The Form Book®

Flat Annual for 2007

Including all the 2006 returns

The HRA's Official Record

Complete record of Flat Racing
from 6 November 2005
to 31 December 2006

Published by Raceform Ltd
Compton, Newbury, Berkshire, RG20 6NL
Raceform Limited is a wholly owned subsidiary of MGN Limited

Printed by William Clowes Ltd, Beccles, Suffolk.

ISBN 1-978-1-905153-23-7

Printed in Great Britain by William Clowes Ltd, Beccles, Suffolk

Full details of all Raceform services and publications are available from:

Raceform Ltd, Compton, Newbury, Berkshire RG20 6NL
Tel: 01635 578080
Fax: 01635 578101
Email: rfsubscription@mgn.co.uk
www.raceform.co.uk

Cover photo: Nayyir (third from right) (L. Dettori) wins the
Vodafone Diomed Stakes at Epsom 3rd June 2006
(Photo: Sean Dempsey/Press Association)

Associated Raceform products

The Form Book, is updated weekly. Subscribers receive a binder, together with all the early racing. Weekly sections and a new index are threaded into the binder to keep it up to date.

The data contained in The Form Book Flat Annual for 2007 is available in paper form or on computer disk. The disk service, Raceform Interactive, contains the same data as Raceform, The Form Book, and operates on any PC within a 'Windows' environment. The database is designed to allow access to the information in a number of different ways, and is extremely quick and easy to use.

CONTENTS

Editor: Graham Dench

Head of Analysis Team: Ashley Rumney

Race Analysts & Notebook Writers:
Dave Bellingham, Mark Brown, Steffan Edwards,
Walter Glynn, Keith Hewitt, Richard Lowther, Lee McKenzie,
David Orton, Ashley Rumney, Desmond Stoneham, David Toft,
Ron Wood, Richard Young.

Production: Ashley Rumney & Richard Lowther

This landmark and exclusive publication is available only through the *Racing Post*. Priced at £99 (with free p&p in the UK), this is a rare opportunity to acquire a truly special collector's item.
'This is no mere travelogue. It is a racing journey with as intelligent and entertaining a companion as anyone could wish to have.'
BROUGH SCOTT
ORDER ONLINE AT
www.racingpost.co.uk/shop
OR CALL OUR ORDERLINE ON
01635 578080
and quote ref WGR06
THE WORLD'S GREATEST RACECOURSES
SANTA AN
ASCOT
GOODWOO
SHA TIN

The Form Book

Flat Racing Annual for **2007**

Welcome to the 2007 edition of *The Form Book,* extended to include the complete year's results from 2006.

Race details contain Racing Post Ratings assessing the merit of each individual performance, speed figures for every horse that clocks a worthwhile time, weight-for-age allowances, stall positions for every race and the starting price percentage, in addition to the traditional features.

Race Focus comments are printed below each race along with officialexplanations and notebook commentsfor all `british races of Class 3 and above, all two-year-old races and foreign races. The comments provide an analysis of the winning performance and, where applicable, explain possible reasons for improvement or attempt to explain why any horse failed to run to its best. More importantly, our team will also indicate the conditions under which horses are likely to be seen to best advantage.

The official record

THE FORM BOOK records comprehensive race details of every domestic race, every major European Group race and every foreign event in which a British-trained runner participated. In the **NOTEBOOK** section, extended interpretation is provided for all runners worthy of a mention, including all placed horses and all favourites. Generally speaking, the higher the class of race, the greater the number of runners noted.

MEETING BACK REFERENCE NUMBER is the Raceform number of the last meeting run at the track and is shown to the left of the course name. Abandoned meetings are signified by a dagger.

THE GOING, The Official going, shown at the head of each meeting, is recorded as follows: Turf: Hard; Firm; Good to firm; Good; Good to soft; Soft; Heavy. All-Weather: Fast; Standard to fast; Standard; Standard to slow; Slow. There may be variations for non-British meetings

Where appropriate, a note is included indicating track bias and any differences to the official going indicated by race times.

THE WEATHER is shown below to th e date for selected meetings.

THE WIND is given as a strength and direction at the Winning Post, classified as follows:
Strength: gale; v.str; str; fresh; mod; slt; almost nil; nil.
Direction: (half) against; (half) bhd; (half) across from or towards stands.

VISIBILITY is good unless otherwise stated.

RACE NUMBERS for Foreign races carry the suffix 'a' in the race header and in the index.

RACE TITLE is the name of the race as shown in the Racing Calendar.

COMPETITIVE RACING CLASSIFICATIONS are shown on a scale from Class 1 to Class 7. All Pattern races are Class 1.

THE RACE DISTANCE is given for all races, and is accompanied by (s) for races run on straight courses and (r) for courses where there is a round track of comparable distance. On All-Weather courses (F) for Fibresand or (P) for Polytrack indicates the nature of the artificial surface on which the race is run.

OFFICIAL RACE TIME as published in the Racing Calendar is followed in parentheses by the time when the race actually started. This is followed by the race class, age restrictions, handicap restrictions and the official rating of the top weight.

PRIZE MONEY shows penalty values down to sixth place (where applicable).

THE POSITION OF THE STARTING STALLS is shown against each race, in the form of: High (H), Centre (C) or Low (L). If one stands at the start facing towards the finish, the stalls are numbered from left to right. If the stalls are placed adjacent to the left rail they are described as low, if against the right rail they are described as high. Otherwise they are central.

IN THE RACE RESULT, the figures to the far left of each horse (under FORM) show the most recent form figures. The figure in bold is the finishing position in this race as detailed below.

1...40 - finishing positions first to fortieth; **b** - brought down; **c** - carried out; **f** - fell; **p** - pulled up; **r** - refused; **ro** - ran out; **s** - slipped up; **u** - unseated rider; **v** - void race.

THE OFFICIAL DISTANCES between the horses are shown on the left-hand side immediately after their position at the finish.

NUMBER OF DAYS SINCE PREVIOUS RUN is the superscript figure immediately following the horse name and suffix.

PREVIOUS RACEFORM RACE NUMBER is the boxed figure to the right of the horse's name.

THE HORSE'S AGE is shown immediately before the weight carried.

WEIGHTS shown are actual weights carried.

OFFICIAL RATING is the figure in bold type directly after the horse's name in the race result. This figure indicates the Official BHB rating, at entry, after the following adjustments had been made:
(i) Overweight carried by the rider.
(ii) The number of pounds out of the handicap (if applicable).
(iii) Penalties incurred after the publication of the weights.
However, no adjustments have been made for:
(i) Weight-for-age.
(ii) Riders' claims.

HEADGEAR is shown immediately befoe the jockey's name and in parentheses and expressed as: **b** (blinkers); **v** (visor); **h** (hood); **e** (eyeshield); **c** (eyecover); **p** (sheepskin cheekpieces).

THE JOCKEY is shown for every runner followed, in superscript, by apprentice allowances in parentheses.

APPRENTICE ALLOWANCES The holders of apprentice jockeys' licences under the provisions of Rule 60(iii) are permitted to claim the following allowances in Flat races:
7lb until they have won 20 Flat races run under the Rules of any recognised Turf Authority; thereafter 5lb until they have won 50 such Flat races; thereafter 3lb until they have won 95 such Flat races.These allowances can be claimed in the Flat races set out below, with the exception of races confined to apprentice jockeys:
(a) All handicap handicaps other than those Rated stakes which are classified as listed races.
(b) All selling and claiming races.
(b) All weight-for-age races classified 3, 4, 5, 6 and 7.

THE DRAW for places at the start is shown after each jockey's name.

RACING POST RATINGS, which record the level of performance attained in this race for each horse, appear in the end column after each horse. These are the work of handicappers Simon Turner, Sam Walker and Paul Curtis, who head a dedicated team dealing with Flat races for Raceform and sister publication, the *Racing Post*.

THE TRAINER is shown for every runner.

COMMENT-IN-RUNNING is shown for each horse in an abbreviated form. Details of abbreviations appear later in this section.

STARTING PRICES appear below the jockey in the race result. The favourite indicator appears to the right of the Starting Price; 1 for the favourite, 2 for the second-favourite and 3 for third-favourite. Joint favourites share the same number.

RACE TIMES in Great Britain are official times which are electronically recorded and shown to 100th of a second. Figures in parentheses following the time show the number of seconds faster or slower than the Raceform Median Time for the course and distance.

RACEFORM MEDIAN TIMES are compiled from all races run over the course and distance in the preceding five years. Times equal to the median are shown as (0.00). Times under the median are preceded by minus, for instance, 1.8 seconds under the median would be shown (-1.8). Record times are displayed either referring to the juvenile record (1.2 under 2y best) or to the overall record (1.2 under best).

GOING CORRECTION appears against each race to allow for changing conditions of the ground. It is shown to a hundredth of a second and indicates the adjustment per furlong against the median time. The going based on the going correction is shown in parentheses and is recorded in the following stages:
Turf: HD (Hard); F (Firm); GF (Good to firm); G (Good); GS (Good to soft); S (Soft); HVY (Heavy). All-Weather: FST (Fast); SF (Standard to fast); STD (Standard); SS (Standard to slow); SLW (Slow)

WEIGHT-FOR-AGE allowances are given where applicable for mixed-age races.

STARTING PRICE PERCENTAGE follows the going correction and weight-for-age details, and gives the total SP percentage of all runners that competed. It precedes the number of runners taking part in the race.

SELLING DETAILS (where applicable) and details of any claim are given. Friendly claims are not detailed.

SPEED RATINGS appear below the race time and going correction. They are the work of time expert Dave Bellingham and differ from conventional ratings systems in that they are an expression of a horse's ability in terms of lengths-per-mile, as opposed to pounds in weight. They are not directly comparable with BHB and Racing Post ratings.

The ratings take no account of the effect of weight, either historically or on the day, and this component is left completely to the user's discretion. What is shown is a speed rating represented in its purest form, rather than one that has been altered for weight using a mathematical formula that treats all types of horses as if they were the same.

A comparison of the rating achieved with the 'par' figure for the grade of race - the rating that should be achievable by an average winner in that class of race- will both provide an at-a-glance indication of whether or not a race was truly run and also highlight the value of the form from a time perspective.

In theory, if a horse has a best speed figure five points superior to another and both run to their best form in a race over a mile, the first horse should beat the second by five lengths. In a race run over two miles, the margin should be ten lengths and so on.

Before the speed figures can be calculated, it is necessary to establish a set of standard or median times for every distance at every track, and this is done by averaging the times of all winners over a particular trip going back several years. No speed ratings are produced when insufficient races have been run over a distance for a reliable median time to be calculated.

Once a meeting has taken place, a raw unadjusted speed rating is calculated for each winner by calculating how many lengths per mile the winning time was faster or slower than the median for the trip. A difference of 0.2 of a second equals one length. The raw speed ratings of all winners on the card are then compared to the 'par' figure for the class of race. The difference between the 'raw' speed rating and the 'par' figure for each race is then noted, and both the fastest and slowest races are discarded before the rest are averaged to produce the going allowance or track variant. This figure gives an idea as to how much the elements, of which the going is one, have affected the final times of each race.

The figure representing the going allowance is then used to adjust the raw speed figures and produce the final ratings, which represent how fast the winners would have run on a perfectly good surface with no external influences, including the weather. The ratings for beaten horses are worked out by taking the number of lengths they were behind the winner, adjusting that to take into account the distance of the race, and deducting that figure from the winner's rating. The reader is left with a rating which provides an instant impression of the value of a time performance.

The speed 'pars' below act as benchmark with which to compare the speed figures earned by each horse in each race. A horse that has already exceeded the 'par' for the class he is about to run in, is of special interest, especially if he has done it more than once, as are horses that have consistently earned higher figures than their rivals.

Class	Par
Class 1 Group One	117
Class 1 Group Two	115
Class 1 Group Three	113
Class 1 Listed	111
Class 2	109
Class 3	107
Class 4	105
Class 5	103
Class 6	101
Class 7	97

Allowances need to be made for younger horses and for fillies. These allowances are as follows.

MONTH	2yo	3yo
Jan / Feb	n/a	-6
Mar / Apr	-11	-5
May / Jun	-10	-4
Jul / Aug	-9	-3
Sep / Oct	-8	-2
Nov / Dec	-7	-1
Races contested by fillies only		-3

Allowances are cumulative. For example, using a combination of the above pars and allowances, the par figure for the Epsom Oaks would be 110. The Group One par is 117, then deduct 4 because the race is confined to three year olds and run in June, then subtract another 3 because the race is confined to fillies.

TOTE prices include £1 stake. Exacta dividends are shown in parentheses. The Computer Straight Forecast dividend is preceded by the letters CSF, Computer Tricast is preceded by CT and Tote Trio dividend is preceded by the word Trio. Jackpot, Placepot and Quadpot details appear at the end of the meeting to which they refer.

OWNER is followed by the breeder's name and the trainer's location.

STEWARDS' INQUIRIES are included with the result, and any suspensions and/or fines incurred. Objections by jockeys and officials are included, where relevant.

HISTORICAL FOCUS details occasional points of historical significance.

FOCUS The Focus section has been enhanced to help readers distinguish good races from bad races and reliable form from unreliable form, by drawing together the opinions of handicapper, time expert and paddock watcher and interpreting their views in a punter-friendly manner.

NOTEBOOK horses marked with the diamond symbol are those deemed by our racereaders especially worthy of note in future races.

OFFICIAL EXPLANATIONS, where the horse is deemed to have run well above or below expectations

Abbreviations and their meanings

Paddock comments

gd sort - well made, above average on looks
h.d.w - has done well, improved in looks
wl grwn - well grown, has filled to its frame
lengthy - longer than average for its height
tall - tall
rangy - lengthy and tall but in proportion.
cl cpld - close coupled
scope - scope for physical development
str - strong, powerful looking
w'like - workmanlike, ordinary in looks
lt-f - light-framed, not much substance
cmpt - compact
neat - smallish, well put together
leggy - long legs compared with body
angular ` unfurnished behind the saddle, not filled to frame
unf - unfurnished in the midriff, not filled to frame
narrow - not as wide as side appearance would suggest
small - lacks any physical scope
nt grwn - not grown
lw - looked fit and well
bkwd - backward in condition
t - tubed
swtg - sweating
b (off fore or nr fore) - bandaged in front
b.hind (off or nr) - bandaged behind

At the start

stdd s - jockey purposely reins back the horse
dwlt - missed the break and left for a short time
s.s - slow to start, left longer than a horse that dwelt
s.v.s - started very slowly
s.i.s - started on terms but took time to get going
ref to r - either does not jump off, or travels a few yards and then stops
rel to r - tries to pull itself up in mid-race
w.r.s - whipped round start

Position in the race

led - in lead on its own
disp ld - upsides the leader

w ldr - almost upsides the leader
w ldrs - in a line of three or more disputing the lead
prom - on the heels of the leaders, in the front third of the field
trckd ldr(s) - just in behind the leaders giving impression that it could lead if asked
chsd ldr - horse in second place
chsd clr ldrs - horse heads main body of field behind two clear leaders
chsd ldrs - horse is in the first four or five but making more of an effort to stay close to the pace than if it were tracking the leaders.
clsd - closed
in tch - close enough to have a chance
hdwy - making ground on the leader
gd hdwy - making ground quickly on the leader, could be a deliberate move
sme hdwy - making some ground but no real impact on the race
stdy hdwy - gradually making ground
ev ch - upsides the leaders when the race starts in earnest
rr - at the back of main group but not detached
bhd - detached from the main body of runners
hld up - restrained as a deliberate tactical move
nt rcvr - lost all chance after interference, mistake etc.
wknd - stride shortened as it began to tire
lost tch - had been in the main body but a gap appeared as it tired
lost pl - remains in main body of runners but lost several positions quickly

Riding

effrt - short-lived effort
pushed along - received urgings with hands only, jockey not using legs
rdn - received urgings from the saddle, including use of the whip
hrd rdn - received maximum assistance from the saddle including use of whip
drvn - received forceful urgings, jockey putting in a lot of effort and using whip
hrd drvn - jockey very animated, plenty of kicking, pushing and reminders

Finishing comments

jst failed - closing rapidly on the winner and probably would have led a stride after the line
r.o - jockey's efforts usually involved to produce an increase in pace without finding an appreciable turn of speed
r.o wl - jockey's efforts usually involved to produce an obvious increase in pace without finding an appreciable turn of speed
unable qckn - not visibly tiring but does not possess a sufficient change of pace
one pce - not tiring but does not find a turn of speed, from a position further out than unable qckn
nt r.o. - did not consent to respond to pressure
styd on - going on well towards the end, utilising stamina
nvr able to chal - unable to produce sufficient to reach a challenging position
nvr nr to chal - in the opinion of the racereader, the horse was never in a suitable position to challenge.
nrst fin - nearer to the winner in distance beaten than at any time since the race had begun in earnest
nvr nrr - nearer to the winner position-wise than at any time since the race had begun in earnest
rallied - responded to pressure to come back with a chance having lost its place
no ex - unable to sustain its run
bttr for r - likely to improve for the run and experience
rn green - inclined to wander and falter through inexperience
too much to do - left with too much leeway to make up

Winning comments

v.easily - a great deal in hand
easily - plenty in hand
comf - something in hand, always holding the others
pushed out - kept up to its work with hands and heels without jockey resorting to whip or kicking along and wins fairly comfortably
rdn out - pushed and kicked out to the line, with the whip employed
drvn out - pushed and kicked out to the line, with considerable effort and the whip employed
all out - nothing to spare, could not have found any more
jst hld on - holding on to a rapidly diminishing lead, could not have found any more if passed
unchal - must either make all or a majority of the running and not be challenged from an early stage

Complete list of abbreviations

a - always
gng - going
qckn - quicken
a.p - always prominent
gp - group
r - race
abt - about
grad - gradually
racd - raced
appr - approaching
grnd - ground
rch - reach
awrdd - awarded
hd - head
rcvr - recover
b.b.v - broke blood-vessel
hdd - headed
rdn - ridden
b.d - brought down
hdwy - headway
rdr - rider
bdly - badly
hld - held
reard - reared
bef - before
hmpd - hampered
ref - refused
bhd - behind
imp - impression
rn - ran
bk - back
ins - inside
rnd - round
blkd - baulked
j.b - jumped badly
r.o - ran on
blnd - blundered
j.w - jumped well
rr - rear
bmpd - bumped

jnd - joined
rspnse - response
bnd - bend
jst - just
rt - right
btn- beaten
kpt - kept
s - start
bttr - better
l - length
sddle - saddle
c - came
ld - lead
shkn - shaken
ch - chance
ldr - leader
slt - slight
chal - challenged
lft - left
sme - some
chse - chase
m - mile
sn - soon
chsd - chased
m.n.s - made no show
spd- speed
chsng - chasing
mde - made

st - straight
circ - circuit
mod - moderate
stmbld - stumbled
cl - close
mid div - mid division
stdd - steadied
clr - clear
mstke - mistake
stdy - steady
clsd - closed
n.d - never dangerous
strly - strongly
comf - comfortably
n.g.t - not go through
styd - stayed
cpld - coupled
n.m.r - not much room
styng - staying
crse - course
nk - neck
s. u - slipped up
ct - caught
no ex - no extra
swtchd - switched
def - definite
nr - near
swvd - swerved

dismntd - dismounted
nrr - nearer
tk - took
disp - disputed
nrst fin - nearest finish
t.k.h - took keen hold
dist - distance
nt - not
t.o - tailed off
div - division
nvr - never
tch - touch
drvn - driven
one pce - one pace
thrght - throughout
dwlt - dwelt
out - from finish
trbld - troubled
edgd - edged
outpcd - outpaced
trckd - tracked
effrt - effort
p.u - pulled up
u.p - under pressure
ent - entering
pce - pace
u.str.p- under strong pressure

ev ch - every chance
pckd - pecked
w - with
ex - extra
pl - place
w.r.s - whipped round start
f - furlong
plcd - placed
wd - wide
fin - finished
plld - pulled
whn - when
fnd - found
press - pressure
wknd - weakened
fnl - final
prog - progress
wl - well
fr - from
prom - prominent
wnr - winner
gd - good
qckly - quickly
wnt - went
fi-wy ß- halfway

Racing Post Ratings

Racing Post Ratings for each horse are shown in the right hand column, headed RPR, and indicate the actual level of performance attained in that race. The figure in the back index represents the BEST public form that Raceform's Handicappers still believe the horse capable of reproducing.

To use the ratings constructively in determining those horses best-in in future events, the following procedure should be followed:

(i) In races where all runners are the same age and are set to carry the same weight, no calculations are necessary. The horse with the highest rating is best-in.

(ii) In races where all runners are the same age but are set to carry different weights, add one point to the Raceform Rating for every pound less than 10 stone to be carried; deduct one point for every pound more than 10 stone.

For example,

Horse	Age & wt	Adjustment from 10st	Base rating	Adjusted rating
Treclare	3-10-1	-1	78	77
Buchan	3-9-13	+1	80	81
Paper Money	3-9-7	+7	71	78
Archaic	3-8-11	+17	60	77

Therefore Buchan is top-rated (best-in)

(iii) In races concerning horses of different ages the procedure in (ii) should again be followed, but reference must also be made to the Official Scale of Weight-For-Age.

For example,

12 furlongs, July 20th

Horse	Age & wt	Adjustment from 10st	Base rating	Adjusted rating	W-F-A deduct	Final rating
Orpheus	5-10-0	0	90	90	Nil	90
Lemonora	4-9-9	+5	88	88	Nil	88
Tamar	3-9-4	+10	85	95	-12	83
Craigangower	4-8-7	+21	73	94	Nil	94

Therefore Craigangower is top-rated (best-in)

(A 3-y-o is deemed 12lb less mature than a 4-y-o or older horse on 20th July over 12f. Therefore, the deduction of 12 points is necessary.)

The following symbols are used in conjunction with the ratings:

++: almost certain to prove better

+: likely to prove better

d: disappointing (has run well below best recently)

?: form hard to evaluate

t: tentative rating based on race-time rating may prove unreliable

Weight adjusted ratings for every race are published daily in Raceform Private Handicap and our new service Raceform Private handicap ONLINE (www.raceform.co.uk).

For subscription terms please contact the Subscription Department on (01635) 578080.

The Official Scale of Weight, Age & Distance (Flat)

The following scale should only be used in conjunction with the Official ratings published in this book. Use of any other scale will introduce errors into calculations. The allowances are expressed as the number of pounds that is deemed the average horse in each group falls short of maturity at different dates and distances.

Dist		Jan		Feb		Mar		Apr		May		Jun		Jul		Aug		Sep		Oct		Nov		Dec	
(fur)	Age	1-15	16-31	1-14	15-28	1-15	16-31	1-15	16-30	1-15	16-31	1-15	16-30	1-15	16-31	1-15	16-31	1-15	16-30	1-15	16-31	1-15	16-30	1-15	16-31
5	2	-	-	-	-	-	47	44	41	38	36	34	32	30	28	26	24	22	20	19	18	17	17	16	16
	3	15	15	14	14	13	12	11	10	9	8	7	6	5	4	3	2	1	1	-	-	-	-	-	-
6	2	-	-	-	-	-	-	-	-	44	41	38	36	33	31	28	26	24	22	21	20	19	18	17	17
	3	16	16	15	15	14	13	12	11	10	9	8	7	6	5	4	3	2	2	1	1	-	-	-	-
7	2	-	-	-	-	-	-	-	-	-	-	-	-	38	35	32	30	27	25	23	22	21	20	19	19
	3	18	18	17	17	16	15	14	13	12	11	10	9	8	7	6	5	4	3	2	2	1	1	-	-
8	2	-	-	-	-	-	-	-	-	-	-	-	-	-	-	37	34	31	28	26	24	23	22	21	20
	3	20	20	19	19	18	17	15	14	13	12	11	10	9	8	7	6	5	4	3	3	2	2	1	1
9	3	22	22	21	21	20	19	17	15	14	13	12	11	10	9	8	7	6	5	4	4	3	3	2	2
	4	1	1	-	-	-	-	-	-	-	-	-	-	-	-	-	-	-	-	-	-	-	-	-	-
10	3	23	23	22	22	21	20	19	17	15	14	13	12	11	10	9	8	7	6	5	5	4	4	3	3
	4	2	2	1	1	-	-	-	-	-	-	-	-	-	-	-	-	-	-	-	-	-	-	-	-
11	3	24	24	23	23	22	21	20	19	17	15	14	13	12	11	10	9	8	7	6	6	5	5	4	4
	4	3	3	2	2	1	1	-	-	-	-	-	-	-	-	-	-	-	-	-	-	-	-	-	-
12	3	25	25	24	24	23	22	21	20	19	17	15	14	13	12	11	10	9	8	7	7	6	6	5	5
	4	4	4	3	3	2	2	1	1	-	-	-	-	-	-	-	-	-	-	-	-	-	-	-	-
13	3	26	26	25	25	24	23	22	21	20	19	17	15	14	13	12	11	10	9	8	8	7	7	6	6
	4	5	5	4	4	3	3	2	1	-	-	-	-	-	-	-	-	-	-	-	-	-	-	-	-
14	3	27	27	26	26	25	24	23	22	21	20	19	17	15	14	13	12	11	10	9	9	8	8	7	7
	4	6	6	5	5	4	4	3	2	1	-	-	-	-	-	-	-	-	-	-	-	-	-	-	-
15	3	28	28	27	27	26	25	24	23	22	21	20	19	17	15	14	13	12	11	10	9	8	8	7	7
	4	6	6	5	5	4	4	3	3	2	1	-	-	-	-	-	-	-	-	-	-	-	-	-	-
16	3	29	29	28	28	27	26	25	24	23	22	21	20	19	17	15	14	13	12	11	10	9	9	8	8
	4	7	7	6	6	5	5	4	4	3	2	1	-	-	-	-	-	-	-	-	-	-	-	-	-
18	3	31	31	30	30	29	28	27	26	25	24	23	22	21	20	18	16	14	13	12	11	10	10	9	9
	4	8	8	7	7	6	6	5	5	4	3	2	1	-	-	-	-	-	-	-	-	-	-	-	-
20	3	33	33	32	32	31	30	29	28	27	26	25	24	23	22	20	18	16	14	13	12	11	11	10	10
	4	9	9	8	8	7	7	6	6	5	4	3	2	1	-	-	-	-	-	-	-	-	-	-	-

Effect of the draw

(R.H.) denotes right-hand and (L.H.) left-hand courses.

RULES OF RACING No. 28 (v): The Starter shall check the runners and riders and, for Flat races, assign the horses to the places drawn by lot, all horses taking their place at the Start in the order drawn for them. The rider who has drawn No. 1 must always be placed on the left and the other riders must take their places in consecutive numbers from the left. Presuming the Stands are on the outside of the course, on right-handed courses, low numbers will be towards the stands' rail at the start of the race. On left-handed courses, high numbers will be towards the stands' rail.

* Draw biases shown below apply to straight-course races unless otherwise stipulated.

** Most races (outside Festival meetings) are now restricted to 20 runners under a recently introduced BHB rule, which means it's now particularly worth looking at the stalls position, as many courses can accommodate more than that number.

ASCOT (R-H) - The course has been re-developed during 2005 and the racing surface re-sited, so previous draw biases may change.

AYR (L-H) - The draw only usually becomes a major issue in sprints at the Western Meeting, with fields rarely big enough the rest of the season for groups to form. Throughout the 90s high numbers were massively favoured in the Gold and Silver Cups, but this has changed lately, with the far side (low) again dominating both races last year. The centre of the course usually rides slower, meaning low numbers are often favoured over 7f50y and 1m.
STALLS: Usually go up the stands' side (high) in sprints, but occasionally go on the other side (normally in the run-up to the Western Meeting to preserve the ground).
BIASES: There's ultimately not a lot between the two sides in big fields now.
SPLITS: Fields only usually split in the Silver and Gold Cups.

BATH (L-H) - The draw is basically of far less importance than the pace at which races are run. In big fields, runners drawn low are often inclined to go off too fast to hold a rail position (the course turns left most of the way, including one major kink) and this can see hold-up horses drawn wide coming through late. Conversely, in smaller fields containing little pace, up front and on the inside is often the place to be.
STALLS: Always go on the inside (low).
SPLITS: Fields almost always stick together, but soft ground can see a split, with the outside rail (high) favoured.

BEVERLEY (R-H) - A high draw is essential on good to soft or faster ground over 5f and also on the round course, particularly in races of 7f100y and 1m100y. In sprints, runners have to negotiate a right-handed jink not long after the start and it seems harder here than at probably any course for runners drawn low to get over to the favoured rail (there's also a camber).
The course management experimented with moving stalls to the stands' side over 5f in 2002 (unsuccessfully, as it led to a huge low bias) and haven't done so since.
STALLS: Go on the inside (high) at all distances.
BIASES: High numbers are massively favoured at 5f on good to soft or faster ground and are also best on the round course.
SPLITS: Splits are very rare, and only likely over 5f on soft ground.

BRIGHTON (L-H) - Much depends on the going and time of year; on good to soft or slower ground runners often head for the outside rail (high), while in late season it's usually just a case of whichever jockey finds the least cut-up strip of ground. Otherwise, low-drawn prominent-racers tend to hold sway in fast-ground sprints, with double figures always facing an uphill task over 5f59y.
STALLS: Always go on the inside (low) in sprints.
SPLITS: These occur frequently in the second half of the season, as jockeys look for a fresh strip on ground that seems to churn up easily.

CARLISLE (R-H) - For the past few seasons, runners racing with the pace and hardest against the inside rail (high) have done well in big fields on decent ground. This is largely down to the fact that the Flat course and NH course are one and the same, and that those racing nearest the fence are running where the hurdle wings were positioned, while those wider out are on the raced-on surface. On soft ground, the bias swings completely, with runners racing widest (low) and grabbing the stands' rail in the straight favoured at all distances.
STALLS: Normally go on the inside (high) but can go down the middle in sprints (usually on slow ground).
BIASES: High numbers are best in early-season sprints as long as the ground is no slower than good. Look to back low numbers on soft/heavy ground.
SPLITS: Rarely will two groups form but, on easy ground, runners often spread out.

CATTERICK (L-H) - When the ground is testing, the stands' rail is definitely the place to be, which suits high numbers in 5f races, and high-drawn prominent-racers at all other distances. However, when the ground is good to firm or faster, horses drawn on the inside (low) often hold the edge, and there have been several meetings over the last few seasons in which those racing prominently hardest against the inside rail have dominated (over all distances, presumably as a result of watering).
STALLS: Go on the inside (low) at all distances these days (they often used to go on the outer over 5f212y).
BIASES: Low numbers are best in sprints on fast ground (particularly watered firm going) but the stands' rail (high) rides faster under slower conditions.
SPLITS: Are common over 5f.

CHEPSTOW (L-H) - High numbers enjoyed a massive advantage in straight-course races in 2000 and the course management duly took steps to eradicate the faster strip, using the same 'earthquake' machine as had been employed at Goodwood in the late 90s. This led to little in the way of a draw bias for the next two years, and it's been patchy since.
STALLS: Always go on the stands' side (high) on the straight course.
BIASES: Have become hard to predict in recent times.
SPLITS: Splits are common, as jockeys drawn low often head far side in the realisation that it's hard to win down the middle.

CHESTER (L-H) - It's well known that low numbers are favoured at all distances here, even in the 2m2f Chester Cup, and the bias is factored into the prices these days. That said sprints (and in particular handicaps) are still playable, as it almost always pays to stick to a runner drawn 1-3.
STALLS: Go on the inside (low) at all distances bar 1m2f75y and 2m2f117y (same starting point) when they go on the outside. Certain starters ask for the stalls to come off the inside rail slightly in sprints.
BIASES: Low numbers are favoured at all distances. Soft ground seems to accentuate the bias until a few races have been staged, when a higher draw becomes less of a disadvantage as the ground on the inside becomes chewed up.

DONCASTER (L-H) - The course closed at the end of 2005 for re-development and will not re-open until 2007.

EPSOM (L-H) - When the going is on the soft side, jockeys tack over to the stands' side for the better ground (this strip rides quicker in such conditions as the course cambers away from the stands' rail towards the far side). In 5f races, the stalls are invariably placed on the stands' side, so when the going is soft the majority of the runners are on the best ground from the outset. Prominent racers drawn low in round-course races are able to take the shortest route around Tattenham Corner, and on faster ground have a decisive edge over 6f, 7f and 1m114y. Over 5f, high numbers used to hold quite an advantage, but the bias is not so great these days.
STALLS: Always go on the outside (high) over 5f and 6f (races over the latter trip start on a chute) and inside (low) at other distances, bar 1m4f10y (centre).
BIASES: Low-drawn prominent racers are favoured at between 6f and 1m114y.
SPLITS: Good to soft ground often leads to a few trying the stands'-side route.

FOLKESTONE (R-H) - Prior to 1998, Folkestone was never thought to have much in the way of a bias, but nowadays the draw is often crucial on the straight course (up to 7f). Whatever the ground, the far rail (high) rides faster than the stands' rail, which in turn rides quicker than the middle of the track. Runners now usually go across to the far side over 6f and 7f (jockeyship often playing a part, with several races going to whichever horse had secured the front up the rail). However, over 5f, when the stalls are up the stands' rail, fields often split, with low numbers just about holding sway (it seems the ground lost by switching across over the mini-

mum trip can't be regained from racing on the faster surface). Slow ground swings things even more in favour of high numbers.
STALLS: Usually go up the stands' side (low) on the straight track, but occasionally down the centre (they can't go up the far side as the ambulance needs access).
BIASES: High numbers are favoured over 6f and 7f, and also over the minimum trip when 14 or more line up. However, very low numbers have a good record in smaller fields over 5f. Front-runners are well worth considering at all distances.
SPLITS: Often occur over 5f and 6f.

GOODWOOD (R-H) & (L-H) - The course management took steps to end the major high bias seen in the Stewards' Cup throughout the late 90s by breaking up the ground by machine in 1998. This led to the stands' side (low) dominating the race in 1999 before the far side gradually took over again.
STALLS: Invariably go on the stands' side (low).
BIASES: High numbers are best at between 7f-1m1f, and the faster the ground, the more pronounced the bias (keep an eye out for the rail on the home turn being moved during Glorious week).
SPLITS: Although fields tend not to break into groups in most sprints, runners often spread out to about two-thirds of the way across in fields of around 20.

HAMILTON (R-H) - Extensive drainage work was carried out in winter 2002 in a bid to level up the two sides of the track but, after encouraging early results, the natural bias in favour of high numbers (far side) kicked in again. Basically the course is stuck with this bias, which can only be altered by watering on faster going (be careful after a dry spell, as things can often swing in favour of low numbers). High numbers are also best over 1m65y, thanks to runners encountering a tight right-handed loop soon after the start.
STALLS: It's not uncommon for the ground to become too soft for the use of stalls, but otherwise they go either side.
BIASES: High draws are best in soft/heavy-ground sprints, but the bias becomes middle to high otherwise (often switching to low on watered fast ground). Front-runners do particularly well at all distances.
SPLITS: Look for high numbers to peel off in fields of 8+ when the stalls are stands' side, unless the ground is fast.

HAYDOCK (L-H) - High numbers used to enjoy a major advantage in soft-ground sprints, but that seems to have been turned full circle by drainage work carried out in the late 90s, with the far side (low) now best on very bad ground. Otherwise, runners usually head for the centre these days, the draw rarely making much of a difference (although very high numbers can be worst off in big fields on faster going).
STALLS: Usually go down the centre in the straight.

KEMPTON (R-H) - The course closed for re-development in 2005 and the Flat turf track has been replaced by a Polytrack All-Weather surface.

LEICESTER (R-H) - There was a four-year spell between 1998 and 2001 when the centre-to-far-side strip (middle to high) enjoyed a decisive advantage over the stands' rail, jockeys eventually choosing to avoid the near side. However, that's changed recently, with very low numbers more than holding their own.
STALLS: Invariably go up the stands' side (low).
SPLITS: Still occur occasionally.

LINGFIELD Turf (L-H) - The draw advantage is nothing like as defined as in years past, but the stands' rail (high) again went through a good spell in the second half of last season, as was the case the year before. The one factor that can have a massive effect on the draw is heavy rainfall on to firm ground. Presumably because of the undulating nature of the track and the fact that the far rail on the straight course is towards the bottom of a slope where it joins the round course, rainfall seems to make the middle and far side ride a deal slower. In these conditions, the top three or four stalls have a massive edge.
STALLS: Go up the stands' side (high) at between 5f and 7f and down the middle over 7f140y.
BIASES: High numbers are massively favoured on fast ground after recent rain, but otherwise the most recent meeting is often the best guide.
SPLITS: It's unusual to see two distinct groups, but runners often fan out centre to stands' side in big fields.

LINGFIELD All-Weather, Polytrack surface (L-H) – There is little bias over most trips, but it is an advantage to be drawn low over 6f and 1m 2f with both starts being situated very close to the first bend. A low to middle draw is preferable over 5f even with a safety limit of just ten, though the very inside stall has a poor recent record. No horse managed to win from stall one over that trip in 2004, which suggests the ground right against the inside rail is slower than elsewhere.
STALLS: Are against the outside rail (high) over 5f and 1m, but against the inside rail (low) for all other distances.
SPLITS: Due to the nature of the circuit, the fields never split though some horses can be forced very wide on the home bend.

MUSSELBURGH (R-H) - The bias in favour of low numbers over 5f isn't as pronounced as many believe. It could be that a few more trying going to the far side (inside) this year on genuinely fast ground. The bias in favour of high numbers at 7f and 1m also isn't that big.
STALLS: Usually go up the stands' side (low) over 5f nowadays, but they can be rotated.
SPLITS: Look out for runners drawn very high in big-field 5f races on fast ground, as they occasionally go right to the far rail.

NEWBURY (L-H) - There's basically little between the two sides these days, apart from on soft ground, in which case the stands' rail (high) is definitely the place to be. When the ground is testing it's not uncommon to see runners race wide down the back straight and down the side at between 1m3f56y and 2m (particularly over 1m5f61y). In such circumstances, a high draw becomes a huge advantage.
STALLS: Can go anywhere for straight-course races.
SPLITS: It's not often fields are big enough for a split to occur.

NEWCASTLE (L-H) - It's always been a case of high numbers best at up to and including 7f on good or firmer, and low numbers having the advantage when the ground is good to soft or softer. Over the straight 1m, the stands' rail (high) is the place to be apart from on bad ground.
STALLS: Invariably go on the stands' side (high), only being switched to the inside under exceptional circumstances.
SPLITS: Two groups are usually formed when 14+ go to post, and often when 8-13 line up.

NEWMARKET July Course (R-H) - The major draw biases seen under the former Clerk of the Course have become a thing of the past since Michael Prosser took over and now only the occasional meeting will be affected. The course is permanently divided into two halves by a rail (the Racing Post now carry information regarding which side is to be used) and, as a rule of thumb, the two outside rails (stands' rail when they're on the stands'-side half, far rail when they're on the far-side half) ride faster than the dividing rail.
Stands'-side half - On fast ground (particularly watered) very high numbers are often favoured at up to 1m, when there's a narrow strip hard against the fence that rides quicker. However, on good to soft or slower ground, runners racing down the centre are favoured.
Far-side half - There's rarely much in the draw, apart from on slow ground, when the far side (low) rides faster.
STALLS: Can go either side on either half of the track.
SPLITS: Runners just about tend to form two groups in capacity fields, but are more likely to run to their draw here than at tracks such as Newcastle.

NEWMARKET Rowley Mile (R-H) - Similarly to the July Course, the draw seems to have been evened out since the Clerk of the Course change. Occasionally a bias will appear, but they're hard to predict these days.
STALLS: Can go anywhere and are rotated.
BIASES: High numbers have dominated the 2m2f Cesarewitch in recent years, the logic here being that those on the inside can be switched off early, while low numbers have to work to get into position before the sole right-handed turn.
SPLIT: It's not unusual for jockeys to come stands' side on slow ground in round-course races.

NOTTINGHAM (L-H) - On the straight course, it used to be a case of low numbers being favoured when the stalls were on the far rail and high numbers when they were stands' side, with low being best when the stalls spanned the entire course. These days, though, it's less clear-cut and the going makes the biggest difference. On soft ground low numbers are best but high tend to be favoured on good to firm or faster.
STALLS: Tend to go on the stands' side (high) unless the ground is very soft.
SPLITS: Fields usually split in sprints when 14+ line up.

PONTEFRACT (L-H) - Low numbers have always been considered best here for the same reason as at Chester, in that the course has several distinct left-hand turns with a short home straight, but this is not always true. High numbers at least hold their own over 6f now, whatever the ground, but massively so on soft/heavy. Drainage work was carried out in the late 90s to try and eradicate the outside-rail bias on slow ground, and this worked immediately afterwards, but during the last few seasons there have been definite signs that it's now riding much faster.
STALLS: Go on the inside (low) unless the ground is very soft, when they're switched to the outside rail.
SPLITS: Although it's uncommon to see distinct groups, high numbers usually race wide these days on good to soft or slower ground.

REDCAR (L-H) - It's not unusual to see big fields throughout the season here, but the draw rarely plays a part, with runners inclined to converge towards the centre.
STALLS: Go towards the stands' side (high).
SPLITS: Splits are unusual and usually of little consequence when they are seen.

RIPON (R-H) - The draw is often the sole deciding factor in big-

field sprints and watering plays a major part. As a general rule, low numbers are best when the ground is good to firm or faster, while the far side is always best on softer going but, ultimately, the best guide here these days is the most recent meeting.
STALLS: Go on the stands' side (low) apart from under exceptional circumstances.
BIASES: Front-runners (particularly from high draws over 1m) have an excellent record and any horse trying to make ground from behind and out wide is always facing a tough task.
SPLITS: Fields tend to stay together in races of 12 or fewer, but a split is near guaranteed when 15 or more line up. Look for 'draw' jockeys who might chance going far side in fields of 13-14.

SALISBURY (R-H) - It's difficult to win from a single-figure draw in big-field fast-ground sprints, and also over 7f, but proven stamina and race suitability become the most important factors over the testing straight 1m. This far-side bias is at its greatest early and late season, before and after the erection of a temporary rail (which usually goes up in July). The draw swings full circle on slower ground, as jockeys then invariably head towards the stands' rail (good to soft seems to be the cut-off point).
STALLS: Go on the far side (high) unless the ground is soft, when they're often moved to the near side.
BIASES: High numbers are best on the straight course on fast ground, there's not much in it on good to soft, while low take over on soft/heavy.
SPLITS: Fields only tend to divide on good to soft ground; otherwise they all converge towards either rail, dependant upon going.

SANDOWN (R-H) - On the 5f chute, when the going is on the soft side and the stalls are on the far side (high), high numbers enjoy a decisive advantage. On the rare occasions that the stalls are placed on the stands' side, low numbers enjoy a slight advantage when all the runners stay towards the stands' rail, but when a few break off and go to the far side high numbers comfortably hold the upper hand again. High numbers enjoy a decent advantage in double-figure fields over 7f and 1m on good going or faster, but jockeys invariably head for the stands' side on slow ground.
STALLS: Usually go far side (high) over 5f, as the course is more level that side.
SPLITS: It's unusual for runners to split over 5f, with capacity fields rare and jockeys all inclined to head for the far rail.

SOUTHWELL All-Weather, Fibresand surface (L-H) – Over most trips on the round track it is preferable to be drawn away from the extreme inside or outside. The exceptions are over 6f and 1m 3f, which both start close to the first bend and therefore it is better to be drawn low to middle. At most meetings the centre of the track rides faster than against either rail, though that can change in extreme weather when power-harrowing can even out the bias. A low to middle draw is preferable over the straight 5f and it is noticeable that even when a high draw wins, the horse concerned almost always giving the stands' rail a wide berth having been angled to its left to race more towards the centre.
STALLS: Are placed next to the inside rail (low), except over 5f where they are placed next to the stands' rail (high).
SPLITS: The fields do not tend to split into groups as such, but can fan right out and take varied routes once into the home straight. Even in big fields over the straight 5f, the runners basically stick to their draw and race as straight as they can from start to finish.

THIRSK (L-H) - This used to be the biggest draw course in the country, back in the days of the old watering system (which was badly affected by the wind) but, while biases still often show up, they're not as predictable as used to be the case. Field sizes, watering and going always have to be taken into account in fields of 12 or more (11 or fewer runners and it's rare to see anything bar one group up the stands' rail, with high numbers best). Otherwise, either rail can enjoy the edge on watered fast ground (the one place not to be under any circumstances is down the middle). Low-drawn prominent-racers are well worth considering whatever the distance on the round course.
STALLS: Always go up the stands' side (high).
BIASES: High numbers are best in sprints when 11 of fewer line up, but it's hard to know which side is likely to do best in bigger fields on fast ground. The far (inside) rail is always best on slow going (the softer the ground, the greater the advantage).
SPLITS: Runners invariably stay towards the stands' side in sprints containing 12 or fewer runners (unless the ground is soft) and frequently when 13-14 line up. Any more and it becomes long odds-on two groups.

WARWICK (L-H) - Low numbers are favoured in fast-ground sprints, but not by as much as many believe, and the prices often over-compensate. However, when the ground is genuinely soft, high numbers can enjoy an advantage.
STALLS: Always go on the inside (low).

WINDSOR (Fig. 8) - It's typical to see large fields all season, and the draw almost always plays a part. In sprints, things are set in stone, with high numbers best on good or faster going (particularly watered fast ground), not much between the two sides on good to soft, and the far side (low) taking over on soft or heavy ground. It can be difficult for runners who switch off the stands' rail to make up the leeway (because the course turns sharply left soon after the finish, those pulled wide must think they're being asked to quicken up into a dead-end). On slower ground, jockeys head centre to far side, and right over to the far rail on genuine soft/heavy (again it's difficult to make ground from behind under such conditions).
STALLS: Can be positioned anywhere for sprints.
BIASES: High-drawn prominent-racers are favoured in fast-ground sprints, and also over 1m67y. On good to soft going, there's rarely much between the two sides, but it's a case of nearer to the far rail (low) the better on bad ground.
SPLITS: Splits only tend to occur on good to soft ground, and even then it's rare to see two defined groups.

WOLVERHAMPTON All-Weather, Polytrack surface since October 2004 (L-H) – The huge bias that used to exist towards those horses that raced away from the inside rail on the old Fibresand is a fading memory, but even though the Polytrack is relatively new, some biases are emerging. A low draw is a big advantage over 5f and 6f and low to middle is preferable over 7f. Beyond that it doesn't seem to matter, though it is never a good idea to race too wide on the home bends and those that do so rarely seem to make up the lost ground.
STALLS: Are placed against the outside rail (high) over 7f and against the inside rail (low) at all other distances.
SPLITS: Splits do not happen and most of the time the runners stay as close as they can next to the inside rail unless traffic problems force them wide.

YARMOUTH (L-H) - High numbers enjoyed a major advantage for much of the 90s, but this was put an end to by the course switching from pop-up sprinklers (which were affected by the off-shore breeze) to a Briggs Boom in '99. These days a bias will appear occasionally but it's hard to predict, and runners often head for the centre whatever the going.
STALLS: Go one side or the other.
SPLITS: It's common to see groups form, often including one down the centre, in big fields.

YORK (L-H) - The draw is nothing like as unpredictable in sprints as many believe, although things are never quite as clear-cut in September/October as earlier in the season. Essentially, on good or faster ground, the faster strip is to be found centre to far side, which means in capacity fields, the place to be is stall 6-12, while in fields of 12-14 runners drawn low are favoured (the course is only wide enough to house 20 runners). On soft/heavy ground, the stands' side (high) becomes the place to be, and high numbers often get the rail to themselves, as this is not a bias well known among jockeys. Low numbers are best on fast ground on the round course, although watering can reduce the bias.
STALLS: Can go anywhere.
BIASES: Prominent-racers drawn down the centre are favoured in fast-ground sprints, but high numbers take over on genuine soft/heavy ground. Low numbers are best in big fields on the round course, apart from on slower going, when runners leave the inside in the home straight.
SPLITS: Defined groups are rare.

Key to racereaders' initials

WG ....Walter Glynn
KH ....Keith Hewitt
RL ....Richard Lowther
LM...................Lee McKenzie
TM ....Tim Mitchell
JN.............Jonathan Neesom
DO ....Darren Owen
SP ....Steve Payne
CR ....Colin Roberts
JR ....Joe Rowntree
JS........................John Santer
ST ....Steve Taylor
RY ....Richard Young

ADDENDA TO PREVIOUS ANNUALS

2005

Race 2010 Vicious Prince (IRE) finished 2nd, disqualified: prohibited substance (morphine) in post-race sample.

Race 3178 Cape Unknown (USA) finished 11th, disqualified: prohibited substance (hydroxyethylpromazine) in post-race sample.

Race 4422 Mystical Land (IRE) finished 1st, disqualified: prohibited substance (phenylbutazone) in post-race sample.

The Form Book ®

Winter Racing 2005

The HRA's Official Record

Complete record of All-Weather Racing
and principal foreign turf races
from 6 November to 31 December 2005

6268 - 6269a (Foreign Racing) - See Raceform Interactive

6204 LEOPARDSTOWN (L-H)

Sunday, November 6

OFFICIAL GOING: Soft to heavy

6270a KNOCKAIRE STKS (LISTED RACE) 7f
1:35 (1:35) 3-Y-0+ £23,085 (£6,773; £3,226; £1,099)

			RPR
1		**Sugarhoneybaby (IRE)**^{21} [5928] 4-8-12 97 JMurtagh 9 (Noel Meade, Ire) *trckd ldrs: 4th early st: 3rd and rdn to chal fr over 1f out: led ins fnl f: sn strly pressed: kpt on wl* **12/1**	104
2	*nk*	**Hard Rock City (USA)**^{28} [5776] 5-9-1 108 NGMcCullagh 6 (M J Grassick, Ire) *sn settled mid-div: rdn to go 4th on inner 1f out: sn chal and almost on terms: no ex and kpt on same pce cl home* **9/2^{2}**	106
3	*nk*	**Turnkey**^{5} [6221] 3-9-0 103 (b) TonyCulhane 13 (M R Channon) *a.p: rdn to chal and ld 1f out: sn strly pressed: hdd and dropped to 3rd ins fnl f: kpt on same pce* **10/1**	106
4	*2*	**Eklim (IRE)**^{14} [6048] 5-9-1 103 KFallon 4 (C A Murphy, Ire) *mid-div: 10th appr st: rdn and kpt on wout threatening fr over 1f out* **4/1^{1}**	101
5	*1*	**Sweet Treat (IRE)**^{21} [5928] 3-8-11 101 (b^{1}) MJKinane 2 (John M Oxx, Ire) *led: strly pressed and hdd 1f out: no ex and kpt on same pce* **6/1**	96
6	*1 ½*	**Indian's Feather (IRE)**^{21} [5928] 4-8-12 92 (b) TPO'Shea 14 (M J Grassick, Ire) *trckd ldrs: mainly 3rd: no imp u.p fr over 1f out* **16/1**	92
7	*½*	**Adaala (USA)**^{21} [5928] 3-9-0 102 DPMcDonogh 8 (Kevin Prendergast, Ire) *chsd ldrs: 5th early st: no imp u.p fr 1 1/2f out* **10/1**	94
8	*hd*	**Alone He Stands (IRE)**^{14} [6043] 5-9-1 96 JohnEgan 3 (J C Hayden, Ire) *towards rr: no imp u.p st: kpt on same pce* **12/1**	94
9	*shd*	**Common World (USA)**^{7} [6189] 6-9-6 107 JAHeffernan 7 (T Hogan, Ire) *mid-div: 7th appr st: no imp u.p fr 2f out* **10/1**	98
10	*½*	**Caprarola (USA)**^{21} [5928] 3-8-6 82 JamieMoriarty$^{(5)}$ 5 (John M Oxx, Ire) *towards rr: rdn bef 1/2-way: swished tail and no imp fr wl bef st* **25/1**	89
11	*1*	**Moyenne (IRE)**^{28} [5776] 3-9-0 98 CatherineGannon 10 (Timothy Doyle, Ire) *mid-div: 8th appr st: sn no imp u.p* **25/1**	90
12	*3 ½*	**Tolpuddle (IRE)**^{168} [1940] 5-9-4 108 (t) WMLordan 12 (T Stack, Ire) *chsd ldrs: 6th early st: rdn and sn no ex* **11/2^{3}**	85
13	*4 ½*	**Sanfrancullinan (IRE)**^{14} [6043] 3-8-11 83 (b) RPCleary 11 (M Halford, Ire) *towards rr: no ex u.p st* **20/1**	69
14	*1 ½*	**Mount Eliza (IRE)**^{392} [6101] 3-8-11 87 PJSmullen 15 (Charles O'Brien, Ire) *a towards rr: rdn and no imp st* **33/1**	65

1m 35.0s **Going Correction** +0.65s/f (Yiel)
WFA 3 from 4yo+ 1lb **14** Ran SP% **131.8**
Speed ratings: 110,109,109,107,105 104,103,103,103,102 101,97,92,90
CSF £68.69 TOTE £10.90: £2.70, £2.20, £3.00; DF 228.50.
Owner Liam Queally **Bred** Mrs Bill O'Neill **Trained** Castletown, Co Meath
■ Stewards' Enquiry : J Murtagh caution: improper use of the whip

NOTEBOOK
Sugarhoneybaby(IRE), three times successful in handicaps last season, made a belated start this term but has been progressive again, quickening to lead a half furlong down. (op 10/1)
Hard Rock City(USA) was bidding for a fourth course success but could not quite quicken with the winner. (op 4/1)
Turnkey challenged from early in the straight and led over a furlong out. He ran on well when headed but the fuse was spent. (op 8/1)
Eklim(IRE) might have had the waiting tactics overdone but he is not really enamoured by this really heavy ground. (op 9/2 tchd 7/2)
Sweet Treat(IRE) ran in front but, joined in the straight, found little when headed over a furlong down (op 11/2)
Common World(USA) was never able to get in any sort of an effective challenge. (op 7/1)
Tolpuddle(IRE) had his ground conditions but faded in the straight. (op 5/1)

6271a EYREFIELD STKS (LISTED RACE) 1m 1f
2:05 (2:05) 2-Y-0 £23,085 (£6,773; £3,226; £1,099)

			RPR
1		**Wovoka (IRE)**^{15} [6024] 2-9-0 TonyCulhane 6 (M R Channon) *mid-div: impr into 5th and rdn 2f out: styd on wl to ld ins fnl f: sn clr* **11/1**	99
2	*2*	**Danehill Music (IRE)**^{13} [6084] 2-8-11 91 WMLordan 9 (David Wachman, Ire) *mid-div: prog into 6th bef st: sn rdn to chal: led 1 1/2f out: strly pressed and hdd ins fnl f: no ex and kpt on same pce* **12/1**	92
3	*2 ½*	**Royal Intrigue (IRE)**^{35} [5643] 2-9-0 PJSmullen 4 (D K Weld, Ire) *mid-div: rdn in 6th fr 2f out: kpt on wout threatening* **9/2^{2}**	91
4	*½*	**Mountain (IRE)**^{11} [6116] 2-9-0 KFallon 3 (A P O'Brien, Ire) *chsd ldrs: clsr in 3rd fr 2f out: sn no imp u.p* **1/1^{1}**	90
5	*1 ½*	**Rhythm'n Roots (IRE)**^{21} [5927] 2-9-3 103 (t) KJManning 5 (J S Bolger, Ire) *trckd ldrs: clsr in 2nd 2f out: sn rdn and no imp* **5/1^{3}**	90
6	*2*	**Bahrain Storm (IRE)**^{15} [6036] 2-9-0 75 DMGrant 2 (Patrick J Flynn, Ire) *trckd ldrs: impr to ld fr early st: strly pressed and hdd 1 1/2f out: sn no ex* **33/1**	84
7	*6*	**Kalmez (IRE)**^{25} [5843] 2-9-0 MJKinane 1 (John M Oxx, Ire) *mid-div: dropped towards rr bef 1/2-way: no imp u.p st* **6/1**	73
8	*1 ½*	**Flyingit (USA)**^{6} [6204] 2-8-11 80 (bt^{1}) JMurtagh 11 (Thomas Mullins, Ire) *towards rr: sme hdwy appr st: sn no imp u.p* **25/1**	67
9	*3 ½*	**Convincing**^{11} [6116] 2-9-0 TPO'Shea 7 (John Joseph Murphy, Ire) *a towards rr: nvr a factor* **66/1**	64
10	*3*	**Ditzy Chick (IRE)**^{11} [6116] 2-8-11 CatherineGannon 8 (Timothy Doyle, Ire) *led: strly pressed and hdd early st: sn wknd* **25/1**	56
11	*8*	**Aleksandr Pushkin (IRE)**^{11} [6115] 2-9-0 JAHeffernan 10 (A P O'Brien, Ire) *trckd ldr in 2nd: rdn fr 1/2-way: no ex st: eased ins fnl f* **25/1**	44

2m 4.10s **Going Correction** +0.825s/f (Soft) **11** Ran SP% **131.1**
Speed ratings: 104,102,100,99,98 96,91,89,86,84 76
CSF £139.54 TOTE £8.40: £2.20, £3.10, £1.90; DF 89.40.
Owner Mrs T Burns **Bred** Rathasker Stud **Trained** West Ilsley, Berks

NOTEBOOK
Wovoka(IRE), successful in a Newbury nursery off 85, made it four out of 16 with an emphatic win here after going to the front inside the last. (op 10/1)
Danehill Music(IRE) looked to have stolen it until reeled in by the winner. (op 10/1)
Royal Intrigue(IRE) took an age to get his effort underway in the straight.
Mountain(IRE) looked pretty slow over the last quarter. (op 5/4 tchd 11/8)
Rhythm'n Roots(IRE) found little under his penalty. (op 9/2 tchd 11/2)
Kalmez(IRE) must have been flattered by his Navan success. (op 5/1)

6272 - 6275a (Foreign Racing) - See Raceform Interactive

6222 CAPANNELLE (R-H)

Sunday, November 6

OFFICIAL GOING: Heavy

6276a PREMIO RIBOT (GROUP 2) 1m
1:30 (1:31) 3-Y-0+ £47,858 (£21,877; £12,174; £6,087)

			RPR
1		**Distant Way (USA)**^{22} [5915] 4-9-2 MPasquale 5 (L Brogi, Italy) *raced in 3rd to straight, led 1 1/2f out, driven out* **289/100^{2}**	110
2	*2 ½*	**Kill Cat (IRE)**^{7} [6193] 4-9-2 GBietolini 6 (A Peraino, Italy) *reared up start, soon recovered, 6th straight, headway 2f out, chased winner final furlong, no imp* **38/1**	105
3	*1 ½*	**Ceprin (IRE)**^{157} [2242] 4-9-2 EBotti 3 (A & G Botti, Italy) *led to 1 1/2f out, kept on same pace* **29/1**	102
4	*1 ½*	**Salselon**^{7} [6193] 6-9-2 AParravani 2 (M Ciciarelli, Italy) *held up in rear, still last approaching final f, driven to take 4th closing stages* **64/10**	99
5	*½*	**Nordhal**^{22} [5915] 6-9-2 MDemuro 1 (B Grizzetti, Italy) *raced in 4th to straight, weakened well over 1f out* **17/1**	98
6	*snk*	**Jader (IRE)**^{14} 3-9-1 MEsposito 10 (D Ducci, Italy) *held up, 9th straight, some progress over 1f out, never near to challenge* **111/1**	99
7	*1 ½*	**Needlecraft (IRE)**^{21} [5936] 3-8-12 MBlancpain 7 (H-A Pantall, France) *raced in mid-div, 5th str, hdwy on outside, going wl whn disp 2nd over 2f out, rdn & wknd 1 1/2f out* **52/10**	93
8	*3 ½*	**De Sica (IRE)**^{22} [5915] 3-9-1 MMonteriso 4 (E Borromeo, Italy) *tracked leader, 2nd straight, beaten 3f out* **49/10^{3}**	89
9	*4*	**Martillo (GER)**^{22} [5915] 5-9-2 THellier 8 (R Suerland, Germany) *held up, 7th straight, ridden 2f out, soon beaten* **11/10^{1}**	80
10	*8*	**Le Giare (IRE)**^{14} 3-9-1 OFancera 9 (R Brogi, Italy) *pulled hard early, 8th straight, always behind* **22/1**	65

1m 40.0s
WFA 3 from 4yo+ 2lb **10** Ran SP% **136.6**
(including 1 euro stake): WIN 3.89; PL 2.24, 7.50, 5.40; DF 59.67.
Owner Allevamento La Nuova Sbarra **Bred** Grundy Bloodstock Ltd **Trained** Italy

6277a PREMIO UMBRIA (GROUP 3) 6f
2:00 (2:05) 2-Y-0+ £30,748 (£14,157; £7,906; £3,953)

			RPR
1		**St Paul House**^{120} [3369] 7-9-12 PAragoni 4 (G Di Chio, Italy) *always prominent on stands rails, led over 1f out, pushed clear, comfortably* **188/100^{1}**	113
2	*4*	**Golden Stravinsky (USA)**^{14} 3-9-9 DVargiu 6 (G Fratini, Italy) *led to over 1f out, kept on same pace under pressure* **215/10**	98
3	*1 ½*	**Key To Pleasure (GER)**^{14} [6049] 5-9-9 WMongil 10 (Mario Hofer, Germany) *towards rear on stands rails til headway from 2f out, reached 3rd 100yds out, no chance with first two* **59/10**	94
4	*1 ½*	**Polish Magic** 5-9-9 (b) THellier 11 (A Wohler, Germany) *always prominent on outside, ridden & every chance over 1f out, one pace final f* **21/1**	89
5	*1*	**Dream Impact (USA)**^{49} 4-9-12 MDemuro 7 (L Riccardi, Italy) *tracked leaders, 4th & hard ridden over 1f out, one pace* **11/2**	89
6	*2*	**Glad To Be Fast (IRE)**^{7} [6193] 5-9-9 (b) AStarke 9 (Mario Hofer, Germany) *never near to challenge* **42/10^{3}**	80
7	*4*	**Crucial**^{21} [5938] 5-9-9 PConvertino 8 (Frank Sheridan, Italy) *tracked leaders, hard ridden well over 1f out, eased when beaten inside final f* **116/10**	68
8	*½*	**Stoxx (IRE)**^{112} [3577] 4-9-5 GMarcelli 13 (L Riccardi, Italy) *prominent on outside til weakening over 1f out* **63/1**	63
9	*3*	**Krisman (IRE)**^{21} [5938] 6-9-12 DPorcu 12 (M Ciciarelli, Italy) *in touch towards outside 4f* **41/10^{2}**	61
10	*1*	**White Arrow (IRE)**^{364} [6586] 4-9-9 MPasquale 1 (L Camici, Italy) *never nearer than mid-division* **98/10**	55
11	*6*	**San Dany (IRE)**^{112} [3577] 5-9-9 MTellini 3 (M Massimi Jr, Italy) *prominent to over 2f out* **36/1**	37
12	*8*	**Blu Delta Force** 3-9-9 MEsposito 5 (V Caruso, Italy) *always outpaced* **46/1**	13
13	*1*	**Shifting Place**^{112} [3577] 3-9-5 CFiocchi 2 (R Menichetti, Italy) *always behind* **115/1**	6

1m 10.4s **13** Ran SP% **136.9**
WIN 2.88; PL 1.63, 5.04, 2.33; DF 37.38.
Owner San Paolo Agri Stud **Bred** San Paolo Agri Stud Srl **Trained** Italy

6278a PREMIO ROMA AT THE RACES (GROUP 1) 1m 2f
2:30 (2:39) 3-Y-0+ £106,894 (£53,787; £31,319; £15,660)

			RPR
1		**Soldier Hollow**^{34} [5678] 5-9-2 WMongil 1 (P Schiergen, Germany) *raced in 3rd to straight, led 2f out, quickened clear, ran on strongly* **558/100**	118
2	*2 ½*	**Without Connexion (IRE)**^{21} [5937] 6-9-2 DVargiu 4 (M Guarnieri, Italy) *held up, 7th str, hdwy wl over 2f out, chased wnr fr appr fnl f, kept on same pace under pressure* **48/1**	114
3	*5*	**Epalo (GER)**^{175} [1738] 6-9-2 AStarke 10 (A Schutz, Germany) *led to 2f out, kept on same pace* **107/10**	105
4	*1*	**Manduro (GER)**^{34} [5678] 3-9-2 THellier 7 (P Schiergen, Germany) *raced in 4th to straight, headway over 3f out, ridden & disputed 3rd 2f out, one pace* **19/10^{1}**	105
5	*shd*	**Delfos (IRE)**^{36} [5641] 4-9-2 MBlancpain 2 (C Laffon-Parias, France) *pushed along at half-way, 5th straight, one pace final 2f* **19/4^{3}**	103
6	*10*	**Nonno Carlo (IRE)**^{175} [1736] 5-9-2 MTellini 5 (M Grassi, Italy) *tracked leader to straight, ridden over 3f out, eased when beaten well over 1f out* **35/1**	85

7 2 **Groom Tesse**[504] 3136 4-9-2 ....(b) MManueddu 3 81
(L Camici, Italy) *held up in rear, last straight, some progress on outside well over 2f out, soon beaten* **64/10**
8 15 **Vol De Nuit**[21] 5937 4-9-2 .... MDemuro 9 54
(L Brogi, Italy) *6th straight, beaten over 2f out, eased* **48/10**
9 hd **Altieri**[22] 5915 7-9-2 .... MEsposito 8 54
(V Caruso, Italy) *held up in rear, 8th straight, beaten well over 2f out (lost off fore plate during the race)* **34/10**[2]

2m 4.20s
WFA 3 from 4yo+ 4lb 9 Ran SP% **133.9**
WIN 6.58; PL 2.72, 9.81, 4.19; DF 136.82.
Owner Gestut Park Wiedingen **Bred** Car Colston Hall Stud **Trained** Germany

NOTEBOOK
Soldier Hollow reversed recent form with Manduro in no uncertain terms to land this race for the second consecutive year. He should now gain an invitation to the Hong Kong Cup, in which he finished 11th last year, although the suspicion is that he is at his best with more cut in the ground than he is likely to get at Sha Tin.
Without Connexion(IRE) was returning from a long absence and, adopting his usual forcing tactics, should be all the better for this run. Another hoping for a Hong Kong invite, he will be fresher than some in that field and, granted an uncontested lead, could be a danger to all.
Epalo(GER) is widely accepted as the best German three-year-old colt but lost his unbeaten record here without having any excuse other than the testing ground.

5930 COLOGNE (R-H)
Sunday, November 6

OFFICIAL GOING: Soft

6279a KOLNER HERBST-STUTEN-MEILE (GROUP 3) (F&M) 1m
2:55 (3:02) 3-Y-O+ £22,695 (£7,092; £3,546; £2,128)

RPR
1 **Marine Bleue (IRE)**[21] 5936 3-8-13 .... TThulliez 6 106
(N Clement, France) *always in touch, 6th straight, led approaching final f, headed 150yds out, ran on well to lead close home* **23/10**[1]
2 nk **Free Dreams (GER)**[42] 5499 3-8-13 .... PHeugl 2 105
(Mario Hofer, Germany) *s.s, last halfway, strong run on outside from 2f out, hard rdn to ld 150yds out, hdd & unable to qckn cl home* **26/1**
3 2 **River Melody (GER)**[16] 3-8-13 .... AHelfenbein 5 101
(Mario Hofer, Germany) *towards rear, stayed on final 2f, nearest at finish* **22/1**
4 1 **Nightdance Forest (IRE)**[21] 5936 4-9-2 .... FilipMinarik 10 100
(P Schiergen, Germany) *mid-division, headway 2f out, kept on one pace from over 1f out* **74/10**
5 2 **Nouvelle Noblesse (GER)**[21] 5936 3-8-13 .... APietsch 12 95
(Mario Hofer, Germany) *5th straight, every chance well over 1f out, one pace* **31/1**
6 nk **The Spring Flower (GER)**[42] 3-8-13 .... ADeVries 1 95
(Andreas Lowe, Germany) *started slowly, behind to straight, stayed on from over 1f out, nearest at finish* **29/2**
7 hd **Grantsville (GER)**[28] 5786 3-8-13 .... TMundry 3 94
(P Rau, Germany) *disputed lead, close 3rd on inside straight, led well over 2f out to approaching final f, one pace* **25/1**
8 1½ **Arlecchina (GER)**[57] 5142 5-9-2 .... JBojko 9 92
(U Stoltefuss, Germany) *broke well, soon outpaced and towards rear, never a factor* **29/1**
9 1½ **Seraphine (GER)**[21] 5936 5-9-2 .... EPedroza 8 89
(A Wohler, Germany) *prominent, 4th straight, weakened well over 1f out* **48/10**[3]
10 1¼ **Golden Island (IRE)**[21] 5936 4-9-2 .... MichaelHills 7 87
(J W Hills) *narrow leader on outside, headed & weakened well over 2f out* **81/10**
11 2½ **Kitcat (GER)**[21] 5936 4-9-2 .... JPalik 13 82
(P Schiergen, Germany) *disputed lead, 2nd straight, beaten 2f out* **15/1**
12 1½ **Auengunst (GER)**[21] 5930 3-8-13 .... ABoschert 14 78
(U Ostmann, Germany) *never a factor* **41/10**[2]
13 ¾ **Indian View (GER)**[21] 5930 3-8-13 .... NRichter 4 76
(A Schutz, Germany) *always towards rear* **13/1**
14 15 **Isarca (GER)**[21] 5936 3-8-13 ....(b) BDCook 11 46
(H Blume, Germany) *well behind final 2f* **46/1**

1m 44.04s
WFA 3 from 4yo+ 2lb 14 Ran SP% **130.4**
PARI-MUTUEL (including 10 euro stakes): WIN 33; PL 17, 49, 44; SF 708.
Owner Lady O'Reilly **Bred** Petra Bloodstock Agency Ltd **Trained** Chantilly, France

NOTEBOOK
Golden Island(IRE) was not allowed her own way in front and was beaten soon after straightening for home.

6262 WOLVERHAMPTON (A.W) (L-H)
Monday, November 7

OFFICIAL GOING: Standard
Wind: Moderate, behind

6280 ALL WEATHER RACING STARTS WITH BETDIRECT AMATEUR RIDERS' H'CAP 1m 5f 194y(P)
1:20 (1:22) (Class 6) (0-65,65) 3-Y-O+ £2,849 (£876; £438) Stalls Low

Form RPR
2212 1 **Our Choice (IRE)**[40] 5550 3-10-12 **64** .... MrsEmmaLittmoden 13 76+
(N P Littmoden) *mid-div: hdwy to ld 3f out: fnd ex whn chal fnl f* **11/4**[1]
03/0 2 ¾ **Activist**[18] 5789 7-10-13 **57** ....(p) KellyHarrison 9 68
(D Carroll) *mid-div: hdwy to chse wnr 3f out: chal 1f out: kpt on but no imp* **50/1**
2334 3 7 **Bid For Fame (USA)**[66] 4920 8-11-0 **65** .... MrSPearce(7) 6 66
(J Pearce) *hld up: hdwy over 2f out: styd on but nvr nr to chal* **9/2**[2]
0062 4 4 **Precious Mystery (IRE)**[7] 6195 5-10-6 **55** .... GerardTumelty(5) 2 51
(A King) *trckd ldrs: pushed along 6f out: hrd rdn over 2f out: no hdwy and wknd over 1f out* **11/4**[1]
5064 5 6 **Jadeeron**[2] 6267 6-10-3 **52** ....(v) MrSRees(5) 5 39
(Miss D A McHale) *trckd ldrs: led 4f out to 3f out: rdn and wknd wl over 1f out* **11/1**
1026 6 10 **Stolen Song**[43] 5321 5-10-8 **59** ....(e) MrJBurdon(7) 12 32
(J Ryan) *mid-div: no hdwy fnl 3f* **33/1**
4000 7 1 **Jidiya (IRE)**[37] 5628 6-10-11 **60** ....(p) MrTFWoodside(5) 4 32
(S Gollings) *sn led: hdd 4f out: wknd sn after* **12/1**
-005 8 ¾ **Wise Tale**[22] 5126 6-10-1 **50** ....(v) MissLHaagensen(5) 7 21
(P D Niven) *a wl in rr* **33/1**
0000 9 5 **Active Account (USA)**[51] 5321 8-10-2 **53** .... ChrisGlenister(7) 8 17
(J R Holt) *a bhd* **66/1**
5002 10 4 **Darko Karim**[9] 6153 3-10-8 **60** ....(v) MrSWalker 10 18
(R J Hodges) *trckd ldrs: rdn and wknd 5f out* **20/1**
4-0 11 10 **Shamsada (IRE)**[28] 5789 5-10-12 **56** .... MrPRoche 11 —
(R H Macnabb, Ire) *mid-div: rdn over 4f out: sn wknd* **8/1**[3]
2100 12 ¾ **Alexander Sapphire (IRE)**[259] 432 4-10-2 **53** .... MrsFleurHawes(7) 3 —
(N B King) *in tch tl wknd over 6f out* **66/1**
0000 13 12 **Santiburi Lad (IRE)**[6] 6218 8-9-13 **50** .... MissSLWatson(7) 1 —
(N Wilson) *broke wl: prom tl wknd over 5f out* **100/1**

3m 4.79s (-2.58) **Going Correction** -0.20s/f (Stan)
WFA 3 from 4yo+ 8lb 13 Ran SP% **115.2**
Speed ratings (Par 101):99,98,94,92,88 83,82,82,79,77 71,70,64
CSF £171.13 CT £606.35 TOTE £3.60: £1.30, £13.70, £1.60; EX 183.50.
Owner A A Goodman **Bred** Islanmore Stud **Trained** Newmarket, Suffolk

FOCUS
A moderate staying handicap and very few ever got in a serious blow. The form is not totally convincing although there may be more to come from the winner.

6281 BETDIRECT.CO.UK EBF MAIDEN STKS (DIV I) 5f 216y(P)
1:55 (1:57) (Class 5) 2-Y-O £3,795 (£1,129; £564; £281) Stalls Low

Form RPR
3642 1 **Jimmy The Guesser**[16] 6024 2-8-11 70 .... RichardThomas(3) 1 76+
(N P Littmoden) *a.p: wnt 2nd 2f out: hung lft bef ld 1f out: rdn out* **6/4**[1]
0306 2 1½ **Rapsgate (IRE)**[33] 5695 2-8-9 68 .... DaneO'Neill 3 67
(R Hannon) *led tl rdn and hdd 1f out: kpt on* **11/2**[3]
00 3 ¾ **Capistrano**[10] 6128 2-9-0 .... JamieSpencer 5 69
(B W Hills) *outpcd on ins tl hdwy on ins over 2f out: swtchd rt over 1f out: styd on wl* **11/2**[3]
5663 4 5 **Mistatake (IRE)**[34] 5682 2-9-0 65 .... NCallan 8 54
(K A Ryan) *chsd ldrs to 2f out: wknd fnl f* **9/2**[2]
5200 5 5 **Sandwith**[34] 5680 2-8-9 68 .... PatrickMathers(5) 9 39
(James Moffatt) *chsd ldrs tl rdn and wknd over 1f out* **16/1**
0 6 1 **Penang Cinta**[108] 3689 2-9-0 .... FrancisNorton 11 36+
(G A Butler) *outpcd: nvr on terms* **9/1**
7 nk **Came Back (IRE)** 2-9-0 .... ShaneKelly 12 35
(J A Osborne) *prom on outside tl wknd over 1f out* **25/1**
0035 8 9 **Macs All Heart (IRE)**[38] 5583 2-8-9 52 ....(t) TonyCulhane 4 3
(A B Coogan) *outpcd and nvr on terms* **33/1**
0050 9 4 **Paddy's Place (IRE)**[57] 5151 2-8-9 52 .... FergusSweeney 10 —
(M Blanshard) *mid-div tl rdn and wknd over 2f out* **40/1**
0 10 2½ **Little Trinket**[7] 6196 2-8-4 .... NataliaGemelova(5) 6 —
(M J Polglase) *outpcd and a bhd* **100/1**
11 5 **Phills Pearl** 2-8-9 .... MichaelTebbutt 7 —
(D Burchell) *v.s.a: a wl bhd* **66/1**

1m 14.69s (-1.12) **Going Correction** -0.20s/f (Stan) 11 Ran SP% **116.5**
Speed ratings (Par 96):99,97,96,89,82 81,80,68,63,60 53
CSF £9.44 TOTE £2.50: £1.20, £2.00, £2.20; EX 12.20.
Owner Miss Vanessa Church **Bred** Mrs P Lewis **Trained** Newmarket, Suffolk

FOCUS
A modest maiden and not that competitive, but the first three were clear and the form could be reasonable.

NOTEBOOK
Jimmy The Guesser, who had shown plenty of ability in this sort of company, and more recently in nurseries, found this a good opportunity and was able to get off the mark at the sixth attempt despite hanging to his left under pressure. Possibly a touch awkward, he could be one to take on in a more competitive race. (op 7-4)
Rapsgate(IRE) was rated 87 earlier in the season but she has regressed since then and first-time blinkers failed to help at Nottingham on her previous start. Without the headgear, back up in trip and switched to Polytrack for the first time, this was a little better than of late, but did not put up much resistance when challenged by the eventual winner. She clearly has the ability to win a small race, and may be worth a try over a little further, but she is not one to be following. (op 6-1 tchd 13-2)
Capistrano, making his debut on Polytrack, looked to find things happening a little too quickly but stepped up on his previous efforts nonetheless. Now qualified for a handicap mark, he will have more options and could improve over a little further. (op 7-1)
Mistatake(IRE), third in a Catterick nursery off a mark of 63 on his previous start, ran below that form returned to Polytrack and connections seem to be struggling a little to establish his optimum conditions. (op 7-2)
Sandwith, back up to six furlongs for the first time since he made his debut, and switched to Polytrack for the first time, ran well below his official mark of 68. (op 18-1)
Penang Cinta seemed to step up on the form he showed when last on his debut at Newbury, but is likely to do better when handicapped and needs one more run. (op 14-1 tchd 17-2)
Paddy's Place(IRE) Official explanation: jockey said filly had no more to give

6282 BETDIRECT.CO.UK EBF MAIDEN STKS (DIV II) 5f 216y(P)
2:30 (2:32) (Class 5) 2-Y-O £3,785 (£1,126; £562; £281) Stalls Low

Form RPR
3200 1 **Balik Pearls**[24] 5871 2-8-9 70 ....(b¹) SteveDrowne 2 66+
(N A Callaghan) *mid-div on outside: hdwy over 2f out: rdn to ld ins fnl f: qcknd clr* **5/1**[3]
0430 2 3½ **Charming Ballet (IRE)**[62] 5030 2-9-0 73 .... JimmyQuinn 10 60+
(N P Littmoden) *sn trckd ldrs: rdn over 1f out: r.o to go 2nd cl home* **7/1**
00 3 hd **Obergurgl (IRE)**[23] 5888 2-9-0 .... TonyCulhane 9 60
(Mrs A Duffield) *led tl rdn and hdd ins fnl f: lost 2nd cl home* **40/1**
0006 4 1¼ **Wednesdays Boy (IRE)**[6] 6213 2-8-11 47 .... PaulMulrennan(3) 8 56
(P D Niven) *mid-div: styd on fnl f: nvr nrr* **66/1**
600 5 ¾ **Alwariah**[18] 5993 2-8-9 60 .... EddieAhern 4 49
(C E Brittain) *s.i.s: styd on fnl f: nvr nr to chal* **16/1**
5 6 ½ **Melody Maker**[9] 6156 2-8-9 .... IanMongan 1 47
(W R Swinburn) *in tch on ins: rdn 2f out: no hdwy after* **4/1**[2]
4 7 ½ **Lisfannon**[19] 5969 2-8-9 .... JamieSpencer 5 46
(B W Hills) *hld up in rr: effrt 2f out: nvr on terms* **11/10**[1]
0506 8 shd **Imperial Gem (IRE)**[21] 5944 2-8-9 61 .... ChrisCatlin 6 45
(Rae Guest) *trckd ldrs tl wknd over 1f out* **20/1**
9 3 **Vino** 2-8-9 .... MartinDwyer 7 36
(B W Hills) *in tch tl wknd 2f out* **40/1**
10 2½ **Alistair John** 2-9-0 ....(t) DeanMcKeown 3 33
(Mrs G S Rees) *v.s.a: a bhd* **40/1**

0506 **11** *4* **Tequila Rose (IRE)**[45] 5427 2-8-4 55...................... PatrickMathers(5) 11 16
(A Bailey) *chsd ldr tl wknd over 2f out* **50/1**

1m 15.85s (0.04) **Going Correction** -0.20s/f (Stan) **11** Ran SP% **118.2**

Speed ratings (Par 96):91,86,86,84,83 82,82,81,77,74 69

CSF £37.30 TOTE £6.80: £1.60, £1.90, £10.40; EX 32.00.

Owner Alan Brazil Racing Club **Bred** T K And Mrs P A Knox **Trained** Newmarket, Suffolk

FOCUS

This was admittedly a modest maiden, but it was still probably a little better that it looks at first glance as both the slow time (over a second slower than the first division) and the proximity of the fourth can be explained by the surprisingly steady early pace.

NOTEBOOK

Balik Pearls ◆ looked to run her best race yet when midfield in a decent nursery at Newmarket on her previous start and, with blinkers fitted for the first time and switched to Polytrack, she stepped up on that effort to run out a quite taking winner. It would be unwise to get carried away given this was a weak race, but the way she picked up from off such a steady pace was impressive in the context of this sort of company and she looked a natural on sand. If the headgear can continue to have a positive effect, she can be followed in better company. (op 9-2 tchd 11-2)

Charming Ballet(IRE), without the blinkers on her return from a 62-day break, seemed to handle the Polytrack well but the steady pace did not look to suit and he was no match whatsoever for the winner. A stronger-run race, or even a return to five furlongs, should bring around improvement and there is a race or two in him. (op 9-1 tchd 10-1 and 13-2)

Obergurgl(IRE), upped in trip on his Polytrack debut, stepped up on his two previous efforts with an encouraging third. A horse with plenty of scope, he can do better again and is now qualified for a handicap mark. (op 33-1)

Wednesdays Boy(IRE), twice beaten in sellers and rated just 47, could be used to hold the form down, but his proximity should not be taken too literally given how steady the pace was early on.

Alwariah, dropped a furlong in trip, was able to recover from a very slow start thanks to the steady pace and ran respectably in the circumstances.

Melody Maker failed to confirm the promise she showed on her debut in a course and distance maiden and may not have been suited by the steady pace. (op 9-2)

Lisfannon ran nowhere near the level of form she showed when an encouraging forth in a five-furlong Bath maiden on her debut, and is another who may have been undone by the steady pace. (op 5-4 tchd 11-8)

6283 PRESS RED TO BET ON ITVI H'CAP — 1m 4f 50y(P)

3:05 (3:05) (Class 6) (0-65,69) 3-Y-O+ **£2,917** (£861; £430) **Stalls** Low

Form RPR

0202 **1** **Stretton (IRE)**[31] 5720 7-9-4 **65**.................................... GrahamGibbons 5 74
(J D Bethell) *hld up in mid-div: rdn over 2f out: styd on to ld jst ins fnl f: kpt on* **3/1**[1]

331 **2** *1 1/2* **War Owl (USA)**[7] 6195 8-9-5 **69** 6ex...................................... DNolan(3) 1 76
(Ian Williams) *a in tch: led 2f out: rdn and hdd jst ins fnl f: kpt on but nt qckn* **9/2**[3]

6212 **3** *hd* **Taxman (IRE)**[20] 5959 3-8-8 **61**....................................(p) FrancisNorton 4 68
(C E Brittain) *a in tch: styd on fnl f* **7/2**[2]

0040 **4** *1 3/4* **King Of Music (USA)**[3] 6247 4-9-1 **62**............................... ChrisCatlin 9 66
(G Prodromou) *s.i.s: in rr: hdwy on ins over 2f out: nvr nrr* **14/1**

5314 **5** *4* **Ocean Rock**[26] 5837 4-8-8 **55**... OscarUrbina 11 52
(C A Horgan) *hld up: rdn 3f out: nvr nr nr to chal* **5/1**

0040 **6** *1 3/4* **Efrhina (IRE)**[28] 5807 5-8-9 **56**.. MickyFenton 7 51
(Stef Liddiard) *mid-div tl wknd 2f out* **12/1**

0160 **7** *nk* **Newcorp Lad**[24] 5884 5-8-9 **56**.......................................(p) TonyCulhane 3 50
(Mrs G S Rees) *led tl hdd 2f out: wknd appr fnl f* **16/1**

000/ **8** *11* **Protection Money**[156] 5928 5-8-13 **60**............................... VinceSlattery 2 37
(L P Grassick) *mid-div: bhd fr 6f out* **100/1**

0600 **9** *3 1/2* **Petite Paramour (IRE)**[30] 5749 4-8-13 **65**..................... AdamKirby(5) 6 36
(Miss Gay Kelleway) *trckd ldr tl wknd over 2f out* **50/1**

2000 **10** *9* **Noble Mind**[6] 3804 4-9-2 **63**...(v1) SteveDrowne 8 20
(P G Murphy) *trckd ldrs tl wknd over 3f out* **40/1**

6000 **11** *2 1/2* **Mi Odds**[28] 5807 9-9-2 **63**.. PhillipMakin 12 16
(Mrs N Macauley) *mid-div: rdn over 3f out: sn btn* **16/1**

3400 **12** *23* **Don Pasquale**[19] 5990 3-8-9 **65**...............................(vt) RobertMiles(3) 10 —
(J T Stimpson) *slowly away: a bhd* **33/1**

2m 39.86s (-2.56) **Going Correction** -0.20s/f (Stan)
WFA 3 from 4yo+ 6lb **12** Ran SP% **116.5**

Speed ratings (Par 101):100,99,98,97,95 93,93,86,84,78 76,61

CSF £15.87 CT £48.94 TOTE £4.30: £1.50, £2.10, £1.90; EX 12.00.

Owner M J Dawson **Bred** Burton Agnes Stud Co Ltd **Trained** Middleham Moor, N Yorks

FOCUS

A decent race that is likely to produce winners and the form looks straightforward rated through the placed horses.

Don Pasquale Official explanation: jockey said gelding had a breathing problem

6284 TEXT "BETDIRECT" TO 88600 NOVICE STKS — 7f 32y(P)

3:40 (3:42) (Class 5) 2-Y-O **£3,500** (£1,041; £520; £259) **Stalls** High

Form RPR

032 **1** **Bomber Command (USA)**[14] 6068 2-8-12 .... EddieAhern 6 78
(J W Hills) *trckd ldr: led appr fnl f: drvn out* **2/1**[1]

30 **2** *1 1/2* **Dean's Yard**[77] 4634 2-8-12 .... JamieSpencer 4 74
(Sir Michael Stoute) *sn in tch: rdn and hung lft ins fnl f: r.o to go 2nd nr fin* **2/1**[1]

1505 **3** *1* **Porters (USA)**[49] 5367 2-9-5 83... DaneO'Neill 2 79
(R Hannon) *trckd ldr: led over 2f out: hdd appr fnl f: kpt on but lost 2nd nr fin* **9/1**[3]

06 **4** *5* **Light Mozart**[11] 6122 2-8-7 .... FrancisNorton 8 54
(C E Brittain) *bhd: kpt on past btn horses fr over 1f out* **50/1**

100 **5** *2 1/2* **Certain Circles (USA)**[37] 5613 2-9-0 79............................ MartinDwyer 5 55
(A M Balding) *a bhd* **10/3**[2]

0064 **6** *2* **Tour D'Amour (IRE)**[29] 5761 2-8-11 66........................... MickyFenton 1 47
(Stef Liddiard) *led tl hdd over 2f out: wkng whn hmpd on ins sn after* **25/1**

1300 **7** *2 1/2* **Luna Landing**[51] 5289 2-9-0 76.. DaleGibson 3 44
(Jedd O'Keeffe) *prom on outside tl wknd sn after 1/2-way* **20/1**

0 **8** *3/4* **Murrumbidgee (IRE)**[11] 6123 2-8-12 .... SteveDrowne 7 40
(J W Hills) *racd wd: sn bhd* **50/1**

1m 29.24s (-1.16) **Going Correction** -0.20s/f (Stan) **8** Ran SP% **112.3**

Speed ratings (Par 96):98,96,95,89,86 84,81,80

CSF £5.70 TOTE £2.50: £1.10, £1.10, £1.80; EX 7.40.

Owner G Woodward **Bred** J B Feins **Trained** Upper Lambourn, Berks

FOCUS

Fair form and basically sound, and the winner looks a nice prospect for three-year-old handicaps.

NOTEBOOK

Bomber Command(USA), who twice ran well in defeat on the Lingfield Polytrack last month, was ideally positioned throughout and he was always holding he reluctant runner up on the run-in. He is clearly a decent sort and will reportedly be put away now until next season. (op 9-4 tchd 15-8)

Dean's Yard bounced back from a disappointing effort at Leicester (softish ground), but he looked far from keen to go by under pressure and was comfortably held. He undoubtedly has a race in him, but is one to tread carefully with. (tchd 9-4)

Porters(USA) kept battling away, but his winning chance had gone as they raced inside the final furlong. He has not really built on his Newmarket maiden win, but seems to be holding his form well enough. (op 7-1)

Light Mozart plugged on late to claim a never-nearer fourth and is now qualified for a handicap mark, a sphere she should do well in. (op 33-1)

Certain Circles(USA) was back down to a more realistic level having contested Listed races on both starts since winning his maiden, but he proved most disappointing and never featured. He has done little to warrant his rating of 79 and will continue to struggle. (op 4-1 tchd 9-2)

6285 BET DIRECT FREEPHONE 0800 211 222 H'CAP — 2m 119y(P)

4:15 (4:15) (Class 4) (0-85,91) 3-Y-O+ **£5,704** (£1,697; £848; £423) **Stalls** Low

Form RPR

021 **1** **Monte Cristo (FR)**[26] 5837 7-8-7 **66** oh4..........................(v) ChrisCatlin 9 73
(Mrs L C Taylor) *trckd ldr: led 1/2-way: rdn over 2f out: kpt on u.p* **12/1**

2010 **2** *3/4* **Annambo**[93] 4159 5-9-2 **75**... DaneO'Neill 7 81
(D Morris) *a in tch: wnt 2nd wl over 1f out: no imp fnl f* **16/1**

2060 **3** *5* **Night Sight (USA)**[33] 4954 8-8-4 **66** oh4...........(b) RichardThomas(3) 12 67+
(Mrs S Lamyman) *s.i.s: hdwy on outside whn hmpd over 2f out: kpt one one pce* **25/1**

1541 **4** *1 3/4* **Ellina**[28] 5807 4-8-12 **71**.. JimmyQuinn 6 70
(J Pearce) *mid-div whn rdn over 3f out: wknd over 2f out* **3/1**[1]

330- **5** *1 1/2* **Polar Dancer**[22] 4-8-9 **68** oh7 ow2... NCallan 8 65
(H Steinmetz, Germany) *led: hdd 1/2-way: rdn over 2f out: sn wknd* **14/1**

/500 **B** **Tender Trap (IRE)**[124] 3247 7-9-9 **82**................................. IanMongan 1 —
(T G Mills) *mid-div whn b.d over 2f out* **16/1**

1041 **B** **Garden Society (IRE)**[8] 6179 8-9-13 **91** 6ex.................. AdamKirby(5) 4 —
(T T Clement) *hld up: mid-div whn b.d over 2f out* **7/2**[2]

0600 **B** **Come What July (IRE)**[29] 5770 4-9-10 **83**........................ PhillipMakin 2 —
(Mrs N Macauley) *bhd whn hmpd and b.d over 2f out* **25/1**

4100 **B** **Beauchamp Trump**[11] 6127 3-8-0 **68** ow1...............(bt) FrancisNorton 10 —
(G A Butler) *hld up in rr: no hdwy whn b.d over 2f out* **7/1**

0300 **U** **Wotchalike (IRE)**[37] 5610 3-8-9 **77**...................................... ShaneKelly 5 —
(R J Price) *mid-div: no hdwy whn hmpd on ins and uns rdr over 2f out* **33/1**

0213 **F** **Skye's Folly (USA)**[17] 6012 5-9-3 **76**................................ MickyFenton 3 —
(Mrs P Sly) *a racing in tch tl broke leg and fell over 2f out: dead* **9/2**[3]

6604 **U** **Templet (USA)**[9] 6141 5-8-13 **72**..............................(b) DerekMcGaffin 11 —
(W G Harrison) *in rr: hdwy over 4f out: in tch whn hmpd and uns rdr over over 2f out* **33/1**

3m 42.08s (-1.05) **Going Correction** -0.20s/f (Stan)
WFA 3 from 4yo+ 9lb **12** Ran SP% **117.6**

Speed ratings (Par 105):94,93,91,90,89 —,—,—,—,— —,—

CSF £178.73 CT £4619.74 TOTE £12.30: £3.60, £4.20, £7.80; EX 159.40 Trifecta £601.50 Part won. Pool: £847.24 - 0.10 winning tickets..

Owner Mrs L C Taylor **Bred** C Cohen **Trained** Upper Lambourn, Berks

■ Incredibly none of the seven jockeys involved in the spectacular pile-up on the home bend was seriously injured.

FOCUS

Just as the pace began to increase on the final bend, Sky's Folly broke a leg and caused serious trouble in behind as she fell - six jockeys parted company with their mounts in the resulting pile-up. That left just five or the original 12 to fight out the finish and the form, rated through the second, is obviously seriously devalued.

6286 IN RUNNING TONIGHT ON SKYTEXT 293 H'CAP (DIV I) — 1m 1f 103y(P)

4:45 (5:07) (Class 6) (0-58,58) 3-Y-O+ **£2,581** (£762; £381) **Stalls** Low

Form RPR

2432 **1** **Qualitair Wings**[21] 5940 6-8-12 **54**................................. DerekMcGaffin 4 61+
(J Hetherton) *hld up in rr tl gd hdwy over 1f out: r.o strly to ld wl ins fnl f* **9/2**[2]

2010 **2** *1 1/2* **Stevedore (IRE)**[29] 5758 4-9-1 **57**... NCallan 11 61
(J R Boyle) *trckd ldr: led 6f out to 3f out: kpt on ins fnl f* **6/1**[3]

/000 **3** *nk* **Harare**[31] 5714 4-8-6 **55**... JamesDoyle(7) 6 59
(R J Price) *led tl hdd 6f out: styd prom and ev ch tl rdn andr rdr dropped whip ins fnl f* **50/1**

0030 **4** *1* **Hashima (USA)**[48] 5386 3-8-10 **55**................................... EddieAhern 13 57
(C E Brittain) *trckd ldrs: ev ch tl nt qckn ins fnl f* **25/1**

4101 **5** *hd* **Band**[77] 4647 5-9-2 **58**.. GrahamGibbons 2 60
(E S McMahon) *in tch tl rdn and one pce fnl f* **7/2**[1]

3124 **6** *1/2* **Zarova (IRE)**[46] 5423 3-8-11 **56**... DaleGibson 7 57+
(M W Easterby) *in rr tl hdwy over 1f out: r.o: nvr nrr* **11/1**

5466 **7** *1/2* **Prince Of Gold**[24] 5884 5-9-0 **56**..................................... GeorgeBaker 3 56
(R Hollinshead) *in tch: rdn over 3f out: one pce ins fnl 2f* **13/2**

2256 **8** *1 1/2* **Dara Mac**[91] 4213 6-8-11 **53**... VinceSlattery 1 50
(L P Grassick) *hld up in tch: no hdwy ins fnl 2f* **25/1**

3300 **9** *1* **Mobo-Baco**[8] 6177 8-8-12 **54**.. SteveDrowne 10 49
(R J Hodges) *in tch: rdn over 2f out: sn wknd* **12/1**

5040 **10** *1* **Shaheer (IRE)**[21] 5940 3-8-13 **58**... ChrisCatlin 5 51
(Mrs L J Mongan) *mid-div: wknd over 2f out* **33/1**

0206 **11** *shd* **Trevian**[8] 6177 4-8-12 **54**.. DaneO'Neill 8 47
(J M Bradley) *hld up: a in rr* **8/1**

6000 **12** *1 1/4* **Riska King**[28] 5794 5-8-10 **57**.................................(p) PatrickMathers(5) 12 48
(James Moffatt) *in tch tl wknd over 2f out* **25/1**

0000 **13** *hd* **Legacy (JPN)**[52] 5281 5-8-8 **55**.. AdamKirby(5) 9 45
(T T Clement) *slowly away: a bhd* **8/1**

2m 1.25s (-1.37) **Going Correction** -0.20s/f (Stan)
WFA 3 from 4yo+ 3lb **13** Ran SP% **122.7**

Speed ratings (Par 101):98,96,96,95,95 94,94,93,92,91 91,90,89

CSF £30.74 CT £1223.39 TOTE £7.30: £2.20, £3.40, £13.40; EX 37.10.

Owner PSB Holdings Ltd **Bred** C S Tateson **Trained** Norton, N Yorks

FOCUS

A moderate contest and the form is not that solid, but a decent effort by Qualitair Wings, who came from behind to win cosily.

6287 IN RUNNING TONIGHT ON SKYTEXT 293 H'CAP (DIV II) — 1m 1f 103y(P)

5:15 (5:35) (Class 6) (0-58,58) 3-Y-O+ **£2,574** (£760; £380) **Stalls** Low

Form RPR

0055 **1** **Western Roots**[56] 5176 4-9-2 **57**....................................... GeorgeBaker 11 67+
(M Appleby) *hld up in rr: hdwy on outside over 2f out led on bit appr fnl f: easily* **12/1**

0301 **2** *2 1/2* **Danzare**[35] 5670 3-9-0 **58**... ChrisCatlin 8 63
(Mrs A J Hamilton-Fairley) *led tl hdd appr fnl f: nt pce of wnr* **11/1**

0000 **3** *3/4* **Charnock Bates One (IRE)**[19] 5980 4-8-11 **52**........ GrahamGibbons 2 56
(J J Quinn) *mid-div: r.o appr fnl f: nvr nrr* **13/2**[3]

2440 **4** *1 1/4* **We'll Meet Again**[77] 4647 5-8-10 **54**........................... PaulMulrennan(3) 6 55
(M W Easterby) *in tch: rdn over 2f out: kpt on but nvr nr to chal* **12/1**

0600 **5** 1 1/2 **Sriology (IRE)**[5] 6231 4-8-6 54 ow1 ChrisCavanagh(7) 3 52
(G Prodromou) *s.i.s: in rr tl styd on appr fnl f: nvr nrr* **14/1**
1000 **6** shd **Lawaaheb (IRE)**[8] 6184 4-8-9 55 RoryMoore(5) 5 53
(B R Johnson) *trckd ldrs. 2nd over 4f out to 2f out: wknd appr fnl f* **9/1**
0402 **7** 1 **Baby Barry**[19] 5979 8-8-13 54 TonyHamilton 9 50
(R A Fahey) *racd wd: in tch tl wknd over 1f out* **9/2[1]**
2243 **8** 1 1/4 **Risk Free**[256] 475 8-8-12 53 (b) VinceSlattery 13 47
(P D Evans) *hld up: rdn and hdwy over 2f out: wknd over 1f out* **9/1**
6111 **9** 3/4 **Magic Warrior**[51] 5303 5-9-2 57 EddieAhern 12 49
(J C Fox) *hld up: hdwy on outside over 2f out: sn rdn and wknd over 1f out* **5/1[2]**
6205 **10** 1 1/2 **Colonel Bilko (IRE)**[25] 5281 3-9-0 58 SteveDrowne 4 48
(Miss S J Wilton) *mid-div: wknd over 2f out* **20/1**
0002 **11** 1 **Barons Spy (IRE)**[34] 5687 4-8-9 57 JamesDoyle(7) 1 45
(R J Price) *chsd ldrs: wkng whn n.m.r over 2f out* **9/1**
5030 **12** 8 **Artful Whisper (USA)**[71] 4794 3-8-13 57 DaneO'Neill 7 30
(M A Buckley) *mid-div whn hmpd over 2f out: no ch after* **16/1**
0000 **13** 10 **Fortiszamo**[7] 6202 3-9-0 58 (v[1]) MartinDwyer 10 12
(A W Carroll) *in tch: wkng whn n.m.r over 2f out* **40/1**

2m 0.69s (-1.93) **Going Correction** -0.20s/f (Stan)
WFA 3 from 4yo+ 3lb 13 Ran SP% **121.6**
Speed ratings (Par 101):100,97,97,96,94 94,93,92,91,90 89,82,73
CSF £140.21 CT £947.47 TOTE £15.10: £4.60, £3.50, £6.90; EX 184.60 Place 6 £152.05, Place 5 £78.87.
Owner Sarnian Racing **Bred** Stratford Place Stud **Trained** Shrewley, Warwicks

FOCUS
This looked marginally the better of the two divisions and Western Roots simply destroyed them. The form is best rated through the third.
Barons Spy(IRE) Official explanation: jockey said gelding was denied a clear run
T/Jkpt: Part won. £7,100.00 to a £1 stake. Pool: £10,000.00. 0.50 winning tickets. T/Plt: £166.20 to a £1 stake. Pool: £88,726.35. 389.65 winning tickets. T/Qpdt: £48.90 to a £1 stake. Pool: £7,623.20. 115.30 winning tickets. JS

6256 SOUTHWELL (L-H)
Tuesday, November 8

OFFICIAL GOING: Standard
The ground was described as 'the usual deep and slow'.
Wind: Fresh, half-against Weather: Fine

6288 FIRST PAST THE POST AT BETDIRECT MAIDEN CLAIMING STKS 5f (F)
1:20 (1:20) (Class 7) 3-Y-0+ **£1,395** (£412; £206) **Stalls** High

Form RPR
320 **1** **Rapid River**[29] 5793 3-8-4 56 EmmettStack(5) 5 62+
(P D Evans) *w ldr: led over 2f out: hrd rdn: drew clr ins last: eased towards fin* **11/10[1]**
0000 **2** 5 **Blendon Belle (FR)**[24] 5898 3-8-9 35 LPKeniry 2 45
(A G Newcombe) *dwlt: sn chsng ldrs: hung lft 2f out: kpt on: no ch w wnr* **50/1**
0003 **3** hd **Ben Casey**[38] 5618 3-9-0 55 (p) PaulEddery 6 49
(B Smart) *led tl over 2f out: kpt on same pce appr fnl f* **7/4[2]**
0004 **4** hd **Lady Hopeful (IRE)**[17] 6031 3-8-7 45 (b) RobbieFitzpatrick 7 41
(Peter Grayson) *dwlt: hdwy to chse ldrs over 2f out: kpt on ins last* **10/1[3]**
5500 **5** 3 **Palatine Dancer (IRE)**[3] 6256 3-8-7 40 (p) JimmyQuinn 1 31
(R W Price) *w ldrs: wknd over 1f out* **20/1**
0040 **6** 2 1/2 **Limited Magician**[80] 4564 4-8-9 30 MichaelTebbutt 8 25
(C Smith) *nvr wnt pce* **25/1**
0-06 **7** 5 **Old Harry**[30] 5766 5-9-0 35 StephenCarson 3 13
(E A Wheeler) *chsd ldrs: hung lft and lost pl 2f out* **20/1**
0206 **8** 2 1/2 **Rock Fever (IRE)**[17] 6035 3-8-4 45 (b) DuranFentiman(5) 4 —
(Peter Grayson) *s.i.s: a detached in last and sn rdn along* **12/1**

60.10 secs (-0.20) **Going Correction** -0.10s/f (Stan) 8 Ran SP% **116.1**
Speed ratings (Par 97):97,89,88,88,83 79,71,67
CSF £76.63 TOTE £2.00: £1.10, £6.60, £1.40; EX 63.10.
Owner Diamond Racing Ltd **Bred** Matthew Sharkey **Trained** Pandy, Abergavenny
■ This race was hand timed.
■ Stewards' Enquiry : Emmett Stack one-day ban: used whip with excessive frequency (Nov 19)

FOCUS
A weak maiden that looked a good opportunity for Rapid River and she made no mistake. The form looks poor and not that solid.
Rock Fever(IRE) Official explanation: jockey said filly was slowly away and never travelled

6289 NO 5P RULE 4'S AT BETDIRECT BANDED STKS 1m 4f (F)
1:50 (1:51) (Class 7) 3-Y-0+ **£1,446** (£427; £213) **Stalls** Low

Form RPR
1000 **1** **Jackie Kiely**[42] 5538 4-9-4 49 TonyCulhane 5 58
(P Howling) *hld up: hdwy to trck ldrs 8f out: led wl over 2f out: hrd rdn and hld on gamely* **5/1[2]**
3363 **2** 1/2 **Tharua (IRE)**[15] 6081 3-8-11 48 (p) BrianReilly 7 56
(Ernst Oertel) *mid-div: hdwy over 3f out: chal 1f out: no ex nr fin* **7/1[3]**
3030 **3** 6 **Staff Nurse (IRE)**[3] 6257 5-9-0 45 (b[1]) ChrisCatlin 13 44
(N Wilson) *mid-div: hdwy to chse ldrs over 3f out: one pce fnl f* **20/1**
0061 **4** 3/4 **Bongoali**[10] 6153 3-8-8 45 LisaJones 9 43
(Mrs C A Dunnett) *chsd ldrs: led 3f out: sn hdd: wknd appr fnl f* **10/1**
0406 **5** 1/2 **Sachin**[36] 5654 4-9-2 47 (p) PatCosgrave 4 44
(J R Boyle) *mid-div: stmbld bnd after 2f: styd on fnl 2f: nvr nr ldrs* **16/1**
4120 **6** 17 **Iamback**[10] 6152 5-8-10 46 (t) AdamKirby(5) 6 18
(Miss Gay Kelleway) *chsd ldrs: wknd fnl 2f* **11/1**
0602 **7** 10 **Bill Bennett (FR)**[10] 6152 4-9-2 47 GeorgeBaker 14 4
(J Jay) *sn bhd: drvn 7f out: nvr a factor* **5/2[1]**
5644 **8** 1/2 **Joey**[83] 4475 3-8-12 49 GrahamGibbons 2 5
(R Hollinshead) *chsd ldrs: sn drvn along: lost pl 3f out* **11/1**
1500 **9** 1 3/4 **Surdoue**[21] 5960 5-9-4 49 NCallan 3 2
(P Howling) *led tl 3f out: sn lost pl* **12/1**
0000 **10** 1/2 **Comical Errors (USA)**[37] 4885 3-8-6 50 RussellKennemore(7) 1 3
(P C Haslam) *chsd ldrs: sn drvn along: lost pl over 4f out* **8/1**
024 **11** 3/4 **Molly's Secret**[145] 2625 7-9-5 50 (p) JimmyQuinn 10 —
(Miss S J Wilton) *prom: lost pl over 3f out* **16/1**
100 **12** 6 **Miss Bear (IRE)**[21] 5959 3-8-13 50 PaulEddery 11 —
(B Smart) *s.i.s: sme hdwy on outside over 3f out: sn lost pl* **25/1**
0/00 **13** 3 **Protagonist**[21] 5959 7-8-12 50 TomMessenger(7) 8 —
(B N Pollock) *sn bhd: detached 7f out: t.o 5f out* **66/1**
4000 **14** 1/2 **Game Guru**[10] 6151 6-8-11 47 PatrickMathers(5) 12 —
(M J Attwater) *rr-div: sn drvn along: t.o 4f out* **20/1**

2m 40.96s (-1.13) **Going Correction** -0.10s/f (Stan)
WFA 3 from 4yo+ 6lb 14 Ran SP% **128.9**
Speed ratings (Par 97):99,98,94,94,93 82,75,75,74,74 73,69,67,67
CSF £41.27 TOTE £4.70: £2.10, £3.90, £8.30; EX 73.70.
Owner P S J Croft **Bred** Mrs M Chaworth Musters **Trained** Newmarket, Suffolk

FOCUS
An above-average contest for the grade, rated positively through the second. The first five finished a long way clear, nothing making any serious inroads from off the pace.
Bill Bennett(FR) Official explanation: jockey said gelding never travelled
Surdoue Official explanation: jockey said gelding had no more to give
Game Guru Official explanation: jockey said gelding never travelled

6290 BETDIRECT.CO.UK MAIDEN AUCTION STKS 6f (F)
2:20 (2:22) (Class 7) 2-Y-O **£1,423** (£420; £210) **Stalls** Low

Form RPR
3602 **1** **The City Kid (IRE)**[6] 6224 2-8-4 72 (v) JohnEgan 11 75+
(P D Evans) *trckd ldrs: led over 2f out: rdn: hung lft and clr over 1f out: eased fnl strides* **7/4[1]**
554 **2** 9 **Lasting Love**[21] 5955 2-8-6 60 ow1 NCallan 3 50
(K A Ryan) *led tl over 2f out: kpt on: no ch w wnr* **15/8[2]**
6600 **3** 2 **Miss Mujahid Times**[21] 5961 2-7-11 47 DuranFentiman(5) 12 40
(A D Brown) *chsd ldrs: edgd lft and one pce fnl 2f* **40/1**
5030 **4** nk **Crush On You**[74] 4734 2-8-2 48 PaulQuinn 10 39
(R Hollinshead) *chsd ldrs: outpcd over 2f out: kpt on wl fnl f* **16/1**
000 **5** 3 **Mythical River**[31] 5737 2-8-2 52 ChrisCatlin 4 30
(J J Quinn) *prom: outpcd over 4f out: kpt on one pce fnl 2f* **9/1**
0030 **6** 1 3/4 **Smoking Star**[15] 6077 2-8-3 58 StephenCarson 5 26
(C E Brittain) *outpcd and lost pl over 4f out: sn bhd: styd on fnl 2f* **13/2[3]**
7 2 1/2 **Pedlar Of Luck** 2-8-8 LPKeniry 6 23
(A G Newcombe) *s.v.s: t.o 4f out: sme hdwy fnl 2f* **20/1**
4000 **8** 3/4 **Spitzensparkes (IRE)**[17] 6030 2-8-6 45 JimmyQuinn 2 19
(J J Quinn) *s.i.s: nvr on terms* **16/1**
00 **9** 1/2 **Scattered Empire (IRE)**[17] 6030 2-8-9 RobbieFitzpatrick 9 21
(Peter Grayson) *trckd ldrs: lost pl 2f out* **80/1**
4000 **10** 1/2 **Little Whitesox**[17] 6030 2-8-5 45 MatthewHenry 7 15
(J Hetherton) *sn outpcd and in rr* **40/1**
0 **11** 5 **Polish Effigy**[29] 5801 2-8-11 PatCosgrave 8 6
(B W Duke) *chsd ldrs: outpcd over 3f out: hung rt and sn lost pl* **50/1**

1m 17.64s (0.74) **Going Correction** -0.10s/f (Stan) 11 Ran SP% **119.1**
Speed ratings (Par 90):91,79,76,75,71 69,66,65,64,63 57
CSF £5.07 TOTE £2.40: £1.10, £1.50, £9.30; EX 5.00.
Owner Mrs S J Lawrence **Bred** T B And Mrs T B Russell **Trained** Pandy, Abergavenny

FOCUS
The winner broke her duck in contemptuous style on her eighth career start but her first on the All-Weather. The form is not that strong behind the winner.

NOTEBOOK
The City Kid(IRE), drawn wide, was soon in the thick of the action towards the inner. Travelling best on her All-Weather debut, she went on and came right away, her rider leaving nothing to chance. She had a stone in hand judged on official ratings but clearly appreciated the track, a surface on which her dam also scored. (op 9-4)
Lasting Love, threatening a first success, was the danger to the winner on official ratings but it was soon clear that the only thing in doubt was the margin of defeat. (op 7-4 tchd 2-1)
Miss Mujahid Times, worst drawn and making her All-Weather bow, seemed to turn in an improved effort. (op 33-1)
Crush On You, absent since August and having her first try on an artificial surface, looks to be crying out for a stiffer test. (op 20-1)
Mythical River, absent for a month and making her All-Weather bow, and looks to need a mile. (op 8-1)
Smoking Star, well adrift turning in, stuck on in her own time and will appreciate a much stiffer test. (op 15-2 tchd 8-1)

6291 PRESS RED TO BET ON ITVI BANDED STKS 6f (F)
2:50 (2:52) (Class 7) 3-Y-O+ **£1,450** (£428; £214) **Stalls** Low

Form RPR
0002 **1** **Ace Club**[3] 6260 4-8-11 40 (b) TonyHamilton 7 51
(J Hetherton) *chsd ldrs: edgd rt and led over 1f out: drvn out* **13/2[3]**
4244 **2** 2 **Jacks Delight**[33] 5702 5-8-11 40 SamHitchcott 13 45
(C N Kellett) *prom: swtchd lft 1f out: kpt on: no real imp* **11/2[2]**
4060 **3** 1 1/4 **Westborough (IRE)**[21] 5966 4-8-11 40 KimTinkler 5 41
(N Tinkler) *w ldr: led over 2f out: hdd over 1f out: no ex* **8/1**
0030 **4** 1/2 **Lizzie Rocket**[26] 5858 5-8-9 40 ow5 (b[1]) JamesO'Reilly(7) 3 45
(J O'Reilly) *s.i.s: hdwy 3f out: kpt on same pce appr fnl f* **20/1**
6150 **5** hd **Sergeant Slipper**[33] 5706 8-8-11 40 (v) RobbieFitzpatrick 1 39
(C Smith) *sn bhd: edgd rt and hdwy over 2f out: styd on fnl f* **16/1**
5300 **6** 2 **Sam The Sorcerer**[241] 605 4-8-11 35 DarrenWilliams 11 33
(J R Norton) *prom: effrt over 2f out: one pce* **40/1**
0500 **7** 1/2 **Forzenuff**[66] 4932 4-8-11 40 (vt) PatCosgrave 10 32
(J R Boyle) *chsd ldrs: one pce fnl 2f* **10/1**
0005 **8** nk **Jakeal (IRE)**[33] 5702 6-8-4 35 MichaelJStainton(7) 6 31
(R M Whitaker) *chsd ldrs: one pce fnl 2f* **11/1**
0030 **9** 3 **Super Canyon**[3] 6260 7-8-11 40 (t) MichaelTebbutt 8 22
(J Pearce) *bhd: sme hdwy over 2f out: nvr on terms* **10/1**
6000 **10** hd **Laurel Dawn**[146] 2583 7-8-11 40 (e) PaulEddery 12 21
(C N Kellett) *s.i.s: nvr on terms* **25/1**
0006 **11** 1/2 **Cleveland Way**[168] 1982 5-8-11 40 (v) FergalLynch 4 20
(D Carroll) *mde most tl hdd & wknd over 2f out* **11/1**
0000 **12** 1 1/2 **Marabar**[28] 5828 7-8-6 40 (b) DuranFentiman(5) 9 15
(D W Chapman) *a in rr* **11/1**
0025 **13** 1/2 **Faithisflying**[26] 5856 3-8-11 40 (b) TonyCulhane 2 14
(D W Chapman) *chsd ldrs: hrd drvn over 3f out: lost pl 2f out* **12/1**
0030 **14** 7 **Secret Vision (USA)**[10] 6155 4-8-11 40 (e[1]) ChrisCatlin 14 —
(R M H Cowell) *fractious in stalls: s.s: sme hdwy on outer over 3f out: lost pl over 2f out: eased whn no ch ins last* **5/1[1]**

1m 17.46s (0.56) **Going Correction** -0.10s/f (Stan) 14 Ran SP% **124.3**
Speed ratings (Par 97):92,89,87,87,86 84,83,83,79,78 78,76,75,66
CSF £42.63 TOTE £7.70: £2.80, £2.50, £3.40; EX 37.30.
Owner K C West **Bred** Helescane Stud **Trained** Norton, N Yorks

FOCUS
A poor event but the form makes sense rated through the runner-up and fourth and is average for the grade.
Secret Vision(USA) Official explanation: jockey said filly panicked in stalls, missed break, and was unable to get into race

The Form Book, Raceform Ltd, Compton, RG20 6NL

6292 **ALLIANCE & LEICESTER PREMIER CURRENT ACCOUNT BANDED STKS** **7f (F)**
3:20 (3:22) (Class 7) 3-Y-O+ **£1,457** (£430; £215) **Stalls** Low

Form RPR
005 1 **Speakerboxxx**[30] 5766 3-9-4 50 NCallan 11 60
(P F I Cole) *sn chsng ldrs: led and hung lft 3f out: led appr fnl f: styd on wl* **8/1**[3]
0020 2 1 1/4 **Blushing Russian (IRE)**[15] 6078 3-8-8 47 GaryBartley[(7)] 13 54
(P C Haslam) *hld up: hdwy 3f out: sn chalng: no ex fnl f* **8/1**[3]
4211 3 hd **Doctor Dennis (IRE)**[3] 6261 8-9-7 46 (v) MichaelTebbutt 1 58
(J Pearce) *s.i.s: bhd tl hdwy on outer over 2f out: styd on wl ins last: nt quite rch ldrs* **9/4**[1]
0400 4 3 **Hollow Jo**[72] 4792 5-9-5 50 FergalLynch 7 49
(J R Jenkins) *sltly hmpd sn after s: sn chsng ldrs: led over 2f out: hdd appr fnl f: sn wknd* **8/1**[3]
0 5 3 1/2 **Glenviews Oldport (USA)**[15] 6070 3-9-4 50 RobbieFitzpatrick 5 40
(Peter Grayson) *mid-div: sn drvn along: kpt on fnl 2f: nvr a threat* **80/1**
2432 6 1 1/4 **Show Me The Lolly (FR)**[24] 5895 5-9-0 50 (v[1]) AdamKirby[(5)] 2 36
(P J McBride) *sn in rr: kpt on fnl 2f: nvr on terms* **3/1**[2]
0000 7 1/2 **Pawn In Life (IRE)**[21] 5960 7-9-2 47 (v) TonyCulhane 6 32
(M J Polglase) *mid-div: rdn over 3f out: nvr a threat* **25/1**
4000 8 1 1/2 **Queenstown (IRE)**[8] 5587 4-9-5 50 JohnEgan 3 31
(B A Pearce) *sn bhd: nvr a factor* **12/1**
0-06 9 shd **Phlaunt**[22] 5950 3-9-4 50 StephenCarson 10 31
(R F Johnson Houghton) *in tch: lost pl over 4f out: n.d after* **20/1**
0000 10 1 3/4 **Mytton's Dream**[21] 5957 3-9-4 50 ChrisCatlin 12 26
(R Brotherton) *chsd ldrs: lost pl over 2f out* **66/1**
0346 11 3 **Treble Seven (USA)**[15] 6082 3-9-1 47 JimmyQuinn 4 16
(C E Brittain) *uns rdr gng to s: prom: lost pl over 4f out* **8/1**[3]
2000 12 2 1/2 **Sharoura**[3] 6261 9-9-4 49 (p) TonyHamilton 8 11
(R A Fahey) *chsd ldrs: lost pl over 2f out* **16/1**
3000 13 7 **Hugo The Boss (IRE)**[198] 1231 3-9-4 50 (v) DarrenWilliams 14 —
(J R Boyle) *led tl 3f out: wknd over 1f out: sn eased* **20/1**

1m 31.4s (0.60) **Going Correction** -0.10s/f (Stan)
WFA 3 from 4yo+ 1lb 13 Ran SP% **129.9**
Speed ratings (Par 97):92,90,90,86,82 81,80,79,79,77 73,70,62
CSF £73.12 TOTE £11.00: £3.40, £3.40, £1.30; EX 62.10.
Owner Christopher Wright & W H Carson **Bred** Minster Enterprises Ltd **Trained** Whatcombe, Oxon

FOCUS
The form of the first three makes the form appear solid and the unexposed winner may be capable of better.
Show Me The Lolly(FR) Official explanation: trainer said mare was unsuited by fibresand

6293 **BET DIRECT ON SKY ACTIVE TRI-BANDED STKS** **1m (F)**
3:50 (3:50) (Class 7) 3-Y-O **£1,412** (£417; £208) **Stalls** Low

Form RPR
0000 1 **Legal Lover (IRE)**[21] 5957 3-8-12 45 GrahamGibbons 5 53
(R Hollinshead) *w ldrs: led over 4f out: styd on u.p fnl 2f: hld on wl* **12/1**
4030 2 3/4 **Starcross Maid**[20] 5979 3-8-12 45 MichaelTebbutt 8 52
(J F Coupland) *trckd ldrs: chal over 1f out: no ex ins last* **10/1**
0635 3 1 3/4 **Canary Dancer**[15] 6069 3-8-2 40 RoryMoore[(5)] 4 43
(B A Pearce) *led 1f: chsd ldrs: chal 3f out: edgd rt and nt qckn fnl f* **14/1**
0003 4 nk **Alcott (FR)**[10] 6153 3-8-12 45 (t) GeorgeBaker 11 47
(J Jay) *trckd ldrs on outer: effrt 2f out: sn rdn: styd on same pce fnl f* **7/2**[1]
0044 5 10 **Preskani**[10] 6154 3-7-11 35 (p) DuranFentiman[(5)] 1 17
(Mrs N Macauley) *chsd ldrs: wknd fnl 2f* **18/1**
6621 6 1 1/4 **Venetian Princess (IRE)**[3] 6258 3-9-4 45 6ex TonyCulhane 14 31
(P Howling) *s.i.s: in rr tl sme hdwy fnl 2f: nvr on terms* **4/1**[2]
1500 7 10 **Sunny Times (IRE)**[21] 5963 3-8-12 45 NCallan 13 5
(J M P Eustace) *chsd ldrs: rdn 3f out: lost pl over 1f out* **5/1**[3]
0056 8 1 **Polesworth**[10] 6154 3-8-12 45 (b) SamHitchcott 12 3
(C N Kellett) *mid-div: effrt 3f out: sn wknd* **18/1**
0000 9 2 1/2 **Saffa Garden (IRE)**[3] 6256 3-8-12 45 StephenCarson 9 —
(C E Brittain) *s.i.s: a bhd: detached 3f out* **50/1**
0000 10 1 **Choreographic (IRE)**[10] 6154 3-8-12 45 (p) TonyHamilton 2 —
(R A Fahey) *led after 1f: rdn and hdd over 4f out: lost pl over 2f out* **28/1**
0532 11 5 **Ginger Cookie**[10] 6154 3-8-7 40 PaulEddery 10 —
(B Smart) *s.i.s: sme hdwy on outer over 4f out: lost pl 3f out* **5/1**[3]
-306 12 3 1/2 **Lighthorne Lad**[56] 5208 3-8-12 45 FergalLynch 6 —
(J R Jenkins) *s.i.s: a in rr* **40/1**

1m 43.91s (-0.69) **Going Correction** -0.10s/f (Stan) 12 Ran SP% **117.4**
Speed ratings (Par 96):99,98,96,96,86 84,74,73,71,70 65,61
CSF £123.66 TOTE £17.50: £4.70, £3.60, £4.70; EX 174.60 Place 6 £133.16, Place 5 £108.93.
Owner Tim Leadbeater **Bred** Ballyhane Stud **Trained** Upper Longdon, Staffs

FOCUS
Ordinary form with only three previous winners in the line-up and the first four a long way clear. The runner-up sets the standard.
Venetian Princess(IRE) Official explanation: trainer said filly resented the kick back; jockey said filly was outpaced throughout
Sunny Times(IRE) Official explanation: jockey said filly had no more to give
Polesworth Official explanation: jockey said filly failed to stay 8f
T/Plt: £431.10 to a £1 stake. Pool: £39,305.05. 66.55 winning tickets. T/Qpdt: £110.90 to a £1 stake. Pool: £3,538.30. 23.60 winning tickets. WG

6280 WOLVERHAMPTON (A.W) (L-H)
Wednesday, November 9

OFFICIAL GOING: Standard
Wind: Moderate, half-behind

6294 **FIRST PAST THE POST AT BET DIRECT CLAIMING STKS** **5f 20y(P)**
1:20 (1:21) (Class 6) 3-Y-O+ **£2,921** (£862; £431) **Stalls** Low

Form RPR
0056 1 **He's A Rocket (IRE)**[21] 5975 4-8-9 52 (b) JohnEgan 4 66
(K R Burke) *mde all: rdn over 1f out: kpt up to work fnl f* **4/1**[2]
0U46 2 1/2 **Sir Sandrovitch (IRE)**[4] 6264 9-8-7 62 (v[1]) MartinDwyer 1 62+
(R A Fahey) *s.i.s: sn mid-div: rdn 1/2-way: hdwy to chse wnr over 1f out: r.o* **5/1**[3]
2030 3 1 **Imperium**[26] 5869 4-8-7 57 (p) NickyMackay 10 59
(Stef Liddiard) *slowly away: hdwy over 1f out: r.o wl fnl f: nvr nrr* **11/1**
4400 4 4 **Byo (IRE)**[4] 6264 7-9-5 60 SteveDrowne 2 56
(P Howling) *chsd ldrs tl rdn and wknd fnl f* **25/1**
0000 5 3/4 **Blue Maeve**[4] 6264 5-9-5 62 DaneO'Neill 9 54
(A D Brown) *chsd wnr tl rdn and wknd over 1f out* **33/1**
5003 6 1/2 **Red Sovereign**[4] 6264 4-8-6 67 RobbieFitzpatrick 3 39
(D G Bridgwater) *chsd ldrs tl wknd over 1f out* **7/2**[1]
3555 7 1 1/2 **Nisr**[49] 5413 8-8-8 61 (t) RonanKeogh[(7)] 8 42
(Miss Gay Kelleway) *bhd: rdn 1/2-way: nvr on terms* **12/1**
5031 8 1 1/2 **On The Trail**[18] 6035 8-8-5 46 EddieAhern 5 27
(D W Chapman) *in tch tl rdn and wknd over 1f out* **8/1**
U000 9 nk **Global Achiever**[53] 5327 4-8-12 61 (p) DeanWilliams[(7)] 12 40
(G C H Chung) *hld up: a in rr* **20/1**
6000 10 3/4 **Almaty Express**[4] 6264 3-8-11 61 (p) AdrianMcCarthy 7 29
(J R Weymes) *bhd: effrt 1/2-way: nvr on terms* **7/1**
3660 11 2 1/2 **Exit Smiling**[188] 1480 3-9-5 61 PaulEddery 13 28
(G C H Chung) *stdd and swtchd lft s: a bhd* **50/1**
6530 12 3 1/2 **Malahide Express (IRE)**[77] 4679 5-9-9 54 JimmyQuinn 11 20
(E J Alston) *slowly away: a struggling in rr* **25/1**

61.11 secs (-1.71) **Going Correction** -0.35s/f (Stan) 12 Ran SP% **115.9**
Speed ratings (Par 101):99,98,96,90,89 88,85,83,82,81 77,72
CSF £22.02 TOTE £4.60: £1.80, £2.50, £4.10; EX 26.40.
Owner Keelings 10 **Bred** Lemongrove Stud **Trained** Middleham Moor, N Yorks

FOCUS
Fast and furious stuff as one has come to expect of races around here over the minimum trip. An ordinary claimer in which the winner got the run of the race, but the placed horses sugges the form is pretty solid for the grade.
Exit Smiling Official explanation: jockey said gelding reared as stalls opened

6295 **NO 5P RULE 4'S AT BET DIRECT (S) STKS** **5f 216y(P)**
1:50 (2:01) (Class 6) 2-Y-O **£2,600** (£767; £384) **Stalls** Low

Form RPR
1 1 **Mr Rigsby**[53] 5323 2-9-2 FergalLynch 2 66
(P Howling) *trckd ldr: led 1/2-way: edgd rt and rdn out fnl f* **13/8**[1]
5542 2 2 1/2 **Lasting Love**[1] 6290 2-8-7 60 ow1 NCallan 1 50
(K A Ryan) *led to 1/2-way: kpt on u.p fnl f* **3/1**[2]
5250 3 1/2 **Phinerine**[69] 4886 2-8-11 63 RobbieFitzpatrick 12 52
(Peter Grayson) *towards rr: hdwy over 2f out: hung rt but kpt on fnl f* **16/1**
5066 4 1 **Mad Professor (IRE)**[25] 5886 2-8-11 68 (b) AdrianMcCarthy 4 49
(P W Chapple-Hyam) *sn chsd ldrs: kpt on one pce fnl f* **10/1**
5510 5 hd **Magnolia Blossom**[33] 5716 2-8-11 62 TonyHamilton 7 48
(R A Fahey) *in tch: rdn 1/2-way: kpt on one pce fnl f* **6/1**
3365 6 7 **Anemone**[9] 6198 2-8-6 59 (b[1]) FrankieMcDonald 11 22
(B J Meehan) *sn chsd ldrs: wknd over 1f out* **14/1**
0650 7 1 **Teddy Monty (IRE)**[23] 5944 2-8-11 60 MartinDwyer 6 24
(M Quinn) *outpcd: nvr on terms* **25/1**
00 8 3/4 **My Reflection**[7] 6225 2-8-6 (v[1]) PatrickMathers[(5)] 9 22
(D Shaw) *v.s.a: a bhd* **66/1**
1356 9 2 1/2 **Half Pint Bill**[15] 6098 2-8-11 58 MarcHalford[(5)] 10 20
(W G M Turner) *mid-div: wl bhd fnl 2f* **20/1**
5506 10 2 **Papaspyros (IRE)**[9] 6197 2-8-11 60 EddieAhern 8 9
(J J Quinn) *in tch: rdn 1/2-way: sn bhd* **4/1**[3]
05 11 2 **Key Of Magic (IRE)**[117] 3496 2-8-11 MichaelTebbutt 3 3
(Peter Grayson) *outpcd thrght* **66/1**

1m 15.09s (-0.72) **Going Correction** -0.35s/f (Stan) 11 Ran SP% **130.6**
Speed ratings (Par 94):90,86,86,84,84 75,73,72,69,66 64
CSF £7.21 TOTE £3.20: £1.10, £1.80, £4.50; EX 9.50.The winner was bought in for 9,500gns. Lasting Love was claimed by Mr C. R. Dore for £6,000.
Owner Mark Entwistle **Bred** P Balding **Trained** Newmarket, Suffolk

FOCUS
Well clear on adjusted official ratings, Figaro Flyer looked to hold outstanding claims in this seller, but he was withdrawn less than half an hour before the race took place having apparently got upset on the way to the course, which left the way clear for his stable-companion Mr Rigsby. The form looks very strong for the grade.

NOTEBOOK
Mr Rigsby was catapulted into favouritism when his stablemate Figaro Flyer was withdrawn in the minutes before the race. A winner on his only previous start in similar grade over seven furlongs here in September, he showed good speed from the gate and, in a race in which very few got competitive, he asserted on the final bend and drew clear in the straight. (op 7-4 tchd 6-4, 15-8 and 2-1 in places)
Lasting Love had finished runner-up, albeit well held, in a maiden at Southwell 24 hours earlier and was well drawn to adopt her favoured front-running tactics on her first encounter with Polytrack. She ran well, showing plenty of early pace, but once again had to settle for second as the winner saw the trip out better. (tchd 7-2)
Phinerine was drawn out in stall 12 but had managed to get over to the rail by the time they got to the bend out of the back straight. Considering he has been running over five furlongs lately, he stayed on well in the straight. Official explanation: jockey said gelding hung right (op 25-1 tchd 33-1)
Mad Professor(IRE) did not find the re-application of headgear doing the trick on his first start on Polytrack. (op 12-1 tchd 9-1)
Magnolia Blossom lost her good early position as they went to the bend out of the back straight and struggled to get back into it thereafter. (op 7-1 tchd 9-1)

6296 **WEATHERBYS BANK NURSERY (DIV I)** **5f 20y(P)**
2:20 (2:26) (Class 5) (0-75,72) 2-Y-O **£3,746** (£1,114; £557; £278) **Stalls** Low

Form RPR
640 1 **Magidene**[212] 961 2-8-8 **59** ow1 SteveDrowne 1 66
(J R Best) *mid-div: hdwy on ins to chse ldrs 2f out: rdn and r.o to ld ins fnl f: readily* **8/1**[3]
5353 2 2 **Don't Tell Sue**[7] 6226 2-9-5 **70** MichaelHills 8 70
(B W Hills) *trckd ldr 1/2-way: led over 1f out: rdn and hdd ins fnl f: nt pce of wnr* **5/2**[1]
6023 3 3/4 **Canina**[7] 6225 2-9-1 **66** NCallan 4 63
(Ms Deborah J Evans) *chsd ldrs: rdn and swtchd lft ent fnl f: r.o* **8/1**[3]
0342 4 3/4 **Whipper In**[30] 5791 2-8-3 **54** MartinDwyer 6 49
(P C Haslam) *led tl hdd over 1f out: edgd rt ins fnl f* **5/2**[1]
4200 5 3/4 **Succeed (IRE)**[31] 5755 2-8-7 **63** RichardKingscote[(5)] 13 55
(Mrs H Sweeting) *raced wd and effrt on outside 2f out: kpt on one pce fnl f* **10/1**
4600 6 3/4 **Alugat (IRE)**[30] 5791 2-9-0 **70** GregFairley[(5)] 12 59
(Mrs A Duffield) *mid-div: r.o fnl f but nvr nr to chal* **14/1**
5563 7 1/2 **First Byte**[76] 4696 2-8-5 **56** (b[1]) JimmyQuinn 5 43
(Miss D A McHale) *slowly away: a towards rr* **25/1**
0100 8 3/4 **Abbielou**[105] 3857 2-9-7 **72** (p) KFallon 7 57
(B J Meehan) *trckd ldr to 1/2-way: wknd over 1f out* **15/2**[2]
1050 9 5 **First Among Equals**[51] 5363 2-8-9 **60** PaulFitzsimons 9 27
(Miss J R Tooth) *in tch for 3f* **40/1**
0100 10 6 **Miss Lovat**[31] 5755 2-9-1 **66** EddieAhern 3 11
(A Bailey) *a struggling in rr* **14/1**

62.16 secs (-0.66) **Going Correction** -0.35s/f (Stan) 10 Ran SP% **119.8**
Speed ratings (Par 96):91,87,86,85,84 83,82,81,73,63
CSF £29.13 CT £176.61 TOTE £10.20: £3.00, £1.80, £2.50; EX 40.60.

Owner The Little Tiny Partnership **Bred** Simon Tindall **Trained** Hucking, Kent

FOCUS

This looked a fairly open nursery and the winner was the least exposed in the field. This is solid enough form if not that special.

NOTEBOOK

Magidene, who was well drawn, was the least exposed in the line-up. He had looked far from straightforward in his three starts in maiden company but clearly connections were expecting better from him on his handicap debut and return from a seven-month absence as he was well supported in the market. Tracking the leader on the rail in the early stages, he picked up well in the straight and ran out a clear winner. There should be more to come from him. (op 7-1)

Don't Tell Sue has been in good form on turf lately and did not look badly rated for his debut on the All-Weather. He ran a sound race in second and gives the form a solid look. (op 11-4 tchd 3-1)

Canina did not get the best of runs as the field charged around the bend into the straight, and she may have given Don't Tell Sue more of a fight for second place with a smoother passage. (op 10-1)

Whipper In, runner-up in a soft-ground nursery at Ayr last time over six furlongs, was not found out for speed over this shorter trip. Indeed, he led them into the straight before giving best. (op 3-1)

Succeed(IRE) did not run badly given that she was stuck out wide most of the way. (op 11-1)

Alugat(IRE) was attempting the impossible in trying to make ground from off the pace.

First Byte Official explanation: jockey said filly suffered slight interference leaving stalls

6297 WEATHERBYS BANK NURSERY (DIV II) 5f 20y(P)

2:50 (2:51) (Class 5) (0-75,71) 2-Y-O £3,746 (£1,114; £557; £278) Stalls Low

Form RPR

600 1 **Stoneacre Lad (IRE)**[155] 2357 2-8-10 60 RobbieFitzpatrick 5 71+
(Peter Grayson) *mde all: clr over 1f out: unchal* **14/1**

3030 2 4 **Musical Romance (IRE)**[51] 5363 2-9-2 66 KFallon 1 63
(B J Meehan) *chsd ldrs: r.o to go 2nd wl ins fnl f* **7/2**[2]

0002 3 ½ **Amber Glory**[7] 6226 2-9-5 69 (b) NCallan 4 64
(K A Ryan) *trckd wnr: rdn over 1f out: one pce and lost 2nd wl ins fnl f* **2/1**[1]

2012 4 ¾ **Lucayos**[15] 6098 2-8-11 66 RichardKingscote(5) 7 58
(Mrs H Sweeting) *in tch: rdn and hung lft appr fnl f: one pce after* **5/1**[3]

0000 5 1 ¾ **Blue Minx (IRE)**[79] 4638 2-8-7 57 (b) JohnEgan 2 43
(J S Moore) *mid-div: r.o fnl f: nvr nr to chal* **20/1**

2100 6 ¾ **Young Flavio**[20] 5994 2-9-1 65 DaneO'Neill 3 48
(J M Bradley) *short of room sn after s: outpcd: kpt on fnl f: n.d* **10/1**

0001 7 3 **Soviet Legend (IRE)**[18] 6030 2-8-12 62 (b) TomEaves 6 34
(T J Etherington) *in tch: rdn 1/2-way: sn btn* **16/1**

6403 8 ½ **Signor Whippee**[18] 6030 2-8-3 58 PatrickMathers(5) 8 29
(A Berry) *sn outpcd* **40/1**

4400 9 nk **Hardy Norseman (IRE)**[42] 5540 2-9-7 71 (b) SteveDrowne 10 40
(W Jarvis) *racd wd: effrt on outside 2f out: nvr on terms* **9/1**

0500 10 1 ½ **Mytton's Pride**[46] 5466 2-8-13 70 MichaelJStainton(7) 9 34
(A Bailey) *mid-div: rdn 1/2-way: sn btn* **14/1**

4252 11 2 **Tombalina**[18] 6030 2-8-2 55 ow1 BenSwarbrick(3) 11 12
(J L Spearing) *in tch on outside for 2f: sn bhd* **14/1**

61.52 secs (-1.30) **Going Correction** -0.35s/f (Stan) 11 Ran SP% **124.4**

Speed ratings (Par 96):96,89,88,87,84 83,78,78,77,75 71

CSF £66.29 CT £147.07 TOTE £15.90: £4.80, £1.50, £2.10; EX 226.00 Trifecta £284.90 Part won. Pool: £401.30 - 0.10 winning tickets..

Owner Richard Teatum **Bred** Mrs Annie Hughes **Trained** Formby, Lancs

FOCUS

The quicker of the two divisions by 0.64sec once again the winner was the least exposed runner in the line-up. The form could rate higher but the placed horses have been rated slightly below their best.

NOTEBOOK

Stoneacre Lad(IRE), making his handicap debut having shown ability on only one of his three starts in maiden company, was the subject of some shrewd support in the market at big prices on his first run since May. Fast away from the gate, his rider was keen to grab the inside rail and that he did, before seeing off the attentions of Amber Glory and running out a most decisive winner. Connections will no doubt now be keen to get him out under a penalty as the Handicapper will not take kindly to this wide-margin success. (op 33-1)

Musical Romance(IRE) chased the pace and looked a danger on the turn into the straight, but she found it impossible to make up ground on the leader. There was nothing wrong with this effort, though. (op 4-1)

Amber Glory had won on her only previous start on the All-Weather on Fibresand and was ridden to have every chance, being up at the front from the start. She was unlucky to run into a winner who was very well handicapped. (op 15-8 tchd 9-4)

Lucayos has been in good form on turf this autumn but he struggled to negotiate the bend and perhaps he would be more at home at Southwell. Official explanation: jockey said colt hung right back straight and both ways home straight (op 6-1)

Blue Minx(IRE) won a seller over the course and distance in the spring but he struggled to go the early pace in this better contest and was checked slightly on the bend into the straight.

Young Flavio was always going to struggle after going into the first bend in last place. (op 14-1)

No Overtime(IRE) Official explanation: vet said filly was lame

6298 BETDIRECT.CO.UK MAIDEN STKS (DIV I) 7f 32y(P)

3:20 (3:23) (Class 5) 3-Y-O £3,044 (£905; £452; £226) Stalls High

Form RPR

5350 1 **Actuality**[59] 5157 3-9-0 62 MartinDwyer 2 79+
(M P Tregoning) *mde virually all: rdn clr over 1f out: edgd rt but r.o: eased nr fin* **4/1**[2]

-430 2 5 **Nazaaha (USA)**[32] 5734 3-8-9 65 LPKeniry 3 59
(A G Newcombe) *chsd ldrs: wnt 2nd over 2f out: nt pce of wnr fr over 1f out* **33/1**

353 3 1 ¼ **Chicken Soup**[57] 5204 3-8-11 63 DNolan(3) 8 61
(D Carroll) *chsd ldrs: outpcd 2f out: styd on fnl f* **4/1**[2]

0004 4 5 **Latin Express (IRE)**[16] 6069 3-9-0 60 KFallon 11 48
(W R Muir) *towards rr: styd on appr fnl f: nvr nr to chal* **14/1**

5 nk **The Rebound Kid** 3-9-0 NCallan 1 47
(G A Huffer) *s.i.s: sn prom: btn whn hung lft appr fnl f* **10/1**

3522 6 hd **Sincerely**[16] 6074 3-8-9 62 MichaelHills 5 41
(B W Hills) *prom on outside tl rdn and wknd over 1f out* **7/2**[1]

0400 7 2 **Lay A Whisper**[36] 5686 3-8-4 60 AdamKirby(5) 9 36
(C G Cox) *in tch tl wknd over 2f out* **13/2**[3]

5403 8 nk **Ringarooma**[22] 5964 3-8-9 56 OscarUrbina 10 35
(C N Allen) *a towards rr* **25/1**

0052 9 6 **Resistance Heroine**[50] 5387 3-8-9 62 SteveDrowne 4 20
(W Jarvis) *w wnr early: wknd wl over 1f out* **10/1**

020 10 6 **Beauchamp Tiger**[18] 6028 3-9-0 68 (t) JohnEgan 12 9
(G A Butler) *slowly away: a bhd* **13/2**[3]

0 11 3 ½ **Ernmoor**[36] 5693 3-9-0 TPQueally 7 —
(J R Best) *broke wl: lost pl sn after 1f: bhd after* **33/1**

1m 27.79s (-2.61) **Going Correction** -0.35s/f (Stan) 11 Ran SP% **123.5**

Speed ratings (Par 102):100,94,92,87,86 86,84,83,77,70 66

CSF £138.26 TOTE £5.50: £2.40, £7.90, £1.50; EX 145.70.

Owner Stanley J Sharp **Bred** Stanley J Sharp **Trained** Lambourn, Berks

■ Stewards' Enquiry : N Callan caution: careless riding

FOCUS

Yet again the place to be was at the front end in this ordinary maiden. The form is not easy to rate but perhaps the third is the best guide.

Beauchamp Tiger Official explanation: jockey said gelding moved badly throughout

6299 WEATHERBYS INSURANCE H'CAP 7f 32y(P)

3:50 (3:51) (Class 6) (0-55,55) 3-Y-O+ £2,888 (£852; £426) Stalls High

Form RPR

3046 1 **Sarraaf (IRE)**[25] 5893 9-9-0 55 TomEaves 6 65
(I Semple) *a in tch: rdn and hdwy to ld wl ins fnl f* **9/1**

4040 2 1 ¼ **I Wish**[10] 6177 7-8-13 54 PaulFitzsimons 3 61
(Miss J R Tooth) *trckd ldrs: rdn 1/2-way: ev ch ins fnl f: nt qckn* **16/1**

0040 3 1 **Londoner (USA)**[78] 4654 7-8-13 54 DaneO'Neill 4 58
(S Dow) *led tl rdn and hdd wl ins fnl f: no ex* **12/1**

0000 4 ½ **Snow Bunting**[58] 5188 7-9-0 55 TPQueally 2 58+
(Jedd O'Keeffe) *hld up in rr: hdwy over 1f out: r.o: nvr nrr* **14/1**

3326 5 ¾ **St Ivian**[22] 5966 5-8-9 55 DuranFentiman(5) 9 56
(Mrs N Macauley) *chsd ldrs: rdn 3f out: one pce fnl f* **7/1**

0000 6 1 **Mount Royale (IRE)**[41] 5566 7-9-0 55 (v) KimTinkler 8 54
(N Tinkler) *mid-div: rdn and hdwy over 1f out: sn one pce* **25/1**

2112 7 1 ½ **Brave Chief**[22] 5960 4-8-8 54 (b) MarcHalford(5) 5 49
(S R Bowring) *trckd ldr tl wknd over 1f out* **11/4**[1]

0000 8 5 **Locombe Hill (IRE)**[25] 5893 9-8-9 55 AndrewMullen(5) 11 37
(N Wilson) *prom: rdn over 2f out: wknd over 1f out* **16/1**

0000 9 2 ½ **Sydneyroughdiamond**[11] 6140 3-8-13 55 LeeEnstone 1 30
(M Mullineaux) *a towards rr* **40/1**

0032 10 2 ½ **Craic Sa Ceili (IRE)**[72] 4813 5-9-0 55 NCallan 7 24
(M S Saunders) *s.i.s: a bhd* **11/2**[3]

0054 11 shd **Temper Tantrum**[10] 6177 7-8-9 55 (p) TravisBlock(5) 10 23
(J R Best) *slowly away: a bhd* **9/2**[2]

-500 12 8 **Piroetta**[58] 5179 3-8-13 55 SteveDrowne 12 3
(J A Osborne) *racd wd: prom to 1/2-way* **33/1**

1m 28.53s (-1.87) **Going Correction** -0.35s/f (Stan)

WFA 3 from 4yo+ 1lb 12 Ran SP% **118.1**

Speed ratings (Par 101):96,94,93,92,92 90,89,83,80,77 77,68

CSF £140.60 CT £1736.40 TOTE £8.80: £3.80, £5.40, £3.70; EX 129.30.

Owner Gordon McDowall **Bred** Joseph O'Brien **Trained** Carluke, S Lanarks

FOCUS

Going against the general trend of the afternoon, this was set up for those in behind as Londoner and Brave Chief matched strides up front. The runner-up is a consistent performer so his effort makes this form pretty straightforward to rate.

6300 BET DIRECT ON SKY ACTIVE H'CAP 1m 4f 50y(P)

4:20 (4:21) (Class 6) (0-55,55) 3-Y-O+ £2,877 (£849; £424) Stalls Low

Form RPR

1 **Gentle Peace (IRE)**[46] 5472 4-8-9 55 AdamKirby(5) 5 65
(J W Unett) *sn led: mde rest: rdn over 1f out: styd on wl* **10/1**[3]

0201 2 2 ½ **Intavac Boy**[31] 5770 4-9-0 55 NCallan 4 61
(C W Thornton) *trckd ldrs: chsd wnr over 3f out: no imp fnl f* **7/2**[1]

2231 3 1 **Pharaoh Prince**[16] 6081 4-9-0 55 (v) ChrisCatlin 2 59
(G Prodromou) *trckd ldrs: kpt on one pce ins fnl 2f* **9/2**[2]

0340 4 ½ **Red Sail**[20] 5998 4-8-12 53 LPKeniry 8 57
(Dr J D Scargill) *mid-div: rdn and hdwy over 2f out: kpt on: nvr nrr* **12/1**

1200 5 shd **Galley Law**[81] 4580 5-8-12 53 TomEaves 6 56
(R Craggs) *hld up: hdwy over 1f out: nvr nr to chal* **25/1**

6462 6 2 **J R Stevenson (USA)**[10] 6184 9-8-13 54 BrianReilly 12 54
(Ernst Oertel) *bhd: effrt over 1f out: nvr on terms* **9/2**[2]

1500 7 ¾ **Arabian Moon (IRE)**[20] 5996 9-8-11 52 DaneO'Neill 1 51
(R Brotherton) *a in rr: and nvr on terms* **12/1**

0004 8 2 **Giunchiglio**[10] 6184 6-8-9 50 KFallon 10 46
(W M Brisbourne) *a bhd* **9/2**[2]

-545 9 2 ½ **High Frequency (IRE)**[15] 6099 4-8-10 51 MartinDwyer 9 43
(W R Muir) *w wnr: rdn over 4f out: wknd 3f out* **20/1**

0520 10 29 **Etching (USA)**[20] 5998 5-8-11 52 DarrenWilliams 7 —
(W M Brisbourne) *trckd ldrs: rdn and wknd over 3f out: eased over 1f out* **25/1**

2m 37.57s (-4.85) **Going Correction** -0.35s/f (Stan) 10 Ran SP% **113.7**

Speed ratings (Par 101):102,100,99,99,99 97,97,96,94,75

CSF £40.86 CT £157.06 TOTE £13.90: £3.30, £1.10, £2.00; EX 64.80.

Owner John Malone **Bred** John Malone **Trained** Preston, Shropshire

FOCUS

Yet again those who raced prominently dominated throughout. The winner's effort has been rated as an improved performance on his debut for his new yard with those immediately behind close to previous form.

6301 BETDIRECT.CO.UK MAIDEN STKS (DIV II) 7f 32y(P)

4:50 (4:56) (Class 5) 3-Y-O £3,037 (£903; £451; £225) Stalls High

Form RPR

4322 1 **Elizabethan Age (FR)**[23] 5952 3-8-9 67 (b) EddieAhern 2 69+
(W J Haggas) *w.w in mid-div: a gng wl: hdwy over 2f out: led on bit jst ins fnl f: v easily* **5/4**[1]

5043 2 1 ¾ **White Bear (FR)**[31] 5754 3-9-0 58 JohnEgan 5 64
(P D Evans) *trckd ldrs: led 2f out: hdd jst ins fnl f: nt pce of wnr* **6/1**

063 3 ½ **Fajr (IRE)**[23] 5950 3-9-0 55 JamieMackay 8 63
(N B King) *mid-div: rdn over 2f out: styd on fnl f: nvr nrr* **10/1**

0 4 ¾ **Baba Ghanoush**[32] 5734 3-8-9 PaulDoe 7 56
(W Jarvis) *hld up in mid-div: hdwy over 2f out: styd on fnl f* **25/1**

0360 5 ½ **Cost Analysis (IRE)**[26] 5880 3-9-0 61 (bt) NCallan 6 60
(M A Jarvis) *t.k.h: prom: nt qckn ent fnl f* **4/1**[2]

6 8 **Woodwool** 3-8-9 DaneO'Neill 3 34
(H Candy) *slowly away: styd on past btn horses fnl f but nvr nr to chal* **20/1**

7 2 ½ **Orenay (USA)**[33] 5723 3-9-0 72 (t) KFallon 10 32
(M J Wallace) *hld up: hdwy over 2f out: n.m.r and wknd over 1f out* **9/2**[3]

00- 8 2 ½ **Rapid Flow**[438] 5118 3-9-0 MartinDwyer 4 26
(W M Brisbourne) *led tl hdd 2f out: wknd over 1f out* **25/1**

0 9 3 ½ **Miss Shontaine**[31] 5756 3-8-9 LPKeniry 11 12
(B G Powell) *trckd ldr to over 2f out: sn wknd* **100/1**

The Form Book, Raceform Ltd, Compton, RG20 6NL

004 **10** 2 ½ **Kirstys Lad**[7] 6229 3-9-0 DarrenWilliams 9 10
(M Mullineaux) *mid-div: rdn 1/2-way: sn bhd* **66/1**
11 5 **Billy's Brother** 3-9-0 DavidAllan 1 —
(M A Buckley) *outpcd: a bhd* **66/1**
12 3 **Barachois Gaudy** 3-8-9 JimmyQuinn 12 —
(R Hollinshead) *outpcd thrght* **33/1**

1m 28.18s (-2.22) **Going Correction** -0.35s/f (Stan) **12** Ran SP% **125.4**
Speed ratings (Par 102):98,96,95,94,94 84,82,79,75,72 66,63
CSF £9.46 TOTE £2.20: £1.10, £2.30, £2.50; EX 12.00 Place 6 £130.08, Place 5 £59.89.
Owner W J Gredley **Bred** W S Farish Jr **Trained** Newmarket, Suffolk

FOCUS
The slower of the two divisions by 0.39sec and pretty modest form, but the winner appeared to score with any amount in hand, looking in a completely different class to the rest.
T/Jkpt: Not won. T/Plt: £90.30 to a £1 stake. Pool: £56,821.75. 459.30 winning tickets. T/Qpdt: £49.80 to a £1 stake. Pool: £3,937.50. 58.40 winning tickets. JS

6177 LINGFIELD (L-H)
Thursday, November 10

OFFICIAL GOING: Standard
Wind: Overcast Weather: Strong behind

6302 BETDIRECT FREEPHONE 0800 211 222 H'CAP (DIV 1) 1m (P)
12:50 (12:51) (Class 5) (0-75,77) 3-Y-O+ **£3,072** (£913; £456; £228) **Stalls** High

Form RPR
6050 **1** **Dr Thong**[55] 5273 4-9-3 **74** JimmyFortune 9 84
(P F I Cole) *trckd ldrs: sltly hmpd over 2f out: effrt over 1f out: drvn to ld ins fnl f: kpt on wl* **8/1**
2003 **2** 1 **Zalkani (IRE)**[17] 6075 5-8-13 **70** MichaelHills 5 78
(B G Powell) *dwlt: hld up in rr: prog over 2f out: nt qckn over 1f out: styd on to take 2nd wl ins fnl f* **9/2**[1]
6410 **3** 1 ½ **Glencalvie (IRE)**[22] 5974 4-8-10 **70** (v) RobertMiles(3) 6 75
(J Akehurst) *w ldr: led 1/2-way to jst over 2f out: stl upsides 1f out: one pce* **7/1**[3]
0600 **4** nk **Arctic Desert**[10] 6201 5-9-2 **73** (t) NCallan 1 77
(A M Balding) *s.v.s: sn in tch in rr and t.k.h: rdn and gd prog to ld 2f out: hdd & wknd ins fnl f* **8/1**
5106 **5** nk **Lizarazu (GER)**[10] 6201 6-9-4 **75** LPKeniry 3 78
(R A Harris) *trckd ldrs: rdn and nt qckn wl over 1f out: one pce after* **15/2**
2103 **6** nk **Anchor Date**[12] 6161 3-9-1 **74** (t) NickyMackay 7 76
(Stef Liddiard) *settled midfield: effrt over 2f out: nt look keen over 1f out: one pce* **11/2**[2]
0000 **7** hd **Quantum Leap**[29] 5834 8-8-13 **70** (v) JimmyQuinn 12 72
(S Dow) *hld up in last trio: shuffled along over 2f out: kpt on fr over 1f out: nvr nrr* **20/1**
0060 **8** 1 ½ **Seneschal**[16] 6101 4-9-3 **74** (p) GeorgeBaker 8 73
(A B Haynes) *dwlt: t.k.h and jnd ldrs 5f out: led briefly jst over 2f out: wknd rapidly fnl f* **18/1**
6001 **9** 1 **Corky (IRE)**[6] 6245 4-9-3 **77** 6ex StephaneBreux(3) 11 73
(R Hannon) *hld up in last trio: rdn on outer over 2f out: no prog* **16/1**
0000 **10** hd **Savoy Chapel**[32] 5758 3-9-0 **73** ChrisCatlin 2 69
(A W Carroll) *hld up in last pair: effrt on inner over 2f out: n.m.r: sn btn* **40/1**
5031 **11** 6 **Princelywallywogan**[24] 5940 3-9-2 **75** TPQueally 4 57
(I A Wood) *led to 1/2-way: wknd 3f out* **8/1**
1006 **12** 14 **Joy And Pain**[167] 2041 4-9-1 **72** EddieAhern 10 22
(J R Boyle) *nvr beyond midfield: wknd over 2f out: t.o* **20/1**

1m 38.06s (-1.37) **Going Correction** -0.075s/f (Stan)
WFA 3 from 4yo+ 2lb **12** Ran SP% **114.3**
Speed ratings (Par 103):103,102,100,100,99 99,99,97,96,96 90,76
CSF £41.07 CT £265.60 TOTE £11.70: £4.70, £1.80, £3.10; EX 59.20.
Owner Frank Stella **Bred** Mascalls Stud **Trained** Whatcombe, Oxon

FOCUS
Just a fair handicap in which Dr Thong proved good enough to make a winning debut on Polytrack. The form looks pretty solid with the scond, fourth and fifth all close to their marks.

6303 PLAY NOW AT BETDIRECTPOKER.COM MEDIAN AUCTION MAIDEN STKS 5f (P)
1:20 (1:21) (Class 5) 2-Y-O **£3,432** (£1,021; £510; £254) **Stalls** High

Form RPR
6430 **1** **Spearit (IRE)**[20] 6004 2-9-0 78 JohnEgan 5 78
(D R C Elsworth) *trckd ldrs: effrt to ld wl over 1f out: in command ins fnl f: rdn out* **2/1**[1]
0623 **2** 1 **Best Double**[7] 6233 2-8-9 73 (b) NickyMackay 8 69
(G A Butler) *s.s: hld up in last: plld out and prog over 1f out: r.o to take 2nd last 50yds and gaining on wnr at fin* **4/1**[2]
3 ¾ **Macademy Royal (USA)** 2-9-0 SteveDrowne 4 71
(H Morrison) *pressed ldrs on outer: upsides 2f out: nt qckn over 1f out: chsd wnr ins fnl f: one pce and lost 2nd last 50yds* **11/2**
6 **4** ¾ **Yellow Card**[13] 6128 2-9-0 JimmyFortune 1 69
(N A Callaghan) *w ldr on inner: upsides fr 1/2-way to over 1f out: one pce* **8/1**
3 **5** 1 **Endless Night**[22] 5985 2-9-0 RobertHavlin 3 65
(H Morrison) *dwlt: hld up: trckd ldrs: over 2f out: outpcd over 1f out: n.d after* **25/1**
5560 **6** shd **Sands Crooner (IRE)**[131] 3142 2-9-0 81 (t) NCallan 2 65
(D Shaw) *pressed ldrs: squeezed out after 1f: effrt 2f out: no prog fnl f* **10/1**
5340 **7** 1 **Overwing (IRE)**[22] 5969 2-8-9 73 DaneO'Neill 7 56
(R Hannon) *t.k.h and hanging bdly thrght: hld up: rn v wd bnd 2f out: n.d after* **5/1**[3]
4500 **8** 10 **Wizard Prince**[98] 4086 2-9-0 53 (b[1]) EddieAhern 6 25
(R A Harris) *mde most to 2f out: wknd rapidly over 1f out* **66/1**

58.98 secs (-0.80) **Going Correction** -0.075s/f (Stan) **8** Ran SP% **110.9**
Speed ratings (Par 96):103,101,100,99,97 97,95,79
CSF £9.32 TOTE £2.10: £1.10, £2.50, £1.80; EX 14.90.
Owner Raymond Tooth **Bred** Raymond Clive Tooth **Trained** Newmarket, Suffolk

FOCUS
Just an ordinary sprint maiden in which Spearit coped with the drop back to five furlongs and denied the frustrating Best Double, although the pair were close to their marks.

NOTEBOOK
Spearit(IRE), who had run to a fair level of form in five runs over six furlongs, including when in mid-division in a sales race at Doncaster on his most recent start, coped with the drop back in trip and found this a good opportunity to get off the mark. Things are likely to be tougher in future, but he is consistent and should continue to give a good account. (op 5-2)
Best Double, dropped to the minimum trip for the first time having raced over seven furlongs on her latest outing, ran a creditable race in defeat. Although a frustrating sort, she should eventually win a similar race and may just prove best over another furlong. (tchd 9-2)
Macademy Royal(USA) ◆, an 18,000gns first foal of a half-sister to the smart French miler Hudo, ran a creditable race in his debut and was just found out by his inexperience. He should get further and, almost sure to be sharper next time, looks well up to winning a similar race. (op 9-2)
Yellow Card, under a positive ride, seemed to step up on the form he showed on his debut at Newmarket. (op 6-1)
Endless Night was ridden by Drowne when third in a weak Nottingham maiden on his debut, but he opted to ride the stable's newcomer, and this one looks more of a handicap prospect. (tchd 33-1)
Sands Crooner(IRE) ran nowhere near his official mark of 81. (op 12-1 tchd 9-1)
Overwing(IRE) looked an awkward ride, again giving the impression she is one to avoid. Official explanation: jockey said filly hung badly right throughout (op 9-2)

6304 BETDIRECT.CO.UK NURSERY 7f (P)
1:50 (1:52) (Class 4) 2-Y-O **£5,149** (£1,531; £765; £382) **Stalls** Low

Form RPR
4133 **1** **Seven Samurai**[24] 5949 2-9-1 **80** RHills 11 85
(J W Hills) *wl plcd bhd ldrs: effrt 2f out: rdn to ld last 100yds: styd on wl* **7/2**[2]
2451 **2** 1 ½ **Broken Spur (FR)**[43] 5542 2-8-9 **74** MichaelHills 6 75
(B W Hills) *pressed ldr: led 2f out: kicked on wl over 1f out: worn down last 100yds* **8/1**[3]
0410 **3** 1 **Kaveri (USA)**[20] 6005 2-9-4 **83** JimmyFortune 8 82
(C E Brittain) *n.m.r on outer over 5f out and dropped to rr: prog over 2f out: drvn to take 3rd ent fnl f: styd on* **10/1**
0046 **4** shd **Salvestro**[21] 5994 2-8-1 **66** ow1 ChrisCatlin 2 65
(Mrs A J Perrett) *hld up in last pair: drvn over 2f out: prog but hanging over 1f out: r.o wl fnl f* **17/2**
3600 **5** 1 **Blu Manruna**[32] 5761 2-8-0 **65** (b[1]) JamieMackay 14 61
(J Akehurst) *stdd s: t.k.h and hld up in last trio: rdn on outer over 2f out: r.o fnl f: n.d* **33/1**
2161 **6** ¾ **King Alfie**[27] 5879 2-8-6 **71** (b) NickyMackay 9 65
(A B Haynes) *hld up towards rr: plenty to do whn nt clr run over 1f out: r.o ins fnl f* **12/1**
5210 **7** hd **Cape Of Luck (IRE)**[19] 6023 2-9-7 **86** EddieAhern 5 85+
(P Mitchell) *hld up wl in rr on inner: nt clr run repeatedly fr 3f out tl styd on fnl f: no ch* **11/4**[1]
0503 **8** 1 **Earl Kraul (IRE)**[21] 5994 2-8-0 **68** ow3 (p) RichardThomas(3) 4 59
(G L Moore) *led to 2f out: wknd and lost several pls fnl f* **12/1**
466 **9** ½ **Dancing Storm**[24] 5945 2-7-13 **64** oh1 ow1 JimmyQuinn 13 54
(W S Kittow) *stdd s: t.k.h: hld up in last trio: prog on inner over 1f out: n.d to ldrs: fdd last 100yds* **25/1**
5005 **10** nk **George The Second**[23] 5953 2-7-7 **63** oh4 DuranFentiman(5) 10 52
(Mrs H Sweeting) *nvr beyond midfield: drvn and struggling on wd outside over 2f out* **33/1**
200 **11** 1 ¼ **Wee Charlie Castle (IRE)**[54] 5325 2-8-4 **69** (v) PaulEddery 12 55
(G C H Chung) *prog on outer to press ldrs 1/2-way: wknd over 1f out: eased ins fnl f* **66/1**
0500 **12** 1 **Surf City**[47] 5464 2-8-6 **71** (p) LPKeniry 7 55
(R A Harris) *chsd ldrs: rdn wl over 2f out: wknd wl over 1f out* **33/1**
0630 **13** 1 ¾ **Shannon House**[44] 5524 2-8-4 **69** ow4 JohnEgan 1 48
(M J McGrath) *dwlt: sn rcvrd to press ldrs: wknd rapidly over 2f out* **14/1**
1660 **14** shd **Pelham Crescent (IRE)**[19] 6016 2-8-9 **74** DaneO'Neill 3 53
(R Hannon) *prom 1f: lost pl on inner and midfield 3f out: nt clr run over 1f out: eased* **12/1**

1m 25.46s (-0.43) **Going Correction** -0.075s/f (Stan) **14** Ran SP% **123.5**
Speed ratings (Par 98):99,97,96,96,94 94,93,92,92,91 90,89,87,87
CSF £31.22 CT £266.47 TOTE £4.90: £1.20, £2.80, £5.20; EX 22.60.
Owner Amity Finance,Chris New,Miss Wendy Hall **Bred** Gilridge Bloodstock Ltd **Trained** Upper Lambourn, Berks

FOCUS
The form of this nursery may not be as strong as one might have expect for the grade, but still a good effort from Seven Samuari to defy a mark of 80.

NOTEBOOK
Seven Samurai ◆, dropped a furlong in trip and returned to Polytrack, produced his best effort yet to run out a ready winner. Progressing, he could develop into a very useful sort and may be put away until next year. (op 9-2)
Broken Spur(FR), off the mark in a course and distance maiden on his previous start, would have found this much tougher but ran a good race behind the improving winner. (op 11-2)
Kaveri(USA), dropped in trip and switched to Polytrack for the first time, returned to the sort of form that saw her win her maiden at Leicester two starts previously and can have few excuses. (tchd 11-1)
Salvestro did not help his chance by appearing to hang under pressure, but still stayed on well and could do better again over a mile. (op 14-1)
Blu Manruna, with blinkers replacing cheekpieces and returned to Polytrack, ran a little better than of late and ought to do even better in a slightly lower grade. (op 25-1)
King Alfie, claimed out of Kevin Ryan's yard after winning at Redcar on his previous start, would have found this tougher but ran well considering he met trouble having been in an unpromising position when the race got serious. Official explanation: jockey said gelding was denied a clear run (op 14-1)
Cape Of Luck(IRE) ◆, ninth of 13 in the Horris Hill last time having won a course and distance conditions event prior to that, can be considered most unlucky on his return to Polytrack as he was continually denied a clear run in the straight. Official explanation: jockey said colt was denied a clear run (op 3-1 tchd 5-2, 10-3 in places)
Pelham Crescent(IRE) Official explanation: jockey said colt was denied a clear run

6305 BETDIRECT FREEPHONE 0800 211 222 H'CAP (DIV II) 1m (P)
2:20 (2:22) (Class 5) (0-75,77) 3-Y-O+ **£3,079** (£916; £457; £228) **Stalls** High

Form RPR
21 **1** **Hits Only Heaven (IRE)**[37] 5693 3-8-13 **72** (be) JimmyQuinn 10 84
(J Pearce) *puled hrd: hld up bhd ldrs: stl pulling over 2f out: effrt over 1f out: led jst ins fnl f: r.o wl* **9/1**
6143 **2** 1 ¼ **Boundless Prospect (USA)**[41] 5588 6-9-0 **71** JohnEgan 11 80
(Miss Gay Kelleway) *hld up in rr: prog on outer 2f out: r.o to take 2nd wl ins fnl f: no imp on wnr* **9/2**[2]
1236 **3** 1 ¼ **Logsdail**[12] 6159 5-9-4 **75** (p) GeorgeBaker 1 81
(G L Moore) *trckd ldrs: effrt over 1f out: got through to chal ent fnl f: one pce* **4/1**[1]
6500 **4** nk **Missed A Beat**[48] 5439 3-8-13 **72** FergusSweeney 6 77
(M Blanshard) *hld up in rr: gng strly but nt wl plcd over 2f out or over 1f out: styd on fnl f: nrst fin* **33/1**
0304 **5** 1 ¼ **Caragh Mia (IRE)**[29] 5834 3-9-0 **73** NickyMackay 2 76+
(G A Butler) *hld up in rr on inner: effrt 2f out: nt clr run jst over 1f out: kpt on but no ch* **11/1**

3300 **6** *shd* **Sonny Parkin**[31] [5799] 3-8-11 **75**....(p) AdamKirby(5) 8 77
(G A Huffer) *dwlt: t.k.h: hld up in last pair: rdn over 2f out: styng on whn nt clr run on inner 1f out: nrst fin* **20/1**
3446 **7** *shd* **Yawmi**[14] [6127] 5-9-1 **72**.... EddieAhern 12 74
(R A Harris) *w ldr: stl upsides 1f out: wknd ins fnl f* **11/2**[3]
6402 **8** *½* **Law Breaker (IRE)**[10] [6201] 7-9-3 **74**.... BrianReilly 4 75
(Miss J Feilden) *trckd ldrs: nt clr run over 1f out: nt qckn and sn btn* **8/1**
0611 **9** *1 ½* **African Sahara (USA)**[10] [6201] 6-8-13 **77** 6ex....(t) ChrisCavanagh(7) 7 74
(Miss D Mountain) *hld up in rr: outpcd over 2f out: rdn wl over 1f out: no ch* **8/1**
1136 **10** *¾* **Deeper In Debt**[32] [5758] 7-9-1 **72**.... DaneO'Neill 3 68
(J Akehurst) *mde most to 1f out: wknd rapidly* **9/1**
255 **11** *¾* **Danger Zone**[81] [4603] 3-8-11 **70**.... IanMongan 5 64
(Mrs A J Perrett) *t.k.h: w ldr to jst over 1f out: wknd rapidly* **20/1**
/00- **12** *17* **Salisbury Plain**[541] [2202] 4-9-3 **74**.... LPKeniry 9 29
(N I M Rossiter) *dwlt: a in last pair: t.o over 2f out* **80/1**

1m 37.5s (-1.93) **Going Correction** -0.075s/f (Stan)
WFA 3 from 4yo+ 2lb **12** Ran SP% **117.8**
Speed ratings (Par 103):106,104,103,103,101 101,101,101,99,99 98,81
CSF £47.00 CT £193.45 TOTE £11.70: £2.80, £1.70, £1.40; EX 38.20.
Owner Clive Whiting **Bred** Waterside Stud **Trained** Newmarket, Suffolk

FOCUS
Possibly a slightly stronger handicap than the first division - the time was quicker - and Hits Only Heaven continued his progression in decent style. The fourth and seventh set the standard and the form looks pretty solid.

6306 EUROPEAN BREEDERS FUND FILLIES' H'CAP 1m 2f (P)
2:50 (2:51) (Class 3) (0-90,87) 3-Y-O
£9,607 (£2,876; £1,438; £719; £359; £180) **Stalls** Low

Form RPR
5540 **1** **Mizz Tee (IRE)**[9] [6216] 3-8-11 **80**.... DavidAllan 3 88
(T D Easterby) *mostly trckd ldr: led wl over 2f out: drvn over 1f out: r.o wl fnl f* **22/1**
1402 **2** *1 ½* **Missatacama (IRE)**[20] [6003] 3-8-9 **78**.... DaneO'Neill 5 83
(D J Daly) *hld up in last: prog over 3f out: drvn to chse wnr wl over 1f out: looked dangerous ent fnl f: readily hld after* **7/2**[2]
1121 **3** *1 ¾* **Dance Partner**[32] [5763] 3-9-4 **87**.... JimmyFortune 6 89
(J H M Gosden) *trckd ldrs: lost pl over 3f out: rdn over 2f out: effrt u.p wl over 1f out: nt qckn* **8/11**[1]
5652 **4** *hd* **Nice Tune**[29] [5834] 3-8-6 **75**.... EddieAhern 2 76
(C E Brittain) *cl up: rdn and nt qckn over 2f out: hanging over 1f out: styd on again ins fnl f* **6/1**[3]
5003 **5** *1 ¾* **Ma'Am (USA)**[22] [5971] 3-8-7 **76**....(p) LPKeniry 4 74
(I A Wood) *hld up in rr: outpcd over 2f out: no ch after* **20/1**
4-50 **6** *1 ¾* **Donyana**[12] [6147] 3-9-0 **83**....(p) PhilipRobinson 1 78
(M A Jarvis) *sn led: pushed along 4f out: hdd wl over 2f out: wknd wl over 1f out* **14/1**
-104 **7** *7* **Penny Wedding (IRE)**[20] [6003] 3-8-4 **73**.... BrianReilly 7 54
(Miss J Feilden) *racd wd: in tch: effrt 3f out: wknd over 2f out* **66/1**

2m 8.51s (0.72) **Going Correction** -0.075s/f (Stan) **7** Ran SP% **111.7**
Speed ratings (Par 103):94,92,91,91,89 88,82
CSF £92.56 TOTE £25.90: £8.80, £1.40; EX 161.20.
Owner Salifix **Bred** Dr Dean Harron **Trained** Great Habton, N Yorks

FOCUS
This looked like a reasonable fillies' handicap, but the pace was steady which resulted in a surprise winner. The runner-up ran to her mark but the form is unconvincing and may not prove reliable.

NOTEBOOK
Mizz Tee(IRE), racing beyond a mile for the first time and making her debut on Polytrack, appeared to produce a career-best effort and was clearly well suited by the conditions. Her overall record is uninspiring, but she is unexposed over this sort of trip and there could be even more to come. (op 20-1)
Missatacama(IRE) was probably not far off her best in second, but she just lacked a decisive finishing kick and may prove even better back over slightly shorter. (op 5-1 tchd 10-3)
Dance Partner, the winner of four of her last five starts, was dropping back two furlongs in trip and was 3lb higher than when just getting home at Goodwood on her previous start. Although this was a creditable effort, she was well held and appears to have finished improving for the year. (tchd 5-6 and 4-5 in places)
Nice Tune, racing over a trip this far for the first time, could not build on the promise she showed when second over a mile here on her previous start and did not help her chance by hanging when put under pressure. (op 9-2 tchd 7-1)
Ma'Am(USA) got outpaced when the tempo increased and gives the impression much more positive tactics will suit better. (op 16-1)

6307 PLAY NOW AT BETDIRECTCASINO.COM MAIDEN STKS 1m 4f (P)
3:20 (3:28) (Class 5) 3-Y-O+ **£3,549** (£1,056; £527; £263) **Stalls** Low

Form RPR
400 **1** **Garibaldi (GER)**[31] [5799] 3-9-0 72.... LPKeniry 6 66
(D R C Elsworth) *t.k.h: hld up in tch: prog to chse ldr over 3f out: narrow ld fr 2f out: drvn out* **5/1**[2]
3406 **2** *½* **Newnham (IRE)**[22] [5972] 4-9-6 73.... EddieAhern 15 65
(J R Boyle) *dwlt: rcvrd to ld after 2f: narrowly hdd 2f out: pressed wnr after: hld last 75yds* **9/4**[1]
4043 **3** *2* **Trials 'n Tribs**[61] [5132] 3-8-9 46.... TPQueally 5 57
(C A Cyzer) *t.k.h: hld up in rr: prog on outer 4f out: rdn to chal over 2f out: one pce over 1f out* **33/1**
2-30 **4** *¾* **Webbswood Lad (IRE)**[20] [6015] 4-9-6 63.... NickyMackay 4 61
(Stef Liddiard) *t.k.h: trckd ldrs: cl up 3f out: outpcd over 2f out: kpt on* **14/1**
5623 **5** *nk* **Rose Bien**[66] [5008] 3-8-4 52.... AdamKirby(5) 2 55
(P J McBride) *hld up wl in rr on inner: lost tch w ldrs over 3f out: sme prog over 2f out: r.o wl fnl f: gaining fast at fin* **12/1**
0 **6** *3 ½* **Townsville (IRE)**[31] [5800] 3-9-0.... JohnEgan 14 55
(D J Daly) *hld up in last trio: lost tch w ldrs over 3f out: rdn and kpt on fr over 2f out: n.d* **33/1**
3530 **7** *shd* **Avicia**[10] [6195] 3-8-9 65.... OscarUrbina 10 50
(C A Horgan) *dwlt: nt gng wl early: prog fr rr 6f out: outpcd by ldrs over 3f out and nt clr run sn after: no ch* **10/1**[3]
0003 **8** *4* **Mujimac (IRE)**[26] [5896] 3-9-0 53.... FergusSweeney 7 48
(J R Boyle) *hld up wl in rr: outpcd over 3f out: n.d after* **66/1**
0 **9** *3* **Escoffier**[19] [6028] 3-9-0.... IanMongan 8 43
(Mrs A J Perrett) *chsd ldrs: outpcd u.p over 3f out: grad wknd* **20/1**
000 **10** *6* **Tipes**[32] [5765] 3-9-0 55.... PaulEddery 1 34
(C J Down) *hmpd on inner 9f out and dropped to rr: wl outpcd over 3f out: no ch after* **80/1**
00 **11** *16* **Smokin Grey**[9] [4864] 5-8-12.... NeilChalmers(3) 11 —
(L Wells) *prom tl wknd 5f out: t.o* **100/1**
03 **12** *1 ¾* **Xacobeo (IRE)**[9] [6215] 3-9-0.... DaneO'Neill 3 5
(R Hannon) *led for 2f: chsd ldr to over 3f out: wknd v rapidly: t.o* **5/1**[2]
00- **13** *½* **Stunning Spark**[395] [6127] 3-8-9.... ChrisCatlin 9 —
(S Dow) *rdn towards rr 7f out: sn struggling: t.o* **100/1**
0 **14** *nk* **Another Mistress**[19] [6028] 3-8-6.... RichardThomas(3) 13 —
(R M Flower) *t.k.h: in tch: rdn and wknd 5f out: t.o* **100/1**

2m 32.69s (-1.70) **Going Correction** -0.075s/f (Stan)
WFA 3 from 4yo+ 6lb **14** Ran SP% **103.9**
Speed ratings (Par 103):102,101,100,99,99 97,97,94,92,88 77,76,76,76
CSF £11.77 TOTE £5.70: £1.70, £1.40, £7.20; EX 19.00.
Owner The Bramfield Racing Syndicate **Bred** Gestut Hof Eichenstein **Trained** Newmarket, Suffolk
■ Stewards' Enquiry : Richard Thomas two-day ban: careless riding (Nov 21-22)

FOCUS
Although the first two home in this maiden are rated in the 70s, the proximity of the 46-rated third suggests the form is modest at best.

6308 TEXT "BETDIRECT" TO 88600 APPRENTICE H'CAP 1m 5f (P)
3:50 (3:53) (Class 5) (0-75,74) 3-Y-O+ **£3,378** (£1,005; £502; £250) **Stalls** Low

Form RPR
3430 **1** **Maystock**[20] [6012] 5-9-7 **72**.... RonanKeogh 3 82
(B G Powell) *trckd ldrs: wnt 2nd 2f out: rdn and kpt on wl to ld last 75yds* **7/2**[1]
0020 **2** *nk* **Santando**[20] [6008] 5-8-11 **69**.... DebraEngland(7) 9 79
(C E Brittain) *trckd ldr: led over 2f out: kicked on wl over 1f out: worn down last 75yds* **8/1**
040 **3** *3 ½* **Mad Carew (USA)**[48] [5437] 6-9-9 **74**.... LiamJones 10 78
(J R Boyle) *hld up in last: outpcd whn nt clr run over 2f out: rapid prog over 1f out: r.o wl: hopeless task* **11/1**
3563 **4** *2* **Bucks**[19] [6029] 8-9-6 **74**.... ChrisCavanagh(3) 2 75+
(D K Ivory) *trckd ldrs: lost pl on inner over 4f out: trapped after: nt clr run over 1f out: r.o strly fnl f: hopeless task* **7/2**[1]
2006 **5** *1 ¾* **Wait For The Will (USA)**[17] [6073] 9-9-9 **74**....(b) JamesDoyle 8 73
(G L Moore) *hld up: smooth prog 4f out: poised to chal over 2f out: wknd tamely over 1f out* **6/1**[3]
0-00 **6** *4* **Indian Solitaire (IRE)**[26] [5890] 6-9-2 **67**....(p) ThomasO'Brien 7 60
(B P J Baugh) *hld up in last pair: reminder over 4f out: outpcd fr 3f out: no ch after* **50/1**
3403 **7** *1 ¼* **Desert Island Disc**[13] [6133] 8-8-9 **60**.... MichaelJStainton 5 51
(Dr J R J Naylor) *in tch: rdn wl over 3f out: sn outpcd and btn* **5/1**[2]
0210 **8** *3* **Willhego**[38] [5671] 4-8-11 **67**.... JamesMillman(5) 4 53
(J R Best) *rdr lost irons after 1f and passenger after: in tch to over 2f out* **10/1**
0000 **9** *shd* **Tuning Fork**[40] [5603] 5-8-4 **60**....(t) MarkCoumbe(5) 6 46
(J Akehurst) *led to over 2f out: wknd* **25/1**
00-0 **10** *5* **Dolzago**[14] [6127] 5-8-11 **65**....(b) JemmaMarshall(3) 1 44
(G L Moore) *trckd ldrs tl wknd u.p 3f out* **25/1**

2m 47.4s (-0.90) **Going Correction** -0.075s/f (Stan) **10** Ran SP% **113.6**
Speed ratings (Par 103):99,98,96,95,94 91,91,89,89,86
CSF £30.61 CT £275.92 TOTE £3.90: £1.70, £3.00, £3.60; EX 37.40 Place 6 £65.27, Place 5 £34.04.
Owner Stock Hill Racing **Bred** Stock Hill Stud **Trained** Morestead, Hants
■ Maystock was winning this race for the third year in succession.

FOCUS
Just an ordinary apprentice handicap rated through the winner with the third and fourth giving the form a sound look.
T/Plt: £155.80 to a £1 stake. Pool: £39,264.60. 183.95 winning tickets. T/Qpdt: £59.70 to a £1 stake. Pool: £3,416.30. 42.30 winning tickets. JN

6294 WOLVERHAMPTON (A.W) (L-H)
Friday, November 11

OFFICIAL GOING: Standard
Earlier in the week there was an advantage to those racing prominently, but a strong wind in the back straight helped negate that at this meeting.
Wind: strong, behind

6309 PLAY INSTANT WIN GAMES AT BETDIRECT.CO.UK NURSERY (DIV I) 7f 32y(P)
1:25 (1:26) (Class 5) (0-75,75) 2-Y-O **£3,737** (£1,111; £555; £277) **Stalls** High

Form RPR
6152 **1** **Soothsay (IRE)**[22] [5994] 2-8-13 **67**.... EddieAhern 9 74+
(J W Hills) *a in tch: wnt 2nd over 2f out: led over 1f out: rdn out* **8/1**[3]
0404 **2** *2* **Moi Aussi (USA)**[7] [6244] 2-8-12 **66**....(b[1]) JamieMackay 10 68+
(Sir Mark Prescott) *slowly away: hdwy 3f out: hung lft over 1f out: r.o to go 2nd ins fnl f* **14/1**
0660 **3** *3* **Ballybeg (IRE)**[33] [5761] 2-8-10 **64**.... ChrisCatlin 12 59
(R Hannon) *racd wd in tch: hdwy on outside over 2f out: carried lft over 1f out: r.o ins fnl f* **14/1**
000 **4** *shd* **Song Of Silence (USA)**[15] [6120] 2-8-8 **62**.... MartinDwyer 8 56
(E A L Dunlop) *bhd tl hdwy over 1f out: r.o: nvr nrr* **8/1**[3]
054 **5** *nk* **Baklawa**[66] [5031] 2-9-1 **69**....(b[1]) JimmyFortune 1 63
(B J Meehan) *led tl rdn and hdd over 1f out: wknd ins fnl f* **11/1**
4045 **6** *5* **Lenoir (GER)**[13] [6158] 2-8-13 **67**....(v[1]) MichaelTebbutt 4 48
(V Smith) *slowly away: nvr on terms* **25/1**
3000 **7** *hd* **Commander Wish**[6] [6249] 2-8-10 **67** ow2.... DNolan(3) 5 48
(Lucinda Featherstone) *a towards rr* **66/1**
3003 **8** *½* **Mocha Java**[18] [6072] 2-9-0 **71**.... NelsonDeSouza(3) 3 50
(P F I Cole) *mid-div: sn rdn: bhd fr 1/2-way* **8/1**[3]
0215 **9** *5* **Il Castagno (IRE)**[20] [6016] 2-9-7 **75**.... PaulEddery 6 42
(B Smart) *trckd ldr tl wknd wl over 1f out* **2/1**[1]
2005 **10** *1* **Sandwith**[4] [6281] 2-8-9 **68**.... PatrickMathers(5) 2 32
(James Moffatt) *prom on ins tl wknd 2f out* **50/1**
3001 **11** *2 ½* **Astorygoeswithit**[18] [6077] 2-9-2 **70**....(p) JohnEgan 11 28
(Julian Poulton) *mid-div tl 1/2-way* **25/1**
11 **12** *9* **Mr Rigsby**[2] [6295] 2-9-4 **72** 7ex.... FergalLynch 7 8
(P Howling) *chsd ldrs tl rdn and wknd 2f out* **10/3**[2]

1m 29.61s (-0.79) **Going Correction** -0.20s/f (Stan) **12** Ran SP% **122.6**
Speed ratings (Par 96):96,93,90,90,89 84,83,83,77,76 73,63
CSF £114.22 CT £1040.10 TOTE £7.60: £2.50, £4.50, £6.30; EX 93.40.
Owner Mrs F Hills **Bred** Maurice Burns **Trained** Upper Lambourn, Berks

FOCUS
A modest nursery in which the leaders seemed to go too fast into the headwind and the principals came from behind. The runner-up sets the standard for the form, which may not be totally reliable.

NOTEBOOK

Soothsay(IRE), who ran quite well on a similar surface earlier in the season, got a good run through on the rail as the leaders weakened and took full advantage. She was kept up to her work but did it well in the end and may be able to follow up. (op 7-1)

Moi Aussi(USA) had plenty of previous Polytrack experience but had not won and the first-time blinkers seemed to help. She missed the break and then hung left at the finish, but was keeping on well to the line and a step back up in trip should suit her. (op 12-1)

Ballybeg(IRE), making his debut on this surface, had been dropped 4lb since his last run. He was on the heels of the leaders turning in, then ran on despite being done no favours by the runner-up. He will need to improve some more to win in this grade.

Song Of Silence(USA), making her handicap debut, ran on steadily in the straight without ever threatening. (op 6-1)

Baklawa has not really gone on from her debut in a Newbury maiden that has produced six subsequent winners. Fitted with blinkers for the first time, she was very keen into the headwind and paid the penalty from the turn in. She can be given another chance, and a drop back to six furlongs may help. (op 10-1)

Il Castagno(IRE)raced up with the early pace, but was struggling from the turn in and was disappointing. (op 11-4)

Mr Rigsby, winner of a seller here two days previously, was stepping up in class. He raced three wide and faded off the turn, so possibly the race came too soon. Official explanation: jockey said gelding ran flat (op 3-1)

6310 PLAY NOW AT BETDIRECTCASINO.COM CLAIMING STKS 5f 216y(P)

2:00 (2:01) (Class 6) 3-5-Y-O **£2,914** (£860; £430) **Stalls** Low

Form				RPR
0020	**1**		**Norcroft**[25] 5951 3-9-5 70 ....(p) IanMongan 9 (Mrs C A Dunnett) *hld up: rdn and hdwy over 1f out: r.o to ld ins fnl f* **9/2**[1]	74
0430	**2**	*1*	**Chilly Cracker**[24] 5954 3-9-0 62 .... GeorgeBaker 4 (R Hollinshead) *mid-div: hdwy on ins over 1f out: kpt on to go 2nd ins fnl f* **11/2**[3]	66
5530	**3**	*nk*	**Willheconquertoo**[122] 3422 5-9-1 69 ....(tp) JohnEgan 10 (Andrew Reid) *trckd ldrs: led over 1f out: rdn and hdd ins fnl f: no ex* **5/1**[2]	66
0000	**4**	*1 1/4*	**Namir (IRE)**[8] 6238 3-9-5 80 ....(v[1]) JimmyFortune 1 (T D Barron) *in tch on ins: rdn over 1f out: nt qckn ins fnl f* **5/1**[2]	66
6005	**5**	*1 1/4*	**Nova Tor (IRE)**[6] 6264 3-8-10 65 .... RobbieFitzpatrick 12 (Peter Grayson) *t.k.h: prom: nt qcknd fnl f* **12/1**	54
5550	**6**	*1/2*	**Speed Dial Harry (IRE)**[96] 4193 3-9-1 62 ....(v) DPMcDonogh 13 (K R Burke) *mid-div: rdn over 2f out: no hdwy after* **20/1**	57
3060	**7**	*1/2*	**Born For Dancing (IRE)**[24] 5954 3-8-10 65 .... MartinDwyer 8 (B W Hills) *mid-div: rdn 2f out: one pce after* **9/2**[1]	51
0000	**8**	*nk*	**Almaty Express**[2] 6294 3-8-11 61 ....(p) EddieAhern 6 (J R Weymes) *trckd ldrs: rdn and wknd over 1f out* **16/1**	51
0-0	**9**	*1 1/4*	**Diamond Dan (IRE)**[178] 1785 3-8-11 .... AdrianMcCarthy 7 (P D Evans) *outpcd: a bhd* **66/1**	47
0	**10**	*hd*	**Its Alex (IRE)**[20] 6031 4-8-7 .... PaulEddery 2 (R J Hodges) *s.i.s: a bhd* **50/1**	42
0100	**11**	*3/4*	**Harrys House**[10] 6217 3-8-11 62 ....(v) TonyHamilton 5 (J J Quinn) *slowly away: a bhd* **14/1**	44
	12	*5*	**In A Fit** 4-9-0 .... FergalLynch 11 (P Howling) *slowly away: racd wd: a bhd* **33/1**	32
/00-	**13**	*1/2*	**Efistorm**[412] 5786 4-9-2 83 .... JasonEdmunds[(3)] 3 (J Balding) *led tl hdd over 1f out: wknd rapidly* **25/1**	36

1m 15.42s (-0.39) **Going Correction** -0.20s/f (Stan) **13** Ran SP% **120.3**

Speed ratings (Par 101):94,92,92,90,88 88,87,87,85,85 84,77,76

CSF £27.76 TOTE £5.00: £2.00, £1.60, £2.00; EX 34.70.Willheconquertoo (no.5) was claimed by I. W. McInnes for £10,000.

Owner John Purcell **Bred** Norcroft Park Stud **Trained** Hingham, Norfolk

■ Stewards' Enquiry : John Egan caution: careless riding

Robbie Fitzpatrick one-day ban: failed to keep straight from stalls (Nov 22)

FOCUS

A modest claimer run slower than the later nursery, and the form has not been rated positively. Once again the winner came from off the pace.

Its Alex(IRE) Official explanation: jockey said gelding hung badly right

6311 BETDIRECTPOKER.COM MAIDEN AUCTION STKS 5f 20y(P)

2:35 (2:36) (Class 6) 2-Y-O **£2,839** (£838; £419) **Stalls** Low

Form				RPR
3	**1**		**Glenviews Youngone (IRE)**[11] 6196 2-8-6 .... RobbieFitzpatrick 1 (Peter Grayson) *mde all: rdn out fnl f* **4/1**[3]	70+
0233	**2**	*1*	**Canina**[2] 6296 2-8-6 66 .... EddieAhern 8 (Ms Deborah J Evans) *mid-div: hdwy over 1f out: rdn and r.o to go 2nd cl home* **6/1**	63
2500	**3**	*nk*	**Twinned (IRE)**[23] 5969 2-8-2 65 ....(p) JosephWalsh[(7)] 6 (J S Moore) *chsd ldr: rdn to chse wnr 1f out: lost 2nd cl home* **22/1**	65
	4	*1 1/2*	**Targer Place** 2-8-11 .... TPQueally 4 (T T Clement) *outpcd: hdwy over 1f out: styd on: nvr nrr* **50/1**	62
42	**5**	*2*	**Exexel**[11] 6196 2-8-5 .... NelsonDeSouza[(3)] 2 (P F I Cole) *chsd wnr tl wknd over 1f out* **9/4**[1]	51
003	**6**	*2 1/2*	**Obergurgl (IRE)**[4] 6282 2-8-13 .... JimmyFortune 9 (Mrs A Duffield) *hld up: rdn 1/2-way: sme late hdwy* **9/1**	47
2020	**7**	*1/2*	**Spirit Of Coniston**[11] 6197 2-8-4 63 .... DuranFentiman[(5)] 5 (M Wellings) *in tch: rdn 1/2-way: wknd over 1f out* **16/1**	42
330	**8**	*2*	**Slipperfoot**[21] 6004 2-8-2 60 .... MartinDwyer 12 (J J Quinn) *a bhd* **25/1**	27
4	**9**	*hd*	**Penny Thoughts**[48] 5465 2-8-4 .... ChrisCatlin 3 (E S McMahon) *trckd ldrs tl wknd wl over 1f out* **3/1**[2]	29
2520	**10**	*4*	**Tombalina**[2] 6297 2-7-11 54 .... MarcHalford[(5)] 10 (J L Spearing) *chsd ldrs: rdn 1/2-way: sn bhd* **25/1**	12

62.21 secs (-0.61) **Going Correction** -0.20s/f (Stan) **10** Ran SP% **119.9**

Speed ratings (Par 94):96,94,93,91,88 84,83,80,80,73

CSF £27.82 TOTE £4.30: £1.60, £1.90, £7.60; EX 30.90.

Owner Mrs M Shaughnessy and Mrs S Grayson **Bred** Leslie Young **Trained** Formby, Lancs

FOCUS

A modest maiden but a somewhat strange race with the first two in the market unable to hold on after being up with the pace early. However, the runner-up and third suggest the form is reasonably solid.

NOTEBOOK

Glenviews Youngone(IRE), easy in the market, showed the benefit of her recent debut, setting the pace and kicking clear off the bend. Despite tiring in the last furlong she ran on well to hold off the placed horses and her pace should continue to prove an asset. (op 11-4)

Canina, has been running well of late both on turf and sand. She tracked the leaders early and picked up well in the straight, but could not reach the winner. Her turn should come, possibly back in nursery company over another furlong. (op 5-1)

Twinned(IRE), making his sand debut, tracked the leaders into the straight and kept on well. He looks to have a small race in him. (op 20-1)

Targer Place ◆, by a sprinter but with more stamina on the dam's side, ran a nice race on this debut having been taken off his feet early. He can be expected to improve for the experience.

Exexel, having her third race in a fortnight, raced up with the winner, who she had beaten here at the end of last month, but was left behind when that rival kicked off the turn. She may need a short break now. (tchd 2-1)

Penny Thoughts the gamble of the race on her Polytrack debut, was up with the pace but had to race three wide and was in trouble coming off the bend. This was a disappointing effort but, out of a winner on sand, can be given another chance. (op 7-1)

6312 PLAY NOW AT BETDIRECTCASINO.COM NURSERY 5f 216y(P)

3:10 (3:11) (Class 5) (0-75,77) 2-Y-O **£4,417** (£1,314; £656; £328) **Stalls** Low

Form				RPR
361	**1**		**Ocean Of Dreams (FR)**[24] 5955 2-9-7 75 .... GrahamGibbons 4 (J D Bethell) *mde all: rdn clr fnl f* **11/4**[1]	80+
2230	**2**	*1 1/4*	**Grenane (IRE)**[66] 5029 2-8-11 65 .... JohnEgan 5 (P D Evans) *mid-div: nt clr run over 2f out: swtchd rt: r.o to go 2nd ins fnl f* **12/1**	66+
2001	**3**	*1*	**Balik Pearls**[4] 6282 2-9-9 77 7ex ....(b) JimmyFortune 6 (N A Callaghan) *stdd s: racd wd: rdn and hdwy 2f out: chsd wnr over 1f out: lost 2nd nr fin* **11/4**[1]	75
U001	**4**	*1 3/4*	**Thoughtsofstardom**[41] 5627 2-9-3 71 .... EddieAhern 7 (W M Brisbourne) *chsd ldrs: nt qckn but kpt on ins fnl f* **12/1**	64
302	**5**	*2*	**Miss Dixie**[37] 5696 2-8-13 67 .... TomEaves 13 (Miss J A Camacho) *hld up: rdn 2f out: styd on fnl f* **20/1**	54
5105	**6**	*5*	**Magnolia Blossom**[2] 6295 2-8-8 62 .... TonyHamilton 1 (R A Fahey) *in tch tl rdn and wknd over 1f out* **14/1**	34
056	**7**	*3*	**Monte Mayor Junior**[15] 6123 2-8-10 64 .... IanMongan 9 (D Haydn Jones) *outpcd: styd on appr fnl f: nvr nr to chal* **20/1**	27
021	**8**	*hd*	**Mimiteh (USA)**[47] 5486 2-9-3 74 .... NelsonDeSouza[(3)] 3 (R M Beckett) *mid-div tl rdn and wknd over 1f out* **5/1**[2]	36
4004	**9**	*1 1/4*	**Optical Seclusion (IRE)**[55] 5293 2-8-8 62 .... PaulFitzsimons 8 (T J Etherington) *a bhd* **66/1**	20+
0100	**10**	*3 1/2*	**Savannah Pride (IRE)**[14] 6129 2-8-6 65 .... AdamKirby[(3)] 2 (Ernst Oertel) *trckd wnr tl wknd 2f out* **50/1**	13
1036	**11**	*17*	**Maggie Minx (IRE)**[9] 6226 2-8-10 64 .... ChrisCatlin 12 (M J Wallace) *a bhd* **11/1**[3]	—
5000	**P**		**Colourpoint (USA)**[17] 6098 2-9-2 70 ....(p) MartinDwyer 11 (C E Brittain) *sddle slipped sn after s: bhd whn p.u over 2f out* **25/1**	—

1m 15.06s (-0.75) **Going Correction** -0.20s/f (Stan) **12** Ran SP% **117.2**

Speed ratings (Par 96):97,95,94,91,89 82,78,78,76,71 49,—

CSF £35.81 CT £99.79 TOTE £4.40: £1.50, £3.40, £1.50; EX 79.20.

Owner R G Toes **Bred** And Mrs E Le Pivert **Trained** Middleham Moor, N Yorks

FOCUS

Three runners dominated the market in what looks a solid nursery. The time was reasonable, being 0.36sec faster than the earlier claimer. The winner brought solid nursery form into the race, and the runner-up has been rated to his best.

NOTEBOOK

Ocean Of Dreams(FR) ◆, who won well on his Fibresand debut, was backed against the favourite, raced up with the pace and, getting a slight advantage at halfway, was clear over a furlong out and kept on well to hold off the late challengers.He looks progressive. (op 7-2)

Grenane(IRE), whose only previous outing on this surface was back in May, tracked the leaders, but did not have much room turning for home. He picked up well in the clear, and while he could never get in a blow at the winner he looks capable of picking up a similar contest. Official explanation: jockey said colt was denied a clear run (op 14-1 tchd 16-1)

Balik Pearls, an easy-to-back favourite, played up and had to be walked to the start. She effectively lost her winning chance\n\x\x by being slowly into her stride, and although she made up a good deal of ground on the outside of the field, the effort ultimately told and cost her second place. She does not look the most straightforward filly. (op 2-1)

Thoughtsofstardom, bought after winning a seller here over a furlong shorter, ran quite well in this better contest without ever threatening to win. He should continue to pay his way in plating company back at the minimum trip. (tchd 14-1)

Miss Dixie ran just a fair race on this sand debut and may be better off in handicaps. (op 33-1)

Magnolia Blossom raced up with the early pace. (op 11-1)

Mimiteh(USA), a fast-ground winner on turf, did not appear to take to the surface, but may be worth a try at Lingfield. (op 9-2 tchd 11-2)

Maggie Minx(IRE) Official explanation: jockey said filly lost its action

Colourpoint(USA) Official explanation: jockey said saddle slipped

6313 PLAY INSTANT WIN GAMES ON ITVI CLAIMING STKS 1m 141y(P)

3:45 (3:45) (Class 6) 2-Y-O **£2,886** (£852; £426) **Stalls** Low

Form				RPR
4030	**1**		**Fusili (IRE)**[25] 5939 2-8-10 74 .... EddieAhern 7 (M G Quinlan) *a.p: wnt 2nd over 2f out: r.o to wl to ld ins fnl f: sn clr* **7/4**[1]	63
6064	**2**	*1 1/2*	**Tafilah**[11] 6198 2-8-4 55 .... JohnEgan 6 (P W D'Arcy) *led after 2f: hdd and outpcd ins fnl f* **14/1**	54
06	**3**	*3/4*	**Divisive**[11] 6199 2-8-4 .... JimmyQuinn 2 (M Blanshard) *mid-div: outpcd over 2f out: r.o and styd on wl ins fnl f* **40/1**	52
0022	**4**	*nk*	**Cool Isle**[11] 6198 2-8-1 55 ....(p) AndrewMullen[(5)] 5 (K A Ryan) *hld up in tch: outpcd over 2f out: edgd lft app fnl f: r.o ins* **12/1**	54
0041	**5**	*nk*	**Angelina Bankes**[11] 6198 2-8-6 54 .... LPKeniry 4 (R A Harris) *lefor 2f: n.m.r over 2f out: swtchd rt over 1f out: kpt on ins fnl f* **7/1**	53
0004	**6**	*nk*	**Scroll**[18] 6072 2-9-7 70 ....(v) FergalLynch 1 (P Howling) *bhd tl hdwy 2f out: swtchd rt over 1f out: r.o* **6/1**[3]	67
0050	**7**	*1 3/4*	**Night Groove (IRE)**[39] 5659 2-8-9 60 .... SamHitchcott 11 (C Tinkler) *trckd ldr: hmpd on ins whn wknd over 1f out* **20/1**	53+
0	**8**	*1 1/4*	**Sahara Style**[34] 5746 2-8-13 .... GrahamGibbons 12 (R Hollinshead) *a bhd* **14/1**	53
0646	**9**	*hd*	**Tour D'Amour (IRE)**[4] 6284 2-8-8 66 .... ChrisCatlin 3 (Stef Liddiard) *hld up: a bhd* **9/2**[2]	47
4604	**10**	*3 1/2*	**Bob's Your Uncle**[18] 6077 2-9-4 59 .... JimmyFortune 13 (J G Portman) *prom tl wknd over 2f out* **12/1**	50
000	**11**	*5*	**Lewis Lloyd (IRE)**[35] 5708 2-9-2 60 ....(t) AdamKirby[(5)] 8 (I A Wood) *racd wd: a bhd* **33/1**	42
00	**P**		**Chase The Lady (USA)**[27] 5886 2-8-0 .... FrankieMcDonald 10 (D J S Ffrench Davis) *sddle slipped: mid-div but sn bhd: p.u over 2f out* **66/1**	—

1m 51.13s (-0.63) **Going Correction** -0.20s/f (Stan) **12** Ran SP% **121.7**

Speed ratings (Par 94):94,92,92,91,91 91,89,88,88,85 80,—

CSF £29.96 TOTE £2.60: £1.20, £3.00, £6.70; EX 44.90.Chase The Lady was claimed by P. D. Evans for £6,000. Fusili was claimed by Nigel Shields for £11,000.

Owner W P Flynn **Bred** Gestut Romerhof **Trained** Newmarket, Suffolk

■ Stewards' Enquiry : Andrew Mullen six-day ban (includes five deferred days): careless riding (Nov 22, 25-30)

FOCUS

Ordinary race run at a modest pace but the winner scored in decent style on her sand debut. The form is held down by the time and the proximity of the runner-up.

NOTEBOOK

Fusili(IRE) ◆, making her sand debut, tracked the leaders before delivering a challenge early in the straight. Once in front she had matters in control and won a shade comfortably. She was claimed by Nigel Shields and should win more races on this surface. (op 2-1 tchd 9-4)

Tafilah set the pace and kicked off the home turn, but could not get away from the winner, although she stuck on well once headed and reversed recent form with the fourth and fifth. Using her and the fourth as a guide the form looks ordinary. (op 16-1)

Divisive ◆ was held up on the inside and was short of room at a crucial stage. She ran on well once switched and would have finished closer wioth a clear passage. She now qualifies for a handicap mark, which should enable her to be competitive. (op 33-1)

Cool Isle reversed recent form with Angelina Bankes on the same terms, but with the apprentice allowances in her favour. With that filly she helps set a modest standard. (op 9-1)

Angelina Bankes, winner of a seller over seven here last time, tracked the pacemakers but failed to pick up in the straight and was unable to confirm that form with the runner-up and fourth.. (tchd 6-1)

Scroll, dropping in class, was running on without ever posing a threat. (op 11-2 tchd 5-1)

Night Groove(IRE) showed up until weakening in the straight.

Tour D'Amour(IRE), stepping up in trip, has shown little in three efforts on Polytrack and a return to Fibresand may help. (op 5-1)

6314 PLAY NOW AT BETDIRECTPOKER.COM H'CAP — 1m 141y(P)

4:20 (4:21) (Class 2) (0-100,102) 3-Y-0+

£11,656 (£3,490; £1,745; £873; £435; £218) **Stalls** Low

Form			Horse	Jockey	RPR
2040	1		**Cimyla (IRE)**[41] 5607 4-8-12 **94** (C F Wall) *w.w: gng wl: led over 1f out: r.o wl and in command fnl f* **7/2**[2]	GeorgeBaker 1	107+
0661	2	3	**Appalachian Trail (IRE)**[90] 4360 4-9-0 **96** (I Semple) *bhd tl hdwy over 2f out: kpt on to chse wnr fnl f* **10/1**	(b) TomEaves 12	103
6060	3	½	**Master Theo (USA)**[34] 5743 4-8-5 **87** oh3 ow1 (Julian Poulton) *bhd tl hdwy on outside 2f out: styd on nvr nrr* **20/1**	(tp) JohnEgan 6	93
6402	4	1	**Brindisi**[12] 6181 4-9-1 **97** (B W Hills) *in tch: n.m.r 2f out: r.o fnl f* **11/2**	MartinDwyer 4	101
0031	5	1¼	**Nevada Desert (IRE)**[13] 6159 5-8-4 **86** oh7 (R M Whitaker) *led over 4f out: rdn and hdd over 1f out: no ex* **12/1**	DeanMcKeown 3	87
2225	6	1½	**Del Mar Sunset**[13] 6159 6-7-11 **86** oh3 (W J Haggas) *in tch: rdn and swtchd rt over 1f out: no ex* **11/1**	LiamJones(7) 13	84
3000	7	1¾	**Bahiano (IRE)**[56] 5269 4-8-11 **93** (C E Brittain) *a bhd* **14/1**	JimmyFortune 10	87
0-06	8	nk	**Hail The Chief**[7] 6247 8-8-8 **90** (R Hannon) *chsd ldrs tl wknd over 1f out* **14/1**	ChrisCatlin 11	84
0051	9	3½	**Cardinal Venture (IRE)**[6] 6248 7-8-8 **95** (K A Ryan) *led tl hdd over 4f out: rdn over 2f out: sn wknd* **5/1**[3]	AndrewMullen(5) 5	81
300	10	16	**Aldora**[6] 6253 6-9-6 **102** (J Ryan) *chsd ldrs tl rdn and wknd 4f out* **25/1**	IanMongan 9	55
0005	11	hd	**Te Quiero**[244] 613 7-8-13 **95** (Miss Gay Kelleway) *sn bhd* **33/1**	(t) FergalLynch 8	47
000	P		**Night Air (IRE)**[90] 4360 4-8-12 **94** (J J Quinn) *in tch tl broke down and p.u 5f out* **10/3**[1]	EddieAhern 7	—

1m 46.71s (-5.05) **Going Correction** -0.20s/f (Stan)
WFA 3 from 4yo+ 3lb — **12** Ran SP% **127.4**
Speed ratings (Par 109):114,111,110,110,108 107,106,105,102,88 88,—
CSF £41.02 CT £652.50 TOTE £3.80: £1.30, £4.50, £6.30; EX 74.60.
Owner Peter Botham **Bred** Dr D G St John And Mrs Sherry Collier **Trained** Newmarket, Suffolk

FOCUS

A good handicap, run at a decent pace from the start, and the first three came from behind. The winner came clear in a very good time and the form looks strong.

NOTEBOOK

Cimyla(IRE) ◆, who won his maiden on his only previous try on Polytrack back in 2003, was backed down to joint favourite and was given a typically well-judged Baker ride. Held up on the inside travelling smoothly, he did not have much room on the bend but taking the brave route paid off and, once in front, he picked up in the manner of an improver. He looks one to keep on the right side this winter. (op 11-2)

Appalachian Trail(IRE) is a good yardstick in this sort of contest and tracked the winner throughout. Following him through on the inside, he tried to deliver a challenge but was always being held. He should win more good races on this surface. (op 9-1)

Master Theo(USA), a three-time winner here last winter, was another held up off the pace but had to come wide to deliver his challenge and never looked like reaching the winner. This was a fair effort nonetheless, and although not especially well handicapped at present, is always one to consider around here. (tchd 25-1)

Brindisi, runner-up in a fillies' Listed race on her Polytrack debut, sat on the heels of the pacemakers and looked a big danger turning in, but did not pick up as well as seemed likely. However, she did best of those to race close to the pace so the effort may have been better than it looked. A return to Lingfield's faster surface may be in her favour. (tchd 6-1)

Nevada Desert(IRE), a winner here last month, was racing from 7lb out of the handicap so was effectively 13lb higher. He was unable to lead with Cardinal Venture in the race and no sooner had he got the better of that rival than the winner swept by on his inside. He will be better off racing from his correct mark. (tchd 14-1)

Del Mar Sunset, who used to make the running but has done quite well this season under waiting tactics, never got into a challenging position. (op 10-1)

Bahiano(IRE) came from the rear at the end of the back straight and was merely staying on past beaten horses.

Hail The Chief, a star in his younger days, ran quite well under a positive ride and suggested he has the ability to win again, although possibly not in races as competitive as this. (op 10-1)

Cardinal Venture(IRE) tried to make the running but got no peace in front and was on the retreat turning in. He seems more effective on Fibresand. (op 11-2)

Aldora Official explanation: jockey said mare ran flat

Night Air(IRE) who was well backed before late money came for the favourite, was on the heels of the leaders when sadly breaking down with fatal consequences at around the halfway mark. (op 9-2 tchd 5-2)

6315 GLOW-WORM HIGH EFFICIENCY H'CAP — 7f 32y(P)

4:50 (4:50) (Class 5) (0-70,70) 3-Y-0+ **£3,453** (£1,027; £513; £256) **Stalls** High

Form			Horse	Jockey	RPR
3300	1		**Nephetriti Way (IRE)**[90] 4357 4-9-3 **69** (P R Chamings) *a.p: led over 2f out: r.o wl fnl f* **40/1**	IanMongan 12	77
1220	2	1	**Summer Recluse (USA)**[32] 5802 6-9-3 **69** (J M Bradley) *stdd in rr: gd hdwy over 1f out: r.o wl to chse wnr ins fnl f* **10/1**	(t) GeorgeBaker 3	74+
5104	3	¾	**Out For A Stroll**[68] 4972 6-9-4 **70** (S C Williams) *hld up: hdwy 2f out: edgd lft and swtchd rt over 1f out: r.o ins fnl f* **8/1**	JamieMackay 2	73+
0000	4	hd	**Petardias Magic (IRE)**[32] 5802 4-8-10 **67** (G A Huffer) *led for 1f: a.p: nt qckn fnl f* **14/1**	AdamKirby(5) 6	70
0060	5	½	**No Grouse**[27] 5893 5-9-1 **67** (E J Alston) *in tch: rdn over 2f out: wknd ins fnl f* **7/1**[3]	DavidAllan 4	69
4051	6	¾	**Vienna's Boy (IRE)**[15] 6126 4-9-3 **69** (W J Musson) *mid-div: styd on appr fnl f but nt qckn* **5/1**[2]	PatCosgrave 8	69
3403	7	3	**Kindlelight Debut**[6] 6266 5-9-2 **68** (N P Littmoden) *in tch tl wknd over 1f out* **11/4**[1]	JimmyFortune 11	60
2040	8	hd	**Benny The Bus**[27] 5893 3-9-2 **69** (Mrs G S Rees) *in tch on outside: rdn 2f out: wknd over 1f out* **20/1**	(p) NickyMackay 5	60
5036	9	2½	**Tequila Sheila (IRE)**[30] 5835 3-9-1 **68** (K R Burke) *hld up: nt clr run over 2f out: sn bhd* **12/1**	DPMcDonogh 1	53
0504	10	shd	**General Feeling (IRE)**[13] 6161 4-9-3 **69** (S Kirk) *mid-div: wknd over 1f out* **5/1**[2]	(t) JohnEgan 10	54
0100	11	3½	**Warden Warren**[38] 5687 7-8-13 **70** (Mrs C A Dunnett) *racd wd: nvr on terms* **25/1**	(b) MarcHalford(5) 9	46
020-	12	15	**How's Things**[363] 6645 5-8-12 **67** (R A Harris) *led after 1f: hdd over 2f out: sn wknd* **25/1**	AmirQuinn(3) 7	4

1m 29.0s (-1.40) **Going Correction** -0.20s/f (Stan)
WFA 3 from 4yo+ 1lb — **12** Ran SP% **122.0**
Speed ratings (Par 103):100,98,98,97,97 96,92,92,89,89 85,68
CSF £396.35 CT £3580.03 TOTE £47.40: £12.60, £3.20, £3.00; EX 264.20.
Owner Mrs Alexandra J Chandris **Bred** Glashare House Stud **Trained** Baughurst, Hants

FOCUS

A modest handicap run at a steady pace and a surprise result, although the form looks reasonably sound.

Kindlelight Debut Official explanation: jockey said mare ran flat

6316 PLAY INSTANT WIN GAMES AT BETDIRECT.CO.UK NURSERY (DIV II) — 7f 32y(P)

5:20 (5:21) (Class 5) (0-75,73) 2-Y-O **£3,730** (£1,109; £554; £277) **Stalls** High

Form			Horse	Jockey	RPR
5430	1		**Flylowflylong (IRE)**[13] 6136 2-9-2 **68** (I Semple) *in tch: rdn over 2f out: r.o strly to ld post* **4/1**[2]	TomEaves 2	71
0500	2	hd	**Gattuso**[9] 6226 2-8-10 **62** (Ms Deborah J Evans) *in tch: hdwy to ld ent fnl f: edgd rt: hdd last strides* **12/1**	SamHitchcott 6	65
2001	3	2½	**Colmar Supreme**[22] 5993 2-9-7 **73** (R Hannon) *in tch: rdn over 2f out: one pce ins fnl f* **7/2**[1]	EddieAhern 5	69
5030	4	1¾	**Global Guardian**[13] 6136 2-8-13 **65** (Mrs G S Rees) *in tch: rdn and hdd ent fnl f: no ex* **15/2**	NickyMackay 1	57
530	5	2	**Almowj**[30] 5833 2-9-2 **68** (C E Brittain) *s.i.s: sn mid-div: one pce ent fnl f* **12/1**	(p) JimmyFortune 10	55
005	6	5	**Blandford Flyer**[30] 5832 2-8-10 **67** (W R Swinburn) *hld up: no hdwy fr wl over 1f out* **5/1**[3]	AdamKirby(5) 3	41
500	7	nk	**Carrietau**[69] 4941 2-8-13 **65** (J G Given) *a bhd* **22/1**	MartinDwyer 7	39
0300	8	¾	**Atticus Trophies (IRE)**[6] 6249 2-8-10 **69** (K McAuliffe) *chsd ldr tl 3f out: sn wknd* **12/1**	(b[1]) JamesDoyle(7) 4	41
6440	9	nk	**Mambo Sun**[33] 5755 2-8-13 **65** (P A Blockley) *a bhd* **14/1**	FergalLynch 9	36
000	10	hd	**Show Thyme**[44] 5547 2-8-11 **63** (K A Ryan) *prom: chsd ldr 3f out: wknd wl over 1f out* **16/1**	JimmyQuinn 11	34+
3043	11	½	**Mujelle**[24] 5955 2-9-1 **67** (D K Ivory) *mid-div: wknd 2f out* **8/1**	ChrisCatlin 12	36

1m 29.84s (-0.56) **Going Correction** -0.20s/f (Stan) — **11** Ran SP% **121.7**
Speed ratings (Par 96):95,94,91,89,87 81,81,80,80,80 79
CSF £53.57 CT £188.71 TOTE £5.00: £2.10, £2.80, £2.00; EX 69.30 Place 6 £303.23, Place 5 £53.25.
Owner G L S Partnership **Bred** Mrs A C Peters **Trained** Carluke, S Lanarks

FOCUS

A modest nursery run fractionally slower than the first division. The first two came clear.

NOTEBOOK

Flylowflylong(IRE), making his sand debut from a reasonable mark, came from off the pace and, striking the front halfway up the straight, had to dig deep to hold the persistent runner-up. (op 7-2 tchd 10-3)

Gattuso, who had run well on his debut on this surface but had played up in the stalls on his last visit, came through on the rail to deliver his challenge and proved as tenacious as his namesake, but the angle favoured the winner. He looks more than capable of gaining compensation. (tchd 14-1)

Colmar Supreme, another making his debut on sand and off a mark 8lb higher than for his maiden win, stayed on in the final furlong without troubling the principals. (tchd 11-2)

Global Guardian, whose best efforts on turf were on sharp, left-handed tracks, made most of the running and looked like holding on when kicking into a clear advantage off the turn. However, his legs turned to jelly just inside the last furlong and he was swallowed up by the strong finishers. (op 8-1 tchd 10-1)

Almowj, with cheekpieces replacing blinkers on this handicap debut, missed the break but, after making up the deficit, did not pick up in the straight. (op 14-1)

Blandford Flyer, well backed on this handicap debut, never got into contention. (op 13-2 tchd 9-2)

T/Plt: £516.90 to a £1 stake. Pool: £36,224.05. 51.15 winning tickets. T/Qpdt: £30.80 to a £1 stake. Pool: £3,831.65. 92.00 winning tickets. JS

5831 TOULOUSE

Friday, November 11

OFFICIAL GOING: Soft

6317a PRIX FILLE DE L'AIR (GROUP 3) (F&M) — 1m 2f 110y

1:50 (1:51) 3-Y-0+ **£26,596** (£10,638; £7,979; £5,319; £2,660)

		Horse	Jockey	RPR
1		**Antioquia**[31] 5831 4-8-11 (C Laffon-Parias, France) *mid-div on inside, 4th and pushed along straight, driven to lead 1 1/2f out, ran on well final furlong, driven out* **59/10**	MBlancpain 2	105
2	½	**Russian Hill**[17] 6104 5-8-11 (A Fabre, France) *raced in 6th, driven straight, finished strongly final furlong to challenge close home, nearest at finish* **53/10**[3]	TGillet 11	104
3	½	**Amie De Mix (FR)**[29] 5863 4-8-11 (A Fabre, France) *led to 1 1/2f out, lost place over 1f out but rallied and went 2nd 1f out, kept on but lost 2nd close home* **13/10**[1]	CSoumillon 6	103
4	1	**Hideaway (FR)**[46] 5522 3-8-8 (R Gibson, France) *in touch, 5th straight, driven to go 2nd over 1f out, ran on til no extra final 100 yards* **11/2**	TJarnet 1	103
5	1	**Olimpic Girl (IRE)**[51] 5417 3-8-8 (F Rohaut, France) *close 2nd, driven 1 1/2f out, one pace final furlong* **53/10**[3]	F-XBertras 10	102
6	¾	**Law Of Chance**[31] 5831 3-8-8 (H-A Pantall, France) *held up in touch, kept on steadily straight* **11/2**	MAndrouin 7	100

7 1 ½ **Maredsous (FR)**[17] 6104 5-8-11 ....(b) SPasquier 5 96
(D Sepulchre, France) *in touch, 7th and driven straight, unable to quicken* **46/10**[2]

8 nk **Quilanga (GER)**[439] 5168 4-8-11 .... EPedroza 3 95
(A Wohler, Germany) *prominent in 3rd, ridden over 1f out, weakened final furlong* **9/1**

9 6 **Lady In Grey (FR)**[19] 6056 3-8-8 .... PSogorb 4 87
(H Carlus, France) *held up, never dangerous* **36/1**

10 5 **All Woman**[96] 3-8-8 .... PFredericks 9 79
(E J Creighton) *towards rear, last and beaten straight* **68/1**

P **Brogue Lanterns (IRE)**[166] 3-8-8 .... EdwardCreighton 8 —
(E J Creighton) *towards rear, dropped to last when rider lost irons at half-way, pulled up* **89/1**

2m 9.78s
WFA 3 from 4yo+ 4lb 11 Ran SP% **153.6**
PARI-MUTUEL (including 1 euro stake): WIN 6.90; PL 1.80, 2.00, 1.20; DF 31.60.
Owner Felipe Hinojosa **Bred** The Kingwood Partnership **Trained** Chantilly, France

NOTEBOOK
Antioquia, very much an improving filly, landed the hat-trick as well as winning her first Group event. She took the lead over a furlong out and ran on really well, and now retires to her owner's stud in England.\n\x\x , very much an improving filly, landed the hat-trick as well as winning her first Group event. She took the lead over a furlong out and ran on really well, and now retires to her owner's stud in England.\n\x\x , very much an improving filly, landed the hat-trick as well as winning her first Group event. She took the lead over a furlong out and ran on really well, and now retires to her owner's stud in England.
Russian Hill, never far from the leading group, looked outpaced early in the straight before running on really well in the closing stages. A longer trip may well be beneficial to her.
Amie De Mix(FR), at the head of affairs soon after the start, was still at the same position on entering the straight and after looking beaten ran on again close home.
Hideaway(FR) was always well up near the rail and was given every possible chance in the straight, but she could not quicken inside the final furlong.

6302 LINGFIELD (L-H)
Saturday, November 12

OFFICIAL GOING: Standard
Wind: Virtually nil

6318 EUROPEAN BREEDERS FUND MAIDEN STKS (DIV I) 1m (P)
12:05 (12:08) (Class 5) 2-Y-O **£3,912** (£1,163; £581; £290) **Stalls** High

Form RPR

02 **1** **I'm In Love (USA)**[57] 5272 2-8-9 .... EddieAhern 12 73+
(M A Magnusson) *b: lw: broke wl: restrained in tch: rdn to ld jst ins fnl f: r.o wl: readily* **10/11**[1]

2 2 **Fyvie** 2-8-9 .... JamieSpencer 2 69
(E A L Dunlop) *w'like: scope: trckd ldrs: led over 3f out: rdn over 1f out: hdd jst ins fnl f: edgd rt and nt pce of wnr* **6/1**[3]

0 **3** 1 **Veronica's Girl**[22] 6009 2-8-9 .... JohnEgan 6 66
(P R Hedger) *t.k.h bhd ldrs: rdn and ev ch over 1f out: kpt on same pce* **50/1**

4 shd **Profitable** 2-8-9 .... OscarUrbina 11 66
(B W Hills) *w'like: str: b.bkwd: hld up: stdy hdwy into midfield over 3f out: sn rdn: styd on ins fnl f* **14/1**

5 2 **Starship (IRE)** 2-8-9 .... KFallon 10 66+
(W J Haggas) *w'like: b.bkwd: w ldr: rdn and effrt over 2f out: chalng whn n.m.r and snatched up 2f out: kpt on same pce but no ch after* **5/1**[2]

0 **6** 2 **Storm Prospect**[24] 5987 2-9-0 .... ChrisCatlin 1 62
(C Tinkler) *leggy: b.bkwd: hld up: rdn over 3f out: styd fr 2f out: nvr a danger* **20/1**

0 **7** nk **Valerie**[29] 5870 2-8-9 .... NickyMackay 8 56
(L M Cumani) *mid div: rdn 3f out: one pced fnl 2f* **14/1**

8 hd **Lord Laing (USA)** 2-9-0 .... JimmyQuinn 5 61
(H J Collingridge) *s.i.s: sn mid div: rdn 3f out: wknd 1f out* **25/1**

0 **9** ¾ **Katsumoto (IRE)**[29] 5870 2-9-0 .... JimmyFortune 7 59
(N P Littmoden) *sn led: hdd 3f out: sn rdn: in tch whn n.m.r and snatched up jst over 2f out: wknd* **25/1**

10 3 **Carpeting** 2-9-0 .... DerekMcGaffin 4 52
(D Morris) *wlike: chsd ldrs: pushed along 4f out: wknd over 2f out* **33/1**

11 23 **Cannygo (IRE)** 2-9-0 .... LPKeniry 9 —
(R M Flower) *b.bkwd: a bhd: lost tch over 2f out* **66/1**

1m 39.29s (-0.14) **Going Correction** -0.15s/f (Stan) 11 Ran SP% **115.5**
Speed ratings (Par 96):94,92,91,90,88 86,86,86,85,82 59
CSF £5.63 TOTE £1.80: £1.10, £1.80, £10.10; EX 7.30.
Owner East Wind Racing Ltd **Bred** W Lazy T Ltd **Trained** Upper Lambourn, Berks

FOCUS
A fair maiden containing some unexposed runners with decent pedigrees. The level of the form is difficult to assess, but has been rated through the winner to previous mark, but could go higher.

NOTEBOOK
I'm In Love(USA) took to the surface well, living up to the promise shown in two races on turf. She looks a useful recruit to the All-Weather scene. (op Evens tchd 5-6)
Fyvie, a Grand Lodge filly from a winning family around a mile and ten furlongs, made a pleasing debut. She can find a similar race. (op 5-1 tchd 13-2)
Veronica's Girl showed much more than she had done on her debut, which was on turf. She should be up to finding a race of this type.
Profitable, a Daylami filly making her debut, is bred to be more effective over longer trips. In the circumstances, she ran well and there should be more to come. (op 12-1 tchd 16-1)
Starship(IRE), a Galileo filly, is related to winners around this trip, though she may get a bit more stamina from her sire. She did not get the best of luck in running, and can improve on this debut effort. (op 9-2)
Storm Prospect has shown promise in her two races to date, and could be heading for handicaps. (tchd 25-1)
Valerie is not living up to her pedigree, but her trainer should get a bit more out of her as she gains experience. (op 12-1 tchd 16-1)

6319 EUROPEAN BREEDERS FUND MAIDEN STKS (DIV II) 1m (P)
12:35 (12:38) (Class 5) 2-Y-O **£3,899** (£1,160; £434; £434) **Stalls** High

Form RPR

03 **1** **Cactus King**[13] 6178 2-9-0 .... JimmyFortune 4 82+
(J H M Gosden) *rangy: scope: prom: led 6f out: qcknd clr over 1f out: comf* **2/1**[1]

22 **2** 4 **Queen's Composer (IRE)**[14] 6135 2-9-0 .... PaulEddery 11 73
(B Smart) *trckd ldrs: rdn and effrt over 2f out: kpt on to go 2nd 1f out: no ch w wnr* **8/1**[3]

0 **3** ½ **Gower Song**[22] 6011 2-8-9 .... JohnEgan 5 67
(D R C Elsworth) *lw: chsd ldrs: rdn 3f out: kpt on same pce* **11/4**[2]

3 dht **Materialize (USA)** 2-8-9 .... ChrisCatlin 7 67
(P J McBride) *slowly away: bhd: styd on fr 2f out: wnt 3rd fnl stride: nvr trbld ldrs* **66/1**

6 **5** 1 **Eclipse Park**[31] 5833 2-9-0 .... EddieAhern 8 70
(M J McGrath) *mid div: hdwy over 2f out: sn rdn: kpt on same pce* **16/1**

0 **6** 2 **Mayden Dawn**[31] 5833 2-8-9 .... DarryllHolland 6 60
(D K Ivory) *hld up towards rr: sme late hdwy: nvr a danger* **100/1**

7 1 **Danamour (IRE)** 2-9-0 .... MartinDwyer 1 63
(M P Tregoning) *str: s.i.s: a towards rr* **8/1**[3]

8 ¾ **Daneway** 2-8-9 ....(b[1]) JimmyQuinn 2 56
(H R A Cecil) *w'like: s.i.s: sn mid div: rdn 4f out: wknd over 1f out* **33/1**

0 **9** nk **King's Ransom**[94] 4262 2-8-11 .... NeilChalmers(3) 3 61
(A M Balding) *trckd ldrs: chsd wnr 3f out tl 1f out: wknd qckly* **20/1**

10 nk **Marachi Band (USA)** 2-8-9 .... JamieSpencer 9 55
(E A L Dunlop) *w'likw: b.bkwd: hld up and a towards rr* **14/1**

0 **11** 2 ½ **Titus Lumpus (IRE)**[16] 6123 2-9-0 .... LPKeniry 10 55
(R M Flower) *led for 2f: prom: rdn over 2f out: wknd over 1f out* **100/1**

0 **12** 3 **Oh Glory Be (USA)**[14] 6143 2-8-9 .... KFallon 12 43
(R Hannon) *a towards rr* **8/1**[3]

1m 38.1s (-1.33) **Going Correction** -0.15s/f (Stan) 12 Ran SP% **117.1**
Speed ratings (Par 96):100,96,95,95,94 92,91,90,90,90 87,84
CSF £17.98 TOTE £2.80: £1.60, £2.40; EX 12.80 Place: Gower Song: £0.70, Materialize £10.00.
Owner A E Oppenheimer **Bred** Hascombe And Valiant Studs **Trained** Newmarket, Suffolk

FOCUS
Another fair maiden, with a progressive winner in a decent time and sound form, rated through the runner-up.

NOTEBOOK
Cactus King gained his reward for a good effort two weeks earlier. He goes well on the surface and is improving, which bodes well for the future. (op 7-4 tchd 9-4)
Queen's Composer(IRE) finished second for the third time in as many runs, but the winner was a tough act to beat. This was a good first effort on sand, and a similar race should be within reach. (op 15-2 tchd 7-1)
Gower Song is coming on gradually, and this trip should suit. She should be placed to win before long. (op 3-1 tchd 10-3 in places)
Materialize(USA), unraced for Khalid Abdulla, and sold out of his ownership for 15,000 guineas, made a satisfactory debut. She should be suited by at least ten furlongs. (op 3-1 tchd 10-3 in places)
Eclipse Park ran another fair race, looking well at home over the trip. He is worth keeping an eye on in this sort of company.
Mayden Dawn ran better than on her debut, but a bit more is needed. (op 66-1)
Danamour(IRE), a half-brother to course winner Londoner, should improve for the outing. (op 7-1)
Daneway, a 23,000gns daughter of Danehill Dancer, was blinkered for this debut, She ran well for a long way but is one to monitor to see if she goes on from here. (op 28-1)
King's Ransom Official explanation: jockey said colt ran too free early
Titus Lumpus(IRE) Official explanation: jockey said gelding hung left
Oh Glory Be(USA) Official explanation: jockey said filly hung right throughout

6320 BET ON RUGBY AT BETDIRECT NURSERY 6f (P)
1:10 (1:12) (Class 4) (0-85,85) 2-Y-O **£4,818** (£1,433; £716; £357) **Stalls** Low

Form RPR

1035 **1** **Secret Night**[22] 6004 2-9-2 **80** .... EddieAhern 9 85
(J A R Toller) *mid div: tk clsr order over 2f out: rdn to ld jst ins fnl f: jst hld on* **10/1**

3102 **2** hd **Brandywell Boy (IRE)**[31] 5836 2-9-7 **85** .... JohnEgan 8 89
(D J S Ffrench Davis) *t.k.h bhd ldrs: stdd after 2f in tch: hdwy and hung lft over 1f out: r.o strly: jst failed* **6/1**[2]

2501 **3** shd **Orpsie Boy (IRE)**[45] 5540 2-9-4 **82** ....(t) JamieSpencer 1 86
(N P Littmoden) *lw: hld up: hdwy on inner over 2f out: swtchd rt over 1f out: r.o strly ins fnl f* **7/4**[1]

3000 **4** 1 **Lyrical Blues (IRE)**[7] 6249 2-8-3 **74** ow2 .... JamesMillman(7) 6 75
(B R Millman) *trckd ldrs: sltly outpcd 2f out: hmpd over 1f out: styd on* **33/1**

1304 **5** 1 **Charlie Delta**[11] 6214 2-8-10 **77** .... DNolan(3) 2 75
(D Carroll) *towards rr: styd on fnl f: nvr trbld ldrs* **20/1**

0124 **6** nk **Lucayos**[3] 6297 2-8-2 **66** .... ChrisCatlin 3 63
(Mrs H Sweeting) *led: rdn 2f out: hdd jst ins fnl f: no ex* **12/1**

4160 **7** ½ **Cheap N Chic**[42] 5613 2-9-5 **83** .... JimmyFortune 10 79
(B J Meehan) *bhd: sme late hdwy: nvr trbld ldrs* **6/1**[2]

0422 **8** hd **Azygous**[40] 5668 2-9-7 **85** .... KFallon 7 80
(J Akehurst) *lw: w ldr: rdn and ev ch over 1f out: wknd ins fnl f* **13/2**[3]

1412 **9** 1 ¼ **Grimes Faith**[16] 6124 2-9-4 **82** .... RichardHughes 5 73
(R Hannon) *trckd ldrs: gd run on inner over 2f out: sn rdn and ev ch: one pced fnl f* **8/1**

0500 **10** 2 ½ **Perfect Order (USA)**[39] 5682 2-7-12 **62** oh2 .... FrankieMcDonald 11 46
(N A Callaghan) *hld up and a towards rr* **50/1**

061 **11** hd **Xaluna Bay (IRE)**[12] 6196 2-9-0 **78** .... MartinDwyer 12 61
(W R Muir) *chsd ldrs: rdn and effrt 2f out: wkng whn short of room over 1f out* **14/1**

0000 **12** dist **Double Valentine**[12] 6197 2-7-13 **63** oh5 ow1 .... DaleGibson 4 —
(R Ingram) *b.hind: sn wl bhd: t.o* **50/1**

1m 11.87s (-0.94) **Going Correction** -0.15s/f (Stan) 12 Ran SP% **124.5**
Speed ratings (Par 98):100,99,99,98,96 96,95,95,93,90 90,—
CSF £70.43 CT £160.60 TOTE £16.20: £3.60, £2.60, £1.30; EX 88.00.
Owner John Drew **Bred** Worksop Manor Stud **Trained** Newmarket, Suffolk
■ Stewards' Enquiry : John Egan three-day ban: careless riding (Nov 25-26,28)
Jamie Spencer two day ban: careless riding (Nov 25-26)

FOCUS
A competitive nursery producing a close finish, and although the field were quite bunched at the finish the form should prove sound.

NOTEBOOK
Secret Night made a winning debut for her new stable, though six furlongs is as far as she wants to go at present. This was a good All-Weather debut, and her handicap mark should not be too badly affected. (op 11-1)
Brandywell Boy(IRE) made a smart handicap debut, and would have won in a few more strides. His mark looks about right, and he should continue to be dangerous in similar company. Official explanation: jockey said colt hung badly left (op 7-1 tchd 9-1)
Orpsie Boy(IRE) did well off a 7lb higher mark than last time, so is one to keep on the short-list in the near future. (op 9-4)
Lyrical Blues(IRE) came back to form with a fine first run on sand. He got the trip well, and will be at home in similar contests. Official explanation: jockey said gelding did not handle track
Charlie Delta made an encouraging All-Weather debut, though - just as on turf - he looked as if seven furlongs would suit these days. (op 22-1)
Lucayos is probably best at five furlongs, especially if ridden like this. (tchd 11-1)
Cheap N Chic was poorly drawn on this All-Weather debut, so ran satisfactorily in the circumstances. (op 8-1)

Azygous goes well on this surface, but is best at five furlongs. (op 6-1)
Perfect Order(USA) Official explanation: jockey said filly hung left
Double Valentine Official explanation: jockey said filly never travelled

6321 LITTLEWOODS BETDIRECT H'CAP — 5f (P)
1:40 (1:42) (Class 4) (0-85,85) 3-Y-O+ **£5,702** (£1,696; £847; £423) Stalls High

Form RPR
0001 **1** **Fromsong (IRE)**[13] 6182 7-9-4 **85** .... JohnEgan 4 — 97
(D K Ivory) *lw: trckd ldr: rdn to ld jst ins fnl f: r.o: edgd rt cl home* **5/2**[2]
-211 **2** ¾ **Fyodor (IRE)**[14] 6157 4-8-11 **78** .... JamieSpencer 8 — 88
(W J Haggas) *lw: b.hind: hld up: hdwy over 1f out: wnt 2nd ins fnl f: kpt on but hung in bhd wnr fnl 50yds* **7/4**[1]
5066 **3** 1 ¼ **Whitbarrow (IRE)**[21] 6021 6-8-10 **77** .... JimmyFortune 1 — 82
(A W Carroll) *led: rdn and hdd jst ins fnl f: no ex* **7/1**
3000 **4** 2 **Little Ridge (IRE)**[26] 5941 4-8-7 **79** .... TravisBlock(5) 6 — 77
(H Morrison) *in tch: rdn to go 3rd over 1f out: kpt on same pce fnl f* **16/1**
0020 **5** nk **Sir Desmond**[23] 5999 7-9-1 **82** ....(p) ChrisCatlin 5 — 79
(Rae Guest) *sn outpcd in rr: styd on ins fnl f: nvr trbld ldrs* **12/1**
0000 **6** 1 **Romany Nights (IRE)**[14] 6149 5-8-8 **75** ....(b) JimmyQuinn 2 — 68
(Miss Gay Kelleway) *b.hind: s.i.s: sn in tch: rdn and effrt 2f out: one pced fnl f* **16/1**
3003 **7** shd **Peopleton Brook**[9] 6238 3-8-12 **79** .... KFallon 7 — 72
(J M Bradley) *trckd ldrs: rdn and effrt 2f out: one pced after* **11/2**[3]
410 **8** 1 ½ **Harrison's Flyer (IRE)**[9] 6238 4-8-12 **79** ....(p) GeorgeBaker 10 — 66
(J M Bradley) *lw: b.hind: hld up and a towards rr* **12/1**

58.30 secs (-1.48) **Going Correction** -0.15s/f (Stan) 8 Ran SP% **120.0**
Speed ratings (Par 105):105,103,101,98,98 96,96,93
CSF £7.73 CT £26.99 TOTE £4.10: £1.30, £1.20, £1.90; EX 7.80.
Owner Dean Ivory **Bred** Mrs Teresa Bergin **Trained** Radlett, Herts
■ Intriguing Glimpse (7/1) was withdrawn (lost shoe on way to s.) R4 applies, deduct 10p in the £.

FOCUS
A decent-quality sprint and the form looks sound with the third running to recent form.
Peopleton Brook Official explanation: jockey said colt coughed pre-race

6322 BETDIRECT.CO.UK H'CAP — 1m (P)
2:15 (2:16) (Class 4) (0-85,85) 3-Y-O+ **£5,780** (£1,719; £859; £429) Stalls Low

Form RPR
3003 **1** **Obrigado (USA)**[59] 5235 5-8-11 **78** .... DarryllHolland 7 — 86
(W J Haggas) *hld up towards rr: hdwy 3f out to trck ldrs: hrd rdn over 1f out: styd on strly ins fnl f: led fnl strides* **13/2**[3]
0010 **2** shd **Red Romeo**[36] 5713 4-9-2 **83** .... DaleGibson 12 — 91
(G A Swinbank) *led for 1f: trckd ldr: drvn to ld ins fnl f: kpt on: hdd fnl strides* **16/1**
0040 **3** nk **Vicious Warrior**[42] 5612 6-8-12 **79** .... DeanMcKeown 10 — 86
(R M Whitaker) *towards rr: hdwy over 1f out: styd on ins fnl f: tk 3rd cl home: nrst fin* **16/1**
4301 **4** hd **Davenport (IRE)**[15] 6134 3-8-4 **80** .... JamesMillman(7) 4 — 87
(B R Millman) *hld up bhd: stdy hdwy over 1f out: r.o strly ins fnl f: tk 4th cl home: nrst fin* **8/1**
3443 **5** nk **Waterside (IRE)**[96] 4221 6-8-11 **78** .... GeorgeBaker 3 — 84
(G L Moore) *led after 1f: clr 4f out: rdn over 1f out: no ex whn hdd ins fnl f* **6/1**[2]
0006 **6** ½ **Sea Storm (IRE)**[27] 5923 7-8-13 **80** ....(p) JamieSpencer 8 — 85
(D R MacLeod) *chsd ldrs: rdn and effrt 2f out: kpt on same pce* **12/1**
0000 **7** ¾ **Blue Trojan (IRE)**[14] 6159 5-8-11 **78** .... JohnEgan 1 — 81
(S Kirk) *lw: in tch: drvn along 4f out: kpt on same pce fnl 2f* **4/1**[1]
6013 **8** shd **Trifti**[14] 6159 4-8-11 **78** .... LPKeniry 9 — 81+
(C A Cyzer) *s.i.s: bhd: hdwy and nt clr run on rails over 1f out: swtchd rt: styd on: nrst fin* **7/1**
0601 **9** ½ **Namroud (USA)**[14] 6138 6-9-0 **81** .... TonyHamilton 6 — 83
(R A Fahey) *lw: mid div: rdn and hdwy over 2f out: hung lft over 1f out: wknd* **8/1**
0620 **10** 1 **Desert Imp**[72] 4897 3-9-2 **85** .... MartinDwyer 2 — 84
(B W Hills) *hld up and a towards rr* **16/1**
100 **11** ½ **Will He Wish**[43] 5593 9-9-4 **85** ....(b) JimmyFortune 11 — 83
(S Gollings) *in tch tl over 1f out* **25/1**
2000 **12** 5 **Wessex (USA)**[23] 5999 5-8-10 **77** .... PatCosgrave 5 — 64
(P A Blockley) *mid div tl over 2f out* **12/1**

1m 37.47s (-1.96) **Going Correction** -0.15s/f (Stan)
WFA 3 from 4yo+ 2lb 12 Ran SP% **119.2**
Speed ratings (Par 105):103,102,102,102,102 101,100,100,100,99 98,93
CSF £106.43 CT £1624.31 TOTE £5.70: £1.90, £6.60, £8.60; EX 97.20.
Owner B Haggas **Bred** Bradyleigh Farms Inc **Trained** Newmarket, Suffolk

FOCUS
An ordinary handicap, but a Handicapper's delight with a blanket finish. The form looks sound with the first five close to their marks.
Trifti Official explanation: jockey said gelding was denied a clear run

6323 STANMORE LAW PRACTICE H'CAP — 1m 4f (P)
2:50 (2:51) (Class 6) (0-60,60) 3-Y-O+ **£2,594** (£766; £383) Stalls Low

Form RPR
0405 **1** **Captain Margaret**[53] 5388 3-8-11 **59** .... JimmyQuinn 10 — 67
(J Pearce) *lw: mid div: hdwy over 2f out: rdn over 1f out: styd on wl to ld cl home* **20/1**
5031 **2** ¾ **Amwell Brave**[13] 6184 4-9-4 **60** .... EddieAhern 4 — 67
(J R Jenkins) *lw: in tch: led wl over 1f out: sn rdn: kpt on but no ex whn hdd cl home* **13/2**[2]
5324 **3** hd **Bienheureux**[12] 6195 4-9-0 **56** ....(t) JohnEgan 13 — 63
(Miss Gay Kelleway) *b.hind: hld up towards rr: nt clr run briefly over 3f out: hdwy and nt clr run over 1f out: styd on strly: nrst fin* **4/1**[1]
1005 **4** shd **Free Style (GER)**[13] 6184 5-8-5 **50** .... NeilChalmers(3) 5 — 57
(Mrs H Sweeting) *b: mid div: hdwy 3f out: rdn wl over 1f out: styd on* **9/1**
3013 **5** ½ **Lady Taverner**[56] 5321 4-8-5 **52** .... NataliaGemelova(5) 14 — 58
(J E Long) *hld up towards rr: hdwy over 2f out into midfield: rdn over 1f out : styd on* **25/1**
1213 **6** 1 **Cup Of Love (USA)**[53] 5388 3-8-11 **59** .... ChrisCatlin 11 — 63
(Rae Guest) *trckd ldr: led briefly jst over 2f out: sn rdn: kpt on same pce* **10/1**
0033 **7** shd **Mad**[13] 6184 4-8-7 **49** .... LPKeniry 15 — 53
(Andrew Reid) *hld up towards rr: rdn 2f out: styd on fnl f: nvr trbld ldrs* **14/1**
2500 **8** nk **Rare Coincidence**[33] 5789 4-8-13 **58** ....(p) DNolan(3) 9 — 62
(R F Fisher) *prom: led after 1f: rdn 4f out: hdd over 2f out: kpt on same pce* **8/1**[3]
3402 **9** shd **Star Welcome**[19] 6081 4-8-8 **50** .... PatCosgrave 1 — 54
(W J Musson) *mid div: n.m.r over 3f out: hdwy over 2f out: rdn over 1f out: kpt on same pce* **9/1**
5560 **10** 1 ¼ **Serramanna**[15] 6130 4-8-8 **57** .... SladeO'Hara(7) 6 — 59
(Dr J R J Naylor) *in tch: rdn to chse ldrs over 2f out: wknd fnl f* **14/1**
-000 **11** hd **Competitor**[19] 6073 4-9-1 **60** ....(bt[1]) RobertMiles(3) 2 — 61
(J Akehurst) *hld up: hdwy over 2f out: rdn and hung lft over 1f out: wknd* **25/1**
0000 **12** 3 **Tata Naka**[13] 6184 5-8-1 **50** .... KirstyMilczarek(7) 16 — 46
(Mrs C A Dunnett) *lw: mid div tl 2f out* **33/1**
0 **13** 19 **Moondancer (GER)**[13] 6177 6-8-8 **50** .... DarryllHolland 7 — 16
(B G Powell) *chsd ldrs tl wknd over 2f out* **40/1**
1063 **14** 2 ½ **Balletomaine (IRE)**[42] 5615 3-8-9 **57** .... MartinDwyer 3 — 19
(B W Hills) *lw: led for 1f: trckd ldr: losing pl whn bdly hmpd over 3f out: no ch and eased after* **13/2**[2]
6050 **15** 4 **Opera Belle**[21] 6029 3-8-12 **60** .... JamieSpencer 12 — 16
(A P Jarvis) *a bhd: t.o fnl 3f* **14/1**

2m 32.35s (-2.04) **Going Correction** -0.15s/f (Stan)
WFA 3 from 4yo+ 6lb 15 Ran SP% **124.7**
Speed ratings (Par 101):100,99,99,99,98 98,98,98,97,97 97,95,82,80,78
CSF £142.19 CT £645.71 TOTE £31.40: £6.10, £2.90, £1.90; EX 142.80.
Owner Mrs Margaret Baxter **Bred** J Wilson **Trained** Newmarket, Suffolk
■ Stewards' Enquiry : Darryll Holland caution: careless riding

FOCUS
A modest race with a packed field at the finish. The form is only ordinary rated through the fifth and sixth, but looks reliable enough.
Bienheureux Official explanation: jockey said gelding was denied a clear run
Competitor Official explanation: jockey said colt missed the break

6324 PAIGE SYMNS H'CAP — 1m 2f (P)
3:25 (3:26) (Class 6) (0-60,60) 3-Y-O+ **£2,897** (£855; £428) Stalls Low

Form RPR
6142 **1** **Ramsgill (USA)**[23] 5423 3-9-0 **60** .... JimmyFortune 9 — 69
(N P Littmoden) *chsd ldrs: drvn along over 2f out: led over 1f out: r.o wl: rdn out* **5/2**[1]
4056 **2** 1 ¾ **Jomus**[70] 4937 4-9-0 **56** ....(p) MartinDwyer 3 — 62
(L Montague Hall) *hld up mid div: rdn and no imp 2f out: styd on strly ins fnl f to go 2nd cl home* **14/1**
4321 **3** nk **Qualitair Wings**[5] 6286 6-9-4 **60** 6ex .... DerekMcGaffin 6 — 65
(J Hetherton) *mid div: hdwy over 3f out: rdn to chse wnr over 1f out: kpt on: lost 2nd cl home* **4/1**[2]
1110 **4** 1 **Magic Warrior**[5] 6287 5-9-1 **57** .... PaulEddery 8 — 61
(J C Fox) *chsd ldrs: rdn over 2f out: kpt on same pce* **14/1**
-065 **5** ½ **Always Mine**[29] 5866 3-9-0 **60** ....(b[1]) ChrisCatlin 7 — 63
(N A Callaghan) *in tch: rdn over 2f out: kpt on ins fnl f* **20/1**
0010 **6** nk **Dinner Date**[75] 4842 3-8-12 **58** .... LPKeniry 10 — 60
(T Keddy) *b: lw: in tch: rdn over 2f out: styd on ins fnl f* **33/1**
2046 **7** hd **Polar Dawn**[12] 6202 3-8-6 **59** .... JamesMillman(7) 14 — 61
(B R Millman) *hld up towards rr: hdwy on outer over 2f out: rdn and hung lft: clipped heels and stmbld over 1f out: styd on* **14/1**
0 **8** 1 ¼ **Olivino (GER)**[16] 6126 4-9-4 **60** .... JohnEgan 2 — 59
(S Dow) *sn led: rdn and hdd over 1f out: wknd* **33/1**
0000 **9** 1 ¼ **Easter Ogil (IRE)**[176] 1862 10-8-13 **58** .... AmirQuinn(3) 1 — 55
(Jane Southcombe) *b: hld up: sme late hdwy: nvr a factor* **25/1**
3502 **10** shd **Blue Quiver (IRE)**[70] 4962 5-8-12 **54** .... GeorgeBaker 5 — 51
(C A Horgan) *b.hind: b.bkwd: stdd s: hld up bhd: rdn and hung lft over 1f out: no imp* **13/2**[3]
5000 **11** nk **Balearic Star (IRE)**[60] 5201 4-9-4 **60** .... KFallon 12 — 56
(B R Millman) *a towards rr* **8/1**
0000 **12** 3 ½ **Rasid (USA)**[98] 4165 7-9-0 **56** ....(v) EddieAhern 4 — 45
(C A Dwyer) *b: a towards rr* **16/1**
-041 **13** 22 **Fossgate**[32] 5824 4-9-4 **60** .... JamieSpencer 11 — 8
(J D Bethell) *mid div tl over 2f out* **13/2**[3]
00-0 **14** nk **Mount Ephram (IRE)**[15] 337 3-9-0 **60** ....(b) JimmyQuinn 13 — 7
(R F Fisher) *plld hrd: sn trcking ldr: rdn 3f out: sn wknd* **66/1**

2m 6.28s (-1.51) **Going Correction** -0.15s/f (Stan)
WFA 3 from 4yo+ 4lb 14 Ran SP% **128.2**
Speed ratings (Par 101):100,98,98,97,97 96,96,95,94,94 94,91,74,73
CSF £41.58 CT £147.86 TOTE £3.20: £1.40, £5.50, £2.30; EX 56.50.
Owner Neil Ryan **Bred** C L Kidder, J K Griggs And N M Cole **Trained** Newmarket, Suffolk

FOCUS
A moderate race, but with a winner in top form the race looks straightforward and pretty sound.
Polar Dawn Official explanation: jockey said filly clipped heels
Fossgate Official explanation: jockey said gelding suffered interference
Mount Ephram(IRE) Official explanation: jockey said gelding lost its action

6325 BETDIRECT ON AT THE RACES INTERACTIVE APPRENTICE H'CAP — 1m 2f (P)
3:50 (3:55) (Class 5) (0-75,75) 3-Y-O+ **£3,564** (£1,060; £530; £264) Stalls Low

Form RPR
2534 **1** **Stargazer Jim (FR)**[8] 6247 3-8-9 **75** .... LiamJones(5) 7 — 83
(W J Haggas) *chsd ldrs: pushed along over 2f out: led 1f out: r.o wl: comf* **5/1**[2]
6110 **2** 2 **African Sahara (USA)**[2] 6305 6-8-9 **73** ....(t) ChrisCavanagh(7) 6 — 77
(Miss D Mountain) *mid div: rdn and hdwy wl over 1f out: styd on ins fnl f to go 2nd cl home* **10/1**
0021 **3** hd **Fasylitator (IRE)**[31] 5838 3-8-11 **72** .... AmirQuinn 2 — 76
(D K Ivory) *chsd ldrs: rdn to ld briefly over 1f out: kpt on: lost 2nd cl home* **4/1**[1]
3452 **4** ¾ **Burgundy**[16] 6127 8-9-4 **75** ....(b) LPKeniry 5 — 78+
(P Mitchell) *hld up towards rr: rdn and hdwy over 1f out: styd on* **5/1**[2]
651- **5** ½ **Croon**[337] 6842 3-8-8 **74** .... AshleyHamblett(5) 3 — 76
(L M Cumani) *sn led: rdn 2f out: hdd over 1f out: kpt on same pce* **7/1**
2466 **6** 1 **Mexican Pete**[31] 4389 5-9-3 **74** .... DNolan 9 — 74
(A W Carroll) *a mid div* **11/2**[3]
0000 **7** ½ **Karaoke (IRE)**[32] 5824 5-8-7 **69** .... RonanKeogh(5) 8 — 68
(S Kirk) *hld up towards rr: hdwy fr 3f out: rdn 2f out: kpt on same pce* **16/1**
0604 **8** 2 ½ **Scottish River (USA)**[12] 6201 6-8-7 **71** .... KMay(7) 13 — 65
(M D I Usher) *stdd s: plld hrd: w ldrs after 2f: rdn over 2f out: wknd over 1f out* **14/1**
3606 **9** 1 **Sri Lipis**[52] 5405 3-9-0 **75** ....(b) NelsonDeSouza 10 — 67
(P F I Cole) *chsd ldrs: rdn over 2f out: wknd over 1f out* **25/1**
2500 **10** hd **Kaymich Perfecto**[22] 6008 5-8-5 **67** .... MichaelJStainton(5) 1 — 59
(R M Whitaker) *mid div tl lost pl 4f out: nt a danger after* **16/1**

160U **11** *hd* **Wujood**^{15} [6134] 3-8-7 **73**.. TravisBlock(5) 4 64
(H Morrison) *chsd ldrs tl lost pl over 4f out: hdwy over 2f out: sn rdn: wknd fnl f* **20/1**

0054 **12** *¾* **Jazrawy**^{133} [3144] 3-8-13 **74**.. NeilChalmers 12 64
(Miss Gay Kelleway) *a towards rr* **25/1**

2m 7.39s (-0.40) **Going Correction** -0.15s/f (Stan)
WFA 3 from 5yo+ 4lb **12** Ran SP% **121.2**
Speed ratings (Par 103):95,93,93,92,92 91,91,89,88,88 87,87
CSF £54.15 CT £220.81 TOTE £6.00: £2.20, £3.90, £1.50; EX 69.40 Place 6 £27.53, Place 5 £19.58.
Owner Nicholas J Hughes **Bred** Sarl Le Lieu Calice And Peter Kavanagh **Trained** Newmarket, Suffolk

FOCUS
A routine race of its type rated through the third to form, although the winner should rate higher.
T/Plt: £47.70 to a £1 stake. Pool: £27,683.70. 423.30 winning tickets. T/Qpdt: £51.90 to a £1 stake. Pool: £1,658.10. 23.60 winning tickets. TM

6288 SOUTHWELL (L-H)
Saturday, November 12

OFFICIAL GOING: Standard
The surface was described as 'the usual deep and slow, even harder work than usual'.
Wind: Almost nil Weather: Fine and sunny

6326 LIVE FOOTBALL CASHBACKS AT BETDIRECT BANDED STKS 5f (F)
11:00 (11:01) (Class 7) 3-Y-0+ **£1,416** (£418; £209) **Stalls** High

Form RPR
0133 **1** **Orchestration (IRE)**^{19} [6076] 4-8-11 45................(v) RobbieFitzpatrick 10 61
(M J Attwater) *sn drvn along in mid-field: hdwy over 1f out: r.o wl to ld nr fin* **13/2**^{2}

0131 **2** *½* **Dellagio (IRE)**^{7} [6256] 4-8-12 49................................ RichardThomas(3) 8 63
(Rae Guest) *hld up: hdwy over 2f out: led jst ins last: edgd lft: hdd nr fin* **11/10**^{1}

4450 **3** *4* **Amanda's Lad (IRE)**^{7} [6261] 5-8-11 45................................ BrianReilly 9 45
(M C Chapman) *chsd ldrs: kpt on same pce fnl 2f* **16/1**

0402 **4** *½* **Desert Light (IRE)**^{19} [6076] 4-8-11 50..........................(v) GregFairley(5) 2 48+
(D Shaw) *w ldrs: hung bdly lft and led 2f out: hdd jst ins last: sn wknd* **13/2**^{2}

3050 **5** *¾* **Kiss The Rain**^{35} [5738] 5-8-13 47.......................................(b) TomEaves 7 42
(R Brotherton) *mid-div: sn drvn along: kpt on fnl 2f: nvr a threat* **33/1**

3060 **6** *shd* **Torrent**^{19} [6076] 10-8-13 47.......................................(p) DarrenWilliams 12 42
(D W Chapman) *s.i.s: hld up: hdwy 2f out: nvr nr ldrs* **28/1**

0050 **7** *hd* **Pulse**^{102} [4024] 7-8-12 46...(p) PaulFitzsimons 14 40
(Miss J R Tooth) *racd stands' side: kpt on fnl 2f: nvr on terms* **12/1**^{3}

0310 **8** *2* **On The Trail**^{3} [6294] 8-8-12 46..(p) PhillipMakin 6 33
(D W Chapman) *chsd ldrs: wknd over 1f out* **20/1**

0006 **9** *1 ¾* **Black Oval**^{19} [6079] 4-8-6 40.. AdamKirby(5) 11 26
(M J Polglase) *prom: sn drvn along: outpcd fnl 2f* **66/1**

0030 **10** *2 ½* **Mr Spliffy (IRE)**^{7} [6256] 6-8-4 40..........................(b) JemmaMarshall(7) 4 17
(M C Chapman) *t.k.h: trckd ldrs: lost pl over 1f out* **33/1**

001U **11** *hd* **Aintnecessarilyso**^{25} [5966] 7-8-12 46............................(p) FergalLynch 1 17
(J M Bradley) *s.i.s: racd far side: nvr on terms* **14/1**

0500 **12** *½* **Prime Recreation**^{42} [5616] 8-8-13 47.................................. LisaJones 3 16
(P S Felgate) *led tl hdd & wknd 2f out* **20/1**

0034 **13** *3 ½* **Molotov**^{40} [5657] 5-8-9 48.. NataliaGemelova(5) 13 —
(I W McInnes) *prom: lost pl 2f out* **16/1**

5005 **14** *¾* **Legal Set (IRE)**^{35} [5738] 9-8-8 47 ow2...........................(t) AnnStokell(7) 5 —
(Miss A Stokell) *outpcd and bhd fnl 2f* **18/1**

58.90 secs (-1.40) **Going Correction** -0.35s/f (Stan) **14** Ran SP% **126.0**
Speed ratings (Par 97):97,96,89,89,87 87,87,84,81,77 77,76,70,69
CSF £13.51 TOTE £8.40: £1.90, £1.10, £5.80; EX 29.20.
Owner Brooklands Racing **Bred** Mrs Anita Rothschild **Trained** Wysall, Notts

FOCUS
Decent form for the grade, the first two pulling clear and the winner back to something like his best two-year-old form.
Aintnecessarilyso Official explanation: jockey said gelding missed the break

6327 FIRST PAST THE POST AT BETDIRECT BANDED STKS 1m (F)
11:30 (11:31) (Class 7) 3-Y-0+ **£1,423** (£420; £210) **Stalls** Low

Form RPR
0052 **1** **Witchcraft**^{14} [6151] 4-8-9 45......................................(v^{1}) BenSwarbrick(3) 6 62
(D Shaw) *trckd ldrs: drvn over 3f out: hdwy u.p on outer to ld over 1f out: clr ins last: eased nr fin* **11/4**^{1}

0023 **2** *6* **Filey Buoy**^{14} [6154] 3-8-12 50....................................... PaulMulrennan(3) 8 55
(R M Whitaker) *w ldrs: led over 2f out: hdd over 1f out: no ch w wnr* **11/1**

054 **3** *hd* **Lake Wakatipu**^{14} [6139] 3-9-1 50... DarrenWilliams 7 54
(M Mullineaux) *chsd ldrs: upsides 2f out: kpt on same pce* **16/1**

U003 **4** *nk* **Fleet Anchor**^{14} [6151] 4-8-7 45.. GregFairley(5) 14 49
(J M Bradley) *stdd and swtchd lft s: hld up in rr: hdwy 3f out: kpt on fnl f* **8/1**

4103 **5** *1* **Anissati**^{7} [6261] 3-8-12 47.. StephenCarson 3 49
(C E Brittain) *s.i.s: hdwy on ins over 4f out: effrt and nt clr run over 2f out: kpt on same pce* **11/2**^{2}

3000 **6** *1 ¼* **Essex Star (IRE)**^{10} [6231] 4-8-10 48.................................. RoryMoore(5) 11 47
(Miss J Feilden) *chsd ldrs: outpcd and n.m.r over 2f out: hrd rdn and styd on fnl f* **25/1**

7 *2* **Ivory Key (IRE)**^{181} [1734] 3-8-6 46.............................(b^{1}) AdamKirby(5) 10 41
(Patrick Morris, Ire) *sn outpcd and bhd: detached over 3f out: kpt on fnl 2f* **25/1**

5410 **8** *1* **Elms Schoolboy**^{25} [5962] 3-8-12 47.........................(b) MichaelTebbutt 12 40
(J M P Eustace) *chsd ldrs: wknd over 1f out* **9/1**

2261 **9** *2 ½* **Tacid**^{25} [5962] 3-8-11 46... RobbieFitzpatrick 13 33
(Dr J D Scargill) *chsd ldrs on outer: lost pl 2f out* **15/2**^{3}

0001 **10** *2 ½* **Ballyrush (IRE)**^{7} [6259] 5-8-6 46................................ StephanieBancroft(7) 1 28
(Miss D A McHale) *led tl over 2f out: lost pl over 1f out* **16/1**

0000 **11** *shd* **Pawn In Life (IRE)**^{4} [6292] 7-9-0 47..........................(v) GrahamGibbons 2 29
(M J Polglase) *s.i.s: sn trcking ldrs on inner: lost pl over 1f out* **28/1**

0035 **12** *nk* **Feast Of Romance**^{7} [6261] 8-9-1 48.............................(b) SamHitchcott 5 29
(C R Dore) *trckd ldrs: wknd 2f out* **14/1**

00-6 **13** *4* **Enborne Again (IRE)**^{205} [1175] 3-8-12 47......................... GylesParkin 4 20
(R A Fahey) *s.i.s: a bhd: detached 3f out* **66/1**

0000 **14** *½* **Senor Eduardo**^{100} [4110] 8-9-0 47......................................(p) TomEaves 9 19
(S Gollings) *chsd ldrs: outpcd over 4f out: lost pl over 2f out* **25/1**

1m 42.18s (-2.42) **Going Correction** -0.325s/f (Stan)
WFA 3 from 4yo+ 2lb **14** Ran SP% **118.2**
Speed ratings (Par 97):99,93,92,92,91 90,88,87,84,82 82,81,77,77
CSF £31.05 TOTE £5.00: £1.10, £3.30, £5.80; EX 20.50.
Owner Danethorpe Racing Ltd **Bred** Brook Stud Ltd **Trained** Danethorpe, Notts

FOCUS
The winner was overdue a first win and the runner-up and third give the form a very sound look.

6328 BETDIRECT FREEPHONE 0800 211 222 MAIDEN CLAIMING STKS 7f (F)
12:00 (12:00) (Class 7) 3-Y-0+ **£1,429** (£422; £211) **Stalls** Low

Form RPR
0202 **1** **Blushing Russian (IRE)**^{4} [6292] 3-8-2 47.................(p) GregFairley(5) 11 54
(P C Haslam) *hld up in tch: hdwy on outer over 2f out: led appr fnl f: styd on wl* **9/4**^{2}

0002 **2** *1 ½* **Queue Up**^{32} [5827] 3-8-8 58...................................... StephenDonohoe(5) 4 56
(J G Given) *led tl over 4f out: led 2f out: hdd appr fnl f: kpt on same pce* **2/1**^{1}

-000 **3** *1 ¼* **Swords**^{57} [5280] 3-8-13 60.. LisaJones 13 53
(P Howling) *sn outpcd and bhd: hdwy on outer 2f out: styd on wl ins last* **8/1**

0 **4** *2* **Gandiloo Gully**^{76} [4781] 4-8-8 ow1............................... GrahamGibbons 5 42
(J D Bethell) *s.i.s: hdwy over 3f out: kpt on wl fnl f* **33/1**

0000 **5** *½* **Dunnett Again (IRE)**^{8} [6245] 4-8-3 40..........................(b^{1}) MarcHalford(5) 9 40
(Mrs C A Dunnett) *mid-div: hdwy over 4f out: sn chsng ldrs: one pce fnl 2f* **50/1**

6006 **6** *2 ½* **Firebird Rising (USA)**^{78} [4707] 4-8-9 35................................ TomEaves 1 35
(R Brotherton) *chsd ldrs: outpcd and hung lft over 2f out: kpt on fnl f* **40/1**

0004 **7** *¾* **Yours Sincerely (IRE)**^{32} [5827] 3-8-13 47........................... FergalLynch 3 38
(P A Blockley) *chsd ldrs: outpcd fnl 2f* **20/1**

0 **8** *nk* **Annitas Dream (IRE)**^{19} [6089] 4-8-9 58................(t) RobbieFitzpatrick 14 32
(T Hogan, Ire) *prom: hdwy to ld over 4f out: hdd 2f out: sn wknd* **6/1**^{3}

0604 **9** *2* **Make It Snappy**^{97} [4189] 3-8-2 60 ow1........................(b^{1}) AdamKirby(5) 6 26
(M Wigham) *chsd ldrs: lost pl over 2f out* **6/1**^{3}

0 **10** *1* **Chingola**^{187} [1569] 3-8-5 .... PaulMulrennan(3) 10 24
(R M Whitaker) *chsd ldrs: lost pl over 3f out: sme late hdwy* **40/1**

0000 **11** *4* **Amazing Grace Mary**^{187} [1573] 3-8-7 30 ow1.................... VHalliday 12 13
(S R Bowring) *chsd ldrs: lost pl over 4f out* **66/1**

0000 **12** *1 ¾* **Danehill Angel**^{61} [5189] 3-8-8 30.. PaulDoe 8 9
(M J Polglase) *sn outpcd and bhd* **80/1**

000 **13** *8* **Fern Valley**^{285} [238] 3-8-13 30...................................... MichaelTebbutt 7 —
(M J Attwater) *s.s: a bhd* **150/1**

1m 29.89s (-0.92) **Going Correction** -0.325s/f (Stan)
WFA 3 from 4yo 1lb **13** Ran SP% **121.7**
Speed ratings (Par 97):92,90,88,86,86 83,82,81,79,78 73,71,62
CSF £6.90 TOTE £4.70: £2.00, £1.50, £1.50; EX 8.60.Blushing Russian (no.11) was claimed by Clifton Hunt for £2,000; Queue Up (no.3) was claimed by A. G. Newcombe for £5,000.
Owner Blue Lion Racing VI **Bred** The Rouge Partnership **Trained** Middleham Moor, N Yorks
■ Stewards' Enquiry : Robbie Fitzpatrick one-day ban: careless riding (Nov 25)

FOCUS
A modest claimer but the first two both ran to their previous form making the form look straightforward, and they both changed hands after successful claims.
Chingola Official explanation: jockey said filly didn't handle bend

6329 BETDIRECT.CO.UK BANDED STKS 2m (F)
12:30 (12:31) (Class 7) 3-Y-0+ **£1,443** (£426; £213) **Stalls** Low

Form RPR
3632 **1** **Tharua (IRE)**^{4} [6289] 3-8-7 48.......................................(p) AdamKirby(5) 8 55
(Ernst Oertel) *hld up in rr: hdwy over 5f out: sn chsng ldrs: led 1f out: styd on* **10/3**^{1}

6020 **2** *1 ¼* **Bill Bennett (FR)**^{4} [6289] 4-9-6 47................................ MichaelTebbutt 5 53
(J Jay) *chsd ldrs: shkn up 6f out: led over 1f out: sn hdd and no ex* **4/1**^{2}

0001 **3** *3* **Jackie Kiely**^{4} [6289] 4-10-0 49.. LisaJones 2 57
(P Howling) *hld up in mid-div: hdwy over 4f out: chal on ins 2f out: kpt on same pce* **7/1**

5000 **4** *nk* **All Bleevable**^{22} [5707] 8-9-1 45.................................. RichardThomas(3) 4 47
(Mrs S Lamyman) *trckd ldr: led over 5f out tl over 1f out: fdd* **16/1**

45-1 **5** *2 ½* **Make My Hay**^{214} [187] 6-9-0 46..............................(b) EmmettStack(5) 13 45
(J Gallagher) *hld up: hdwy on outer over 5f out: sn chsng ldrs: fdd fnl f* **5/1**^{3}

6055 **6** *6* **Ulshaw**^{14} [6152] 8-8-13 35.. GregFairley(5) 10 36
(J M Bradley) *hld up in rr: hdwy 7f out: chsng ldrs over 3f out: wknd 2f out* **13/2**

0006 **7** *4* **Sungio**^{37} [5707] 7-9-4 45..(b) PhillipMakin 11 32
(B P J Baugh) *hld up in rr: hdwy 7f out: sn chsng ldrs: rdn and wknd over 2f out* **12/1**

065 **8** *2* **It Must Be Speech**^{42} [5620] 4-9-4 45............................ DarrenWilliams 12 29
(S L Keightley) *trckd ldrs: chal 4f out: hrd rdn and wknd 2f out* **33/1**

0000 **9** *15* **Jamaican Flight (USA)**^{92} [4316] 12-9-4 35................ GrahamGibbons 9 11
(Mrs S Lamyman) *led tl over 5f out: sn lost pl and bhd* **66/1**

0 **10** *1* **Sandhill Jack**^{56} [5301] 4-9-4 40.. SamHitchcott 1 10
(A G Newcombe) *trckd ldrs: lost pl 5f out: sn bhd* **50/1**

15-0 **11** *1 ¼* **Regal Fantasy (IRE)**^{231} [725] 5-9-4 35............................ FergalLynch 7 8
(P A Blockley) *chsd ldrs: lost pl over 5f out: sn bhd* **25/1**

500/ **12** *12* **Just The Job Too (IRE)**^{657} [1520] 8-9-4 45....................... VinceSlattery 6 —
(L Corcoran) *mid-div: lost pl 7f out: sn bhd* **25/1**

00 **13** *dist* **Hawksmoor (IRE)**^{14} [6160] 3-8-9 35......................................(t) PaulDoe 3 —
(L A Dace) *s.i.s: bhd and drvn along 9f out: t.o 4f out: btn 47l* **66/1**

3m 43.65s (-0.89) **Going Correction** -0.325s/f (Stan)
WFA 3 from 4yo+ 9lb **13** Ran SP% **114.7**
Speed ratings (Par 97):89,88,86,86,85 82,80,79,71,71 70,64,—
CSF £14.60 TOTE £3.00: £1.60, £1.80, £2.80; EX 18.20.
Owner Winning Colours Racing Club **Bred** Finbar Cahill And Dermot O'Rourke **Trained** Newmarket, Suffolk

FOCUS
A modest time but the winner and third ran to their previous encounter. The runner-up ran a lot better but is still not back to last winter's form.

6330 HAPPY 50TH BIRTHDAY STEVE GILES BANDED STKS 6f (F)
1:00 (1:02) (Class 7) 3-Y-0+ **£1,433** (£423; £211) **Stalls** Low

Form RPR
3004 **1** **Mambazo**^{7} [6256] 3-8-6 45...(e) AdamKirby(5) 3 59
(S C Williams) *trckd ldrs: led 2f out: kpt on wl* **9/2**^{2}

0505 **2** *1 ¾* **Desert Lover (IRE)**^{21} [6031] 3-8-11 45.............................. PhillipMakin 4 54
(R J Price) *chsd ldrs: wnt 2nd over 1f out: no real imp* **10/1**

4003 **3** 2 ½ **Jalouhar**[14] 6155 5-8-4 45 .... JemmaMarshall(7) 5 46
(B P J Baugh) *mid-div: styd on fnl 2f: nt trble 1st 2* **4/1**[1]
0540 **4** 2 ½ **Mind Alert**[19] 6078 4-8-6 45 .... (v[1]) GregFairley(5) 13 39
(D Shaw) *trckd ldrs: led over 3f out tl 2f out: wknd appr fnl f* **8/1**
0655 **5** hd **Jedeydd**[21] 6032 8-8-8 45 .... (v) PaulMulrennan(3) 8 38
(J S Wainwright) *rr-div: kpt on fnl 2f: nvr trbld ldrs* **9/1**
2035 **6** hd **Radlett Lady**[7] 6256 4-8-11 45 .... DavidKinsella 12 38
(D K Ivory) *chsd ldrs: wknd appr fnl f* **9/2**[2]
000 **7** 1 **Christian Bendix**[19] 6069 3-8-11 45 .... LisaJones 2 35
(P Howling) *led tl over 3f out: wknd 1f out* **50/1**
2040 **8** ½ **Polar Haze**[14] 6155 8-8-11 40 .... (v) MichaelTebbutt 9 33
(J Pearce) *mid-div: effrt 3f out: nvr on terms* **15/2**[3]
5/00 **9** 3 ½ **To Be Fare (IRE)**[49] 5447 5-8-11 45 .... FergalLynch 10 23
(J Pearce) *dwlt: effrt on wd outside over 2f out: nvr on terms* **28/1**
6000 **10** nk **Rainbow Iris**[30] 5854 3-8-11 45 .... GylesParkin 7 22
(B Smart) *chsd ldrs: lost pl over 3f out* **14/1**
0-00 **11** hd **Bennanabaa**[35] 5736 6-8-11 40 .... (t) VinceSlattery 6 21
(S C Burrough) *s.i.s: effrt on inner over 2f out: nvr nrr* **80/1**
0205 **12** 1 **Saucepot**[14] 6155 3-8-11 45 .... PaulFitzsimons 11 18
(Miss J R Tooth) *trckd ldrs: rdn on outer 3f out: sn lost pl* **16/1**
0105 **13** 12 **Frenchmans Lodge**[25] 5966 5-8-11 40 .... (b) PaulDoe 1 —
(L A Dace) *s.s: a in rr: bhd and eased over 1f out* **14/1**

1m 15.68s (-1.22) **Going Correction** -0.325s/f (Stan) 13 Ran SP% **124.2**
Speed ratings (Par 97):95,92,89,86,85 85,84,83,78,78 78,76,60
CSF £50.94 TOTE £4.10: £1.10, £4.40, £1.30; EX 72.00.
Owner D G Burge **Bred** Barry Taylor **Trained** Newmarket, Suffolk

FOCUS
Not a strong race but the second looks the key to the overall value of the form, which appears straightforward. The winner may be capable of a bit better.
Frenchmans Lodge Official explanation: jockey said gelding never travelled

6331 PRESS RED TO BET ON ITVI TRI-BANDED STKS 1m 3f (F)
1:30 (1:31) (Class 7) 3-Y-O £1,429 (£422; £211) **Stalls** Low

Form RPR
0035 **1** **Zoripp (IRE)**[19] 6081 3-8-7 45 .... (b) StephenDonohoe(5) 12 57
(J G Given) *trckd ldrs: led on bit over 2f out: clr whn ducked rt ins last* **4/1**[2]
5260 **2** 3 ½ **Finnegans Rainbow**[11] 6215 3-8-7 45 .... AdamKirby(5) 11 52
(M C Chapman) *trckd ldrs: led over 5f out: rdn 3f out: sn hdd: kpt on: no ch w wnr* **6/1**
U020 **3** 5 **Degree Of Honor (FR)**[35] 5741 3-8-5 40 ow1 .... PaulMulrennan(3) 9 40
(J G Given) *outpcd over 4f out: kpt on fnl 2f* **9/2**[3]
-000 **4** shd **Liquid Lover (IRE)**[47] 5519 3-8-9 45 .... (b[1]) BenSwarbrick(3) 3 44
(W M Brisbourne) *led tl over 7f out: outpcd over 3f out: wandered: put hd in air and kpt on fnl 2f* **20/1**
3432 **5** 1 ¾ **Tanning**[8] 6241 3-8-2 35 .... StephenCarson 2 31
(A W Carroll) *trckd ldrs: drvn and outpcd 6f out: kpt on fnl 2f* **3/1**[1]
0003 **6** 4 **Katana**[8] 6241 3-8-8 40 ow1 .... (b) LeeEnstone 1 31
(I A Wood) *sn drvn along: hdwy to chse 1st 2 over 5f out: wknd 2f out* **9/1**
0004 **7** 5 **Ingleby Cross**[14] 6153 3-8-7 40 .... GrahamGibbons 6 23
(J D Bethell) *chsd ldrs: rdn and lost pl 2f out* **11/2**
000 **8** 25 **Meikle Beoch**[73] 4863 3-7-11 30 .... DuranFentiman(5) 10 —
(Mrs H Sweeting) *sn bhd and drvn along: t.o 3f out* **25/1**
0500 **9** shd **Hamburg Springer (IRE)**[6] 5697 3-8-12 45 .... (b) PaulDoe 5 —
(M J Polglase) *s.i.s: sn drvn along: led over 7f out: hdd over 5f out: sn lost pl: t.o 3f out* **25/1**
0560 **10** 13 **Dancing Moonlight (IRE)**[30] 5856 3-7-11 30 .... MarcHalford(5) 4 —
(Mrs N Macauley) *w ldrs: lost pl over 4f out: t.o 3f out: virtually p.u over 1f out* **40/1**
5666 **P** **Lord Mayfair (USA)**[9] 6237 3-8-8 40 ow8 .... AnnStokell(7) 8 —
(Miss A Stokell) *stmbld sltly s: sn bhd: t.o 6f out: sn p.u* **20/1**

2m 25.88s (-3.02) **Going Correction** -0.325s/f (Stan) 11 Ran SP% **122.5**
Speed ratings (Par 96):97,94,90,90,89 86,82,64,64,55 —
CSF £27.23 TOTE £4.80: £1.60, £1.20, £3.20; EX 45.30 Place 6 £18.34, Place 5 £12.41.
Owner P A Horton **Bred** Bryan Ryan **Trained** Willoughton, Lincs

FOCUS
Just modest form despite a fair time. The winner could rate a fraction higher through the fourth.
Lord Mayfair(USA) Official explanation: jockey said gelding slipped leaving stalls and never travelled
T/Plt: £62.80 to a £1 stake. Pool: £23,912.40. 277.80 winning tickets. T/Qpdt: £25.10 to a £1 stake. Pool: £1,611.80. 47.50 winning tickets. WG

6309 WOLVERHAMPTON (A.W) (L-H)
Saturday, November 12

OFFICIAL GOING: Standard
Wind: Virtually nil.

6332 "STOVES" AT WATERLINE E B F MAIDEN STKS 7f 32y(P)
7:00 (7:00) (Class 5) 2-Y-O £4,303 (£1,280; £639; £319) **Stalls** High

Form RPR
1 **After You** 2-8-9 .... MartinDwyer 3 76+
(B W Hills) *trckd ldr: led 4f out: rdn out and r.o wl fnl f* **16/1**
2 2 ½ **Well Guarded (IRE)** 2-9-0 .... JohnEgan 5 75
(C R Egerton) *w.w: rdn and hdwy 1/2-way: wnt 2nd wl over 1f out: styd on but no imp on wnr fnl f* **6/1**
3 nk **Chasing A Dream** 2-8-9 .... DeanMcKeown 11 69
(B W Hills) *hld up in in rr: hdwy on ins over 2f out: styd on fnl f* **22/1**
44 **4** 4 **Finsbury**[14] 6156 2-9-0 .... GeorgeBaker 9 64
(C F Wall) *hld up in mid-div: hdwy on outside over 2f out bef carried rt ent st: hung lft bef kpt on fnl f* **9/4**[1]
5 nk **Ennobling** 2-8-9 .... KFallon 6 58
(E F Vaughan) *slowly away: rdn and sn mid-div: u.p bef wknd over 1f out* **11/1**
3 **6** 5 **Zorooni**[12] 6200 2-8-9 .... MatthewHenry 8 46
(M A Jarvis) *trckd ldrs: rdn 4f out: carried rt 2f out: styd on fnl f* **9/2**[3]
02 **7** 2 **Ohana**[16] 6121 2-9-0 .... JimmyFortune 2 46
(N A Callaghan) *in tch: rdn 3f out: wknd over 1f out* **5/2**[2]
8 4 **Valentino Taffi** 2-8-7 .... EstherRemmerswaal(7) 7 36
(S C Williams) *slowly away: a bhd* **66/1**
9 1 **Wings Of Speed** 2-8-9 .... ChrisCatlin 10 28
(H Morrison) *outpcd thrght* **40/1**
10 5 **Stoneacre Fred (IRE)** 2-9-0 .... RobbieFitzpatrick 4 21
(Peter Grayson) *led to 4f out: hung rt and wknd qckly over 2f out* **25/1**

1m 28.85s (-1.55) **Going Correction** -0.275s/f (Stan) 10 Ran SP% **118.1**
Speed ratings (Par 96):97,94,93,89,88 83,80,76,75,69
CSF £106.38 TOTE £11.70: £2.90, £2.10, £3.60; EX 95.30.
Owner Guy Reed **Bred** G Reed **Trained** Lambourn, Berks

FOCUS
An interesting maiden featuring a number of nicely-bred debutants run in a respectable time for the grade.

NOTEBOOK
After You had reportedly been working well but was weak in the market. She belied her price with a convincing success as she travelled well throughout and was well in command at the line. Time will tell what she beat, but the time suggests this was an above-average affair. (op 12-1)
Well Guarded(IRE), a 170,000gns Derby entrant, is related to an All-Weather winner and should progress for this first start. He lacked the natural pace of the winner, but did little wrong and will appreciate a stiffer test. (op 11-1)
Chasing A Dream took the eye with a promising first effort. Easy to back, she stayed on to good effect inside the distance from a wide draw and will be a lot sharper mentally and physically next time. (op 20-1)
Finsbury was done few favours when a rival carried him wide on the home turn, but he again hung left under pressure and may be tough to win with even if he is now handicapped. Official explanation: jockey said colt was hampered on turn into home straight (op 11-4)
Ennobling hails from a yard that traditionally leaves a bit to work on with their newcomers and this half-sister to Let It Be will be better over further in time, especially as she was a late foal. (op 8-1)
Ohana attracted good support, but was ultimately disappointing and his future probably lies in handicaps. (op 9-4)
Stoneacre Fred(IRE) Official explanation: jockey said gelding hung right off turn into home straight

6333 "BELLING" AT WATERLINE MAIDEN STKS 1m 141y(P)
7:30 (7:31) (Class 5) 3-Y-O+ £3,432 (£1,021; £510; £254) **Stalls** Low

Form RPR
03 **1** **Oh Danny Boy**[38] 5699 4-9-3 .... KFallon 1 69
(Julian Poulton) *a.p: short of room ent fnl f: strly rdn to ld cl home* **7/1**
4000 **2** nk **Lord Of Dreams (IRE)**[15] 6134 3-9-0 69 .... FergalLynch 5 68
(D W P Arbuthnot) *led: rdn over 1f out: no ex whn hdd cl home* **9/2**[3]
5232 **3** 2 **Rock Chick**[14] 6160 3-8-9 67 .... JimmyFortune 6 59
(J H M Gosden) *trckd ldrs: wnt 2nd 3f out: edgd lft ent fnl f: wknd wl ins* **7/4**[1]
0 **4** 8 **Miss Inch**[211] 1027 3-8-9 .... JohnEgan 8 42
(G Wragg) *in tch tl outpcd over 2f out: nvr on terms w first 3 after* **4/1**[2]
4303 **5** 1 ¼ **Constructor**[16] 6126 4-9-3 64 .... LPKeniry 10 44
(C A Cyzer) *trckd ldrs tl wknd over 2f out* **13/2**
6 hd **Hilversum** 3-8-2 .... DawnRankin(7) 12 39
(Miss J A Camacho) *bhd: rdn 4f out: nvr on terms* **66/1**
7 shd **Loyalist (USA)** 3-9-0 .... MartinDwyer 13 44
(J G Given) *mid-div: rdn 1/2-way: sn no ch* **40/1**
8 3 **Arpetcheeo (USA)**[388] 6316 3-8-11 .... DNolan(3) 4 37
(D Carroll) *s.i.s: rdn 4f out: rdn but nvr on terms* **66/1**
00- **9** 1 ½ **Bodfari Dream**[396] 6141 4-8-12 .... DarrenWilliams 11 29
(M Mullineaux) *s.i.s: sn mid-div: lost tch over 3f out* **100/1**
0 **10** 5 **Drumroll (IRE)**[301] 123 3-9-0 .... BrianReilly 3 24
(Miss J Feilden) *mid-div: rdn 1/2-way: sn bhd* **50/1**
6 **11** 2 **Numanthia (IRE)**[161] 2304 3-8-6 .... NeilChalmers(3) 7 15
(Miss J R Gibney) *s.i.s: sn in tch: rdn 4f out: wknd* **50/1**
12 6 **California Bay (IRE)** 5-8-12 .... AdamKirby(5) 9 7
(C P Donoghue, Ire) *slowly away: a bhd* **40/1**
0-60 **13** 11 **Ustad (IRE)**[194] 1407 3-9-0 70 .... (b[1]) ChrisCatlin 2 —
(P L Gilligan) *a bhd* **25/1**

1m 49.11s (-2.65) **Going Correction** -0.275s/f (Stan)
WFA 3 from 4yo+ 3lb 13 Ran SP% **117.0**
Speed ratings (Par 103):100,99,97,90,89 89,89,86,85,81 79,73,64
CSF £36.09 TOTE £5.00: £1.70, £2.30, £1.20; EX 38.20.
Owner Danny Berry **Bred** Whitsbury Manor Stud **Trained** Caterham, Surrey

FOCUS
A modest maiden featuring some exposed types, although the form is sounder than most with the placed horses to form.
Miss Inch Official explanation: jockey said filly had no more to give

6334 "NEFF" AT WATERLINE E B F MAIDEN STKS 1m 1f 103y(P)
8:00 (8:02) (Class 5) 2-Y-O £4,197 (£1,248; £624; £311) **Stalls** Low

Form RPR
0 **1** **Entranced**[24] 5976 2-8-9 .... TomEaves 1 69+
(Miss J A Camacho) *mid-div: hdwy on outside 2f out: shkn up and r.o strly to ld cl home* **20/1**
03 **2** hd **Green Lemon (USA)**[19] 6068 2-9-0 .... JimmyFortune 10 74
(G A Butler) *trckd ldrs: ev ch ins fnl f: passed by wnr cl home* **15/8**[1]
3 ¾ **Born Wild (GER)** 2-8-9 .... KFallon 11 68
(Sir Michael Stoute) *trckd ldr: led 3f out: rdn fnl f: hdd and passed by first 2 nr fin* **5/2**[2]
0 **4** 1 **Tower Hill (IRE)**[78] 4720 2-9-0 .... MatthewHenry 6 71
(M A Jarvis) *led tl hdd 3f out: rdn wl over 1f out: kpt on one pce* **11/2**[3]
00 **5** shd **Ogee**[18] 6102 2-9-0 .... NickyMackay 7 70
(Sir Michael Stoute) *trckd ldrs: rdn 3f out: kpt on one pce fnl f* **15/2**
00 **6** 6 **Gaelic Games (UAE)**[32] 5821 2-8-9 .... GregFairley(5) 13 59
(M Johnston) *t.k.h: in tch: rdn 1/2-way: wknd over 1f out* **14/1**
0 **7** ½ **French Opera**[13] 6178 2-9-0 .... MartinDwyer 9 58
(J A Osborne) *slowly away: rdn 3f out: a towards rr* **20/1**
0 **8** ½ **Machhapuchhare**[12] 6200 2-9-0 .... DarrenWilliams 5 57
(W M Brisbourne) *mid-div: rdn 4f out: wknd 2f out* **100/1**
00 **9** ½ **King Of Chav's (IRE)**[71] 4916 2-9-0 .... VinceSlattery 2 56
(A Bailey) *mid-div tl lost pl 3f out* **66/1**
0 **10** ½ **Benjum**[32] 5821 2-9-0 .... LPKeniry 3 55
(B I Case) *rdn 3f out: a in rr* **66/1**
11 4 **Digger Girl (USA)** 2-8-9 .... ChrisCatlin 12 43
(N A Callaghan) *a bhd* **25/1**
00 **12** 5 **Sunny Disposition (IRE)**[10] 6227 2-9-0 .... GeorgeBaker 4 38
(E F Vaughan) *s.i.s: a bhd* **100/1**

2m 2.49s (-0.13) **Going Correction** -0.275s/f (Stan) 12 Ran SP% **115.5**
Speed ratings (Par 96):89,88,88,87,87 81,81,80,80,80 76,72
CSF £54.53 TOTE £18.70: £3.00, £1.50, £2.00; EX 80.30.
Owner Elite Racing Club **Bred** Elite Racing Club **Trained** Norton, N Yorks
■ Stewards' Enquiry : Jimmy Fortune one-day ban: used whip without giving colt time to respond (Nov 25)

FOCUS
An ordinary maiden and the slowest time of the night pro-rata. The runner-up sets the standard for the form.

NOTEBOOK

Entranced was green and backward in a soft-ground Newcastle maiden on her debut, but left that form behind with a pleasing effort. She knuckled down to her task well after travelling well and can build on this if her connections keep her going this winter. (tchd 22-1)

Green Lemon(USA) has a dirt pedigree and is now handicapped following another solid run. He was slightly unlucky not to win as he was only passed late on and appeared to take the step up in trip in his stride. (op 9-4)

Born Wild(GER) was weak in the market, but shaped with promise as she only tired close home after kicking for home three furlongs out. This was a fine initial effort and it will be a surprise if she does not win shortly. (op 7-4)

Tower Hill(IRE) got stirred up prior to his debut at Newmarket, but took the preliminaries calmly on this occasion. He did not go off unfancied and, after making the running to the three-furlong marker, kept on well when passed. (op 9-1)

Ogee stepped up on his previous efforts on heavy and fast ground to post a more encouraging run. He is nicely bred, from a good family so it would be no surprise to see him make his mark in handicaps. (tchd 8-1)

6335 "HOTPOINT" AT WATERLINE H'CAP 5f 20y(P)

8:30 (8:32) (Class 5) (0-70,70) 3-Y-O+ **£4,080** (£1,214; £606; £303) **Stalls** Low

Form RPR

4203 **1** **Gilded Cove**[25] 5954 5-9-1 **67** .... GrahamGibbons 6 78
(R Hollinshead) *mid-div: rdn and hdwy over 1f out: r.o to ld wl ins fnl f* **6/1**[3]

00-1 **2** ½ **After The Show**[25] 5954 4-9-3 **69** .... ChrisCatlin 13 78
(Rae Guest) *towards rr: rdn and hdwy over 1f out: r.o strly fnl f to go 2nd cl home* **16/1**

6001 **3** *nk* **Wicked Uncle**[7] 6264 6-9-4 **70** ....(v) JimmyFortune 2 78
(S Gollings) *trckd ldr: stongly rdn to ld appr fnl f: hdd wl ins: no ex* **6/1**[3]

0530 **4** ¾ **Divine Spirit**[9] 6238 4-9-1 **67** ....(b) KFallon 5 72
(M Dods) *in tch: rdn and n.m.r ent fnl f: kpt on after* **4/1**[1]

1504 **5** 1 ¾ **Law Maker**[56] 5327 5-8-9 **68** ....(v) MichaelJStainton[(7)] 4 67
(A Bailey) *a in tch on ins: rdn 1/2-way: nt qckn fnl f* **5/1**[2]

0004 **6** ¾ **Wainwright (IRE)**[29] 5868 5-9-2 **68** .... FergalLynch 10 64
(P A Blockley) *in rr: hdwy outside over 1f out: nvr nr to chal* **16/1**

4403 **7** ½ **Dixieanna**[24] 5986 3-9-4 **70** .... MartinDwyer 1 65
(B W Hills) *led rdn 2f out: hdd appr fnl f: wkng whn n.m.r ins* **5/1**[2]

0010 **8** *hd* **The Fisio**[59] 5222 5-9-4 **70** ....(v) TomEaves 11 64
(S Gollings) *prom: rdn 2f out: sn btn* **33/1**

6530 **9** *nk* **Trick Cyclist**[25] 5956 4-9-3 **69** .... DaleGibson 8 62
(M W Easterby) *mid-div: bhd fnl 2f* **33/1**

0654 **10** ¾ **Talcen Gwyn (IRE)**[29] 5869 3-8-12 **67** ....(v) RichardThomas[(3)] 9 57
(M F Harris) *a bhd* **25/1**

0400 **11** ½ **Four Amigos (USA)**[24] 5986 4-8-13 **68** .... SilvestreDeSousa[(3)] 7 56
(D Nicholls) *sn mid-div: dropped out fr 1/2-way* **25/1**

050 **12** *nk* **Salon Prive**[14] 6157 5-9-4 **70** .... LPKeniry 12 57
(C A Cyzer) *trckd ldrs on outside: rdn 2f out: wknd qckly ent fnl f* **14/1**

61.36 secs (-1.46) **Going Correction** -0.275s/f (Stan) 12 Ran SP% **113.9**
Speed ratings (Par 103):100,99,98,97,94 93,92,92,91,90 89,89
CSF £88.80 CT £601.59 TOTE £6.60: £2.30, £4.00, £2.20; EX 84.60.
Owner M Johnson **Bred** R Hollinshead And M Johnson **Trained** Upper Longdon, Staffs

FOCUS
A modest but typically competitive sprint that look solids with the winner producing a career best and the third to his best.

6336 "FRANKE" AT WATERLINE H'CAP 1m 141y(P)

9:00 (9:00) (Class 6) (0-60,69) 3-Y-O+ **£2,966** (£875; £438) **Stalls** Low

Form RPR

5500 **1** **Bijou Dan**[108] 3849 4-9-3 **59** ....(b) TomEaves 2 68
(I Semple) *a in tch: chsd ldr 2f out: edgd rt u.p fr 1f out: r.o to ld last strides* **16/1**

5021 **2** *hd* **Stellite**[44] 5566 5-9-4 **60** .... FergalLynch 1 69
(J S Goldie) *led to over 6f out: led again over 3f out: strly rdn fnl f: hdd last strides* **9/1**

4502 **3** ¾ **Sling Back (IRE)**[34] 5774 4-9-4 **60** .... MartinDwyer 3 67
(Eamon Tyrrell, Ire) *towards rr tl hdwy on ins over 2f out: r.o wl fnl f* **12/1**

254 **4** 3 **Welsh Wind (IRE)**[253] 557 9-8-12 **59** ....(p) AdamKirby[(5)] 11 60
(M Wigham) *in rr tl hdwy on ins over 1f out: r.o: nvr nrr* **28/1**

6021 **5** 1 **Burhaan (IRE)**[12] 6202 3-9-10 **69** ....(t) JimmyFortune 9 68
(J H M Gosden) *trckd ldrs: hung lft appr fnl f: one pce after* **1/1**[1]

4000 **6** ¾ **Shifty Night (IRE)**[25] 5956 4-8-13 **60** ....(v) MarcHalford[(5)] 7 57
(Mrs C A Dunnett) *t.k.h: hld up: rdn over 3f out: no hdwy fnl 2f* **50/1**

2440 **7** ¾ **Joshua's Gold (IRE)**[29] 5884 4-9-0 **59** ....(v) DNolan[(3)] 8 54
(D Carroll) *outpcd: hdwy over 2f out: edgd lft appr fnl f: no ex* **16/1**

1015 **8** 2 ½ **Band**[5] 6286 5-9-2 **58** .... GrahamGibbons 10 48
(E S McMahon) *mid-div: hdwy 3f out: wknd fnl f* **7/1**[3]

-000 **9** 1 **Skip Of Colour**[28] 5893 5-9-4 **60** .... PatCosgrave 4 48
(P A Blockley) *in tch tl wknd 2f out* **80/1**

4020 **10** 6 **Zafarshah (IRE)**[23] 5997 6-9-1 **60** ....(b) AmirQuinn[(3)] 6 36
(R A Harris) *in tch tl wknd over 2f out* **50/1**

0000 **11** *nk* **Winning Venture**[45] 5544 8-9-4 **60** ....(p) ChrisCatlin 5 35
(A W Carroll) *led over 6f out: hdd over 3f out: rdn and wknd 2f out* **50/1**

3024 **12** 9 **Zhitomir**[11] 6216 7-9-4 **60** .... PhillipMakin 13 16
(M Dods) *in tch on outside tl wknd over 3f out* **6/1**[2]

0-00 **13** *hd* **Diamond Shannon (IRE)**[200] 1295 4-9-2 **58** .... AdrianMcCarthy 12 14
(D Carroll) *mid-div: hdwy 3f out: hung lft and wknd qckly fnl f* **100/1**

1m 48.61s (-3.15) **Going Correction** -0.275s/f (Stan)
WFA 3 from 4yo+ 3lb 13 Ran SP% **117.8**
Speed ratings (Par 101):103,102,102,99,98 97,97,95,94,88 88,80,80
CSF £145.96 CT £1171.31 TOTE £19.00: £3.80, £3.00, £2.60; EX 151.70.
Owner Belstane Park Racing - Greens Committee **Bred** James Thom And Sons **Trained** Carluke, S Lanarks

FOCUS
A modest but relatively strong handicap with the first three pulling clear of their rivals. The time was good for the grade and the form should pay to follow.

6337 "RANGEMASTER" AT WATERLINE H'CAP 1m 1f 103y(P)

9:30 (9:31) (Class 5) (0-70,70) 3-Y-O+ **£3,524** (£1,048; £523; £261) **Stalls** Low

Form RPR

6203 **1** **Desert Leader (IRE)**[14] 6160 4-9-1 **67** .... MartinDwyer 2 77
(W M Brisbourne) *mid-div: rdn and hdwy over 2f out: r.o to ld 1f out: drvn out* **9/2**[3]

5643 **2** 1 ½ **Khanjar (USA)**[12] 6201 5-9-4 **70** .... JimmyFortune 10 77
(K R Burke) *sn led: rdn 2f out: hdd 1f out: kpt on one pce* **7/2**[1]

2061 **3** *nk* **Easy Laughter (IRE)**[7] 6265 4-9-1 **67** ....(bt) KFallon 8 73
(C P Morlock) *mid-div: rdn over 1f out: kpt on u.p: nt rch first 2* **4/1**[2]

6002 **4** 1 ½ **Oldenway**[14] 6137 6-9-1 **67** .... TonyHamilton 3 71
(R A Fahey) *trckd ldrs: rdn 2f out: one pce fnl f* **8/1**

5006 **5** ½ **Sorbiesharry (IRE)**[42] 5624 6-8-12 **69** .... AdamKirby[(5)] 4 72
(Mrs N Macauley) *mid-div: styd on one pce fnl f* **6/1**

1000 **6** ½ **Weet A Head (IRE)**[10] 6230 4-9-1 **67** .... GrahamGibbons 12 69
(R Hollinshead) *slowly away: hdwy on outside over 2f out: one pce fnl f* **40/1**

1603 **7** 6 **Charlie Kennet**[22] 6015 7-9-4 **70** .... GeorgeBaker 5 60
(Mrs H Sweeting) *in tch: hdwy 3f out: rdn 2f out: wknd fnl f* **11/2**

3000 **8** *nk* **Cherished Number**[42] 5624 6-9-2 **68** ....(b) TomEaves 13 58
(I Semple) *in rr: mde sme late hdwy* **14/1**

6000 **9** *hd* **She's Our Lass (IRE)**[35] 5743 4-8-11 **70** .... MarkCoumbe[(7)] 7 59
(D Carroll) *a in rr* **33/1**

0310 **10** 2 **Tony Tie**[34] 5772 9-9-3 **69** .... FergalLynch 6 55
(J S Goldie) *trckd ldrs: wnt 2nd 2f out: rdn and wknd rapidly appr fnl f* **16/1**

3000 **11** 2 **Marajuana**[14] 6161 3-8-10 **70** ....(e[1]) MarcHalford[(5)] 9 52
(J Ryan) *hld up: hdwy over 3f out: sn rdn: wknd over 1f out* **40/1**

20-0 **12** *dist* **How's Things**[1] 6315 5-8-12 **67** .... AmirQuinn[(3)] 11 —
(R A Harris) *trckd ldr to 4f out: sn lost pl: t.o* **50/1**

1m 59.43s (-3.19) **Going Correction** -0.275s/f (Stan)
WFA 3 from 4yo+ 3lb 12 Ran SP% **123.5**
Speed ratings (Par 103):103,101,101,100,99 99,93,93,93,91 89,—
CSF £21.14 CT £71.00 TOTE £5.70: £2.60, £2.80, £1.90; EX 27.90 Place 6 £505.40, Place 5 £65.25.
Owner R Rickett **Bred** Shadwell Estate Company Limited **Trained** Great Ness, Shropshire

FOCUS
A well-contested handicap, run at a good pace which produced a winner that will pay to follow this winter as he loves the Polytrack. The runner-up sets the standard while the third is not yet exposed on this surface and ran up to his old mark.

T/Plt: £243.30 to a £1 stake. Pool: £41,589.85. 124.75 winning tickets. T/Qpdt: £30.10 to a £1 stake. Pool: £2,593.40. 63.70 winning tickets. JS

6188 SAINT-CLOUD (L-H)

Saturday, November 12

OFFICIAL GOING: Heavy

6338a CRITERIUM DE SAINT-CLOUD (GROUP 1) (ENTIRE COLTS & FILLIES) 1m 2f

1:20 (1:29) 2-Y-O **£81,050** (£32,426; £16,213; £8,099; £4,057)

RPR

1 **Linda's Lad**[27] 5933 2-9-0 .... CSoumillon 4 110+
(A Fabre, France) *raced in 2nd, led over 1 1/2f out, soon driven, hdd 100 yards out, rallied to lead again close home, driven out* **7/10**[1]

2 *1* **Fauvelia (FR)**[27] 5933 2-8-11 .... TJarnet 2 105
(Y De Nicolay, France) *raced in 3rd, pushed along 1 1/2f out, challenged 1f out, led 100 yards out til headed close home* **13/1**

3 *2* **Flashing Numbers (USA)**[38] 2-9-0 .... ABoschert 1 105
(Mario Hofer, Germany) *held up in last, stayed on from over 1f out to take 3rd* **6/1**

4 *2 ½* **Salsalava (FR)**[9] 6240 2-9-0 .... DBoeuf 5 100
(P Demercastel, France) *raced in 4th, never challenged leaders* **42/10**[3]

5 *4* **Customary**[27] 2-9-0 ....(b) SPasquier 3 93
(Mme C Head-Maarek, France) *led, driven approaching straight, headed over 1 1/2f out, weakened* **28/10**[2]

2m 23.3s **Going Correction** +0.70s/f (Yiel) 5 Ran SP% **125.8**
Speed ratings: 98,97,95,93,90
PARI-MUTUEL: WIN 1.70; PL 1.10, 2.40; SF 8.30.
Owner S Mulryan **Bred** The Niarchos Family **Trained** Chantilly, France

NOTEBOOK

Linda's Lad took control two furlongs out and then had to hold off a challenge from the runner-up at the furlong marker. He pulled out a little more in the final stages but did have a tendency to look to his right. A very consistent individual, he is will be aimed at the Vodafone Derby next year, and his breeding suggests that the trip should be well within his capabilities.

Fauvelia(FR), who is tiny, settled in third place behind the winner. She quickened well a furlong and a half out and nearly took the lead a little later, but the winner was going away from her at the end. She has plenty of stamina on her dam's side and looks likely to stay distances longer than a mile next year.

Flashing Numbers(USA) put up a decent performance considering this was just his second racecourse performance. He made progress from a furlong and a half out but never looked like pressing the winner and runner-up, and his trainer felt that better ground would have been an advantage. He is now to be aimed at next year's French Derby.

Salsalava(FR) did not appear to stay the distance so it would be no surprise to see him return to a mile.

6339a PRIX DENISY (LISTED RACE) 1m 7f 110y

2:20 (2:23) 3-Y-O+ **£16,667** (£6,667; £5,000; £3,333; £1,667)

RPR

1 **Le Carre (USA)**[33] 5809 7-9-4 .... CSoumillon 4 110
(A De Royer-Dupre, France)

2 *2* **Vinando**[13] 6191 4-9-1 ....(b) SPasquier 8 105
(C R Egerton) *prominent, 2nd straight, ridden to lead stands side group 1f out, kept on*

3 *2* **Frank Sonata**[21] 6026 4-9-4 .... IanMongan 1 106
(M G Quinlan) *in touch on outside, 3rd half-way, led over 4f out, pushed along straight, headed over 1 1/2f out, stayed on*

4 *1 ½* **Soterio (GER)**[49] 5482 5-9-4 .... ABoschert 7 105
(W Baltromei, Germany)

5 *nse* **Albanov (IRE)**[15] 5-9-1 .... TThulliez 11 101
(M Rolland, France)

6 *2* **Grey Plover (IRE)**[11] 6218 3-8-4 .... TJarnet 5 97
(J L Dunlop) *disputing lead early, close 4th half-way, 5th and pushed along straight, one pace from well over 1f out*

7 *snk* **Winter Silence**[72] 4907 3-8-4 .... JVictoire 6 97
(A Fabre, France)

8 *2 ½* **Soreze (FR)**[36] 7-9-1 .... FGeroux 3 97
(D Sepulchre, France)

9 *8* **Zenato (GER)**[49] 4-9-4 .... IMendizabal 10 92
(F Reuterskiold, Sweden) **17/1**[1]

10 20 **Double Green (IRE)**[72] 4907 4-8-12 .... MBlancpain 2 66
(F Head, France)

3m 43.2s
WFA 3 from 4yo+ 8lb 11 Ran SP% **5.6**
PARI-MUTUEL: WIN 2.40; PL 1.30, 2.00, 3.00; DF 9.00.
Owner J-R De Aragao Bozano **Bred** Haras Santa Maria De Araras **Trained** Chantilly, France

NOTEBOOK
Vinando, always in the leading group, was brought over to the stands' rail to make his challenge. He was still at the head of affairs passing the post but the race went to the only horse who was brought up the far rail.
Frank Sonata was always well placed and led running into the final turn before staying on one-paced. His rider was fined 200 euros for abusive use of the whip.
Grey Plover(IRE) was always thereabouts and given every possible chance. She was one-paced in the straight, though, and had no chance of a place in the frame from the furlong marker.

1660 JAGERSRO (R-H)
Sunday, November 13

OFFICIAL GOING: Good

6340a JOCKEYKLUBBENS AVESLOPNING (LISTED RACE) (F&M) (DIRT) 1m 4f
2:09 (2:11) 3-5-Y-0 **£9,796** (£4,937; £2,351; £1,567; £940)

RPR
1 **Oblique (IRE)**[58] 5278 3-9-1 .... FJohansson 6 —
(Sir Mark Prescott) *1.54-1* **154/100**[1]
2 ½ **Halfsong (SWE)**[63] 5-9-6 .... SaraSlot 3 —
(K Anderson)
3 ½ **La Petite Chinoise**[464] 4518 4-9-6 .... LHammer-Hansen 2 —
(L Kelp, Sweden)
4 1 **Gryngolette**[28] 5-9-6 .... (b) ESki 7 —
(R A Kvisla)
5 ½ **Shangri La (DEN)** 3-9-1 .... NCordrey 1 —
(Hanne Bechmann)
6 12 **Azolla**[63] 4-9-6 .... YvonneDurant 5 —
(M Khan)
7 1 **Feaat**[470] 4321 4-9-6 .... JJohansen 10 —
(B Olsen, Norway)
8 2 **New Business (USA)**[826] 4038 5-9-6 .... MSantos 8 —
(F Castro, Sweden)
9 5 **Pinwinnie (SWE)** 4-9-6 .... (b) MLarsen 9 —
(Bruno Nilsson, Sweden)

2m 33.1s
WFA 3 from 4yo+ 6lb 10 Ran SP% **39.4**
(Including 1 SKr stake): WIN 2.54; PL 1.49, 1.66, 1.96; DF 17.78.
Owner Lady O'Reilly **Bred** Dr A J O'Reilly And Skymarc Farm **Trained** Newmarket, Suffolk

NOTEBOOK
Oblique(IRE) was well placed to gain a valuable black type success, clearly the aim of connections. She will undoubtedly find life tougher next year if she remains in training with a Listed penalty.

KYOTO (R-H)
Sunday, November 13

OFFICIAL GOING: Firm

6341a QUEEN ELIZABETH II COMMEMORATIVE CUP (GRADE 1) (F&M) 1m 3f
6:40 (6:40) 3-Y-0+ **£528,166** (£208,997; £129,914; £76,247; £50,831)

RPR
1 **Sweep Tosho (JPN)**[14] 4-8-11 .... Kenichilkezoe 8 119
(A Tsurudome, Japan) **18/10**[2]
2 ½ **Osumi Haruka (JPN)**[364] 5-8-11 .... SKawashima 1 118
(M Ando, Japan) **154/10**
3 2½ **Admire Groove (JPN)**[14] 5-8-11 .... HUemura 3 114
(M Hashida, Japan) **101/10**
4 ¾ **Yamanin Sucre (JPN)**[392] 4-8-11 .... HShii 14 113
(Hidekazu Asami, Japan) **36/1**
5 nk **Air Messiah (JPN)**[28] 3-8-7 .... YTake 11 114
(Y Ito, Japan) **6/4**[1]
6 1½ **Lailaps (JPN)**[28] 3-8-7 .... MikioMatsunaga 2 111
(K Matsuda, Japan) **53/1**
7 nk **Osumi Cosmo (JPN)**[364] 6-8-11 .... YIwata 5 110
(T Nakao, Japan) **143/1**
8 ½ **Yamanin Alabaster (JPN)**[364] 4-8-11 .... TEda 12 109
(S Hoshino, Japan) **64/10**[3]
9 hd **Best Album (JPN)**[756] 5-8-11 .... KWatanabe 18 109
(Yoshio Oki, Japan) **62/1**
10 ½ **Winglet (JPN)**[392] 4-8-11 .... KTake 15 108
(Y Munakata) **117/1**
11 nk **Kuroyuri Jo (JPN)**[343] 3-8-7 .... OPeslier 9 108
(I Okada, Japan) **50/1**
12 ¾ **Mighty Collar (JPN)** 5-8-11 .... KUchida 7 106
(Toru Miya, Japan) **69/1**
13 hd **Memory Keanu (JPN)**[364] 5-8-11 .... KTsunoda 6 106
(S Yukubo, Japan) **182/1**
14 nse **Meine Samantha (JPN)**[756] 5-8-11 .... C-PLemaire 16 106
(H Nakamura, Japan) **60/1**
15 nk **Shonan Peintre (JPN)**[28] 3-8-7 .... YYoshida 4 106
(Y Okubo, Japan) **85/1**
16 ½ **Summitville**[21] 6053 5-8-11 .... SebSanders 13 104
(J G Given) *outpaced early stages, never better than mid-division* **35/1**
17 3 **Les Clefs D'Or (JPN)**[364] 4-8-11 .... MEbina 17 100
(Y Ikee, Japan) **30/1**
18 1½ **Brian's Letter (JPN)** 6-8-11 .... YFukunaga 10 97
(M Okubo, Japan) **120/1**

2m 12.5s
WFA 3 from 4yo+ 5lb 18 Ran SP% **125.6**
(Including Y100 stake): WIN 280; PL 150, 380, 360; DF 1,650.
Owner Tosho Sangyo **Bred** Tosho Sangyo Corporation Tosho Bokujo **Trained** Japan

NOTEBOOK
Sweep Tosho(JPN) had been in good form this year, including at the top level against the colts, and gained her second Grade One success of the year here. She would be a definite contender for the big Hong Kong meeting next month.
Summitville was never able to get involved. The strong early pace meant her jockey could not get the position he wanted, and she never threatened to land a blow.

6332 WOLVERHAMPTON (A.W) (L-H)
Monday, November 14

OFFICIAL GOING: Standard changing to standard to fast after race 2 (2.00)
Wind: Slight, behind Weather: Fine

6342 NEW ACCOUNT FREE BET AT BET DIRECT MEDIAN AUCTION MAIDEN STKS 1m 1f 103y(P)
1:30 (1:33) (Class 7) 2-Y-0 **£1,446** (£427; £213) **Stalls** Low

Form RPR
003 1 **Mr Excel (IRE)**[18] 6121 2-9-0 73 .... JamieSpencer 12 68+
(J A Osborne) *a.p: led wl over 1f out: r.o wl* **4/1**[3]
50 2 2 **Party Belle**[32] 5857 2-8-2 .... WilliamCarson(7) 11 59
(C E Brittain) *hld up towards rr: rdn and hdwy on outside 2f out: chsd wnr and hung lft ins fnl f: nt qckn* **33/1**
0000 3 3½ **Punjabi**[16] 6150 2-9-0 55 .... GrahamGibbons 2 58
(Mrs G S Rees) *led early: a.p: rdn over 1f out: one pce fnl f* **33/1**
4523 4 ½ **Is It Me (USA)**[49] 5503 2-9-0 69 .... PatCosgrave 7 57
(P A Blockley) *sn led: rdn and hdd 2f out: no ex fnl f* **14/1**
0 5 1¾ **Lynford Lady**[16] 6150 2-8-9 .... LPKeniry 6 48
(P W D'Arcy) *mid-div: rdn over 3f out: no real prog fnl 2f* **33/1**
5600 6 hd **Rambling Socks**[32] 5857 2-8-9 50 .... PaulEddery 8 48
(S R Bowring) *chsd ldr: rdn 3f out: led briefly 2f out: wknd ins fnl f* **40/1**
2 7 3 **Mighty Kitchener (USA)**[16] 6150 2-9-0 .... KFallon 4 49+
(P Howling) *s.i.s: sn chsng ldrs: pushed along over 6f out: rdn over 2f out: wknd over 1f out* **4/5**[1]
0360 8 1¾ **Flying Penne**[69] 5029 2-8-9 54 .... SamHitchcott 5 39
(M R Channon) *mid-div: rdn over 3f out: wknd over 1f out* **25/1**
0 9 9 **Alistair John**[7] 6282 2-9-0 .... (t) DeanMcKeown 3 27
(Mrs G S Rees) *s.i.s: a bhd* **33/1**
00 10 3½ **Allouette**[10] 6246 2-8-6 .... AdamKirby(3) 13 15
(J M P Eustace) *s.i.s: rdn over 4f out: a bhd* **33/1**
404 11 nk **Beauchamp United**[11] 6233 2-9-0 72 .... SteveDrowne 10 20
(G A Butler) *hld up towards rr: rdn over 3f out: no rspnse* **3/1**[2]
12 5 **Fairytale Of York (IRE)** 2-8-9 .... ChrisCatlin 1 5
(D Carroll) *s.i.s: a bhd* **66/1**
00 13 22 **Becky's Dancer**[14] 6199 2-8-6 .... BenSwarbrick(3) 9 —
(W M Brisbourne) *dwlt: a bhd: t.o* **66/1**

2m 0.76s (-1.86) **Going Correction** -0.30s/f (Stan) 13 Ran SP% **131.2**
Speed ratings (Par 90):96,94,91,90,89 88,86,84,76,73 73,68,49
CSF £138.46 TOTE £4.40: £1.30, £13.80, £8.30; EX 176.40.
Owner A Taylor **Bred** Ellesmere Bloodstock Ltd **Trained** Upper Lambourn, Berks

FOCUS
A decent winning time for the type of contest and a two-year-old course record, but this was only the sixth race of its type run over the trip since the Polytrack was laid. Sound but limited form.

NOTEBOOK
Mr Excel(IRE) relished this stamina test and confirmed his liking for this surface with a decisive victory. Described as big and weak by his trainer, he will now be put away for the winter. (op 7-2)
Party Belle, another who stayed the trip well, looked much more at home on this surface than the Fibresand, although she did lug over to the far rail.
Punjabi, who also appeared to handle the Polytrack better than Fibresand, was going as well as any on the home turn but he failed to raise his game. He may do better back at a mile.
Is It Me(USA) made sure there would be no hanging about but rather cut his own throat on this switch to sand. (op 10-1)
Lynford Lady at least showed some improvement on her Fibresand debut last month.
Rambling Socks appeared to get found out by what was a stiff test for two-year-olds.
Mighty Kitchener(USA) found this surface a totally different kettle of fish to the Fibresand at Southwell. (op 6-5)

6343 TEXT "BETDIRECT" TO 88600 BANDED STKS (DIV I) 1m 1f 103y(P)
2:00 (2:00) (Class 7) 3-Y-0+ **£1,436** (£424; £212) **Stalls** Low

Form RPR
6042 1 **Rotuma (IRE)**[26] 5980 6-9-3 48 .... (b) TomEaves 3 55
(M Dods) *broke wl: stdd and lost pl sn after s: rdn and hdwy over 2f out: r.o to ld last strides* **9/2**[2]
4326 2 shd **Show Me The Lolly (FR)**[6] 6292 5-9-5 50 .... KFallon 8 57
(P J McBride) *hld up in tch: rdn wl over 1f out: led ins fnl f: hdd last strides* **6/1**[3]
4030 3 1¼ **Adobe**[65] 5131 10-9-2 47 .... GeorgeBaker 11 52
(W M Brisbourne) *hld up in rr: rdn and hdwy over 2f out: kpt on ins fnl f* **25/1**
4212 4 hd **Shekan Star**[23] 6034 3-8-11 45 .... PaulEddery 4 49
(K G Reveley) *a.p: rdn to ld wl over 1f out: hdd and nt qckn ins fnl f* **8/1**
00-1 5 1¾ **Mad Maurice**[42] 5656 4-9-4 49 .... JamieSpencer 1 53+
(B J Curley) *hld up in mid-div: rdn and hdwy on ins whn nt clr run briefly 2f out: one pce fnl f* **11/8**[1]
-000 6 1¾ **Amberlina (IRE)**[51] 5471 3-8-12 49 .... AdamKirby(3) 2 47
(Patrick Morris, Ire) *hld up and bhd: hdwy on ins whn nt clr run briefly 2f out: sn rdn: no imp* **25/1**
5030 7 1 **Guadiana (GER)**[30] 5895 3-8-12 49 .... DNolan(3) 5 45
(A W Carroll) *mid-div: rdn over 2f out: no hdwy* **25/1**
0000 8 7 **My Boo**[87] 4555 3-9-2 50 .... (t) SteveDrowne 7 32
(T Keddy) *nvr nr ldrs* **50/1**
1060 9 1¼ **Wanna Shout**[126] 3405 7-9-2 47 .... LisaJones 12 27
(R Dickin) *hld up in mid-div: rdn on outside over 2f out: sn bhd* **50/1**
0040 10 1¼ **Yours Sincerely (IRE)**[2] 6328 3-8-6 47 .... KevinGhunowa(7) 9 25
(P A Blockley) *chsd ldr tl rdn over 2f out: sn wknd* **40/1**
-300 11 2½ **Zantero**[279] 320 3-9-1 49 .... GrahamGibbons 6 22
(W M Brisbourne) *led: rdn and hdd wl over 1f out: sn wknd* **16/1**
3031 12 3½ **Phoenix Eye**[23] 6033 4-9-2 47 .... DarrenWilliams 13 13
(M Mullineaux) *keen early: prom: rdn over 3f out: wkng whn n.m.r over 2f out* **7/1**

2m 0.46s (-2.16) **Going Correction** -0.30s/f (Stan)
WFA 3 from 4yo+ 3lb 12 Ran SP% **122.0**
Speed ratings (Par 97):97,96,95,95,94 92,91,85,84,83 80,77
CSF £30.38 TOTE £10.10: £1.90, £1.90, £5.80; EX 44.30.

Owner Denton Hall Racing Ltd **Bred** Sean Twomey **Trained** Denton, Co Durham

FOCUS

A stronger pace meant this was run in a faster time than the second division. Pretty straightforward form to rate through the runner-up.

6344 BET DIRECT ON AT THE RACES INTERACTIVE BANDED STKS 1m 4f 50y(P)

2:30 (2:31) (Class 7) 3-Y-O+ **£1,419** (£419; £209) **Stalls** Low

Form RPR

6 **1** **Mickmacmagoole (IRE)**[37] 5741 3-8-9 40 JamieSpencer 7 51
(Seamus G O'Donnell, Ire) *hld up: rdn and hdwy on outside over 2f out: hung lft 1f out: r.o to ld wl ins fnl f* **7/4**[1]

0433 **2** *1 1/4* **Brennie (IRE)**[41] 5683 4-9-1 40 (v) DaneO'Neill 12 49
(V Smith) *prom: chsd ldr 8f out: led 5f out: rdn over 2f out: hdd and no ex wl ins fnl f* **7/2**[3]

5502 **3** *1/2* **Bulberry Hill**[32] 5855 4-9-1 40 SamHitchcott 8 48
(R W Price) *hld up and bhd: stdy hdwy 6f out: rdn to chse ldr over 2f out: nt qckn ins fnl f* **3/1**[2]

6203 **4** *1 1/2* **Lucefer (IRE)**[25] 5996 7-9-1 40 PaulEddery 6 46
(G C H Chung) *hld up and bhd: hdwy 2f out: styd on ins fnl f* **9/1**

0-00 **5** *2* **Ice And Fire**[30] 5892 6-8-12 40 AdamKirby(3) 9 43
(J T Stimpson) *a.p: rdn over 4f out: no hdwy fnl 2f* **40/1**

2053 **6** *nk* **Bobering**[23] 6033 5-8-8 40 JemmaMarshall(7) 2 42
(B P J Baugh) *hld up in mid-div: lost pl 6f out: sme hdwy over 1f out: n.d* **14/1**

510- **7** *1 3/4* **Courant D'Air (IRE)**[188] 5451 4-8-12 40 DNolan(3) 4 39
(Lucinda Featherstone) *hld up in tch: rdn to chse ldr over 3f out tl over 2f out: wknd fnl f* **16/1**

0000 **8** *1* **Dancing Shirl**[13] 6215 3-8-9 40 DeanMcKeown 3 38
(C W Fairhurst) *prom: bhd fnl 4f* **40/1**

4054 **9** *6* **Susiedil (IRE)**[21] 6079 4-8-12 40 SilvestreDeSousa(3) 1 28
(D Nicholls) *plld hrd: led 2f: prom tl wknd 4f out* **20/1**

0006 **10** *1* **Ewar Finch (FR)**[20] 6099 3-8-6 40 NeilChalmers(3) 5 27
(K O Cunningham-Brown) *s.s: a bhd* **25/1**

4006 **11** *1* **Danger Bird (IRE)**[21] 6080 5-8-8 40 HugoFellows(7) 10 25
(R Hollinshead) *plld hrd: sddle sn slipped: led after 2f to 5f out: wknd 3f out* **20/1**

2m 40.91s (-1.51) **Going Correction** -0.30s/f (Stan)
WFA 3 from 4yo+ 6lb 11 Ran SP% **124.4**
Speed ratings (Par 97):93,92,91,90,89 89,88,87,83,82 82
CSF £7.89 TOTE £2.70: £1.30, £1.40, £1.70; EX 12.80.
Owner J Roberts **Bred** Tower Bloodstock **Trained** Ballinalard, Co Tipperary
■ The first winner in Britain for Seamus O'Donnell.

FOCUS

A modest winning time, even for a race like this, and the form does not look strong.
Danger Bird(IRE) Official explanation: jockey said saddle slipped

6345 BET DIRECT FREEPHONE ON 0800 211 222 BANDED STKS 5f 216y(P)

3:00 (3:02) (Class 7) 3-Y-O+ **£1,470** (£434; £217) **Stalls** Low

Form RPR

3443 **1** **Magic Amour**[21] 6082 7-8-8 46 (b) KevinGhunowa(7) 1 54
(P A Blockley) *sn prom: rdn over 2f out: led and edgd lft 1f out: r.o* **11/4**[1]

620 **2** *1/2* **Musiotal**[70] 4999 4-9-5 50 TomEaves 5 57
(J S Goldie) *s.i.s: bhd tl hdwy on ins wl over 1f out: r.o ins fnl f* **7/1**

2555 **3** *1/2* **Multahab**[21] 6076 6-8-12 46 (t) AdamKirby(3) 7 51
(Miss Gay Kelleway) *hld up and bhd: swtchd rt over 2f out and over 1f out: gd hdwy fnl f: fin wl* **6/1**[3]

2030 **4** *1 3/4* **Taipan Tommy (IRE)**[102] 4083 3-9-5 50 (v) PaulDoe 2 50
(S Dow) *hld up in tch: rdn over 2f out: one pce fnl f* **25/1**

01U0 **5** *1/2* **Aintnecessarilyso**[2] 6326 7-9-1 46 (p) GeorgeBaker 3 44
(J M Bradley) *a.p: rdn and one pce fnl 2f* **9/1**

0004 **6** *3* **Auentraum (GER)**[21] 6070 5-9-5 50 (b) JamieSpencer 9 39
(K McAuliffe) *hld up in tch: rdn over 2f out: wknd 1f out* **9/1**

6052 **7** *3/4* **Sholto**[37] 5736 7-8-10 48 (b) JamesO'Reilly(7) 10 35
(J O'Reilly) *led early: prom: rdn over 2f out: wknd fnl f* **25/1**

0010 **8** *nk* **Largs**[27] 5966 5-9-1 46 (p) RobbieFitzpatrick 11 32
(J Balding) *nvr trbld ldrs* **20/1**

0062 **9** *1* **Leah's Pride**[23] 6031 4-9-1 46 KFallon 4 29
(P Howling) *sn led: rdn and hdd whn nt clr run on ins 1f out: eased whn btn* **7/1**

0000 **10** *shd* **Melaina**[26] 5975 4-9-1 46 (p) PhillipMakin 6 29
(M S Saunders) *sn mid-div: lost pl after 2f: n.d after* **40/1**

5112 **11** *nk* **Desertina (IRE)**[9] 6261 3-8-9 47 MichaelJStainton(7) 12 29
(R M Whitaker) *bhd fnl 3f* **12/1**

6452 **12** *1/2* **Golden Spectrum (IRE)**[21] 6082 6-8-12 46 (b) AmirQuinn(3) 13 26
(R A Harris) *a bhd* **11/2**[2]

6025 **13** *6* **Bold Maggie**[117] 3636 3-8-9 47 RussellKennemore(7) 8 9
(J A Pickering) *prom tl wknd wl over 1f out* **33/1**

1m 14.35s (-1.46) **Going Correction** -0.30s/f (Stan) 13 Ran SP% **126.9**
Speed ratings (Par 97):97,96,95,93,92 88,87,87,85,85 85,84,76
CSF £22.05 TOTE £4.00: £1.50, £2.50, £2.30; EX 49.80.
Owner Mrs Joanna Hughes **Bred** Juddmonte Farms **Trained** Lambourn, Berks
■ Stewards' Enquiry : Kevin Ghunowa one day ban: careless riding (Nov 25)

FOCUS

Not a bad race for its type and the fastest time of the meeting compared with standard.

6346 BETDIRECT.CO.UK BANDED STKS 7f 32y(P)

3:30 (3:30) (Class 7) 3-Y-O+ **£1,470** (£434; £217) **Stalls** High

Form RPR

4636 **1** **Cayman Breeze**[21] 6078 5-9-3 48 GeorgeBaker 3 59+
(J M Bradley) *hld up: hdwy over 2f out: nt clr run ins fnl f: rdn to ld last strides* **11/2**[3]

0052 **2** *hd* **Fulvio (USA)**[49] 5521 5-9-5 50 (v) KFallon 8 58
(P Howling) *t.k.h: sn chsng ldr: led wl over 1f out: hdd last strides* **10/3**[1]

0501 **3** *1 1/4* **Humility**[21] 6074 4-9-5 50 LPKeniry 7 55
(C A Cyzer) *a.p: rdn over 1f out: nt qckn ins fnl f* **10/1**

0000 **4** *3/4* **Vibe**[9] 6262 4-9-0 48 RichardThomas(3) 1 51
(R J Price) *prom: lost pl over 3f out: rdn over 2f out: rallied and hung lft fr over 1f out: kpt on ins fnl f* **13/2**

0000 **5** *1 1/4* **Mytton's Dream**[6] 6292 3-9-4 50 ChrisCatlin 11 50
(R Brotherton) *hld up: hdwy on outside over 1f out: r.o ins fnl f* **33/1**

0601 **6** *3/4* **Dane's Rock (IRE)**[70] 4991 3-9-2 48 (p) PhillipMakin 4 46
(M S Saunders) *chsd ldr early: prom: rdn over 2f out: wknd over 1f out* **10/1**

0000 **7** *1 1/4* **Lucky Emerald (IRE)**[34] 5819 3-9-1 50 RobertMiles(3) 2 45
(B Palling) *led: rdn and hdd wl over 1f out: wknd ins fnl f* **33/1**

500 **8** *nk* **Orpen Quest (IRE)**[93] 4376 3-9-4 50 RobbieFitzpatrick 6 44
(M J Attwater) *bhd tl hdwy on ins over 1f out: nt rch ldrs* **11/2**[3]

0060 **9** *4* **Rafters Music (IRE)**[10] 6243 10-9-2 50 (p) AdamKirby(3) 5 33
(Julian Poulton) *a bhd* **14/1**

0000 **10** *1/2* **Awarding**[37] 5738 5-8-10 48 (vt[1]) PatriciaStainton(7) 12 30
(Dr J R J Naylor) *plld hrd in rr: hdwy over 4f out: wknd over 2f out* **50/1**

4400 **11** *1* **Sierra**[114] 3726 4-9-4 49 JamieSpencer 10 29
(A W Carroll) *swtchd lft sn after s: a bhd* **16/1**

0021 **12** *4* **Colloseum**[23] 6032 4-9-3 48 GrahamGibbons 9 17
(T J Etherington) *prom: rdn over 3f out: wknd 2f out* **9/2**[2]

1m 29.32s (-1.08) **Going Correction** -0.30s/f (Stan)
WFA 3 from 4yo+ 1lb 12 Ran SP% **123.9**
Speed ratings (Par 97):94,93,92,91,90 89,87,87,82,82 81,76
CSF £25.03 TOTE £7.50: £2.80, £1.60, £4.60; EX 38.40.
Owner G & L Johnson **Bred** M P B Bloodstock Ltd **Trained** Sedbury, Gloucs

FOCUS

A somewhat controversial affair with some aggrieved favourite backers thinking Fallon was too easy on the runner-up. The form looks sound enough for the grade.
Lucky Emerald(IRE) Official explanation: jockey said filly ran too keenly early

6347 PLAY INSTANT WIN GAMES ON ITVI BANDED STKS 1m 1f 103y(P)

4:00 (4:01) (Class 7) 4-Y-O+ **£1,433** (£423; £211) **Stalls** Low

Form RPR

546- **1** **Scorchio (IRE)**[491] 3371 4-8-11 45 DerekMcGaffin 2 50
(B Smart) *led early: a.p: rdn over 2f out: r.o u.p to ld cl home* **20/1**

0300 **2** *1/2* **Fortunes Favourite**[42] 5655 5-8-6 45 NataliaGemelova(5) 1 49
(J E Long) *chsd ldrs: led wl ins fnl f: hrd rdn and edgd rt: hdd cl home* **50/1**

0663 **3** *nk* **Now Look Away (IRE)**[9] 6258 4-8-11 45 (p) GrahamGibbons 4 48
(E S McMahon) *sn led: hrd rdn and hdd wl ins fnl f* **7/2**[2]

6664 **4** *1/2* **Peace Emblem (IRE)**[37] 5740 4-8-11 45 (p) AdrianMcCarthy 5 47
(J W Unett) *a.p: rdn and ev ch 2f out: nt qckn ins fnl f* **14/1**

0000 **5** *1* **Successor**[30] 5895 5-8-11 45 (t) DaneO'Neill 11 46
(M D I Usher) *hld up and bhd: hdwy over 2f out: edgd lft ins fnl f: no ex* **20/1**

0000 **6** *1 1/4* **Tropical Son**[49] 5519 6-8-6 45 (v) PatrickMathers(5) 13 43
(D Shaw) *hld up in rr: c wd bnd 3f out: hdwy over 1f out: nvr able to chal* **40/1**

0462 **7** *1 1/4* **Louve Heureuse (IRE)**[12] 6231 4-8-5 45 ow1 JamesMillman(7) 9 42
(B R Millman) *nvr nrr* **5/1**[3]

0034 **8** *hd* **Fleet Anchor**[2] 6327 4-8-11 45 SteveDrowne 12 40
(J M Bradley) *plld hrd in rr: hdwy over 2f out: rdn wl over 1f out: no imp* **10/1**

5000 **9** *7* **Another Con (IRE)**[98] 4229 4-8-11 45 LisaJones 7 27
(P Howling) *sn mid-div: bhd fnl 3f* **14/1**

0005 **10** *2* **Single Track Mind**[30] 5897 7-8-8 45 (e[1]) AmirQuinn(3) 3 23
(J R Boyle) *s.i.s: sn chsng ldrs: rdn over 3f out: wknd wl over 1f out* **25/1**

0-00 **11** *5* **Inescapable (USA)**[49] 5521 4-8-4 45 JackDean(7) 6 14
(A W Carroll) *plld hrd: prom: wnt 2nd over 5f out: wknd over 2f out* **33/1**

2021 **12** *13* **Bold Phoenix (IRE)**[32] 5858 4-8-11 45 JamieSpencer 8 —
(B J Curley) *hld up: hdwy over 3f out: wknd over 2f out* **11/4**[1]

2m 1.47s (-1.15) **Going Correction** -0.30s/f (Stan) 12 Ran SP% **108.7**
Speed ratings (Par 97):93,92,92,91,90 89,88,88,82,80 76,64
CSF £580.14 TOTE £23.60: £6.00, £22.00, £1.40; EX 788.80.
Owner B Smart **Bred** Joe Foley and Jeff O'Callaghan **Trained** Hambleton, N Yorks

FOCUS

A steadily-run affair made even weaker by the withdrawal of the third favourite at the start.
Bold Phoenix(IRE) Official explanation: trainer had no explanation for the poor form shown

6348 TEXT "BETDIRECT" TO 88600 BANDED STKS (DIV II) 1m 1f 103y(P)

4:30 (4:30) (Class 7) 3-Y-O+ **£1,436** (£424; £212) **Stalls** Low

Form RPR

-502 **1** **Awaaser (USA)**[21] 6080 3-9-0 48 KFallon 2 54
(J A Osborne) *w ldr: led over 3f out: rdn over 1f out: jst hld on* **2/1**[1]

1400 **2** *hd* **Magari**[16] 6151 4-9-2 47 GrahamGibbons 7 53
(W M Brisbourne) *a.p: rdn over 2f out: r.o ins fnl f jst failed* **11/2**[3]

-100 **3** *2* **Big Mystery (IRE)**[91] 4437 4-9-2 47 GeorgeBaker 8 49
(S C Williams) *hld up in mid-div: smooth hdwy over 3f out: chsd wnr over 2f out: sn rdn: no ex ins fnl f* **16/1**

5400 **4** *3* **My Lilli (IRE)**[83] 4657 5-9-2 47 DarrenWilliams 10 44
(P Mitchell) *hld up in mid-div: rdn 4f out: hdwy over 2f out: one pce appr fnl f* **10/1**

0030 **5** *1 1/4* **Hollywood Henry (IRE)**[49] 5515 5-9-3 48 (b) PatCosgrave 11 42
(P A Blockley) *s.i.s: bhd tl hdwy over 3f out: one pce fnl 2f* **25/1**

3006 **6** *nk* **Gallas (IRE)**[10] 6245 4-8-12 50 (v) DeanWilliams(7) 3 44
(G C H Chung) *bhd: hdwy on ins wl over 1f out: no further prog fnl f* **25/1**

0060 **7** *1 1/4* **Showtime Annie**[8] 6139 4-9-2 47 (p) JoeFanning 9 38
(A Bailey) *hld up: hdwy 6f out: wknd 3f out* **9/1**

8 *1 1/2* **Cockney Tai (IRE)**[51] 5472 5-8-12 46 AdamKirby(3) 6 34
(Patrick Morris, Ire) *hld up and bhd: sme hdwy on outside over 1f out: n.d* **9/2**[2]

6005 **9** *3/4* **Cautiously (USA)**[30] 5895 4-9-4 49 (b[1]) DaneO'Neill 4 36
(M Blanshard) *hld up in mid-div: lost pl over 3f out: n.d after* **16/1**

0003 **10** *nk* **Super King**[9] 6262 4-9-5 50 LPKeniry 12 36
(A D Brown) *hld up: hdwy 6f out: rdn over 3f out: wknd over 1f out* **16/1**

1000 **11** *3* **River Of Diamonds**[42] 5654 4-9-2 47 ChrisCatlin 5 28
(R A Harris) *prom tl wknd 3f out* **8/1**

0000 **12** *1* **Tiggers Touch**[35] 5804 3-8-13 47 (v[1]) SteveDrowne 1 26
(A W Carroll) *led: hdd over 3f out: wknd 2f out* **50/1**

0004 **13** *2* **Edict**[21] 6081 3-8-13 47 PaulEddery 13 22
(C J Down) *a bhd* **20/1**

2m 0.74s (-1.88) **Going Correction** -0.30s/f (Stan)
WFA 3 from 4yo+ 3lb 49 Ran SP% **129.2**
Speed ratings (Par 97):96,95,94,91,90 90,88,87,86,86 83,83,81
CSF £13.26 TOTE £2.80: £1.20, £2.20, £6.40; EX 17.00 Place 6 £191.16, Place 5 £37.54.
Owner Jerry Jamgotchian **Bred** Skymarc Farm Inc And Castlemartin Stud **Trained** Upper Lambourn, Berks

FOCUS

The fact that they went no pace was reflected in a time slower than the first division. Straightforward average form for the grade.
Cockney Tai(IRE) Official explanation: jockey said mare pulled up lame
T/Plt: £830.00 to a £1 stake. Pool: £40,650.50. 35.75 winning tickets. T/Qpdt: £83.60 to a £1 stake. Pool: £4,614.30. 40.80 winning tickets. KH

[6318] LINGFIELD (L-H)
Tuesday, November 15

OFFICIAL GOING: Standard
Wind: Light, against Weather: Overcast becoming fine

6349 DAILY OFFERS FROM BETDIRECT MAIDEN STKS (DIV I) 6f (P)
12:20 (12:22) (Class 5) 2-Y-O **£3,873** (£1,152; £575; £287) **Stalls** Low

Form RPR
6 **1** **Nyarhini**[45] 5609 2-8-9 .... SteveDrowne 8 69
(G Wragg) *bit bkwd: trckd ldng pair: effrt over 1f out: urged along and narrow ld ins fnl f: hld on wl* **5/1**[3]
04 **2** *shd* **Radius**[55] 5407 2-9-0 .... KDarley 5 74
(H Morrison) *trckd ldr: led 2f out: idled in front over 1f out: hdd ins fnl f: rallied: jst hld* **16/1**
3 *1 1/4* **Music By Mozart** 2-9-0 .... JimmyFortune 9 70
(P W Chapple-Hyam) *w'like: trckd ldrs: cl up over 1f out: hanging bdly lft after: r.o nr fin* **8/1**
4 *hd* **Clafoutis (USA)** 2-8-9 .... KFallon 7 64
(Sir Michael Stoute) *w'like: scope: s.s: wl in rr tl prog 2f out: clsd on ldrs ins fnl f: one pce nr fin* **9/2**[2]
0222 **5** *1* **Danawi (IRE)**[10] 6251 2-9-0 76 .... RichardHughes 1 66
(R Hannon) *lw: trckd ldng pair: effrt to chal jst over 1f out: sn rdn and fnd nil* **10/11**[1]
6 *1/2* **Red Cape (FR)** 2-9-0 .... DarryllHolland 12 65+
(N A Callaghan) *unf: scope: lengthy: bit bkwd: racd wd in last trio: pushed along and prog wl over 1f out: styd on fnl f: bttr for r* **33/1**
0 **7** *hd* **Gibbs Camp**[70] 5031 2-8-9 .... NickyMackay 2 59+
(E A L Dunlop) *stdd s: hld up towards rr: pushed along and effrt on inner 2f out: one pce over 1f out* **50/1**
0 **8** *nk* **Imperial Soldier**[15] 6199 2-9-0 .... EddieAhern 10 63
(M J Wallace) *unf: chsd ldrs on outer: rdn and rn wd bnd 2f out: kpt on same pce after* **66/1**
0 **9** *5* **Satin Doll**[19] 6120 2-8-9 .... RHills 3 43
(M P Tregoning) *led to 2f out: n.m.r on inner 1f out: wknd rapidly* **25/1**
10 *nk* **Simpsons Ross (IRE)** 2-8-11 .... RichardThomas(3) 6 47
(R M Flower) *leggy: in tch towards rr: stl at rr of main gp whn squeezed out 1f out : wknd* **100/1**
11 *2 1/2* **Mucho Loco (IRE)** 2-8-11 .... NelsonDeSouza(3) 4 40
(J G Portman) *w'like: bit bkwd: s.s: rn v green in last: a bhd* **66/1**
0 **12** *7* **Steve Austin**[62] 5231 2-9-0 .... GrahamGibbons 11 19
(S C Williams) *w'like: s.s: sn rdn in last pair: a wl bhd* **100/1**

1m 12.25s (-0.56) **Going Correction** -0.125s/f (Stan) **12** Ran SP% **117.9**
Speed ratings (Par 96):98,97,96,95,94 93,93,93,86,86 82,73
CSF £75.92 TOTE £7.00: £1.60, £3.70, £2.00; EX 90.10.
Owner Mrs Hugo Morris **Bred** Hascombe And Valiant Studs **Trained** Newmarket, Suffolk

FOCUS
A fair maiden, run at a sound pace, but the overall form should be treated with a degree of caution. It was the sort of winning time you would expect for a race like this despite being more than a second quicker than the second division.

NOTEBOOK
Nyarhini, despite drifting in the betting, was handy throughout and confirmed the promise of her debut fifth at Newmarket, doing just enough to lose her maiden tag at the second attempt. As a half-sister to top-class miler Rebecca Sharp, she can be expected to improve to a higher level, and with her sire's influence she ought to get further next year. (op 3-1)
Radius ◆, without the visor for this first start since leaving David Loder, only failed narrowly and turned in by far his best display to date. Having shown temperament on both his previous outings this year, it was little surprise that he was subsequently gelded, and the decision looks to have paid dividends. He is well suited by this trip and is clearly capable of going one better on this surface if kept going through the winter.
Music By Mozart, related to plenty of winners from five to 12 furlongs, hung left when asked to win his race entering the final furlong and was not given too hard a time thereafter. This was a pleasing debut effort, he looked suited by the trip, and should be up to finding a maiden during the winter. (op 12-1)
Clafoutis(USA) ◆, a half-sister to high-class miler Slip Stream out of a mare who was smart over a mile in France, proved easy in the betting and looked in need of the experience. She did well to recover from her sluggish start and, with this outing under her belt, will surely get closer next time. (op 4-1 tchd 5-1, 11-2 in places)
Danawi(IRE), a well-backed runner-up on his three previous outings, was again strongly supported ahead of this All-Weather debut. However, having been in with every chance against the rail approaching the final furlong, he found nothing when push came to shove, and ultimately proved disappointing. He may have found this one race too many this term. (op 11-10 tchd 6-5 in places)
Red Cape(FR), a half-brother to six winners from five to 12 furlongs out of a mare who was a dual winner in France, was given time to find his stride and, having raced wide throughout, ultimately finished his race in eye-catching fashion. He should improve a deal for this debut experience and has a future.
Gibbs Camp, who ran distinctly green on her Newbury debut 70 days previously, may have been better served by a more positive ride over this shorter trip and can be rated better than the bare form. She would have finished closer with a clearer passage in the straight and, given that her dam was a four-time winner over 12 furlongs at three, better can be expected of her when she is handicapped and faced with a stiffer test next season.

6350 BETDIRECT FREEPHONE 0800 211 222 H'CAP (DIV I) 7f (P)
12:50 (12:53) (Class 4) (0-85,85) 3-Y-O+ **£5,524** (£1,643; £821; £410) **Stalls** Low

Form RPR
0203 **1** **Goodenough Mover**[16] 6182 9-9-4 85 .... KFallon 10 94
(Andrew Turnell) *lw: pressed ldr: led wl over 2f out: drvn fnl f: hld on wl* **3/1**[1]
6601 **2** *hd* **Wyatt Earp (IRE)**[14] 6216 4-9-0 81 .... DarryllHolland 3 89
(R A Fahey) *trckd ldrs: effrt 2f out: chsd wnr jst over 1f out: swtchd ins to chal fnl f: styd on: jst hld* **9/2**[2]
0103 **3** *1 1/4* **Pinchbeck**[74] 4915 6-8-10 77 ....(p) PhilipRobinson 13 82
(M A Jarvis) *lw: t.k.h: hld up midfield: effrt 2f out: rdn and nt qckn over 1f out: styd on fnl f* **10/1**
0110 **4** *1* **Jayanjay**[16] 6182 6-8-12 82 .... RichardThomas(3) 2 84+
(Miss B Sanders) *hld up towards rr: nt clr run over 2f out: prog wl over 1f out: swtchd ins and styd on fnl f* **12/1**
2040 **5** *hd* **Big Bradford**[22] 6075 4-8-4 71 oh6........(b) StephenCarson 11 73
(W R Muir) *prom: pushed along over 4f out: u.p over 2f out: kpt on* **14/1**
300 **6** *nk* **Cheese 'n Biscuits**[21] 6103 5-8-11 78 ....(p) JimmyFortune 12 79+
(M Wigham) *dwlt: hld up in last pair: stl in last pair whn rn wd bnd 2f out: shkn up and styd on wl fr over 1f out* **8/1**
4310 **7** *1/2* **Why Now**[29] 5941 3-8-9 77 .... GrahamGibbons 4 77
(K A Ryan) *racd v freely: led to wl over 2f out: wknd jst over 1f out* **33/1**
2504 **8** *3* **Clara Bow (IRE)**[45] 5603 3-8-9 77 .... MichaelHills 7 69
(B W Hills) *s.s: hld up in last pair: stl in last pair 2f out: shuffled along and styd on fr over 1f out: n.d* **13/2**[3]
3200 **9** *1 1/2* **Easy Feeling (IRE)**[59] 5313 3-8-0 71 .... StephaneBreux(3) 6 59
(R Hannon) *chsd ldrs: pushed along over 4f out: lost pl over 2f out: no prog after* **66/1**
3460 **10** *nk* **Alta Petens**[16] 6180 3-9-3 85 .... JimmyQuinn 1 72
(Jane Chapple-Hyam) *hld up in rr: n.m.r on inner 5f out and again over 2f out: rdn and no prog* **9/1**
100 **11** *1 1/2* **Raza Cab (IRE)**[97] 4256 3-8-4 75 .... NeilChalmers(3) 9 58
(Karen George) *a towards rr: rdn and no prog over 2f out* **33/1**
0260 **12** *1/2* **She's My Outsider**[24] 6022 3-8-8 76 .... KDarley 14 58
(I A Wood) *racd on outer in midfield: rdn over 2f out: no prog* **20/1**
1020 **13** *12* **Indebted**[34] 5834 3-8-6 74 .... EddieAhern 5 25
(P W D'Arcy) *trckd ldng pair: rdn over 3f out: wknd over 2f out: eased: t.o* **20/1**

1m 23.6s (-2.29) **Going Correction** -0.125s/f (Stan)
WFA 3 from 4yo+ 1lb **13** Ran SP% **118.0**
Speed ratings (Par 105):108,107,106,105,104 104,104,100,98,98 96,96,82
CSF £14.33 CT £124.41 TOTE £3.70: £1.80, £2.10, £3.50; EX 14.00.
Owner D Goodenough Removals & Transport **Bred** G Foster **Trained** Broad Hinton, Wilts

FOCUS
A fair handicap and the form looks sound for the class. The winning time was marginally faster than the second division.
Why Now Official explanation: jockey said filly hung right throughout

6351 DAILY OFFERS FROM BETDIRECT MAIDEN STKS (DIV II) 6f (P)
1:20 (1:23) (Class 5) 2-Y-O **£3,860** (£1,148; £573; £286) **Stalls** Low

Form RPR
1 **Easy Air** 2-9-0 .... KFallon 1 75+
(E A L Dunlop) *w'like: scope: lw: s.s: rapid rcvry over 4f out to trck ldrs over 2f out: green 1f out: shkn up and qcknd last 100yds to ld fnl strides* **5/2**[1]
62 **2** *hd* **Rebellious Spirit**[15] 6199 2-9-0 .... KDarley 8 71
(J G Given) *leggy: scope: led: kicked on 2f out: drvn fnl f: hdd fnl strides* **4/1**[2]
0 **3** *3/4* **Pleasing**[10] 6251 2-8-9 .... EddieAhern 4 64
(J L Dunlop) *w'like: prom: chsd ldr wl over 1f out: kpt on same pce fnl f* **8/1**
35 **4** *1 1/2* **Endless Night**[5] 6303 2-9-0 .... DarryllHolland 6 64
(H Morrison) *mostly chsd ldr to wl over 1f out: shkn up and nt qckn sn after: kpt on* **6/1**[3]
5 *hd* **Some Diva** 2-8-9 .... MichaelHills 9 59
(W R Swinburn) *w'like: prom: cl up on outer 2f out: nt qckn over 1f out: kpt on* **25/1**
6 *1/2* **Tawaaf** 2-9-0 .... JimmyFortune 7 62+
(P W Chapple-Hyam) *unf: tall: s.s: t.k.h and green in rr: sme prog 2f out: styd on fnl f: nrst fin* **16/1**
7 *1 3/4* **Usk Poppy** 2-8-9 .... FrankieMcDonald 5 52
(D R C Elsworth) *leggy: unf: s.s: wl bhd in last pair: kpt on fr over 1f out: nvr nrr* **14/1**
0 **8** *hd* **Freeze The Flame (GER)**[15] 6200 2-9-0 .... SteveDrowne 2 56
(C R Egerton) *in tch in midfield: outpcd 2f out: shkn up and one pce over 1f out* **25/1**
60 **9** *1 3/4* **Old Time Dancing**[19] 6120 2-8-9 .... DaneO'Neill 10 46
(M J Wallace) *leggy: chsd ldrs: nt on terms over 2f out: fdd* **50/1**
5 **10** *1 1/2* **Girandola**[29] 5945 2-9-0 .... StephenCarson 11 47
(R F Johnson Houghton) *leggy: dwlt and swtchd to inner fr wd draw: n.m.r in rr over 2f out: no prog* **4/1**[2]
11 *28* **The Lady Mandarin** 2-8-9 .... JimmyQuinn 3 —
(G Wragg) *leggy: rn v green and sn t.o* **50/1**

1m 13.28s (0.47) **Going Correction** -0.125s/f (Stan) **11** Ran SP% **118.1**
Speed ratings (Par 96):91,90,89,87,87 86,84,84,81,79 42
CSF £11.92 TOTE £3.00: £1.60, £1.50, £2.40; EX 12.10.
Owner Maktoum Al Maktoum **Bred** Gainsborough Stud Management Ltd **Trained** Newmarket, Suffolk

FOCUS
A modest winning time, over a second slower than the first division, but the winner can be rated value for plenty further and looks sure to rate higher in due course.

NOTEBOOK
Easy Air ◆, a half-brother to his owner's Group winners Maybe Forever and Court Masterpiece, produced a remarkable display to score at the first time of asking under a top-class ride from Fallon. He looked all at sea coming out of the stalls and lost many lengths, but recovered quickly when asked to join the pack and, despite still looking green in the straight, quickened smartly when in the clear to mow down his rivals and score cosily. He is clearly a colt of some potential, should improve plenty for this experience and is one to note for next year. (tchd 11-4)
Rebellious Spirit, who just failed to last home over seven at Wolverhampton last time, only just failed to make all over this shorter trip and turned in another solid effort. He now qualifies for handicaps, looks best kept to this distance and can pick up a race during the winter. (op 9-2 tchd 5-1)
Pleasing, well backed, had her chance and improved on her recent debut seventh at Doncaster. She is clearly going the right way and should be placed to score as she becomes more streetwise. (op 10-1)
Endless Night was handy throughout and, while he lacked the pace to stay with the principals, he posted an improvemed effort on his recent debut at this track. The return to this trip was in his favour and he is now eligible for handicaps. (op 13-2)
Some Diva, a half-sister to Middle Park winner Primo Valentino and high-class juvenile spinter Dora Carrington, shaped with certain ability and is entitled to improve a deal for this debut experience.
Tawaaf, a cheap purchase for his yard, ran far too freely after making a sluggish start and did well to finish so close in the circumstances. He ought to be a lot wiser next time.
Freeze The Flame(GER) Official explanation: vet said colt was coughing after the race and finished slightly lame
Girandola failed to improve on her Windsor debut and still looked in need of the experience. Official explanation: jockey said colt hung right (op 7-2)
The Lady Mandarin Official explanation: jockey said filly ran very green

6352 BETDIRECT.CO.UK NURSERY 1m (P)
1:50 (1:52) (Class 4) (0-85,85) 2-Y-O **£4,844** (£1,441; £720; £359) **Stalls** High

Form RPR
431 **1** **Natural Force (IRE)**[37] 5753 2-9-5 83 .... DaneO'Neill 8 90+
(Saeed Bin Suroor) *lw: mde virtually all: kicked on over 2f out: clr over 1f out: unchal after* **9/2**[2]
054 **2** *1* **Salute The General**[22] 6068 2-8-10 74 .... SteveDrowne 7 79
(W R Muir) *lw: t.k.h early: hld up towards rr: rdn 3f out: prog 2f out: styd on to take 2nd wl ins fnl f: nt rch wnr* **12/1**

001 **3** ½ **Fregate Island (IRE)**[15] [6200] 2-8-10 **74**................................ KFallon 10 78
(W J Haggas) *trckd ldrs: effrt over 2f out: drvn on outer over 1f out: styd on fnl f: nvr able to chal* **4/1**[1]

010 **4** 2 **Montreux (UAE)**[31] [5904] 2-9-3 **81**................................ JimmyFortune 9 80
(J H M Gosden) *prom: chsd wnr over 2f out: no imp: wknd ins fnl f* **8/1**

0641 **5** hd **Scarlet Knight**[22] [6071] 2-9-7 **85**................................ EddieAhern 11 84
(P Mitchell) *lw: racd wd in tch: rdn over 2f out and v wd bnd sn after: kpt on fnl f: no real danger* **13/2**

1110 **6** 1¼ **Quince (IRE)**[33] [5852] 2-9-4 **82**................................(p) JimmyQuinn 2 78
(J Pearce) *hld up in rr: drvn 2f out: styd on same pce fr over 1f out* **5/1**[3]

2203 **7** ¾ **King's Revenge**[14] [6213] 2-9-1 **79**................................ GrahamGibbons 4 73
(T D Easterby) *settled midfield: rdn over 3f out: outpcd over 2f out: one pce after* **8/1**

044 **8** nk **Grand Jour (IRE)**[13] [6225] 2-8-11 **75**................................(t) DarryllHolland 12 69
(K McAuliffe) *hld up in last: rdn 3f out: kpt on but nvr a factor* **25/1**

4016 **9** ¾ **Sands Of Barra (IRE)**[11] [6244] 2-8-6 **73**................................ RichardThomas(3) 5 65
(N A Callaghan) *dwlt: t.k.h and sn chsd ldrs: rdn 3f out: wknd over 1f out* **9/1**

1530 **10** ¾ **Norman Beckett**[109] [3898] 2-8-2 **73** ow3................................ ThomasO'Brien(7) 3 64
(M R Channon) *hld up: detached in last pair over 2f out: no ch* **25/1**

3306 **11** 5 **Manouche**[46] [5582] 2-8-6 **70**................................ PatCosgrave 1 50
(K A Ryan) *w wnr to over 2f out: wknd rapidly* **25/1**

1m 37.73s (-1.70) **Going Correction** -0.125s/f (Stan) 11 Ran SP% **119.6**
Speed ratings (Par 98):103,102,101,99,99 98,97,97,96,95 90
CSF £56.96 CT £230.11 TOTE £4.30: £1.50, £3.20, £1.90; EX 58.00.
Owner Godolphin **Bred** Derek Veitch **Trained** Newmarket, Suffolk

FOCUS
A fair winning time for a race of its type and the form looks solid for the grade, so the race should produce winners.

NOTEBOOK
Natural Force(IRE), off the mark at the third attempt when upped to this trip at Bath last time, was given a positive ride by O'Neill and followed up with a decisive success on this All-Weather bow. He clearly has more stamina than his smart half-brother Moss Vale, and further improvement next season looks likely. (op 5-1 tchd 11-2 in a place)
Salute The General, making his handicap debut, did well to bag second considering he was too free early on. He has begun handicap life on a fair mark, but must learn to settle if he is to take advantage.
Fregate Island(IRE), making his handicap bow having won at Wolverhampton last time, lacked the pace required to trouble the winner yet was not disgraced from his wide draw. He got the extra furlong well. (op 10-3 tchd 9-2 in a place)
Montreux(UAE), outclassed in the Rockfel last time, suprisingly failed to see out the trip on this return to the All-Weather. She still ran well enough, however, and has found her level now. (op 10-1)
Scarlet Knight looked a player turning for home, but failed to sustain his effort and was ultimately well held. He was at a disadvantage in racing wide throughout over this extra furlong, however, and is not one to write off yet. (op 5-1)
Quince(IRE), making his All-Weather debut, did not find that much when produced from off the pace and looks held by the Handicapper at present. (op 15-2)

6353 BETDIRECT ON AT THE RACES INTERACTIVE CLAIMING STKS 7f (P)
2:20 (2:21) (Class 5) 2-Y-0 **£3,575** (£1,063; £531; £265) **Stalls** Low

Form RPR

0405 **1** **Casablanca Minx (IRE)**[64] [5171] 2-7-13 56 ow1 EdwardCreighton(3) 12 60
(Mrs H Sweeting) *hld up: prog on outer fr 1/2-way: chsd ldng pair 2f out: rdn to ld ins fnl f: styd on* **33/1**

0040 **2** 1 **Fangorn Forest (IRE)**[10] [6249] 2-8-6 84................................(p) JimmyQuinn 8 62+
(K A Ryan) *s.i.s: hld up in last pair: stl in last pair over 2f out: v wd bnd after: storming run fnl f: hopeless task* **5/2**[1]

0013 **3** ½ **Colmar Supreme**[4] [6316] 2-8-3 73................................ StephaneBreux(3) 1 60
(R Hannon) *hld up towards rr: prog on inner 2f out: swtchd rt jst ins fnl f: styd on: unable to chal* **4/1**[2]

6110 **4** shd **Outlook**[31] [5887] 2-9-7 79................................(b) GrahamGibbons 11 75
(N P Littmoden) *hld up: prog on outer fr 3f out: chsd ldrs 2f out: rdn and nt qckn over 1f out: kpt on* **5/2**[1]

0235 **5** nk **Neardown Beauty (IRE)**[22] [6072] 2-8-11 64................................(t) KDarley 13 64
(I A Wood) *hld up in rr: prog on wd outside over 2f out: drvn and nt qckn over 1f out: styd on u.p* **11/1**

6500 **6** 2½ **Teddy Monty (IRE)**[6] [6295] 2-7-13 60................................ RoryMoore(5) 5 51
(M Quinn) *mde most tl hdd & wknd ins fnl f* **66/1**

0500 **7** ½ **Psycho Cat**[17] [6136] 2-8-1 65................................ AurelioMedeiros(5) 9 52
(M R Channon) *pressed ldr: upsides over 1f out: wknd ent fnl f* **25/1**

6002 **8** nk **Zizou (IRE)**[29] [5947] 2-9-0 64................................ DaneO'Neill 3 59
(P R Hedger) *trckd ldrs: effrt on inner and cl up over 1f out: wknd* **6/1**[3]

00 **9** nk **Murrumbidgee (IRE)**[8] [6284] 2-9-2................................ EddieAhern 4 60+
(J W Hills) *hld up in last trio: nt clr run over 2f out: nudged along and kpt on steadily fr over 1f out: do bttr* **25/1**

10 ¾ **Dolce Maria (IRE)**[58] [5350] 2-8-1................................ FrankieMcDonald 6 43
(Michael Cunningham, Ire) *t.k.h: hld up in midfield: cl up over 1f out: hld whn hmpd jst ins fnl f: wknd* **33/1**

5520 **11** ½ **Angie And Liz (IRE)**[70] [5030] 2-8-1 53 ow5................................ RichardThomas(3) 10 45
(P D Evans) *chsd ldrs: pushed along and n.m.r over 2f out: wknd* **50/1**

050 **12** ½ **Prince Algarhoud**[76] [4861] 2-7-13 35................................(b[1]) RobynBrisland(5) 2 44
(G L Moore) *t.k.h: hld up in rr: pushed along and no prog fnl 2f* **100/1**

1m 25.8s (-0.09) **Going Correction** -0.125s/f (Stan) 12 Ran SP% **117.8**
Speed ratings (Par 96):95,93,93,93,92 89,89,89,88,87 87,86
CSF £110.89 TOTE £39.90: £5.50, £1.50, £1.70; EX 247.20.
Owner P Sweeting **Bred** Airlie Stud And Widden Stud **Trained** Lockeridge, Wilts

FOCUS
A moderate claimer run at a steady early pace.

NOTEBOOK
Casablanca Minx(IRE) had quite a bit to do at the weights and her rider put up 1lb overweight as well, but she runs well at this level and appreciated the step up to seven furlongs. She was recording her third success of the year and her first on the All-Weather, and looks to have put up a personal best. (tchd 40-1)
Fangorn Forest(IRE) had plenty in hand on adjusted figures, but she was not particularly strong in the market and ran a strange race on this drop in grade. She missed the break, never seemed to be travelling at the back of the field and, swinging wide into the straight, took a good while to get into top gear. She stayed on strongly once in line for home, but it was all too late, and she might be happier on a more galloping track. Official explanation: jockey said filly moved badly throughout (op 2-1 tchd 11-4)
Colmar Supreme, who ran well in a nursery at Wolverhampton four days earlier and was second-best in at the weights on adjusted figures, did not get the clearest of runs next to the inside rail in the straight. A stronger all-round pace would have probably suited her better.
Outlook, successful three times on the sand at Wolverhampton and on the turf at this venue, was expected to appreciate the drop back into claiming company, but he took a while to pick up and was another to give the impression that he would have been better suited by a stronger pace. (op 3-1)
Neardown Beauty(IRE), down in grade having failed to get off the mark in five starts in maiden company, challenged widest of all rounding the turn into the straight and did not look the most willing under pressure. (op 12-1 tchd 10-1)
Teddy Monty(IRE), well held in a seller at Wolverhampton last time, made the running in this stronger heat but could not hold off the pack inside the final furlong.
Murrumbidgee(IRE), having his third run for a mark, was shuffled along from some way out and ran as though he can do better than this bare form suggests once he makes the move into handicap company. Official explanation: jockey said colt suffered interference in running (op 33-1)

6354 BETDIRECT FREEPHONE 0800 211 222 H'CAP (DIV II) 7f (P)
2:50 (2:52) (Class 4) (0-85,84) 3-Y-0+ **£5,508** (£1,638; £819; £409) **Stalls** Low

Form RPR

1233 **1** **Perfect Story (IRE)**[18] [6132] 3-8-8 **75**................................ OscarUrbina 1 83
(J A R Toller) *hld up in tch: effrt 2f out: hit over hd by rival's whip 1f out: squeezed through to ld last 150yds: hld on wl* **6/1**[3]

0045 **2** hd **Binanti**[49] [5526] 5-9-1 **81**................................(v) GeorgeBaker 11 88
(P R Chamings) *hld up towards rr: prog on outer wl over 1f out: rdn to press wnr ins fnl f: clsd but jst hld: nt keen* **4/1**[2]

4600 **3** 1¼ **Screwdriver**[45] [5603] 3-8-10 **77**................................ RichardHughes 6 81
(R Hannon) *hld up towards rr: effrt 2f out: swtchd lft jst over 1f out: styd on: nt pce to chal nr fin* **16/1**

0000 **4** hd **Takes Tutu (USA)**[104] [4043] 6-8-8 **74**................................ PatCosgrave 10 77+
(K R Burke) *hld up in rr and racd wd: effrt over 1f out: nt clr run and swtchd rt 1f out: r.o: nrst fin* **12/1**

5065 **5** shd **Loupho1e**[34] [5835] 3-8-6 **76**................................ EdwardCreighton(3) 3 79
(P J Makin) *lw: dwlt: t.k.h: hld up in last pair: effrt over 1f out: rdn and styd on fnl f: nt pce to chal* **20/1**

0004 **6** 1 **Queens Rhapsody**[17] [6140] 5-8-11 **77**................................ SamHitchcott 7 77
(A Bailey) *prom: rdn 3f out: chal 2f out: one pce ins fnl f* **12/1**

0045 **7** hd **Idle Power (IRE)**[16] [6180] 7-9-1 **84**................................(p) AmirQuinn(3) 5 84
(J R Boyle) *lw: t.k.h: trckd ldr: led over 2f out: hdd & wknd last 150yds* **7/2**[1]

2100 **8** 1¼ **Hurricane Coast**[10] [6248] 6-8-10 **76**................................(b) DarryllHolland 4 73
(K McAuliffe) *trckd ldrs: effrt to chal on outer 2f out: hld whn n.m.r 1f out: hanging and wknd* **12/1**

1130 **9** 7 **Neon Blue**[51] [5488] 4-8-6 **72**................................ NickyMackay 2 50
(R M Whitaker) *lw: s.i.s: pushed along in last pair: nvr a factor* **14/1**

0020 **10** 2 **Material Witness (IRE)**[52] [5460] 8-9-1 **81**................................(v) KFallon 13 54
(W R Muir) *lw: led at decent pce: hdd over 2f out: btn whn snatched up jst over 1f out: eased* **6/1**[3]

-000 **11** 1½ **Sahara Prince (IRE)**[37] [5778] 5-9-4 **84**................................(p) KDarley 8 53
(Michael Cunningham, Ire) *chsd ldrs: rdn and wknd 3f out* **16/1**

1m 23.76s (-2.13) **Going Correction** -0.125s/f (Stan)
WFA 3 from 4yo+ 1lb 11 Ran SP% **117.1**
Speed ratings (Par 105):107,106,105,105,105 103,103,102,94,91 90
CSF £30.06 CT £375.60 TOTE £6.10: £2.00, £1.80, £5.50; EX 27.00 Trifecta £405.90 Part won. Pool: £571.72 - 0.20 winning tickets..
Owner John Drew and Dr Bridget Drew **Bred** Airlie Stud **Trained** Newmarket, Suffolk
■ Stewards' Enquiry : Richard Hughes 22-day ban (takes into account previous offences, five days deferred): careless riding (Dec 9-29)

FOCUS
There was a decent pace on in this competitive handicap and, despite the winning time being a little slower than the first division, it was still more than acceptable for the grade.

6355 BETDIRECTCASINO.COM MAIDEN STKS 1m 2f (P)
3:20 (3:24) (Class 5) 3-Y-0+ **£4,167** (£1,240; £619; £309) **Stalls** Low

Form RPR

4 **1** **Mohafazaat (IRE)**[27] [5971] 3-8-9................................(v[1]) RHills 3 65
(M P Tregoning) *w'like: scope: lw: mde all: clr and gng easily over 2f out: rdn over 1f out: jst hld on* **8/11**[1]

5 **2** shd **Kyles Prince (IRE)**[24] [6028] 3-8-11................................ AmirQuinn(3) 1 75+
(P J Makin) *lw: hld up midfield: prog 4f out: 4th whn hmpd over 2f out: chsd wnr over 1f out: clsd fnl f: needed one more stride* **3/1**[2]

00 **3** 3 **Escoffier**[5] [6307] 3-9-0................................ JimmyQuinn 2 64
(Mrs A J Perrett) *lw: prom: drvn over 3f out: chsd wnr over 2f out to jst over 1f out: one pce* **14/1**

6 **4** 5 **Scamperdale**[43] [5664] 3-9-0................................ DarryllHolland 11 55
(Karen George) *chsd wnr 8f out to over 2f out: wknd over 1f out* **20/1**

0 **5** ¾ **Blaenavon**[37] [5756] 3-8-9................................ KDarley 8 48
(D W P Arbuthnot) *unf: dwlt: wl in rr: sme prog on outer fr 3f out: hanging but kpt on fr over 1f out: nrst fin* **50/1**

00 **6** 4 **Almisq (USA)**[43] [5666] 4-8-13................................(p) OscarUrbina 6 41
(J Ryan) *w'like: t.k.h: hld up bhd ldrs: rdn over 3f out: sn struggling* **40/1**

00 **7** shd **War Feather**[24] [6028] 3-8-11................................ EdwardCreighton(3) 14 45
(T D McCarthy) *b: in tch: prog to dispute 2nd 1/2-way: wknd 3f out* **66/1**

8 2½ **Ashwell Rose** 3-8-9................................ SteveDrowne 9 36
(R T Phillips) *str: bit bwkd: hld up and sn in midfield: struggling u.p over 3f out* **12/1**[3]

9 1½ **Monteleone (IRE)** 3-8-9................................ DaneO'Neill 13 33
(R Hannon) *w'like: bit bkwd: dwlt: a towards rr: n.d fnl 3f* **20/1**

00 **10** 1 **Panadin (IRE)**[29] [5950] 3-9-0................................ JimmyFortune 10 36
(V Smith) *cmpt: chsd wnr for 2f: pushed along and lost pl 6f out: sn btn* **20/1**

00 **11** 2½ **Miss Shontaine**[6] [6301] 3-8-9................................ SamHitchcott 5 26
(B G Powell) *w'like: settled wl in rr: nvr a factor: sme prog on inner over 2f out: wknd wl over 1f out* **100/1**

0 **12** 2 **Life Is Rosie (IRE)**[239] [671] 3-8-2................................ LauraReynolds(7) 4 22
(D K Ivory) *hld up in rr: struggling fr 4f out* **100/1**

2m 6.57s (-1.22) **Going Correction** -0.125s/f (Stan)
WFA 3 from 4yo 4lb 12 Ran SP% **119.4**
Speed ratings (Par 103):99,98,96,92,91 88,88,86,85,84 82,81
CSF £2.55 TOTE £1.80: £1.10, £1.40, £2.90; EX 3.60.
Owner Hamdan Al Maktoum **Bred** Shadwell Estate Company Limited **Trained** Lambourn, Berks

FOCUS
Pretty weak maiden form and the runner-up has been rated a clear winner.

6356 BETDIRECT NO Q ON 08000 93 66 93 AMATEUR RIDERS' H'CAP 1m 4f (P)
3:50 (3:51) (Class 5) (0-70,70) 3-Y-0+ **£3,397** (£1,053; £526; £263) **Stalls** Low

Form RPR

060 **1** **Prime Powered (IRE)**[29] [5598] 4-10-9 **63**................................ MrDHutchison(5) 10 74
(G L Moore) *wl plcd: prog over 2f out: pushed into ld over 1f out: kpt on wl* **25/1**

0600 **2** ½ **Countrywide Luck**[24] [6029] 4-11-4 **67**................................ MrsEmmaLittmoden 3 77+
(N P Littmoden) *wl in rr: prog over 2f out: nt clr run over 2f out: hdwy over 1f out: chsd wnr ins fnl f: kpt on but hld* **11/2**[2]

0032 **3** *2* **Zalkani (IRE)**[5] 6302 5-11-0 **70** .... MrRElliott(7) 6 77
(B G Powell) *t.k.h: hld up in rr: prog fr over 2f out: bmpd along and styd on fr over 1f out* **7/1**[3]
5051 **4** *shd* **Typhoon Tilly**[64] 5185 8-11-0 **66** .... MissRDavidson(3) 1 73
(C R Egerton) *trckd ldng pair: led briefly wl over 1f out: one pce fnl f* **7/1**[3]
0344 **5** *1 ½* **Resonate (IRE)**[62] 5233 7-11-4 **67** .... MissCHannaford 8 71+
(A G Newcombe) *lw: hld up in rr: trapped on inner fr 3f out: got out over 1f out: r.o wl fnl f: no ch* **3/1**[1]
0260 **6** *1 ¾* **El Chaparral (IRE)**[19] 6127 5-11-2 **70** .... CJCallow(5) 16 71
(W J Haggas) *s.s: t.k.h and sn prom: cl up 2f out: fdd* **12/1**
2100 **7** *shd* **Willhego**[5] 6308 4-10-13 **67** .... KylieManser(5) 9 68+
(J R Best) *hld up in last pair: stl same pce 2f out: urged along frantically and r.o fr over 1f out: hopeless task* **20/1**
3343 **8** *¾* **Bid For Fame (USA)**[8] 6280 8-10-9 **65** .... MrSPearce(7) 4 65
(J Pearce) *lw: nvr beyond midfield: in tch over 2f out: sn outpcd* **10/1**
1061 **9** *nk* **Platinum Charmer (IRE)**[12] 6236 5-10-11 **65** ....(p) MissKellyBurke(5) 12 65
(K R Burke) *pressed ldr to 2f out: wknd over 1f out* **12/1**
6630 **10** *¾* **Kirin**[27] 5981 3-10-10 **70** .... MrNPearce(5) 13 68
(D E Cantillon) *dwlt: hld up in last trio: pushed along and kpt on fnl 2f: no ch* **25/1**
0266 **11** *1 ½* **Stolen Song**[8] 6280 5-10-3 **59** ....(e) MrJBurdon(7) 2 55
(J Ryan) *hld up midfield: effrt on inner over 2f out: no prog over 1f out: wknd* **40/1**
1530 **12** *shd* **Slavonic (USA)**[24] 6029 4-10-7 **63** ....(p) MissARyan(7) 15 59
(K A Ryan) *racd v wd: in tch tl rn wdst of all bnd 2f out: wknd* **16/1**
5400 **13** *½* **Isle De Maurice**[37] 5760 3-11-1 **70** .... MrSDobson 14 65
(D B Feek) *a wl in rr: rdn and struggling 3f out* **33/1**
0060 **14** *nk* **Rafelite**[108] 3956 3-10-6 **61** .... MrSWalker 5 56
(Lady Herries) *led to wl over 1f out: wknd* **10/1**
55-0 **15** *5* **Team-Mate (IRE)**[227] 843 7-10-13 **69** .... MrRBirkett(7) 7 56
(Miss J Feilden) *settled in midfield: n.m.r and lost pl over 2f out: wknd* **66/1**
0000 **16** *½* **Tricky Venture**[11] 6247 5-10-6 **62** .... MissKJewell(7) 11 48
(Mrs L C Jewell) *racd wd: in tch to over 2f out: wd bnd sn after and wknd* **40/1**

2m 35.17s (0.78) **Going Correction** -0.125s/f (Stan)
WFA 3 from 4yo+ 6lb **16** Ran SP% **126.6**
Speed ratings (Par 103):92,91,90,90,89 88,88,87,87,86 85,85,85,85,81 81
CSF £155.48 CT £1105.96 TOTE £35.10: £5.20, £1.70, £2.40, £2.20; EX 360.80 Place 6 £71.55, Place 5 £15.26.
Owner Prime Power GB Ltd **Bred** Caribbean Quest Partnership **Trained** Woodingdean, E Sussex

FOCUS
Probably not a bad race for the grade and the form could work out alright.
T/Jkpt: Not won. T/Plt: £75.60 to a £1 stake. Pool: £33,709.65. 325.25 winning tickets. T/Qpdt: £12.50 to a £1 stake. Pool: £4,402.55. 258.70 winning tickets. JN

6326 SOUTHWELL (L-H)
Tuesday, November 15

OFFICIAL GOING: Standard
Wind: Light, half-behind

6357 BETDIRECTPOKER.COM NURSERY (DIV I) 7f (F)
12:10 (12:10) (Class 6) (0-65,65) 2-Y-O **£3,089** (£919; £459; £229) **Stalls** Low

Form RPR
0020 **1** **Rainbows Guest (IRE)**[10] 6249 2-9-5 **63** ....(v[1]) MartinDwyer 11 73+
(A M Balding) *chsd ldrs on outer: gd hdwy 2f out: rdn to ld over 1f out: clr ins last* **9/2**[2]
0604 **2** *5* **Royal Embrace**[13] 6224 2-8-6 **55** .... PatrickMathers(5) 5 53
(D Shaw) *chsd ldrs: rdn 2f out: styd on appr last* **25/1**
0030 **3** *1 ½* **Egyptian Lord**[65] 5145 2-8-12 **56** .... RobbieFitzpatrick 7 52+
(Peter Grayson) *led 2f: cl up: ev ch whn rdn: hung lft and lost action over 1f out: kpt on same pce* **28/1**
040 **4** *hd* **Caribbean Nights (IRE)**[14] 6213 2-9-2 **60** .... DavidAllan 2 53
(T D Easterby) *sn cl up: led after 2f: rdn 2f out: hdd over 1f out: sn drvn and one pce ent last* **10/1**
0456 **5** *nk* **Inchdhuaig (IRE)**[17] 6136 2-8-11 **60** .... GregFairley(5) 1 53
(P C Haslam) *chsd ldrs on inner: effrt 2f out: sn rdn and kpt on same pce appr last* **5/1**[3]
6634 **6** *1 ½* **Mistatake (IRE)**[8] 6281 2-9-7 **65** .... NCallan 4 54
(K A Ryan) *cl up: effrt 2f out: sn rdn and ev ch: wkng whn hmpd appr last* **7/2**[1]
005 **7** *4* **Emotive**[52] 5446 2-8-8 **52** .... LeeEnstone 9 31
(I A Wood) *midfield: rdn along over 2f out: n.d* **33/1**
0560 **8** *¾* **Ridgeway Cross (IRE)**[18] 6128 2-8-10 **59** ow1.... StephenDonohoe(5) 3 36
(Ernst Oertel) *keen: towards rr: sme hdwy on inner 2f out: nvr a factor* **25/1**
5130 **9** *4* **Montini Royale (IRE)**[99] 4227 2-8-7 **58** .... StacyRenwick(7) 6 25
(M J Attwater) *chsd ldrs: rdn along 3f out: sn wknd* **10/1**
0000 **10** *2 ½* **Spasiba**[49] 5536 2-8-10 **54** .... JamieMackay 8 15
(Sir Mark Prescott) *sn chsd along: bhd fr 1/2-way* **16/1**
5405 **11** *1 ½* **Bincrafty**[29] 5947 2-8-5 **56** ....(b) JosephWalsh(7) 13 13
(J S Moore) *a towards rr* **25/1**
0600 **12** *shd* **Wizby**[36] 5791 2-8-10 **54** ....(t) RobertHavlin 12 11
(P D Evans) *a rr* **14/1**
5060 **13** *7* **Imperial Gem (IRE)**[8] 6282 2-9-3 **61** .... ChrisCatlin 14 —
(Rae Guest) *s.i.s: a rr* **25/1**
4252 **14** *1 ¾* **Gymbolini**[102] 4125 2-8-13 **57** .... MickyFenton 10 —
(N P Littmoden) *chsd ldrs: rdn along halfwy: sn wknd* **17/2**

1m 29.6s (-1.20) **Going Correction** -0.275s/f (Stan) **14** Ran SP% **120.1**
Speed ratings (Par 94):95,89,87,87,87 85,80,79,75,72 70,70,62,60
CSF £122.54 CT £2899.14 TOTE £8.00: £1.80, £13.10, £9.70; EX 124.00.
Owner Winterbeck Manor Stud **Bred** Mrs M Purcell **Trained** Kingsclere, Hants

FOCUS
Probably not the strongest of nurseries and few ever got into it. The winning time was marginally slower than the second division.

NOTEBOOK
Rainbows Guest(IRE), who had already shown ability on this surface when finishing second in a course and distance maiden last month, was sporting a first-time visor. She was never far off the pace and, after hitting the front a furlong out, powered right away from her rivals. She is now likely to be put away until next season. (op 4-1 tchd 5-1)
Royal Embrace, making his sand debut, was another always within striking distance and stayed on well to snatch the runner-up spot. He shaped as though an extra furlong would not come amiss on this surface and his trainer is likely to find an opportunity for him here this winter.
Egyptian Lord ran an extraordinary race. Up with the pace from the start, he was still battling away, though the winner seemed to have his measure, when he faltered crossing some ruts in the track just inside the last furlong and his rider eased him off. Despite that he still managed to hold on to third, but was subsequently found to be unsound. Official explanation: jockey said gelding lost its action final furlong; vet said gelding returned unsound (op 25-1)
Caribbean Nights(IRE) helped force the pace from his low stall, but was inclined to run about down the home straight and was unable to see it out. He still has a little bit of scope. (op 9-1 tchd 17-2)
Inchdhuaig(IRE), from a yard with a fine record at this track, was probably not helped by being forced to race on the inside from his rails draw, but showed enough to suggest he is worth another try here. (op 4-1)
Mistatake(IRE) was well backed to make a successful Fibresand debut after showing some promise on Polytrack, but faded out of it late on after showing up for a long way. (op 6-1)

6358 MORE OFFERS AT BETDIRECT.CO.UK CLAIMING STKS 1m (F)
12:40 (12:41) (Class 6) 2-Y-O **£2,852** (£842; £421) **Stalls** Low

Form RPR
0000 **1** **Countrywide Belle**[25] 6004 2-8-10 58 ....(p) NCallan 8 56
(K A Ryan) *chsd ldrs: led 2f out: kpt on wl ins last* **3/1**[2]
0100 **2** *1 ¾* **Captivate**[11] 6244 2-9-0 49 .... PaulDoe 12 56
(M J Polglase) *chsd ldrs on outer: reminders after s: styd on to take 2nd nr fin* **22/1**
4003 **3** *shd* **Pix**[52] 5446 2-8-4 50 .... ChrisCatlin 2 46
(S Kirk) *trckd ldrs: led 3f out: hdd 2f out: kpt on same pce* **11/1**
400 **4** *¾* **Stolen Glance**[99] 4225 2-8-7 50 .... PaulMulrennan(3) 5 50
(M W Easterby) *s.i.s: hdwy over 2f out: styd on same pce fnl f* **25/1**
0602 **5** *½* **Secret Tender (IRE)**[82] 4696 2-8-9 63 .... PhillipMakin 10 48
(J R Weymes) *chsd ldrs: outpcd over 2f out: styd on strly ins last* **6/1**[3]
0020 **6** *hd* **Aboyne (IRE)**[11] 6244 2-9-1 71 .... DavidMcCabe 7 54+
(M G Quinlan) *towards rr: hdwy on ins over 2f out: sn rdn and hung lft: kpt on: nvr a threat* **9/4**[1]
0400 **7** *nk* **Devon Ruby**[28] 5953 2-9-0 50 ....(p) PaulFessey 1 52
(Mrs A Duffield) *sn chsng ldrs: one pce fnl 2f* **40/1**
006 **8** *4* **Yeoman's Girl**[32] 5864 2-8-10 52 .... MartinDwyer 4 39+
(A M Balding) *chsd ldrs: hung lft and wknd over 1f out* **20/1**
0000 **9** *2* **Mullzima (IRE)**[37] 5753 2-8-6 50 ow9........ JBrennan(7) 9 38
(P D Evans) *sn in rr: sme hdwy 2f out: nvr on terms* **20/1**
10 *hd* **Lady Lynch (IRE)**[58] 5350 2-8-8 .... TonyHamilton 14 32
(Michael Cunningham, Ire) *mde most: hdd 3f out: lost pl over 1f out* **7/1**
P0 **11** *11* **Jamie's Princess (IRE)**[52] 5446 2-7-11 ....(t) JamesDoyle(7) 3 4
(I A Wood) *w ldrs: lost pl 3f out* **50/1**
0025 **12** *15* **Oblo (IRE)**[169] 2118 2-8-7 49 ow3........ RobertMiles(3) 13 —
(B Palling) *chsd ldrs on outer: lost pl and sltly hmpd 4f out: sn bhd: t.o* **33/1**
13 *6* **Ardkeel Boy (IRE)** 2-8-6 .... MarcHalford(5) 11 —
(B Palling) *s.v.s: a wl bhd: t.o* **20/1**
P0 **14** *12* **Taggin'Along (IRE)**[169] 2118 2-8-5 .... JamieMackay 6 —
(M D I Usher) *s.i.s: sn drvn along in rr: t.o 2f out* **100/1**

1m 44.64s (0.04) **Going Correction** -0.275s/f (Stan) **14** Ran SP% **121.7**
Speed ratings (Par 94):88,86,86,85,84 84,84,80,78,78 67,52,46,34
CSF £74.30 TOTE £4.00: £1.60, £7.30, £2.60; EX 115.40.Secret Tender was the subject of a friendly claim.
Owner Countrywide Racing **Bred** W G B Hungerford **Trained** Hambleton, N Yorks

FOCUS
This looked a modest claimer and the time was moderate to boot.

NOTEBOOK
Countrywide Belle, who had faced some very stiff tasks since winning over the minimum trip here in the spring, proved far too good for this field and may be able to find something a little better on this surface. (op 11-4 tchd 5-2)
Captivate ◆, making her sand debut, stayed on to snatch the runner-up spot and posted by far her best effort on her third appearance for her new stable, especially as she was badly in at the weights. A modest race can probably be found for her on this surface. (op 25-1 tchd 20-1)
Pix ran her race over this longer trip and probably matched the best of her form on turf and Polytrack. (op 8-1)
Stolen Glance ◆ is one of few to take out of this race. Reappearing from a three-month break, she gave away a lot of ground at the start and did well to finish as close on a track that so favours front-runners. (op 18-1)
Secret Tender(IRE) was another to finish well on this sand debut having been well backed and shapes as though he will get even further. (op 12-1)
Aboyne(IRE) was given a lot to do and had the extra burden of being asked to make his effort tight against the inside rail. On the face of it this was disappointing considering he was best in at the weights, but given the way the race was run he might be worth one more chance. (tchd 11-4)
Lady Lynch(IRE) did far too much too soon. Official explanation: jockey said filly ran too free (tchd 13-2)

6359 BETDIRECTPOKER.COM NURSERY (DIV II) 7f (F)
1:10 (1:11) (Class 6) (0-65,66) 2-Y-O **£3,083** (£917; £458; £228) **Stalls** Low

Form RPR
3000 **1** **George's Flyer (IRE)**[17] 6150 2-8-13 **57** ....(b) TonyHamilton 9 63
(R A Fahey) *prom: wd st: rdn to ld wl over 1f out: kpt on u.p fnl f* **8/1**
000 **2** *¾* **Mighty Dancer (IRE)**[27] 5970 2-8-12 **56** .... MartinDwyer 11 60
(S Kirk) *midfield: wd st: hdwy 2f out: sn rdn and styd on wl u.p ins last* **20/1**
2002 **3** *nk* **Snake Skin**[11] 6244 2-8-11 **55** .... ChrisCatlin 13 58
(J Gallagher) *in tch: wd st: hdwy over 2f out: rdn and ev ch wl over 1f out: drvn and one pce ins last* **10/1**
060 **4** *2* **Baltic Rhapsody**[17] 6156 2-9-3 **61** .... NCallan 6 59
(M A Jarvis) *in tch: hdwy to chse ldrs wl over 1f out: one pce ins last* **13/2**[2]
0601 **5** *1* **Fateful Attraction**[33] 5857 2-9-2 **60** .... LeeEnstone 2 56+
(I A Wood) *in tch on inner: hdwy 2f out: sn rdn and kpt on same pce appr last* **6/1**[1]
500 **6** *1 ½* **Samsouma (IRE)**[70] 5031 2-9-0 **58** .... JoeFanning 8 50
(C E Brittain) *cl up: rdn to ld over 2f out: drvn and hdd over 1f out: wknd* **20/1**
0565 **7** *1 ¼* **Bellini Star**[13] 6227 2-9-2 **60** ....(v) PhillipMakin 3 49
(P D Evans) *towards rr: hdwy 2f out: sn rdn and kpt on appr last: nrst fin* **25/1**
6002 **8** *1* **Taras Tornado**[17] 6136 2-8-8 **52** .... LPKeniry 14 39
(J J Quinn) *in tch on outer: hdwy to chal 2f out: sn rdn and hung lft wl over 1f out: wknd* **8/1**
660 **9** *½* **Final Bid (IRE)**[62] 5231 2-9-7 **65** ....(b[1]) DavidMcCabe 12 50
(M G Quinlan) *s.i.s: bhd and v wd st: n.d* **7/1**[3]
0303 **10** *¾* **Charlien**[33] 5857 2-8-7 **54** .... BenSwarbrick(3) 7 37
(E S McMahon) *a midfield* **14/1**

6001 **11** 2 ½ **Stoneacre Lad (IRE)**^{6} [6297] 2-9-8 **66** 6ex................. RobbieFitzpatrick 5 43+
(Peter Grayson) *led on inner: rdn along and hdd over 2f out: drvn and wknd wl over 1f out* **6/1**^{1}

6510 **12** nk **Buzzin'Boyzee (IRE)**^{80} [4757] 2-8-10 **54**........................ RobertHavlin 10 30
(P D Evans) *prominet: rdn along over 2f out: wknd wl over 1f out* **28/1**

0404 **13** 2 **Nico's Girl**^{32} [5879] 2-8-7 **54**.. PaulMulrennan(3) 1 25
(M W Easterby) *s.i.s on inner: a rr* **50/1**

600 **14** shd **National Dress**^{125} [3441] 2-8-13 **57**................................. JamieMackay 4 28
(Sir Mark Prescott) *s.i.s and sn rdn along: a bhd* **14/1**

1m 29.49s (-1.31) **Going Correction** -0.275s/f (Stan) **14** Ran SP% **117.8**
Speed ratings (Par 94):96,95,94,92,91 89,88,87,86,85 82,82,80,80
CSF £163.59 CT £1617.07 TOTE £10.00: £3.30, £8.40, £3.00; EX 293.80.
Owner P D Smith Holdings Ltd **Bred** H De Bromhead **Trained** Musley Bank, N Yorks

FOCUS
The winning time was marginally quicker than the first division and, as is usually the case here, those that raced down the centre of the track held the advantage over those that kept towards the inside.

NOTEBOOK
George's Flyer(IRE), who had cut little ice in a maiden on his sand debut here last month, had shown some ability on turf and was off a handy mark here if able to translate it, which he did with a cosy victory. Now that he has hit the target, he looks worth persevering with on sand. (op 12-1)
Mighty Dancer(IRE) ◆, making his sand and nursery debuts, left his previous form well behind and was staying on very nicely at the end. With further improvement likely, he should not take long in going one better. (op 25-1)
Snake Skin had run very well on heavy ground on turf last time, which did suggest she might take to this surface, and she duly ran with plenty of credit on her first attempt. (op 12-1 tchd 9-1)
Baltic Rhapsody, another making her nursery debut, was not disgraced and seemed more suited by this surface than the Polytrack she ran on last time. (op 8-1 tchd 17-2)
Fateful Attraction had already shown her liking for this surface when winning a course-and-distance maiden last time, but she was always being forced to race closer to the inside rail than ideal from her low draw and probably performed with credit under the circumstances. (op 8-1)
Stoneacre Lad(IRE) made the majority of the running, but a combination of a 6lb penalty, an extra two furlongs and racing tight against the inside rail ultimately proved all too much. (op 4-1)

6360 TEXT BETDIRECT TO 88600 MEDIAN AUCTION MAIDEN STKS 7f (F)
1:40 (1:42) (Class 5) 2-Y-O **£3,426** (£1,019; £509; £254) **Stalls** Low

Form RPR

0 **1** **Solicitude**^{36} [5801] 2-8-9 .... RobertHavlin 14 69
(D Haydn Jones) *chsd ldrs on outer: effrt over 2f out: led over 1f out: rdn clr ins last: eased towards fin* **66/1**

6 **2** 4 **Al Rayanah**^{40} [5703] 2-8-9 .... ChrisCatlin 10 59
(G Prodromou) *w ldrs: wnt 2nd over 1f out: kpt on: no ch w wnr* **12/1**

00 **3** 2 ½ **Primo Gold**^{17} [6156] 2-9-0 ....(t) JoeFanning 1 58
(W R Swinburn) *w ldrs on inner: led over 4f out tl over 1f out: one pce* **9/1**^{3}

4 shd **Esthlos (FR)** 2-9-0 .... MichaelTebbutt 12 58
(J Jay) *sn in rr on outer and pushed along: hdwy over 2f out: styd on fnl f* **28/1**

02 **5** 2 **Lady Lochinver (IRE)**^{14} [6213] 2-8-9 .... DeanMcKeown 3 48
(M D Hammond) *w ldrs: wknd over 1f out* **11/2**^{2}

6 nk **Ruse** 2-8-9 .... JDSmith 2 47+
(J R Fanshawe) *s.i.s: outpcd and wl bhd: gd hdwy fnl 2f: will improve* **11/1**

7 3 **Mrs Diniver (IRE)** 2-8-9 .... NCallan 8 39
(Liam Roche, Ire) *prom: rdn 3f out: lost pl over 1f out* **14/1**

8 1 ¾ **Skylarking (IRE)** 2-8-9 .... JamieSpencer 5 35
(J R Fanshawe) *hld up: hdwywto trck ldrs over 4f out: swtchd ins over 2f out: wknd over 1f out* **8/11**^{1}

9 3 ½ **Iopes (IRE)** 2-8-6 .... BenSwarbrick(3) 9 26
(Liam Roche, Ire) *chsd ldrs: lost pl 2f out* **66/1**

00 **10** 2 **El Alamein (IRE)**^{11} [6242] 2-9-0 .... JamieMackay 13 26+
(Sir Mark Prescott) *sn outpcd: bhd and drvn along: nvr on terms* **20/1**

11 3 **Dark Night (IRE)** 2-9-0 .... TomEaves 7 19
(D W Barker) *s.s: a bhd: hung lft fnl 2f* **40/1**

0 **12** nk **Boppys Pride**^{22} [6077] 2-9-0 .... TonyHamilton 4 18
(R A Fahey) *chsd ldrs: lost pl over 2f out* **28/1**

00 **13** 1 **Tatsthesticket**^{41} [5695] 2-8-11 .... JasonEdmunds(3) 6 15
(J Balding) *t.k.h: led tl over 4f out: lost pl 2f out* **100/1**

1m 29.64s (-1.16) **Going Correction** -0.275s/f (Stan) 13 Ran SP% **124.1**
Speed ratings (Par 96):95,90,87,87,85 84,81,79,75,73 69,69,68
CSF £725.15 TOTE £150.30: £15.00, £2.80, £1.60; EX 460.30.
Owner The Preseli Partnership **Bred** Mrs M L Parry **Trained** Efail Isaf, Rhondda C Taff

FOCUS
This did not look a great maiden and the winning time was fractionally slower than both divisions of the nursery.

NOTEBOOK
Solicitude, who had apparently benefited from a racecourse gallop at Wolverhampton, left the form of her Windsor racecourse debut well behind on this Fibresand debut and should give connections plenty of fun if persevered with on this surface.
Al Rayanah stepped up from her debut effort here last month, despite being well beaten by the winner, and the extra two furlongs was probably the key. She needs one more run for a handicap mark and that is probably where her future lies. (op 16-1)
Primo Gold ◆ was given a positive ride on this third outing and posted his best effort yet. He can now be handicapped and is one to watch out for in that sphere. (op 15-2 tchd 13-2)
Esthlos(FR) ◆, from a yard not noted for producing first-time-out winners, ran a most encouraging racecourse debut, and with improvement likely he should be able to find a similar contest in the near future. (op 25-1 tchd 33-1)
Lady Lochinver(IRE) was well backed for this sand debut and ran with credit without improving on her recent Catterick second. (op 8-1)
Ruse ◆ demonstrated some ability after taking a while to realise what was required and should improve a good deal for the experience. (op 12-1)
Skylarking(IRE) was very disappointing. After appearing to be travelling well enough on the heels of the leaders turning in, she was then rather surprisingly switched to the deeper ground on the inside and was soon floundering. She is obviously thought capable of much better than this and should be given another chance. (tchd Evens, 4-6 in places)

6361 PRESS RED TO BET ITVI (S) STKS 1m (F)
2:10 (2:11) (Class 6) 3-Y-O+ **£2,559** (£755; £378) **Stalls** Low

Form RPR

0500 **1** **Spitfire Bob (USA)**^{73} [4956] 6-8-9 50...........................(p) GregFairley(5) 8 55
(M E Sowersby) *midfield: hdwy over 2f out: rdn over 1f out: led ins last: kpt on wl* **28/1**

5500 **2** nk **Pending (IRE)**^{26} [5997] 4-9-6 53...................................... TonyHamilton 5 61
(R A Fahey) *dwlt: hld up in rr: hdwy on inner 2f out: rdn to chal ent last: and ev ch tl no ex nr fin* **6/1**^{3}

6000 **3** 1 ½ **Nevsky Bridge**^{36} [5794] 3-8-7 48... LPKeniry 4 47
(J J Quinn) *midfield: hdwy 3f out: rdn to chse ldrs over 1f out: drvn and kpt on ins last* **28/1**

3000 **4** nk **Sister Eugenie (IRE)**^{50} [5506] 3-8-7 47.............................. JoeFanning 9 46
(S Kirk) *midfield: hdwy over 2f out: swtchd wd and rdn over 1f out: styd on ins last: nrst fin* **16/1**

0510 **5** 1 ¼ **Castanza**^{27} [5991] 3-8-13 66.. MickyFenton 11 50
(H Morrison) *cl up: effrt 2f out: rdn wl over 1f out and ev ch tl drvn and one pce ent last* **7/2**^{1}

1200 **6** shd **Aswan (IRE)**^{167} [2184] 7-9-6 64...(t) PhillipMakin 3 54
(S R Bowring) *led 1f: cl up tl led again over 4f out: rdn 2f out: drvn and hdd ins last: wknd* **10/1**

0500 **7** 1 **Musical Gift**^{127} [3405] 5-9-0 51...(p) ChrisCatlin 14 46
(P A Blockley) *in tch on outer: hdwy wl over 2f out: sn ridde: drvn over 1f out: grad wknd* **4/1**^{2}

8 shd **Greenbelt**^{496} 4-9-0 86.. DarrenWilliams 6 46
(D W Chapman) *trckd ldrs: hdwy to chal 2f out and ev ch tl rdn: edgd lft and wknd ent last* **14/1**

2050 **9** 2 **Colonel Bilko (IRE)**^{8} [6287] 3-8-12 58.................................. NCallan 13 42
(Miss S J Wilton) *trckd ldrs: hdwy and wd st: rdn wl over 1f out and grad wknd* **13/2**

2520 **10** 1 **Priorina (IRE)**^{35} [5819] 3-8-7 52.......................................(p) MartinDwyer 7 35
(D Haydn Jones) *a rr* **17/2**

0602 **11** hd **Terraquin (IRE)**^{26} [5996] 5-9-0 48...(v) AlanDaly 2 40
(J J Bridger) *a rr* **20/1**

0000 **12** 9 **Pawn In Life (IRE)**^{3} [6327] 7-9-6 47.......................................(v) PaulDoe 1 28
(M J Polglase) *led after 1f: pushed along and hdd over 4f out: rdn and wknd 3f out* **28/1**

0000 **13** 2 **Zinging**^{31} [5898] 6-9-6 40..(b) LisaJones 12 24
(J J Bridger) *chsd ldrs on outer: rdn along 3f out: sn wknd* **40/1**

1m 44.18s (-0.42) **Going Correction** -0.275s/f (Stan)
WFA 3 from 4yo+ 2lb **13** Ran SP% **119.6**
Speed ratings (Par 101):91,90,89,88,87 87,86,86,84,83 83,74,72
CSF £180.29 TOTE £42.00: £11.90, £2.10, £6.70; EX 355.80.There was no bid for the winner. Castanza was claimed by Mark Wellings for £6,000.
Owner A E & K E Searby **Bred** Jim & Pam Robinson **Trained** Goodmanham, E Yorks

FOCUS
A poor seller, run in a moderate time even for this grade, that is unlikely to linger long in the memory and there were nine horses in a line across the track passing the furlong pole.
Terraquin(IRE) Official explanation: jockey said gelding hung right straight

6362 BETDIRECT.CO.UK H'CAP 1m (F)
2:40 (2:41) (Class 5) (0-70,70) 3-Y-O+ **£3,996** (£1,188; £594; £296) **Stalls** Low

Form RPR

5000 **1** **Elrafa Mujahid**^{22} [6075] 3-8-13 **67**... NCallan 12 76
(Ernst Oertel) *w ldrs: led 3f out: edgd rt fnl f: styd on wl* **25/1**

1000 **2** 2 **Nimello (USA)**^{15} [6201] 9-9-3 **69**... LPKeniry 2 73
(A G Newcombe) *sn bhd: hdwy 2f out: styd on to go 2nd ins last: no imp* **14/1**

2300 **3** ¾ **Bessemer (JPN)**^{60} [5266] 4-8-11 **66**....................................(p) DNolan(3) 6 68
(D Carroll) *trckd ldrs: wnt 2nd over 2f out: nt qckn fnl f* **20/1**

0065 **4** 2 **Sorbiesharry (IRE)**^{3} [6337] 6-8-12 **69**...................(p) DuranFentiman(5) 9 67
(Mrs N Macauley) *mid-div: sn drvn along: styd on wl fnl f* **13/2**

2040 **5** ½ **Samuel Charles**^{22} [6075] 7-9-0 **66**...................................... RobertHavlin 1 63
(C R Dore) *chsd ldrs: one pce fnl 2f* **14/1**

4450 **6** 1 **Lord Links (IRE)**^{38} [5730] 4-9-4 **70**.............................. JamieSpencer 5 65
(D J Daly) *sn led: hdd 3f out: styd ins: wknd ins fnl f* **10/3**^{1}

1000 **7** nk **Warden Warren**^{4} [6315] 7-8-13 **70**..............................(p) MarcHalford(5) 8 64
(Mrs C A Dunnett) *best away: led early: chsd ldrs: drvn along over 3f out: one pce fnl 2f* **20/1**

-106 **8** 6 **Sol Rojo**^{145} [2845] 3-8-13 **67**....................................... RobbieFitzpatrick 10 49
(M J Attwater) *sn mid-div: drvn 3f out: sn btn* **28/1**

1150 **9** ¾ **Llamadas**^{17} [6161] 3-8-11 **70**.................................... PatrickMathers(5) 11 51
(Andrew Reid) *chsd ldrs on outer: sn drvn along: lost pl over 2f out* **6/1**^{3}

0400 **10** hd **Blue Java**^{22} [6075] 4-8-13 **65**...(v^{1}) MickyFenton 3 46
(H Morrison) *mid-div on inner: swtchd to wd outside over 2f out: nvr on terms* **4/1**^{2}

0504 **11** 1 ¾ **Dudley Docker (IRE)**^{22} [6075] 3-8-6 **67**............... MarkCoumbe(7) 14 44
(D Carroll) *s.v.s: a bhd* **14/1**

2500 **12** 11 **Entailment**^{18} [6134] 3-9-0 **68**... MartinDwyer 7 23
(Miss Gay Kelleway) *sn in rr and pushed along: bhd whn eased over 1f out* **14/1**

3000 **13** 11 **Set Alight**^{17} [6161] 4-9-1 **67**...(p) PhillipMakin 4 —
(Mrs C A Dunnett) *sn in rr and drvn along: eased whn t.o 2f out* **16/1**

1m 41.35s (-3.25) **Going Correction** -0.275s/f (Stan)
WFA 3 from 4yo+ 2lb **13** Ran SP% **120.1**
Speed ratings (Par 103):105,103,102,100,99 98,98,92,91,91 89,78,67
CSF £327.38 CT £7166.23 TOTE £26.60: £6.50, £5.20, £6.90; EX 287.80.
Owner Giovanni Favarulo **Bred** R S A Urquhart **Trained** Newmarket, Suffolk

FOCUS
This was probably not a bad handicap and the winning time was almost three seconds quicker than the preceding seller.
Llamadas Official explanation: jockey said gelding hung right in straight
Dudley Docker(IRE) Official explanation: jockey said gelding missed the break
Set Alight Official explanation: jockey said filly never travelled

6363 BETDIRECT FREEPHONE 0800 211 222 H'CAP 6f (F)
3:10 (3:12) (Class 6) (0-55,55) 3-Y-O+ **£2,893** (£854; £427) **Stalls** Low

Form RPR

0000 **1** **Cool Sands (IRE)**^{11} [6243] 3-8-7 **53**......................... PatrickMathers(5) 4 63
(D Shaw) *sn chsng ldrs: hdwy 2f out: rdn over 1f out: led ent last and hung lft: drvn and styd on* **25/1**

1120 **2** nk **Brave Chief**^{6} [6299] 4-8-8 **54**...(b) MarcHalford(5) 3 63
(S R Bowring) *mde most tl rdn and hdd ent last: rallied wl u.p and jst hld* **3/1**^{1}

3265 **3** 2 **St Ivian**^{6} [6299] 5-8-9 **55**.......................................(p) DuranFentiman(5) 12 58
(Mrs N Macauley) *cl up[on outer: effrt 2f out and ev ch tl rdn over 1f out and grad wknd* **6/1**^{3}

/060 **4** nk **High Swainston**^{140} [3006] 4-8-12 **53**................................. TomEaves 8 55
(R Craggs) *chsd ldrs: rdn along and sltly outpcd 1/2-way: styd on wl appr last* **22/1**

-002 **5** 1 **Carnivore**^{57} [5360] 3-9-0 **55**... PhillipMakin 2 54+
(T D Barron) *sn pushed along towards rr: rdn and hdwy on inenr 2f out: kpt on ins last: nrst fin* **9/2**^{2}

5500 **6** 3/4 **Monkey Madge**^{36} [5803] 3-8-12 **53** .... PaulEddery 9 50
(B Smart) *towards rr: hdwy over 2f out: sn rdn and kpt on ins last: nrst fin* **25/1**

4000 **7** 1 1/4 **George The Best (IRE)**^{14} [6217] 4-9-0 **55** .... DeanMcKeown 14 48
(M D Hammond) *racd wd: in tch: rdn along over 2f out and grad wknd* **25/1**

0021 **8** 5 **Lady Pekan**^{33} [5854] 6-9-0 **55** .... (v) MartinDwyer 6 33
(P Howling) *cl up: rdn along over 2f out and grad wknd* **10/1**

3215 **9** 1 **Gaudalpin (IRE)**^{16} [6177] 3-8-13 **54** .... MickyFenton 10 29
(Ernst Oertel) *in tch: rdn along 1/2-way: sn wknd* **7/1**

4056 **10** 5 **Paddywack (IRE)**^{104} [4060] 8-8-13 **54** .... (b) DarrenWilliams 7 14
(D W Chapman) *in tch: hdwy to chse ldrs 2f out: sn rdn and grad wknd appr last* **14/1**

1200 **11** 1 1/2 **Eforetta (GER)**^{131} [3280] 3-8-13 **54** .... VinceSlattery 13 10
(D J Wintle) *s.i.s: a rr* **25/1**

0500 **12** 1 1/2 **Wizardmicktee (IRE)**^{52} [5469] 3-8-12 **53** .... ChrisCatlin 11 4
(A Bailey) *bhd fr 1/2-way* **80/1**

0060 **13** 1 **Tiger Hunter**^{86} [4604] 3-8-12 **53** .... JoeFanning 5 1
(P Howling) *a bhd* **66/1**

2100 **14** 7 **Labelled With Love**^{11} [6243] 5-9-0 **55** .... (t) NCallan 1 —
(J R Boyle) *dwlt: sn chsng ldrs on inner: rdn along and wknd qckly 1/2-way: eased wl over 1f out* **10/1**

1m 15.65s (-1.25) **Going Correction** -0.275s/f (Stan) **14** Ran SP% **117.3**
Speed ratings (Par 101):97,96,93,93,92 91,89,82,81,74 72,70,69,60
CSF £91.75 CT £542.48 TOTE £35.20: £5.60, £1.50, £2.20; EX 192.60.
Owner Peter Swann **Bred** Rathasker Stud **Trained** Danethorpe, Notts

FOCUS
This modest handicap was about as tight as you can get with the whole field separated by just 2lb. The early pace was decent, though the final time was ordinary.
Labelled With Love Official explanation: jockey said saddle slipped

6364 BET DIRECT H'CAP 1m 3f (F)
3:40 (3:40) (Class 6) (0-65,65) 3-Y-0+ **£3,408** (£1,013; £506; £253) **Stalls** Low

Form RPR

0406 **1** **Efrhina (IRE)**^{8} [6283] 5-8-9 **56** .... MickyFenton 8 67
(Stef Liddiard) *hld up in rr: hdwy 8f out: c wdst of all over 2f out: styd on to ld last 75yds* **7/1**

0000 **2** nk **Mi Odds**^{8} [6283] 9-9-2 **63** .... MartinDwyer 9 74
(Mrs N Macauley) *trckd ldrs: led 5f out: hdd and no ex ins last* **20/1**

6600 **3** 6 **Je Suis Belle**^{16} [6183] 3-8-11 **63** .... PhillipMakin 2 64
(Miss Gay Kelleway) *hld up in rr: hdwy to chse ldrs over 5f out: one pce appr fnl f* **12/1**

0050 **4** 2 1/2 **Arinos (GER)**^{200} [1344] 5-8-10 **57** .... JamieSpencer 3 54
(B J Curley) *trckd ldrs: chal over 2f out: wknd over 1f out* **7/4**^{1}

0532 **5** 1/2 **Jakarmi**^{10} [6265] 4-9-1 **65** .... RobertMiles(3) 1 61
(B Palling) *w ldrs: chal over 2f out: fdd over 1f out* **6/1**^{3}

0600 **6** 5 **Futoo (IRE)**^{13} [6230] 4-8-13 **60** .... DavidAllan 6 48
(G M Moore) *chsd ldrs: rdn and outpcd over 3f out: sn btn* **14/1**

0404 **7** 3/4 **King Of Music (USA)**^{8} [6283] 4-8-13 **60** .... ChrisCatlin 14 47
(G Prodromou) *mid-div: effrt over 4f out: nvr on terms* **9/2**^{2}

0060 **8** 7 **Simply The Guest (IRE)**^{15} [6195] 6-9-1 **62** .... (t) KimTinkler 13 38
(N Tinkler) *sn outpcd and in rr: nvr on terms* **33/1**

0000 **9** 3 **Senor Set (GER)**^{36} [5807] 4-8-10 **57** .... (b^{1}) DeanMcKeown 7 28
(P A Blockley) *led tl 5f out: styd far side and lost pl over 2f out* **33/1**

0523 **10** 9 **Bundaberg**^{43} [5655] 5-9-2 **63** .... DarrenWilliams 4 20
(P W Hiatt) *chsd ldrs: rdn over 5f out: lost pl 3f out* **14/1**

/4-0 **11** 9 **Bluefield (IRE)**^{180} [1031] 4-8-13 **60** .... (p) LeeEnstone 12 2
(Mrs K Walton) *s.i.s: sme hdwy 6f out: sn lost pl* **100/1**

12 3/4 **Balasari (IRE)**^{3} [5963] 5-9-3 **64** .... LisaJones 10 5
(Miss Kariana Key) *sn bhd and drvn along: t.o 5f out* **50/1**

6-32 **13** dist **Mansiya**^{159} [2427] 3-8-11 **63** .... JoeFanning 5 —
(C E Brittain) *hld up towards rr: sme hdwy 7f out: rdn and lost pl over 4f out: t.o 2f out: virtually p.u* **16/1**

2m 24.48s (-4.42) **Going Correction** -0.275s/f (Stan)
WFA 3 from 4yo+ 5lb **13** Ran SP% **121.8**
Speed ratings (Par 101):105,104,100,98,98 94,94,88,86,80 73,73,—
CSF £146.56 CT £1668.64 TOTE £9.40: £2.30, £4.70, £3.60; EX 79.50 Place 6 £31,796.05, Place 5 £7,183.24.
Owner John Liddiard **Bred** Sheikh Ahmed Bin Rashid Al Maktoum **Trained** Great Shefford, Berks

FOCUS
A race run at a rapid pace in a fair time thanks to Senor Set going off quickly in the first-time blinkers, and they finished very well spread out as a result.
Bluefield(IRE) Official explanation: jockey said gelding moved badly throughout
Mansiya Official explanation: jockey said filly hung left from 6f out
T/Plt: Part won. £19,297.90 to a £1 stake. Pool: £26,435.60. 0.05 winning tickets. T/Qpdt: Part won. £2,028.70 to a £1 stake. Pool: £2,741.60. 0.10 winning tickets. JR

6357 SOUTHWELL (L-H)
Wednesday, November 16

OFFICIAL GOING: Standard to fast
Wind: Light, behind Weather: Fine

6365 BET DIRECT H'CAP (DIV I) 1m (F)
12:00 (12:01) (Class 6) (0-60,61) 3-Y-0+ **£2,533** (£747; £374) **Stalls** Low

Form RPR

600U **1** **Monte Mayor Boy**^{16} [6202] 3-9-2 **60** .... (p) RobertHavlin 2 71
(D Haydn Jones) *s.s: hdwy over 6f out: rdn to ld and hung rt 2f out: styd on* **50/1**

0100 **2** 2 **Parkview Love (USA)**^{20} [6126] 4-8-13 **60** .... (v) PatrickMathers(5) 11 67
(D Shaw) *chsd ldrs: led 3f out: rdn and hdd 2f out: styd on same pce fnl f* **10/1**

065 **3** 1/2 **Bavarica**^{61} [5280] 3-8-6 **57** .... DonnaCaldwell(7) 8 63
(Miss J Feilden) *mid-div: hdwy 1/2-way: nt clear run 2f out: soon rdn: no ex ins fnl f* **14/1**

0461 **4** 3/4 **Sarraaf (IRE)**^{7} [6299] 9-9-5 **61** 6ex .... TomEaves 7 66
(I Semple) *prom: outpcd 1/2-way: hdwy over 1f out: nt rch ldrs* **6/1**^{3}

050- **5** 2 1/2 **Rood Boy (IRE)**^{240} [6343] 4-8-10 **52** .... ChrisCatlin 13 52
(Andrew Turnell) *mid-div: lost pl over 4f out: hdwy over 1f out: nt trble ldrs* **13/2**

1002 **6** 1 **Abstract Folly (IRE)**^{16} [6202] 3-9-2 **60** .... (b) GrahamGibbons 9 58+
(J D Bethell) *sn outpcd: hdwy u.p over 1f out: nt trble ldrs* **11/2**^{2}

0-60 **7** 7 **Bob Baileys**^{104} [4095] 3-8-11 **55** .... StephenCarson 4 39
(P R Chamings) *sn outpcd* **40/1**

3140 **8** 3/4 **Ruman (IRE)**^{146} [2843] 3-9-1 **59** .... NCallan 12 41
(M J Attwater) *prom: hung rt over 3f out: wknd over 1f out* **14/1**

0046 **9** 3 **Yashin (IRE)**^{27} [5997] 4-8-13 **55** .... GeorgeBaker 10 31
(P A Blockley) *s.s: hdwy 5f out: wknd over 2f out* **9/2**^{1}

0000 **10** 3 1/2 **Locombe Hill (IRE)**^{7} [6299] 9-8-8 **55** .... AndrewMullen(5) 3 24
(N Wilson) *led 5f: wknd wl over 1f out* **20/1**

0000 **11** hd **Blue Empire (IRE)**^{73} [4972] 4-9-2 **58** .... MickyFenton 1 27
(C R Dore) *sn outpcd: bhd whn swtchd wd 1/2-way* **12/1**

0-50 **12** 1 3/4 **Follow The Game**^{79} [4840] 3-8-11 **55** .... JoeFanning 5 20
(W R Swinburn) *chsd ldrs over 5f* **33/1**

0001 **13** nk **Topton (IRE)**^{11} [6262] 11-9-1 **57** .... (b) SteveDrowne 6 22
(P Howling) *prom: rdn over 3f out: wknd over 2f out* **9/2**^{1}

2000 **14** 5 **Grumpyintmorning**^{178} [1919] 6-8-12 **54** .... SamHitchcott 14 9
(M J Gingell) *hld up: bhd fr 1/2-way* **33/1**

1m 42.54s (-2.06) **Going Correction** -0.20s/f (Stan)
WFA 3 from 4yo+ 2lb **14** Ran SP% **124.5**
Speed ratings (Par 101):102,100,99,98,96 95,88,87,84,81 80,79,78,73
CSF £493.47 CT £7465.06 TOTE £57.50: £11.60, £5.00, £5.00; EX 436.60.
Owner R Phillips **Bred** W H Joyce **Trained** Efail Isaf, Rhondda C Taff

FOCUS
A moderate handicap, run at a fair pace, and the form makes sense. The winning time was 0.36sec slower than the second division.
Ruman(IRE) Official explanation: jockey said gelding hung right
Yashin(IRE) Official explanation: jockey said gelding was slowly away
Topton(IRE) Official explanation: vet said gelding bled from the nose
Grumpyintmorning Official explanation: jockey said gelding hung left

6366 PRESS RED TO BET ON ITVI CLAIMING STKS 6f (F)
12:30 (12:31) (Class 6) 2-Y-O **£2,866** (£846; £423) **Stalls** Low

Form RPR

6000 **1** **Woodwee**^{31} [5921] 2-8-7 56 ow1 .... DarrylHolland 5 58
(J R Weymes) *chsd ldrs: hmpd over 4f out: rdn to ld wl ins fnl f* **8/1**^{3}

605 **2** nk **Our Mary (IRE)**^{33} [5881] 2-8-5 60 .... GregFairley(5) 7 60
(Robert Gray) *chsd ldrs: rdn to ld 1f out: edgd lft and hdd wl ins fnl f* **16/1**

000 **3** 2 **Diktalex (IRE)**^{11} [6251] 2-8-1 58 .... (t) MarcHalford(5) 4 50
(W G M Turner) *in rr: hdwy over 2f out: r.o* **11/1**

0420 **4** 1 **Axis Shield (IRE)**^{103} [4125] 2-8-3 54 .... NelsonDeSouza(3) 10 47
(J G Portman) *chsd ldrs: led over 2f out: sn rdn and edgd rt: hdd and no ex 1f out* **12/1**

0003 **5** hd **Ten Shun**^{16} [6198] 2-8-8 56 .... (b^{1}) GrahamGibbons 2 49
(M J Polglase) *chsd ldrs: ev ch fr over 2f out tl no ex ins fnl f* **9/1**

0600 **6** 1/2 **Bold Tiger (IRE)**^{16} [6196] 2-8-9 55 .... (b^{1}) TomEaves 12 48
(Mrs L Stubbs) *dwlt: plld hrd and hdwy 4f out: sn barged through rivals: rdn and swtchd lft over 2f out: no ex fnl f* **20/1**

0 **7** hd **Lady Josh**^{16} [6200] 2-7-11 .... LiamJones(7) 9 42
(W G M Turner) *dwlt: hdwy over 1f out: nt clr run ins fnl f: nvr nrr* **50/1**

6410 **8** 6 **Lucys Lady**^{86} [4642] 2-7-12 55 ow2 .... AndrewElliott(7) 8 25
(K R Burke) *dwlt: sn pushed along in rr: n.d* **8/1**^{3}

000 **9** 4 **Why Whisper**^{151} [2694] 2-8-6 56 .... PaulEddery 13 14
(B Smart) *prom: rdn whn hmpd wl over 3f out: sn wknd* **8/1**^{3}

3400 **10** 1/2 **Sapphire Storm (IRE)**^{29} [5961] 2-8-4 54 .... (v) JimmyQuinn 1 11
(Miss D A McHale) *dwlt: outpcd* **14/1**

0 **11** 2 **Lake Suprima (IRE)**^{42} [5695] 2-8-2 .... NickyMackay 11 3
(R M Whitaker) *plld hrd and prom: hmpd wl over 3f out: sn wknd* **16/1**

10 **12** 1 1/4 **No Overtime (IRE)**^{71} [5017] 2-8-1 56 .... FrankieMcDonald 3 —
(M D I Usher) *s.s and rel to r: a wl bhd* **7/1**^{2}

44 **13** 2 **Indian Agent (IRE)**^{16} [6197] 2-8-5 .... ChrisCatlin 6 —
(M D I Usher) *led over 3f: edgd lft and wknd over 1f out* **5/2**^{1}

1m 17.22s (0.32) **Going Correction** -0.20s/f (Stan) **13** Ran SP% **125.6**
Speed ratings (Par 94):89,88,85,84,84 83,83,75,70,69 66,65,62
CSF £136.15 TOTE £12.20: £2.50, £5.10, £6.40; EX 149.20.
Owner Dandyjack Racing **Bred** Richard William Floyd **Trained** Middleham Moor, N Yorks
■ Stewards' Enquiry : Chris Catlin two-day ban: careless riding (Nov 28-29)

FOCUS
A modest time, even for a race like this, and the form is weak.

NOTEBOOK
Woodwee, whose best effort previously came when he was narrowly denied on his second start over five at this track back in April, eventually just did enough to repel the runner-up close home and score. Considering he met trouble approaching the turn for home, he could be rated value for a touch further, and it is worth noting that his rider carried 1lb overweight. (op 17-2)
Our Mary(IRE), making her All-Weather debut, was just held at the finish and posted a personal-best on this drop in class. This was a fair effort under top weight, and with a little bit of improvement she can win in this grade.
Diktalex(IRE), having her first outing on the Fibresand, showed the benefit of a drop in grade and turned in a more encouraging effort. She may need further to be seen at her best. (tchd 12-1)
Axis Shield(IRE) had her chance and shaped as though she may improve for the outing. She seems at her best when granted an uncontested lead.
No Overtime(IRE) Official explanation: jockey said filly had been reluctant to race
Indian Agent(IRE), well backed, had her chance and failed to see out the extra furlong. She may prove best back over the minimum trip, but could get closer under a more conservative ride at this distance in the future. Official explanation: jockey said filly lost her action in the final furlong (op 10-3 tchd 7-2 in places)

6367 TEXT BETDIRECT TO 88600 MAIDEN STKS 6f (F)
1:00 (1:02) (Class 5) 3-Y-0+ **£3,361** (£1,000; £499; £249) **Stalls** Low

Form RPR

2000 **1** **Middle Eastern**^{33} [5865] 3-9-0 59 .... NCallan 13 68
(P A Blockley) *s.i.s: sn chsng ldrs: led 3f out: rdn over 1f out: edgd rt ins fnl f: jst hld on* **9/1**

4 **2** nk **Generator**^{23} [6074] 3-9-0 .... MickyFenton 2 67
(Dr J D Scargill) *s.i.s: sn chsng ldrs: rdn over 1f out: hung rt and r.o ins fnl f* **11/2**^{3}

0432 **3** 3 1/2 **White Bear (FR)**^{7} [6301] 3-9-0 58 .... JamieSpencer 9 57
(P D Evans) *chsd ldrs: outpcd over 3f out: hdwy u.p and hung lft over 1f out: r.o* **10/3**^{2}

6252 **4** 3/4 **Art Elegant**^{28} [5981] 3-9-0 64 .... (b^{1}) TomEaves 8 54
(I Semple) *hld up: hdwy 1/2-way: rdn over 1f out: styd on same pce ins fnl f* **3/1**^{1}

0200 **5** 3/4 **Hidden Star**^{28} [5991] 3-9-0 62 .... GeorgeBaker 3 52
(F Jordan) *hld up: styd on appr fnl f: nvr nrr* **10/1**

5002 **6** 1/2 **Silent Spring (USA)**^{11} [6263] 3-8-9 58 .... MichaelHills 14 46
(B W Hills) *chsd ldrs: rdn and ev ch over 2f out: wknd over 1f out* **11/2**^{3}

0050 **7** 1 1/4 **Keon (IRE)**^{16} [6202] 3-9-0 57 .... DarryllHolland 7 47
(R Hollinshead) *outpcd: nvr nrr* **25/1**

8 1 1/4 **Legal Dram** 4-9-0 .... PhillipMakin 5 43
(M Dods) *sn outpcd: nvr nrr* **40/1**

2-00 **9** *1* **Westlake Bond (IRE)**[13] 6235 3-8-4 60 GregFairley(5) 4 35
(B Smart) *prom: lost pl over 4f out: n.d after* **12/1**
0050 **10** *hd* **As Handsome Does**[110] 3919 3-9-0 55 JoeFanning 10 40
(N Tinkler) *prom: rdn 1/2-way: sn wknd* **33/1**
0 **11** *5* **Wolfman**[181] 1824 3-9-0 EddieAhern 6 25
(D W Barker) *dwlt: outpcd* **16/1**
0 **12** *hd* **Lucky Lil**[29] 5957 3-8-3 ow1 MichaelJStainton(7) 11 20
(R M Whitaker) *chsd ldrs: lost pl over 3f out: sn bhd* **66/1**
00 **13** *hd* **Vintage Times (IRE)**[11] 6263 3-9-0 TonyHamilton 1 23
(R A Fahey) *prom to 1/2-way* **40/1**
0 **14** *5* **Fir Tree**[65] 5187 5-9-0 VHalliday 12 8
(S R Bowring) *racd keenly and sn led: hdd 3f out: sn rdn and wknd* **50/1**

1m 15.66s (-1.24) **Going Correction** -0.20s/f (Stan) **14** Ran SP% **126.6**
Speed ratings (Par 103):100,99,94,93,92 92,90,88,87,87 80,80,80,73
CSF £58.42 TOTE £12.90: £3.10, £1.90, £1.40; EX 97.00.
Owner Isla & Colin Cage **Bred** Mrs L A Sadler **Trained** Lambourn, Berks

FOCUS
A weak maiden as such contests for older horses usually are at this time of year, full of disappointing or exposed sorts.

6368 BETDIRECT ON AT THE RACES INTERACTIVE H'CAP 2m (F)
1:30 (1:31) (Class 5) (0-75,71) 3-Y-O+ **£3,322** (£988; £494; £246) **Stalls** Low

Form RPR
0000 **1** **Peak Park (USA)**[72] 5007 5-9-8 **67** ChrisCatlin 5 75
(P L Gilligan) *hld up: hdwy 1/2-way: rdn over 5f out: led over 1f out: styd on* **5/1**[3]
4030 **2** *1 ½* **Saffron Fox**[11] 6267 4-8-12 **60** NelsonDeSouza(3) 11 66
(J G Portman) *a.p: rdn over 1f out: styd on* **10/1**
0211 **3** *hd* **Monte Cristo (FR)**[9] 6285 7-9-9 **68** 6ex (v) DaneO'Neill 13 74
(Mrs L C Taylor) *chsd ldrs: led over 5f out: rdn: edgd lft and hdd over 1f out: styd on* **9/2**[2]
0000 **4** *2 ½* **Bank On Benny**[28] 5973 3-8-3 **57** JamieMackay 8 60
(P W D'Arcy) *hld up in tch: outpcd and hmpd over 4f out: styd on u.p fnl 2f* **18/1**
4300 **5** *4* **Sun Hill**[15] 6218 5-9-1 **65** GregFairley(5) 3 63
(C W Fairhurst) *chsd ldrs: rdn over 3f out: hung lft and wknd over 1f out* **10/1**
2040 **6** *5* **Reminiscent (IRE)**[16] 6195 6-8-12 **57** (v) PaulEddery 1 49
(B P J Baugh) *s.s: hld up: hdwy over 3f out: sn rdn: wknd over 2f out* **20/1**
3565 **7** *2 ½* **Just Waz (USA)**[15] 6218 3-8-3 **57** NickyMackay 10 46
(R M Whitaker) *chsd ldrs: rdn over 3f out: wknd over 2f out* **8/1**
4626 **8** *2* **J R Stevenson (USA)**[7] 6300 9-8-12 **57** JimmyQuinn 12 44
(Ernst Oertel) *hld up in tch: rdn over 3f out: sn wknd* **14/1**
0465 **9** *4* **Macaroni Gold (IRE)**[67] 5105 5-9-12 **71** JamieSpencer 9 53
(D J Daly) *dwlt: hld up: hdwy 7f out: rdn over 2f out: sn wknd* **7/2**[1]
0000 **10** *18* **Mungo Jerry (GER)**[39] 5747 4-9-9 **68** MickyFenton 4 28
(J G Given) *hld up: hdwy over 4f out: wknd over 2f out* **33/1**
0000 **11** *11* **Senor Set (GER)**[1] 6364 4-8-12 **57** (p) DeanMcKeown 7 4
(P A Blockley) *led over 10f: wkng whn hmpd over 4f out* **33/1**
050 **12** *1 ½* **Amir Zaman**[107] 4003 7-9-6 **65** EddieAhern 6 10
(J R Jenkins) *mid-div: wknd over 4f out* **10/1**
/010 **13** *dist* **Vanishing Dancer (SWI)**[11] 6267 8-8-10 **55** (t) TomEaves 2 —
(B Ellison) *s.s: rel to r: sn t.o* **20/1**

3m 41.98s (-2.56) **Going Correction** -0.20s/f (Stan)
WFA 3 from 4yo+ 9lb **13** Ran SP% **122.8**
Speed ratings (Par 103):98,97,97,95,93 91,90,89,87,78 72,71,—
CSF £53.24 CT £245.13 TOTE £6.50: £2.10, £3.20, £1.80; EX 70.90.
Owner Alan Fletcher **Bred** Kenneth L Ramsey And Sarah K Ramsey **Trained** Newmarket, Suffolk
■ Stewards' Enquiry : Jamie Mackay one-day ban: careless riding (Nov 28)

FOCUS
Not the stamina test that races over this trip here usually are, as the early pace was not that strong and several still had a chance turning for home. As a result the winning time was modest for the grade.

6369 MORE OFFERS AT BETDIRECT.CO.UK (S) STKS 7f (F)
2:05 (2:07) (Class 6) 3-Y-O+ **£2,586** (£763; £382) **Stalls** Low

Form RPR
4306 **1** **Sweet Pickle**[36] 5819 4-9-2 60 (e[1]) EddieAhern 5 63
(J R Boyle) *trckd ldrs: led on bit 1/2-way: shkn up over 1f out: r.o* **4/1**[1]
5200 **2** *1 ½* **Priorina (IRE)**[1] 6361 3-8-9 52 (p) RobertHavlin 13 53
(D Haydn Jones) *chsd ldrs: rdn and hung lft over 1f out: styd on same pce* **16/1**
0035 **3** *2* **Mister Elegant**[58] 5368 3-9-0 53 SteveDrowne 11 53
(J L Spearing) *chsd ldrs: rdn 1/2-way: styd on same pce appr fnl f* **5/1**[2]
5550 **4** *nk* **Nisr**[7] 6294 8-9-1 61 (t[1]) MickyFenton 8 52
(Miss Gay Kelleway) *s.i.s: rn in snatches: hdwy 5f out: outpcd over 3f out: styd on u.p fr over 1f out: hung rt ins fnl f* **4/1**[1]
0006 **5** *2 ½* **Essex Star (IRE)**[4] 6327 4-8-11 48 RoryMoore(5) 9 47
(Miss J Feilden) *sn outpcd: hdwy u.p over 1f out: nrst fin* **12/1**
3046 **6** *½* **Dane Rhapsody (IRE)**[25] 6031 4-8-7 45 RobertMiles(3) 14 39
(B Palling) *chsd ldrs over 5f* **50/1**
5000 **7** *2* **Barzak (IRE)**[160] 2425 5-9-7 62 (b) PhillipMakin 7 45
(S R Bowring) *chsd ldrs: rdn over 2f out: wknd over 1f out* **8/1**[3]
000 **8** *1 ½* **Sapphire Dream**[15] 6217 3-8-9 56 DavidAllan 6 30
(A Bailey) *led to 1/2-way: wknd over 1f out* **16/1**
0022 **9** *1* **Queue Up**[4] 6328 3-9-0 58 LPKeniry 3 33
(A G Newcombe) *chsd ldrs over 4f* **5/1**[2]
0005 **10** *5* **Lady Ellendune**[23] 6074 4-8-10 40 ChrisCatlin 4 15
(Andrew Turnell) *dwlt: outpcd* **16/1**
5000 **11** *3 ½* **Stagnite**[15] 6217 5-9-0 53 (be) JamesDoyle(7) 1 16
(K McAuliffe) *prom over 4f* **40/1**
0005 **12** *nk* **Ahaz**[18] 6154 3-9-0 40 DarryllHolland 2 10
(J F Coupland) *starting slowly: outpcd* **28/1**
0000 **13** *4* **King Eric**[34] 5854 3-9-0 45 RobbieFitzpatrick 12 —
(C Smith) *sn outpcd* **100/1**
0000 **14** *nk* **Entertain**[58] 5368 3-9-1 45 NCallan 10 —
(Ms Deborah J Evans) *sn outpcd* **33/1**

1m 29.42s (-1.38) **Going Correction** -0.20s/f (Stan)
WFA 3 from 4yo+ 1lb **14** Ran SP% **121.6**
Speed ratings (Par 101):99,97,95,94,91 91,88,87,86,80 76,76,71,71
CSF £69.78 TOTE £4.20: £2.00, £4.20, £2.30; EX 77.70.The winner was bought in for 7,200gns.
Owner M Khan X2 **Bred** C T Van Hoorn **Trained** Epsom, Surrey

FOCUS
An ordinary affair, run at a sound pace and the winner won as she was entitled to at the weights.
Entertain Official explanation: jockey said filly had no more to give

6370 LITTLEWOODS BET DIRECT H'CAP 5f (F)
2:40 (2:40) (Class 2) (0-100,97) 3-Y-O+ **£13,413** (£3,990; £1,994; £996) **Stalls** High

Form RPR
F303 **1** **Celtic Mill**[17] 6180 7-9-4 **97** EddieAhern 9 107
(D W Barker) *chsd ldrs: r.o to ld wl ins fnl f* **7/2**[2]
3546 **2** *1* **Yomalo (IRE)**[48] 5575 5-9-0 **93** ChrisCatlin 14 99+
(Rae Guest) *s.i.s: outpcd: nt clr run and swtchd rt ins fnl f: fin wl* **12/1**
3000 **3** *shd* **Polish Emperor (USA)**[17] 6180 5-9-0 **93** (e) JoeFanning 1 99
(W R Swinburn) *s.i.s: sn chsng ldrs: rdn and hung rt over 1f out : led ins fnl f: sn hdd and unable qck* **25/1**
0020 **4** *nk* **Desperate Dan**[31] 5922 4-8-7 **86** (b) DarryllHolland 4 91
(J A Osborne) *led: rdn over 1f out: hdd and unable qck ins fnl f* **12/1**
0 **5** *½* **Lake Andre (IRE)**[56] 5416 4-8-10 **94** AndrewMullen(5) 2 97+
(K A Ryan) *chsd ldrs: rdn over 1f out: styd on* **9/1**
3025 **6** *1 ¼* **Frascati**[31] 5922 5-8-1 **85** oh1 ow2 PatrickMathers(5) 3 84
(A Berry) *chsd ldrs: outpcd 1/2-way: nt clr run over 1f out: styd on* **16/1**
0000 **7** *nk* **Piccled**[13] 6238 7-8-5 **84** JimmyQuinn 10 82
(E J Alston) *hld up: hdwy u.p over 1f out: sn edgd rt: styd on same pce ins fnl f* **8/1**[3]
3460 **8** *½* **Dancing Mystery**[17] 6180 11-9-4 **97** StephenCarson 11 93
(E A Wheeler) *prom: rdn 3f out: nt clr run and swtchd lft 1f out: hmpd sn after: nvr able to chal* **12/1**
0004 **9** *nk* **Quiet Times (IRE)**[17] 6180 6-8-11 **90** (b) NCallan 5 85
(K A Ryan) *chsd ldrs: rdn 1/2-way: no ex fnl f* **3/1**[1]
0000 **10** *hd* **The Lord**[11] 6252 5-8-1 **85** MarcHalford(5) 8 80
(W G M Turner) *rrd s: hung lft and outpcd: n.d* **16/1**
4040 **11** *hd* **Magic Glade**[102] 4147 6-8-8 **87** DaneO'Neill 7 81
(R Brotherton) *chsd ldrs: rdn over 1f out: wknd ins fnl f* **16/1**
3531 **12** *2 ½* **Cornus**[57] 5379 3-8-6 **85** GrahamGibbons 12 70
(M J Polglase) *hld up: hdwy 1/2-way: wknd over 1f out* **20/1**
0300 **13** *7* **Smokin Beau**[17] 6180 8-9-0 **96** NelsonDeSouza(3) 13 58
(N P Littmoden) *prom to 1/2-way: bhd whn hung lft over 1f out* **10/1**

57.82 secs (-2.48) **Going Correction** -0.25s/f (Stan) **13** Ran SP% **126.8**
Speed ratings (Par 109):109,107,107,106,105 103,103,102,102,101 101,97,86
CSF £48.88 CT £984.13 TOTE £3.60: £1.60, £4.80, £9.80; EX 78.90 Trifecta £411.00 Part won. Pool: £578.90 - 0.10 winning tickets..
Owner P Asquith **Bred** P Asquith **Trained** Scorton, N Yorks

FOCUS
A very competitive and classy sprint handicap run at a true gallop. The action unfolded centre to stands' side, although those that raced tight against the stands' rail never had a chance.

NOTEBOOK
Celtic Mill, rated a stone lower on sand than he is on turf, has won over a longer trip on the old Wolverhampton Fibresand, but this was his first appearance here and his first try over the minimum trip on sand. Although handy, he was not able to get the overall early lead yet still found enough to come through and take the race well inside the last furlong. There are not too many options open to him on sand over the winter, but given his ability on turf connections are unlikely to be too bothered by that. (op 3-1)
Yomalo(IRE), not well drawn, ran a remarkable race. Slowly away, she looked set to finish tailed off at halfway, but she eventually finished with such a rattle that she eventually mowed down all her rivals apart from the winner. On the face of it she would be one to side with if returned here, but her style of running will always be a liability on this surface, especially over the minimum trip.
Polish Emperor(USA), starting from the best draw, was always up with the pace and kept battling away despite edging continually to his right as the race progressed. He is kept very busy, but shows no ill-effects.
Desperate Dan ◆, a winner on Polytrack on his racecourse debut and running on sand for the first time since, travelled well in front down the middle of the track and was not swamped until the very closing stages. He may be better suited by six furlongs and looks well worth another try here if an opportunity can be found. (op 11-1)
Lake Andre(IRE), an Irish import making his debut on sand and for the yard, was backed in from 33-1 and certainly ran with credit considering his three wins had all been in very soft ground over seven furlongs. That will be of little comfort to those who backed him each-way, though. Official explanation: jockey said gelding hung left (op 33-1)
Frascati, a winner over course and distance a couple of winters ago, looks to be on a stiff mark considering she has not won a race since the summer of 2004, but she nonetheless ran with credit from a good draw. Unfortunately, she might not get the help from the Handicapper she needs as a result.
Piccled ◆, winner of his last five starts over this course and distance, is rated 15lb higher on sand than on turf but was still able to race off an 8lb lower mark than for his last victory here almost three years ago. He travelled well enough just behind the leaders and might have done even better had he not made his effort tight against the stands' rail. He would be of great interest back under these conditions granted a lower draw. Official explanation: jockey said gelding hung right (op 9-1)
Quiet Times(IRE), off the same mark as when winning this race last year, broke well enough, but it was not long before he was feeling the pinch and he dropped away rather tamely. (op 11-4 tchd 10-3)
Smokin Beau Official explanation: vet said gelding had bled from the nose

6371 BETDIRECT.CO.UK H'CAP 1m 4f (F)
3:15 (3:15) (Class 5) (0-75,74) 3-Y-O+ **£4,074** (£1,212; £605; £302) **Stalls** Low

Form RPR
1412 **1** **Bethanys Boy (IRE)**[37] 5807 4-8-7 **68** GregFairley(5) 12 78
(B Ellison) *dwlt: hld up: racd keenly: hdwy over 3f out: led 2f out: r.o* **7/2**[1]
3200 **2** *nk* **Pass The Port**[26] 6006 4-9-3 **73** JamieSpencer 4 83
(D Haydn Jones) *a.p: rdn and swtchd rt to chal over 1f out: r.o* **15/2**
1032 **3** *1 ¼* **Heathyards Pride**[38] 5759 5-8-13 **69** GeorgeBaker 3 77
(R Hollinshead) *s.i.s: hld up: hdwy over 1f out: r.o* **13/2**[3]
03 **4** *1* **Mad Carew (USA)**[6] 6308 6-9-1 **74** (e) AmirQuinn(3) 11 80
(J R Boyle) *hld up: nt clr run 3f out: hdwy over 1f out: nrst fin* **14/1**
1400 **5** *6* **Newtonian (USA)**[214] 1053 6-8-7 **68** MarcHalford(5) 14 65
(J Parkes) *chsd ldrs: rdn over 2f out: wknd over 1f out* **33/1**
1116 **6** *hd* **Ti Adora (IRE)**[44] 5669 3-8-12 **74** EddieAhern 8 70
(P W D'Arcy) *prom: jnd ldr 7f out: rdn over 2f out: sn wknd* **7/1**
6003 **7** *hd* **Dovedon Hero**[123] 3526 5-9-3 **73** (b) ChrisCatlin 13 69
(P J McBride) *hld up: hdwy over 3f out: led over 2f out: sn hdd: wknd over 1f out* **14/1**
606- **8** *1* **Bienvenue**[434] 5402 4-9-2 **72** MartinDwyer 2 67
(M P Tregoning) *hld up i tch: lost pl over 4f out: n.d after* **10/1**
0010 **9** *1 ¾* **Yenaled**[15] 6218 8-8-10 **73** DonnaCaldwell(7) 10 65
(N Wilson) *hld up: rdn over 3f out: n.d* **14/1**
1044 **10** *2 ½* **Ballet Ballon (USA)**[20] 6127 3-8-10 **72** NCallan 5 60
(M A Jarvis) *led: hdd over 2f out: wknd over 1f out* **9/1**
0-00 **11** *3 ½* **Movie King (IRE)**[45] 5281 6-8-11 **67** MichaelTebbutt 1 49
(S R Bowring) *prom over 9f* **33/1**

2021 **12** *shd* **Stretton (IRE)**[9] 6283 7-9-1 **71** 6ex.............................. GrahamGibbons 6 53
(J D Bethell) *chsd ldr 4f: wknd wl over 1f out* **5/1**[2]

2m 38.1s (-3.99) **Going Correction** -0.20s/f (Stan)
WFA 3 from 4yo+ 6lb **12** Ran SP% **121.5**
Speed ratings (Par 103):105,104,103,103,99 99,99,98,97,95 93,93
CSF £30.48 CT £166.15 TOTE £5.10: £2.00, £2.10, £2.80; EX 32.70.
Owner Get Into Racing UK **Bred** K And Mrs Cullen **Trained** Norton, N Yorks

FOCUS
A fair handicap, run at a decent pace and the first four came clear. The form looks sound enough for the grade.

6372 BET DIRECT H'CAP (DIV II) 1m (F)
3:45 (3:46) (Class 6) (0-60,60) 3-Y-0+ **£2,533** (£747; £374) **Stalls** Low

Form RPR
0102 **1** **Stevedore (IRE)**[9] 6286 4-9-1 **57**.................................... MartinDwyer 13 69
(J R Boyle) *chsd ldrs: led 3f out: edgd lft over 1f out: drvn out* **4/1**[1]
1000 **2** *2* **Simply St Lucia**[28] 5981 3-9-2 **60**.................................. DarryllHolland 7 68
(J R Weymes) *led 5f: sn rdn: styd on same pce fnl f* **16/1**
-050 **3** *3½* **Roman Empire**[265] 474 5-9-3 **59**...................................(b) NCallan 10 60
(K A Ryan) *hld up in tch: rdn over 2f out: wknd fnl f* **8/1**[3]
6005 **4** *3½* **Sriology (IRE)**[9] 6287 4-8-7 **56** ow4.......................... ChrisCavanagh(7) 2 50
(G Prodromou) *s.s: outpcd: r.o ins fnl f: nvr nrr* **10/1**
5560 **5** *2½* **Aberdeen Park**[55] 5423 3-8-12 **56**.................................... GeorgeBaker 3 45
(Mrs H Sweeting) *s.i.s: styd on fnl f: nvr nrr* **16/1**
0104 **6** *1¼* **Machinate (USA)**[16] 6202 3-8-13 **57**................................. EddieAhern 8 44
(W M Brisbourne) *mid-div: effrt over 3f out: wknd over 2f out* **8/1**[3]
0010 **7** *nk* **Phi Phi (IRE)**[11] 6266 3-9-2 **60**... ChrisCatlin 14 46
(Rae Guest) *chsd ldrs over 5f* **10/1**
2163 **8** *1½* **My Michelle**[14] 6229 4-8-13 **55**..................................... StephenCarson 1 38
(B Palling) *chsd ldrs over 4f* **16/1**
-000 **9** *2½* **Diamond Shannon (IRE)**[4] 6336 4-8-11 **58**............ EmmettStack(5) 11 36
(D Carroll) *prom to 1/2-way* **40/1**
0210 **10** *5* **Mademoiselle**[14] 6231 3-8-11 **55**..................................... MichaelHills 5 23
(B W Hills) *chsd ldrs tl wknd over 3f out* **5/1**[2]
4005 **11** *1¼* **Yorker (USA)**[20] 5246 7-8-9 **51**.. SamHitchcott 6 16
(Ms Deborah J Evans) *chsd ldrs over 4f* **28/1**
3420 **12** *2* **Mink Mitten**[69] 5061 3-8-12 **56**...(t) DaneO'Neill 4 17
(D J Daly) *sn outpcd* **12/1**
0-00 **P** **The Best Yet**[29] 5956 7-9-4 **60**... LPKeniry 12 —
(A G Newcombe) *s.s: hld up: p.u over 4f out* **28/1**
0600 **P** **Cavan Gael (FR)**[17] 6183 3-9-2 **60**................................. SteveDrowne 9 —
(P Howling) *chsd ldrs: lost pl 5f out: sn bhd: t.o whn p.u and dismntd fnl f* **9/1**

1m 42.18s (-2.42) **Going Correction** -0.20s/f (Stan)
WFA 3 from 4yo+ 2lb **14** Ran SP% **121.7**
Speed ratings (Par 101):104,102,98,95,92 91,90,89,86,81 80,78,—,—
CSF £69.82 CT £514.50 TOTE £3.80: £1.90, £4.60, £3.60; EX 62.50 Place 6 £1,905.35, Place 5 £152.65.
Owner M Khan X2 **Bred** C J Foy **Trained** Epsom, Surrey

FOCUS
This looked the stronger of the two divisions, backed up by the winning time being 0.36sec faster than the first division, and the field came home fairly strung out.
Cavan Gael(FR) Official explanation: vet said colt had bled from the nose
T/Jkpt: Not won. T/Plt: £5,898.90 to a £1 stake. Pool: £77,979.85. 9.65 winning tickets. T/Qpdt: £42.90 to a £1 stake. Pool: £9,694.13. 167.10 winning tickets. CR

6349 LINGFIELD (L-H)
Saturday, November 19

OFFICIAL GOING: Standard
Wind: Nil Weather: Sunny and crisp

6373 DAILY OFFERS FROM BETDIRECT H'CAP 1m (P)
12:40 (12:41) (Class 4) (0-80,78) 3-Y-0+ **£5,816** (£1,730; £864; £431) **Stalls** High

Form RPR
0001 **1** **Obezyana (USA)**[47] 5664 3-9-3 **78**..............................(bt) MartinDwyer 2 90
(G A Huffer) *trckd ldng pair: effrt 2f out: chsd ldr over 1f out: styd on wl to ld last strides* **5/1**
0421 **2** *hd* **Mina A Salem**[26] 6075 3-8-12 **73**.................................. JimmyFortune 10 85
(C E Brittain) *lw: trckd ldr gng wl: led wl over 1f out: drvn fnl f: worn down last strides* **4/1**[3]
3006 **3** *3½* **Sonny Parkin**[9] 6305 3-8-13 **74**....................................(p) PatCosgrave 8 78
(G A Huffer) *t.k.h: hld up in rr: effrt 2f out: squeezed through to take 3rd ins fnl f: no ch w ldng pair* **20/1**
1524 **4** *½* **Hand Chime**[23] 6126 8-7-11 **63**.. LiamJones(7) 6 66
(Ernst Oertel) *b: b.hind: t.k.h: trckd ldrs: pushed along and one pce fnl 2f* **25/1**
4524 **5** *nk* **Burgundy**[7] 6325 8-9-2 **75**...(b) TPQueally 12 77+
(P Mitchell) *sn last: rdn on outer 3f out: v wd bnd 2f out: styd on fnl f: no ch* **11/1**
4030 **6** *hd* **Kindlelight Debut**[8] 6315 5-8-8 **67**................................... HayleyTurner 7 69+
(N P Littmoden) *hld up bhd ldrs: outpcd 2f out: kpt on fnl f: n.d* **20/1**
1432 **7** *nk* **Boundless Prospect (USA)**[9] 6305 6-9-1 **74**............. MickyFenton 11 75
(Miss Gay Kelleway) *lw: hld up in last trio: rdn over 2f out: one pce and no imp* **7/2**[2]
1425 **8** *½* **Habshan (USA)**[84] 4760 5-9-4 **77**.. KFallon 1 77
(C F Wall) *led to wl over 1f out: wknd* **11/4**[1]
6101 **9** *½* **Midnight Lace**[14] 6266 3-8-5 **66**.. ChrisCatlin 9 65
(J R Boyle) *settled in midfield: pushed along over 3f out: outpcd 2f out: no ch after* **20/1**
0000 **10** *2* **Savoy Chapel**[9] 6302 3-8-9 **70**.. JimmyQuinn 4 64
(A W Carroll) *hld up in midfield: effrt on inner over 2f out: wknd over 1f out* **66/1**
0/ **L** **Battling Mac (IRE)**[43] 5728 7-9-4 **77**...........................(b) DarryllHolland 3 —
(L A Dace) *reluctant to go to post: restless stalls: ref to r: tk no part* **66/1**

1m 37.09s (-2.34) **Going Correction** -0.175s/f (Stan)
WFA 3 from 5yo+ 2lb **11** Ran SP% **115.0**
Speed ratings (Par 105):104,103,100,99,99 99,99,98,98,96 —
CSF £22.35 CT £368.32 TOTE £6.20: £2.20, £2.20, £5.10; EX 21.10.
Owner T P Ramsden **Bred** Stone Canyon Thoroughbreds **Trained** Newmarket, Suffolk

FOCUS
A modest but competitive heat, with half of the field in good recent form. The form could rate higher but is limited by the proximity of the fourth.

6374 BETDIRECT NO Q ON 08000 93 66 93 MAIDEN STKS 5f (P)
1:10 (1:12) (Class 5) 2-Y-0 **£4,145** (£1,233; £616; £307) **Stalls** High

Form RPR
3400 **1** **Overwing (IRE)**[9] 6303 2-8-9 70.. DaneO'Neill 7 71
(R Hannon) *chsd ldr: rdn to ld 1f out: jst hld on* **3/1**[2]
2 *shd* **Stonecrabstomorrow (IRE)** 2-9-0 .... SteveDrowne 8 76
(P F I Cole) *unf: scope: chsd ldrs: rdn 2f out: styd on wl to cl on wnr fnl f: jst failed* **16/1**
65 **3** *1¼* **Cativo Cavallino**[17] 6225 2-9-0 .... IanMongan 1 71
(Julian Poulton) *lw: trckd ldng pair: nt clr run jst over 1f out and swtchd rt: styd on same pce fnl 150yds* **7/1**
64 **4** *1¼* **Yellow Card**[9] 6303 2-9-0 .... JimmyFortune 3 67
(N A Callaghan) *fractious bef s: chsd ldrs: effrt 2f out: hanging fr over 1f out: styng on but hld whn n.m.r last 100yds* **9/4**[1]
5606 **5** *¾* **Sands Crooner (IRE)**[9] 6303 2-9-0 75................(t) FrankieMcDonald 10 64
(D Shaw) *off the pce in last quartet: rdn 1/2-way: styd on fnl f: nvr nrr* **10/1**
04 **6** *nk* **Somoya**[19] 6196 2-8-9 .... PhilipRobinson 2 58
(M A Jarvis) *led to 1f out: wknd* **6/1**[3]
7 *1* **Perfect Treasure (IRE)** 2-8-9 .... KFallon 9 54
(J A R Toller) *w'like: b.bkwd: dwlt: racd wd in last quartet: wl adrift whn rn wd bnd 2f out: one pce after* **8/1**
00 **8** *1* **Lambency (IRE)**[14] 6251 2-8-9 .... MickyFenton 6 51
(J G Given) *chsd ldrs: rdn and struggling fr 1/2-way* **33/1**
05 **9** *¾* **Jessica Wigmo**[19] 6197 2-8-6 .... RichardThomas(3) 5 48
(A W Carroll) *off the pce in last quartet: nvr a factor* **33/1**
06 **10** *1¼* **Penang Cinta**[12] 6281 2-9-0 .... DarryllHolland 4 48
(G A Butler) *squeezed out after 1f: a in rr after: last and hanging over 2f out* **20/1**

59.16 secs (-0.62) **Going Correction** -0.175s/f (Stan) **10** Ran SP% **119.3**
Speed ratings (Par 96):97,96,94,92,91 91,89,87,86,84
CSF £49.80 TOTE £5.70: £2.30, £3.70, £2.00; EX 130.00.
Owner Cathal M Ryan **Bred** Noel Finegan And Noel Cogan **Trained** East Everleigh, Wilts

FOCUS
An interesting maiden, with the winner having shown some decent turf form and the runner-up making a promising debut. The fourth and fifth set a fair standard.

NOTEBOOK
Overwing(IRE) had the best turf form, and put a poor All-Weather debut behind her. Now she has got the hang of the game, she should continue to acquit herself well. (op 10-3 tchd 7-2 and 4-1 in places)
Stonecrabstomorrow(IRE), a 50,000gns Fasliyev colt out of an unraced mare, made a fine debut and only failed by a whisker. With the experience behind him, a similar race is there for the taking. (op 20-1)
Cativo Cavallino made a good All-Weather debut. He showed promise in two races on turf, and is capable of winning. (tchd 11-2)
Yellow Card has ability, but has fallen a little short in his two races on sand. He possesses plenty of speed, but may be worth a try at six furlongs. (tchd 11-4)
Sands Crooner(IRE) may be suited by an extra furlong. (op 12-1 tchd 9-1)
Somoya is quite highly thought-of by connections, but so far she has fallen short of expectations. Plenty of use has been made of her, so maybe a change of tactics is required. (op 13-2 tchd 7-1)
Perfect Treasure(IRE), a 32,000 guinea Night Shift colt, will improve with a stiffer test. In the circumstances, this was a satisfactory debut. (op 7-1 tchd 9-1)

6375 BETDIRECT 0800 211222 (S) STKS 1m (P)
1:40 (1:42) (Class 6) 2-Y-0 **£2,559** (£755; £378) **Stalls** High

Form RPR
0456 **1** **Lenoir (GER)**[8] 6309 2-8-11 62....................................(v) DarryllHolland 1 64+
(V Smith) *t.k.h: trckd ldrs: hmpd over 2f out: drvn and effrt over 1f out: r.o to ld last 75yds: sn clr* **7/2**[1]
5004 **2** *1½* **Bathwick Rox (IRE)**[33] 5947 2-8-11 58........................(v[1]) DaneO'Neill 11 61
(B R Millman) *t.k.h: trckd ldrs: led over 3f out: rdn over 1f out: hdd and outpcd last 75yds* **9/2**[2]
0033 **3** *1* **Pix**[4] 6358 2-8-6 50.. ChrisCatlin 9 54
(S Kirk) *wl in tch: prog to chse ldr over 2f out: rdn over 1f out: nt qckn and lost 2nd last 100yds* **9/2**[2]
4005 **4** *½* **Ms Rainbow Runner**[32] 5958 2-8-6 56.................... FrankieMcDonald 7 52
(B J Meehan) *hld up in rr: hmpd on inner over 2f out: effrt over 1f out: kpt on : nvr able to chal* **11/2**[3]
0000 **5** *2* **La Via Ferrata (IRE)**[75] 4990 2-8-8 52.................... NelsonDeSouza(3) 4 53
(P F I Cole) *sn pushed along in last pair: struggling 3f out: styd on fr over 1f out: nrst fin* **6/1**
0350 **6** *2½* **Macs All Heart (IRE)**[12] 6281 2-8-6 47..........................(t) HayleyTurner 5 43
(A B Coogan) *racd freely: pressed ldr to over 3f out: wknd over 1f out* **20/1**
4050 **7** *4* **Bincrafty**[4] 6357 2-8-4 56..(b) JosephWalsh(7) 8 39
(J S Moore) *wl in rr: no prog over 2f out* **20/1**
P00 **8** *nk* **Jamie's Princess (IRE)**[4] 6358 2-7-13 ....(t) JamesDoyle(7) 2 33
(I A Wood) *chsd ldrs tl wknd 3f out* **33/1**
0640 **9** *5* **Fashion Chic**[179] 1980 2-8-8 50 ow2................................ MickyFenton 3 24
(Stef Liddiard) *led to over 3f out: wknd over 2f out* **14/1**
2000 **10** *18* **Anyone Can Whistle**[33] 5947 2-8-11 53........................ JamieMackay 10 —
(G G Margarson) *lw: dwlt: wl in rr: prog on wd outside over 3f out: sn wknd: t.o* **9/1**

1m 39.19s (-0.24) **Going Correction** -0.175s/f (Stan) **10** Ran SP% **117.4**
Speed ratings (Par 94):94,92,91,91,89 86,82,82,77,59
CSF £18.70 TOTE £3.90: £1.60, £2.00, £1.70; EX 26.70.The winner was bought in for 7,200gns.
Owner The Contretemps Partnership **Bred** Graf And Grafin Von Stauffenberg **Trained** Exning, Suffolk
■ Stewards' Enquiry : Chris Catlin caution: careless riding

FOCUS
A weak seller producing a comfortable winner. The remainder are very modest and set the standard for the form which is average for the grade.

NOTEBOOK
Lenoir(GER) was the highest rated of these, and comfortably overcame trouble in running around the final bend. In similarly weak company, there is no reason why he cannot repeat the dose. (op 9-2)
Bathwick Rox(IRE) is suited by this trip, and made a solid All-Weather debut. However, he was comfortably outpaced by the winner, and should be kept to this level. Official explanation: jockey said gelding hung badly right throughout (op 5-1 tchd 11-2)
Pixhad every chance, but was not good enough in the final furlong. Sellers are her game. (op 4-1)
Ms Rainbow Runner was trying a longer trip, but it was lack of tactical speed, rather than any stamina deficiency, that beat her. Official explanation: jockey said filly was denied a clear run (op 4-1)
La Via Ferrata(IRE) did not achieve a great deal, but there was a hint of potential in the way he was keeping on at the finish after getting well back. With this All-Weather debut behind him, he would not be out of the reckoning in a similar contest. (tchd 11-2)
Macs All Heart(IRE) raced too freely, but was easily left behind even at this lowly level. (op 16-1)

The Form Book, Raceform Ltd, Compton, RG20 6NL

Anyone Can Whistle Official explanation: jockey said gelding missed the break

6376 EUROPEAN BREEDERS FUND BETDIRECT 0800 211222 FILLIES' H'CAP 1m (P)
2:10 (2:11) (Class 4) (0-85,82) 3-Y-O+ £6,760 (£2,011; £1,005; £502) Stalls High

Form RPR
-312 1 **Three Wrens (IRE)**[45] 5701 3-8-11 76 KFallon 5 86+
(D J Daly) *lw: t.k.h: hld up in midfield: clsd over 1f out: shkn up to ld last 100yds: comf* 1/1[1]
6524 2 1 1/4 **Nice Tune**[9] 6306 3-8-10 75 JimmyFortune 1 82
(C E Brittain) *mostly pressed ldr: led 2f out: styd on u.p: hdd and outpcd last 100yds* 8/1[3]
1000 3 hd **Boot 'n Toot**[57] 5436 4-9-1 78 MichaelHills 10 85+
(C A Cyzer) *dwlt: t.k.h and hld up in detached last: stl last 2f out: rapid prog over 1f out: fin strly* 25/1
3045 4 2 **Caragh Mia (IRE)**[9] 6305 3-8-7 72 (b[1]) DarryllHolland 9 74
(G A Butler) *lw: s.s: hld up wl in rr: sme prog over 2f out: rdn and styd on: nt pce to rch ldrs* 12/1
304 5 hd **Zerlina (USA)**[40] 5806 4-9-3 80 JimmyQuinn 8 81
(J Ryan) *trckd ldrs: effrt to chal 2f out: hanging and nt qckn fr over 1f out* 15/2[2]
0050 6 nk **Khe Sanh**[60] 5382 3-8-7 72 LPKeniry 4 73
(R A Harris) *hld up wl in rr: prog over 2f out: chsd ldrs over 1f out: one pce after* 16/1
220 7 2 1/2 **Fantaisiste**[50] 5585 3-9-3 82 SteveDrowne 3 77
(P F I Cole) *lw: hld up on inner: n.m.r 5f out: rdn and no prog 2f out* 10/1
5004 8 2 **Missed A Beat**[9] 6305 3-8-7 72 MartinDwyer 7 69+
(M Blanshard) *prom: cl up 2f out: wknd over 1f out: eased fnl f* 10/1
0040 9 3/4 **Munaawashat (IRE)**[21] 6161 4-8-8 71 PatCosgrave 2 60
(K R Burke) *prom tl wknd u.p over 1f out* 25/1
210- 10 3 **Baboosh (IRE)**[378] 6571 4-8-13 76 DaneO'Neill 6 58
(M Wigham) *hld up and racd wd: rdn and no prog over 2f out* 33/1
0100 11 11 **Sabrina Brown**[21] 6149 4-9-4 81 (t) StephenCarson 12 38
(J A Geake) *lw: led to 2f out: wknd v rapidly: t.o* 14/1

1m 36.89s (-2.54) **Going Correction** -0.175s/f (Stan)
WFA 3 from 4yo 2lb 11 Ran SP% 121.9
Speed ratings (Par 102):105,103,103,101,101 101,98,96,95,92 81
CSF £9.73 CT £140.86 TOTE £1.80: £1.10, £2.00, £6.30; EX 12.40.
Owner Mrs James Wigan **Bred** Mrs James Wigan **Trained** Newmarket, Suffolk

FOCUS
A fair fillies' race, but the winner looked a cut above her rivals. The runner-up sets an ordinary standard and the form is reasonable.
Caragh Mia(IRE) Official explanation: jockey said filly missed the break
Missed A Beat Official explanation: jockey said filly hung left throughout

6377 BETDIRECT "TODAY'S BEST BETS" H'CAP 1m 4f (P)
2:40 (2:41) (Class 2) (0-100,97) 3-Y-O+
£11,628 (£3,481; £1,740; £871; £434; £218) Stalls Low

Form RPR
1410 1 **Sri Diamond**[28] 6025 5-9-2 91 KFallon 6 101
(S Kirk) *hld up in midfield: effrt 2f out: drvn and r.o fnl f to ld last 100yds* 10/1
016 2 1 1/4 **Wild Savannah**[63] 5309 3-9-2 97 (v) JimmyFortune 11 105
(J H M Gosden) *led: styd on wl fr 2f out: hdd and no ex last 100yds* 4/1[2]
1003 3 1 3/4 **Millville**[54] 5512 5-9-4 93 PhilipRobinson 12 98
(M A Jarvis) *lw: trckd ldng trio: gng easily over 2f out: effrt over 1f out: kpt on same pce* 7/2[1]
6510 4 nk **Go Tech**[43] 5715 5-9-2 91 DavidAllan 2 96
(T D Easterby) *lw: trckd ldng pair on inner: rdn wl over 2f out: kpt on u.p fr over 1f out* 14/1
3060 5 nk **Wellington Hall (GER)**[14] 6254 7-8-4 79 oh1 AdrianMcCarthy 8 84
(P W Chapple-Hyam) *trckd ldr: rdn and hld over 1f out: fdd ins fnl f* 16/1
3342 6 1 **Pagan Sky (IRE)**[26] 6073 6-8-10 85 (v) ChrisCatlin 1 88
(Miss Venetia Williams) *trckd ldrs: effrt over 2f out: one pce fr over 1f out* 9/2[3]
0504 7 nk **The Violin Player (USA)**[26] 6073 4-8-9 84 DarryllHolland 3 86
(H J Collingridge) *hld up in last trio: plenty to do over 2f out: styd on fr over 1f out: nt rch ldrs* 7/1
0524 8 1 1/4 **Wingman (IRE)**[14] 6254 3-8-6 87 FrankieMcDonald 10 87
(J W Hills) *hld up towards rr: rdn and one pce fr over 2f out* 7/1
0102 9 hd **Annambo**[12] 6285 5-8-4 79 oh3 MartinDwyer 7 79
(D Morris) *hld up in 9th: rdn and no prog over 2f out* 14/1
6600 10 1/2 **Skidmark**[50] 5588 4-8-13 88 SteveDrowne 5 87
(Miss J R Tooth) *stdd s: hld up in last pair: rdn and no prog over 2f out* 33/1
0000 11 3/4 **Easter Ogil (IRE)**[7] 6324 10-8-7 85 oh23 ow6 AmirQuinn(3) 4 83?
(Jane Southcombe) *b: a in last pair: no prog over 2f out* 100/1
450 12 11 **Colinca's Lad (IRE)**[14] 6255 3-7-11 85 DeanWilliams(7) 9 66
(G C H Chung) *dwlt: sn chsd ldrs: rdn over 4f out: wknd over 2f out: t.o* 66/1

2m 30.52s (-3.87) **Going Correction** -0.175s/f (Stan)
WFA 3 from 4yo+ 6lb 12 Ran SP% 119.1
Speed ratings (Par 109):105,104,103,102,102 101,101,100,100,100 99,92
CSF £49.81 CT £172.69 TOTE £11.50: £3.70, £2.80, £1.40; EX 36.50.
Owner Ascot Brew Racing **Bred** B J And Mrs Crangle **Trained** Upper Lambourn, Berks

FOCUS
A decent race, with some useful performers on show and a winner who looks like one to follow. The race was not that strongly run but the form appears sound enough.

NOTEBOOK
Sri Diamond ◆ impressed with his turn of foot, and looks one to keep on the right side this winter. He got the trip well, and looks a smart All-Weather performer in the making. (op 8-1)
Wild Savannah ended up setting it up for the smart-looking winner, but went down gamely. This was a good All-Weather debut, and he should continue to run well on the surface in the coming months. (op 7-2)
Millville had his share of weight, and was anchored by it in the closing stages. Nonetheless, he put up a creditable effort. (op 9-2 tchd 5-1)
Go Tech kept on well enough to indicate that he gets this trip, but he was just run out of the first three in a decent sort of race. (op 12-1)
Wellington Hall(GER) ran satisfactorily, finally proving that he does act on the surface.
Pagan Sky(IRE), recently sold for 25,000 guineas out of James Toller's stable, was found wanting in the home straight. He is a bit better than this, and may have needed time to acclimatise to his new surroundings. (op 5-1)
The Violin Player(USA) was given quite a bit to do, and is worth another chance on a surface that suits him. (op 15-2 tchd 8-1)

6378 BETDIRECT.CO.UK CHURCHILL STKS (LISTED RACE) 1m 2f (P)
3:15 (3:18) (Class 1) 3-Y-O+
£22,712 (£8,608; £4,308; £2,148; £1,076; £540) Stalls Low

Form RPR
1100 1 **Kew Green (USA)**[49] 5607 7-9-0 100 DaneO'Neill 7 110
(P R Webber) *trckd ldng trio: effrt to chse ldr 2f out: sustained chal fr over 1f out to ld last 75yds* 9/1
5336 2 hd **Boule D'Or (IRE)**[27] 6050 4-9-0 107 NigelDay 6 110
(J Akehurst) *lw: t.k.h: trckd ldng pair: wnt 2nd 1/2-way: led over 2f out: battled on wl whn chal over 1f out: hdd last 75yds* 10/1
4413 3 1 1/4 **Compton Bolter (IRE)**[55] 5493 8-9-4 110 DarryllHolland 1 111
(G A Butler) *trckd ldrs: effrt 2f out: styd on fr over 1f out: nt pce to chal* 9/2[1]
1251 4 hd **Zayn Zen**[20] 6181 3-8-7 99 PhilipRobinson 9 104
(M A Jarvis) *trckd ldrs on outer: effrt 2f out: styd on fr over 1f out: nt pce to chal* 5/1[2]
0500 5 nk **Kandidate**[35] 5900 3-8-10 106 JimmyFortune 2 106
(C E Brittain) *chsd ldr to 1/2-way: lost pl over 2f out: rdn and styd on same pce fr over 1f out* 14/1
-300 6 nk **Simple Exchange (IRE)**[97] 4404 4-9-0 PJSmullen 13 106+
(D K Weld, Ire) *hld up in rr: effrt on outer over 2f out: r.o fnl f: nt rch ldrs* 9/1
0400 7 nk **Helm Bank**[35] 5906 5-9-0 98 EddieAhern 12 105
(J L Dunlop) *lw: chsd ldrs: rdn 3f out: kpt on u.p but no imp* 10/1
0403 8 3/4 **Lord Mayor**[28] 6025 4-9-0 102 ChrisCatlin 10 104
(R M H Cowell) *hld up midfield: rdn 2f out: kpt on same pce and no imp* 12/1
5024 9 1/2 **Colisay**[22] 6131 6-9-0 102 KFallon 4 103
(Mrs A J Perrett) *b.hind: hld up midfield: effrt 2f out: one pce and no prog fnl f* 7/1[3]
0200 10 hd **Moayed**[36] 5874 6-9-0 102 (bt) HayleyTurner 11 102+
(N P Littmoden) *dwlt: t.k.h: hld up in last: prog on inner wl over 1f out: nt clr run sn after: no ch* 16/1
0/ 11 2 1/2 **Lights Out (DEN)**[23] 5-9-0 (t) ESki 8 98?
(Ms C Erichsen, Norway) *rangy: squeezed out after 1f: in rr after: rdn and one pce fnl 2f* 33/1
605 12 hd **Jath**[14] 6253 4-8-9 88 SteveDrowne 14 92?
(Julian Poulton) *stdd s: hld up in last trio: rdn and no prog over 2f out* 50/1
1000 13 nk **Hurricane Coast**[4] 6354 6-9-0 76 (b) JamesDoyle 3 97?
(K McAuliffe) *hld up in last trio: rdn and no prog over 2f out* 66/1
6052 14 nk **St Petersburg**[21] 6147 5-9-0 88 MichaelHills 5 96?
(M H Tompkins) *led at stdy pce: hdd & wknd over 2f out* 12/1

2m 5.21s (-2.58) **Going Correction** -0.175s/f (Stan)
WFA 3 from 4yo+ 4lb 14 Ran SP% 119.9
Speed ratings (Par 111):103,102,101,101,101 101,100,100,99,99 97,97,97,97
CSF £94.85 TOTE £12.50: £4.40, £3.10, £1.80; EX 62.90 Trifecta £199.40 Pool: £983.20 - 3.50 winning units..
Owner Peter S Jensen **Bred** Tim Foreman **Trained** Mollington, Oxon

FOCUS
A good Listed contest with several performers who will be back for more valuable prizes this winter. The winning time was moderate for an event of this grade, however, which makes the form slightly questionable despite the principals being close to their marks.

NOTEBOOK
Kew Green(USA) bounced back to form on a surface that suited him well last winter. Though nearly eight years old now, this was probably his best performance to date. (op 10-1)
Boule D'Or(IRE) ran much better than he had done on his only previous attempt on this surface. He is a smart performer at his best, and can hold his own in decent races around here this winter.
Compton Bolter(IRE) is a standing dish around here in races like this. On this evidence, there is plenty of life left in him yet but, now rising nine, he is becoming more vulnerable than in the past. (op 4-1)
Zayn Zen has been on a steady upward curve, and ran really well against the colts. She gets this trip well and will be one to consider in similar company. (tchd 6-1)
Kandidate was more at home here after having some tough assigments on turf during the summer. Yet again, he showed that he is happy on dirt or sand surfaces. (op 12-1)
Simple Exchange(IRE), who should improve for the run, was not ideally drawn and, stuck out wide, sat a long way off the pace. He gave the impression that he will do better if returning here later in the winter. (op 8-1)
Helm Bank ran reasonably, but has yet to fully fire on the All-Weather. (op 14-1)
Lord Mayor was stuck wide from a poor draw, and can do a bit better than this. He has already proved that this surface suits him, having won his maiden here as a juvenile. (op 14-1)
Colisay, making his All-Weather debut, was not beaten far but needs to do a bit better to make an impact at this level. (tchd 8-1)

6379 BETDIRECT ON CHANNEL 4 TEXT PAGE 613 H'CAP 7f (P)
3:45 (3:46) (Class 2) (0-100,109) 3-Y-O+
£11,759 (£3,521; £1,760; £881; £439; £220) Stalls Low

Form RPR
3602 1 **Red Spell (IRE)**[23] 6125 4-8-7 89 DarryllHolland 12 101
(R Hannon) *hld up in midfield: gng easily over 2f out: prog to chse ldr over 1f out: r.o to ld last 100yds* 8/1
2004 2 1 1/4 **King's Caprice**[23] 6125 4-8-4 86 (t) StephenCarson 8 95
(J A Geake) *sn chsd ldr: led over 2f out and kicked on: worn down last 100yds* 8/1
2000 3 2 1/2 **Lygeton Lad**[127] 3508 7-8-13 95 (t) MickyFenton 4 97
(Miss Gay Kelleway) *b: b.hind: hld up wl in rr: prog and swtchd rt wl over 1f out: hanging but styd on to take 3rd wl ins fnl f* 12/1
0600 4 hd **Psychiatrist**[23] 6125 4-8-9 91 JimmyFortune 3 92
(R Hannon) *b: t.k.h: hld up: n.m.r on inner 5f out: prog 2f out: styd on fnl f: nvr able to chal* 16/1
6000 5 1 **Party Boss**[43] 5717 3-9-5 109 WilliamCarson(7) 6 108
(C E Brittain) *in tch: prog on inner to chse ldrs 3f out: rdn whn hit rail over 1f out: kpt on* 10/1
4603 6 hd **Marshman (IRE)**[23] 6125 6-8-4 86 NickyMackay 7 84+
(M H Tompkins) *hld up wl in rr: prog wl over 1f out: nt clr run briefly sn after: r.o ins fnl f: no ch* 7/1[2]
6202 7 1/2 **Russian Symphony (USA)**[20] 6180 4-8-8 90 (b) SteveDrowne 10 87
(C R Egerton) *trckd ldrs: effrt 2f out: disp 2nd over 1f out: wknd ins fnl f: eased nr fin* 9/4[1]
020- 8 1/2 **Leoballero**[400] 6193 5-8-4 86 (t) ChrisCatlin 1 82
(D J Daly) *dwlt: hld up in last and wl off the pce: styd on fr over 1f out: no ch* 25/1
-000 9 1 1/4 **Claret And Amber**[21] 6147 3-8-3 86 oh1 MartinDwyer 9 79
(R A Fahey) *b: a wl in rr: rdn and struggling fr 1/2-way* 16/1

0102 **10** 3 1/2 **Red Romeo**[7] 6322 4-8-4 86 oh2.. DaleGibson 2 69
(G A Swinbank) *chsd ldrs: rdn 3f out: stl wl in tch 2f out: wknd over 1f out* **15/2**[3]

0030 **11** 3 1/2 **Acomb**[40] 5806 5-7-13 86 oh8.. RoryMoore(5) 5 60
(N Wilson) *free to post: led at fast pce: hdd & wknd over 2f out* **33/1**

0000 **12** 3/4 **Chateau Nicol**[14] 6248 6-8-4 86 oh1..........................(b) JimmyQuinn 11 58
(B G Powell) *lw: hld up towards rr: effrt over 2f out: rdn and wknd over 1f out: eased fnl f* **16/1**

1m 22.19s (-3.70) **Going Correction** -0.175s/f (Stan) course record
WFA 3 from 4yo+ 1lb **12** Ran SP% **118.5**
Speed ratings (Par 109):114,112,109,109,108 108,107,106,105,101 97,96
CSF £70.61 CT £782.61 TOTE £9.40: £2.80, £2.40, £4.40; EX 84.10 Place 6 £59.13, Place 5 £16.78.
Owner Mrs John Lee **Bred** Tom Darcy And Vincent McCarthy **Trained** East Everleigh, Wilts

FOCUS
A fair handicap and a decent race for the track and a smart winning time. The time was good and the form looks solid.

NOTEBOOK
Red Spell(IRE) is very much at home on this surface, and did particularly well to overcome an outside draw. He quickened well, and is one to follow until beaten. (op 15-2)
King's Caprice has now run well in two consecutive races over this course and distance. The winner looks progressive, so this was a good effort, and he can win a similar contest.
Lygeton Lad made a fine reappearance after four months off. With this sharpener behind him, he will again be one to consider around here this winter. (op 10-1 tchd 14-1)
Psychiatrist is high in the weights at present, but this represented a return to form after a spell in the doldrums. On this evidence, he might be even more effective over a mile.
Party Boss is more effective on sand than turf, but he could do with a bit of help from the Handicapper after a good spell round here last winter. (op 12-1)
Marshman(IRE), winner of this race three years ago, put in some good late work. Timing is the essence with him. (tchd 13-2)
Russian Symphony(USA) is equally effective at this trip and a furlong shorter, so it was disappointing to see him fading quickly in the final furlong after being handy throughout. In his defence, he did not have a great draw. Official explanation: vet said gelding returned slightly lame in front (op 11-4)
Leoballero did quite well considering a 400 day absence and the tardy start. His only win was over this course and distance, so there could be more to come around here.
T/Plt: £83.50 to a £1 stake. Pool: £40,172.50. 350.85 winning tickets. T/Qpdt: £7.80 to a £1 stake. Pool: £3,649.50. 342.50 winning tickets. JN

6365 SOUTHWELL (L-H)

Saturday, November 19

OFFICIAL GOING: Standard to slow

The course was riding on the slow side after deep harrowing overnight due to frost, and the use of 16 tons of salt on Friday.
Wind: Nil

6380 IN RUNNING BETTING ON SKYTEXT 293 BANDED STKS 5f (F)
11:00 (11:02) (Class 7) 3-Y-0+ **£1,429** (£422; £211) **Stalls** High

Form RPR

0240 **1** **Ardkeel Lass (IRE)**[28] 6035 4-8-4 40.......................... JBrennan(7) 2 51
(P D Evans) *mde all: rdn and edgd rt ins last: kpt on* **5/1**[2]

0050 **2** 2 1/2 **Off Hire**[44] 5702 9-8-11 35..........................(v) RobbieFitzpatrick 5 43
(C Smith) *chsd wnr: rdn wl over 1f out: kpt on same pce* **12/1**

6606 **3** shd **Hello Roberto**[14] 6256 4-8-11 40..........................(v[1]) KimTinkler 11 42
(R A Harris) *chsd ldrs: rdn along wl over 1f out: kpt on same pce* **7/2**[1]

5000 **4** 1 3/4 **Forzenuff**[11] 6291 4-8-11 40..........................(b) FergalLynch 9 36
(J R Boyle) *midfield: hdwy over 1f out: sn rdn and kpt on ins last: nrst fin* **6/1**[3]

5 2 **Chiltai (IRE)**[24] 6113 4-8-11 40.......................... GrahamGibbons 3 29
(Mervyn Torrens, Ire) *chsd ldrs: rdn 2f out: drvn and one pce appr last* **7/1**

2000 **6** 1 1/4 **Mad Marty Wildcard**[40] 5804 3-8-11 35..........................(t) TomEaves 6 25
(R Brotherton) *s.i.s: swtchd lft and hdwy to chse ldrs after 1f: rdn 2f out and sn one pce* **25/1**

0066 **7** shd **Avit (IRE)**[35] 5898 5-8-11 40..........................(e[1]) JoeFanning 12 25
(P L Gilligan) *midfield: rdn along and outpcd 1/2-way: styd on ins last* **8/1**

0300 **8** nk **Mr Spliffy (IRE)**[7] 6326 6-8-11 40..........................(b) BrianReilly 13 24
(M C Chapman) *bhd tl styd on fnl 2f: nvr a factor* **14/1**

0050 **9** 2 **Jakeal (IRE)**[11] 6291 6-8-4 35..........................(v) MichaelJStainton(7) 14 17
(R M Whitaker) *a rr* **16/1**

3660 **10** nk **Safranine (IRE)**[14] 6256 8-8-7 40 ow3.......................... AnnStokell(7) 7 19
(Miss A Stokell) *chsd ldrs: rdn 1/2-way: sn wknd* **20/1**

4000 **11** 2 **Levelled**[37] 5854 11-8-11 40.......................... PhillipMakin 1 9
(D W Chapman) *trckd ldrs: rdn 2f out: sn wknd and eased* **16/1**

0000 **12** hd **Balthasar**[28] 6031 3-8-11 40..........................(b[1]) VinceSlattery 4 9
(K G Wingrove) *a bhd* **50/1**

-600 **13** nk **Run On**[56] 5450 7-8-8 35.......................... DNolan(3) 10 7
(D G Bridgwater) *bhd fr 1/2-way* **20/1**

00/0 **14** 4 **Nifty Major**[35] 5898 8-8-6 35.......................... RobynBrisland(5) 8 —
(N E Berry) *a bhd* **66/1**

62.66 secs (2.36) **Going Correction** +0.40s/f (Slow) **14** Ran SP% **119.7**
Speed ratings (Par 97):97,93,92,90,86 84,84,84,81,80 77,77,76,70
CSF £59.31 TOTE £9.50: £3.40, £4.70, £1.10; EX 86.10.
Owner Merthyr Motor Auctions **Bred** J Campbell **Trained** Pandy, Abergavenny
■ John Brennan's first winning ride.

FOCUS
Only Ardkeel Lass looked like winning at any stage, and nothing came from off the pace. The first two are rated close to this season's best form, but the ordinary time tempers enthusiasm.

6381 BETDIRECT FOOTBALL ON ITV TEXT P367 BANDED STKS 1m 4f (F)
11:30 (11:30) (Class 7) 3-Y-0+ **£1,457** (£430; £215) **Stalls** Low

Form RPR

4561 **1** **Royal Axminster**[37] 5855 10-8-12 50.......................... AmyBaker(7) 8 56
(Mrs P N Dutfield) *hld up in midfield: stdy hdwy over 4f out: led 2f out: styd on* **13/2**[3]

0351 **2** 1 1/2 **Zoripp (IRE)**[7] 6331 3-8-10 50 ow2..........................(b) StephenDonohoe(5) 10 56
(J G Given) *midfield: hdwy to trck ldrs over 5f out: chal 3f out: sn rdn and ev ch tl drvn and one pce appr last* **11/4**[1]

5000 **3** 12 **Surdoue**[11] 6289 5-9-2 47.......................... J-PGuillambert 7 33
(P Howling) *a.p: led 1/2-way: rdn along 3f out: hdd and drvn 2f out: grad wknd* **10/1**

0005 **4** 1 3/4 **East Cape**[37] 5855 8-9-0 35.......................... KimTinkler 2 28
(N Tinkler) *s.i.s and bhd tl styd on fnl 3f: nvr a factor* **28/1**

0645 **5** 10 **Jadeeron**[12] 6280 6-9-4 49..........................(v) DarrenWilliams 4 17
(Miss D A McHale) *chsd ldrs: rdn along 4f out: sn outpcd* **9/1**

4020 **6** 3 1/2 **Star Welcome**[7] 6323 4-9-4 49.......................... FergalLynch 3 12
(W J Musson) *trckd ldrs: rdn along 3f out: sn wknd* **7/2**[2]

0330 **7** 1 1/2 **Zandeed (IRE)**[14] 6259 7-9-0 45..........................(p) TomEaves 13 6
(A C Whillans) *towards rr: hdwy on outer over 5f out: sn rdn along and nvr nr ldrs* **20/1**

1000 **8** 16 **Muqarrar (IRE)**[21] 6152 6-9-2 50..........................(vt) PaulMulrennan(3) 14 —
(T J Fitzgerald) *chsd ldrs: rdn along over 4f out: sn wknd* **25/1**

466 **9** 1 3/4 **College Rebel**[14] 6258 4-9-0 40.......................... PhillipMakin 11 —
(J F Coupland) *in tch: pushed along 1/2-way: wknd over 4f out* **50/1**

-005 **10** 15 **Paradise Valley**[14] 6267 5-9-2 50..........................(t) BenSwarbrick(3) 6 —
(Stef Liddiard) *sn pushed along in rr: a bhd* **13/2**[3]

000- **11** 2 1/2 **Venetian Romance (IRE)**[399] 6231 4-9-0 35.......................... JoeFanning 5 —
(D J S Ffrench Davis) *chsd ldrs: rdn along over 5f out and sn wknd* **16/1**

0-00 **12** 1 1/4 **Southburgh (IRE)**[236] 770 4-8-9 35..........................(p) MarcHalford(5) 9 —
(Mrs C A Dunnett) *led to 1/2-way: sn wknd* **50/1**

0054 **13** 13 **Tip Toes (IRE)**[15] 6241 3-8-1 45.......................... KirstyMilczarek(7) 1 —
(Mrs C A Dunnett) *in tch: rdn along over 5f out and sn wknd* **40/1**

000/ **14** 30 **Lady Sunrize**[809] 4635 6-8-7 35..........................(t) JBrennan(7) 12 —
(P D Evans) *a rr: bhd fr 1/2-way* **66/1**

2m 47.35s (5.26) **Going Correction** +0.275s/f (Slow)
WFA 3 from 4yo+ 6lb **14** Ran SP% **120.4**
Speed ratings (Par 97):93,92,84,82,76 73,72,62,61,51 49,48,39,19
CSF £23.14 TOTE £9.20: £2.30, £1.70, £5.40; EX 19.20.
Owner Axminster Carpets Ltd **Bred** Meon Valley Stud **Trained** Axmouth, Devon

FOCUS
The horses were strung out like three-mile chasers down the straight, so the form is not likely to be reliable. The front two, however, look capable of holding their form, with the runner-up the best guide to the level.
Star Welcome Official explanation: jockey said filly never travelled
Tip Toes(IRE) Official explanation: jockey said filly finished lame

6382 LIVE FOOTBALL CASHBACKS AT BETDIRECT BANDED STKS 1m (F)
12:00 (12:00) (Class 7) 3-Y-0+ **£1,433** (£423; £211) **Stalls** Low

Form RPR

0001 **1** **Legal Lover (IRE)**[11] 6293 3-8-11 47.......................... GrahamGibbons 6 59
(R Hollinshead) *cl up: led wl over 2f out: rdn over 1f out and kpt on wl* **4/1**[2]

2320 **2** 1 1/4 **Sonderborg**[26] 6082 4-8-11 45..........................(p) DaleGibson 8 54
(J Mackie) *in tch: hdwy to chse ldrs 3f out: riudden to chse wnr and ch over 1f out: drvn and one pce ins last* **7/1**

3504 **3** 2 **Kumakawa**[14] 6259 7-8-4 45.......................... LauraReynolds(7) 3 50
(D K Ivory) *hld up: hdwy on inner 3f out: rdn and hung rt over 1f out: sn drvn and no imp* **6/1**[3]

2602 **4** 5 **Finnegans Rainbow**[7] 6331 3-8-9 45.......................... BrianReilly 11 40
(M C Chapman) *in tch: hdwy on outer 3f out: rdn and hung lft wl over 1f out: kpt on ins last: nvr rch ldrs* **15/2**

0060 **5** nk **Bojangles (IRE)**[21] 6152 6-8-11 45.......................... TomEaves 4 39
(R Brotherton) *in tch: rdn along and outpcd 1/2-way: kpt on u.p fnl 2f: nvr a factor* **12/1**

0305 **6** 1 **Inchdura**[14] 6259 7-8-11 45.......................... KimTinkler 9 37
(N Tinkler) *chsd ldrs: rdn along 3f out: sn outpcd* **14/1**

0302 **7** 2 1/2 **Starcross Maid**[11] 6293 3-8-9 45.......................... MichaelTebbutt 1 32
(J F Coupland) *led: rdn along over 3f out: hdd wl over 2f out and sn wknd* **10/1**

0023 **8** 1 3/4 **Star Fern**[39] 5828 4-8-11 45.......................... RobbieFitzpatrick 2 29
(M J Attwater) *s.i.s and sn rdn along: hdwy to chse ldrs after 3f riudden over 2f out and sn wknd* **3/1**[1]

0030 **9** 2 1/2 **Semper Paratus (USA)**[32] 5966 6-8-11 45..........(b) MatthewHenry 7 24
(V Smith) *a rr* **14/1**

0040 **10** dist **Robin Sharp**[14] 6259 7-8-8 40..........................(p) RobertMiles(3) 10 —
(J Akehurst) *in tch on outer: rdn along and wknd 1/2-way: sn bhd and virtually p.u fnl 2f* **40/1**

1m 46.19s (1.59) **Going Correction** +0.275s/f (Slow)
WFA 3 from 4yo+ 2lb **10** Ran SP% **116.1**
Speed ratings (Par 97):103,101,99,94,94 93,90,89,86,—
CSF £32.08 TOTE £5.80: £1.70, £1.90, £1.90; EX 30.50.
Owner Tim Leadbeater **Bred** Ballyhane Stud **Trained** Upper Longdon, Staffs

FOCUS
A fair race for the grade and a good time. The winner is improving and rarely looked in trouble and the form looks solid rated through the placed horses.
Robin Sharp Official explanation: jockey said horse never travelled

6383 BETDIRECT FREEPHONE 0800 211 222 BANDED STKS 1m (F)
12:30 (12:31) (Class 7) 3-Y-0+ **£1,450** (£428; £214) **Stalls** Low

Form RPR

5424 **1** **Tirailleur (IRE)**[14] 6260 5-8-13 40.......................... FergalLynch 5 51
(J R Boyle) *hld up towards rr: hdwy on inenr 3f out: rdn over 1f out: styd on to ld ins last: drvn out* **9/2**[2]

1243 **2** 2 1/2 **Caerphilly Gal**[17] 6231 5-8-13 40.......................... BrianReilly 10 46
(P L Gilligan) *cl up: effrt over 2f out: rdn to ld over 1f out: drvn and hdd ins last: kpt on same pce* **10/3**[1]

0300 **3** 2 **Wodhill Gold**[14] 6257 4-8-13 40..........................(b[1]) DerekMcGaffin 6 42
(D Morris) *hld up: hdwy 3f out: rdn to chse ldrs 2f: drvn and ev ch over 1f out: one pce ins last* **18/1**

0-03 **4** 3/4 **Uno Mente**[14] 6260 6-8-13 40.......................... GrahamGibbons 12 41
(E S McMahon) *towards rr: pushed along and hdwy 3f out: rdn 2f out: kpt on same pce* **7/1**

0304 **5** 1 3/4 **Lizzie Rocket**[11] 6291 5-8-6 40..........................(b) JamesO'Reilly(7) 7 37
(J O'Reilly) *led: rdn along over 2f out: hdd over 1f out and grad wknd* **14/1**

0540 **6** shd **Susiedil (IRE)**[5] 6344 4-8-10 40.......................... SilvestreDeSousa(3) 8 37
(D Nicholls) *in tch: rdn along over 2f out: sn rdn and no imp* **12/1**

0066 **7** 1 1/2 **Firebird Rising (USA)**[7] 6328 4-8-13 35.......................... TomEaves 2 34
(R Brotherton) *s.i.s and bhd tl styd on fnl 2f: nrst fin* **50/1**

0550 **8** shd **Pride Of Kinloch**[17] 6231 5-8-8 40..........................(p) AndrewMullen(5) 14 34
(K A Ryan) *chsd ldrs: rdn 2f out: wknd over 1f out* **11/2**[3]

-046 **9** hd **Just Wiz**[207] 1301 9-8-13 40.......................... MichaelTebbutt 11 33
(J Jay) *bhd: rdn along over 3f out: n.d* **8/1**

00-0 **10** 15 **Jamestown**[37] 5858 8-8-13 40.......................... RobbieFitzpatrick 1 3
(C Smith) *bhd fr 1/2-way* **40/1**

0500 **11** 16 **Heartbeat**[56] 5448 4-8-13 35.......................... LeeEnstone 4 —
(I A Wood) *a bhd* **100/1**

06-0 **12** 1/2 **Ariesanne (IRE)**[21] 6141 4-8-10 40.......................... PatrickMathers(3) 9 —
(A C Whillans) *prom: rdn along 1/2-way: sn wknd* **66/1**

000- **13** *14* **Xeight Express (IRE)**[449] 5097 3-8-11 40........................ JoeFanning 3 —
(A Bailey) *a bhd* **80/1**

14 *1* **Lateforbingo (IRE)**[24] 6113 4-8-13 40........................... PhillipMakin 13 —
(Michael Cunningham, Ire) *prom: rdn along and wknd qckly 1/2-way: sn bhd* **22/1**

1m 47.65s (3.05) **Going Correction** +0.275s/f (Slow)
WFA 3 from 4yo+ 2lb **14** Ran SP% **112.3**
Speed ratings (Par 97):95,92,90,89,88 87,86,86,86,71 55,54,40,39
CSF £17.58 TOTE £5.40: £2.10, £1.70, £3.10; EX 16.30.

Owner All The Rubbish **Bred** Iain And Miss Ciara Burns **Trained** Epsom, Surrey

FOCUS
This was the first race of the day where the winner came off the pace and down the 'wrong' side. The second is the benchmark to the form and along with the runner-up makes the form look sound, although the time was slower than the earlier race over the same distance.

Xeight Express(IRE) Official explanation: jockey said filly never travelled

6384 PEGGY LOCKE 70TH BIRTHDAY BANDED STKS 7f (F)
1:00 (1:00) (Class 7) 3-Y-0+ **£1,457** (£430; £215) **Stalls** Low

Form RPR
5052 **1** **Desert Lover (IRE)**[7] 6330 3-8-11 45................................ PhillipMakin 5 54
(R J Price) *trckd ldrs: hdwy 3f out: led 2f out: rdn over 1f out: kpt on wl* **7/2**[2]

5304 **2** *1* **The Job**[75] 4991 4-8-12 45...(v) JoeFanning 9 52
(A D Smith) *hld up: gd hdwy on outer 3f out: chal over 1f out: sn rdn and ev ch tl drvn and kpt on same pce ins last* **11/2**[3]

0445 **3** *2* **Preskani**[11] 6293 3-8-11 35..(p) AlanDaly 3 46
(Mrs N Macauley) *chsd ldr: rdn along over 2f out and ch tl rdn and kpt on same pce ent last* **25/1**

0004 **4** *nk* **Travelling Times**[44] 5706 6-8-12 45............................(b) DavidMcCabe 4 46
(Julian Poulton) *towards rr: hewadway over 2f out: sn rdn: styd on wl u.p ins last: nrst fin* **14/1**

1406 **5** *3 ½* **Wodhill Be**[14] 6259 5-8-12 45.. MichaelTebbutt 2 36
(D Morris) *s.i.s and bhd: hdwy 1/2-way: swtchd outside and rdn to chse ldrs 2f out: wknd over 1f out* **11/2**[3]

0560 **6** *4* **Polesworth**[11] 6293 3-8-6 45.......................................(b) MarcHalford(5) 6 26
(C N Kellett) *sn led: rdn along and hdd 2f out: sn wknd* **50/1**

0000 **7** *5* **Zanderido**[83] 4776 3-8-11 40...(v) TomEaves 8 13
(B S Rothwell) *sn outpcd and bhd* **50/1**

0021 **8** *nk* **Ace Club**[11] 6291 4-8-12 45.......................................(b) TonyHamilton 10 12
(J Hetherton) *prom:rdn along 1/2-way: sn btn* **3/1**[1]

0000 **9** *1 ¼* **Repeat (IRE)**[37] 5859 5-8-12 45... BrianReilly 7 9
(J W Unett) *a rr* **40/1**

0501 **10** *7* **Princess Arwen**[21] 6154 3-8-11 45............................... RobertHavlin 11 —
(Mrs Barbara Waring) *chsd ldrs: rdn along wl 3f outr and sn wknd* **8/1**

4006 **11** *15* **Free Wheelin (IRE)**[14] 6261 5-8-9 45......................... RobertMiles(3) 12 —
(J Akehurst) *v.s.a and rel to r: a t.o* **10/1**

5600 **12** *5* **Dancing Moonlight (IRE)**[7] 6331 3-8-6 30............. DuranFentiman(5) 1 —
(Mrs N Macauley) *s.i.s: a rr* **100/1**

1m 32.77s (1.97) **Going Correction** +0.275s/f (Slow)
WFA 3 from 4yo+ 1lb **12** Ran SP% **116.1**
Speed ratings (Par 97):99,97,95,95,91 86,80,80,79,71 54,48
CSF £21.82 TOTE £5.60: £3.10, £1.90, £2.70; EX 55.30.

Owner Multi Lines Partnership **Bred** Penfold Bloodstock And Mr D B Clark **Trained** Ullingswick, H'fords

FOCUS
A fair event for the grade with the first two and fourth close to their marks. The winner could turn out to be better than this class.

Ace Club Official explanation: trainer had no explanation for the poor form shown

Princess Arwen Official explanation: vet said filly finished lame

6385 CASHBACKS ON SKY TEXT PAGE 371 BANDED STKS 6f (F)
1:30 (1:30) (Class 7) 3-Y-0+ **£1,429** (£422; £211) **Stalls** Low

Form RPR
5404 **1** **Mind Alert**[7] 6330 4-8-8 45......................................(v) PatrickMathers(3) 1 53
(D Shaw) *prom: gd hdwy on inner 2f out: qcknd to ld ins last: kpt on* **7/1**[3]

0041 **2** *1* **Mambazo**[7] 6330 3-9-2 50..(e) J-PGuillambert 4 55
(S C Williams) *cl up: led 1/2-way: rdn ent last: sn hdd and nt qckn* **10/11**[1]

0400 **3** *1 ½* **Polar Haze**[7] 6330 8-8-11 40...(v) FergalLynch 5 46
(J Pearce) *rr: hdwy over 2f out: sn rdn and kpt on u.p appr last: nrst fin* **6/1**[2]

2-00 **4** *1 ¼* **Mr Uppity**[35] 5897 6-8-11 45..(e) DavidMcCabe 3 42
(Julian Poulton) *led: pushed along and hdd 1/2-way: rdn over 2f out and kpt on same pce* **11/1**

0000 **5** *½* **Morag**[47] 5653 4-8-11 35.. LeeEnstone 9 40
(I A Wood) *dwlt: hdwy to chse ldrs 3f out: rdn 2f out: hld in 4th whn n.m.r over 1f out* **20/1**

6 *9* **Whispering Melody**[94] 4489 4-8-11 45...................... GrahamGibbons 6 13
(Mervyn Torrens, Ire) *chsd ldrs: rdn along 3f out: wknd over 2f out* **9/1**

01-0 **7** *1 ¼* **John O'Groats (IRE)**[54] 5508 7-8-4 45....................... RonanKeogh(7) 7 10
(B Mactaggart) *chsd ldrs: rdn along 3f out: wknd over 2f out* **22/1**

4206 **8** *1 ¾* **Doughty**[163] 2427 3-8-11 45.. VinceSlattery 2 4
(D J Wintle) *chsd ldrs: rdn along 3f out: sn wknd* **10/1**

1m 19.0s (2.10) **Going Correction** +0.275s/f (Slow) **8** Ran SP% **115.7**
Speed ratings (Par 97):97,95,93,92,91 79,77,75
CSF £13.97 TOTE £5.30: £2.30, £1.20, £1.40; EX 19.60 Place 6 £34.27, Place 5 £18.22.

Owner Simon Mapletoft Racing IV **Bred** P T Tellwright **Trained** Danethorpe, Notts

■ Stewards' Enquiry : Fergal Lynch caution: careless riding

Lee Enstone caution: used whip without allowing filly time to respond

FOCUS
An average race for the grade with the first three close to previous form.

T/Plt: £32.40 to a £1 stake. Pool: £22,902.40. 515.45 winning tickets. T/Qpdt: £10.40 to a £1 stake. Pool: £1,840.50. 130.60 winning tickets. JR

6342 WOLVERHAMPTON (A.W) (L-H)
Saturday, November 19

OFFICIAL GOING: Standard (meeting abandoned after race 2 (7.30) due to heavy fog)
Last four races abandoned due to fog.
Wind: Nil Weather: Foggy

6386 STRATSTONE JAGUAR CLAIMING STKS 1m 141y(P)
7:00 (7:10) (Class 6) 2-Y-0 **£2,893** (£854; £427) **Stalls** Low

Form RPR
0500 **1** **Night Groove (IRE)**[8] 6313 2-8-7 58.............................. SamHitchcott 5 63
(C Tinkler) *mde all: rdn out* **6/1**[3]

0001 **2** *3* **Countrywide Belle**[4] 6358 2-8-4 58..........................(b[1]) JimmyQuinn 11 53
(K A Ryan) *chsd wnr: rdn over 2f out: styd on same pce appr fnl f* **4/1**[2]

1000 **3** *nk* **Twentyfirst Dansar**[19] 6198 2-8-7 53................................(v[1]) LPKeniry 2 56
(A D Smith) *chsd ldrs: rdn over 3f out: styd on same pce appr fnl f* **28/1**

4 *3* **Bigalo's Banjo** 2-9-0 .... GrahamGibbons 12 56
(J J Quinn) *s.s: plld hrd and hdwy over 6f out: stdd and sn lost pl: hdwy over 2f out: no imp appr fnl f* **20/1**

6625 **5** *1 ¾* **Aysgarth Flyer (IRE)**[70] 5125 2-8-9 51...........................(p) TomEaves 10 47
(I Semple) *mid-div: hdwy 5f out: styd on same pce fnl 2f* **9/1**

0304 **6** *½* **Crush On You**[11] 6290 2-8-1 48.. PaulQuinn 9 38
(R Hollinshead) *sn outpcd: styd on fnl f: nvr nrr* **20/1**

0206 **7** *hd* **Aboyne (IRE)**[4] 6358 2-8-10 71.. TPQueally 7 47
(M G Quinlan) *hld up: hdwy 5f out: lost pl over 3f out: n.d after* **4/1**[2]

0010 **8** *½* **Danse Du Flambe**[15] 6244 2-8-1 54..........................(b) JamieMackay 4 37
(D J S Ffrench Davis) *prom 6f* **10/1**

0 **9** *1 ¾* **Wings Of Speed**[7] 6332 2-8-2 .... HayleyTurner 3 34
(H Morrison) *prom to 1/2-way* **25/1**

0046 **10** *7* **Scroll**[8] 6313 2-9-0 70...(v) FergalLynch 8 30
(P Howling) *hld up: hdwy 5f out: rdn over 2f out: wknd and eased over 1f out* **5/2**[1]

0 **11** *17* **Amber Spirit**[40] 5805 2-7-9 .... DuranFentiman(5) 6 —
(Peter Grayson) *s.i.s: sn prom: lost pl 7f out: sn bhd* **50/1**

0 **12** *2* **Ardkeel Boy (IRE)**[4] 6358 2-8-6 .... FrancisFerris 13 —
(B Palling) *s.i.s: sn chsng ldrs: wknd 3f out* **66/1**

1m 51.35s (-0.41) **Going Correction** -0.075s/f (Stan) **12** Ran SP% **122.2**
Speed ratings (Par 94):98,95,95,92,90 90,90,89,88,82 66,65
CSF £28.80 TOTE £6.80: £2.20, £1.60, £5.30; EX 87.30.The winner was claimed by Nick Littmoden for £8,000.

Owner George Ward **Bred** Illuminatus Investments **Trained** Compton, Berks

FOCUS
A routine claimer run in a modest time with the principals close up throughout. The form is best rated through the runner-up and appears sound enough.

NOTEBOOK
Night Groove(IRE) had met some trouble in running at the track a week ago, but was prominent throughout on this occasion and won with a fair bit in hand. He was claimed by a stable that traditionally does well with his type and appears a likely type for handicaps. (op 10-1 tchd 11-1)
Countrywide Belle, blinkered first time, is versatile as both All-Weather surfaces come alike to her. This was her first attempt at the trip and she seemed to see it out okay, but it was a weak race. (op 3-1)
Twentyfirst Dansar was another sporting headgear for the first time and the visor may have induced a small amount of improvement. A winner over the minimum trip at Bath in the summer, this was his first attempt at the trip and he appeared to stay well enough. (op 25-1 tchd 33-1)
Bigalo's Banjo shaped well enough on debut and should improve for the experience. He was slowly away and keen early on prior to making ground on the home turn. Although his effort petered out in the straight, he displayed some promise in the run and could be better than the bare form. (op 25-1 tchd 16-1)
Aysgarth Flyer(IRE) is already exposed as modest and even found this company to hot. He may need to drop another grade to become competitive. (op 8-1)
Aboyne(IRE) was rated to win this but was never competitive once he lost his place three out. His better performances have come over shorter, however he is clearly not capable of winning off his current mark. (op 9-2 tchd 5-1)

6387 TEXT "BETDIRECT" TO 88600 (S) STKS 1m 141y(P)
7:30 (7:39) (Class 6) 3-5-Y-0 **£2,634** (£777; £389) **Stalls** Low

Form RPR
0135 **1** **La Viola**[46] 5689 3-8-9 59...(b[1]) PatCosgrave 7 61+
(K R Burke) *a.p: led 2f out: rdn clr 1f out: all out* **4/1**[2]

0 **2** *hd* **Greenbelt**[4] 6361 4-8-10 86... TonyCulhane 9 56
(D W Chapman) *hld up in tch: led over 2f out: sn hdd: r.o u.p ins fnl f* **8/1**

5000 **3** *1* **Musical Gift**[4] 6361 5-8-10 51..(v) HayleyTurner 8 53
(P A Blockley) *hld up: hdwy 1/2-way: ev ch 2f out: styd on* **5/1**[3]

0000 **4** *3 ½* **Look At The Stars (IRE)**[30] 3752 3-8-7 57............... GrahamGibbons 1 46
(R Hollinshead) *w ldr to 1/2-way: rdn and nt clr run over 2f out: styd on same pce appr fnl f* **11/1**

4360 **5** *1* **White Star Magic**[173] 2124 3-8-7 45..................................(bt) LPKeniry 3 44
(K G Wingrove) *hld up: nt clr run wl over 2f out: sn swtchd rt: styd on fnl f: nvr nrr* **40/1**

6016 **6** *½* **Dane's Rock (IRE)**[5] 6346 3-9-0 48..............................(p) GeorgeBaker 5 50
(M S Saunders) *chsd ldrs: rdn over 2f out: wknd over 1f out* **11/1**

0010 **7** *7* **Owed**[14] 6264 3-9-0 58..(t) J-PGuillambert 6 35
(P A Blockley) *chsd ldrs: led over 5f out: hdd over 2f out: wknd over 1f out* **9/1**

0204 **8** *2 ½* **Raul Sahara**[49] 5629 3-8-7 52.. MartinDwyer 4 23
(J W Unett) *chsd ldrs: rdn over 2f out: sn wknd* **3/1**[1]

0030 **9** *3* **Diatonic**[3] 5826 3-8-7 45..(v) FrancisFerris 10 17
(D Carroll) *sn outpcd* **25/1**

2000 **10** *19* **Princess Karla (IRE)**[169] 2273 3-8-2 49............................. ChrisCatlin 2 —
(J W Unett) *led: hdd over 5f out: wknd 1/2-way* **33/1**

0010 **11** *3* **Mytton's Bell (IRE)**[15] 6243 3-8-9 53.............................(p) DavidAllan 13 —
(A Bailey) *sn outpcd* **16/1**

00 **12** *21* **Bold Arrow**[202] 1392 3-8-7 .... PaulQuinn 11 —
(B J Llewellyn) *s.i.s: outpcd* **66/1**

1m 51.88s (0.12) **Going Correction** -0.075s/f (Stan)
WFA 3 from 4yo+ 3lb **12** Ran SP% **116.0**
Speed ratings (Par 101):96,95,94,91,90 90,84,82,79,62 59,41
CSF £34.13 TOTE £5.00: £1.80, £3.10, £1.90; EX 22.80.The winner was bought in for 3,250gns. Greenbelt was claimed by George Moore for £6,000. Raul Sahara was claimed by Paul Blockley for £6,000.

Owner A Polignone **Bred** R Howe **Trained** Middleham Moor, N Yorks

FOCUS
A moderate race, but the front three pulled clear and the form looks solid enough for the grade.

Raul Sahara Official explanation: trainer had no explanation for the poor form shown

6388 **RUGBY UNION AT BETDIRECT H'CAP** **1m 4f 50y(P)**
() (Class 6) (0-55,) 3-Y-0+ £

6389 **BETDIRECTPOKER.COM MAIDEN STKS** **1m 141y(P)**
() (Class 5) 2-Y-0 £

6390 **BETDIRECT.CO.UK NURSERY** **7f 32y(P)**
() (Class 4) (0-85,) 2-Y-0 £

6391 **LIVE FOOTBALL CASHBACKS AT BET DIRECT H'CAP** **5f 216y(P)**
() (Class 5) (0-75,) 4-Y-0+ £

T/Plt: £4.00 to a £1 stake. Pool: £43,136.90. 7,745.50 winning tickets. T/Qpdt: Void. CR

MARSEILLE BORELY (L-H)

Saturday, November 19

OFFICIAL GOING: Very soft

6392a **PRIX DELAHANTE (LISTED RACE)** **1m 1f**
1:05 (1:04) 2-Y-0 **£16,667** (£6,667; £5,000; £3,333; £1,667)

RPR
1 **Danzon (USA)**[28] 2-8-8 .... IMendizabal 4 96
(J-C Rouget, France)
2 1 1/2 **Lounaos (FR)**[10] 2-8-8 .... LDeLaRosa 7 93
(Mlle F Forneron, France)
3 1 1/2 **Fabuleux Concept (FR)** 2-8-11 .... TDalBalcon 2 93
(Mme J Laurent-Joye Rossi, France)
4 1 1/2 **Mister Des Aigles (FR)**[31] 2-8-11 ....(b) RMarchelli 5 90
(Mme C Barande-Barbe, France)
5 1 **April San**[23] 2-8-11 .... CEscuder 9 88
(P Khozian, France)
6 1 1/2 **Poquelin (FR)**[23] 2-8-11 .... SPasquier 1 85
(F-X de Chevigny, France)
7 1 1/2 **Dream Day (FR)**[18] 6219 2-8-8 .... J-LCambet 8 79
(Mlle F Forneron, France)
8 5 **Araschan (FR)**[51] 5577 2-8-11 .... WMLordan 3 72
(T Stack, Ire) *mid-division, 6th and niggled half-way, driven approaching straight, unable to quicken* **27/1**[2]
9 8 **Midnight Traveller**[25] 6102 2-8-11 .... TThulliez 6 56
(G C H Chung) *in touch, 5th on outside half-way, soon driven along, 9th and beaten straight* **20/1**[1]
10 10 **Peintre Bere (FR)**[114] 2-8-11 .... FBlondel 10 36
(Mme J Laurent-Joye Rossi, France)

1m 54.49s **10** Ran SP% **8.3**
PARI-MUTUEL (Including 1 Euro stake); WIN 2.00; PL 1.30, 4.70, 1.50;DF 18.80.
Owner N Radwan **Bred** Ecurie Woodcote Stud **Trained** Pau, France

NOTEBOOK
Midnight Traveller, stepping up in class following his second in a Yarmouth maiden, should have had no problem with the testing ground but was probably out of his depth.

6373 LINGFIELD (L-H)

Monday, November 21

OFFICIAL GOING: Standard
Wind: Nil Weather: Fine and crisp

6394 **IN RUNNING TONIGHT ON SKYTEXT 293 APPRENTICE BANDED STKS** **1m 2f (P)**
1:10 (1:11) (Class 7) 3-Y-0+ **£1,429** (£422; £211) **Stalls** Low

Form RPR
5024 **1** **Revolve**[37] 5894 5-8-9 45........(p) JamesDoyle(5) 5 51
(Mrs L J Mongan) *trckd ldr: led narrowly wl over 1f out: hung rt ins fnl f: hld on* **7/2**[1]
-044 **2** nk **Mister Completely (IRE)**[16] 6257 4-8-7 45........ WilliamCarson(7) 13 51
(J R Best) *sn led: rdn and narrowly hdd wl over 1f out: kpt on and upsides ins fnl f: no ex nr fin* **7/1**[3]
5040 **3** 1 **Prince Valentine**[34] 5962 4-8-9 45........(be) JemmaMarshall(5) 6 49
(G L Moore) *t.k.h: hld up in tch: prog to chse ldng pair over 1f out: cl enough ins fnl f: nt qckn* **10/1**
0242 **4** 3/4 **Tojoneski**[44] 5740 6-9-0 40........ DuranFentiman 3 48+
(I W McInnes) *hld up: last over 4f out: prog 3f out but only 9th 2f out: rdn and r.o wl fr over 1f out: hopeless task* **5/1**[2]
4620 **5** 1 1/2 **Louve Heureuse (IRE)**[7] 6347 4-8-9 45........ JamesMillman(5) 11 45
(B R Millman) *chsd ldng pair: bmpd along and fdd over 1f out* **5/1**[2]
004P **6** hd **Oktis Morilious (IRE)**[39] 5855 4-8-11 40........ SladeO'Hara(3) 8 44
(A W Carroll) *hld up towards rr: prog to chse ldrs 2f out: no imp over 1f out* **14/1**
5600 **7** 3/4 **Isabella Rossini**[30] 6033 3-8-5 40........ ThomasO'Brien(5) 7 43
(A M Hales) *hld up towards rr: prog to chse ldrs 2f out: one pce and no imp over 1f out* **20/1**
0300 **8** 2 1/2 **Gran Clicquot**[61] 5400 10-8-9 40........ JosephWalsh(5) 2 38
(G P Enright) *dwlt: t.k.h: hld up wl in rr: nt clr run over 2f out: rdn and no real prog over 1f out* **14/1**
1440 **9** 3 **Halcyon Magic**[30] 6034 7-8-9 45........(b) StephanieBancroft(5) 12 32
(M Wigham) *racd wd: hld up: prog to trck ldrs 1/2-way: wknd 2f out* **12/1**
0000 **10** 1 3/4 **Somewhere My Love**[8] 6033 4-8-9 40........(p) LiamJones(5) 1 29
(P Butler) *settled midfield: wknd over 2f out* **40/1**
5630 **11** 1/2 **Lyric Dances (FR)**[79] 4935 3-8-10 45........ StephenDonohoe 9 28
(M Blanshard) *chsd ldrs: rdn over 3f out: wknd over 2f out* **16/1**
4350 **12** 11 **Shamwari Fire (IRE)**[13] 6033 5-9-0 40........ RoryMoore 4 7
(I W McInnes) *chsd ldrs: rdn wl over 3f out: wknd rapidly over 2f out* **12/1**
5000 **13** nk **E Bride (USA)**[16] 6257 3-8-6 40 ow1........ RonanKeogh(5) 10 8
(T T Clement) *nvr beyond midfield: u.p over 4f out: sn wknd* **66/1**
0000 **14** 7 **Falcon Goer (USA)**[182] 1956 3-8-8 45 ow1........ TravisBlock(3) 14 —
(Miss B Sanders) *hld up in last trio: rdn over 4f out: sn wknd* **25/1**

2m 6.61s (-1.18) **Going Correction** -0.225s/f (Stan)
WFA 3 from 4yo+ 4lb **14** Ran SP% **124.3**
Speed ratings (Par 97):95,94,93,93,92 92,91,89,87,85 85,76,76,70
CSF £27.56 TOTE £4.70: £1.40, £2.80, £5.90; EX 32.30.
Owner Mrs P J Sheen **Bred** Wickfield Farm Partnership **Trained** Epsom, Surrey
■ Laura Mongan's first winner on the Flat.

FOCUS
A steadily-run affair and typically modest form with the third setting the standard.
E Bride(USA) Official explanation: jockey said filly lost her action

6395 **SUE HARGREAVES MEMORIAL MEDIAN AUCTION MAIDEN STKS** **7f (P)**
1:40 (1:44) (Class 7) 2-Y-0 **£1,426** (£421; £210) **Stalls** Low

Form RPR
1 **Fun Time** 2-8-9 .... SamHitchcott 11 61
(M R Channon) *chsd ldrs: effrt and rn green over 2f out: prog over 1f out: rdn and styd on to ld last strides* **16/1**
5 **2** nk **Opal Warrior**[121] 3723 2-8-9 .... JohnEgan 7 60
(P W D'Arcy) *prom: chsd ldr over 2f out: urged along to ld 1f out: hanging and nt look keen: hdd last strides* **10/1**
05 **3** 1 1/4 **Farne Island**[33] 5984 2-9-0 .... NickyMackay 10 62
(L M Cumani) *prom: rdn to chal on inner over 1f out: one pce fnl f* **7/2**[2]
0026 **4** hd **Divine White**[16] 6249 2-8-9 62........ OscarUrbina 1 57
(Mrs A J Perrett) *led: rdn 2f out: hdd and nt qckn 1f out* **1/1**[1]
6005 **5** 1/2 **Blu Manruna**[11] 6304 2-9-0 63........(b) JamieMackay 6 60
(J Akehurst) *plld hrd: hld up bhd ldrs: rdn and nt qckn 2f out: r.o again ins fnl f* **4/1**[3]
0500 **6** 5 **Prince Algarhoud**[6] 6353 2-9-0 35........(b) GeorgeBaker 5 48
(G L Moore) *chsd ldr to over 2f out: wknd over 1f out* **33/1**
60 **7** hd **Bekoning (IRE)**[17] 6242 2-8-7 .... ChrisCavanagh(7) 9 47
(M Quinn) *off the pce in midfield: pushed along fr 1/2-way: no prog* **50/1**
8 1 **Nettlebed** 2-8-9 .... SteveDrowne 2 40
(G L Moore) *s.i.s: settled in rr and wl off the pce: nudged along over 2f out: nvr nr ldrs* **20/1**
9 2 1/2 **Lady Evi** 2-8-9 .... DaneO'Neill 3 34
(D K Ivory) *a wl off the pce in rr: shkn up and no real prog over 2f out* **50/1**
000 **10** 1/2 **Count The Trees**[39] 5857 2-8-2 35........ LiamJones(7) 4 32+
(W G M Turner) *prom: n.m.r and snatched up 5f out: wknd over 2f out* **50/1**
0 **11** 2 1/2 **Marinero**[70] 5184 2-9-0 .... PaulDoe 13 31
(Lady Herries) *s.s and threw hd in air: reminders over 4f out: sme prog 3f out: sn wknd* **16/1**
12 5 **Mr Bilbo Baggins** 2-9-0 .... MartinDwyer 14 19
(J S Moore) *a wl bhd* **25/1**
13 hd **Master Malarkey** 2-8-7 .... KirstyMilczarek(7) 8 18
(Mrs C A Dunnett) *a wl bhd* **40/1**

1m 25.47s (-0.42) **Going Correction** -0.225s/f (Stan) **13** Ran SP% **132.9**
Speed ratings (Par 90):93,92,91,91,90 84,84,83,80,79 77,71,71
CSF £174.43 TOTE £31.70: £7.90, £2.70, £1.10; EX 156.80.
Owner Billy Parish **Bred** Mike Channon Bloodstock Ltd **Trained** West Ilsley, Berks

FOCUS
The first five finished clear in this ordinary maiden but the form looks moderate and is rated near selling class.

NOTEBOOK
Fun Time, is out of a winning sprinter for the Channon yard, including on Polytrack, who was a half-sister to smart sprinter Acclamation. She showed signs of inexperience and was still only fifth passing the furlong pole, but then came with a sustained run to lead close home. She should have improvement in her over a mile. (op 14-1 tchd 20-1)
Opal Warrior, stepped up to seven for this second run, edged ahead with a furlong to run but did not help her rider once in front and was worried out of it. (op 11-1 tchd 12-1)
Farne Island stayed on the inside rail in the straight and failed to find a quickening touch in the final furlong. Now eligible for handicaps, he should improve over a mile plus. (op 9-2)
Divine White, proven on this track, forced the pace but could not counter when tackled with a furlong to run. (op 5-4 tchd 11-8 in a place)
Blu Manruna, the most experienced in the line-up, could not take advantage of a decent opportunity. He has ability but is a tricky ride. (tchd 9-2)
Nettlebed is a half-sister to mile winner and listed-placed Allergy and ten-furlong handicapper Night Spot. She could not go the early pace, but picked up in the latter stages as she found her feet. Modest improvement can be expected. (op 18-1)

6396 **FIRST PAST THE POST AT BETDIRECT TRI-BANDED STKS** **6f (P)**
2:10 (2:12) (Class 7) 3-Y-0 **£1,412** (£417; £208) **Stalls** Low

Form RPR
0 **1** **Segoria (IRE)**[16] 6261 3-8-12 45........ DaneO'Neill 10 53+
(A M Hales) *hld up midfield: trckd ldrs 2f out: swtchd rt over 1f out: led ins fnl f: edgd rt: hld on* **13/2**[3]
0405 **2** shd **Beverley Beau**[30] 6035 3-8-5 45........ KristinStubbs(7) 11 53
(Mrs L Stubbs) *hld up off the pce: smooth prog over 1f out: jnd wnr ins fnl f: bmpd along and nt qckn nr fin* **9/1**
0000 **3** 2 **Christian Bendix**[9] 6330 3-8-12 45........ SteveDrowne 9 47
(P Howling) *settled midfield: rdn and effrt on outer over 2f out: styd on to take 3rd ins fnl f* **15/2**
0605 **4** 1 **Angel River**[16] 6260 3-8-7 40........(e[1]) MartinDwyer 12 39
(J Ryan) *outpcd in last pair and sn detached: prog u.p on outer over 1f out: r.o fnl f* **5/1**[2]
0044 **5** 1 3/4 **Lady Hopeful (IRE)**[13] 6288 3-8-7 45........(b) DuranFentiman(5) 6 39
(Peter Grayson) *disp ld at fast pce to 1f out: wknd* **14/1**
0005 **6** 1/2 **Tipsy Lillie**[41] 5825 3-8-12 45........(b) DavidMcCabe 1 37+
(Julian Poulton) *mde most at fast pce tl hdd & wknd ins fnl f* **9/1**
2060 **7** 1 **Rock Fever (IRE)**[13] 6288 3-8-7 40........(b) PaulDoe 8 34+
(Peter Grayson) *dwlt: outpcd in last pair and detached: prog on inner 2f out: styng on whn r.o of room jst ins fnl f: nt rcvr* **14/1**
000 **8** 1 **Tennessee Belle (IRE)**[42] 5804 3-8-12 45........(e[1]) OscarUrbina 4 31
(C N Allen) *chsd ldrs: rdn and in tch over 2f out: wknd fnl f* **14/1**
6353 **9** nk **Canary Dancer**[13] 6293 3-8-2 40........(p) RoryMoore(5) 5 25+
(B A Pearce) *disp ld at fast pce to 2f out: wknd over 1f out* **7/2**[1]
0000 **10** shd **Question Mark**[37] 5899 3-8-12 45........ JohnEgan 2 30+
(Andrew Reid) *disp ld at fast pce to 1f out: wknd rapidly* **14/1**
2050 **11** 5 **Saucepot**[9] 6330 3-8-7 40........ PaulFitzsimons 7 10
(Miss J R Tooth) *chsd ldrs to 1/2-way: wknd u.p* **12/1**

1m 12.56s (-0.25) **Going Correction** -0.225s/f (Stan) **11** Ran SP% **118.3**
Speed ratings (Par 96):92,91,89,87,85 84,83,82,81,81 75
CSF £64.28 TOTE £8.70: £3.20, £2.00, £3.90; EX 92.50.
Owner A M Hales **Bred** Tom Darcy And Vincent McCarthy **Trained** Quainton, Bucks

FOCUS
This was run at a fast early pace which set this up for those coming from behind. The overall time was ordinary but the form looks reasonable with the placed horses close to their marks.
Rock Fever(IRE) Official explanation: jockey said filly was denied a clear run
Canary Dancer Official explanation: jockey said filly lost her action

The Form Book, Raceform Ltd, Compton, RG20 6NL

6397 CASHBACKS ON SKY TEXT PAGE 371 BANDED STKS 5f (P)
2:40 (2:41) (Class 7) 3-Y-O+ **£1,416** (£418; £209) **Stalls High**

Form RPR

0303 **1** **Zazous**[28] 6069 4-9-0 48 SteveDrowne 9 54
(J J Bridger) *sn pushed along in rr: effrt on outer over 1f out: drvn and r.o to ld last stride* **8/1**

4024 **2** *shd* **Desert Light (IRE)**[9] 6326 4-9-2 50 (v) FrankieMcDonald 6 56
(D Shaw) *pressed ldr: drvn to ld jst ins fnl f: kpt on: hdd last stride* **11/4**[1]

0000 **3** *½* **Stephanie's Mind**[67] 5256 3-9-2 50 MartinDwyer 7 54
(M Quinn) *chsd ldrs: effrt over 1f out: ch ins fnl f: styd on* **12/1**

0046 **4** *nk* **Auentraum (GER)**[7] 6345 5-8-9 50 JamesDoyle(7) 4 53
(K McAuliffe) *trckd ldng pair: rdn to chal and upsides over 1f out: nt qckn ins fnl f* **5/1**[2]

0304 **5** *½* **Taipan Tommy (IRE)**[7] 6345 3-9-2 50 (v) PaulDoe 2 51
(S Dow) *chsd ldrs: rdn 2f out: kpt on fnl f: nvr able to chal* **12/1**

0006 **6** *nk* **Strathclyde (IRE)**[44] 5736 6-8-11 45 JamieMackay 10 45
(A M Hales) *racd wd: hld up in last pair: pushed along and wd bnd 2f out: r.o ins fnl f: gaining at fin* **12/1**

0500 **7** *shd* **Pulse**[9] 6326 7-8-12 46 (p) PaulFitzsimons 1 45
(Miss J R Tooth) *chsd ldrs: rdn over 1f out: kpt on same pce* **11/2**[3]

0620 **8** *½* **Leah's Pride**[7] 6345 4-8-12 46 JohnEgan 5 43
(P Howling) *mde most on inner: hdd and fdd jst ins fnl f* **6/1**

4004 **9** *½* **Petana**[28] 6076 5-8-6 45 (p) DuranFentiman(5) 8 40
(Peter Grayson) *a towards rr: rdn over 2f out: kpt on same pce: no imp* **20/1**

60-0 **10** *½* **Princess Kai (IRE)**[28] 6070 4-9-2 50 (b) DaneO'Neill 3 46+
(R Ingram) *s.v.s: last pair tl sme prog on inner 2f out: styng on but no ch whn nt clr run last 100yds* **25/1**

58.80 secs (-0.98) **Going Correction** -0.225s/f (Stan) 10 Ran SP% **115.8**
Speed ratings (Par 97):98,97,97,96,95 95,95,94,93,92
CSF £30.04 TOTE £7.40: £1.90, £1.50, £3.70; EX 26.50.
Owner J J Bridger **Bred** Lordship Stud **Trained** Liphook, Hants

FOCUS
A typically tight banded sprint in which a couple did not see much daylight and the whole field were separated by a little over three lengths at the line. The form looks reasonably solid with the first four close to their marks.
Princess Kai(IRE) Official explanation: jockey said filly missed the break

6398 BETDIRECT.CO.UK BANDED STKS 1m (P)
3:10 (3:13) (Class 7) 3-Y-O+ **£1,453** (£429; £214) **Stalls High**

Form RPR

000- **1** **Homebred Star**[323] 4478 4-8-7 45 RobynBrisland(5) 2 51
(G P Enright) *dwlt: t.k.h: hld up: last over 2f out: prog on wd outside sn after: pushed along and r.o wl to ld last strides* **33/1**

2212 **2** *½* **Young Kate**[16] 6259 4-8-5 45 WilliamCarson(7) 8 50
(J R Best) *trckd ldrs: plld out and effrt over 1f out: rdn to ld last 100yds: hdd fnl strides* **2/1**[1]

0350 **3** *1 ½* **Never Away**[49] 5654 3-8-10 45 (p) JohnEgan 3 47
(N A Callaghan) *chsd ldrs: rdn and effrt 2f out: prog to chal ins fnl f: nt qckn* **12/1**

0053 **4** *shd* **Nebraska City**[37] 5897 4-8-12 45 DaneO'Neill 11 46
(B Gubby) *mde most tl hdd & wknd last 100yds* **9/2**[2]

0000 **5** *1 ¼* **One Last Time**[107] 4172 5-8-12 45 SteveDrowne 12 43
(Miss B Sanders) *t.k.h: hld up and racd wd: prog over 2f out: pressed ldrs ent fnl f: nt qckn* **11/2**[3]

4-00 **6** *shd* **Boogie Magic**[41] 5828 5-8-12 40 RobertHavlin 10 43
(T T Clement) *chsd ldrs: rdn and nt qckn over 2f out: kpt on same pce* **20/1**

0002 **7** *hd* **Wilford Maverick (IRE)**[30] 6032 3-8-3 45 StacyRenwick(7) 4 43
(M J Attwater) *dwlt: plld hrd and hld up wl in rr: effrt over 2f out: n.m.r over 1f out: kpt on: no ch* **6/1**

0000 **8** *1 ¼* **Debs Broughton**[32] 5996 3-8-10 45 (t) DavidMcCabe 7 40
(W J Musson) *hld up towards rr: hmpd over 2f out and dropped to last pair: renewed effrt over 1f out: one pce* **18/1**

000- **9** *nk* **Dara Girl (IRE)**[499] 3748 3-8-10 45 MartinDwyer 5 39
(L Montague Hall) *s.s: t.k.h and hld up in last pair: effrt over 2f out : hanging bdly over 1f out: no prog* **25/1**

5000 **10** *1 ¼* **Zolash (IRE)**[17] 6241 3-8-5 45 RoryMoore(5) 9 36
(Mrs L C Jewell) *t.k.h: pressed ldrs tl wknd wl over 1f out* **40/1**

0030 **11** *½* **Binnion Bay (IRE)**[49] 5655 4-8-12 45 (v) TPQueally 1 39+
(J J Bridger) *hld up and racd on inner: nt clr run over 2f out and over 1f out: no ch* **6/1**

0000 **12** *1 ½* **Bahama Reef (IRE)**[121] 3726 4-8-12 45 SamHitchcott 6 32
(B Gubby) *w ldr: rdn 3f out: stl upsides over 1f out: wknd rapidly* **20/1**

1m 39.18s (-0.25) **Going Correction** -0.225s/f (Stan)
WFA 3 from 4yo+ 2lb 12 Ran SP% **127.2**
Speed ratings (Par 97):92,91,90,89,88 88,88,87,86,85 85,83
CSF £100.85 TOTE £71.40: £7.50, £1.30, £3.30; EX 230.30.
Owner Homebred Racing **Bred** Chris Wall **Trained** Lewes, E Sussex

FOCUS
A poor contest run in a modest time, even for a banded race, and the form is rated around the second and fourth and unconvincing.

6399 BETDIRECT FREEPHONE 0800 211 222 BANDED STKS 1m 2f (P)
3:40 (3:44) (Class 7) 3-Y-O+ **£1,453** (£429; £214) **Stalls Low**

Form RPR

4004 **1** **My Lilli (IRE)**[7] 6348 5-9-2 47 GeorgeBaker 7 52
(P Mitchell) *hld up in midfield: prog over 2f out: chsd ldr over 1f out: urged along and kpt on to ld ins fnl f: jst hld on* **5/1**[2]

05 **2** *shd* **Glenviews Oldport (USA)**[13] 6292 3-8-8 48 DuranFentiman(5) 9 53
(Peter Grayson) *hld up wl in rr: prog 3f out: drvn over 1f out: r.o ins fnl f: jst failed* **25/1**

0330 **3** *½* **Mad**[9] 6323 4-9-1 46 JohnEgan 6 50
(Andrew Reid) *trckd ldrs gng wl: effrt to ld 2f out: drvn and hdd ins fnl f: one pce* **11/8**[1]

660- **4** *1 ½* **Whenwillitwin**[487] 4065 4-8-11 49 (p) JosephWalsh(7) 3 50
(J S Moore) *dwlt: t.k.h: hld up midfield: rdn over 2f out: kpt on same pce* **33/1**

5-00 **5** *1 ¾* **King's Minstrel (IRE)**[207] 1316 4-9-0 45 (t) PaulDoe 2 43+
(R Rowe) *hld up: stl last but gng easily over 2f out: prog whn nt clr run over 1f out and swtchd lft: styd on: no ch* **16/1**

4230 **6** *1* **Emerald Dancer**[37] 5895 3-8-13 48 SteveDrowne 14 44
(H Morrison) *towards rr: rdn on outer over 4f out: struggling 3f out: plugged on fnl 2f* **7/1**[3]

0006 **7** *nk* **Spanish Music**[37] 5899 3-8-12 47 (t) RobertHavlin 5 42
(R Ingram) *settled midfield: rdn over 3f out: nvr on terms w ldrs* **16/1**

0004 **8** *¾* **Norman Norman**[37] 5895 3-9-1 50 DaneO'Neill 11 44
(W S Kittow) *reluctant to enter stalls: hld up in rr: effrt on wd outside over 3f out: one pce and no imp* **10/1**

4000 **9** *½* **Kinsman (IRE)**[65] 5303 8-8-13 47 RobertMiles(3) 4 40
(T D McCarthy) *t.k.h: w ldrs: stl upsides 2f out: wknd over 1f out* **16/1**

0000 **10** *½* **Queenstown (IRE)**[13] 6292 4-8-12 48 (p) RoryMoore(5) 10 40
(B A Pearce) *led after 3f to 2f out: wknd* **25/1**

0003 **11** *1 ¾* **Mythical Charm**[32] 5997 6-9-4 49 (t) FrankieMcDonald 8 44+
(J J Bridger) *hld up wl in rr: trapped on inner fr over 3f out: no ch* **8/1**

1200 **12** *10* **Senor Bond (USA)**[32] 5997 4-9-4 49 JamieMackay 12 19
(A M Hales) *chsd ldrs: rdn 1/2-way: wkng whn bdly hmpd over 2f out* **16/1**

6-00 **13** *3 ½* **Riviera Red (IRE)**[280] 378 5-9-0 45 MartinDwyer 1 8
(L Montague Hall) *led for 3f: styd w ldrs tl wknd rapidly over 2f out* **25/1**

0000 **14** *3* **Legacy (JPN)**[14] 6286 5-9-5 50 TPQueally 13 7
(T T Clement) *dwlt: sn chsd ldrs: rdn over 4f out: sn wknd* **20/1**

2m 6.00s (-1.79) **Going Correction** -0.225s/f (Stan)
WFA 3 from 4yo+ 4lb 14 Ran SP% **134.2**
Speed ratings (Par 97):98,97,97,96,94 94,93,93,92,92 91,83,80,77
CSF £141.32 TOTE £7.40: £2.40, £9.30, £2.00; EX 311.30 Place 6 £171.97, Place 5 £73.35.
Owner M Vickers **Bred** Dr Dean Harron **Trained** Epsom, Surrey

FOCUS
A fair race of its type, but they went an ordinary early pace and the contest developed into something of a sprint. The race could rate higher but has been treated cautiously.
T/Plt: £361.80 to a £1 stake. Pool: £49,814.70. 100.50 winning tickets. T/Qpdt: £23.30 to a £1 stake. Pool: £6,103.50. 193.30 winning tickets. JN

6380 SOUTHWELL (L-H)
Monday, November 21

OFFICIAL GOING: Standard to slow
The surface was particularly testing, but there did not appear to be any track bias.
Wind: Virtually nil

6400 TEXT "BETDIRECT" TO 88600 AMATEUR RIDERS' H'CAP (DIV I) 1m (F)
12:00 (12:01) (Class 6) (0-55,60) 3-Y-O+ **£2,415** (£743; £371) **Stalls Low**

Form RPR

0000 **1** **Active Account (USA)**[14] 6280 8-10-9 **50** (b) ChrisGlenister(7) 12 58
(J R Holt) *s.i.s and bhd: gd hdwy on inner 3f out: rdn over 1f out: styd on to ld ins last* **25/1**

006 **2** *2* **Layed Back Rocky**[53] 5564 3-10-9 **52** MissMMullineaux(7) 7 56
(M Mullineaux) *sn led: pushed clr over 2f out: rdn wl over 1f out: hdd and one pce ins last* **11/1**

6414 **3** *¾* **Ragasah**[30] 6032 7-10-5 **46** (p) MissAlexWells(7) 5 49
(Ernst Oertel) *towards rr: hdwy 3f out: rdn to chse ldrs and edgd lft over 1f out: kpt on ins last* **8/1**

0602 **4** *nk* **Sugitani (USA)**[7] 3615 3-11-3 **60** ow8 MrMBailey(7) 3 62
(N B King) *b ehind: hdwy on inner 3f out: rdn 2f out: kpt on appr last: nrst fin* **18/1**

4600 **5** *4* **Quiet Reading (USA)**[227] 929 8-11-4 **52** (v) MrsSBosley 4 46
(M R Bosley) *prom: rdn along 2f out: grad wknd* **13/2**[2]

0004 **6** *nk* **Didnt Tell My Wife**[19] 6231 6-10-13 **54** MrAChahal(7) 6 47
(Julian Poulton) *dwlt and towards rr: hdwy 3f out: rdn along 2f out: kpt on same pce* **9/2**[1]

0003 **7** *1 ¼* **Harare**[14] 6286 4-11-0 **55** MrMPrice(7) 11 46
(R J Price) *towards rr: carried wd and swtchd lft 3f out: rdn and hdwy 2f out: kpt on u.p appr last: nrst fin* **7/1**[3]

3356 **8** *hd* **Hows That**[207] 1330 3-11-0 **55** MissKellyBurke(5) 1 45
(K R Burke) *cl up: rdn along over 2f out: grad wknd* **12/1**

5001 **9** *¾* **Spitfire Bob (USA)**[6] 6361 6-11-1 **56** 6ex (p) MissKSearby(7) 13 45
(M E Sowersby) *hld up and bhd: hdwy on inner 3f out: rdn 2f out and sn no imp* **14/1**

0400 **10** *1 ½* **Shaheer (IRE)**[14] 6286 3-10-12 **55** MissSSawyer(7) 14 41
(Mrs L J Mongan) *a rr* **25/1**

6000 **11** *1 ¼* **Crux**[38] 5880 3-11-4 **54** MrSDobson 9 37
(C W Thornton) *midfield: poushed along 1/2-way: sn wknd* **8/1**

004 **12** *2 ½* **Cape Venus (IRE)**[137] 3263 3-11-4 **54** MrSWalker 2 32
(R Curtis) *chsd ldrs: rdn along 3f out: sn wknd* **8/1**

0350 **13** *shd* **Feast Of Romance**[9] 6327 8-10-9 **46** (b) MrJOwen(3) 8 24
(C R Dore) *chsd ldrs on outer: rdn along 3f out and sn wknd* **14/1**

0250 **14** *7* **Bold Maggie**[7] 6345 3-10-4 **47** MissKJames(7) 10 11
(J A Pickering) *in tch: lost pl after 3f: sn bhd* **33/1**

1m 49.63s (5.03) **Going Correction** +0.325s/f (Slow)
WFA 3 from 4yo+ 2lb 14 Ran SP% **122.6**
Speed ratings (Par 101):87,85,84,83,79 79,78,78,77,75 74,72,72,65
CSF £279.49 CT £2485.87 TOTE £46.40: £12.30, £5.20, £2.80; EX 709.90.
Owner Mr & Mrs R M Glenister **Bred** White Fox Farm **Trained** Peckleton, Leics
■ The first winner under Rules for both John Holt and Chris Glenister.

FOCUS
A moderate amateur riders' handicap but, despite the eventual winner coming from well off the pace, few of these were ever that competitive. The winning time was 0.47 seconds slower than the second division. The exposed runner-up ran to his mark but this is not strong form.

6401 TEXT "BETDIRECT" TO 88600 AMATEUR RIDERS' H'CAP (DIV II) 1m (F)
12:30 (12:31) (Class 6) (0-55,55) 3-Y-O+ **£2,415** (£743; £371) **Stalls Low**

Form RPR

4404 **1** **We'll Meet Again**[14] 6287 5-11-4 **52** MissSBrotherton 11 61
(M W Easterby) *sn pushed along in rr: hdwy over 3f out: chsd ldr and hung lft over 1f out: styd on to ld wl ins fnl f* **7/2**[2]

2335 **2** *1 ¾* **Sound And Vision (IRE)**[40] 5431 3-11-5 **55** (v[1]) MrSDobson 13 61
(M Dods) *chsd ldrs: led over 3f out: rdn over 1f out: sn hung lft: hdd wl ins fnl f* **12/1**

0522 **3** *6* **Fulvio (USA)**[7] 6346 5-10-9 **50** (v) MissFGuillambert(7) 10 44
(P Howling) *chsd ldrs: led 5f out: hdd over 3f out: wknd fnl f* **9/1**[3]

00-1 **4** *2 ½* **Mutared (IRE)**[23] 6151 7-10-12 **46** MrsEmmaLittmoden 5 35
(N P Littmoden) *hld up: hdwy over 3f out: sn rdn: wknd over 1f out* **3/1**[1]

0051 **5** *1* **Speakerboxxx**[13] 6292 3-11-4 **54** MrSWalker 14 41
(P F I Cole) *prom: rdn over 2f out: sn hung lft and wknd* **7/2**[2]

5006 **6** *¾* **Intended**[43] 5756 3-11-0 **55** (t) MissMSowerby(5) 4 40
(A M Balding) *hld up: rdn over 2f out: n.d* **25/1**

0000 **7** *2* **Sydneyroughdiamond**[12] 6299 3-10-7 **50** (p) MissMMullineaux(7) 12 31
(M Mullineaux) *prom over 5f* **66/1**

0000 **8** *shd* **Majehar**[16] 6263 3-11-2 **52** .... MissCHannaford 8 33
(A G Newcombe) *dwlt: outpcd: nvr nrr* **28/1**

0050 **9** *3* **Yorker (USA)**[5] 6372 7-10-10 **51** .... (b) MrCEllingham(7) 2 26
(Ms Deborah J Evans) *dwlt: hdwy 6f out: wknd 3f out* **50/1**

0415 **10** *1 ½* **Vettorious**[6] 5131 3-10-6 **47** .... MrSFMagee(5) 6 19
(Mrs P Sly) *sn led: hdd 5f out: wknd 3f out* **9/1**[3]

00-0 **11** *dist* **Dave (IRE)**[74] 5063 4-10-13 **52** .... KylieManser(5) 1 —
(J R Best) *chsd ldrs to 1/2-way* **25/1**

1m 49.16s (4.56) **Going Correction** +0.325s/f (Slow)
WFA 3 from 4yo+ 2lb 11 Ran SP% **111.7**
Speed ratings (Par 101):90,88,82,79,78 78,76,75,72,71 —
CSF £35.86 CT £261.65 TOTE £6.60: £1.60, £3.20, £2.20; EX 55.80.
Owner K Wreglesworth **Bred** Nasrullah Holdings **Trained** Sheriff Hutton, N Yorks
■ Barons Spy (9/1, unruly in stalls) was withdrawn. R4 applies, deduct 10p in the £.

FOCUS

Like the first division, a moderate handicap for amateur riders, and few got competitive despite the winner coming from quite a way off the pace. The winning time was 0.47 seconds faster than the first race. The first two were clear, but both are exposed and are unlikely to have improved.

6402 EUROPEAN BREEDERS FUND NOVICE STKS 1m (F)

1:00 (1:00) (Class 5) 2-Y-O **£4,012** (£1,193; £596; £297) **Stalls** Low

Form RPR

00 **1** **Twill (IRE)**[22] 6178 2-8-12 .... DarryllHolland 4 80+
(H Morrison) *a promient: led wl over 2f out: rdn clr and edgd lft over 1f out: rdn out* **8/1**

222 **2** *8* **Queen's Composer (IRE)**[9] 6319 2-8-12 75 .... PaulEddery 2 62
(B Smart) *cl up: led after 3f: rdn along 3f out and sn hdd: drvn and one pce fr over 1f out* **15/8**[1]

00 **3** *4* **Sahara Style**[10] 6313 2-8-12 .... GrahamGibbons 8 54
(R Hollinshead) *in tch: pushed along 1/2-way: rdn to chse ldng pair wl over 1f out: sn one pce* **33/1**

2043 **4** *2 ½* **Makai**[19] 6224 2-8-12 70 .... JoeFanning 3 48
(M Johnston) *led 3f: cl up tl rdn along wl over 2f out and sn wknd* **9/1**

432 **5** *½* **Katchit (IRE)**[32] 5995 2-8-12 79 .... TonyCulhane 7 47
(M R Channon) *chsd ldrs: rdn along 3f out: drvn over 2f out and sn wknd* **9/4**[2]

4400 **6** *2 ½* **Mambo Sun**[10] 6316 2-8-12 60 .... FergalLynch 9 42
(P A Blockley) *a towards rr* **25/1**

1002 **7** *5* **Captivate**[6] 6358 2-8-9 49 .... (b[1]) DeanMcKeown 6 28
(M J Polglase) *a rr* **28/1**

5234 **8** *14* **Is It Me (USA)**[7] 6342 2-8-12 69 .... NCallan 10 —
(P A Blockley) *outpcd and bhd fr 1/2-way* **13/2**[3]

9 *nk* **Boucheen** 2-8-8 .... EddieAhern 5 —
(Ms Deborah J Evans) *in tch: rdn along 3f out: sn wknd* **50/1**

0000 **10** *20* **Kooks (IRE)**[124] 3625 2-8-12 40 .... (v[1]) HayleyTurner 1 —
(Miss Kariana Key) *sn outpcd and bhd fr 1/2-way* **150/1**

11 *nk* **Blue Danielle (IRE)** 2-8-3 .... ChrisCatlin 11 —
(A D Brown) *s.i.s: sn outpcd and wl bhd fr 1/2-way* **66/1**

1m 46.0s (1.40) **Going Correction** +0.325s/f (Slow) 11 Ran SP% **114.3**
Speed ratings (Par 96):106,98,94,91,91 88,83,69,69,49 48
CSF £21.89 TOTE £12.70: £3.30, £1.70, £4.50; EX 33.30.
Owner de La Warr Racing **Bred** Rathbarry Stud **Trained** East Ilsley, Berks

FOCUS

Hard to know what to make of the form but, while Twill probably just handled the testing conditions better than most, he was quite impressive and recorded a very smart time indeed for a race of its type. The form is rated through the third to form, but the going may have affected the distances.

NOTEBOOK

Twill(IRE) ◆ had run to just a modest level of form on his two previous starts, including over this trip on Polytrack last time but, switched to Fibresand for the first time, he showed early speed to hold a good position and found plenty when asked to sustain his effort in the straight. It is hard to know what to make of the form, and he has clearly just handled the conditions better than the others, but he was impressive and could be followed with confidence to follow up round here. Elsewhere, he still has something to prove. (op 11-2)

Queen's Composer(IRE), runner-up on his previous three career starts, including over this trip on the Polytrack last time, ran respectably on his first run on this particular surface, but was left behind by the impressive winner and the slow surface did not look to bring out the very best in him. (tchd 85-40 in a place)

Sahara Style was well beaten in a claimer at Wolverhampton on his previous start, so his proximity does not do a great deal for the form, but this testing surface clearly brought about improvement, and he could find his level in handicap company now he is qualified for a mark. (op 28-1)

Makai travelled well into the straight, but this was his first run beyond six furlongs and he was basically outstayed. (op 11-1)

Katchit(IRE) was beaten quite a way from home and did not appear suited by the surface. (op 11-4)

Is It Me(USA) Official explanation: jockey said the colt had no more to give

6403 DAILY OFFERS AT BETDIRECT (S) STKS 7f (F)

1:30 (1:33) (Class 6) 2-Y-O **£2,518** (£743; £371) **Stalls** Low

Form RPR

5000 **1** **Psycho Cat**[6] 6353 2-8-12 65 .... ChrisCatlin 9 68
(M R Channon) *chsd ldrs: rdn over 2f out: styd on u.p to ld post* **11/1**

6460 **2** *hd* **Tour D'Amour (IRE)**[10] 6313 2-8-12 59 .... MickyFenton 10 67
(Stef Liddiard) *led: hdd over 4f out: led over 2f out: rdn and edgd rt 1f out: hdd post* **3/1**[1]

0224 **3** *6* **Cool Isle**[10] 6313 2-8-9 55 ow2 .... (b[1]) NCallan 1 49
(K A Ryan) *dwlt: sn drvn along: hdwy over 4f out: wknd fnl f* **4/1**[2]

4000 **4** *1 ¼* **Devon Ruby**[6] 6358 2-8-7 50 .... (p) PaulFessey 11 44
(Mrs A Duffield) *dwlt: hld up: outpcd 3f out: styd on u.p fr over 1f out* **14/1**

0000 **5** *3 ½* **Mytass**[36] 5921 2-8-6 48 ow1 .... RussellKennemore(7) 4 41
(J A Pickering) *hld up: hdwy u.p over 1f out: nt clr run ins fnl f: nvr trbld ldrs* **100/1**

1060 **6** *5* **Garlogs**[66] 5265 2-9-3 57 .... JoeFanning 6 33+
(A Bailey) *w ldrs tl led over 4f out: hdd over 2f out: lost action and wknd fnl f* **11/1**

6025 **7** *¾* **Secret Tender (IRE)**[6] 6358 2-8-12 63 .... DarryllHolland 14 26
(J R Weymes) *s.i.s: outpcd* **8/1**

6000 **8** *6* **Saxon Star (IRE)**[76] 5023 2-8-12 49 .... HayleyTurner 8 11
(M D I Usher) *hld up: rdn and wknd over 2f out* **40/1**

2244 **9** *1* **Noble Edge**[159] 2582 2-8-12 55 .... (p) FergalLynch 12 8
(P A Blockley) *hld up: rdn and wknd over 2f out* **16/1**

6003 **10** *2 ½* **Miss Mujahid Times**[13] 6290 2-8-7 48 .... EddieAhern 13 —
(A D Brown) *w ldrs tl rdn 1/2-way: hung lft and wknd 2f out* **25/1**

4204 **11** *hd* **Axis Shield (IRE)**[5] 6366 2-8-4 54 .... NelsonDeSouza(3) 3 —
(J G Portman) *w ldrs 4f: sn rdn: wknd over 1f out* **9/1**

045 **12** *6* **Cumberland Road**[38] 5879 2-8-12 62 .... LeeEnstone 2 —
(P C Haslam) *s.i.s: hdwy 4f out: wknd 3f out* **11/2**[3]

0006 **13** *7* **Cuesta Canyon (IRE)**[84] 4829 2-8-12 46 .... (b) LukeFletcher 5 —
(M J Polglase) *s.s: outpcd* **80/1**

1m 33.92s (3.12) **Going Correction** +0.325s/f (Slow) 13 Ran SP% **119.2**
Speed ratings (Par 94):95,94,87,86,82 76,75,69,67,65 64,57,49
CSF £43.22 TOTE £12.70: £2.60, £1.70, £2.30; EX 51.70.The winner was sold to Paul Blockley for 6,200gns.
Owner M Channon **Bred** Peter Taplin **Trained** West Ilsley, Berks

FOCUS

A good race by selling standards and the form looks pretty sound, rated through the runner-up.

NOTEBOOK

Psycho Cat, dropped into a seller for the first time, and making his debut on Fibresand, responded well to a good, strong ride from Chris Catlin to nail the long-time leader close home. The eventual runner-up did not exactly look to be stopping - a view backed up by the fact the pair finished six lengths clear of the remainder - so this was a decent enough effort and he must be respected in better company. (op 14-1 tchd 10-1)

Tour D'Amour(IRE), dropped into selling company for the first time, and returned to Fibresand, looked all over the winner at the furlong pole but was ultimately just denied. She looks well up to winning at this level. (op 4-1 tchd 9-2)

Cool Isle, with blinkers replacing cheekpieces, did not appear ideally suited by this drop in trip, but she should find easier sellers in any case.

Devon Ruby would have appreciated the return to selling company, but she did not help her chance with a slow start, especially considering she was dropping back a furlong in trip, and could never get seriously competitive. A return to a mile should suit. (tchd 16-1)

Mytass was having his 12th career start, but his first on Fibresand and the surface seemed to suit. He may have been closer with a clearer run and is not without hope. (op 66-1)

Garlogs ◆, upped to his furthest trip to date on his Fibresand debut, travelled strongly into the straight, but his stamina soon gave way and then he lost his action. The way he moved into contention was quite taking in the context of this grade, and he looks one to be with when returned to shorter. (op 12-1 tchd 14-1)

Cumberland Road, switched to Fibresand for the first time, never really looked happy and failed to confirm the modest level of ability he showed on turf and Polytrack. (op 9-2 tchd 4-1)

6404 BETDIRECT.CO.UK FILLIES' H'CAP 6f (F)

2:00 (2:01) (Class 5) (0-70,70) 3-Y-O+ **£3,993** (£1,188; £593; £296) **Stalls** Low

Form RPR

0062 **1** **Nan Jan**[65] 5322 3-8-10 **62** .... (t) ChrisCatlin 2 73
(R Ingram) *led to 1/2-way: cl up: rdn 2f out: drvn over 1f out: styd on to ld ins last* **11/2**[2]

0520 **2** *¾* **Look Of Eagles**[48] 5687 3-8-5 **60** .... NelsonDeSouza(3) 8 69+
(P F I Cole) *prom: lost pl after 1f: sn outpcd and bhd: hdwy 2f out: sn rdn: styd on strly ent last* **8/1**[3]

000 **3** *hd* **Lady Algarhoud (FR)**[79] 4963 3-8-10 **62** .... EddieAhern 1 70
(D K Ivory) *cl up: led 1/2-way: rdn 2f out: drvn over 1f out: hdd and no ex ins last* **22/1**

3035 **4** *3 ½* **Cerebus**[18] 6235 3-8-13 **65** .... GrahamGibbons 6 63
(M J Polglase) *in tch on inner: pushed along 1/2-way: rdn along 2f out: kpt on same pce* **5/2**[1]

0430 **5** *1 ¾* **Tapa**[38] 5869 3-8-5 **60** .... (b) NeilChalmers(3) 4 52
(A M Balding) *chsd ldrs: rdn along wl over 2f out: drvn over 1f out and kpt on same pce* **16/1**

0500 **6** *nk* **Clove (USA)**[34] 5954 3-9-0 **66** .... MickyFenton 3 57
(J A Osborne) *keen: trckd ldrs tl n.m.r and lost pl after: hdwy and hung rt 2f out: sn rdn and no imp appr last* **28/1**

0360 **7** *1 ¾* **Tequila Sheila (IRE)**[10] 6315 3-9-0 **66** .... (p) PatCosgrave 5 52
(K R Burke) *hmpd s and bhd tl styd on fnl 2f* **12/1**

4302 **8** *½* **Chilly Cracker**[10] 6310 3-8-10 **62** .... PaulQuinn 11 47
(R Hollinshead) *chsd ldrs: hdwy on outer over 2f out: sn rdn: edgd lft and kpt on same pce* **9/1**

5-00 **9** *½* **Tizzy's Law**[48] 5686 4-8-9 **61** .... NCallan 7 44
(E F Vaughan) *chsd ldrs: rdn whn n.m.r 2f out: sn drvn and wknd over 1f out* **11/1**

6000 **10** *nk* **Mitchelland**[125] 3610 3-8-10 **62** .... HayleyTurner 14 44
(James Moffatt) *s.i.s: a rr* **40/1**

1020 **11** *10* **Marinaite**[21] 6201 4-9-4 **70** .... MichaelTebbutt 9 22
(S R Bowring) *cl up: rdn wl over 2f out: sn wknd* **9/1**

4000 **12** *2 ½* **Karashino (IRE)**[18] 6235 3-8-10 **62** .... (p) TonyHamilton 10 7
(R A Fahey) *prom: rdn along 1/2-way: wknd over 2f out* **20/1**

0030 **13** *17* **Dematraf (IRE)**[120] 3786 3-8-8 **60** .... J-PGuillambert 13 —
(Ms Deborah J Evans) *a rr* **10/1**

1m 18.56s (1.66) **Going Correction** +0.325s/f (Slow) 13 Ran SP% **121.1**
Speed ratings (Par 100):101,100,99,95,92 92,90,89,88,88 74,71,48
CSF £47.45 CT £947.77 TOTE £8.00: £2.40, £5.40, £7.60; EX 55.70 Trifecta £341.90 Part won. Pool: £481.66 - 0.60 winning tickets..
Owner The Waltons **Bred** Mrs S Ingram **Trained** Epsom, Surrey

FOCUS

A modest but competitive fillies' handicap. The winner has slipped to a potentially good mark and the form seems sound enough.

6405 BETDIRECT FREEPHONE 0800 211 222 MAIDEN STKS 1m 4f (F)

2:30 (2:31) (Class 5) 3-Y-O+ **£3,393** (£1,009; £504; £252) **Stalls** Low

Form RPR

3530 **1** **Piper General (IRE)**[109] 4104 3-8-12 56 .... DaleGibson 3 74+
(J Mackie) *chsd ldrs: rdn to ld over 1f out: styd on strly* **20/1**

6032 **2** *12* **Silsong (USA)**[37] 5896 3-8-4 53 .... (b[1]) NelsonDeSouza(3) 5 51
(Miss Gay Kelleway) *led: hdd over 8f out: led 5f out: rdn and hdd over 1f out: sn outpcd* **11/1**

-304 **3** *7* **Webbswood Lad (IRE)**[11] 6307 4-9-4 63 .... MickyFenton 9 46
(Stef Liddiard) *hld up: hdwy 1/2-way: rdn over 3f out: wknd over 2f out* **5/2**[1]

0035 **4** *5* **Ma'Am (USA)**[11] 6306 3-8-8 72 ow1 .... (b[1]) LeeEnstone 13 34
(I A Wood) *prom: chsd ldr over 4f out: rdn over 2f out: sn wknd* **5/1**[3]

60- **5** *8* **I'll Do It Today**[286] 6519 4-8-11 .... PaulPickard(7) 2 26
(J M Jefferson) *hld up: sme hdwy over 3f out: sn wknd* **66/1**

6-3 **6** *8* **Swindon (USA)**[164] 2449 3-8-7 .... JoeFanning 4 9
(P F I Cole) *prom 8f* **3/1**[2]

7 *12* **Amoli (IRE)**[136] 3327 3-8-9 ow2 .... NCallan 8 —
(K A Ryan) *chsd ldrs: rdn over 7f out: wknd over 5f out* **9/1**

0000 **8** *2* **Naivety**[17] 6247 3-8-7 54 .... J-PGuillambert 6 —
(G G Margarson) *hld up: sme hdwy 1/2-way: sn wknd* **9/1**

/63- **9** *4* **Fourswainby (IRE)**[558] 2037 4-9-4 45 .... TomEaves 14 —
(B Ellison) *outpcd* **50/1**

0-0 **10** *11* **Feel The Need**[190] 1726 3-8-12 .... DeanMcKeown 1 —
(G A Swinbank) *outpcd* **66/1**

4500 **11** *12* **Royal Sailor (IRE)**[22] 6184 3-8-12 53........................(b) DarryllHolland 10 —
(Julian Poulton) *trckd ldr: racd keenly: led over 8f out: hdd 5f out: sn wknd* **18/1**

-600 **P** **Ustad (IRE)**[9] 6333 3-8-12 60.. ChrisCatlin 12 —
(P L Gilligan) *outpcd: t.o whn p.u over 4f out* **25/1**

2m 42.74s (0.65) **Going Correction** +0.325s/f (Slow)
WFA 3 from 4yo 6lb **12** Ran SP% **117.4**
Speed ratings (Par 103):110,102,97,94,88 83,75,74,71,64 56,—
CSF £214.45 TOTE £29.80: £5.20, £2.40, £1.70; EX 231.80.

Owner Fools Who Dream **Bred** Edward And Mrs S Hannigan **Trained** Church Broughton , Derbys

FOCUS
A moderate maiden and, with the pace strong from the start, very few of these saw their race out. Although the form may not be worth a great deal, and it probably did not take much winning, the time was smart for a race of this type.

Amoli(IRE) Official explanation: jockey said filly had no more to give

Ustad(IRE) Official explanation: jockey said gelding lost its action

6406 LIVE FOOTBALL CASHBACKS AT BETDIRECT H'CAP 1m 6f (F)
3:00 (3:00) (Class 5) (0-75,74) 3-Y-0+ **£3,336** (£992; £496; £247) **Stalls** Low

Form RPR

3005 **1** **Sun Hill**[5] 6368 5-9-0 **65**.. PaulMulrennan(3) 10 71
(C W Fairhurst) *cl up: led over 5f out: rdn along 2f out: drvn over 1f out: edgd lft ins last: hld on gamely* **8/1**

0026 **2** *nk* **He's A Star**[7] 5998 3-7-13 **55** oh3....................................... JimmyQuinn 5 60
(Miss Gay Kelleway) *hld up in tch: hdwy 3f out: rdn wl over 1f out: drvn to chal ins last and ev ch tl no ex nr fin* **14/1**

2660 **3** *3/4* **Stolen Song**[6] 6356 5-8-4 **57**.......................................(e) MarcHalford(5) 9 61
(J Ryan) *hld up in rr: hdwy 4f out and sn pushed along: rdn and styng on whn hmpd over 1f out: sn drvn and styd on wl fnl f* **25/1**

0001 **4** *shd* **Peak Park (USA)**[5] 6368 5-9-11 **73** 6ex.............................. ChrisCatlin 8 77
(P L Gilligan) *hld up in tch: hdwy 4f out: sn pushed along: rdn 2f out: drvn over 1f out: styd on ins last* **7/4**[1]

0603 **5** *1/2* **Night Sight (USA)**[14] 6285 8-9-0 **62**..............................(b) TonyCulhane 4 65
(Mrs S Lamyman) *trckd ldrs gng wl: smooth hdwy 3f out: chal 2f out: sn rdn and ev ch tl drvn and wknd ent last* **16/1**

0533 **6** *shd* **Queen's Dancer**[17] 6247 3-7-12 **57** oh1 ow2......... EdwardCreighton(3) 2 60
(M R Channon) *hld up in rr: hdwy on inner over 3f out: rdn 2f out: drvn over 1f out and kpt on ins last* **4/1**[2]

0020 **7** *9* **Red Forest (IRE)**[16] 6267 6-8-12 **60**................................(t) DaleGibson 1 51
(J Mackie) *keen: cl up: rdn along over 2f out: drvn and hung rt over 1f out: sn wknd* **5/1**[3]

/12- **8** *10* **Great As Gold (IRE)**[562] 1958 6-9-0 **62**.............................. TomEaves 6 39
(B Ellison) *a rr* **12/1**

0010 **9** *dist* **Palamedes**[58] 5451 6-9-12 **74**... NCallan 7 —
(Robert Gray) *led: rdn along and hdd over 5f out: wknd qckly and virtually p.u fnl 2f* **12/1**

3m 11.75s (2.15) **Going Correction** +0.325s/f (Slow)
WFA 3 from 5yo+ 8lb **9** Ran SP% **115.9**
Speed ratings (Par 103):106,105,105,105,105 105,99,94,—
CSF £112.26 CT £2653.25 TOTE £8.90: £2.50, £3.20, £6.00; EX 99.70.

Owner William Hill **Bred** London Thoroughbred Services Ltd **Trained** Middleham Moor, N Yorks

■ Stewards' Enquiry : Tom Eaves caution: used whip when out of contention

FOCUS
They usually finish well strung out in races over this sort of distance round here, especially when the surface is so testing, but there was around just a length and a half separating the front six this time, suggesting they did not go a great pace, and the form may want treating with a little caution.

6407 IN RUNNING TONIGHT ON SKYTEXT 293 H'CAP 5f (F)
3:30 (3:33) (Class 6) (0-55,59) 3-Y-0+ **£2,878** (£849; £425) **Stalls** High

Form RPR

0561 **1** **He's A Rocket (IRE)**[12] 6294 4-8-7 **55**......................(b) AndrewElliott(7) 7 64
(K R Burke) *chsd ldrs: outpcd 1/2-way: rallied and nt clr run over 1f out: swtchd rt: r.o to ld wl ins fnl f* **10/3**[1]

1360 **2** *1/2* **Elvina**[48] 5686 4-9-0 **55**... LPKeniry 14 61
(A G Newcombe) *chsd ldrs: rdn to ld 1f out: hdd wl ins fnl f: fin 3rd, plcd 2nd* **16/1**

0005 **3** *1/2* **Dutch Key Card (IRE)**[67] 5256 4-8-11 **52**................. RobbieFitzpatrick 4 56
(C Smith) *chsd ldrs: rdn and ev ch ins fnl f: unable qck nr fin: pl 3rd* **10/1**

2653 **4** *1/2* **St Ivian**[6] 6363 5-8-7 **53**... MarcHalford(5) 8 56
(Mrs N Macauley) *chsd ldrs: rdn 1/2-way: styd on: fin 5th, plcd 4th* **5/1**[2]

4004 **5** *1* **Byo (IRE)**[12] 6294 7-9-0 **55**.. TonyCulhane 2 54
(P Howling) *chsd ldrs: rdn and ev ch ins fnl f: unable qckn: fin 6th, plcd 5th* **8/1**

0210 **6** *1/2* **Lady Pekan**[6] 6363 6-9-0 **55**..(v) J-PGuillambert 5 53
(P Howling) *mde most 4f: no ex ins fnl f: fin 7th, plcd 6th* **7/1**[3]

2000 **7** *1 1/2* **Henry Tun**[42] 5803 7-8-10 **54**.......................................(b) JasonEdmunds(3) 9 46
(J Balding) *s.i.s: sn chsng ldrs: rdn ev ch 1f out: wknd fnl f: fin 8th, plcd 7th* **20/1**

0000 **8** *1/2* **Trace Clip**[33] 5975 7-8-12 **53**... VinceSlattery 6 44
(N I M Rossiter) *s.i.s: hdwy over 3f out: wknd ins fnl f: fin 9th, plcd 8th* **14/1**

5300 **9** *nk* **Malahide Express (IRE)**[12] 6294 5-8-11 **52**.................... JimmyQuinn 3 42
(E J Alston) *s.i.s: sn w ldr: rdn and ev ch 1f out: sn wknd: fin 10th, plcd 9th* **16/1**

2600 **10** *2 1/2* **Cayman King**[81] 4888 3-9-0 **55**... TomEaves 12 36
(R Craggs) *s.s: outpcd: fin 11th, plcd 10th* **66/1**

0120 **11** *1 1/4* **Vlasta Weiner**[34] 5966 5-8-11 **52**......................................(b) ChrisCatlin 13 29
(J M Bradley) *chsd ldrs: outpcd over 3f out: sn bhd: fin 12th, plcd 11th* **9/1**

5400 **12** *shd* **Petite Mac**[61] 5413 5-8-4 **52**...................................... SuzzanneFrance(7) 11 29
(N Bycroft) *sn outpcd: fin 13th, plcd 12th* **33/1**

0001 **D** *1/2* **Cool Sands (IRE)**[6] 6363 3-9-1 **59** 6ex................... PatrickMathers(3) 10 67+
(D Shaw) *outpcd: hdwy over 1f out: r.o: fin 2nd,½l: disq* **15/2**

60.60 secs (0.30) **Going Correction** +0.10s/f (Slow) **13** Ran SP% **121.8**
Speed ratings (Par 101):101,99,98,97,96 95,93,92,91,87 85,85,100
CSF £28.20 CT £374.93 TOTE £3.30: £1.40, £2.70, £3.30; EX 36.20 Place 6 £453.25, Place 5 £67.47. STEWARDS ENQUIRY Cool Sands disq; rider did not hold a licence at the time.

Owner Keelings 10 **Bred** Lemongrove Stud **Trained** Middleham Moor, N Yorks

FOCUS
Just a moderate sprint handicap, but solid form for the grade. The winner did not need to reproduce the form of his claiming victory while the second ran a career best.

T/Jkpt: Not won. T/Plt: £428.70 to a £1 stake. Pool: £40,055.20. 68.20 winning tickets. T/Qpdt: £31.30 to a £1 stake. Pool: £5,381.80. 127.00 winning tickets. JR

6219 MAISONS-LAFFITTE (R-H)
Monday, November 21

OFFICIAL GOING: Very soft

6408a PRIX CONTESSINA (LISTED RACE) (STRAIGHT) 6f (S)
1:50 (1:54) 3-Y-0+ **£16,667** (£6,667; £5,000; £3,333; £1,667)

RPR

1 **Crossover**[9] 3-8-8 ....(b) RonanThomas 11 104
(H-A Pantall, France)

2 *1/2* **Matrix (GER)**[20] 6221 4-9-2 .... CSoumillon 12 110
(W Baltromei, Germany)

3 *2* **Satchmo Bay (FR)**[20] 4-8-11 ....(b) DBoeuf 1 99
(C Boutin, France)

4 *1 1/2* **Love Green (FR)**[51] 4-8-8 .... J-BEyquem 7 92
(F Rohaut, France)

5 *1/2* **Pout (IRE)**[16] 6252 3-8-8 .... TJarnet 8 90
(John Joseph Murphy, Ire) *towards rear of centre group, stayed on steadily final 1 1/2f* **39/1**[1]

6 *1* **Tremar**[38] 5873 3-8-11 .... IanMongan 2 90
(T G Mills) *led stands side group briefly early, remained prominent til ridden and one pace from over 1f out*

7 *1* **Soave (GER)**[20] 6221 6-9-6 .... ADeVries 3 96
(A Trybuhl, Germany)

8 *1 1/2* **Beautifix (GER)**[17] 3-8-8 .... MBlancpain 9 80
(C Laffon-Parias, France)

9 *nk* **Bischoff's Boy (GER)**[142] 3161 4-8-11 .... JVictoire 5 82
(N Sauer, Germany)

10 *shd* **Donatello (GER)**[85] 4804 4-9-2 .... ABoschert 4 86
(W Baltromei, Germany)

0 **Dolma (FR)**[20] 6221 4-8-8 .... TThulliez 10 —
(N Clement, France)

0 **Kasali (IRE)**[22] 6189 4-8-11 .... FSpanu 13 —
(J-P Gallorini, France)

0 **Kuaicoss (IRE)**[36] 5938 3-8-8 .... MEsposito 6 —
(A Renzoni, Italy)

0 **Risque De Verglas (FR)**[13] 4-8-8 .... YLerner 14 —
(Mme R-W Allen, France)

1m 13.9s **14** Ran SP% **2.5**
PARI-MUTUEL: WIN 11.40; PL 3.20, 2.40, 2.40; DF 29.00.
Owner Sheikh Mohammed **Bred** Darley **Trained** France

NOTEBOOK
Tremar showed up with the leaders until fading in the closing stages. He had beaten the winner in a Group Three at Chantilly last autumn, but has not gone on from that.

6400 SOUTHWELL (L-H)
Tuesday, November 22

OFFICIAL GOING: Standard to slow
The track was worked until the frost went at 3am. After that it was harrowed and rolled and the surface was described as 'very slow'.
Wind: Almost nil Weather: Fine but dull and cold.

6409 BET ON CHAMPIONS LEAGUE FOOTBALL @ BETDIRECT BANDED STKS 5f (F)
1:10 (1:10) (Class 7) 3-Y-0+ **£1,416** (£418; £209) **Stalls** High

Form RPR

0100 **1** **Largs**[8] 6345 5-8-8 45...(b[1]) JasonEdmunds(3) 6 51
(J Balding) *sn drvn along: hdwy over 2f out: styd on to ld last stride* **20/1**

5300 **2** *shd* **Empress Josephine**[17] 6256 5-8-11 45......................(vt) FergalLynch 2 51
(J R Jenkins) *w ldrs: led and edgd lft over 1f out: jst ct* **7/1**

0252 **3** *3* **Innclassic (IRE)**[31] 6035 4-8-11 45................................(b) LeeEnstone 1 40
(Jane Southcombe) *led: hdd over 1f out: hung lft: wknd last 100yds* **13/2**

4503 **4** *1/2* **Amanda's Lad (IRE)**[10] 6326 5-8-11 45................................ NCallan 12 39
(M C Chapman) *chsd ldrs: outpcd over 2f out: styd on fnl f* **6/1**[3]

3063 **5** *3/4* **Beamsley Beacon**[17] 6256 4-8-11 45...............................(b) TomEaves 9 36
(M Dods) *chsd ldrs: carried hd high over 1f out: no ex* **3/1**[1]

0430 **6** *1 3/4* **Velvet Touch**[125] 3640 4-8-11 45.....................................(t) MickyFenton 4 30
(D M Simcock) *sn chsng ldrs: one pce fnl 2f* **12/1**

4041 **7** *1 3/4* **Mind Alert**[3] 6385 4-9-3 45.......................................(v) TonyHamilton 11 30
(D Shaw) *w ldrs: wknd over 1f out* **4/1**[2]

0606 **8** *1 1/2* **Torrent**[10] 6326 10-8-11 45..(p) TonyCulhane 10 19
(D W Chapman) *stdd s: hld up in rr: effrt over 2f out: nvr on terms* **9/1**

0002 **9** *7* **Blendon Belle (FR)**[14] 6288 3-8-11 40................................. LPKeniry 5 —
(A G Newcombe) *prom: sn drvn along: lost pl over 2f out: eased* **33/1**

6040 **10** *2 1/2* **Misty Princess**[115] 3930 3-8-11 45...................................(v) JoeFanning 3 —
(D Shaw) *s.i.s: sn prom on outside: edgd lft and lost pl over 2f out: eased* **33/1**

0000 **11** *dist* **Shaymee's Girl**[45] 5736 4-8-6 45...........................(e[1]) MarcHalford(5) 7 —
(J Ryan) *sn outpcd and bhd: virtually p.u over 1f out: t.o: btn 31 l* **33/1**

61.24 secs (0.94) **Going Correction** +0.125s/f (Slow) **11** Ran SP% **116.4**
Speed ratings (Par 97):97,96,92,91,90 87,84,82,70,66 —
CSF £147.57 TOTE £17.80: £5.20, £3.40, £2.40; EX 151.10.

Owner Hollinbridge Racing **Bred** Mrs Gillian A R Jones And John Balding **Trained** Scrooby, Notts

FOCUS
A run-of-the mill banded event with just two figuring at the finish but both running to their best marks.

Shaymee's Girl Official explanation: vet said filly had bled from the nose

6410 BET IN-RUNNING TONIGHT AT BETDIRECT.CO.UK BANDED STKS 1m 6f (F)
1:40 (1:40) (Class 7) 3-Y-0+ **£1,419** (£419; £209) **Stalls** Low

Form RPR

-005 **1** **Ice And Fire**[8] 6344 6-9-3 40..(b) MickyFenton 5 51
(J T Stimpson) *hld up in mid-field: hdwy 6f out: led and edgd rt over 1f out: styd on* **80/1**

0004 **2** *1* **All Bleevable**[10] 6329 8-9-3 45... TonyCulhane 7 50
(Mrs S Lamyman) *mid-div: hdwa 3f out: chal over 1f out: unable qckn* **9/1**

5-15 **3** *6* **Make My Hay**[10] 6329 6-9-4 46...(b) NCallan 9 42
(J Gallagher) *s.i.s: hdwy 7f out: effrt on outer to ld 3f out: hdd over 1f out: wknd ins last* **8/1**

6321 **4** *4* **Tharua (IRE)**[10] 6329 3-8-9 50 (p) StephenDonohoe(5) 6 41
(Ernst Oertel) *hld up in rr: hdwy 8f out: prom 5f out: outpcd and c wd over 2f out: kpt on fnl f* **7/2**[2]
2512 **5** *4* **Medjugorje Message (IRE)**[17] 6257 3-9-0 50 (b) TonyHamilton 10 35
(R A Fahey) *trckd ldrs: t.k.h: rdn over 3f out: lost pl over 1f out* **5/2**[1]
0000 **6** *½* **Handa Island (USA)**[12] 5206 6-9-0 45 PaulMulrennan(3) 11 29
(M W Easterby) *trckd ldrs on outer: reminders over 5f out: wknd over 1f out* **16/1**
0000 **7** *8* **Jamaican Flight (USA)**[10] 6329 12-9-3 35 JimmyQuinn 1 18
(Mrs S Lamyman) *drvn to ld: hdd 3f out: sn lost pl* **66/1**
0202 **8** *17* **Bill Bennett (FR)**[10] 6329 4-9-5 47 MichaelTebbutt 4 —
(J Jay) *trckd ldrs: drvn along 7f out: lost pl 3f out: sn bhd* **5/1**[3]
2106 **9** *7* **Beaumont Girl (IRE)**[5] 5790 3-8-10 46 TomEaves 3 —
(Miss M E Rowland) *chsd ldrs: sn drvn along: lost pl 7f out: sn bhd* **28/1**
6455 **10** *3½* **Jadeeron**[3] 6381 6-9-7 49 (e) DarrenWilliams 2 —
(Miss D A McHale) *w ldrs: chal over 4f out: lost pl over 2f out: sn bhd* **20/1**
5026 **11** *7* **Keltic Rainbow (IRE)**[31] 6034 4-9-3 45 (v) RobertHavlin 8 —
(D Haydn Jones) *in rr: ppushed along after 5f: lost tch over 4f out* **8/1**

3m 12.39s (2.79) **Going Correction** +0.15s/f (Slow)
WFA 3 from 4yo+ 8lb **11** Ran SP% **116.5**
Speed ratings (Par 97):98,97,94,91,89 89,84,74,70,68 64
CSF £676.41 TOTE £61.60: £11.20, £2.80, £2.80; EX 271.20.
Owner J T Stimpson & B Trubshaw **Bred** Abdullah Saeed Bul Hab **Trained** Newcastle-Under-Lyme, Staffs
■ A first training success for John Stimpson.

FOCUS
Ice And Fire bounced back from the dead scoring in a good time with the runner-up the yardstick. The placed horses ran to their marks and set the level.
Keltic Rainbow(IRE) Official explanation: jockey said filly hung left

6411 BETDIRECT.CO.UK MAIDEN CLAIMING STKS 6f (F)
2:10 (2:13) (Class 7) 3-Y-0+ **£1,412** (£417; £208) **Stalls** Low

Form RPR
0042 **1** **Mulberry Lad (IRE)**[17] 6258 3-9-0 47 DarrenWilliams 5 54
(P W Hiatt) *mde all: 3 l clr 1f out: hld on towards fin* **3/1**[1]
0033 **2** *¾* **Ben Casey**[14] 6288 3-9-0 54 (p) PaulEddery 4 52+
(B Smart) *dwlt: hld up gng wl: stdy hdwy 3f out: wnt 2nd jst ins last: rdn and r.o: nt quite rch wnr: too much too do* **10/3**[2]
0250 **3** *1¼* **Faithisflying**[14] 6291 3-8-10 40 (p) TonyCulhane 1 44
(D W Chapman) *mid-div: lost pl over 4f out: hdwy over 2f out: kpt on same pce fnl f* **15/2**
0442 **4** *3½* **Tree Roofer**[197] 1573 6-8-12 45 (b) HayleyTurner 3 36
(N P Littmoden) *t.k.h: w wnr: wknd appr fnl f* **15/2**
5000 **5** *1¾* **Piroetta**[13] 6299 3-8-9 50 (b[1]) JoeFanning 10 27
(J A Osborne) *mid-div: effrt on outer over 2f out: hung violenty lft over 1f out: nvr trbld ldrs* **9/1**
0600 **6** *1* **Danaatt (USA)**[17] 6258 3-8-9 35 (b[1]) PatCosgrave 6 24
(K R Burke) *sn drvn along: outpcd over 4f out: kpt on fnl 2f* **16/1**
00 **7** *2½* **Chingola**[10] 6328 3-8-2 MichaelJStainton(7) 8 17
(R M Whitaker) *s.i.s: sn wl bhd: styd on fnl 2f* **18/1**
0400 **8** *nk* **Yours Sincerely (IRE)**[8] 6343 3-8-13 45 (p) FergalLynch 11 20
(P A Blockley) *sn drvn along: lost pl over 4f out: n.d after* **7/1**[3]
0400 **9** *3* **Isle Dream**[50] 5662 3-8-0 30 MarcHalford(5) 7 3
(John A Harris) *prom: hrd rdn and outpcd over 3f out: sn lost pl* **66/1**
400- **10** *hd* **Raetihi**[400] 6275 4-8-7 35 DeanMcKeown 9 4
(P S Felgate) *in tch: lost pl over 3f out: sn bhd* **25/1**
0000 **11** *2½* **Amazing Grace Mary**[10] 6328 3-8-8 30 ow1 (b) VHalliday 2 —
(S R Bowring) *chsd ldng pair: lost pl 2f out* **40/1**
0406 **12** *5* **Limited Magician**[14] 6288 4-8-9 30 DeanMernagh 12 —
(C Smith) *racd wd: lost pl over 4f out: sn bhd* **33/1**

1m 19.3s (2.40) **Going Correction** +0.15s/f (Slow) **12** Ran SP% **116.0**
Speed ratings (Par 97):90,89,87,82,80 79,75,75,71,71 67,61
CSF £12.11 TOTE £3.90: £1.60, £1.80, £2.90; EX 14.30.
Owner P W Hiatt **Bred** Mountarmstrong Stud **Trained** Hook Norton, Oxon

FOCUS
A poor claimer and a moderate time, even for a race like this. The third looks the key to the value of the form and the ride given to Ben Casey came under the microscope.
Piroetta Official explanation: jockey said filly hung left

6412 BETDIRECT FREEPHONE 0800 211 222 BANDED STKS 7f (F)
2:40 (2:41) (Class 7) 3-Y-0+ **£1,429** (£422; £211) **Stalls** Low

Form RPR
2432 **1** **Caerphilly Gal**[3] 6383 5-8-4 40 LukeMorris(7) 13 56+
(P L Gilligan) *w ldrs: led over 4f out: rdn clr over 1f out: eased towards fin* **7/2**[1]
2442 **2** *5* **Jacks Delight**[14] 6291 5-8-11 40 MickyFenton 2 42+
(C N Kellett) *mid-div: hdwy over 2f out: styd on to take 2nd last 75yds: no ch w wnr* **9/2**[2]
3045 **3** *1½* **Lizzie Rocket**[3] 6383 5-8-6 40 ow2 (v[1]) JamesO'Reilly(7) 10 40
(J O'Reilly) *w ldrs: wnt 2nd over 2f out: one pce fnl f* **8/1**
5026 **4** *1* **Tiny Tim (IRE)**[84] 4851 7-8-4 40 (b) JamesRogers(7) 4 35
(A M Balding) *rr-div: hdwy over 2f out: kpt on fnl f* **10/1**
5 *4* **Mescalera (GER)**[65] 4-8-11 40 LPKeniry 3 25
(B G Powell) *sn chsng ldrs: lost pl over 1f out* **8/1**
6400 **6** *1¼* **Dominer (IRE)**[35] 5962 3-8-10 40 (b[1]) TonyCulhane 12 22
(J M Bradley) *hld up on outside: effrt over 3f out: nvr nr ldrs* **12/1**
-000 **7** *nk* **Madame Guillotine**[113] 3995 3-8-7 40 PaulMulrennan(3) 6 21
(P T Midgley) *chsd ldrs: rdn over 3f out: lost pl over 2f out* **33/1**
0060 **8** *6* **Cleveland Way**[14] 6291 5-8-9 40 ow1 (b) DNolan(3) 7 6
(D Carroll) *led tl over 4f out: wknd and eased over 1f out* **18/1**
6004 **9** *3½* **Red Lantern**[31] 6033 4-8-11 40 NCallan 9 —
(M J Attwater) *chsd ldrs: lost pl over 2f out* **7/1**[3]
6506 **10** *2* **Garnock Venture (IRE)**[24] 6155 4-8-11 40 (b) FergalLynch 5 —
(A Berry) *s.i.s: sn detached in rr: nvr a factor* **8/1**
00-0 **11** *2½* **Xeight Express (IRE)**[3] 6383 3-8-10 40 (b[1]) JoeFanning 1 —
(A Bailey) *s.i.s: sn chsng ldrs: lost pl over 3f out* **66/1**
-000 **12** *9* **Mytori**[84] 4848 3-8-10 40 TonyHamilton 8 —
(D Shaw) *sn drvn along in rr: bhd fnl 4f* **50/1**
3006 **13** *1½* **Sam The Sorcerer**[14] 6291 4-8-11 40 DarrenWilliams 14 —
(J R Norton) *sn outpcd and in rr: bhd fnl 4f* **25/1**

1m 32.76s (1.96) **Going Correction** +0.15s/f (Slow)
WFA 3 from 4yo+ 1lb **13** Ran SP% **118.5**
Speed ratings (Par 97):94,88,86,85,80 79,79,72,68,65 63,52,51
CSF £17.82 TOTE £3.20: £2.10, £2.20, £3.20; EX 15.00.
Owner T Williams **Bred** D J And Mrs Deer **Trained** Newmarket, Suffolk
■ A first riding success for 17-year-old Luke Morris having just his eighth ride.

FOCUS
A modest time and a weak race with the winner easily the best on the day and running near her best turf mark.

6413 10% BONUS IN-RUNNING ON ITVI BANDED STKS 1m (F)
3:10 (3:10) (Class 7) 3-Y-0+ **£1,429** (£422; £211) **Stalls** Low

Form RPR
4645 **1** **Thornaby Green**[24] 6141 4-8-12 45 (v) JamieSpencer 4 52
(T D Barron) *trckd ldrs: hrd rdn and hung lft over 1f out: styd on to ld nr fin* **3/1**[1]
3000 **2** *½* **Captain Darling (IRE)**[29] 6082 5-8-13 46 JimmyQuinn 6 52
(R W Price) *led: rdn over 1f out: kpt on: hdd towards fin* **20/1**
5000 **3** *1* **Orpen Quest (IRE)**[8] 6346 3-9-1 50 MickyFenton 2 54
(M J Attwater) *chsd ldrs: rdn and lost pl over 3f out: hdwy 2f out: kpt on same pce fnl f* **3/1**[1]
0010 **4** *5* **Ballyrush (IRE)**[10] 6327 5-8-6 46 StephanieBancroft(7) 9 40
(Miss D A McHale) *trckd ldrs: effrt 3f out: wknd over 1f out* **25/1**
0326 **5** *shd* **Tommytyler (IRE)**[24] 6151 6-8-12 48 DNolan(3) 8 42
(D Carroll) *sn trcking ldrs: effrt over 2f out: one pce* **9/2**[3]
0340 **6** *5* **Fleet Anchor**[8] 6347 4-8-12 45 LPKeniry 5 29
(J M Bradley) *hld up: hdwy to trck ldrs over 4f out: lost pl 3f out* **4/1**[2]
0305 **7** *1* **Hollywood Henry (IRE)**[8] 6348 5-9-1 48 (b) PatCosgrave 3 30
(P A Blockley) *s.i.s: a dectached in rr* **16/1**
4100 **8** *5* **Elms Schoolboy**[10] 6327 3-8-11 46 (b) MichaelTebbutt 7 18
(J M P Eustace) *sn trcking ldrs: rdn and lost pl 3f out: sn bhd* **17/2**

1m 45.13s (0.53) **Going Correction** +0.15s/f (Slow)
WFA 3 from 4yo+ 2lb **8** Ran SP% **113.2**
Speed ratings (Par 97):103,102,101,96,96 91,90,85
CSF £62.41 TOTE £4.20: £1.30, £5.20, £1.80; EX 45.70.
Owner K J Alderson **Bred** Mrs S Broadhurst **Trained** Maunby, N Yorks

FOCUS
The winning time was fair for a race of its type. The winner ran to his handicap mark but the runner-up, who has slid down the ratings, has recorded both his career wins on Lingfield's Polytrack surface. The form is not totally solid.

6414 WATCH FOOTBALL WHILST YOU BET ON ITVI BANDED STKS 1m 3f (F)
3:40 (3:41) (Class 7) 3-Y-0+ **£1,436** (£424; £212) **Stalls** Low

Form RPR
0216 **1** **Kentucky Bullet (USA)**[35] 5959 9-9-0 45 LPKeniry 1 51
(A G Newcombe) *hld up in rr: stdy hdwy over 3f out: styd on to ld jst ins last: r.o* **9/4**[1]
-260 **2** *1¾* **Melograno (IRE)**[139] 1103 5-8-11 45 DNolan(3) 14 48
(Mark Campion) *chsd ldrs: led over 2f out: hdd and no ex jst ins last* **20/1**
6024 **3** *½* **Finnegans Rainbow**[3] 6382 3-8-9 45 NCallan 5 48
(M C Chapman) *mid-div: hdwy 5f out: chal over 2f out: kpt on same pce fnl f* **9/2**[3]
0034 **4** *3½* **Alcott (FR)**[14] 6293 3-8-9 45 (t) MichaelTebbutt 12 42
(J Jay) *hld up: hdwy on outside over 4f out: sn outpcd: kpt on fnl 2f* **8/1**
6503 **5** *nk* **Aggi Mac**[17] 6257 4-8-7 40 SuzzanneFrance(7) 13 42
(N Bycroft) *trckd ldr: led over 4f out tl over 2f out: wknd jst ins last* **16/1**
0050 **6** *2* **Printsmith (IRE)**[17] 6259 8-9-0 40 DarrenWilliams 8 39
(J R Norton) *chsd ldrs: wknd over 1f out* **66/1**
/000 **7** *hd* **Cotton Eyed Joe (IRE)**[112] 4026 4-9-0 30 DeanMcKeown 10 39
(G A Swinbank) *hld up towards rr: hdwy on outer over 3f out: nvr rchd ldrs* **50/1**
61 **8** *½* **Mickmacmagoole (IRE)**[8] 6344 3-9-1 40 JamieSpencer 4 44
(Seamus G O'Donnell, Ire) *hld up in rr: effrt 3f out: hung lft over 1f out: nvr on terms* **3/1**[2]
1206 **9** *½* **Iamback**[14] 6289 5-8-7 45 (t) RonanKeogh(7) 6 37
(Miss Gay Kelleway) *hld up in rr: hdwy on outer over 2f out: nvr a factor* **20/1**
0005 **10** *4* **Blue Streak (IRE)**[17] 6257 8-9-0 35 GeorgeBaker 2 31
(Mrs H Sweeting) *hld up in mid-div: effrt over 3f out: sn wknd* **25/1**
6465 **11** *hd* **Airedale Lad (IRE)**[17] 6258 4-9-0 45 HayleyTurner 7 31
(R M Whitaker) *chsd ldrs: lost pl over 2f out* **16/1**
0004 **12** *3½* **Liquid Lover (IRE)**[10] 6331 3-8-6 40 (b) BenSwarbrick(3) 3 26
(W M Brisbourne) *mid-divsion: drvn over 3f out: nvr a factor* **50/1**
0-60 **13** *16* **Enborne Again (IRE)**[10] 6327 3-8-9 45 TonyHamilton 11 2
(R A Fahey) *led tl over 4f out: lost pl over 2f out: bhd whn eased ins last* **66/1**
0-00 **14** *21* **Cabopino Lad (USA)**[21] 6215 3-8-9 45 TomEaves 9 —
(Mrs L Stubbs) *sn chsng ldrs: hrd rdn 4f out: sn lost pl: bhd whn eased ins last* **80/1**

2m 30.85s (1.95) **Going Correction** +0.15s/f (Slow)
WFA 3 from 4yo+ 5lb **14** Ran SP% **118.3**
Speed ratings (Par 97):98,96,96,93,93 92,92,91,91,88 88,85,74,58
CSF £54.74 TOTE £3.10: £1.40, £4.10, £2.00; EX 72.10 Place 6 £231.28, Place 5 £39.27.
Owner Mrs B J Sherwin **Bred** Foxfield **Trained** Yarnscombe, Devon

FOCUS
Standard form for the grade, although not the most solid, with the third possibly the best guide to the overall value.
Liquid Lover(IRE) Official explanation: jockey said gelding resented the kickback
T/Jkpt: Not won. T/Plt: £645.00 to a £1 stake. Pool: £45,636.85. 51.65 winning tickets. T/Qpdt: £6.60 to a £1 stake. Pool: £4,765.60. 534.10 winning tickets. WG

6338 SAINT-CLOUD (L-H)
Tuesday, November 22
OFFICIAL GOING: Very soft

6416a PRIX BELLE DE NUIT (LISTED RACE) (F&M) 1m 4f 110y
1:50 (2:03) 3-Y-0+ **£16,667** (£6,667; £5,000; £3,333; £1,667)

RPR
1 **Pilgrim Of Grace (FR)**[10] 4-9-0 SMaillot 2 104
(F Cohen, France)
2 *½* **Pink Cloud (FR)**[58] 5-9-0 TThulliez 18 103
(J-M Beguigne, France)
3 *½* **Milwaukee (FR)**[82] 4907 5-9-0 DBoeuf 6 102
(D Smaga, France)
4 *5* **Kiswahili**[19] 6237 3-8-8 J-BEyquem 19 96
(Sir Mark Prescott) *pressed leader, ridden and outpaced 3f out, stayed on under stong pressure from over 2f out*
5 *1* **New Destiny (FR)**[20] 4-9-0 FSpanu 10 93
(J-P Gallorini, France)

The Form Book, Raceform Ltd, Compton, RG20 6NL

6	3/4	**Petite Speciale (USA)**[19] 6-9-0 ... HPaimblanc 5 (E Lecoiffier, France)		92
7	3/4	**Ammo (IRE)**[42] 5831 3-8-8 ... JAuge 17 (R Gibson, France)		92
8	1	**Whazzat**[17] 6253 3-8-8 ... IMendizabal 13 (B W Hills) *tracked leaders, ridden and one pace final 3f*		91
9	10	**Lunathea (IRE)**[20] 3-8-8 ... CSoumillon 8 (A Fabre, France)		76
10	2 1/2	**Pony Girl (IRE)**[131] 4-9-0 ... MBlancpain 12 (C Laffon-Parias, France)		71
11		**Night Dhu**[89] 3-8-8 ... TGillet 11 (P Bary, France)		72
12		**Gloirez (FR)**[47] 4-9-4 ... (b) RonanThomas 7 (P Demercastel, France)		75
13		**Lady Sagamix (FR)**[20] 3-8-8 ... THuet 14 (R Pritchard-Gordon, France)		72
14		**Reynosa (IRE)**[20] 3-8-8 ... SPasquier 16 (J De Roualle, France)		72
15		**Subtle Affair (IRE)**[17] 6250 3-8-8 ... (b) TPQueally 15 (M G Quinlan) *never a factor*		72
16		**Segesta (IRE)**[62] 5417 3-8-8 ... (b) TJarnet 1 (R Gibson, France)		72
17		**Novarra (IRE)**[23] 6192 3-8-8 ... AStarke 9 (A Schutz, Germany)	96/1[1]	72
18		**Mpenzi**[34] 5972 3-8-8 ... (b) FBlondel 4 (J L Dunlop) *in touch, ridden along over 5f out, weakened 4f out*		72

2m 56.5s
WFA 3 from 4yo+ 6lb — **19** Ran SP% **1.0**
PARI-MUTUEL: WIN 8.30; PL 2.70, 4.20, 3.10; DF 61.60.
Owner W Green **Bred** Fularton Lodge Stud Ltd **Trained** France

NOTEBOOK
Kiswahili, dropping back in trip, was again ridden positively, but stayed on after getting outpaced. She has yet to prove she is truly up to this level, but is lightly raced and open to improvement.
Whazzat, who ran her best race of the season last time on similar ground, did not follow that up but may not have stayed this longer trip.
Subtle Affair(IRE), who was dropping back in trip, once again did not look up to this class.
Mpenzi, a 73-rated handicapper, was out of her depth and probably found the ground against her.

6386 WOLVERHAMPTON (A.W) (L-H)

Friday, November 25

OFFICIAL GOING: Standard changing to standard to fast after race 3 (2.20)
Wind: Slight, across Weather: Fine

6417 FIRST PAST POST AT BETDIRECT MEDIAN AUCTION MAIDEN STKS (DIV I) — 1m 141y(P)

1:10 (1:11) (Class 6) 2-Y-O — **£2,497** (£737; £368) **Stalls** Low

Form				RPR
	1		**Monashee Gold (IRE)** 2-9-0 ... EddieAhern 2 (E J O'Neill) *a.p: rdn to ld wl over 1f out: edgd rt ins fnl f: r.o wl* **9/1**	73
0542	2	1/2	**Salute The General**[10] 6352 2-9-0 74 ... SteveDrowne 9 (W R Muir) *hld up in tch: chal gng wl 2f out: rdn and ev ch ins fnl f: nt qckn* **5/6**[1]	72
60	3	3 1/2	**Ansells Joy**[144] 3192 2-8-10 ow1 ... DerekMcGaffin 3 (B Smart) *chsd ldrs: rdn over 3f out: one pce fnl 2f* **66/1**	60+
	4	3	**Spanish Lace** 2-8-9 ... TomEaves 6 (Miss J A Camacho) *s.s: bhd tl hdwy over 1f out: edgd lft jst ins fnl f: nvr nrr* **6/1**[2]	52
2	5	1	**Baileys Polka**[22] 6233 2-8-9 ... MickyFenton 13 (J G Given) *led 1f: remained prom: led over 3f out: rdn and hdd wl over 1f out: wknd fnl f* **7/1**[3]	50
	6	6	**Supa Tramp** 2-9-0 ... JDSmith 8 (J R Fanshawe) *hld up and bhd: sme hdwy over 1f out: nvr nr ldrs* **16/1**	42
00	7	1/2	**Katsumoto (IRE)**[13] 6318 2-9-0 ... HayleyTurner 1 (N P Littmoden) *t.k.h: led after 1f tl over 3f out: wknd wl over 1f out* **20/1**	41
00	8	nk	**Machhapuchhare**[13] 6334 2-9-0 ... DarrenWilliams 10 (W M Brisbourne) *mid-div: rdn and short-lived effrt over 2f out* **66/1**	40
	9	1 3/4	**Prima Markova** 2-8-9 ... DaneO'Neill 12 (D J Daly) *sn pushed along towards rr: rdn over 3f out: hdwy on ins over 2f out: wknd over 1f out* **25/1**	31
00	10	1 3/4	**Guanyin**[22] 6234 2-8-9 ... (p) NCallan 5 (J G Given) *prom tl wknd over 2f out* **40/1**	28
0	11	2	**Mucho Loco (IRE)**[10] 6349 2-9-0 ... TonyCulhane 7 (J G Portman) *hld up in mid-div: rdn 3f out: sn struggling* **66/1**	28
00	12	7	**Alistair John**[11] 6342 2-9-0 ... J-PGuillambert 4 (Mrs G S Rees) *a bhd* **80/1**	13
	13	8	**Curbridge Bell** 2-8-9 ... ChrisCatlin 11 (M R Channon) *sn pushed along and bhd* **25/1**	—

1m 51.06s (-0.70) **Going Correction** -0.125s/f (Stan) — **13** Ran SP% **117.8**
Speed ratings (Par 94):98,97,94,91,90 85,85,84,83,81 79,73,66
CSF £15.67 TOTE £10.90: £2.90, £1.10, £14.90; EX 24.20.
Owner Roadmate Racing **Bred** Paul Moroney **Trained** Averham Park, Notts

FOCUS
A modest maiden run in a reasonable time for the grade. The winner won with a little in hand and looks a decent prospect and the form is best rated through the runner-up.

NOTEBOOK
Monashee Gold(IRE) ended a quiet spell for his trainer with a cosy debut victory, achieved without his rider asking for everything. Travelling marginally worse that the runner-up turning for home, he edged right under pressure in the straight, but was good value for his win at the line. (tchd 10-1 and 11-1 in a place)
Salute The General moved well for the majority of the contest and looked virtually certain to shed his maiden tag when moving to the head of affairs on the bridle turning in. However, he could not find a way past the game winner inside the distance and he may require a drop in trip as he showed plenty of pace. (op 10-11 tchd evens in places)
Ansells Joy had displayed a glimmer of ability and again showed promise with a decent effort. However, she tried to pull herself up inside the distance and is not one to trust implicitly. Official explanation: jockey said filly hung right
Spanish Lace was the big eye-catcher as she lost lengths at the start and was trapped behind tiring rivals two furlongs out when making ground. She stayed on nicely in the straight and will be much sharper for the experience, both mentally and physically. (op 7-1)
Baileys Polka had shaped well on her debut and was in the firing line on the home turn on this switch to sand before fading disappointingly inside the distance. (op 11-2 tchd 17-2)
Supa Tramp was another for the future as he was green in the early stages before making late headway. He is bred to appreciate further, being a half-brother to Oaks winner Lady Carla, and will be seen to better effect over middle distances.

Katsumoto(IRE) Official explanation: jockey said gelding ran green and did not handle the first bend

6418 NO 5P RULE 4S AT BETDIRECT MAIDEN STKS — 1m 1f 103y(P)

1:45 (1:47) (Class 5) 3-Y-O — **£3,374** (£1,003; £501; £250) **Stalls** Low

Form				RPR
525	1		**Bazelle**[74] 5174 3-8-9 77 ... TonyCulhane 12 (D Shaw) *hld up in mid-div: hdwy over 5f out: led 2f out: r.o wl* **5/1**[1]	58
	2	1 1/2	**John Charles (IRE)** 3-9-0 ... LPKeniry 10 (D R C Elsworth) *s.s: hld up and bhd: stdy hdwy over 2f out: rdn and edgd lft jst over 1f out: r.o ins fnl f: nt trble winne* **7/1**[3]	60+
00	3	3/4	**Drumroll (IRE)**[13] 6333 3-9-0 ... BrianReilly 4 (Miss J Feilden) *led: rdn and hdd 2f out: nt qckn ins fnl f* **66/1**	59
263	4	1 1/4	**High Arctic**[175] 2259 3-9-0 70 ... SamHitchcott 9 (A Bailey) *s.i.s: hld up: hdwy over 3f out: rdn wl over 1f out: one pce fnl f* **5/1**[1]	57
4600	5	shd	**King Forever**[153] 2937 3-9-0 75 ... NCallan 11 (D E Cantillon) *stdd s: hld up and bhd: hdwy over 3f out: rdn wl over 1f out: one pce fnl f* **5/1**[1]	56
4500	6	nk	**Colinca's Lad (IRE)**[6] 6377 3-8-7 85 ... DeanWilliams(7) 3 (G C H Chung) *t.k.h: hld up in tch: lost pl over 3f out: hung bdly rt ent st: styd on ins fnl f* **12/1**	56
06	7	nk	**Townsville (IRE)**[15] 6307 3-9-0 ... DaneO'Neill 8 (D J Daly) *prom: wnt 2nd over 5f out: rdn 3f out: wknd ins fnl f* **11/2**[2]	55
0	8	2	**Arpetcheeo (USA)**[13] 6333 3-8-11 ... DanielTudhope(3) 5 (D Carroll) *hld up in mid-div: dropped rr 4f out: n.d after* **33/1**	51
0	9	8	**Monteleone (IRE)**[10] 6355 3-8-9 ... PaulFitzsimons 6 (R Hannon) *s.i.s: sn prom: rdn and wknd 2f out* **25/1**	31
	10	6	**Ginger For Pluck**[22] 3-8-9 ... MickyFenton 13 (J G Given) *sn prom: rdn and wknd 3f out* **40/1**	20
	11	1/2	**Oriental Way (GR)** 3-8-9 ... IanMongan 7 (P R Chamings) *s.i.s: hld up and bhd: hdwy over 5f out: rdn over 3f out: sn wknd* **14/1**	19

2m 4.20s (1.58) **Going Correction** -0.125s/f (Stan) — **11** Ran SP% **103.0**
Speed ratings (Par 102):87,85,85,83,83 83,83,81,74,69 68
CSF £30.19 TOTE £3.80: £1.40, £4.00, £13.50; EX 34.10.
Owner Mrs Jackie Cornwell **Bred** Loughbrown Stud **Trained** Danethorpe, Notts
■ The 1,000th winner in Britain for Tony Culhane. The first was in April 1986.

FOCUS
A steady early gallop contributed to a modest time for this maiden which did not take a lot of winning. The form is best rated through the winner.
Colinca's Lad(IRE) Official explanation: jockey said gelding hung right around the bottom bend

6419 TEXT 'BETDIRECT' TO 88600 (S) STKS — 1m 4f 50y(P)

2:20 (2:20) (Class 6) 3-Y-O+ — **£2,545** (£751; £375) **Stalls** Low

Form				RPR
0001	1		**Sea Map**[21] 6241 3-9-5 57 ... GeorgeBaker 2 (S Kirk) *a.p: led wl over 1f out: sn rdn: r.o* **11/4**[1]	62
0550	2	hd	**Champion Lion (IRE)**[36] 5996 6-9-6 59 ... TonyCulhane 4 (M R Channon) *hld up towards rr: hdwy on ins over 3f out: rdn over 1f out: r.o ins fnl f* **7/2**[2]	57
0643	3	4	**York Cliff**[98] 4556 7-9-6 57 ... EddieAhern 12 (W M Brisbourne) *stdd s: sn swtchd lft: hdwy on ins 3f out: sn rdn: n.m.r briefly over 1f out: one pce fnl f* **9/2**[3]	50
2005	4	hd	**Moon Shot**[98] 4556 9-9-6 63 ... NCallan 3 (A G Juckes) *t.k.h in tch: rdn 3f out: no ex fnl f* **12/1**	50
240	5	5	**Molly's Secret**[17] 6289 7-9-1 48 ... (p) JimmyQuinn 5 (Miss S J Wilton) *prom: led over 2f out: rdn and hdd wl over 1f out: wknd fnl f* **14/1**	37
5450	6	nk	**High Frequency (IRE)**[16] 6300 4-9-6 48 ... (v[1]) SteveDrowne 1 (W R Muir) *led: rdn and hdd over 2f out: wknd fnl f* **16/1**	41
00-	7	7	**Greatest By Phar**[20] 739 4-9-6 ... ChrisCatlin 9 (J Akehurst) *hld up in mid-div: wknd 3f out* **33/1**	30
5000	8	3	**Arabian Moon (IRE)**[16] 6300 9-9-11 50 ... DaneO'Neill 6 (R Brotherton) *rdn over 3f out: a towards rr* **8/1**	30
1500	9	1 1/4	**Regency Red (IRE)**[47] 5770 7-9-8 50 ... BenSwarbrick(3) 11 (W M Brisbourne) *hld up in mid-div: rdn over 3f out: sn struggling* **12/1**	28
6300	10	18	**Lyric Dances (FR)**[4] 6394 3-8-9 45 ... FergusSweeney 8 (M Blanshard) *chsd ldr tl rdn and wknd over 3f out: t.o* **40/1**	—
5-00	11	7	**Team-Mate (IRE)**[10] 6356 7-9-6 69 ... OscarUrbina 7 (Miss J Feilden) *a bhd: t.o* **16/1**	—
0/	12	7	**Beauchamp Spark**[741] 6003 4-9-6 ... VinceSlattery 10 (D G Bridgwater) *rdn 4f out: a towards rr: t.o* **66/1**	—

2m 40.29s (-2.13) **Going Correction** -0.125s/f (Stan)
WFA 3 from 4yo+ 6lb — **12** Ran SP% **118.9**
Speed ratings (Par 101):102,101,99,99,95 95,90,88,88,76 71,66
CSF £11.91 TOTE £3.60: £1.60, £2.00, £1.70; EX 17.80.The winner was sold to Peter Hart for 10,500gns. Champion Lion was claimed by M Khan for £6,000. Lyric Dances was claimed by Keith Wills for £6,000.
Owner The www.mortgages.tv Partnership **Bred** Slatch Farm Stud **Trained** Upper Lambourn, Berks

FOCUS
An average seller, but run in a good time and the first four home should all continue to prove competitive at this level.
Team-Mate(IRE) Official explanation: jockey said gelding had a breathing problem

6420 BET DIRECT FREEPHONE ON 0800 211 222 NURSERY (DIV I) — 7f 32y(P)

2:50 (2:51) (Class 5) (0-75,75) 2-Y-O — **£3,746** (£1,114; £557; £278) **Stalls** High

Form				RPR
1000	1		**Pommes Frites**[20] 6249 2-9-5 **73** ... SteveDrowne 2 (W R Muir) *led early: a.p: rdn to ld over 1f out: r.o wl* **16/1**	81
6600	2	2 1/2	**Final Bid (IRE)**[10] 6359 2-8-11 **65** ... (b) TPQueally 1 (M G Quinlan) *stdd and lost pl sn after s: hdwy over 2f out: rdn wl over 1f out: kpt on ins fnl f: nt trble wnr* **12/1**	67
4051	3	2	**Casablanca Minx (IRE)**[10] 6353 2-8-6 **63** 7ex.... EdwardCreighton(3) 12 (Mrs H Sweeting) *hld up: rdn and lost pl 3f out: hdwy on outside fnl f: r.o* **14/1**	60
5540	4	1/2	**Cresta Gold**[83] 4942 2-9-6 **74** ... SamHitchcott 11 (A Bailey) *s.i.s: bhd: rdn 3f out: hdwy on ins wl over 1f out: one pce fnl f* **28/1**	70
602	5	hd	**Cape Win (IRE)**[29] 6123 2-9-6 **74** ... GeorgeBaker 6 (S Kirk) *mid-div: rdn over 3f out: sme hdwy over 1f out: kpt on ins fnl f: n.d* **11/4**[1]	69
2302	6	nk	**Grenane (IRE)**[14] 6312 2-8-6 **67** ... JBrennan(7) 9 (P D Evans) *hld up: sn in tch: rdn and c wd wl ent st: edgd lft ins fnl f: no ex* **6/1**[3]	62

0404 **7** *1* **Caribbean Nights (IRE)**[10] 6357 2-8-6 **60**......................... DavidAllan 3 52
(T D Easterby) *n.m.r and lost pl bnd after 1f: rdn and hdwy over 2f out: no imp fnl f* **12/1**

3045 **8** *shd* **Charlie Delta**[13] 6320 2-9-4 **75**.................... DanielTudhope(3) 10 67
(D Carroll) *s.i.s: hld up: nt clr run over 3f out: nvr nr ldrs* **11/2**[2]

0302 **9** *1 ½* **Musical Romance (IRE)**[16] 6297 2-9-1 **69**....................... DaneO'Neill 5 57
(B J Meehan) *sn led: rdn and hdd wl over 1f out: wknd ins fnl f* **11/1**

5002 **10** *1 ¾* **Gattuso**[14] 6316 2-8-11 **65**.. NCallan 4 49
(Ms Deborah J Evans) *sn chsng ldrs: rdn over 3f out: wknd wl over 1f out* **11/2**[2]

1006 **11** *10* **Young Flavio**[16] 6297 2-8-7 **61**.. LPKeniry 7 20
(J M Bradley) *plld hrd: prom tl rdn and wknd wl over 1f out* **25/1**

6320 **12** *5* **Roonah (FR)**[24] 6212 2-8-13 **67**.. ChrisCatlin 8 14
(Karen McLintock) *sn chsng ldr: rdn over 3f out: wknd over 2f out* **33/1**

1m 29.81s (-0.59) **Going Correction** -0.125s/f (Stan) **12** Ran SP% **118.2**
Speed ratings (Par 96):98,95,92,92,92 91,90,90,88,86 75,69
CSF £190.50 CT £2789.37 TOTE £27.80: £4.60, £6.00, £7.20; EX 138.20.
Owner Dulverton Equine **Bred** Dulverton Equine **Trained** Lambourn, Berks

FOCUS
A competitive nursery settled by a decisive turn of foot by Pommes Frites. The third caught the eye staying on well from off the pace, and the form is sound rated through the winner.

NOTEBOOK
Pommes Frites has been shown some leniency by the Handicapper and took full advantage with a comfortable success. She quickened nicely when afforded a dream run two furlongs out and looks capable of defying a rise in the weights. (op 12-1)
Final Bid(IRE) has some talent but may not be straightforward. He arguably travelled best into the straight, but could not cope with the turn of foot displayed by the winner. He may appreciate a drop to six furlongs as he does not lack pace. (op 11-1)
Casablanca Minx(IRE) ran a cracker considering she was parked wide throughout and lost her position three furlongs out. She appears a candidate for a step up to seven furlongs and can win again soon. (op 12-1)
Cresta Gold showed promise on her Polytrack debut and should appreciate a stiffer test of stamina. A sluggish start did not aid her cause, but she made good headway a furlong out and should improve for the outing - her first for 83 days.
Cape Win(IRE) was a shade disappointing as he moved menacingly until coming under pressure three out. He kept on at one pace in the straight and looks to need further to be competitive. (op 9-2)
Grenane(IRE) is pretty exposed and was unplaced for the first time in three runs over seven furlongs. He raced wide into the straight and will relish a return to six, even if the Handicapper still looks to have him in his grip. (op 9-2)

6421 BETDIRECT.CO.UK H'CAP 5f 216y(P)
3:25 (3:30) (Class 4) (0-85,85) 3-Y-0+ **£5,787** (£1,721; £860; £429) **Stalls** Low

Form RPR

0000 **1** **Chateau Nicol**[6] 6379 6-9-4 **85**...(v) JoeFanning 4 93
(B G Powell) *a.p: rdn to ld over 1f out: edgd rt ins fnl f: r.o* **9/1**

2330 **2** *½* **Looks Could Kill (USA)**[55] 5599 3-9-2 **83**.......................... JimmyQuinn 2 90
(E J Alston) *s.i.s: hdwy on ins wl over 1f out: ev ch ins fnl f: r.o* **13/2**[3]

5-00 **3** *nk* **Countdown**[34] 6022 3-8-12 **79**..(v[1]) TomEaves 9 85
(Miss J A Camacho) *led after 1f: rdn over 2f out: hdd over 1f out: nt qckn ins fnl f* **33/1**

000 **4** *shd* **Will He Wish**[13] 6322 9-9-1 **82**.. IanMongan 12 88+
(S Gollings) *a.p: rdn 3f out: r.o ins fnl f* **20/1**

5310 **5** *hd* **Cornus**[9] 6370 3-9-4 **85**... LukeFletcher 7 90
(M J Polglase) *led 1f: a.p: rdn over 2f out: n.m.r briefly over 1f out: nt qckn ins fnl f* **25/1**

4100 **6** *nk* **Prince Tum Tum (USA)**[26] 6182 5-9-1 **82**........................ FergalLynch 6 86+
(D W Barker) *bhd: hdwy over 2f out: c wd st: r.o ins fnl f* **11/2**[2]

1423 **7** *1* **Balakiref**[20] 6248 6-8-10 **77**.. TonyCulhane 10 78
(M Dods) *hld up: sn bhd: hdwy 1f out: nrst fin* **8/1**

0205 **8** *1* **Sir Desmond**[13] 6321 7-9-0 **81**...(p) ChrisCatlin 3 79
(Rae Guest) *broke wl: sn lost pl: rdn over 3f out: sme hdwy fnl f: n.d* **7/1**

0046 **9** *½* **Queens Rhapsody**[10] 6354 5-8-10 **77**............................ SamHitchcott 1 74
(A Bailey) *prom: rdn 3f out: ev ch over 1f out: nt clr run briefly ins fnl f: wknd towards fin* **9/2**[1]

0450 **10** *½* **Idle Power (IRE)**[10] 6354 7-9-0 **84**...............................(p) AmirQuinn(3) 11 79
(J R Boyle) *t.k.h: prom: rdn 2f out: wknd fnl f* **10/1**

100 **11** *1* **Harrison's Flyer (IRE)**[13] 6321 4-8-10 **77**...........................(p) NCallan 5 69
(J M Bradley) *mid-div: rdn and hdwy over 2f out: nt clr run briefly over 1f out: wknd ins fnl f* **9/1**

0000 **12** *½* **Endless Summer**[35] 6014 8-8-11 **78**................................. EddieAhern 13 69
(A W Carroll) *s.i.s: a bhd* **25/1**

01-0 **13** *2 ½* **Exponential (IRE)**[34] 6022 3-8-11 **78**......................(be) J-PGuillambert 8 61
(S C Williams) *t.k.h in mid-div: bhd fnl 2f* **25/1**

1m 14.15s (-1.66) **Going Correction** -0.125s/f (Stan) **13** Ran SP% **118.8**
Speed ratings (Par 105):106,105,104,104,104 104,102,101,100,100 98,98,94
CSF £61.26 CT £1917.73 TOTE £12.40: £3.50, £2.40, £7.90; EX 108.90.
Owner Basingstoke Commercials **Bred** Aston House Stud **Trained** Morestead, Hants
■ Stewards' Enquiry : Joe Fanning caution: careless riding

FOCUS
A well-contested handicap run at a true pace. The winner scored with a little in hand, while both the runner-up and Prince Tum Tum looked prospective future winners in a solid handicap.
Chateau Nicol Official explanation: trainer said, regarding the improved form shown, gelding had been badly drawn last time out and had been dropped in class for this race
Cornus Official explanation: jockey said gelding was denied a clear run

6422 PLAY INSTANT WIN GAMES AT BETDIRECT.CO.UK H'CAP 5f 20y(P)
3:55 (3:56) (Class 5) (0-70,70) 3-Y-0+ **£3,463** (£1,030; £515; £257) **Stalls** Low

Form RPR

5045 **1** **Law Maker**[13] 6335 5-8-8 **67**...................................(v) MichaelJStainton(7) 2 78
(A Bailey) *w ldr: led over 3f out: rdn and edgd lft over 1f out: edgd rt and hdd wl ins fnl f: sn led again: r.o* **7/1**[3]

2031 **2** *shd* **Gilded Cove**[13] 6335 5-9-4 **70**....................................... GrahamGibbons 6 81
(R Hollinshead) *s.i.s: hdwy on ins over 2f out: rdn whn swtchd rt over 1f out: led briefly wl ins fnl f: r.o* **7/2**[1]

0013 **3** *1 ¾* **Wicked Uncle**[13] 6335 6-9-4 **70**...(v) IanMongan 7 75
(S Gollings) *bhd: rdn and hdwy on ins wl over 1f out: kpt on ins fnl f* **11/2**[2]

0-12 **4** *½* **After The Show**[13] 6335 4-9-4 **70**.. ChrisCatlin 3 73
(Rae Guest) *t.k.h: a.p: rdn wl over 1f out: one pce fnl f* **7/2**[1]

0100 **5** *1* **The Fisio**[13] 6335 5-9-2 **68**...(v) EddieAhern 13 67+
(S Gollings) *bhd: hdwy on outside over 2f out: r.o ins fnl f* **20/1**

0100 **6** *½* **Ashes (IRE)**[22] 6238 3-9-1 **67**... NCallan 8 65
(K R Burke) *chsd ldrs: nt clr run over 2f out: rdn over 1f out: one pce fnl f* **16/1**

/00- **7** *1* **Bahamian Breeze**[54] 2181 4-8-13 **65**.................................... LPKeniry 10 59
(D M Simcock) *s.i.s: outpcd: sme late prog: nvr nrr* **50/1**

0021 **8** *hd* **Campeon (IRE)**[22] 6235 3-8-13 **65**.................................. GeorgeBaker 5 58
(J M Bradley) *led over 1f: rdn and wknd over 1f out* **9/1**

6000 **9** *shd* **Gone'N'Dunnett (IRE)**[46] 5802 6-8-9 **66**.....................(v) MarcHalford(5) 4 59
(Mrs C A Dunnett) *chsd ldrs: rdn over 1f out: sn btn* **14/1**

0000 **10** *3* **Oakbridge (IRE)**[45] 5824 3-9-1 **67**................................ VinceSlattery 11 49
(D J Wintle) *outpcd* **33/1**

1004 **11** *2 ½* **Vague Star (ITY)**[38] 5954 3-9-0 **66**..............................(b) RobertHavlin 12 39
(R Ingram) *prom tl rdn and wknd wl over 1f out* **20/1**

0661 **12** *2* **Dizzy In The Head**[24] 6217 6-8-13 **65**..............................(b) LeeEnstone 9 31
(I Semple) *prom tl rdn and wknd wl over 1f out* **10/1**

61.96 secs (-0.86) **Going Correction** -0.125s/f (Stan) **12** Ran SP% **118.4**
Speed ratings (Par 103):101,100,98,97,95 94,93,92,92,87 83,80
CSF £30.25 CT £150.18 TOTE £10.80: £2.10, £1.40, £1.80; EX 35.70.
Owner North Cheshire Trading & Storage Ltd **Bred** North Cheshire Trading And Storage Ltd **Trained** Cotebrook, Cheshire

FOCUS
A typically congested handicap fought out by the two course specialists. The time stacked up well enough, the result corresponds to previous races and the form looks solid.

6423 BET DIRECT FREEPHONE ON 0800 211 222 NURSERY (DIV II) 7f 32y(P)
4:25 (4:26) (Class 5) (0-75,75) 2-Y-O **£3,737** (£1,111; £555; £277) **Stalls** High

Form RPR

065 **1** **Aravalli (IRE)**[49] 5711 2-8-10 **64**.. ChrisCatlin 9 69
(D J Daly) *hld up: rdn and hdwy over 2f out: led wl ins fnl f: drvn out* **10/1**

000 **2** *¾* **Royle Dancer**[53] 5659 2-8-6 **60**.................................... GrahamGibbons 4 63
(R Hollinshead) *s.i.s: hld up: rdn and hdwy over 2f out: edgd lft ins fnl f: r.o wl* **50/1**

614 **3** *nk* **Pressure Putt**[20] 6249 2-9-7 **75**.. TonyCulhane 3 78
(W J Haggas) *a.p: rdn to ld jst over 1f out: hdd and nt qckn wl ins fnl f* **1/1**[1]

0004 **4** *3 ½* **Song Of Silence (USA)**[14] 6309 2-8-6 **60**........................ NickyMackay 5 54
(E A L Dunlop) *s.s: bhd tl hdwy over 1f out: nvr trbld ldrs* **11/2**[3]

0004 **5** *2* **Lyrical Blues (IRE)**[13] 6320 2-8-13 **74**...................... JamesMillman(7) 2 63
(B R Millman) *led: rdn and hdd jst over 1f out: wknd ins fnl f* **10/1**

2403 **6** *1* **Squadron Leader (IRE)**[24] 6214 2-9-4 **72**......................... DaneO'Neill 1 59
(R Hannon) *chsd ldrs: rdn over 3f out: wknd over 2f out* **9/2**[2]

3120 **7** *nk* **Upthedowns (IRE)**[46] 5791 2-8-11 **65**..................................(v[1]) NCallan 10 51
(T D Barron) *w ldr tl rdn and wknd wl over 1f out* **22/1**

1003 **8** *½* **Mystified (IRE)**[40] 5921 2-8-8 **65**............................. PaulMulrennan(3) 11 50
(R F Fisher) *sn bhd* **40/1**

046 **9** *11* **Flash And Dazzle (IRE)**[29] 6120 2-8-13 **67**.................... RobertHavlin 6 25
(J H M Gosden) *chsd ldrs tl rdn and wknd over 3f out* **16/1**

2045 **10** *nk* **Miss Sure Bond (IRE)**[27] 6136 2-9-0 **68**.......................(b[1]) PaulEddery 12 25
(B Smart) *s.i.s: sn prom: wknd 3f out* **33/1**

1m 29.83s (-0.57) **Going Correction** -0.125s/f (Stan) **10** Ran SP% **119.3**
Speed ratings (Par 96):98,97,96,92,90 89,88,88,75,75
CSF £427.14 CT £937.94 TOTE £13.00: £2.60, £7.80, £1.40; EX 347.80.
Owner Gold Ace Racing **Bred** River Downs Stud **Trained** Newmarket, Suffolk

FOCUS
A weak nursery run at a strong gallop with the first four home all finishing from off the pace. The time was reasonable and the form rated through the third looks pretty sound.

NOTEBOOK
Aravalli(IRE) benefited from a strong ride to score at the fourth time of asking. She was off the bridle and pumped along heading out of the back straight, but found plenty for pressure and will relish an extra furlong. Official explanation: trainer said, regarding the improved form shown, this was filly's first run on an all-weather surface (op 11-1)
Royle Dancer ran the best race of his embryonic career, especially after he lost ground due to a tardy start. He is another that should enjoy a stiffer test of stamina. (op 40-1)
Pressure Putt looked to have the race in safe keeping when threaded through a narrow gap turning for home However, he found disappointingly little. (op 10-11 tchd 11-10 in places)
Song Of Silence(USA) was detached from the word go thanks to another tardy start, attributed to the fact she banged her head on the stalls. In the circumstances, she did well to finish so close to the principals, but will find life tough unless she can jump on terms. Official explanation: trainer said filly had hit her head on the stalls (op 6-1 tchd 5-1)
Lyrical Blues(IRE) cut out a generous pace, which was a surprise as he was stepping up in trip with his stamina far from assured. It was therefore not a shock to see him fade in the straight. (op 9-1)

6424 FIRST PAST POST AT BETDIRECT MEDIAN AUCTION MAIDEN STKS (DIV II) 1m 141y(P)
4:55 (4:59) (Class 6) 2-Y-O **£2,497** (£737; £368) **Stalls** Low

Form RPR

03 **1** **Prime Meridian**[27] 6158 2-9-0 .... NCallan 5 69
(J Nicol) *hld up in tch: rdn over 2f out: r.o to ld cl home* **11/10**[1]

0 **2** *nk* **Reem Three**[29] 6122 2-8-9 .... NickyMackay 6 63
(L M Cumani) *a.p: rdn 2f out: led over 1f out: hdd cl home* **5/1**[2]

3 *2* **Very Agreeable** 2-8-9 .... StephenCarson 1 59
(W R Swinburn) *a.p: ev ch over 1f out: sn rdn: no ex towards fin* **8/1**

4 *3* **De La Rue (USA)** 2-9-0 .... TPQueally 13 58+
(M G Quinlan) *s.s and wnt rt: hdwy over 2f out: hung lft fr over 1f out: r.o* **14/1**

0 **5** *1 ¼* **Under Fire (IRE)**[25] 6199 2-9-0 .... HayleyTurner 2 55?
(A W Carroll) *led: rdn 2f out: hdd over 1f out: wknd fnl f* **50/1**

00 **6** *2 ½* **French Opera**[13] 6334 2-9-0 .... EddieAhern 8 50
(J A Osborne) *sn prom: rdn over 2f out: wknd wl over 1f out* **13/2**[3]

7 *2* **Making Moves** 2-8-6 .... PaulMulrennan(3) 4 41
(Ms Deborah J Evans) *prom: rdn over 3f out: sn wknd* **50/1**

8 *3 ½* **True Ruby** 2-8-9 .... DaneO'Neill 9 33
(S Kirk) *s.s: a bhd* **7/1**

0 **9** *½* **Stoneacre Fred (IRE)**[13] 6332 2-9-0 .... GylesParkin 12 37
(Peter Grayson) *plld hrd: sn mid-div: short-lived effrt over 3f out* **50/1**

0 **10** *1* **Fairytale Of York (IRE)**[11] 6342 2-8-9 .... GrahamGibbons 7 30
(D Carroll) *rdn 4f out: a bhd* **100/1**

0 **11** *2 ½* **Xenia**[35] 6002 2-8-9 .... MickyFenton 3 25
(J G Given) *bhd fnl 6f* **20/1**

00 **12** *13* **Bertie Bear**[38] 5961 2-9-0 ....(t) JamieMackay 11 —
(G G Margarson) *hld up in tch: rdn and wknd over 3f out* **50/1**

1m 53.22s (1.46) **Going Correction** -0.125s/f (Stan) **12** Ran SP% **121.5**
Speed ratings (Par 94):88,87,85,83,82 79,78,75,74,73 71,59
CSF £6.57 TOTE £1.70: £1.30, £2.80, £3.90; EX 9.60 Place 6 £358.31, Place 5 £236.59.
Owner J P Hill **Bred** Gilridge Bloodstock Ltd **Trained** Newmarket, Suffolk

FOCUS
A weak maiden and the time was modest. The form can be rated through the winner but the form is not that solid.

NOTEBOOK

Prime Meridian, well backed to score, duly landed a modest event, albeit by a narrow margin. He is entitled to improve with racing and showed a willing attitude when required, but is no star and will find life tougher now. (op 7-4)

Reem Three looked in need of the experience first time at Lingfield and saw her race out better on this occasion. She looks capable of winning a maiden of his nature. (op 9-2 tchd 6-1)

Very Agreeable hails from a stable that has very few first-time out winners, but shaped with promise for the future. She was a little nervy in the stalls but that did not stop her posting an encouraging effort and she should be sharper next time. (op 5-1)

De La Rue(USA), a half-brother to the talented Priolo, was friendless in the market and very green through the early stages. He kept on past some tiring rivals in the straight and will have more of an idea of what is required next time. (op 11-2)

Under Fire(IRE) cut out the early running before fading and his future will surely lie in handicaps. (op 40-1)

French Opera was punted at long odds, but weakened at the distance and can now be handicapped. (op 10-1)

Stoneacre Fred(IRE) Official explanation: jockey said gelding had run too freely

T/Plt: £621.70 to a £1 stake. Pool: £45,055.70. 52.90 winning tickets. T/Qpdt: £164.30 to a £1 stake. Pool: £3,865.50. 17.40 winning tickets. KH

6394 LINGFIELD (L-H)

Saturday, November 26

OFFICIAL GOING: Standard

Wind: Moderate against

6425 BETDIRECT.CO.UK MAIDEN STKS (DIV I) — 1m 2f (P)

12:00 (12:04) (Class 4) 2-Y-O — **£5,129** (£1,526; £762; £380) **Stalls** Low

Form — RPR

4240 **1** **Well Armed (USA)**[35] 6023 2-9-0 95 ... RichardHughes 3 — 78
(C E Brittain) *mde all: shkn up over 1f out: qcknd clr: comf* **4/1**[3]

2 **2** 1 1/4 **Bull Market (IRE)**[27] 6178 2-9-0 ... EddieAhern 13 — 76
(J A Osborne) *lw: a.p: chsd wnr over 2f out: no imp fnl f* **2/1**[1]

0 **3** 1/2 **Remember Ramon (USA)**[133] 3541 2-9-0 ... ChrisCatlin 10 — 75
(M J Wallace) *lw: hld up in rr tl rapid hdwy on outside over 3f out: kpt on one pce ins fnl 2f* **33/1**

4 1 1/4 **Snoqualmie Boy** 2-9-0 ... LPKeniry 6 — 77+
(D R C Elsworth) *w'like: lw: slowly away and rn green: hdwy on outside over 2f out: hung lft in st but styd on* **3/1**[2]

0 **5** 3 1/2 **Christmas Player (USA)**[50] 5708 2-8-9 ... RobertHavlin 2 — 61
(J H M Gosden) *trckd ldrs: rdn 2f out: fdd appr fnl f* **50/1**

0522 **6** 1 1/4 **Opera Comica**[40] 5939 2-8-9 75 ... (v) JimmyFortune 5 — 59
(J H M Gosden) *in rr: mde sme late hdwy on outside* **5/1**

0440 **7** 1/2 **Grand Jour (IRE)**[11] 6352 2-8-7 71 ... (t) JamesDoyle(7) 1 — 63
(K McAuliffe) *in tch on ins: rdn over 2f out: sn outpcd* **25/1**

0 **8** 3/4 **Patoma (IRE)**[33] 6072 2-9-0 ... MickyFenton 8 — 62
(Miss E C Lavelle) *t.k.h: prom: rdn over 2f out: wknd over 1f out* **50/1**

054 **9** 5 **Basiliko (USA)**[38] 5987 2-9-0 75 ... AdrianMcCarthy 4 — 53
(P W Chapple-Hyam) *bhd fr 1/2-way* **20/1**

0020 **10** 1 1/4 **Zizou (IRE)**[11] 6353 2-9-0 64 ... DaneO'Neill 9 — 51
(P R Hedger) *prom on outside: rdn over 2f out: sn btn* **66/1**

65 **11** 3/4 **King's Fable (USA)**[22] 6246 2-9-0 ... KDarley 7 — 49
(M Johnston) *w'like: trckd wnr tl wknd qckly over 2f out* **20/1**

50 **12** 7 **Rubileo**[30] 6122 2-8-9 ... SteveDrowne 11 — 32
(Mrs A J Perrett) *a bhd* **40/1**

0 **13** 3 1/2 **Little Erhaab**[44] 5850 2-8-9 ... IanMongan 12 — 25
(G L Moore) *slowly away: a bhd* **80/1**

2m 5.93s (-1.86) **Going Correction** -0.225s/f (Stan) — **13** Ran SP% **120.4**

Speed ratings (Par 98):98,97,96,95,92 91,91,90,86,85 85,79,76

CSF £11.34 TOTE £5.50: £2.00, £1.40, £7.80; EX 18.40.

Owner Winstar Farm Llc **Bred** WinStar Farm Llc **Trained** Newmarket, Suffolk

FOCUS

A modest pace for this maiden and the winning time was 0.62 seconds slower than the second division. Not many got into this and the winner showed that you can make all over this trip if you judge the pace right. The runner-up sets the standard and the race should produce winners.

NOTEBOOK

Well Armed(USA), trying this trip for the first time on this switch to sand, has typically been plying his trade in Group company in his last few starts on turf, although not entirely disgraced. Given a decent front-running ride, an injection of pace rounding the home bend won him the race as his rivals had insufficient time to make up the leeway. He is likely to struggle to find opportunities from now on however, as he looks to be on a stiff-enough mark. (op 5-1 tchd 11-2)

Bull Market(IRE), up two furlongs from his debut, had to do quite a bit of running early to take a handy position from his wide draw but whether that limited his finishing effort is debatable. He was staying on well at the line which suggests the trip was not a problem and it seems likely he just ran into a better rival on the day. (op 9-4 tchd 7-4)

Remember Ramon(USA) ◆, not seen since his debut in July, got into the race with a swift mid-race move on the outside of the field and deserves credit for keeping on right to the line. This was encouraging.

Snoqualmie Boy ◆, a half-brother to three winners including Seattle Express and Seattle Robber, broke slowly but gradually crept closer as the race progressed. Although unable to get on terms with the front three in the latter stages, he still comes out of the race with plenty of credit. The stable have unleashed some decent types in races like this in recent years, so he is one to watch. (op 5-2)

Christmas Player(USA) is bred to be better than she has shown so far, but did show some ability on this second start and may not have stayed. She looks to have some sort of future, if not necessarily for this yard.

Opera Comica has already shown enough ability on turf, though she may not be totally straightforward, to suggest that she should have finished ahead of her stable companion at least. The fact that she did not even manage that and did not get going until too late made this a disappointing effort. (tchd 11-2)

Rubileo Official explanation: jockey said filly hung left

6426 FIRST PAST THE POST AT BETDIRECT H'CAP (DIV I) — 6f (P)

12:30 (12:32) (Class 5) (0-70,70) 3-Y-O+ — **£3,031** (£901; £450; £225) **Stalls** Low

Form — RPR

-010 **1** **Lake Chini (IRE)**[28] 6157 3-9-4 70 ... (p) PhilipRobinson 5 — 77
(M A Jarvis) *mde all: r.o gamely whn rdn and chal appr fnl f* **11/1**

1221 **2** 3/4 **Dance To The Blues (IRE)**[53] 5686 4-9-0 66 ... (p) DaneO'Neill 11 — 71
(B De Haan) *trckd wnr: chal and ev ch appr fnl f: kpt on but nt quixcken ins* **5/1**[2]

3200 **3** 3/4 **Aggravation**[29] 6132 3-9-0 66 ... (t) LPKeniry 7 — 69
(D R C Elsworth) *hld up: rdn 2f out: styd on wl fnl f* **8/1**[3]

2202 **4** 1/2 **Summer Recluse (USA)**[15] 6315 6-9-4 70 ... (t) GeorgeBaker 1 — 71+
(J M Bradley) *slowly away tl hdwy on ins: r.o wl fnl f* **4/1**[1]

3035 **5** shd **Constructor**[14] 6333 4-8-12 64 ... HayleyTurner 8 — 65+
(C A Cyzer) *hld up: hdwy on ins whn nt clr run appr fnl f. r.o wl towards fin* **10/1**

2146 **6** hd **Kennington**[43] 5869 5-8-4 63 ... (b) KirstyMilczarek(7) 4 — 63
(Mrs C A Dunnett) *prom tl fdd ins fnl f* **9/1**

1366 **7** hd **Sweetest Revenge (IRE)**[97] 4605 4-8-7 66 ... KMay(7) 9 — 66
(M D I Usher) *lw: in rr tl hdwy on outside wl over 1f out: r.o wl fnl f* **12/1**

6540 **8** 1 **Talcen Gwyn (IRE)**[14] 6335 3-8-13 65 ... (v) SteveDrowne 10 — 62
(M F Harris) *t.k.h: prom tl rdn appr fnl f: wknd ins* **25/1**

2100 **9** hd **Attorney**[39] 5954 7-8-10 67 ... MarcHalford(5) 12 — 63
(N E Berry) *trckd ldrs: rdn 2f out: wknd appr fnl f* **10/1**

6050 **10** hd **Monashee Prince (IRE)**[49] 5735 3-8-10 69 ... WilliamCarson(7) 3 — 65
(J R Best) *hld up: rdn 1/2-way: hdwy over 1f out: wknd ins fnl f* **8/1**[3]

1604 **11** nk **Patternmaker (USA)**[59] 5539 3-9-3 69 ... (b) EddieAhern 2 — 64
(W Jarvis) *s.i.s: hdwy 1/2-way: wknd appr fnl f* **8/1**[3]

1m 11.55s (-1.26) **Going Correction** -0.225s/f (Stan) — **11** Ran SP% **118.1**

Speed ratings (Par 103):99,98,97,96,96 95,95,94,94,93 93

CSF £65.49 CT £481.54 TOTE £15.80: £4.10, £1.90, £4.50; EX 90.40.

Owner H R H Sultan Ahmad Shah **Bred** Paul McEnery **Trained** Newmarket, Suffolk

FOCUS

A routine sprint handicap for the track with little separating the whole field at the line. The winning time was identical to the second division.

Lake Chini(IRE) Official explanation: trainer said, regarding the improved form shown, gelding had been suited by wearing cheekpieces for the first time and for being given a more positive ride

Summer Recluse(USA) Official explanation: jockey said gelding had been denied a clear run

6427 RUGBY UNION AT BETDIRECT NOVICE STKS — 7f (P)

1:00 (1:01) (Class 5) 2-Y-O — **£4,287** (£1,275; £637; £318) **Stalls** Low

Form — RPR

0 **1** **Snark (IRE)**[84] 4941 2-8-12 ... FergusSweeney 2 — 76+
(P J Makin) *w'like: str: lw: a gng wl and in tch: qcknd to ld ins fnl f: r.o wl* **20/1**

5053 **2** 1 1/2 **Porters (USA)**[19] 6284 2-9-5 82 ... RichardHughes 4 — 79
(R Hannon) *led tl rdn and hdd ins fnl f: kpt on* **7/2**[2]

5 **3** nk **Rembrandt Quality (USA)**[36] 6013 2-8-12 ... KDarley 5 — 71
(Mrs A J Perrett) *trckd ldr tl nt qckn ins fnl f* **5/2**[1]

1005 **4** 1/2 **Certain Circles (USA)**[19] 6284 2-8-11 75 ... NeilChalmers(3) 9 — 72
(A M Balding) *trckd ldrs: rdn 1/2-way: r.o fnl f* **12/1**

04 **5** shd **Vodkatini**[28] 6148 2-8-12 ... (v[1]) ChrisCatlin 10 — 70
(P J Makin) *in tch: rdn over 1f out: styd on fnl f* **33/1**

30 **6** 5 **Bitter Chill**[38] 5988 2-8-12 ... AdrianMcCarthy 7 — 57
(P W Chapple-Hyam) *prom on outside: rdn 1/2-way: one pce ins fnl 2f* **8/1**

7 1/2 **Appreciated** 2-7-10 ... LiamJones(7) 12 — 47
(W J Haggas) *w'like: leggy: bit bkwd: mid-div: pushed along 1/2-way: mde sme late hdwy* **50/1**

8 nk **Misterbianco (IRE)** 2-8-9 ow1 ... JimmyFortune 6 — 52
(B J Meehan) *unf: scope: rangy: a towards rr* **6/1**[3]

9 3/4 **Great Composer (IRE)** 2-8-8 ... EddieAhern 8 — 49
(Mrs A J Perrett) *leggy: slowly away: sn pushed along: nvr on terms* **20/1**

10 1/2 **Black Sea Pearl** 2-8-3 ... JimmyQuinn 13 — 43
(P W D'Arcy) *w'like: slowly away: a bhd* **40/1**

0 **11** 1 1/2 **Miss Champagne (IRE)**[22] 6242 2-8-2 ... RoryMoore(5) 14 — 43
(M Quinn) *w'like: neat: hld up: racd wd: nvr on terms* **66/1**

12 9 **Island Myth (IRE)** 2-8-8 ... SteveDrowne 1 — 22
(M P Tregoning) *w'like: slowly away: a bhd* **14/1**

13 1 3/4 **Brabinger (IRE)** 2-8-8 ... LPKeniry 11 — 18
(B G Powell) *leggy: a struggling in rr* **33/1**

1616 **P** **King Alfie**[16] 6304 2-9-4 70 ... (b) DaneO'Neill 3 — —
(A B Haynes) *chsd ldrs tl wknd rapidly 2f out: p.u and dismntd over 1f out* **7/1**

1m 25.07s (-0.82) **Going Correction** -0.225s/f (Stan) — **14** Ran SP% **124.3**

Speed ratings (Par 96):95,93,92,92,92 86,85,85,84,84 82,72,70,—

CSF £87.66 TOTE £28.70: £6.00, £1.60, £1.70; EX 223.30.

Owner Brian Brackpool **Bred** Anthony Rafferty **Trained** Ogbourne Maisey, Wilts

FOCUS

This looked a fair contest of its type and the pace was decent. The front five pulled well clear of the others, the form looks sound rated through the runner-up and third and it is amongst that quintet that the interest lies with the future in mind.

NOTEBOOK

Snark(IRE) ◆, a 28,000gns colt out of a winning half-sister to World Premiere and Shiny, had not shown much on his turf debut in September, but may have had excuses for that and was a different proposition here. Always travelling well just behind the leaders, he found plenty when asked to go and win his race and, highly regarded by his trainer, could be a nice handicapper for the yard at around a mile next season. (op 14-1)

Porters(USA) tried to make every yard, but was unable to hold the progressive winner late on. He is consistent and time may show that he faced a stiff task in trying to concede the winner 7lb, but this looks to be as good as he is. (tchd 4-1)

Rembrandt Quality(USA), who showed promise on his debut at Newbury last month, had every chance but lacked a turn of foot and this furlong-shorter trip may not have been ideal. (op 3-1)

Certain Circles(USA) ran better than he did at Wolverhampton and, using Porters as a guide, probably ran very close to his mark. He did not take the home bend as well as some which means that the performance could be rated a length or so better, but he lacks the scope of a couple of those that finished ahead of him. (op 10-1)

Vodkatini, with the visor replacing the blinkers for this sand debut, finished strongly up the inside without getting on terms with his stable companion, but still showed enough to suggest a race could be found on this surface. It will be interesting to see what sort of a mark he gets.

Appreciated Official explanation: jockey said filly suffered interference in running

Misterbianco(IRE) Official explanation: jockey said colt had run green

Great Composer(IRE) Official explanation: jockey said colt suffered interference in running

King Alfie was still in with a shout when appearing to go wrong soon after turning for home. (op 10-1)

6428 BETDIRECT.CO.UK MAIDEN STKS (DIV II) — 1m 2f (P)

1:30 (1:35) (Class 4) 2-Y-O — **£5,129** (£1,526; £762; £380) **Stalls** Low

Form — RPR

5 **1** **All The Good (IRE)**[36] 6009 2-9-0 ... KDarley 4 — 80+
(G A Butler) *lw: trckd eladers: led 2f out: clr whn veered sharply rt cl home* **11/2**

2 1 1/4 **Pigeon Island** 2-9-0 ... DaneO'Neill 3 — 77+
(H Candy) *neat: bit bkwd: hld up: hdwy over 3f out: styd on to chse wnr over 1f out* **9/2**[2]

0 **3** 1 3/4 **Dimelight**[70] 5306 2-8-9 ... LPKeniry 2 — 69+
(D R C Elsworth) *t.k.h: settled in mid-sivision: hdwy 2f out: styd on: nvr nrr* **5/1**[3]

04 **4** 1 3/4 **Tower Hill (IRE)**[14] 6334 2-9-0 ... PhilipRobinson 13 — 71+
(M A Jarvis) *lw: led after 2f: hdd 2f out: wknd ins fnl f* **10/1**

505 **5** ½ **Rajaall**[49] 5748 2-9-0 76 ChrisCatlin 12 70
(M R Channon) *hld up: hdwy 1/2-way: rdn 3f out: one pce ins fnl 2f* **10/1**

5 **6** 3½ **Raydiation (USA)**[50] 5709 2-9-0 RichardHughes 9 64
(B J Meehan) *lw: prom tl lost pl 4f out: rdn and n.d after* **5/2**[1]

000 **7** 7 **Peephole**[38] 5968 2-9-0 61 FergusSweeney 6 51
(P J Makin) *nvr bttr than mid-div* **50/1**

8 1½ **Leeson Street (IRE)** 2-8-9 TPQueally 14 44
(M G Quinlan) *neat: slowly away: sme hdwy over 3f out: nvr on terms* **66/1**

0 **9** 1¼ **Regal Magic (IRE)**[23] 6234 2-8-9 JimmyFortune 5 41
(J H M Gosden) *led for 2f: wknd qckly wl over 1f out* **33/1**

10 1 **Radical Attraction (USA)** 2-8-9 EddieAhern 10 39
(R Hannon) *w'like: leggy: s.i.s: a bhd* **25/1**

0 **11** 7 **Bournonville**[64] 5435 2-9-0 NickyMackay 11 32
(J Ryan) *trckd ldrs:m rdn 4f out: sn wknd* **14/1**

12 shd **Sky High Guy (IRE)** 2-9-0 GeorgeBaker 7 32
(S Kirk) *leggy: slowly away: a bhd* **25/1**

05 **13** 8 **Unasuming (IRE)**[28] 6150 2-8-9 JimmyQuinn 1 12
(J Pearce) *a bhd: eased ins fnl f* **20/1**

05 **14** 11 **Lynford Lady**[12] 6342 2-8-9 IanMongan 8 —
(P W D'Arcy) *chsd ldrs tl wknd qckly 4f out: eased ins fnl f* **66/1**

2m 5.31s (-2.48) **Going Correction** -0.225s/f (Stan) **14** Ran SP% **124.0**
Speed ratings (Par 98):100,99,97,96,95 93,87,86,85,84 78,78,72,63
CSF £29.50 TOTE £7.60: £1.50, £2.40, £2.30; EX 32.20.
Owner Future In Mind Partnership **Bred** Mount Coote Partnership **Trained** Blewbury, Oxon

FOCUS
A fair maiden in which the front half-dozen came clear of the others and there were a few encouraging performances for the future. The winning time was 0.62 seconds faster than the first division and the form looks pretty strong, rated through the fourth.

NOTEBOOK
All The Good(IRE) ◆ appreciated this longer trip, just as his debut effort at Newbury last month suggested he might. Staying on strongly down the straight, he may have won by even further had he not shown signs of greenness late on and there is every chance he will improve again from this. (op 5-1 tchd 9-2 and 6-1)
Pigeon Island ◆, a 75,000gns half-brother to five winners including Mons and Inforapenny, ran a debut full of promise and never stopped trying at any stage. He should not take long in going one better and on this evidence will stay a bit further. (op 7-2)
Dimelight, stepping up three furlongs from her debut, ran her race and is going the right way. Her breeding and her style of running suggest she may be suited by going up in trip again. (tchd 6-1)
Tower Hill(IRE) had to race four-wide around the first bend in order to get to the front and that may have contributed to his capitulation in the home straight. He may do better now that he can be handicapped. (op 8-1)
Rajaall did not improve much for this longer trip. He will remain vulnerable in races like this and may be better off in a handicap. (op 9-1)
Raydiation(USA) was close enough for the early part of the contest, but he came under pressure at the top bend and looked very awkward thereafter. Hopefully it was just a case of greenness and his next outing should tell us more. Official explanation: jockey said colt hung badly left early on (op 3-1)
Bournonville, 11th of 13 after showing up until halfway on his debut here in September, was a springer in the market on this occasion but was one of the first beaten. (op 40-1 tchd 50-1)

6429 FOOTBALL CASHBACKS AT BETDIRECT H'CAP 7f (P)
2:00 (2:03) (Class 6) (0-52,54) 3-Y-0+ **£3,378** (£1,005; £502; £250) **Stalls** Low

Form RPR

1200 **1** **Vlasta Weiner**[5] 6407 5-8-12 52 (b) LPKeniry 12 60
(J M Bradley) *trckd ldrs: hung lft over 1f out: squeezed through to ld wl ins fnl f* **20/1**

6125 **2** nk **Tipsy Lad**[21] 6262 3-8-11 52 (bt) DavidMcCabe 14 59
(D J S Ffrench Davis) *a.p: wnt 2nd 2f out: rdn and kpt on ins fnl f* **14/1**

3500 **3** 1¼ **High Rhythm**[58] 5564 3-8-11 52 J-PGuillambert 10 56
(S C Williams) *hld up in mis-div: rdn 2f out: r.o wl fnl f* **14/1**

0421 **4** shd **Mulberry Lad (IRE)**[4] 6411 3-8-12 53 6ex DarrenWilliams 11 56
(P W Hiatt) *trckd ldr: led 3f out: rdn and hdd wl ins fnl f: no ex* **9/1**

2113 **5** shd **Doctor Dennis (IRE)**[18] 6292 8-8-12 52 (v) JimmyQuinn 6 55
(J Pearce) *hld up: hdwy over 1f out: fin wl: nvr nrr* **6/1**[2]

0006 **6** 1½ **Lawaaheb (IRE)**[19] 6287 4-8-7 52 (v) RoryMoore(5) 9 51
(B R Johnson) *chsd ldrs: rdn 2f out: wknd ins fnl f* **9/1**

2461 **7** nk **Smirfys Night**[33] 6078 6-8-12 52 FergalLynch 8 51
(E S McMahon) *mid-div: rdn over 3f out: kpt on but nvr nr to chal after* **11/4**[1]

3031 **8** shd **Zazous**[5] 6397 4-9-0 54 6ex SteveDrowne 3 52
(J J Bridger) *b: towards rr: stqayed on fnl f: nvr nrr* **10/1**

1306 **9** ¾ **Noble Mount**[33] 6070 4-8-12 52 (p) DaneO'Neill 1 48
(A B Haynes) *b.hind: slowly away: a towards rr* **12/1**

2361 **10** nk **Lucius Verrus (USA)**[61] 5520 5-8-9 52 (v) PatrickMathers(3) 7 48
(D Shaw) *slowly away: a bhd* **10/1**

3660 **11** 3½ **Lord Lahar**[255] 632 6-8-11 51 TPQueally 4 37
(M A Buckley) *bit bkwd: chsd ldrs tl wknd qckly over 2f out* **25/1**

035 **12** 3 **Inherit (IRE)**[74] 5210 3-8-11 52 TonyHamilton 13 31
(R A Fahey) *wl bhd whn rn ver wd into home st* **8/1**[3]

0120 **13** 4 **My Girl Pearl (IRE)**[38] 5975 5-8-12 52 MickyFenton 5 20
(M S Saunders) *led tl hdd 3f out: wknd qckly* **14/1**

0000 **14** 3½ **We'Re Stonybroke (IRE)**[25] 6217 6-8-12 52 (p) ChrisCatlin 2 11
(G C H Chung) *a bhd* **33/1**

1m 24.23s (-1.66) **Going Correction** -0.225s/f (Stan)
WFA 3 from 4yo+ 1lb **14** Ran SP% **129.5**
Speed ratings (Par 101):100,99,98,98,98 96,95,95,94,94 90,87,82,78
CSF £290.67 CT £2390.22 TOTE £30.60: £8.30, £4.80, £5.80; EX 478.40.
Owner Miss Diane Hill **Bred** C J Hill **Trained** Sedbury, Gloucs

FOCUS
A modest handicap, but run at a decent gallop and not many were able to get into the race from off the pace. Those drawn wide held sway, but that may just be coincidence, and the form looks pretty solid rated through the placed horses.
Doctor Dennis(IRE) Official explanation: jockey said gelding suffered interference in running
Lucius Verrus(USA) Official explanation: jockey said gelding stumbled at the start
Lord Lahar Official explanation: jockey said gelding hung right
Inherit(IRE) Official explanation: jockey said gelding hung right

6430 FIRST PAST THE POST AT BETDIRECT H'CAP (DIV II) 6f (P)
2:35 (2:35) (Class 5) (0-70,70) 3-Y-0+ **£3,024** (£899; £449; £224) **Stalls** Low

Form RPR

040 **1** **General Feeling (IRE)**[15] 6315 4-9-2 68 GeorgeBaker 9 77
(S Kirk) *lw: hld up in rr: hdwy on outside wl over 1f out: rdn and r.o to ld nr fin gng away* **9/2**[2]

0060 **2** 1¼ **Joy And Pain**[16] 6302 4-9-3 69 RichardHughes 12 74+
(J R Boyle) *b: trckd ldrs: ev ch ins fnl f: kpt on cl home* **6/1**

0052 **3** nk **Tag Team (IRE)**[21] 6264 4-8-11 63 (v[1]) PaulEddery 8 67
(John A Harris) *b: b.hind: trckd ldr: rdn and led jst ins fnl f: hdd and lost 2nd nr fin* **5/1**[3]

2404 **4** ¾ **Kew The Music**[32] 6103 5-9-0 66 ChrisCatlin 1 68
(M R Channon) *lw: slowly away and in rr tl rapid hdwy appr fnl f: nvr nrr* **4/1**[1]

4004 **5** ¾ **Kempsey**[29] 6132 3-8-13 65 (b) J-PGuillambert 4 65
(J J Bridger) *led tl rdn and hdd jst ins fnl f: no ex* **14/1**

-056 **6** hd **Extra Mark**[99] 4534 3-8-4 63 WilliamCarson(7) 6 62
(J R Best) *t.k.h: in rr: mde sme late hdwy* **10/1**

1000 **7** nk **Turibius**[66] 5406 6-9-0 66 JimmyQuinn 7 64
(T E Powell) *hld up in mid-div: effrt over 1f out: nvr nr to chal* **15/2**

0000 **8** 1½ **Windy Prospect**[25] 6216 3-9-4 70 MickyFenton 5 64
(C R Dore) *trckd ldrs: rdn 2f out: wknd appr fnl f* **10/1**

020 **9** 1 **Revien (IRE)**[77] 5119 3-8-11 63 PaulFitzsimons 3 54
(Miss J R Tooth) *mid-div on ins: bhd fnl 2f* **12/1**

1m 11.55s (-1.26) **Going Correction** -0.225s/f (Stan) **9** Ran SP% **113.4**
Speed ratings (Par 103):99,97,96,95,94 94,94,92,90
CSF £31.01 CT £125.16 TOTE £5.70: £1.90, £2.70, £2.10; EX 23.10.
Owner The So Long Partnership **Bred** John Graham And Leslie Laverty **Trained** Upper Lambourn, Berks

FOCUS
As with the first division, an ordinary sprint handicap for the track and the time was exactly the same. The form looks reasonably sound with the third, fourth and fifth close to their marks.

6431 BETDIRECTPOKER.COM H'CAP 1m (P)
3:10 (3:10) (Class 3) (0-95,94) 3-Y-0+ **£8,313** (£2,473; £1,236; £617) **Stalls** High

Form RPR

6021 **1** **Red Spell (IRE)**[7] 6379 4-9-4 94 RichardHughes 7 108+
(R Hannon) *lw: hld up in tch: sustained run in fnl 2f to ld fnl 50yds: cleverly* **7/4**[1]

6004 **2** ¾ **Psychiatrist**[7] 6379 4-9-0 90 JimmyFortune 10 99
(R Hannon) *b: trckd ldrs: wnt 2nd over 2f out: rdn to ld 100yds out: hdd fnl 50yds* **11/1**

0000 **3** ¾ **Bahiano (IRE)**[15] 6314 4-9-0 90 SteveDrowne 3 97
(C E Brittain) *a in tch: rdn and r.o fnl f* **12/1**

5302 **4** ¾ **San Antonio**[27] 6182 5-8-12 88 (b) MickyFenton 4 94
(Mrs P Sly) *lw: led tl hdd 100yds out: no ex* **13/2**[2]

6012 **5** ½ **Wyatt Earp (IRE)**[11] 6350 4-8-7 83 JimmyQuinn 1 87
(R A Fahey) *hld up: kpt on one pce fnl f* **8/1**[3]

0403 **6** nk **Vicious Warrior**[14] 6322 6-8-4 80 oh1 DeanMcKeown 9 84
(R M Whitaker) *lw: t.k.h: sn in tch: effrt over 1f out: nt qckn after* **8/1**[3]

6036 **7** 2 **Marshman (IRE)**[7] 6379 6-8-10 86 EddieAhern 5 85
(M H Tompkins) *hld up: rdn whn short of room over 2f out: n.d after* **8/1**[3]

0042 **8** shd **King's Caprice**[7] 6379 4-8-12 88 (t) StephenCarson 2 87
(J A Geake) *lw: v.s.a: nvr on terms* **8/1**[3]

6000 **9** ¾ **Skidmark**[7] 6377 4-8-8 84 (p) PaulFitzsimons 12 81
(Miss J R Tooth) *s.i.s: a in rr* **25/1**

20-0 **10** 2½ **Leoballero**[7] 6379 5-8-8 84 (t) ChrisCatlin 8 75
(D J Daly) *b: lw: racd wd: in tch: rdn 3f out: wknd over 1f out* **16/1**

0050 **11** 10 **Te Quiero**[15] 6314 7-8-11 90 (t) NelsonDeSouza(3) 6 58
(Miss Gay Kelleway) *b: b.hind: trckd ldr tl wknd qckly over 2f out* **50/1**

1m 35.77s (-3.66) **Going Correction** -0.225s/f (Stan) course record **11** Ran SP% **121.9**
Speed ratings (Par 107):109,108,107,106,106 105,103,103,103,100 90
CSF £23.85 CT £194.32 TOTE £2.20: £1.40, £3.90, £3.70; EX 26.70.
Owner Mrs John Lee **Bred** Tom Darcy And Vincent McCarthy **Trained** East Everleigh, Wilts

FOCUS
A cracking race run at a rapid pace resulting in a course record. The form looks strong and could rate higher although the runner-up's promimity tempers enthusiasm.

NOTEBOOK
Red Spell(IRE), 5lb higher than when winning here seven days ago, was never going to have a problem with the extra furlong. Switched off in the pack, he had to be brought wide for his effort turning in but although he had a bit of ground to make up, he always gave the impression he was going to make it. He was given an excellent ride and he has now lowered two of this track's course records within a week. (op 2-1 tchd 9-4)
Psychiatrist ◆, 6lb better off with Red Spell for a four-length beating here last week, duly got closer over this extra furlong having been close to the pace from the start, but was unable to withstand his old rival's devastating late burst. He deserves to win a race on this surface. (op 10-1 tchd 12-1)
Bahiano(IRE), without a win since scoring here in the February of last year, has run some decent races in defeat since then and this was another, but he probably needs to drop a bit further in the weights and after this effort the Handicapper may not be inclined to accommodate him.
San Antonio blasted off in front as usual and hung on in typically game fashion for as long as he could. He is still lightly raced on sand, but he remains 9lb higher than for his last win on turf and this effort is unlikely to help his cause. (op 9-2)
Wyatt Earp(IRE), trying a mile for the first time in his 24th start, stayed on down the straight and was not beaten far. It would be hard to say that he did not stay. (tchd 7-1)
Vicious Warrior was not completely disgraced, but neither did he build on his promising return to this track two weeks ago. (op 10-1 tchd 12-1)
Marshman(IRE), making a rare appearance over this trip, finished behind Red Spell and Psychiatrist here seven days ago and was 5lb better off with the former, but 1lb worse off with the latter. He was just trying to get into the race when running into bother on the home bend and for a horse that needs delivering with precision timing that was the last thing he needed. Official explanation: jockey said gelding suffered interference in running (op 9-1)
King's Caprice, runner-up to Red Spell here the previous week and 3lb better off for just over a length, was trying this trip for the very first time, but whether it suited or not became academic when he completely lost all chance at the start. This effort is best ignored. Official explanation: jockey said gelding had been slowly away (op 9-1)
Te Quiero has a wretched record on Polytrack, so the way he capitulated after showing up for a long way was no great surprise. It will probably be a different matter if or when he returns to Fibresand.

6432 BETDIRECT 0800 211222 H'CAP 1m 4f (P)
3:40 (3:42) (Class 5) (0-70,70) 3-Y-0+ **£4,103** (£1,220; £610; £304) **Stalls** Low

Form RPR

4650 **1** **Wise Owl**[25] 6218 3-8-12 70 JimmyQuinn 10 84
(J Pearce) *t.k.h: mid-div tl stdy hdwy fr 4f out: led over 2f out: sn clr: kpt up to work fnl f* **10/1**

0000 **2** 5 **Karaoke (IRE)**[14] 6325 5-9-0 66 GeorgeBaker 1 72
(S Kirk) *hld up: hdwy 2f out: styd on to go 2nd ins fnl f* **7/1**[3]

3035 **3** ½ **Trew Style**[25] 6215 3-8-10 68 EddieAhern 11 73
(M H Tompkins) *mid-div: rdn over 2f out: styd on fnl f: nvr nrr* **7/1**[3]

0613 **4** shd **Easy Laughter (IRE)**[14] 6337 4-9-1 67 (bt) AlanDaly 9 72
(C P Morlock) *hld up in mid-vision: hdwy to go 2nd 2f out: no ex and lost 2nd ins fnl f* **12/1**

0060 **5** *1* **King Of Knight (IRE)**[21] 6265 4-8-11 63......................(v[1]) ChrisCatlin 16 66
(G Prodromou) *slowly away: in rr tl hdwy over 1f out: styd on: nvr nrr* **14/1**
6060 **6** *1 3/4* **Sri Lipis**[14] 6325 3-8-12 70.. TPQueally 6 71
(P F I Cole) *lw: s.i.s: rdn 3f out: nvr nr to chal* **33/1**
43/0 **7** *3* **Sphinx (FR)**[36] 6012 7-9-4 70.. IanMongan 8 66
(Jamie Poulton) *b: in tch: rdn 3f out: wknd wl over 1f out* **14/1**
0024 **8** *shd* **Oldenway**[14] 6337 6-8-13 65.. TonyHamilton 13 61
(R A Fahey) *trckd ldrs tl wknd 2f out* **5/1**[2]
0006 **9** *1/2* **Duelling Banjos**[24] 6230 6-9-3 69................................ StephenCarson 2 64+
(J Akehurst) *in tch tl wknd 2f out* **12/1**
-066 **10** *1/2* **Rome (IRE)**[40] 3751 6-8-11 68...............................(b) RobynBrisland(5) 12 62
(G P Enright) *a towards rr* **20/1**
3143 **11** *hd* **Perfidious (USA)**[43] 5867 7-8-10 65..............................(v) AmirQuinn(3) 7 59
(J R Boyle) *trckd ldr: rdn 5f out: wknd qckly 2f out* **10/1**
601 **12** *1/2* **Prime Powered (IRE)**[11] 6356 4-9-2 68.......................... JimmyFortune 5 61+
(G L Moore) *in tch tl wknd over 3f out* **4/1**[1]
4235 **13** *3/4* **Hawkit (USA)**[135] 3473 4-9-0 66.................................. AdrianMcCarthy 4 58
(P D Evans) *s.i.s: a in rr* **20/1**
0004 **14** *3/4* **Border Edge**[36] 6015 7-8-10 62..................................(v) J-PGuillambert 3 53
(J J Bridger) *plld hrd: led tl hdd over 2f out: wknd qckly* **25/1**
/00- **15** *9* **Grey Admiral (USA)**[42] 3695 4-8-6 63.......................... RoryMoore(5) 15 39
(B R Johnson) *a bhd* **66/1**
0000 **16** *12* **Dickie Deadeye**[35] 6029 8-9-0 66.................................. SteveDrowne 14 23
(J A Geake) *lw: mid-div tl wknd sn after 1/2-way* **25/1**

2m 30.95s (-3.44) **Going Correction** -0.225s/f (Stan)
WFA 3 from 4yo+ 6lb **16** Ran SP% **130.2**
Speed ratings (Par 103):102,98,98,98,97 96,94,94,94,93 93,93,92,92,86 78
CSF £77.16 CT £544.84 TOTE £16.80: £3.60, £2.20, £2.30, £3.40; EX 132.00 Place 6 £300.96, Place 5 £170.95.
Owner S Birdseye **Bred** Darley **Trained** Newmarket, Suffolk

FOCUS
A competitive if modest handicap. The early pace was decent thanks to Border Edge tearing off in front, though the final time was average and the form, although sound, is not particularly strong.
Perfidious(USA) Official explanation: jockey said gelding had no more to give
Prime Powered(IRE) Official explanation: jockey said gelding was hampered on the bend
Border Edge Official explanation: jockey said gelding had run too freely
T/Plt: £622.70 to a £1 stake. Pool: £36,297.20. 42.55 winning tickets. T/Qpdt: £67.60 to a £1 stake. Pool: £1,918.50. 21.00 winning tickets. JS

6417 WOLVERHAMPTON (A.W) (L-H)
Saturday, November 26

OFFICIAL GOING: Standard to fast
Wind: Slight, across Weather: Fine

6433 NO 5P RULE 4S AT BETDIRECT MAIDEN STKS 5f 20y(P)
7:00 (7:00) (Class 5) 2-Y-O **£3,413** (£1,015; £507; £253) **Stalls** Low

Form RPR
4302 **1** **Charming Ballet (IRE)**[19] 6282 2-9-0 67......................(p) JimmyQuinn 1 73
(N P Littmoden) *mde all: rdn wl over 1f out: all out* **7/2**[2]
2332 **2** *1/2* **Canina**[15] 6311 2-8-9 68.. EddieAhern 11 66
(Ms Deborah J Evans) *hld up in mid-div: rdn over 2f out: swtchd rt ent st: hdwy fnl f: nt rch wnr* **9/1**
6232 **3** *nk* **Best Double**[16] 6303 2-8-9 72..(b) NCallan 12 65
(G A Butler) *mid-div: hdwy over 2f out: rdn wl over 1f out: r.o ins fnl f* **9/4**[1]
6065 **4** *shd* **Sands Crooner (IRE)**[7] 6374 2-8-11 70................(t) PatrickMathers(3) 5 70
(D Shaw) *a.p: rdn and ev ch whn n.m.r and hit rails ins fnl f: r.o* **8/1**[3]
2200 **5** *1* **Deserving**[22] 6242 2-8-9 69.. TonyCulhane 3 61
(W J Haggas) *outpcd and bhd: hdwy u.p over 1f out: r.o ins fnl f* **8/1**[3]
6623 **6** *1/2* **Gavarnie Beau (IRE)**[124] 3792 2-9-0 69.......................... FergusSweeney 9 64
(M Blanshard) *bhd: hdwy fnl f: nvr nrr* **33/1**
0 **7** *1/2* **Charley's Aunt (IRE)**[26] 6197 2-8-9 .... MickyFenton 2 58
(N P Littmoden) *sn bhd: c wd ent st: hdwy fnl f: r.o* **16/1**
0230 **8** *hd* **Bel Cantor**[26] 6197 2-9-0 75.. FergalLynch 13 62
(W J H Ratcliffe) *prom: rdn over 2f out: wknd ins fnl f* **22/1**
5003 **9** *2* **Twinned (IRE)**[15] 6311 2-8-7 70..................................(p) JosephWalsh(7) 8 55
(J S Moore) *prom: rdn over 1f out: wknd ins fnl f* **22/1**
3025 **10** *2 1/2* **Miss Dixie**[15] 6312 2-8-9 65.. TomEaves 7 41
(Miss J A Camacho) *mid-div: rdn over 3f out: bhd fnl 2f* **9/1**
0 **11** *2* **Ames Souer (IRE)**[29] 6128 2-8-2 .... DanielleMcCreery(7) 10 33
(D Carroll) *bmpd s: plld hrd: a bhd* **50/1**
00 **12** *3* **Aeronaut**[50] 5711 2-9-0 .... DaneO'Neill 4 28
(J M Bradley) *outpcd* **33/1**
40 **13** *1 1/4* **Penny Thoughts**[15] 6311 2-8-9 .... ChrisCatlin 6 18
(E S McMahon) *w wnr: rdn 2f out: sn wknd* **25/1**

62.26 secs (-0.56) **Going Correction** -0.20s/f (Stan) **13** Ran SP% **121.5**
Speed ratings (Par 96):96,95,94,94,92 92,91,91,87,83 80,75,73
CSF £32.49 TOTE £4.30: £1.60, £2.10, £1.80; EX 43.10.
Owner Ivan Allan **Bred** Brian Donlon **Trained** Newmarket, Suffolk

FOCUS
A moderate maiden but sound enough form rated through the consistent placed horses.

NOTEBOOK
Charming Ballet(IRE) found the combination of cheekpieces and front-running tactics back over the minimum trip paying off with a hard-fought victory. (tchd 3-1 and 4-1)
Canina continues to knock on the door in this sort of company and would certainly not mind a return to six. (op 8-1)
Best Double was back up to six furlongs having already confirmed that she stays seven. (op 2-1)
Sands Crooner(IRE) may well have been just beginning to get the worst of the argument when tightened up on the inside rail. He was probably second best on merit. (op 12-1)
Deserving ◆, who showed plenty of promise on her first two starts, gave the impression that she will do better when tackling further on this first outing on sand. (op 6-1)
Gavarnie Beau(IRE), returning after a four-month break, is another to bear in mind when reverting to a longer distance.
Bel Cantor Official explanation: jockey said gelding hung left
Ames Souer(IRE) Official explanation: jockey said saddle slipped

6434 BETDIRECT ON CHANNEL 4 TEXT PAGE 613 CLAIMING STKS 1m 5f 194y(P)
7:30 (7:30) (Class 6) 3-Y-0+ **£2,900** (£856; £428) **Stalls** Low

Form RPR
2000 **1** **Tedstale (USA)**[57] 5594 7-10-0 80..(b) NCallan 4 72+
(K A Ryan) *hld up and bhd: hdwy over 3f out: rdn 2f out: hung lft and bmpd over 1f out: led ins fnl f: r.o wl* **2/1**[2]
2220 **2** *2* **Missie Baileys**[81] 5034 3-8-9 52.. IanMongan 9 58
(Mrs L J Mongan) *plld hrd: led 1f: remained prom: led 4f out: rdn over 2f out: edgd rt and bmpd over 1f out: hdd and no ex ins fnl furlon* **16/1**
-000 **3** *3* **Movie King (IRE)**[10] 6371 6-9-8 62..........................(t) MichaelTebbutt 11 59
(S R Bowring) *hld up in tch: hdwy over 5f out: rdn over 3f out: nt clr run ent st: sn edgd lft: one pce fnl f* **25/1**
0514 **4** *3/4* **Typhoon Tilly**[11] 6356 8-10-0 66.. SteveDrowne 3 64
(C R Egerton) *hld up in tch: hdwy over 5f out: wnt 2nd over 2f out: sn rdn: one pce* **11/8**[1]
04P6 **5** *3* **Oktis Morilious (IRE)**[5] 6394 4-8-12 40........................... JimmyQuinn 2 44
(A W Carroll) *hld up in mid-div: hdwy over 3f out: sn rdn: wknd fnl f* **33/1**
0050 **6** *2 1/2* **Paradise Valley**[7] 6381 5-9-8 48......................................(t) MickyFenton 1 50
(Stef Liddiard) *hld up in rr: sme hdwy over 1f out: nvr nr ldrs* **20/1**
4325 **7** *2* **Tanning**[14] 6331 3-7-8 35.. DuranFentiman(5) 7 32
(A W Carroll) *hld up towards rr: rdn over 3f out: n.d* **16/1**
8 *1/2* **Nabir (FR)**[22] 5-9-6 79... TomEaves 12 45
(P D Niven) *hld up: hdwy 4f out: rdn and wknd 3f out* **20/1**
0003 **9** *17* **Ben Bacchus (IRE)**[46] 5822 3-9-0 47....................................(b) FergalLynch 8 23
(P A Blockley) *s.i.s: hld up and bhd: stdy hdwy 5f out: rdn and wknd over 3f out* **12/1**[3]
0060 **10** *7* **Ewar Finch (FR)**[12] 6344 3-7-13 35.................................. FrancisFerris 5 —
(K O Cunningham-Brown) *s.i.s: hdwy to ld over 12f out: hdd over 6f out: wknd 4f out* **66/1**
00- **11** *21* **Naval Attache**[395] 6441 3-9-6 .... GrahamGibbons 6 —
(P A Blockley) *plld hrd: led briefly after 1f: chsd ldr: led over 6f out to 4f out: sn wknd: t.o* **40/1**

3m 4.98s (-2.39) **Going Correction** -0.20s/f (Stan)
WFA 3 from 4yo+ 8lb **11** Ran SP% **115.1**
Speed ratings (Par 101):98,96,95,94,93 91,90,90,80,76 64
CSF £28.49 TOTE £3.70: £2.30, £1.50, £7.10; EX 22.90.
Owner Yorkshire Racing Club & Derek Blackhurst **Bred** Gainesway Thoroughbreds Limited **Trained** Hambleton, N Yorks
■ Stewards' Enquiry : Steve Drowne one-day ban: careless riding (Dec 7)

FOCUS
Plenty of dead wood in this slowly-run claimer. The form makes sense on paper but the time suggests this is shaky.
Ben Bacchus(IRE) Official explanation: trainer said gelding had a breathing problem
Naval Attache Official explanation: jockey said saddle slipped

6435 BETTER OFFERS AT BETDIRECT.CO.UK MAIDEN STKS 5f 216y(P)
8:00 (8:00) (Class 5) 2-Y-O **£4,216** (£1,254; £626; £313) **Stalls** Low

Form RPR
53 **1** **Heaven Knows**[21] 6251 2-9-0 .... TonyCulhane 4 76+
(W J Haggas) *hld up in tch: pushed into ld nr fin: cleverly* **5/2**[2]
2 **2** *1/2* **Stonecrabstomorrow (IRE)**[7] 6374 2-9-0 .... EddieAhern 7 74
(P F I Cole) *led over 1f: w ldrs: rdn wl over 1f out: led wl ins fnl f: hdd and nt qckn nr fin* **13/8**[1]
3 *3/4* **Star Crowned (USA)** 2-9-0 ....(t) JimmyFortune 2 72
(B J Meehan) *prom: led over 4f out: rdn wl over 1f out: hdd and nt qckn wl ins fnl f* **5/1**[3]
4 *1 3/4* **Siwa** 2-8-9 .... SteveDrowne 1 62+
(E A L Dunlop) *chsd ldrs: n.m.r on ins and lost pl over 4f out: hdwy wl over 1f out: nt qckn ins fnl f* **9/1**
5 *nk* **Jenise (IRE)** 2-8-4 .... DuranFentiman(5) 8 61?
(Mark Campion) *bhd: hmpd over 4f out: rdn and hdwy on ins wl over 1f out: sn swtchd rt: edgd lft ins fnl f: kpt on* **66/1**
6 *shd* **Creme Brulee** 2-8-9 .... DaneO'Neill 11 61+
(C R Egerton) *s.s: hdwy 2f out: r.o one pce fnl f: bttr for r* **16/1**
7 *3/4* **Bellabelini (IRE)** 2-8-9 .... ChrisCatlin 3 58
(S Kirk) *prom: rdn 3f out: no ex fnl f* **25/1**
04 **8** *2 1/2* **Jakeini (IRE)**[21] 6251 2-9-0 .... GrahamGibbons 13 56
(E S McMahon) *prom: ev ch 2f out: sn rdn: wknd 1f out* **28/1**
9 *5* **Hand Of Destiny (USA)** 2-9-0 ....(t) IanMongan 12 40
(N P Littmoden) *plld hrd: sn prom: rdn 2f out: sn wknd* **25/1**
10 *hd* **Kartikeya (USA)** 2-8-9 .... JDSmith 6 35
(J R Fanshawe) *chsd ldrs tl wknd over 2f out* **25/1**
11 *3/4* **Late Night Love** 2-8-9 .... DaleGibson 9 33
(K R Burke) *outpcd* **66/1**
12 *9* **Lily On A Hill** 2-8-9 .... PaulEddery 5 5
(B Smart) *rdn over 3f out: a bhd* **50/1**

1m 15.54s (-0.27) **Going Correction** -0.20s/f (Stan) **12** Ran SP% **119.1**
Speed ratings (Par 96):93,92,91,89,88 88,87,84,77,77 76,64
CSF £6.47 TOTE £3.60: £1.70, £1.20, £1.90; EX 8.90.
Owner B Haggas **Bred** Southcourt Stud **Trained** Newmarket, Suffolk

FOCUS
The first two home had the benefit of previous experience in this interesting maiden full of newcomers despite the time of the year. The first two set the standard.

NOTEBOOK
Heaven Knows ◆, who had shown promise in a couple of back-end runs on soft ground, came through under a very confident ride for a cheeky win. The margin of victory does not reflect his superiority and he can continue to go the right way. (op 9-4 tchd 11-4)
Stonecrabstomorrow(IRE) ran another sound race after his short-head defeat at Lingfield a week earlier but the winner was just biding his time in the closing stages. (op 6-4 tchd 7-4)
Star Crowned(USA) is a half-brother to Eddington who finished third in last year's Preakness and fourth in the Belmont. Well backed on his debut, he looks a ready-made future winner. (op 10-1)
Siwa ◆ is a half-sister to three winners including the useful filly Candice. She seemed not to enjoy being trapped on the inside after a furlong and a half and should benefit from the experience. (op 10-1 tchd 11-1)
Jenise(IRE) ◆ is a half-sister to a couple of successful juveniles and the multiple winner Fort McHenry. Apparently totally unfancied, she did not have things go her way and improvement can be expected.
Creme Brulee ◆, out of a half-sister to the smart sprinter Blyton Lad, showed plenty of promise for the future after blowing the start. (op 20-1 tchd 14-1)

6436 BETDIRECT ON AT THE RACES INTERACTIVE (S) STKS 1m 141y(P)
8:30 (8:31) (Class 6) 3-Y-0+ **£2,600** (£767; £384) **Stalls** Low

Form RPR
2006 **1** **Aswan (IRE)**[11] 6361 7-9-2 62..(t) AmirQuinn(3) 1 69
(S R Bowring) *broke wl: mde all: clr over 2f out: rdn over 1f out: r.o wl* **8/1**
4000 **2** *4* **Shaheer (IRE)**[5] 6400 3-8-11 55..(p) IanMongan 6 56
(Mrs L J Mongan) *a.p: chsd wnr over 6f out: rdn over 3f out: no imp fnl 2f* **33/1**
-110 **3** *1 1/2* **The Prince**[126] 3759 11-9-5 87... ChrisCatlin 3 57+
(Ian Williams) *s.i.s: rdn and hdwy over 2f out: nt clr run wl over 1f out: swtchd rt ins fnl f: r.o* **3/1**[1]
1060 **4** *2* **Sol Rojo**[11] 6362 3-9-2 65... MickyFenton 4 53
(M J Attwater) *a.p: rdn over 3f out: one pce* **10/1**
0540 **5** *nk* **Wiltshire (IRE)**[151] 3004 3-9-2 60.................................(v) FergalLynch 10 53
(P A Blockley) *bhd: rdn over 2f out: hdwy over 1f out: nvr trbld ldrs* **20/1**

5105 **6** *5* **Castanza**[11] 6361 3-8-11 60 AlanDaly 5 37
(M Wellings) *chsd wnr to 6f out: rdn over 2f out: wknd over 1f out* **20/1**
0560 **7** *hd* **Distant Country (USA)**[86] 4900 6-9-5 66 (b) EddieAhern 8 42
(R A Harris) *s.i.s: hdwy on ins over 2f out: sn rdn: eased whn btn ins fnl f* **3/1**[1]
1351 **8** *2 ½* **La Viola**[7] 6387 3-8-11 59 (b) PatCosgrave 12 31
(K R Burke) *hld up towards rr: rdn and short-lived effor 3f out* **6/1**[3]
544 **9** *½* **Welsh Wind (IRE)**[14] 6336 9-9-5 59 (tp) DaneO'Neill 9 35
(M Wigham) *nvr nr ldrs* **11/2**[2]
6000 **10** *½* **Mirasol Princess**[21] 6264 4-8-2 56 LauraReynolds(7) 11 24
(D K Ivory) *hld up in mid-div: wknd over 2f out* **20/1**
00 **11** *7* **Holly Rocket**[99] 4556 4-8-4 NataliaGemelova(5) 2 10
(J E Long) *broke wl: sn mid-div: bhd fnl 6f* **100/1**
00 **12** *21* **Its Alex (IRE)**[15] 6310 4-9-0 PaulEddery 7 —
(R J Hodges) *sn chsng ldrs: rdn over 3f out: sn wknd: t.o* **50/1**

1m 49.19s (-2.57) **Going Correction** -0.20s/f (Stan)
WFA 3 from 4yo+ 3lb 12 Ran SP% **120.1**
Speed ratings (Par 101):103,99,98,96,96 91,91,89,88,88 82,63
CSF £254.71 TOTE £8.80: £2.00, £9.70, £2.10; EX 520.00.The winner was bought in for 6,500gns.
Owner Paul Bacon **Bred** G Strawbridge And London Thoroughbred Services Lt **Trained** Edwinstowe, Notts

FOCUS
There was no hanging about in this seller as a result of which the form has been rated positively through the first two.
Distant Country(USA) Official explanation: jockey said gelding lost its action
Its Alex(IRE) Official explanation: jockey said gelding felt wrong behind

6437 BETDIRECT FREEPHONE 0800 211 222 H'CAP 1m 1f 103y(P)
9:00 (9:00) (Class 4) (0-85,85) 3-Y-0+ **£5,741** (£1,708; £853; £426) **Stalls** Low

Form RPR
0130 **1** **Trifti**[14] 6322 4-9-0 **78** FrancisFerris 3 86+
(C A Cyzer) *hld up in tch: wnt 2nd ent st: swtchd rt jst over 1f out: rdn to ld cl home: jst hld on* **10/1**
1000 **2** *shd* **Crail**[36] 6015 5-8-13 **77** GeorgeBaker 8 86+
(C F Wall) *hld up and bhd: hdwy on ins 2f out: swtchd rt 1f out: fin wl* **8/1**
5401 **3** *1* **Mizz Tee (IRE)**[16] 6306 3-9-4 **85** DavidAllan 2 91
(T D Easterby) *led early: a.p: led 2f out: sn rdn: hdd and nt qckn cl home* **14/1**
0000 **4** *2 ½* **Blue Trojan (IRE)**[14] 6322 5-8-13 **77** SteveDrowne 9 78
(S Kirk) *hld up in mid-div: rdn and lost pl over 3f out: hdwy on outside fnl f: r.o* **5/1**[2]
3503 **5** *2 ½* **Danelor (IRE)**[58] 5565 7-8-13 **77** (p) TonyHamilton 11 74
(R A Fahey) *a.p: wnt 2nd over 6f out: rdn and ev ch over 2f out: wknd fnl f* **16/1**
0044 **6** *½* **True Companion**[32] 6101 6-8-13 **77** HayleyTurner 6 73
(N P Littmoden) *prom: rdn 4f out: no hdwy fnl 3f* **12/1**
2030 **7** *hd* **Toshi (USA)**[28] 6159 3-8-13 **80** TomEaves 4 75
(I Semple) *prom: rdn over 3f out: nt clr run and swtchd lft jst over 1f out: one pce* **11/1**
0315 **8** *hd* **Nevada Desert (IRE)**[15] 6314 5-9-2 **80** DeanMcKeown 5 75
(R M Whitaker) *mid-div: lost pl 3f out: n.d after* **10/3**[1]
1300 **9** *½* **Northside Lodge (IRE)**[28] 6159 7-9-0 **78** (t) JimmyFortune 10 72
(W R Swinburn) *bhd: rdn over 2f out: nvr nr ldrs* **20/1**
2210 **10** *½* **Overlord Way (GR)**[57] 5585 3-9-3 **84** IanMongan 7 77
(P R Chamings) *sn led: rdn and hdd 2f out: wknd over 1f out* **14/1**
3014 **11** *3 ½* **Davenport (IRE)**[14] 6322 3-8-6 **80** JamesMillman(7) 12 66
(B R Millman) *t.k.h: hdwy over 6f out: wknd wl over 1f out* **7/1**[3]
3045 **12** *5* **Zerlina (USA)**[7] 6376 4-8-9 **78** MarcHalford(5) 1 55
(J Ryan) *s.v.s: plld hrd in rr: rdn 3f out: eased whn no ch ins fnl f* **25/1**

1m 59.61s (-3.01) **Going Correction** -0.20s/f (Stan)
WFA 3 from 4yo+ 3lb 12 Ran SP% **116.3**
Speed ratings (Par 105):105,104,104,101,99 99,98,98,98,97 94,90
CSF £86.04 CT £1125.42 TOTE £12.40: £3.90, £2.20, £3.20; EX 133.40.
Owner Mrs Charles Cyzer **Bred** C A Cyzer **Trained** Maplehurst, W Sussex

FOCUS
Quite a competitive handicap with the principals the best guide to the level of the form.
Nevada Desert(IRE) Official explanation: jockey said gelding lost its off-fore plate

6438 PLAY NOW AT BETDIRECTPOKER.CO.UK FILLIES' H'CAP 7f 32y(P)
9:30 (9:30) (Class 6) (0-55,55) 3-Y-0+ **£2,862** (£845; £422) **Stalls** High

Form RPR
6050 **1** **Miskina**[70] 5299 4-9-0 **55** EddieAhern 2 63
(W M Brisbourne) *hld up: hdwy 3f out: r.o u.p to ld ins fnl f: drvn out* **11/2**[2]
0402 **2** *¾* **I Wish**[17] 6299 7-9-0 **55** PaulFitzsimons 1 61
(Miss J R Tooth) *led early: a.p: rdn 2f out: ev ch 1f out: r.o* **4/1**[1]
1450 **3** *2 ½* **Limonia (GER)**[70] 5319 3-8-13 **55** FergalLynch 11 55
(D K Ivory) *sn led: rdn 2f out: hdd and no ex ins fnl f* **10/1**[3]
0100 **4** *½* **Monda**[26] 6202 3-8-11 **53** TomEaves 10 51
(Miss J A Camacho) *a.p: wnt 2nd 4f out: rdn and ev ch 1f out: one pce* **16/1**
5662 **5** *1 ¼* **Flying Dancer**[145] 3179 3-8-3 **52** TolleyDean(7) 7 47
(R A Harris) *bhd: rdn and hdwy on ins 2f out: one pce fnl f* **20/1**
0000 **6** *1* **Party Princess (IRE)**[46] 5819 4-8-11 **52** DeanMcKeown 8 44
(J A Glover) *hld up and bhd: rdn and hdwy 2f out: no imp fnl f* **25/1**
4251 **7** *1 ¼* **Spark Up**[148] 3100 5-9-0 **55** (b) GeorgeBaker 5 44
(J W Unett) *bhd: sme hdwy over 1f out: n.d* **4/1**[1]
0030 **8** *1 ¼* **Eskimo's Nest**[26] 6202 3-8-10 **55** PatrickMathers(3) 9 41
(D Shaw) *hld up and bhd: rdn wl over 1f out: nvr nr ldrs* **10/1**[3]
2150 **9** *¾* **Gaudalpin (IRE)**[11] 6363 3-8-10 **52** (t) JimmyQuinn 4 36
(Ernst Oertel) *hld up: hdwy over 3f out: rdn over 2f out: wknd wl over 1f out* **4/1**[1]
10 *7* **Rain Holly (IRE)**[79] 5078 3-8-11 **53** LPKeniry 3 19
(R A Harris) *sn w ldrs: wknd over 3f out* **12/1**
0200 **11** *1 ¾* **Zimbali**[71] 5277 3-8-13 **55** (p) ChrisCatlin 6 16
(J M Bradley) *hld up: hdwy 4f out: sn rdn and wknd* **22/1**

1m 29.35s (-1.05) **Going Correction** -0.20s/f (Stan)
WFA 3 from 4yo+ 1lb 11 Ran SP% **120.1**
Speed ratings (Par 98):98,97,94,93,92 91,89,88,87,79 77
CSF £27.62 CT £223.20 TOTE £6.00: £2.30, £1.50, £3.20; EX 20.40 Place 6 £110.93, Place 5 £73.30.
Owner The Blacktoffee Partnership **Bred** Darley **Trained** Great Ness, Shropshire
■ Stewards' Enquiry : Paul Fitzsimons one-day ban: used whip without allowing mare time to respond (Dec 7)

FOCUS
This competitive low-grade affair was run at a decent early pace, and the form is modest but sound.

T/Plt: £109.10 to a £1 stake. Pool: £50,022.95. 334.50 winning tickets. T/Qpdt: £29.20 to a £1 stake. Pool: £2,652.70. 67.20 winning tickets. KH

TOKYO (L-H)
Saturday, November 26

OFFICIAL GOING: Fast

6439a JAPAN CUP DIRT (GRADE 1) 1m 2f 110y
6:20 (6:20) 3-Y-0+
£678,951 (£269,506; £170,335; £101,662; £66,080; £46,256)

RPR
1 **Kane Hekili (JPN)**[28] 3-8-10 YTake 10 117
(Katsuhiko Sumii, Japan) **11/10**[1]
2 *nse* **Seeking The Dia (USA)**[195] 1738 4-9-0 NYokoyama 7 116
(Hideyuki Mori, Japan) **51/1**
3 *nk* **Star King Man (USA)**[53] 6-9-0 KDesormeaux 6 115
(Hideyuki Mori, Japan) **82/1**
4 *1 ¼* **Time Paradox (JPN)**[23] 7-9-0 OPeslier 5 113
(H Matsuda, Japan) **53/10**[3]
5 *nse* **Sunrise Bacchus (JPN)**[28] 3-8-10 TSato 3 114
(H Otonashi, Japan) **159/10**
6 *5* **Shirokita God Run (JPN)**[363] 6760 6-9-0 MDemuro 1 104
(H Nakao, Japan) **182/1**
7 *1 ¼* **Saqalat (JPN)**[64] 5-9-0 LDettori 11 102
(S Ishizaka, Japan) **43/10**[2]
8 *1 ½* **Utopia (JPN)**[23] 5-9-0 (b) KAndo 4 99
(K Hashiguchi, Japan) **29/1**
9 *6* **Higher Game (JPN)**[209] 4-9-0 (b) KatsuharuTanaka 9 88
(Y Okubo, Japan) **34/1**
10 *nk* **Adjudi Mitsuo (JPN)**[64] 4-9-0 HUchida 14 88
(M Kawashima, Japan) **102/10**
11 *1 ¾* **Lava Man (USA)**[56] 4-9-0 (b) CNakatani 2 85
(Doug O'Neill, U.S.A) **166/10**
12 *5* **Gene Crisis (USA)**[363] 6760 4-9-0 YShibata 13 76
(M Tsuchida, Japan) **87/1**
13 *nk* **Tap Day (USA)**[50] 4-9-0 (b) ECoa 8 75
(M Hennig, U.S.A) **31/1**
14 *2 ½* **Personal Rush (USA)**[279] 4-9-0 SFujita 12 71
(K Yamauchi, Japan) **172/10**
15 *½* **Hishi Atlas (JPN)**[28] 5-9-0 MEbina 16 70
(T Nakano, Japan) **75/1**
16 *dist* **Eccentric**[42] 5906 4-9-0 DarryllHolland 15 —
(Andrew Reid) *niggled along early from outside draw to dispute 8th on outside, weakened 3f out, 15th and beaten straight, eased final f* **123/1**

2m 8.00s
WFA 3 from 4yo+ 4lb 16 Ran SP% **124.6**
(including Y100 stake): WIN 210; PL 130, 910, 1450; DF 5900; SF 6980.
Owner Kaneko Makoto Holdings Co Ltd **Bred** Northern Farm **Trained** Japan

NOTEBOOK
Eccentric, whose Winter Derby win crowned a fine season on Polytrack last winter, had since been progressive on turf. However, this was a step up in grade and, not helped by racing around the outside of the field, he dropped away tamely before the turn and was eased.

6439 TOKYO (L-H)
Sunday, November 27

OFFICIAL GOING: Firm

6440a JAPAN CUP (GROUP 1) 1m 4f
6:20 (6:20) 3-Y-0+
£1,290,418 (£513,923; £323,042; £193,158; £127,078; £88,954)

RPR
1 **Alkaased (USA)**[43] 5902 5-8-13 LDettori 14 125
(L M Cumani) *missed break, raced in 12th, headway 5f out, 5th straight, ridden under 2f out, led 1f out, driven out, just held on* **96/10**[3]
2 *nse* **Heart's Cry (JPN)**[28] 4-8-13 C-PLemaire 16 125
(K Hashiguchi, Japan) *held up in 16th, 14th straight towards inside, 8th 1f out, ran on strongly while edging left final f, just failed* **62/10**[2]
3 *1 ¾* **Zenno Rob Roy (JPN)**[28] 5-8-13 KDesormeaux 8 122
(Kazuo Fujisawa, Japan) *racd in 13th, 10th str, strong run down outside to disp ld briefly jst over 1f out, sn hdd, stayed on same pace* **11/10**[1]
4 *nse* **Lincoln (JPN)**[28] 5-8-13 YTake 5 122
(H Otonashi, Japan) *raced in 7th, 11th straight, headway to go 4th inside final f, kept on, just missed 3rd* **195/10**
5 *nk* **Ouija Board**[29] 6164 4-8-9 KFallon 6 118
(E A L Dunlop) *racd in 10th, hdwy 5f out, 3rd str, wnt 2nd over 2f out, lost 2nd jst over 1f out, staying on one pace whn carried lft 80y* **118/10**
6 *1 ½* **Sunrise Pegasus (JPN)**[28] 7-8-13 HGoto 13 119
(S Ishizaka, Japan) *held up in 15th, 16th straight, headway widest of all to go 6th 1f out, one pace final f* **71/1**
7 *½* **Heavenly Romance (JPN)**[28] 5-8-9 (b) MikioMatsunaga 10 115
(S Yamamoto, Japan) *raced in 8th, 7th straight on outside, stayed on same pace* **185/10**
8 *½* **Bago (FR)**[29] 6168 4-8-13 TGillet 12 118
(J E Pease, France) *raced in 11th, 12th straight, ridden 2f out, stayed on same pace* **119/10**
9 *nk* **Suzuka Mambo (JPN)**[28] 4-8-13 KAndo 17 117
(M Hashida, Japan) *detached from main field in 17th, brought wide entering straight, stayed on steadily* **25/1**
10 *1 ¼* **Tap Dance City (USA)**[28] 8-8-13 TSato 2 115
(S Sasaki, Japan) *set strong pace, still 4 lengths clear 2f out, headed just over 1f out, weakened* **162/10**
11 *¾* **Admire Japan (JPN)**[35] 3-8-9 NYokoyama 4 116
(H Matsuda, Japan) *raced in 4th, 8th straight, soon ridden and one pace* **109/10**
12 *1 ¼* **Better Talk Now (USA)**[29] 6168 6-8-13 (b) RADominguez 7 112
(H G Motion, U.S.A) *raced in 14th, 15th straight, never a factor* **33/1**
13 *nse* **Warrsan (IRE)**[56] 5651 7-8-13 JamieSpencer 3 112
(C E Brittain) *raced in 9th, 13th straight, never a factor* **96/1**

14 ½ **Cosmo Bulk (JPN)**[154] 4-8-13 DBonilla 11 112
(K Tabe, Japan) *raced in 5th, 4th straight, soon weakened* **49/1**
15 3 **My Sole Sound (JPN)**[210] 6-8-13 MHonda 1 107
(Katsuichi Nishiura, Japan) *detached in last, always behind* **137/1**
16 6 **King's Drama (IRE)**[15] 5-8-13 EPrado 15 98
(R J Frankel, U.S.A) *raced in 6th, weakened over 2f out* **59/1**
17 3½ **Big Gold (JPN)**[154] 7-8-13 RWada 18 93
(T Nakao, Japan) *led chasing pack in 3rd, weakened 3f out* **134/1**
18 ¾ **Stormy Cafe (JPN)**[28] 3-8-9 HShii 9 94
(F Kojima, Japan) *chased leader 5 lengths clear of remainder, weakened over 2f out* **70/1**

2m 22.1s
WFA 3 from 4yo+ 6lb **18** Ran SP% **126.5**
(including Y100 stake): WIN 1060; PL 260, 180, 110; DF 3310; SF 6330.
Owner M R Charlton **Bred** Clovelly Farms **Trained** Newmarket, Suffolk
■ New track record.

NOTEBOOK
Alkaased(USA) appreciated the return to a mile and a half on a fast surface and narrowly held on by the shortest margin to record Britain's first win in the race since Pilsudski in 1997. His success came in a track record time and was his second win of the season at the top level.
Zenno Rob Roy(JPN), who won this last year and finished runner-up in the International Stakes at York in the summer, was a well-supported favourite and ran a gallant race in his repeat attempt.
Ouija Board, runner-up at the Breeders' Cup on her previous start, appeared to run her race and has been rated as having run to her Filly & Mare form. Connections have the option of running her in the Hong Kong International Vase on December 11.
Warrsan(IRE) might have found the ground quicker than ideal but he did not look good enough anyway.

6409 SOUTHWELL (L-H)

Monday, November 28

OFFICIAL GOING: Standard
The riders reckoned the recent wet weather had quickened up the surface a notch.
Wind: Light, half-behind Weather: Overcast, sleet and snow from race 3 onwards

6441 PLAY INSTANT WIN GAMES AT BETDIRECT.CO.UK BANDED STKS 5f (F)

1:10 (1:10) (Class 7) 3-Y-O+ **£1,423** (£420; £210) **Stalls** High

Form RPR
0300 1 **Secret Vision (USA)**[20] 6291 4-8-11 40 (p) GrahamGibbons 4 47
(R M H Cowell) *mde all: kpt on wl fnl f* **9/2**[2]
0453 2 1¼ **Lizzie Rocket**[6] 6412 5-8-8 40 ow4 (v) JamesO'Reilly(7) 1 47
(J O'Reilly) *dwlt: sn chsng wnr on outer: no ex fnl f* **5/1**[3]
0000 3 hd **Mac The Knife (IRE)**[147] 3179 4-8-4 35 MichaelJStainton(7) 6 42
(M Appleby) *mid-div: hdwy over 1f out: styd on ins last* **25/1**
6063 4 3 **Hello Roberto**[9] 6380 4-8-8 40 (b[1]) AmirQuinn(3) 12 32+
(R A Harris) *mid-div: styd on fnl f: nvr on terms* **11/4**[1]
0000 5 ½ **King Marrakech (IRE)**[4] 5858 3-8-11 35 (v[1]) HayleyTurner 3 30
(M D I Usher) *chsd ldrs on outer: wknd appr fnl f* **22/1**
3000 6 ¾ **Mr Spliffy (IRE)**[9] 6380 6-8-4 40 (b) JemmaMarshall(7) 7 28
(M C Chapman) *hld up: hdwy 2f out: nvr nr ldrs* **14/1**
5606 7 ¾ **Polesworth**[9] 6384 3-8-6 40 (b) MarcHalford(5) 13 25
(C N Kellett) *s.i.s: sme hdwy and hung lft 2f out: nvr on terms* **25/1**
0502 8 1¾ **Off Hire**[9] 6380 9-8-11 40 (v) RobbieFitzpatrick 10 19
(C Smith) *chsd ldrs: sn drvn along: wknd fnl 2f* **5/1**[3]
00-0 9 1¾ **Raetihi**[6] 6411 4-8-11 35 DeanMcKeown 8 13
(P S Felgate) *chsd ldrs: lost pl over 1f out* **50/1**
0300 10 2½ **Starlight River (IRE)**[23] 6256 3-8-11 40 TonyHamilton 9 5
(J Parkes) *mid-div: effrt whn hmpd over 1f out: nvr on terms* **40/1**
0000 11 2½ **Levelled**[9] 6380 11-8-11 40 (p) DarrenWilliams 2 —
(D W Chapman) *chsd ldrs on outer: lost pl 2f out* **16/1**
0000 12 6 **Laurel Dawn**[20] 6291 7-8-11 40 FrancisFerris 14 —
(C N Kellett) *s.s: a bhd* **18/1**

59.05 secs (-1.25) **Going Correction** -0.325s/f (Stan) **12** Ran SP% **112.4**
Speed ratings (Par 97):97,95,94,89,89 87,86,83,81,77 73,63
CSF £23.94 TOTE £4.00: £1.40, £1.40, £9.30; EX 30.50.
Owner Allen Rix **Bred** Juddmonte Farms Inc **Trained** Six Mile Bottom, Cambs
FOCUS
Races do not come much worse than this, even at banded level, with this lot rated between 35 and 40. This straight five furlongs rode to type, suiting those that raced down the centre of the track from the lower stalls, whilst those drawn closest to the stands' rail may as well have stayed at home.

6442 BETDIRECTPOKER.COM BANDED STKS 1m 3f (F)

1:40 (1:40) (Class 7) 3-Y-O+ **£1,426** (£421; £210) **Stalls** Low

Form RPR
5500 1 **Spanish Star**[238] 863 8-9-0 35 HayleyTurner 9 45
(Mrs N Macauley) *in rr: hdwy over 5f out: wnt 2nd over 2f out: edgd lft and led jst ins last: styd on* **12/1**
5035 2 2 **Aggi Mac**[6] 6414 4-8-7 40 SuzzanneFrance(7) 14 42
(N Bycroft) *in rr: hdwy on outer over 7f out: led over 4f out: styd ins in st: hdd and no ex jst ins last* **15/2**[3]
0460 3 3½ **Just Wiz**[9] 6383 9-9-0 40 MichaelTebbutt 7 36
(J Jay) *hld up in rr: hdwy over 3f out: kpt on to take modest 3rd 1f out* **9/1**
0203 4 3 **Degree Of Honor (FR)**[16] 6331 3-8-9 40 J-PGuillambert 2 31
(J G Given) *prom: outpcd over 4f out: hdwy over 2f out: edgd rt and kpt on fnl f* **6/1**[2]
1423 5 hd **Quest On Air**[194] 1808 6-9-0 40 (p) FergalLynch 8 31
(J R Jenkins) *chsd ldrs: chal over 4f out: one pce fnl 2f* **15/8**[1]
0054 6 ½ **East Cape**[9] 6381 8-9-0 35 KimTinkler 12 30
(N Tinkler) *in rr and sn drvn along: kpt on fnl 3f: nvr rchd ldrs* **15/2**[3]
0506 7 8 **Printsmith (IRE)**[6] 6414 8-9-0 40 DarrenWilliams 11 17
(J R Norton) *edgd lft after s: chsd ldrs: lost pl over 1f out* **11/1**
-000 8 9 **Justice Jones**[48] 5826 4-8-11 35 NeilChalmers(3) 13 3
(Mrs P Ford) *mid-div: racd wd: lost pl over 4f out* **50/1**
060 9 2 **Eastfields Lad**[182] 2123 3-8-9 40 PaulEddery 10 —
(S R Bowring) *prom: reminders and hung rt over 5f out: lost pl 4f out* **33/1**
0000 10 1½ **Casalese**[17] 6257 3-8-9 35 (b[1]) DeanMcKeown 4 —
(M D Hammond) *dwlt: a in rr: bhd fnl 4f* **33/1**
240- 11 dist **Leyaaly**[516] 3412 6-8-7 40 JemmaMarshall(7) 6 —
(Miss Z C Davison) *led tl over 4f out: bhd and eased 2f out: t.o* **22/1**
0050 12 dist **Louisville Prince**[23] 6260 4-9-0 35 (e[1]) FergusSweeney 1 —
(A P Jones) *chsd ldrs: drvn along 7f out: lost pl over 4f out: virtually p.u: t.o* **16/1**

2m 30.18s (1.28) **Going Correction** +0.025s/f (Slow)
WFA 3 from 4yo+ 5lb **12** Ran SP% **116.7**
Speed ratings (Par 97):96,94,92,89,89 89,83,76,75,74 —,—
CSF £94.25 TOTE £21.60: £3.90, £2.60, £3.60; EX 130.00.
Owner Mrs N Macauley **Bred** Granham Farm **Trained** Sproxton, Leics
■ Stewards' Enquiry : Darren Williams one-day ban: failed to keep straight from stalls (Dec 9)
FOCUS
Another dire contest with several of these having seen better days, and they finished well spread out.
Quest On Air Official explanation: trainer's representative said gelding lost a near front shoe and finished lame

6443 PLAY NOW AT BETDIRECTPOKER.COM MAIDEN CLAIMING STKS 1m (F)

2:10 (2:10) (Class 7) 3-Y-O+ **£1,436** (£424; £212) **Stalls** Low

Form RPR
6205 1 **Louve Heureuse (IRE)**[7] 6394 4-8-1 45 ow2 JamesMillman(7) 9 56
(B R Millman) *hld up towards rr: swtchd ins and gd hdwy over 2f out: led 1f out: sn clr: readily* **4/1**[3]
50 2 2½ **Sea Heir (IRE)**[197] 1726 3-8-9 TonyHamilton 11 54
(R A Fahey) *chsd ldrs: hung lft and led appr fnl f: sn hdd: no ex* **10/1**
0003 3 3 **Swords**[16] 6328 3-8-9 55 J-PGuillambert 4 48
(P Howling) *s.v.s: swtchd wd outside after 1 1/2f: hdwy on wd outside over 2f out: kpt on: nvr nrr* **3/1**[1]
2503 4 1½ **Faithisflying**[6] 6411 3-8-6 40 (p) DaleGibson 6 42
(D W Chapman) *led: hdd appr fnl f: wknd ins last* **16/1**
0000 5 1 **Small Time Blues (IRE)**[23] 6258 3-7-9 30 (t) DuranFentiman(5) 13 34
(J Parkes) *chsd ldrs: one pce fnl 2f* **125/1**
000/ 6 ½ **Merlins Pride**[825] 4482 4-7-13 45 LiamJones(7) 8 37
(W M Brisbourne) *prom: rdn 3f out: one pce* **25/1**
0000 7 shd **Crux**[7] 6400 3-8-5 54 DeanMcKeown 14 38
(C W Thornton) *hld up on outer: effrt on outer over 2f out: nvr trbld ldrs* **8/1**
000 8 5 **Valentine's Pet**[63] 5517 5-8-6 35 FergusSweeney 10 27
(A W Carroll) *in tch: effrt over 2f out: sn wknd* **20/1**
04 9 6 **Gandiloo Gully**[16] 6328 4-8-3 NelsonDeSouza(3) 12 15
(J D Bethell) *s.i.s: a in rr* **16/1**
-600 10 2 **Seven Shirt**[14] 5699 4-8-0 40 JamesDoyle(7) 2 12
(E G Bevan) *mid-div: drvn over 3f out: sn lost pl* **40/1**
0 11 dist **Gozetan Lace**[27] 6215 3-8-4 RobbieFitzpatrick 3 —
(D W Barker) *in rr: bhd fnl 3f: tailed of: btn 33 l* **50/1**
0-00 12 5 **Mystic Promise (IRE)**[41] 5964 4-8-11 30 (v) HayleyTurner 1 —
(Mrs N Macauley) *s.i.s: a bhd: t.o 3f out* **100/1**
6633 P **Now Look Away (IRE)**[14] 6347 4-8-11 45 (p) GrahamGibbons 5 —
(E S McMahon) *p.u after 2f* **10/3**[2]

1m 45.47s (0.87) **Going Correction** +0.025s/f (Slow)
WFA 3 from 4yo+ 2lb **13** Ran SP% **114.8**
Speed ratings (Par 97):96,93,90,89,88 87,87,82,76,74 —,—,—
CSF £39.25 TOTE £5.20: £1.70, £4.30, £1.60; EX 78.00.The winner was claimed by M. Khan for £5,000.
Owner Alan Whitton **Bred** Dayton Investments Ltd **Trained** Kentisbeare, Devon
FOCUS
The classiest race on the card with horses rated up to 55, though as a contest it may have been weakened by the favourite giving so much ground away at the start and the second-favourite breaking a leg early, but the winner still scored with real authority.
Swords Official explanation: jockey said gelding did not face the kickback, having dwelt leaving the stalls
Gozetan Lace Official explanation: jockey said filly had a breathing problem

6444 PLAY NOW AT BETDIRECTCASINO.COM BANDED STKS 1m (F)

2:40 (2:41) (Class 7) 3-Y-O+ **£1,433** (£423; £211) **Stalls** Low

Form RPR
5043 1 **Kumakawa**[9] 6382 7-8-7 45 LauraReynolds(7) 7 52
(D K Ivory) *mid-div: hdwy 3f out: edgd rt over 1f out: led appr fnl f: pushed out* **8/1**
3202 2 ¾ **Sonderborg**[9] 6382 4-9-0 45 (p) DaleGibson 8 50
(J Mackie) *chsd ldrs on outer: drvn and outpcd over 3f out: styd on fnl 2f: tk 2nd ins last: no real imp* **5/1**[2]
0003 3 1¾ **Orpen Quest (IRE)**[6] 6413 3-8-12 45 (v[1]) RobbieFitzpatrick 4 47
(M J Attwater) *sn chsng ldrs on inner: chal 2f out: nt qckn fnl f* **15/8**[1]
0003 4 6 **Surdoue**[9] 6381 5-9-0 45 J-PGuillambert 11 41+
(P Howling) *w ldr: led over 2f out tl appr last: wknd last 100yds* **11/2**[3]
3056 5 ½ **Inchdura**[9] 6382 7-9-0 45 KimTinkler 1 34
(N Tinkler) *s.i.s: bhd tl sme hdwy 2f out: nvr a factor* **25/1**
3642 6 1¼ **Danettie**[114] 4171 4-8-11 45 BenSwarbrick(3) 9 31
(W M Brisbourne) *mde most tl over 2f out: wknd over 1f out* **12/1**
0000 7 1¾ **Pawn In Life (IRE)**[13] 6361 7-9-0 40 (v) FergusSweeney 10 28
(M J Polglase) *racd wd: rdn and lost pl over 3f out* **40/1**
2530 8 3 **Mexican (USA)**[20] 6259 6-9-0 40 (b) DeanMcKeown 12 22
(M D Hammond) *in tch on outer: lost pl over 2f out* **14/1**
0000 9 ¾ **Bontadini**[23] 6260 6-9-0 35 (v) GrahamGibbons 6 20
(D Morris) *chsd ldrs: lost pl over 1f out* **66/1**
10 4 **Woolett (FR)**[28] 6203 5-9-0 45 PaulEddery 5 12
(Daniel Mark Loughnane, Ire) *wl in tch: rdn and lost pl 5f out: sn bhd* **12/1**
0003 11 shd **Mister Aziz (IRE)**[13] 6031 3-8-12 45 FergalLynch 3 12
(J R Jenkins) *dwlt: a in rr* **18/1**

1m 44.93s (0.33) **Going Correction** +0.025s/f (Slow)
WFA 3 from 4yo+ 2lb **11** Ran SP% **113.0**
Speed ratings (Par 97):99,98,96,90,90 88,87,84,83,79 79
CSF £45.21 TOTE £8.10: £2.20, £1.60, £1.80; EX 30.70.
Owner R D Hartshorn **Bred** Carlton Consultants Ltd **Trained** Radlett, Herts
FOCUS
A routine banded contest though it was run at a fair pace. Several of these are regulars in this type of race at this track and it was Kumakawa's turn to score this time.

6445 BETDIRECTCASINO.COM BANDED STKS 7f (F)

3:10 (3:11) (Class 7) 3-Y-O+ **£1,453** (£429; £214) **Stalls** Low

Form RPR
0232 1 **Filey Buoy**[16] 6327 3-8-9 50 MichaelJStainton(7) 9 56
(R M Whitaker) *chsd ldrs: led over 1f out: styd on wl ins last* **9/1**
4520 2 1 **Golden Spectrum (IRE)**[14] 6345 6-8-10 46 (b) AmirQuinn(3) 14 50
(R A Harris) *mid-div: hdwy on outer over 2f out: edgd rt: styd on to take 2nd wl ins last* **7/1**[3]

4004 **3** 1 1/4 **Hollow Jo**[20] 6292 5-9-1 48 FergalLynch 10 48
(J R Jenkins) *w ldrs: led over 4f out: hdd over 1f out: wknd ins last* **5/1**[2]
4143 **4** nk **Ragasah**[7] 6400 7-8-6 46 (p) LiamJones(7) 8 46
(Ernst Oertel) *hdwy on outer over 3f out: c wd: kpt on fnl 2f: nt rch ldrs* **8/1**
6555 **5** 1 1/2 **Shielaligh**[48] 5819 4-8-7 47 JamesMillman(7) 13 43
(B R Millman) *sn bhd: hdwy on outside 2f out: nt rch ldrs* **12/1**
0011 **6** 2 1/2 **Legal Lover (IRE)**[9] 6382 3-9-2 50 GrahamGibbons 3 40
(R Hollinshead) *chsd ldrs on inner: hmpd and lost pl over 3f out: kpt on fnl 2f* **9/4**[1]
0104 **7** 5 **Ballyrush (IRE)**[6] 6413 5-8-6 46 StephanieBancroft(7) 7 23
(Miss D A McHale) *w ldrs: lost pl over 1f out* **20/1**
0-00 **8** nk **Diamond Dan (IRE)**[17] 6310 3-8-11 50 EmmettStack(5) 12 26
(P D Evans) *chsd ldrs on outer: lost pl over 2f out* **20/1**
0543 **9** 4 **Lake Wakatipu**[16] 6327 3-9-2 50 DarrenWilliams 6 16
(M Mullineaux) *sn outpcd and in rr: nvr on terms* **14/1**
0030 **10** 2 1/2 **Super King**[14] 6348 4-9-0 47 J-PGuillambert 2 7
(A D Brown) *s.i.s: bhd tl sme hdwy 2f out: nvr on terms* **28/1**
3500 **11** 1 **Feast Of Romance**[7] 6400 8-8-13 46 (b) FergusSweeney 5 —
(C R Dore) *chsd ldrs: lost pl over 3f out* **20/1**
6000 **12** 29 **On The Waterline (IRE)**[91] 4813 3-8-9 50 (b) JBrennan(7) 4 —
(P D Evans) *led tl over 4f out: lost pl over 3f out: sn bhd: virtually p.u: t.o* **33/1**
0400 **13** 19 **Drury Lane (IRE)**[35] 6078 5-8-13 46 (p) DaleGibson 1 —
(D W Chapman) *s.i.s: a in rr: virtually p.u: t.o* **25/1**

1m 30.58s (-0.22) **Going Correction** +0.025s/f (Slow) **13** Ran SP% **119.9**
WFA 3 from 4yo+ 1lb
Speed ratings (Par 97):102,100,99,99,97 94,88,88,83,81 79,46,25
CSF £63.32 TOTE £10.50: £1.90, £2.60, £2.30; EX 99.90.
Owner The Barflys **Bred** J F Day **Trained** Scarcroft, W Yorks

FOCUS
This race was run in a blizzard and the Fibresand had turned almost white. This looked a reasonable race of its type and the winning time was fair for the grade.
Legal Lover(IRE) Official explanation: jockey said colt was denied a clear run
Drury Lane(IRE) Official explanation: jockey said gelding was never travelling

6446 PLAY INSTANT WIN GAMES ON ITVI BANDED STKS 6f (F)
3:40 (3:40) (Class 7) 4-Y-0+ **£1,412** (£417; £208) **Stalls** Low

Form RPR
5034 **1** **Amanda's Lad (IRE)**[6] 6409 5-8-4 45 LiamJones(7) 3 53
(M C Chapman) *w ldrs: led over 1f out: kpt on wl ins last* **9/1**
0033 **2** 1 **Jalouhar**[16] 6330 5-8-4 45 (p) JemmaMarshall(7) 9 50
(B P J Baugh) *trckd ldrs: outpcd over 2f out: styd on wl fnl f: nt rch wnr* **7/2**[1]
0210 **3** shd **Ace Club**[9] 6384 4-8-11 45 (b) TonyHamilton 2 50
(J Hetherton) *led tl over 3f out: rallied and upsides 1f out: no ex ins last* **7/1**[3]
0356 **4** hd **Radlett Lady**[16] 6330 4-8-11 45 GrahamGibbons 1 49
(D K Ivory) *dwlt: hdwy on ins to ld over 3f out: hdd over 1f out: kpt on same pce ins last* **5/1**[2]
1505 **5** 1/2 **Sergeant Slipper**[20] 6291 8-8-11 40 (v) RobbieFitzpatrick 10 48
(C Smith) *s.i.s: hdwy on outer 2f out: kpt on wl ins last* **11/1**
0003 **6** 3/4 **Fitzwarren**[37] 6032 4-8-11 45 J-PGuillambert 7 45
(A D Brown) *in rr whn swtchd v wd after 1f: hdwy on outer 2f out: styd on fnl f* **7/1**[3]
0500 **7** 1 3/4 **Jakeal (IRE)**[9] 6380 6-8-4 35 (b[1]) MichaelJStainton(7) 6 40
(R M Whitaker) *chsd ldrs: outpcd over 2f out: hdwy to chse ldrs over 1f out: wknd and eased ins last* **20/1**
8 3 1/2 **The Crunch (IRE)**[163] 2727 4-8-11 40 (t) PaulEddery 11 30
(Daniel Mark Loughnane, Ire) *racd wd: nvr nr ldrs* **12/1**
4003 **9** 2 **Polar Haze**[9] 6385 8-8-11 45 (v) FergalLynch 8 24
(J Pearce) *chsd ldrs: lost pl 2f out* **5/1**[2]
000 **10** 19 **Instinct**[118] 4032 4-8-11 45 DeanMcKeown 5 —
(M D Hammond) *s.i.s: hdwy on inner to chse ldrs over 4f out: lost pl 3f out: sn bhd and eased: t.o* **14/1**

1m 17.62s (0.72) **Going Correction** +0.025s/f (Slow) **10** Ran SP% **118.0**
Speed ratings (Par 97):96,94,94,94,93 92,90,85,82,57
CSF £41.10 TOTE £10.50: £2.80, £1.60, £2.30; EX 37.80 Place 6 £109.85, Place 5 £46.48.
Owner Eric Knowles **Bred** Mrs Helen Smith **Trained** Market Rasen, Lincs

FOCUS
A moderate race full of horses that find it very hard to win. Those that raced up with the pace dominated and very few got into it.
T/Plt: £163.80 to a £1 stake. Pool: £31,885.75. 142.10 winning tickets. T/Qpdt: £15.90 to a £1 stake. Pool: £9,948.90. 460.90 winning tickets. WG

6433 WOLVERHAMPTON (A.W) (L-H)
Monday, November 28

OFFICIAL GOING: Standard (meeting abandoned after race 3 (2.20) due to unsafe track conditions)
Wind: Fresh, across Weather: Snowing

6447 NEW ACCOUNT FREE BET AT BETDIRECT H'CAP 5f 20y(P)
1:20 (1:31) (Class 6) (0-60,60) 3-Y-0+ **£2,867** (£846; £423) **Stalls** Low

Form RPR
0000 **1** **Almaty Express**[17] 6310 3-9-1 57 (b) JoeFanning 7 64
(J R Weymes) *chsd ldr: led over 3f out: clr 2f out: jst hld on* **22/1**
6400 **2** nk **Majestical (IRE)**[77] 5172 3-9-3 59 (p) GeorgeBaker 2 69+
(J M Bradley) *hld up in tch: nt clr run 1/2-way: hmpd over 1f out: rdn to chse wnr ins fnl f: r.o wl* **9/2**[1]
4506 **3** 1 1/2 **Cashel Mead**[158] 2843 5-9-4 60 (b) SteveDrowne 3 61
(J L Spearing) *a.p: rdn to chse wnr over 1f out: styd on same pce ins fnl f* **8/1**[3]
2060 **4** 1 1/2 **Cloann (IRE)**[79] 5119 3-9-1 57 (b) StephenCarson 1 52
(E A Wheeler) *outpcd: nt clr run over 3f out: r.o ins fnl f: nvr nrr* **16/1**
0055 **5** 2 **Nova Tor (IRE)**[17] 6310 3-9-2 58 GylesParkin 12 46
(Peter Grayson) *chsd ldrs: rdn 1/2-way: wknd fnl f* **14/1**
3 **6** hd **Cookie Cutter (IRE)**[23] 6263 3-9-4 60 PatCosgrave 10 47
(K R Burke) *led: hdd over 3f out: rdn 1/2-way: wknd fnl f* **14/1**
0035 **7** 1 **Snow Wolf**[27] 6217 4-9-4 60 DaneO'Neill 9 44
(J M Bradley) *mid-div: rdn 1/2-way: nvr trbld ldrs* **6/1**[2]
0120 **8** nk **Clearing Sky (IRE)**[55] 5686 4-9-3 59 EddieAhern 11 42
(J R Boyle) *chsd ldrs over 3f* **6/1**[2]
0000 **9** nk **Sundried Tomato**[252] 677 6-9-2 58 (p) TonyCulhane 5 39
(D W Chapman) *outpcd* **14/1**
-100 **10** 2 1/2 **Young Valentino**[89] 4862 3-9-4 60 TPQueally 6 32
(A W Carroll) *mid-div: n.m.r over 3f out: n.d* **50/1**
3006 **11** 1 3/4 **Park Approach (IRE)**[23] 6263 3-9-2 58 (p) JimmyQuinn 4 24
(D J Daly) *mid-div: rdn 1/2-way: sn wknd* **11/1**
0134 **12** 5 **Never Without Me**[75] 5222 5-9-4 60 MickyFenton 8 8
(J F Coupland) *s.i.s: outpcd: rdn and hung lft over 1f out: a in rr* **6/1**[2]
166- **13** 6 **Why Harry**[559] 2194 3-9-4 60 LPKeniry 13 —
(J J Quinn) *s.i.s: sn prom: wknd 1/2-way* **50/1**

62.07 secs (-0.75) **Going Correction** -0.15s/f (Stan) **13** Ran SP% **114.6**
Speed ratings (Par 101):100,99,97,94,91 91,89,89,88,84 81,73,64
CSF £112.64 CT £872.68 TOTE £25.50: £5.20, £2.00, £2.40; EX 73.60.
Owner Sporting Occasions Racing No 5 **Bred** P G Airey **Trained** Middleham Moor, N Yorks

FOCUS
This was a modest sprint, in which half of the field were making their return from a break, and once again a low draw proved a real advantage.
Never Without Me Official explanation: jockey said gelding bled from the nose

6448 TEXT "BETDIRECT" TO 88600 H'CAP (AMATEUR RIDERS) 1m 5f 194y(P)
1:50 (2:00) (Class 6) (0-65,65) 3-Y-0+ **£2,787** (£857; £428) **Stalls** Low

Form RPR
0405 **1** **Cumbrian Knight (IRE)**[44] 5890 7-10-4 55 MissNJefferson(7) 2 71
(J M Jefferson) *dwlt: hld up: hdwy over 4f out: led over 1f out: styd on wl* **25/1**
0350 **2** 4 **Principal Witness (IRE)**[40] 5983 4-10-11 60 MissMSowerby(5) 8 70
(Tom Dascombe) *chsd ldrs: hmpd over 3f out: ev ch 2f out: styd on same pce appr fnl f* **16/1**
0354 **3** 2 **Robbie Can Can**[38] 6008 6-10-12 61 ow4 MrMJJSmith(5) 12 68
(A W Carroll) *dwlt: hld up: hdwy over 3f out: rdn over 1f out: styd on same pce* **8/1**[3]
3/02 **4** 2 1/2 **Activist**[21] 6280 7-11-2 60 (p) KellyHarrison 4 64
(D Carroll) *s.i.s: hld up: hdwy over 4f out: wknd over 1f out* **17/2**
544- **5** hd **Luxi River (USA)**[22] 6275 5-11-2 60 MissNCarberry 13 63
(Michael McElhone, Ire) *led: rdn over 3f out: hdd over 1f out: wknd fnl f* **5/2**[1]
3430 **6** 2 1/2 **Bid For Fame (USA)**[13] 6356 8-10-12 63 MrSPearce(7) 6 63
(J Pearce) *prom: lost pl after 2f: n.d after* **17/2**
0406 **7** 5 **Reminiscent (IRE)**[12] 6368 6-10-6 55 (v) MrPCollington(5) 10 48
(B P J Baugh) *s.i.s: sn prom: chsd ldr 8f out: rdn and ev ch 2f out: sn wknd* **22/1**
2313 **8** 8 **Pharaoh Prince**[19] 6300 4-10-11 55 (vt) MrSWalker 7 37
(G Prodromou) *mid-div: hdwy 1/2-way: wknd 2f out* **6/1**[2]
1 **9** 3 **Gentle Peace (IRE)**[19] 6300 4-10-13 62 MrJBond(5) 11 40
(J W Unett) *chsd ldrs tl wknd over 2f out* **12/1**
0130 **10** 1 1/2 **Explosive Fox (IRE)**[36] 3354 4-10-9 58 (p) GerardTumelty(5) 1 33
(C P Morlock) *mid-div: rdn 1/2-way: wknd 5f out* **12/1**
0001 **11** 5 **Active Account (USA)**[7] 6400 8-10-7 56 6ex (b) ChrisGlenister(5) 9 24
(J R Holt) *chsd ldr 6f: wknd over 4f out* **40/1**
0254 **12** 6 **Royal Atalza (FR)**[64] 4926 8-11-1 59 MrSDobson 5 19
(G A Huffer) *hld up: bhd fr 1/2-way* **11/1**
0-0S **13** 9 **Tilla**[61] 5559 5-11-2 65 MissGDGracey-Davison(5) 3 12
(Mrs A J Hamilton-Fairley) *s.s: a in rr* **50/1**

3m 5.34s (-2.03) **Going Correction** -0.15s/f (Stan) **13** Ran SP% **117.2**
Speed ratings (Par 101):99,96,95,94,94 92,89,85,83,82 79,76,71
CSF £363.10 CT £3469.16 TOTE £38.30: £8.30, £7.60, £2.60; EX 737.70.
Owner J M Jefferson **Bred** John P A Kenny **Trained** Norton, N Yorks
■ The first winner for Nicola Jefferson, daughter of winning trainer Malcolm.

FOCUS
A modest staying handicap, confined to amateur riders, which saw the field finish fairly strung out behind the emphatic winner. The form looks straightforward.

6449 BETDIRECT ON AT THE RACES INTERACTIVE (S) STKS 7f 32y(P)
2:20 (2:29) (Class 6) 3-Y-0+ **£2,586** (£763; £382) **Stalls** High

Form RPR
0004 **1** **Snow Bunting**[19] 6299 7-9-0 53 TPQueally 1 59
(Jedd O'Keeffe) *chsd ldrs: stdd and lost pl over 5f out: hdwy over 2f out: led over 1f out: rdn out* **7/1**
6220 **2** 1 **Quincannon (USA)**[72] 5322 4-9-6 55 EddieAhern 5 63
(W M Brisbourne) *hld up: hdwy over 1f out: r.o* **7/2**[2]
0353 **3** nk **Mister Elegant**[12] 6369 3-8-13 50 SteveDrowne 4 55
(J L Spearing) *chsd ldrs: led wl over 1f out: sn hdd: styd on* **12/1**
0200 **4** hd **Zafarshah (IRE)**[16] 6336 6-9-6 58 (b) LPKeniry 2 61
(R A Harris) *led 1f: remained handy: rdn over 1f out: styd on* **25/1**
0305 **5** 2 **Ever Cheerful**[32] 6126 4-9-3 61 AdamKirby(3) 8 56
(G C H Chung) *prom: lost pl 1/2-way: hdwy u.p over 1f out: r.o* **9/2**[3]
0014 **6** 4 **Shadow Jumper (IRE)**[23] 6261 4-8-13 52 (v) StacyRenwick(7) 12 46
(M J Attwater) *s.i.s: hdwy to ld 6f out: rdn and hdd wl over 1f out: wknd fnl f* **33/1**
2/6- **7** 1 1/4 **Incline (IRE)**[29] 6186 6-9-0 73 JimmyQuinn 10 37
(R McGlinchey, Ire) *s.i.s: hdwy 1/2-way: wknd over 2f out* **3/1**[1]
0060 **8** 1 1/2 **Albashoosh**[131] 3629 7-8-11 62 SilvestreDeSousa(3) 7 33
(D Nicholls) *chsd ldrs 5f* **25/1**
3510 **9** shd **La Viola**[2] 6436 3-9-0 59 (b) PatCosgrave 3 33
(K R Burke) *chsd ldrs: rdn and ev ch over 1f out: sn wknd* **12/1**
4600 **10** 20 **Mister Mal (IRE)**[69] 5380 9-9-6 59 DaneO'Neill 9 —
(B Ellison) *chsd ldrs 4f* **20/1**
5504 **11** 5 **Nisr**[12] 6369 8-9-0 55 (bt) MickyFenton 11 —
(Miss Gay Kelleway) *hdwy over 5f out: wknd and eased over 2f out* **12/1**

1m 29.8s (-0.60) **Going Correction** -0.15s/f (Stan) **11** Ran SP% **116.4**
WFA 3 from 4yo+ 1lb
Speed ratings (Par 101):97,95,95,95,93 88,87,85,85,62 56
CSF £29.83 TOTE £9.30: £2.60, £2.20, £3.00; EX 49.00 Place 6 £46.07, Place 5 £14.84.There was no bid for the winner. Ever Cheerful was the subject of a friendly claim. Incline was the subject of a friendly claim.
Owner W R B Racing 49 (wrbracingcom) **Bred** The Queen **Trained** Middleham Moor, N Yorks

FOCUS
A moderate affair, run at a strong gallop in driving snow, and those to come from off the pace were at an advantage. The form is fair for the grade.

6450 **BETDIRECT FREEPHONE 0800 211 222 NURSERY** **1m 141y(P)**
() (Class 5) (0-75,) 2-Y-O £

6451 **BETDIRECT.CO.UK H'CAP** **2m 119y(P)**
() (Class 5) (0-75,) 3-Y-O+ £

6452 **PLAY INSTANT WIN GAMES ON ITVI H'CAP (DIV I)** **1m 1f 103y(P)**
() (Class 6) (0-60,) 3-Y-O+ £

6453 **PLAY INSTANT WIN GAMES ON ITVI H'CAP (DIV II)** **1m 1f 103y(P)**
() (Class 6) (0-60,) 3-Y-O+ £

6454 **LITTLEWOODS BETDIRECT H'CAP** **5f 20y(P)**
() (Class 5) (0-75,) 3-Y-O+ £

T/Plt: £38.00 to a £1 stake. Pool: £36,890.80. 746.80 winning tickets. T/Qpdt: £2.40 to a £1 stake. Pool: £3,931.60. 1,207.20 winning tickets. CR

6425 LINGFIELD (L-H)

Tuesday, November 29

OFFICIAL GOING: Standard

Wind: Almost nil Weather: Sunny

6455 **FIRST PAST THE POST AT BETDIRECT H'CAP (DIV I)** **6f (P)**
12:20 (12:21) (Class 6) (0-60,60) 3-Y-O+ **£3,045** (£906; £452; £226) **Stalls** Low

Form				RPR
2001	**1**		**Vlasta Weiner**[3] 6429 5-9-2 **58** 6ex.....(b) GeorgeBaker 3 (J M Bradley) *trckd ldrs: rdn to ld 1f out: hld on wl* **7/2**[1]	64
1122	**2**	½	**Kallista's Pride**[73] 5319 5-8-12 **54**..... HayleyTurner 8 (J R Best) *hld up towards rr: hdwy and wd st: pressed wnr in centre fnl f: kpt on* **9/2**[3]	59+
4305	**3**	*nk*	**Tapa**[8] 6404 3-9-1 **60**.....(b) NeilChalmers(3) 5 (A M Balding) *in tch: rdn to press ldrs over 1f out: kpt on* **16/1**	64
0000	**4**	½	**Marsad (IRE)**[99] 4641 11-9-1 **57**..... PaulDoe 12 (J Akehurst) *dwlt: bhd: gd hdwy over 1f out: styd on fnl f* **25/1**	60
0000	**5**	*shd*	**State Dilemma (IRE)**[63] 5532 4-9-1 **60**.....(v) BenSwarbrick(3) 2 (D Shaw) *prom: led over 2f out tl 1f out: one pce* **25/1**	62
0000	**6**	1¾	**Transaction (IRE)**[57] 5662 3-9-4 **60**..... LukeFletcher 11 (J M P Eustace) *dwlt: bhd: rdn over 2f out: nrst fin* **20/1**	57
5000	**7**	½	**Bodden Bay**[48] 5835 3-9-2 **58**..... J-PGuillambert 10 (C A Dwyer) *v wd and pushed along thrght: in tch: no hdwy fnl 2f* **40/1**	53
201	**8**	*hd*	**Rapid River**[21] 6288 3-8-9 **56**..... EmmettStack(5) 7 (P D Evans) *hld up towards rr: effrt over 1f out: nvr able to chal* **13/2**	51
5002	**9**	½	**Cyfrwys (IRE)**[56] 5686 4-9-1 **57**.....(p) FrancisFerris 9 (B Palling) *prom: hrd rdn over 1f out: sn wknd* **7/1**	50
4004	**10**	*nk*	**Flaran**[69] 5406 5-9-2 **58**..... JimmyFortune 1 (J A R Toller) *led tl over 2f out: wknd 1f out* **4/1**[2]	50
0100	**11**	2½	**Lady Londra**[62] 5539 3-9-4 **60**..... JohnEgan 4 (D K Ivory) *prom tl wknd over 1f out* **14/1**	45
	12	*8*	**Fontaine House**[133] 3-8-13 **55**..... SteveDrowne 6 (T T Clement) *mid-div: outpcd 1/2-way: sn bhd* **40/1**	16

1m 12.09s (-0.72) **Going Correction** -0.175s/f (Stan) **12** Ran SP% **116.1**
Speed ratings (Par 101):97,96,95,95,95 92,92,91,91,90 87,76
CSF £17.32 CT £221.09 TOTE £3.80: £1.70, £1.80, £4.10; EX 19.60.
Owner Miss Diane Hill **Bred** C J Hill **Trained** Sedbury, Gloucs

FOCUS
Just a moderate handicap, but still pretty competitive and it should produce winners at a similar level.

6456 **PLAY INSTANT WIN GAMES AT BETDIRECT.CO.UK NOVICE STKS** **6f (P)**
12:50 (12:54) (Class 5) 2-Y-O **£4,158** (£1,237; £618; £308) **Stalls** Low

Form				RPR
	1		**Matuza (IRE)** 2-8-8..... SteveDrowne 4 (W R Muir) *str: rangy: scope: sn in tch: effrt and wd st: rdn to ld fnl 50 yds* **12/1**	69
0	**2**	½	**Perfect Treasure (IRE)**[10] 6374 2-8-7..... JimmyQuinn 7 (J A R Toller) *prom: rdn to narrow ld ins fnl f: hdd and nt qckn fnl 50 yds* **16/1**	66
0643	**3**	*1*	**Highland Song (IRE)**[31] 6136 2-9-2 59..... LukeFletcher 6 (R F Fisher) *led tl ins fnl f: one pce* **14/1**	72
1	**4**	*shd*	**Hogmaneigh (IRE)**[61] 5562 2-9-2 87..... J-PGuillambert 5 (S C Williams) *b.hind; t.k.h: stdd towards rr after 2f: shkn up and r.o fnl 2f: gng on at fin* **5/1**[3]	72+
4301	**5**	½	**Spearit (IRE)**[19] 6303 2-9-2 78..... JohnEgan 1 (D R C Elsworth) *chsd ldrs: hrd rdn over 1f out: no ex fnl f* **7/4**[1]	70
0	**6**	2½	**Salisbury World (IRE)**[47] 5847 2-8-12..... IanMongan 2 (D R C Elsworth) *hld up in midfield to rr: stdy hdwy on rail 2f out: shkn up over 1f out: no imp* **16/1**	59+
0351	**7**	¾	**Secret Night**[17] 6320 2-9-2 83..... EddieAhern 9 (J A R Toller) *dwlt: towards rr: mod effrt 2f out: nvr able to chal* **9/4**[2]	60
0	**8**	*5*	**Valhar**[47] 5847 2-8-7..... HayleyTurner 8 (J R Jenkins) *prom to 1/2-way: btn whn rn v wd home turn* **50/1**	36
0	**9**	*shd*	**Pink Pyjamas**[76] 5230 2-8-7..... FergusSweeney 12 (J A R Toller) *dwlt: a bhd* **40/1**	36
0	**10**	1½	**Simpsons Ross (IRE)**[14] 6349 2-8-12..... DaneO'Neill 3 (R M Flower) *s.s: a bhd* **66/1**	37

1m 12.48s (-0.33) **Going Correction** -0.175s/f (Stan) **10** Ran SP% **115.8**
Speed ratings (Par 96):95,94,93,92,92 88,87,81,81,79
CSF £181.73 TOTE £16.40: £3.40, £3.30, £2.30; EX 196.30.
Owner The Eastwood Partnership **Bred** Round Hill Stud **Trained** Lambourn, Berks

FOCUS
A fair event of its type, run at a solid pace, and the form appears sound enough. The winner can rate higher.

NOTEBOOK
Matuza(IRE) ◆, a 200,000gns half-brother to high-class sprinter Resplendent Glory, got his career off to a perfect start by outclassing his rivals with a ready debut success. It should be little surprise that he took to this surface as his illustrious half-brother won his first two outings over the course and distance, and this trip should prove to be his optimum. With further improvement assured, he has the potential to progress into a decent sprinter next year, and will likely be put away for a turf campaign.
Perfect Treasure(IRE) ◆ showed the benefit of her recent debut over the minimum trip and had every chance. The extra furlong proved much to her liking, she ought to have no trouble landing a maiden in the coming weeks and, as time will likely tell, there was no disgrace in this defeat.
Highland Song(IRE) showed decent pace on this return to Polytrack and was only found wanting inside the final furlong. This has to rate as a much-improved display, especially considering that he was giving weight to the first two. If he is able to reproduce this effort he will go close back in a handicap off his current rating. (op 20-1)
Hogmaneigh(IRE), a ready winner on his debut at Ayr in September, ran too freely on this return to action and still looked green. He finished his race well, however, and will be capable of better when consenting to settle. (op 11-4)
Spearit(IRE), well backed to follow up his recent maiden success at this track, had his chance but failed to see out the extra furlong that well. He looks on a high enough mark at present, but should prove happier when reverting to the minimum trip. (op 11-4)
Salisbury World(IRE), unplaced on his debut at Newmarket over this trip 47 days previously, lacked the pace to play a part but still shaped with ability. He ought to fare better when upped in trip. (op 10-1)
Secret Night, raised 3lb for making a winning debut for her current yard over course and distance last time, was always playing catch-up after a sluggish start and disappointed. She should be capable of a good deal better when breaking on terms. Official explanation: vet said filly suffered a cut to left hind leg (op 5-2 tchd 11-4)

6457 **BETDIRECT FREEPHONE 0800 211 222 NURSERY** **1m (P)**
1:20 (1:21) (Class 4) (0-85,85) 2-Y-O **£5,100** (£1,517; £758; £378) **Stalls** High

Form				RPR
0013	**1**		**Fregate Island (IRE)**[14] 6352 2-8-12 **76**..... JohnEgan 6 (W J Haggas) *chsd ldrs: wnt 2nd 3f out: led over 1f out: drvn out* **5/2**[1]	84
6600	**2**	1¼	**Pelham Crescent (IRE)**[19] 6304 2-8-6 **70**.....(b[1]) EddieAhern 7 (R Hannon) *chsd ldr: led over 3f out tl over 1f out: kpt on* **16/1**	75
622	**3**	1¼	**Annabelle Ja (FR)**[62] 5555 2-9-7 **85**..... GeorgeBaker 9 (D R C Elsworth) *chsd ldrs: effrt 2f out: nt qckn fnl f* **6/1**[3]	88
2135	**4**	1¼	**Time For Life (USA)**[36] 6071 2-9-2 **80**..... JimmyFortune 8 (H J Collingridge) *s.i.s: outpcd and bhd: gd late hdwy* **4/1**[2]	80+
241	**5**	*shd*	**Possessed**[73] 5325 2-8-10 **74**..... DaneO'Neill 3 (T D McCarthy) *mid-div: rdn to chse ldrs 2f out: one pce appr fnl f* **12/1**	74
0160	**6**	½	**Sands Of Barra (IRE)**[14] 6352 2-8-3 **70**..... NeilChalmers(3) 11 (N A Callaghan) *s.i.s: hld up and bhd: promising hdwy to chse ldrs 2f out: no ex fnl f* **10/1**	68
1106	**7**	*3*	**Quince (IRE)**[14] 6352 2-9-2 **80**..... JimmyQuinn 2 (J Pearce) *chsd ldrs: rdn and dropped towards rr over 3f out: n.d after* **9/1**	72
3210	**8**	2½	**Dream Mountain**[39] 6005 2-8-7 **71**..... JoeFanning 12 (M Johnston) *mid-div and wd: rdn 3f out: sn outpcd* **10/1**	57
1104	**9**	*nk*	**Outlook**[14] 6353 2-9-1 **79**.....(b) HayleyTurner 10 (N P Littmoden) *mid-div: rdn over 2f out: sn btn* **20/1**	65
0513	**10**	*nk*	**Casablanca Minx (IRE)**[4] 6420 2-8-0 **64**..... NickyMackay 1 (Mrs H Sweeting) *mid-div: hmpd on rail after 2f and again 1f later: dropped to rr: nt rcvr* **20/1**	49
0010	**11**	*20*	**Astorygoeswithit**[18] 6309 2-8-6 **70**.....(p) PaulDoe 5 (Julian Poulton) *led at str pce tl over 3f out: sn wknd and qckly lost pl* **66/1**	11
0140	**12**	*14*	**Cnoc Na Gaoithe (USA)**[96] 4692 2-9-2 **80**..... SteveDrowne 4 (E A L Dunlop) *prom: drvn along over 3f out: sn lost pl: wl bhd fnl 2f* **20/1**	—

1m 37.36s (-2.07) **Going Correction** -0.175s/f (Stan) **12** Ran SP% **120.4**
Speed ratings (Par 98):103,101,100,99,99 98,95,93,92,92 72,58
CSF £44.41 CT £226.57 TOTE £2.90: £1.40, £3.30, £1.90; EX 81.50.
Owner Mr & Mrs G Middlebrook **Bred** G And Mrs Middlebrook **Trained** Newmarket, Suffolk

FOCUS
A fair nursery run at a decent pace, and the form looks solid enough.

NOTEBOOK
Fregate Island(IRE) got back to winning ways in ready fashion and could have been called the winner at the top of the straight. He stays this trip very well, clearly enjoys the Polytrack and further improvement cannot be ruled out despite a future weight rise. (op 11-4 tchd 3-1 in places)
Pelham Crescent(IRE), equipped with first-time blinkers, showed much-improved form and the headgear clearly had a positive effect. He may go up again in the weights now, but providing the headgear has a similar effect in the future, he can build on this and find a race at around this distance during the winter. (op 20-1)
Annabelle Ja(FR), making her handicap and All-Weather debut off top weight, had her chance but failed to see out the race as well as the first two. On this evidence she has begun handicap life on a high enough mark, but she may be ready to tackle a stiffer test now and is not one to write off. (tchd 11-2)
Time For Life(USA) lost his chance with a sluggish start and, judging by the way he finished his race, can be rated better than the bare form. He has a race in him off this mark, but may not be all that straightforward. Official explanation: jockey said colt was hampered leaving stalls (op 10-3 tchd 9-2)
Possessed, making her debut for new connections after a 73-day break, shaped as though she will come on for the run and will most likely be best suited by further in due course. (op 10-1)
Sands Of Barra(IRE) was made to sit and suffer on this inside rail after missing the break, and was tight for room when trying to improve on the home turn, but he still found just the one pace when eventually in the clear. He is capable of a little better, but is not one to have any great faith in.
Cnoc Na Gaoithe(USA) Official explanation: vet said gelding bled from the nose

6458 **LITTLEWOODS BETDIRECT H'CAP** **1m (P)**
1:50 (1:51) (Class 4) (0-85,85) 3-Y-O+ **£5,742** (£1,708; £853; £426) **Stalls** High

Form				RPR
4435	**1**		**Waterside (IRE)**[17] 6322 6-8-11 **78**..... HayleyTurner 6 (G L Moore) *chsd ldrs: wnt 2nd over 1f out: styd on to ld fnl 75 yds: rdn out* **8/1**	88
-060	**2**	1¼	**Hail The Chief**[18] 6314 8-9-4 **85**..... DaneO'Neill 11 (R Hannon) *chsd ldr: led 3f out: hrd rdn over 1f out: hdd and nt qckn fnl 75 yds* **22/1**	92
0452	**3**	*1*	**Binanti**[14] 6354 5-9-2 **83**.....(v) GeorgeBaker 5 (P R Chamings) *mid-div: hdwy to chse ldrs over 1f out: kpt on fnl f* **6/1**[2]	88
0120	**4**	*1*	**Hayyani (IRE)**[50] 5799 3-8-9 **78**..... JohnEgan 4 (K McAuliffe) *plld hrd: stdd in rr: rdn and r.o wl fnl 2f: nrst fin* **9/1**	81+
0501	**5**	½	**Dr Thong**[19] 6302 4-8-12 **79**..... JimmyFortune 3 (P F I Cole) *hld up in midfield: effrt and nt clr run over 1f out: styd on fnl f* **5/1**[1]	81+
4505	**6**	*shd*	**Stoic Leader (IRE)**[31] 6138 5-8-8 **75**..... JimmyQuinn 2 (R F Fisher) *chsd ldrs: hrd rdn and one pce fnl 2f* **8/1**	76
0655	**7**	¾	**Louphole**[14] 6354 3-8-7 **76**..... FergusSweeney 7 (P J Makin) *rrd s and missed break: hdwy into midfield after 1f: rdn and no prog fnl 2f* **14/1**	76
0321	**8**	¾	**Top Man Tee**[38] 6028 3-8-2 **78**..... LiamJones(7) 10 (D J Daly) *towards rr and wd: pushed along over 4f out: nvr able to chal* **9/1**	76
1522	**9**	*shd*	**Wavertree Warrior (IRE)**[38] 6022 3-8-10 **79**..... IanMongan 12 (N P Littmoden) *prom tl wknd over 1f out* **7/1**[3]	77
6003	**10**	1¾	**Screwdriver**[14] 6354 3-8-8 **77**..... EddieAhern 8 (R Hannon) *towards rr: rdn over 2f out: n.d* **8/1**	71

0000 **11** *shd* **Hurricane Coast**[10] 6378 6-8-9 **76** .... SteveDrowne 1 69
(K McAuliffe) *led tl 3f out: wknd over 1f out* **16/1**
0/L **12** *1 ½* **Battling Mac (IRE)**[10] 6373 7-8-10 **77** .... J-PGuillambert 9 67
(L A Dace) *s.s: a bhd: no ch whn wd st* **100/1**
1m 36.11s (-3.32) **Going Correction** -0.175s/f (Stan) course record
WFA 3 from 4yo+ 2lb **12** Ran SP% **114.7**
Speed ratings (Par 105):109,107,106,105,105 105,104,103,103,101 101,100
CSF £164.65 CT £1143.51 TOTE £9.30: £3.00, £7.20, £2.60; EX 190.00.
Owner Nigel Shields **Bred** Yeomanstown Stud **Trained** Woodingdean, E Sussex
FOCUS
A fair handicap run at a solid gallop, and the form, rated around the third, appears sound enough for the class.

6459 TEXT "BETDIRECT" TO 88600 H'CAP 1m 2f (P)
2:20 (2:20) (Class 2) (0-100,102) 3-Y-0+
£11,635 (£3,483; £1,741; £871; £435; £218) **Stalls** Low

Form RPR
0401 **1** **Cimyla (IRE)**[18] 6314 4-9-6 **102** .... GeorgeBaker 4 109+
(C F Wall) *hld up in rr: smooth hdwy on outside over 2f out: led 1f out: rdn out* **9/4**[1]
0- **2** *1 ¼* **Activo (FR)**[79] 4-8-5 **87** .... PaulDoe 3 90
(S Dow) *hld up in tch: n.m.r on rail over 6f out: hdwy and nt clr run 2f out: swtchd lft and chal 1f out: nt qckn* **50/1**
162 **3** *nk* **Wild Savannah**[10] 6377 3-8-13 **99** ....(v) JimmyFortune 8 101
(J H M Gosden) *prom: led after 2f tl 1f out: one pce* **10/3**[2]
0003 **4** *shd* **Boot 'n Toot**[10] 6376 4-8-4 **86** oh8........ FrancisFerris 2 88
(C A Cyzer) *towards rr: rdn and styd on fnl 2f: nvr nrr* **18/1**
4101 **5** *nk* **Sri Diamond**[10] 6377 5-9-0 **96** .... DaneO'Neill 9 97
(S Kirk) *wd: hld up in tch: rdn to chal 2f out: no ex fnl f* **7/2**[3]
0-00 **6** *1* **Zonergem**[126] 3823 7-8-7 **89** ....(p) JohnEgan 10 88
(Lady Herries) *hld up and bhd: hmpd over 3f out: shkn up and r.o fnl 2f: nrst fin* **16/1**
1606 **7** *½* **Desert Cristal (IRE)**[32] 6131 4-8-4 **86** oh4........ EddieAhern 5 84
(J R Boyle) *plld hrd: chsd ldrs: outpcd and drvn along over 3f out: n.d after* **25/1**
5104 **8** *¾* **Go Tech**[10] 6377 5-8-8 **90** .... DavidAllan 1 87
(T D Easterby) *led 2f: remained prom: outpcd over 2f out: btn over 1f out* **6/1**
0/0 **9** *23* **Lights Out (DEN)**[10] 6378 5-9-2 **98** ....(t) ESki 11 51
(Ms C Erichsen, Norway) *sn prom: wknd rapidly over 3f out* **50/1**
6050 **10** *hd* **Jath**[10] 6378 4-8-8 **90** ow2........ SteveDrowne 6 43
(Julian Poulton) *in tch: n.m.r 3f out: wknd over 2f out* **25/1**
2m 3.38s (-4.41) **Going Correction** -0.175s/f (Stan)
WFA 3 from 4yo+ 4lb **10** Ran SP% **113.1**
Speed ratings (Par 109):110,109,108,108,108 107,107,106,88,88
CSF £136.24 CT £368.31 TOTE £3.40: £1.60, £4.60, £2.00; EX 114.50 Trifecta £592.70 Pool: £918.34 - 1.10 winning tickets..
Owner Peter Botham **Bred** Dr D G St John And Mrs Sherry Collier **Trained** Newmarket, Suffolk
■ Stewards' Enquiry : Francis Ferris two-day ban: careless riding (Dec 10,12)
FOCUS
A decent handicap for the class but the early pace was not that strong.
NOTEBOOK
Cimyla(IRE), an impressive winner at Wolverhampton 18 days previously, was given a fine ride from off the pace by Baker and followed up to defy an 8lb higher mark. He has clearly come good now, possesses a neat turn of foot and clearly enjoys the surface. This also proves he stays the trip, and enhances his claims for the Winter Derby over course and distance next year, but he still has to improve to be involved in that, and his handicap days will most likely be behind him now after another rise in the weights. (op 2-1 tchd 5-2)
Activo(FR), last seen posting back-to-back successes in the French Provinces and making his All-Weather debut for new connections, turned in a solid effort and would have given the winner more to think about with a better run in the straight. His new connections look to have a decent performer on their hands, clearly capable of winning races, but they may have to turn him out before the Handicapper can react, as a hike in the weights looks certain now.
Wild Savannah proved suited by racing up with the pace and turned in another sound effort, reversing recent course form with Sri Diamond in the process. He is in good heart at present, but does look held by the Handicapper all the same. (op 3-1)
Boot 'n Toot, 8lb out of the handicap, was doing all of her best work at the finish and posted yet another improved effort. She deserves extra credit as she did not get the decent pace she requires over this trip and her turn may not be far off. (op 20-1)
Sri Diamond, who posted a personal best when scoring over 12 furlongs on his return to this track ten days previously, would not have been suited by the lack of real early pace on this drop back in trip. He was not disgraced off his 5lb higher mark and can do better when getting the decent pace he requires. (op 4-1)
Zonergem, third in this event from a 1lb higher mark in 2003, was another who would have preferred a stronger pace and can be rated better than the bare form.
Go Tech failed to really improve for the drop in trip and is another who is capable of improving when faced with a stronger early pace. (op 7-1)
Jath Official explanation: jockey said filly was hampered 3f out and lost action

6460 FIRST PAST THE POST AT BETDIRECT H'CAP (DIV II) 6f (P)
2:50 (2:51) (Class 6) (0-60,60) 3-Y-0+ **£3,040** (£904; £452; £225) **Stalls** Low

Form RPR
5403 **1** **Shade Cozy (USA)**[29] 6202 3-9-1 **57** ....(t) JimmyFortune 10 74+
(A M Balding) *chsd ldrs: led over 1f out: sn qcknd clr* **5/1**[1]
0000 **2** *2 ½* **Mirasol Princess**[3] 6436 4-8-7 **56** .... LauraReynolds(7) 9 60
(D K Ivory) *n.m.r leaving stalls: rdn along in midfield: hdwy over 1f out: styd on to take 2nd fnl 100 yds* **16/1**
5460 **3** *hd* **California Laws**[62] 5552 3-9-2 **58** .... JoeFanning 11 61+
(T D Barron) *sn bhd: effrt and nt clr run over 1f out: weaved through and fin wl* **6/1**[3]
0 **4** *½* **Sunny Afternoon**[24] 6266 5-9-1 **57** ....(v[1]) SteveDrowne 2 59
(Miss E C Lavelle) *prom: sn pushed along: briefly wnt 2nd ins fnl f: one pce* **14/1**
5250 **5** *½* **Times Review (USA)**[28] 6217 4-9-4 **60** .... JimmyQuinn 7 60
(C A Dwyer) *in tch: hdwy to press ldrs 3f out: wd st: one pce* **8/1**
0/5 **6** *1* **Renegade (IRE)**[24] 6263 4-8-13 **55** .... IanMongan 1 52
(Mrs L J Mongan) *led 2f: remained prom: sltly outpcd and rdn 2f out: fdd fnl f* **10/1**
3000 **7** *nk* **Music Teacher**[51] 5754 3-9-0 **56** .... JohnEgan 12 53+
(N A Callaghan) *t.k.h: hld up and bhd: hdwy and gng wl whn nt clr run fnl 2f: nt rcvr* **28/1**
0004 **8** *nk* **Taminoula (IRE)**[24] 6266 4-9-4 **60** .... DaneO'Neill 6 56
(P Mitchell) *in tch: hdwy to join ldrs over 2f out: wknd over 1f out* **11/2**[2]
3061 **9** *1 ¼* **Sweet Pickle**[13] 6369 4-9-4 **60** ....(e) EddieAhern 3 52
(J R Boyle) *chsd ldr: led after 2f tl wknd over 1f out* **11/2**[2]

0014 **10** *1* **Hadath (IRE)**[179] 2271 8-9-2 **58** .... GeorgeBaker 4 52+
(B G Powell) *bhd: sme hdwy on rail whn nt clr run early st: unable to chal* **5/1**[1]
1m 11.54s (-1.27) **Going Correction** -0.175s/f (Stan) **10** Ran SP% **114.6**
Speed ratings (Par 101):101,97,97,96,96 94,94,93,92,90
CSF £82.88 CT £387.17 TOTE £4.80: £2.70, £4.00, £2.50; EX 134.70.
Owner Mr & Mrs A Hogarth **Bred** London Thoroughbred Services Ltd **Trained** Kingsclere, Hants
FOCUS
A moderate handicap and, while run in a faster time than the first division, the overall form appears weaker.
Music Teacher Official explanation: jockey said filly was denied a clear run
Hadath(IRE) Official explanation: jockey said gelding was denied a clear run

6461 BETDIRECTPOKER.COM AMATEUR RIDERS' H'CAP 2m (P)
3:20 (3:20) (Class 6) (0-65,63) 3-Y-0+ **£2,819** (£867; £433) **Stalls** Low

Form RPR
0046 **1** **Cayman Calypso (IRE)**[24] 6257 4-9-12 **45** .... MissLAllan(5) 13 52
(Mrs P Sly) *in tch: led 4f out: rdn 3 l ahd 1f out: jst hld on* **12/1**
1332 **2** *shd* **Reggae Rhythm (IRE)**[24] 6267 11-10-11 **60** .... MissZoeLilly(7) 2 67
(A J Lidderdale) *t.k.h: hdwy on outside 3f out: wd st: styd on wl to chse wnr fnl f: clsd steadily: jst failed* **7/1**[3]
3520 **3** *2 ½* **Makarim (IRE)**[45] 5894 9-10-4 **46** ....(p) MrsSBosley 6 50
(M R Bosley) *hld up in rr: hdwy 3f out: kpt on fnl 2f: nt pce to chal* **12/1**
0002 **4** *½* **Montosari**[48] 5837 6-11-2 **63** .... MrDHutchison(5) 4 66
(P Mitchell) *mid-div: hdwy 4f out: chsd wnr 3f out tl ins fnl f: one pce* **3/1**[1]
4306 **5** *2 ½* **Bid For Fame (USA)**[1] 6448 8-11-0 **63** .... MrSPearce(7) 9 63
(J Pearce) *prom tl wknd over 1f out* **8/1**
0530 **6** *1 ½* **Zaffeu**[130] 3679 4-10-6 **48** .... MrsEmmaLittmoden 3 47
(N P Littmoden) *s.s: hdwy into midfield after 6f: outpcd fnl 3f* **9/1**
2003 **7** *4* **Airgusta (IRE)**[24] 6267 4-10-11 **53** .... MissEJJones 14 47
(C P Morlock) *t.k.h: prom: outpcd over 2f out: steadily fdd* **14/1**
0065 **8** *1 ¾* **Redspin (IRE)**[17] 4934 5-10-1 **46** .... MrsSMoore(3) 7 38
(J S Moore) *towards rr: rdn 6f out: n.d fnl 4f* **6/1**[2]
4400 **9** *½* **Mr Dip**[16] 5965 5-9-11 **44** oh9........ MissLBrewer(5) 10 35
(L A Dace) *stdd s: plld hrd in rr: sme hdwy 1/2-way: wknd 3f out* **10/1**
0302 **10** *½* **Saffron Fox**[13] 6368 4-11-4 **60** .... MrSWalker 1 51
(J G Portman) *prom tl wknd 4f out* **7/1**[3]
0005 **11** *22* **Wavertree One Off**[116] 4130 3-9-13 **55** ....(b) JackMitchell(5) 5 19
(D R C Elsworth) *sddle slipped early: chsd ldrs 6f: sn towards rr: lost tch over 3f out: eased over 1f out* **14/1**
0000 **12** *25* **Tuning Fork**[19] 6308 5-11-2 **58** ....(t) MrsACooke 11 —
(J Akehurst) *led and set mod pce: increased tempo 9f out: hdd 4f out: wknd rapidly 3f out* **16/1**
3m 28.75s (-0.04) **Going Correction** -0.175s/f (Stan)
WFA 3 from 4yo+ 9lb **12** Ran SP% **122.4**
Speed ratings (Par 101):93,92,91,91,90 89,87,86,86,86 75,62
CSF £96.73 CT £1052.83 TOTE £18.90: £3.80, £2.90, £2.50; EX 215.60 Place 6 £445.68, Place 5 £231.10.
Owner Terry Pryke **Bred** Jamestown House Stud **Trained** Thorney, Cambs
■ Stewards' Enquiry : Miss L Brewer one-day ban: used whip when out of contention (Dec 19)
FOCUS
They went a modest pace early on and the form looks pretty weak, rated through the third.
Wavertree One Off Official explanation: jockey said saddle slipped
T/Jkpt: Not won. T/Plt: £2,245.20 to a £1 stake. Pool: £36,293.35. 11.80 winning tickets. T/Qpdt: £32.20 to a £1 stake. Pool: £3,874.60. 88.80 winning tickets. LM

6441 SOUTHWELL (L-H)
Tuesday, November 29

OFFICIAL GOING: Standard
Wind: Light, across Weather: Fine

6462 NO 5P RULE 4'S AT BETDIRECT MAIDEN STKS 5f (F)
12:00 (12:02) (Class 5) 3-Y-0+ **£3,348** (£996; £497; £248) **Stalls** High

Form RPR
4364 **1** **El Potro**[24] 6263 3-9-0 56........ GrahamGibbons 1 67
(E S McMahon) *chsd ldrs: rdn to ld ins fnl f: r.o* **7/2**[2]
3-00 **2** *½* **Clipper Hoy**[24] 6263 3-9-0 57........ RobertHavlin 2 65
(Mrs H Sweeting) *led over 3f out: rdn and hdd ins fnl f: styd on* **12/1**
3 *3* **Rogue** 3-8-9 .... LPKeniry 8 50+
(A M Balding) *s.i.s: sn chsng ldrs: rdn over 1f out: styd on same pce* **20/1**
2000 **4** *2* **Muktasb (USA)**[103] 4507 4-8-11 53........(v[1]) PatrickMathers(3) 4 48
(D Shaw) *chsd ldrs: rdn over 1f out: wknd ins fnl f* **10/1**
3605 **5** *½* **Cost Analysis (IRE)**[20] 6301 3-9-0 57........(bt) MatthewHenry 9 47
(M A Jarvis) *sn outpcd: styd on ins fnl f: nvr nrr* **15/2**
4304 **6** *1* **Briery Lane (IRE)**[46] 5883 4-8-9 50........ GregFairley(5) 6 43
(Mrs K Walton) *sn outpcd: styd on fnl f: nrst fin* **5/1**[3]
0000 **7** *1 ¼* **Zambezi River**[175] 2371 6-8-7 30........ MichaelJStainton(7) 3 39?
(J M Bradley) *sn outpcd* **100/1**
0 **8** *½* **Mustang Lil**[24] 6263 4-8-6 .... AdamKirby(3) 5 32
(M Wigham) *s.s: outpcd: styd on ins fnl f: nrst fin* **20/1**
2333 **9** *1 ¼* **Montana**[25] 6243 5-9-0 54........ SamHitchcott 7 33
(J L Spearing) *sn outpcd* **11/4**[1]
00 **10** *nk* **Pack Of Lies**[24] 6263 3-8-9 .... TonyCulhane 12 27
(Rae Guest) *chsd ldrs over 3f* **50/1**
0060 **11** *2 ½* **Detonate**[46] 5869 3-8-9 56........ MarcHalford(5) 10 23
(Mrs C A Dunnett) *s.i.s: outpcd* **14/1**
00 **12** *5* **Fir Tree**[13] 6367 5-9-0 ....(t) PaulEddery 11 6
(S R Bowring) *led: hdd over 3f out: wknd over 1f out* **66/1**
4424 **13** *6* **Tree Roofer**[7] 6411 6-9-0 45........(b) MickyFenton 13 —
(N P Littmoden) *wnt lft s: chsd ldrs to 1/2-way* **25/1**
0006 **14** *2 ½* **Ninja Storm (IRE)**[131] 3674 3-8-9 60........(e[1]) RobynBrisland(5) 14 —
(G L Moore) *sn outpcd* **20/1**
59.67 secs (-0.63) **Going Correction** -0.05s/f (Stan) **14** Ran SP% **123.3**
Speed ratings (Par 103):103,102,97,94,93 91,89,89,87,86 82,74,64,60
CSF £42.68 TOTE £3.80: £2.00, £4.30, £6.40; EX 77.50.
Owner R J H Ltd, G Pickering & J P Hames **Bred** L A C Ashby **Trained** Hopwas, Staffs
FOCUS
Moderate maiden form highlighted by the poor seventh only being beaten just over eight lengths.
Montana Official explanation: jockey said gelding was outpaced throughout

6463 BETDIRECT ON AT THE RACES INTERACTIVE CLAIMING STKS 1m 4f (F)
12:30 (12:30) (Class 6) 3-Y-0+ £2,866 (£846; £423) Stalls Low

Form RPR

0604 **1** **Romil Star (GER)**[31] [6152] 8-8-8 55 (v) PatrickDonaghy(7) 10 71
(K R Burke) *chsd ldrs: led 9f out: rdn over 1f out: styd on* **11/2**

0002 **2** ¾ **Mi Odds**[14] [6364] 9-9-5 67 AlanDaly 2 74
(Mrs N Macauley) *a.p: chsd wnr over 4f out: rdn over 1f out: styd on* **2/1**[1]

2010 **3** 2 **Daring Affair**[27] [6230] 4-9-6 71 PatCosgrave 3 72
(K R Burke) *hld up in tch: rdn over 1f out: styd on same pce* **11/2**

0010 **4** 11 **Spitfire Bob (USA)**[8] [6400] 6-8-10 53 (p) GregFairley(5) 9 51
(M E Sowersby) *s.s: hld up: hdwy u.p over 3f out: wknd over 2f out* **18/1**

0100 **5** 3 **Yenaled**[13] [6371] 8-8-10 68 DonnaCaldwell(7) 1 48
(N Wilson) *s.s: hld up: hdwy over 3f out: wknd over 2f out* **4/1**[2]

0000 **6** ¾ **Mungo Jerry (GER)**[13] [6368] 4-9-11 64 MickyFenton 8 55
(J G Given) *chsd ldrs tl rdn and wknd over 2f out* **9/2**[3]

0000 **7** 26 **Muqarrar (IRE)**[10] [6381] 6-8-13 48 (vt) TomEaves 5 4
(T J Fitzgerald) *led after 1f: hdd 9f out: chsd wnr tl rdn over 4f out: sn wknd* **20/1**

8 dist **Grunzig**[21] 3-8-4 AdamKirby(3) 4 —
(Mrs C A Dunnett) *led 1f: lost pl 8f out: sn bhd* **50/1**

2m 40.86s (-1.23) **Going Correction** -0.025s/f (Stan)
WFA 3 from 4yo+ 6lb 8 Ran SP% **114.3**
Speed ratings (Par 101):103,102,101,93,91 91,74,—
CSF £16.91 TOTE £6.80: £2.20, £1.10, £2.00; EX 21.90.
Owner Mrs Elaine M Burke **Bred** J H A Baggen **Trained** Middleham Moor, N Yorks
■ Patrick Donaghy's first winner.

FOCUS
Not a bad claimer and the form looks sound enough, but very few got competitive.
Mungo Jerry(GER) Official explanation: jockey said, regarding the running and riding, his orders were to be handy early without pressurising gelding too much, to settle gelding, and to do his best thereafter, adding that gelding met with slight interference early on, and suffered a recurrence of past breathing problems and tired rapidly when challenging turning for home; trainer added that no tongue-strap was fitted as gelding had resented it in the past; vet said gelding finished slightly lame on the near fore

6464 BETDIRECTPOKER.COM H'CAP (DIV I) 7f (F)
1:00 (1:02) (Class 6) (0-60,60) 3-Y-0+ £2,559 (£755; £378) Stalls Low

Form RPR

0400 **1** **Paso Doble**[85] [5008] 7-8-10 **59** JamesMillman(7) 8 72+
(B R Millman) *outpcd: nt clr run over 1f out: swtchd rt: r.o to ld last strides* **18/1**

0050 **2** ½ **Scuba (IRE)**[25] [6243] 3-8-6 **54** (v) TravisBlock(5) 10 64
(H Morrison) *chsd ldrs: rdn over 1f out: r.o* **10/1**

4125 **3** hd **Yorkie**[25] [6243] 6-9-1 **57** DeanMcKeown 7 66
(J Pearce) *trckd ldrs: racd keenly: led over 1f out: sn hdd: rdn to ld and hung lft wl ins fnl f: hdd last strides* **11/2**[2]

0012 **4** ½ **Cool Sands (IRE)**[8] [6407] 3-8-10 **56** PatrickMathers(3) 3 64+
(D Shaw) *chsd ldrs: rdn to ld 1f out: hdd and unable qck wl ins fnl f* **9/2**[1]

1400 **5** 3 **Ruman (IRE)**[13] [6365] 3-9-1 **58** RobbieFitzpatrick 5 58
(M J Attwater) *hld up: hdwy over 2f out: rdn and ev ch over 1f out: no ex ins fnl f* **18/1**

0604 **6** ½ **High Swainston**[14] [6363] 4-8-10 **52** TomEaves 13 51
(R Craggs) *chsd ldrs: outpcd 1/2-way: styd on u.p fnl f* **11/1**

0006 **7** 1¼ **Mount Royale (IRE)**[20] [6299] 7-8-8 **50** (v) KimTinkler 1 46
(N Tinkler) *chsd ldrs: led over 4f out: hdd over 2f out: rdn to ld 2f out: hdd over 1f out: wknd fnl f* **12/1**

0604 **8** 7 **Larky's Lob**[50] [5803] 6-8-7 **56** JamesO'Reilly(7) 2 34
(J O'Reilly) *chsd ldrs: led over 2f out: sn rdn and hdd: wknd over 1f out* **11/1**

0006 **9** 2½ **Shifty Night (IRE)**[17] [6336] 4-8-12 **59** (v) MarcHalford(5) 6 30
(Mrs C A Dunnett) *led: hdd over 4f out: rdn and wknd over 2f out* **7/1**[3]

0004 **10** ¾ **Piccolo Prince**[42] [5956] 4-8-10 **55** DonnaCaldwell(7) 4 28
(E J Alston) *w ldrs to 1/2-way: wknd over 2f out* **10/1**

0506 **11** ½ **Blythe Spirit**[42] [5956] 6-9-4 **60** MickyFenton 14 28
(C R Dore) *chsd ldrs: rdn over 2f out: wknd over 1f out* **17/2**

1000 **12** 3 **Young Valentino**[1] [6447] 3-9-3 **60** TonyCulhane 12 20
(A W Carroll) *prom over 4f* **40/1**

030- **13** hd **General Nuisance (IRE)**[462] [5022] 3-8-9 **52** JamieMackay 11 12
(A J Chamberlain) *dwlt: outpcd* **50/1**

1m 30.87s (0.07) **Going Correction** -0.025s/f (Stan)
WFA 3 from 4yo+ 1lb 13 Ran SP% **114.8**
Speed ratings (Par 101):98,97,97,96,93 92,91,83,80,79 78,75,75
CSF £180.65 CT £1128.73 TOTE £28.40: £6.80, £3.40, £2.00; EX 240.50.
Owner B R Millman **Bred** P Cutler **Trained** Kentisbeare, Devon

FOCUS
This ordinary handicap was run at a strong pace early and the final time was slower than the second division by 0.54sec.

6465 BETDIRECT.CO.UK H'CAP 6f (F)
1:30 (1:33) (Class 5) (0-75,75) 3-Y-0+ £4,037 (£1,201; £600; £299) Stalls Low

Form RPR

0000 **1** **Wessex (USA)**[17] [6322] 5-9-4 **75** (t) GrahamGibbons 1 84
(P A Blockley) *dwlt: hdwy over 3f out: rdn over 1f out: r.o to ld nr fin* **7/1**[1]

5406 **2** ¾ **My Gacho (IRE)**[31] [6157] 3-9-0 **71** (v) PaulFessey 2 78
(T D Barron) *sn led: rdn and hdd over 1f out: rallied to ld ins fnl f: edgd lft and hdd nr fin* **15/2**[2]

0460 **3** ¾ **Queens Rhapsody**[4] [6421] 5-9-4 **75** SamHitchcott 6 80
(A Bailey) *mid-div: rdn 1/2-way: hdwy over 1f out: r.o* **8/1**[3]

0600 **4** shd **Anfield Dream**[106] [4436] 3-9-2 **73** FergalLynch 4 77
(J R Jenkins) *dwlt: sn chsng ldrs: rdn 2f out: edgd rt and ev ch ins fnl f: styng on same pce whn nt clr run nr fin* **25/1**

2005 **5** 1 **Harry Up**[43] [5941] 4-9-4 **75** PatCosgrave 5 76
(K A Ryan) *chsd ldr: led over 1f out: sn rdn: hdd and no ex ins fnl f* **9/1**

0201 **6** 1½ **Norcroft**[18] [6310] 3-8-9 **71** (p) MarcHalford(5) 11 68
(Mrs C A Dunnett) *mid-div: rdn and hung lft over 1f out: styd on: nt rch ldrs* **12/1**

0352 **7** ½ **Pawan (IRE)**[26] [6238] 5-8-11 **75** AnnStokell(7) 13 70
(Miss A Stokell) *s.i.s: hdwy over 1f out: one pce ins fnl f* **12/1**

5004 **8** ½ **High Ridge**[31] [6157] 6-8-9 **71** (p) GregFairley(5) 10 65
(J M Bradley) *prom: rdn 1/2-way: wknd ins fnl f* **8/1**[3]

0006 **9** ¾ **Romany Nights (IRE)**[17] [6321] 5-9-0 **71** (b) MickyFenton 8 63
(Miss Gay Kelleway) *s.i.s: hdwy over 2f out: wknd over 1f out* **8/1**[3]

6004 **10** 2 **Arctic Desert**[19] [6302] 5-9-1 **72** (t) LPKeniry 3 58
(A M Balding) *dwlt: hld up: plld hrd: rdn over 2f out: no rspnse* **15/2**[2]

6140 **11** nk **Hits Only Cash**[94] [4755] 3-9-0 **71** DeanMcKeown 14 56
(J Pearce) *n.d* **8/1**[3]

6100 **12** 5 **Orpen Wide (IRE)**[28] [6216] 3-9-1 **75** AdamKirby(3) 9 45
(M C Chapman) *sn outpcd* **14/1**

-005 **13** 9 **Hermitage Court (USA)**[31] [6161] 4-9-0 **71** DarrenWilliams 12 14
(M J McGrath) *chsd ldrs over 3f out: sn wknd* **25/1**

0000 **14** 2½ **Cherokee Nation**[125] [3847] 4-9-3 **74** TonyCulhane 7 9
(P W D'Arcy) *sn outpcd* **40/1**

1m 16.47s (-0.43) **Going Correction** -0.025s/f (Stan) 14 Ran SP% **122.7**
Speed ratings (Par 103):101,100,99,98,97 95,94,94,93,90 90,83,71,68
CSF £58.02 CT £440.05 TOTE £7.00: £2.70, £3.20, £2.70; EX 96.10.
Owner Nigel Shields **Bred** Darley Stud Management, L L C **Trained** Lambourn, Berks
■ Stewards' Enquiry : Graham Gibbons three-day ban: used whip with excessive frequency without giving gelding time to respond (Dec 10-13)

FOCUS
An open handicap in which they went 7-1 the field, and probably fair form for the grade.
Wessex(USA) Official explanation: trainer said, regarding the improved form shown, gelding was suited by the drop in class and distance
Pawan(IRE) Official explanation: jockey said gelding missed the break

6466 BET DIRECT FREEPHONE 0800 211 222 (S) STKS 6f (F)
2:00 (2:02) (Class 6) 2-Y-O £2,518 (£743; £371) Stalls Low

Form RPR

0001 **1** **Psycho Cat**[8] [6403] 2-9-6 61 FergalLynch 7 69
(P A Blockley) *s.i.s: hdwy over 3f out: rdn over 1f out: r.o to ld post* **6/1**[3]

406 **2** hd **Inaminute (IRE)**[29] [6196] 2-8-9 53 PaulFessey 6 57
(Mrs A Duffield) *chsd ldr 5f out: rdn and ev ch fr over 1f out: r.o* **33/1**

642 **3** hd **Quote Unquote**[29] [6197] 2-8-9 65 JamieMackay 4 57
(Sir Mark Prescott) *led 5f out: rdn over 1f out: hdd post* **4/1**[2]

0001 **4** 3 **Woodwee**[13] [6366] 2-9-3 61 PaulMulrennan(3) 11 59
(J R Weymes) *trckd ldrs: racd keenly: rdn over 1f out: hung lft ins fnl f: styd on* **12/1**

1300 **5** 2 **Montini Royale (IRE)**[14] [6357] 2-9-1 55 GrahamGibbons 3 48
(M J Attwater) *led 1f: remained handy: rdn over 2f out: wknd fnl f* **25/1**

1056 **6** ½ **Magnolia Blossom**[18] [6312] 2-9-1 58 TonyHamilton 2 46
(R A Fahey) *dwlt: hdwy 1/2-way: wknd over 1f out* **16/1**

2503 **7** 5 **Phinerine**[20] [6295] 2-9-0 63 RobbieFitzpatrick 5 30
(Peter Grayson) *prom: rdn over 3f out: wknd 2f out* **8/1**

0035 **8** shd **Ten Shun**[13] [6366] 2-8-11 56 (b) AdamKirby(3) 13 30
(M J Polglase) *hld up in tch: rdn over 2f out: sn hung lft and wknd* **22/1**

4602 **9** 1 **Tour D'Amour (IRE)**[8] [6403] 2-9-1 59 MickyFenton 9 28
(Stef Liddiard) *sn pushed along and prom: hung lft and wknd over 2f out* **11/4**[1]

5422 **10** 6 **Lasting Love**[20] [6295] 2-8-9 59 AlanDaly 8 4
(C R Dore) *s.s: outpcd* **16/1**

0 **11** 2½ **Washabul**[27] [6227] 2-8-4 StephanieHollinshead(5) 1 —
(R Hollinshead) *dwlt: outpcd* **66/1**

000 **12** 3 **Wee Charlie Castle (IRE)**[19] [6304] 2-9-0 63 (v) PaulEddery 10 —
(G C H Chung) *mid-div: rdn and wknd 3f out* **11/1**

1m 17.56s (0.66) **Going Correction** -0.025s/f (Stan) 12 Ran SP% **112.5**
Speed ratings (Par 94):94,93,93,89,86 86,79,79,78,70 66,62
CSF £190.86 TOTE £4.80: £2.70, £5.20, £1.70; EX 312.40.There was no bid for the winner. Inaminute was claimed by R. A. Harris for £6,000. Quote Unquote was claimed by M. Khan for £6,000.
Owner Mrs Joanna Hughes **Bred** Peter Taplin **Trained** Lambourn, Berks

FOCUS
An average seller but the first three came nicely clear and the form looks solid enough for the grade.

NOTEBOOK
Psycho Cat followed up his recent course success by the narrowest of margins, and gave the impression that a return to seven furlongs will suit. He deserves to be stepped up to handicap company now. (op 5-1)
Inaminute(IRE) ran well on her first start outside of maiden company. She was just in the process of getting the better of Quote Unquote when Psycho Cat charged past them both.
Quote Unquote, dropping into a seller for the first time, got the longer trip well enough. Her official rating continues to flatter her, though. (op 5-2)
Woodwee, a winner of a weak claimer over the course and distance on his last start, was not as well drawn this time. He probably ran to a similar level given the circumstances.
Montini Royale(IRE) was seen to better effect back in this grade, but she still appears to be struggling to find her best form. (op 33-1)
Magnolia Blossom had a decent draw but she has yet to run to the best of her turf form on sand. (op 14-1)
Tour D'Amour(IRE) had run as though she would be suited by the drop back to six last time so it was disappointing to see her having to be scrubbed along to hold a prominent pitch. (op 4-1)
Lasting Love Official explanation: jockey said filly stumbled leaving stalls; vet said filly bled from nose

6467 DAILY SPECIAL OFFERS AT BETDIRECT NURSERY 1m (F)
2:30 (2:34) (Class 5) (0-75,75) 2-Y-O £4,028 (£1,198; £598; £299) Stalls Low

Form RPR

4042 **1** **Moi Aussi (USA)**[18] [6309] 2-9-1 **69** (b) JamieMackay 14 78+
(Sir Mark Prescott) *s.s: hdwy 1/2-way: rdn to ld over 1f out: r.o: edgd lft towards fin* **10/1**

4006 **2** 2 **Mambo Sun**[8] [6402] 2-8-6 **60** (b[1]) GrahamGibbons 12 63
(P A Blockley) *chsd ldrs: led over 2f out: rdn and hdd over 1f out: hung lft ins fnl f: styd on same pce* **10/1**

0023 **3** 3 **Snake Skin**[14] [6359] 2-8-0 **57** PatrickMathers(3) 6 57+
(J Gallagher) *mid-div: hmpd and lost pl over 6f out: hdwy over 1f out: nt rch ldrs* **10/1**

002 **4** nk **Mighty Dancer (IRE)**[14] [6359] 2-8-2 **59** NelsonDeSouza(3) 3 54+
(S Kirk) *hld up: nt clr run over 3f out: hdwy over 2f out: shkn up over 1f out: edgd rt: nvr nr to chal* **5/1**[2]

6143 **5** 2 **Pressure Putt**[4] [6423] 2-9-7 **75** TonyCulhane 10 66+
(W J Haggas) *broke wl: hmpd and lost pl over 6f out: hdwy over 3f out: styd on same pce appr fnl f* **3/1**[1]

0433 **6** 5 **Siakira**[39] [6004] 2-9-2 **70** MickyFenton 9 50
(I A Wood) *hld up: nvr nrr* **25/1**

0001 **7** shd **George's Flyer (IRE)**[14] [6359] 2-8-8 **62** (b) TonyHamilton 13 42
(R A Fahey) *prom: rdn 1/2-way: wknd over 1f out* **7/1**[3]

5000 **8** nk **Carrietau**[18] [6316] 2-8-7 **61** ow1 DeanMcKeown 11 40
(J G Given) *prom: jnd ldr 1/2-way: rdn and ev ch over 2f out: sn wknd* **33/1**

0560 **9** 2½ **Monte Mayor Junior**[18] [6312] 2-8-7 **61** RobertHavlin 8 35
(D Haydn Jones) *hld up: a in rr* **12/1**

0012 **10** ¾ **Countrywide Belle**[10] [6386] 2-8-4 **58** (p) PaulFessey 1 30
(K A Ryan) *led: hdd over 6f out: rdn over 3f out: sn weakeneed* **14/1**

5001 **11** 1 1/4 **Night Groove (IRE)**[10] 6386 2-8-11 **65**............................ FergalLynch 2 34
(N P Littmoden) *led over 6f out: rdn and hdd over 2f out: sn wknd* **9/1**
0440 **12** 1 3/4 **Herninski**[43] 5939 2-8-11 **65**............................ LeeEnstone 7 30
(P C Haslam) *hld up: n.d* **20/1**
505 **13** hd **Cecchetti (IRE)**[84] 5031 2-8-1 **58**............................ EdwardCreighton(3) 4 23
(Mrs H Sweeting) *s.s: hld up: a in rr* **50/1**
6300 **14** 18 **Shannon House**[19] 6304 2-8-8 **62**............................ LPKeniry 5 —
(M J McGrath) *chsd ldrs over 5f* **33/1**

1m 43.92s (-0.68) **Going Correction** -0.025s/f (Stan) 14 Ran SP% **122.2**
Speed ratings (Par 96):102,100,97,96,94 89,89,89,86,86 84,83,82,64
CSF £101.89 CT £1067.56 TOTE £11.30: £5.50, £3.80, £2.00; EX 175.50.
Owner Miss K Rausing **Bred** K Rausing **Trained** Newmarket, Suffolk

FOCUS
A fair race run in a decent time for a nursery, 0.72 seconds faster than the following handicap over the same trip for older horses, and the form should work out.

NOTEBOOK
Moi Aussi(USA), blinkered again, did not break well but she saw her race out very strongly and coped well with this slower surface. She likes some give in the ground on turf so it should not have come as a surprise that she took to this track, and she looks sure to record further success here. (op 9-1)
Mambo Sun, binkered for the first time, travelled well into the straight and finished a clear second. A reproduction of this effort should see him off the mark in the near future. (op 16-1)
Snake Skin, who was hampered in the early stages and dropped back in the field, stayed on again late in the day to record another third-place finish. The longer trip was no problem at all.
Mighty Dancer(IRE) ran quite well considering he challenged nearest the unfavoured far-side rail in the straight. (tchd 11-2)
Pressure Putt, squeezed up in the early stages, lost his position and struggled to get back into it. He was not knocked about in pursuit of third place and is better than the bare form suggests. (op 10-3)
Siakira was never nearer than at the finish on this All-Weather debut. (op 28-1)

6468 BETDIRECTCASINO.COM H'CAP 1m (F)
3:00 (3:02) (Class 6) (0-60,60) 3-Y-0+ **£2,971** (£877; £438) **Stalls** Low

Form RPR
1214 **1** **Abbeygate**[42] 5960 4-8-11 **53**............................ BrianReilly 10 57
(T Keddy) *chsd ldrs: rdn over 3f out: styd on to ld nr fin* **5/1**[1]
5000 **2** hd **Ming Vase**[50] 5794 3-8-9 **53**............................(p) LeeEnstone 8 57
(D Carroll) *mde most 6f: rallied to ld wl ins fnl f: hdd nr fin* **16/1**
0000 **3** shd **Balearic Star (IRE)**[17] 6324 4-8-8 **57**............................ JamesMillman(7) 13 61
(B R Millman) *prom: lost pl over 6f out: hdwy over 1f out: r.o* **9/1**
0150 **4** 1/2 **Band**[17] 6336 5-9-1 **57**............................ GrahamGibbons 12 60
(E S McMahon) *chsd ldr: led 2f out: sn rdn: hdd and no ex wl ins fnl f* **11/2**[2]
5002 **5** 3/4 **Pending (IRE)**[14] 6361 4-9-2 **58**............................(p) TonyHamilton 3 61+
(R A Fahey) *s.s: hld up: hdwy u.p over 1f out: styd on same pce nr fin* **8/1**
5605 **6** 2 1/2 **Aberdeen Park**[13] 6372 3-8-10 **54**............................(b[1]) RobertHavlin 11 50
(Mrs H Sweeting) *s.s: hdwy over 6f out: rdn and hung lft over 2f out: styd on same pce fnl f* **12/1**
0054 **7** 2 **Sriology (IRE)**[13] 6372 4-8-6 **55** ow3............................ ChrisCavanagh(7) 7 47+
(G Prodromou) *s.s: outpcd: styd on ins fnl f: nrst fin* **15/2**[3]
0500 **8** 1 1/2 **Keon (IRE)**[13] 6367 3-8-11 **55**............................ TonyCulhane 5 44
(R Hollinshead) *hld up: hdwy over 3f out: wknd over 1f out* **12/1**
02 **9** nk **Greenbelt**[10] 6387 4-9-1 **57**............................ LPKeniry 1 46
(G M Moore) *hld up: hdwy and nt clr run over 3f out: rdn and wknd over 1f out* **9/1**
5406 **10** 1/2 **Turner's Touch**[70] 5388 3-8-10 **54**............................ GylesParkin 2 42
(G L Moore) *hld up: nt clr run over 3f out: rdn over 1f out: nt run on* **25/1**
0460 **11** 3 1/2 **Yashin (IRE)**[13] 6365 4-8-10 **52**............................ MickyFenton 14 33
(P A Blockley) *chsd ldrs: rdn 1/2-way: wknd 2f out* **10/1**
0600 **12** 5 **Simply The Guest (IRE)**[14] 6364 6-9-4 **60**............................(t) KimTinkler 4 31
(N Tinkler) *sn pushed along: a in rr* **16/1**
0030 **13** 1 1/4 **Bahamian Spring (IRE)**[25] 6243 3-8-5 **52**............................(v) PatrickMathers(3) 6 20
(D Shaw) *chsd ldrs: sn drvn along: wknd 3f out* **40/1**
0000 **14** 3 **Veneer (IRE)**[24] 6265 3-8-9 **60**............................(b) RonanKeogh(7) 9 22
(Miss Gay Kelleway) *chsd ldrs over 5f* **22/1**

1m 44.64s (0.04) **Going Correction** -0.025s/f (Stan)
WFA 3 from 4yo+ 2lb 14 Ran SP% **121.8**
Speed ratings (Par 101):98,97,97,97,96 93,91,90,90,89 86,81,79,76
CSF £84.55 CT £715.14 TOTE £5.40: £2.70, £7.00, £1.80; EX 253.40.
Owner Mrs H Keddy **Bred** I A Southcott **Trained** Newmarket, Suffolk

FOCUS
Modest form and the race has been rated negatively.
Sriology(IRE) Official explanation: jockey said gelding jumped awkwardly from stalls and saddle slipped, causing him to lose an iron

6469 BETDIRECTPOKER.COM H'CAP (DIV II) 7f (F)
3:30 (3:32) (Class 6) (0-60,60) 3-Y-0+ **£2,547** (£752; £376) **Stalls** Low

Form RPR
5202 **1** **Look Of Eagles**[8] 6404 3-9-0 **60**............................ NelsonDeSouza(3) 7 73+
(P F I Cole) *mid-div: outpcd 4f out: hdwy over 1f out: led ins fnl f: edgd lft: r.o* **4/1**[2]
1252 **2** 1 1/2 **Tipsy Lad**[3] 6429 3-8-9 **52**............................(bt) GrahamGibbons 5 61
(D J S Ffrench Davis) *chsd ldrs: rdn to ld over 1f out: hdd and unable qck ins fnl f* **11/2**[3]
3025 **3** 1/2 **Amorist (IRE)**[27] 6231 3-8-11 **54**............................ JamieMackay 1 62
(Sir Mark Prescott) *hld up: hdwy over 4f out: rdn over 2f out: styd on* **7/1**
0250 **4** 5 **Guadaloup**[102] 4534 3-9-0 **60**............................ DanielTudhope(3) 12 55
(M Brittain) *hld up: hdwy 1/2-way: styd on same pce fnl 2f* **20/1**
6000 **5** shd **New England**[59] 5629 3-8-11 **54**............................ FergalLynch 4 49
(W M Brisbourne) *stmbld s: hld up: plld hrd: nvr nrr* **16/1**
1202 **6** 3/4 **Brave Chief**[14] 6363 4-8-8 **55**............................(b) MarcHalford(5) 13 48
(S R Bowring) *chsd ldr tl rdn over 2f out: sn wknd* **7/2**[1]
0350 **7** 3/4 **Savernake Brave (IRE)**[24] 6262 4-8-8 **50**............................ RobertHavlin 11 41
(Mrs H Sweeting) *s.s: bhd tl styd on appr fnl f: nrst fin* **18/1**
4214 **8** 2 **Mulberry Lad (IRE)**[3] 6429 3-8-10 **53** 6ex............................ DarrenWilliams 6 39
(P W Hiatt) *led: rdn and hdd over 1f out: wknd ins fnl f* **7/1**
0004 **9** 1 3/4 **Lets Get It On (IRE)**[151] 3096 4-9-4 **60**............................ LPKeniry 8 42
(J J Quinn) *chsd ldrs over 4f* **8/1**
3500 **10** 13 **Siraj**[35] 6103 6-9-2 **58**............................(p) MichaelTebbutt 10 7
(J Ryan) *prom over 4f* **14/1**
0300 **11** 1 1/4 **Dematraf (IRE)**[8] 6404 3-9-3 **60**............................ TonyCulhane 2 6
(Ms Deborah J Evans) *s.i.s: hld up: a in rr* **33/1**
0500 **12** 3/4 **As Handsome Does**[13] 6367 3-8-7 **50**............................ KimTinkler 9 —
(N Tinkler) *mid-div: rdn and wknd 1/2-way* **40/1**
-000 **13** 4 **Miss Hermione**[150] 3135 3-8-11 **57**............................ AdamKirby(3) 14 —
(Mrs C A Dunnett) *sn outpcd* **40/1**
040/ **14** 7 **Batool (USA)**[898] 2392 6-8-12 **57**............................ SilvestreDeSousa(3) 3 —
(D Nicholls) *dwlt: outpcd* **66/1**

1m 30.33s (-0.47) **Going Correction** -0.025s/f (Stan)
WFA 3 from 4yo+ 1lb 14 Ran SP% **125.6**
Speed ratings (Par 101):101,99,98,93,92 92,91,88,86,72 70,69,65,57
CSF £26.42 CT £161.13 TOTE £5.10: £1.60, £1.50, £2.40; EX 17.40 Place 6 £427.84, Place 5 £142.91.
Owner R Wilson, L Martin and P Jones **Bred** Mrs G Kindersley **Trained** Whatcombe, Oxon

FOCUS
The leaders went off too fast here and the race was presented to the hold-up performers. The quicker of the two divisions, it looks fair form for the grade.
New England Official explanation: jockey said gelding stumbled leaving stalls
T/Plt: £667.30 to a £1 stake. Pool: £28,384.50. 31.05 winning tickets. T/Qpdt: £138.50 to a £1 stake. Pool: £2,416.10. 12.90 winning tickets. CR

6447 WOLVERHAMPTON (A.W) (L-H)
Wednesday, November 30

OFFICIAL GOING: Standard
Wind: Slight, behind Weather: Misty and damp

6470 NEW ACCOUNT FREE BET AT BETDIRECT BANDED STKS 5f 216y(P)
1:20 (1:20) (Class 7) 3-Y-0+ **£1,521** (£449; £224) **Stalls** Low

Form RPR
1331 **1** **Orchestration (IRE)**[18] 6326 4-9-1 49............................(v) RobbieFitzpatrick 5 57
(M J Attwater) *chsd ldrs: rdn 2f out: r.o to ld nr fin* **4/1**[1]
6361 **2** nk **Cayman Breeze**[16] 6346 5-9-2 50............................ GeorgeBaker 12 57
(J M Bradley) *hld up: hdwy on outside over 2f out: rdn over 1f out: r.o ins fnl f* **7/1**[3]
0410 **3** nk **Mind Alert**[8] 6409 4-8-12 49............................(v) PatrickMathers(3) 4 55
(D Shaw) *t.k.h: a.p: rdn over 1f out: r.o ins fnl f* **14/1**
4431 **4** 1/2 **Magic Amour**[16] 6345 7-8-7 48............................(b) KevinGhunowa(7) 10 53
(P A Blockley) *hdwy to ld over 4f out: rdn over 2f out: hdd and no ex nr fin* **6/1**[2]
3045 **5** 1 1/4 **Taipan Tommy (IRE)**[9] 6397 3-9-1 49............................(v) JohnEgan 9 50
(S Dow) *hld up: hdwy over 4f out: rdn over 2f out: one pce fnl f* **11/1**
0-00 **6** 1/2 **Princess Kai (IRE)**[9] 6397 4-9-2 50............................(b) DaneO'Neill 8 49
(R Ingram) *s.i.s: hld up: hdwy over 2f out: rdn 1f out: one pce* **16/1**
6100 **7** 3 1/2 **Ligne D'Eau**[50] 5819 4-9-2 50............................(b) RobertHavlin 3 39
(P D Evans) *sn bhd: rdn and hung lft over 1f out: nvr nrr* **6/1**[2]
0560 **8** 1 **Paddywack (IRE)**[15] 6363 8-9-2 50............................(b) TonyCulhane 13 41+
(D W Chapman) *bhd tl hdwy over 2f out: eased whn btn ins fnl f* **12/1**
0521 **9** shd **Desert Lover (IRE)**[11] 6384 3-8-13 47............................ IanMongan 7 32
(R J Price) *prom: rdn over 3f out: wknd over 2f out* **4/1**[1]
2504 **10** 3 1/2 **Pragmatica**[37] 6078 4-9-0 48............................(p) ChrisCatlin 1 23
(R M H Cowell) *prom 2f* **8/1**
0600 **11** 4 **Tiger Hunter**[15] 6363 3-9-2 50............................ J-PGuillambert 11 13
(P Howling) *prom tl rdn and wknd over 3f out* **33/1**
1000 **12** 4 **Feminist (IRE)**[142] 3401 3-9-0 48............................ LPKeniry 6 —
(J M Bradley) *led over 1f: rdn and wknd over 2f out* **33/1**

1m 15.8s (-0.01) **Going Correction** -0.05s/f (Stan) 12 Ran SP% **126.6**
Speed ratings (Par 97):98,97,97,96,94 94,89,88,88,83 78,72
CSF £34.37 TOTE £4.50: £1.50, £1.90, £6.00; EX 25.00.
Owner Brooklands Racing **Bred** Mrs Anita Rothschild **Trained** Wysall, Notts

FOCUS
The fact that three-quarters of the field wore some sort of headgear just about sums this race up. The third looks a good guide to the form.
Ligne D'Eau Official explanation: jockey said gelding hung left-handed

6471 TEXT "BETDIRECT" TO 88600 BANDED STKS 5f 20y(P)
1:50 (1:50) (Class 7) 3-Y-0+ **£1,474** (£435; £217) **Stalls** Low

Form RPR
0445 **1** **Lady Hopeful (IRE)**[9] 6396 3-8-11 45............................(b) RobbieFitzpatrick 8 52
(Peter Grayson) *jockey slow to remove blindfold and swtchd lft s: rdn and hdwy wl over 1f out: r.o wl to ld nr fin* **14/1**
6060 **2** hd **Torrent**[8] 6409 10-8-11 45............................(p) TonyCulhane 1 52
(D W Chapman) *chsd ldrs: rdn and swtchd rt ins fnl f: r.o* **7/1**[2]
6200 **3** 1 1/4 **Leah's Pride**[9] 6397 4-8-11 45............................ IanMongan 10 47
(P Howling) *w ldr: rdn wl over 1f out: led ins fnl f: hdd and no ex nr fin* **8/1**[3]
0050 **4** shd **Legal Set (IRE)**[18] 6326 9-8-10 45 ow6............................(bt[1]) AnnStokell(7) 3 53
(Miss A Stokell) *dwlt: sn mid-div: hdwy over 2f out: rdn and swtchd lft 1f out: kpt on* **12/1**
0004 **5** 1/2 **Indian Bazaar (IRE)**[39] 6035 9-8-6 45............................ MarcHalford(5) 2 45
(R A Harris) *led: rdn wl over 1f out: hdd ins fnl f: no ex* **10/1**
0066 **6** 3/4 **Strathclyde (IRE)**[9] 6397 6-8-11 45............................ ChrisCatlin 13 42
(A M Hales) *bhd tl hdwy fnl f: nrst fin* **9/1**
4052 **7** 1 **Beverley Beau**[9] 6396 3-8-4 45............................ KristinStubbs(7) 12 39+
(Mrs L Stubbs) *bhd: swtchd rt over 1f out: late hdwy: nvr nrr* **20/1**
2401 **8** 1 1/4 **Ardkeel Lass (IRE)**[11] 6380 4-8-5 45 ow1............................ JBrennan(7) 5 35
(P D Evans) *chsd ldrs: rdn over 2f out: wknd over 1f out* **8/1**[3]
0210 **9** nk **Cark**[25] 6256 7-8-8 45............................(p) JasonEdmunds(3) 11 33
(J Balding) *prom: rdn over 2f out: wknd ins fnl f* **10/1**
1510 **10** 1 **Urban Calm**[81] 5130 4-8-11 45............................ BrianReilly 7 29
(J W Unett) *bhd: rdn and hdwy on ins over 1f out: no further prog fnl f* **7/1**[2]
1U05 **11** shd **Aintnecessarilyso**[16] 6345 7-8-11 45............................(p) LPKeniry 6 29
(J M Bradley) *mid-div: rdn 3f out: bhd fnl 2f* **7/1**[2]
0060 **12** nk **Hymn Of Victory (IRE)**[78] 5207 3-8-11 45............................(b) JoeFanning 4 28
(T J Etherington) *a towards rr* **14/1**
2523 **13** 12 **Inclassic (IRE)**[8] 6409 4-8-8 45............................(b) AmirQuinn(3) 9 —
(Jane Southcombe) *mid-div: rdn 3f out: bhd fnl 2f* **6/1**[1]

62.56 secs (-0.26) **Going Correction** -0.05s/f (Stan) 13 Ran SP% **128.0**
Speed ratings (Par 97):100,99,97,97,96 95,93,91,91,89 89,89,70
CSF £116.57 TOTE £22.90: £4.60, £3.50, £3.50; EX 257.70.
Owner Peter Grayson Racing Clubs Limited **Bred** Raymond P Doyle **Trained** Formby, Lancs

FOCUS
They went 6-1 the field in a wide-open affair. The time was reasonable and the third and fourth set the level.
Inclassic(IRE) Official explanation: jockey said filly missed break and never travelled

The Form Book, Raceform Ltd, Compton, RG20 6NL

6472 TREND CONTROL SYSTEMS BANDED STKS 2m 119y(P)
2:20 (2:21) (Class 7) 3-Y-0+ **£1,494** (£441; £220) **Stalls** Low

Form RPR

0421 **1** **Tycheros**[39] 6034 3-8-10 49 AmirQuinn(3) 12 57+
(S C Williams) *sn w ldr: led after 2f: rdn 2f out: styd on* **9/2**[1]

4332 **2** 1 ½ **Brennie (IRE)**[16] 6344 4-9-4 45 (v) DaneO'Neill 3 49
(V Smith) *a.p: chsd wnr over 3f out: rdn over 2f out: styd on same pce fnl f* **9/1**

6032 **3** 1 ¼ **Toni Alcala**[6] 5518 6-9-7 48 (p) LukeFletcher 11 51
(R F Fisher) *hld up in mid-div: rdn 4f out: hdwy over 2f out: edgd lft jst over 1f out: styd on towards fin* **13/2**[3]

2000 **4** 1 ½ **Lysander's Quest (IRE)**[31] 6184 7-9-5 46 FergusSweeney 5 47
(R Ingram) *hld up in mid-div: hdwy over 3f out: sn rdn: one pce fnl f* **13/2**[3]

6004 **5** ½ **Top Trees**[20] 5760 7-9-6 47 ChrisCatlin 13 47
(W S Kittow) *hld up towards rr: rdn and hdwy over 2f out: swtchd rt over 1f out: styd on ins fnl f* **8/1**

4550 **6** 3 ½ **Jadeeron**[8] 6410 6-9-6 47 (p) DarrenWilliams 4 43
(Miss D A McHale) *hld up in mid-div: hdwy 3f out: one pce fnl 2f* **20/1**

3214 **7** 2 ½ **Tharua (IRE)**[8] 6410 3-8-11 50 (p) AdamKirby(3) 7 43
(Ernst Oertel) *hld up and bhd: rdn and hdwy on outside over 3f out: no imp fnl f* **11/2**[2]

3461 **8** 2 ½ **Zeydnaa (IRE)**[49] 5683 5-9-9 50 TonyHamilton 2 40
(C R Wilson) *led early: prom tl wknd 3f out* **8/1**

0000 **9** 3 **My Boo**[16] 6343 3-8-3 46 (t) LiamJones(7) 8 32
(T Keddy) *bhd: rdn over 3f out: nvr nr ldrs* **40/1**

5405 **10** 1 **Trackattack**[15] 3615 3-8-10 46 J-PGuillambert 1 31
(P Howling) *sn led: hdd after 2f: chsd wnr tl rdn over 3f out: sn wknd* **25/1**

5/00 **11** 16 **Brunston Castle**[145] 3294 5-9-6 47 JimmyQuinn 9 13
(A W Carroll) *s.i.s: t.k.h: a bhd* **50/1**

-153 **12** 5 **Make My Hay**[8] 6410 6-9-5 46 (b) TPQueally 10 6
(J Gallagher) *t.k.h in rr: hdwy over 5f out: rdn over 3f out: sn wknd* **8/1**

0000 **13** 4 **Day One**[164] 2747 4-9-8 49 GeorgeBaker 6 4
(R J Price) *a bhd* **16/1**

3m 43.83s (0.70) **Going Correction** -0.05s/f (Stan)
WFA 3 from 4yo+ 9lb 13 Ran SP% **122.5**
Speed ratings (Par 97):96,95,94,94,93 92,90,89,88,87 80,78,76
CSF £44.68 TOTE £3.80: £1.50, £3.00, £3.00; EX 56.30.
Owner Stuart C Williams **Bred** London Thoroughbred Services Ltd **Trained** Newmarket, Suffolk

FOCUS
This basement level contest for stayers was run at a muddling pace and, although the winner can rate higher, the runner-up limits the form.

6473 BETDIRECT.CO.UK BANDED STKS 1m 1f 103y(P)
2:50 (2:50) (Class 7) 3-Y-0+ **£1,521** (£449; £224) **Stalls** Low

Form RPR

0450 **1** **Three Ships**[175] 1707 4-9-4 49 DarrenWilliams 2 57
(Miss J Feilden) *a.p: rdn to ld wl over 1f out: r.o* **8/1**

2560 **2** nk **Dara Mac**[23] 6286 6-9-5 50 VinceSlattery 5 57
(L P Grassick) *hld up in mid-div: hdwy over 2f out: hrd rdn and ev ch ins fnl f: r.o* **12/1**

0303 **3** 1 **Adobe**[16] 6343 10-9-2 47 GeorgeBaker 8 52
(W M Brisbourne) *swtchd lft s: hld up: sn mid-div: hdwy over 1f out: rdn and swtchd rt ins fnl f: r.o* **15/2**

052 **4** 1 **Glenviews Oldport (USA)**[9] 6399 3-9-0 48 RobbieFitzpatrick 9 53+
(Peter Grayson) *hld up and bhd: nt clr run on ins over 2f out: sn rdn: hdwy 1f out: r.o* **6/1**[3]

6440 **5** 1 ¼ **Joey**[22] 6289 3-8-13 47 GrahamGibbons 4 48
(R Hollinshead) *w ldr: led wl over 2f out: sn rdn: hdd wl over 1f out: fdd ins fnl f* **12/1**

3100 **6** nk **Hiawatha (IRE)**[25] 6262 6-9-5 50 ChrisCatlin 1 50
(A M Hales) *hld up in mid-div: rdn and hdwy on ins wl over 1f out: one pce fnl f* **5/1**[1]

6605 **7** ½ **Milk And Sultana**[30] 5655 5-9-1 49 AdamKirby(3) 6 48
(G A Ham) *hld up and bhd: hdwy 2f out: no imp fnl f* **12/1**

4002 **8** 1 **Magari**[16] 6348 4-9-1 49 BenSwarbrick(3) 12 46
(W M Brisbourne) *prom: rdn over 2f out: wknd fnl f* **7/1**

0004 **9** 1 ¼ **Vibe**[16] 6346 4-9-2 47 LukeFletcher 11 42
(R J Price) *hld up in mid-div: rdn 3f out: hdwy over 2f out: hung lft fr over 1f out: sn wknd* **9/1**

1003 **10** 2 **Big Mystery (IRE)**[16] 6348 4-8-13 47 NeilChalmers(3) 13 38
(S C Williams) *hld up and bhd: short-lived effrt on outside over 2f out* **11/2**[2]

0000 **11** 15 **Montcalm (IRE)**[32] 6141 3-9-2 50 TonyCulhane 3 13
(J G Given) *led: hdd wl over 2f out: wknd qckly* **25/1**

2m 3.39s (0.77) **Going Correction** -0.05s/f (Stan)
WFA 3 from 4yo+ 3lb 11 Ran SP% **118.6**
Speed ratings (Par 97):94,93,92,91,90 90,90,89,88,86 73
CSF £100.85 TOTE £8.80: £2.60, £4.70, £3.20; EX 109.90.
Owner Ocean Trailers Ltd **Bred** Juddmonte Farms **Trained** Exning, Suffolk

FOCUS
A steadily-run affair and only ordinary form for the grade, rated through the placed horses.
Adobe Official explanation: jockey said gelding was denied a clear run on home bend

6474 MCMAHON CONTRACTORS SERVICES LTD BANDED STKS 1m 1f 103y(P)
3:20 (3:21) (Class 7) 3-Y-0+ **£1,501** (£443; £221) **Stalls** Low

Form RPR

0202 **1** **Tuscan Treaty**[39] 6033 5-8-11 40 (t) AdamKirby(3) 5 50
(P J McBride) *s.i.s: hld up: hdwy over 3f out: rdn over 2f out: led 1f out: r.o* **4/1**[2]

0060 **2** ½ **Danger Bird (IRE)**[16] 6344 5-8-7 40 HugoFellows(7) 4 49
(R Hollinshead) *hld up: hdwy 3f out: swtchd rt over 2f out: rdn over 1f out: r.o ins fnl f: nt rch wnr* **6/1**[3]

4626 **3** 2 ½ **Mister Clinton (IRE)**[58] 5655 8-9-0 40 JohnEgan 10 44
(D K Ivory) *hld up in mid-div: hdwy 4f out: rdn over 2f out: one pce fnl f* **8/1**

3003 **4** ½ **Wodhill Gold**[11] 6383 4-9-0 40 DerekMcGaffin 1 43
(D Morris) *led 1f: chsd ldr tl rdn over 3f out: sltly outpcd wl over 1f out: kpt on ins fnl f* **7/2**[1]

0040 **5** nk **Liquid Lover (IRE)**[8] 6414 3-8-8 40 (b) BenSwarbrick(3) 2 43
(W M Brisbourne) *chsd ldrs: rdn over 4f out: outpcd 3f out: styd on fnl f* **14/1**

0000 **6** hd **Repeat (IRE)**[11] 6384 5-8-7 40 KirbyHarris(7) 11 42
(J W Unett) *led after 1f: clr over 5f out: rdn and hdd 1f out: wknd wl ins fnl f* **33/1**

0500 **7** 8 **Wandering Act (IRE)**[25] 5865 3-8-11 40 JimmyQuinn 13 27
(A W Carroll) *hld up in mid-div: rdn over 3f out: sn struggling* **14/1**

0000 **8** ½ **David's Symphony (IRE)**[13] 5897 3-8-11 40 TPQueally 12 26
(A W Carroll) *bhd: rdn over 3f out: nvr nr ldrs* **14/1**

-000 **9** ½ **Flying Spud**[13] 5707 4-9-0 40 DeanMcKeown 8 25
(A J Chamberlain) *bhd: rdn over 3f out: nvr nr ldrs* **25/1**

0503 **10** 1 ¼ **Indian's Landing (IRE)**[37] 6079 4-9-0 40 JoeFanning 6 23
(Jennie Candlish) *prom: wnt 2nd over 3f out: wknd over 2f out* **4/1**[2]

00-0 **11** 5 **Bodfari Dream**[18] 6333 4-9-0 40 DarrenWilliams 9 13
(M Mullineaux) *rdn over 4f out: a bhd* **25/1**

600 **12** 8 **Rhuby River (IRE)**[32] 6160 3-8-11 40 TonyCulhane 7 —
(R Dickin) *a bhd* **20/1**

000 **13** dist **Victoriana**[43] 5966 4-9-0 40 ChrisCatlin 3 —
(H J Collingridge) *chsd ldrs tl wknd 4f out: t.o* **20/1**

2m 3.24s (0.62) **Going Correction** -0.05s/f (Stan)
WFA 3 from 4yo+ 3lb 13 Ran SP% **127.8**
Speed ratings (Par 97):95,94,92,91,91 91,84,83,83,82 77,70,—
CSF £28.21 TOTE £5.90: £1.60, £2.30, £2.70; EX 40.90.
Owner Future Electrical Services Ltd **Bred** Paul L Coe **Trained** Newmarket, Suffolk

FOCUS
A dire contest but marginally the faster of the two races over the distance. The form has been rated through the fourth and fifth.

6475 PLAY INSTANT WIN GAMES ON ITVI BANDED STKS 1m 4f 50y(P)
3:50 (3:51) (Class 7) 3-Y-0+ **£1,535** (£453; £226) **Stalls** Low

Form RPR

0055 **1** **Saameq (IRE)**[173] 2465 4-8-13 45 PatrickMathers(3) 11 56
(A C Whillans) *hld up and bhd: hdwy on outside over 3f out: rdn over 1f out: led jst ins fnl f: drvn out* **8/1**

1000 **2** 1 ½ **Little Richard (IRE)**[190] 1983 6-9-2 45 (p) AlanDaly 5 54
(M Wellings) *w ldr: led over 2f out: sn rdn: hdd jst ins fnl f: nt qckn* **10/1**

2124 **3** 1 ¾ **Shekan Star**[16] 6343 3-8-10 45 PaulEddery 6 53+
(K G Reveley) *hld up in mid-div: rdn and hdwy over 2f out: styd on ins fnl f* **2/1**[1]

0442 **4** 1 **Mister Completely (IRE)**[9] 6394 4-8-9 45 WilliamCarson(7) 8 50
(J R Best) *prom: led briefly 6f out: rdn over 3f out: fdd ins fnl f* **8/1**

0040 **5** shd **Summer Bounty**[28] 6230 9-9-2 45 TonyCulhane 4 49
(F Jordan) *hld up in mid-div: hdwy 4f out: rdn over 2f out: one pce fnl f* **6/1**[3]

46-1 **6** 3 **Scorchio (IRE)**[16] 6347 4-9-2 45 DerekMcGaffin 2 45
(B Smart) *s.s: hld up and bhd: rdn and hdwy over 2f out: nvr trbld ldrs* **9/1**

3500 **7** 2 **Emma Lilley (USA)**[24] 5741 3-8-10 45 JoeFanning 10 41
(J G M O'Shea) *hld up in mid-div: hdwy 4f out: rdn over 2f out: wknd over 1f out* **40/1**

4400 **8** shd **Halcyon Magic**[9] 6394 7-9-2 45 (b) DarrenWilliams 3 41
(M Wigham) *t.k.h: hld up and bhd: rdn and hdwy on ins over 1f out: n.d* **20/1**

3050 **9** ¾ **Hollywood Henry (IRE)**[8] 6413 5-9-2 45 (b) PatCosgrave 7 40
(P A Blockley) *hld up: stdy hdwy over 5f out: rdn and wknd over 2f out* **20/1**

5023 **10** 4 **Bulberry Hill**[16] 6344 4-9-2 45 SamHitchcott 9 34
(R W Price) *t.k.h in tch: hdwy to ld over 5f out: rdn and hdd over 2f out: wknd wl over 1f out* **4/1**[2]

300- **11** 20 **Lahob**[323] 6782 5-8-13 45 AdamKirby(3) 1 2
(P Howling) *led: hdd 6f out: rdn 4f out: wknd 3f out: t.o* **25/1**

0054 **12** 4 **Blackthorn**[13] 3743 6-9-2 45 GeorgeBaker 12 —
(M Appleby) *sn prom: wknd over 5f out: t.o* **14/1**

2m 42.42s **Going Correction** -0.05s/f (Stan)
WFA 3 from 4yo+ 6lb 12 Ran SP% **131.4**
Speed ratings (Par 97):98,97,95,95,95 93,91,91,91,88 75,72
CSF £90.53 TOTE £9.50: £2.90, £4.60, £1.60; EX 138.70 Place 6 £675.46, Place 5 £220.59.
Owner Mrs L Irving **Bred** Shadwell Estate Company Limited **Trained** Newmill-On-Slitrig, Borders

FOCUS
This moderately-run race turned out to be quite competitive and the form looks pretty sound.
T/Plt: £187.90 to a £1 stake. Pool: £43,302.25. 168.20 winning tickets. T/Qpdt: £12.70 to a £1 stake. Pool: £5,173.30. 300.40 winning tickets. KH

6470 WOLVERHAMPTON (A.W) (L-H)
Friday, December 2

OFFICIAL GOING: Standard
Wind: Moderate, across

6477 FIRST PAST THE POST AT BETDIRECT MAIDEN STKS (DIV I) 1m 141y(P)
12:50 (12:52) (Class 5) 2-Y-0 **£3,737** (£1,111; £555; £277) **Stalls** Low

Form RPR

1 **Demon Docker (IRE)** 2-9-0 EddieAhern 8 72
(P W Chapple-Hyam) *sn prom: led over 3f out: hdd wl over 1f out: edgd lft but led again ins fnl f: rdn out* **11/4**[1]

0 **2** ¾ **Island Myth (IRE)**[6] 6427 2-9-0 DaneO'Neill 3 70
(M P Tregoning) *mid-div: rdn over 3f out: hdwy to ld wl over 1f out: rdn and hdd ins fnl f: no ex nr fin* **16/1**

32 **3** 7 **Disco Lights**[49] 5864 2-8-9 ChrisCatlin 6 50
(D J Daly) *bmpd s: sn prom: chsd wnr over 3f out to 2f out: sn one pce* **7/2**[2]

4 1 **Markington** 2-9-0 GrahamGibbons 7 59+
(J D Bethell) *slowly away and wl in rr tl hdwy on ins over 1f out: styd on: nvr nrr* **33/1**

54 **5** ½ **Roslea Lady (IRE)**[43] 5995 2-8-9 JDSmith 5 47
(J R Fanshawe) *mid-div: hdwy on ins 4f out: rdn and wknd appr fnl f* **13/2**

0 **6** ¾ **Marachi Band (USA)**[20] 6319 2-8-9 IanMongan 12 45
(E A L Dunlop) *prom to 3f out: rdn and wknd over 2f out* **12/1**

7 2 **Precious Dancer** 2-9-0 SteveDrowne 13 46
(W R Muir) *a towards rr* **12/1**

8 1 ½ **Duty (IRE)** 2-9-0 NickyMackay 1 42
(Sir Michael Stoute) *slowly away: sn rdn: a towards rr* **9/2**[3]

9 1 ½ **Carmona** 2-8-9 TPQueally 10 34
(M G Quinlan) *trckd ldr to over 3f out: wknd over 2f out* **20/1**

0 **10** 7 **Premier Cru**[44] 5968 2-9-0 DeanMcKeown 11 24
(Andrew Turnell) *led tl hdd over 3f out: wknd qckly* **33/1**

11 2 **Subsidise (IRE)** 2-9-0 MickyFenton 2 19
(J G Given) *prom for 3f: sn bhd* **25/1**

0 **12** *20* **Master Malarkey**[11] [6395] 2-8-7 .... KirstyMilczarek(7) 9 —
(Mrs C A Dunnett) *sn outpcd: t.o 1/2-way* **100/1**

1m 51.77s (0.01) **Going Correction** -0.075s/f (Stan) **12** Ran SP% **117.2**

Speed ratings (Par 96):96,95,89,88,87 87,85,84,82,76 74,56

CSF £45.61 TOTE £4.20: £1.70, £5.20, £1.60; EX 62.10.

Owner Mrs Sue Catt & Partners **Bred** Airlie Stud **Trained** Newmarket, Suffolk

FOCUS

Probably a reasonable maiden, although the time was nothing special The front two both look worth following as they pulled seven lengths clear of the third after a good duel from the home turn.

NOTEBOOK

Demon Docker(IRE) was backed as if straight enough to score first time out and so it proved as he battled on gamely after a protracted duel in the straight. Although displaying signs of greenness, he also showed a terrific attitude and can go on from this, possibly over further. (op 7-2)

Island Myth(IRE), driven along leaving the back straight, found plenty for pressure and looked the leader turning for home when he nipped up the inside of the winner. However, his effort in getting to the front may have taken its toll as he faded close home. This was still a marked improvement on his debut run and a similar maiden should fall his way. (op 10-1)

Disco Lights, related to Ebor winner Tuning, was left behind when the main protagonists quickened in the straight. Given her breeding, it was no surprise to see her lacking in pace over this trip and middle-distance handicaps will be her target now. (op 10-3)

Markington shaped with some promise as he is expected to need much further in time. He should be better mentally and physically for the experience and it will be interesting to see how he is campaigned.

Roslea Lady(IRE) enjoyed a return to the Polytrack after disappointing on soft ground at Brighton. She is now handicapped and should be placed to score by connections. (tchd 6-1)

Duty(IRE), a Derby entry, was never competitive or that strongly fancied in the market. There is plenty of stamina in his pedigree and he is sure to be seen to better effect over further. (op 5-1)

6478 PRESS RED TO BET ON ITVI CLAIMING STKS 1m 4f 50y(P)

1:20 (1:21) (Class 6) 3-Y-O+ **£2,914** (£860; £430) **Stalls** Low

Form RPR

0013 **1** **Tranquilizer**[53] [5808] 3-9-0 62 ....(t) EddieAhern 10 70
(D J Coakley) *alway in tch: hdwy to go 2nd wl over 1f out: sn rdn: styd on strly ins fnl f to ld nr fin* **7/1**[3]

4460 **2** *½* **Yawmi**[22] [6305] 5-9-7 70 .... AmirQuinn(3) 3 74
(R A Harris) *led tl hdd 9f out: led again over 2f out: rdn clr appr fnl f: hdd nr fin* **7/2**[1]

0006 **3** *3* **Weet A Head (IRE)**[20] [6337] 4-9-10 64 ....(p) GrahamGibbons 7 69
(R Hollinshead) *slowly away: hld up in rr: hdwy over 2f out: styd on to go 3rd ins fnl f* **20/1**

0003 **4** *¾* **Movie King (IRE)**[6] [6434] 6-9-6 62 ....(t) MichaelTebbutt 5 64
(S R Bowring) *led 9f out: hdd over 2f out: rdn and fdd ins fnl f* **25/1**

5502 **5** *1* **Champion Lion (IRE)**[7] [6419] 6-8-5 59 .... GregFairley(5) 2 53
(J R Boyle) *hld up in tch: rdn over 2f out: one pce and no imp after* **7/2**[1]

0001 **6** *shd* **Tedstale (USA)**[6] [6434] 7-9-3 80 ....(b) CDTimmons(7) 8 66
(K A Ryan) *hld up in rr: hdwy over 3f out: hung lft over 1f out: no hdwy after* **5/1**[2]

0610 **7** *3 ½* **Platinum Charmer (IRE)**[17] [6356] 5-9-3 65 ....(p) AndrewElliott(7) 9 61
(K R Burke) *hld up: nvr nr to chal* **12/1**

6003 **8** *1 ¼* **Je Suis Belle**[17] [6364] 3-8-11 61 .... NelsonDeSouza(3) 12 54
(Miss Gay Kelleway) *mid-div: hdwy 5f out: rdn over 2f out: sn btn* **20/1**

0030 **9** *3* **Mujimac (IRE)**[22] [6307] 3-8-7 53 .... FergusSweeney 6 42
(J R Boyle) *hld up: rdn 4f out: a bhd* **16/1**

600B **10** *1 ¼* **Come What July (IRE)**[25] [6285] 4-9-10 83 .... HayleyTurner 1 52
(Mrs N Macauley) *trckd ldrs: rdn over 5f out: wknd over 3f out* **8/1**

3600 **11** *16* **Marsh Orchid**[57] [2974] 4-9-6 63 .... TonyCulhane 11 22
(C C Bealby) *hld up: a bhd* **66/1**

040- **P** **Epaminondas (USA)**[466] [5006] 4-9-2 65 .... SteveDrowne 4 —
(A J Chamberlain) *prom tl boke down over 5f out: p.u and dismntd* **40/1**

2m 43.18s (0.76) **Going Correction** -0.075s/f (Stan)

WFA 3 from 4yo+ 5lb **12** Ran SP% **115.6**

Speed ratings (Par 101):94,93,91,91,90 90,88,87,85,84 73,—

CSF £28.86 TOTE £8.40: £2.40, £1.30, £8.10; EX 47.20.The winner was the subject of a friendly claim. Yawmi was the subject of a friendly claim.

Owner Count Calypso Racing **Bred** Highclere Stud Ltd **Trained** West Ilsley, Berks

FOCUS

Quite a competitive event for the grade, but a pedestrian early gallop suited Tranquilizer who used his mile speed to quicken past the well-supported Yawmi in the last 50 yards. It would seem unwise to follow the form implicitly.

6479 BETDIRECT.CO.UK NURSERY 5f 216y(P)

1:55 (1:55) (Class 4) (0-85,79) 2-Y-O **£5,751** (£1,711; £855; £427) **Stalls** Low

Form RPR

3611 **1** **Ocean Of Dreams (FR)**[21] [6312] 2-9-7 **79** .... GrahamGibbons 6 81
(J D Bethell) *a in tch: rdn to ld jst ins fnl f: hld on wl* **11/4**[1]

3362 **2** *½* **Hits Only Jude (IRE)**[31] [6214] 2-9-5 **77** .... DeanMcKeown 3 77
(J Pearce) *a in tch: rdn over 1f out: r.o to go 2nd post* **5/1**[3]

2036 **3** *shd* **Scooby Dude (IRE)**[47] [5920] 2-9-6 **78** .... GeorgeBaker 10 78
(Ms Deborah J Evans) *hld up in rr: hdwy on ins over 2f out: squeezed through to dispute 2nd wl ins fnl f* **33/1**

6200 **4** *½* **Daaweitza**[27] [6249] 2-8-8 **66** .... DeanMernagh 9 65
(B Ellison) *outpcd and in rr tl gd hdwy appr fnl f: r.o wl: nvr nrr* **25/1**

0303 **5** *nk* **Egyptian Lord**[17] [6357] 2-7-11 **60** .... DuranFentiman(5) 4 58+
(Peter Grayson) *a.p: rdn and ev ch ent fnl f: no ex whn short of room and hmpd cl home* **18/1**

6421 **6** *nk* **Jimmy The Guesser**[25] [6281] 2-9-5 **77** .... HayleyTurner 7 74
(N P Littmoden) *chsd ldrs: rdn 1/2-way: nt qckn fnl f* **9/2**[2]

3322 **7** *½* **Canina**[6] [6433] 2-8-10 **68** .... EddieAhern 8 63+
(Ms Deborah J Evans) *hld up: rdn and hdwy whn n.m.r appr fnl f: one pce after* **7/1**

516 **8** *nk* **Ochre Bay**[31] [6214] 2-9-6 **78** .... TonyCulhane 11 72
(R Hollinshead) *hld up in tch: effrt over 1f out: nvr nr to chal* **50/1**

0050 **9** *shd* **Sandwith**[21] [6309] 2-8-3 **64** ow4 ....(p) PatrickMathers(3) 1 58
(James Moffatt) *a.p: led over 3f out: hdd jst ins fnl f and fdd* **33/1**

0020 **10** *5* **Gattuso**[7] [6420] 2-8-7 **65** .... JimmyQuinn 2 44
(Ms Deborah J Evans) *slowly away: a bhd* **14/1**

1246 **11** *nk* **Lucayos**[20] [6320] 2-8-6 **64** .... ChrisCatlin 13 42
(Mrs H Sweeting) *w ldrs on outside: rdn whn wknd over 1f out* **20/1**

3062 **12** *1 ¾* **Rapsgate (IRE)**[25] [6281] 2-8-9 **67** .... JohnEgan 12 40
(R Hannon) *w ldrs: rdn 1/2-way: sn bhd* **11/1**

425 **13** *½* **Exexel**[21] [6311] 2-8-4 **65** .... NelsonDeSouza(3) 5 36
(P F I Cole) *led tl hdd over 3f out: rdn and wknd over 2f out* **12/1**

1m 15.77s (-0.04) **Going Correction** -0.075s/f (Stan) **13** Ran SP% **118.4**

Speed ratings (Par 98):97,96,96,95,95 94,94,93,93,86 86,84,83

CSF £14.62 CT £390.65 TOTE £3.40: £1.20, £3.20, £6.80; EX 22.10.

Owner R G Toes **Bred** And Mrs E Le Pivert **Trained** Middleham Moor, N Yorks

■ Stewards' Enquiry : Dean McKeown one-day ban: used whip with excessive frequency (Dec 13)

FOCUS

A messy and rough race. Ocean Of Dreams continued his fantastic run of form with a third successive victory, however with the first nine home separated by little more than two lengths it is questionable what the form is worth.

NOTEBOOK

Ocean Of Dreams(FR), raised 4lb for his win over course and distance last month, duly completed the hat-trick. However, in a race where one or two of his rivals struggled for a run in the straight, he was given the percentage ride and enjoyed the perfect trip in behind the front-runners. (tchd 3-1)

Hits Only Jude(IRE) ran well on his Polytrack debut and was a little inconvenienced when the winner crossed him inside the distance. He does look high enough in the weights for what he has achieved, but he is capable of finding a similar event this winter. (op 9-2 tchd 11-2)

Scooby Dude(IRE) made an encouraging start to life on the All-Weather, finishing well from off a modest gallop. A poor draw did not aid his cause and he took this step up to six furlongs in his stride so should find races in the forthcoming months. (tchd 40-1)

Daaweitza ran without the headgear and posted his best effort on the sand. He was placed over six furlongs with cut in the ground at Haydock in the summer and shaped as though a stiffer test of stamina would have suited here.

Egyptian Lord was on the front end throughout and was weakening when hampered close home. Given the fact he returned unsound from his previous start at Southwell, it may have been a lack of fitness which caught him out and he is not one to write off. (op 20-1)

Jimmy The Guesser, raised 7lb for a win over course and distance at the track on his previous start, ran respectably but failed to find a change of gear when required. He was another that would have preferred a more end-to-end gallop. (op 4-1)

Canina Official explanation: jockey said filly was denied a clear run

6480 TEXT "BETDIRECT" TO 88600 H'CAP (DIV I) 5f 216y(P)

2:25 (2:25) (Class 5) (0-70,70) 3-Y-O+ **£4,396** (£980; £980; £326) **Stalls** Low

Form RPR

5303 **1** **Willheconquertoo**[21] [6310] 5-9-1 **67** ....(tp) TomEaves 4 76
(I W McInnes) *a.p: led ent fnl f: r.o wl* **10/1**

0000 **2** *1 ¼* **Gone'N'Dunnett (IRE)**[7] [6422] 6-8-7 **66** ....(v) KirstyMilczarek(7) 3 71
(Mrs C A Dunnett) *led for 1f: led again 2f out: hdd ent fnl f: kpt on but nt qckn* **14/1**

0312 **2** *dht* **Gilded Cove**[7] [6422] 5-9-4 **70** .... GrahamGibbons 5 75
(R Hollinshead) *in rr tl hdwy over 1f out: swtchd rt ins fnl f: r.o to join for 2nd post* **2/1**[1]

0001 **4** *2 ½* **Middle Eastern**[16] [6367] 3-9-0 **66** ow2 .... FergalLynch 7 64
(P A Blockley) *s.i.s: hld up: gd hdwy on outside over 2f out: fdd ins fnl f* **5/1**[2]

5000 **5** *1* **Alexia Rose (IRE)**[53] [5793] 3-9-3 **69** .... EddieAhern 10 64
(A Berry) *in tch: rn wd ent st: n.d after but r.o fnl f* **40/1**

0566 **6** *shd* **Extra Mark**[6] [6430] 3-8-11 **63** .... HayleyTurner 1 57
(J R Best) *hld up in tch: rdn over 1f out: one pce after* **14/1**

2003 **7** *¾* **Aggravation**[6] [6426] 3-9-0 **66** ....(t) JohnEgan 2 58
(D R C Elsworth) *hld up: rdn over 2f out: no hdwy after* **6/1**[3]

1000 **8** *nk* **Attorney**[6] [6426] 7-8-10 **67** .... MarcHalford(5) 6 58
(N E Berry) *hld up: sme hdwy whn short of room oer 1f out* **14/1**

4000 **9** *2 ½* **Four Amigos (USA)**[20] [6335] 4-8-9 **64** .... SilvestreDeSousa(3) 9 48
(D Nicholls) *led after 1f: hdd 2f out: wknd over 1f out* **33/1**

0110 **10** *1 ¼* **Desert Opal**[27] [6248] 5-9-3 **69** .... TonyCulhane 12 49
(D W Chapman) *hld up: a in rr* **8/1**

0004 **11** *4* **Namir (IRE)**[21] [6310] 3-9-4 **70** ....(v) JoeFanning 13 38
(T D Barron) *prom tl wknd wl over 1f out* **20/1**

0210 **12** *nk* **Campeon (IRE)**[7] [6422] 3-8-13 **65** .... SteveDrowne 11 32
(J M Bradley) *prom tl wknd wl over 1f out* **16/1**

1m 15.03s (-0.78) **Going Correction** -0.075s/f (Stan) **12** Ran SP% **120.5**

Speed ratings (Par 103):102,100,100,97,95 95,94,94,90,89 83,83

WIN: Willheconquertoo £12.90. PL: Willheconquertoo £2.90, Gilded Cove £1.20, Gone'n'dunnett £5.60. EX: W/GC £17.20, W/G'N'D £50.90. CSF: W/GC £15.08, W/G'N'D £70.57. TRIC: W/GC/G'N'D £148.12, W/G'N'D/GC £198.63..

Owner Stephen Hackney And Martin Higgins **Bred** A S Reid **Trained** Catwick, E Yorks

FOCUS

A decent time for the grade and a return to winning ways for Willheconquertoo who scored for the first time in 12 months on his first start for new connections. The form looks solid with Gilded Cove again running his race.

6481 LITTLEWOODS BETDIRECT H'CAP 5f 216y(P)

3:00 (3:01) (Class 2) (0-100,102) 3-Y-O+

£11,571 (£3,464; £1,732; £867; £432; £217) **Stalls** Low

Form RPR

6041 **1** **Bonus (IRE)**[109] [4428] 5-8-7 **89** .... NickyMackay 3 103
(G A Butler) *hld up: hdwy on ins over 1f out: swtchd rt ins fnl f: r.o to ld last strides* **9/1**

410 **2** *nk* **Kostar**[133] [3687] 4-8-2 **87** ow1 .... AdamKirby(3) 1 100
(C G Cox) *a.p: rdn to ld 1f out: kpt on: hdd last strides* **7/1**[3]

3302 **3** *3 ½* **Looks Could Kill (USA)**[7] [6421] 3-8-4 **86** oh3 .... JimmyQuinn 6 89
(E J Alston) *mid-div: hdwy over 2f out: r.o fnl f: nvr nrr* **9/1**

2010 **4** *½* **Green Manalishi**[50] [5853] 4-9-2 **98** .... EddieAhern 2 99
(D W P Arbuthnot) *led tl rdn and hdd 1f out: one pce after* **8/1**

2000 **5** *½* **Moayed**[13] [6378] 6-9-6 **102** ....(bt) HayleyTurner 13 102
(N P Littmoden) *hld up: hdwy over 1f out: nvr nr to chal* **14/1**

0204 **6** *shd* **Desperate Dan**[16] [6370] 4-8-1 **86** ....(b) NelsonDeSouza(3) 4 85
(J A Osborne) *prom: rdn over 1f out: fdd ins fnl f* **9/2**[1]

0011 **7** *½* **Fromsong (IRE)**[20] [6321] 7-8-10 **92** .... DaneO'Neill 5 90
(D K Ivory) *prom: rdn 2f out: wknd ins fnl f* **8/1**

4021 **8** *1 ½* **Middleton Grey**[111] [4369] 7-8-9 **91** ....(b) FergusSweeney 7 84
(A G Newcombe) *hld up in rr: effrt over 2f out: nvr on terms* **12/1**

5462 **9** *shd* **Yomalo (IRE)**[16] [6370] 5-8-12 **94** .... ChrisCatlin 8 87
(Rae Guest) *outpcd: sme hdwy whn swtchd lft over 1f out: n.d* **11/2**[2]

05 **10** *3 ½* **Lake Andre (IRE)**[16] [6370] 4-8-5 **94** .... DeanHeslop(7) 12 76
(K A Ryan) *racd wd: prom tl wknd wl over 1f out* **25/1**

0040 **11** *1* **Quiet Times (IRE)**[16] [6370] 6-8-6 **88** ....(b) JoeFanning 10 67
(K A Ryan) *s.i.s: rdn 1/2-way: bhd fnl 2f* **16/1**

35 **12** *4* **Lindbergh**[35] [6132] 3-8-5 **87** .... JohnEgan 9 54
(R Hannon) *in tch: rdn over 2f out: wknd over 1f out* **20/1**

210- **13** *9* **Newsround**[419] [6068] 3-8-12 **94** .... TonyCulhane 11 34
(D W Chapman) *racd wd in mid-div: lost tch 1/2-way* **40/1**

1m 13.48s (-2.33) **Going Correction** -0.075s/f (Stan) **13** Ran SP% **119.6**

Speed ratings (Par 109):112,111,106,106,105 105,104,102,102,98 96,91,79

CSF £69.24 CT £593.62 TOTE £12.60: £3.50, £2.30, £3.70; EX 116.10.

Owner The Bonus Partnership **Bred** A Stroud And J Hanly **Trained** Blewbury, Oxon

FOCUS

Unsurprisingly, the best race of the day on the clock with Bonus narrowly outside the course record in beating Kostar. The pair put good daylight between themselves and solid yardstick Looks Could Kill in third and the form looks sound.

NOTEBOOK

Bonus(IRE), a Group Three winner in his youth, looks a shrewd claim by his current connections who are sure to map out an extensive campaign on the All-Weather for their new charge. He produced a terrific turn of foot to pick off the runner-up close home and looks set for a good winter, maybe in Dubai. (op 10-1)

Kostar would not gain any medals for consistency, but this was a sound effort and he was unlucky not to score. He did little wrong in defeat and, although he was favoured by the draw, this was his best effort on the Polytrack. He has yet to finish out of the frame on the All-Weather and should find compensation soon. (op 8-1)

Looks Could Kill(USA) has found some consistency of late but remains a tough horse to win with - his career stats are now 1-18. That said, he has run two solid races in warm handicaps lately and six furlongs at Wolverhampton seems to be his optimum conditions. (op 11-1)

Green Manalishi has done most of his winning at the minimum trip so it was perhaps a surprise to see him forcing the issue over six furlongs. In the circumstances he posted an excellent effort and a drop in distance should see him score this winter - he was beaten a short-head on his last All-Weather outing over 5f. (op 10-1)

Moayed stayed on well from off the pace, but probably finds this trip on the short side for him nowadays. He is of course a tricky ride, but a return to seven furlongs on the Polytrack could see him get his head in front as this is his time of year. (op 9-1)

Desperate Dan was having his first start on the All-Weather and was not disgraced. He faded inside the distance and may be better served by a return to the minimum trip as he has displayed plenty of pace in hot handicaps during the summer. (op 6-1)

6482 BETDIRECT ON SKY ACTIVE H'CAP 1m 4f 50y(P)

3:30 (3:31) (Class 4) (0-85,85) 3-Y-0+ **£5,625** (£1,673; £836; £417) **Stalls** Low

Form RPR

2002 **1** **Pass The Port**[16] 6371 4-8-8 **75** EddieAhern 6 82
(D Haydn Jones) *trckd ldrs: wnt 2nd 2f out: rdn to ld ins fnl f: all out* **7/1**

1230 **2** *hd* **Gibraltar Bay (IRE)**[169] 2622 3-8-8 **80** IanMongan 7 87
(T G Mills) *led after 2f: rdn over 2f out: hdd ins fnl f: kpt on* **8/1**

5040 **3** *nk* **The Violin Player (USA)**[13] 6377 4-9-2 **83** TonyCulhane 9 89+
(H J Collingridge) *mid-div: rdn and hdwy over 1f out: r.o wl fnl f* **6/1**[2]

1560 **4** *shd* **Dower House**[46] 5948 10-9-4 **85** (t) ChrisCatlin 2 91
(Andrew Turnell) *t.k.h: hld up: rdn over 2f out: n.m.r and sn swtchd rt: r.o wl fnl f* **8/1**

4121 **5** *hd* **Bethanys Boy (IRE)**[16] 6371 4-8-2 **72** PatrickMathers(3) 4 78
(B Ellison) *t.k.h: mid-div: hdwy on ins over 2f out: kpt on fnl f* **4/1**[1]

5634 **6** *½* **Bucks**[22] 6308 8-8-7 **74** JohnEgan 11 79
(D K Ivory) *a.p: rdn and ev ch 2f out: edgd lft and nt qckn ins fnl f* **7/1**

3351 **7** *½* **Top Spec (IRE)**[74] 5371 4-8-7 **74** JimmyQuinn 10 78
(J Pearce) *s.i.s: sn mid-div: rdn over 3f out: hdwy over 2f out: no imp fnl f* **13/2**[3]

4320 **8** *4* **Boundless Prospect (USA)**[13] 6373 6-8-3 **73** NelsonDeSouza(3) 1 71
(Miss Gay Kelleway) *a in rr* **9/1**

1000 **9** *nk* **Salute (IRE)**[62] 4819 6-9-3 **84** RobertHavlin 3 81
(P G Murphy) *led for 2f: prom tl wknd over 2f out* **20/1**

0/2- **10** *shd* **Afadan (IRE)**[353] 6891 7-8-10 **77** MickyFenton 8 74
(J R Jenkins) *slowly away: in rr: brief effrt over 1f out: nvr on terms* **40/1**

300U **11** *3 ½* **Wotchalike (IRE)**[25] 6285 3-8-5 **77** HayleyTurner 5 69
(R J Price) *tokk t.k.h: in front rnk tl wknd over 2f out* **66/1**

1020 **12** *9* **Annambo**[13] 6377 5-8-9 **76** DaneO'Neill 12 53
(D Morris) *chsd ldrs: rdn over 3f out: wknd over 2f out* **20/1**

2m 42.64s (0.22) **Going Correction** -0.075s/f (Stan)
WFA 3 from 4yo+ 5lb **12** Ran SP% **118.3**
Speed ratings (Par 105):96,95,95,95,95 95,94,92,91,91 89,83
CSF £59.28 CT £360.26 TOTE £9.80: £3.00, £3.90, £2.20; EX 72.00.
Owner The Porters **Bred** Meon Valley Stud **Trained** Efail Isaf, Rhondda C Taff

FOCUS
A moderate time for this event, run at a modest gallop, and it remains to be seen how the form works out with the bare form ordinary at best. Less than two lengths separated the first seven home and it could be a race to treat with caution.

Wotchalike(IRE) Official explanation: jockey said saddle slipped

Annambo Official explanation: vet said gelding had a haematoma on its left shoulder

6483 TEXT "BETDIRECT" TO 88600 H'CAP (DIV II) 5f 216y(P)

4:00 (4:01) (Class 5) (0-70,70) 3-Y-0+ **£4,404** (£1,310; £654; £327) **Stalls** Low

Form RPR

0621 **1** **Nan Jan**[11] 6404 3-9-2 **68** 6ex (t) DaneO'Neill 2 79
(R Ingram) *trckd ldr: led 2f out: in command fnl f* **9/2**[2]

0046 **2** *1 ½* **Wainwright (IRE)**[20] 6335 5-9-0 **66** FergalLynch 1 72
(P A Blockley) *trckd eladers: chsd wnr over 1f out: r.o* **6/1**[3]

5500 **3** *nk* **Savile's Delight (IRE)**[45] 5956 6-8-12 **64** TomEaves 3 69+
(R Brotherton) *hld up in tch: hdwy over 1f out: r.o wl* **14/1**

030 **4** *1* **Joyeaux**[27] 6252 3-8-13 **65** MickyFenton 5 67
(S L Keightley) *trckd ldrs: kpt on one pce ins fnl 2f* **33/1**

2024 **5** *shd* **Summer Recluse (USA)**[6] 6426 6-9-4 **70** (t) GeorgeBaker 4 72
(J M Bradley) *hld up: hdwy on ins 2f out: r.o one pce fnl f* **4/1**[1]

4044 **6** *1 ¼* **Kew The Music**[6] 6430 5-9-0 **66** ChrisCatlin 8 64+
(M R Channon) *slowly away: wl bhd and stl last ent fnl f: fin strly: nvr nr to chal* **15/2**

5023 **7** *hd* **Sling Back (IRE)**[20] 6336 4-8-11 **63** PatCosgrave 12 60
(Eamon Tyrrell, Ire) *prom: rdn over 2f out: no hdwy ent fnl f* **10/1**

31 **8** *nk* **Bahamian Ballet**[60] 5666 3-9-4 **70** GrahamGibbons 13 67
(E S McMahon) *trckd ldrs: rdn and edgd lft over 1f out: wknd ins* **8/1**

0605 **9** *nk* **No Grouse**[21] 6315 5-9-0 **66** JimmyQuinn 7 62
(E J Alston) *hld up: rdn over 1f out: no hdwy* **10/1**

0500 **10** *1 ¼* **Monashee Prince (IRE)**[6] 6426 3-8-10 **69** WilliamCarson(7) 10 61
(J R Best) *hld up: rdn 1/2-way: nvr on terms* **25/1**

0014 **11** *1 ¼* **Jilly Why (IRE)**[72] 5411 4-8-13 **65** EddieAhern 6 53
(Ms Deborah J Evans) *led tl hdd 2f out: wknd over 1f out* **14/1**

0000 **12** *nk* **Alpaga Le Jomage (IRE)**[45] 5954 3-8-9 **64** AdamKirby(3) 11 51
(M J Polglase) *a bhd* **66/1**

2550 **13** *6* **Merdiff**[220] 1284 6-8-12 **67** BenSwarbrick(3) 9 36
(W M Brisbourne) *chsd ldrs tl lost pl over 3f out: sn bhd* **25/1**

1m 14.32s (-1.49) **Going Correction** -0.075s/f (Stan) **65** Ran SP% **119.0**
Speed ratings (Par 103):106,104,103,102,102 100,100,99,99,97 96,95,87
CSF £30.43 CT £284.09 TOTE £4.90: £2.20, £2.60, £4.70; EX 37.20.
Owner The Waltons **Bred** Mrs S Ingram **Trained** Epsom, Surrey

FOCUS
The versatile Nan Jan duly followed up her recent Southwell success with a cosy win under a penalty, recording her best effort on the clock to date. She coped well with the change in surface and this win opens up plenty of options for her. This looks particularly solid form for the grade.

6484 FIRST PAST THE POST AT BETDIRECT MAIDEN STKS (DIV II) 1m 141y(P)

4:30 (4:31) (Class 5) 2-Y-O **£3,727** (£1,108; £554; £276) **Stalls** Low

Form RPR

0 **1** **Danamour (IRE)**[20] 6319 2-9-0 DaneO'Neill 9 75
(M P Tregoning) *in tch: hdwy over 3f out: led wl over 1f out: wnt lft u.p: r.o ins fnl f* **3/1**[1]

2 *½* **Whatizzit** 2-8-9 EddieAhern 4 69
(E A L Dunlop) *a.p: rdn and swtchd rt over 1f out: r.o strly to go 2nd ins fnl f* **4/1**[2]

53 **3** *1 ¾* **Genau (IRE)**[34] 6135 2-9-0 TomEaves 10 70
(Mrs L Stubbs) *prom: led over 6f out: hdd wl over 1f out: n.m.r 1f out: kpt on ins* **9/1**

03 **4** *1 ¼* **Bouzouki (USA)**[36] 6123 2-9-0 JoeFanning 12 69+
(W R Swinburn) *a.p: wnt 2nd over 3f out: ev ch whn bdly hmpd 1f out: nt rcvr* **4/1**[2]

0 **5** *4* **Uandi**[30] 6225 2-8-6 RobertMiles(3) 8 54
(J Akehurst) *slowly baway: in rr tl hdwy on outside 4f out: one pce fnl 2f* **50/1**

6 *5* **That Look** 2-9-0 TPQueally 7 48
(D E Cantillon) *hld up: rdn 3f out: nvr on terms* **50/1**

7 *½* **Being There** 2-9-0 SteveDrowne 6 46
(P F I Cole) *nvr bttr than mid-div* **25/1**

8 *1* **Kinetic Power (IRE)** 2-9-0 JohnEgan 2 44
(D R C Elsworth) *slowly away: hld up: nvr on terms* **15/2**[3]

9 *1 ¼* **Dance A Daydream** 2-8-9 JDSmith 3 36
(J R Fanshawe) *hld up: a bhd* **8/1**

00 **10** *2 ½* **Xenia**[7] 6424 2-8-9 MickyFenton 5 31
(J G Given) *trckd ldrs: rdn over 3f out: sn wknd* **40/1**

11 *22* **Artists Touch (IRE)** 2-9-0 HayleyTurner 1 —
(N P Littmoden) *a bhd* **25/1**

12 *11* **Tina's Magic** 2-8-9 GrahamGibbons 13 —
(Mrs G S Rees) *led tl hdd over 6f out: short of room and wknd rapidly 3f out* **40/1**

1m 51.64s (-0.12) **Going Correction** -0.075s/f (Stan) **52** Ran SP% **114.4**
Speed ratings (Par 96):97,96,95,93,90 85,85,84,83,81 61,51
CSF £13.19 TOTE £3.60: £1.50, £1.80, £3.20; EX 17.10 Place 6 £141.37, Place 5 £82.35.
Owner Byculla Thoroughbreds **Bred** Tullamaine Castle Stud And Partners **Trained** Lambourn, Berks

■ Stewards' Enquiry : Dane O'Neill two-day ban: careless riding (Dec 13-14)

FOCUS
Some nice prospects and Danamour was the second horse on the afternoon from Marcus Tregoning's stable to improve significantly on his debut effort, even if the time was modest. There is sure to be a race in the well-bred Whatizzit, while Genau is now handicapped and should be placed to good effect this winter. The form looks pretty sound.

NOTEBOOK

Danamour(IRE) looked green and backward on debut, but overcame his lack of racing to put his head in front, even if he did hang left under pressure. That was probably more inexperience than temperament and he looks the type to continue progressing. (tchd 10-3)

Whatizzit, a half-sister to Chesham Stakes winner Whazzat, should find a similar race as she stuck on gamely inside the distance to chase the winner. Her stable often leave plenty to work on with the debutants and she appears a ready-made winner in waiting. (op 9-2 tchd 7-2)

Genau(IRE) was easy to back and is now handicapped. He emerged with some credit considering this was a marked step up in trip and he should find a little handicap, especially if ridden with a little more restraint. (op 7-1)

Bouzouki(USA) is no star, but he was a shade unfortunate as the winner went across him at the distance and he might have been second but for the interference. He is another that is now handicapped and that will be his best opportunity of success. (op 7-2 tchd 9-2)

Uandi, a daughter of Singspiel, is always going to be better once she is handicapped and stepped up in trip. She is still learning, but showed a little promise and will be better for the experience.

Xenia Official explanation: jockey said filly had been struck into

T/Plt: £224.10 to a £1 stake. Pool: £38,571.15. 125.60 winning tickets. T/Qpdt: £41.80 to a £1 stake. Pool: £3,955.70. 70.00 winning tickets. JS

6477 WOLVERHAMPTON (A.W) (L-H)

Saturday, December 3

OFFICIAL GOING: Standard

Wind: Moderate, behind

6485 NO 5P RULE 4'S AT BETDIRECT MAIDEN STKS 1m 4f 50y(P)

7:00 (7:07) (Class 5) 3-Y-O+ **£3,471** (£1,032; £516; £257) **Stalls** Low

Form RPR

52 **1** **Kyles Prince (IRE)**[18] 6355 3-9-0 FergusSweeney 4 77+
(P J Makin) *a front rnk: led 3f out: rn clr over 1f out: styd on wl* **13/8**[2]

2 *1 ¾* **Lady Gregory (IRE)**[115] 4279 3-8-9 EddieAhern 5 66
(John M Oxx, Ire) *a in tch: rdn to chse wnr 3f out: no imp appr fnl f* **11/10**[1]

00 **3** *5* **Golo Gal**[156] 3046 3-9-0 IanMongan 2 63
(Mrs L J Mongan) *a in tch: rdn and edgd lft appr fnl f: no ch w first 2* **50/1**

04 **4** *2 ½* **Medora Leigh (USA)**[136] 3643 3-8-9 TPQueally 1 54
(J A R Toller) *prom tl wknd over 1f out* **25/1**[3]

5 *9* **Tara King** 3-8-9 LPKeniry 7 40
(A B Haynes) *hld up: sme hdwy 4f out: nvr on terms* **100/1**

6 *2 ½* **Blackbury**[11] 3-8-6 AdamKirby(3) 8 36
(J W Unett) *bhd and nvr on terms* **100/1**

0/- **7** *½* **Kuka**[757] 5938 4-9-5 GrahamGibbons 6 40
(R Hollinshead) *led tl hdd 3f out: wknd over 2f out* **80/1**

05 **8** *8* **Blaenavon**[18] 6355 3-8-9 DaneO'Neill 10 22
(D W P Arbuthnot) *unruly in stalls: bhd and nvr on terms* **40/1**

/50- **9** *shd* **Skelligs Rock (IRE)**[579] 1832 5-9-5 **75** TonyCulhane 9 27
(A W Carroll) *bhd whn rdn 5f out: nvr on terms* **25/1**[3]

50- **10** *dist* **Taj India (USA)**[36] 5347 3-9-0 VinceSlattery 3 —
(N J Hawke) *bhd whn rdn over 4f out: sn lost tch: t.o* **80/1**

11 *2* **Arthurs Legacy** 3-8-7 RonanKeogh(7) 12 —
(J A R Toller) *a bhd: t.o* **80/1**

2m 41.21s (-1.21) **Going Correction** -0.10s/f (Stan)
WFA 3 from 4yo+ 5lb **11** Ran SP% **103.5**
Speed ratings (Par 103):100,98,95,93,87 86,85,80,80,— —
CSF £2.70 TOTE £2.50: £1.10, £1.30, £6.40; EX 5.00.
Owner Weldspec Glasgow Limited **Bred** Norelands Bloodstock **Trained** Ogbourne Maisey, Wilts

■ Custodian (15/2) was withdrawn (refused to enter stalls). R4 applies, deduct 10p in the £.

FOCUS
Very little strength in depth, but Kyles Prince and Lady Gregory finished clear.

6486 TEXT "BETDIRECT" TO 88600 CLAIMING STKS 5f 216y(P)

7:30 (7:33) (Class 6) 3-Y-0+ **£2,927** (£864; £432) **Stalls** Low

Form RPR

0130 **1** **Mystic Man (FR)**[48] 5923 7-9-3 80 FergalLynch 4 73+
(K A Ryan) *hld up on ins: hdwy whn short of room and swtchd rt over 1f out: hung lft but led ins fnl f and r.o wl* **2/1**[1]

0000 **2** *1 ½* **Alpaga Le Jomage (IRE)**[1] 6483 3-8-8 64 AdamKirby(3) 1 63
(M J Polglase) *chsd ldrs: c wd into st r.o to go 2nd ins fnl f* **28/1**

1466 **3** *½* **Kennington**[7] 6426 5-9-9 62 (b) JohnEgan 7 73
(Mrs C A Dunnett) *chsd ldrs: rdn 1/2-way: kpt on fnl f* **7/1**[2]

0344 **4** *hd* **Million Percent**[108] 4471 6-9-3 74 PatCosgrave 12 66
(K R Burke) *broke wl: styd prom: led over 1f out: hdd ins fnl f: no ex* **10/1**

0110 **5** *3 ½* **Ballybunion (IRE)**[77] 5319 6-8-11 64 DaneO'Neill 8 50
(N E Berry) *mid-div: rdn 2f out: kpt on one pce* **9/1**

0040 **6** *nk* **Namir (IRE)**[1] 6480 3-8-13 70 (v) JoeFanning 6 51
(T D Barron) *trckd ldrs: wkng whn sltly hmpd ent fnl f* **11/1**

0000 **7** *½* **Endless Summer**[8] 6421 8-9-9 74 JimmyQuinn 13 60
(A W Carroll) *hld up: rdn over 2f out: nvr nr to chal* **12/1**

6000 **8** *1 ¾* **Doctor's Cave**[54] 5802 3-8-13 62 ChrisCatlin 3 44
(K O Cunningham-Brown) *hld up: nvr on terms* **28/1**

0 **9** *½* **In A Fit**[22] 6310 4-8-12 TonyCulhane 9 42
(P Howling) *nvr on terms* **100/1**

6610 **10** *¾* **Dizzy In The Head**[8] 6422 6-8-13 63 (b) TomEaves 2 41
(I Semple) *sn led: hdd over 1f out: wknd qckly fnl f* **8/1**[3]

5546 **11** *1* **Ulysees (IRE)**[78] 5266 6-8-13 62 LeeEnstone 5 38
(I Semple) *hld up: a bhd* **7/1**[2]

3020 **12** *1 ¼* **Chilly Cracker**[12] 6404 3-9-0 62 GeorgeBaker 10 35
(R Hollinshead) *hld up: a bhd* **16/1**

0 **13** *10* **Ginger For Pluck**[8] 6418 3-8-0 JamieMackay 11 —
(J G Given) *a struggling in rr* **80/1**

1m 14.77s (-1.04) **Going Correction** -0.10s/f (Stan) 13 Ran SP% **119.6**
Speed ratings (Par 101):102,100,99,99,94 94,93,91,90,89 88,86,73
CSF £73.86 TOTE £3.40: £1.30, £8.80, £3.50; EX 130.40.
Owner R J H Limited **Bred** Gainsborough Stud Management Ltd **Trained** Hambleton, N Yorks
■ Stewards' Enquiry : Pat Cosgrave one-day ban: failed to keep straight from the stalls (Dec 14)

FOCUS
A reasonable enough race for the grade, rated through the third, but Mystic Man did not have to be at his best.

6487 BETDIRECTPOKER.COM H'CAP 1m 141y(P)

8:00 (8:00) (Class 6) (0-55,55) 3-Y-0+ **£2,922** (£862; £431) **Stalls** Low

Form RPR

0020 **1** **Barons Spy (IRE)**[26] 6287 4-9-0 55 DarrenWilliams 5 60
(R J Price) *a.p and gng wl: rdn over 2f out: led over 1f out: rdn out* **14/1**

2 *nk* **Glenree**[40] 6089 4-9-0 55 (b) PatCosgrave 7 59
(Eamon Tyrrell, Ire) *mid-div: hdwy 2f out: ev ch 1f out: r.o fnl f* **16/1**

5020 **3** *nk* **Blue Quiver (IRE)**[21] 6324 5-8-12 53 SteveDrowne 12 57+
(C A Horgan) *slowly away: hdwy on outside over 1f out: r.o strly fnl f: nvr nrr* **9/1**

5000 **4** *shd* **Young Mick**[54] 5794 3-8-12 55 (b[1]) JamieMackay 6 59
(G G Margarson) *hld up: hdwy on outside over 2f out: r.o wl fnl f* **40/1**

4041 **5** *nk* **We'll Meet Again**[12] 6401 5-9-0 55 DaleGibson 1 58
(M W Easterby) *prom on ins: ev ch 1f out: nt qckn ins fnl f* **5/1**[1]

0403 **6** *1 ¼* **Londoner (USA)**[24] 6299 7-8-12 53 DaneO'Neill 4 53
(S Dow) *trckd ldr tl rdn and nt qckn appr fnl f* **11/2**[2]

4660 **7** *½* **Prince Of Gold**[26] 6286 5-8-13 54 GrahamGibbons 10 53
(R Hollinshead) *hld up: effrt whn n.m.r over 1f out: n.d* **13/2**[3]

0000 **8** *nk* **Blue Empire (IRE)**[17] 6365 4-9-0 55 GeorgeBaker 2 54
(C R Dore) *led tl hdd over 1f out: wknd ins fnl f* **8/1**

0200 **9** *3* **Gem Bien (USA)**[54] 5794 7-9-0 55 (p) TonyCulhane 3 47
(D W Chapman) *mid-div: rdn over 1f out: sn btn* **7/1**

0320 **10** *1* **Craic Sa Ceili (IRE)**[24] 6299 5-8-13 54 (p) MickyFenton 13 44
(M S Saunders) *racd wd: a bhd* **14/1**

0020 **11** *5* **Frank's Quest (IRE)**[34] 6177 5-8-13 54 FergusSweeney 11 34
(A B Haynes) *mid-div: rdn over 3f out: sn btn* **16/1**

2510 **12** *2* **Spark Up**[7] 6438 5-8-11 55 (b) AdamKirby(3) 9 30
(J W Unett) *trckd ldrs: rdn 3f out: wknd 2f out* **8/1**

1m 50.5s (-1.26) **Going Correction** -0.10s/f (Stan)
WFA 3 from 4yo+ 2lb 12 Ran SP% **117.6**
Speed ratings (Par 101):101,100,100,100,100 99,98,98,95,94 90,88
CSF £217.93 CT £2151.61 TOTE £24.10: £5.20, £5.90, £4.50; EX 452.10.
Owner Barry Veasey **Bred** Tally-Ho Stud **Trained** Ullingswick, H'fords

FOCUS
Just a moderate handicap and the form is limited.
We'll Meet Again Official explanation: jockey said gelding hung right straight
Blue Empire(IRE) Official explanation: jockey said gelding hung right throughout

6488 BETDIRECT FREEPHONE 0800 211 222 H'CAP 1m 1f 103y(P)

8:30 (8:31) (Class 5) (0-70,70) 3-Y-0+ **£3,396** (£1,010; £505; £252) **Stalls** Low

Form RPR

2031 **1** **Desert Leader (IRE)**[21] 6337 4-9-4 70 EddieAhern 1 84+
(W M Brisbourne) *trckd ldrs: gng wl: led jst ins fnl f: r.o strly* **9/4**[1]

2606 **2** *2* **El Chaparral (IRE)**[18] 6356 5-9-2 68 JohnEgan 5 78
(W J Haggas) *hld up on outside: hdwy over 2f out: edgd lft but r.o wl to chse wnr ins fnl f* **4/1**[2]

6432 **3** *2* **Khanjar (USA)**[21] 6337 5-9-4 70 PatCosgrave 7 76
(K R Burke) *led tl rdn and hdd jst ins fnl f: no ex* **9/2**[3]

6040 **4** *nk* **Scottish River (USA)**[21] 6325 6-9-4 70 HayleyTurner 2 76
(M D I Usher) *mid-div: hdwy over 2f out: rdn over 1f out: kpt on one pce* **17/2**

0000 **5** *½* **Silent Storm**[33] 6201 5-9-1 67 J-PGuillambert 9 72
(C A Cyzer) *plld hard: trckd ldr: rdn 2f out: wknd ins fnl f* **12/1**

0510 **6** *2* **Midshipman**[180] 2345 7-8-8 67 WilliamCarson(7) 12 68
(A W Carroll) *bhd and nvr nr to chal* **16/1**

0002 **7** *hd* **Nimello (USA)**[18] 6362 9-9-4 70 LPKeniry 13 71
(A G Newcombe) *a bhd* **10/1**

0000 **8** *2* **She's Our Lass (IRE)**[21] 6337 4-8-8 67 DanielleMcCreery(7) 4 64
(D Carroll) *bhd and nvr on terms* **25/1**

2634 **9** *3* **High Arctic**[8] 6418 3-9-2 70 SamHitchcott 8 61
(A Bailey) *slowly away: t.k.h and sn chsd ldrs: wknd over 2f out* **20/1**

0046 **10** *2* **My Pension (IRE)**[40] 6075 4-9-1 67 TonyCulhane 10 54
(P Howling) *hld up in tch: wknd over 2f out* **12/1**

-000 **11** *3* **Shami**[56] 5743 6-9-4 70 DarrenWilliams 6 52
(D W Chapman) *mid-div: rdn over 3f out: sn btn* **33/1**

2m 0.78s (-1.84) **Going Correction** -0.10s/f (Stan)
WFA 3 from 4yo+ 2lb 11 Ran SP% **121.4**
Speed ratings (Par 103):104,102,100,100,99 97,97,96,93,91 88
CSF £10.97 CT £38.81 TOTE £1.90: £1.50, £2.30, £2.40; EX 9.80.
Owner R Rickett **Bred** Shadwell Estate Company Limited **Trained** Great Ness, Shropshire

FOCUS
A modest handicap, but sound form for the grade and Desert Leader won well, looking worth his place in better company.
She's Our Lass(IRE) Official explanation: jockey said filly made a noise on pulling up

6489 BETDIRECT.CO.UK H'CAP 5f 20y(P)

9:00 (9:00) (Class 4) (0-85,85) 3-Y-0+ **£5,653** (£1,681; £840; £419) **Stalls** Low

Form RPR

4030 **1** **Ok Pal**[42] 6021 5-8-13 80 IanMongan 1 91
(T G Mills) *mid-div: hdwy on ins over 2f out: led ins fnl f: drvn out* **9/2**[1]

0000 **2** *1 ¼* **Piccled**[17] 6370 7-9-1 82 JimmyQuinn 2 88
(E J Alston) *s.i.s: sn chsd ldrs: led 2f out: rdn and hdd ins fnl f: r.o* **10/1**

3105 **3** *¾* **Cornus**[8] 6421 3-9-4 85 EddieAhern 7 88
(M J Polglase) *mid-div: rdn and hdwy over 1f out: r.o fnl f* **10/1**

0663 **4** *nk* **Whitbarrow (IRE)**[21] 6321 6-8-10 77 DaleGibson 3 79
(A W Carroll) *a.p: ev ch 2f out: rdn and no ex ins fnl f* **6/1**[3]

0000 **5** *¾* **The Lord**[17] 6370 5-9-1 82 AlanDaly 11 82+
(W G M Turner) *swtchd lft fr wd draw to centre s: bhd tl hdwy over 1f out: nvr nr to chal* **33/1**

-000 **6** *1 ¼* **Premier Fantasy**[168] 2692 3-8-8 75 JohnEgan 12 70+
(W J Haggas) *swtchd lft fr outside draw to ins sn after s: bhd: swtchd rt 1/2-way: hdwy over 1f out: nvr nr to chal* **9/2**[1]

0060 **7** *1 ½* **Whistler**[42] 6021 8-9-0 81 (p) PaulFitzsimons 6 71
(Miss J R Tooth) *outpcd: nvr on terms* **18/1**

-001 **8** *½* **Maktavish**[30] 6238 6-8-10 77 (p) TomEaves 5 65
(I Semple) *trckd ldr to over 2f out: one pce after* **7/1**

0044 **9** *nk* **The Jobber (IRE)**[34] 6182 4-9-2 83 DaneO'Neill 8 70
(M Blanshard) *hld up: nvr on terms* **11/2**[2]

00-0 **10** *3* **Efistorm**[22] 6310 4-8-8 78 JasonEdmunds(3) 4 54
(J Balding) *led tl hdd 2f out: wknd over 1f out* **66/1**

0400 **11** *2* **Magic Glade**[17] 6370 6-9-4 85 ChrisCatlin 9 54
(R Brotherton) *prom to 1/2-way* **20/1**

0004 **12** *2 ½* **Little Ridge (IRE)**[21] 6321 4-8-11 78 SteveDrowne 10 38
(H Morrison) *chsd ldrs on outside tl wknd wl over 1f out* **20/1**

61.47 secs (-1.35) **Going Correction** -0.10s/f (Stan) 12 Ran SP% **115.9**
Speed ratings (Par 105):106,104,102,102,101 99,96,95,95,90 87,83
CSF £46.60 CT £434.61 TOTE £6.00: £1.60, £2.70, £2.50; EX 34.30.
Owner Sherwoods Transport Ltd **Bred** Sherwoods Transport Ltd **Trained** Headley, Surrey

FOCUS
A decent sprint handicap and straightforward form to rate. The draw played a big part as usual, with stall one beating stall two, and Whitbarrow only narrowly failing to complete an inside draw tricast.
Magic Glade Official explanation: trainer had no explanation for the poor form shown

6490 BETDIRECTCASINO.COM H'CAP 2m 119y(P)

9:30 (9:36) (Class 6) (0-65,62) 3-Y-0+ **£2,912** (£860; £430) **Stalls** Low

Form RPR

3322 **1** **Reggae Rhythm (IRE)**[4] 6461 11-9-6 60 RichardThomas(3) 4 72+
(A J Lidderdale) *hld up in rr: hdwy on outside 2f out: led over 1f out: styd on strly* **13/2**

0004 **2** *2 ½* **Bank On Benny**[17] 6368 3-8-12 57 JohnEgan 2 65
(P W D'Arcy) *hld up: hdwy 2f out: edgd lft but styd on to go 2nd ins fnl f* **5/1**[2]

5044 **3** *1* **Countback (FR)**[43] 635 6-8-13 50 JimmyQuinn 9 57
(A W Carroll) *bhd tl hdwy wl over 2f out: ev ch over 1f out: no ex fnl f* **16/1**

0013 **4** *1 ¼* **Jackie Kiely**[21] 6329 4-9-1 52 TonyCulhane 6 57
(P Howling) *hld up: hdwy to go 3rd 3f out: rdn over 1f out: wknd ins fnl f* **8/1**

2301 **5** *hd* **Spitting Image (IRE)**[28] 6267 5-9-5 61 GregFairley(5) 3 66
(M Johnston) *in tch: rdn over 2f out: one pce after* **11/8**[1]

3043 **6** *3 ½* **Webbswood Lad (IRE)**[12] 6405 4-9-11 62 MickyFenton 10 63
(Stef Liddiard) *in tch: wnt 2nd 4f out: led wl over 2f out: hdd over 1f out: wknd fnl f* **16/1**

/024 **7** *4* **Activist**[5] 6448 7-9-6 60 (p) DanielTudhope(3) 12 56
(D Carroll) *hld up in rr: nvr on terms* **20/1**

000/ **8** *5* **Coppermalt (USA)**[20] 3860 7-8-13 50 LPKeniry 5 40
(R Curtis) *trckd ldrs: led over 5f out: hdd wl over 2f out: wknd wl over 1f out* **66/1**

/43- **9** *8* **High Policy (IRE)**[535] 2987 9-9-4 60 StephanieHollinshead(5) 8 40
(R Hollinshead) *hld up in rr: a bhd* **40/1**

0624 **10** *15* **Precious Mystery (IRE)**[26] 6280 5-9-6 57 EddieAhern 11 19
(A King) *trckd ldrs: rdn 4f out: sn wknd* **6/1**[3]

00/0 **11** *8* **Protection Money**[26] 6283 5-9-6 57 VinceSlattery 1 10
(L P Grassick) *led tl hdd over 5f out: wknd qckly* **100/1**

3m 42.26s (-0.87) **Going Correction** -0.10s/f (Stan)
WFA 3 from 4yo+ 8lb 11 Ran SP% **119.0**
Speed ratings (Par 101):98,96,96,95,95 94,92,89,86,78 75
CSF £38.63 CT £506.87 TOTE £5.80: £1.90, £2.50, £3.40; EX 63.40 Place 6 £179.58, Place 5 £150.41.
Owner Mrs A Lidderdale **Bred** Liffeyside Stud **Trained** Eastbury, Berks

FOCUS
A modest staying handicap.
T/Plt: £279.10 to a £1 stake. Pool: £60,171.80. 157.35 winning tickets. T/Qpdt: £149.30 to a £1 stake. Pool: £2,462.30. 12.20 winning tickets. JS

6415 SAINT-CLOUD (L-H)

Saturday, December 3

OFFICIAL GOING: Very soft

6492a PRIX PETITE ETOILE (LISTED RACE) (FILLIES) 1m 2f 110y

2:25 (2:26) 3-Y-0 **£16,667** (£6,667; £5,000; £3,333; £1,667)

RPR

1 **Alvarita**[34] 6181 3-8-11 J-BEyquem 6 105
(Sir Mark Prescott) *raced in 2nd behind clear leader, progress and brought field stands side straight, led 2f out, stayed on well to line*

2 *2* **Gift Range (IRE)**27 6274 3-8-11 RonanThomas 3 101
(John M Oxx, Ire) *raced in 3rd, driven 2f out, ridden over 1f out, stayed on finished 3rd, placed 2nd*
3 *nk* **Afaf (FR)**25 3-8-11 SMaillot 8 100
(M Delzangles, France) *finished 4th, placed 3rd*
4 *2 ½* **Pyrana (USA)**26 3-8-11 MCherel 4 101
(Y De Nicolay, France) *finished 2nd, placed 4th*
5 *2 ½* **First Charm (FR)**21 3-8-11 THuet 2 91
(G Cherel, France)
6 *3* **Attirina**164 3-8-11 NGuesdon 7 86
(Mme C Head-Maarek, France)
7 *8* **Misdirect**68 5522 3-8-11 TGillet 1 72
(P Bary, France)
8 *10* **Mahima (FR)** 3-8-11 FSpanu 9 54
(J E Hammond, France)
9 *5* **Lady Bountiful**48 3-8-11 TJarnet 5 45
(H-A Pantall, France)

2m 30.1s 9 Ran
PARI-MUTUEL: WIN 29.50; PL 8.30, 3.10, 1.90; DF 5.60.
Owner Miss K Rausing **Bred** Miss K Rausing **Trained** Newmarket, Suffolk

NOTEBOOK
Alvarita, fourth in a Listed contest on the Polytrack last time, rewarded another spot of good overseas placing by her trainer to grab some valuable black type. Appreciating the step up in trip, she saw the extended ten furlongs out really well.

6462 SOUTHWELL (L-H)
Sunday, December 4

OFFICIAL GOING: Standard
Wind: Almost nil Weather: Mostly fine

6493 FIRST PAST THE POST AT BETDIRECT BANDED STKS 5f (F)
1:00 (1:00) (Class 7) 3-Y-0+ £1,409 (£416; £208) Stalls High

Form RPR
3311 **1** **Orchestration (IRE)**4 6470 4-9-7 49 (v) RobbieFitzpatrick 1 62
(M J Attwater) *w ldrs: led over 2f out: r.o wl: readily* **2/1**1
1001 **2** *1* **Largs**12 6409 5-8-9 46 (b) JasonEdmunds(3) 8 50
(J Balding) *hld up: effrt over 2f out: edgd rt and hdwy over 1f out: wnt 2nd ins last: no real imp* **8/1**
0056 **3** *¾* **Tipsy Lillie**13 6396 3-8-11 45 (b) JohnEgan 2 46
(Julian Poulton) *s.i.s: sn chsng ldrs: kpt on same pce fnl f* **12/1**
3002 **4** *1 ¼* **Empress Josephine**12 6409 5-8-13 47 (vt) FergalLynch 3 44
(J R Jenkins) *sltly hmpd s: outpcd and swtchd wd outside over 3f out: hdwy 2f out: kpt on same pce* **10/3**3
000 **5** *nk* **Sapphire Dream**18 6369 3-8-9 50 MichaelJStainton(7) 6 46
(A Bailey) *trckd ldrs: one pce appr fnl f* **16/1**
0242 **6** *nk* **Desert Light (IRE)**13 6397 4-9-0 51 (v) PatrickMathers(3) 4 46
(D Shaw) *sn trcking ldrs: one pce appr fnl f* **3/1**2
0400 **7** *4* **Misty Princess**12 6409 3-8-11 45 (v) TonyCulhane 5 27
(D Shaw) *led tl over 2f out: lost pl over 1f out* **33/1**
0000 **8** *3* **Make Us Flush**31 6235 3-8-13 47 GrahamGibbons 7 18
(A Berry) *prom: lost pl 2f out* **33/1**

59.83 secs (-0.47) **Going Correction** -0.15s/f (Stan) 8 Ran SP% **112.0**
Speed ratings (Par 97):97,95,94,92,91 91,84,80
CSF £18.18 TOTE £4.00: £1.10, £4.00, £3.30; EX 10.90.
Owner Brooklands Racing **Bred** Mrs Anita Rothschild **Trained** Wysall, Notts
FOCUS
The winner ruled himself out of Banded racing, the runner-up sets the standard and the form has a sound look about it.

6494 NO 5P RULE 4'S AT BETDIRECT MAIDEN CLAIMING STKS 1m 4f (F)
1:30 (1:30) (Class 7) 3-Y-0+ £1,419 (£419; £209) Stalls Low

Form RPR
4506 **1** **High Frequency (IRE)**9 6419 4-9-0 45 (b1) JohnEgan 3 51
(W R Muir) *mde all: styd on wl u.p fnl f* **7/4**1
0003 **2** *2* **Nevsky Bridge**19 6361 3-8-8 46 LPKeniry 8 47
(J J Quinn) *trckd ldrs: wnt 2nd 4f out: rdn 1f out: kpt on same pce* **13/2**
0033 **3** *13* **Swords**6 6443 3-8-13 55 J-PGuillambert 6 31
(P Howling) *hld up: hdwy to chse ldrs 7f out: wnt mod 3rd over 2f out: no ch w 1st 2* **5/2**2
0430 **4** *10* **Danum**195 1946 5-9-4 35 (p) GrahamGibbons 5 15
(R Hollinshead) *hld up in rr: drvn along and prom over 4f out: sn wl outpcd: kpt on ins last* **10/1**
006 **5** *¾* **Amberlina (IRE)**20 6343 3-8-8 EddieAhern 2 9
(Patrick Morris, Ire) *trckd ldrs: drvn and lost pl 3f out* **6/1**3
6000 **6** *7* **Isabella Rossini**13 6394 3-8-6 40 ChrisCatlin 4 —
(A M Hales) *hld up in mid-div: effrt 4f out: sn btn* **8/1**
000 **7** *18* **Holly Rocket**8 6436 4-8-8 35 NataliaGemelova(5) 7 —
(J E Long) *hld up towards rr: effrt over 5f out: sn lost pl and bhd* **80/1**
060/ **8** *18* **The Roan Runner**1149 2677 7-8-11 30 JemmaMarshall(7) 1 —
(B P J Baugh) *trckd ldrs: lost pl over 7f out: t.o 4f out* **80/1**

2m 40.08s (-2.01) **Going Correction** -0.225s/f (Stan)
WFA 3 from 4yo+ 5lb 8 Ran SP% **115.2**
Speed ratings (Par 97):97,95,87,80,79 75,63,51
CSF £14.13 TOTE £2.50: £1.30, £1.40, £1.50; EX 39.60.The winner was claimed by T. D. Barron for £3,000. Nevsky Bridge was claimed by D. McCain for £5,000.
Owner M J Caddy **Bred** Laurent Cottrell **Trained** Lambourn, Berks
FOCUS
A very weak seller rated through the runner-up.

6495 BETDIRECT.CO.UK BANDED STKS 1m 3f (F)
2:00 (2:00) (Class 7) 3-Y-0+ £1,419 (£419; £209) Stalls Low

Form RPR
50-5 **1** **Rood Boy (IRE)**18 6365 4-9-5 50 ChrisCatlin 8 61
(Andrew Turnell) *rr-div on outer: hdwy over 5f out: rdn to chse ldr 3f out: kpt on fnl f: led last strides* **9/2**1
0034 **2** *hd* **Surdoue**6 6444 5-9-0 45 J-PGuillambert 7 56
(P Howling) *led 2f: led over 5f out: kpt on fnl f: hdd nr fin* **7/1**
0040 **3** *10* **Giunchiglio**25 6300 6-9-3 48 EddieAhern 11 43
(W M Brisbourne) *hld up in rr: hdwy over 4f out: tk mod 3rd 1f out* **6/1**2
4100 **4** *4* **Power Glory**45 5998 3-8-13 48 TonyHamilton 9 37
(R A Fahey) *sn chsng ldrs: drvn over 3f out: one pce* **13/2**3
0303 **5** *½* **Staff Nurse (IRE)**26 6289 5-8-11 45 (b) DanielTudhope(3) 5 33
(N Wilson) *trckd ldrs: one pce fnl 3f* **13/2**3
0243 **6** *3* **Finnegans Rainbow**12 6414 3-8-3 45 LiamJones(7) 2 28
(M C Chapman) *w ldrs: wknd fnl 2f* **9/2**1
0 **7** *4* **Ivory Key (IRE)**22 6327 3-8-7 45 (b) AdamKirby(3) 1 22
(Patrick Morris, Ire) *mid-div whn hmpd on inner and lost pl bnd after 2f: hdwy u.p on wd outside over 4f out: wknd 2f out* **28/1**
0000 **8** *3 ½* **Queenstown (IRE)**13 6399 4-9-1 46 BrianReilly 6 17
(B A Pearce) *mid-div: drvn along over 5f out: nvr a factor* **20/1**
0-00 **9** *23* **Diequest (USA)**108 4509 4-8-11 47 GregFairley(5) 10 —
(Mrs P Ford) *mid-div: drvn along 7f out: lost pl over 5f out: sn bhd* **66/1**
0000 **10** *½* **River Of Diamonds**20 6348 4-8-11 45 (b1) AmirQuinn(3) 4 —
(R A Harris) *mid-div: drvn along 6f out: sn lost pl and bhd* **16/1**
0300 **11** *6* **Guadiana (GER)**20 6343 3-8-11 46 HayleyTurner 3 —
(A W Carroll) *mid-div: drvn along over 7f out: sn lost pl and bhd* **22/1**
0006 **12** *dist* **Handa Island (USA)**12 6410 6-8-11 35 (b) PaulMulrennan(3) 12 —
(M W Easterby) *reminders after s: led after 2f: hdd over 5f out: t.o 3f out: virtually p.u: btn 60 l* **14/1**

2m 26.38s (-2.52) **Going Correction** -0.225s/f (Stan)
WFA 3 from 4yo+ 4lb 12 Ran SP% **116.4**
Speed ratings (Par 97):100,99,92,89,89 87,84,81,64,64 60,—
CSF £33.45 TOTE £4.00: £1.70, £3.30, £2.00; EX 42.00.
Owner Dajam Ltd **Bred** Mrs Stephen Nolan, Miss Sandra Nolan, And Noel Lyo **Trained** Broad Hinton, Wilts
FOCUS
Just two in at at the finish but the gallop was strong and the pair look above average for this low grade.

6496 PRESS RED TO BET ON ITVI MEDIAN AUCTION MAIDEN STKS 6f (F)
2:30 (2:33) (Class 7) 2-Y-0 £1,423 (£420; £210) Stalls Low

Form RPR
52 **1** **Opal Warrior**13 6395 2-8-9 JohnEgan 2 64
(P W D'Arcy) *swvd lft s: mde all: r.o wl fnl f: readily* **15/8**1
6006 **2** *1* **Rambling Socks**20 6342 2-8-9 52 (b1) PaulEddery 5 61
(S R Bowring) *trckd wnr: chalr over 1f out: rdn and no ex ins last* **10/1**
0054 **3** *5* **Mister Incredible**32 6226 2-9-0 58 PatCosgrave 14 51
(C A Dwyer) *trckd ldrs: effrt over 2f out: kpt on same pce appr fnl f* **11/2**3
004 **4** *hd* **Left Nostril (IRE)**116 4268 2-8-2 51 DonnaCaldwell(7) 4 45
(P S McEntee) *chsd ldrs: one pce appr fnl f* **20/1**
0 **5** *1 ½* **Parazone**36 6150 2-9-0 EddieAhern 9 46
(E J O'Neill) *chsd ldrs: kpt on same pce fnl 2f* **7/1**
4 **6** *5* **Bigalo's Banjo**15 6386 2-9-0 GrahamGibbons 3 31+
(J J Quinn) *slowly inbto stride: sn chsng ldrs: wknd over 1f out* **4/1**2
6040 **7** *¾* **Genoa Star**84 5145 2-8-2 45 (v1) JamesO'Reilly(7) 1 30+
(T J Pitt) *mid-div: n.m.r on inner and lost pl over 3f out: n.d after* **16/1**
6400 **8** *3* **Fashion Chic**15 6375 2-8-9 45 MickyFenton 13 15
(Stef Liddiard) *dwlt: sn chsng ldrs on outer: outpcd over 3f out: no threat after* **40/1**
00 **9** *nk* **Boppys Pride**19 6360 2-8-7 NSLawes(7) 6 19
(R A Fahey) *rr-div: hmpd and lost pl over 3f out: sme hdwy 2f out: nvr on terms* **33/1**
000 **10** *2 ½* **Sanders Boy**165 2813 2-9-0 48 DarrenWilliams 12 11
(J R Norton) *s.i.s: rr div whn hmpd over 3f out* **66/1**
3000 **11** *2 ½* **Shopfitter**54 5823 2-8-9 48 MarcHalford(5) 10 —
(Mrs C A Dunnett) *chsd ldrs: lost pl over 4f out* **25/1**
12 *1 ¾* **Superior Bay** 2-8-9 TonyHamilton 11 —
(R A Fahey) *s.v.s: swtchd lft after s: a bhd* **28/1**
5000 **13** *2 ½* **Wizard Prince**24 6303 2-8-11 53 (b) AmirQuinn(3) 7 —
(R A Harris) *mid-div: lost pl over 3f out* **33/1**
0 **14** *1 ¾* **Sahara Secret (IRE)**107 4553 2-8-6 PatrickMathers(3) 8 —
(D Shaw) *mid-div: hmpd and lost pl over 3f out: sn bhd* **100/1**

1m 16.88s (-0.02) **Going Correction** -0.225s/f (Stan) 14 Ran SP% **120.5**
Speed ratings (Par 90):91,89,83,82,80 74,73,69,68,65 62,59,56,54
CSF £20.25 TOTE £2.50: £1.30, £4.10, £2.10; EX 26.40.
Owner Mrs Jan Harris **Bred** Mrs Maureen Barbara Walsh **Trained** Newmarket, Suffolk
■ Genoa Star was 31-year-old Tim Pitt's first runner as a trainer.
FOCUS
A weak maiden no better than a seller, but the winner was cleraly the best in the line-up and can progress.
NOTEBOOK
Opal Warrior, forced wide when narrowly denied at Lingfield, had a favourable draw and in the end did more than enough, even though this trip is her bare minimum and she may be happier on the quicker Polytrack surface. (op 6-4 tchd 2-1)
Rambling Socks, blinkered for the first time, travelled equally well but in the end was very much second best. (op 14-1)
Mister Incredible, very warm on quite a cold day, had the worst of the draw. (op 8-1 tchd 5-1)
Left Nostril(IRE), absent since August, was having just her second try on the All-Weather. (tchd 22-1)
Parazone, absent for five weeks, showed a fair bit more than he had done on his debut. (tchd 11-2)
Bigalo's Banjo missed a beat at the start and did not improve on his initial effort. Perhaps Polytrack suits him better at this stage. (op 9-2)
Genoa Star, her trainer's first runner, lost whatever chance she had when knocked right back on the inner at the halfway mark. (op 22-1)

6497 FOOTBALLER-DRIVES.CO.UK BANDED STKS 7f (F)
3:00 (3:01) (Class 7) 3-Y-0+ £1,429 (£422; £211) Stalls Low

Form RPR
3042 **1** **The Job**15 6384 4-8-11 45 (v) TonyCulhane 13 54
(A D Smith) *chsd ldrs: led over 1f out: hld on wl* **7/2**1
4453 **2** *1* **Preskani**15 6384 3-8-11 40 (p) AlanDaly 1 51
(Mrs N Macauley) *rr-div: effrt over 2f out: hdwy over 1f out: styd on wl ins last to take 2nd last 50yds: nt rch wnr* **22/1**
4321 **3** *1* **Caerphilly Gal**12 6412 5-8-9 50 JosephWalsh(7) 8 54
(P L Gilligan) *trckd ldrs: led over 2f out: hdd over 1f out: no ex ins last* **7/2**1
2054 **4** *¾* **Wings Of Morning (IRE)**200 1812 4-8-8 45 (v) DanielTudhope(3) 6 47
(D Carroll) *s.i.s: hdwy on outer over 2f out: styd on fnl f* **10/1**
0230 **5** *½* **Star Fern**15 6382 4-8-11 45 RobbieFitzpatrick 3 45
(M J Attwater) *s.i.s: hdwy over 2f out: styd on fnl f* **6/1**2
0341 **6** *3* **Amanda's Lad (IRE)**6 6446 5-8-10 45 LiamJones(7) 7 44
(M C Chapman) *led tl over 4f out: outpcd over 3f out: no threat after* **12/1**
0431 **7** *½* **Kumakawa**6 6444 7-8-10 45 LauraReynolds(7) 2 43
(D K Ivory) *slowly into s: sn given remeinders: hdwy on wd outside 2f out: kpt on fnl f* **8/1**3
2103 **8** *4* **Ace Club**6 6446 4-8-11 45 (b) TonyHamilton 12 27
(J Hetherton) *w ldr: led over 4f out tl over 2f out: hung lft and lost pl over 1f out* **8/1**3

-000 **9** ½ **Inescapable (USA)**[20] 6347 4-8-4 45 .... TolleyDean[(7)] 11 25
(A W Carroll) *stdd s: tk fierce hold in rr: sddle slipped over 4f out: nt rcvr* **33/1**
0030 **10** ¾ **Mister Aziz (IRE)**[6] 6444 3-8-11 45 .... (p) EddieAhern 10 24
(J R Jenkins) *bhd and pushed along: nvr on terms* **20/1**
0-30 **11** ½ **Government (IRE)**[7] 682 4-8-11 45 .... GrahamGibbons 4 22
(M C Chapman) *in tch: outpcd 4f out: n.d after* **33/1**
0000 **12** 9 **Tiggers Touch**[20] 6348 3-8-11 45 .... HayleyTurner 5 —
(A W Carroll) *in tch: lost pl over 3f out: sn bhd* **80/1**
-355 **13** ¾ **Wares Home (IRE)**[313] 190 4-8-11 45 .... (v) PatCosgrave 9 —
(K R Burke) *in tch: sn drvn along: lost pl over 3f out: sn bhd* **25/1**

1m 30.3s (-0.50) **Going Correction** -0.225s/f (Stan) **13** Ran SP% **117.8**
Speed ratings (Par 97):93,91,90,89,89 85,85,80,80,79 78,68,67
CSF £90.71 TOTE £4.40: £2.10, £6.30, £1.80; EX 80.80.
Owner Duckhaven Stud **Bred** A Smith **Trained** Westward Ho!, Devon

FOCUS
Ordinary form with the first two both stepping up a fraction on recent efforts.
Inescapable(USA) Official explanation: jockey said saddle slipped

6498 BETDIRECTCASINO.COM BANDED STKS 1m (F)
3:30 (3:32) (Class 7) 3-Y-O+ **£1,423** (£420; £210) **Stalls** Low

Form RPR
3400 **1** **Night Warrior (IRE)**[29] 6257 5-8-12 40 .... (b[1]) PaulDoe 3 47
(K McAuliffe) *chsd ldrs: effrt on outer over 2f out: edgd lft and styd on to ld nr fin* **5/1**[3]
4422 **2** *hd* **Jacks Delight**[12] 6412 5-8-12 40 .... MickyFenton 8 47
(C N Kellett) *trckd ldrs: edgd lft over 1f out: carried lft ins last: no ex nr fin* **10/3**[1]
0300 **3** ½ **Semper Paratus (USA)**[15] 6382 6-8-12 40 .... (v) MatthewHenry 6 46
(V Smith) *chsd ldrs: led on inner over 2f out: hdd and no ex towards fin* **6/1**
3530 **4** 7 **Canary Dancer**[13] 6396 3-8-6 40 .... RoryMoore[(5)] 7 32
(B A Pearce) *w ldrs: led 3f out: sn hdd: wknd appr fnl f* **4/1**[2]
4450 **5** *shd* **Paper Doll**[220] 1319 3-8-4 40 .... SoniaEaton[(7)] 5 32
(B P J Baugh) *in tch: effrt on inner over 2f out: wknd over 1f out* **25/1**
6006 **6** 6 **Danaat (USA)**[12] 6411 3-8-4 35 .... (b) AndrewElliott[(7)] 9 20
(K R Burke) *chsd ldrs: lost pl over 1f out* **9/1**
0600 **7** 6 **Eastfields Lad**[6] 6442 3-8-11 40 .... PaulEddery 4 8
(S R Bowring) *sn drvn along in rr: nvr on terms* **28/1**
0600 **8** 2½ **Cleveland Way**[12] 6412 5-8-9 40 .... (b) DanielTudhope[(3)] 11 3
(D Carroll) *led tl 3f out: wknd and eased over 1f out* **16/1**
5060 **9** 2½ **Garnock Venture (IRE)**[12] 6412 4-8-12 40 .... (b) GrahamGibbons 13 —
(A Berry) *s.i.s: nvr on terms* **14/1**
0000 **10** 1¼ **Pawn In Life (IRE)**[6] 6444 7-8-12 40 .... (v) TonyCulhane 1 —
(M J Polglase) *mid-div: lost pl over 4f out* **14/1**
000- **11** 2½ **Munaahej (IRE)**[347] 6977 4-8-12 40 .... AlanDaly 14 —
(Mrs N Macauley) *s.i.s: a bhd* **40/1**
4000 **12** *shd* **Isle Dream**[12] 6411 3-8-8 30 .... PatrickMathers[(3)] 12 —
(John A Harris) *mid-div on outer: lost pl over 4f out: sn bhd* **100/1**
040U **13** ½ **Sadlers Senor (IRE)**[139] 3589 3-8-4 40 .... (b[1]) JamesO'Reilly[(7)] 10 —
(J O'Reilly) *mid-div: lost pl over 4f out: sn bhd* **66/1**

1m 44.92s (0.32) **Going Correction** -0.225s/f (Stan)
WFA 3 from 4yo+ 1lb **13** Ran SP% **115.5**
Speed ratings (Par 97):89,88,88,81,81 75,69,66,64,62 60,60,59
CSF £20.35 TOTE £6.30: £2.00, £1.40, £2.40; EX 29.60 Place 6 £11.60, Place 5 £5.65.
Owner Barrie Kirby **Bred** Sean Collins **Trained** Fernham, Oxon

FOCUS
A moderate winning time, even for a banded race. Straightforward form for the grade, rated through the third.
Canary Dancer Official explanation: jockey said filly hung right
T/Plt: £14.00 to a £1 stake. Pool: £40,055.90. 2,082.30 winning tickets. T/Qpdt: £9.10 to a £1 stake. Pool: £3,185.10. 257.15 winning tickets. WG

6455 LINGFIELD (L-H)
Monday, December 5

OFFICIAL GOING: Standard
Wind: Light; half behind Weather: Overcast

6499 BETDIRECT FREEPHONE 0800 211 222 H'CAP (DIV I) 1m (P)
12:10 (12:11) (Class 5) (0-75,75) 3-Y-O+ **£3,044** (£905; £452; £226) **Stalls** High

Form RPR
0213 **1** **Fasylitator (IRE)**[23] 6325 3-9-0 72 .... JohnEgan 3 86
(D K Ivory) *trckd ldrs: effrt over 2f out: pressed ldr over 1f out: led ins fnl f: drvn and hld on gamely* **7/2**[2]
3501 **2** *nk* **Actuality**[26] 6298 3-8-10 68 .... MartinDwyer 5 82
(M P Tregoning) *prom: wnt 2nd 1/2-way: led over 2f out: wd bnd sn after: hdd ins fnl f: kpt on but outbattled by wnr* **2/1**[1]
2600 **3** 5 **All A Dream**[116] 4297 3-9-0 72 .... TomEaves 8 74
(Mrs L Williamson) *s.i.s: hld up wl in rr: effrt on inner over 2f out: styd on fr over 1f out: nrst fin* **100/1**
0004 **4** ½ **Just Fly**[58] 5735 5-9-3 74 .... DaneO'Neill 10 75
(Dr J R J Naylor) *hld up wl in rr: gng wl but nt clr run over 2f out: prog over 1f out: styd on* **12/1**
0000 **5** *nk* **Quantum Leap**[25] 6302 8-8-13 70 .... (v) JimmyQuinn 7 70
(S Dow) *sn shuffled along in last: gng bttr over 2f out but stl last: prog over 1f out: drvn and r.o: no ch* **16/1**
6055 **6** ¾ **Gaelic Princess**[35] 6201 5-9-1 72 .... FergusSweeney 6 70
(A G Newcombe) *hld up in rr: pushed along 1/2-way: effrt and nowhere to go wl over 1f out: swtchd ins and styd on: no ch* **11/1**
0040 **7** 1¼ **Resplendent Prince**[77] 5365 3-8-11 69 .... IanMongan 2 65
(T G Mills) *t.k.h: hld up in midfield: prog on outer 3f out: nt qckn u.p over 1f out: wknd fnl f* **20/1**
6006 **8** ½ **Consonant (IRE)**[65] 5603 8-9-4 75 .... PaulDoe 11 69
(D G Bridgwater) *led for 1f: styd chsng ldrs: rdn 1/2-way: struggling over 2f out* **20/1**
5100 **9** 1 **Danielle's Lad**[63] 5671 9-8-10 67 .... (b) FrancisFerris 4 59
(B Palling) *led after 1f to over 2f out: wknd* **50/1**
001 **10** 5 **Elrafa Mujahid**[20] 6362 3-9-2 74 .... ChrisCatlin 12 55
(Ernst Oertel) *prog on wd outside to chse ldrs 3f out: wd bnd 2f out: wknd* **14/1**
0 **11** *shd* **Orenay (USA)**[26] 6301 3-8-11 69 .... (t) EddieAhern 1 49
(M J Wallace) *dwlt: sn chsd ldrs: rdn and no prog over 2f out: heavily eased fnl f* **25/1**
0002 **12** 5 **Lord Of Dreams (IRE)**[23] 6333 3-8-12 70 .... JamieSpencer 9 39
(D W P Arbuthnot) *prom to wl over 2f out: sn eased and lost all ch* **13/2**[3]

1m 36.26s (-3.17) **Going Correction** -0.20s/f (Stan) course record
WFA 3 from 5yo+ 1lb **12** Ran SP% **113.8**
Speed ratings (Par 103):107,106,101,101,100 100,98,98,97,92 92,87
CSF £9.63 CT £569.51 TOTE £5.10: £1.30, £1.20, £13.40; EX 9.80.
Owner Mrs A Shone **Bred** Gerard Callanan **Trained** Radlett, Herts
■ Stewards' Enquiry : Francis Ferris one-day ban: careless riding (Dec 16)

FOCUS
A modest handicap, run at a solid pace, and the first two came clear. The form appears sound enough.
Gaelic Princess Official explanation: jockey said mare was denied a clear run
Lord Of Dreams(IRE) Official explanation: jockey said colt hung badly left throughout

6500 LITTLEWOODS BETDIRECT (S) STKS 6f (P)
12:40 (12:40) (Class 6) 2-Y-O **£2,484** (£733; £366) **Stalls** Low

Form RPR
6065 **1** **She Whispers (IRE)**[79] 5323 2-8-6 54 .... ChrisCatlin 12 52
(G C H Chung) *rr of main gp: prog 2f out: drvn to chse ldr ins fnl f: r.o to ld last stride* **7/1**[3]
5030 **2** *hd* **Phinerine**[6] 6466 2-8-11 63 .... (b) JoeFanning 4 56
(Peter Grayson) *t.k.h: trckd ldr: led over 1f out: 2 l clr ins fnl f: collared last stride* **4/1**[2]
0 **3** ½ **Dolce Maria (IRE)**[20] 6353 2-8-6 .... JimmyQuinn 7 50
(Michael Cunningham, Ire) *trckd ldrs: effrt 2f out: drvn to dispute 2nd ins fnl f: styd on but jst outpcd* **12/1**
3005 **4** 1 **Montini Royale (IRE)**[6] 6466 2-8-11 55 .... IanMongan 2 52
(M J Attwater) *led to over 1f out: fdd ins fnl f* **4/1**[2]
5 1¼ **Miss A Bargain (IRE)** 2-8-6 .... FranciscoDaSilva 6 43
(K R Burke) *green to post: wl in rr: lost tch 1/2-way: rdn and styd on wl fr over 1f out: nrst fin* **25/1**
5006 **6** 1¼ **Teddy Monty (IRE)**[20] 6353 2-8-6 56 .... RoryMoore[(5)] 11 44
(M Quinn) *dwlt: rcvrd and prom on outer: cl up 2f out: wknd over 1f out* **9/1**
5000 **7** 1¼ **Surf City**[25] 6304 2-8-11 67 .... (b[1]) DaneO'Neill 5 41
(R A Harris) *chsd ldng pair: rdn 1/2-way: wknd 2f out* **3/1**[1]
1000 **8** 1¼ **Miss Lovat**[26] 6296 2-8-11 60 .... SamHitchcott 10 37
(A Bailey) *chsd ldrs to 1/2-way: sn struggling u.p* **8/1**
00 **9** 29 **Ardkeel Boy (IRE)**[16] 6386 2-8-11 .... FrancisFerris 3 —
(B Palling) *dwlt: sn t.o* **66/1**

1m 12.67s (-0.14) **Going Correction** -0.20s/f (Stan) **9** Ran SP% **111.6**
Speed ratings (Par 94):92,91,91,89,88 86,84,83,44
CSF £33.48 TOTE £6.00: £2.40, £1.40, £3.70; EX 29.60.There was no bid for the winner.
Owner J T Developments UK **Bred** Dermot Cantillon And Forenaghts Stud **Trained** Newmarket, Suffolk

FOCUS
A moderate race, even by selling standards.

NOTEBOOK
She Whispers(IRE) had a far from convincing profile for Richard Hannon but, dropped in trip on her debut for a new yard, she responded well to an impressively strong ride from Chris Catlin to gain her first success at the eighth attempt. Things will be tougher under a penalty in this grade. (tchd 15-2)
Phinerine, with the blinkers back on, returned to form and was just denied. (tchd 9-2)
Dolce Maria(IRE), Irish trained, appreciated the drop into selling company and achieved her best finishing position yet. (op 9-1)
Montini Royale(IRE) seemed to have her chance. Maybe she could be worth another try at Southwell. (tchd 9-2)
Miss A Bargain(IRE), out of a half-sister to high-class sprinter Piccolo, showed ability on her racecourse debut and is open to a fair amount of improvement.
Surf City, with blinkers replacing cheekpieces, ran well below his mark on this drop in grade. He has it all to prove now. (op 10-3 tchd 11-4)
Miss Lovat Official explanation: jockey said filly ran flat

6501 BETDIRECTPOKER.COM NURSERY 7f (P)
1:10 (1:10) (Class 5) (0-85,80) 2-Y-O **£4,320** (£1,285; £642; £320) **Stalls** Low

Form RPR
1606 **1** **Sands Of Barra (IRE)**[6] 6457 2-8-11 70 .... JohnEgan 5 75
(N A Callaghan) *sn wl in rr: trapped bhd wall of horses over 2f out: prog over 1f out: swtchd to inner and r.o to ld last stride* **9/2**[2]
0610 **2** *shd* **Orchard Supreme**[31] 6244 2-8-9 68 .... DaneO'Neill 8 73
(R Hannon) *t.k.h: trckd ldr 5f out: narrow ld 2f out: kpt on wl fnl f: hdd last stride* **11/1**
4561 **3** ¾ **Lenoir (GER)**[16] 6375 2-8-5 64 .... (v) ChrisCatlin 10 67
(V Smith) *s.i.s: last tl rdn and gd prog on outer to chal 2f out: nt qckn over 1f out: styd on again nr fin* **14/1**
0055 **4** *nk* **Blu Manruna**[14] 6395 2-8-5 64 .... (b) PaulDoe 2 66
(J Akehurst) *pressed ldrs: rdn and nt qckn 2f out: renewed effrt fnl f: styd on but a hld* **20/1**
0001 **5** ½ **Pommes Frites**[10] 6420 2-9-7 80 .... SteveDrowne 6 81
(W R Muir) *trckd ldrs: rdn and effrt over 1f out: styd on same pce fnl f* **6/1**[3]
0200 **6** *nk* **Chia (IRE)**[45] 6005 2-8-10 69 .... RobertHavlin 11 69
(D Haydn Jones) *hld up bhd ldrs: n.m.r over 2f out: rdn and hanging over 1f out: r.o last 150yds* **16/1**
0450 **7** 1 **Charlie Delta**[10] 6420 2-8-13 75 .... DanielTudhope[(3)] 12 72
(D Carroll) *led for 1f: pressed ldrs after: upsides 2f out: fdd fnl f* **14/1**
0460 **8** ¾ **Scroll**[16] 6386 2-8-10 69 .... (v) RobertWinston 7 64
(P Howling) *t.k.h: hld up in rr: hmpd over 5f out: prog 2f out: styng on whn nowhere to go and snatched up 150yds out* **25/1**
5130 **9** *hd* **Casablanca Minx (IRE)**[6] 6457 2-8-0 62 .... EdwardCreighton[(3)] 13 57
(Mrs H Sweeting) *forced to r wd: lost pl and in rr 4f out: prog to chse ldrs over 2f out: wd bnd sn after: n.d* **20/1**
0464 **10** 1¼ **Salvestro**[25] 6304 2-8-6 65 .... MartinDwyer 4 57
(Mrs A J Perrett) *led after 1f to 2f out: wknd fnl f* **4/1**[1]
21 **11** ½ **Pearly Poll**[33] 6224 2-9-2 78 .... NelsonDeSouza[(3)] 9 68
(R M Beckett) *sn pushed along towards rr: struggling in last pair over 2f out* **8/1**
000 **12** 1½ **Murrumbidgee (IRE)**[20] 6353 2-8-5 64 .... EddieAhern 1 50
(J W Hills) *a wl in rr: shkn up and no prog over 2f out* **9/1**
300 **13** 1¼ **Thomas A Beckett (IRE)**[83] 5196 2-8-8 67 .... JimmyQuinn 3 50
(P R Chamings) *hld up in midfield: no prog 2f out: wknd over 1f out* **40/1**

1m 24.17s (-1.72) **Going Correction** -0.20s/f (Stan) **13** Ran SP% **116.9**
Speed ratings (Par 96):101,100,100,99,99 98,97,96,96,95 94,92,91
CSF £49.19 CT £644.75 TOTE £5.60: £2.50, £2.60, £4.30; EX 62.10.
Owner Alan Brazil Racing Club Ltd **Bred** Sunderland Holdings Inc **Trained** Newmarket, Suffolk

FOCUS
A reasonable nursery run in a fair time.

NOTEBOOK

Sands Of Barra(IRE), dropped a furlong in trip, overcame trouble in-running to get up on the line and double his career tally. He is likely to be put away for the winter now and may be gelded, as connections see him as a potential juvenile hurdler. (op 5-1)
Orchard Supreme, dropped a furlong in trip on his Polytrack debut, returned to his very best and was just denied. He looks well up to winning a similar event. (op 14-1)
Lenoir(GER) would have found this much tougher than the mile seller he won here on his previous start, but acquitted himself most creditably in third. He can clearly remain competitive in this sort of company. (op 12-1)
Blu Manruna is still a maiden, but he was probably not far off his best in fourth and should find a race eventually.
Pommes Frites, 7lb higher than when winning at Wolverhampton on her previous start, did not run badly in fifth but did not look as well suited by this particular surface. (op 5-1)
Salvestro failed to build on the promise he showed when fourth on his debut on this surface last time. (op 5-1)

6502 TEXT "BETDIRECT" TO 88600 MEDIAN AUCTION MAIDEN STKS 1m (P)
1:40 (1:45) (Class 5) 2-Y-O **£3,387** (£1,007; £503; £251) **Stalls High**

Form RPR
5 **1** **Katies Tuitor**[47] 5968 2-9-0 .... JamieSpencer 5 72
(B W Duke) *mde virtually all: rdn and green wl over 1f out: kpt on wl fnl f* **17/2**
2 *1 ¼* **First Slip** 2-9-0 .... JoeFanning 6 69
(Mrs A J Perrett) *chsd wnr fr 5f out: rdn to chal over 1f out: hld fnl f* **7/1**[3]
3 *1 ¼* **Servillia (IRE)** 2-8-9 .... StephenCarson 1 62
(W R Swinburn) *s.s: rcvrd whn hmpd on inner 5f out and lost pl: prog whn hmpd over 1f out: styd on: gd effrt* **7/1**[3]
03 **4** *nk* **Pleasing**[20] 6351 2-8-9 .... EddieAhern 2 61
(J L Dunlop) *prom: drvn 3f out: effrt u.p and swtchd rt over 1f out: one pce* **2/1**[1]
0 **5** *1* **Lord Laing (USA)**[23] 6318 2-9-0 .... JimmyQuinn 8 64
(H J Collingridge) *prom: chal 3f out: nt qckn wl over 1f out: fdd* **8/1**
6 *1 ½* **Exotic Venture** 2-8-6 .... NelsonDeSouza(3) 7 55
(R M Beckett) *pushed along towards rr over 4f out: rdn and nt on terms w ldng gp over 2f out: plugged on* **20/1**
5 **7** *hd* **Ennobling**[23] 6332 2-8-9 .... DaneO'Neill 9 55
(E F Vaughan) *hld up in midfield: nt on terms 3f out: shkn up and one pce after* **4/1**[2]
8 *3 ½* **Smart Golden Boy (IRE)** 2-9-0 .... SamHitchcott 10 52
(Mrs L C Jewell) *a towards rr: wl off the pce fr over 2f out* **66/1**
9 *½* **Bahhmirage (IRE)** 2-8-9 .... FrancisFerris 11 46
(C N Kellett) *rn green: a in rr: struggling fnl 3f* **66/1**
0 **10** *1* **Health Spa**[53] 5850 2-8-4 .... RoryMoore(5) 4 44
(B R Johnson) *sn prom: rdn and wknd wl over 2f out* **25/1**
11 *2* **Duka** 2-9-0 .... MartinDwyer 12 45
(W R Muir) *rn green and a in last pair* **25/1**
12 *nk* **Bold Pioneer (USA)** 2-9-0 .... RobertHavlin 3 44
(C P Morlock) *hld up: in tch tl wknd over 3f out* **50/1**

1m 39.21s (-0.22) **Going Correction** -0.20s/f (Stan) 12 Ran SP% **117.4**
Speed ratings (Par 96):93,91,90,90,89 87,87,84,83,82 80,80
CSF £61.46 TOTE £7.90: £2.60, £3.00, £2.40; EX 61.90.
Owner Kevin Cooke **Bred** Brendan W Duke **Trained** Lambourn, Berks
■ Stewards' Enquiry : Eddie Ahern two-day ban: careless riding (Dec 16-17)

FOCUS
Just an ordinary maiden, but a decent enough effort from Katies Tuitor considering he is very much bred to improve with both time and distance.

NOTEBOOK
Katies Tuitor, not without promise over this trip at Bath on his debut, stepped up on that effort under a positive ride to gain a clear-cut success. Given his breeding suggests he will get better with age and, when stepped up in trip, he looks a nice enough prospect. (op 15-2 tchd 9-1)
First Slip, a 16,000gns half-brother to Faiza, a five-furlong winner at three, was always being held but made a pleasing debut nonetheless. He ought to improve and should find a similar race. (op 13-2 tchd 6-1)
Servillia(IRE), a 52,000gns first foal, out of a dual seven furlong/mile winner who was also successful in the US, missed the break and met with trouble in running, but she finished to good effect to pick up a place and offered promise. Almost sure to be better for the experience, it will be disappointing if she does not go on from this. (op 9-1)
Pleasing offered promise on both her previous starts, including over six furlongs here on her previous outing, but she was well held in fourth and may not have been suited by such a significant step up in trip. (tchd 5-2)
Lord Laing(USA) was not beaten all that far and seems to be going the right way.
Exotic Venture, a half-sister to Firewire, a triple mile to ten-furlong winner, was not without promise and ought to improve. (op 16-1)
Ennobling did not really improve on her debut effort and may be best watched until she is handicapped. (op 7-2 tchd 9-2)
Bold Pioneer(USA) Official explanation: jockey said colt ran green and keen

6503 BETDIRECT FREEPHONE 0800 211 222 H'CAP (DIV II) 1m (P)
2:10 (2:12) (Class 5) (0-75,74) 3-Y-O+ **£3,039** (£904; £451; £225) **Stalls High**

Form RPR
1500 **1** **Llamadas**[20] 6362 3-8-11 **68** .... J-PGuillambert 1 75
(Andrew Reid) *trckd ldr: pushed along 3f out: sustained chal fr 2f out to ld last 100yds: hld on* **20/1**
4500 **2** *hd* **Island Rapture**[116] 4311 5-9-0 **70** .... EddieAhern 2 77
(J A R Toller) *hld up midfield: prog over 2f out: drvn and r.o to press wnr nr fin: jst hld* **14/1**
4103 **3** *½* **Glencalvie (IRE)**[25] 6302 4-9-0 **70** ....(v) MartinDwyer 10 76
(J Akehurst) *racd freely: led: rdn 2f out: hdd and no ex last 100yds* **7/1**[3]
4600 **4** *2 ½* **Admiral Compton**[85] 5157 4-8-13 **69** .... SteveDrowne 4 69
(J R Boyle) *s.s: hld up in rr: prog 2f out: drvn and kpt on one pce fnl f* **7/1**[3]
0004 **5** *shd* **Takes Tutu (USA)**[20] 6354 6-9-4 **74** .... PatCosgrave 7 74
(K R Burke) *hld up towards rr: prog over 2f out: rdn and nt qckn over 1f out: one pce after* **8/1**
0323 **6** *2* **Zalkani (IRE)**[20] 6356 5-9-3 **73** .... JamieSpencer 8 68+
(B G Powell) *v s.i.s: hld up in last trio: effrt and sme prog 2f out: nt qckn and no imp fr over 1f out* **4/1**[2]
1065 **7** *2 ½* **Lizarazu (GER)**[25] 6302 6-8-10 **73** .... TolleyDean(7) 3 63
(R A Harris) *t.k.h: trckd ldrs: cl up over 1f out: wknd rapidly fnl f* **9/1**
6563 **8** *1* **Almanshood (USA)**[57] 5756 3-8-10 **67** .... ChrisCatlin 5 54
(P L Gilligan) *hld up in last trio: pushed along 3f out: no real prog* **12/1**
5510 **9** *hd* **Hey Presto**[73] 5439 5-8-12 **68** .... PaulDoe 9 55
(R Rowe) *hld up in last trio: brief effrt over 2f out: nvr nr ldrs* **40/1**
031 **10** *1 ½* **Oh Danny Boy**[23] 6333 4-9-2 **72** .... JohnEgan 6 55
(Julian Poulton) *trckd ldrs: pushed along and lost pl 2f out: eased fnl f* **7/2**[1]
0060 **11** *1* **Love Affair (IRE)**[57] 5758 3-8-11 **68** .... DaneO'Neill 12 49
(R Hannon) *chsd ldrs: rdn on outer over 2f out: sn wknd: eased* **25/1**
0540 **12** *2 ½* **Jazrawy**[23] 6325 3-8-12 **72** ....(t) NelsonDeSouza(3) 11 47
(Miss Gay Kelleway) *t.k.h: prom: drvn 3f out: sn wknd* **33/1**

1m 36.32s (-3.11) **Going Correction** -0.20s/f (Stan) course record
WFA 3 from 4yo+ 1lb 12 Ran SP% **116.7**
Speed ratings (Par 103):107,106,106,103,103 101,99,98,98,96 95,93
CSF £261.42 CT £2196.38 TOTE £29.80: £6.10, £4.30, £2.60; EX 248.00.
Owner K Tyre **Bred** Burton Agnes Stud Co Ltd **Trained** Mill Hill, London NW7

FOCUS
A fair handicap in which Llamadas returned to form to gain his first success for his current stable.
Oh Danny Boy Official explanation: jockey said gelding hung left throughout

6504 BETDIRECT.CO.UK H'CAP 7f (P)
2:40 (2:43) (Class 4) (0-85,83) 3-Y-O+ **£5,752** (£1,711; £855; £427) **Stalls Low**

Form RPR
2331 **1** **Perfect Story (IRE)**[20] 6354 3-8-13 **78** .... OscarUrbina 13 87
(J A R Toller) *trckd ldng pair: rdn to chal over 1f out: led ins fnl f: hld on nr fin* **10/1**
3121 **2** *hd* **Three Wrens (IRE)**[16] 6376 3-9-3 **82** .... JamieSpencer 2 93+
(D J Daly) *hld up bhd ldrs: effrt 2f out: n.m.r fr over 1f out: squeezed through ins fnl f: gaining on wnr at fin* **2/1**[1]
4523 **3** *½* **Binanti**[6] 6458 5-9-4 **83** ....(v) JohnEgan 8 90
(P R Chamings) *trckd ldrs: effrt to chal over 1f out: ref to go by ins fnl f* **13/2**[3]
054 **4** *shd* **Chief Exec**[96] 4865 3-8-13 **81** .... NelsonDeSouza(3) 3 88
(C A Cyzer) *led for 1f: pressed ldr: rdn to ld narrowly over 1f out: hdd ins fnl f: no ex* **16/1**
0000 **5** *hd* **Northern Desert (IRE)**[171] 2656 6-8-13 **78** .... ChrisCatlin 12 86+
(P W Hiatt) *t.k.h: hld up in rr: prog 2f out: clsng on ldrs whn nt clr run wl ins fnl f* **50/1**
211 **6** *¾* **Hits Only Heaven (IRE)**[25] 6305 3-8-13 **78** .... JimmyQuinn 5 82
(J Pearce) *s.i.s: plld hrd: hld up in tch: rdn and nt qckn wl over 1f out: r.o again last 100yds* **5/1**[2]
F012 **7** *hd* **Alchemist Master**[37] 6161 6-8-5 **77** .... MichaelJStainton(7) 11 81
(R M Whitaker) *t.k.h: hld up in rr: effrt wl over 1f out: rdn and r.o ins fnl f: too much to do* **25/1**
0405 **8** *hd* **Big Bradford**[20] 6350 4-8-4 **69** oh1 ....(b) MartinDwyer 1 72
(W R Muir) *racd freely: led after 1f to over 1f out: wknd ins fnl f* **14/1**
1033 **9** *½* **Pinchbeck**[20] 6350 6-8-12 **77** ....(p) MatthewHenry 6 79
(M A Jarvis) *t.k.h: hld up jst bhd ldrs: nt qckn 2f out: one pce after* **14/1**
1104 **10** *2 ½* **Jayanjay**[20] 6350 6-9-0 **82** .... RichardThomas(3) 10 77
(Miss B Sanders) *racd on outer: wl in tch: outpcd 2f out: wknd fnl f* **12/1**
4060 **11** *hd* **Smokin Joe**[84] 5188 4-8-12 **77** ....(b) SteveDrowne 4 72
(J R Best) *hld up: a in same pce: shuffled along and no prog fnl 2f* **25/1**
3006 **12** *5* **Cheese 'n Biscuits**[20] 6350 5-8-9 **77** ....(p) AdamKirby(3) 7 59
(M Wigham) *s.s: hld up in last: lost tch 3f out: wl bhd after* **11/1**

1m 24.53s (-1.36) **Going Correction** -0.20s/f (Stan) 12 Ran SP% **117.3**
Speed ratings (Par 105):99,98,98,98,97 97,96,96,95,93 92,87
CSF £29.34 CT £147.84 TOTE £13.90: £3.80, £1.10, £2.20; EX 36.80 Trifecta £302.70 Part won. Pool: £426.42 - 0.70 winning units - £127.92 rolled over to Saturday (10/12).
Owner John Drew and Dr Bridget Drew **Bred** Airlie Stud **Trained** Newmarket, Suffolk

FOCUS
A good handicap for the grade and very competitive, but the winning time was only modest.

6505 FRED GIBSON MEMORIAL CLAIMING STKS 7f (P)
3:10 (3:11) (Class 6) 3-Y-O+ **£2,921** (£862; £431) **Stalls Low**

Form RPR
3055 **1** **Ever Cheerful**[7] 6449 4-8-13 61 .... J-PGuillambert 6 73
(G C H Chung) *plld hrd: prom: led 3f out: drvn 4 l clr wl over 1f out : unchal* **14/1**
5040 **2** *1 ¼* **Marko Jadeo (IRE)**[34] 6216 7-9-2 77 .... RobertWinston 10 76+
(K A Morgan) *hld up wl in rr: plenty to do over 2f out: gd prog over 1f out: wnt 2nd ins fnl f: clsng at fin but no ch* **4/1**[2]
0600 **3** *hd* **Seneschal**[25] 6302 4-9-2 72 .... SamHitchcott 4 72
(A B Haynes) *hld up in midfield: plenty to do 2f out: prog over 1f out: disp 2nd ins fnl f: r.o but no ch* **11/1**
0010 **4** *¾* **Corky (IRE)**[25] 6302 4-8-12 71 .... DaneO'Neill 3 66
(R Hannon) *chsd ldrs: rdn 3f out: kpt on same pce u.p fnl 2f* **11/2**[3]
401 **5** *1 ¼* **General Feeling (IRE)**[9] 6430 4-9-2 74 .... JohnEgan 8 67+
(S Kirk) *hld up in rr: nt wl plcd on inner and plenty to do over 2f out: prog whn hmpd jst over 1f out: nt rcvr* **9/4**[1]
3600 **6** *½* **Tequila Sheila (IRE)**[14] 6404 3-8-11 63 .... PatCosgrave 5 61
(K R Burke) *trckd ldrs: effrt over 2f out: no imp over 1f out: fdd ins fnl f* **14/1**
0000 **7** *nk* **Sahara Prince (IRE)**[20] 6354 5-8-11 ....(p) NelsonDeSouza(3) 2 63
(Michael Cunningham, Ire) *t.k.h: prom: wknd 2f out* **12/1**
2004 **8** *¾* **Zafarshah (IRE)**[7] 6449 6-8-5 58 ....(b) TolleyDean(7) 11 59
(R A Harris) *hld up in midfield: effrt over 2f out: no prog wl over 1f out* **20/1**
0140 **9** *1* **Hadath (IRE)**[6] 6460 8-8-13 58 ....(b) JamieSpencer 7 57
(B G Powell) *racd on outer: hld up towards rr: rdn and no real prog over 2f out* **8/1**
2400 **10** *7* **Acorazado (IRE)**[199] 1844 6-8-12 62 .... StephenCarson 9 38
(C P Morlock) *a towards rr: wknd over 2f out* **20/1**
11 *shd* **Cinder Maid** 3-8-11 .... JimmyQuinn 14 37
(J G Portman) *dwlt: a in last trio: bhd fnl 2f* **100/1**
0 **12** *1 ¾* **Justcallmehandsome**[31] 6245 3-8-8 ....(v) AdamKirby(3) 1 32
(D J S Ffrench Davis) *prom: wkng whn hmpd on inner over 2f out: sn bhd* **66/1**
1300 **13** *2 ½* **Missed Turn**[121] 4156 3-8-9 52 .... SteveDrowne 12 24
(J M P Eustace) *mde most to 3f out: wkng rapidly whn hmpd on inner over 1f out* **66/1**

1m 24.08s (-1.81) **Going Correction** -0.20s/f (Stan) 13 Ran SP% **120.1**
Speed ratings (Par 101):102,100,100,99,98 97,97,96,95,87 87,85,82
CSF £67.18 TOTE £12.20: £3.10, £2.30, £3.00; EX 90.90.Marko Jadeo was claimed by S.Dow for £12,000. Corky was claimed by I.McInnes for £8,000.
Owner K L Man **Bred** Southill Stud **Trained** Newmarket, Suffolk
■ Stewards' Enquiry : Dane O'Neill one-day ban: careless riding (Dec 16)

FOCUS
This looked like a reasonable enough claimer, but Ever Cheerful got the run of things up front and the from is suspect.

6506 MORE OFFERS AT BETDIRECT.CO.UK H'CAP 1m 2f (P)
3:40 (3:41) (Class 6) (0-52,52) 3-Y-O+ £2,882 (£851; £425) Stalls Low

Form RPR

0401 1 **Augustine**278 542 4-8-9 49 JoeFanning 14 56
(P W Hiatt) *prom: effrt 2f out: disp ld on outer 1f out: gained upper hand last 75yds* 20/1

0302 2 nk **Hoh Bleu Dee**30 6262 4-8-11 51 (p) J-PGuillambert 8 57
(T Keddy) *t.k.h: hld up in midfield: prog 2f out: rdn to dispute ld 1f out: nt qckn llast 75yds* 5/1²

0421 3 nk **Rotuma (IRE)**21 6343 6-8-11 51 (b) EddieAhern 12 57
(M Dods) *prom: effrt on inner 2f out: disp ld 1f out: no ex last 75yds* 7/2¹

0101 4 ½ **So Elegant (IRE)**51 5894 3-8-9 52 ChrisCatlin 13 57+
(J Jay) *hld up in rr: effrt over 2f out: drvn to chse ldng trio ins fnl f: too much to do* 8/1

0003 5 ½ **Charnock Bates One (IRE)**28 6287 4-8-12 52 RobertWinston 9 56
(J J Quinn) *prom: chal 3f out: nt qckn over 1f out: nt clr run sn after: styd on again nr fin* 11/2³

052- 6 nk **Clare Galway**350 6940 4-8-9 49 JimmyQuinn 11 52
(B G Powell) *trckd ldrs: cl enough over 2f out: hanging and nt qckn over 1f out: kpt on* 25/1

0066 7 shd **Intended**14 6401 3-8-9 52 (t) MartinDwyer 10 55
(A M Balding) *led after 2f and set modest pce: rdn over 2f out: hdd & wknd 1f out* 20/1

0540 8 hd **Sriology (IRE)**6 6468 4-8-12 52 DaneO'Neill 3 55
(G Prodromou) *hld up in last pair: effrt on outer 2f out: styd on fnl f: no ch* 13/2

040 9 ½ **Double Ransom**47 5980 6-8-12 52 (b) TomEaves 7 54
(Mrs L Stubbs) *hld up in midfield: rdn on inner over 2f out: one pce and no imp* 10/1

0000 10 ½ **Larad (IRE)**36 6184 4-8-11 51 (b) JohnEgan 6 52
(J S Moore) *hld up towards rr: rdn and one pce fnl 2f* 20/1

0550 11 hd **Azreme**41 6103 5-8-12 52 JamieSpencer 1 53
(P Howling) *hld up in last pair: shkn up 2f out: nvr a factor* 9/1

-600 12 1¼ **Bob Baileys**19 6365 3-8-9 52 StephenCarson 4 50
(P R Chamings) *pushed up to ld: hdd after 3f: rdn 3f out: wknd 2f out* 33/1

0000 13 ¾ **Naivety**14 6405 3-8-9 52 JamieMackay 5 49
(G G Margarson) *s.s and rousted along early: in tch tl wknd over 2f out* 66/1

2m 10.54s (2.75) **Going Correction** -0.20s/f (Stan)
WFA 3 from 4yo+ 3lb 13 Ran SP% 120.4
Speed ratings (Par 101):81,80,80,80,79 79,79,79,78,78 78,77,76
CSF £110.28 CT £446.86 TOTE £26.10: £6.90, £3.40, £1.70; EX 174.60 Place 6 £288.08, Place 5 £192.62.
Owner Phil Kelly **Bred** Darley **Trained** Hook Norton, Oxon

FOCUS
A moderate handicap and a pedestrian time, but competitive enough and reasonable form for the grade.
T/Jkpt: Not won. T/Plt: £464.20 to a £1 stake. Pool: £31,924.00. 50.20 winning tickets. T/Qpdt: £109.40 to a £1 stake. Pool: £2,677.50. 18.10 winning tickets. JN

6485 WOLVERHAMPTON (A.W) (L-H)
Monday, December 5

OFFICIAL GOING: Standard
Wind: Fresh, across Weather: Overcast

6507 BETDIRECT ON SNOOKER CLAIMING STKS 7f 32y(P)
1:00 (1:00) (Class 7) 3-Y-O+ £1,457 (£430; £215) Stalls High

Form RPR

1200 1 **My Girl Pearl (IRE)**9 6429 5-8-9 50 MickyFenton 2 53
(M S Saunders) *hld up in tch: rdn to ld over 1f out: r.o* 10/1

0000 2 nk **Stagnite**19 6369 5-9-0 50 TonyCulhane 3 57
(K McAuliffe) *led early: chsd ldrs: rdn over 1f out: r.o* 14/1

6202 3 nk **Musiotal**21 6345 4-8-12 50 FergalLynch 9 55+
(J S Goldie) *s.i.s: hld up: hdwy 2f out: nt clr run and swtchd rt over 1f out: r.o* 7/4¹

5040 4 2½ **Nisr**7 6449 8-8-7 55 (t) RonanKeogh(7) 8 50
(Miss Gay Kelleway) *chsd ldrs: rdn over 2f out: hmpd over 1f out: styd on same pce* 16/1

4100 5 hd **Samson Quest**35 6202 3-8-12 58 (p) HayleyTurner 11 47
(N P Littmoden) *s.i.s: sn pushed along: swtchd lft and r.o ins fnl f: nvr nrr* 11/2³

0500 6 1¾ **Lady Vee (IRE)**109 4507 3-8-6 51 PaulMulrennan(3) 10 40
(P D Niven) *trckd ldrs: rdn over 2f out: styd on same pce appr fnl f* 16/1

0500 7 2 **Colonel Bilko (IRE)**20 6361 3-9-0 52 (p) TPQueally 4 40
(Miss S J Wilton) *hld up: rdn over 2f out: n.d* 12/1

6000 8 2 **Tiger Hunter**5 6470 3-9-0 50 LPKeniry 12 34
(P Howling) *chsd ldrs: led 5f out: rdn and hdd 2f out: wknd fnl f* 40/1

040 9 1 **Gandiloo Gully**7 6443 4-8-9 GrahamGibbons 1 27
(J D Bethell) *dwlt: sn w ldrs: rdn to ld 2f out: hdd over 1f out: sn wknd* 20/1

1056 10 1¼ **Castanza**9 6436 3-8-9 55 AlanDaly 7 24
(M Wellings) *sn led: hdd 5f out: rdn over 2f out: sn wknd* 12/1

1000 11 shd **Ligne D'Eau**5 6470 4-9-0 50 (b) GeorgeBaker 6 28
(P D Evans) *s.i.s: hld up: rdn over 2f out: a in rr* 9/2²

1m 30.15s (-0.25) **Going Correction** -0.10s/f (Stan) 11 Ran SP% 120.0
Speed ratings (Par 97):97,96,96,93,93 91,88,86,85,84 83
CSF £144.26 TOTE £14.50: £3.90, £3.20, £1.30; EX 111.40.
Owner T A Godbert **Bred** Loan And Development Corporation **Trained** Green Ore, Somerset

FOCUS
A weak claimer and little to get excited about outside the front three.
My Girl Pearl(IRE) Official explanation: trainer said, regarding improved form shown, mare benefited from a change of tactics, in that she was dropped in
Ligne D'Eau Official explanation: vet said gelding finished lame

6508 GOOD LUCK PETER EBDON BANDED STKS 1m 141y(P)
1:30 (1:30) (Class 7) 3-Y-O+ £1,440 (£425; £212) Stalls Low

Form RPR

3033 1 **Adobe**5 6473 10-9-0 47 GeorgeBaker 9 54
(W M Brisbourne) *hld up: hdwy over 2f out: rdn to ld wl ins fnl f: jst hld on* 6/1

0000 2 shd **Fantasy Defender (IRE)**48 5960 3-9-0 49 (v) LPKeniry 3 56
(J J Quinn) *hld up: hdwy over 1f out: r.o wl* 25/1

0003 3 1½ **Musical Gift**16 6387 5-9-3 50 (v) HayleyTurner 10 54
(P A Blockley) *trckd ldrs: racd keenly: led over 6f out: rdn and hdd wl ins fnl f* 4/1¹

0116 4 1¼ **Legal Lover (IRE)**7 6445 3-9-1 50 GrahamGibbons 12 51
(R Hollinshead) *chsd ldrs: rdn over 2f out: hung lft over 1f out: styd on same pce fnl f* 9/2²

0166 5 1¼ **Dane's Rock (IRE)**16 6387 3-8-13 48 (p) MickyFenton 1 47
(M S Saunders) *hld up: r.o ins fnl f: nrst fin* 20/1

3550 6 hd **Able Mind**32 6236 5-9-0 50 (p) PatrickMathers(3) 11 48
(A C Whillans) *hld up: hdwy over 2f out: styd on u.p ins fnl f* 7/1

0030 7 ½ **Big Mystery (IRE)**5 6473 4-8-11 47 AmirQuinn(3) 6 44
(S C Williams) *led after 1f: hdd over 6f out: rdn over 2f out: wknd ins fnl f* 15/2

5006 8 2 **Triffid**185 2273 3-9-1 50 TonyHamilton 4 43
(R A Fahey) *chsd ldrs: rdn over 2f out: wknd fnl f* 11/1

0350 9 hd **Extemporise (IRE)**31 6243 5-9-2 49 TPQueally 5 42
(T T Clement) *led 1f: chsd ldrs: rdn over 2f out: wknd fnl f* 5/1³

3656 10 2½ **Pharoah's Gold (IRE)**224 1268 7-9-0 47 (v) VinceSlattery 2 34
(D Burchell) *s.i.s: rdn over 2f out: a in rr* 33/1

430 11 2 **Lake Wakatipu**7 6445 3-9-1 50 DarrenWilliams 8 33
(M Mullineaux) *prom: rdn over 3f out: wknd over 2f out* 40/1

0025 12 1¼ **Fools Entire**8 3100 4-9-1 48 AlanDaly 7 28
(Miss J Feilden) *chsd ldrs: hmpd 7f out: wknd over 3f out* 25/1

0300 13 5 **Super King**7 6445 4-9-0 47 TonyCulhane 13 17
(A D Brown) *hld up: rdn over 3f out: wknd over 2f out* 40/1

1m 50.74s (-1.02) **Going Correction** -0.10s/f (Stan)
WFA 3 from 4yo+ 2lb 13 Ran SP% 122.0
Speed ratings (Par 97):100,99,98,97,96 96,95,93,93,91 89,88,84
CSF £157.31 TOTE £5.10: £1.50, £20.00, £2.30; EX 237.70.
Owner P R Kirk **Bred** Sheikh Mohammed Bin Rashid Al Maktoum **Trained** Great Ness, Shropshire

FOCUS
As banded races come, this was not bad and a few winners at this level could come out of the contest.

6509 BETDIRECT.CO.UK BANDED STKS 1m 1f 103y(P)
2:00 (2:01) (Class 7) 3-Y-O+ £1,433 (£423; £211) Stalls Low

Form RPR

0300 1 **Super Dominion**42 6080 8-9-0 45 (p) VinceSlattery 5 52
(R Hollinshead) *hld up in tch: rdn to chse ldr over 1f out: styd on u.p to ld post* 10/1

00-0 2 hd **Naval Attache**9 6434 3-8-12 45 GrahamGibbons 10 52
(P A Blockley) *son led: rdn over 1f out: hdd post* 14/1

0066 3 1¼ **Heathyards Joy**58 5740 4-8-9 45 StephanieHollinshead(5) 2 49
(R Hollinshead) *hld up: hdwy over 2f out: nt clr run over 1f out: r.o* 7/1³

-006 4 2 **Boogie Magic**14 6398 5-8-9 40 MarcHalford(5) 1 45
(T T Clement) *chsd ldrs: rdn over 2f out: no ex fnl f* 20/1

00-0 5 1¾ **Lahob**5 6475 5-9-0 45 LPKeniry 11 42
(P Howling) *chsd ldr: rdn over 3f out: wknd fnl f* 22/1

-001 6 shd **Artzola (IRE)**70 5517 5-9-0 45 GeorgeBaker 7 42
(C A Horgan) *s.s: hld up: hdwy on outside over 2f out: rdn and hung lft over 1f out: nt run on* 9/4¹

0000 7 nk **Sydneyroughdiamond**14 6401 3-8-12 45 (p) DarrenWilliams 6 41
(M Mullineaux) *hld up: hdwy u.p over 1f out: nt rch ldrs* 25/1

3605 8 1 **White Star Magic**16 6387 3-8-9 45 (bt) NeilChalmers(3) 8 39
(K G Wingrove) *hld up in tch: rdn over 2f out: hung lft and wknd over 1f out* 12/1

005 9 1¾ **Successor**21 6347 5-9-0 45 (t) HayleyTurner 13 36
(M D I Usher) *prom: rdn over 3f out: wknd over 1f out* 9/2²

0000 10 1½ **Another Con (IRE)**21 6347 4-9-0 45 TonyCulhane 9 33
(P Howling) *chsd ldrs 7f* 7/1³

0050 11 3½ **Eidsfoss (IRE)**53 5856 3-8-12 45 TPQueally 12 27
(T T Clement) *hld up: rdn and wknd over 2f out* 40/1

500- 12 5 **The Footballresult**33 3190 4-9-0 45 (b) MickyFenton 3 17
(C N Kellett) *hld up: hdwy 1/2-way: wknd over 2f out* 40/1

0000 13 10 **Flying Spud**5 6474 4-9-0 40 FergalLynch 4 —
(A J Chamberlain) *hld up: rdn over 3f out: sn wknd* 16/1

2m 2.85s (0.23) **Going Correction** -0.10s/f (Stan)
WFA 3 from 4yo+ 2lb 13 Ran SP% 121.1
Speed ratings (Par 97):94,93,92,90,89 89,89,88,86,85 82,77,68
CSF £133.84 TOTE £10.70: £4.20, £5.10, £2.10; EX 122.60.
Owner Mrs Norman Hill **Bred** Norman Hill Plant Hire Ltd **Trained** Upper Longdon, Staffs

FOCUS
Unlike the previous contest, this looked a below-average banded race run at an ordinary pace and it seems unlikely to produce many winners.
Lahob Official explanation: jockey said gelding hung left-handed
Artzola(IRE) Official explanation: jockey said mare missed break and hung left-handed under pressure

6510 BETDIRECT FREEPHONE 0800 211 222 BANDED STKS 1m 5f 194y(P)
2:30 (2:31) (Class 7) 3-Y-O+ £1,443 (£426; £213) Stalls Low

Form RPR

-003 1 **Michaels Dream (IRE)**24 5826 6-9-4 40 (b) DavidMcCabe 4 49
(N Wilson) *led: hdd over 4f out: edgd rt and led over 1f out: all out* 8/1

0000 2 hd **Tipes**25 6307 3-8-11 50 StephenDonohoe(5) 5 54
(C J Down) *chsd wnr over 7f: rdn and hung lft over 1f out: sn ev ch: styd on* 25/1

0002 3 5 **Little Richard (IRE)**5 6475 6-9-4 45 (p) AlanDaly 8 42
(M Wellings) *a.p: rdn and swtchd lft fnl f: styd on same pce* 5/1¹

503- 4 1½ **Dancing Pearl**87 3518 7-9-1 45 BenSwarbrick(3) 2 40
(C J Price) *hld up: rdn over 2f out: styd on fnl f: nrst fin* 16/1

0042 5 hd **All Bleevable**13 6410 8-9-5 46 TonyCulhane 1 40
(Mrs S Lamyman) *chsd ldrs: rdn over 3f out: styd on same pce fnl 2f* 5/1¹

6-03 6 1½ **Claradotnet**227 1183 5-9-2 48 GregFairley(5) 6 40
(Mrs L Williamson) *hld up: stmbld over 11f out: rdn over 2f out: styd on fnl f: nvr nrr* 16/1

0066 7 1¾ **Gallas (IRE)**21 6348 4-9-7 48 (v) FergalLynch 9 38
(P A Blockley) *s.i.s: hld up: hdwy over 2f out: wknd over 1f out* 9/1

0051 8 shd **Ice And Fire**13 6410 6-9-7 48 (b) MickyFenton 10 38
(J T Stimpson) *hld up in tch: plld hrd: led over 4f out: sn clr: hung rt and hdd over 1f out: sn wknd* 7/1³

0045 9 ½ **Top Trees**5 6472 7-9-1 47 MarcHalford(5) 12 36
(W S Kittow) *hld up: plld hrd: hdwy 4f out: rdn and wknd over 1f out* 5/1¹

4405 10 1¼ **Joey**5 6473 3-8-13 47 GrahamGibbons 3 34
(R Hollinshead) *hld up in tch: rdn over 3f out: wknd 2f out* 13/2²

0-06 11 2½ **Magic Charm**227 1183 7-9-1 30 (t) NeilChalmers(3) 13 29
(K G Wingrove) *s.i.s: hld up: rdn over 2f out: a in rr* 66/1

610/ 12 *dist* **Secret Dell (IRE)**[274] 4381 9-9-9 50..............................(b[1]) VinceSlattery 7 —
(R Brotherton) *hld up: rdn and wknd 4f out* 50/1
3m 7.75s (0.38) **Going Correction** -0.10s/f (Stan)
WFA 3 from 4yo+ 7lb 12 Ran SP% **116.0**
Speed ratings (Par 97):94,93,91,90,90 89,88,88,87,87 85,—
CSF £189.39 TOTE £12.20: £4.70, £8.50, £3.00; EX 142.40.
Owner Mrs Michael John Paver **Bred** M J Paver **Trained** Upper Helmsley, N Yorks
FOCUS
A moderate race of its type and a rather messy contest. The pace for the first ten furlongs or so was ordinary, resulting in a sprint finish.

6511 LITTLEWOODS BETDIRECT BANDED STKS 5f 216y(P)
3:00 (3:00) (Class 7) 3-Y-0+ **£1,440** (£425; £212) **Stalls** Low

Form RPR
3001 1 **Secret Vision (USA)**[7] 6441 4-9-3 40..........................(p) GrahamGibbons 9 58
(R M H Cowell) *dwlt: hdwy over 4f out: ev ch over 1f out: hrd riden to ld nr fin* 6/1[2]
2620 2 *nk* **Boanerges (IRE)**[37] 6155 8-8-6 40.............................. GregFairley(5) 10 51
(J M Bradley) *chsd ldrs: led and hung lft over 1f out: rdn and hdd nr fin* 7/2[1]
5 3 *3* **Mescalera (GER)**[13] 6412 4-8-11 40.............................. HayleyTurner 5 42
(B G Powell) *chsd ldrs: rdn and ev ch over 1f out: styd on same pce ins fnl f* 10/1
4000 4 *hd* **Princeable Lady (IRE)**[42] 6080 3-8-5 40 ow1.... RussellKennemore(7) 4 43
(J A Pickering) *hld up: hdwy over 2f out: nt clr run over 1f out: styd on* 25/1
0600 5 *hd* **Rock Fever (IRE)**[14] 6396 3-8-11 40......................(b) RobbieFitzpatrick 3 41
(Peter Grayson) *dwlt: in rr tl r.o ins fnl f: nt rch ldrs* 7/2[1]
5000 6 *3* **Tappit (IRE)**[37] 6155 6-8-11 40..................................(vt) TonyHamilton 6 32
(L R James) *led over 4f: wknd fnl f* 33/1
0300 7 *1* **Obe Bold (IRE)**[55] 5825 4-8-11 40.............................. DavidAllan 8 29
(A Berry) *chsd ldrs over 4f* 9/1
0323 8 *¾* **Fenwicks Pride (IRE)**[70] 5514 7-8-11 40......................... GylesParkin 7 27
(J S Wainwright) *hld up: rdn over 2f out: n.d* 8/1[3]
5404 9 *3* **The Baroness (IRE)**[51] 5898 5-8-11 40....................(b[1]) MickyFenton 11 18
(Ernst Oertel) *chsd ldrs 4f* 14/1
6054 10 *shd* **Angel River**[14] 6396 3-8-6 40....................................(e) MarcHalford(5) 12 17
(J Ryan) *broke wl: lost pl 4f out: rdn and wknd over 2f out* 12/1
0- 11 *¾* **Mustgodowntothesea (IRE)**[40] 6113 3-8-11 40............(bt) TPQueally 2 15
(F J Bowles, Ire) *chsd ldrs: lost pl 4f out: rdn and wknd over 2f out* 14/1
0 12 *nk* **Lateforbingo (IRE)**[16] 6383 4-8-11 40..........................(p) TonyCulhane 1 14
(Michael Cunningham, Ire) *dwlt: outpcd* 20/1
1m 15.37s (-0.44) **Going Correction** -0.10s/f (Stan) 12 Ran SP% **121.5**
Speed ratings (Par 97):98,97,93,93,93 89,87,86,82,82 81,81
CSF £27.32 TOTE £6.70: £1.70, £2.60, £1.30; EX 35.00.
Owner Allen Rix **Bred** Juddmonte Farms Inc **Trained** Six Mile Bottom, Cambs
FOCUS
A fair banded contest, but at least the pace was strong and the front pair pulled clear.
The Baroness(IRE) Official explanation: jockey said mare kept changing its legs

6512 WOLVERHAMPTON & DUDLEY BREWERIES TRI-BANDED STKS 1m 141y(P)
3:30 (3:32) (Class 7) 3-Y-0 **£1,429** (£422; £211) **Stalls** Low

Form RPR
0064 1 **Joe Jo Star**[42] 6080 3-8-12 45..(p) FergalLynch 5 50
(P A Blockley) *trckd ldr: led 1/2-way: rdn over 1f out: styd on u.p* 5/2[1]
5000 2 *nk* **Taylor Maid**[37] 6154 3-8-7 40....................................(p) GrahamGibbons 2 44
(R M H Cowell) *led to 1/2-way: rdn and ev ch ins fnl f: styd on* 14/1
2610 3 *1 ¼* **Tacid**[23] 6327 3-8-12 45... MickyFenton 7 47
(Dr J D Scargill) *hld up: hdwy over 2f out: rdn over 1f out: styd on* 7/2[2]
000 4 *½* **Miss Shontaine**[20] 6355 3-8-2 35.............................. HayleyTurner 6 36+
(B G Powell) *hld up: hdwy over 1f out: r.o* 20/1
0440 5 *1 ¼* **Cross My Shadow (IRE)**[52] 5865 3-8-9 45.........(t) PaulMulrennan(3) 12 43
(M F Harris) *plld hrd and prom: rdn over 2f out: styd on same pce fnl f* 5/1[3]
-000 6 *nk* **Ready Teddy Go**[88] 5062 3-8-7 45.............................. MarcHalford(5) 1 42
(J Ryan) *chsd ldrs: rdn over 2f out: no ex fnl f* 33/1
2060 7 *1 ½* **Doughty**[16] 6385 3-8-12 45.. VinceSlattery 9 39
(D J Wintle) *hld up: hdwy u.p over 1f out: nt rch ldrs* 20/1
0000 8 *nk* **Madame Guillotine**[13] 6412 3-8-7 40........................ RobbieFitzpatrick 8 34
(P T Midgley) *hld up: rdn over 2f out: n.d* 50/1
5000 9 *½* **Wizardmicktee (IRE)**[20] 6363 3-8-12 45............................ DavidAllan 3 38
(A Bailey) *prom: rdn over 3f out: wknd 2f out* 12/1
3020 10 *1* **Starcross Maid**[16] 6382 3-8-12 45............................... TonyCulhane 11 36
(J F Coupland) *hld up: nvr nrr* 6/1
0040 11 *nk* **Kirstys Lad**[26] 6301 3-8-12 45.. TPQueally 4 35
(M Mullineaux) *chsd ldrs to 1/2-way* 33/1
0000 12 *21* **Zanderido**[16] 6384 3-8-4 40 ow2..................................(v) GregFairley(5) 13 —
(B S Rothwell) *hld up: a in rr* 50/1
660- 13 *2 ½* **Imperatrice**[430] 5910 3-8-4 35 ow2...................................... AlanDaly 10 —
(G A Ham) *s.s: alwyas in rr* 33/1
1m 52.01s (0.25) **Going Correction** -0.10s/f (Stan) 13 Ran SP% **118.4**
Speed ratings (Par 96):94,93,92,92,91 90,89,89,88,87 87,68,66
CSF £36.35 TOTE £2.80: £1.20, £4.70, £1.60; EX 42.70 Place 6 £130.64, Place 5 £65.14.
Owner Joe Singh **Bred** B J And Mrs Crangle **Trained** Lambourn, Berks
FOCUS
A very moderate race of its type and very few got into it with the front pair dominating throughout.
Starcross Maid Official explanation: jockey said, regarding running and riding, his orders were to drop filly in because of her bad draw then come through horses to win race, adding that filly was never travelling and he was unable to lie up any closer or improve his position; trainer's representative said filly may have been unsuited by the surface and would probably be rested after a busy season to date
T/Plt: £121.10 to a £1 stake. Pool: £33,939.65. 204.45 winning tickets. T/Qpdt: £31.40 to a £1 stake. Pool: £3,211.00. 75.60 winning tickets. CR

6493 SOUTHWELL (L-H)
Tuesday, December 6

OFFICIAL GOING: Standard
Wind: Light, behind Weather: Cloudy

6513 BET DIRECT ON SNOOKER H'CAP (DIV I) 7f (F)
12:00 (12:03) (Class 6) (0-65,71) 3-Y-0+ **£2,888** (£852; £426) **Stalls** Low

Form RPR
0014 1 **Middle Eastern**[4] 6480 3-9-3 64.................................. GrahamGibbons 4 71
(P A Blockley) *dwlt: hdwy over 3f out: rdn to ld over 1f out: r.o* 5/1[2]
0354 2 *¾* **Cerebus**[15] 6404 3-8-13 63.. AdamKirby(3) 13 68
(M J Polglase) *a.p: rdn over 1f out: r.o* 13/2[3]
0124 3 *shd* **Cool Sands (IRE)**[7] 6464 3-8-12 62........................ PatrickMathers(3) 12 67
(D Shaw) *hld up: hdwy over 1f out: r.o* 7/1
1303 4 *¾* **Silver Visage (IRE)**[97] 4862 3-8-11 58 ow1......................... BrianReilly 8 61
(Miss J Feilden) *chsd ldrs: rdn over 2f out: styd on same pce ins fnl f* 12/1
6211 5 *½* **Nan Jan**[4] 6483 3-9-10 71 6ex..................................(t) ChrisCatlin 10 73
(R Ingram) *sn pushed along in rr: hdwy u.p over 1f out: nt rch ldrs* 9/4[1]
0501 6 *hd* **Miskina**[10] 6438 4-8-12 59.. EddieAhern 14 60
(W M Brisbourne) *sn led: rdn and hdd over 1f out: no ex ins fnl f* 11/1
0104 7 *1 ¼* **Lord Chamberlain**[31] 6265 12-9-1 62...........................(b) LPKeniry 1 60
(J M Bradley) *dwlt: bhd: hdwy u.pr over 1f out: nt rch ldrs* 20/1
5000 8 *nk* **Contented (IRE)**[183] 2336 3-9-4 65.................................. HayleyTurner 7 62
(Mrs L C Jewell) *chsd ldrs: rdn over 2f out: no ex fnl f* 50/1
0300 9 *1 ¾* **Soba Jones**[125] 4060 8-8-10 60.............................. JasonEdmunds(3) 11 53
(J Balding) *plld hrd and prom: wknd over 1f out* 33/1
5600 10 *nk* **Distant Country (USA)**[10] 6436 6-8-13 63..................... AmirQuinn(3) 3 55
(R A Harris) *hld up in tch: rdn over 1f out: wknd fnl f* 10/1
-200 11 *1 ¼* **Overjoy Way**[124] 4094 3-8-13 60.. MickyFenton 5 49
(P R Chamings) *prom over 4f* 50/1
5560 12 *¾* **Lowestoft Playboy**[42] 6103 3-9-0 61........................... MichaelTebbutt 6 48
(J Jay) *hld up: rdn over 2f out: n.d* 14/1
1300 13 *1 ¼* **Bogaz (IRE)**[42] 6103 3-9-4 65... GeorgeBaker 2 48
(Mrs H Sweeting) *s.i.s: a in rr* 33/1
0000 14 *13* **Mitchelland**[15] 6404 3-8-13 60.. JimmyQuinn 9 10
(James Moffatt) *dwlt: a in rr: eased over 1f out* 66/1
1m 29.6s (-1.20) **Going Correction** -0.20s/f (Stan) 14 Ran SP% **121.1**
Speed ratings (Par 101):98,97,97,96,95 95,93,93,91,91 89,88,87,72
CSF £35.61 CT £238.37 TOTE £4.50: £1.70, £2.10, £3.00; EX 28.80.
Owner Isla & Colin Cage **Bred** Mrs L A Sadler **Trained** Lambourn, Berks
■ Stewards' Enquiry : L P Keniry one-day ban: used whip without giving gelding time to respond (Dec 17)
FOCUS
A modest handicap run in a marginally slower time than the second division.
Lowestoft Playboy Official explanation: jockey said gelding resented the kickback
Mitchelland Official explanation: jockey said filly reared at the start

6514 BET DIRECT ON SNOOKER H'CAP (DIV II) 7f (F)
12:30 (12:31) (Class 6) (0-65,66) 3-Y-0+ **£2,888** (£852; £426) **Stalls** Low

Form RPR
1002 1 **Parkview Love (USA)**[20] 6365 4-8-11 61............(v) PatrickMathers(3) 14 71
(D Shaw) *dwlt: hdwy over 5f out: rdn to ld and hung lft over 1f out: hung rt ins fnl f: r.o* 8/1
1253 2 *nk* **Yorkie**[7] 6464 6-8-10 57.. DeanMcKeown 11 66+
(J Pearce) *hld up: hdwy over 1f out: nt clr run ins fnl f: r.o* 9/2[2]
2021 3 *hd* **Look Of Eagles**[7] 6469 3-9-2 66 6ex...................... NelsonDeSouza(3) 13 74
(P F I Cole) *chsd ldrs: lost pl over 4f out: hdwy over 1f out: rdn and ev ch ins fnl f: unable qck nr fin* 2/1[1]
0000 4 *5* **Barzak (IRE)**[20] 6369 5-8-10 60.................................(b) AmirQuinn(3) 3 55
(S R Bowring) *led: rdn and hdd over 1f out: wknd ins fnl f* 16/1
3000 5 *2 ½* **Count Cougar (USA)**[49] 5956 5-8-13 60............................ DaleGibson 8 49
(S P Griffiths) *chsd ldrs: rdn over 1f out: wknd fnl f* 33/1
0405 6 *½* **Samuel Charles**[21] 6362 7-9-3 64................................ RobertWinston 6 52
(C R Dore) *mid-div: rdn 1/2-way: hdwy and nt clr run over 1f out: nt run on* 7/1[3]
0000 7 *1 ½* **Panshir (FR)**[42] 6103 4-9-4 65.. JohnEgan 4 49
(Julian Poulton) *chsd ldrs: rdn over 2f out: wknd over 1f out* 33/1
0000 8 *½* **Sundried Tomato**[8] 6447 6-8-11 58..............................(p) TonyCulhane 7 40
(D W Chapman) *chsd ldrs over 5f* 14/1
-000 9 *nk* **Tizzy's Law**[15] 6404 4-8-13 60.. TPQueally 9 42
(E F Vaughan) *chsd ldrs to 1/2-way* 40/1
3530 10 *2 ½* **Bamzooki**[47] 5997 3-9-0 61.. DaneO'Neill 5 36
(D J Daly) *s.i.s: rdn 1/2-way: n.d* 22/1
0600 11 *1 ¼* **Mossmann Gorge**[70] 5538 3-9-4 65..................................(v[1]) AlanDaly 10 37
(M Wellings) *sn outpcd* 50/1
304 12 *7* **Pertemps Magus**[82] 5247 5-9-2 63................................(v) MickyFenton 2 17
(A D Smith) *chsd ldrs: rdn over 4f out: hung lft and wknd 2f out* 12/1
0040 13 *2 ½* **Bond Diamond**[69] 5549 8-9-2 63.................................. DarrenWilliams 1 10
(P T Midgley) *hld up: rdn 1/2-way: sn wknd* 25/1
5244 14 *1* **Hand Chime**[17] 6373 8-8-12 62.. AdamKirby(3) 12 7
(Ernst Oertel) *stasrted slowly: outpcd* 8/1
1m 29.42s (-1.38) **Going Correction** -0.20s/f (Stan) 14 Ran SP% **125.0**
Speed ratings (Par 101):99,98,98,92,89 89,87,87,86,83 82,74,71,70
CSF £42.71 CT £103.54 TOTE £10.60: £3.20, £2.20, £1.30; EX 55.50.
Owner Danethorpe Racing Ltd **Bred** Mark Johnston Racing Ltd **Trained** Danethorpe, Notts
FOCUS
Slightly the quicker of the two divisions but there was little strength in depth to this handicap and the form looks modest.
Pertemps Magus Official explanation: vet said mare bled from the nose

6515 BET ON CHAMPIONS LEAGUE AT BETDIRECT.CO.UK (S) STKS 6f (F)
1:00 (1:01) (Class 6) 3-Y-0+ **£2,545** (£751; £375) **Stalls** Low

Form RPR
3300 1 **Far Note (USA)**[116] 4343 7-8-11 61..............................(bt) AmirQuinn(3) 4 61
(S R Bowring) *mde virtually all: rdn and edgd lft over 1f out: r.o* 9/2[2]
0100 2 *¾* **Owed**[17] 6387 3-9-7 57...(t) GrahamGibbons 1 65
(P A Blockley) *chsd ldrs: rdn over 1f out: r.o* 6/1
0146 3 *1 ¼* **Shadow Jumper (IRE)**[8] 6449 4-9-7 52................(v) RobbieFitzpatrick 2 61
(M J Attwater) *chsd ldrs: rdn over 2f out: styd on: eased whn hld nr fin* 4/1[1]
4314 4 *3 ½* **Magic Amour**[6] 6470 7-9-0 48..............................(b) KevinGhunowa(7) 14 51
(P A Blockley) *s.i.s: hld up: hdwy 2f out: rdn over 1f out: no ex fnl f* 7/1
0005 5 *2 ½* **Dunnett Again (IRE)**[24] 6328 4-9-0 40..............................(b) JohnEgan 6 36
(Mrs C A Dunnett) *mid-div: rdn over 2f out: sn outpcd* 25/1
5060 6 *1 ¼* **Blythe Spirit**[7] 6464 6-9-0 60.. RobertWinston 11 33
(C R Dore) *hld up: effrt over 2f out: wknd over 1f out* 6/1
0502 7 *2 ½* **Mynd**[35] 6217 5-9-0 56.. DeanMcKeown 3 25
(R M Whitaker) *chsd ldrs 5f* 5/1[3]
005 8 *shd* **Sapphire Dream**[2] 6493 3-8-2 50.................................. LiamJones(7) 13 20
(A Bailey) *s.i.s: in rr whn hmpd 4f out: n.d* 33/1
3000 9 *1 ¼* **Online Investor**[161] 3005 6-9-0 53.................................. MickyFenton 8 21
(C Smith) *dwlt: hdwy 1/2-way: rdn and wknd wl over 1f out* 25/1
6000 10 *3 ½* **Mister Mal (IRE)**[8] 6449 9-9-7 59.................................. DaneO'Neill 5 17
(B Ellison) *sn pushed along and prom: wknd 2f out* 14/1
5000 11 *2* **Jakeal (IRE)**[8] 6446 6-9-0 35....................................(b) VHalliday 7 4
(R M Whitaker) *bhd fr 1/2-way* 100/1

0400 **12** *5* **Hiamovi (IRE)**[195] 1999 3-9-7 58....................................(b) ChrisCatlin 10 —
(R M H Cowell) *dwlt: hld up: plld hrd: bhd fr 1/2-way* **16/1**

600 **13** *2* **Albashoosh**[8] 6449 7-8-11 62................................ SilvestreDeSousa(3) 12 —
(D Nicholls) *hld up: edgd rt 4f out: sn bhd* **20/1**

0000 **14** *8* **Make Us Flush**[2] 6493 3-8-9 47.. FergalLynch 9 —
(A Berry) *mid-div: rdn over 3f out: sn wknd* **50/1**

1m 15.59s (-1.31) **Going Correction** -0.20s/f (Stan) **14** Ran SP% **126.8**

Speed ratings (Par 101):100,99,97,92,89 87,84,84,82,77 75,68,65,55

CSF £31.34 TOTE £6.20: £2.50, £2.70, £1.70; EX 35.60.The winner was bought in for 4,400gns. Owed was claimed by Naughty Diesel Ltd for £6,000.

Owner Mrs Ann Potts **Bred** Juddmonte Farms **Trained** Edwinstowe, Notts

FOCUS

A pretty straightforward seller and about average form for the grade.

Sapphire Dream Official explanation: jockey said filly was hampered leaving back straight bend

Online Investor Official explanation: jockey said gelding hung right

6516 10% BONUS IN-RUNNING ON ITVI H'CAP 6f (F)

1:30 (1:32) (Class 6) (0-55,61) 3-Y-0+ **£2,895** (£854; £427) **Stalls** Low

Form RPR

3610 **1** **Lucius Verrus (USA)**[10] 6429 5-8-8 **52**................(v) PatrickMathers(3) 11 61
(D Shaw) *trckd ldrs: rdn over 2f out: r.o u.p to ld post* **14/1**

0502 **2** *nk* **Scuba (IRE)**[7] 6464 3-8-13 **54**..(v) SteveDrowne 8 62
(H Morrison) *chsd ldrs: rdn to ld 1f out: hdd post* **10/3**[1]

2522 **3** *1/2* **Tipsy Lad**[7] 6469 3-8-13 **54**..(bt) DavidMcCabe 7 61+
(D J S Ffrench Davis) *stmbld s: hld up: hdwy u.p over 1f out: edgd lft ins fnl f: r.o* **4/1**[2]

4503 **4** *3 1/2* **Limonia (GER)**[10] 6438 3-8-13 **54**...................................... FergalLynch 1 50
(D K Ivory) *w ldr: rdn over 2f out: wknd ins fnl f* **12/1**

0005 **5** *nk* **Blue Maeve**[27] 6294 5-9-0 **55**... DaneO'Neill 13 50
(A D Brown) *chsd ldrs: rdn over 1f out: wknd ins fnl f* **50/1**

2140 **6** *nk* **Mulberry Lad (IRE)**[7] 6469 3-8-12 **53**.............................. DarrenWilliams 2 47
(P W Hiatt) *mde most 5f: wknd ins fnl f* **9/1**

0011 **7** *3 1/2* **Vlasta Weiner**[7] 6455 5-9-6 **61** 6ex...............................(b) GeorgeBaker 14 45
(J M Bradley) *hld up: hdwy over 3f out: rdn and wkng whn hung lft over 1f out* **13/2**[3]

-060 **8** *nk* **Davids Mark**[100] 4793 5-8-11 **52**.......................................(e[1]) EddieAhern 3 35
(J R Jenkins) *hld up: nvr trbld ldrs* **25/1**

0002 **9** *hd* **Mirasol Princess**[7] 6460 4-8-6 **54**............................ LauraReynolds(7) 5 36
(D K Ivory) *s.s: outpcd* **14/1**

0-12 **10** *8* **Nevinstown (IRE)**[122] 4172 5-9-0 **55**.................................. TPQueally 12 13
(C Grant) *s.s: outpcd* **4/1**[2]

3560 **11** *3/4* **Hows That**[15] 6400 3-8-12 **53**.. RobertWinston 4 9
(K R Burke) *mid-div: rdn and lost pl 4f out: sn bhd* **20/1**

00-4 **12** *1 1/2* **Chillin Out**[165] 2894 3-8-11 **52**.. PaulDoe 10 4
(W Jarvis) *chsd ldrs 4f* **20/1**

5000 **13** *7* **Long Weekend (IRE)**[99] 4817 7-8-9 **53**...................(p) BenSwarbrick(3) 9 —
(D Shaw) *stsarted slowly: outpcd* **40/1**

1m 15.89s (-1.01) **Going Correction** -0.20s/f (Stan) **13** Ran SP% **125.2**

Speed ratings (Par 101):98,97,96,92,91 91,86,86,86,75 74,72,63

CSF £59.80 CT £234.39 TOTE £23.60: £5.50, £1.60, £1.80; EX 109.40.

Owner Danethorpe Racing Ltd **Bred** Pacelco S A **Trained** Danethorpe, Notts

FOCUS

There was a good pace on here and the first three came clear, but the form looks nothing out of the ordinary.

Nevinstown(IRE) Official explanation: jockey said gelding was slowly away

6517 LITTLEWOODS BET DIRECT NURSERY 5f (F)

2:00 (2:01) (Class 4) (0-85,78) 2-Y-0 **£6,719** (£1,999; £999; £499) **Stalls** High

Form RPR

0010 **1** **Stoneacre Lad (IRE)**[21] 6359 2-9-2 **73**..................... RobbieFitzpatrick 7 75
(Peter Grayson) *chsd ldrs: rdn to ld and hung lft ins fnl f: r.o* **11/2**[3]

2460 **2** *nk* **Lucayos**[4] 6479 2-8-6 **63**.. ChrisCatlin 2 64
(Mrs H Sweeting) *chsd ldrs: rdn over 1f out: r.o* **13/2**

0606 **3** *1/2* **Garlogs**[15] 6403 2-7-5 **55** oh3.. LiamJones(7) 6 54
(A Bailey) *led: rdn over 1f out: edgd lft and hdd ins fnl f: unable qck nr fin* **16/1**

2300 **4** *1 3/4* **Bel Cantor**[10] 6433 2-8-6 **70**.. JosephWalsh(7) 8 63
(W J H Ratcliffe) *hld up: rdn and hung lft over 1f out: r.o ins fnl f: nrst fin* **12/1**

6040 **5** *shd* **Tiber Tilly**[53] 5871 2-9-6 **77**... HayleyTurner 9 69
(N P Littmoden) *chsd ldrs: outpcd 1/2-way: r.o ins fnl f* **6/1**

0363 **6** *1/2* **Scooby Dude (IRE)**[4] 6479 2-9-7 **78**.............................. GeorgeBaker 10 69
(Ms Deborah J Evans) *w ldr over 3f: sn rdn: hung lft and wknd ins fnl f* **3/1**[1]

0654 **7** *shd* **Sands Crooner (IRE)**[10] 6433 2-8-12 **72**...........(vt[1]) PatrickMathers(3) 4 62
(D Shaw) *s.i.s and hmpd s: sn w ldrs: rdn over 1f out: wknd ins fnl f* **8/1**

3220 **8** *1 3/4* **Canina**[4] 6479 2-8-11 **68**.. EddieAhern 3 52
(Ms Deborah J Evans) *chsd ldrs: rdn over 1f out: wknd ins fnl f* **4/1**[2]

5650 **9** *4* **Jazz At The Sands (USA)**[34] 6226 2-7-13 **56** ow1........... DaleGibson 5 26
(D Shaw) *dwlt: sn sushed along and prom: wknd 1/2-way* **25/1**

0006 **10** *2* **Twilight Avenger (IRE)**[36] 6198 2-8-0 **57** oh3 ow2......(p) JimmyQuinn 1 19
(M J Polglase) *s.i.s: sn pushed along and prom: wknd 1/2-way* **33/1**

0005 **11** *1/2* **Blue Minx (IRE)**[27] 6297 2-7-12 **55** oh1................(b) FrankieMcDonald 11 16
(J S Moore) *dwlt: outpcd* **33/1**

59.08 secs (-1.22) **Going Correction** -0.25s/f (Stan) **11** Ran SP% **122.4**

Speed ratings (Par 98):99,98,97,94,94 93,93,91,84,81 80

CSF £42.23 CT £555.17 TOTE £6.60: £1.90, £3.50, £4.80; EX 68.40.

Owner Richard Teatum **Bred** Mrs Annie Hughes **Trained** Formby, Lancs

FOCUS

A fair nursery for the track and as is usually the case those that raced down the centre of the track enjoyed a major advantage.

NOTEBOOK

Stoneacre Lad(IRE), who failed to see out seven furlongs here last time, proved well suited by this return to the trip he won over at Wolverhampton despite a 13lb higher mark. Even though he hung markedly to his left in the second half of the contest, he was always just about doing enough and won this on merit. His early pace will always be an asset over this trip both here and at Dunstall Park. (op 5-1)

Lucayos, always there or thereabouts, ran his best race on sand so far from his decent draw and is now only 1lb higher than for his sole win on turf. (op 15-2)

Garlogs duly appreciated the return to the minimum trip and showed tremendous speed down the centre of the track. He was carried slightly to his left by the hanging winner inside the last furlong, but his jockey never had to stop riding and he was third-best on merit. (op 20-1)

Bel Cantor is usually ridden more positively and was up against it in trying to come from off the pace here, especially as he raced close to the stands' rail from his draw. He deserves some credit for finishing where he did, but his previous form was not exactly progressive. (op 10-1)

Tiber Tilly rather found everything happening too quickly for her on this sand debut and ideally needs an extra furlong. (op 5-1 tchd 7-1)

Scooby Dude(IRE) was forced to race against the stands' rail from his high draw and that almost certainly helped seal his downfall. (op 7-2)

Sands Crooner(IRE), visored for the first time, got into a bit of a mess leaving the stalls and though he was able to get back into contention fairly soon, he had nothing left towards the end. He is worth another chance under these conditions. (tchd 17-2)

6518 BET DIRECT FREEPHONE 0800 211 222 STKS (H'CAP) 5f (F)

2:30 (2:31) (Class 2) (0-100,95) 3-Y-0+ **£13,381** (£3,981; £1,989; £993) **Stalls** High

Form RPR

2112 **1** **Fyodor (IRE)**[24] 6321 4-8-6 83 ow1.................................. TonyCulhane 3 92+
(W J Haggas) *hld up in tch: swtchd rt over 1f out: qcknd to ld wl ins fnl f: comf* **11/4**[1]

0020 **2** *1 1/2* **Rydal (USA)**[149] 3371 4-8-10 87.............................. GrahamGibbons 8 91
(E J Alston) *s.i.s: sn w ldrs: led 1/2-way: rdn and hdd wl ins fnl f* **10/1**

0005 **3** *1/2* **The Lord**[3] 6489 5-8-5 82... AlanDaly 2 84
(W G M Turner) *chsd ldrs: rdn 1/2-way: ev ch ins fnl f: unable qck* **6/1**

3520 **4** *1/2* **Pawan (IRE)**[7] 6465 5-8-6 90 oh6 ow9............................ AnnStokell(7) 4 91
(Miss A Stokell) *s.s: hdwy over 1f out: nt rch ldrs* **22/1**

0256 **5** *1/2* **Frascati**[20] 6370 5-8-5 82... EddieAhern 5 81
(A Berry) *w ldrs: rdn and ev ch ins fnl f: styd on same pce* **15/2**

0523 **6** *1 3/4* **Tag Team (IRE)**[10] 6430 4-8-4 81 oh18............................(v) PaulEddery 6 74
(John A Harris) *led to 1/2-way: wknd ins fnl f* **40/1**

0003 **7** *shd* **Polish Emperor (USA)**[20] 6370 5-9-0 94.....................(e) AdamKirby(3) 9 87
(W R Swinburn) *chsd ldrs: outpcd 3f out: n.d after* **5/1**[3]

4600 **8** *shd* **Dancing Mystery**[20] 6370 11-9-4 95.........................(b) StephenCarson 7 87
(E A Wheeler) *chsd ldrs over 3f* **8/1**

0002 **R** **Piccled**[3] 6489 7-8-5 82... JimmyQuinn 1 —
(E J Alston) *ref to r* **7/2**[2]

58.00 secs (-2.30) **Going Correction** -0.25s/f (Stan) **9** Ran SP% **118.6**

Speed ratings (Par 109):108,105,104,104,103 100,100,100,—

CSF £32.45 CT £156.74 TOTE £3.60: £1.20, £2.70, £2.50; EX 36.10 Trifecta £344.80 Part won. Pool: £485.64 - 0.90 winning tickets..

Owner The Fyodor Partnership **Bred** E J Banks And D I Scott **Trained** Newmarket, Suffolk

FOCUS

A very decent sprint handicap, despite a couple apparently running extremely well at disadvantageous terms, and again the centre of the track was the place to be.

NOTEBOOK

Fyodor(IRE) ♦, making his Fibresand debut and racing off a 10lb higher mark than when successful at Wolverhampton two starts ago, travelled like a dream just behind the leaders before delivering a turn of foot that is not seen very often on this surface. Still unexposed on sand, there should be other opportunities for him if connections decide to persevere with him through the winter. (op 3-1 tchd 10-3)

Rydal(USA) ♦, reappearing from a five-month break and without any of the various headgear he usually sports on this debut for the yard, was able to edge away to his left from his high draw and by halfway was travelling very well in a narrow lead. Like all the others, he could do nothing to withstand the winner's devastating turn of foot, but this was a decent effort nonetheless on his Fibresand debut and, as he stays further and acts on Polytrack too, an opportunity seems very likely to be found. (op 12-1 tchd 14-1)

The Lord, well backed, was drawn better than at Wolverhampton three days earlier and ran another highly creditable race. He is yet to win on sand, but if he maintains this level of form that will surely change before too long. (op 8-1)

Pawan(IRE), effectively 15lb wrong including his rider's overweight, stayed on very well over a trip probably short of his best, but it would be unwise to take this form at face value given his overall record and he cannot expect any favours from the Handicapper after this. (op 25-1)

Frascati, without a win since June of last year but proven under these conditions, was not disgraced but is apparently bound for the paddocks. (op 7-1 tchd 8-1)

Tag Team(IRE), backed at fancy odds despite being 18lb out of the handicap, has never been short of early pace but it was asking a lot for him to maintain it the whole way at this level.

Polish Emperor(USA), who had four of these behind him when starting from the plum number one draw here last time, had the coffin box against the stands' rail this time around and it showed. (op 9-2)

Dancing Mystery, winner of this race last year off a 2lb lower mark, was not best drawn but continues to perform a little way below his best and perhaps his age is starting to show. (tchd 10-1)

Piccled, who has refused to race a couple of times on turf, disgraced himself for the first time on sand after running so well at Wolverhampton just three days earlier. It seems that he cannot be trusted now. (op 11-4)

6519 PRESS RED TO BET ON ITVI H'CAP 1m 6f (F)

3:00 (3:00) (Class 4) (0-85,73) 3-Y-0+ **£6,661** (£1,981; £990; £494) **Stalls** Low

Form RPR

0323 **1** **Heathyards Pride**[20] 6371 5-9-6 69................................ GeorgeBaker 2 84+
(R Hollinshead) *hld up: hdwy over 2f out: led over 1f out: styd on* **3/1**[1]

060 **2** *nk* **Trance (IRE)**[35] 6218 5-9-7 70.. HayleyTurner 3 82+
(T D Barron) *hld up: hdwy over 3f out: nt clr run 2f out: rdn to chse wnr over 1f out: styd on* **5/1**[3]

0014 **3** *6* **Peak Park (USA)**[15] 6406 5-9-10 73.................................... ChrisCatlin 1 77
(P L Gilligan) *chsd ldrs: lost pl 7f out: outpcd over 4f out: styd on u.p appr fnl f* **9/2**[2]

6035 **4** *3/4* **Night Sight (USA)**[15] 6406 8-8-12 61...........................(b) TonyCulhane 4 64
(Mrs S Lamyman) *hld up: hdwy over 2f out: sn rdn: wknd fnl f* **8/1**

0030 **5** *1/2* **Dovedon Hero**[20] 6371 5-9-9 72..................................(b) RobertWinston 7 74
(P J McBride) *hld up in tch: rdn over 2f out: wknd fnl f* **13/2**

0051 **6** *5* **Sun Hill**[15] 6406 5-9-1 67... PaulMulrennan(3) 9 62
(C W Fairhurst) *chsd ldrs: led 2f out: edgd lft and hdd over 1f out: sn wknd* **11/2**

6041 **7** *1/2* **Romil Star (GER)**[7] 6463 8-8-4 60 5ex..................(v) PatrickDonaghy(7) 5 54
(K R Burke) *chsd ldrs: rdn over 3f out: wknd over 2f out* **10/1**

1430 **8** *hd* **Perfidious (USA)**[10] 6432 7-8-12 64...........................(v) AmirQuinn(3) 6 58
(J R Boyle) *led: rdn over 4f out: hdd over 2f out: sn wknd* **14/1**

0500 **9** *8* **Amir Zaman**[10] 6368 7-9-0 63.. TPQueally 8 46
(J R Jenkins) *chsd ldr: led over 2f out: sn hdd: wkng whn hmpd over 1f out* **50/1**

3m 4.77s (-4.83) **Going Correction** -0.20s/f (Stan) **9** Ran SP% **117.4**

Speed ratings (Par 105):105,104,101,100,100 97,97,97,92

CSF £18.39 CT £67.00 TOTE £2.60: £1.60, £2.30, £1.70; EX 17.90.

Owner L A Morgan **Bred** L A Morgan **Trained** Upper Longdon, Staffs

FOCUS

A decent staying handicap, but the pace was no more than ordinary which would not have suited a few.

6520 BETDIRECT.CO.UK H'CAP 1m 3f (F)

3:30 (3:31) (Class 5) (0-75,75) 3-Y-0+ **£4,121** (£1,226; £612; £306) **Stalls** Low

Form RPR

0022 **1** **Mi Odds**[7] 6463 9-8-10 **67**.. AlanDaly 14 73
(Mrs N Macauley) *hld up in tch: rdn over 1f out: r.o to ld nr fin* **11/1**

5035 **2** *nk* **Danelor (IRE)**[10] 6437 7-9-4 **75**....................(p) TonyHamilton 11 81
(R A Fahey) *led: rdn over 1f out: hdd nr fin* **8/1**
34 **3** *nk* **Mad Carew (USA)**[20] 6371 6-8-13 **73**....................(e) AmirQuinn(3) 6 78
(J R Boyle) *hld up: hdwy 2f out: swtchd rt over 1f out: r.o* **6/1**
1601 **4** *1* **Kylkenny**[71] 5511 10-9-3 **74**....................(t) SteveDrowne 5 77
(H Morrison) *hld up: hdwy over 2f out: r.o* **5/1**[3]
1246 **5** *½* **Eloquent Knight (USA)**[177] 2513 3-8-6 **67**.................... JohnEgan 8 70
(W R Muir) *chsd ldrs: rdn over 2f out: no ex ins fnl f* **14/1**
0 **6** *½* **Nabir (FR)**[10] 6434 5-8-13 **70**.................... TomEaves 10 72?
(P D Niven) *chsd ldr 9f out: rdn over 2f out: no ex fnl f* **100/1**
6000 **7** *nk* **Sir Haydn**[52] 5437 5-9-4 **75**....................(e[1]) FergalLynch 4 76
(J R Jenkins) *hld up: hdwy on outside over 3f out: nt rch ldrs* **33/1**
1102 **8** *½* **African Sahara (USA)**[24] 6325 6-8-9 **73**....................(t) ChrisCavanagh(7) 3 74
(Miss D Mountain) *hld up: nt clr run over 3f out: swtchd stands' side over 2f out: nt rch ldrs* **16/1**
0654 **9** *2 ½* **Sorbiesharry (IRE)**[21] 6362 6-8-9 **66**.................... HayleyTurner 12 63
(Mrs N Macauley) *hld up: n.d* **10/1**
0530 **10** *2 ½* **Bentley Brook (IRE)**[73] 5467 3-9-0 **75**.................... GrahamGibbons 1 68
(P A Blockley) *hld up: effrt over 2f out: hung lft and wknd over 1f out* **25/1**
0000 **11** *2 ½* **Intricate Web (IRE)**[38] 6159 9-9-0 **71**.................... JimmyQuinn 2 60
(E J Alston) *hld up: effrt over 3f out: wknd wl over 1f out* **40/1**
1165 **12** *1* **Tromp**[43] 6073 4-9-0 **71**.................... EddieAhern 7 58
(D J Coakley) *hld up in tch: rdn over 3f out: wknd 2f out* **10/3**[1]
1013 **13** *2* **Summer Charm**[60] 5714 3-8-10 **71**.................... RobertWinston 9 55
(W Jarvis) *chsd ldrs: rdn over 2f out: wkng whn nt clr run over 1f out* **4/1**[2]

2m 25.04s (-3.86) **Going Correction** -0.20s/f (Stan)
WFA 3 from 4yo+ 4lb **13** Ran SP% **125.3**
Speed ratings (Par 103):106,105,105,104,104 104,103,103,101,99 98,97,95
CSF £98.82 CT £594.62 TOTE £18.70: £4.60, £2.60, £2.20; EX 102.80 Place 6 £75.07, Place 5 £24.50.
Owner Mrs N Macauley **Bred** G Wiltshire **Trained** Sproxton, Leics

FOCUS
A fairly competitive handicap run at a true pace thanks to Danelor. Despite that, several had a chance down the home straight and there was not much separating the front eight at the line.
T/Jkpt: Not won. T/Plt: £154.60 to a £1 stake. Pool: £34,787.20. 164.25 winning tickets. T/Qpdt: £86.00 to a £1 stake. Pool: £2,825.70. 24.30 winning tickets. CR

6499 LINGFIELD (L-H)
Wednesday, December 7

OFFICIAL GOING: Standard
Wind: Nil Weather: Fine becoming cloudy

6521 CUSTOM ADVERTISING MAIDEN CLAIMING STKS 1m 2f (P)
1:10 (1:12) (Class 7) 2-Y-O **£1,423** (£420; £210) **Stalls** Low

Form RPR
0054 **1** **Ms Rainbow Runner**[18] 6375 2-8-7 54.................... EddieAhern 11 58
(B J Meehan) *trckd ldr to over 6f out: styd prom: led over 3f out: shkn up and clr wl over 1f out: unchal* **11/4**[1]
040 **2** *5* **Stoneacre Lil (IRE)**[103] 4713 2-8-7 40....................(b[1]) RobbieFitzpatrick 3 49
(Peter Grayson) *s.s: t.k.h: hld up in rr: lost tch w ldrs 3f out: urged along and r.o fnl 2f: tk 2nd nr fin* **33/1**
0250 **3** *1 ¼* **Secret Tender (IRE)**[16] 6403 2-8-10 50.................... J-PGuillambert 4 50
(J R Weymes) *hld up in midfield: prog over 3f out: chsd wnr over 2f out: no imp: lost 2nd nr fin* **4/1**[2]
0333 **4** *¾* **Pix**[18] 6375 2-8-7 52.................... ChrisCatlin 14 46
(S Kirk) *hld up in midfield: prog over 2f out: effrt on inner over 1f out: one pce* **9/2**[3]
0000 **5** *2* **Count The Trees**[16] 6395 2-8-0 35.................... MarcHalford(5) 2 40
(W G M Turner) *chsd ldrs: rdn over 3f out: nt clr run over 2f out: one pce after* **33/1**
000 **6** *2 ½* **Guanyin**[12] 6417 2-8-8 45 ow1.................... MickyFenton 5 39
(J G Given) *nvr beyond midfield: u.p and struggling 3f out* **12/1**
0060 **7** *1 ¾* **Fitzsimons (IRE)**[54] 5879 2-8-10 48.................... DaneO'Neill 9 37
(A M Hales) *wl in rr: rdn over 4f out: sn lost tch: n.d* **13/2**
00 **8** *nk* **Amber Spirit**[18] 6386 2-8-6 ow1.................... PaulDoe 6 33
(Peter Grayson) *led to over 3f out: wknd rapidly 2f out* **50/1**
9 *4* **Ten For Fun (FR)** 2-8-3....................(b[1]) AdamKirby(3) 8 26
(M J Polglase) *s.v.s: rapid prog to press ldr over 6f out: led briefly over 3f out: wknd rapidly 2f out* **50/1**
0000 **10** *1 ¾* **Paris Power**[35] 6227 2-8-12 45.................... MichaelTebbutt 13 28
(D Morris) *racd on outer: hld up: rdn and struggling 3f out: wknd* **33/1**
00 **11** *4* **Little Erhaab**[11] 6425 2-8-6 ow1....................(t) LPKeniry 7 15
(G L Moore) *s.s: a wl in rr: wl btn over 3f out* **25/1**
0000 **12** *½* **Mullzima (IRE)**[22] 6358 2-8-5 50.................... JimmyQuinn 10 13
(P D Evans) *a wl in rr: rdn and struggling over 4f out* **10/1**
4000 **13** *hd* **Skezahra**[47] 6004 2-8-5 40.................... HayleyTurner 1 13
(T M Jones) *plld v hrd: in tch tl wknd rapidly over 3f out* **50/1**

2m 8.98s (1.19) **Going Correction** -0.225s/f (Stan) **13** Ran SP% **113.5**
Speed ratings (Par 90):86,82,81,80,78 76,75,75,71,70 67,66,66
CSF £98.98 TOTE £2.90: £1.70, £8.10, £1.80; EX 85.50.The winner was claimed by P. Butler for £5,000.
Owner Tony Tunstall & Peter Clark **Bred** D J Brown And Mrs J Berry **Trained** Manton, Wilts
■ Plough Maite (12/1, ref to enter stalls) was withdrawn. R4 applies, deduct 5p in the £.

FOCUS
A very weak contest run in a modest time, which saw the field trail home behind the decisive winner.

NOTEBOOK
Ms Rainbow Runner, stepping up in trip once again, outlcassed her rivals and finally lost her maiden tag in decisive fashion. She saw out the longer trip really well, had plenty in hand at the finish, and should be high on confidence now. However, it must be noted that this took very little winning. (tchd 10-3)
Stoneacre Lil(IRE), having her first outing on the All-Weather and equipped with first-time blinkers, spoilt her chance with a sluggish start and by then refusing to settle under restraint through the first half of the contest. The fact she finished her race well suggests she was suited by the longer trip, however, and this still rates by far her best effort to date.
Secret Tender(IRE), making her Polytrack debut, had her chance yet failed to see out the longer trip. She is worth a chance back over a mile on this surface. (op 9-2)
Pix failed to improve for the longer trip, and never looked like reversing her recent selling form with the winner, but was not disgraced considering her wide stall. She helps set the level of this form. (op 4-1 tchd 11-2)
Count The Trees would have finished a touch closer with a clear passage around two out and turned in a more encouraging effort.

6522 BIFFA WASTE SERVICES BANDED STKS 1m 2f (P)
1:40 (1:43) (Class 7) 3-Y-O+ **£1,450** (£428; £214) **Stalls** Low

Form RPR
0030 **1** **Mythical Charm**[16] 6399 6-9-2 48....................(t) J-PGuillambert 7 56
(J J Bridger) *hld up in rr: smooth prog to trck ldrs 3f out: rdn 2f out: effrt on outer over 1f out: kpt on u.p to ld last 100yds* **25/1**
1006 **2** *¾* **Hiawatha (IRE)**[7] 6473 6-9-4 50.................... ChrisCatlin 13 56
(A M Hales) *hld up in rr: prog 3f out: nt clr run 2f out: hrd rdn and styd on to take 2nd nr fin* **25/1**
0610 **3** *hd* **Fantasy Crusader**[32] 6262 6-9-3 49.................... DaneO'Neill 14 55
(R M H Cowell) *hld up wl in rr: prog to trck ldrs 3f out: drvn to ld 1f out: hdd and no ex last 100yds* **14/1**
4430 **4** *nk* **Ten-Cents**[70] 5544 3-9-0 49.................... GeorgeBaker 12 59+
(C F Wall) *hld up in rr: prog 3f out: nt clr run after and lost pl bdly: wd bnd 2f out: str run fnl f: nt rcvr* **11/2**[2]
2122 **5** *nk* **Young Kate**[16] 6398 4-8-13 45.................... HayleyTurner 3 50
(J R Best) *hld up in midfield: prog on inner over 2f out: rdn to chal over 1f out: kpt on same pce* **6/1**[3]
0000 **6** *1 ¼* **Kinsman (IRE)**[16] 6399 8-8-11 46.................... RobertMiles(3) 1 48
(T D McCarthy) *s.v.s: hld up in detached last: nudged along and prog over 2f out: styd on wl fnl f: no ch* **33/1**
60-4 **7** *¾* **Whenwillitwin**[16] 6399 4-8-10 49....................(p) JosephWalsh(7) 2 50
(J S Moore) *dwlt: plld hrd: hld up in midfield: hrd rdn fnl 2f: kpt on: n.d* **25/1**
3303 **8** *shd* **Mad**[16] 6399 4-9-0 46.................... EddieAhern 11 47
(Andrew Reid) *sn prom: disp ld 3f out to 1f out: wknd* **7/2**[1]
6600 **9** *2* **Lord Lahar**[11] 6429 6-9-3 49.................... MickyFenton 4 46
(M A Buckley) *t.k.h: led for 2f: disp ld again 3f out to 1f out: wknd rapidly* **33/1**
0020 **10** *2 ½* **Magari**[7] 6473 4-9-0 49.................... BenSwarbrick(3) 5 41
(W M Brisbourne) *trckd ldrs: rdn and losing pl whn squeezed out over 2f out* **20/1**
0524 **11** *nk* **Glenviews Oldport (USA)**[7] 6473 3-9-0 49.................... RobbieFitzpatrick 8 41
(Peter Grayson) *racd wd in midfield: u.p and losing pl whn hmpd over 2f out* **11/2**[2]
3106 **12** *3 ½* **Parsley's Return**[53] 5894 3-8-7 45....................(b) AdamKirby(3) 6 30
(M Wigham) *disp ld after 2f to 3f out: sn btn* **8/1**
4501 **13** *½* **Three Ships**[7] 6473 4-9-6 49.................... AmirQuinn(3) 10 39
(Miss J Feilden) *disp ld after 2f to 3f out: sn wknd u.p* **6/1**[3]
6644 **14** *5* **Peace Emblem (IRE)**[23] 6347 4-8-13 45....................(p) BrianReilly 9 20
(J W Unett) *chsd ldrs tl wknd over 3f out* **25/1**

2m 5.91s (-1.88) **Going Correction** -0.225s/f (Stan)
WFA 3 from 4yo+ 3lb **14** Ran SP% **125.4**
Speed ratings (Par 97):98,97,97,97,96 95,95,95,93,91 91,88,88,84
CSF £532.31 TOTE £25.60: £5.30, £7.40, £4.80; EX 436.60.
Owner Tommy Ware **Bred** B J And Mrs Crangle **Trained** Liphook, Hants

FOCUS
A weak event, but the pace was fair and the form appears sound enough for the class.
Ten-Cents Official explanation: jockey said filly suffered interference on final bend
Kinsman(IRE) Official explanation: jockey said, regarding the running and riding, his orders were to jump out, be handy but not too close to the pace, however gelding missed break losing many lengths, and being of a quirky disposition and reluctant to race if put under pressure early, it needs to be coaxed long to obtain the best performance; he added gelding likes to come through horses and at 1 1/2f out he tried to improve his position with a run up the inner
Lord Lahar Official explanation: jockey said gelding hung right and suffered interference on final bend
Magari Official explanation: jockey said filly suffered interference on final bend
Three Ships Official explanation: jockey said gelding suffered interference on final bend

6523 LYNHURST PRESS BANDED STKS 1m 4f (P)
2:10 (2:11) (Class 7) 3-Y-O+ **£1,450** (£428; £214) **Stalls** Low

Form RPR
6000 **1** **Mostarsil (USA)**[47] 6012 7-9-5 50....................(p) IanMongan 5 62+
(G L Moore) *hld up midfield: prog 3f out: rdn to chse ldr 2f out: led jst over 1f out: forged clr* **8/1**
0433 **2** *4* **Trials 'n Tribs**[27] 6307 3-9-0 50.................... FergusSweeney 12 56
(C A Cyzer) *hld up in midfield: prog on outer over 5f out: led 3f out: kicked on 2f out : hdd and outpcd jst over 1f out: wkng nr fin* **7/1**[3]
5000 **3** *1 ½* **Regency Red (IRE)**[12] 6419 7-8-13 47.................... BenSwarbrick(3) 7 51
(W M Brisbourne) *hld up in midfield: effrt and sme prog over 2f out: sn rdn: kpt on to take 3rd nr fin* **20/1**
1040 **4** *nk* **Mustang Ali (IRE)**[53] 5892 4-9-4 49.................... BrianReilly 6 52
(Dr J R J Naylor) *in tch on outer: rdn 3f out: prog to chse ldrs 2f out: one pce after* **7/1**[3]
2060 **5** *¾* **Iamback**[15] 6414 5-8-11 45....................(t) AdamKirby(3) 13 47
(Miss Gay Kelleway) *dwlt: t.k.h: hld up in rr: last 4f out: hanging and nt keen but styd on fnl 2f* **16/1**
0054 **6** *1* **Free Style (GER)**[25] 6323 5-9-5 50.................... GeorgeBaker 2 50
(Mrs H Sweeting) *dwlt: sn prom: rdn wl over 2f out: fdd over 1f out* **10/3**[1]
3322 **7** *shd* **Brennie (IRE)**[7] 6472 4-9-0 45.................... DaneO'Neill 15 45
(V Smith) *trckd ldrs: drvn over 2f out: btn over 1f out* **9/2**[2]
5443 **8** *1 ¼* **Zeena**[64] 5689 3-8-12 48.................... OscarUrbina 16 46
(C A Horgan) *wnt rt s: hld up wl in rr: prog on outer over 3f out: jst in tch 2f out: sn wknd* **16/1**
0000 **9** *1* **My Boo**[7] 6472 3-8-10 46....................(tp) ChrisCatlin 1 43
(T Keddy) *a towards rr: u.p over 3f out: n.d* **66/1**
0-00 **10** *1 ¾* **Stolen**[196] 1997 3-9-0 50.................... JimmyQuinn 14 44
(W R Muir) *nvr beyond midfield: wl in rr and rdn over 3f out: n.d* **50/1**
0405 **11** *6* **Summer Bounty**[7] 6475 9-9-0 45.................... J-PGuillambert 9 29
(F Jordan) *cl up: effrt to dispute ld 3f out to over 2f out: wknd on inner wl over 1f out* **15/2**
5040 **12** *1 ¼* **Sweet Sioux**[38] 6184 3-9-0 50.................... StephenCarson 8 32
(W R Swinburn) *led for 3f: led again 5f out to 3f out: sn wknd* **20/1**
0040 **13** *1 ¾* **Edict**[23] 6348 3-8-9 45.................... PaulEddery 10 24
(C J Down) *trckd ldrs tl wknd u.p over 3f out* **40/1**
0000 **14** *9* **Viniyoga**[105] 4673 3-8-10 46.................... EddieAhern 3 11
(M H Tompkins) *hld up towards rr: drvn over 4f out: struggling after* **33/1**
0 **15** *27* **Rain Holly (IRE)**[11] 6438 3-9-0 50.................... LPKeniry 11 —
(R A Harris) *t.k.h: led after 3f to 5f out: wknd rapidly over 3f out: t.o* **50/1**

2m 31.87s (-2.52) **Going Correction** -0.225s/f (Stan)
WFA 3 from 4yo+ 5lb **15** Ran SP% **121.2**
Speed ratings (Par 97):99,96,95,95,94 93,93,93,92,91 87,86,85,79,61
CSF £59.08 TOTE £9.30: £2.40, £3.00, £5.50; EX 91.80.

Owner G A Jackman **Bred** Shadwell Farm Inc **Trained** Woodingdean, E Sussex

FOCUS
Sound form for the class, the pace was solid, and the winner outclassed his rivals on his banded debut.

6524 P & M ELECTRICAL BANDED STKS — 1m (P)
2:40 (2:40) (Class 7) 3-Y-O+ — **£1,433** (£423; £211) **Stalls** High

Form — RPR

6426 **1** **Danettie**[9] 6444 4-8-12 45 EddieAhern 2 — 59
(W M Brisbourne) *trckd ldrs: effrt to ld over 2f out: hrd rdn and styd on fr over 1f out* **7/1**

0600 **2** 1 ¾ **Wanna Shout**[23] 6343 7-8-12 45 JimmyQuinn 7 — 55
(R Dickin) *hld up in midfield: prog and swtchd rt wl over 2f out: chsd wnr 2f out: hrd rdn and nt qckn fnl f* **14/1**

0000 **3** 2 ½ **Zolash (IRE)**[16] 6398 3-8-11 45 DaneO'Neill 8 — 49
(Mrs L C Jewell) *settled in last trio: prog on inner fr 3f out: wnt 3rd jst ins fnl f: no ch w ldng pair* **40/1**

0403 **4** 2 **Prince Valentine**[16] 6394 4-8-12 45 (be) IanMongan 1 — 45
(G L Moore) *hld up midfield: n.m.r over 6f out: drvn and outpcd over 2f out: plugged on* **11/2**[3]

0605 **5** ½ **First Of May**[50] 5962 4-8-12 45 ChrisCatlin 12 — 43
(Miss Z C Davison) *settled in last trio: pushed along over 3f out: nt clr run over 2f out and over 1f out: kpt on* **20/1**

4405 **6** ¾ **Cross My Shadow (IRE)**[2] 6512 3-8-8 45 (t) RichardThomas(3) 3 — 42
(M F Harris) *mde most to over 2f out: wknd rapidly fnl f* **13/2**

00-0 **7** 1 ½ **Dream Of Dubai (IRE)**[53] 5897 4-8-12 45 HayleyTurner 4 — 38
(P Mitchell) *chsd ldrs: rdn 3f out: sn struggling and btn* **50/1**

0200 **8** 1 **Endless Peace (IRE)**[46] 6032 4-8-9 45 AdamKirby(3) 6 — 36
(J W Unett) *w ldr to over 2f out: sn wknd* **16/1**

5202 **9** 1 **Golden Spectrum (IRE)**[9] 6445 6-8-5 45 (b) TolleyDean(7) 9 — 34
(R A Harris) *nvr beyond midfield: wl in rr and u.p 3f out* **9/2**[2]

0060 **10** 1 ¾ **Dexileos (IRE)**[204] 1783 6-8-12 45 (t) FergusSweeney 11 — 30
(David Pinder) *chsd ldrs: drvn sn after 1/2-way: wknd 2f out* **25/1**

4241 **11** ¾ **Tirailleur (IRE)**[18] 6383 5-8-12 45 OscarUrbina 5 — 28
(J R Boyle) *nvr beyond midfield: rdn in rr 3f out: no prog on inner fnl 2f* **3/1**[1]

0060 **12** ½ **Spanish Music**[16] 6399 3-8-11 45 (t) RobertHavlin 10 — 27
(R Ingram) *sn towards rr: drvn and struggling 3f out* **10/1**

1m 37.44s (-1.99) **Going Correction** -0.225s/f (Stan)
WFA 3 from 4yo+ 1lb — **12** Ran SP% **119.0**
Speed ratings (Par 97):100,98,95,93,93 92,91,90,89,87 86,86
CSF £96.61 TOTE £9.70: £2.30, £4.60, £11.80; EX 63.60.
Owner J Oldknow A & H Johnstone & B Carter **Bred** John E Oldknow **Trained** Great Ness, Shropshire

FOCUS
A poor event, but the time was fair and the form does appear solid enough for the class rated through the runner-up.
Cross My Shadow(IRE) Official explanation: jockey said gelding hung right

6525 BIFFA BANDED STKS — 7f (P)
3:10 (3:10) (Class 7) 3-Y-O+ — **£1,457** (£430; £215) **Stalls** Low

Form — RPR

0043 **1** **Hollow Jo**[9] 6445 5-9-0 48 MickyFenton 3 — 56
(J R Jenkins) *hld up in midfield: effrt on outer 2f out: drvn and r.o to ld narrowly last 100yds* **8/1**

5013 **2** nk **Humility**[23] 6346 4-9-1 49 LPKeniry 6 — 57
(C A Cyzer) *t.k.h: hld up: prog 2f out: n.m.r but r.o to press wnr last 100yds: jst hld* **9/1**

01 **3** 1 **Segoria (IRE)**[16] 6396 3-9-1 49 DaneO'Neill 4 — 54
(A M Hales) *hld up in last trio: effrt towards inner 2f out: drvn to chal fnl f: nt qckn nr fin* **20/1**

0464 **4** hd **Auentraum (GER)**[16] 6397 5-9-0 48 (b) PaulDoe 2 — 52
(K McAuliffe) *hld up in last trio: effrt on inner 2f out: prog whn hmpd over 1f out: r.o last 150yds* **16/1**

5223 **5** hd **Fulvio (USA)**[16] 6401 5-9-2 50 (v) J-PGuillambert 10 — 54
(P Howling) *t.k.h: pressed ldrs: chal 2f out: led jst over 1f out: hdd and one pce last 100yds* **7/2**[2]

3612 **6** ¾ **Cayman Breeze**[7] 6470 5-9-2 50 GeorgeBaker 1 — 52
(J M Bradley) *trckd ldrs: poised to chal 2f out: nt clr run over 1f out: rdn and fnd nil* **2/1**[1]

0310 **7** 1 ¾ **Zazous**[11] 6429 4-9-2 50 EddieAhern 14 — 47
(J J Bridger) *t.k.h: led at modest pce for 2f: rdn to ld again 2f out: hdd and fdd over 1f out* **11/2**[3]

1100 **8** ½ **Coronado Forest (USA)**[53] 5895 6-8-13 47 IanMongan 8 — 43
(M R Hoad) *hld up tl plld way to ld after 2f: hdd 2f out: sn btn* **12/1**

3500 **9** nk **Savernake Brave (IRE)**[8] 6469 4-9-2 50 ChrisCatlin 5 — 45
(Mrs H Sweeting) *s.i.s: hld up in last pair: outpcd 2f out: styd on nr fin* **16/1**

6625 **10** 5 **Flying Dancer**[11] 6438 3-8-9 50 TolleyDean(7) 11 — 32
(R A Harris) *plld hrd: prom tl wknd 3f out* **33/1**

1m 25.91s (0.02) **Going Correction** -0.225s/f (Stan) — **10** Ran SP% **119.2**
Speed ratings (Par 97):90,89,88,88,88 87,85,84,84,78
CSF £79.55 TOTE £9.70: £2.30, £2.20, £3.50; EX 87.40.
Owner Jim McCarthy **Bred** K J Reddington **Trained** Royston, Herts
■ Stewards' Enquiry : Eddie Ahern one day ban: careless riding (Dec 19)

FOCUS
A modest time, even for a banded contest.
Cayman Breeze Official explanation: jockey said gelding was denied clear run

6526 FORMARK SCAFFOLDING BANDED STKS — 6f (P)
3:40 (3:40) (Class 7) 3-Y-O+ — **£1,419** (£419; £209) **Stalls** Low

Form — RPR

0000 **1** **Park Star**[203] 1811 5-8-8 45 PatrickMathers(3) 1 — 51
(D Shaw) *trckd ldrs gng easily: effrt on inner to ld jst over 1f out: sn drvn clr* **20/1**

0054 **2** 1 ½ **Rosiella**[88] 5128 3-8-11 45 (b) FergusSweeney 2 — 46
(M Blanshard) *chsd ldrs: rdn and effrt 2f out: styd on to take 2nd jst ins fnl f: nt rch wnr* **16/1**

0005 **3** 1 **One Last Time**[16] 6398 5-8-8 45 RichardThomas(3) 8 — 43
(Miss B Sanders) *rrd s: towards rr: rdn over 2f out: no prog tl styd on wl on outer fnl f: tk 3rd nr fin* **7/2**[2]

0000 **4** ¾ **Sunset Dreamer (USA)**[95] 4933 4-8-11 45 (p) HayleyTurner 3 — 41
(P Mitchell) *sn rdn in rr: prog over 2f out: kpt on one pce fr over 1f out* **33/1**

0040 **5** shd **Shirley Oaks (IRE)**[50] 5966 7-8-11 45 ChrisCatlin 6 — 40
(Miss Z C Davison) *settled in last trio: no prog tl rdn and styd on fr over 1f out: nvr nrr* **8/1**

5100 **6** shd **Urban Calm**[7] 6471 4-8-11 45 BrianReilly 12 — 40
(J W Unett) *trckd ldrs: rdn and one pce fnl 2f* **14/1**

5553 **7** 2 **Multahab**[23] 6345 6-8-8 45 (t) AdamKirby(3) 9 — 34
(Miss Gay Kelleway) *stdd s: hld up in rr and racd on outer: wd bnd 2f out: modest late prog* **2/1**[1]

0466 **8** ½ **Dane Rhapsody (IRE)**[21] 6369 4-8-4 45 JamesDoyle(7) 11 — 33
(B Palling) *pressed ldng pair tl wknd over 1f out* **20/1**

0003 **9** nk **Christian Bendix**[16] 6396 3-8-11 45 J-PGuillambert 5 — 32
(P Howling) *t.k.h: pressed ldr to over 1f out: wknd* **11/2**[3]

0000 **10** 1 **Lucky Emerald (IRE)**[23] 6346 3-8-11 45 FrancisFerris 4 — 29
(B Palling) *led: rdn 1/2-way: hdd & wknd jst over 1f out* **25/1**

0000 **11** 1 ½ **Hugo The Boss (IRE)**[29] 6292 3-8-11 45 (v) IanMongan 7 — 24
(J R Boyle) *pressed ldrs tl wknd 1/2-way* **25/1**

6020 **12** 1 ¼ **Yamato Pink**[46] 6032 4-8-8 45 NeilChalmers(3) 10 — 21
(Mrs H Sweeting) *s.i.s: a in rr: v wd bnd 2f out: no ch* **11/1**

1m 12.22s (-0.59) **Going Correction** -0.225s/f (Stan) — **12** Ran SP% **123.1**
Speed ratings (Par 97):94,92,90,89,89 89,86,86,85,84 82,80
CSF £295.90 TOTE £29.20: £6.10, £4.00, £1.90; EX 112.10 Place 6 £34,985.41, Place 5 £19,960.87.
Owner N P Franklin **Bred** D R Tucker **Trained** Danethorpe, Notts

FOCUS
Park Star ran out a cosy winner of what was a fair race for the grade.
T/Jkpt: Not won. T/Plt: £9,320.90 to a £1 stake. Pool: £53,627.50. 4.20 winning tickets. T/Qpdt: £256.10 to a £1 stake. Pool: £5,260.70. 15.20 winning tickets. JN

6507 WOLVERHAMPTON (A.W) (L-H)
Friday, December 9

OFFICIAL GOING: Standard
Wind: Light behind. Weather: Fine.

6527 PRESS RED TO BET ON ITVI H'CAP — 5f 20y(P)
12:35 (12:35) (Class 6) (0-52,52) 3-Y-O+ — **£2,854** (£842; £421) **Stalls** Low

Form — RPR

0412 **1** **Mambazo**[20] 6385 3-8-7 **50** (e) AdamKirby(3) 3 — 61
(S C Williams) *s.i.s: nt clr run over 2f out: swtchd rt and hdwy whn n.m.r 1f out: r.o wl to ld nr fin* **4/1**[1]

0000 **2** ¾ **Henry Tun**[18] 6407 7-8-8 **51** (v) JasonEdmunds(3) 1 — 59
(J Balding) *a.p: rdn 2f out: led 1f out: hdd nr fin* **11/1**

6535 **3** ½ **St Ivian**[18] 6407 5-8-12 **52** AlanDaly 6 — 58
(Mrs N Macauley) *mid-div: rdn over 2f out: hdwy wl over 1f out: kpt on ins fnl f* **11/2**[2]

4103 **4** 1 **Mind Alert**[9] 6470 4-8-6 **49** (v) PatrickMathers(3) 5 — 52
(D Shaw) *bhd: hdwy on ins 1f out: swtchd rt ins fnl f: nrst fin* **9/1**

2426 **5** ½ **Desert Light (IRE)**[5] 6493 4-8-11 **51** (v) TonyCulhane 11 — 52
(D Shaw) *s.i.s: rdn over 2f out: hdwy on outside fnl f: nt rch ldrs* **8/1**

-005 **6** hd **Urban Rose**[190] 2217 4-8-12 **52** BrianReilly 13 — 52
(J W Unett) *hdwy over 2f out: rdn and edgd lft 1f out: one pce* **25/1**

2100 **7** ½ **Lady Pekan**[18] 6407 6-8-12 **52** (v) J-PGuillambert 2 — 50
(P Howling) *led: rdn over 2f out: hdd 1f out: wknd towards fin* **7/1**

6565 **8** 1 ¼ **New Options**[60] 5803 8-8-12 **52** (b) RobbieFitzpatrick 4 — 46
(Peter Grayson) *towards rr: nt clr run on ins over 3f out: rdn and hdwy over 2f out: cl 3rd whn n.m.r ins fnl f: eased* **13/2**[3]

3000 **9** ¾ **Blue Power (IRE)**[177] 2589 4-8-10 **50** (v) PatCosgrave 7 — 41
(K R Burke) *chsd ldrs: rdn over 2f out: hld whn hmpd 1f out: sn wknd* **25/1**

3265 **10** hd **Blue Moon Hitman (IRE)**[141] 3658 4-8-12 **52** (b) ChrisCatlin 10 — 42
(R Brotherton) *chsd ldr: rdn 2f out: wknd fnl f* **11/1**

2000 **11** 3 ½ **Zimbali**[13] 6438 3-8-10 **50** (p) LPKeniry 9 — 28
(J M Bradley) *bhd fnl 2f* **50/1**

3000 **12** hd **Malahide Express (IRE)**[18] 6407 5-8-10 **50** (tp) JimmyQuinn 8 — 27
(E J Alston) *chsd ldrs: rdn 3f out: sn wknd* **20/1**

62.06 secs (-0.76) **Going Correction** -0.20s/f (Stan) — **12** Ran SP% **113.4**
Speed ratings (Par 101):98,96,96,94,93 93,92,90,89,88 83,83
CSF £44.08 CT £244.03 TOTE £3.30: £1.90, £3.70, £2.00; EX 36.50.
Owner D G Burge **Bred** Barry Taylor **Trained** Newmarket, Suffolk
■ Stewards' Enquiry : Jason Edmunds one-day ban: careless riding (Dec 20)

FOCUS
A moderate contest with only two of the runners not equipped with some kind of headgear. The form looks sound enough with the fourth the best guide.
Mind Alert Official explanation: jockey said gelding was outpaced early

6528 BETDIRECTPOKER.COM MEDIAN AUCTION MAIDEN STKS — 5f 216y(P)
1:10 (1:10) (Class 6) 2-Y-O — **£2,880** (£850; £425) **Stalls** Low

Form — RPR

6 **1** **Tawaaf**[24] 6351 2-9-0 EddieAhern 9 — 67
(P W Chapple-Hyam) *s.i.s: hld up: hdwy on outside over 1f out: sn hung lft: r.o wl to ld cl home* **2/1**[1]

0 **2** ¾ **Bellabelini (IRE)**[13] 6435 2-8-9 JohnEgan 2 — 60
(S Kirk) *a.p: rdn over 2f out: edgd lft and led 1f out: hdd cl home* **4/1**[3]

05 **3** 1 ½ **Night Rainbow (IRE)**[84] 5272 2-8-9 SteveDrowne 3 — 56
(A J Lidderdale) *s.i.s: sn mid-div: hdwy over 2f out: rdn and hung lft over 1f out: nt qckn ins fnl f* **12/1**

00 **4** ¾ **Xpres Boy (IRE)**[128] 4053 2-8-11 AmirQuinn(3) 6 — 58
(S R Bowring) *dwlt: hld up: hdwy over 2f out: rdn whn swtchd rt over 1f out: r.o one pce fnl f* **50/1**

0 **5** ¾ **Coltchester (IRE)**[182] 2468 2-9-0 RobbieFitzpatrick 1 — 56
(Peter Grayson) *s.s: in rr whn rdn 4f out: hdwy wl over 1f out: swtchd lft ins fnl f: r.o* **50/1**

6 1 **Higher Option (IRE)**[47] 6042 2-8-9 PatCosgrave 7 — 48
(Declan Gillespie, Ire) *led after 1f: rdn and hdd 1f out: wknd wl ins fnl f* **14/1**

6 **7** hd **Desert Dust**[41] 6156 2-9-0 ChrisCatlin 10 — 52
(R M H Cowell) *led 1f: w ldr: ev ch over 2f out: sn rdn: wknd 1f out* **10/1**

8 nk **Devine Dancer** 2-8-9 DaneO'Neill 5 — 47
(H Candy) *s.s: late prog: nrst fin* **14/1**

0 **9** 1 **Skylarking (IRE)**[24] 6360 2-8-9 OscarUrbina 8 — 44
(J R Fanshawe) *t.k.h in tch: rdn 2f out: wknd 1f out* **10/3**[2]

00 **10** 1 ¾ **Trick Or Treat**[84] 5275 2-8-9 MickyFenton 13 — 38
(J G Given) *chsd ldrs 2f* **20/1**

00 **11** 12 **Pink Pyjamas**[10] 6456 2-8-9 JoeFanning 12 —
(J A R Toller) *prom 3f* **66/1**

00 **12** 1/2 **Ames Souer (IRE)**13 6433 2-8-6 .... JohnMcAuley(3) 11 —
(D Carroll) stdd s: plld hrd: sn prom: rdn and wknd over 2f out **66/1**

1m 16.19s (0.38) **Going Correction** -0.20s/f (Stan) **12** Ran SP% **118.2**
Speed ratings (Par 94):89,88,86,85,84 82,82,82,80,78 62,61
CSF £9.47 TOTE £2.70: £1.20, £1.70, £2.60; EX 10.90.
Owner Saleh Al Homeizi **Bred** Saleh Al Homaizi **Trained** Newmarket, Suffolk

FOCUS
The best part of a second slower than the following nursery, this was probably only an ordinary maiden with the first two rated as having improved a little on their debut efforts.

NOTEBOOK
Tawaaf built on the promise of his debut last month at Lingfield but again lost some ground at the start and showed signs of inexperience. He eventually got on top with Ahern having to contend with his mount wanting to lean on the runner-up. (op 15-8 tchd 7-4)
Bellabelini(IRE) ◆ was supported by the offices having finished seventh when unfancied on her recent debut over course and distance in what had looked a hot race at the time. She did not let that form down and is clearly going the right way. (op 6-1)
Night Rainbow(IRE) was dropping back from seven having been highly tried on her two outings on turf. This is much more her level.
Xpres Boy(IRE) had shown signs of ability over seven here on his debut in July and a return to a longer trip may help. (op 33-1)
Coltchester(IRE) ◆ stepped up considerably on his course and distance debut in June and further improvement can be expected when he tackles a longer trip. (op 33-1)
Higher Option(IRE), not disgraced in a big field at the Curragh in October, did not quite get home after having far more use made of her this time. (op 20-1)

6529 BETDIRECTCASINO.COM NURSERY 5f 216y(P)
1:45 (1:47) (Class 5) (0-75,70) 2-Y-O **£4,119** (£1,225; £612; £305) **Stalls** Low

Form RPR
3026 **1** **Grenane (IRE)**14 6420 2-9-3 **66** .... JohnEgan 4 68
(P D Evans) hld up in mid-div: n.m.r over 4f out: swtchd rt and hdwy wl over 1f out: r.o u.p to ld cl home **4/1**2
6102 **2** *nk* **Orchard Supreme**4 6501 2-9-2 **68** .... StephaneBreux(3) 9 69
(R Hannon) hld up in tch: rdn and hung lft over 1f out: led ent fnl f: hdd cl home **3/1**1
000 **3** *shd* **Catbang (IRE)**43 6123 2-8-12 **61** .... SteveDrowne 11 62
(N A Callaghan) outpcd: rdn and hdwy on ins wl over 1f out: swtchd rt ins fnl f: r.o wl **9/1**
1430 **4** *1* **Trombone Tom**38 6214 2-9-0 **66** .... PaulMulrennan(3) 13 64
(J R Norton) led after 1f: rdn 2f out: hdd ent fnl f: no ex towards fin **66/1**
6236 **5** *nk* **Gavarnie Beau (IRE)**13 6433 2-9-6 **69** .... FergusSweeney 2 66
(M Blanshard) hld up in mid-div: swtchd rt and hdwy ins fnl f: r.o **7/1**3
3035 **6** *nk* **Egyptian Lord**7 6479 2-8-11 **60** .... RobbieFitzpatrick 7 56
(Peter Grayson) prom: rdn over 2f out: ev ch 1f out: no ex ins fnl f **8/1**
5440 **7** *1* **Make My Dream**37 6226 2-9-1 **64** .... J-PGuillambert 10 57
(J Gallagher) sn chsng ldr: rdn over 2f out: sltly outpcd whn n.m.r over 1f out: swtchd rt ins fnl f: kpt on **33/1**
0014 **8** *hd* **Thoughtsofstardom**28 6312 2-9-7 **70** .... EddieAhern 8 63
(W M Brisbourne) led 1f: prom: rdn and hung lft over 1f out: one pce **7/1**3
2005 **9** *2 1/2* **Deserving**13 6433 2-9-2 **65** .... TonyCulhane 12 50
(W J Haggas) mid-div: rdn over 2f out: sn btn **9/1**
5500 **10** *5* **Scherzo A La Russe (USA)**88 5183 2-8-13 **62** .... LPKeniry 5 32
(A G Newcombe) s.i.s: a bhd **50/1**
1200 **11** *1 3/4* **Upthedowns (IRE)**14 6423 2-8-12 **61** ....(v) ChrisCatlin 1 26
(T D Barron) n.m.r over 4f out: a bhd **8/1**
663 **12** *3/4* **Lady Synthia**39 6197 2-9-2 **65** ....(v1) DaneO'Neill 6 28
(B Palling) a bhd **16/1**
450 **13** *1 1/2* **Mr Cheers**220 1445 2-9-0 **63** .... TomEaves 3 21
(Miss J A Camacho) prom: hmpd and lost pl over 4f out: sn bhd **25/1**

1m 15.36s (-0.45) **Going Correction** -0.20s/f (Stan) **13** Ran SP% **128.3**
Speed ratings (Par 96):95,94,94,93,92 92,91,90,87,80 78,77,75
CSF £17.37 CT £112.85 TOTE £4.40: £1.60, £1.40, £4.90; EX 17.10.
Owner Trevor Gallienne **Bred** Kilnamoragh Stud **Trained** Pandy, Abergavenny
■ Stewards' Enquiry : Paul Mulrennan one-day ban: failed to keep straight from stalls (Dec 20)

FOCUS
This nursery was 0.85 seconds faster than the preceding maiden and the form is sound enough although the field finished in something of a heap.

NOTEBOOK
Grenane(IRE) duly took advantage of the shorter trip but the manner of his victory suggests he will not mind a return to seven. (op 9-2 tchd 7-2)
Orchard Supreme, just touched off over seven at Lingfield earlier in the week, again had to settle for the role of bridesmaid. His young French rider seemed unable to pull his whip through to the correct hand when his mount hung left. (op 7-2 tchd 9-2)
Catbang(IRE) appears to be getting the hang of things and is one to keep an eye on when reverting to seven. (op 6-1 tchd 10-1)
Trombone Tom, dropped 6lb on his sand debut, gave a good account of himself. However, his rider received a one-day ban for not riding to his wide draw.
Gavarnie Beau(IRE) was duly back up to six after his run here last time. He shaped as though he now wants even further. (op 14-1)
Egyptian Lord had no excuses after putting up a personal best in a maiden over course and distance last time. (op 12-1 tchd 15-2)

6530 BETDIRECT.CO.UK H'CAP 7f 32y(P)
2:20 (2:21) (Class 2) (0-100,110) 3-Y-0+ **£12,031** (£3,579; £1,788; £893) **Stalls** High

Form RPR
0612 **1** **Suggestive**69 5614 7-9-12 **108** ....(b) TonyCulhane 7 117
(W J Haggas) s.i.s: sn in tch: led 2f out: sn rdn: r.o wl **5/1**2
6612 **2** *2* **Appalachian Trail (IRE)**28 6314 4-9-0 **96** ....(b) TomEaves 9 100+
(I Semple) hld up: hdwy over 2f out: rdn wl over 1f out: r.o ins fnl f: nt trble wnr **9/2**1
0005 **3** *1 1/2* **Moayed**7 6481 6-9-6 **102** ....(bt) HayleyTurner 4 102
(N P Littmoden) s.i.s: sn in tch: rdn wl over 1f out: one pce fnl f **17/2**
3023 **4** *hd* **Looks Could Kill (USA)**7 6481 3-8-4 **86** oh2................. JimmyQuinn 1 85+
(E J Alston) chsd ldr: led over 5f out: rdn and hdd 2f out: no ex fnl f **15/2**
0001 **5** *1/2* **Chateau Nicol**14 6421 6-8-6 **88** ....(v) JoeFanning 5 86
(B G Powell) a.p: rdn 2f out: one pce fnl f **16/1**
0211 **6** *shd* **Red Spell (IRE)**13 6431 4-9-4 **100** .... DaneO'Neill 11 98+
(R Hannon) hld up: rdn wl over 1f out: kpt on ins fnl f: nt trble ldrs **5/1**2
-266 **7** *1/2* **One More Round (USA)**90 5136 7-9-8 **104** .... IanMongan 8 101
(N P Littmoden) bhd: rdn and hdwy on ins wl over 1f out: no further prog fnl f **25/1**
1053 **8** *3 1/2* **Cornus**6 6489 3-8-4 **86** oh1 .... ChrisCatlin 12 73
(M J Polglase) a bhd **33/1**
6105 **9** *1 1/4* **Rafferty (IRE)**38 6216 6-8-1 **86** oh1 .... NelsonDeSouza(3) 3 70
(T D Barron) led over 1f: rdn over 3f out: wknd over 2f out **10/1**
022 **10** *3/4* **Vortex**84 5269 6-10-0 **110** ....(t) MickyFenton 6 92
(Miss Gay Kelleway) hld up: sn mid-div: towards rr whn nt clr run over 2f out: n.d after **6/1**3
2300 **11** *10* **King Marju (IRE)**34 6252 3-9-0 **96** .... RobertWinston 10 52
(K R Burke) prom: rdn over 3f out: wknd over 2f out **14/1**

1m 27.44s (-2.96) **Going Correction** -0.20s/f (Stan) **11** Ran SP% **116.5**
Speed ratings (Par 109):108,105,104,103,103 103,102,98,97,96 84
CSF £27.49 CT £191.60 TOTE £6.60: £2.40, £1.60, £3.30; EX 40.90.
Owner Mrs Barbara Bassett **Bred** Keith Freeman **Trained** Newmarket, Suffolk

FOCUS
A classy turnout for some decent prizemoney and the track record was broken despite an apparent lack of pace early on. The form seems sound enoughrated through the first two.

NOTEBOOK
Suggestive, making his All-Weather debut, was on a fact-finding mission with regard to a trip to the UAE. This triple Listed winner came through with flying colours and now heads to Dubai for the winter. (op 13-2)
Appalachian Trail(IRE) stuck to his task without causing the winner much anxiety and ran as if he will not mind a return to a mile. (op 4-1 tchd 5-1)
Moayed, set to drop 2lb in future handicaps, was back up to a more suitable distance but he was taking on some useful sorts. (op 8-1 tchd 9-1)
Looks Could Kill(USA), again just out of the handicap proper, had finished a length in front of Moayed on identical terms over six here last week. (op 12-1)
Chateau Nicol had been raised 3lb for beating Looks Could Kill by half a length over six here last time. (tchd 20-1)
Red Spell(IRE) was trying to complete a hat-trick having been raised a total of 11lb after breaking the course records over both seven furlongs and a mile at Lingfield. (op 7-2)
One More Round(USA) Official explanation: vet said gelding returned unsound
Vortex Official explanation: trainer said gelding injured its back

6531 BIG CHIEF T-BOX AT RUMMY'S BAR MAIDEN STKS (DIV I) 7f 32y(P)
2:55 (2:56) (Class 5) 2-Y-0 **£3,698** (£1,100; £549; £274) **Stalls** High

Form RPR
6 **1** **Red Cape (FR)**24 6349 2-9-0 .... JohnEgan 9 84
(N A Callaghan) a.p: rdn over 2f out: hung lft fr over 1f out: led ins fnl f: r.o **15/8**1
4 **2** *shd* **Lunar Express (USA)**121 4267 2-8-9 .... TonyCulhane 4 79
(W J Haggas) led: rdn wl over 1f out: hdd ins fnl f: r.o **5/2**2
3 *5* **Summertime Parkes** 2-8-9 .... DaneO'Neill 8 66
(H Candy) s.i.s: t.k.h: hdwy over 5f out: one pce fnl 2f **9/2**3
00 **4** *1 1/4* **Gibbs Camp**24 6349 2-8-9 .... SteveDrowne 12 63
(E A L Dunlop) hld up: hdwy over 3f out: rdn and edgd lft wl over 1f out: one pce **14/1**
0 **5** *10* **Boucheen**18 6402 2-9-0 .... J-PGuillambert 10 43
(Ms Deborah J Evans) prom: rdn over 3f out: wknd over 2f out **66/1**
0 **6** *shd* **Mussorgsky (USA)**41 6148 2-9-0 ....(t) RobertWinston 1 43
(Sir Michael Stoute) s.i.s: bhd: rdn 3f out: sme hdwy over 1f out: nvr nr ldrs **9/1**
0 **7** *3/4* **Great Composer (IRE)**13 6427 2-9-0 .... EddieAhern 7 41
(Mrs A J Perrett) s.i.s: bhd: sme hdwy over 1f out: n.d **14/1**
0 **8** *shd* **Dark Night (IRE)**24 6360 2-9-0 .... TomEaves 3 41
(D W Barker) hld up in mid-div: rdn 3f out: sn struggling **50/1**
9 *1* **Sorrel Point** 2-9-0 .... JimmyQuinn 5 38
(H J Collingridge) s.i.s: bhd: short-lived effrt over 2f out **40/1**
10 *1 1/2* **Go Amwell** 2-9-0 .... LPKeniry 2 35
(J R Jenkins) s.s: a bhd **66/1**
0 **11** *3* **Kissimee**196 2039 2-8-9 .... MickyFenton 6 22
(N P Littmoden) w ldr: rdn over 3f out: wknd over 2f out **50/1**
00 **12** *10* **Bournonville**13 6428 2-9-0 .... HayleyTurner 11 —
(J Ryan) mid-div: rdn over 3f out: sn bhd **40/1**

1m 29.41s (-0.99) **Going Correction** -0.20s/f (Stan) **12** Ran SP% **116.7**
Speed ratings (Par 96):97,96,91,89,78 78,77,77,76,74 70,59
CSF £6.17 TOTE £3.20: £2.00, £1.30, £1.70; EX 7.40.
Owner Franconson Partners **Bred** G And Mrs Forien **Trained** Newmarket, Suffolk
■ John Egan's 100th winner of the season, his first century.
■ Stewards' Enquiry : John Egan caution: careless riding

FOCUS
This maiden was over a second faster than the following division and the form looks sound and fairly strong.

NOTEBOOK
Red Cape(FR) ◆, who had shaped promisingly over six at Lingfield last month, just managed to hold on after showing signs of inexperience. He is going the right way and there should be further improvement to come. (tchd 7-4)
Lunar Express(USA) ◆ had shown ability on her debut at Yarmouth back in August. She lost no caste in defeat and should have little difficulty going one better. (op 10-3 tchd 7-2)
Summertime Parkes, who has plenty of speed on her dam's side, may have been unable to go with the two principals but there was still a lot to like about this debut. (op 3-1)
Gibbs Camp had finished a whisker behind Red Cape over six furlongs at Lingfield last month. (op 12-1)

6532 BIG CHIEF T-BOX AT RUMMY'S BAR MAIDEN STKS (DIV II) 7f 32y(P)
3:30 (3:34) (Class 5) 2-Y-0 **£3,698** (£1,100; £549; £274) **Stalls** High

Form RPR
1 **Bentong (IRE)** 2-9-0 .... JoeFanning 11 72+
(P F I Cole) a.p: led over 2f out: clr over 1f out: eased cl home **5/1**3
2 *3 1/2* **Flying Rani (IRE)**55 5909 2-8-9 .... PatCosgrave 10 56
(Declan Gillespie, Ire) hld up in tch: rdn and wnt 2nd over 1f out: no ch w wnr **14/1**
06 **3** *nk* **Hilltop Destiny**41 6148 2-9-0 .... MichaelTebbutt 6 61
(V Smith) s.i.s: hld up and bhd: hdwy over 3f out: rdn wl over 1f out: kpt on ins fnl f **16/1**
0 **4** *1/2* **Making Moves**14 6424 2-8-9 .... JohnEgan 12 54
(Ms Deborah J Evans) hld up in tch: rdn wl over 1f out: one pce **66/1**
0 **5** *3/4* **Malakiya (IRE)**67 5667 2-9-0 .... AlanDaly 8 57
(G A Butler) s.s: hld up in rr: hdwy fnl f: nrst fin **9/2**2
06 **6** *nk* **Swayze (IRE)**35 6242 2-9-0 .... MickyFenton 7 57
(N P Littmoden) hld up: hdwy over 2f out: one pce fnl f **7/1**
06 **7** *1 1/4* **Marachi Band (USA)**7 6477 2-8-9 .... SteveDrowne 4 49
(E A L Dunlop) chsd ldrs: rdn over 2f out: wknd over 1f out **4/1**1
0 **8** *3/4* **Red Vixen (IRE)**43 6122 2-8-9 .... OscarUrbina 4 47
(C N Allen) prom tl wknd fnl f **25/1**
9 *2* **Trimlestown (IRE)** 2-9-0 .... DaneO'Neill 2 47
(H Candy) hld up in mid-div: rdn over 2f out: eased whn btn fnl f **5/1**3
0 **10** *3 1/2* **Brabinger (IRE)**13 6427 2-9-0 .... LPKeniry 1 38
(B G Powell) sn led: rdn and hdd over 2f out: wknd jst over 1f out **33/1**
0 **11** *3/4* **Valentino Taffi**27 6332 2-8-7 .... EstherRemmerswaal(7) 9 36
(S C Williams) s.i.s: a bhd **33/1**

12 3 ½ **Billy Bling (IRE)** 2-9-0 ChrisCatlin 3 27
(R Hannon) *led early: chsd ldr: wknd 2f out* **6/1**

1m 30.68s (0.28) **Going Correction** -0.20s/f (Stan) 12 Ran SP% **122.1**
Speed ratings (Par 96):90,86,85,85,84 83,82,81,79,75 74,70
CSF £72.60 TOTE £5.10: £2.00, £4.80, £4.00; EX 87.20.
Owner H R H Sultan Ahmad Shah **Bred** J Egan, J Corcoran And J Judd **Trained** Whatcombe, Oxon

FOCUS
This was 1.27 seconds slower than the first division and despite the winner scoring well it is hard to set the level for the form.

NOTEBOOK
Bentong(IRE) ◆, a half-brother to a six-furlong juvenile winner in France, had been taught his job well and made a highly satisfactory debut. He could have won by a wider margin and despite the fact the time was slow he appears to have a bright future. (op 4-1)
Flying Rani(IRE) got the better of the separate battle for the runner-up spot but is flattered by her proximity to the winner. A step up to a mile could help. (op 12-1)
Hilltop Destiny, a half-brother to mile winner Hilltop Rhapsody, had been highly tried in a couple of back-end maidens at Newmarket. He will not mind a return to a mile. (tchd 20-1)
Making Moves improved on her debut over the stretch mile here a fortnight earlier.
Malakiya(IRE) ◆ is a brother to mile and a half winner Time Crystal and ten-furlong winner True Crystal. Not knocked about after again losing ground at the start, he is being brought along quietly and should come into his own when stepped up in distance. (op 8-1)
Swayze(IRE) appeared to handle the surface after a couple of outings over six on soft ground late in the turf season. (op 13-2 tchd 6-1)

6533 LITTLEWOODS BETDIRECT H'CAP 1m 141y(P)
4:00 (4:00) (Class 4) (0-85,85) 3-Y-O+ £5,748 (£1,710; £854; £426) Stalls Low

Form				RPR
0602	1		**Hail The Chief**[10] [6458] 8-9-2 **85** DaneO'Neill 3 (R Hannon) *sn led: rdn clr wl over 1f out: drvn out* **11/2**[3]	93
0000	2	1	**Claret And Amber**[20] [6379] 3-8-9 **80** (b¹) TonyHamilton 10 (R A Fahey) *hld up and bhd: hdwy on outside 3f out: sn rdn: r.o ins fnl f: nt rch wnr* **25/1**	86
0603	3	½	**Master Theo (USA)**[28] [6314] 4-9-2 **85** (p) JohnEgan 6 (Julian Poulton) *hld up in mid-div: hdwy on ins 3f out: rdn 2f out: kpt on ins fnl f* **9/2**[2]	90
0031	4	hd	**Obrigado (USA)**[27] [6322] 5-8-11 **80** TonyCulhane 13 (W J Haggas) *hld up and bhd: hdwy over 2f out: rdn and hung lft fr over 1f out: kpt on towards fin* **8/1**	84
0200	5	1	**Following Flow (USA)**[41] [6159] 3-8-7 **78** (p) LPKeniry 9 (R Hollinshead) *bhd: sn pushed along: rdn and hdwy over 2f out: bmpd ins fnl f: one pce* **50/1**	80
5015	6	2 ½	**Dr Thong**[10] [6458] 4-8-10 **79** EddieAhern 1 (P F I Cole) *led early: prom: rdn to chse wnr over 2f out tl over 1f out: sn wknd* **13/2**	76
5056	7	1 ¼	**Stoic Leader (IRE)**[10] [6458] 5-8-6 **75** JimmyQuinn 2 (R F Fisher) *hld up in mid-div: rdn and lost pl whn nt clr run briefly on ins 3f out: hdwy over 2f out: sn no imp* **16/1**	69
1330	8	hd	**Eastborough (IRE)**[117] [4389] 6-8-8 **77** FergusSweeney 4 (B G Powell) *s.i.s: bhd: styd on fnl f: n.d* **66/1**	71
0500	9	½	**Te Quiero**[13] [6431] 7-9-2 **85** (t) SteveDrowne 12 (Miss Gay Kelleway) *hld up and bhd: short-lived effrt over 1f out* **40/1**	78
0066	10	10	**Sea Storm (IRE)**[27] [6322] 7-8-5 **79** GregFairley(5) 7 (D R MacLeod) *prom: rdn over 3f out: wknd over 2f out* **20/1**	51
2100	11	1 ½	**Overlord Way (GR)**[13] [6437] 3-8-9 **80** IanMongan 11 (P R Chamings) *w ldr tl rdn and wknd qckly over 2f out* **16/1**	49
2565	12	3	**Libre**[65] [4183] 5-8-8 **77** ow1 MickyFenton 5 (F Jordan) *prom: rdn over 3f out: wknd over 2f out* **25/1**	39
1-6	13	4	**Zarabad (IRE)**[67] [5660] 3-8-11 **82** RobertWinston 8 (K R Burke) *hld up in mid-div: lost pl 3f out: sn bhd* **5/2**[1]	36

1m 47.93s (-3.83) **Going Correction** -0.20s/f (Stan)
WFA 3 from 4yo+ 2lb 13 Ran SP% **116.7**
Speed ratings (Par 105):109,108,107,107,106 104,103,103,102,93 92,89,86
CSF £143.00 CT £698.81 TOTE £6.30: £1.90, £5.60, £1.90; EX 134.20.
Owner Peter M Crane **Bred** Green Meadow Stud And P Crane **Trained** East Everleigh, Wilts
■ Stewards' Enquiry : Ian Mongan caution: allowed colt to coast home without assistance

FOCUS
A decent handicap and a strong pace led to a fast time. The third sets the standard, backed up by those immediately behind him..
Zarabad(IRE) Official explanation: trainer had no explanation for the poor form shown

6534 BETDIRECT FREEPHONE 0800 211 222 APPRENTICE H'CAP 1m 5f 194y(P)
4:30 (4:32) (Class 6) (0-65,65) 3-Y-O+ £2,926 (£864; £432) Stalls Low

Form				RPR
5301	1		**Piper General (IRE)**[18] [6405] 3-9-7 **65** TomEaves 11 (J Mackie) *t.k.h early in mid-div: hdwy over 5f out: rdn over 2f out: led jst over 1f out: styd on wl* **4/1**[3]	81+
6433	2	3 ½	**York Cliff**[14] [6419] 7-9-4 **55** PatrickMathers 5 (W M Brisbourne) *s.s: hld up in rr: stdy hdwy over 4f out: rdn whn carried rt over 1f out: styd on ins fnl f: nt trble winn* **12/1**	61
6000	3	1 ½	**Petite Paramour (IRE)**[32] [6283] 4-9-9 **60** AdamKirby 3 (Miss Gay Kelleway) *s.i.s: sn in tch: rdn over 2f out: edgd rt over 1f out: kpt on ins fnl f* **50/1**	64
4600	4	¾	**Lady Misha**[51] [5983] 3-9-1 **59** PaulMulrennan 9 (Jedd O'Keeffe) *chsd ldrs: rdn to ld over 2f out: hdd jst over 1f out: one pce* **22/1**	62
240-	5	1 ¼	**Valeureux**[8] [4015] 7-8-6 **50** AdamCarter(7) 4 (J Hetherton) *s.i.s: bhd: rdn over 4f out: hdwy over 1f out: styd on ins fnl f* **33/1**	51
3015	6	shd	**Spitting Image (IRE)**[6] [6490] 5-9-7 **61** GregFairley(3) 6 (M Johnston) *hld up in tch: rdn and no hdwy fnl 2f* **9/4**[1]	62
5000	7	½	**Entailment**[24] [6362] 3-9-2 **65** RonanKeogh(5) 12 (Miss Gay Kelleway) *hld up: hdwy over 5f out: wnt 2nd over 2f out: edgd lft over 1f out: wknd fnl f* **28/1**	65
6024	8	1 ½	**Sugitani (USA)**[18] [6400] 3-8-4 **55** JamesMillman(7) 8 (N B King) *nvr nr ldrs* **11/1**	53
6000	9	nk	**Pearson Glen (IRE)**[14] [5770] 6-8-8 **52** (tp) KatieHales(7) 13 (James Moffatt) *s.i.s: hdwy over 3f out: sn no imp* **50/1**	50
4051	10	3 ½	**Cumbrian Knight (IRE)**[11] [6448] 7-9-3 **61** 6ex PaulPickard(7) 7 (J M Jefferson) *sn prom: wkng whn n.m.r over 3f out* **11/4**[2]	54
0034	11	1 ¼	**Movie King (IRE)**[7] [6478] 6-9-8 **59** (t) AmirQuinn 2 (S R Bowring) *led: rdn over 4f out: hdd and hmpd on ins over 2f out: sn wknd* **12/1**	50
006	12	13	**Almisq (USA)**[24] [6355] 4-8-1 **45** MarvinCheung(7) 10 (J Ryan) *a bhd* **66/1**	18
0663	P		**Mischief**[41] [6152] 9-8-5 **42** oh2 NeilChalmers 1 (Mrs H Sweeting) *a bhd: t.o 6f out: p.u 4f out* **20/1**	—

3m 2.96s (-4.41) **Going Correction** -0.20s/f (Stan)
WFA 3 from 4yo+ 7lb 13 Ran SP% **122.1**
Speed ratings (Par 101):104,102,101,100,100 99,99,98,98,96 95,88,—
CSF £48.45 CT £2122.02 TOTE £6.00: £1.70, £2.40, £9.10; EX 43.10 Place 6 £33.89, Place 5 £17.53.
Owner Fools Who Dream **Bred** Edward And Mrs S Hannigan **Trained** Church Broughton , Derbys

FOCUS
A distinctly moderate handicap although the time was fair.
Mischief Official explanation: jockey said gelding badly lost its action; vet said gelding returned lame in both front legs
T/Plt: £48.00 to a £1 stake. Pool: £36,462.55. 553.70 winning tickets. T/Qpdt: £17.40 to a £1 stake. Pool: £3,637.70. 154.40 winning tickets. KH

6513 SOUTHWELL (L-H)
Saturday, December 10

OFFICIAL GOING: Standard
The surface was described as 'the usual slow and hard work'.
Wind: Almost nil Weather: Fine

6535 BETDIRECTCASINO.COM H'CAP (DIV I) 1m (F)
11:30 (11:32) (Class 6) (0-65,68) 3-Y-O+ £3,046 (£906; £453; £226) Stalls Low

Form				RPR
3533	1		**Chicken Soup**[31] [6298] 3-8-10 **62** DanielTudhope(3) 14 (D Carroll) *trckd ldrs on outer: led 2f out: hld on wl towards fin* **10/1**	70
0021	2	¾	**Parkview Love (USA)**[4] [6514] 4-9-3 **68** 7ex (v) PatrickMathers(3) 8 (D Shaw) *trckd ldrs: effrt over 2f out: no ex ins last* **6/1**[2]	74
0000	3	1	**Blue Empire (IRE)**[7] [6487] 4-8-5 **53** AlanDaly 2 (C R Dore) *t.k.h: trckd ldrs: outpcd 4f out: kpt on to chse ldrs 2f out: styd on same pce fnl f* **20/1**	57
6005	4	nk	**Quiet Reading (USA)**[19] [6400] 8-8-2 **50** (v) HayleyTurner 4 (M R Bosley) *mid-div: hdwy to chse ldrs 2f out: kpt on same pce fnl f* **12/1**	53
250	5	3	**Highliner**[37] [6236] 3-8-11 **60** TomEaves 6 (Mrs L Williamson) *s.i.s: hdwy over 2f out: styd on fnl f* **40/1**	57
6020	6	4	**Bridgewater Boys**[46] [6103] 4-8-2 **57** (b) DeanHeslop(7) 5 (K A Ryan) *s.s: hdwy on ins over 2f out: nvr rchd ldrs* **6/1**[2]	46+
0061	7	3	**Aswan (IRE)**[14] [6436] 7-8-13 **64** (t) AmirQuinn(3) 7 (S R Bowring) *led tl 2f out: sn wknd* **8/1**[3]	47
0605	8	shd	**King Of Knight (IRE)**[14] [6432] 4-9-0 **62** (v) ChrisCatlin 11 (G Prodromou) *s.i.s: racd wd: nvr nrr* **14/1**	45+
-066	9	1 ½	**Play Master (IRE)**[218] [1510] 4-9-2 **64** PaulEddery 12 (B Smart) *w ldrs on outer: wknd 2f out* **12/1**	44
0653	10	1 ¼	**Bavarica**[24] [6365] 3-8-1 **57** DonnaCaldwell(7) 13 (Miss J Feilden) *sn in rr* **8/1**[3]	35
1420	11	3 ½	**Burnley Al (IRE)**[62] [5773] 3-8-12 **61** (p) PaulHanagan 9 (R A Fahey) *trckd ldrs: effrt 3f out: sn lost pl* **10/1**	32
2200	12	1 ¼	**Friends Hope**[82] [5359] 4-8-13 **61** FergalLynch 3 (P A Blockley) *s.s: a bhd* **16/1**	29+
2011	13	3	**Formidable Will (FR)**[53] [5960] 3-9-1 **64** (p) DaleGibson 10 (M W Easterby) *sn pushed along: a in rr* **9/2**[1]	26
-010	14	3 ½	**Lobengula (IRE)**[25] [3355] 3-8-13 **62** RobertWinston 1 (I W McInnes) *s.i.s: sn chsng ldrs: wknd over 2f out: eased fnl f* **25/1**	17

1m 44.31s (-0.29) **Going Correction** -0.125s/f (Stan)
WFA 3 from 4yo+ 1lb 14 Ran SP% **126.1**
Speed ratings (Par 101):96,95,94,93,90 86,83,83,82,81 77,76,73,69
CSF £70.82 CT £1245.09 TOTE £13.60: £3.20, £2.10, £7.90; EX 110.40.
Owner Fishlake Commercial Motors Ltd **Bred** Limestone Stud **Trained** Warthill, N Yorks

FOCUS
Sound but limited form rated through the third. It was difficult to make ground from off the pace.
Friends Hope Official explanation: jockey said filly missed break and was bumped on leaving stalls
Formidable Will(FR) Official explanation: jockey said gelding never travelled
Lobengula(IRE) Official explanation: jockey said gelding never travelled and hung right-handed straight

6536 BETDIRECT NO Q ON 08000 93 66 93 CLAIMING STKS 1m 3f (F)
12:00 (12:00) (Class 6) 3-4-Y-O £2,839 (£838; £419) Stalls Low

Form				RPR
	1		**Chater Knight (IRE)**[643] 4-8-11 SteveDrowne 2 (W R Muir) *chsd ldrs: outpcd over 3f out: rallied over 1f out: styd on to ld last 75yds* **10/1**[3]	63
5220	2	¾	**Desperation (IRE)**[78] [5431] 3-9-7 70 RobertWinston 1 (K R Burke) *led 1f: chsd ldr: effrt over 3f out: led over 2f out tl hdd and no ex wl ins last* **4/1**[2]	76
0063	3	8	**Weet A Head (IRE)**[8] [6478] 4-9-7 64 (p) TonyCulhane 8 (R Hollinshead) *mid-div: pushed along 7f out: one pce fnl 4f: tk modest 3rd wl ins last* **7/2**[1]	59
4600	4	1	**Yashin (IRE)**[11] [6468] 4-8-9 49 (b¹) HayleyTurner 7 (P A Blockley) *led after 1f: hdd over 2f out: wknd fnl f* **16/1**	46
00B0	5	5	**Come What July (IRE)**[8] [6478] 4-9-2 80 (v) MarcHalford(5) 3 (Mrs N Macauley) *hld up in rr: rdn 4f out: nvr on terms* **12/1**	50
1010	6	2 ½	**Midnight Lace**[21] [6373] 3-9-0 65 EddieAhern 9 (J R Boyle) *in rr: hdwy on outside 5f out: lost pl over 3f out* **4/1**[2]	43
0030	7	3	**Je Suis Belle**[8] [6478] 3-8-6 60 ow2 JohnEgan 5 (Miss Gay Kelleway) *mid-div: drvn along 7f out: lost pl over 3f out* **7/2**[1]	30
0250	8	21	**Fools Entire**[5] [6508] 4-8-9 48 (p) AlanDaly 4 (Miss J Feilden) *chsd ldrs: rdn and lost pl over 5f out: t.o 3f out* **50/1**	—
1053	9	8	**Bellalou**[37] [2976] 3-8-4 52 (t) ChrisCatlin 6 (Mrs S A Watt) *bhd and drvn along 5f out: t.o 3f out* **16/1**	—

2m 26.5s (-2.40) **Going Correction** -0.125s/f (Stan)
WFA 3 from 4yo 4lb 9 Ran SP% **115.0**
Speed ratings (Par 101):103,102,96,95,92 90,88,73,67
CSF £49.58 TOTE £10.90: £2.80, £1.40, £1.60; EX 56.10.The winner was claimed by M D Hammond for £7,000
Owner M J Caddy **Bred** John McLoughlin **Trained** Lambourn, Berks

FOCUS
An uncompetitive claimer but the runner-up looked back to something like his old self and sets the standard.
Desperation(IRE) Official explanation: jockey said gelding hung right-handed straight
Midnight Lace Official explanation: jockey said filly never travelled

The Form Book, Raceform Ltd, Compton, RG20 6NL

6537 BETDIRECT.CO.UK MAIDEN STKS — 1m 4f (F)
12:30 (12:30) (Class 5) 3-4-Y-O — **£3,303** (£982; £491; £245) **Stalls** Low

Form — RPR

0606 **1** **Sri Lipis**[14] 6432 3-9-0 68 ......(b) JoeFanning 1 — 73+
(P F I Cole) *trckd ldr: shkn up to ld 2f out: clr whn heavily eased wl ins last* **3/1**[2]

4062 **2** *4* **Newnham (IRE)**[30] 6307 4-9-5 71 ...... EddieAhern 6 — 63
(J R Boyle) *trckd ldrs: drvn along over 3f out: kpt on to take 2nd 1f out: no ch w wnr* **10/11**[1]

0240 **3** *¾* **Sugitani (USA)**[1] 6534 3-9-0 55 ...... JamieMackay 5 — 62
(N B King) *hld up in rr: drvn along over 4f out: kpt on fnl 2f* **16/1**

0322 **4** *6* **Silsong (USA)**[19] 6405 3-8-9 51 ......(b) JohnEgan 4 — 47
(Miss Gay Kelleway) *led: hdd 2f out: wknd fnl f* **6/1**[3]

5 *24* **Antrim (IRE)** 3-9-0 ...... PaulHanagan 2 — 14
(R A Fahey) *trckd ldrs: shkn up 7f out: rdn and outpcd over 4f out: sn bhd* **7/1**

6 *7* **Kalaam** 3-8-9 ...... RobynBrisland(5) 3 — 3
(G P Enright) *s.s: hdwy on outside to chse ldrs 7f out: rdn over 4f out: sn wknd and bhd* **66/1**

2m 42.77s (0.68) **Going Correction** -0.125s/f (Stan)
WFA 3 from 4yo 5lb — **6** Ran SP% **111.5**
Speed ratings (Par 103):92,89,88,84,68 64
CSF £6.03 TOTE £4.50: £1.70, £1.50; EX 9.00.
Owner H R H Sultan Ahmad Shah **Bred** Lordship Stud **Trained** Whatcombe, Oxon

FOCUS
A moderate winning time and the 55-rated third holds down the level of the form.
Antrim(IRE) Official explanation: vet said gelding returned lame

6538 EUROPEAN BREEDERS FUND MAIDEN STKS — 1m (F)
1:05 (1:06) (Class 5) 2-Y-O — **£4,061** (£1,208; £603; £301) **Stalls** Low

Form — RPR

22 **1** **Bull Market (IRE)**[14] 6425 2-9-0 ...... EddieAhern 7 — 76
(J A Osborne) *led after 1f: qcknd 3f out: styd on wl fnl f* **10/11**[1]

5422 **2** *1 ¼* **Salute The General**[15] 6417 2-9-0 77 ...... SteveDrowne 4 — 73
(W R Muir) *trckd ldrs: wnt 2nd over 2f out: kpt on same pce fnl f: no real imp* **11/8**[2]

020 **3** *3 ½* **Ohana**[28] 6332 2-9-0 72 ......(p) JohnEgan 5 — 66
(N A Callaghan) *trckd ldrs: outpcd over 2f out: styd on to take mod 3rd 1f out* **12/1**[3]

0 **4** *5* **Subsidise (IRE)**[8] 6477 2-9-0 ...... FergalLynch 8 — 55
(J G Given) *trckd ldrs: edgd rt 2f out: sn wknd* **66/1**

06 **5** *1 ¼* **Bond Cruz**[37] 6234 2-9-0 ...... PaulEddery 6 — 52
(B Smart) *sn trckng ldrs: lost pl over 1f out* **33/1**

3506 **6** *18* **Macs All Heart (IRE)**[21] 6375 2-8-9 45 ...... HayleyTurner 3 — 7
(A B Coogan) *led 1f: t.k.h: outpcd over 4f out: lost pl 3f out: sn bhd* **100/1**

7 *dist* **Keenstar** 2-8-9 ...... PaulHanagan 1 — —
(Jedd O'Keeffe) *s.i.s: in rr and drvn along: t.o 3f out: virtualy p.u: btn 95l* **125/1**

1m 43.8s (-0.80) **Going Correction** -0.125s/f (Stan) — **7** Ran SP% **108.4**
Speed ratings (Par 96):99,97,94,89,88 70,—
CSF £2.07 TOTE £1.70: £1.10, £1.50; EX 2.50.
Owner Michael Tabor **Bred** King Bloodstock **Trained** Upper Lambourn, Berks

FOCUS
The first two proved much too good in a fair maiden by Southwell-race standards and set the level for the form.

NOTEBOOK
Bull Market(IRE), making his Fibresand debut, looked a couple of sizes bigger than the runner-up. He stepped up the pace turning in and always looked like coming out on top. (op 5-6 tchd Evens)
Salute The General, another having his first outing on Fibresand, went in pursuit of the much bigger winner but in truth never really looked like finishing anything but second best. (op 13-8 tchd 5-4)
Ohana, in first-time cheekpieces, kept on in his own time after being left behind and will be suited by an even stiffer test. (op 9-1)
Subsidise(IRE) showed a fair bit more than on his Polytrack debut a week ago. (op 50-1)
Bond Cruz had shown little in two backend outings on turf. (op 25-1)

6539 BETDIRECTPOKER.COM NURSERY — 1m (F)
1:40 (1:42) (Class 5) (0-75,77) 2-Y-O — **£3,393** (£1,009; £504; £252) **Stalls** Low

Form — RPR

0420 **1** **Magical Music**[36] 6244 2-7-13 53 ow1 ...... JimmyQuinn 6 — 62
(J Pearce) *w ldrs: led over 2f out: edgd lft: styd on wl fnl f* **16/1**

0044 **2** *¾* **Song Of Silence (USA)**[15] 6423 2-8-6 60 ...... PaulHanagan 2 — 67
(E A L Dunlop) *trckd ldrs: kpt on wl appr fnl f: no ex towards fin* **9/1**

0062 **3** *3* **Mambo Sun**[11] 6467 2-8-10 64 ......(p) FergalLynch 9 — 65
(P A Blockley) *w ldrs on outer: kpt on same pce appr fnl f* **9/2**[2]

024 **4** *2 ½* **Mighty Dancer (IRE)**[11] 6467 2-8-5 59 ...... EddieAhern 7 — 54
(S Kirk) *sn mid-div: effrt on inner and sltly hmpd over 2f out: styd on fnl f* **9/2**[2]

0421 **5** *1 ¾* **Moi Aussi (USA)**[11] 6467 2-9-7 77 ......(b) JamieMackay 1 — 68
(Sir Mark Prescott) *w ldrs: edgd lft over 1f out: edgd rt and one pce fnl f* **5/1**[3]

0350 **6** *½* **Ten Shun**[11] 6466 2-8-0 54 ...... HayleyTurner 4 — 44
(M J Polglase) *chsd ldrs: wknd over 1f out* **66/1**

0604 **7** *3 ½* **Baltic Rhapsody**[25] 6359 2-8-2 59 ...... AdamKirby(3) 14 — 42
(M A Jarvis) *prom on outer: outpcd over 2f out: kpt on fnl f* **14/1**

0040 **8** *¾* **Macs Ransom (USA)**[117] 4420 2-8-9 63 ...... JohnEgan 10 — 44
(N A Callaghan) *reluctant to enter stalls: hld up in tch: effrt on outer over 2f out: sn rdn and btn* **4/1**[1]

5600 **9** *2* **Monte Mayor Junior**[11] 6467 2-8-1 58 ...... RichardThomas(3) 11 — 35
(D Haydn Jones) *in rr: sme hdwy on outer 2f out: nvr on terms* **33/1**

0050 **10** *4* **George The Second**[30] 6304 2-8-2 56 ...... ChrisCatlin 12 — 24
(Mrs H Sweeting) *chsd ldrs: lost pl 2f out* **18/1**

603 **11** *1 ¼* **Ansells Joy**[15] 6417 2-8-13 67 ...... DerekMcGaffin 13 — 32
(B Smart) *mid-div on outer: nvr a threat* **66/1**

0003 **12** *6* **Twentyfirst Dansar**[21] 6386 2-8-0 57 ......(v) EdwardCreighton(3) 8 — 9
(A D Smith) *mde most: hdd over 2f out: sn wknd* **33/1**

003 **13** *3* **Sahara Style**[19] 6402 2-8-10 64 ...... TonyCulhane 5 — 9
(R Hollinshead) *in rr: detached 3f out* **20/1**

6042 **14** *4* **Royal Embrace**[25] 6357 2-8-0 57 ...... PatrickMathers(3) 3 — —
(D Shaw) *bhd and drvn along: detached 3f out* **18/1**

1m 43.28s (-1.32) **Going Correction** -0.125s/f (Stan) — **14** Ran SP% **119.7**
Speed ratings (Par 96):101,100,97,94,93 92,89,88,86,82 81,75,72,68
CSF £146.30 CT £788.08 TOTE £20.00: £4.10, £2.90, £1.40; EX 185.70.
Owner Killarney Glen & Mrs E M Clarke **Bred** Peter Taplin **Trained** Newmarket, Suffolk

FOCUS
A decent pace and the first three finished well strung out with the runner-up perhaps the best guide to the overall value of the form, which is pretty solid.

NOTEBOOK
Magical Music, having just her second outing for this stable, took this under bottom weight showing a willing attitude.
Song Of Silence(USA), who banged her head in the stalls last time, proved suited by the step up in trip and went down fighting. (tchd 8-1)
Mambo Sun, in cheekpieces rather than blinkers, turned the tables on Moi Aussi on the revised terms. (op 15-2)
Mighty Dancer(IRE), renewing rivalry with Moi Aussie and Mambo Sun, did well considering he raced on the slower part of the track and met trouble in running. (tchd 7-2)
Moi Aussi(USA) found the 8lb hike in the ratings too much. (op 7-2 tchd 6-1)
Ten Shun, with the blinkers left off, ran his best race so far on his third start for this yard. (op 50-1)
Macs Ransom(USA), very awkward to load, was having her first outing since August and the market confidence was misplaced. Official explanation: jockey said filly unsuited by the fibresand (op 5-1)
Ansells Joy Official explanation: jockey said filly hung right-handed throughout
Royal Embrace Official explanation: jockey said gelding never travelled

6540 TEXT "BETDIRECT" TO 88600 H'CAP — 1m 6f (F)
2:10 (2:10) (Class 5) (0-75,70) 3-Y-O+ — **£3,343** (£994; £497; £248) **Stalls** Low

Form — RPR

602 **1** **Trance (IRE)**[4] 6519 5-9-10 70 ...... HayleyTurner 3 — 83+
(T D Barron) *hld up in last: hdwy to trck ldrs over 7f out: drvn along over 4f out: led over 2f out: forged clr ins last: readily* **11/8**[1]

0410 **2** *3* **Romil Star (GER)**[4] 6519 8-8-12 65 ......(v) AndrewElliott(7) 5 — 74
(K R Burke) *sn trcking ldr: led and qcknd over 4f out: hdd over 1f out: no ex* **20/1**

0262 **3** *5* **He's A Star**[9] 6406 3-8-3 56 ...... JimmyQuinn 7 — 58
(Miss Gay Kelleway) *hld up in tch: effrt over 4f out: wnt mod 3rd over 2f out: one pce* **7/1**

3502 **4** *8* **Principal Witness (IRE)**[12] 6448 4-9-2 62 ...... SteveDrowne 4 — 53
(Tom Dascombe) *trckd ldrs: outpcd over 3f out: hung lft and wknd over 2f out* **6/1**[3]

0312 **5** *1 ¾* **Amwell Brave**[28] 6323 4-9-0 60 ...... EddieAhern 8 — 48
(J R Jenkins) *hld up in tch: effrt over 3f out: sn lost pl* **9/2**[2]

0200 **6** *1 ¼* **Red Forest (IRE)**[19] 6406 6-8-11 57 ......(t) DaleGibson 2 — 44
(J Mackie) *led: hdd over 4f out: lost pl 3f out* **9/1**

0500 **7** *3 ½* **Boris The Spider**[16] 5789 4-8-10 56 ...... DeanMcKeown 1 — 38
(M D Hammond) *chsd ldrs: pushed along over 4f out: lost pl over 3f out* **33/1**

1110 **8** *1 ¾* **Woolstone Boy (USA)**[16] 6081 4-8-10 56 ......(t) MichaelTebbutt 6 — 35
(J Jay) *hld up in tch: drvn along over 5f out: lost pl over 3f out* **11/1**

3m 6.40s (-3.20) **Going Correction** -0.125s/f (Stan)
WFA 3 from 4yo+ 7lb — **8** Ran SP% **113.1**
Speed ratings (Par 103):104,102,99,94,93 93,91,90
CSF £32.48 CT £146.63 TOTE £2.40: £1.10, £5.40, £2.10; EX 16.00.
Owner Nigel Shields **Bred** Forenaghts Stud Co Ltd **Trained** Maunby, N Yorks

FOCUS
Solid form in this staying handicap which was run at a sound gallop.

6541 BETDIRECT 0800 211 222 H'CAP — 7f (F)
2:45 (2:45) (Class 6) (0-55,55) 3-Y-O+ — **£2,923** (£863; £431) **Stalls** Low

Form — RPR

0020 **1** **Chickado (IRE)**[47] 6078 4-8-4 48 ...... RichardThomas(3) 6 — 57
(D Haydn Jones) *chsd ldrs: wnt 2nd over 1f out: styd on to ld last 50yds* **10/1**

1135 **2** *1 ¼* **Doctor Dennis (IRE)**[14] 6429 8-8-11 52 ......(v) JimmyQuinn 4 — 57+
(J Pearce) *dwlt: hld up in rr: nt clr run over 3f out: hdwy and hung lft over 2f out: styd on: tk 2nd nr fin* **4/1**[1]

3213 **3** *shd* **Caerphilly Gal**[6] 6497 5-8-2 50 ...... NicolPolli(7) 9 — 55
(P L Gilligan) *wnt lft s: led: styd ins in home st: hdd and no ex nr fin* **11/2**[2]

0060 **4** *3* **Mount Royale (IRE)**[11] 6464 7-8-7 48 ......(v) KimTinkler 10 — 45
(N Tinkler) *w ldr: fdd appr fnl f* **6/1**[3]

3352 **5** *1 ¼* **Sound And Vision (IRE)**[19] 6401 3-9-0 55 ......(v) TomEaves 13 — 49
(M Dods) *dwlt: sn chsng ldrs on outside: wknd over 1f out* **11/2**[2]

0005 **6** *1 ¼* **New England**[11] 6469 3-8-11 52 ...... FergalLynch 1 — 43
(W M Brisbourne) *s.i.s: sme hdwy on inner over 2f out: nvr nr ldrs* **11/1**

0002 **7** *8* **Ming Vase**[11] 6468 3-8-13 54 ......(p) TonyCulhane 3 — 24
(P T Midgley) *chsd ldrs: sn drvn along: lost pl 3f out* **6/1**[3]

0350 **8** *5* **Inherit (IRE)**[14] 6429 3-8-9 50 ...... PaulHanagan 2 — 7
(R A Fahey) *hld up in rr-div: drvn over 3f out: sn btn* **12/1**

0150 **9** *¾* **Grezie**[112] 4576 3-9-0 55 ...... ChrisCatlin 5 — 10
(T D McCarthy) *sltly hmpd s: bhd and swtchd outside after 1f: sn chsng ldrs: lost pl 3f out* **20/1**

0300 **10** *¾* **Eskimo's Nest**[14] 6438 3-8-8 52 ......(v[1]) PatrickMathers(3) 12 — 5
(D Shaw) *in tch on outer: lost pl over 3f out* **16/1**

1m 30.42s (-0.38) **Going Correction** -0.125s/f (Stan) — **10** Ran SP% **115.1**
Speed ratings (Par 101):97,95,95,92,90 89,80,74,73,72
CSF £49.17 CT £245.83 TOTE £14.10: £3.50, £2.20, £2.30; EX 55.80.
Owner Monolithic Refractories Ltd **Bred** M Channon **Trained** Efail Isaf, Rhondda C Taff

FOCUS
In effect a banded handicap with the winner and the third running to their previous marks, and the form is sound but ordinary.

6542 BETDIRECTCASINO.COM H'CAP (DIV II) — 1m (F)
3:20 (3:20) (Class 6) (0-65,65) 3-Y-O+ — **£3,051** (£908; £453; £226) **Stalls** Low

Form — RPR

0253 **1** **Amorist (IRE)**[11] 6469 3-8-5 54 ...... JamieMackay 9 — 65+
(Sir Mark Prescott) *mde virtually all: styd on wl fnl 2f: readily* **11/4**[1]

0000 **2** *2* **Blueberry Tart (IRE)**[67] 5686 3-8-13 62 ...... SteveDrowne 11 — 69
(J M P Eustace) *sn in rr and drvn along: hdwy on outside over 3f out: edgd lft over 1f out: kpt on to take 2nd nr fin* **16/1**

1021 **3** *nk* **Stevedore (IRE)**[24] 6372 4-9-1 63 ...... EddieAhern 13 — 69
(J R Boyle) *w ldrs on outside: wnt 2nd 2f out: kpt on same pce ins last* **3/1**[2]

0604 **4** *2 ½* **Sol Rojo**[14] 6436 3-8-11 60 ...... RobbieFitzpatrick 4 — 61
(M J Attwater) *chsd ldrs: outpcd over 2f out: kpt on fnl f* **9/1**

5040 **5** *¾* **Dudley Docker (IRE)**[25] 6362 3-8-13 65 ...... DanielTudhope(3) 8 — 65
(D Carroll) *s.s: bhd tl styd on fnl 2f: nt rch ldrs* **20/1**

6451 **6** *3 ½* **Thornaby Green**[18] 6413 4-8-2 50 oh4 ......(v) ChrisCatlin 10 — 43
(T D Barron) *w ldrs on outer: wknd over 1f out* **6/1**[3]

2504 **7** *3 ½* **Guadaloup**[11] 6469 3-8-9 **58** .... DeanMcKeown 6 44
(M Brittain) *chsd ldrs: wknd fnl 2f* **33/1**

-010 **8** *shd* **Qobtaan (USA)**[184] 2425 6-8-13 **61** .... (t) HayleyTurner 2 46
(M R Bosley) *hld up in rr: sme hdwy over 2f out: lost pl over 1f out* **33/1**

0004 **9** *6* **Barzak (IRE)**[4] 6514 5-8-12 **60** .... (b) PaulEddery 12 33
(S R Bowring) *w ldrs on outside: lost pl 2f out* **12/1**

0044 **10** *shd* **Latin Express (IRE)**[31] 6298 3-8-5 **57** .... RichardThomas(3) 7 30
(W R Muir) *mid-div: drvn along 3f out: sn btn* **8/1**

6000 **11** *hd* **Simply The Guest (IRE)**[11] 6468 6-8-9 **57** .... (t) KimTinkler 1 30
(N Tinkler) *chsd ldrs on inner: reminders after 2f: lost pl over 4f out: sn bhd* **66/1**

4560 **12** *14* **King Nicholas (USA)**[38] 6231 6-9-2 **64** .... (tp) TonyCulhane 14 9
(J Parkes) *w ldrs on wd outside: lost pl over 3f out: bhd and eased fnl f* **14/1**

51-5 **13** *4* **Suffolk House**[302] 350 3-9-0 **63** .... JimmyQuinn 5 —
(K A Ryan) *t.k.h: in tch: lost pl and eased over 2f out: sn bhd* **28/1**

1m 42.94s (-1.66) **Going Correction** -0.125s/f (Stan)
WFA 3 from 4yo+ 1lb **13 Ran SP% 122.9**
Speed ratings (Par 101):103,101,100,98,97 93,90,90,84,84 84,70,66
CSF £47.07 CT £146.71 TOTE £3.40: £1.70, £5.80, £1.50; EX 57.70 Place 6 £46.01, Place 5 £7.86.
Owner W E Sturt - Osborne House Iv **Bred** Ian Fair **Trained** Newmarket, Suffolk

FOCUS
Just ordinary form but the winner will progress and the third did well from an outside draw.
Dudley Docker(IRE) Official explanation: jockey said gelding hung left throughout
Suffolk House Official explanation: jockey said gelding had no more to give in straight
T/Plt: £49.40 to a £1 stake. Pool: £29,909.70. 441.65 winning tickets. T/Qpdt: £6.20 to a £1 stake. Pool: £2,921.70. 344.20 winning tickets. WG

6527 WOLVERHAMPTON (A.W) (L-H)

Saturday, December 10

OFFICIAL GOING: Standard
Wind: Almost nil. Weather: Fine

6543 BET IN RUNNING ON SKYTEXT 293 CLAIMING STKS 1m 141y(P)
7:00 (7:00) (Class 5) 2-Y-O **£3,400** (£1,011; £505; £252) **Stalls** Low

Form RPR

6062 **1** **Ruffie (IRE)**[84] 5323 2-9-0 57 .... JimmyQuinn 8 66
(Miss Gay Kelleway) *hld up and bhd: rdn over 3f out: hdwy on outside over 1f out: r.o wl u.str.p to ld last strides* **14/1**

0011 **2** *nk* **Psycho Cat**[11] 6466 2-8-13 69 .... FergalLynch 12 64
(P A Blockley) *hld up and bhd: rdn over 3f out: hdwy over 2f out: ev ch whn hung bdly rt to stands' rail ins fnl f: r.o* **7/2**[1]

0120 **3** *shd* **Countrywide Belle**[11] 6467 2-8-8 57 .... (p) RobertWinston 4 59
(K A Ryan) *a.p: rdn to ld wl over 1f out: hdd last strides* **11/2**[2]

3540 **4** *½* **Chookie Windsor**[37] 6234 2-8-7 59 .... TomEaves 13 57
(I Semple) *stdd s: rdn over 4f out: hdwy on ins over 1f out: kpt on ins fnl f* **14/1**

0642 **5** *nk* **Tafilah**[29] 6313 2-8-6 56 .... EddieAhern 3 55
(P W D'Arcy) *a.p: rdn over 2f out: ev ch wl ins fnl f: no ex* **7/2**[1]

4040 **6** *¾* **Nico's Girl**[25] 6359 2-8-2 50 .... DaleGibson 9 50
(M W Easterby) *hld up towards rr: hdwy whn nt clr run briefly and swtchd rt over 2f out: sn rdn: r.o ins fnl f* **20/1**

0415 **7** *3* **Angelina Bankes**[29] 6313 2-8-8 57 .... LPKeniry 10 49
(R A Harris) *w ldr: led over 2f out: rdn and hdd wl over 1f out: wknd ins fnl f* **10/1**[3]

0030 **8** *½* **Mystified (IRE)**[15] 6423 2-9-1 61 .... (p) TonyCulhane 2 55
(R F Fisher) *chsd ldrs: rdn and sltly outpcd over 3f out: rallied on ins over 2f out: wknd ins fnl f* **10/1**[3]

3334 **9** *2 ½* **Pix**[3] 6521 2-8-3 52 ow1 .... (b) ChrisCatlin 7 38
(S Kirk) *hld up in mid-div: hdwy over 3f out: rdn over 2f out: wknd over 1f out* **11/1**

0010 **10** *shd* **Night Groove (IRE)**[11] 6467 2-9-3 64 .... MickyFenton 11 52
(N P Littmoden) *chsd ldrs: rdn over 2f out: wknd wl over 1f out* **14/1**

3046 **11** *5* **Crush On You**[21] 6386 2-8-1 48 .... StephanieHollinshead(5) 1 30
(R Hollinshead) *led: hdd over 2f out: wknd wl over 1f out* **33/1**

5630 **12** *8* **First Byte**[31] 6296 2-8-5 55 .... AdamKirby(3) 6 16
(Miss D A McHale) *hld up towards rr: rdn over 3f out: sn struggling* **40/1**

0 **13** *2 ½* **Ten For Fun (FR)**[3] 6521 2-8-6 ow1 .... DeanMcKeown 5 8
(M J Polglase) *hld up in mid-div: rdn over 3f out: sn bhd* **66/1**

1m 50.5s (-1.26) **Going Correction** -0.175s/f (Stan) **13 Ran SP% 118.0**
Speed ratings (Par 96):98,97,97,97,96 96,93,93,90,90 86,79,77
CSF £59.99 TOTE £11.00: £2.00, £1.70, £2.80; EX 46.20.
Owner Johnfarleypatticrookrosemaryedwards **Bred** F Jones **Trained** Exning, Suffolk

FOCUS
This modest claimer produced a cracking finish.

NOTEBOOK
Ruffie(IRE) was a springer in the market and it subsequently turned out that she had been laid out for this. Appreciating the longer trip, she came through to land a gamble under liberal use of the whip. (op 25-1)
Psycho Cat was trying to supplement his back-to-back wins in sellers at Southwell. He may well have completed the hat-trick over the longer trip on this faster surface had he kept straight. Official explanation: jockey said gelding hung right (op 3-1 tchd 4-1)
Countrywide Belle, again in cheekpieces instead of blinkers, was returning to the right sort of grade and only got worn down at the death. (op 5-1 tchd 9-2)
Chookie Windsor, whose best run on turf was when fourth in a seven-furlong Musselburgh seller, gave the impression he would not have minded the slightly longer trip here on his sand debut. (op 16-1)
Tafilah just got run out of the money in a tight finish. (op 4-1)
Nico's Girl did not appear to be inconvenienced by the step up in distance. (op 16-1)

6544 BETDIRECT FREEPHONE 0800 211 222 H'CAP 7f 32y(P)
7:30 (7:30) (Class 5) (0-75,79) 3-Y-O+ **£3,426** (£1,019; £509; £254) **Stalls** High

Form RPR

015 **1** **General Feeling (IRE)**[5] 6505 4-9-3 **74** .... GeorgeBaker 12 83
(S Kirk) *s.i.s: sn swtchd lft: hld up and bhd: hdwy whn n.m.r over 2f out: sn rdn: led ins fnl f: drvn ou* **15/2**[3]

1360 **2** *¾* **Deeper In Debt**[30] 6305 7-8-13 **70** .... DaneO'Neill 4 77
(J Akehurst) *sn bhd: rdn and hdwy wl over 1f out: ev ch ins fnl f: nt qckn* **16/1**

4603 **3** *nk* **Queens Rhapsody**[11] 6465 5-9-4 **75** .... SamHitchcott 7 81
(A Bailey) *bhd: hdwy on ins over 3f out: rdn to ld over 2f out: hdd ins fnl f: nt qckn* **8/1**

0001 **4** *nk* **Wessex (USA)**[11] 6465 5-9-3 **79** .... (t) GregFairley(5) 1 84+
(P A Blockley) *s.s: hdwy on outside over 2f out: r.o ins fnl f* **11/4**[1]

3-54 **5** *shd* **Connotation**[294] 424 3-8-13 **70** .... EddieAhern 9 75
(P W Chapple-Hyam) *hld up: nt clr run on ins over 3f out: hdwy over 2f out: sn rdn: ev ch ins fnl f: no ex* **6/1**[2]

6003 **6** *5* **Seneschal**[5] 6505 4-9-1 **72** .... FergusSweeney 5 64
(A B Haynes) *chsd ldrs: rdn and wknd over 1f out* **14/1**

3001 **7** *1 ½* **Nephetriti Way (IRE)**[29] 6315 4-9-3 **74** .... IanMongan 2 62
(P R Chamings) *chsd ldrs: rdn over 2f out: wknd fnl f* **8/1**

4050 **8** *¾* **Big Bradford**[5] 6504 4-8-11 **68** .... StephenCarson 8 54
(W R Muir) *chsd ldrs tl wknd over 3f out* **14/1**

0560 **9** *2* **Stoic Leader (IRE)**[1] 6533 5-9-2 **73** .... JimmyQuinn 11 54
(R F Fisher) *s.i.s: sn swtchd lft: hld up and bhd: hdwy over 3f out: rdn over 2f out: wknd wl over 1f out* **6/1**[2]

2000 **10** *1* **Easy Feeling (IRE)**[25] 6350 3-8-8 **68** .... StephaneBreux(3) 10 46
(R Hannon) *bhd fnl 4f* **50/1**

1-00 **11** *1* **Exponential (IRE)**[15] 6421 3-9-3 **74** .... J-PGuillambert 3 50
(S C Williams) *led: rdn over 3f out: hdd over 2f out: wknd wl over 1f out* **40/1**

0000 **12** *13* **Totally Yours (IRE)**[42] 6149 4-9-1 **72** .... (p) SteveDrowne 6 14
(W R Muir) *w ldr: wkng whn hmpd over 2f out* **20/1**

1m 29.07s (-1.33) **Going Correction** -0.175s/f (Stan) **12 Ran SP% 117.6**
Speed ratings (Par 103):100,99,98,98,98 92,90,87,86 85,70
CSF £117.64 CT £1002.30 TOTE £11.40: £4.40, £4.20, £3.20; EX 195.00.
Owner The So Long Partnership **Bred** John Graham And Leslie Laverty **Trained** Upper Lambourn, Berks

FOCUS
A competitve low grade handicap.

6545 FIRST PAST THE POST AT BETDIRECT MAIDEN STKS 7f 32y(P)
8:00 (8:02) (Class 5) 3-Y-O+ **£3,355** (£998; £498; £249) **Stalls** High

Form RPR

04 **1** **Baba Ghanoush**[31] 6301 3-8-9 .... PaulDoe 1 71
(W Jarvis) *led over 2f: w ldr: led over 2f out: sn rdn: clr 1f out: r.o* **7/2**[2]

060- **2** *2 ½* **Perez (IRE)**[453] 5507 3-8-9 70 .... (b[1]) EmmettStack(5) 5 69
(Pat Eddery) *wnt lft s: plld hrd: a.p: rdn over 2f out: wnt 2nd and hung lft 1f out: no imp* **4/1**[3]

02- **3** *4* **Duxford**[430] 6015 4-9-0 .... JimmyQuinn 4 59
(D K Ivory) *bmpd s: hld up and bhd: hdwy over 2f out: styd on ins fnl f* **5/1**

4/ **4** *1 ½* **Hilltop Fantasy**[724] 6203 4-8-9 .... MichaelTebbutt 2 50
(V Smith) *hld up in tch: rdn over 2f out: one pce* **20/1**

5 *2* **John Bratby (USA)** 3-9-0 .... FergusSweeney 6 50
(P J Makin) *t.k.h: sn w ldr: led over 4f out: rdn and hdd over 2f out: wknd fnl f* **2/1**[1]

6 *1 ¼* **Strobinia (IRE)** 3-8-6 .... NelsonDeSouza(3) 11 41
(R M Beckett) *plld hrd in rr: hdwy over 4f out: wknd over 2f out* **12/1**

00 **7** *shd* **In A Fit**[7] 6486 4-8-10 ow1 .... TonyCulhane 8 42
(P Howling) *nvr nr ldrs* **40/1**

0 **8** *shd* **Legal Dram**[24] 6367 4-9-0 .... TomEaves 10 46
(M Dods) *plld hrd: hdwy over 4f out: wknd over 3f out* **20/1**

9 *3* **Freshwinds** 3-9-0 .... DarrenWilliams 9 38
(S L Keightley) *plld hrd: sn mid-div: hdwy over 3f out: wknd wl over 1f out* **66/1**

00 **10** *1* **Life Is Rosie (IRE)**[25] 6355 3-8-2 .... LauraReynolds(7) 3 30
(D K Ivory) *chsd ldrs tl wknd over 3f out* **50/1**

11 *14* **Belrose (IRE)** 3-8-4 .... MarcHalford(5) 12 —
(Mrs C A Dunnett) *s.s: a bhd* **66/1**

00- **12** *4* **Livvies Lady (IRE)**[408] 6446 3-8-9 .... ChrisCatlin 7 —
(D K Ivory) *a bhd* **66/1**

1m 29.9s (-0.50) **Going Correction** -0.175s/f (Stan) **12 Ran SP% 118.3**
Speed ratings (Par 103):95,92,87,85,83 82,82,81,78,77 61,56
CSF £16.84 TOTE £5.40: £1.30, £1.70, £2.20; EX 20.70.
Owner Canisbay Bloodstock **Bred** Canisbay Bloodstock Ltd **Trained** Newmarket, Suffolk
■ Perez was Pat Eddery's first runner as a trainer.

FOCUS
A poor maiden with several refusing to settle because of the lack of pace.
John Bratby(USA) Official explanation: jockey said colt had a breathing problem; vet said colt returned lame near fore

6546 BETDIRECT ON SNOOKER H'CAP 5f 216y(P)
8:30 (8:32) (Class 5) (0-70,73) 3-Y-O+ **£3,361** (£1,000; £499; £249) **Stalls** Low

Form RPR

3003 **1** **Bessemer (JPN)**[25] 6362 4-8-11 **66** .... (p) DanielTudhope(3) 1 80+
(D Carroll) *hld up in tch: n.m.r on ins over 3f out: swtchd rt over 1f out: rdn to ld ins fnl f: r.o wl* **13/2**

0002 **2** *2 ½* **Gone'N'Dunnett (IRE)**[8] 6480 6-8-9 **68** .... (v) KirstyMilczarek(7) 12 74
(Mrs C A Dunnett) *led: hrd rdn over 1f out: hdd ins fnl f: nt qckn* **16/1**

5220 **3** *1 ½* **Hard To Catch (IRE)**[78] 5439 7-8-8 **67** .... LauraReynolds(7) 4 69
(D K Ivory) *hld up and bhd: hdwy over 1f out: r.o ins fnl f* **14/1**

003 **4** *shd* **Lady Algarhoud (FR)**[19] 6404 3-8-12 **64** .... EddieAhern 13 65
(D K Ivory) *a.p: rdn over 2f out: kpt on ins fnl f* **13/2**

3031 **5** *shd* **Willheconquertoo**[8] 6480 5-9-7 **73** .... (tp) TomEaves 5 74
(I W McInnes) *s.i.s: hdwy wl over 1f out: kpt on ins fnl f* **4/1**[1]

0133 **6** *nk* **Wicked Uncle**[15] 6422 6-9-4 **70** .... (v) IanMongan 7 70
(S Gollings) *sn prom: rdn over 2f out: one pce fnl f* **11/2**[3]

1000 **7** *hd* **Green Pirate**[113] 4557 3-8-13 **65** .... RobertWinston 9 64
(R Craggs) *s.i.s: hdwy over 4f out: rdn over 2f out: one pce fnl f* **50/1**

0000 **8** *1 ½* **Attorney**[8] 6480 7-8-12 **64** .... DaneO'Neill 3 59
(N E Berry) *hld up: sn in tch: n.m.r and lost pl over 3f out: n.d after* **12/1**

3344 **9** *nk* **Holly Springs**[129] 4047 3-8-8 **65** .... (p) MarcHalford(5) 2 59
(Mrs C A Dunnett) *w ldr: rdn over 2f out: wknd ins fnl f* **20/1**

4620 **10** *shd* **Arnie De Burgh**[177] 2621 3-8-7 **66** .... JamieHamblett(7) 11 60
(D J Daly) *chsd ldrs tl wknd over 2f out* **20/1**

3660 **11** *½* **Sweetest Revenge (IRE)**[14] 6426 4-8-6 **65** .... KMay(7) 8 57
(M D I Usher) *a bhd* **20/1**

0606 **12** *1 ½* **Yorkshire Lad (IRE)**[114] 4508 3-8-13 **68** .... AdamKirby(3) 6 56
(Miss Gay Kelleway) *a bhd* **11/1**

5003 **13** *2* **Savile's Delight (IRE)**[8] 6483 6-8-11 **63** .... ChrisCatlin 10 45
(R Brotherton) *broke wl: sn mid-div: bhd fnl 2f* **9/2**[2]

1m 14.35s (-1.46) **Going Correction** -0.175s/f (Stan) **13 Ran SP% 125.1**
Speed ratings (Par 103):102,98,96,96,96 96,95,93,93,93 92,90,87
CSF £104.97 CT £1479.39 TOTE £8.80: £2.40, £4.50, £6.10; EX 227.10.
Owner Mrs B Ramsden **Bred** Darley Stud **Trained** Warthill, N Yorks

FOCUS
They went 4/1 the field in this tight little handicap, which is rated through the runner-up.
Willheconquertoo Official explanation: trainer said gelding lost a plate and finished lame

6547 BETDIRECT.CO.UK H'CAP 1m 1f 103y(P)
9:00 (9:00) (Class 4) (0-85,79) 3-Y-0+ £5,733 (£1,705; £852; £425) Stalls Low

Form RPR

3230 **1** **Boo**[84] 5292 3-9-1 78........................(v) RobertWinston 4 87
(K R Burke) *hld up in tch: rdn to ld and edgd lft jst over 1f out: r.o* **7/1**[3]

0311 **2** 1 1/4 **Desert Leader (IRE)**[7] 6488 4-9-3 78........................ EddieAhern 2 85
(W M Brisbourne) *a.p: rdn wl over 1f out: r.o ins fnl f* **9/4**[1]

0002 **3** 1/2 **Crail**[14] 6437 5-9-4 79........................ GeorgeBaker 6 85
(C F Wall) *hld up: rdn 2f out: hdwy 1f out: kpt on* **9/4**[1]

251 **4** 1 3/4 **Bazelle**[15] 6418 3-9-0 77........................ TonyCulhane 1 80
(D Shaw) *led: rdn and hdd jst over 1f out: sn edgd lft: no ex* **20/1**

3236 **5** 1/2 **Zalkani (IRE)**[5] 6503 5-8-12 73........................ JimmyQuinn 7 78+
(B G Powell) *hld up in rr: hdwy on ins wl over 1f out: cl up whn nt clr run and hmpd on ins ent fnl f: nt rcvr* **22/1**

0300 **6** 3/4 **Toshi (USA)**[14] 6437 3-9-0 77........................(p) TomEaves 5 77
(I Semple) *w ldr: rdn and ev ch wl over 1f out: wknd fnl f* **16/1**

4022 **7** 1 3/4 **Missatacama (IRE)**[30] 6306 3-9-2 79........................ DaneO'Neill 8 76
(D J Daly) *hld up: rdn over 2f out: sn wknd* **8/1**

0004 **8** 1/2 **Blue Trojan (IRE)**[14] 6437 5-9-1 76........................(b[1]) SteveDrowne 3 72
(S Kirk) *hld up: rdn over 4f out: bhd fnl 3f* **6/1**[2]

1m 59.76s (-2.86) **Going Correction** -0.175s/f (Stan)
WFA 3 from 4yo+ 2lb **8** Ran SP% **114.4**
Speed ratings (Par 105):105,103,103,101,101 100,99,98
CSF £23.20 CT £46.80 TOTE £7.20: £1.70, £1.70, £1.50; EX 29.30.
Owner Mrs M Gittins **Bred** J Purcell **Trained** Middleham Moor, N Yorks
■ Robert Winston's first winner since breaking his jaw in a fall in August.
■ Stewards' Enquiry : Tony Culhane two-day ban: careless riding (Dec 21-22)

FOCUS
Quite an interesting event with a few in form and with the pace decent the form looks reasonable.
Missatacama(IRE) Official explanation: jockey said filly ran flat

6548 BETDIRECT ON AT THE RACES INTERACTIVE H'CAP 1m 4f 50y(P)
9:30 (9:30) (Class 6) (0-60,58) 3-Y-0+ £2,955 (£872; £436) Stalls Low

Form RPR

0135 **1** **Lady Taverner**[28] 6323 4-8-8 52........................ NataliaGemelova(5) 1 58
(J E Long) *hld up in tch: wnt 2nd 2f out: rdn to ld 1f out: drvn out* **20/1**

4332 **2** nk **York Cliff**[1] 6534 7-9-2 55........................ EddieAhern 6 61
(W M Brisbourne) *hld up and bhd: hdwy on ins over 3f out: rdn wl over 1f out: styd on ins fnl f* **4/1**[2]

3243 **3** 1/2 **Bienheureux**[28] 6323 4-9-4 57........................(t) FergalLynch 9 62
(Miss Gay Kelleway) *hld up and bhd: rdn and hdwy on outside 2f out: kpt on ins fnl f* **7/2**[1]

2012 **4** 2 **Intavac Boy**[31] 6300 4-8-12 54........................ DanielTudhope(3) 12 56
(C W Thornton) *chsd ldr: rdn to ld over 2f out: hdd 1f out: no ex* **9/2**[3]

031- **5** 3 **Smoothie (IRE)**[397] 6596 7-9-5 58........................ FergusSweeney 2 55
(Ian Williams) *hld up in mid-div: stdy hdwy over 5f out: no imp fnl f* **20/1**

0106 **6** 2 **Dinner Date**[28] 6324 3-8-12 56........................ J-PGuillambert 7 50
(T Keddy) *hld up in mid-div: rdn and hdwy on outside over 2f out: wknd ins fnl f* **20/1**

4040 **7** 2 1/2 **King Of Music (USA)**[25] 6364 4-9-5 58........................ ChrisCatlin 10 48
(G Prodromou) *hld up: rdn over 2f out: nvr trbld ldrs* **11/1**

5000 **8** 3/4 **Rare Coincidence**[10] 6323 4-9-2 55........................(p) SteveDrowne 8 44
(R F Fisher) *led: rdn and hdd over 2f out: wknd wl over 1f out* **9/2**[3]

2005 **9** 1 1/2 **Galley Law**[31] 6300 5-9-0 53........................ TomEaves 4 39
(R Craggs) *hld up in tch: wknd 3f out* **12/1**

0335 **10** 5 **Farnborough (USA)**[128] 4104 4-9-3 56........................ DarrenWilliams 5 34
(R J Price) *a towards rr* **14/1**

0000 **11** 5 **Competitor**[28] 6323 4-9-4 57........................(bt) JimmyQuinn 11 27
(J Akehurst) *s.s: a in rr* **25/1**

1104 **12** 3 **Magic Warrior**[28] 6324 5-9-3 56........................ MickyFenton 3 22
(J C Fox) *prom: rdn over 3f out: wknd over 2f out* **20/1**

2m 39.15s (-3.27) **Going Correction** -0.175s/f (Stan)
WFA 3 from 4yo+ 5lb **12** Ran SP% **124.2**
Speed ratings (Par 101):103,102,102,101,99 97,96,95,94,91 87,85
CSF £96.09 CT £363.26 TOTE £30.20: £4.40, £2.60, £1.60; EX 241.90 Place 6 £271.73, Place 5 £139.48.
Owner The Chantilly Partnership **Bred** Highclere Stud Ltd **Trained** Caterham, Surrey

FOCUS
A good finish to this low-grade affair and the form looks fairly solid.
Competitor Official explanation: jockey said colt had a breathing problem
T/Plt: £269.30 to a £1 stake. Pool: £46,964.25. 127.30 winning tickets. T/Qpdt: £20.20 to a £1 stake. Pool: £2,841.20. 104.00 winning tickets. KH

1721 SHA TIN (R-H)
Sunday, December 11

OFFICIAL GOING: Good to firm

6549a CATHAY PACIFIC HONG KONG VASE (GROUP 1) 1m 4f
6:10 (6:11) 3-Y-0+
£536,193 (£201,072; £100,536; £53,619; £30,161; £16,756)

RPR

1 **Ouija Board**[14] 6440 4-8-10........................ KFallon 7 119+
(E A L Dunlop) *hld up towards rr, 10th str, hdwy 2f out, qcknd through gap to ld just ins fnl f, driven clr, ran on wl* **5/2**[2]

2 2 3/4 **Six Sense (JPN)**[49] 3-8-9........................ HShii 11 119
(H Nagahama, Japan) *raced in mid-div, headway on outside over 3f out, 5th straight on outside, stayed on, ridden to take 2nd last strides* **33/1**

3 shd **Best Gift (NZ)**[28] 4-9-0........................ DWhyte 8 119
(J Moore, Hong Kong) *reared start, soon prominent, 4th straight, reached 2nd 120yds out, lost 2nd last strides* **16/1**

4 1/2 **Shamdala (IRE)**[49] 6055 3-8-7........................ CSoumillon 4 114
(A De Royer-Dupre, France) *mid-div, 7th straight, 4th but caught behind leader well over 1f out, 7th 1f out, switched out & kept on steadily* **16/1**

5 1/2 **Westerner**[70] 5651 6-9-0........................ OPeslier 6 117
(E Lellouche, France) *mid-div, close 8th on outside straight, ridden appr final f, stayed on under pressure but never able to chal* **9/4**[1]

6 nk **Reefscape**[49] 6055 4-9-0........................ RichardHughes 2 117
(A Fabre, France) *raced in 3rd to straight, disputing 5th well over 1f out, ridden & outpaced approaching final f, rallied closing stages* **16/1**

7 shd **Samando (FR)**[49] 6055 5-8-10........................ ELegrix 9 113
(F Doumen, France) *held up in rear, 11th straight, effort on outside, kept on, nearest at finish* **25/1**

8 shd **Sweet Stream (ITY)**[95] 5045 5-8-10........................ TGillet 3 113
(J E Hammond, France) *hld up in rr, 9th str, cl 7th when not clear run on rail appr fnl f, switched out & stayed on again close home* **9/1**

9 3/4 **Cherry Mix (FR)**[56] 5937 4-9-0........................ LDettori 12 115
(Saeed Bin Suroor) *tracked leader after 2 1/2f, 2nd straight, hard ridden & every chance 1f out, soon beaten* **8/1**[3]

10 shd **Saturn (IRE)**[28] 5-9-0........................ RFradd 5 115
(C Fownes, Hong Kong) *led to just inside final furlong* **40/1**

11 2 1/4 **Norse Dancer (IRE)**[70] 5651 5-9-0........................ MartinDwyer 1 112
(D R C Elsworth) *held up, slipped through on ins to be 6th str, hard rdn & disp 2nd 1 1/2f out, hmpd distance, no chance after* **20/1**

12 7 **Warrsan (IRE)**[14] 6440 7-9-0........................ JamieSpencer 10 101
(C E Brittain) *prominent early, 5th over 3f out, weakened well over 2f out, last straight* **16/1**

2m 28.9s
WFA 3 from 4yo+ 5lb **12** Ran SP% **118.0**
(including $HK10 stakes): WIN 44.50; PL 20.00, 55.00, 26.00; DF 526.00.
Owner Lord Derby **Bred** Stanley Estate & Stud Co **Trained** Newmarket, Suffolk

NOTEBOOK
Ouija Board was held up some way off a steady pace, Fallon clearly wary of a repeat of the Japan Cup where he felt that he had kicked for home too soon. It looked as if she might not get a run when caught in tight quarters early in the home straight, but the gaps came perfectly for her and, slicing through to lead at the furlong pole, she quickened clear in most impressive fashion. The style of this triumph may convince connections to let her race on in 2006.
Shamdala(IRE) was about to be produced when she was caught behind the toiling leader with over a furlong to run. Losing her place completely, she did well to rally in the closing stages.
Westerner was compromised by the slow pace and firm ground. He is now due to retire to stud and signs off as the winner of five Group 1 races and one of the outstanding stayers of recent times.
Reefscapeneeds a stiffer test of stamina than this.
Cherry Mix(FR) had the run of the race, in behind the leader, but did not quicken when asked and needs softer ground.
Norse Dancer(IRE) was driven up the inside to momentarily dispute second early in the straight but was already beaten when tightened up a furlong out.
Warrsan(IRE) has lost his form completely and was beaten before the home turn.

6550a CATHAY PACIFIC HONG KONG SPRINT (GROUP 1) 5f (S)
7:20 (7:21) 3-Y-0+
£382,038 (£147,453; £67,024; £38,204; £22,118; £13,405)

RPR

1 **Natural Blitz I (AUS)**[21] 5-9-0........................ GSchofield 3 119
(D Cruz, Hong Kong) *fast away on far side, led over 3f out, ridden clear from 1f out, ran on well* **16/1**

2 1 3/4 **Planet Ruler (AUS)**[21] 6-9-0........................ GMosse 1 113
(A Lee, Hong Kong) *always chasing winner on far side, challenged well over 1f out, one pace final f* **6/1**

3 nk **Able Prince (AUS)**[21] 4-9-0........................(b) DWhyte 11 112
(J Moore, Hong Kong) *outpaced early, headway from half-way, reached 3rd 1f out, kept on steadily* **9/1**

4 shd **Country Music (AUS)**[21] 4-9-0........................ FCoetzee 10 112
(A S Cruz, Hong Kong) *last early, headway half-way, kept on under strong pressure final 1 1/2f, just missed 3rd* **25/1**

5 1 1/2 **Cape Of Good Hope**[36] 7-9-0........................(b) MJKinane 7 106
(D Oughton, Hong Kong) *always prominent on far side, ridden 1 1/2f out, no extra final f* **10/3**[1]

6 shd **Benbaun (IRE)**[70] 5647 4-9-0........................(v) KFallon 12 106
(M J Wallace) *outpaced to half-way, ridden 2f out, stayed on, never nearer* **8/1**

7 1 1/4 **Absolute Champion (AUS)**[21] 4-9-0........................ RFradd 8 101
(A Lee, Hong Kong) *prominent to 2f out, kept on one pace* **40/1**

8 shd **Chineur (FR)**[40] 6221 4-9-0........................ C-PLemaire 4 101
(M Delzangles, France) *slowly into stride, last half-way, headway & switched to far rail to dispute 5th over 1f out, soon ridden & beaten* **11/2**[3]

9 1 3/4 **Warcat (NZ)** 4-9-0........................ WHo 9 95
(Choy Yu Yee, Macau) *speed to half-way, ridden & beaten 2f out* **33/1**

10 shd **Nipping (IRE)**[70] 5647 3-8-10........................ CSoumillon 6 90
(Robert Collet, France) *mid-division, headway 2f out, switched right, beaten 1f out* **12/1**

11 shd **Admire Max (JPN)**[21] 6-9-0........................ HUemura 5 94
(M Hashida, Japan) *always outpaced* **5/1**[2]

12 2 1/4 **Nicole's Dream (USA)** 5-8-10........................ EBaird 13 82
(L Rivelli, U.S.A) *led on stands side over 1f, beaten over 2f out* **14/1**

57.60 secs **12** Ran SP% **120.0**
WIN 282.00; PL 46.50, 18.00, 22.00; DF 552.00.
Owner Lam Yin Kee **Bred** R & Mrs J V Williamson **Trained** Hong Kong

NOTEBOOK
Natural Blitz I(AUS) showed terrific pace and was a worthy winner on the day, but the absence of the brilliant Silent Witness, who had him back in third 12 months previously, robbed the race of much of its significance and none of the European challengers were at the top of their game.
Benbaun(IRE) started slowly and Fallon was hard at work soon after halfway. His perseverance began to pay off in the closing stages and he almost snatched fifth place from Cape Of Good Hope.

6551a CATHAY PACIFIC HONG KONG MILE (GROUP 1) 1m
8:30 (8:45) 3-Y-0+
£536,193 (£201,072; £100,536; £53,619; £30,161; £16,756)

RPR

1 **Hat Trick (JPN)**[21] 4-9-0........................ OPeslier 11 119
(Katsuhiko Sumii, Japan) *held up in mid-div, close 11th straight on outside, headway well over 1f out, driven to lead well inside final f, ran on* **11/2**

2 1 1/4 **The Duke (AUS)**[21] 5-9-0........................ DBeadman 13 116
(C Fownes, Hong Kong) *soon tracking leader, 2nd straight, driven to lead appr final f, hard ridden & headed well inside final f, ran on* **33/1**

3 1/2 **Dave's Best**[21] 5-9-0........................ CSoumillon 4 115
(C H Yip, Hong Kong) *started slowly, last straight, tracking winner on outside 2f out, kept on under pressure to take 3rd well inside final f* **16/1**

4 1/2 **Bullish Luck (USA)**[21] 6-9-0........................(b) GMosse 5 114
(A S Cruz, Hong Kong) *dwelt, 10th straight, headway well over 1f out, 8th 1f out, ran on, nearest at finish* **3/1**[1]

5 nk **Court Masterpiece**[71] 5638 5-9-0........................ KFallon 12 113
(E A L Dunlop) *held up towards rear, 9th straight on inside, stayed on up rails but never reached challenging position* **14/1**

6 *nse* **Asakusa Den'En**[42] 6-9-0 ....(b) SFujita 14 113
(Michifumi Kono, Japan) *held up, headway on outside over 3f out, 6th straight, 5th 1 1/2f out, kept on same pace* **4/1**[3]

7 *1 1/4* **Perfect Partner (AUS)**[21] 5-9-0 .... FCoetzee 6 110
(A S Cruz, Hong Kong) *always prominent, 4th straight, disputed 3rd 1 1/2f out, kept on same pace* **16/1**

8 *shd* **High Intelligent (AUS)**[21] 5-9-0 .... DWhyte 2 110
(J Size, Hong Kong) *always prominent, 3rd straight, ridden 1 1/2f out, beaten when slightly hampered inside final f, kept on* **20/1**

9 *hd* **Wealthy (AUS)**[21] 5-9-0 .... ODoleuze 7 109
(C H Yip, Hong Kong) *in rear, 12th straight, never a factor* **40/1**

10 *nk* **Scintillation (AUS)**[21] 5-9-0 .... ESaint-Martin 1 109
(C S Shum, Hong Kong) *led to approaching final f* **25/1**

11 *nse* **Rakti**[57] 5902 6-9-0 .... PhilipRobinson 3 109
(M A Jarvis) *slowly into stride, soon racing in 6th, 7th on inside straight, one pace final 1 1/2f* **7/2**[2]

12 *2 1/2* **Super Kid (NZ)**[43] 6-9-0 .... SDye 9 103
(J Moore, Hong Kong) *mid-division, 8th straight, one pace* **33/1**

13 *2 3/4* **Town Of Fionn (AUS)**[21] 4-9-0 .... GSchofield 10 96
(C S Shum, Hong Kong) *prominent, 5th straight, weakened well over 1f out* **40/1**

1m 34.8s **13** Ran SP% **120.4**
WIN 48.00; PL 21.00, 77.00, 40.00;DF 1,198.

Owner U Carrot Farm **Bred** Oiwake Farm **Trained** Japan

NOTEBOOK
Hat Trick(JPN) recorded a second Group One win in three weeks, following last month's Kyoto success. While the opposition was not the strongest, his win underlines the growing strength of the Japanese within the international arena. It was also another feather in the cap of his trainer, who earlier in the year landed a first Japanese Grade One win in America with Cesario in the American Oaks and also has charge of the brilliant Japanese three-year-old Deep Impact and the outstanding dirt three-year-old Kane Hekili.

Court Masterpiece was dropped out and switched to the inside from his outside draw. Getting all the splits hard up against the running rail in the last quarter mile, he plugged on gamely but only snatched fifth because the Japanese jockey on Asakusa Den'en stopped riding too soon and was fined.

Rakti rounded off his up and down career on a low note, not getting much room at the crucial stage early in the straight but not really picking up when he did find some space. Though temperamental throughout, he was brilliant on his day and won Group One races in four successive seasons - six of them all.

6552a CATHAY PACIFIC HONG KONG CUP (GROUP 1) 1m 2f
9:10 (9:25) 3-Y-0+
£683,646 (£268,097; £120,643; £67,024; £40,214; £26,810)

RPR

1 **Vengeance Of Rain (NZ)**[28] 4-9-0 .... ADelpech 4 127
(D Ferraris, Hong Kong) *raced in 5th to straight, headway from well over 1f out to lead 150yds out, ran on well* **3/1**[1]

2 *nk* **Pride (FR)**[57] 5902 5-8-10 .... CSoumillon 3 122
(A De Royer-Dupre, France) *held up, 9th straight, headway on outside from 2f out, took 2nd 100yds out, ran on* **9/2**[3]

3 *1* **Maraahel (IRE)**[57] 5902 4-9-0 ....(v) RHills 5 124
(Sir Michael Stoute) *held up, 8th straight, headway on outside from well over 1f out, ridden 1f out, no extra last 50yds* **5/1**

4 *1 1/2* **Russian Pearl (NZ)**[231] 1247 5-9-0 .... FCoetzee 7 122
(A S Cruz, Hong Kong) *in rear & pulling early, 7th straight, headway well over 1f out, one pace last 150yds* **14/1**

5 *shd* **Touch Of Land (FR)**[57] 5902 5-9-0 .... C-PLemaire 6 121
(H-A Pantall, France) *always close up, went 3rd 4f out, disputed 2nd over 1f out, kept on same pace* **12/1**

6 *hd* **Epalo (GER)**[35] 6278 6-9-0 .... AStarke 10 121
(A Schutz, Germany) *tracked leader, led entering straight, headed 150yds out, one pace* **25/1**

7 *nk* **Green Treasure (AUS)**[28] 4-9-0 .... ODoleuze 9 120
(D Cruz, Hong Kong) *last to straight, stayed on but never a factor* **25/1**

8 *1/2* **Alexander Goldrun (IRE)**[57] 5902 4-8-10 .... KJManning 1 116
(J S Bolger, Ire) *held up in 6th to straight, switched to inside 2f out, close 6th when not clear run 1 1/2f out, no chance after* **7/2**[2]

9 *1/2* **Willow O Wisp (USA)**[97] 3-8-11 .... KFallon 8 119
(V Cerin, U.S.A) *led to entering straight (over 2f out), not much room on inside well over 1f out, one pace* **16/1**

10 *2 3/4* **River Dancer (IRE)**[21] 6-9-0 .... DWhyte 2 114
(J Size, Hong Kong) *raced in 3rd to 4f out, 4th straight, disputing 4th when squeezed up over 1f out, not recover* **25/1**

2m 4.50s
WFA 3 from 4yo+ 3lb **10** Ran SP% **113.9**
WIN 18.50; PL 12.00, 24.50, 22.50; DF 108.50.

Owner Exors of the late Chow Nam & Raymond Gianco **Bred** K Biggs Enterprise Pty Ltd Et Al **Trained** Hong Kong

NOTEBOOK
Vengeance Of Rain(NZ) has been improving all year and put up another career-best effort in recording his fourth Group One win of the year. He was a thoroughly deserving winner from an international field, and his late charge earned him the additional accolade of the World Racing Championship.

Pride(FR) retires to the paddocks following another mighty display and she might have won with a stronger pace. Last but one on the turn, she stayed on well down the outside but could not quite reel in the winner.

Maraahel(IRE) repeated his Champion Stakes form with Pride almost to the pound and is set to stay in training.

Alexander Goldrun(IRE) was forced back to the inside when looking for a run on the home turn and found a gap closing on top of her with a furlong and a half to run, losing all chance of a place in the frame. No decision has yet been made about possible retirement.

6535 SOUTHWELL (L-H)
Monday, December 12

OFFICIAL GOING: Standard
Wind: Almost nil

6554 TEXT BETDIRECT TO 88600 MAIDEN CLAIMING STKS 5f (F)
1:00 (1:01) (Class 7) 3-Y-0+ **£1,409** (£416; £208) **Stalls** High

Form RPR

0005 1 **King Marrakech (IRE)**[14] 6441 3-8-10 35....(v) HayleyTurner 1 40
(M D I Usher) *cl up: led over 2f out: rdn over 1f out: wandered ins last: kpt on* **5/1**[3]

000 2 *1 3/4* **Fir Tree**[13] 6462 5-9-0 40.... MichaelTebbutt 2 38
(S R Bowring) *hld up: hdwy 1/2-way: rdn to chse wnr over 1f out: kpt on same pce ins last* **22/1**

000 3 *1/2* **Pack Of Lies**[13] 6462 3-8-9 40.... ChrisCatlin 3 31
(Rae Guest) *stdd s: hld up towards rr: hdwy 2f out: rdn and kpt on ins last* **9/1**

4306 4 *3* **Velvet Touch**[20] 6409 4-8-9 45....(t) J-PGuillambert 5 21
(D M Simcock) *prom: rdn along over 2f out: drvn and wknd wl over 1f out* **3/1**[1]

4060 5 *1 1/4* **Limited Magician**[20] 6411 4-8-9 30....(v[1]) GylesParkin 4 17
(C Smith) *sn outpcd and bhd: swtchd lft 2f out: styd on u.p appr lastr: n.d* **50/1**

0-00 6 *nk* **Raetihi**[14] 6441 4-8-7 35.... DeanMcKeown 7 14
(P S Felgate) *led to 1/2-way: sn rdn along and wknd wl over 1f out* **40/1**

4240 7 *1 1/4* **Tree Roofer**[13] 6462 6-8-8 40....(p) JoeFanning 8 11
(N P Littmoden) *dwlt: sn cl up: led briefly 1/2-way: sn rdn and grad wknd* **11/2**

2500 8 *hd* **Bold Maggie**[21] 6400 3-8-10 45 ow1.... FergalLynch 9 12
(J A Pickering) *cl up: rdn along 2f out: grad wknd* **9/1**

2023 9 *2* **Alzarma**[147] 3593 3-8-11 50.... JohnMcAuley[(3)] 6 9
(J Gallagher) *chsd ldrs: rdn along 1/2-way: sn outpcd and bhd* **4/1**[2]

0020 10 *6* **Blendon Belle (FR)**[20] 6409 3-8-9 40.... FergusSweeney 10 —
(A G Newcombe) *dwlt: sn in tch: rdn along 1/2-way: sn wknd* **8/1**

59.80 secs (-0.50) **Going Correction** -0.175s/f (Stan) **10** Ran SP% **116.9**
Speed ratings (Par 97):97,94,93,88,86 86,84,83,80,71
CSF £108.40 TOTE £3.70: £1.40, £12.60, £3.70; EX 90.40.The winner was claimed by B. P. J. Baugh for £3,000
Owner I Sheward **Bred** Haras D'Etreham **Trained** Upper Lambourn, Berks

FOCUS
A very weak sprint which saw those drawn low dominate.

6555 PRESS RED TO BET ON ITVI BANDED STKS 1m 3f (F)
1:30 (1:31) (Class 7) 3-Y-0+ **£1,419** (£419; £209) **Stalls** Low

Form RPR

610 1 **Mickmacmagoole (IRE)**[20] 6414 3-8-10 45 ow1.... JamieSpencer 7 69+
(Seamus G O'Donnell, Ire) *trckd ldrs: smooth hdwy 3f out: led on bit wl over 1f out: v cheekily* **13/8**[1]

0000 2 *1/2* **Cotton Eyed Joe (IRE)**[20] 6414 4-8-13 35.... DeanMcKeown 6 60
(G A Swinbank) *trckd ldrs: hdwy on inner to ld 3f out: sn rdn: drvn and hdd wl over 1f out: kpt on u.p: no ch w wnr* **18/1**

0342 3 *10* **Surdoue**[8] 6495 5-8-13 45.... J-PGuillambert 9 44
(P Howling) *trckd ldrs: hdwy to ld over 4f out: hdd 3f out: sn rdn and wknd* **15/8**[2]

2436 4 *2 1/2* **Finnegans Rainbow**[8] 6495 3-8-2 45.... LiamJones[(7)] 5 40
(M C Chapman) *cl up: led after 3f: rdn along and hdd over 4f out: drvn and wknd over 3f out* **5/1**[3]

0600 5 *5* **Showtime Annie**[20] 6348 4-8-13 45....(p) JoeFanning 3 32
(A Bailey) *cl up: rdn along over 4f out and sn wknd* **14/1**

0500 6 *9* **Hollywood Henry (IRE)**[12] 6475 5-8-13 45....(b) FergalLynch 12 18
(P A Blockley) *rr whn rn wd bnd after 1f: a bhd* **14/1**

5001 7 *1/2* **Spanish Star**[14] 6442 8-8-13 45.... HayleyTurner 4 17
(Mrs N Macauley) *in tch: rdn along over 4f out: sn wknd* **10/1**

5-00 8 *13* **Regal Fantasy (IRE)**[30] 6329 5-8-13 30.... PatCosgrave 10 —
(P A Blockley) *rr whn rn wd bnd after 1f: a bhd* **66/1**

0000 9 *23* **Sydneyroughdiamond**[7] 6509 3-8-11 45 ow2....(p) DarrenWilliams 2 —
(M Mullineaux) *chsd ldrs: rdn along 1/2-way: sn wknd* **25/1**

0006 10 *18* **Queen Nefitari**[11] 4583 3-8-6 45....(bt[1]) PaulMulrennan[(3)] 1 —
(M W Easterby) *led 3f: rdn along and wknd qckly 1/2-way: sn bhd* **33/1**

2m 26.52s (-2.38) **Going Correction** -0.20s/f (Stan)
WFA 3 from 4yo+ 4lb **10** Ran SP% **125.5**
Speed ratings (Par 97):100,99,92,90,86 80,80,70,53,40
CSF £36.31 TOTE £2.90: £1.60, £4.60, £1.10; EX 40.60.
Owner J Roberts **Bred** Tower Bloodstock **Trained** Ballinalard, Co Tipperary

FOCUS
A fair event for the class, run at a sound pace, and the first two came well clear. The winner did the job easily and can be rated value for much further with the runner-up the best guide to the level.
Regal Fantasy(IRE) Official explanation: trainer said mare found to have mucus on its lungs
Sydneyroughdiamond Official explanation: jockey said gelding hung left-handed

6556 MORE OFFERS AT BETDIRECT.CO.UK BANDED STKS 1m (F)
2:00 (2:01) (Class 7) 3-Y-0+ **£1,433** (£423; £211) **Stalls** Low

Form RPR

5203 1 **Desert Fury**[70] 5656 8-8-11 40....(b) RobertWinston 12 51
(R Bastiman) *hld up: gd hdwy on outer over 3f out: rdn to ld over 1f out: kpt on* **7/2**[2]

650 2 *2 1/2* **It Must Be Speech**[30] 6329 4-8-11 40....(v) DarrenWilliams 3 46
(S L Keightley) *t.k.h: trckd ldrs: hdwy 3f out: swtchd rt 2f out: rdn and ev ch over 1f out: kpt on same pce ins last* **9/1**

0000 3 *nk* **Pawn In Life (IRE)**[8] 6498 7-8-11 40....(p) DeanMcKeown 7 45
(M J Polglase) *cl up: led over 3f out: rdn over 2f out: drvn and hdd over 1f out: kpt on same pce* **14/1**

0536 4 *3 1/2* **Bobering**[28] 6344 5-8-8 40.... PatrickMathers[(3)] 4 38
(B P J Baugh) *bhd: hdwy on inner 3f out: rdn 2f out: styd on appr last: nrst fin* **7/1**[3]

3003 5 *1/2* **Semper Paratus (USA)**[8] 6498 6-8-11 40....(v) MichaelTebbutt 13 37
(V Smith) *hung lft thrght: sn pushed along in midfield: hdwy 3f out: rdn and hung bdly lft wl over 1f out: sn rdn and no imp* **11/4**[1]

5406 6 *hd* **Susiedil (IRE)**[23] 6383 4-8-8 35.... SilvestreDeSousa[(3)] 5 37
(D Nicholls) *chsd ldrs: rdn along 3f out: kpt on same pce fnl 2f* **9/1**

0660 7 *6* **Firebird Rising (USA)**[23] 6383 4-8-11 35....(b[1]) ChrisCatlin 1 25
(R Brotherton) *chsd ldrs: rdn along over 3f out: wknd over 2f out* **18/1**

The Form Book, Raceform Ltd, Compton, RG20 6NL

6-00 **8** 12 **Pearl Island (USA)**[65] [5736] 4-8-11 40 .... VinceSlattery 11 —
(D J Wintle) *a rr* **8/1**

0000 **9** 2 1/2 **Madame Guillotine**[7] [6512] 3-8-7 40 .... PaulMulrennan(3) 2 —
(P T Midgley) *led: rdn along and hdd over 3f out: sn wknd* **50/1**

0000 **10** 4 **Blake Hall Lad (IRE)**[34] [6245] 4-8-11 40 ....(bt) J-PGuillambert 14 —
(P S McEntee) *bhd fr 1/2-way* **16/1**

40-0 **11** 12 **Leyaaly**[14] [6442] 6-8-11 40 ....(t) HayleyTurner 8 —
(Miss Z C Davison) *chsd ldng pair: rdn along and wkng whn stmbld 2f out: sn lost pl* **28/1**

-020 **12** 1 **Showtime Faye**[271] [634] 3-8-10 40 .... JoeFanning 9 —
(A Bailey) *a bhd* **25/1**

0000 **13** 6 **King Eric**[26] [6369] 3-8-10 40 .... GylesParkin 6 —
(C Smith) *cl up: rdn along over 4f out and wknd qckly* **66/1**

0000 **14** 5 **High Window (IRE)**[37] [6258] 5-8-4 40 .... AdeleRothery(7) 10 —
(G P Kelly) *sn rdn along and bhd* **40/1**

1m 44.09s (-0.51) **Going Correction** -0.20s/f (Stan)
WFA 3 from 4yo+ 1lb **14** Ran SP% **123.5**
Speed ratings (Par 97):94,91,91,87,87 87,81,69,66,62 50,49,43,38
CSF £34.77 TOTE £4.20: £2.40, £4.30, £3.10; EX 58.30.
Owner Robin Bastiman **Bred** Meon Valley Stud **Trained** Cowthorpe, N Yorks
■ Stewards' Enquiry : Darren Williams two-day ban: careless riding (Dec 26-27)

FOCUS
Typical form for the grade and not that strong.
Semper Paratus(USA) Official explanation: jockey said gelding hung left-handed and bit slipped through mouth
Leyaaly Official explanation: jockey said mare suffered interference and briefly lost its action

6557 BET DIRECT FREEPHONE 0800 211 222 MEDIAN AUCTION MAIDEN STKS 7f (F)
2:30 (2:31) (Class 7) 2-Y-O **£1,433** (£423; £211) **Stalls** Low

Form RPR

0430 **1** **Mujelle**[31] [6316] 2-9-0 67 .... FergalLynch 2 65
(D K Ivory) *mde most: rdn 2f out: drvn and hung lft ins last: kpt on* **3/1**[2]

0434 **2** 1 **Makai**[21] [6402] 2-9-0 65 .... JoeFanning 11 63
(M Johnston) *midfield:hdwy over 2f out: sn rdn and edgd lft: swtchd rt over 1f out: styd on strly ins last* **2/1**[1]

4 **3** 1/2 **Esthlos (FR)**[27] [6360] 2-9-0 .... MichaelTebbutt 10 61
(J Jay) *prom: hdwy 3f out: effrt and ev ch 2f out: sn rdn and kpt on fnl f* **7/1**

0 **4** hd **Appreciated**[16] [6427] 2-8-2 .... LiamJones(7) 8 56
(W J Haggas) *trckd ldrs: hdwy over 2f out: swtchd lft and rdn over 1f out: styng on whn nt clr run and swtchd rt ins last: kpt on* **11/2**[3]

62 **5** 3 1/2 **Al Rayanah**[27] [6360] 2-8-9 .... ChrisCatlin 4 47
(G Prodromou) *s.i.s: hdwy on inner 1/2-way: rdn over 2f out and sn no imp* **11/2**[3]

4500 **6** 1/2 **Dangermouse**[53] [5994] 2-8-9 50 .... FergusSweeney 6 46
(A G Newcombe) *cl up: rdn wl over 2f out: wknd over 1f out* **25/1**

00 **7** 3 1/2 **Marinero**[21] [6395] 2-9-0 .... DarrenWilliams 9 42
(Lady Herries) *s.i.s: a rr* **25/1**

0005 **8** 1/2 **Mytass**[21] [6403] 2-8-11 45 .... DanielTudhope(3) 7 41
(J A Pickering) *chsd ldrs: rdn along 3f out: sn wknd* **33/1**

0 **9** 1 **Milton's Keen**[38] [6242] 2-9-0 .... J-PGuillambert 5 38
(P S McEntee) *cl up: rdn along 3f out: wknd over 2f out* **12/1**

10 14 **Star Of Erhaab** 2-9-0 .... VinceSlattery 3 3
(E A Wheeler) *s.i.s: a rr* **66/1**

1m 30.97s (0.17) **Going Correction** -0.20s/f (Stan) **10** Ran SP% **121.4**
Speed ratings (Par 90):91,89,89,89,85 84,80,79,78,62
CSF £9.56 TOTE £3.70: £1.30, £1.40, £1.60; EX 10.90.
Owner Mrs J A Cornwell **Bred** Mrs J A Cornwell **Trained** Radlett, Herts
■ Stewards' Enquiry : Fergal Lynch two-day ban: careless riding (Dec 26-27)

FOCUS
A fair maiden for the class and the form makes sense rated through the winner.

NOTEBOOK
Mujelle belatedly lost his maiden tag at the tenth attempt under a positive ride and scored as his official rating entitled her to do. He seems best on this surface, and got the trip well, so may build on this now that he has managed to get his head in front. (op 4-1)
Makai took an age to hit his full stride and did not prove suited by this drop back in trip. He still ran close to his official rating, however, and should prove happier back over a mile in the future. (op 11-4 tchd 3-1 in places)
Esthlos(FR), fourth on his recent debut over this course and distance, had every chance and posted another creditable effort. He will be eligible for a handicap mark after his next outing and could prove to be the best of these in the longer term. (op 13-2 tchd 8-1)
Appreciated stepped up on the form of her recent debut at Lingfield and would have most likely bagged a place with a clearer passage in the final furlong. She is clearly going the right way, will be qualified for handicaps after her next outing, and ought to get another furlong in due course. (op 4-1)
Al Rayanah did not help her cause with a sluggish start and failed to rate a serious threat. She was not disgraced, however, and should fare better now she is eligible for a handicap mark. (op 5-1)
Dangermouse ran his race and helps set the level for this form. (op 28-1)

6558 BETDIRECT FOOTBALL ON ITV TEXT P367 BANDED STKS 7f (F)
3:00 (3:01) (Class 7) 3-Y-O+ **£1,423** (£420; £210) **Stalls** Low

Form RPR

4065 **1** **Wodhill Be**[23] [6384] 5-8-11 45 .... MichaelTebbutt 6 48
(D Morris) *hld up in tch: smooth hdwy over 2f out: led wl over 1f out: rdn and styd on ins last* **9/4**[2]

0000 **2** 1 1/4 **Inescapable (USA)**[8] [6497] 4-8-4 45 .... TolleyDean(7) 4 45
(A W Carroll) *dwlt: hld up: hdwy over 2f out: rdn wl over 1f out: drvn to chse wnr ins last: kpt on* **6/1**

0-02 **3** 3 **Naval Attache**[7] [6509] 3-8-11 45 .... FergalLynch 3 37
(P A Blockley) *cl up: led after 2f: rdn over 2f out: hdd wl over 1f out and wknd ins last* **7/4**[1]

0000 **4** 2 1/2 **Jakeal (IRE)**[6] [6515] 6-8-11 40 ....(v) VHalliday 8 31
(R M Whitaker) *chsd ldrs on outer: rdn along over 2f out: sn one pce* **14/1**

0060 **5** 1 **Sam The Sorcerer**[20] [6412] 4-8-11 40 .... DarrenWilliams 5 28
(J R Norton) *trckd ldrs: hdwy 3f out: rdn over 2f out and sn btn* **20/1**

0000 **6** 4 **Pearl Fisher (IRE)**[234] [1185] 4-8-8 45 ....(v[1]) DanielTudhope(3) 1 18
(D Carroll) *trckd ldrs on inner: rdn along 1/2-way: sn wknd* **3/1**[3]

0000 **7** 3/4 **Catheriniski (IRE)**[58] [5899] 3-8-11 45 .... PatCosgrave 7 16
(P A Blockley) *led 2f: cl up tl rdn wl over 2f out and sn wknd* **80/1**

00-0 **8** 3/4 **Just Dashing**[331] [125] 6-8-6 30 .... NataliaGemelova(5) 2 14
(J E Long) *dwlt: sn outpcd and a bhd* **80/1**

1m 31.4s (0.60) **Going Correction** -0.20s/f (Stan) **8** Ran SP% **120.3**
Speed ratings (Par 97):88,86,83,80,79 74,73,72
CSF £17.05 TOTE £3.40: £1.10, £2.20, £1.10; EX 19.30.
Owner Miss S Graham **Bred** Wodhill Stud **Trained** Newmarket, Suffolk

FOCUS
A very moderate winning time even for a banded race, 0.43 seconds slower than the preceding two-year-old maiden, but the form looks straightforward rated through the first two.

6559 IN RUNNING TONIGHT ON SKYTEXT 293 BANDED STKS 6f (F)
3:30 (3:31) (Class 7) 3-Y-O+ **£1,433** (£423; £211) **Stalls** Low

Form RPR

1034 **1** **Mind Alert**[3] [6527] 4-8-13 50 ....(v) PatrickMathers(3) 5 58
(D Shaw) *hld up: smooth hdwy 2f out: shkn up and qcknd to ld ins last: sn rdn and kpt on* **3/1**[1]

6000 **2** nk **Cayman King**[21] [6407] 3-9-1 49 .... RobertWinston 10 56
(R Craggs) *cl up: led over 2f out: rdn wl over 1f out: drvn and hdd ins last: kpt on wl u.p* **16/1**

3144 **3** 2 **Magic Amour**[6] [6515] 7-8-7 48 ....(b) KevinGhunowa(7) 4 49
(P A Blockley) *hld up: hdwy on outer 2f out: sn rdn and kpt on wl fnl f* **7/2**[2]

3416 **4** 3/4 **Amanda's Lad (IRE)**[8] [6497] 5-8-5 46 .... LiamJones(7) 12 45
(M C Chapman) *cl up: rdn along 2f out: ev ch tl drvn and one pce ins last* **7/1**

4010 **5** 2 1/2 **Ardkeel Lass (IRE)**[12] [6471] 4-8-5 45 ow1 .... JBrennan(7) 6 37
(P D Evans) *chsd ldrs: rdn 2f out: wknd over 1f out* **12/1**

0000 **6** hd **Donegal Shore (IRE)**[55] [5960] 6-9-2 50 ....(vt) SamHitchcott 11 41
(Jennie Candlish) *s.i.s and bhd tl styd on fnl 2f* **33/1**

1120 **7** 1 **Desertina (IRE)**[28] [6345] 3-8-6 47 .... MichaelJStainton(7) 8 35
(R M Whitaker) *in tch: hdwy to chse ldrs over 2f out: sn rdn and btn* **6/1**[3]

5040 **8** 3/4 **Pragmatica**[12] [6470] 4-8-12 46 ....(p) ChrisCatlin 13 32
(R M H Cowell) *midfield: effrt and sme hdwy over 2f out: sn rdn and nvr a factor* **14/1**

0000 **9** 3 **Blakeshall Quest**[37] [6261] 5-8-13 47 ....(b) HayleyTurner 7 24
(R Brotherton) *a towards rr* **22/1**

0000 **10** 4 **Huxley (IRE)**[40] [6231] 6-9-2 50 ....(t) VinceSlattery 9 15
(D J Wintle) *s.i.s: a rr* **22/1**

0006 **11** hd **Party Princess (IRE)**[16] [6438] 4-9-2 50 .... DeanMcKeown 2 14
(S Parr) *chsd ldrs on inner: rdn along 3f out: sn wknd* **10/1**

3100 **12** 12 **On The Trail**[30] [6326] 8-8-12 46 ....(p) DarrenWilliams 1 —
(D W Chapman) *led: rdn along and hdd over 2f out: sn wknd* **16/1**

0500 **13** 2 1/2 **Saucepot**[21] [6396] 3-8-11 40 ....(b[1]) VHalliday 3 —
(Miss J R Tooth) *a rr* **20/1**

1m 15.99s (-0.91) **Going Correction** -0.20s/f (Stan) **13** Ran SP% **125.6**
Speed ratings (Par 97):98,97,94,93,90 90,89,88,84,78 78,62,59
CSF £53.37 TOTE £4.40: £1.50, £5.60, £2.10; EX 84.30 Place 6 £51.90, Place 5 £8.81.
Owner Simon Mapletoft Racing IV **Bred** P T Tellwright **Trained** Danethorpe, Notts

FOCUS
A typical sprint for the class and the form looks sound rated through the third.
T/Plt: £123.00 to a £1 stake. Pool: £30,558.80. 181.35 winning tickets. T/Qpdt: £4.80 to a £1 stake. Pool: £2,925.60. 449.00 winning tickets. JR

6543 WOLVERHAMPTON (A.W) (L-H)
Monday, December 12

OFFICIAL GOING: Standard
Wind: Almost nil. Weather: Fine

6560 BETDIRECT ON SNOOKER H'CAP (DIV I) 1m 141y(P)
1:10 (1:11) (Class 6) (0-55,55) 3-Y-O+ **£2,548** (£752; £376) **Stalls** Low

Form RPR

2000 **1** **Gem Bien (USA)**[9] [6487] 7-8-13 **54** ....(p) TonyCulhane 13 62
(D W Chapman) *hld up and bhd: rdn and hdwy on outside 2f out: r.o u.p to ld wl ins fnl f* **12/1**

2305 **2** nk **Star Fern**[8] [6497] 4-8-5 **46** oh1 .... JimmyQuinn 12 53
(M J Attwater) *dwlt: hld up and bhd: rdn and hdwy on outside 2f out: led ins fnl f: sn hdd: r.o* **9/1**

0004 **3** 1 3/4 **Young Mick**[9] [6487] 3-8-12 **55** ....(b) JamieMackay 7 59
(G G Margarson) *hld up in mid-div: rdn and hdwy over 2f out: ev ch 1f out: nt qckn* **10/1**

6055 **4** nk **Cost Analysis (IRE)**[13] [6462] 3-8-11 **54** ....(t) MatthewHenry 1 57
(M A Jarvis) *s.i.s: hld up and bhd: hdwy over 2f out: swtchd rt over 1f out: edgd lft ins fnl f: kpt on* **5/1**[1]

4351 **5** 3/4 **Sonntag Blue (IRE)**[130] [4107] 3-8-1 **51** ....(b) DonnaCaldwell(7) 9 52
(Miss J Feilden) *a.p: rdn 3f out: led over 1f out tl ins fnl f: no ex* **20/1**

5602 **6** 3/4 **Dara Mac**[12] [6473] 6-8-11 **52** .... LPKeniry 8 52
(L P Grassick) *hld up in mid-div: rdn and hdwy whn nt clr run 2f out: ev ch 1f out: wknd towards fin* **11/2**[2]

0002 **7** shd **Shaheer (IRE)**[16] [6436] 3-8-10 **53** .... IanMongan 2 53
(Mrs L J Mongan) *sn led: hdd 6f out: led over 3f out: rdn over 2f out: hdd over 1f out: wknd wl ins fnl f* **7/1**[3]

5500 **8** 1 3/4 **Azreme**[7] [6506] 5-8-11 **52** .... SteveDrowne 5 48
(P Howling) *hld up in mid-div: hdwy over 3f out: rdn over 2f out: edgd lft over 1f out: wknd ins fnl f* **8/1**

0030 **9** 3 **Harare**[21] [6400] 4-8-13 **54** .... PaulHanagan 3 44
(R J Price) *prom: lost pl 5f out: n.d after* **11/2**[2]

5540 **10** 1/2 **Padre Nostro (IRE)**[40] [5321] 6-9-0 **55** .... BrianReilly 11 44
(J R Holt) *bhd fnl 5f* **40/1**

6003 **11** 3 1/2 **Lady Suesanne (IRE)**[55] [5957] 3-8-6 **49** ....(b) DavidMcCabe 4 30
(N Wilson) *led early: led 6f out tl over 3f out: rdn and wknd wl over 1f out* **20/1**

3000 **12** 16 **Zantero**[28] [6343] 3-8-4 **47** .... EddieAhern 6 —
(W M Brisbourne) *plld hrd: prom: rdn 3f out: sn wknd* **9/1**

1m 50.0s (-1.76) **Going Correction** -0.225s/f (Stan)
WFA 3 from 4yo+ 2lb **12** Ran SP% **119.8**
Speed ratings (Par 101):98,97,96,95,95 94,94,92,90,89 86,72
CSF £114.05 CT £1150.86 TOTE £21.40: £5.40, £2.80, £3.30; EX 229.90.
Owner J M Chapman **Bred** George Pruette **Trained** Stillington, N Yorks

FOCUS
A moderate handicap, though competitive enough with seven in a line across the track passing the furlong pole and the form looks sound. Unusually for this track, the front two dominated the finish despite coming very wide around the home bend.
Lady Suesanne(IRE) Official explanation: jockey said filly ran too freely

6561 FIRST PAST THE POST AT BETDIRECT MAIDEN AUCTION STKS 5f 20y(P)
1:40 (1:40) (Class 6) 2-Y-O **£2,846** (£840; £420) **Stalls** Low

Form RPR

2564 **1** **Prettilini**[51] [6030] 2-8-0 60 ow1 .... RichardThomas(3) 4 60
(A W Carroll) *wnt lft s: mde virtually all: rdn wl over 1f out: r.o* **3/1**[2]

653 **2** *1* **Cativo Cavallino**[23] 6374 2-8-9 74 .... IanMongan 6 62
(Julian Poulton) *a.p: rdn and ev ch wl over 1f out: j. path ins fnl f: nt qckn* **5/6**[1]

3 *shd* **Radiator Rooney (IRE)**[61] 5840 2-8-11 .... LPKeniry 9 64
(Patrick Morris, Ire) *s.i.s: sn w wnr: rdn and ev ch 2f out: kpt on towards fin* **10/1**

2005 **4** *1 ¼* **Succeed (IRE)**[33] 6296 2-7-13 60 .... DuranFentiman(5) 7 52
(Mrs H Sweeting) *a.p: rdn over 2f out: r.o one pce fnl f* **13/2**[3]

0000 **5** *nk* **Drink To Me Only**[56] 5944 2-8-7 45 .... DavidAllan 8 54?
(J R Weymes) *bhd: rdn 2f out: hdwy fnl f: nt rch wnrs* **40/1**

0 **6** *3 ½* **Ballyhooligan (IRE)**[124] 4254 2-8-9 .... SteveDrowne 5 43
(Jamie Poulton) *s.i.s: hld up and bhd: late prog: n.d* **33/1**

5600 **7** *1* **Stoneacre Girl (IRE)**[205] 1883 2-8-7 30 ow3 .... RobbieFitzpatrick 2 38?
(Peter Grayson) *hmpd s: a bhd* **66/1**

000 **8** *nk* **Scattered Empire (IRE)**[34] 6290 2-8-7 40 .... PaulDoe 1 37
(Peter Grayson) *hld up in tch: rdn and wknd 2f out* **66/1**

0000 **9** *1 ¾* **No Inkling (IRE)**[54] 5984 2-8-4 50 .... (v) JimmyQuinn 3 27
(M J Attwater) *carried lft and bmpd s: hld up: short-lived effrt over 2f out* **16/1**

62.45 secs (-0.37) **Going Correction** -0.225s/f (Stan) **9** Ran SP% **116.2**
Speed ratings (Par 94):93,91,91,89,88 83,81,81,78
CSF £5.79 TOTE £3.70: £1.30, £1.10, £2.60; EX 10.70.
Owner David Shorthouse **Bred** G W Turner And Miss S J Turner **Trained** Cropthorne, Worcs
■ Stewards' Enquiry : Richard Thomas one-day ban: used whip with excessive frequency (Dec 26)

FOCUS
An ordinary maiden dominated by those that helped force the pace and the order changed little during the contest. The form could rate higher but is held down by the time and the proximity of the fifth.

NOTEBOOK
Prettilini, better drawn than here last time, shifted left leaving the stalls and caused problems for the pair drawn immediately on her inside, but it did mean that she was able to grab the coveted spot next to the inside rail before the bend. Taking the shortest route home of the front trio as a result, that probably made a big difference and she showed the right attitude to get off the mark at the 12th attempt. Her future now depends on the how the Handicapper interprets her beating a horse with whom she would have been 8lb better off in a handicap. (op 4-1 tchd 9-2 and 11-4)
Cativo Cavallino, best in by upwards of 8lb on adjusted official ratings, was always up there but appeared to get unbalanced when shying at the tracks left by the stalls in the first race and there was no way back from there. It is impossible to say whether it affected the result, but he still seems to be learning and certainly has more potential for improvement than the winner. (op 8-11 tchd Evens)
Radiator Rooney(IRE), who has only one eye, was making his British and sand debuts. He broke well enough from the worst draw and showed good speed but he was always losing ground on the two other pacesetters by racing so wide and the amount of ground he lost was probably about the same he was beaten by. He is nothing special, but has the ability to win a race like this when better drawn. (tchd 11-1)
Succeed(IRE) was again not best drawn and so was not totally disgraced. Her best effort on turf came on very fast ground so she may prefer the Lingfield Polytrack to this. (op 6-1)
Drink To Me Only, made a little late headway in a race dominated by the pacesetters, but never looked like winning. He faced a stiff task at the weights and would probably be better off in a tri-banded event in the New Year. (op 33-1)
Stoneacre Girl(IRE), reappearing after a seven-month break, had little chance after getting buffeted at the start. (op 40-1)
No Inkling(IRE), who has shown nothing in four previous starts, was done few favours by the eventual winner after leaving the gates. (op 20-1)

6562 BETDIRECT ON CHANNEL 4 TEXT PAGE 613 (S) STKS 5f 216y(P)
2:10 (2:10) (Class 6) 2-Y-O **£2,552** (£753; £376) **Stalls** Low

Form RPR
5200 **1** **Angie And Liz (IRE)**[27] 6353 2-8-7 53 .... PaulHanagan 6 56
(P D Evans) *plld hrd: a.p: rdn over 3f out: led over 1f out: r.o* **20/1**

5100 **2** *nk* **Buzzin'Boyzee (IRE)**[27] 6359 2-8-12 52 .... SteveDrowne 2 60
(P D Evans) *hld up in mid-div: hdwy whn nt clr run briefly over 2f out: sn rdn: ev ch 1f out: r.o* **8/1**

6346 **3** *¾* **Mistatake (IRE)**[27] 6357 2-8-12 63 .... (p) JimmyQuinn 1 58
(K A Ryan) *led early: a.p: rdn to ld 2f out: edgd rt over 1f out: nt qckn ins fnl f* **2/1**[1]

0302 **4** *3 ½* **Phinerine**[7] 6500 2-8-12 60 .... (b) RobbieFitzpatrick 4 48
(Peter Grayson) *s.i.s: hdwy 4f out: rdn over 2f out: wkng whn hung rt ins fnl f* **3/1**[2]

0060 **5** *1 ¼* **Twilight Avenger (IRE)**[6] 6517 2-8-9 52 .... (p) AdamKirby(3) 11 44
(M J Polglase) *outpcd: hdwy fnl f: nrst fin* **33/1**

0600 **6** *½* **Imperial Gem (IRE)**[27] 6357 2-8-7 54 .... (b1) EddieAhern 10 37
(Rae Guest) *hld up: rdn over 2f out: no hdwy whn edgd lft 1f out* **10/1**

0000 **7** *½* **Surf City**[7] 6500 2-8-12 67 .... (p) DaneO'Neill 9 41
(R A Harris) *hld up: rdn 4f out: sme late prog* **9/1**

0000 **8** *1* **Why Whisper**[26] 6366 2-8-12 52 .... PaulEddery 8 38
(B Smart) *sn outpcd: sme late prog* **40/1**

0 **9** *5* **Threeball (IRE)**[42] 6196 2-8-7 .... TonyHamilton 12 18
(J J Quinn) *bhd fnl 3f* **33/1**

0054 **10** *shd* **Montini Royale (IRE)**[7] 6500 2-8-12 53 .... IanMongan 7 22
(M J Attwater) *sn led: hdd over 4f out: wknd wl over 1f out* **7/1**[3]

0500 **11** *5* **First Among Equals**[33] 6296 2-8-10 56 ow1 .... (b1) DNolan(3) 3 8
(Miss J R Tooth) *sn prom: led over 4f out: rdn 3f out: hdd 2f out: sn wknd* **16/1**

0000 **12** *2 ½* **Miss Lovat**[7] 6500 2-8-12 60 .... (b1) MickyFenton 5 —
(A Bailey) *sn outpcd* **33/1**

1m 15.14s (-0.67) **Going Correction** -0.225s/f (Stan) **12** Ran SP% **122.9**
Speed ratings (Par 94):95,94,93,88,87 86,85,84,77,77 71,67
CSF £170.44 TOTE £24.00: £5.10, £3.00, £1.80; EX 268.30.There was no bid for the winner.
Owner G M McGuinness **Bred** John Perotta **Trained** Pandy, Abergavenny
■ Stewards' Enquiry : Paul Eddery two-day ban: used whip with excessive force and frequency (Dec 26-27)

FOCUS
An ordinary seller in which the first four home came from the six lowest stalls and the form is very limited. The race provided a one-two for trainer David Evans and the front three pulled clear of the rest.

NOTEBOOK
Angie And Liz(IRE), who had run her best race when runner-up in a course-and-distance claimer in August, appreciated the return to this trip after failing to stay seven last time and battled on well to edge out her stable-companion. She had been beaten at this level a few times in her early starts, but seems to have improved since as she beat several rivals here with whom she would have been a lot worse off in a nursery.
Buzzin'Boyzee(IRE), the stable's first string according to the market, may just have needed her outing at Southwell last month following a three-month break and performed much better here, just finding her stablemate too strong. She is not the most consistent though and her penalty does her few favours in races like this. (op 7-1)
Mistatake(IRE), dropping back a furlong with the cheekpieces on for the first time, was well backed to win at Southwell last time and it was a similar story here but he again fell short after seemingly holding every chance. (op 7-4 tchd 9-4)
Phinerine, well backed, was tucked in just behind the three leaders turning for home and looked sure to play a big part in the finish, but he found less under pressure than had looked likely and was soon getting left behind. He does not look entirely straightforward. (op 5-1)
Twilight Avenger(IRE), who has shown bits and pieces of form, deserves a little credit for finishing where he did from a disadvantageous draw, but he is still looking for his first win after 16 attempts.
Surf City Official explanation: jockey said colt hung left

6563 IN RUNNING TONIGHT ON SKY TEXT 293 H'CAP 1m 5f 194y(P)
2:40 (2:41) (Class 6) (0-55,55) 3-Y-O+ **£2,878** (£849; £425) **Stalls** Low

Form RPR
3065 **1** **Sovereign Spirit (IRE)**[58] 5892 3-8-8 **54** .... (t) IanMongan 12 63
(W R Swinburn) *hld up in tch: wnt 2nd over 5f out: rdn over 3f out: led 2f out: edgd rt ins fnl f: drvn out* **11/1**

5 **2** *¾* **Ocean King (USA)**[102] 4903 4-9-2 **55** .... EddieAhern 6 63
(M G Holden, Ire) *hld up in tch: rdn over 2f out: styd on ins fnl f* **33/1**

5306 **3** *1 ¾* **Zaffeu**[13] 6461 4-8-4 **46** .... RichardThomas(3) 3 51+
(N P Littmoden) *hld up and bhd: hdwy over 4f out: nt clr run and lost pl 3f out: rallying whn hung lft 1f out: swtchd lft ins fnl f:* **8/1**

0443 **4** *1* **Countback (FR)**[9] 6490 6-8-4 **50** .... JackDean(7) 8 54
(A W Carroll) *s.i.s: hld up and bhd: swtchd lft over 2f out: hdwy wl over 1f out: styd on fnl f* **20/1**

00/0 **5** *hd* **Coppermalt (USA)**[9] 6490 7-8-7 **46** .... LPKeniry 2 50
(R Curtis) *hld up and bhd: hdwy over 2f out: styd on ins fnl f* **50/1**

0510 **6** *½* **Ice And Fire**[7] 6510 6-8-9 **48** .... (b) MickyFenton 9 51
(J T Stimpson) *hld up in mid-div: hdwy over 4f out: rdn over 2f out: wknd ins fnl f* **25/1**

4211 **7** *hd* **Tycheros**[12] 6472 3-8-3 **52** .... AdamKirby(3) 13 55
(S C Williams) *led: rdn 3f out: hdd 2f out: wknd ins fnl f* **9/4**[1]

0030 **8** *shd* **Airgusta (IRE)**[13] 6461 4-8-12 **51** .... JamieMackay 4 54
(C P Morlock) *hld up in mid-div: rdn over 2f out: no hdwy* **25/1**

0002 **9** *4* **Selika (IRE)**[72] 5629 3-8-8 **54** .... BrianReilly 1 51
(K F Clutterbuck) *nvr nr ldrs* **16/1**

3306 **10** *5* **Barella (IRE)**[54] 5980 6-8-13 **52** .... JimmyQuinn 11 42
(E J Alston) *s.i.s: a bhd* **16/1**

0134 **11** *2 ½* **Jackie Kiely**[9] 6490 4-8-12 **51** .... TonyCulhane 7 38
(P Howling) *prom: wnt 2nd briefly 6f out: rdn and wknd over 2f out* **7/1**[3]

0031 **12** *11* **Michaels Dream (IRE)**[7] 6510 6-8-7 **46** 6ex .... (b) DavidMcCabe 5 17
(N Wilson) *chsd ldr 8f: wknd qckly 4f out* **14/1**

0124 **13** *11* **Intavac Boy**[2] 6548 4-9-1 **54** .... PaulHanagan 10 10
(C W Thornton) *hld up in mid-div: stdy hdwy over 6f out: rdn and edgd lft over 4f out: wknd over 2f out* **10/3**[2]

3m 2.22s (-5.15) **Going Correction** -0.225s/f (Stan)
WFA 3 from 4yo+ 7lb **13** Ran SP% **121.6**
Speed ratings (Par 101):105,104,103,103,102 102,102,102,100,97 95,89,83
CSF £343.94 CT £3056.09 TOTE £11.30: £2.60, £7.40, £3.90; EX 272.70.
Owner Cunnane, Godfrey, Kirkland & Winter **Bred** Exors Of The Late Mrs I Morris **Trained** Aldbury, Herts

FOCUS
A decent pace for this low-key if competitive handicap resulting in a fair winning time for a race of its class. The form looks sound rated through those in the frame behind the winner.
Ice And Fire Official explanation: jockey said gelding lost its action final furlong
Michaels Dream(IRE) Official explanation: jockey said gelding ran flat

6564 BETDIRECT.CO.UK H'CAP (DIV I) 1m 1f 103y(P)
3:10 (3:10) (Class 5) (0-75,75) 3-Y-O+ **£3,032** (£902; £450; £225) **Stalls** Low

Form RPR
0551 **1** **Western Roots**[35] 6287 4-8-7 **64** .... JimmyQuinn 6 70+
(M Appleby) *hld up: hdwy on ins 3f out: swtchd rt over 2f out: led jst ins fnl f: drvn out* **7/2**[2]

0060 **2** *½* **Consonant (IRE)**[7] 6499 8-9-4 **75** .... MickyFenton 8 80
(D G Bridgwater) *hld up towards rr: hdwy on outside over 1f out: fin wl* **20/1**

0200 **3** *¾* **Indebted**[27] 6350 3-8-13 **72** .... EddieAhern 2 76
(P W D'Arcy) *hld up in tch: rdn wl over 1f out: nt qckn fnl f* **11/1**

6003 **4** *½* **All A Dream**[7] 6499 3-8-13 **72** .... TomEaves 5 75
(Mrs L Williamson) *hld up: hdwy on ins over 3f out: sn rdn: swtchd rt and lft over 1f out: nt qckn ins fnl f* **20/1**

10 **5** *shd* **Gentle Peace (IRE)**[14] 6448 4-8-3 **63** oh1 ow2 .... AdamKirby(3) 3 66
(J W Unett) *chsd ldr: rdn over 2f out: led and edgd rt over 1f out: hdd jst ins fnl f: no ex* **10/1**

5106 **6** *2 ½* **Midshipman**[9] 6488 7-8-3 **67** ow1 .... WilliamCarson(7) 1 65
(A W Carroll) *s.i.s: hdwy on ins over 2f out: rdn and edgd rt over 1f out: no further prog* **8/1**

1020 **7** *¾* **African Sahara (USA)**[6] 6520 6-8-9 **73** .... (t) ChrisCavanagh(7) 7 70
(Miss D Mountain) *nvr nrr* **10/3**[1]

1626 **8** *¾* **Buscador (USA)**[240] 1066 6-7-13 **61** oh1 .... DuranFentiman(5) 11 56
(W M Brisbourne) *led: rdn over 2f out: hdd over 1f out: eased whn btn towards fin* **6/1**[3]

0221 **9** *1 ¾* **Mi Odds**[6] 6520 9-9-2 **73** 6ex .... AlanDaly 10 65
(Mrs N Macauley) *s.i.s: sn prom: rdn over 3f out: wknd over 2f out* **7/1**

0000 **10** *9* **Shami**[9] 6488 6-8-7 **64** .... PaulHanagan 9 39
(D W Chapman) *a bhd* **40/1**

0020 **11** *1 ½* **Penwell Hill (USA)**[132] 4032 6-9-3 **74** .... RobbieFitzpatrick 12 46
(M J Attwater) *hld up in tch: wknd over 3f out* **25/1**

2m 0.26s (-2.36) **Going Correction** -0.225s/f (Stan)
WFA 3 from 4yo+ 2lb **11** Ran SP% **116.4**
Speed ratings (Par 103):101,100,99,99,99 97,96,95,94,86 84
CSF £75.83 CT £702.89 TOTE £3.30: £2.10, £3.40, £2.90; EX 160.40 Trifecta £235.10 Part won. Pool £331.20 - 0.10 winning units..
Owner Sarnian Racing **Bred** Stratford Place Stud **Trained** Shrewley, Warwicks

FOCUS
A strongly-run race in which the first two came off the pace. The form is modest being limited by the fourth and fifth.
African Sahara(USA) Official explanation: jockey said, regarding the running and riding, his orders were to get cover in early stages and not make a move until 2f out, but that he mistakenly made ground too early in back straight and got stuck behind slower horses on final bend; trainer's representative added that horse is always held up in its races

6565 BETDIRECT FREEPHONE 0800 211 222 MAIDEN STKS 1m 1f 103y(P)
3:40 (3:43) (Class 5) 3-Y-O+ £3,439 (£1,023; £511; £255) Stalls Low

Form RPR
5630 1 **Almanshood (USA)**[7] 6503 3-9-0 67 DaneO'Neill 3 69
(P L Gilligan) *sn led: clr over 4f out: rdn over 2f out: r.o* 9/2[3]
0002 2 ½ **Blueberry Tart (IRE)**[2] 6542 3-8-9 62 RobertHavlin 7 63
(J M P Eustace) *a.p: rdn to chse wnr 2f out: kpt on ins fnl f* 4/1[2]
3435 3 2½ **Kryena**[37] 6266 3-8-9 63 SteveDrowne 2 58
(R F Johnson Houghton) *t.k.h in mid-div: hdwy over 2f out: rdn wl over 1f out: swtchd rt ins fnl f: one pce* 2/1[1]
60 4 3½ **Numanthia (IRE)**[30] 6333 3-8-9 IanMongan 5 52
(Miss J R Gibney) *s.i.s: rdn and hdwy on ins over 2f out: no imp fnl f* 50/1
6300 5 nk **Kirin**[27] 6356 3-9-0 67 (t) EddieAhern 12 56
(D E Cantillon) *hld up in tch: rdn over 3f out: no real prog fnl 2f* 5/1
003 6 ½ **Drumroll (IRE)**[17] 6418 3-9-0 70 BrianReilly 11 55+
(Miss J Feilden) *sn chsng ldr: rdn and lost 2nd 2f out: wkng whn eased ins fnl f* 20/1
64 7 nk **Scamperdale**[27] 6355 3-8-11 AdamKirby(3) 4 55
(Karen George) *hld up: rdn over 3f out: nvr trbld ldrs* 25/1
5306 8 1¼ **Linden Lime**[61] 5838 3-8-9 63 PaulDoe 1 47
(Jamie Poulton) *led early: hld up in tch: rdn over 3f out: wknd wl over 1f out* 8/1
050- 9 shd **Trew Flight (USA)**[380] 6741 3-9-0 65 GeorgeBaker 10 52
(M H Tompkins) *s.i.s: bhd: short-lived effrt on ins wl over 1f out* 12/1
10 ¾ **Hometomammy** 3-9-0 LPKeniry 9 51
(P W Hiatt) *dwlt: a bhd* 33/1
50-0 11 1½ **Skelligs Rock (IRE)**[9] 6485 5-9-2 70 TonyCulhane 8 48
(A W Carroll) *a bhd* 33/1
0 12 14 **Loyalist (USA)**[30] 6333 3-9-0 MickyFenton 6 21
(J G Given) *hld up in mid-div: rdn 4f out: wl bhd fnl 3f* 50/1

2m 1.16s (-1.46) **Going Correction** -0.225s/f (Stan)
WFA 3 from 4yo+ 2lb 12 Ran SP% **125.4**
Speed ratings (Par 103):97,96,94,91,90 90,90,89,89,88 87,74
CSF £22.74 TOTE £8.00: £3.00, £1.30, £1.10; EX 36.20.
Owner Mrs Mary Roche **Bred** Shadwell Farm LLC **Trained** Newmarket, Suffolk

FOCUS
An ordinary maiden that took little winning and a modest winning time for the grade, being slower than both divisions of the 61-75 handicap over the same trip.
Drumroll(IRE) Official explanation: jockey said he thought gelding was wrong behind

6566 BETDIRECT.CO.UK H'CAP (DIV II) 1m 1f 103y(P)
4:10 (4:11) (Class 5) (0-75,75) 3-Y-O+ £3,037 (£903; £451; £225) Stalls Low

Form RPR
1033 1 **Shankly Bond (IRE)**[152] 3431 3-8-10 **69** PaulEddery 2 76
(B Smart) *a.p: rdn 2f out: led 1f out: r.o wl* 14/1
1100 2 1¾ **Dragon Slayer (IRE)**[88] 5250 3-8-13 **72** IanMongan 9 76
(M J Attwater) *led 1f: chsd ldr: rdn to ld 2f out: edgd lft and hdd 1f out: nt qckn* 5/1[2]
5410 3 nk **Gramada (IRE)**[69] 5685 3-7-11 **61** DuranFentiman(5) 12 64
(P A Blockley) *led after 1f: rdn and hdd 2f out: nt qckn fnl f* 50/1
1421 4 hd **Ramsgill (USA)**[30] 6324 3-8-3 **65** RichardThomas(3) 7 68+
(N P Littmoden) *hld up: rdn and hdwy on ins over 2f out: r.o ins fnl f* 9/4[1]
0000 5 shd **Sir Haydn**[6] 6520 5-9-4 **75** (v) EddieAhern 4 78
(J R Jenkins) *hld up in tch: rdn over 2f out: sltly outpcd over 1f out: rallied ins fnl f* 5/1[2]
4000 6 shd **Nautical**[27] 5402 7-9-2 **73** GeorgeBaker 6 76
(A W Carroll) *hld up in mid-div: hdwy over 2f out: rdn wl over 1f out: one pce fnl f* 8/1[3]
6540 7 1 **Sorbiesharry (IRE)**[6] 6520 6-8-9 **66** AlanDaly 5 67
(Mrs N Macauley) *hld up and bhd: hdwy on ins wl over 1f out: nvr trbld ldrs* 5/1[2]
1010 8 2 **Tanforan**[95] 5070 3-9-2 **75** (b[1]) TonyCulhane 1 72
(K McAuliffe) *hld up in mid-div: hdwy over 3f out: rdn over 2f out: wknd fnl f* 12/1
0000 9 2½ **Sandy's Legend (USA)**[86] 5317 3-8-4 **63** ow1 PaulDoe 10 55
(Jamie Poulton) *a towards rr* 28/1
0000 10 1½ **Savoy Chapel**[23] 6373 3-8-7 **66** JimmyQuinn 3 55
(A W Carroll) *a bhd* 25/1
0340 11 12 **Border Tale**[17] 6008 5-9-1 **72** (p) MickyFenton 11 39
(James Moffatt) *hld up in mid-div: rdn over 3f out: sn bhd* 33/1
000- 12 5 **Bayadere (GER)**[14] 6573 5-8-13 **70** BrianReilly 8 27
(K F Clutterbuck) *prom tl rdn and wknd over 3f out* 50/1

1m 59.92s (-2.70) **Going Correction** -0.225s/f (Stan)
WFA 3 from 5yo+ 2lb 12 Ran SP% **120.4**
Speed ratings (Par 103):103,101,101,101,100 100,99,98,95,94 83,79
CSF £80.54 CT £3422.80 TOTE £11.90: £3.40, £2.00, £10.80; EX 100.10.
Owner R C Bond **Bred** John Nolan **Trained** Hambleton, N Yorks
■ Stewards' Enquiry : George Baker caution: careless riding

FOCUS
A moderate handicap which looks solid enough through the first two, although those immediately behind raise doubts.
Ramsgill(USA) Official explanation: jockey said gelding hung left

6567 BETDIRECT ON SNOOKER H'CAP (DIV II) 1m 141y(P)
4:40 (4:40) (Class 6) (0-55,55) 3-Y-O+ £2,552 (£753; £376) Stalls Low

Form RPR
0203 1 **Blue Quiver (IRE)**[9] 6487 5-8-13 **54** SteveDrowne 3 62
(C A Horgan) *dwlt: rdn & hdwy wl over 1f out: rdn to ld ins fnl f: r.o* 11/4[1]
0036 2 1 **Bauhinia**[37] 6262 3-8-7 **50** PaulDoe 4 56
(J A R Toller) *hld up and bhd: hdwy whn nt clr run on ins over 1f out: fin wl* 14/1
0002 3 nk **Captain Darling (IRE)**[20] 6413 5-8-2 **46** EdwardCreighton(3) 6 51
(R W Price) *mde most: rdn over 2f out: hdd and nt qckn ins fnl f* 12/1
0033 4 nk **Orpen Quest (IRE)**[14] 6444 3-8-4 **47** PaulHanagan 11 51
(M J Attwater) *mid-div: pushed along over 6f out: lost pl 4f out: hdwy over 1f out: edgd lft ins fnl f: fin wl* 5/1[3]
1046 5 shd **Machinate (USA)**[26] 6372 3-8-12 **55** EddieAhern 1 59
(W M Brisbourne) *hld up: hdwy over 3f out: rdn over 2f out: nt qckn ins fnl f* 9/2[2]
6600 6 1¼ **Prince Of Gold**[9] 6487 5-8-11 **52** (b) TonyCulhane 8 54
(R Hollinshead) *dwlt: hld up and bhd: hdwy over 2f out: sn rdn: one pce fnl f* 8/1
4036 7 2 **Londoner (USA)**[9] 6487 7-8-11 **52** (v[1]) DaneO'Neill 2 49
(S Dow) *w ldr: hung lft over 4f out: wknd over 1f out* 10/1
2000 8 1 **Endless Peace (IRE)**[5] 6524 4-8-3 **47** oh1 ow1 AdamKirby(3) 10 42
(J W Unett) *nvr trbld ldrs* 66/1
0/56 9 ½ **Renegade (IRE)**[13] 6460 4-8-11 **52** IanMongan 13 46
(Mrs L J Mongan) *chsd ldrs: rdn over 3f out: wknd over 2f out* 20/1
0005 10 1 **Weet Yer Tern (IRE)**[42] 6202 3-8-12 **55** MickyFenton 9 47
(P A Blockley) *a bhd* 20/1
3113 11 3½ **Glendale**[256] 813 4-8-11 **52** JimmyQuinn 12 37
(D K Ivory) *hld up: rdn over 3f out: wknd wl over 1f out* 10/1
0660 12 3½ **Intended**[7] 6506 3-8-9 **52** (vt[1]) LPKeniry 7 29
(A M Balding) *chsd ldrs: rdn over 4f out: wknd over 3f out* 33/1

1m 50.17s (-1.59) **Going Correction** -0.225s/f (Stan)
WFA 3 from 4yo+ 2lb 12 Ran SP% **122.1**
Speed ratings (Par 101):98,97,96,96,96 95,93,92,92,91 88,85
CSF £42.53 CT £408.09 TOTE £4.20: £1.60, £4.90, £2.30; EX 54.40 Place 6 £417.23, Place 5 £54.13.
Owner Mrs Wendy Gillings **Bred** Mrs B Sumner **Trained** Uffcott, Wilts

FOCUS
This low-grade handicap was run at a strong pace, which set things up for those coming from behind. The form looks sound enough rated through the third and fourth.
Orpen Quest(IRE) Official explanation: jockey said gelding hung left
Renegade(IRE) Official explanation: jockey said gelding hung right throughout
T/Jkpt: Not won. T/Plt: £415.00 to a £1 stake. Pool: £39,369.70. 69.25 winning tickets. T/Qpdt: £86.00 to a £1 stake. Pool: £3,243.00. 27.90 winning tickets. KH

6554 SOUTHWELL (L-H)
Tuesday, December 13

OFFICIAL GOING: Standard
Wind: Light, half-behind Weather: Cloudy

6568 SARAH MITCHELL 21 TODAY BANDED STKS 5f (F)
12:50 (12:51) (Class 7) 3-Y-O+ £1,423 (£420; £210) Stalls High

Form RPR
4630 1 **Soul Provider (IRE)**[50] 6079 4-8-11 40 J-PGuillambert 2 47
(G Prodromou) *sn outpcd: hdwy over 1f out: led ins fnl f: r.o* 15/2[3]
6035 2 1¼ **Comic Tales**[203] 1982 4-8-11 40 DarrenWilliams 1 43
(M Mullineaux) *chsd ldrs: rdn 1/2-way: led over 1f out: hdd and unable qck ins fnl f* 12/1
0000 3 nk **Four Kings**[99] 5000 4-8-11 40 PaulHanagan 4 42
(R Allan) *chsd ldrs: outpcd 3f out: hdwy over 1f out: r.o* 9/1
0300 4 hd **Straffan (IRE)**[45] 6155 3-8-11 40 (b) DaleGibson 12 41
(J Hetherton) *chsd ldrs: led over 3f out: rdn and hdd over 1f out: edgd lft and styd on same pce ins fnl f* 14/1
5020 5 ¾ **Off Hire**[15] 6441 9-8-11 40 (v) RobbieFitzpatrick 8 39
(C Smith) *chsd ldrs: sn drvn along: styd on* 7/1[2]
0006 6 ¾ **Mr Spliffy (IRE)**[15] 6441 6-8-4 40 (b) LiamJones(7) 11 36
(M C Chapman) *s.i.s: outpcd: rdn and hung lft over 1f out: styd on: nrst fin* 10/1
0500 7 ¾ **A Teen**[231] 1298 7-8-11 40 RobertWinston 6 33
(P Howling) *led: hdd over 3f out: sn rdn: btn whn nt clr run over 1f out* 9/1
0003 8 shd **Mac The Knife (IRE)**[15] 6441 4-8-11 40 EddieAhern 7 33
(M Appleby) *chsd ldrs: rdn 3f out: wknd fnl f* 11/4[1]
0006 9 ½ **Mad Marty Wildcard**[24] 6380 3-8-11 35 (bt[1]) ChrisCatlin 5 31
(R Brotherton) *s.i.s: sn drvn along: outpcd over 3f out: sme hdwy whn nt clr run ins fnl f: n.d* 17/2
0400 10 ¾ **Sion Hill (IRE)**[133] 4025 4-8-8 35 (b) JohnMcAuley(3) 9 29
(M C Chapman) *s.i.s: hdwy to join ldrs over 3f out: rdn over 1f out: wknd ins fnl f* 11/1
0000 11 4 **Levelled**[15] 6441 11-8-11 40 (p) TonyCulhane 3 15
(D W Chapman) *w ldrs to 1/2-way: sn rdn: wknd over 1f out* 16/1
0600 12 9 **Grasslandik**[123] 4319 9-8-6 35 ow2 (b) AnnStokell(7) 10 —
(Miss A Stokell) *s.i.s: sn outpcd* 50/1

60.24 secs (-0.06) **Going Correction** -0.075s/f (Stan) 12 Ran SP% **121.1**
Speed ratings (Par 97):97,95,94,94,93 91,90,90,89,88 82,67
CSF £96.36 TOTE £8.50: £2.30, £3.50, £4.40; EX 78.60.
Owner F & Mrs A Butler **Bred** Eamon Kelly **Trained** East Harling, Norfolk

FOCUS
A weak sprint, which again saw those drawn low at an advantage, and the form looks fair for the class rated through the placed horses.

6569 PRESS RED TO BET ON ITVI MAIDEN CLAIMING STKS 6f (F)
1:20 (1:23) (Class 7) 2-Y-O £1,457 (£430; £215) Stalls Low

Form RPR
6255 1 **Aysgarth Flyer (IRE)**[24] 6386 2-8-7 51 (b[1]) GregFairley(5) 7 62
(I Semple) *s.i.s: hld up: hdwy over 2f out: swtchd rt over 1f out: r.o u.p to ld towards fin* 8/1[3]
0003 2 1¼ **Diktalex (IRE)**[27] 6366 2-8-0 55 (t) LiamJones(7) 10 53
(W G M Turner) *chsd ldrs: rdn to ld 2f out: edgd lft ins fnl f: hdd towards fin* 8/1[3]
0000 3 3 **Musical City**[109] 4734 2-8-7 45 PaulEddery 3 44
(B Smart) *chsd ldrs: rdn 1/2-way: no ex fnl f* 25/1
2040 4 2 **Axis Shield (IRE)**[22] 6403 2-8-8 52 ow1 RobertWinston 6 39
(J G Portman) *led 4f: wknd fnl f* 16/1
3000 5 shd **Lucky Celts (IRE)**[108] 4757 2-8-7 35 (p) RobertHavlin 8 38
(D Haydn Jones) *trckd ldrs: plld hrd: rdn over 1f out: wknd fnl f* 25/1
423 6 1½ **Quote Unquote**[14] 6466 2-8-7 62 EddieAhern 1 33
(J R Boyle) *w ldr tl rdn over 2f out: wknd fnl f* 1/1[1]
0664 7 ½ **Mad Professor (IRE)**[34] 6295 2-8-10 62 (b) TonyCulhane 4 35
(P W Chapple-Hyam) *prom: rdn over 2f out: wknd over 1f out* 7/2[2]
044 8 ¾ **Left Nostril (IRE)**[9] 6496 2-8-0 51 DonnaCaldwell(7) 13 30
(P S McEntee) *chsd ldrs over 4f* 25/1
000 9 3½ **Canary Girl**[71] 5667 2-8-7 40 PaulHanagan 2 19
(P D Evans) *hld up: rdn and wknd over 2f out* 50/1
0030 10 3 **Miss Mujahid Times**[22] 6403 2-7-10 48 DuranFentiman(5) 5 4
(A D Brown) *s.i.s: outpcd* 33/1
000 11 2½ **Tatstheticket**[28] 6360 2-8-9 35 JasonEdmunds(3) 12 8
(J Balding) *s.i.s: hld up: rdn and wknd over 2f out* 80/1
000 12 4 **La Bomba Veloce**[40] 6233 2-8-7 45 TomEaves 11 —
(Mrs L Williamson) *sn outpcd* 50/1

1m 17.43s (0.53) **Going Correction** -0.125s/f (Stan) 12 Ran SP% **120.0**
Speed ratings (Par 90):91,89,85,82,82 80,79,78,74,70 66,61
CSF £66.45 TOTE £9.10: £2.30, £1.90, £6.70; EX 77.40.The winner was claimed by John Parkes for £5,000.

Owner A R M Galbraith **Bred** Denis Phelan **Trained** Carluke, S Lanarks

FOCUS

A very poor heat, run at a fair pace, and the field came home fairly strung out. The third sets the level for the form.

NOTEBOOK

Aysgarth Flyer(IRE), with first-time blinkers replacing cheekpieces, lost his maiden tag at the eighth time of asking despite losing ground with a sluggish start. The headgear looked to have the desired effect, as did the drop back in trip, and he ultimately scored with a bit up his sleeve. While he is tricky, his yard tends to do well with this type, and he could have a bit more to offer yet. (tchd 7-1)

Diktalex(IRE) had every chance and, while she was eventually put in her place by the winner, she turned in another sound effort in defeat. She still has to convince that she is worthy of her current official rating, but is slowly going the right way and has a race of this nature within her compass. (op 13-2)

Musical City, making her All-Weather bow after a 109-day absence from the track, showed her best form to date and shaped as though she would benefit for the outing. She could build on this during the winter and looked suited by the trip. (op 20-1)

Axis Shield(IRE) had her chance from the front and improved on her recent effort back over this more suitable distance. (tchd 20-1)

Lucky Celts(IRE) did not shape that badly on this return from her 108-day break, considering she ran too keenly through the early parts.

Quote Unquote, making her debut for new connections, was again found wanting at the business end of the race and really is proving a very frustrating customer. She is probably happiest over the minimum trip, however. Official explanation: jockey said filly became upset in stalls (op 5-4 tchd 11-8)

Mad Professor(IRE) dropped out tamely when it mattered and did not look overly suited by this surface. He is only moderate, but could do better when reverting to Polytrack. (op 4-1)

6570 DAILY OFFERS FROM BETDIRECT BANDED STKS — 6f (F)

1:50 (1:54) (Class 7) 3-Y-O+ — **£1,429** (£422; £211) **Stalls** Low

Form — RPR

0105 **1** — **Ardkeel Lass (IRE)**[1] 6559 4-8-11 45 — PaulHanagan 1 — 54
(P D Evans) *led 1f: remained w ldr tl led and hung rt over 2f out: styd on* **13/2**[3]

0635 **2** *1* — **Beamsley Beacon**[21] 6409 4-8-11 45 — (b) TomEaves 2 — 51
(M Dods) *a.p: chsd wnr 2f out: sn rdn: styd on* **6/1**[2]

0030 **3** *¾* — **Christian Bendix**[6] 6526 3-8-11 45 — RobertWinston 11 — 49
(P Howling) *hld up: hdwy over 1f out: r.o* **14/1**

0332 **4** *hd* — **Jalouhar**[15] 6446 5-8-11 45 — (p) ChrisCatlin 5 — 49
(B P J Baugh) *mid-div: sn pushed along: hdwy over 2f out: styd on same pce fnl f* **11/4**[1]

0030 **5** *1* — **Polar Haze**[15] 6446 8-8-11 45 — (v) JimmyQuinn 6 — 46
(J Pearce) *chsd ldrs: rdn over 2f out: styd on same pce fnl f* **12/1**

0036 **6** *1* — **Fitzwarren**[15] 6446 4-8-11 45 — EddieAhern 7 — 43
(A D Brown) *chsd ldrs: rdn 1/2-way: no ex fnl f* **7/1**

5055 **7** *½* — **Sergeant Slipper**[15] 6446 8-8-11 40 — (v) RobbieFitzpatrick 3 — 41
(C Smith) *dwlt: hdwy u.p over 1f out: no ex ins fnl f* **11/1**

0602 **8** *2½* — **Torrent**[13] 6471 10-8-11 45 — (p) TonyCulhane 9 — 34
(D W Chapman) *hld up: rdn over 1f out: wknd fnl f* **13/2**[3]

0400 **9** *shd* — **Efimac**[38] 6259 5-8-4 45 — (v) SuzzanneFrance(7) 8 — 33
(N Bycroft) *s.s: outpcd* **33/1**

0641 **10** *2½* — **Joe Jo Star**[8] 6512 3-9-3 45 — (p) FergalLynch 10 — 32
(P A Blockley) *hld up: shkn up over 2f out: nvr nr to chal* **17/2**

5000 **11** *5* — **Saucepot**[1] 6559 3-8-11 40 — (b) SamHitchcott 4 — 11
(Miss J R Tooth) *led 5f out: hdd over 2f out: wknd wl over 1f out* **50/1**

1m 17.54s (0.64) **Going Correction** -0.125s/f (Stan) — 11 Ran SP% **118.2**

Speed ratings (Par 97):90,88,87,87,86 84,84,80,80,77 70

CSF £45.57 TOTE £7.70: £2.50, £2.20, £6.80; EX 42.00.

Owner Merthyr Motor Auctions **Bred** J Campbell **Trained** Pandy, Abergavenny

FOCUS

A moderate winning time even for a banded race, slightly slower than the preceding two-year-old maiden claimer. The form looks fairly straightforward rated through the runner-up.

Joe Jo Star Official explanation: jockey said, regarding the running and riding, gelding resents kickback and does not respond to vigourous riding, so his orders were to ride accordingly, adding that he was somewhat outpaced over this 6f trip, having run over a mile previously

6571 TEXT BETDIRECT TO 88600 BANDED STKS — 1m 4f (F)

2:20 (2:20) (Class 7) 3-Y-O+ — **£1,440** (£425; £212) **Stalls** Low

Form — RPR

0230 **1** — **Bulberry Hill**[13] 6475 4-9-0 40 — SamHitchcott 5 — 52
(R W Price) *s.i.s: hld up: hdwy on bit over 3f out: rdn to ld 1f out: edgd lft: styd on* **7/4**[1]

0405 **2** *shd* — **Liquid Lover (IRE)**[13] 6474 3-8-9 40 — EddieAhern 11 — 52
(W M Brisbourne) *chsd ldrs: rdn to ld over 1f out: sn edgd lft and hdd: styd on u.p* **9/2**[3]

4000 **3** *7* — **Mr Dip**[14] 6461 5-9-0 35 — TonyCulhane 9 — 41
(L A Dace) *hld up: hdwy 1/2-way: led 3f out: sn rdn: hung rt and hdd over 1f out: sn wknd* **12/1**

3000 **4** *3* — **Lyric Dances (FR)**[18] 6419 3-8-9 40 — MichaelTebbutt 14 — 36
(J Jay) *outpcd: hdwy over 4f out: rdn over 2f out: sn wknd* **25/1**

0600 **5** *1¼* — **Shotley Dancer**[42] 6218 6-8-7 40 — SuzzanneFrance(7) 4 — 34
(N Bycroft) *mid-div: hdwy over 3f out: wknd 2f out* **16/1**

0000 **6** *1¾* — **Jamaican Flight (USA)**[21] 6410 12-9-0 30 — RobertWinston 3 — 31
(Mrs S Lamyman) *w ldr tl led 9f out: hdd over 3f out: sn wknd* **25/1**

4235 **7** *1* — **Quest On Air**[15] 6442 6-9-0 40 — (p) FergalLynch 2 — 29
(J R Jenkins) *led 1f: chsd ldrs tl wknd over 2f out* **7/2**[2]

00/0 **8** *5* — **Ball Games**[13] 3609 7-8-7 40 — (p) KatieHales(7) 6 — 21
(James Moffatt) *outpcd* **25/1**

0546 **9** *1* — **East Cape**[15] 6442 8-9-0 35 — KimTinkler 12 — 20
(N Tinkler) *prom: led over 3f out: sn hdd & wknd* **15/2**

000- **10** *dist* — **Allez Mousson**[37] 4778 7-8-7 40 — (b) MichaelJStainton(7) 13 — —
(A Bailey) *s.s: outpcd* **16/1**

00/0 **11** *13* — **Lady Sunrize**[24] 6381 6-9-0 35 — (vt[1]) PaulHanagan 7 — —
(P D Evans) *led after 1f: hdd 9f out: wknd over 4f out* **66/1**

00-0 **12** *dist* — **Charlieslastchance**[101] 4936 3-8-2 30 — (p) JamesDoyle(7) 1 — —
(Ms J S Doyle) *prom: lost pl 8f out: sn bhd* **66/1**

2m 41.52s (-0.57) **Going Correction** -0.125s/f (Stan)

WFA 3 from 4yo+ 5lb — 12 Ran SP% **122.5**

Speed ratings (Par 97):96,95,91,89,88 87,86,83,82,— —,—

CSF £9.45 TOTE £3.00: £1.30, £2.60, £4.00; EX 14.30.

Owner Miss D Hutchinson **Bred** Mrs Ian Pilkington **Trained** Newmarket, Suffolk

■ The first training success for former jockey Russell Price.

FOCUS

A weak heat, but it was run at a sound gallop, and the first two came clear. The form appears sound enough for the grade rated through the winner.

Bulberry Hill Official explanation: trainer said, regarding improved form shown, gelding was possibly better suited by the absence of a cross noseband, which it wore in its last race

Quest On Air Official explanation: jockey said gelding lost its off-fore shoe

6572 BETDIRECT FREEPHONE 0800 211 222 TRI-BANDED STKS — 7f (F)

2:50 (2:51) (Class 7) 3-Y-O — **£1,429** (£422; £211) **Stalls** Low

Form — RPR

4532 **1** — **Preskani**[9] 6497 3-8-7 40 — (p) AlanDaly 10 — 57+
(Mrs N Macauley) *trckd ldrs: led over 2f out: clr fnl f: eased towards fin* **85/40**[1]

5034 **2** *5* — **Faithisflying**[15] 6443 3-8-7 40 — (p) DaleGibson 4 — 44
(D W Chapman) *chsd ldrs: ev ch over 2f out: styd on same pce appr fnl f* **13/2**

6103 **3** *¾* — **Tacid**[8] 6512 3-8-12 45 — MickyFenton 2 — 47
(Dr J D Scargill) *chsd ldrs: ev ch over 2f out: sn rdn and hmpd: styd on same pce* **9/2**[2]

4050 **4** *nk* — **Trackattack**[13] 6472 3-8-12 45 — RobertWinston 12 — 46+
(P Howling) *prom: rdn and lost pl over 4f out: styd on appr fnl f* **10/1**

0050 **5** *¾* — **Ahaz**[27] 6369 3-8-7 40 — JimmyQuinn 9 — 40
(J F Coupland) *hld up: styd on appr fnl f: nvr nrr* **28/1**

5320 **6** *2½* — **Ginger Cookie**[35] 6293 3-8-7 40 — PaulEddery 6 — 33
(B Smart) *dwlt: hdwy 5f out: wknd 2f out* **5/1**[3]

600 **7** *½* — **Son Of Sophie**[178] 2718 3-8-7 40 — (b[1]) RobbieFitzpatrick 8 — 32
(C N Kellett) *led over 4f: wknd over 1f out* **50/1**

0005 **8** *1¾* — **Small Time Blues (IRE)**[15] 6443 3-7-11 35 — (t) DuranFentiman(5) 7 — 23
(J Parkes) *mid-div: rdn 1/2-way: wknd over 2f out* **66/1**

0600 **9** *1¼* — **Doughty**[8] 6512 3-8-12 45 — VinceSlattery 11 — 30
(D J Wintle) *s.s: hld up: rdn and wknd over 2f out* **9/1**

6060 **10** *2½* — **Polesworth**[15] 6441 3-8-7 40 — (b) FrancisFerris 1 — 18
(C N Kellett) *w ldr: racd keenly: rdn and ev ch over 2f out: sn hung rt and wknd* **20/1**

0600 **11** *5* — **Young Thomas (IRE)**[13] 2226 3-8-12 45 — (p) HayleyTurner 5 — 11
(James Moffatt) *bhd fr 1/2-way* **25/1**

66-0 **12** *3½* — **Kashtanka (IRE)**[246] 973 3-8-9 45 — JasonEdmunds(3) 13 — 2
(J Balding) *mid-div: rdn 1/2-way: sn wknd* **40/1**

1m 30.9s (0.10) **Going Correction** -0.125s/f (Stan) — 12 Ran SP% **117.2**

Speed ratings (Par 96):94,88,87,87,86 83,82,80,79,76 70,66

CSF £14.71 TOTE £2.80: £1.20, £2.00, £1.50; EX 14.30.

Owner Godfrey Horsford **Bred** P And Mrs Venner **Trained** Sproxton, Leics

FOCUS

A very weak affair which saw the field trail home behind the decisive winner. The runner-up sets a sound level and the form looks sound.

6573 MORE OFFERS AT BETDIRECT.CO.UK BANDED STKS — 1m (F)

3:20 (3:20) (Class 7) 3-Y-O+ — **£1,429** (£422; £211) **Stalls** Low

Form — RPR

1206 **1** — **Dispol Foxtrot**[38] 6253 7-8-6 45 — GregFairley(5) 4 — 57+
(Miss V Scott) *trckd ldrs: led over 4f out: rdn clr over 1f out: eased nr fin* **5/4**[1]

0360 **2** *2* — **Sea Frolic (IRE)**[50] 6080 4-8-11 45 — (v) RobbieFitzpatrick 9 — 51
(Jennie Candlish) *chsd ldrs: rdn over 3f out: no ex fnl f* **20/1**

2410 **3** *shd* — **Tirailleur (IRE)**[6] 6524 5-8-11 45 — FergalLynch 7 — 51
(J R Boyle) *chsd ldrs: rdn over 3f out: styd on same pce fnl f* **9/1**

0565 **4** *3* — **Inchdura**[15] 6444 7-8-11 45 — KimTinkler 11 — 45
(N Tinkler) *sn pushed along in rr: hdwy over 3f out: rdn over 2f out: styd on same pce* **14/1**

2022 **5** *nk* — **Sonderborg**[15] 6444 4-8-11 45 — (p) DaleGibson 2 — 44
(J Mackie) *chsd ldrs: rdn and lost pl over 3f out: n.d after* **10/3**[2]

0544 **6** *shd* — **Wings Of Morning (IRE)**[9] 6497 4-8-8 45 — (v) DanielTudhope(3) 6 — 44
(D Carroll) *chsd ldrs: rdn over 2f out:: wknd over 1f out* **8/1**

5555 **7** *1* — **Shielaligh**[15] 6445 4-8-4 45 — JamesMillman(7) 5 — 42
(B R Millman) *s.s: bhd: hdwy u.p over 1f out: nvr nrr* **13/2**[3]

3000 **8** *20* — **Super King**[8] 6508 4-8-11 45 — (v[1]) EddieAhern 8 — 2
(A D Brown) *dwlt: hdwy over 5f out: wknd over 2f out* **40/1**

4660 **9** *10* — **College Rebel**[24] 6381 4-8-11 40 — MickyFenton 1 — —
(J F Coupland) *sn led: rdn and hdd over 4f out: wknd 3f out* **66/1**

6-00 **10** *7* — **Sinjaree**[187] 296 7-8-11 40 — (p) JimmyQuinn 3 — —
(Mrs S Lamyman) *s.i.s: outpcd* **33/1**

5000 **11** *4* — **Golden Remedy**[9] 5181 4-8-11 35 — (b[1]) VinceSlattery 10 — —
(A R Dicken) *chsd ldrs: lost pl 5f out: bhd fr 1/2-way* **100/1**

1m 44.0s (-0.60) **Going Correction** -0.125s/f (Stan) — 11 Ran SP% **121.3**

Speed ratings (Par 97):98,96,95,92,92 92,91,71,61,54 50

CSF £35.93 TOTE £2.20: £1.40, £3.00, £2.10; EX 47.60 Place 6 £181.02, Place 5 £45.91.

Owner Miss Victoria Scott Jnr **Bred** B N And Mrs Toye **Trained** Elsdon, Northumberland

FOCUS

A fair event for the class in which the winner took advantage of a 25lb lower All-Weather rating. The form looks sound rated through the placed horses.

Sinjaree Official explanation: trainer said gelding lost its action

T/Plt: £653.50 to a £1 stake. Pool: £36,216.00. 40.45 winning tickets. T/Qpdt: £19.90 to a £1 stake. Pool: £4,291.30. 159.00 winning tickets. CR

6521 LINGFIELD (L-H)

Wednesday, December 14

OFFICIAL GOING: Standard

Wind: Light against Weather: Fine & cloudy

6574 PLAY GAMES AT BETDIRECT.CO.UK BANDED STKS (DIV I) — 1m (P)

12:10 (12:14) (Class 7) 3-Y-O+ — **£1,433** (£423; £211) **Stalls** High

Form — RPR

3030 **1** — **Mad**[7] 6522 4-8-12 46 — JohnEgan 3 — 54
(Andrew Reid) *settled in midfield: rdn and effrt wl over 1f out: r.o to ld last 150yds: sn clr* **4/1**[1]

0301 **2** *1¾* — **Mythical Charm**[7] 6522 6-9-6 48 — (t) J-PGuillambert 8 — 58
(J J Bridger) *hld up in last trio: gng easily but stl wl in rr 2f out: rdn and r.o fr over 1f out: tk 2nd nr fin* **6/1**[3]

0-14 **3** *½* — **Mutared (IRE)**[23] 6401 7-8-9 46 — RichardThomas(3) 11 — 49
(N P Littmoden) *mde most: drvn on inner 2f out: hdd and outpcd last 150yds* **12/1**

0045 **4** *nk* — **Wind Chime (IRE)**[66] 5758 8-9-0 48 — FergusSweeney 12 — 50
(A G Newcombe) *pressed ldr: rdn to chal 2f out: upsides ent fnl f: nt qckn* **8/1**

6103 **5** *¾* — **Fantasy Crusader**[7] 6522 6-9-1 49 — GrahamGibbons 9 — 49
(R M H Cowell) *racd wd: hld up towards rr: effrt wl over 1f out: flashed tail u.p: r.o ins fnl f* **9/2**[2]

6 *shd* **Hillfield Flyer (IRE)**[135] 4012 5-8-13 47 .... JimmyQuinn 1 47
(Samuel Murphy, Ire) *racd on inner in midfield: effrt 2f out: nt clr run jst over 1f out: styd on ins fnl f* **10/1**

2021 7 *nk* **Blushing Russian (IRE)**[32] 6328 3-9-1 50 .... SteveDrowne 7 49
(J M Bradley) *pressed ldng pair: rdn to chal and upsides 1f out: wknd last 150yds* **14/1**

1000 8 *1 ¼* **Coronado Forest (USA)**[7] 6525 6-8-13 47 .... IanMongan 10 45+
(M R Hoad) *hld up: hmpd on inner 5f out: effrt on inner 2f out: nt clr run over 1f out: styd on: no ch* **20/1**

0003 9 *½* **Zolash (IRE)**[7] 6524 3-8-10 45 .... EddieAhern 6 40
(Mrs L C Jewell) *hld up midfield: shuffled along and no rspnse wl over 1f out* **16/1**

00-1 10 *½* **Homebred Star**[23] 6398 4-8-8 47 .... RobynBrisland(5) 5 41
(G P Enright) *dwlt: hld up in last trio: shkn up over 1f out: one pce and no prog* **9/1**

004 11 *hd* **Sister Eugenie (IRE)**[29] 6361 3-8-11 46 .... TonyCulhane 4 40
(S Kirk) *chsd ldrs: cl up over 1f out: wknd ins fnl f* **25/1**

12 *2 ½* **Junebug Symphony (IRE)**[103] 4929 3-9-1 50 .... DManning 2 38
(V Smith) *pressed ldng pair: rdn and ch jst over 1f out: wknd rapidly* **16/1**

1m 38.47s (-0.96) **Going Correction** -0.125s/f (Stan)
WFA 3 from 4yo+ 1lb **12 Ran SP% 117.4**
Speed ratings (Par 97):99,97,96,96,95 95,95,94,93,93 92,90
CSF £27.30 TOTE £4.40: £2.00, £2.10, £4.70; EX 30.40.
Owner A S Reid **Bred** A S Reid **Trained** Mill Hill, London NW7

FOCUS
A very ordinary banded contest run at just a fair pace, but the form looks reliable and fair for the grade.

6575 NO 5P RULE 4S AT BETDIRECT BANDED STKS 1m 2f (P)
12:40 (12:51) (Class 7) 3-Y-O+ **£1,423** (£420; £210) **Stalls** Low

Form RPR

050 1 **Successor**[9] 6509 5-8-12 45 .... (t) JamieMackay 13 54
(M D I Usher) *hld up wl in rr: plenty to do over 2f out: gd prog over 1f out: r.o to ld last 100yds: sn clr* **33/1**

2021 2 *1 ¼* **Tuscan Treaty**[14] 6474 5-8-9 45 .... (t) AdamKirby(3) 3 51+
(P J McBride) *dwlt: hld up wl in rr: rdn 3f out: no prog tl hung rt and r.o fr over 1f out: fin strly* **10/1**

4034 3 *shd* **Prince Valentine**[7] 6524 4-8-12 45 .... (be) IanMongan 6 51
(G L Moore) *prog to ld over 6f out and increased pce: rdn over 2f out: hdd ins fnl f: kpt on* **8/1**

4424 4 *shd* **Mister Completely (IRE)**[14] 6475 4-8-12 45 .... ChrisCatlin 4 51
(J R Best) *trckd ldrs: rdn over 2f out: effrt on inner over 1f out: led briefly ins fnl f: nt qckn sn after* **9/2**[1]

-005 5 *1 ¼* **King's Minstrel (IRE)**[23] 6399 4-8-12 45 .... (t) PaulDoe 8 48
(R Rowe) *trckd ldrs: rdn and effrt over 2f out: cl up 1f out: nt qckn* **11/2**[2]

000R 6 *½* **Opera Knight**[67] 5740 5-8-12 45 .... MickyFenton 9 47
(A W Carroll) *dwlt: hld up in tch: prog to trck ldrs 2f out and gng wl: rdn and fnd nil over 1f out* **25/1**

0-00 7 *1* **Dream Of Dubai (IRE)**[7] 6524 4-8-12 45 .... HayleyTurner 10 46
(P Mitchell) *w ldr: led over 7f out to over 6f out: styd prom tl wknd fnl f* **50/1**

2424 8 *nk* **Tojoneski**[23] 6394 6-8-12 45 .... TomEaves 12 45
(I W McInnes) *hld up in rr: rdn and no prog wl over 2f out: plugged on fnl f: no ch* **7/1**[3]

00-0 9 *3* **Dara Girl (IRE)**[23] 6398 3-8-6 45 .... RobertMiles(3) 7 39
(L Montague Hall) *mounted on crse: reluctant to enter stalls: s.s: hld up in detached last: rdn over 1f out: kpt on* **40/1**

1225 10 *nk* **Young Kate**[7] 6522 4-8-12 45 .... SteveDrowne 5 42+
(J R Best) *trckd ldrs: rdn and effrt on inner 2f out: hanging and nt qckn over 1f out: eased ins fnl f* **11/2**[2]

0540 11 *6* **Tip Toes (IRE)**[25] 6381 3-8-9 45 .... TonyCulhane 1 27
(Mrs C A Dunnett) *chsd ldrs tl wknd 3f out* **50/1**

0000 12 *7* **Hugo The Boss (IRE)**[7] 6526 3-8-9 45 .... FergusSweeney 14 14
(J R Boyle) *a in rr: rdn over 4f out: sn btn* **50/1**

0241 13 *dist* **Revolve**[23] 6394 5-8-5 45 .... (p) JamesDoyle(7) 2 —
(Mrs L J Mongan) *led at stdy pce to over 7f out: virtually ref to r fr over 4f out: sn t.o: walked in* **9/2**[1]

2m 8.90s (1.11) **Going Correction** -0.125s/f (Stan)
WFA 3 from 4yo+ 3lb **13 Ran SP% 114.9**
Speed ratings (Par 97):90,89,88,88,87 87,86,86,84,83 78,73,—
CSF £311.36 TOTE £42.90: £11.90, £3.20, £3.40; EX 407.90.
Owner G A Summers **Bred** Juddmonte Farms **Trained** Upper Lambourn, Berks

FOCUS
They went no pace at all in the early stages of this contest and the tempo did not pick up until Prince Valentine was rushed into the lead after three furlongs. The winning time was therefore moderate, even for a banded race and the form is not particularly solid with the third the best guide.
Young Kate Official explanation: jockey said filly hung badly left
Revolve Official explanation: vet said gelding bled from the nose

6576 PLAY GAMES AT BETDIRECT.CO.UK BANDED STKS (DIV II) 1m (P)
1:10 (1:11) (Class 7) 3-Y-O+ **£1,433** (£423; £211) **Stalls** High

Form RPR

0006 1 **Kinsman (IRE)**[7] 6522 8-8-9 46 .... RobertMiles(3) 1 53
(T D McCarthy) *hld up: last and plenty to do over 2f out: taken wd and prog wl over 1f out: responded wl to press and r.o to ld last 50yds* **13/2**[3]

00 2 *¾* **Moondancer (GER)**[22] 6323 6-8-13 47 .... HayleyTurner 3 52
(B G Powell) *led at fast pce to 5f out: led again over 3f out: kicked 2 l clr over 1f out: worn down last 50yds* **20/1**

2000 3 *1 ¼* **Senor Bond (USA)**[23] 6399 4-8-13 47 .... EddieAhern 12 49
(A M Hales) *chsd ldrs: u.p fr 3f out: kpt on fnl f: nt pce to chal* **8/1**

4644 4 *¾* **Auentraum (GER)**[7] 6525 5-9-0 48 .... (b) TonyCulhane 11 49
(K McAuliffe) *hld up: smooth prog to trck ldrs 2f out: urged along to chse ldr 1f out: fnd little* **5/2**[1]

0065 5 *1* **Major Speculation (IRE)**[175] 2807 5-9-2 50 .... ChrisCatlin 10 48
(J M Bradley) *hld up in rr: rdn and sme prog over 2f out: one pce and nvr rchd ldrs* **13/2**[3]

002 6 *shd* **Fantasy Defender (IRE)**[9] 6508 3-9-0 49 .... (v) LPKeniry 6 47
(J J Quinn) *hld up in midfield: rdn over 2f out: kpt on same pce: n.d* **5/1**[2]

5000 7 *nk* **Royal Sailor (IRE)**[23] 6405 3-9-1 50 .... JohnEgan 9 47
(Julian Poulton) *hld up in last trio: rdn and sme prog into midfield over 2f out: kpt on same pce fr over 1f out* **9/1**

0000 8 *½* **Awarding**[30] 6346 5-8-4 45 .... (vt) MichaelJStainton(7) 8 41
(Dr J R J Naylor) *t.k.h: prom: rdn to chse ldr briefly over 1f out: wknd fnl f* **33/1**

4310 9 *1 ¼* **Kumakawa**[10] 6497 7-8-6 47 .... LauraReynolds(7) 4 40
(D K Ivory) *a towards rr: rdn and no prog over 2f out* **10/1**

6000 10 *nk* **Lord Lahar**[7] 6522 6-9-1 49 .... (p) MickyFenton 7 42
(M A Buckley) *t.k.h: w ldr: led 5f out to over 2f out: wknd over 1f out* **16/1**

0000 11 *8* **Princess Karla (IRE)**[25] 6387 3-8-10 45 .... BrianReilly 2 19
(J W Unett) *chsd ldrs to 1/2-way: sn wknd* **40/1**

1m 38.32s (-1.11) **Going Correction** -0.125s/f (Stan)
WFA 3 from 4yo+ 1lb **11 Ran SP% 118.1**
Speed ratings (Par 97):100,99,98,97,96 96,95,95,94,93 85
CSF £130.18 TOTE £8.50: £2.50, £4.10, £3.30; EX 109.60.
Owner Brickmakers Arms Tandridge Partnership **Bred** Elsdon Farms **Trained** Godstone, Surrey

FOCUS
Very much like the first division, this was a very routine banded contest even though the pace was solid and the winning time was slightly quicker, suggesting the form is sound enough.

6577 BETDIRECTCASINO.COM BANDED STKS 7f (P)
1:45 (1:45) (Class 7) 3-Y-O+ **£1,443** (£426; £213) **Stalls** Low

Form RPR

0-00 1 **Beneking**[51] 6080 5-8-11 40 .... (p) ChrisCatlin 7 46
(D Burchell) *w ldr: led over 4f out: abt 2 l clr fr 3f out: hrd rdn over 1f out: kpt on wl* **20/1**

0055 2 *1 ¾* **Dunnett Again (IRE)**[8] 6515 4-8-11 40 .... (b) SteveDrowne 6 41
(Mrs C A Dunnett) *prom: chsd wnr wl over 2f out: drvn and no imp fnl f: jst hld on for 2nd* **6/1**[3]

0006 3 *hd* **Repeat (IRE)**[14] 6474 5-8-11 40 .... BrianReilly 3 41
(J W Unett) *prom: rdn 3f out: chsd ldng pair 2f out: kpt on but no imp wnr* **10/1**

0000 4 *nk* **Tennessee Belle (IRE)**[23] 6396 3-8-11 40 .... (e) OscarUrbina 10 40
(C N Allen) *chsd ldrs: rdn wl over 2f out: n.m.r briefly sn after: styd on u.p fnl f* **16/1**

/000 5 *nk* **To Be Fare (IRE)**[32] 6330 5-8-11 40 .... DeanMcKeown 13 39
(J Pearce) *off the pce towards rr: rdn over 2f out: styd on fnl f: nrst fin* **9/2**[1]

0060 6 *hd* **Black Oval**[32] 6326 4-8-8 40 .... AdamKirby(3) 4 39
(M J Polglase) *racd on inner in midfield: effrt 2f out: styd on same pce fnl f: n.d* **20/1**

0006 7 *nk* **Good Wee Girl (IRE)**[72] 5653 3-8-11 40 .... (b) IanMongan 5 38
(S Woodman) *wl in rr: rdn over 2f out: no prog tl r.o fnl f: nrst fin* **11/1**

6263 8 *2 ½* **Mister Clinton (IRE)**[14] 6474 8-8-11 40 .... (p) TonyCulhane 8 32
(D K Ivory) *hld up wl in rr: shuffled along fr 2f out: nvr nr ldrs* **7/1**

0004 9 *nk* **Ravel (IRE)**[95] 5129 4-8-11 40 .... (t) FergusSweeney 12 31
(M R Bosley) *racd on outer in midfield: sharp reminders 1/2-way: struggling over 2f out* **8/1**

0006 10 *hd* **Isabella Rossini**[10] 6494 3-8-4 40 .... (p) ThomasO'Brien(7) 9 30
(A M Hales) *s.i.s and rousted along early: prog to chse ldrs over 2f out: wknd over 1f out* **16/1**

0002 11 *1 ½* **Taylor Maid**[9] 6512 3-8-11 40 .... (p) GrahamGibbons 11 26
(R M H Cowell) *led to over 4f out: styd prom tl wknd over 1f out* **11/2**[2]

0U00 12 *23* **Eden Star (IRE)**[72] 5653 3-8-11 40 .... JohnEgan 1 —
(D K Ivory) *a wl in rr: lost tch over 2f out: eased over 1f out: t.o* **11/1**

0400 13 *28* **Robin Sharp**[25] 6382 7-8-11 40 .... (p) PaulDoe 2 —
(J Akehurst) *sn detached and drvn: t.o fr 1/2-way* **25/1**

1m 25.41s (-0.48) **Going Correction** -0.125s/f (Stan) **13 Ran SP% 122.4**
Speed ratings (Par 97):97,95,94,94,94 93,93,90,90,90 88,62,30
CSF £135.84 TOTE £38.80: £8.20, £2.20, £5.40; EX 184.00.
Owner B M G Group **Bred** Helshaw Grange Stud And Mrs M Mason **Trained** Briery Hill, Blaenau Gwent

FOCUS
A very poor contest, even for a banded race, and dominated by those that raced up with the pace. The runner-up, fourth and sixth set the standard.
Mister Clinton(IRE) Official explanation: jockey said, regarding running and riding, his orders were to kid gelding along and do his best, adding that gelding jumped well and he kicked it into a good position, but he was out wider than ideal in early stages and at 3 1/2f out he was hampered, resulting in being shuffled back, so entering final bend he was flat out; he rode hands and heels in straight as he could never have got into a challenging position

6578 BRICKFARMRACING.CO.UK MAIDEN CLAIMING STKS 6f (P)
2:15 (2:15) (Class 7) 3-Y-O+ **£1,429** (£422; £211) **Stalls** Low

Form RPR

2000 1 **Dorn Hill**[57] 5966 3-8-9 45 .... (p) MickyFenton 6 47
(D G Bridgwater) *off the pce in last pair early: prog over 3f out: v wd bnd 2f out: drvn to ld jst over 1f out: kpt on* **4/1**[2]

0000 2 *1 ¼* **Question Mark**[23] 6396 3-8-10 40 .... JohnEgan 4 44
(Andrew Reid) *hld up bhd ldrs: prog 2f out: w wnr jst over 1f out: nt qckn fnl f* **9/2**[3]

5000 3 *1 ¾* **Silver Reign**[14] 4369 4-8-10 40 .... (v) SteveDrowne 3 39
(J A Geake) *hld up bhd ldrs: effrt on inner 2f out: chsd ldng pair fnl f: nt qckn* **7/1**

0-00 4 *1* **Duncanbil (IRE)**[11] 146 4-8-9 35 .... (v[1]) J-PGuillambert 1 35
(J J Bridger) *prom: drvn and lost pl over 2f out: plugged on again fnl f* **14/1**

0000 5 *½* **Victoriana**[14] 6474 4-8-6 35 .... (p) AdamKirby(3) 8 34
(H J Collingridge) *cl up: rdn to ld wl over 1f out to jst over 1f out: fdd* **16/1**

0000 6 *shd* **Speedy Spirit**[81] 5449 3-8-9 30 .... (bt) HayleyTurner 9 33
(M Salaman) *prom on outer: lost pl and struggling over 2f out: n.d fr over 1f out* **50/1**

6-00 7 *shd* **Ariesanne (IRE)**[25] 6383 4-8-6 35 .... PatrickMathers(3) 5 33
(A C Whillans) *prom for 2f: sn lost pl and struggling in rr: kpet on again fnl f* **20/1**

0455 8 *½* **Taipan Tommy (IRE)**[14] 6470 3-9-0 46 .... (v) PaulDoe 7 36
(S Dow) *s.s: mostly in last: kpt on fnl f but no ch* **2/1**[1]

0060 9 *4* **Ninja Storm (IRE)**[15] 6462 3-8-9 54 .... RobynBrisland(5) 2 24
(G L Moore) *mde most to wl over 1f out: wknd rapidly* **7/1**

1m 13.64s (0.83) **Going Correction** -0.125s/f (Stan) **9 Ran SP% 115.8**
Speed ratings (Par 97):89,87,85,83,83 82,82,82,76
CSF £22.46 TOTE £5.60: £2.30, £1.70, £2.30; EX 40.30.
Owner D A Thorpe **Bred** Cotswold Stud **Trained** Icomb, Gloucs

FOCUS
The only non-banded race on the card, but still a poor event and a very moderate time, 1.24 seconds slower than the following banded race and the form is very weak.
Taipan Tommy(IRE) Official explanation: jockey said, regarding running and riding, his orders were to track leaders and pick off horses through the race, but gelding shook its head vigorously in stalls and jumped awkwardly and slowly; he added that he pushed it from the gate, was beaten early on, and was not helped in straight by gelding, who was reluctant to go forward

6579 BETDIRECTPOKER.COM BANDED STKS 6f (P)
2:50 (2:50) (Class 7) 3-Y-0+ £1,457 (£430; £215) Stalls Low

Form RPR

0002 1 **Stagnite**[9] [6507] 5-9-2 50 TonyCulhane 9 55
(K McAuliffe) *wl in rr: effrt on wd outside ent st: str run fnl f to ld last stride* **12/1**

013 2 *shd* **Segoria (IRE)**[7] [6525] 3-9-1 49 ChrisCatlin 12 54
(A M Hales) *dwlt: last early: prog fr 1/2-way: forced way through 1f out: led nr fin: hdd last stride* **14/1**

3100 3 ½ **Zazous**[7] [6525] 4-9-2 50 SteveDrowne 5 53
(J J Bridger) *towards rr: effrt over 1f out: styd on wl fnl f: jst outpcd* **5/1**[2]

0520 4 *shd* **Beverley Beau**[14] [6471] 3-8-7 48 KristinStubbs[(3)] 3 51
(Mrs L Stubbs) *mde most: looked like holding on ent fnl f: bmpd along and hdd nr fin* **16/1**

0603 5 *shd* **Smirfys Party**[130] [4172] 7-8-13 47 (v) EddieAhern 8 53+
(W M Brisbourne) *wl in rr: effrt on outer whn hmpd over 1f out: last ent fnl f: fin strly* **6/1**[3]

0001 6 *hd* **Park Star**[7] [6526] 5-9-0 45 PatrickMathers[(3)] 11 53
(D Shaw) *hld up in last trio: stdy prog on inner fr 2f out: styd on ins fnl f: nt quite able to chal* **12/1**

3060 7 *hd* **Noble Mount**[18] [6429] 4-9-2 50 (p) SamHitchcott 2 51
(A B Haynes) *sn prom: hrd rdn 2f out: bmpd 1f out: kpt on* **8/1**

-006 8 *hd* **Princess Kai (IRE)**[14] [6470] 4-8-13 47 (p) FergusSweeney 10 48
(R Ingram) *chsd ldrs: rdn over 1f out: styd on ins fnl f: nvr able to chal* **16/1**

0-21 9 *shd* **Midmaar (IRE)**[289] [522] 4-8-10 47 AdamKirby[(3)] 7 47
(M Wigham) *hld up in last trio: effrt wl over 1f out: hanging and nt clr run sn after: r.o fnl f: nt rch ldrs* **2/1**[1]

0003 10 *hd* **Stephanie's Mind**[23] [6397] 3-9-1 49 MickyFenton 4 49
(M Quinn) *pressed ldr tl ins fnl f: lost several pls nr fin* **12/1**

00/5 11 ¾ **Amber Nectar Two**[60] [5898] 5-8-11 40 (b) LPKeniry 1 42
(A G Newcombe) *chsd ldrs: stl cl up ent fnl f: lost several pls last 75yds* **33/1**

0000 12 1 ¾ **Tiger Hunter**[9] [6507] 3-8-11 45 IanMongan 6 37
(P Howling) *prom tl wknd 1f out* **33/1**

1m 12.4s (-0.41) **Going Correction** -0.125s/f (Stan) 12 Ran SP% **122.8**
Speed ratings (Par 97):97,96,96,96,95 95,95,95,94,94 93,91
CSF £174.98 TOTE £15.40: £3.80, £3.90, £2.10; EX 109.60.
Owner Nadeem Ahmad **Bred** D A And Mrs Hicks **Trained** Fernham, Oxon
■ Stewards' Enquiry : Chris Catlin one-day ban: careless riding (Dec 26)

FOCUS
A fair race of its type, run at a solid pace and the winning time was over a second quicker than the preceding maiden claimer with the form looking sound. However, it was a very messy contest in the home straight and there was only just over a length covering the first ten horses at the line.
Park Star Official explanation: jockey said mare was denied a clear run

6580 BETDIRECT ON CHANNEL 4 TEXT PAGE 613 BANDED STKS 5f (P)
3:20 (3:21) (Class 7) 3-Y-0+ £1,409 (£416; £208) Stalls High

Form RPR

2003 1 **Leah's Pride**[14] [6471] 4-8-11 45 IanMongan 4 51
(P Howling) *mde all: kicked clr over 1f out: a holding on nr fin* **5/1**[3]

0200 2 ½ **Chantelle's Dream**[72] [5657] 3-8-4 45 (t) JamesDoyle[(7)] 2 49
(Ms J S Doyle) *s.i.s: last tl prog on outer 3f out: hanging over 1f out: r.o to chse wnr ins fnl f: gaining at fin* **33/1**

0666 3 1 ¾ **Strathclyde (IRE)**[14] [6471] 6-8-11 45 ChrisCatlin 7 43
(A M Hales) *hld up in last trio: effrt over 1f out: r.o last 150yds: no threat to wnr* **3/1**[1]

0504 4 ½ **Legal Set (IRE)**[14] [6471] 9-8-4 45 (bt) AnnStokell[(7)] 1 41
(Miss A Stokell) *prom: rdn 2f out: nt qckn over 1f out: one pce after* **11/2**

5230 5 *nk* **Innclassic (IRE)**[14] [6471] 4-8-8 45 (b) AmirQuinn[(3)] 8 40
(Jane Southcombe) *mostly chsd wnr tl ins fnl f: one pce* **12/1**

1006 6 *nk* **Urban Calm**[7] [6526] 4-8-11 45 BrianReilly 6 39
(J W Unett) *pushed along to stay in tch early: effrt 2f out: one pce fnl f* **7/1**

0563 7 *nk* **Tipsy Lillie**[10] [6493] 3-8-11 45 (b) JohnEgan 9 38
(Julian Poulton) *in tch: effrt towards outer 2f out: one pce over 1f out* **16/1**

0300 8 *nk* **Binnion Bay (IRE)**[23] [6398] 4-8-11 45 (v) J-PGuillambert 3 37
(J J Bridger) *sn in last trio: v wd bnd 2f out: kpt on ins fnl f: no ch* **8/1**

0011 9 1 ¾ **Secret Vision (USA)**[9] [6511] 4-9-3 45 (p) GrahamGibbons 10 36
(R M H Cowell) *pressed ldrs tl wknd jst over 1f out* **4/1**[2]

4000 10 ½ **Misty Princess**[10] [6493] 3-8-8 45 (v) PatrickMathers[(3)] 5 29
(D Shaw) *nvr bttr than midfield: wknd over 1f out* **33/1**

58.98 secs (-0.80) **Going Correction** -0.125s/f (Stan) 10 Ran SP% **120.1**
Speed ratings (Par 97):101,100,97,96,96 95,95,94,91,91
CSF £154.99 TOTE £5.60: £2.40, £8.70, £1.50; EX 138.30 Place 6 £3,172.16, Place 5 £1,460.41.
Owner Oaks Racing **Bred** F A Dickinson **Trained** Newmarket, Suffolk

FOCUS
A decent pace for this banded sprint in which the first two horses home received very different rides. the form looks solid enough.
Strathclyde(IRE) Official explanation: jockey said gelding was denied a clear run
T/Plt: £9,521.70 to a £1 stake. Pool: £35,869.70. 2.75 winning tickets. T/Qpdt: £181.00 to a £1 stake. Pool: £3,571.70. 14.60 winning tickets. JN

6568 SOUTHWELL (L-H)
Thursday, December 15

OFFICIAL GOING: Standard
Wind: Moderate behind.

6581 BETDIRECT ONLY 10 DAYS TIL XMAS NURSERY 5f (F)
12:30 (12:30) (Class 5) (0-75,75) 2-Y-0 £4,010 (£1,193; £596; £297) Stalls High

Form RPR

0356 1 **Egyptian Lord**[6] [6529] 2-8-6 60 (b[1]) RobbieFitzpatrick 4 66
(Peter Grayson) *cl up: led after 2f out: rdn over 1f out and kpt on wl* **11/2**

6063 2 1 ¼ **Garlogs**[9] [6517] 2-7-5 52 LiamJones[(7)] 9 54
(A Bailey) *trckd ldrs:hdwy 2f out: sn rdn and chsd wnr over 1f out: drvn and no imp ins last* **4/1**[2]

4500 3 1 ¾ **Charlie Delta**[10] [6501] 2-9-4 75 DanielTudhope[(3)] 3 71
(D Carroll) *a.p: rdn along 2f out: kpt on same pce appr last* **8/1**

0023 4 1 ¼ **Amber Glory**[36] [6297] 2-9-2 70 (b) NCallan 5 62
(K A Ryan) *led 2f: cl up tl rdn along wl over 1f out and grad wknd* **7/2**[1]

4602 5 ½ **Lucayos**[9] [6517] 2-8-8 62 ChrisCatlin 10 52
(Mrs H Sweeting) *midfield: rdn along 2f out: kpt on ins last: nrst fin* **9/2**[3]

6500 6 1 ¼ **Jazz At The Sands (USA)**[9] [6517] 2-8-1 58 ow3.(v[1]) PatrickMathers[(3)] 1 44
(D Shaw) *towards rr: rdn along 1/2-way: styd on appr last: nrst fin* **33/1**

005 7 1 ¾ **Nilsatisoptimum (USA)**[61] [5889] 2-8-9 63 (t) JimmyQuinn 7 43
(M Mullineaux) *chsd ldrs: rdn along 1/2-way: grad wknd* **20/1**

4100 8 ¾ **Pauvic (IRE)**[43] [6226] 2-8-7 61 PaulFessey 2 38
(Mrs A Duffield) *nvr nr ldrs* **25/1**

000 9 1 **Sarah's Art (IRE)**[66] [5801] 2-7-12 52 oh2 HayleyTurner 6 26
(N A Callaghan) *s.i.s: a rr* **16/1**

600 10 1 **Old Time Dancing**[30] [6351] 2-8-5 59 ow1 EddieAhern 8 30
(M J Wallace) *bhd fr 1/2-way* **20/1**

0040 11 5 **John Claude (IRE)**[43] [6226] 2-8-13 67 MickyFenton 11 21
(Ronald Thompson) *s.i.s: a rr* **20/1**

4325 12 9 **Dream Factor (IRE)**[61] [5888] 2-8-9 63 RobertWinston 12 —
(J O'Reilly) *bhd fr 1/2-way* **16/1**

57.89 secs (-2.41) **Going Correction** -0.575s/f (Fast) 2y crse rec 12 Ran SP% **119.7**
Speed ratings (Par 96):96,94,91,89,88 86,83,82,80,79 71,56
CSF £25.67 CT £181.81 TOTE £8.90: £2.00, £1.70, £4.70; EX 46.30.
Owner D & R Rhodes & Mrs S Grayson **Bred** I A N Wight And Mrs D M Wight **Trained** Formby, Lancs

FOCUS
Just a modest nursery and, as is currently the theme with five-furlong races at Southwell, those drawn low were at an advantage. The for m is ordinary and the placed horses set the standard for the form.

NOTEBOOK
Egyptian Lord had been running creditably enough in defeat recently and, taking well to first-time blinkers, he took advantage of his low draw to get off the mark at ninth attempt. Things fell just right for him and, unless he is well drawn over this course and distance again next time, he looks one to take on. (op 7-1)
Garlogs appreciated the drop to this trip when third here on his previous start, and this was another fine effort in defeat. Given he was drawn in stall nine, and those around him were in stalls four, three and five, this effort is all the more creditable and he should eventually find a race. (op 6-1)
Charlie Delta, dropped back two furlongs, had a good draw and ran creditably. (op 15-2)
Amber Glory, who won her maiden on her only previous run over this course and distance, did not have a bad draw and can have few excuses. Her stable know a thing or two about the claiming system, and she would be hard to beat if dropped into that grade. (op 11-4)
Lucayos had a poor draw and ran well in the circumstances. (tchd 5-1)
Jazz At The Sands(USA) had the best draw but seemed to take forever to get going.
John Claude(IRE) Official explanation: jockey said gelding lost its action on leaving stalls

6582 PRESS RED TO BET ON ITVI H'CAP 1m 4f (F)
1:00 (1:00) (Class 5) (0-75,76) 3-Y-0+ £3,330 (£990; £495; £247) Stalls Low

Form RPR

3011 1 **Piper General (IRE)**[6] [6534] 3-8-8 65 DaleGibson 9 77+
(J Mackie) *trckd ldrs: hdwy 4f out: rdn to chal 2f out: drvn to ld ins last: kpt on wl* **6/4**[1]

0240 2 *nk* **Oldenway**[19] [6432] 6-8-10 62 PaulHanagan 6 73
(R A Fahey) *led: pushed along 3f out: rdn and hdd 2f out: drvn and rallied ins last: jst hld* **12/1**

4323 3 *nk* **Khanjar (USA)**[12] [6488] 5-9-4 70 PatCosgrave 7 81
(K R Burke) *trckd ldr: hdwy over 3f out: rdn to ld 2f out: drvn and hdd ins last: kpt on wl* **12/1**

021 4 13 **Trance (IRE)**[5] [6540] 5-9-10 76 6ex HayleyTurner 1 68
(T D Barron) *towards rr and sn pushed along: hdwy over 5f out: rdn to chse ldng trio 3f out: drvn and no imp fnl 2f* **2/1**[2]

06 5 4 **Nabir (FR)**[9] [6520] 5-9-4 70 TomEaves 5 56
(P D Niven) *chsd ldng pair: rdn along 4f out: wknd 3f out* **33/1**

6000 6 1 ¾ **Mossmann Gorge**[9] [6514] 3-8-8 65 (v) AlanDaly 3 48
(M Wellings) *hld up: stdy hdwy over 4f out: rdn along over 3f out and sn btn* **66/1**

4061 7 1 ¼ **Efrhina (IRE)**[30] [6364] 5-8-9 61 MickyFenton 8 42
(Stef Liddiard) *hld up: a rr* **7/1**[3]

100B 8 20 **Beauchamp Trump**[38] [6285] 3-8-7 67 (bt) AdamKirby[(3)] 2 18
(G A Butler) *in tch: pushed along 1/2-way: sn wknd* **16/1**

0610 9 *dist* **Sovietta (IRE)**[206] [1973] 4-8-8 60 LPKeniry 4 —
(A G Newcombe) *in tch: rdn along 1/2-way: sn lost pl and bhd* **40/1**

2m 36.86s (-5.23) **Going Correction** -0.05s/f (Stan)
WFA 3 from 4yo+ 5lb 9 Ran SP% **114.0**
Speed ratings (Par 103):115,114,114,105,103 102,101,87,—
CSF £20.63 CT £159.40 TOTE £3.10: £1.30, £3.90, £2.60; EX 28.20.
Owner Fools Who Dream **Bred** Edward And Mrs S Hannigan **Trained** Church Broughton , Derbys

FOCUS
A fair handicap run at a good pace and a very smart winning time for a race of its class, rated though the runner-up to his All-Weather best.

6583 BETDIRECT FREEPHONE 0800 211 222 MAIDEN STKS 1m 3f (F)
1:30 (1:31) (Class 5) 3-Y-0+ £3,342 (£994; £496; £248) Stalls Low

Form RPR

-400 1 **Blue Opal**[184] [2567] 3-8-12 52 MickyFenton 5 54
(Miss S E Hall) *cl up: rdn to ld 2f out: drvn and edgd rt ins last: hld on wl* **22/1**

2 *nk* **Dance Troupe**[43] 3-8-12 MichaelTebbutt 4 54
(J Jay) *hld up: hdwy over 4f out: rdn 3f out: hdwy whn nt clr run over 2f out: ev ch ent last: sn drvn and kpt on same pce* **6/5**[1]

0-06 3 6 **Antley Court (IRE)**[47] [6160] 3-9-3 54 RobertWinston 7 49
(R Hollinshead) *led: rdn along and hung rt over 2f out: sn hdd and hung lft wl over 1f out: drvn and one pce appr last* **7/1**

0660 4 ¾ **Gallas (IRE)**[10] [6510] 4-9-7 48 (v) FergalLynch 6 48
(P A Blockley) *prom: effrt 3f out: rdn and ev ch 2f out: sn drvn and wknd* **13/2**[3]

0/4- 5 2 **Whole Grain**[224] 4-9-2 GeorgeBaker 11 40
(B R Millman) *midfield: hdwy to chse ldrs over 4f out: rdn 3f out and sn wknd* **11/2**[2]

0/-0 6 7 **Kuka**[12] [6485] 4-9-7 GrahamGibbons 1 34
(R Hollinshead) *chsd ldrs: rdn along 4f out: drvn and wknd 3f out* **28/1**

3000 7 19 **Miss Monica (IRE)**[296] [446] 4-9-2 48 DarrenWilliams 10 —
(P W Hiatt) *in tch: hdwy to trck ldrs 5f out: rdn along 3f out and sn wknd* **25/1**

8 1 ¼ **Rectangle Blue**[18] 3-9-3 DeanMcKeown 9 1
(M D Hammond) *a rr: bhd frn 1/2-way* **66/1**

0440 9 *shd* **Expression Echo (IRE)**[56] [5998] 3-8-12 53 LPKeniry 2 —
(A G Newcombe) *a rr: bhd fr 1/2-way* **8/1**

640 **10** *dist* **Penway**[243] 1068 4-9-7 50....................(t) BrianReilly 8 —
(A Sadik) *a bhd: t.o fr 1/2-way* **16/1**

2m 29.09s (0.19) **Going Correction** -0.05s/f (Stan)
WFA 3 from 4yo 4lb **10** Ran SP% **116.8**
Speed ratings (Par 103):97,96,92,91,90 85,71,70,70,—
CSF £47.82 TOTE £20.20: £4.50, £1.10, £1.80; EX 48.10.
Owner C Platts **Bred** Miss S E Hall **Trained** Middleham Moor, N Yorks

FOCUS
A very moderate maiden run in a modest time. The third sets the level, which is basically plating class.
Antley Court(IRE) Official explanation: jockey said gelding hung right

6584 BETDIRECT.CO.UK (S) STKS 7f (F)
2:00 (2:01) (Class 6) 3-Y-O+ **£2,566** (£757; £379) **Stalls** Low

Form RPR
1002 **1** **Owed**[9] 6515 3-9-1 57....................(t) GregFairley(5) 7 69
(Robert Gray) *cl up: led 3f out: rdn and hung bdly lft wl over 1f out: drvn ins last: kpt on* **11/2**[3]
4323 **2** *1* **White Bear (FR)**[29] 6367 3-9-0 57.................... SteveDrowne 8 60
(P D Evans) *in tch: hdwy 3f out: rdn to chse wnr ent last: sn drvn and kpt on* **4/1**[2]
3001 **3** *5* **Far Note (USA)**[9] 6515 7-9-3 61....................(bt) AmirQuinn(3) 4 54
(S R Bowring) *a prom: effrt over 2f out: sn rdn and kpt on same pce fr over 1f out* **13/2**
6000 **4** *1 3/4* **Distant Country (USA)**[9] 6513 6-9-6 63....................(b) LPKeniry 12 49
(R A Harris) *hld up towards rr: hdwy on outer 3f out: rdn to chse ldrs 2f out: sn no imp* **14/1**
0033 **5** *2 1/2* **Musical Gift**[10] 6508 5-9-0 50....................(v) HayleyTurner 11 37
(P A Blockley) *hld up towards rr: hdwy on ouetr 3f out: sn rdn and nvr rch ldrs* **10/3**[1]
0040 **6** *1 1/2* **Zafarshah (IRE)**[10] 6505 6-8-13 56....................(b) TolleyDean(7) 3 39
(R A Harris) *in tch on inner: hdwy 3f out: rdn to chse ldrs 2f out: sn drvn and btn* **33/1**
-240 **7** *1 1/2* **Smith N Allan Oils**[136] 652 6-9-0 58.................... RobbieFitzpatrick 10 29
(C Smith) *bhd tl styd on fnl 2f: nvr a factor* **28/1**
F660 **8** *1 1/2* **Champagne Rossini (IRE)**[6] 4633 3-8-7 45.................... LiamJones(7) 1 26
(M C Chapman) *bhd tl sme late hdwy* **100/1**
0220 **9** *8* **Queue Up**[29] 6369 3-9-0 53.................... MickyFenton 5 6
(A G Newcombe) *a rr* **14/1**
0000 **10** *1 1/4* **Locombe Hill (IRE)**[29] 6365 9-9-3 52.................... DanielTudhope(3) 13 9
(N Wilson) *chsd ldrs on outer: rdn along 3f out and sn wknd* **25/1**
5-0 **11** *2 1/2* **Gorgeous Boy (IRE)**[93] 5210 3-8-7 .... NicolPolli(7) 14 —
(P L Gilligan) *a bhd* **50/1**
0000 **12** *3/4* **Coleorton Dane**[34] 4867 3-9-0 67....................(b[1]) NCallan 2 —
(K A Ryan) *led: rdn along and hdd 3f out: sn drvn and wknd* **7/1**
0100 **13** *7* **Mytton's Bell (IRE)**[26] 6387 3-9-1 52....................(v[1]) DavidAllan 9 —
(A Bailey) *chsd ldrs: rdn along over 3f out: sn wknd* **18/1**
5600 **14** *18* **Hows That**[9] 6516 3-9-1 53.................... RobertWinston 6 —
(K R Burke) *chsd ldrs: rdn and lost action over 2f out and immediately eased* **28/1**

1m 29.89s (-0.91) **Going Correction** -0.05s/f (Stan) **14** Ran SP% **119.5**
Speed ratings (Par 101):103,101,96,94,91 89,87,86,77,75 72,71,63,43
CSF £25.84 TOTE £7.80: £2.50, £1.70, £2.70; EX 33.20.The winner was bought in for 5,250gns. White Bear was claimed by Mrs C R Dore for £6,000.
Owner Naughty Diesel Ltd **Bred** Helshaw Grange Stud, N Kent And H Phillips **Trained** Malton, N Yorks

FOCUS
A competitive race and probably not too bad form by selling standards with the winner achieving a slight personal best.
Coleorton Dane Official explanation: jockey said gelding hung right throughout
Hows That Official explanation: jockey said filly lost its action home straight

6585 TEXT BETDIRECT TO 88600 MAIDEN AUCTION STKS 7f (F)
2:30 (2:31) (Class 5) 2-Y-O **£3,316** (£986; £493; £246) **Stalls** Low

Form RPR
004 **1** **Xpres Boy (IRE)**[6] 6528 2-8-7 .... PaulEddery 9 56
(S R Bowring) *a.p: led over 2f out: rdn clr over 1f out: kpt on* **7/2**[2]
062 **2** *1/2* **Inaminute (IRE)**[16] 6466 2-8-2 57.................... ChrisCatlin 4 50
(R A Harris) *hld up in tch: hdwy over 2f out: sn rdn and n.m.r wl over 1f out: sn drvn and styd on ins last* **5/4**[1]
00 **3** *1* **Mucho Loco (IRE)**[20] 6417 2-8-11 .... J-PGuillambert 8 56
(J G Portman) *cl up on outer: effrt and ev ch over 2f out: sn rdn: drvn and one pce fnl f* **14/1**
5560 **4** *1 1/4* **Dream Of Paradise (USA)**[44] 6213 2-8-6 50 ow1.................... TomEaves 3 48
(Mrs L Williamson) *chsd ldrs: hdwy over 2f out: sn rdn and ev ch tl drvn and one pce appr last* **12/1**
5000 **5** *5* **Scherzo A La Russe (USA)**[6] 6529 2-8-6 62 ow1.................... LPKeniry 7 36
(A G Newcombe) *a towards rr* **20/1**
004 **6** *nk* **Ullah Pendragon (IRE)**[171] 2970 2-8-9 60.................... DeanMcKeown 2 38
(M J Polglase) *cl up: ev ch over 2f out: sn rdn:edgd rt wl over 1f out and sn wknd* **14/1**
7 *7* **Tesoro** 2-8-11 .... FergalLynch 6 22
(P A Blockley) *dwlt: a rr* **11/2**[3]
0000 **8** *1* **Millbrook Star (IRE)**[44] 6212 2-8-3 35.................... LiamJones(7) 5 19
(M C Chapman) *led: rdn along and hdd wl over 2f out: sn wknd* **66/1**
9 *dist* **Monte Carrio** 2-8-7 .... RobbieFitzpatrick 1 —
(C Drew) *towards rr: pushed along and hung bdly rt 3f out: sn bhd and virtually p.u fnl f* **33/1**

1m 31.76s (0.96) **Going Correction** -0.05s/f (Stan) **9** Ran SP% **112.3**
Speed ratings (Par 96):92,91,90,88,83 82,74,73,—
CSF £7.80 TOTE £5.00: £1.60, £1.20, £2.60; EX 10.50.
Owner Charterhouse Holdings Plc **Bred** Gerard Phelan **Trained** Edwinstowe, Notts

FOCUS
A moderate juvenile maiden, run at an ordinary early pace. The form looks fair for the class, but is limited by the moderate time.

NOTEBOOK
Xpres Boy(IRE) was given a prominent ride over this extra furlong and knuckled down under pressure to repel the runner-up and broke his duck at the fourth attempt. The step-up to this trip was clearly much to his liking, he had no trouble with this deeper surface, and should have more to offer over this trip during the winter. A mile should be well within his compass as a three-year-old. (op 4-1 tchd 9-2)
Inaminute(IRE), making her debut for new connections, found trouble approaching the final furlong, yet still had every chance when clear, and it made little difference to the overall result. She got the extra furlong well, and would have ideally preferred a stronger early pace, so can be given another chance to atone if found a similar event in the coming weeks. (tchd Evens and 11-8 in places)
Mucho Loco(IRE), dropping back a furlong, met support in the betting and duly turned in his best effort to date. While he enjoyed racing on the early pace, he did not look totally suited by the drop back to this trip, and the return to a mile on this surface should prove more to his liking. He now has the options of handicaps. (op 28-1)
Dream Of Paradise(USA) showed improved form on this switch to Fibresand and had every chance. She may look better off in low-grade handicaps from her current mark. Official explanation: jockey said filly hung right-handed
Scherzo A La Russe(USA), making her Fibresand debut, ran no sort of race and continues to look greatly flattered by her official rating. She may be better of when reverting to the Polytrack. (op 16-1)
Ullah Pendragon(IRE) held every chance, before hanging under pressure and doing the runner-up no favours, and shaped as though this race would bring her on fitness wise. She was at an advantage by racing up with the modest early pace, however, and still has to prove she is worthy of her current official mark. Official explanation: jockey said gelding hung right throughout (op 10-1)
Tesoro, an 8,200gns purchase out of an unraced half-sister to a top-class ten furlong performer in Italy, proved easy to back ahead of this debut and was never a factor after missing the break. He is surely capable of better. Official explanation: jockey said gelding ran green (op 9-2)
Monte Carrio Official explanation: jockey said colt hung right-handed

6586 DAILY OFFERS FROM BETDIRECT H'CAP 1m (F)
3:00 (3:01) (Class 5) (0-70,66) 3-Y-O+ **£3,401** (£1,012; £505; £252) **Stalls** Low

Form RPR
0213 **1** **Stevedore (IRE)**[5] 6542 4-9-1 **63**.................... EddieAhern 10 75
(J R Boyle) *cl up on outer: hdwy to ld 3f out: sn clr: rdn over 1f out and styd on strly* **10/3**[1]
0025 **2** *3 1/2* **Pending (IRE)**[16] 6468 4-8-10 **58**....................(p) PaulHanagan 13 63
(R A Fahey) *dwlt: towards rr: hdwy 1/2-way: rdn to chse wnr over 1f out: drvn ins last and no imp* **11/2**[2]
0003 **3** *2 1/2* **Balearic Star (IRE)**[16] 6468 4-8-3 **58**.................... JamesMillman(7) 3 58+
(B R Millman) *hld up in tch: hdwy 2f out: swtchd wd and rdn wl over 1f out: styd on ins last: nrst fin* **6/1**[3]
4-00 **4** *nk* **Iberus (GER)**[43] 4975 7-9-0 **62**.................... GeorgeBaker 11 61
(S Gollings) *hld up towards rr: hdwy to chse ldrs over 2f out: sn rdn and one pce* **20/1**
0022 **5** *2 1/2* **Blueberry Tart (IRE)**[3] 6565 3-8-13 **62**.................... SteveDrowne 14 56
(J M P Eustace) *chsd ldrs on outer: rdn over 2f out: sn one pce* **6/1**[3]
4532 **6** *3 1/2* **Cantarna (IRE)**[40] 6266 4-9-4 **66**.................... DaleGibson 2 53
(J Mackie) *led: rdn along and hdd 3f out: sn drvn and wknd 2f out* **11/2**[2]
000 **7** *13* **Set Alight**[30] 6362 4-9-3 **65**....................(v[1]) PhillipMakin 9 26
(Mrs C A Dunnett) *dwlt: a rr* **25/1**
0000 **8** *1 3/4* **Windy Prospect**[19] 6430 3-9-3 **66**.................... MickyFenton 8 24
(C R Dore) *cl up: rdn along 3f out: sn wknd* **40/1**
5066 **9** *shd* **Wrenlane**[184] 2566 4-8-11 **59**.................... TonyHamilton 1 17
(R A Fahey) *cl up on inner: rdn along 3f out: wknd 2f out* **33/1**
0000 **10** *1 3/4* **Warden Warren**[30] 6362 7-9-4 **66**....................(p) HayleyTurner 6 20
(Mrs C A Dunnett) *cl up: rdn along 3f out: sn drvn and wknd* **20/1**
3600 **11** *5* **Wychbury (USA)**[39] 5743 4-9-4 **66**.................... RobertWinston 12 10
(Heather Dalton) *a rr* **7/1**

1m 42.97s (-1.63) **Going Correction** -0.05s/f (Stan)
WFA 3 from 4yo+ 1lb **11** Ran SP% **113.7**
Speed ratings (Par 103):106,102,100,99,97 93,80,78,78,77 72
CSF £18.87 CT £105.76 TOTE £3.10: £1.50, £1.70, £2.80; EX 25.30.
Owner M Khan X2 **Bred** C J Foy **Trained** Epsom, Surrey

FOCUS
A modest handicap, run at a sound pace, and the form looks fair, rated through the runner-up to recent form.

6587 BET DIRECT H'CAP 1m (F)
3:30 (3:30) (Class 6) (0-55,60) 3-Y-O+ **£2,895** (£854; £427) **Stalls** Low

Form RPR
2531 **1** **Amorist (IRE)**[5] 6542 3-9-4 **60** 6ex.................... JamieMackay 2 71+
(Sir Mark Prescott) *trckd ldrs on inner: smooth hdwy to ld over 2f out: sn clr: rdn ins last and styd on* **13/8**[1]
5400 **2** *1 1/4* **Sriology (IRE)**[10] 6506 4-8-11 **52**.................... ChrisCatlin 7 58
(G Prodromou) *s.i.s: swtchd wd and rdn along in rr: hdwy and wd st: drvn 2f out: styd on ins last: nrst fin* **9/1**[3]
0054 **3** *1/2* **Quiet Reading (USA)**[5] 6535 8-8-9 **50**....................(v) HayleyTurner 13 55
(M R Bosley) *chsd ldrs: hdwy and ev ch 2f out: sn rdn and kpt on u.p fnl f* **9/1**[3]
0415 **4** *2* **We'll Meet Again**[12] 6487 5-8-11 **55**.................... PaulMulrennan(3) 4 56
(M W Easterby) *towards rr: hdwy 1/2-way: st: hdwy over 2f out: rdn to chse ldrs over 1f out: drvn and one pce ent last* **11/1**
2141 **5** *1/2* **Abbeygate**[16] 6468 4-9-0 **55**.................... J-PGuillambert 1 55
(T Keddy) *bhd: rdn and hdwy on inner over 2f out: sn rdn and kpt on same pce* **11/2**[2]
0000 **6** *1 3/4* **Veneer (IRE)**[16] 6468 3-8-6 **55**....................(b) RonanKeogh(7) 3 52
(Miss Gay Kelleway) *chsd ldrs: rdn over 2f out: sn drvn and wknd wl over 1f out* **66/1**
3525 **7** *3* **Sound And Vision (IRE)**[5] 6541 3-8-13 **55**....................(v) TomEaves 11 46
(M Dods) *midfield: rdn along 3f out: sn no imp* **25/1**
2321 **8** *2 1/2* **Filey Buoy**[17] 6445 3-8-4 **53**.................... MichaelJStainton(7) 10 39
(R M Whitaker) *prom: rdn along 3f out: drvn over 2f out and sn wknd* **11/1**
2040 **9** *7* **Raul Sahara**[26] 6387 3-8-11 **53** ow1.................... FergalLynch 9 25
(P A Blockley) *a towards rr* **50/1**
0065 **10** *1/2* **Dubai Dreams**[23] 1289 5-8-11 **55**....................(b) AmirQuinn(3) 12 26
(S R Bowring) *chsd ldrs: rdn along wl over 2f out and sn wknd* **22/1**
062 **11** *1/2* **Layed Back Rocky**[24] 6400 3-8-3 **52**.................... LiamJones(7) 8 22
(M Mullineaux) *led: rdn along 3f out: hdd & wknd 2f out* **33/1**
2051 **12** *3 1/2* **Louve Heureuse (IRE)**[8] 6443 4-8-9 **50**.................... EddieAhern 14 13
(J R Boyle) *a towards rr* **10/1**
-120 **13** *5* **Nevinstown (IRE)**[9] 6516 5-9-0 **55**.................... TPQueally 6 8
(C Grant) *a bhd* **33/1**
4200 **14** *4* **Crusoe (IRE)**[220] 1589 8-8-12 **53**....................(bt) BrianReilly 5 —
(A Sadik) *cl up: rdn and edgd lft 3f out: drvn and wknd over 2f out* **50/1**

1m 44.08s (-0.52) **Going Correction** -0.05s/f (Stan)
WFA 3 from 4yo+ 1lb **14** Ran SP% **118.7**
Speed ratings (Par 101):100,98,98,96,95 94,91,88,81,81 80,77,72,68
CSF £15.11 CT £108.37 TOTE £2.50: £1.60, £3.80, £2.60; EX 21.90 Place 6 £27.81, Place 5 £8.33.
Owner W E Sturt - Osborne House Iv **Bred** Ian Fair **Trained** Newmarket, Suffolk

FOCUS
A moderate affair, but the early pace was generous and the winner did the job nicely. The form is weak though, with the runner-up's previous banded form the best guide to the level.
Nevinstown(IRE) Official explanation: jockey said gelding missed the break
T/Plt: £39.10 to a £1 stake. Pool: £30,980.65. 577.10 winning tickets. T/Qpdt: £3.30 to a £1 stake. Pool: £2,920.60. 647.00 winning tickets. JR

6560

WOLVERHAMPTON (A.W) (L-H)

Friday, December 16

OFFICIAL GOING: Standard
Wind: Fresh across.

6588 MORE OFFERS AT BETDIRECT.CO.UK MAIDEN STKS (DIV I) 1m 141y(P)
1:10 (1:12) (Class 5) 2-Y-O **£3,727** (£1,108; £554; £276) **Stalls** Low

Form RPR
2 **1** **Whatizzit**[14] 6484 2-8-9 .... SteveDrowne 2 66+
(E A L Dunlop) *a in tch: wnt 2nd over 2f out: hrd rdn to ld last strides* **13/8**[2]
2 **2** *nk* **Pigeon Island**[20] 6428 2-9-0 .... FergusSweeney 8 70+
(H Candy) *traked ldr: led 5f out: rdn over 1f out: hdd last strides* **6/4**[1]
4 **3** *½* **Spanish Lace**[21] 6417 2-8-9 .... TomEaves 5 64+
(Miss J A Camacho) *hld up in mid-div: rdn and hdwy 3f out: styd on fnl f* **7/1**[3]
4 *3 ½* **Fisher Bridge (IRE)** 2-9-0 .... IanMongan 13 62
(W R Swinburn) *s.i.s: bhd tl gd hdwy 4f out: styd on one pce ins fnl 2f* **33/1**
0 **5** *1* **Tender The Great (IRE)**[48] 6143 2-8-9 .... MichaelTebbutt 11 55
(V Smith) *in tch: rdn over 2f out: wknd appr fnl f* **100/1**
00 **6** *shd* **Pocket Too**[172] 2990 2-9-0 .... JimmyQuinn 10 59
(Jean-Rene Auvray) *hld up: rdn over 3f out: nvr nr to chal* **66/1**
4 **7** *hd* **Markington**[14] 6477 2-9-0 .... GrahamGibbons 12 59
(J D Bethell) *in rr tl rdn and hdwy over 3f out: wknd over 1f out* **25/1**
8 *3 ½* **Jumanji (IRE)** 2-8-2 .... StacyRenwick[(7)] 7 47
(M J Attwater) *a towards rr* **100/1**
36 **9** *2* **Asbury Park**[83] 5455 2-9-0 .... PhillipMakin 6 53+
(E S McMahon) *in tch tl rdn and wknd over 2f out* **16/1**
0 **10** *23* **Galaxy King (IRE)**[69] 5746 2-9-0 .... JoeFanning 9 —
(M Johnston) *mid-div: wknd wl over 2f out* **16/1**
00 **11** *½* **Fairytale Of York (IRE)**[21] 6424 2-8-9 ow3 .... DanielTudhope[(3)] 1 —
(D Carroll) *hld up: a bhd* **100/1**
0 **12** *3* **Tina's Magic**[14] 6484 2-8-9 .... J-PGuillambert 3 —
(Mrs G S Rees) *led to 5f out: wknd qckly sn after* **100/1**

1m 51.7s (-0.06) **Going Correction** -0.175s/f (Stan) **12** Ran SP% **114.6**
Speed ratings (Par 96):93,92,92,89,88 88,88,84,83,62 62,59
CSF £4.06 TOTE £2.40: £1.30, £1.10, £1.60; EX 5.30.
Owner Eurostrait Ltd **Bred** Eurostrait Ltd **Trained** Newmarket, Suffolk

FOCUS
An ordinary maiden run at a steady early pace and the winning time was only modest for the grade as a result, 0.62 seconds slower than the second division. The form is difficult to weigh up and has been rated cautiously for the time being.

NOTEBOOK
Whatizzit, who would not have been suited by the way the race was run as she is bred to need middle distances next year, took time to claw back the leader and only got on top close home, but she has scope for improvement and will be seen to much better effect in a faster-run race and, of course, when stepped up in trip. (tchd 6-4 and 7-4)
Pigeon Island, who made his debut over a mile and a quarter at Lingfield, would also have probably preferred a stronger pace at this shorter trip, but his rider tried to make the best of the situation and take advantage of the steady early pace by going to the front around five furlongs out. He kicked on the home turn and the tactic almost paid off. (op 13-8 tchd 7-4)
Spanish Lace was back in the pack for most of the race and that put her at a disadvantage when the sprint to the line in this steadily-run affair began. She finished nicely clear of the rest, though. (op 9-2)
Fisher Bridge(IRE) ran a promising race on his debut as he was poorly drawn, broke badly and was last in the early stages. He was forced to make his ground around the outside and was running on at the finish so there should be better to come with this experience behind him.
Tender The Great(IRE), well held in a Newmarket maiden on her debut, ran a better race on her All-Weather bow, although she did benefit from racing fairly prominently in a steadily-run race.
Pocket Too ran her best race so far and now qualifies for a handicap mark.

6589 BETDIRECT.CO.UK (S) STKS 5f 216y(P)
1:40 (1:41) (Class 6) 3-Y-O+ **£2,545** (£751; £375) **Stalls** Low

Form RPR
0500 **1** **Tiviski (IRE)**[43] 6235 3-8-7 59 .... JimmyQuinn 2 53
(E J Alston) *chsd ldrs: hrd rdn to ld wl ins fnl f: jst hld on* **16/1**
0606 **2** *hd* **Blythe Spirit**[10] 6515 6-8-12 57 .... (p) RobertWinston 1 58
(C R Dore) *bhd tl hdwy over 1f out: swtchd rt: r.o strly fnl f: jst failed* **7/2**[1]
1463 **3** *hd* **Shadow Jumper (IRE)**[10] 6515 4-9-5 52 .... (v) RobbieFitzpatrick 6 64
(M J Attwater) *led tl rdn and hdd wl ins fnl f: lost 2nd nr post* **4/1**[2]
0634 **4** *1* **Madrasee**[41] 6264 7-8-7 61 .... TolleyDean[(7)] 5 56
(R A Harris) *mid-div: hdwy on ins 2f out: kpt on one pce fnl f* **9/2**[3]
U462 **5** *1* **Sir Sandrovitch (IRE)**[37] 6294 9-9-5 57 .... (p) PaulHanagan 12 58
(R A Fahey) *in tch: hdwy whn short of room over 1f out: kpt on fnl f* **7/1**
1100 **6** *3* **Desert Opal**[14] 6480 5-9-5 68 .... TonyCulhane 8 49
(D W Chapman) *towards rr: rdn 2f out: nvr nr to chal* **7/2**[1]
0036 **7** *4* **Red Sovereign**[37] 6294 4-9-0 58 .... MickyFenton 7 32
(D G Bridgwater) *disp ld tl rdn and wknd qckly appr fnl f* **12/1**
4030 **8** *2* **Ringarooma**[37] 6298 3-8-7 55 .... DeanMcKeown 4 19
(C N Allen) *v.s.a: a bhd* **33/1**
4000 **9** *1 ½* **Hiamovi (IRE)**[10] 6515 3-9-5 58 .... (b) ChrisCatlin 13 27
(R M H Cowell) *a in rr* **25/1**
1000 **10** *9* **Molly Dancer**[44] 6231 3-9-0 52 .... NCallan 10 —
(M Meade) *trckd ldrs tl rdn and wknd qckly over 2f out* **40/1**

1m 14.45s (-1.36) **Going Correction** -0.175s/f (Stan) **10** Ran SP% **117.9**
Speed ratings (Par 101):102,101,101,100,98 94,89,86,84,72
CSF £71.29 TOTE £23.90: £4.50, £1.70, £1.60; EX 73.10.There was no bid for the winner. Blythe Spirit was claimed by R. A. Fahey for £6,000. Madrasee was claimed by Ms P. M. Marks for £6,000.
Owner The Selebians **Bred** Patrick J Fadden **Trained** Longton, Lancs
■ Stewards' Enquiry : Robbie Fitzpatrick one-day ban: failed to keep straight from stalls (Dec 27)

FOCUS
A fairly competitive seller and once again those drawn low came through at the finish. The third is the best guide to the level of the form.
Sir Sandrovitch(IRE) Official explanation: jockey said gelding hung left
Molly Dancer Official explanation: jockey said filly had a breathing problem

6590 LITTLEWOODS BET DIRECT H'CAP 5f 216y(P)
2:15 (2:15) (Class 4) (0-85,85) 3-Y-O+
£5,571 (£1,668; £834; £417; £208; £104) **Stalls** Low

Form RPR
0004 **1** **Will He Wish**[21] 6421 9-9-1 82 .... JohnEgan 3 94
(S Gollings) *chsd ldrs: rdn to ld ent fnl f: drvn out* **13/2**[3]
1006 **2** *½* **Prince Tum Tum (USA)**[21] 6421 5-9-1 82 .... FergalLynch 4 100+
(D W Barker) *in rr tl hdwy over 2f out: edgd lft but r.o to cl on wnr fnl f* **5/2**[1]
-003 **3** *1 ½* **Countdown**[21] 6421 3-8-12 79 .... (v) TomEaves 9 85
(Miss J A Camacho) *trckd ldr: ev ch ent fnl f: nt qckn ins* **12/1**
4230 **4** *½* **Balakiref**[21] 6421 6-8-9 76 .... PhillipMakin 2 81
(M Dods) *s.i.s: sn in tch: hdwy on ins 2f out: kpt on one pce fnl f* **13/2**[3]
2050 **5** *1 ½* **Sir Desmond**[21] 6421 7-8-12 79 .... (p) ChrisCatlin 13 79
(Rae Guest) *outpcd: rdn and hdwy over 1f out: nvr nr to chal* **16/1**
0000 **6** *hd* **Kingsmaite**[95] 5188 4-8-10 80 .... (b) AmirQuinn[(3)] 7 79
(S R Bowring) *led tl rdn and hdd 1f out: wknd ins* **10/1**
6550 **7** *1 ½* **Louphole**[17] 6458 3-8-7 74 .... FergusSweeney 6 69
(P J Makin) *hld up: rdn and hdwy on outside over 2f out: one pce appr fnl f* **9/1**
6600 **8** *nk* **Mistral Sky**[155] 3481 6-8-7 74 .... (p) MickyFenton 8 68
(Stef Liddiard) *prom: rdn 1/2-way: wknd wl over 1f out* **40/1**
3122 **9** *1 ½* **Gilded Cove**[14] 6480 5-8-8 75 .... GrahamGibbons 10 65
(R Hollinshead) *chsd ldrs: rdn 1/2-way: wknd over 1f out* **4/1**[2]
1000 **10** *4* **Harrison's Flyer (IRE)**[21] 6421 4-8-3 75 .... (p) GregFairley[(5)] 11 53
(J M Bradley) *a in rr* **20/1**
10-0 **11** *1 ¾* **Newsround**[14] 6481 3-9-4 85 .... (b[1]) TonyCulhane 5 57
(D W Chapman) *slowly away: a struggling in rr* **40/1**

1m 13.66s (-2.15) **Going Correction** -0.175s/f (Stan) **11** Ran SP% **117.5**
Speed ratings (Par 105):107,106,104,103,101 101,99,99,97,91 89
CSF £22.63 CT £194.60 TOTE £9.00: £2.60, £1.90, £4.00; EX 28.50.
Owner Mrs D Dukes **Bred** Mrs C Buckland **Trained** Scamblesby, Lincs

FOCUS
Over half the field ran last time out in a similar course and distance handicap three weeks earlier, and those six provided the first five home here. The form, too, was more or less confirmed, with only Countdown failing to maintain his position relative to the others and looks sound.

6591 BETDIRECTPOKER.COM NURSERY 5f 216y(P)
2:50 (2:51) (Class 4) (0-85,77) 2-Y-O **£4,718** (£1,403; £701; £350) **Stalls** Low

Form RPR
4216 **1** **Jimmy The Guesser**[14] 6479 2-9-3 76 .... (b[1]) RichardThomas[(3)] 4 85
(N P Littmoden) *led over 4f out: rdn clr over 1f out: tired but hld on wl fnl f* **6/1**[2]
1022 **2** *¾* **Orchard Supreme**[7] 6529 2-8-9 68 .... (v[1]) StephaneBreux[(3)] 3 75+
(R Hannon) *mid-div tl hdwy over 2f out: r.o to chse wnr fnl f* **10/3**[1]
0003 **3** *hd* **Catbang (IRE)**[7] 6529 2-8-5 61 .... JohnEgan 10 67+
(N A Callaghan) *mid-div: rdn 1/2-way: hdwy over 1f out: r.o wl fnl f* **10/3**[1]
5160 **4** *2* **Ochre Bay**[14] 6479 2-9-5 75 .... GrahamGibbons 5 75
(R Hollinshead) *slowly away: sn mid-div: c wd into st: r.o one pce fnl f* **12/1**
4304 **5** *2* **Trombone Tom**[7] 6529 2-8-10 66 .... DarrenWilliams 7 60
(J R Norton) *led tl hdd over 4f out: styd prom tl wknd ins fnl f* **16/1**
0632 **6** *1* **Garlogs**[1] 6581 2-7-5 54 oh2 .... LiamJones[(7)] 9 45
(A Bailey) *chsd ldrs: rdn over 2f out: sn outpcd* **7/1**[3]
2004 **7** *½* **Daaweitza**[14] 6479 2-8-10 66 .... (p) DeanMernagh 2 56
(B Ellison) *in rr: sme hdwy over 1f out: nvr nr to chal* **11/1**
0405 **8** *½* **Tiber Tilly**[10] 6517 2-9-7 77 .... HayleyTurner 6 65
(N P Littmoden) *chsd ldrs: rdn 1/2-way: bhd fnl 2f* **16/1**
050 **9** *4* **Jessica Wigmo**[27] 6374 2-8-3 59 .... ChrisCatlin 11 35
(A W Carroll) *sn bhd* **50/1**
0000 **10** *1 ½* **Lady Fas (IRE)**[144] 3792 2-7-7 54 oh4 .... DuranFentiman[(5)] 1 26
(A W Carroll) *sn bhd and outpcd* **50/1**
110 **11** *5* **Mr Rigsby**[35] 6309 2-9-3 73 .... TonyCulhane 12 30
(P Howling) *in tch on outside: rdn over 3f out: wknd 2f out* **25/1**
1000 **12** *¾* **Capital Lass**[101] 5017 2-7-12 54 oh2 .... JimmyQuinn 8 8
(M J Wallace) *a bhd* **8/1**

1m 14.2s (-1.61) **Going Correction** -0.175s/f (Stan) **12** Ran SP% **119.6**
Speed ratings (Par 98):103,102,101,99,96 95,94,93,88,86 79,78
CSF £26.18 CT £79.73 TOTE £9.50: £3.20, £1.70, £1.90; EX 29.40.
Owner Miss Vanessa Church **Bred** Mrs P Lewis **Trained** Newmarket, Suffolk

FOCUS
Times of earlier races suggested the surface was riding fast and that was confirmed when a new course record was set in this race. The form appears solid with those in the frame behind the winner close to previous form.

NOTEBOOK
Jimmy The Guesser, who set a new course record, made most of the running in his first-time blinkers. He got tired in the closing stages, as he was entitled to, but he had enough in reserve to hold on from the closing pack. Connections plan to give him a bit of a break now but he will be an interesting candidate for early-season three-year-old handicaps next year. (op 9-2)
Orchard Supreme , who was equipped with a visor for the first time and, well drawn in three, travelled well off the pace but his rider gave him a bit too much to do and the winner always looked like holding on. This was third time in a row he has finished runner-up but there is nothing wrong with the horse's attitude. (op 7-2 tchd 3-1)
Catbang(IRE) ran well from his double-figure stall, giving the impression that he will appreciate a return to seven furlongs. (op 3-1 tchd 7-2)
Ochre Bay had the benefit of the rail but could not find the pace to throw down a challenge in the straight.
Trombone Tom has plenty of pace and should not mind a drop back to five furlongs.
Garlogs, who ran well from a poor draw at Southwell the previous day, failed to reproduce that form on this quicker surface. (op 9-1)
Capital Lass Official explanation: jockey said filly ran free early stages

6592 BETDIRECT FREEPHONE 0800 211 222 H'CAP 1m 4f 50y(P)
3:20 (3:20) (Class 2) (0-100,107) 3-Y-O+
£11,458 (£3,431; £1,715; £858; £428; £215) **Stalls** Low

Form RPR
2003 **1** **Cold Turkey**[26] 6179 5-8-10 91 .... J-PGuillambert 7 98+
(G L Moore) *hld up in rr: smooth hdwy on outside to go 2nd over 2f out: led appr fnl f: fnd ex cl home* **6/1**[3]
4133 **2** *hd* **Compton Bolter (IRE)**[27] 6378 8-9-12 107 .... JamieSpencer 5 114
(G A Butler) *led tl rdn and hdd appr fnl f: rallied nr fin* **9/4**[1]
-330 **3** *½* **Rehearsal**[21] 5309 4-8-11 92 .... PaulHanagan 2 98
(L Lungo) *trckd ldrs: rdn 2f out: r.o fnl f* **3/1**[2]

3540 **4** 1 **Tiger Tiger (FR)**[77] 5589 4-8-8 **89** .... JohnEgan 6 93
(Jamie Poulton) *hld up in tch: rdn 3f out: kpt on fnl f* **8/1**
0403 **5** ½ **The Violin Player (USA)**[14] 6482 4-8-5 **86** oh3........ JimmyQuinn 4 90
(H J Collingridge) *hld up: hdwy 7f out: rdn over 1f out: kpt on one pce* **13/2**
0605 **6** 3½ **Wellington Hall (GER)**[27] 6377 7-8-5 **86** oh8........ ChrisCatlin 3 84
(P W Chapple-Hyam) *trckd ldr to over 2f out: rdn and wknd sn after* **14/1**
041B **7** 1¾ **Garden Society (IRE)**[39] 6285 8-8-7 **88**........ HayleyTurner 8 83
(T T Clement) *prom: rdn over 3f out: wknd over 2f out* **12/1**
226- **8** ¾ **Putra Sas (IRE)**[565] 2510 4-9-7 **102**........ JoeFanning 1 96
(P F I Cole) *t.k.h: in tch tl wknd 2f out* **20/1**

2m 39.27s (-3.15) **Going Correction** -0.175s/f (Stan) **8** Ran SP% **113.6**
Speed ratings (Par 109):103,102,102,101,101 99,98,97
CSF £19.66 CT £48.01 TOTE £6.10: £1.30, £1.60, £1.40; EX 12.90.
Owner A Grinter **Bred** Worksop Manor Stud **Trained** Woodingdean, E Sussex

FOCUS
A decent handicap but lack of early pace resulted in something of a sprint finish. The placed horse set the standard for the form.

NOTEBOOK
Cold Turkey, a winner over timber last time out, found the best turn of foot off the steady gallop, confirming he is a very useful performer on Polytrack. Given that he stays two miles, he has surprising speed when required, but the plan is to go back over hurdles next, with a race at Newbury on December 28th pencilled in. (op 4-1)
Compton Bolter(IRE) arguably should have won as the absence of a natural front-runner led to his rider taking the wise tactical decision to make the running. He set just a steady pace but he did not make the best of the situation, failing to kick on and make the rest chase him down but allowing the race to develop into a sprint from the turn into the straight. (op 2-1)
Rehearsal, another who was last seen over hurdles, did not run badly in defeat but he was probably not alone in finding the way the race was run against him. (op 7-2)
Tiger Tiger(FR) is a hold-up performer best seen in a race run at a decent pace. Given that, he did not run badly on his first outing for 11 weeks. (op 9-1)
The Violin Player(USA) had a stiff task from out of the handicap and, as a hold-up performer, did not have the race run to suit either. (op 7-1)
Wellington Hall(GER) was another who had plenty on his plate as he was 8lb wrong at the weights. (op 16-1)

6593 BETDIRECTCASINO.COM H'CAP (DIV I) 1m 1f 103y(P)
3:50 (3:50) (Class 6) (0-65,70) 3-Y-0+ **£2,560** (£756; £378) **Stalls** Low

Form RPR
4366 **1** **Ronsard (IRE)**[49] 6134 3-9-2 **65**........ JohnEgan 3 71
(Heather Dalton) *a in tch: rdn over 1f out: r.o strly to ld cl home* **10/1**
5001 **2** nk **Bijou Dan**[34] 6336 4-9-3 **64**........(b) TomEaves 5 69
(I Semple) *sn led: rdn over 1f out: kpt on: hdd nr fin* **9/2**[2]
5511 **3** ½ **Western Roots**[4] 6564 4-9-9 **70** 6ex........ GeorgeBaker 13 74+
(M Appleby) *racd wd in mid-div: r.o strly fnl f: nvr nrr* **11/4**[1]
1040 **4** hd **Lord Chamberlain**[10] 6513 12-9-1 **62**........(b) LPKeniry 12 66+
(J M Bradley) *hld up in rr: hdwy on outside over 1f out: r.o wl fnl f* **25/1**
6010 **5** 1 **Sforzando**[41] 6266 4-8-9 **63**........ KristinStubbs(7) 8 65
(Mrs L Stubbs) *slowly away: in rr tl hdwy on ins over 1f out: r.o wl: nvr nrr* **25/1**
2350 **6** hd **Hawkit (USA)**[20] 6432 4-9-0 **64**........(t) DanielTudhope(3) 7 65
(P D Evans) *chsd ldr 7f out: ev ch ent fnl f: wknd ins fnl f* **9/2**[2]
0460 **7** ½ **My Pension (IRE)**[13] 6488 4-9-4 **65**........ TonyCulhane 4 65
(P Howling) *trckd ldr to 7f out: styd prom tl wknd ins fnl f* **9/1**
5460 **8** 6 **Ulysees (IRE)**[13] 6486 6-8-13 **60**........ PaulHanagan 6 49
(I Semple) *mid-div: wknd wl over 1f out* **20/1**
5325 **9** 1¼ **Jakarmi**[31] 6364 4-9-1 **65**........ RobertMiles(3) 9 57+
(B Palling) *mid-div: wknd over 1f out* **8/1**[3]
200 **10** 1½ **Sting Like A Bee (IRE)**[58] 5979 6-8-13 **60**........ FergalLynch 10 44
(J S Goldie) *sn bhd and nvr on terms* **16/1**
00 **11** nk **Portacarron (IRE)**[175] 2902 3-9-2 **65**........ MCHussey 11 48
(Eamon Tyrrell, Ire) *a bhd* **16/1**
4000 **12** 5 **Acorazado (IRE)**[11] 6505 6-9-1 **62**........ JamieMackay 1 36
(C P Morlock) *a bhd* **50/1**
500/ **13** 2 **Secret's Out**[62] 2060 9-8-13 **60**........ JamieSpencer 2 30
(W M Brisbourne) *mid-div: rdn 1/2-way: wknd over 2f out* **12/1**

2m 1.93s (-0.69) **Going Correction** -0.175s/f (Stan)
WFA 3 from 4yo+ 2lb **13** Ran SP% **127.1**
Speed ratings (Par 101):96,95,95,95,94 94,93,88,87,85 85,81,79
CSF £55.97 CT £165.35 TOTE £11.50: £3.60, £2.80, £1.80; EX 115.90.
Owner R Edwards And W J Swinnerton **Bred** Liscannor Stud Ltd **Trained** Norton, Shropshire

FOCUS
The pace was only steady in this routine handicap and those held up were disadvantaged. The race was run in a modest time for the grade, 1.59 seconds slower than the second division. The form does not look totally solid with the runner-up the best guide to the level.
Jakarmi Official explanation: jockey said gelding ran flat

6594 BETDIRECTCASINO.COM H'CAP (DIV II) 1m 1f 103y(P)
4:20 (4:21) (Class 6) (0-65,65) 3-Y-0+ **£2,559** (£755; £378) **Stalls** Low

Form RPR
3005 **1** **Blue Patrick**[66] 5824 5-9-2 **63**........ NCallan 3 76+
(K A Ryan) *a in tch on ins: rdn to ld appr fnl f: sn clr* **5/2**[1]
0605 **2** 3 **Mollyputtheketelon (USA)**[48] 6160 4-9-2 **63**........ JamieSpencer 1 68
(M J Wallace) *a.p: led over 2f out: hdd appr fnl f: kpt on but nt pce of wnr* **14/1**
4614 **3** ½ **Sarraaf (IRE)**[30] 6365 9-8-13 **60**........ TomEaves 8 64
(I Semple) *mid-div: rdn and hdwy 2f out: r.o fnl f* **7/1**[2]
0306 **4** 1¾ **Kindlelight Debut**[27] 6373 5-9-4 **65**........ MickyFenton 13 66+
(N P Littmoden) *a.p: rdn over 1f out: kpt on one pce* **8/1**[3]
1420 **5** 1¼ **Seattle Robber**[99] 5061 3-9-0 **63**........(p) FergalLynch 9 61
(P A Blockley) *hld up in rr: hdwy on ins over 1f out: nvr nrr* **20/1**
0106 **6** hd **Tokewanna**[82] 5491 5-8-12 **62**........ PatrickMathers(3) 5 60
(W M Brisbourne) *mid-div: rdn 2f out: kpt on one pce fnl f* **14/1**
0000 **7** 1¾ **She's Our Lass (IRE)**[13] 6488 4-9-1 **65**........ DanielTudhope(3) 7 60
(D Carroll) *a towards rr: effrt over 2f out: sn btn* **7/1**[2]
-500 **8** ½ **Pittsburgh**[50] 6127 3-8-13 **65**........(t) NeilChalmers(3) 11 59
(A M Balding) *in rr: sme hdwy over 1f out: nvr on terms* **25/1**
6006 **9** 2 **Piano Man**[41] 6265 3-8-13 **62**........ LPKeniry 12 52
(J C Fox) *chsd ldrs: rdn 3f out: wknd over 1f out* **12/1**
0220 **10** 2 **Barking Mad (USA)**[31] 6101 7-9-3 **64**........ RobertWinston 2 50
(C R Dore) *led tl hdd over 5f out: wknd over 2f out* **17/2**
5600 **11** 5 **King Nicholas (USA)**[6] 6542 6-9-3 **64**........(tp) TonyCulhane 6 41
(J Parkes) *led over 5f out: hdd over 2f out: wknd qckly* **20/1**
50-0 **12** 15 **Trew Flight (USA)**[4] 6565 3-9-2 **65**........ JoeFanning 10 13
(M H Tompkins) *racd wd in mid-div: wknd over 2f out* **20/1**
654 **13** ¾ **Carvoeiro**[107] 4864 3-8-13 **62**........ GeorgeBaker 4 9
(C F Wall) *slowly away: a bhd* **10/1**

2m 0.34s (-2.28) **Going Correction** -0.175s/f (Stan)
WFA 3 from 4yo+ 2lb **13** Ran SP% **123.5**
Speed ratings (Par 101):103,100,99,98,97 97,95,95,93,91 87,73,73
CSF £39.67 CT £230.46 TOTE £3.00: £1.40, £5.10, £2.50; EX 48.70.
Owner S R H Turner **Bred** Finbar Kent **Trained** Hambleton, N Yorks

FOCUS
There was a more solid gallop on in this division which resulted in a fair time for the grade, 1.59 seconds quicker than division one. The placed horses provide the best guide to the level of the form.

6595 MORE OFFERS AT BETDIRECT.CO.UK MAIDEN STKS (DIV II) 1m 141y(P)
4:50 (4:53) (Class 5) 2-Y-O **£3,717** (£1,106; £552; £276) **Stalls** Low

Form RPR
32 **1** **Hard To Explain (IRE)**[61] 5919 2-9-0........ JamieSpencer 3 76+
(E J O'Neill) *chsd ldrs: led 4f out: clr whn rn green over 1f out: kpt on* **1/1**[1]
2 ¾ **Dream Champion** 2-9-0........ TonyCulhane 4 74
(M R Channon) *mid-div: rdn 3f out: styd on to chse wnr fnl f* **12/1**
3 ½ **Country Affair (USA)**[76] 5636 2-9-0........ JimmyQuinn 6 73
(John A Quinn, Ire) *in rr tl rdn and hdwy over 2f out: styd on fnl f* **16/1**
02 **4** 2 **Island Myth (IRE)**[14] 6477 2-9-0........ ChrisCatlin 10 69+
(M P Tregoning) *in rr: rdn 3f out: styd on wl fnl f: nvr nrr* **2/1**[2]
0 **5** 1¼ **Blue Beacon**[87] 5391 2-8-9........ NCallan 5 61
(K A Ryan) *a.p: rdn to chse wnr over 2f out: edgd lft and wknd fnl f* **16/1**
0 **6** 9 **Black Sea Pearl**[20] 6427 2-8-9........ JohnEgan 7 42+
(P W D'Arcy) *mid-div: rdn over 3f out: btn whn eased ins fnl f* **33/1**
7 1 **Questive** 2-9-0........ SteveDrowne 2 45+
(E A L Dunlop) *hld up in tch: chsd wnr 3f out tl wknd over 1f out* **9/1**[3]
00 **8** 1¼ **Stoneacre Fred (IRE)**[21] 6424 2-9-0........ RobbieFitzpatrick 11 43
(Peter Grayson) *outpcd: a bhd* **66/1**
06 **9** 2 **Berties Brother**[104] 4961 2-9-0........ MickyFenton 13 38
(D G Bridgwater) *a bhd* **50/1**
00 **10** 1½ **Dark Night (IRE)**[7] 6531 2-9-0........ RobertWinston 8 35
(D W Barker) *led tl hdd 4f out: wknd wl over 1f out* **40/1**
0 **11** ½ **Light Of Day (IRE)**[48] 6143 2-8-6........ AdamKirby(3) 12 29
(Miss Diana Weeden) *v.s.a: hdwy on outside over 3f out: wknd over 2f out* **66/1**
12 28 **Frantastik Lady (IRE)** 2-8-9........ FranciscoDaSilva 9 —
(A Kinsella, Ire) *prom tl wknd 4f out* **66/1**

1m 51.08s (-0.68) **Going Correction** -0.175s/f (Stan) **12** Ran SP% **124.6**
Speed ratings (Par 96):96,95,94,93,92 84,83,82,80,78 78,53
CSF £16.39 TOTE £2.00: £1.30, £2.30, £3.90; EX 17.90 Place 6 £6.45, Place 5 £5.94.
Owner J C Fretwell **Bred** Hirschmann Nolan And Sullivan Partnership **Trained** Averham Park, Notts

FOCUS
An average maiden and the winning time was about par for a race like this, despite being 0.62 seconds faster than division one. Despite that the form is modest and not that solid.

NOTEBOOK
Hard To Explain(IRE) raced a touch keenly in the early stages on his All-Weather debut and did not handle the first bend well, but he eventually scored with a bit more in hand than the margin of victory would suggest. Still a touch green despite this being his third start, there should be better to come in handicap company. (op 11-10 tchd 6-5 and 10-11)
Dream Champion ◆, who is related to winners, posted a promising debut effort, responding well to pressure. He will be hard to beat in a similar contest next time with this experience behind him. (tchd 14-1)
Country Affair(USA) looked an interesting player as he had finished in midfield in a decent maiden at The Curragh on his debut. The market did not suggest that much was expected on his first outing for 76 days, though, and it was only late in the day that he got involved. He should get further in time and one more run will make him eligible for handicaps. (op 10-1)
Island Myth(IRE) had run well over the course and distance on his last start but got little luck with the draw this time. Handicaps are now open to him. (op 5-2)
Blue Beacon, sold out of Ed Dunlop's stable for 28,000gns since her debut at Newmarket, does not have the ability to match her pedigree. (op 12-1)
Questive, who is a brother to useful middle-distance handicapper Blaze Of Colour, was making her racecourse debut and looks the type who will do better in time when granted a stiffer test. Official explanation: jockey said colt had a breathing problem (op 10-1)
Dark Night(IRE) Official explanation: jockey said gelding hung left
T/Plt: £17.70 to a £1 stake. Pool: £43,613.25. 1,797.40 winning tickets. T/Qpdt: £3.50 to a £1 stake. Pool: £3,385.30. 712.90 winning tickets. JS

6574 LINGFIELD (L-H)
Saturday, December 17

OFFICIAL GOING: Standard
Wind: Moderate, against

6596 NO 5P RULE 4S AT BETDIRECT H'CAP (DIV I) 1m 2f (P)
11:50 (11:51) (Class 5) (0-70,70) 3-Y-0+ **£3,122** (£929; £464; £231) **Stalls** Low

Form RPR
1000 **1** **Willhego**[32] 6356 4-9-0 **66**........ HayleyTurner 12 77
(J R Best) *trckd ldr to over 4f out: styd prom: rallied to ld wl ins fnl f: jst hld on* **8/1**
0002 **2** nk **Karaoke (IRE)**[21] 6432 5-9-1 **67**........ GeorgeBaker 3 78
(S Kirk) *lw: w.w early hdwy to go 2nd over 4f out: led 2f out: kpt on u.p whn haded wl ins fnl f* **4/1**[1]
0355 **3** 3 **Constructor**[21] 6426 4-8-12 **64**........ MickyFenton 11 69
(C A Cyzer) *hld up in mid-div: hdwy 2f out: styd on wl fnl f: nvr nrr* **16/1**
2132 **4** ¾ **Oakley Absolute**[167] 3165 3-8-7 **65**........ StephaneBreux(3) 6 69
(R Hannon) *lw: trckd ldrs: rdn and one pce fnl f* **9/1**
1036 **5** ¾ **Blackmail (USA)**[64] 5867 7-8-8 **63**........(b) RichardThomas(3) 8 65
(Miss B Sanders) *hmpered 6f out: in rr tl hdwy on outside 2f out: fin wl fnl f* **13/2**[3]
2465 **6** nk **Eloquent Knight (USA)**[11] 6520 3-8-12 **67**........ JimmyQuinn 13 69
(W R Muir) *slowly away: hdwy wl over 1f out: nt pce to chal* **8/1**
3000 **7** shd **Fortune Point (IRE)**[47] 4042 7-8-7 **59**........(v) RobertWinston 9 60
(A W Carroll) *led tl hdd 2f out: rdn and wknd appr fnl f* **14/1**
4020 **8** hd **Jubilee Dream**[81] 5528 3-8-9 **64**........ IanMongan 7 65
(Mrs L J Mongan) *mid-div: rdn over 3f out: sn outpcd* **33/1**
0/L0 **9** 2 **Battling Mac (IRE)**[18] 6458 7-9-4 **70**........ J-PGuillambert 5 67
(L A Dace) *lw: hld up: a in rr* **66/1**
6004 **10** 1½ **Admiral Compton**[12] 6503 4-9-1 **67**........ SteveDrowne 10 61
(J R Boyle) *in tch tl wknd wl over 1f out* **6/1**[2]
2606 **11** ¾ **In The Pink (IRE)**[42] 6266 5-8-10 **62**........ PaulHanagan 2 55
(M A Buckley) *t.k.h: a bhd* **10/1**

0000 **12** *6* **Cherokee Nation**[18] [6465] 4-9-2 **68**............................(e) TonyCulhane 14 50
(P W D'Arcy) *t.k.h: hdwy over 4f out: wknd 3f out* **66/1**
-200 **13** *1 1/2* **Fabulous Emperor (IRE)**[120] [4545] 3-9-1 **70**........................ JohnEgan 1 49
(Jamie Poulton) *lw: a bhd* **14/1**
0000 **14** *1* **Postmaster**[61] [5940] 3-8-8 **63** ow3..................................(t) RobertHavlin 4 40
(R Ingram) *in tch tl rdn and wknd over 2f out* **50/1**

2m 6.72s (-1.07) **Going Correction** -0.125s/f (Stan)
WFA 3 from 4yo+ 3lb **14** Ran SP% **116.0**
Speed ratings (Par 103):99,98,96,95,95 94,94,94,93,91 91,86,85,84
CSF £37.83 CT £502.18 TOTE £11.60: £2.90, £1.70, £6.30; EX 50.60.
Owner G G Racing **Bred** J R Wills **Trained** Hucking, Kent
■ Stewards' Enquiry : George Baker one-day ban: careless riding (Dec 28)

FOCUS
There was no pace on at all until halfway, resulting in several taking a fierce hold. The winning time was 0.64 seconds slower than the second division.
Postmaster Official explanation: vet said gelding had bled from the nose

6597 BETDIRECT FREEPHONE 0800 211 222 H'CAP (DIV I) 5f (P)
12:20 (12:24) (Class 5) (0-70,70) 3-Y-0+ **£3,031** (£901; £450; £225) **Stalls** High

Form RPR
4663 **1** **Kennington**[14] [6486] 5-8-12 **64**......................................(b) TonyCulhane 5 77
(Mrs C A Dunnett) *trckd ldrs: led ins fnl f: r.o wl* **6/1**[3]
304 **2** *1 1/4* **Joyeaux**[15] [6483] 3-8-11 **63**.. MickyFenton 6 71
(S L Keightley) *b.hind: towards rr: hdwy and swtchd rt over 1f out: fin strly* **12/1**
1005 **3** *1 3/4* **The Fisio**[22] [6422] 5-9-1 **67**...(v) IanMongan 2 69+
(S Gollings) *led after 1f: rdn and hdd insd fnl f: kpt on* **6/1**[3]
5236 **4** *1/2* **Tag Team (IRE)**[11] [6518] 4-8-13 **65**...(v) PaulEddery 8 65
(John A Harris) *b: hld up in tch: rdn over 1f out: r.o fnl f* **6/1**[3]
0000 **5** *shd* **Turibius**[21] [6430] 6-8-13 **65**.. JohnEgan 4 65
(T E Powell) *a in tch: hdwy on ins and ever ch ins fnl f: no ex fnl 50yds* **8/1**
0005 **6** *hd* **Alexia Rose (IRE)**[15] [6480] 3-9-1 **67**................................. FergalLynch 9 66
(A Berry) *in rr: r.o fnl f: nvr nrr* **33/1**
1105 **7** *3/4* **Ballybunion (IRE)**[14] [6486] 6-8-11 **63**.............................. DaneO'Neill 10 59
(N E Berry) *outpcd thrght* **20/1**
0500 **8** *1/2* **Salon Prive**[35] [6335] 5-8-13 **68**.................................. NelsonDeSouza(3) 3 62
(C A Cyzer) *led for 1f: styd prom tl wknd qckly fnl f* **5/1**[2]
0200 **9** *5* **One Way Ticket**[62] [5922] 5-8-10 **62**...............................(p) SteveDrowne 7 38
(J M Bradley) *trckd ldrs tl wknd over 1f out* **9/2**[1]

58.38 secs (-1.40) **Going Correction** -0.125s/f (Stan) **9** Ran SP% **104.2**
Speed ratings (Par 103):106,104,101,100,100 99,98,97,89
CSF £60.89 CT £330.79 TOTE £8.30: £2.30, £3.60, £2.00; EX 48.60.
Owner Mrs Christine Dunnett **Bred** C J R Trotter **Trained** Hingham, Norfolk
■ Justalord (8/1, refused to enter stalls) was withdrawn. R4 applies, deduct 10p in the £.

FOCUS
An ordinary sprint, but the pace was very decent and the winning time was 0.61 seconds faster than the second division.
One Way Ticket Official explanation: jockey said horse never travelled

6598 NO 5P RULE 4S AT BETDIRECT H'CAP (DIV II) 1m 2f (P)
12:50 (12:50) (Class 5) (0-70,70) 3-Y-0+ **£3,120** (£928; £463; £231) **Stalls** Low

Form RPR
0230 **1** **Night Storm**[51] [6126] 4-8-10 **62**... JohnEgan 6 69
(S Dow) *lw: slowly away: hdwy on outside over 1f out: r.o wl u.p to ld cl home* **20/1**
2550 **2** *hd* **Danger Zone**[37] [6305] 3-8-12 **67**.. IanMongan 7 74
(Mrs A J Perrett) *hld up on outside: r.o strly fnl f: jst failed* **25/1**
3445 **3** *nk* **Resonate (IRE)**[32] [6356] 7-9-1 **67**...................................... DaneO'Neill 3 73
(A G Newcombe) *a.p: rdn to ld ins fnl f: hdd and lost 2nd cl home* **2/1**[1]
0060 **4** *shd* **Duelling Banjos**[21] [6432] 6-8-11 **66**.............................. RobertMiles(3) 14 72
(J Akehurst) *lw: chsd ldrs: rdn over 2f out: r.o fnl f* **16/1**
0404 **5** *1 1/4* **Scottish River (USA)**[14] [6488] 6-9-4 **70**............................ HayleyTurner 1 74
(M D I Usher) *b: b.hind: lw: mid-div: r.o fnl f: nvr nr to chal* **7/1**
0000 **6** *1 1/4* **Tricky Venture**[32] [6356] 5-8-6 **58**...................................... JimmyQuinn 11 59
(Mrs L C Jewell) *trckd ldrs: led over 2f out: hdd & wknd ins fnl f* **20/1**
4214 **7** *5* **Ramsgill (USA)**[5] [6566] 3-8-10 **65**.................................... FergalLynch 10 57
(N P Littmoden) *trckd ldr to over 2f out: wknd over 1f out* **11/4**[2]
0040 **8** *2* **Border Edge**[21] [6432] 7-8-8 **60**.....................................(v) J-PGuillambert 8 48
(J J Bridger) *b: sn led: hdd over 2f out: wknd over 1f out* **16/1**
9 *1/2* **Tignasse (FR)**[45] 4-8-5 **57**..(p) ChrisCatlin 13 44
(G L Moore) *a bhd* **33/1**
345 **10** *5* **Swainson (USA)**[134] [4129] 4-9-2 **68**..................................... JoeFanning 2 46
(P Mitchell) *bit bkwd: in tch tl rdn and wknd over 1f out* **11/2**[3]
6005 **11** *1 3/4* **King Forever**[22] [6418] 3-9-1 **70**.....................................(e[1]) MickyFenton 5 44
(D E Cantillon) *t.k.h: a bhd* **20/1**
4000 **12** *dist* **Comeintothespace (IRE)**[68] [5808] 3-8-10 **65**............. SamHitchcott 12 —
(A Bailey) *a in rr: t.o* **33/1**

2m 6.08s (-1.71) **Going Correction** -0.125s/f (Stan)
WFA 3 from 4yo+ 3lb **51** Ran SP% **123.7**
Speed ratings (Par 103):101,100,100,100,99 98,94,92,92,88 87,—
CSF £427.60 CT £1452.84 TOTE £15.70: £3.90, £6.10, £1.40; EX 296.50.
Owner W Thornton & R E Anderson **Bred** The Lavington Stud **Trained** Epsom, Surrey
■ Stewards' Enquiry : Dane O'Neill two-day ban: used whip with excessive frequency (Dec 28-29)

FOCUS
A more solid all-round pace than the first division and the winning time was 0.64 seconds faster. Despite that, the front four still finished in a heap.
Ramsgill(USA) Official explanation: jockey said gelding hung left and ran flat
Swainson(USA) Official explanation: jockey said colt lost its action
Comeintothespace(IRE) Official explanation: jockey said gelding moved poorly throughout and hung left

6599 BETDIRECT ON FOOTBALL NOVICE STKS 1m (P)
1:20 (1:20) (Class 4) 2-Y-0 **£4,792** (£1,425; £712; £355) **Stalls** High

Form RPR
0 **1** **Before You Go (IRE)**[88] [5392] 2-8-12 .... IanMongan 10 79
(T G Mills) *hld up: hdwy on outside over 1f out: styd on wl to ld fnl 50yds: won gng away* **14/1**
61 **2** *1 1/4* **Red Cape (FR)**[8] [6531] 2-9-5 85.. JohnEgan 9 83
(N A Callaghan) *lw: chsd ldrs: led ins fnl f: edgd lft: nt qckn and hdd fnl 50yds* **2/1**[1]
1354 **3** *3/4* **Time For Life (USA)**[18] [6457] 2-9-2 80............................ SteveDrowne 5 78+
(H J Collingridge) *slowly away: in rr: rdn 1/2-way: fin fast fnl f: nvr nrr* **3/1**[2]
0301 **4** *shd* **Fusili (IRE)**[36] [6313] 2-8-9 72.. HayleyTurner 12 71
(N P Littmoden) *in tch tl outpcd over 3f out: rallied and r.o strly fnl f* **14/1**
53 **5** *nk* **Rembrandt Quality (USA)**[21] [6427] 2-8-12 .... RobertWinston 1 73
(Mrs A J Perrett) *chsd ldrs: kpt on one pce fnl f* **9/2**[3]
2415 **6** *2* **Possessed**[18] [6457] 2-9-0 73... MatthewHenry 8 71
(T D McCarthy) *b: trckd ldr: ev ch appr fnl f: one pce ins* **20/1**
0541 **7** *1 1/4* **Ms Rainbow Runner**[10] [6521] 2-8-0 57.......................... LiamJones(7) 11 61
(P Butler) *hld up: 1/2-way: rdn and hdd ins fnl f: fdd* **50/1**
1 **8** *hd* **Fun Time**[26] [6395] 2-8-7 .... SamHitchcott 7 61
(M R Channon) *trckd ldrs: rdn and one pce fnl f* **7/1**
6 **9** *4* **That Look**[15] [6484] 2-8-12 .... TPQueally 4 56
(D E Cantillon) *leggy: a bhd* **100/1**
0233 **10** *5* **Snake Skin**[18] [6467] 2-8-11 57.. J-PGuillambert 2 44
(J Gallagher) *led to 1/2-way: wknd 2f out* **33/1**
11 *13* **Earth Master (IRE)**[54] [6084] 2-9-5 .... GeorgeBaker 6 22
(S Kirk) *s.i.s: a bhd: virtually p.u fnl f* **33/1**

1m 38.09s (-1.34) **Going Correction** -0.125s/f (Stan) **11** Ran SP% **115.9**
Speed ratings (Par 98):101,99,99,98,98 96,95,95,91,86 73
CSF £40.32 TOTE £17.20: £3.60, £1.50, £1.30; EX 61.50.
Owner Mrs Tina Smith **Bred** The Niarchos Family **Trained** Headley, Surrey

FOCUS
A decent little contest even though a few of these had little chance. The pace was solid and resulted in a fair winning time for a race of its type.

NOTEBOOK
Before You Go(IRE) ◆, beaten out of sight in a Newmarket maiden that has produced a couple of winners in his only previous outing, was much more the finished article. He showed a smart turn of foot to cut down the favourite and, if building on this, could be quite decent. (tchd 16-1)
Red Cape(FR), stepping up another furlong, was produced at just the right time, but no sooner had he hit the front than he appeared to run green, hanging right over to the inside rail, and was run out of it. Time may show that he faced a stiff task in trying to concede 7lb to the winner, but he also had the edge in experience. Given their respective attitudes in the last furlong one would be fooled for thinking it was the other way around. (op 6-4 tchd 9-4 in places)
Time For Life(USA) again gave away too much ground at the start and it was only his rider's persistence that got him into third. If he can learn to break on terms, there are more races to be won with him. (op 7-2 tchd 11-4)
Fusili(IRE) ◆ may have found things happening too quickly for her on this quicker track, yet kept on trying and was far from disgraced. A longer trip or a return to a slower surface should see her winning again. (op 12-1)
Rembrandt Quality(USA) seemed to have every chance, but was never doing enough. His ideal trip is still to be identified, but he now qualifies for a handicap mark and that could be his best option now. (op 4-1 tchd 5-1)
Possessed was 4lb worse off with Time For Life after finishing just behind him in a nursery here last time, so she probably ran to form. (op 25-1)
Fun Time was a little disappointing over this extra furlong, especially as the form of her debut victory here was boosted by the subsequent success of the runner-up. (op 8-1 tchd 17-2)

6600 FIRST PAST THE POST AT BETDIRECT (S) STKS 6f (P)
1:50 (1:52) (Class 6) 2-Y-0 **£2,504** (£739; £369) **Stalls** Low

Form RPR
2636 **1** **Figaro Flyer (IRE)**[96] [5178] 2-9-2 87................................ TonyCulhane 5 72+
(P Howling) *sn led: mde rest: rdn clr over 1f out: comf* **4/6**[1]
3024 **2** *1 1/4* **Phinerine**[5] [6562] 2-8-4 59..(b) RonanKeogh(7) 9 63
(Peter Grayson) *hld up in tch: hdwy to chse wnr over 1f out: r.o* **10/1**[3]
0651 **3** *3* **She Whispers (IRE)**[12] [6500] 2-8-6 56.................................. ChrisCatlin 7 49
(G C H Chung) *lw: mid-div tl hdwy over 1f out: kpt on but no ch w first 2 fnl f* **11/2**[2]
6006 **4** *1 3/4* **Imperial Gem (IRE)**[5] [6562] 2-8-6 54............................... FrancisFerris 6 44
(Rae Guest) *hld up: rdn 1/2-way: r.o fnl f* **25/1**
0032 **5** *shd* **Diktalex (IRE)**[4] [6569] 2-7-13 55......................................(t) LiamJones(7) 1 43+
(W G M Turner) *sn bhd: mde sme late hdwy* **10/1**[3]
1504 **6** *nk* **Bermuda Beauty (IRE)**[88] [5384] 2-8-11 55.................... SteveDrowne 3 48
(J M Bradley) *chsd ldrs: one pce appr fnl f* **20/1**
00 **7** *1 1/2* **Lady Josh**[31] [6366] 2-8-6 .... AlanDaly 2 38
(W G M Turner) *chsd ldrs to 1/2-way* **40/1**
2006 **8** *2* **Straight As A Die**[120] [4543] 2-8-6 50................................. JimmyQuinn 10 32
(R J Hodges) *trckd ldr: rdn over 2f out: wknd over 1f out* **16/1**
03 **9** *3/4* **Dolce Maria (IRE)**[12] [6500] 2-8-6 .... PaulHanagan 12 30
(Michael Cunningham, Ire) *prom: wnt 2nd 1/2-way: wknd wl over 1f out* **14/1**
00 **10** *6* **Health Spa**[12] [6502] 2-8-1 .... RoryMoore(5) 4 12
(B R Johnson) *a bhd* **50/1**
11 *18* **Saint Nick** 2-8-11 .... J-PGuillambert 11 —
(J J Bridger) *w'like: slowly away: a bhd* **50/1**

1m 12.9s (0.09) **Going Correction** -0.125s/f (Stan) **11** Ran SP% **121.1**
Speed ratings (Par 94):94,92,88,86,85 85,83,80,79,71 47
CSF £8.18 TOTE £1.70: £1.10, £2.30, £1.80; EX 9.80.The winner was bought in for 15,000gns. Phinerine was claimed by R. A. Harris for £6,000.
Owner Mark Entwistle **Bred** Mohammad Al Qatami **Trained** Newmarket, Suffolk

FOCUS
A poor seller and won in predictable style by the favourite who had a ton in hand on official ratings and made every yard.

NOTEBOOK
Figaro Flyer(IRE), a three-time winner on turf, even with his penalty had upwards of 21lb in hand of his rivals on adjusted official ratings. Given a positive ride, he never saw another rival and won with plenty in hand, but connections had to go to 15,000gns to keep him and it will be interesting to see where they go with him now. (op 4-5 tchd 10-11 and 5-6 in a place)
Phinerine, already placed a few times on turf and sand including at this level, emphatically reversed recent course form with She Whispers and stayed on to the line to get within a respectable distance of the winner. On the other hand he already looks exposed in moderate company and connections will be hoping the Handicapper does not take the form with the favourite too literally. (op 9-1 tchd 8-1 and 11-1)
She Whispers(IRE) found this a better seller than the one she landed over course and distance two weeks earlier, but she could not confirm the form of that race with Phinerine despite being no worse off. She is not going to be easy to place from now on. (op 7-1)
Imperial Gem(IRE), unplaced in all seven of her previous starts including at this level, did not get going until too late. She may need further, but is only very moderate. (op 20-1)
Diktalex(IRE), placed on Fibresand in her last two starts, found everything happening too quickly for her on this quicker track and should be given another chance back a slower surface. (op 9-1)

6601 BETDIRECT.CO.UK CONDITIONS STKS 1m (P)
2:25 (2:25) (Class 4) 3-Y-0+ **£5,647** (£1,680; £839; £419) **Stalls** High

Form RPR
0042 **1** **Psychiatrist**[21] [6431] 4-8-12 92.. SteveDrowne 3 99
(R Hannon) *b: sn trckd ldr: rdn to ld ins fnl f: r.o* **9/4**[2]
1300 **2** *nk* **Azarole (IRE)**[64] [5873] 4-9-8 106.. JohnEgan 6 108
(J S Moore) *hld up towards rr: hdwy over 1f out: r.o wl to cl on wnr nr fin* **7/1**

6021 **3** *1* **Hail The Chief**[8] 6533 8-8-12 85 DaneO'Neill 2 96
(R Hannon) *b: b.hind: lw: led tl hdd and nt qckn ins fnl f* **5/1**[3]
1212 **4** *hd* **Three Wrens (IRE)**[12] 6504 3-8-6 82 RobertWinston 4 91
(D J Daly) *t.k.h: trckd ldrs: rdn and nt qckn fnl f* **7/4**[1]
0-2 **5** *3* **Activo (FR)**[18] 6459 4-8-12 88 PaulDoe 1 89
(S Dow) *b: lw: a in tch: one pce ent fnl f* **10/1**
0360 **6** *2* **James Caird (IRE)**[71] 5717 5-8-12 88 JoeFanning 5 84
(M H Tompkins) *a bhd and nvr on terms* **14/1**
1m 37.25s (-2.18) **Going Correction** -0.125s/f (Stan)
WFA 3 from 4yo+ 1lb **6** Ran SP% **112.1**
Speed ratings (Par 105):105,104,103,103,100 98
CSF £17.79 TOTE £2.90: £1.60, £3.30; EX 21.90.
Owner Raymond Tooth **Bred** Downclose Stud **Trained** East Everleigh, Wilts
FOCUS
A decent little conditions event and even though the early pace was steady, they must have quickened appreciably in the second half of the contest as the final time was perfectly acceptable for a race like this.

6602 LITTLEWOODS BETDIRECT H'CAP 6f (P)
3:00 (3:04) (Class 2) (0-100,97) 3-Y-0+ **£12,021** (£3,576; £1,787; £892) **Stalls** Low

Form RPR
2040 **1** **Les Arcs (USA)**[51] 6125 5-8-4 90 JamesO'Reilly(7) 3 102
(T J Pitt) *slowly away: t.k.h: hld up: hdwy on outside over 1f out: r.o strly to ld ins fnl f* **11/2**[2]
0110 **2** *½* **Fromsong (IRE)**[15] 6481 7-8-13 **92** JohnEgan 4 103
(D K Ivory) *chsd ldrs: ev ch ins fnl f: kpt on to line* **8/1**
0530 **3** *1 ½* **Cornus**[8] 6530 3-8-5 **84** PaulHanagan 5 90
(M J Polglase) *b: chsd ldrs: rdn 2f out: r.o fnl f* **14/1**
0104 **4** *nk* **Green Manalishi**[15] 6481 4-9-4 **97** DaneO'Neill 1 102
(D W P Arbuthnot) *bhd tl hdwy on ins over 1f out: r.o fnl f* **10/1**
3311 **5** *1 ½* **Perfect Story (IRE)**[12] 6504 3-8-1 **83** oh2 NelsonDeSouza(3) 9 84
(J A R Toller) *lw: racd wd towards rr tl r.o fnl f* **6/1**[3]
3403 **6** *½* **Katiypour (IRE)**[81] 5526 8-8-6 **88** RichardThomas(3) 11 87
(Miss B Sanders) *lw: s.i.s: hld up in rr: r.o one pce fnl f* **7/1**
0015 **7** *hd* **Chateau Nicol**[8] 6530 6-8-9 **88** (v) JoeFanning 10 87
(B G Powell) *lw: chsd ldrs tl wknd fnl f* **12/1**
0030 **8** *nk* **Polish Emperor (USA)**[11] 6518 5-8-11 **93** (p) AdamKirby(3) 7 91
(W R Swinburn) *w ldr: rdn over 2f out: wknd appr fnl f* **20/1**
0053 **9** *½* **The Lord**[11] 6518 5-8-4 **83** oh3 AlanDaly 2 79
(W G M Turner) *led tl hdd & wknd ins fnl f* **16/1**
50 **10** *1 ¾* **Lindbergh**[15] 6481 3-8-2 **84** StephaneBreux(3) 6 75
(R Hannon) *mid-div whn short of room over 4f out: bhd and nvr on terms after* **33/1**
2020 **11** *1 ¼* **Russian Symphony (USA)**[28] 6379 4-8-11 **90** (b) SteveDrowne 8 77
(C R Egerton) *hld up in tch: lost pl 1/2-way and a bhd after* **5/2**[1]
1m 10.65s (-2.16) **Going Correction** -0.125s/f (Stan) **11** Ran SP% **118.9**
Speed ratings (Par 109):109,108,106,105,103 103,103,102,101,99 97
CSF £49.72 CT £592.19 TOTE £7.10: £2.10, £3.20, £3.20; EX 53.00.
Owner Willie McKay **Bred** Elk Manor Farm **Trained** Bawtry, S Yorks
■ A first winner with only his second runner for Tim Pitt.
FOCUS
A decent quality sprint handicap run at a good pace and dominated by those drawn low, with the first four coming from the five lowest stalls. The proximity of the third limits the form.
NOTEBOOK
Les Arcs(USA), who usually races over further than this, was held up for a late run which seems to suit him and, receiving plenty of encouragement from the saddle, was brought with a perfectly-timed effort. He did not look particularly well handicapped, so may well have improved for the change of yards and is still relatively unexposed over sprint trips. (op 7-1)
Fromsong(IRE), a winner on his last two visits here, did nothing wrong at all off a 7lb higher mark than for his last win and does look happier here than at Wolverhampton, where he finished unplaced last time. (op 7-1 tchd 9-1 and 10-1 in a place)
Cornus , who had run well in his only previous try here, did so again back over a much more suitable trip. He goes well at Wolverhampton too and perhaps the only negative is that he is yet to win a handicap. (op 20-1)
Green Manalishi was ridden much more patiently than last time and finished well but was never going to get there in time. He does look capable of winning over this trip when ridden this way. (op 9-1 tchd 8-1)
Perfect Story(IRE), bidding for a hat-trick, ran as though her wide draw and the drop in trip were more of a handicap than the 5lb higher mark. (op 5-1 tchd 13-2)
Katiypour(IRE) ◆, reappearing from a three-month break, ran with plenty of credit from the outside stall and is only 2lb higher than for his last win on sand. This should have put him right. (tchd 8-1)
Russian Symphony(USA) was a disappointing favourite here last time, but this was even worse as he was beaten a very long way out. Obviously all is not well. Official explanation: jockey said gelding suffered interference in running (op 3-1 tchd 7-2)

6603 BETDIRECT FREEPHONE 0800 211 222 H'CAP (DIV II) 5f (P)
3:30 (3:32) (Class 5) (0-70,69) 3-Y-0+ **£3,031** (£901; £450; £225) **Stalls** High

Form RPR
-124 **1** **After The Show**[22] 6422 4-9-4 **69** ChrisCatlin 10 73
(Rae Guest) *hld up in rr: hdwy appr fnl f: r.o wl to ld post* **4/1**[1]
0551 **2** *shd* **Ever Cheerful**[12] 6505 4-9-2 **67** J-PGuillambert 3 71
(G C H Chung) *mid-div: strly rdn and hdwy on ins 1f out: r.o: jst failed* **4/1**[1]
5400 **3** *nk* **Talcen Gwyn (IRE)**[21] 6426 3-8-13 **64** (v) SteveDrowne 7 67
(M F Harris) *in tch: rdn and squeezed through to ld ins fnl f: hdd and lost 2nd last strides* **12/1**
6030 **4** *¾* **Oceanico Dot Com (IRE)**[44] 6235 3-8-12 **63** FergalLynch 2 63
(A Berry) *led tl hdd ins fnl f: no ex nr fin* **25/1**
0022 **5** *shd* **Gone'N'Dunnett (IRE)**[7] 6546 6-9-3 **68** (v) DaneO'Neill 6 68
(Mrs C A Dunnett) *trckd ldr: ev ch ins fnl f: no ex fnl 50yds* **9/2**[2]
6040 **6** *nk* **Patternmaker (USA)**[21] 6426 3-9-1 **66** RobertWinston 4 67+
(W Jarvis) *slowly away: in rr: hdwy whn n.m.r and swtchd rt appr fnl f: r.o* **8/1**
0045 **7** *hd* **Kempsey**[21] 6430 3-8-11 **62** (v) MickyFenton 8 60
(J J Bridger) *prom on outside tl one pce fnl f* **12/1**
0002 **8** *½* **Alpaga Le Jomage (IRE)**[14] 6486 3-8-11 **62** PaulHanagan 9 58
(M J Polglase) *in tch: rdn 2f out: nt qckn fnl f* **9/1**
3440 **9** *2 ½* **Holly Springs**[7] 6546 3-8-11 **62** (p) TonyCulhane 1 49
(Mrs C A Dunnett) *in tch tl wknd over 1f out* **12/1**
0040 **10** *1 ¼* **Vague Star (ITY)**[22] 6422 3-9-0 **65** (b) RobertHavlin 5 47
(R Ingram) *rrd up in stalls and lost several l: a bhd* **15/2**[3]
58.99 secs (-0.79) **Going Correction** -0.125s/f (Stan) **10** Ran SP% **118.0**
Speed ratings (Par 103):101,100,100,99,99 98,98,97,93,91
CSF £20.07 CT £182.62 TOTE £5.20: £2.00, £1.80, £4.00; EX 31.90 Place 6 £60.47, Place 5 £25.61.
Owner Michael Ng Miss L Thompson **Bred** Michael Ng **Trained** Newmarket, Suffolk
FOCUS
An ordinary sprint handicap and the winning time was 0.61 seconds slower than the first division. The form looks ordinary, with the runner-up the key.
Vague Star(ITY) Official explanation: jockey said colt missed the break
T/Plt: £56.10 to a £1 stake. Pool: £57,025.30. 741.95 winning tickets. T/Qpdt: £7.70 to a £1 stake. Pool: £5,465.70. 519.20 winning tickets. JS

6581 SOUTHWELL (L-H)
Sunday, December 18

OFFICIAL GOING: Standard to slow
It was -5c overnight and the track had to be continually worked and as a result the surface was described as 'deep and exceptionally slow'.
Wind: Almost nil Weather: Fine but cold

6604 BETDIRECT ONLY A WEEK TIL XMAS BANDED STKS 5f (F)
1:00 (1:00) (Class 7) 3-Y-0+ **£917** (£917; £209) **Stalls** High

Form RPR
0012 **1** **Largs**[14] 6493 5-8-12 46 (b) RobertWinston 3 51+
(J Balding) *wnt rt and bmpd s: outpcd over 2f out: hdwy and edgd lft over 1f out: kpt on to dead-heat on line* **9/4**[1]
4532 **1** *dht* **Lizzie Rocket**[20] 6441 5-8-6 40 ow2 (v) JamesO'Reilly(7) 1 52
(J O'Reilly) *led: hrd rdn over 2f out: kpt on fnl f: jnd on line* **6/1**
0110 **3** *nk* **Secret Vision (USA)**[4] 6580 4-8-12 46 (p) PaulHanagan 4 50+
(R M H Cowell) *swvd lft s and bmpd s: outpcd over 2f out: hdwy and edgd lft over 1f out: styd on ins last* **3/1**[2]
1051 **4** *nk* **Ardkeel Lass (IRE)**[5] 6570 4-8-10 45 JBrennan(7) 5 54
(P D Evans) *missed break sltly: sn chsng ldrs: hdwy 2f out: styd on strly ins last: fin best* **7/2**[3]
2100 **5** *2 ½* **Cark**[18] 6471 7-8-11 45 (p) TonyCulhane 2 40
(J Balding) *chsd ldr: wknd fnl f* **11/2**
6250 **6** *2* **Flying Dancer**[11] 6525 3-8-6 47 TolleyDean(7) 7 35
(R A Harris) *sn outpcd and in rr: kpt on fnl 2f: nvr on terms* **20/1**
0060 **7** *3* **Piccleyes**[83] 5521 4-8-4 45 (b) ManavNem(7) 6 23
(M J Polglase) *trckd ldrs: lost pl over 1f out* **16/1**
0000 **8** *5* **Percy Douglas**[75] 5684 5-8-6 45 ow2 AnnStokell(7) 8 8
(Miss A Stokell) *outpcd and in rr after 2f: sn bhd* **25/1**
63.03 secs (2.73) **Going Correction** +0.325s/f (Slow) **8** Ran SP% **122.2**
Speed ratings (Par 97):91,91,90,90,86 82,78,70
Win: Largs £1.50, Lizzie Rocket £3.60; PL: L £1.10, LR £2.20, SV £1.70; Exacta: L/LR £8.80, LR/L £6.50; CSF: L/LR £8.95, LR/L £10.72.
Owner Hollinbridge Racing **Bred** Mrs Gillian A R Jones And John Balding **Trained** Scrooby, Notts
Owner Mrs K Morrell **Bred** Keith Morrell **Trained** Doncaster, S Yorks
■ Stewards' Enquiry : James O'Reilly one-day ban: used whip with excessive frequency (Dec 29)
FOCUS
A tight if very modest affair with the first four closely matched at the line. The winning time was half a second slower than the following two-year-old maiden and the form does not look that solid.

6605 PLAY INSTANT WIN GAMES AT BETDIRECT.CO.UK MEDIAN AUCTION MAIDEN STKS 5f (F)
1:30 (1:32) (Class 7) 2-Y-0 **£1,405** (£415; £207) **Stalls** High

Form RPR
5200 **1** **Tombalina**[37] 6311 2-8-3 50 ow1 MarkCoumbe(7) 1 55
(C J Teague) *mde all: rdn and edgd lft 2f out: edgd rt fnl f: hld on towards fin* **14/1**
430 **2** *¾* **Luloah**[48] 6197 2-8-9 62 DaleGibson 9 51
(J G Given) *chsd ldrs: styd on to go 2nd ins last: no ex* **11/2**
6540 **3** *1* **Sands Crooner (IRE)**[12] 6517 2-8-11 71 (t) PatrickMathers(3) 6 53
(D Shaw) *sn outpcd: hdwy over 1f out: styd on to take 3rd nr line* **6/4**[1]
0543 **4** *nk* **Mister Incredible**[14] 6496 2-9-0 55 PatCosgrave 3 52
(C A Dwyer) *chsd wnr: sn drvn along and hung lft: kpt on same pce fnl 2f* **4/1**[3]
0300 **5** *½* **Miss Mujahid Times**[5] 6569 2-8-4 48 DuranFentiman(5) 2 45
(A D Brown) *chsd ldrs: one pce fnl 2f* **33/1**
00 **6** *7* **Bollywood (IRE)**[146] 3801 2-9-0 MatthewHenry 8 27
(M A Jarvis) *s.i.s: nvr on terms* **7/2**[2]
0 **7** *nk* **Marvin Gardens**[44] 6242 2-9-0 BrianReilly 5 26
(P S McEntee) *sn outpcd and in rr: nvr on terms* **50/1**
8 *½* **Sir Mikeale** 2-9-0 J-PGuillambert 4 24
(G Prodromou) *dwlt: wnt lft s s: nvr on terms* **22/1**
0200 **9** *5* **Dispol Valentine**[87] 5418 2-8-10 51 ow1 TonyCulhane 7 —
(P T Midgley) *outpcd and in rr after 2f* **25/1**
0000 **10** *9* **Scattered Empire (IRE)**[6] 6561 2-9-0 40 (b[1]) RobbieFitzpatrick 10 —
(Peter Grayson) *s.i.s: racd stands' rail: sn bhd* **50/1**
62.53 secs (2.23) **Going Correction** +0.325s/f (Slow) **10** Ran SP% **119.3**
Speed ratings (Par 90):95,93,92,91,90 79,79,78,70,56
CSF £86.01 TOTE £18.20: £3.10, £2.10, £1.10; EX 96.80.
Owner Shaun Taylor **Bred** B A Beale & Bbb Computer Services Ltd **Trained** Station Town, Co Durham
FOCUS
A very modest sprint maiden with the winner rated just 50 compared with the third's inflated 71. The placed horses ran below their official marks and the form is not convincing.
NOTEBOOK
Tombalina, having her first run since leaving John Spearing, is all speed, and despite going both ways under pressure she did just enough. (op 12-1)
Luloah, bred to handle the All-Weather, was having her first outing for seven weeks. She was closing the gap all the way to the line but never quickly enough, and will appreciate a sixth furlong. (tchd 5-1)
Sands Crooner(IRE), with the visor left off, ran very lethargically but stayed on in good style very late in the day. Six furlongs suits him much better. (op 13-8 tchd 7-4 and 2-1 in a place)
Mister Incredible chased the winner, but carried his head high and does not look the most enthusastic. (op 11-2 tchd 7-2)
Miss Mujahid Times , very awkward to load, was always in about the same place.
Bollywood(IRE) was unplaced in two Windsor maidens in July. Having his third career run, he made a tardy start and never figured. (tchd 4-1)

6606 BETDIRECT ON AT THE RACES INTERACTIVE BANDED STKS 1m 4f (F)
2:00 (2:00) (Class 7) 3-Y-0+ **£1,429** (£422; £211) **Stalls** Low

Form RPR
4001 **1** **Night Warrior (IRE)**[10] 6498 5-9-0 45 (b) TonyCulhane 10 56+
(K McAuliffe) *hld up gng wl: smooth hdwy over 7f out: led on bit over 2f out: shkn up 1f out: sn rdn and kpt on wl* **3/1**[2]

2020 **2** *3* **Bill Bennett (FR)**[26] 6410 4-9-0 45 .... RobertWinston 3 — 49
(J Jay) *chsd ldrs: sn pushed along: upsides appr fnl f: kpt on same pce* **85/40**[1]

0403 **3** *6* **Reflex Blue**[19] 4509 8-8-7 45 .... JamesDoyle(7) 7 — 39
(R J Price) *sn chsng ldrs: wnt 2nd over 4f out: kpt on one pce fnl 2f* **5/1**[3]

00/0 **4** *½* **Dextrous**[18] 5828 8-9-0 40 .... (p) MickyFenton 8 — 39
(P T Midgley) *trckd ldr: led over 5f out tl over 2f out: one pce* **33/1**

0010 **5** *6* **Spanish Star**[6] 6555 8-9-0 45 .... HayleyTurner 5 — 29
(Mrs N Macauley) *mid-div: effrt over 4f out: kpt on one pce: eased whn wl hld ins last* **13/2**

4000 **6** *16* **Gravardlax**[200] 2204 4-8-7 45 .... (p) StephanieBancroft(7) 1 — 3
(Miss D A McHale) *sn outpcd in last: racd wd: bhd fnl 5f* **9/1**

3410 **7** *7* **Dimashq**[57] 6034 3-8-9 45 .... PhillipMakin 4 — —
(Ronald Thompson) *led: hdd over 5f out: lost pl over 3f out: bhd whn eased over 1f out* **11/1**

0406 **8** *3* **Brother Cadfael**[236] 1299 4-9-0 45 .... PaulEddery 2 — —
(John A Harris) *chsd ldrs: lost pl over 5f out: sn bhd* **16/1**

406- **P** **Golden Fields (IRE)**[372] 6849 5-9-0 30 .... (b) RobbieFitzpatrick 9 — —
(Jennie Candlish) *in rr: drvn along 6f out: sn lost pl: t.o over 3f out: p.u 2f out* **40/1**

2m 44.59s (2.50) **Going Correction** +0.20s/f (Slow)
WFA 3 from 4yo+ 5lb — **9** Ran SP% **116.6**
Speed ratings (Par 97):99,97,93,92,88 78,73,71,—
CSF £9.90 TOTE £3.50: £1.50, £1.50, £1.80; EX 15.30.
Owner Barrie Kirby **Bred** Sean Collins **Trained** Fernham, Oxon

FOCUS
The winner had won a handicap in the past from an official mark of 64 and he travelled easily best. The runner-up sets the standard.
Golden Fields(IRE) Official explanation: jockey said mare started whinnying

6607 FOOTBALLERS-DRIVES.CO.UK TRI-BANDED STKS — 6f (F)
2:30 (2:32) (Class 7) 3-Y-O — £1,409 (£416; £208) Stalls Low

Form — RPR

5321 **1** **Preskani**[5] 6572 3-9-4 45 6ex .... (p) AlanDaly 1 — 64+
(Mrs N Macauley) *trckd ldrs: rdn over 1f out: led jst ins last: kpt on wl* **4/5**[1]

3004 **2** *1¼* **Straffan (IRE)**[5] 6568 3-8-7 40 .... (p) DaleGibson 2 — 49
(J Hetherton) *swvd rt s: trckd ldrs: led over 4f out: rdn and carried hd high over 1f out: hdd jst ins last: no ex* **4/1**[2]

0600 **3** *1¾* **Polesworth**[5] 6572 3-8-7 40 .... FrancisFerris 6 — 44
(C N Kellett) *swvd lft s: in rr whn sltly hmpd and lost pl over 4f out: hdwy 2f out: styd on wl ins last* **22/1**

6000 **4** *nk* **Doughty**[5] 6572 3-8-4 40 .... EdwardCreighton(3) 4 — 43
(D J Wintle) *swvd rt s: mid-div: effrt over 2f out: styd on fnl f* **10/1**

0303 **5** *1* **Christian Bendix**[5] 6570 3-8-12 45 .... (p) RobertWinston 5 — 45+
(P Howling) *hmpd s: in rr tl styd on fnl 2f: nt rch ldrs* **5/1**[3]

1000 **6** *1¼* **Make It Happen Now**[43] 6252 3-8-2 35 .... MatthewHenry 3 — 31
(S L Keightley) *s.i.s and hmpd s: hdwy on ins over 2f out: wknd over 1f out* **22/1**

3000 **7** *½* **Starlight River (IRE)**[20] 6441 3-8-7 40 .... MickyFenton 8 — 35
(J Parkes) *trckd ldrs: effrt on outer over 2f out: one pce* **80/1**

5000 **8** *1½* **As Handsome Does**[19] 6469 3-8-12 45 .... KimTinkler 10 — 35
(N Tinkler) *s.i.s: racd wd: hdwy over 4f out: nvr on terms* **16/1**

6-00 **9** *14* **Kashtanka (IRE)**[5] 6572 3-8-12 45 .... (p) RobbieFitzpatrick 9 — —
(J Balding) *swtchd lft after s and led over 1f: lost pl 2f out: bhd whn eased* **66/1**

0000 **10** *5* **Amazing Grace Mary**[26] 6411 3-8-3 30 ow1 .... PaulEddery 7 — —
(S R Bowring) *reminders after s: chsd ldrs: lost pl over 2f out: bhd whn eased ins last* **100/1**

1m 19.74s (2.84) **Going Correction** +0.20s/f (Slow) — **10** Ran SP% **119.6**
Speed ratings (Par 96):89,87,85,84,83 81,80,78,60,53
CSF £4.16 TOTE £1.80: £1.10, £1.50, £3.50; EX 6.00.
Owner Godfrey Horsford **Bred** P And Mrs Venner **Trained** Sproxton, Leics

FOCUS
A moderate time, even for a banded contest. The fourth sets the standard which overall looks weak.
Christian Bendix Official explanation: jockey said gelding was squeezed out start

6608 FASTSIGNS 10TH ANNIVERSARY BANDED STKS — 7f (F)
3:00 (3:01) (Class 7) 3-Y-O+ — £1,443 (£426; £213) Stalls Low

Form — RPR

0023 **1** **Captain Darling (IRE)**[6] 6567 5-8-9 46 .... EdwardCreighton(3) 1 — 60
(R W Price) *mde all: qcknd 3f out: styd on wl: readily* **7/1**

0604 **2** *2* **Mount Royale (IRE)**[8] 6541 7-8-13 47 .... (v) KimTinkler 9 — 56
(N Tinkler) *chsd ldrs: wnt 2nd over 4f out: hung lft over 1f out: kpt on ins last: no imp* **11/1**

5210 **3** *1¾* **Desert Lover (IRE)**[18] 6470 3-8-13 47 .... PhillipMakin 10 — 51
(R J Price) *chsd ldrs: kpt on same pce fnl 2f* **8/1**

3100 **4** *3½* **Kumakawa**[4] 6576 7-8-6 47 .... LauraReynolds(7) 5 — 42
(D K Ivory) *sn bhd and rdn along: kpt on fnl 2f: nvr trbld ldrs* **16/1**

0006 **5** *½* **Donegal Shore (IRE)**[6] 6559 6-9-2 50 .... (vt) RobbieFitzpatrick 6 — 44
(Jennie Candlish) *s.v.s: hdwy on outer 2f out: kpt on ins last* **16/1**

2133 **6** *nk* **Caerphilly Gal**[8] 6541 5-8-9 50 .... NicolPolli(7) 13 — 43
(P L Gilligan) *w ldrs on outer: outpcd over 3f out: kpt on fnl 2f* **9/1**

0421 **7** *7* **The Job**[14] 6497 4-9-1 49 .... (v) TonyCulhane 7 — 24
(A D Smith) *mid-div: hrd rdn 2f out: nvr a threat* **11/4**[1]

0521 **8** *1½* **Spy Gun (USA)**[43] 6260 5-9-1 49 .... J-PGuillambert 2 — 20
(T Wall) *s.i.s: sn chsng ldrs on inner: lost pl over 1f out* **9/2**[2]

0060 **9** *1¾* **Triffid**[13] 6508 3-8-11 45 .... (p) PaulHanagan 12 — 11
(R A Fahey) *in tch on outer: lost pl over 4f out* **14/1**

0002 **10** *1¼* **Cayman King**[6] 6559 3-9-1 49 .... RobertWinston 11 — 12
(R Craggs) *s.i.s: nvr a factor* **5/1**[3]

2060 **11** *1¾* **Rocky Reppin**[214] 1811 5-8-13 47 .... (p) DeanMcKeown 4 — 5
(J Balding) *prom: lost pl over 3f out* **22/1**

0000 **12** *10* **Sudden Impulse**[55] 6069 4-8-6 45 .... DuranFentiman(5) 3 — —
(A D Brown) *s.i.s: sn chsng ldrs on inner: lost pl over 4f out: bhd whn eased ins last* **80/1**

0 **13** *1¾* **Fontaine House**[19] 6455 3-8-13 50 .... AdamKirby(3) 8 — —
(T T Clement) *chsd ldrs: lost pl over 4f out: bhd whn eased ins last* **125/1**

1m 32.25s (1.45) **Going Correction** +0.20s/f (Slow) — **13** Ran SP% **128.3**
Speed ratings (Par 97):99,96,94,90,90 89,81,80,78,76 74,63,61
CSF £87.46 TOTE £9.20: £2.30, £3.50, £3.00; EX 63.40.
Owner A Dunmore **Bred** Knocktoran Stud **Trained** Newmarket, Suffolk

FOCUS
A fair contest for the grade and it could well rate a couple of pounds higher.
Donegal Shore(IRE) Official explanation: jockey said horse missed the break
Spy Gun(USA) Official explanation: jockey said gelding ran flat

6609 HEART 106 BANDED STKS — 1m (F)
3:30 (3:30) (Class 7) 3-Y-O+ — £1,429 (£422; £211) Stalls Low

Form — RPR

3602 **1** **Sea Frolic (IRE)**[5] 6573 4-8-11 45 .... (v) RobbieFitzpatrick 7 — 51
(Jennie Candlish) *chsd ldrs: drvn and outpcd over 3f out: styd on to ld over 1f out: kpt on strly* **2/1**[2]

0044 **2** *3* **Travelling Times**[29] 6384 6-8-11 40 .... (be) DavidMcCabe 1 — 45
(Julian Poulton) *led tl over 4f out: led over 2f out: hdd over 1f out: no ex* **7/1**[3]

4103 **3** *2½* **Tirailleur (IRE)**[5] 6573 5-8-11 45 .... FergalLynch 3 — 40
(J R Boyle) *stdd s: sn trcking ldrs on ins: effrt 3f out: edgd rt and one pce fnl f* **5/4**[1]

5654 **4** *nk* **Inchdura**[5] 6573 7-8-11 45 .... (p) KimTinkler 2 — 39
(N Tinkler) *chsd ldrs: sn drvn along: lost pl after 2f: kpt on appr fnl f* **8/1**

1040 **5** *4* **Ballyrush (IRE)**[20] 6445 5-8-4 45 .... StephanieBancroft(7) 6 — 31
(Miss D A McHale) *racd wd: w ldrs: led over 4f out tl over 2f out: lost pl over 1f out* **12/1**

0000 **6** *6* **River Of Diamonds**[14] 6495 4-8-4 45 .... TolleyDean(7) 4 — 19
(R A Harris) *trckd ldrs: lost pl over 1f out: eased towards fin* **14/1**

0004 **7** *23* **Cheeky Chi (IRE)**[216] 1767 4-8-4 40 .... DonnaCaldwell(7) 5 — —
(P S McEntee) *sn w ldrs on outer: hung rt and lost pl 3f out: sn wl bhd* **33/1**

1m 47.16s (2.56) **Going Correction** +0.20s/f (Slow) — **7** Ran SP% **118.7**
Speed ratings (Par 97):95,92,89,89,85 79,56
CSF £17.47 TOTE £2.80: £1.20, £3.10; EX 25.00 Place 6 £43.08, Place 5 £27.82.
Owner Mrs Judith Ratcliff **Bred** Donal Turner **Trained** Basford Green, Staffs

FOCUS
Just a steady gallop but the winner, who came from just off the pace, scored in very ready fashion and is the key to the overall value of the form.
T/Plt: £37.80 to a £1 stake. Pool: £50,988.75. 984.25 winning tickets. T/Qpdt: £14.60 to a £1 stake. Pool: £3,796.90. 191.80 winning tickets. WG

6596 LINGFIELD (L-H)
Monday, December 19

OFFICIAL GOING: Standard
Wind: Almost nil Weather: Sunny and mild

6610 TEXT "BETDIRECT" TO 88600 MEDIAN AUCTION MAIDEN STKS — 7f (P)
1:00 (1:02) (Class 7) 2-Y-O — £1,423 (£420; £210) Stalls Low

Form — RPR

00 **1** **Beauchamp Unique**[59] 6013 2-8-6 .... AdamKirby(3) 5 — 63+
(G A Butler) *trckd ldrs: prog 2f out: led jst over 1f out: edgd rt but drew clr fnl f* **9/2**[3]

6425 **2** *3½* **Tafilah**[9] 6543 2-8-9 56 .... (v[1]) IanMongan 9 — 54
(P W D'Arcy) *pushed along in midfield early: trckd ldrs and gng bttr 3f out: effrt 2f out: rdn and styd on to take 2nd nr fin* **4/1**[2]

05 **3** *nk* **Parazone**[15] 6496 2-9-0 .... EddieAhern 2 — 58
(E J O'Neill) *trckd ldr: rdn 2f out: upsides over 1f out: nt qckn and hld by wnr fnl f: lost 2nd nr fin* **10/3**[1]

0 **4** *2½* **Assumption (IRE)**[60] 5993 2-8-9 .... OscarUrbina 6 — 47
(S C Williams) *hld up in rr: prog 3f out: c wd bnd 2f out: shkn up over 1f out: kpt on: nvr nr ldrs* **12/1**

440 **5** *1¾* **Left Nostril (IRE)**[6] 6569 2-8-9 50 .... BrianReilly 3 — 42
(P S McEntee) *led at fast pce: drvn over 2f out: hdd & wknd jst over 1f out* **14/1**

6060 **6** *½* **Seattle Spy (USA)**[135] 4153 2-9-0 63 .... PatCosgrave 4 — 46
(G A Huffer) *reluctant to go out on to the crse: reluctant to enter the stalls: sn drvn to stay in tch: wl in rr 3f out: plodded on* **5/1**

0 **7** *1¾* **Smart Golden Boy (IRE)**[14] 6502 2-9-0 .... SamHitchcott 1 — 41
(Mrs L C Jewell) *prom: rdn 3f out: wknd wl over 1f out* **33/1**

0 **8** *nk* **Emily's Pet (IRE)**[69] 5823 2-9-0 .... FergusSweeney 10 — 41
(B W Duke) *chsd ldrs: rdn 4f out: effrt u.p over 2f out: sn wknd* **50/1**

9 *1* **Safaah** 2-9-0 .... J-PGuillambert 7 — 38
(G Prodromou) *s.i.s: a struggling in rr* **9/1**

000 **10** *1¾* **Lady Josh**[2] 6600 2-8-9 .... SteveDrowne 11 — 28
(W G M Turner) *racd on outer: in tch to 1/2-way: sn btn u.p* **20/1**

00 **11** *¾* **Sahara Secret (IRE)**[15] 6496 2-8-6 .... PatrickMathers(3) 8 — 26
(D Shaw) *sn outpcd and rdn: nvr a factor* **66/1**

1m 25.48s (-0.41) **Going Correction** -0.05s/f (Stan) — **11** Ran SP% **113.4**
Speed ratings (Par 90):100,96,95,92,90 90,88,87,86,84 83
CSF £21.23 TOTE £6.60: £2.00, £1.10, £1.80; EX 14.90.
Owner Erik Penser **Bred** E Penser **Trained** Blewbury, Oxon

FOCUS
A modest maiden with one obvious horse standing out - the winner - and the winning time was 0.29 seconds faster than the following banded stakes for older horses. The form is limited by the runner-up and fifth and the rest will have to keep their sights very low.

NOTEBOOK
Beauchamp Unique had showed minor promise in turf maidens during the autumn, and that was more than enough in a weak race. She should do at least as well over a mile, and even farther, in due course, and ought to be capable of winning better contests than this one. (op 3-1)
Tafilah had shown a fair level of form but was well exposed, and vulnerable to an improver like the winner. In addition, she looked in need of a return to a stiffer test. (op 7-2)
Parazone only just gets this trip at present, but is probably better at six furlongs. He is now qualified for handicaps, where he would be one to consider if not too highly tested. (op 4-1 tchd 3-1)
Assumption(IRE) is a late developer, but she has shown a little on both her outings and this showed she acts on sand. There a bit more improvement in her too. (tchd 14-1)
Left Nostril(IRE) was a doubtful stayer, and riding her like this gave her little chance of lasting out.
Seattle Spy(USA) will probably be suited by longer trips, but he is only moderate, and looks a bit of a character too. (op 7-1)

6611 PRESS RED TO BET ON ITVI BANDED STKS — 7f (P)
1:30 (1:32) (Class 7) 3-Y-O+ — £1,446 (£427; £213) Stalls Low

Form — RPR

1434 **1** **Ragasah**[21] 6445 7-8-11 45 .... (p) EddieAhern 6 — 49
(Ernst Oertel) *chsd ldrs: rdn over 2f out: effrt on outer over 1f out: styd on u.p to ld last strides* **10/3**[1]

U050 **2** *nk* **Aintnecessarilyso**[19] 6471 7-8-11 45 .... (p) LPKeniry 3 — 48
(J M Bradley) *hld up in midfield: prog over 2f out: rdn to ld ins fnl f: hdd last strides* **16/1**

0000 **3** *¾* **Awarding**[5] 6576 5-8-4 45 .... (vt) MichaelJStainton(7) 11 — 46
(Dr J R J Naylor) *rrd s: towards rr: prog over 2f out: drvn to press ldrs ins fnl f: kpt on same pce nr fin* **25/1**

0053 **4** *hd* **One Last Time**[12] [6526] 5-8-11 45 SteveDrowne 5 45
(Miss B Sanders) *led after 1f: rdn over 2f out: hanging and hdd ins fnl f: nt qckn* **7/2**[2]

0212 **5** *½* **Tuscan Treaty**[5] [6575] 5-8-8 45 (t) AdamKirby(3) 2 44
(P J McBride) *cl up: gng easily over 2f out: to chse ldr over 1f out: nt qckn and hld ins fnl f* **6/1**[3]

30- **6** *nk* **Margaret's Dream (IRE)**[54] [6113] 4-8-8 45 DanielTudhope(3) 4 43
(D Carroll) *towards rr: prog wl over 1f out: drvn to chse ldrs ins fnl f: one pce* **9/1**

0542 **7** *1 ¼* **Rosiella**[12] [6526] 3-8-8 45 (b) EdwardCreighton(3) 13 40
(M Blanshard) *led for 1f: w ldr tl over 1f out: wknd last 100yds* **12/1**

000 **8** *1* **In A Fit**[9] [6545] 4-8-11 45 IanMongan 9 38
(P Howling) *hld up in last: prog on inner 2f out: chsd ldrs 1f out: one pce after* **20/1**

0030 **9** *½* **Zolash (IRE)**[5] [6574] 3-8-11 45 HayleyTurner 14 36
(Mrs L C Jewell) *prom tl wknd wl over 1f out* **20/1**

0651 **10** *2* **Wodhill Be**[7] [6558] 5-9-3 45 MichaelTebbutt 1 46+
(D Morris) *trckd ldrs on inner: shkn up and cl up over 1f out: wknd and heavily eased last 75yds* **9/1**

-050 **11** *4* **Ballare (IRE)**[112] 6-8-11 45 FergusSweeney 10 21
(P J Makin) *a towards rr: u.p and struggling 1/2-way* **14/1**

0060 **12** *4* **Free Wheelin (IRE)**[30] [6384] 5-8-6 45 RoryMoore(5) 7 10
(J Akehurst) *late on to the trck: s.s: rapid prog and prom 5f out: wknd 3f out: reluctant on bnd 2f out* **20/1**

000- **13** *1 ½* **She's My Dream (IRE)**[567] [2515] 3-8-8 45 RichardThomas(3) 12 6
(A J Lidderdale) *a wl in rr: struggling fr 3f out* **100/1**

500 **14** *5* **Mephistos Kick**[104] [5036] 4-8-11 45 J-PGuillambert 8 —
(Jean-Rene Auvray) *hld up wl in rr: no prog 3f out: wknd* **50/1**

1m 25.77s (-0.12) **Going Correction** -0.05s/f (Stan) 14 Ran SP% **120.9**
Speed ratings (Par 97):98,97,96,96,96 95,94,93,92,90 85,81,79,73
CSF £51.95 TOTE £3.60: £1.20, £6.50, £9.60; EX 53.00.
Owner Winning Colours Racing Club **Bred** Miss Sarah Kelleway **Trained** Newmarket, Suffolk

FOCUS
A moderate banded race, but a competitive one with a close finish between the first six and the fourth to recent form sets the standard.
One Last Time Official explanation: jockey said gelding hung right
Free Wheelin(IRE) Official explanation: jockey said gelding hung badly right off the bend
Mephistos Kick Official explanation: trainer said gelding bled internally

6612 MORE OFFERS AT BETDIRECT.CO.UK BANDED STKS 2m (P)
2:05 (2:06) (Class 7) 3-Y-O+ **£1,433** (£423; £211) **Stalls** Low

Form RPR

0002 **1** **Tipes**[14] [6510] 3-8-10 46 (p) SteveDrowne 2 53
(C J Down) *trckd ldrs: prog 3f out: rdn to ld over 1f out: idled ins fnl f: jnd nr fin: won on the nod* **13/2**[3]

0004 **2** *shd* **Lysander's Quest (IRE)**[19] [6472] 7-9-3 45 (b[1]) EddieAhern 14 52
(R Ingram) *trckd ldrs: prog over 2f out: pressed wnr on inner 1f out: rallied and upsides last strides: jst hld* **11/2**[2]

4332 **3** *¾* **Trials 'n Tribs**[12] [6523] 3-9-0 50 FergusSweeney 8 56
(C A Cyzer) *t.k.h: hld up wl in rr: stdy prog on outer 3f out: drvn and styd on wl fnl f: gaining at fin* **5/1**[1]

0/05 **4** *1 ½* **Coppermalt (USA)**[7] [6563] 7-9-4 46 LPKeniry 5 50
(R Curtis) *prom: led 1/2-way: drvn over 2f out: hdd and one pce over 1f out* **9/1**

5506 **5** *¾* **Jadeeron**[19] [6472] 6-9-3 45 (p) OscarUrbina 12 48
(Miss D A McHale) *hld up in rr: prog fr 3f out: rdn and kpt on same pce fnl 2f: nvr able to chal* **16/1**

2140 **6** *shd* **Tharua (IRE)**[19] [6472] 3-8-12 48 (p) BrianReilly 7 51
(Ernst Oertel) *trckd ldrs: effrt over 2f out: hrd rdn and nt qckn over 1f out: one pce after* **9/1**

0605 **7** *shd* **Iamback**[12] [6523] 5-9-0 45 (t) AdamKirby(3) 4 48
(Miss Gay Kelleway) *hld up towards rr: effrt 3f out: nvr on terms w ldrs: kpt on fnl f* **11/1**

5203 **8** *nk* **Makarim (IRE)**[20] [6461] 9-9-3 45 (p) IanMongan 3 48
(M R Bosley) *t.k.h: hld up in last trio: prog fr 3f out: nvr on terms w ldrs: styd on fnl f: nvr nrr* **13/2**[3]

0546 **9** *3* **Free Style (GER)**[12] [6523] 5-9-6 48 GeorgeBaker 10 47
(Mrs H Sweeting) *led to 1/2-way: pressed ldr tl over 2f out: wknd over 1f out* **8/1**

0506 **10** *5* **Paradise Valley**[23] [6434] 5-9-6 48 (t) HayleyTurner 1 41
(Stef Liddiard) *s.v.s: t.k.h and hld up in last trio: brief effrt over 3f out: sn no prog* **33/1**

0650 **11** *7* **Briannie (IRE)**[7] [5447] 3-8-6 45 (p) RichardThomas(3) 6 30
(P Butler) *towards rr: rdn 4f out: struggling 3f out: eased fnl f* **50/1**

0650 **12** *2* **Redspin (IRE)**[20] [6461] 5-8-10 45 JosephWalsh(7) 11 27
(J S Moore) *s.s: racd wd and sn chsd ldrs: rdn and lost pl over 4f out: no ch after* **14/1**

/000 **13** *nk* **Brunston Castle**[19] [6472] 5-9-3 45 J-PGuillambert 13 27
(A W Carroll) *dwlt: rcvrd to press ldr to 1/2-way: u.p and wkng over 4f out* **66/1**

000 **14** *6* **Panadin (IRE)**[34] [6355] 3-8-12 48 (p) MichaelTebbutt 9 23
(V Smith) *racd on outer in midfield: rdn and wknd 5f out* **25/1**

3m 29.62s (0.83) **Going Correction** -0.05s/f (Stan)
WFA 3 from 5yo+ 8lb 14 Ran SP% **121.0**
Speed ratings (Par 97):95,94,94,93,93 93,93,93,91,89 85,84,84,81
CSF £41.28 TOTE £7.90: £3.60, £2.70, £1.50; EX 64.80.
Owner Birchwood Stud Limited **Bred** John Jess And Graham Palmer **Trained** Mutterton, Devon
■ Stewards' Enquiry : L P Keniry one-day ban: used whip with excessive frequency (Dec 30)

FOCUS
A modest banded race containing some paceless types - hence the distance. The form is very ordinary but solid enough.
Panadin(IRE) Official explanation: vet said gelding bled from the nose

6613 BETDIRECT FREEPHONE 0800 211 222 BANDED STKS 6f (P)
2:40 (2:41) (Class 7) 3-Y-O+ **£1,429** (£422; £211) **Stalls** Low

Form RPR

6202 **1** **Boanerges (IRE)**[14] [6511] 8-8-11 40 SteveDrowne 10 41
(J M Bradley) *trckd ldrs: prog 2f out: rdn to ld narrowly 1f out: kpt on wl* **9/4**[1]

0/50 **2** *½* **Amber Nectar Two**[5] [6579] 5-8-11 40 (b) LPKeniry 6 42+
(A G Newcombe) *hld up in midfield: prog 2f out: clsng on ldrs whn nt clr run 1f out: r.o to take 2nd last strides: unlucky* **11/1**

-000 **3** *shd* **Bennanabaa**[37] [6330] 6-8-4 40 (tp) DonnaCaldwell(7) 2 39
(S C Burrough) *s.s: rn in snatches in rr: prog 2f out: urged along and r.o ins fnl f: jst hld* **66/1**

0050 **4** *nk* **Harbour House**[36] [5653] 6-8-11 40 J-PGuillambert 7 38
(J J Bridger) *trckd ldrs: rdn over 2f out: effrt on inner to press wnr fnl f: hld and lost 2 pls nr fin* **11/1**

0660 **5** *¾* **Avit (IRE)**[30] [6380] 5-8-11 40 (e) BrianReilly 3 36
(P L Gilligan) *w ldr: led 2f out: drvn and hdd 1f out: wknd nr fin* **10/1**

0400 **6** *¾* **Fizzy Lizzy**[132] [4237] 5-8-11 40 DavidMcCabe 12 37+
(H E Haynes) *taken down early: hld up in last: prog wl over 1f out: nt clr run 1f out: fnd little whn in the clr last 150yds* **20/1**

4040 **7** *hd* **The Baroness (IRE)**[14] [6511] 5-8-11 40 (p) EddieAhern 5 33
(Ernst Oertel) *chsd ldrs on inner: drvn and effrt over 1f out: wknd ins fnl f* **14/1**

0040 **8** *nk* **Ravel (IRE)**[5] [6577] 4-8-11 40 (v[1]) IanMongan 11 32
(M R Bosley) *s.i.s: a towards rr: rdn bef 1/2-way: kpt on fnl f: n.d* **10/1**

0606 **9** *shd* **Black Oval**[5] [6577] 4-8-8 40 AdamKirby(3) 1 32
(M J Polglase) *taken down early: led to 2f out: wknd fnl f* **14/1**

0264 **10** *1 ¼* **Tiny Tim (IRE)**[27] [6412] 7-8-4 40 (b) JamesRogers(7) 9 28
(A M Balding) *racd wd: nvr on terms w ldrs: bmpd along and no prog over 1f out* **7/1**[3]

5304 **11** *shd* **Canary Dancer**[15] [6498] 3-8-6 40 RoryMoore(5) 4 28
(Miss Z C Davison) *chsd ldng pair to 2f out: fdd u.p* **14/1**

53 **12** *2 ½* **Mescalera (GER)**[14] [6511] 4-8-11 40 HayleyTurner 8 20
(B G Powell) *nvr gng wl: a wl in rr* **13/2**[2]

1m 13.03s (0.22) **Going Correction** -0.05s/f (Stan) 12 Ran SP% **117.7**
Speed ratings (Par 97):96,95,95,94,93 92,92,92,92,90 90,86
CSF £27.93 TOTE £2.40: £1.20, £3.40, £10.70; EX 35.20.
Owner E A Hayward **Bred** Clare Dore Ltd **Trained** Sedbury, Gloucs

FOCUS
A routine banded event won a by a former decent handicapper. The form is weak with the placed horses setting the standard.
Canary Dancer Official explanation: jockey said saddle slipped

6614 BETDIRECT.CO.UK BANDED STKS 1m 2f (P)
3:10 (3:10) (Class 7) 3-Y-O+ **£1,453** (£429; £214) **Stalls** Low

Form RPR

4244 **1** **Mister Completely (IRE)**[5] [6575] 4-8-12 45 SteveDrowne 3 51
(J R Best) *trckd ldrs: prog to chse ldr over 1f out: rdn to ld narrowly ins fnl f: hld on* **5/1**[2]

002 **2** *nk* **Moondancer (GER)**[5] [6576] 6-9-0 47 HayleyTurner 10 52
(B G Powell) *t.k.h: led at modest pce: tried to kick on 2f out: narrowly hdd ins fnl f: kpt on but jst hld* **12/1**

4060 **3** *hd* **Turner's Touch**[20] [6468] 3-9-0 50 (be) GeorgeBaker 4 55
(G L Moore) *trckd ldrs: hanging fr 3f out: effrt over 1f out: nt looking keen but styd on: jst hld* **4/1**[1]

0206 **4** *½* **Star Welcome**[30] [6381] 4-8-10 48 StephenDonohoe(5) 2 53+
(W J Musson) *hld up in midfield: prog 2f out: styng on to press ldrs but hld whn nt clr run wl ins fnl f* **11/2**[3]

0055 **5** *½* **King's Minstrel (IRE)**[5] [6575] 4-8-12 45 (t) PaulDoe 13 48+
(R Rowe) *dwlt: hld up in last: gng wl enough but stl last over 2f out: r.o fr over 1f out: too much to do* **10/1**

050 **6** *½* **Murrieta**[72] [5734] 3-9-0 50 OscarUrbina 6 52?
(Miss J R Gibney) *racd on outer in midfield: rdn 4f out: prog u.p 2f out: kpt on but nvr able to chal* **50/1**

501 **7** *nk* **Successor**[5] [6575] 5-9-4 45 (t) JamieMackay 12 52+
(M D I Usher) *dwlt: hld up in last pair: effrt 2f out: nt clr run briefly over 1f out: kpt on: no ch* **12/1**

52-6 **8** *2 ½* **Clare Galway**[14] [6506] 4-9-1 48 IanMongan 9 44
(B G Powell) *settled midfield: nt qckn 3f out: struggling and no prog after* **14/1**

0000 **9** *nk* **Larad (IRE)**[14] [6506] 4-9-3 50 (b) EddieAhern 11 46
(J S Moore) *nvr beyond midfield: u.p and struggling 3f out* **8/1**

0000 **10** *½* **Naivety**[14] [6506] 3-8-11 47 (b[1]) J-PGuillambert 1 42
(G G Margarson) *dwlt: t.k.h: hld up in rr: prog on inner and nt clr run over 2f out: n.d after: running on at fin* **50/1**

6055 **11** *nk* **First Of May**[12] [6524] 4-8-12 45 SamHitchcott 7 39
(Miss Z C Davison) *prom: chsd ldr over 3f out to over 1f out: wknd rapidly* **20/1**

1035 **12** *2* **Fantasy Crusader**[5] [6574] 6-9-3 50 FergusSweeney 14 41
(R M H Cowell) *racd wd: towards rr: rdn over 3f out: sn btn* **7/1**

0431 **13** *11* **Bella Pavlina**[230] [1454] 7-8-9 49 TolleyDean(7) 5 19
(R A Harris) *chsd ldr to over 3f out: sn wknd: t.o* **16/1**

2m 8.54s (0.75) **Going Correction** -0.05s/f (Stan)
WFA 3 from 4yo+ 3lb 13 Ran SP% **121.4**
Speed ratings (Par 97):95,94,94,94,93 93,93,91,90,90 90,88,79
CSF £64.00 TOTE £5.30: £1.80, £4.90, £2.00; EX 72.00.
Owner G G Racing **Bred** Eamonn Griffin **Trained** Hucking, Kent

FOCUS
A typically low-grade banded contest, run at a confusing pace, but the first two are better than average at this level and set the standard.
Fantasy Crusader Official explanation: jockey said gelding ran flat

6615 BETDIRECTCASINO.COM BANDED STKS 1m (P)
3:40 (3:40) (Class 7) 3-Y-O+ **£1,470** (£434; £217) **Stalls** High

Form RPR

4261 **1** **Danettie**[12] [6524] 4-9-1 49 EddieAhern 7 51
(W M Brisbourne) *tk fierce hold: trckd ldrs: effrt 2f out: rdn to ld narrowly 1f out: hld on* **5/6**[1]

0404 **2** *½* **Nisr**[14] [6507] 8-8-11 48 (t) AdamKirby(3) 11 49
(Miss Gay Kelleway) *prom: chsd ldr 3f out: rdn to ld 2f out: narrowly hdd 1f out: kpt on wl but a jst hld* **8/1**[3]

0000 **3** *2* **Debs Broughton**[28] [6398] 3-8-10 45 DavidMcCabe 9 41
(W J Musson) *stdd s: hld up in last: pushed along and prog 2f out: wnt 3rd ins fnl f: nvr nr ldng pair* **20/1**

0004 **4** *¾* **Tennessee Belle (IRE)**[5] [6577] 3-8-10 40 (e) OscarUrbina 2 39
(C N Allen) *led to 2f out: one pce u.p over 1f out* **12/1**

5 **5** *2* **Live And Dangerous**[226] [1555] 4-8-13 50 DanielTudhope(3) 8 40
(D Carroll) *t.k.h: hld up towards rr: effrt over 2f out: rdn and nt qckn over 1f out* **8/1**[3]

0655 **6** *1 ½* **Major Speculation (IRE)**[5] [6576] 5-9-2 50 SteveDrowne 10 36
(J M Bradley) *dwlt: hld up in rr: rdn and no prog 2f out* **4/1**[2]

3000 **7** *½* **Eskimo's Nest**[9] [6541] 3-8-11 49 PatrickMathers(3) 1 34
(D Shaw) *rousted along to chse ldr: lost pl 3f out: wknd over 1f out* **16/1**

4000 **8** *2 ½* **Robin Sharp**[5] [6577] 7-8-11 40 (p) MichaelTebbutt 5 24
(J Akehurst) *in tch: effrt on inner over 2f out: wknd over 1f out* **50/1**

0000 **9** *nk* **Bahama Reef (IRE)**[28] 6398 4-8-11 40........................ SamHitchcott 12 24
(B Gubby) *racd on outer: in tch: rdn 1/2-way: wknd 2f out* **20/1**

1m 39.74s (0.31) **Going Correction** -0.05s/f (Stan)
WFA 3 from 4yo+ 1lb 9 Ran SP% **121.8**
Speed ratings (Par 97):96,95,93,92,90 89,88,86,85
CSF £8.97 TOTE £1.80: £1.10, £1.80, £4.40; EX 10.50 Place 6 £26.04, Place 5 £19.17.
Owner J Oldknow A & H Johnstone & B Carter **Bred** John E Oldknow **Trained** Great Ness, Shropshire

FOCUS
A weak banded contest with the third and fourth the best guides to the level, but the winner was landing her second victory here in 12 days.
T/Plt: £16.30 to a £1 stake. Pool: £36,654.25. 1,631.85 winning tickets. T/Qpdt: £5.70 to a £1 stake. Pool: £2,888.40. 368.60 winning tickets. JN

6588 WOLVERHAMPTON (A.W) (L-H)
Monday, December 19

OFFICIAL GOING: Standard
Wind: Light behind Weather: Fine

6616 DAILY OFFERS FROM BETDIRECT AMATEUR RIDERS' H'CAP (DIV I) 5f 216y(P)
1:10 (1:10) (Class 5) (0-75,75) 3-Y-0+ **£2,910** (£902; £451; £225) **Stalls** Low

Form RPR
0000 **1** **Ryedane (IRE)**[46] 6238 3-11-2 **73**............................(e) GerardTumelty(3) 9 81
(T D Easterby) *a.p: chsd ldr over 4f out: rdn 2f out: edgd rt and r.o to ld wl ins fnl f* **7/1**
5550 **2** *3/4* **Willhewiz**[107] 4945 5-11-4 **72**... MrSDobson 3 78
(M S Saunders) *led: rdn over 1f out: hdd wl ins fnl f* **9/2**
0031 **3** *3/4* **Bessemer (JPN)**[9] 6546 4-11-2 **75**..............................(p) MrSFMagee(5) 8 79
(D Carroll) *a.p: rdn and hung lft over 1f out: styd on* **4/1**[3]
0505 **4** *shd* **Witchry**[71] 5754 3-11-5 **73**.. MissCHannaford 1 76
(A G Newcombe) *hld up: hdwy and swtchd lft over 1f out: sn rdn: styd on* **12/1**
1006 **5** *1/2* **Ashes (IRE)**[24] 6422 3-10-6 **65**................................ MissKellyBurke(5) 10 67
(K R Burke) *chsd ldrs: rdn over 1f out: no ex ins fnl f* **20/1**
200 **6** *1* **Revien (IRE)**[23] 6430 3-10-0 **61** oh1.............................. MrJDNolan(7) 2 60
(Miss J R Tooth) *s.i.s: styd on ins fnl f: nvr nrr* **22/1**
-044 **7** *1/2* **Jun Fan (USA)**[240] 1214 3-10-4 **61** oh1....................(p) MissLEllison(3) 6 58
(B Ellison) *prom: rdn over 2f out: no ex fnl f* **50/1**
0010 **8** *1* **Sand Iron (IRE)**[165] 3280 3-10-3 **62**............................ MissALTurner(5) 4 56
(S L Keightley) *hld up: n.d* **33/1**
1222 **9** *1 3/4* **Kallista's Pride**[20] 6455 5-10-2 **61** oh4.......................... KylieManser(5) 7 50
(J R Best) *dwlt: a in rr* **11/4**[1]
0141 **10** *3/4* **Middle Eastern**[13] 6513 3-10-10 **67**...................... MissFayeBramley(3) 5 54
(P A Blockley) *hld up: nt clr run 4f out: a in rr* **7/2**[2]

1m 15.66s (-0.15) **Going Correction** -0.125s/f (Stan) **10** Ran SP% **121.3**
Speed ratings (Par 103):96,95,94,93,93 91,91,89,87,86
CSF £38.55 CT £150.45 TOTE £9.90: £3.10, £2.40, £1.60; EX 57.30.
Owner Ryedale Partners No 5 **Bred** Tally-Ho Stud **Trained** Great Habton, N Yorks

FOCUS
The time compared unfavourably with the second division and this is only ordinary form.

6617 FIRST PAST THE POST AT BETDIRECT CLAIMING STKS 1m 141y(P)
1:45 (1:46) (Class 6) 2-Y-0 **£2,927** (£864; £432) **Stalls** Low

Form RPR
0010 **1** **George's Flyer (IRE)**[20] 6467 2-9-1 62......................(b) PaulHanagan 12 65
(R A Fahey) *hld up: hdwy 3f out: rdn to ld and hung rt 1f out: styd on* **13/2**
0300 **2** *1/2* **Mystified (IRE)**[9] 6543 2-8-12 58.......................................(b[1]) DNolan(3) 7 64
(R F Fisher) *sn pushed along and prom: rdn over 2f out: hung rt over 1f out: styd on* **25/1**
0054 **3** *1/2* **Ivans Ride (IRE)**[51] 6158 2-9-1 64.. DaneO'Neill 3 63
(S Kirk) *chsd ldrs: outpcd 3f out: rallied over 1f out: styd on* **10/1**
1203 **4** *hd* **Countrywide Belle**[9] 6543 2-8-8 60..........................(b) RobertWinston 10 56
(K A Ryan) *chsd ldr tl led over 2f out: sn rdn: hdd 1f out: no ex towards fin* **11/2**[3]
000 **5** *1 3/4* **Wee Charlie Castle (IRE)**[20] 6466 2-8-13 59.................. ChrisCatlin 4 57
(G C H Chung) *hld up: hdwy over 1f out: nt rch ldrs* **33/1**
0402 **6** *1 1/4* **Fangorn Forest (IRE)**[34] 6353 2-8-9 75..................(p) AndrewMullen(5) 1 55
(K A Ryan) *hld up: rdn 1/2-way: no imp fnl 2f* **2/1**[1]
0030 **7** *nk* **Sahara Style**[9] 6539 2-9-1 60... DaleGibson 11 56
(R Hollinshead) *s.i.s: styd on ins fnl f: nvr nrr* **40/1**
2503 **8** *1 1/2* **Secret Tender (IRE)**[12] 6521 2-8-5 50............................ JimmyQuinn 8 42
(J R Weymes) *hld up: effrt over 3f out: n.d* **16/1**
46 **9** *1* **Bigalo's Banjo**[15] 6496 2-9-1 .... JamieSpencer 6 50
(J J Quinn) *led 6f: wknd fnl f* **20/1**
0112 **10** *nk* **Psycho Cat**[9] 6543 2-8-12 69... FergalLynch 9 47
(P A Blockley) *prom: rdn over 2f out: hung rt and wknd over 1f out* **11/4**[2]
000 **11** *2* **Dashfa Baileys**[167] 3214 2-8-8 58 ow1................................ MickyFenton 5 39
(C A Dwyer) *chsd ldrs 7f* **66/1**
5 **12** *5* **Miss A Bargain (IRE)**[14] 6500 2-8-4 .... FranciscoDaSilva 13 24
(K R Burke) *hld up: rdn over 3f out: wknd over 2f out* **40/1**
00 **13** *2* **Washabul**[20] 6466 2-8-1 ow6......................... StephanieHollinshead(5) 2 22
(R Hollinshead) *hld up: rdn and wknd over 3f out* **100/1**

1m 50.71s (-1.05) **Going Correction** -0.125s/f (Stan) 13 Ran SP% **122.6**
Speed ratings (Par 94):99,98,98,97,96 95,95,93,92,92 90,86,84
CSF £163.61 TOTE £8.30: £3.10, £7.30, £3.00; EX 151.10.Ivans Ride was claimed by Mr C. Lee for £10,000.
Owner P D Smith Holdings Ltd **Bred** H De Bromhead **Trained** Musley Bank, N Yorks

FOCUS
This looks remarkably solid for the grade with the first three all running to form.

NOTEBOOK
George's Flyer(IRE), stepping up in trip, is an in-and-out performer, but he handled the surface well and knuckled down willingly to score. (op 9-1 tchd 10-1)
Mystified(IRE) was tried in blinkers for the first time but has worn cheekpieces before. He veered badly over to the stands' rail in the home straight but did prove he acts on Polytrack. Official explanation: jockey said gelding drifted badly right (op 16-1)
Ivans Ride(IRE), down in grade, stayed on quite well once in line for home to reach a place for the first time. (op 14-1 tchd 16-1)
Countrywide Belle, a stablemate of the favourite, was fitted with blinkers instead of cheekpieces. She had plenty of use made of her from her high draw and, after showing ahead on the home turn, was cut down entering the last. (op 5-1 tchd 9-2 and 6-1)
Wee Charlie Castle(IRE), without the visor, showed a little more than on his previous visits.
Fangorn Forest(IRE), tackling her longest trip to date, was unable to pick up once in line for home. She has become expensive to follow. (op 9-4 tchd 15-8)
Psycho Cat again hung once in line for home. Official explanation: jockey said gelding hung left (op 5-2)

6618 DAILY OFFERS FROM BETDIRECT AMATEUR RIDERS' H'CAP (DIV II) 5f 216y(P)
2:20 (2:20) (Class 5) (0-75,74) 3-Y-0+ **£2,905** (£901; £450; £225) **Stalls** Low

Form RPR
0055 **1** **Harry Up**[20] 6465 4-11-0 **74**.. MissARyan(7) 9 86+
(K A Ryan) *disp ld tl led 4f out: shkn up ins fnl f: r.o* **4/1**[2]
3611 **2** *1* **Kensington (IRE)**[50] 6177 4-10-4 **60** oh1..................(p) MissEFolkes(3) 1 69
(P D Evans) *chsd ldrs: rdn over 1f out: r.o* **2/1**[1]
5000 **3** *1* **Monashee Prince (IRE)**[17] 6483 3-10-8 **66**............... KylieManser(5) 10 72
(J R Best) *disp ld 2f: chsd wnr: rdn over 1f out: no ex ins fnl f* **16/1**
0110 **4** *3 1/2* **Vlasta Weiner**[13] 6516 5-10-10 **63**......................(b) MrsEmmaLittmoden 5 59
(J M Bradley) *mid-div: hdwy over 2f out: styd on same pce appr fnl f* **15/2**
3444 **5** *5* **Million Percent**[16] 6486 6-11-0 **72**........................... MissKellyBurke(5) 7 53
(K R Burke) *chsd ldrs: rdn over 2f out: wknd over 1f out* **11/2**[3]
1400 **6** *1 1/4* **Hadath (IRE)**[14] 6505 8-10-2 **60** oh3.............................. MrsRPowell(5) 2 37
(B G Powell) *sn outpcd* **12/1**
062- **7** *3 1/2* **White Ledger (IRE)**[427] 6274 6-10-2 **62**......................... MrLRPayter(7) 3 28
(R E Peacock) *dwlt: a in rr* **33/1**
0315 **8** *1* **Willheconquertoo**[9] 6546 5-10-13 **73**...................(tp) MrTGardham(7) 8 36
(I W McInnes) *s.s: hld up: hung rt and eased wl over 1f out* **8/1**
0000 **9** *2 1/2* **Acorazado (IRE)**[3] 6593 6-10-0 **60**.............................(b) MissCGrime(7) 4 16
(C P Morlock) *s.s: a in rr* **33/1**

1m 14.47s (-1.34) **Going Correction** -0.125s/f (Stan) **33** Ran SP% **111.1**
Speed ratings (Par 103):103,101,100,95,89 87,82,81,78
CSF £11.63 CT £106.46 TOTE £4.90: £2.00, £1.30, £4.20; EX 16.40.
Owner The Fishermen **Bred** J E Rose **Trained** Hambleton, N Yorks
■ A first winner on only her third ride for 16-year-old Amy Ryan, daughter of winning trainer Kevin Ryan.

FOCUS
The winning time was 1.19 seconds faster than the first division and this is solid form with the third setting the standard.
Willheconquertoo Official explanation: vet said gelding returned lame

6619 BETDIRECT ON CHANNEL 4 TEXT PAGE 613 MAIDEN STKS (DIV I) 1m 141y(P)
2:50 (2:50) (Class 5) 3-Y-0+ **£2,998** (£892; £445; £222) **Stalls** Low

Form RPR
1 **Heartcrusher (IRE)**[71] 5778 3-8-9 62.................................. DaleGibson 1 51
(G A Swinbank) *hld up: hdwy u.p over 2f out: styd on to ld nr fin* **16/1**
640 **2** *1/2* **Scamperdale**[7] 6565 3-9-0 .... ChrisCatlin 8 55
(Karen George) *mid-div: hdwy 1/2-way: rdn and edgd lft over 3f out: hung rt ins fnl f: styd on* **14/1**
0020 **3** *shd* **Lord Of Dreams (IRE)**[14] 6499 3-9-0 70.............................. FergalLynch 9 54
(D W P Arbuthnot) *led: rdn over 1f out: hdd nr fin* **2/1**[1]
300 **4** *hd* **Lake Wakatipu**[14] 6508 3-8-9 47.................................... DarrenWilliams 5 49
(M Mullineaux) *hld up: hdwy over 1f out: r.o* **33/1**
00 **5** *1/2* **Legal Dram**[9] 6545 4-9-2 .... PhillipMakin 7 53
(M Dods) *chsd ldrs: rdn over 2f out: edgd rt ins fnl f: styd on* **33/1**
0 **6** *11* **Dayoff (IRE)**[104] 5039 4-8-11 63..................................... RobertWinston 3 25
(P D Evans) *hld up: rdn 1/2-way: wknd 3f out* **4/1**[3]
3364 **7** *3/4* **Rowan Warning**[77] 5664 3-8-11 63................................. AmirQuinn(3) 10 28
(J R Boyle) *chsd ldr 5f: sn rdn: wknd over 1f out* **11/4**[2]
8 *8* **Flaming Shot (IRE)**[181] 2803 3-9-0 58............................. JamieSpencer 4 11
(Jennie Candlish) *trckd ldrs: rdn whn hmpd over 3f out: sn wknd* **6/1**
60-0 **9** *dist* **Imperatrice**[14] 6512 3-8-9 35... AlanDaly 6 —
(G A Ham) *stdd s: hld up: bhd fnl 3f* **100/1**

1m 49.39s (-2.37) **Going Correction** -0.125s/f (Stan)
WFA 3 from 4yo 2lb 9 Ran SP% **113.7**
Speed ratings (Par 103):105,104,104,104,103 94,93,86,—
CSF £207.24 TOTE £17.50: £2.40, £3.20, £1.30; EX 124.40.
Owner J P Porter **Bred** E O'Leary **Trained** Melsonby, N Yorks
■ Stewards' Enquiry : Chris Catlin caution: careless riding

FOCUS
A modest maiden, the form limited by the fourth.
Imperatrice Official explanation: jockey said gelding lost its action but returned sound

6620 BETDIRECTPOKER.COM (S) STKS 1m 4f 50y(P)
3:20 (3:20) (Class 6) 3-Y-0+ **£2,504** (£739; £369) **Stalls** Low

Form RPR
0006 **1** **Mungo Jerry (GER)**[20] 6463 4-9-8 60.............................. MickyFenton 3 54
(J G Given) *hld up: hdwy 3f out: rdn over 1f out: edgd lft ins fnl f: styd on u.p to ld post* **12/1**
0054 **2** *nk* **Moon Shot**[24] 6419 9-9-4 60... VinceSlattery 1 50
(A G Juckes) *trckd ldrs: racd keenly: led 2f out: sn rdn: hdd post* **11/1**
3322 **3** *shd* **York Cliff**[9] 6548 7-9-4 57.. RobertWinston 4 50
(W M Brisbourne) *s.i.s: hld up: hdwy u.p over 2f out: n.m.r ins fnl f: styd on* **6/4**[1]
0003 **4** *1* **Regency Red (IRE)**[12] 6523 7-9-1 45............................... LiamJones(7) 12 52
(W M Brisbourne) *hld up: hdwy over 2f out: rdn and hung lft over 1f out: styd on* **20/1**
503/ **5** *3/4* **Thorpeness (IRE)**[12] 4685 6-9-4 .... DaneO'Neill 2 47
(P D Cundell) *chsd ldrs: rdn over 2f out: styd on* **33/1**
0403 **6** *1/2* **Giunchiglio**[15] 6495 6-9-4 46.. FergalLynch 5 46
(W M Brisbourne) *prom: rdn over 2f out: styd on same pce ins fnl f* **10/1**
0300 **7** *2* **Harare**[7] 6560 4-9-4 54.. PhillipMakin 9 43
(R J Price) *led 10f: wknd ins fnl f* **13/2**[3]
5025 **8** *1 3/4* **Champion Lion (IRE)**[17] 6478 6-9-4 53.............................. TonyCulhane 8 40
(J R Boyle) *hld up in tch: rdn over 3f out: styd on same pce appr fnl f* **7/2**[2]
-000 **9** *1 1/4* **Team-Mate (IRE)**[24] 6419 7-9-1 67................................ AmirQuinn(3) 10 38
(Miss J Feilden) *hld up: rdn over 3f out: styd on appr fnl f: nvr trbld ldrs* **33/1**
0663 **10** *3* **Heathyards Joy**[14] 6509 4-8-8 45................. StephanieHollinshead(5) 6 28
(R Hollinshead) *s.i.s and hmpd s: hld up: hdwy over 3f out: wknd over 2f out* **28/1**
0560 **11** *4* **Castanza**[14] 6507 3-8-12 50.. AlanDaly 7 26
(M Wellings) *hld up: plld hrd: wknd 4f out* **50/1**
0-0 **12** *17* **Topple**[20] 5800 4-8-13 ....(p) DarrenWilliams 11 —
(P W Hiatt) *racd keenly: trckd ldr tl wknd over 2f out* **100/1**

2m 44.1s (1.68) **Going Correction** -0.125s/f (Stan)
WFA 3 from 4yo+ 5lb 12 Ran SP% **117.7**
Speed ratings (Par 101):89,88,88,88,87 87,85,84,83,81 79,67
CSF £125.18 TOTE £11.80: £2.70, £4.50, £1.10; EX 121.20.The winner was sold to Ben Pollock for 7,000gns.

The Form Book, Raceform Ltd, Compton, RG20 6NL

Owner Mrs Ann Harrison **Bred** Gestut Trona **Trained** Willoughton, Lincs

FOCUS

A weak seller in which they went no pace and the time was slow. The form looks dubious and is rated negatively through the second and fourth.

Team-Mate(IRE) Official explanation: jockey said gelding had a breathing problem

6621 BETDIRECT.CO.UK H'CAP — 1m 1f 103y(P)

3:50 (3:50) (Class 5) (0-75,75) 3-Y-0+ — £4,119 (£1,225; £612; £305) Stalls Low

Form				RPR
0602	1		**Consonant (IRE)**[7] 6564 8-9-1 **72** ... MickyFenton 4 (D G Bridgwater) *trckd ldrs: led 1f out: rdn out* **4/1**[2]	79+
1002	2	1 ¾	**Dragon Slayer (IRE)**[7] 6566 3-8-13 **72** ... ChrisCatlin 2 (M J Attwater) *led: rdn and hdd 1f out: styd on same pce* **9/4**[1]	75
6000	3	2	**Poppys Footprint (IRE)**[51] 6161 4-8-13 **70** ... RobertWinston 1 (K A Ryan) *mid-div: hdwy over 2f out: rdn over 1f out: styd on same pce* **11/1**	70
5321	4	nk	**Celtique**[51] 6160 3-9-2 **75** ... JamieSpencer 8 (M Wigham) *s.i.s: hld up: hdwy over 1f out: styd on same pce ins fnl f* **6/1**[3]	74
000	5	1 ¾	**Raza Cab (IRE)**[34] 6350 3-8-11 **70** ... DaneO'Neill 6 (Karen George) *chsd ldr over 7f out: rdn and ev ch 2f out: wknd fnl f* **33/1**	66
6006	6	½	**Tequila Sheila (IRE)**[14] 6505 3-8-2 **61** oh1 ... PaulHanagan 5 (K R Burke) *hld up: plld hrd: rdn over 1f out: nvr nrr* **12/1**	56
6521	7	shd	**Monkstown Road**[69] 5819 3-8-2 **61** ... (b) FrancisFerris 9 (E S McMahon) *hld up: styd on ins fnl f: nrst fin* **20/1**	56
5600	8	2 ½	**Stoic Leader (IRE)**[9] 6544 5-8-13 **70** ... JimmyQuinn 11 (R F Fisher) *hld up: plld hrd: hdwy over 2f out: rdn and wknd over 1f out* **9/1**	60
05-0	9	¾	**Sunisa (IRE)**[16] 2285 4-9-4 **75** ... (t) DaleGibson 3 (J Mackie) *prom: rdn over 3f out: n.m.r and wknd over 2f out* **8/1**	63
604U	10	8	**Templet (USA)**[13] 6285 5-9-1 **72** ... (b) DerekMcGaffin 10 (W G Harrison) *chsd ldrs 7f* **16/1**	45

2m 0.47s (-2.15) **Going Correction** -0.125s/f (Stan)
WFA 3 from 4yo+ 2lb — **10** Ran SP% **115.8**
Speed ratings (Par 103):104,102,100,100,98 98,98,96,95,88
CSF £13.27 CT £90.55 TOTE £5.60: £1.50, £1.30, £2.60; EX 14.90.
Owner The Rule Racing Syndicate **Bred** Kilfrush Stud Ltd **Trained** Icomb, Gloucs

FOCUS

This fair contest was run at a modest pace and the form is only ordinary.

6622 BETDIRECT FREEPHONE 0800 211 222 H'CAP — 1m 141y(P)

4:20 (4:20) (Class 5) (0-75,75) 3-Y-0+ — £3,413 (£1,015; £507; £253) Stalls Low

Form				RPR
3602	1		**Deeper In Debt**[9] 6544 7-9-1 **71** ... DaneO'Neill 13 (J Akehurst) *a.p: chsd ldr 6f out: rdn to ld 2f out: styd on u.p* **10/1**	80
0000	2	1 ¼	**Hurricane Coast**[16] 6458 6-8-10 **73** ... (b) JamesDoyle(7) 1 (K McAuliffe) *chsd ldr over 2f: remained handy: chsd wnr fnl f: sn rdn and hung lft: nt run on* **12/1**	79
0104	3	1 ¾	**Corky (IRE)**[14] 6505 4-8-13 **69** ... TomEaves 8 (I W McInnes) *hld up: rdn 1/2-way: r.o ins fnl f: nrst fin* **11/2**[3]	71+
0045	4	shd	**Takes Tutu (USA)**[14] 6503 6-9-3 **73** ... RobertWinston 12 (K R Burke) *hld up: r.o ins fnl f: nt rch ldrs* **5/1**[2]	75+
1000	5	3 ½	**Danielle's Lad**[14] 6499 9-8-9 **65** ... (b) TonyCulhane 7 (B Palling) *led over 6f: wknd fnl f* **16/1**	60
00-0	6	¾	**Hit's Only Money (IRE)**[240] 1197 5-9-3 **73** ... DeanMcKeown 2 (P A Blockley) *hld up in tch: wknd over 1f out* **20/1**	66
00U0	7	shd	**Wotchalike (IRE)**[9] 6482 3-9-0 **75** ... (v[1]) AmirQuinn(3) 5 (R J Price) *s.i.s: hld up: styd on ins fnl f: nvr nrr* **12/1**	68
0310	8	1 ½	**Oh Danny Boy**[14] 6503 4-9-2 **72** ... JamieSpencer 4 (Julian Poulton) *chsd ldrs: rdn over 2f out: wknd over 1f out* **4/1**[1]	62
2115	9	1 ¼	**Nan Jan**[13] 6513 3-9-2 **74** ... (t) ChrisCatlin 6 (R Ingram) *chsd ldrs: rdn over 3f out: wknd 2f out* **11/2**[3]	61
0200	10	2 ½	**Penwell Hill (USA)**[7] 6564 6-9-4 **74** ... RobbieFitzpatrick 10 (M J Attwater) *dwlt: hld up: a in rr* **66/1**	56
0000	11	nk	**Union Jack Jackson (IRE)**[139] 4021 3-8-13 **71** ... FergalLynch 11 (J G Given) *hld up: a in rr* **12/1**	52
0000	12	nk	**Savoy Chapel**[7] 6566 3-8-8 **66** ... JimmyQuinn 9 (A W Carroll) *hld up: effrt over 3f out: wknd over 2f out* **20/1**	47

1m 49.22s (-2.54) **Going Correction** -0.125s/f (Stan)
WFA 3 from 4yo+ 2lb — **12** Ran SP% **116.5**
Speed ratings (Par 103):106,104,103,103,100 99,99,98,96,94 94,94
CSF £119.09 CT £741.68 TOTE £11.10: £2.60, £4.00, £2.40; EX 114.60.
Owner Tipp-Ex Rapid Racing II **Bred** P And Mrs Venner **Trained** Epsom, Surrey

FOCUS

This was run at a modest pace and not many got into it, with the winner back to his old form.

Hurricane Coast Official explanation: jockey said gelding lost a near-fore shoe

Danielle's Lad Official explanation: jockey said gelding had a breathing problem

Hit's Only Money(IRE) Official explanation: jockey said, regarding the running and riding, his orders were to jump out handy, hunt the gelding along and keep pushing, but not to knock it around as this was its first run since April, adding that he was able to settle gelding in mid-division but when asked a question gelding could not quicken, appeared to blow up, and would not have finished closer for more vigorous riding; trainer said gelding has been operated on twice for a wind problem and may benefit from a slight drop in trip in the future

6623 BETDIRECT ON CHANNEL 4 TEXT PAGE 613 MAIDEN STKS (DIV II) — 1m 141y(P)

4:50 (4:50) (Class 5) 3-Y-0+ — £2,998 (£892; £445; £222) Stalls Low

Form				RPR
30	1		**Ninth House (USA)**[61] 5990 3-9-0 ... (t) JamieSpencer 10 (D J Daly) *hld up: hdwy over 2f out: led over 1f out: eased wl ins fnl f* **8/13**[1]	68+
0252	2	2 ½	**Grande Roche (IRE)**[71] 5756 3-9-0 63 ... DeanMcKeown 7 (G A Swinbank) *a.p: rdn to chse ldr over 2f out: hung lft ins fnl f: styd on same pce* **5/2**[2]	56
0040	3	1 ¾	**Bold Trump**[84] 5518 4-9-2 40 ... VinceSlattery 9 (Mrs N S Evans) *chsd ldr 6f: styng on same pce whn hmpd ins fnl f* **100/1**	52?
620	4	¾	**Layed Back Rocky**[4] 6587 3-8-7 52 ... LiamJones(7) 3 (M Mullineaux) *hld up: hdwy over 2f out: rdn over 1f out: styd on same pce* **20/1**	50
6	5	1 ¼	**Woodwool**[40] 6301 3-8-9 ... DaneO'Neill 2 (H Candy) *mid-div: rdn over 2f out: sn outpcd: swtchd lft and nt clr run ins fnl f: styd on* **12/1**[3]	43
0050	6	¾	**Weet Yer Tern (IRE)**[7] 6567 3-9-0 55 ... FergalLynch 1 (P A Blockley) *led: rdn and hdd over 1f out: wkng whn hmpd ins fnl f* **16/1**	52+
00	7	2	**Arpetcheeo (USA)**[24] 6418 3-8-11 60 ... DNolan(3) 6 (D Carroll) *chsd ldrs 7f* **33/1**	42
	8	3	**Naemi (GER)**[41] 3-8-9 ... MickyFenton 8 (S L Keightley) *dwlt: hld up: a in rr* **50/1**	31
6	9	19	**Blackbury**[16] 6485 3-8-9 ... AlanDaly 5 (J W Unett) *dwlt: hld up: rdn over 3f out: sn wknd* **40/1**	—

1m 49.6s (-2.16) **Going Correction** -0.125s/f (Stan)
WFA 3 from 4yo 2lb — **26** Ran SP% **117.2**
Speed ratings (Par 103):104,101,100,99,98 97,96,93,76
CSF £2.20 TOTE £1.50: £1.10, £1.40, £8.30; EX 3.40 Place 6 £141.87, Place 5 £44.10.
Owner Gold Ace Racing **Bred** Juddmonte Farms Inc **Trained** Newmarket, Suffolk

FOCUS

Just a moderate maiden but quite an impressive winner who passed all his rivals to score easily. The form is limited by the proximity of the third.

T/Plt: £387.70 to a £1 stake. Pool: £36,918.50. 69.50 winning tickets. T/Qpdt: £5.80 to a £1 stake. Pool: £4,333.80. 550.90 winning tickets. CR

6610 LINGFIELD (L-H)

Tuesday, December 20

OFFICIAL GOING: Standard

Wind: Nil Weather: Misty becoming fine

6624 BETDIRECT.CO.UK MAIDEN STKS (DIV I) — 1m (P)

12:00 (12:02) (Class 5) 2-Y-0 — £3,785 (£1,126; £562; £281) Stalls Low

Form				RPR
66	1		**Royal Reservation**[70] 5823 2-9-0 ... JamieSpencer 6 (P W Chapple-Hyam) *lw: hld up in midfield: smooth prog to trck ldrs 2f out: effrt 1f out: pushed into ld last 100yds: readily* **9/2**[2]	73
240	2	nk	**Abstract Art (USA)**[115] 4745 2-9-0 75 ... SteveDrowne 5 (N A Callaghan) *t.k.h: trckd ldrs: pushed along 3f out: no imp tl r.o wl fnl f to take 2nd nr fin* **11/2**[3]	72
2	3	nk	**First Slip**[15] 6502 2-9-0 ... EddieAhern 2 (Mrs A J Perrett) *lw: trckd ldng pair: effrt 2f out: rdn over 1f out: styd on wl fnl f: a hld* **9/2**[2]	71
045	4	½	**Vodkatini**[24] 6427 2-9-0 73 ... (v) FergusSweeney 10 (P J Makin) *sn trckd ldr: rdn to ld over 1f out: hanging lft after: hdd and nt qckn last 100yds: lost 2 pls nr fin* **14/1**	70
	5	1 ¾	**Airbuss (IRE)** 2-9-0 ... TonyCulhane 12 (M R Channon) *unf: lw: trckd ldng pair: pushed along and green fr 3f out: one pce u.p over 1f out* **6/4**[1]	66
323	6	½	**Disco Lights**[18] 6477 2-8-9 73 ... DaneO'Neill 4 (D J Daly) *leggy: s.i.s: pushed up to ld and set stdy pce: hdd over 1f out: wknd ins fnl f* **10/1**	60
	7	3	**Startengo (IRE)** 2-9-0 ... JohnEgan 9 (D R C Elsworth) *unf: dwlt: wl in rr: pushed along and nt on terms 3f out: kpt on steadily fr over 1f out* **25/1**	58
	8	3	**Henry Holmes** 2-8-11 ... RichardThomas(3) 3 (Mrs L Richards) *cmpt: bit bkwd: s.v.s: wl in rr tl sme prog on inner over 2f out: nvr on terms* **100/1**	51
	9	½	**Broadway Calling** 2-9-0 ... LPKeniry 11 (A M Balding) *leggy: bit bkwd: dwlt: mostly last: pushed along over 3f out: no real prog* **100/1**	50
0	10	6	**Lady Evi**[29] 6395 2-8-9 ... ChrisCatlin 7 (D K Ivory) *chsd ldrs: rdn over 4f out: wknd 3f out* **100/1**	31
05	11	3	**Uandi**[18] 6484 2-8-6 ... RobertMiles(3) 8 (J Akehurst) *leggy: racd wd: in tch tl wknd over 3f out* **50/1**	24

1m 39.4s (-0.03) **Going Correction** -0.10s/f (Stan) — **11** Ran SP% **116.3**
Speed ratings (Par 96):96,95,95,94,93 92,89,86,86,80 77
CSF £28.57 TOTE £7.20: £2.00, £1.90, £1.90; EX 34.00.
Owner Colin Mercer **Bred** Mountgrange Stud Ltd **Trained** Newmarket, Suffolk

FOCUS

The winning time was 0.73 seconds slower than the second division, but this still looked a reasonable maiden with a few fancied, the runner-up and fourth set the standard and the form should work out.

NOTEBOOK

Royal Reservation, who showed a little ability in two turf maidens, was given a patient ride and was always travelling well before being produced with his effort off the home bend. He eventually scored with a little bit in hand, despite the narrow margin, and his future now lies in the hands of the Handicapper, but there is probably still some improvement in him. (op 7-2)

Abstract Art(USA), reappearing from a four-month break and making his sand debut, took a while to find top gear but was finishing best of all though he may be a little flattered by his proximity to the winner. There should be a race in him on this surface, perhaps over further. (tchd 6-1)

First Slip was always in a prominent position and tried his best, but was lacking a decisive turn of foot when it mattered and probably did not improve on the form of his debut. He may do better once handicapped. (op 4-1)

Vodkatini was given every chance this time and hit the front soon after turning in, but he could never get away from his rivals and was swamped inside the last furlong. He is yet to show that he stays the mile, but in any case he may be better off switching to handicaps now. (op 11-1)

Airbuss(IRE), an athletic 160,000gns half-brother to King's County and Deuxieme, was very well backed to make a winning debut but was off the bridle some way out and could never quite get on terms down the home straight. The four in front of him all had previous racecourse experience, so it may be wise to give him the benefit of the doubt on this occasion and he is obviously held in some regard. (op 2-1 tchd 9-4 in places)

Disco Lights ◆, a springer in the market, set an ordinary pace before being easily picked off. This trip on a faster surface was never going to play to her strengths given her breeding, especially given the modest tempo she set, and she remains of interest when stepped up in distance, especially if switched to handicaps. (op 16-1)

6625 INFO@HORSESFORCAUSES.COM H'CAP (DIV I) — 7f (P)

12:30 (12:31) (Class 6) (0-60,60) 3-Y-0+ — £2,540 (£749; £375) Stalls Low

Form				RPR
3004	1		**Holiday Cocktail**[53] 6134 3-9-4 **60** ... HayleyTurner 13 (S C Williams) *sn prom: rdn and effrt 2f out: disp ld 1f out: narrow ld last strides* **9/2**[2]	68
4022	2	hd	**I Wish**[24] 6438 7-9-1 **57** ... LPKeniry 5 (Miss J R Tooth) *trckd ldrs: rdn and effrt 2f out: disp ld 1f out: narrowly hdd last strides* **14/1**	64
6112	3	1	**Kensington (IRE)**[1] 6618 4-9-3 **59** ... (p) JamieSpencer 7 (P D Evans) *hld up towards rr: nt clr run and dropped to last trio 2f out: nt clr run and swtchd rt over 1f out: r.o wl last 100yds* **2/1**[1]	63+
5022	4	nk	**Scuba (IRE)**[14] 6516 3-9-1 **57** ... (v) SteveDrowne 10 (H Morrison) *settled midfield: rdn wl over 2f out: prog u.p jst over 1f out: styd on* **9/2**[2]	61

0060 **5** ½ **Charlie Bear**[77] 5687 4-9-1 **57**........................ ChrisCatlin 6 59
(Miss Z C Davison) *t.k.h: hld up in midfield: nt clr run 2f out: hrd rdn and styd on fnl f: nvr able to chal* **12/1**

-003 **6** *shd* **Cold Climate**[73] 5738 10-9-2 **58**........................ OscarUrbina 8 60+
(Bob Jones) *hld up in last trio: effrt on inner and nt clr run over 2f out: nvr much room after but styng on wl nr fin* **25/1**

0004 **7** *shd* **Marsad (IRE)**[21] 6455 11-9-2 **58**........................ PaulDoe 9 60
(J Akehurst) *dwlt: hld up in last trio: promising effrt on outer over 1f out: fnd nil ins fnl f* **20/1**

0021 **8** ¾ **Stagnite**[6] 6579 5-9-0 **56** 6ex........................(b) TonyCulhane 2 56
(K McAuliffe) *trckd ldng pair: rdn and stl cl up 1f out: fdd ins fnl f* **14/1**

0000 **9** *1* **Double M**[54] 6126 8-9-1 **60**........................(v) RichardThomas(3) 11 57
(Mrs L Richards) *dwlt: hld up wl in rr: no prog tl styd on fnl f: n.d* **20/1**

0100 **10** ½ **Qobtaan (USA)**[10] 6542 6-9-4 **60**........................ GeorgeBaker 3 56
(M R Bosley) *hld up towards rr on inner: prog over 2f out: cl up 1f out: sn btn* **33/1**

004 **11** *hd* **Grand Design**[125] 4464 3-9-2 **58**........................ J-PGuillambert 12 53
(C A Cyzer) *lw: racd wd in midfield: effrt and rdn over 2f out: fdd fnl f* **33/1**

6600 **12** 1½ **Exit Smiling**[41] 6294 3-9-2 **58**........................(v) DaneO'Neill 1 50
(G C H Chung) *drvn to ld: hdd & wknd 1f out* **66/1**

6140 **13** *nk* **Spindor (USA)**[113] 4836 6-9-4 **60**........................(b) EddieAhern 14 51
(M A Magnusson) *b: b.hind: lw: t.k.h: hld up in rr: no prog fnl 2f* **10/1**[3]

0000 **14** *8* **Young Valentino**[21] 6464 3-8-13 **55**........................ TPQueally 4 25
(A W Carroll) *b.hind: pressed ldr: rdn 3f out: wknd rapidly over 1f out* **100/1**

1m 25.28s (-0.61) **Going Correction** -0.10s/f (Stan) **14** Ran SP% **121.5**
Speed ratings (Par 101):99,98,97,97,96 96,96,95,94,93 93,91,91,82
CSF £61.36 CT £172.13 TOTE £5.60: £1.80, £4.00, £1.10; EX 76.00.
Owner The B52's **Bred** Mrs W H Gibson Fleming **Trained** Newmarket, Suffolk
■ Stewards' Enquiry : L P Keniry caution: used whip in an incorrect place

FOCUS
A typically tight Lingfield handicap in which racing room was a premium over the last couple of furlongs, and while some enjoyed uninterrupted runs, others did not. The winning time was about half a second faster than the second division and the form looks solid enough, rated through the runner-up.
Kensington(IRE) Official explanation: jockey said gelding was denied a clear run
Cold Climate Official explanation: jockey said gelding was denied a clear run

6626 BETDIRECT FREEPHONE 0800 211 222 H'CAP 1m 2f (P)
1:00 (1:02) (Class 6) (0-58,60) 3-Y-O+ **£2,886** (£852; £426) **Stalls** Low

Form RPR

0600 **1** **Red Birr (IRE)**[48] 6230 4-9-2 **58**........................ DaneO'Neill 8 70+
(P R Webber) *trckd ldng trio: effrt to dispute 2nd 3f out: rdn over 2f out: led jst over 1f out: drvn clr* **15/2**[3]

0562 **2** 2½ **Jomus**[38] 6324 4-9-1 **57**........................(p) EddieAhern 14 64
(L Montague Hall) *led to post: settled in 6th: clsd on ldrs fr 3f out: rdn to chal over 1f out: outpcd by wnr* **8/1**

1351 **3** 1¼ **Lady Taverner**[10] 6548 4-8-8 **55**........................ NataliaGemelova(5) 4 64+
(J E Long) *trckd ldng trio: clsd up over 2f out: nowhere to go on inner over 1f out: r.o last 100yds: nt rcvr* **8/1**

00 **4** *nk* **Olivino (GER)**[38] 6324 4-9-1 **57**........................ PaulDoe 5 61
(S Dow) *led at decent pce: kicked on again wl over 2f out: hdd and no ex jst over 1f out* **25/1**

0006 **5** ¾ **Tricky Venture**[3] 6598 5-9-2 **58**........................ JimmyQuinn 9 61
(Mrs L C Jewell) *chsd ldr: stl disputing 2nd wl over 1f out: nt qckn u.p* **13/2**[2]

0103 **6** *nk* **Bishops Finger**[117] 4689 5-8-13 **55**........................(b) JohnEgan 7 57
(Jamie Poulton) *b: settled in midfield: effrt over 3f out: nt on terms w ldrs fr over 2f out: one pce* **11/1**

2000 **7** *nk* **Friends Hope**[10] 6535 4-9-2 **58**........................ PatCosgrave 11 59
(P A Blockley) *hld up in midfield: nt on terms w ldrs fr over 3f out: hrd rdn and kpt on same pce fnl 2f* **20/1**

5300 **8** *2* **Bamzooki**[14] 6514 3-8-13 **58**........................ JamieSpencer 6 56
(D J Daly) *t.k.h and restrained in last pair: wl off the pce over 3f out: sme prog 2f out: swtchd rt over 1f out: nvr nr ldrs* **16/1**

2031 **9** ¾ **Blue Quiver (IRE)**[8] 6567 5-9-4 **60** 6ex........................ SteveDrowne 1 56
(C A Horgan) *s.s: hld up wl in rr: pushed along over 3f out: kpt on steadily fnl 2f: nvr nr ldrs* **6/1**[1]

0201 **10** 1¾ **Barons Spy (IRE)**[17] 6487 4-9-1 **57**........................ DarrenWilliams 13 50
(R J Price) *lw: hld up in midfield: rdn and no prog 3f out: kpt on same pce after* **14/1**

56-5 **11** *5* **Cultured**[232] 1427 4-9-2 **58**........................ GeorgeBaker 12 41
(Mrs A J Bowlby) *stdd s: hld up wl in rr: hrd rdn and no prog over 3f out* **20/1**

4234 **12** ½ **Port 'n Starboard**[94] 5326 4-9-2 **58**........................ J-PGuillambert 2 40
(C A Cyzer) *lw: racd on outer: hld up in midfield: shkn up and no prog over 2f out: wknd over 1f out* **6/1**[1]

3012 **13** *3* **Danzare**[43] 6287 3-8-13 **58**........................ ChrisCatlin 10 35
(Mrs A J Hamilton-Fairley) *chsd ldr to 3f out: wknd* **11/1**

5000 **14** 3½ **Primed Up (IRE)**[139] 4045 3-8-13 **58**........................ TonyCulhane 3 28
(G L Moore) *hld up wl in rr: rdn and btn over 3f out* **25/1**

2m 4.82s (-2.97) **Going Correction** -0.10s/f (Stan)
WFA 3 from 4yo+ 3lb **14** Ran SP% **122.3**
Speed ratings (Par 101):107,105,104,103,103 102,102,101,100,99 95,94,92,89
CSF £63.74 CT £499.34 TOTE £10.70: £3.20, £2.90, £3.60; EX 112.90.
Owner John Nicholls (Trading) Ltd **Bred** Mrs Ellen Lyons **Trained** Mollington, Oxon

FOCUS
A race run at a true pace and dominated by those that raced handily. As a result the winning time was decent for a race of its class and the form could prove above average.

6627 DIO-UK.COM DEAD CERT FOR OFFICE SUPPLIES NURSERY 7f (P)
1:30 (1:30) (Class 4) (0-85,82) 2-Y-O **£4,699** (£1,398; £698; £348) **Stalls** Low

Form RPR

4400 **1** **Grand Jour (IRE)**[24] 6425 2-8-10 **71**........................(t) TonyCulhane 6 75
(K McAuliffe) *led on sufferance and set stdy pce: kicked on 2f out: hrd pressed fnl f: hld on wl* **14/1**

0532 **2** ½ **Porters (USA)**[24] 6427 2-9-7 **82**........................ DaneO'Neill 5 85
(R Hannon) *trckd ldrs: effrt over 2f out: chsd wnr over 1f out: chal fnl f: nt qckn and hld last 100yds* **11/4**[2]

4600 **3** *1* **Scroll**[15] 6501 2-8-8 **69**........................(v) J-PGuillambert 3 69
(P Howling) *hld up in last pair: rdn and prog 2f out: nt that keen but kpt on to take 3rd nr fin* **14/1**

0261 **4** *nk* **Grenane (IRE)**[11] 6529 2-8-9 **70**........................ JohnEgan 4 69
(P D Evans) *b: b.hind: plld hrd early: trckd wnr to over 1f out: nt qckn* **9/2**[3]

0015 **5** *1* **Pommes Frites**[15] 6501 2-9-5 **80**........................ SteveDrowne 2 77
(W R Muir) *hld up bhd ldrs: rdn 2f out: nt qckn and hld fr over 1f out* **7/1**

6002 **6** *1* **Pelham Crescent (IRE)**[21] 6457 2-8-11 **72**........................ EddieAhern 1 66
(R Hannon) *t.k.h early: trckd ldng pair to over 2f out: sn btn* **5/2**[1]

5003 **7** *nk* **Charlie Delta**[5] 6581 2-8-9 **73**........................ DanielTudhope(3) 8 66
(D Carroll) *hld up and racd wd: outpcd fr 2f out: one pce after* **12/1**

0001 **8** ¾ **Deserted Prince (IRE)**[64] 5947 2-8-4 **65**........................ ChrisCatlin 7 56
(M J Wallace) *hld up in last: outpcd over 2f out: no ch after* **20/1**

1m 26.09s (0.20) **Going Correction** -0.10s/f (Stan) **8** Ran SP% **111.7**
Speed ratings (Par 98):94,93,92,91,90 89,89,88
CSF £50.18 CT £551.20 TOTE £16.80: £3.70, £1.40, £3.30; EX 73.20.
Owner John Reed **Bred** Islanmore Stud **Trained** Fernham, Oxon

FOCUS
A messy race in which the winner was allowed to dictate at a modest pace and he took full advantage. As a result the winning time was modest for a race of its type and the form may not be totally reliable.

NOTEBOOK
Grand Jour(IRE), tried over distances ranging from six to ten furlongs in his last three outings, was gifted a soft lead and that enabled him to keep enough in reserve for the final sprint for home. Although the form of this race is dodgy, he has hinted at ability in the past so it is not impossible he can add to this. (op 16-1)
Porters(USA) is very consistent and tried his hardest under top weight, but could never quite get to grips with the winner who was rather gifted the race from the front. He remains vulnerable to an unexposed type and his consistency is not getting him any help from the Handicapper. (op 4-1)
Scroll, ran his usual sort of race, staying on in the straight without giving the impression that he was giving it 100%. He remains a maiden after 12 attempts. (op 9-1)
Grenane(IRE), raised 4lb for his Wolverhampton victory, should have had no problem with the extra furlong but it all became irrelevant when he pulled his chance away thanks to the pedestrian early pace. He should be forgiven this. (op 4-1)
Pommes Frites would not have been helped by the moderate early tempo, though she was not alone there, and it was fairly obvious soon after turning for home that she had had her chips. She does look better suited by a slower surface. (op 11-2)
Pelham Crescent(IRE), surprisingly without the blinkers he ran so well in here last time, never seemed to be travelling that well and never picked up at all. (op 9-4 tchd 11-4 and 3-1 in a place)

6628 BETDIRECT.CO.UK MAIDEN STKS (DIV II) 1m (P)
2:00 (2:01) (Class 5) 2-Y-O **£3,776** (£1,123; £561; £280) **Stalls** Low

Form RPR

1 **It's A Dream (FR)** 2-9-0........................ LPKeniry 8 79+
(D R C Elsworth) *w'like: scope: tall: lw: s.s: hld up in last: prog on outer over 2f out: led over 1f out: shkn up and styd on wl: v promisi* **33/1**

506 **2** 1¼ **Billich**[140] 4020 2-9-0 **71**........................ JamieSpencer 10 76
(E J O'Neill) *sn led: kicked 2l clr 2f out: hdd over 1f out: kpt on but no ch w wnr* **20/1**

0006 **3** *nk* **Mr Floodlight (IRE)**[123] 4542 2-9-0 **77**........................ DaneO'Neill 6 75
(R Hannon) *trckd ldrs: rdn fr 3f out: styd on wl u.p to chal over 1f out: kpt on* **6/1**[3]

4 **4** *1* **Snoqualmie Boy**[24] 6425 2-9-0........................ JohnEgan 1 73
(D R C Elsworth) *lw: hld up in midfield: effrt over 2f out: nt qckn and bdly outpcd sn after: rdn and r.o fnl f: nt rch ldrs* **4/6**[1]

0203 **5** *5* **Ohana**[10] 6538 2-9-0 **72**........................(p) SteveDrowne 4 61
(N A Callaghan) *hld up in rr: effrt over 2f out: sn outpcd: n.d after* **14/1**

000 **6** 1¼ **Million All Day (IRE)**[113] 4809 2-8-9 **55**........................ SamHitchcott 3 53
(W R Muir) *in tch: rdn over 3f out: struggling on outer fr over 2f out* **100/1**

04 **7** *nk* **Appreciated**[8] 6557 2-8-9........................ TonyCulhane 7 53
(W J Haggas) *t.k.h: hld up in rr: prog to dispute 2nd 2f out: wknd rapidly over 1f out* **20/1**

5300 **8** *5* **Symphonia (IRE)**[77] 5688 2-8-9 **50**........................ HayleyTurner 11 41
(N P Littmoden) *chsd ldr to 2f out: wknd rapidly* **100/1**

00 **9** *5* **Mo Chroi**[143] 3946 2-8-9........................ ChrisCatlin 9 30
(C G Cox) *chsd ldrs to 3f out: sn wknd* **50/1**

306 **10** *5* **Bitter Chill**[24] 6427 2-9-0 **75**........................ EddieAhern 2 23
(P W Chapple-Hyam) *hld up: shkn up over 3f out: sn btn and eased* **4/1**[2]

00 **11** *8* **Brabinger (IRE)**[11] 6532 2-9-0........................ GeorgeBaker 5 5
(B G Powell) *prom tl wknd rapidly wl over 2f out* **100/1**

1m 38.67s (-0.76) **Going Correction** -0.10s/f (Stan) **45** Ran SP% **118.3**
Speed ratings (Par 96):99,97,97,96,91 90,89,84,79,74 66
CSF £520.88 TOTE £28.00: £5.20, £3.00, £1.60; EX 282.80.
Owner Matthew Green **Bred** Serge Bernereau Sarl **Trained** Newmarket, Suffolk

FOCUS
A fair maiden in which the winning time was 0.73 seconds faster than the first division and probably an above-average contest for the time of year, and rated positively as a result.

NOTEBOOK
It's A Dream(FR) ◆, an attractive, scopey colt who is a half-brother to winners in France, was the stable second-string according to the market. However, he overcame a slow start to win in good style from horses with official ratings in the 70s. He showed signs of greenness when in front and looks the type to go on to better things. (tchd 40-1)
Billich, having his first start on Polytrack, was last seen running in a Brighton maiden which has produced four subsequent winner. He did his best to make virtually all, but could not respond when the winner swept by. He kept going for second though and should be able to win a race on this surface.
Mr Floodlight(IRE), another Polytrack debutant, had shown fair form at up to a mile on turf. He acted on the track and had every chance, but like the runner-up ran into a colt who looks better than average for the time of year. He has races in him, possibly back at seven furlongs. (op 7-2)
Snoqualmie Boy, the favourite and stable companion of the winner, was dropping back two furlongs from his debut run. He tracked the leaders but got left behind on the run down to the straight before keeping on well once in line for home. He looks better than the bare result and the return to ten furlongs should be in his favour. (tchd 4-5)
Ohana, with more previous experience than most, was held up off the pace and kept on in the latter stages, but was well behind the first four. He is bred to need middle-distances and handicaps look a better option for him. (tchd 12-1)
Bitter Chill, who was well backed, was quite disappointing but ran as if something was amiss. (op 5-1 tchd 6-1)

6629 £10 FREE BET H'CAP 1m (P)
2:30 (2:31) (Class 4) (0-85,82) 3-Y-O+ **£5,764** (£1,715; £857; £428) **Stalls** Low

Form RPR

2116 **1** **Hits Only Heaven (IRE)**[15] 6504 3-8-13 **78**........................(be) JimmyQuinn 12 87
(J Pearce) *plld hrd and trckd ldr after 1f: effrt to ld 2f out: hrd pressed 1f out: drvn and styd on wl* **6/1**[2]

5002 **2** 1¼ **Island Rapture**[15] 6503 5-8-9 **73**........................ EddieAhern 10 79
(J A R Toller) *trckd ldrs: effrt 2f out: drvn to press wnr 1f out: styd on but no imp* **7/1**

0005 **3** *nk* **Northern Desert (IRE)**[15] 6504 6-9-0 **78**........................ ChrisCatlin 3 83
(P W Hiatt) *plld hrd early: trckd ldrs: effrt 2f out: rdn to press wnr 1f out: styd on but a hld* **7/1**

4351 **4** ¾ **Waterside (IRE)**[21] 6458 6-9-4 **82** HayleyTurner 11 86
(G L Moore) *t.k.h: sn led: rdn and hdd 2f out: styd cl up: one pce ins fnl f* **13/2**[3]

5220 **5** *nk* **Wavertree Warrior (IRE)**[21] 6458 3-8-9 **77** RichardThomas(3) 7 80
(N P Littmoden) *hld up towards rr: effrt 2f out: styd on fnl f: no ch of rching ldrs* **10/1**

0030 **6** *1* **Screwdriver**[21] 6458 3-8-10 **75** (b) LPKeniry 6 76
(Miss J R Tooth) *rrd s: hld up in rr: effrt over 2f out: styng on but no ch whn hanging fr over 1f out* **50/1**

0402 **7** ¾ **Marko Jadeo (IRE)**[15] 6505 7-8-11 **75** DaneO'Neill 2 74
(S Dow) *dwlt: hld up wl in rr: nt wl plcd and outpcd 2f out: shkn up and styd on: no ch* **20/1**

0544 **8** ¾ **Chief Exec**[15] 6504 3-9-2 **81** J-PGuillambert 8 78
(C A Cyzer) *t.k.h: trckd ldrs: rdn 2f out: wknd jst over 1f out* **16/1**

4-56 **9** *2* **Magic Merlin**[84] 5526 4-8-13 **77** StephenCarson 4 70
(W R Swinburn) *t.k.h: hld up in midfield: outpcd over 2f out: n.d after* **6/1**[2]

0-00 **10** *nk* **Leoballero**[24] 6431 5-9-2 **80** (tp) JamieSpencer 1 72
(D J Daly) *dwlt: hld up in rr: effrt on inner over 2f out: wknd over 1f out* **12/1**

0600 **11** *3* **Smokin Joe**[15] 6504 4-8-11 **75** (b) SteveDrowne 5 60
(J R Best) *dwlt: a wl in rr: rdn and struggling 3f out* **14/1**

1204 **12** *10* **Hayyani (IRE)**[21] 6458 3-8-12 **77** JohnEgan 9 39
(K McAuliffe) *t.k.h: racd on outer: chsd ldrs tl wknd wl over 2f out: t.o* **11/2**[1]

1m 37.28s (-2.15) **Going Correction** -0.10s/f (Stan)
WFA 3 from 4yo+ 1lb 12 Ran SP% **118.3**
Speed ratings (Par 105):106,104,104,103,103 102,101,100,98,98 95,85
CSF £47.63 CT £307.73 TOTE £9.60: £3.10, £2.50, £3.50; EX 63.40 Trifecta £298.20 Part won. Pool: £420.10 - 0.20 winning tickets..
Owner Clive Whiting **Bred** Waterside Stud **Trained** Newmarket, Suffolk

FOCUS
A decent and competitive handicap, and though the early pace was modest, resulting in several taking a keen hold, they quickened up appreciably late on and the final time was perfectly acceptable. Again those that raced prominently were favoured with the front four always up with the pace which suggests the form may not be solid.
Hayyani(IRE) Official explanation: jockey said gelding pulled too hard and hung right

6630 INFO@HORSESFORCAUSES.COM H'CAP (DIV II) 7f (P)
3:00 (3:03) (Class 6) (0-60,60) 3-Y-O+ **£2,545** (£751; £375) **Stalls** Low

Form RPR

4006 **1** **Hadath (IRE)**[1] 6618 8-9-1 **57** GeorgeBaker 12 65
(B G Powell) *hld up in last trio: stdy prog fr over 2f out: effrt over 1f out: r.o to ld nr fin* **8/1**

2220 **2** *nk* **Kallista's Pride**[1] 6616 5-9-1 **57** HayleyTurner 6 64
(J R Best) *t.k.h: pressed ldr: led over 2f out: drvn fnl f: hdd nr fin* **6/1**[2]

5016 **3** 1 ½ **Miskina**[14] 6513 4-9-3 **59** EddieAhern 2 62
(W M Brisbourne) *hld up bhd ldrs on inner: effrt over 2f out: cl up jst over 1f out: nt qckn: styd on again ins fnl f* **7/1**

3600 **4** *nk* **Manic**[77] 5686 3-9-4 **60** JohnEgan 7 62
(Andrew Reid) *trckd ldrs: effrt over 2f out: rdn to chse wnr briefly ent fnl f: one pce* **11/1**

0201 **5** *hd* **Night Wolf (IRE)**[91] 5386 5-8-12 **54** PaulDoe 1 56
(Jamie Poulton) *trckd ldrs: cl up 2f out: nt qckn over 1f out: kpt on* **8/1**

4041 **6** ½ **Bollin Billy**[57] 6070 3-9-2 **58** JamieSpencer 10 58
(R Brotherton) *hld up in midfield: nt qckn over 2f out: prog over 1f out: kpt on : nvr able to chal* **9/2**[1]

0034 **7** ½ **Tregarron**[46] 6245 4-9-4 **60** DaneO'Neill 8 59+
(R Hannon) *hld up towards rr: nt clr run wl over 1f out: n.d after: styng on nr fin* **13/2**[3]

1100 **8** ¾ **Secam (POL)**[161] 3420 6-9-0 **59** (b) EdwardCreighton(3) 14 56
(Mrs P Townsley) *prom: jnd ldr over 2f out: wknd jst over 1f out* **12/1**

0000 **9** *nk* **Music Teacher**[21] 6460 3-8-13 **55** SteveDrowne 9 51
(N A Callaghan) *hld up wl in rr: hung lft briefly 2f out: shuffled along and nvr nr ldrs* **12/1**

1000 **10** ½ **Lady Londra**[21] 6455 3-9-2 **58** JimmyQuinn 4 53
(D K Ivory) *hld up in midfield and racd on inner: shkn up wl over 1f out: one pce and nvr on terms* **50/1**

0000 **11** 1 ½ **Oakbridge (IRE)**[25] 6422 3-9-4 **60** VinceSlattery 3 51
(D J Wintle) *s.i.s: a wl in rr: struggling 2f out* **20/1**

0006 **12** *1* **Transaction (IRE)**[21] 6455 3-9-1 **57** StephenCarson 11 46
(J M P Eustace) *racd wd in rr: rdn 3f out: sn btn* **10/1**

0460 **13** 1 ½ **Zorn**[197] 2341 6-9-0 **56** TonyCulhane 5 41
(P Howling) *led to over 2f out: wknd* **25/1**

1m 25.77s (-0.12) **Going Correction** -0.10s/f (Stan) 67 Ran SP% **123.9**
Speed ratings (Par 101):96,95,93,93,93 92,92,91,91,90 88,87,85
CSF £56.46 CT £376.18 TOTE £9.20: £3.10, £2.60, £2.70; EX 72.50.
Owner Seamus Mannion **Bred** Shadwell Estate Company Limited **Trained** Morestead, Hants

FOCUS
Another highly competitive if low-key handicap run at a fair pace. The winning time was about half a second slower than the first division and the form is very ordinary.

6631 BETDIRECTCASINO.COM H'CAP 6f (P)
3:30 (3:32) (Class 5) (0-70,70) 3-Y-O+ **£3,452** (£1,027; £513; £256) **Stalls** Low

Form RPR

0005 **1** **Silent Storm**[17] 6488 5-9-0 **66** ChrisCatlin 3 77
(C A Cyzer) *off the pce towards rr: prog fr 1/2-way: str run over 1f out to ld last 150yds: sn clr* **7/1**[3]

2203 **2** 1 ¾ **Hard To Catch (IRE)**[10] 6546 7-8-6 **65** LauraReynolds(7) 6 71
(D K Ivory) *settled in rr and wl off the pce: effrt over 2f out: r.o fr over 1f out to take 2nd nr fin* **14/1**

0036 **3** *1* **Seneschal**[10] 6544 4-9-4 **70** SamHitchcott 2 73
(A B Haynes) *chsd ldrs: rdn 2f out: styd on fnl f to take 3rd nr fin* **10/1**

5512 **4** ½ **Ever Cheerful**[3] 6603 4-9-1 **67** J-PGuillambert 10 69
(G C H Chung) *lw; prom: chsd ldr over 3f out: led over 2f out and kicked 2l clr: hdd & wknd last 150yds* **10/3**[1]

0402 **5** *shd* **Ivory Lace**[54] 6126 4-8-13 **65** HayleyTurner 4 66
(S Woodman) *lw: hld up in last pair: plenty to do whn nt clr run 2f out: pushed along and styd on fnl f: nvr nrr* **8/1**

0060 **6** *hd* **Romany Nights (IRE)**[21] 6465 5-9-2 **68** (b) JimmyQuinn 12 69
(Miss Gay Kelleway) *towards rr and off the pce: effrt on outer over 2f out: nt qckn wl over 1f out: styd on ins fnl f* **12/1**

0000 **7** 1 ½ **Endless Summer**[17] 6486 8-9-4 **70** TonyCulhane 8 66
(A W Carroll) *hld up in last pair: no ch 2f out: styd on fnl f* **16/1**

034 **8** 2 ½ **Lady Algarhoud (FR)**[10] 6546 3-8-11 **63** EddieAhern 9 52
(D K Ivory) *prom: chsd ldr 4f out to over 3f out: chsd new ldr 2f out to over 1f out: wknd* **14/1**

0400 **9** *shd* **Vague Star (ITY)**[3] 6603 3-8-13 **65** (b) SteveDrowne 5 53
(R Ingram) *prom: drvn to chse ldr briefly over 1f out: sn wknd* **12/1**

0602 **10** *2* **Joy And Pain**[24] 6430 4-9-4 **70** GeorgeBaker 1 52
(J R Boyle) *chsd ldr for 2f: lost pl: struggling whn hmpd on inner 2f out: no ch after* **7/2**[2]

6060 **11** 1 ¼ **Yorkshire Lad (IRE)**[10] 6546 3-8-13 **65** (t) JohnEgan 7 44
(Miss Gay Kelleway) *led at fast pce to over 2f out: wknd* **33/1**

6200 **12** *15* **Arnie De Burgh**[10] 6546 3-8-12 **64** ow1 (t) JamieSpencer 11 —
(D J Daly) *a in rr: wknd 1/2-way: t.o* **14/1**

1m 11.42s (-1.39) **Going Correction** -0.10s/f (Stan) 12 Ran SP% **122.2**
Speed ratings (Par 103):105,102,101,100,100 100,98,94,94,92 90,70
CSF £104.22 CT £994.47 TOTE £7.20: £1.70, £4.90, £5.60; EX 112.80 Place 6 £408.63, Place 5 £203.61.
Owner Mrs Charles Cyzer **Bred** Middle Park Stud Ltd **Trained** Maplehurst, W Sussex

FOCUS
A fairly competitive sprint handicap run at a solid pace and the form looks solid rated through the paced horses.
Joy And Pain ◆ Official explanation: jockey said gelding was denied a clear run
Yorkshire Lad(IRE) Official explanation: jockey said gelding felt wrong behind
T/Jkpt: Not won. T/Plt: £493.40 to a £1 stake. Pool: £45,894.95. 67.90 winning tickets. T/Qpdt: £126.10 to a £1 stake. Pool: £2,556.50. 15.00 winning tickets. JN

6604 SOUTHWELL (L-H)
Tuesday, December 20

OFFICIAL GOING: Standard
Wind: Light, half-behind Weather: Overcast

6632 BETDIRECT FREEPHONE 0800 211 222 H'CAP (DIV I) 7f (F)
12:20 (12:20) (Class 5) (0-70,70) 3-Y-O+ **£3,717** (£1,106; £552; £276) **Stalls** Low

Form RPR

4001 **1** **Paso Doble**[21] 6464 7-8-4 **63** JamesMillman(7) 2 73
(B R Millman) *hld up: hdwy over 1f out: r.o to ld nr fin* **5/1**[3]

4060 **2** *shd* **Certain Justice (USA)**[45] 6248 7-9-4 **70** MickyFenton 6 79
(Stef Liddiard) *a.p: rdn to ld ins fnl f: hdd nr fin* **4/1**[2]

6050 **3** *2* **Second Reef**[62] 5981 3-8-10 **62** PaulQuinn 7 66
(E J Alston) *sn led: rdn over 1f out: edgd rt and hdd ins fnl f: styd on same pce* **16/1**

0000 **4** 1 ¾ **Contented (IRE)**[14] 6513 3-8-11 **63** RobertWinston 9 63
(Mrs L C Jewell) *hld up: hdwy over 1f out: hung lft and no ex ins fnl f* **20/1**

0212 **5** *hd* **Parkview Love (USA)**[10] 6535 4-9-0 **69** (v) PatrickMathers(3) 8 69
(D Shaw) *trckd ldrs: hmpd over 4f out: sn rdn: styd on* **11/4**[1]

5500 **6** *2* **Merdiff**[18] 6483 6-8-13 **65** FergalLynch 1 60
(W M Brisbourne) *chsd ldrs: rdn over 2f out: wknd fnl f* **33/1**

0000 **7** ½ **Windy Prospect**[5] 6586 3-9-0 **66** AlanDaly 11 59
(C R Dore) *bhd: rdn over 2f out: styd on ins fnl f: nrst fin* **22/1**

2440 **8** *2* **Hand Chime**[14] 6514 8-8-10 **62** NCallan 3 50
(Ernst Oertel) *chsd ldrs: rdn over 2f out: wknd fnl f* **20/1**

0402 **9** ¾ **Majik**[46] 6243 6-8-9 **68** (p) LiamJones(7) 5 54
(D J S Ffrench Davis) *s.s: hld up: effrt over 2f out: n.d* **10/1**

3600 **10** *6* **Marshallspark (IRE)**[72] 5774 6-8-5 **57** (v[1]) PaulHanagan 10 28
(R A Fahey) *plld hrd and prom: rdn over 2f out: sn edgd lft and wknd* **10/1**

00 **11** *5* **Orenay (USA)**[15] 6499 3-8-8 **65** (v[1]) DerekNolan(5) 4 24
(M J Wallace) *s.i.s: hld up: hdwy 1/2-way: wknd wl over 1f out* **50/1**

0005 **12** *10* **Count Cougar (USA)**[14] 6514 5-8-7 **59** DaleGibson 12 —
(S P Griffiths) *prom: rdn over 2f out: sn wknd* **12/1**

1m 31.84s (1.04) **Going Correction** +0.125s/f (Slow) 12 Ran SP% **113.9**
Speed ratings (Par 103):99,98,96,94,94 92,91,89,88,81 75,64
CSF £22.26 CT £300.18 TOTE £5.40: £1.30, £2.00, £4.40; EX 35.50.
Owner B R Millman **Bred** P Cutler **Trained** Kentisbeare, Devon

FOCUS
A modest handicap producing a good finish with the third and fourth setting the standard. The winning time was 1.64 seconds slower than the second division and fairly modest for the grade.
Count Cougar(USA) Official explanation: vet said gelding finished lame

6633 BETDIRECT ON AT THE RACES INTERACTIVE CLAIMING STKS 1m 3f (F)
12:50 (12:50) (Class 6) 3-Y-O+ **£2,900** (£856; £428) **Stalls** Low

Form RPR

6014 **1** **Kylkenny**[14] 6520 10-9-0 74 (t) TravisBlock(5) 7 84+
(H Morrison) *a.p: chsd ldr 3f out: led on bit over 1f out: shkn up and r.o: eased nr fin* **3/1**[2]

0352 **2** *1* **Danelor (IRE)**[14] 6520 7-9-4 77 (p) PaulHanagan 6 81
(R A Fahey) *sn led: rdn over 2f out: hdd over 1f out: styd on same pce* **7/4**[1]

0103 **3** *6* **Daring Affair**[21] 6463 4-9-1 67 RobertWinston 5 68
(K R Burke) *prom: chsd ldr 8f out tl rdn 3f out: wknd over 1f out* **13/2**[3]

5400 **4** 1 ½ **Padre Nostro (IRE)**[8] 6560 6-9-0 55 BrianReilly 8 65
(J R Holt) *hld up: hdwy over 5f out: rdn over 2f out: sn hung lft and wknd* **66/1**

2210 **5** *hd* **Mi Odds**[8] 6564 9-9-2 70 AlanDaly 4 67
(Mrs N Macauley) *chsd ldrs: rdn over 4f out: wknd over 2f out* **13/2**[3]

4102 **6** *10* **Romil Star (GER)**[10] 6540 8-8-7 65 (v) PatrickDonaghy(7) 1 49
(K R Burke) *sn bhd: racd wd down far side: n.d* **12/1**

0000 **7** *5* **Salute (IRE)**[18] 6482 6-9-7 82 RobertHavlin 2 48
(P G Murphy) *chsd ldrs to 1/2-way* **8/1**

6603 **8** *dist* **Stolen Song**[29] 6406 5-9-0 57 (e) NCallan 3 —
(J Ryan) *sn outpcd* **22/1**

2m 27.65s (-1.25) **Going Correction** +0.125s/f (Slow) 8 Ran SP% **112.7**
Speed ratings (Par 101):109,108,103,102,102 95,91,—
CSF £8.36 TOTE £4.30: £1.80, £1.10, £1.60; EX 8.40.
Owner W R B Racing 59 (wrbracing.com) **Bred** R M , P J And S R Payne **Trained** East Ilsley, Berks

FOCUS
A fair race of its type featuring a number of regulars at the track and run in a very decent time for the class, but an easy win for the most prolific. The form is rated through winner and fourth to this year's marks.
Romil Star(GER) Official explanation: jockey said, regarding the running and riding, his orders were to jump out and ride gelding positively, adding that gelding stumbled slightly at start, was unable to hold a prominent position and resented the kickback; trainer added that gelding would probably be better suited by further
Stolen Song Official explanation: jockey said gelding was never travelling

6634 TEXT "BETDIRECT" TO 88600 NURSERY — 7f (F)

1:20 (1:20) (Class 5) (0-75,72) 2-Y-O — **£4,090** (£1,216; £608; £303) **Stalls** Low

Form — RPR

0623 **1** **Mambo Sun**^{10} [6539] 2-8-12 **63**....(p) FergalLynch 10 — 68
(P A Blockley) *chsd ldrs: rdn to ld over 1f out: hung lft: r.o* **3/1**^{2}

0010 **2** 1 ¾ **Glenbuck (IRE)**^{46} [6244] 2-9-0 **72**....(v) MichaelJStainton$^{(7)}$ 7 — 73
(A Bailey) *w ldr tl hung rt and led 1/2-way: sn rdn: hdd over 1f out: styng on same pce whn hmpd ins fnl f* **11/1**

01 **3** 1 ¼ **Solicitude**^{35} [6360] 2-9-5 **70**.... RobertHavlin 6 — 69+
(D Haydn Jones) *chsd ldrs: rdn over 1f out: styng on same pce whn nt clr run ins fnl f* **5/1**^{3}

0442 **4** 1 ¼ **Song Of Silence (USA)**^{10} [6539] 2-8-13 **64**.... PaulHanagan 4 — 58
(E A L Dunlop) *prom: rdn and hung lft 2f out: styd on same pce fnl f* **5/2**^{1}

2100 **5** 5 **Dream Mountain**^{21} [6457] 2-9-3 **68**.... RobertWinston 8 — 50
(M Johnston) *sn drvn along in rr: hdwy 4f out: outpcd 3f out: n.d after* **5/1**^{3}

0000 **6** 5 **Dylan (IRE)**^{106} [4996] 2-8-2 **53**.... KimTinkler 9 — 22
(N Tinkler) *mid-div: sn pushed along: wknd 3f out* **40/1**

5600 **7** shd **Ridgeway Cross (IRE)**^{35} [6357] 2-8-4 **55**.... AlanDaly 1 — 24
(Ernst Oertel) *s.s: outpcd* **33/1**

0100 **8** 1 **Astorygoeswithit**^{21} [6457] 2-8-13 **67**....(p) AdamKirby$^{(3)}$ 5 — 34
(Julian Poulton) *mid-div: lost pl over 4f out: sn bhd* **25/1**

3060 **9** 1 **Manouche**^{35} [6352] 2-9-0 **65**....(p) NCallan 3 — 29
(K A Ryan) *led to 1/2-way: wknd over 2f out* **14/1**

4150 **10** 2 ½ **Angelina Bankes**^{10} [6543] 2-7-12 **56**.... TolleyDean$^{(7)}$ 2 — 14
(R A Harris) *sn outpcd* **25/1**

1m 32.93s (2.13) **Going Correction** +0.125s/f (Slow) — **10** Ran SP% **115.0**
Speed ratings (Par 96):92,90,88,87,81 75,75,74,73,70
CSF £33.37 CT £159.96 TOTE £4.50: £1.90, £3.30, £1.90; EX 55.80.
Owner Market Avenue Racing Club Ltd **Bred** Michael John Williamson **Trained** Lambourn, Berks

FOCUS
A modest nursery run in an ordinary time for the grade and the form does not look solid.

NOTEBOOK
Mambo Sun, who has run well of late in similar events at the track, was dropped a furlong in trip and that seemed to do the trick, although he did drift across the placed horses after hitting the front. Cheekpieces, and before that blinkers, have definitely helped him and there may be more to come now he has got his head in front. (op 7-2)
Glenbuck(IRE), giving weight away all round, not counting his rider's allowance, on this All-Weather debut, handled the surface well enough. He was done no favours by the drifting winner in the closing stages, but was already held and the result was not affected. He is a soft-ground winner on turf, and this testing surface seems to play to his strengths. (op 12-1 tchd 10-1)
Solicitude, a surprise winner of her maiden over course and distance last month, raced just off the pace and had every chance, but was held in the last furlong. This looks as good as she is and she probably needs to be eased a few pounds in the handicap. (op 4-1 tchd 11-2)
Song Of Silence(USA), who had today's winner behind when second in a similar race here earlier in the month, was 5lb worse off but ran below that form, hanging early in the straight. (op 3-1)
Dream Mountain, a winner on fast ground earlier in the year, was being ridden along at an early stage on this Fibresand debut and may be better off back on Polytrack. (op 7-1)
Manouche Official explanation: jockey said gelding hung right-handed

6635 BETDIRECT.CO.UK (S) STKS — 7f (F)

1:50 (1:51) (Class 6) 2-Y-O — **£2,518** (£743; £371) **Stalls** Low

Form — RPR

6020 **1** **Tour D'Amour (IRE)**^{21} [6466] 2-8-11 61.... MickyFenton 13 — 64
(Stef Liddiard) *chsd ldrs: led 2f out: drvn out* **9/1**

0014 **2** 3 ½ **Woodwee**^{21} [6466] 2-9-2 61.... RobertWinston 2 — 60
(J R Weymes) *hld up: hdwy over 2f out: sn rdn: edgd lft over 1f out: styd on same pce* **5/1**^{3}

3463 **3** shd **Mistatake (IRE)**^{8} [6562] 2-8-11 63....(b^{1}) NCallan 8 — 55
(K A Ryan) *chsd ldrs: rdn over 2f out: no ex fnl f* **5/2**^{1}

0042 **4** 8 **Bathwick Rox (IRE)**^{31} [6375] 2-8-5 59 ow1....(v) JamesMillman$^{(7)}$ 14 — 36
(B R Millman) *chsd ldrs: rdn over 2f out: sn wknd* **9/2**^{2}

060 **5** hd **Smile For Us**^{148} [3807] 2-8-11 58.... BrianReilly 3 — 35
(C Drew) *chsd ldrs: rdn over 2f out: sn wknd* **20/1**

2440 **6** 1 ¼ **Noble Edge**^{29} [6403] 2-8-11 50....(p) FergalLynch 7 — 31
(P A Blockley) *s.i.s: hld up: hdwy 1/2-way: rdn and wknd 2f out* **12/1**

0100 **7** shd **Danse Du Flambe**^{31} [6386] 2-8-8 50....(v^{1}) AdamKirby$^{(3)}$ 10 — 31
(D J S Ffrench Davis) *mid-div: rdn 4f out: wknd 3f out* **16/1**

0406 **8** 5 **Nico's Girl**^{10} [6543] 2-8-6 50.... DaleGibson 1 — 14
(M W Easterby) *led over 4f: wknd over 1f out* **14/1**

6300 **9** ¾ **First Byte**^{10} [6543] 2-8-4 50....(v^{1}) StephanieBancroft$^{(7)}$ 9 — 17
(Miss D A McHale) *hld up: hdwy 1/2-way: wknd over 2f out* **50/1**

00 **10** 8 **The Great Delaney**^{81} [5583] 2-8-11....(p) IanMongan 4 — —
(Miss D A McHale) *s.i.s: outpcd* **25/1**

0 **11** 3 ½ **Bahhmirage (IRE)**^{15} [6502] 2-8-6.... FrancisFerris 5 — —
(C N Kellett) *hmpd s: outpcd* **40/1**

00 **12** 2 ½ **Ten For Fun (FR)**^{10} [6543] 2-8-11....(b) DeanMcKeown 12 — —
(M J Polglase) *chsd ldrs over 4f* **66/1**

1m 32.06s (1.26) **Going Correction** +0.125s/f (Slow) — **12** Ran SP% **108.2**
Speed ratings (Par 94):97,93,92,83,83 82,81,76,75,66 62,59
CSF £41.84 TOTE £7.40: £2.70, £2.10, £1.50; EX 33.50.The winner was sold to Ray Craggs for 6,200gns. Mistatake was claimed by A. Haynes for £6,000.
Owner Christopher Shankland **Bred** Peter McCutcheon **Trained** Great Shefford, Berks

FOCUS
Moderate fare but the winner did it in good style and the first two set the standard.

NOTEBOOK
Tour D'Amour(IRE), returning to seven furlongs, came clear in the straight. Her previous run might have come a bit quick but she showed her true form here. Whether she can handle a step up into handicap company remains to be seen, though. (op 11-2)
Woodwee did not run badly from his low draw. He did not get home over seven furlongs on his only previous try at the distance at Musselburgh in October, but he got it well enough this time. (op 6-1)
Mistatake(IRE), wearing blinkers instead of cheekpieces this time, looked to be a big threat turning into the straight but failed to go through with his effort. He might not be one to trust. (op 3-1 tchd 9-4)
Bathwick Rox(IRE), dropping back from a mile on his first outing on Fibresand, had his chance turning in but hung right in the straight. (op 6-1)
Smile For Us, missing the headgear and dropping into a seller for the first time, did not fare too badly given that he raced on the slower ground next to the inside rail.
Noble Edge has yet to convince that he stays this trip. (op 11-1)

6636 LITTLEWOODS BETDIRECT H'CAP — 5f (F)

2:20 (2:21) (Class 4) (0-85,85) 3-Y-0+ — **£6,758** (£2,010; £1,004; £501) **Stalls** High

Form — RPR

0301 **1** **Ok Pal**^{17} [6489] 5-9-4 **85**.... IanMongan 12 — 97
(T G Mills) *outpcd: hdwy 1/2-way: rdn to ld ins fnl f: r.o wl* **9/2**^{1}

6004 **2** 2 ½ **Anfield Dream**^{21} [6465] 3-8-7 **74** ow1.... RobertWinston 6 — 77
(J R Jenkins) *disp ld tl led over 1f out: hdd and unable qckn ins fnl f* **6/1**^{3}

0-00 **3** 1 **Efistorm**^{17} [6489] 4-8-7 **74**.... GrahamGibbons 2 — 74
(J Balding) *disp ld over 3f: no ex ins fnl f* **20/1**

5204 **4** 1 ½ **Pawan (IRE)**^{14} [6518] 5-8-6 **80**.... AnnStokell$^{(7)}$ 7 — 75
(Miss A Stokell) *s.i.s: outpcd: r.o ins fnl f: nrst fin* **8/1**

4006 **5** hd **Fizzlephut (IRE)**^{109} [4915] 3-8-11 **81** ow2.... DNolan$^{(3)}$ 3 — 75
(Miss J R Tooth) *hmpd s: sn chsng ldrs: rdn over 1f out: styd on same pce* **33/1**

1605 **6** ½ **Tartatartufata**^{127} [4427] 3-8-9 **79**....(v) PatrickMathers$^{(3)}$ 13 — 71
(D Shaw) *trckd ldrs: rdn and wknd ins fnl f* **14/1**

2660 **7** nk **Bonne De Fleur**^{100} [5146] 4-9-1 **82**.... DerekMcGaffin 5 — 73
(B Smart) *outpcd: sme hdwy over 1f out: n.d* **25/1**

0140 **8** 1 ½ **Jilly Why (IRE)**^{18} [6483] 4-7-11 **71** oh9.... LiamJones$^{(7)}$ 10 — 57
(Ms Deborah J Evans) *outpcd: nvr nrr* **40/1**

0040 **9** 1 ¾ **Little Ridge (IRE)**^{17} [6489] 4-8-7 **74**.... MickyFenton 4 — 54
(H Morrison) *wnt lft s: chsd ldrs over 3f* **9/2**^{1}

0020 **10** ½ **Alpaga Le Jomage (IRE)**^{3} [6603] 3-8-1 **71** oh9.... NelsonDeSouza$^{(3)}$ 9 — 49
(M J Polglase) *chsd ldrs to 1/2-way* **25/1**

0065 **11** 1 **Ashes (IRE)**^{1} [6616] 3-8-4 **71** oh6.... PaulHanagan 8 — 46
(K R Burke) *chsd ldrs to 1/2-way* **25/1**

0010 **12** hd **Maktavish**^{17} [6489] 6-8-9 **76**....(p) TomEaves 11 — 50
(I Semple) *disp ld 3f: sn wknd* **17/2**

0101 **13** 1 ¾ **Lake Chini (IRE)**^{24} [6426] 3-8-9 **76** ow1....(p) NCallan 1 — 44
(M A Jarvis) *chsd ldrs: sn drvn along: wknd over 1f out* **5/1**^{2}

59.55 secs (-0.75) **Going Correction** -0.025s/f (Stan) — **13** Ran SP% **117.3**
Speed ratings (Par 105):105,101,99,97,96 95,95,93,90,89 87,87,84
CSF £27.60 CT £509.33 TOTE £3.80: £1.60, £2.60, £9.20; EX 39.10.
Owner Sherwoods Transport Ltd **Bred** Sherwoods Transport Ltd **Trained** Headley, Surrey

FOCUS
A fair handicap run at a decent pace, and a reversal of a recent trend for those drawn low to dominate over this trip. The form does not look as strong as it could have been.
Pawan(IRE) Official explanation: jockey said gelding was slow away
Ashes(IRE) Official explanation: trainer said filly was unsuited by the fibresand surface

6637 PRESS RED TO BET ON ITVI H'CAP — 2m (F)

2:50 (2:50) (Class 5) (0-75,70) 3-Y-0+ — **£3,947** (£1,174; £586; £293) **Stalls** Low

Form — RPR

0156 **1** **Spitting Image (IRE)**^{11} [6534] 5-9-1 **60**.... RobertWinston 3 — 71
(M Johnston) *hld up in tch: rdn over 4f out: led wl ins fnl f: styd on strly* **7/1**

0016 **2** 3 **Tedstale (USA)**^{18} [6478] 7-9-11 **70**....(b) NCallan 2 — 77
(K A Ryan) *hld up: hdwy over 4f out: rdn to ld over 1f out: edgd lft: hdd wl ins fnl f* **6/1**

0042 **3** 1 **Bank On Benny**^{17} [6490] 3-8-5 **58**.... PaulHanagan 7 — 64
(P W D'Arcy) *hld up: hdwy 8f 1/2-way: led over 4f out: rdn and hdd over 1f out : styd on same pce* **5/2**^{1}

3604 **4** 1 ¾ **Woodford Consult**^{15} [5959] 3-8-2 **55**.... DaleGibson 4 — 59
(M W Easterby) *chsd ldrs: led over 5f out: hdd over 4f out: rdn over 2f out: no ex fnl f* **8/1**

0B05 **5** 2 **Come What July (IRE)**^{10} [6536] 4-9-11 **70**....(v) AlanDaly 6 — 72
(Mrs N Macauley) *hld up: rdn and hung lft over 2f out: n.d* **25/1**

2623 **6** nk **He's A Star**^{10} [6540] 3-8-0 **56** ow1....(b^{1}) NelsonDeSouza$^{(3)}$ 1 — 57
(Miss Gay Kelleway) *plld hrd: led 14f out: hdd over 10f out: lost pl over 5f out: son rdn: hung lft over 2f out: sn wknd* **9/2**^{2}

3020 **7** 11 **Saffron Fox**^{21} [6461] 4-8-11 **59**.... AdamKirby$^{(3)}$ 5 — 47
(J G Portman) *led 2f: led over 10f out: hdd over 5f out: rdn and wknd over 2f out* **11/1**

0516 **8** 5 **Sun Hill**^{14} [6519] 5-9-7 **66**.... DavidAllan 9 — 48
(C W Fairhurst) *hld up: hdwy over 5f out: rdn and wknd over 2f out* **11/2**^{3}

3m 48.21s (3.67) **Going Correction** +0.125s/f (Slow)
WFA 3 from 4yo+ 8lb — **8** Ran SP% **112.2**
Speed ratings (Par 103):95,93,93,92,91 90,85,82
CSF £46.39 CT £132.54 TOTE £6.90: £1.80, £2.50, £1.90; EX 35.00.
Owner J Shack **Bred** Denis McDonnell **Trained** Middleham Moor, N Yorks

FOCUS
They did not go a great pace early on and the result was a moderate winning time for a race of its class. The form is best rated through the third.

6638 BETDIRECT FREEPHONE 0800 211 222 H'CAP (DIV II) — 7f (F)

3:20 (3:22) (Class 5) (0-70,69) 3-Y-0+ — **£3,708** (£1,103; £551; £275) **Stalls** Low

Form — RPR

6506 **1** **Local Poet**^{52} [6140] 4-9-0 **65**....(bt^{1}) TomEaves 9 — 81
(I Semple) *chsd ldrs: rdn to ld over 1f out: edgd lft ins fnl f : r.o* **7/1**

5506 **2** ¾ **Speed Dial Harry (IRE)**^{39} [6310] 3-8-10 **61**....(v) NCallan 3 — 75
(K R Burke) *a.p: rdn to chse wnr over 1f out: edgd rt ins fnl f: r.o* **28/1**

0462 **3** 3 **Wainwright (IRE)**^{18} [6483] 5-9-1 **66**.... FergalLynch 4 — 73
(P A Blockley) *hld up: hdwy u.p over 1f out: nt rch ldrs* **9/2**^{2}

0400 **4** hd **Resplendent Prince**^{15} [6499] 3-9-1 **66**.... IanMongan 5 — 72
(T G Mills) *chsd ldr: led 3f out: rdn and hdd over 1f out: no ex fnl f* **10/1**

0213 **5** 3 **Look Of Eagles**^{14} [6514] 3-9-0 **68**.... NelsonDeSouza$^{(3)}$ 1 — 67
(P F I Cole) *mid-div: sn drvn along: lost pl 4f out: rdn over 2f out: no imp appr fnl f* **15/8**^{1}

0000 **6** 1 ¼ **Green Pirate**^{10} [6546] 3-8-11 **62**.... RobertWinston 7 — 58
(R Craggs) *sn led: hdd 3f out: wknd fnl f* **16/1**

2600 **7** ¾ **Mister Benji**^{229} [1477] 6-8-7 **58**.... DeanMcKeown 2 — 52
(B P J Baugh) *s.i.s: hld up: hdwy 3f out: sn rdn and wknd* **40/1**

1243 **8** 5 **Cool Sands (IRE)**^{14} [6513] 3-8-9 **63**.... PatrickMathers$^{(3)}$ 12 — 44
(D Shaw) *hld up: edgd lft over 4f out: hdwy over 2f out: sn rdn and wknd* **11/2**^{3}

6050 **9** 14 **No Grouse**^{18} [6483] 5-8-13 **64**.... GrahamGibbons 11 — 10
(E J Alston) *hld up: hmpd over 1f out: n.d* **14/1**

0000 **10** 29 **Karashino (IRE)**^{29} [6404] 3-8-6 **57**....(p) PaulHanagan 8 — —
(R A Fahey) *chsd ldrs: rdn 1/2-way: sn wknd* **33/1**

0506 **F** **Khe Sanh**^{31} [6376] 3-8-11 **69**.... TolleyDean$^{(7)}$ 6 — —
(R A Harris) *hld up: clipped heels and fell over 4f out* **25/1**

4056 **P** **Samuel Charles**^{14} [6514] 7-8-11 **62**.... MickyFenton 10 — —
(C R Dore) *s.i.s: bhd whn hmpd over 4f out: sn p.u* **14/1**

1m 30.2s (-0.60) **Going Correction** +0.125s/f (Slow) **31** Ran SP% **121.8**
Speed ratings (Par 103):108,107,103,103,100 98,97,92,76,42 —,—
CSF £197.06 CT £1000.83 TOTE £6.20: £2.50, £6.70, £1.90; EX 264.30 Place 6 £39.13, Place 5 £12.42.
Owner newkeylets **Bred** Richard Brunger **Trained** Carluke, S Lanarks

FOCUS
A modest handicap but run in a decent winning time for the grade, 1.64 seconds quicker than the first division, and the form looks above average.
T/Plt: £46.50 to a £1 stake. Pool: £33,358.95. 522.90 winning tickets. T/Qpdt: £11.70 to a £1 stake. Pool: £2,205.90. 138.80 winning tickets. CR

6624 LINGFIELD (L-H)
Wednesday, December 21

OFFICIAL GOING: Standard
Wind: Light, behind Weather: Cloudy

6639 TEXT "BETDIRECT" TO 88600 H'CAP (DIV I) 6f (P)
12:00 (12:01) (Class 6) (0-55,55) 3-Y-0+ **£2,158** (£637; £318) **Stalls** Low

Form				RPR
0431	**1**		**Hollow Jo**[14] [6525] 5-8-9 **50** ... MickyFenton 7 (J R Jenkins) *lw: in tch: effrt 2f out: led 1f out: drvn out* **6/1**[2]	61
0055	**2**	1	**Blue Maeve**[15] [6516] 5-8-11 **52** ... DaneO'Neill 12 (A D Brown) *pressed ldr: led briefly over 1f out: kpt on same pce fnl f* **20/1**	60
6126	**3**	½	**Cayman Breeze**[14] [6525] 5-8-11 **52** ... JamieSpencer 8 (J M Bradley) *lw: towards rr tl r.o wl u.p fnl f: gng on at fin* **5/1**[1]	59
6200	**4**	½	**Taboor (IRE)**[68] [5869] 7-8-13 **54** ... EddieAhern 10 (R M H Cowell) *s.s: bhd tl gd hdwy on ins rail over 1f out: kpt on: no imp fnl 100 yds* **11/1**	59
3111	**5**	hd	**Orchestration (IRE)**[17] [6493] 4-9-0 **55** ...(v) ChrisCatlin 2 (M J Attwater) *broke wl: chsd ldrs: rdn over 2f out: styd on same pce* **6/1**[2]	59
1003	**6**	1 ¼	**Zazous**[7] [6579] 4-8-9 **50** ... SteveDrowne 4 (J J Bridger) *in rr: outpcd 1/2-way: styd on wl fnl f: nvr nrr* **8/1**	51
5034	**7**	1	**Limonia (GER)**[15] [6516] 3-8-12 **53** ... JohnEgan 1 (D K Ivory) *dwlt: sn prom: no ex fnl f* **9/1**	51
5630	**8**	1	**Kitchen Sink (IRE)**[52] [6177] 3-8-10 **54** ...(b) AmirQuinn(3) 11 (P J Makin) *sn led: hdd & wknd over 1f out* **16/1**	49
1406	**9**	½	**Mulberry Lad (IRE)**[15] [6516] 3-8-11 **52** ... HayleyTurner 5 (P W Hiatt) *chsd ldrs tl wknd over 1f out* **14/1**	45
6444	**10**	1 ½	**Auentraum (GER)**[7] [6576] 5-8-7 **48** ...(b) PaulDoe 6 (K McAuliffe) *mid-div: effrt on outside 3f out: wd st: sn wknd* **13/2**[3]	37
0555	**11**	2 ½	**Nova Tor (IRE)**[23] [6447] 3-8-7 **55** ... RonanKeogh(7) 3 (Peter Grayson) *mid-div tl wknd over 2f out* **8/1**	36

1m 11.86s (-0.95) **Going Correction** -0.10s/f (Stan) **11** Ran SP% **116.4**
Speed ratings (Par 101):102,100,100,99,99 97,96,94,94,92 88
CSF £117.23 CT £645.52 TOTE £6.10: £2.50, £8.10, £2.00; EX 148.50.
Owner Jim McCarthy **Bred** K J Reddington **Trained** Royston, Herts
■ Stewards' Enquiry : Jamie Spencer one-day ban: used whip with whip arm above shoulder height (Jan 1)

FOCUS
A moderate handicap with only a modest gallop until halfway - hence it was hard to come from too far behind. The form looks sound with the third the best guide to the level.
Taboor(IRE) Official explanation: jockey said gelding reared leaving stalls and was hampered on first bend

6640 BETDIRECT FREEPHONE 0800 211 222 MAIDEN FILLIES' STKS (DIV I) 7f (P)
12:30 (12:30) (Class 5) 2-Y-0 **£3,727** (£1,108; £554; £276) **Stalls** Low

Form				RPR
03	**1**		**Veronica's Girl**[39] [6318] 2-8-11 ... DaneO'Neill 1 (P R Hedger) *t.k.h: prom: drvn to ld over 1f out: jst hld on* **4/1**[2]	60
4003	**2**	hd	**Korikancha (IRE)**[57] [6102] 2-8-11 68 ... JamieSpencer 7 (J Noseda) *lw: hld up in tch: n.m.r and swvd rt bnd after 2f: effrt 2f out: styd on wl fnl f: jst failed* **6/4**[1]	59
235	**3**	1 ¾	**Precautionary**[117] [4732] 2-8-11 69 ... BrianReilly 3 (Miss J Feilden) *leggy: wnt rt s: t.k.h: chsd ldrs: wd st: styd on same pce* **4/1**[2]	54
0	**4**	¾	**Attitude Annie**[170] [3192] 2-8-11 ... PaulDoe 2 (S Dow) *w'like: bit bkwd: dwlt: hld up in rr: hrd rdn and hdwy on ins over 1f out: one pce fnl f* **50/1**	53
6034	**5**	1 ¼	**In Hope**[121] [4644] 2-8-11 52 ... J-PGuillambert 9 (Andrew Reid) *led tl over 1f out: wknd fnl f* **16/1**	49
00	**6**	nk	**Valhar**[22] [6456] 2-8-11 ... MickyFenton 8 (J R Jenkins) *wnt lft s: plld hrd early: sn chsng ldr: wknd fnl f* **40/1**	48
	7	2	**Compton Express** 2-8-11 ... JohnEgan 6 (Jamie Poulton) *unf: scope: bit bkwd: dwlt: t.k.h in rr: hmpd bnd after 2f: pushed along and nt rch ldrs fnl 2f* **16/1**	43
0	**8**	4	**Cape Gigi (IRE)**[163] [3402] 2-8-11 ... ChrisCatlin 4 (B J Meehan) *leggy: unf: dwlt: sn pushed along and bhd: hrd rdn 2f out: nvr trbld ldrs* **14/1**	33
00	**9**	3	**Red Vixen (IRE)**[12] [6532] 2-8-11 ... OscarUrbina 5 (C N Allen) *towards rr: hmpd bnd after 2f: n.d after* **10/1**[3]	25
00	**10**	½	**Southgate Lady (IRE)**[82] [5581] 2-8-11 ...(t) HayleyTurner 10 (N P Littmoden) *t.k.h: in tch tl rdn and wknd 3f out* **40/1**	24

1m 26.15s (0.26) **Going Correction** -0.10s/f (Stan) **10** Ran SP% **114.4**
Speed ratings (Par 93):94,93,91,90,89 89,86,82,78,78
CSF £10.02 TOTE £4.40: £1.30, £1.10, £1.80; EX 11.00.
Owner J J Whelan **Bred** J J Whelan **Trained** Nyton, W Sussex
■ Stewards' Enquiry : J-P Guillambert one-day ban: careless riding (Jan 1)

FOCUS
Likely to prove a moderate maiden, run at a steady early pace, causing a number of the runners to pull hard for the first three furlongs. The winning time was 1.14 seconds slower than the second division and the proximity of the fifth anchors the form.

NOTEBOOK
Veronica's Girl was edgy and on her toes in the paddock and was still too keen early on, but the pedestrian early pace was partly to blame for that. Though only just holding on, she battled well and has the option of returning to a mile if required. (op 3-1)
Korikancha(IRE) lost ground when nearly caught on heels on the first turn, and that may have made all the difference. Still very unfurnished, she is - in theory - good enough to win a routine maiden, but her head carriage is not ideal. (op 11-8 tchd 7-4)
Precautionary, sold for 10,000 guineas in October, had not run since, and would be one to consider in a similarly modest maiden. However, the form is nothing special. (op 6-1)
Attitude Annie stepped up on her solitary turf effort in July, and ran well enough to give connections some hope of success at a minor level. (op 33-1)
In Hope set a weak early pace, and was done for speed by less-exposed rivals in the home straight.
Valhar was too headstrong in the face of a poor early tempo, but ran with some credit until finally capitulating a furlong from home. This was a bit more promising than her previous two efforts. (op 50-1)
Compton Express was too keen early, but shaped well enough on this debut. (op 25-1)
Red Vixen(IRE) Official explanation: jockey said filly was hampered shortly after start

6641 BETDIRECT FREEPHONE 0800 211 222 MAIDEN FILLIES' STKS (DIV II) 7f (P)
1:00 (1:00) (Class 5) 2-Y-0 **£3,717** (£1,106; £552; £276) **Stalls** Low

Form				RPR
6223	**1**		**Annabelle Ja (FR)**[22] [6457] 2-8-11 85 ... JohnEgan 7 (D R C Elsworth) *lw: mde all: edgd rt fnl f: rdn out* **1/2**[1]	79
5	**2**	1 ½	**Starship (IRE)**[39] [6318] 2-8-11 ... JamieSpencer 1 (W J Haggas) *chsd ldrs: wnt 2nd over 2f out: nt qckn fnl f* **9/2**[2]	75
	3	1 ¼	**Miss Highjinks (USA)**[51] [6204] 2-8-11 ... EddieAhern 2 (E J O'Neill) *w'like: t.k.h: in tch: hmpd bnd after 2f: rallied on ins 2f out: one pce fnl f* **11/1**[3]	72
	4	9	**Nikki Bea (IRE)** 2-8-11 ... PaulDoe 4 (Jamie Poulton) *leggy: s.s: bhd: mod effrt and hung lft ent st: tk modest 4th fnl f* **66/1**	48
	5	1 ¼	**Shardia (IRE)** 2-8-11 ... ChrisCatlin 9 (J Jay) *w'like: bit bkwd: s.s: bhd: sme hdwy and wnt mod 4th ent st: no further prog* **50/1**	45
0	**6**	2	**Carefree Girl**[240] [1260] 2-8-11 ... StephenCarson 3 (E A Wheeler) *w'like: towards rr: rdn 3f out: n.d after* **100/1**	40
0	**7**	3 ½	**Devine Dancer**[12] [6528] 2-8-11 ... DaneO'Neill 5 (H Candy) *unf: b.hind: t.k.h: chsd ldrs: sltly hmpd bnd after 2f: wknd over 2f out* **20/1**	31
053	**8**	12	**Night Rainbow (IRE)**[12] [6528] 2-8-11 66 ... SteveDrowne 8 (A J Lidderdale) *pressed wnr over 5f: losing pl whn eased ent st* **20/1**	—

1m 25.01s (-0.88) **Going Correction** -0.10s/f (Stan) **33** Ran SP% **107.1**
Speed ratings (Par 93):101,99,97,87,86 83,79,66
CSF £2.20 TOTE £1.40: £1.10, £1.40, £1.90; EX 2.20.
Owner Mcdowell Racing **Bred** S C De Moubray Et Al **Trained** Newmarket, Suffolk

FOCUS
An above-average maiden for the track, with the first three acquitting themselves well and the winning time was 1.14 seconds faster than the first division.

NOTEBOOK
Annabelle Ja(FR) put up a spirited performance and looks a cut above the average around here. She is a decent-looking sort, and there is more to come. (op 4-9 tchd 8-15 in a place)
Starship(IRE) had come on for her first outing, and did well against a more experienced and above-average rival. She still looked a bit green, and is capable of winning a maiden if progressing. (op 7-2)
Miss Highjinks(USA) had to regain her momentum after being hampered on the far side, and acquitted herself well. Ex-Irish, and bought for 110,000 guineas earlier this year, she can win a maiden. (op 9-1)
Nikki Bea(IRE), a cheap purchase, was well beaten in an above-average maiden. She should improve for the experience but will probably operate in more routine company. (op 50-1 tchd 80-1)
Shardia(IRE) is bred to stay middle-distances, so this was a satisfactory if unspectacular debut.
Carefree Girl needs to improve to become competitive in any company. (op 66-1)
Night Rainbow(IRE) Official explanation: jockey said filly lost its action

6642 ROBERT LEECH MAIDEN STKS 7f (P)
1:30 (1:31) (Class 5) 2-Y-0 **£4,138** (£1,231; £615; £307) **Stalls** Low

Form				RPR
0	**1**		**Sigismundus (IRE)**[128] [4426] 2-8-8 ... AmirQuinn(3) 11 (J R Boyle) *leggy: w ldr: led over 2f out: drvn out* **33/1**	67
	2	½	**Chief Commander (FR)** 2-8-11 ... JohnEgan 6 (Jane Chapple-Hyam) *unf: chsd ldng pair: drvn to press wnr over 1f out: kpt on* **9/2**[1]	66
0	**3**	2	**Trimlestown (IRE)**[12] [6532] 2-8-11 ... DaneO'Neill 2 (H Candy) *unf: chsd ldrs: rdn over 2f out: kpt on fnl f* **9/2**[1]	61
00	**4**	2	**Premier Cru**[19] [6477] 2-8-11 ... ChrisCatlin 8 (Andrew Turnell) *w'like: broke wl: slt ld tl over 2f out: no ex over 1f out* **16/1**	55
	5	hd	**Boss Mak (IRE)** 2-8-11 ... MichaelTebbutt 10 (V Smith) *w'like: mid-div: rdn 3f out: styd on appr fnl f: nt rch ldrs* **20/1**	55
0	**6**	½	**Hand Of Destiny (USA)**[25] [6435] 2-8-11 ... TPQueally 1 (N P Littmoden) *w'like: towards rr: hmpd on rail bnd after 2f: styd on fnl 2f* **14/1**	53+
00	**7**	1 ¼	**Titus Lumpus (IRE)**[39] [6319] 2-8-8 ... RichardThomas(3) 3 (R M Flower) *hld up in midfield: n.m.r on rail over 4f out: shkn up and nt in chalng position fnl 2f* **9/1**[3]	50
0	**8**	nk	**Go Amwell**[12] [6531] 2-8-11 ... MickyFenton 4 (J R Jenkins) *w'like: cl cpld: in tch: outpcd over 2f out: sn btn* **66/1**	49
00	**9**	nk	**Great Composer (IRE)**[12] [6531] 2-8-11 ... EddieAhern 14 (Mrs A J Perrett) *chsd ldrs: drvn along over 3f out: sn outpcd* **11/2**[2]	49
	10	1	**Husam (IRE)** 2-8-11 ... LPKeniry 13 (P W Chapple-Hyam) *unf: s.i.s: sn rdn along and bhd: nvr rchd ldrs* **9/2**[1]	46
06	**11**	shd	**Ballyhooligan (IRE)**[9] [6561] 2-8-11 ... IanMongan 9 (Jamie Poulton) *settled in midfield: rdn and n.d fnl 3f* **20/1**	46
	12	nk	**Hits Only Life (USA)** 2-8-11 ... DeanMcKeown 7 (J Pearce) *w'like: bit bkwd: dwlt: outpcd and bhd: nvr trbld ldrs* **16/1**	45
	13	dist	**Kolibre** 2-8-11 ... SteveDrowne 12 (Mrs C A Dunnett) *w'like: str: bit bkwd: plld hrd towards rr on outside: nt handle bnd and nrly rn off trck over 4f out: t.o after* **20/1**	—

1m 25.6s (-0.29) **Going Correction** -0.10s/f (Stan) **30** Ran SP% **117.1**
Speed ratings (Par 96):97,96,94,91,91 91,89,89,88,87 87,87,—
CSF £164.71 TOTE £41.50: £7.10, £2.30, £2.10; EX 631.60.
Owner Inside Track Racing Club **Bred** Liam Queally **Trained** Epsom, Surrey

FOCUS
A fair maiden with some unexposed types, probably containing several future winners at a realistic level.

NOTEBOOK
Sigismundus(IRE) showed much more than on his only other race, which was on turf four months earlier. It helped to be up with the pace in this race, but there was no fluke about it.
Chief Commander(FR) made a good debut and looks set to find a similar event. Trips around seven furlongs and a mile look ideal. (op 4-1 tchd 5-1)
Trimlestown(IRE) is going the right way, and getting close to finding a similar race. This was much more encouraging than his debut at Wolverhampton. (op 11-2)
Premier Cru stepped up on his previous two efforts, with the shorter trip appearing to suit. (op 10-1)

Boss Mak(IRE), whose sire Shinko Forest was a high-class sprinter in Japan, shaped well on this debut, and is open to improvement. (op 16-1)
Hand Of Destiny(USA), a chunky colt, ran well, particularly considering the traffic problem early on. He should be even sharper in future, with handicaps an option after one more run. (op 12-1)
Titus Lumpus(IRE), who got warm beforehand, is now ready for handicaps, and is likely to be very much at home in them on this evidence. Official explanation: jockey said gelding hung left (op 10-1 tchd 15-2)
Husam(IRE), a debutant who is a full-brother to the decent miler Resplendent One, was struggling from the word go. Another run is needed to assess his prospects. (op 11-2 tchd 6-1)
Kolibre Official explanation: jockey said colt hung violently right-handed from the start

6643 POWER 2000 CLAIMING STKS — 1m 2f (P)
2:00 (2:00) (Class 6) 3-Y-O+ — **£2,893** (£854; £427) **Stalls** Low

Form — RPR
5650 **1** **Libre**[12] [6533] 5-9-4 74 ... EddieAhern 4 — 62
(F Jordan) *prom: hrd rdn over 1f out: r.o to ld nr fin* **14/1**
0022 **2** *nk* **Karaoke (IRE)**[4] [6596] 5-9-0 67 ... GeorgeBaker 7 — 58
(S Kirk) *hld up in tch: disp 2nd fr 3f out: hrd rdn over 1f out: kpt on: lame* **2/1**[1]
4602 **3** *hd* **Yawmi**[19] [6478] 5-9-8 69 ... DaneO'Neill 10 — 66
(R A Harris) *lw: led: wnt 5l clr 1/2-way: hrd rdn over 1f out: no ex fnl 100 yds: hdd nr fin* **6/1**[2]
4000 **4** *1 1/4* **Barton Sands (IRE)**[84] [5545] 8-8-13 66 ...(t) J-PGuillambert 1 — 54
(Andrew Reid) *mid-div: rdn and hdwy 3f out: styd on same pce fnl 2f* **8/1**[3]
0011 **5** *nk* **Night Warrior (IRE)**[3] [6606] 5-9-2 45 ...(b) JamieSpencer 11 — 57
(K McAuliffe) *hld up towards rr: stdy hdwy over 2f out: rdn to chse ldrs over 1f out: kpt on same pce* **8/1**[3]
3310 **6** *nk* **Treetops Hotel (IRE)**[62] [5998] 6-9-1 52 ... RoryMoore(5) 6 — 60
(B R Johnson) *hld up in rr: stdy hdwy 2f out: shkn up and r.o wl fnl f: clsng at fin* **22/1**
0306 **7** *6* **Kristinor (FR)**[18] [5506] 3-8-11 55 ...(be) IanMongan 14 — 43
(G L Moore) *plld hrd: in tch: rdn and btn 2f out* **14/1**
0030 **8** *1 1/2* **Dagola (IRE)**[186] [2699] 4-8-10 52 ... JohnEgan 8 — 36
(C A Dwyer) *lw: chsd ldrs: n.m.r 4f out: n.d after* **33/1**
540 **9** *1 1/2* **Temper Tantrum**[42] [6299] 7-8-8 53 ...(p) HayleyTurner 9 — 31
(J R Best) *hld up towards rr: effrt 3f out: n.d* **16/1**
0100 **10** *2* **Millkom Elegance**[243] [1183] 6-8-3 40 ...(v) ChrisCatlin 2 — 22
(G A Ham) *s.s: hld up towards rr: rdn and n.d fnl 3f* **66/1**
11 *16* **Rose Amber**[24] 4-8-4 ow1 ... StephenCarson 5 — —
(J J Bridger) *prom tl rdn and wknd over 4f out* **100/1**
0000 **12** *2 1/2* **Rasid (USA)**[39] [6324] 7-8-10 55 ...(v) TPQueally 12 — —
(C A Dwyer) *wd: mid-div tl wknd 4f out: no ch fnl 3f* **33/1**
2003 **R** **Keshya**[47] [6245] 4-8-13 67 ... MickyFenton 3 — —
(N P Littmoden) *ref to r: rrd and uns rdr in stalls* **6/1**[2]

2m 6.71s (-1.08) **Going Correction** -0.10s/f (Stan)
WFA 3 from 4yo+ 3lb — **13** Ran SP% **116.1**
Speed ratings (Par 101):100,99,99,98,98 98,93,92,90,89 76,74,—
CSF £39.57 TOTE £14.60: £3.90, £1.40, £2.60; EX 40.80.The winner was claimed by A. S. Reid for £10,000. Night Warrior was claimed by Nigel Shields for £9,000. Yawmi was claimed by Barry Leavy for £12,000. Karaoke was claimed by D. G. Bridgwater for £8,000.
Owner Brian Taylor **Bred** J C S Wilson Bloodstock **Trained** Adstone, Northants

FOCUS
Only a claimer, but not a bad one, with some fair former handicappers in the line-up. The sixth sets the standard but limits the form.
Karaoke(IRE) Official explanation: vet said gelding finished lame
Rasid(USA) Official explanation: jockey said gelding was never travelling

6644 BETDIRECT ON ATTHERACES INTERACTIVE H'CAP — 1m 4f (P)
2:30 (2:30) (Class 5) (0-75,75) 3-Y-O+ — **£3,504** (£1,042; £521; £260) **Stalls** Low

Form — RPR
4051 **1** **Captain Margaret**[39] [6323] 3-7-13 61 ... JimmyQuinn 6 — 69
(J Pearce) *lw: t.k.h: chsd ldrs: led over 1f out: drvn to hold on fnl f* **6/1**[2]
0446 **2** *nk* **True Companion**[25] [6437] 6-9-4 75 ... JamieSpencer 9 — 83
(N P Littmoden) *chsd ldrs: effrt 2f out: drvn to chse wnr ins fnl f: clsng at fin* **5/1**[1]
6002 **3** *3/4* **Countrywide Luck**[36] [6356] 4-8-13 70 ... HayleyTurner 1 — 76+
(N P Littmoden) *plld hrd in midfield: rdn and hdwy over 1f out: fin wl* **13/2**[3]
3/00 **4** *3/4* **Sphinx (FR)**[25] [6432] 7-8-10 67 ... JohnEgan 15 — 72
(Jamie Poulton) *b: t.k.h: prom: drvn to chse wnr 1f out: nt qckn* **25/1**
1540 **5** *nk* **Isa'Af (IRE)**[151] [3728] 6-8-8 65 ... ChrisCatlin 8 — 70
(P W Hiatt) *prom: chsd ldr after 3f tl 1f out: one pce* **25/1**
2365 **6** *1 1/4* **Zalkani (IRE)**[11] [6547] 5-9-0 71 ... SteveDrowne 11 — 74
(B G Powell) *hld up towards rr: hdwy on bit over 1f out: shkn up and r.o wl fnl f: gng on at fin* **7/1**
3000 **7** *shd* **Northside Lodge (IRE)**[25] [6437] 7-9-4 75 ...(t) DaneO'Neill 10 — 77
(W R Swinburn) *lw: sn led and set solid pce: hdd and hrd rdn 2f out: no ex over 1f out* **16/1**
0130 **8** *shd* **Summer Charm**[15] [6520] 3-8-1 70 ... BRoper(7) 14 — 72
(W Jarvis) *bhd: rdn and styd on wl fnl 2f: nvr nrr* **16/1**
0305 **9** *nk* **Dovedon Hero**[15] [6519] 5-8-13 70 ...(b) EddieAhern 2 — 72
(P J McBride) *dwlt: sn in midfield: rdn and no hdwy fnl 2f* **15/2**
/2-0 **10** *2 1/2* **Afadan (IRE)**[19] [6482] 7-9-4 75 ... MickyFenton 12 — 73
(J R Jenkins) *dwlt: hld up towards rr: effrt on ins 2f out: n.d* **40/1**
0000 **11** *nk* **Entailment**[12] [6534] 3-8-4 66 ow3 ... StephenCarson 7 — 63
(Miss Gay Kelleway) *dwlt: sn in midfield: effrt 3f out: wknd wl over 1f out* **25/1**
-000 **12** *1* **Lewis Island (IRE)**[12] [2816] 6-9-1 72 ... GeorgeBaker 5 — 68
(G L Moore) *lw: stdd s: hld up and bhd: plld outside and rdn 3f out: no rspnse* **6/1**[2]
3506 **13** *2 1/2* **Hawkit (USA)**[5] [6593] 4-8-2 64 ...(t) EmmettStack(5) 13 — 56
(P D Evans) *wd: hld up in rr: sme hdwy on outside 3f out: wknd 2f out* **16/1**
61 **14** *3* **Shakerattleandroll (IRE)**[88] [5468] 4-9-1 75 ... RichardThomas(3) 4 — 62
(Mrs L Richards) *in tch tl wknd 2f out* **20/1**
1100 **15** *1/2* **Wild Pitch**[112] [4873] 4-8-7 64 ...(b) TPQueally 3 — 50
(P Mitchell) *dwlt: sn in midfield: wknd over 2f out* **16/1**

2m 32.38s (-2.01) **Going Correction** -0.10s/f (Stan)
WFA 3 from 4yo+ 5lb — **15** Ran SP% **125.1**
Speed ratings (Par 103):102,101,101,100,100 99,99,99,99,97 97,96,95,93,92
CSF £34.69 CT £209.82 TOTE £6.00: £2.90, £2.50, £2.40; EX 49.30.
Owner Mrs Margaret Baxter **Bred** J Wilson **Trained** Newmarket, Suffolk

FOCUS
An ordinary handicap, with several of these still trying to recapture their best form. The form looks ordinary with the placed horses rated to recent form.

Zalkani(IRE) Official explanation: jockey said gelding was denied a clear run
Dovedon Hero Official explanation: jockey said gelding was denied a clear run
Lewis Island(IRE) Official explanation: jockey said gelding hung right

6645 BETDIRECT.CO.UK H'CAP — 1m 2f (P)
3:00 (3:00) (Class 4) (0-85,85) 3-Y-O+ — **£5,717** (£1,701; £850; £424) **Stalls** Low

Form — RPR
5604 **1** **Dower House**[19] [6482] 10-9-4 85 ... ChrisCatlin 3 — 92
(Andrew Turnell) *hld up in midfield: rdn and hdwy ent st: r.o u.str.p to ld fnl stride* **17/2**
0005 **2** *shd* **Sir Haydn**[9] [6566] 5-8-6 73 ...(v) EddieAhern 6 — 80
(J R Jenkins) *lw: t.k.h: trckd ldrs: drvn to ld 1f out: kpt on u.p: jst ct* **8/1**
0040 **3** *nk* **Admiral Compton**[4] [6596] 4-8-4 71 oh4 ...(b) JimmyQuinn 9 — 77+
(J R Boyle) *hld up towards rr: promising hdwy to trck ldrs whn nt clr run 1f out: fnd room and r.o wl fnl 75 yds* **16/1**
0044 **4** *hd* **Just Fly**[16] [6499] 5-8-2 72 ... RichardThomas(3) 2 — 78
(Dr J R J Naylor) *chsd ldrs: rdn 3f out: squeezed through on rail to chal ins fnl f: nt qckn nr fin* **16/1**
1100 **5** *hd* **Gingko**[61] [6015] 8-8-9 76 ... DaneO'Neill 5 — 81
(P R Webber) *cl up: drvn to press ldrs over 1f out: nt qckn fnl 100 yds* **12/1**
5245 **6** *hd* **Burgundy**[32] [6373] 8-8-7 74 ...(b) TPQueally 11 — 79
(P Mitchell) *hld up and bhd: swtchd v wd and effrt ent st: fin wl: lame* **8/1**
0000 **7** *3/4* **Skidmark**[25] [6431] 4-8-10 80 ... DNolan(3) 7 — 84
(Miss J R Tooth) *dwlt: sn in midfield: rdn and styd on same pce fnl 2f* **20/1**
343 **8** *shd* **Mad Carew (USA)**[15] [6520] 6-8-1 75 ...(e) LiamJones(7) 8 — 78
(J R Boyle) *chsd ldr tl wknd wl over 1f out* **7/1**[3]
3110 **9** *hd* **South O'The Border**[91] [5404] 3-8-6 76 ... IanMongan 4 — 79
(T G Mills) *led: rdn and hdd 1f out: n.m.r and wknd ins fnl f* **3/1**[1]
3300 **10** *3/4* **Eastborough (IRE)**[12] [6533] 6-8-9 76 ... HayleyTurner 10 — 78
(B G Powell) *dwlt: t.k.h towards rr on outside: rdn and styd on fnl 2f: nt rch ldrs* **33/1**
0034 **11** *6* **Boot 'n Toot**[22] [6459] 4-8-13 80 ... J-PGuillambert 12 — 70
(C A Cyzer) *lw: plld hrd and wd: chsd ldrs: rdn 3f out: sn wknd* **9/2**[2]
5000 **12** *1/2* **Te Quiero**[12] [6533] 7-9-1 82 ...(t) SteveDrowne 1 — 71
(Miss Gay Kelleway) *lw: a towards rr: rdn and lost tch 2f out* **50/1**

2m 6.19s (-1.60) **Going Correction** -0.10s/f (Stan)
WFA 3 from 4yo+ 3lb — **12** Ran SP% **117.6**
Speed ratings (Par 105):102,101,101,101,101 101,100,100,100,99 94,94
CSF £72.85 CT £1074.53 TOTE £12.50: £2.70, £3.00, £5.90; EX 86.10.
Owner Mrs Claire Hollowood **Bred** Lord Howard De Walden **Trained** Broad Hinton, Wilts
■ Stewards' Enquiry : T P Queally one-day ban: whip arm raised above shoulder height (Jan 1)
Dane O'Neill four-day ban: used whip with excessive frequency and without giving gelding time to respond (Jan 1-4)

FOCUS
A spectacular blanket finish between the first nine, and of fair quality for the track, but the form is ordinary.
Admiral Compton Official explanation: jockey said gelding was denied a clear run
Burgundy Official explanation: vet said gelding was lame

6646 TEXT "BETDIRECT" TO 88600 H'CAP (DIV II) — 6f (P)
3:30 (3:30) (Class 6) (0-55,56) 3-Y-O+ — **£2,156** (£636; £318) **Stalls** Low

Form — RPR
-401 **1** **Edin Burgher (FR)**[67] [5899] 4-8-11 52 ... SamHitchcott 9 — 59
(T T Clement) *lw: in tch: rdn along 3f out: styd on wl to ld nr fin* **11/2**[3]
1500 **2** *nk* **Gaudalpin (IRE)**[25] [6438] 3-8-9 50 ...(t) JimmyQuinn 3 — 56
(Ernst Oertel) *chsd ldrs: rdn to ld 1f out: kpt on u.p: hdd nr fin* **16/1**
0210 **3** *nk* **Stagnite**[1] [6625] 5-9-1 56 6ex ...(b) JamieSpencer 2 — 61
(K McAuliffe) *prom: rdn to join ldrs 1f out: kpt on* **4/1**[1]
0000 **4** *3/4* **Global Achiever**[42] [6294] 4-9-0 55 ...(p) OscarUrbina 1 — 58
(G C H Chung) *chsd ldr: lft in ld ent st: hdd 1f out: kpt on same pce* **16/1**
0016 **5** *3/4* **Park Star**[7] [6579] 5-8-8 49 ... DeanMcKeown 11 — 50
(D Shaw) *mid-div: rdn and styd on fnl 2f: nvr nrr* **10/1**
0600 **6** *1/2* **Davids Mark**[15] [6516] 5-8-9 50 ... EddieAhern 8 — 51+
(J R Jenkins) *b: mid-div: hdwy to chse ldrs over 1f out: n.m.r & no ex fnl 100 yds* **5/1**[2]
0303 **7** *shd* **Imperium**[42] [6294] 4-9-0 55 ...(p) MickyFenton 12 — 54
(Stef Liddiard) *s.i.s: towards rr: rdn and wd st: gd late hdwy* **8/1**
5040 **8** *nk* **Pheckless**[195] [2412] 6-8-10 51 ... ChrisCatlin 7 — 49
(J M Bradley) *b: dwlt: hld up in rr: swtchd lft and hdwy over 1f out: no imp fnl f* **7/1**
0020 **9** *1 1/2* **Mirasol Princess**[15] [6516] 4-8-13 54 ... DaneO'Neill 4 — 49+
(D K Ivory) *towards rr: hdwy on ins ent st: no ex fnl f* **8/1**
/560 **10** *3/4* **Renegade (IRE)**[9] [6567] 4-8-11 52 ...(b[1]) IanMongan 10 — 43
(Mrs L J Mongan) *led tl hung bdly rt and rn wd home turn: sn hdd: nt rcvr* **16/1**
0046 **11** *4* **Byo (IRE)**[30] [6407] 7-8-12 53 ... SteveDrowne 6 — 32
(P Howling) *wd: in tch: rdn 3f out: wknd 2f out* **16/1**
0600 **12** *3/4* **Sound That Alarm**[122] [4604] 3-8-11 52 ... TPQueally 5 — 29
(P Mitchell) *chsd ldrs: hrd rdn 3f out: wknd 2f out* **33/1**

1m 11.99s (-0.82) **Going Correction** -0.10s/f (Stan) — **39** Ran SP% **122.3**
Speed ratings (Par 101):101,100,100,99,98 97,97,97,95,94 88,87
CSF £93.34 CT £403.46 TOTE £7.70: £2.10, £4.70, £1.60; EX 93.50 Place 6 £9.71, Place 5 £4.28.
Owner Rothmere Racing Limited **Bred** Classic Breeding Sarl And Scea Le Lieu Marmion **Trained** Newmarket, Suffolk
■ Stewards' Enquiry : Oscar Urbina caution careless riding

FOCUS
A low-grade, but competitive, handicap - little better than a seller - but the form appears sound.
Renegade(IRE) Official explanation: jockey said gelding hung right

T/Plt: £9.80 to a £1 stake. Pool: £37,288.95. 2,756.25 winning tickets. T/Qpdt: £4.80 to a £1 stake. Pool: £2,290.20. 352.25 winning tickets. LM

6616 WOLVERHAMPTON (A.W) (L-H)

Wednesday, December 21

OFFICIAL GOING: Standard

Wind: Moderate, behind

6647 WINVIC CONSTRUCTION BANDED STKS 5f 20y(P)

12:50 (12:51) (Class 7) 3-Y-O+ £1,446 (£427; £213) Stalls Low

Form RPR

4451 1 **Lady Hopeful (IRE)**[21] 6471 3-8-11 45..................(b) RobbieFitzpatrick 9 54+
(Peter Grayson) *slowly away: in rr tl hdwy on ins fr 2f out: squeezed through and r.o wl to ld fnl 50yds* **9/2**[1]

1005 2 1 1/4 **Cark**[3] 6604 7-8-11 45..................(p) RobertWinston 1 50
(J Balding) *led: rdn over 1f out: kpt on but hdd fnl 50yds* **5/1**[2]

2650 3 hd **Blue Moon Hitman (IRE)**[12] 6527 4-9-2 50..................(b) PaulHanagan 5 54
(R Brotherton) *in tch: carried lft over 1f out: r.o ins fnl f* **6/1**

2002 4 1 **Chantelle's Dream**[7] 6580 3-8-4 45..................(t) JamesDoyle(7) 4 45
(Ms J S Doyle) *in rr: hdwy on ins 2f out: hung lft over 1f out: r.o ins fnl f* **10/1**

0505 5 3/4 **Kiss The Rain**[39] 6326 5-8-13 47..................(b) TomEaves 7 44
(R Brotherton) *in rr and sn rdn: mde hdwy fnl f* **16/1**

0040 6 shd **Petana**[30] 6397 5-8-6 45..................(p) DuranFentiman(5) 3 42
(Peter Grayson) *a.p: sn pushed along: no ex fnl f* **12/1**

0031 7 hd **Leah's Pride**[7] 6580 4-9-3 45.................. FergalLynch 8 47
(P Howling) *trckd ldr tl rdn and edgd lft appr fnl f: one pce after* **8/1**

4265 8 1/2 **Desert Light (IRE)**[12] 6527 4-8-13 50..................(v) PatrickMathers(3) 6 45
(D Shaw) *in rr: hdwy whn swtchd rt over 1f out: r.o* **11/2**[3]

5044 9 3/4 **Legal Set (IRE)**[7] 6580 9-8-4 45..................(bt) AnnStokell(7) 10 37
(Miss A Stokell) *in rr: c wd into st: nvr nr to chal* **14/1**

0000 10 nk **Feminist (IRE)**[21] 6470 3-8-11 45.................. GrahamGibbons 11 36
(J M Bradley) *chsd ldrs tl rdn and wknd over 1f out* **25/1**

0060 11 1 1/2 **Princess Kai (IRE)**[7] 6579 4-8-13 47..................(p) FergusSweeney 12 32
(R Ingram) *racd on outside towards rr: carried v wd into st and no ch after* **25/1**

1000 12 3 **On The Trail**[9] 6559 8-8-12 46..................(p) PhillipMakin 2 21
(D W Chapman) *chsd ldrs tl rdn and wknd qckly over 1f out* **11/2**[3]

62.58 secs (-0.24) **Going Correction** -0.125s/f (Stan) 12 Ran SP% **128.0**

Speed ratings (Par 97):96,94,93,92,90 90,90,89,88,87 85,80

CSF £29.01 TOTE £4.80: £2.20, £2.40, £2.60; EX 42.20.

Owner Peter Grayson Racing Clubs Limited **Bred** Raymond P Doyle **Trained** Formby, Lancs

FOCUS

A routine banded sprint featuring the usual suspects, but a fine tactical ride aboard the favourite. The form is just ordinary for the grade.

Legal Set(IRE) Official explanation: jockey said gelding hung right on the bend

6648 UNIVERSAL MOULDINGS LTD MAIDEN AUCTION STKS 1m 141y(P)

1:20 (1:21) (Class 7) 2-Y-O £1,405 (£415; £207) Stalls Low

Form RPR

1 **Cragganmore Creek** 2-8-10 ow1.................. DerekMcGaffin 4 53
(D Morris) *slowly away: hdwy whn swtchd lft over 1f out: r.o to ld ins fnl f: hld on* **22/1**

0050 2 nk **Duel In The Sands**[102] 5111 2-8-5 57.................. PatrickMathers(3) 6 50
(D Shaw) *bhd: hdwy on outside 2f out: c wd into st: hung lft over 1f out but r.o to cl on wnr wl ins* **7/1**

0000 3 1 1/4 **Peephole**[25] 6428 2-8-11 61..................(v[1]) FergusSweeney 5 50
(P J Makin) *chsd ldr: led over 5f out: rdn and hdd ins fnl f: nt qckn* **3/1**[1]

3340 4 shd **Pix**[11] 6543 2-8-1 49.................. NelsonDeSouza(3) 9 43
(S Kirk) *a.p: ev ch whn hung rt ent fnl f: one pce after* **7/2**[2]

0460 5 1 1/4 **Crush On You**[11] 6543 2-8-2 45.................. PaulQuinn 7 39
(R Hollinshead) *t.k.h: prom: rdn 3f out: hmpd ent fnl f: one pce after* **12/1**

0050 6 2 **Mytass**[9] 6557 2-8-8 45 ow1.................. DanielTudhope(3) 2 48+
(J A Pickering) *trckd ldrs: rdn and outpcd 1/2-way: swtchd to ins: hld whn hmpd over 1f out* **9/2**[3]

000 7 1 3/4 **Vertigo Blue**[113] 4847 2-8-8 45.................. TomEaves 11 37
(C W Thornton) *a towards rr* **10/1**

060 8 nk **Master Ben (IRE)**[113] 4847 2-8-9 48..................(b[1]) PhillipMakin 8 41+
(S R Bowring) *in tch: rdn over 2f out: wkng whn hmpd appr fnl f* **16/1**

0000 9 2 1/2 **La Bomba Veloce**[8] 6569 2-8-2 45..................(b[1]) PaulHanagan 3 25
(Mrs L Williamson) *led tl hdd over 5f out: wknd 2f out* **20/1**

00 10 1 1/2 **Wings Of Speed**[32] 6386 2-8-3.................. JamieMackay 10 23
(H Morrison) *mid-div: rdn 3f out: sn bhd* **12/1**

1m 52.89s (1.13) **Going Correction** -0.125s/f (Stan) 10 Ran SP% **117.4**

Speed ratings (Par 90):89,88,87,87,86 84,83,82,80,79

CSF £169.40 TOTE £30.30: £10.30, £3.50, £1.50; EX 230.90.

Owner Stag And Huntsman **Bred** Grovewood Stud **Trained** Newmarket, Suffolk

FOCUS

A very moderate contest and something of a rough race. The first two home occupied the last two positions for most of the way which suggests the leaders may have gone off too quick.

NOTEBOOK

Cragganmore Creek, who cost only 2,200gns as a yearling, is out of a half-sister to a multiple winner in Italy. Switched off right out the back, he made for the inside rail to deliver his effort soon after turning in, probably a shrewd move considering the trouble that occurred towards the outside, and he found enough to score all-out. He probably beat nothing, but is entitled to progress from this debut. (op 20-1)

Duel In The Sands, making his sand debut after finishing unplaced in four outings on turf, like the winner was patiently ridden but unlike that rival he circled the field on the wide outside turning for home. He hung left under pressure in the straight, causing problems on his inside, and was just outbattled. This was a poor race and he may need to drop in class to break his duck. (tchd 8-1)

Peephole was given a positive ride in the first-time visor but did not get home. He looks very moderate. (op 5-2)

Pix, an exposed filly, had every chance but hung right under pressure in the home straight and was never doing enough. Her proximity does nothing for the form and she would probably be better off in banded company come the new year. (op 3-1 tchd 5-2)

Crush On You, already exposed as moderate, had every chance starting up the home straight and though she got messed about entering the last furlong she was not really going anywhere at the time. She looks destined for banded company. (op 7-1)

Mytass, the gamble of the race despite only having made the frame once in his 13 previous outings, got into plenty of trouble a furlong from home but only appeared to be fighting for places at the time. Official explanation: jockey said gelding suffered interference in running (op 11-1)

Master Ben(IRE), blinkered for the first time on this sand debut having finished unplaced in three outings on turf, was already on the retreat when getting seriously hampered a furlong from home. (tchd 20-1)

6649 PLAY NOW AT BETDIRECTPOKER.COM BANDED STKS 1m 141y(P)

1:50 (1:50) (Class 7) 3-Y-O+ £1,440 (£425; £212) Stalls Low

Form RPR

0034 1 **Wodhill Gold**[21] 6474 4-8-10 40..................(v[1]) DerekMcGaffin 4 46
(D Morris) *towards rr: rdn 4f out: styd on on ins to ld ins fnl f* **11/4**[1]

0002 2 1 1/4 **Fir Tree**[9] 6554 5-8-10 40.................. PhillipMakin 11 43
(S R Bowring) *led to 6f out: led again over 3f out: hdd over 1f out bef led again ins fnl f: hdd nr fin* **16/1**

0004 3 1/2 **Princeable Lady (IRE)**[16] 6511 3-8-5 40.................. EdwardCreighton(3) 12 42
(J A Pickering) *in rr tl hdwy 5f out: rdn 2f out: r.o wl fnl f: nvr nrr* **16/1**

2031 4 1/2 **Desert Fury**[9] 6556 8-9-1 40..................(b) RobertWinston 6 46
(R Bastiman) *slowly away: rdn and hdwy on outside over 2f out: r.o one pce ins fnl f* **3/1**[2]

4505 5 3/4 **Paper Doll**[17] 6498 3-8-8 40.................. PaulEddery 7 40
(B P J Baugh) *in rr: rdn and hdwy 5f out: ev ch 1f out: nt qckn* **16/1**

-004 6 nk **Mr Uppity**[32] 6385 6-8-7 40..................(be) AdamKirby(3) 1 39
(Julian Poulton) *trckd ldr: led 6f out to over 3f out: led again over 1f out tl wknd and hdd ins fnl f* **14/1**

0050 7 nk **Viking Star (IRE)**[17] 6260 4-8-5 40.................. DuranFentiman(5) 2 38
(A D Brown) *in rr tl hdwy over 1f out: nvr nr to chal* **25/1**

0063 8 shd **Repeat (IRE)**[7] 6577 5-8-10 40.................. FergusSweeney 8 38
(J W Unett) *prom tl wknd appr fnl f* **12/1**

0040 9 nk **Red Lantern**[29] 6412 4-8-10 40.................. RobbieFitzpatrick 10 38
(M J Attwater) *in tch: rdn 3f out: no ex fnl f* **9/1**

0505 10 5 **Ahaz**[8] 6572 3-8-8 40.................. GrahamGibbons 9 27
(J F Coupland) *a in rr* **40/1**

060- 11 14 **Nopleazinu**[373] 6878 5-8-10 40..................(t) DaleGibson 3 —
(A W Carroll) *trckd ldrs tl rdn 4f out: sn bhd* **6/1**[3]

0605 12 9 **Sam The Sorcerer**[9] 6558 4-8-11 40 ow1..................(v[1]) DarrenWilliams 13 —
(J R Norton) *prom tl rdn 4f out: sn bhd* **33/1**

0003 13 19 **Four Kings**[8] 6568 4-8-10 40.................. PaulHanagan 5 —
(R Allan) *a bhd* **9/1**

1m 51.53s (-0.23) **Going Correction** -0.125s/f (Stan)

WFA 3 from 4yo+ 2lb 13 Ran SP% **127.2**

Speed ratings (Par 97):96,94,94,94,93 93,92,92,92,88 75,67,50

CSF £51.63 TOTE £4.00: £1.30, £5.90, £5.70; EX 79.90.

Owner Miss S Graham **Bred** Wodhill Stud **Trained** Newmarket, Suffolk

FOCUS

A routine banded contest and trouble in running for a couple, including the winner.

Mr Uppity Official explanation: jockey said gelding hung right

Nopleazinu Official explanation: jockey said mare had a breathing problem

Four Kings Official explanation: jockey said colt had a breathing problem

6650 DARREN HAYCOCK BUILDING CONTRACTORS BANDED STKS 1m 1f 103y(P)

2:20 (2:20) (Class 7) 3-Y-O+ £1,463 (£432; £216) Stalls Low

Form RPR

2630 1 **Mister Clinton (IRE)**[7] 6577 8-8-11 40..................(p) FergalLynch 9 53
(D K Ivory) *hld up in rr: rdn 3f out: hdwy on ins over 1f out: r.o to ld ins fnl f* **11/2**[3]

4000 2 1 1/2 **Halcyon Magic**[21] 6475 7-8-8 40..................(b) AdamKirby(3) 5 50
(M Wigham) *in rr tl hdwy on outside over 2f out: r.o wl fnl f to go 2nd nr fin* **7/2**[1]

5364 3 3/4 **Bobering**[9] 6556 5-8-8 40.................. PatrickMathers(3) 6 49
(B P J Baugh) *mid-div: hdwy 3f out: led 1f out: hdd ins fnl f: nt qckn* **7/1**

4P65 4 2 1/2 **Oktis Morilious (IRE)**[25] 6434 4-8-11 40.................. PaulHanagan 2 44
(A W Carroll) *bhd tl rdn and hdwy over 3f out: kpt on one pce fnl f* **5/1**[2]

0600 5 shd **Spanish Music**[14] 6524 3-8-9 40..................(t) RobertHavlin 1 44
(R Ingram) *trckd ldrs: rdn over 2f out: ev ch appr fnl f: fdd ins* **7/1**

6600 6 3 **College Rebel**[8] 6573 4-8-11 40.................. RobbieFitzpatrick 3 38
(J F Coupland) *in tch: rdn 3f out: wknd appr fnl f* **25/1**

0020 7 1 1/2 **Taylor Maid**[7] 6577 3-8-9 40..................(p) GrahamGibbons 11 36
(R M H Cowell) *sn led: wknd and hdd 1f out* **14/1**

0-05 8 1 1/4 **Lahob**[16] 6509 5-8-11 40.................. RobertWinston 12 33
(P Howling) *trckd ldr: ev ch over 1f out: wknd ins fnl f* **12/1**

5060 9 3 1/2 **Printsmith (IRE)**[23] 6442 8-8-11 40..................(v[1]) DarrenWilliams 8 26
(J R Norton) *prom: rdn over 3f out: wknd over 2f out* **14/1**

0602 10 5 **Danger Bird (IRE)**[21] 6474 5-8-4 40.................. HugoFellows(7) 7 17
(R Hollinshead) *in rr: hdwy 5f out: rdn and wknd 3f out* **5/1**[2]

6040 11 9 **Dejeeje (IRE)**[211] 1983 4-8-11 40..................(p) PhillipMakin 10 —
(D W Chapman) *a in rr* **20/1**

5060 12 1 1/4 **Mustakhlas (USA)**[60] 6034 4-8-11 40..................(p) PaulEddery 13 —
(B P J Baugh) *prom on outside tl lost pl 4f out* **25/1**

2m 0.88s (-1.74) **Going Correction** -0.125s/f (Stan)

WFA 3 from 4yo+ 2lb 12 Ran SP% **129.4**

Speed ratings (Par 97):102,100,100,97,97 95,93,92,89,85 77,75

CSF £26.91 TOTE £7.80: £2.50, £2.00, £2.20; EX 31.60.

Owner J B Waterfall **Bred** C N Hart **Trained** Radlett, Herts

FOCUS

Probably a fair little contest of its type run at a true gallop. The winning time was 1.23 seconds faster than the following contest over the same trip and the principals all came from off the pace. The winner and third set the level for the form.

Lahob Official explanation: jockey said gelding hung left-handed

Dejeeje(IRE) Official explanation: jockey said gelding had no more to give

Mustakhlas(USA) Official explanation: jockey said gelding had no more to give

6651 FATSPANNER BANDED STKS 1m 1f 103y(P)

2:50 (2:50) (Class 7) 3-Y-O+ £1,443 (£426; £213) Stalls Low

Form RPR

3052 1 **Star Fern**[9] 6560 4-8-12 45.................. PaulHanagan 1 53
(M J Attwater) *bhd tl rdn and hdwy on outside over 2f out: r.o to ld ins fnl f: won gng away* **2/1**[1]

4440 2 2 **Bond Millennium**[11] 3867 7-9-1 48.................. PaulEddery 7 52
(B Smart) *a.p: rdn to ld over 1f out: all out whn hdd ins fnl f* **8/1**

3001 3 nk **Super Dominion**[16] 6509 8-9-1 48..................(p) VinceSlattery 2 52
(R Hollinshead) *hld up in rr: rdn 3f out: hdwy on ins over 1f out: r.o fnl f: nvr nrr* **14/1**

5240 4 3/4 **Glenviews Oldport (USA)**[14] 6522 3-8-12 47.......... RobbieFitzpatrick 5 49
(Peter Grayson) *trckd ldrs: rdn 2f out: kpt on one pce fnl f* **7/1**

0331 5 3/4 **Adobe**[16] 6508 10-9-3 50.................. DarrenWilliams 3 51
(W M Brisbourne) *mid-div: rdn over 1f out: r.o one pce* **13/2**[3]

0050 6 3 1/2 **Dysonic (USA)**[134] 4237 3-8-10 45.................. GrahamGibbons 6 39
(D Burchell) *led: rdn over 2f out: hdd & wknd over 1f out* **33/1**

0000 7 1/2 **Lord Lahar**[7] 6576 6-9-0 47.................. TomEaves 10 40
(M A Buckley) *in rr: rdn and hdwy over 3f out: nvr nr to chal* **20/1**

0454 **8** 3 **Wind Chime (IRE)**[7] 6574 8-9-1 48 FergusSweeney 11 35
(A G Newcombe) *in rr: hdwy 4f out: rdn 3f out: sn wknd* **6/1**[2]
6000 **9** 1 3/4 **Insignia (IRE)**[81] 5629 3-8-12 50 PatrickMathers(3) 12 34
(W M Brisbourne) *swtchd lft s: a in rr* **10/1**
0260 **10** 1 **Tintac**[204] 2151 4-8-13 46 PhillipMakin 13 28
(E J O'Neill) *t.k.h: trckd ldr: rdn and wknd over 1f out* **14/1**
0205 **11** 5 **Gala Sunday (USA)**[28] 5516 5-9-0 47 (t) DaleGibson 8 20
(M W Easterby) *trckd ldrs: rdn over 3f out: sn wknd* **10/1**
0000 **12** 1 1/2 **Blendon Boy (IRE)**[62] 5998 3-9-0 49 FrancisFerris 4 19
(A G Newcombe) *t.k.h: mid-div: rdn 3f out: sn bhd* **25/1**
400 **13** 5 **Penway**[6] 6583 4-9-0 50 (b[1]) AdamKirby(3) 9 10
(A Sadik) *a in rr* **40/1**

2m 2.11s (-0.51) **Going Correction** -0.125s/f (Stan)
WFA 3 from 4yo+ 2lb **13** Ran SP% **130.1**
Speed ratings (Par 97):97,95,94,94,93 90,90,87,85,84 80,79,74
CSF £19.60 TOTE £3.20: £1.10, £3.20, £6.20; EX 45.30.
Owner Miss Vivian Pratt **Bred** Miss Heather Pratt **Trained** Wysall, Notts

FOCUS
In theory a slightly better-class contest than the preceding one, but the winning time was 1.23 seconds slower and the form looks weak.

6652 CHAMBERLAINS ESTATE AGENTS FESTIVE TRI-BANDED STKS 1m 4f 50y(P)
3:20 (3:21) (Class 7) 3-Y-0 **£1,405** (£415; £207) **Stalls** Low

Form RPR
0000 **1** **My Boo**[14] 6523 3-8-4 40 (tp) AdamKirby(3) 6 44
(T Keddy) *a in tch: edgd lft fr over 1f out but r.o u.p to ld last stride* **16/1**
04 **2** hd **Goldstar Dancer (IRE)**[21] 5132 3-8-12 45 GrahamGibbons 2 49
(J J Quinn) *led: kicked clr 2f out: kpt on but hdd last stride* **11/8**[1]
4052 **3** 1 **Liquid Lover (IRE)**[8] 6571 3-8-4 40 PatrickMathers(3) 1 42
(W M Brisbourne) *trckd ldrs: rdn 3f out: wnt 2nd appr fnl f: no ex fnl 50yds* **9/4**[2]
0004 **4** 1 **Lyric Dances (FR)**[8] 6571 3-8-7 40 (t) RobertWinston 9 40
(J Jay) *in rr tl hdwy 3f out: rdn and styd on fnl f* **12/1**
00 **5** 2 1/2 **Ivory Key (IRE)**[17] 6495 3-8-9 45 DanielTudhope(3) 10 41
(Patrick Morris, Ire) *t.k.h: chsd ldr over 2f out tl wknd over 1f out* **16/1**
0400 **6** 3 1/2 **Edict**[14] 6523 3-8-12 45 PaulEddery 4 36
(C J Down) *bhd: rdn 3f out: nvr on terms* **25/1**
250 **7** 3/4 **Tanning**[25] 6434 3-8-2 35 PaulHanagan 5 25
(A W Carroll) *a bhd* **12/1**
0-02 **8** 1 **Legend Of Dance**[219] 1762 3-8-5 45 KMay(7) 7 33
(J L Spearing) *in tch tl rdn and wknd 2f out* **40/1**
065 **9** 7 **Amberlina (IRE)**[17] 6494 3-8-12 45 FergalLynch 8 22
(Patrick Morris, Ire) *in rr tl hdwy over 4f out: rdn over 2f out: sn wknd* **13/2**[3]
5000 **10** 8 **Emma Lilley (USA)**[21] 6475 3-8-7 40 (v[1]) TomEaves 3 4
(J G M O'Shea) *a bhd* **14/1**
0-00 **11** 13 **Imperioli**[205] 2120 3-7-11 35 DuranFentiman(5) 11 —
(P A Blockley) *trckd ldrs: rdn over 4f out: wknd 4f out* **40/1**

2m 43.73s (1.31) **Going Correction** -0.125s/f (Stan) **11** Ran SP% **128.7**
Speed ratings (Par 96):90,89,89,88,86 84,84,83,78,73 64
CSF £41.64 TOTE £42.60: £5.70, £1.10, £1.30; EX 143.90 Place 6 £39.75, Place 5 £19.24.
Owner NewmarketConnections.com **Bred** M E Wates **Trained** Newmarket, Suffolk

FOCUS
A poor contest and the pace was ordinary which resulted in a moderate winning time, even for a race like this. The form looks a shade below average with the first two setting the standard.
T/Plt: £31.60 to a £1 stake. Pool: £34,564.80. 797.50 winning tickets. T/Qpdt: £9.80 to a £1 stake. Pool: £2,993.80. 224.70 winning tickets. JS

6632 SOUTHWELL (L-H)
Thursday, December 22

OFFICIAL GOING: Standard
Wind: Nil

6653 BETDIRECT ONLY 3 DAYS 'TIL XMAS NOVICE STKS 5f (F)
11:40 (11:41) (Class 5) 2-Y-0 **£4,022** (£1,196; £598; £298) **Stalls** High

Form RPR
1 **1** **Matuza (IRE)**[23] 6456 2-9-5 SteveDrowne 2 77+
(W R Muir) *trckd ldrs gng wl: shkn up and qcknd to ld ent last: sn clr: easily* **10/11**[1]
06 **2** 3 1/2 **Eeshee**[75] 5737 2-8-7 MickyFenton 1 53
(S L Keightley) *cl up: led after 1f: rdn wl over 1f out: drvn and hdd ent last: kpt on same pce* **50/1**
0650 **3** shd **Smooch**[84] 5570 2-9-5 89 EddieAhern 6 65
(R M H Cowell) *chsd ldrs: rdn 2f out and ev ch tl drvn and one pce ent last* **3/1**[3]
31 **4** 2 **Glenviews Youngone (IRE)**[41] 6311 2-8-2 71 RonanKeogh(7) 3 48
(Peter Grayson) *trckd ldrs: rdn along and outpcd after 1f: swtchd rt and hdwy u.p 2f out: nt rch ldrs* **11/4**[2]
0000 **5** 1/2 **No Inkling (IRE)**[10] 6561 2-8-7 50 (v) FrancisFerris 5 44
(M J Attwater) *led 1f: cl up tl rdn 2f out and grad wknd* **100/1**
6 11 **Charming Princess** 2-8-3 PaulFessey 7 3
(P T Midgley) *s.i.s: a bhd* **66/1**
7 10 **Balfour House** 2-8-8 (b[1]) RobbieFitzpatrick 4 —
(R A Harris) *s.i.s and wnt rt s: a outpcd and bhd* **66/1**

60.37 secs (0.07) **Going Correction** -0.075s/f (Stan) **7** Ran SP% **110.0**
Speed ratings (Par 96):96,90,90,87,86 68,52
CSF £43.06 TOTE £1.90: £1.10, £7.20; EX 24.90.
Owner The Eastwood Partnership **Bred** Round Hill Stud **Trained** Lambourn, Berks

FOCUS
Normal service was resumed over this straight five with stall two beating stall one. The winner still looks a nice sort though.

NOTEBOOK
Matuza(IRE), confidently ridden over this shorter trip, was taken right out to the middle of the track and was running all over his rivals from a long way out. He may not have beaten much and the draw was in his favour, but it is hard to argue with an unbeaten record and there should be more to come. (op 11-10 tchd 11-8)
Eeshee, unplaced in two six-furlong turf maidens in the autumn, was a different proposition here and though she was favoured by the draw she still travelled very well out in front until the favourite cruised past. This was a huge improvement and if she can maintain it there is a race in her, though connections will be hoping the Handicapper does not interpret the form literally through the third horse.
Smooch, who faced some very stiff tasks during a busy campaign on turf, was always making hard work of it from her modest draw. She might have just needed it, but is still going to remain hard to place, even on sand. (op 5-2 tchd 2-1)
Glenviews Youngone(IRE), who made full use of a brilliant draw when winning at Wolverhampton last time, had a fair draw here but was soon struggling on this slower surface. To be fair, she managed to get into a challenging position passing the two-furlong pole but she was trying to make her effort in the slower ground against the stands' rail and that was one handicap too many. (op 10-3 tchd 7-2)
No Inkling(IRE) faced an impossible task, but did at least match strides with some far superior horses until well past halfway.
Charming Princess Official explanation: jockey said filly hung left

6654 JEREMY GLOVER RETIREMENT H'CAP (DIV I) 1m (F)
12:10 (12:10) (Class 6) (0-60,65) 3-Y-0+ **£2,512** (£741; £371) **Stalls** Low

Form RPR
2061 **1** **Dispol Foxtrot**[9] 6573 7-8-10 51 6ex EddieAhern 9 65
(Miss V Scott) *trckd ldrs: hdwy on outer over 2f out: rdn over 1f out: styd on strly ins last to ld nr line* **3/1**[2]
0206 **2** hd **Bridgewater Boys**[12] 6535 4-8-13 54 (b) NCallan 10 68
(K A Ryan) *trckd ldrs: hdwy to chal 2f out: rdn wl over 1f out: drvn to ld ins last: hdd nr line* **9/2**[3]
4011 **3** 1 1/4 **Augustine**[17] 6506 4-8-11 52 DarrenWilliams 11 63
(P W Hiatt) *cl up: led wl over 2f out: sn rdn: drvn over 1f out: hdd ins last: no ex last 100 yds* **9/1**
5311 **4** 1/2 **Amorist (IRE)**[7] 6587 3-9-9 65 6ex JamieMackay 12 75
(Sir Mark Prescott) *cl up: effrt 2f out: sn rdn and ev ch tl drvn and one pce fnl f* **11/4**[1]
1504 **5** 1 1/4 **Band**[23] 6468 5-9-2 57 GrahamGibbons 2 65
(E S McMahon) *midfield: hdwy 3f out: rdn to chse ldrs 2f out: drvn and one pce appr last* **16/1**
0521 **6** nk **Witchcraft**[40] 6327 4-8-11 55 (v) PatrickMathers(3) 6 62
(D Shaw) *towards rr: hdwy 3f out: rdn 2f out: kpt on appr last: nrst fin* **11/1**
2136 **7** 1/2 **Cup Of Love (USA)**[40] 6323 3-9-3 59 ChrisCatlin 4 65
(Rae Guest) *chsd ldrs: rdn along 2f out: drvn and one pce appr last* **22/1**
0033 **8** 1 1/4 **Balearic Star (IRE)**[7] 6586 4-8-10 58 JamesMillman(7) 3 61
(B R Millman) *hld up: hdwy over 2f out: sn rdn and no imp* **12/1**
3034 **9** nk **Silver Visage (IRE)**[16] 6513 3-9-2 58 BrianReilly 5 61
(Miss J Feilden) *sn led: rdn along and hdd wl over 2f out: grad wknd* **33/1**
3200 **10** 7 **Craic Sa Ceili (IRE)**[19] 6487 5-8-11 52 (b[1]) MickyFenton 7 41
(M S Saunders) *s.i.s: a rr* **33/1**
0000 **11** 7 **Simply The Guest (IRE)**[12] 6542 6-8-12 53 KimTinkler 1 28
(N Tinkler) *s.i.s: a rr* **80/1**
2400 **12** 10 **Shesthebiscuit**[86] 5537 3-9-4 60 DeanMcKeown 8 15
(J Parkes) *chsd ldrs: rdn along 1/2-way: sn wknd* **100/1**
-060 **13** 13 **Missin Margot**[162] 3432 3-8-3 45 PaulHanagan 13 —
(P D Evans) *a rr* **100/1**

1m 44.15s (-0.45) **Going Correction** +0.025s/f (Slow)
WFA 3 from 4yo+ 1lb **13** Ran SP% **115.2**
Speed ratings (Par 101):103,102,101,101,99 99,99,97,97,90 83,73,60
CSF £15.44 CT £99.84 TOTE £3.60: £1.50, £1.90, £3.00; EX 15.40.
Owner Ms V Scott **Bred** B N And Mrs Toye **Trained** Elsdon, Northumberland

FOCUS
A very tight handicap in which there were virtually eight in a line across the track passing the furlong pole, but those that raced wide were favoured and it was significant that the first four home came from the five highest stalls. The winning time was 0.61 seconds faster than the second division.

6655 ARCHER ELECTRICAL H'CAP 1m 4f (F)
12:40 (12:40) (Class 5) (0-70,70) 3-Y-0+ **£3,388** (£1,008; £503; £251) **Stalls** Low

Form RPR
3233 **1** **Khanjar (USA)**[7] 6582 5-9-4 70 (p) PatCosgrave 6 79
(K R Burke) *cl up: led after 2f: rdn along 2f out: drvn and hdd ins last: rallied to ld nr fin* **5/2**[2]
1005 **2** hd **Yenaled**[23] 6463 8-8-3 62 DonnaCaldwell(7) 4 71
(P S McEntee) *hld up: hdwy to trck ldrs 1/2-way: chal 2f out: rdn and styd on to ld briefly ins last: hdd and no ex nr fin* **20/1**
2402 **3** nk **Oldenway**[7] 6582 6-8-10 62 PaulHanagan 3 70
(R A Fahey) *led 2f: cl up: rdn along over 2f out: drvn over 1f out and kpt on towards fin* **85/40**[1]
4001 **4** 8 **Blue Opal**[7] 6583 3-8-2 59 6ex ow1 ChrisCatlin 1 55
(Miss S E Hall) *a.p: hdwy to chal 3f out and ev ch tl rdn 2f out and grad wknd* **14/1**
5400 **5** 5 **Sorbiesharry (IRE)**[10] 6566 6-8-10 65 AdamKirby(3) 2 54
(Mrs N Macauley) *hld up in rr: hdwy 4f out: rdn along 3f out and sn outpcd* **15/2**
0610 **6** 5 **Efrhina (IRE)**[7] 6582 5-8-9 61 (p) MickyFenton 7 42
(Stef Liddiard) *hld up in rr: hdwy over 4f out: rdn along 3f out and sn btn* **11/2**[3]
6260 **7** dist **J R Stevenson (USA)**[36] 6368 9-8-4 56 oh1 (e[1]) JimmyQuinn 5 —
(Ernst Oertel) *trckd ldrs: rdn along 1/2-way: sn wknd* **11/1**
6036 **8** 21 **Victory Quest (IRE)**[260] 912 5-9-4 70 (v) DaneO'Neill 8 —
(Mrs S Lamyman) *prom: pushed along 1/2-way: sn wknd* **25/1**

2m 40.44s (-1.65) **Going Correction** +0.025s/f (Slow)
WFA 3 from 5yo+ 5lb **8** Ran SP% **111.3**
Speed ratings (Par 103):106,105,105,100,97 93,—,—
CSF £46.70 CT £117.45 TOTE £3.10: £1.40, £5.60, £1.10; EX 79.00.
Owner Alan Draper **Bred** Alexander-Groves Thoroughbreds **Trained** Middleham Moor, N Yorks

FOCUS
A decent pace for this handicap and it paid to race handily. There was little separating the front three all the way up the home straight.
Victory Quest(IRE) Official explanation: jockey said gelding lost its action

6656 PRESS RED TO BET ON ITVI "PREMIER" CLAIMING STKS 6f (F)
1:10 (1:10) (Class 4) 2-Y-0 **£5,337** (£1,587; £793; £396) **Stalls** Low

Form RPR
6021 **1** **The City Kid (IRE)**[44] 6290 2-8-1 76 (v) PaulHanagan 2 65
(P D Evans) *cl up: led after 1 1/2f: rdn wl over 1f out: drvn ins last and kpt on* **13/8**[1]
0234 **2** 1 1/4 **Amber Glory**[7] 6581 2-7-12 70 ow4 (p) DeanHeslop(7) 9 66
(K A Ryan) *trckd ldrs: hdwy over 2f out: rdn to chse wnr over 1f out: ev ch ent last: kpt on same pce* **3/1**[2]
0325 **3** 1 1/2 **Diktalex (IRE)**[5] 6600 2-7-6 55 ow1 (t) LiamJones(7) 6 55
(W G M Turner) *hld up in tch: hdwy chse ldrs 2f out: sn rdn and one pce appr last* **10/1**
2551 **4** 1 **Aysgarth Flyer (IRE)**[9] 6569 2-8-0 51 (b) PatrickMathers(3) 5 56
(I Semple) *s.i.s and sn bhd: rdn along 1/2-way: hdwy u.p on inner over 2f out: sn drvn and kpt on: nrst fin* **5/1**[3]

0142 **5** 3 1/2 **Woodwee**[2] 6635 2-8-3 61 ..... JimmyQuinn 1 46
(J R Weymes) *a rr* **5/1**[3]

0 **6** 1 **Musicmaestroplease (IRE)**[54] 6156 2-8-11 ..... DeanMcKeown 4 51
(S Parr) *trckd ldrs: hdwy 3f out: rdn and wandered 2f out: sn wknd* **50/1**

0005 **7** 6 **Lucky Celts (IRE)**[9] 6569 2-8-0 35 ow5 .....(p) RichardThomas(3) 8 25
(D Haydn Jones) *led 11/2f: cl up tl rdn 3f out and sn wknd* **66/1**

8 5 **Lake Bonneville (USA)** 2-8-1 ..... HayleyTurner 7 8
(Robert Gray) *chsd ldrs on outer: rdn along over 2f out and sn wknd* **25/1**

1m 17.45s (0.55) **Going Correction** +0.025s/f (Slow) 8 Ran SP% **112.8**
Speed ratings (Par 98):97,95,93,92,87 86,78,71
CSF £6.36 TOTE £2.50: £1.10, £1.60, £2.20; EX 7.30.
Owner Mrs S J Lawrence **Bred** T B And Mrs T B Russell **Trained** Pandy, Abergavenny
■ Stewards' Enquiry : Patrick Mathers three-day ban: used whip with excessive frequency (Jan 2-4)

FOCUS
A decent little juvenile claimer in which the pace was solid and again it paid to race handily. The result was very much as adjusted official ratings would have suggested.

NOTEBOOK
The City Kid(IRE) has really taken to this surface and followed up her course-and-distance victory last month with another decent front-running display. Admittedly she had upwards of 12lb in hand of her rivals on adjusted official ratings and it remains to be seen what else there is for her on this surface. As yet she is unproven on Polytrack. (op 7-4 tchd 2-1)
Amber Glory was second-best in at the weights, but with her rider's overweight she was 12lb badly in with the winner so probably achieved at least as much as could be expected. (op 4-1)
Diktalex(IRE) had a mountain to climb at the weights as she would have been a massive 19lb better off with the favourite in a handicap including the overweight, so she was far from disgraced in the circumstances and this performance did confirm that she seems to prefer this surface to the Polytrack. There should be a modest race in her. (op 8-1)
Aysgarth Flyer(IRE) ◆ took a broadside from Musicmaestroplease leaving the gates and soon found himself detached in last place as a result. His rider then made for the disadvantaged inside rail on reaching the home straight, so he did well to put himself in with any sort of chance. He can be forgiven this performance, even though he in theory had absolutely no chance at the weights. (op 4-1 tchd 7-2)
Woodwee was another of those badly in at the weights and was struggling from a very early stage. (op 9-2)

6657 CLARENCE CONTRACTORS LIMITED H'CAP 6f (F)
1:40 (1:42) (Class 4) (0-85,85) 3-Y-0+ **£6,596** (£1,962; £980; £489) **Stalls** Low

Form RPR
0330 **1** **Pinchbeck**[17] 6504 6-8-9 **76** .....(p) MatthewHenry 10 87
(M A Jarvis) *hld up in rr: gd hdwy on outer 2rf out: rdn and edgd lft ent last: led last 10o yds* **10/1**

0400 **2** 1 1/4 **Quiet Times (IRE)**[20] 6481 6-9-4 **85** .....(b) NCallan 11 92
(K A Ryan) *prom: hdwy to chal over 2f out: rdn to ld 11/2f out: drvn ent last: hdd and no ex last 100 yds* **15/2**

0006 **3** 1/2 **Kingsmaite**[6] 6590 4-8-13 **80** .....(b) PhillipMakin 14 86
(S R Bowring) *in tch: hdwy to chse ldr over 1f out: sn rdn and ev ch whn n.m.r ins last and snatched up ins last: kpt on* **20/1**

2044 **4** 3 **Pawan (IRE)**[2] 6636 5-8-6 **80** ..... AnnStokell(7) 8 77
(Miss A Stokell) *in rr: rdn and hdwy 2f out: kpt on ins last: nrst fin* **11/1**

4062 **5** 3/4 **My Gacho (IRE)**[23] 6465 3-8-6 **73** .....(v) PaulFessey 9 68
(T D Barron) *trckd ldrs: effrt and ev ch over 2f out: sn rdn and kpt on same pce appr last* **11/2**[2]

5050 **6** 1 **Flint River**[54] 6149 7-8-8 **75** ..... SteveDrowne 7 67
(H Morrison) *chsd ldrs: rdn along 2f out: kpt on same pce appr last* **6/1**[3]

4000 **7** 3/4 **Magic Glade**[19] 6489 6-9-1 **82** ..... TomEaves 5 71
(R Brotherton) *led: rdn along over 2f out: drvn and hdd over 11/2f out: grad wknd* **33/1**

0313 **8** 1 3/4 **Bessemer (JPN)**[3] 6616 4-8-5 **75** .....(p) DanielTudhope(3) 13 59
(D Carroll) *racd wd: a towards rr* **10/1**

0-00 **9** 1 3/4 **Russian Rocket (IRE)**[66] 5941 3-8-9 **76** ..... HayleyTurner 2 55
(Mrs C A Dunnett) *chsd ldrs on inner: rdn along over 2f out: grad wknd* **66/1**

1000 **10** 4 **Sabrina Brown**[33] 6376 4-8-7 **77** .....(t) RichardThomas(3) 3 44
(J A Geake) *midfield: rdn along over 2f out: sn btn* **16/1**

0006 **11** 1 1/4 **Premier Fantasy**[19] 6489 3-8-6 **73** ..... JohnEgan 6 36
(W J Haggas) *hld up towards rr: pushed along and hdwy on inner 2f out: sn rdn and hung lft wl over 1f out: sn wknd* **9/2**[1]

151 **12** 4 **General Feeling (IRE)**[12] 6544 4-8-10 **77** ..... DaneO'Neill 12 28
(S Kirk) *dwlt: a rr* **6/1**[3]

0110 **13** 3 1/2 **Polar Force**[76] 5719 5-8-5 **72** ..... ChrisCatlin 1 13
(Mrs C A Dunnett) *cl up: rdn along wl over 2f out: sn wknd* **20/1**

2004 **14** 3 1/2 **Caustic Wit (IRE)**[108] 4995 7-8-5 **72** .....(p) FrancisFerris 4 2
(M S Saunders) *a rr* **28/1**

1m 16.76s (-0.14) **Going Correction** +0.025s/f (Slow) 14 Ran SP% **123.7**
Speed ratings (Par 105):101,99,98,94,93 92,91,89,86,81 79,74,69,65
CSF £80.41 CT £995.48 TOTE £16.40: £4.40, £3.30, £9.40; EX 145.40.
Owner T G Warner **Bred** Red House Stud **Trained** Newmarket, Suffolk
■ Stewards' Enquiry : Matthew Henry one-day ban: careless riding (Jan 2)

FOCUS
A very competitive handicap and the field were spread right across the track in the home straight, but the time was ordinary when compared to the preceding two-year-old claimer. Again those drawn high were favoured.
Premier Fantasy Official explanation: trainer's representative said gelding would not face the kickback

6658 BETDIRECT FREEPHONE 0800 211 222 (S) STKS 7f (F)
2:10 (2:11) (Class 6) 3-Y-0+ **£2,484** (£733; £366) **Stalls** Low

Form RPR
0021 **1** **Owed**[7] 6584 3-9-4 57 .....(t) HayleyTurner 1 64
(Robert Gray) *chsd ldrs: hdwy to ld 2f out: rdn over 1f out: styd on u.p ins last* **13/8**[1]

0030 **2** 1 1/4 **Lady Suesanne (IRE)**[10] 6560 3-8-10 49 .....(b) DNolan(3) 2 56
(N Wilson) *cl up: led 1/2-way: rdn and hdd 2f out: drvn over 1f out: kpt on ins last* **25/1**

0004 **3** 1/2 **Distant Country (USA)**[7] 6584 6-9-4 60 .....(b) DaneO'Neill 7 60
(R A Harris) *towards rr: hdwy on inner over 2f out: rdn to chse ldrs over 1f out: drvn and one pce ins last* **16/1**

0000 **4** nk **Coleorton Dane**[7] 6584 3-8-12 67 ..... NCallan 3 53
(K A Ryan) *led: hdd 1/2-way and sn edgd lft: cl up and rdn over 2f out: drvn and kpt on same pce fnl f* **11/1**

0610 **5** 1 1/2 **Sweet Pickle**[23] 6460 4-8-13 60 .....(e) EddieAhern 8 50
(J R Boyle) *cl up on outer: effrt and ev ch over 2f out: sn rdn and one pce fr over 1f out* **15/8**[2]

5550 **6** 1 **Shielaligh**[9] 6573 4-8-5 45 ow5 .....(p) JamesMillman(7) 5 46
(B R Millman) *in tch and poushed along 1/2-way: hdwy on outer 2f out: sn rdn and hun bdly rt: kpt on ins last: nrst fin* **12/1**

0013 **7** 5 **Far Note (USA)**[7] 6584 7-9-4 61 .....(bt) PhillipMakin 6 39
(S R Bowring) *chsd ldrs: rdn over 2f out and sn wknd* **13/2**[3]

410- **8** 19 **Grub Street**[648] 1026 9-8-7 ..... DuranFentiman(5) 4 —
(J Parkes) *sn outpcd and bhd fr 1/2-way* **66/1**

1m 32.47s (1.67) **Going Correction** +0.025s/f (Slow) 8 Ran SP% **113.5**
Speed ratings (Par 101):91,89,89,88,86 85,80,58
CSF £42.61 TOTE £2.50: £1.10, £4.30, £3.70; EX 33.70.The winner was bought in for 7,800gns. Lady Suesanne was claimed by M. Attwater for £6,000.
Owner Naughty Diesel Ltd **Bred** Helshaw Grange Stud, N Kent And H Phillips **Trained** Malton, N Yorks
■ Stewards' Enquiry : Dane O'Neill seven-day ban: used whip with excessive frequency and without giving gelding time to respond (Jan 2-7, 9)

FOCUS
A moderate seller in which the form of an identical contest here seven days earlier was confirmed with Owed going in again. Despite there only being eight runners, the field used the whole width of the track in the home straight. The winning time was moderate, even for a seller.
Shielaligh Official explanation: jockey said filly hung right

6659 MORE OFFERS AT BETDIRECT.CO.UK MAIDEN AUCTION STKS 1m (F)
2:40 (2:41) (Class 6) 2-Y-0 **£2,832** (£836; £418) **Stalls** Low

Form RPR
4222 **1** **Salute The General**[12] 6538 2-8-9 78 ..... SteveDrowne 6 69
(W R Muir) *hld up in tch: pushed along 3f out: wd st and rdn 2f out: styd on u.p to ld ins last* **4/11**[1]

00 **2** 1 3/4 **Crazy Bear (IRE)**[145] 3954 2-8-5 ..... JimmyQuinn 10 62
(K A Ryan) *chsd ldrs: rdn along 2f out: drvn and kpt on ins last* **66/1**

3004 **3** 3/4 **Bel Cantor**[16] 6517 2-8-1 67 ..... JosephWalsh(7) 2 63
(W J H Ratcliffe) *cl up: effrt 2f out: rdn to ld over 1f out: hdd and one pce ins last* **12/1**[3]

3506 **4** 1 1/2 **Ten Shun**[12] 6539 2-8-11 50 ..... DeanMcKeown 8 63
(M J Polglase) *led: rdn along over 2f out: drvn and hdd over 1f out: sn one pce* **20/1**

00 **5** 5 **Miss Champagne (IRE)**[26] 6427 2-7-13 ..... RoryMoore(5) 7 46
(M Quinn) *chsd ldrs: rdn along over 2f out: wknd wl over 1f out* **100/1**

00 **6** hd **Patoma (IRE)**[26] 6425 2-8-12 ..... MickyFenton 9 54
(Miss E C Lavelle) *in tch on outer: rdn along 3f out: sn btn* **14/1**

04 **7** 3/4 **Subsidise (IRE)**[12] 6538 2-8-9 ..... J-PGuillambert 5 49
(J G Given) *chsd ldrs: rdn along 1/2-way: sn wknd* **28/1**

00 **8** 12 **Katie Lawson (IRE)**[56] 6122 2-8-2 ..... RichardThomas(3) 3 21
(D Haydn Jones) *dwlt: a rr* **100/1**

0 **9** nk **Precious Dancer**[20] 6477 2-8-10 ..... MartinDwyer 4 26
(W R Muir) *a rr* **11/1**[2]

0 **10** 5 **Late Night Love**[26] 6435 2-8-4 ..... DaleGibson 1 —
(K R Burke) *a rr* **100/1**

0 **11** 12 **Grammaticus**[211] 2008 2-8-9 ..... NCallan 11 —
(K A Ryan) *chsd ldrs: rdn along over 3f out: sn wknd* **25/1**

1m 45.35s (0.75) **Going Correction** +0.025s/f (Slow) 11 Ran SP% **112.5**
Speed ratings (Par 94):97,95,94,93,88 87,87,75,74,69 57
CSF £50.86 TOTE £1.30: £1.10, £10.30, £2.30; EX 31.30.
Owner Mrs D Edginton **Bred** Foursome Thoroughbreds **Trained** Lambourn, Berks

FOCUS
A poor maiden lacking strength in depth, and though the long odds-on winner scored he made rather hard work of it. The front four finished well clear and the others are really going to struggle.

NOTEBOOK
Salute The General, runner-up in his last three starts, looked to face a straightforward task but he never seemed to be travelling that comfortably. After making laboured progress to challenge, he hung over to the stands' rail but was always just about doing enough. There is a strong possibility that the Fibresand is not ideal for him and he may be seen in a better light back on a faster surface. (tchd 2-5)
Crazy Bear(IRE) ◆, well beaten in two turf maidens for Nick Littmoden in the summer, left that form behind and emerged a clear second best on this sand debut. Any further progress should find him a race and he now qualifies for a mark. (op 50-1)
Bel Cantor, trying a trip two furlongs further than anything he has tackled before, saw it out better than might have been expected, but he is now a maiden after 12 attempts and lacks anything in the way of scope. (op 14-1 tchd 11-1)
Ten Shun was not disgraced, but will always be vulnerable to higher-class horses in races like this and would surely be better off back in moderate handicap company. (op 40-1)
Miss Champagne(IRE), well held in both outings so far, probably achieved little here either. (op 66-1)
Katie Lawson(IRE) Official explanation: jockey said filly hung left-handed
Precious Dancer, who showed nothing on his debut earlier in the month, was nonetheless thought by his trainer to be the biggest danger to his stable-companion, but he ran no sort of race and obviously much better was expected. (op 15-2)

6660 JEREMY GLOVER RETIREMENT H'CAP (DIV II) 1m (F)
3:10 (3:11) (Class 6) (0-60,60) 3-Y-0+ **£2,506** (£739; £370) **Stalls** Low

Form RPR
0543 **1** **Quiet Reading (USA)**[7] 6587 8-8-8 **49** .....(v) HayleyTurner 9 61
(M R Bosley) *trckd ldrs: effrt over 2f out: hdwy and rdn over 1f out: styd on ins last to ld last 100 yds* **11/2**[3]

020 **2** 3/4 **Greenbelt**[23] 6468 4-8-11 **52** ..... RobertWinston 5 62
(G M Moore) *cl up: led after 2f: rdn wl over 1f out: edgd rt and drvn ins last: hdd and no ex last 100 yds* **9/1**

0002 **3** 2 **Simply St Lucia**[36] 6372 3-9-4 **60** ..... PhillipMakin 3 66
(J R Weymes) *led 2f: cl up: rdn along 2f out: drvn over 1f out and kpt on same pce* **6/1**

1244 **4** shd **Seldemosa**[244] 1188 4-9-0 **55** ..... MickyFenton 10 61
(M S Saunders) *dwlt and bhd: stdy hdwy opn inner over 2f out: rdn to chse ldrs over 1f out: drvn and one pce ins last* **10/1**

0503 **5** 3 1/2 **Roman Empire**[36] 6372 5-9-3 **58** .....(b) NCallan 6 57
(K A Ryan) *trckd ldrs: hdwy over 2f out and ev ch tl rdn and one pce appr last* **15/2**

5600 **6** 3 **Lowestoft Playboy**[16] 6513 3-8-13 **58** ..... DominicFox(3) 12 51
(J Jay) *cl up on outer: effrt and ev ch over 2f out: sn rdn and wknd wl over 1f out* **25/1**

6044 **7** 3 **Sol Rojo**[12] 6542 3-9-2 **58** ..... RobbieFitzpatrick 4 45
(M J Attwater) *chsd ldrs: rdn along 3f out: sn wknd* **9/2**[1]

0201 **8** hd **Chickado (IRE)**[12] 6541 4-8-7 **51** ..... RichardThomas(3) 7 37
(D Haydn Jones) *a towards rr* **11/1**

4200 **9** 5 **Burnley Al (IRE)**[12] 6535 3-9-4 **60** .....(p) PaulHanagan 1 36
(R A Fahey) *dwlt: a bhd* **20/1**

0000 **10** 3/4 **Tizzy's Law**[16] 6514 4-9-0 **55** ..... EddieAhern 11 30
(E F Vaughan) *a bhd* **33/1**

0515 **11** *1* **Speakerboxxx**[31] 6401 3-8-11 **53**.................................. SteveDrowne 2 26
(P F I Cole) *chsd ldrs on inner: rdn along wl over 2f out: sn wknd* **5/1**[2]
0020 **12** *1 3/4* **Ming Vase**[12] 6541 3-8-12 **54**.................................. LeeEnstone 8 23
(P T Midgley) *prom:rdn along 1/2-way: sn wknd* **33/1**
1m 44.76s (0.16) **Going Correction** +0.025s/f (Slow)
WFA 3 from 4yo+ 1lb **12** Ran SP% **118.2**
Speed ratings (Par 101):100,99,97,97,93 90,87,87,82,81 80,78
CSF £51.52 CT £310.93 TOTE £4.70: £2.10, £2.60, £2.30; EX 70.60 Place 6 £75.12, Place 5 £48.75.
Owner Mrs Jean M O'Connor **Bred** European Thoroughbreds Ltd **Trained** Lockeridge, Wilts
FOCUS
An ordinary handicap run at just an average pace and the winning time was 0.61 seconds slower than the first division. There were five in a line across the track with every chance a furlong out.
Chickado(IRE) Official explanation: jockey said filly was never travelling
Speakerboxxx Official explanation: jockey said gelding had no more to give
T/Plt: £58.00 to a £1 stake. Pool: £30,457.50. 382.75 winning tickets. T/Qpdt: £15.50 to a £1 stake. Pool: £3,183.40. 151.50 winning tickets. JR

6647 WOLVERHAMPTON (A.W) (L-H)

Monday, December 26

OFFICIAL GOING: Standard
The Clerk of the Course felt that the ground may have just on the slow side.
Wind: Light; against Weather: Light showers

6661 MERRY CHRISTMAS FROM BETDIRECT MAIDEN STKS 5f 216y(P)
1:35 (1:38) (Class 5) 2-Y-0 **£3,500** (£1,041; £520; £259) **Stalls** Low

Form RPR
34 **1** **Foreplay (IRE)**[90] 5529 2-8-9 .... PaulHanagan 2 66
(E A L Dunlop) *a.p: rdn to ld wl over 1f out: flashed tail whn hit w whip ins fnl f: r.o* **7/4**[1]
2200 **2** *1 1/2* **Canina**[20] 6517 2-8-9 66.. EddieAhern 5 61
(Ms Deborah J Evans) *a.p: rdn and ev ch over 2f out: r.o one pce fnl f* **4/1**[2]
0 **3** *1/2* **Billy Bling (IRE)**[17] 6532 2-9-0 .... DaneO'Neill 1 65
(R Hannon) *w ldr: led over 3f out: rdn and hdd wl over 1f out: kpt on same pce fnl f* **7/1**
06 **4** *hd* **Black Sea Pearl**[10] 6595 2-8-9 .... JimmyQuinn 11 59
(P W D'Arcy) *hld up in mid-div: rdn and lost pl over 3f out: hdwy over 2f out: r.o one pce fnl f* **50/1**
5 *1 1/2* **Miss Lopez (IRE)** 2-8-9 .... RobertWinston 8 61+
(K R Burke) *hld up and bhd: nt clr run over 1f out: hdwy fnl f: bttr for r* **14/1**
0 **6** *hd* **Sendinpost**[58] 6143 2-8-9 .... RobbieFitzpatrick 9 54+
(S C Williams) *hld up and bhd: rdn wl over 1f out: hdwy fnl f: r.o* **33/1**
0 **7** *hd* **Noble Minstrel**[76] 5817 2-9-0 .... J-PGuillambert 13 58+
(S C Williams) *racd wd: hld up and bhd: rdn over 2f out: kpt on fnl f: nt rch ldrs* **50/1**
60 **8** *1* **Desert Dust**[17] 6528 2-9-0 .... PatCosgrave 12 55
(R M H Cowell) *t.k.h: prom: rdn over 2f out: wknd over 1f out* **40/1**
9 *2 1/2* **Alice Amelia** 2-8-9 .... MickyFenton 3 43
(C R Egerton) *s.i.s: sn hld up in mid-div: rdn over 3f out: sn struggling* **14/1**
06 **10** *1 3/4* **Hand Of Destiny (USA)**[5] 6642 2-9-0 .... HayleyTurner 7 42
(N P Littmoden) *chsd ldrs: lost pl after 1f: wkng whn hung lft over 1f out* **10/1**
0050 **11** *1* **Deserving**[17] 6529 2-8-9 63.......................................(t) TomEaves 6 34
(W J Haggas) *s.i.s: hdwy over 3f out: rdn wl over 1f out: sn wknd* **11/2**[3]
503P **12** *3* **Ashburnham (IRE)**[93] 5446 2-8-9 70.. AlanDaly 4 25
(N I M Rossiter) *led over 2f: wknd 2f out: hmpd over 1f out* **14/1**
1m 16.82s (1.01) **Going Correction** -0.025s/f (Stan) **12** Ran SP% **122.6**
Speed ratings (Par 96):92,90,89,89,87 86,86,85,81,79 78,74
CSF £8.49 TOTE £2.30: £1.20, £1.70, £2.40; EX 10.00.
Owner St Albans Bloodstock LLP **Bred** Gainsborough Stud Management Ltd **Trained** Newmarket, Suffolk
FOCUS
A modest maiden with the exposed 66-rated runner-up a good yardstick.
NOTEBOOK
Foreplay(IRE), whose two previous starts came within a week in September, has been given some time and took to the sand well. Her rider thought she idled after hitting the front and that she will get further in time. (op 5-2)
Canina, a shade disappointing on Fibresand last time, met one too good for the fourth time in her career on this return to six. (op 3-1)
Billy Bling(IRE) stepped up considerably on his debut here earlier in the month and may appreciate a return to seven. (op 11-1)
Black Sea Pearl showed improvement on this drop back in distance but, as her breeding suggests, she will probably need further next year.
Miss Lopez(IRE) is a half-sister to several winners at up to just short of two miles. Shaping promisingly on her debut, she is one to keep an eye on when tackling further. (op 12-1)
Sendinpost ◆, a half-sister to the multiple winning staying handicapper Sendintank, is another who will come into her own over longer trips next year.

6662 BETDIRECT FOOTBALL CASHBACKS NURSERY 5f 20y(P)
2:10 (2:10) (Class 4) (0-85,78) 2-Y-0 **£4,631** (£1,377; £688; £343) **Stalls** Low

Form RPR
0620 **1** **Rapsgate (IRE)**[24] 6479 2-8-5 **65**.................................. StephaneBreux(3) 2 70
(R Hannon) *a.p: rdn over 1f out: r.o to ld nr fin* **7/1**[3]
3561 **2** *nk* **Egyptian Lord**[11] 6581 2-8-8 **65**..................................(b) RobbieFitzpatrick 3 69
(Peter Grayson) *sn led: rdn over 1f out: hdd nr fin* **7/2**[1]
5403 **3** *3/4* **Sands Crooner (IRE)**[8] 6605 2-8-11 **71**..................(t) PatrickMathers(3) 1 72
(D Shaw) *s.i.s: hld up: hdwy 2f out: sn rdn: edgd lft ins fnl f: kpt on* **7/1**[3]
3636 **4** *2* **Scooby Dude (IRE)**[20] 6517 2-9-7 **78**.................................. GeorgeBaker 5 72
(Ms Deborah J Evans) *hld up and bhd: hdwy on ins 2f out: sn rdn: one pce fnl f* **7/2**[1]
0140 **5** *3/4* **Thoughtsofstardom**[17] 6529 2-8-11 **68**.................................. EddieAhern 7 59
(W M Brisbourne) *led early: prom: rdn over 2f out: edgd lft over 1f out: one pce* **8/1**
3021 **6** *1* **Charming Ballet (IRE)**[30] 6433 2-9-3 **74**..................(p) JimmyQuinn 6 62
(N P Littmoden) *t.k.h in rr: rdn and hung lft over 1f out: nvr trbld ldrs* **4/1**[2]
3045 **7** *1/2* **Trombone Tom**[10] 6591 2-8-6 **66**.................................. PaulMulrennan(3) 4 52
(J R Norton) *chsd ldr: rdn over 2f out: wknd 1f out* **7/1**[3]
0050 **8** *5* **Blue Minx (IRE)**[20] 6517 2-7-9 **55** oh5..........................(b) DominicFox(3) 8 23
(J S Moore) *chsd ldrs tl wknd 2f out* **25/1**
62.49 secs (-0.33) **Going Correction** -0.025s/f (Stan) **8** Ran SP% **116.9**
Speed ratings (Par 98):101,100,99,96,94 93,92,84
CSF £32.49 CT £160.84 TOTE £10.40: £2.50, £1.50, £2.10; EX 11.70.
Owner Team Havana **Bred** J F O'Malley **Trained** East Everleigh, Wilts
■ The first winner in Britain for French rider Stephane Breux.
FOCUS
A competitive little nursery but probably only ordinary form.
NOTEBOOK
Rapsgate(IRE), dropped 2lb, finally got off the mark on this return to the minimum trip. This should have boosted her confidence and she is likely to be out again soon. (op 8-1)
Egyptian Lord lost nothing in defeat having gone up 5lb for his win in first-time blinkers at Southwell.
Sands Crooner(IRE) has been exclusively campaigned at this trip but again ran as if he is ready to tackle six furlongs. (tchd 8-1)
Scooby Dude(IRE) may do better back at six furlongs. (tchd 3-1)
Thoughtsofstardom was dropping back from six having landed a seller over course and distance in October. (tchd 9-1)
Charming Ballet(IRE) adopted different tactics after the Handicapper had not taken too many chances with him for his win in a maiden over course and distance a month earlier. (tchd 9-2)

6663 BETDIRECT NO Q ON 08000 93 66 93 NOVICE STKS 7f 32y(P)
2:45 (2:46) (Class 5) 2-Y-0 **£4,061** (£1,208; £603; £301) **Stalls** High

Form RPR
0000 **1** **Reveur**[101] 5265 2-8-7 54.. JimmyQuinn 3 70+
(M Mullineaux) *n.m.r s: hld up and bhd: nt clr run whn swtchd lft and hdwy over 1f out: led wl ins fnl f: r.o wl* **50/1**
5322 **2** *1 3/4* **Porters (USA)**[6] 6627 2-9-5 82.. DaneO'Neill 5 75
(R Hannon) *a.p: rdn to ld 2f out: hdd and nt qckn wl ins fnl f* **8/11**[1]
3 *2 1/2* **Kokila** 2-8-3 .... HayleyTurner 2 52
(W J Haggas) *a.p: rdn 2f out: one pce* **10/1**
0200 **4** *1 1/4* **Gattuso**[24] 6479 2-8-12 63.. EddieAhern 9 58
(Ms Deborah J Evans) *hld up: rdn wl over 1f out: late hdwy on outside: nt rch ldrs* **16/1**
0242 **5** *nk* **Phinerine**[9] 6600 2-8-12 65.. MickyFenton 1 57
(R A Harris) *led early: prom: rdn over 1f out: wknd ins fnl f* **8/1**[3]
521 **6** *1 3/4* **Opal Warrior**[22] 6496 2-8-7 63.. PaulHanagan 4 47
(P W D'Arcy) *sn led: rdn and hdd 2f out: wknd ins fnl f* **10/3**[2]
3250 **7** *6* **Dream Factor (IRE)**[11] 6581 2-8-6 60.......................... PatrickMathers(3) 6 34
(J O'Reilly) *prom: rdn over 3f out: wkng whn edgd lft 1f out* **33/1**
1500 **8** *1 1/4* **Angelina Bankes**[6] 6634 2-8-9 56.......................... RobbieFitzpatrick 8 31
(R A Harris) *rdn over 3f out: a bhd* **20/1**
0400 **9** *12* **Double Oh Seven (IRE)**[72] 5887 2-8-12 65.................. RobertWinston 7 2
(J W Unett) *sn prom: rdn and wknd over 3f out* **20/1**
1m 31.04s (0.64) **Going Correction** -0.025s/f (Stan) **9** Ran SP% **121.5**
Speed ratings (Par 96):95,93,90,88,88 86,79,78,64
CSF £90.07 TOTE £53.70: £6.50, £1.10, £2.60; EX 161.30.
Owner A Jones **Bred** Bishopswood Bloodstock And Trickledown Stud **Trained** Alpraham, Cheshire
FOCUS
Run at a modest pace, this was not a great race of its type and the form looks dubious.
NOTEBOOK
Reveur, previously trained by Richard Fahey, was having her first outing for three months and showed tremendous improvement on this sand debut.
Porters(USA) had no answer to the shock winner and made it a hat-trick of seconds. (tchd 4-5)
Kokila made a satisfactory start to her career and it will be interesting to see if she is kept going on the All-Weather. (op 8-1 tchd 7-1)
Gattuso is fully exposed and had something to find on official figures. (op 14-1)
Phinerine again failed to get home having run in a seller over this course and distance back in June. (op 12-1)
Opal Warrior should not have been beaten for stamina and may have been better off setting a stronger gallop. (op 7-2 tchd 3-1)
Double Oh Seven(IRE) Official explanation: jockey said colt hung left throughout

6664 BETDIRECT.CO.UK CLAIMING STKS 7f 32y(P)
3:20 (3:23) (Class 6) 3-Y-0+ **£2,941** (£868; £434) **Stalls** High

Form RPR
03-1 **1** **Atlantic Quest (USA)**[353] 62 6-9-5 82..................(p) RobertWinston 3 79
(K R Burke) *hld up: hdwy over 2f out: shkn up to ld wl ins fnl f: r.o* **9/4**[2]
1301 **2** *1/2* **Mystic Man (FR)**[23] 6486 7-9-5 80.. NCallan 2 78
(K A Ryan) *hld up: hdwy 3f out: led wl over 1f out: sn rdn: hdd wl ins fnl f: nt qckn* **11/10**[1]
0340 **3** *3 1/2* **Tregarron**[6] 6630 4-8-8 60.. StephaneBreux(3) 1 61+
(R Hannon) *hld up in mid-div: lost pl over 4f out: hdwy over 2f out: rdn wl over 1f out: kpt on ins fnl f* **13/2**[3]
4030 **4** *2 1/2* **Iced Diamond (IRE)**[125] 4657 6-9-1 60.......................... EddieAhern 5 58
(W M Brisbourne) *sn prom: rdn to ld jst over 2f out: hdd wl over 1f out: wknd ins fnl f* **12/1**
0000 **5** *6* **Sahara Prince (IRE)**[21] 6505 5-8-11 75..................(p) PaulHanagan 6 38
(K A Morgan) *s.s: bhd: hrd rdn and hdwy on outside 3f out: n.d* **12/1**
0005 **6** *1/2* **Prospect Court**[114] 4959 3-8-2 55.......................... JosephWalsh(7) 8 35
(J W Unett) *nvr nr ldrs* **33/1**
0506 **7** *1 3/4* **Weet Yer Tern (IRE)**[7] 6623 3-9-1 53..................(p) PatCosgrave 10 42+
(P A Blockley) *led after 1f: hdd over 2f out: sn hmpd on ins: wknd wl over 1f out* **33/1**
5000 **8** *1* **Shrine Mountain (USA)**[100] 5324 3-9-1 62.......................... BrianReilly 9 34
(J R Holt) *prom tl wknd over 2f out* **40/1**
0200 **9** *5* **Chilly Cracker**[23] 6486 3-8-6 60.. TomEaves 7 12
(R Hollinshead) *broke wl: sn lost pl: hdwy 5f out: rdn over 3f out: wknd over 2f out* **16/1**
550- **10** *3 1/2* **Weet N Measures**[74] 6600 3-8-9 54.......................... J-PGuillambert 4 6
(T Wall) *led 1f: wknd over 3f out* **40/1**
1m 29.63s (-0.77) **Going Correction** -0.025s/f (Stan) **10** Ran SP% **123.7**
Speed ratings (Par 101):103,102,98,95,88 88,86,85,79,75
CSF £5.30 TOTE £3.20: £1.40, £1.10, £2.00; EX 6.90.Atlantic Quest was claimed by R. A. Harris for £12,000.
Owner A Polignone **Bred** Bemark N V & Bon Marche **Trained** Middleham Moor, N Yorks
FOCUS
An uncompetitive claimer with the two at the head of the market fighting out the finish.
Sahara Prince(IRE) Official explanation: jockey said horse missed break

6665 LITTLEWOODS BETDIRECT H'CAP 1m 4f 50y(P)
3:50 (3:50) (Class 4) (0-85,83) 3-Y-O+ £5,704 (£1,697; £848; £423) Stalls Low

Form RPR
3231 1 Heathyards Pride[20] 6519 5-9-3 75 GeorgeBaker 5 83
(R Hollinshead) *hld up and bhd: rdn and hdwy on outside wl over 1f out: led wl ins fnl f: r.o* 11/2
0021 2 nk Pass The Port[24] 6482 4-9-4 76 EddieAhern 7 84
(D Haydn Jones) *hld up in tch: led on bit jst over 2f out: rdn and hdd wl ins fnl f: r.o* 7/2[1]
1215 3 1 3/4 Bethanys Boy (IRE)[24] 6482 4-9-0 72 TomEaves 6 77
(B Ellison) *hld up: rdn and hdwy over 2f out: one pce fnl f* 9/2[3]
0023 4 3 1/2 Countrywide Luck[5] 6644 4-8-12 70 HayleyTurner 4 70
(N P Littmoden) *hld up in mid-div: rdn 2f out: styd on one pce fnl f* 4/1[2]
514 5 nk Bazelle[16] 6547 3-8-9 75 PatrickMathers(3) 8 74
(D Shaw) *hld up and bhd: hdwy on ins wl over 1f out: no further prog fnl f* 25/1
0U00 6 3/4 Wotchalike (IRE)[7] 6622 3-8-9 75 (v) AmirQuinn(3) 1 73
(R J Price) *chsd ldr: rdn over 3f out: wknd over 1f out* 16/1
3000 7 nk Eastborough (IRE)[5] 6645 6-9-4 76 NCallan 9 73
(B G Powell) *sn led: set slow pce: qcknd over 4f out: rdn 3f out: hdd jst over 2f out: wknd 1f out* 10/1
6021 8 8 Consonant (IRE)[7] 6621 8-9-11 83 6ex MickyFenton 2 76+
(D G Bridgwater) *led early: prom: rdn over 4f out: wknd wl over 1f out* 15/2
0020 U Fiddlers Creek (IRE)[22] 1664 6-9-0 72 (v) JimmyQuinn 3 —
(R Allan) *stmbld and uns rdr s* 7/1

2m 40.21s (-2.21) **Going Correction** -0.025s/f (Stan)
WFA 3 from 4yo+ 5lb 9 Ran SP% **118.9**
Speed ratings (Par 105):106,105,104,102,102 101,101,96,—
CSF £25.91 CT £95.72 TOTE £5.60: £1.80, £1.90, £1.80; EX 21.00.
Owner L A Morgan **Bred** L A Morgan **Trained** Upper Longdon, Staffs
FOCUS
They went no gallop for the best part of a mile in this tightly-knit handicap. The winner is progressive.

6666 IN RUNNING TONIGHT ON SKYTEXT 293 FILLIES' H'CAP 1m 1f 103y(P)
4:20 (4:20) (Class 5) (0-70,70) 3-Y-O+ £3,371 (£1,003; £501; £250) Stalls Low

Form RPR
-545 1 Connotation[16] 6544 3-9-4 70 EddieAhern 10 78
(P W Chapple-Hyam) *hld up in mid-div: hdwy over 2f out: sn rdn: led ins fnl f: flashed tail: drvn out* 5/1[2]
1033 2 nk Daring Affair[6] 6633 4-9-3 67 NCallan 12 74
(K R Burke) *a.p: rdn over 3f out: led over 1f out tl ins fnl f: r.o* 9/2[1]
0105 3 1 1/2 Sforzando[10] 6593 4-8-5 62 KristinStubbs(7) 5 66+
(Mrs L Stubbs) *hld up and bhd: rdn and hdwy over 1f out: r.o ins fnl f* 12/1
2301 4 shd Night Storm[9] 6598 4-9-1 65 JimmyQuinn 1 69
(S Dow) *hld up in mid-div: hdwy wl over 1f out: sn swtchd rt: r.o ins fnl f* 9/2[1]
6060 5 nk In The Pink (IRE)[9] 6596 5-8-10 60 PaulHanagan 9 63
(M A Buckley) *hld up: hdwy over 3f out: rdn over 2f out: ev ch over 1f out: no ex ins fnl f* 14/1
4150 6 3 Littleton Zephir (USA)[182] 2985 6-9-3 67 TomEaves 11 65
(Mrs P Townsley) *hld up and bhd: rdn and hdwy over 2f out: no imp fnl f* 14/1
0066 7 2 Tequila Sheila (IRE)[7] 6621 3-8-8 60 PatCosgrave 8 54
(K R Burke) *hld up in tch: rdn 2f out: wknd ins fnl f* 16/1
2040 8 1 House Martin[84] 5662 3-9-1 67 MickyFenton 4 59
(C R Dore) *chsd ldr: led over 3f out: rdn and hdd over 1f out: wknd fnl f* 33/1
1066 9 1/2 Tokewanna[10] 6594 5-8-7 60 (t) PatrickMathers(3) 7 51
(W M Brisbourne) *t.k.h in mid-div: lost pl on ins over 3f out: n.d after* 8/1
604 10 1 3/4 Numanthia (IRE)[14] 6565 3-8-6 58 J-PGuillambert 13 46
(Miss J R Gibney) *hld up and bhd: rdn 4f out: hdwy on outside 3f out: wknd wl over 1f out* 33/1
6052 11 9 Mollyputtheketelon (USA)[10] 6594 4-8-9 64 DerekNolan(5) 6 35
(M J Wallace) *bhd fnl 3f* 13/2[3]
0600 12 1 3/4 Love Affair (IRE)[21] 6503 3-8-10 65 StephaneBreux(3) 2 32
(R Hannon) *prom: lost pl on ins over 3f out: sn bhd* 14/1
310- 13 dist Chorus Beauty[391] 6773 4-8-12 62 RobertWinston 3 —
(N I M Rossiter) *led: rdn and hdd over 3f out: wknd qckly over 2f out: eased whn no ch fnl f* 20/1

2m 2.41s (-0.21) **Going Correction** -0.025s/f (Stan)
WFA 3 from 4yo+ 2lb 13 Ran SP% **121.7**
Speed ratings (Par 100):99,98,97,97,97 94,92,91,91,89 81,80,—
CSF £27.70 CT £260.31 TOTE £5.30: £1.60, £1.60, £5.70; EX 25.40 Place 6 £10.17, Place 5 £6.95.
Owner Hyperion Bloodstock **Bred** Millsec Limited **Trained** Newmarket, Suffolk
FOCUS
This wide-open looking handicap was run at a steady pace but the form looks sound enough. The winner is not fully exposed.
T/Plt: £12.50 to a £1 stake. Pool: £30,926.40. 1,792.55 winning tickets. T/Qpdt: £3.20 to a £1 stake. Pool: £1,807.60. 417.40 winning tickets. KH

6653 SOUTHWELL (L-H)
Tuesday, December 27

OFFICIAL GOING: Standard
The track had to be worked because of the snow showers and the surface was described as 'deep, very slow and hard work'.
Wind: Light, half-behind Weather: Frequent heavy snow showers

6667 MORE OFFERS AT BETDIRECT.CO.UK H'CAP (DIV I) 1m (F)
11:35 (11:36) (Class 6) (0-55,57) 3-Y-O+ £2,485 (£733; £367) Stalls Low

Form RPR
3211 1 Preskani[9] 6607 3-9-1 57 7ex (p) AlanDaly 10 65
(Mrs N Macauley) *hld up in rr: hdwy over 3f out: rdn over 2f out: led 1f out: edgd rt: hld on wl* 10/1
2002 2 nk Priorina (IRE)[41] 6369 3-8-7 49 (v) RobertHavlin 8 56
(D Haydn Jones) *chsd ldrs: chal over 2f out: no ex towards fin* 16/1
0003 3 2 1/2 Blue Empire (IRE)[17] 6535 4-8-11 52 RobertWinston 7 54
(C R Dore) *chsd ldrs: effrt 3f out: kpt on same pce fnl f* 11/2[3]
0231 4 1 1/4 Captain Darling (IRE)[9] 6608 5-8-10 54 7ex EdwardCreighton(3) 6 54
(R W Price) *led: rdn and hung rt over 2f out: hdd 1f out: sn fdd* 5/1[2]
1415 5 5 Abbeygate[12] 6587 4-9-0 55 J-PGuillambert 1 45
(T Keddy) *s.i.s: hdwy 4f out: hrd rdn on outer over 2f out: nvr nr ldrs* 7/2[1]
0006 6 4 Veneer (IRE)[12] 6587 3-8-11 53 (b) JimmyQuinn 2 35
(Miss Gay Kelleway) *chsd ldrs: lost pl over 1f out* 16/1
0026 7 1 1/4 Fantasy Defender (IRE)[13] 6576 3-8-10 52 (v) ChrisCatlin 9 31
(J J Quinn) *mid-div: hrd drvn 4f out: nvr a threat* 20/1
4154 8 1 1/4 We'll Meet Again[12] 6587 5-8-10 54 PaulMulrennan(3) 12 31
(M W Easterby) *sn drvn along and bhd: hrd rdn and hung lft over 2f out: nvr on terms* 5/1[2]
0060 9 8 Noul (USA)[210] 2148 6-8-4 52 JosephWalsh(7) 5 13
(J S Moore) *s.i.s: sme hdwy on inner over 2f out: nvr a factor* 20/1
0004 10 1 1/2 Jakeal (IRE)[15] 6558 6-8-6 47 oh6 ow1 (b) DeanMcKeown 4 5
(R M Whitaker) *chsd ldrs: rdn 3f out: sn lost pl* 66/1
66 11 4 Two Chimneys (USA)[87] 5629 3-8-10 52 (t) NCallan 3 2
(K A Ryan) *chsd ldrs: lost pl over 2f out* 11/2[3]
1200 12 24 Nevinstown (IRE)[12] 6587 5-8-12 53 TonyHamilton 11 —
(C Grant) *s.v.s: a detached in last: t.o 3f out* 33/1

1m 45.62s (1.02) **Going Correction** -0.025s/f (Stan)
WFA 3 from 4yo+ 1lb 12 Ran SP% **121.1**
Speed ratings (Par 101):93,92,90,88,83 79,78,77,69,67 63,39
CSF £154.51 CT £980.93 TOTE £11.10: £3.30, £4.60, £1.90; EX 127.60.
Owner Godfrey Horsford **Bred** P And Mrs Venner **Trained** Sproxton, Leics
FOCUS
A slow time and a modest contest rated through the runner-up.
Nevinstown(IRE) Official explanation: trainer said gelding was reluctant to race

6668 FIRST PAST THE POST AT BETDIRECT CLAIMING STKS 5f (F)
12:05 (12:08) (Class 6) 3-Y-O+ £2,852 (£842; £421) Stalls High

Form RPR
2364 1 Tag Team (IRE)[10] 6597 4-9-3 63 NCallan 7 74
(John A Harris) *mde all: hld on gamely* 15/2
1312 2 nk Dellagio (IRE)[45] 6326 4-8-7 51 EddieAhern 3 63
(Rae Guest) *stdd and swtchd rt s: hdwy over 2f out: chal 1f out: no ex towards fin* 10/3[1]
4625 3 1 3/4 Sir Sandrovitch (IRE)[11] 6589 9-8-3 57 (v) PaulHanagan 1 53
(R A Fahey) *s.i.s: hdwy on outer over 2f out: kpt on wl fnl f* 9/2[2]
3000 4 1 1/4 Soba Jones[21] 6513 8-8-8 58 JasonEdmunds(3) 9 57
(J Balding) *chsd ldrs: kpt on same pce appr fnl f* 20/1
5020 5 1 Mynd[21] 6515 5-8-6 55 ow1 (v[1]) DeanMcKeown 8 48
(R M Whitaker) *chsd ldrs: one pce fnl 2f* 16/1
5611 6 nk He's A Rocket (IRE)[36] 6407 4-8-4 60 (b) AndrewElliott(7) 6 52
(K R Burke) *sn in rr: hdwy over 1f out: styd on ins last* 9/2[2]
0600 7 5 Yorkshire Lad (IRE)[7] 6631 3-8-13 65 (t) JimmyQuinn 4 37
(Miss Gay Kelleway) *chsd ldrs on outer: fdd over 1f out* 40/1
0200 8 hd Mirasol Princess[6] 6646 4-7-11 54 LauraReynolds(7) 14 28
(D K Ivory) *restless stalls: bhd and edgd lft: ended up on far side: nvr on terms* 33/1
0200 9 shd Marinaite[36] 6404 4-8-12 68 PhillipMakin 2 35
(S R Bowring) *prom on outer: wknd over 1f out* 12/1
4060 10 3/4 Mulberry Lad (IRE)[6] 6639 3-8-3 52 ChrisCatlin 11 24
(P W Hiatt) *chsd ldrs: lost pl over 1f out* 28/1
6100 11 2 1/2 Dizzy In The Head[24] 6486 6-8-11 62 (b) TomEaves 10 23
(I Semple) *a in rr* 14/1
0406 12 1 1/4 Namir (IRE)[24] 6486 3-9-9 66 (v) MickyFenton 12 31
(Stef Liddiard) *a in rr* 25/1
0460 13 nk Byo (IRE)[6] 6646 7-8-13 53 RobertWinston 5 20
(P Howling) *in tch: hung rt and heavily eased fnl f* 25/1
2010 14 1 1/2 Rapid River[28] 6455 3-7-12 56 HayleyTurner 13 —
(P D Evans) *sn bhd* 7/1[3]

59.88 secs (-0.42) **Going Correction** +0.05s/f (Slow) 14 Ran SP% **125.2**
Speed ratings (Par 101):105,104,101,99,98 97,89,89,89,87 83,81,81,79
CSF £31.29 TOTE £9.60: £2.60, £1.70, £2.30; EX 49.00.Dellagio was claimed by Russell Price for £7,000.
Owner Clearthern Glass Sealed Units Ltd **Bred** Miss Sally Hodgins **Trained** Eastwell, Leics
■ Neil Callan's 150th winner this year.

Marinaite Official explanation: jockey said filly hung violently right all the way
Byo(IRE) Official explanation: jockey said gelding suffered an overreach
Rapid River Official explanation: jockey said filly was never travelling

6669 PRESS RED TO BET ON ITVI H'CAP 1m 4f (F)
12:35 (12:36) (Class 5) (0-75,81) 3-Y-O+ £3,960 (£1,178; £588; £294) Stalls Low

Form RPR
0141 1 Kylkenny[7] 6633 10-9-5 81 7ex (t) TravisBlock(5) 4 88
(H Morrison) *sn trcking ldr: led over 4f out: rdn and hld on gamely* 10/3[1]
3430 2 1 1/4 Mad Carew (USA)[6] 6645 6-9-1 75 (e) AmirQuinn(3) 8 80
(J R Boyle) *trckd ldrs gng wl: smooth hdwy over 3f out: effrt over 1f out: no ex ins last* 7/2[2]
3050 3 3/4 Dovedon Hero[6] 6644 5-8-13 70 (b) NCallan 2 74
(P J McBride) *mid-div: effrt 4f out: sn chsng ldrs: kpt on same pce fnl f* 6/1[3]
0052 4 6 Yenaled[5] 6655 8-7-12 62 DonnaCaldwell(7) 1 57
(P S McEntee) *hld up in rr: t.k.h and hdwy on outside to trck ldrs 6f out: wknd over 1f out* 10/3[1]
B055 5 17 Come What July (IRE)[7] 6637 4-8-13 70 (v) AlanDaly 6 40
(Mrs N Macauley) *hld up in rr: hdwy on outer 6f out: effrt on inner over 2f out: sn btn* 16/1
2200 6 5 Barking Mad (USA)[11] 6594 7-8-5 62 PaulHanagan 5 24
(C R Dore) *led: sn clr: hdd over 4f out: lost pl over 2f out* 9/1
2003 7 1/2 Indebted[15] 6564 3-8-10 72 EddieAhern 3 33
(P W D'Arcy) *chsd ldrs: lost pl over 2f out* 10/1
5224 8 2 1/2 Hue[228] 1665 4-9-1 72 (p) TomEaves 7 30
(B Ellison) *mid-div: rdn and outpcd over 4f out: lost pl 3f out* 14/1

2m 40.98s (-1.11) **Going Correction** -0.025s/f (Stan)
WFA 3 from 4yo+ 5lb 8 Ran SP% **114.3**
Speed ratings (Par 103):102,101,100,96,85 82,81,80
CSF £15.24 CT £65.75 TOTE £4.30: £1.50, £2.00, £1.80; EX 19.20.
Owner W R B Racing 59 (wrbracing.com) **Bred** R M , P J And S R Payne **Trained** East Ilsley, Berks
FOCUS
Veteran Kylkenny rolled back the years to record his nineteenth career win, helped it must be said by the reluctance of the runner-up.

6670 BETDIRECT FREEPHONE 0800 211 222 (S) STKS 5f (F)
1:05 (1:07) (Class 6) 2-Y-O £2,504 (£739; £369) Stalls High

Form				RPR
4302	1		**Luloah**[9] 6605 2-8-7 62 .... DaleGibson 7 (J G Given) *mde all: rdn and hld on* 7/4[1]	49
2001	2	¾	**Angie And Liz (IRE)**[15] 6562 2-8-5 55 .... JBrennan(7) 8 (P D Evans) *sn trcking wnr: styd on fnl f: no ex towards fin* 7/2[2]	52
00	3	1¼	**Lake Suprima (IRE)**[41] 6366 2-8-3 ow3 .... MichaelJStainton(7) 3 (R M Whitaker) *chsd ldrs: outpcd 2f out: styd on ins last: tk 3rd nr line* 16/1	46
1000	4	nk	**Pauvic (IRE)**[12] 6581 2-9-3 57 .... PaulFessey 1 (Mrs A Duffield) *w wnr: rdn over 2f out: kpt on same pce* 8/1	52
0000	5	¾	**Tatstheticket**[14] 6569 2-8-9 35 ....(b[1]) JasonEdmunds(3) 2 (J Balding) *chsd ldrs on outer: kpt on same pce fnl 2f* 40/1	44
	6	1	**Sweet Rosella** 2-8-0 .... NicolaTopper(7) 4 (G M Moore) *dwlt: hdwy on outer 3f out: fdd over 1f out* 25/1	36
5066	7	½	**Macs All Heart (IRE)**[17] 6538 2-8-7 45 .... RobertWinston 6 (A B Coogan) *sn outpcd: kpt on fnl 2f: nvr a threat* 9/1	34
3300	8	5	**In The Fountain (IRE)**[144] 4132 2-8-7 47 .... HayleyTurner 5 (C A Dwyer) *dwlt: a outpcd and in rr* 14/1	17
63	9	dist	**Follow Me In (IRE)**[136] 4355 2-8-7 ....(b[1]) PatCosgrave 9 (K R Burke) *ref to r: virtually tk no part* 4/1[3]	—

61.88 secs (1.58) **Going Correction** +0.05s/f (Slow) 9 Ran SP% **118.5**
Speed ratings (Par 94):89,87,85,85,84 82,81,73,—
CSF £8.09 TOTE £2.60: £1.30, £1.50, £6.40; EX 10.50.The winner was sold to P. McEntee for 7,000gns. Angie And Liz was claimed by Mr P. M. Grayson for £6,000.
Owner Mrs Susan M Lee **Bred** Mrs S M Lee **Trained** Willoughton, Lincs

FOCUS
A poor seller run in a slow time and rated through the fifth.

NOTEBOOK
Luloah, who never entered the parade ring, looks a real madam but to her credit once underway she did nothing at all wrong. She changed hands at the auction. (tchd 9-4)
Angie And Liz(IRE) looked a real threat but in the end the winner proved just the tougher. She was claimed. (op 9-2)
Lake Suprima(IRE), having her third outing, stayed on after getting outpaced and can do better in handicap company over six furlongs plus. (op 20-1)
Pauvic(IRE) had 15lb to find with the winner on official rtaings. The Polytrack surface at Lingfield seems to suit him slightly better. (op 11-2)
Tatstheticket, in first-ime blinkers, seemed to run a lot better on just his fifth career start.
Follow Me In(IRE), absent since August, stood still when the traps opened and virtually took no part. (op 7-2 tchd 10-3)

6671 LITTLEWOODS BET DIRECT H'CAP 1m (F)
1:40 (1:42) (Class 5) (0-70,70) 3-Y-O+ £5,796 (£1,724; £861; £430) Stalls Low

Form				RPR
0242	1		**Byron Bay**[59] 6138 3-9-1 70 .... TomEaves 11 (I Semple) *trckd ldrs: led jst ins last: hld on gamely* 6/1[3]	83
0051	2	nk	**Blue Patrick**[11] 6594 5-9-2 70 .... NCallan 12 (K A Ryan) *trckd ldrs: rdn to ld wl over 1f out: hdd jst ins last: no ex towards fin* 5/1[2]	82
0000	3	6	**Windy Prospect**[7] 6632 3-8-7 62 .... AlanDaly 8 (C R Dore) *s.i.s: hdwy on inner over 2f out: kpt on same pce* 25/1	62
00U1	4	2½	**Monte Mayor Boy**[41] 6365 3-8-11 66 ....(p) RobertHavlin 7 (D Haydn Jones) *chsd ldrs: rdn 3f out: kpt on one pce* 7/1	61
3114	5	1¼	**Amorist (IRE)**[5] 6654 3-8-11 66 .... JamieMackay 2 (Sir Mark Prescott) *w ldrs: led over 2f out: hdd wl over 1f out: sn btn* 5/2[1]	59
5400	6	shd	**Jazrawy**[22] 6503 3-8-3 65 ....(t) RonanKeogh(7) 9 (Miss Gay Kelleway) *mid-div: effrt over 3f out: one pce* 50/1	57
0011	7	hd	**Paso Doble**[7] 6632 7-8-9 70 7ex .... JamesMillman(7) 5 (B R Millman) *outpcd and in rr over 4f out: kpt on fnl 2f: nvr nr ldrs* 15/2	62
2125	8	1	**Parkview Love (USA)**[7] 6632 4-8-12 69 ....(v) PatrickMathers(3) 1 (D Shaw) *led tl hdd wl over 2f out: hung lft and lost pl over 1f out* 11/1	59
1000	9	¾	**Secam (POL)**[7] 6630 6-8-2 59 ....(b) EdwardCreighton(3) 13 (Mrs P Townsley) *racd on outer: sn in rr: kpt on fnl 2f: nvr on terms* 25/1	47
6301	10	9	**Almanshood (USA)**[15] 6565 3-9-0 69 .... DaneO'Neill 10 (P L Gilligan) *mid-div: outpcd over 4f out: nvr a factor* 12/1	39
4140	11	3	**John Forbes**[164] 2928 3-9-1 70 .... RobertWinston 4 (B Ellison) *mid-div: outpcd 4f out: sn btn* 14/1	34
0110	12	hd	**Formidable Will (FR)**[17] 6535 3-8-9 64 ....(p) DaleGibson 14 (M W Easterby) *chsd ldrs: rdn 3f out: sn btn* 14/1	28
-300	13	2½	**Diction (IRE)**[326] 278 3-8-2 64 .... AndrewElliott(7) 6 (K R Burke) *w ldrs: lost pl over 2f out* 66/1	23
0500	14	7	**Edge Fund**[74] 5868 3-8-6 61 .... ChrisCatlin 3 (Miss Gay Kelleway) *chsd ldrs on inner: drvn over 4f out: lost pl over 3f out* 33/1	6

1m 42.91s (-1.69) **Going Correction** -0.025s/f (Stan)
WFA 3 from 4yo+ 1lb 14 Ran SP% **127.2**
Speed ratings (Par 103):107,106,100,98,96 96,96,95,94,85 82,82,80,73
CSF £36.72 CT £731.09 TOTE £7.90: £2.00, £2.50, £9.90; EX 49.80.
Owner Ian Murray Tough **Bred** Ian Murray Tough **Trained** Carluke, S Lanarks

FOCUS
Fair form, the first two both improving and pulling clear in a race run at a strong gallop. Thr third is the best guide to the value of the form.

6672 RICHARD LITCHFIELD 50TH BIRTHDAY MAIDEN STKS 6f (F)
2:15 (2:15) (Class 5) 3-Y-O+ £3,309 (£984; £492; £245) Stalls Low

Form				RPR
222	1		**Aegean Dancer**[192] 2712 3-9-0 70 .... DerekMcGaffin 3 (B Smart) *trckd ldr gng wl: shkn up: wnt bdly rt and led over 1f out: rdn clr ins last: heavily eased towards fin* 5/6[1]	59+
3035	2	1¾	**Christian Bendix**[9] 6607 3-9-0 45 ....(p) RobertWinston 7 (P Howling) *chsd ldrs: outpcd 3f out: hung rt and kpt on to take 2nd ins last: no ch w wnr* 5/1[3]	49
0	3	3	**Freshwinds**[17] 6545 3-9-0 .... MickyFenton 2 (S L Keightley) *wnt lft s: led tl over 1f out: wknd ins last* 25/1	40
0000	4	1	**Fayrz Please (IRE)**[77] 5830 4-8-7 35 .... LiamJones(7) 5 (M C Chapman) *chsd ldrs: wknd appr fnl f* 50/1	37
4000	5	10	**Sion Hill (IRE)**[14] 6568 4-9-0 35 ....(b) HayleyTurner 1 (M C Chapman) *sltly hmpd s: sn chsng ldrs: hung lft over 2f out: lost pl over 1f out* 20/1	7
000	6	6	**Life Is Rosie (IRE)**[17] 6545 3-8-2 40 .... LauraReynolds(7) 4 (D K Ivory) *s.i.s: sn outpcd and bhd* 40/1	—
	7	22	**Ash The Cash (IRE)** 3-8-7 .... TJHowell(7) 6 (K F Clutterbuck) *sn outpcd and bhd: virtually p.u* 33/1	—
3405	8	¾	**Agilete**[64] 6075 3-8-11 67 .... AmirQuinn(3) 8 (J R Boyle) *chsd ldrs: rdn and lost pl over 4f out: eased over 2f out: virtually p.u* 9/4[2]	—

1m 18.07s (1.17) **Going Correction** -0.025s/f (Stan) 8 Ran SP% **117.9**
Speed ratings (Par 103):91,88,84,83,70 62,32,31
CSF £5.49 TOTE £1.90: £1.10, £1.50, £4.80; EX 7.20.
Owner Pinnacle Piccolo Partnership **Bred** Theobalds Stud **Trained** Hambleton, N Yorks

FOCUS
A weak maiden and an easy winner. The form has been rated through the runner-up who is only Banded class.
Agilete Official explanation: jockey said, regarding the running and riding, his orders were to ride positively from the start but gelding went down to the start freely, was never travelling in the race and was beaten before reaching the home straight; trainer had no further explanation for the poor form shown, adding that gelding was fully prepared for this race despite coming back from a nine-week absence

6673 BETDIRECT.CO.UK NURSERY 1m (F)
2:50 (2:50) (Class 4) (0-85,81) 2-Y-O £6,645 (£1,977; £988; £493) Stalls Low

Form				RPR
4215	1		**Moi Aussi (USA)**[17] 6539 2-9-6 76 ....(b) JamieMackay 9 (Sir Mark Prescott) *hld up in tch: smooth hdwy over 2f out: shkn up to ld over 1f out: pushed clr jst ins last: readily* 7/2[2]	82+
1040	2	3	**Outlook**[28] 6457 2-9-7 77 ....(b) MickyFenton 1 (N P Littmoden) *drvn to ld after 1f: hdd over 1f out: kpt on: no ch w wnr* 16/1	76
2006	3	½	**Chia (IRE)**[22] 6501 2-8-12 68 .... RobertHavlin 2 (D Haydn Jones) *led 1f: trckd ldrs: effrt over 2f out: kpt on same pce appr fnl f* 9/1	66
0040	4	1¾	**Daaweitza**[11] 6591 2-8-9 65 .... TomEaves 3 (B Ellison) *trckd ldrs: outpcd over 2f out: styd on fnl f* 14/1	60
4342	5	½	**Makai**[15] 6557 2-8-9 65 .... RobertWinston 8 (M Johnston) *chsd ldrs on outer: effrt over 2f out: one pce* 9/4[1]	59
0211	6	7	**The City Kid (IRE)**[5] 6656 2-9-4 81 5ex ....(v) JBrennan(7) 7 (P D Evans) *stmbld s: sn chsng ldrs: rdn and hung lft over 2f out: lost pl over 1f out* 8/1	61
6025	7	3½	**Cape Win (IRE)**[32] 6420 2-9-4 74 .... TonyCulhane 4 (W J Haggas) *t.k.h: sn trcking ldrs: effrt 3f out: wknd over 1f out: eased ins last* 4/1[3]	47
0420	8	16	**Royal Embrace**[17] 6539 2-8-0 59 ow2 .... PatrickMathers(3) 6 (D Shaw) *in tch: drvn and lost pl over 4f out: sn bhd: eased* 33/1	—
0300	9	8	**Hill Of Howth (IRE)**[96] 5422 2-9-7 77 .... NCallan 5 (K A Ryan) *chsd ldrs: drvn over 4f out: lost pl over 3f out: sn bhd: eased* 13/2	2

1m 44.56s (-0.04) **Going Correction** -0.025s/f (Stan) 9 Ran SP% **122.9**
Speed ratings (Par 98):99,96,95,93,93 86,82,66,58
CSF £61.38 CT £484.88 TOTE £4.80: £1.70, £4.30, £2.80; EX 77.80.
Owner Miss K Rausing **Bred** K Rausing **Trained** Newmarket, Suffolk
■ Stewards' Enquiry : J Brennan caution: used whip in the forehand position down the neck

FOCUS
An improved effort from the winner.

NOTEBOOK
Moi Aussi(USA) came there on the bridle and took this with the minimum of fuss. In this frame of mind she is much better than a 76-rated filly. (op 11-4)
Outlook, a former stablemate of the winner, was very keen to lead but in the end it was like Chelsea playing Sunderland !
Chia(IRE), having just her second taste of the All-Weather and her first try on Fibresand, if anything proved suited by the step up to a mile. (op 10-1 tchd 11-1)
Daaweitza, making his Fibresand debut, looks welll worth a try over further. (op 11-1)
Makai, making his handicap debut, found himself trapped wide and never looked like justifying the market confidence. (op 10-3 tchd 7-2 in places)
Cape Win(IRE), who has changed stables, was far too keen to get on with it and as a result didn't remotely see out the extra furlong. (op 5-1)
Hill Of Howth(IRE) Official explanation: jockey said colt was never travelling

6674 MORE OFFERS AT BETDIRECT.CO.UK H'CAP (DIV II) 1m (F)
3:20 (3:21) (Class 6) (0-55,55) 3-Y-O+ £2,491 (£735; £367) Stalls Low

Form				RPR
0202	1		**Greenbelt**[5] 6660 4-8-11 52 .... RobertWinston 7 (G M Moore) *chsd ldr: led over 3f out: kpt on fnl f: hld on towards fin* 4/1[2]	64
0113	2	1	**Augustine**[5] 6654 4-8-11 52 .... PhillipMakin 5 (P W Hiatt) *chsd ldrs: wnt 2nd over 1f out: kpt on ins last* 4/1[2]	62
2062	3	9	**Bridgewater Boys**[5] 6654 4-8-13 54 ....(b) NCallan 9 (K A Ryan) *chsd ldrs: rdn and outpcd over 3f out: styd on fnl 2f: tk mod 3rd nr line* 7/4[1]	46
1004	4	nk	**Kumakawa**[9] 6608 7-7-13 47 .... LauraReynolds(7) 3 (D K Ivory) *rr-div: hdwy on inner over 2f out: one pce* 20/1	38
1164	5	6	**Legal Lover (IRE)**[22] 6508 3-8-8 50 .... MickyFenton 11 (R Hollinshead) *led tl over 3f out: wknd over 1f out* 15/2	29
5216	6	2½	**Witchcraft**[5] 6654 4-8-11 55 ....(v) PatrickMathers(3) 6 (D Shaw) *rr-div: effrt over 3f out: nvr nr ldrs* 6/1[3]	29
0046	7	1¾	**Didnt Tell My Wife**[36] 6400 6-8-12 53 ....(p) EddieAhern 4 (Julian Poulton) *chsd ldrs: drvn over 3f out: wknd fnl 2f* 12/1	24
0000	8	½	**Shami**[15] 6564 6-9-0 55 .... TonyCulhane 2 (D W Chapman) *in rr: nvr a factor* 50/1	25
2000	9	1	**Eforetta (GER)**[42] 6363 3-8-11 53 ow1 .... VinceSlattery 10 (D J Wintle) *sn in rr* 40/1	21
2000	10	17	**Crusoe (IRE)**[12] 6587 8-8-11 52 ....(b) BrianReilly 8 (A Sadik) *sn bhd: virtually p.u ins last* 50/1	—
0000	11	18	**Grumpyintmorning**[20] 6365 6-8-6 54 ....(v[1]) LiamJones(7) 1 (M J Gingell) *sn detached in last: virtually p.u: t.o* 50/1	—

1m 44.2s (-0.40) **Going Correction** -0.025s/f (Stan)
WFA 3 from 4yo+ 1lb 30 Ran SP% **123.2**
Speed ratings (Par 101):101,100,91,90,84 82,80,79,78,61 43
CSF £20.72 CT £38.03 TOTE £6.40: £2.10, £1.70, £1.20; EX 25.80 Place 6 £73.65, Place 5 £11.35.
Owner Mrs A Roddis **Bred** Juddmonte Farms **Trained** Middleham Moor, N Yorks

FOCUS
This race was run in a snow storm with precious little visible from the stands.
Witchcraft Official explanation: jockey said gelding hung right-handed on bend
Crusoe(IRE) Official explanation: jockey said gelding missed break
Grumpyintmorning Official explanation: jockey said gelding was never travelling
T/Plt: £48.30 to a £1 stake. Pool: £30,569.75. 461.60 winning tickets. T/Qpdt: £9.50 to a £1 stake. Pool: £3,851.40. 299.90 winning tickets. WG

6661 WOLVERHAMPTON (A.W) (L-H)

Wednesday, December 28

OFFICIAL GOING: Standard to slow

Wind: Almost nil Weather: Fine

6675 BETDIRECT ON FOOTBALL MAIDEN CLAIMING STKS 1m 141y(P)

1:00 (1:00) (Class 7) 3-Y-0+ £1,433 (£423; £211) Stalls Low

Form RPR

0023 1 **Velocitas**[65] 6080 4-9-0 45 (b[1]) EddieAhern 8 52
(W M Brisbourne) *bhd: reminders sn after s: rdn and hdwy over 2f out: led wl over 1f out: r.o* 7/2[2]

0333 2 hd **Swords**[24] 6494 3-8-12 48 RobertWinston 1 52+
(P Howling) *s.i.s: hld up in rr: bdly hmpd on ins and swtchd rt over 3f out: hdwy on outside over 1f out: rdn and hung lft ins fnl f: r* 9/2[3]

3000 3 shd **Harare**[9] 6620 4-8-7 52 JamesDoyle(7) 10 52
(R J Price) *a.p: rdn and ev ch fr wl over 1f out: r.o* 11/2

0000 4 1 **Miss Monica (IRE)**[13] 6583 4-8-7 46 HayleyTurner 7 43
(P W Hiatt) *t.k.h: a.p: rdn 2f out: kpt on ins fnl f* 22/1

0000 5 1 3/4 **Crux**[30] 6443 3-8-6 45 DeanMcKeown 11 40
(C W Thornton) *hld up and bhd: hdwy 2f out: sn rdn: one pce fnl f* 14/1

5250 6 1/2 **Sound And Vision (IRE)**[13] 6587 3-8-12 53 (p) PhillipMakin 6 45
(M Dods) *hld up in mid-div: hdwy over 5f out: rdn over 2f out: one pce fnl f* 11/4[1]

0004 7 1 **Doughty**[10] 6607 3-8-12 40 VinceSlattery 2 43
(D J Wintle) *stdd sn after s: hdwy 2f out: sn hrd rdn: edgd lft 1f out: no imp* 20/1

6050 8 1 **White Star Magic**[23] 6509 3-8-9 45 (bt) AdamKirby(3) 3 41
(K G Wingrove) *prom: hung lft over 3f out: lost pl over 2f out: rdn and rallied wl over 1f out: eased whn btn wl ins fnl f* 33/1

0344 9 13 **Alcott (FR)**[19] 6414 3-8-12 45 (bt[1]) ChrisCatlin 13 13
(J Jay) *hld up in mid-div: rdn over 3f out: sn wknd* 12/1

000 10 2 **Penway**[7] 6651 4-8-12 47 (b) BrianReilly 9 7
(A Sadik) *prom: led over 3f out: rdn over 2f out: hdd wl over 1f out: sn wknd* 50/1

3636 11 nk **Haenertsburg (IRE)**[165] 3138 3-8-7 45 (p) PaulEddery 4 4
(A L Forbes) *led: hdd over 3f out: sn rdn: wknd over 2f out* 20/1

0-55 12 3 **Perianth (IRE)**[350] 97 3-8-12 50 RobertHavlin 5 2
(J G M O'Shea) *prom: lost pl over 6f out: rdn 4f out: sn bhd* 33/1

0 13 28 **Billy's Brother**[49] 6301 3-8-12 PaulHanagan 12 —
(M A Buckley) *bhd fnl 5f: t.o* 66/1

1m 52.9s (1.14) **Going Correction** +0.10s/f (Slow)
WFA 3 from 4yo 2lb 13 Ran SP% **120.0**
Speed ratings (Par 97):98,97,97,96,95 94,93,93,81,79 79,76,51
CSF £18.05 TOTE £3.60: £1.50, £2.10, £1.90; EX 11.40.Swords was the subject of a friendly claim (£5,000).
Owner P Wright-Bevans **Bred** Southill Stud **Trained** Great Ness, Shropshire

FOCUS
A fair race of its type producing a close finish.
White Star Magic Official explanation: jockey said gelding hung left-handed
Haenertsburg(IRE) Official explanation: jockey said filly was struck into

6676 BETDIRECT.CO.UK BANDED STKS 7f 32y(P)

1:35 (1:35) (Class 7) 3-Y-0+ £1,463 (£432; £216) Stalls High

Form RPR

6006 1 **Prince Of Gold**[16] 6567 5-9-2 50 (b) VinceSlattery 2 57
(R Hollinshead) *s.s: hdwy wl over 1f out: sn rdn: r.o to ld cl home* 5/1[3]

6042 2 nk **Mount Royale (IRE)**[10] 6608 7-8-13 47 (v) KimTinkler 9 53
(N Tinkler) *sn led: rdn wl over 1f out: hdd wl ins fnl f: r.o* 8/1

0210 3 nk **Blushing Russian (IRE)**[14] 6574 3-9-1 49 LPKeniry 6 54
(J M Bradley) *hld up in tch: lost pl over 4f out: rdn and hdwy wl over 1f out: r.o ins fnl f* 40/1

5006 4 shd **Monkey Madge**[43] 6363 3-9-2 50 PaulEddery 5 55
(B Smart) *led early: a.p: rdn 2f out: led wl ins fnl f: hdd cl home* 14/1

2023 5 1 1/4 **Musiotal**[23] 6507 4-9-2 50 FergalLynch 4 51
(P A Blockley) *s.s: bhd: rdn and hdwy over 1f out: nt qckn ins fnl f* 3/1[1]

2235 6 3/4 **Fulvio (USA)**[21] 6525 5-9-1 49 (v) RobertWinston 8 49
(P Howling) *chsd ldrs: rdn over 2f out: one pce fnl f* 7/2[2]

5210 7 1 3/4 **Spy Gun (USA)**[10] 6608 5-9-1 49 J-PGuillambert 10 44
(T Wall) *jnd ldrs after 1f: rdn and ev ch 2f out: wknd fnl f* 25/1

6204 8 2 1/2 **Layed Back Rocky**[9] 6623 3-9-2 50 (p) DarrenWilliams 7 38
(M Mullineaux) *s.i.s: rdn and sme hdwy on outside over 2f out: c wd st: sn wknd* 16/1

2001 9 1 **My Girl Pearl (IRE)**[23] 6507 5-9-2 50 MickyFenton 3 36
(M S Saunders) *hld up in mid-div: rdn over 2f out: sn bhd* 7/1

0 10 3 1/2 **Junebug Symphony (IRE)**[14] 6574 3-9-0 48 MichaelTebbutt 1 25
(V Smith) *prom tl rdn and wknd over 1f out* 25/1

6035 11 1 1/4 **Smirfys Party**[14] 6579 7-8-13 47 (v) EddieAhern 11 21
(W M Brisbourne) *t.k.h: prom: hung bdly rt to outside rail over 5f out: rejnd main gp over 4f out: rdn and wknd 2f out* 12/1

0230 12 6 **Alzarma**[16] 6554 3-8-13 47 PaulHanagan 12 5
(P D Evans) *hld up in mid-div: rdn over 3f out: sn bhd* 33/1

1m 31.08s (0.68) **Going Correction** +0.10s/f (Slow) 12 Ran SP% **120.8**
Speed ratings (Par 97):100,99,99,99,97 96,94,92,90,86 85,78
CSF £43.89 TOTE £8.50: £3.20, £3.10, £7.40; EX 55.10.
Owner Horne, Hollinshead, Johnson **Bred** Longdon Stud Ltd **Trained** Upper Longdon, Staffs
■ Stewards' Enquiry : L P Keniry one-day ban: used whip with excessive frequency (Jan 9)

FOCUS
A moderate event that produced a blanket finish.
Smirfys Party Official explanation: jockey said gelding hung right-handed

6677 BETDIRECT FOOTBALL CASHBACKS BANDED STKS 5f 216y(P)

2:05 (2:06) (Class 7) 3-Y-0+ £1,433 (£423; £211) Stalls Low

Form RPR

3324 1 **Jalouhar**[15] 6570 5-8-4 45 SoniaEaton(7) 1 53
(B P J Baugh) *hld up and bhd: hdwy on ins over 2f out: rdn to ld ent fnl f: edgd rt cl home: r.o* 15/2

6663 2 3/4 **Strathclyde (IRE)**[14] 6580 6-8-11 45 ChrisCatlin 9 51
(A M Hales) *hld up and bhd: hdwy 2f out: sn swtchd rt and rdn: r.o u.str.p ins fnl f* 4/1[2]

6352 3 1 **Beamsley Beacon**[15] 6570 4-8-11 45 (b) TomEaves 12 48
(M Dods) *sn led: hdd over 3f out: rdn to ld wl over 1f out: edgd rt and hdd ent fnl f: nt qckn* 6/1[3]

5530 4 1/2 **Multahab**[21] 6526 6-8-8 45 (t) AdamKirby(3) 2 46
(Miss Gay Kelleway) *hld up in mid-div: hdwy on ins over 3f out: rdn wl over 1f out: carried rt ent fnl f: nt qckn* 7/2[1]

0502 5 2 1/2 **Aintnecessarilyso**[9] 6611 7-8-11 45 (p) LPKeniry 7 39
(J M Bradley) *hld up and bhd: hdwy 2f out: rdn over 1f out: no ex ins fnl f* 8/1

5-00 6 1 3/4 **Gorgeous Boy (IRE)**[13] 6584 3-8-11 45 BrianReilly 10 34
(P L Gilligan) *led early: prom: rdn over 3f out: one pce whn hmpd ent fnl f* 66/1

0405 7 nk **Shirley Oaks (IRE)**[21] 6526 7-8-11 45 SamHitchcott 8 33
(Miss Z C Davison) *sn outpcd and bhd: hdwy 1f out: nvr nr ldrs* 12/1

0330 8 1 1/2 **Juwwi**[239] 1456 11-8-11 45 PhillipMakin 5 28
(J M Bradley) *sn outpcd: late hdwy: n.d* 16/1

0000 9 1 3/4 **Melaina**[44] 6345 4-8-11 45 (p) MickyFenton 6 23
(M S Saunders) *sn prom: rdn and ev ch over 2f out: wknd wl over 1f out* 50/1

6501 10 2 **Vaudevire**[250] 1184 4-8-11 45 (p) RobbieFitzpatrick 4 17
(Peter Grayson) *prom tl rdn and wknd 2f out* 16/1

0600 11 1 3/4 **Lakeside Guy (IRE)**[182] 3020 4-8-8 45 RichardThomas(3) 13 12
(M Appleby) *racd wd: hld up in tch: rdn wl over 1f out: sn wknd* 33/1

0001 12 1/2 **Dorn Hill**[14] 6578 3-8-11 45 (p) VinceSlattery 11 10
(D G Bridgwater) *chsd ldrs: rdn 3f out: wknd 2f out* 16/1

0000 13 4 **Zantero**[16] 6560 3-8-11 45 EddieAhern 3 —
(W M Brisbourne) *prom: led over 3f out: rdn and hdd wl over 1f out: eased whn btn fnl f* 9/1

1m 16.11s (0.30) **Going Correction** +0.10s/f (Slow) 13 Ran SP% **121.1**
Speed ratings (Par 97):102,101,99,99,95 93,92,90,88,85 83,82,77
CSF £37.75 TOTE £8.90: £3.10, £2.20, £2.70; EX 44.60.
Owner Miss S M Potts **Bred** Roy Matthews **Trained** Audley, Staffs
■ A first winner on only her third ride for Sonia Eaton.
■ Stewards' Enquiry : Adam Kirby one-day ban: careless riding (Jan 9)

FOCUS
A typically moderate contest but run at a decent gallop.

6678 BETDIRECT FREEPHONE 0800 211 222 BANDED STKS 1m 5f 194y(P)

2:35 (2:40) (Class 7) 4-Y-0+ £1,440 (£425; £212) Stalls Low

Form RPR

0000 1 **Blue Hills**[24] 5959 4-9-2 50 (p) DarrenWilliams 10 57
(P W Hiatt) *led after 2f: rdn clr 2f out: jst hld on* 25/1

0023 2 nk **Little Richard (IRE)**[23] 6510 6-8-11 45 (p) AlanDaly 4 52
(M Wellings) *hld up in mid-div: swtchd rt 2f out: sn rdn: chsd wnr fnl f: jst failed* 4/1[1]

0500 3 4 **Magic Red**[2] 4866 5-8-8 47 (b) MarcHalford(5) 5 48
(J Ryan) *sn led: hdd after 2f: chsd wnr: rdn 3f out: wknd ins fnl f* 33/1

0450 4 3/4 **Top Trees**[23] 6510 7-8-11 45 ChrisCatlin 11 45
(W S Kittow) *hld up and bhd: hdwy 3f out: rdn over 1f out: styd on fnl f: nt rch ldrs* 7/1

0300 5 2 **Airgusta (IRE)**[16] 6563 4-9-2 50 HayleyTurner 13 48
(C P Morlock) *a.p: rdn over 3f out: hung lft wl over 1f out: wknd ins fnl f* 8/1

5106 6 nk **Ice And Fire**[16] 6563 6-8-13 47 (b) RobbieFitzpatrick 2 44
(J T Stimpson) *hld up and bhd: rdn and hdwy wl over 1f out: nvr nr ldrs* 13/2

0360 7 2 1/2 **Desert Hawk**[98] 5400 4-9-2 50 EddieAhern 3 44
(W M Brisbourne) *hld up towards rr: sme hdwy over 1f out: n.d* 8/1

/054 8 5 **Coppermalt (USA)**[9] 6612 7-8-12 46 LPKeniry 8 33
(R Curtis) *hld up and bhd: stdy hdwy over 5f out: rdn over 2f out: wknd over 1f out* 6/1[3]

-036 9 2 1/2 **Claradotnet**[23] 6510 5-8-11 45 TomEaves 1 28
(Mrs L Williamson) *s.i.s: hld up in mid-div: bhd fnl 4f* 14/1

/-06 10 5 **Kuka**[13] 6583 4-8-11 45 VinceSlattery 6 21
(R Hollinshead) *led early: t.k.h in tch: rdn over 4f out: wknd 3f out* 66/1

/602 11 3 **Midnight Creek**[66] 5829 7-9-1 49 BrianReilly 7 21
(A Sadik) *hld up: sn mid-div: hdwy 6f out: rdn and wknd 3f out* 9/2[2]

5060 12 1 3/4 **Paradise Valley**[9] 6612 5-9-0 48 (t) MickyFenton 12 17
(Stef Liddiard) *s.i.s: a bhd* 10/1

3m 6.96s (-0.41) **Going Correction** +0.10s/f (Slow) 12 Ran SP% **124.6**
Speed ratings (Par 97):105,104,102,102,100 100,99,96,95,92 90,89
CSF £127.52 TOTE £37.80: £8.50, £1.90, £6.90; EX 151.10 TRIFECTA Not won..
Owner Tom Pratt **Bred** Darley **Trained** Hook Norton, Oxon

FOCUS
A fair event for the class, run at a sound gallop, and the first two came clear.
Blue Hills Official explanation: trainer said, regarding the improved form shown, gelding had benefited from being able to dominate
Airgusta(IRE) Official explanation: jockey said gelding hung left-handed
Midnight Creek Official explanation: trainer said gelding was unsuited by surface

6679 BACK LIVERPOOL OR EVERTON BANDED STKS 1m 141y(P)

3:10 (3:15) (Class 7) 3-Y-0+ £1,481 (£437; £218) Stalls Low

Form RPR

0056 1 **New England**[18] 6541 3-9-2 50 RobbieFitzpatrick 12 55
(W M Brisbourne) *hld up in rr: rdn and hdwy on outside 1f out: r.o wl to ld cl home* 16/1

2611 2 1/2 **Danettie**[9] 6615 4-9-9 49 EddieAhern 4 59
(W M Brisbourne) *a.p: rdn 2f out: led wl ins fnl f: hdd cl home* 11/4[1]

0000 3 1 **Insignia (IRE)**[7] 6651 3-9-2 50 (p) RobertWinston 5 52
(W M Brisbourne) *led early: a.p: rdn wl over 1f out: led ent fnl f: hdd and nt qckn towards fin* 14/1

0000 4 1 1/4 **Majehar**[37] 6401 3-8-13 47 LPKeniry 6 46
(A G Newcombe) *a.p: rdn whn edgd lft and led wl over 1f out: hdd ent fnl f: no ex towards fin* 8/1

0521 5 1 **Star Fern**[7] 6651 4-9-9 49 JimmyQuinn 11 52
(M J Attwater) *s.i.s: bhd: rdn over 3f out: hdwy over 1f out: one pce ins fnl f* 7/2[2]

2103 6 nk **Desert Lover (IRE)**[10] 6608 3-8-13 47 PhillipMakin 2 44
(R J Price) *t.k.h in mid-div: rdn and hdwy 2f out: no imp fnl f* 13/2[3]

3315 7 hd **Adobe**[7] 6651 10-8-11 50 LiamJones(7) 3 46
(W M Brisbourne) *hld up in mid-div: hdwy on ins over 1f out: one pce ins fnl f* 8/1

502 8 5 **Sea Heir (IRE)**[30] 6443 3-9-2 50 PaulHanagan 8 36
(R A Fahey) *hld up in mid-div: rdn over 3f out: short-lived effrt over 2f out* 8/1

00-0 9 2 1/2 **Beautiful Noise**[74] 5907 4-9-0 46 MickyFenton 7 26
(M G Quinlan) *prom: led over 3f out: rdn over 2f out: hdd wl over 1f out: sn wknd* 25/1

3004 **10** *1 ½* **Lake Wakatipu**[9] 6619 3-8-13 47 VinceSlattery 1 24
(M Mullineaux) *a bhd* **12/1**
2000 **11** *16* **Glasson Lodge**[188] 2845 3-8-13 47 PaulEddery 10 —
(A L Forbes) *a bhd* **50/1**
000- **12** *4* **Rambo Blue**[394] 6767 5-9-4 50 SamHitchcott 13 —
(G J Smith) *sn led: hdd over 3f out: sn rdn and wknd: eased whn no ch wl over 1f out* **50/1**

1m 51.74s (-0.02) **Going Correction** +0.10s/f (Slow)
WFA 3 from 4yo+ 2lb 12 Ran SP% **123.6**
Speed ratings (Par 97):104,103,102,101,100 100,100,95,93,92 78,74
CSF £61.78 TOTE £21.00: £4.20, £2.00, £4.10; EX 97.20.
Owner Stephen Walker **Bred** Darley **Trained** Great Ness, Shropshire

FOCUS
Another fair event for the grade, run at a decent pace, and the Brisbourne yard bagged the first three places.
Desert Lover(IRE) Official explanation: jockey said gelding ran too free early on
Rambo Blue Official explanation: jockey said gelding hung left-handed

6680 MERSEYSIDE DERBY IN-RUNNING SKY PAGE 293 BANDED STKS 1f 103y(P)
3:45 (3:45) (Class 7) 4-Y-0+ **£1,433** (£423; £211) **Stalls** Low

Form RPR
0034 **1** **Regency Red (IRE)**[9] 6620 7-8-4 45 LiamJones(7) 13 52
(W M Brisbourne) *s.i.s: hld up: sn swtchd lft: hdwy over 5f out: rdn to ld and hung lft jst ins fnl f: wandered towards fin: r.o* **9/1**[3]
0115 **2** *1 ¼* **Night Warrior (IRE)**[7] 6643 5-9-3 45 (b) ChrisCatlin 3 56
(N P Littmoden) *a.p: rdn and ev ch 2f out: kpt on towards fin* **11/10**[1]
3 *shd* **Level Par (IRE)**[428] 6434 5-8-11 45 (t) MickyFenton 9 49
(J A Supple) *sn led: hdd 6f out: led over 3f out: rdn wl over 1f out: hdd jst ins fnl f: kpt on* **66/1**
2602 **4** *nk* **Melograno (IRE)**[36] 6414 5-8-6 45 DerekNolan(5) 12 50+
(Mark Campion) *s.i.s: sn swtchd lft: hld up and bhd: rdn over 2f out: hdwy wl over 1f out: carried lft 1f out: nt clr run and swtchd lft i* **9/1**[3]
0040 **5** *1* **Vibe**[14] 6473 4-8-8 45 RichardThomas(3) 11 47
(R J Price) *hld up and bhd: hdwy over 3f out: rdn and hung lft fr over 1f out: one pce* **22/1**
6440 **6** *1* **Peace Emblem (IRE)**[21] 6522 4-8-8 45 (p) AdamKirby(3) 5 45
(J W Unett) *led early: prom: rdn over 2f out: no ex towards fin* **16/1**
0340 **7** *¾* **Cryfield**[11] 5979 8-8-11 45 (v) KimTinkler 2 44
(N Tinkler) *broke wl: stdd after 1f: sn mid-div: no hdwy fnl 2f* **12/1**
8 *½* **Settle (IRE)**[40] 4876 6-8-11 45 (p) LPKeniry 7 43
(M Flannery, Ire) *hld up in mid-div: rdn and lost pl over 3f out* **22/1**
6-16 **9** *1 ¼* **Scorchio (IRE)**[28] 6475 4-8-4 45 GaryWales(7) 6 40
(B Smart) *s.i.s: hdwy on outside over 5f out: rdn and wknd 3f out* **7/1**[2]
6630 **10** *½* **Heathyards Joy**[9] 6620 4-8-6 45 StephanieHollinshead(5) 1 39
(R Hollinshead) *hld up and bhd: rdn 3f out: no rspnse* **16/1**
3002 **11** *4* **Fortunes Favourite**[44] 6347 5-8-6 45 NataliaGemelova(5) 4 32
(J E Long) *a bhd* **9/1**[3]
0000 **12** *8* **Sudden Impulse**[10] 6608 4-8-6 45 DuranFentiman(5) 10 17
(A D Brown) *w ldr: led 6f out: rdn and hdd over 3f out: wknd 2f out* **66/1**
0030 **13** *4* **Get To The Point**[53] 6259 4-8-11 45 BrianReilly 8 9
(Miss J Feilden) *hld up in tch: wknd 2f out* **33/1**

2m 4.76s (2.14) **Going Correction** +0.10s/f (Slow) 13 Ran SP% **124.2**
Speed ratings (Par 97):94,92,92,92,91 90,90,89,88,88 84,77,73
CSF £19.15 TOTE £10.00: £2.50, £1.30, £8.40; EX 27.40 Place 6 £216.47, Place 5 £128.14..
Owner Mrs J M Russell **Bred** Patrick J Burke **Trained** Great Ness, Shropshire

FOCUS
This was run at a decent early pace and the form looks sound for the class.
Settle(IRE) Official explanation: jockey said gelding hung left-handed in home straight
T/Jkpt: Not won. T/Plt: £90.20 to a £1 stake. Pool: £108,116.15. 874.20 winning tickets. T/Qpdt: £15.10 to a £1 stake. Pool: £8,305.00. 406.80 winning tickets. KH

6639 LINGFIELD (L-H)
Thursday, December 29

OFFICIAL GOING: Standard
Wind: Nil Weather: Cloudy and cold

6681 MORE OFFERS AT BETDIRECT.CO.UK BANDED STKS 1m 4f (P)
1:00 (1:00) (Class 7) 3-Y-0+ **£1,460** (£431; £215) **Stalls** Low

Form RPR
1406 **1** **Tharua (IRE)**[10] 6612 3-8-9 48 (v) AdamKirby(3) 10 52
(Ernst Oertel) *cl up gng wl: effrt over 1f out: squeezed through to ld ins fnl f: hld on wl* **6/1**[2]
0343 **2** *hd* **Prince Valentine**[15] 6575 4-9-0 45 (be) IanMongan 5 49
(G L Moore) *hld up in midfield: prog over 2f out: rdn to chal over 1f out: w wnr ins fnl f: nt qckn and hld nr fin* **7/1**[3]
0404 **3** *1* **Mustang Ali (IRE)**[22] 6523 4-8-13 47 (b[1]) RichardThomas(3) 7 49
(Dr J R J Naylor) *hld up in midfield: gng easily over 2f out: effrt over 1f out: sn rdn and nt qckn: styd on last 100yds* **7/2**[1]
0000 **4** *nk* **Larad (IRE)**[10] 6614 4-9-5 50 (b) LPKeniry 16 52
(J S Moore) *hld up in rr: trapped on inner 3f out: prog over 1f out to press ldrs ins fnl f: one pce last 100yds* **8/1**
4430 **5** *1* **Zeena**[22] 6523 3-8-10 46 MickyFenton 11 46
(C A Horgan) *w ldr: led after 4f: narrowly hdd 1f out: wknd last 100yds* **20/1**
3224 **6** *nk* **Silsong (USA)**[19] 6537 3-8-13 49 (b) JimmyQuinn 6 49
(Miss Gay Kelleway) *t.k.h: led for 4f: w ldr tl led again narrowly 1f out: sn hdd & wknd* **9/1**
0555 **7** *hd* **King's Minstrel (IRE)**[10] 6614 4-9-0 45 (t) PaulDoe 14 45
(R Rowe) *dwlt: hld up in last: prog on wd outside over 3f out: drvn over 2f out: nt qckn over 1f out: kpt on* **8/1**
0506 **8** *½* **Murrieta**[10] 6614 3-9-0 50 ChrisCatlin 1 49
(Miss J R Gibney) *t.k.h: hld up in midfield: pushed along 5f out: hrd drvn and effrt on inner over 1f out: nt qckn* **16/1**
0000 **9** *¾* **Eskimo's Nest**[10] 6615 3-8-10 49 PatrickMathers(3) 8 47
(D Shaw) *t.k.h: hld up in rr: nt wl plcd over 2f out: hrd rdn on outer over 1f out: kpt on: no ch* **33/1**
0-40 **10** *shd* **Whenwillitwin**[22] 6522 4-8-9 47 JosephWalsh(7) 3 44
(J S Moore) *dwlt: t.k.h: hld up in rr: last and rdn over 3f out: n.d after* **12/1**
0000 **11** *1* **Just Beware**[51] 5302 3-8-9 40 (p) AdrianMcCarthy 12 41
(Miss Z C Davison) *hld up: prog to press ldrs 4f out: wknd over 1f out* **66/1**
5005 **12** *5* **Longing For Cindy (USA)**[101] 5366 3-8-13 49 EddieAhern 13 37
(W M Brisbourne) *in tch: rdn over 4f out: wknd over 2f out* **15/2**
0040 **13** *5* **Bansha Bandit (IRE)**[122] 4811 3-8-9 40 SamHitchcott 9 25
(A B Haynes) *prom: rdn over 4f out: wknd 3f out* **80/1**

2m 34.88s (0.49) **Going Correction** -0.10s/f (Stan)
WFA 3 from 4yo+ 5lb 13 Ran SP% **117.0**
Speed ratings (Par 97):94,93,93,93,92 92,92,91,91,91 90,87,83
CSF £45.33 TOTE £7.20: £2.10, £2.50, £1.30; EX 73.50.
Owner Winning Colours Racing Club **Bred** Finbar Cahill And Dermot O'Rourke **Trained** Newmarket, Suffolk

FOCUS
Moderate form with the runner-up setting the standard, but the winner had a little up her sleeve at the finish.

6682 PRESS RED TO BET ON ITVI MAIDEN CLAIMING STKS 1m 2f (P)
1:30 (1:30) (Class 7) 3-Y-0+ **£1,446** (£427; £213) **Stalls** Low

Form RPR
500 **1** **Tanning**[8] 6652 3-8-0 35 (v[1]) PaulHanagan 5 44
(A W Carroll) *mde virtually all: set stdy pce to 4f out: kicked on 2f out: hrd pressed fnl f: hld on* **15/2**[3]
0300 **2** *hd* **Mujimac (IRE)**[27] 6478 3-8-8 50 ow1 FergusSweeney 8 52
(J R Boyle) *hld up in rr: prog on outer over 3f out: chsd wnr wl over 2f out: drvn to chal 1f out: kpt on but hld nr fin* **4/1**[1]
0020 **3** *½* **Shaheer (IRE)**[17] 6560 3-8-11 51 (p) IanMongan 1 54
(Mrs L J Mongan) *settled in midfield: rdn over 2f out: styd on fr over 1f out: nvr nrr* **4/1**[1]
3060 **4** *shd* **Kristinor (FR)**[8] 6643 3-8-11 55 J-PGuillambert 13 53
(G L Moore) *hld up in rr: cajoled along and prog over 2f out: chal on inner fnl f: ref to go by* **9/2**[2]
0-50 **5** *3* **Isleofhopeantears (IRE)**[49] 6-8-12 45 LPKeniry 4 46
(A E Jones) *trckd ldrs: rdn to chse ldng pair 2f out: hanging and fnd little over 1f out: btn after* **12/1**
0050 **6** *2* **Karrnak**[7] 5533 3-8-11 60 (bt) MickyFenton 2 44
(Miss J Feilden) *sn detached in last: drvn on outer over 3f out: styd on fr over 1f out: nrst fin* **11/1**
0000 **7** *nk* **Naivety**[10] 6614 3-8-6 47 (b) JamieMackay 3 38
(G G Margarson) *hld up in tch: chsng ldrs whn hmpd on inner over 2f out: nt rcvr* **15/2**[3]
-004 **8** *2* **Duncanbil (IRE)**[15] 6578 4-8-9 35 SteveDrowne 7 35
(J J Bridger) *broke wl: restrained: trckd wnr to over 6f out: disp 2nd again over 3f out: wknd over 2f out* **25/1**
0000 **9** *1 ¾* **Valentine's Pet**[31] 6443 5-8-9 35 RobertWinston 9 31
(A W Carroll) *hld up in midfield: rdn over 2f out: wknd wl over 1f out* **25/1**
6400 **10** *4* **Tintawn Gold (IRE)**[75] 5896 5-8-9 40 HayleyTurner 6 24
(S Woodman) *t.k.h: hld up towards rr: rdn and struggling 3f out* **16/1**
0600 **11** *5* **Ewar Finch (FR)**[33] 6434 3-8-1 35 ow4 EdwardCreighton(3) 11 12
(K O Cunningham-Brown) *prom: chsd wnr over 6f out to wl over 2f out: wknd* **66/1**
0 **12** *4* **Cinder Maid**[24] 6505 3-8-6 JimmyQuinn 10 7
(J G Portman) *in tch: wknd 3f out* **40/1**

2m 7.26s (-0.53) **Going Correction** -0.10s/f (Stan)
WFA 3 from 4yo+ 3lb 12 Ran SP% **115.2**
Speed ratings (Par 97):98,97,97,97,94 93,93,91,90,86 82,79
CSF £35.28 TOTE £9.30: £2.60, £1.80, £1.80; EX 56.50.Mujimac was claimed by Michael James Oxton for £3,000. Shaheer was claimed by Paul Howling for £5,000. Tanning was the subject of a friendly claim of £2,000.
Owner Dennis Deacon **Bred** Genesis Green Stud Ltd **Trained** Cropthorne, Worcs

FOCUS
Not form to rely on as the winner set just a modest pace in front.

6683 BETDIRECT FREEPHONE 0800 211 222 BANDED STKS 1m 2f (P)
2:00 (2:01) (Class 7) 3-Y-0+ **£1,460** (£431; £215) **Stalls** Low

Form RPR
0603 **1** **Turner's Touch**[10] 6614 3-9-0 50 (be) GeorgeBaker 13 61
(G L Moore) *dwlt: hld up in last: prog on wd outside 3f out: hanging bdly lft and reluctant over 1f out: forced ahd last 100yds* **9/1**[3]
5010 **2** *½* **Successor**[10] 6614 5-9-0 47 (t) JamieMackay 4 57
(M D I Usher) *hld up towards rr: smooth prog 3f out: drvn to ld jst ins fnl f: hdd and outpcd last 100yds* **10/1**
0003 **3** *½* **Senor Bond (USA)**[15] 6576 4-9-0 47 ChrisCatlin 2 56
(A M Hales) *hld up in midfield: prog on inner to trck ldr 3f out: drvn to ld over 1f out: hdd jst ins fnl f: nt qckn* **14/1**
4042 **4** *3* **Nisr**[10] 6615 8-9-1 48 (t) JimmyQuinn 10 51
(Miss Gay Kelleway) *hld up in rr: gng easily but stl wl in rr over 2f out: drvn and r.o fr over 1f out: no ch* **12/1**
4050 **5** *1* **Summer Bounty**[22] 6523 9-8-12 40 LPKeniry 9 46
(F Jordan) *dwlt: hld up wl in rr: gng easily but stl wl in rr over 2f out: drvn and styd on fr over 1f out: no ch* **11/1**
0066 **6** *1* **Lawaaheb (IRE)**[33] 6429 4-8-12 50 (b[1]) RoryMoore(5) 3 50
(B R Johnson) *w ldr: led 1/2-way: kicked on over 2f out: hdd over 1f out: wknd fnl f* **9/2**[1]
6400 **7** *½* **Piquet**[75] 5895 7-9-0 47 J-PGuillambert 11 46
(J J Bridger) *hld up wl in rr: prog on outer over 3f out: chsd ldrs 2f out: wknd over 1f out* **20/1**
0061 **8** *shd* **Kinsman (IRE)**[15] 6576 8-9-0 50 RobertMiles(3) 6 48
(T D McCarthy) *hld up wl in rr: prog on outer 3f out: rdn and nt qckn whn wd bnd 2f out: btn after* **11/1**
502 **9** *2 ½* **It Must Be Speech**[17] 6556 4-8-12 40 (v) RobertWinston 12 39
(S L Keightley) *forced to r wd thrght: in tch: prog and prom 3f out: wknd 2f out* **25/1**
4036 **10** *shd* **Giunchiglio**[10] 6620 6-8-13 46 (p) EddieAhern 5 39
(W M Brisbourne) *chsd ldrs: rdn 3f out: sn lost pl and btn* **9/2**[1]
P654 **11** *3 ½* **Oktis Morilious (IRE)**[8] 6650 4-8-12 40 MickyFenton 7 32
(A W Carroll) *trckd ldrs: rdn and wknd over 2f out* **33/1**
0022 **12** *7* **Moondancer (GER)**[10] 6614 6-9-2 49 HayleyTurner 8 23
(B G Powell) *prom: rdn and lost pl over 3f out: sn wknd: b.b.v* **7/1**[2]
0360 **13** *1 ¼* **Londoner (USA)**[17] 6567 7-9-3 50 IanMongan 14 21
(S Dow) *taken down early: prom tl wknd 3f out* **12/1**
3010 **14** *1 ¾* **Icannshift (IRE)**[70] 5998 5-8-12 40 FergusSweeney 1 13
(T M Jones) *led to 1/2-way: styd prom tl wknd 2f out: eased fnl f* **20/1**

2m 4.65s (-3.14) **Going Correction** -0.10s/f (Stan)
WFA 3 from 4yo+ 3lb 14 Ran SP% **123.0**
Speed ratings (Par 97):108,107,107,104,104 103,102,102,100,100 97,92,91,89
CSF £93.20 TOTE £10.30: £3.70, £3.90, £4.10; EX 93.30 Trifecta £276.20 Pool £817.22 - 2.10 winning units..
Owner The Wacko Partnership **Bred** Hedgeholme Stud **Trained** Woodingdean, E Sussex

FOCUS
A reasonable event for its class, being run 2.61sec faster than the preceding claimer and solid form rated through the runner-up and fourth.

Moondancer(GER) Official explanation: jockey said gelding bled from nose
Londoner(USA) Official explanation: jockey said gelding hung left throughout

6684 TEXT "BETDIRECT" TO 88600 BANDED STKS — 1m (P)
2:30 (2:30) (Class 7) 3-Y-0+ — **£1,423** (£420; £210) — **Stalls** High

Form — RPR

-000 **1** **Riviera Red (IRE)**[38] 6399 5-8-11 45.....................(v[1]) RobertWinston 12 — 51
(L Montague Hall) *stdd s: hld up in last: prog on outer wl over 1f out: hanging lft but drvn to ld last 75yds: won gng away* **33/1**

-001 **2** 1 ¼ **Beneking**[15] 6577 5-8-11 45.....................(p) ChrisCatlin 2 — 48
(D Burchell) *mde most: drvn 2f out: hdd and outpcd last 75yds* **9/2**

5050 **3** ½ **Mr Belvedere**[129] 4639 4-8-8 45.....................(p) RichardThomas(3) 7 — 47
(A J Lidderdale) *trckd ldrs: effrt 2f out: drvn to try to chal 1f out: kpt on same pce* **16/1**

30-6 **4** hd **Margaret's Dream (IRE)**[10] 6611 4-8-8 45............. DanielTudhope(3) 4 — 49+
(D Carroll) *hld up in rr: trapped on inner in last pair over 2f out: effrt whn nt clr run jst over 1f out: r.o: nrst fin* **11/4**[1]

-000 **5** 1 ½ **Dream Of Dubai (IRE)**[15] 6575 4-8-11 45..................... HayleyTurner 3 — 43
(P Mitchell) *pressed ldr: upsides over 2f out: nt qckn over 1f out: wknd ins fnl f* **14/1**

-000 **6** shd **Diamond Dan (IRE)**[31] 6445 3-8-10 45..................... PaulHanagan 8 — 46+
(P D Evans) *hld up in rr: effrt 2f out: styng on to press ldrs whn rn out of room last 150yds: nt rcvr* **20/1**

0003 **7** shd **Miss Glory Be**[54] 6259 7-8-11 45.....................(p) EddieAhern 11 — 42
(Ernst Oertel) *hld up: prog to chse ldrs over 2f out: drvn to try to chal 1f out: fnd nil* **7/2**[2]

0550 **8** hd **First Of May**[10] 6614 4-8-11 45..................... SamHitchcott 1 — 42
(Miss Z C Davison) *trckd ldrs: rdn and cl up 1f out: wknd* **16/1**

0064 **9** 1 ½ **Boogie Magic**[24] 6509 5-8-8 45.....................(p) AdamKirby(3) 6 — 39
(T T Clement) *in tch: rdn over 2f out: sn wknd* **14/1**

0000 **10** 7 **Coronado Forest (USA)**[15] 6574 6-8-11 45..................... IanMongan 9 — 22
(M R Hoad) *plld hrd: racd on outer: trckd ldrs: rdn 3f out: wknd 2f out* **4/1**[3]

1m 37.97s (-1.46) **Going Correction** -0.10s/f (Stan)
WFA 3 from 4yo+ 1lb — **10** Ran SP% **119.9**
Speed ratings (Par 97):103,101,101,101,99 99,99,99,97,90
CSF £181.04 TOTE £32.00: £5.80, £2.10, £3.90; EX 237.10.
Owner Michael S Green & Partners **Bred** Abergwaun Farms **Trained** Epsom, Surrey

FOCUS
An ordinary contest run at a fair gallop and the form looks sound enough despite the surprise winner.
Diamond Dan(IRE) Official explanation: jockey said gelding was denied a clear run
Coronado Forest(USA) Official explanation: jockey said gelding was never travelling

6685 PLAY INSTANT WIN GAMES AT BETDIRECT.CO.UK BANDED STKS — 6f (P)
3:05 (3:05) (Class 7) 3-Y-0+ — **£1,446** (£427; £213) — **Stalls** Low

Form — RPR

0132 **1** **Segoria (IRE)**[15] 6579 3-9-2 50..................... ChrisCatlin 8 — 58
(A M Hales) *trckd ldrs gng wl: prog on inner 2f out: led ent fnl f: drvn and styd on wl* **7/2**[1]

5002 **2** 1 ½ **Gaudalpin (IRE)**[8] 6646 3-9-2 50.....................(t) JimmyQuinn 4 — 54
(Ernst Oertel) *prom: chsd ldr over 2f out: drvn and kpt on same pce fr over 1f out* **4/1**[2]

0036 **3** hd **Zazous**[8] 6639 4-9-2 50..................... J-PGuillambert 7 — 53
(J J Bridger) *chsd ldrs: pushed along fr 1/2-way: urged along over 1f out: styd on fnl f* **6/1**

0300 **4** ½ **Enjoy The Buzz**[139] 4335 6-9-0 48..................... SteveDrowne 9 — 50
(J M Bradley) *chsd ldrs: effrt on outer 2f out: one pce fr over 1f out* **5/1**[3]

0000 **5** shd **Hiamovi (IRE)**[13] 6589 3-9-2 50.....................(v[1]) RobertWinston 1 — 51
(R M H Cowell) *racd freely: led: hdd & wknd ent fnl f* **16/1**

2650 **6** ½ **Desert Light (IRE)**[8] 6647 4-8-13 50.....................(v) PatrickMathers(3) 11 — 50
(D Shaw) *s.s: rdn in last pair over 2f out: hanging lft over 1f out: r.o ins fnl f* **13/2**

0600 **7** 1 **Noble Mount**[15] 6579 4-9-1 49.....................(p) SamHitchcott 2 — 46
(A B Haynes) *chsd ldr to over 2f out: wknd over 1f out* **6/1**

0-40 **8** nk **Chillin Out**[23] 6516 3-9-2 50..................... PaulDoe 12 — 46
(W Jarvis) *racd wd: hld up in tch: rdn and no prog over 2f out: sn btn* **16/1**

0300 **9** 3 **Ringarooma**[13] 6589 3-9-2 50..................... VinceSlattery 3 — 37
(C N Allen) *dwlt: a in rr: rdn and no prog over 2f out* **25/1**

1m 12.39s (-0.42) **Going Correction** -0.10s/f (Stan) — **9** Ran SP% **116.4**
Speed ratings (Par 97):98,96,95,95,94 94,92,92,88
CSF £17.69 TOTE £3.70: £1.50, £1.90, £2.20; EX 9.70.
Owner A M Hales **Bred** Tom Darcy And Vincent McCarthy **Trained** Quainton, Bucks

FOCUS
Modest fare but sound enough form for the grade.

6686 LITTLEWOODS £2M POOLS ON 0800 500 000 BANDED STKS — 5f (P)
3:40 (3:45) (Class 7) 3-Y-0+ — **£1,412** (£417; £208) — **Stalls** High

Form — RPR

6005 **1** **Rock Fever (IRE)**[24] 6511 3-8-4 40.....................(b) RonanKeogh(7) 6 — 51
(Peter Grayson) *chsd ldng pair: clr of rest fr 1/2-way: drvn to chal on inner 1f out: kpt on to ld nr fin* **14/1**

0440 **2** hd **Legal Set (IRE)**[8] 6647 9-8-4 45.....................(bt) AnnStokell(7) 1 — 50
(Miss A Stokell) *mde most at str pce: urged along over 1f out: worn down nr fin* **8/1**

5000 **3** 1 ¼ **A Teen**[16] 6568 7-8-11 40..................... RobertWinston 2 — 46
(P Howling) *off the pce in midfield: rdn 3f out: styd on wl fnl f to take 3rd nr fin* **16/1**

4511 **4** ¾ **Lady Hopeful (IRE)**[8] 6647 3-9-3 45.....................(b) RobbieFitzpatrick 5 — 49+
(Peter Grayson) *s.i.s: wl off the pce in last trio: bustled along fnl 2f: styd on ins fnl f: no ch* **7/4**[1]

/502 **5** shd **Amber Nectar Two**[10] 6613 5-8-11 40.....................(b) EddieAhern 10 — 43
(A G Newcombe) *chsd clr ldrs: rdn 2f out: hanging and no imp over 1f out: plugged on* **10/3**[2]

2305 **6** nk **Innclassic (IRE)**[15] 6580 4-8-8 45.....................(b) AmirQuinn(3) 4 — 42
(Jane Southcombe) *w ldr at str pce to wl over 1f out: wknd ins fnl f* **20/1**

0630 **7** 1 ½ **Jasmine Pearl (IRE)**[87] 5657 4-8-11 45..................... FergusSweeney 7 — 36
(T M Jones) *chsd clr ldrs: rdn and no imp over 2f out: fdd* **14/1**

4550 **8** ¾ **Taipan Tommy (IRE)**[15] 6578 3-8-11 45.....................(v) JimmyQuinn 8 — 34
(S Dow) *s.i.s: wl off the pce in last trio: struggling fr 1/2-way : n.d* **11/2**[3]

0002 **9** 1 ¾ **Question Mark**[15] 6578 3-8-11 40..................... J-PGuillambert 9 — 27
(Andrew Reid) *walked to s: hanging and off the pce in last trio: nvr a factor* **12/1**

58.64 secs (-1.14) **Going Correction** -0.10s/f (Stan) — **9** Ran SP% **117.6**
Speed ratings (Par 97):105,104,102,101,101 100,98,97,94
CSF £122.52 TOTE £16.90: £3.40, £2.30, £3.50; EX 130.90 Place 6 £1,179.65, Place 5 £698.84..
Owner Lol Ogburn **Bred** Liam Phelan **Trained** Formby, Lancs
■ Stewards' Enquiry : Ronan Keogh two-day ban: used whip with excessive frequency (Jan 9-10)

FOCUS
This was run at a strong pace and few got into it, but the form looks sound enough.
T/Jkpt: Not won. . T/Plt: £782.20 to a £1 stake. Pool: £107,317.05. 100.15 winning tickets. T/Qpdt: £253.30 to a £1 stake. Pool: £7,669.50. 22.40 winning tickets. JN

6681 LINGFIELD (L-H)
Friday, December 30

OFFICIAL GOING: Standard
Wind: Fresh, behind

6687 FIRST PAST THE POST AT BETDIRECT MAIDEN STKS — 1m 2f (P)
12:30 (12:35) (Class 5) 3-Y-0 — **£4,070** (£1,211; £605; £302) — **Stalls** Low

Form — RPR

1 **Danse Spectre (IRE)**[88] 5674 3-8-9..................... RobertWinston 10 — 56+
(E J O'Neill) *hld up: hdwy on outside over 2f out: str run to ld wl ins fnl f: won gng away* **14/1**

6030 **2** 1 ½ **Lady Pilot**[55] 6265 3-8-6 62..................... RichardThomas(3) 12 — 53
(Dr J R J Naylor) *in rr: hdwy 3f out: sn short of room: rallied fnl f and r.o to go 2nd cl home* **12/1**

423 **3** nk **A Thousand Smiles (IRE)**[72] 5982 3-8-9 70............. MatthewHenry 14 — 53
(M A Jarvis) *sn chsd ldr: led tl hdd 2f out: rdn and hdd wl ins fnl f: nt pce of wnr and lost 2nd cl home* **3/1**[1]

3-4 **4** hd **Red Sans**[356] 67 3-9-0..................... MartinDwyer 11 — 57
(P Mitchell) *mid-div: hdwy on outside over 2f out: kpt on one pce fnl f* **11/1**

0050 **5** shd **Wavertree One Off**[31] 6461 3-9-0 55.....................(b) GeorgeBaker 5 — 57
(D R C Elsworth) *bhd tl hdwy over 2f out: styd on fnl f* **20/1**

6 ½ **Esprit De Corps** 3-9-0..................... JamieMackay 7 — 56+
(Sir Mark Prescott) *slowly away and rn green in rr: picked up wl and r.o strly fnl f: nvr nrr* **7/2**[2]

003 **7** ½ **Golo Gal**[27] 6485 3-9-0 59..................... IanMongan 13 — 57+
(Mrs L J Mongan) *hld up: hdwy over 4f out: rdn and ev ch 1f out: hld whn hmpd nr fin* **7/1**[3]

2505 **8** hd **Highliner**[20] 6535 3-9-0 57..................... TomEaves 8 — 55
(Mrs L Williamson) *chsd ldrs: rdn over 1f out: hld whn n.m.r ins fnl f* **10/1**

0330 **9** ¾ **Madhavi**[63] 6134 3-8-9 65..................... DaneO'Neill 1 — 48
(R Hannon) *in tch tl wknd fnl f* **7/1**[3]

3500 **10** ½ **Paddys Tern**[221] 1958 3-9-0 60..................... FergusSweeney 4 — 52
(N M Babbage) *sn led: hdd after 2f: styd prom tl rdn and wknd fnl f* **33/1**

6530 **11** 6 **Bavarica**[20] 6535 3-8-2 57..................... DonnaCaldwell(7) 9 — 36
(Miss J Feilden) *led after 2f: hdd 2f out: wknd appr fnl f* **20/1**

12 1 ¾ **Elleray (IRE)** 3-8-9..................... MickyFenton 2 — 33
(J G Given) *slowly away: a bhd* **40/1**

0-40 **13** 8 **Swell Lad**[8] 1778 3-9-0 65.....................(b) SteveDrowne 3 — 22
(S Gollings) *broke wl: prom tl wknd over 3f out* **33/1**

00 **14** dist **Dancing Beauty (IRE)**[67] 6069 3-8-9..................... SamHitchcott 6 — —
(T T Clement) *slowly away: rn wd: t.o 1/2-way* **100/1**

2m 5.87s (-1.92) **Going Correction** -0.125s/f (Stan) — **14** Ran SP% **122.8**
Speed ratings (Par 102):102,100,100,100,100 99,99,99,98,98 93,92,85,—
CSF £162.80 TOTE £18.20: £5.50, £3.90, £1.70; EX 213.00.
Owner Miss A H Marshall **Bred** Kilcarn Stud **Trained** Averham Park, Notts
■ Stewards' Enquiry : Matthew Henry caution: careless riding

FOCUS
A routine maiden that is limited by the fifth although could still be rated on the high side, but containing a few interesting contenders at this level.
Esprit De Corps ◆ Official explanation: vet said colt was lame on left fore
Golo Gal Official explanation: jockey said gelding suffered interference in final furlong
Dancing Beauty(IRE) Official explanation: jockey said filly hung badly right throughout

6688 BETDIRECT FREEPHONE 0800 211 222 NURSERY — 6f (P)
1:00 (1:07) (Class 4) (0-85,83) 2-Y-0 — **£4,663** (£1,387; £693; £346) — **Stalls** Low

Form — RPR

0222 **1** **Orchard Supreme**[14] 6591 2-8-8 **70**..................... RobertWinston 2 — 75
(R Hannon) *trckd ldrs: shkn up to ld ins fnl f: r.o wl* **13/8**[1]

3510 **2** ½ **Secret Night**[31] 6456 2-9-7 **83**..................... SteveDrowne 8 — 86
(J A R Toller) *hld up in rr: hdwy over 2f out: r.o to go 2nd wl ins fnl f* **6/1**[3]

0640 **3** 1 ¼ **African Concerto (IRE)**[63] 6128 2-8-6 **68**..................... StephenCarson 6 — 67
(S Kirk) *bhd tl hdwy on outside over 1f out: r.o strly: nvr nrr* **25/1**

1 **4** 1 ¼ **What Do You Know**[62] 6156 2-8-12 **77**..................... AdamKirby(3) 3 — 73+
(G A Butler) *t.k.h and hmpd sn after s: hdwy whn n.m.r appr fnl f: styd on one pce ins* **5/1**[2]

0101 **5** shd **Stoneacre Lad (IRE)**[24] 6517 2-8-12 **74**..................... RobbieFitzpatrick 7 — 69
(Peter Grayson) *chsd ldr: rdn to ld appr fnl f: hdd ins and no ex* **5/1**[2]

5000 **6** 3 **Perfect Order (USA)**[48] 6320 2-7-12 **60** oh5.....................(p) HayleyTurner 5 — 46
(N A Callaghan) *racd wd in tch: wknd over 1f out* **33/1**

3635 **7** ½ **Kings Cavalier (USA)**[139] 4356 2-9-1 **77**..................... DaneO'Neill 4 — 62
(S Dow) *bhd: rdn whn n.m.r over 1f out* **11/1**

6433 **8** 1 ¼ **Highland Song (IRE)**[31] 6456 2-8-11 **73**..................... PaulHanagan 1 — 54
(R F Fisher) *led tl hdd appr fnl f: wknd qckly ins* **8/1**

1m 12.12s (-0.69) **Going Correction** -0.125s/f (Stan) — **8** Ran SP% **111.9**
Speed ratings (Par 98):99,98,96,95,94 90,90,88
CSF £11.17 CT £168.29 TOTE £2.70: £1.20, £2.10, £5.20; EX 17.10.
Owner Brian C Oakley **Bred** Mrs M H Goodrich **Trained** East Everleigh, Wilts

FOCUS
A medium-grade, but competitive, nursery and the form looks ordinary, rated through the placed horses.

NOTEBOOK
Orchard Supreme was winning for the first time on the sand after being runner-up three times in succession. He has taken to the surface well, and only the Handicapper can stop him winning again. (op 2-1 tchd 9-4)
Secret Night had a stiff task conceding so much weight to the winner, but did well. She is proving to be useful around here. (op 5-1 tchd 13-2)
African Concerto(IRE), making his All-Weather debut, showed he has a future on it. He also got the trip better than he appeared to on turf.

What Do You Know appeared to fall a bit short of the promise he showed when winning at Wolverhampton on his debut. However, to be fair, this was a better race and the Handicapper took no chances. (op 4-1)
Stoneacre Lad(IRE) still looks to be more effective over five furlongs. (op 6-1)
Perfect Order(USA), 5lb out of the handicap, was too wide to hold her place in the straight. However, she continues to show signs of minor ability.
Kings Cavalier(USA) is bred to go on artificial surfaces, but this was not a great debut on Polytrack. His turf form suggests he can do better following this first outing for four months. (op 9-1)
Highland Song(IRE) could do with dropping a few pounds. (op 7-1)

6689 BETDIRECTPOKER.COM CLAIMING STKS 6f (P)
1:30 (1:35) (Class 6) 3-Y-O+ £2,873 (£848; £424) Stalls Low

Form RPR
5346 **1** **Franksalot (IRE)**[108] 5201 5-8-12 71 RichardThomas(3) 9 76
(Miss B Sanders) *stdd s and swtchd lft fr outside draw: in rr tl rdn and r.o strly fnl f to ld nr fin* **4/1**[1]
1510 **2** ½ **General Feeling (IRE)**[8] 6657 4-9-2 77 GeorgeBaker 11 76
(S Kirk) *swtchd lft s fr outside draw: hdwy on outside appr fnl f: fin wl to go 2nd nr fin* **5/1**[2]
0061 **3** hd **Hadath (IRE)**[10] 6630 8-8-7 57 RobertWinston 8 66
(B G Powell) *hld up in rr: rdn and hdwy on ins 1f out: pressed ldrs ins fnl f* **6/1**[3]
5500 **4** ½ **Louphole**[14] 6590 3-8-11 72 FergusSweeney 6 68
(P J Makin) *slowly away: sn mid-div: rdn and ld briefly jst ins fnl f: no ex* **4/1**[1]
4445 **5** 1 **Million Percent**[11] 6618 6-8-9 72 (v) PatCosgrave 3 63
(K R Burke) *prom: rdn over 1f out: kpt on one pce* **5/1**[2]
0000 **6** ½ **Easy Feeling (IRE)**[20] 6544 3-8-4 65 (b[1]) MartinDwyer 2 57
(R Hannon) *led tl hdd & wknd jst ins fnl f* **16/1**
0000 **7** nk **Music Teacher**[10] 6630 3-8-4 55 HayleyTurner 7 56
(N A Callaghan) *in tch: rdn over 2f out: no imp appr fnl f* **12/1**
6004 **8** ½ **Manic**[10] 6630 3-8-2 60 ChrisCatlin 1 53
(Andrew Reid) *trckd ldrs: rdn over 1f out: wknd ins fnl f* **12/1**
0000 **9** 1 **Doctor's Cave**[27] 6486 3-8-9 60 DaneO'Neill 5 57
(K O Cunningham-Brown) *trckd ldr: rdn over 2f out: wknd appr fnl f* **50/1**
6344 **10** 2 **Madrasee**[14] 6589 7-8-8 60 ow1 AmirQuinn(3) 4 53
(Jane Southcombe) *prom tl wknd qckly ins fnl f* **14/1**

1m 11.3s (-1.51) **Going Correction** -0.125s/f (Stan) 10 Ran SP% **117.5**
Speed ratings (Par 101):105,104,104,103,102 101,101,100,99,96
CSF £24.06 TOTE £5.40: £1.80, £2.00, £1.80; EX 28.90.
Owner Peter Crate And Jane Byers **Bred** J P Hardiman **Trained** Headley, Surrey

FOCUS
Just a fair claimer but run in a decent time and the form looks sound, rated through the third and seventh.

6690 LITTLEWOODS BETDIRECT H'CAP 1m (P)
2:00 (2:05) (Class 4) (0-80,78) 3-Y-O+ £5,754 (£1,711; £855; £427) Stalls High

Form RPR
1033 **1** **Glencalvie (IRE)**[25] 6503 4-8-12 72 (v) DaneO'Neill 6 84
(J Akehurst) *mde all: rdn and kpt up to work fnl f: unchal* **6/1**[2]
0053 **2** 1½ **Northern Desert (IRE)**[10] 6629 6-9-4 78 ChrisCatlin 3 87
(P W Hiatt) *mid-div: in tch: rdn 2f out: styd on to chse wnr appr fnl f* **6/1**[2]
0002 **3** 1½ **Hurricane Coast**[11] 6622 6-8-6 73 (b) JamesDoyle(7) 2 79
(K McAuliffe) *bhd tl hdwy over 1f out: styd on fnl f: nvr nrr* **12/1**
0220 **4** 1 **Missatacama (IRE)**[20] 6547 3-9-3 78 MickyFenton 12 81
(D J Daly) *chsd wnr tl rdn appr fnl f: one pce after* **16/1**
6000 **5** nk **Stoic Leader (IRE)**[11] 6621 5-8-10 70 PaulHanagan 10 73
(R F Fisher) *in rr tl styd on fnl f: nvr nrr* **16/1**
0063 **6** ¾ **Sonny Parkin**[41] 6373 3-8-10 74 (p) AdamKirby(3) 7 75
(G A Huffer) *prom: rdn and nt qckn appr fnl f* **12/1**
0034 **7** nk **All A Dream**[18] 6564 3-8-10 71 TomEaves 4 71
(Mrs L Williamson) *s.i.s: t.k.h: in rr: effrt 2f out: nt qckn fr over 1f out* **33/1**
3656 **8** ¾ **Zalkani (IRE)**[9] 6644 5-8-11 71 RobertWinston 9 69
(B G Powell) *slowly away: racd wd: a bhd* **17/2**[3]
-560 **9** ½ **Magic Merlin**[10] 6629 4-9-3 77 IanMongan 1 74
(W R Swinburn) *chsd ldrs tl rdn and wknd fnl f* **9/1**
1043 **10** ¾ **Out For A Stroll**[49] 6315 6-8-10 70 (e[1]) HayleyTurner 5 66
(S C Williams) *a in rr* **6/1**[2]
0022 **11** ½ **Island Rapture**[10] 6629 5-8-13 73 SteveDrowne 8 67
(J A R Toller) *bhd: rdn over 2f out: nvr got into r* **4/1**[1]
0454 **12** 3 **Takes Tutu (USA)**[11] 6622 6-8-13 73 PatCosgrave 11 60
(K R Burke) *t.k.h: in tch tl rdn and wknd over 2f out* **12/1**

1m 36.87s (-2.56) **Going Correction** -0.125s/f (Stan)
WFA 3 from 4yo+ 1lb 12 Ran SP% **121.2**
Speed ratings (Par 105):107,105,104,103,102 101,101,100,100,99 99,96
CSF £42.92 CT £428.62 TOTE £6.60: £2.10, £2.00, £3.60; EX 70.60 Trifecta £326.00 Pool: £688.84 - 1.50 winning tickets..
Owner Tattenham Corner Racing **Bred** Top Of The Form Syndicate **Trained** Epsom, Surrey

FOCUS
A modest but competitive handicap with the runner-up the best guide to the value of the form.
Island Rapture Official explanation: trainer was unable to offer any explanation for poor form shown
Takes Tutu(USA) Official explanation: jockey said gelding ran too free

6691 BETDIRECTCASINO.COM (S) STKS 1m 2f (P)
2:30 (2:35) (Class 6) 3-Y-O+ £2,518 (£743; £371) Stalls Low

Form RPR
0000 **1** **Competitor**[20] 6548 4-9-0 55 (vt[1]) DaneO'Neill 2 63
(J Akehurst) *chsd ldr: led over 3f out: drvn clr over 1f out: kpt on* **6/1**
0004 **2** 1¾ **Barton Sands (IRE)**[9] 6643 8-9-6 66 (t) J-PGuillambert 9 66
(Andrew Reid) *hld up in tch: hdwy to chse wnr 2f out: no imp fnl f* **2/1**[1]
0660 **3** 2½ **Salinger (USA)**[11] 6103 3-9-3 67 ChrisCatlin 11 61
(Andrew Turnell) *in rr tl hdwy over 2f out: styd on to go 3rd ins fnl f: no ch w first 2* **6/1**
0300 **4** 1¾ **Je Suis Belle**[20] 6536 3-8-6 59 (p) JimmyQuinn 4 47
(Miss Gay Kelleway) *prom: rdn whn n.m.r over 2f out: kpt on one pce* **11/2**[3]
0000 **5** 3½ **Senor Eduardo**[30] 6327 8-9-0 45 (p) GeorgeBaker 1 45
(S Gollings) *led for 3f: hung lft and fdd over 1f out* **14/1**
0000 **6** ¾ **Rasid (USA)**[9] 6643 7-9-0 55 RobertWinston 10 44
(C A Dwyer) *mid-div: rdn and chsd ldrs over 2f out: nt qckn fr over 1f out* **16/1**
0203 **7** 3 **Shaheer (IRE)**[1] 6682 3-8-11 51 (p) IanMongan 7 38
(P Howling) *bhd tl rapid hdwy to ld after 3f: hdd over 3f out: wknd 2f out* **5/1**[2]
0000 **8** 2 **Somewhere My Love**[39] 6394 4-8-6 35 (v[1]) RobertMiles(3) 5 29
(P Butler) *hld up in mid-div: lost pl 3f out: n.d after* **50/1**
0000 **9** ½ **Naivety**[1] 6682 3-8-6 47 (b) JamieMackay 12 28
(G G Margarson) *racd wd: a bhd* **20/1**
6560 **10** 6 **Pharoah's Gold (IRE)**[17] 6508 7-9-6 45 (v) AlanDaly 8 28
(D Burchell) *trckd ldrs tl wknd 2f out* **28/1**
0066 **11** 2 **Teutonic (IRE)**[63] 4623 4-8-9 35 PaulHanagan 6 13
(R F Fisher) *slowly away: a bhd* **50/1**

2m 5.75s (-2.04) **Going Correction** -0.125s/f (Stan)
WFA 3 from 4yo+ 3lb 11 Ran SP% **118.6**
Speed ratings (Par 101):103,101,99,98,95 94,92,90,90,85 84
CSF £17.94 TOTE £7.00: £2.50, £1.20, £2.20; EX 25.10.There was no bid for the winner. Salinger was claimed by Mrs L. J. Mongan for £6,000.
Owner Who Cares Who Wins **Bred** Cheveley Park Stud Ltd **Trained** Epsom, Surrey

FOCUS
An ordinary seller rated through the winner to recent form, but the second and third ran well at the weights.
Shaheer(IRE) Official explanation: jockey said gelding had no more to give

6692 FOOTBALLPOOLS.COM H'CAP (DIV I) 7f (P)
3:00 (3:08) (Class 6) (0-55,55) 3-Y-O+ £2,171 (£641; £320) Stalls Low

Form RPR
3515 **1** **Sonntag Blue (IRE)**[18] 6560 3-8-3 51 DonnaCaldwell(7) 9 59
(Miss J Feilden) *sn trckd ldr: rdn to ld ins fnl f: hld on nr fin* **16/1**
0003 **2** nk **Awarding**[11] 6611 5-8-2 46 oh6 (vt) RichardThomas(3) 12 53
(Dr J R J Naylor) *a in tch on outside: str run to hold ev ch fnl f: no ex last strides* **16/1**
1263 **3** nk **Cayman Breeze**[9] 6639 5-8-11 52 SteveDrowne 2 58
(J M Bradley) *hld up: str run on ins over 1f out: pressed ldrs cl home* **3/1**[1]
0000 **4** 1¼ **Bodden Bay**[31] 6455 3-8-11 55 DanielTudhope(3) 3 59+
(D Carroll) *chsd ldrs: rdn whn short of room ins fnl f* **16/1**
2103 **5** shd **Stagnite**[9] 6646 5-8-4 52 JamesDoyle(7) 4 54
(K McAuliffe) *hld up in mid-div: rdn over 1f out: kpt on ins fnl f* **11/2**[2]
5003 **6** nk **High Rhythm**[34] 6429 3-8-11 52 (e[1]) J-PGuillambert 8 54
(S C Williams) *t.k.h: led tl hdd ins fnl f: no ex* **11/2**[2]
3012 **7** 1 **Mythical Charm**[16] 6574 6-8-13 54 (t) StephenCarson 11 53
(J J Bridger) *s.i.s: bhd tl mde sme late hdwy* **10/1**
3030 **8** nk **Imperium**[9] 6646 4-9-0 55 (p) MickyFenton 7 53
(Stef Liddiard) *mid-div: rdn and one pce ins fnl 2f* **9/1**
0165 **9** 1 **Park Star**[9] 6646 5-8-5 49 PatrickMathers(3) 6 45
(D Shaw) *hld up in tch: wknd over 1f out* **12/1**
1500 **10** ¾ **Grezie**[20] 6541 3-8-10 54 RobertMiles(3) 10 56+
(T D McCarthy) *t.k.h: trckd ldrs: wknd and eased whn btn ins fnl f* **25/1**
0440 **11** ½ **Latin Express (IRE)**[20] 6542 3-8-12 53 (t) MartinDwyer 1 45
(W R Muir) *a in rr* **8/1**[3]
6060 **12** shd **Even Hotter**[209] 2306 4-8-5 46 oh1 ChrisCatlin 14 38
(D W P Arbuthnot) *in rr: rdn over 1f out: nvr on terms* **40/1**
0003 **13** 3 **Bennanabaa**[11] 6613 6-8-0 46 oh6 (tp) NataliaGemelova(5) 5 30
(S C Burrough) *mid-div tl wknd 2f out* **33/1**
0004 **14** 6 **Sunset Dreamer (USA)**[23] 6526 4-8-5 46 oh1 (p) HayleyTurner 13 15
(P Mitchell) *racd wd in mid-div: wknd 2f out* **40/1**

1m 24.58s (-1.31) **Going Correction** -0.125s/f (Stan) 14 Ran SP% **123.0**
Speed ratings (Par 101):102,101,101,99,99 99,98,97,96,95 95,95,91,84
CSF £247.68 CT £1013.68 TOTE £15.70: £5.00, £5.40, £2.00; EX 324.50.
Owner DD & N Associates **Bred** B Kennedy **Trained** Exning, Suffolk
■ Stewards' Enquiry : Richard Thomas one-day ban: careless riding (Jan 10)

FOCUS
A very moderate handicap, not much better than a seller and the form looks far from solid.
Bodden Bay Official explanation: jockey said gelding was hampered on run to line
Mythical Charm Official explanation: jockey said mare missed break
Grezie Official explanation: jockey said filly was hampered at furlong marker

6693 FOOTBALLPOOLS.COM H'CAP (DIV II) 7f (P)
3:30 (3:37) (Class 6) (0-55,55) 3-Y-O+ £2,177 (£642; £321) Stalls Low

Form RPR
2314 **1** **Captain Darling (IRE)**[3] 6667 5-8-9 53 6ex EdwardCreighton(3) 7 62
(R W Price) *t.k.h: in tch: r.o strly fnl f to ld last strides* **6/1**[1]
0012 **2** nk **Beneking**[1] 6684 5-8-5 46 oh1 (p) ChrisCatlin 6 54
(D Burchell) *led: rdn over 1f out: kpt on: hdd last strides* **8/1**
1352 **3** 1¾ **Doctor Dennis (IRE)**[20] 6541 8-8-11 52 (v) JimmyQuinn 13 56
(J Pearce) *racd wd in mid-div: r.o wl fnl f: nvr nrr* **6/1**[1]
0400 **4** ¾ **Pheckless**[9] 6646 6-8-10 51 SteveDrowne 2 53
(J M Bradley) *slowly away: hdwy on outside over 1f out: r.o: nvr nrr* **8/1**
0534 **5** ½ **One Last Time**[11] 6611 5-8-2 46 oh1 RichardThomas(3) 12 46
(Miss B Sanders) *towards rr tl hdwy appr fnl f: r.o: nvr nrr* **15/2**[3]
2534 **6** shd **Pearl Farm**[102] 5364 4-8-13 54 MickyFenton 9 54
(C A Horgan) *in rr tl hdwy appr fnl f: nvr nrr* **7/1**[2]
5353 **7** hd **St Ivian**[21] 6527 5-8-11 52 AlanDaly 5 52
(Mrs N Macauley) *chsd ldrs on ins: fdd ins fnl f* **8/1**
0301 **8** 1¼ **Mad**[16] 6574 4-8-9 50 J-PGuillambert 14 46
(Andrew Reid) *s.i.s: rdn and sn prom: chsd ldrs 3f out tl wknd 1f out* **7/1**[2]
4006 **9** 1¼ **Fizzy Lizzy**[11] 6613 5-8-5 46 oh6 PaulHanagan 3 39
(H E Haynes) *t.k.h: in tch: rdn 3f out: wknd 2f out* **50/1**
0043 **10** ½ **Young Mick**[18] 6560 3-9-0 55 (b) JamieMackay 8 47
(G G Margarson) *trckd ldrs: rdn 2f out: sn bhd* **16/1**
0006 **11** ½ **Vizulize**[153] 3945 6-8-5 53 JackDean(7) 4 44
(A W Carroll) *a bhd* **33/1**
0004 **12** 2½ **Global Achiever**[9] 6646 4-9-0 55 (p) RobertWinston 10 39
(G C H Chung) *t.k.h: a bhd* **14/1**
0060 **13** ½ **Good Wee Girl (IRE)**[16] 6577 3-8-5 46 oh6 (b) HayleyTurner 1 29
(S Woodman) *t.k.h: rdn 3f out: sn wknd* **50/1**

1m 24.54s (-1.35) **Going Correction** -0.125s/f (Stan) 13 Ran SP% **118.1**
Speed ratings (Par 101):102,101,99,98,98 98,97,96,95,94 93,91,90
CSF £51.96 CT £311.85 TOTE £5.90: £2.30, £3.50, £2.00; EX 54.60 Place 6 £13.27, Place 5 £4.13.
Owner A Dunmore **Bred** Knocktoran Stud **Trained** Newmarket, Suffolk

FOCUS
Another low-grade handicap, like the first division, and with those immediately behind the winner to recent marks the form looks sound.
Pearl Farm Official explanation: trainer said mare was found to be in season
T/Jkpt: Not won. T/Plt: £81.00 to a £1 stake. Pool: £81,334.65. 732.25 winning tickets. T/Qpdt: £22.50 to a £1 stake. Pool: £6,184.50. 203.30 winning tickets. JS

6675 WOLVERHAMPTON (A.W) (L-H)
Saturday, December 31

OFFICIAL GOING: Standard
Wind: Fresh, behind Weather: Overcast

6694 BETDIRECT.CO.UK MAIDEN STKS (DIV I) 7f 32y(P)
12:05 (12:06) (Class 5) 2-Y-O **£3,756** (£1,117; £558; £278) **Stalls** High

Form | | | | RPR
42 **1** **Lunar Express (USA)**[22] 6531 2-8-9 ... TonyCulhane 1 87+
(W J Haggas) *mde all: pushed clr over 1f out: edgd rt fnl f: eased nr fin* **1/2**[1]
0063 **2** 3½ **Mr Floodlight (IRE)**[11] 6628 2-9-0 77 ... DaneO'Neill 8 76+
(R Hannon) *prom: rdn to chse wnr 2f out: no imp* **4/1**[2]
00 **3** 1¼ **Bin Rahy (IRE)**[59] 6227 2-9-0 ... ChrisCatlin 5 68
(M R Channon) *prom: outpcd over 2f out: styd on ins fnl f* **11/1**[3]
530 **4** ¾ **Merchant Bankes**[68] 6068 2-9-0 75 ... SteveDrowne 7 66
(W G M Turner) *chsd wnr 5f: wknd over 1f out* **22/1**
02 **5** nk **Pab Special (IRE)**[191] 2846 2-9-0 ... RobertWinston 11 65
(K R Burke) *chsd ldrs: rdn over 2f out: wknd over 1f out* **12/1**
60 **6** 15 **That Look**[14] 6599 2-9-0 ... MickyFenton 12 26
(D E Cantillon) *sn outpcd* **66/1**
000 **7** 1 **Southgate Lady (IRE)**[10] 6640 2-8-9 40 ... (t) HayleyTurner 10 18
(N P Littmoden) *hld up: wknd 1/2-way* **100/1**
8 1¾ **Silvabella (IRE)** 2-8-9 ... RobertHavlin 6 14
(D Haydn Jones) *s.i.s: hdwy 6f out: wknd 4f out* **40/1**
0 **9** 1 **Hits Only Life (USA)**[10] 6642 2-9-0 ... DeanMcKeown 2 16
(J Pearce) *s.s: outpcd* **50/1**
00 **10** 1 **Vehari**[63] 6150 2-9-0 ... VinceSlattery 9 14
(M Scudamore) *dwlt: outpcd* **100/1**
0 **11** 1¼ **Tesoro**[16] 6585 2-9-0 ... FergalLynch 3 10
(P A Blockley) *s.s: outpcd* **40/1**
12 2 **Marron Flore** 2-8-6 ... RichardThomas(3) 4 —
(A J Lidderdale) *prom over 4f* **66/1**

1m 30.26s (-0.14) **Going Correction** -0.05s/f (Stan) **12 Ran SP% 118.8**
Speed ratings (Par 96):98,94,92,91,91 74,73,71,69,68 67,65
CSF £2.46 TOTE £1.40: £1.02, £1.20, £2.90; EX 3.10.
Owner Wentworth Racing (pty) Ltd **Bred** Wentworth Racing **Trained** Newmarket, Suffolk

FOCUS
This was a fair maiden, in which the first five were well clear on the remainder. The first two are value for more than the official margins and the form looks solid enough.

NOTEBOOK
Lunar Express(USA), a half-sister to the German 2000 Guineas winner Dupont, had shown plenty of promise previously and had the best of the draw. Pushed straight into the lead, she never looked in any danger and it remains to be seen what connections decide to do with her, as she now has increased paddock value. (op 4-7 after early 4-6 in a place)
Mr Floodlight(IRE), dropping down a furlong, had more than enough decent form behind him on both the turf and All Weather to go very close. He chased the leader home throughout the final stages, but was never getting to her, and will surely find an easier opportunity next time.
Bin Rahy(IRE), who is a son of a Molyglare winner, had not shown a great deal previously, although his debut run was in a hot-looking maiden. He came under pressure fairly early in the race, but stayed on well in the home straight, and shaped as though another furlong will pose no problems. He does have the option of handicaps now. (op 8-1)
Merchant Bankeshas an official rating of 75 and gives the form a fairly solid look. (op 20-1)
Pab Special(IRE), not seen since June due to an injury at home, had been gelded since his last run and raced a bit too keen on his return to the track to be a factor in the final stages. (op 14-1)
Tesoro Official explanation: jockey said gelding missed break
Marron Flore did not shape without promise on her debut despite being well beaten.

6695 LIVE FOOTBALL CASHBACKS AT BETDIRECT H'CAP (DIV I) 5f 20y(P)
12:35 (12:36) (Class 6) (0-60,60) 3-Y-O+ **£2,527** (£746; £373) **Stalls** Low

Form | | | | RPR
-002 **1** **Clipper Hoy**[32] 6462 3-9-1 57 ... GeorgeBaker 3 74+
(Mrs H Sweeting) *mde all: clr fnl 2f: eased ins fnl f* **7/2**[1]
2026 **2** 3 **Brave Chief**[32] 6469 4-8-13 55 ... (b) PhillipMakin 4 62
(S R Bowring) *hld up: hdwy over 1f out: nt rch wnr* **9/2**[2]
6300 **3** 3 **Kitchen Sink (IRE)**[10] 6639 3-8-10 52 ... (e[1]) FergusSweeney 8 48
(P J Makin) *dwlt: sn chsng ldrs: rdn over 2f out: sn outpcd: nt clr run ins fnl f* **12/1**
5600 **4** nk **Paddywack (IRE)**[31] 6470 8-8-2 47 ... (b) SilvestreDeSousa(3) 13 42+
(D W Chapman) *hld up: hdwy over 1f out: hung rt and wknd fnl f* **20/1**
6116 **5** nk **He's A Rocket (IRE)**[4] 6668 4-8-11 60 ... (b) AndrewElliott(7) 12 54+
(K R Burke) *prom: chsd wnr 1/2-way: wknd fnl f* **13/2**[3]
5063 **6** ½ **Cashel Mead**[33] 6447 5-9-2 58 ... (b) SteveDrowne 2 50
(J L Spearing) *mid-div: sn drvn along: nt clr run over 2f out: nvr trbld ldrs* **9/2**[2]
0440 **7** 1½ **Jun Fan (USA)**[12] 6616 3-9-2 58 ... (p) TomEaves 1 45
(B Ellison) *s.i.s: sn outpcd: nvr nrr* **9/1**
1035 **8** 1 **Stagnite**[1] 6692 5-8-8 57 ... JamesDoyle(7) 10 40
(K McAuliffe) *mid-div: rdn over 2f out: sn wknd* **15/2**
-000 **9** ½ **Kashtanka (IRE)**[13] 6607 3-8-6 51 oh6 ow5 ... (p) JasonEdmunds(3) 6 32
(J Balding) *chsd wnr to 1/2-way: sn rdn and wknd* **66/1**
006 **10** 2 **Revien (IRE)**[12] 6616 3-9-3 59 ... EddieAhern 11 33
(Miss J R Tooth) *swtchd lft sn after s: outpcd* **16/1**
4400 **11** ½ **Holly Springs**[14] 6603 3-8-12 59 ... (p) MarcHalford(5) 7 31
(Mrs C A Dunnett) *chsd ldrs: rdn 1/2-way: hung lft and wknd 2f out* **20/1**
0/00 **12** 6 **Nifty Major**[42] 6380 8-7-11 46 oh11 ... JosephWalsh(7) 9 —
(N E Berry) *s.s: outpcd* **100/1**

62.12 secs (-0.70) **Going Correction** -0.05s/f (Stan) **12 Ran SP% 119.3**
Speed ratings (Par 101):103,98,93,92,92 91,89,87,86,83 82,73
CSF £18.31 CT £173.00 TOTE £3.20: £1.10, £2.30, £5.30; EX 21.20.
Owner P Sweeting **Bred** P Sweeting **Trained** Lockeridge, Wilts

FOCUS
This was a low-grade sprint won in very easy style by Clipper Hoy, who had it all his own way in front. The time was slightly quicker than the second division and the form has been rated at face value through the runner-up.

6696 LIVE FOOTBALL CASHBACKS AT BETDIRECT H'CAP (DIV II) 5f 20y(P)
1:05 (1:06) (Class 6) (0-60,60) 3-Y-O+ **£2,515** (£742; £371) **Stalls** Low

Form | | | | RPR
3641 **1** **El Potro**[32] 6462 3-9-2 58 ... GrahamGibbons 2 68
(E S McMahon) *chsd ldr: rdn over 1f out: edgd lft and styd on to ld wl ins fnl f* **9/2**[2]
0001 **2** 1¼ **Almaty Express**[33] 6447 3-9-4 60 ... (b) RobertWinston 1 65
(J R Weymes) *chsd ldrs: rdn 1/2-way: nt clr run ins fnl f: styd on* **7/2**[1]
-001 **3** nk **Coconut Moon**[56] 6263 3-8-13 55 ... PaulQuinn 11 59+
(E J Alston) *led: clr 2f out: sn rdn: hdd wl ins fnl f* **7/1**[3]
6253 **4** nk **Sir Sandrovitch (IRE)**[4] 6668 9-9-1 57 ... (v) PaulHanagan 5 60
(R A Fahey) *chsd ldrs: rdn 1/2-way: styd on* **7/2**[1]
2505 **5** ½ **Times Review (USA)**[32] 6460 4-9-2 58 ... JimmyQuinn 9 59+
(C A Dwyer) *hld up: hdwy over 1f out: nt rch ldrs* **10/1**
5550 **6** ½ **Nova Tor (IRE)**[10] 6639 3-8-3 58 ... RonanKeogh(7) 10 51
(Peter Grayson) *chsd ldrs: rdn 1/2-way: no ex fnl f* **16/1**
0604 **7** ¾ **Cloann (IRE)**[33] 6447 3-8-13 55 ... (b) StephenCarson 6 52
(E A Wheeler) *dwlt: outpcd: r.o ins fnl f: nvr nrr* **25/1**
0050 **8** nk **Sapphire Dream**[25] 6515 3-8-7 49 ... DavidAllan 3 44
(A Bailey) *prom: sn pushed along: rdn 1/2-way: styd on same pce appr fnl f* **50/1**
0000 **9** 5 **Sundried Tomato**[25] 6514 6-8-12 54 ... (b) TonyCulhane 7 31
(D W Chapman) *n.d* **12/1**
2200 **10** hd **Gallego**[153] 3969 3-9-1 57 ... GeorgeBaker 4 34
(R J Price) *dwlt: outpcd* **14/1**
100 **11** 2 **Edged In Gold**[101] 5406 3-9-3 59 ... FergusSweeney 8 29
(P J Makin) *hld up: n.d* **25/1**
0002 **12** nk **Henry Tun**[22] 6527 7-8-8 53 ... (v) JasonEdmunds(3) 12 21
(J Balding) *a in rr* **14/1**

62.58 secs (-0.24) **Going Correction** -0.05s/f (Stan) **12 Ran SP% 120.8**
Speed ratings (Par 101):99,97,96,96,95 94,93,92,84,84 81,80
CSF £20.64 CT £113.33 TOTE £5.10: £1.90, £1.70, £2.30; EX 19.60.
Owner R J H Ltd, G Pickering & J P Hames **Bred** L A C Ashby **Trained** Hopwas, Staffs
■ Stewards' Enquiry : Ronan Keogh one-day ban: failed to keep straight from stalls (Jan 11)

FOCUS
This was probably the more competitive of the two divisions of the low-grade sprint, but was slightly slower on the clock. The form looks sound enough rated through the runner-up and fourth.

6697 BETDIRECT 0800 211 222 (S) STKS 1m 141y(P)
1:35 (1:35) (Class 6) 2-Y-O **£2,880** (£850; £425) **Stalls** Low

Form | | | | RPR
4406 **1** **Noble Edge**[11] 6635 2-8-12 48 ... (p) FergalLynch 10 57
(P A Blockley) *chsd ldr: led 4f out: rdn over 1f out: edgd lft: all out* **20/1**
005 **2** hd **Wee Charlie Castle (IRE)**[12] 6617 2-8-12 57 ... ChrisCatlin 3 57
(G C H Chung) *hld up: hdwy over 2f out: rdn over 1f out: r.o* **11/4**[2]
0424 **3** 1 **Bathwick Rox (IRE)**[11] 6635 2-8-12 58 ... (b[1]) DaneO'Neill 8 54
(B R Millman) *hld up in tch: rdn and ev ch over 1f out: unable qckn ins fnl f* **3/1**[3]
5001 **4** hd **Indian Wizard (IRE)**[76] 5921 2-9-4 64 ... SamHitchcott 6 60+
(M R Channon) *s.s: hld up: hdwy over 2f out: chsd wnr over 1f out: sn ev ch: hung lft and no ex fnl f* **5/2**[1]
0600 **5** ¾ **Master Ben (IRE)**[10] 6648 2-8-12 48 ... (b) PhillipMakin 1 52
(S R Bowring) *hld up: hdwy over 2f out: sn rdn: styd on* **33/1**
4060 **6** ¾ **Nico's Girl**[11] 6635 2-8-7 50 ... DaleGibson 4 46
(M W Easterby) *prom: lost pl whn hmpd over 3f out: hdwy over 2f out: no ex fnl f* **8/1**
0005 **7** 6 **Count The Trees**[24] 6521 2-8-7 40 ... AlanDaly 13 33
(W G M Turner) *led over 4f: wknd over 1f out* **66/1**
0506 **8** 3½ **Mytass**[10] 6648 2-8-12 52 ... DeanMcKeown 9 31
(J A Pickering) *hld up: rdn whn n.m.r and wknd over 2f out* **20/1**
0000 **9** ¾ **Vertigo Blue**[10] 6648 2-8-12 45 ... TomEaves 7 29
(C W Thornton) *chsd ldrs 7f* **40/1**
004 **10** ½ **Take No Notice (IRE)**[82] 5805 2-8-7 45 ... RobertWinston 11 23
(K R Burke) *prom: n.m.r 2f out: sn wknd: eased fnl f* **14/1**
00 **11** 3 **Late Night Love**[9] 6659 2-8-7 ... PaulHanagan 2 17
(K R Burke) *a in rr* **33/1**
0000 **12** 26 **Shopfitter**[27] 6496 2-8-7 45 ... MarcHalford(5) 12 —
(Mrs C A Dunnett) *chsd ldrs 6f* **40/1**
0050 **13** 10 **Lucky Celts (IRE)**[9] 6656 2-8-7 40 ... (p) RobertHavlin 5 —
(D Haydn Jones) *prom: rdn over 3f out: sn wknd* **22/1**

1m 53.25s (1.49) **Going Correction** -0.05s/f (Stan) **13 Ran SP% 124.1**
Speed ratings (Par 94):91,90,89,89,89 88,83,79,79,78 76,53,44
CSF £72.72 TOTE £24.80: £6.70, £1.80, £1.30; EX 55.40.There was no bid for the winner. Indian Wizard was claimed by P.Howling for £6,000.
Owner Mrs Joanna Hughes **Bred** A P Jones **Trained** Lambourn, Berks
■ Stewards' Enquiry : Dane O'Neill 18-day ban (takes into account previous offences - four days deferred): Jan 13-28

FOCUS
A seller of varied abilities on official figures, and the time was pretty ordinary. The form is limited by the winner and the fifth.

NOTEBOOK
Noble Edge, stepping up in trip and trying Polytrack for the first time, did enough when getting back to the front, after being briefly headed, to hold on as the line approached, reversing Fibresand form with Bathwick Rox on better terms. He did not attract any bids at the subsequent auction. (op 11-1)
Wee Charlie Castle(IRE) had looked a none-too reliable sort in the past and only got going as the line approached. He is not one to totally trust. (op 7-2)
Bathwick Rox(IRE), blinkered for the first time, probably did not appreciate Southwell's surface last time and ran a lot better. He appeared to have every chance up the rail but never quite threatened to win. (tchd 11-4 and 10-3)
Indian Wizard(IRE), winner of a seller when last seen at Musselburgh in October, held every chance down the middle of the course, after missing the break at the stalls, but did not quite get home. He was claimed by Paul Howling after the race. (op 3-1 after early 7-2)
Master Ben(IRE) ran his best race to date without looking like a winner about to happen. (op 25-1)
Nico's Girl could not reverse form with both Noble Edge and Bathwick Rox on their running at Southwell, despite having every chance to do so. (op 7-1 tchd 9-1)
Mytass Official explanation: jockey said gelding was denied a clear run
Take No Notice(IRE) Official explanation: jockey said filly lost her action

6698 HAVE A LUCKY NEW YEAR FROM BETDIRECT H'CAP 7f 32y(P)
2:05 (2:05) (Class 4) (0-85,81) 3-Y-O+ **£5,787** (£1,721; £860; £429) **Stalls** High

Form | | | | RPR
0014 **1** **Wessex (USA)**[21] 6544 5-9-2 79 ... NCallan 6 94+
(P A Blockley) *chsd ldrs: rdn to ld over 1f out: r.o wl* **7/2**[2]
4103 **2** 4 **Councellor (FR)**[91] 5599 3-8-13 76 ... MickyFenton 4 81
(Stef Liddiard) *chsd ldrs: rdn and edgd lft over 1f out: styd on same pce* **7/1**[3]
0002 **3** ½ **Claret And Amber**[22] 6533 3-9-4 81 ... (b) PaulHanagan 2 85
(R A Fahey) *s.i.s: hld up: hdwy over 2f out: sn rdn: styd on: nt rch ldrs* **11/4**[1]
0063 **4** 3 **Kingsmaite**[9] 6657 4-9-1 81 ... (b) AmirQuinn(3) 10 77
(S R Bowring) *chsd ldr: rdn and ev ch over 1f out: wknd ins fnl f* **8/1**

6033 **5** 2 **Queens Rhapsody**[21] 6544 5-8-12 **75** SamHitchcott 11 66
(A Bailey) *hld up: rdn over 2f out: n.d* **16/1**
0306 **6** 3/4 **Screwdriver**[11] 6629 3-8-10 **73** (b) EddieAhern 5 62
(Miss J R Tooth) *s.i.s: rdn 1/2-way: n.d* **9/1**
0023 **7** 1/2 **Hurricane Coast**[1] 6690 6-8-4 **74** (b) JamesDoyle(7) 7 61
(K McAuliffe) *led over 5f: wknd fnl f* **7/1**[3]
2304 **8** 3/4 **Balakiref**[15] 6590 6-8-12 **75** PhillipMakin 9 61
(M Dods) *dwlt: a in rr* **10/1**
0600 **9** 9 **Whistler**[28] 6489 8-9-1 **78** (p) ChrisCatlin 1 40
(Miss J R Tooth) *prom: lost pl 6f out: n.d after* **25/1**
2005 **10** 3/4 **Following Flow (USA)**[22] 6533 3-8-13 **76** (p) GrahamGibbons 12 36
(R Hollinshead) *chsd ldrs: rdn 1/2-way: wknd over 2f out* **25/1**

1m 28.81s (-1.59) **Going Correction** -0.05s/f (Stan) **10** Ran SP% **117.7**
Speed ratings (Par 105):107,102,101,98,96 95,94,93,83,82
CSF £28.68 CT £75.48 TOTE £4.90: £1.80, £1.90, £1.60; EX 49.50.
Owner Nigel Shields **Bred** Darley Stud Management, L L C **Trained** Lambourn, Berks

FOCUS
A competitive handicap run in a much quicker time than the opening seven-furlong maiden. The winner is value for more than the official margin with the placed horses giving the form a solid look.
Hurricane Coast Official explanation: jockey said gelding went left after leaving the stalls
Balakiref Official explanation: jockey said gelding was never travelling

6699 BETDIRECT.CO.UK MAIDEN STKS (DIV II) 7f 32y(P)
2:35 (2:36) (Class 5) 2-Y-O **£3,746** (£1,114; £557; £278) **Stalls** High

Form RPR
52 **1** **Starship (IRE)**[10] 6641 2-8-9 TonyCulhane 8 71
(W J Haggas) *chsd ldr: rdn and ev ch fr over 1f out: styd on u.p to ld wl ins fnl f* **1/2**[1]
2 **2** shd **Chief Commander (FR)**[10] 6642 2-9-0 JimmyQuinn 11 76
(Jane Chapple-Hyam) *a.p: led over 1f out: edgd lft and hdd wl ins fnl f* **5/2**[2]
502 **3** 6 **Party Belle**[47] 6342 2-8-9 62 EddieAhern 1 55
(C E Brittain) *led: rdn: hung lft and hdd over 1f out: sn wknd* **5/1**[3]
0 **4** 3/4 **Jumanji (IRE)**[15] 6588 2-8-2 StacyRenwick(7) 4 53
(M J Attwater) *chsd ldrs: rdn over 2f out: nt clr run and wknd over 1f out* **33/1**
5 6 **Keelings Donabate** 2-9-0 RobertWinston 3 43
(K R Burke) *s.s: hdwy over 2f out: sn wknd* **12/1**
6 3 1/2 **Skye Boat Song** 2-8-11 DominicFox(3) 6 34
(J Jay) *prom: pushed along 6f out: lost pl 4f out: sn bhd* **40/1**
05 **7** 8 **Under Fire (IRE)**[36] 6424 2-9-0 HayleyTurner 5 13
(A W Carroll) *prom to 1/2-way* **25/1**

1m 30.93s (0.53) **Going Correction** -0.05s/f (Stan) **7** Ran SP% **128.8**
Speed ratings (Par 96):94,93,87,86,79 75,66
CSF £2.60 TOTE £1.50: £1.10, £2.00; EX 3.10.
Owner Mrs Magnier/Scott/Hirschfeld & Piggott **Bred** L K Piggott And A Hirschfeld **Trained** Newmarket, Suffolk

FOCUS
Little strength in depth, and the first two home had by far the best form in the book. The time was slower than the opening division of the race and the form does not look as solid.

NOTEBOOK
Starship(IRE) showed admirable battling qualities up the home straight to get in front just as the line approached. She is very much like her half-sister, Superstar Leo, in that she lacks any size, but has a brave heart. It is not easy to predict which way connections will go with her now, as she is qualified for handicaps, but they may want to try for some black type when those sort of races start appearing again. (new market op 8-11)
Chief Commander(FR) is definitely go going the right way and only lost out in a driving finish. He has plenty of size and should keep finding improvement. (new market op 11-4 tchd 4-1)
Party Belle made good use of her decent draw to take the field along early. However, she could not resist the challenge of the front two, and was firmly put in her place by the end. Official explanation: jockey said filly hung left (new market op 13-2)
Jumanji(IRE) shaped really well just behind the fancied runners, and would pick up an ordinary maiden if the effort can be believed. (new market op 50-1)
Keelings Donabate missed the break badly but did get back into contention coming around the home turn, before finding his earlier exertions taking their toll. He has the ability to go close next time if getting away from the stalls more quickly. (new market op 28-1)

6700 BETDIRECT FREEPHONE 0800 211 222 H'CAP 1m 1f 103y(P)
3:10 (3:11) (Class 2) (0-100,100) 3-Y-O+
£11,446 (£3,427; £1,713; £857; £427; £214) **Stalls** Low

Form RPR
2301 **1** **Boo**[21] 6547 3-7-12 **89** oh4 ow3 (v) AndrewElliott(7) 3 98
(K R Burke) *hld up: hdwy 1/2-way: chsd ldr and hung lft over 1f out: rdn to ld ins fnl f: r.o wl* **9/2**[2]
4013 **2** 2 1/2 **Mizz Tee (IRE)**[35] 6437 3-7-11 **86** oh1 DuranFentiman(5) 1 91
(T D Easterby) *chsd ldrs: rdn over 1f out: nt clr run ins fnl f: swtchd rt: styd on* **5/1**[3]
0213 **3** nk **Hail The Chief**[14] 6601 8-8-7 **89** DaneO'Neill 2 93
(R Hannon) *led: rdn over 1f out: hdd and no ex ins fnl f* **11/4**[1]
110 **4** 1/2 **Gavroche (IRE)**[70] 6025 4-8-12 **94** IanMongan 6 97
(J R Boyle) *s.i.s: hld up: hdwy over 1f out: nt rch ldrs* **13/2**
0053 **5** 1 3/4 **Moayed**[22] 6530 6-9-4 **100** (bt) NCallan 8 100
(N P Littmoden) *hld up: hdwy over 2f out: rdn over 1f out: styd on same pce* **7/1**
3112 **6** 4 **Desert Leader (IRE)**[21] 6547 4-7-11 **86** oh8 LiamJones(7) 5 78
(W M Brisbourne) *chsd ldr over 7f: wknd over 1f out* **7/1**
003 **7** 2 1/2 **Lygeton Lad**[42] 6379 7-8-12 **94** (t) SteveDrowne 4 81
(Miss Gay Kelleway) *chsd ldrs 7f* **12/1**
2040 **8** nk **Shahzan House (IRE)**[147] 4174 6-9-0 **96** MickyFenton 7 83
(Stef Liddiard) *mid-div: lost pl over 3f out: sn bhd* **14/1**

2m 0.55s (-2.07) **Going Correction** -0.05s/f (Stan)
WFA 3 from 4yo+ 2lb **8** Ran SP% **114.2**
Speed ratings (Par 109):107,104,104,104,102 98,96,96
CSF £27.11 CT £72.29 TOTE £5.50: £2.00, £2.00, £1.10; EX 35.10.
Owner Mrs M Gittins **Bred** J Purcell **Trained** Middleham Moor, N Yorks

FOCUS
A very competitive handicap run at a solid pace. The first two home are improving quickly and the proximity of the third makes the form look sound.

NOTEBOOK
Boo, still unbeaten at the track and carrying overweight due to being out of the handicap and his jockey not being able to claim his full amount, forged clear of his rivals when asked to quicken, and won in good style. Such is his progress, connections are now looking at a possible tilt at the Winter Derby. (op 11-2)
Mizz Tee(IRE), running from out of the handicap, gave the impression that she is still improving, and may be able to find a race of this stature during the winter. (tchd 9-2 and 11-2)
Hail The Chief found the concession on weight to a couple of improving three-year-olds too much. He has risen in the weights for his recent upturn in form, and also would have preferred a bit shorter to be at his very best. (op 7-2)
Gavroche(IRE), returning from a break, ran reasonably well but has nothing in hand on the Handicapper at the moment, and is likely to struggle unless he finds some improvement from somewhere. (op 7-1 tchd 11-2)
Moayed travelled nicely during the race, but again found less than expected at the business end of the race. He is on a winning handicap mark - but the top end of it - and might be better suited by slightly shorter. (op 5-1)
Desert Leader(IRE) is now high enough in the weights after his winning spell, and was beaten much further by Boo this time than on their last meeting. (op 15-2 tchd 9-1)

6701 BETDIRECT "SEE YOU IN 2006" H'CAP 1m 5f 194y(P)
3:45 (3:46) (Class 6) (0-60,60) 3-Y-O+ **£2,987** (£882; £441) **Stalls** Low

Form RPR
60-5 **1** **I'll Do It Today**[40] 6405 4-8-11 **50** PaulHanagan 4 58
(J M Jefferson) *s.i.s: hld up: hdwy over 3f out: rdn over 1f out: styd on to ld post* **33/1**
0651 **2** shd **Sovereign Spirit (IRE)**[19] 6563 3-8-12 **58** (t) IanMongan 6 66
(W R Swinburn) *plld hrd and prom: trckd ldr 8f out: led over 3f out: rdn over 1f out: hdd post* **4/1**[2]
3513 **3** nk **Lady Taverner**[11] 6626 4-8-11 **55** NataliaGemelova(5) 1 63
(J E Long) *chsd ldrs: rdn and ev ch ins fnl f: styd on* **7/1**
3063 **4** 2 1/2 **Zaffeu**[19] 6563 4-8-5 **47** RichardThomas(3) 3 51
(N P Littmoden) *s.i.s: hld up: hdwy and hung lft over 1f out: nt rch ldrs* **7/1**
0003 **5** 3/4 **Petite Paramour (IRE)**[22] 6534 4-9-2 **58** AdamKirby(3) 11 61
(Miss Gay Kelleway) *chsd ldr 6f: remained handy: rdn and ev ch over 1f out: no ex ins fnl f* **25/1**
52 **6** 1 3/4 **Ocean King (USA)**[19] 6563 4-9-5 **58** EddieAhern 7 59
(W M Brisbourne) *plld hrd and prom: stdd and lost pl after 2f: hdwy 6f out: rdn over 3f out: styd on same pce appr fnl f* **7/2**[1]
3500 **7** 1/2 **Wembury Point (IRE)**[21] 2309 3-8-9 **55** (b) RobertWinston 2 55
(B G Powell) *hld up: rdn over 1f out: styd on ins fnl f: nvr trbld ldrs* **12/1**
3223 **8** nk **York Cliff**[12] 6620 7-8-13 **55** PatrickMathers(3) 5 54
(W M Brisbourne) *hld up: rdn over 2f out: n.d* **12/1**
2 **9** 1 3/4 **Dance Troupe**[16] 6583 3-8-10 **56** (p) ChrisCatlin 13 53
(J Jay) *hld up: rdn over 3f out: n.d* **8/1**
2433 **10** 3 **Bienheureux**[21] 6548 4-9-5 **58** (t) SteveDrowne 8 51
(Miss Gay Kelleway) *hld up: hdwy 6f out: wknd over 1f out* **5/1**[3]
-006 **11** 26 **Indian Solitaire (IRE)**[22] 6308 6-9-7 **60** (p) PhillipMakin 12 16
(B P J Baugh) *chsd ldrs: rdn 4f out: wknd 3f out* **40/1**
31-5 **12** 5 **Smoothie (IRE)**[21] 6548 7-9-4 **57** FergusSweeney 9 6
(Ian Williams) *sn led: rdn and hdd over 3f out: wknd over 2f out* **18/1**

3m 6.53s (-0.84) **Going Correction** -0.05s/f (Stan)
WFA 3 from 4yo+ 7lb **12** Ran SP% **124.9**
Speed ratings (Par 101):100,99,99,98,97 96,96,96,95,93 78,76
CSF £167.54 CT £1078.77 TOTE £35.20: £10.40, £2.60, £3.20; EX 560.10 Place 6 £6.71, Place 5 £6.25.
Owner Mr & Mrs J M Davenport **Bred** Mrs D W Davenport **Trained** Norton, N Yorks

FOCUS
A very competitive low-grade staying event, run in a moderate time. The form is only ordinary rated through the third and fifth.
Zaffeu Official explanation: jockey said gelding missed the break
Smoothie(IRE) Official explanation: jockey said gelding lost its action
T/Plt: £16.00 to a £1 stake. Pool: £39,997.10. 1,814.75 winning tickets. T/Qpdt: £4.40 to a £1 stake. Pool: £3,121.50. 524.40 winning tickets. CR

The Form Book

TURF AND ALL-WEATHER
FLAT RACING 2006

Complete record of Turf and All-Weather Racing from
1st January to 31st December 2006

SOUTHWELL (L-H)

Sunday, January 1

OFFICIAL GOING: Standard to fast

Wind: Fresh, behind Weather: Cloudy with sunny spells

1 PLAY NOW AT BETDIRECTPOKER.COM H'CAP (DIV I) 6f (F)

12:00 (12:02) (Class 5) (0-70,73) 4-Y-0+ **£2,914** (£867; £433; £216) **Stalls** Low

Form RPR

200- **1** **Alpaga Le Jomage (IRE)**[12] 6636 4-8-8 **60**.................. DeanMcKeown 13 69
(M J Polglase) *led: hdd over 4f out: chsd ldr: rdn over 1f out: r.o to ld towards fin* **40/1**

224- **2** ¾ **Scuba (IRE)**[12] 6625 4-8-5 **57**.. PaulHanagan 11 64
(H Morrison) *mid-div: sn drvn along: hdwy over 2f out: hung lft ins fnl f: hung rt towards fin: r.o* **4/1**[2]

030- **3** *hd* **Savile's Delight (IRE)**[22] 6546 7-8-10 **62**.........................(b) TomEaves 6 68
(R Brotherton) *led over 4f out: rdn and hung lft over 1f out: hdd towards fin* **14/1**

225- **4** 2 ½ **Gone'N'Dunnett (IRE)**[15] 6603 7-8-9 **68**.............(v) KirstyMilczarek(7) 14 67
(Mrs C A Dunnett) *chsd ldrs: rdn over 2f out: styd on same pce fnl f* **16/1**

135- **5** ¾ **Blue Knight (IRE)**[79] 5869 7-8-11 **63**........................... AdrianTNicholls 7 59
(D Nicholls) *hld up: hdwy u.p 2f out: styd on* **16/1**

040- **6** 1 ½ **Piccolo Prince**[33] 6464 5-8-5 **57**....................................(p) JimmyQuinn 4 49
(E J Alston) *prom: rdn 1/2-way: wknd fnl f* **9/1**

050- **7** *shd* **Canadian Danehill (IRE)**[113] 5119 4-8-8 **60**...................(p) ChrisCatlin 5 52
(R M H Cowell) *chsd ldrs: rdn over 2f out: wknd fnl f* **33/1**

602- **8** *nk* **Certain Justice (USA)**[12] 6632 8-9-7 **73**......................... MickyFenton 2 64
(Stef Liddiard) *sn outpcd and bhd: r.o ins fnl f: nvr nrr* **10/3**[1]

645- **9** *1* **Sahara Silk (IRE)**[128] 4738 5-8-7 **62**......................(v) PatrickMathers(3) 8 50
(D Shaw) *chsd ldrs: rdn over 2f out: wknd over 1f out* **25/1**

163- **10** *2* **Miskina**[12] 6630 5-8-0 **59**.. LiamJones(7) 12 41
(W M Brisbourne) *hld up: rdn over 2f out: n.d* **16/1**

160- **11** *1* **Dash Of Lime**[126] 4784 4-8-8 **63**.................................... RobertMiles(3) 9 42
(J Akehurst) *prom: rdn 1/2-way: sn wknd* **14/1**

050- **12** ¾ **Count Cougar (USA)**[12] 6632 6-8-6 **58**............................. DaleGibson 1 34
(S P Griffiths) *mid-div: wknd 1/2-way* **25/1**

223/ **13** 2 ½ **Shannon Arms (USA)**[177] 3325 5-9-3 **69**............................... NCallan 3 38
(K A Ryan) *s.s: effrt and nt clr run over 3f out: sn wknd* **8/1**[3]

000- **14** ½ **Xpres Digital**[96] 5532 5-8-12 **64**..................................... PhillipMakin 10 31
(S R Bowring) *s.s: hdwy 4f out: sn rdn: wknd 1/2-way* **8/1**[3]

1m 15.08s (-1.82) **Going Correction** -0.325s/f (Stan) **14** Ran SP% **119.4**
Speed ratings (Par 103):99,98,97,94,93 91,91,90,89,86 85,84,81,80
CSF £188.47 CT £2475.03 TOTE £53.80: £11.60, £1.60, £8.10; EX 563.10.
Owner Paul J Dixon,J Kennerley,F Cody **Bred** Patrick M Ryan **Trained** Babworth, Notts

FOCUS
A modest handicap in which nothing was able to get into the race from off the pace, but the form looks sound enough rated through the runner-up.
Certain Justice(USA) Official explanation: jockey said gelding was outpaced in early stages
Shannon Arms(USA) Official explanation: jockey said gelding was slowly away from stalls

2 BETDIRECT.CO.UK APPRENTICE MEDIAN AUCTION MAIDEN STKS 1m 3f (F)

12:30 (12:30) (Class 6) 4-6-Y-0 **£2,388** (£705; £352) **Stalls** Low

Form RPR

063- **1** **Sonic Anthem (USA)**[112] 5149 4-8-13 52................. SilvestreDeSousa 9 73
(D Nicholls) *chsd ldrs: led over 4f out: pushed clr fr over 2f out* **4/1**[3]

050- **2** *16* **Sand Repeal (IRE)**[92] 5610 4-8-8 66......................... DonnaCaldwell(5) 3 47
(Miss J Feilden) *hld up in tch: racd keenly: rdn to go remote 2nd 2f out: no ch w wnr* **11/10**[1]

\- **3** *10* **City Of Manchester (IRE)**[35] 4-8-6 .... VictoriaBehan(7) 7 31
(D Nicholls) *led 2f: chsd ldr tl led over 7f out: hdd over 4f out: wknd over 2f out* **10/1**

000- **4** *10* **High Window (IRE)**[20] 6556 6-9-2 35............................ PaulMulrennan 6 15
(G P Kelly) *hld up: a bhd* **50/1**

364- **5** *7* **Finnegans Rainbow**[20] 6555 4-8-8 40........... StephanieHollinshead(5) 1 4
(M C Chapman) *chsd ldr tl led 9f out: hdd over 7f out: rdn and wknd over 3f out* **3/1**[2]

0- **6** *3* **Naemi (GER)**[13] 6623 4-8-1 .... MarkCoumbe(7) 5 —
(S L Keightley) *s.i.s: hld up: plld hrd: rdn and wknd over 3f out* **20/1**

500- **7** *11* **Eidsfoss (IRE)**[27] 6509 4-8-13 40.. AdamKirby 4 —
(T T Clement) *prom over 7f* **20/1**

8 *16* **Pearl Oyster**[418] 4-8-13 .... EdwardCreighton 8 —
(D J Wintle) *s.i.s: hld up: bhd fnl 7f* **14/1**

2m 24.21s (-4.69) **Going Correction** -0.325s/f (Stan)
WFA 4 from 6yo 3lb **8** Ran SP% **119.9**
Speed ratings: 104,92,85,77,72 70,62,50
CSF £9.10 TOTE £4.20: £1.20, £1.10, £3.20; EX 7.50.
Owner Middleham Park Racing Xvii **Bred** The Thoroughbred Corporation **Trained** Sessay, N Yorks
■ The first winner in Britain for Brazilian Silvestre De Sousa.

FOCUS
A very moderate maiden in which they came home strung out like three-mile chasers, but the time was reasonable and the winner is value for even further.
Naemi(GER) Official explanation: jockey said filly lost its action
Pearl Oyster Official explanation: jockey said gelding had breathing problem and never travelled

3 NO 5P RULE 4S AT BET DIRECT (S) STKS 1m (F)

12:55 (12:56) (Class 6) 4-Y-0+ **£2,388** (£705; £352) **Stalls** Low

Form RPR

302- **1** **Lady Suesanne (IRE)**[10] 6658 4-8-7 49..............(b) RobbieFitzpatrick 13 54
(M J Attwater) *hld up in tch: led over 1f out: rdn clr* **3/1**[1]

600- **2** *6* **Castanza**[13] 6620 4-8-7 47.. JimmyQuinn 12 42
(M Wellings) *prom: lost pl over 4f out: hdwy over 3f out: rdn to chse wnr and edgd lft 1f out: styd on same pce* **16/1**

035- **3** ½ **Semper Paratus (USA)**[20] 6556 7-8-12 40...........................(v) NCallan 3 46
(V Smith) *sn pushed along in rr: hdwy u.p over 2f out: styd on same pce fnl f* **5/1**[3]

000- **4** 1 ½ **King Nicholas (USA)**[16] 6594 7-8-12 59.....................(tp) TonyCulhane 9 43
(J Parkes) *prom: rdn over 2f out: wknd over 1f out* **5/1**[3]

000- **5** *nk* **Flying Spud**[27] 6509 5-8-12 30...................................... DeanMcKeown 8 42
(A J Chamberlain) *sn led: rdn and hdd over 1f out: sn wknd* **28/1**

665- **6** *2* **Dane's Rock (IRE)**[27] 6508 4-8-12 46.........................(p) MickyFenton 11 38
(M S Saunders) *chsd ldrs: rdn 1/2-way: wknd over 1f out* **4/1**[2]

544- **7** *nk* **Inchdura**[14] 6609 8-8-12 40...(p) KimTinkler 2 38
(N Tinkler) *sn outpcd: styd on ins fnl f: nvr nrr* **11/1**

600- **8** 1 ½ **Pharoah's Gold (IRE)**[2] 6691 8-8-12 45...........................(v) AlanDaly 10 35
(D Burchell) *sn chsng ldr: ev ch fr 3f out tl rdn and wknd over 1f out* **10/1**

300- **9** *9* **Headland (USA)**[111] 5181 8-8-12 53..............................(be) PhillipMakin 5 17
(D W Chapman) *dwlt: hdwy over 3f out: rdn and wknd over 1f out* **11/1**

000- **10** *3* **Lady Predominant**[23] 5890 5-8-7 30.............................(b[1]) HayleyTurner 4 6
(Robert Gray) *s.s: rdn over 4f out: a bhd* **40/1**

600- **11** *7* **Champagne Rossini (IRE)**[17] 6584 4-8-9 45............... AdamKirby(3) 6 —
(M C Chapman) *dwlt: sn chsng ldrs: lost pl over 4f out: sn bhd* **50/1**

550- **12** *5* **Perianth (IRE)**[4] 6675 4-8-12 50...(b) TomEaves 7 —
(J G M O'Shea) *sn pushed along and prom: wknd 3f out* **22/1**

1m 42.82s (-1.78) **Going Correction** -0.325s/f (Stan) **12** Ran SP% **122.2**
Speed ratings (Par 101):95,89,88,87,86 84,84,82,73,70 63,58
CSF £54.28 TOTE £3.50: £1.70, £7.40, £1.60; EX 96.30.The winner was bought in for 9,200gns.
Owner Phones Direct Partnership **Bred** Larry Ryan **Trained** Wysall, Notts

FOCUS
A poor seller with the form anchored by the proximity of the fifth, but a decisive winner.
Dane's Rock(IRE) Official explanation: jockey said gelding hung to right
Lady Predominant Official explanation: jockey said mare was reluctant to jump out of stalls, rendering her slowly away

4 PLAY NOW AT BETDIRECTPOKER.COM H'CAP (DIV II) 6f (F)

1:30 (1:32) (Class 5) (0-70,70) 4-Y-0+ **£2,914** (£867; £433; £216) **Stalls** Low

Form RPR

211- **1** **Owed**[10] 6658 4-8-11 **63**..(t) HayleyTurner 3 76
(Robert Gray) *mde virtually all: rdn and edgd lft over 1f out: r.o wl* **9/2**[1]

005- **2** *3* **Ruman (IRE)**[33] 6464 4-8-4 **56**...................................... ChrisCatlin 9 60
(M J Attwater) *hld up: hdwy over 1f out: nt rch wnr* **9/1**

305- **3** ¾ **Lincolneurocruiser**[71] 6022 4-8-11 **70**............... RussellKennemore(7) 7 72
(Mrs N Macauley) *outpcd: hdwy over 1f out: nrst fin* **10/1**

631- **4** *nk* **Kennington**[15] 6597 6-9-3 **69**.......................................(b) TonyCulhane 12 70
(Mrs C A Dunnett) *chsd ldrs: rdn over 1f out: styd on same pce* **5/1**[2]

430- **5** ¾ **Cool Sands (IRE)**[12] 6638 4-8-8 **63**.....................(v) PatrickMathers(3) 13 62
(D Shaw) *hld up: hdwy over 2f out: rdn and hung lft over 1f out: nt trble ldrs* **10/1**

340- **6** ¾ **Lady Algarhoud (FR)**[12] 6631 4-8-8 **60**.......................... MickyFenton 4 56
(D K Ivory) *chsd ldrs: rdn over 2f out: wknd fnl f* **11/1**

040- **7** ¾ **Barzak (IRE)**[22] 6542 6-7-13 **58**..................................(b) LiamJones(7) 11 52
(S R Bowring) *chsd ldrs over 4f* **20/1**

542- **8** *1* **Cerebus**[26] 6513 4-8-9 **64**... AdamKirby(3) 1 55
(M J Polglase) *w wnr tl rdn over 2f out: wknd fnl f* **7/1**

000- **9** *2* **Attorney**[22] 6546 8-8-2 **61**... JosephWalsh(7) 6 46
(N E Berry) *hld up: n.d* **18/1**

340- **10** *1* **Silver Visage (IRE)**[10] 6654 4-8-5 **57**................................ BrianReilly 8 39
(Miss J Feilden) *prom 4f* **6/1**[3]

503- **11** 1 ¼ **Second Reef**[12] 6632 4-8-10 **62**.. PaulQuinn 14 40
(E J Alston) *hld up: hdwy 1/2-way: rdn and wknd 2f out* **17/2**

526/ **12** *shd* **Winning Pleasure (IRE)**[719] 515 8-8-10 **65**.......(b) JasonEdmunds(3) 2 43
(J Balding) *hld up in tch: racd keenly: wknd over 2f out* **25/1**

100- **13** *shd* **Sand Iron (IRE)**[13] 6616 4-8-7 **59**.............................. RobbieFitzpatrick 5 37
(S L Keightley) *s.i.s: hld up: wknd over 2f out* **33/1**

000- **14** *1* **Four Amigos (USA)**[30] 6480 5-8-5 **60**............(v[1]) SilvestreDeSousa(3) 10 35
(D Nicholls) *prom: hmpd and lost pl 5f out: wknd 1/2-way* **33/1**

1m 14.76s (-2.14) **Going Correction** -0.325s/f (Stan) **14** Ran SP% **128.4**
Speed ratings (Par 103):101,97,96,95,94 93,92,91,88,87 85,85,85,84
CSF £46.31 CT £410.28 TOTE £4.50: £1.90, £3.60, £6.40; EX 78.90.
Owner Naughty Diesel Ltd **Bred** Helshaw Grange Stud, N Kent And H Phillips **Trained** Malton, N Yorks

FOCUS
A modest contest but a decisive winner who was completing a hat-trick and the form behind appears sound.
Kennington Official explanation: jockey said gelding lost hind plate

5 PLAY £1/4M SPOT THE BALL ON 0800 500 000 H'CAP 2m (F)

2:05 (2:05) (Class 5) (0-75,71) 4-Y-0+ **£3,238** (£963; £481; £240) **Stalls** Low

Form RPR

561- **1** **Spitting Image (IRE)**[12] 6637 6-9-7 **66**......................... RobertWinston 4 80+
(M Johnston) *a.p: led on bit over 3f out: clr over 2f out: styd on strly* **15/8**[1]

143- **2** *13* **Peak Park (USA)**[26] 6519 6-9-12 **71**................................. ChrisCatlin 3 68
(P L Gilligan) *hld up: hdwy 8f out: rdn over 4f out: outpcd over 2f out: wnt mod 2nd 1f out* **9/4**[2]

162- **3** ¾ **Tedstale (USA)**[12] 6637 8-9-12 **71**..(b) NCallan 7 67
(K A Ryan) *hld up: hdwy 4f out: rdn over 2f out: sn outpcd* **7/2**[3]

026- **4** 1 ½ **Romil Star (GER)**[12] 6633 9-8-13 **65**.....................(v) PatrickDonaghy(7) 6 59
(K R Burke) *led: hdd over 14f out: chsd ldr: led over 4f out: hdd over 3f out: sn outpcd* **14/1**

360- **5** *18* **Victory Quest (IRE)**[10] 6655 6-9-9 **68**...........................(v) TonyCulhane 1 41
(Mrs S Lamyman) *chsd ldrs: ev ch over 3f out: wknd over 2f out* **16/1**

030- **6** *nk* **Stolen Song**[12] 6633 6-8-5 **55**.......................................(e) MarcHalford(5) 2 27
(J Ryan) *chsd ldrs over 12f* **14/1**

006- **7** *9* **Barking Mad (USA)**[5] 6669 8-9-3 **62**................................ MickyFenton 5 23
(C R Dore) *s.s: rcvrd to ld over 14f out: hdd over 4f out: sn wknd* **18/1**

3m 39.69s (-4.85) **Going Correction** -0.325s/f (Stan) **7** Ran SP% **112.3**
Speed ratings (Par 103):99,92,92,91,82 82,77
CSF £6.06 TOTE £2.20: £1.80, £2.10; EX 9.30.
Owner J Shack **Bred** Denis McDonnell **Trained** Middleham Moor, N Yorks

FOCUS
A modest handicap and, thanks to only an ordinary early pace, not the test of stamina it might have been but it still proved too much for several of these. The winner was very impressive.

6 HAPPY NEW YEAR FROM BET DIRECT H'CAP 5f (F)

2:40 (2:41) (Class 2) (0-100,94) 4-Y-0+ **£12,954** (£3,854; £1,926; £962) **Stalls** High

Form RPR

121- **1** **Fyodor (IRE)**[26] 6518 5-9-2 **89**.. TonyCulhane 2 103+
(W J Haggas) *chsd ldrs: led over 1f out: pushed out* **8/11**[1]

620- **2** ¾ **Yomalo (IRE)**[30] 6481 6-9-7 **94**... ChrisCatlin 7 99+
(Rae Guest) *outpcd: r.o u.p ins fnl f: nt rch wnr* **9/1**

410- **3** *nk* **Trinculo (IRE)**[99] 5453 9-8-10 **83**................................ AdrianTNicholls 3 87
(D Nicholls) *chsd ldr: rdn 1/2-way: styd on* **12/1**

000- **4** 1 ¼ **Dancing Mystery**[26] 6518 12-9-6 **93**.......................(b) StephenCarson 1 93
(E A Wheeler) *chsd ldrs: rdn over 1f out: no ex ins fnl f* **18/1**

444- **5** 1 ¼ **Pawan (IRE)**[10] 6657 6-8-3 **83** oh2 ow3............................ AnnStokell(7) 10 78
(Miss A Stokell) *sn outpcd: hdwy 1/2-way: rdn and hung lft over 1f out: nt rch ldrs* **18/1**

000- **6** ¾ **Magic Glade**[10] 6657 7-8-7 **80** oh1...................................(b[1]) TomEaves 9 73
(R Brotherton) *led over 3f: wknd ins fnl f* **20/1**

202- **7** 5 **Rydal (USA)**^{26} [6518] 5-9-0 **87** .... JimmyQuinn 5 63
(E J Alston) *dwlt: hdwy over 3f out: wknd over 1f out* **15/2**^{3}
056- **8** 3 **Tartatartufata**^{12} [6636] 4-8-4 **80** oh3.......... (v) PatrickMathers$^{(3)}$ 6 46
(D Shaw) *chsd ldrs 3f* **25/1**
002- **9** 2½ **Quiet Times (IRE)**^{10} [6657] 7-9-0 **87** .... (b) NCallan 8 44
(K A Ryan) *s.i.s: outpcd* **7/1**^{2}
/00- **10** 4 **Newsround**^{16} [6590] 4-8-4 **80** .... SilvestreDeSousa$^{(3)}$ 4 24
(D W Chapman) *outpcd* **66/1**

57.35 secs (-2.95) **Going Correction** -0.35s/f (Stan) course record **10** Ran SP% **120.5**
Speed ratings (Par 109):109,107,107,105,103 102,94,89,85,78
CSF £8.42 CT £51.98 TOTE £1.60: £1.10, £3.30, £4.30; EX 11.00.
Owner The Fyodor Partnership **Bred** E J Banks And D I Scott **Trained** Newmarket, Suffolk

FOCUS
A very decent race but a comfortable winner who broke the track record in the process. The runner-up sets the standard.

NOTEBOOK
Fyodor(IRE) ◆ has really progressed since returning from nearly 11 months off in the autumn, and took his score to four wins and two seconds in six runs with an emphatic success from some battle-hardened sprinters. The impressive thing was how comfortably he was travelling at halfway while some fast horses were flat out and, already 25lb high than for his return to action, he will be rated in the mid-90s after this but looks capable of further success. (op Evens)
Yomalo(IRE) ran her usual race, being outpaced early before keeping on strongly in the closing stages. A six-furlong performer on turf, she has run two fine races over this trip here this winter and looks capable of winning a similar race if she can avoid the winner. (op 8-1)
Trinculo(IRE) ◆, returning from a three-month break after having a good spell on turf in the summer, is now rated 5lb lower on sand as a result. He looks reasonably treated and can win a similar contest, possibly on Polytrack, with this under his belt. (op 14-1)
Dancing Mystery. last year's winner of this event, was 8lb better of with today's winner compared with their meeting here a month ago and closed the gap. There is life in the old boy yet. (op 16-1)
Pawan(IRE) keeps running well and has crept up the handicap without getting his head in front. He is capable of winning races in slightly lesser company, and may be helped by having a top jockey aboard. (op 20-1)
Magic Glade goes well on this track but probably went too fast for his own good, as he got some speedy rivals off the bridle in the early stages, and could not sustain the effort.
Rydal(USA) Official explanation: jockey said gelding finished distressed
Tartatartufata Official explanation: jockey said filly was outpaced and changed her legs

7 BET DIRECT FREEPHONE 0800 211 222 H'CAP 1m (F)
3:15 (3:15) (Class 2) (0-100,102) 4-Y-0+ **£12,954** (£3,854; £1,926; £962) **Stalls** Low

Form RPR
411/ **1** **Gentleman's Deal (IRE)**^{440} [6279] 5-8-7 **86** oh6.......... DaleGibson 6 95+
(M W Easterby) *hld up: hdwy over 2f out: led over 2f out: r.o wl* **7/1**^{3}
514- **2** 3 **Waterside (IRE)**^{12} [6629] 7-8-7 **86** oh4.......... HayleyTurner 2 89
(G L Moore) *dwlt: plld hrd: led 7f out: hdd over 4f out: led over 2f out: rdn and hdd over 1f out: styd on same pce* **4/1**^{2}
535- **3** 4 **Moayed**^{1} [6700] 7-9-7 **100** .... (bt) ChrisCatlin 4 95
(N P Littmoden) *hld up: hdwy 1/2-way: rdn over 1f out: wknd fnl f* **4/1**^{2}
510- **4** 6 **Cardinal Venture (IRE)**^{51} [6314] 8-8-13 **92** .... NCallan 3 75
(K A Ryan) *s.s: sn chsng ldrs: led over 4f out: rdn and hdd over 2f out: wknd over 1f out* **7/4**^{1}
000- **5** shd **Te Quiero**^{11} [6645] 8-8-7 **86** oh7.......... (bt) JimmyQuinn 1 69
(Miss Gay Kelleway) *led 1f: racd keenly: remained handy tl rdn and wknd over 1f out* **10/1**
540- **6** 1½ **Takes Tutu (USA)**^{2} [6690] 7-8-0 **86** oh15.......... AndrewElliott$^{(7)}$ 5 66
(K R Burke) *chsd ldrs: rdn over 3f out: hung rt over 2f out: sn wknd* **16/1**
660- **7** 6 **One More Round (USA)**^{23} [6530] 8-9-9 **102** .... (p) MickyFenton 7 70
(N P Littmoden) *hld up in tch: hung rt 3f out: sn rdn and wknd* **12/1**

1m 40.7s (-3.90) **Going Correction** -0.325s/f (Stan) **7** Ran SP% **111.5**
Speed ratings (Par 109):106,103,99,93,92 91,85
CSF £33.12 TOTE £6.50: £2.50, £2.10; EX 28.20.
Owner Stephen J Curtis **Bred** C H Wacker Iii **Trained** Sheriff Hutton, N Yorks

FOCUS
A decent prize, but a race spoiled by a pedestrian early pace and not the most solid form.

NOTEBOOK
Gentleman's Deal(IRE), previously trained by Ed Dunlop and not seen out for 15 months, was also 6lb out of the handicap. Held up early in a slowly-run race, he found a smart turn of foot in the home straight to score and even though the form may not be totally reliable given the way the race was run, he obviously has retained plenty of ability. (tchd 6-1)
Waterside(IRE), 4lb wrong, is often a front-runner and found himself in front here, but it looked as though his rider did not want him to be there as he was pulling her arms out. He could never get any cover though, and did well to keep on for second though he had no answer to the winner's turn of foot. This was his first try on Fibresand and perhaps being allowed to stride on over a shorter trip here could produce dividends, otherwise he will be reliant on getting a lead. (op 6-1 tchd 7-2)
Moayed was given a patient ride and was brought to hold every chance halfway up the home straight, but this testing mile seemed to find him out even in a race run at a crawl early. (tchd 7-2)
Cardinal Venture(IRE) is an effective performer from the front so his race was effectively over when he completely missed the break. He managed to get to the front at halfway, but the effort to do so eventually told. He is much better than this. (op 15-8 tchd 2-1)
Te Quiero, back on his favoured surface, was 7lb out of the handicap. He broke well, perhaps too well, and found himself in front in the very early stages and was then nailed against the slower inside rail. He could never quite get away from the inside after that and though he still had a chance of sorts turning in, it was not long before he was beaten. He is worth one more chance to show that the spark still remains. (op 8-1)
Takes Tutu(USA), already faced a huge task from 15lb out of the handicap even before he made things worse by hanging right over to the stands' rail after turning in. Official explanation: jockey said gelding hung to right (tchd 18-1)
One More Round(USA) did not improve for the switch to Fibresand and hung badly to his right after turning for home. He has not won for three and a half years and will remain hard to place. Official explanation: jockey said gelding hung to right (op 7-1)

8 DAILY OFFERS FROM BETDIRECT H'CAP 1m (F)
3:45 (3:46) (Class 6) (0-60,60) 4-Y-0+ **£2,388** (£705; £352) **Stalls** Low

Form RPR
033- **1** **Blue Empire (IRE)**^{5} [6667] 5-8-10 **52** .... RobertWinston 11 71+
(C R Dore) *chsd ldr: led over 5f out: clr over 2f out: eased ins fnl f* **9/2**^{1}
431- **2** 10 **Quiet Reading (USA)**^{10} [6660] 9-8-11 **53** .... (v) HayleyTurner 2 49
(M R Bosley) *hld up in tch: racd keenly: rdn to chse wnr over 1f out: no imp* **9/2**^{1}
660- **3** nk **Wrenlane**^{17} [6586] 5-9-1 **57** .... TonyHamilton 7 52
(R A Fahey) *prom: chsd wnr 1/2-way: outpcd fnl 2f* **25/1**
200- **4** 1 **Ming Vase**^{10} [6660] 4-8-10 **52** .... LeeEnstone 12 45
(P T Midgley) *chsd ldrs: rdn over 2f out: sn outpcd* **33/1**
000- **5** hd **Mister Benji**^{12} [6638] 7-9-0 **56** .... DeanMcKeown 9 49
(B P J Baugh) *hld up: effrt over 2f out: nvr trbld ldrs* **16/1**
111- **6** 1 **Preskani**^{5} [6667] 4-9-4 **60** 6ex.......... (p) AlanDaly 8 51
(Mrs N Macauley) *hld up: swtchd rt and styd on ins fnl f: nvr nrr* **9/2**^{1}
000- **7** 2½ **Chairman Rick (IRE)**^{110} [5207] 4-8-7 **52** .... SilvestreDeSousa$^{(3)}$ 13 38
(D Nicholls) *s.i.s: hld up: hdwy over 3f out: wknd over 2f out* **33/1**
252- **8** ½ **Pending (IRE)**^{17} [6586] 5-9-2 **58** .... (p) PaulHanagan 1 43
(R A Fahey) *started slowly: hdwy over 3f out: rdn and wknd 2f out* **11/2**^{2}
130- **9** ½ **Glendale**^{20} [6567] 5-8-10 **52** .... JimmyQuinn 3 36
(D K Ivory) *hld up: plld hrd: rdn over 2f out: n.d* **10/1**
005- **10** ¾ **Kirin**^{20} [6565] 4-8-11 **60** .... (t) JosephWalsh$^{(7)}$ 5 43
(D E Cantillon) *sn outpcd* **8/1**^{3}
000- **11** nk **Crusoe (IRE)**^{5} [6674] 9-8-10 **52** .... (b) BrianReilly 6 34
(A Sadik) *led: hdd over 4f out: rdn and wknd 3f out* **40/1**
001- **12** 6 **Gem Bien (USA)**^{20} [6560] 8-9-2 **58** .... (b) TonyCulhane 10 28
(D W Chapman) *hld up: wknd 3f out* **11/1**
340- **13** 1¾ **Movie King (IRE)**^{23} [6534] 7-9-2 **58** .... (t) NCallan 14 24
(S R Bowring) *prom: rdn over 4f out: sn lost pl: eased fnl 2f* **11/1**
0- **14** dist **Flaming Shot (IRE)**^{13} [6619] 4-8-13 **55** .... (v^{1}) RobbieFitzpatrick 4 —
(Jennie Candlish) *plld hrd and prom: wknd 1/2-way* **40/1**

1m 41.03s (-3.57) **Going Correction** -0.325s/f (Stan) **14** Ran SP% **127.3**
Speed ratings (Par 101):104,94,93,92,92 91,89,88,88,87 86,80,79,—
CSF £24.35 CT £486.20 TOTE £5.20: £1.80, £1.70, £14.70; EX 25.50 Place 6 £34.47, Place 5 £7.00.
Owner Mrs Jennifer Marsh **Bred** Yeomanstown Stud **Trained** West Pinchbeck, Lincs

FOCUS
A competitive if low-grade handicap on paper, but the winner made a complete mockery of it in a reasoanble time and is rated to his best in the last year.
Kirin Official explanation: jockey said colt would not face kick-back
Movie King(IRE) Official explanation: jockey said gelding had a breathing problem
T/Plt: £67.80 to a £1 stake. Pool: £31,021.90. 333.70 winning tickets. T/Qpdt: £6.90 to a £1 stake. Pool: £2,455.90. 260.90 winning tickets. CR

1SOUTHWELL (L-H)
Monday, January 2

OFFICIAL GOING: Standard
Wind: Virtually nil

9 BETDIRECT IN-RUNNING SKYTEXT P293 CLAIMING STKS 6f (F)
12:30 (12:30) (Class 6) 4-Y-0+ **£2,388** (£705; £352) **Stalls** Low

Form RPR
004- **1** **Soba Jones**^{6} [6668] 9-8-6 58.......... JasonEdmunds$^{(3)}$ 4 62
(J Balding) *cl up: led 2f out: rdn over 1f out: drvn ins last and kpt on* **12/1**
633- **2** ½ **Shadow Jumper (IRE)**^{17} [6589] 5-8-7 55.......... (v) RobbieFitzpatrick 5 58
(M J Attwater) *cl up: effrt over 2f out: sn rdn: styd on u.p ins last* **3/1**^{1}
000- **3** 3 **Ariesanne (IRE)**^{19} [6578] 5-8-0 35 ow2.......... PaulHanagan 8 42
(A C Whillans) *sn led: rdn along and hdd 2f out: kpt on same pce u.p appr last* **100/1**
306/ **4** ¾ **Miracle Ridge (IRE)**^{68} [6113] 11-8-3 45.......... (b) ChrisCatlin 2 43
(Adrian McGuinness, Ire) *in tch: rdn and hdwy over 2f out: sn drvn and kpt on same pce appr last* **25/1**
530- **5** 1¾ **St Ivian**^{3} [6693] 6-8-4 52.......... (v) DuranFentiman$^{(5)}$ 10 44
(Mrs N Macauley) *chsd ldrs wd: st: rdn 2f out and sn no imp* **6/1**
000- **6** ½ **Penwell Hill (USA)**^{14} [6622] 7-8-10 72.......... StacyRenwick$^{(7)}$ 11 50
(M J Attwater) *stdd s and bhd tl styd on fnl 2f: nrst fin* **14/1**
000- **7** 2 **Colonel Cotton (IRE)**^{108} [5262] 7-9-4 82.......... SilvestreDeSousa$^{(3)}$ 3 48
(D Nicholls) *towards rr: pushed along 1/2-way: no imp* **11/1**
035- **8** nk **Roman Empire**^{11} [6660] 6-9-3 56.......... (b) NCallan 7 43
(K A Ryan) *chsd ldrs: wd st: rdn 2f out and sn btn* **11/2**^{3}
000- **9** 4 **Native Title**^{128} [4755] 8-9-7 82.......... AdrianTNicholls 6 35
(D Nicholls) *dwlt: hdwy and in tch 1/2-way: wd st: rdn 2f out and sn btn* **10/3**^{2}
332- **10** 7 **Ben Casey**^{41} [6411] 4-8-7 54.......... PaulEddery 1 18
(B Smart) *a rr* **15/2**

1m 17.07s (0.17) **Going Correction** 0.0s/f (Stan) **10** Ran SP% **117.0**
Speed ratings (Par 101):98,97,93,92,90 89,86,86,80,79
CSF £48.22 TOTE £37.40: £4.10, £1.50, £24.50; EX 81.40.
Owner R L Crowe **Bred** Mrs M J Hills **Trained** Scrooby, Notts

FOCUS
An ordinary claimer dominated by those that raced close to the pace and the third sets the level.

10 BETDIRECT FOOTBALL SKYTEXT P372 H'CAP 6f (F)
1:00 (1:01) (Class 6) (0-65,65) 3-Y-0 **£2,388** (£705; £352) **Stalls** Low

Form RPR
434- **1** **Mister Incredible**^{15} [6605] 3-8-8 **55** .... (p) EddieAhern 5 64
(C A Dwyer) *cl up: effrt 2f out: rdn to ld over 1f out: kpt on ins last* **7/1**^{2}
3- **2** 1½ **Radiator Rooney (IRE)**^{21} [6561] 3-9-3 **64** .... (b) LPKeniry 12 69
(Patrick Morris, Ire) *sn led: rdn along 2f out: hdd over 1f out: drvn and kpt on ins last* **8/1**^{3}
421- **3** 4 **Babeth (IRE)**^{63} [6197] 3-9-4 **65** .... MartinDwyer 4 58
(A M Balding) *chsd ldng pair: rdn 2f out and sn hung bdly rt: drvn over 1f out and kpt on same pce* **2/1**^{1}
002- **4** 1 **Buzzin'Boyzee (IRE)**^{21} [6562] 3-8-12 **59** .... RobertWinston 9 49+
(P D Evans) *towards rr: hdwy over 2f out: styng on whn hmpd over 1f out: sn rdn and kpt on wl fnl f: nrst fin* **9/1**
60- **5** 1¼ **Money Mate (IRE)**^{135} [4579] 3-8-11 **65** .... MarkCoumbe$^{(7)}$ 3 51
(C J Teague) *chsd ldrs: rdn and edgd rt wl over 1f out: sn one pce* **12/1**
060- **6** 1 **Royal Moon (USA)**^{136} [4528] 3-8-13 **60** .... PhillipMakin 2 43
(T D Barron) *towards rr: hdwy on inner 2f out: sn rdn and kpt on ins last: nrst fin* **8/1**^{3}
643- **7** nk **Smart Ass (IRE)**^{146} [4236] 3-7-11 **51** .... JosephWalsh$^{(7)}$ 11 33
(J S Moore) *s.i.s and bhd: gd hdwy wl over 1f out: styd on ins last: nrst fin* **20/1**
006- **8** 4 **Jazz At The Sands (USA)**^{18} [6581] 3-8-4 **51** oh1.......... (v) PaulHanagan 8 27+
(D Shaw) *in tch: rdn along 2f out: wkng whn hmpd over 1f out* **12/1**
440- **9** 3 **Garstang**^{144} [4295] 3-8-9 **56** .... RobbieFitzpatrick 10 17
(Peter Grayson) *chsd ldrs: rdn along 2f out: hmpd over 1f out and sn wknd* **18/1**
042- **10** hd **Lady Palma Nova**^{161} [3796] 3-8-12 **59** .... DaleGibson 13 19
(M W Easterby) *s.i.s: a rr* **14/1**
006- **11** 4 **Dylan (IRE)**^{13} [6634] 3-8-4 **51** oh4.......... KimTinkler 1 —
(N Tinkler) *a rr* **28/1**
236- **12** 8 **Quote Unquote**^{20} [6569] 3-8-13 **60** .... TonyCulhane 6 —
(J Parkes) *bhd fr 1/2-way* **12/1**
000- **13** 2 **Dispol Valentine**^{15} [6605] 3-7-13 **51** oh3.......... DuranFentiman$^{(5)}$ 14 —
(P T Midgley) *chsd ldrs on outer: rdn along 1/2-way: sn wknd* **66/1**

1m 17.44s (0.54) **Going Correction** 0.0s/f (Stan) **13** Ran SP% **122.8**
Speed ratings (Par 95):96,94,88,87,85 84,83,78,74,74 69,58,55
CSF £62.75 CT £161.34 TOTE £7.70: £2.30, £3.00, £1.40; EX 99.80.

The Form Book, Raceform Ltd, Compton, RG20 6NL

Owner R West **Bred** R J H West **Trained** Burrough Green, Cambs

FOCUS
An ordinary sprint handicap and again those that raced up with the pace held a big advantage and the form is not rock solid. The first three home were the leading trio throughout.

11 FIRST PAST THE POST AT BETDIRECT (S) STKS — 7f (F)
1:30 (1:30) (Class 6) 3-Y-0+ — **£2,388** (£705; £352) **Stalls** Low

Form — RPR

004- **1** **Resplendent Prince**[13] 6638 4-9-7 65 ....(v[1]) NCallan 2 — 72
(T G Mills) *sn led: pushed clr 2f out: rdn out* **4/11**[1]

000- **2** *10* **Colonel Bilko (IRE)**[12] 6507 4-9-7 49 .... ChrisCatlin 4 — 48
(Miss S J Wilton) *in tch and rdn along 3f out: styd on u.p to take 2nd ins last: no ch w wnr* **14/1**[3]

443- **3** *3* **Magic Amour**[21] 6559 8-9-12 47 ....(v) FergalLynch 1 — 46
(P A Blockley) *prom on inner: hdwy to chse wnr 3f out: sn rdn: drvn and one pce fr wl over 1f out* **9/2**[2]

000- **4** *5* **Hows That**[18] 6584 4-9-2 50 ....(p) RobertWinston 7 — 24
(K R Burke) *chsd ldrs: rdn along 3f out: sn outpcd* **20/1**

000- **5** *½* **Cleveland Way**[29] 6498 6-9-7 40 ....(v) LeeEnstone 8 — 28
(D Carroll) *chsd wnr: rdn along over 3f out and sn wknd* **33/1**

0- **6** *3* **Lily On A Hill**[37] 6435 3-7-7 .... NataliaGemelova(5) 3 — 15
(B Smart) *a rr: bhd fr 1/2-way* **50/1**

00-0 **7** *19* **Lady Predominant**[1] 3 5-9-2 30 ....(b) HayleyTurner 9 — —
(Robert Gray) *a rr: bhd fr 1/2-way* **50/1**

1m 30.66s (-0.14) **Going Correction** 0.0s/f (Stan)
WFA 3 from 4yo+ 18lb — **7** Ran SP% **109.8**
Speed ratings (Par 101):100,88,85,79,78 75,53
CSF £5.71 TOTE £1.40: £1.10, £5.50; EX 9.30.The winner was bought in for 11,400gns.
Owner Resplendent Racing Limited **Bred** Miss K Rausing **Trained** Headley, Surrey

FOCUS
A nondescript seller with a totally predictable outcome and rated around the winner to his previous run and the runner-up.
Magic Amour Official explanation: trainer's representative said gelding had lost a front shoe

12 LITTLEWOODSPOOLS.CO.UK H'CAP — 1m 6f (F)
2:00 (2:00) (Class 6) (0-65,65) 4-Y-0+ — **£2,388** (£705; £352) **Stalls** Low

Form — RPR

236- **1** **He's A Star**[13] 6637 4-8-8 **54** .... PaulHanagan 3 — 63
(Miss Gay Kelleway) *in tch: psuhed along over 6f out: swtchd outside and gd hdwy 4f out: rdn to ld over 2fg out: drvn clr ent last* **9/2**[2]

340- **2** *6* **Jackie Kiely**[21] 6563 5-8-11 **51** .... TonyCulhane 8 — 52
(P Howling) *trckd ldrs: hdwy 4f out: rdn to chse wnr 2f out: drvn and one pce ent last* **7/1**

160- **3** *½* **Sun Hill**[13] 6637 6-9-8 **65** ....(v[1]) PaulMulrennan(3) 5 — 66
(C W Fairhurst) *led 6f: cl up tl led again over 6f out: rdn along 3 f out: hdd over 2f out: sn drvn and kpt on same pce* **8/1**

600- **4** *1½* **Moon Emperor**[61] 5837 9-9-6 **60** ....(v) EddieAhern 7 — 59
(J R Jenkins) *trckd ldrs: rdn along over 3f out: drvn and kpt on same pce fnl 2f* **14/1**

425- **5** *1* **All Bleevable**[7] 6510 9-8-7 **47** oh1 ow1 .... GrahamGibbons 4 — 44
(Mrs S Lamyman) *prom: rdn along 4f out: drvn and one pce over 2f out* **6/1**[3]

26-4 **6** *nk* **Romil Star (GER)**[1] 5 9-9-4 **65** ....(v) PatrickDonaghy(7) 6 — 62
(K R Burke) *cl up: rdn along over 4f out: wknd 4f out* **11/1**

260- **7** *27* **Keltic Rainbow (IRE)**[41] 6410 5-8-7 **47** oh6 ow1 ....(p) RobertHavlin 2 — 9
(D Haydn Jones) *a rr: bhd fnl 4f* **25/1**

460- **8** *1* **East Cape**[20] 6571 9-8-6 **46** oh11 .... KimTinkler 9 — 7
(N Tinkler) *a rr: bhd fnl 4f* **50/1**

001- **9** *dist* **Le Soleil (GER)**[98] 5519 5-9-2 **56** .... JamieSpencer 1 — —
(B J Curley) *cl up: led after 6f: rdn along and hdd over 6f out: wknd qckly and bhd whn heavily eased fnl 3f* **7/4**[1]

3m 8.76s (-0.84) **Going Correction** 0.0s/f (Stan)
WFA 4 from 5yo+ 6lb — **9** Ran SP% **113.2**
Speed ratings (Par 101):102,98,98,97,96 96,81,80,—
CSF £35.16 CT £242.15 TOTE £5.20: £1.90, £2.70, £4.00; EX 37.40.
Owner Miss Gay Kelleway **Bred** Arnfin Lund And John James **Trained** Exning, Suffolk
■ Stewards' Enquiry : Jamie Spencer two-day ban: used whip with excessive force (Jan 13-14)

FOCUS
A fair pace for this stayers' event and the ability to see out the trip was of paramount importance. The winner and third set the standard and suggest the form is reasonable.
Le Soleil(GER) Official explanation: trainer had no explanation for the poor form shown

13 TEXT "BETDIRECT" TO 88600 H'CAP — 1m 4f (F)
2:30 (2:30) (Class 6) (0-60,60) 4-Y-0+ — **£2,388** (£705; £352) **Stalls** Low

Form — RPR

004- **1** **Padre Nostro (IRE)**[13] 6633 7-9-1 **57** .... BrianReilly 6 — 65
(J R Holt) *trckd ldrs:hdwy 3f out: rdn to chse ldrs 2f out: rdr dropped whip over 1f out: styd on to ld ent last* **12/1**

543- **2** *1¼* **Robbie Can Can**[35] 6448 7-9-3 **59** .... RobertWinston 1 — 65
(A W Carroll) *towards rr and rdn along 1/2-way: hdwy u.p over 2f out: drvn and wandered over 1f out: kpt on ins last: nt rch wnr* **11/4**[1]

006- **3** *½* **Mossmann Gorge**[18] 6582 4-9-0 **60** ....(v) EddieAhern 10 — 66
(M Wellings) *in tch: hdwy 4f out: rdn to chse ldr over 2f out: drvn and ev ch over 1f out: one pce ins last* **25/1**

000- **4** *¾* **Amir Zaman**[27] 6519 8-9-4 **60** ....(v[1]) JamieSpencer 2 — 65
(J R Jenkins) *prom: hdwy to chse clr ldr over 4f out: led 3f out: drvn over 1f out: hdd ent last and sn no ex* **15/2**

000- **5** *3½* **Polish Power (GER)**[127] 4789 6-8-4 **53** .... JosephWalsh(7) 8 — 53
(J S Moore) *s.i.s: rr tl hdwy 4f out: styd on fnl 2f: nrst fin* **14/1**

061- **6** *2½* **High Frequency (IRE)**[29] 6494 5-8-8 **50** .... PhillipMakin 9 — 46
(T D Barron) *chsd clr ldr: rdn along 5f out: drvn and outpcd fnl 3f* **3/1**[2]

600- **7** *6* **J R Stevenson (USA)**[11] 6655 10-8-11 **53** .... GrahamGibbons 13 — 41
(Ernst Oertel) *hld up: hdwy 1/2-way: rdn to chse ldrs wl over 2f out: drvn and no imp fr wl over 1f out* **12/1**

200- **8** *8* **Extra Cover (IRE)**[23] 5959 5-8-9 **51** .... J-PGuillambert 14 — 28
(Ronald Thompson) *a towards rr* **14/1**

440- **9** *4* **Sol Rojo**[11] 6660 4-8-10 **56** .... PaulHanagan 12 — 27
(M J Attwater) *chsd ldrs: rdn along over 4f out and sn wknd* **6/1**[3]

000- **10** *2* **Miss Bear (IRE)**[55] 6289 4-8-4 **50** ow2 ....(b[1]) PaulEddery 4 — 18
(B Smart) *chsd ldrs: rdn along 5f out: sn wknd* **33/1**

4/5- **11** *1* **Whole Grain**[18] 6583 5-9-4 **60** ....(b) MartinDwyer 3 — 27
(B R Millman) *a rr* **20/1**

004- **12** *23* **Coleorton Dane**[11] 6658 4-8-9 **55** .... NCallan 7 — —
(K A Ryan) *led: clr after 4f: rdn along 4f out: sn hdd & wknd* **20/1**

000- **13** *dist* **Shesthebiscuit**[11] 6654 4-8-10 **56** ow1 .... TonyCulhane 5 — —
(J Parkes) *midsfield: rdn along and lost pl opver 7f out: t.o fnl 4f* **33/1**

2m 41.8s (-0.29) **Going Correction** 0.0s/f (Stan)
WFA 4 from 5yo+ 4lb — **13** Ran SP% **125.7**
Speed ratings (Par 101):100,99,98,98,96 94,90,85,82,81 80,65,—
CSF £44.43 CT £852.42 TOTE £24.40: £6.40, £1.02, £14.30; EX 43.50.
Owner J R Holt **Bred** Mrs G P Gaffney **Trained** Peckleton, Leics

FOCUS
A furious early gallop with Coleorton Dane virtually bolting, but they were not travelling very quickly over the last couple of furlongs in what became a war of attrition. The second sets the standard but the form does not look sound.
Coleorton Dane Official explanation: jockey said gelding hung badly right
Shesthebiscuit Official explanation: jockey said filly would not face the kickback

14 BETDIRECT.CO.UK MAIDEN STKS — 6f (F)
3:00 (3:03) (Class 5) 3-Y-0+ — **£3,238** (£963; £481; £240) **Stalls** Low

Form — RPR

422/ **1** **Cummiskey (IRE)**[477] 5490 4-9-12 80 .... EddieAhern 1 — 77+
(J A Osborne) *trckd ldrs: hdwy to chse ldr 2f out: rdn: flashed tail and led over 1f out: edgd rt and rdr dropped whip ins last: kpt on* **10/11**[1]

36- **2** *3* **Cookie Cutter (IRE)**[35] 6447 4-9-7 57 ....(p) RobertWinston 3 — 63
(K R Burke) *led: rdn 2f out: drvn and hdd appr last: kpt on same pce* **4/1**[2]

000- **3** *6* **Madame Guillotine**[21] 6556 4-9-4 35 ....(p) PaulMulrennan(3) 2 — 45
(P T Midgley) *midfield: hdwy to chse ldrs over 2f out: sn rdn and kpt on same pce* **66/1**

060- **4** *3* **Weet Yer Tern (IRE)**[7] 6664 4-9-12 50 .... FergalLynch 5 — 41
(P A Blockley) *chsd ldr: rdn along over 2f out and sn one pce* **14/1**

33- **5** *7* **Stylistic (IRE)**[112] 5192 5-9-7 62 .... LPKeniry 7 — 15+
(Patrick Morris, Ire) *s.i.s and towards rr: hdwy on outer and hmpd 3f out: nvr nr ldrs* **8/1**

6- **6** *½* **Strobinia (IRE)**[23] 6545 4-9-7 .... MartinDwyer 8 — 14
(R M Beckett) *towards rr: hdwy: n.m.r and hung rt 1/2-way: sn rdn and nvr nr ldrs* **12/1**

506- **7** *7* **Dysonic (USA)**[12] 6651 4-9-12 45 .... GrahamGibbons 9 — —
(D Burchell) *chsd ldrs: rdn over 2f out: grad wknd* **25/1**

04- **8** *3* **Hillbilly Cat (USA)**[248] 1335 3-8-10 .... PaulFessey 6 — —
(T D Barron) *chsd ldrs: pushed along 1/2-way: sn wknd* **14/1**

0/ **9** *2* **Starling (IRE)**[124] 4875 4-9-7 62 .... AdrianTNicholls 10 — —
(D Nicholls) *racd wd: in tch: rdn along 1/2-way and sn wknd* **7/1**[3]

10 *1* **Opening Line** 4-9-9 .... AdamKirby(3) 4 — —
(Ernst Oertel) *sn outpcd and a bhd* **25/1**

1m 16.37s (-0.53) **Going Correction** 0.0s/f (Stan)
WFA 3 from 4yo+ 16lb — **10** Ran SP% **126.2**
Speed ratings (Par 103):103,99,91,87,77 77,67,63,61,59
CSF £5.14 TOTE £1.90: £1.30, £1.20, £9.20; EX 5.90.
Owner Harry Redknapp **Bred** Schwindibode Ag **Trained** Upper Lambourn, Berks

FOCUS
A very uncompetitive maiden predictably won by the odds-on favourite. The proximity of the third raises doubts about the strength of the form. For the second race in a row, the winning rider dropped his whip over a furlong from home.
Starling(IRE) Official explanation: jockey said filly had had no more to give
Opening Line Official explanation: jockey said gelding was had been outpaced

15 NO 5P RULE 4'S AT BETDIRECT H'CAP — 1m (F)
3:30 (3:31) (Class 5) (0-70,69) 4-Y-0+ — **£3,238** (£963; £481; £240) **Stalls** Low

Form — RPR

062- **1** **Speed Dial Harry (IRE)**[13] 6638 4-9-0 **64** ....(v) NCallan 11 — 77
(K R Burke) *prom on outer: hdwy 3f out: sn led: rdn clr ent last: kpt on strly* **8/1**

041- **2** *3½* **Out Of India**[80] 5880 4-9-3 **67** .... PaulEddery 10 — 73
(B Smart) *trckd ldrs: smooth hdwy over 2f out: rdn and ev ch over 1f out: drvn and one pce ins last* **12/1**

021- **3** *shd* **Greenbelt**[6] 6674 5-8-10 **60** 6ex .... RobertWinston 2 — 66
(G M Moore) *sn led: rdn along 3f out: sn hdd: drvn and kpt on same pce fr wl over 1f out* **11/4**[1]

450- **4** *1¼* **True Night**[93] 5612 9-9-4 **68** .... AdrianTNicholls 7 — 71
(D Nicholls) *hld up: hdwy 3f out: rdn to chse ldrs wl over 1f out: kpt on same pce* **33/1**

U14- **5** *2½* **Monte Mayor Boy**[6] 6671 4-9-2 **66** ....(p) RobertHavlin 6 — 64
(D Haydn Jones) *s.i.s: towards rr and wd st: hdwy 2f out: sn rdn and kpt on fnl f: nrst fin* **9/1**

023- **6** *1¾* **Simply St Lucia**[11] 6660 4-8-10 **60** .... PhillipMakin 1 — 55
(J R Weymes) *cl up on inner: ev ch 3f out: sn rdn and wknd fnl 2f* **12/1**

005- **7** *1½* **Sorbiesharry (IRE)**[11] 6655 7-8-7 **62** ....(v) DuranFentiman(5) 8 — 54
(Mrs N Macauley) *bhd tl styd on fnl 2f: nvr a factor* **12/1**

326- **8** *½* **Cantarna (IRE)**[18] 6586 5-9-1 **65** .... DaleGibson 3 — 56
(J Mackie) *cl up: rdn along 3f out: sn wknd* **25/1**

11-1 **9** *1¾* **Owed**[1] 4 4-9-5 **69** 6ex ....(t) HayleyTurner 4 — 56
(Robert Gray) *cl up: rdn along 3f out: sn wknd* **6/1**[3]

053- **10** *3* **Lockstock (IRE)**[58] 6265 8-8-13 **63** ....(p) MickyFenton 5 — 44
(M S Saunders) *chsd ldrs on outer: n.m.r over 3f out: sn rdn and wknd* **8/1**

500/ **11** *3* **Devil's Island**[453] 6011 4-8-9 **59** .... JamieMackay 9 — 34
(Sir Mark Prescott) *s.i.s: a rr* **4/1**[2]

1m 42.86s (-1.74) **Going Correction** 0.0s/f (Stan) — **11** Ran SP% **123.0**
Speed ratings (Par 103):108,104,104,103,100 98,97,96,95,92 89
CSF £104.67 CT £342.47 TOTE £7.30: £2.80, £3.70, £1.50; EX 63.50 Place 6 £39.34, Place 5 £12.82.
Owner Nigel Shields **Bred** Brendan Lavery **Trained** Middleham Moor, N Yorks

FOCUS
A solid pace on for this ordinary handicap and the winning time was decent for the class of contest. The form looks sound enough and the winner could rate higher.
True Night Official explanation: jockey said gelding hung right in home straight

T/Plt: £35.90 to a £1 stake. Pool: £40,845.65. 830.50 winning tickets. T/Qpdt: £7.00 to a £1 stake. Pool: £3,337.50. 352.30 winning tickets. JR

LINGFIELD (L-H)

Tuesday, January 3

OFFICIAL GOING: Standard

Wind: Light behind becoming almost nil Weather: Dull and damp

16 FIRST PAST THE POST AT BETDIRECT MAIDEN STKS 1m (P)

12:10 (12:19) (Class 5) 3-Y-O **£3,886** (£1,156; £577; £288) **Stalls** High

Form RPR

3- **1** **Miss Highjinks (USA)**[13] 6641 3-8-9 .... EddieAhern 12 78+
(E J O'Neill) *lw: trckd ldrs: led 3f out: sn clr: v easily* **2/1**[2]

2 *7* **Kasumi** 3-8-9 .... SteveDrowne 11 57
(H Morrison) *leggy: bit bkwd: in tch: wnt 2nd 2f out: no ch w wnr* **25/1**

06- **3** *1* **Salisbury World (IRE)**[35] 6456 3-9-0 .... LPKeniry 3 59+
(D R C Elsworth) *plld hrd in midfield: eased wd and shkn up ent st: styd on steadily: improve* **8/1**[3]

0- **4** *½* **Questive**[18] 6595 3-9-0 .... (t) PaulHanagan 2 58+
(E A L Dunlop) *lw: plld hrd: disp 2nd tl 3f out: one pce* **16/1**

- **5** *nk* **Hazium (IRE)**[71] 6086 3-8-9 .... ChrisCatlin 9 52
(Patrick Morris, Ire) *leggy: bit bkwd: mid-div and wd: effrt 3f out: one pce* **40/1**

6 *1 ¾* **Blushing Thief (USA)** 3-9-0 .... MartinDwyer 6 53+
(W Jarvis) *w'like: bit bkwd: s.s: hld up in midfield: rdn 3f out: styd on same pce* **25/1**

7 *shd* **Iberian Light (USA)** 3-9-0 .... NCallan 5 53
(N A Callaghan) *str: bit bkwd: s.s: bhd: rdn 3f out: sme late hdwy* **25/1**

00- **8** *½* **Smart Golden Boy (IRE)**[15] 6610 3-9-0 .... HayleyTurner 4 52
(Mrs L C Jewell) *led tl 3f out: wknd wl over 1f out* **100/1**

5- **9** *½* **Airbuss (IRE)**[14] 6624 3-9-0 .... TonyCulhane 8 51+
(M R Channon) *lw: t.k.h towards rr: rdn 3f out: n.d* **7/4**[1]

0- **10** *hd* **Kinetic Power (IRE)**[32] 6484 3-9-0 .... FrankieMcDonald 1 50
(D R C Elsworth) *hld up in tch: outpcd 3f out: sn btn* **33/1**

0- **11** *hd* **Startengo (IRE)**[14] 6624 3-9-0 .... MickyFenton 10 50
(D R C Elsworth) *chsd ldrs: rdn 1/2-way: sn lost pl* **10/1**

- **12** *7* **Jeudi** 3-9-0 .... JamieMackay 7 34
(Sir Mark Prescott) *leggy: s.s: rn green: a bhd* **16/1**

1m 40.33s (0.90) **Going Correction** -0.15s/f (Stan) **12** Ran SP% **119.6**

Speed ratings (Par 97):89,82,81,80,80 78,78,77,77,77 76,69

CSF £61.85 TOTE £2.90: £1.30, £7.40, £2.30; EX 94.80.

Owner Miss A H Marshall **Bred** C Chan **Trained** Averham Park, Notts

FOCUS

A race delayed by nine minutes when the outside ten stalls failed to open at the first attempt. When they finally did get under way, the early pace was modest resulting in a moderate winning time for a race of its type and the form does not look solid despite the preformance of the winner.

Airbuss(IRE) Official explanation: jockey said, regarding the running and riding, his orders were to ride colt patiently as too much use had been made of it on its debut, adding that colt was unsuited by the slow pace and the track and, in his opinion, it needs a longer trip; trainer's representative added that colt ran in snatches

17 INSTANT WIN GAMES AT BETDIRECT.CO.UK H'CAP 7f (P)

12:40 (12:47) (Class 5) (0-70,69) 4-Y-O+ **£3,238** (£963; £481; £240) **Stalls** Low

Form RPR

005- **1** **Stoic Leader (IRE)**[4] 6690 6-9-1 **66** .... MartinDwyer 10 76
(R F Fisher) *disp ld: led over 2f out: hrd rdn and flashed tail fnl f: drvn out* **11/2**[1]

000- **2** *½* **Cherokee Nation**[17] 6596 5-9-1 **66** .... (p) TonyCulhane 4 74
(P W D'Arcy) *cl up: drvn to chse wnr over 1f out: kpt on: jst hld* **25/1**

032- **3** *1 ½* **Hard To Catch (IRE)**[14] 6631 8-8-7 **65** .... LauraReynolds(7) 7 70
(D K Ivory) *prom: outpcd and lost pl over 2f out: r.o again fnl f* **10/1**

335- **4** *hd* **Glad Big (GER)**[245] 1449 4-9-3 **68** .... EddieAhern 14 72+
(J A Osborne) *hld up and bhd: v wd st: shkn up and hdwy over 1f out: hung lft: gng on wl at fin* **14/1**

005- **5** *½* **Quantum Leap**[29] 6499 9-9-3 **68** .... (v) JamieSpencer 12 71
(S Dow) *s.i.s: hld up towards rr: hdwy on ins ent st: kpt on same pce* **7/1**[3]

020- **6** *1 ¾* **Joy And Pain**[14] 6631 5-9-4 **69** .... NCallan 9 67
(J R Boyle) *b: lw: plld hrd in midfield: hdwy to chse wnr 2f out tl over 1f out: no ex fnl f* **8/1**

030- **7** *¾* **Aggravation**[32] 6480 4-8-13 **64** .... (t) LPKeniry 11 60
(D R C Elsworth) *towards rr: effrt and wd st: nvr able to chal* **14/1**

600- **8** *shd* **Tuscarora (IRE)**[59] 6266 7-8-13 **64** .... PaulHanagan 3 60
(A W Carroll) *dwlt: t.k.h towards rr: shkn up and styd on appr fnl f: nt rch ldrs* **25/1**

212- **9** *shd* **Cormorant Wharf (IRE)**[308] 540 6-9-4 **69** .... GeorgeBaker 1 65
(G L Moore) *dwlt: sn in tch: hung rt and rdn over 2f out: wknd over 1f out* **7/1**[3]

135- **10** *1 ¼* **Look Of Eagles**[14] 6638 4-9-3 **68** .... (b[1]) ChrisCatlin 2 60
(P F I Cole) *dwlt: sn in midfield: rdn 1/2-way: hrd drvn and no imp fnl f* **10/1**

025- **11** *2 ½* **Ivory Lace**[14] 6631 5-8-13 **64** .... SteveDrowne 8 50+
(S Woodman) *mid-div: rdn over 2f out: n.m.r and snatched up home turn: no ch after* **6/1**[2]

506- **12** *1* **Littleton Zephir (USA)**[8] 6666 7-8-13 **67** .... EdwardCreighton(3) 13 50
(Mrs P Townsley) *chsd ldrs 5f* **25/1**

100- **13** *1 ¾* **Hey Presto**[29] 6503 6-9-2 **67** .... PaulDoe 6 46
(R Rowe) *lw: s.s: bhd: rdn 1/2-way: v wd st: n.d* **25/1**

000- **14** *5* **Warden Warren**[19] 6586 8-8-13 **64** .... (b) HayleyTurner 5 30
(Mrs C A Dunnett) *dwlt: hdwy to dispute ld after 1f tl over 2f out: wknd wl over 1f out* **40/1**

1m 24.34s (-1.55) **Going Correction** -0.15s/f (Stan) **14** Ran SP% **115.1**

Speed ratings (Par 103):102,101,99,99,98 96,96,95,95,94 91,90,88,82

CSF £145.65 CT £1370.36 TOTE £5.20: £2.40, £6.00, £3.40; EX 131.10.

Owner Alan Willoughby **Bred** P J Higgins **Trained** Ulverston, Cumbria

FOCUS

An ordinary but typically competitive handicap for the track and, with little room to play with, a few did not enjoy the clearest of runs. As a result those that raced up with the pace were favoured and the form does not look straightforward.

Glad Big(GER) ◆ Official explanation: jockey said gelding had been hanging left

Cormorant Wharf(IRE) Official explanation: jockey said gelding had been hanging badly right

Ivory Lace Official explanation: jockey said mare sufferd interference on final bend

18 NO 5P RULE 4S AT BETDIRECT MEDIAN AUCTION MAIDEN STKS 1m 4f (P)

1:10 (1:21) (Class 6) 4-6-Y-O **£2,388** (£705; £352) **Stalls** Low

Form RPR

055- **1** **Jack Rolfe**[90] 5699 4-9-0 55 .... GeorgeBaker 4 65
(G L Moore) *b.hind: lw: hld up towards rr: effrt and hrd rdn 3f out: styd on to ld ins fnl f* **5/2**[1]

436- **2** *2 ½* **Webbswood Lad (IRE)**[31] 6490 5-9-4 60 .... (p) MickyFenton 8 61
(Stef Liddiard) *prom: led 4f out tl ins fnl f: no ex* **3/1**[2]

000- **3** *1 ¼* **Fabulous Emperor (IRE)**[17] 6596 4-9-0 67 .... PaulDoe 9 59
(Jamie Poulton) *lw: mid-div: hdwy 5f out: rdn to dispute 2nd over 2f out: one pce appr fnl f* **10/1**

4 *3* **Ihuru**[20] 4-9-0 .... NCallan 2 54
(J G Portman) *w'like: leggy: dwlt: sn in tch: drvn to chse ldrs 3f out: no ex over 1f out* **20/1**

036- **5** *2 ½* **Drumroll (IRE)**[22] 6565 4-9-0 65 .... (v[1]) BrianReilly 7 50
(Miss J Feilden) *t.k.h: prom: led over 4f out tl 3f out: wknd fnl f* **9/1**[3]

/00- **6** *8* **Skelligs Rock (IRE)**[22] 6565 6-9-4 60 .... TonyCulhane 1 37
(A W Carroll) *wd most of way: hld up in rr: lost tch over 3f out* **20/1**

000- **7** *13* **Stolen**[27] 6523 4-9-0 45 .... MartinDwyer 3 17
(W R Muir) *led tl over 4f out: sn hrd rdn and losing pl: wknd over 3f out* **20/1**

6- **8** *nk* **Kalaam**[24] 6537 4-8-9 .... RobynBrisland(5) 10 16
(G P Enright) *w'like: sn wl bhd* **66/1**

P- **9** *6* **Maarees**[94] 4123 5-8-13 .... (b[1]) ChrisCatlin 6 2
(G P Enright) *sn towards rr: no ch fnl 5f* **25/1**

000- **10** *17* **Mystic Promise (IRE)**[36] 6443 5-9-4 30 .... (b) HayleyTurner 5 —
(Mrs N Macauley) *prom tl wknd qckly 5f out* **100/1**

2m 32.9s (-1.49) **Going Correction** -0.15s/f (Stan)

WFA 4 from 5yo+ 4lb **10** Ran SP% **93.3**

Speed ratings: 98,96,95,93,91 86,77,77,73,62

CSF £5.32 TOTE £2.50: £1.30, £1.30, £1.90; EX 7.60.

Owner Mrs Sarah Diamandis & Mrs Celia Woollett **Bred** W H F Carson **Trained** Woodingdean, E Sussex

■ Rose Bien (3/1, ref to enter stalls) was withdrawn. R4 applies, deduct 25p in the £.

FOCUS

A modest maiden that is unlikely to produce many future winners, on the Flat at least, with the runner-up the best guide. The finish was almost in slow motion and the ability to see out the trip was paramount.

19 BETDIRECT FREEPHONE 0800 211 222 H'CAP 1m 2f (P)

1:40 (1:45) (Class 4) (0-85,82) 3-Y-O **£6,477** (£1,927; £963; £481) **Stalls** Low

Form RPR

014- **1** **Fusili (IRE)**[17] 6599 3-8-9 **73** .... NCallan 6 82
(N P Littmoden) *prom: led 3f out: rdn out: readily* **9/2**[2]

01- **2** *2* **Before You Go (IRE)**[17] 6599 3-9-4 **82** .... JamieSpencer 1 87+
(T G Mills) *lw: dwlt: hld up towards rr: sltly outpcd whn pce qcknd 1/2-way: hdwy over 2f out: styd on u.p to take 2nd fnl 75 yds* **1/2**[1]

613- **3** *1* **Lenoir (GER)**[29] 6501 3-8-4 **68** oh3 .... (v) ChrisCatlin 3 71
(V Smith) *lw: hld up in 5th: hdwy to chse wnr over 2f out: one pce fnl f: lost 2nd fnl 75 yds* **8/1**[3]

300- **4** *12* **Norman Beckett**[49] 6352 3-8-1 **68** oh1 .... EdwardCreighton(3) 5 48
(M R Channon) *led and set modest pce: hdd 1/2-way: wknd 3f out* **33/1**

0- **5** *½* **Earth Master (IRE)**[17] 6599 3-8-11 **75** .... StephenCarson 7 54
(S Kirk) *hld up and bhd: pushed along 1/2-way: nvr nr ldrs* **66/1**

035- **6** *1 ½* **Ohana**[14] 6628 3-8-2 **71** .... (p) RoryMoore(5) 4 47
(N A Callaghan) *cl up: jnd ldr after 2f: led and qcknd tempo 5f out: hdd 3f out: wknd 2f out* **20/1**

653- **7** *4* **Bacharach (IRE)**[130] 4731 3-8-8 **72** .... MartinDwyer 2 41
(R F Fisher) *prom tl wknd 3f out* **33/1**

2m 5.37s (-2.42) **Going Correction** -0.15s/f (Stan) **7** Ran SP% **108.1**

Speed ratings (Par 99):103,101,100,91,90 89,86

CSF £6.41 TOTE £4.10: £1.80, £1.10; EX 11.50.

Owner Nigel Shields **Bred** Gestut Romerhof **Trained** Newmarket, Suffolk

FOCUS

A rather messy contest with the early pace not strong, but nothing should be taken away from the winner who seemed to score on merit and it has been rated positively through the third.

20 BETDIRECT FREEPHONE 0800 211 222 (S) STKS 1m (P)

2:15 (2:16) (Class 6) 3-Y-O **£2,388** (£705; £352) **Stalls** High

Form RPR

014- **1** **Indian Wizard (IRE)**[3] 6697 3-9-2 64 .... TonyCulhane 7 64
(P Howling) *rrd s and lost 6l: hld up in rr: hdwy 3f out: drvn to chal fnl f: led nr fin* **15/8**[1]

064- **2** *nk* **Ten Shun**[12] 6659 3-8-11 60 .... EddieAhern 4 58
(M J Polglase) *b.hind: led: rdn and kpt on fnl f: hdd and jst outpcd nr fin* **7/2**[3]

000- **3** *3 ½* **King's Charter (USA)**[66] 6142 3-8-11 50 .... SteveDrowne 8 50
(S Dow) *hld up in 5th: effrt on outside 3f out: hrd rdn and swished tail 2f out: hung bdly lft: kpt on to take 3rd ins fnl f* **2/1**[2]

066- **4** *1 ½* **Teddy Monty (IRE)**[29] 6500 3-8-6 53 .... (p) RoryMoore(5) 5 47
(M Quinn) *cl up: wnt 2nd over 3f out: hung lft and no ex over 1f out* **20/1**

04- **5** *hd* **Assumption (IRE)**[15] 6610 3-8-3 .... AdamKirby(3) 9 41
(S C Williams) *b: lw: hld up towards rr: hdwy 4f out: outpcd fnl 2f* **5/1**

000- **6** *dist* **Skezahra**[27] 6521 3-8-6 35 .... HayleyTurner 1 —
(T M Jones) *prom tl wknd rapidly over 3f out* **66/1**

00- **7** *5* **Cape Gigi (IRE)**[13] 6640 3-8-6 .... (b[1]) PaulHanagan 2 —
(B J Meehan) *t.k.h: prom 3f: wknd rapidly: wl bhd and eased fnl 2f* **20/1**

1m 39.3s (-0.13) **Going Correction** -0.15s/f (Stan) **7** Ran SP% **118.0**

Speed ratings (Par 95):94,93,90,88,88 —,—

CSF £9.18 TOTE £3.50: £1.50, £2.20; EX 9.80.The winner was bought in for 6,800gns. King's Charter was the subject of a friendly claim.

Owner Mark Entwistle **Bred** Epona Bloodstock Ltd **Trained** Newmarket, Suffolk

FOCUS

An ordinary seller in which the winner is value for further having given away so much ground at the start and the runner-up sets the level.

21 PLAY LITTLEWOODS POOLS ON 0800 500 000 H'CAP (DIV I) 6f (P)

2:50 (2:51) (Class 6) (0-58,58) 4-Y-O+ **£2,047** (£604; £302) **Stalls** Low

Form RPR

311- **1** **Hollow Jo**[13] 6639 6-8-13 **55** .... MickyFenton 3 62+
(J R Jenkins) *hld up in tch: effrt 2f out: chal fnl f: drvn to ld fnl strides* **7/4**[1]

065- **2** *hd* **Soft Focus (IRE)**[106] 5364 4-8-12 **54** .... (b) EddieAhern 4 60
(J A Osborne) *prom: rdn to ld ins fnl f: kpt on: hdd fnl strides* **11/2**[2]

605- **3** *1* **Charlie Bear**[14] 6625 5-9-0 **56** .... AdrianMcCarthy 10 59
(Miss Z C Davison) *chsd ldrs: led over 2f out tl ins fnl f: one pce* **10/1**

105- 4 3/4 **Sweet Pickle**[12] 6658 5-9-2 **58**.......... GeorgeBaker 7 59
(J R Boyle) *dwlt: sn rcvrd and hld up in midfield: effrt 2f out: styd on fnl f* **8/1**

000- 5 1 **Mirasol Princess**[7] 6668 5-8-10 **52**.......... ChrisCatlin 2 50
(D K Ivory) *broke wl: sn outpcd towards rr: rallied over 1f out: kpt on same pce* **14/1**

000- 6 hd **Siraj**[35] 6469 7-9-0 **56**.......... (p) MichaelTebbutt 1 53
(J Ryan) *hld up and bhd: shkn up and r.o fnl 2f: nrst fin* **16/1**

555- 7 2 1/2 **Border Artist**[82] 5322 7-9-2 **58**.......... HayleyTurner 12 48
(B G Powell) *wd: hld up towards rr: effrt into midfield 2f out: no further prog* **14/1**

400- 8 1/2 **Chillin Out**[5] 6685 4-8-8 **50**.......... PaulDoe 11 38
(W Jarvis) *hld up in midfield: hdwy to dispute 2nd 2f out: hrd rdn and wknd 1f out* **33/1**

/03- 9 2 1/2 **Red Finesse**[91] 5686 4-9-1 **57**.......... NCallan 8 38
(M A Jarvis) *outpcd towards rr: nvr a factor* **6/1**[3]

600- 10 3 **Zorn**[14] 6630 7-8-11 **53**.......... SteveDrowne 5 25
(P Howling) *prom: rdn and lost pl over 3f out: sn struggling* **25/1**

41- 11 5 **Montillia (IRE)**[160] 3850 4-8-10 **52**.......... MartinDwyer 9 9+
(C F Wall) *led tl over 2f out: 2nd and rdn whn hmpd on bnd sn after: nt rcvr* **8/1**

1m 11.75s (-1.06) **Going Correction** -0.15s/f (Stan) 11 Ran SP% **123.4**
Speed ratings (Par 101):101,100,99,98,97 96,93,92,89,85 78
CSF £11.80 CT £81.70 TOTE £2.90: £1.40, £2.00, £5.20; EX 12.20.
Owner Jim McCarthy **Bred** K J Reddington **Trained** Royston, Herts

FOCUS
A modest sprint handicap in which the winning time was 0.39 seconds slower than the second division and this race does not look as strong.

22 PLAY LITTLEWOODS POOLS ON 0800 500 000 H'CAP (DIV II) 6f (P)
3:20 (3:22) (Class 6) (0-58,58) 4-Y-0+ **£2,047** (£604; £302) **Stalls** Low

Form RPR

416- 1 **Bollin Billy**[14] 6630 4-9-2 **58**.......... PaulHanagan 10 68
(R Brotherton) *sn rdn along towards rr: gd hdwy over 1f out: r.o to ld fnl 75 yds* **8/1**

121- 2 1 **Mambazo**[25] 6527 4-8-12 **57**.......... (e) AdamKirby[(3)] 1 64
(S C Williams) *chsd ldrs: hrd rdn over 1f out: r.o wl fnl f* **4/1**[1]

633- 3 shd **Cayman Breeze**[4] 6692 6-8-10 **52**.......... SteveDrowne 3 59
(J M Bradley) *lw: hld up in tch: rdn to press ldrs over 1f out: kpt on same pce* **4/1**[1]

004- 4 hd **Taboor (IRE)**[13] 6639 8-8-11 **53**.......... JamieSpencer 2 59
(R M H Cowell) *dwlt: hld up in midfield: hdwy on rail 2f out: rdn to ld ins fnl f: hdd and nt qckn fnl 75 yds* **6/1**[3]

060- 5 1 **Transaction (IRE)**[14] 6630 4-8-12 **54**.......... NCallan 11 57
(J M P Eustace) *s.s: sn in midfield: rdn 1/2-way: n.m.r and hdwy ent st: styd on same pce fnl f* **12/1**

321- 6 shd **Segoria (IRE)**[5] 6685 4-9-0 **56** 6ex.......... ChrisCatlin 7 59+
(A M Hales) *hld up in tch: effrt over 1f out: squeezed for room ins fnl f: kpt on nr fin* **11/2**[2]

200- 7 hd **Clearing Sky (IRE)**[36] 6447 5-9-1 **57**.......... EddieAhern 5 60
(J R Boyle) *led tl ins fnl f: no ex* **10/1**

030- 8 shd **Stephanie's Mind**[20] 6579 4-8-6 **48**.......... MartinDwyer 6 50
(M Quinn) *prom: str chal ent fnl f: no ex fnl 100 yds* **25/1**

000- 9 2 **Lady Londra**[14] 6630 4-8-13 **55**.......... TonyCulhane 9 51
(D K Ivory) *towards rr: mod effrt on outside 2f out: nvr rchd ldrs* **25/1**

040- 10 1 **Marsad (IRE)**[14] 6625 12-9-1 **57**.......... PaulDoe 4 50
(J Akehurst) *dwlt: bhd: mod hdwy over 1f out: no imp* **14/1**

022- 11 1 1/4 **Gaudalpin (IRE)**[5] 6685 4-8-10 **52**.......... MickyFenton 8 41
(Ernst Oertel) *b.hind: prom tl wknd over 1f out* **12/1**

000- 12 2 1/2 **Oakbridge (IRE)**[14] 6630 4-8-13 **55**.......... VinceSlattery 12 37
(D J Wintle) *s.s: sn rdn along: a bhd* **33/1**

1m 11.36s (-1.45) **Going Correction** -0.15s/f (Stan) 49 Ran SP% **122.6**
Speed ratings (Par 101):103,101,101,101,99 99,99,99,96,95 93,90
CSF £40.60 CT £154.46 TOTE £9.90: £3.10, £1.60, £2.20; EX 42.90.
Owner J R Hall **Bred** Sir Neil And Lady Westbrook **Trained** Elmley Castle, Worcs

FOCUS
A moderate handicap run at a decent early pace, but those that set it paid for it late on. The winning time was 0.39 seconds faster than the first division but the form looks solid, rated through the third, fourth and sixth.

23 PLAY NOW AT BETDIRECTPOKER.COM H'CAP 5f (P)
3:50 (3:52) (Class 5) (0-75,74) 4-Y-0+ **£3,238** (£963; £481; £240) **Stalls** High

Form RPR

124- 1 **Ever Cheerful**[14] 6631 5-9-0 **70**.......... GeorgeBaker 2 79
(G C H Chung) *chsd ldrs: rdn 1/2-way: r.o to ld 100 yds out: drvn out* **11/2**

451- 2 1 **Law Maker**[39] 6422 6-8-10 **73**.......... (v) MichaelJStainton[(7)] 3 78
(A Bailey) *broke wl: disp ld: rdn and hdd 100 yds out: kpt on* **5/1**[3]

336- 3 hd **Wicked Uncle**[24] 6546 7-8-13 **69**.......... (v) NCallan 5 73
(S Gollings) *prom: disp ld 2f out tl 100 yds out: kpt on* **6/1**

000- 4 shd **Salon Prive**[17] 6597 6-8-9 **65**.......... ChrisCatlin 4 69
(C A Cyzer) *in tch: pushed along after 2f: rdn to chse ldrs over 1f out: styd on fnl f* **6/1**

060- 5 nk **Namir (IRE)**[7] 6668 4-8-10 **66**.......... MickyFenton 9 69
(Stef Liddiard) *lw: bhd and wd: rdn and hdwy over 1f out: fin wl* **40/1**

100- 6 1/2 **Polar Force**[12] 6657 6-9-1 **71**.......... SteveDrowne 6 72
(Mrs C A Dunnett) *towards rr: sme hdwy on rail ent st: styd on same pce* **20/1**

406- 7 3/4 **Patternmaker (USA)**[17] 6603 4-8-9 **65**.......... MichaelTebbutt 7 63
(W Jarvis) *sn outpcd and bhd: styd on fnl 2f: nt rch ldrs* **10/1**

053- 8 1 **The Fisio**[17] 6597 6-8-9 **65**.......... (v) MartinDwyer 1 60
(S Gollings) *reluctant to load: disp ld tl 2f out: no ex fnl f* **10/3**[1]

000- 9 3/4 **Russian Rocket (IRE)**[12] 6657 4-9-2 **72**.......... HayleyTurner 10 64
(Mrs C A Dunnett) *in tch: effrt on outside 2f out: wknd over 1f out* **50/1**

042- 10 shd **Anfield Dream**[14] 6636 4-9-4 **74**.......... EddieAhern 8 66
(J R Jenkins) *a bhd* **4/1**[2]

58.31 secs (-1.47) **Going Correction** -0.15s/f (Stan) 10 Ran SP% **122.0**
Speed ratings (Par 103):105,103,103,102,102 101,100,98,97,97
CSF £34.27 CT £175.75 TOTE £5.10: £1.90, £2.40, £2.10; EX 36.00 Trifecta £388.60 Pool: £711.60 - 1.30 winning tickets. Place 6 £19.23, Place 5 £6.55.
Owner K L Man **Bred** Southill Stud **Trained** Newmarket, Suffolk

FOCUS
A typically tight Lingfield sprint and, with three horses taking each other on for the lead, there was no hanging about. The form looks sound with placed horses close to form.
Anfield Dream Official explanation: jockey said colt had lost a shoe
T/Jkpt: £3,006.20 to a £1 stake. Pool: £19,053.50. 4.50 winning tickets. T/Plt: £14.90 to a £1 stake. Pool: £46,227.85. 2,253.50 winning tickets. T/Qpdt: £2.10 to a £1 stake. Pool: £3,507.60. 1,182.10 winning tickets. LM

[9]SOUTHWELL (L-H)
Tuesday, January 3

OFFICIAL GOING: Standard
Wind: Nil

24 FOOTBALLPOOLS.COM BANDED STKS 5f (F)
12:50 (12:51) (Class 7) 3-Y-0+ **£1,365** (£403; £201) **Stalls** High

Form RPR

06/4 1 **Miracle Ridge (IRE)**[1] 9 11-8-13 45.......... (b) PatCosgrave 1 57
(Adrian McGuinness, Ire) *chsd ldrs: hdwy 2f out: rdn to ld over 1f out: clr ins last* **14/1**

000- 2 3 **Blue Power (IRE)**[25] 6527 5-9-1 47.......... RobertWinston 14 49
(K R Burke) *trckd ldrs: hdwy 1/2-way: led wl over 1f out: sn rdn and hdd appr last: kpt on same pce* **7/1**[3]

000- 3 nk **On The Trail**[13] 6647 9-8-13 45.......... (p) PhillipMakin 7 46+
(D W Chapman) *trckd ldrs: hdwy 2f out: rdn over 1f out: kpt on same pce ins last* **40/1**

514- 4 1 **Ardkeel Lass (IRE)**[16] 6604 5-8-11 50.......... JBrennan[(7)] 2 47
(P D Evans) *cl up: rdn along 2f out: drvn and wknd ent last* **15/2**

340- 5 nk **Limonia (GER)**[13] 6639 4-9-4 50.......... (b[1]) FergalLynch 8 46
(D K Ivory) *dwlt: pushed along and hdwy 1/2-way: rdn 2f out: kpt on u.p ins last: nrst fin* **8/1**

121- 6 nk **Largs**[16] 6604 6-8-12 47.......... (b) JasonEdmunds[(3)] 4 42
(J Balding) *wnt rt and bmpd s: sn pushed along to chse ldrs: swtchd lft and rdn wl over 1f out: no imp ins last* **9/2**[1]

164- 7 nk **Amanda's Lad (IRE)**[22] 6559 6-8-6 45.......... LiamJones[(7)] 3 39
(M C Chapman) *led: rdn along 2f out: sn hdd and wkng whn n.m.r over 1f out* **6/1**[2]

000- 8 shd **Lakeside Guy (IRE)**[6] 6677 5-8-13 45.......... RobbieFitzpatrick 5 39
(M Appleby) *dwlt and hmpd s: towards rr tl sme late hdwy* **33/1**

103- 9 1 3/4 **Secret Vision (USA)**[16] 6604 5-9-0 46.......... (p) GrahamGibbons 6 34+
(R M H Cowell) *bmpd s: in tch tl rdn along 1/2-way and sn wknd* **9/2**[1]

500- 10 nk **Katie Killane**[179] 3316 4-8-13 40.......... (v[1]) AlanDaly 13 32
(M Wellings) *cl up: rdn along 2f out: sn edgd lft and wknd* **66/1**

000- 11 3 1/2 **Lady Pekan**[25] 6527 7-9-4 50.......... (v) J-PGuillambert 11 25
(P Howling) *cl up: rdn along and wkng whn n.m.r wl over 1f out* **10/1**

321- 12 1 **Lizzie Rocket**[16] 6604 6-8-9 48.......... (v) JamesO'Reilly[(7)] 9 20
(J O'Reilly) *dwlt: squeezed out and hmpd sn after s: lost action and a bhd* **12/1**

000- 13 1 3/4 **Percy Douglas**[16] 6604 6-8-6 45.......... (v) AnnStokell[(7)] 10 11
(Miss A Stokell) *a bhd* **50/1**

006- 14 4 **Gorgeous Boy (IRE)**[6] 6677 4-8-10 45.......... DominicFox[(3)] 12 —
(P L Gilligan) *a bhd* **40/1**

59.00 secs (-1.30) **Going Correction** -0.325s/f (Stan) 14 Ran SP% **120.7**
Speed ratings (Par 97):97,92,91,90,89 89,88,88,85,85 79,78,75,68
CSF £106.35 TOTE £12.70: £4.10, £3.10, £12.30; EX 154.90.
Owner Adrian McGuinness **Bred** K Prendergast & Con Harrington **Trained** Lusk, Co Dublin

FOCUS
Hand-timed. A competitive race of its type, but won in decisive fashion by the Irish raider, but not easy to set the level of the form.
Lizzie Rocket Official explanation: jockey said mare never travelled

25 TEXT "BETDIRECT" TO 88600 BANDED STKS 1m 4f (F)
1:20 (1:20) (Class 7) 4-Y-0+ **£1,706** (£503; £252) **Stalls** Low

Form RPR

002- 1 **Cotton Eyed Joe (IRE)**[22] 6555 5-8-13 45.......... DeanMcKeown 12 67+
(G A Swinbank) *chsd ldrs: hdwy to ld wl over 2f out: sn rdn clr: drvn out* **3/1**[2]

301- 2 10 **Bulberry Hill**[21] 6571 5-8-13 45.......... SamHitchcott 2 47
(R W Price) *in rr: hdwy over 4f out: rdn over 2f out: drvn to chse wnr fnl 2f: no imp* **11/4**[1]

505- 3 5 **Trappeto (IRE)**[45] 5957 4-8-6 49.......... LiamJones[(7)] 7 44
(C Smith) *towards rr: stdy hdwy 1/2-way: rdn to chse ldrs over 2f out: sn drvn and one pce* **16/1**

005- 4 1 **Shotley Dancer**[21] 6571 7-8-6 40.......... (p) SuzzanneFrance[(7)] 10 38
(N Bycroft) *chsd ldrs: hdwy to ld over 4f out: rdn 3f out: sn hdd and grad wknd* **40/1**

/04- 5 1 1/4 **Dextrous**[16] 6606 9-8-13 40.......... (p) LeeEnstone 6 36
(P T Midgley) *chsd ldrs: rdn along and n.m.r over 4f out: drvn along over 3f out and plugged on* **40/1**

423- 6 9 **Surdoue**[22] 6555 6-8-13 45.......... J-PGuillambert 1 23
(P Howling) *hld up: hdwy and in tch over 4f out: rdn along 3f out: sn no imp* **5/1**

044- 7 6 **Lyric Dances (FR)**[13] 6652 4-8-6 40.......... (t) DominicFox[(3)] 4 14
(J Jay) *chsd ldrs: rdn along over 4f out and sn wknd* **25/1**

420- 8 dist **The Beduth Navi**[238] 1600 6-8-13 45.......... RobbieFitzpatrick 3 —
(D G Bridgwater) *sn rdn along in rr: a bhd* **14/1**

060/ 9 3 **Inmom (IRE)**[400] 6762 5-8-13 45.......... PhillipMakin 8 —
(S R Bowring) *sn led: hdd after 4f: rdn along over 5f out and sn wknd* **66/1**

365/ 10 2 **Interstice**[21] 800 9-8-13 45.......... AdrianTNicholls 9 —
(M J Gingell) *cl up: led after 4f: rdn along and hdd over 4f out: sn wknd* **25/1**

042- 11 3 **Goldstar Dancer (IRE)**[13] 6652 4-8-9 45.......... RobertWinston 11 —
(J J Quinn) *in tch: hdwy to chse ldrs over 5f out: sn rdn along and wknd qckly 3f out: sn eased and dismntd after line* **10/3**[3]

310- 12 13 **Bella Pavlina**[15] 6614 8-9-3 49.......... FrancisFerris 5 —
(R A Harris) *a rr: bhd fnl 4f* **12/1**

2m 37.76s (-4.33) **Going Correction** -0.175s/f (Stan)
WFA 4 from 5yo+ 4lb 12 Ran SP% **125.7**
Speed ratings (Par 97):107,100,97,96,95 89,85,—,—,— —,—
CSF £11.99 TOTE £4.60: £2.00, £1.80, £6.40; EX 11.00.
Owner Mrs S Sanbrook **Bred** Tally-Ho Stud **Trained** Melsonby, N Yorks

FOCUS
An ordinary event on paper but a runaway winner in a very smart winning time indeed for a banded contest. The form looks solid with the placed horses and fifth close to form.
Goldstar Dancer(IRE) Official explanation: jockey said colt pulled up lame

26 BETDIRECT.CO.UK MAIDEN CLAIMING STKS 1m (F)
1:55 (1:58) (Class 7) 4-Y-0+ **£1,365** (£403; £201) **Stalls** Low

Form RPR

506- 1 **Sound And Vision (IRE)**[6] 6675 4-9-0 53.......... (b) PhillipMakin 4 46
(M Dods) *sn led: rdn 3l clr 2f out: edgd lft and drvn ins last: kpt on* **85/40**[1]

/40- **2** ½ **Crocodile Kiss (IRE)**[335] 257 4-8-9 54 .... RobertWinston 7 40
(J A Osborne) *midfield and pushed along over 3f out: rdn and hdwy 2f out: drvn and kpt on fnl f: jst hld* **9/2**[3]

005- **3** 2 **Sion Hill (IRE)**[7] 6672 5-9-0 35 .... J-PGuillambert 8 41
(M C Chapman) *in tch: hdwy over 3f out: rdn to chse ldrs over 2f out: sn drvn and kpt on same pce* **14/1**

00- **4** 2 ½ **Justcallmehandsome**[29] 6505 4-8-7 .... DonnaCaldwell(7) 9 36
(D J S Ffrench Davis) *prom: rdn along 3f out: drvn and one pce fnl 2f* **28/1**

022- **5** 1 ¾ **Fir Tree**[13] 6649 6-9-0 40 .... PaulEddery 12 33
(S R Bowring) *prom: hdwy to chse wnr 1/2-way: rdn wl over 2f out and grad wknd* **3/1**[2]

400- **6** 2 **High (IRE)**[262] 1055 4-9-0 57 .... DavidMcCabe 1 29+
(W J Musson) *broke wl: hld up and bhd: swtchd rt after 2f: taken v wd home turn: styd on steadily fnl 2f: nvr nr ldrs* **11/2**

000- **7** 8 **Valentine's Pet**[5] 6682 6-8-9 35 .... (v¹) JimmyQuinn 11 8
(A W Carroll) *in tch on outer: hdwy to chse ldrs over 3f out: sn rdn along and wknd over 2f out* **20/1**

000- **8** 2 ½ **Son Of Sophie**[21] 6572 4-9-0 40 .... (b) RobbieFitzpatrick 2 8
(C N Kellett) *a bhd* **33/1**

00- **9** 1 ¼ **Rain Holly (IRE)**[27] 6523 4-8-9 46 .... FrancisFerris 3 —
(R A Harris) *chsd leaders: rdn along after 3f: sn lost pl and bhd* **18/1**

0/0- **10** 13 **Livvies Lady (IRE)**[24] 6545 4-8-9 35 .... FergalLynch 6 —
(D K Ivory) *chsd ldrs: rdn along after 3f and sn bhd* **50/1**

000- **11** 8 **Between Friends**[87] 5741 4-8-8 40 ow1 .... GylesParkin 5 —
(A Berry) *s.i.s: a bhd* **28/1**

0- **12** 20 **Ash The Cash (IRE)**[7] 6672 4-8-3 ow1 .... TJHowell(7) 10 —
(K F Clutterbuck) *s.i.s: a bhd* **100/1**

1m 44.02s (-0.58) **Going Correction** -0.175s/f (Stan) 12 Ran SP% **120.0**
Speed ratings (Par 97):95,94,92,90,88 86,78,75,74,61 53,33
CSF £11.19 TOTE £3.20: £1.30, £2.10, £3.60; EX 16.00.The winner was claimed by J. K. Price for £5,000.
Owner The Idol Partnership **Bred** Mrs Valerie Dalgetty And Joan Heary **Trained** Denton, Co Durham

FOCUS
A typically moderate contest and a time to match.
High(IRE) Official explanation: jockey said gelding jumped out well but was soon outpaced and in dropping back became affected by the kickback and soon became detached; he added that gelding hung left throughout the home straight and was ridden hands and heels to keep it balanced

27 BETDIRECT FREEPHONE 0800 211 222 BANDED STKS 7f (F)
2:30 (2:32) (Class 7) 4-Y-0+ **£1,365** (£403; £201) **Stalls** Low

Form RPR

446- **1** **Wings Of Morning (IRE)**[21] 6573 5-8-9 45 ow1...(v) DanielTudhope(3) 1 50
(D Carroll) *trckd ldrs on inner: hdwy over 2f out: rdn to chal over 1f out: drvn ins last: styd on gamely to ld nr line* **6/1**[1]

000- **2** nk **Feast Of Romance**[36] 6445 9-8-11 45 .... (b) RobertWinston 12 49
(C R Dore) *chsd ldrs on outer: hdwy to chal over 2f out and ev ch: drvn ent last: kpt on* **7/1**[3]

000- **3** shd **Sierra**[50] 6346 5-8-11 45 .... JimmyQuinn 5 48
(A W Carroll) *sn pushed along towards rr: hdwy on inner 3f out: rdn wl over 1f out: hrd drvn ins last and kpt on* **12/1**

030- **4** hd **Ace Club**[30] 6497 5-8-11 45 .... (b) TonyHamilton 4 48
(J Hetherton) *led: rdn along 2f out: drvn ent last: hdd and no ex nr fin* **8/1**

000- **5** nk **Penel (IRE)**[8] 6151 5-8-11 40 .... (p) LeeEnstone 8 47
(P T Midgley) *chsd ldrs: rdn 2f out: drvn and kpt on ins last: nt qckn towards fin* **13/2**[2]

055- **6** nk **Paper Doll**[13] 6649 4-8-11 40 .... (p) PaulEddery 9 47
(B P J Baugh) *chsd ldr: rdn along wl over 2f out: drvn ent last: no ex last 100 yds* **10/1**

053- **7** 5 **Tally (IRE)**[132] 4671 6-8-11 45 .... RobbieFitzpatrick 6 35
(D G Bridgwater) *midfield: hdwy over 2f out: rdn to chse ldrs over 1f out: drvn and no imp ent last* **6/1**[1]

600- **8** ¾ **Rocky Reppin**[16] 6608 6-8-6 45 .... (b) JasonEdmunds(3) 10 33
(J Balding) *s.i.s: a towards rr* **10/1**

000- **9** 2 ½ **Tiger Hunter**[20] 6579 4-8-11 40 .... J-PGuillambert 13 27
(P Howling) *towards rr: sme hdwy over 2f out: sn rdn and no imp* **33/1**

002- **10** 2 ½ **Inescapable (USA)**[22] 6558 5-8-11 45 .... TomEaves 3 21
(A W Carroll) *keen: hld up towards rr: effrt and sme hdwy 3f out: sn rdn and n.d* **15/2**

060- **11** ½ **Earthling**[122] 4962 5-8-11 45 .... PhillipMakin 7 20
(D W Chapman) *s.i.s and sn rdn along: a rr* **28/1**

000- **12** 1 ¾ **Efimac**[21] 6570 6-8-4 40 .... SuzzanneFrance(7) 2 15
(N Bycroft) *a towards rr* **25/1**

006/ **13** 11 **Night Market**[479] 5450 8-8-11 45 .... DeanMcKeown 11 —
(Ronald Thompson) *keen: chsd ldrs: rdn along 3f out and wknd qckly* **33/1**

000- **14** 15 **Eden Star (IRE)**[20] 6577 4-8-11 40 .... FergalLynch 14 —
(D K Ivory) *sn outpcd and wl bhd fr 1/2-way* **20/1**

1m 30.29s (-0.51) **Going Correction** -0.175s/f (Stan) 14 Ran SP% **121.1**
Speed ratings (Par 97):95,94,94,94,93 93,87,87,84,81 80,78,66,49
CSF £44.23 TOTE £6.20: £2.70, £2.80, £5.60; EX 55.30.
Owner L Ibbotson **Bred** Limestone Stud **Trained** Warthill, N Yorks

FOCUS
A very ordinary contest that produced a blanket finish with the runner-up and fourth close to recent form.

28 PLAY NOW AT BETDIRECTPOKER.COM BANDED STKS 2m (F)
3:00 (3:01) (Class 7) 4-Y-0+ **£1,365** (£403; £201) **Stalls** Low

Form RPR

/00- **1** **Smart Boy Prince (IRE)**[12] 4217 5-8-9 45 .... LiamJones(7) 9 53
(C Smith) *mde most to 7f out: cl up: led again over 5f out: rdn 2f out: kpt on wl fnl f* **6/1**

001- **2** ½ **Blue Hills**[6] 6678 5-9-12 50 .... (p) DarrenWilliams 6 62
(P W Hiatt) *trckd ldrs: hdwy over 6f out: cl up 3f out: rdn wl over 1f out and ev ch tl drvn and no ex wl ins last* **6/1**

220- **3** 3 ½ **Brennie (IRE)**[27] 6523 5-9-2 45 .... (p¹) J-PGuillambert 5 48
(V Smith) *hld up and bhd: stdy hdwy over 5f out: rdn to chse ldrs 2f out: sn drvn and one pce appr last* **11/2**[3]

265- **4** nk **Maunby Reveller**[42] 5683 4-8-9 45 .... LeeEnstone 7 47
(P C Haslam) *trckd ldrs: hdwy over 4f out: rdn along over 2f out: drvn and one pce appr last* **4/1**[2]

003- **5** 16 **Magic Red**[6] 6678 6-9-4 47 .... (e¹) DaleGibson 4 30
(J Ryan) *towards rr: pushed along over 7f out: rdn 5f out: drvn and outpcd 4f out* **8/1**

202- **6** 12 **Bill Bennett (FR)**[16] 6606 5-9-2 45 .... RobertWinston 8 14
(J Jay) *hld up: hdwy to trck ldrs 6f out: rdn along 3f out: sn drvn and wknd* **11/4**[1]

25-5 **7** 5 **All Bleevable**[1] 12 9-9-2 45 .... GrahamGibbons 3 8
(Mrs S Lamyman) *trckd ldrs: rdn along and n.m.r on inner 4f out: drvn and wknd 3f out* **6/1**

006- **8** 19 **Jamaican Flight (USA)**[21] 6571 13-9-2 30 .... JimmyQuinn 10 —
(Mrs S Lamyman) *cl up: rdn along over 7f out and sn wknd* **33/1**

400- **9** 29 **Dejeeje (IRE)**[13] 6650 5-9-2 35 .... (p) PhillipMakin 2 —
(D W Chapman) *prom: rdn along 1/2-way: sn lost pl and bhd fnl 5f* **66/1**

050- **P** **Small Time Blues (IRE)**[21] 6572 4-8-4 35 .... (t) DuranFentiman(5) 1 —
(J Parkes) *a rr: bhd 1/2-way: t.o whn p.u over 4f out* **100/1**

3m 42.73s (-1.81) **Going Correction** -0.175s/f (Stan)
WFA 4 from 5yo+ 7lb 10 Ran SP% **121.4**
Speed ratings (Par 97):97,96,95,94,86 80,78,68,54,—
CSF £43.49 TOTE £10.90: £3.60, £2.20, £1.90; EX 83.00.
Owner Phil Martin **Bred** J Kennedy **Trained** Temple Bruer, Lincs

FOCUS
A typical stayers' event here, run at an even pace, and a real test of stamina. The form is sound enough with those in the frame behind the winner close to form.
Dejeeje(IRE) Official explanation: jockey said gelding had a breathing problem
Small Time Blues(IRE) Official explanation: jockey said saddle slipped

29 BETDIRECT IN-RUNNING SKYTEXT P293 BANDED STKS 6f (F)
3:30 (3:34) (Class 7) 3-Y-0+ **£1,365** (£403; £201) **Stalls** Low

Form RPR

042- **1** **Straffan (IRE)**[16] 6607 4-9-0 40 .... (p) DaleGibson 4 52
(J Hetherton) *mde all: rdn wl over 1f out: drvn ins last and styd on wl* **8/1**

241- **2** 1 ½ **Jalouhar**[6] 6677 6-8-13 45 .... SoniaEaton(7) 8 53
(B P J Baugh) *towards rr: wd st: hdwy 2f out: sn rdn: styd on strly ins last: nrst fin* **7/1**[3]

352- **3** ¾ **Christian Bendix**[7] 6672 4-9-0 45 .... (p) RobertWinston 5 45
(P Howling) *chsd ldrs: rdn 2f out: drvn to chse wnr over 1f out: one pce ins last* **5/2**[1]

523- **4** shd **Beamsley Beacon**[6] 6677 5-9-0 45 .... (b) TomEaves 11 45
(M Dods) *prom: effrt over 2f out: sn rdn and ev ch tl drvn and one pce ent last* **10/3**[2]

342- **5** 1 ¼ **Faithisflying**[21] 6572 4-9-0 40 .... (p) PhillipMakin 9 41
(D W Chapman) *cl up: rdn over 2f out: sn drvn and wknd over 1f out* **20/1**

051- **6** nk **King Marrakech (IRE)**[22] 6554 4-9-0 40 .... (v) GrahamGibbons 12 40
(B P J Baugh) *towards rr: hdwy to chse ldrs 1/2-way: drvn and one pce fnl 2f* **12/1**

506- **7** ½ **Flying Dancer**[16] 6604 4-9-0 45 .... (p) FrancisFerris 10 39
(R A Harris) *prom: rdn along wl over 2f out: sn wknd* **40/1**

305- **8** nk **Polar Haze**[21] 6570 9-9-0 45 .... (v) JimmyQuinn 2 38
(J Pearce) *towards rr: hdwy on inner over 2f out: rdn over 1f out: kpt on same pce ins last* **10/1**

352- **9** ¾ **Comic Tales**[21] 6568 5-9-0 40 .... DeanMcKeown 6 35
(M Mullineaux) *a towards rr* **22/1**

230- **10** 2 ½ **Fenwicks Pride (IRE)**[29] 6511 8-9-0 40 .... (v) GylesParkin 14 28
(A Berry) *s.i.s: a rr* **33/1**

301- **11** 7 **Soul Provider (IRE)**[21] 6568 5-9-0 45 .... J-PGuillambert 7 7
(G Prodromou) *in rr: v wd st and sn bhd* **7/1**[3]

000- **12** 3 **Night Reveller (IRE)**[77] 5953 3-7-9 40 .... DominicFox(3) 1 —
(M C Chapman) *towards rr: bhd fr 1/2-way* **66/1**

1m 16.79s (-0.11) **Going Correction** -0.175s/f (Stan)
WFA 3 from 4yo+ 16lb 12 Ran SP% **120.5**
Speed ratings (Par 97):93,91,90,89,88 87,87,86,85,82 73,69
CSF £60.50 TOTE £9.30: £2.70, £2.40, £1.70; EX 77.70 Place 6 £252.63, Place 5 £26.62.
Owner K C West **Bred** Mountarmstrong Stud **Trained** Norton, N Yorks

FOCUS
An ordinary sprint but the runner-up and fourth ran to previous form and give it a solid enough appearance.
T/Plt: £315.50 to a £1 stake. Pool: £40,757.25. 94.30 winning tickets. T/Qpdt: £39.40 to a £1 stake. Pool: £5,372.60. 100.70 winning tickets. JR

[16]LINGFIELD (L-H)
Wednesday, January 4

OFFICIAL GOING: Standard
Wind: Light, against

30 BETDIRECT FREEPHONE 0800 211 222 H'CAP (DIV I) 7f (P)
12:10 (12:12) (Class 6) (0-60,60) 3-Y-O **£2,047** (£604; £302) **Stalls** Low

Form RPR

065- **1** **Super Frank (IRE)**[63] 6224 3-8-13 **58** .... (b¹) AdamKirby(3) 10 64+
(G A Butler) *a.p: hdwy on ins to go 2nd 1f out: edgd rt but r.o to ld ins fnl f* **7/2**[1]

410- **2** ½ **Ms Rainbow Runner**[18] 6599 3-9-4 **60** .... EddieAhern 11 63
(P Butler) *racd wd in tch: rdn to ld over 2f out: no ex u.p and hdd ins fnl f* **11/2**[2]

000- **3** 1 **Prince Charlemagne (IRE)**[120] 5029 3-8-13 **55** .... NCallan 1 55
(N P Littmoden) *slowly away: sn mid-div: swtchd rt over 1f out: kpt on fnl f* **11/2**[2]

605- **4** ½ **Twilight Avenger (IRE)**[23] 6562 3-8-8 **50** .... (p) JimmyQuinn 12 49
(M J Polglase) *racd wd: rdn and styd on fnl f: nvr nrr* **33/1**

000- **5** ½ **Paris Power**[28] 6521 3-8-4 **46** oh1 .... (v¹) JamieMackay 9 43
(D Morris) *prom: swtchd rt wl over 1f out: kpt on one pce fnl f* **50/1**

605- **6** ½ **Smile For Us**[15] 6635 3-8-11 **53** .... JoeFanning 2 49
(C Drew) *led tl hdd over 2f out: nt qckn fnl f* **33/1**

000- **7** ½ **Titus Lumpus (IRE)**[14] 6642 3-8-13 **58** .... RichardThomas(3) 3 53
(R M Flower) *bhd: outpcd over 2f out: styd on fnl f: nvr nrr* **16/1**

000- **8** ½ **Old Time Dancing**[20] 6581 3-8-8 **55** .... DerekNolan(5) 6 49
(M J Wallace) *a towards rr* **25/1**

006- **9** nk **Perfect Order (USA)**[5] 6688 3-8-13 **55** .... (p) SteveDrowne 4 51+
(N A Callaghan) *in tch: hmpd on ins wl over 1f out: no hdwy after* **10/1**

003- **10** hd **Peephole**[14] 6648 3-9-4 **60** .... (v) FergusSweeney 13 52
(P J Makin) *swtchd lft s fr outside draw: nvr on terms* **10/1**

060- **11** 1 **Cape Latina**[210] 2396 3-8-10 **52** .... HayleyTurner 8 42
(J R Best) *plld hrd: trckd ldr tl wknd over 2f out* **12/1**

404- **12** ¾ **Pix**[14] 6648 3-8-10 **52** .... LPKeniry 5 40
(S Kirk) *in tch: wkng whn hmpd 3f out* **9/1**

625- **13** 1 ½ **Al Rayanah**[23] 6557 3-9-4 **60** .... ChrisCatlin 7 44
(G Prodromou) *slowly away: a bhd* **13/2**[3]

1m 26.93s (1.04) **Going Correction** -0.05s/f (Stan) 13 Ran SP% **119.8**
Speed ratings (Par 95):92,91,90,89,89 88,88,87,87,86 85,84,83
CSF £21.11 CT £109.47 TOTE £4.30: £1.50, £2.40, £1.80; EX 21.90.
Owner A D Spence **Bred** A Butler **Trained** Blewbury, Oxon
■ Stewards' Enquiry : N Callan one-day ban: careless riding (Jan 16)

The Form Book, Raceform Ltd, Compton, RG20 6NL

FOCUS
The winning time was 0.43 seconds faster than the second division, though still ordinary for the grade. The form is probably sound, though.
Super Frank(IRE) Official explanation: trainer had no explanation for the improved form shown other than that colt was wearing first-time blinkers
Titus Lumpus(IRE) Official explanation: jockey said gelding hung left throughout
Perfect Order(USA) Official explanation: jockey said filly suffered interference in running
Pix Official explanation: jockey said filly suffered interference in running

31 BETDIRECT FREEPHONE 0800 211 222 H'CAP (DIV II) 7f (P)
12:40 (12:41) (Class 6) (0-60,60) 3-Y-O £2,047 (£604; £302) Stalls Low

Form RPR
500- 1 **Welsh Dragon**[123] 4941 3-8-10 **52** MartinDwyer 4 56
(A M Balding) *mde all: rdn and r.o wl fnl f* **12/1**
006- 2 1 1/4 **Bollywood (IRE)**[17] 6605 3-8-10 **52** MatthewHenry 9 53
(M A Jarvis) *a in tch: rdn over 1f out: r.o to go 2nd ins fnl f* **13/2**
300- 3 hd **Casablanca Minx (IRE)**[30] 6501 3-9-4 **60** GeorgeBaker 8 60
(Mrs H Sweeting) *a.p: outpcd over 1f out: r.o ins fnl f* **5/2**[1]
0P4- 4 1 1/4 **Next Ness (IRE)**[67] 6135 3-9-2 **58** SteveDrowne 6 55
(R F Fisher) *in tch: rdn over 1f out: styd on ins fnl f* **14/1**
005- 5 shd **Miss Champagne (IRE)**[13] 6659 3-8-5 **52** RoryMoore(5) 11 48
(M Quinn) *w wnr: rdn over 1f out: wknd ins fnl f* **16/1**
050- 6 nk **Nilsatisoptimum (USA)**[20] 6581 3-9-4 **60** (t) JimmyQuinn 3 56
(M Mullineaux) *t.k.h: chsd ldrs on ins: no ex fnl f* **11/2**[2]
500- 7 1/2 **Mine The Balance (IRE)**[114] 5183 3-8-8 **50** HayleyTurner 2 44
(J R Best) *t.k.h: mid-div: outpcd over 2f out: styd on ins fnl f* **6/1**[3]
500- 8 1 1/4 **Jessica Wigmo**[19] 6591 3-8-10 **55** RichardThomas(3) 12 46
(A W Carroll) *t.k.h: hld up in rr: rdn over 1f out: no hdwy* **33/1**
562- 9 1 **Sky At Night (IRE)**[111] 5251 3-8-12 **54** EddieAhern 1 43
(P Mitchell) *slowly away: in rr: brief hdwy over 1f out: nvr on terms* **7/1**
000- 10 1 3/4 **Ridgeway Cross (IRE)**[15] 6634 3-8-10 **55** AdamKirby(3) 5 39
(Ernst Oertel) *a outpcd in rr* **20/1**
520- 11 shd **Gymbolini**[50] 6357 3-9-1 **57** (t) NCallan 10 41
(N P Littmoden) *s.i.s: a bhd* **10/1**
1m 27.36s (1.47) **Going Correction** -0.05s/f (Stan) 11 Ran SP% **121.1**
Speed ratings (Par 95):89,87,87,85,85 85,84,83,82,80 80
CSF £90.64 CT £263.85 TOTE £20.80: £5.90, £2.50, £1.50; EX 92.40.
Owner Welsh Dragon Partnership **Bred** Usk Valley Stud **Trained** Kingsclere, Hants
FOCUS
The weaker of the two divisions and the winning time was moderate for the grade, 0.43 seconds slower than the first division. The form has been rated around the third and fourth.
Mine The Balance(IRE) Official explanation: jockey said gelding ran too free
Ridgeway Cross(IRE) Official explanation: jockey said filly ran too free
Gymbolini Official explanation: jockey said filly suffered interference in running

32 FIRST PAST THE POST AT BETDIRECT MAIDEN STKS 1m 2f (P)
1:10 (1:11) (Class 5) 4-Y-0+ £3,238 (£963; £481; £240) Stalls Low

Form RPR
340- 1 **Port 'n Starboard**[15] 6626 5-9-2 57 MartinDwyer 7 66
(C A Cyzer) *s.i.s: bhd tl gd hdwy on outside 4f out: led over 2f out: rdn clr over 1f out: styd on* **3/1**[2]
200/ 2 2 1/2 **Kirkstone (IRE)**[829] 5250 5-9-2 70 EddieAhern 3 61
(J A Osborne) *led for 2f: styd prom: rdn to chse wnr 2f out: no imp fnl f* **13/8**[1]
0- 3 2 1/2 **Dubai Ace (USA)**[32] 35 5-8-13 50 EdwardCreighton(3) 5 56
(Miss Sheena West) *bhd tl hdwy over 1f out: styd on to go 3rd ins fnl f* **12/1**
00- 4 3 1/2 **Ernmoor**[56] 6298 4-9-0 SteveDrowne 8 50
(J R Best) *in tch: hdwy over 3f out: plugged on one pce fr over 1f out* **66/1**
060- 5 2 1/2 **Linden Lime**[23] 6565 4-8-9 60 PaulDoe 10 40
(Jamie Poulton) *in tch tl ins fnl 3f* **7/1**
050- 6 1 1/2 **Blaenavon**[32] 6485 4-8-9 49 JoeFanning 2 37
(D W P Arbuthnot) *mid-div: wknd over 2f out* **16/1**
056- 7 1/2 **Height Of Spirits**[82] 5866 4-8-11 54 RobertMiles(3) 11 41
(T D McCarthy) *led after 2f: hdd over 2f out: wknd over 1f out* **14/1**
505- 8 hd **Wavertree One Off**[5] 6687 4-9-0 55 (b) LPKeniry 12 41
(D R C Elsworth) *2nd after 2f tl 2f out: rdn and wknd over 1f out* **11/2**[3]
0- 9 3 1/2 **Samuel John Peploe (IRE)**[247] 1412 4-9-0 GeorgeBaker 6 34
(G L Moore) *hld up in rr: rn green: a bhd* **14/1**
2m 5.65s (-2.14) **Going Correction** -0.05s/f (Stan)
WFA 4 from 5yo 2lb 9 Ran SP% **119.4**
Speed ratings (Par 103):106,104,102,99,97 96,95,95,92
CSF £8.59 TOTE £4.00: £1.10, £1.10, £4.10; EX 12.40.
Owner Mrs Charles Cyzer **Bred** C A Cyzer **Trained** Maplehurst, W Sussex
FOCUS
A moderate maiden for older horses but the winning time was slightly faster than the following Class 5 handicap. The winner limits the form, although it appears fairly reliable.
Port 'n Starboard Official explanation: trainer said, regarding the improved form shown, gelding benefited from its previous run, which came after a lay-off

33 NO 5P RULE 4'S AT BETDIRECT H'CAP 1m 2f (P)
1:40 (1:41) (Class 5) (0-75,75) 4-Y-0+ £3,238 (£963; £481; £240) Stalls Low

Form RPR
052- 1 **Sir Haydn**[14] 6645 6-9-3 **74** (v) EddieAhern 14 82
(J R Jenkins) *mid-div: hdwy 2f out: rdn to ld jst ins fnl f: hld on cl home* **9/1**
000- 2 nk **Eastborough (IRE)**[9] 6665 7-9-4 **75** FergusSweeney 11 82
(B G Powell) *hld up in rr: hdwy over 4f out: short of room and swtchd lft over 1f out: r.o u.p to go cl nr fin* **50/1**
560- 3 nk **Zalkani (IRE)**[5] 6690 6-9-0 **71** GeorgeBaker 2 77
(B G Powell) *hld up in mid-div: hdwy 2f out: ev ch 1f out: no ex nr fin* **4/1**[1]
001- 4 1 1/2 **Willhego**[18] 6596 5-9-0 **71** HayleyTurner 4 75
(J R Best) *a.p: led wl over 1f out: hdd jst ins fnl f: no ex fnl 50yds* **13/2**[3]
453- 5 hd **Resonate (IRE)**[18] 6598 8-8-12 **69** LPKeniry 13 72
(A G Newcombe) *hld up in rr: hdwy and styd on fnl f: nvr nrr* **10/1**
444- 6 shd **Just Fly**[14] 6645 6-8-12 **72** RichardThomas(3) 6 75
(Dr J R J Naylor) *sn trckd ldr: lft in ld wl over 1f out: hdd jst ins fnl f: wkng whn short of room ins fnl f* **14/1**
200- 7 nk **African Sahara (USA)**[23] 6564 7-8-9 **73** (t) ChrisCavanagh(7) 1 75
(Miss D Mountain) *hld up in mid-div: effrt over 1f out: nvr nr to chal* **12/1**
636- 8 1 1/2 **Sonny Parkin**[5] 6690 4-8-12 **74** (v) AdamKirby(3) 12 74
(G A Huffer) *outpcd: sme hdwy whn carried wd on bnd wl over 1f out: nvr on terms* **14/1**
403- 9 shd **Admiral Compton**[14] 6645 5-9-1 **72** (b) JimmyQuinn 7 71
(J R Boyle) *hld up: rdn over 3f out: nvr on terms* **12/1**
501- 10 1 **Libre**[14] 6643 6-9-3 **74** J-PGuillambert 5 72
(Andrew Reid) *racd wd: in tch whn stmbld bdly over 2f out: nt rcvr* **16/1**
062- 11 3/4 **El Chaparral (IRE)**[32] 6488 6-8-13 **70** JoeFanning 8 71+
(W J Haggas) *led tl hung bdly rt on bend wl over 1f out: sn btn and eased fnl f* **6/1**[2]
0/0- 12 6 **Baboosh (IRE)**[46] 6376 5-9-4 **75** JamieMackay 10 60
(M Wigham) *outpcd and a bhd* **66/1**
300- 13 1 1/2 **Harcourt (USA)**[21] 4639 6-9-2 **73** ChrisCatlin 9 55
(M Madgwick) *prom: wnt 2nd over 4f out: wknd over 2f out* **100/1**
S23- 14 2 1/2 **Toparudi**[63] 6230 5-9-1 **72** NCallan 3 49
(M H Tompkins) *in tch: wnt 2nd 4f out: rdn and wknd over 2f out* **9/1**
2m 5.83s (-1.96) **Going Correction** -0.05s/f (Stan)
WFA 4 from 5yo+ 2lb 14 Ran SP% **115.8**
Speed ratings (Par 103):105,104,104,103,103 103,102,101,101,100 100,95,94,92
CSF £387.82 CT £2070.85 TOTE £9.00: £2.20, £10.20, £1.40; EX 132.50.
Owner Alan Sowle **Bred** D Leggate, Miss N Kent And Helshaw Grange Stud **Trained** Royston, Herts
■ Stewards' Enquiry : Hayley Turner caution: careless riding
FOCUS
The winning time was slightly slower than the preceding maiden, but still more than acceptable for the class. The form looks ordinary rated through the third and is not that solid.
Libre Official explanation: jockey said gelding clipped heels
El Chaparral(IRE) Official explanation: jockey said gelding hung right

34 PLAY NOW AT BETDIRECTCASINO.COM H'CAP 1m (P)
2:10 (2:10) (Class 4) (0-85,82) 3-Y-O £6,477 (£1,927; £963; £481) Stalls High

Form RPR
632- 1 **Mr Floodlight (IRE)**[4] 6694 3-9-1 **77** StephaneBreux(3) 5 80
(R Hannon) *trckd ldr: led over 4f out: rdn clr over 1f out: hld on wl fr fast finishers* **7/2**[1]
325- 2 nk **Katchit (IRE)**[44] 6402 3-8-11 **73** EdwardCreighton(3) 6 75
(M R Channon) *hld up in rr: racd wd: r.o strly appr fnl f: fin fast: nvr nrr* **12/1**
151- 3 hd **Moi Aussi (USA)**[8] 6673 3-9-9 **82** 6ex (b) JamieMackay 4 86+
(Sir Mark Prescott) *s.i.s: in rr tl hdwy over 1f out: styd on strly fnl f: nvr nrr* **4/1**[2]
003- 4 3/4 **Scroll**[15] 6627 3-8-11 **70** (v) J-PGuillambert 1 70
(P Howling) *in rr tl hdwy over 1f out: r.o fnl f: nvr nrr* **11/1**
031- 5 nk **Veronica's Girl**[14] 6640 3-8-12 **71** NCallan 9 70
(P R Hedger) *in tch: wnt 2nd wl over 1f out: wknd ins fnl f* **12/1**
054- 6 3 **Certain Circles (USA)**[39] 6427 3-9-2 **75** MartinDwyer 7 67
(A M Balding) *prom: wnt 2nd over 2f out: tl over 1f out: wknd fnl f* **9/2**[3]
133- 7 1 1/2 **Colmar Supreme**[50] 6353 3-8-13 **72** EddieAhern 3 61
(R Hannon) *hld up in tch: wknd over 2f out* **7/1**
01- 8 3 1/2 **Sigismundus (IRE)**[14] 6642 3-8-9 **71** AmirQuinn(3) 2 52+
(J R Boyle) *plld hrd: led tl hdd over 2f out: rdn over 1f out: wknd appr fnl f* **5/1**
1m 38.64s (-0.79) **Going Correction** -0.05s/f (Stan) 8 Ran SP% **113.3**
Speed ratings (Par 99):101,100,100,99,99 96,94,91
CSF £44.51 CT £172.94 TOTE £6.10: £2.20, £3.80, £1.90; EX 74.80.
Owner N A Woodcock & Simon Leech **Bred** Mrs Celine Collins **Trained** East Everleigh, Wilts
FOCUS
A decent handicap but an ordinary time for the grade and producing a close finish although the form looks sound.
Certain Circles(USA) Official explanation: jockey said colt hung right

35 BETDIRECT.CO.UK (S) STKS 1m (P)
2:40 (2:43) (Class 6) 4-Y-0+ £2,388 (£705; £352) Stalls High

Form RPR
042- 1 **Barton Sands (IRE)**[5] 6691 9-9-0 65 (t) J-PGuillambert 2 64
(Andrew Reid) *prom in chsng gp: hdwy over 2f out: led 1f out: rdn out: jst hld on* **13/8**[1]
005- 2 shd **Samson Quest**[30] 6507 4-9-0 56 (b[1]) ChrisCatlin 1 64
(N P Littmoden) *v.s.a: in rr tl hdwy on outside over 1f out: kpt on u.p: jst failed* **14/1**
440- 3 3 **Welsh Wind (IRE)**[39] 6436 10-9-0 57 (tp) JamieMackay 6 57
(M Wigham) *bhd tl hdwy on ins tl short of room over 1f out: kpt on one pce ins fnl f* **14/1**
403- 4 3/4 **Tregarron**[9] 6664 5-9-0 59 EddieAhern 3 55
(R Hannon) *in tch tl rdn and fdd wl over 1f out* **2/1**[2]
400- 5 nk **Temper Tantrum**[14] 6643 8-8-9 52 (p) TravisBlock(5) 5 55
(J R Best) *outpcd: in rr: mde sme late hdwy* **16/1**
666- 6 1 **Extra Mark**[33] 6480 4-9-0 61 GeorgeBaker 8 52
(J R Best) *s.i.s: nvr on terms* **7/1**[3]
040- 7 3 1/2 **Sunset Dreamer (USA)**[5] 6692 5-8-9 45 (v[1]) JoeFanning 11 39+
(P Mitchell) *sn trckd ldr: rdn and wknd over 1f out* **50/1**
000- 8 5 **Missed Turn**[30] 6505 4-8-9 50 HayleyTurner 10 28
(J M P Eustace) *chsd ldrs tl rdn and wknd 2f out* **33/1**
0- 9 shd **Rose Amber**[14] 6643 5-8-9 SteveDrowne 12 28
(J J Bridger) *a bhd* **100/1**
550- 10 2 **Indigo Sky (IRE)**[79] 3296 5-9-0 55 (b) NCallan 7 28+
(B G Powell) *sn led: rdn and hdd 1f out: wknd qckly* **16/1**
000- 11 3 **Penway**[7] 6675 5-8-11 45 (bt) AdamKirby(3) 4 21
(A Sadik) *s.i.s: a bhd* **66/1**
/00- 12 7 **Markusha**[115] 5157 8-9-0 47 PaulDoe 9 5
(Jamie Poulton) *mid-div: rdn 1/2-way: sn bhd* **40/1**
1m 38.15s (-1.28) **Going Correction** -0.05s/f (Stan) 12 Ran SP% **118.9**
Speed ratings (Par 101):104,103,100,100,99 98,95,90,90,88 85,78
CSF £26.13 TOTE £2.50: £1.60, £3.30, £3.40; EX 36.10.There was no bid for the winner.
Owner A S Reid **Bred** Patrick Cassidy **Trained** Mill Hill, London NW7
FOCUS
A fair time for a seller and an average but fairly sound race for the grade.
Extra Mark Official explanation: jockey said gelding hung right

36 BETDIRECT IN-RUNNING SKYTEXT P293 H'CAP 7f (P)
3:10 (3:12) (Class 4) (0-80,80) 4-Y-0+ £5,505 (£1,637; £818; £408) Stalls Low

Form RPR
440- 1 **Chief Exec**[15] 6629 4-9-4 **80** MartinDwyer 10 88
(C A Cyzer) *w.w: hdwy over 1f out: qcknd to ld ins fnl f: hld on fin* **8/1**[3]
020- 2 hd **Marko Jadeo (IRE)**[15] 6629 8-8-11 **73** SteveDrowne 2 80
(S Dow) *slowly away: r.o strly: clsng nr fin* **11/2**[2]
000- 3 1 1/4 **Smokin Joe**[15] 6629 5-8-10 **72** (b) HayleyTurner 12 76
(J R Best) *t.k.h: racd wd: hdwy and r.o wl fnl f* **14/1**
400- 4 nk **Alfridini**[125] 4900 5-8-6 **68** ow1 LPKeniry 1 71
(D R C Elsworth) *led tl rdn and hdd ins fnl f: no ex* **16/1**

060- **5** nk **Cheese 'n Biscuits**[30] 6504 6-8-13 **75**........................(p) JamieMackay 7 80+
(M Wigham) *slowly away: hld up: hdwy over 1f out: kpt on fnl f* **12/1**
634- **6** 1 ½ **Whitbarrow (IRE)**[32] 6489 7-9-0 **76**........................ NCallan 5 75
(A W Carroll) *plld hrd: a in tch: wnt 2nd 1f out: wknd ins fnl f* **8/1**[3]
05-1 **7** shd **Stoic Leader (IRE)**[1] 17 6-8-10 **72** 6ex........................ ChrisCatlin 11 71
(R F Fisher) *prom: rdn and chal over 1f out: wknd ins fnl f* **7/4**[1]
335- **8** ½ **Queens Rhapsody**[4] 6698 6-8-13 **75**........................(v[1]) EddieAhern 9 72
(A Bailey) *t.k.h: chsd ldrs: rdn 2f out: wknd 1f out* **10/1**
/10- **9** ¾ **Star Magnitude (USA)**[277] 840 5-8-11 **73**........................ JimmyQuinn 4 68
(S Dow) *chsd ldrs: pushed along 3f out: wknd 2f out* **25/1**
300- **10** nk **Curtain Bluff**[103] 5440 4-8-9 **78**........................ ThomasO'Brien(7) 6 72
(M R Channon) *mid-div: wknd over 2f out* **20/1**
600- **11** 2 **Physical (IRE)**[69] 6126 4-8-4 **66** oh4........................(t) JoeFanning 3 55
(Mrs A J Perrett) *chsd ldr tl wknd qckly over 1f out* **12/1**

1m 24.59s (-1.30) **Going Correction** -0.05s/f (Stan) 11 Ran SP% **119.6**
Speed ratings (Par 105):105,104,103,103,102 100,100,100,99,99 96
CSF £52.55 CT £627.16 TOTE £13.40: £2.00, £1.40, £4.60; EX 67.00.
Owner Mrs Charles Cyzer **Bred** C A Cyzer **Trained** Maplehurst, W Sussex

FOCUS
A decent handicap run at a fair pace and rated around the principals. The runner-up sets the standard but the form behind is not solid.
Cheese 'n Biscuits Official explanation: jockey said, regarding the running and riding, his orders were to have mare handy but he missed the break and was unable to do so, and he was also outpaced early on; trainer said mare has leg problems and is difficult to train; vet said mare finished sore and stiff
Queens Rhapsody Official explanation: jockey said gelding suffered a cut right fore-leg

37 LITTLEWOODS LOTTO4 0800 500 000 H'CAP 1m 5f (P)
3:40 (3:41) (Class 5) (0-70,69) 4-Y-0+ £3,238 (£963; £481; £240) Stalls Low

Form RPR
024- **1** **Principal Witness (IRE)**[25] 6540 5-8-9 **60**........................ SteveDrowne 14 66
(Tom Dascombe) *trckd ldrs: led 1f out: r.o wl* **10/1**
43-2 **2** ½ **Robbie Can Can**[2] 13 7-8-8 **59**........................ MartinDwyer 6 64+
(A W Carroll) *s.i.s: hld up: hdwy whn short of room and swtchd rt over 1f out: r.o wl: nvr nrr* **4/1**[1]
365- **3** hd **Blackmail (USA)**[18] 6596 8-8-12 **63**........................(b) FrankieMcDonald 2 69+
(Miss B Sanders) *in tch: swtchd rt appr fnl f: r.o ins last* **12/1**
450- **4** ½ **Swainson (USA)**[18] 6598 5-9-0 **65**........................ JoeFanning 1 69
(P Mitchell) *led to over 6f out: led again over 2f out: hdd 1f out: nt qckn ins fnl f* **10/1**
503- **5** shd **Dovedon Hero**[8] 6669 6-9-4 **69**........................(b) NCallan 9 73
(P J McBride) *hld up in rr: hdwy over 2f out: nt qckn ins fnl f* **6/1**[2]
604- **6** hd **Duelling Banjos**[18] 6598 7-9-3 **68**........................ EddieAhern 11 72
(J Akehurst) *bhd tl hdwy on ins over 1f out: nt qckn ins fnl f* **6/1**[2]
150- **7** 3 **Bendarshaan**[88] 5747 6-8-7 **61**........................ StephaneBreux(3) 3 61
(R Hannon) *trckd ldr: wkng whn hmpd jst ins fnl f* **6/1**[2]
405- **8** ¾ **Isa'Af (IRE)**[14] 6644 7-9-0 **65**........................ ChrisCatlin 8 64
(P W Hiatt) *t.k.h: mid-div tl gd hdwy to ld over 6f out tl hdd 2f out: wknd fnl f* **14/1**
001- **9** 3 ½ **Mostarsil (USA)**[28] 6523 8-8-9 **60**........................(p) HayleyTurner 7 54
(G L Moore) *mid-div tl bhd fr over 4f out* **9/1**[3]
010- **10** hd **Prime Powered (IRE)**[39] 6432 5-9-3 **68**........................(p) GeorgeBaker 12 61
(G L Moore) *hld up in tch: rdn over 1f out: hung lft and wknd* **12/1**
0- **11** hd **Eamon An Chnoic (IRE)**[9] 5635 5-8-9 **60**........................ FergusSweeney 10 53
(B W Duke) *trckd ldrs tl wknd over 3f out* **66/1**
004- **12** ½ **Sphinx (FR)**[14] 6644 8-9-2 **67**........................ PaulDoe 13 59
(Jamie Poulton) *s.i.s: bhd: hdwy on ins over 2f out: rdn and sn wknd* **16/1**
L00- **R** **Battling Mac (IRE)**[18] 6596 8-9-2 **67**........................(p) J-PGuillambert 4 —
(L A Dace) *ref to r* **66/1**

2m 49.78s (1.48) **Going Correction** -0.05s/f (Stan) 13 Ran SP% **122.0**
Speed ratings (Par 103):93,92,92,92,92 92,90,89,87,87 87,87,—
CSF £50.73 CT £500.36 TOTE £11.60: £4.30, £2.10, £3.70; EX 49.30 Place 6 £22.59, Place 5 £14.60.
Owner G J Dascombe **Bred** Yeomanstown Stud **Trained** Lambourn, Berks
■ A first winner as a trainer for former jump jockey Tom Dascombe.

FOCUS
A steady early pace and a very moderate winning time for a race of its class, which suggests the form will not prove reliable.
T/Plt: £21.20 to a £1 stake. Pool: £33,569.25. 1,152.80 winning tickets. T/Qpdt: £10.10 to a £1 stake. Pool: £3,442.10. 251.90 winning tickets. JS

WOLVERHAMPTON (A.W) (L-H)
Wednesday, January 4
OFFICIAL GOING: Standard
Wind: Almost nil

38 BETDIRECT.CO.UK BANDED STKS 5f 216y(P)
1:20 (1:21) (Class 7) 4-Y-0+ £1,365 (£403; £201) Stalls Low

Form RPR
43-3 **1** **Magic Amour**[2] 11 8-8-6 47........................(b) KevinGhunowa(7) 10 62
(P A Blockley) *led early: a.p: led 2f out: rdn clr over 1f out: r.o wl* **8/1**
330- **2** 3 ½ **Trouble Maker**[61] 6243 5-8-13 50........................ NeilChalmers(3) 6 55+
(A M Balding) *sn mid-div: rdn and hdwy 2f out: r.o ins fnl f: nt trble wnr* **9/2**[2]
310- **3** 3 **Leah's Pride**[14] 6647 5-8-12 46........................ FergalLynch 13 42
(P Howling) *a.p: rdn and edgd lft wl over 1f out: one pce fnl f* **16/1**
000- **4** nk **Malahide Express (IRE)**[26] 6527 6-8-13 47........................ MickyFenton 8 42
(E J Alston) *led: rdn and hdd 2f out: no ex ins fnl f* **33/1**
004- **5** shd **Pheckless**[5] 6693 7-9-1 49........................ PaulHanagan 5 43
(J M Bradley) *s.i.s: rdn and hdwy 2f out: one pce fnl f* **6/1**[3]
204- **6** shd **Beverley Beau**[21] 6579 4-8-7 48........................ KristinStubbs(7) 3 42
(Mrs L Stubbs) *prom: rdn wl over 1f out: carried sltly lft ent fnl f: one pce* **7/1**
350- **7** ¾ **Smirfys Party**[7] 6676 8-8-10 47........................(p) PaulMulrennan(3) 4 39
(W M Brisbourne) *outpcd: late hdwy: nvr nrr* **12/1**
005- **8** ½ **Hiamovi (IRE)**[6] 6685 4-9-2 50........................(v) RobertWinston 11 40
(R M H Cowell) *s.i.s: hdwy over 2f out: sn rdn: one pce fnl f* **14/1**
056- **9** hd **Urban Rose**[26] 6527 5-9-2 50........................ BrianReilly 7 40
(J W Unett) *chsd ldrs: rdn over 2f out: wknd fnl f* **10/1**
160- **10** nk **Carcinetto (IRE)**[72] 6076 4-8-13 47........................(v) FrancisFerris 2 41+
(B Palling) *mid-div: hdwy whn edgd lft 1f out: nt clr run ins fnl f: eased* **16/1**
040- **11** 5 **Layed Back Rocky**[7] 6676 4-9-2 50........................ DeanMcKeown 9 24
(M Mullineaux) *mid-div: wkng whn n.m.r over 2f out* **33/1**
004- **12** 5 **Enjoy The Buzz**[6] 6685 7-9-0 48........................ RobbieFitzpatrick 1 50+
(J M Bradley) *broke wl: lost pl after 1f: hdwy on ins whn hmpd 1f out: sn eased* **7/2**[1]

1m 14.91s (-0.90) **Going Correction** -0.025s/f (Stan) 12 Ran SP% **119.4**
Speed ratings (Par 97):105,100,96,95,95 95,94,94,93,93 86,80
CSF £44.18 TOTE £7.70: £1.80, £2.40, £4.80; EX 53.90.
Owner Mrs Joanna Hughes **Bred** Juddmonte Farms **Trained** Lambourn, Berks
■ Stewards' Enquiry : Francis Ferris two-day ban: careless riding (Jan 16-17)

FOCUS
Plenty of pace on here and a very smart winning time indeed for a banded contest. Those that raced up with the pace were very much favoured and the form may not prove that solid.

39 HOTEL & CONFERENCING AT DUNSTALL PARK TRI-BANDED STKS 5f 216y(P)
1:50 (1:51) (Class 7) 3-Y-O £1,365 (£403; £201) Stalls Low

Form RPR
000- **1** **My Reflection**[56] 6295 3-8-7 40........................ RobertWinston 6 43
(D Shaw) *chsd ldrs: rdn to ld wl over 1f out: sn edgd lft: drvn out* **16/1**
000- **2** 1 ¾ **Chalice Welcome**[111] 5251 3-8-8 40 ow1........................ MickyFenton 8 39
(J A Supple) *s.i.s: outpcd: rdn and hdwy over 2f out: r.o to take 2nd nr fin* **12/1**
000- **3** nk **Saxon Star (IRE)**[44] 6403 3-8-12 45........................(v[1]) RobertHavlin 9 42
(M D I Usher) *w ldrs: rdn over 3f out: kpt on and edgd lft towards fin* **9/1**[3]
000- **4** 1 **Sanders Boy**[31] 6496 3-8-12 45........................ DarrenWilliams 10 39
(J R Norton) *outpcd: rdn and hdwy over 2f out: nt qckn ins fnl f* **20/1**
000- **5** ½ **Sarah's Art (IRE)**[20] 6581 3-8-12 45........................ FergalLynch 3 38
(N A Callaghan) *led over 4f out tl over 3f out: rdn and ev ch wl over 1f out: no ex fnl f* **2/1**[2]
000- **6** nk **Three Feathers**[83] 5857 3-8-12 45........................ AlanDaly 5 37
(M Salaman) *chsd ldrs: outpcd over 3f out: rallied on ins wl over 1f out: no imp fnl f* **16/1**
003- **7** 2 ½ **Musical City**[22] 6569 3-8-12 45........................ PaulEddery 7 29
(B Smart) *led over 1f: w ldrs: rdn over 3f out: wknd wl ins fnl f* **15/8**[1]
000- **8** nk **Shopfitter**[4] 6697 3-8-7 45........................(b[1]) MarcHalford(5) 1 28
(Mrs C A Dunnett) *prom: led over 3f out: rdn and hdd wl over 1f out: sn wknd* **9/1**[3]
050- **9** 1 **Key Of Magic (IRE)**[56] 6295 3-8-2 30........................ DaleGibson 4 15
(J Hetherton) *sn outpcd* **22/1**
000- **10** 5 **La Bomba Veloce**[14] 6648 3-8-7 40........................(b) PaulHanagan 2 5
(Mrs L Williamson) *s.i.s: outpcd* **16/1**

1m 17.13s (1.32) **Going Correction** -0.025s/f (Stan) 10 Ran SP% **122.6**
Speed ratings (Par 91):90,87,87,85,85 84,81,81,79,73
CSF £202.26 TOTE £18.50: £4.30, £2.90, £2.60; EX 159.70.
Owner Danethorpe Racing Ltd **Bred** D R Tucker **Trained** Danethorpe, Notts

FOCUS
A poor race in which the leaders may have gone off too quickly.
My Reflection Official explanation: trainer had no explanation for the improved form shown other than that gelding travelled better during today's race

40 BETDIRECT FREEPHONE 0800 211 222 BANDED STKS 1m 5f 194y(P)
2:20 (2:20) (Class 7) 4-Y-0+ £1,365 (£403; £201) Stalls Low

Form RPR
232- **1** **Little Richard (IRE)**[7] 6678 7-9-1 45........................(p) AlanDaly 2 53+
(M Wellings) *hld up in mid-div: swtchd rt and hdwy over 1f out: r.o u.p to ld last strides* **7/2**[2]
542- **2** nk **Moon Shot**[16] 6620 10-9-6 50........................ VinceSlattery 4 57
(A G Juckes) *t.k.h in tch: rdn to ld 1f out: hdd last strides* **9/1**[3]
434- **3** 1 **Countback (FR)**[23] 6563 7-9-6 50........................ PaulHanagan 3 56
(A W Carroll) *hld up and bhd: hdwy over 2f out: edgd lft fr over 1f out: ev ch ins fnl f: nt qckn* **2/1**[1]
461- **4** 2 ½ **Cayman Calypso (IRE)**[36] 6461 5-9-3 47........................ MickyFenton 5 50
(Mrs P Sly) *led: rdn over 2f out: hdd 1f out: wknd towards fin* **7/2**[2]
065- **5** nk **Jadeeron**[16] 6612 7-9-1 45........................(p) DarrenWilliams 11 47
(Miss D A McHale) *hld up and bhd: hdwy over 3f out: sn rdn: wknd 1f out* **12/1**
3/5- **6** 5 **Thorpeness (IRE)**[16] 6620 7-9-1 45........................ RobertHavlin 1 40
(P D Cundell) *prom: rdn over 3f out: wknd over 2f out* **12/1**
646- **7** ½ **Power Strike (USA)**[67] 6152 5-9-2 46........................ TomEaves 8 40
(Mrs L B Normile) *w ldr tl rdn over 3f out: wknd 2f out* **33/1**
600- **8** shd **Paradise Valley**[7] 6678 6-9-2 46........................(tp) RobbieFitzpatrick 10 40
(Stef Liddiard) *hld up and bhd: rdn over 3f out: no rspnse* **25/1**
005- **9** 16 **Airgusta (IRE)**[7] 6678 5-9-6 50........................(p) DaleGibson 9 22
(C P Morlock) *t.k.h in tch: rdn over 3f out: sn wknd* **16/1**

3m 8.03s (0.66) **Going Correction** -0.025s/f (Stan) 9 Ran SP% **115.8**
Speed ratings (Par 97):97,96,96,94,94 91,91,91,82
CSF £35.08 TOTE £4.00: £1.30, £1.90, £1.30; EX 20.00.
Owner Mark Wellings Racing **Bred** Rathbarry Stud **Trained** Six Ashes, Shropshire

FOCUS
Not the stamina test that it might have been, as the pace for the first mile was moderate and the contest developed into something of a sprint. The third sets the standard on recent handicap form.

41 DAILY OFFERS FROM BETDIRECT BANDED STKS 1m 1f 103y(P)
2:50 (2:50) (Class 7) 4-Y-0+ £1,706 (£503; £252) Stalls Low

Form RPR
4/0- **1** **Itcanbedone Again (IRE)**[81] 5131 7-9-2 49........................ FrancisFerris 5 58
(Ian Williams) *mde all: rdn over 2f out: r.o wl* **9/1**
0/0- **2** 1 ¼ **Basinet**[34] 5381 8-9-2 49........................(p) PaulHanagan 13 56
(J J Quinn) *hld up and bhd: hdwy over 2f out: hung lft and wnt 2nd over 2f out: r.o ins fnl f: nt rch wnr* **11/1**
013- **3** 4 **Super Dominion**[14] 6651 9-9-1 48........................(p) VinceSlattery 10 47
(R Hollinshead) *hld up towards rr: hdwy on ins over 2f out: kpt on towards fin* **12/1**
003- **4** hd **Insignia (IRE)**[7] 6679 4-9-0 48........................(p) RobertWinston 6 47
(W M Brisbourne) *chsd wnr: rdn 3f out: wknd fnl f* **6/1**[3]
000- **5** nk **Azreme**[23] 6560 6-9-2 49........................(b[1]) TonyCulhane 11 47
(P Howling) *hld up and bhd: hdwy over 2f out: hung lft over 1f out: one pce* **12/1**
334- **6** 1 **Orpen Quest (IRE)**[23] 6567 4-8-13 47........................ RobbieFitzpatrick 4 43
(M J Attwater) *hld up in mid-div: rdn over 3f out: hdwy over 2f out: no imp whn bmpd 1f out* **11/4**[1]
002- **7** hd **Mujimac (IRE)**[6] 6682 4-9-2 50........................ FergalLynch 9 46
(P A Blockley) *swtchd lft sn after s: hld up in mid-div: sme hdwy fnl f: n.d* **15/2**
150- **8** ½ **Adobe**[7] 6679 11-8-10 50........................ LiamJones(7) 12 45
(W M Brisbourne) *swtchd lft sn after s: hld up in rr: hdwy fnl f: nvr nrr* **12/1**

402- **9** *5* **Bond Millennium**[14] 6651 8-9-1 48 .... PaulEddery 2 33
(B Smart) *hld up in tch: wknd 1f out: eased whn btn ins fnl f* **11/2**[2]
400- **10** *1* **Raul Sahara**[20] 6587 4-8-9 50 .... KevinGhunowa(7) 1 33
(P A Blockley) *prom tl wknd over 3f out* **33/1**
403- **11** *½* **Bold Trump**[16] 6623 5-9-3 50 .... MickyFenton 8 32
(Mrs N S Evans) *prom tl wknd over 2f out* **33/1**
300- **12** *25* **Dagola (IRE)**[14] 6643 5-9-1 48 .... AdrianTNicholls 7 —
(C A Dwyer) *hld up towards rr: hdwy over 5f out: rdn over 3f out: sn wknd: eased whn no ch fnl 2f* **20/1**

2m 2.82s (0.20) **Going Correction** -0.025s/f (Stan)
WFA 4 from 5yo+ 1lb **12** Ran SP% **120.2**
Speed ratings (Par 97):98,96,93,93,92 92,91,91,86,86 85,63
CSF £103.19 TOTE £9.40: £2.70, £2.30, £3.60; EX 129.00.
Owner Ian Williams **Bred** R Hollinshead **Trained** Portway, Worcs

FOCUS
Probably a fair race of its type and the front pair pulled well clear of the others. The form is above average for the grade and looks sound.
Insignia(IRE) Official explanation: jockey said gelding hung left
Orpen Quest(IRE) Official explanation: jockey said gelding hung left
Dagola(IRE) Official explanation: jockey said gelding lost its action

42 WOLVERHAMPTON-RACECOURSE.CO.UK BANDED STKS 1m 1f 103y(P)
3:20 (3:21) (Class 7) 4-Y-0+ **£1,365** (£403; £201) **Stalls** Low

Form RPR
0R6- **1** **Opera Knight**[21] 6575 6-8-12 45 .... TonyCulhane 7 51
(A W Carroll) *hld up and bhd: hdwy 3f out: rdn to ld 1f out: drvn out* **16/1**
341- **2** *½* **Regency Red (IRE)**[7] 6680 8-8-11 45 .... LiamJones(7) 12 56
(W M Brisbourne) *hld up in mid-div: hdwy over 3f out: rdn over 2f out: edgd lft ins fnl f: r.o* **4/1**[2]
006- **3** *nk* **Diamond Dan (IRE)**[6] 6684 4-8-11 45 .... PaulHanagan 11 49
(P D Evans) *hld up: rdn and hdwy 3f out: r.o ins fnl f* **13/2**[3]
0/5- **4** *2* **Schinken Otto (IRE)**[19] 1377 5-8-5 45 .... PaulPickard(7) 10 45
(J M Jefferson) *hld up and bhd: hdwy on outside over 2f out: swtchd lft and styd on towards fin* **25/1**
023- **5** *shd* **Naval Attache**[23] 6558 4-8-11 45 .... FergalLynch 13 45
(P A Blockley) *led: rdn and edgd lft whn hdd 1f out: one pce* **8/1**
3- **6** *hd* **Level Par (IRE)**[7] 6680 6-8-12 45 .... (t) MickyFenton 8 45
(J A Supple) *a.p: ev ch 2f out: rdn 1f out: wknd ins fnl f* **7/1**
125- **7** *½* **Tuscan Treaty**[16] 6611 6-8-5 45 .... (t) AndrewElliott(7) 3 44+
(P J McBride) *mid-div: lost pl over 4f out: nt clr run on ins wl over 2f out: hdwy on outside fnl f: r.o* **7/2**[1]
600- **8** *1* **Tintac**[14] 6651 5-8-12 45 .... PhillipMakin 6 42
(E J O'Neill) *hld up in tch: rdn over 3f out: no hdwy fnl 2f* **20/1**
400- **9** *½* **Pragmatica**[23] 6559 5-8-12 45 .... RobertWinston 9 41
(R M H Cowell) *nvr trbld ldrs* **12/1**
406- **10** *1 ¼* **Peace Emblem (IRE)**[7] 6680 5-8-12 45 .... (p) BrianReilly 1 38
(J W Unett) *hld up in tch: rdn over 3f out: sn wknd* **11/1**
005- **11** *9* **Mytton's Dream**[51] 6346 4-8-11 45 .... TomEaves 4 21
(R Brotherton) *a bhd* **33/1**
500- **12** *9* **Be Bop Aloha**[142] 4417 4-8-11 45 .... RobbieFitzpatrick 2 4
(John Berry) *prom: rdn over 3f out: wknd over 2f out* **20/1**
/00- **13** *13* **Topple**[16] 6620 5-8-12 45 .... (p) DarrenWilliams 5 —
(P W Hiatt) *prom tl rdn and wknd over 3f out: eased whn no ch over 1f out* **66/1**

2m 3.16s (0.54) **Going Correction** -0.025s/f (Stan)
WFA 4 from 5yo+ 1lb **13** Ran SP% **118.9**
Speed ratings (Par 97):96,95,95,93,93 93,92,91,91,90 82,74,62
CSF £73.98 TOTE £24.30: £4.70, £1.30, £1.90; EX 137.40.
Owner Frontrunner Syndicate **Bred** M Bin Hendi **Trained** Cropthorne, Worcs

FOCUS
An ordinary banded contest with the winning time 0.34 seconds slower than the preceding event. The form looks sound with those in the frame behind the winner closr to form.
Level Par(IRE) Official explanation: jockey said gelding had a breathing problem
Tuscan Treaty Official explanation: jockey said mare was denied a clear run
Topple Official explanation: jockey said mare had a breathing problem

43 PLAY NOW AT BETDIRECTPOKER.COM APPRENTICE BANDED STKS 1m 141y(P)
3:50 (3:51) (Class 7) 4-Y-0+ **£1,365** (£403; £201) **Stalls** Low

Form RPR
000- **1** **Legacy (JPN)**[44] 6399 6-8-9 47 .... JBrennan(5) 7 54
(P D Evans) *s.i.s: hld up and bhd: rdn and hdwy on outside over 1f out: r.o to ld last strides* **14/1**
561- **2** *hd* **New England**[7] 6679 4-9-8 50 .... LiamJones 10 63
(W M Brisbourne) *hld up: hdwy on outside whn forced wd over 2f out: rdn wl over 1f out: led cl home: hdd last strides* **13/8**[1]
003- **3** *1 ¾* **Harare**[7] 6675 5-9-0 50 .... JamesDoyle(3) 9 53
(R J Price) *hld up: rdn over 3f out: rdn and hdwy whn carried rt over 2f out: led ins fnl f: hdd and no ex cl home* **6/1**[3]
100- **4** *1 ½* **Spy Gun (USA)**[7] 6676 6-9-2 49 .... SladeO'Hara 1 49
(T Wall) *led: rdn and edgd lft over 1f out: hdd ins fnl f: one pce* **18/1**
020- **5** *½* **Wilford Maverick (IRE)**[44] 6398 4-8-8 45 .... StacyRenwick(3) 5 44
(M J Attwater) *t.k.h: hdwy 2f out: n.m.r on ins fnl f: one pce* **12/1**
235- **6** *nk* **Musiotal**[7] 6676 5-9-0 50 .... KevinGhunowa(3) 11 48
(P A Blockley) *hld up: hdwy over 3f out: rdn and swtchd rt over 2f out: one pce fnl f* **9/2**[2]
405- **7** *shd* **Ballyrush (IRE)**[17] 6609 6-8-7 45 .... StephanieBancroft(5) 2 43
(Miss D A McHale) *chsd ldr: rdn over 1f out: wknd ins fnl f* **33/1**
103- **8** *1 ¼* **Blushing Russian (IRE)**[7] 6676 4-9-1 49 .... AndrewElliott 6 44
(J M Bradley) *prom early: sn mid-div: hdwy and carried rt over 2f out: rdn and wknd over 1f out* **13/2**
000- **9** *nk* **Guadiana (GER)**[31] 6495 4-8-4 45 .... JackDean(7) 13 40
(A W Carroll) *hld up and bhd: hdwy on outside and swtchd lft jst over 1f out: no further prog* **28/1**
320- **10** *shd* **Indian Edge**[214] 2284 5-8-7 47 .... WilliamCarson(7) 12 44+
(B Palling) *s.i.s: hld up and bhd: rdn over 2f out: hdwy and swtchd lft over 1f out: nt clr run and hit rail ins fnl f:* **10/1**
044- **11** *¾* **Kumakawa**[8] 6674 8-8-8 46 .... LauraReynolds(5) 8 39
(D K Ivory) *a bhd* **28/1**
00- **12** *4* **Junebug Symphony (IRE)**[7] 6676 4-8-7 48 .... (p[1]) TJHowell(7) 4 33
(V Smith) *hld up: rdn over 3f out: sn struggling* **33/1**
0/0- **13** *8* **Elsinora**[205] 2554 5-8-11 47 .... (v) JamesMillman(3) 3 15
(A G Juckes) *chsd ldrs tl wknd over 2f out* **50/1**

1m 51.99s (0.23) **Going Correction** -0.025s/f (Stan)
WFA 4 from 5yo+ 1lb **13** Ran SP% **127.3**
Speed ratings (Par 97):97,96,95,93,93 93,93,92,91,91 91,87,80
CSF £38.03 TOTE £30.80: £6.20, £1.60, £2.40; EX 131.40 Place 6 £529.67, Place 5 £171.35.
Owner P D Evans **Bred** Darley Stud **Trained** Pandy, Abergavenny

FOCUS
An ordinary race, but the early pace was solid and suited those that came from behind. The third sets the standard.
Wilford Maverick(IRE) Official explanation: jockey said gelding was denied a clear run
T/Plt: £659.90 to a £1 stake. Pool: £37,652.65. 41.65 winning tickets. T/Qpdt: £31.20 to a £1 stake. Pool: £4,723.40. 111.80 winning tickets. KH

[38] WOLVERHAMPTON (A.W) (L-H)
Thursday, January 5

OFFICIAL GOING: Standard
Wind: Almost nil Weather: Overcast and cold

44 PLAY NOW AT BETDIRECTCASINO.COM CLAIMING STKS 7f 32y(P)
12:35 (12:35) (Class 5) 4-Y-0+ **£3,412** (£1,007; £504) **Stalls** High

Form RPR
012- **1** **Mystic Man (FR)**[10] 6664 8-9-5 80 .... NCallan 8 75
(K A Ryan) *hld up in tch: wnt 2nd 2f out: rdn to ld 1f out: edgd lft wl ins fnl f: r.o* **4/5**[1]
000- **2** *¾* **Doctor's Cave**[6] 6689 4-9-1 60 .... (b) ChrisCatlin 4 69
(K O Cunningham-Brown) *led: rdn and hdd 1f out: nt qckn* **50/1**
404- **3** *¾* **Lord Chamberlain**[20] 6593 13-9-1 61 .... (b) SteveDrowne 5 67
(J M Bradley) *s.i.s: hld up and bhd: rdn and hdwy over 2f out: hung lft 1f out: r.o wl towards fin* **14/1**
004- **4** *2* **Louphole**[6] 6689 4-9-1 72 .... FergusSweeney 9 62
(P J Makin) *dwlt: hld up: hdwy over 3f out: rdn wl over 1f out: one pce fnl f* **15/2**[3]
016- **5** *¾* **Norcroft**[37] 6465 4-9-4 71 .... (p) TonyCulhane 3 63
(Mrs C A Dunnett) *hld up: hdwy over 2f out: rdn wl over 1f out: one pce* **11/2**[2]
010- **6** *1* **Chickado (IRE)**[14] 6660 5-8-7 51 .... RobertHavlin 11 49
(D Haydn Jones) *prom: chsd ldr 4f out tl rdn 2f out: wknd fnl f* **40/1**
150- **7** *1 ½* **Speakerboxxx**[14] 6660 4-8-13 52 .... (b[1]) JoeFanning 12 51
(P F I Cole) *hld up in mid-div: hdwy over 4f out: rdn over 2f out: wknd over 1f out* **33/1**
000- **8** *2* **Riska King**[59] 6286 6-9-3 54 .... FergalLynch 7 50
(P A Blockley) *s.s: nvr nr ldrs* **33/1**
613- **9** *¾* **Hadath (IRE)**[6] 6689 9-8-12 60 .... EddieAhern 6 43
(B G Powell) *a bhd* **9/1**
000- **10** *½* **Craic Sa Ceili (IRE)**[14] 6654 6-9-0 50 .... (p) MickyFenton 2 44
(M S Saunders) *chsd ldrs tl pushed along and wknd over 3f out* **40/1**
100/ **11** *7* **Vandal**[370] 5001 6-8-12 70 .... RobbieFitzpatrick 10 24
(M Appleby) *chsd ldr 4f: sn rdn: wknd over 2f out* **66/1**
0/6- **12** *5* **Camp Commander (IRE)**[283] 765 7-9-5 83 .... RobertWinston 1 18
(C R Dore) *a in rr* **12/1**

1m 29.3s (-1.10) **Going Correction** -0.05s/f (Stan) **12** Ran SP% **121.3**
Speed ratings (Par 103):104,103,102,100,99 98,96,94,93,92 84,78
CSF £76.85 TOTE £1.70: £1.10, £11.60, £3.40; EX 84.20.
Owner R J H Limited **Bred** Gainsborough Stud Management Ltd **Trained** Hambleton, N Yorks

FOCUS
This ordinary claimer was run at a decent pace and turned out to be more competitive than expected. The form looks reasonable rated through the third.
Camp Commander(IRE) Official explanation: jockey said horse had a breathing problem

45 HOTEL & CONFERENCING AT DUNSTALL PARK MAIDEN STKS 5f 20y(P)
1:10 (1:10) (Class 5) 3-Y-0+ **£3,238** (£963; £481; £240) **Stalls** Low

Form RPR
033- **1** **Sands Crooner (IRE)**[10] 6662 3-8-8 67 .... (t) PatrickMathers(3) 7 61
(D Shaw) *chsd ldrs: rdn over 2f out: struck on hd by rival jockey's whip wl over 1f out: led wl ins fnl f: r.o* **3/1**[2]
002- **2** *1 ¼* **Canina**[10] 6661 3-8-6 65 .... EddieAhern 3 51
(Ms Deborah J Evans) *chsd ldrs: rdn over 2f out: ev ch wl ins fnl f: nt qckn* **11/4**[1]
36-2 **3** *nk* **Cookie Cutter (IRE)**[3] 14 4-9-7 57 .... (p) RobertWinston 5 56
(K R Burke) *led 1f: w. ldr: led wl over 1f out: sn rdn: hdd wl ins fnl f: nt qckn* **11/4**[1]
000- **4** *2 ½* **Holly Springs**[5] 6695 4-9-0 59 .... (b) KirstyMilczarek(7) 6 47
(Mrs C A Dunnett) *a.p: rdn wl over 1f out: no ex ins fnl f* **28/1**
52-0 **5** *½* **Comic Tales**[2] 29 5-9-12 40 .... JimmyQuinn 11 50
(M Mullineaux) *s.s: hrd rdn and hdwy wl over 1f out: r.o* **20/1**
6 *1 ½* **Royal Crescent (IRE)** 3-8-6 .... JamieMackay 10 39+
(Sir Mark Prescott) *s.i.s: rdn and hdwy over 1f out: nvr trbld ldrs* **20/1**
03- **7** *1 ¼* **Freshwinds**[9] 6672 4-9-12 .... DarrenWilliams 13 40
(S L Keightley) *led after 1f: rdn and hdd wl over 1f out: wknd ins fnl f* **66/1**
062- **8** *1 ¾* **Eeshee**[14] 6653 3-8-7 62 ow1 .... MickyFenton 2 24
(S L Keightley) *dwlt: rdn and hdwy on ins 3f out: wknd wl over 1f out* **13/2**[3]
0- **9** *nk* **Sir Mikeale**[18] 6605 3-8-11 .... J-PGuillambert 4 27
(G Prodromou) *s.i.s: a bhd* **40/1**
06-0 **10** *1 ½* **Gorgeous Boy (IRE)**[2] 24 4-9-12 45 .... BrianReilly 12 28
(P L Gilligan) *outpcd* **66/1**
006- **11** *½* **Raetihi**[24] 6554 5-9-7 35 .... DeanMcKeown 9 21
(P S Felgate) *chsd ldrs: lost pl over 3f out: sn bhd* **100/1**

62.68 secs (-0.14) **Going Correction** -0.05s/f (Stan)
WFA 3 from 4yo+ 15lb **11** Ran SP% **111.1**
Speed ratings (Par 103):99,97,96,92,91 89,87,84,84,81 80
CSF £10.10 TOTE £4.10: £1.40, £1.40, £1.90; EX 12.40.
Owner Danethorpe Racing Ltd **Bred** Peter Molony **Trained** Danethorpe, Notts

FOCUS
A poor maiden with the form held down by the fifth.
Comic Tales Official explanation: jockey said gelding missed the break
Eeshee Official explanation: jockey said filly missed the break

46 DINE AT DUNSTALL PARK (S) STKS 5f 216y(P)
1:45 (1:45) (Class 6) 4-Y-0+ **£2,388** (£705; £352) **Stalls** Low

Form RPR
33-2 **1** **Shadow Jumper (IRE)**[3] 9 5-8-11 55 .... (v) RobbieFitzpatrick 3 58
(M J Attwater) *a.p: rdn to ld jst over 1f out: r.o wl* **2/1**[1]
000- **2** *3* **Exit Smiling**[16] 6625 4-9-2 55 .... ChrisCatlin 10 54
(G C H Chung) *bhd: swtchd lft and hdwy over 1f out: r.o ins fnl f: nt trble wnr* **20/1**
001- **3** *hd* **Tiviski (IRE)**[20] 6589 4-8-11 59 .... JimmyQuinn 8 48
(E J Alston) *hld up in tch: rdn over 2f out: edgd lft ins fnl f: nt qckn* **8/1**[3]

006- **4** *hd* **Desert Opal**[20] 6589 6-9-2 65 TonyCulhane 9 53
(D W Chapman) *led early: prom: rdn and outpcd over 2f out: rallied ins fnl f* **8/1**[3]
060- **5** *½* **Party Princess (IRE)**[24] 6559 5-9-2 47 DeanMcKeown 5 51
(S Parr) *prom: nt clr run over 1f out: rdn and nt qckn ins fnl f* **33/1**
00-4 **6** *¾* **Malahide Express (IRE)**[1] 38 6-8-9 47 DonnaCaldwell(7) 2 49
(E J Alston) *s.i.s: hld up: hdwy over 1f out: swtchd rt ins fnl f: kpt on* **14/1**
60-4 **7** *½* **Weet Yer Tern (IRE)**[3] 14 4-8-11 50 FergalLynch 11 43
(P A Blockley) *prom: rdn over 2f out: wknd ins fnl f* **16/1**
360- **8** *1* **Red Sovereign**[20] 6589 5-9-2 55 PaulDoe 4 45
(D G Bridgwater) *sn led: rdn and hdd jst over 1f out: edgd lft and wknd ins fnl f* **10/1**
0/0- **9** *3 ½* **Weet N Measures**[10] 6664 4-8-11 54 J-PGuillambert 13 29
(T Wall) *bhd: short-lived effrt on outside over 2f out: wknd wl over 1f out* **66/1**
053- **10** *2* **Tapa**[37] 6455 4-8-11 62 (b) MartinDwyer 1 23
(A M Balding) *hmpd on ins after 1f: sn bhd* **3/1**[2]
6/0- **11** *20* **Why Harry**[38] 6447 4-9-2 57 JamieSpencer 7 —
(J J Quinn) *a bhd: rdn over 1f out: sn eased* **25/1**

1m 15.56s (-0.25) **Going Correction** -0.05s/f (Stan) 11 Ran SP% **115.2**
Speed ratings (Par 101):99,95,94,94,93 92,92,90,86,83 56
CSF £48.98 TOTE £3.10: £1.40, £6.90, £2.10; EX 58.70.There was no bid for the winner.
Owner Brooklands Racing **Bred** Newtown Stud **Trained** Wysall, Notts

FOCUS
A fair seller but anchored by the fifth and sixth.
Tapa Official explanation: jockey said filly suffered interference shortly after start

47 BETDIRECT FREEPHONE 0800 211 222 H'CAP (DIV I) 5f 216y(P)
2:15 (2:16) (Class 5) (0-70,69) 4-Y-0+ **£2,914** (£867; £433; £216) **Stalls** Low

Form RPR
123- **1** **Kensington (IRE)**[16] 6625 5-8-9 60 (p) RobertWinston 5 73
(P D Evans) *broke wl: sn stdd: rdn over 3f out: hdwy 2f out: r.o to ld nr fin* **11/4**[2]
031- **2** *hd* **Shade Cozy (USA)**[37] 6460 4-8-12 63 (t) MartinDwyer 6 75+
(A M Balding) *s.i.s: hdwy after 1f: wnt 2nd 2f out: rdn to ld 1f out: hdd nr fin* **15/8**[1]
30-3 **3** *1 ½* **Savile's Delight (IRE)**[4] 1 7-8-11 62 (b) TomEaves 11 70
(R Brotherton) *led: rdn and hdd 1f out: no ex towards fin* **20/1**
31-4 **4** *nk* **Kennington**[4] 4 6-9-4 69 (b) TonyCulhane 7 76
(Mrs C A Dunnett) *a.p: rdn over 2f out: r.o one pce fnl f* **8/1**
30-5 **5** *1 ½* **Cool Sands (IRE)**[4] 4 4-8-9 63 (v) PatrickMathers(3) 2 66
(D Shaw) *hld up: rdn and hdwy on ins wl over 1f out: one pce fnl f* **12/1**
600- **6** *1 ½* **Disguise**[78] 5986 4-9-2 67 JamieSpencer 1 65
(J J Quinn) *a.p: n.m.r 2f out: sn rdn: one pce fnl f* **9/2**[3]
056- **7** *hd* **Alexia Rose (IRE)**[19] 6597 4-8-13 64 FergalLynch 10 61
(A Berry) *hld up and bhd: hdwy on outside over 2f out: no further prog* **50/1**
40-6 **8** *hd* **Piccolo Prince**[4] 1 5-8-6 57 (p) JimmyQuinn 9 54
(E J Alston) *s.i.s: mid-div: rdn over 3f out: hdwy over 2f out: no imp fnl f* **20/1**
130- **9** *nk* **Greenwood**[70] 6126 8-8-13 64 (t) SteveDrowne 4 60
(P G Murphy) *hld up and bhd: bmpd and swtchd rt wl over 1f out: sn rdn: no rspnse* **16/1**
500- **10** *1 ½* **Sweet Namibia (IRE)**[155] 4064 4-8-12 63 EddieAhern 3 54
(J W Hills) *bhd fnl 3f* **33/1**
040- **11** *6* **Caustic Wit (IRE)**[14] 6657 8-9-4 69 (p) MickyFenton 8 42
(M S Saunders) *prom: n.m.r 2f out: sn rdn and wknd* **50/1**

1m 14.69s (-1.12) **Going Correction** -0.05s/f (Stan) 11 Ran SP% **120.7**
Speed ratings (Par 103):105,104,102,102,100 98,98,97,97,95 87
CSF £8.03 CT £86.89 TOTE £4.00: £1.80, £1.10, £5.60; EX 8.90.
Owner Derek Buckley **Bred** Mountarmstrong Stud **Trained** Pandy, Abergavenny

FOCUS
This was 0.33 seconds faster than the other division and the proximity of the third and fourth give the form a sound look.
Disguise Official explanation: jockey said gelding hung left-handed home straight

48 WOLVERHAMPTON-RACECOURSE.CO.UK CLAIMING STKS 1m 4f 50y(P)
2:50 (2:50) (Class 6) 4-Y-0+ **£2,730** (£806; £403) **Stalls** Low

Form RPR
202- **1** **Desperation (IRE)**[26] 6536 4-9-3 70 RobertWinston 9 74
(K R Burke) *hld up: hdwy 5f out: rdn over 2f out: led ins fnl f: r.o* **6/1**
522- **2** *hd* **Danelor (IRE)**[16] 6633 8-9-5 77 (p) PaulHanagan 7 71
(R A Fahey) *led after 1f: rdn 3f out: hdd ins fnl f: r.o* **3/1**[1]
302- **3** *1 ¼* **Mad Carew (USA)**[9] 6669 7-9-13 74 (e) MartinDwyer 4 77
(J R Boyle) *hld up in mid-div: rdn and hdwy over 2f out: hung lft over 1f out: swtchd rt ins fnl f: r.o* **7/2**[2]
430- **4** *2* **Eton (GER)**[112] 5244 10-8-9 54 AdrianTNicholls 12 56
(D Nicholls) *led 1f: chsd ldr: rdn over 3f out: no ex ins fnl f* **33/1**
060- **5** *¾* **Reminiscent (IRE)**[27] 6448 7-8-13 53 (v) TonyCulhane 8 59
(B P J Baugh) *s.v.s: hld up in rr: rdn and hdwy over 1f out: nrst fin* **33/1**
000- **6** *1* **Cherished Number**[54] 6337 7-8-11 66 (b) TomEaves 5 55
(I Semple) *hld up and bhd: rdn and hdwy 2f out: edgd lft over 1f out: no imp fnl f* **16/1**
214- **7** *¾* **Trance (IRE)**[21] 6582 6-9-13 76 PhillipMakin 2 73+
(T D Barron) *hld up and bhd: rdn over 3f out: nt clr run over 2f out and over 1f out: nvr nrr* **9/2**[3]
506- **8** *½* **Karrnak**[7] 6682 4-8-3 60 (t) ChrisCatlin 3 49?
(Miss J Feilden) *prom: rdn and lost pl over 3f out: n.d after* **100/1**
633- **9** *½* **Weet A Head (IRE)**[26] 6536 5-9-7 62 (p) GrahamGibbons 1 62
(R Hollinshead) *hld up and bhd: rdn over 3f out: hdwy over 1f out: no further prog fnl f* **16/1**
202- **10** *3* **Missie Baileys**[40] 6434 4-8-12 56 LPKeniry 11 53
(Mrs L J Mongan) *prom tl rdn and wknd over 2f out* **33/1**
144- **11** *8* **Typhoon Tilly**[40] 6434 9-9-1 66 SteveDrowne 10 39
(C R Egerton) *hld up in tch: rdn and wknd over 2f out* **8/1**
034- **12** *6* **Lucefer (IRE)**[52] 6344 8-8-2 40 DeanWilliams(7) 6 23
(G C H Chung) *a bhd* **33/1**

2m 40.05s (-2.37) **Going Correction** -0.05s/f (Stan)
WFA 4 from 5yo+ 4lb 12 Ran SP% **120.2**
Speed ratings (Par 101):105,104,104,102,102 101,101,100,100,98 93,89
CSF £23.90 TOTE £3.90: £2.20, £1.60, £1.30; EX 31.10.The winner was the subject of a friendly claim.
Owner J C S Wilson **Bred** Bernard Colclough **Trained** Middleham Moor, N Yorks

FOCUS
An ordinary claimer run at a modest pace. The third and fifth are the best guides to the form, which seems sound enough.
Reminiscent(IRE) Official explanation: jockey said gelding would not jump out of stalls

49 BETDIRECT.CO.UK H'CAP 1m 1f 103y(P)
3:25 (3:26) (Class 6) (0-58,60) 3-Y-0 **£2,388** (£705; £352) **Stalls** Low

Form RPR
001- **1** **Reveur**[10] 6663 3-9-2 60 6ex JamieSpencer 7 62
(M Mullineaux) *hld up and bhd: hdwy over 2f out: rdn wl over 1f out: led jst ins fnl f: hung rt cl home: r.o* **10/3**[2]
052- **2** *½* **Wee Charlie Castle (IRE)**[5] 6697 3-8-13 57 ChrisCatlin 4 58
(G C H Chung) *hld up in mid-div: hdwy 3f out: rdn and wnt 2nd 2f out: ev ch 1f out: carried rt cl home: r.o* **7/2**[3]
650- **3** *nk* **King's Fable (USA)**[40] 6425 3-9-0 58 JoeFanning 13 58
(M Johnston) *led: rdn and hung rt over 2f out: hdd jst ins fnl f: carried rt cl home: kpt on* **13/2**
430- **4** *2* **Youralittlemiller**[147] 4301 3-8-12 56 RobertWinston 3 53
(P G Murphy) *a.p: rdn 4f out: one pce fnl f* **10/1**
000- **5** *nk* **Crocodile Star (USA)**[134] 4670 3-8-13 57 EddieAhern 11 53
(J A Osborne) *hld up and bhd: hdwy 2f out: nt rch ldrs* **14/1**
000- **6** *¾* **Katie Lawson (IRE)**[14] 6659 3-8-12 56 (v[1]) RobertHavlin 12 51
(D Haydn Jones) *chsd ldr: rdn over 3f out: hung lft and lost 2nd 2f out: wknd ins fnl f* **50/1**
200- **7** *½* **Royal Embrace**[9] 6673 3-8-10 57 (v[1]) PatrickMathers(3) 8 51
(D Shaw) *hld up in rr: rdn over 3f out: nvr trbld ldrs* **25/1**
404- **8** *2* **Chookie Windsor**[26] 6543 3-9-0 58 TomEaves 2 48
(I Semple) *prom: rdn over 3f out: wknd 2f out* **11/4**[1]
606- **9** *5* **Seattle Spy (USA)**[17] 6610 3-8-13 57 (b[1]) PatCosgrave 10 37
(G A Huffer) *prom: rdn over 3f out: sn wknd* **14/1**
050- **10** *5* **Unasuming (IRE)**[40] 6428 3-8-13 57 JimmyQuinn 5 28
(J Pearce) *prom tl n.m.r and lost pl bnd 7f out: hrd rdn 4f out: sn bhd* **14/1**

2m 3.91s (1.29) **Going Correction** -0.05s/f (Stan) 10 Ran SP% **120.2**
Speed ratings (Par 95):92,91,91,89,89 88,88,86,81,77
CSF £16.04 CT £73.62 TOTE £3.80: £1.70, £2.30, £2.30; EX 9.20.
Owner A Jones **Bred** Bishopswood Bloodstock And Trickledown Stud **Trained** Alpraham, Cheshire
■ Stewards' Enquiry : Jamie Spencer one-day ban: careless riding (Jan 16)

FOCUS
A moderate handicap and the slow pace was reflected in the time. The runner-up and seventh help set the standard for the form.

50 WIN £2M @ CLASSICVALUEPOOLS.COM APPRENTICE H'CAP 1m 141y(P)
4:00 (4:00) (Class 5) (0-75,76) 4-Y-0+ **£3,238** (£963; £481; £240) **Stalls** Low

Form RPR
021- **1** **Deeper In Debt**[17] 6622 8-9-4 75 RoryMoore 7 83
(J Akehurst) *a.p: rdn over 2f out: led 1f out: r.o* **6/1**[3]
066- **2** *1* **Midshipman**[24] 6564 8-8-1 65 (vt) WilliamCarson(7) 8 70
(A W Carroll) *hld up and bhd: hdwy over 1f out: sn hung lft: r.o ins fnl f: nt rch wnr* **9/1**
512- **3** *½* **Blue Patrick**[9] 6671 6-8-13 70 AndrewMullen 2 74
(K A Ryan) *hld up in mid-div: rdn and hdwy over 2f out: r.o ins fnl f* **13/8**[1]
230- **4** *hd* **Hurricane Coast**[5] 6698 7-8-12 74 (b) JamesDoyle(5) 1 78
(K McAuliffe) *led: rdn over 2f out: hdd 1f out: no ex towards fin* **9/1**
045- **5** *½* **Scottish River (USA)**[19] 6598 7-8-8 70 KMay(5) 6 73
(M D I Usher) *s.s: hld up: hdwy 4f out: rdn and sltly outpcd over 2f out: edgd lft 1f out: one pce* **9/1**
063- **6** *½* **Scotty's Future (IRE)**[112] 5239 8-8-4 66 VictoriaBehan(5) 5 68
(D Nicholls) *hld up in mid-div: rdn and hdwy over 1f out: styng on whn nt clr run on ins towards fin* **16/1**
332- **7** *1* **Daring Affair**[10] 6666 5-8-5 65 AndrewElliott(3) 9 65
(K R Burke) *prom tl rdn and wknd over 2f out* **11/2**[2]
340- **8** *1 ½* **High Arctic**[33] 6488 4-8-5 68 MichaelJStainton(5) 3 65
(A Bailey) *s.i.s: hdwy 7f out: rdn and outpcd 2f out: wknd 1f out* **25/1**
342- **9** *½* **Monash Lad (IRE)**[76] 6008 4-8-1 66 PatrickHills(7) 12 62
(M H Tompkins) *dwlt: racd wd: t.k.h: hdwy 6f out: lost pl over 3f out* **14/1**
0/0- **10** *nk* **Flying Pass**[365] 38 4-8-6 67 LiamJones(3) 10 62
(D J S Ffrench Davis) *hld up in tch: lost pl over 3f out: sn bhd* **50/1**
250/ **11** *1 ½* **Honest Injun**[135] 6858 5-8-10 72 JamesMillman(5) 11 64
(A G Juckes) *plld hrd early: a bhd* **50/1**

1m 51.24s (-0.52) **Going Correction** -0.05s/f (Stan)
WFA 4 from 5yo+ 1lb 11 Ran SP% **118.1**
Speed ratings (Par 103):100,99,98,98,98 97,96,95,94,94 93
CSF £58.44 CT £129.65 TOTE £8.40: £2.30, £1.90, £1.50; EX 72.60.
Owner Tipp-Ex Rapid Racing II **Bred** P And Mrs Venner **Trained** Epsom, Surrey

FOCUS
A modest handicap run at an ordinary pace and therefore may not be that reliable.

51 BETDIRECT FREEPHONE 0800 211 222 H'CAP (DIV II) 5f 216y(P)
4:30 (4:30) (Class 5) (0-70,69) 4-Y-0+ **£2,914** (£867; £433; £216) **Stalls** Low

Form RPR
042- **1** **Joyeaux**[19] 6597 4-8-13 64 EddieAhern 7 71
(S L Keightley) *a.p: rdn and swtchd rt over 1f out: r.o to ld cl home* **4/1**[1]
35-5 **2** *½* **Blue Knight (IRE)**[4] 1 7-8-12 63 (v) AdrianTNicholls 9 69
(D Nicholls) *hld up: hdwy over 2f out: rdn to ld jst over 1f out: hdd cl home* **10/1**
623- **3** *1 ½* **Wainwright (IRE)**[16] 6638 6-9-1 66 FergalLynch 8 67
(P A Blockley) *s.i.s: hld up and bhd: rdn over 1f out: hdwy fnl f: r.o* **4/1**[1]
400- **4** *shd* **Hits Only Cash**[37] 6465 4-9-4 69 DeanMcKeown 2 72+
(J Pearce) *hld up and bhd: hdwy fnl f: r.o* **6/1**[2]
60-0 **5** *nk* **Dash Of Lime**[4] 1 4-8-12 63 JimmyQuinn 1 63
(J Akehurst) *a.p: rdn and swtchd rt over 1f out: kpt on ins fnl f* **8/1**[3]
650- **6** *¾* **Ashes (IRE)**[16] 6636 4-8-12 63 RobertWinston 10 61
(K R Burke) *plld hrd: sn bhd: hdwy over 2f out: sn rdn: one pce fnl f* **25/1**
0/0- **7** *hd* **Bahamian Breeze**[41] 6422 5-8-12 63 LPKeniry 6 60
(D M Simcock) *s.i.s: hld up and bhd: c wd st: rdn over 1f out: nvr trbld ldrs* **25/1**
25-4 **8** *¾* **Gone'N'Dunnett (IRE)**[4] 1 7-8-10 68 (v) KirstyMilczarek(7) 5 63
(Mrs C A Dunnett) *led: rdn and edgd lft whn hdd jst over 1f out: wknd wl ins fnl f* **9/1**
060- **9** *¾* **Revien (IRE)**[5] 6695 4-8-8 59 (b[1]) ChrisCatlin 3 52
(Miss J R Tooth) *s.i.s: t.k.h in mid-div: rdn over 2f out: sn bhd* **40/1**
002- **10** *1* **Majestical (IRE)**[38] 6447 4-8-9 60 (p) SteveDrowne 4 50
(J M Bradley) *t.k.h: w ldrs: ev ch wl over 1f out: sn hmpd on ins: swtchd rt ent fnl f: wknd* **4/1**[1]

1m 15.02s (-0.79) **Going Correction** -0.05s/f (Stan) 10 Ran SP% **114.6**
Speed ratings (Par 103):103,102,100,100,99 98,98,97,96,95
CSF £43.68 CT £152.68 TOTE £5.50: £1.20, £3.70, £1.60; EX 29.50 Place 6 £9.20, Place 5 £5.63 .

Owner Mrs C C Regalado-Gonzalez **Bred** Mrs Ann Jarvis **Trained** Waltham-On-The-Wolds, Leics
FOCUS
This open-looking handicap was a third of a second slower than the first division.
Wainwright(IRE) Official explanation: jockey said, regarding the running and riding, his orders were to get a good break, get a position and make his effort in the home straight, adding that gelding anticipated the start and therefore broke more slowly than expected; he was also held up in his run entering the home straight and thereafter gelding could only stay on at one pace under hard riding
T/Plt: £5.60 to a £1 stake. Pool: £38,762.70. 5,013.80 winning tickets. T/Qpdt: £3.80 to a £1 stake. Pool: £3,319.70. 638.40 winning tickets. KH

[44]WOLVERHAMPTON (A.W) (L-H)
Friday, January 6

OFFICIAL GOING: Standard
Wind: Almost nil Weather: Overcast with some drizzle

52 SUPPORT RETRAINING OF RACEHORSES AMATEUR RIDERS' H'CAP (DIV I) 2m 119y(P)
1:00 (1:00) (Class 6) (0-60,60) 4-Y-0+ **£1,977** (£608; £304) **Stalls** Low

Form RPR
510- **1** **Cumbrian Knight (IRE)**[5] [6534] 8-11-2 **60**............ MissNJefferson(5) 10 67
(J M Jefferson) *t.k.h in tch: wnt 2nd after 5f: led over 1f out: pushed out* **4/1**[3]
34-3 **2** ¾ **Countback (FR)**[2] [40] 7-10-7 **51** ow1......................... MrMJJSmith(5) 1 57
(A W Carroll) *hld up and bhd: hdwy 4f out: wnt 2nd ins fnl f: rdn and nt qckn* **7/2**[2]
004- **3** ½ **Olivino (GER)**[17] [6626] 5-10-11 **55**.............................. MrDHutchison(5) 8 60
(S Dow) *a.p: rdn and edgd lft ins fnl f: nt qckn* **15/2**
441- **4** ¾ **Mister Completely (IRE)**[18] [6614] 5-10-2 **46**............. KylieManser(5) 11 50
(J R Best) *hld up in mid-div: hdwy over 1f out: styd on ins fnl f* **16/1**
030- **5** ½ **Makarim (IRE)**[18] [6612] 10-10-7 **46** oh1.........................(p) MrsSBosley 12 50
(M R Bosley) *hld up and bhd: stdy hdwy over 8f out: rdn wl over 1f out: one pce fnl f* **12/1**
240- **6** *shd* **Activist**[34] [6490] 8-11-5 **58**..(p) KellyHarrison 3 61
(D Carroll) *a.p: rdn over 1f out: one pce* **10/1**
423- **7** ½ **Bank On Benny**[17] [6637] 4-10-7 **58**........................... MrMD'Arcy(5) 7 61
(P W D'Arcy) *stmbld sn after s: hld up in rr: rdn and hdwy on ins over 1f out: nt rch ldrs* **11/4**[1]
/50- **8** 3 ½ **Smoothie (IRE)**[6] [6701] 8-10-11 **57**............................(p) MrJRavenall(7) 9 56
(Ian Williams) *led: rdn and hdd over 1f out: wknd ins fnl f* **16/1**
2/0- **9** ½ **Great As Gold (IRE)**[11] [6406] 7-11-7 **60**........................(p) MrSDobson 6 58
(B Ellison) *hld up and bhd: reminder 9f out: hdwy 7f out: rdn and lost pl 5f out: n.d after* **16/1**
/00- **10** 25 **Ressource (FR)**[230] [255] 7-10-2 **46** oh11..................(b) MrWRussell(5) 4 14
(G L Moore) *bhd fnl 7f: t.o* **40/1**
200- **11** *dist* **Vrubel (IRE)**[129] [4850] 7-10-0 **46** oh6........................ MissJessicaHolt(7) 2 —
(J R Holt) *chsd ldr over 4f: wknd over 8f out: t.o* **66/1**

3m 46.39s (3.26) **Going Correction** -0.025s/f (Stan)
WFA 4 from 5yo+ 7lb 11 Ran SP% **119.0**
Speed ratings (Par 101):91,90,90,90,89 89,89,87,87,75 —
CSF £18.66 CT £102.63 TOTE £5.90: £2.20, £1.50, £2.40; EX 24.80.
Owner J M Jefferson **Bred** John P A Kenny **Trained** Norton, N Yorks
■ Stewards' Enquiry : Mr M D'Arcy seven-day ban: in breach of Rule 156 - rode an ill-judged race (Jan 20-21, Feb 2-3,7,20, Mar 6)
FOCUS
A moderate event, confined to amateur riders, which was run at a modest early pace and saw the first seven fairly closely covered at the finish.

53 PARADE RESTAURANT CLAIMING STKS 5f 216y(P)
1:30 (1:32) (Class 6) 3-Y-0 **£2,730** (£806; £403) **Stalls** Low

Form RPR
00- **1** **Charley's Aunt (IRE)**[41] [6433] 3-8-3 .... RichardThomas(3) 5 64+
(N P Littmoden) *led early: prom: led over 1f out: sn edgd lft: r.o wl* **14/1**
034- **2** 2 ½ **Countrywide Belle**[18] [6617] 3-8-9 59 ow2..............................(b) NCallan 3 59
(K A Ryan) *sn led: rdn and hdd over 1f out: one pce* **11/2**[3]
02-4 **3** 1 ¼ **Buzzin'Boyzee (IRE)**[4] [10] 3-8-4 59.................................. PaulHanagan 9 50
(P D Evans) *rdn and hdwy on outside over 2f out: no ex fnl f* **6/1**
500- **4** *nk* **Dream Factor (IRE)**[11] [6663] 3-8-3 60....................... PatrickMathers(3) 8 51
(J O'Reilly) *rdn and hdwy whn hung lft fr over 1f out: nt rch ldrs* **25/1**
05-4 **5** 1 **Twilight Avenger (IRE)**[2] [30] 3-8-9 50..................(p) DeanMcKeown 2 51
(M J Polglase) *a.p: rdn over 2f out: one pce* **12/1**
053- **6** ¾ **Parazone**[18] [6610] 3-8-10 60... EddieAhern 6 50
(E J O'Neill) *prom: lost pl after 2f: sme late prog* **11/4**[2]
602- **7** ¾ **Sounds Simla (IRE)**[130] [4835] 3-8-9 82.................................. ChrisCatlin 7 47
(Rae Guest) *broke wl: settled in tch: rdn over 2f out: sn btn* **9/4**[1]
000- **8** 1 ½ **Midge's Girl (IRE)**[90] [5737] 3-8-1 51..................................... PaulFessey 12 34
(Mrs A Duffield) *hdwy 4f out: rdn over 2f out: wknd wl over 1f out* **50/1**
046- **9** 1 ¼ **Bermuda Beauty (IRE)**[20] [6600] 3-8-6 55 ow1............ RobertWinston 1 41+
(J M Bradley) *sn bhd* **25/1**
100- **10** 7 **Lucys Lady**[51] [6366] 3-8-4 52... JoeFanning 4 12
(K R Burke) *prom: rdn over 3f out: wkng whn hmpd wl over 2f out* **20/1**
630- **R** **Follow Me In (IRE)**[10] [6670] 3-8-0 .... FranciscoDaSilva 11 —
(K R Burke) *ref to r: tk no part* **50/1**

1m 15.4s (-0.41) **Going Correction** -0.025s/f (Stan) 11 Ran SP% **117.8**
Speed ratings (Par 95):101,97,96,95,94 93,92,90,88,79 —
CSF £84.26 TOTE £23.20: £5.60, £1.90, £2.10; EX 96.20.The winner was claimed by Mr M. Khan for £9,000.
Owner Miss Vanessa Church **Bred** James And Joe Brannigan **Trained** Newmarket, Suffolk
■ Stewards' Enquiry : Richard Thomas one-day ban: careless riding (Jan 17)
FOCUS
A modest event, but run at a decent pace. The form has been rated through the second and fifth.
Dream Factor(IRE) Official explanation: jockey said filly hung badly left
Bermuda Beauty(IRE) Official explanation: jockey said filly suffered interference in running

54 TEXT "BETDIRECT" TO 88600 H'CAP 5f 216y(P)
2:00 (2:07) (Class 2) (0-100,96) 4-Y-0+ **£11,658** (£3,468; £1,733; £865) **Stalls** Low

Form RPR
401- **1** **Les Arcs (USA)**[20] [6602] 6-9-0 **96**.............................. JamesO'Reilly(7) 2 108
(T J Pitt) *chsd ldrs: rdn and edgd lft over 1f out: led ent fnl f: drvn out* **10/3**[2]
102- **2** 1 ¼ **Kostar**[35] [6481] 5-9-0 **92**... AdamKirby(3) 4 100
(C G Cox) *s.i.s: hdwy over 3f out: rdn over 1f out: r.o ins fnl f: nt rch wnr* **3/1**[1]
036- **3** *nk* **Katiypour (IRE)**[20] [6602] 9-8-8 **86**............................ RichardThomas(3) 9 93
(Miss B Sanders) *bhd: hdwy over 1f out: r.o ins fnl f* **16/1**
062- **4** *shd* **Prince Tum Tum (USA)**[21] [6590] 6-8-10 **85**..................... EddieAhern 10 92
(D W Barker) *outpcd: hdwy on ins over 2f out: rdn wl over 1f out: r.o ins fnl f* **7/2**[3]
10-3 **5** ½ **Trinculo (IRE)**[5] [6] 9-8-8 **83**.. AdrianTNicholls 1 88
(D Nicholls) *led: rdn over 1f out: hdd ent fnl f: one pce* **14/1**
303- **6** ¾ **Cornus**[20] [6602] 4-8-9 **84**.. DeanMcKeown 7 87
(M J Polglase) *chsd ldr: rdn wl over 1f out: wknd ins fnl f* **25/1**
003- **7** ½ **Bahiano (IRE)**[41] [6431] 5-9-1 **90**.. MartinDwyer 13 91
(C E Brittain) *bhd tl late hdwy on outside: nvr nrr* **16/1**
210- **8** *nk* **Middleton Grey**[35] [6481] 8-9-0 **89**............................(b) FergusSweeney 12 90
(A G Newcombe) *outpcd: hdwy fnl f: n.d* **40/1**
200- **9** 2 **Russian Symphony (USA)**[20] [6602] 5-9-0 **89**.............(b) SteveDrowne 5 84
(C R Egerton) *chsd ldrs: rdn over 2f out: wknd wl over 1f out* **8/1**
050- **10** *shd* **Lake Andre (IRE)**[35] [6481] 5-8-13 **93**........................ AndrewMullen(5) 6 87
(K A Ryan) *hld up in tch: rdn and wknd over 2f out* **25/1**
402- **11** 3 **Legal Set (IRE)**[8] [6686] 10-8-0 **82** oh37........................(bt) AnnStokell(7) 3 67
(Miss A Stokell) *bhd fnl 2f* **100/1**
150- **12** 1 ½ **Chateau Nicol**[20] [6602] 7-8-12 **87**..(v) JoeFanning 11 68
(B G Powell) *mid-div: hdwy over 2f out: rdn and wknd over 1f out* **33/1**
02-0 **13** 1 ¾ **Quiet Times (IRE)**[5] [6] 7-8-12 **87**......................................(p) NCallan 8 63
(K A Ryan) *sn rdn along and bhd: eased whn no ch fnl f* **33/1**

1m 13.76s (-2.05) **Going Correction** -0.025s/f (Stan) 13 Ran SP% **116.8**
Speed ratings (Par 109):112,110,109,109,109 108,107,107,104,104 100,98,95
CSF £12.43 CT £142.95 TOTE £3.30: £1.40, £1.60, £5.00; EX 14.30 Trifecta £155.00 Pool: £676.82 - 3.10 winning units..
Owner Willie McKay **Bred** Elk Manor Farm **Trained** Bawtry, S Yorks
■ Stewards' Enquiry : James O'Reilly four-day ban: used whip in the wrong place on the flank (Jan 17-20)
FOCUS
A decent event for the class. The winner is progressive and the form looks sound.
NOTEBOOK
Les Arcs(USA), raised 6lb for resuming winning ways at Lingfield last time, advertised his current rude health and followed up with a decisive success under top weight. He has clearly been improved for a recent change of trainer, plus for being dropped to this trip, and despite the fact he will go up again in the ratings for this, probably has more to offer at sprint trips. (op 7-2)
Kostar ◆ ran on well in the final furlong only to find the winner gone beyond recall. Things may well have been different had he broken on terms, however, and he does look capable of scoring from this mark when things go his way. (op 11-4 tchd 9-4)
Katiypour(IRE) was doing his best work at the finish and posted a much more encouraging effort. He can build on this and is weighted to win at present. (op 14-1)
Prince Tum Tum(USA) ◆ was always up against it from his wide draw and was not at all disgraced in the circumstances. He is another who is weighted to score at present and will be of real interest when getting a low draw over this course and distance. (tchd 4-1)
Trinculo(IRE) showed decent early dash and turned in another solid effort. He can find easier opportunities.
Bahiano(IRE) should be rated better than the bare form, as he was forced to race wide from his draw, and he is one to bear in mind on this surface granted a lower berth in the future. (op 20-1)
Russian Symphony(USA), while showing improvement on his latest effort, is just struggling for form at present. (op 9-1)
Legal Set(IRE) Official explanation: jockey said gelding hung right

55 SUPPORT RETRAINING OF RACEHORSES AMATEUR RIDERS' H'CAP (DIV II) 2m 119y(P)
2:30 (2:31) (Class 6) (0-60,60) 4-Y-0+ **£1,977** (£608; £304) **Stalls** Low

Form RPR
504- **1** **Red Sun**[120] [5081] 9-10-13 **59**...........................(t) MrStephenHarrison(7) 12 66
(J Mackie) *a.p: wnt 2nd after 5f: led over 5f out: rdn over 1f out: styd on wl* **10/1**
110- **2** 1 ¾ **Tycheros**[25] [6563] 4-10-5 **51**.. MrSWalker 1 56
(S C Williams) *t.k.h: led: hdd over 5f out: chsd wnr: rdn 2f out: styd on same pce fnl f* **11/10**[1]
004- **3** 1 **Lady Misha**[28] [6534] 4-10-5 **58**....................................... MissJWaring(7) 2 62
(Jedd O'Keeffe) *prom: outpcd 3f out: rallied over 1f out: styd on ins fnl f* **10/1**
000- **4** *nk* **Spectested (IRE)**[10] [6195] 5-10-8 **52**..........................(p) MrMJJSmith(5) 9 56
(A W Carroll) *s.s: bhd: hdwy on ins wl over 1f out: edgd rt ins fnl f: styd on* **8/1**[3]
105- **5** *hd* **Bobby Kennard**[80] [5959] 7-10-12 **58**............................ MissAGarner(7) 4 61
(J A Osborne) *hld up: hdwy over 1f out: bmpd ins fnl f: styd on* **5/1**[2]
006- **6** 5 **Chocolate Boy (IRE)**[54] [5837] 7-10-13 57.........(be) MrDHutchison(5) 11 54
(G L Moore) *hld up: hdwy over 2f out: wknd 1f out* **8/1**[3]
/00- **7** 5 **Margarets Wish**[16] [2549] 6-10-1 **47** oh16 ow1............... LeeEdwards(7) 6 38
(T Wall) *nvr nr ldrs* **33/1**
000- **8** *hd* **Team-Mate (IRE)**[18] [6620] 8-11-2 **60**..................(t) MrMatthewSmith(5) 10 51
(Miss J Feilden) *hld up: hdwy over 5f out: rdn over 3f out: wknd over 1f out* **50/1**
000- **9** 4 **Alexander Sapphire (IRE)**[31] [6280] 5-10-5 **51**...(tp) MrsFleurHawes(7) 5 37
(N B King) *chsd ldr 5f: lost pl over 9f out: bhd fnl 6f* **33/1**
300- **10** 4 **Late Arrival**[111] [5298] 9-10-7 **53** oh11 ow7...........(b) MrTWThompson(7) 7 35
(Micky Hammond) *a in rr* **25/1**
/50- **11** 2 ½ **Radiant Bride**[209] [2480] 6-10-4 **46** oh1..................... MissFayeBramley(3) 3 25
(P A Blockley) *hld up in mid-div: rdn over 4f out: sn struggling* **33/1**
04/ **12** 1 **Sullivan's Cascade (IRE)**[6] [5204] 8-10-0 **46** oh16...... MissIPickard(7) 8 23
(E G Bevan) *bhd fnl 3f* **66/1**

3m 48.82s (5.69) **Going Correction** -0.025s/f (Stan)
WFA 4 from 5yo+ 7lb 12 Ran SP% **120.8**
Speed ratings (Par 101):85,84,83,83,83 81,78,78,76,74 73,73
CSF £20.88 CT £124.64 TOTE £17.70: £4.90, £1.10, £3.30; EX 32.40.
Owner Bulls Head Racing Club **Bred** Paul L Coe **Trained** Church Broughton , Derbys
■ Steve Harrison's first winner.
■ Stewards' Enquiry : Mr M J J Smith one-day ban: careless riding (Jan 20)
FOCUS
The first two were prominent throughout here, but there is little suggestion they were flattered, with the winner well in on last year's form and the runner-up unexposed at the trip.
Late Arrival Official explanation: jockey said, regarding running and riding, his orders were to hold gelding up and come late, adding that having dropped gelding in, he made an effort on final bend, but gelding didn't respond and felt lame on pulling up; vet said gelding was lame

56 DAILY OFFERS FROM BETDIRECT (S) STKS 1m 141y(P)
3:00 (3:02) (Class 6) 4-Y-0+ **£2,388** (£705; £352) **Stalls** Low

Form RPR
430- **1** **Risk Free**[60] [6287] 9-8-7 53...(bt) JBrennan(7) 11 59
(P D Evans) *hld up and bhd: hdwy on outside over 2f out: c wd st: rdn to ld ins fnl f: r.o* **14/1**

205- **2** *hd* **Seattle Robber**[21] 6594 4-8-13 62....................(v) FergalLynch 8 59
(P A Blockley) *hld up and bhd: rdn over 3f out: hdwy over 2f out: rdn and hung lft ins fnl f: r.o* **4/1**[1]

143- **3** *¾* **Sarraaf (IRE)**[21] 6594 10-9-5 60.................... TomEaves 6 62
(I Semple) *hld up: hdwy on ins over 2f out: rdn and ev ch ins fnl f: r.o* **9/2**[2]

004- **4** *hd* **Look At The Stars (IRE)**[28] 6387 4-8-13 50.........(b) GrahamGibbons 13 57
(R Hollinshead) *hld up and bhd: rdn over 5f out: hdwy over 2f out: ev ch ins fnl f: r.o* **25/1**

00-2 **5** *¾* **Colonel Bilko (IRE)**[4] 11 4-8-13 49.................... ChrisCatlin 1 55
(Miss S J Wilton) *led early: prom: lost pl over 4f out: rallied on ins to ld wl over 1f out: hdd ins fnl f: nt qckn* **14/1**

043- **6** *¾* **Distant Country (USA)**[15] 6658 7-9-0 58....................(b) LPKeniry 3 53
(R A Harris) *hld up: hdwy wl over 1f out: sn swtchd lft: ev ch ins fnl f: no ex towards fin* **6/1**

000- **7** *6* **Shrine Mountain (USA)**[11] 6664 4-8-13 62.................... BrianReilly 5 41
(J R Holt) *prom: rdn and lost pl on ins over 3f out: nt clr run over 2f out: n.d after* **50/1**

405- **8** *1* **Wiltshire (IRE)**[41] 6436 4-8-6 55....................(v) KevinGhunowa(7) 4 39
(P A Blockley) *hld up: rdn and hdwy over 2f out: ev ch wl over 1f out: wknd ent fnl f* **12/1**

360- **9** *nk* **Haenertsburg (IRE)**[9] 6675 4-8-8 45....................(p) PaulEddery 12 33
(A L Forbes) *a bhd* **100/1**

/00- **10** *12* **Familiar Affair**[337] 262 5-9-0 66.................... NCallan 2 13+
(T D Barron) *sn led: rdn over 2f out: hdd wl over 1f out: sn wknd* **5/1**[3]

610- **11** *2* **Aswan (IRE)**[27] 6535 8-9-2 64....................(t) AmirQuinn(3) 10 14+
(S R Bowring) *sn chsng ldr: rdn and ev ch 2f out: sn wknd* **4/1**[1]

000- **12** *1¼* **Locombe Hill (IRE)**[22] 6584 10-8-11 49.................... DanielTudhope(3) 9 6
(N Wilson) *hld up: hdwy over 5f out: rdn over 3f out: wknd over 2f out* **50/1**

100- **13** *8* **La Viola**[39] 6449 4-8-13 55....................(b) PatCosgrave 7 —
(K R Burke) *hld up: rdn and short-lived effrt 3f out* **25/1**

1m 50.96s (-0.80) **Going Correction** -0.025s/f (Stan)
WFA 4 from 5yo+ 1lb **13** Ran SP% **122.8**
Speed ratings (Par 101):102,101,101,100,100 99,94,93,93,82 80,79,72
CSF £69.12 TOTE £18.70: £4.60, £2.30, £1.80; EX 136.10.There was no bid for the winner. Seattle Robber was claimed by Lucinda Featherstone for £6,000.
Owner P D Evans **Bred** Roldvale Ltd **Trained** Pandy, Abergavenny

FOCUS
A weak event, run at a fair pace. The form is held down by the fourth and fifth, and the first three have all been rated below their best.

57 BETDIRECT.CO.UK CONDITIONS STKS 1m 141y(P)
3:30 (3:30) (Class 2) 4-Y-0+
£11,217 (£3,358; £1,679; £840; £419; £210) **Stalls** Low

Form RPR

6/0- **1** **Putra Sas (IRE)**[21] 6592 5-9-0 100.................... JoeFanning 1 93
(P F I Cole) *led: rdn and hdd wl over 1f out: led wl ins fnl f: r.o* **12/1**

301- **2** *hd* **Trifti**[41] 6437 5-9-0 81.................... FrancisFerris 2 93
(C A Cyzer) *a.p: rdn to ld wl over 1f out: edgd rt and hdd wl ins fnl f: r.o* **9/1**[3]

421- **3** *½* **Psychiatrist**[20] 6601 5-9-0 92.................... SteveDrowne 5 92
(R Hannon) *chsd ldr: rdn 2f out: ev ch over 1f out: kpt on ins fnl f* **5/2**[2]

122- **4** *1¼* **Appalachian Trail (IRE)**[28] 6530 5-9-0 96....................(b) TomEaves 6 89
(I Semple) *hld up in rr: hdwy on outside over 2f out: rdn and ev ch over 1f out: nt qckn ins fnl f* **10/11**[1]

033- **5** *3* **Master Theo (USA)**[28] 6533 5-9-0 85....................(p) AdamKirby 3 83
(Lucinda Featherstone) *hld up: rdn wl over 1f out: no hdwy* **14/1**

60-0 **6** *7* **One More Round (USA)**[5] 7 8-9-0 102.................... NCallan 4 75
(N P Littmoden) *hld up in tch: rdn 3f out: wknd wl over 1f out* **14/1**

1m 49.9s (-1.86) **Going Correction** -0.025s/f (Stan) **6** Ran SP% **112.0**
Speed ratings (Par 109):107,106,106,105,102 96
CSF £104.73 TOTE £14.50: £5.60, £2.80; EX 67.00.
Owner H R H Sultan Ahmad Shah **Bred** Hrh Sultan Ahmad Shah **Trained** Whatcombe, Oxon

FOCUS
A decent little conditions event, but the early pace was only average, and the form should be treated with caution.

NOTEBOOK
Putra Sas(IRE), well backed to improve on his recent return to action over 12 furlongs at this venue last time, duly did so and landed a gamble in the process. He was given a typically well judged front-running ride by Fanning, really enjoyed dictating matters over this shorter trip, and showed a decent attitude to repel the runner-up close home. He had a leading chance on official figures, however, and while this proves he retains his ability, he is most likely flattered by this. (op 11-1)
Trifti ran a blinder at the weights and went down with all guns blazing. He loves this track, and this was a personal-best effort, but the Handicapper is likely to make his life much harder after this. (op 10-1 tchd 8-1)
Psychiatrist, who resumed winning ways at Lingfield last time, posted another solid effort and probably enjoyed the easy pace over this slightly longer trip. He is probably best kept to this type of event, as he could struggle in handicaps off his current mark. (tchd 11-4)
Appalachian Trail(IRE), runner-up on his previous two outings, emerged to have every chance yet failed to quicken when it mattered. He would have been unsuited by the tactical nature of this race. (op Evens tchd 11-10 in places)
Master Theo(USA), having his first start for a new yard, ran his race and again hinted that he needs a stiffer test. (op 12-1)

58 BETDIRECT ON CHANNEL 4 TEXT PAGE 613 H'CAP 7f 32y(P)
4:00 (4:01) (Class 4) (0-85,88) 4-Y-0+ **£5,505** (£1,637; £818; £408) **Stalls** High

Form RPR

100- **1** **Wahoo Sam (USA)**[90] 5743 6-8-9 **76**.................... NCallan 9 83
(K A Ryan) *sn led: rdn wl over 1f out: r.o* **20/1**

050- **2** *nk* **Rafferty (IRE)**[28] 6530 7-9-4 **85**.................... PaulFessey 8 91
(T D Barron) *led early: chsd ldr: rdn over 2f out: r.o ins fnl f* **25/1**

066- **3** *1½* **Screwdriver**[6] 6698 4-8-6 **73**....................(b) LPKeniry 12 78+
(Miss J R Tooth) *stdd s: sn swtchd lft: hld up in rr: hdwy whn nt clr run 1f out: r.o* **40/1**

44-5 **4** *nk* **Pawan (IRE)**[5] 6 6-8-4 **78**.................... AnnStokell(7) 4 79
(Miss A Stokell) *hld up and bhd: hdwy 2f out: r.o one pce fnl f* **20/1**

141- **5** *¾* **Wessex (USA)**[6] 6698 6-9-4 **85** 6ex.................... GrahamGibbons 1 84
(P A Blockley) *hld up in tch: rdn over 2f out: one pce fnl f* **6/4**[1]

023- **6** *¾* **Claret And Amber**[6] 6698 4-9-0 **81**....................(b) PaulHanagan 3 78
(R A Fahey) *hld up: rdn over 3f out: hdwy over 2f out: nt much briefly ins fnl f: one pce* **11/4**[2]

34-6 **7** *nk* **Whitbarrow (IRE)**[2] 36 7-8-9 **76**.................... RobertWinston 6 73
(A W Carroll) *hld up and bhd: rdn and hdwy 1f out: n.d* **25/1**

/11- **8** *1* **Atlantic Quest (USA)**[11] 6664 7-9-7 **88** 6ex............(p) DarrenWilliams 11 82
(R A Harris) *prom tl rdn and wknd 3f out* **20/1**

205- **9** *nk* **Wavertree Warrior (IRE)**[17] 6629 4-8-6 **76**......... RichardThomas(3) 10 69
(N P Littmoden) *prom: rdn 3f out: wknd 2f out* **10/1**

400- **10** *1¼* **Mr Lambros**[132] 4744 5-9-4 **85**.................... MartinDwyer 7 75
(A M Balding) *a bhd* **8/1**[3]

304- **11** *1¼* **Outer Hebrides**[91] 5713 5-9-1 **82**....................(t) MickyFenton 2 69
(Stef Liddiard) *hld up: rdn and hdwy on ins over 2f out: wknd fnl f* **8/1**[3]

1m 28.3s (-2.10) **Going Correction** -0.025s/f (Stan) **11** Ran SP% **122.4**
Speed ratings (Par 105):111,110,108,108,107 106,106,105,105,103 102
CSF £419.40 CT £17997.70 TOTE £20.60: £4.50, £7.90, £7.80; EX 434.30.
Owner Blackhurst,Bridge,Moll,O'Brien **Bred** Stonereath Farms Inc **Trained** Hambleton, N Yorks
■ Stewards' Enquiry : N Callan caution: used whip with arm above shoulder height

FOCUS
A fair handicap which saw the winner make just about all from his modest draw. The form looks sound.
Mr Lambros Official explanation: jockey said gelding was hampered at start
Outer Hebrides Official explanation: jockey said gelding was hampered at start

59 WIN £2M @ FOOTBALLPOOLS.COM MAIDEN STKS 1m 4f 50y(P)
4:30 (4:32) (Class 5) 4-Y-0+ **£3,238** (£963; £481; £240) **Stalls** Low

Form RPR

3- **1** **Caraman (IRE)**[11] 562 8-9-4.................... RobertWinston 1 62
(J J Quinn) *a.p: rdn 2f out: carried rt over 1f out: led wl ins fnl f: r.o* **10/3**[2]

622- **2** *nk* **Newnham (IRE)**[27] 6537 5-9-4 67....................(p) NCallan 10 62
(J R Boyle) *a.p: wnt 2nd over 6f out: led 3f out: sn rdn: edgd rt over 1f out: hdd wl ins fnl f: nt qckn* **8/11**[1]

040- **3** *1¾* **Lake Wakatipu**[9] 6679 4-8-9 50.................... DeanMcKeown 8 54
(M Mullineaux) *stdd and swtchd lft sn after s: hld up and bhd: hdwy wl over 1f out: r.o ins fnl f* **66/1**

4 *2½* **Candarli (IRE)**[29] 4087 10-9-1.................... NeilChalmers(3) 9 55
(D R Gandolfo) *hld up: rdn over 3f out: hdwy over 2f out: swtchd lft over 1f out: one pce fnl f* **33/1**

040- **5** *2* **Grand Design**[17] 6625 4-8-9 55.................... EddieAhern 12 47
(C A Cyzer) *hld up towards rr: hdwy 4f out: rdn over 2f out: wknd fnl f* **7/1**[3]

004- **6** *9* **Nutley Queen (IRE)**[37] 3400 7-8-13 35....................(t) FergusSweeney 2 32
(M Appleby) *nvr nr ldrs* **40/1**

7 *3* **Rose Thistle (UAE)**[236] 1729 4-8-9.................... LPKeniry 6 28
(John A Quinn, Ire) *bhd fnl 6f* **20/1**

0- **8** *12* **Pips Assertive Way**[41] 4191 5-8-13.................... PaulHanagan 5 8
(A W Carroll) *led: hdd 7f out: hrd rdn 4f out: wknd 3f out* **40/1**

404- **9** *½* **Glenviews Oldport (USA)**[16] 6651 4-8-9 46........... RobbieFitzpatrick 7 8
(Peter Grayson) *chsd ldr: led 7f out to 3f out: wknd 2f out* **20/1**

0/0- **10** *dist* **She's My Dream (IRE)**[18] 6611 4-8-6 40................ RichardThomas(3) 4 —
(A J Lidderdale) *hld up in tch: wknd 4f out: t.o* **100/1**

11 *dist* **Pampamee** 4-8-9.................... AlanDaly 11 —
(M Wellings) *stdd and swtchd lft sn after s: a bhd: rdn over 4f out: t.o* **100/1**

2m 40.82s (-1.60) **Going Correction** -0.025s/f (Stan)
WFA 4 from 5yo+ 4lb **11** Ran SP% **114.3**
Speed ratings (Par 103):104,103,102,100,99 93,91,83,83,— —
CSF £5.50 TOTE £4.20: £1.60, £1.10, £6.70; EX 7.70 Place 6 £303.94, Place 5 £159.43.
Owner Alan Mann **Bred** His Highness The Aga Khan's Studs S C **Trained** Settrington, N Yorks

FOCUS
A weak maiden and the form, which has been rated through the banded third, may be suspect.
T/Jkpt: Not won. T/Plt: £448.40 to a £1 stake. Pool: £46,039.85. 74.95 winning tickets. T/Qpdt: £113.40 to a £1 stake. Pool: £3,725.70. 24.30 winning tickets. KH

30 LINGFIELD (L-H)
Saturday, January 7

OFFICIAL GOING: Standard
Wind: Nil Weather: Dank

60 BETDIRECT FOOTBALL SKYTEXT P372 MAIDEN STKS 6f (P)
12:40 (12:41) (Class 5) 3-Y-0 **£3,238** (£963; £481; £240) **Stalls** Low

Form RPR

033- **1** **Dingaan (IRE)**[227] 2004 3-9-0 84.................... JamieSpencer 3 84+
(A M Balding) *mde all: drew 3l clr over 1f out: urged along and kpt on fnl f: unchal* **7/2**[2]

006- **2** *1½* **Trans Sonic**[113] 5265 3-9-0 74.................... NCallan 5 76
(A P Jarvis) *trckd wnr after 2f: rdn and no imp wl over 1f out: kpt on fnl f* **6/1**

3 *shd* **His Master's Voice (IRE)** 3-9-0.................... JoeFanning 6 76
(D W P Arbuthnot) *s.s: sn in tch: smooth prog to chse ldng pair 2f out: shkn up to dispute 2nd fnl f: kpt on: n.d to wnr* **33/1**

04- **4** *5* **Attitude Annie**[17] 6640 3-8-9.................... PaulDoe 4 56
(S Dow) *hld up in rr: detached in last trio 1/2-way: sme prog 2f out: one pce and no hdwy fr over 1f out* **50/1**

02- **5** *¾* **Perfect Treasure (IRE)**[39] 6456 3-8-9.................... EddieAhern 1 54
(J A R Toller) *chsd wnr for 2f: rdn on inner 1/2-way: struggling 2f out: wknd fnl f* **9/2**[3]

00- **6** *¾* **Simpsons Ross (IRE)**[39] 6456 3-9-0.................... JimmyQuinn 12 57
(R M Flower) *s.s: detached in last tl rdn and plugged on fnl 2f: no ch* **66/1**

7 *½* **Coastal Breeze** 3-9-0.................... J-PGuillambert 8 55
(J W Hills) *rn green: chsd ldrs: rdn over 3f out: struggling fnl 2f* **25/1**

042- **8** *2* **Radius**[53] 6349 3-9-0 82.................... ChrisCatlin 7 49
(H Morrison) *prom: rdn 1/2-way: sn struggling: wknd 2f out* **11/8**[1]

0- **9** *1* **Marron Flore**[7] 6698 3-8-6.................... RichardThomas(3) 2 41
(A J Lidderdale) *t.k.h early: hld up in last trio: detached 1/2-way: nvr a factor* **100/1**

532- **10** *5* **Cativo Cavallino**[26] 6561 3-9-0 71....................(p) RobertWinston 10 31
(Julian Poulton) *racd wd: in tch to over 2f out: wknd rapidly* **12/1**

1m 11.6s (-1.21) **Going Correction** -0.075s/f (Stan) **10** Ran SP% **115.7**
Speed ratings (Par 97):105,103,102,96,95 94,93,90,89,82
CSF £23.60 TOTE £5.40: £1.70, £2.30, £5.60; EX 33.60.
Owner Lady C S Cadbury **Bred** Mrs Gill Wilson **Trained** Kingsclere, Hants

FOCUS
With both Perfect Treasure and Radius below their previous best, the form of this maiden is not as strong as it might have been. The winning time, though, was smart for the type of race.
Simpsons Ross(IRE) Official explanation: jockey said gelding hung left
Radius Official explanation: jockey said gelding ran flat

61 BET NOW AT BETDIRECT.CO.UK H'CAP 1m 2f (P)
1:10 (1:10) (Class 5) (0-70,69) 3-Y-O **£3,238** (£963; £481; £240) **Stalls** Low

Form RPR

005- **1** **La Via Ferrata (IRE)**[49] 6375 3-8-4 **55** oh3 JoeFanning 4 54
(P F I Cole) *hld up in midfield: pushed along 3f out: prog on inner over 1f out: chsd ldr jst ins fnl f: r.o to ld last 75yds* **7/1**

100- **2** *½* **Night Groove (IRE)**[28] 6543 3-8-10 **61** ow1 NCallan 7 59
(N P Littmoden) *led: rdn 2f out: kpt on wl: hdd and no ex last 75yds* **5/1**[3]

200- **3** *¾* **Zizou (IRE)**[42] 6425 3-8-12 **63** ChrisCatlin 10 60
(P R Hedger) *trckd ldrs: rdn 2f out: effrt to chal 1f out: nt qckn ins fnl f* **14/1**

236- **4** *1* **Disco Lights**[18] 6624 3-9-4 **69** RobertWinston 9 64
(D J Daly) *hld up in midfield: sme prog over 2f out: shkn up and hanging over 1f out: nt qckn* **11/2**

1- **5** *shd* **Cragganmore Creek**[17] 6648 3-8-11 **62** DerekMcGaffin 8 57
(D Morris) *hld up in last: rdn and struggling 3f out: nt clr run over 1f out and swtchd rt: styd on wl last 150yds* **10/1**

046- **6** *¾* **Ullah Pendragon (IRE)**[23] 6585 3-8-4 **55** PaulDoe 2 48
(M J Polglase) *rrd s: hld up in last pair: rdn over 2f out: no prog on outer over 1f out: kpt on ins fnl f* **28/1**

00-5 **7** *½* **Crocodile Star (USA)**[2] 49 3-8-6 **57** EddieAhern 5 50
(J A Osborne) *hld up in midfield: pushed along 3f out: nt far off the pce but nt qckn 1f out: plugged on* **9/2**[2]

006- **8** *shd* **Pocket Too**[22] 6588 3-9-0 **65** J-PGuillambert 3 57
(Jean-Rene Auvray) *chsd ldr to wl over 1f out: wknd ins fnl f* **8/1**

010- **9** *shd* **Deserted Prince (IRE)**[18] 6627 3-8-12 **63** JamieSpencer 1 55
(M J Wallace) *t.k.h: trckd ldng pair: chsd ldr wl over 1f out tl jst ins fnl f: fnd nil and sn btn* **7/2**[1]

2m 7.30s (-0.49) **Going Correction** -0.075s/f (Stan) **9** Ran SP% **115.3**
Speed ratings (Par 97):98,97,97,96,96 95,95,95,94
CSF £41.79 CT £478.59 TOTE £9.70: £2.70, £2.10, £3.80; EX 51.80.
Owner P F I Cole Ltd **Bred** Roland H Alder **Trained** Whatcombe, Oxon

FOCUS
Just a moderate handicap in which La Via Ferrata showed improved form to get off the mark.
Crocodile Star(USA) Official explanation: jockey said gelding was denied a clear run
Pocket Too Official explanation: jockey said gelding was denied a clear run

62 BETDIRECT NO Q ON 08000 93 66 93 MAIDEN STKS 1m 2f (P)
1:40 (1:42) (Class 5) 3-Y-O **£3,886** (£1,156; £577; £288) **Stalls** Low

Form RPR

402- **1** **Abstract Art (USA)**[18] 6624 3-9-0 76 JamieSpencer 2 74+
(N A Callaghan) *led after 2f: mde rest: shuffled along and drew clr over 1f out: 4l ahd ins fnl f: eased nr fin* **8/15**[1]

0- **2** *1½* **Sky High Guy (IRE)**[42] 6428 3-9-0 EddieAhern 4 65
(S Kirk) *settled towards rr: outpcd over 3f out: drvn and prog over 2f out: styd on to take 2nd ins fnl f: no ch w wnr* **14/1**

226- **3** *½* **Opera Comica**[42] 6425 3-8-9 75 (v) JimmyQuinn 6 59
(J H M Gosden) *t.k.h: trckd ldrs: rdn and nt qckn over 2f out: styd on fr over 1f out* **3/1**[2]

0- **4** *¾* **Henry Holmes**[18] 6624 3-8-11 RichardThomas(3) 3 63
(Mrs L Richards) *hld up in rr: prog 4f out: chsd wnr over 2f out: sn drvn and no imp: lost 2nd ins fnl f: one pce* **33/1**

0- **5** *6* **Being There**[36] 6484 3-9-0 JoeFanning 8 51
(P F I Cole) *prom: trckd wnr 1/2-way to over 2f out: wknd over 1f out* **20/1**

6 *5* **Bariloche** 3-9-0 PaulDoe 5 42
(J H M Gosden) *s.s: rn green in last: lost tch fr 4f out: no ch after* **12/1**[3]

00- **7** *11* **Lady Evi**[18] 6624 3-8-9 ChrisCatlin 1 16
(D K Ivory) *a in rr: rdn 7f out: wknd 4f out: sn bhd* **66/1**

0- **8** *8* **Safaah**[19] 6610 3-9-0 J-PGuillambert 7 6
(G Prodromou) *drvn to ld: hdd after 2f: chsd wnr to 1/2-way: wknd: t.o* **50/1**

2m 7.18s (-0.61) **Going Correction** -0.075s/f (Stan) **8** Ran SP% **115.7**
Speed ratings (Par 97):99,97,97,96,92 88,79,72
CSF £9.89 TOTE £1.60: £1.10, £2.40, £1.10; EX 12.70.
Owner Matthew Green **Bred** Ms J L Mills **Trained** Newmarket, Suffolk

FOCUS
A very uncompetitive maiden and Abstract Art was a class apart.

63 BETDIRECT FOOTBALL CASHBACKS SKYTEXT P372 (S) STKS 1m 2f (P)
2:15 (2:16) (Class 6) 4-Y-O+ **£2,388** (£705; £352) **Stalls** Low

Form RPR

400- **1** **Whenwillitwin**[9] 6681 5-9-2 45 (p) LPKeniry 8 53
(J S Moore) *trckd ldng trio: rdn and effrt over 2f out: chsd ldr over 1f out: drvn and r.o to ld last stride* **20/1**

001- **2** *shd* **Competitor**[8] 6691 5-9-7 60 (v) ChrisCatlin 3 58
(J Akehurst) *trckd ldr: led over 2f out: drvn fnl f: kpt on: hdd last stride* **11/4**[1]

102- **3** *2* **Successor**[9] 6683 6-9-7 47 (t) JamieMackay 11 54
(M D I Usher) *hld up in last pair: gng wl 3f out: stdy prog on outer over 2f out: rdn fnl f: wnt 3rd last 100yds: no ch to chal* **9/2**[3]

001- **4** *1¼* **Tanning**[9] 6682 4-9-0 45 (v) PaulHanagan 10 47
(A W Carroll) *led to over 2f out: wknd fnl f* **25/1**

00-5 **5** *2* **Temper Tantrum**[3] 35 8-8-11 52 (p) TravisBlock(5) 9 43
(J R Best) *settled in 6th: effrt over 2f out: sn outpcd: no imp ldrs after* **6/1**

006- **6** *nk* **Night Explosion (IRE)**[63] 6260 8-8-9 35 (t) JamesDoyle(7) 1 42
(D J S Ffrench Davis) *settled in 5th: rdn and outpcd over 2f out: one pce and n.d after* **50/1**

000- **7** *½* **Orenay (USA)**[18] 6632 4-9-0 60 (t) JamieSpencer 7 41
(M J Wallace) *hld up in 7th: gng wl 3f out: brief effrt on inner and nt clr run over 1f out: shuffled along and nvr nr ldrs* **10/1**

332- **8** *¾* **Swords**[10] 6675 4-9-0 50 RobertWinston 4 40
(P Howling) *dwlt: a wl in rr: rdn and one pce over 2f out* **3/1**[2]

205- **9** *nk* **Strathtay**[17] 2359 4-8-9 56 JimmyQuinn 5 34
(M Appleby) *trckd ldng pair to over 2f out: wknd* **12/1**

000- **10** *12* **Blake Hall Lad (IRE)**[26] 6556 5-8-9 35 DeanWilliams(7) 12 17
(P S McEntee) *stdd s: hld up in last trio: brief effrt over 4f out: sn wknd: t.o* **66/1**

2m 6.90s (-0.89) **Going Correction** -0.075s/f (Stan)
WFA 4 from 5yo+ 2lb **10** Ran SP% **113.0**
Speed ratings (Par 101):100,99,98,97,95 95,95,94,94,84
CSF £70.83 TOTE £20.10: £4.10, £1.50, £2.00; EX 131.80.There was no bid for the winner.
Owner Mitchell Block **Bred** Mrs Gail Gaisford **Trained** Upper Lambourn, Berks

FOCUS
A typical seller in which Whenwillitwin seemed to produce a career-best effort.

64 BETDIRECT.CO.UK H'CAP 1m (P)
2:45 (2:47) (Class 4) (0-85,85) 4-Y-O+ **£6,477** (£1,927; £963; £481) **Stalls** High

Form RPR

532- **1** **Northern Desert (IRE)**[8] 6690 7-8-11 **78** ChrisCatlin 6 86
(P W Hiatt) *t.k.h: hld up in rr: prog over 2f out: rdn to ld jst over 1f out: r.o wl* **4/1**[2]

000- **2** *nk* **Farewell Gift**[70] 6149 5-8-2 **72** (b) StephaneBreux(3) 7 79
(R Hannon) *t.k.h: led at stdy pce on inner: hdd jst over 1f out: kpt on wl but a hld* **25/1**

161- **3** *¾* **Hits Only Heaven (IRE)**[18] 6629 4-9-1 **82** (be) JimmyQuinn 1 87+
(J Pearce) *dwlt: t.k.h: hld up in tch: at bk of main gp whn sprint sed 2f out: drvn over 1f out: r.o strly last 100yds* **4/1**[2]

605- **4** *nk* **Swift Oscar**[112] 5313 4-8-13 **80** EddieAhern 4 85
(J W Hills) *t.k.h: hld up in cl tch: prog to join ldr 2f out: nt qckn 1f out: one pce after* **8/1**

331- **5** *nk* **Glencalvie (IRE)**[8] 6690 5-8-11 **78** (v) JoeFanning 3 82+
(J Akehurst) *t.k.h: hld up in tch: effrt on inner 2f out: nt clr run over 1f out: kpt on but nvr able to chal* **9/2**[3]

100- **6** *½* **Tanforan**[26] 6566 4-7-13 **73** JamesDoyle(7) 9 76
(K McAuliffe) *t.k.h: pressed ldr to 2f out: one pce over 1f out* **33/1**

006- **7** *1* **Nautical**[26] 6566 8-8-5 **72** PaulHanagan 5 72
(A W Carroll) *t.k.h: hld up in tch: effrt on outer 2f out: one pce over 1f out* **20/1**

316/ **8** *nk* **Polonius**[546] 3751 5-9-4 **85** JamieSpencer 8 85+
(P R Webber) *started awkwardly: hld up in last: stl last and nt clr run wl over 1f out to ins fnl f: nudged along and kpt on* **7/2**[1]

/60- **9** *2* **Zarabad (IRE)**[29] 6533 4-8-13 **80** RobertWinston 2 75
(K R Burke) *plld hrd: hld up in tch: effrt on wd outside over 2f out: sn btn* **7/1**

1m 38.92s (-0.51) **Going Correction** -0.075s/f (Stan) **9** Ran SP% **115.6**
Speed ratings (Par 105):99,98,97,97,97 96,95,95,93
CSF £99.04 CT £428.27 TOTE £5.20: £1.70, £4.90, £1.60; EX 107.00.
Owner Clive Roberts **Bred** J P Hardiman **Trained** Hook Norton, Oxon

FOCUS
A decent enough handicap, but they went a very steady pace pretty much until they turned into the straight and finished in a bunch.
Zarabad(IRE) Official explanation: jockey said colt ran too free

65 BETDIRECT FREEPHONE 0800 211 222 H'CAP 1m 4f (P)
3:20 (3:20) (Class 2) (0-100,95) 4-Y-O+ **£12,954** (£3,854; £1,926; £962) **Stalls** Low

Form RPR

006- **1** **Polygonal (FR)**[203] 2709 6-8-12 **89** EddieAhern 5 95
(Ernst Oertel) *dwlt: hld up in 6th: prog over 3f out to trck ldrs: rdn 2f out : r.o fnl f to ld last strides* **33/1**

303- **2** *nk* **Rehearsal**[22] 6592 5-9-1 **92** PaulHanagan 6 98
(L Lungo) *led: kicked on over 2f out: drvn and kpt on wl fr over 1f out: hdd last strides* **3/1**[2]

124- **3** *shd* **Cristoforo (IRE)**[104] 5496 9-9-4 **95** JamieSpencer 1 101
(B J Curley) *trckd ldr: rdn to chal wl over 1f out: nrly upsides ins fnl f: nt qckn nr fin* **11/4**[1]

031- **4** *¾* **Cold Turkey**[22] 6592 6-9-2 **93** J-PGuillambert 7 98
(G L Moore) *dwlt: hld up in last: effrt over 2f out: nt qckn wl over 1f out: r.o ins fnl f: nrst fin* **11/4**[1]

501- **5** *hd* **Wise Owl**[42] 6432 4-8-0 **81** JimmyQuinn 2 87+
(J Pearce) *t.k.h: trckd ldng pair: tried to chal on inner over 1f out: cl up whn nt clr run ent fnl f: nt rcvr* **11/2**[3]

041- **6** *1¾* **Dower House**[17] 6645 11-8-9 **86** (t) ChrisCatlin 8 88
(Andrew Turnell) *hld up in last pair: outpcd over 2f out: styd on same pce fr over 1f out* **14/1**

340- **7** *1¼* **Boot 'n Toot**[17] 6645 5-8-4 **81** oh3 FrancisFerris 3 81
(C A Cyzer) *dwlt: hld up in 5th: gng wl enough 3f out: sn outpcd and btn* **12/1**

400- **8** *2* **Shahzan House (IRE)**[7] 6700 7-9-1 **92** (p) MickyFenton 4 88
(Stef Liddiard) *trckd ldng trio: outpcd over 2f out: wknd* **33/1**

2m 32.7s (-1.69) **Going Correction** -0.075s/f (Stan)
WFA 4 from 5yo+ 4lb **8** Ran SP% **114.0**
Speed ratings (Par 109):102,101,101,101,101 99,99,97
CSF £129.41 CT £372.32 TOTE £25.60: £5.90, £1.60, £1.70; EX 186.00.
Owner E Oertel **Bred** Ecurie Ferdane **Trained** Newmarket, Suffolk

FOCUS
A good handicap in which Polygonal just proved good enough to make a winning debut for new connections having been bought out of Luca Cumani's yard for £15,000 since he was last seen.

NOTEBOOK
Polygonal(FR) went winless through 2005, but was picked up from Luca Cumani's yard for 15,000gns at the Horses In Training Sales in October and proved good enough to take this decent prize on his debut for new connections. Given this was his first start in 203 days, there could well be more to come and Polytrack clearly suits. (op 25-1)
Rehearsal, just behind Cold Turkey in a similar race at Wolverhampton on his previous start, reversed placings with that rival and was just held. He looks well capable of landing one of these valuable handicaps. (tchd 4-1)
Cristoforo(IRE), returned to Polytrack off the back of a 104-day break, was given every chance under a really determined ride from the Champion and was just held. He is apparently being readied for a trip to Dubai for their Carnival. (op 3-1)
Cold Turkey, 2lb higher than when winning a similar race over course and distance on his previous start, was not ideally placed turning in and that proved his undoing. (tchd 3-1)
Wise Owl, 11lb higher than when winning a weaker race over course and distance on his previous start, would have gone very close had he got a run against the far rail when looking to make his move. Official explanation: jockey said gelding was denied a clear run (op 7-1)

66 PLAY LITTLEWOODS POOLS ON 0800 500 000 H'CAP 5f (P)
3:50 (3:51) (Class 5) (0-70,70) 3-Y-O **£3,238** (£963; £481; £240) **Stalls** High

Form RPR

612- **1** **Egyptian Lord**[12] 6662 3-9-1 **67** (b) RobbieFitzpatrick 2 72
(Peter Grayson) *mde virtually all and racd on inner: hrd pressed fr over 1f out: jst hld on* **3/1**[2]

021- **2** *shd* **Luloah**[11] 6670 3-8-5 **57** BrianReilly 4 61
(P S McEntee) *trckd ldng pair: effrt to chal and upsides fr over 1f out: hanging lft after: jst pipped* **14/1**

400- **3** *1½* **Developer (IRE)**[80] 5969 3-9-4 **70** (p) NCallan 1 69
(T G Mills) *chsd ldrs: rdn 2f out: styd on on fnl f to take 3rd last 100yds* **11/4**[1]

054- **4** *nk* **Succeed (IRE)**[26] 6561 3-8-7 **59** ChrisCatlin 9 57
(Mrs H Sweeting) *hld up in last: prog on inner 1/2-way: styd on fnl f: nvr nrr* **11/1**

000- **5** ¾ **Hardy Norseman (IRE)**[59] 6297 3-9-1 **67** .... RobertWinston 3 62
(W Jarvis) *pressed wnr: upsides wl over 1f out: nt qckn ent fnl f: wknd last 100yds* **13/2**

201- **6** shd **Rapsgate (IRE)**[12] 6662 3-8-13 **68** .... StephaneBreux(3) 7 63+
(R Hannon) *hld up: last over 2f out: pushed along over 1f out: styd on ins fnl f: no ch* **9/2**[3]

330- **7** 1 **Lady Zanzara (USA)**[110] 5363 3-8-11 **63** .... EddieAhern 8 54
(J W Hills) *missed the break: t.k.h and sn chsd ldrs: nt qckn wl over 1f out: one pce* **14/1**

000- **8** 6 **Wotavadun (IRE)**[192] 3016 3-8-4 **56** oh1 ....(be[1]) PaulHanagan 5 26
(K McAuliffe) *restrained in rr sn after s: effrt 1/2-way: no prog 2f out: wknd rapidly over 1f out* **25/1**

000- **9** 2 **Capital Lass**[22] 6591 3-8-4 **56** oh6 .... HayleyTurner 6 18
(M J Wallace) *a in rr: wknd 2f out* **25/1**

59.16 secs (-0.62) **Going Correction** -0.075s/f (Stan) 9 Ran SP% **112.5**
Speed ratings (Par 97):101,100,98,97,96 96,95,85,82
CSF £42.71 CT £125.32 TOTE £2.90: £1.60, £3.70, £1.90; EX 46.20 Place 6 £65.41, Place 5 £22.24.
Owner D & R Rhodes & Mrs S Grayson **Bred** I A N Wight And Mrs D M Wight **Trained** Formby, Lancs

FOCUS
A modest sprint handicap but sound form rated through the third.
T/Plt: £127.30 to a £1 stake. Pool: £39,905.90. 228.80 winning tickets. T/Qpdt: £6.10 to a £1 stake. Pool: £3,880.20. 470.40 winning tickets. JN

[52]WOLVERHAMPTON (A.W) (L-H)

Monday, January 9

OFFICIAL GOING: Standard
Wind: Light, behind Weather: Overcast

67 LITTLEWOODS £2M POOLS ON 0800 500 000 H'CAP 5f 216y(P)
1:00 (1:02) (Class 6) (0-58,64) 4-Y-0+ **£2,388** (£705; £352) **Stalls** Low

Form RPR

05-2 **1** **Ruman (IRE)**[8] 4 4-9-0 **56** .... ChrisCatlin 6 65
(M J Attwater) *hld up and bhd: hdwy over 2f out: hrd rdn to ld cl home* **6/1**[2]

601- **2** nk **Diamond Josh**[79] 6031 4-9-2 **58** .... JamieSpencer 11 66
(P D Evans) *sn led: rdn wl over 1f out: edgd rt ins fnl f: hdd cl home* **12/1**

35-0 **3** nk **Roman Empire**[7] 9 6-9-0 **56** ....(b) NCallan 3 63
(K A Ryan) *chsd ldrs: rdn over 2f out: r.o wl towards fin* **9/1**

16-1 **4** 1 ½ **Bollin Billy**[6] 22 4-9-1 **64** 6ex .... LiamJones(7) 7 67
(R Brotherton) *bhd: rdn over 2f out: hdwy and edgd lft over 1f out: kpt on ins fnl f* **7/1**[3]

05-3 **5** shd **Charlie Bear**[6] 21 5-9-0 **56** .... AdrianMcCarthy 1 58
(Miss Z C Davison) *a.p: rdn 3f out: no ex ins fnl f* **8/1**

21-2 **6** ½ **Mambazo**[6] 22 4-8-10 **57** ....(e) GregFairley(5) 2 58+
(S C Williams) *t.k.h: sn prom: wnt 2nd over 2f out: rdn and edgd lft jst over 1f out: one pce* **5/2**[1]

101- **7** ½ **Lucius Verrus (USA)**[34] 6516 6-8-11 **56** ....(v) PatrickMathers(3) 10 55
(D Shaw) *outpcd in rr: hdwy on ins over 1f out: no further prog fnl f* **11/1**

55-0 **8** 2 ½ **Border Artist**[6] 21 7-9-2 **58** .... HayleyTurner 8 50
(B G Powell) *hld up towards rr: hdwy over 2f out: rdn over 1f out: fdd fnl f* **25/1**

04-1 **9** 1 **Soba Jones**[7] 9 9-9-4 **63** 6ex .... JasonEdmunds(3) 4 52
(J Balding) *led early: prom tl rdn and wknd over 1f out* **14/1**

055- **10** 2 **Times Review (USA)**[9] 6696 5-9-1 **57** .... JimmyQuinn 9 40
(C A Dwyer) *bhd fnl 2f* **12/1**

000- **11** hd **Marshallspark (IRE)**[20] 6632 7-8-13 **55** ....(v) PaulHanagan 5 37
(R A Fahey) *prom tl rdn and wknd over 1f out* **25/1**

0-60 **12** shd **Piccolo Prince**[4] 47 5-8-8 **57** .... DonnaCaldwell(7) 12 39
(E J Alston) *hld up: rdn over 3f out: no rspnse* **28/1**

1m 14.68s (-1.13) **Going Correction** -0.05s/f (Stan) 12 Ran SP% **118.0**
Speed ratings (Par 101):105,104,104,102,102 101,100,97,96,93 93,93
CSF £73.70 CT £657.36 TOTE £7.80: £2.30, £3.40, £3.10; EX 107.70.
Owner Brooklands Racing **Bred** Noel And Michael Buckley **Trained** Wysall, Notts

FOCUS
A tight race on paper and the field finished well bunched up with Ruman narrowly coming out on top. The form looks solid for the grade ratred through runner-up, fourth and fifth.

68 FIRST PAST THE POST AT BETDIRECT H'CAP 5f 216y(P)
1:30 (1:31) (Class 5) (0-70,70) 3-Y-0 **£3,238** (£963; £481; £240) **Stalls** Low

Form RPR

614- **1** **Grenane (IRE)**[20] 6627 3-9-4 **70** .... RobertWinston 5 77+
(P D Evans) *hld up: hdwy over 2f out: rdn over 1f out: led wl ins fnl f: r.o wl* **2/1**[1]

02-2 **2** 1 ¾ **Canina**[4] 45 3-8-13 **65** .... NCallan 10 67
(Ms Deborah J Evans) *hld up: hdwy over 2f out: rdn over 1f out: r.o to take 2nd last strides* **9/1**[3]

450- **3** hd **Trombone Tom**[14] 6662 3-8-11 **63** .... DarrenWilliams 6 64
(J R Norton) *a.p: rdn to ld and edgd lft over 1f out: hdd and nt qckn wl ins fnl f* **9/1**[3]

216- **4** 2 **Opal Warrior**[14] 6663 3-8-11 **63** .... TonyCulhane 4 58
(P W D'Arcy) *mid-div: rdn over 3f out: hdwy on ins over 2f out: one pce fnl f* **9/1**[3]

040- **5** 2 ½ **Correct Time (IRE)**[143] 4553 3-8-8 **60** .... JimmyQuinn 1 48
(N P Littmoden) *led after 1f: sn hung rt: rdn and hdd over 1f out: wknd ins fnl f* **12/1**

00-5 **6** ½ **Hardy Norseman (IRE)**[2] 66 3-8-8 **67** .... BRoper(7) 11 53
(W Jarvis) *hld up in mid-div: hdwy on outside 2f out: sn rdn and hung lft: one pce* **12/1**

041- **7** nk **Xpres Boy (IRE)**[25] 6585 3-8-13 **65** .... PaulEddery 12 51
(S R Bowring) *s.i.s: n.m.r 3f out: hdwy over 1f out: n.d* **25/1**

641- **8** 2 ½ **Prettilini**[28] 6561 3-8-10 **65** .... RichardThomas(3) 7 43
(A W Carroll) *broke wl: hld up in tch: rdn over 3f out: wknd over 2f out* **7/1**[2]

200- **9** ¾ **Spirit Of Coniston**[59] 6311 3-8-8 **60** ow1 .... MickyFenton 2 36
(M Wellings) *led 1f: prom: rdn over 3f out: wknd over 1f out* **14/1**

403- **10** 1 **African Concerto (IRE)**[10] 6688 3-9-2 **68** .... ChrisCatlin 8 41
(S Kirk) *s.i.s: a bhd* **9/1**[3]

640- **11** 2 **Reality Time (IRE)**[143] 4543 3-9-2 **68** .... EddieAhern 3 35
(J A Osborne) *a bhd* **14/1**

100- **12** ½ **Mr Rigsby**[24] 6591 3-9-2 **68** .... FergalLynch 13 33
(P Howling) *prom: rdn over 2f out: wknd over 1f out* **22/1**

1m 15.4s (-0.41) **Going Correction** -0.05s/f (Stan) 12 Ran SP% **122.7**
Speed ratings (Par 97):100,97,97,94,91 90,90,87,86,84 82,81
CSF £21.21 CT £141.31 TOTE £2.60: £1.50, £2.30, £2.20; EX 18.00.
Owner Trevor Gallienne **Bred** Kilnamoragh Stud **Trained** Pandy, Abergavenny

FOCUS
A fair early gallop and Grenane won tidily. The winner should rate higher and the form appears sound enough.

69 WOLVERHAMPTON-RACECOURSE.CO.UK (S) STKS 1m 141y(P)
2:00 (2:01) (Class 6) 3-Y-0 **£2,388** (£705; £352) **Stalls** Low

Form RPR

64-2 **1** **Ten Shun**[6] 20 3-8-11 60 .... DeanMcKeown 12 63+
(M J Polglase) *mde all: clr 2f out: sn rdn: r.o wl* **5/1**[2]

513- **2** 3 ½ **She Whispers (IRE)**[23] 6600 3-8-6 54 .... ChrisCatlin 1 49
(G C H Chung) *hld up and bhd: rdn and hdwy over 2f out: r.o to take 2nd nr fin: no ch w wnr* **7/1**[3]

061- **3** nk **Noble Edge**[9] 6697 3-8-11 61 ....(p) FergalLynch 5 54
(P A Blockley) *sn prom: rdn over 2f out: edgd lft over 1f out: kpt on same pce* **7/1**[3]

05-5 **4** nk **Miss Champagne (IRE)**[5] 31 3-8-1 52 .... RoryMoore(5) 9 48
(M Quinn) *sn chsng wnr: rdn 3f out: one pce fnl 2f* **12/1**

243- **5** 2 ½ **Cool Isle**[49] 6403 3-8-1 55 ....(p) AndrewMullen(5) 6 43
(K A Ryan) *hld up in mid-div: rdn and lost pl over 3f out: rallied on ins wl over 1f out: one pce* **9/2**[1]

450- **6** 3 **Cumberland Road**[49] 6403 3-8-11 60 .... LeeEnstone 4 41
(P C Haslam) *hld up: rdn and hdwy 3f out: wknd wl over 1f out* **10/1**

243- **7** 1 ¾ **Bathwick Rox (IRE)**[9] 6697 3-8-5 58 ow1 ....(p) JamesMillman(7) 11 39
(B R Millman) *nvr nr ldrs* **7/1**[3]

00- **8** nk **Grove Cherry (IRE)**[129] 4923 3-8-6 .... EddieAhern 2 32
(M H Tompkins) *dwlt: nvr nr ldrs* **5/1**[2]

000- **9** 2 ½ **Bright**[132] 4847 3-8-11 48 .... BrianReilly 3 32
(Miss J Feilden) *prom 3f* **25/1**

030- **10** 1 ¾ **Secret Tender (IRE)**[21] 6617 3-8-11 50 .... RobertWinston 13 28
(J R Weymes) *hld up in mid-div: stdy hdwy over 5f out: rdn over 3f out: wknd over 2f out* **16/1**

005- **11** 7 **Master Ben (IRE)**[9] 6697 3-8-11 55 ....(b) PaulEddery 8 14
(S R Bowring) *s.i.s: sn prom: rdn over 3f out: wknd over 2f out* **25/1**

00- **12** 18 **Bahhmirage (IRE)**[20] 6635 3-8-6 .... FrancisFerris 7 —
(C N Kellett) *s.i.s: a bhd: rdn 4f out: t.o* **66/1**

1m 52.31s (0.55) **Going Correction** -0.05s/f (Stan) 12 Ran SP% **120.9**
Speed ratings (Par 95):95,91,91,91,89 86,84,84,82,80 74,58
CSF £40.16 TOTE £6.30: £1.90, £3.60, £2.90; EX 35.90.The winner was bought in for 6,500gns.
Owner Paul J Dixon **Bred** R J Cornelius **Trained** Babworth, Notts
■ Stewards' Enquiry : Dean McKeown two-day ban: careless riding (Jan 20-21)

FOCUS
A typically moderate contest and an easy win for Ten Shun who received a fine front-running ride by McKeown. The winner is the best guide to the level.
Bathwick Rox(IRE) Official explanation: jockey said gelding hung violently right-handed

70 BETDIRECT FREEPHONE 0800 211 222 MAIDEN STKS 7f 32y(P)
2:30 (2:33) (Class 5) 3-Y-0 **£3,886** (£1,156; £577; £288) **Stalls** High

Form RPR

234- **1** **Critic (IRE)**[93] 5746 3-9-0 86 .... JamieSpencer 5 74+
(M L W Bell) *a gng wl: led on bit over 2f out: shkn up over 1f out: sn clr: easily* **1/2**[1]

05- **2** 5 **Blue Beacon**[24] 6595 3-8-9 .... NCallan 9 56
(K A Ryan) *sn prom: ev ch over 2f out: sn rdn: one pce* **14/1**[3]

3 nk **Pretty Sister** 3-8-2 .... LiamJones(7) 4 55+
(W J Haggas) *hld up and bhd: rdn and hdwy wl over 1f out: sn edgd rt: r.o ins fnl f* **20/1**

24- **4** shd **Didn't We (IRE)**[101] 5584 3-9-0 .... PaulDoe 7 60
(T G Mills) *a.p: rdn over 2f out: one pce fnl f* **11/4**[2]

00- **5** 2 **Valentino Taffi**[31] 6532 3-9-0 .... GrahamGibbons 2 55
(S C Williams) *hld up: rdn over 3f out: hdwy over 2f out: wknd over 1f out* **66/1**

5- **6** 1 ¾ **Shardia (IRE)**[19] 6641 3-8-2 .... TJHowell(7) 1 45
(J Jay) *led early: prom: rdn over 3f out: wknd fnl f* **50/1**

7 ½ **Rudry World (IRE)** 3-9-0 .... FergalLynch 3 49
(P A Blockley) *s.s: bhd tl hdwy and hung lft fr over 1f out: n.d* **33/1**

8 1 **King's Melody** 3-8-7 .... JamesMillman(7) 6 46
(B R Millman) *bhd: sme hdwy on ins whn hung lft wl over 1f out: nvr nr ldrs* **33/1**

00- **9** 4 **Tesoro**[9] 6694 3-8-7 .... KevinGhunowa(7) 10 36
(P A Blockley) *s.i.s: t.k.h: sn prom: rdn and wknd over 2f out* **100/1**

10 ½ **Palm Desert (IRE)** 3-9-0 .... JoeFanning 12 35
(M H Tompkins) *s.i.s: a bhd* **40/1**

05- **11** 1 ½ **Boucheen**[31] 6531 3-8-11 .... NeilChalmers(3) 11 31
(Ms Deborah J Evans) *prom tl rdn and wknd over 2f out* **66/1**

0- **12** 4 **Blue Danielle (IRE)**[49] 6402 3-8-9 .... MickyFenton 8 15
(A D Brown) *sn led: rdn and hdd over 2f out: wkng whn n.m.r ent st* **66/1**

1m 31.51s (1.11) **Going Correction** -0.05s/f (Stan) 12 Ran SP% **120.5**
Speed ratings (Par 97):91,85,84,84,82 80,79,78,74,73 71,67
CSF £9.41 TOTE £1.60: £1.10, £2.50, £3.00; EX 11.10.
Owner Highclere Thoroughbred Racing XXX **Bred** Tullamaine Castle Stud **Trained** Newmarket, Suffolk

FOCUS
No strength in depth to this maiden and the winner won as he was entitled to on official figures. It was a moderate winning time for the type of contest and by far the slowest of the three races over the trip on the day.
Rudry World(IRE) Official explanation: jockey said gelding ran green and hung left

71 TEXT "BETDIRECT" TO 88600 APPRENTICE H'CAP (DIV I) 7f 32y(P)
3:00 (3:01) (Class 6) (0-65,66) 4-Y-0+ **£2,047** (£604; £302) **Stalls** High

Form RPR

56P- **1** **Samuel Charles**[20] 6638 8-8-13 **62** .... AndrewMullen(3) 4 74
(C R Dore) *hld up in mid-div: hdwy over 2f out: rdn whn carried hd high and edgd lft over 1f out: led ins fnl f: r.o wl* **13/2**[2]

00-1 **2** 3 ½ **Alpaga Le Jomage (IRE)**[8] 1 4-9-6 **66** 6ex .... BrianReilly 5 69
(M J Polglase) *sn chsng ldr: rdn over 2f out: ev ch 1f out: one pce* **7/1**[3]

03-0 **3** hd **Second Reef**[8] 4 4-8-11 **62** .... DonnaCaldwell(5) 3 64
(E J Alston) *sn led: rdn over 2f out: hdd and no ex ins fnl f* **7/1**[3]

04-3 **4** 1 ½ **Lord Chamberlain**[4] 44 13-8-10 **61** ....(b) KellyHarrison(5) 6 60
(J M Bradley) *bhd: hdwy over 2f out: rdn wl over 1f out: one pce fnl f* **4/1**[1]

63-0 **5** *nk* **Miskina**^{8} [1] 5-8-13 **59** .... PatrickMathers 1 57
(W M Brisbourne) *t.k.h: led early: prom: rdn over 2f out: wknd ins fnl f* **13/2**^{2}

66-6 **6** *nk* **Extra Mark**^{5} [35] 4-8-8 **61** .... (e^{1}) WilliamCarson$^{(7)}$ 11 58
(J R Best) *bhd: hdwy on ins wl over 1f out: one pce fnl f* **20/1**

006- **7** *5* **Taranaki**^{156} [4154] 8-8-9 **60** .... TravisBlock$^{(5)}$ 10 44
(P D Cundell) *nvr nr ldrs* **8/1**

050- **8** *3/4* **Agilete**^{13} [6672] 4-9-3 **63** .... AmirQuinn 8 45
(J R Boyle) *sn prom: rdn over 3f out: sn wknd* **16/1**

000- **9** *hd* **Savoy Chapel**^{21} [6622] 4-9-0 **60** .... DNolan 9 42
(A W Carroll) *hld up towards rr: hdwy over 3f out: wknd wl over 1f out* **10/1**

435- **10** *1* **Storm Centre**^{84} [5952] 4-9-4 **64** .... NeilChalmers 7 43
(A M Balding) *sn prom: rdn over 2f out: wknd wl over 1f out* **8/1**

600- **11** *8* **Sweetest Revenge (IRE)**^{30} [6546] 5-8-9 **62** .... KMay$^{(7)}$ 12 20
(M D I Usher) *bhd fnl 3f* **33/1**

1m 29.2s (-1.20) **Going Correction** -0.05s/f (Stan) 11 Ran SP% **116.6**
Speed ratings (Par 101):104,100,99,98,97 97,91,90,90,89 80
CSF £51.05 CT £264.59 TOTE £5.90: £2.00, £2.50, £2.80; EX 76.80.
Owner Chris Marsh **Bred** Sheikh Mohammed Obaid Al Maktoum **Trained** West Pinchbeck, Lincs

FOCUS
Modest stuff, but Samuel Charles won emphatically and is clearly on good terms with himself at present. The form is rated around the first two.
Agilete Official explanation: jockey said gelding was never travelling
Storm Centre Official explanation: jockey said gelding hung left in home straight

72 HOLIDAY INN GARDEN COURT WOLVERHAMPTON H'CAP 1m 4f 50y(P)
3:30 (3:31) (Class 6) (0-55,54) 4-Y-0+ **£2,388** (£705; £352) **Stalls** Low

Form RPR

32-1 **1** **Little Richard (IRE)**^{5} [40] 7-8-9 **52** 6ex .... (p) NeilChalmers$^{(3)}$ 6 60+
(M Wellings) *hld up: sn mid-div: stdy hdwy on ins 7f out: n.m.r wl over 1f out: r.o wl to ld cl home* **9/1**

064- **2** *1* **Star Welcome**^{21} [6614] 5-8-9 **49** ow1 .... NCallan 11 53
(W J Musson) *hld up and bhd: hdwy 3f out: rdn and ev ch whn carried rt fr over 1f out: r.o* **8/1**^{2}

316- **3** *nk* **Iftikhar (USA)**^{315} [530] 7-9-0 **54** .... JamieSpencer 12 58
(W M Brisbourne) *led: rdn over 2f out: edgd rt fr over 1f out: hdd cl home* **8/1**^{2}

230- **4** *1* **York Cliff**^{9} [6701] 8-8-13 **53** .... EddieAhern 3 55
(W M Brisbourne) *hld up towards rr: rdn and hdwy on ins wl over 1f out: kpt on ins fnl f* **4/1**^{1}

000- **5** *2* **Shami**^{13} [6674] 7-8-10 **50** .... TonyCulhane 8 49
(D W Chapman) *a.p: rdn over 2f out: edgd rt over 1f out: one pce* **25/1**

600- **6** *shd* **Desert Hawk**^{12} [6678] 5-8-8 **48** .... RobbieFitzpatrick 2 47
(W M Brisbourne) *hld up and bhd: rdn and hdwy 1f out: nvr trbld ldrs* **25/1**

010- **7** *3/4* **Three Ships**^{33} [6522] 5-8-13 **53** .... DarrenWilliams 7 50
(Miss J Feilden) *plld hrd early: prom: rdn over 2f out: wknd fnl f* **22/1**

350- **8** *nk* **Farnborough (USA)**^{30} [6548] 5-8-7 **54** .... JamesDoyle$^{(7)}$ 1 51
(R J Price) *s.i.s: hdwy over 5f out: rdn over 2f out: nt clr run and lost pl wl over 1f out: n.d after* **12/1**

002- **9** *1 1/2* **Sriology (IRE)**^{25} [6587] 5-8-12 **52** .... ChrisCatlin 10 46
(G Prodromou) *hld up in mid-div: rdn over 2f out: no hdwy* **17/2**^{3}

130- **10** *7* **Pharaoh Prince**^{42} [6448] 5-9-0 **54** .... (v) RobertWinston 9 37
(G Prodromou) *prom: rdn over 3f out: wkng whn wl over 1f out* **8/1**^{2}

014- **11** *7* **So Elegant (IRE)**^{35} [6506] 4-8-8 **52** .... HayleyTurner 4 24
(J Jay) *hld up in mid-div: pushed along and sme hdwy 6f out: rdn over 3f out: sn bhd* **4/1**^{1}

155- **12** *1* **Abbeygate**^{13} [6667] 5-9-0 **54** .... BrianReilly 5 24
(T Keddy) *s.i.s: hld up and bhd: hdwy over 5f out: rdn 3f out: sn lost pl and eased* **11/1**

2m 43.75s (1.33) **Going Correction** -0.05s/f (Stan)
WFA 4 from 5yo+ 4lb 12 Ran SP% **121.9**
Speed ratings (Par 101):93,92,92,91,90 90,89,89,88,83 79,78
CSF £79.50 CT £607.26 TOTE £7.60: £2.90, £4.00, £3.20; EX 92.40.
Owner Mark Wellings Racing **Bred** Rathbarry Stud **Trained** Six Ashes, Shropshire

FOCUS
A very moderate winning time for the class and the form is modest, with the runner-up the best guide.
Abbeygate Official explanation: jockey said gelding was injured leaving stalls

73 BETDIRECT.CO.UK H'CAP 1m 1f 103y(P)
4:00 (4:03) (Class 6) (0-58,59) 4-Y-0+ **£2,388** (£705; £352) **Stalls** Low

Form RPR

360- **1** **Cup Of Love (USA)**^{18} [6654] 4-9-0 **57** .... ChrisCatlin 11 62
(Rae Guest) *a.p: led over 2f out: sn rdn: r.o* **9/1**

300- **2** *hd* **Bavarica**^{10} [6687] 4-8-7 **57** .... JamesDoyle$^{(7)}$ 10 62
(Miss J Feilden) *hld up and bhd: rdn and hdwy over 2f out: r.o ins fnl f* **33/1**

40-0 **3** *3/4* **Sol Rojo**^{7} [13] 4-8-13 **56** .... (b) RobbieFitzpatrick 5 60
(M J Attwater) *led: hdd 7f out: sn hit rail: rdn over 3f out: ev ch ins fnl f: nt qckn* **12/1**

30-1 **4** *1/2* **Risk Free**^{3} [56] 9-8-10 **59** 6ex .... (bt) JBrennan$^{(7)}$ 3 62
(P D Evans) *s.i.s: hld up: rdn and hdwy over 2f out: r.o ins fnl f* **5/1**^{1}

0- **5** *1 3/4* **Adarila (IRE)**^{77} [6089] 5-8-13 **55** .... AdrianTNicholls 2 54
(James Leavy, Ire) *hld up in mid-div: hdwy on ins over 2f out: edgd rt wl over 1f out: one pce* **20/1**

010- **6** *1/2* **Barons Spy (IRE)**^{20} [6626] 5-9-1 **57** .... DarrenWilliams 4 55
(R J Price) *hld up in tch: rdn over 2f out: no ex ins fnl f* **8/1**

000- **7** *3/4* **Friends Hope**^{20} [6626] 5-8-13 **55** .... PatCosgrave 12 52
(P A Blockley) *s.s: bhd: hdwy fnl f: nrst fin* **14/1**

310- **8** *1 1/2* **Blue Quiver (IRE)**^{20} [6626] 6-9-2 **58** .... MickyFenton 13 52
(C A Horgan) *s.v.s: hdwy on ins wl over 1f out: no further prog fnl f* **7/1**

000- **9** *hd* **Fortune Point (IRE)**^{23} [6596] 8-9-2 **58** .... (v) TonyCulhane 7 52
(A W Carroll) *led 7f out: hdd over 2f out: sn rdn: wknd ins fnl f* **12/1**

01- **10** *3 1/2* **La Gessa**^{117} [5232] 4-9-0 **57** .... JamieSpencer 9 44
(John Berry) *hld up in mid-div: lost pl over 6f out: nt clr run 4f out: n.d after* **11/2**^{2}

050- **11** *1/2* **Highliner**^{10} [6687] 4-9-0 **57** .... TomEaves 6 43
(Mrs L Williamson) *hld up in tch: rdn over 3f out: wknd over 2f out* **8/1**

000- **12** *6* **Sting Like A Bee (IRE)**^{24} [6593] 7-8-13 **55** .... FergalLynch 8 30
(J S Goldie) *hld up: hdwy over 4f out: rdn over 3f out: wkng whn n.m.r wl over 1f out* **16/1**

065- **13** *6* **Tricky Venture**^{20} [6626] 6-8-13 **55** .... HayleyTurner 1 18
(Mrs L C Jewell) *prom: sltly hmpd over 6f out: lost pl over 3f out* **6/1**^{3}

2m 2.26s (-0.36) **Going Correction** -0.05s/f (Stan)
WFA 4 from 5yo+ 1lb 13 Ran SP% **126.7**
Speed ratings (Par 101):99,98,98,97,96 95,95,93,93,90 89,84,79
CSF £286.21 CT £3585.78 TOTE £11.10: £3.60, £9.20, £6.40; EX 184.50.
Owner Adrian Smith **Bred** A Smith **Trained** Newmarket, Suffolk

FOCUS
A modest handicap run at only an ordinary pace with the placed horses setting a sound enough standard.
La Gessa Official explanation: jockey said filly suffered interference in running
Tricky Venture Official explanation: jockey said gelding lost its action

74 TEXT "BETDIRECT" TO 88600 APPRENTICE H'CAP (DIV II) 7f 32y(P)
4:30 (4:31) (Class 6) (0-65,65) 4-Y-0+ **£2,047** (£604; £302) **Stalls** High

Form RPR

064- **1** **Kindlelight Debut**^{24} [6594] 6-8-12 **64** .... JamesDoyle$^{(5)}$ 11 77
(N P Littmoden) *hld up and bhd: hdwy 2f out: sn rdn: led wl ins fnl f: r.o wl* **7/2**^{2}

041- **2** *1 1/2* **Holiday Cocktail**^{20} [6625] 4-8-13 **63** .... GregFairley$^{(3)}$ 5 72
(S C Williams) *t.k.h: chsd ldr: led 2f out: rdn and edgd lft wl over 1f out: hdd wl ins fnl f: nt qckn* **2/1**^{1}

400- **3** *1 1/4* **Hand Chime**^{20} [6632] 9-8-8 **60** .... LiamJones$^{(5)}$ 4 66
(Ernst Oertel) *led early: a.p: carried sltly lft wl over 1f out: nt qckn ins fnl f* **10/1**

640- **4** *1/2* **Rowan Warning**^{21} [6619] 4-8-13 **60** .... AmirQuinn 10 65
(J R Boyle) *hld up and bhd: hdwy over 1f out: r.o ins fnl f* **22/1**

222- **5** *nk* **I Wish**^{20} [6625] 8-8-12 **59** .... DNolan 8 63
(Miss J R Tooth) *hld up in mid-div: rdn and hdwy over 1f out: kpt on ins fnl f* **8/1**

202- **6** *4* **Kallista's Pride**^{20} [6630] 6-8-5 **59** .... WilliamCarson$^{(7)}$ 12 53
(J R Best) *hld up and bhd: rdn and hdwy on outside 2f out: hung lft over 1f out: wknd ins fnl f* **8/1**

100- **7** *3* **Lobengula (IRE)**^{18} [6535] 4-8-10 **60** .... AndrewMullen$^{(3)}$ 3 46
(I W McInnes) *sn led: rdn and hdd 2f out: carried sltly lft wl over 1f out: eased whn btn wl ins fnl f* **33/1**

103- **8** *1 3/4* **Gramada (IRE)**^{28} [6566] 4-8-8 **60** .... KevinGhunowa$^{(5)}$ 1 41
(P A Blockley) *hld up in mid-div: t.k.h and hdwy over 4f out: rdn over 2f out: hmpd over 1f out: nt rcvr* **16/1**

006- **9** *1 1/2* **Merdiff**^{20} [6632] 7-9-2 **63** .... PatrickMathers 2 40+
(W M Brisbourne) *prom: rdn 2f out: hmpd on ins wl over 1f out: nt rcvr* **5/1**^{3}

104- **10** *6* **Vlasta Weiner**^{21} [6618] 6-9-1 **62** .... (b) PhillipMakin 9 24
(J M Bradley) *hld up in mid-div: rdn over 3f out: short-lived effrt on outside over 2f out* **16/1**

1m 29.58s (-0.82) **Going Correction** -0.05s/f (Stan) 10 Ran SP% **122.6**
Speed ratings (Par 101):102,100,98,98,97 93,89,87,86,79
CSF £11.55 CT £68.31 TOTE £6.60: £2.40, £1.30, £2.50; EX 16.50 Place 6 £157.80, Place 5 £46.29 .
Owner Kindlelight Ltd **Bred** Cheveley Park Stud Ltd **Trained** Newmarket, Suffolk

FOCUS
Just an ordinary pace for this handicap and the whole field were only covered by just a couple of lengths turning in before the tempo quickened. The winning time was 0.38 seconds slower than the first division, but the form looks sound enough rated through the third, fourth and fifth.
Rowan Warning Official explanation: jockey said gelding suffered interference
Lobengula(IRE) Official explanation: jockey said gelding hung throughout
Gramada(IRE) Official explanation: jockey said filly suffered interference in home straight
Merdiff Official explanation: jockey said gelding suffered interference in home straight
T/Plt: £133.70 to a £1 stake. Pool: £37,018.65. 202.10 winning tickets. T/Qpdt: £34.30 to a £1 stake. Pool: £3,472.80. 74.80 winning tickets. KH

^{24}SOUTHWELL (L-H)
Tuesday, January 10

OFFICIAL GOING: Standard
Wind: Moderate, across

75 PLAY NOW AT BETDIRECTPOKER.COM APPRENTICE H'CAP 1m 4f (F)
12:50 (12:50) (Class 5) (0-70,65) 4-Y-0+ **£3,238** (£963; £481; £240) **Stalls** Low

Form RPR

05-0 **1** **Isa'Af (IRE)**^{6} [37] 7-9-2 **65** .... JosephWalsh$^{(5)}$ 3 73
(P W Hiatt) *chsd ldng pair: hdwy 1/2-way: led 4f out: rdn clr 2f out: kpt on u.p ins last* **5/1**^{2}

6-46 **2** *2* **Romil Star (GER)**^{8} [12] 9-9-2 **65** .... (v) PatrickDonaghy$^{(5)}$ 1 70
(K R Burke) *towards rr: pushed along 1/2-way: rdn along 4f out: styd on u.p to chse wnr ent last: kpt on* **12/1**

524- **3** *6* **Yenaled**^{14} [6669] 9-9-4 **65** .... DonnaCaldwell$^{(3)}$ 4 62
(P S McEntee) *hld up in tch: hdwy 1/2-way: rdn along over 2f out: sn one pce* **8/1**^{3}

152- **4** *2 1/2* **Night Warrior (IRE)**^{13} [6680] 6-8-2 **51** .... (b) KevinGhunowa$^{(5)}$ 6 44
(N P Littmoden) *hld up in tch: hdwy 4f out: rdn to chse wnr 3f out: drvn and wknd wl over 1f out* **7/2**^{1}

003- **5** *3 1/2* **Windy Prospect**^{14} [6671] 4-9-0 **62** .... AndrewMullen 8 50
(C R Dore) *towards rr: pushed along and sme hdwy 4f out: rdn 3f out: drvn and no imp fnl 2f* **8/1**^{3}

61-6 **6** *3/4* **High Frequency (IRE)**^{8} [13] 5-8-2 **51** oh1 .... (b) JamesDoyle$^{(5)}$ 7 38
(T D Barron) *cl up: led after 1f and set str pce: rdn along over 4f out: sn hdd & wknd 3f out* **7/2**^{1}

000- **7** *24* **Rare Coincidence**^{19} [6548] 5-8-9 **53** .... (p) GregFairley 2 7
(R F Fisher) *led 1f: chsd ldr tl rdn along 1/2-way: sn lost pl and bhd whn eased over 2f out* **7/2**^{1}

2m 46.2s (4.11) **Going Correction** +0.125s/f (Slow)
WFA 4 from 5yo+ 4lb 7 Ran SP% **113.2**
Speed ratings (Par 103):91,89,85,84,81 81,65
CSF £58.63 CT £469.06 TOTE £7.00: £3.30, £5.60; EX 59.40.
Owner Phil Kelly **Bred** T Monaghan **Trained** Hook Norton, Oxon
■ Stewards' Enquiry : Andrew Mullen two-day ban: used whip with excessive frequency (Jan 21, 23)

FOCUS
Just a modest apprentice handicap but, although they went a good pace, those who were held up struggled to get competitive. The winning time was very moderate for the class, 3.5 seconds slower than the seller and the form does not appear that reliable.
Rare Coincidence Official explanation: jockey said gelding had run flat

76 PLAY NOW ON BETDIRECTCASINO.COM "PREMIER" CLAIMING STKS 7f (F)
1:20 (1:22) (Class 5) 3-Y-O **£5,181** (£1,541; £770; £384) **Stalls** Low

Form RPR

5- **1** **Drawback (IRE)**[71] 6199 3-8-11 .... EddieAhern 5 75
(J A Osborne) *dwlt: hld up in tch: hdwy on outer 3f out: rdn to chal and edgd lft over 1f out: styd on to ld ins last: rdn out* **9/1**

026- **2** ½ **Fangorn Forest (IRE)**[22] 6617 3-8-9 70 .... (p) NCallan 1 72
(K A Ryan) *cl up: led ½-wy: rdn and hdd 2f out: sn drvn: ev ch tl no ex wl ins last* **9/2**[3]

116- **3** 1¼ **The City Kid (IRE)**[14] 6673 3-8-9 75 .... (v) RobertWinston 3 71+
(P D Evans) *trckd ldrs: hdwy to chal 2f out: sn led: rdn over 1f out: drvn and hdd ins last: wknd towards fin* **15/8**[2]

402- **4** 3½ **Outlook**[14] 6673 3-9-7 78 .... (b) MickyFenton 8 72
(N P Littmoden) *led to 1/2-way: cl up tl led again 2f out: sn rdn and hdd over 1f out: drvn and wknd ent last* **6/4**[1]

233- **5** 1 **Rosthwaite (IRE)**[97] 5694 3-8-9 72 .... DeanMcKeown 4 57
(Ronald Thompson) *prom: rdn along wl over 2f out: grad wknd* **11/1**

6- **6** 22 **Sweet Rosella**[14] 6670 3-7-6 .... NicolaTopper(7) 7 —
(G M Moore) *rdn along and bhd fr 1/2-way* **66/1**

200- **7** 5 **Roonah (FR)**[46] 6420 3-8-10 60 .... (b[1]) ChrisCatlin 2 —
(Karen McLintock) *s.i.s: a rr: bhd fr 3f out* **28/1**

1m 33.17s (2.37) **Going Correction** +0.125s/f (Slow) **7** Ran SP% **116.2**
Speed ratings (Par 97):91,90,89,85,83 58,53
CSF £50.12 TOTE £7.20: £3.00, £3.10; EX 37.20.The winner was claimed by R. A. Harris for £12,000.
Owner J A Osborne **Bred** Mrs H B Raw **Trained** Upper Lambourn, Berks
■ Stewards' Enquiry : Robert Winston caution: careless riding

FOCUS
Not a bad race for the grade - the prizemoney was respectable - and it proved to be pretty competitive and has been rated at face value. That said, the winning time was moderate.

77 BETDIRECT.CO.UK H'CAP 1m (F)
1:50 (1:53) (Class 6) (0-65,70) 4-Y-O+ **£2,266** (£674; £337; £168) **Stalls** Low

Form RPR

62-1 **1** **Speed Dial Harry (IRE)**[8] 15 4-9-9 70 6ex .... (v) HayleyTurner 13 81
(K R Burke) *in tch: hdwy over 2f out: rdn to ld over 1f out: hdd ins last: drvn and rallied to ld nr fin* **4/1**[2]

00-5 **2** hd **Mister Benji**[9] 8 7-8-9 56 .... DeanMcKeown 11 67
(B P J Baugh) *hld up towards rr: hdwy over 2f out: rdn over 1f out: edgd lft and led ins last: hdd and no ex nr fin* **25/1**

21-3 **3** 2½ **Greenbelt**[8] 15 5-8-11 58 .... EddieAhern 4 64
(G M Moore) *chsd ldrs: hdwy over 2f out: sn rdn and kpt on same pce u.p ent last* **11/2**[3]

331- **4** 2½ **Chicken Soup**[31] 6535 4-9-1 65 .... DanielTudhope(3) 9 66
(D Carroll) *prom: effrt to ld wl over 2f out: sn rdn and hdd over 1f out: sn drvn and wknd* **8/1**

33-1 **5** ½ **Blue Empire (IRE)**[9] 8 5-8-11 58 6ex .... RobertWinston 8 58
(C R Dore) *cl up: led 1/2-way: rdn along and hdd wl over 2f out: sn drvn and wknd* **7/4**[1]

31-2 **6** ½ **Quiet Reading (USA)**[9] 8 9-8-6 53 .... (v) JimmyQuinn 12 52
(M R Bosley) *in tch: hdwy to chse ldrs wl over 2f out: sn rdn and kpt on same pce* **14/1**

623- **7** 1¾ **Bridgewater Boys**[14] 6674 5-8-9 56 .... (bt) NCallan 2 52
(K A Ryan) *sn pushed along on inner to chse ldrs: hdwy on inner 3f out: rdn over 2f out: sn drvn and wknd* **9/1**

005- **8** 13 **Legal Dram**[22] 6619 5-8-7 54 .... PhillipMakin 7 24
(M Dods) *towards rr tl sme hdwy fnl 2f: nvr a factor* **40/1**

11-6 **9** nk **Preskani**[9] 8 4-8-9 61 .... (p) DuranFentiman(5) 14 30
(Mrs N Macauley) *racd wd: hdwy over 3f out: rdn to chse ldrs over 2f out: sn wknd* **25/1**

045- **10** 6 **Knock Bridge (IRE)**[19] 6134 4-8-8 62 .... JBrennan(7) 1 19
(P D Evans) *s.i.s: a rr* **40/1**

/50- **11** nk **Suffolk House**[31] 6542 4-8-13 60 .... AdrianTNicholls 10 16
(K A Ryan) *chsd ldrs: rdn along 3f out: sn wknd* **100/1**

000- **12** 2 **Qobtaan (USA)**[21] 6625 7-8-12 59 .... TonyCulhane 3 11
(M R Bosley) *slwoly into stride: a rr* **50/1**

100- **13** ½ **Formidable Will (FR)**[14] 6671 4-9-1 62 .... (tp) DaleGibson 5 13
(M W Easterby) *s.i.s: a rr* **22/1**

53-0 **14** 13 **Lockstock (IRE)**[8] 15 8-9-2 63 .... MickyFenton 6 —
(M S Saunders) *led: pushed along and hdd 1/2-way: sn rdn and wknd* **16/1**

1m 44.48s (-0.12) **Going Correction** +0.125s/f (Slow) **14** Ran SP% **125.3**
Speed ratings (Par 101):105,104,102,99,99 98,97,84,83,77 77,75,74,61
CSF £110.05 CT £590.19 TOTE £3.80: £1.70, £6.30, £1.80; EX 209.10.
Owner Nigel Shields **Bred** Brendan Lavery **Trained** Middleham Moor, N Yorks

FOCUS
A modest but competitive handicap and, with so many of these seemingly keen to make the running, the pace was fast. The form looks sound enough overall.
Preskani Official explanation: jockey said gelding hung right-handed throughout
Qobtaan(USA) Official explanation: trainer said gelding would not face the kickback

78 LITTLEWOODSPOOLS.CO.UK (S) STKS 1m 4f (F)
2:20 (2:21) (Class 6) 4-6-Y-O **£2,388** (£705; £352) **Stalls** Low

Form RPR

650- **1** **Macaroni Gold (IRE)**[55] 6368 6-9-3 70 .... JamieSpencer 8 74+
(D J Daly) *trckd ldrs gng wl: smooth hdwy on outer over 3f out: led over 2f out: rdn and edgd lft over 1f out: styd on* **5/6**[1]

060- **2** 6 **Hawkit (USA)**[20] 6644 5-9-0 60 .... (t) DanielTudhope(3) 4 62
(P D Evans) *trckd ldrs: smooth hdwy on inner to ld 3f out: rdn and hdd over 2f out: sn drvn and kpt on same pce appr last* **9/2**[3]

00-0 **3** 8 **Extra Cover (IRE)**[8] 13 5-9-3 51 .... MickyFenton 6 51
(Ronald Thompson) *s.i.s and bhd: hdwy on outer 5f out: rdn along 3f out: no imp fnl 2f* **20/1**

1- **4** 5 **Chater Knight (IRE)**[31] 6536 5-9-8 62 .... DeanMcKeown 3 49
(Micky Hammond) *cl up: rdn along over 3f out: sn drvn and one pce* **7/2**[2]

000- **5** 11 **Noble Mind**[64] 6283 5-9-3 60 .... (p) RobertWinston 5 29
(P G Murphy) *chsd ldrs: rdn along over 4f out: sn wknd* **16/1**

030- **6** 6 **Shaheer (IRE)**[11] 6691 4-8-13 53 .... TonyCulhane 2 20
(P Howling) *led: rdn along over 4f out: hdd over 3f out and sn wknd* **22/1**

00-0 **7** 1¼ **Dejeeje (IRE)**[7] 28 5-9-3 35 .... PhillipMakin 7 18
(D W Chapman) *a towards rr* **80/1**

00-0 **8** 16 **Penway**[6] 35 5-9-3 40 .... (b) BrianReilly 9 —
(A Sadik) *keen: chsd ldrs: rdn along 5f out and sn wknd* **66/1**

540- **9** 3½ **Oktis Morilious (IRE)**[12] 6683 5-9-3 35 .... JimmyQuinn 1 —
(A W Carroll) *in tch: rdn along 1/2-way: sn wknd* **20/1**

2m 42.7s (0.61) **Going Correction** +0.125s/f (Slow)
WFA 4 from 5yo+ 4lb **9** Ran SP% **117.4**
Speed ratings: 102,98,92,89,82 78,77,66,64
CSF £4.64 TOTE £2.20: £1.30, £1.30, £5.70; EX 8.80.The winner was bought in for 10,200gns. Extra Cover was claimed by Ms V. Scott for £6,000. Hawkit was the subject of a friendly claim.
Owner Gold Ace Racing **Bred** Thomas Stacey **Trained** Newmarket, Suffolk

FOCUS
A fair seller in which Macaroni Gold totally outclassed his eight rivals. The third sets the level with the winner improving on recent efforts in this lower grade.
Extra Cover(IRE) Official explanation: jockey said gelding hung left-handed from halfway

79 BET NOW AT BETDIRECT.CO.UK H'CAP 5f (F)
2:50 (2:52) (Class 4) (0-85,85) 4-Y-O+ **£6,477** (£1,927; £963; £481) **Stalls** High

Form RPR

530- **1** **The Lord**[24] 6602 6-8-13 80 .... TonyCulhane 6 92
(W G M Turner) *a prom: rdn and edgd lft ent last: sn led and kpt on wl* **7/1**

241- **2** 1½ **After The Show**[24] 6603 5-8-5 72 .... ChrisCatlin 8 79
(Rae Guest) *trckd ldrs: swtchd lft after 1f: hdwy 2f out: sn rdn and kpt on ins last* **6/1**[3]

046- **3** nk **Desperate Dan**[39] 6481 5-9-4 85 .... (b) EddieAhern 7 91
(J A Osborne) *trckd ldrs: hdwy to chal 2f out: rdn to ld briefly 1f out sn drvn: hdd and one pce* **7/2**[2]

502- **4** ½ **Willhewiz**[22] 6616 6-8-8 75 .... PhillipMakin 1 79
(M S Saunders) *cl up: ev ch 2f out: sn rdn and kpt on same pce fnl f* **25/1**

220- **5** ½ **Gilded Cove**[25] 6590 6-8-7 74 .... GrahamGibbons 5 77+
(R Hollinshead) *dwlt: hmpd after 1f: swtchd wd and hdwy 2f out: sn rdn and kpt on ins last: nrst fin* **18/1**

00-6 **6** 1 **Magic Glade**[9] 6 7-8-12 79 .... (b) TomEaves 10 78
(R Brotherton) *led: rdn along 2fg out: drvn and hdd 1f out: wknd* **20/1**

551- **7** 1¾ **Harry Up**[22] 6618 5-8-11 78 .... NCallan 12 71
(K A Ryan) *cl up: rdn along 2f out: sn rdn and wknd over 1f out* **11/4**[1]

001- **8** 3½ **Ryedane (IRE)**[22] 6616 4-8-5 77 .... (e) DuranFentiman(5) 9 58
(T D Easterby) *sn rdn along and a towards rr* **28/1**

000- **9** 1 **Whinhill House**[129] 4938 6-9-4 85 .... RobertWinston 3 63
(D W Barker) *hmpd s: sn chsng ldrs on outer: rdn wl over 1f out and grad wknd* **14/1**

003- **10** 1¼ **Efistorm**[21] 6636 5-8-5 72 .... JoeFanning 2 46
(J Balding) *cl up: rdn along 2f out: sn wknd* **11/1**

400- **11** 5 **Little Ridge (IRE)**[21] 6636 5-8-5 72 .... AdrianTNicholls 4 29
(H Morrison) *dwlt and hmpd s: a rr* **10/1**

101/ **12** 2½ **Lady Bahia (IRE)**[668] 1008 5-8-4 71 oh6 .... (p) JimmyQuinn 11 19
(Peter Grayson) *s.i.s: a rr* **66/1**

59.62 secs (-0.68) **Going Correction** 0.0s/f (Stan) **12** Ran SP% **118.6**
Speed ratings (Par 105):105,102,102,101,100 98,96,90,88,86 78,74
CSF £46.70 CT £174.41 TOTE £9.10: £2.40, £1.90, £1.70; EX 58.30.
Owner Mrs M S Teversham **Bred** Mrs M S Teversham **Trained** Sigwells, Somerset

FOCUS
As is usually the case with sprint handicaps, a very competitive contest and the form look sound with those in the frame behind the winner close to their marks. There has been a significant advantage to low-drawn runners over this course and distance in recent months, but while that was not quite the case this time, it still seems as though those drawn very high are at a disadvantage.
Ryedane(IRE) Official explanation: jockey said gelding had been unsuited by the fibresand surface

80 LITTLEWOODS BETDIRECT H'CAP 6f (F)
3:20 (3:22) (Class 4) (0-85,84) 4-Y-O+ **£6,477** (£1,927; £963; £481) **Stalls** Low

Form RPR

301- **1** **Pinchbeck**[19] 6657 7-9-2 82 .... (p) MatthewHenry 3 89
(M A Jarvis) *towards rr: pushed along and gd hdwy over 2f out: chsd ldrs ocver 1f out: rdn to ld ins last: edgd lft and styd on wl* **9/2**[2]

020- **2** ¾ **Majik**[21] 6632 7-7-11 70 oh4 .... (p) JamesDoyle(7) 5 75
(D J S Ffrench Davis) *towards rr: gd hdwy on outer 2f out: rdn to ld over 1f out: hdd ins last: kpt on* **18/1**

505- **3** nk **Sir Desmond**[25] 6590 8-8-11 77 .... (p) ChrisCatlin 10 81
(Rae Guest) *bhd tl hdwy 2f out: rdn and styd on strly ins last* **12/1**

461- **4** nk **Poker Player (IRE)**[99] 5672 4-8-12 78 .... TonyCulhane 8 81
(G C Bravery) *s.i.s and bhd: hdwy 2f out: sn rdn and kpt on ins last: nrst fin* **9/1**

14-2 **5** shd **Waterside (IRE)**[9] 7 7-9-2 82 .... NCallan 9 85
(G L Moore) *chased ldrs: effrt 2f out: sn rdn and kpt on same pce appr last* **10/3**[1]

634- **6** 1½ **Kingsmaite**[10] 6698 5-8-11 80 .... (b) AmirQuinn(3) 7 78
(S R Bowring) *cl up: effrt to chal 2f out: sn rdn and ev ch tl wknd ent last* **11/2**[3]

221- **7** 3 **Aegean Dancer**[14] 6672 4-8-4 70 .... PaulEddery 6 59
(B Smart) *cl up: led 1/2-way: rdn 2f out: hdd over 1f out: wknd* **10/1**

42-0 **8** ½ **Cerebus**[9] 4 4-7-11 70 oh6 .... ManavNem(7) 4 58
(M J Polglase) *led to 1/2-way: rdn along over 2f out and sn wknd* **50/1**

03-6 **9** 1 **Cornus**[4] 54 4-9-4 84 .... DeanMcKeown 2 69
(M J Polglase) *midfield: hdwy on inner over 2f out: sn rdn and btn wl over 1f out* **8/1**

42-0 **10** 4 **Anfield Dream**[7] 23 4-8-8 74 .... RobertWinston 1 47
(J R Jenkins) *in tch: hdwy to chse ldrs 2f out: sn rdn and wknd over 1f out* **15/2**

000- **11** ½ **Orpen Wide (IRE)**[42] 6465 4-8-7 73 ow1 .... BrianReilly 11 44
(M C Chapman) *bhd fr 1/2-way* **28/1**

065- **12** 2 **Fizzlephut (IRE)**[21] 6636 4-8-13 79 .... LPKeniry 12 44
(Miss J R Tooth) *chsd ldrs: rdn over 2f out and sn wknd* **40/1**

1m 16.62s (-0.28) **Going Correction** +0.125s/f (Slow) **12** Ran SP% **119.4**
Speed ratings (Par 105):106,105,104,104,104 102,98,97,96,90 90,87
CSF £81.88 CT £934.21 TOTE £5.40: £1.90, £5.40, £4.20; EX 140.50.
Owner T G Warner **Bred** Red House Stud **Trained** Newmarket, Suffolk

FOCUS
A competitive sprint handicap, but the leaders looked to go off a little too fast and set the race up for those coming from behind. The form is rated through the first two.

81 TEXT "BETDIRECT" TO 88600 H'CAP 6f (F)
3:50 (3:52) (Class 6) (0-52,52) 4-Y-O+ **£2,388** (£705; £352) **Stalls** Low

Form RPR

523- **1** **Doctor Dennis (IRE)**[11] 6693 9-8-12 52 .... (v) JimmyQuinn 5 61
(J Pearce) *held up towards rr: gd hdwy on inner wl over 1f out: swtchd rt and rdn to ld ins last: kpt on* **5/1**[2]

300- **2** *nk* **Imperium**[11] 6692 5-8-12 **52**..........(p) MickyFenton 12 60
(Stef Liddiard) *sn outpcd and bhd: hdwy on outer 2f out: sn rdn and kpt on strly ins last: jst failed* **14/1**
650- **3** *1 ¾* **Park Star**[11] 6692 6-8-7 **47**.......... RobertWinston 14 50
(D Shaw) *hld up towards rr: hdwy over 2f out: sn rdn and styd on wl fnl f: nrst fin* **16/1**
046- **4** *nk* **High Swainston**[42] 6464 5-8-5 **50**.......... GregFairley(5) 1 52+
(R Craggs) *chsd ldng pair: hdwy 2f out: rdn to ld ent last: sn hdd and one pce* **9/1**
41-2 **5** *½* **Jalouhar**[7] 29 6-7-13 **46**..........(e1) SoniaEaton(7) 10 46
(B P J Baugh) *midfield: hdwy and in tch 2f out: sn rdn and kpt ins last: nrst fin* **6/1**[3]
35-6 **6** *nk* **Musiotal**[6] 43 5-8-9 **49**..........(v1) NCallan 7 49
(P A Blockley) *s.i.s and bhd: wd st: hdwy 2f out: swtchd rt over 1f out: kpt on u.p ins last: nrst fin* **7/1**
40-5 **7** *2* **Limonia (GER)**[7] 24 4-8-10 **50**..........(b) FergalLynch 9 44
(D K Ivory) *led and sn clr: rdn wl over 1f out: hdd & wknd ent last* **11/1**
600- **8** *nk* **Mulberry Lad (IRE)**[14] 6668 4-8-11 **51** ow1.......... DarrenWilliams 2 44
(P W Hiatt) *chsd ldr: rdn 2f out: drvn and wknd appr last* **33/1**
30-5 **9** *1 ½* **St Ivian**[8] 9 6-8-7 **52**.......... DuranFentiman(5) 11 40
(Mrs N Macauley) *bhd tl sme late hdwy* **12/1**
341- **10** *2 ½* **Mind Alert**[29] 6559 5-8-9 **52**..........(v) PatrickMathers(3) 4 33
(D Shaw) *towards rr: gd hdwy on inner to chse ldrs 2f out: sn rdn and btn over 1f out* **9/2**[1]
054- **11** *3* **Dutch Key Card (IRE)**[50] 6407 5-8-12 **52**.......... GylesParkin 6 24
(C Smith) *chsd ldrs: rdn over 2f out: drvn and wknd over 1f out* **9/1**
00-0 **12** *6* **Crusoe (IRE)**[9] 8 9-8-8 **48**..........(b) BrianReilly 3 2
(A Sadik) *a rr* **40/1**
0/0- **13** *6* **Cheeney Basin (IRE)**[314] 547 8-8-1 **48**.......... LiamJones(7) 8 —
(M C Chapman) *chsd ldrs: rdn along wl over 2f out and sn wknd* **66/1**
000- **14** *nk* **Baymist**[68] 6235 4-8-12 **52**.......... DaleGibson 13 —
(M W Easterby) *chsd ldrs to 1/2-way: sn lost pl and bhd* **50/1**

1m 17.12s (0.22) **Going Correction** +0.125s/f (Slow) 14 Ran SP% **119.0**
Speed ratings (Par 101):103,102,100,99,99 98,96,95,93,90 86,78,70,70
CSF £70.92 CT £1079.45 TOTE £2.90: £1.10, £6.20, £7.20; EX 50.00 Place 6 £1,173.09, Place 5 £147.06.
Owner Mrs Jennifer Marsh **Bred** David Allan **Trained** Newmarket, Suffolk

FOCUS
A moderate sprint handicap in which they went a very fast pace from the start and were soon well strung out. The winner is rated to his best form in the last two years.
Mind Alert Official explanation: jockey said gelding hung right-handed in the straight
Crusoe(IRE) Official explanation: jockey said gelding missed the break and would not face the kickback
T/Plt: £694.70 to a £1 stake. Pool: £36,163.90. 38.00 winning tickets. T/Qpdt: £27.50 to a £1 stake. Pool: £3,830.70. 103.00 winning tickets. JR

60 LINGFIELD (L-H)
Wednesday, January 11

OFFICIAL GOING: Standard
Wind: Light, across Weather: Sunny

82 DAILY OFFERS FROM BETDIRECT H'CAP (DIV I) 1m (P)
12:05 (12:05) (Class 6) (0-58,58) 4-Y-0+ **£2,047** (£604; £302) **Stalls** High

Form RPR
400- **1** **Border Edge**[25] 6598 8-9-0 **56**..........(v) NCallan 6 68
(J J Bridger) *b: prom: drvn and effrt 2f out: chsd ldr 1f out: styd on gamely to ld last strides* **10/1**
006- **2** *nk* **Lowestoft Playboy**[20] 6660 4-8-8 **55**.......... GregFairley(5) 7 66
(J Jay) *cl up: prog over 2f out: led wl over 1f out and kicked 2 l clr: worn down last strides* **10/1**
112- **3** *2 ½* **Danettie**[14] 6679 5-8-13 **55**.......... ChrisCatlin 1 61
(W M Brisbourne) *hld up towards rr: prog 3f out: drvn 2f out: chsd ldng pair ins fnl f: no imp* **7/1**
622- **4** *½* **Jomus**[22] 6626 5-9-1 **57**..........(p) RobertWinston 5 61+
(L Montague Hall) *taken down early: s.s: wl in rr: nt clr run over 3f out: prog over 2f out: kpt on u.p fr over 1f out: no ch* **3/1**[1]
00-0 **5** *1 ¾* **Fortune Point (IRE)**[2] 73 8-9-2 **58**..........(v) TonyCulhane 10 58
(A W Carroll) *pressed ldr: led over 2f out: hdd wl over 1f out: wknd tamely* **16/1**
040- **6** *3* **Magic Warrior**[32] 6548 6-8-12 **54**.......... MickyFenton 3 47
(J C Fox) *hld up in rr: effrt on outer over 3f out: sn outpcd: n.d after* **20/1**
151- **7** *hd* **Sonntag Blue (IRE)**[12] 6692 4-8-5 **54**.......... DonnaCaldwell(7) 2 47
(Miss J Feilden) *b: chsd ldrs: lost pl on inner 1/2-way: sn rdn: no prog after* **7/1**
141- **8** *¾* **Captain Darling (IRE)**[12] 6693 6-8-13 **58**.......... EdwardCreighton(3) 9 49
(R W Price) *taken down early: led to over 2f out: wknd rapidly over 1f out* **9/2**[2]
000- **9** *hd* **Gallego**[11] 6696 4-8-11 **53**.......... LPKeniry 11 44
(R J Price) *s.v.s: last tl 3f out: nvr a factor: one pce u.p fnl 2f* **6/1**[3]
000- **10** *4* **Acorazado (IRE)**[23] 6618 7-8-13 **55**..........(v) HayleyTurner 4 37
(C P Morlock) *b: s.s: wl in rr: pushed along on inner 3f out: no prog* **33/1**
000- **11** *20* **Primed Up (IRE)**[22] 6626 4-9-0 **56**..........(be) PaulHanagan 12 —
(G L Moore) *chsd ldrs for 3f: wknd rapidly over 3f out: t.o* **33/1**

1m 37.37s (-2.06) **Going Correction** -0.10s/f (Stan) 11 Ran SP% **117.2**
Speed ratings (Par 101):106,105,103,102,100 97,97,97,96,92 72
CSF £103.00 CT £761.72 TOTE £15.60: £2.80, £5.20, £1.70; EX 114.60.
Owner Allsorts **Bred** R Hutt **Trained** Liphook, Hants

FOCUS
They did not appear to go that fast in the first part of the race, but the time suggests they really quickened in the final half of the race and the winning time was just over a second quicker than the second division. It is probably solid form for the grade.

83 NO 5P RULE 4S AT BETDIRECT APPRENTICE CLAIMING STKS 6f (P)
12:35 (12:36) (Class 6) 3-Y-0 **£2,388** (£705; £352) **Stalls** Low

Form RPR
21-2 **1** **Luloah**[4] 66 3-8-10 57.......... DonnaCaldwell(3) 6 63
(P S McEntee) *lw: mde all: clr fr over 2f out: 4 l ahd over 1f out: shkn up and unchal* **10/3**[1]
2 *2 ½* **Stamford Street (IRE)** 3-8-10 .... JosephWalsh(5) 2 58
(J S Moore) *dwlt: sn midfield: prog over 2f out: hanging rt over 1f out: rdn and r.o to take 2nd nr fin* **33/1**
2-43 **3** *nk* **Buzzin'Boyzee (IRE)**[5] 53 3-8-3 59 ow1.......... JBrennan(5) 9 50
(P D Evans) *dwlt: hld up wl in rr: prog on inner over 2f out: chsd wnr u.str.p ent fnl f: kpt on same pce* **7/2**[2]
04-0 **4** *1* **Pix**[7] 30 3-8-1 52.......... DuranFentiman 3 40
(S Kirk) *chsd clr ldrs: rdn to cl over 2f out: one pce fr over 1f out* **12/1**
02-0 **5** *3* **Sounds Simla (IRE)**[5] 53 3-8-11 82.......... RobbieMills(5) 5 46
(Rae Guest) *lw: towards rr: bmpd along and no prog 1/2-way: kpt on fnl f* **7/2**[2]
345- **6** *hd* **In Hope**[21] 6640 3-8-1 60.......... LiamJones(3) 4 33
(Andrew Reid) *mostly chsd wnr tl wknd ent fnl f* **5/1**[3]
00-3 **7** *1 ¼* **Saxon Star (IRE)**[7] 39 3-8-4 45..........(v) KMay(5) 8 35
(M D I Usher) *prom tl wknd wl over 1f out* **14/1**
060- **8** *3* **Ballyhooligan (IRE)**[21] 6642 3-9-4 53..........(b1) MarcHalford 7 35
(Jamie Poulton) *a towards rr: u.p bef 1/2-way: no ch after* **20/1**
000- **9** *hd* **Dashfa Baileys**[23] 6617 3-8-9 50.......... GregFairley 1 25
(C A Dwyer) *prom tl wknd rapidly over 1f out* **25/1**
000- **10** *7* **First Byte**[22] 6635 3-8-2 45..........(v) StephanieBancroft(5) 11 2
(Miss D A McHale) *hld up in last pair: lost tch fr 1/2-way: t.o* **50/1**
000- **11** *3 ½* **In The Fountain (IRE)**[15] 6670 3-8-2 47 ow6..........(p) MarkWaite(5) 10 —
(C A Dwyer) *lw: outpcd and sn t.o* **40/1**

1m 12.51s (-0.30) **Going Correction** -0.10s/f (Stan) 11 Ran SP% **114.5**
Speed ratings (Par 95):98,94,94,92,88 88,87,83,82,73 68
CSF £119.42 TOTE £3.60: £1.60, £7.90, £1.70; EX 94.40.The winner was the subject of a friendly claim.
Owner Eventmaker Partnership **Bred** Mrs S M Lee **Trained** Newmarket, Suffolk

FOCUS
The winner apart, this was a very moderate race, and the runner-up's performance casts doubt on the level of the form.

84 BETDIRECT FREEPHONE 0800 211 222 MAIDEN STKS 1m (P)
1:10 (1:12) (Class 5) 4-Y-0+ **£3,238** (£963; £481; £240) **Stalls** High

Form RPR
35-4 **1** **Glad Big (GER)**[8] 17 4-9-0 68.......... RobertWinston 5 63+
(J A Osborne) *lw: cl up: led wl over 1f out: sn clr: easily* **1/2**[1]
4- **2** *2* **Melee**[160] 4080 4-8-2 .... TJHowell(7) 9 51
(J Jay) *hld up towards rr: prog on inner whn sltly hmpd over 2f out: rdn and r.o to take 2nd last 100yds: no ch w wnr* **33/1**
56-0 **3** *1 ½* **Height Of Spirits**[7] 32 4-8-11 54.......... RobertMiles(3) 10 52
(T D McCarthy) *b: mde most: rdn over 2f out: hdd and one pce wl over 1f out* **25/1**
400- **4** *¾* **House Martin**[16] 6666 4-8-9 63.......... MickyFenton 11 46
(C R Dore) *t.k.h: in tch on wd outside: effrt over 2f out: kpt on same pce fr over 1f out* **7/1**[3]
000- **5** *3* **In A Fit**[23] 6611 5-8-10 45 ow1.......... TonyCulhane 6 40
(P Howling) *hld up in last trio: shuffled along and kpt on fnl 2f: nvr nr ldrs* **33/1**
0- **6** *¾* **Barachois Gaudy**[63] 6301 4-8-9 .... LPKeniry 4 37
(Mrs N Smith) *b.bkwd: s.s: mostly in last pair tl styd on u.p fr 2f out: no ch* **50/1**
000- **7** *1 ¼* **Zambezi River**[43] 6462 7-8-9 35.......... GregFairley(5) 3 39
(J M Bradley) *plld hrd: hld up in tch: wknd wl over 1f out* **66/1**
8 *1 ½* **Mary Anastatia (USA)**[242] 1719 4-8-9 68.......... MCHussey 1 31
(Eamon Tyrrell, Ire) *s.i.s: pushed up to join ldr: u.p fr 1/2-way: wknd rapidly wl over 1f out* **12/1**
0- **9** *1 ½* **Megalala (IRE)**[208] 2652 5-8-11 .... NeilChalmers(3) 12 32
(J J Bridger) *b.bkwd: chsd ldrs tl wknd over 2f out* **40/1**
2/3- **10** *2 ½* **Duxford**[32] 6545 5-9-0 65.......... JimmyQuinn 7 26
(D K Ivory) *t.k.h: hld up in tch: wknd over 2f out* **11/2**[2]
040- **11** *nk* **Duncanbil (IRE)**[13] 6682 5-8-9 35.......... ChrisCatlin 2 21
(J J Bridger) *b.hind: t.k.h early: a last: lost tch over 2f out* **50/1**

1m 38.97s (-0.46) **Going Correction** -0.10s/f (Stan) 11 Ran SP% **119.8**
Speed ratings (Par 103):98,96,94,93,90 90,88,87,85,83 82
CSF £32.28 TOTE £1.40: £1.10, £4.50, £4.80; EX 21.00.
Owner Mountgrange Stud **Bred** Gestut Auenquelle **Trained** Upper Lambourn, Berks

FOCUS
Probably only a poor maiden and the time was modest for the class when compared to the two divisions of the handicap for older horses.

85 BETDIRECT.CO.UK H'CAP 1m (P)
1:45 (1:47) (Class 6) (0-65,70) 3-Y-0 **£2,388** (£705; £352) **Stalls** High

Form RPR
00-3 **1** **Casablanca Minx (IRE)**[7] 31 3-8-10 **60**.......... EdwardCreighton(3) 8 64
(Mrs H Sweeting) *hld up in rr: prog on outer fr 3f out: rdn and r.o to ld last 150yds: in command after* **12/1**
023- **2** *1 ¼* **Party Belle**[11] 6699 3-9-1 **62**.......... JoeFanning 3 63
(C E Brittain) *hld up in midfield: effrt 2f out: cl up 1f out: kpt on same pce to take 2nd last strides* **10/1**
10-2 **3** *nk* **Ms Rainbow Runner**[7] 30 3-8-13 **60**.......... HayleyTurner 1 60
(P Butler) *t.k.h: hld up midfield: got through on inner 2f out to join ldr over 1f out: upsides ent fnl f: nt qckn* **4/1**[1]
252- **4** *shd* **Tafilah**[23] 6610 3-8-9 **56**..........(v) RobertWinston 9 56
(P W D'Arcy) *lw: prom: rdn to ld wl over 1f out: sn jnd: hdd and nt qckn last 150yds* **7/1**
000- **5** *1 ¼* **Murrumbidgee (IRE)**[37] 6501 3-9-0 **61**.......... MichaelHills 7 58
(J W Hills) *lw: dwlt: hld up towards rr: effrt 2f out: nt qckn wl over 1f out: styd on ins fnl f* **10/1**
330- **6** *½* **Snake Skin**[25] 6599 3-8-8 **55**.......... JimmyQuinn 11 51
(J Gallagher) *chsd ldrs: effrt 2f out: cl up over 1f out: sn rdn and fnd nil* **14/1**
00-0 **7** *hd* **Titus Lumpus (IRE)**[7] 30 3-8-8 **58**.......... RichardThomas(3) 2 54
(R M Flower) *dwlt: hld up in last pair: prog on inner wl over 1f out: one pce and no imp ins fnl f* **14/1**
14-1 **8** *2* **Indian Wizard (IRE)**[8] 20 3-9-9 **70** 6ex.......... TonyCulhane 10 61
(P Howling) *hld up wl in rr: effrt and in tch 2f out: rdn and one pce after* **5/1**[2]
00-3 **9** *4* **Zizou (IRE)**[4] 61 3-9-2 **63**.......... ChrisCatlin 4 45
(P R Hedger) *pushed up to press ldrs: drvn over 2f out: wknd jst over 1f out* **13/2**[3]
21-3 **10** *8* **Babeth (IRE)**[9] 10 3-9-4 **65**.......... LPKeniry 5 29
(A M Balding) *pressed ldr: upsides 2f out: wknd rapidly jst over 1f out* **13/2**[3]
050- **11** *½* **Caan**[149] 4435 3-8-11 **58**.......... MickyFenton 12 20
(D K Ivory) *hld up in last: rdn wl over 3f out: sn struggling and bhd* **33/1**
000- **12** *nk* **Astorygoeswithit**[22] 6634 3-9-3 **64**..........(p) NCallan 6 26
(Lucinda Featherstone) *mde most to wl over 1f out: wknd rapidly and eased* **25/1**

1m 39.04s (-0.39) **Going Correction** -0.10s/f (Stan) 12 Ran SP% **121.8**
Speed ratings (Par 95):97,95,95,95,94 93,93,91,87,79 78,78
CSF £130.16 CT £583.14 TOTE £12.60: £3.00, £3.30, £1.60; EX 120.30.

Owner P Sweeting **Bred** Airlie Stud And Widden Stud **Trained** Lockeridge, Wilts

FOCUS

A low-grade handicap won by a horse who did not have any solid form at the trip. Most of the runners have form in selling company which confirms the stature of the race.

Babeth(IRE) Official explanation: vet said filly was lame

86 DAILY OFFERS FROM BETDIRECT H'CAP (DIV II) 1m (P)

2:15 (2:17) (Class 6) (0-58,58) 4-Y-O+ **£2,047** (£604; £302) **Stalls** High

Form RPR

000- **1** **Burnley Al (IRE)**[20] 6660 4-9-2 **57**....(b) PaulHanagan 10 66
(R A Fahey) mde all: clr early: stdd after 3f: kicked on again 2f out: 3l clr fnl f: in no real danger after **7/1**

05-2 **2** ¾ **Samson Quest**[7] 35 4-9-1 **56**....(v) MickyFenton 1 63
(A W Carroll) dwlt: t.k.h: hld up in last trio: prog 2f out: hemmed in over 1f out: chsd wnr ins fnl f: clsng fast at fin **4/1**[1]

600- **3** 2 **Dennick**[33] 4647 4-8-11 **52**....(t) ChrisCatlin 4 54
(P C Haslam) t.k.h: hld up in midfield: effrt 2f out: rdn and nt qckn over 1f out: styd on ins fnl f **6/1**[3]

015- **4** 1 ¾ **Night Wolf (IRE)**[22] 6630 6-8-12 **53**.... MichaelHills 6 51
(Jamie Poulton) prom: rdn to chse wnr wl over 1f out: no imp: one pce fnl f **9/2**[2]

000- **5** ¾ **Bragadino**[79] 6089 7-9-2 **57**.... TonyCulhane 2 54
(Lindsay Woods, Ire) hld up in midfield: prog on inner over 2f out: rdn and one pce fr over 1f out **8/1**

120- **6** nk **Mythical Charm**[12] 6692 7-8-13 **54**....(t) NCallan 5 50
(J J Bridger) b: plld hrd: hld up in rr: rdn 3f out: nt qckn and no imp fnl 2f **6/1**[3]

50-0 **7** hd **Indigo Sky (IRE)**[7] 35 5-9-0 **55**.... HayleyTurner 9 51
(B G Powell) reluctant to go to post: a in rr: shkn up over 3f out: no prog **25/1**

350- **8** shd **Stagnite**[11] 6695 6-8-11 **55**.... AmirQuinn(3) 12 50
(K McAuliffe) t.k.h: hld up in last: nvr a factor: kpt on fnl f **16/1**

2- **9** ¾ **Glenree**[15] 6487 5-9-1 **56**....(b) MCHussey 7 50
(Eamon Tyrrell, Ire) t.k.h: trckd ldrs on outer: rdn over 2f out: wknd over 1f out **9/1**

00-0 **10** ¾ **Lady Londra**[8] 22 4-9-0 **55**.... JimmyQuinn 11 47
(D K Ivory) mostly chsd wnr to wl over 1f out: wknd **50/1**

036- **11** 5 **Cold Climate**[22] 6625 11-9-2 **57**.... JoeFanning 8 37
(Bob Jones) prom tl wknd rapidly wl over 1f out **12/1**

1m 38.39s (-1.04) **Going Correction** -0.10s/f (Stan) 11 Ran SP% **119.7**

Speed ratings (Par 101):101,100,98,96,95 95,95,95,94,93 88

CSF £35.80 CT £185.81 TOTE £11.80: £3.80, £1.70, £1.50; EX 47.90.

Owner The Matthewman Partnership **Bred** James Mahon **Trained** Musley Bank, N Yorks

■ Stewards' Enquiry : Micky Fenton one-day ban: careless riding (Jan 23)

FOCUS

The winning time was more than a second slower than the first division, but still acceptable for the grade. The race has been rated around the runner-up and third.

Burnley Al(IRE) Official explanation: trainer's representative said, regarding the improved form shown, gelding was better suited by the Polytrack and by the re-fitting of blinkers

87 BETDIRECT.CO.UK H'CAP 1m 2f (P)

2:50 (2:51) (Class 4) (0-85,85) 3-Y-O **£6,477** (£1,927; £963) **Stalls** Low

Form RPR

01-2 **1** **Before You Go (IRE)**[8] 19 3-9-1 **82**.... JoeFanning 3 96+
(T G Mills) lw: hld up in last: rdn 2f out: r.o to ld jst ins fnl f: in command whn edgd rt nr fin **4/5**[1]

543- **2** 2 **Time For Life (USA)**[25] 6599 3-8-13 **80**.... JimmyQuinn 4 85
(H J Collingridge) led after 3f and maintained stdy pce: rdn 3f out: kpt on tl hdd and one pce jst ins fnl f **11/4**[2]

14-1 **3** 1 ½ **Fusili (IRE)**[8] 19 3-8-12 **79** 6ex.... NCallan 5 81
(N P Littmoden) led at stdy pce for 3f: trckd ldr after: chal 3f out: upsides over 1f out: nt qckn **11/4**[2]

2m 12.26s (4.47) **Going Correction** -0.10s/f (Stan) 3 Ran SP% **108.9**

Speed ratings (Par 99):78,76,75

CSF £3.26 TOTE £1.70; EX 4.90.

Owner Mrs Tina Smith **Bred** The Niarchos Family **Trained** Headley, Surrey

FOCUS

All of three rivals look to have futures, but the race was ruined due to a very pedestrian winning time for a race of its class.

88 CLASSICVALUEPOOLS.COM H'CAP 1m 4f (P)

3:20 (3:20) (Class 4) (0-85,83) 4-Y-O+ **£6,477** (£1,927; £963; £481) **Stalls** Low

Form RPR

01-4 **1** **Willhego**[7] 33 5-8-6 **71**.... HayleyTurner 2 78
(J R Best) lw: prom: trckd ldr gng easily over 3f out: rdn over 1f out: kpt on fnl f: led last stride and won on the nod **12/1**

302- **2** shd **Gibraltar Bay (IRE)**[40] 6482 4-8-13 **82**.... NCallan 7 89
(T G Mills) led: kicked on 4f out: drvn 2f out: kpt on gamely fnl f: pipped on the post **6/1**[2]

/R1- **3** hd **Champagne Shadow (IRE)**[214] 2488 5-8-13 **78**....(b) DarrenWilliams 4 85
(G L Moore) wl in tch: prog on inner 4f out: clsd on ldr and swtchd rt 1f out: styd on: jst hld **50/1**

462- **4** ½ **True Companion**[21] 6644 7-8-7 **77**.... GregFairley(5) 3 83+
(N P Littmoden) prom: lost pl sltly over 4f out: drvn and nt qckn 2f out: styd on again fnl f: a hld **15/2**

035- **5** nk **The Violin Player (USA)**[26] 6592 5-9-4 **83**.... JimmyQuinn 13 88
(H J Collingridge) hld up wl in rr: nt clr run briefly 3f out: prog after: clsd on ldrs over 1f out: nt qckn and no imp last 150yds **11/2**[1]

311- **6** nk **Heathyards Pride**[16] 6665 6-9-0 **79**.... GrahamGibbons 12 84+
(R Hollinshead) lw: hld up in last trio: nt clr run on inner fr 3f out tl jst over 1f out: str run fnl f: nt rch ldrs **10/1**

00-2 **7** 1 ¼ **Eastborough (IRE)**[7] 33 7-8-8 **73**.... MichaelHills 15 76
(B G Powell) lw: hld up and mostly last: rdn and effrt over 2f out: styd on fnl f: no ch **10/1**

456- **8** ¾ **Burgundy**[21] 6645 9-8-6 **74**....(b) RichardThomas(3) 9 76
(P Mitchell) wl in rr: rdn wl over 2f out: plugged on fr over 1f out: n.d **8/1**

212- **9** ½ **Pass The Port**[16] 6665 5-8-11 **76**.... MickyFenton 8 77
(D Haydn Jones) prom: rdn to press ldrs 2f out: wknd fnl f **7/1**[3]

354- **10** nk **Nawow**[218] 1702 6-8-7 **72**.... LPKeniry 6 72
(P D Cundell) chsd ldr to 6f out: styd prom: rdn over 2f out: wknd jst over 1f out **25/1**

000- **11** 3 **Northside Lodge (IRE)**[21] 6644 8-8-9 **74**....(tp) JoeFanning 11 70
(W R Swinburn) settled midfield: rdn over 2f out: no real prog: fdd fnl f **25/1**

010- **12** ½ **Malibu (IRE)**[59] 1784 5-8-6 **71**.... ChrisCatlin 1 66
(S Dow) hld up in rr: rdn 3f out: no prog **50/1**

100- **13** 2 **Paparaazi (IRE)**[20] 5292 4-8-3 **72**.... PaulHanagan 5 64
(R A Fahey) t.k.h: hld up in midfield: rdn over 3f out: wknd over 1f out **12/1**

000- **14** ½ **Salute (IRE)**[22] 6633 7-8-13 **78**....(p) RobertWinston 14 69
(P G Murphy) hld up in last pair: rdn 4f out: sn struggling **33/1**

000- **15** 5 **Golano**[52] 6073 6-8-10 **75**.... TonyCulhane 16 58
(P R Webber) prom: chsd ldr 6f out to over 3f out: wknd rapidly **14/1**

2m 31.95s (-2.44) **Going Correction** -0.10s/f (Stan)

WFA 4 from 5yo+ 4lb 15 Ran SP% **119.8**

Speed ratings (Par 105):104,103,103,103,103 103,102,101,101,101 99,98,97,97,93

CSF £77.72 CT £3471.72 TOTE £17.50: £5.30, £2.70, £8.10; EX 169.30.

Owner G G Racing **Bred** J R Wills **Trained** Hucking, Kent

FOCUS

A fair race run at only a reasonable pace. The first four home were always prominent during the race, while the third and fourth are on harsh-looking handicap marks. Heathyards Pride caught the eye behind the placed horses.

Eastborough(IRE) Official explanation: jockey said gelding hung left throughout

Paparaazi(IRE) Official explanation: jockey said gelding suffered interference in running

89 BETDIRECT.CO.UK FOR IN-RUNNING FOOTBALL H'CAP 6f (P)

3:50 (3:50) (Class 5) (0-75,76) 4-Y-O+ **£3,238** (£963; £481; £240) **Stalls** Low

Form RPR

051- **1** **Silent Storm**[22] 6631 6-9-1 **72**.... ChrisCatlin 6 81
(C A Cyzer) lw: chsd clr ldng quartet: rdn 1/2-way: clsd 2f out: styd on to ld last 150yds: in command after **5/1**[1]

24-1 **2** 1 ½ **Ever Cheerful**[8] 23 5-9-5 **76** 6ex.... MickyFenton 8 80
(G C H Chung) wl off the pce in midfield: drvn and effrt 2f out: r.o to take 2nd wl ins fnl f: nt rch wnr **12/1**

600- **3** 1 ½ **Saviours Spirit**[246] 1605 5-9-2 **73**.... NCallan 11 72+
(T G Mills) w ldr at furious pce: led wl over 1f out: hdd and fdd last 150yds **14/1**

20-6 **4** hd **Joy And Pain**[8] 17 5-8-12 **69**.... PaulHanagan 9 67
(J R Boyle) wl off the pce in rr: rdn wl over 2f out: no prog tl r.o fnl f: nrst fin **14/1**

150- **5** 1 **Willheconquertoo**[23] 6618 6-9-1 **72**....(tp) TomEaves 4 67
(I W McInnes) dwlt: off the pce in midfield: nvr on terms w ldrs: kpt on fnl f **20/1**

461- **6** nk **Franksalot (IRE)**[12] 6689 6-8-11 **71**.... RichardThomas(3) 2 77+
(Miss B Sanders) sn outpcd and towards rr: prog on inner 2f out: clsng on ldrs and ch whn hmpd ent fnl f: nt rcvr **8/1**

51-2 **7** hd **Law Maker**[8] 23 6-8-9 **73**....(v) MichaelJStainton(7) 7 67
(A Bailey) w ldr at furious pce to 2f out: wknd fnl f **12/1**

00-3 **8** ½ **Smokin Joe**[7] 36 5-9-1 **72**.... HayleyTurner 1 64
(J R Best) a wl in rr: last pair and wl off the pce 1/2-way: no ch: kpt on **5/1**[1]

040- **9** nk **Hayyani (IRE)**[22] 6629 4-9-4 **75**....(b[1]) RobertWinston 3 67
(K McAuliffe) s.s: wl off the pce in rr: urged along and one pce over 1f out **7/1**[3]

20-2 **10** 1 **Marko Jadeo (IRE)**[7] 36 8-8-13 **73**.... RobertMiles(3) 10 62
(S Dow) lw: outpcd and wl in rr: kpt on fnl f: n.d **6/1**[2]

021- **11** 11 **Clipper Hoy**[11] 6695 4-8-11 **68**.... DarrenWilliams 5 24
(Mrs H Sweeting) lw: mde most at furious pce to 2f out: wknd rapidly **6/1**[2]

004- **12** ¾ **Stargem**[151] 4374 5-8-10 **67**.... JimmyQuinn 12 20
(J Pearce) w ldrs to 1/2-way: sn wknd rapidly **33/1**

1m 11.62s (-1.19) **Going Correction** -0.10s/f (Stan) 12 Ran SP% **121.9**

Speed ratings (Par 103):103,101,99,98,97 97,96,96,95,94 79,78

CSF £67.89 CT £816.75 TOTE £6.00: £2.20, £3.30, £5.50; EX 65.90 Place 6 £94.56, Place 5 £13.78.

Owner Mrs Charles Cyzer **Bred** Middle Park Stud Ltd **Trained** Maplehurst, W Sussex

■ Stewards' Enquiry : N Callan two-day ban: careless riding (Jan 23-24)

FOCUS

Four horses went off in front and led at a furious pace, which played into the hands of Silent Storm.

T/Plt: £29.40 to a £1 stake. Pool: £30,114.85. 746.00 winning tickets. T/Qpdt: £5.90 to a £1 stake. Pool: £3,397.90. 422.40 winning tickets. JN

[75]SOUTHWELL (L-H)

Wednesday, January 11

OFFICIAL GOING: Standard

All six races were restricted to jockeys who did not ride more than 30 winners in 2005.

Wind: Fresh, half-behind Weather: Cloudy with sunny spells

90 BET NOW AT BETDIRECT.CO.UK BANDED STKS 5f (F)

12:55 (12:56) (Class 7) 3-Y-O+ **£1,365** (£403; £201) **Stalls** High

Form RPR

64-0 **1** **Amanda's Lad (IRE)**[8] 24 6-8-13 45.... AdrianMcCarthy 3 53
(M C Chapman) chsd ldrs: r.o to ld wl ins fnl f **13/2**[3]

00-3 **2** ¾ **On The Trail**[8] 24 9-8-13 45....(p) DaleGibson 6 51
(D W Chapman) w ldrs: led over 1f out: sn hdd: ev ch wl ins fnl f: styd on **7/1**

23-4 **3** 1 ¼ **Beamsley Beacon**[8] 29 5-8-13 45....(b) PaulFessey 1 47
(M Dods) w ldrs: rdn to ld 1f out: hdd wl ins fnl f **11/4**[1]

003- **4** ¾ **A Teen**[13] 6686 8-8-13 40.... PatCosgrave 12 44
(P Howling) mid-div: hdwy 1/2-way: rdn and nt clr run over 1f out: styd on **16/1**

000- **5** 1 ¼ **Kashtanka (IRE)**[11] 6695 4-8-10 40....(b[1]) JasonEdmunds(3) 2 40
(J Balding) sn outpcd: hdwy u.p over 1f out: nt rch ldrs **25/1**

000- **6** ½ **Keresforth**[20] 6261 4-8-13 45....(p) PaulEddery 4 38
(Mrs L C Jewell) sn outpcd: hrd rdn over 1f out: r.o ins fnl f: nt rch ldrs **25/1**

600- **7** 1 **Piccleyes**[24] 6604 5-8-13 45.... PaulDoe 14 35
(M J Polglase) chsd ldrs: rdn 1/2-way: wknd fnl f **16/1**

00-0 **8** shd **Lakeside Guy (IRE)**[8] 24 5-8-13 45.... VinceSlattery 7 34
(M Appleby) chsd ldrs to 1/2-way **16/1**

51-6 **9** nk **King Marrakech (IRE)**[8] 29 4-8-13 40....(v) MatthewHenry 5 33
(B P J Baugh) sn outpcd **3/1**[2]

020- **10** 1 ¼ **Torrent**[29] 6570 11-8-13 45....(b) GylesParkin 10 29
(D W Chapman) sn outpcd **9/1**

00-0 **11** nk **Percy Douglas**[8] 24 6-8-6 45....(vt) AnnStokell(7) 13 28
(Miss A Stokell) chsd ldrs: edgd lft and wknd over 1f out **50/1**

010- **12** *2* **Vaudevire**[14] 6677 5-8-13 45..............................(b) LeeEnstone 8 21
(Peter Grayson) *led over 3f: sn wknd* **20/1**

59.26 secs (-1.04) **Going Correction** -0.275s/f (Stan) **12** Ran SP% **119.6**
Speed ratings (Par 97):97,95,93,92,90 89,88,88,87,85 85,81
CSF £49.64 TOTE £7.00: £3.30, £2.40, £1.40; EX 27.20.
Owner Eric Knowles **Bred** Mrs Helen Smith **Trained** Market Rasen, Lincs

FOCUS
A typical banded sprint although, as has been the case over this trip in recent months, those drawn high were at a disadvantage.

91 BETDIRECT FREEPHONE 0800 211 222 BANDED STKS 1m 6f (F)
1:30 (1:32) (Class 7) 4-Y-0+ **£1,365** (£403; £201) **Stalls** Low

Form RPR
02-1 **1** **Cotton Eyed Joe (IRE)**[8] 25 5-9-6 45.............................. GylesParkin 5 71+
(G A Swinbank) *trckd ldrs: led over 2f out: edgd lft and clr over 1f out: eased ins fnl f* **8/11**[1]
061- **2** *13* **Tharua (IRE)**[13] 6681 4-8-11 48..............................(v) FrancisFerris 4 49
(Ernst Oertel) *hld up: hdwy over 4f out: rdn over 2f out: sn outpcd* **6/1**[2]
066- **3** *1* **Ice And Fire**[14] 6678 7-8-12 46..............................(b) JasonEdmunds(3) 2 46
(J T Stimpson) *s.i.s: hld up: hdwy over 4f out: rdn over 2f out: sn outpcd* **6/1**[2]
000- **4** *½* **Tiegs (IRE)**[79] 6081 4-8-8 45.............................. PaulDoe 12 44
(P W Hiatt) *s.s: hdwy 12f out: led over 3f out: rdn and hdd over 2f out: wknd over 1f out* **25/1**
000- **5** *1 ½* **Robbie Will**[16] 4085 5-9-0 45.............................. AdrianMcCarthy 11 42
(F Jordan) *hld up: outpcd and bhd 10f out: nvr nrr* **50/1**
060- **6** *½* **Brother Cadfael**[24] 6606 5-9-0 40.............................. PaulEddery 3 42
(John A Harris) *chsd ldr 5f: lost pl 7f out: hdwy over 3f out: sn rdn and wknd* **50/1**
050/ **7** *1 ¾* **Lough Bow (IRE)**[813] 5692 8-9-0 45..............................(b) DaleGibson 6 40
(M W Easterby) *prom: racd keenly: rdn over 3f out: wknd 2f out* **40/1**
000- **8** *½* **Kerry's Blade (IRE)**[52] 5244 4-8-8 45..............................(p) LeeEnstone 10 39
(P C Haslam) *hld up: hdwy 1/2-way: wknd over 3f out* **12/1**[3]
660- **9** *17* **Two Chimneys (USA)**[15] 6667 4-8-12 49.............................. PaulFessey 9 23
(K A Ryan) *prom: chsd ldr 9f out: led over 7f out: hdd & wknd over 3f out* **14/1**
050/ **10** *dist* **Starry Mary**[12] 5258 8-9-0 45..............................(p) VinceSlattery 13 —
(R J Price) *mid-div: sn drvn along: lost pl 10f out: sn bhd* **40/1**
020- **11** *¾* **Legend Of Dance**[21] 6652 4-8-8 45.............................. DeanMernagh 8 —
(J L Spearing) *hld up: a bhd* **66/1**
565- **12** *2* **True To Yourself (USA)**[66] 5826 5-9-0 45..............................(v) MatthewHenry 1 —
(J G Given) *led over 6f: sn rdn: wknd 5f out* **6/1**[2]
50-0 **13** *1 ¼* **Radiant Bride**[5] 55 6-9-0 45..............................(b) PatCosgrave 7 —
(P A Blockley) *mid-div: hrd rdn 1/2-way: wknd over 5f out* **50/1**

3m 9.56s (-0.04) **Going Correction** -0.20s/f (Stan)
WFA 4 from 5yo+ 6lb **13** Ran SP% **131.2**
Speed ratings (Par 97):92,84,84,83,82 82,81,81,71,— —,—,—
CSF £6.18 TOTE £1.40: £1.10, £2.40, £2.40; EX 7.50.
Owner Mrs S Sanbrook **Bred** Tally-Ho Stud **Trained** Melsonby, N Yorks

FOCUS
Cotton Eyed Joe totally outclassed his rivals and is clearly quite a bit better than a banded-class performer, although the winning time was just modest.

92 LITTLEWOODS BETDIRECT BANDED STKS 1m 3f (F)
2:05 (2:06) (Class 7) 4-Y-0+ **£1,365** (£403; £201) **Stalls** Low

Form RPR
200- **1** **Beauchamp Star**[271] 1037 5-9-5 50.............................. PaulFessey 6 59
(Mrs A Duffield) *chsd ldrs: rdn to ld and edgd lft over 1f out: r.o* **40/1**
23-6 **2** *3 ½* **Surdoue**[8] 25 6-9-0 45.............................. DaleGibson 2 49
(P Howling) *led: rdn and hdd 2f out: ev ch over 1f out: styd on same pce fnl f* **11/2**
41-4 **3** *nk* **Mister Completely (IRE)**[5] 52 5-9-1 46.............................. AdrianMcCarthy 12 49
(J R Best) *chsd ldr: rdn to ld 2f out: hdd over 1f out: styd on same pce* **4/1**[2]
004- **4** *2 ½* **Yashin (IRE)**[32] 6536 5-9-2 47.............................. LeeEnstone 7 47
(P A Blockley) *hld up: hdwy over 5f out: rdn and edgd lft over 1f out: sn wknd* **10/1**
161- **5** *4* **Kentucky Bullet (USA)**[50] 6414 10-9-2 47.............................. FrancisFerris 9 41
(A G Newcombe) *hld up: hdwy over 2f out: edgd lft and no imp fr over 1f out* **10/3**[1]
34-6 **6** *2 ½* **Orpen Quest (IRE)**[7] 41 4-8-13 47..............................(p) PaulDoe 4 37
(M J Attwater) *hld up: rdn over 2f out: n.d* **9/2**[3]
02-0 **7** *1 ¼* **Mujimac (IRE)**[7] 41 4-9-2 50.............................. PatCosgrave 8 38
(P A Blockley) *chsd ldrs over 7f* **12/1**
600- **8** *3* **Triffid**[24] 6608 4-8-11 45.............................. GylesParkin 3 28
(R A Fahey) *chsd ldrs: rdn over 4f out: wknd over 3f out* **16/1**
200- **9** *4* **Queue Up**[27] 6584 4-9-2 50.............................. MatthewHenry 11 27
(A G Newcombe) *hld up: racd keenly: hdwy over 5f out: wknd over 3f out* **25/1**
00-0 **10** *2* **Miss Bear (IRE)**[9] 13 4-9-0 48..............................(b) PaulEddery 10 22
(B Smart) *chsd ldrs: effrt over 3f out: sn wknd* **66/1**
504- **11** *nk* **Trackattack**[20] 6572 4-8-11 45.............................. DerekMcGaffin 14 19
(P Howling) *s.i.s: hdwy over 6f out: wknd over 4f out* **33/1**
000- **12** *hd* **Simply The Guest (IRE)**[20] 6654 7-9-4 49..............................(t) KimTinkler 13 23
(N Tinkler) *s.i.s: a in rr* **14/1**
000- **13** *½* **Eforetta (GER)**[15] 6674 4-9-1 49.............................. VinceSlattery 5 22
(D J Wintle) *mid-div: hdwy 7f out: rdn and wknd 4f out* **33/1**

2m 26.76s (-2.14) **Going Correction** -0.20s/f (Stan)
WFA 4 from 5yo+ 3lb **13** Ran SP% **119.6**
Speed ratings (Par 97):99,96,96,94,91 89,88,86,83,82 82,81,81
CSF £242.71 TOTE £63.40: £9.90, £2.40, £1.40; EX 400.30.
Owner Diamond Racing Ltd **Bred** E Penser **Trained** Constable Burton, N Yorks

FOCUS
A standard banded contest in which Beauchamp Star ran out a convincing winner on her debut for a new trainer. The runner-up and third ran close to the level of their recent form.
Mujimac(IRE) Official explanation: trainer said gelding had a breathing problem
Trackattack Official explanation: jockey said gelding hung severely right-handed throughout

93 TEXT "BETDIRECT" TO 88600 TRI-BANDED STKS 1m (F)
2:35 (2:40) (Class 7) 3-Y-O **£1,365** (£302; £302) **Stalls** Low

Form RPR
000- **1** **Petrichan (IRE)**[145] 4539 3-8-12 45.............................. PaulFessey 11 59
(K A Ryan) *chsd ldrs: led over 4f out: rdn clr over 2f out* **10/1**
00-5 **2** *8* **Paris Power**[7] 30 3-8-12 45..............................(v) DerekMcGaffin 7 43
(D Morris) *chsd ldrs: rdn over 2f out: sn edgd lft and outpcd* **5/1**[2]
000- **2** *dht* **Mykeyta**[128] 4996 3-8-12 45.............................. DaleGibson 5 43
(J G Given) *dwlt: hld up: drvn along 1/2-way: sn outpcd: styd on fnl f: n.d* **20/1**
400- **4** *1 ¼* **Genoa Star**[38] 6496 3-8-12 45.............................. VinceSlattery 14 40
(T J Pitt) *prom: outpcd 6f out: hdwy and edgd lft over 3f out: wknd over 1f out* **4/1**[1]
000- **5** *3 ½* **Xenia**[40] 6484 3-8-12 45..............................(b[1]) PaulDoe 13 33
(J G Given) *dwlt: effrt over 2f out: n.d* **16/1**
000- **6** *nk* **Ever Special (IRE)**[121] 5184 3-8-12 45.............................. LeeEnstone 3 32
(P C Haslam) *chsd ldrs: lost pl after 2f out: sn bhd: mod late prog* **7/1**
000- **7** *6* **Late Night Love**[11] 6697 3-8-7 40..............................(b[1]) NeilPollard 9 15
(K R Burke) *sn led: hdd over 4f out: rdn and wknd over 2f out* **50/1**
8 *1 ½* **Beginners Luck (IRE)**[109] 5474 3-8-12 45.............................. FrancisFerris 12 17+
(D Carroll) *hld up in tch: rdn 1/2-way: sn hmpd and eased* **8/1**
040- **9** *4* **Take No Notice (IRE)**[11] 6697 3-8-12 45.............................. PatCosgrave 10 9
(K R Burke) *chsd ldrs: rdn over 2f out: wknd wl over 1f out* **6/1**[3]
000- **10** *12* **Southgate Lady (IRE)**[11] 6694 3-8-7 40..............................(t) AdrianMcCarthy 2 —
(N P Littmoden) *chsd ldrs: lost pl 6f out: bhd fr 1/2-way* **20/1**
000- **11** *10* **Tilen (IRE)**[70] 6227 3-8-12 45.............................. MatthewHenry 6 —
(S Parr) *chsd ldrs to 1/2-way* **9/1**
005- **12** *½* **Skin Sure Thing**[93] 5805 3-8-7 40 ow3.............................. JasonEdmunds(3) 1 —
(A D Smith) *sn outpcd* **50/1**
000- **13** *2* **Amber Spirit**[35] 6521 3-8-7 40.............................. GylesParkin 4 —
(Peter Grayson) *chsd ldrs 3f* **16/1**

1m 45.09s (0.49) **Going Correction** -0.20s/f (Stan) **13** Ran SP% **118.9**
Speed ratings (Par 91):89,81,81,79,76 75,69,68,64,52 42,41,39
WIN: £12.90. PL: Petrichan £4.20, Mykeyta £5.40, Paris Power £1.80. EX: P/M £89.10, P/PP £24.10. CSF: P/M £86.55, P/PP £25.89..
Owner Peter & Richard Foden Racing Partnership **Bred** Fortbarrington Stud **Trained** Hambleton, N Yorks
■ Stewards' Enquiry : Vince Slattery caution: careless riding

FOCUS
Very little strength in depth in this banded contest and Petrichan, who had previously shown very little, bolted up. The runner-up, fourth and fifth all appear to have run close to their pre-race marks.
Petrichan(IRE) Official explanation: trainer's representative had no explanation for the improved form shown other than that gelding was very green as a two-year-old
Mykeyta Official explanation: jockey said filly hung left

94 WIN £2M @ LITTLEWOODSPOOLS.CO.UK BANDED STKS 1m (F)
3:10 (3:12) (Class 7) 4-Y-0+ **£884** (£884; £201) **Stalls** Low

Form RPR
00-3 **1** **Sierra**[8] 27 5-8-11 45.............................. PaulFessey 8 53
(A W Carroll) *a.p: rdn over 1f out: edgd rt and led wl ins fnl f: jnd post* **7/1**
225- **1** *dht* **Sonderborg**[29] 6573 5-8-11 45..............................(p) DaleGibson 12 53
(J Mackie) *in rr: hdwy over 2f out: rdn to ld 1f out: hung lft: hdd wl ins fnl f: edgd rt and r.o to join wnr post* **9/2**[1]
250- **3** *3* **Young Kate**[28] 6575 5-8-11 45.............................. PaulDoe 4 47
(J R Best) *hld up: hdwy over 3f out: rdn over 1f out: no ex ins fnl f* **11/2**[3]
030- **4** *1 ½* **Miss Glory Be**[13] 6684 8-8-11 45..............................(p) FrancisFerris 14 48+
(Ernst Oertel) *hld up: hdwy over 4f out: led over 2f out: rdn and hdd 1f out: hmpd and no ex ins fnl f* **9/1**
314- **5** *1 ¾* **Desert Fury**[21] 6649 9-8-11 45..............................(b) LeeEnstone 10 41+
(R Bastiman) *s.s: hdwy over 3f out: hung lft and wknd over 1f out* **7/1**
060- **6** *2 ½* **True (IRE)**[144] 4565 5-8-11 45.............................. MatthewHenry 13 36
(Mrs S Lamyman) *in rr: hdwy 1/2-way: hung lft and wknd over 1f out* **20/1**
000- **7** *1* **Heversham (IRE)**[32] 6262 5-8-11 45.............................. DeanMernagh 5 34
(J Hetherton) *led early: nt clr run and lost pl over 4f out: n.d after* **20/1**
216- **8** *8* **Venetian Princess (IRE)**[64] 6293 4-8-11 45.............................. VinceSlattery 2 18
(P Howling) *chsd ldrs over 6f* **12/1**
9 *1 ½* **Cabrillo (IRE)**[20] 5470 5-8-11 45..............................(t) NeilPollard 6 15
(John A Quinn, Ire) *dwlt: outpcd* **25/1**
001- **10** *1 ¼* **Naughty Girl (IRE)**[232] 1986 6-8-11 45.............................. PaulEddery 3 12
(John A Harris) *chsd ldrs over 5f* **14/1**
003- **11** *nk* **Pawn In Life (IRE)**[30] 6556 8-8-11 40.............................. PatCosgrave 7 11
(M J Polglase) *chsd ldrs 6f* **9/1**
006- **12** *¾* **Ready Teddy Go**[37] 6512 4-8-11 45.............................. DerekMcGaffin 9 10
(J Ryan) *outpcd* **40/1**
000- **13** *7* **Napapijri (FR)**[114] 5364 4-8-11 45.............................. AdrianMcCarthy 11 —
(W G M Turner) *chsd ldrs over 4f* **33/1**
000- **14** *4* **Vintage Times (IRE)**[56] 6367 4-8-11 45.............................. GylesParkin 1 —
(R A Fahey) *sn led: hdd & wknd over 2f out* **5/1**[2]

1m 44.01s (-0.59) **Going Correction** -0.20s/f (Stan) **14** Ran SP% **128.3**
Speed ratings (Par 97):94,94,91,89,87 85,84,76,74,73 73,72,65,61
WIN: Sierra £4.90, Sonderborg £2.60. PL: Sierra £3.30, Sond'g £2.10, Young Kate £2.00. EX: Sierra/Sond'g £18.00, Sond'g/Sierra £21.10. CSF: Sierra/Sond'g £19.29, Sond'g/Sierra £17.91..
Owner Hugh Le Fanu **Bred** M S Griffiths **Trained** Church Broughton , Derbys
■ Sierra was the third leg of a treble for jockey Paul Fessey.
Owner Wyck Hall Stud **Bred** Meon Valley Stud **Trained** Cropthorne, Worcs
■ Sierra was the third leg of a treble for jockey Paul Fessey.

FOCUS
A reasonable enough banded contest with the first two running to the level of their recent form.
Desert Fury Official explanation: jockey said gelding was slow away
Ready Teddy Go Official explanation: jockey said gelding resented the kick-back

95 BETDIRECT.CO.UK BANDED STKS 7f (F)
3:40 (3:43) (Class 7) 4-Y-0+ **£1,706** (£503; £252) **Stalls** Low

Form RPR
3-31 **1** **Magic Amour**[7] 38 8-9-5 47..............................(b) PatCosgrave 7 63+
(P A Blockley) *w ldrs: led over 2f out: rdn clr over 1f out: eased nr fin* **13/2**
210- **2** *1 ½* **The Job**[24] 6608 5-9-1 49..............................(v) AdrianMcCarthy 3 54
(A D Smith) *dwlt: outpcd: hdwy over 1f out: hung lft ins fnl f: nt rch wnr* **16/1**
510- **3** *1 ¾* **Wodhill Be**[23] 6611 6-9-0 48.............................. DerekMcGaffin 10 49
(D Morris) *s.i.s: outpcd: hdwy 1/2-way: rdn over 1f out: styd on* **50/1**
064- **4** *shd* **Monkey Madge**[14] 6676 4-9-2 50.............................. PaulEddery 12 50
(B Smart) *in rr: hdwy u.p over 1f out: nt rch ldrs* **16/1**
210- **5** *½* **Midmaar (IRE)**[28] 6579 5-8-12 46.............................. JamieMackay 4 45
(M Wigham) *mid-div: hdwy over 1f out: hrd rdn over 1f out: styd on* **5/1**[2]
036- **6** *1 ¾* **Desert Lover (IRE)**[14] 6679 4-8-12 46.............................. LeeEnstone 2 41
(R J Price) *w ldrs: led 4f out: hdd over 2f out: wknd fnl f* **5/1**[2]
02-1 **7** *¾* **Lady Suesanne (IRE)**[10] 3 4-9-7 49..............................(b) PaulDoe 8 48
(M J Attwater) *hld up in tch: outpcd 4f out: n.d after* **11/2**[3]
00-4 **8** *hd* **Spy Gun (USA)**[7] 43 6-9-0 48.............................. MatthewHenry 14 40
(T Wall) *w ldrs to 1/2-way: wknd over 1f out* **12/1**
422- **9** *hd* **Mount Royale (IRE)**[14] 6676 8-9-0 48..............................(v) KimTinkler 9 40
(N Tinkler) *w ldrs tl rdn over 2f out: wknd over 1f out* **9/4**[1]

0-00 **10** 3 ½ **Crusoe (IRE)**[1] [81] 9-9-0 48..........(b) DaleGibson 13 31
(A Sadik) *hdwy 1/2-way: rdn and wknd 2f out* **25/1**
010- **11** 3 ½ **Princess Arwen**[53] [6384] 4-8-11 45.......... VinceSlattery 11 19
(Mrs Barbara Waring) *chsd ldrs over 4f* **66/1**
00-2 **12** nk **Castanza**[10] [3] 4-8-13 47.......... DeanMernagh 5 21
(M Wellings) *led 3f: wknd over 2f out* **50/1**
021- **13** 1 **Sea Frolic (IRE)**[24] [6609] 5-8-13 47..........(v) FrancisFerris 6 18
(Jennie Candlish) *s.i.s: rdn over 4f out: a in rr* **7/1**
00-4 **14** 6 **Hows That**[9] [11] 4-9-2 50.......... NeilPollard 1 6
(K R Burke) *prom: rdn over 4f out: sn lost pl* **66/1**
1m 29.46s (-1.34) **Going Correction** -0.20s/f (Stan) **14** Ran SP% **135.5**
Speed ratings (Par 97):99,97,95,95,94 92,91,91,91,87 83,82,81,74
CSF £116.52 TOTE £7.40: £2.30, £6.10, £9.00; EX 202.30 Place 6 £330.97, Place 5 £175.96.
Owner Mrs Joanna Hughes **Bred** Juddmonte Farms **Trained** Lambourn, Berks
FOCUS
A decent, competitive banded contest and solid form for the grade.
T/Plt: £49.60 to a £1 stake. Pool: £33,503.90. 492.15 winning tickets. T/Qpdt: £33.30 to a £1 stake. Pool: £2,449.60. 54.30 winning tickets. CR

[90]SOUTHWELL (L-H)
Thursday, January 12

OFFICIAL GOING: Standard
As is so often the case, the surface looked to be riding quickest middle to stands' side. A high draw on the round course was therefore no disadvantage.
Wind: Virtually nil

96 NO 5P RULE 4S AT BETDIRECT APPRENTICE CLAIMING STKS 5f (F)
12:40 (12:41) (Class 6) 4-Y-O+ **£2,388** (£705; £352) **Stalls** High

Form RPR
100- **1** **Maktavish**[23] [6636] 7-9-7 75..........(b[1]) PhillipMakin 1 84
(I Semple) *qckly away: pushed clr 1/2-way: comf* **13/2**
00-0 **2** 3 ½ **Native Title**[10] [9] 8-9-0 82.......... VictoriaBehan(7) 3 72
(D Nicholls) *in tch: hdwy to chse wnr 2f out: sn rdn: edgd rt and no imp ent last* **10/1**
534- **3** 1 ½ **Sir Sandrovitch (IRE)**[12] [6696] 10-8-0 57..........(v) AndrewMullen(3) 10 49
(R A Fahey) *s.i.s and bhd: hdwy 2f out: sn rdn and kpt on same pce ins last* **9/2**[3]
040- **4** 1 ¼ **Larky's Lob**[47] [6464] 7-8-8 54.......... JamesO'Reilly(5) 8 55
(J O'Reilly) *in tch: rdn along 2f out: styd on ins last* **25/1**
115- **5** 1 **Orchestration (IRE)**[22] [6639] 5-8-12 55..........(v) StacyRenwick(5) 5 55
(M J Attwater) *in tch: hdwy 2f out: sn rdn and kpt on same pce* **4/1**[2]
641- **6** shd **Tag Team (IRE)**[16] [6668] 5-9-0 63.......... GregFairley(3) 4 55
(John A Harris) *chsd ldrs: rdn along 2f out: drvn wl over 1f out and sn btn* **9/4**[1]
205- **7** 1 **Mynd**[16] [6668] 6-8-6 55.......... MichaelJStainton(5) 7 46
(R M Whitaker) *chsd ldrs: rdn over 2f out: sn wknd* **11/1**
055- **8** 2 ½ **Little Biscuit (IRE)**[267] [1136] 4-7-9 49 ow4.......... PatrickDonaghy(7) 2 28
(K R Burke) *in tch: rdn along halfway and sn wknd* **33/1**
00-0 **9** 2 ½ **Colonel Cotton (IRE)**[10] [9] 7-9-3 82..........(v) SilvestreDeSousa 9 35
(D Nicholls) *in tch: hdwy to chse ldrs 1/2-way: sn rdn and wknd* **14/1**
/0-0 **10** 3 **Cheeney Basin (IRE)**[2] [81] 8-8-8 48.......... LiamJones(5) 6 20
(M C Chapman) *dwlt: sn outpcd and bhd fr 1/2-way* **66/1**
59.41 secs (-0.89) **Going Correction** -0.15s/f (Stan) **10** Ran SP% **114.7**
Speed ratings (Par 101):101,95,93,91,89 89,87,83,79,74
CSF £66.97 TOTE £7.10: £1.90, £4.30, £1.90; EX 64.10.
Owner D G Savala **Bred** V Robin Lawson **Trained** Carluke, S Lanarks
FOCUS
A fair claimer contested by a mix of in-form and highly-rated horses. Those drawn low-to-middle were at an advantage.
Sir Sandrovitch(IRE) Official explanation: jockey said gelding hung left-handed
Cheeney Basin(IRE) Official explanation: jockey said gelding hung right-handed

97 DAILY OFFERS FROM BETDIRECT MAIDEN STKS 1m 3f (F)
1:10 (1:11) (Class 5) 4-Y-O+ **£3,238** (£963; £481; £240) **Stalls** Low

Form RPR
50-2 **1** **Sand Repeal (IRE)**[11] [2] 4-9-0 66.......... ChrisCatlin 14 63
(Miss J Feilden) *trckd ldrs: hdwy 3f out: chsd ldr 2f out: rdn to ld ent last: drvn and hld on towards fin* **16/1**
403- **2** nk **Sugitani (USA)**[33] [6537] 4-9-0 56.......... MickyFenton 11 63
(N B King) *hld up towards rr: hdwy over 4f out: rdn 2f out: styd on strly ins last* **14/1**
000- **3** 3 **Bamzooki**[23] [6626] 4-8-9 54.......... NCallan 6 53
(D J Daly) *cl up: led after 3f: pushed clr over 2f out: rdn and hdd ent last: kpt on same pce* **10/1**
063- **4** 3 **Antley Court (IRE)**[28] [6583] 4-9-0 52.......... GrahamGibbons 10 53
(R Hollinshead) *chsd ldng pair: rdn along 3f out: drvn and one pce fnl 2f* **40/1**
400- **5** 3 ½ **Orange Blue (GER)**[134] [4879] 4-9-0.......... JamieSpencer 8 52+
(C Von Der Recke, Germany) *trckd ldrs: pushed along 4f out: rdn along 3f out: sn one pce* **2/1**[2]
233- **6** 7 **Waterloo Corner**[248] [1571] 4-9-0 68.......... RobertWinston 4 37
(R Craggs) *towards rr: hdwy 3f out: sn rdn and no imp fnl 2f* **5/1**[3]
-3 **7** hd **City Of Manchester (IRE)**[11] [2] 4-9-0.......... AdrianTNicholls 7 36
(D Nicholls) *led 3f: cl up tl rdn along over 4f out and grad wknd* **33/1**
600- **8** 5 **The Plainsman**[68] [6257] 4-9-0 40.......... DarrenWilliams 5 28
(P W Hiatt) *chsd ldrs: rdn along 4f out: n.m.r and wknd 3f out* **66/1**
6- **9** ¾ **Esprit De Corps**[13] [6687] 4-9-0.......... JamieMackay 13 27
(Sir Mark Prescott) *s.i.s: pushed along 1/2-way: a rr* **15/8**[1]
0/0- **10** 2 ½ **Jeune Loup**[366] [82] 4-9-0 65.......... LeeEnstone 12 23
(P C Haslam) *midfield: rdn along 5f out: nvr a factor* **40/1**
64-5 **11** 2 **Finnegans Rainbow**[11] [2] 4-8-10 40 ow1.......... StephenDonohoe(5) 2 21
(M C Chapman) *a rr* **66/1**
0/0- **12** 5 **General Nuisance (IRE)**[44] [6464] 4-9-0 45.......... DeanMcKeown 9 12
(A J Chamberlain) *a b ehind* **66/1**
13 6 **Must Be Keen**[43] 7-9-0.......... AdamKirby(3) 1 2
(Ernst Oertel) *in tch: rdn along 1/2-way: sn lost pl and bhd* **100/1**
14 shd **Rythm N Rhyme (IRE)**[53] 7-9-3.......... PaulEddery 3 2
(John A Harris) *a bhd* **100/1**
2m 26.18s (-2.72) **Going Correction** -0.25s/f (Stan)
WFA 4 from 7yo 3lb **14** Ran SP% **120.7**
Speed ratings (Par 103):99,98,96,94,91 86,86,83,82,80 79,75,71,71
CSF £213.37 TOTE £13.00: £2.90, £3.30, £3.40; EX 115.30.
Owner The Sultans of Speed **Bred** Don Commins **Trained** Exning, Suffolk
FOCUS
A very moderate maiden, no better than fair selling level.
Orange Blue(GER) Official explanation: jockey said colt never travelled

98 PLAY NOW AT BETDIRECTCASINO.COM H'CAP 1m 6f (F)
1:40 (1:40) (Class 5) (0-75,74) 4-Y-O+ **£3,238** (£963; £481; £240) **Stalls** Low

Form RPR
023- **1** **Oldenway**[21] [6655] 7-9-2 65.......... PaulHanagan 8 77
(R A Fahey) *sn prom: cl up after 4f: led over 3f out and sn clr: rdn over 1f out and styd on wl* **7/1**[3]
61-1 **2** 8 **Spitting Image (IRE)**[11] [5] 6-9-9 72 6ex.......... RobertWinston 3 76+
(M Johnston) *in tch: pushed along and outpcd after 4f: sn rdn: drvn and hdwy over 3f out: chsd wnr fnl 2f: no imp* **1/2**[1]
331- **3** 10 **Khanjar (USA)**[21] [6655] 6-9-11 74.......... PatCosgrave 7 63
(K R Burke) *led: rdn along and hdd over 3f out: drvn over 2f out and sn one pce* **9/2**[2]
60-3 **4** 1 ¼ **Sun Hill**[10] [12] 6-8-9 65..........(v) MichaelJStainton(7) 2 52
(C W Fairhurst) *trckd ldrs: pushed along 5f out: rdn 4f out and sn btn* **12/1**
002- **5** 1 ¼ **Muntami (IRE)**[59] [6230] 5-9-4 67.......... PaulEddery 1 52
(John A Harris) *hld up in rr: hdwy 5f out: rdn along 4f out: sn drvn and wknd 3f out* **28/1**
555- **6** 6 **Come What July (IRE)**[16] [6669] 5-9-3 66..........(v) PhillipMakin 5 44
(Mrs N Macauley) *hld up: a rr* **20/1**
60-5 **7** dist **Victory Quest (IRE)**[11] [5] 6-9-5 68..........(v) TonyCulhane 6 —
(Mrs S Lamyman) *prom: rdn along 5f out and sn wknd* **33/1**
3m 6.14s (-3.46) **Going Correction** -0.25s/f (Stan) **7** Ran SP% **116.2**
Speed ratings (Par 103):99,94,88,88,87 83,—
CSF £11.18 CT £18.77 TOTE £7.90: £2.50, £1.50; EX 19.80.
Owner J J Staunton **Bred** Snailwell Stud Co Ltd **Trained** Musley Bank, N Yorks
■ Stewards' Enquiry : Pat Cosgrave one-day ban: careless riding (Jan 23)
FOCUS
A fair staying handicap and, with the pace decent throughout, it proved a good test.

99 PLAY NOW AT BETDIRECTPOKER.COM (S) STKS 7f (F)
2:10 (2:11) (Class 6) 3-Y-O **£2,388** (£705; £352) **Stalls** Low

Form RPR
605- **1** **Crush On You**[22] [6648] 3-8-7 47.......... GrahamGibbons 5 53
(R Hollinshead) *chsd ldrs: hdwy 2f out: swtchd rt and effrt to ld over 1f out: rdn clr ent last: styd on* **10/1**
61-3 **2** 3 ½ **Noble Edge**[3] [69] 3-9-4 61..........(p) FergalLynch 11 54
(P A Blockley) *cl up: led over 2f out: sn rdn and hdd over 1f out: kpt on same pce* **9/2**[3]
5-45 **3** ¾ **Twilight Avenger (IRE)**[6] [53] 3-8-12 50..........(p) DeanMcKeown 8 46
(M J Polglase) *cl up: ev ch 2f out tl rdn and one pce appr last* **8/1**
425- **4** ½ **Woodwee**[21] [6656] 3-9-4 61.......... RobertWinston 9 51
(J R Weymes) *keen: in tch tl pushed along and outpcd 3f out: rdn 2f out: kpt on appr last: nrst fin* **10/3**[2]
622- **5** ½ **Inaminute (IRE)**[28] [6585] 3-8-0 57.......... TolleyDean(7) 2 38
(R A Harris) *towards rr: pushed along on inner 3f out: hdwy to chse ldesr 2f out sn rdn and btn over 1f out* **6/4**[1]
03-0 **6** 3 **Musical City**[8] [39] 3-8-7 45.......... PaulEddery 4 31
(B Smart) *led: rdn along and hdd over 2f out: sn drvn and wknd* **25/1**
003- **7** 3 **Lake Suprima (IRE)**[16] [6670] 3-8-2 50 ow2.......... MichaelJStainton(7) 3 25
(R M Whitaker) *chsd ldrs: rdn along wl over 2f out: sn wknd* **12/1**
50-0 **8** 4 **Key Of Magic (IRE)**[8] [39] 3-8-12 30..........(b[1]) DaleGibson 1 17
(J Hetherton) *a rr* **100/1**
6- **9** 6 **Charming Princess**[21] [6653] 3-8-7.......... PaulFessey 10 —
(P T Midgley) *dwlt: hdwy on outer to chse ldrs after 2f: rdn along 3f out and sn wknd* **33/1**
1m 30.39s (-0.41) **Going Correction** -0.25s/f (Stan) **9** Ran SP% **116.9**
Speed ratings (Par 95):92,88,87,86,86 82,79,74,67
CSF £54.55 TOTE £16.60: £3.50, £1.70, £2.60; EX 77.40.There was no bid for the winner. Inaminute was claimed by K. R. Burke for £6,000. Noble Edge was claimed by Naughty Diesel Ltd for £6,000.
Owner D Coppenhall **Bred** Tweenhills Stud And Stuart McPhee **Trained** Upper Longdon, Staffs
FOCUS
Just an ordinary seller rated through the runner-up.
Lake Suprima(IRE) Official explanation: jockey said filly lost its action

100 BETDIRECT FREEPHONE 0800 211 222 H'CAP 7f (F)
2:40 (2:41) (Class 5) (0-75,74) 4-Y-O+ **£3,412** (£1,007; £504) **Stalls** Low

Form RPR
061- **1** **Local Poet**[23] [6638] 5-9-0 70..........(bt) TomEaves 12 83
(I Semple) *trckd ldrs on outer: hdwy 2f out: rdn to ld 1f out: styd on wl* **7/2**[1]
506- **2** 1 ¾ **Flint River**[21] [6657] 8-8-11 72.......... TravisBlock(5) 9 80
(H Morrison) *chsd ldrs: hdwy 2f out: swtchd lft and rdn over 1f out: ev ch tl nt qckn ent last* **5/1**[2]
156- **3** ¾ **Mission Affirmed (USA)**[167] [3915] 5-9-3 73..........(v[1]) RobertWinston 8 79
(T P Tate) *towards rr: pushed along 3f out: swtchd lft and hdwy wl over 1f out: sn rdn and styd on u.p: nrst fin* **8/1**
130- **4** nk **Bessemer (JPN)**[21] [6657] 5-9-1 74..........(p) DanielTudhope(3) 4 79
(D Carroll) *trckd ldrs: hdwy 2f out: swtchd lft and rdn to ld briefly over 1f out: sn hdd and one pce* **20/1**
04-1 **5** 1 ¾ **Resplendent Prince**[10] [11] 4-9-1 71 6ex..........(v) NCallan 5 72
(T G Mills) *cl up: led 2f out: sn rdn: drvn and hdd over 1f out: wknd ent last* **5/1**[2]
05-3 **6** 1 ¼ **Lincolneurocruiser**[11] [4] 4-8-7 70.......... RussellKennemore(7) 10 67
(Mrs N Macauley) *prom: effrt and ev ch 2f out: sn rdn and one pce* **14/1**
30-4 **7** 2 **Hurricane Coast**[7] [50] 7-9-3 73..........(b) TonyCulhane 7 65
(K McAuliffe) *hld up towards rr: hdwy over 2f out: sn rdn and no imp* **7/1**
02-0 **8** 1 **Certain Justice (USA)**[11] [1] 8-9-3 73..........(e[1]) MickyFenton 11 63
(Stef Liddiard) *hld up in rr whn hmpd after 2f: kpt on fnl 2f: nvr a factor* **20/1**
000- **9** 2 ½ **Diction (IRE)**[16] [6671] 4-8-4 60.......... HayleyTurner 13 43
(K R Burke) *in tch: rdn along over 2f out: no hdwy* **66/1**
625- **10** nk **My Gacho (IRE)**[21] [6657] 4-9-2 72..........(v) PaulFessey 2 54
(T D Barron) *led: rdn along and hdd over 2f out: sn wknd* **10/1**
41-2 **11** 3 **Out Of India**[10] [15] 4-8-11 67.......... PaulEddery 6 42
(B Smart) *dwlt: sn in tch: rdn along 2f out and sn btn* **13/2**[3]
00-6 **12** 8 **Penwell Hill (USA)**[10] [9] 7-9-2 72.......... RobbieFitzpatrick 1 26
(M J Attwater) *sn rdn along in rr: a bhd* **25/1**

00-0 **13** *1* **Chairman Rick (IRE)**[11] [8] 4-8-1 **60** oh8.......... SilvestreDeSousa(3) 3 11
(D Nicholls) *s.i.s: a bhd* **100/1**
1m 28.21s (-2.59) **Going Correction** -0.25s/f (Stan) **13** Ran SP% **124.1**
Speed ratings (Par 103):104,102,101,100,98 97,95,93,91,90 87,78,77
CSF £20.18 CT £136.91 TOTE £5.20: £2.10, £1.80, £2.50; EX 32.80.
Owner newkeylets **Bred** Richard Brunger **Trained** Carluke, S Lanarks
■ Stewards' Enquiry : Russell Kennemore caution: used whip with excessive force
FOCUS
A fair handicap and solid form.
Flint River ◆ Official explanation: jockey said gelding lost its near-fore plate

101 TEXT "BETDIRECT" TO 88600 H'CAP — 1m (F)
3:10 (3:15) (Class 5) (0-75,73) 4-Y-0+ **£3,238** (£963; £481; £240) **Stalls** Low

Form RPR
6P-1 **1** **Samuel Charles**[3] [71] 8-8-2 **62**................................ AndrewMullen(5) 5 76
(C R Dore) *trckd ldrs: hdwy 2f out: rdn to chse ldr and put hd in air over 1f out: drvn to ld and hung lft ins last: kpt on* **7/1**[3]
2-11 **2** *1 ¼* **Speed Dial Harry (IRE)**[2] [77] 4-9-1 **70** 6ex.......................(v) NCallan 9 81
(K R Burke) *cl up: led over 2f out: jnd and rdn over 1f out: hdd ins last: kpt on* **2/1**[1]
00-0 **3** *5* **Orpen Wide (IRE)**[2] [80] 4-9-3 **72**...................................... BrianReilly 7 73
(M C Chapman) *led: rdn alon g and hdd over 2f out: drvn and one pce fr wl over 1f out* **40/1**
010- **4** *hd* **Elrafa Mujahid**[38] [6499] 4-9-0 **72**..................................... AdamKirby(3) 4 73
(Ernst Oertel) *cl up on inner: rdn along over 2df out and kpt on same pce* **10/1**
00-0 **5** *¾* **African Sahara (USA)**[8] [33] 7-8-11 **73**............(vt[1]) ChrisCavanagh(7) 1 72
(Miss D Mountain) *towards rr: hdwy on inner 2f out: sn rdn: drvn and kpt on ins last* **18/1**
022- **6** *2 ½* **Dragon Slayer (IRE)**[24] [6621] 4-9-3 **72**............................ ChrisCatlin 10 66
(M J Attwater) *cl up: rdn over 2f out and sn btn* **4/1**[2]
043- **7** *2 ½* **Corky (IRE)**[24] [6622] 5-8-12 **67**.. TomEaves 3 56
(I W McInnes) *towards rr: hdwy 2f out: sn rdn and kpt on appr last: nt rch ldrs* **8/1**
110- **8** *3* **Paso Doble**[16] [6671] 8-8-5 **67**...................................... JamesMillman(7) 2 50
(B R Millman) *a towards rr* **11/1**
506- **9** *2* **Lord Links (IRE)**[58] [6362] 5-8-13 **68**.............................. VinceSlattery 14 47
(D J Daly) *nvr nr ldrs* **33/1**
551- **10** *¾* **Forest Of Love**[131] [4963] 4-8-12 **67**..................................... DaleGibson 8 45
(M W Easterby) *midfield: rdn along 1/2-way: sn wknd* **28/1**
000- **11** *3 ½* **Union Jack Jackson (IRE)**[24] [6622] 4-8-11 **66**............. FergalLynch 13 37
(J G Given) *racd wd: a rr* **40/1**
645/ **12** *2* **Pagan Prince**[53] 9-8-11 **66**.. LPKeniry 11 33
(J Gallagher) *bhd fr 1/2-way* **16/1**
030- **13** *5* **Indebted**[16] [6669] 4-9-1 **70**.. RobertWinston 12 27
(P W D'Arcy) *chsd ldrs on outer: rdn wl over 2f out and sn wknd* **28/1**
000- **14** *4* **Wistman (UAE)**[118] [5266] 5-9-4 **73**.............................. AdrianTNicholls 6 22
(D Nicholls) *s.i.s: a bhd* **40/1**
1m 41.4s (-3.20) **Going Correction** -0.25s/f (Stan) **14** Ran SP% **122.7**
Speed ratings (Par 103):106,104,99,99,98 96,93,90,88,88 84,82,77,73
CSF £20.44 CT £536.33 TOTE £7.50: £2.40, £1.10, £12.70; EX 22.30.
Owner Chris Marsh **Bred** Sheikh Mohammed Obaid Al Maktoum **Trained** West Pinchbeck, Lincs
FOCUS
A fair handicap and the form looks sound for the grade.

102 BETDIRECT.CO.UK H'CAP — 5f (F)
3:40 (3:43) (Class 6) (0-60,61) 3-Y-O **£2,388** (£705; £352) **Stalls** High

Form RPR
326- **1** **Garlogs**[27] [6591] 3-9-1 **54**.. NCallan 6 57
(A Bailey) *cl up: led over 2f out: rdn over 1f out: edgd lft and kpt on ins last* **7/4**[2]
000- **2** *1* **Stoneacre Fred (IRE)**[27] [6595] 3-8-13 **52**...........(p) RobbieFitzpatrick 10 52
(Peter Grayson) *chsd ldrs: rdn 2f out: drvn and hung lft ins last: kpt on* **11/2**[3]
34-1 **3** *1* **Mister Incredible**[10] [10] 3-9-3 **61** 6ex.......................(p) GregFairley(5) 3 57
(C A Dwyer) *bmpd s: sn trcking ldrs: hdwy to chse wnr wl over 1f out: sn rdn and kpt on same pce ins last* **13/8**[1]
005- **4** *4* **No Inkling (IRE)**[21] [6653] 3-8-11 **50**................................. PaulHanagan 7 33
(John A Harris) *chsd ldrs: rdn along and outpcd 1/2-way: kpt on u.p ins last* **25/1**
00-1 **5** *nk* **My Reflection**[8] [39] 3-8-4 **46** 6ex............................ PatrickMathers(3) 1 28
(D Shaw) *racd wd: in tch: rdn along 2f out: kpt on same pce appr last* **12/1**
00-0 **6** *1* **Wotavadun (IRE)**[5] [66] 3-8-9 **55**.............................(b) JamesDoyle(7) 8 33
(K McAuliffe) *led: rdn along and hdd over 2f out: sn wknd* **40/1**
000- **7** *6* **Wise Kid**[119] [5245] 3-7-12 **44** oh13 ow1......................(p) MarkCoumbe(7) 4 2
(P T Midgley) *bmpd s: a bhd* **66/1**
000- **8** *2* **Moraadi**[117] [5323] 3-8-1 **43** oh13............................. SilvestreDeSousa(3) 5 —
(D W Chapman) *wnt lft s: chsd ldrs to 1/2-way: sn wknd* **66/1**
60.12 secs (-0.18) **Going Correction** -0.15s/f (Stan) **8** Ran SP% **106.8**
Speed ratings (Par 95):95,93,91,85,84 83,73,70
CSF £9.62 CT £12.75 TOTE £2.70: £1.10, £1.10, £1.20; EX 13.10 Place 6 £273.24, Place 5 £99.89.
Owner Peter G Freeman **Bred** Peter Taplin **Trained** Cotebrook, Cheshire
FOCUS
A moderate sprint handicap rated around the third's five-furlong form.
Wise Kid Official explanation: trainer said gelding was hampered leaving stalls
T/Plt: £471.20 to a £1 stake. Pool: £35,476.50. 54.95 winning tickets. T/Qpdt: £34.60 to a £1 stake. Pool: £3,477.40. 74.30 winning tickets. JR

67 WOLVERHAMPTON (A.W) (L-H)
Friday, January 13

OFFICIAL GOING: Standard
The Clerk of the Course thought the ground may have been a shade on the slow side.
Wind: Moderate, half behind Weather: Fine

103 NO 5P RULE 4S AT BETDIRECT (S) STKS — 1m 5f 194y(P)
1:20 (1:20) (Class 6) 4-Y-0+ **£2,388** (£705; £352) **Stalls** Low

Form RPR
40-6 **1** **Activist**[7] [52] 8-9-0 **58**...(p) DanielTudhope(3) 2 63
(D Carroll) *hld up in tch: lost pl 6f out: hdwy over 3f out: rdn over 2f out: edgd lft and led over 1f out: styd on wl* **7/2**[2]
42-2 **2** *6* **Moon Shot**[9] [40] 10-9-3 **50**.. VinceSlattery 1 55
(A G Juckes) *hld up in tch: hdwy on ins 6f out: ev ch whn n.m.r over 1f out: sn rdn: one pce* **7/2**[2]
30-4 **3** *2 ½* **Eton (GER)**[8] [48] 10-9-3 **54**.. AdrianTNicholls 4 52
(D Nicholls) *led 2f: prom: led over 6f out: rdn and hdd over 1f out: one pce* **9/1**
0/6- **4** *4* **Ambersong**[45] [309] 8-9-3 **45**... HayleyTurner 10 46
(A W Carroll) *s.s: hld up and bhd: rdn and hdwy over 4f out: one pce fnl 2f* **20/1**
05-0 **5** *10* **Strathtay**[6] [63] 4-8-6 **56**..(b[1]) JimmyQuinn 7 27
(M Appleby) *hld up in tch: wnt 2nd over 4f out: rdn and wknd over 2f out* **16/1**
30-4 **6** *6* **York Cliff**[4] [72] 8-9-3 **53**... RobertWinston 9 43+
(W M Brisbourne) *s.s: hld up and bhd: hdwy over 4f out: rdn over 3f out: eased whn btn ins fnl f* **5/2**[1]
60-0 **7** *18* **Haenertsburg (IRE)**[7] [56] 4-8-6 **45**................................(p) PaulEddery 6 —
(A L Forbes) *s.s: a bhd: t.o* **66/1**
/00- **8** *1 ½* **Bodfari Dream**[44] [6474] 5-8-12 **40**.................................... JamieMackay 3 —
(M Mullineaux) *s.s: a bhd: t.o* **20/1**
50-P **9** *5* **Small Time Blues (IRE)**[10] [28] 4-8-8 **35** ow2..........(t) MickyFenton 11 —
(J Parkes) *t.k.h: prom: rdn over 5f out: wknd 4f out: t.o* **100/1**
10-0 **10** *dist* **Bella Pavlina**[10] [25] 8-8-5 **49**... TolleyDean(7) 8 —
(R A Harris) *led after 2f tl over 6f out: rdn and wknd over 4f out: t.o* **33/1**
001- **11** *19* **Southern Shore (IRE)**[110] [4493] 4-8-11 **58**.................(bt) TonyCulhane 5 —
(D Burchell) *prom tl wknd over 5f out: t.o* **7/1**[3]
3m 9.21s (1.84) **Going Correction** +0.10s/f (Slow)
WFA 4 from 5yo+ 6lb **11** Ran SP% **116.3**
Speed ratings (Par 101):98,94,93,90,85 81,71,70,67,— —
CSF £15.10 TOTE £5.30: £1.50, £1.20, £2.90; EX 16.00.There was no bid for the winner.
Owner Dreams **Bred** Slatch Farm Stud **Trained** Warthill, N Yorks
FOCUS
A weak and slowly-run seller.
York Cliff Official explanation: jockey said gelding lost its action and hung right-handed in straight
Bella Pavlina Official explanation: jockey said mare hung badly right throughout

104 BE LUCKY @ LITTLEWOODSPOOLS.CO.UK MAIDEN STKS (DIV I) — 7f 32y(P)
1:50 (1:52) (Class 5) 3-Y-0+ **£2,914** (£867; £433; £216) **Stalls** High

Form RPR
626- **1** **Keel (IRE)**[143] [4652] 3-8-8 **73**... MickyFenton 7 75
(J A Osborne) *s.i.s: hld up: stdy hdwy over 5f out: rdn to ld wl over 1f out: edgd rt fnl f: drvn out* **11/2**[3]
025- **2** *2 ½* **Pab Special (IRE)**[13] [6694] 3-8-8 **74**............................. RobertWinston 6 69+
(K R Burke) *bhd: rdn and hdwy on outside over 2f out: hung lft and wnt 2nd 1f out: one pce* **7/2**[2]
063- **3** *4* **Ockums Razor (IRE)**[101] [5680] 3-8-8 **65**.................................. NCallan 4 58
(N A Callaghan) *hld up in tch: hdwy on ins over 3f out: rdn over 2f out: wkng whn edgd lft wl ins fnl f* **7/2**[2]
030- **4** *2* **Nut (IRE)**[96] [5755] 3-8-3 **67**.. ChrisCatlin 8 48
(J W Hills) *hld up and bhd: rdn and hdwy over 2f out: wknd fnl f* **9/1**
20-0 **5** *1 ½* **Indian Edge**[9] [43] 5-9-12 **47**... FrancisFerris 3 53
(B Palling) *led: rdn and hdd wl over 1f out: wknd ins fnl f* **16/1**
203- **6** *nk* **Lord Of Dreams (IRE)**[25] [6619] 4-9-12 **67**.....................(p) FergalLynch 1 52
(D W P Arbuthnot) *broke wl: sn mid-div: rdn and hdwy on ins wl over 1f out: no further prog* **3/1**[1]
600- **7** *3* **Feathergrass (IRE)**[177] [3639] 4-9-4 **61**.................. RichardThomas(3) 5 39
(B S Rothwell) *hld up in mid-div: rdn 3f out: n.d after* **25/1**
006- **8** *½* **Pearl Fisher (IRE)**[32] [6558] 5-9-4 **40**......................... DanielTudhope(3) 10 38
(D Carroll) *sn prom: rdn over 3f out: wknd 2f out* **33/1**
50-6 **9** *6* **Nilsatisoptimum (USA)**[9] [31] 3-8-8 **60**.......................(p) JimmyQuinn 9 24
(M Mullineaux) *sn chsng ldr: rdn over 2f out: wknd wl over 1f out* **12/1**
060- **10** *hd* **Mad Marty Wildcard**[31] [6568] 4-9-12 **35**............................ TomEaves 2 27
(R Brotherton) *broke wl: sn bhd* **66/1**
-0 **11** *15* **Jeudi**[10] [16] 3-8-8 .... JamieMackay 11 —
(Sir Mark Prescott) *s.i.s: outpcd: t.o fnl 4f* **50/1**
1m 30.58s (0.18) **Going Correction** +0.10s/f (Slow)
WFA 3 from 4yo+ 18lb **11** Ran SP% **118.6**
Speed ratings (Par 103):102,99,94,92,90 90,86,86,79,79 62
CSF £24.72 TOTE £6.70: £2.10, £2.00, £1.90; EX 30.40.
Owner Mountgrange Stud **Bred** Oak Lodge Bloodstock **Trained** Upper Lambourn, Berks
FOCUS
This poor maiden was run at a fast pace and the time was slightly quicker than the other division.
Lord Of Dreams(IRE) Official explanation: jockey said, regarding the running and riding, his orders were to try and jump well, get a soft lead, see how the race developed and make his best way home but colt missed the break and veered left at the start; trainer added that colt is a difficult ride and has a history of hanging, and would also appear not to have the pace to make the running over 7f
Nilsatisoptimum(USA) Official explanation: trainer said colt ran without the declared tongue-strap, which had come adrift and could not be refitted

105 WOLVERHAMPTON-RACECOURSE.CO.UK (S) STKS — 5f 20y(P)
2:20 (2:22) (Class 6) 3-Y-O **£2,388** (£705; £352) **Stalls** Low

Form RPR
405- **1** **Thoughtsofstardom**[18] [6662] 3-9-3 **66**......................... RobertWinston 7 58
(W M Brisbourne) *s.i.s: rdn over 3f out: hdwy whn nt clr run wl over 1f out: sn swtchd rt: edgd lft and led wl ins fnl furl* **2/1**[2]
005- **2** *1 ¼* **Tatstheticket**[17] [6670] 3-8-9 **45**..............................(b) JasonEdmunds(3) 3 48
(J Balding) *chsd ldrs: rdn to ld ins fnl f: sn hdd: nt qckn* **40/1**
46-0 **3** *1 ½* **Bermuda Beauty (IRE)**[7] [53] 3-8-12 **55**.............................. LPKeniry 2 43
(J M Bradley) *chsd ldr: rdn 2f out: ev ch ins fnl f: one pce* **16/1**
000- **4** *hd* **Sweet Cherokee**[120] [5245] 3-8-8 **35** ow1.......................... MickyFenton 4 38
(C N Kellett) *chsd ldrs: rdn and stly outpcd 2f out: rallied towards fin* **50/1**
060- **5** *hd* **Straight As A Die**[27] [6600] 3-8-7 **47**................................ JimmyQuinn 6 36
(R J Hodges) *hld up towards rr: hdwy on ins wl over 1f out: one pce fnl f* **40/1**
004- **6** *nk* **Pauvic (IRE)**[17] [6670] 3-9-3 **56**.. PaulFessey 9 45
(Mrs A Duffield) *chsd ldrs: rdn over 2f out: no hdwy* **12/1**[3]
00-0 **7** *shd* **Lucys Lady**[7] [53] 3-8-12 **52**... PaulHanagan 10 40
(K R Burke) *s.i.s: hdwy whn hung lft ins fnl f: sn swtchd rt: nt rch ldrs* **40/1**
00-1 **7** *dht* **Charley's Aunt (IRE)**[7] [53] 3-8-12 .... NCallan 1 40
(J R Boyle) *led: rdn 2f out: hdd ins fnl f: wknd towards fin* **10/11**[1]
000- **9** *1 ½* **Stoneacre Girl (IRE)**[32] [6561] 3-8-7 **40**..................... RobbieFitzpatrick 5 29
(Peter Grayson) *t.k.h: prom: rdn over 2f out: wknd over 1f out* **33/1**

405- **10** 1½ **Left Nostril (IRE)**[25] 6610 3-8-8 49 ow1 .... BrianReilly 8 25
(P S McEntee) *wnt lft s: chsd ldrs: rdn over 2f out: wkng whn hung lft over 1f out* **25/1**

64.62 secs (1.80) **Going Correction** +0.10s/f (Slow) **10** Ran SP% **115.4**
Speed ratings (Par 95):89,87,84,84,83 83,83,83,80,78
CSF £87.25 TOTE £3.30: £1.40, £4.40, £2.60; EX 77.90.The winner was sold to P. S. McEntee for 10,000gns. Charley's Aunt was claimed by Christine Dunnett for £6,000.
Owner Weetman Wardle & Brown **Bred** B Bargh **Trained** Great Ness, Shropshire

FOCUS
A modest seller and an ordinary time, even for a race like this.
Charley's Aunt(IRE) Official explanation: vet said filly finished lame

106 FIRST PAST THE POST AT BETDIRECT H'CAP 1m 1f 103y(P)
2:50 (2:50) (Class 6) (0-65,65) 4-Y-0+ **£2,388** (£705; £352) **Stalls** Low

Form RPR

64-1 **1** **Kindlelight Debut**[4] 74 6-8-10 **64** .... JamesDoyle(7) 6 80
(N P Littmoden) *hld up towards rr: hdwy over 4f out: rdn over 2f out: led ins fnl f: r.o* **6/1[2]**

001- **2** *hd* **Red Birr (IRE)**[24] 6626 5-9-3 **64** .... ChrisCatlin 11 79+
(P R Webber) *chsd ldrs: rdn over 3f out: ev ch ins fnl f: r.o* **5/2[1]**

4-34 **3** *5* **Lord Chamberlain**[4] 71 13-9-0 **61** ....(b) LPKeniry 12 67
(J M Bradley) *s.s: hdwy over 2f out: swtchd lft over 1f out and ins fnl f: one pce* **16/1**

600- **4** *hd* **My Pension (IRE)**[28] 6593 5-9-2 **63** .... RobertWinston 1 68
(P Howling) *led early: lost pl over 7f out: hdwy on ins wl over 1f out: one pce fnl f* **8/1**

250- **5** *hd* **Jakarmi**[28] 6593 5-9-2 **63** .... FrancisFerris 13 68
(B Palling) *sn led: rdn over 2f out: hdd ins fnl f: wknd* **20/1**

012- **6** ½ **Bijou Dan**[28] 6593 5-9-3 **64** ....(b) TomEaves 8 68
(I Semple) *sn chsng ldr: ev ch over 2f out: rdn wl over 1f out: wknd ins fnl f* **6/1[2]**

66-2 **7** 1½ **Midshipman**[8] 50 8-8-11 **65** ....(vt) WilliamCarson(7) 10 66
(A W Carroll) *s.i.s: nvr nrr* **7/1[3]**

24-3 **8** ½ **Yenaled**[3] 75 9-8-11 **65** ....(p) DonnaCaldwell(7) 4 65
(P S McEntee) *hld up and bhd: hdwy 5f out: rdn wl over 1f out: no imp* **16/1**

1- **9** 3½ **Heartcrusher (IRE)**[25] 6619 4-9-0 **62** .... DeanMcKeown 5 56
(G A Swinbank) *prom: rdn over 3f out: wknd wl over 1f out* **16/1**

053- **10** *4* **Sforzando**[18] 6666 5-8-8 **62** .... KristinStubbs(7) 7 48
(Mrs L Stubbs) *s.i.s: hdwy over 5f out: wknd over 2f out* **16/1**

000- **11** *13* **Farriers Charm**[69] 6266 5-8-13 **60** .... PaulHanagan 3 21
(D J Coakley) *hld up in tch: wknd over 5f out* **20/1**

225- **12** 1½ **Blueberry Tart (IRE)**[29] 6586 4-9-0 **62** .... NCallan 9 20
(J M P Eustace) *prom tl rdn and wknd over 2f out* **16/1**

106- **13** 3½ **Midnight Lace**[34] 6536 4-9-2 **64** .... FergalLynch 2 16
(J R Boyle) *bhd fnl 5f* **33/1**

2m 0.91s (-1.71) **Going Correction** +0.10s/f (Slow)
WFA 4 from 5yo+ 1lb **13** Ran SP% **122.6**
Speed ratings (Par 101):111,110,106,106,106 105,104,103,100,97 85,84,81
CSF £21.26 CT £239.17 TOTE £5.70: £2.10, £1.90, £4.60; EX 31.50.
Owner Kindlelight Ltd **Bred** Cheveley Park Stud Ltd **Trained** Newmarket, Suffolk

FOCUS
The fastest of the three races over the trip at the meeting and this appeared to be a decent event for its type.
Sforzando Official explanation: jockey said mare had been in season
Blueberry Tart(IRE) Official explanation: jockey said filly had never been travelling

107 HOTEL AND CONFERENCING AT DUNSTALL PARK CLAIMING STKS 1m 1f 103y(P)
3:20 (3:21) (Class 6) 4-Y-0+ **£2,730** (£806; £403) **Stalls** Low

Form RPR

22-2 **1** **Danelor (IRE)**[8] 48 8-9-2 78 ....(p) PaulHanagan 6 74
(R A Fahey) *sn chsng wnr: led over 7f out: rdn 2f out: r.o wl* **11/8[1]**

12-1 **2** *5* **Mystic Man (FR)**[8] 44 8-9-8 80 .... NCallan 7 71
(K A Ryan) *hld up and bhd: hdwy on outside over 3f out: rdn over 2f out: chsd wnr fnl f: one pce* **13/2[3]**

03R- **3** *shd* **Keshya**[23] 6643 5-8-4 67 .... RichardThomas(3) 3 56
(N P Littmoden) *s.i.s: t.k.h: hdwy over 2f out: hung lft over 1f out: r.o ins fnl f* **12/1**

04-4 **4** *nk* **Look At The Stars (IRE)**[7] 56 4-8-7 50 .... GrahamGibbons 12 56
(R Hollinshead) *chsd ldrs: rdn over 3f out: one pce fnl f* **25/1**

63-6 **5** 1¼ **Scotty's Future (IRE)**[8] 50 8-9-8 66 .... AdrianTNicholls 5 68
(D Nicholls) *hld up in mid-div: rdn over 3f out: styd on fnl f* **20/1**

05-2 **6** *nk* **Seattle Robber**[7] 56 4-9-1 62 ....(v) FergalLynch 9 61
(Lucinda Featherstone) *hld up and bhd: hdwy over 4f out: rdn over 3f out: no imp fnl f* **14/1**

0-14 **7** *3* **Risk Free**[4] 73 9-8-7 53 ow1 ....(bt) RobertWinston 10 51+
(P D Evans) *prom: chsd ldr over 6f out: ev ch over 2f out: sn rdn: wknd 1f out* **5/1[2]**

00-6 **8** 2½ **Cherished Number**[8] 48 7-8-8 66 ....(b) TomEaves 11 43
(I Semple) *nvr nr ldrs* **9/1**

0/0 **9** *nk* **Starling (IRE)**[11] 14 4-7-13 62 .... SilvestreDeSousa(3) 1 37
(D Nicholls) *t.k.h: led: hdd over 7f out: rdn and wknd 2f out* **40/1**

020- **10** 3½ **Nimello (USA)**[41] 6488 10-9-2 69 .... LPKeniry 8 43
(A G Newcombe) *a bhd* **10/1**

11 *shd* **Jomelamin**[9] 4-8-4 .... JimmyQuinn 4 32
(R J Hodges) *bhd fnl 4f* **66/1**

/06- **12** *5* **Tashkandi (IRE)**[18] 1580 6-9-8 100 .... ChrisCatlin 2 40
(P Bowen) *prom: rdn over 4f out: sn wknd* **25/1**

2m 3.09s (0.47) **Going Correction** +0.10s/f (Slow)
WFA 4 from 5yo+ 1lb **12** Ran SP% **121.9**
Speed ratings (Par 101):101,96,96,96,95 94,92,89,89,86 86,82
CSF £10.06 TOTE £2.20: £1.80, £1.50, £5.30; EX 11.30.Seattle Robber was claimed by R. A. Harris for £10,000.
Owner Mark A Leatham **Bred** Barronstown Stud And Orpendale **Trained** Musley Bank, N Yorks

FOCUS
An uncompetitive claimer run at an even pace, though the time was unremarkable.
Risk Free Official explanation: jockey said gelding hung left in the home straight

108 BETDIRECT.CO.UK H'CAP 1m 1f 103y(P)
3:50 (3:52) (Class 4) (0-85,86) 4-Y-0+ **£5,505** (£1,637; £818; £408) **Stalls** Low

Form RPR

11/1 **1** **Gentleman's Deal (IRE)**[12] 7 5-9-5 **86** 6ex .... DaleGibson 8 99+
(M W Easterby) *sltly hmpd s: hld up: hdwy on outside 3f out: sn rdn: hung lft fr over 1f out: led wl ins fnl f: r.o wl* **1/1[1]**

010- **2** *2* **Almanshood (USA)**[17] 6671 4-8-3 **71** oh3 .... PaulHanagan 1 75
(P L Gilligan) *led: rdn over 2f out: hdd and no ex wl ins fnl f* **28/1**

126- **3** *1* **Desert Leader (IRE)**[13] 6700 5-8-11 **78** .... RobertWinston 10 80
(W M Brisbourne) *stdd s: hld up and bhd: rdn wl over 1f out: hdwy fnl f: r.o* **10/1**

11-0 **4** *hd* **Atlantic Quest (USA)**[7] 58 7-8-8 **82** ....(p) TolleyDean(7) 9 84
(R A Harris) *prom: rdn whn n.m.r ent st: kpt on ins fnl f* **33/1**

421- **5** *shd* **Byron Bay**[17] 6671 4-8-8 **76** .... TomEaves 2 78
(I Semple) *t.k.h: chsd ldr: rdn over 2f out: no ex ins fnl f* **9/2[2]**

01-0 **6** 1½ **Libre**[9] 33 6-8-7 **74** .... HayleyTurner 3 73
(Andrew Reid) *prom: rdn wl over 1f out: wknd ins fnl f* **20/1**

023- **7** *nk* **Crail**[34] 6547 6-8-5 **79** .... SladeO'Hara(7) 6 77
(C F Wall) *hld up and bhd: hdwy wl over 1f out: no imp fnl f* **5/1[3]**

000- **8** *2* **Dance World**[22] 5972 6-9-4 **85** .... DarrenWilliams 11 79
(Miss J Feilden) *nvr trbld ldrs* **20/1**

030- **9** *hd* **Arry Dash**[22] 5432 6-8-13 **80** ....(v) NCallan 5 74
(M J Wallace) *hld up in mid-div: hdwy on ins over 2f out: rdn wl over 1f out: wknd fnl f* **10/1**

005- **10** *hd* **Gingko**[23] 6645 9-8-9 **76** .... ChrisCatlin 4 70
(P R Webber) *bhd fnl 3f* **25/1**

331- **11** 1½ **Shankly Bond (IRE)**[32] 6566 4-8-6 **74** .... PaulEddery 7 65
(B Smart) *hld up: hdwy 6f out: rdn 3f out: n.m.r wl over 1f out: sn wknd* **16/1**

2m 1.75s (-0.87) **Going Correction** +0.10s/f (Slow)
WFA 4 from 5yo+ 1lb **11** Ran SP% **128.7**
Speed ratings (Par 105):107,105,104,104,104 102,102,100,100,100 99
CSF £49.40 CT £227.88 TOTE £1.80: £1.10, £6.90, £2.50; EX 54.30.
Owner Stephen J Curtis **Bred** C H Wacker Iii **Trained** Sheriff Hutton, N Yorks
■ Stewards' Enquiry : Tolley Dean one-day ban: failed to keep straight from the stalls (Jan 24)

FOCUS
This was more competitive than expected considering that they went 10/1 bar three.
Shankly Bond(IRE) Official explanation: jockey said gelding suffered interference in the home straight and had no more to give thereafter

109 BETDIRECT FREEPHONE ON 0800 211 222 FILLIES' H'CAP 1m 4f 50y(P)
4:20 (4:20) (Class 5) (0-70,69) 4-Y-0+ **£3,238** (£963; £481; £240) **Stalls** Low

Form RPR

342- **1** **Millagros (IRE)**[26] 6236 6-8-13 **63** .... PaulHanagan 5 70
(I Semple) *hld up towards rr: hdwy whn n.m.r 1f out: rdn to ld cl home* **4/1[2]**

131- **2** ¾ **Tranquilizer**[42] 6478 4-8-12 **66** ....(t) RobertWinston 7 72+
(D J Coakley) *hld up in mid-div: nt clr run and hdwy over 1f out: ev ch wl ins fnl f: r.o* **4/1[2]**

511- **3** *shd* **Captain Margaret**[23] 6644 4-8-10 **64** .... JimmyQuinn 3 69
(J Pearce) *a.p: rdn whn nt clr run and swtchd rt over 1f out: rdn to ld ins fnl f: hdd cl home* **3/1[1]**

32-0 **4** 2½ **Daring Affair**[8] 50 5-9-4 **68** .... NCallan 11 69
(K R Burke) *a.p: rdn and ev ch over 2f out: r.o one pce fnl f* **11/2[3]**

660- **5** ¾ **Tokewanna**[18] 6666 6-8-4 **57** ....(t) PatrickMathers(3) 2 57
(W M Brisbourne) *s.s: t.k.h: hdwy over 3f out: rdn 2f out: one pce fnl f* **33/1**

300- **6** *1* **Summer Charm**[23] 6644 4-8-8 **69** .... BRoper(7) 10 67
(W Jarvis) *hld up towards rr: hdwy over 3f out: led 2f out: edgd lft over 1f out: hdd ins fnl f: wknd* **8/1**

035- **7** *nk* **Charnock Bates One (IRE)**[39] 6506 5-8-4 **54** oh2 ....(p) ChrisCatlin 6 52
(J J Quinn) *hld up in mid-div: stdy hdwy over 5f out: rdn and btn whn n.m.r jst over 1f out* **12/1**

340- **8** *hd* **All A Dream**[14] 6690 4-9-1 **69** .... TomEaves 4 67
(Mrs L Williamson) *stdd s: hdwy on ins 1f out: swtchd rt ins fnl f: one pce* **25/1**

23-6 **9** *shd* **Simply St Lucia**[11] 15 4-8-6 **60** .... HayleyTurner 8 57
(J R Weymes) *chsd ldr: ev ch over 2f out: sn rdn: wknd fnl f* **20/1**

001- **10** *shd* **My Boo**[23] 6652 4-7-9 **54** oh18 ....(tp) DuranFentiman(5) 9 51
(T Keddy) *hld up and bhd: short-lived effrt on outside over 2f out* **25/1**

520- **11** *4* **Mollyputtheketelon (USA)**[18] 6666 5-9-0 **64** .... GrahamGibbons 1 55
(M J Wallace) *led: hdd 2f out: sn rdn: wknd qckly fnl f* **25/1**

2m 42.81s (0.39) **Going Correction** +0.10s/f (Slow)
WFA 4 from 5yo+ 4lb **11** Ran SP% **118.4**
Speed ratings (Par 100):102,101,101,99,99 98,98,98,98,98 95
CSF £18.94 CT £55.03 TOTE £5.20: £1.40, £2.00, £1.50; EX 21.00.
Owner James A Cringan **Bred** Elsdon Farms **Trained** Carluke, S Lanarks

FOCUS
There were stamina doubts over some of these in this open-looking handicap which was only run at a modest pace.

110 BE LUCKY @ LITTLEWOODSPOOLS.CO.UK MAIDEN STKS (DIV II) 7f 32y(P)
4:50 (4:52) (Class 5) 3-Y-0+ **£2,914** (£867; £433; £216) **Stalls** High

Form RPR

22- **1** **Chief Commander (FR)**[13] 6699 3-8-8 .... JimmyQuinn 3 76
(Jane Chapple-Hyam) *broke wl: stdd and lost pl over 5f out: rdn and hdwy 2f out: edgd lft and ld ins fnl f: drvn out* **1/2[1]**

524- **2** 2½ **Art Elegant**[58] 6367 4-9-12 64 .... RobertWinston 2 73
(G A Swinbank) *hld up: hdwy 3f out: ev ch 2f out: sn rdn: ld jst over 1f out: hdd ins fnl f: one pce* **7/1[2]**

0- **3** ½ **Kut (IRE)**[139] 4750 3-8-8 .... NCallan 4 68
(J Noseda) *sn prom: rdn over 2f out: r.o one pce fnl f* **7/1[2]**

406- **4** 2½ **Donna Giovanna**[141] 4692 3-8-3 70 .... PaulHanagan 7 56
(J A Osborne) *ld after 1f: rdn over 2f out: hdd jst over 1f out: wknd ins fnl f* **7/1[2]**

5- **5** *8* **Miss Lopez (IRE)**[18] 6661 3-8-3 .... HayleyTurner 8 35
(K R Burke) *t.k.h: sn chsng ldr: rdn 2f out: sn wknd* **25/1**

302- **6** *3* **Nazaaha (USA)**[65] 6298 4-9-7 62 .... LPKeniry 9 32
(A G Newcombe) *plld hrd: sn chsng ldrs: wknd over 2f out* **22/1[3]**

00-0 **7** 1¾ **Zambezi River**[2] 84 7-9-12 35 .... ChrisCatlin 5 32
(J M Bradley) *a bhd* **200/1**

060- **8** *shd* **Berties Brother**[28] 6595 3-8-8 50 .... MickyFenton 6 28
(D G Bridgwater) *led 1f: prom: rdn 3f out: sn wknd* **300/1**

0 **9** *dist* **Opening Line**[11] 14 4-9-9 .... AdamKirby(3) 10 —
(Ernst Oertel) *sn prom: hung rt over 5f out: wknd 4f out: t.o fnl 3f* **200/1**

1m 30.69s (0.29) **Going Correction** +0.10s/f (Slow)
WFA 3 from 4yo+ 18lb **9** Ran SP% **113.7**
Speed ratings (Par 103):102,99,98,95,86 83,81,81,—
CSF £4.34 TOTE £1.50: £1.10, £1.90, £2.10; EX 5.40 Place 6 £39.11, Place 5 £19.69.
Owner Franconson Partners **Bred** Vinery Stud Pty Ltd **Trained** Newmarket, Suffolk
■ Jane Chapple-Hyam's first training success.

FOCUS
A very ordinary maiden run in a slightly slower time than the first division.
Donna Giovanna Official explanation: jockey said filly hung right-handed throughout
Miss Lopez(IRE) Official explanation: jockey said filly had run too freely
Opening Line Official explanation: jockey said gelding hung right-handed throughout
T/Plt: £42.90 to a £1 stake. Pool: £39,441.25. 670.10 winning tickets. T/Qpdt: £18.10 to a £1 stake. Pool: £3,112.00. 127.10 winning tickets. KH

[82] LINGFIELD (L-H)
Saturday, January 14

OFFICIAL GOING: Standard
Wind: Fresh, behind

111 BETDIRECT IN-RUNNING SKYTEXT P293 H'CAP (DIV I) 1m 2f (P)
12:10 (12:11) (Class 5) (0-70,69) 4-Y-0+ **£2,914** (£867; £433; £216) **Stalls** Low

Form RPR
505- **1** **Bonnabee (IRE)**[92] [5867] 4-8-7 **60** .... JamieMackay 2 67
(C F Wall) *s.i.s: sn trckd ldrs: rdn to ld 1f out: hld on wl* **9/1**
40-1 **2** *nk* **Port 'n Starboard**[10] [32] 5-8-9 **60** .... JoeFanning 6 66
(C A Cyzer) *hld up: rdn and hdwy over 2f out: chsd wnr ins fnl f: no imp nr fin* **9/2**[1]
113- **3** *1 1/4* **Western Roots**[29] [6593] 5-9-4 **69** .... JimmyQuinn 11 73
(M Appleby) *swtg: hld up: hdwy on outside over 1f out: styd on: nvr nr to chal* **5/1**[2]
014- **4** *hd* **Night Storm**[19] [6666] 5-8-13 **64** .... ChrisCatlin 10 67
(S Dow) *bhd tl hdwy on ins to chal ent fnl f: no ex ins* **13/2**
136/ **5** *nk* **Shirazi**[15] [3336] 8-8-13 **67** .... NeilChalmers(3) 3 70
(D R Gandolfo) *mid-div: kpt on one pce fnl f* **16/1**
65-3 **6** *1/2* **Blackmail (USA)**[10] [37] 8-8-13 **64** .... (b) FrankieMcDonald 5 66
(Miss B Sanders) *mid-div: rdn over 3f out: outpcd 2f out: r.o fnl f* **11/2**[3]
/44- **7** *1 3/4* **Red Sans**[15] [6687] 4-8-8 **61** .... MartinDwyer 1 59
(P Mitchell) *led: rdn 2f out: hdd 1f out: wknd* **6/1**
500- **8** *3/4* **Blue Hedges**[130] [5035] 4-8-1 **57** .... EdwardCreighton(3) 8 54
(H J Collingridge) *b: t.k.h: trckd ldr: wknd appr fnl f* **33/1**
65-0 **9** *shd* **Tricky Venture**[5] [73] 6-8-4 **55** .... HayleyTurner 12 52
(Mrs L C Jewell) *prom tl wknd over 1f out* **11/1**
04-0 **10** *7* **Sphinx (FR)**[10] [37] 8-9-0 **65** .... MichaelHills 7 48
(Jamie Poulton) *lw: b: mid-div tl wknd over 2f out* **14/1**

2m 8.37s (0.58) **Going Correction** +0.05s/f (Slow)
WFA 4 from 5yo+ 2lb **10 Ran SP% 111.7**
Speed ratings (Par 103):99,98,97,97,97 96,95,94,94,89
CSF £47.10 CT £222.52 TOTE £14.50: £4.00, £1.90, £1.80; EX 91.70.
Owner T J Wells **Bred** C Lilburn **Trained** Newmarket, Suffolk
■ Stewards' Enquiry : Jamie Mackay two-day ban: used whip without allowing sufficient time for mount to respond (Jan 25-26)

FOCUS
A moderate ten-furlong race spoilt by the lack of pace early. The form is slightly dubious.

112 FOOTBALLPOOLS.COM MEDIAN AUCTION MAIDEN STKS 1m (P)
12:45 (12:47) (Class 6) 3-Y-0 **£3,071** (£906; £453) **Stalls** High

Form RPR
5- **1** **Direct Debit (IRE)**[141] [4735] 3-9-0 .... HayleyTurner 9 76+
(M L W Bell) *w'like: trckd ldrs: wnt 2nd 2f out: shkn up over 1f out: rdn and kpt on to ld nr fin* **9/4**[2]
2- **2** *shd* **Dream Champion**[29] [6595] 3-9-0 .... TonyCulhane 8 76+
(M R Channon) *w'like: lw: led tl rdn and hdd nr fin* **4/5**[1]
3 *3 1/2* **Babcary** 3-8-9 .... MartinDwyer 5 63+
(M P Tregoning) *unf: mid-div tl outpcd 3f out: r.o fnl f* **10/1**[3]
4 *2* **Russian Mist (IRE)** 3-8-9 .... DerekNolan(5) 4 63
(M J Wallace) *w'like: str: b.bkwd: s.i.s: sn in tch: rdn 3f out: swtchd lft over 1f out: kpt on one pce* **25/1**
5 *1* **Laheen (IRE)** 3-8-9 .... MichaelHills 6 56
(M H Tompkins) *w'like: cmpt: lw: mid-div: outpcd over 2f out: kpt on fnl f* **20/1**
0- **6** *3/4* **Black Beauty**[107] [5574] 3-9-0 .... TPQueally 7 59
(M G Quinlan) *lengthy: unf: bhd tl hdwy over 1f out: nvr nr to chal* **16/1**
0- **7** *shd* **Broadway Calling**[25] [6624] 3-9-0 .... LPKeniry 10 59
(A M Balding) *trckd ldr to 2f out: wknd appr fnl f* **25/1**
0- **8** *5* **Bold Pioneer (USA)**[40] [6502] 3-9-0 .... RobertHavlin 3 48
(C P Morlock) *t.k.h: in tch: bhd fr 1/2-way* **66/1**
9 *1 1/2* **Lanfredo** 3-9-0 .... JoeFanning 11 44
(D W P Arbuthnot) *w'like: b.bkwd: slowly away: sn in tch: bhd fr 1/2-way* **33/1**
10 *nk* **Batchworth Fleur** 3-8-9 .... VinceSlattery 2 38
(E A Wheeler) *leggy: slowly away: a in rr* **50/1**
00- **11** *nk* **Go Amwell**[24] [6642] 3-9-0 .... MickyFenton 12 43
(J R Jenkins) *racd wd: chsd ldrs tl wknd 2f out* **33/1**
0- **12** *dist* **Saint Nick**[28] [6600] 3-8-11 .... NeilChalmers(3) 1 —
(J J Bridger) *slowly away: a bhd: t.o* **100/1**

1m 40.91s (1.48) **Going Correction** +0.05s/f (Slow) **12 Ran SP% 124.1**
Speed ratings (Par 95):94,93,90,88,87 86,86,81,80,79 79,—
CSF £4.22 TOTE £3.00: £1.60, £1.10, £2.50; EX 7.40.
Owner Billy Maguire **Bred** Hawthorn Villa Stud **Trained** Newmarket, Suffolk
■ Stewards' Enquiry : Michael Hills caution: careless riding

FOCUS
A fair maiden run at a reasonable pace. The first two had racing experience, which made all the difference as some in behind ran as though the run was required.
Babcary Official explanation: jockey said filly ran green
Lanfredo Official explanation: jockey said colt hung left
Saint Nick Official explanation: jockey said gelding pulled up lame

113 BETDIRECT FOOTBALL CASHBACKS SKYTEXT P372 CLAIMING STKS 1m 2f (P)
1:20 (1:21) (Class 6) 4-Y-0+ **£2,388** (£705; £352) **Stalls** Low

Form RPR
036- **1** **Bishops Finger**[25] [6626] 6-8-11 53 .... (b) SimonWhitworth 7 56
(Jamie Poulton) *b: hld up in rr: racd on ins: hdwy wl over 1f out: squeezed through to ld wl ins fnl f: drvn out* **14/1**[3]
02-3 **2** *1/2* **Mad Carew (USA)**[9] [48] 7-9-9 76 .... (e) MartinDwyer 1 67
(J R Boyle) *trckd ldrs: wnt 2nd 1/2-way: led wl over 1f out: rdn and hdd wl ins f* **5/2**[1]
42-1 **3** *nk* **Barton Sands (IRE)**[10] [35] 9-8-7 63 .... (t) LPKeniry 8 50
(Andrew Reid) *hld up in rr: hdwy on outside into st: r.o fnl f: nvr nrr* **11/4**[2]
050- **4** *1/2* **Milk And Sultana**[45] [6473] 6-8-6 47 .... JimmyQuinn 5 48
(G A Ham) *a in tch: rdn appr fnl f: kpt on one pce* **40/1**
02-1 **5** *shd* **Desperation (IRE)**[9] [48] 4-9-7 73 .... RobertWinston 4 65
(K R Burke) *a.p on outside: rdn 2f out: kpt on one pce fnl f* **5/2**[1]
106- **6** *1 3/4* **Treetops Hotel (IRE)**[24] [6643] 7-8-12 52 .... RichardThomas(3) 2 54
(B R Johnson) *trckd ldrs tl rdn and wknd 2f out* **16/1**
000- **7** *1* **Piquet**[16] [6683] 8-8-10 45 .... TonyCulhane 3 47
(J J Bridger) *mid-div: wknd over 1f out* **33/1**
02-0 **8** *2 1/2* **Sriology (IRE)**[5] [72] 5-9-5 52 .... ChrisCatlin 6 51
(G Prodromou) *a towards rr* **33/1**
220- **9** *hd* **Moondancer (GER)**[16] [6683] 7-8-5 47 .... HayleyTurner 10 37
(B G Powell) *led: rdn over 2f out: hdd & wknd wl over 1f out* **25/1**
000- **10** *14* **Heartbeat**[56] [6383] 5-8-0 35 .... FrancisFerris 13 5
(I A Wood) *hld up: racd wd: a bhd* **100/1**
11 *4* **Crystal Ka (FR)**[13] 4-8-7 60 .... JoeFanning 9 7
(M R Hoad) *t.k.h: trckd ldr tl wknd rapidly 1/2-way* **100/1**

2m 7.66s (-0.13) **Going Correction** +0.05s/f (Slow)
WFA 4 from 5yo+ 2lb **11 Ran SP% 110.5**
Speed ratings (Par 101):102,101,101,100,100 99,98,96,96,85 82
CSF £42.46 TOTE £10.50: £2.30, £1.50, £1.70; EX 36.80.Mad Carew was the subject of a friendly claim.
Owner Jamie Poulton **Bred** Cheveley Park Stud Ltd And Mrs J Druce **Trained** Telscombe, E Sussex
■ Hoh Bleu Dee was withdrawn (12/1, vet's advice). R4 applies, deduct 5p in the £.
■ Stewards' Enquiry : Simon Whitworth caution: careless riding

FOCUS
A claimer of mixed ability. The time was quicker than all of the handicaps over the same distance on the card.

114 TEXT "BETDIRECT" TO 88600 MAIDEN STKS 1m 2f (P)
1:50 (1:52) (Class 5) 4-Y-0+ **£3,562** (£1,059; £529; £264) **Stalls** Low

Form RPR
22-2 **1** **Newnham (IRE)**[8] [59] 5-9-2 65 .... JoeFanning 9 68
(J R Boyle) *lw: hld up in tch: hdwy over 1f out: rdn to ld wl ins fnl f* **11/4**[1]
\- **2** *nk* **Custodian (IRE)** 4-9-0 .... SteveDrowne 12 67
(H R A Cecil) *w'like: t.k.h: a.p: led over 2f out: hung rt and hdd wl ins fnl f* **7/2**[2]
433- **3** *hd* **Measured Response**[121] [5250] 4-9-0 67 .... NCallan 6 67
(J G M O'Shea) *mid-div: hdwy wl over 1f out to hold ev ch ente4ring fnl f: nt qckn cl home* **11/2**
302- **4** *1* **Lady Pilot**[15] [6687] 4-8-6 60 .... RichardThomas(3) 8 60
(Dr J R J Naylor) *chsd ldrs: rdn 3f out: r.o fnl f* **14/1**
053- **5** *1/2* **Master'n Commander**[136] [4863] 4-9-0 72 .... ChrisCatlin 13 64+
(C A Cyzer) *lw: in rr: rdn 4f out: kpt on fnl f: nvr nr to chal* **9/2**[3]
6 *shd* **Grey Report (IRE)**[63] 9-9-2 .... VinceSlattery 10 64
(R H Buckler) *slowly away: wl in rr: styd on appr fnl f: fin wl* **33/1**
65- **7** *3/4* **Woodwool**[26] [6623] 4-8-9 .... SimonWhitworth 4 57
(H Candy) *towards rr: hdwy on outside over 1f out: hung lft: no ex* **25/1**
8 *hd* **Stage Manager (IRE)** 4-8-9 .... DerekNolan(5) 1 65+
(M J Wallace) *w'like: towards rr whn bdly hmpd over 2f out* **50/1**
004- **9** *1 1/4* **Contented (IRE)**[25] [6632] 4-9-0 61 .... HayleyTurner 5 60
(Mrs L C Jewell) *t.k.h: led for 1f: wnt lft over 2f out: wknd* **33/1**
42-0 **10** *3 1/2* **Monash Lad (IRE)**[9] [50] 4-9-0 65 .... MichaelHills 11 53
(M H Tompkins) *in tch: led over 3f out: hdd over 2f out: wknd appr fnl f* **9/1**
000- **11** *4* **Postmaster**[28] [6596] 4-9-0 60 .... (t) RobertHavlin 3 45
(R Ingram) *bhd: no ch whn hmpd over 2f out* **33/1**
006- **12** *nk* **Whitsbury Common**[110] [5504] 4-8-9 58 .... LPKeniry 14 40
(D R C Elsworth) *a bhd* **40/1**
13 *18* **Busy Man (IRE)**[32] 7-9-2 .... MickyFenton 7 11+
(J R Jenkins) *led after 1f: hdd over 3f out: wkng whn bdly hmpd over 2f out* **100/1**
0-0 **14** *11* **Rose Amber**[10] [35] 5-8-11 .... TonyCulhane 2 —
(J J Bridger) *a bhd* **100/1**

2m 7.96s (0.17) **Going Correction** +0.05s/f (Slow)
WFA 4 from 5yo+ 2lb **14 Ran SP% 118.2**
Speed ratings (Par 103):101,100,100,99,99 99,98,98,97,94 91,91,76,68
CSF £11.08 TOTE £3.50: £1.30, £2.30, £2.60; EX 16.00.
Owner M Khan X2 **Bred** Ballygallon Stud **Trained** Epsom, Surrey

FOCUS
An interesting maiden with a couple of unknown quantities making their Flat debuts. The time was slower than the preceding claimer and the form should be treated with caution until a few of these run again. The fourth is probably the benchmark to the form.
Custodian(IRE) Official explanation: jockey said colt hung right home straight

115 BETDIRECT IN-RUNNING SKYTEXT P293 H'CAP (DIV II) 1m 2f (P)
2:25 (2:26) (Class 5) (0-70,69) 4-Y-0+ **£2,914** (£867; £433; £216) **Stalls** Low

Form RPR
00-4 **1** **Alfridini**[10] [36] 5-9-2 **67** .... LPKeniry 2 76
(D R C Elsworth) *lw: mde all: qcknd clr over 2f out: r.o wl fnl f* **9/2**[2]
003- **2** *2 1/2* **Monashee Prince (IRE)**[26] [6618] 4-8-11 **64** .... NCallan 12 69
(J R Best) *lw: trckd wnr for most of r: hung lft over 1f out: nt qckn ins fnl f* **8/1**
560- **3** *nk* **Unrestricted**[120] [5281] 4-8-4 **57** .... JamieMackay 4 61
(C F Wall) *in rr: outpcd 1/2-way: hdwy on ins to go 3rd 1f out: styd on* **15/2**
502- **4** *nk* **Danger Zone**[28] [6598] 4-9-2 **69** .... JoeFanning 11 72
(Mrs A J Perrett) *lw: t.k.h: in tch tl outpcd over 2f out: styd on fnl f* **3/1**[1]
300- **5** *1 1/2* **Madhavi**[15] [6687] 4-8-4 **60** .... StephaneBreux(3) 9 61
(R Hannon) *lw: trckd ldrs: rdn 3f out: wknd over 1f out* **33/1**
500- **6** *hd* **Opera Belle**[63] [6323] 4-8-4 **57** .... ChrisCatlin 3 57
(A P Jarvis) *trckd ldrs til; l wknd 2f out* **25/1**
45-5 **7** *1/2* **Scottish River (USA)**[9] [50] 7-9-4 **69** .... HayleyTurner 7 68
(M D I Usher) *b.hind: t.k.h: hld up in rr: hdwy over 3f out on outside: nvr on terms* **5/1**[3]
420- **8** *1 1/2* **Birthday Star (IRE)**[168] [3956] 4-8-7 **60** .... MickyFenton 5 56
(W J Musson) *hld up in tch: wknd 2f out* **10/1**
640/ **9** *1/2* **Ground Patrol**[429] [6624] 5-8-7 **58** .... (p) PaulHanagan 6 53
(G L Moore) *a in rr* **14/1**
661- **10** *3/4* **Ronsard (IRE)**[29] [6593] 4-8-13 **66** .... RobertWinston 10 60
(Heather Dalton) *t.k.h: sn prom: wknd 2f out* **6/1**

2m 11.38s (3.59) **Going Correction** +0.05s/f (Slow)
WFA 4 from 5yo+ 2lb **10 Ran SP% 119.6**
Speed ratings (Par 103):87,85,84,84,83 83,82,81,81,80
CSF £41.56 CT £269.07 TOTE £6.60: £2.40, £2.20, £3.10; EX 47.90.
Owner A Heaney **Bred** Miss K Rausing **Trained** Newmarket, Suffolk
■ Stewards' Enquiry : N Callan one-day ban: failed to keep straight from stalls (Jan 25)

FOCUS
A competitive handicap, but marred by a very slow gallop, resulting in a time some three seconds slower than the first division. The winning jockey should take credit for dictating the pace from the front, but the form is not likely to be reliable.
Unrestricted Official explanation: jockey said filly lost right-fore shoe and hung right

116 BETDIRECT.CO.UK H'CAP 1m 2f (P)
2:55 (2:56) (Class 2) (0-100,98) 4-Y-0+
£12,464 (£3,732; £1,866; £934; £466; £234) **Stalls** Low

Form				RPR
404-	**1**		**Tiger Tiger (FR)**[29] 6592 5-8-9 **89** ... MichaelHills 4 (Jamie Poulton) *lw: a.p on ins rail: r.o to ld ins fnl f* **9/2**[3]	96
011-	**2**	*nk*	**Boo**[14] 6700 4-8-13 **95** ... (v) RobertWinston 6 (K R Burke) *hld up in tch: swtchd rt over 1f out: r.o wl to go 2nd fnl 50yds* **4/1**[2]	101
124-	**3**	*3/4*	**Royal Island (IRE)**[99] 5717 4-9-2 **98** ... JoeFanning 7 (M Johnston) *chsd ldrs: rdn 2f out: ev ch 1f out: no ex fnl 50yds* **10/3**[1]	103
133-	**4**	*2 1/2*	**Hail The Chief**[14] 6700 9-8-6 **89** ... StephaneBreux(3) 5 (R Hannon) *lw: b: b.hind: led tl hdd wl ins fnl f: no ex* **12/1**	89
/25-	**5**	*shd*	**Activo (FR)**[28] 6601 5-8-7 **87** ... PaulDoe 1 (S Dow) *v slowly: bhd tl hdwy on ins over 1f out: nvr nr to chal* **12/1**	87
132-	**6**	*2 1/2*	**Mizz Tee (IRE)**[14] 6700 4-7-13 **86** ... DuranFentiman(5) 8 (T D Easterby) *trckd ldr tl wknd over 1f out* **6/1**	81
043-	**7**	*8*	**Mustang Ali (IRE)**[16] 6681 5-8-1 **84** oh37 ... (b) RichardThomas(3) 2 (Dr J R J Naylor) *a bhd* **100/1**	64?
430-	**8**	*6*	**Qadar (IRE)**[126] 5114 4-8-11 **93** ... NCallan 9 (N P Littmoden) *in tch tl wknd 2f out* **20/1**	62
500-	**9**	*20*	**Howle Hill (IRE)**[13] 4478 6-9-4 **98** ... (v) SteveDrowne 10 (A King) *trckd ldrs: rdn 4f out: sn wknd* **11/2**	29

2m 4.52s (-3.27) **Going Correction** +0.05s/f (Slow)
WFA 4 from 5yo+ 2lb **9** Ran SP% **112.1**
Speed ratings (Par 109):115,114,114,112,112 110,103,98,82
CSF £21.92 CT £65.81 TOTE £5.60: £1.80, £2.00, £1.30; EX 23.30.
Owner R W Huggins **Bred** Pierre Talvard And Jean-Claude Seroul **Trained** Telscombe, E Sussex

FOCUS
The best race on the card won in a very good time. The first three home are decent performers and the form should work out.

NOTEBOOK
Tiger Tiger(FR), better handicapped on an All-Weather surface than grass, has done really well on the Polytrack given that his best turf form has been with plenty of cut. He sneaked up the rail in the last furlong and won nicely once striking the front. He would appear on course for a tilt at the Winter Derby. (op 5-1 tchd 4-1)
Boo has been on an upward curve recently and continued that improvement with a decent effort in defeat off a 6lb higher mark than his success at Wolverhampton last time. He never quite reeled in the leaders from off the pace but went down fighting, and his improvement may not be quite over yet. (tchd 9-2)
Royal Island(IRE), who had some solid form in good turf handicaps throughout 2005, ran another good race after his absence, responding to strong driving all the way to the line. This was his first attempt on Polytrack and one would presume that the Winter Derby is his objective, which, with a little improvement, might be within his grasp. (op 4-1 tchd 3-1)
Hail The Chief took his customary place at the head of affairs and set the race up for the horses in behind. He has been in fine form during the winter but a slight ease in grade is required to give him a clear winning chance. (op 8-1)
Activo(FR) ◆ completely missed the break but soon recovered to travel nicely at the back of the field. Going really nicely off the final turn, he never quite got to the leaders and was probably slightly outclassed. Lesser opposition would make him interesting next time. (op 10-1)
Mizz Tee(IRE), who tracked Hail The Chief throughout the race, found nothing for pressure in the home straight and proved most disappointing given her recent good efforts. (op 13-2 tchd 7-1)
Qadar(IRE), making his debut for shrewd All-Weather connections, travelled smoothly in the early stages but dropped right out when the pressure was fully applied. He had improvement in him on paddock inspection, but is one to be wary of for the time being.
Howle Hill(IRE), winner of the race last year off a 4lb higher mark, dropped himself out at the mid-point of the race and showed no interest after coming under pressure. He did not seem to like the visor being refitted. Official explanation: jockey said gelding never travelled (op 5-1)

117 BETDIRECT FREEPHONE 0800 211 222 CONDITIONS STKS 6f (P)
3:25 (3:26) (Class 2) 3-Y-0+
£12,464 (£3,732; £1,866; £934; £466; £234) **Stalls** Low

Form				RPR
35-3	**1**		**Moayed**[13] 7 7-9-11 99 ... (bt) NCallan 3 (N P Littmoden) *hld up: hdwy on ins wl over 1f out: led ins fnl f: r.o strly* **11/4**[1]	82
102-	**2**	*1 1/2*	**Secret Night**[15] 6688 3-7-12 86 ... JimmyQuinn 7 (J A R Toller) *a in tch: r.o to go 2nd i9nside fnl f* **4/1**[3]	67
00-6	**3**	*1*	**Polar Force**[11] 23 6-9-5 71 ... SteveDrowne 6 (Mrs C A Dunnett) *trckd ldr: led briefly 1f out: o ex fnl 100yds* **20/1**	69
50-0	**4**	*nk*	**Chateau Nicol**[8] 54 7-9-5 87 ... JoeFanning 4 (B G Powell) *hld up: hdwy on outside appr fnl f: r.o* **8/1**	68
36-3	**5**	*nk*	**Katiypour (IRE)**[8] 54 9-9-5 86 ... RichardThomas 8 (Miss B Sanders) *chsd ldrs: rdn and one pce appr fnl f* **3/1**[2]	67
450-	**6**	*nk*	**Kempsey**[28] 6603 4-9-5 60 ... (v) J-PGuillambert 5 (J J Bridger) *led tl rdn and hdd 1f out: wknd ins fnl f* **66/1**	66
000-	**7**	*2*	**Who's Winning (IRE)**[99] 5713 5-9-5 81 ... MichaelHills 9 (B G Powell) *racd wd: wknd appr fnl f* **9/1**	60
16-5	**8**	*2*	**Norcroft**[9] 44 4-9-5 71 ... TonyCulhane 1 (Mrs C A Dunnett) *hld up in tch: rdn 2f out: no hdwy after* **20/1**	54
1-44	**9**	*1*	**Kennington**[9] 47 6-9-5 69 ... (b) HayleyTurner 10 (Mrs C A Dunnett) *chsd ldrs: rdn 2f out: sn btn* **14/1**	51
032-	**10**	*1 3/4*	**Awarding**[15] 6692 6-9-5 48 ... (vt) MichaelJStainton 11 (Dr J R J Naylor) *swtchd leaft fr outside draw: a bhd* **100/1**	46
503-	**11**	*4*	**Smooch**[23] 6653 3-8-4 84 ... ChrisCatlin 2 (R M H Cowell) *chsd ldrs tl wknd qckly 2f out* **20/1**	35

1m 11.79s (-1.02) **Going Correction** +0.05s/f (Slow)
WFA 3 from 4yo+ 16lb **11** Ran SP% **116.2**
Speed ratings (Par 109):108,106,104,104,103 103,100,98,96,94 89
CSF £12.81 TOTE £4.50: £2.10, £1.70, £5.60; EX 22.30.
Owner Nigel Shields **Bred** Sentinal Bloodstock And Wong Chung Mat **Trained** Newmarket, Suffolk

FOCUS
A race of mixed ability won by a talented All-Weather performer. The pace was good throughout.

NOTEBOOK
Moayed, dropping back to six furlongs, landed his first success since the start of 2005 with an easy victory. Everything dropped in place for him and there is no doubt he is a classy All-Weather performer at his best, but he is not easy to catch right and will need placing carefully to win again. (tchd 3-1 and 10-3 in places)
Secret Night, one of only two three-year-olds in the race, ran a cracker against her older opposition and would be of interest next time if returned to her own age group. She should stay a seventh furlong. (op 11-2)
Polar Force made his bid for success off the final turn and looked the likely winner at the top of the home straight. He weakened in the final stages but ran a solid race in defeat given his official rating.
Chateau Nicol was forced wide off the final turn and also suffered slight interference at that point. He finished well but did not threaten to win at any stage. (op 6-1)
Katiypour(IRE) became outpaced as the tempo increased three furlongs from home, but finished well in the final stages. (op 9-4)

118 PLAY NOW AT BETDIRECTCASINO.COM H'CAP 7f (P)
3:55 (3:55) (Class 4) (0-85,82) 3-Y-0 **£6,477** (£1,927; £963; £481) **Stalls** Low

Form				RPR
001-	**1**		**Grand Jour (IRE)**[25] 6627 3-8-11 **75** ... TonyCulhane 2 (K McAuliffe) *mde all: qcknd clr over 1f out: easily* **6/1**	82+
01-0	**2**	*2 1/2*	**Sigismundus (IRE)**[10] 34 3-8-5 **69** ... MartinDwyer 1 (J R Boyle) *chsd ldrs: wnt 2nd 3f out: rdn and no imp appr fnl f* **9/1**	70
333-	**3**	*nk*	**Power Assisted**[124] 5171 3-8-8 **72** ... JimmyQuinn 6 (C F Wall) *s.i.s: hld up: hdwy on ins over 1f out: nvr nrr* **16/1**	72
32-1	**4**	*nk*	**Mr Floodlight (IRE)**[10] 34 3-9-1 **82** ... StephaneBreux(3) 9 (R Hannon) *in tch tl outpcd over 2f out: swtchd rt over 1f out:l r.o strly* **5/1**[2]	81
03-4	**5**	*1/2*	**Scroll**[10] 34 3-8-6 **70** ... (v) JoeFanning 4 (P Howling) *in tch: short of room ent fnl f: one pce after* **13/2**	68
026-	**6**	*3/4*	**Pelham Crescent (IRE)**[25] 6627 3-8-8 **72** ... RobertWinston 8 (R Hannon) *chsd ldrs: rdn and hung lft bef wknd fnl f* **11/2**[3]	68
111-	**7**	*3/4*	**Ocean Of Dreams (FR)**[43] 6479 3-9-4 **82** ... GrahamGibbons 7 (J D Bethell) *in tch tl rdn and outpcd wl over 1f out* **3/1**[1]	76
021-	**8**	*1/2*	**Isphahan**[112] 5446 3-9-1 **79** ... LPKeniry 3 (A M Balding) *in tch tl outpcd 2f out* **10/1**	72
350-	**9**	*9*	**Kings Cavalier (USA)**[15] 6688 3-8-9 **73** ... ChrisCatlin 5 (S Dow) *plld hrd: trckd ldr to 3f out: wknd qckly* **16/1**	42

1m 25.71s (-0.18) **Going Correction** +0.05s/f (Slow) **9** Ran SP% **115.5**
Speed ratings (Par 99):103,100,99,99,98 98,97,96,86
CSF £58.54 CT £824.02 TOTE £8.40: £1.60, £2.40, £4.00; EX 74.40 Place 6 £10.96, Place 5 £5.61.
Owner John Reed **Bred** Islanmore Stud **Trained** Fernham, Oxon

FOCUS
A fair handicap run at a good gallop. The form should be solid for the grade.
Pelham Crescent(IRE) Official explanation: jockey said colt hung left home straight
T/Plt: £27.40 to a £1 stake. Pool: £40,350.30. 1,074.90 winning tickets. T/Qpdt: £12.20 to a £1 stake. Pool: £3,013.50. 181.50 winning tickets. JS

103 WOLVERHAMPTON (A.W) (L-H)
Monday, January 16

OFFICIAL GOING: Standard
Wind: Moderate, behind Weather: Fine

119 BETDIRECT ON THE MASTERS SNOOKER H'CAP FOR AMATEUR RIDERS (DIV I) 5f 20y(P)
1:10 (1:11) (Class 6) (0-65,65) 4-Y-0+ **£1,977** (£608; £304) **Stalls** Low

Form				RPR
636-	**1**		**Cashel Mead**[16] 6695 6-10-10 **54** ... (b) MissEJJones 2 (J L Spearing) *a.p: led on bit over 1f out: drvn out* **4/1**[2]	63
45-0	**2**	*1 1/4*	**Sahara Silk (IRE)**[15] 1 5-11-2 **60** ... (v) MrsMMorris 12 (D Shaw) *mid-div: hdwy 2f out: rdn and hung lft over 1f out: r.o ins fnl f* **20/1**	64
-311	**3**	*nk*	**Magic Amour**[5] 95 8-11-0 **61** 6ex ... (b) MissFayeBramley(3) 5 (P A Blockley) *hld up in tch: rdn over 2f out: kpt on ins fnl f* **4/1**[2]	64
50-6	**4**	*1*	**Ashes (IRE)**[11] 51 4-10-13 **62** ... MissKellyBurke(5) 11 (K R Burke) *led early: sn edgd lft and hdd: ev ch wl over 1f out: sn rdn: no ex towards fin* **12/1**	61
000-	**5**	*3/4*	**Edged In Gold**[16] 6696 4-10-13 **57** ... MrSWalker 10 (P J Makin) *hld up in tch: rdn wl over 1f out: one pce fnl f* **16/1**	54
02-6	**6**	*3/4*	**Kallista's Pride**[7] 74 6-10-10 **59** ... KylieManser(5) 13 (J R Best) *bhd: hdwy and hung lft 1f out: nvr trbld ldrs* **10/1**[3]	53
500-	**7**	*1/2*	**Miss Porcia**[72] 6252 5-10-2 **51** oh11 ... MissALTurner(5) 4 (S L Keightley) *chsd ldrs: no hdwy fnl 2f* **12/1**	43
60-0	**8**	*1 1/2*	**Revien (IRE)**[11] 51 4-10-4 **55** ... MrJDNolan(7) 7 (Miss J R Tooth) *outpcd: nvr nrr* **12/1**	42
04-0	**9**	*shd*	**Enjoy The Buzz**[12] 38 7-10-0 **51** oh6 ... MissSBradley(7) 9 (J M Bradley) *wnt lft s: sn bhd* **14/1**	37
0-33	**10**	*shd*	**Savile's Delight (IRE)**[11] 47 7-11-2 **63** ... (b) MrMSeston(3) 6 (R Brotherton) *rdn to sn ld: saddle slipped and hdd over 1f out: rdr lost irons ins fnl f: eased* **5/2**[1]	49+
2/0-	**11**	*3/4*	**White Ledger (IRE)**[28] 6618 7-10-7 **58** ... MrLRPayter(7) 8 (R E Peacock) *n.m.r s: a bhd* **40/1**	41

62.96 secs (0.14) **Going Correction** -0.10s/f (Stan) **11** Ran SP% **120.5**
Speed ratings (Par 101):94,92,91,89,88 87,86,84,84,84 82
CSF £83.06 CT £352.18 TOTE £6.80: £1.70, £6.00, £2.00; EX 105.50.
Owner Masonaires **Bred** D R Tucker **Trained** Kinnersley, Worcs

FOCUS
This weak event is fractionally faster than the other division.
Savile's Delight(IRE) Official explanation: jockey said saddle slipped

120 BETDIRECT FREEPHONE 0800 211 222 H'CAP 5f 216y(P)
1:40 (1:42) (Class 6) (0-55,57) 3-Y-0 **£2,388** (£705; £352) **Stalls** Low

Form				RPR
005-	**1**		**Drink To Me Only**[35] 6561 3-8-9 **50** ... DaleGibson 4 (J R Weymes) *prom: outpcd over 2f out: rallied over 1f out: led wl ins fnl f: r.o* **6/1**[3]	56
40-0	**2**	*1/2*	**Garstang**[14] 10 3-8-10 **51** ... GylesParkin 9 (Peter Grayson) *bhd: rdn and hdwy over 1f out: swtchd lft jst ins fnl f: sn ev ch: r.o* **20/1**	56
012-	**3**	*nk*	**Angie And Liz (IRE)**[20] 6670 3-8-7 **55** ... RonanKeogh(7) 3 (Peter Grayson) *sn chsng ldrs: hung rt and led 1f out: hdd wl ins fnl f: nt qckn* **11/4**[1]	59
43-0	**4**	*1/2*	**Smart Ass (IRE)**[14] 10 3-8-9 **50** ... FergalLynch 13 (J S Moore) *bhd: hmpd and swtchd lft after 1f: hdwy whn nt clr run and swtchd lft over 1f out: r.o ins fnl f* **10/1**	53+
060-	**5**	*2*	**Tequila Rose (IRE)**[70] 6282 3-8-9 **50** ... SamHitchcott 6 (A Bailey) *mid-div: rdn over 3f out: hdwy to chse ldr 2f out: carried rt ins fnl f: one pce* **40/1**	47

424- **6** 3/4 **Whipper In**[68] 6296 3-8-4 **52**.......... RussellKennemore(7) 1 46
(P C Haslam) *sn led: rdn clr 2f out: hung rt and hdd 1f out: wknd ins fnl f* **4/1**[2]

00-0 **7** shd **Jessica Wigmo**[12] 31 3-8-9 **53**.......... RichardThomas(3) 12 47
(A W Carroll) *bhd: edgd lft over 1f out: hdwy fnl f: nvr trbld ldrs* **33/1**

006- **8** 1 **Dangermouse**[35] 6557 3-8-9 **50**.......... FergusSweeney 11 41
(A G Newcombe) *sn outpcd: hdwy on ins wl over 1f out: wknd wl ins fnl f* **14/1**

000- **9** 3 **Mid Valley**[81] 6121 3-8-9 **50**.......... MickyFenton 8 32
(J R Jenkins) *bhd fnl 3f* **25/1**

500- **10** shd **Mr Cheers**[38] 6529 3-9-0 **55**..........(b[1]) TomEaves 10 37
(Miss J A Camacho) *sn bhd: rdn and hung lft wl over 1f out: nvr nr ldrs* **12/1**

05-4 **11** 1/2 **No Inkling (IRE)**[4] 102 3-8-9 **50**.......... PaulHanagan 5 30
(John A Harris) *sn chsng ldrs: rdn over 2f out: edgd lft over 1f out: sn wknd* **9/1**

00-4 **12** 1 3/4 **Dream Factor (IRE)**[10] 53 3-8-9 **57** ow4..........(v[1]) JamesO'Reilly(7) 7 32
(J O'Reilly) *prom: rdn over 2f out: sn wknd* **8/1**

1m 16.04s (0.23) **Going Correction** -0.10s/f (Stan) **12** Ran SP% **119.5**
Speed ratings (Par 95):94,93,92,92,89 88,88,87,83,83 82,80
CSF £125.06 CT £411.68 TOTE £7.10: £2.30, £6.80, £1.50; EX 162.50.
Owner Lovely Bubbly Racing **Bred** Mrs Deborah O'Brien **Trained** Middleham Moor, N Yorks

FOCUS
A tightly-knit low grade handicap.

121 WOLVERHAMPTON-RACECOURSE.CO.UK (S) STKS 7f 32y(P)
2:10 (2:11) (Class 6) 4-Y-0+ **£2,388** (£705; £352) **Stalls** High

Form RPR

130- **1** **Vancouver Gold (IRE)**[270] 1160 4-8-7 73.......... RobertWinston 8 60
(K R Burke) *hld up in tch: wnt 2nd over 3f out: rdn 2f out: led wl ins fnl f: r.o* **9/2**[2]

10-0 **2** 1 **Aswan (IRE)**[10] 56 8-9-0 64..........(t) AmirQuinn(3) 1 67
(S R Bowring) *led: rdn over 2f out: hdd wl ins fnl f: nt qckn* **5/1**[3]

533- **3** 2 **Mister Elegant**[49] 6449 4-8-12 50.......... SteveDrowne 5 57
(J L Spearing) *chsd ldrs: rdn 3f out: one pce fnl f* **4/1**[1]

43-6 **4** 1 **Distant Country (USA)**[10] 56 7-8-12 55..........(b) TonyCulhane 7 54
(R A Harris) *hld up: hdwy 3f out: sn rdn: one pce fnl f* **9/2**[2]

00-0 **5** 2 1/2 **Savoy Chapel**[7] 71 4-8-12 60..........(vt[1]) JimmyQuinn 2 48
(A W Carroll) *s.i.s: hld up and bhd: hdwy over 2f out: no further prog* **7/1**

00-2 **6** 4 **Exit Smiling**[11] 46 4-8-12 54.......... ChrisCatlin 4 38
(G C H Chung) *hld up: hdwy 3f out: wknd over 1f out* **7/1**

600- **7** 3 **Dexileos (IRE)**[40] 6524 7-8-12 45..........(t) FergusSweeney 9 30
(David Pinder) *mid-div: rdn 3f out: no rspnse* **50/1**

000- **8** nk **Belle Encore**[84] 6070 4-8-7 50..........(v) JamieMackay 10 24
(A P Jarvis) *a bhd* **33/1**

20-5 **9** 1 1/2 **Wilford Maverick (IRE)**[12] 43 4-8-12 45.......... MickyFenton 11 25
(M J Attwater) *dwlt: a bhd* **16/1**

06-0 **10** 1 3/4 **Dysonic (USA)**[14] 14 4-8-12 45.......... GrahamGibbons 12 20
(D Burchell) *sn prom: rdn over 3f out: wknd over 2f out* **40/1**

05-0 **11** 1 **Mytton's Dream**[12] 42 4-8-7 45.......... TomEaves 6 13
(R Brotherton) *s.i.s: outpcd* **40/1**

410- **12** 7 **Joe Jo Star**[34] 6570 4-9-3 45..........(p) FergalLynch 3 5
(P A Blockley) *chsd ldr tl rdn over 3f out: wkng whn n.m.r over 2f out* **16/1**

1m 29.42s (-0.98) **Going Correction** -0.10s/f (Stan) **12** Ran SP% **119.6**
Speed ratings (Par 101):101,99,97,96,93 89,85,85,83,81 80,72
CSF £26.92 TOTE £4.90: £1.60, £2.00, £2.10; EX 43.90.The winner was bought in for 6,500gns.
Owner Bigwigs Bloodstock II **Bred** Ballinacurra Stud **Trained** Middleham Moor, N Yorks

FOCUS
A strongly-run seller which had the fastest time of the day compared with standard.

122 HOTEL & CONFERENCING AT DUNSTALL PARK CLAIMING STKS 1m 141y(P)
2:40 (2:41) (Class 6) 3-Y-0 **£2,730** (£806; £403) **Stalls** Low

Form RPR

0-31 **1** **Casablanca Minx (IRE)**[5] 85 3-8-5 61.......... EdwardCreighton(3) 10 73+
(Mrs H Sweeting) *hld up and bhd: hdwy over 3f out: led wl over 1f out: sn clr: easily* **7/2**[1]

0-50 **2** 8 **Crocodile Star (USA)**[9] 61 3-8-5 56..........(b[1]) PaulHanagan 1 53
(J A Osborne) *hld up in tch: rdn over 2f out: hung lft fr jst over 1f out: wnt 2nd nr fin: no ch w wnr* **5/1**

000- **3** 1/2 **Angelina Bankes**[21] 6663 3-8-6 51.......... AdrianMcCarthy 4 53
(R A Harris) *a.p: rdn over 3f out: chsd wnr over 1f out: no impresssion* **20/1**

13-2 **4** 1 3/4 **She Whispers (IRE)**[7] 69 3-8-2 54.......... ChrisCatlin 9 45
(G C H Chung) *hld up and bhd: hdwy over 4f out: rdn and one pce fnl 2f* **7/1**

4-21 **5** 1/2 **Ten Shun**[7] 69 3-9-3 58.......... DeanMcKeown 5 59
(M J Polglase) *led: rdn and hdd wl over 1f out: wknd ins fnl f* **9/2**[3]

00-2 **6** 3 **Night Groove (IRE)**[9] 61 3-8-12 62.......... JamesDoyle(7) 3 55
(N P Littmoden) *prom: rdn over 3f out: wknd 2f out* **4/1**[2]

000- **7** 4 **Sahara Secret (IRE)**[28] 6610 3-8-1 30.......... PatrickMathers(3) 12 32
(D Shaw) *nvr nr ldrs* **66/1**

000- **8** 2 **Bournonville**[38] 6531 3-8-6 50..........(t) MarcHalford(5) 6 34
(J Ryan) *a bhd* **40/1**

000- **9** 2 1/2 **Hill Of Howth (IRE)**[20] 6673 3-9-5 74..........(b) RobertWinston 11 37
(K A Ryan) *hld up in tch: rdn and wknd over 3f out* **8/1**

000- **10** 6 **Mo Chroi**[27] 6628 3-8-2 40.......... JimmyQuinn 8 7
(C G Cox) *prom: lost pl over 5f out: sn bhd* **28/1**

000- **11** 4 **Amorada**[186] 3464 3-8-10 50.......... SteveDrowne 7 7
(H Morrison) *s.i.s: bhd fnl 5f* **40/1**

1m 50.98s (-0.78) **Going Correction** -0.10s/f (Stan) **11** Ran SP% **115.3**
Speed ratings (Par 95):99,91,91,89,89 86,83,81,79,73 70
CSF £19.55 TOTE £4.80: £1.60, £2.50, £5.20; EX 29.80.The winner was claimed by Mustafa Khan for £9,000. She Whispers was claimed by Ed Weetman for £6,000.
Owner P Sweeting **Bred** Airlie Stud And Widden Stud **Trained** Lockeridge, Wilts

FOCUS
Casablanca Minx turned this claimer into a one-horse race.

123 BETDIRECT.CO.UK H'CAP 1m 1f 103y(P)
3:10 (3:11) (Class 5) (0-70,70) 3-Y-0 **£3,238** (£963; £481; £240) **Stalls** Low

Form RPR

101- **1** **George's Flyer (IRE)**[28] 6617 3-8-13 **65**..........(b) PaulHanagan 3 70
(R A Fahey) *hld up in tch: rdn over 3f out: led over 1f out: drvn out* **10/3**[2]

000- **2** 1 1/2 **Mae Cigan (FR)**[169] 3973 3-8-4 **56**.......... JimmyQuinn 5 58
(M Blanshard) *mid-div: rdn and hdwy whn edgd lft 3f out: r.o ins fnl f* **25/1**

604- **3** 2 1/2 **Busy Shark (IRE)**[99] 5752 3-9-4 **70**.......... TonyCulhane 4 67
(M R Channon) *hld up in mid-div: hdwy on ins 4f out: rdn over 2f out: no ex ins fnl f* **16/1**

50-3 **4** 1/2 **King's Fable (USA)**[11] 49 3-8-8 **60**.......... JoeFanning 2 57
(M Johnston) *led: rdn over 2f out: hdd over 1f out: wkng whn hung rt ins fnl f* **2/1**[1]

502- **5** 1/2 **Duel In The Sands**[26] 6648 3-8-6 **58**.......... RobertWinston 10 54
(D Shaw) *stdd s: sn swtchd lft: hld up and bhd: rdn over 2f out: hdwy over 1f out: styng on whn nt clr run and swtchd rt wl* **9/1**

00-0 **6** nk **Royal Embrace**[11] 49 3-8-1 **56** oh3..........(v) PatrickMathers(3) 9 51
(D Shaw) *bhd: rdn over 3f out: hdwy wl over 1f out: one pce fnl f* **25/1**

360- **7** 2 1/2 **Asbury Park**[31] 6588 3-8-13 **65**.......... PhillipMakin 12 55
(E S McMahon) *t.k.h in mid-div: rdn over 2f out: btn whn c wd ent st* **16/1**

000- **8** 1 1/2 **Capitalise (IRE)**[89] 5988 3-8-4 **56** oh4..........(t) AdrianMcCarthy 1 43
(V Smith) *prom: rdn over 2f out: wknd fnl f* **22/1**

1-5 **9** 2 **Cragganmore Creek**[9] 61 3-8-9 **61**.......... DerekMcGaffin 7 45
(D Morris) *s.i.s: hld up: n.m.r on ins over 3f out: hmpd on ins wl over 2f out: hdwy wl over 1f out: eased whn btn* **5/1**[3]

00-4 **10** 2 **Norman Beckett**[13] 19 3-8-8 **63**.......... EdwardCreighton(3) 8 43
(M R Channon) *bhd fnl 3f* **14/1**

040- **11** 1 3/4 **Baltic Rhapsody**[37] 6539 3-8-6 **58**..........(p) MatthewHenry 13 34
(M A Jarvis) *prom: rdn over 3f out: wknd over 2f out* **12/1**

030- **12** 9 **Drawn Out (IRE)**[124] 5217 3-7-13 **56** oh2..........(p) MarcHalford(5) 6 15
(P C Haslam) *pushed along 7f out: a bhd* **20/1**

040- **13** 13 **Subsidise (IRE)**[25] 6659 3-8-5 **57**.......... DaleGibson 11 —
(J G Given) *prom tl wknd over 3f out* **50/1**

2m 2.56s (-0.06) **Going Correction** -0.10s/f (Stan) **13** Ran SP% **128.0**
Speed ratings (Par 97):96,94,92,92,91 91,89,87,85,84 82,74,63
CSF £97.39 CT £1232.35 TOTE £4.00: £1.90, £14.60, £5.30; EX 128.80.
Owner P D Smith Holdings Ltd **Bred** H De Bromhead **Trained** Musley Bank, N Yorks
■ Stewards' Enquiry : Jimmy Quinn three-day ban: careless riding (Jan 27-29)

FOCUS
They went an even pace in this ordinary handicap.
Subsidise(IRE) Official explanation: jockey said gelding lost its action

124 LITTLEWOODSPOOLS.CO.UK MAIDEN STKS 1m 1f 103y(P)
3:40 (3:43) (Class 5) 3-Y-0 **£3,886** (£1,156; £577; £288) **Stalls** Low

Form RPR

4- **1** **De La Rue (USA)**[52] 6424 3-9-0.......... TPQueally 13 80
(M G Quinlan) *hld up in mid-div: hdwy over 3f out: rdn over 2f out: led wl ins fnl f: r.o* **9/1**

062- **2** 1 1/4 **Billich**[27] 6628 3-9-0 78.......... RobertWinston 11 78
(E J O'Neill) *sn chsng ldr: rdn over 2f out: ev ch ins fnl f: nt qckn* **2/1**[2]

25-2 **3** hd **Katchit (IRE)**[12] 34 3-8-11 77.......... EdwardCreighton(3) 2 78
(M R Channon) *led: rdn wl over 1f out: hdd and nt qckn wl ins fnl f* **6/5**[1]

6 **4** 6 **Bariloche**[9] 62 3-9-0..........(b[1]) SteveDrowne 3 66
(J H M Gosden) *prom: rdn and one pce fnl 3f: edgd lft over 1f out* **25/1**

5 2 **Fantastic Promise (USA)** 3-8-9.......... RobertHavlin 9 57
(J H M Gosden) *bmpd s: bhd tl rdn and hdwy over 2f out: no further prog* **25/1**

6 6 **Lightning Strike (GER)** 3-9-0.......... JoeFanning 4 51+
(T G Mills) *s.i.s: sn mid-div: lost pl over 5f out: n.d after* **6/1**[3]

0 **7** 3 **Rudry World (IRE)**[7] 70 3-9-0.......... FergalLynch 7 45
(P A Blockley) *nvr nr ldrs* **50/1**

06- **8** nk **Carefree Girl**[26] 6641 3-8-9.......... StephenCarson 8 40
(E A Wheeler) *mid-div: reminder 7f out: rdn over 5f out: bhd fnl 4f* **150/1**

04- **9** nk **Jumanji (IRE)**[16] 6699 3-8-9.......... AdrianMcCarthy 1 39
(M J Attwater) *prom: rdn over 3f out: wknd over 2f out* **28/1**

0- **10** 6 **Flashing Floozie**[147] 4630 3-8-9.......... JamieMackay 10 28
(M F Harris) *carried lft s: t.k.h: prom: rdn over 3f out: wknd over 2f out* **50/1**

- **11** 1 1/2 **Fantasy Legend (IRE)** 3-8-11.......... RichardThomas(3) 12 30
(N P Littmoden) *rdn over 4f out: a bhd* **40/1**

00- **12** 1 1/4 **Red Tsarina**[164] 4132 3-8-2.......... TJHowell(7) 5 23
(V Smith) *a bhd* **100/1**

2m 2.19s (-0.43) **Going Correction** -0.10s/f (Stan) **12** Ran SP% **122.2**
Speed ratings (Par 97):97,95,95,90,88 83,80,80,80,74 73,72
CSF £27.11 TOTE £11.10: £3.00, £1.20, £1.20; EX 39.30.
Owner Miss J E Moore **Bred** Skymarc Farm Inc **Trained** Newmarket, Suffolk

FOCUS
With the first three finishing clear, this form may stand the test of time.

125 NO 5P RULE 4S AT BETDIRECT H'CAP 1m 4f 50y(P)
4:10 (4:12) (Class 5) (0-75,74) 4-Y-0+ **£3,238** (£963; £481; £240) **Stalls** Low

Form RPR

153- **1** **Bethanys Boy (IRE)**[21] 6665 5-8-11 **72**.......... GregFairley(5) 10 83
(B Ellison) *hld up and bhd: stdy hdwy over 5f out: rdn to ld wl over 1f out: r.o* **7/2**[2]

650- **2** 1 **Tromp**[41] 6520 5-9-0 **70**.......... TPQueally 3 79
(D J Coakley) *hld up in tch: rdn over 2f out: chsd wnr fnl f: r.o* **4/1**[3]

23-1 **3** 3 1/2 **Oldenway**[4] 98 7-9-1 **71** 6ex.......... PaulHanagan 5 74
(R A Fahey) *a.p: rdn 3f out: one pce fnl f* **5/2**[1]

023- **4** 3 1/2 **Yawmi**[26] 6643 6-9-4 **74**.......... RobertWinston 7 72
(B D Leavy) *hld up in tch: led over 5f out: rdn and hdd wl over 1f out: wknd ins fnl f* **14/1**

001- **5** nk **Garibaldi (GER)**[9] 6307 4-8-12 **72**.......... FrankieMcDonald 8 69
(D R C Elsworth) *bhd: hdwy over 1f out: n.d* **15/2**

100- **6** 3/4 **Cordier**[98] 5799 4-8-13 **73**.......... DaleGibson 4 69
(J Mackie) *hld up: rdn and hdwy on outside over 2f out: no further prog* **33/1**

62-3 **7** 1 1/2 **Tedstale (USA)**[15] 5 8-8-10 **71**..........(b) AndrewMullen(5) 1 65
(K A Ryan) *sn prom: rdn over 3f out: wknd over 2f out* **8/1**

006- **8** nk **Wotchalike (IRE)**[21] 6665 4-8-3 **70**.......... JamesDoyle(7) 9 63
(R J Price) *a towards rr* **25/1**

50-4 **9** 1/2 **Swainson (USA)**[12] 37 5-8-9 **65**.......... JoeFanning 6 57
(P Mitchell) *prom: rdn over 3f out: wknd over 2f out* **12/1**

20U- **10** 13 **Fiddlers Creek (IRE)**[21] 6665 7-9-2 **72**..........(v) JimmyQuinn 12 44
(R Allan) *hld up: hdwy over 6f out: wknd 3f out* **12/1**

/00- **11** 14 **Afadan (IRE)**[26] 6644 8-9-0 **70**.......... FergalLynch 11 19
(J R Jenkins) *dwlt: sn swtchd lft: a bhd: t.o* **33/1**

0-60 **12** 10 **Penwell Hill (USA)**[4] 100 7-8-7 **66**.......... PatrickMathers(3) 2 —
(M J Attwater) *t.k.h: led: rdn over 3f out: wkng whn n.m.r on ins over 3f out: t.o* **66/1**

2m 39.09s (-3.33) **Going Correction** -0.10s/f (Stan)
WFA 4 from 5yo+ 4lb **12** Ran SP% **126.9**
Speed ratings (Par 103):107,106,104,101,101 100,99,99,99,90 81,74
CSF £18.91 CT £43.35 TOTE £3.90: £1.10, £2.00, £1.80; EX 34.40.

Owner Get Into Racing UK **Bred** K And Mrs Cullen **Trained** Norton, N Yorks
FOCUS
The time suggested that this was run at a decent pace.
Cordier Official explanation: jockey said gelding hung badly left final 2f

126 BETDIRECT ON THE MASTERS SNOOKER H'CAP FOR AMATEUR RIDERS (DIV II) — 5f 20y(P)
4:40 (4:43) (Class 6) (0-65,63) 4-Y-0+ **£1,977** (£608; £304) **Stalls** Low

Form — RPR
1-26 **1** **Mambazo**[7] 67 4-11-2 **58**......(e) MrSWalker 11 — 69+
(S C Williams) *hld up: swtchd lft sn after s: hdwy on ins over 2f out: rdn over 1f out: r.o to ld cl home* **10/3**[1]
012- **2** 1 ¼ **Almaty Express**[16] 6696 4-11-6 **62**......(b) MrsSBosley 2 — 68
(J R Weymes) *sn led: clr whn rdn wl over 1f out: hdd and no ex cl home* **7/2**[2]
50-0 **3** ¾ **Canadian Danehill (IRE)**[15] 1 4-10-11 **58**......(p) MrPCollington(5) 1 — 61
(R M H Cowell) *a.p: rdn over 2f out: kpt on ins fnl f* **7/1**
00-0 **4** 4 **Mulberry Lad (IRE)**[6] 81 4-10-1 **50**...... MissDawnBridgewater(7) 8 — 39
(P W Hiatt) *s.i.s and carried rt: outpcd and bhd: c wd st: hdwy and edgd lft fnl f: r.o* **20/1**
53-0 **5** 1 ½ **The Fisio**[13] 23 6-11-2 **63**......(v) MrTFWoodside(5) 6 — 47
(S Gollings) *wnt rt and nrly uns rdr s: bhd: carried wd ent st: hdwy and edgd lft 1f out: nvr trbld ldrs* **9/2**[3]
2-05 **6** hd **Comic Tales**[11] 45 5-10-0 **49** oh9......(p) MissMMullineaux(7) 12 — 32
(M Mullineaux) *s.s: outpcd and wl bhd: late hdwy: nvr nrr* **33/1**
621- **7** ¾ **Boisdale (IRE)**[147] 4645 8-10-8 **55**...... MissALTurner(5) 5 — 35
(S L Keightley) *prom: n.m.r and lost pl over 3f out: sme late prog* **20/1**
300- **8** ¾ **Missperon (IRE)**[98] 5793 4-10-12 **57**......(p) MrMSeston(3) 7 — 34
(K A Ryan) *hmpd s: hld up: hdwy over 2f out: carried rt ent st: sn rdn: no imp fnl f* **14/1**
010- **9** 1 ½ **Best Lead**[145] 4679 7-11-5 **61**......(b) MrSDobson 10 — 33
(Ian Emmerson) *sn chsng ldr: rdn over 2f out: wknd over 1f out* **20/1**
165- **10** shd **He's A Rocket (IRE)**[16] 6695 5-10-12 **59**......(b) MissKellyBurke(5) 9 — 31
(K R Burke) *prom tl n.m.r and lost pl over 3f out: n.d after* **13/2**
304- **11** 2 ½ **Oceanico Dot Com (IRE)**[30] 6603 4-11-0 **63**...... MrKGundowry(7) 3 — 26
(A Berry) *a bhd* **16/1**
10-0 **12** nk **Vaudevire**[5] 90 5-10-2 **49** oh4......(b) JackMitchell(5) 4 — 11
(Peter Grayson) *tried to get under stalls and anticipated s: led: sn hdd: prom: rdn whn edgd rt ent st: sn edgd lft* **33/1**

62.89 secs (0.07) **Going Correction** -0.10s/f (Stan) — **40** Ran SP% **122.0**
Speed ratings (Par 101):95,93,91,85,83 82,81,80,77,77 73,73
CSF £14.29 CT £78.86 TOTE £4.90: £1.80, £1.80, £1.70; EX 20.80 Place 6 £66.69, Place 5 £22.63.
Owner D G Burge **Bred** Barry Taylor **Trained** Newmarket, Suffolk
FOCUS
An eventful amateur riders contest, slightly slower than the first division.
Best Lead Official explanation: jockey said gelding pulled up slightly lame on left fore
T/Plt: £71.00 to a £1 stake. Pool: £34,608.85. 355.70 winning tickets. T/Qpdt: £14.60 to a £1 stake. Pool: £3,432.80. 173.70 winning tickets. KH

96 SOUTHWELL (L-H)
Tuesday, January 17

OFFICIAL GOING: Standard
Wind: Light, behind Weather: Cloudy

127 PLAY NOW AT BETDIRECTPOKER.COM H'CAP (DIV I) — 7f (F)
12:20 (12:22) (Class 6) (0-55,61) 4-Y-0+ **£2,047** (£604; £302) **Stalls** Low

Form — RPR
5-03 **1** **Roman Empire**[8] 67 6-9-0 **55**......(b) JamieSpencer 4 — 63
(K A Ryan) *chsd ldrs: hrd rdn fr over 1f out: styd on to ld nr fin* **3/1**[1]
3113 **2** nk **Magic Amour**[1] 119 8-8-13 **61** 6ex......(b) KevinGhunowa(7) 6 — 69
(P A Blockley) *hld up in tch: rdn to ld ins fnl f: hdd nr fin* **5/1**[2]
100- **3** 1 **Mademoiselle**[62] 6372 4-8-12 **53**...... MichaelHills 12 — 58
(B W Hills) *chsd ldrs: rdn to ld over 1f out: edgd lft and hdd ins fnl f: no ex towards fin* **8/1**
00-0 **4** 2 ½ **Zorn**[14] 21 7-8-9 **50**...... RobertWinston 7 — 51+
(P Howling) *led: rdn over 2f out: hdd over 1f out: styng on same pce whn nt clr run ins fnl f* **22/1**
00-0 **5** 1 ½ **Shrine Mountain (USA)**[11] 56 4-8-6 **54**...... KirstyMilczarek(7) 8 — 49
(J R Holt) *chsd ldrs: rdn 1/2-way: styd on same pce fnl 2f* **50/1**
400- **6** nk **Fiore Di Bosco (IRE)**[115] 5469 5-9-0 **55**...... PhillipMakin 3 — 49
(T D Barron) *sn pushed along in rr: styd on fnl 2f: nvr nrr* **12/1**
004- **7** 3 **Bodden Bay**[18] 6692 4-8-9 **53**...... DanielTudhope(3) 5 — 39
(D Carroll) *in rr whn hmpd 6f out: rdn 1/2-way: n.d* **6/1**[3]
10-6 **8** 2 **Chickado (IRE)**[12] 44 5-8-9 **50**...... RobertHavlin 10 — 31
(D Haydn Jones) *chsd ldr: rdn over 2f out: wknd over 1f out* **5/1**[2]
000- **9** 3 **Sundried Tomato**[17] 6696 7-8-9 **50**...... JoeFanning 2 — 23
(D W Chapman) *s.i.s: sn prom: wknd 2f out* **16/1**
000- **10** 1 ¼ **Huxley (IRE)**[36] 6559 7-8-3 **47**...... EdwardCreighton(3) 11 — 17
(D J Wintle) *s.i.s: a in rr* **50/1**
30-4 **11** 9 **Ace Club**[14] 27 5-8-5 **46** oh1......(b) DaleGibson 1 — —
(J Hetherton) *sn pushed along and prom: wknd over 4f out* **14/1**

1m 28.74s (-2.06) **Going Correction** -0.225s/f (Stan) — **11** Ran SP% **112.2**
Speed ratings (Par 101):102,101,100,97,95 95,92,89,86,85 74
CSF £16.20 CT £107.36 TOTE £3.00: £1.30, £1.60, £2.50; EX 11.20.
Owner Yorkshire Racing Syndicates **Bred** Mervyn Ayers And Richard Brunger **Trained** Hambleton, N Yorks
FOCUS
An ordinary handicap and the winning time was 0.36 seconds slower than the second division.
Ace Club Official explanation: jockey said gelding never travelled

128 BETDIRECT ON THE MASTERS SNOOKER AW JOCKEYS CHAMPIONSHIP H'CAP — 6f (F)
12:50 (12:50) (Class 5) (0-75,74) 3-Y-0 **£3,238** (£963; £481; £240) **Stalls** Low

Form — RPR
41-0 **1** **Prettilini**[8] 68 3-8-9 **65**...... RobertWinston 4 — 68
(A W Carroll) *led 1f: sn lost pl: hdwy over 2f out: rdn to ld 1f out: r.o* **5/1**[3]
60-5 **2** 1 ½ **Money Mate (IRE)**[15] 10 3-8-0 **63**...... MarkCoumbe(7) 6 — 62
(C J Teague) *chsd ldrs: led 1/2-way: rdn and hdd 1f out: styd on same pce* **8/1**
00-3 **3** 5 **Developer (IRE)**[10] 66 3-9-0 **70**......(p) JoeFanning 5 — 54
(T G Mills) *trckd ldrs: rdn over 2f out: sn outpcd* **5/4**[1]
342- **4** 6 **Amber Glory**[26] 6656 3-8-7 **68**......(p) AndrewMullen(5) 1 — 34
(K A Ryan) *led 5f out: rdn and hdd 1/2-way: wknd over 1f out* **2/1**[2]
455- **5** 24 **She's Our Beauty (IRE)**[180] 3661 3-8-12 **68**...... AdrianTNicholls 3 — —
(D Nicholls) *disp ld 2f: rdn: hung lft and wknd over 2f out* **22/1**

1m 16.38s (-0.52) **Going Correction** -0.225s/f (Stan) — **5** Ran SP% **109.9**
Speed ratings (Par 97):94,92,85,77,45
CSF £38.78 TOTE £5.20: £2.20, £4.20; EX 50.50.
Owner David Shorthouse **Bred** G W Turner And Miss S J Turner **Trained** Cropthorne, Worcs
FOCUS
A modest handicap and unusually for this track, the field stayed against the inside rail after turning for home. However, the track bias was again in evidence as the horse that raced widest was the eventual winner.
She's Our Beauty(IRE) Official explanation: jockey said filly hung badly left

129 FIRST PAST THE POST AT BETDIRECT H'CAP — 2m (F)
1:20 (1:20) (Class 6) (0-65,63) 4-Y-0+ **£2,388** (£705; £352) **Stalls** Low

Form — RPR
00-4 **1** **Moon Emperor**[15] 12 9-9-9 **57**......(b[1]) JamieSpencer 8 — 68+
(J R Jenkins) *hld up: hdwy 1/2-way: jnd ldr over 4f out: led 2f out: shkn up and r.o: eased nr fin* **12/1**
01-2 **2** 3 **Blue Hills**[14] 28 5-9-7 **55**......(p) DarrenWilliams 4 — 62
(P W Hiatt) *led: rdn and hdd 2f out: styd on same pce fnl f* **7/2**[2]
2-11 **3** 1 **Cotton Eyed Joe (IRE)**[6] 91 5-10-1 **63** 6ex...... DeanMcKeown 2 — 69
(G A Swinbank) *trckd ldrs: rdn and hung lft fr over 1f out: no ex fnl f* **10/11**[1]
4-32 **4** 1 **Countback (FR)**[11] 52 7-9-4 **52**...... PaulHanagan 7 — 57
(A W Carroll) *hld up: hdwy over 3f out: rdn over 2f out: styd on* **5/1**[3]
5-50 **5** 11 **All Bleevable**[14] 28 9-8-11 **45**...... RobertWinston 5 — 36
(Mrs S Lamyman) *hld up: hdwy u.p over 3f out: sn wknd* **12/1**
000- **6** 5 **Logger Rhythm (USA)**[199] 3126 6-8-7 **41** oh1...... JimmyQuinn 3 — 26
(R Dickin) *chsd ldr to 1/2-way: wknd over 4f out* **66/1**
0-0 **7** 5 **Eamon An Chnoic (IRE)**[13] 37 5-9-7 **55**...... FergusSweeney 9 — 34
(B W Duke) *prom: chsd ldr 1/2-way to over 4f out: sn wknd* **40/1**
/00- **8** 5 **Mystic Forest**[73] 6267 7-9-12 **60**......(v[1]) TomEaves 6 — 33
(Miss J A Camacho) *hld up: rdn over 4f out: sn wknd* **33/1**
000- **9** dist **Viniyoga**[41] 6523 4-8-4 **45**......(b[1]) ChrisCatlin 1 — —
(M H Tompkins) *hld up: rdn and wknd over 4f out* **66/1**

3m 46.34s (1.80) **Going Correction** -0.225s/f (Stan)
WFA 4 from 5yo+ 7lb — **9** Ran SP% **115.0**
Speed ratings (Par 101):86,84,84,83,78 75,73,70,—
CSF £52.81 CT £76.67 TOTE £11.30: £2.50, £1.50, £1.10; EX 33.50.
Owner R M Ellis **Bred** Fares Stables Ltd **Trained** Royston, Herts
■ Stewards' Enquiry : Dean McKeown caution: careless riding
FOCUS
An incredibly slow early pace that did not increase until around five furlongs from home. As a result, this was not the test of stamina it might have been and the winning time was very slow for the class.

130 BETDIRECT.CO.UK (S) STKS — 5f (F)
1:50 (1:50) (Class 6) 4-Y-0+ **£2,388** (£705; £352) **Stalls** High

Form — RPR
020- **1** **Henry Tun**[17] 6696 8-8-11 52......(b) JasonEdmunds(3) 5 — 61
(J Balding) *a.p: chsd ldr over 1f out: sn rdn: r.o to ld post* **4/1**[2]
550/ **2** shd **Borzoi Maestro**[458] 6222 5-9-0 63......(p) SteveDrowne 6 — 60
(J L Spearing) *led: rdn ins fnl f: hdd post* **11/2**[3]
00-2 **3** 3 **Blue Power (IRE)**[14] 24 5-9-0 45...... RobertWinston 1 — 50
(K R Burke) *chsd ldrs: rdn and hung lft fr 1/2-way: no ex ins fnl f* **13/8**[1]
03-4 **4** 2 ½ **A Teen**[6] 90 8-9-0 40...... PatCosgrave 2 — 42
(P Howling) *chsd ldrs: rdn over 1f out: wknd ins fnl f* **14/1**
000- **5** 1 ½ **Online Investor**[42] 6515 7-9-0 50...... RobbieFitzpatrick 9 — 36
(C Smith) *dwlt: outpcd: hdwy 1/2-way: styd on same pce appr fnl f* **14/1**
60-0 **6** ¾ **Red Sovereign**[12] 46 5-8-9 52...... MickyFenton 3 — 29
(D G Bridgwater) *w ldr 2f: rdn and wknd over 1f out* **7/1**
00-3 **7** 5 **Ariesanne (IRE)**[15] 9 5-8-9 40...... PaulHanagan 8 — 12
(A C Whillans) *chsd ldrs to 1/2-way* **11/1**
000- **8** 2 ½ **Grasslandik**[35] 6568 10-8-7 35......(p) AnnStokell(7) 7 — 8
(Miss A Stokell) *chsd ldrs: sn pushed along: hung lft and wknd 1/2-way* **66/1**

58.27 secs (-2.03) **Going Correction** -0.375s/f (Stan) — **8** Ran SP% **109.1**
Speed ratings (Par 101):101,100,96,92,89 88,80,76
CSF £23.69 TOTE £4.30: £1.30, £1.50, £1.30; EX 24.80.There was no bid for the winner. Borzoi Maestro was claimed by Mark Wellings for £6,000.
Owner Terry Reffell **Bred** T Tunstall **Trained** Scrooby, Notts
FOCUS
A moderate seller and the form does not amount to much.
Blue Power(IRE) Official explanation: jockey said gelding hung left

131 BETDIRECT FREEPHONE 0800 211 222 H'CAP — 1m 4f (F)
2:20 (2:20) (Class 6) (0-65,61) 4-Y-0+ **£2,388** (£705; £352) **Stalls** Low

Form — RPR
512- **1** **Sovereign Spirit (IRE)**[17] 6701 4-9-3 **61**......(t) JoeFanning 9 — 69
(W R Swinburn) *hld up inn tch: trckd ldr over 7f out: led over 2f out: styd on* **15/2**[3]
1-66 **2** shd **High Frequency (IRE)**[7] 75 5-8-8 **48**...... PaulFessey 2 — 56
(T D Barron) *hld up: hdwy over 3f out: rdn over 1f out: r.o* **22/1**
1-33 **3** ½ **Greenbelt**[7] 77 5-9-6 **60**...... RobertWinston 3 — 67
(G M Moore) *mid-divsion: hdwy and edgd lft 3f out: rdn and nt clr run over 1f out: r.o* **9/1**
03-2 **4** shd **Sugitani (USA)**[5] 97 4-8-12 **56**...... MickyFenton 4 — 64+
(N B King) *hld up: effrt and nt clr run over 3f out: hdwy and nt clr run over 1f out: r.o: nvr able to chal* **9/1**
63-1 **5** 4 **Sonic Anthem (USA)**[16] 2 4-8-11 **55**...... AdrianTNicholls 1 — 55
(D Nicholls) *led: plld hrd: hdd over 2f out: rdn and hung lft over 1f out: wknd ins fnl f* **6/5**[1]
014- **6** 1 ¼ **Blue Opal**[26] 6655 4-8-8 **52**...... ChrisCatlin 8 — 50
(Miss S E Hall) *prom: rdn over 2f out: styd on same pce* **25/1**
40-2 **7** nk **Jackie Kiely**[15] 12 5-8-11 **51**...... DaleGibson 6 — 49
(P Howling) *prom: rdn over 3f out: styd on same pce fnl 2f* **8/1**
3-22 **8** 6 **Robbie Can Can**[13] 37 7-9-6 **60**...... HayleyTurner 11 — 48
(A W Carroll) *hld up: rdn over 4f out: a in rr* **11/1**
006- **9** 9 **Futoo (IRE)**[26] 6364 5-9-4 **58**...... FergalLynch 7 — 32
(G M Moore) *chsd ldr over 4f: wkng whn nt clr run over 3f out* **66/1**
00-4 **10** 1 ½ **Amir Zaman**[15] 13 8-9-5 **59**......(v) JamieSpencer 5 — 31
(J R Jenkins) *prom: edgd lft and wknd over 3f out* **7/1**[2]

06-3 **11** 2 1/2 **Mossmann Gorge**15 [13] 4-9-2 **60**............(p) JimmyQuinn 10 28
(M Wellings) *hld up: hdwy over 4f out: wknd over 3f out* **50/1**
2m 37.07s (-5.02) **Going Correction** -0.225s/f (Stan)
WFA 4 from 5yo+ 4lb 11 Ran SP% **120.8**
Speed ratings (Par 101):107,106,106,106,103 103,102,98,92,91 90
CSF £164.43 CT £1518.28 TOTE £8.10: £2.60, £7.50, £3.50; EX 305.20.
Owner Cunnane, Godfrey, Kirkland & Winter **Bred** Exors Of The Late Mrs I Morris **Trained** Aldbury, Herts

FOCUS
With the favourite Sonic Anthem setting a searching pace, the winning time was decent for the class.
Futoo(IRE) Official explanation: jockey said gelding suffered interference
Amir Zaman Official explanation: jockey said gelding stopped quickly

132 BETDIRECT ON TENNIS MAIDEN STKS 1m (F)
2:50 (2:51) (Class 5) 3-Y-O **£3,238** (£963; £481; £240) **Stalls** Low

Form RPR
404- **1** **Daaweitza**21 [6673] 3-9-0 63............ TomEaves 2 75
(B Ellison) *chsd ldrs: rdn to ld ins fnl f: r.o* **7/1**
002- **2** 3/4 **Crazy Bear (IRE)**26 [6659] 3-8-9 66............ PaulHanagan 9 68
(K A Ryan) *chsd ldrs: rdn 1/2-way: r.o* **4/1**3
032- **3** nk **Korikancha (IRE)**27 [6640] 3-8-10 70 ow1............ JamieSpencer 1 68
(J Noseda) *trckd ldrs: led over 3f out: rdn over 1f out: hdd and nt qckn inbside fnl f* **5/4**1
2 **4** 9 **Kasumi**14 [16] 3-8-9............ SteveDrowne 8 49
(H Morrison) *chsd ldrs: rdn over 1f out: sn wknd and eased* **7/2**2
5 2 1/2 **Mind Out (USA)** 3-9-0............ RobertWinston 4 49+
(J A Osborne) *led 7f out: hdd over 3f out: wknd 2f out* **12/1**
6 2 **Tip Top Style** 3-9-0............ DaleGibson 3 45
(J Mackie) *s.i.s: nvr nrr* **80/1**
7 2 **Grand Assault** 3-9-0............ NeilPollard 12 41
(Lucinda Featherstone) *s.i.s: sn chsng ldrs: wknd over 2f out* **50/1**
06-0 **8** 3/4 **Dylan (IRE)**15 [10] 3-9-0 45............ KimTinkler 7 40
(N Tinkler) *led 1f: wknd 1/2-way* **80/1**
0 **9** 5 **Beginners Luck (IRE)**6 [93] 3-8-6 45............ DanielTudhope(3) 5 25
(D Carroll) *hld up: bhd fr 1/2-way* **100/1**
10 1 1/4 **Maxemull** 3-8-6............ EdwardCreighton(3) 11 22
(D J Wintle) *s.i.s: outpcd* **66/1**
-00 **11** 4 **Jeudi**4 [104] 3-9-0............ JamieMackay 6 19
(Sir Mark Prescott) *bhd fr 1/2-way* **66/1**
0- **12** 10 **Cannygo (IRE)**66 [6318] 3-9-0............(b1) BrianReilly 13 —
(R M Flower) *chsd ldrs over 4f* **100/1**
1m 43.45s (-1.15) **Going Correction** -0.225s/f (Stan) 12 Ran SP% **116.3**
Speed ratings (Par 97):96,95,94,85,83 81,79,78,73,72 68,58
CSF £34.30 TOTE £9.90: £2.30, £1.50, £1.10; EX 41.60.
Owner Mrs Andrea M Mallinson **Bred** C Mallinson **Trained** Norton, N Yorks

FOCUS
An ordinary maiden in which the front three pulled miles clear of the rest.

133 PLAY NOW AT BETDIRECTCASINO.COM FILLIES' H'CAP 7f (F)
3:20 (3:20) (Class 5) (0-70,61) 4-Y-O+ **£3,238** (£963; £481; £240) **Stalls** Low

Form RPR
000- **1** **Dispol Isle (IRE)**80 [6139] 4-8-13 **56**............ PhillipMakin 8 65
(T D Barron) *a.p: rdn to ld ins fnl f: r.o* **9/2**3
65-2 **2** 3/4 **Soft Focus (IRE)**14 [21] 4-9-1 **58**............(b) RobertWinston 2 65
(J A Osborne) *hld up in tch: rdn and ev ch ins fnl f: unable qck nr fin* **9/4**1
336- **3** 2 1/2 **Caerphilly Gal**30 [6608] 6-8-0 **50**............ NicolPolli(7) 4 51
(P L Gilligan) *led: hdd over 4f out: led 2f out: sn rdn: hdd and no ex ins fnl f* **11/4**2
03-0 **4** 1/2 **Red Finesse**14 [21] 4-8-13 **56**............ MatthewHenry 7 55
(M A Jarvis) *chsd ldrs: rdn 1/2-way: styd on same pce fnl 2f* **16/1**
05-4 **5** 1/2 **Sweet Pickle**14 [21] 5-9-1 **58**............(e) JoeFanning 1 56
(J R Boyle) *trckd ldrs: racd keenly: led over 4f out: hdd 2f out: rdn and ev ch ins fnl f: wknd towards fin* **9/2**3
660- **6** 3 **Tequila Sheila (IRE)**22 [6666] 4-8-12 **55**............ FranciscoDaSilva 3 45
(K R Burke) *hld up: rdn over 2f out: n.d* **6/1**
160- **7** 5 **Ballycroy Girl (IRE)**53 [5240] 4-9-2 **59**............ MickyFenton 6 36
(A Bailey) *chsd ldrs: lost pl 5f out: bhd fnl 3f* **20/1**
1m 28.53s (-2.27) **Going Correction** -0.225s/f (Stan) 7 Ran SP% **118.7**
Speed ratings (Par 100):103,102,99,98,98 94,89
CSF £15.95 CT £33.36 TOTE £6.70: £3.20, £1.40; EX 26.70.
Owner W B Imison **Bred** Mrs I A Balding **Trained** Maunby, N Yorks

FOCUS
A modest contest, but a fair pace and the winning time split the two divisions of the handicap open to both sexes.

134 PLAY NOW AT BETDIRECTPOKER.COM H'CAP (DIV II) 7f (F)
3:50 (3:50) (Class 6) (0-55,55) 4-Y-O+ **£2,047** (£604; £302) **Stalls** Low

Form RPR
032- **1** **Golden Square**17 [5704] 4-8-12 **53**............ RobertWinston 8 65
(A W Carroll) *a.p: rdn to ld over 1f out: r.o* **7/1**3
132- **2** 1 1/2 **Augustine**21 [6674] 5-9-0 **55**............ DarrenWilliams 10 63
(P W Hiatt) *led 1f: chsd ldrs: rdn and ev ch over 1f out: styd on same pce ins fnl f* **11/4**1
0-52 **3** nk **Mister Benji**7 [77] 7-9-0 **55**............ DeanMcKeown 5 62
(B P J Baugh) *hld up: hdwy 1/2-way: rdn over 1f out: styd on same pce* **10/3**2
061- **4** 3 **Prince Of Gold**20 [6676] 6-8-11 **52**............(b) GrahamGibbons 7 52
(R Hollinshead) *mid-div: hmpd 6f out: sn drvn along: hdwy over 2f out: no ex fnl f* **7/1**3
000- **5** 1/2 **Zariano**232 [2131] 6-8-10 **51**............ PhillipMakin 6 49
(T D Barron) *chsd ldrs: led over 4f out: rdn and hdd over 1f out: wknd ins fnl f* **15/2**
2-10 **6** 1 **Lady Susanne (IRE)**6 [95] 4-8-9 **50**............(b) RobbieFitzpatrick 11 46
(M J Attwater) *chsd ldrs over 5f* **9/1**
10-3 **7** 2 **Wodhill Be**6 [95] 6-8-8 **49** ow1............ DerekMcGaffin 1 39
(D Morris) *hld up: rdn over 2f out: nvr trbld ldrs* **16/1**
50-0 **8** nk **Speakerboxxx**12 [44] 4-8-9 **50**............(t) JoeFanning 4 40
(P F I Cole) *s.i.s: hdwy 3f out: wknd over 1f out* **11/1**
400- **9** 6 **Smith N Allan Oils**33 [6584] 7-9-0 **55**............ MickyFenton 9 29
(C Smith) *s.i.s: outpcd* **40/1**
000- **10** 3 1/2 **Nevinstown (IRE)**21 [6667] 6-8-12 **53**............ TonyHamilton 12 18
(C Grant) *led 6f out: hung rt and hdd over 4f out: wknd 1/2-way* **66/1**

02P- **11** 8 **Waltzing Wizard**263 [1334] 7-8-6 **47**............ AlanDaly 2 —
(A Berry) *hld up: a bhd* **50/1**
1m 28.38s (-2.42) **Going Correction** -0.225s/f (Stan) 33 Ran SP% **116.6**
Speed ratings (Par 101):104,102,101,98,97 96,94,94,87,83 74
CSF £26.13 CT £78.50 TOTE £11.20: £2.20, £1.40, £1.40; EX 36.60 Place 6 £93.19, Place 5 £55.77.
Owner Mr & Mrs J B **Bred** J R And Mrs P Good **Trained** Cropthorne, Worcs

FOCUS
A modest event and not many got into it. The winning time was 0.36 seconds faster than the first division. The form looks pretty sound.
Wodhill Be Official explanation: jockey said mare pulled up lame
T/Plt: £135.50 to a £1 stake. Pool: £28,662.15. 154.40 winning tickets. T/Qpdt: £16.20 to a £1 stake. Pool: £3,140.00. 143.10 winning tickets. CR

111 LINGFIELD (L-H)
Wednesday, January 18

OFFICIAL GOING: Standard
Wind: Almost nil Weather: Overcast

135 LITTLEWOODS BETDIRECT H'CAP (DIV I) 1m 2f (P)
12:40 (12:41) (Class 4) (0-85,85) 4-Y-O+ **£6,153** (£1,830; £914; £456) **Stalls** Low

Form RPR
000- **1** **El Tiger (GER)**81 [6147] 5-9-4 **85**............ JamieSpencer 5 94+
(B J Curley) *hld up in rr: smooth prog over 2f out: led over 1f out: idled fnl f and hdd: hung rt but drvn to ld again nr fin* **14/1**
210- **2** shd **Consonant (IRE)**23 [6665] 9-8-10 **77**............ MickyFenton 3 84
(D G Bridgwater) *trckd ldng pair: rdn over 2f out: effrt on inner u.p to ld ins fnl f: hung bdly rt and hdd nr fin* **7/1**
05-0 **3** 1 1/4 **Gingko**5 [108] 9-8-9 **76**............ ChrisCatlin 4 81
(P R Webber) *settled midfield: rdn 3f out: effrt u.p over 1f out: styd on to take 3rd nr fin: nvr able to chal* **11/1**
03-0 **4** nk **Admiral Compton**14 [33] 5-8-4 **71** oh1............(b) MartinDwyer 6 75
(J R Boyle) *trckd ldr to 2f out: stl chalng ent fnl f: hld whn carried rt last 100yds* **5/1**2
56-0 **5** 1/2 **Burgundy**7 [88] 9-8-7 **74**............(b) PaulHanagan 2 77
(P Mitchell) *rousted along in last trio early: drvn 3f out: styd on fr over 1f out : nrst fin* **13/2**3
000- **6** 1/2 **Skidmark**28 [6645] 5-8-12 **79**............ SamHitchcott 10 83+
(Miss J R Tooth) *dwlt: hld up in last: prog on inner and nt clr run over 1f out: swtchd rt: styng on but hld whn squeezed out last 50yds* **9/1**
204- **7** 7 **Missatacama (IRE)**19 [6690] 4-8-8 **77**............ JoeFanning 8 66
(D J Daly) *trckd ldrs: rdn over 2f out: wknd rapidly over 1f out* **5/1**2
35-5 **8** shd **The Violin Player (USA)**7 [88] 5-9-2 **83**............(p) SteveDrowne 7 72
(H J Collingridge) *hld up in tch: rdn over 2f out: wknd rapidly wl over 1f out* **4/1**1
000- **9** 1 3/4 **Selective**19 [3829] 7-9-0 **81**............(t) RobertWinston 1 66
(A W Carroll) *led: pushed along over 2f out: hdd over 1f out: eased ins fnl f* **20/1**
005- **10** 8 **Forthright**250 [1356] 5-8-1 **73**............ RobynBrisland(5) 11 43
(G L Moore) *racd wd: in tch tl wknd 3f out: t.o* **16/1**
2m 6.44s (-1.35) **Going Correction** -0.075s/f (Stan)
WFA 4 from 5yo+ 2lb 10 Ran SP% **114.8**
Speed ratings (Par 105):102,101,100,100,100 99,94,94,92,86
CSF £106.85 CT £1124.40 TOTE £13.00: £2.90, £2.40, £4.30; EX 65.90.
Owner Curley Leisure **Bred** Gestut Wittekindshof **Trained** Newmarket, Suffolk
■ Stewards' Enquiry : Micky Fenton three-day ban: careless riding (Jan 29-31)

FOCUS
A competitive handicap won by a horse that had decent Group One form in his native Germany in 2004. There was a typically modest pace for the course-and-distance and a bunch finish, and the form, rated through the third, is not rock solid.

136 BETDIRECT ON THE MASTERS SNOOKER H'CAP 5f (P)
1:10 (1:11) (Class 5) (0-75,74) 3-Y-O+ **£3,238** (£963; £481; £240) **Stalls** High

Form RPR
1-20 **1** **Law Maker**7 [89] 6-9-6 **74**............(v) MichaelJStainton(7) 3 83
(A Bailey) *trckd ldng pair: effrt over 1f out: rdn to ld last 100yds: sn in command* **6/1**
36-3 **2** 1 1/2 **Wicked Uncle**15 [23] 7-9-9 **70**............(v) NCallan 1 74
(S Gollings) *mde most: rdn and def advantage over 1f out: hdd and one pce last 100yds* **3/1**2
003- **3** 2 **Talcen Gwyn (IRE)**32 [6603] 4-9-4 **65**............(v) SteveDrowne 5 62
(M F Harris) *in tch: rdn 2f out: kpt on fnl f to take 3rd nr fin: nvr pce to rch ldrs* **5/1**3
21-0 **4** nk **Clipper Hoy**7 [89] 4-9-7 **68**............ GeorgeBaker 2 64
(Mrs H Sweeting) *w ldr tl 2f out: hanging rt after: nt qckn 1f out: btn after* **2/1**1
001- **5** 1 1/2 **Overwing (IRE)**60 [6374] 3-8-6 **71**............ StephaneBreux(3) 4 61
(R Hannon) *in tch: rdn over 2f out: one pce and no imp* **10/1**
01/0 **6** shd **Lady Bahia (IRE)**8 [79] 5-9-4 **65**............(p) RobbieFitzpatrick 8 55
(Peter Grayson) *outpcd in last: nvr a factor* **25/1**
005- **7** 2 1/2 **Turibius**32 [6597] 7-9-2 **63**............(b) JimmyQuinn 7 44
(T E Powell) *racd wd: in tch: rdn 2f out: fnd nil* **8/1**
58.37 secs (-1.41) **Going Correction** -0.075s/f (Stan)
WFA 3 from 4yo+ 15lb 7 Ran SP% **113.3**
Speed ratings (Par 103):108,105,102,101,99 99,95
CSF £23.86 CT £95.90 TOTE £6.20: £2.50, £2.10; EX 19.50.
Owner North Cheshire Trading & Storage Ltd **Bred** North Cheshire Trading And Storage Ltd **Trained** Cotebrook, Cheshire

FOCUS
A fair handicap for its grade run at a strong pace. This was the fourth time the first two have met in the last two months, and the form should be reliable.
Lady Bahia(IRE) Official explanation: jockey said mare hung badly left throughout

137 BETDIRECT ON TENNIS H'CAP 6f (P)
1:40 (1:43) (Class 6) (0-60,60) 4-Y-O+ **£2,388** (£705; £352) **Stalls** Low

Form RPR
2-66 **1** **Kallista's Pride**2 [119] 6-9-3 **59**............ HayleyTurner 2 67
(J R Best) *hld up in midfield: prog on inner wl over 1f out: threaded through to ld ins fnl f: jst hld on* **4/1**1
02-0 **2** shd **Majestical (IRE)**13 [51] 4-9-3 **59**............(p) RobertWinston 1 67
(J M Bradley) *hld up in last: stl last 2f out: gd prog on outer jst over 1f out : r.o wl: jst failed* **8/1**

30-0 **3** *shd* **Greenwood**[13] [47] 8-9-4 **60**...(t) SteveDrowne 7 68
(P G Murphy) *hld up towards rr: prog 2f out: drvn to chal 1f out: r.o nr fin: jst hld* **7/1**[2]

0-03 **4** *½* **Canadian Danehill (IRE)**[2] [126] 4-9-2 **58**.......................(p) ChrisCatlin 9 64
(R M H Cowell) *trckd ldr after 1f: rdn to chal 2f out: disp ld ent fnl f: edgd rt and nt qckn* **8/1**

33-5 **5** *½* **Stylistic (IRE)**[16] [14] 5-9-4 **60**.. TPQueally 5 65
(Patrick Morris, Ire) *trckd ldrs: effrt 2f out: drvn to dispute ld ent fnl f: nt qckn* **25/1**

06-0 **6** *1* **Taranaki**[9] [71] 8-9-4 **60**.. SimonWhitworth 3 62
(P D Cundell) *s.s: wl in rr: prog 2f out: chsd ldrs 1f out: one pce after* **20/1**

000- **7** *½* **Double M**[29] [6625] 9-9-2 **58**...(v) NCallan 8 58
(Mrs L Richards) *prog fr rr wl over 3f out: drvn over 2f out: effrt on inner to dispute ld ent fnl f: wknd last 100yds* **15/2**[3]

01-2 **8** *2* **Diamond Josh**[9] [67] 4-9-2 **58**.................................... JamieSpencer 11 55+
(P D Evans) *led: rdn 2f out: hdd ent fnl f: eased whn btn* **4/1**[1]

000- **9** *¾* **Jennverse**[200] [3135] 4-9-4 **60**.. JimmyQuinn 6 52
(D K Ivory) *a wl in rr: rdn and no prog on inner wl over 1f out* **40/1**

53-0 **10** *nk* **Tapa**[13] [46] 4-9-4 **60**...(b) MartinDwyer 4 51
(A M Balding) *chsd ldr for 1f: styd prom tl wknd u.p over 1f out* **12/1**

22-5 **11** *hd* **I Wish**[9] [74] 8-9-3 **59**.. PaulFitzsimons 10 49
(Miss J R Tooth) *chsd ldrs: rdn wl over 2f out: wknd wl over 1f out* **14/1**

00-0 **12** *5* **Physical (IRE)**[14] [36] 4-9-4 **60**.. JoeFanning 12 35
(Mrs A J Perrett) *racd wd: in tch tl wknd 2f out: t.o* **14/1**

1m 11.94s (-0.87) **Going Correction** -0.075s/f (Stan) **12** Ran SP% **118.6**
Speed ratings (Par 101):102,101,101,101,100 99,98,95,94,94 94,87
CSF £35.16 CT £223.22 TOTE £4.90: £1.70, £2.40, £2.40; EX 52.90.
Owner G G Racing **Bred** Miss K S Buckley And J S Middleton **Trained** Hucking, Kent

FOCUS
A competitive sprint handicap run at a solid pace. The race involved some frustrating types, so the form may not be entirely reliable although the time suggest that it is sound enough.
Diamond Josh Official explanation: jockey said gelding had no more to give

138 BETDIRECT.CO.UK MAIDEN STKS 6f (P)
2:10 (2:11) (Class 5) 3-Y-0+ **£3,238** (£963; £481; £240) **Stalls** Low

Form RPR
24-4 **1** **Didn't We (IRE)**[9] [70] 3-8-10 .... JoeFanning 7 60
(T G Mills) *pushed along to stay prom: rdn 2f out: chal 1f out: forced ahd last 100yds* **5/2**[1]

3-2 **2** *nk* **Radiator Rooney (IRE)**[16] [10] 3-8-10 69...........................(b) NCallan 5 60
(Patrick Morris, Ire) *trckd ldng pair: rdn to ld 1f out: hdd and hld last 100yds* **4/1**[2]

003- **3** *1½* **Kitchen Sink (IRE)**[18] [6695] 4-9-12 50......................(e) FergusSweeney 2 59
(P J Makin) *chsd ldrs: effrt and rdn 2f out: styd on fnl f to take 3rd nr fin* **14/1**

500- **4** *1* **Lauren Louise**[123] [5305] 4-9-2 47.................................. MarcHalford(5) 3 51
(T T Clement) *chsd ldrs: effrt on inner 2f out: tried to chal 1f out: one pce after* **66/1**

5-35 **5** *1¾* **Charlie Bear**[9] [67] 5-9-12 57..................................... AdrianMcCarthy 9 51
(Miss Z C Davison) *led to 1f out: wknd ins fnl f* **7/1**

03- **6** *¾* **Billy Bling (IRE)**[23] [6661] 3-8-7 .... StephaneBreux(3) 11 45
(R Hannon) *pressed ldr to over 1f out: wknd ins fnl f* **12/1**

024- **7** *½* **Chantelle's Dream**[28] [6647] 4-9-0 45............................ JamesDoyle(7) 8 42
(Ms J S Doyle) *dwlt: hld up towards rr: prog on wd outside 1/2-way: wd bnd 2f out: hanging and no imp after* **33/1**

3- **8** *nk* **Kokila**[23] [6663] 3-8-5 .... HayleyTurner 12 37
(W J Haggas) *towards rr: drvn 2f out: plugged on same pce* **6/1**[3]

9 *2½* **Billy Wizz (IRE)** 3-8-10 .... MartinDwyer 10 35
(A M Balding) *dwlt: last trio and off the pce by 1/2-way: nvr a factor* **14/1**

10 *5* **King's College (USA)** 3-8-3 .... JamieJones(7) 1 20
(G L Moore) *dwlt: sn struggling and wl in rr: wknd over 1f out* **33/1**

11 *1¼* **Island Green (USA)** 3-8-10 .... JamieSpencer 6 16
(B J Curley) *s.s: detached in last: virtually t.o fr 1/2-way* **4/1**[2]

12 *½* **Hello Molly** 5-9-0 .... JamesMillman(7) 4 13
(E A Wheeler) *dwlt: a wl bhd* **66/1**

1m 12.25s (-0.56) **Going Correction** -0.075s/f (Stan)
WFA 3 from 4yo+ 16lb **12** Ran SP% **125.3**
Speed ratings (Par 103):100,99,97,96,93 92,92,91,88,81 80,79
CSF £12.85 TOTE £3.30: £1.40, £1.70, £3.10; EX 16.10.
Owner T G Mills **Bred** Mrs John McEnery **Trained** Headley, Surrey

FOCUS
A very moderate maiden run at a reasonable pace.
Island Green(USA) Official explanation: jockey said gelding was slowly away

139 BETDIRECT FREEPHONE 0800 211 222 CLAIMING STKS 7f (P)
2:40 (2:41) (Class 6) 3-Y-0 **£2,388** (£705; £352) **Stalls** Low

Form RPR
06-2 **1** **Bollywood (IRE)**[14] [31] 3-9-7 54.................................... MatthewHenry 1 71
(M A Jarvis) *led after 1f: mde rest: drvn into def advantage over 1f out: kpt on wl* **10/1**

52-4 **2** *1* **Tafilah**[7] [85] 3-8-4 55...(v) JimmyQuinn 5 51
(P W D'Arcy) *in tch: prog to chse ldng pair 1/2-way: drvn and nt qckn over 1f out: styd on to take 2nd last 100yds: unable to chal* **5/1**[3]

33-0 **3** *hd* **Colmar Supreme**[14] [34] 3-8-12 70........................... RobertWinston 11 58
(R Hannon) *in tch towards outer: rdn over 2f out: no prog tl styd on fnl f: nrst fin* **7/1**

45-6 **4** *1¾* **In Hope**[7] [83] 3-7-11 60 ow6....................................... JamieJones(7) 10 46
(Andrew Reid) *prom: chsd wnr 4f out: rdn to chal 2f out: nt qckn and hld over 1f out: wknd and lost 2 pls last 100yds* **40/1**

02-4 **5** *nk* **Outlook**[8] [76] 3-9-7 78...(b) ChrisCatlin 6 62
(N P Littmoden) *sn lost pl and in rr: rdn wl over 2f out: no prog tl styd on fnl f: no ch* **4/1**[2]

40-0 **6** *¾* **Reality Time (IRE)**[9] [68] 3-8-4 68..............................(b[1]) MartinDwyer 4 44+
(J A Osborne) *v s.i.s: rcvrd and midfield by 1/2-way: prog to chse ldng trio over 1f out: wkng whn nt clr run last 75yds* **14/1**

2-05 **7** *2½* **Sounds Simla (IRE)**[7] [83] 3-8-7 77.............................. RobbieMills(7) 8 47
(Rae Guest) *hld up and sn last: no prog over 2f out: no ch after* **14/1**

26-2 **8** *nk* **Fangorn Forest (IRE)**[8] [76] 3-8-9 70 ow1..........................(p) NCallan 2 49+
(K A Ryan) *chsd ldrs: drvn on inner 1/2-way: struggling whn hmpd over 2f out: no ch after* **7/4**[1]

-453 **9** *½* **Twilight Avenger (IRE)**[6] [99] 3-8-7 53......................(p) HayleyTurner 9 38
(M J Polglase) *hld up: a wl in rr: no ch wl over 1f out* **33/1**

05-6 **10** *3½* **Smile For Us**[14] [30] 3-8-8 51.. BrianReilly 7 30
(C Drew) *led for 1f: chsd wnr to 4f out: hanging bdly after and sn lost pl: eased over 1f out* **66/1**

1m 26.03s (0.14) **Going Correction** -0.075s/f (Stan) **10** Ran SP% **114.8**
Speed ratings (Par 95):96,94,94,92,92 91,88,88,87,83
CSF £57.89 TOTE £10.30: £2.60, £1.60, £2.90; EX 71.20.Wnr claimed M.R.Hoad £14,000
Colmar Supreme claimed Claes Bjorling £12,000 Fangorn Forest claimed R.A.Harris £10,000
Owner Charles Cain and Michael Jarvis **Bred** Glashare House Stud **Trained** Newmarket, Suffolk

FOCUS
A race that featured many out-of-form or frustrating characters. The form is hard to rate and may not be reliable, but it is doubtful that the winner is flattered.
Reality Time(IRE) Official explanation: jockey said filly was denied a clear run in final furlong
Smile For Us Official explanation: jockey said gelding hung badly left

140 LITTLEWOODS BETDIRECT H'CAP (DIV II) 1m 2f (P)
3:10 (3:10) (Class 4) (0-85,85) 4-Y-0+ **£6,153** (£1,830; £914; £456) **Stalls** Low

Form RPR
1-41 **1** **Willhego**[7] [88] 5-8-10 **76** 6ex.. HayleyTurner 1 82+
(J R Best) *trckd ldng pair: effrt and nt clr run jst over 1f out: squeezed through to ld ins fnl f: drvn out* **10/1**

02-4 **2** *½* **Danger Zone**[4] [115] 4-8-2 **70** oh1.. JimmyQuinn 8 75
(Mrs A J Perrett) *prog to trck ldng pair 7f out: chsd ldr over 1f out: rdn to ld briefly ins fnl f: hld nr fin* **4/1**[2]

121- **3** *shd* **Bobby Charles**[85] [6101] 5-9-1 **81**....................................... PaulHanagan 3 86
(Dr J D Scargill) *hld up in rr in slowly run r: prog 2f out: swtchd rt over 1f out: chal ins fnl f: hld nr fin* **11/2**[3]

050/ **4** *shd* **Alekhine (IRE)**[93] [6332] 5-8-9 **75**... JoeFanning 4 80
(J R Boyle) *hld up in last in slowly run r: swtchd lft and prog over 1f out: tried to chal ins fnl f: styd on* **33/1**

44-6 **5** *nk* **Just Fly**[14] [33] 6-8-2 **71**... RichardThomas(3) 10 75
(Dr J R J Naylor) *hld up towards rr: reminders 3f out: nt qckn 2f out: r.o fnl f: a hld* **16/1**

011- **6** *½* **Obezyana (USA)**[60] [6373] 4-9-3 **85**...............................(t) MartinDwyer 9 88
(G A Huffer) *chsd ldrs: shkn up 3f out: no prog 2f out: edgd rt but r.o ins fnl f* **15/8**[1]

4-25 **7** *nk* **Waterside (IRE)**[8] [80] 7-9-4 **84**.. NCallan 7 86
(G L Moore) *t.k.h: led at stdy pce: increased tempo over 2f out: hdd & wknd ins fnl f* **11/1**

23-0 **8** *¾* **Crail**[5] [108] 6-8-13 **79**... GeorgeBaker 6 80
(C F Wall) *trckd ldr to over 1f out: wknd ins fnl f* **15/2**

00-0 **9** *nk* **Northside Lodge (IRE)**[7] [88] 8-8-3 **74**...................(t[1]) GregFairley(5) 5 74
(W R Swinburn) *hld up in last trio in slowly run r: one pce fnl 2f* **16/1**

6/0- **10** *nk* **Fame**[19] [5800] 6-8-9 **75**.. ChrisCatlin 2 75
(P J Hobbs) *t.k.h: hld up towards rr: nt qckn 2f out: one pce after* **50/1**

2m 7.33s (-0.46) **Going Correction** -0.075s/f (Stan)
WFA 4 from 5yo+ 2lb **10** Ran SP% **116.0**
Speed ratings (Par 105):98,97,97,97,97 96,96,95,95,95
CSF £49.58 CT £246.66 TOTE £9.10: £2.10, £1.80, £1.80; EX 41.00 Trifecta £97.20 Pool: £630.16 - 4.60 winning tickets..
Owner G G Racing **Bred** J R Wills **Trained** Hucking, Kent
■ Stewards' Enquiry : George Baker two-day ban: careless riding (Jan 29-30)

FOCUS
A competitive handicap run at a slow early pace, resulting in a bunch finish and a slower time than division one. The form is questionable, rated around the fifth.
Obezyana(USA) Official explanation: vet said gelding returned lame

141 NO 5P RULE 4S AT BETDIRECT (S) STKS 2m (P)
3:40 (3:41) (Class 6) 4-Y-0+ **£2,388** (£705; £352) **Stalls** Low

Form RPR
1-43 **1** **Mister Completely (IRE)**[7] [92] 5-9-9 45.................................. NCallan 7 57
(J R Best) *hld up: prog to trck ldrs 1/2-way: led and kicked on 3f out: sn jnd gained upper hand over 1f out: hld on nr fin* **7/2**[2]

000- **2** *nk* **Another Con (IRE)**[44] [6509] 5-8-13 45.......................... MickyFenton 5 47
(A M Hales) *hld up towards rr: lost pl and rdn 5f out: prog 4f out to join wnr wl over 2f out: nt qckn over 1f out: kpt on nr fin* **14/1**

000- **3** *6* **Mujazaf**[74] [4748] 4-8-8 57.. EdwardCreighton(3) 8 47+
(Miss Sheena West) *hld up in rr: trapped on inner whn pce qcknd 3f out: modest 6th 2f out: styd on to take 3rd ins fnl f: no ch* **9/2**[3]

060- **4** *2* **Sungio**[19] [6329] 8-9-4 40...(b) JoeFanning 6 42
(B P J Baugh) *trckd ldrs: trapped on inner whn pce qcknd 3f out: no ch after: kpt on fr over 1f out* **9/1**

06-6 **5** *nk* **Chocolate Boy (IRE)**[12] [55] 7-9-4 55........................(be) GeorgeBaker 9 42
(G L Moore) *hld up in rr: prog 4f out: chsd ldng pair wl over 2f out but immediately outpcd: wknd fnl f* **2/1**[1]

000- **6** *8* **Buz Kiri (USA)**[16] [4041] 8-9-4 35....................................(t) PaulHanagan 11 32
(A W Carroll) *hld up in rr: u.p and losing tch 4f out: no ch after* **20/1**

000- **7** *8* **Tintawn Gold (IRE)**[20] [6682] 6-8-13 35................................ TPQueally 1 17
(S Woodman) *led at stdy pce to 3f out: immediately btn* **40/1**

666- **8** *8* **Lawaaheb (IRE)**[20] [6683] 5-9-1 48.........................(v) RichardThomas(3) 3 13
(B R Johnson) *plld hrd: w ldng pair 10f out to over 3f out: wknd rapidly* **5/1**

00-0 **9** *2* **The Plainsman**[6] [97] 4-8-11 40.................................... HayleyTurner 10 10
(P W Hiatt) *t.k.h: w ldr to 4f out: wknd rapidly* **25/1**

00- **10** *21* **Another Mistress**[37] [6307] 4-8-6 .... JimmyQuinn 2 —
(R M Flower) *t.k.h: prom to 1/2-way: sn wknd: t.o* **66/1**

3m 26.37s (-2.42) **Going Correction** -0.075s/f (Stan)
WFA 4 from 5yo+ 7lb **10** Ran SP% **119.6**
Speed ratings (Par 101):103,102,99,98,98 94,90,86,85,75
CSF £49.79 TOTE £3.80: £1.30, £4.30, £1.70; EX 53.20.The winner was sold to Gerald West for 5,800gns
Owner G G Racing **Bred** Eamonn Griffin **Trained** Hucking, Kent

FOCUS
A very weak seller run at only a modest pace. The winner has been rated back to his old level but the form does not look solid.
Sungio Official explanation: jockey said gelding was denied a clear run
Lawaaheb(IRE) Official explanation: jockey said gelding hung right throughout
Another Mistress Official explanation: jockey said filly ran too free

142 FREE £25 WITH LITTLEWOODSPOKER.COM APPRENTICE H'CAP 1m (P)
4:10 (4:11) (Class 5) (0-75,71) 3-Y-0 **£3,238** (£963; £481; £240) **Stalls** High

Form RPR
00-3 **1** **Prince Charlemagne (IRE)**[14] [30] 3-8-1 **57** oh1....... JamesDoyle(3) 3 67+
(N P Littmoden) *hld up in last pair: rdn and looked struggling 3f out: gd prog over 2f out: led over 1f out: sn clr* **5/2**[1]

The Form Book, Raceform Ltd, Compton, RG20 6NL

00-6 **2** 3½ **Simpsons Ross (IRE)**[11] [60] 3-8-9 62 SladeO'Hara 9 61
(R M Flower) *in tch: effrt over 2f out: n.m.r on inner over 1f out: wnt 2nd jst ins fnl f: no ch w wnr* 33/1
040- **3** 1 **Stellenbosch (USA)**[127] [5195] 3-9-4 71 DerekNolan 2 68
(J W Hills) *hld up in last: rdn over 3f out and struggling: gd prog over 1f out: one pce ins fnl f* 8/1
0-40 **4** 2 **Norman Beckett**[2] [123] 3-8-7 63 ThomasO'Brien(3) 6 55
(M R Channon) *rn in snatches: in tch: struggling whn hit rail and rdr unbalanced over 2f out: one pce after* 16/1
002- **5** ½ **Final Bid (IRE)**[54] [6420] 3-9-0 67 (b) JamieJones 7 58
(M G Quinlan) *t.k.h: trckd ldng pair: brushed aside fr 2f out* 7/2[3]
0-23 **6** 1¾ **Ms Rainbow Runner**[7] [85] 3-8-10 63 LiamJones 1 50
(P Butler) *t.k.h: led: set str pce after 2f: hdd & wknd over 1f out* 5/1
13-3 **7** 1¾ **Lenoir (GER)**[15] [19] 3-8-8 68 (v) TJHowell(7) 8 51
(V Smith) *plld hrd: w ldr to over 1f out: wknd rapidly* 11/4[2]

1m 39.35s (-0.08) **Going Correction** -0.075s/f (Stan) 7 Ran SP% 114.1
Speed ratings (Par 97):97,93,92,90,90 88,86
CSF £72.69 CT £579.75 TOTE £3.30: £2.50, £7.50; EX 48.80 Place 6 £352.37, Place 5 £56.28.
Owner Neil Ryan **Bred** Michael O'Mahony **Trained** Newmarket, Suffolk

FOCUS
A low-grade apprentice handicap in which the leaders appeared to go off too fast. The winner should rate higher and the placed form looks solid enough.
T/Jkpt: £158,960.30 to a £1 stake. Pool: £223,887.75. 1.00 winning ticket. T/Plt: £408.50 to a £1 stake. Pool: £59,748.30. 106.75 winning tickets. T/Qpdt: £22.60 to a £1 stake. Pool: £6,362.40. 207.80 winning tickets. JN

127 SOUTHWELL (L-H)
Thursday, January 19

OFFICIAL GOING: Standard
Wind: Light, across Weather: Fine becoming cloudy

143 PLAY NOW AT BETDIRECTPOKER.COM APPRENTICE BANDED STKS 1m (F)
1:40 (1:43) (Class 7) 4-Y-0+ **£1,365** (£403; £201) **Stalls** Low

Form RPR
020- **1** **Golden Spectrum (IRE)**[43] [6524] 7-8-6 47 (b) WilliamCarson(7) 1 52
(R A Harris) *trckd ldrs: racd keenly: led over 4f out: clr over 2f out: sn rdn: styd on* 20/1
0-40 **2** ½ **Spy Gun (USA)**[8] [95] 6-8-9 46 SladeO'Hara(3) 2 50
(T Wall) *led 1f: remained handy tl outpcd over 3f out: rallied to chse wnr over 1f out: styd on* 22/1
020- **3** shd **It Must Be Speech**[21] [6683] 5-8-6 40 (v) MarkCoumbe(5) 8 49
(S L Keightley) *hld up: hdwy over 1f out: n.m.r ins fnl f: r.o* 14/1
645- **4** 1 **Legal Lover (IRE)**[23] [6674] 4-8-11 48 StephanieHollinshead(3) 13 50
(R Hollinshead) *hld up in tch: chsd wnr over 3f out: sn rdn: styd on same pce fnl f* 5/1[3]
143- **5** shd **Mutared (IRE)**[36] [6574] 8-8-7 46 JamesDoyle(5) 3 48
(N P Littmoden) *hld up: outpcd over 3f out: hdwy 2f out: styd on* 9/2[2]
10-2 **6** 1¼ **The Job**[8] [95] 5-9-1 49 (v) MarcHalford 12 48
(A D Smith) *hld up in tch: rdn over 1f out: styd on same pce* 11/2
00-4 **7** 1 **Justcallmehandsome**[16] [26] 4-8-8 40 DonnaCaldwell(3) 7 42
(D J S Ffrench Davis) *led 7f out: hdd over 4f out: no ex ins fnl f* 80/1
03-0 **8** 3½ **Pawn In Life (IRE)**[8] [94] 8-8-6 40 (b) RobbieMills(5) 5 35
(M J Polglase) *s.i.s: sme hdwy over 1f out: nvr nrr* 40/1
00-1 **9** hd **Legacy (JPN)**[15] [43] 6-8-8 47 JBrennan(5) 10 37
(P D Evans) *dwlt: hdwy 1/2-way: rdn over 2f out: sn hung lft and btn* 7/2[1]
0-00 **10** 3½ **Chairman Rick (IRE)**[7] [100] 4-8-12 49 KellyHarrison(3) 9 32
(D Nicholls) *s.i.s: effrt 1/2-way: sn wknd* 50/1
556- **11** 1¼ **Major Speculation (IRE)**[31] [6615] 6-8-12 46 GregFairley 14 26
(J M Bradley) *chsd ldrs over 5f* 16/1
03-0 **12** 2 **Blushing Russian (IRE)**[15] [43] 4-8-10 49 JamesMillman(5) 6 25
(J M Bradley) *s.i.s: outpcd* 8/1
40-2 **13** 8 **Crocodile Kiss (IRE)**[16] [26] 4-9-2 50 AndrewMullen 4 10
(J A Osborne) *sn outpcd* 16/1
0-00 **14** 3½ **Cheeney Basin (IRE)**[7] [96] 8-8-11 48 LiamJones(3) 11 —
(M C Chapman) *plld hrd and prom: wknd 1/2-way* 100/1

1m 44.13s (-0.47) **Going Correction** -0.20s/f (Stan) 14 Ran SP% 117.7
Speed ratings (Par 97):94,93,93,92,92 91,90,86,86,82 81,79,71,68
CSF £375.25 TOTE £33.30: £7.20, £6.20, £8.10; EX 302.60.
Owner Peter A Price **Bred** Orpendale And Global Investments **Trained** Earlswood, Monmouths
■ The first winner for William Carson, grandson of former champion jockey Willie Carson.
■ Stewards' Enquiry : James Doyle one-day ban: careless riding (Feb 21)

FOCUS
A competitive banded event but only ordinary form.

144 PLAY NOW AT BETDIRECTCASINO.COM MAIDEN CLAIMING STKS 6f (F)
2:10 (2:14) (Class 7) 4-Y-0+ **£1,365** (£403; £201) **Stalls** Low

Form RPR
430- **1** **Favouring (IRE)**[206] [2987] 4-9-0 53 (v) PaulHanagan 10 59
(R A Fahey) *s.i.s and hmpd s: hdwy u.p over 3f out: hung lft fr over 2f out: led 1f out: r.o wl* 4/1[1]
22-5 **2** 4 **Fir Tree**[16] [26] 6-9-0 40 PhillipMakin 8 47
(S R Bowring) *led: rdn 2f out: sn hung rt: hdd 1f out: sn outpcd* 9/2[2]
064- **3** 1¾ **Velvet Touch**[38] [6554] 5-8-7 40 (t) ChrisCatlin 13 35
(D M Simcock) *chsd ldr: rdn over 2f out: no ex fnl f* 8/1
06-0 **4** 2½ **Flying Dancer**[16] [29] 4-8-9 45 (b[1]) NCallan 9 29
(R A Harris) *s.i.s and edgd rt s: sn chsng ldrs: rdn over 2f out: wknd fnl f* 6/1
600- **5** 2½ **Missin Margot**[28] [6654] 4-8-7 40 ow2 (v[1]) RobertWinston 4 20
(P D Evans) *hld up in tch: rdn over 2f out: sn btn* 20/1
605- **6** 1¾ **Limited Magician**[38] [6554] 5-8-9 30 RobbieFitzpatrick 12 17
(C Smith) *sn outpcd: nvr nrr* 50/1
42-5 **7** 1¾ **Faithisflying**[16] [29] 4-8-9 40 (b) TonyCulhane 2 11
(D W Chapman) *sn pushed along and prom: wknd over 1f out* 5/1[3]
60-0 **8** 2½ **Mad Marty Wildcard**[6] [104] 4-9-0 35 TomEaves 11 9
(R Brotherton) *sn outpcd* 20/1
32-0 **9** nk **Ben Casey**[17] [9] 4-9-0 53 (p) PaulEddery 5 8
(B Smart) *s.i.s: sn mid-div: n.m.r and lost pl over 4f out: sn bhd* 9/2[2]
/0-0 **10** 1 **Weet N Measures**[14] [46] 4-9-0 49 J-PGuillambert 6 5
(T Wall) *chsd ldrs over 3f* 25/1
40-0 **11** 1 **Duncanbil (IRE)**[8] [84] 5-8-7 35 (v) AlanDaly 7 —
(J J Bridger) *sn pushed along and prom: hmpd and lost pl over 4f out: sn bhd* 33/1
000- **12** 7 **Silloth Spirit**[35] [3126] 6-8-9 30 ow1 (p) MickyFenton 3 —
(Mrs A M Naughton) *s.i.s: outpcd* 200/1
/06- **13** 5 **Dispol Charm (IRE)**[310] [626] 4-8-0 30 SilvestreDeSousa(3) 1 —
(D W Chapman) *sn outpcd* 66/1

1m 15.92s (-0.98) **Going Correction** -0.20s/f (Stan) 13 Ran SP% 118.7
Speed ratings (Par 97):98,92,90,87,83 81,79,75,75,73 72,63,56
CSF £20.23 TOTE £5.30: £1.60, £1.60, £3.20; EX 22.70.The winner was claimed by M. C. Chapman for £5,000.
Owner Colin Jarvis **Bred** Christopher John Strain **Trained** Musley Bank, N Yorks

FOCUS
They went a fair pace in this moderate claimer for horses who had not won a race before.

145 LITTLEWOODS BETDIRECT BANDED STKS 6f (F)
2:40 (2:42) (Class 7) 3-Y-0+ **£1,365** (£403; £201) **Stalls** Low

Form RPR
0-30 **1** **Ariesanne (IRE)**[2] [130] 5-9-0 40 AdrianTNicholls 11 51
(A C Whillans) *mde all: rdn over 2f out: styd on gamely* 16/1
440- **2** 1¼ **Auentraum (GER)**[29] [6639] 6-9-0 45 (b) TonyCulhane 4 47
(K McAuliffe) *hld up in tch: rdn over 2f out: hung lft ins fnl f: styd on* 6/1
160- **3** hd **Teyaar**[87] [6076] 10-9-0 45 AlanDaly 2 46
(M Wellings) *chsd ldrs: rdn over 2f out: styd on* 25/1
3-43 **4** 1¼ **Beamsley Beacon**[8] [90] 5-8-9 45 (b) AndrewMullen(5) 10 43
(M Dods) *a.p: rdn to chse wnr 2f out: no ex fnl f* 3/1[1]
52-3 **5** 2 **Christian Bendix**[16] [29] 4-9-0 45 (p) RobertWinston 5 37
(P Howling) *s.i.s: in rr whn snatched up over 4f out: nt clr run and swtchd lft over 1f out: nvr nr to chal* 4/1[2]
003- **6** hd **Polesworth**[32] [6607] 4-9-0 40 MickyFenton 1 36
(C N Kellett) *chsd wnr tl rdn 2f out: wknd fnl f* 16/1
564- **7** 3 **Radlett Lady**[52] [6446] 5-9-0 45 JimmyQuinn 7 27
(D K Ivory) *chsd ldrs over 4f* 9/2[3]
00-3 **8** shd **Madame Guillotine**[17] [14] 4-8-11 40 (p) PaulMulrennan(3) 8 27
(P T Midgley) *s.i.s: n.d* 16/1
000- **9** 1 **Blakeshall Quest**[38] [6559] 6-9-0 45 (b) TomEaves 6 24
(R Brotherton) *mid-div: rdn and dropped rr over 4f out: sn bhd* 16/1
300- **10** ½ **Juwwi**[22] [6677] 12-9-0 45 NCallan 14 22
(J M Bradley) *s.i.s: sn outpcd and bhd* 16/1
00-0 **11** hd **Midge's Girl (IRE)**[13] [53] 3-7-12 45 PaulFessey 3 22
(Mrs A Duffield) *mid-div: rdn over 3f out: wknd over 2f out* 33/1
0-00 **12** nk **Lakeside Guy (IRE)**[8] [90] 5-9-0 45 RobbieFitzpatrick 12 21
(M Appleby) *prom over 3f* 25/1
1-60 **13** ½ **King Marrakech (IRE)**[8] [90] 4-9-0 40 (p) MichaelTebbutt 9 19
(B P J Baugh) *s.i.s: hdwy over 3f out: sn wknd* 20/1

1m 16.81s (-0.09) **Going Correction** -0.20s/f (Stan)
WFA 3 from 4yo+ 16lb 13 Ran SP% 122.3
Speed ratings (Par 97):92,90,90,88,85 85,81,81,80,79 79,78,78
CSF £106.89 TOTE £17.90: £5.80, £2.40, £9.50; EX 99.80.
Owner James Baxter **Bred** Drumhass Stud **Trained** Newmill-On-Slitrig, Borders

FOCUS
A very moderate contest run in a modest time in which a return to front-running tactics did the trick for the winner.

146 TEXT "BETDIRECT" TO 88600 BANDED STKS 5f (F)
3:10 (3:10) (Class 7) 3-Y-0+ **£1,706** (£503; £252) **Stalls** High

Form RPR
4-01 **1** **Amanda's Lad (IRE)**[8] [90] 6-9-5 45 AdrianMcCarthy 5 58
(M C Chapman) *trckd ldrs: rdn to ld ins fnl f: r.o* 8/1
600- **2** nk **Byo (IRE)**[23] [6668] 8-9-4 50 RobertWinston 10 56
(P Howling) *chsd ldrs: rdn 3f out: sn lost pl: swtchd rt and hdwy over 1f out: r.o* 14/1
00-5 **3** ½ **Mirasol Princess**[16] [21] 5-9-4 50 FergalLynch 3 54
(D K Ivory) *sn pushed along and prom: rdn and ev ch ins fnl f: styd on* 16/1
021- **4** nk **Boanerges (IRE)**[31] [6613] 9-8-13 45 NCallan 13 48
(J M Bradley) *chsd ldrs: led over 1f out: sn rdn: hdd and unable qckn ins fnl f* 12/1
004- **5** nk **Muktasb (USA)**[51] [6462] 5-9-1 50 (v) PatrickMathers(3) 7 52
(D Shaw) *s.i.s: hdwy 1/2-way: styd on* 15/2[3]
05-0 **6** 2 **Hiamovi (IRE)**[15] [38] 4-9-0 46 (v) ChrisCatlin 14 41
(R M H Cowell) *chsd ldrs: led 1/2-way: rdn and hdd over 1f out: no ex fnl f* 25/1
363- **7** shd **Zazous**[21] [6685] 5-9-4 50 SteveDrowne 8 45
(J J Bridger) *prom: outpcd over 3f out: r.o ins fnl f* 9/1
42-1 **8** 1½ **Straffan (IRE)**[16] [29] 4-9-0 46 (p) DaleGibson 9 36
(J Hetherton) *prom: lost pl 4f out: n.d after* 8/1
0-23 **9** 1 **Blue Power (IRE)**[2] [130] 5-8-13 45 PatCosgrave 2 32
(K R Burke) *chsd ldrs: rdn over 1f out: wknd ins fnl f* 9/2[1]
21-0 **10** nk **Lizzie Rocket**[16] [24] 6-9-2 48 (v) JimmyQuinn 6 34
(J O'Reilly) *s.i.s: sn outpcd* 18/1
21-6 **11** hd **Largs**[16] [24] 6-8-12 47 (b) JasonEdmunds(3) 11 32
(J Balding) *edgd rt s: sn outpcd* 12/1
0-32 **12** nk **On The Trail**[8] [90] 9-8-13 45 (p) TonyCulhane 1 29
(D W Chapman) *chsd ldrs: rdn over 1f out: wknd fnl f* 6/1[2]
00-0 **13** ¾ **Lady Pekan**[16] [24] 7-9-2 48 J-PGuillambert 4 29
(P Howling) *led to 1/2-way: ev ch whn rdn and hung lft over 1f out: sn wknd and eased* 10/1
55-0 **14** 10 **Little Biscuit (IRE)**[7] [96] 4-8-10 49 PatrickDonaghy(7) 12 —
(K R Burke) *s.i.s and hmpd s: outpcd* 100/1

59.05 secs (-1.25) **Going Correction** -0.325s/f (Stan) 14 Ran SP% 123.6
Speed ratings (Par 97):97,96,95,95,94 91,91,89,87,86 86,86,84,68
CSF £118.44 TOTE £9.20: £3.70, £5.30, £4.40; EX 121.20.
Owner Eric Knowles **Bred** Mrs Helen Smith **Trained** Market Rasen, Lincs

FOCUS
A competitive banded sprint featuring the usual names.
Lizzie Rocket Official explanation: jockey said mare was slowly away from starting stalls
Lady Pekan Official explanation: jockey said mare was struck into

147 FIRST PAST THE POST AT BETDIRECT BANDED STKS 1m 4f (F)
3:40 (3:40) (Class 7) 4-Y-0+ **£1,365** (£403; £201) **Stalls** Low

Form RPR
2-22 **1** **Moon Shot**[6] [103] 10-9-4 50 NCallan 4 60
(A G Juckes) *trckd ldrs: led over 1f out: sn rdn and hung rt: styd on* 5/1[3]
01-2 **2** 1½ **Bulberry Hill**[16] [25] 5-8-13 45 SamHitchcott 10 53
(R W Price) *hld up: racd keenly: hdwy over 3f out: rdn over 1f out: styd on* 4/1[2]

523- **3** *1* **Liquid Lover (IRE)**[29] [6652] 4-8-9 40 .... RobertWinston 5 51
(W M Brisbourne) *chsd ldrs: led 3f out: sn rdn and edgd lft: hdd over 1f out: sn hmpd: styd on same pce ins fnl f* **6/1**

000- **4** *nk* **Figurative (IRE)**[257] [1552] 4-9-0 50 .... DeanMcKeown 14 56
(G A Swinbank) *dwlt: hld up in tch: plld hrd: rdn and edgd rt over 1f out: styd on* **9/4**[1]

00-1 **5** *7* **Beauchamp Star**[8] [92] 5-9-10 50 .... PaulFessey 6 51
(Mrs A Duffield) *chsd ldrs: rdn over 2f out: wknd fnl f* **5/1**[3]

66-3 **6** *1 ½* **Ice And Fire**[8] [91] 7-9-0 46 .... (b) MickyFenton 12 39
(J T Stimpson) *hld up: effrt and hung rt fr over 3f out: nt trble ldrs* **12/1**

040- **7** *7* **Lujain Rose**[162] [4266] 4-8-9 45 .... FergusSweeney 9 28
(N M Babbage) *hld up: rdn over 3f out: n.d* **66/1**

446/ **8** *3* **Dancing Bear**[407] [6832] 5-9-1 47 .... NeilPollard 13 25
(Lucinda Featherstone) *s.s: hld up: rdn over 4f out: n.d* **50/1**

060- **9** *2 ½* **Beaumont Girl (IRE)**[58] [6410] 4-8-9 45 .... AdrianTNicholls 11 19
(Miss M E Rowland) *prom over 8f* **50/1**

000- **10** *1* **Muqarrar (IRE)**[51] [6463] 7-8-10 45 .... (vt) PaulMulrennan(3) 7 18
(T J Fitzgerald) *chsd ldrs: led over 8f out: rdn and hdd over 3f out: sn wknd* **50/1**

345- **11** *¾* **Tinian**[32] [872] 8-8-13 40 .... MichaelTebbutt 2 17
(Miss Tracy Waggott) *chsd ldrs 9f* **50/1**

050- **12** *18* **Longing For Cindy (USA)**[21] [6681] 4-8-10 46 .... TonyCulhane 1 —
(W M Brisbourne) *led over 3f: rdn over 4f out: sn wknd* **20/1**

0 **13** *dist* **Cabrillo (IRE)**[8] [94] 5-8-13 45 .... (t) FergalLynch 3 —
(John A Quinn, Ire) *sn outpcd and bhd* **66/1**

2m 39.01s (-3.08) **Going Correction** -0.20s/f (Stan) **13** Ran SP% **121.7**
WFA 4 from 5yo+ 4lb
Speed ratings (Par 97):102,101,100,100,95 94,89,87,86,85 84,72,—
CSF £24.87 TOTE £5.30: £1.90, £1.90, £1.90; EX 20.20.
Owner Whistlejacket Partnership **Bred** Societe Aland **Trained** Abberley, Worcs
■ Stewards' Enquiry : N Callan one-day ban: careless riding (Jan 30)

FOCUS
An ordinary race notable for the gamble of Figurative which came unstuck. The first four came clear and the form looks solid for the grade.

148 BETDIRECT.CO.UK BANDED STKS 7f (F)
4:10 (4:12) (Class 7) 4-Y-0+ **£1,365** (£403; £201) **Stalls** Low

Form RPR

0-31 **1** **Sierra**[8] [94] 5-9-3 45 .... PaulFessey 1 56
(A W Carroll) *a.p: led over 1f out: drvn out* **5/1**[3]

025- **2** *1* **Aintnecessarilyso**[22] [6677] 8-8-11 45 .... (p) NCallan 11 47
(J M Bradley) *hld up in tch: rdn over 1f out: r.o* **16/1**

55-6 **3** *shd* **Paper Doll**[16] [27] 4-8-11 45 .... (p) PaulEddery 5 47
(B P J Baugh) *chsd ldrs: rdn over 2f out: r.o* **16/1**

44-0 **4** *shd* **Kumakawa**[15] [43] 8-8-4 45 .... DonnaCaldwell(7) 12 47
(D K Ivory) *dwlt: outpcd: hdwy over 1f out: r.o* **16/1**

00-0 **5** *1 ½* **Dexileos (IRE)**[3] [121] 7-8-11 45 .... (t) FergusSweeney 4 43
(David Pinder) *led 3f: w ldr tl led 2f out: rdn and hdd over 1f out: no ex ins fnl f* **80/1**

000- **6** *nk* **Binnion Bay (IRE)**[36] [6580] 5-8-11 45 .... (v) SteveDrowne 2 42
(J J Bridger) *trckd ldrs: led 4f out: hdd 2f out: sn rdn: styd on same pce fnl f* **18/1**

53-0 **7** *1 ¼* **Tally (IRE)**[16] [27] 6-8-11 45 .... RobbieFitzpatrick 7 39
(D G Bridgwater) *sn pushed along and prom: rdn over 1f out: wknd fnl f* **7/1**

222- **8** *nk* **Jacks Delight**[46] [6498] 6-8-11 45 .... MickyFenton 9 38
(C N Kellett) *chsd ldrs: nt clr run and lost pl over 4f out: n.d after* **7/2**[1]

00-5 **9** *1 ½* **Penel (IRE)**[16] [27] 5-8-8 45 .... (b) PaulMulrennan(3) 6 34
(P T Midgley) *s.i.s: hdwy u.p over 2f out: wknd fnl f* **7/1**

30-4 **10** *5* **Miss Glory Be**[8] [94] 8-8-11 45 .... (p) TonyCulhane 14 22
(Ernst Oertel) *hld up: effrt over 2f out: sn wknd* **8/1**

0-20 **11** *1 ¾* **Castanza**[8] [95] 4-8-11 45 .... JimmyQuinn 3 18
(M Wellings) *hld up: hdwy over 2f out: rdn and wknd over 1f out* **33/1**

00-2 **12** *shd* **Feast Of Romance**[16] [27] 9-8-11 45 .... (b) RobertWinston 8 17
(C R Dore) *hld up: rdn over 3f out: sn bhd* **4/1**[2]

200- **13** *21* **Taylor Maid**[29] [6650] 4-8-11 40 .... (v) ChrisCatlin 10 —
(R M H Cowell) *chsd ldrs over 4f* **33/1**

1m 30.0s (-0.80) **Going Correction** -0.20s/f (Stan) **13** Ran SP% **125.0**
Speed ratings (Par 97):96,94,94,94,92 92,91,90,89,83 81,81,57
CSF £85.73 TOTE £4.60: £2.30, £4.70, £5.50; EX 71.00 Place 6 £8,416.88, Place 5 £588.59.
Owner Wyck Hall Stud **Bred** Meon Valley Stud **Trained** Cropthorne, Worcs

FOCUS
A fairly open contest.
Penel(IRE) Official explanation: jockey said gelding was slowly away from stalls
T/Plt: £29,096.20 to a £1 stake. Pool: £39,857.85. 0.80 winning tickets. £7,971.57 carried over to Musselburgh today T/Qpdt: £403.30 to a £1 stake. Pool: £4,360.10. 8.00 winning tickets. CR

NAD AL SHEBA (L-H)
Thursday, January 19
OFFICIAL GOING: Dirt course - fast; turf course - good to firm

149a SHADWELL FARM CUP (H'CAP) (TURF) 7f 110y(D)
3:15 (3:15) (90-105,105) 3-Y-0+ **£41,569** (£12,790; £6,395; £3,197)

RPR

1 **King Jock (USA)**[29] 5-9-4 **102** .... TPO'Shea 12 113
(E Charpy, UAE) *hld up in rr: mid-div early st: prog 2 1/2f out: disp 2f out: sn clr: comf* **5/1**[2]

2 *4* **Azarole (IRE)**[33] [6601] 5-9-6 **105** .... JohnEgan 2 107
(J S Moore) *trckd ldrs: chal 2f out: led briefly: no ch w wnr: r.o* **9/2**[1]

3 *nk* **Pentecost**[177] [3823] 7-9-3 **101** .... SO'Gorman 5 103
(A M Balding) *hld up last: keen prog rail 3f out: swtchd wd 2f out: r.o wl: nrst fin* **9/1**

4 *1 ¼* **Berlioz (IND)**[25] 5-8-10 **95** .... (bt) RyanMoore 3 94
(S Padmanabhan, India) *hld up in rr: travelled strly early st: ev ch 2f out: r.o one pce* **14/1**

5 *4 ½* **Red Crescent (SAF)**[27] 9-8-4 **91** .... (bt) RPCleary(3) 1 82
(A Selvaratnam, UAE) *disp early: ev ch 3 1/2f out: fdd* **25/1**

6 *¾* **Amandus (USA)**[70] 6-8-10 **95** .... PatDobbs 8 83
(Doug Watson, UAE) *mid-div early on: n.d* **16/1**

7 *2 ¼* **Millennium Force**[166] [4162] 8-8-10 **95** .... TedDurcan 10 79
(M R Channon) *trckd ldrs: ev ch top st: nt qckn* **6/1**[3]

8 *1* **Little Good Bay**[89] [6025] 6-8-10 **95** .... (b) RichardMullen 11 77
(A Laird, UAE) *slowly away: racd rr on rail: prog 4f out to trck ldrs: fdd 2f out* **12/1**

9 *shd* **Egyptian (USA)**[29] 7-9-2 **100** .... PDillon 4 83
(R Bouresly, Kuwait) *disp early: ev ch 3 1/2f out: wknd* **7/1**

10 *3 ½* **John Falstaff (BRZ)**[133] [5083] 5-8-6 **90** .... (t) MAlmeida 6 66
(C Morgado, Brazil) *prom early on: wknd 4f out* **33/1**

11 *4 ¾* **Summoner**[29] 9-9-2 **100** .... (bt) RoystonFfrench 7 66
(A Al Raihe, UAE) *in rr early: wd home turn: nvr a factor* **10/1**

12 *21* **Harb (IRE)**[50] 6-8-8 **93** .... (t) RHills 9 16
(Doug Watson, UAE) *prom but wd: virtually p.u 4f out* **7/1**

1m 29.92s **Going Correction** +0.30s/f (Good) **12** Ran SP% **120.3**
Speed ratings: 114,110,109,108,103 103,100,99,99,96 91,70

Owner James Mearns Long **Bred** Kenneth L Ramsey & Sarah K Ram **Trained** United Arab Emirates

FOCUS
This looked like a pretty competitive handicap, but King Jock ran away with this and looked as though he would be well worth his place back in Pattern company at some stage this season.

NOTEBOOK
King Jock(USA) ◆, 9lb higher than when winning a similar race over course and distance for Dermot Weld last year, appeared to produce a career-best effort with an emphatic success. He has been placed in Listed company and, on this evidence, could well make his mark at an even higher level.
Azarole(IRE), formerly trained by James Fanshawe, made a pleasing debut for his new trainer when second on the Polytrack at Lingfield, and this was another decent effort. It would not be surprising if he prove up to winning a similar race.
Pentecost ◆'s trainer does very well with his foreign raiders and this was a very pleasing performance. He can do even better with the benefit of this first run in 177 days.
Millennium Force could not take advantage of a 7lb lower mark than when winning at last year's Carnival, but can be expected to come on for this first run in 166 days.

150a SHADWELL FARM TROPHY (DIRT) 7f (D)
3:45 (3:45) 3-Y-O **£11,337** (£3,488; £1,744; £872)

RPR

1 **Well Armed (USA)**[54] [6425] 3-8-9 95 .... RyanMoore 9 95
(C E Brittain) *nvr far away: disp into st: led 2 1/2f out: clr 1 1/2f out: easily* **11/1**

2 *3 ½* **Testimony (USA)**[75] 3-8-9 90 .... (t) KerrinMcEvoy 3 86+
(Saeed Bin Suroor) *in rr of main gp: no room 3f out: swtchd wd: r.o wl once clr: no ch w wnr* **9/2**[1]

3 *shd* **Nomoretaxes (BRZ)**[131] 4-9-4 90 .... KShea 12 85
(M F De Kock, South Africa) *racd in 3rd: trckd ldrs into st* **5/1**[2]

4 *1 ¾* **Wovoka (IRE)**[74] [6271] 3-8-9 100 .... JAHeffernan 11 81
(M R Channon) *mid-div: trckd ldrs into st: ev ch: 2f out r.o but no ch w wnr* **10/1**

5 *1 ¾* **National Captain (SAF)**[201] 4-9-4 98 .... TedDurcan 10 76
(A Laird, UAE) *mid-div: trckd ldrs early st: one pce* **5/1**[2]

6 *2 ¾* **Golden Acer (IRE)**[125] [5261] 3-8-9 99 .... PatDobbs 8 69
(Doug Watson, UAE) *prom early on: disp tl 2 1/2f out: fdd* **12/1**

7 *½* **Jet Express (SAF)**[190] 4-9-4 95 .... SRandolph 7 67
(H J Brown, South Africa) *n.d: sme prog 3f out* **12/1**

8 *1 ¾* **Villa Sciarra (IRE)**[39] 3-8-9 93 .... (t) MJKinane 4 64
(A Peraino, Italy) *trckd ldrs on rail: mid-div: home turn: nvr threatened* **16/1**

9 *shd* **Figjam**[95] [5920] 3-8-9 89 .... KJManning 16 63
(S Seemar, UAE) *prom early: wd into st: one pce: n.d* **33/1**

10 *shd* **Land Before Time (IRE)**[99] [5843] 3-8-9 .... TPO'Shea 2 63
(E Charpy, UAE) *in rr main gp: short of room after 3f: nt rcvr* **8/1**[3]

11 *3 ¾* **Emirates Gold (IRE)**[146] [4728] 3-8-9 94 .... PJSmullen 5 53
(Saeed Bin Suroor) *hld up in rr: nvr involved* **8/1**[3]

12 *2 ½* **Renderoc (USA)**[108] [5679] 3-8-9 90 .... JohnEgan 13 47
(J S Moore) *in rr main gp home turn: n.d* **9/1**

13 *¾* **Gadahar (USA)**[125] 3-8-9 75 .... RichardMullen 15 45
(S Seemar, UAE) *in rr of main gp ent st: nvr a factor* **25/1**

14 *1 ¼* **Krischera (USA)**[93] [5953] 3-8-9 66 .... GHind 6 42
(S Seemar, UAE) *trckd ldrs on rail tl top of st: fdd* **100/1**

15 *4 ½* **Global Leader (AUS)**[28] 4-9-1 65 .... (t) RPCleary(3) 14 29
(S Seemar, UAE) *a in rr* **66/1**

16 *2 ¾* **Getbuzzin**[244] [1845] 3-8-9 74 .... (t) RoystonFfrench 1 23
(M Al Muhairi, UAE) *slowly away: a in rr* **50/1**

1m 24.57s **Going Correction** +0.15s/f (Slow)
WFA 3 from 4yo 18lb **16** Ran SP% **133.7**
Speed ratings: 110,106,105,103,101 98,98,96,96,95 91,88,87,86,81 78

Owner Winstar Farm Llc **Bred** WinStar Farm Llc **Trained** Newmarket, Suffolk

FOCUS
A competitive contest, and a good performance from the dirt-bred former Lingfield winner Well Armed.

NOTEBOOK
Well Armed(USA) ◆ showed very useful form on turf as a juvenile, including when fourth in the Group Three Autumn Stakes, but it was not until he was switched to Polytrack that he got off the mark in a ten-furlong maiden. Dropped back significantly in trip on his debut in Dubai, he showed good early speed to hold a handy position and drew right away from his rivals in the straight. By dual Breeders' Cup Classic winner Tiznow, he is very much dirt bred and clearly looks capable of fulfilling his undoubted potential. With his stamina for further already proven, his ambitious trainer has every right to aim him at both the UAE 2000 Guineas, and Derby.
Testimony(USA), a mile winner on the dirt in his native US, ran respectably from his low draw on his debut for the Godolphin operation.
Nomoretaxes(BRZ), ex-Brazilian, ran well on his debut in Dubai off the back of a 131-day break.
Wovoka(IRE), a really tough juvenile who landed a Listed race in Ireland on his 16th start of last year, ran a fine race on his debut in Dubai.
Emirates Gold(IRE), a maiden winner and placed in Listed company on the turf as a juvenile, was his trainer's second string and was well held on his debut on dirt.
Renderoc(USA), a winner on Polytrack at Lingfield on his only previous start on sand, failed to prove as effective on this surface.

151a SHADWELL FARM (H'CAP) (TURF) 7f 110y(D)
4:15 (4:16) (90-105,105) 4-Y-0+ **£41,569** (£12,790; £6,395; £3,197)

RPR

1 **Kandidate**[61] [6378] 4-9-6 **105** .... EddieAhern 6 110
(C E Brittain) *trckd ldr: asked to cl 4f out: u.p top st: led 2f out: kicked clr* **9/1**

2 *3 ¾* **Tajseed (IRE)**[336] [411] 6-8-6 **90** .... RichardMullen 3 89
(A Manuel, UAE) *mid-div on rail: short of room top st and 2 1/2f out: swtchd 1 1/2f out: r.o* **18/1**

			RPR
3	¾	**Hidden Dragon (USA)**^{128} [5212] 7-8-6 **90** .... MJKinane 7 (J Pearce) *hld up in rr: trckd ldrs on rail: gap opened 2f out: r.o* **20/1**	87
4	½	**Pango**^{90} [6014] 7-8-12 **97** .... RyanMoore 2 (H Morrison) *settled in rr: 2nd last ent st: prog 3f out: no room 2f out: r.o once in clr* **13/2**^{3}	92
5	2 ¾	**Sabirli (TUR)**^{56} 5-9-5 **104** .... JamieSpencer 10 (C Kurt, Turkey) *slowly away: racd in rr: last top of st: r.o late* **7/2**^{1}	94
6	½	**Mercury Chief (SAF)**^{257} 5-8-6 **90** ....(t) KerrinMcEvoy 11 (H J Brown, South Africa) *slowly away: rr main gp: n.d: sme late hdwy* **16/1**	80
7	½	**King Marju (IRE)**^{41} [6530] 4-8-11 **96** ....(v^{1}) RoystonFfrench 5 (K R Burke) *led early: hdd 2f out: one pce afterwards* **14/1**	84
8	2	**Leicester Square (IRE)**^{50} 5-9-2 **100** .... TPO'Shea 4 (E Charpy, UAE) *prom on rail: ev ch early st: outpcd 2f out: one pce* **14/1**	85
9	1 ¾	**Alshawameq (IRE)**^{41} 5-8-8 **93** .... RHills 8 (Doug Watson, UAE) *racd 4th in centre: ev ch 3f out: nt qckn: fdd* **7/2**^{1}	73
10	½	**Fez (SAF)**^{217} 5-8-10 **95** .... TedDurcan 9 (A Laird, UAE) *in rr main gp: ev ch 3f out: short of room: swtchd wd: one pce and wknd* **9/2**^{2}	74
11	4 ¼	**Mandobi (IRE)**^{29} 5-8-13 **100** .... RPCleary$^{(3)}$ 12 (D Selvaratnam, UAE) *nt far away early but wd: ev ch 3f out: fdd* **14/1**	72

1m 30.35s **Going Correction** +0.30s/f (Good) **11** Ran SP% **121.9**
Speed ratings: 112,108,107,107,104 103,103,101,99,99 94

.

Owner A J Richards **Bred** Proton Partnership **Trained** Newmarket, Suffolk
■ Kandidate was the second leg of a double for Newmarket trainer Clive Brittain, who had earlier won with Well Armed.

FOCUS
This looked like a typically competitive Carnival handicap, but last year's UAE 2000 Guineas fourth, and English Guineas third, Kandidate, ran out an impressive winner off a mark of 105 without quite reproducing his best form.

NOTEBOOK
Kandidate ◆ acquitted himself with credit on the dirt at the last Carnival but is just as good on turf, if not better, and was third in last year's 2,000 Guineas. He defied top weight in pretty impressive fashion and, on this evidence, deserves his chance back in Group company.
Tajseed(IRE) has not won since taking an Irish maiden in October 2002 but, with the headgear left off on his debut for a new trainer, ran well off the back of a 336-day absence.
Hidden Dragon(USA), upped to his furthest trip to date on his debut for a new trainer, ran well off the back of a 128-day break and should continue to go well at the Carnival.
Pango ◆, making his debut in Dubai off the back of a 90-day break, acquitted himself with credit off a career-high mark and could be considered unlucky not have finished closer. He is just the sort to enjoy success at the Carnival.
Sabirli(TUR) ◆, a multiple winner in his native Turkey, can be considered unlucky not to have finished much closer and looks well worth following in the coming weeks.
King Marju(IRE) only has a maiden win to his name, and is not obviously well handicapped, but this not a bad effort in a first-time visor.
Alshawameq(IRE), 3lb higher than when winning over a mile at last year's Carnival, has since won easily off a lower mark on dirt. Returned to turf, he looked to have an obvious chance but ran disappointingly below form.

152a SHADWELL FARM STKS (H'CAP) (DIRT) 1m 1f (D)
4:45 (4:46) (90-105,105) 4-Y-O+ **£41,569** (£12,790; £6,395; £3,197)

			RPR
1		**Win River Win (USA)**^{54} 7-9-4 **102** .... JamieSpencer 1 (C Kurt, Turkey) *trckd ldrs: u.p long way out: produced to chal 2f out: hit front ins fnl f* **14/1**	112
2	1 ¾	**Dubai Honor**^{27} 7-9-0 **98** ....(e) PatDobbs 10 (Doug Watson, UAE) *mid-div: trckd ldrs into st: led 2f out: chal 1 1/2f out: r.o: nt pce of wnr* **9/1**	104
3	2 ¼	**Curule (USA)**^{41} 9-8-12 **97** .... GBirrer 13 (Doug Watson, UAE) *mid-div: asked to cl home turn: trckd ldrs ent st: short of room 3f out: r.o wl* **12/1**	98
4	3	**Parasol (IRE)**^{41} 7-9-1 **99** ....(vt) KJManning 2 (Doug Watson, UAE) *baulked at s: racd in rr main gp: r.o in st without threatening* **16/1**	95
5	hd	**Deodatus (USA)**^{27} 8-9-4 **102** ....(vt) TPO'Shea 9 (E Charpy, UAE) *in rr of main gp: asked to cl 5f out: r.o one pce: nvr threatened* **15/2**^{3}	98
6	2 ¼	**Elmustanser**^{27} 5-9-6 **105** ....(t) RHills 4 (Doug Watson, UAE) *trckd ldr into st: travelling wl: disp 3f out: wknd qckly* **6/1**^{2}	96
7	1	**Change The Grange (AUS)**^{72} 8-9-2 **100** ....(ve) ELegrix 7 (M C Tam, Macau) *rousted to ld early stages: led into st: chal 3f out: fdd* **14/1**	90
8	2 ¼	**Sapucai (ARG)**^{27} 6-8-10 **95** ....(bt) RyanMoore 14 (S Seemar, UAE) *in mid-div but wd: clsd on ldrs ent st: ev ch 3f out: one pce* **20/1**	79
9	¾	**Surbiton (USA)**^{27} 6-9-1 **99** ....(t) RoystonFfrench 8 (A Al Raihe, UAE) *trckd front 2 early st: wd into st: ev ch: one pce* **10/1**	83
10	15	**Roehampton**^{315} [600] 5-9-1 **99** ....(bt) SRandolph 12 (H J Brown, South Africa) *racd in rr: n.d: sme late prog* **9/1**	55
11	hd	**Clasp**^{63} 4-8-8 **94** ....(bt) TedDurcan 5 (A Laird, UAE) *racd in 4th: u.p ent st: wknd* **11/2**^{1}	48
12	½	**Gypsy Johnny**^{299} [734] 4-8-11 **97** .... RichardMullen 6 (A Laird, UAE) *slowly away: n.d* **20/1**	50
13	¾	**State Shinto (USA)**^{307} 10-8-10 **95** .... PDillon 3 (R Bouresly, Kuwait) *mid-div: short of room home turn: n.d* **16/1**	47
14	4 ½	**Billy Allen (IRE)**^{124} 5-9-6 **105** ....(t) SPasquier 16 (F Chappet, France) *mid-div early: nvr a factor* **20/1**	48
15	5 ½	**Kestrel Cross (IRE)**^{87} [6087] 4-8-9 **95** ....(e^{1}) MJKinane 15 (V Smith) *dropped in rr early on: nvr a threat* **12/1**	28
16	15	**Eclipse West (ARG)**^{474} [5967] 7-8-10 **95** ....(vt^{1}) PJSmullen 11 (S Seemar, UAE) *slowly away: n.d* **25/1**	—

1m 49.99s **Going Correction** +0.15s/f (Slow)
WFA 4 from 5yo+ 1lb **16** Ran SP% **129.1**
Speed ratings: 109,107,105,102,102 100,99,97,97,83 83,83,82,78,73 60

.

Owner Y Gelgin **Bred** James G Bell **Trained** Turkey

FOCUS
A competitive handicap and Win River Win did very well to score on his debut in Dubai from the inside stall.

NOTEBOOK
Win River Win(USA) ◆, a winner on the dirt in Turkey, gave a lot of trouble at the start and did very well to win from his inside draw on his debut in Dubai. On this evidence, he can rate a fair bit higher and must have a serious chance of following up.
Clasp can throw in the odd poor performance.
Kestrel Cross(IRE), ex-Irish, offered nothing on his debut for a new trainer on his first start on dirt.

153a SHADWELL FARM PLATE (H'CAP) (TURF) 1m 194y
5:15 (5:16) 4-Y-O+ **£66,133** (£20,348; £10,174; £5,087)

			RPR
1		**Iqte Saab (USA)**^{315} [596] 5-8-9 **102** .... PatDobbs 9 (Doug Watson, UAE) *racd in rr: rail in st: plld out 2f out: led 1f out: r.o wl* **8/1**	110
2	1 ¾	**Shanty Star (IRE)**^{329} [480] 6-8-8 **101** ow1 .... PDillon 7 (R Bouresly, Kuwait) *a.p: led into st: chal 3f out: r.o gamely to reclaim 2nd* **33/1**	106
3	½	**Shakis (IRE)**^{299} [737] 6-9-5 **112** ....(t) RHills 6 (Doug Watson, UAE) *mid-div: trckd ldrs into st: short of room: r.o once gap opened* **13/2**^{2}	116
4	1 ¼	**Boule D'Or (IRE)**^{61} [6378] 5-9-0 **107** .... NigelDay 8 (J Akehurst) *hld up in rr: slipped ent st then travelled wl: racd wd: r.o wl* **9/1**	108
5	shd	**Lundy's Lane (IRE)**^{50} 6-8-9 **102** .... RyanMoore 4 (S Seemar, UAE) *in rr of main gp: buffeted top of st: no room: r.o once gap opened* **9/1**	103
6	1	**Trademark (SAF)**^{50} 10-9-2 **109** ....(t) TedDurcan 13 (A Laird, UAE) *tacked across to rail: trckd ldrs into st: no room 2f out: r.o again* **15/2**	108
7	1	**Democratic Deficit (IRE)**^{96} [5906] 4-9-1 **109** .... KJManning 3 (J S Bolger, Ire) *in mid-div: travelling wl: short of room top st: swtchd wd: no room 1f out* **7/1**^{3}	106
8	1 ¼	**Terfel**^{27} 7-8-9 **102** ....(t) JohnEgan 12 (Daniel J Murphy, Singapore) *in mid-div: ev ch ent st: nt threaten* **16/1**	97
9	shd	**Bailador (IRE)**^{27} 6-8-4 **100** .... SaleemGolam$^{(3)}$ 15 (A Laird, UAE) *hld up last: nvr involved: sme late prog but short of room* **25/1**	95
10	½	**Excellento (USA)**^{41} 6-8-7 **100** ....(b^{1}) TPO'Shea 2 (E Charpy, UAE) *trckd ldrs on rail: ev ch top of st: nt qckn* **40/1**	94
11	1 ½	**Destinate (IRE)**^{27} 4-8-11 **106** ....(t) JAHeffernan 14 (I Jory, Saudi Arabia) *trckd ldr: ev ch top st: chal 2 1/2f out one pce* **20/1**	96
12	1	**Key Of Destiny (SAF)**^{299} [737] 8-9-6 **113** .... KerrinMcEvoy 5 (M F De Kock, South Africa) *prom: 3rd on home turn: disp 2 1/2f out: one pce* **14/1**	102
13	1 ¾	**Full Speed (IND)**^{25} 5-8-5 **95** .... SNarredu 10 (Pesi Shroff, India) *hld up in rr: n.d* **50/1**	84
14	5 ¾	**Wolf Whistle (SAF)**^{299} [737] 8-9-6 **113** ....(bt) KShea 11 (M F De Kock, South Africa) *racd mid-div but wd: ev ch ent st: fdd* **9/2**^{1}	88
15	5 ¾	**Tahreeb (FR)**^{50} 5-8-8 **105** .... RPCleary$^{(3)}$ 1 (D Selvaratnam, UAE) *disp into st: wknd rapidly* **25/1**	68

1m 49.46s **Going Correction** +0.30s/f (Good)
WFA 4 from 5yo+ 1lb **15** Ran SP% **119.2**
Speed ratings: 108,106,106,104,104 103,103,101,101,101 100,99,97,92,87

.

Owner Hamdan Al Maktoum **Bred** Shadwell Farm LLC **Trained** United Arab Emirates

FOCUS
A very high-class handicap.

NOTEBOOK
Iqte Saab(USA) did not really fulfil his potential when trained in Britain by John Dunlop, and found one too good on both his starts at the Carnival last season, but after finally consenting to go in the stalls, he proved good enough to defy a 315-day absence. He has always promised to develop into a Pattern-class performer but, given the length of time he had off, it is hard to know what he could be capable of next time.
Shanty Star(IRE), just as he did when campaigned on the dirt at last year's Carnival, ran better than anyone could surely expect for a horse who won the Queen Vase (two miles) as a three-year-old for Mark Johnston. Given he could place off a mark of 100 over this trip, just imagine what he could achieve over his optimum distance.
Shakis(IRE) ◆, down the field in the Group One Dubai Duty Free following some good efforts in handicap company at last year's Carnival, ran well off the back of a 299-day break and could have been even closer to his winning stablemate with better luck in running. A promising return and there should be better to come.
Boule D'Or(IRE) ◆, 8lb higher than when gaining the second of two wins at last year's Carnival, ran a fine race on his return to Dubai and this should put him right for further success.
Lundy's Lane(IRE) had no easy task off a mark 12lb higher than when winning a similar race at last year's Carnival, but did not get the best of luck in-running.
Trademark(SAF) fared best of those in double-figure stalls.
Democratic Deficit(IRE), last year's Craven Stakes winner who also won a Group Three in his native Ireland, had quite a task off a mark of 109 but may have been closer with a clearer run. Better can be expected in future.
Wolf Whistle(SAF) twice enjoyed success at last year's Carnival, but this was a disappointing return to action.

154a SHADWELL FARM SH MAKTOUM BIN RASHID AL MAKTOUM CHALLENGE R1 (GROUP 3) (DIRT) 1m (D)
5:45 (5:45) 4-Y-O+ **£75,581** (£23,255; £11,627; £5,813)

			RPR
1		**Blatant**^{82} [6146] 7-9-0 115 ....(t) RHills 6 (I Mohammed, UAE) *sn disp then led outrt after 1 1/2f: 2 l clr ent st: skipped clr easily* **9/1**	115
2	9 ¾	**Cherry Pickings (USA)**^{21} 9-9-0 110 ....(t) TedDurcan 7 (A Laird, UAE) *in rr of main gp: prog early st: r.o one pce* **12/1**	95
3	1 ½	**Lundy's Liability (BRZ)**^{299} [738] 6-9-0 115 ....(t) KShea 5 (M F De Kock, South Africa) *mid-div: trckd ldrs into st: wd: r.o: no ch w wnr* **13/8**^{1}	92
4	6 ¼	**Blue On Blues (ARG)**^{21} 5-9-0 101 ....(t) RyanMoore 1 (S Seemar, UAE) *mid-div on rail: u.p top st: one pce* **9/1**	80
5	1	**Kill Cat (IRE)**^{74} [6276] 5-9-0 107 ....(t) JamieSpencer 2 (A Peraino, Italy) *in rr of main gp: nvr threatened* **18/1**	78
6	¾	**Baldaquin**^{27} 9-9-0 104 .... PDillon 3 (R Bouresly, Kuwait) *slowly away: rdn to r in mid-div: n.d* **10/1**	76
7	nk	**Brunel (IRE)**^{131} [5142] 5-9-0 111 ....(bt) KerrinMcEvoy 9 (I Mohammed, UAE) *trckd ldrs out wd: 2nd into st: wknd* **6/1**^{2}	75
8	½	**Petit Paris (CHI)**^{35} 6-9-0 106 ....(t) JohnEgan 4 (I Jory, Saudi Arabia) *led early: hdd after 1 1/2f: trckd ldr into st u.p: fdd* **8/1**^{3}	74
9	¾	**Near Dock (GER)**^{96} [5915] 5-9-0 108 .... MJKinane 8 (V Smith) *settled in rr: nvr threat* **12/1**	73
10	16	**Party Boss**^{61} [6379] 4-9-0 108 .... EddieAhern 10 (C E Brittain) *mid-div early: sn dropped in rr: n.d* **20/1**	41

1m 36.71s **Going Correction** +0.15s/f (Slow) **10** Ran SP% **118.0**
Speed ratings: 109,99,97,91,90 89,89,88,88,72

.

Owner H R H Princess Haya Of Jordan **Bred** Sh Mohd Bin Rashid Al Maktoum **Trained** UAE
FOCUS
With the 2004 UAE Derby winner Lundy's Liability running below form on his return to Dubai, this was by no means a strong Group Three, but Blatant has form at the highest level and ran out an impressive winner on his debut for a new trainer.
NOTEBOOK
Blatant ◆ was not the most consistent when trained by Saeed Bin Suroor, but had shown glimpses of high-class form when fourth in the 2003 Queen Elizabeth II Stakes, second in the an Italian Group One that same year, and most recently when third in the 2005 running of the Queen Elizabeth II Stakes. Switched to dirt, and without the visor on his debut for a new trainer, he produced an effort pretty much up there with his best to run out a very comfortable winner. When part of the Godolphin operation he was just one of many, so he could enjoy being one of the stars of his new stable, and will surely have a major target on Dubai World Cup night. He could well develop into a contender for the World Cup itself, but has to prove his stamina for the extra two furlongs, and the Godolphin Mile is an alternative.
Cherry Pickings(USA) improved on the form he showed on his reappearance, but was still below the form he showed in handicap company at last year's Carnival.
Lundy's Liability(BRZ), winner of the 2004 UAE Derby and subsequently successful in the US, made a disappointing return to Dubai. He is better than this.
Near Dock(GER), ex-German and placed in a Group Two on turf last year, offered little on his debut for a new trainer on his first start on dirt. He always has the option of returning to turf.
Party Boss had proven his effectiveness on both Fibresand and Polytrack in England, and is a prolific winner, but he ran no sort of race on his first start on Dubai's dirt surface.

155a SHADWELL FARM (H'CAP) (TURF) (F&M) 7f 110y(D)
6:15 (6:15) 3-Y-O+ **£41,569** (£12,790; £6,395; £3,197)

RPR
1 **Clinet (IRE)**[116] [5492] 4-8-9 **98**.................... EddieAhern 11 100
(J W Hills) *mid-div: in rr of main gp: swtchd wd: r.o: led dying strides* **10/1**[3]
2 *nk* **Satwa Queen (FR)**[109] [5648] 4-9-6 **109**.................... ELegrix 4 110
(J De Roualle, France) *trckd ldr on rail: moved smoothly to ld 1 1/2f out: ct last strides* **10/1**[3]
3 *1/2* **Rock Opera (SAF)**[235] 4-8-6 **105**.................... TedDurcan 1 95
(A Laird, UAE) *nt far away: on rail st: short of room 2f out: r.o wl once in clr* **5/2**[1]
4 *nk* **Brindisi**[69] [6314] 5-8-4 **96**.................... RPCleary[(3)] 6 95
(D Selvaratnam, UAE) *hld up in rr: wd into st: r.o wl: nrst fin* **10/1**[3]
5 *1 1/4* **Quality Special (BRZ)**[29] 4-8-5 **100**.................... MAlmeida 5 91
(C Morgado, Brazil) *trckd ldrs: asked to cl 3f out: disp 1 1/2f out: r.o* **14/1**
6 *3/4* **Venus Arising (IND)**[46] 5-8-7 **96**....................(t) RyanMoore 2 91
(V Gaekwad, India) *nt far off pce: ev ch in st: n.m.r fnl 2f* **25/1**
7 *3/4* **Shersha (IRE)**[102] [5776] 7-8-9 **98**.................... PJSmullen 10 92
(Kevin F O'Donnell, Ire) *trckd ldrs but wd: u.p 2 1/2f out: nt qckn* **28/1**
8 *nk* **Emerald Beauty (ARG)**[299] [733] 6-9-0 **102**.................... KShea 9 96
(M F De Kock, South Africa) *racd in mid-div: travelled wl into st: short room: r.o* **11/4**[2]
9 *shd* **Festive Style (SAF)**[284] 6-8-6 **95**.................... MJKinane 7 88
(J Noseda) *hld up last: n.d* **14/1**
10 *4 3/4* **Imperial Ice (SAF)**[166] 4-8-5 **91**.................... KerrinMcEvoy 3 78
(H J Brown, South Africa) *hld up in rr: rail top of st: no racing room: n.d* **10/1**[3]
11 *1/2* **Queleden Candela (ARG)**[27] 5-8-6 **95**....................(t) JohnEgan 12 78
(I Jory, Saudi Arabia) *t.k.h: led early: chal 3f out: hdd 2f out: fdd* **12/1**
1m 32.54s **Going Correction** +0.30s/f (Good) **11** Ran SP% **119.9**
Speed ratings: 101,100,100,99,98 97,97,96,96,92 91

Owner Wood Hall Stud Limited **Bred** Mrs J Costelloe **Trained** Upper Lambourn, Berks
■ Clinet was the second leg of a double for English-based jockey Eddie Ahern, who earlier won on Kandidate.
FOCUS
A good, competitive handicap for fillies and mares.
NOTEBOOK
Clinet(IRE) held her form well and improved throughout 2005, so it was no surprise to see her take so well to racing in Dubai at the first attempt. She should not go up too much for this and could enjoy further Carnival success.
Satwa Queen(FR), three times a winner in France at up to ten furlongs last year, ran well over a trip shorter than may have been ideal, and on ground that would have been fast enough. She is clearly versatile and there could be even better to come.
Rock Opera(SAF) ◆, a multiple winner in her native South Africa, would have found this a tough enough ask on her debut in Dubai off a mark of 105, and emerges with plenty of credit in third.
Brindisi, ex Barry Hills, ran well on her return to Dubai.
Shersha(IRE), Irish trained, should be better for her first run in Dubai.
Emerald Beauty(ARG) was not the only De Kock horse to run below its best on the opening night of the Carnival but, in her defence, she did not get much luck in running.
Festive Style(SAF), formerly trained by a Dubai-based trainer, looked interesting given she was switched to a yard that did so well at last year's Carnival, but she was well held.

[119]WOLVERHAMPTON (A.W) (L-H)
Friday, January 20
OFFICIAL GOING: Standard
Wind: Fresh, half-behind

156 WOLVERHAMPTON-RACECOURSE.CO.UK AMATEUR RIDERS' H'CAP 1m 1f 103y(P)
1:10 (1:10) (Class 6) (0-58,58) 4-Y-O+ **£2,186** (£677; £338; £169) **Stalls** Low

Form RPR
32-2 1 **Augustine**[3] [134] 5-10-13 **55**.................... MrsMarieKing[(5)] 11 64
(P W Hiatt) *mde all: rdn out fnl f* **7/2**[1]
52-0 2 *1 1/2* **Pending (IRE)**[19] [8] 5-10-13 **57**....................(p) MrBMcHugh[(7)] 8 64
(R A Fahey) *slowly away: t.k.h: sn in tch: wnt 2nd over 2f out: rdn and no imp fnl f* **9/1**
035- 3 *nk* **Petite Paramour (IRE)**[20] [6701] 5-10-13 **57**.................... MissAlexWells[(7)] 1 63
(Miss Gay Kelleway) *trckd ldrs: rdn over 2f out: styd on fnl f* **10/1**
23-0 4 *1* **Bridgewater Boys**[10] [77] 5-11-0 **56**....................(b) MissARyan[(5)] 2 60
(K A Ryan) *trckd ldrs: outpcd over 2f out: styd on but no imp after* **8/1**[3]
00-2 5 *3/4* **Bavarica**[11] [73] 4-10-12 **57**.................... MrRBirkett[(7)] 13 60
(Miss J Feilden) *hld up: hdwy over 2f out: rdn and kpt on one pce fnl f* **10/1**
553- 6 *8* **Choristar**[221] [2539] 5-10-13 **55**.................... MrStephenHarrison[(5)] 4 42
(J Mackie) *trckd wnr tl rdn over 2f out: wknd over 1f out* **5/1**[2]
00-0 7 *2 1/2* **Sting Like A Bee (IRE)**[11] [73] 7-10-13 **57** ow2.................... MrGGoldie[(7)] 6 40
(J S Goldie) *outpcd and bhd fr 1/2-way: kpt on but nvr nr to chal* **33/1**
55-0 8 *hd* **Abbeygate**[11] [72] 5-11-3 **54**.................... MrsSBosley 7 36
(T Keddy) *in tch: rdn over 3f out: sn wknd* **12/1**
354- 9 *3* **Zonic Boom (FR)**[59] [4425] 6-11-7 **58**.................... MrSWalker 9 35
(Heather Dalton) *mid-div: reminders 1/2-way: sn bhd* **7/2**[1]
-140 10 *1/2* **Risk Free**[7] [107] 9-10-13 **57**....................(bt) MissABevan[(7)] 3 33
(P D Evans) *bhd whn c wd over 2f out: nvr on terms* **20/1**
010- 11 *hd* **Active Account (USA)**[53] [6448] 9-10-12 **54**..........(b) ChrisGlenister[(5)] 12 29
(J R Holt) *prom tl wknd over 3f out* **50/1**
00-0 12 *17* **Acorazado (IRE)**[9] [82] 7-10-11 **55**.................... MissCGrime[(7)] 10 —
(C P Morlock) *trckd wnr early: wknd qckly over 3f out: t.o* **50/1**
560/ 13 *1 3/4* **Fubos**[616] [2097] 5-10-11 **55**.................... MrAChahal[(7)] 5 —
(Lucinda Featherstone) *mid-div tl rdn and wknd over 3f out: t.o* **66/1**
2m 1.81s (-0.81) **Going Correction** -0.175s/f (Stan)
WFA 4 from 5yo+ 1lb **13** Ran SP% **121.2**
Speed ratings (Par 101):96,94,94,93,92 85,83,83,80,80 80,64,63
CSF £35.19 CT £296.44 TOTE £3.70: £1.60, £3.20, £3.40; EX 43.30.
Owner Phil Kelly **Bred** Darley **Trained** Hook Norton, Oxon
■ Stewards' Enquiry : Mrs Marie King one-day ban: failed to keep straight from stalls (Feb 2)
FOCUS
A moderate contest in which the front five pulled well clear of the rest. The form looks pretty sound.

157 WIN £2M @ FOOTBALLPOOLS.COM H'CAP (DIV I) 1m 141y(P)
1:40 (1:41) (Class 6) (0-60,63) 4-Y-O+ **£2,047** (£604; £302) **Stalls** Low

Form RPR
400- 1 **King Of Music (USA)**[41] [6548] 5-8-13 **55**....................(v[1]) TonyCulhane 1 62
(G Prodromou) *hld up in rr: hdwy on ins over 2f out: r.o to ld ins fnl f: rdn out* **9/2**[2]
61-2 2 *3/4* **New England**[16] [43] 4-8-12 **55**.................... RobbieFitzpatrick 8 60
(W M Brisbourne) *hld up: rdn and hdwy over 2f out: r.o strly fnl f to go 2nd cl home* **4/1**[1]
004- 3 *hd* **Iberus (GER)**[36] [6586] 8-9-4 **60**....................(p) GeorgeBaker 2 65
(S Gollings) *trckd ldr: rdn and led briefly 1f out: kpt on: lost 2nd nr fin* **14/1**
41-0 4 *1* **Captain Darling (IRE)**[9] [82] 6-8-13 **58**.................... EdwardCreighton[(3)] 3 61
(R W Price) *led tl rdn and hdd 1f out: no ex ins fnl f* **14/1**
00-1 5 *nk* **Burnley Al (IRE)**[9] [86] 4-9-6 **63** 6ex....................(b) PaulHanagan 9 65
(R A Fahey) *slowly away: sn mid-divisio: kpt on one pce ins fnl 2f* **7/1**[3]
03-4 6 *3/4* **Tregarron**[16] [35] 5-8-13 **58**.................... StephaneBreux[(3)] 6 58
(R Hannon) *a in tch: styd on one pce ins fnl 2f* **14/1**
210- 7 *1 1/4* **Monkstown Road**[32] [6621] 4-9-3 **60**....................(b) GrahamGibbons 4 58
(E S McMahon) *trckd ldrs tl rdn 2f out: one pce after* **15/2**
12-3 8 *nk* **Danettie**[9] [82] 5-8-13 **55**.................... RobertWinston 7 52
(W M Brisbourne) *hld up in tch: rdn over 2f out: no hdway after* **9/2**[2]
00-3 9 *hd* **Hand Chime**[11] [74] 9-8-11 **60**.................... LiamJones[(7)] 11 57
(Ernst Oertel) *in tch tl rdn and fdd ent fnl f* **16/1**
36-5 10 *6* **Drumroll (IRE)**[17] [18] 4-9-3 **60**....................(v) BrianReilly 5 44
(Miss J Feilden) *prom tl wknd over 1f out* **22/1**
000- 11 *8* **Edge Fund**[24] [6671] 4-9-1 **58**.................... TomEaves 12 25
(Miss Gay Kelleway) *a towards rr* **22/1**
/44- 12 *2* **Atlantic Ace**[310] [631] 9-9-4 **60**.................... PaulEddery 10 23
(B Smart) *bhd tl hdwy on outside over 4f out: wknd over 2f out* **20/1**
1m 50.39s (-1.37) **Going Correction** -0.175s/f (Stan)
WFA 4 from 5yo+ 1lb **12** Ran SP% **120.0**
Speed ratings (Par 101):99,98,98,97,97 96,95,94,94,89 82,80
CSF £22.42 CT £236.13 TOTE £6.30: £2.30, £2.40, £4.80; EX 50.50.
Owner Mrs B Macalister **Bred** B Laue **Trained** East Harling, Norfolk
FOCUS
A modest handicap and the winning time was slightly slower than the second division. The form looks generally sound, with the second, fourth and fifth all close to recent form.

158 HOLIDAY INN GARDEN COURT WOLVERHAMPTON (S) H'CAP 1m 4f 50y(P)
2:15 (2:16) (Class 6) (0-60,57) 4-Y-O+ **£2,388** (£705; £352) **Stalls** Low

Form RPR
41-2 1 **Regency Red (IRE)**[16] [42] 8-8-4 **50**.................... LiamJones[(7)] 10 58
(W M Brisbourne) *hld up: gd hdwy on outside over 3f out: led 2f out: clr whn edgd lft ins fnl f* **9/2**[2]
634- 2 *2* **Zaffeu**[20] [6701] 5-8-5 **47**.................... RichardThomas[(3)] 6 53+
(N P Littmoden) *hld up: hdwy whn denied clr run over 1f out: swtchd lft: fin wl to go 2nd nr fin* **7/2**[1]
250- 3 *shd* **Champion Lion (IRE)**[32] [6620] 7-8-13 **52**.................... NCallan 11 57
(J R Boyle) *mid-div: strly rdn and hdwy over 2f out: kpt on u.p: nvr nrr* **13/2**
00-0 4 *3/4* **J R Stevenson (USA)**[18] [13] 10-8-11 **50**..........(p) GrahamGibbons 3 54
(Ernst Oertel) *trckd ldrs: one pce fnl f* **14/1**
0-46 5 *nk* **York Cliff**[7] [103] 8-9-0 **53**.................... RobertWinston 7 56
(W M Brisbourne) *slowly away: in rr: hrd rdn 2f out: styd on: nvr nr to chal* **6/1**[3]
006- 6 *2* **Rasid (USA)**[21] [6691] 8-8-9 **48** ow1.................... J-PGuillambert 9 48
(C A Dwyer) *bhd whn outpcd 3f out: sme late hdwy: nvr on terms* **25/1**
50-4 7 *3* **Milk And Sultana**[6] [113] 6-8-8 **47**.................... JimmyQuinn 8 42
(G A Ham) *trckd ldrs: rdn and ev ch 2f out: wknd over 1f out* **12/1**
0-03 8 *3 1/2* **Sol Rojo**[11] [73] 4-8-10 **53**....................(b) RobbieFitzpatrick 1 43
(M J Attwater) *led tl rdn and hdd 2f out: sn wknd* **6/1**[3]
0-43 9 *2 1/2* **Eton (GER)**[7] [103] 10-9-3 **56**.................... AdrianTNicholls 5 42
(D Nicholls) *disp ld tl wknd over 1f out* **10/1**
004- 10 *1* **Je Suis Belle**[21] [6691] 4-8-12 **55**....................(b[1]) PaulHanagan 12 39
(Miss Gay Kelleway) *a towards rr: wl bhd fnl 3f* **16/1**
00-0 11 *dist* **Team-Mate (IRE)**[14] [55] 8-9-4 **57**....................(t) DarrenWilliams 2 —
(Miss J Feilden) *in tch tl wknd over 3f out: eased over 1f out: t.o* **33/1**
2m 40.45s (-1.97) **Going Correction** -0.175s/f (Stan)
WFA 4 from 5yo+ 4lb **11** Ran SP% **118.4**
Speed ratings (Par 101):99,97,97,97,96 95,93,91,89,88 —
CSF £20.78 CT £103.49 TOTE £6.10: £1.60, £1.80, £2.80; EX 26.60.The winner was bought in for 3,750gns. Zaffeu was claimed by Nigel I. P. Brown for £6,000.
Owner Mrs J M Russell **Bred** Patrick J Burke **Trained** Great Ness, Shropshire
■ Stewards' Enquiry : Richard Thomas two-day ban: careless riding (Jan 31-Feb 1)
FOCUS
A modest seller in which the early pace was fair, but the pace-setters did not get home and set the race up for the closers. Modest form, rated through the third.
Team-Mate(IRE) Official explanation: trainer said gelding had a breathing problem

159 BETDIRECT ON TENNIS CLAIMING STKS 5f 216y(P)
2:50 (2:51) (Class 6) 4-Y-0+ £2,730 (£806; £403) Stalls Low

Form RPR
401- 1 Graze On[103] [5754] 4-9-3 70 ....(v) GrahamGibbons 11 77
(J J Quinn) *trckd ldr: rdn to ld 1f out: drvn out* 10/1
4-60 2 1 Whitbarrow (IRE)[14] [58] 7-9-7 74 .... RobertWinston 7 78
(A W Carroll) *led tl rdn and hdd 1f out: kpt on but nt qckn ins* 9/2[2]
0-02 3 1½ Native Title[8] [96] 8-9-3 77 .... AdrianTNicholls 4 70
(D Nicholls) *s.i.s: in rr tl hdwy over 3f out: kpt on fnl f but nvr nr to chal* 7/2[1]
102- 4 ½ General Feeling (IRE)[21] [6689] 5-9-9 76 .... GeorgeBaker 13 74
(S Kirk) *slowly away: styd on appr fnl f: nvr nrr* 9/2[2]
0-40 5 1 Hurricane Coast[8] [100] 7-9-2 73 ....(v[1]) JamesDoyle[(7)] 3 71
(K McAuliffe) *trckd ldrs: rdn over 2f out: one pce after* 11/2[3]
006- 6 ½ Louisiade (IRE)[121] [5413] 5-9-5 61 ....(b) NCallan 10 66
(K A Ryan) *chsd ldrs: ridde over 2f out: sn btn* 6/1
55-0 7 3 Times Review (USA)[11] [67] 5-8-9 57 ....(v[1]) JimmyQuinn 5 47
(C A Dwyer) *towards rr: nvr on terms* 16/1
0-00 8 ½ Colonel Cotton (IRE)[8] [96] 7-8-10 78 ....(v) SilvestreDeSousa[(3)] 6 49
(D Nicholls) *mid-div: rdn and wknd over 2f out* 25/1
26/0 9 1¾ Winning Pleasure (IRE)[19] [4] 8-8-8 62 ....(b) JasonEdmunds[(3)] 12 42
(J Balding) *racd wd in tch: wknd over 2f out* 33/1
000- 10 2 Dematraf (IRE)[52] [6469] 4-8-4 57 .... ChrisCatlin 2 29
(Ms Deborah J Evans) *a towards rr* 33/1
006- 11 7 Easy Feeling (IRE)[21] [6689] 4-8-7 63 ....(b) StephaneBreux[(3)] 9 14
(R Hannon) *prom tl rdn and wknd 1/2-way* 33/1
000- 12 3½ Oeuf A La Neige[153] [4563] 6-9-2 63 .... DeanWilliams[(7)] 1 16
(G C H Chung) *s.i.s: a bhd* 66/1
130- 13 7 Far Note (USA)[29] [6658] 8-8-9 58 ....(bt) PhillipMakin 8 —
(S R Bowring) *outpcd thrght* 20/1

1m 14.37s (-1.44) **Going Correction** -0.175s/f (Stan) 13 Ran SP% 122.2
Speed ratings (Par 101):102,100,98,98,96 96,92,91,89,86 77,72,63
CSF £52.16 TOTE £12.70: £3.30, £2.10, £1.70; EX 67.60.The winner was claimed by P. A. Blockley for £12,000. General Feeling was claimed by Michael Mullineaux for £15,000.
Owner J R Rowbottom **Bred** Mrs Sandra Cooper **Trained** Settrington, N Yorks

FOCUS
A competitive claimer in which a couple were very well backed including the winner, but very few got into it. The runner-up is probably the best guide to the form.
Times Review(USA) Official explanation: jockey said horse hung right throughout
Far Note(USA) Official explanation: jockey said gelding hung right

160 PLAY NOW AT BETDIRECTPOKER.COM H'CAP 1m 141y(P)
3:25 (3:25) (Class 4) (0-85,85) 3-Y-0 £5,505 (£1,637; £818; £408) Stalls Low

Form RPR
01-1 1 Grand Jour (IRE)[6] [118] 3-9-0 81 6ex .... TonyCulhane 4 86
(K McAuliffe) *mde all: ridde over 1f out: drvn out* 5/2[2]
51-3 2 1 Moi Aussi (USA)[16] [34] 3-9-4 85 ....(b) JamieMackay 3 88
(Sir Mark Prescott) *trckd wnr to 6f out: remained in cl tch: wnt 2nd again over 1f out: no imp ins fnl f* 9/4[1]
4-13 3 1½ Fusili (IRE)[9] [87] 3-8-12 79 .... NCallan 7 79
(N P Littmoden) *trckd wnr 6f out: to over 1f out: rdn and no hdwy ins fnl f* 9/2[3]
5-23 4 nk Katchit (IRE)[4] [124] 3-8-7 77 .... EdwardCreighton[(3)] 6 76
(M R Channon) *in rr tl hdwy over 2f out: nt pce to chal* 9/2[3]
01-1 5 nk Reveur[15] [49] 3-8-4 71 oh2 .... JimmyQuinn 5 69
(M Mullineaux) *hld up in tch: rdn 2f out: no further hdwy* 9/1
105- 6 3 Archimboldo (USA)[127] [5252] 3-8-13 80 .... J-PGuillambert 2 72
(T Wall) *a towards rr: outpcd over 2f out* 14/1

1m 50.62s (-1.14) **Going Correction** -0.175s/f (Stan) 6 Ran SP% 112.4
Speed ratings (Par 99):98,97,95,95,95 92
CSF £8.58 TOTE £3.60: £1.90, £1.70; EX 11.60.
Owner John Reed **Bred** Islanmore Stud **Trained** Fernham, Oxon

FOCUS
A decent little handicap in which the majority came into the race in decent form. The winner had his own way out in front and the order changed little during the contest. He and the runner-up may be getting a bit high in the weights now. The race has been rated through the fourth.

161 BETDIRECT FREEPHONE 0800 211 222 H'CAP 1m 141y(P)
3:55 (3:56) (Class 4) (0-85,85) 4-Y-0+ £5,505 (£1,637; £818; £408) Stalls Low

Form RPR
500- 1 Bravo Maestro (USA)[119] [5436] 5-8-13 80 .... HayleyTurner 13 93
(N P Littmoden) *trckd ldrs: rdn to ld jst ins fnl f: r.o wl* 18/1
1-04 2 2 Atlantic Quest (USA)[7] [108] 7-8-12 82 ....(p) AmirQuinn[(3)] 9 91
(R A Harris) *trckd ldr tl led 2f out: rdn and hdd jst ins fnl f: nt pce of wnr* 28/1
61-3 3 1¾ Hits Only Heaven (IRE)[13] [64] 4-9-0 82 ....(be) JimmyQuinn 11 87
(J Pearce) *chsd ldrs: rdn and outpcd over 2f out: r.o fnl f* 4/1[1]
000- 4 3 Alfonso[112] [5588] 5-8-10 77 .... TomEaves 6 76
(I Semple) *mid-div: styd on ins fnl 2f: nvr nr to chal* 6/1
00-1 5 nk Wahoo Sam (USA)[14] [58] 6-8-12 79 .... NCallan 5 77
(K A Ryan) *led tl hdd 2f out: wknd ent fnl f* 5/1[3]
40-6 6 ¾ Takes Tutu (USA)[19] [7] 7-8-4 71 .... ChrisCatlin 12 68
(K R Burke) *hld up: hdwy over 2f out: styd on: no imp* 14/1
233- 7 1 Binanti[46] [6504] 6-9-2 83 ....(b[1]) GeorgeBaker 4 78
(P R Chamings) *hld up: rdn over 2f out: no imp* 9/1
10-4 8 1 Elrafa Mujahid[8] [101] 4-7-13 72 ....(b[1]) MarcHalford[(5)] 2 65
(Ernst Oertel) *nvr on terms* 33/1
23-6 9 2 Claret And Amber[14] [58] 4-8-12 80 .... PaulHanagan 8 68
(R A Fahey) *a towards rr and nvr on terms* 9/2[2]
21-1 10 3 Deeper In Debt[15] [50] 8-8-12 79 .... SimonWhitworth 10 61
(J Akehurst) *chsd ldrs tl wknd qckly over 1f out* 10/1
01-2 11 1¼ Trifti[14] [57] 5-9-4 85 .... FrancisFerris 7 64
(C A Cyzer) *hld up: lost t0uch over 2f out* 8/1
214- 12 9 Celtique[32] [6621] 4-8-5 73 .... JamieMackay 3 34
(M Wigham) *slowly away: a bhd* 20/1
00-0 13 2 Wistman (UAE)[8] [101] 5-8-3 73 .... SilvestreDeSousa[(3)] 1 29
(D Nicholls) *a bhd* 100/1

1m 48.27s (-3.49) **Going Correction** -0.175s/f (Stan)
WFA 4 from 5yo+ 1lb 13 Ran SP% 119.7
Speed ratings (Par 105):108,106,104,102,101 101,100,99,97,94 93,85,83
CSF £456.05 CT £1689.82 TOTE £26.50: £6.50, £9.80, £1.30; EX 373.20.
Owner Nigel Shields **Bred** Pacelco S A & Partners **Trained** Newmarket, Suffolk
■ A welcome winner on this track for Hayley Turner who had gone almost three years and 107 rides since her last winner here.

FOCUS
A very competitive handicap and the fastest of the five races run over the trip on the day, but the exposed runner-up limits the form. The pace was strong and very few got into it with the first three home prominent throughout.
Binanti Official explanation: jockey said gelding hung left throughout

162 TEXT "BETDIRECT" TO 88600 MAIDEN STKS 1m 141y(P)
4:25 (4:26) (Class 5) 4-Y-0+ £3,238 (£963; £481; £240) Stalls Low

Form RPR
000- 1 Orpendonna (IRE)[148] [4700] 4-8-10 61 ow1 ....(p) NCallan 6 63
(K A Ryan) *trckd ldr: led over 2f out: drvn out fnl f* 12/1
24-2 2 ½ Art Elegant[7] [110] 4-9-0 64 .... RobertWinston 2 66
(G A Swinbank) *trckd ldrs: wnt 2nd 2f out: ev ch ins fnl f: nt go by* 1/1[1]
4-2 3 3½ Melee[9] [84] 4-8-9 .... ChrisCatlin 3 54
(J Jay) *mid-div: rdn and hdwy 2f out: kpt on: no ch w first 2* 8/1[3]
03-0 4 3 Bold Trump[16] [41] 5-9-1 45 .... GrahamGibbons 8 52
(Mrs N S Evans) *mid-div: rdn over 3f out: kpt on but nvr nr to chal* 50/1
03-6 5 3 Lord Of Dreams (IRE)[7] [104] 4-9-0 67 .... FergalLynch 1 46
(D W P Arbuthnot) *led tl hdd over 2f out: wknd over 1f out* 4/1[2]
6 1¾ Discord[131] 5-9-1 .... PaulHanagan 5 42
(T H Caldwell) *towards rr: sme hdwy over 2f out: nvr on terms* 66/1
0/0- 7 ¾ Grey Admiral (USA)[55] [6432] 5-8-12 60 .... RichardThomas[(3)] 7 41
(B R Johnson) *towards rr: sme hdwy over 2f out: nvr on terms y* 50/1
-30 8 shd City Of Manchester (IRE)[8] [97] 4-9-0 .... AdrianTNicholls 12 41
(D Nicholls) *in tch: rdn 4f out: no hdwy after* 25/1
430- 9 1¾ Young Mick[21] [6693] 4-9-0 54 ....(b) JamieMackay 9 37
(G G Margarson) *a in rr* 9/1
040- 10 7 Rock Haven (IRE)[129] [5215] 4-9-0 60 ....(p) DaleGibson 10 22
(J Mackie) *a wl bhd* 14/1
03-4 11 nk Insignia (IRE)[16] [41] 4-9-0 48 ....(p) DarrenWilliams 13 22
(W M Brisbourne) *trckd ldrs: rdn and wknd over 3f out* 20/1
0- 12 18 Elleray (IRE)[21] [6687] 4-8-9 .... TonyCulhane 11 —
(J G Given) *mid-div: outpcd and bhd fr 1/2-way* 50/1
13 dist Superior Dream[73] 4-9-0 .... AdrianMcCarthy 4 —
(J W Unett) *a bhd: t.o* 100/1

1m 49.37s (-2.39) **Going Correction** -0.175s/f (Stan)
WFA 4 from 5yo 1lb 13 Ran SP% 122.4
Speed ratings (Par 103):103,102,99,96,94 92,91,91,90,84 83,67,—
CSF £24.11 TOTE £11.80: £2.20, £1.50, £1.90; EX 31.50.
Owner Mrs C Reilly & Mrs J Ryan **Bred** Lodge Park Stud **Trained** Hambleton, N Yorks

FOCUS
A weak maiden contested by horses of varying ability and very few got into it. They finished well spread out and there is little to get excited about outside the front three.
Elleray(IRE) Official explanation: vet said filly finished lame

163 WIN £2M @ FOOTBALLPOOLS.COM H'CAP (DIV II) 1m 141y(P)
4:55 (4:56) (Class 6) (0-60,60) 4-Y-0+ £2,047 (£604; £302) Stalls Low

Form RPR
00/0 1 Devil's Island[18] [15] 4-8-12 55 .... JamieMackay 9 66+
(Sir Mark Prescott) *hld up in tch: hdwy over 2f out: led ins fnl f: drvn out* 12/1
00/2 2 hd Kirkstone (IRE)[16] [32] 5-9-4 60 .... RobertWinston 10 70+
(J A Osborne) *hld yp: hdwy over 2f out: led over 2f out: rdn and hdd ins fnl f: kpt on* 7/2[1]
10-0 3 4 Blue Quiver (IRE)[11] [73] 6-9-2 58 .... SteveDrowne 7 60
(C A Horgan) *hld up in tch: hdwy on outside over 2f out: r.o fnl f* 5/1[3]
40-4 4 3 Rowan Warning[11] [74] 4-9-3 60 .... NCallan 13 56
(J R Boyle) *in tch: strly rdn over 1f out: kpt on u.p* 14/1
10-6 5 1 Barons Spy (IRE)[11] [73] 5-9-1 57 .... DarrenWilliams 12 51
(R J Price) *in tch: led over 2f out: hdd over 1f out: wknd ins fnl f* 22/1
400- 6 1½ Swell Lad[21] [6687] 4-9-2 59 .... TonyCulhane 5 49?
(S Gollings) *trckd ldr: chal 2f out: rdn and wknd over 1f out* 66/1
002- 7 ½ Danzolin[116] [5506] 5-8-13 55 .... JimmyQuinn 4 44
(W R Muir) *slowly away: nvr on terms* 14/1
40-0 8 hd Barzak (IRE)[19] [4] 6-8-10 55 ....(b) AmirQuinn[(3)] 2 44
(S R Bowring) *in tch: rdn over 2f out: sn btn* 15/2
60-3 9 1¾ Wrenlane[19] [8] 5-9-1 57 .... PaulHanagan 3 42
(R A Fahey) *prom early: sn mid-div: wknd wl over 1f out* 4/1[2]
260- 10 5 Buscador (USA)[39] [6564] 7-9-1 60 .... PatrickMathers[(3)] 1 35
(W M Brisbourne) *sn led: hdd over 2f out: wknd wl over 1f out* 6/1
600- 11 1¼ Best Game[18] [5880] 4-8-10 56 ....(p) DanielTudhope[(3)] 6 28
(D W Thompson) *in tch tl wknd wl over 1f out* 25/1
00-0 12 3½ Lobengula (IRE)[11] [74] 4-9-3 60 ....(p) TomEaves 11 25
(I W McInnes) *trckd ldrs tl rdn and wknd 3f out* 66/1

1m 50.15s (-1.61) **Going Correction** -0.175s/f (Stan)
WFA 4 from 5yo+ 1lb 12 Ran SP% 117.1
Speed ratings (Par 101):100,99,96,93,92 91,90,90,89,84 83,80
CSF £51.72 CT £242.70 TOTE £16.50: £4.60, £1.10, £2.30; EX 64.20 Place 6 £40.55, Place 5 £16.16.
Owner The Coursing Partnership **Bred** Miss K Rausing **Trained** Newmarket, Suffolk

FOCUS
Another modest handicap though the winning time was slightly faster than the first division and the front pair look better than the grade. The early leaders may have gone off too quick as the front three all came from off the pace.
Devil's Island ◆ Official explanation: trainer's representative had no expalanation for the improved form shown other than that gelding missed the break at Southwell last time out
T/Plt: £148.10 to a £1 stake. Pool: £42,538.00. 209.65 winning tickets. T/Qpdt: £8.70 to a £1 stake. Pool: £4,475.10. 377.90 winning tickets. JS

[156]WOLVERHAMPTON (A.W) (L-H)
Saturday, January 21

OFFICIAL GOING: Standard
Wind: Almost nil Weather: Fine

164 HOTEL & CONFERENCING AT DUNSTALL PARK AMATEUR RIDERS' H'CAP 5f 216y(P)
12:55 (12:55) (Class 5) (0-70,69) 4-Y-0+ £3,123 (£968; £484; £242) Stalls Low

Form RPR
5-52 1 Blue Knight (IRE)[16] [51] 7-11-5 67 ....(v) MrSDobson 9 78
(D Nicholls) *hld up: hdwy 3f out: rdn 2f out: hung lft and led over 1f out: r.o* 6/1[3]

04-4 **2** *1 1/4* **Louphole**[16] 44 4-11-4 **66** ... MrSWalker 10 73
(P J Makin) *hld up: hdwy 3f out: rdn and swtchd rt 1f out: r.o one pce* **4/1**[1]

00-0 **3** *1 1/2* **Sweetest Revenge (IRE)**[12] 71 5-10-7 **60** ... JackMitchell(5) 7 63
(M D I Usher) *hld up: rdn and hdwy over 2f out: kpt on same pce fnl f* **33/1**

230- **4** *hd* **Tyrone Sam**[99] 5880 4-11-2 **69** ... (b) MissARyan(5) 4 71
(K A Ryan) *hld up and bhd: rdn and hdwy over 2f out: c wd st: r.o ins fnl f* **6/1**[3]

005- **5** *1* **State Dilemma (IRE)**[53] 6455 5-10-12 **60** ... (v) MrsMMorris 5 59
(D Shaw) *led early: a.p: one pce fnl 2f* **20/1**

-661 **6** *1 1/4* **Kallista's Pride**[3] 137 6-10-12 **65** 6ex ... KylieManser(5) 8 60
(J R Best) *t.k.h: chsd ldrs tl lost pl over 3f out: kpt on fnl f* **8/1**

6-50 **7** *hd* **Norcroft**[7] 117 4-11-2 **69** ... (p) MrPCollington(5) 1 64
(Mrs C A Dunnett) *sn led: rdn over 2f out: hdd over 1f out: wknd ins fnl f* **11/2**[2]

02-6 **8** *1 1/2* **Nazaaha (USA)**[8] 110 4-10-9 **57** ... MissCHannaford 3 47
(A G Newcombe) *hld up and bhd: short-lived effrt on ins wl over 1f out* **16/1**

23-3 **9** *1/2* **Wainwright (IRE)**[16] 51 6-11-1 **66** ... MissFayeBramley(3) 2 55
(P A Blockley) *w ldr: ev ch over 2f out: sn rdn: wknd over 1f out* **4/1**[1]

40-0 **10** *5* **Silver Visage (IRE)**[20] 4 4-10-1 **56** ... MrRBirkett(7) 12 30
(Miss J Feilden) *prom over 3f:* **16/1**

/0-0 **11** *10* **White Ledger (IRE)**[5] 119 7-10-3 **58** ... MrLRPayter(7) 6 2
(R E Peacock) *prom over 3f* **80/1**

1m 15.52s (-0.29) **Going Correction** -0.125s/f (Stan) 11 Ran SP% **115.8**
Speed ratings (Par 103):96,94,92,92,90 89,88,86,86,79 66
CSF £29.22 CT £732.11 TOTE £6.00: £1.80, £1.70, £11.20; EX 34.70.
Owner M Barber **Bred** Mrs Ann Egan **Trained** Sessay, N Yorks
FOCUS
A typically modest amateurs' event, rated through the winner and fourth, and the form looks reliable enough.

165 BETDIRECT IN RUNNING SKYTEXT PAGE 293 MAIDEN STKS 5f 216y(P)
1:25 (1:28) (Class 5) 3-Y-O **£3,886** (£1,156; £577; £288) **Stalls** Low

Form RPR

1 **Hypocrisy** 3-8-9 ... J-PGuillambert 4 72
(S C Williams) *sn prom: rdn 2f out: led wl ins fnl f: r.o* **100/1**

22- **2** *hd* **Stonecrabstomorrow (IRE)**[56] 6435 3-9-0 ... JoeFanning 1 76
(P F I Cole) *led: rdn over 1f out: hdd wl ins fnl f: r.o* **1/2**[1]

0- **3** *2 1/2* **Came Back (IRE)**[75] 6281 3-9-0 ... MickyFenton 9 69
(J A Osborne) *hld up: sn mid-div: hdwy on ins 3f out: rdn 2f out: swtchd lft ins fnl f: no ex towards fin* **20/1**

5- **4** *1/2* **Keelings Donabate**[21] 6699 3-9-0 ... RobertWinston 8 67
(K R Burke) *w ldr: rdn and ev ch 2f out: one pce fnl f* **14/1**

5 *shd* **Ten Prophets (IRE)** 3-9-0 ... EddieAhern 6 67
(J A Osborne) *a.p: rdn over 2f out: one pce fnl f* **11/2**[2]

0 **6** *6* **Coastal Breeze**[14] 60 3-9-0 ... MichaelHills 3 49+
(J W Hills) *sn bhd: hdwy wl over 1f out: nvr nr ldrs* **7/1**[3]

0- **7** *2* **Sorrel Point**[43] 6531 3-9-0 ... JimmyQuinn 13 43
(H J Collingridge) *hld up in mid-div: rdn and wknd over 2f out* **200/1**

00- **8** *1* **Sea Of Serenity (IRE)**[227] 2396 3-8-2 ... KevinGhunowa(7) 12 35
(P A Blockley) *prom over 2f* **100/1**

9 *nk* **Beverley Bell** 3-8-9 ... TomEaves 11 34
(Miss J A Camacho) *s.i.s: hdwy wl over 1f out: sn swtchd lft: n.d* **33/1**

0- **10** *2 1/2* **Pedlar Of Luck**[74] 6290 3-9-0 ... SimonWhitworth 7 32
(A G Newcombe) *s.i.s: outpcd: a bhd* **100/1**

0- **11** *1 1/2* **Alice Amelia**[26] 6661 3-8-9 ... SteveDrowne 10 22
(C R Egerton) *hld up in mid-div: wknd over 2f out* **40/1**

00- **12** *9* **Hits Only Life (USA)**[21] 6694 3-9-0 ... FergalLynch 2 —
(J Pearce) *s.i.s: outpcd* **66/1**

0-0 **13** *hd* **Blue Danielle (IRE)**[12] 70 3-8-4 ... DuranFentiman(5) 5 —
(A D Brown) *prom: rdn after 1f: sn lost pl* **200/1**

1m 15.06s (-0.75) **Going Correction** -0.125s/f (Stan) 13 Ran SP% **116.8**
Speed ratings (Par 97):100,99,96,95,95 87,84,83,83,79 77,65,65
CSF £151.02 TOTE £108.30: £14.30, £1.10, £3.50; EX 185.80.
Owner Fighttheban Partnership I **Bred** Hyperion Bloodstock **Trained** Newmarket, Suffolk
FOCUS
There were plenty available at fancy prices in this maiden.

166 FOOTBALLPOOLS.COM MAIDEN STKS 1m 4f 50y(P)
2:00 (2:01) (Class 5) 4-Y-O+ **£3,238** (£963; £481; £240) **Stalls** Low

Form RPR

233- **1** **A Thousand Smiles (IRE)**[22] 6687 4-8-9 60 ... NCallan 6 67+
(M A Jarvis) *prom: led 7f out: rdn clr over 2f out: edgd rt fr over 1f out: eased towards fin* **1/1**[1]

06- **2** *8* **Dayoff (IRE)**[16] 6619 5-8-13 60 ... RobertWinston 9 50
(P D Evans) *rdn and hdwy after 2f: chsd wnr 6f out: rdn over 4f out: no imp fnl 3f: edgd lft ins fnl f* **7/1**[3]

5- **3** *1 1/4* **Tara King**[49] 6485 4-8-9 ... SamHitchcott 3 48
(A B Haynes) *hld up in mid-div: rdn and hdwy on ins over 3f out: one pce fnl 2f* **33/1**

4 **4** *1 1/4* **Candarli (IRE)**[15] 59 10-9-1 ... NeilChalmers(3) 7 51
(D R Gandolfo) *hld up in mid-div: hdwy 6f out: rdn over 3f out: one pce fnl 2f* **12/1**

63-4 **5** *shd* **Antley Court (IRE)**[9] 97 4-9-0 52 ... GrahamGibbons 1 51
(R Hollinshead) *led 1f: prom: rdn over 3f out: one pce fnl 2f: fin lame* **7/1**[3]

6 *1/2* **Real Chief (IRE)**[379] 8-9-1 ... EdwardCreighton(3) 5 50
(Miss M E Rowland) *hld up and bhd: hdwy 5f out: rdn over 3f out: no imp whn hung lft over 1f out* **100/1**

7 *1/2* **Mr Jawbreaker (IRE)**[160] 7-9-4 ... MickyFenton 10 49
(J T Stimpson) *s.s: bhd tl hdwy fnl f: nvr nrr* **40/1**

6-0 **8** *hd* **Esprit De Corps**[9] 97 4-9-0 ... JamieMackay 8 49
(Sir Mark Prescott) *hld up in mid-div: hdwy 6f out: rdn over 5f out: no imp fnl 3f* **7/2**[2]

0 **9** *7* **Rythm N Rhyme (IRE)**[9] 97 7-9-4 ... PaulEddery 2 38
(John A Harris) *hld up and bhd: hdwy over 5f out: wknd over 3f out* **100/1**

U20- **10** *16* **Giant's Rock (IRE)**[189] 1202 4-9-0 67 ... (b) RobertHavlin 11 12
(B J Llewellyn) *s.i.s: a bhd* **12/1**

0-0 **11** *dist* **Pips Assertive Way**[15] 59 5-8-13 ... PaulHanagan 12 —
(A W Carroll) *led after 1f: hung rt and hdd 7f out: wknd 5f out: t.o* **40/1**

2m 40.08s (-2.34) **Going Correction** -0.125s/f (Stan)
WFA 4 from 5yo+ 4lb 11 Ran SP% **122.4**
Speed ratings (Par 103):102,96,95,95,94 94,94,94,89,78 —
CSF £9.22 TOTE £2.00: £1.10, £2.50, £9.20; EX 13.30.
Owner N R A Springer **Bred** Barronstown Stud And Ron Con **Trained** Newmarket, Suffolk
FOCUS
The well-backed favourite turned this weak maiden into a one-horse race.
Antley Court(IRE) Official explanation: vet said gelding finished lame
Pips Assertive Way Official explanation: jockey said he had steering problems

167 BETDIRECT NO Q ON 08000 93 66 93 H'CAP 1m 141y(P)
2:30 (2:30) (Class 5) (0-75,75) 4-Y-O+ **£3,238** (£963; £481; £240) **Stalls** Low

Form RPR

145- **1** **Bazelle**[26] 6665 4-8-12 **73** ... PatrickMathers(3) 5 80
(D Shaw) *hld up: nt clr run on ins and swtchd rt over 3f out: rdn and hdwy over 2f out: r.o to ld last strides* **14/1**

22-6 **2** *nk* **Dragon Slayer (IRE)**[9] 101 4-9-0 **72** ... J-PGuillambert 2 78
(M J Attwater) *led: rdn 3f out: hdd last strides* **11/2**[2]

451- **3** *hd* **Connotation**[26] 6666 4-9-0 **72** ... EddieAhern 3 78+
(P W Chapple-Hyam) *a.p: rdn to chse ldr over 2f out: ev ch whn hung rt and flashed tail ins fnl f: kpt on* **4/1**[1]

-112 **4** *nk* **Speed Dial Harry (IRE)**[3] 101 4-9-3 **75** ... (v) NCallan 6 80
(K R Burke) *hld up: rdn and hdwy over 2f out: r.o ins fnl f* **6/1**[3]

06-0 **5** *3 1/2* **Nautical**[14] 64 8-8-13 **70** ... PaulHanagan 12 68
(A W Carroll) *hld up and bhd: rdn and hdwy wl over 1f out: nt rch ldrs* **11/1**

60-3 **6** *1 1/2* **Zalkani (IRE)**[17] 33 6-9-0 **71** ... MichaelHills 8 65
(B G Powell) *hld up and bhd: rdn and hdwy over 2f out: no imp fnl f* **13/2**

600- **7** *5* **Magic Merlin**[22] 6690 5-9-2 **73** ... (e[1]) StephenCarson 7 57
(W R Swinburn) *w ldr tl rdn and wknd over 2f out* **9/1**

064- **8** *5* **Carry On Doc**[151] 4656 5-8-10 **70** ... AdamKirby(3) 1 43
(Ernst Oertel) *hld up in tch: lost pl over 5f out: hmpd on ins over 3f out: n.d after* **11/1**

100- **9** *1/2* **Amazin**[96] 5941 4-9-1 **73** ... HayleyTurner 13 45
(N P Littmoden) *plld hrd: hdwy 6f out: wknd 3f out* **25/1**

50/0 **10** *3 1/2* **Honest Injun**[17] 50 5-9-0 **71** ... TonyCulhane 4 36
(A G Juckes) *chsd ldrs tl rdn and wknd 3f out* **66/1**

130- **11** *23* **Desert Lightning (IRE)**[146] 4783 4-9-1 **73** ... RobertWinston 9 —
(K R Burke) *hld up and bhd: short-lived effrt over 3f out: eased over 1f out: t.o* **9/1**

300- **12** *1/2* **Bentley Brook (IRE)**[46] 6520 4-9-1 **73** ... FergalLynch 11 —
(P A Blockley) *a bhd: t.o: fin lame* **14/1**

/6-0 **13** *2* **Camp Commander (IRE)**[16] 44 7-9-4 **75** ... (t) MickyFenton 10 —
(C R Dore) *chsd ldrs tl wknd over 3f out: t.o* **50/1**

1m 49.41s (-2.35) **Going Correction** -0.125s/f (Stan)
WFA 4 from 5yo+ 1lb 13 Ran SP% **120.3**
Speed ratings (Par 103):105,104,104,104,101 99,95,90,90,87 66,66,64
CSF £88.97 CT £310.82 TOTE £18.90: £4.40, £2.20, £2.10; EX 130.60.
Owner Mrs Jackie Cornwell **Bred** Loughbrown Stud **Trained** Danethorpe, Notts
FOCUS
An ordinary handicap.
Desert Lightning(IRE) Official explanation: jockey said gelding had no more to give
Bentley Brook(IRE) Official explanation: vet said colt finished lame
Camp Commander(IRE) Official explanation: trainer said horse had a breathing problem

168 BETDIRECT.CO.UK H'CAP 2m 119y(P)
3:00 (3:00) (Class 5) (0-75,71) 4-Y-O+ **£3,238** (£963; £481; £240) **Stalls** Low

Form RPR

0-41 **1** **Moon Emperor**[4] 129 9-9-4 **63** 6ex ... (b) EddieAhern 5 76
(J R Jenkins) *hld up in tch: led wl over 1f out: drew clr fnl f: readily* **7/1**[3]

3-1 **2** *5* **Caraman (IRE)**[15] 59 8-9-8 **67** ... RobertWinston 3 74
(J J Quinn) *led early: a.p: rdn over 1f out: r.o one pce fnl f* **6/1**[2]

2-11 **3** *1/2* **Little Richard (IRE)**[12] 72 7-8-10 **55** ... (p) AlanDaly 12 61
(M Wellings) *hld up: rdn and hdwy 2f out: one pce fnl f* **12/1**

/51- **4** *1* **I'll Do It Today**[21] 6701 5-8-9 **54** ... PaulHanagan 2 59
(J M Jefferson) *hld up in mid-div: rdn and hdwy on ins over 2f out: ev ch wl over 1f out: one pce fnl f* **11/2**[1]

01-0 **5** *3/4* **Mostarsil (USA)**[17] 37 8-8-13 **58** ... (p) IanMongan 8 62
(G L Moore) *hld up in mid-div: rdn and hdwy over 2f out: no imp fnl f* **16/1**

526- **6** *1/2* **Ocean King (USA)**[21] 6701 5-8-13 **58** ... FergalLynch 1 61
(W M Brisbourne) *hld up and bhd: hdwy 2f out: no further prog fnl f* **8/1**

113- **7** *1* **Monte Cristo (FR)**[44] 6368 8-9-9 **68** ... (v) ChrisCatlin 9 70
(Mrs L C Taylor) *a.p: ev ch over 2f out: rdn and wknd over 1f out* **8/1**

150- **8** *3 1/2* **Golden Boot**[126] 5291 7-9-5 **64** ... SamHitchcott 10 62
(A Bailey) *s.i.s: nvr trbld ldrs* **16/1**

50-0 **9** *3* **Bendarshaan**[17] 37 6-9-1 **60** ... SteveDrowne 4 57+
(R Hannon) *sn led: rdn and hdd wl over 1f out: sn wknd* **7/1**[3]

04-1 **10** *6* **Red Sun**[15] 55 9-9-4 **63** ... (t) DaleGibson 7 50
(J Mackie) *prom: rdn 4f out: wknd over 2f out* **8/1**

054/ **11** *5* **Sono**[594] 2409 9-9-3 **62** ... TomEaves 6 43
(P D Niven) *s.i.s: a bhd* **66/1**

43-2 **12** *3* **Peak Park (USA)**[20] 5 6-9-12 **71** ... NCallan 11 49
(P L Gilligan) *hld up in mid-div: rdn and hdwy over 5f out: wknd 3f out* **9/1**

3m 40.1s (-3.03) **Going Correction** -0.125s/f (Stan) 12 Ran SP% **119.0**
Speed ratings (Par 103):102,99,99,98,98 98,97,96,94,92 89,88
CSF £48.86 CT £503.72 TOTE £5.60: £1.80, £2.70, £4.50; EX 80.90.
Owner R M Ellis **Bred** Fares Stables Ltd **Trained** Royston, Herts
FOCUS
They went 11/2 the field in what had looked to be a wide-open handicap.
Peak Park(USA) Official explanation: jockey said gelding was unsuited by the track

169 BETDIRECT FREEPHONE 0800 211 222 H'CAP (DIV I) 7f 32y(P)
3:30 (3:31) (Class 5) (0-70,70) 4-Y-O+ **£2,914** (£867; £433; £216) **Stalls** High

Form RPR

4-11 **1** **Kindlelight Debut**[8] 106 6-8-11 **70** ... JamesDoyle(7) 4 83
(N P Littmoden) *hld up in mid-div: hdwy 2f out: rdn to ld 1f out: r.o wl* **4/1**[1]

41-2 **2** *2* **Holiday Cocktail**[12] 74 4-8-13 **65** ... J-PGuillambert 1 73
(S C Williams) *hld up and bhd: hdwy on ins over 2f out: squeezed through ent st: sn rdn: r.o one pce fnl f* **4/1**[1]

264- **3** *nk* **Winthorpe (IRE)**[78] 6243 6-8-4 **56** ... JimmyQuinn 5 63
(J J Quinn) *hld up in mid-div: hdwy over 2f out: rdn and ev ch 1f out: nt qckn* **9/2**[2]

23-1 **4** *1 3/4* **Kensington (IRE)**[16] 47 5-9-0 **66** ... (p) RobertWinston 10 69
(P D Evans) *hld up and bhd: hdwy 2f out: swtchd rt over 1f out: kpt on ins fnl f* **4/1**[1]

500- **5** *1* **Storm Chase (USA)**[109] 5687 4-8-10 **62** ... NCallan 3 62
(A P Jarvis) *chsd ldr: led over 2f out: sn rdn: hdd 1f out: wknd wl ins fnl f* **16/1**

300- **6** *3 1/2* **Soviet Threat (IRE)**[155] 4557 5-9-0 **66** ... FergusSweeney 12 57
(A G Juckes) *hld up and bhd: rdn over 2f out: nvr trbld ldrs* **33/1**

06-0 **7** *nk* **Patternmaker (USA)**[18] 23 4-8-11 **63**......................... SteveDrowne 7 53
(W Jarvis) *hld up in mid-div: hdwy over 2f out: rdn and wknd over 1f out* **13/2**[3]

6-14 **8** *nk* **Bollin Billy**[12] 67 4-8-10 **62**.. PaulHanagan 8 51
(R Brotherton) *bhd: rdn 4f out: n.d* **9/1**

005- **9** *5* **Danielle's Lad**[33] 6622 10-8-11 **63**.............................(b) FrancisFerris 2 39
(B Palling) *led: rdn and hdd over 2f out: hmpd ent st: sn wknd* **25/1**

00-2 **10** *nk* **Cherokee Nation**[18] 17 5-9-2 **68**..........................(p) TonyCulhane 6 44
(P W D'Arcy) *prom: rdn over 2f out: sn wknd* **14/1**

11 *19* **Lilly Hawk (IRE)**[25] 4740 5-8-7 **56** oh11 ow3...................(b[1]) AlanDaly 11 —
(Adrian Sexton, Ire) *t.k.h: sn prom: wknd over 3f out: bbv* **100/1**

1m 28.66s (-1.74) **Going Correction** -0.125s/f (Stan) 11 Ran SP% **121.8**
Speed ratings (Par 103):104,101,101,99,98 94,93,93,87,87 65
CSF £20.49 CT £77.18 TOTE £5.30: £1.90, £1.50, £2.50; EX 13.30.
Owner Kindlelight Ltd **Bred** Cheveley Park Stud Ltd **Trained** Newmarket, Suffolk
■ Stewards' Enquiry : J-P Guillambert one-day ban: careless riding (Feb 1)

FOCUS
This was much quicker than the other division with the time only fractionally outside the standard.
Lilly Hawk(IRE) Official explanation: trainer said mare had bled from the nose

170 WOLVERHAMPTON-RACECOURSE.CO.UK H'CAP 7f 32y(P)
4:05 (4:05) (Class 6) (0-60,60) 4-Y-0+ **£2,388** (£705; £352) **Stalls** High

Form RPR
000- **1** **Arnie De Burgh**[32] 6631 4-9-4 **60**.................................... JoeFanning 4 74
(D J Daly) *led 1f: chsd ldr: rdn over 2f out: led over 1f out: edgd lft ins fnl f: r.o wl* **15/2**

5-22 **2** *2 ½* **Soft Focus (IRE)**[4] 133 4-9-2 **58**..............................(b) EddieAhern 3 65
(J A Osborne) *hld up in mid-div: hdwy 4f out: rdn and ev ch over 1f out: nt qckn* **7/2**[1]

11-1 **3** *1 ¼* **Hollow Jo**[18] 21 6-9-4 **60**.. MickyFenton 11 64
(J R Jenkins) *sn prom: rdn over 2f out: kpt on ins fnl f* **8/1**

43-3 **4** *shd* **Sarraaf (IRE)**[15] 56 10-9-4 **60**.................................. TomEaves 1 63
(I Semple) *hld up in mid-div: n.m.r on ins over 3f out: hdwy over 1f out: kpt on ins fnl f* **11/2**[2]

00-2 **5** *½* **Doctor's Cave**[16] 44 4-9-4 **60**...................................(b) ChrisCatlin 2 62
(K O Cunningham-Brown) *broke wl: sn lost pl: rdn and hdwy over 2f out: one pce fnl f* **7/1**

1-04 **6** *1 ½* **Captain Darling (IRE)**[1] 157 6-8-13 **58**...........(p) EdwardCreighton[(3)] 8 56
(R W Price) *led after 1f: rdn and hdd over 1f out: wknd ins fnl f* **6/1**[3]

00-0 **7** *nk* **Sweet Namibia (IRE)**[16] 47 4-9-3 **59**......................... MichaelHills 12 57
(J W Hills) *nvr trbld ldrs* **22/1**

050- **8** *1 ¾* **Balerno**[93] 5997 7-9-4 **60**.. PaulEddery 7 53
(R Ingram) *nvr nr ldrs* **11/1**

00/0 **9** *½* **Vandal**[16] 44 6-9-4 **60**.. GeorgeBaker 10 52
(M Appleby) *a bhd* **33/1**

0 **10** *hd* **Rose Thistle (UAE)**[15] 59 4-9-4 **60**.............................. JimmyQuinn 5 51
(John A Quinn, Ire) *prom: rdn 2f out: sn wknd* **50/1**

040- **11** *1* **Taminoula (IRE)**[53] 6460 5-9-3 **59**............................ RobertWinston 6 48
(P Mitchell) *prom: lost pl over 5f out: rdn over 3f out: sn bhd* **7/2**[1]

1m 29.33s (-1.07) **Going Correction** -0.125s/f (Stan) 11 Ran SP% **127.1**
Speed ratings (Par 101):101,98,96,96,96 94,93,91,91,91 90
CSF £36.32 CT £232.09 TOTE £8.70: £2.80, £2.00, £2.80; EX 69.00.
Owner Gregory Way **Bred** Wyck Hall Stud Ltd **Trained** Newmarket, Suffolk

FOCUS
This tightly-knit handicap was significantly slower than the previous race.
Arnie De Burgh Official explanation: trainer said, regarding the improved form shown, colt was better suited by today's 7f trip and a more favourable draw
Taminoula(IRE) Official explanation: jockey said mare had lost its action

171 BETDIRECT FREEPHONE 0800 211 222 H'CAP (DIV II) 7f 32y(P)
4:35 (4:35) (Class 5) (0-70,69) 4-Y-0+ **£2,914** (£867; £433; £216) **Stalls** High

Form RPR
00-0 **1** **Tuscarora (IRE)**[18] 17 7-8-11 **62**.............................. RobertWinston 5 72
(A W Carroll) *hld up and bhd: rdn 3f out: hdwy on ins wl over 1f out: led ins fnl f: r.o wl* **6/1**

5-36 **2** *1 ¾* **Lincolneurocruiser**[9] 100 4-9-3 **68**............................. JimmyQuinn 11 73
(Mrs N Macauley) *hld up: rdn and hdwy over 2f out: c wd st: r.o ins fnl f* **7/1**

06-0 **3** *½* **Merdiff**[12] 74 7-8-11 **62**.. EddieAhern 9 66
(W M Brisbourne) *a.p: rdn over 3f out: kpt on ins fnl f* **11/2**[3]

0-12 **4** *½* **Alpaga Le Jomage (IRE)**[12] 71 4-9-0 **65**...................... ChrisCatlin 6 67
(M J Polglase) *led: rdn over 2f out: edgd rt and hdd ins fnl f: one pce* **9/2**[1]

6/ **5** *shd* **Luna Tacumana (IRE)**[203] 3154 6-8-12 **63**..................... TonyCulhane 2 65
(J J Lambe, Ire) *hld up in mid-div: hdwy wl over 1f out: nt qckn ins fnl f* **11/1**

/0-0 **6** *shd* **Flying Pass**[16] 50 4-8-8 **66**.. LiamJones[(7)] 7 68
(D J S Ffrench Davis) *outpcd in rr: hdwy on ins wl over 1f out: nt rchd ldrs* **33/1**

600- **7** *nk* **Celtic Thunder**[145] 4836 5-8-12 **63**............................. RobertHavlin 1 64
(T J Etherington) *prom: rdn over 2f out: one pce fnl f* **11/1**

041- **8** *½* **Snow Bunting**[54] 6449 8-7-11 **55** oh1....................... LeanneKershaw[(7)] 4 55
(Jedd O'Keeffe) *nvr nrr* **5/1**[2]

40-0 **9** *¾* **Marsad (IRE)**[18] 22 12-8-6 **57** ow1.................................. PaulDoe 3 55
(J Akehurst) *hld up: rdn and hdwy whn nt clr run fr over 1f out: nt rcvr* **16/1**

23/0 **10** *1 ½* **Shannon Arms (USA)**[20] 1 5-9-2 **67**............................... NCallan 10 61
(K A Ryan) *t.k.h: chsd ldr: rdn and ev ch 2f out: wknd 1f out* **6/1**

1m 29.48s (-0.92) **Going Correction** -0.125s/f (Stan) 66 Ran SP% **116.8**
Speed ratings (Par 103):100,98,97,96,96 96,96,95,94,93
CSF £47.71 CT £252.26 TOTE £8.50: £2.30, £2.40, £2.80; EX 55.20 Place 6 £42.88, Place 5 £15.97.
Owner Oliver Ryan **Bred** Yeomanstown Stud **Trained** Cropthorne, Worcs

FOCUS
This was the best part of a second slower than the first division.
Shannon Arms(USA) Official explanation: jockey said gelding hung right throughout

T/Plt: £62.20 to a £1 stake. Pool: £44,309.80. 519.40 winning tickets. T/Qpdt: £12.30 to a £1 stake. Pool: £2,788.70. 167.20 winning tickets. KH

[164]WOLVERHAMPTON (A.W) (L-H)
Monday, January 23

OFFICIAL GOING: Standard
Wind: Almost nil Weather: Fine but cold

172 BETDIRECT ON THE MASTERS SNOOKER APPRENTICE BANDED STKS 1m 1f 103y(P)
1:50 (1:51) (Class 7) 4-Y-0+ **£1,365** (£403; £201) **Stalls** Low

Form RPR
424- **1** **Nisr**[25] 6683 9-8-12 50...(t) RonanKeogh[(5)] 3 56
(Miss Gay Kelleway) *hld up in mid-div: hdwy 2f out: sn rdn: r.o to ld last strides* **8/1**

30-0 **2** *shd* **Glendale**[22] 8 5-9-3 50.. MarcHalford 5 56
(D K Ivory) *a.p: led over 3f out: rdn over 2f out: hung rt wl over 1f out: hdd last strides* **16/1**

/0-2 **3** *hd* **Basinet**[19] 41 8-9-3 50..(p) DuranFentiman 2 55
(J J Quinn) *hld up and bhd: rdn and hdwy on ins wl over 1f out: ev ch ins fnl f: r.o* **7/1**[3]

304- **4** *hd* **Ten-Cents**[47] 6522 4-8-13 50.. JamieJones[(3)] 8 55
(C F Wall) *hld up in mid-div: hdwy over 3f out: rdn over 2f out: ev ch ins fnl f: r.o* **11/4**[1]

060- **5** *1 ½* **Vizulize**[24] 6693 7-8-10 50.. JackDean[(7)] 4 52
(A W Carroll) *hld up: rdn and hdwy wl over 1f out: kpt on ins fnl f* **16/1**

004- **6** *nk* **Larad (IRE)**[25] 6681 5-8-8 46......................................(b) JosephWalsh[(5)] 6 48
(J S Moore) *hld up and bhd: hdwy 5f out: rdn over 2f out: kpt on ins fnl f* **8/1**

215- **7** *¾* **Star Fern**[26] 6679 5-8-13 49.. JamesDoyle[(3)] 10 49
(M J Attwater) *hld up and bhd: rdn and hdwy on outside over 2f out: c wd st: one pce fnl f* **7/2**[2]

00-0 **8** *¾* **Dagola (IRE)**[19] 41 5-8-13 46.. GregFairley 13 45
(C A Dwyer) *prom tl rdn and wknd 2f out* **33/1**

50-0 **9** *hd* **Adobe**[19] 41 11-8-12 48... LiamJones[(3)] 1 46
(W M Brisbourne) *hld up in tch: rdn and ev ch over 1f out: wknd ins fnl f* **12/1**

61-5 **10** *nk* **Kentucky Bullet (USA)**[12] 92 10-8-9 47.............. JamesMillman[(5)] 7 45
(A G Newcombe) *a bhd* **12/1**

400- **11** *1 ¼* **Expression Echo (IRE)**[39] 6583 4-8-11 50........... ThomasO'Brien[(5)] 11 45
(A G Newcombe) *s.i.s: sme hdwy over 6f out: rdn over 3f out: sn wknd* **66/1**

00/ **12** *1 ½* **Darling River (FR)**[452] 6452 7-9-0 50......................... JamesO'Reilly[(3)] 9 43
(R Brotherton) *led 1f: prom: rdn over 2f out: wknd over 1f out* **100/1**

060- **13** *½* **Rock Concert**[305] 697 8-9-0 47....................................... MarkLawson 12 39
(I W McInnes) *led after 1f: hdd over 3f out: sn rdn: wknd wl over 1f out* **66/1**

2m 4.10s (1.48) **Going Correction** -0.15s/f (Stan)
WFA 4 from 5yo+ 1lb 13 Ran SP% **117.7**
Speed ratings (Par 97):87,86,86,86,85 84,84,83,83,83 82,80,80
CSF £125.15 TOTE £10.40: £2.20, £4.90, £2.50; EX 111.10.
Owner W R B Racing 52 (wrbracing.com) **Bred** Downclose Stud **Trained** Exning, Suffolk
■ Stewards' Enquiry : Ronan Keogh two-day ban: used whip with excessive frequency and without giving time to respond (Feb 3-4)

FOCUS
A very slow time, even for a banded race. The third sets the standard but the form does not look particularly reliable.
Vizulize Official explanation: vet said mare returned lame behind

173 WOLVERHAMPTON-RACECOURSE.CO.UK MAIDEN CLAIMING STKS 1m 1f 103y(P)
2:25 (2:26) (Class 7) 4-Y-0+ **£1,365** (£403; £201) **Stalls** Low

Form RPR
30-0 **1** **Young Mick**[3] 162 4-8-11 54....................................(v[1]) RobertWinston 11 60
(G G Margarson) *hld up in mid-div: hdwy 3f out: sn rdn: led ins fnl f: r.o wl* **6/1**[3]

32-0 **2** *3 ½* **Swords**[16] 63 4-8-11 49.. TonyCulhane 12 53
(P Howling) *hld up and bhd: hdwy over 4f out: sn rdn: led 1f out: hdd and one pce ins fnl* **8/1**

30-6 **3** *1* **Shaheer (IRE)**[13] 78 4-8-12 50 ow1................................ FergalLynch 6 52
(P Howling) *hld up and bhd: rdn and hdwy wl over 1f out: styd on wl towards fin* **12/1**

246- **4** *shd* **Silsong (USA)**[25] 6681 4-8-6 47....................................(b) PaulHanagan 8 46
(Miss Gay Kelleway) *led: rdn 3f out: hdd 1f out: one pce* **5/1**[2]

00-5 **5** *1 ¼* **Noble Mind**[13] 78 5-8-12 57..(p) SteveDrowne 4 49
(P G Murphy) *prom: rdn and lost pl 4f out: rallied wl over 1f out: styd on fnl f* **16/1**

600- **6** *2* **Intended**[42] 6567 4-8-6 49..(t) MartinDwyer 5 40
(A M Balding) *hld up and bhd: rdn and hdwy wl over 1f out: no further prog fnl f* **9/1**

-000 **7** *3 ½* **Chairman Rick (IRE)**[4] 143 4-8-11 49...................(v) AdrianTNicholls 10 38
(D Nicholls) *s.i.s: hdwy 6f out: wnt 2nd over 4f out: rdn over 3f out: wknd over 2f out* **25/1**

003- **8** *2* **Debs Broughton**[35] 6615 4-8-6 45.................................. DavidMcCabe 7 29
(W J Musson) *nvr nr ldrs* **14/1**

534- **9** *hd* **Nebraska City**[63] 6398 5-8-12 45.................................. TonyHamilton 13 34
(D W Thompson) *prom tl rdn and wknd over 2f out* **40/1**

3-6 **10** *nk* **Level Par (IRE)**[19] 42 6-8-8 45...............................(t) RobbieFitzpatrick 1 29
(J A Supple) *hld up in mid-div: nt clr run on ins and lost pl over 3f out: n.d after* **6/1**[3]

5- **11** *2* **Tuckerman**[22] 5896 5-8-12 .... EddieAhern 2 30
(F J Bowles, Ire) *prom: rdn 4f out: sn wknd* **7/2**[1]

005- **12** *¾* **Crux**[26] 6675 4-8-5 45.. DeanMcKeown 3 22
(C W Thornton) *hld up in mid-div: rdn 3f out: wknd wl over 1f out* **25/1**

00- **13** *18* **Billy's Brother**[26] 6675 4-8-11 ....(b[1]) HayleyTurner 9 —
(M A Buckley) *chsd ldr tl over 4f out: sn rdn: wknd 3f out* **100/1**

2m 1.17s (-1.45) **Going Correction** -0.15s/f (Stan)
WFA 4 from 5yo+ 1lb 13 Ran SP% **119.9**
Speed ratings (Par 97):100,96,96,95,94 93,89,88,87,87 85,85,69
CSF £52.06 TOTE £8.60: £2.70, £2.30, £3.30; EX 50.60.The winner was the subject of a friendly claim.
Owner M F Kentish **Bred** M F Kentish **Trained** Newmarket, Suffolk

FOCUS
A weak race won in good style by Young Mick. The form looks surprisingly sound, however, with most of the first seven close to form, an exception being the sixth.
Silsong(USA) Official explanation: jockey said filly became unbalanced close home

174 CLASSICVALUEPOOLS.COM BANDED STKS — 2m 119y(P)
2:55 (2:56) (Class 7) 4-Y-0+ £1,365 (£403; £201) Stalls Low

Form RPR

-431 **1** **Mister Completely (IRE)**^{5} [141] 5-9-5 45 EdwardCreighton$^{(3)}$ 9 60+
(Miss Sheena West) *hld up and bhd: stdy hdwy over 5f out: led over 2f out: rdn over 1f out: styd on wl* 9/2^{2}

43-0 **2** 2 **Mustang Ali (IRE)**^{9} [116] 5-9-4 47 (b) TonyCulhane 5 53
(Dr J R J Naylor) *hld up and bhd: hdwy 3f out: rdn and ev ch 2f out: edgd rt fr over 1f out: nt qckn* 6/1^{3}

40-3 **3** 1½ **Lake Wakatipu**^{17} [59] 4-9-0 50 DeanMcKeown 10 54
(M Mullineaux) *hld up and bhd: rdn and hdwy over 2f out: edgd lft over 1f out: one pce* 14/1

042- **4** nk **Lysander's Quest (IRE)**^{35} [6612] 8-9-3 46 EddieAhern 11 50
(R Ingram) *hld up in mid-div: rdn and hdwy over 2f out: one pce fnl f* 5/2^{1}

30-5 **5** 1¾ **Makarim (IRE)**^{17} [52] 10-9-2 45 (p) GeorgeBaker 2 47
(M R Bosley) *prom: rdn over 2f out: wknd ins fnl f* 15/2

61-2 **6** 5 **Tharua (IRE)**^{12} [91] 4-8-9 48 (v) AdamKirby$^{(3)}$ 7 44
(Ernst Oertel) *hld up in mid-div: nt clr run over 2f out: styd on fr over 1f out: n.d* 6/1^{3}

064- **7** 1 **Gaelic Roulette (IRE)**^{151} [4229] 6-9-7 50 ChrisCatlin 8 44
(J Jay) *hld up in tch: rdn 4f out: wknd over 2f out* 16/1

06-0 **8** 3 **Karrnak**^{18} [48] 4-8-12 48 SimonWhitworth 13 39
(Miss J Feilden) *hld up in mid-div: hdwy 4f out: rdn over 2f out: wknd over 1f out* 25/1

00-0 **9** 2 **Tintac**^{19} [42] 5-9-2 45 PhillipMakin 12 33
(E J O'Neill) *hld up in mid-div: rdn and hdwy over 2f out: wknd over 1f out* 33/1

20-0 **10** 8 **The Beduth Navi**^{20} [25] 6-8-13 45 DNolan$^{(3)}$ 1 24
(D G Bridgwater) *led: rdn and hdd over 2f out: wknd qckly* 50/1

03-5 **11** hd **Magic Red**^{6} [28] 6-8-11 45 (b) MarcHalford$^{(5)}$ 4 24
(J Ryan) *prom: rdn over 3f out: wkng whn n.m.r over 2f out* 14/1

405- **12** ¾ **Viscount Rossini**^{270} [1333] 4-8-9 45 (p) GrahamGibbons 3 23
(E S McMahon) *w ldr: rdn over 4f out: wknd wl over 2f out* 33/1

600- **13** 5 **Key In**^{10} [2711] 5-9-3 46 (b^{1}) TomEaves 6 18
(I W McInnes) *hld up: hdwy after 5f: wknd 6f out* 50/1

3m 41.78s (-1.35) **Going Correction** -0.15s/f (Stan)
WFA 4 from 5yo+ 7lb 13 Ran SP% **120.0**
Speed ratings (Par 97):97,96,95,95,94 92,91,90,89,85 85,85,82
CSF £30.41 TOTE £5.20: £1.90, £2.90, £4.30; EX 47.00.
Owner Michael Moriarty **Bred** Eamonn Griffin **Trained** Falmer, E Sussex

FOCUS
A competitive contest likely to produce the odd winner. The time was decent for stayers here and the form has been rated at face value, with the second and third to form.
Karrnak Official explanation: jockey said gelding had no more to give

175 FIRST PAST THE POST AT BETDIRECT BANDED STKS — 1m 141y(P)
3:30 (3:31) (Class 7) 4-Y-0+ £1,365 (£403; £201) Stalls Low

Form RPR

063- **1** **Latif (USA)**^{91} [6078] 5-8-12 45 SamHitchcott 8 55
(Ms Deborah J Evans) *s.i.s: hld up and bhd: rdn and hdwy 2f out: led ins fnl f: r.o wl* 6/1^{2}

0-05 **2** 1½ **Indian Edge**^{10} [104] 5-8-12 45 FrancisFerris 9 52
(B Palling) *led: rdn over 2f out: edgd rt over 1f out: hdd and edgd lft ins fnl f: nt qckn* 14/1

503- **3** ¾ **Mr Belvedere**^{25} [6684] 5-8-9 45 (p) RichardThomas$^{(3)}$ 2 50
(A J Lidderdale) *w ldr: rdn over 1f out: r.o one pce fnl f* 8/1^{3}

50-3 **4** ½ **Young Kate**^{12} [94] 5-8-7 45 GregFairley$^{(5)}$ 1 50+
(J R Best) *a.p: rdn 2f out: nt qckn whn nt clr run wl ins fnl f* 9/4^{1}

0-40 **5** nk **Miss Glory Be**^{4} [148] 8-8-12 45 (p) EddieAhern 11 49
(Ernst Oertel) *a.p: rdn over 1f out: one pce whn n.m.r on ins wl ins fnl f* 8/1^{3}

000- **6** shd **Ringarooma**^{25} [6685] 4-8-11 45 (t) MartinDwyer 12 52+
(C N Allen) *s.i.s: hld up and bhd: hdwy over 1f out: nt clr run ins fnl f: swtchd rt and r.o cl home* 16/1

004- **7** 1 **Miss Monica (IRE)**^{26} [6675] 5-8-12 45 HayleyTurner 5 49+
(P W Hiatt) *hld up and bhd: hdwy on ins over 1f out: styng on whn nt clr run and eased wl ins fnl f* 16/1

04-0 **8** shd **Glenviews Oldport (USA)**^{17} [59] 4-8-11 45 (b^{1}) RobbieFitzpatrick 4 46
(Peter Grayson) *hld up: sn towards rr: rdn over 2f out: kpt on fnl f: nt rch ldrs* 14/1

0-50 **9** 1 **Wilford Maverick (IRE)**^{7} [121] 4-8-11 45 ChrisCatlin 13 44
(M J Attwater) *nvr trbld ldrs* 20/1

500- **10** ½ **Ballare (IRE)**^{35} [6611] 7-8-12 45 (v) FergusSweeney 7 43
(P J Makin) *hld up in tch: rdn 2f out: wknd fnl f* 66/1

50-0 **11** ¾ **Smirfys Party**^{19} [38] 8-8-9 45 (p) PaulMulrennan$^{(3)}$ 3 42
(W M Brisbourne) *plld hrd in mid-div: rdn and hdwy over 2f out: wknd wl over 1f out* 10/1

002- **12** 1¾ **Wanna Shout**^{47} [6524] 8-8-12 45 TonyCulhane 6 38
(R Dickin) *bhd fnl 3f* 8/1^{3}

00-0 **13** 3 **Guadiana (GER)**^{19} [43] 4-8-11 45 RobertWinston 10 32
(A W Carroll) *mid-div: rdn over 3f out: bhd fnl 2f* 14/1

1m 51.1s (-0.66) **Going Correction** -0.15s/f (Stan)
WFA 4 from 5yo+ 1lb 13 Ran SP% **125.5**
Speed ratings (Par 97):96,94,94,93,93 93,92,92,91,90 90,88,86
CSF £92.08 TOTE £8.90: £2.60, £5.20, £3.30; EX 93.30.
Owner Paddy Mason **Bred** Shadwell Farm LLC **Trained** Lydiate, Merseyside

FOCUS
A standard banded contest with the second to fifth all running close to their marks.
Ringarooma Official explanation: jockey said filly was unlucky in running
Miss Monica(IRE) Official explanation: jockey said mare was unlucky in running
Smirfys Party Official explanation: jockey said gelding hung right throughout

176 HOLIDAY INN GARDEN COURT TRI-BANDED STKS — 7f 32y(P)
4:00 (4:01) (Class 7) 3-Y-0 £1,365 (£403; £201) Stalls High

Form RPR

00-0 **1** **Tilen (IRE)**^{12} [93] 3-8-12 45 (b^{1}) MatthewHenry 5 50
(S Parr) *hld up in mid-div: rdn and hdwy wl over 1f out: sn edgd lft: edgd rt and led ins fnl f: sn edgd lft: r.o* 33/1

60-0 **2** 1¾ **Berties Brother**^{10} [110] 3-8-10 45 ow1 DNolan$^{(3)}$ 2 46
(D G Bridgwater) *led: rdn over 2f out: hung rt and hdd ins fnl f: kpt on* 12/1

00-6 **3** nk **Three Feathers**^{19} [39] 3-8-12 45 AlanDaly 9 44
(M Salaman) *chsd ldrs: sltly hmpd after 1f: rdn over 2f out: edgd lft over 1f out: r.o ins fnl f* 20/1

00-4 **4** nk **Genoa Star**^{12} [93] 3-8-7 45 ow2 (b) JamesO'Reilly$^{(7)}$ 4 45
(T J Pitt) *s.i.s: bhd tl rdn and hdwy wl over 1f out: r.o ins fnl f* 11/2^{3}

0-15 **5** nk **My Reflection**^{11} [102] 3-8-9 45 PatrickMathers$^{(3)}$ 3 46+
(D Shaw) *hld up in tch: n.m.r after 1f: rdn over 2f out: nt clr run on ins and swtchd rt over 1f out: kpt on ins fnl f* 7/2^{1}

00-0 **6** ½ **Bahhmirage (IRE)**^{14} [69] 3-8-12 45 (b^{1}) ChrisCatlin 7 41
(C N Kellett) *s.i.s: sn mid-div: rdn and lost pl over 3f out: late hdwy: nrst fin* 33/1

0-52 **7** 1 **Paris Power**^{12} [93] 3-8-12 45 (v) TonyCulhane 1 39
(D Morris) *led early: prom: rdn over 3f out: ev ch 1f out: wknd wl ins fnl f* 4/1^{2}

00-2 **8** nk **Chalice Welcome**^{19} [39] 3-8-12 45 RobbieFitzpatrick 6 38
(J A Supple) *chsd ldrs: rdn over 2f out: edgd lft fnl f: no imp* 8/1

00-4 **9** shd **Sanders Boy**^{19} [39] 3-8-12 45 DarrenWilliams 11 38
(J R Norton) *prom: rdn and ev ch 2f out: wknd ins fnl f* 12/1

00-0 **10** 2 **In The Fountain (IRE)**^{12} [83] 3-8-12 45 (v^{1}) RobertWinston 10 39+
(C A Dwyer) *s.i.s: bhd: hung lft and hdwy 1f out: no imp whn hmpd wl ins fnl f* 16/1

00-0 **11** 1¼ **First Byte**^{12} [83] 3-8-12 45 (v) EddieAhern 8 38+
(Miss D A McHale) *w ldr: rdn and ev ch 2f out: wkng whn bdly hmpd wl ins fnl f* 16/1

0-30 **12** 10 **Saxon Star (IRE)**^{12} [83] 3-8-12 45 (v) HayleyTurner 12 —
(M D I Usher) *plld hrd: a in rr* 11/2^{3}

1m 31.27s (0.87) **Going Correction** -0.15s/f (Stan) 12 Ran SP% **121.9**
Speed ratings (Par 91):89,87,86,86,85 85,84,83,83,81 80,68
CSF £391.03 TOTE £46.30: £9.10, £4.70, £6.00; EX 747.40.
Owner Tilen Electrics Ltd **Bred** Rory O'Brien **Trained** Carburton, Notts
■ A first winner for Stewart Parr, who took over the licence on the retirement of Jeremy Glover.

FOCUS
A weak tri-banded contest which took little winning. The form should prove reliable.
Tilen(IRE) Official explanation: trainer said, regarding the improved form shown, gelding was suited by the Polytrack and benefited from the fitting of blinkers

177 BETDIRECT.CO.UK BANDED STKS (DIV I) — 5f 216y(P)
4:30 (4:34) (Class 7) 3-Y-0+ £1,876 (£554; £277) Stalls Low

Form RPR

30-2 **1** **Trouble Maker**^{19} [38] 5-9-4 49 MartinDwyer 4 58+
(A M Balding) *a.p: rdn over 2f out: led jst over 1f out: r.o wl* 1/1^{1}

1-25 **2** 1½ **Jalouhar**^{13} [81] 6-8-10 48 SoniaEaton$^{(7)}$ 9 49+
(B P J Baugh) *hld up in mid-div: hdwy whn nt clr run and swtchd lft over 1f out: swtchd rt wl ins fnl f: nt rch wnr* 10/1

506- **3** nk **Nova Tor (IRE)**^{23} [6696] 4-9-5 50 (b) RobbieFitzpatrick 12 50
(Peter Grayson) *s.i.s: rdn and hdwy on outside wl over 1f out: edgd lft ins fnl f: r.o* 25/1

0-04 **4** ½ **Mulberry Lad (IRE)**^{7} [126] 4-9-3 48 DarrenWilliams 11 47
(P W Hiatt) *outpcd and bhd: rdn and hdwy over 1f out: edgd lft wl ins fnl f: nvr nrr* 25/1

50-3 **5** ½ **Park Star**^{13} [81] 6-9-1 46 RobertWinston 13 43
(D Shaw) *broke wl: sn mid-div: rdn and hdwy whn n.m.r jst over 2f out: one pce fnl f* 8/1^{3}

46-4 **6** 2 **High Swainston**^{13} [81] 5-9-3 48 PaulFessey 6 39
(R Craggs) *prom: rdn over 3f out: edgd lft jst over 2f out: sn wknd* 10/1

0-06 **7** nk **Wotavadun (IRE)**^{11} [102] 3-8-0 47 (be) AdrianMcCarthy 7 37
(K McAuliffe) *led: rdn and hdd jst over 1f out: wknd wl ins fnl f* 66/1

60-5 **8** 1¾ **Party Princess (IRE)**^{18} [46] 5-9-2 47 (v^{1}) DeanMcKeown 1 34+
(S Parr) *chsd ldr tl wl over 1f out: wkng whn bdly hmpd wl ins fnl f* 16/1

0-53 **9** nk **Mirasol Princess**^{4} [146] 5-9-5 50 (b^{1}) FergalLynch 2 34
(D K Ivory) *s.s: bhd: short-lived effrt on outside ent st* 6/1^{2}

020- **10** 2 **Taras Tornado**^{69} [6359] 3-8-0 47 JimmyQuinn 10 25
(J J Quinn) *a bhd* 14/1

/50- **11** 1½ **La Musique**^{172} [4109] 4-9-3 48 PaulHanagan 8 22
(P J McBride) *prom tl rdn and wknd over 2f out* 25/1

00-0 **12** 4 **Headland (USA)**^{22} [3] 8-9-5 50 (be) TonyCulhane 3 12+
(D W Chapman) *mid-div: rdn over 3f out: sme hdwy whn hmpd on ins jst over 2f out: nt rcvr: sn eased* 16/1

000- **13** 27 **Long Weekend (IRE)**^{48} [6516] 8-9-2 50 (p) PatrickMathers$^{(3)}$ 5 —
(D Shaw) *s.i.s: rdn over 3f out: a bhd* 50/1

1m 15.2s (-0.61) **Going Correction** -0.15s/f (Stan)
WFA 3 from 4yo+ 16lb 13 Ran SP% **127.0**
Speed ratings (Par 97):98,96,95,94,94 91,91,88,88,85 83,78,42
CSF £12.43 TOTE £2.20: £1.30, £3.30, £6.40; EX 15.50.
Owner Fred Yeung **Bred** Hamilton Nash Inc **Trained** Kingsclere, Hants

FOCUS
Trouble Maker won as expected and is probably a bit better than banded-class. The race has been rated through the runner-up but does not look rock solid.
Mirasol Princess Official explanation: jockey said he was unable to remove blinds in time at start
Long Weekend(IRE) Official explanation: vet said gelding bled from the nose

178 BETDIRECT.CO.UK BANDED STKS (DIV II) — 5f 216y(P)
5:00 (5:03) (Class 7) 3-Y-0+ £1,876 (£554; £277) Stalls Low

Form RPR

122- **1** **Beneking**^{24} [6693] 6-9-5 50 (p) ChrisCatlin 6 59
(D Burchell) *a.p: led 2f out: sn rdn: drvn out* 7/1^{3}

006- **2** ½ **Davids Mark**^{33} [6646] 6-9-3 48 EddieAhern 7 56
(J R Jenkins) *hld up in mid-div: hdwy over 3f out: rdn and ev ch ins fnl f: nt qckn* 5/1^{1}

506- **3** nk **Desert Light (IRE)**^{25} [6685] 5-9-2 47 (v) RobertWinston 4 54
(D Shaw) *hld up: hdwy wl over 1f out: sn rdn: hung lft ins fnl f: r.o* 11/2^{2}

000- **4** nk **Karashino (IRE)**^{34} [6638] 4-9-5 50 (b^{1}) PaulHanagan 8 56
(R A Fahey) *chsd ldrs: rdn over 1f out: kpt on towards fin* 25/1

020- **5** 1¾ **Cayman King**^{36} [6608] 4-9-5 50 PaulFessey 13 50
(R Craggs) *prom: rdn and ev ch over 2f out: wknd ins fnl f* 33/1

114- **6** ½ **Lady Hopeful (IRE)**^{25} [6686] 4-9-3 48 (b) RobbieFitzpatrick 1 47+
(Peter Grayson) *rdr slow to remove blindfold and s.s: hdwy whn nt clr run and plld out over 1f out: nrst fin* 5/1^{1}

04-5 **7** 1½ **Muktasb (USA)**^{4} [146] 5-9-2 50 (v) PatrickMathers$^{(3)}$ 11 44
(D Shaw) *mid-div: rdn and no hdwy fnl 2f* 8/1

22-0 **8** ½ **Gaudalpin (IRE)**^{20} [22] 4-9-5 50 (t) JimmyQuinn 5 43
(Ernst Oertel) *prom tl rdn and wknd fnl f* 10/1

006- **9** 1½ **Lady Vee (IRE)**^{49} [6507] 4-9-4 49 (p) TomEaves 3 37+
(P D Niven) *bhd: rdn over 2f out: short-lived effrt on ins wl over 1f out: eased whn btn wl ins fnl f* 16/1

0-04 **10** nk **Zorn**^{6} [127] 7-9-5 50 SteveDrowne 12 38
(P Howling) *led 2f: rdn and ev ch over 2f out: wknd wl over 1f out* 14/1

005- **11** 2½ **Scherzo A La Russe (USA)**^{39} [6585] 3-8-3 50 SimonWhitworth 9 30
(A G Newcombe) *s.i.s: a bhd* 40/1

The Form Book, Raceform Ltd, Compton, RG20 6NL

55- **12** *1 ¼* **Live And Dangerous**[35] [6615] 5-9-2 47 FergalLynch 2 23+
(D Carroll) *w ldr: led 4f out to 2f out: sn rdn: eased whn btn ins fnl f* **7/1**[3]

00-0 **13** *1 ¾* **Sundried Tomato**[6] [127] 7-9-5 50 (b) TonyCulhane 10 21
(D W Chapman) *bhd fnl 2f: b.b.v* **16/1**

1m 15.0s (-0.81) **Going Correction** -0.15s/f (Stan)
WFA 3 from 4yo+ 16lb **13** Ran SP% **121.6**
Speed ratings (Par 97):99,98,97,97,95 94,92,91,89,89 86,84,82
CSF £41.97 TOTE £5.50: £2.60, £2.40, £2.30; EX 48.60 Place 6 £2,750.00, Place 5 £684.13 .
Owner B M G Group **Bred** Helshaw Grange Stud And Mrs M Mason **Trained** Briery Hill, Blaenau Gwent

FOCUS
An ordinary but competitive banded sprint, slightly better than division one with the winner running to a similar level. The form looks solid.
Live And Dangerous Official explanation: jockey said mare lost its action but returned sound
Sundried Tomato Official explanation: jockey said gelding hung right
T/Plt: £6,145.70 to a £1 stake. Pool: £44,198.65. 5.25 winning tickets. T/Qpdt: £472.50 to a £1 stake. Pool: £4,342.40. 6.80 winning tickets. KH

143 SOUTHWELL (L-H)
Tuesday, January 24

OFFICIAL GOING: Standard
Wind: Nil

179 BETDIRECT ON TENNIS BANDED STKS 5f (F)
1:30 (1:31) (Class 7) 3-Y-O+ **£1,365** (£403; £201) **Stalls** High

Form RPR

21-4 **1** **Boanerges (IRE)**[5] [146] 9-8-13 45 RobertWinston 1 48
(J M Bradley) *trckd ldrs: hdwy 1/2-way: rdn tpo chal over 1f out: drvn to ld ins last: kpt on* **7/2**[2]

03-0 **2** *1 ¼* **Freshwinds**[19] [45] 4-8-13 45 DarrenWilliams 3 44
(S L Keightley) *cl up: led 1/2-way: rdn wl over 1f out: hdd ins last: no ex towards fin* **7/1**

050- **3** *shd* **Shirley Oaks (IRE)**[27] [6677] 8-8-13 45 AdrianMcCarthy 4 43
(Miss Z C Davison) *in tch tl rdn along and outpcd 1/2-way: swtchd lft and hdwy wl over 1f out: styd on u.p ins last: nrst fin* **50/1**

-434 **4** *½* **Beamsley Beacon**[5] [145] 5-8-13 45 (b) PhillipMakin 11 42
(M Dods) *chsd ldrs: hdwy 2f out: rdn and ev ch ent last: kpt on same pce* **4/1**[3]

10-3 **5** *1 ½* **Leah's Pride**[20] [38] 5-8-13 45 FergalLynch 7 37
(P Howling) *cl up: led after 1f: hdd 1/2-way: sn rdn along and grad wknd appr last* **6/1**

205- **6** *½* **Off Hire**[42] [6568] 10-8-13 40 (v) MickyFenton 5 35
(C Smith) *chsd ldrs: rdn along 2f out: gradyually wknd* **33/1**

00-0 **7** *1* **Katie Killane**[21] [24] 4-8-13 40 (v) AlanDaly 6 32
(M Wellings) *dwlt and bhd tl sme late hdwy* **80/1**

550- **8** *¾* **Sergeant Slipper**[42] [6570] 9-8-13 40 (v) RobbieFitzpatrick 9 29
(C Smith) *s.i.s and bhd tl sme late hdwy* **18/1**

000- **9** *2* **Feminist (IRE)**[34] [6647] 4-8-13 45 ChrisCatlin 8 22
(J M Bradley) *led 1f: cl up tl rdn along 1/2-way and sn wknd* **40/1**

00-0 **10** *½* **Juwwi**[5] [145] 12-8-13 45 TonyCulhane 12 20
(J M Bradley) *s.i.s: a rr* **33/1**

0/4- **11** *2 ½* **Unprecedented (IRE)**[120] [5514] 5-8-13 40 (v) SamHitchcott 10 12
(T T Clement) *bmpd s: sn chsng ldrs: rdn along 1/2-way: wknd wl over 1f out* **50/1**

000- **12** *2 ½* **Bold Maggie**[43] [6554] 4-8-6 40 RussellKennemore(7) 14 3
(J A Pickering) *towards rr whn hmpd after 1f: a bhd* **66/1**

6/41 **13** *20* **Miracle Ridge (IRE)**[21] [24] 11-8-13 45 (b) PatCosgrave 13 —
(Adrian McGuinness, Ire) *dwlt: sn rdn along towards rr and hung rt after 1f: lost action and virtually p.u 1/2-way* **9/4**[1]

60.90 secs (0.60) **Going Correction** +0.05s/f (Slow) **13** Ran SP% **120.0**
Speed ratings (Par 97):97,95,94,94,91 90,89,88,84,84 80,76,44
CSF £27.33 TOTE £5.10: £1.40, £2.90, £10.30; EX 34.10.
Owner E A Hayward **Bred** Clare Dore Ltd **Trained** Sedbury, Gloucs

FOCUS
The three drawn lowest filled the first three places, with the horse drawn 2 an absentee. Unconvincing form, not as strong a race as the one in which the winner was fourth in at Wolverhampton last time.
Off Hire Official explanation: jockey said gelding hung right-handed
Miracle Ridge(IRE) Official explanation: jockey said gelding lost its action

180 BETDIRECT MAIDEN CLAIMING STKS 7f (F)
2:00 (2:01) (Class 7) 4-Y-O+ **£1,365** (£403; £201) **Stalls** Low

Form RPR

0-40 **1** **Justcallmehandsome**[5] [143] 4-8-4 40 (v) DonnaCaldwell(7) 13 51
(D J S Ffrench Davis) *trckd ldrs: hdwy to ld 2f out: rdn over 1f out: kpt on wl u.p ins last* **4/1**[1]

000- **2** *nk* **Pearl Island (USA)**[43] [6556] 5-8-7 35 (b[1]) GrahamGibbons 9 47
(D J Wintle) *in tch: hdwy over 2f out: rdn to chal ent last and ev ch tl no ex towards fin* **5/1**[2]

050- **3** *5* **King Forever**[38] [6598] 4-8-11 67 MickyFenton 11 37
(D E Cantillon) *midfield on outer: hdwy and wd st: rdn wl over 1f out: no imp fnl f* **4/1**[1]

64-3 **4** *¾* **Velvet Touch**[5] [144] 5-8-4 40 (t) ChrisCatlin 2 28
(D M Simcock) *led: rdn along over 2f out: sn hdd and grad wknd over 1f out* **5/1**[2]

0000 **5** *nk* **Chairman Rick (IRE)**[1] [173] 4-8-11 49 (v) AdrianTNicholls 7 34
(D Nicholls) *s.i.s and bhd: hdwy 1/2-way: styd on fnl 2f: nrst fin* **8/1**

000- **6** *5* **Catheriniski (IRE)**[43] [6558] 4-8-0 40 ow2 RichardThomas(3) 10 13
(P A Blockley) *chsd ldrs: rdn along 3f out: sn wknd* **66/1**

00-0 **7** *1* **Son Of Sophie**[21] [26] 4-8-11 35 RobbieFitzpatrick 5 19
(C N Kellett) *chsd ldrs: rdn along 3f out: sn wknd* **66/1**

205- **8** *½* **Cooleycall Star (IRE)**[260] [1573] 5-8-9 45 (p) RobertWinston 12 16
(A G Juckes) *towards rr: hdwy 1/2-way: rdn and in tch wl over 1f out: sn wknd and eased ins last* **15/2**[3]

000- **9** *11* **Chingola**[63] [6411] 4-8-0 35 HayleyTurner 6 —
(R M Whitaker) *chsd ldrs: rdn along after 3f and sn wknd* **20/1**

066- **10** *2* **Danaatt (USA)**[51] [6498] 4-8-0 35 (b) DaleGibson 8 —
(K R Burke) *a rr* **16/1**

11 *½* **Jennyfromtheblock (IRE)**[176] [4015] 5-7-13 40 (p) DanielleMcCreery(7) 3 —
(Samuel Murphy, Ire) *s.i.s: a rr* **16/1**

000- **12** *3* **Seven Shirt**[57] [6443] 5-8-5 35 (bt[1]) AdrianMcCarthy 1 —
(E G Bevan) *chsd ldrs on inner: rdn along 3f out and sn wknd* **80/1**

006- **13** *2* **Speedy Spirit**[41] [6578] 4-8-6 30 (bt) AlanDaly 4 —
(M Salaman) *chsd ldrs to 1/2-way: sn wknd* **66/1**

0/6- **14** *17* **Bjorling**[48] [455] 5-7-12 (p) JosephWalsh(7) 14 —
(M J Gingell) *a bhd* **80/1**

1m 31.2s (0.40) **Going Correction** -0.05s/f (Stan) **23** Ran SP% **119.7**
Speed ratings (Par 97):95,94,88,88,87 82,80,80,67,65 64,61,59,39
CSF £22.81 TOTE £6.40: £2.20, £2.70, £1.90; EX 41.00.
Owner Mrs J E Taylor **Bred** Mrs J E Taylor **Trained** Lambourn, Berks

FOCUS
A weak event which could be rated 6lb higher through the runner-up's best form.
Jennyfromtheblock(IRE) Official explanation: jockey said mare ran green
Seven Shirt Official explanation: jockey said gelding hung left-handed throughout

181 BET NOW AT BETDIRECT.CO.UK BANDED STKS 7f (F)
2:30 (2:30) (Class 7) 4-Y-O+ **£1,706** (£503; £252) **Stalls** Low

Form RPR

200- **1** **Only If I Laugh**[162] [4437] 5-8-13 47 GrahamGibbons 1 52
(M J Attwater) *in tch: hdwy 3f out: rdn to chse ldrs 2f out: drvn and styd on to ld ins last* **10/1**

64-4 **2** *½* **Monkey Madge**[13] [95] 4-9-1 49 PaulEddery 6 53
(B Smart) *chsd ldrs: hdwy 3f out: rdn to ld wl over 1f out: drvn and hdd ins last* **5/1**[3]

22-0 **3** *1 ¼* **Mount Royale (IRE)**[13] [95] 8-9-0 48 (v) KimTinkler 3 49
(N Tinkler) *sn led: rdn over 2f out: hdd wl over 1f out: sn drvn and kpt on same pce* **8/1**

/46- **4** *hd* **Bronx Bomber**[81] [6243] 8-9-0 48 (b) MickyFenton 8 48
(Dr J D Scargill) *trckd ldrs: hdwy 3f out: ev ch 2f out: sn rdn and grad wknd appr last* **10/1**

5-66 **5** *3 ½* **Musiotal**[14] [81] 5-8-12 46 (v) FergalLynch 5 37
(P A Blockley) *s.i.s and bhd: hdwy on inner over 2f out: sn rdn and no imp fr over 1f out* **9/2**[2]

000- **6** *5* **Old Bailey (USA)**[86] [6177] 6-9-1 49 (be) GeorgeBaker 10 27
(G L Moore) *towards rr and rdn along 1/2-way: nvr a factor* **3/1**[1]

R6-1 **7** *nk* **Opera Knight**[20] [42] 6-8-12 46 TonyCulhane 12 23
(A W Carroll) *stdd s: hld up and bhd: hdwy over 2f out: no imp and eased over 1f out* **9/2**[2]

040- **8** *¾* **Canary Dancer**[36] [6613] 4-8-6 40 RoryMoore(5) 2 20
(Miss Z C Davison) *prom: rdn along 1/2-way: sn wknd* **50/1**

10-0 **9** *1* **Princess Arwen**[13] [95] 4-8-11 45 FrankieMcDonald 4 18
(Mrs Barbara Waring) *cl up: rdn along 3f out: drvn and wknd 2f out* **20/1**

-000 **10** *8* **Cheeney Basin (IRE)**[5] [143] 8-8-4 45 LiamJones(7) 7 —
(M C Chapman) *a rr* **100/1**

030- **11** *25* **Four Kings**[34] [6649] 5-8-11 40 (t) JoeFanning 9 —
(R Allan) *midfield: rdn along 3f out: sn wknd* **40/1**

1m 31.31s (0.51) **Going Correction** -0.05s/f (Stan) **11** Ran SP% **117.5**
Speed ratings (Par 97):95,94,93,92,88 83,82,81,80,71 43
CSF £57.96 TOTE £14.10: £3.40, £1.50, £2.20; EX 83.70.
Owner Phones Direct Partnership **Bred** The Lavington Stud **Trained** Wysall, Notts
■ Stewards' Enquiry : Graham Gibbons three-day ban: used whip with excessive frequency (Feb 4-6)

FOCUS
A reasonably competitive event of its type, and the form looks sound.
Old Bailey(USA) Official explanation: jockey said gelding never travelled
Canary Dancer Official explanation: jockey said filly hung right-handed throughout
Cheeney Basin(IRE) Official explanation: jockey said gelding moved poorly throughout

182 PLAY NOW AT BETDIRECTPOKER.COM BANDED STKS 1m 3f (F)
3:00 (3:00) (Class 7) 4-Y-O+ **£1,365** (£403; £201) **Stalls** Low

Form RPR

3-62 **1** **Surdoue**[13] [92] 6-9-0 45 J-PGuillambert 2 52
(P Howling) *mde all: rdn 2f out: drvn ins last: jst hld on* **9/2**[2]

23-3 **2** *hd* **Liquid Lover (IRE)**[5] [147] 4-8-11 40 EddieAhern 11 52
(W M Brisbourne) *midfield: hdwy 4f out: rdn wl over 1f out: drvn and edgd rt ent last: kpt on: jst hld* **9/4**[1]

04-4 **3** *7* **Yashin (IRE)**[13] [92] 5-9-0 45 HayleyTurner 3 41
(P A Blockley) *prom: hdwy to chse wnr 3f out: drvn wl over 1f out and kpt on same pce* **5/1**[3]

024- **4** *6* **Melograno (IRE)**[27] [6680] 6-8-13 45 ow2 DNolan(3) 14 33
(Mark Campion) *racd wd: in tch: hdwy 4f out: rdn wl over 2f out: drvn and wknd wl over 1f out* **8/1**

6-36 **5** *3 ½* **Ice And Fire**[5] [147] 7-9-0 45 (b) MickyFenton 13 26
(J T Stimpson) *bhd: hdwy over 4f out: wd st: rdn to chse ldrs 2f out: sn no imp* **11/1**

030- **6** *½* **Alqaayid**[98] [6704] 5-8-7 45 RussellKennemore(7) 6 25
(P W Hiatt) *chsd ldrs: rdn along 3f out: drvn over 2f out and sn wknd* **8/1**

00-0 **7** *¾* **Simply The Guest (IRE)**[13] [92] 7-9-0 45 (t) KimTinkler 4 24
(N Tinkler) *s.i.s: a rr* **28/1**

000- **8** *5* **Brunston Castle**[36] [6612] 6-9-0 45 (t) RobertWinston 10 16
(A W Carroll) *s.i.s: a rr* **20/1**

105- **9** *10* **Spanish Star**[37] [6606] 9-8-7 40 KellyHarrison(7) 1 —
(Mrs N Macauley) *bhd fr 1/2-way* **22/1**

300- **10** *1* **Isitloveyourafter (IRE)**[34] [5965] 4-8-11 45 (be) TonyCulhane 7 —
(G L Moore) *a bhd* **25/1**

006- **11** *3* **Hollywood Henry (IRE)**[43] [6555] 6-9-0 40 (v[1]) FergalLynch 12 —
(P A Blockley) *chsd ldrs: rdn along over 4f out and sn wknd* **40/1**

200- **12** *¾* **Showtime Faye**[43] [6556] 4-8-11 40 SamHitchcott 8 —
(A Bailey) *prom: rdn along 1/2-way: sn wknd* **100/1**

50/0 **13** *15* **Lough Bow (IRE)**[13] [91] 8-9-0 45 (b) DaleGibson 5 —
(M W Easterby) *cl up: rdn along 1/2-way: sn wknd* **40/1**

050- **14** *7* **Crimson Bow (GER)**[6] [5206] 4-8-11 40 JoeFanning 9 —
(J G Given) *a bhd* **50/1**

2m 28.37s (-0.53) **Going Correction** -0.05s/f (Stan)
WFA 4 from 5yo+ 3lb **14** Ran SP% **120.4**
Speed ratings (Par 97):99,98,93,89,86 86,85,82,75,74 72,71,60,55
CSF £13.62 TOTE £6.40: £1.60, £1.40, £2.20; EX 17.90.
Owner Les Amis Partners **Bred** R A G Robinson **Trained** Newmarket, Suffolk

FOCUS
Ordinary form for the grade, with the winner running close to his recent level.
Isitloveyourafter(IRE) Official explanation: jockey said filly resented kick-back
Hollywood Henry(IRE) Official explanation: jockey said gelding weakened quickly and felt amiss; jockey said, regarding the apparent tender ride, his orders were to ride gelding in a handy position, adding that on leaving back straight gelding weakened quickly and felt amiss so he decided to hold gelding together; trainer said gelding has finished distressed in the past

183 BETDIRECT.CO.UK BANDED STKS — 1m (F)
3:30 (3:32) (Class 7) 4-Y-0+ — **£1,365** (£403; £201) **Stalls** Low

Form — RPR

00-5 **1** **Azreme**[20] 41 6-9-0 48 (b) TonyCulhane 9 — 53
(P Howling) *in tch: hdwy 3f out: rdn to chal over 1f out: drvn to ld ins last: hld on wl* **15/2**

-106 **2** *shd* **Lady Suesanne (IRE)**[7] 134 4-9-2 50 (b) RobbieFitzpatrick 4 — 55
(M J Attwater) *led: rdn wl over 1f out: drvn and hdd ins last: rallied wl u.p towards fin* **11/2**[3]

-311 **3** *shd* **Sierra**[5] 148 5-9-8 50 PaulFessey 13 — 61
(A W Carroll) *trckd ldng pair: hdwy 2f out: rdn over 1f out: drvn and styd on wl fnl f: jst hld* **5/1**[2]

45-4 **4** *2½* **Legal Lover (IRE)**[5] 143 4-9-0 48 GrahamGibbons 2 — 48
(R Hollinshead) *trckd ldrs: pushed along 3f out: rdn 2f out and kpt on same pce appr last* **11/4**[1]

065- **5** *½* **Donegal Shore (IRE)**[37] 6608 7-8-13 47 (vt) HayleyTurner 5 — 46
(Jennie Candlish) *midfield: hdwy 3f out: rdn 2f out: drvn and kpt on ins last: nrst fin* **14/1**

000- **6** *2½* **Elms Schoolboy**[63] 6413 4-8-11 45 (b) MichaelTebbutt 7 — 39
(J M P Eustace) *chsd ldr: rdn along over 2f out: drvn and wknd over 1f out* **22/1**

05-0 **7** *1* **Legal Dram**[14] 77 5-9-2 50 PhillipMakin 14 — 42
(M Dods) *chsd ldrs: rdn along over 2f out: sn wknd* **16/1**

066- **8** *¾* **Susiedil (IRE)**[43] 6556 5-8-11 40 AdrianTNicholls 3 — 35
(D Nicholls) *in tch on inner: rdn along 1/2-way: sn wknd* **25/1**

25-1 **9** *1¼* **Sonderborg**[13] 94 5-9-2 50 (p) DaleGibson 1 — 38
(J Mackie) *a rr* **7/1**

400- **10** *1* **Cryfield**[27] 6680 9-8-11 40 (v) KimTinkler 8 — 31
(N Tinkler) *chsd ldrs: rdn along 1/2-way: drvn 3f out and sn wknd* **18/1**

6- **11** *15* **Hillfield Flyer (IRE)**[41] 6574 6-8-8 45 (p) DanielTudhope(3) 10 — —
(Samuel Murphy, Ire) *chsd ldrs tl rdn along 1/2-way and sn wknd* **11/1**

00-0 **12** *¾* **Riska King**[19] 44 6-9-2 50 FergalLynch 6 — 4
(P A Blockley) *v.s.a: a bhd* **14/1**

1m 44.65s (0.05) **Going Correction** -0.05s/f (Stan) — 12 Ran SP% **124.0**
Speed ratings (Par 97):97,96,96,94,93 91,90,89,88,87 72,71
CSF £50.81 TOTE £10.90: £2.80, £2.00, £1.60; EX 44.60.

Owner Halcyon Partnership **Bred** Miss Helen Mary Ann Omersa **Trained** Newmarket, Suffolk

■ Stewards' Enquiry : Tony Culhane one-day ban: used whip down the shoulder in the forehand position (Feb 4)

Robbie Fitzpatrick three-day ban: used whip with excessive frequency (Feb 4-6)

FOCUS
Fairly solid form for the grade taking the third's performance as a guide.

184 BETDIRECT FREEPHONE 0800 211 222 BANDED STKS — 1m (F)
4:00 (4:02) (Class 7) 4-Y-0+ — **£1,365** (£403; £201) **Stalls** Low

Form — RPR

033- **1** **Tacid**[42] 6572 4-8-11 45 MickyFenton 1 — 53
(Dr J D Scargill) *cl up: led over 4f out: rdn wl over 1f out: drvn and kpt on wl fnl f* **8/1**

005- **2** *1* **To Be Fare (IRE)**[41] 6577 6-8-11 40 DeanMcKeown 14 — 51
(J Pearce) *trckd ldrs towards outer: hdwy 3f out: rdn to chse ldng pair 2f out: drvn and kpt on ins last* **7/2**[1]

-000 **3** *1* **Crusoe (IRE)**[13] 95 9-8-11 45 (b) BrianReilly 8 — 49
(A Sadik) *a.p: effrt 3f out: rdn 2f out: drvn over 1f out and ev ch tl no ex ins last* **33/1**

0-50 **4** *3* **Penel (IRE)**[5] 148 5-8-11 45 (p) TonyCulhane 4 — 43
(P T Midgley) *midfield: pushed along and outpcd 1/2-way: hdwy over 2f out: sn rdn and kpt on same pce appr last* **9/1**

3-00 **5** *¾* **Pawn In Life (IRE)**[5] 143 8-8-11 40 (v) EddieAhern 11 — 42
(M J Polglase) *in tch: pushed along and outpcd 1/2-way: wd st and sn rdn: kpt on ins last: nrst fin* **12/1**

000- **6** *2½* **Lord Lahar**[34] 6651 7-8-11 45 (p) RobertWinston 12 — 37
(M A Buckley) *hld up in tch gng wl: effrt 3f out: rdn over 2f out and sn one pce* **8/1**

0-00 **7** *hd* **The Plainsman**[6] 141 4-8-11 40 (p) HayleyTurner 6 — 36
(P W Hiatt) *chsd ldrs: rdn along 3f out: wknd over 2f out* **18/1**

/64- **8** *2½* **Margaret's Dream (IRE)**[26] 6684 5-8-8 45 DanielTudhope(3) 10 — 31
(D Carroll) *keen: racd wd: cl up tl rdn over 2f out and sn wknd* **4/1**[2]

4-04 **9** *½* **Kumakawa**[5] 148 8-8-4 45 DonnaCaldwell(7) 3 — 30
(D K Ivory) *v.s.a: a bhd* **9/2**[3]

020- **10** *1¾* **Danger Bird (IRE)**[34] 6650 6-8-4 40 (p) HugoFellows(7) 13 — 27
(R Hollinshead) *stdd and swtchd lft s: a rr* **33/1**

00-0 **11** *1½* **Tiger Hunter**[21] 27 4-8-11 40 PatCosgrave 5 — 24
(P Howling) *chsd ldrs: rdn along over 3f out: sn wknd* **66/1**

16-0 **12** *hd* **Venetian Princess (IRE)**[13] 94 4-8-11 45 FergalLynch 7 — 23
(P Howling) *led: pushed along and hdd over 4f out: sn rdn and wknd* **12/1**

13 *28* **Princess Rioja**[507] 6-8-11 40 ChrisCatlin 2 — —
(J M Bradley) *a rr: bhd fr 1/2-way* **66/1**

1m 44.71s (0.11) **Going Correction** -0.05s/f (Stan) — 13 Ran SP% **122.1**
Speed ratings (Par 97):97,96,95,92,91 88,88,86,85,83 82,82,54
CSF £36.31 TOTE £9.50: £2.50, £1.90, £8.00; EX 47.10 Place 6 £160.22, Place 5 £45.78.

Owner Derek W Johnson **Bred** J P T Partnership **Trained** Newmarket, Suffolk

■ Stewards' Enquiry : Dean McKeown two-day ban: used whip with excessive frequency (Feb 4-5)

FOCUS
A weak affair which Tacid did well to win from stall one.

The Plainsman Official explanation: jockey said gelding was denied a clear run

Margaret's Dream(IRE) Official explanation: jockey said mare ran too freely early

Kumakawa Official explanation: jockey said saddle slipped

Venetian Princess(IRE) Official explanation: jockey said filly hung right-handed throughout

T/Jkpt: Part won. £7,100.00 to a £1 stake. Pool: £10,000.00. 0.50 winning tickets. T/Plt: £159.40 to a £1 stake. Pool: £47,349.05. 216.80 winning tickets. T/Qpdt: £20.50 to a £1 stake. Pool: £3,793.40. 136.60 winning tickets. JR

[135]LINGFIELD (L-H)
Wednesday, January 25

OFFICIAL GOING: Standard
Wind: Almost nil Weather: Sunny becoming cloudy

185 LITTLEWOODSPOOLS.CO.UK H'CAP (DIV I) — 1m 2f (P)
12:50 (12:52) (Class 6) (0-65,65) 4-Y-0+ — **£2,047** (£604; £302) **Stalls** Low

Form — RPR

00-0 **1** **Blue Hedges**[11] 111 4-7-12 54 JamesDoyle(7) 10 — 62
(H J Collingridge) *b: hld up in last: prog over 2f out: gd hdwy jst over 1f out: got through ins fnl f: r.o to ld last 50yds* **25/1**

0/22 **2** *¾* **Kirkstone (IRE)**[5] 163 5-8-13 60 EddieAhern 9 — 66
(J A Osborne) *lw: trckd ldrs gng wl: prog to ld 2f out: rdn over 1f out: fnd little: hdd and nt qckn last 50yds* **13/8**[1]

22-4 **3** *hd* **Jomus**[14] 82 5-8-10 57 (p) RobertWinston 5 — 63
(L Montague Hall) *hld up towards rr: prog over 2f out: rdn to chal over 1f out: upsides ins fnl f: fnd nil and hld after* **5/1**[2]

404- **4** *hd* **Red Sail**[77] 6300 5-8-5 52 (b[1]) PaulHanagan 12 — 58
(Dr J D Scargill) *b.hind: hld up in rr: nt clr run 3f out: effrt on outer over 1f out: r.o ins fnl f: nt rch ldrs* **10/1**

01-2 **5** *1¾* **Competitor**[18] 63 5-8-13 60 (vt) ChrisCatlin 3 — 62
(J Akehurst) *lw: chsd ldrs: rdn wl over 3f out: stl wl in tch jst over 1f out: one pce* **9/1**

2-13 **6** *¾* **Barton Sands (IRE)**[11] 113 9-8-7 61 (t) JamieJones(7) 7 — 62
(Ernst Oertel) *lw: hld up towards rr: prog over 2f out: cl up over 1f out: one pce fnl f* **8/1**[3]

411- **7** *1¼* **Granary Girl**[102] 5895 4-8-5 54 JimmyQuinn 4 — 52
(J Pearce) *prom: rdn over 2f out: nt qckn over 1f out: fdd ins fnl f* **12/1**

050- **8** *4* **Coronado's Gold (USA)**[71] 5317 5-9-4 65 JoeFanning 2 — 56
(W R Swinburn) *trckd ldr: led briefly over 2f out: wknd fnl f* **12/1**

25-0 **9** *nk* **Blueberry Tart (IRE)**[12] 106 4-8-11 60 (p) SteveDrowne 11 — 50
(J M P Eustace) *chsd ldrs: rdn over 5f out: stl in tch u.p 2f out: wknd over 1f out* **33/1**

00-1 **10** *2* **Border Edge**[14] 82 8-9-0 61 (v) TonyCulhane 1 — 48
(J J Bridger) *b: led at decent pce: rdn and hdd over 2f out: hld whn hmpd on inner over 1f out: wknd* **12/1**

00-6 **11** *22* **Swell Lad**[5] 163 4-8-10 59 MartinDwyer 6 — 4
(S Gollings) *chsd ldrs: rdn over 5f out: wknd rapidly 3f out: t.o* **66/1**

45/0 **12** *¾* **Pagan Prince**[13] 101 9-9-3 64 JamieSpencer 8 — 7
(J Gallagher) *restless in stalls: hld up in rr: in tch whn snatched up on inner over 2f out: eased: t.o* **25/1**

00-0 **13** *8* **Warden Warren**[22] 17 8-8-10 62 (p) MarcHalford(5) 13 — —
(Mrs C A Dunnett) *racd wd: in tch to 1/2-way: sn wknd and t.o* **33/1**

2m 5.61s (-2.18) **Going Correction** -0.15s/f (Stan)
WFA 4 from 5yo+ 2lb — 13 Ran SP% **123.1**
Speed ratings (Par 101):102,101,101,101,99 99,98,94,94,93 75,74,68
CSF £65.55 CT £261.33 TOTE £49.00: £10.10, £1.20, £1.80; EX 198.30.

Owner N H Gardner **Bred** S C E A Des Bissons **Trained** Exning, Suffolk

FOCUS
They went a good pace in this modest handicap and it led to the finish being dominated by those held up. The third and fifth set the standard for the form.

186 TEXT "BETDIRECT" TO 88600 H'CAP — 1m 4f (P)
1:20 (1:23) (Class 5) (0-70,70) 4-Y-0+ — **£3,238** (£963; £481; £240) **Stalls** Low

Form — RPR

234- **1** **Countrywide Luck**[30] 6665 5-8-11 70 JamesDoyle(7) 10 — 80
(N P Littmoden) *lw: settled wl in rr: rdn and sustained prog fr 4f out: chal fnl f: edgd lft but ld nr fin* **9/2**[2]

24-1 **2** *shd* **Principal Witness (IRE)**[21] 37 5-8-10 62 SteveDrowne 15 — 72
(Tom Dascombe) *trckd ldrs: prog 5f out: led 3f out: drvn and jnd fnl f: hanging lft and hdd nr fin* **7/1**

1-05 **3** *3* **Mostarsil (USA)**[4] 168 8-8-6 58 (p) EddieAhern 16 — 63
(G L Moore) *wl in rr: pushed along 7f out: prog u.p over 3f out: nt qckn over 2f out: r.o fr over 1f out to take 3rd nr fin* **10/1**

11-3 **4** *½* **Captain Margaret**[12] 109 4-8-11 67 JimmyQuinn 7 — 71
(J Pearce) *lw: in tch: prog 5f out: trckd ldrs 3f out: drvn to chse ldng pair fnl f: no imp: lost 3rd nr fin* **13/2**[3]

0-40 **5** *4* **Swainson (USA)**[9] 125 5-8-13 65 (b[1]) JoeFanning 9 — 63
(P Mitchell) *trckd ldr: led over 6f out and maintained str pce: hdd 3f out: styd cl up on inner tl wknd over 1f out* **12/1**

000- **6** *3* **Sandy's Legend (USA)**[44] 6566 4-8-4 60 SimonWhitworth 13 — 53
(Jamie Poulton) *dwlt: hld up wl in rr: sme prog 8f out: outpcd over 3f out: no ch after: plugged on* **50/1**

2-42 **7** *½* **Danger Zone**[7] 140 4-8-12 68 IanMongan 5 — 60
(Mrs A J Perrett) *prom: chsd ldr 5f out: chal 3f out: wknd rapidly over 1f out* **4/1**[1]

04-6 **8** *3* **Duelling Banjos**[21] 37 7-9-2 68 MartinDwyer 11 — 55
(J Akehurst) *hld up in last: outpcd whn sltly hmpd 4f out: nvr on terms* **10/1**

050- **9** *hd* **King Of Knight (IRE)**[46] 6535 5-8-10 62 ow2 (v) TonyCulhane 12 — 60+
(G Prodromou) *wl in tch: prog 4f out: jnd ldr 3f out: losing pl whn hmpd wl over 1f out and eased* **16/1**

344/ **10** *2* **Open Arms**[1134] 5937 10-7-13 58 oh1 ow2 MarkCoumbe(7) 4 — 42
(Mrs A L M King) *b.bkwd: wl in rr: outpcd whn hmpd over 4f out: nvr on terms* **50/1**

36/5 **11** *½* **Shirazi**[11] 111 8-8-11 66 NeilChalmers(3) 14 — 49
(D R Gandolfo) *towards rr: outpcd over 3f out: nt on terms w ldng gp over 2f out: wknd* **14/1**

4-30 **12** *6* **Yenaled**[12] 106 9-8-10 62 HayleyTurner 6 — 35
(P S McEntee) *chsd ldrs: rdn 5f out: wknd over 3f out* **14/1**

0S4- **13** *10* **Persona (IRE)**[192] 3565 4-8-8 64 ow2 MickyFenton 2 — 21
(B J McMath) *chsd ldrs: rdn and wknd over 5f out: t.o* **66/1**

000/ **14** *shd* **Christmas Truce (IRE)**[271] 483 7-8-4 56 oh1 PaulHanagan 3 — 13
(Ms J S Doyle) *a wl in rr: bhd fnl 4f: t.o* **66/1**

300- **15** *nk* **Private Benjamin**[50] 3751 6-8-4 56 oh4 ChrisCatlin 8 — 13
(M R Hoad) *a wl in rr: bhd over 3f out: t.o* **33/1**

20-0 **16** *dist* **Mollyputtheketelon (USA)**[12] 109 5-8-10 62 (v) JamieSpencer 1 — —
(M J Wallace) *led at furious pce: hdd over 6f out: wknd 5f out: sn wl t.o* **25/1**

2m 31.25s (-3.14) **Going Correction** -0.15s/f (Stan)
WFA 4 from 5yo+ 4lb — **16** Ran SP% **122.8**
Speed ratings (Par 103):104,103,101,101,98 96,96,94,94,93 92,88,82,82,81 —
CSF £34.77 CT £307.00 TOTE £5.60: £1.50, £2.80, £2.40, £1.70; EX 69.80.

The Form Book, Raceform Ltd, Compton, RG20 6NL

Owner Countrywide Steel & Tubes Ltd **Bred** Miss Nicola Kent **Trained** Newmarket, Suffolk

FOCUS

Another race run at a strong early gallop, and once again the winner came from well off the pace. The first two both showed slightly improved form, and the third and fourth ran to their marks, so the form looks reliable.

Duelling Banjos Official explanation: jockey said gelding was hampered

King Of Knight(IRE) Official explanation: jockey said gelding had no more to give

Persona(IRE) Official explanation: jockey said filly had breathing problem

187 LITTLEWOODSPOOLS.CO.UK H'CAP (DIV II) 1m 2f (P)

1:50 (1:52) (Class 6) (0-65,65) 4-Y-0+ £2,047 (£604; £302) Stalls Low

Form RPR

0-01 1 **Young Mick**[2] [173] 4-8-12 **60** 6ex....(v) JimmyQuinn 7 67
(G G Margarson) *trckd ldrs: effrt over 2f out: rdn to press ldr jst over 1f out: styd on to ld last stride* **12/1**

35-3 2 shd **Petite Paramour (IRE)**[5] [156] 5-8-8 **57**.... AdamKirby(3) 10 63
(Miss Gay Kelleway) *led for 1f: trckd ldr: led again over 2f out: hrd rdn fnl f: hdd last stride* **10/1**

36-1 3 1 1/4 **Bishops Finger**[11] [113] 6-9-2 **62**....(b) SimonWhitworth 1 66
(Jamie Poulton) *b: hld up midfield: rdn over 2f out: clsd on ldrs over 1f out: styd on fnl f* **20/1**

140- 4 1 1/4 **Ramsgill (USA)**[39] [6598] 4-9-3 **65**.... EddieAhern 11 67
(N P Littmoden) *trckd ldrs: rdn and nt qckn 2f out: kpt on again fnl f* **6/1**[2]

14-4 5 3/4 **Night Storm**[11] [111] 5-9-4 **64**.... JamieSpencer 5 67+
(S Dow) *s.s: wl in rr: sme prog 2f out: shkn up and kpt on fnl f: nvr nrr* **6/1**[2]

02-4 6 3/4 **Lady Pilot**[11] [114] 4-8-8 **59**.... RichardThomas(3) 6 58
(Dr J R J Naylor) *hld up towards rr: rdn and no prog 2f out: kpt on fnl f* **33/1**

60-1 7 1/2 **Cup Of Love (USA)**[16] [73] 4-8-11 **59**.... ChrisCatlin 13 57
(Rae Guest) *racd freely: led after 1f and sn clr: hdd over 2f out: wknd rapidly fnl f* **11/1**

00-4 8 1/2 **My Pension (IRE)**[12] [106] 5-9-1 **61**.... TonyCulhane 8 58
(P Howling) *hld up in last pair: pushed along and no prog 4f out: last over 2f out : styd on steadily fr over 1f out: nvr nrr* **8/1**[3]

04-3 9 nk **Iberus (GER)**[5] [157] 8-9-0 **60**....(p) GeorgeBaker 14 56
(S Gollings) *hld up in last: pushed along over 2f out: kpt on steadily: nvr nrr* **20/1**

0-55 10 shd **Temper Tantrum**[18] [63] 8-8-5 **51**....(p) HayleyTurner 2 47
(J R Best) *b: t.k.h: hld up in midfield: no prog over 2f out: wknd over 1f out* **33/1**

603- 11 2 **Salinger (USA)**[26] [6691] 4-8-12 **60**.... IanMongan 3 52
(Mrs L J Mongan) *plld v hrd: chsd ldrs tl wknd over 2f out* **14/1**

50-0 12 nk **Farnborough (USA)**[16] [72] 5-7-13 **52**.... JamesDoyle(7) 12 44
(R J Price) *hld up in rr: rdn and no prog over 2f out: wknd* **16/1**

1- 13 7 **Danse Spectre (IRE)**[26] [6687] 4-9-0 **62**.... RobertWinston 9 40
(E J O'Neill) *lw: trckd ldrs on outer: rdn 3f out: wknd over 2f out* **2/1**[1]

2m 7.67s (-0.12) **Going Correction** -0.15s/f (Stan)

WFA 4 from 5yo+ 2lb 13 Ran SP% **126.1**

Speed ratings (Par 101):94,93,92,91,91 90,90,89,89,89 88,87,82

CSF £127.75 CT £2402.04 TOTE £15.00: £4.00, £4.70, £5.80; EX 244.30.

Owner M F Kentish **Bred** M F Kentish **Trained** Newmarket, Suffolk

FOCUS

The slower of the two divisions by over two seconds but the form looks reasonable as the principals were always well placed.

Danse Spectre(IRE) Official explanation: jockey said filly hung right throughout; vet said filly was lame

188 BETDIRECT FREEPHONE 0800 211 222 H'CAP 1m 2f (P)

2:20 (2:25) (Class 5) (0-75,73) 3-Y-0 £3,238 (£963; £481; £240) Stalls Low

Form RPR

0-31 1 **Prince Charlemagne (IRE)**[7] [142] 3-7-11 **59** oh3.... JamesDoyle(7) 4 69+
(N P Littmoden) *trckd ldrs: prog to ld over 2f out: rdn clr fr over 1f out: r.o wl* **7/4**[1]

3-30 2 5 **Lenoir (GER)**[7] [142] 3-8-13 **68**....(v) EddieAhern 10 69
(V Smith) *hld up towards rr: smooth prog over 3f out: chsd wnr 2f out: brushed aside fr over 1f out* **10/1**

001- 3 1 **Beauchamp Unique**[37] [6610] 3-8-7 **65**.... AdamKirby(3) 14 69+
(G A Butler) *reluctant to enter stalls: hld up wl in rr: pushed along 5f out: prog 3f out: r.o to take 3rd 1f out: nvr able to chal* **7/1**[3]

304- 4 1 **Merchant Bankes**[25] [6694] 3-9-4 **73**.... TonyCulhane 13 70
(W G M Turner) *wl in tch: rdn to chse ldrs over 2f out: sn outpcd: fdd ins fnl f* **40/1**

04-1 5 3 **Daaweitza**[8] [132] 3-9-0 **69** 6ex.... TomEaves 7 60
(B Ellison) *wl in rr and sn pushed along: struggling u.p over 3f out: styd on fnl 2f* **8/1**

003- 6 1 1/4 **Bin Rahy (IRE)**[25] [6694] 3-9-4 **73**.... ChrisCatlin 9 62
(M R Channon) *unruly bef gng in stalls: wl in rr: rdn and effrt over 3f out: outpcd over 2f out: no ch after* **13/2**[2]

500- 7 nk **Galaxy Bound (IRE)**[117] [5582] 3-8-11 **66**.... RobertWinston 12 54
(D Shaw) *dwlt: wl in rr: rdn and lost tch 3f out: plugged on* **33/1**

156- 8 shd **Possessed**[39] [6599] 3-9-4 **73**.... MatthewHenry 6 61
(T D McCarthy) *b: uns rdr on way to post: cl up: led 3f out to over 2f out: nt run on and sn btn* **12/1**

02-5 9 nk **Duel In The Sands**[9] [123] 3-8-1 **59** oh1.... PatrickMathers(3) 5 47
(D Shaw) *pushed along early then t.k.h in rr: lost tch w ldrs 3f out: wknd* **40/1**

0-30 10 9 **Zizou (IRE)**[14] [85] 3-8-8 **63**....(p) JimmyQuinn 1 34
(P R Hedger) *lw: prom tl wknd 3f out: sn bhd* **25/1**

46-6 11 7 **Ullah Pendragon (IRE)**[18] [61] 3-8-2 **60** oh8 ow1(p) RichardThomas(3) 3 17
(M J Polglase) *trckd ldrs: hmpd by wkng rival fr over 4f out to over 3f out: no ch after* **66/1**

26-3 12 8 **Opera Comica**[18] [62] 3-9-1 **70**....(v) RobertHavlin 11 12
(J H M Gosden) *pressed ldr tl wknd rapidly 4f out: t.o* **14/1**

0-26 13 shd **Night Groove (IRE)**[9] [122] 3-8-7 **62**....(p) PaulHanagan 2 4
(N P Littmoden) *led to 3f out: wknd rapidly and eased: t.o* **16/1**

00-0 14 nk **Smart Golden Boy (IRE)**[22] [16] 3-8-5 **60**.... HayleyTurner 8 1
(Mrs L C Jewell) *pressed ldr tl wknd rapidly over 4f out: t.o* **100/1**

2m 6.69s (-1.10) **Going Correction** -0.15s/f (Stan) 14 Ran SP% **116.8**

Speed ratings (Par 97):98,94,93,92,90 89,88,88,88,81 75,69,69,68

CSF £18.15 CT £101.76 TOTE £2.40: £1.60, £3.30, £2.40; EX 25.90.

Owner Neil Ryan **Bred** Michael O'Mahony **Trained** Newmarket, Suffolk

■ Prince Charlemagne completed a treble on the card for 17-year-old James Doyle, a notable achievement for a 7lb claimer.

■ Stewards' Enquiry : Chris Catlin two-day ban: improper riding - appeared to strike colt whilst on the ground (Feb 5-6)

FOCUS

A modest handicap and those who forced the decent pace paid the price in the latter stages. The form looks sound rated through the runner-up and fourth.

Galaxy Bound(IRE) Official explanation: jockey said gelding hung left

189 NO 5P RULE 4S AT BETDIRECT (S) STKS 6f (P)

2:50 (2:52) (Class 6) 3-Y-0 £2,388 (£705; £352) Stalls Low

Form RPR

253- 1 **Diktalex (IRE)**[34] [6656] 3-8-2 **60**....(t) MarcHalford(5) 6 55+
(W G M Turner) *dwlt: hld up in tch: prog 1/2-way: led wl over 1f out: kicked 2l clr fnl f: tired nr fin and all out* **8/1**[3]

50-0 2 1/2 **Kings Cavalier (USA)**[11] [118] 3-8-12 **68**....(v[1]) PaulFitzsimons 1 55
(S Dow) *dwlt: pushed up to join ldr: rdn and nt qckn over 2f out: chsd wnr jst over 1f out: gaining at fin* **7/2**[2]

00-0 3 1 1/2 **Mr Rigsby**[16] [68] 3-9-3 **64**.... TonyCulhane 5 58+
(P Howling) *chsd ldrs: rdn 1/2-way: outpcd 2f out: hmpd on inner jst over 1f out: r.o last 100yds* **8/1**[3]

50- 4 1/2 **Miss A Bargain (IRE)**[37] [6617] 3-8-7.... FranciscoDaSilva 7 44
(K R Burke) *chsd ldrs: rdn 1/2-way: reluctant and lost pl wl over 1f out: styd on again last 100yds* **25/1**

60-5 5 1/2 **Straight As A Die**[12] [105] 3-8-7 **45**.... JimmyQuinn 9 42
(R J Hodges) *detached in last and pushed along: reminder wl over 1f out: nt clr run fnl f: r.o last 75yds* **33/1**

0-06 6 1 **Reality Time (IRE)**[7] [139] 3-8-7 **63**....(b) EddieAhern 3 39
(J A Osborne) *dwlt: in tch in last pair: rdn and no prog fnl 2f* **8/1**[3]

5-64 7 shd **In Hope**[7] [139] 3-8-0 **57**.... JamieJones(7) 2 39
(Ernst Oertel) *mde most to 1/2-way: wknd over 1f out* **16/1**

1-21 8 1/2 **Luloah**[14] [83] 3-8-12 **69**.... BrianReilly 8 42
(P S McEntee) *trckd ldrs: prog to ld 1/2-way: hanging and hdd wl over 1f out: sn btn* **11/10**[1]

1m 13.93s (1.12) **Going Correction** -0.15s/f (Stan) 8 Ran SP% **115.8**

Speed ratings (Par 95):86,85,83,82,82 80,80,79

CSF £36.65 TOTE £9.10: £2.00, £1.50, £3.50; EX 50.80.There was no bid for the winner. Kings Cavalier (USA) was claimed by I. W. McInnes for £6,000. Luloah was the subject of a friendly claim.

Owner Miss D M Harding **Bred** G B Turnbull Ltd **Trained** Sigwells, Somerset

FOCUS

A poor sprint seller and a slow time after the leaders went off too fast.

Straight As A Die Official explanation: jockey said filly was denied a clear run in final furlong

190 PLAY NOW AT BETDIRECTPOKER.COM H'CAP 6f (P)

3:20 (3:21) (Class 4) (0-85,84) 3-Y-0 £6,477 (£1,927; £963; £481) Stalls Low

Form RPR

33-1 1 **Dingaan (IRE)**[18] [60] 3-9-4 **84**.... MartinDwyer 3 89+
(A M Balding) *lw: pressed ldr: led 2f out: drvn and styd on wl fnl f* **15/8**[1]

05-1 2 3/4 **Thoughtsofstardom**[12] [105] 3-8-4 **70** oh4.... HayleyTurner 7 68
(P S McEntee) *off the pce in last quartet: prog over 2f out: r.o fnl f to snatch 2nd last stride* **33/1**

31-5 3 shd **Veronica's Girl**[21] [34] 3-8-5 **71**.... ChrisCatlin 2 69
(P R Hedger) *mounted on crse: pressed ldng pair: rdn to chse wnr 1f out: no real imp last 100yds: lost 2nd last stride* **16/1**

33-1 4 1 1/4 **Sands Crooner (IRE)**[20] [45] 3-8-3 **72**....(t) PatrickMathers(3) 9 66
(D Shaw) *lw: dwlt: wl off the pce in last trio: styd on fr over 1f out: nvr nrr* **16/1**

01-6 5 1/2 **Rapsgate (IRE)**[18] [66] 3-8-1 **70** oh2....(b) StephaneBreux(3) 1 63
(R Hannon) *led at fast pce: hdd 2f out: wknd fnl f* **20/1**

1-02 6 nk **Sigismundus (IRE)**[11] [118] 3-8-4 **70**.... PaulHanagan 10 62
(J R Boyle) *wnt rt s: wl off the pce in last trio: kpt on fr over 1f out: n.d* **8/1**

212- 7 hd **Littledodayno (IRE)**[179] [3958] 3-8-13 **79**.... JamieSpencer 4 70
(J Noseda) *in tch: prog and poised to chal 2f out: rdn wl over 1f out: edgd rt and fnd nil* **9/4**[2]

14-1 8 1 **Grenane (IRE)**[16] [68] 3-8-10 **76**.... RobertWinston 6 64
(P D Evans) *bdly outpcd in last and looked reluctant: styd on fnl f: no ch* **6/1**[3]

430- 9 3/4 **Grecianette (IRE)**[92] [6098] 3-8-4 **70** oh2.... JoeFanning 8 56
(J A R Toller) *wl in tch: rdn whn veered rt bnd 2f out: no ch after* **50/1**

421- 10 3 1/2 **Bellsbank (IRE)**[88] [6135] 3-8-7 **73**.... SamHitchcott 5 49
(A Bailey) *prom tl wknd 2f out* **25/1**

1m 12.18s (-0.63) **Going Correction** -0.15s/f (Stan) 10 Ran SP% **116.2**

Speed ratings (Par 99):98,97,96,95,94 94,93,92,91,86

CSF £75.83 CT £802.55 TOTE £2.90: £1.20, £3.20, £2.90; EX 62.60.

Owner Lady C S Cadbury **Bred** Mrs Gill Wilson **Trained** Kingsclere, Hants

FOCUS

A fair little handicap run at a good pace, and the form looks pretty sound rated through the third.

Grenane(IRE) Official explanation: jockey said colt ran without both hind shoes and was suffering from a sore mouth; vet said colt was sensitive around mouth

191 BETDIRECT.CO.UK FOR IN-RUNNING FOOTBALL MAIDEN STKS 1m (P)

3:50 (3:52) (Class 5) 3-Y-0 £3,886 (£1,156; £577; £288) Stalls High

Form RPR

3 1 **Babcary**[11] [112] 3-8-9.... MartinDwyer 6 70
(M P Tregoning) *lw: led for 1f: trckd ldr: led again jst over 2f out: drvn and hrd pressed fnl f: hld on wl* **5/2**[1]

2 nk **Just Logic (IRE)** 3-9-0.... JamieSpencer 9 74+
(J Noseda) *unf: lengthy: b.bkwd: rn green early: wl in tch: effrt 2f out: chsd wnr fnl f: hrd rdn and clsd grad: jst hld* **7/2**[2]

3 1 1/2 **Airbound (USA)** 3-9-0.... JoeFanning 2 71+
(M Johnston) *leggy: scope: prom: effrt 2f out: rdn and styd on same pce fr over 1f out* **9/2**[3]

- 4 1 1/4 **Westport** 3-9-0.... RobertHavlin 1 73+
(J H M Gosden) *w'like: lw: rn green early in midfield: prog and cl up 2f out: nowhere to go on inner over 1f out to ins fnl f: kpt on* **20/1**

0-4 5 hd **Questive**[22] [16] 3-9-0....(t) PaulHanagan 5 68
(E A L Dunlop) *lw: led after 1f to jst over 2f out: fdd fnl f* **10/1**

6 6 6 **Blushing Thief (USA)**[22] [16] 3-9-0.... RobertWinston 8 54
(W Jarvis) *lw: trckd ldrs: cl up over 1f out: wknd rapidly ins fnl f* **9/2**[3]

7 2 **Bobby Rose** 3-9-0.... MickyFenton 12 49
(D K Ivory) *w'like: a towards rr: lost tch 3f out: no ch after* **66/1**

0- 8 1/2 **Compton Express**[35] [6640] 3-8-9.... SimonWhitworth 10 43
(Jamie Poulton) *racd wd: chsd ldrs: rdn 3f out: wknd over 2f out* **33/1**

9 1/2 **Beauchamp Ultra** 3-8-6.... AdamKirby(3) 11 42
(G A Butler) *hld up in last: lost tch w ldng gp over 3f out: no ch after* **16/1**

10 1 3/4 **Lethal** 3-9-0.... J-PGuillambert 7 43
(Ernst Oertel) *unf: b: s.s: plld hrd early: hld up: lost tch 3f out* **33/1**

0 11 1 **King's College (USA)**[7] [138] 3-8-7.... JamieJones(7) 4 41
(G L Moore) *in tch: hrd rdn and wknd 3f out* **100/1**

\- **12** *2* **The Lady Ermyn** 3-8-9 .... JimmyQuinn 3 31
(T G Mills) *unf: dwlt: a in rr: rdn and lost tch over 3f out* **16/1**

1m 38.6s (-0.83) **Going Correction** -0.15s/f (Stan) **12** Ran SP% **121.1**
Speed ratings (Par 97):98,97,96,94,94 88,86,86,85,84 83,81
CSF £10.90 TOTE £3.20: £1.50, £2.00, £2.10; EX 13.70.
Owner Major & Mrs R B Kennard And Partner **Bred** Stowell Hill Ltd And Major And Mrs R B Kennard **Trained** Lambourn, Berks

FOCUS
Probably a fair maiden that should produce winners with those in the frame behind the winner making promising debuts. the fifth and sixth are the best guides to the level.
Westport ◆ Official explanation: jockey said colt was denied a clear run
Beauchamp Ultra Official explanation: jockey said filly ran green
Lethal Official explanation: jockey said colt ran too free

192 PLAY SLOTS AT LITTLEWOODSCASINO.COM H'CAP 7f (P)
4:20 (4:21) (Class 5) (0-75,75) 4-Y-0+ **£3,238** (£963; £481; £240) **Stalls** Low

Form				RPR
005-	**1**		**Raza Cab (IRE)**[37] 6621 4-8-9 **66** .... ChrisCatlin 8 (Karen George) *trckd ldr: rdn to ld over 1f out: drvn and jst hld on* **16/1**	73
0-20	**2**	*shd*	**Marko Jadeo (IRE)**[14] 89 8-9-4 **75** .... PaulFitzsimons 4 (S Dow) *b: dwlt: hld up in rr: nt clr run 1/2-way and again over 2f out: prog wl over 1f out: r.o fnl f: jst failed* **9/1**	82
05-5	**3**	*hd*	**Quantum Leap**[22] 17 9-8-10 **67** ....(v) JimmyQuinn 5 (S Dow) *trckd ldrs: effrt 2f out: rdn and r.o fnl f: jst hld* **8/1**[3]	73
00-6	**4**	*1*	**Tanforan**[18] 64 4-8-7 **71** .... JamesDoyle(7) 14 (K McAuliffe) *lw: b.hind: led and crossed to inner fr wd draw: rdn and hdd over 1f out: one pce ins fnl f* **7/1**[2]	74
66-3	**5**	*½*	**Screwdriver**[19] 58 4-8-12 **72** ....(b) DNolan(3) 9 (Miss J R Tooth) *lw: dwlt: sn chsd ldrs: effrt 2f out: tried to cl 1f out: one pce ins fnl f* **7/1**[2]	74
0-30	**6**	*½*	**Hand Chime**[5] 157 9-8-1 **61** oh1 .... PatrickMathers(3) 1 (Ernst Oertel) *chsd ldrs: n.m.r on inner 2f out: kpt on same pce after* **25/1**	62
010-	**7**	*nk*	**Lake Chini (IRE)**[36] 6636 4-9-4 **75** ....(b[1]) MatthewHenry 6 (M A Jarvis) *prom: rdn on inner 3f out: kpt on and stl cl up 1f out: fdd* **10/1**	75
6616	**8**	*1*	**Kallista's Pride**[4] 164 6-8-8 **65** 6ex .... HayleyTurner 2 (J R Best) *t.k.h: hld up towards rr on inner: n.m.r over 2f out: n.d after: kpt on fnl f* **9/1**	62
1-06	**9**	*1 ¾*	**Libre**[12] 108 6-9-1 **72** .... J-PGuillambert 7 (Ernst Oertel) *t.k.h: prom: rdn 2f out: wknd over 1f out* **14/1**	65
50-5	**10**	*1 ½*	**Willheconquertoo**[14] 89 6-8-13 **70** ....(tp) TomEaves 11 (I W McInnes) *dwlt: a towards rr: rdn and no prog 2f out* **14/1**	59
35-0	**11**	*¾*	**Queens Rhapsody**[21] 36 6-9-2 **73** .... SamHitchcott 10 (A Bailey) *towards rr whn stmbld bdly over 5f out: no ch after* **12/1**	60
233-	**12**	*shd*	**Age Of Kings (USA)**[205] 3191 4-9-2 **73** .... SteveDrowne 3 (A B Haynes) *b: dwlt: outpcd in detached last: nvr a factor* **16/1**	60
0-64	**13**	*shd*	**Joy And Pain**[14] 89 5-8-9 **66** .... EddieAhern 13 (J R Boyle) *b: hld up towards rr: effrt on wd outside 3f out: wknd 2f out* **5/1**[1]	53

1m 23.88s (-2.01) **Going Correction** -0.15s/f (Stan) **13** Ran SP% **118.5**
Speed ratings (Par 103):105,104,104,103,102 102,102,100,98,97 96,96,96
CSF £151.99 CT £1251.96 TOTE £24.20: £5.90, £3.90, £3.00; EX 366.50 Place 6 £205.63, Place 5 £124.46.
Owner B R Phillips **Bred** Rathyork Stud **Trained** Higher Easington, Devon

FOCUS
A competitive handicap run at a solid gallop but there are doubts about the value of the form.
Queens Rhapsody Official explanation: jockey said gelding clipped heels a furlong after start
T/Plt: £429.30 to a £1 stake. Pool: £48,261.35. 82.05 winning tickets. T/Qpdt: £386.10 to a £1 stake. Pool: £4,226.90. 8.10 winning tickets. JN

[179]SOUTHWELL (L-H)
Thursday, January 26

OFFICIAL GOING: Standard
Wind: Fresh, across Weather: Cloudy with sunny spells

193 TEXT "BETDIRECT" TO 88600 H'CAP (DIV I) 1m (F)
12:30 (12:31) (Class 6) (0-60,59) 3-Y-0 **£2,047** (£604; £302) **Stalls** Low

Form				RPR
00-1	**1**		**Petrichan (IRE)**[15] 93 3-9-4 **59** ....(p) NCallan 7 (K A Ryan) *mde all: rdn over 2f out: styd on gamely* **13/8**[1]	68+
06-0	**2**	*¾*	**Perfect Order (USA)**[22] 30 3-8-12 **53** ....(p) SteveDrowne 8 (N A Callaghan) *a.p: rdn to chse wnr over 2f out: styd on u.p* **6/1**[3]	61
000-	**3**	*1 ¼*	**Monte Mayor Junior**[47] 6539 3-8-11 **52** ....(v[1]) RobertHavlin 6 (D Haydn Jones) *chsd wnr over 5f: sn rdn: no ex ins fnl f* **6/1**[3]	57
563-	**4**	*10*	**Franky'N'Jonny**[101] 5947 3-9-1 **56** .... FergalLynch 9 (J Pearce) *s.i.s: hld up: sme hdwy over 2f out: n.d* **7/1**	41
003-	**5**	*1 ½*	**Tirol Livit (IRE)**[108] 5805 3-8-8 **52** .... DanielTudhope(3) 4 (N Wilson) *mid-div: rdn 1/2-way: wknd over 3f out* **16/1**	34
05-0	**6**	*2 ½*	**Master Ben (IRE)**[17] 69 3-9-0 **55** ....(b) PaulEddery 2 (S R Bowring) *chsd ldrs over 5f* **25/1**	32
30-0	**7**	*2 ½*	**Drawn Out (IRE)**[10] 123 3-8-6 **54** ....(b[1]) RussellKennemore(7) 3 (P C Haslam) *bhd fr 1/2-way* **33/1**	26
66-4	**8**	*3 ½*	**Teddy Monty (IRE)**[23] 20 3-8-4 **50** ....(p) RoryMoore(5) 10 (M Quinn) *chsd ldrs 5f* **10/1**	15
05-1	**9**	*10*	**Crush On You**[14] 99 3-9-2 **57** .... GrahamGibbons 1 (R Hollinshead) *broke wl: sn outpcd: bhd fr 1/2-way* **5/1**[2]	—
000-	**10**	*6*	**Baron De Hoyland**[120] 5546 3-7-13 **45** oh10 .... DuranFentiman(5) 5 (J R Norton) *s.i.s: bhd fr 1/2-way* **100/1**	—

1m 44.59s (-0.01) **Going Correction** -0.10s/f (Stan) **10** Ran SP% **118.6**
Speed ratings (Par 95):96,95,94,84,82 80,77,74,64,58
CSF £11.76 CT £48.73 TOTE £2.10: £1.10, £2.20, £2.50; EX 13.60.
Owner Peter & Richard Foden Racing Partnership **Bred** Fortbarrington Stud **Trained** Hambleton, N Yorks

FOCUS
A moderate handicap in which and the first three home, who had this race to themselves from some way out, finished well clear.
Crush On You Official explanation: jockey said filly was never travelling

194 BETDIRECT.CO.UK H'CAP 1m 4f (F)
1:00 (1:00) (Class 4) (0-85,85) 4-Y-0+ **£5,505** (£1,637; £818; £408) **Stalls** Low

Form				RPR
12-0	**1**		**Pass The Port**[15] 88 5-8-9 **76** .... EddieAhern 9 (D Haydn Jones) *hld up in tch: led over 1f out: edgd rt: rdn out* **7/2**[1]	83
411-	**2**	*1*	**Kylkenny**[30] 6669 11-9-4 **85** ....(t) SteveDrowne 1 (H Morrison) *chsd ldrs: rdn and ev ch over 1f out: edgd rt: styd on* **12/1**	91
14-0	**3**	*½*	**Trance (IRE)**[21] 48 6-8-7 **74** .... PhillipMakin 8 (T D Barron) *sn pushed along in rr: hdwy over 5f out: sn rdn: styd on* **15/2**	79
11-6	**4**	*shd*	**Heathyards Pride**[15] 88 6-8-13 **80** .... GeorgeBaker 5 (R Hollinshead) *hld up and bhd: hdwy over 4f out: rdn and swtchd lft 2f out: sn ev ch: no ex ins fnl f* **4/1**[2]	85+
53-1	**5**	*1 ½*	**Bethanys Boy (IRE)**[10] 125 5-8-6 **78** 6ex .... GregFairley(5) 3 (B Ellison) *s.i.s: bhd: hdwy over 2f out: sn rdn: nt clr run ins fnl f: no imp* **7/2**[1]	80+
31-3	**6**	*6*	**Khanjar (USA)**[14] 98 6-8-7 **74** ....(p) PatCosgrave 7 (K R Burke) *chsd ldr tl led over 5f out: rdn and hdd over 1f out: wknd fnl f* **15/2**	67
220-	**7**	*13*	**Torrid Kentavr (USA)**[82] 6254 9-8-8 **75** .... TomEaves 4 (B Ellison) *prom over 6f* **20/1**	49
000-	**8**	*16*	**Paddys Tern**[27] 6687 4-7-8 **72** oh11 ow1 .... JosephWalsh(7) 6 (N M Babbage) *chsd ldrs to 1/2-way* **150/1**	22
2-21	**9**	*5*	**Danelor (IRE)**[13] 107 8-8-11 **78** ....(p) PaulHanagan 2 (R A Fahey) *led over 6f: wknd wl over 2f out* **6/1**[3]	20

2m 39.54s (-2.55) **Going Correction** -0.10s/f (Stan)
WFA 4 from 5yo+ 4lb **9** Ran SP% **115.4**
Speed ratings (Par 105):104,103,103,102,101 97,89,78,75
CSF £46.30 CT £297.06 TOTE £3.20: £1.60, £2.50, £2.80; EX 30.70.
Owner The Porters **Bred** Meon Valley Stud **Trained** Efail Isaf, Rhondda C Taff

FOCUS
A good, fiercely competitive handicap for the grade and they went a strong pace throughout. The fifth sets the level and was close to form.
Danelor(IRE) Official explanation: vet said gelding was lame

195 BETDIRECT FREEPHONE 0800 211 222 MAIDEN STKS 6f (F)
1:30 (1:31) (Class 5) 3-Y-0+ **£3,238** (£963; £481; £240) **Stalls** Low

Form				RPR
6-23	**1**		**Cookie Cutter (IRE)**[21] 45 4-9-7 57 ....(p) RobertWinston 1 (K R Burke) *mde all: rdn over 1f out: r.o* **11/4**[1]	77
63-3	**2**	*3*	**Ockums Razor (IRE)**[13] 104 3-8-10 65 .... NCallan 10 (N A Callaghan) *trckd wnr: racd keenly: rdn over 1f out: no ex fnl f* **7/2**[2]	68
-	**3**	*4*	**Crimson King (IRE)** 5-9-9 .... AdamKirby(3) 4 (T T Clement) *s.s: in rr: r.o ins fnl f: nrst fin* **33/1**	61
040-	**4**	*1*	**Tuckers Point (IRE)**[131] 5318 3-8-5 70 .... EddieAhern 9 (J A Osborne) *prom: rdn over 3f out: no imp fnl 2f* **11/2**[3]	48
06-	**5**	*3 ½*	**Musicmaestroplease (IRE)**[35] 6656 3-8-10 .... DeanMcKeown 2 (S Parr) *chsd ldrs over 3f* **8/1**	43
2-35	**6**	*1 ½*	**Christian Bendix**[7] 145 4-9-12 45 .... SteveDrowne 6 (P Howling) *prom: rdn 4f out: wknd 2f out* **12/1**	43
4-50	**7**	*¾*	**Muktasb (USA)**[3] 178 5-9-9 50 ....(be) PatrickMathers(3) 11 (D Shaw) *hld up: effrt over 3f out: n.d* **12/1**	41
5	**8**	*shd*	**Ten Prophets (IRE)**[5] 165 3-8-10 .... MickyFenton 8 (J A Osborne) *chsd ldrs over 3f* **7/1**	35
0-30	**9**	*3*	**Madame Guillotine**[7] 145 4-9-4 40 ....(p) PaulMulrennan(3) 3 (P T Midgley) *mid-div: rdn over 4f out: wknd 1/2-way* **66/1**	26
6	**10**	*12*	**Royal Crescent (IRE)**[21] 45 3-8-5 .... JimmyQuinn 5 (Sir Mark Prescott) *sn outpcd* **8/1**	—
00-	**11**	*9*	**Bold Havana**[180] 3948 4-9-7 .... TPQueally 7 (T T Clement) *dwlt: outpcd* **80/1**	—

1m 15.91s (-0.99) **Going Correction** -0.10s/f (Stan)
WFA 3 from 4yo+ 16lb **11** Ran SP% **120.0**
Speed ratings (Par 103):102,98,92,91,86 84,83,83,79,63 51
CSF £12.43 TOTE £2.80: £1.50, £1.40, £14.90; EX 14.00.
Owner G Mullins **Bred** Limestone Stud **Trained** Middleham Moor, N Yorks

FOCUS
The front two went off very fast and looked as though they might be doing a bit too much up front, but this maiden lacked strength in depth and basically nothing could get to them. The runner-up sets the standard.
Ten Prophets(IRE) Official explanation: jockey said gelding lost its action in final furlong

196 PLAY NOW AT BETDIRECTCASINO.COM H'CAP 6f (F)
2:00 (2:01) (Class 6) (0-55,55) 4-Y-0+ **£2,388** (£705; £352) **Stalls** Low

Form				RPR
3-21	**1**		**Shadow Jumper (IRE)**[21] 46 5-9-0 **55** ....(v) RobbieFitzpatrick 1 (M J Attwater) *s.i.s: hdwy over 4f out: led 1/2-way: drvn out* **11/4**[1]	67+
4-10	**2**	*¾*	**Soba Jones**[17] 67 9-8-11 **55** .... JasonEdmunds(3) 7 (J Balding) *a.p: rdn and ev ch ins fnl f: unable qck nr fin* **15/2**	62
15-5	**3**	*½*	**Orchestration (IRE)**[14] 96 5-8-13 **54** ....(v) ChrisCatlin 5 (M J Attwater) *chsd ldrs: rdn over 1f out: no ex towards fin* **11/2**[3]	60
41-0	**4**	*1*	**Mind Alert**[16] 81 5-8-8 **52** ....(be) PatrickMathers(3) 11 (D Shaw) *hld up in tch: effrt over 1f out: styd on same pce ins fnl f* **12/1**	55
005-	**5**	*2*	**Massey**[161] 4508 10-8-6 **52** .... AndrewMullen(5) 8 (C R Dore) *led to 1/2-way: rdn and ev ch over 1f out: no ex ins fnl f* **33/1**	49
00-5	**6**	*¾*	**Zariano**[9] 134 6-8-10 **51** .... PaulFessey 13 (T D Barron) *sn pushed along in rr: hdwy over 1f out: nt trble ldrs* **10/1**	45
-040	**7**	*1 ¼*	**Zorn**[3] 178 7-8-9 **50** .... SteveDrowne 2 (P Howling) *chsd ldr tl rdn 1/2-way: wknd fnl f* **7/1**	41
062-	**8**	*1 ¼*	**Blythe Spirit**[41] 6589 7-8-13 **54** ....(t) PaulHanagan 9 (R A Fahey) *chsd ldrs: rdn over 2f out: wknd fnl f* **5/1**[2]	41
400-	**9**	*2*	**Jun Fan (USA)**[26] 6695 4-8-9 **55** ....(be[1]) GregFairley(5) 4 (B Ellison) *s.s: n.d* **12/1**	36
21-0	**10**	*½*	**Boisdale (IRE)**[10] 126 8-9-0 **55** .... MickyFenton 6 (S L Keightley) *chsd ldrs over 4f* **20/1**	34
0-00	**11**	*shd*	**Headland (USA)**[3] 177 8-8-9 **50** ....(be) PhillipMakin 3 (D W Chapman) *hld up: effrt over 2f out: a in rr* **20/1**	29
0-00	**12**	*1 ½*	**Lady Londra**[15] 86 4-8-9 **50** .... JimmyQuinn 12 (D K Ivory) *a in rr* **40/1**	24
50-0	**13**	*3*	**Suffolk House**[16] 77 4-8-13 **54** ....(p) NCallan 10 (K A Ryan) *s.i.s: hdwy over 3f out: wknd over 2f out* **16/1**	19

1m 16.61s (-0.29) **Going Correction** -0.10s/f (Stan) **13** Ran SP% **128.2**
Speed ratings (Par 101):97,96,95,94,91 90,88,87,84,83 83,81,77
CSF £24.45 CT £117.96 TOTE £2.70: £1.50, £2.90, £1.90; EX 23.30.
Owner Brooklands Racing **Bred** Newtown Stud **Trained** Wysall, Notts

FOCUS
Just a moderate handicap, but still very competitive and the form looks solid for the grade rated through the runner-up.
Suffolk House Official explanation: jockey said gelding had no more to give

The Form Book, Raceform Ltd, Compton, RG20 6NL

197 FIRST PAST THE POST AT BETDIRECT (S) STKS 7f (F)
2:30 (2:33) (Class 6) 3-Y-O £2,388 (£705; £352) Stalls Low

Form RPR
22-5 1 **Inaminute (IRE)**[14] 99 3-8-9 55 PatCosgrave 9 57
(K R Burke) *chsd ldrs: led over 2f out: rdn and edgd lft over 1f out: hdd ins fnl f: rallied to ld nr fin* **8/1**
215 2 ½ **Ten Shun**[10] 122 3-9-5 66 EddieAhern 1 66
(M J Polglase) *hld up in tch: rdn to join wnr and edgd rt over 1f out: led ins fnl f: hdd nr fin* **15/2**
43-5 3 1 ¼ **Cool Isle**[17] 69 3-8-9 53 (b) NCallan 2 52
(K A Ryan) *chsd ldrs: led 1/2-way: rdn and hdd over 2f out: nt clr run over 1f out: styd on same pce* **16/1**
2-42 4 1 ¼ **Tafilah**[8] 139 3-8-9 56 (v) JimmyQuinn 13 49
(P W D'Arcy) *hld up in tch: rdn over 2f out: hung lft over 1f out: styd on same pce* **7/1[3]**
1-32 5 ¾ **Noble Edge**[14] 99 3-9-5 61 (p) RobertWinston 4 57
(Robert Gray) *hld up in tch: rdn 1/2-way: styd on* **9/1**
514- 6 ½ **Aysgarth Flyer (IRE)**[35] 6656 3-9-0 60 (b) GregFairley(5) 10 56
(I Semple) *chsd ldrs: rdn over 2f out: styd on same pce appr fnl f* **7/2[1]**
04-0 7 2 ½ **Chookie Windsor**[21] 49 3-9-0 57 (p) TomEaves 14 44
(I Semple) *sn outpcd: styd on appr fnl f: nvr nrr* **12/1**
000- 8 3 **Tolinis Girl**[97] 6004 3-8-9 56 (b[1]) PaulEddery 12 32
(B Smart) *sn outpcd: nvr nrr* **66/1**
000- 9 nk **Upthedowns (IRE)**[48] 6529 3-9-0 58 (b) PhillipMakin 3 36
(T D Barron) *chsd ldrs: rdn 1/2-way: wknd over 2f out* **25/1**
060- 10 ¾ **Mytass**[26] 6697 3-8-7 52 RussellKennemore(7) 11 34
(J A Pickering) *sn outpcd* **66/1**
42-0 11 shd **Lady Palma Nova**[24] 10 3-8-9 59 (b[1]) DaleGibson 8 29
(M W Easterby) *s.i.s: hdwy 5f out: wknd over 2f out* **7/1[3]**
4-10 12 1 ¼ **Indian Wizard (IRE)**[15] 85 3-9-5 65 TonyCulhane 6 35
(P Howling) *prom over 4f* **5/1[2]**
0-6 13 7 **Lily On A Hill**[24] 11 3-8-4 NataliaGemelova(5) 5 7
(B Smart) *sn led: hdd 1/2-way: wknd 2f out* **150/1**
00-0 14 14 **Grove Cherry (IRE)**[17] 69 3-8-9 51 ChrisCatlin 7 —
(M H Tompkins) *sn outpcd and bhd* **50/1**

1m 30.89s (0.09) **Going Correction** -0.10s/f (Stan) 14 Ran SP% **119.8**
Spd rtgs (Par 95):95,94,93,91,90 90,87,83,83,82 82,81,73,57 CSF £65.26 TOTE £9.80: £3.50, £2.10, £4.70; EX 80.40 Indian Wizard clmd D. Rees £6,000; Ten Shun clmd P. D. Evans £6,000
Owner Mrs Elaine M Burke **Bred** R Bailey **Trained** Middleham Moor, N Yorks

FOCUS
Quite a competitive seller and the form looks sound and reliable with four of the first five close to their marks.
Lady Palma Nova Official explanation: jockey said filly hung throughout race

198 LITTLEWOODS BETDIRECT H'CAP 5f (F)
3:00 (3:01) (Class 2) (0-100,92) 4-Y-O+ £12,954 (£3,854; £1,926; £962) Stalls High

Form RPR
011- 1 **Ok Pal**[37] 6636 6-9-7 92 IanMongan 9 102
(T G Mills) *chsd ldrs: rdn to ld over 1f out: edgd lft ins fnl f : r.o* **7/2[1]**
00-4 2 1 **Dancing Mystery**[25] 6 12-9-6 91 (b) StephenCarson 2 98
(E A Wheeler) *chsd ldrs: rdn over 1f out: edgd rt ins fnl f: styd on* **11/1**
46-3 3 nk **Desperate Dan**[16] 79 5-9-0 85 (b) EddieAhern 4 91
(J A Osborne) *s.i.s: sn chsng ldrs: rdn and ev ch whn edgd lft ins fnl f: unable qck* **5/1[3]**
4-54 4 ¾ **Pawan (IRE)**[20] 58 6-8-2 80 oh1 ow2 AnnStokell(7) 1 83
(Miss A Stokell) *sn chsng ldrs: rdn over 1f out: styd on same pce ins fnl f* **14/1**
000- 5 1 **Zarzu**[195] 3515 7-9-2 87 RobbieFitzpatrick 6 87+
(C R Dore) *hld up in tch: rdn 1/2-way: styng on whn nt clr run ins fnl f: nvr able to chal* **50/1**
040- 6 4 **Glaramara**[171] 4222 5-9-5 90 SamHitchcott 10 76
(A Bailey) *in tch: sn rdn along: no imp fnl 2f* **18/1**
00-0 7 shd **Whinhill House**[16] 79 6-8-12 83 (p) RobertWinston 3 69
(D W Barker) *led over 3f: wknd fnl f* **13/2**
30-1 8 shd **The Lord**[16] 79 6-9-2 87 TonyCulhane 5 73
(W G M Turner) *chsd ldrs: rdn 1/2-way: wknd over 1f out* **4/1[2]**
00-1 9 4 **Maktavish**[14] 96 7-8-7 78 oh3 (b) PaulHanagan 8 50
(I Semple) *chsd ldrs to 1/2-way* **9/1**
0-35 10 nk **Trinculo (IRE)**[20] 54 9-9-0 85 AdrianTNicholls 7 56
(D Nicholls) *chsd ldrs: lost pl over 3f out: sn bhd* **11/2**

59.58 secs (-0.72) **Going Correction** +0.10s/f (Slow) 10 Ran SP% **119.8**
Speed ratings (Par 109):109,107,106,105,104 97,97,97,91,90
CSF £44.35 CT £200.60 TOTE £3.90: £1.60, £3.20, £1.90; EX 57.80 Trifecta £355.40 Part won. Pool: £500.60 - 0.70 winning tickets..
Owner Sherwoods Transport Ltd **Bred** Sherwoods Transport Ltd **Trained** Headley, Surrey

FOCUS
With the top weight rated 8lb below the ceiling of 100 for this valuable sprint handicap, the form could be stronger for the grade, but still this was another fine effort from Ok Pal.

NOTEBOOK
Ok Pal, successful from an unfavourably high draw over course and distance on his previous start, defied a 7lb higher mark to follow up from what was another poor draw. He has clearly been winning with a little bit in hand and is a progressive sprinter worth keeping on the right side of. (tchd 4-1 in places)
Dancing Mystery had a good draw and ran creditably behind the progressive winner. (op 14-1)
Desperate Dan ran his usual race, travelling well before failing to find enough to win. (op 9-2)
Pawan(IRE) is an admirable performer and ran about as well as could have been expected, especially as he is almost certainly better over further. (op 12-1)
Zarzu kept on from off the pace to make a promising return from a 195-day break, and should pop up at least once or twice in the coming months.
Glaramara had a bad draw and can be expected to come on for this first run in 171 days. (op 40-1)
Whinhill House was again below the pick of his form. (tchd 7-1)
The Lord could not repeat the form of his recent course-and-distance success off a 7lb higher mark.
Maktavish would have found this tougher than the course-and-distance claimer he won on his previous start, and could not dominate from his poor draw. (op 10-1 tchd 12-1)
Trinculo(IRE) had run creditably on his two starts this year, but was disappointing this time.

199 TEXT "BETDIRECT" TO 88600 H'CAP (DIV II) 1m (F)
3:30 (3:30) (Class 6) (0-60,60) 3-Y-O £2,047 (£604; £302) Stalls Low

Form RPR
006- 1 **Hi Dancer**[138] 5125 3-8-7 49 LeeEnstone 5 58
(P C Haslam) *prom: lost pl and hmpd over 5f out: hdwy over 3f out: rdn and hung lft fr over 2f out: r.o to ld wl ins fnl f* **13/2[3]**
060- 2 1 ¾ **Marachi Band (USA)**[48] 6532 3-9-2 58 (b[1]) SteveDrowne 8 63
(E A L Dunlop) *a.p: rdn to chse ldr over 2f out: led over 1f out: hdd wl ins fnl f* **5/1[1]**
25-4 3 2 ½ **Woodwee**[14] 99 3-8-13 60 AndrewMullen(5) 3 60
(J R Weymes) *chsd ldrs: led 1/2-way: hdd over 2f out: no ex fnl f* **11/2[2]**
060- 4 6 **Chicherova (IRE)**[138] 5122 3-8-10 52 PaulFessey 2 40
(T D Barron) *chsd ldrs over 6f* **13/2[3]**
000- 5 5 **Spasiba**[72] 6357 3-8-8 50 (b[1]) J-PGuillambert 1 28
(Sir Mark Prescott) *rdn to ld 7f out: hdd over 5f out: rdn and wknd 2f out* **10/1**
600- 6 3 **Bekoning (IRE)**[66] 6395 3-8-12 54 RobertWinston 9 26
(M Quinn) *dwlt: hdwy to ld over 5f out: hdd 1/2-way: rdn and wknd over 1f out* **10/1**
00-0 7 5 **Sahara Secret (IRE)**[10] 122 3-8-1 46 oh16 (v[1]) PatrickMathers(3) 10 8
(D Shaw) *sn pushed along in rr: n.d* **66/1**
060- 8 5 **Guideline**[85] 6226 3-8-10 55 PaulMulrennan(3) 7 7
(M W Easterby) *sn outpcd and bhd* **13/2[3]**
50-0 9 2 ½ **Caan**[15] 85 3-8-10 52 (p) ChrisCatlin 4 —
(D K Ivory) *led 1f: wknd over 4f out* **25/1**
000- 10 22 **Show Thyme**[76] 6316 3-9-0 56 NCallan 6 —
(K A Ryan) *sn outpcd: hdwy over 3f out: sn wknd* **5/1[1]**

1m 44.35s (-0.25) **Going Correction** -0.10s/f (Stan) 10 Ran SP% **112.2**
Speed ratings (Par 95):97,95,92,86,81 78,73,68,66,44
CSF £37.44 CT £193.69 TOTE £9.50: £2.30, £2.50, £1.10; EX 51.60.
Owner Middleham Park Racing Viii **Bred** Mrs E Roberts **Trained** Middleham Moor, N Yorks

FOCUS
Just a moderate handicap, but a few of these came into this unexposed. The form could be rated higher through the third.

200 PLAY NOW AT BETDIRECTPOKER.COM H'CAP 1m (F)
4:00 (4:00) (Class 6) (0-65,65) 4-Y-O+ £2,388 (£705; £352) Stalls Low

Form RPR
31-4 1 **Chicken Soup**[16] 77 4-9-1 65 DanielTudhope(3) 3 73
(D Carroll) *hld up: hdwy over 3f out: led over 1f out: rdn out* **10/3[2]**
50-5 2 1 ¼ **Jakarmi**[13] 106 5-9-0 61 FrancisFerris 7 67
(B Palling) *chsd ldrs: rdn over 3f out: styd on same pce fnl f* **5/1[3]**
-600 3 3 **Penwell Hill (USA)**[10] 125 7-9-4 65 (b) ChrisCatlin 4 65
(M J Attwater) *chsd ldrs: led over 2f out: rdn and hdd over 1f out: no ex fnl f* **20/1**
32-1 4 4 **Golden Square**[9] 134 4-8-12 59 6ex RobertWinston 5 51
(A W Carroll) *sn pushed along in rr: hdwy over 3f out: nvr trbld ldrs* **11/4[1]**
650- 5 2 ½ **Triple Jump**[184] 3818 5-9-1 62 NCallan 6 49
(K A Ryan) *hld up: hdwy over 3f out: wknd over 1f out* **6/1**
06-0 6 ½ **Lord Links (IRE)**[14] 101 5-9-4 65 PatCosgrave 8 51
(D J Daly) *s.s: styd on fnl f: nvr nrr* **16/1**
55-6 7 2 **Come What July (IRE)**[14] 98 5-8-10 64 (p) KellyHarrison(7) 2 46
(Mrs N Macauley) *sn outpcd and bhd: nvr nrr* **40/1**
600- 8 1 ¼ **Fraternity**[99] 5991 9-8-8 62 RussellKennemore(7) 13 41
(J A Pickering) *led over 5f: sn wknd* **25/1**
405- 9 hd **Dudley Docker (IRE)**[47] 6542 4-8-9 63 DanielleMcCreery(7) 12 42
(D Carroll) *s.s: a bhd* **14/1**
0-00 10 2 ½ **Warden Warren**[1] 185 8-8-10 62 (p) MarcHalford(5) 11 36
(Mrs C A Dunnett) *prom to 1/2-way* **40/1**
00-0 11 1 **Union Jack Jackson (IRE)**[14] 101 4-9-0 61 FergalLynch 1 33
(J G Given) *chsd ldrs over 3f* **22/1**
01-0 12 15 **Gem Bien (USA)**[25] 8 8-8-11 58 (b) TonyCulhane 10 —
(D W Chapman) *prom to 1/2-way* **20/1**
00-0 13 2 **Familiar Affair**[20] 56 5-9-4 65 PhillipMakin 14 3
(T D Barron) *chsd ldrs over 4f* **20/1**

1m 43.48s (-1.12) **Going Correction** -0.10s/f (Stan) 13 Ran SP% **120.6**
Speed ratings (Par 101):101,99,96,92,90 89,87,86,86,83 82,67,65
CSF £18.33 CT £291.28 TOTE £6.20: £2.00, £2.10, £5.50; EX 28.80 Place 6 £80.71, Place 5 £55.93.
Owner Fishlake Commercial Motors Ltd **Bred** Limestone Stud **Trained** Warthill, N Yorks

FOCUS
A moderate handicap in which the leaders went off very fast and the overall time was ordinary. The runner-up sets the standard.
Dudley Docker(IRE) Official explanation: jockey said gelding hung left
T/Jkpt: £3,550.00 to a £1 stake. Pool: £10,000.00. 2.00 winning tickets. T/Plt: £90.50 to a £1 stake. Pool: £46,797.10. 377.40 winning tickets. T/Qpdt: £15.50 to a £1 stake. Pool: £4,710.20. 223.70 winning tickets. CR

149 NAD AL SHEBA (L-H)
Thursday, January 26
OFFICIAL GOING: Dirt course - fast; turf course - good to firm

201a ZAWAJ STKS (H'CAP) (TURF) 6f 110y(T)
3:05 (3:10) (95-110,108) 3-Y-O+ £45,348 (£13,953; £6,976; £3,488)

RPR
1 **Compton's Eleven**[91] 6125 5-8-10 98 TedDurcan 13 103
(M R Channon) *racd in mid-div: swtchd wd early st: smooth prog 2f out: led 1f out: r.o* **10/1**
2 shd **Slip Dance (IRE)**[119] 5573 4-8-9 97 MCHussey 11 102
(Eamon Tyrrell, Ire) *t.k.h: hld up in rr: chal wd in st: ev ch: jst failed* **18/1**
3 1 ¼ **So Will I**[36] 5-9-2 104 (t) RHills 4 105
(Doug Watson, UAE) *trckd ldrs: short of room 3f out: swtchd to rail 2 1/2f out: r.o* **10/1**
4 ½ **T-Bird (SAF)**[36] 5-9-6 108 (t) TPO'Shea 12 107
(E Charpy, UAE) *hld up in rr: clsd on rail 1 1/2f out: r.o wl once clr* **10/3[1]**
5 ½ **Ned Kelly (SAF)**[306] 734 5-8-7 95 (bt[1]) JBekker 6 93
(D Maroun, South Africa) *racd in mid-div on rail: no room: swtchd wd 2f out: r.o wl: nrst fin* **33/1**
6 1 ½ **Stetchworth Prince**[140] 5065 4-9-2 104 KerrinMcEvoy 1 97
(Saeed Bin Suroor) *trckd ldrs on rail: led 1 1/2f out: one pce* **9/2[3]**
7 1 ½ **Montgomery's Arch (USA)**[151] 4805 4-9-3 105 MJKinane 8 94
(J Noseda) *trckd ldrs: ev ch 2 1/2f out: nt qckn* **4/1[2]**
8 1 ¼ **Millbag (IRE)**[56] 5-8-12 100 JMurtagh 2 85
(D Selvaratnam, UAE) *trckd ldrs: prom top of st: ev ch 1 1/2f out: nt qckn* **16/1**
9 6 **Hinterland (SAF)**[36] 8-9-3 105 RyanMoore 5 72
(S Seemar, UAE) *led early: secured rail: disp into st: kicked on 3f out: passed 1 1/2f out: eased* **13/2**

10 4 **Damachida (IRE)**[91] 7-9-1 **102**....(t) JamieSpencer 10 58
(Eva Sundbye, Sweden) *n.d* **11/1**

11 2 ¾ **Prince Charming**[122] [5508] 4-8-12 **100**.... PDillon 3 47
(R Bouresly, Kuwait) *prom: disp into st: fdd 3f out* **33/1**

P **Sleipner (BRZ)**[314] 5-9-1 **102**....(v¹) RPCleary 9 —
(A Selvaratnam, UAE) *mid-div early: wknd 4f out: broke down 2f out and p.u* **20/1**

1m 17.25s **Going Correction** +0.20s/f (Good) **12** Ran SP% **122.9**
Speed ratings: 106,105,104,103,103 101,99,98,91,87 83,—

Owner PCM Racing **Bred** Lady Cobham **Trained** West Ilsley, Berks

FOCUS
A very competitive handicap and the form is strong.

NOTEBOOK
Compton's Eleven was winless since taking a similar race at last year's Carnival, but was only 2lb higher than when gaining that success and did enough to end his losing run. Although he only held on by a short-head, he never looked like actually being caught and was a worthy winner. He can be expected to be sharper next time given this was his first run in 91 days, but his overall record suggests he could be worth opposing. (op 11/1)
Slip Dance(IRE) ◆, an Irish-trained performer who won a five-furlong Listed race at Hamilton last season, ran a fine race on her return to Dubai (she was fifth in the UAE 1000 Guineas on only start out here last year). Given that this was her first run in 119 days, there could be even better to come and she should win at this year's Carnival. (op 16/1)
So Will I, despite winning a Listed race at three, never fulfilled his potential when trained in England by Marcus Tregoning. This was a creditable performance and it would be no surprise to see him find a race or two for his current connections.
T-Bird(SAF), a seven-furlong Listed winner on his previous start, gives the form a solid look. (op 7/2 tchd 3/1)
Ned Kelly(SAF), not seen since finishing fourth in the UAE Derby on the dirt at last year's Carnival, made a most encouraging return to action off the back of a 306-day absence.
Stetchworth Prince, a smart performer for David Loder, made an unspectacular debut for Godolphin off the back of a 140-day break.
Montgomery's Arch(USA), ex Peter Chapple-Hyam, was well held off the back of a 151-day break.

202a MUSTAQBALI CUP (FILLIES) (DIRT) 7f (D)
3:35 (3:41) 3-Y-O **£11,337** (£3,488; £1,744; £872)

RPR

1 **Vague (USA)**[172] [4206] 3-8-9 106.... MJKinane 2 91
(J Noseda) *a.p on rail: led 2f out: clr 1f out: r.o: comf* **5/6¹**

2 1 ½ **Swan Maiden (USA)**[150] [4816] 3-8-9 77.... TedDurcan 10 87
(A Laird, UAE) *disp ld tl st: led briefly 3f out: hdd 2f out: no ch w wnr* **8/1³**

3 3 ½ **Give Me The Night (IRE)**[103] [5888] 3-8-9 90.... WSupple 12 78
(Doug Watson, UAE) *mid-div: trckd ldrs into st: ev ch 2f out: nt qckn* **14/1**

4 ½ **Fair Rosamond (IRE)**[35] 3-8-9 75.... RichardMullen 7 77
(A Laird, UAE) *mid-div: outpcd 3f out: r.o one pce* **25/1**

5 1 ¼ **Dont Dili Dali**[119] [5570] 3-8-9 93.... JohnEgan 6 74
(J S Moore) *in rr: last into st: swtchd centre: sme late hdwy: nrst fin* **8/1³**

6 1 ¼ **Lindus Atenor**[142] [5017] 3-8-9 80....(t) JAHeffernan 1 71
(M Al Muhairi, UAE) *trckd ldrs in early stages: 3rd 3f out: one pce* **33/1**

7 hd **Imperial Ice (SAF)**[7] [155] 4-9-4 91.... SRandolph 8 61
(H J Brown, South Africa) *trckd ldrs into st: ev ch 2 1/2f out: nt qckn* **25/1**

8 1 ½ **Blue Grouse (USA)**[106] [5833] 3-8-9 80.... KerrinMcEvoy 9 66
(Saeed Bin Suroor) *mid-div: dropped to rr 3f out: n.d* **9/2²**

9 1 ¼ **Donia Dubai (IRE)** 3-8-9.... PDillon 5 63
(R Bouresly, Kuwait) *mid-div: wknd 3f out* **33/1**

10 2 ½ **Princess Woodman (BRZ)**[320] 4-9-4 90.... MAlmeida 11 47
(C Morgado, Brazil) *disp ld early stages: wknd 3f out* **16/1**

11 3 **Zeina Of Arabia** 3-8-9.... PatDobbs 4 49
(Doug Watson, UAE) *slowly away: a bhd* **40/1**

12 24 **Bakhoor (IRE)** 3-8-9.... RoystonFfrench 3 —
(A Al Raihe, UAE) *v.s.a: a in rr* **33/1**

1m 25.38s **Going Correction** +0.125s/f (Slow)
WFA 3 from 4yo 18lb **12** Ran SP% **126.5**
Speed ratings: 105,103,99,98,97 95,95,93,92,89 86,58

Owner J Paul Reddam **Bred** Dr N M Cole And Christopher Kline **Trained** Newmarket, Suffolk

FOCUS
This was one of the first trials for the UAE 1,000 Guineas, but it was not a very strong race and Vague, who showed very useful form on turf last year without being Group class, outclassed her opponents.

NOTEBOOK
Vague(USA), a very useful juvenile on the turf last season but just short of Group class, took to dirt at the first attempt and basically outclassed her rivals from an unfavourably low draw, winning well without needing to run to her best. The plan now is to go for the UAE 1,000 Guineas, where the step up to a mile is likely to suit but her chance will basically depend on the strength of opposition. She also has enough stamina in her pedigree to warrant an entry in the UAE Oaks. Connections probably made the right decision sending her out here, as she would face more strength in depth back in England. (tchd 10/11)
Swan Maiden(USA), an Epsom maiden winner for Jeremy Noseda when last seen 150 days previously, took well to dirt at the first attempt and ran as well as could have been expected behind her former stablemate, given their respective form on turf back in England. (op 9/1)
Give Me The Night(IRE), 90-rated and three times a winner over five furlongs for Ed Dunlop last year, ran respectably stepped up to her furthest trip to date and is clearly effective on dirt (she won a Wolverhampton maiden on her only previous start on sand).
Fair Rosamond(IRE), the stable second string, is rated just 75 in England so this effort could be considered her best yet.
Dont Dili Dali, a very useful, tough and consistent juvenile at up to a mile on the turf last year, was not at her best switched to dirt off the back of a 119-day break.
Blue Grouse(USA) won a Lingfield maiden from the front when last seen 106 days previously, so it was a surprise to see her ridden with some restraint.

203a AMAN TROPHY (H'CAP) (TURF) 6f 110y(T)
4:05 (4:11) (95-110,107) 3-Y-O+ **£45,348** (£13,953; £6,976; £3,488)

RPR

1 **Obe Gold**[110] [5745] 4-9-0 **100**.... RyanMoore 2 107
(M R Channon) *mid-div on rail: prog 3f out: swtchd outside 1 1/2f out: rdn to ld fnl 110yds* **10/1**

2 1 **Kodiac**[138] [5117] 5-9-0 **100**.... TPO'Shea 1 104
(E Charpy, UAE) *settled in rr of main gp on rail: short of room 3f out and again 2f out: r.o wl once clr* **10/1**

3 nk **Bygone Days**[124] [5452] 5-9-2 **102**.... KerrinMcEvoy 13 105
(I Mohammed, UAE) *mid-div: wd into st: ev ch 2f out: r.o: nrst fin* **9/2²**

4 ½ **Sevillano**[69] 5-9-3 **104**....(t) TedDurcan 3 105
(A Laird, UAE) *disp ld on rail: 2nd into st: led 1 1/2f out: r.o* **4/1¹**

5 1 ¼ **Three Graces (GER)**[161] [4510] 6-9-6 **107**....(vt) WSupple 6 104
(I Mohammed, UAE) *prom in centre: led 4f out: hdd 1 1/2f out: one pce* **7/1**

6 ¾ **Jet Express (SAF)**[7] [150] 4-8-5 **95**.... SRandolph 11 87
(H J Brown, South Africa) *in rr: short of room on turn: sme prog on rail early st: n.d* **20/1**

7 ½ **Shersha (IRE)**[7] [155] 7-8-9 **96**.... MJKinane 4 89
(Kevin F O'Donnell, Ire) *trckd ldrs: ev ch 3f out: one pce* **25/1**

8 nk **Rockets 'n Rollers (IRE)**[314] 6-9-5 **106**.... RoystonFfrench 9 98
(M Al Muhairi, UAE) *mid-div: clsd 3f out: ev ch 2f out: nt qckn* **12/1**

9 1 ¾ **Safe Structure (SAF)**[271] 6-9-3 **104**.... JBekker 5 91
(D Maroun, South Africa) *in rr: hmpd on turn: nvr involved* **5/1³**

10 1 **Mokabra (IRE)**[42] 5-9-0 **100**.... JMurtagh 8 85
(D Selvaratnam, UAE) *mid-div: t.k.h: asked for effrt 3f out: fdd* **40/1**

11 11 **Golden Stravinsky (USA)**[81] [6277] 4-9-1 **101**.... MDemuro 7 53
(A Peraino, Italy) *racd in 3rd: fdd 2 1/2f out* **9/1**

P **Cedarberg (UAE)**[912] [3671] 5-9-2 **102**.... PDillon 12 —
(R Bouresly, Kuwait) *slowly away: in rr: racd v keenly: stmbld 2f out: p.u 1 1/2f out* **33/1**

1m 17.27s **Going Correction** +0.20s/f (Good) **12** Ran SP% **117.2**
Speed ratings: 106,104,104,103,102 101,101,100,98,97 85,—

Owner BDR Partnership **Bred** Mrs M Mason **Trained** West Ilsley, Berks
■ Obe Gold completed a double for Mick Channon following the earlier success of Compton's Eleven.

FOCUS
A typically competitive handicap and the form look solid enough.

NOTEBOOK
Obe Gold was not the easiest to place in England last season, but he is still a very smart performer and proved good enough to make a successful debut in Dubai off the back of a 110-day break. He should remain very competitive in similar company. (op 12/1)
Kodiac ◆, no less than 18lb higher than when he won at Newbury for John Dunlop last season, ran a fine race on his debut in Dubai off the back of a 138-day break. He may have been even closer with a clearer run and there should be even better to come.
Bygone Days, a progressive sprinter who won a competitive handicap off a mark of 94 on his last start for Willie Haggas 124 days previously, ran to a smart level of form on his debut in Dubai, but could still be considered disappointing. Despite racing wide for much of the way, he still had every chance in the straight and did not totally convince that he was going through with his effort. (op 5/1)
Sevillano, a winner on the dirt over five furlongs at Jebal Ali on his previous start, looked to run pretty much up to his best on this return to turf. (op 9/2)
Three Graces(GER) has done all his winning over further but ran much better than on his only previosu try at this trip.
Shersha(IRE) did not really improve on the form she showed over an extended seven furlongs the previous week.

204a SHAHRAZADE TROPHY (H'CAP) (DIRT) 7f (D)
4:35 (4:42) (90-105,105) 3-Y-O+ **£41,569** (£12,790; £6,395; £3,197)

RPR

1 **Happy Pearl (AUS)**[79] 6-8-6 **90**....(b) MJKinane 11 98
(G Moore, Macau) *disp early ld: trckd ldr: led 2f out: r.o* **8/1**

2 1 ½ **Sea Hunter**[124] [5460] 4-8-9 **94**....(v) RichardMullen 3 97
(Saeed Bin Suroor) *in rr on rail: prog on turn to tch ldrs 3f out: ev ch 2f out: r.o: nrst fin* **7/1³**

3 1 ¾ **Marbush (IRE)**[34] 5-9-3 **101**....(e) JMurtagh 4 100
(D Selvaratnam, UAE) *mid-div: outpcd 4f out: n.m.r on home turn: hrd rdn 3f out: r.o late: nrst fin* **20/1**

4 ½ **Aleutian**[314] 6-8-10 **95**.... WSupple 1 92
(Doug Watson, UAE) *nt far off pce: ev ch 3f out: rdn to cl 2f out: r.o: one pce* **16/1**

5 2 ½ **Glad To Be Fast (IRE)**[26] 6-9-6 **105**....(b) AStarke 2 96
(Mario Hofer, Germany) *trckd ldng pair: ev ch 2f out: one pce* **6/1²**

6 4 ¼ **Kill Cat (IRE)**[7] [154] 5-9-4 **102**....(t) MDemuro 13 82
(A Peraino, Italy) *settled in rr: wd into st: prog 2 1/2f out: r.o: nrst fin* **14/1**

7 nse **Egyptian (USA)**[7] [149] 7-9-0 **98**.... PDillon 7 78
(R Bouresly, Kuwait) *in rr: n.d* **12/1**

8 nk **At Once (GER)**[75] 5-9-2 **100**.... JamieSpencer 8 80
(Frau E Mader, Germany) *impeded s: hld up in rr: wd into st: n.d* **12/1**

9 7 ¾ **Jersey Bounce (IRE)**[123] 5-8-12 **97**....(t) SRandolph 5 55
(H J Brown, South Africa) *slowly away: a in rr* **28/1**

10 1 ¼ **Hidden Dragon (USA)**[7] [151] 7-9-6 **105**.... RyanMoore 10 60
(J Pearce) *mid-div: rdn along 5f out: n.d* **8/1**

11 ¾ **Master Robbie**[97] [6014] 7-8-6 **90**.... TPO'Shea 14 44
(R Bouresly, Kuwait) *racd in 4th: rdn 4f out: ev ch 2 1/2f out: fdd 1 1/2f out* **33/1**

12 1 ½ **Hoy Soy Usted (BRZ)**[56] 5-8-6 **90**.... MAlmeida 9 40
(C Morgado, Brazil) *broke awkwardly: sn led: set fast pce into st: fdd 2 1/2f out* **33/1**

13 1 ½ **Masquerader (USA)**[89] [6159] 4-8-8 **93**....(t) KerrinMcEvoy 12 38
(I Mohammed, UAE) *mid-div: wknd 3f out* **7/2¹**

14 5 ½ **Delude (IRE)**[70] 8-8-7 **91**.... TedDurcan 6 23
(A Laird, UAE) *outpcd early: a bhd* **7/1³**

1m 24.06s **Going Correction** +0.125s/f (Slow) **14** Ran SP% **125.8**
Speed ratings: 112,110,108,107,104 100,99,99,90,89 88,86,85,78

Owner Ye Hanoiang & Partners **Bred** Mr & Mrs Hine **Trained** Macau

FOCUS
Probably just an ordinary handicap for the grade, but solid enough form.

NOTEBOOK
Happy Pearl(AUS), a mile winner on the dirt in Macau, made a successful debut in Dubai with a pretty decisive success. He looks worth keeping on the right side of in similar company.
Sea Hunter, a tough and progressive handicapper on the turf for Mick Channon last season, proved just as effective on dirt and ran a fine race on his debut for Godolphin. He thrives on his racing and there could be even better to come.
Marbush(IRE) ◆ ran a fine race over a distance that would have been short enough and is one to look out for when stepping back up in trip.
Hidden Dragon(USA) shaped well on his debut in Dubai on turf the previous week, but failed to prove as effective on this dirt surface.
Masquerader(USA), a useful performer on Polytrack for the Godolphin operation last year, ran well below form on his debut for a new trainer on this much faster dirt surface. (op 4/1)

205a TASAHEEL CUP (H'CAP) (TURF) 1m 4f (T)
5:05 (5:12) (95-110,110) 4-Y-0+ £45,348 (£13,953; £6,976; £3,488)

RPR

1 **Encinas (GER)**[69] 5-8-11 **101** ow2 WMongil 15 107
(P Schiergen, Germany) *settled in rr: travelled v wl: smooth prog in st: disp ld 1f out: r.o* **25/1**

2 ½ **Excalibur (IRE)**[256] 1738 6-9-5 **109** (t) KShea 3 114
(M F De Kock, South Africa) *trckd ldrs: on rail in st: led 2f out: chal 1f out: r.o wl* **7/2**[1]

3 1 **Grand Ekinoks (TUR)**[88] 8-9-4 **108** (b) JamieSpencer 13 112
(C Kurt, Turkey) *settled in last: stl last ent st: swtchd wd: r.o late: nrst fin* **10/1**

4 2½ **Remaadd (USA)**[28] 5-8-12 **102** JMurtagh 16 102
(D Selvaratnam, UAE) *hld up in rr: trckd wnr in st: r.o: nrst fin* **20/1**

5 2½ **Daring Ransom (USA)**[116] 5645 4-8-8 **102** (v[1]) MJKinane 5 98
(J Noseda) *trckd ldrs: ev ch 3f out: disp ld 2f out: one pce* **12/1**

6 4¾ **Shanty Star (IRE)**[7] 153 6-8-11 **101** PDillon 4 90
(R Bouresly, Kuwait) *led tl 2 1/2f out: outpcd* **13/2**[3]

7 2¾ **Zaajel (IRE)**[371] 166 7-8-8 **98** (t) RHills 8 83
(E Charpy, UAE) *mid-div: travelling wl ent st: hmpd 3f out: r.o wl fr 2f out* **14/1**

8 3¼ **Land 'n Stars**[103] 5903 6-8-12 **102** PaulDoe 10 82
(Jamie Poulton) *mid-div: n.d* **25/1**

9 1 **Surbiton (USA)**[7] 152 6-8-7 **97** (t) RoystonFfrench 2 75
(A Al Raihe, UAE) *on rail in mid-div: trckd ldrs 2 1/2f out: ev ch: outpcd and fdd* **25/1**

10 3½ **One Little David (GER)**[88] 6191 6-8-10 **100** ASuborics 6 73
(P Vovcenko, Germany) *mid-div: travlling wl 4f out: rdn 3f out: nt qckn* **16/1**

11 shd **Omikron (IRE)**[28] 5-9-6 **110** (t) JAHeffernan 9 83
(I Jory, Saudi Arabia) *mid-div: short of room 3f out: in clr 2f out: nt qckn* **14/1**

12 1¾ **Punch Punch (BRZ)**[256] 5-8-10 **100** (b) MAlmeida 7 70
(C Morgado, Brazil) *in rr of main gp: n.d* **25/1**

13 ½ **Oratory (SAF)**[322] 600 9-8-10 **100** TedDurcan 11 70
(A Laird, UAE) *nt far off pce: ev ch 2 1/2f out: fdd 1 1/2f out* **12/1**

14 1¾ **Blue Corrig (IRE)**[11] 5781 6-8-11 **101** (b) PJSmullen 14 68
(Joseph Crowley, Ire) *slowly away: swtchd to rail: n.d* **25/1**

15 1¼ **Fantastic Love (USA)**[439] 6652 6-9-3 **107** (bt) KerrinMcEvoy 1 72
(I Mohammed, UAE) *settled in rr: prog on rail 3f out: n.m.r 2f out: n.d* **11/2**[2]

16 1¼ **Velodrome (BRZ)**[137] 7-9-1 **105** (t) TPO'Shea 12 68
(E Charpy, UAE) *trckd ldrs: rdn 4f out: fdd* **10/1**

2m 29.5s **Going Correction** +0.20s/f (Good)
WFA 4 from 5yo+ 4lb **16** Ran SP% **127.7**
Speed ratings: 110,109,109,107,105 102,100,98,97,95 95,94,93,92,91 91

Owner Stiftung Gestut Fahrhof **Bred** Stiftung Gestut Fahrhof **Trained** Germany

FOCUS
A good handicap and, with the pace decent, the form looks strong.

NOTEBOOK
Encinas(GER), a German raider who has been placed in Listed company in France, made a winning debut in Dubai, travelling strongly throughout and finding plenty when asked. Clearly well suited by these sort of conditions, there should be more to come.
Excalibur(IRE), not seen since finishing fifth in a Group One at Kranji 256 days previously, ran well on his return to handicap company and was just held by the surprise winner. His stable later completed a double at the Carnival and, now they are in full swing, this one must be respected.
Grand Ekinoks(TUR) ◆, a multiple winner over this trip in Turkey, ran well on his debut in Dubai and could be considered a little unlucky not to have finished even closer. His stable, from three runners at this year's Carnival, have had one winner, and two horses who could be considered unlucky, so they could be worth following.
Remaadd(USA), ex-Marcus Tregoning, ran third in a mile conditions race on the dirt off the back of a long absence last time, and acquitted himself most creditably stepped back up in trip and switched to turf.
Daring Ransom(USA), a beaten favourite when only fifth in the German St Leger on his last start 116 days previously, looked to have every chance in the first-time visor.
Shanty Star(IRE) failed to build on the definite promise he showed when second over a mile here the previous week.
Land 'n Stars has never won over shorter than a mile five, and four of his five career wins came over two miles, so this trip may not have been ideal for his first run back after 103 days off. He was well held.
Blue Corrig(IRE), a Listed winner on the Flat in Ireland last year, has since had a few unsuccessful spins over hurdles. Returned to the Flat, he should not have minded the conditions, but failed to produce his best.

206a NAJAH AL SHINDAGHA SPRINT (GROUP 3) (DIRT) 6f (D)
5:35 (5:46) 3-Y-0+ £75,581 (£23,255; £11,627; £5,813)

RPR

1 **Heart Alone (BRZ)**[75] 5-9-7 100 MJKinane 5 115
(A Cintra, Brazil) *broke awkwardly: sn prom: disp 3f out: clr 1 1/2f out: easily* **25/1**

2 3¾ **Conroy (USA)**[306] 736 8-9-1 112 JMurtagh 6 98
(A Selvaratnam, UAE) *prom: swtchd to rail: r.o wl but no ch w wnr* **7/1**[3]

3 3½ **Thajja (IRE)**[56] 5-9-1 100 (v) RHills 7 88
(Doug Watson, UAE) *trckd ldrs early: ev ch 2f out: one pce* **9/1**

4 nse **Safsoof (USA)**[118] 5593 4-9-1 90 RichardMullen 2 87
(I Mohammed, UAE) *outpcd early stages: r.o wl fr 2 1/2f out: nrst fin* **33/1**

5 ½ **Tropical Star (IRE)**[306] 736 6-9-1 109 (vt) RoystonFfrench 13 86
(A Al Raihe, UAE) *u.p 3f out: hrd rdn 2f out: r.o late* **7/2**[2]

6 2¼ **Conceal**[412] 8-9-1 106 PDillon 9 79
(R Bouresly, Kuwait) *mid-div: trckd ldrs 2f out: fdd* **20/1**

7 1¾ **Karlo Guitar (BRZ)**[173] 6-9-1 98 MAlmeida 3 74
(C Morgado, Brazil) *slowly away: tacked on to main gp 5f out in centre: outpcd 2f out* **33/1**

8 ½ **Sleeping Weapon (USA)**[28] 7-9-1 95 (vt) WSupple 8 72
(Doug Watson, UAE) *sn outpcd* **20/1**

9 ½ **Candidato Roy (ARG)**[306] 734 5-9-1 105 KShea 14 71
(M F De Kock, South Africa) *prom on rail: outpcd 2f out* **16/1**

10 2 **Tableau (USA)**[514] 5194 5-9-1 85 TPO'Shea 4 65
(R Bouresly, Kuwait) *impeded at s: nvr involved* **66/1**

11 hd **Starpix (FR)**[173] 4179 4-9-1 113 SRandolph 11 64
(H J Brown, South Africa) *outpcd* **12/1**

12 1¼ **Botanical (USA)**[143] 5-9-1 109 (vt) KerrinMcEvoy 10 61
(I Mohammed, UAE) *mid-div: n.m.r 2f out: n.d* **2/1**[1]

13 5 **Kay Two (IRE)**[103] 5910 4-9-1 101 PJSmullen 1 46
(Ms F M Crowley, Ire) *prom early: fdd 3f out* **33/1**

14 1 **Commandocourageous (SAF)**[196] 5-9-1 100 (t) JBekker 12 43
(D Maroun, South Africa) *mid-div early: sn wknd* **8/1**

1m 10.17s **Going Correction** +0.125s/f (Slow) **14** Ran SP% **126.4**
Speed ratings: 107,102,97,97,96 93,91,90,89,87 87,85,78,77

Owner Stud C & T **Bred** Haras Rosa Do Sul **Trained** Brazil

FOCUS
The sprinting division is weak in Dubai and, with both Tropical Star and Botanical below form, this was a very ordinary contest by Group Three standards. Nevertheless, Heart Alone certainly won in style.

NOTEBOOK
Heart Alone(BRZ) ◆, a winning sprinter in his native Brazil, took well to racing in Dubai at the first attempt and ran out an impressive winner. Until the Americans come over for the Group One Golden Shaheen in March, the sprinting division in Dubai is just ordinary and he could well enjoy further success.
Conroy(USA) ◆ is a multiple winner in Dubai and a real favourite amongst racegoers there. Returning from a 306-day break, he made a most promising return to action behind the comfortable winner and is clearly far from done with yet. There should be plenty of options for him, but no doubt his main aim will be the Mahab Al Shimaal in March, a race he has won three times in the last four years.
Thajja(IRE) would have found this tougher than the course and distance handicap he won on his previous start off a mark of 95, but acquitted himself with credit.
Safsoof(USA), ex-Godolphin, finished well after getting outpaced on his debut for a new yard off the back of a 143-day break.
Tropical Star(IRE) would have gone very close on the pick of his form, but this was a substandard effort. (op 100/30)
Botanical(USA) goes well fresh, and is well suited by this course and distance, but he ran a shocker on his first run since leaving Godolphin. (op 9/4)
Kay Two(IRE), Irish trained, ran well below his turf form on his first start on dirt.

207a ATTIJARI PHONE CUP (H'CAP) (TURF) 1m 2f (T)
6:05 (6:14) (90-105,105) 4-Y-0+ £41,569 (£12,790; £6,395; £3,197)

RPR

1 **Oracle West (SAF)**[180] 5-8-10 **95** ow1 KShea 10 100
(M F De Kock, South Africa) *mid-div: rdn to cl 2f out: wnt 2nd 1 1/2f out: hrd rdn: led last strides* **5/1**[3]

2 nk **Earl's Court**[102] 5934 4-8-12 **99** (t) KerrinMcEvoy 1 103
(Saeed Bin Suroor) *led: clr in st: stl a length clr 1f out: hdd last strides* **5/2**[1]

3 3¼ **Desert Anger**[28] 5-8-9 **94** (bt) RyanMoore 3 92
(S Seemar, UAE) *slowly away: racd in mid-div: on rail 3 1/2f out: swtchd outside: r.o: nrst fin* **14/1**

4 1¾ **Bianconi (SAF)**[291] 7-9-6 **105** (t) TedDurcan 4 100
(A Laird, UAE) *trckd ldrs on rail: ev ch in st: one pce* **5/1**[3]

5 ¾ **Courageous Duke (USA)**[162] 4476 7-9-2 **100** MJKinane 9 95
(J Noseda) *hld up in last: sme late hdwy out wd: nrst fin* **4/1**[2]

6 1 **The Carbon Unit (USA)**[48] 4-8-9 **96** TPO'Shea 12 88
(E Charpy, UAE) *in rr of main gp: n.m.r 3f out: nvr threatened but r.o: nrst fin* **9/1**

7 ½ **Sapucai (ARG)**[7] 152 6-8-10 **95** (bt) RichardMullen 2 86
(S Seemar, UAE) *trckd ldrs: 2nd 3f out: nt qckn* **20/1**

8 5¼ **Mustaneer (USA)**[56] 6-8-6 **90** RHills 7 73
(Doug Watson, UAE) *hld up in rr: sme prog wd 3f out: n.d* **25/1**

9 ¾ **Sekula Pata (NZ)**[357] 274 7-8-3 **90** (p) SaleemGolam[(3)] 6 71
(Christian Wroe, UAE) *hld up in rr travelling wl: n.m.r on turn and early st: n.d* **33/1**

10 1¼ **Documento Fiscal (BRZ)**[63] 4-8-5 **90** (p) MAlmeida 5 70
(C Morgado, Brazil) *in rr of main gp: no room early st whn gng wl: nt rcvr* **33/1**

11 ½ **Izdiham (IRE)**[57] 7-8-12 **97** WSupple 8 74
(A Manuel, UAE) *nt far away: wnt 2nd u.p 2f out: fdd 1 1/2f out* **25/1**

12 3½ **Ibn Shaqraan (KSA)**[41] 6-9-2 **100** (t) JAHeffernan 13 72
(I Jory, Saudi Arabia) *trckd ldrs: u.p 3 1/2f out: fdd* **14/1**

13 2 **Happy Diamond (USA)**[1427] 9-9-0 **98** (t) RoystonFfrench 11 66
(A Al Raihe, UAE) *mid-div: fdd 3 1/2f out* **40/1**

2m 3.25s **Going Correction** +0.20s/f (Good)
WFA 4 from 5yo+ 2lb **13** Ran SP% **126.0**
Speed ratings: 110,109,107,105,105 104,103,99,99,98 97,94,93

Owner A Geemooi **Bred** Langeberg Stud **Trained** South Africa

FOCUS
A good handicap, although it proved hard to come from far off the pace.

NOTEBOOK
Oracle West(SAF) defied a 180-day absence to make a winning debut in Dubai under a well-timed ride. There ought to be more to come.
Earl's Court, ex-Andre Fabre, was just held on his debut for Godolphin and first start in Dubai. It will be disappointing if he does not build on this and find a similar race.
Desert Anger had to be switched with his run and basically got going too late.
Bianconi(SAF), twice a winner at last year's Carnival, ran respectably off the back of a 291-day break.
Courageous Duke(USA) was never a serious danger on his return to Dubai off the back of a 162-day absence, and ought to be sharper next time.

208a COMMERCIAL BANK OF DUBAI CUP (H'CAP) (TURF) 1m 2f (T)
6:35 (6:42) (90-105,102) 4-Y-0+ £41,569 (£12,790; £6,395; £3,197)

RPR

1 **Tyson (SAF)**[208] 6-9-6 **102** KShea 2 111
(M F De Kock, South Africa) *trckd ldrs gng wl: n.m.r 2 1/2f out: eased to front 1 1/2f out: won wl* **5/2**[1]

2 1¾ **Mutafanen**[291] 5-9-3 **99** RHills 11 104
(E Charpy, UAE) *settled in rr: wd into st: swtchd centre 2 1/2f out: n.m.r: clr 1 1/2f out: r.o* **11/2**[3]

3 ¾ **Chinkara**[28] 6-8-8 **90** WSupple 10 94
(Doug Watson, UAE) *settled in rr of main gp: no room 2 1/2f out: swtchd and n.m.r 1 1/2f out: r.o wl once clr* **8/1**

4 ½ **Mistongo (URU)**[34] 6-8-8 **90** (t) RyanMoore 4 93
(S Seemar, UAE) *trckd ldrs: ev ch 2f out: nt qckn* **25/1**

5 ¾ **Kestrel Cross (IRE)**[7] 152 4-8-10 **95** MJKinane 7 96
(V Smith) *racd in last: n.d: styd on late: nrst fin* **8/1**

6 1½ **Kitara (GER)**[88] 6192 6-8-12 **95** ASuborics 5 93
(P Vovcenko, Germany) *trckd ldr: disp 2f out: outpcd* **16/1**

7 hd **Terfel**[7] 153 7-9-4 **100** (t) JohnEgan 6 99
(Daniel J Murphy, Singapore) *settled in rr: no room 3 1/2f out: swtchd outside: n.d* **10/1**

8 *nk* **Bailador (IRE)**[7] [153] 6-8-13 **98**................................ SaleemGolam(3) 12 96
(A Laird, UAE) *settled in rr: travelling wl ent st: ev ch 1f out: nt qckn* **25/1**

9 *1* **State Shinto (USA)**[7] [152] 10-8-12 **95**.................................(bt) PDillon 1 90
(R Bouresly, Kuwait) *mid-div: on rail 3f out: short of room* **25/1**

10 *nk* **Realism (FR)**[111] [5715] 6-9-3 **99**.................................... TedDurcan 13 95
(R A Fahey) *mid-div: no room 3f out: asked to cl 2 1/2f out: n.d* **9/2**[2]

11 *nse* **Tipperary All Star (FR)**[109] [5781] 6-9-1 **97**.........................(t) JMurtagh 3 93
(M Halford, Ire) *set mod pce: led to 2f out: one pce: wknd* **11/1**

12 *16* **Eclipse West (ARG)**[7] [152] 7-8-12 **95**.................................(t) RPCleary 9 61
(S Seemar, UAE) *ref to settle: trckd ldrs: asked to qckn 3f out: fdd* **33/1**

2m 7.50s **Going Correction** +0.20s/f (Good)
WFA 4 from 5yo+ 2lb 13 Ran SP% **122.1**
Speed ratings: 93,91,91,90,90 88,88,88,87,87 87,74

Owner M Naidoo, M De Kock, O Leibrandt, R Adair **Bred** M K Naidoo **Trained** South Africa

■ Tyson was the second leg of a double for both Mike De Kock and Kevin Shea following the success of Oracle West.

FOCUS
Another good handicap, but the pace was modest.

NOTEBOOK
Tyson(SAF), a multiple winner from seven to ten furlongs in his native South Africa, took well to racing in Dubai at the first attempt and ran out a clear-cut winner. Given this was his first run in 208 days, there could be even better to come and he does not look too far off pattern class. (op 100/30)
Mutafanen did not get a clear run under Richard Hills and could have been closer. This was a promising return from a 291-day break. (op 5/1)
Chinkara, switched to turf from dirt, ran well but is yet to win in Dubai. (op 7/1)
Mistongo(URU), a Listed winner in Uruguay, ran with credit fourth.
Kestrel Cross(IRE) ran much better than he did on dirt the previous week.
Realism(FR) was making his debut in Dubai off a career-high mark and was well held.
Tipperary All Star(FR), Irish trained, was fitted with a tongue-tie for the first time on his debut in Dubai. He had the run of the race in front, so it was disappointing he could not pick up.

[172]WOLVERHAMPTON (A.W) (L-H)

Friday, January 27

OFFICIAL GOING: Standard
Wind: Light, half-against Weather: Light showers

209 WIN £2M @ CLASSICVALUEPOOLS.COM H'CAP (DIV I) 5f 20y(P)
1:50 (1:51) (Class 6) (0-55,58) 4-Y-0+ **£2,047** (£604; £302) **Stalls** Low

Form RPR

14-6 **1** **Lady Hopeful (IRE)**[4] [178] 4-8-7 **48**......................(b) RobbieFitzpatrick 7 57
(Peter Grayson) *a.p: rdn wl over 1f out: led wl ins fnl f: r.o* **9/2**[1]

0-35 **2** *nk* **Leah's Pride**[3] [179] 5-8-5 **46** oh1.............................. AdrianTNicholls 11 54
(P Howling) *w ldr: rdn 2f out: led ins fnl f: sn hdd: nt qckn* **8/1**

040- **3** *3* **Town House**[156] [4679] 4-7-13 **47**.................................. SoniaEaton(7) 1 44
(B P J Baugh) *led tl hdd and no ex ins fnl f* **20/1**

34-3 **4** *shd* **Sir Sandrovitch (IRE)**[15] [96] 10-9-0 **55**....................(v) PaulHanagan 9 52
(R A Fahey) *mid-div: hdwy over 2f out: kpt on ins fnl f* **6/1**[2]

040- **5** *1* **Cloann (IRE)**[27] [6696] 4-8-11 **52**.................................(b) StephenCarson 5 45
(E A Wheeler) *hld up and bhd: rdn over 2f out: hdwy fnl f: r.o* **11/1**

4-00 **6** *1/2* **Enjoy The Buzz**[11] [119] 7-8-5 **46** oh1.............................. PaulFitzsimons 2 37
(J M Bradley) *mid-div: rdn and hdwy on ins over 2f out: no further prog* **17/2**

632- **7** *nk* **Strathclyde (IRE)**[30] [6677] 7-8-5 **46** oh1............................ ChrisCatlin 12 36
(A M Hales) *hld up in rr: sn swtchd lft: hdwy fnl f: nvr nrr* **7/1**[3]

0/0- **8** *3/4* **Rapid Flow**[79] [6301] 4-9-0 **55**.. RobertWinston 10 43
(W M Brisbourne) *chsd ldrs: rdn 3f out: wknd wl over 1f out* **12/1**

000- **9** *hd* **Monte Major (IRE)**[269] [1450] 5-8-8 **52**.......................(v) PatrickMathers(3) 3 39
(D Shaw) *hld up: sn bhd: swtchd lft and hdwy on ins over 1f out: sn no imp* **33/1**

420- **10** *nk* **Rosiella**[39] [6611] 4-8-2 **46** oh1.............................(b) EdwardCreighton(3) 4 32
(M Blanshard) *keen early: a bhd* **10/1**

552- **11** *3/4* **Blue Maeve**[37] [6639] 6-8-12 **53**.. MickyFenton 6 36
(A D Brown) *n.m.r sn after s: rdn and short-lived effrt on outside over 2f out* **9/2**[1]

61.96 secs (-0.86) **Going Correction** -0.05s/f (Stan) 11 Ran SP% **117.6**
Speed ratings (Par 101):104,103,98,98,96 96,95,94,94,93 92
CSF £40.48 CT £671.39 TOTE £5.80: £2.20, £3.00, £8.90; EX 44.40.
Owner Peter Grayson Racing Clubs Limited **Bred** Raymond P Doyle **Trained** Formby, Lancs

FOCUS
A poor handicap, little better than banded class, but run in faster time than both the second division and the five-furlong claimer and the form looks sound.
Sir Sandrovitch(IRE) Official explanation: jockey said gelding hung left throughout
Blue Maeve Official explanation: jockey said gelding missed the break

210 WOLVERHAMPTON-RACECOURSE.CO.UK (S) STKS 7f 32y(P)
2:25 (2:27) (Class 6) 4-Y-0+ **£2,388** (£705; £352) **Stalls** High

Form RPR

3-64 **1** **Distant Country (USA)**[11] [121] 7-8-12 55...........................(b) NCallan 5 59
(R A Harris) *hld up: hdwy whn nt clr run and swtchd rt wl over 1f out: rdn to ld nr fin* **3/1**[2]

356- **2** *1/2* **Fulvio (USA)**[30] [6676] 6-8-12 49...................................(v) J-PGuillambert 3 58
(P Howling) *led early: a.p: rdn 2f out: led 1f out: hdd nr fin* **9/2**[3]

30-1 **3** *nk* **Vancouver Gold (IRE)**[11] [121] 4-8-13 73.................. RobertWinston 6 58
(K R Burke) *prom: n.m.r over 5f out: rdn 2f out: ev ch 1f out: nt qckn* **13/8**[1]

-500 **4** *3 1/2* **Wilford Maverick (IRE)**[4] [175] 4-8-5 45.................. StacyRenwick(7) 2 48
(M J Attwater) *sn led: hdd over 3f out: led over 2f out: rdn and hdd 1f out: wknd ins fnl f* **25/1**

50-0 **5** *1* **Stagnite**[16] [86] 6-9-1 53.. AmirQuinn(3) 9 51
(K McAuliffe) *hld up: hdwy over 1f out: nvr trbld ldrs* **16/1**

500- **6** *5* **Dundonald**[206] [3215] 7-8-12 45..(bt) MartinDwyer 8 32
(M Appleby) *sn prom: rdn and wknd over 2f out* **25/1**

000- **7** *2 1/2* **Sabo Prince**[159] [4604] 4-8-12 45....................................(p) LPKeniry 7 26
(J M Bradley) *s.i.s: hld up: rdn over 2f out: sn bhd* **40/1**

32-0 **8** *3* **Awarding**[13] [117] 6-8-9 48....................................(vt) RichardThomas(3) 12 18
(Dr J R J Naylor) *sn prom: led over 3f out: tl over 2f out: sn wknd* **12/1**

0-26 **U** **Exit Smiling**[11] [121] 4-8-12 54... ChrisCatlin 4 —
(G C H Chung) *uns rdr leaving stalls* **6/1**

1m 30.58s (0.18) **Going Correction** -0.05s/f (Stan) 9 Ran SP% **119.3**
Speed ratings (Par 101):96,95,95,91,89 84,81,77,—
CSF £17.28 TOTE £4.30: £1.40, £1.80, £1.20; EX 19.50.The winner was sold for 5,000gns to K R Burke.
Owner Peter A Price **Bred** Audubon Farm And D L Martin **Trained** Earlswood, Monmouths

FOCUS
A typically modest seller and, although the first two and the fourth were close to their best, the form is not totally convincing.

211 HOTEL & CONFERENCING AT DUNSTALL PARK H'CAP 7f 32y(P)
2:55 (2:57) (Class 6) (0-55,61) 3-Y-0 **£2,388** (£705; £352) **Stalls** High

Form RPR

060- **1** **Penang Cinta**[69] [6374] 3-8-11 **52**.................................... RobertWinston 3 55+
(G A Butler) *t.k.h towards rr: rdn and hdwy on ins over 2f out: led 1f out: r.o* **11/4**[1]

0-06 **2** *nk* **Royal Embrace**[11] [123] 3-8-9 **53**..........................(v) PatrickMathers(3) 10 55
(D Shaw) *hld up: hdwy over 2f out: rdn wl over 1f out: ev ch ins fnl f: r.o* **14/1**

00-6 **3** *1 1/2* **Katie Lawson (IRE)**[22] [49] 3-8-12 **53**........................(v) RobertHavlin 2 51+
(D Haydn Jones) *prom: sltly hmpd on ins after 1f: rdn whn nt clr run over 1f out: r.o ins fnl f* **10/1**

4530 **4** *3/4* **Twilight Avenger (IRE)**[9] [139] 3-8-12 **53**......................(p) EddieAhern 5 49
(M J Polglase) *a.p: rdn over 2f out: kpt on same pce fnl f* **11/1**

600- **5** *1 1/4* **Danetime Lord (IRE)**[134] [5237] 3-8-12 **53**............................(p) NCallan 7 46
(K A Ryan) *sn w ldr: led 3f out: rdn 2f out: edgd rt and hdd 1f out: wknd wl ins fnl f* **10/1**

00- **6** *shd* **Bella Fiorella (IRE)**[125] [5466] 3-8-8 **54**.......................... GregFairley(5) 1 47
(T J Pitt) *led: hdd 3f out: sn rdn: ev ch 1f out: wknd wl ins fnl f* **20/1**

6-21 **7** *1 1/2* **Bollywood (IRE)**[9] [139] 3-9-6 **61** 6ex.............................. IanMongan 11 50
(M R Hoad) *t.k.h: sn prom: rdn over 3f out: lost pl on outside over 2f out: hung lft over 1f out: n.d after* **3/1**[2]

05-1 **8** *1 1/2* **Drink To Me Only**[11] [120] 3-9-1 **56** 6ex............................ DaleGibson 9 41
(J R Weymes) *prom 3f* **5/1**[3]

000- **9** *2 1/2* **Worldly Pursuit**[88] [6199] 3-9-0 **55**...................................... PaulEddery 8 33
(B Smart) *s.i.s: a bhd* **33/1**

0-40 **10** *6* **Dream Factor (IRE)**[11] [120] 3-8-12 **53**.......................... TonyCulhane 6 16
(J O'Reilly) *hld up in tch: rdn and wknd over 2f out* **14/1**

000- **11** *1 1/2* **Astronova**[100] [5985] 3-9-0 **55**.. MichaelHills 12 14
(M H Tompkins) *a bhd* **25/1**

00-0 **12** *1 1/2* **Roonah (FR)**[17] [76] 3-9-0 **55**......................................(v[1]) ChrisCatlin 4 10
(Karen McLintock) *a bhd* **33/1**

1m 31.06s (0.66) **Going Correction** -0.05s/f (Stan) 12 Ran SP% **122.7**
Speed ratings (Par 95):94,93,91,91,89 89,87,86,83,76 74,72
CSF £42.22 CT £350.33 TOTE £3.20: £1.50, £3.80, £3.30; EX 44.20.
Owner Mrs A K H Ooi **Bred** Mrs A K H Ooi **Trained** Blewbury, Oxon

FOCUS
A moderate contest, but there were some unexposed sorts making their handicap debuts, and the next four behind the winner were close to their marks. The winner can rate higher over further.
Katie Lawson(IRE) Official explanation: jockey said filly hung left
Dream Factor(IRE) Official explanation: jockey said filly hung both ways

212 TEXT "BETDIRECT" TO 88600 CLAIMING STKS 5f 20y(P)
3:30 (3:31) (Class 5) 3-Y-0+ **£3,238** (£963; £481; £240) **Stalls** Low

Form RPR

503- **1** **Blue Moon Hitman (IRE)**[37] [6647] 5-9-8 49..............(b) PaulHanagan 12 61
(R Brotherton) *sn led: rdn wl over 1f out: edgd rt ent fnl f: drvn out* **11/1**

00-2 **2** *1/2* **Byo (IRE)**[8] [146] 8-9-7 50... TonyCulhane 5 58
(P Howling) *chsd ldrs: rdn 2f out: wnt 2nd over 1f out: r.o ins fnl f* **9/2**[2]

114- **3** *1 1/2* **Undeterred**[151] [4836] 10-9-11 79... NCallan 1 57+
(K J Burke) *hld up: nt clr run on ins after 1f: rdn and hdwy on ins wl over 1f out: kpt on ins fnl f* **6/1**[3]

634- **4** *1/2* **Hello Roberto**[60] [6441] 5-8-9 40...............................(p) WilliamCarson(7) 4 46
(R A Harris) *bhd: hdwy on outside fnl f: r.o* **6/1**[3]

00-0 **5** *nk* **Feminist (IRE)**[3] [179] 4-9-3 45... GeorgeBaker 11 46
(J M Bradley) *led early: chsd wnr tl rdn over 1f out: one pce fnl f* **33/1**

65-0 **6** *nk* **He's A Rocket (IRE)**[11] [126] 5-9-3 59..................(b) PatrickDonaghy(7) 2 52
(K R Burke) *mid-div: rdn and hdwy 2f out: one pce fnl f* **11/4**[1]

02-0 **7** *1 1/2* **Legal Set (IRE)**[21] [54] 10-9-4 45..............................(bt) AnnStokell(7) 3 47
(Miss A Stokell) *nvr trbld ldrs* **22/1**

24-0 **8** *nk* **Chantelle's Dream**[9] [138] 4-8-7 45..........................(b[1]) JamesDoyle(7) 8 35
(Ms J S Doyle) *prom: rdn over 2f out: wknd over 1f out* **9/1**

055- **9** *nk* **Kiss The Rain**[37] [6647] 6-9-3 45.....................................(b) TomEaves 9 37
(R Brotherton) *a bhd* **16/1**

0-50 **10** *nk* **Party Princess (IRE)**[4] [177] 5-8-6 47..................(v) KirstyMilczarek(7) 7 32
(S Parr) *bhd fnl 2f* **16/1**

62-0 **11** *1 3/4* **Eeshee**[22] [45] 3-8-3 59.. AdrianMcCarthy 6 31
(S L Keightley) *chsd ldrs tl rdn over 2f out* **14/1**

62.38 secs (-0.44) **Going Correction** -0.05s/f (Stan)
WFA 3 from 4yo+ 15lb 11 Ran SP% **117.5**
Speed ratings (Par 103):101,100,97,97,96 96,93,93,92,92 89
CSF £59.91 TOTE £12.40: £3.60, £2.00, £1.80; EX 54.20.
Owner Steve Cambridge **Bred** Edward Sexton **Trained** Elmley Castle, Worcs

FOCUS
This was slower than both divisions of the five-furlong handicap but the first two set a sound-enough standard.
Chantelle's Dream Official explanation: jockey said filly hung right

213 BETDIRECT.CO.UK CONDITIONS STKS 1m 141y(P)
4:00 (4:00) (Class 2) 3-Y-0+
£11,217 (£3,358; £1,679; £840; £419; £210) **Stalls** Low

Form RPR

011- **1** **Cimyla (IRE)**[59] [6459] 5-9-11 106....................................... GeorgeBaker 5 107+
(C F Wall) *hld up and bhd: rdn and hdwy over 1f out: led and edgd lft ins fnl f: r.o* **4/5**[1]

321- **2** *shd* **Hard To Explain (IRE)**[42] [6595] 3-8-3 83........................... ChrisCatlin 2 99
(E J O'Neill) *a.p: rdn over 3f out: ev ch wl ins fnl f: r.o* **12/1**

22-4 **3** *1 1/4* **Appalachian Trail (IRE)**[21] [57] 5-9-11 95.....................(b) TomEaves 1 101
(I Semple) *hld up: rdn and hdwy on ins wl over 1f out: ev ch ins fnl f: nt qckn* **4/1**[2]

000- **4** *2 1/2* **Always Esteemed (IRE)**[153] [3320] 6-9-11 95.......................(p) NCallan 8 96
(K A Ryan) *chsd ldr 7f out: rdn over 2f out: ev ch 1f out: hld whn hmpd ins fnl f* **25/1**

33-4 **5** *shd* **Hail The Chief**[13] [116] 9-9-11 88.................................. StephaneBreux 7 96
(R Hannon) *led: rdn over 1f out: hdd ins fnl f: wknd* **16/1**

444- **6** *1 3/4* **Grand Passion (IRE)**[175] [4135] 6-9-11 105....................... SteveDrowne 6 92
(G Wragg) *hld up in tch: rdn over 2f out: wknd over 1f out* **11/2**[3]

6/5- **7** *3 1/2* **Berkhamsted (IRE)**[287] [1025] 4-9-10 97............................ EddieAhern 3 85
(J A Osborne) *hld up in tch: wknd over 2f out* **33/1**

0-06 **8** *1 1/2* **One More Round (USA)**[21] [57] 8-9-11 95..................(b) IanMongan 9 82
(N P Littmoden) *a bhd* **22/1**

05-6 **9** *5* **Archimboldo (USA)**[7] 160 3-8-3 80..........................(b[1]) HayleyTurner 4 66
(T Wall) *rdn over 3f out: a bhd* **66/1**

1m 49.35s (-2.41) **Going Correction** -0.05s/f (Stan)
WFA 3 from 4yo 22lb 4 from 5yo+ 1lb **9** Ran SP% **117.1**
Speed ratings (Par 109):108,107,106,104,104 102,99,98,94
CSF £11.95 TOTE £2.00: £1.10, £2.20, £1.70; EX 17.80.
Owner Peter Botham **Bred** Dr D G St John And Mrs Sherry Collier **Trained** Newmarket, Suffolk
■ Stewards' Enquiry : George Baker caution: careless riding

FOCUS
A fair turnout for good prizemoney with Hail The Chief waiting in front. The form is slightly messy and not totally solid.

NOTEBOOK
Cimyla(IRE) came from an unpromising position to retain his unbeaten record on sand and would probably have preferred a stronger gallop. He now heads to Cagnes-sur-Mer for the first leg of the European All-Weather series and the Winter Derby could still be on the agenda. (op 5-6 tchd 10-11 in places)
Hard To Explain(IRE) ◆ must have delighted connections on this big step up in class and should have no problem staying further.
Appalachian Trail(IRE) was meeting the winner on 2lb better terms than when beaten three lengths over course and distance in November. (op 9-2 tchd 5-1)
Always Esteemed(IRE), last seen over hurdles in August, had finished a close third in the Lincoln trial here last March. He would have finished a shade closer had he not been hampered.
Hail The Chief was up against it based on his form behind the winner here in November. (tchd 18-1)
Grand Passion(IRE), who landed the Listed Churchill Stakes at Lingfield in November 2004, was having his first start since last August. (op 4-1)

214 PLAY NOW AT BETDIRECTCASINO.COM H'CAP 1m 1f 103y(P)
4:30 (4:31) (Class 4) (0-85,85) 4-Y-0+ **£5,505** (£1,637; £818; £408) **Stalls** Low

Form RPR
12-3 **1** **Blue Patrick**[22] 50 6-8-8 **74**.. NCallan 7 81
(K A Ryan) *hld up: hdwy over 3f out: rdn over 2f out: led wl ins fnl f: r.o* **9/2**[1]
4-65 **2** *½* **Just Fly**[9] 140 6-8-2 **71**..(v[1]) RichardThomas[(3)] 1 77
(Dr J R J Naylor) *hld up: hdwy over 2f out: rdn and edgd lft over 1f out: r.o ins fnl f* **14/1**
050- **3** *½* **Little Jimbob**[118] 5612 5-8-4 **70**... PaulHanagan 4 75+
(R A Fahey) *chsd ldr: led over 2f out: rdn 1f out: hdd and nt qckn wl ins fnl f* **12/1**
015- **4** *½* **Graham Island**[154] 4737 5-9-2 **82**.................................. SteveDrowne 12 86
(G Wragg) *hld up in rr: hdwy over 1f out: r.o ins fnl f* **12/1**
13-3 **5** *½* **Western Roots**[13] 111 5-8-4 **70** oh1.............................. MartinDwyer 11 73
(M Appleby) *hld up and bhd: hdwy over 2f out: rdn over 1f out: no ex ins fnl f* **7/1**[3]
00-6 **6** *2* **Skidmark**[9] 135 5-8-13 **79**... PaulFitzsimons 3 78
(Miss J R Tooth) *hld up and bhd: hdwy over 2f out: rdn over 1f out: wknd ins fnl f* **9/1**
50/4 **7** *1½* **Alekhine (IRE)**[9] 140 5-8-9 **75**... JoeFanning 9 71
(J R Boyle) *hld up and bhd: sme hdwy over 1f out: nvr trbld ldrs* **12/1**
10-2 **8** *6* **Almanshood (USA)**[14] 108 4-8-6 **73** ow1.................. RobertWinston 6 58
(P L Gilligan) *prom: rdn 3f out: wknd wl over 1f out* **5/1**[2]
32-6 **9** *½* **Mizz Tee (IRE)**[13] 116 4-8-13 **85**.......................... DuranFentiman[(5)] 13 69
(T D Easterby) *hld up: rdn over 2f out: no rspnse* **7/1**[3]
000- **10** *1* **Fair Shake (IRE)**[54] 6248 6-8-4 **70**..................................(v) ChrisCatlin 5 52
(Karen McLintock) *prom: rdn 3f out: sn wknd* **66/1**
26-3 **11** *¾* **Desert Leader (IRE)**[14] 108 5-8-12 **78**............................ EddieAhern 8 59
(W M Brisbourne) *mid-div: rdn over 3f out: lost pl and hmpd over 2f out* **9/2**[1]
100- **12** *2* **Baylaw Star**[126] 5432 5-8-10 **83**.................................... CDTimmons[(7)] 2 60
(K A Ryan) *led: clr 7f out: rdn and hdd over 2f out: wknd wl over 1f out* **33/1**

2m 0.02s (-2.60) **Going Correction** -0.05s/f (Stan)
WFA 4 from 5yo+ 1lb **12** Ran SP% **122.2**
Speed ratings (Par 105):109,108,108,107,107 105,104,98,98,97 96,95
CSF £70.86 CT £724.94 TOTE £4.60: £1.90, £5.80, £6.20; EX 75.60.
Owner S R H Turner **Bred** Finbar Kent **Trained** Hambleton, N Yorks

FOCUS
A fair handicap won in the fastest time of the day compared with standard but the form is not as strong as it might have been with the runner-up the best guide to the form.
Desert Leader(IRE) Official explanation: vet said gelding was lame on its left fore

215 DAILY OFFERS FROM BETDIRECT MAIDEN STKS 1m 1f 103y(P)
5:00 (5:05) (Class 5) 3-Y-0 **£3,238** (£963; £481; £240) **Stalls** Low

Form RPR
43- **1** **Spanish Lace**[42] 6588 3-8-9 .... TomEaves 2 63
(Miss J A Camacho) *led after 1f tl over 6f out: prom: rdn over 2f out: led wl ins fnl f: r.o* **5/4**[1]
2 *½* **Glentaisie (USA)** 3-8-9 .... NCallan 13 62
(J Noseda) *a.p: rdn over 3f out: led 2f out: hdd and nt qckn wl ins fnl f* **13/2**[3]
3- **3** *hd* **Vacation (IRE)**[84] 6242 3-9-0 .... MichaelTebbutt 11 66
(V Smith) *s.i.s: hld up and bhd: nt clr run whn swtchd rt and hdwy 4f out: sn rdn: ev ch 1f out: r.o* **8/1**
64 **4** *1¼* **Bariloche**[11] 124 3-9-0 ....(b) RobertHavlin 8 64
(J H M Gosden) *a.p: led over 6f out: rdn over 3f out: hdd 2f out: edgd lft wl ins fnl f: no ex* **8/1**
4 **5** *1¼* **Russian Mist (IRE)**[13] 112 3-8-9 .... DerekNolan[(5)] 7 65+
(M J Wallace) *hld up in mid-div: hdwy over 3f out: sn rdn: ev ch wl over 1f out: hld whn hmpd ins fnl f* **5/1**[2]
6 *2* **Permanent Way (IRE)** 3-9-0 .... ChrisCatlin 5 58
(B J Meehan) *prom: rdn over 3f out: wknd wl over 1f out* **12/1**
0- **7** *10* **Artists Touch (IRE)**[56] 6484 3-8-7 .... JamesDoyle[(7)] 1 39
(N P Littmoden) *led 1f: prom tl rdn and wknd 4f out* **40/1**
5 **8** *½* **Mind Out (USA)**[10] 132 3-9-0 .... EddieAhern 6 38
(J A Osborne) *hld up in mid-div: rdn 4f out: sn struggling* **14/1**
-0 **9** *shd* **Fantasy Legend (IRE)**[11] 124 3-9-0 .... TPQueally 12 38
(N P Littmoden) *a bhd* **40/1**
0 **10** *dist* **Maxemull**[10] 132 3-8-9 .... AdrianTNicholls 10 —
(D J Wintle) *prom tl rdn and wknd 4f out: t.o* **125/1**
0 **11** *1½* **Palm Desert (IRE)**[18] 70 3-9-0 .... MichaelHills 3 —
(M H Tompkins) *s.i.s: a bhd: t.o fnl 6f* **50/1**
0- **12** *3½* **Silvabella (IRE)**[27] 6694 3-8-9 .... SteveDrowne 9 —
(D Haydn Jones) *hld up: sme hdwy over 5f out: wknd 4f out: t.o* **80/1**

2m 3.50s (0.88) **Going Correction** -0.05s/f (Stan) **12** Ran SP% **119.9**
Speed ratings (Par 97):94,93,93,92,91 89,80,80,79,— —,—
CSF £9.69 TOTE £2.10: £1.20, £2.40, £2.30; EX 13.90.

Owner Elite Racing Club **Bred** Elite Racing Club **Trained** Norton, N Yorks
■ Stewards' Enquiry : Robert Havlin caution: careless riding

FOCUS
Quite an interesting little maiden which may turn out to be above average for the course despite the modest time. The fourth sets a sound-enough standard.

216 WIN £2M @ CLASSICVALUEPOOLS.COM H'CAP (DIV II) 5f 20y(P)
5:30 (5:32) (Class 6) (0-55,55) 4-Y-0+ **£2,047** (£604; £302) **Stalls** Low

Form RPR
5-00 **1** **Times Review (USA)**[7] 159 5-8-9 **55**.........................(b) GregFairley[(5)] 8 64
(C A Dwyer) *mid-div: rdn and hdwy whn hung rt fr over 2f out: c wd st: led under stands' rail wl ins fnl f: r.o* **11/1**
06-3 **2** *1* **Nova Tor (IRE)**[4] 177 4-8-9 **50**.............................(b) RobbieFitzpatrick 10 55
(Peter Grayson) *a.p: rdn wl over 1f out: led and edgd rt ins fnl f: sn hdd: r.o* **5/1**[3]
04-4 **3** *2* **Taboor (IRE)**[24] 22 8-8-12 **53**.. NCallan 3 53+
(R M H Cowell) *mid-div: hdwy whn hmpd over 2f out: rdn wl over 1f out: kpt on ins fnl f* **5/2**[1]
0-00 **4** *1* **Percy Douglas**[16] 90 6-8-2 **50** oh6 ow4....................(vt) AnnStokell[(7)] 9 45
(Miss A Stokell) *s.i.s: hdwy on ins whn nt clr run over 2f out: rdn over 1f out: no ex ins fnl f* **66/1**
03-0 **5** *nk* **Secret Vision (USA)**[24] 24 5-8-5 **46**....................(p) GrahamGibbons 2 40
(R M H Cowell) *n.m.r s: sn outpcd: rdn and hdwy 1f out: kpt on towards fin* **8/1**
41-0 **6** *½* **Montillia (IRE)**[24] 21 4-8-11 **52**..................................... MartinDwyer 1 44
(C F Wall) *led: rdn over 1f out: hdd ins fnl f: fdd* **4/1**[2]
40-4 **7** *nk* **Larky's Lob**[15] 96 7-8-6 **54**...................................... JamesO'Reilly[(7)] 11 45
(J O'Reilly) *prom tl rdn and wknd over 1f out* **14/1**
0-00 **8** *½* **Juwwi**[3] 179 12-7-12 **46** oh1... JamesDoyle[(7)] 4 38+
(J M Bradley) *outpcd: nvr nrr* **20/1**
0-00 **9** *¾* **Lady Pekan**[8] 146 7-8-7 **48**.. J-PGuillambert 7 34
(P Howling) *s.i.s: outpcd: n.d* **22/1**
00-0 **10** *shd* **Clearing Sky (IRE)**[24] 22 5-9-0 **55**.................................. EddieAhern 6 41
(J R Boyle) *w ldr: ev ch over 2f out: sn rdn: wknd fnl f* **5/1**[3]
051- **11** *1* **Rock Fever (IRE)**[29] 6686 4-8-6 **47** ow1.......................(b) GylesParkin 12 29
(Peter Grayson) *chsd ldrs: rdn over 2f out: wknd wl over 1f out* **16/1**

62.10 secs (-0.72) **Going Correction** -0.05s/f (Stan) **11** Ran SP% **124.5**
Speed ratings (Par 101):103,101,98,96,96 95,94,94,92,92 91
CSF £67.88 CT £190.62 TOTE £9.60: £2.50, £1.70, £1.40; EX 124.60 Place 6 £55.81, Place 5 £19.17.
Owner Times Of Wigan **Bred** Charger 6 Ventures **Trained** Burrough Green, Cambs

FOCUS
This weak handicap was a shade slower than the first division and the runner-up sets a moderate standard.
T/Plt: £128.90 to a £1 stake. Pool: £50,173.00. 284.10 winning tickets. T/Qpdt: £38.70 to a £1 stake. Pool: £4,083.20. 77.90 winning tickets. KH

185 LINGFIELD (L-H)
Saturday, January 28

OFFICIAL GOING: Standard
Wind: Moderate, half-against

217 BETDIRECT FOOTBALL ON SKYTEXT P372 MAIDEN STKS (DIV I) 1m (P)
12:25 (12:27) (Class 5) 3-Y-0+ **£2,914** (£867; £433; £216) **Stalls** High

Form RPR
6-03 **1** **Height Of Spirits**[17] 84 4-9-10 48............................. RobertMiles[(3)] 10 60
(T D McCarthy) *b: hld up in rr: hdwy on outside over 2f out: rdn: edgd lft: led ins fnl f: drvn out* **16/1**
4- **2** *1* **Nikki Bea (IRE)**[38] 6641 3-8-2 .... ChrisCatlin 12 48
(Jamie Poulton) *lw: hld up: rdn and hdwy over 1f out: rdn to go 2nd cl home* **33/1**
5- **3** *nk* **The Rebound Kid**[80] 6298 4-9-13 .... NCallan 1 57
(G A Huffer) *w'like: a in tch: led 2f out: rdn and hdd ins fnl f: lost 2nd cl home* **11/2**[2]
36- **4** *¾* **Zorooni**[77] 6332 3-8-2 ....(t) MatthewHenry 9 45
(M A Jarvis) *unf: scope: a.p: rdn over 3f out: nt qkn ins fnl f* **5/2**[1]
0- **5** *nk* **Prince Darius**[134] 5271 3-8-7 .... EddieAhern 11 50+
(P W Chapple-Hyam) *in rr and outpcd: hdfway whn n.m.r over 1f out: swtchd rt and r.o ins fnl f* **10/1**
40-5 **6** *nk* **Grand Design**[22] 59 4-9-8 53...................................... RobertWinston 7 49
(C A Cyzer) *lw: t.k.h: rdn to chse ldrs 2f out: one pce fnl f* **13/2**
5- **7** *¾* **Boss Mak (IRE)**[38] 6642 3-8-8 ow1.............................. MickyFenton 3 48
(V Smith) *outpcd: rdn over 3f out: kpt on ins fnl f: nvr nr to chal* **6/1**[3]
0-0 **8** *¾* **Megalala (IRE)**[17] 84 5-9-10 .... NeilChalmers[(3)] 2 50
(J J Bridger) *b.hind: t.k.h: mid-div: rdn 2f out: fdd ins fnl f* **100/1**
2 **9** *4* **Stamford Street (IRE)**[17] 83 3-8-0 .... JosephWalsh[(7)] 5 36
(J S Moore) *led tl hdd 2f out: sn wknd* **7/1**
0- **10** *hd* **Arthurs Legacy**[56] 6485 4-9-6 .... RonanKeogh[(7)] 8 41
(J A R Toller) *a bhd* **50/1**
0-6 **11** *3* **Barachois Gaudy**[17] 84 4-9-8 .... LPKeniry 4 29
(Mrs N Smith) *bhd whn rdn over 3f out: nvr on terms* **100/1**
0-0 **12** *¾* **Broadway Calling**[14] 112 3-8-7 .... MartinDwyer 6 27
(A M Balding) *trckd ldr tl rdn and wknd over 2f out* **8/1**

1m 39.5s (0.07) **Going Correction** -0.05s/f (Stan)
WFA 3 from 4yo+ 20lb **12** Ran SP% **117.0**
Speed ratings (Par 103):97,96,95,94,94 94,93,92,88,88 85,84
CSF £449.12 TOTE £27.90: £5.10, £3.80, £2.50; EX 264.70.
Owner S R W Brooks **Bred** Whitsbury Manor Stud And Clarendon Farms **Trained** Godstone, Surrey

FOCUS
A modest maiden, run at a true pace, and the form looks reasonable for the class rated around the winner.
Prince Darius Official explanation: jockey said gelding was denied a clear run 1f out

218 FOOTBALLPOOLS.COM MAIDEN STKS 1m 4f (P)
12:55 (12:56) (Class 5) 4-Y-0+ **£3,238** (£963; £481; £240) **Stalls** Low

Form RPR
0 **1** **Stage Manager (IRE)**[14] 114 4-8-9 .... DerekNolan[(5)] 1 67+
(M J Wallace) *a in tch: rdn to ld 1f out: sn clr* **4/1**[2]
0-3 **2** *2½* **Dubai Ace (USA)**[24] 32 5-9-1 50...................... EdwardCreighton[(3)] 6 63
(Miss Sheena West) *hld up: rdn and hdwy 3f out: styd on to go 2nd ins fnl f* **10/1**
53-5 **3** *1½* **Master'n Commander**[14] 114 4-9-0 69.................................. NCallan 3 61
(C A Cyzer) *trckd ldrs: ev ch appr fnl f: rdn: one pce and lost 2nd ins* **7/2**[1]

405- **4** 1 3/4 **River Gypsy**[106] 5877 5-9-4 67 .... JohnEgan 10 58
(D R C Elsworth) *hld up: hdwy over 3f out: n.m.r over 2f out: styd on one pce ins fnl f* **7/2**[1]
00-0 **5** 1/2 **Postmaster**[14] 114 4-9-0 57 .... (t) MatthewHenry 7 57
(R Ingram) *hld up in tch: lost pl over 4f out: hdwy over 2f out: one pce fnl f* **66/1**
3-24 **6** hd **Sugitani (USA)**[11] 131 4-9-0 58 .... (b) MickyFenton 11 57
(N B King) *hld up: hdwy to trck ldrs 6f out: led over 2f out: rdn and hdd 1f out: wknd* **15/2**[3]
7 1 3/4 **Flyingwithoutwings**[28] 7-9-4 .... EddieAhern 15 54
(A King) *mid-div: hdwy over 4f out: wknd fnl f* **33/1**
6-00 **8** 1 1/4 **Esprit De Corps**[7] 166 4-9-0 60 .... JamieMackay 4 52
(Sir Mark Prescott) *mid-div: rdn 3f out: no hdwy ins fnl 2f* **14/1**
003- **9** 3/4 **Escoffier**[74] 6355 4-8-9 64 .... EmmettStack(5) 13 51
(Pat Eddery) *lw: trckd ldr to over 2f out: rdn and wknd entering fnl f* **10/1**
5/0- **10** nk **Daybreaking (IRE)**[287] 1049 4-9-0 62 .... StephenCarson 16 50
(R F Johnson Houghton) *mid-div: rdn 3f out: sn bhd* **80/1**
00-3 **11** 1/2 **Fabulous Emperor (IRE)**[25] 18 4-9-0 60 .... MichaelHills 8 49
(Jamie Poulton) *mid-div tl wknd over 2f out* **14/1**
044- **12** hd **Medora Leigh (USA)**[56] 6485 4-8-9 59 .... RobertWinston 9 44
(J A R Toller) *hld up: rdn 4f out: a bhd* **33/1**
400- **13** 2 1/2 **Latin Express (IRE)**[29] 6692 4-9-0 50 .... MartinDwyer 12 45
(W R Muir) *trckd ldrs tl wknd over 2f out* **33/1**
14 1 3/4 **Dr Flight**[7] 4-9-0 .... (tp) ChrisCatlin 14 42
(H Morrison) *s.i.s: a bhd* **33/1**
00-3 **15** 7 **Bamzooki**[16] 97 4-8-9 52 .... JoeFanning 2 26
(D J Daly) *led tl hdd over 2f out: wknd rapidly* **20/1**

2m 33.09s (-1.30) **Going Correction** -0.05s/f (Stan)
WFA 4 from 5yo+ 4lb **15** Ran SP% **127.0**
Speed ratings (Par 103):102,100,99,98,97 97,96,95,95,95 94,94,92,91,87
CSF £43.55 TOTE £7.10: £2.40, £3.10, £1.60; EX 74.80.
Owner Birchwood Stud Limited **Bred** T Brennan **Trained** Newmarket, Suffolk

FOCUS
A modest maiden, run at an average pace, but the field came home fairly strung out behind the ready winner and it looks more solid that the preceding and following races.

219 BETDIRECT FOOTBALL ON SKYTEXT P372 MAIDEN STKS (DIV II) 1m (P)
1:30 (1:32) (Class 5) 3-Y-0+ **£2,914** (£867; £433; £216) **Stalls** High

Form RPR
0- **1** **Paradise Expected**[95] 6102 3-8-4 ow2 .... EddieAhern 8 60+
(P W Chapple-Hyam) *leggy: scope: lw: bhd and sn pushed along: hdwy on outside over 2f out: edgd lft fnl f but r.o to ld nr fin* **14/1**
420- **2** 1/2 **Fiddlers Wood**[85] 6246 3-8-7 94 .... (v) NCallan 1 61
(V Smith) *trckd ldrs: rdn to ld 1f out: hdd nr fin* **4/1**
4-22 **3** 1 1/2 **Art Elegant**[8] 162 4-9-13 64 .... (b) PaulHanagan 7 63
(G A Swinbank) *b: t.k.h: hld up in tch: rdn 2f out: kpt on one pce fnl f* **11/4**[1]
25-2 **4** 1 3/4 **Pab Special (IRE)**[15] 104 3-8-7 72 .... RobertWinston 3 57+
(K R Burke) *unf: hld up in mid-div: hdwy whn hmpd 1f out: nt qckn* **3/1**[2]
0-0 **5** 2 **Flashing Floozie**[12] 124 3-8-1 ow2 .... RichardThomas(3) 4 46+
(M F Harris) *in rr tl hdwy over 1f out: r.o: nvr nrr* **66/1**
0 **6** 1 **Lanfredo**[14] 112 3-8-7 .... JoeFanning 9 47
(D W P Arbuthnot) *b: in tch: hdwy to trck ldrs 1/2-way: hld whn hmpd appr fnl f* **66/1**
0 **7** 1 **Busy Man (IRE)**[14] 114 7-9-13 .... FergalLynch 12 50
(J R Jenkins) *prom: led 5f out: rdn and hdd 1f out: chkd and wknd* **66/1**
06- **8** shd **Raise The Heights (IRE)**[175] 4153 3-8-10 ow3 .... SamHitchcott 6 48
(C Tinkler) *slowly away and a outpcd* **14/1**
0- **9** 3 1/2 **Hometomammy**[47] 6565 4-9-13 .... DarrenWilliams 2 41
(P W Hiatt) *w'like: b.hind: led tl hdd 5f out: wknd over 2f out* **33/1**
00- **10** 1/2 **War Dancer**[117] 5672 4-9-13 .... StephenCarson 10 40
(E A Wheeler) *mid-div: rdn over 3f out: sn bhd* **100/1**
06-3 **11** 2 **Salisbury World (IRE)**[25] 16 3-8-7 67 .... JohnEgan 11 31+
(D R C Elsworth) *lw: t.k.h: prom tl wknd qckly over 1f out* **7/2**[3]
0- **12** 1 1/4 **Belrose (IRE)**[49] 6545 4-9-8 .... ChrisCatlin 5 28
(Mrs C A Dunnett) *unf: slowly away: a bhd* **150/1**

1m 39.71s (0.28) **Going Correction** -0.05s/f (Stan)
WFA 3 from 4yo+ 20lb **12** Ran SP% **116.3**
Speed ratings (Par 103):96,95,94,92,90 89,88,88,84,84 82,80
CSF £67.55 TOTE £20.40: £4.90, £1.70, £1.10; EX 85.60.
Owner W J Gredley **Bred** Middle Park Stud Ltd **Trained** Newmarket, Suffolk

FOCUS
This looked the stronger of the two divisions, the pace was sound, and the form appears fair, although not that solid.
Art Elegant Official explanation: jockey said gelding ran too free
Busy Man(IRE) Official explanation: jockey said gelding had to be checked approaching final furlong and lost its action

220 BETDIRECT.CO.UK H'CAP 7f (P)
2:05 (2:10) (Class 4) (0-85,85) 4-Y-0+
£6,232 (£1,866; £933; £467; £233; £117) **Stalls** Low

Form RPR
40-0 **1** **Hayyani (IRE)**[17] 89 4-8-6 73 .... (e1) JohnEgan 1 80
(K McAuliffe) *in tch: short of room and swtchd rt 1f out: r.o to ld last strides* **8/1**
04-0 **2** 1/2 **Outer Hebrides**[22] 58 5-9-1 82 .... (vt) MickyFenton 10 88
(Stef Liddiard) *hld up towards rr: hdwy over 1f out: rdn to go 2nd cl home* **33/1**
40-1 **3** 1/2 **Chief Exec**[24] 36 4-9-2 83 .... MartinDwyer 6 88
(C A Cyzer) *lw: mid-div: rdn and hdwy 2f out: drvn to ld ins fnl f: hdd and lost 2nd nr fin* **11/2**[3]
4-12 **4** 1 1/4 **Ever Cheerful**[17] 89 5-8-9 76 .... ChrisCatlin 7 77
(G C H Chung) *t.k.h: prom: rdn over 1f out: no imp fnl f* **10/1**
3-60 **5** hd **Cornus**[18] 80 4-9-1 82 .... RobertWinston 8 83
(M J Polglase) *b: hld up in rr: hdwy over 1f out: r.o: nvr nrr* **14/1**
115- **6** nk **Perfect Story (IRE)**[42] 6602 4-8-7 81 .... RonanKeogh(7) 11 81
(J A R Toller) *prom: rdn 2f out: ev ch 1f out: no ex ins fnl f* **9/2**[2]
00-0 **7** hd **Who's Winning (IRE)**[14] 117 5-8-13 80 .... MichaelHills 9 80
(B G Powell) *t.k.h: sn trckd ldr: ev ch ent fnl f: fdd ins* **25/1**
340- **8** 1 **Ali Bruce**[127] 5439 6-8-11 78 .... NCallan 5 75+
(G L Moore) *bhd tl gd hdwy on ins over 1f out: nt clr run ent fnl f and no ch after* **12/1**
020- **9** nk **Red Romeo**[70] 6379 5-9-3 84 .... DaleGibson 3 80+
(G A Swinbank) *prom tl sltly hmpd 1f out: sn btn* **15/2**
62-4 **10** 1 1/4 **Prince Tum Tum (USA)**[22] 54 6-9-4 85 .... FergalLynch 2 78
(D W Barker) *lw: slowly away: a struggling in rr* **4/1**[1]
33-0 **11** 1/2 **Binanti**[8] 161 6-9-1 82 .... (v) IanMongan 4 74
(P R Chamings) *led tl rdn and hdd ins fnl f: wknd rapidly* **9/1**

1m 24.74s (-1.15) **Going Correction** -0.05s/f (Stan) **11** Ran SP% **116.7**
Speed ratings (Par 105):104,103,102,101,101 100,100,99,99,97 97
CSF £235.35 CT £1599.53 TOTE £11.10: £3.90, £12.00, £3.20; EX 307.10.
Owner Aidan J Ryan **Bred** Sean O'Keeffe **Trained** Fernham, Oxon

FOCUS
A fair handicap for the class, run at a sound pace, and the field were closely bunched at the finish. The form is somewhat messy and does not look anything out of the ordinary.
Cornus Official explanation: jockey said gelding suffered interference in running
Ali Bruce Official explanation: jockey said gelding was denied a clear run
Red Romeo Official explanation: jockey said gelding was denied a clear run
Prince Tum Tum(USA) Official explanation: jockey said gelding ran flat and had a breathing problem
Binanti Official explanation: jockey said gelding hung left-handed in home straight

221 LITTLEWOODS BETDIRECT H'CAP 1m (P)
2:35 (2:41) (Class 4) (0-85,82) 4-Y-0+ **£6,477** (£1,927; £963; £481) **Stalls** High

Form RPR
00-2 **1** **Farewell Gift**[21] 64 5-8-6 73 .... (b) StephaneBreux(3) 7 81
(R Hannon) *a.p: rdn to ld ins fnl f: drvn out* **14/1**
002- **2** 1 **Spring Goddess (IRE)**[113] 5713 5-9-3 81 .... DarrenWilliams 2 87
(A P Jarvis) *a in tch: rdn 2f out: ev ch 1f out: r.o* **16/1**
32-1 **3** hd **Northern Desert (IRE)**[21] 64 7-9-2 80 .... ChrisCatlin 9 87+
(P W Hiatt) *hld up: hdwy over 2f out: r.o fnl f: nvr nrr* **13/2**[3]
05-4 **4** nk **Swift Oscar**[21] 64 4-9-2 80 .... EddieAhern 5 85+
(J W Hills) *hld up: hdwy 3f out: running on whn n.m.r ins fnl f* **13/2**[3]
3-60 **5** 3/4 **Claret And Amber**[8] 161 4-8-13 77 .... (b) PaulHanagan 3 80
(R A Fahey) *hld up in rr: rdn and hdwy over 3f out: one pce appr fnl f* **11/2**[2]
0-64 **6** shd **Tanforan**[3] 192 4-8-0 71 .... JamesDoyle(7) 8 74
(K McAuliffe) *lw: mde most tl rdn and hdd ins fnl f: no ex* **7/1**
220- **7** shd **Island Rapture**[29] 6690 6-8-9 73 .... JohnEgan 10 76
(J A R Toller) *slowly away: bhd: rdn 3f out: hdwy oer 1f out: edgd lft and kpt on ins fnl f* **16/1**
-250 **8** hd **Waterside (IRE)**[10] 140 7-9-4 82 .... NCallan 12 84
(G L Moore) *a.p on outside: rdn 2f out: fdd ins fnl f* **11/1**
51-1 **9** 1 1/2 **Silent Storm**[17] 89 6-9-0 78 .... MartinDwyer 4 77
(C A Cyzer) *lw: mid-div: rdn over 2f out: no ex appr fnl f* **7/1**
250- **10** 1 1/2 **Habshan (USA)**[70] 6373 6-8-12 76 .... MichaelHills 1 71
(C F Wall) *disp ld tl wknd fnl f* **9/2**[1]
14-0 **11** 1 1/2 **Celtique**[8] 161 4-8-7 71 .... JamieMackay 11 63
(M Wigham) *lw: a bhd* **40/1**
/15- **12** 2 1/2 **St Savarin (FR)**[271] 1408 5-9-0 78 .... GylesParkin 6 64
(R A Fahey) *mid-div: rdn 1/2-way: sn bhd* **14/1**

1m 36.18s (-3.25) **Going Correction** -0.05s/f (Stan) course record **12** Ran SP% **121.1**
Speed ratings (Par 105):114,113,112,112,111 111,111,111,109,108 106,104
CSF £223.98 CT £1628.62 TOTE £13.80: £3.90, £4.40, £2.40; EX 150.00.
Owner Lady Whent And Friends **Bred** Lady Whent **Trained** East Everleigh, Wilts

FOCUS
A fair handicap run at a sound pace and the winning time was under half a second outside the course record. Again the field were close together at the finish and the form is again somewhat messy.
Swift Oscar Official explanation: jockey said gelding was denied a clear run

222 BETDIRECT FREEPHONE 0800 211 222 H'CAP 1m 2f (P)
3:10 (3:15) (Class 2) (0-100,98) 4-Y-0+
£15,580 (£4,665; £2,332; £1,167; £582; £292) **Stalls** Low

Form RPR
00-1 **1** **Bravo Maestro (USA)**[8] 161 5-8-8 88 ow1 .... NCallan 9 92
(N P Littmoden) *lw: set stdy pce tl qcknd over 2f out: clr over 1f out: drvn out fnl f* **11/2**[3]
-411 **2** nk **Willhego**[10] 140 5-8-1 84 oh5 .... RichardThomas(3) 7 87
(J R Best) *trckd ldrs: rdn to chse wnr appr fnl f: r.o* **11/1**
06-1 **3** 1 **Polygonal (FR)**[21] 65 6-8-11 91 .... EddieAhern 4 93
(Ernst Oertel) *b.hind: t.k.h: hld up: rdn and hdwy over 1f out: r.o fnl f: nvr nrr* **7/1**
25-5 **4** nk **Activo (FR)**[14] 116 5-8-6 86 ow1 .... JohnEgan 3 87
(S Dow) *mid-div: rdn and hdwy over 1f out: r.o: nvr nrr* **6/1**
11-2 **5** 1 **Boo**[14] 116 4-9-2 98 .... (v) RobertWinston 6 97
(K R Burke) *plld hrd: sn trckd wnr tl no ex appr fnl f* **11/4**[1]
1-20 **6** nk **Trifti**[8] 161 5-8-5 85 .... MartinDwyer 5 84
(C A Cyzer) *hld up: effrt over 1f out: sn btn* **20/1**
41-6 **7** 3 **Dower House**[21] 65 11-8-6 86 .... (t) ChrisCatlin 8 79
(Andrew Turnell) *hld up: sme hdwy over 3f out: nvr on terms* **16/1**
04-1 **8** 3/4 **Tiger Tiger (FR)**[14] 116 5-8-13 93 .... MichaelHills 1 84
(Jamie Poulton) *lw: trckd ldrs tl wknd over 2f out* **10/3**[2]
046/ **9** 5 **Bustan (IRE)**[434] 6694 7-9-4 98 .... MickyFenton 2 80
(G C Bravery) *bkwd: a bhd* **25/1**

2m 7.20s (-0.59) **Going Correction** -0.05s/f (Stan)
WFA 4 from 5yo+ 2lb **9** Ran SP% **114.7**
Speed ratings (Par 109):100,99,98,98,97 97,95,94,90
CSF £63.35 CT £427.92 TOTE £6.30: £2.20, £1.70, £2.30; EX 46.10.
Owner Nigel Shields **Bred** Pacelco S A & Partners **Trained** Newmarket, Suffolk

FOCUS
A decent handicap, run at an uneven gallop in a moderate time, and the winner made all under a shrewd ride, so the form cannot be taken at face value.

NOTEBOOK
Bravo Maestro(USA), raised 8lb for winning at Wolverhampton eight days previously, made all and followed-up in determined fashion under tactically astute ride from Callan. Having swooped late when successful previously, it was a surprise to see him dictating matters, but the decision paid off and he could have been called the winner approaching the final furlong. He is clearly in top form at present. (op 5-1 tchd 6-1)
Willhego, searching for the hat-trick and racing from 5lb out of the handicap, finished his race with gusto, but was always being held by the winner late on. This must rate another improved effort and he is another who appears to be at the top of his game at present. (op 10-1 tchd 12-1)
Polygonal(FR), raised 2lb for his win over further at this venue 21 days previously, was not suited by the tactical nature of this event and emerges with plenty of credit in the circumstances. (op 15-2 tchd 8-1)
Activo(FR) was another who would have ideally been suited by a stronger gallop, yet still posted a solid effort and helps set the level of this form. (tchd 11-2)
Boo was placed to have every chance just in behind Bravo Maestro nearing the final furlong, but he ultimately paid for refusing to settle through the early stages and dropped out disappointingly thereafter. He is better than this. (op 5-2 tchd 3-1 and 10-3 in a place)

Tiger Tiger(FR), raised 4lb for winning over course and distance a fortnight previously, ran well below par and failed to confirm that form with Boo. (op 7-2 tchd 3-1 and 4-1 in a place)

223 PLAY NOW WITH LITTLEWOODSPOKER.COM H'CAP 1m 2f (P)
3:45 (3:50) (Class 5) (0-70,71) 4-Y-0+ **£3,238** (£963; £481; £240) **Stalls** Low

Form RPR

145- **1** **Amorist (IRE)**[32] 6671 4-8-11 **65** JamieMackay 4 83
(Sir Mark Prescott) *mde all: rdn clr over 1f out: unchal* **11/2**[2]

01-2 **2** *3 1/2* **Red Birr (IRE)**[15] 106 5-9-4 **70** ChrisCatlin 5 82
(P R Webber) *lw: trckd ldrs: wnt 2nd over 2f out: no ch w wnr fnl f* **7/4**[1]

0-12 **3** *3 1/2* **Port 'n Starboard**[14] 111 5-8-10 **62** MartinDwyer 11 67
(C A Cyzer) *lw: chsd ldng 3: hrd rdn 2f out: kpt on gamely to go 3rd last strides* **6/1**[3]

656- **4** *shd* **Eloquent Knight (USA)**[42] 6596 4-8-12 **66** JoeFanning 10 71
(W R Muir) *lw: trckd wnr to over 2f out: no ex fnl f and lost 2nd fnl strides* **16/1**

133- **5** *1 1/4* **Lady Taverner**[28] 6701 5-8-1 **58** NataliaGemelova(5) 13 60
(J E Long) *hld up: mde hdwy ins fnl 2f but nvr nr to chal* **12/1**

00-0 **6** *1/2* **Paparaazi (IRE)**[17] 88 4-9-2 **70** (v) PaulHanagan 7 71
(R A Fahey) *hmpd s: in rr: mde sme late hdwy* **33/1**

5-50 **7** *shd* **Scottish River (USA)**[14] 115 7-8-10 **69** JamesDoyle(7) 12 70
(M D I Usher) *b.hind: v.s.a: mde sme hdwy 6f out: kpt on one pce ins fnl 2f* **14/1**

1-22 **8** *nk* **Holiday Cocktail**[7] 169 4-8-12 **66** J-PGuillambert 3 67
(S C Williams) *a towards rr* **15/2**

3-04 **9** *3* **Admiral Compton**[10] 135 5-9-5 **71** (b) EddieAhern 9 66
(J R Boyle) *mid-div: rdn 2f out: sn bhd* **10/1**

0-10 **10** *2 1/2* **Border Edge**[3] 185 8-8-9 **61** (v) RobertWinston 14 51
(J J Bridger) *b: a in rr and nvr on terms* **20/1**

12-0 **11** *3 1/2* **Cormorant Wharf (IRE)**[25] 17 6-8-11 **68** RobynBrisland(5) 2 52
(G L Moore) *in tch tl wknd over 4f out* **25/1**

400- **12** *11* **Innpursuit**[8] 3348 4-9-0 **68** (b) NCallan 1 31
(J M P Eustace) *mid-div: bhd fnl 4f* **100/1**

000- **13** *4* **Rawaabet (IRE)**[89] 5671 4-9-2 **70** JohnEgan 6 25
(P W Hiatt) *a struggling in rr* **50/1**

/0-0 **14** *1 1/2* **Baboosh (IRE)**[24] 33 5-9-4 **70** MichaelTebbutt 8 22
(M Wigham) *a bhd* **100/1**

2m 3.51s (-4.28) **Going Correction** -0.05s/f (Stan)
WFA 4 from 5yo+ 2lb **14** Ran SP% **122.6**
Speed ratings (Par 103):115,112,109,109,108 107,107,107,105,103 100,91,88,87
CSF £14.95 CT £62.79 TOTE £5.90: £3.20, £1.20, £2.50; EX 25.60.
Owner W E Sturt - Osborne House Iv **Bred** Ian Fair **Trained** Newmarket, Suffolk

FOCUS
A competitive handicap for the grade, run at a decent clip and the winning time was under a second outside the course record. The form looks solid, with the third and fourth close to their course marks, and the winner made all to score convincingly.
Cormorant Wharf(IRE) Official explanation: jockey said gelding hung right
Innpursuit Official explanation: jockey said gelding hung left

224 TEXT "BETDIRECT" TO 88600 H'CAP 6f (P)
4:20 (4:25) (Class 5) (0-75,75) 4-Y-0+ **£3,238** (£963; £481; £240) **Stalls** Low

Form RPR

00-3 **1** **Saviours Spirit**[17] 89 5-8-13 **70** JoeFanning 6 79+
(T G Mills) *trckd ldrs: rdn to ld over 1f out: edgd lft but sn clr* **7/2**[1]

10-0 **2** *1 3/4* **Lake Chini (IRE)**[3] 192 4-9-4 **75** (b) NCallan 3 79
(M A Jarvis) *lw: mid-div: rdn and hdwy 2f out: edgd lft u.p but r.o to go 2nd cl home* **4/1**[2]

0-50 **3** *hd* **Willheconquertoo**[3] 192 6-8-13 **70** (v[1]) PaulHanagan 10 73
(I W McInnes) *hld up: hdwy over 2f out on ins: ev ch appr fnl f: sltly short of room but kpt on* **20/1**

61-6 **4** *hd* **Franksalot (IRE)**[17] 89 6-9-0 **71** EddieAhern 11 74
(Miss B Sanders) *in tch: rdn over 2f out: kpt on fnl f* **11/2**[3]

-521 **5** *2* **Blue Knight (IRE)**[7] 164 7-9-1 **72** (v) AdrianTNicholls 8 69
(D Nicholls) *outpcd: hdwy whn short of room and swtchd rt over 1f out: kpt on fnl f* **13/2**

00-0 **6** *1 1/4* **Amazin**[7] 167 4-8-6 **70** (b) JamesDoyle(7) 5 63
(N P Littmoden) *bhd: passed sme btn horses fnl f* **16/1**

-602 **7** *3/4* **Whitbarrow (IRE)**[8] 159 7-9-3 **74** RobertWinston 9 65
(A W Carroll) *lw: chsd ldrs tl wknd fnl f* **10/1**

2-00 **8** *4* **Anfield Dream**[18] 80 4-9-1 **72** FergalLynch 2 51
(J R Jenkins) *led tl hdd & wknd appr fnl f* **12/1**

0-63 **9** *1 1/4* **Polar Force**[14] 117 6-8-13 **70** OscarUrbina 12 45
(Mrs C A Dunnett) *lw: in tch: rdn 1/2-way: wknd over 1f out* **11/1**

-440 **10** *nk* **Kennington**[14] 117 6-8-12 **69** (b) ChrisCatlin 7 43
(Mrs C A Dunnett) *a in rr* **14/1**

240- **11** *3 1/2* **Depressed**[176] 4126 4-9-3 **74** (p) JohnEgan 4 38
(Ernst Oertel) *trckd ldr tl rdn and wknd over 1f out* **25/1**

054- **12** *3* **Witchry**[40] 6616 4-9-1 **72** LPKeniry 1 27
(A G Newcombe) *chsd ldrs tl rdn and wknd wl over 1f out* **16/1**

1m 11.38s (-1.43) **Going Correction** -0.05s/f (Stan) **12** Ran SP% **123.1**
Speed ratings (Par 103):107,104,104,104,101 99,98,93,91,91 86,82
CSF £17.86 CT £257.77 TOTE £4.60: £2.40, £2.50, £6.30; EX 26.10 Place 6 £917.45, Place 5 £182.59..
Owner J E Harley **Bred** Mrs S Shaw **Trained** Headley, Surrey

FOCUS
A competitive sprint for the class and the form looks sound enough with the placed horses setting the standard. The winner can rate higher on this surface.
Anfield Dream Official explanation: jockey said colt hung right
Depressed Official explanation: jockey said filly had no more to give
T/Plt: £1,019.90 to a £1 stake. Pool: £46,875.95. 33.55 winning tickets. T/Qpdt: £119.00 to a £1 stake. Pool: £4,486.90. 27.90 winning tickets. JS

209 WOLVERHAMPTON (A.W) (L-H)
Saturday, January 28

OFFICIAL GOING: Standard
Wind: Light, against Weather: Fine

225 LITTLEWOODSPOOLS.COM H'CAP 5f 216y(P)
2:00 (2:07) (Class 6) (0-65,65) 4-Y-0+ **£2,388** (£705; £352) **Stalls** Low

Form RPR

2-02 **1** **Majestical (IRE)**[10] 137 4-9-0 **61** (p) TonyCulhane 9 71
(J M Bradley) *hld up: rdn 3f out: hdwy over 1f out: led wl ins fnl f: r.o* **7/2**[2]

1-20 **2** *1 1/4* **Diamond Josh**[10] 137 4-8-10 **60** DanielTudhope(3) 3 66
(P D Evans) *prom: led 2f out: rdn over 1f out: hdd wl ins fnl f: hld cl home* **10/3**[1]

-330 **3** *1/2* **Savile's Delight (IRE)**[12] 119 7-9-2 **63** (b) TomEaves 6 68
(R Brotherton) *led early: remained prom: rdn and ev ch ins fnl f: nt qckn cl home* **8/1**[3]

-124 **4** *shd* **Alpaga Le Jomage (IRE)**[7] 171 4-9-4 **65** DeanMcKeown 11 69
(M J Polglase) *chsd ldrs: rdn over 1f out: styd on ins fnl f* **9/1**

0-64 **5** *hd* **Ashes (IRE)**[12] 119 4-8-13 **60** HayleyTurner 10 64
(K R Burke) *in tch: rdn and outpcd over 2f out: r.o ins fnl f* **22/1**

2-00 **6** *hd* **Cerebus**[18] 80 4-9-3 **64** (b) PhillipMakin 12 67
(M J Polglase) *hld up: rdn and hdwy ins fnl f: r.o: nrst fin* **14/1**

0/5- **7** *nk* **Oneiro Way (IRE)**[170] 4302 4-9-4 **65** GeorgeBaker 13 67
(P R Chamings) *racd wd: in tch: rdn ins fnl f: styd on* **16/1**

32-3 **8** *2 1/2* **Hard To Catch (IRE)**[25] 17 8-8-11 **65** LauraReynolds(7) 7 60
(D K Ivory) *towards rr after 1f: hdwy over 1f out: no imp ins fnl f* **8/1**[3]

00-0 **9** *1/2* **Celtic Thunder**[7] 171 5-9-1 **62** RobertHavlin 1 55
(T J Etherington) *chsd ldrs: rdn over 1f out: wknd ins fnl f* **8/1**[3]

0-03 **10** *2 1/2* **Greenwood**[10] 137 8-9-1 **62** (t) SteveDrowne 8 48
(P G Murphy) *a bhd* **9/1**

50-0 **11** *3* **Agilete**[19] 71 4-8-13 **60** (p) FergusSweeney 5 37
(J R Boyle) *s.i.s: rdn 3f out: a bhd* **25/1**

1/06 **12** *1 1/2* **Lady Bahia (IRE)**[10] 136 5-9-1 **62** (p) RobbieFitzpatrick 2 34
(Peter Grayson) *sn led: rdn and hdd 2f out: wknd fnl f* **16/1**

50/2 **13** *1 1/2* **Borzoi Maestro**[11] 130 5-8-13 **60** (p) AlanDaly 4 28
(M Wellings) *chsd ldrs: rdn over 2f out: wknd over 1f out* **10/1**

1m 14.67s (-1.14) **Going Correction** -0.15s/f (Stan) **13** Ran SP% **134.4**
Speed ratings (Par 101):101,99,98,98,98 98,97,94,93,90 86,84,82
CSF £17.87 CT £99.84 TOTE £5.50: £1.80, £1.60, £3.10; EX 27.50.
Owner Raymond Tooth **Bred** Sean Beston **Trained** Sedbury, Gloucs

FOCUS
A competitive sprint in which the well-backed winner came from off the pace. The form looks particularly reliable, with the second, third and fourth all close to their form and the winner improving slightly after a luckless run two starts previously.

226 PLAY TODAY AT LITTLEWOODSCASINO.COM H'CAP 5f 216y(P)
2:30 (2:40) (Class 5) (0-70,68) 3-Y-0 **£3,412** (£1,007; £504) **Stalls** Low

Form RPR

04-6 **1** **Pauvic (IRE)**[15] 105 3-8-6 **56** (v[1]) PaulFessey 3 63
(Mrs A Duffield) *mde all: rdn over 1f out: hld on wl* **12/1**

0-02 **2** *nk* **Garstang**[12] 120 3-8-4 **54** oh2 RobbieFitzpatrick 6 60
(Peter Grayson) *trckd ldrs: rdn over 2f out: wnt 2nd and hung lft 1f out: r.o cl home* **9/2**[3]

340- **3** *1 1/2* **Stoneacre Boy (IRE)**[104] 5920 3-9-3 **67** TonyHamilton 4 68
(Peter Grayson) *s.i.s: towards rr: hdwy over 1f out: sn edgd rt: styd on* **15/2**

314- **4** *2* **Glenviews Youngone (IRE)**[37] 6653 3-8-13 **68** DuranFentiman(5) 2 63
(Peter Grayson) *prom: rdn 2f out: wknd ins fnl f* **4/1**[2]

5-12 **5** *shd* **Thoughtsofstardom**[3] 190 3-9-2 **66** HayleyTurner 5 61
(P S McEntee) *hld up in tch: rdn over 1f out: edgd lft ent fnl f: kpt on: nt trble ldrs* **6/4**[1]

06-0 **6** *3/4* **Jazz At The Sands (USA)**[26] 10 3-8-2 **55** oh6 ow1(v) PatrickMathers(3) 7 47
(D Shaw) *hld up in rr: rdn over 2f out: nvr able to chal* **14/1**

000- **7** *3/4* **Red Vixen (IRE)**[38] 6640 3-7-12 **55** KirstyMilczarek(7) 1 45
(C N Allen) *s.i.s: in rr: nvr on terms* **12/1**

-433 **8** *3* **Buzzin'Boyzee (IRE)**[17] 83 3-8-7 **57** TomEaves 8 38
(P D Evans) *hld up: rdn over 2f out: outpcd over 1f out* **12/1**

5-54 **9** *3/4* **Miss Champagne (IRE)**[19] 69 3-7-13 **54** oh2 RoryMoore(5) 9 33
(M Quinn) *prom: rdn over 2f out: wknd over 1f out* **14/1**

1m 14.8s (-1.01) **Going Correction** -0.15s/f (Stan) **9** Ran SP% **126.4**
Speed ratings (Par 97):100,99,97,94,94 93,92,88,87
CSF £71.45 CT £452.97 TOTE £14.20: £3.30, £2.10, £3.50; EX 81.60.
Owner Middleham Park Racing XLV **Bred** Thomas Stacey **Trained** Constable Burton, N Yorks
■ Stewards' Enquiry : Rory Moore one-day ban: failed to keep straight from stalls (Feb 8)

FOCUS
A modest handicap in which it paid to race close to the pace. Solid enough form of its type nevertheless.

227 BET NOW AT BETDIRECT.CO.UK H'CAP (DIV I) 7f 32y(P)
3:05 (3:11) (Class 6) (0-58,58) 4-Y-0+ **£2,047** (£604; £302) **Stalls** High

Form RPR

-034 **1** **Canadian Danehill (IRE)**[10] 137 4-9-2 **58** (p) FergusSweeney 7 68
(R M H Cowell) *mde virtually all: rdn and hung rt fr over 1f out: r.o* **7/1**[3]

304- **2** *1 3/4* **Iced Diamond (IRE)**[33] 6664 7-9-2 **58** GeorgeBaker 4 63
(W M Brisbourne) *prom for over 1f: sn in midfield: hdwy over 3f out: rdn over 1f out: sn edgd rt: wnt 2nd ins fnl f: styd on* **3/1**[2]

5-00 **3** *2 1/2* **Border Artist**[19] 67 7-8-13 **55** TonyCulhane 3 54
(B G Powell) *cl up: rdn and ev ch wl over 1f out: wknd towards fin* **7/1**[3]

-000 **4** *3/4* **Lakeside Guy (IRE)**[9] 145 5-7-11 **46** oh6 (vt) LiamJones(7) 8 43
(M Appleby) *hld up: rdn and hdwy over 1f out: styd on* **20/1**

33-3 **5** *1* **Cayman Breeze**[25] 22 6-8-11 **53** SteveDrowne 1 47
(J M Bradley) *prom early: sn in midfield: rdn and hdwy 2f out: one pce fr over 1f out* **2/1**[1]

00-0 **6** *1 1/4* **Chillin Out**[25] 21 4-8-5 **47** SimonWhitworth 2 38
(W Jarvis) *racd keenly in midfield: rdn over 2f out: wknd wl over 1f out* **9/1**

4/0- **7** *shd* **String Serenade (IRE)**[81] 4077 5-8-8 **50** DManning 12 41
(V Smith) *hld up: rdn over 2f out: no imp* **20/1**

60-6 **8** *2 1/2* **Tequila Sheila (IRE)**[11] 133 4-8-10 **52** (v[1]) HayleyTurner 5 36
(K R Burke) *trckd ldrs: rdn over 2f out: wknd wl over 1f out* **7/1**[3]

00-0 **9** *2* **Jennverse**[10] 137 4-8-10 **57** MarcHalford(5) 9 36
(D K Ivory) *hmpd s: in rr: rdn over 2f out: nvr on terms* **20/1**

30-0 **10** *25* **Fenwicks Pride (IRE)**[25] 29 8-7-13 **46** oh6 (v) DuranFentiman(5) 10 —
(A Berry) *wnt lft s: sn w wnr: rdn over 3f out: sn wknd* **33/1**

540- **P** **Pauline's Prince**[163] 4503 4-9-2 **58** (t) GrahamGibbons 6 —
(R Hollinshead) *trckd ldrs tl rdn and wknd 4f out: t.o whn p.u over 1f out* **17/2**

1m 29.5s (-0.90) **Going Correction** -0.15s/f (Stan) **11** Ran SP% **133.6**
Speed ratings (Par 101):99,97,94,93,92 90,90,87,85,56 —
CSF £30.93 CT £166.79 TOTE £8.50: £2.20, £1.90, £2.20; EX 40.10.
Owner Blue Metropolis **Bred** Skymarc Farm Inc And Dr A J O'Reilly **Trained** Six Mile Bottom, Cambs
■ Stewards' Enquiry : D Manning three-day ban: careless riding (Feb 8-10)

FOCUS
A moderate handicap, and not the most solid of form, even though it was run slightly faster than the two later events over the same trip. The field came towards the stands side in the straight.

Pauline's Prince Official explanation: vet said colt bled from the nose

228 BETDIRECT.CO.UK H'CAP — 7f 32y(P)
3:40 (3:45) (Class 4) (0-85,79) 3-Y-0 — £5,505 (£1,637; £818; £408) Stalls High

Form — RPR

-026 **1** **Sigismundus (IRE)**[3] 190 3-8-10 **70** .... PatCosgrave 5 — 72
(J R Boyle) *mde all: rdn over 1f out: jst hld on* **13/2**

22-1 **2** *nk* **Chief Commander (FR)**[15] 110 3-9-5 **79** .... TonyCulhane 4 — 80
(Jane Chapple-Hyam) *a.p: rdn 3f out: r.o cl home* **11/8**[1]

61- **3** *½* **Tawaaf**[50] 6528 3-9-2 **76** .... AdrianMcCarthy 3 — 76
(P W Chapple-Hyam) *hld up: rdn and hdwy over 2f out: r.o cl home* **11/4**[2]

26-1 **4** *½* **Keel (IRE)**[15] 104 3-9-3 **77** .... SteveDrowne 1 — 75
(J A Osborne) *hld up: swtchd rt over 4f out: rdn over 2f out: hdwy over 1f out: sn edgd lft: styd on cl home* **4/1**[3]

040- **5** *6* **Tamagin (USA)**[105] 5888 3-8-8 **68** .... TomEaves 2 — 51
(P D Evans) *racd keenly: prom: lost pl 4f out: n.d after* **22/1**

454- **6** *½* **Vodkatini**[39] 6624 3-9-0 **74** ....(v) FergusSweeney 6 — 56
(P J Makin) *cl up: rdn over 2f out: wknd wl over 1f out* **12/1**

1m 29.81s (-0.59) **Going Correction** -0.15s/f (Stan) — 6 Ran SP% **114.1**
Speed ratings (Par 99):97,96,96,95,88 88
CSF £16.41 TOTE £9.90: £3.10, £1.50; EX 21.70.
Owner Inside Track Racing Club **Bred** Liam Queally **Trained** Epsom, Surrey

FOCUS
An interesting handicap, despite the small field, as it featured several lightly raced and improving types. However, the time was slower than both divisions of the Class 6 handicap.
Vodkatini Official explanation: trainer said gelding was later found to be lame on its near hind

229 BETDIRECT FREEPHONE 0800 211 222 H'CAP — 1m 1f 103y(P)
4:10 (4:15) (Class 6) (0-55,58) 4-Y-0+ — £2,388 (£705; £352) Stalls Low

Form — RPR

-011 **1** **Young Mick**[3] 187 4-9-2 **58** 6ex ....(v) GeorgeBaker 5 — 66
(G G Margarson) *prom: led over 1f out: r.o* **11/10**[1]

00-0 **2** *1* **Friends Hope**[19] 73 5-8-12 **53** .... PatCosgrave 13 — 59+
(P A Blockley) *s.s: hld up: hdwy 2f out: wnt 2nd ins fnl f: r.o: nt rch wnr* **13/2**[2]

-030 **3** *1* **Sol Rojo**[8] 158 4-8-11 **53** ....(b) RobbieFitzpatrick 6 — 57
(M J Attwater) *squeezed out s: midfield: rdn over 3f out: forced wd over 2f out: hdwy over 1f out: styd on wl towards fin* **15/2**

100- **4** *2* **Spark Up**[56] 6487 6-8-12 **53** ....(b) AdrianMcCarthy 2 — 53
(J W Unett) *midfield: hdwy whn nt clr run and swtchd rt over 2f out: no ex ins fnl f* **25/1**

30-0 **5** *3 ½* **Pharaoh Prince**[19] 72 5-8-12 **53** ....(v) TonyCulhane 1 — 47
(G Prodromou) *led: rdn and hdd over 1f out: wknd ins fnl f* **14/1**

00-6 **6** *¾* **Fiore Di Bosco (IRE)**[11] 127 5-8-12 **53** .... PhillipMakin 7 — 45
(T D Barron) *hld up: styd on fnl f: nvr nr to chal* **25/1**

0-00 **7** *½* **Farnborough (USA)**[3] 187 5-8-13 **54** .... HayleyTurner 9 — 45
(R J Price) *hld up: forced wd over 2f out: kpt on fnl f* **7/1**[3]

0-05 **8** *1* **Fortune Point (IRE)**[17] 82 8-9-0 **55** ....(v) PaulFessey 4 — 44
(A W Carroll) *prom: rdn over 2f out: wknd over 1f out* **20/1**

0-00 **9** *nk* **Sting Like A Bee (IRE)**[8] 156 7-8-4 **52** .... KellyHarrison(7) 12 — 41
(J S Goldie) *s.s: hld up: rdn over 1f out: nvr on terms* **33/1**

022- **10** *2 ½* **Hoh Bleu Dee**[54] 6506 5-8-6 **52** ....(p) MarcHalford(5) 11 — 36
(T Keddy) *hld up: hdwy 4f out: rdn 3f out: wknd over 1f out* **9/1**

213- **11** *½* **Rotuma (IRE)**[54] 6506 7-8-11 **52** ....(b) TomEaves 8 — 35
(M Dods) *midfield: rdn whn forced wd over 2f out: sn wknd* **8/1**

/00- **12** *5* **Cool Bathwick (IRE)**[110] 5807 7-9-0 **55** .... FergusSweeney 3 — 29
(G H Yardley) *prom: rdn 4f out: wknd over 2f out* **50/1**

2m 3.06s (0.44) **Going Correction** -0.15s/f (Stan)
WFA 4 from 5yo+ 1lb — 12 Ran SP% **130.4**
Speed ratings (Par 101):92,91,90,88,85 84,84,83,83,80 80,75
CSF £9.16 CT £45.23 TOTE £1.90: £1.30, £3.00, £2.80; EX 17.40.
Owner M F Kentish **Bred** M F Kentish **Trained** Newmarket, Suffolk

FOCUS
A moderate handicap run at a steady provided an ideal opportunity for Young Mick to complete a quick hat-trick without needing to improve on his previous form..

230 LITTEWOODS BET DIRECT H'CAP (DIV I) — 1m 4f 50y(P)
4:40 (4:41) (Class 6) (0-60,59) 4-Y-0+ — £2,047 (£604; £302) Stalls Low

Form — RPR

52-4 **1** **Night Warrior (IRE)**[18] 75 6-8-10 **51** ....(b) GrahamGibbons 9 — 59
(N P Littmoden) *hld up: rdn and hdwy over 3f out: edgd rt and led ins fnl f: r.o* **7/2**[2]

65-5 **2** *1* **Jadeeron**[24] 40 7-8-4 **45** ....(v) AlanDaly 1 — 51
(Miss D A McHale) *midfield: hdwy over 3f out: rdn to ld over 1f out: hdd and edgd lft ins fnl f: nt qckn cl home* **12/1**

34-2 **3** *shd* **Zaffeu**[8] 158 5-8-8 **49** .... FergusSweeney 2 — 55
(A G Juckes) *hld up: swtchd rt and hdwy 4f out: rdn and ev ch 1f out: r.o cl home* **11/4**[1]

-465 **4** *6* **York Cliff**[8] 158 8-8-8 **52** .... PatrickMathers(3) 4 — 48
(W M Brisbourne) *midfield: rdn over 3f out: hdwy over 1f out: no ex ins fnl f* **6/1**

000- **5** *¾* **Kirkhammerton (IRE)**[102] 5959 4-8-12 **57** ....(v) DeanMcKeown 7 — 52
(M J Polglase) *chsd ldr: led 3f out: rdn and hdd over 1f out: wknd ins fnl f* **28/1**

1-21 **6** *2* **Regency Red (IRE)**[8] 158 8-8-7 **55** .... LiamJones(7) 11 — 47
(W M Brisbourne) *hld up: hdwy 4f out: rdn over 2f out: wknd over 1f out* **6/1**

/0-0 **7** *1 ¾* **Grey Admiral (USA)**[8] 162 5-9-0 **55** .... SteveDrowne 3 — 44
(B R Johnson) *midfield: rdn and wknd over 3f out* **28/1**

00-1 **8** *nk* **King Of Music (USA)**[8] 157 5-9-4 **59** ....(v) TonyCulhane 12 — 48
(G Prodromou) *hld up: rdn over 2f out: no imp* **11/2**[3]

600- **9** *7* **Methodical**[8] 2377 4-8-8 **53** .... HayleyTurner 8 — 30
(B G Powell) *in tch: rdn over 3f out: wknd over 2f out* **10/1**

06-0 **10** *2* **Barking Mad (USA)**[27] 5 8-9-1 **56** .... RobbieFitzpatrick 10 — 30
(C R Dore) *led: clr after 2f: rdn and hdd 3f out: wknd 2f out* **20/1**

611- **11** *5* **Royal Axminster**[70] 6381 11-8-4 **52** .... AmyBaker(7) 5 — 18
(Mrs P N Dutfield) *chsd ldrs tl wknd over 3f out* **12/1**

500- **12** *20* **Viking Star (IRE)**[38] 6649 5-7-13 **45** oh5.............. DuranFentiman(5) 6 — —
(A D Brown) *midfield: rdn over 4f out: wknd over 3f out: t.o* **50/1**

2m 40.33s (-2.09) **Going Correction** -0.15s/f (Stan)
WFA 4 from 5yo+ 4lb — 12 Ran SP% **130.9**
Speed ratings (Par 101):100,99,99,95,94 93,92,92,87,86 82,69
CSF £48.68 CT £140.46 TOTE £4.80: £1.50, £3.40, £2.00; EX 78.50.
Owner Nigel Shields **Bred** Sean Collins **Trained** Newmarket, Suffolk
■ Stewards' Enquiry : Graham Gibbons one-day ban: careless riding (Feb 8)

FOCUS
A moderate handicap dominated by horses who have recently been competing in banded company.

231 LITTEWOODS BET DIRECT H'CAP (DIV II) — 1m 4f 50y(P)
5:10 (5:11) (Class 6) (0-60,60) 4-Y-0+ — £2,047 (£604; £302) Stalls Low

Form — RPR

0-21 **1** **Sand Repeal (IRE)**[16] 97 4-9-2 **60** .... SimonWhitworth 2 — 69
(Miss J Feilden) *in tch: hdwy over 2f out: led 1f out: r.o* **4/1**[1]

00-6 **2** *½* **Desert Hawk**[19] 72 5-8-6 **46** ....(b) RobbieFitzpatrick 1 — 54
(W M Brisbourne) *s.s: midfield: hdwy over 3f out: led over 1f out: sn hdd: r.o* **9/2**[2]

60-0 **3** *2 ½* **Buscador (USA)**[8] 163 7-8-11 **58** .... LiamJones(7) 8 — 62
(W M Brisbourne) *led: rdn over 3f out: hdd over 1f out: no ex ins fnl f* **20/1**

-324 **4** *1* **Countback (FR)**[11] 129 7-8-5 **52** .... JackDean(7) 11 — 55+
(A W Carroll) *s.s: hld up: hdwy over 1f out: styd on ins fnl f* **12/1**

6-30 **5** *nk* **Mossmann Gorge**[11] 131 4-8-13 **57** ....(v) HayleyTurner 12 — 59
(M Wellings) *hld up: hdwy 3f out: rdn over 1f out: kpt on* **25/1**

-662 **6** *2 ½* **High Frequency (IRE)**[11] 131 5-8-11 **51** .... PaulFessey 7 — 49
(T D Barron) *hld up: rdn 4f out: hdwy on outside 2f out: swtchd lft over 1f out: one pce ins fnl f: eased towards fin* **11/2**[3]

522- **7** *2 ½* **Grande Roche (IRE)**[40] 6623 4-9-0 **58** .... DeanMcKeown 9 — 52
(G A Swinbank) *midfield: rdn over 2f out: sn outpcd* **9/2**[2]

04-3 **8** *¾* **Olivino (GER)**[22] 52 5-9-1 **55** .... SteveDrowne 6 — 48
(S Dow) *prom: rdn over 3f out: wknd wl over 1f out* **4/1**[1]

0-04 **9** *shd* **J R Stevenson (USA)**[8] 158 10-8-2 **49** ....(p) StephanieBancroft(7) 4 — 42
(Ernst Oertel) *chsd ldrs tl wknd over 2f out* **20/1**

000- **10** *3* **Eskimo's Nest**[30] 6681 4-8-2 **49** ow4.............. PatrickMathers(3) 5 — 37
(D Shaw) *midfield: rdn 4f out: wknd 3f out* **40/1**

00-6 **11** *8* **Opera Belle**[14] 115 4-8-9 **53** .... TPQueally 10 — 28
(A P Jarvis) *prom tl rdn and wknd over 2f out* **20/1**

00-5 **12** *dist* **Flying Spud**[27] 3 5-8-4 **44** oh4.............. AdrianMcCarthy 3 — —
(A J Chamberlain) *a bhd: rdn 4f out: t.o* **40/1**

2m 39.36s (-3.06) **Going Correction** -0.15s/f (Stan)
WFA 4 from 5yo+ 4lb — 12 Ran SP% **122.5**
Speed ratings (Par 101):104,103,102,101,101 99,97,97,97,95 89,—
CSF £20.55 CT £327.73 TOTE £6.60: £2.20, £1.70, £7.00; EX 41.00.
Owner The Sultans of Speed **Bred** Don Commins **Trained** Exning, Suffolk

FOCUS
A moderate handicap, but run almost a second faster than the first division and slightly stronger form.

232 BET NOW AT BETDIRECT.CO.UK H'CAP (DIV II) — 7f 32y(P)
5:40 (5:40) (Class 6) (0-58,58) 4-Y-0+ — £2,047 (£604; £302) Stalls High

Form — RPR

01-0 **1** **Lucius Verrus (USA)**[19] 67 6-8-11 **56** ....(v) PatrickMathers(3) 6 — 65
(D Shaw) *midfield: hdwy over 3f out: led over 1f out: r.o wl* **5/1**[2]

6-06 **2** *1 ½* **Taranaki**[10] 137 8-9-2 **58** .... SimonWhitworth 10 — 63
(P D Cundell) *hld up: hdwy 2f out: rdn over 1f out: edgd lft ins fnl f: r.o to take 2nd towards fin* **9/1**

310- **3** *1* **Triple Zero (IRE)**[140] 5119 4-9-2 **58** .... DeanMcKeown 1 — 61
(A P Jarvis) *a.p: rdn and ev ch over 1f out: no ex towards fin* **14/1**

3-05 **4** *1* **Miskina**[19] 71 5-9-2 **58** .... GeorgeBaker 5 — 58
(W M Brisbourne) *in tch: rdn over 1f out: styd on same pce ins fnl f* **4/1**[1]

0-05 **5** *1 ¾* **Savoy Chapel**[12] 121 4-8-11 **53** ....(vt) RobbieFitzpatrick 11 — 48
(A W Carroll) *s.i.s: hld up: hdwy whn nt clr run and hmpd under 2f out: styd on ins fnl f: eased whn hld towards fin* **8/1**

00-4 **6** *nk* **Karashino (IRE)**[5] 178 4-8-8 **50** ....(b) TonyHamilton 4 — 45
(R A Fahey) *cl up: rdn over 1f out: wknd fnl f* **7/1**

000- **7** *5* **Westlake Bond (IRE)**[73] 6367 4-8-12 **54** .... DerekMcGaffin 8 — 36
(B Smart) *hld up: rdn over 3f out: no imp* **25/1**

341- **8** *2* **Ragasah**[40] 6611 8-7-11 **46** ....(p) StephanieBancroft(7) 9 — 22
(Ernst Oertel) *hld up: hdwy to chse ldrs after 2f: wknd over 3f out* **10/1**

305- **9** *½* **Welsh Whisper**[96] 6079 7-8-4 **46** oh6.............. FrancisFerris 2 — 21
(S A Brookshaw) *led: rdn 4f out: rdr dropped whip and hdd over 1f out: wknd fnl f* **33/1**

04-5 **10** *2* **Pheckless**[24] 38 7-8-5 **47** .... HayleyTurner 7 — 17
(J M Bradley) *s.s: racd keenly: a bhd* **13/2**[3]

60-5 **11** *shd* **Transaction (IRE)**[25] 22 4-8-11 **53** .... SteveDrowne 3 — 23
(J M P Eustace) *prom: rdn over 3f out: sn wknd* **4/1**[1]

1m 29.63s (-0.77) **Going Correction** -0.15s/f (Stan) — 11 Ran SP% **126.2**
Speed ratings (Par 101):98,96,95,94,92 91,85,83,83,80 80
CSF £53.58 CT £626.18 TOTE £5.50: £1.80, £4.10, £3.60; EX 89.60 Place 6 £49.36, Place 5 £27.96..
Owner Danethorpe Racing Ltd **Bred** Pacelco S A **Trained** Danethorpe, Notts

FOCUS
A moderate handicap run slightly slower than the first division. Ordinary form, but reasonably sound.
T/Plt: £157.80 to a £1 stake. Pool: £47,692.85. 220.55 winning tickets. T/Qpdt: £14.10 to a £1 stake. Pool: £3,209.00. 167.80 winning tickets. DO

217 LINGFIELD (L-H)
Sunday, January 29

OFFICIAL GOING: Standard
Wind: Moderate, half-against Weather: Sunny and cold

233 PLAY ROULETTE AT LITTLEWOODSCASINO.COM MEDIAN AUCTION MAIDEN STKS — 6f (P)
1:30 (1:32) (Class 6) 3-Y-0 — £2,730 (£806; £403) Stalls Low

Form — RPR

644- **1** **Kingsgate Prince (IRE)**[192] 3673 3-9-0 75.............. SteveDrowne 4 — 80
(J R Best) *trckd ldrs: effrt on inner over 1f out: led jst ins fnl f : r.o wl* **9/2**[2]

330- **2** *2* **Diane's Choice**[88] 6226 3-8-9 71.............. DaneO'Neill 7 — 69
(J Akehurst) *w ldr: led after 2f: drvn and hdd jst ins fnl f: one pce* **10/1**

3 *1 ¾* **Arzaag** 3-9-0 .... LPKeniry 11 — 69
(D M Simcock) *unf: towards rr: outpcd fr 1/2-way: rdn and sme prog over 1f out: r.o to take 3rd last 100yds: fin wl* **66/1**

0-3 **4** *2* **Came Back (IRE)**[8] 165 3-9-0 .... EddieAhern 9 — 63
(J A Osborne) *unf: pressed ldrs: rdn and cl up over 1f out: wknd fnl f* **7/1**[3]

3 **5** *2* **His Master's Voice (IRE)**[22] 60 3-9-0 .... JoeFanning 5 — 57
(D W P Arbuthnot) *lw: led for 2f: w ldr to wl over 1f out: wknd rapidly* **10/11**[1]

	6	2	**Top Shot** 3-9-0 ... JamieMackay 10 — 51+ (M H Tompkins) *w'like: bit bkwd: dwlt: rn green in last trio: wl off the pce 1/2-way: swtchd lft over 1f out: r.o fnl f: nrst fin* **66/1**
0	7	1 1/4	**Billy Wizz (IRE)**[11] [138] 3-9-0 ... MartinDwyer 2 — 47 (A M Balding) *chsd ldrs: outpcd over 2f out: wknd over 1f out* **20/1**
00-	8	1	**Native Tiptoes**[108] [5847] 3-8-6 ... AdamKirby(3) 3 — 39 (Miss Gay Kelleway) *cl up whn hmpd on inner over 4f out: outpcd over 2f out: wknd* **25/1**
354-	9	2 1/2	**Sharp Thrust (IRE)**[183] [3944] 3-9-0 70 ... NCallan 6 — 37 (A P Jarvis) *dwlt: t.k.h and sn midfield: wkng whn hung rt bnd 2f out* **8/1**
0	10	3/4	**Batchworth Fleur**[15] [112] 3-8-9 ... StephenCarson 12 — 30 (E A Wheeler) *racd on outer: in tch to 1/2-way: sn wknd* **100/1**
0-0	11	1	**Pedlar Of Luck**[8] [165] 3-9-0 ... SimonWhitworth 8 — 32 (A G Newcombe) *leggy: dwlt: scrubbed along in last pair 4f out: nvr a factor* **100/1**
	12	7	**Superior Point** 3-8-9 ... J-PGuillambert 1 — 6 (P Howling) *neat: dwlt: a last: detached over 3f out: t.o* **66/1**

1m 11.95s (-0.86) **Going Correction** -0.175s/f (Stan) 12 Ran SP% **118.3**
Speed ratings (Par 95):98,95,93,90,87 85,83,82,78,77 76,67
CSF £46.23 TOTE £6.40: £1.80, £2.40, £9.80; EX 41.60.
Owner John Mayne **Bred** P G Lyons **Trained** Hucking, Kent

FOCUS
An ordinary maiden and a worthy winner despite the disappointing show of the favourite. The form appears fairly sound with the runner-up and fourth close to form.
Sharp Thrust(IRE) Official explanation: jockey said gelding hung right

234 BETDIRECT FREEPHONE 0800 211 222 H'CAP 1m (P)
2:00 (2:02) (Class 5) (0-75,71) 3-Y-O **£3,238** (£963; £481; £240) **Stalls** High

Form				RPR
424-	1		**Song Of Silence (USA)**[40] [6634] 3-8-11 64 ... SteveDrowne 2 (E A L Dunlop) *lw: w ldr: led 1/2-way: drew rt away fr 2f out: rdn out* **13/2**[3]	78+
3-45	2	5	**Scroll**[15] [118] 3-9-2 69 ...(v) J-PGuillambert 10 (P Howling) *hld up: last 3f out: effrt on inner whn nt clr run wl over 1f out: gd prog after: r.o to take 2nd last 75yds* **15/2**	71+
1-53	3	3/4	**Veronica's Girl**[4] [190] 3-9-4 71 ... DaneO'Neill 8 (P R Hedger) *hld up towards rr: rdn and prog 2f out: chsd clr wnr jst over 1f out: no imp: lost 2nd last 75yds* **7/1**	70
00-5	4	shd	**Murrumbidgee (IRE)**[18] [85] 3-8-0 60 ... JamesDoyle(7) 5 (J W Hills) *settled in rr: rdn and prog wl over 1f out: styd on fnl f* **5/1**[2]	59
10-0	5	3	**Deserted Prince (IRE)**[22] [61] 3-8-6 59 ... HayleyTurner 1 (M J Wallace) *lw: trckd ldrs on inner: chsd wnr 2f out to jst over 1f out: wknd* **9/1**	51
-236	6	nk	**Ms Rainbow Runner**[11] [142] 3-8-7 60 ... JohnEgan 12 (P Butler) *s.i.s: t.k.h and racd wd: effrt and v wd bnd 2f out: sme prog over 1f out: no hdwy fnl f* **14/1**	51+
063-	7	1	**Chia (IRE)**[33] [6673] 3-9-0 67 ... RobertHavlin 3 (D Haydn Jones) *t.k.h: trckd ldrs: gng wl enough but lost pl over 2f out: wl in rr whn nt clr run over 1f out: nvr nr ldrs after* **8/1**	56+
300-	8	2 1/2	**Rock Of Cloonavery (IRE)**[101] [5995] 3-9-3 70 ... IanMongan 6 (S C Williams) *dwlt: in tch in rr: prog on inner over 2f out: chal for 2nd over 1f out: wknd sn after* **16/1**	53
0-62	9	shd	**Simpsons Ross (IRE)**[11] [142] 3-8-10 63 ... EddieAhern 11 (R M Flower) *hld up: in last pair 2f out: nt clr run briefly over 1f out: nvr a factor* **12/1**	46
530-	10	2 1/2	**Night Rainbow (IRE)**[39] [6641] 3-8-11 64 ... MartinDwyer 4 (A J Lidderdale) *led to 1/2-way: chsd wnr to 2f out: wknd* **40/1**	41
03-0	11	hd	**African Concerto (IRE)**[20] [68] 3-9-0 67 ... StephenCarson 7 (S Kirk) *t.k.h: trckd ldrs tl wknd 2f out* **16/1**	44
32-3	12	shd	**Korikancha (IRE)**[12] [132] 3-9-2 69 ... NCallan 9 (J Noseda) *t.k.h: racd wd: trckd ldrs: rdn over 3f out: nt keen and sn btn* **4/1**[1]	45

1m 38.11s (-1.32) **Going Correction** -0.175s/f (Stan) 12 Ran SP% **123.9**
Speed ratings (Par 97):99,94,93,93,90 89,88,86,86,83 83,83
CSF £57.35 CT £367.08 TOTE £6.30: £2.40, £2.70, £2.60; EX 81.10.
Owner Gainsborough Stud **Bred** Gainsborough Farm Llc **Trained** Newmarket, Suffolk

FOCUS
This looked a fairly competitive handicap on paper but the winner bolted up and with the placed horses to previous marks the form looks solid.
Chia(IRE) Official explanation: jockey said filly was denied a clear run
Night Rainbow(IRE) Official explanation: jockey said filly lost its action on final bend and was eased
Korikancha(IRE) Official explanation: jockey said filly hung right throughout

235 PLAY NOW AT BETDIRECTPOKER.COM CLAIMING STKS 1m (P)
2:30 (2:30) (Class 6) 4-Y-O+ **£2,388** (£705; £352) **Stalls** High

Form				RPR
2-12	1		**Mystic Man (FR)**[16] [107] 8-9-7 77 ...(b) NCallan 4 (K A Ryan) *hld up in midfield: effrt wl over 1f out: narrow ld last 150yds: drvn and jst hld on* **6/4**[1]	73
-060	2	shd	**Libre**[4] [192] 6-9-5 72 ... EddieAhern 5 (Ernst Oertel) *lw: cl up: trckd ldr 2f out: led over 1f out: narrowly hdd last 150yds: kpt on wl: jst failed* **5/2**[2]	71
002-	3	2	**Rowan Pursuit**[146] [4991] 5-8-2 50 ow2 ...(b) MartinDwyer 6 (J Akehurst) *hld up in rr: prog wl over 1f out: chsd ldng pair jst ins fnl f: sn rdn and no imp* **6/1**[3]	49
0-00	4	1 1/2	**Indigo Sky (IRE)**[18] [86] 5-8-7 50 ... HayleyTurner 1 (B G Powell) *settled towards rr: prog on inner 2f out: chsd ldrs ent fnl f: one pce* **25/1**	51
005-	5	1 1/2	**Sahara Prince (IRE)**[34] [6664] 6-8-13 68 ...(p) SteveDrowne 9 (K A Morgan) *racd on outer: in tch: rdn over 2f out: sn outpcd: one pce after* **16/1**	54
006/	6	3	**Jewel Of India**[538] [4613] 7-9-7 79 ... JoeFanning 8 (Mrs A L M King) *s.i.s: t.k.h: hld up in rr: effrt and swtchd to inner over 1f out: no prog* **16/1**	55
3-04	7	1	**Red Finesse**[12] [133] 4-8-8 55 ... MatthewHenry 12 (M A Jarvis) *t.k.h: trckd ldr after 1f to 2f out: wknd over 1f out* **10/1**	39
00-0	8	1 3/4	**Belle Encore**[13] [121] 4-8-8 45 ... TPQueally 11 (A P Jarvis) *t.k.h: led for 1f: styd prom: wknd bdly jst over 1f out* **33/1**	35
00-0	9	2 1/2	**Missed Turn**[25] [35] 4-8-1 45 ... JamesDoyle(7) 2 (J M P Eustace) *led after 1f to over 1f out: wknd rapidly on inner fnl f: eased* **33/1**	30
030/	10	14	**Canni Thinkaar (IRE)**[62] [5493] 5-8-11 55 ... LPKeniry 3 (P Butler) *last and struggling over 5f out: t.o* **66/1**	—

1m 38.12s (-1.31) **Going Correction** -0.175s/f (Stan) 10 Ran SP% **114.9**
Speed ratings (Par 101):99,98,96,95,93 90,89,88,85,71
CSF £4.89 TOTE £2.30: £1.80, £1.10, £1.70; EX 5.50.The winner was claimed by I. W. McInnes for £12,000. Libre was claimed by F. Jordan for £11,000.

Owner R J H Limited **Bred** Gainsborough Stud Management Ltd **Trained** Hambleton, N Yorks

FOCUS
An uncompetitive claimer which the market called correctly. However, the fourth is the best guide to the level of the form.

236 PLAY NOW AT BETDIRECTCASINO.COM H'CAP 1m (P)
3:00 (3:04) (Class 5) (0-70,70) 4-Y-O+ **£3,886** (£1,156; £577; £288) **Stalls** High

Form				RPR
040-	1		**Arctic Desert**[61] [6465] 6-9-4 70 ... RichardHughes 1 (A M Balding) *dwlt: hld up in midfield: effrt gng wl 2f out: cajoled along and r.o to ld last 100yds* **10/1**[3]	79
5-41	2	1 1/4	**Glad Big (GER)**[18] [84] 4-9-2 68 ... EddieAhern 8 (J A Osborne) *lw: t.k.h: prom: trckd ldr 1/2-way: led wl over 1f out: hanging lft after: hdd and nt qckn last 100yds* **11/4**[1]	74
6/5	3	nk	**Luna Tacumana (IRE)**[8] [171] 6-8-11 63 ... TPQueally 9 (J J Lambe, Ire) *dwlt: wl in rr: rdn 1/2-way: no prog tl r.o fr over 1f out: fin wl* **14/1**	68
14-5	4	nk	**Monte Mayor Boy**[27] [15] 4-8-13 65 ...(p) RobertHavlin 10 (D Haydn Jones) *chsd ldrs: rdn 1/2-way: effrt u.p 2f out: chal 1f out: one pce* **25/1**	69
10-0	5	nk	**Star Magnitude (USA)**[25] [36] 5-9-4 70 ... DaneO'Neill 12 (S Dow) *sn lost pl and wl in rr: effrt 2f out: styd on wl fnl f: nrst fin* **25/1**	74
4-45	6	1	**Night Storm**[4] [187] 5-8-12 64 ... JohnEgan 5 (S Dow) *trckd ldrs: rdn and effrt 2f out: cl up jst over 1f out: fdd last 150yds* **10/1**[3]	65
03-2	7	2	**Monashee Prince (IRE)**[15] [115] 4-8-11 63 ... NCallan 3 (J R Best) *chsd ldr to 1/2-way: losing pl whn nt clr run over 1f out: no ch after* **3/1**[2]	60
43-0	8	nk	**Corky (IRE)**[17] [101] 5-9-0 66 ...(v[1]) HayleyTurner 6 (I W McInnes) *s.v.s: in tch after 2f: rdn in last pair 1/2-way: struggling over 2f out: styd on ins fnl f* **16/1**	62
0/01	9	1/2	**Devil's Island**[9] [163] 4-8-10 62 ... JamieMackay 4 (Sir Mark Prescott) *led to wl over 1f out: wknd rapidly ins fnl f* **3/1**[2]	57
64-0	10	1/2	**Carry On Doc**[8] [167] 5-9-1 70 ... AdamKirby(3) 11 (Ernst Oertel) *racd on outer: t.k.h: in tch: rdn 3f out: wknd over 2f out* **33/1**	64
00-0	11	1/2	**Hey Presto**[26] [17] 6-9-0 66 ... JoeFanning 7 (R Rowe) *dwlt: a wl in rr: rdn and struggling in last pair 3f out: no ch* **50/1**	59

1m 37.71s (-1.72) **Going Correction** -0.175s/f (Stan) 11 Ran SP% **120.0**
Speed ratings (Par 103):101,99,99,99,98 97,95,95,95,94 94
CSF £37.30 CT £407.76 TOTE £14.80: £3.40, £1.60, £2.80; EX 57.40.
Owner Holistic Racing Ltd **Bred** Whatton Manor Stud **Trained** Kingsclere, Hants

FOCUS
Competitive stuff and sound form for the grade with the first two showing margin improvement.
Corky(IRE) Official explanation: jockey said gelding missed the break and didn't face first time visor

237 TEXT "BETDIRECT" TO 88600 H'CAP 2m (P)
3:30 (3:30) (Class 4) (0-85,83) 4-Y-O+ **£6,477** (£1,927; £963; £481) **Stalls** Low

Form				RPR
221-	1		**Reggae Rhythm (IRE)**[57] [6490] 12-8-12 67 ... RichardThomas(3) 10 (A J Lidderdale) *settled in rr: prog fr wl off the pce over 3f out: rdn to ld over 1f out: styd on wl* **8/1**	73
0B0-	2	2	**Beauchamp Trump**[22] [6582] 4-8-4 66 ow1 ...(bt) AdamKirby(3) 7 (G A Butler) *hld up in last pair: u.p in last over 4f out: no prog tl r.o fr over 1f out: tk 2nd last 100yds* **12/1**	70
0-20	3	1 1/4	**Eastborough (IRE)**[18] [88] 7-9-9 75 ... FergusSweeney 6 (B G Powell) *dwlt: hld up in last pair: pushed along 4f out: styd on fr over 1f out to take 3rd nr fin* **12/1**	78
13-0	4	1/2	**Monte Cristo (FR)**[8] [168] 8-9-1 67 ...(v) DaneO'Neill 4 (Mrs L C Taylor) *lw: trckd ldng pair: led over 6f out: sn jnd: duelled w rival and clr of rest over 3f out: tried and hdd over 1f out* **5/1**[3]	69+
-411	5	1/2	**Moon Emperor**[8] [168] 9-9-9 75 ...(b) EddieAhern 5 (J R Jenkins) *hld up bhd clr ldrs: chsd ldng pair 3f out: tried to cl over 1f out: sn rdn and fnd nil: plugged on* **3/1**[2]	76
02-2	6	nk	**Gibraltar Bay (IRE)**[18] [88] 4-9-10 83 ... IanMongan 8 (T G Mills) *lw: trckd ldng trio: jnd ldr 6f out: duelled w that rival after: u.p over 3f out: cracked and btn over 1f out* **5/2**[1]	84+
505-	7	shd	**High Point (IRE)**[93] [6133] 8-9-3 72 ... AmirQuinn(3) 9 (G P Enright) *led to over 6f out: sn rdn: outpcd and looked wl btn 3f out: plugging on again on inner whn nowhere to go fnl f* **12/1**	73
5-36	7	dht	**Blackmail (USA)**[15] [111] 8-8-11 63 ...(b) NCallan 1 (Miss B Sanders) *hld up in rr: rdn over 3f out: no real prog fr over 2f out* **8/1**	64
00-0	9	2	**Salute (IRE)**[18] [88] 7-9-9 75 ... RobertHavlin 2 (P G Murphy) *w ldr to 7f out: u.p in 4th 5f out: wknd over 2f out* **33/1**	73

3m 23.48s (-5.31) **Going Correction** -0.175s/f (Stan)
WFA 4 from 6yo+ 7lb 9 Ran SP% **118.5**
Speed ratings (Par 105):106,105,104,104,103 103,103,103,102
CSF £100.82 CT £1153.45 TOTE £9.40: £2.70, £4.30, £4.80; EX 135.50.
Owner Mrs A Lidderdale **Bred** Liffeyside Stud **Trained** Eastbury, Berks

FOCUS
A fair staying contest run at a proper gallop and in a good time, the race was run to suit the hold-up horses.
Blackmail(USA) Official explanation: jockey said gelding hung right
High Point(IRE) Official explanation: jockey said gelding was denied a clear run

238 LITTLEWOODS WIN £2M @ LITTLEWOODSPOOLS.CO.UK H'CAP 7f (P)
4:00 (4:05) (Class 2) (0-100,100) 4-Y-O+ **£12,954** (£2,890; £2,890; £962) **Stalls** Low

Form				RPR
411-	1		**Bonus (IRE)**[58] [6481] 6-9-0 96 ... EddieAhern 12 (G A Butler) *t.k.h early: hld up on outer: effrt over 1f out: hanging lft but drvn and r.o wl to ld last stride* **5/1**[3]	104
024-	2	shd	**San Antonio**[64] [6431] 6-8-3 88 ...(b) EdwardCreighton(3) 1 (Mrs P Sly) *lw: sn led: clr 1/2-way: rdn 2f out: tired fnl f: collared last stride* **13/2**	96
116-	2	dht	**Red Spell (IRE)**[51] [6530] 5-9-4 100 ... RichardHughes 7 (R Hannon) *lw: hld up in midfield: nt clr run over 1f out and swtchd to inner: r.o fnl f: jst failed* **11/4**[1]	108+
6-35	4	1/2	**Katiypour (IRE)**[15] [117] 9-8-1 86 oh1 ... RichardThomas(3) 4 (Miss B Sanders) *hld up in midfield: effrt on inner 2f out: disp 2nd fnl f: jst outpcd nr fin* **9/1**	93
030-	5	shd	**Lygeton Lad**[29] [6700] 8-8-7 92 ...(t) AdamKirby(3) 3 (Miss Gay Kelleway) *b: b.hind: prom: rdn 2f out: kpt on wl fr over 1f out: jst outpcd* **12/1**	98

5-31 **6** 2 **Moayed**[15] [117] 7-8-9 **98**....(bt) JamesDoyle(7) 8 99
(N P Littmoden) *hld up in rr: effrt 2f out: rdn and styd on fr over 1f out: nt rch ldrs* **4/1**[2]
-605 **7** 3 **Cornus**[1] [220] 4-8-4 **86** oh4.... MartinDwyer 2 79
(M J Polglase) *b: prom: chsd ldr 2f out to 1f out: wknd rapidly* **20/1**
0/ **8** ¾ **Purus (IRE)**[97] 4-8-6 **88**....(t) JohnEgan 11 79
(P Mitchell) *w'like: lw: hld up wl in rr: shkn up 2f out: no real prog* **14/1**
610- **9** nk **Intoxicating**[128] [5438] 4-9-4 **100**.... StephenCarson 10 91
(R F Johnson Houghton) *racd on outer: in tch: hrd rdn and struggling 1/2-way: sn no ch* **20/1**
50-0 **10** 3½ **Lake Andre (IRE)**[23] [54] 5-8-9 **91**.... NCallan 6 73
(K A Ryan) *chsd ldr to 2f out: hanging and wknd rapidly over 1f out* **20/1**
0-04 **11** ¾ **Chateau Nicol**[15] [117] 7-8-4 **86**....(v) JoeFanning 5 66
(B G Powell) *prom: losing pl whn squeezed out over 1f out: wknd* **16/1**
10-0 **12** 3½ **Middleton Grey**[23] [54] 8-8-5 **87**....(b) RobbieFitzpatrick 9 58
(A G Newcombe) *mostly last and sn struggling: wl bhd 3f out* **50/1**

1m 23.04s (-2.85) **Going Correction** -0.175s/f (Stan) **12** Ran SP% **123.2**
Speed ratings (Par 109):109,108,108,108,108 105,102,101,101,97 96,92
WIN: Bonus £5.30. PL: Bonus £1.80, Red Spell 1.60, San Antonio £2.90. EX: B/RS £10.80, B/SA £24.10. CSF: B/RS £9.45, B/SA £18.55. TRIC: B/RS/SA £48.02, B/SA/RS £56.04..
Owner The Bonus Partnership **Bred** A Stroud And J Hanly **Trained** Blewbury, Oxon

FOCUS
A good handicap and extremely competitive with a blanket finish. The form looks solid.

NOTEBOOK
Bonus(IRE), who made a successful debut for this yard when winning a six-furlong handicap at Wolverhampton 58 days previously, defied a 7lb higher mark to follow up over what was the furthest trip he has tackled to date. Given he has spent his whole career competing over sprint distances, it was a surprise to see him take so long to pick up at this trip but, whatever the case, it clearly suited well. Connections should have more options open to them now and he is clearly worth keeping on the right side of. (op 9-2)
Red Spell(IRE) ◆, the course-record holder over seven furlongs and a mile round here, can be considered most unlucky not have gained his fifth Polytrack success. On this evidence, he remains worthy of the utmost respect on this surface. (op 3-1 tchd 7-2 in a place and 100-30 in a place)
San Antonio, given his usual positive ride, was just denied. He is holding his form well, and deserves to find a similar race, but will go up in the weights again for this. (op 3-1 tchd 7-2 in a place and 100-30 in a place)
Katiypour(IRE), beaten just over half a length, was probably not far off his best in fourth. He usually wins his share and is one to keep on the right side of in the coming weeks. (op 10-1)
Lygeton Lad is at his best round here and was not beaten far at all in fifth. It is over a year since his last success, but he is now 9lb lower and it would be no surprise to see him pop up before the All-Weather season is over. (op 9-1)
Moayed, who did not have to be at his best to win a six-furlong conditions event round here on his previous start, found this a whole lot tougher and never really looked like getting seriously involved. (op 7-2 tchd 9-2)
Purus(IRE), a medium-sized gelding who has been successful over seven furlongs and a mile on the continent, was having his first start for the yard. (op 25-1)
Intoxicating looked straight enough for his first outing in 128 days. (op 33-1)
Lake Andre(IRE) Official explanation: jockey said gelding hung left

239 BETDIRECT.CO.UK H'CAP 5f (P)
4:30 (4:31) (Class 6) (0-60,60) 3-Y-O £2,388 (£705; £352) Stalls High

Form RPR
40-5 **1** **Correct Time (IRE)**[20] [68] 3-9-0 **56**.... NCallan 5 64
(N P Littmoden) *lw: hld up in last pair: prog to trck ldrs 1/2-way: effrt over 1f out : rdn to ld last 150yds: styd on* **7/2**[2]
00-0 **2** 1 **Mine The Balance (IRE)**[25] [31] 3-8-8 **50**.... SteveDrowne 4 54
(J R Best) *wl in rr: pushed along 3f out: prog over 1f out: chsd wnr last 100yds: no imp nr fin* **4/1**[3]
00-2 **3** 2 **Stoneacre Fred (IRE)**[17] [102] 3-8-13 **55**....(b[1]) RobbieFitzpatrick 6 52
(Peter Grayson) *prom: chsd ldr over 2f out tl ent fnl f: one pce* **9/2**
54-4 **4** 1½ **Succeed (IRE)**[22] [66] 3-8-10 **59**.... JamesDoyle(7) 1 51
(Mrs H Sweeting) *b: b.hind: mde most: drvn 2l clr jst over 1f out: wknd and hdd last 150yds* **3/1**[1]
-640 **5** 2 **In Hope**[4] [189] 3-8-13 **55**.... JohnEgan 9 39
(Ernst Oertel) *w ldr to 1/2-way: wknd over 1f out* **20/1**
000- **6** 1 **Milky Bar Kid (IRE)**[104] [5945] 3-9-0 **56**....(t) EddieAhern 3 37
(C F Wall) *chsd ldrs: hanging bdly lft and wknd over 1f out* **8/1**
-300 **7** 1¼ **Saxon Star (IRE)**[6] [176] 3-8-4 **46** oh1.... HayleyTurner 2 22
(M D I Usher) *mostly last: u.p 2f out: no ch* **20/1**
265- **8** ¾ **Par Excellence**[209] [3175] 3-8-7 **54**.... MarcHalford(5) 7 28
(W G M Turner) *chsd ldrs: struggling whn wd bnd 2f out: wknd* **25/1**
30-0 **9** 1 **Lady Zanzara (USA)**[22] [66] 3-9-4 **60**.... WandersonD'Avila 8 30
(J W Hills) *rrd s: racd on wd outside: struggling fr 1/2-way: hanging bdly and wknd over 1f out* **16/1**

60.60 secs (6.22) **Going Correction** -0.175s/f (Stan) **9** Ran SP% **115.8**
Speed ratings (Par 95):86,84,81,78,75 74,72,70,69
CSF £17.40 CT £63.51 TOTE £5.50: £1.50, £2.40, £2.10; EX 21.70 Place 6 £356.75, Place 5 £83.93.
Owner Ivan Allan **Bred** A F O'Callaghan **Trained** Newmarket, Suffolk

FOCUS
A pretty moderate sprint handicap and the time was ordinary, but the form look reasonable rated through the third.
Milky Bar Kid(IRE) Official explanation: jockey said colt hung left
T/Plt: £388.30 to a £1 stake. Pool: £55,379.95. 104.10 winning tickets. T/Qpdt: £27.20 to a £1 stake. Pool: £5,497.10. 149.50 winning tickets. JN

193 SOUTHWELL (L-H)
Sunday, January 29

OFFICIAL GOING: Standard
The surface was described as 'the usual slow and hard work'.
Wind: Light, half-against Weather: overcast and cold

240 TEXT "BETDIRECT" TO 88600 H'CAP (DIV I) 1m (F)
12:50 (12:51) (Class 6) (0-55,55) 4-Y-O+ £2,914 (£867; £433; £216) Stalls Low

Form RPR
1062 **1** **Lady Suesanne (IRE)**[5] [183] 4-8-7 **48**....(b) PaulHanagan 11 60
(M J Attwater) *mde all: edgd rt over 1f out: styd on strly: unchal* **11/4**[1]
61-4 **2** 5 **Prince Of Gold**[12] [134] 6-8-11 **52**....(b) GrahamGibbons 4 54
(R Hollinshead) *sn chsng ldrs: hmpd bnd over 4f out: styd on to go 2nd 1f: out: no imp* **9/2**[3]
232- **3** 1¼ **White Bear (FR)**[45] [6584] 4-9-0 **55**.... RobertWinston 8 55
(C R Dore) *trckd ldrs: t.k.h: drvn over 4f out: wnt 2nd 3f out: kpt on same pce* **4/1**[2]
00-3 **4** 2½ **Mademoiselle**[12] [127] 4-8-13 **54**.... MichaelHills 10 49
(B W Hills) *chsd ldrs: edgd lft bnd over 4f out: sn outpcd: one pce fnl 2f* **9/2**[3]
506- **5** 1 **Supreme Salutation**[88] [6231] 10-8-2 **50**.... LauraReynolds(7) 2 43
(D K Ivory) *s.i.s: hld up in rr: kpt on fnl 2f: nvr nr ldrs* **11/1**
05-0 **6** 1 **Ballyrush (IRE)**[25] [43] 6-7-12 **46** oh1....(e) StephanieBancroft(7) 12 37
(Miss D A McHale) *chsd wnr: fdd over 1f out* **33/1**
04-0 **7** 5 **Miss Monica (IRE)**[6] [175] 5-8-5 **46** oh1.... ChrisCatlin 5 27
(P W Hiatt) *mid-div: effrt on outer over 2f out: n.d* **14/1**
104- **8** ½ **Spitfire Bob (USA)**[61] [6463] 7-8-6 **52**....(p) GregFairley(5) 9 32
(M E Sowersby) *s.i.s: sn drvn along: nvr on terms* **14/1**
00-0 **9** 5 **Pharoah's Gold (IRE)**[28] [3] 8-8-5 **46** oh6....(v) AlanDaly 3 16
(Mrs N S Evans) *s.i.s: a in rr* **80/1**
00-0 **10** 7 **Gallego**[18] [82] 4-8-10 **51**.... PhillipMakin 7 7
(R J Price) *mid-div on outer: outpcd over 3f out: sn lost pl* **10/1**
220/ **11** 18 **Shoof (USA)**[1213] [5062] 7-8-12 **53**.... BrianReilly 6 —
(M J Gingell) *prom: sn drvn along: lost pl over 4f out: t.o 3f out* **50/1**

1m 43.84s (-0.76) **Going Correction** -0.075s/f (Stan) **11** Ran SP% **119.9**
Speed ratings (Par 101):100,95,93,91,90 89,84,83,78,71 53
CSF £15.27 CT £51.02 TOTE £4.20: £1.40, £2.10, £1.40; EX 23.30.
Owner Phones Direct Partnership **Bred** Larry Ryan **Trained** Wysall, Notts

FOCUS
A weak event, run at a fair gallop, and the field came home fairly strung out behind the convincing winner, who sets the level for the form.

241 DAILY OFFERS FROM BETDIRECT CLAIMING STKS 1m (F)
1:20 (1:21) (Class 6) 3-Y-O £2,730 (£806; £403) Stalls Low

Form RPR
35-6 **1** **Ohana**[26] [19] 3-9-5 69....(p) JamieSpencer 7 72
(N A Callaghan) *led early: racd wd: led 5f out: pushed out towards fin* **3/1**[2]
2-51 **2** ½ **Inaminute (IRE)**[3] [197] 3-8-7 55 ow1.... PatCosgrave 3 59
(K R Burke) *trckd ldrs: wnt 2nd over 4f out: upsides fnl f: no ex towards fin* **10/3**[3]
-325 **3** 10 **Noble Edge**[3] [197] 3-8-6 61....(p) GregFairley(5) 5 43
(Robert Gray) *chsd ldrs: wknd over 1f out* **10/3**[3]
000- **4** ¾ **Ayala Cove (USA)**[213] [3042] 3-7-13 47....(t) AndrewMullen(5) 8 35
(P C Haslam) *in rr: hdwy to chse ldrs over 3f out: one pce fnl 2f* **40/1**
-502 **5** 2½ **Crocodile Star (USA)**[13] [122] 3-8-3 53....(b) PaulHanagan 9 29
(J A Osborne) *chsd ldrs on wd outside: one pce fnl 2f* **9/4**[1]
40-0 **6** 9 **Take No Notice (IRE)**[18] [93] 3-8-0 45....(v[1]) FranciscoDaSilva 1 8
(K R Burke) *s.i.s: lost pl over 4f out: edgd rt 2f out: sn lost pl* **66/1**
000- **7** 11 **The Great Delaney**[40] [6635] 3-9-1 45....(b[1]) AlanDaly 4 —
(Miss D A McHale) *reminders after s: sn led: hdd 5f out: lost pl over 3f out: sn bhd* **100/1**
030- **8** dist **Twentyfirst Dansar**[50] [6539] 3-8-11 54....(v) TonyCulhane 2 —
(A D Smith) *s.i.s: in rr: virtually p.u 2f out: hopelessly t.o: btn 43l* **20/1**

1m 44.1s (-0.50) **Going Correction** -0.075s/f (Stan) **8** Ran SP% **111.6**
Speed ratings (Par 95):99,98,88,87,85 76,65,—
CSF £12.58 TOTE £3.50: £1.10, £1.30, £1.80; EX 13.70.The winner was claimed by Nick Littmoden for £12,000.
Owner Franconson Partners **Bred** Milton Park Stud Partnership **Trained** Newmarket, Suffolk

FOCUS
A moderate event, run at an average pace, and the first two pulled clear. The winner is value for further.

242 TEXT "BETDIRECT" TO 88600 H'CAP (DIV II) 1m (F)
1:50 (1:50) (Class 6) (0-55,59) 4-Y-O+ £2,914 (£867; £433; £216) Stalls Low

Form RPR
1-26 **1** **Quiet Reading (USA)**[19] [77] 9-8-12 **53**....(v) AlanDaly 7 62
(M R Bosley) *trckd ldrs: led over 1f out: hld on towards fin* **10/1**[3]
00-4 **2** hd **Figurative (IRE)**[10] [147] 4-8-9 **50**.... DeanMcKeown 8 59
(G A Swinbank) *w ldrs: led after 2f tl over 1f out: kpt on wl: no ex towards fin* **13/8**[1]
2-21 **3** 3 **Augustine**[9] [156] 5-9-4 **59**.... DarrenWilliams 6 62
(P W Hiatt) *w ldrs: drvn over 3f out: nt qckn fnl 2f* **15/8**[2]
/5-4 **4** 3 **Schinken Otto (IRE)**[25] [42] 5-8-5 **46** oh1.... PaulHanagan 9 43
(J M Jefferson) *mid-div: hdwy on outer over 2f out: kpt on same pce* **11/1**
2-00 **5** 1½ **Sriology (IRE)**[15] [113] 5-8-11 **52**.... ChrisCatlin 2 46
(G Prodromou) *s.i.s: reminders after s: hdwy over 2f out: nvr rchd ldrs* **12/1**
0003 **6** hd **Crusoe (IRE)**[5] [184] 9-8-7 **48** oh1 ow2....(b) BrianReilly 11 42
(A Sadik) *sn chsng ldrs on outer: one pce fnl 2f* **16/1**
00-4 **7** 1 **House Martin**[18] [84] 4-8-12 **53**.... RobertWinston 4 45
(C R Dore) *s.i.s: hdwy on inner over 3f out: nvr nr ldrs* **16/1**
8 2½ **Bahrain Gold (IRE)**[109] [5839] 6-8-7 **48**....(p) DaleGibson 5 35
(N P McCormack) *chsd ldrs: drvn over 3f out: wknd fnl 2f* **40/1**
050- **9** 3½ **Kalishka (IRE)**[226] [2648] 5-8-9 **50**.... TomEaves 1 30
(R Allan) *s.s: nvr a factor* **66/1**
00-4 **10** 6 **Ming Vase**[28] [8] 4-8-10 **51**....(v[1]) LeeEnstone 3 19
(P T Midgley) *led 2f: chsd ldrs: n.m.r and lost pl 2f out* **40/1**
026- **11** 21 **Dara Mac**[48] [6560] 7-8-11 **52**.... JamieSpencer 10 —
(L P Grassick) *dwlt: lost pl over 4f out: eased over 2f out: virtually p.u* **14/1**

1m 43.79s (-0.81) **Going Correction** -0.075s/f (Stan) **11** Ran SP% **122.8**
Speed ratings (Par 101):101,100,97,94,93 93,92,89,86,80 59
CSF £27.63 CT £47.33 TOTE £18.00: £3.20, £1.20, £1.30; EX 44.60.
Owner Mrs Jean M O'Connor **Bred** European Thoroughbreds Ltd **Trained** Lockeridge, Wilts
■ Stewards' Enquiry : Alan Daly one-day ban: used whip with excessive frequency (Feb 9)

FOCUS
The stronger division rated through the third's previous running here but limited by the proximity of the fourth.

243 BETDIRECT.CO.UK (S) STKS 1m 3f (F)
2:20 (2:21) (Class 6) 4-Y-O+ £2,388 (£705; £352) Stalls Low

Form RPR
60-2 **1** **Hawkit (USA)**[19] [78] 5-8-11 60....(t) DanielTudhope(3) 12 67
(P D Evans) *hld up in mid-div: smooth hdwy over 4f out: led 2f out: pushed out* **5/2**[1]
-462 **2** 2 **Romil Star (GER)**[19] [75] 9-9-6 65....(v) PatCosgrave 11 70
(K R Burke) *w ldrs: led 8f out tl 2f out: kpt on ins last: no real imp* **5/2**[1]
4-44 **3** 6 **Look At The Stars (IRE)**[16] [107] 4-8-11 52....(b) GrahamGibbons 7 54
(R Hollinshead) *chsd ldrs: wnt 2nd over 4f out: wknd ins last* **6/1**[3]
004- **4** 4 **Power Glory**[17] [6495] 4-8-11 45.... PaulHanagan 8 48
(R A Fahey) *chsd ldrs: one pce fnl 2f* **8/1**

360- **5** 3/4 **Giunchiglio**[31] 6683 7-9-0 45 RobertWinston 5 46
(W M Brisbourne) *in rr: hdwy over 5f out: outpcd fnl 3f* **16/1**

5-60 **6** 2 1/2 **Come What July (IRE)**[3] 200 5-8-7 64 (p) KellyHarrison(7) 6 42
(Mrs N Macauley) *bhd: sme hdwy on outer over 4f out: kpt on fnl 2f: nvr on terms* **9/2**[2]

0-00 **7** 1 3/4 **Simply The Guest (IRE)**[5] 182 7-9-0 45 (vt) KimTinkler 1 40
(N Tinkler) *dwlt: hdwy and in tch 8f out: lost pl over 3f out* **40/1**

5-05 **8** 2 **Strathtay**[9] 103 4-7-13 52 (b) JosephWalsh(7) 10 31
(M Appleby) *bhd: hdwy on outer over 7f out: lost pl over 3f out* **25/1**

006- **9** 10 **River Of Diamonds**[42] 6609 5-9-0 40 AdrianMcCarthy 4 20
(R A Harris) *led early: w ldrs: lost pl over 2f out* **50/1**

0-00 **10** 3 1/2 **Haenertsburg (IRE)**[16] 103 4-8-6 45 (t) DaleGibson 3 10
(A L Forbes) *sn led: hdd 8f out: lost pl over 3f out* **100/1**

11 6 **Sandhill Dancer** 4-8-7 ow1 DeanMcKeown 2 1
(S Parr) *in tch: lost pl over 5f out: sn bhd* **80/1**

000- **12** *dist* **Glasson Lodge**[32] 6679 4-8-6 45 (v) ChrisCatlin 13 —
(A L Forbes) *prom 3f: lost pl over 3f out: t.o 3f out: btn 45l* **100/1**

0 **13** *dist* **Pampamee**[23] 59 4-8-6 AlanDaly 14 —
(M Wellings) *w ldrs on outer: lost pl after 3f: sn t.o: virtually p.u: btn 32l* **100/1**

2m 28.32s (-0.58) **Going Correction** -0.075s/f (Stan)
WFA 4 from 5yo+ 3lb 13 Ran SP% **119.1**
Speed ratings (Par 101):99,97,93,90,89 87,86,85,77,75 71,—,—
CSF £8.00 TOTE £3.80: £1.70, £1.40, £2.00; EX 9.10.The winner was sold to Alan Bailey for 8,600gns.
Owner Diamond Racing Ltd **Bred** Hargus Sexton And Sandra Sexton **Trained** Pandy, Abergavenny

FOCUS
A fair race by selling race standards and the first two ran close to their marks.
Glasson Lodge Official explanation: jockey said filly lost its action

244 PLAY NOW AT BETDIRECTPOKER.COM H'CAP 5f (F)
2:50 (2:50) (Class 4) (0-85,85) 4-Y-0+ **£6,477** (£1,927; £963; £481) **Stalls** High

Form RPR

6-33 **1** **Desperate Dan**[3] 198 5-9-4 85 (b) JamieSpencer 5 94+
(J A Osborne) *trckd ldrs gng wl: smooth hdwy to ld on bit jst ins last: smoothly* **2/1**[1]

03-0 **2** 1 3/4 **Efistorm**[19] 79 5-8-4 71 oh1 PaulFessey 1 74
(J Balding) *led tl jst ins last: kpt on: no ch w wnr* **25/1**

5-40 **3** 5 **Gone'N'Dunnett (IRE)**[24] 51 7-7-11 71 oh5 (v) KirstyMilczarek(7) 10 57
(Mrs C A Dunnett) *sn outpcd: hdwy 2f out: styd on fnl f* **40/1**

-544 **4** nk **Pawan (IRE)**[3] 198 6-8-3 77 AnnStokell(7) 8 62
(Miss A Stokell) *s.i.s: edgd lft over 2f out: styd on* **7/1**[3]

4400 **5** 1/2 **Kennington**[1] 224 6-8-4 71 oh2 (b) ChrisCatlin 9 54
(Mrs C A Dunnett) *chsd ldrs: rdn and outpcd over 2f out: n.d after* **12/1**

0-66 **6** nk **Magic Glade**[19] 79 7-8-10 77 TomEaves 3 59
(R Brotherton) *w ldrs: wknd appr fnl f* **7/1**[3]

02-4 **7** 3 1/2 **Willhewiz**[19] 79 6-8-7 74 (b) RobertWinston 4 44
(M S Saunders) *chsd ldrs: lost pl over 1f out* **10/3**[2]

-201 **8** shd **Law Maker**[11] 136 6-8-6 80 (v) MichaelJStainton(7) 2 50
(A Bailey) *s.i.s: nvr on terms* **8/1**

-350 **9** 1 3/4 **Trinculo (IRE)**[3] 198 9-9-4 85 AdrianTNicholls 6 49
(D Nicholls) *s.i.s: carried hd high: a in rr* **12/1**

58.94 secs (-1.36) **Going Correction** -0.125s/f (Stan) 9 Ran SP% **114.2**
Speed ratings (Par 105):105,102,94,93,92 92,86,86,83
CSF £56.38 CT £1532.91 TOTE £2.30: £1.10, £7.20, £8.00; EX 75.50.
Owner Mountgrange Stud **Bred** Sheikh Amin Dahlawi **Trained** Upper Lambourn, Berks

FOCUS
Not a strong handicap for the money on offer. The winner made it look very easy, the first two came clear.
Pawan(IRE) Official explanation: jockey said gelding missed the break

245 LITTLEWOODS BETDIRECT H'CAP 6f (F)
3:20 (3:21) (Class 4) (0-80,80) 4-Y-0+ **£6,477** (£1,927; £963; £481) **Stalls** Low

Form RPR

01-1 **1** **Graze On**[9] 159 4-8-11 73 (b[1]) AdrianMcCarthy 9 87
(R A Harris) *mde all: kpt on wl: unchal* **12/1**

22/1 **2** 1 3/4 **Cummiskey (IRE)**[27] 14 4-9-4 80 JamieSpencer 3 89
(J A Osborne) *sn chsng ldrs: swished tail and wnt 2nd over 1f out: no real imp* **7/2**[1]

032- **3** 1/2 **Councellor (FR)**[29] 6698 4-9-0 76 PaulHanagan 11 83
(Stef Liddiard) *hld up in mid-div: hdwy on inner over 2f out: styd on fnl f* **8/1**[3]

1-10 **4** 1 3/4 **Owed**[27] 15 4-8-6 73 (t) GregFairley(5) 4 75
(Robert Gray) *chsd ldrs: styd on same pce fnl 2f* **13/2**[2]

34-6 **5** 1/2 **Kingsmaite**[19] 80 5-8-10 79 (b) LiamJones(7) 7 80
(S R Bowring) *chsd ldrs: outpcd over 3f out: hdwy 2f out: kpt on* **12/1**

5-00 **6** 2 **Queens Rhapsody**[4] 192 6-8-4 73 (v) MichaelJStainton(7) 12 68
(A Bailey) *s.i.s: styd on fnl 2f: nvr rchd ldrs* **12/1**

20-2 **7** 3/4 **Majik**[19] 80 7-8-8 70 (p) DeanMcKeown 5 62
(D J S Ffrench Davis) *hld up in rr: kpt on fnl 2f: nvr nr ldrs* **9/1**

433- **8** 1/2 **Pamir (IRE)**[121] 5585 4-9-1 77 PhillipMakin 13 68
(P R Chamings) *chsd ldrs: fdd over 1f out* **14/1**

20-5 **9** 1 **Gilded Cove**[19] 79 6-8-11 73 GrahamGibbons 10 61
(R Hollinshead) *lost pl over 4f out: hdwy on wd outside over 2f out: nvr a threat* **25/1**

05-3 **10** 1/2 **Sir Desmond**[19] 80 8-9-1 77 (p) ChrisCatlin 2 63
(Rae Guest) *sn outpcd and bhd: sme hdwy over 2f out: nvr on terms* **12/1**

61-4 **11** 1 **Poker Player (IRE)**[19] 80 4-9-2 78 TonyCulhane 1 61
(G C Bravery) *hld up in rr: nvr a factor* **13/2**[2]

-362 **12** 3 1/2 **Lincolneurocruiser**[8] 171 4-8-7 69 DaleGibson 6 42
(Mrs N Macauley) *s.i.s: in rr: edgd lft over 1f out: nvr a factor* **22/1**

100- **13** 5 **Why Now**[75] 6350 4-9-0 76 RobertWinston 14 34
(K A Ryan) *chsd ldrs: hung lft and wknd 2f out: eased fnl f* **10/1**

1m 15.28s (-1.62) **Going Correction** -0.075s/f (Stan) 13 Ran SP% **124.7**
Speed ratings (Par 105):107,104,104,101,101 98,97,96,95,94 93,88,82
CSF £56.03 CT £385.41 TOTE £14.10: £4.10, £1.50, £3.20; EX 20.80.
Owner Tom Tuohy Paraic Gaffney **Bred** Mrs Sandra Cooper **Trained** Earlswood, Monmouths

FOCUS
A strongly-run race and the form looks solid. The race could be rated 3lb higher and the form should work out.
Councellor(FR) Official explanation: trainer said colt had been struck into

246 NO 5P RULE 4S AT BETDIRECT H'CAP 1m 6f (F)
3:50 (3:51) (Class 5) (0-70,70) 4-Y-0+ **£3,886** (£1,156; £577; £288) **Stalls** Low

Form RPR

-113 **1** **Cotton Eyed Joe (IRE)**[12] 129 5-9-5 64 DeanMcKeown 10 75
(G A Swinbank) *trckd ldrs: swtchd rt over 2f out: sn led: clr over 1f out: styd on strly* **9/2**[3]

36-1 **2** 6 **He's A Star**[27] 12 4-8-12 63 PaulHanagan 11 66
(Miss Gay Kelleway) *trckd ldrs: rdn and wl outpcd over 4f out: styd on fnl 2f: tk 2nd nr fin* **8/1**

1-22 **3** 1 **Blue Hills**[12] 129 5-8-12 57 (p) DarrenWilliams 4 59
(P W Hiatt) *trckd ldrs: chal over 4f out: wnt 2nd over 1f out: kpt on same pce* **9/1**

353- **4** 2 **Trew Style**[64] 6432 4-9-3 68 MichaelHills 7 67
(M H Tompkins) *t.k.h in rr: hdwy on outer over 6f out: kpt on same pce fnl 2f* **16/1**

0-50 **5** hd **Victory Quest (IRE)**[17] 98 6-9-4 63 (v) RobertWinston 5 62
(Mrs S Lamyman) *led tl over 3f out: hung rt over 2f out: one pce* **50/1**

50-1 **6** 1 1/2 **Macaroni Gold (IRE)**[19] 78 6-9-11 70 JamieSpencer 9 66
(D J Daly) *dwlt: in rr: swtchd outside 6f out: kpt on fnl 2f: nvr trbld ldrs* **7/2**[2]

111- **7** hd **Piper General (IRE)**[45] 6582 4-9-0 70 GregFairley(5) 3 66
(J Mackie) *w ldrs: t.k.h: led over 3f out: hdd 2f out: edgd rt whn btn ins last* **13/8**[1]

04-1 **8** 3/4 **Padre Nostro (IRE)**[27] 13 7-9-2 61 BrianReilly 2 56
(J R Holt) *hld up: effrt over 3f out: nvr a threat* **25/1**

105- **9** nk **Mi Odds**[40] 6633 10-9-2 68 RussellKennemore(7) 1 63
(Mrs N Macauley) *trckd ldrs: t.k.h: drvn along 6f out: lost pl over 4f out* **50/1**

60-5 **10** 3 **Reminiscent (IRE)**[24] 48 7-8-11 56 (v) TonyCulhane 6 46
(B P J Baugh) *s.s: a in rr* **33/1**

3m 8.46s (-1.14) **Going Correction** -0.075s/f (Stan)
WFA 4 from 5yo+ 6lb 10 Ran SP% **116.2**
Speed ratings (Par 103):100,96,96,94,94 93,93,93,93,91
CSF £38.65 CT £309.14 TOTE £6.40: £1.70, £2.00, £2.40; EX 49.50.
Owner Mrs S Sanbrook **Bred** Tally-Ho Stud **Trained** Melsonby, N Yorks

FOCUS
A modest but fairly competitive handicap and an improved effort from the winner who was dropping back in trip. The race has been rated through the placed horses.

247 BET NOW AT BETDIRECT.CO.UK H'CAP 7f (F)
4:20 (4:21) (Class 6) (0-55,55) 4-Y-0+ **£3,238** (£963; £481; £240) **Stalls** Low

Form RPR

33-3 **1** **Mister Elegant**[13] 121 4-8-9 50 AdrianTNicholls 9 59
(J L Spearing) *chsd ldrs: wnt 2nd over 2f out: led jst ins last: styd on wl* **5/1**[1]

2-03 **2** 1 1/2 **Mount Royale (IRE)**[5] 181 8-8-7 48 (v) KimTinkler 2 53
(N Tinkler) *s.i.s: sn chsng ldrs: kpt on same pce fnl f* **11/1**

20-1 **3** shd **Golden Spectrum (IRE)**[10] 143 7-8-0 48 (b) WilliamCarson(7) 11 53
(R A Harris) *w ldrs on outer: led after 2f: hdd jst ins last: no ex* **11/2**[2]

-044 **4** 3/4 **Mulberry Lad (IRE)**[6] 177 4-8-6 47 ChrisCatlin 12 50
(P W Hiatt) *chsd ldrs: kpt on same pce fnl f* **13/2**[3]

23-1 **5** 1/2 **Doctor Dennis (IRE)**[19] 81 9-9-0 55 (v) MichaelTebbutt 8 57
(J Pearce) *in rr: hdwy on outer over 2f out: kpt on same pce appr fnl f* **7/1**

0-26 **6** 1 1/4 **The Job**[10] 143 5-8-10 51 ow1 (v) TonyCulhane 3 49
(A D Smith) *stmbld s: bhd: hdwy over 2f out: styd on fnl f: nt rch ldrs* **13/2**[3]

00-0 **7** 8 **Diction (IRE)**[17] 100 4-9-0 55 (p) RobertWinston 4 33
(K R Burke) *mid-div: effrt over 2f out: wknd fnl f* **11/1**

4-42 **8** 1/2 **Monkey Madge**[5] 181 4-8-8 49 PaulEddery 5 25
(B Smart) *chsd ldrs: n.m.r bnd over 4f out: lost pl over 2f out* **11/2**[2]

0004 **9** 1 3/4 **Lakeside Guy (IRE)**[1] 227 5-7-12 46 oh6 (vt) LiamJones(7) 10 18
(M Appleby) *hld up in rr: edgd lft and wknd over 1f out* **28/1**

0-00 **10** 6 **Penway**[19] 78 5-8-7 48 oh16 ow2 (b) BrianReilly 7 4
(A Sadik) *s.i.s: sn drvn along in mid-field: lost pl over 2f out* **100/1**

0-50 **11** 3 1/2 **Flying Spud**[1] 231 5-8-6 47 oh6 ow1 DeanMcKeown 6 —
(A J Chamberlain) *led 2f: n.m.r and lost pl bnd over 4f out* **40/1**

000- **12** 5 **Game Flora**[185] 3866 5-8-3 47 oh11 ow1 PatrickMathers(3) 13 —
(D Shaw) *w ldrs on wd outside: lost pl over 4f out: sn bhd* **80/1**

2- **13** 13 **Apple Wood**[99] 6037 6-8-5 46 oh6 GrahamGibbons 1 —
(Denis P Quinn, Ire) *s.i.s: a bhd: t.o 3f out* **16/1**

1m 30.16s (-0.64) **Going Correction** -0.075s/f (Stan) 13 Ran SP% **117.3**
Speed ratings (Par 101):100,98,98,97,96 95,86,85,83,76 72,67,52
CSF £58.07 CT £324.65 TOTE £5.80: £1.90, £4.00, £1.70; EX 111.70 Place 6 £14.11, Place 5 £9.93.
Owner M Lawrence & W Cooper **Bred** J Spearing And Kate Ive **Trained** Kinnersley, Worcs

FOCUS
In effect a banded handicap but the form has a sound look to it rated through the runner-up and the fourth.
T/Plt: £13.40 to a £1 stake. Pool: £42,554.65. 2,316.80 winning tickets. T/Qpdt: £5.10 to a £1 stake. Pool: £4,133.20. 595.60 winning tickets. WG

225 WOLVERHAMPTON (A.W) (L-H)
Monday, January 30

OFFICIAL GOING: Standard
Wind: Almost nil Weather: Fine

248 PLAY £1/4M SPOT THE BALL ON 0800 500 000 CLAIMING STKS 5f 216y(P)
1:40 (1:41) (Class 6) 3-Y-O **£2,730** (£806; £403) **Stalls** Low

Form RPR

3-32 **1** **Ockums Razor (IRE)**[4] 195 3-9-5 65 SteveDrowne 1 74
(N A Callaghan) *w ldr: led wl over 1f out: sn rdn and hung lft: r.o* **2/1**[1]

53-1 **2** 2 **Diktalex (IRE)**[5] 189 3-7-9 60 (t) MarcHalford(5) 9 49
(W G M Turner) *s.i.s: hdwy on outside over 2f out: rdn and kpt on ins fnl f: nt trble wnr* **11/2**[3]

1-01 **3** nk **Prettilini**[13] 128 3-8-10 71 RobertWinston 8 58
(A W Carroll) *led early: a.p: rdn over 3f out: kpt on same pce fnl f* **5/2**[2]

42-4 **4** nk **Amber Glory**[13] 128 3-8-7 68 (p) DeanHeslop(7) 5 61
(K A Ryan) *sn led: rdn and hdd wl over 1f out: no ex wl ins fnl f* **7/1**

220- **5** 3 1/2 **Lasting Love**[62] 6466 3-8-0 55 HayleyTurner 10 37
(C R Dore) *prom: rdn over 2f out: wknd wl over 1f out* **20/1**

6-03 **6** 4 **Bermuda Beauty (IRE)**[17] 105 3-8-2 51 ChrisCatlin 7 27
(J M Bradley) *prom: rdn over 2f out: wknd wl over 1f out* **25/1**

00- 7 3½ **Kissimee**[52] [6531] 3-7-11 ....(t) JamesDoyle(7) 6 18
(N P Littmoden) *bhd fnl 3f* **20/1**

0-00 8 1¾ **Lucys Lady**[17] [105] 3-8-0 45 .... PaulHanagan 4 9
(K R Burke) *in tch: n.m.r sn after s: rdn over 2f out: sn bhd* **33/1**

606- 9 3½ **Honey Flame**[112] [5805] 3-8-6 45 .... J-PGuillambert 3 —
(A P Jarvis) *prom: sn pushed along: lost pl over 3f out: hmpd on ins over 2f out* **33/1**

1m 15.38s (-0.43) **Going Correction** -0.125s/f (Stan) 9 Ran SP% **109.0**
Speed ratings (Par 95):97,94,93,93,88 83,78,76,71
CSF £11.17 TOTE £2.40: £1.70, £1.70, £1.10; EX 18.10.The winner was claimed by Paul J. Dixon for £12,000. Diktalex was claimed by M. Attwater for £5,000.
Owner Franconson Partners **Bred** Minch Bloodstock **Trained** Newmarket, Suffolk

FOCUS
A reasonable enough claimer in which it proved hard to come from off the pace. The sole colt in the race beat the eight fillies. An improved effort from the winner, but no fluke.
Kissimee Official explanation: jockey said filly hung left-handed throughout

249 NO 5P RULE 4S AT BETDIRECT FILLIES' H'CAP (DIV I) 5f 216y(P)
2:10 (2:11) (Class 6) (0-60,63) 4-Y-0+ **£2,047** (£604; £302) **Stalls** Low

Form RPR

5-02 1 **Sahara Silk (IRE)**[14] [119] 5-9-1 **60** ....(v) PatrickMathers(3) 8 67
(D Shaw) *hld up: rdn over 2f out: hdwy over 1f out: carried sltly rt ins fnl f: r.o to ld cl home* **9/1**

0-03 2 ½ **Sweetest Revenge (IRE)**[9] [164] 5-9-2 **58** .... MartinDwyer 4 67+
(M D I Usher) *chsd ldrs: rdn over 2f out: nt clr run and swtchd rt over 1f out and ins fnl f: sn ev ch: r.o* **5/1**[2]

-231 3 1 **Cookie Cutter (IRE)**[4] [195] 4-9-7 **63** 6ex ....(p) RobertWinston 6 65
(K R Burke) *a.p: rdn over 2f out: led and edgd lft ins fnl f: hdd cl home* **5/2**[1]

060- 4 nk **Fizzy Lizzy**[31] [6693] 6-8-5 **47** oh6 ow1 .... RobbieFitzpatrick 9 48
(H E Haynes) *sn outpcd and bhd: hdwy 2f out: swtchd rt 1f out: no ex towards fin* **33/1**

60-0 5 1¼ **Carcinetto (IRE)**[26] [38] 4-8-4 **46** oh1 ....(v) FrancisFerris 3 43
(B Palling) *sn w ldr: rdn over 2f out: ev ch whn hung lft over 1f out: flashed tail and nt qckn wl ins fnl f* **18/1**

00-0 6 hd **Miss Porcia**[14] [119] 5-7-13 **46** oh6 .... DuranFentiman(5) 1 43
(S L Keightley) *led: rdn wl over 1f out: hdd and no ex ins fnl f* **12/1**

2-10 7 ½ **Straffan (IRE)**[11] [146] 4-8-4 **46** ....(p) DaleGibson 11 41
(J Hetherton) *prom: rdn wl over 1f out: nt qckn whn carried sltly rt ins fnl f* **14/1**

55-0 8 shd **Kiss The Rain**[3] [212] 6-8-4 **46** oh1 ....(b) PaulHanagan 10 41
(R Brotherton) *bhd tl sme late prog on outside: nvr nrr* **8/1**

00-0 9 ¾ **Missperon (IRE)**[14] [126] 4-8-8 **55** ....(p) AndrewMullen(5) 12 48
(K A Ryan) *mid-div: rdn and hdwy on outside 3f out: wknd wl over 1f out* **18/1**

00-0 10 nk **Dematraf (IRE)**[10] [159] 4-8-13 **55** .... ChrisCatlin 5 47
(Ms Deborah J Evans) *mid-div: rdn over 3f out: sn bhd* **40/1**

406- 11 3 **Bint Royal (IRE)**[240] [2287] 8-8-7 **49** .... JimmyQuinn 2 32
(Miss V Haigh) *s.i.s: sn mid-div: rdn and wknd over 2f out* **6/1**[3]

000- 12 5 **Danethorpe Lady (IRE)**[109] [5856] 4-8-4 **46** oh11 ....(v) HayleyTurner 7 14
(D Shaw) *s.i.s: a bhd* **66/1**

1m 15.1s (-0.71) **Going Correction** -0.125s/f (Stan) 12 Ran SP% **112.4**
Speed ratings (Par 98):99,98,97,96,94 94,94,93,92,92 88,81
CSF £50.14 CT £145.86 TOTE £6.20: £1.50, £1.70, £1.50; EX 24.30.
Owner Danethorpe Racing Ltd **Bred** John Cullinan **Trained** Danethorpe, Notts

FOCUS
Just a moderate sprint handicap for fillies. The winner ran to last year's form while the proximity of the fourth is a concern.
Kiss The Rain Official explanation: jockey said mare hung right-handed throughout

250 FIRST PAST THE POST AT BETDIRECT H'CAP 1m 4f 50y(P)
2:40 (2:40) (Class 5) (0-75,74) 4-Y-0+ **£3,238** (£963; £481; £120; £120) **Stalls** Low

Form RPR

2-21 1 **Newnham (IRE)**[16] [114] 5-8-11 **67** .... JoeFanning 8 73
(J R Boyle) *hld up and bhd: hdwy 2f out: edgd lft over 1f out: styd on to ld wl ins fnl f* **13/2**

2-15 2 nk **Desperation (IRE)**[16] [113] 4-8-13 **73** .... RobertWinston 9 78
(K R Burke) *hld up in mid-div: rdn and hdwy over 2f out: hung lft over 1f out: kpt on ins fnl f* **13/2**

2-62 3 nk **Dragon Slayer (IRE)**[9] [167] 4-8-12 **72** .... J-PGuillambert 5 77
(M J Attwater) *t.k.h: a.p: led over 2f out: sn rdn: clr over 1f out: hdd and nt qckn wl ins fnl f* **5/1**[2]

000- 4 1¾ **Compton Drake**[166] [4183] 7-9-4 **74** .... EddieAhern 2 76
(G A Butler) *a.p: carried lft over 1f out: one pce whn swtchd rt ins fnl f* **7/2**[1]

510- 4 dht **Top Spec (IRE)**[59] [6482] 5-9-4 **74** .... JimmyQuinn 4 76
(J Pearce) *s.i.s: hld up and bhd: rdn over 1f out: hdwy and edgd lft ins fnl f: r.o* **11/2**[3]

0-05 6 1½ **African Sahara (USA)**[18] [101] 7-8-8 **71** ....(t) ChrisCavanagh(7) 1 74+
(Miss D Mountain) *t.k.h in mid-div: hdwy wl over 1f out: sn rdn: nt clr run and swtchd rt ins fnl f: one pce* **9/1**

400- 7 1 **John Forbes**[7] [6671] 4-8-8 **68** .... TomEaves 6 66
(B Ellison) *hld up towards rr: rdn over 2f out: nvr nrr* **33/1**

50-0 8 1 **Golden Boot**[9] [168] 7-8-6 **62** .... MartinDwyer 7 59
(A Bailey) *stdd s: hld up and bhd: swtchd rt over 3f out: hdwy on outside over 2f out: c wd st: rdn and wknd over 1f out* **10/1**

5-01 9 1 **Isa'Af (IRE)**[20] [75] 7-8-13 **69** .... ChrisCatlin 10 64
(P W Hiatt) *hld up in tch: led 3f out: rdn and hdd over 2f out: wknd over 1f out* **12/1**

/40- 10 8 **Kingkohler (IRE)**[120] [4187] 7-9-2 **72** .... PaulHanagan 3 54
(K A Morgan) *led: hdd 3f out: sn rdn: wknd wl over 1f out* **25/1**

046- 11 13 **Jamaar**[162] [4607] 4-8-1 **64** ow4 .... EdwardCreighton(3) 11 25
(C N Kellett) *hld up towards rr: hdwy over 5f out: rdn 4f out: wknd 3f out* **66/1**

2m 39.69s (-2.73) **Going Correction** -0.125s/f (Stan)
WFA 4 from 5yo+ 4lb 11 Ran SP% **116.0**
Speed ratings (Par 103):104,103,103,102,102 101,100,100,99,94 85
CSF £46.98 CT £229.85 TOTE £6.90: £2.00, £1.90, £2.00; EX 27.10.
Owner M Khan X2 **Bred** Ballygallon Stud **Trained** Epsom, Surrey
■ Stewards' Enquiry : Robert Winston caution: careless riding

FOCUS
A fair handicap, but they went no more than an ordinary pace for much of the way. The runner-up and the third are pretty exposed and set the standard.
Golden Boot Official explanation: jockey said gelding hung right-handed throughout

251 BETDIRECT FREEPHONE 0800 211 222 CLAIMING STKS 1m 1f 103y(P)
3:10 (3:10) (Class 6) 4-Y-0+ **£2,388** (£705; £352) **Stalls** Low

Form RPR

-405 1 **Hurricane Coast**[10] [159] 7-9-8 72 ....(b) JamieSpencer 8 78
(K McAuliffe) *hld up and bhd: hdwy over 2f out: led wl ins fnl f: r.o* **5/1**[1]

660- 2 nk **Play Master (IRE)**[51] [6535] 5-9-0 62 .... PaulEddery 7 69
(B Smart) *hld up: hdwy over 2f out: rdn to ld over 1f out: hdd wl ins fnl f: r.o* **25/1**

1400 3 1¼ **Risk Free**[10] [156] 9-8-8 56 ....(bt) MartinDwyer 1 61
(P D Evans) *hld up in mid-div: rdn and hdwy wl over 1f out: r.o ins fnl f* **12/1**

0-60 4 shd **Cherished Number**[17] [107] 7-8-10 61 ....(b) TomEaves 2 63
(I Semple) *hld up in tch: rdn over 3f out: ev ch over 1f out: nt qckn ins fnl f* **12/1**

20-0 5 2½ **Nimello (USA)**[17] [107] 10-9-4 67 .... LPKeniry 5 66
(A G Newcombe) *hld up and bhd: hdwy over 1f out: r.o ins fnl f: nrst fin* **16/1**

0-66 6 shd **Takes Tutu (USA)**[10] [161] 7-9-4 69 .... RobertWinston 12 66
(K R Burke) *t.k.h in rr: rdn over 2f out: hdwy fnl f: nvr nrr* **5/1**[1]

3R-3 7 nk **Keshya**[17] [107] 5-8-6 62 .... RichardThomas(3) 9 56
(N P Littmoden) *hld up: lost pl over 3f out: late prog on outside: nt rch ldrs* **9/1**

3-46 8 ½ **Tregarron**[10] [157] 5-8-9 56 .... StephaneBreux(3) 6 58
(R Hannon) *hld up in mid-div: rdn over 3f out: c wd st: no real prog* **9/1**

50-3 9 2½ **King Forever**[6] [180] 4-9-3 67 .... EddieAhern 4 60
(D E Cantillon) *t.k.h: prom: rdn over 3f out: wknd wl over 1f out* **11/1**

3-65 10 ¾ **Scotty's Future (IRE)**[17] [107] 8-9-8 66 .... AdrianTNicholls 10 62
(D Nicholls) *a bhd* **16/1**

00-0 11 hd **Farriers Charm**[17] [106] 5-8-7 56 ....(v) TPQueally 11 47
(D J Coakley) *led: rdn and hdd over 1f out: sn wknd* **25/1**

0303 12 2 **Sol Rojo**[2] [229] 4-8-7 53 ....(b) RobbieFitzpatrick 13 44
(M J Attwater) *prom: rdn over 3f out: wknd wl over 1f out* **6/1**[2]

-443 13 1¾ **Look At The Stars (IRE)**[1] [243] 4-8-9 52 ....(b) GrahamGibbons 3 43
(R Hollinshead) *prom: rdn over 3f out: wknd over 1f out* **7/1**[3]

2m 1.37s (-1.25) **Going Correction** -0.125s/f (Stan)
WFA 4 from 5yo+ 1lb 13 Ran SP% **123.3**
Speed ratings (Par 101):100,99,98,98,96 96,95,95,93,92 92,90,89
CSF £138.90 TOTE £4.00: £1.50, £13.20, £5.10; EX 162.80.
Owner Nadeem Ahmad **Bred** Ian H Wills **Trained** Fernham, Oxon

FOCUS
An ordinary claimer and competitive enough with just 11lb separating the entire field at the weights. The form makes sense. The pace, though, was just fair.

252 BETDIRECT.CO.UK FILLIES' H'CAP 1m 1f 103y(P)
3:40 (3:41) (Class 5) (0-70,70) 4-Y-0+ **£3,238** (£963; £481; £240) **Stalls** Low

Form RPR

00-5 1 **Madhavi**[16] [115] 4-8-1 **57** .... StephaneBreux(3) 3 64
(R Hannon) *hld up towards rr: hdwy on ins 2f out: rdn over 1f out: led wl ins fnl f: r.o* **11/1**

0-25 2 nk **Bavarica**[10] [156] 4-7-11 **57** .... JamesDoyle(7) 2 63
(Miss J Feilden) *a.p: rdn over 1f out: ev ch wl ins fnl f: r.o* **7/2**[1]

320- 3 2 **Mansiya**[76] [6364] 4-8-7 **60** .... J-PGuillambert 6 62
(C E Brittain) *hld up in mid-div: hdwy on ins over 3f out: hrd rdn over 1f out: ev ch wl ins fnl f: nt qckn* **25/1**

03-0 4 nk **Gramada (IRE)**[21] [74] 4-8-7 **60** .... GrahamGibbons 4 62
(P A Blockley) *chsd ldr: ev ch over 2f out: sn rdn: one pce fnl f* **7/1**[3]

53-0 5 hd **Sforzando**[17] [106] 5-8-1 **60** .... KristinStubbs(7) 7 64+
(Mrs L Stubbs) *s.i.s: hld up and bhd: hdwy on ins whn nt clr run wl over 1f out and wl ins fnl f: swtchd rt: r.o* **10/1**

2-30 6 nk **Danettie**[10] [157] 5-8-4 **56** oh2 .... ChrisCatlin 9 57
(W M Brisbourne) *hld up towards rr: rdn over 2f out: hdwy over 1f out: styd on ins fnl f* **8/1**

0-40 7 ½ **Elrafa Mujahid**[10] [161] 4-9-0 **70** ....(b) AdamKirby(3) 1 70
(Ernst Oertel) *led: rdn over 2f out: hdd & wknd wl ins fnl f* **8/1**

556- 8 ¾ **Gaelic Princess**[56] [6499] 6-9-4 **70** .... FergusSweeney 10 68
(A G Newcombe) *hld up and bhd: rdn over 2f out: edgd rt and hdwy 1f out: nt rch ldrs* **14/1**

003- 9 1¾ **Poppys Footprint (IRE)**[42] [6621] 5-8-11 **68** ....(p) AndrewMullen(5) 11 63
(K A Ryan) *hld up towards rr: hdwy over 5f out: rdn over 3f out: wknd fnl f* **6/1**[2]

000- 10 2 **Elsie Hart (IRE)**[94] [6134] 4-9-0 **67** .... DavidAllan 13 58
(T D Easterby) *hld up and bhd: rdn 4f out: nvr nr ldrs* **50/1**

01-0 11 ¾ **La Gessa**[21] [73] 4-8-3 **56** oh1 .... JimmyQuinn 8 46
(John Berry) *bhd fnl 2f* **14/1**

000- 12 hd **Mytori**[69] [6412] 4-8-1 **57** oh21 ow1 .... PatrickMathers(3) 12 46
(D Shaw) *rdn over 4f out: a bhd* **100/1**

30-0 13 4 **Indebted**[18] [101] 4-9-1 **68** .... EddieAhern 5 50
(P W D'Arcy) *prom tl rdn and wkng whn n.m.r wl over 1f out* **7/1**[3]

2m 0.91s (-1.71) **Going Correction** -0.125s/f (Stan)
WFA 4 from 5yo+ 1lb 13 Ran SP% **121.3**
Speed ratings (Par 100):102,101,99,99,99 99,98,98,96,94 94,93,90
CSF £49.62 CT £973.98 TOTE £18.20: £4.10, £1.70, £7.40; EX 90.80 TRIFECTA Not won..
Owner White Beech Farm **Bred** Elsdon Farms **Trained** East Everleigh, Wilts

FOCUS
Just a modest fillies' handicap, the runner-up setting the standard.

253 TEXT "BETDIRECT" TO 88600 H'CAP 7f 32y(P)
4:10 (4:11) (Class 5) (0-75,79) 4-Y-0+ **£3,238** (£963; £481; £240) **Stalls** High

Form RPR

3620 1 **Lincolneurocruiser**[1] [245] 4-8-5 **69** .... RussellKennemore(7) 1 77
(Mrs N Macauley) *a.p: rdn over 1f out: led jst ins fnl f: drvn out* **13/2**

6-05 2 nk **Nautical**[9] [167] 8-8-11 **68** .... RobertWinston 2 75
(A W Carroll) *hld up and bhd: hdwy on ins over 2f out: rdn and ev ch ins fnl f: nt qckn* **6/1**

300- 3 nk **Defi (IRE)**[93] [6159] 4-8-13 **70** ....(bt[1]) TomEaves 6 76
(I Semple) *w ldr: rdn to ld over 1f out: hdd jst ins fnl f: nt qckn* **10/1**

02-4 4 1½ **General Feeling (IRE)**[10] [159] 5-9-4 **75** .... JimmyQuinn 3 77
(M Mullineaux) *s.i.s: hld up in rr: rdn and hdwy wl over 1f out: sn swtchd rt: kpt on ins fnl f* **8/1**

51-3 5 nk **Connotation**[9] [167] 4-9-1 **72** .... EddieAhern 11 74+
(P W Chapple-Hyam) *hld up and bhd: nt clr run and swtchd lft over 1f out: hdwy fnl f: nrst fin* **11/4**[1]

-500 6 ¾ **Norcroft**[9] [164] 4-8-11 **68** ....(p) ChrisCatlin 4 68
(Mrs C A Dunnett) *led: rdn over 2f out: hdd over 1f out: wknd ins fnl f* **20/1**

/06- **7** 1 1/2 **Hit's Only Money (IRE)**[42] [6622] 6-9-0 **71** .... DeanMcKeown 7 67
(P A Blockley) *hld up in tch: rdn over 2f out: wknd over 1f out* **5/1**[2]

000- **8** 1 1/2 **Mistral Sky**[45] [6590] 7-9-0 **71** ....(v) PaulHanagan 10 63
(Stef Liddiard) *hld up: hdwy over 3f out: sn rdn: wknd over 1f out* **25/1**

100- **9** 13 **Onlytime Will Tell**[135] [5285] 8-8-12 **69** .... AdrianTNicholls 8 27
(D Nicholls) *hld up in tch: rdn over 3f out: wknd 2f out* **40/1**

0-01 **10** 1 **Hayyani (IRE)**[2] [220] 4-9-8 **79** 6ex..............................(e[1]) JamieSpencer 9 34
(K McAuliffe) *s.i.s: a bhd* **11/2**[3]

6-00 **11** 5 **Camp Commander (IRE)**[9] [167] 7-8-11 **73**.........(t) AndrewMullen(5) 12 15
(C R Dore) *a bhd* **100/1**

1m 28.71s (-1.69) **Going Correction** -0.125s/f (Stan) **11** Ran SP% **118.6**
Speed ratings (Par 103):104,103,103,101,101 100,98,96,82,80 75
CSF £44.10 CT £392.54 TOTE £9.90: £2.50, £2.10, £3.90; EX 61.60.

Owner Peter Smith P C Coaches Limited **Bred** David Brown, Slatch Farm Stud And G B Turnbull L **Trained** Sproxton, Leics

FOCUS
A close finish with Lincolneurocruiser seeing it out best. The form appears sound but the race is unlikely to produce many winners.

Lincolneurocruiser Official explanation: trainer said, regarding the improved form shown, at Southwell the previous day gelding missed break, got into the kick-back and never got a clear run
Onlytime Will Tell Official explanation: jockey said gelding lost its action
Hayyani(IRE) Official explanation: jockey said gelding ran flat

254 PLAY NOW AT BETDIRECTPOKER.COM MAIDEN STKS 7f 32y(P)
4:40 (4:42) (Class 5) 3-Y-O **£3,238** (£963; £481; £240) **Stalls** High

Form RPR

06-4 **1** **Donna Giovanna**[17] [110] 3-8-9 68.................................(b[1]) EddieAhern 5 70
(J A Osborne) *a.p: led 2f out: rdn over 1f out: r.o* **10/1**

4- **2** nk **Siwa**[65] [6435] 3-8-9 .... SteveDrowne 1 70
(E A L Dunlop) *led over 1f: prom: rdn 2f out: kpt on ins fnl f* **10/3**[3]

522- **3** 1 1/4 **Ludovico**[177] [4140] 3-8-9 76.. AndrewMullen(5) 10 71
(K A Ryan) *prom: led over 5f out: rdn and hdd 2f out: edgd lft 1f out: nt qckn* **7/1**

0-3 **4** 1 1/4 **Kut (IRE)**[17] [110] 3-9-0 .... JamieSpencer 8 68
(J Noseda) *hld up: sn in tch: rdn 2f out: one pce fnl f* **9/4**[1]

5 **5** 2 **Laheen (IRE)**[16] [112] 3-8-9 .... JoeFanning 4 58+
(M H Tompkins) *mid-div: hmpd over 2f out: c wd st: hdwy fnl f: r.o* **20/1**

42- **6** 1 **Kapellmeister (IRE)**[179] [4092] 3-9-0 .... PaulHanagan 6 60+
(C R Egerton) *bmpd sn after s: swtchd rt and rdr lost whip over 4f out: hdwy on outside over 2f out: wknd 1f out* **11/4**[2]

7 1/2 **Living On A Prayer** 3-8-9 .... JimmyQuinn 12 54
(J Pearce) *s.i.s: bhd: hdwy over 1f out: nvr trbld ldrs* **66/1**

8 1 **Ten Tenors (IRE)** 3-8-9 .... ShaneKelly 7 51
(J A Osborne) *hld up towards rr: hdwy 4f out: rdn and hung lft 2f out: sn wknd* **50/1**

0- **9** 2 **Carpeting**[79] [6318] 3-9-0 .... DerekMcGaffin 3 51
(D Morris) *sn outpcd: a bhd* **50/1**

10 1 1/2 **Postage (USA)** 3-9-0 .... RobertWinston 2 47+
(K A Morgan) *hld up: short-lived effrt whn n.m.r jst over 2f out* **12/1**

0 **11** 2 **King's Melody**[21] [70] 3-8-7 .... JamesMillman(7) 9 42
(B R Millman) *sn w ldr: wknd over 2f out* **66/1**

12 3 **Vi's Boy** 3-9-0 .... RobbieFitzpatrick 11 34
(W M Brisbourne) *s.i.s: sn swtchd lft: outpcd* **100/1**

1m 30.53s (0.13) **Going Correction** -0.125s/f (Stan) **12** Ran SP% **122.5**
Speed ratings (Par 97):94,93,92,90,88 87,86,85,83,81 79,75
CSF £43.71 TOTE £10.90: £2.00, £1.90, £2.50; EX 24.90.

Owner Mountgrange Stud **Bred** Mountgrange Stud Ltd **Trained** Upper Lambourn, Berks

FOCUS
A slightly surprise winner in Donna Giovanna, who showed improved form in the first-time blinkers. The bare form is only ordinary.

Carpeting Official explanation: jockey said gelding hung left-handed 3 1/2f out

255 NO 5P RULE 4S AT BETDIRECT FILLIES' H'CAP (DIV II) 5f 216y(P)
5:10 (5:11) (Class 6) (0-60,60) 4-Y-O+ **£2,047** (£604; £302) **Stalls** Low

Form RPR

21-6 **1** **Segoria (IRE)**[27] [22] 4-8-13 **55**... DaneO'Neill 9 62
(A M Hales) *hld up and bhd: smooth hdwy over 2f out: rdn over 1f out: led wl ins fnl f: r.o wl* **4/1**[2]

01-3 **2** 1 1/4 **Tiviski (IRE)**[25] [46] 4-9-0 **56**... JimmyQuinn 11 60
(E J Alston) *sn chsng ldr: rdn to ld over 1f out: hdd and nt qckn wl ins fnl f* **7/1**

10-3 **3** 1/2 **Triple Zero (IRE)**[2] [232] 4-9-2 **58**.................................. J-PGuillambert 6 60
(A P Jarvis) *a.p: rdn 2f out: kpt on towards fin* **10/1**

-222 **4** hd **Soft Focus (IRE)**[9] [170] 4-9-4 **60**.................................(b) EddieAhern 2 61
(J A Osborne) *a.p: rdn wl over 1f out: sn hung lft: one pce fnl f* **13/8**[1]

0-35 **5** nk **Park Star**[7] [177] 6-8-1 **46**.. PatrickMathers(3) 7 47
(D Shaw) *t.k.h in tch: rdn over 2f out: kpt on same pce fnl f* **6/1**[3]

044- **6** 1 **Tennessee Belle (IRE)**[42] [6615] 4-8-4 **46** oh6................ HayleyTurner 5 44
(C N Allen) *prom: lost pl after 2f: kpt on u.p fnl f* **33/1**

50-3 **7** 1 3/4 **Shirley Oaks (IRE)**[6] [179] 8-8-4 **46** oh1..................... AdrianMcCarthy 3 38
(Miss Z C Davison) *sn bhd: sme late prog: n.d* **20/1**

3-05 **8** hd **Secret Vision (USA)**[3] [216] 5-8-4 **46**............................(p) ChrisCatlin 10 38
(R M H Cowell) *bhd fnl 3f* **10/1**

00-4 **9** 1 1/2 **Holly Springs**[25] [45] 4-8-3 **52**..............................(b) KirstyMilczarek(7) 4 39
(Mrs C A Dunnett) *led: rdn and hdd over 1f out: wknd fnl f* **33/1**

006- **10** 3 1/2 **Make It Happen Now**[43] [6607] 4-7-13 **46** oh11......... DuranFentiman(5) 1 23
(S L Keightley) *a bhd* **66/1**

000- **11** 17 **Cayman Mischief**[153] [4851] 6-7-11 **46** oh6.................. JosephWalsh(7) 8 —
(James Moffatt) *s.i.s: a bhd: eased whn no ch 1f out* **66/1**

1m 15.21s (-0.60) **Going Correction** -0.125s/f (Stan) **24** Ran SP% **116.7**
Speed ratings (Par 98):99,97,96,96,96 94,92,92,90,85 62
CSF £30.21 CT £264.99 TOTE £4.70: £2.10, £2.80, £2.20; EX 45.90 Place 6 £212.49, Place 5 £165.65.

Owner A M Hales **Bred** Tom Darcy And Vincent McCarthy **Trained** Quainton, Bucks

FOCUS
A good winner in the shape of Segoria, who picked up well once asked to go and win the race. Very ordinary form, with the ralative time the worst of the three races over the trip, and the form may not prove that solid.

T/Jkpt: Not won. T/Plt: £221.90 to a £1 stake. Pool: £47,192.55. 155.20 winning tickets. T/Qpdt: £216.30 to a £1 stake. Pool: £2,690.00. 9.20 winning tickets. KH

[240]SOUTHWELL (L-H)
Tuesday, January 31

OFFICIAL GOING: Standard
Wind: Almost nil

256 PLAY NOW AT BETDIRECTPOKER.COM BANDED STKS 1m 6f (F)
1:50 (1:50) (Class 7) 4-Y-O+ **£1,365** (£403; £201) **Stalls** Low

Form RPR

0-55 **1** **Makarim (IRE)**[8] [174] 10-9-0 45..(p) AlanDaly 8 52+
(M R Bosley) *stdd s: hld up: hdwy 6f out: wnt 2nd over 4f out: led over 2f out: comf* **5/2**[2]

00-6 **2** 7 **Logger Rhythm (USA)**[14] [129] 6-9-0 40.......................... DaleGibson 7 41
(R Dickin) *in rr tl hdwy over 2f out: styd on to go 2nd ins fnl f* **25/1**

1-26 **3** 1 1/4 **Tharua (IRE)**[8] [174] 4-8-11 48..(v) JamieMackay 4 42
(Ernst Oertel) *hld up: hdwy after 4f: chsd winner 2f out tl wknd ins fnl f* **7/4**[1]

60-6 **4** 8 **Brother Cadfael**[20] [91] 5-9-0 40.. PaulEddery 3 28
(John A Harris) *in tch: rdn over 4f out: wknd fnl 2f* **8/1**

00-0 **5** 8 **Kerry's Blade (IRE)**[20] [91] 4-8-8 45................................... NeilPollard 2 17
(P C Haslam) *led for 1f: trckd ldr: led over 5f out: hdd over 2f out: sn wknd* **6/1**[3]

00-5 **6** 3 **Robbie Will**[20] [91] 5-9-0 40... FrancisFerris 6 13
(F Jordan) *a bhd* **8/1**

00/- **7** shd **Mist Opportunity (IRE)**[13] [5097] 4-8-8 45.....................(vt[1]) LeeEnstone 1 13
(P C Haslam) *led after 1f: hdd over 5f out: rdn and sn btn* **50/1**

0-00 **8** dist **Radiant Bride**[20] [91] 6-9-0 40..................................(p) PatCosgrave 5 —
(P A Blockley) *chsd ldrs tl rdn and wknd over 5f out: t.o* **33/1**

3m 11.52s (1.92) **Going Correction** -0.05s/f (Stan)
WFA 4 from 5yo+ 6lb **8** Ran SP% **110.2**
Speed ratings (Par 97):92,88,87,82,78 76,76,—
CSF £57.57 TOTE £3.40: £1.10, £7.10, £1.10; EX 48.60.

Owner Mrs Jean M O'Connor **Bred** Katom **Trained** Lockeridge, Wilts

■ Stewards' Enquiry : Lee Enstone one day ban: using whip when out of contention (Feb 11)

FOCUS
A weak affair which took no winning with the favourite not running his race, and the field finished fairly strung out behind the emphatic winner. The winning time was modest even for a banded race.

257 PLAY NOW AT BETDIRECTCASINO.COM MAIDEN CLAIMING STKS 1m (F)
2:20 (2:21) (Class 7) 4-Y-O+ **£1,365** (£403; £201) **Stalls** Low

Form RPR

00-2 **1** **Pearl Island (USA)**[7] [180] 5-8-11 35.............................(b) ChrisCatlin 10 51
(D J Wintle) *in tch: rdn over 3f out: kpt up to work: led 1f out: drvn out* **6/1**

46-4 **2** 3 **Silsong (USA)**[8] [173] 4-8-5 47 ow1...........................(v[1]) AdamKirby(3) 9 42
(Miss Gay Kelleway) *led tl rdn and hdd 1f out: nt qckn* **4/1**[3]

300- **3** 1 1/2 **Alzarma**[34] [6676] 4-8-12 45..(p) NCallan 12 43
(J Gallagher) *t.k.h: prom on outside: wnt 2nd over 3f out: no ex fnl f* **14/1**

0-40 **4** 1/2 **Weet Yer Tern (IRE)**[26] [46] 4-8-12 49............................(p) FergalLynch 6 42
(P A Blockley) *trckd ldrs: rdn over 3f out: one pce fnl 2f* **9/2**

0-20 **5** 3 **Crocodile Kiss (IRE)**[12] [143] 4-8-5 45........................(b[1]) EddieAhern 3 29
(J A Osborne) *in rr tl sme hdwy over 2f out: kpt on one pce* **7/2**[2]

2-02 **6** 7 **Swords**[8] [173] 4-8-12 49.. TonyCulhane 8 22
(P Howling) *slowly away: nvr on terms: fin lame* **5/2**[1]

-000 **7** 5 **Penway**[2] [247] 5-8-6 30......................................(bt) J-PGuillambert 4 6
(A Sadik) *trckd ldr to over 3f out: sn btn* **50/1**

0/0- **8** 2 1/2 **Rambo Blue**[34] [6679] 6-8-12 45....................................... SamHitchcott 5 7
(G J Smith) *mid-div: rdn over 5f out: sn bhd* **50/1**

00- **9** 17 **Cinder Maid**[33] [6682] 4-8-5 .... JamieMackay 2 —
(J G Portman) *a bhd* **66/1**

0/0- **10** dist **Lucky Uno**[258] [1807] 10-8-12 30................................ RobbieFitzpatrick 11 —
(C Smith) *slowly away and sn struggling wl in rr: t.o* **100/1**

1m 44.21s (-0.39) **Going Correction** -0.05s/f (Stan) **10** Ran SP% **116.3**
Speed ratings (Par 97):99,96,94,94,91 84,79,76,59,—
CSF £29.98 TOTE £6.30: £1.60, £1.80, £3.40; EX 29.80.The winner was the subject of a friendly claim. Swords was claimed by Ms Heather Dalton for £5,000.

Owner G Havelaar **Bred** Swettenham Stud And Pacelco S A **Trained** Naunton, Gloucs

FOCUS
A poor event which took little winning, run at a fair pace, and the form does not look too solid.

Swords Official explanation: vet said gelding was slightly lame on left fore
Lucky Uno Official explanation: jockey said gelding hung right-handed

258 BETDIRECT.CO.UK BANDED STKS 1m (F)
2:50 (2:51) (Class 7) 4-Y-O+ **£1,706** (£503; £252) **Stalls** Low

Form RPR

/15- **1** **Mad Maurice**[78] [6343] 5-9-0 48.. JamieSpencer 13 53+
(B J Curley) *hld up: stdy hdwy over 2f out: nudged into ld fnl 50yds* **1/1**[1]

335- **2** 3/4 **Musical Gift**[47] [6584] 6-8-9 50.................................(v) KevinGhunowa(7) 4 53
(P A Blockley) *mid-div: hdwy to chse ldr over 2f out: led ins fnl f: rdn and hdd fnl 50yds* **16/1**

00-6 **3** 3/4 **Old Bailey (USA)**[7] [181] 6-9-1 49..................................(b) GeorgeBaker 8 51
(G L Moore) *led tl rdn and hdd ins fnl f: kpt on* **14/1**

24-1 **4** hd **Nisr**[8] [172] 9-8-9 50..(t) RonanKeogh(7) 10 51
(Miss Gay Kelleway) *mid-div: hdwy 3f out: rdn and styd on fnl f* **5/1**[2]

35-3 **5** 1/2 **Semper Paratus (USA)**[30] [3] 7-8-11 40...............................(v) NCallan 5 45
(V Smith) *trckd ldr to over 2f out: kpt on one pce* **16/1**

20-3 **6** 1 3/4 **It Must Be Speech**[12] [143] 5-8-11 45......................... DarrenWilliams 9 41
(S L Keightley) *slowly away: rdn over 3f out: kpt on one pce ins fnl 2f* **8/1**[3]

65-5 **7** 1 **Donegal Shore (IRE)**[7] [183] 7-8-13 47......................(vt) HayleyTurner 7 41
(Jennie Candlish) *in rr tl hdwy 3f out: wknd over 1f out* **12/1**

600- **8** 2 **Noul (USA)**[35] [6667] 7-9-0 48.......................................(b) FrankieMcDonald 1 38
(J S Moore) *slowly away: hdwy 6f out: wknd 2f out* **40/1**

02-0 **9** 4 **Wanna Shout**[8] [175] 8-8-11 45..(b) TonyCulhane 6 26
(R Dickin) *trckd ldr to over 2f out: sn wknd* **33/1**

20-0 **10** 8 **Moondancer (GER)**[17] [113] 7-8-13 47................................ EddieAhern 12 10
(B G Powell) *chsd ldrs tl rdn and wknd over 2f out* **16/1**

540- **11** 1 3/4 **Poirot**[94] [3916] 4-8-9 50..(b[1]) AmbroiseReilly(7) 2 9
(J Howard Johnson) *slowly away: a bhd* **18/1**

00/0 **12** 4 **Darling River (FR)**[8] [172] 7-9-2 50................................... TomEaves 3 —
(R Brotherton) *in tch: rdn over 3f out: wknd 2f out* **150/1**

13-3 **13** 3 ½ **Super Dominion**[27] 41 9-8-13 47........................(p) GrahamGibbons 11 —
(R Hollinshead) *chsd ldrs tl wknd over 3f out* **10/1**

1m 44.85s (0.25) **Going Correction** -0.05s/f (Stan) **13 Ran SP% 130.2**
Speed ratings (Par 97):96,95,94,94,93 92,91,89,85,77 75,71,67
CSF £23.56 TOTE £1.90: £1.50, £5.70, £5.60; EX 39.40.
Owner P Byrne **Bred** M R M Bloodstock **Trained** Newmarket, Suffolk

FOCUS
A fair event for the grade and the winner is value for further, although te form is not too solid.
Moondancer(GER) Official explanation: vet said gelding bled from nose

259 BETDIRECT FREEPHONE 0800 211 222 BANDED STKS 1m 4f (F)
3:20 (3:20) (Class 7) 4-Y-0+ **£1,365** (£403; £201) **Stalls** Low

Form RPR
0-20 **1** **Jackie Kiely**[14] 131 5-9-5 50.. TonyCulhane 7 61
(P Howling) *a in tch: led over 3f out: edgd rt u.p fnl f: hld on* **11/4**[1]
-221 **2** ½ **Moon Shot**[12] 147 10-9-5 50.. NCallan 1 60
(A G Juckes) *chsd ldrs: wnt 2nd over 3f out: kpt on gamely to press wnr fnl f* **3/1**[2]
1-22 **3** 13 **Bulberry Hill**[12] 147 5-9-0 45.. SamHitchcott 3 34+
(R W Price) *hld up: rdn and hdwy over 3f out: no ch w first 2: fnl 2f* **7/2**[3]
260- **4** 1 **Mr Whizz**[150] 4934 9-8-7 30..........................(p) LiamJones(7) 9 33
(A P Jones) *in rr: rdn and kpt on u.p fnl 2f but nvr on terms* **25/1**
00-0 **5** nk **Heversham (IRE)**[20] 94 5-9-0 40.................................. DaleGibson 14 32
(J Hetherton) *nvr bttr than mid-div* **80/1**
0-03 **6** 1 ½ **Extra Cover (IRE)**[21] 78 5-9-0 50.............................. GregFairley(5) 8 35
(Miss V Scott) *bhd: sme hdwy over 3f out: nvr on terms* **12/1**
-300 **7** 3 ½ **City Of Manchester (IRE)**[11] 162 4-8-7 45........ SilvestreDeSousa(3) 2 24
(D Nicholls) *in tch tl wknd over 2f out* **50/1**
432- **8** ½ **Prince Valentine**[33] 6681 5-9-0 45............................(be) GeorgeBaker 12 23
(G L Moore) *hld up: sme hdwy 4f out: nvr on terms* **8/1**
420- **9** 8 **Fillameena**[6] 5894 6-9-1 46...(v[1]) LeeEnstone 13 12
(P T Midgley) *slowly away: hdwy on outside 4f out: wknd over 2f out* **28/1**
00-4 **10** 2 **Tiegs (IRE)**[20] 91 4-8-10 45... ChrisCatlin 4 7
(P W Hiatt) *led to over 3f out: sn wknd* **16/1**
00-5 **11** 10 **Shami**[22] 72 7-9-3 48.. DarrenWilliams 6 —
(D W Chapman) *trckd ldr to over 3f out: wknd qckly* **20/1**
2-00 **12** 9 **Mujimac (IRE)**[20] 92 4-8-6 48..........................(tp) KevinGhunowa(7) 11 —
(P A Blockley) *a bhd* **50/1**
/00- **13** 3 **Just Dashing**[50] 6558 7-8-9 30............................. NataliaGemelova(5) 10 —
(J E Long) *in tch tl wknd 4f out* **150/1**
0- **14** ¾ **Settle (IRE)**[34] 6680 7-9-0 40... EddieAhern 5 —
(W M Brisbourne) *a bhd* **7/1**

2m 40.46s (-1.63) **Going Correction** -0.05s/f (Stan)
WFA 4 from 5yo+ 4lb **14 Ran SP% 128.9**
Speed ratings (Par 97):103,102,94,93,93 92,89,89,84,82 76,70,68,67
CSF £11.40 TOTE £4.00: £2.10, £1.60, £1.70; EX 17.70.
Owner P S J Croft **Bred** Mrs M Chaworth Musters **Trained** Newmarket, Suffolk

FOCUS
A fair event for the class, run at a sound clip in a good time for a banded race, and the first two came well clear to post above-average form for the grade.
Just Dashing Official explanation: trainer said gelding bled from nose

260 BETDIRECT IN RUNNING SKYTEXT P293 BANDED STKS 6f (F)
3:50 (3:52) (Class 7) 3-Y-0+ **£1,365** (£403; £201) **Stalls** Low

Form RPR
-356 **1** **Christian Bendix**[5] 195 4-9-0 45.................................... PatCosgrave 7 54
(P Howling) *chsd ldrs: rdn to ld ins fnl f* **6/1**[2]
00-0 **2** 2 **Blakeshall Quest**[12] 145 6-9-0 45..............................(b) PaulFessey 5 48
(R Brotherton) *led: clr over 1f out: rdn and tired bef hdd ins fnl f* **14/1**
1-41 **3** nk **Boanerges (IRE)**[7] 179 9-9-6 45.............................. JamieMackay 8 53+
(J M Bradley) *in rr and sn pushed along: hdwy over 1f out: r.o: nvr nrr* **7/2**[1]
-230 **4** shd **Blue Power (IRE)**[12] 146 5-9-0 45......................... FranciscoDaSilva 14 47
(K R Burke) *a in tch: rdn and kpt on one pce fnl f* **8/1**
05-0 **5** 4 **Polar Haze**[28] 29 9-9-0 45.......................................(v) MichaelTebbutt 6 35
(J Pearce) *s.i.s: hdwy after 2f: one pce fnl 2f* **10/1**
0-05 **6** 3 **Dexileos (IRE)**[12] 148 7-9-0 45....................................(t) SamHitchcott 1 26
(David Pinder) *towards rr and nvr on terms* **13/2**[3]
60-3 **7** 1 ½ **Teyaar**[12] 145 10-9-0 45... AlanDaly 9 21
(M Wellings) *bhd and nvr on terms* **7/1**
-006 **8** 1 ½ **Enjoy The Buzz**[4] 209 7-9-0 45.............................. PaulFitzsimons 10 17
(J M Bradley) *outpcd and nvr on terms* **8/1**
05-6 **9** 1 ½ **Off Hire**[7] 179 10-8-11 40.....................................(v) JasonEdmunds(3) 12 12
(C Smith) *chsd ldrs tl wknd wl over 1f out* **20/1**
0-00 **10** 3 **Weet N Measures**[12] 144 4-9-0 45.................................. FrancisFerris 2 —
(T Wall) *a bhd* **80/1**
0-40 **11** ½ **Ace Club**[14] 127 5-9-0 45..(b) DaleGibson 11 —
(J Hetherton) *slowly away: a bhd* **13/2**[3]
060- **12** 8 **Teenage Rampage**[180] 4096 4-9-0 40.................................... NeilPollard 3 —
(W M Brisbourne) *chsd ldr tl rdn and wknd over 2f out* **66/1**
066- **13** 3 **Mr Spliffy (IRE)**[49] 6568 7-9-0 40...........................(b) AdrianMcCarthy 13 —
(M C Chapman) *slowly away: a bhd* **25/1**

1m 17.36s (0.46) **Going Correction** -0.05s/f (Stan) **13 Ran SP% 125.0**
Speed ratings (Par 97):94,91,90,90,85 81,79,77,75,71 70,60,56
CSF £88.47 TOTE £10.30: £2.70, £4.70, £1.40; EX 200.60.
Owner Mrs A K Petersen **Bred** C B Petersen **Trained** Newmarket, Suffolk

FOCUS
A poor event, run at a decent early pace, and the form makes sense.

261 FOOTBALLPOOLS.COM BANDED STKS 7f (F)
4:20 (4:21) (Class 7) 4-Y-0+ **£1,365** (£403; £201) **Stalls** Low

Form RPR
36-6 **1** **Desert Lover (IRE)**[20] 95 4-8-11 45.............................. PhillipMakin 2 58
(R J Price) *trckd ldrs on ins: rdn to ld 2f out: rdn out fnl f* **9/2**[2]
-005 **2** 2 ½ **Pawn In Life (IRE)**[7] 184 8-8-11 40......................(v) DeanMcKeown 5 51
(M J Polglase) *led tl hdd 2f out: kpt on one pce fnl f* **28/1**
0036 **3** 1 **Crusoe (IRE)**[2] 242 9-8-11 45.....................................(b) BrianReilly 9 49
(A Sadik) *in tch: racd wd: kpt on one pce ins fnl 2f* **10/1**
-402 **4** 3 ½ **Spy Gun (USA)**[12] 143 6-8-11 45............................. J-PGuillambert 6 40+
(T Wall) *chsd ldrs tl lost pl 3f out: styd on ins fnl 2f* **4/1**[1]
-504 **5** ½ **Penel (IRE)**[7] 184 5-8-11 45...(p) LeeEnstone 13 39
(P T Midgley) *prom: rdn 1/2-way: nt qckn fnl 2f* **20/1**
40-2 **6** 2 **Auentraum (GER)**[12] 145 6-8-11 45...............................(b) TonyCulhane 4 36+
(K McAuliffe) *hld up: hdwy over 3f out: rdn and wknd over 1f out* **4/1**[1]
0-20 **7** nk **Feast Of Romance**[12] 148 9-8-6 45....................(b) AndrewMullen(5) 10 33
(C R Dore) *slowly away: sme hdwy over 2f out: nvr on terms* **16/1**

00-0 **8** ¾ **Eforetta (GER)**[20] 92 4-8-11 45...................................(b[1]) ChrisCatlin 1 31
(D J Wintle) *slowly away: a bhd* **20/1**
-052 **9** 10 **Indian Edge**[8] 175 5-8-11 45... FrancisFerris 11 5
(B Palling) *prom tl wknd over 2f out* **8/1**
5-00 **10** 3 **Mytton's Dream**[15] 121 4-8-11 45.. TomEaves 7 —
(R Brotherton) *s.i.s: a outpcd* **40/1**
25-2 **11** nk **Aintnecessarilyso**[12] 148 8-8-11 45..................................(p) NCallan 3 —
(J M Bradley) *mid-div: rdn over 2f out: wknd wl over 1f out* **6/1**[3]
0-40 **12** nk **Hows That**[20] 95 4-8-11 45..(p) PatCosgrave 8 —
(K R Burke) *prom tl wknd over 3f out* **50/1**
3-00 **13** 5 **Tally (IRE)**[12] 148 6-8-11 45 ow3...................................(v[1]) DNolan(3) 12 —
(D G Bridgwater) *racd wd: wknd wl over 2f out* **25/1**

1m 30.56s (-0.24) **Going Correction** -0.05s/f (Stan) **13 Ran SP% 119.8**
Speed ratings (Par 97):99,96,95,91,90 88,87,86,75,72 71,71,65
CSF £135.07 TOTE £6.50: £2.00, £5.50, £2.70; EX 159.50 Place 6 £61.89, Place 5 £48.99.
Owner Multi Lines Partnership **Bred** Penfold Bloodstock And Mr D B Clark **Trained** Ullingswick, H'fords

FOCUS
Typical form for the class and sound enough. The race was run at a solid pace.
T/Plt: £71.90 to a £1 stake. Pool: £55,862.85. 566.55 winning tickets. T/Qpdt: £33.10 to a £1 stake. Pool: £4,126.30. 92.20 winning tickets. JS

233 LINGFIELD (L-H)
Wednesday, February 1

OFFICIAL GOING: Standard
Wind: Nil Weather: Overcast & cold

262 BET NOW AT BETDIRECT.CO.UK CLASSIFIED CLAIMING STKS (DIV I) 6f (P)
1:00 (1:00) (Class 6) 4-Y-0+ **£2,388** (£705; £352) **Stalls** Low

Form RPR
0-30 **1** **Shirley Oaks (IRE)**[2] 255 8-8-4 45............................ AdrianMcCarthy 5 53
(Miss Z C Davison) *mde virtually all: drvn 2f out: kpt on while several rivals were hmpd fnl f: all out* **33/1**
040- **2** nk **Manic**[33] 6689 4-8-6 56... RobertWinston 4 54
(Ernst Oertel) *trckd ldrs: effrt over 1f out: got through to chse wnr jst ins fnl f: nt qckn nr fin* **11/1**
13-0 **3** ½ **Hadath (IRE)**[27] 44 9-8-3 60.......................................(b) JoeFanning 2 58+
(B G Powell) *hld up in midfield: nt clr run on inner over 1f out: r.o last 150yds : nrst fin* **5/2**[1]
2224 **4** nk **Soft Focus (IRE)**[2] 255 4-8-8 60....................................(b) EddieAhern 1 59+
(J A Osborne) *hld up in last trio: prog over 1f out: denied clr run ent fnl f: r.o nr fin* **3/1**[2]
40-5 **5** ½ **Cloann (IRE)**[5] 209 4-8-4 52....................................(b) StephenCarson 3 48
(E A Wheeler) *dwlt: sn rcvrd and prom: upsides fr 1/2-way tl hanging bdly lft jst over 1f out: fdd nr fin* **16/1**
4-34 **6** shd **Sir Sandrovitch (IRE)**[5] 209 10-8-1 55...................(v) PaulHanagan 10 47+
(R A Fahey) *trckd ldrs on outer: effrt over 1f out: trying to chal whn bmpd jst ins fnl f: nt rcvr* **4/1**[3]
/0-0 **7** 1 ¼ **Bahamian Breeze**[27] 51 5-8-9 60... LPKeniry 9 49
(D M Simcock) *lw: trckd ldng gp: cl up whn nt clr run and swtchd rt 1f out: no imp after* **8/1**
504- **8** 1 ¼ **Harbour House**[44] 6613 7-8-1 40.. ChrisCatlin 8 37
(J J Bridger) *w wnr: stl upsides jst over 1f out: losing pl whn squeezed out ins fnl f* **40/1**
/04- **9** hd **Smokincanon**[12] 5957 4-7-12 60.................................... MarcHalford(5) 7 46+
(W G M Turner) *sltly hmpd s: wl in rr: effrt whn nt clr run 1f out: nt rcvr* **33/1**
00-0 **10** 1 ½ **Oeuf A La Neige**[12] 159 6-8-12 58.............................. DeanWilliams(7) 11 50
(G C H Chung) *a in last trio: no prog over 1f out* **50/1**
160/ **11** 1 ¾ **Galloway Boy (IRE)**[479] 6099 9-8-11 60.........................(t) SamHitchcott 6 37
(J F Panvert) *dwlt: a in last trio: rdn and no prog 2f out* **33/1**

1m 12.54s (-0.27) **Going Correction** -0.15s/f (Stan) **11 Ran SP% 112.1**
Speed ratings (Par 101):95,94,93,93,92 92,91,89,89,87 84
CSF £331.32 TOTE £34.60: £5.70, £3.20, £1.90; EX 149.30.Sir Sandrovitch (IRE) was claimed by R Price for £5,000
Owner The Secret Circle **Bred** Miss Honora Corridan **Trained** Hammerwood, E Sussex
■ Stewards' Enquiry : Eddie Ahern one-day ban: careless riding (Feb 12)

FOCUS
Suspect form, with outsider Shirley Oaks making all at a modest race in a race where it paid to race prominently. There were several hard-luck stories in behind and the field finished well bunched.
Sir Sandrovitch(IRE) Official explanation: jockey said gelding hung left-handed

263 FIRST PAST THE POST AT BETDIRECT H'CAP 1m 2f (P)
1:30 (1:30) (Class 6) (0-58,58) 4-Y-0+ **£2,730** (£806; £403) **Stalls** Low

Form RPR
02-0 **1** **Missie Baileys**[27] 48 4-8-5 **55**............................... JamesDoyle(7) 3 62
(Mrs L J Mongan) *lw: mde all: set stdy pce tl kicked on over 2f out: nrly 3 l clr over 1f out: jst hld on* **25/1**
0111 **2** shd **Young Mick**[4] 229 4-9-1 **58** 6ex......................................(v) NCallan 1 65
(G G Margarson) *trckd ldrs: effrt to chse wnr wl over 1f out: clsd ins fnl f: jst failed* **7/2**[1]
20-0 **3** nk **Birthday Star (IRE)**[18] 115 4-9-0 **57**............................. MickyFenton 4 63
(W J Musson) *hld up in midfield: prog on inner 2f out: r.o to chal wl ins fnl f: no ex last strides* **16/1**
414- **4** 1 ¼ **Thebestisyettocome**[134] 5388 4-9-1 **58**............................ IanMongan 7 62+
(T G Mills) *rn in snatches in rr: prog on inner over 1f out: styd on u.p fnl f: nvr able to chal* **6/1**[3]
40/0 **5** shd **Ground Patrol**[18] 115 5-9-0 **56** ow1.............................(be[1]) GeorgeBaker 6 60+
(G L Moore) *hld up midfield: gng easily but nt wl plcd whn pce qcknd over 2f out: styd on fr over 1f out: nvr able to chal* **50/1**
2-43 **6** 1 **Jomus**[7] 185 5-9-1 **57**..(p) RobertWinston 13 59+
(L Montague Hall) *led to post early: s.i.s: hld up in last: prog 2f out: styd on after: no ch of rching ldrs* **6/1**[3]
11-0 **7** 1 ½ **Granary Girl**[7] 185 4-8-11 **54**...................................... JimmyQuinn 12 53
(J Pearce) *trckd wnr for 2f: styd prom: lost pl sltly 1/2-way: effrt again 2f out: no imp over 1f out: fdd* **33/1**
2-41 **8** nk **Night Warrior (IRE)**[4] 230 6-9-1 **57** 6ex...............(b) GrahamGibbons 10 56
(N P Littmoden) *lw: hld up wl in rr: effrt on wd outside 3f out: no prog over 1f out: one pce* **10/1**
9 2 ½ **My Trip (IRE)**[66] 6409 4-8-12 **55**.......................................(t) LPKeniry 11 49
(Kieran P Cotter, Ire) *trckd wnr after 2f to wl over 1f out: wknd* **40/1**

33-5 **10** *shd* **Lady Taverner**[4] 223 5-8-11 **58** NataliaGemelova(5) 8 52
(J E Long) *prom: nt qckn over 2f out: wknd over 1f out* **8/1**
02-0 **11** *½* **Danzolin**[12] 163 5-8-12 **54** SteveDrowne 5 47
(W R Muir) *a towards rr: pushed along over 3f out: struggling over 2f out* **66/1**
65-0 **12** *hd* **Woodwool**[18] 114 4-9-0 **57** DaneO'Neill 2 49
(H Candy) *dwlt: hld up in rr: hmpd on inner over 2f out and dropped to last: no ch after* **12/1**
60-3 **13** *nk* **Unrestricted**[18] 115 4-9-0 **57** JamieMackay 9 49
(C F Wall) *lw: trckd ldrs: cl enough on outer over 2f out: sn wknd: hanging fnl f* **9/2**[2]

2m 6.40s (-1.39) **Going Correction** -0.15s/f (Stan)
WFA 4 from 5yo+ 1lb 13 Ran SP% **115.4**
Speed ratings (Par 101):99,98,98,97,97 96,95,95,93,93 92,92,92
CSF £104.82 CT £1479.32 TOTE £43.30: £8.10, £1.80, £6.70; EX 147.80.
Owner Mrs P J Sheen **Bred** Mrs J Wotherspoon **Trained** Epsom, Surrey

FOCUS
Just a moderate handicap, and the winner Missie Baileys very much had the run of what was a slowly-run race.
Thebestisyettocome Official explanation: jockey said colt missed break

264 BETDIRECT FREEPHONE 0800 211 222 H'CAP 1m 5f (P)
2:00 (2:01) (Class 5) (0-75,73) 4-Y-O+ **£3,238** (£963; £481; £240) **Stalls** Low

Form RPR
03-5 **1** **Dovedon Hero**[28] 37 6-8-13 **68** (b) TonyCulhane 6 76+
(P J McBride) *hld up: last 4f out: prog on inner over 2f out: taken to outer and effrt over 1f out: led last 150yds: tried to pull up nr fin* **13/2**
-360 **2** *hd* **Blackmail (USA)**[3] 237 8-8-8 **63** (b) EddieAhern 4 70
(Miss B Sanders) *settled in rr: rdn 3f out: no prog tl eased to outer ins fnl f: flashed home: jst failed* **12/1**
051- **3** *hd* **Fen Game (IRE)**[186] 3956 4-8-10 **69** RobertHavlin 3 79+
(J H M Gosden) *lw: dwlt: hld up in rr: prog over 3f out: trckd ldrs 2f out: nowhere to go tl jst over 1f out: r.o fnl f: nrst fin* **6/1**[3]
1-34 **4** *¾* **Captain Margaret**[7] 186 4-8-8 **67** JimmyQuinn 2 73
(J Pearce) *stmbld s: sn trckd ldrs: rdn and cl up 2f out: styd on same pce fnl f* **14/1**
50-2 **5** *1 ¼* **Tromp**[16] 125 5-9-4 **73** TPQueally 1 77
(D J Coakley) *trckd ldng gp: prog to ld 2f out: hdd & wknd last 150yds* **13/2**
33-1 **6** *1 ¾* **A Thousand Smiles (IRE)**[11] 166 4-8-11 **70** NCallan 7 71
(M A Jarvis) *trckd ldr: chal 3f out: upsides 2f out to over 1f out: wknd ins fnl f* **5/1**[2]
54-0 **7** *hd* **Nawow**[21] 88 6-9-1 **70** DaneO'Neill 8 71
(P D Cundell) *hld up in rr: rdn wl over 3f out: no prog and hanging over 1f out: styd on fnl f* **12/1**
3-13 **8** *¾* **Oldenway**[16] 125 7-9-1 **70** PaulHanagan 13 70
(R A Fahey) *led to 2f out: stl cl up on inner 1f out: wknd* **14/1**
60-5 **9** *1 ½* **Linden Lime**[28] 32 4-8-4 **63** oh8 ow4 PaulDoe 9 60
(Jamie Poulton) *reluctant to go to post: trckd ldng gp tl lost pl over 3f out : n.d after* **33/1**
00-6 **10** *½* **Sandy's Legend (USA)**[7] 186 4-8-3 **62** oh3 ow2.. SimonWhitworth 10 59
(Jamie Poulton) *dwlt: prog to trck ldrs after 4f: lost pl u.p wl over 2f out: btn after* **50/1**
4-12 **11** *1 ¾* **Principal Witness (IRE)**[7] 186 5-8-6 **61** FrankieMcDonald 12 55
(Tom Dascombe) *lw: stmbld s: t.k.h: hld up in tch: rdn 4f out: wknd over 2f out* **11/4**[1]
660- **12** *dist* **Rome (IRE)**[67] 6432 7-8-10 **65** (p) HayleyTurner 5 —
(G P Enright) *last whn reminder after 2f: prog on outer 7f out: wknd 4f out: t.o* **66/1**

2m 44.38s (-3.92) **Going Correction** -0.15s/f (Stan)
WFA 4 from 5yo+ 4lb 12 Ran SP% **119.4**
Speed ratings (Par 103):106,105,105,105,104 103,103,102,101,101 100,—
CSF £81.84 CT £498.47 TOTE £8.10: £2.60, £3.40, £2.00; EX 67.80.
Owner Michael C Whatley **Bred** Michael C Whatley And R Ames **Trained** Newmarket, Suffolk

FOCUS
In contrast to the first race those coming from behind were at an advantage here and Dovedon Hero got first run on the two unlucky placed horses. The form looks sound enough, with the first six all running close to their marks.
Nawow Official explanation: jockey said colt had been hanging

265 BET NOW AT BETDIRECT.CO.UK CLASSIFIED CLAIMING STKS (DIV II) 6f (P)
2:30 (2:30) (Class 6) 4-Y-O+ **£2,388** (£705; £352) **Stalls** Low

Form RPR
0444 **1** **Mulberry Lad (IRE)**[3] 247 4-8-1 47 ChrisCatlin 2 49
(P W Hiatt) *trckd ldng pair: rdn over 2f out: effrt on inner to ld jst over 1f out: hld on wl u.p nr fin* **4/1**[1]
4-00 **2** *nk* **Chantelle's Dream**[5] 212 4-7-11 45 (bt) JamesDoyle(7) 5 51
(Ms J S Doyle) *s.v.s: hld up: last to 1/2-way: gd prog on inner over 1f out: pressed wnr last 100yds: nt qckn and hld nr fin* **33/1**
03-3 **3** *nk* **Kitchen Sink (IRE)**[14] 138 4-8-7 55 (e) FergusSweeney 4 53+
(P J Makin) *lw: chsd ldrs: rdn 1/2-way: effrt whn hanging and nt clr run 1f out: r.o last 100yds* **5/1**[2]
40-0 **4** *¾* **Taminoula (IRE)**[11] 170 5-8-8 58 EddieAhern 6 52
(P Mitchell) *wl in rr: rdn over 2f out: effrt on outer over 1f out: r.o ins fnl f: nt rch ldrs* **7/1**
500- **5** *shd* **He's A Diamond**[265] 1645 4-9-5 60 IanMongan 3 63
(T G Mills) *lw: pressed ldr: upsides 3f out to jst over 1f out: styd on same pce* **11/2**[3]
2-00 **6** *½* **Gaudalpin (IRE)**[9] 178 4-8-2 50 (t) JimmyQuinn 1 44
(Ernst Oertel) *trckd ldrs gng easily: rdn and fnd nil over 1f out: kpt on last 100yds* **16/1**
440- **7** *nk* **Madrasee**[33] 6689 8-8-7 57 AmirQuinn(3) 7 51
(P G Murphy) *rrd s: wl in rr: prog on inner 2f out: cl up 1f out: fdd nr fin* **20/1**
000- **8** *2 ½* **Winning Venture**[81] 6336 9-8-6 56 ow1 RobertWinston 8 40
(A W Carroll) *mde most to jst over 1f out: wknd* **16/1**
5-45 **9** *¾* **Sweet Pickle**[15] 133 5-7-8 57 LiamJones(7) 10 32
(J R Boyle) *prom: u.p 1/2-way: wknd over 1f out* **4/1**[1]
3-44 **10** *1 ½* **A Teen**[15] 130 8-8-3 40 JoeFanning 11 30
(P Howling) *nvr on terms w ldrs: u.p 1/2-way: struggling after* **16/1**
00-6 **11** *3 ½* **Binnion Bay (IRE)**[13] 148 5-8-1 45 PaulHanagan 9 17
(J J Bridger) *chsd ldrs for 2f: sn outpcd: last and wl bhd 2f out* **20/1**

1m 11.77s (-1.04) **Going Correction** -0.15s/f (Stan) 11 Ran SP% **114.7**
Speed ratings (Par 101):100,99,99,98,98 97,97,93,92,90 86
CSF £145.16 TOTE £5.70: £1.90, £7.10, £2.00; EX 214.20.
Owner P W Hiatt **Bred** Mountarmstrong Stud **Trained** Hook Norton, Oxon

FOCUS
A moderate claimer and, despite the winning time being 0.77 seconds faster than the first division, the pace through the first couple of furlongs was noticeably steady for a sprint. More reliable form than for division one.
Winning Venture Official explanation: jockey said gelding hung right

266 TEXT "BETDIRECT" TO 88600 MAIDEN STKS 6f (P)
3:00 (3:00) (Class 5) 3-Y-O+ **£3,886** (£1,156; £577; £288) **Stalls** Low

Form RPR
0-34 **1** **Came Back (IRE)**[3] 233 3-8-11 EddieAhern 1 57+
(J A Osborne) *trckd ldrs gng wl: squeezed through to ld jst ins fnl f: r.o wl to hold on* **5/2**[2]
6- **2** *shd* **Creme Brulee**[67] 6435 3-8-6 PaulHanagan 7 52+
(C R Egerton) *lw: trckd ldrs: rdn 2f out: effrt to join wnr jst ins fnl f: r.o: jst hld* **3/1**[3]
0-33 **3** *3 ½* **Developer (IRE)**[15] 128 3-8-11 70 (p) JoeFanning 3 46
(T G Mills) *pressed ldr: drvn to ld jst over 1f out to jst ins fnl f: sn outpcd* **2/1**[1]
4 *nk* **Western Sky** 3-8-8 ow2 ShaneKelly 8 42+
(J Noseda) *unf: bit bkwd: dwlt: rn green early and off the pce in last trio: prog fr 1/2-way : shkn up over 1f out: styd on: nrst fin* **9/1**
005- **5** *shd* **Spanish Music**[42] 6650 4-9-7 40 (t) SteveDrowne 2 44
(R Ingram) *s.i.s: pushed along to stay in tch: kpt on same pce fr over 1f out: n.d* **14/1**
/4-0 **6** *1* **Unprecedented (IRE)**[8] 179 5-9-12 40 (v) SamHitchcott 5 46
(T T Clement) *led to jst over 1f out: wknd ins fnl f* **66/1**
7 *8* **Miss Odd Sox** 3-8-6 RobertHavlin 9 13
(R Ingram) *w'like: plain: s.s and wnt rt s: v green in last and sn wl off the pce* **33/1**
3P0- **8** *¾* **Ashburnham (IRE)**[37] 6661 3-8-6 63 AdrianMcCarthy 4 11
(N I M Rossiter) *prom tl wknd rapidly sn after 1/2-way* **25/1**
006- **9** *1 ¾* **Life Is Rosie (IRE)**[36] 6672 4-9-7 40 DaneO'Neill 6 10
(D K Ivory) *s.v.s: a in last pair and toiling* **66/1**

1m 12.38s (-0.43) **Going Correction** -0.15s/f (Stan)
WFA 3 from 4yo+ 15lb 9 Ran SP% **113.3**
Speed ratings (Par 103):96,95,91,90,90 89,78,77,75
CSF £9.96 TOTE £4.00: £1.30, £1.60, £1.20; EX 14.10.
Owner J A Osborne **Bred** Yeomanstown Stud **Trained** Upper Lambourn, Berks
■ Stewards' Enquiry : Sam Hitchcott one-day ban: improper riding - used whip down the shoulder in the forehand position (Feb 12)

FOCUS
An ordinary maiden, but there were one or two promising performances and the race should produce the odd winner. The fifth and sixth limit the form.

267 BETDIRECT.CO.UK H'CAP 1m (P)
3:30 (3:31) (Class 4) (0-80,80) 4-Y-O+
£5,297 (£1,586; £793; £396; £198; £99) **Stalls** High

Form RPR
2-13 **1** **Northern Desert (IRE)**[4] 221 7-9-4 **80** ChrisCatlin 2 91+
(P W Hiatt) *hld up in rr: t.k.h fr 1/2-way: prog 2f out: got through to ld last 150yds: drvn and r.o wl* **7/2**[2]
-111 **2** *½* **Kindlelight Debut**[11] 169 6-8-7 **76** JamesDoyle(7) 8 86
(N P Littmoden) *settled in midfield: pushed along 3f out: prog 2f out: swtchd to outer and r.o to chse wnr last 75yds: clsng at fin* **15/2**
05-0 **3** *1 ½* **Wavertree Warrior (IRE)**[26] 58 4-8-13 **75** NCallan 3 82
(N P Littmoden) *cl up: rdn to ld over 1f out: hdd and outpcd last 150yds* **9/2**[3]
5-44 **4** *1* **Swift Oscar**[4] 221 4-9-4 **80** EddieAhern 1 84
(J W Hills) *hld up in midfield: effrt on inner 2f out: rdn to chal 1f out: nt qckn* **3/1**[1]
000- **5** *1 ¼* **Luis Melendez (USA)**[116] 5747 4-8-5 **67** (t) PaulHanagan 11 68
(Tom Dascombe) *cl up: prog to chse ldr over 2f out to over 1f out: rdn and fnd nil* **10/1**
5-53 **6** *½* **Quantum Leap**[7] 192 9-8-5 **67** (v) JimmyQuinn 9 67
(S Dow) *lw: towards rr: t.k.h 1/2-way: last of main gp 2f out: styd on fnl f: nt pce to rch ldrs* **9/1**
00-0 **7** *5* **Selective**[14] 135 7-9-1 **77** (t) RobertWinston 7 66
(A W Carroll) *t.k.h: cl up: wknd 2f out* **25/1**
056- **8** *¾* **Kabeer**[233] 2552 8-9-3 **79** (t) DavidMcCabe 5 66
(Lucinda Featherstone) *bit bkwd: racd freely: led over 5f out to over 1f out: wknd rapidly* **33/1**
630- **9** *1 ¾* **Goose Chase**[15] 3193 4-8-7 **69** FrankieMcDonald 10 52
(C J Mann) *racd freely: led to over 5f out: chsd ldr to over 2f out: wknd rapidly* **66/1**
430- **10** *1 ½* **Out For A Stroll**[33] 6690 7-8-7 **69** HayleyTurner 6 49
(S C Williams) *hld up in rr: rdn 1/2-way: sn struggling and bhd* **16/1**
0/1- **11** *8* **Ground Rules (USA)**[149] 5006 4-9-2 **78** DaneO'Neill 4 39
(V Smith) *hld up: t.k.h early and racd on outer: wknd 1/2-way: t.o* **14/1**

1m 36.56s (-2.87) **Going Correction** -0.15s/f (Stan) 11 Ran SP% **117.1**
Speed ratings (Par 105):108,107,106,105,103 103,98,97,95,94 86
CSF £29.45 CT £122.53 TOTE £4.70: £1.60, £3.00, £2.00; EX 29.10.
Owner Clive Roberts **Bred** J P Hardiman **Trained** Hook Norton, Oxon

FOCUS
A good handicap for the grade and the pace was reasonable enough. The form seems sound.

268 WIN £2M @ LITTLEWOODSPOOLS.CO.UK H'CAP 1m (P)
4:00 (4:01) (Class 6) (0-60,60) 4-Y-O+ **£2,730** (£806; £403) **Stalls** High

Form RPR
633- **1** **Fajr (IRE)**[84] 6301 4-8-13 55 MickyFenton 12 69
(N B King) *lw: racd wd: hld up: prog over 2f out: led wl over 1f out: sn clr : comf* **8/1**
06-2 **2** *3* **Lowestoft Playboy**[21] 82 4-8-12 59 GregFairley(5) 1 66
(J Jay) *cl up: effrt on inner 2f out: styd on fnl f to take 2nd last strides: no ch w wnr* **7/2**[2]
0-00 **3** *nk* **Physical (IRE)**[14] 137 4-9-1 57 JoeFanning 11 63
(Mrs A J Perrett) *swtg: racd wd: hld up in last pair: prog over 2f out: drvn to chse wnr over 1f out: no imp: lost 2nd last strides* **40/1**
5-22 **4** *½* **Samson Quest**[21] 86 4-9-4 60 (v) RobertWinston 7 65+
(A W Carroll) *hld up in rr: drvn over 2f out: prog over 1f out: styd on: n.d* **5/2**[1]
0-44 **5** *1 ¼* **Rowan Warning**[12] 163 4-9-2 58 NCallan 10 60
(J R Boyle) *lw: prom: effrt to ld over 2f out: hdd wl over 1f out: sn btn* **10/1**

0-10 **6** *nk* **King Of Music (USA)**[4] 230 5-9-3 59........................(v) TonyCulhane 3 61
(G Prodromou) *s.s: drvn to rcvr: stl last and rdn over 2f out: kpt on fr over 1f out: no ch* **5/1**[3]

-306 **7** *1* **Hand Chime**[7] 192 9-9-4 60.. EddieAhern 6 59
(Ernst Oertel) *settled wl in rr: pushed along 2f out: kpt on steadily at one pce: nvr nr ldrs* **12/1**

-046 **8** *nk* **Captain Darling (IRE)**[11] 170 6-8-12 57............ EdwardCreighton(3) 2 56
(R W Price) *plld hrd: early: cl up: lost pl 3f out: struggling wl over 1f out* **14/1**

03-0 **9** *1* **Salinger (USA)**[7] 187 4-9-4 60.. IanMongan 5 56
(Mrs L J Mongan) *chsd ldr: rdn over 3f out: wknd over 2f out* **14/1**

60-0 **10** *2* **Ballycroy Girl (IRE)**[15] 133 4-9-1 57.............................. JimmyQuinn 4 49
(A Bailey) *a towrds rr: n.m.r on inner 2f out: reminder and no prog* **33/1**

000- **11** *1 3/4* **Overjoy Way**[57] 6513 4-9-1 57... GeorgeBaker 9 45
(P R Chamings) *hld up in midfield: wknd 2f out* **50/1**

0/0- **12** *14* **Chorus Beauty**[37] 6666 5-9-3 59.................................... SteveDrowne 8 14
(N I M Rossiter) *led at decent pce to over 2f out: wknd rapidly* **66/1**

1m 37.87s (-1.56) **Going Correction** -0.15s/f (Stan) **12** Ran SP% **117.5**
Speed ratings (Par 101):101,98,97,97,95 95,94,94,93,91 89,75
CSF £35.17 CT £1087.98 TOTE £11.80: £3.10, £1.70, £9.10; EX 48.30.
Owner C H Huggan **Bred** Shadwell Estate Company Limited **Trained** Newmarket, Suffolk

FOCUS
A good performance by handicap debutant Fajr, who showed a decent change of gear to win going away. This was just an ordinary handicap but the form has a solid look to it.
King Of Music(USA) Official explanation: jockey said gelding suffered interference at 5f marker
Hand Chime Official explanation: jockey said gelding was denied a clear run

269 OVER 60 GAMES AT LITTLEWOODSCASINO.COM H'CAP 7f (P)
4:30 (4:30) (Class 5) (0-75,81) 3-Y-O **£3,238** (£963; £481; £240) **Stalls** Low

Form RPR

44-1 **1** **Kingsgate Prince (IRE)**[3] 233 3-9-10 **81** 6ex................ GeorgeBaker 6 91+
(J R Best) *t.k.h early: trckd ldrs: effrt over 1f out: rdn and r.o wl to ld last 75yds: won gng away* **5/2**[2]

4-41 **2** *3/4* **Didn't We (IRE)**[14] 138 3-9-1 **72**...................................(v[1]) JoeFanning 4 80
(T G Mills) *lw: t.k.h: trckd ldr: rdn to chal 2f out: led over 1f out : hdd and outpcd last 75yds* **4/1**[3]

221- **3** *1 1/2* **Orchard Supreme**[33] 6688 3-9-4 **75**............................ RichardHughes 1 79
(R Hannon) *lw: led: set stdy pce 1st 3f: pressed 2f out: hdd over 1f out: outpcd ins fnl f* **9/4**[1]

400- **4** *3 1/2* **Patavium Prince (IRE)**[181] 4092 3-8-13 **70**............................ NCallan 8 65
(J R Best) *swtg: t.k.h early: hld up in last pair: drvn wl over 2f out: outpcd over 1f out: kpt on fnl f* **14/1**

04-4 **5** *1 1/4* **Attitude Annie**[25] 60 3-8-5 **62**.. PaulDoe 3 54
(S Dow) *cl up: rdn 2f out: wknd over 1f out* **16/1**

004- **6** *1/2* **Gibbs Camp**[54] 6531 3-8-11 **68**.. SteveDrowne 9 59
(E A L Dunlop) *trckd ldrs: pushed along over 2f out: outpcd and nudged along fr over 1f out* **25/1**

02-5 **7** *1 1/4* **Final Bid (IRE)**[14] 142 3-8-10 **67**... TPQueally 7 54
(M G Quinlan) *hld up in rr: outpcd over 1f out: wknd* **11/1**

30-4 **8** *1 1/4* **Nut (IRE)**[19] 104 3-8-5 **62**.. EddieAhern 5 46
(J W Hills) *t.k.h: hld up in rr: no prog 2f out: wknd over 1f out* **33/1**

33-3 **9** *1/2* **Power Assisted**[18] 118 3-9-1 **72**...................................... JimmyQuinn 10 55
(C F Wall) *t.k.h early: racd wd: cl up to 1/2-way: struggling over 2f out* **9/1**

1m 24.82s (-1.07) **Going Correction** -0.15s/f (Stan) **9** Ran SP% **117.0**
Speed ratings (Par 97):100,99,97,93,92 91,90,88,88
CSF £13.26 CT £25.29 TOTE £4.40: £1.80, £1.40, £1.70; EX 19.30 Place 6 £103.33, Place 5 £44.01.
Owner John Mayne **Bred** P G Lyons **Trained** Hucking, Kent

FOCUS
A decent enough race for the grade, especially considering Kingsgate Prince was racing off a mark 6lb higher than the official ceiling of 75, and that one created quite an impression. The third is the most obvious marker to the form.
T/Plt: £169.20 to a £1 stake. Pool: £44,158.40. 190.50 winning tickets. T/Qpdt: £21.50 to a £1 stake. Pool: £4,861.30. 166.80 winning tickets. JN

256 SOUTHWELL (L-H)
Thursday, February 2

OFFICIAL GOING: Standard
Wind: Virtually nil

270 LITTLEWOODS £2M POOLS ON 0800 500 000 AMATEUR RIDERS' H'CAP 2m (F)
1:20 (1:22) (Class 5) (0-70,62) 4-Y-0+ **£3,123** (£968; £484; £242) **Stalls** Low

Form RPR

065- **1** **Bid For Fame (USA)**[65] 6461 9-10-12 **60**....................... MrSPearce(7) 1 67
(J Pearce) *hld up: stdy hdwy 6f out: pushed along to chse ldrs 3f out: rdn to chal over 1f out: led and edgd rt ins last: r.o* **5/1**[3]

-223 **2** *2 1/2* **Blue Hills**[4] 246 5-11-2 **57**..(p) MissEJJones 2 61
(P W Hiatt) *led: rdn along over 2f out: drvn over 1f out: hdd ins last: one pce* **9/4**[1]

-551 **3** *3 1/2* **Makarim (IRE)**[2] 256 10-10-10 **51** 6ex..........................(p) MrsSBosley 4 52
(M R Bosley) *hld up: hdwy to trck ldrs 6f out: effrt over 2f out: sn rdn and no imp fr over 1f out* **11/4**[2]

5/0- **4** *5* **Transit**[61] 5685 7-10-9 **53**..(p) MissLEllison(3) 5 49
(B Ellison) *hld up and bhd: hdwy over 4f out: rdn and kpt on fnl 2f: nrst fin* **12/1**

4-10 **5** *3 1/2* **Red Sun**[12] 168 9-11-2 **62**...(t) MrStephenHarrison(5) 8 54
(J Mackie) *trckd ldrs: hdwy to chse ldr 1/2-way: rdn over 2f out and grad wknd* **10/1**

04-3 **6** *21* **Lady Misha**[27] 55 4-10-4 **58**... MissJWaring(7) 3 29
(Jedd O'Keeffe) *chsd ldrs: rdn along over 4f out and sn wknd* **13/2**

00-0 **7** *10* **Alexander Sapphire (IRE)**[17] 55 5-10-0 **48**..(p) MrsFleurHawes(7) 10 9
(N B King) *keen: hdwy to chse ldr after 6f: rdn along 6f out and sn wknd* **50/1**

005/ **8** *dist* **Grand Prairie (SWE)**[253] 645 10-10-7 **55**.............(b[1]) PietroRomeo(7) 6 —
(G L Moore) *in tch: pushed along after 6f: wknd over 6f out and sn wl bhd* **66/1**

326/ **9** *30* **Delta Force**[598] 2935 7-10-11 **55**.......................... MissFayeBramley(3) 7 —
(P A Blockley) *in tch: pushed along 1/2-way: lost pl and bhd fnl 6f* **22/1**

600- **P** **Cemgraft**[158] 4780 5-9-13 **47**...(t) MissZoeLilly(7) 9 —
(A J Lidderdale) *in tch tl sddle slipped after 4f and sn p.u* **50/1**

3m 47.48s (2.94) **Going Correction** -0.075s/f (Stan)
WFA 4 from 5yo+ 6lb **10** Ran SP% **114.0**
Speed ratings (Par 103):89,87,86,83,81 71,66,—,—,—
CSF £15.88 CT £36.45 TOTE £6.10: £1.60, £1.40, £1.20; EX 20.50.
Owner Simon Pearce **Bred** Swifty Farms, Don Myers And Dana Myers **Trained** Newmarket, Suffolk
■ A first winner for rider Simon Pearce, son of Jeff and Lydia Pearce.

FOCUS
A moderate handicap in which few could be fancied. The runner-up sets the standard and the form appears reasonably sound.
Cemgraft Official explanation: jockey said saddle slipped

271 BETDIRECT ON 0800 211 222 (S) STKS 6f (F)
1:50 (1:50) (Class 6) 3-Y-O+ **£2,388** (£705; £352) **Stalls** Low

Form RPR

6/00 **1** **Winning Pleasure (IRE)**[13] 159 8-9-5 60............. JasonEdmunds(3) 6 69
(J Balding) *a.p: led and hung lft over 1f out: sn rdn and kpt on wl fnl f* **33/1**

0-20 **2** *1/2* **Majik**[4] 245 7-9-1 70...(p) JamesDoyle(7) 8 67
(D J S Ffrench Davis) *bhd and pushed along 1/2-way: gd hdwy 2f out: rdn to chal ins last and ev ch tl no ex towards fin* **11/10**[1]

6-00 **3** *2 1/2* **Patternmaker (USA)**[12] 169 4-9-8 61......................... RobertWinston 2 60
(W Jarvis) *chsd ldrs: hdwy 2f out and ev ch tl rdn and one pce ent last* **7/2**[3]

1132 **4** *nk* **Magic Amour**[16] 127 8-9-6 64...............................(b) KevinGhunowa(7) 4 64
(P A Blockley) *chsd ldrs: rdn along wl over 1f out: drvn and wknd appr last* **10/3**[2]

30-0 **5** *4* **Far Note (USA)**[13] 159 8-9-13 55............................(bt) DeanMcKeown 1 52
(S R Bowring) *led: rdn along over 2f out: hdd wl over 1f out and sn wknd* **33/1**

6 *1 3/4* **Dukestreet**[25] 6186 5-9-8 70...(p) NCallan 3 41
(Michael Cunningham, Ire) *a towards rr* **18/1**

0-02 **7** *12* **Aswan (IRE)**[17] 121 8-9-10 64..(t) AmirQuinn(3) 7 10
(S R Bowring) *chsd ldrs: rdn over 2f out: sn wknd* **10/1**

00-0 **8** *18* **Grasslandik**[16] 130 10-9-1 35.. AnnStokell(7) 5 —
(Miss A Stokell) *a towards rr* **100/1**

1m 16.55s (-0.35) **Going Correction** -0.075s/f (Stan) **8** Ran SP% **114.1**
Speed ratings (Par 101):99,98,95,94,89 86,70,46
CSF £69.98 TOTE £42.90: £7.40, £1.40, £1.40; EX 119.00.There was no bid for the winner. Majik was claimed by P. A. Blockley for £6,000. Patternmaker was claimed by Gary P. Martin for £6,000.
Owner R L Crowe **Bred** Mrs B A Headon **Trained** Scrooby, Notts

FOCUS
Not a bad race for the grade of contest, but there is little solid recent form to go on.
Far Note(USA) Official explanation: jockey said gelding hung right-handed throughout
Grasslandik Official explanation: jockey said gelding had a breathing problem

272 BETDIRECT.CO.UK MAIDEN STKS 1m (F)
2:20 (2:21) (Class 5) 3-Y-0 **£3,238** (£963; £481; £240) **Stalls** Low

Form RPR

-4 **1** **Westport**[8] 191 3-9-0 .... RobertHavlin 3 71+
(J H M Gosden) *a.p: effrt to dispute ld 2f out: rdn and slt ld over 1f out: drvn and kpt on gamely ins last* **11/8**[1]

3 **2** *shd* **Airbound (USA)**[8] 191 3-9-0 .... JoeFanning 10 71+
(M Johnston) *a cl up: led over 2f out: jnd 2f out: sn rdn and hdd over 1f out: drvn and kpt on gamely ins last* **11/8**[1]

3 *9* **Tenini** 3-9-0 .... ShaneKelly 1 53
(J A Osborne) *dwlt: midfield tl hdwy 3f out: rdn 2f out and kpt on same pce* **25/1**

00 **4** *nk* **Rudry World (IRE)**[17] 124 3-8-7 .... KevinGhunowa(7) 8 52
(P A Blockley) *keen: trckd ldrs tl pushed along and outpcd 3f out: swtchd lft and rdn 2f out: kpt on ins last* **50/1**

2-50 **5** *shd* **Duel In The Sands**[8] 188 3-8-11 58......................... PatrickMathers(3) 9 52
(D Shaw) *chsd ldrs: rdn along and outpcd 3f out: styd on wl fnl f* **16/1**

6 **6** *hd* **Tip Top Style**[16] 132 3-9-0 .... DaleGibson 2 52?
(J Mackie) *in tch on inner: rdn along 3f out: sn one pce* **40/1**

00-0 **7** *3/4* **Hits Only Life (USA)**[12] 165 3-9-0 45......................... DeanMcKeown 4 50
(J Pearce) *rr: hdwy 2f out: sn rdn and kpt on appr last* **50/1**

8 *3* **Celtic Sunset (IRE)** 3-8-10 ow1.. NCallan 5 40
(M A Jarvis) *s.i.s: sn rdn along to chse ldrs: wknd over 2f out* **10/1**[2]

646- **9** *1 3/4* **Tallyhobye**[129] 5510 3-9-0 57.. RobertWinston 6 41
(J R Weymes) *sn led: rdn along and hdd over 2f out: sn wknd* **12/1**[3]

6- **10** *3 1/2* **Skye Boat Song**[33] 6699 3-8-7 .... TJHowell(7) 7 34
(J Jay) *chsd ldrs on outer: rdn along 3f out: sn wknd* **66/1**

1m 44.52s (-0.08) **Going Correction** -0.075s/f (Stan) **10** Ran SP% **118.6**
Speed ratings (Par 97):97,96,87,87,87 87,86,83,81,78
CSF £3.11 TOTE £2.30: £1.10, £1.10, £4.90; EX 3.50.
Owner Jumeirah Racing **Bred** Agricola Ficomontanino S R L **Trained** Newmarket, Suffolk

FOCUS
The market made it a two-horse race and so it proved, as the joint-favourites had a battle royal up the home straight. The time was modest and the form was not solid behind the first two.
Rudry World(IRE) Official explanation: jockey said, regarding the apparent tender handling, his orders had been to keep gelding balanced due to it being a poor mover but gelding hung left from 2f out and had been difficult to ride out vigourously towards the end of the race; trainer emphasised gelding's poor action and inclination to hang; vet said although he found gelding to be sound on examination post race, he later found it to be lame

273 BETDIRECT FREEPHONE 0800 211 222 CLAIMING STKS 1m 4f (F)
2:50 (2:50) (Class 6) 4-Y-0+ **£2,388** (£705; £352) **Stalls** Low

Form RPR

-210 **1** **Danelor (IRE)**[7] 194 8-9-2 78......................................(p) PaulHanagan 8 75
(R A Fahey) *led: rdn along 3f out: sn hdd and drvn: rallied wl to ld ins last: kpt on* **11/4**[2]

1-36 **2** *1 3/4* **Khanjar (USA)**[7] 194 6-9-8 73..................................(p) PatCosgrave 6 78
(K R Burke) *trckd ldr: hdwy and cl up over 4f out: rdn to ld wl over 2f out: drvn over 1f out: hdd and one pce ins last* **9/4**[1]

1-4 **3** *1/2* **Chater Knight (IRE)**[23] 78 5-8-4 59 ow1..................... GregFairley(5) 1 64
(Micky Hammond) *in tch: hdwy to chse ldng pair 4f out: rdn along wl over 2f out: drvn and kpt on same pce ins last* **4/1**[3]

4622 **4** *2 1/2* **Romil Star (GER)**[4] 243 9-8-5 65......................(p) PatrickDonaghy(7) 7 64
(K R Burke) *prom: rdn along and outpcd 4f out: drvn and kpt on fnl 2f* **4/1**[3]

405- **5** *11* **Molly's Secret**[69] 6419 8-8-3 45...(p) ChrisCatlin 2 38
(Miss S J Wilton) *a rr* **33/1**

6 *dist* **Abraham (IRE)**[19] 6117 4-9-1 63... NCallan 4 —
(Michael Cunningham, Ire) *chsd ldrs: rdn along 5f out: sn wknd* **10/1**

2m 40.52s (-1.57) **Going Correction** -0.075s/f (Stan)
WFA 4 from 5yo+ 3lb **6** Ran SP% **109.5**
Speed ratings (Par 101):102,100,100,98,91 —
CSF £8.86 TOTE £3.40: £1.50, £2.40; EX 8.90.The winner was claimed by D. Shaw for £9,000.

Owner Mark A Leatham **Bred** Barronstown Stud And Orpendale **Trained** Musley Bank, N Yorks

FOCUS
An ordinary claimer dominated by the two with the highest official marks. The placed horses set the standard.

274 BET NOW AT BETDIRECT.CO.UK H'CAP 6f (F)
3:20 (3:22) (Class 6) (0-60,60) 4-Y-0+ **£2,388** (£705; £352) **Stalls** Low

Form RPR

0400 **1** **Zorn**[7] 196 7-8-8 **50** ow1 ShaneKelly 13 62
(P Howling) *qckly away: mde all: rdn wl over 1f out: kpt on* **33/1**

3-15 **2** ¾ **Doctor Dennis (IRE)**[4] 247 9-8-13 **55** (v) JimmyQuinn 6 65
(J Pearce) *towards rr: hdwy 2f out: sn rdn and kpt on wl fnl f: nt rch wnr* **7/1**[3]

64-3 **3** ½ **Winthorpe (IRE)**[12] 169 6-9-0 **56** GrahamGibbons 5 65
(J J Quinn) *chsd ldrs: rdn wl over 1f out: kpt on same pce ins last* **9/2**[2]

0-25 **4** 1 ¼ **Doctor's Cave**[12] 170 4-9-4 **60** (b) AdrianTNicholls 2 65
(K O Cunningham-Brown) *a.p on inner: rdn along 2f out: drvn and kpt on same pce ent last* **12/1**

-102 **5** ¾ **Soba Jones**[7] 196 9-8-10 **55** JasonEdmunds(3) 1 58
(J Balding) *chsd ldrs: rdn along 2f out: kpt on same pce appr last* **10/1**

00-0 **6** ¾ **Four Amigos (USA)**[32] 4 5-8-12 **57** SilvestreDeSousa(3) 8 57
(D Nicholls) *chsd wnr: rdn along 2f out: wknd appr last* **66/1**

5-21 **7** ¾ **Ruman (IRE)**[24] 67 4-9-3 **59** ChrisCatlin 9 57
(M J Attwater) *towards rr: effrt and sme hdwy 2f out: sn rdn: drvn and kpt on ins last: nvr nr ldrs* **4/1**[1]

006- **8** nk **Green Pirate**[44] 6638 4-9-4 **60** PaulFessey 3 59+
(R Craggs) *s.i.s and bhd: hdwy on inenr 2f out: rdn to chse ldrs over 1f out: sn wknd* **12/1**

30-1 **9** ¾ **Favouring (IRE)**[14] 144 4-8-11 **53** BrianReilly 10 48
(M C Chapman) *in tch: rdn along wl over 2f out: sn wknd* **8/1**

-031 **10** 5 **Roman Empire**[16] 127 6-9-3 **59** (b) NCallan 4 39
(K A Ryan) *midfield: rdn along and lost pl 1/2-way: sn towards rr* **4/1**[1]

-011 **11** 1 **Amanda's Lad (IRE)**[14] 146 6-8-10 **52** AdrianMcCarthy 11 29
(M C Chapman) *chsd ldrs: rdn over 2f out: sn drvn and wknd* **14/1**

05-5 **12** ¾ **Massey**[7] 196 10-8-5 **52** AndrewMullen(5) 7 27
(C R Dore) *in tch: pushed along 1/2-way: sn wknd* **40/1**

05-5 **13** 7 **State Dilemma (IRE)**[12] 164 5-9-0 **59** (v) PatrickMathers(3) 12 13
(D Shaw) *a rr* **25/1**

1m 16.13s (-0.77) **Going Correction** -0.075s/f (Stan) **13** Ran SP% **123.7**

Speed ratings (Par 101):102,101,100,98,97 96,95,95,94,87 86,85,75

CSF £254.15 CT £1305.38 TOTE £44.10: £6.90, £2.00, £2.20; EX 271.50.

Owner Mrs A K Petersen **Bred** C B Petersen **Trained** Newmarket, Suffolk

■ Stewards' Enquiry : Paul Fessey caution: allowed gelding to coast home with no assistance from saddle

FOCUS
Ordinary sprint handicap form, but the pace was true throughout and the form looks solid for the grade, rated through the placed horses.

Zorn Official explanation: trainer's representative said, regarding the improved form shown, gelding was unable to force the pace at Wolverhampton last time and benefited from a positive ride on this occasion

Green Pirate Official explanation: jockey said gelding reared as stalls opened

State Dilemma(IRE) Official explanation: jockey said gelding was never travelling

275 LITTLEWOODS BETDIRECT CONDITIONS STKS 6f (F)
3:50 (3:51) (Class 2) 3-Y-0+ **£12,954** (£3,854; £1,926; £962) **Stalls** Low

Form RPR

2/12 **1** **Cummiskey (IRE)**[4] 245 4-9-8 80 RobertWinston 4 95
(J A Osborne) *in tch on inner: hdwy 2f out: rdn over 1f out: led ent last: flashed tail: styd on* **5/1**[3]

41-5 **2** 1 ½ **Wessex (USA)**[27] 58 6-9-4 87 GrahamGibbons 11 87
(P A Blockley) *in tch: gd hdwy on outer 1/2-way: rdn to chal wl over 1f out and ev ch tl drvn and nt qckn ins last* **11/2**

01-1 **3** 1 ¾ **Pinchbeck**[23] 80 7-9-4 85 (p) MatthewHenry 5 82
(M A Jarvis) *towards rr: hdwy over 2f out: sn rdn and kpt on appr last* **4/1**[2]

50-2 **4** 1 **Rafferty (IRE)**[27] 58 7-9-4 87 NCallan 2 79
(T D Barron) *led: rdn wl over 1f out: drvn and hdd ent last: wknd* **5/1**[3]

5444 **5** ½ **Pawan (IRE)**[4] 244 6-9-4 77 AnnStokell 6 77
(Miss A Stokell) *dwlt and squeezed out s and bhd: hdwy on inner 2f out: sn rdn and kpt on ins last* **12/1**

-331 **6** 1 ½ **Desperate Dan**[4] 244 5-9-4 85 (b) SteveDrowne 12 73
(J A Osborne) *stdd s and bhd tl sme late hdwy* **7/2**[1]

30-0 **7** hd **Qadar (IRE)**[19] 116 4-9-4 89 HayleyTurner 9 72
(N P Littmoden) *bhd: rdn alon g over 2f out: kpt on towards fin* **11/1**

-403 **8** ½ **Gone'N'Dunnett (IRE)**[4] 244 7-9-4 66 (v) AdrianTNicholls 10 70
(Mrs C A Dunnett) *chsd ldrs: rdn over 2f out: grad wknd* **66/1**

-104 **9** 7 **Owed**[4] 245 4-9-4 73 (t) PaulHanagan 3 49
(Robert Gray) *cl up: rdn along over 2f out: grad wknd* **20/1**

3-22 **10** ¾ **Radiator Rooney (IRE)**[15] 138 3-8-3 68 (b) ChrisCatlin 7 43
(Patrick Morris, Ire) *chsd ldrs: rdn along wl over 2f out: sn wknd* **25/1**

0-52 **11** 4 **Money Mate (IRE)**[16] 128 3-8-5 65 MarkCoumbe 8 33
(C J Teague) *a rr* **100/1**

110/ **12** 17 **Gorse**[1666] 2971 11-9-4 JoeFanning 1 —
(Jamie Poulton) *chsd ldrs to 1/2-way: sn wknd* **14/1**

1m 15.52s (-1.38) **Going Correction** -0.075s/f (Stan)
WFA 3 from 4yo+ 15lb **12** Ran SP% **124.7**

Speed ratings (Par 109):106,104,101,100,99 97,97,96,87,86 81,58

CSF £33.63 TOTE £6.90: £1.90, £2.40, £1.50; EX 54.90.

Owner Ian Morgan **Bred** Schwindibode Ag **Trained** Upper Lambourn, Berks

FOCUS
A decent little conditions race and a taking performance from the relatively lightly-raced Cummiskey, who appears to be progressing fast, but the fifth and eighth limit the form.

NOTEBOOK
Cummiskey(IRE), who ran into a rival on a roll last time, put up a personal best to give weight all round and a beating to a number of horses rated as much as 9lb higher than him. His tail was going round like a windmill in the closing stages but he is not ungenuine and continues to progress nicely, although the Handicapper is now likely to take drastic action. (op 11-2)

Wessex(USA) was favoured by the weights and ran a solid race to finish a clear second. Equally effective on this surface as he is on Polytrack, he should continue to run well, although whether he can win in handicap company off this sort of mark is open to question. (op 7-1)

Pinchbeck, chasing a hat-trick, was another who had the weights in his favour. He kept on well from off the pace but he tended to hang left in the closing stages. (op 5-1)

Rafferty(IRE) is ideally suited by seven furlongs and was only running over a sprint distance for the third time in his career. He showed plenty of dash, though, and to his credit kept on quite well after being headed. (op 6-1)

Pawan(IRE) had a tough task at the weights but his style of running ensures he will always be running on at the finish of races. He is probably flattered by this performance simply because others were stopping in front. (op 18-1)

Desperate Dan took a keen hold in the early stages and got stuck in behind in the kickback. A bridle horse, he received a good ride from Spencer last time but is generally one to oppose.

276 FIRST PAST THE POST AT BETDIRECT H'CAP 1m (F)
4:20 (4:22) (Class 5) (0-75,75) 4-Y-0+ **£3,238** (£963; £481; £240) **Stalls** Low

Form RPR

21-5 **1** **Byron Bay**[20] 108 4-9-4 **75** TomEaves 9 85+
(I Semple) *dwlt and towards rr: stdy hdwy to trck ldrs after 3f: effrt to chse ldr 2f out: rdn to ld and hung bdly lft ins last: kpt o* **7/2**[1]

1124 **2** ¾ **Speed Dial Harry (IRE)**[12] 167 4-9-4 **75** (v) HayleyTurner 6 83
(K R Burke) *trckd ldrs: effrt 2f out: sn rdn and kpt on ins last* **9/2**[2]

000- **3** 2 **Set Alight**[49] 6586 5-8-8 **65** (v) PhillipMakin 2 69
(Mrs C A Dunnett) *cl up on inner: led over 4f out: rdn clr 2f out: drvn and hdd ins last: swtchd rt and no ex* **100/1**

P-11 **4** ½ **Samuel Charles**[21] 101 8-8-8 **70** AndrewMullen(5) 5 73
(C R Dore) *hld up: hdwy 2f out: rdn and kpt on appr last: nrst fin* **8/1**

06-2 **5** 5 **Flint River**[21] 100 8-9-2 **73** SteveDrowne 3 66
(H Morrison) *trckd ldrs: effrt and n.m.r over 2f out: sn rdn and no impression* **9/2**[2]

410- **6** 1 ¾ **Middle Eastern**[45] 6616 4-8-10 **67** GrahamGibbons 7 57
(P A Blockley) *chsd ldrs: rdn over 2f out and sn one pce* **14/1**

05-0 **7** 1 **Dudley Docker (IRE)**[7] 200 4-7-13 **63** DanielleMcCreery(7) 11 51+
(D Carroll) *v.s.a and bhd tl styd on fnl 2f* **66/1**

6003 **8** nk **Penwell Hill (USA)**[7] 200 7-8-6 **63** (b) ChrisCatlin 13 50
(M J Attwater) *prom: rdn over 2f out and sn wknd* **12/1**

30-4 **9** 1 ¼ **Tyrone Sam**[12] 164 4-8-10 **67** (b) NCallan 10 51
(K A Ryan) *racd wd: a towards rr* **8/1**

0-03 **10** 2 **Orpen Wide (IRE)**[21] 101 4-9-0 **71** BrianReilly 4 51
(M C Chapman) *bhd and rdn along 1/2-way: nvr a factor* **33/1**

000- **11** ½ **Hezaam (USA)**[10] 5628 5-8-7 **64** DeanMcKeown 8 43
(C W Fairhurst) *bhd fr 1/2-way* **50/1**

56-3 **12** 1 **Mission Affirmed (USA)**[21] 100 5-9-2 **73** (v) RobertWinston 1 50+
(T P Tate) *s.i.s: sn chsng ldrs on inner: rdn along 3f out and sn wknd* **5/1**[3]

50-4 **13** 2 ½ **True Night**[31] 15 9-8-10 **67** AdrianTNicholls 12 39
(D Nicholls) *led 3f: sn rdn along and wknd over 3f out* **20/1**

1m 42.96s (-1.64) **Going Correction** -0.075s/f (Stan) **13** Ran SP% **124.0**

Speed ratings (Par 103):105,104,102,101,96 95,94,93,92,90 89,88,86

CSF £19.08 CT £1416.77 TOTE £5.00: £2.20, £2.10, £16.60; EX 30.10 Place 6 £20.27, Place 5 £16.52.

Owner Ian Murray Tough **Bred** Ian Murray Tough **Trained** Carluke, S Lanarks

FOCUS
Solid handicap form for the grade, rated through the runner-up and fourth.

Dudley Docker(IRE) Official explanation: jockey said gelding hung left-handed

True Night Official explanation: jockey said gelding hung violently right-handed

T/Plt: £22.80 to a £1 stake. Pool: £45,258.05. 1,445.90 winning tickets. T/Qpdt: £12.90 to a £1 stake. Pool: £3,035.60. 173.40 winning tickets. JR

201 NAD AL SHEBA (L-H)
Thursday, February 2

OFFICIAL GOING: Dirt course - fast; turf course - good to firm

277a DUBAL TROPHY (H'CAP) (DIRT) 1m (D)
3:55 (3:56) (90-105,105) 4-Y-0+ **£41,569** (£12,790; £6,395; £3,197)

RPR

1 **Rock Music**[111] 5874 4-8-6 **90** KerrinMcEvoy 6 99
(Saeed Bin Suroor) *sn led: diputed 4f out: stl on bridle 2f out: led 1 1/2f out: comf* **9/4**[1]

2 2 ¾ **Little Jim (ARG)**[313] 733 6-9-6 **105** (vt) RichardMullen 5 107
(A Laird, UAE) *wl away: disp 4f out: hrd rdn 2 1/2f out: nt pce of wnr* **7/1**

3 6 ½ **Curule (USA)**[14] 152 9-8-11 **96** WSupple 3 85
(Doug Watson, UAE) *trckd ldr: ev ch ent st: nt pce of front two* **10/3**[2]

4 5 ¼ **Bo Bid (USA)**[321] 6-8-10 **95** (t) TedDurcan 2 74
(A Laird, UAE) *hld up in rr: t.k.h early on: trckd ldrs 4f out: nvr able to chal* **4/1**

5 2 **Bridge Loan**[130] 5496 4-8-7 **91** RHills 1 67
(Doug Watson, UAE) *broke akwardly: racd in rr but nt far away: rr on rail: n.m.r 3f out: n.d* **7/2**[3]

6 23 **Bold Demand**[334] 569 12-8-7 **91** PJSmullen 4 21
(R Bouresly, Kuwait) *trckd ldr wd: last 3f out: wknd: nvr threatened: virtually p.u* **33/1**

1m 37.14s **Going Correction** +0.375s/f (Slow) **6** Ran SP% **111.5**

Speed ratings: 116,113,106,101,99 76

Owner Godolphin **Bred** Mrs J Chandris **Trained** Newmarket, Suffolk

FOCUS
A disappointing turn out for the money and the form looks ordinary for the grade. Even in such a small field, the draw still looked to play its part with stall six beating five, three, two and one (the horse in four had little chance).

NOTEBOOK
Rock Music failed to progress from a very impressive maiden win on Lingfield's Polytrack when with David Loder last year but, making his debut for Godolphin off the back of a 111-day break, he took well to this fast dirt surface and had this won some way out. He was getting no less than 14lb from the runner-up, so he has a little way to go yet, but he clearly looks capable of fulfilling that initial promise and really should win again.

Little Jim(ARG), giving away upwards of 9lb all round, ran a fine race off the back of a 313-day absence. The winner had his measure early in the straight, but he kept on to the line and finished a long way clear of the remainder.

Curule(USA) shaped quite well when third in a nine-furlong handicap here two weeks previously, so this was pretty disappointing.

Bo Bid(USA) was well below his best on his return from a 321-day absence.

Bridge Loan, very useful when trained by Jeremy Noseda, including on Polytrack, was disappointing on his debut for a new trainer and first run in Dubai, but can be forgiven this. Drawn poorly in stall one, he was soon stuck behind horses on the inside of the track and unsurprisingly failed to pick up. He can do better.

278a DUBAL STKS (H'CAP) (TURF) 1m (T)

4:25 (4:25) (90-105,105) 4-Y-0+ **£41,569** (£12,790; £6,395; £3,197)

RPR

1 **Cashier**[138] [5287] 4-8-9 **94** .... TedDurcan 9 101+
(J H M Gosden) *trckd ldr: rdn to chal 2 1/2f out: led 1 1/2f out: r.o wl* **10/3**[2]

2 1 3/4 **Desert Destiny**[124] [5607] 6-9-3 **101** ....(vt) LDettori 6 102
(Saeed Bin Suroor) *mid-div: trckd ldrs 3f out: n.m.r 2 1/2f out: plld out 1 1/2f out: r.o* **3/1**[1]

3 hd **Azarole (IRE)**[14] [149] 5-9-6 **105** .... JohnEgan 4 105
(J S Moore) *racd in rr: nrly last 3f out: rdn to cl in centre: r.o wl: nrst fin* **5/1**[3]

4 3/4 **Lundy's Lane (IRE)**[14] [153] 6-9-4 **102** .... RyanMoore 14 101
(S Seemar, UAE) *mid-div wd: clsd 4f out: ev ch 3f out: disp 2 1/2f out: nt qckn* **7/1**

5 1 3/4 **Persian Majesty (IRE)**[125] [5589] 6-9-0 **98** .... SRandolph 5 93
(H J Brown, South Africa) *racd in rr: last in st on rail: n.m.r 3f out: r.o without threatening: nrst fin* **40/1**

6 1/2 **Alshawameq (IRE)**[14] [151] 5-8-7 **91** .... RHills 13 85
(Doug Watson, UAE) *racd 4th: ev ch 3f out: one pce* **12/1**

7 3 1/2 **Red Crescent (SAF)**[14] [149] 9-8-7 **91** ....(b) RichardMullen 1 77
(A Selvaratnam, UAE) *led tl 2 1/2f out: wknd* **40/1**

8 nse **Hurricane James (IRE)**[124] [5640] 4-9-5 **104** ....(t) TPO'Shea 10 88
(E Charpy, UAE) *mid-div: rdn 3f out: no prog* **14/1**

9 2 3/4 **Blazing Ability (USA)**[76] 7-8-10 **95** ....(t) WSupple 8 73
(Doug Watson, UAE) *hld up in rr: n.d* **12/1**

10 1 1/2 **Baaridd**[64] 8-9-2 **100** .... JMurtagh 2 76
(D Selvaratnam, UAE) *settled rr on rail: n.m.r 3f out: nt rcvr* **20/1**

11 20 **Legal Approach**[329] [597] 7-8-11 **96** .... ASuborics 11 25
(R Bouresly, Kuwait) *trckd ldrs: ev ch 3f out: wknd: virtually p.u* **66/1**

12 5 3/4 **Pango**[14] [151] 7-8-11 **96** .... MJKinane 3 11
(H Morrison) *mid-div: n.m.r 3f out: wknd: virtually p.u* **13/2**

P **Royal Beacon**[693] [1001] 6-8-10 **95** ....(b) GBirrer 12 —
(Christian Wroe, UAE) *slowly away: racd in rr: p.u early on* **100/1**

1m 39.24s **Going Correction** +0.525s/f (Yiel) 14 Ran SP% **124.8**
Speed ratings: 108,106,106,105,103 103,99,99,96,95 75,69,—

Owner Sheikh Mohammed **Bred** Lord Vestey **Trained** Newmarket, Suffolk

FOCUS
A very good handicap and a reasonable pace from the start resulted in a winning time over a second faster than the race won by Pentecost later on the card.

NOTEBOOK
Cashier ◆ progressed nicely in England last season and continued his improvement on his first run in Dubai by readily defying a 3lb higher mark than when winning the Ayrshire Handicap on his last start 138 days previously. Given this was just the sixth outing of his career, there should be plenty more to come and he must be kept on the right side of.
Desert Destiny, a very respectable sixth of 30 in the Cambridgeshire on his last start 124 days previously, was racing off a mark 1lb lower than when winning at last year's Carnival. Having travelled throughout, it initially looked as though his jockey had waited too long to ask for an effort, but he did not close as one might have hoped in the last furlong in any case. He may have needed this first run back, but this effort did raise questions about his attitude.
Azarole(IRE) confirmed the promise he showed when second over seven and half furlongs on his debut in Dubai two weeks previously, but basically got going too late and was never in a winning position. Ridden more positively, he should do better again.
Lundy's Lane(IRE), a little unlucky in a similar event two weeks previously, did not look to have any excuses this time.
Persian Majesty(IRE) ◆ did not progress as one might have hoped for Peter Harris/Walter Swinburn after winning the Listed Hampton Court Stakes at Royal Ascot on just his second start, but this was an eye-catching introduction to racing in Dubai. Going very well at the top of the straight, he appeared to have had to wait for a gap and basically got going far too late over a trip shorter than he usually races over. He should be better for this outing, and is one to follow this Carnival.
Pango shaped so well on his debut in Dubai, but something must have been amiss.

279a DUBAL CUP (H'CAP) (DIRT) 1m 4f (D)

4:55 (4:55) (90-105,102) 4-Y-0+ **£41,569** (£12,790; £6,395; £3,197)

RPR

1 **Muhareb (USA)**[35] 7-8-10 **93** ....(t) WSupple 8 103
(Doug Watson, UAE) *racd ldr's quarters: disp 3f out: led 2f out: r.o* **10/3**[2]

2 1 **Clasp**[14] [152] 4-8-6 **91** ....(t) TedDurcan 4 101
(A Laird, UAE) *trckd ldr centre: chal wd: disp 2 1/2f out: one pce* **12/1**

3 4 1/2 **Change The Grange (AUS)**[14] [152] 8-9-1 **97** ....(ve) EddieAhern 9 100
(M C Tam, Macau) *led tl hdd 2f out: r.o for press: one pce* **16/1**

4 5 1/2 **Forty Hablador (ARG)**[41] 5-8-10 **93** .... RyanMoore 3 87
(S Seemar, UAE) *hld up in rr: rdn to cl ent st: wknd* **16/1**

5 6 3/4 **Craft Fair (IRE)**[162] 4-8-12 **98** ....(t) LDettori 2 81
(Saeed Bin Suroor) *trckd ldr rail early: moved off rail ent st: wknd* **6/5**[1]

6 4 1/4 **Zenato (GER)**[82] [6339] 5-9-6 **102** .... JMurtagh 1 80
(F Reuterskiold, Sweden) *hld up rr: prog on rail to trck ldrs 4f out: wknd* **12/1**

7 7 1/2 **Sekula Pata (NZ)**[7] [207] 7-8-9 **91** ow1 ....(p) GBirrer 7 58
(Christian Wroe, UAE) *broke akwardly & stmbld: settled in rr: wd: reminders 6f and 5f out: nvr involved* **40/1**

8 5 **Zabeel Palace**[193] [3782] 4-8-6 **91** ow1 ....(t) KerrinMcEvoy 6 50
(I Mohammed, UAE) *hld up last: wd: n.d* **7/1**[3]

9 8 3/4 **Kalibanos (BRZ)**[63] 5-8-10 **93** .... MAlmeida 5 38
(C Morgado, Brazil) *mid-div: wknd 5f out* **7/1**[3]

2m 31.46s
WFA 4 from 5yo+ 3lb 9 Ran SP% **123.1**

Owner Prince Turky Bin Bader **Bred** Katalpa Farm **Trained** United Arab Emirates
■ Muhareb completed a double for Doug Watson following his success with Dubai Honor earlier on the card.

FOCUS
Not that strong a race for the grade, and those drawn high were again at an advantage.

NOTEBOOK
Muhareb(USA) came down a long way in the weights on his first few starts in Dubai, but is taking advantage now and once again showed his liking for this fast dirt surface to complete the hat-trick off a mark 13lb higher than when starting his winning run. This was a very good effort and he seems to be thriving.
Clasp did not have things go his way when a beaten favourite over nine furlongs here on his previous start, but this longer trip gave him more time to find his stride and the smaller field would also have suited better. In the end, though, he was basically outstayed and probably did well to finish as close as he did given his only previous success came over an extended six furlongs.
Change The Grange(AUS) got his own way out in front from his favourable wide draw, but he usually races over shorter and did not appear to stay.
Craft Fair(IRE), a ten-furlong winner on easy ground in France for Andre Fabre, failed to show his best on his first start on dirt and debut for Godolphin. His inside draw would have been far from ideal.

280a DUBAL AL RASHIDIYA (GROUP 3) (TURF) 1m 194y(T)

5:25 (5:25) 4-Y-0+ **£75,581** (£23,255; £11,627; £5,813)

RPR

1 **Linngari (IRE)**[152] [4943] 4-9-0 **113** .... RyanMoore 4 115
(H J Brown, South Africa) *disp ld early: kicked clr 2 1/2f out: r.o wl: jst hld on* **7/1**

2 1/2 **Greys Inn (USA)**[93] [6223] 6-9-0 **117** .... KShea 8 114
(M F De Kock, South Africa) *in rr of main gp: 2nd last ent st: prog wd 2 1/2f out: chal fnl f: nrst fin* **4/1**[2]

3 1 **Latino Magic (IRE)**[95] 6-9-0 **109** .... LDettori 1 112
(R J Osborne, Ire) *hld up in last on rail: trckd ldrs 2 1/2f out: n.m.r: rdn to cl 1 1/2f out: r.o* **14/1**

4 1 3/4 **Trademark (SAF)**[14] [153] 10-9-0 **109** ....(bt) TedDurcan 5 109
(A Laird, UAE) *slowly away: hld up in rr: prog to trck ldrs 3f out: rdn 2 1/2f out: one pce* **14/1**

5 shd **Shakis (IRE)**[14] [153] 6-9-0 **112** ....(t) RHills 9 108
(Doug Watson, UAE) *mid-div travelling wl: ev ch 3f out: one pce* **9/2**[3]

6 shd **Etesaal (USA)**[134] [5403] 6-9-0 **110** ....(t) KerrinMcEvoy 7 108
(I Mohammed, UAE) *trckd ldrs: dropped to rr 3f out: n.m.r 2f out: n.d* **11/2**

7 3/4 **Near Dock (GER)**[14] [154] 5-9-0 **108** .... ASuborics 3 107
(V Smith) *trckd ldrs: plld hrd: rdn 2 1/2f out: nt qckn* **18/1**

8 nk **Alayan (IRE)**[124] [5641] 4-9-0 **113** .... MJKinane 6 106
(John M Oxx, Ire) *disp ld early: rdn 3f out: ev ch: outpcd and wknd* **3/1**[1]

9 3 3/4 **Key Of Destiny (SAF)**[14] [153] 8-9-0 **113** .... JMurtagh 10 99
(M F De Kock, South Africa) *trckd ldrs wd: 3rd 2 1/2f out: nt qckn* **18/1**

10 2 3/4 **Boule D'Or (IRE)**[14] [153] 5-9-0 **107** .... NigelDay 2 94
(J Akehurst) *hld up in rr: last and wd into st: n.d* **14/1**

1m 51.27s **Going Correction** +0.525s/f (Yiel) 10 Ran SP% **121.6**
Speed ratings: 109,108,107,106,106 105,105,105,101,99

Owner Jim Atkinson & P Walraninski **Bred** Hh Aga Khan's Stud **Trained** South Africa

FOCUS
A good Group Three and very competitive, but the pace was just steady for most of the way and that would not have suited a few of these. The progressive Linngari got the run of the race under a good ride and just held off the fellow South African-trained Greys Inn to record his first success at this level.

NOTEBOOK
Linngari(IRE) ◆ was most progressive when trained by Sir Michael Stoute for the Aga Khan last season and certainly looked to have Group-race potential, so it was a surprise to see him off-loaded by that trainer/owner combination, but their loss is clearly his new connections' gain. Ideally placed given the gallop was steady, he showed a decent change of pace when asked for his effort and had just enough left to hold off the runner-up. Given he got the run of the race, and several of those in behind would have been better suited by a stronger pace, he could be considered a somewhat fortunate winner, but his jockey thinks he can improve again. That would make sense given his RPR's - 64, 90, 92+, 103, 68, 112, 119, 119 (latest) - point to pretty consistent improvement throughout his career, and he must be kept on the right side of.
Greys Inn(USA) ◆, a high-class South African-trained runner, was below form when an 80/1 shot in the Melbourne Cup on his last start three months previously. Given he tends to race over further, and gained his last success at the previous Carnival over a mile and a half, he did very well to get so close to the winner, who enjoyed the run of the race in a steadily-run affair. On this evidence, he could well win over this distance at this sort of level providing the gallop is strong, but he will also have the option of stepping back up in trip.
Latino Magic(IRE), who ran several good races at last year's Carnival without managing to win, picked up a handicap in his native Ireland off a mark of 102 last summer. Returned to Dubai, he ran yet another good race in defeat and is most admirable.
Trademark(SAF), now ten, is still very capable, as he showed when winning a Listed race at Abu Dhabi towards the end of last year. This was another very creditable effort.
Shakis(IRE), a promising third and unlucky not to have finished closer in a handicap off a mark of a 112 on his reappearance, would have found this tougher and ran respectably.
Etesaal(USA), a Listed winner at Goodwood on his last start for Godolphin 134 days previously, might not have minded the steady pace as much as most, but did not get a clear run when looking to pick up and was well held.
Near Dock(GER) would have appreciated the switch to turf having run poorly on dirt on his debut for these connections, but the steady pace would not have suited.
Alayan(IRE), a little disappointing in a Group Two in France when last seen 124 days previously, again failed to run to best. His potential was there for all to see on a number of occasions last season, but he has something to prove off the back of this effort.
Boule D'Or(IRE) shaped well when fourth on his return to Dubai in a handicap off a mark of 107, but this would have been tougher and the steady pace was totally against him.

281a DUBAL POTLINE CUP (H'CAP) (TURF) 7f 110y(D)

5:55 (5:55) 4-Y-0+ **£66,133** (£20,348; £10,174; £5,087)

RPR

1 **Caesar Beware (IRE)**[147] [5073] 4-8-11 **105** .... TedDurcan 3 116
(A Laird, UAE) *slowly away: hld up in rr: 2nd last 3f out: swtchd wd: r.o wl: led fnl 110yds* **14/1**

2 3 3/4 **Suggestive**[55] [6530] 8-9-1 **108** ....(b) NickyMackay 2 112
(W J Haggas) *racd in 3rd on rail: t.k.h: prog on rail 2 1/2f out: r.o to take 2nd* **11/2**[3]

3 1/2 **Sabbeeh (USA)**[103] [6017] 5-9-0 **107** ....(t) LDettori 7 110
(Saeed Bin Suroor) *led main gp: ev ch 3f out: outpcd* **11/2**[3]

4 nse **Brunel (IRE)**[14] [154] 5-9-4 **111** ....(bt) KerrinMcEvoy 9 114
(I Mohammed, UAE) *led: clr early stages: stl clr 2f out: hdd fnl 110yds: wknd* **10/1**

5 3/4 **King Jock (USA)**[14] [149] 5-9-1 **108** .... TPO'Shea 4 109
(E Charpy, UAE) *mid-div: travelling wl 4f out: rapid prog to chal 1 1/2f out: nt qckn* **7/2**[1]

6 2 1/4 **Kandidate**[14] [151] 4-9-5 **112** .... RyanMoore 5 108
(C E Brittain) *mid-div: ev ch 3f out: nt qckn* **5/1**[2]

7 1 1/2 **Starpix (FR)**[7] [206] 4-9-6 **113** .... JMurtagh 10 106
(H J Brown, South Africa) *settled in last: n.d* **16/1**

8 4 1/4 **Democratic Deficit (IRE)**[14] [153] 4-9-2 **109** .... MJKinane 1 92
(J S Bolger, Ire) *mid-div on rail: n.m.r 2 1/2f out: swtchd: nvr a threat* **6/1**

9 9 **National Icon (SAF)**[313] [736] 6-9-3 **110** ....(t) JBekker 11 73
(D Maroun, South Africa) *in rr out wd: n.d* **25/1**

10 7 1/4 **So Will I**[7] [201] 5-8-10 **104** ....(t) RHills 8 51
(Doug Watson, UAE) *trckd ldrs: ev ch wd 3f out: nt qckn: eased fnl 1 1/2f out* **10/1**

11 17 **Coral Gables (IND)**[165] 6-8-7 **100** .... RichardMullen 6 10
(L D'Silva, India) *slowly away: n.d: virtually p.u* **25/1**

1m 31.18s **Going Correction** +0.525s/f (Yiel) 11 Ran SP% **122.4**
Speed ratings: 117,113,112,112,111 109,108,103,94,87 70

Owner H E Sheikh Rashid Bin Mohammed **Bred** Glending Bloodstock **Trained** United Arab Emirates

■ Caesar Beware was the second leg of a double for Ted Durcan, who had earlier won on Cashier.

FOCUS

A high-class handicap in which the former classy juvenile Caesar Beware produced a Group-class performance to trounce some smart rivals. Despite Brunel leading at what looked a reasonable pace, the chasing pack did not actually seem to go that fast, so Caesar Beware had quite a lot of ground to make up in the straight.

NOTEBOOK

Caesar Beware(IRE) ◆ looked potentially high-class when trained by Henry Candy as a juvenile, but failed to confirm that last year off the back of a far from ideal preparation - his was prepared to race on the dirt at last year's Carnival but did not take to the surface and was returned to Candy. However, given another chance in Dubai, he has presumably done a fair bit of his work on turf this time and, clearly training well enough to make the course, looked the horse he once promised to be with a mightily-impressive performance. Although there was a clear leader, the chasing pack did not look to be going all that fast and he still had a lot to do in the straight but, once switched wide for a run, he was able to sustain quite a taking change of pace to draw clear of some pretty smart rivals. He is quite clearly a Group horse and the Dubai Duty Free Stakes on World Cup night could a worthwhile target - his winning RPR of 118 would have put him second in last season's renewal - although he would have to prove his stamina for an extended mile.

Suggestive, racing off the same mark as when winning quite a competitive handicap on his Polytrack debut at Wolverhampton last time, ran well behind the impressive winner. He should continue to go well, while connections will also have the option of trying the dirt surface out here.

Sabbeeh(USA), who ran consistently well in defeat throughout last season, ran another good race on his return to Dubai off the back of a 103-day break.

Brunel(IRE), returned to turf, got his own way in front and can have no excuses whatsoever.

King Jock(USA), an impressive winner over course and distance on his previous start, would have found this tougher off a 6lb higher mark and ran well. His effort is all the more creditable given he was one of the first horses to try and reel in the long-time leader Brunel, and he remains one to have on your side.

Kandidate, like King Jock, won well in a similar race on his previous start, but would have found this tougher off a 7lb higher mark.

Democratic Deficit(IRE) failed to step up on the form he showed on his first run in Dubai.

282a DUBAL PLATE (H'CAP) (TURF) 1m (T)

6:25 (6:26) (90-105,105) 4-Y-O+ £41,569 (£12,790; £6,395; £3,197)

RPR

1 **Pentecost**[14] [149] 7-9-3 **101** .... LDettori 11 107
(A M Balding) *t.k.h in mid-div: swtchd wd 2 1/2f out: rdn 1 1/2f out: prog to ld last strides* **5/1**[3]

2 *nse* **Spirit Of France (IRE)**[111] [5874] 4-8-8 **93** .... GBirrer 8 98
(Christian Wroe, UAE) *led early: trckd ldr: 3rd into st: nt qckn 2 1/2f out: hdd last strides* **9/1**

3 *1 ½* **Falstaff (IRE)**[242] [2328] 4-9-4 **102** .... KShea 10 105
(M F De Kock, South Africa) *hld up in last: 4th into st: stl last 1 1/2f out: r.o wl: nrst fin* **4/1**[1]

4 *nk* **Little Good Bay**[14] [149] 6-8-8 **93** .... (b) RichardMullen 2 94
(A Laird, UAE) *settled in rr: n.m.r on rail 3f out: nt clr run 2f out: nvr able to chal* **16/1**

5 *½* **Bahiano (IRE)**[27] [54] 5-8-6 **90** .... EddieAhern 1 91
(C E Brittain) *mid-div on rail: ev ch 2 1/2f out: n.m.r: r.o* **14/1**

6 *2* **Excellento (USA)**[14] [153] 6-8-12 **97** .... (b) TPO'Shea 7 93
(E Charpy, UAE) *settled in rr: rdn 3f out: sme late prog: nrst fin* **33/1**

7 *nk* **Festive Style (SAF)**[14] [155] 6-8-10 **95** .... TedDurcan 3 91
(J Noseda) *slowly away: in rr of main gp: n.m.r 3f out: n.d* **16/1**

8 *nk* **Jader (IRE)**[72] 4-9-1 **99** .... (b[1]) RyanMoore 4 95
(S Seemar, UAE) *mid-div: n.m.r 2 1/2f out: swtchd wd: n.d* **25/1**

9 *nk* **Amandus (USA)**[14] [149] 6-8-10 **95** .... (be) WSupple 6 90
(Doug Watson, UAE) *trckd ldrs: disp 2 1/2f out: ev ch 1f out: wknd* **28/1**

10 *nk* **Jalamid (IRE)**[124] [5612] 4-9-2 **100** .... (t) RHills 9 95
(J H M Gosden) *settled in rr: n.m.r 3f out: nvr able to chal* **9/2**[2]

11 *1 ¼* **Wazir (USA)**[179] [4184] 4-8-7 **91** .... KerrinMcEvoy 5 84
(J H M Gosden) *settled in rr: t.k.h: rdn to cl 3f out: n.m.r 1 1/2f out: nt rcvr* **16/1**

12 *1* **Setembro Chove (BRZ)**[89] 5-9-6 **105** .... MJKinane 12 95
(P Nickel Filho, Brazil) *mid-div out wd: sme prog 3f out: ev ch 1 1/2f out: btn whn hmpd 1f out* **11/2**

13 *2 ¼* **Cat Belling (IRE)**[364] [273] 6-9-3 **101** .... PJSmullen 14 87
(R Bouresly, Kuwait) *prom: led after 1f: hdd 1f out: wknd* **25/1**

14 *½* **Walmooh**[49] 10-9-6 **105** .... (vt) JMurtagh 13 89
(D Selvaratnam, UAE) *trckd ldrs: 4th into st: ev ch 2 1/2f out: one pce* **16/1**

1m 40.38s **Going Correction** +0.525s/f (Yiel) **14** Ran SP% **124.5**

Speed ratings: 103,102,101,101,100 98,98,98,97,97 96,95,92,92

Owner J C, J R And S R Hitchins **Bred** Miss S N Ralphs **Trained** Kingsclere, Hants

FOCUS

A good handicap, but the early pace was pretty ordinary and the winning time was over a second slower than that taken by Cashier earlier on the card.

NOTEBOOK

Pentecost shaped well on his debut in Dubai when third in a similar event over seven and a half furlongs two weeks previously and built on that promise under a fine ride from the ever-brilliant Frankie Dettori. He should be raised too much for this and should remain competitive.

Spirit Of France(IRE), a very useful handicapper and noticeably tough when trained by Mark Johnston, ran right up to his best on his debut for a new trainer and first run in Dubai. While this was promising, he will inevitably go up in the weights and things will not get any easier.

Falstaff(IRE) ◆, a smart performer when trained by Aidan O'Brien, had not been seen since finishing last in the 2005 French Derby. Returning from a 242-day absence and both making his debut for a new yard and having his first start in Dubai, he finished well from a long way off the pace and offered plenty of encouragement in third. He can be expected to improve for the run and could well find success at the Carnival.

Little Good Bay is not that easy to win with these days, but this was a solid effort and he may have been even closer with a clearer run.

Bahiano(IRE) ran a very respectable race and is another who would have been even closer with a clear run.

Festive Style(SAF) ran better than on her first run for this stable and is going the right way.

Jalamid(IRE) was pretty progressive for these connections in England last year but, switched to Dubai off the back of a 124-day break, he proved a little disappointing, even allowing for him not getting that clear a run when initially trying to pick up. Perhaps a stronger-run race will suit better.

Wazir(USA), upped to a mile for the first time on his debut in Dubai, lost any chance he may have had when meeting trouble in the last couple of furlongs.

[248] WOLVERHAMPTON (A.W) (L-H)

Friday, February 3

OFFICIAL GOING: Standard

Wind: Nil Weather: Dull with some drizzle

283 JOAN COOPER 80TH BIRTHDAY AMATEUR RIDERS' H'CAP 1m 4f 50y(P)

1:50 (1:51) (Class 5) (0-70,75) 4-Y-O+ £3,123 (£968; £484; £242) Stalls Low

Form RPR

65-1 1 **Bid For Fame (USA)**[1] [270] 9-10-9 **65** 5ex .... MrSPearce[(7)] 4 66
(J Pearce) *hld up: hdwy 3f out: r.o to ld post* **5/1**[2]

34-1 2 *shd* **Countrywide Luck**[9] [186] 5-11-12 **75** 5ex .... MrsEmmaLittmoden 3 76
(N P Littmoden) *set slow pce: hdd over 9f out: chsd clr ldr: rdn over 1f out: led ins fnl f: hdd post* **6/1**[3]

0-33 3 *2 ½* **Lake Wakatipu**[11] [174] 4-9-11 **56** oh6 .... MissMMullineaux[(7)] 1 53
(M Mullineaux) *hld up and bhd: hdwy on ins wl over 1f out: kpt on ins fnl f* **10/1**

0-00 4 *nk* **Golden Boot**[4] [250] 7-10-13 **62** .... MrSWalker 2 58
(A Bailey) *hld up and bhd: hdwy over 2f out: one pce fnl f* **9/2**[1]

00-5 5 *nk* **Polish Power (GER)**[32] [13] 6-10-4 **56** oh6 .... (p) MrsSMoore[(3)] 10 52
(J S Moore) *hld up: hdwy over 3f out: one pce fnl f* **12/1**

130- 6 *hd* **Court Of Appeal**[160] [4762] 9-11-2 **68** .... (tp) MissLEllison[(3)] 6 64
(B Ellison) *hld up: hdwy 3f out: rdn and edgd lft wl over 1f out: one pce fnl f* **12/1**

0-61 7 *4* **Activist**[21] [103] 8-10-7 **61** .... (p) MissDAllman[(5)] 7 50
(D Carroll) *nvr trbld ldrs* **11/1**

10-1 8 *1* **Cumbrian Knight (IRE)**[28] [52] 8-10-9 **63** .... MissNJefferson[(5)] 8 51
(J M Jefferson) *s.i.s: hld up and bhd: hdwy over 3f out: wknd wl over 1f out* **5/1**[2]

0-36 9 *½* **Zalkani (IRE)**[13] [167] 6-11-0 **70** .... MrRElliott[(7)] 12 57
(B G Powell) *plld hrd: sn chsng ldr: led over 9f out: wl clr over 6f out: stl 30l ahd 3f out: wknd and hdd ins fnl f* **10/1**

6/5- 10 *1 ¼* **Bolshoi Ballet**[182] [275] 8-10-1 **57** .... (b) MrBMcHugh[(7)] 11 42
(R A Fahey) *nvr nr ldrs* **20/1**

00-0 11 *10* **Cool Bathwick (IRE)**[6] [229] 7-10-2 **56** oh1 .... MrStephenHarrison[(5)] 9 25
(G H Yardley) *hld up: rdn over 4f out: sn bhd* **66/1**

2m 47.15s (4.73) **Going Correction** -0.075s/f (Stan)

WFA 4 from 5yo+ 3lb **11** Ran SP% **114.0**

Speed ratings (Par 103):81,80,79,79,78 78,76,75,75,74 67

CSF £33.92 CT £286.99 TOTE £6.30: £2.00, £1.80, £1.80; EX 36.80.

Owner Simon Pearce **Bred** Swifty Farms, Don Myers And Dana Myers **Trained** Newmarket, Suffolk

FOCUS

An extraordinary race with Zalkani pulling his way into a big lead after they had crawled for the first quarter-mile. The form looks messy and the proximity of the third and fifth emphasises the point.

Court Of Appeal Official explanation: jockey said gelding had breathing problem

284 BETDIRECT ON 0800 211 222 (S) H'CAP 2m 119y(P)

2:20 (2:20) (Class 6) (0-60,58) 4-Y-O+ £2,388 (£705; £352) Stalls Low

Form RPR

05-5 1 **Bobby Kennard**[28] [55] 7-9-7 **58** .... ShaneKelly 4 63
(J A Osborne) *led 12f out: rdn and hung lft over 1f out: r.o* **15/8**[1]

164- 2 *½* **Three Boars**[132] [4683] 4-8-11 **54** .... (b) NCallan 5 58
(S Gollings) *t.k.h: hdwy on ins to chse wnr over 2f out: sn rdn: styd on towards fin* **7/1**[2]

4-23 3 *5* **Zaffeu**[6] [230] 5-8-12 **49** .... FergusSweeney 2 47
(A G Juckes) *hld up: hdwy over 5f out: rdn over 2f out: wknd over 1f out* **15/8**[1]

00-2 4 *hd* **Another Con (IRE)**[16] [141] 5-8-9 **46** ow1 .... DaneO'Neill 3 44
(A M Hales) *prom: wnt 2nd 9f out: rdn over 3f out: wknd over 1f out* **15/2**[3]

/6-4 5 *13* **Ambersong**[21] [103] 8-8-8 **45** .... RobertWinston 6 28
(A W Carroll) *dwlt: rdn over 4f out: a bhd* **8/1**

00/0 6 *9* **Christmas Truce (IRE)**[9] [186] 7-8-11 **55** .... JamesDoyle[(7)] 1 27
(Ms J S Doyle) *led over 4f: prom: rdn 4f out: wknd over 3f out* **33/1**

3m 40.89s (-2.24) **Going Correction** -0.075s/f (Stan)

WFA 4 from 5yo+ 6lb **6** Ran SP% **107.9**

Speed ratings (Par 101):102,101,99,99,93 88

CSF £14.55 TOTE £3.10: £1.20, £2.70; EX 11.90.The winner was bought in for 4,750gns.

Owner J A Osborne **Bred** Stowell Hill Ltd And Major And Mrs R B Kennard **Trained** Upper Lambourn, Berks

FOCUS

A weak seller that could be rated higher but the form is not convincing.

285 BETDIRECT.CO.UK H'CAP (DIV I) 1m 141y(P)

2:50 (2:51) (Class 6) (0-58,58) 4-Y-O+ £2,388 (£705; £352) Stalls Low

Form RPR

-306 1 **Danettie**[4] [252] 5-8-12 **54** .... ShaneKelly 8 59
(W M Brisbourne) *a.p: rdn to ld over 2f out: drvn out* **9/1**

-000 2 *hd* **Farnborough (USA)**[6] [229] 5-8-5 **54** .... JamesDoyle[(7)] 3 59
(R J Price) *hld up in mid-div: rdn and hdwy on ins over 2f out: ev ch wl ins fnl f: r.o* **7/1**[2]

4003 3 *½* **Risk Free**[4] [251] 9-9-0 **56** .... (bt) JamieSpencer 7 60
(P D Evans) *hld up and bhd: rdn and hdwy whn hung lft fr over 1f out: r.o ins fnl f* **7/1**[2]

4-23 4 *shd* **Melee**[14] [162] 4-8-11 **53** .... NCallan 2 57
(J Jay) *led early: a.p: rdn over 2f out: swtchd rt ins fnl f: kpt on* **7/1**[2]

63-1 5 *nk* **Latif (USA)**[11] [175] 5-8-2 **51** 6ex .... LiamJones[(7)] 11 54
(Ms Deborah J Evans) *hld up: rdn and hdwy over 2f out: r.o ins fnl f* **9/2**[1]

5-26 6 *shd* **Seattle Robber**[21] [107] 4-9-2 **58** .... (p) FergalLynch 6 61
(P A Blockley) *hld up and bhd: rdn and hdwy on ins over 1f out: r.o* **9/1**

062- 7 *nk* **Hiawatha (IRE)**[58] [6522] 7-8-10 **52** .... ChrisCatlin 5 54+
(A M Hales) *hld up and bhd: hdwy fnl f: nrst fin* **16/1**

0-30 8 *shd* **Wrenlane**[14] [163] 5-8-13 **55** .... (b[1]) TonyHamilton 1 57
(R A Fahey) *led over 7f out: rdn and hdd over 2f out: no ex ins fnl f* **16/1**

4-50 9 *3* **Pheckless**[6] [232] 7-8-6 **48** ow1 .... RobertWinston 9 44
(J M Bradley) *s.i.s: nvr trbld ldrs* **20/1**

1-42 10 *hd* **Prince Of Gold**[5] [240] 6-8-10 **52** .... (b) GrahamGibbons 13 51+
(R Hollinshead) *hld up in tch: rdn over 2f out: wkng whn hmpd ins fnl f* **8/1**[3]

35-2 11 *nk* **Musical Gift**[3] [258] 6-8-1 **50** .... (v) KevinGhunowa[(7)] 12 45
(P A Blockley) *t.k.h in tch: rdn over 2f out: wknd wl over 1f out* **7/1**[2]

00-0 12 *6* **Feathergrass (IRE)**[21] [104] 4-8-10 **55** .... RichardThomas[(3)] 4 37
(B S Rothwell) *hld up in mid-div: rdn over 4f out: wknd 3f out* **80/1**

010/ **13** *8* **Mujarad (USA)**[95] 6208 6-8-8 **57**........................(t) RDEgan(7) 10 22
(P M Mooney, Ire) *sn led: hdd over 7f out: prom tl rdn and wknd 3f out* **80/1**

1m 50.55s (-1.21) **Going Correction** -0.075s/f (Stan) 13 Ran SP% **118.3**
Speed ratings (Par 101):102,101,101,101,101 100,100,100,97,97 97,92,85
CSF £69.26 CT £471.90 TOTE £13.70: £3.60, £2.10, £2.60; EX 94.50.
Owner J Oldknow A & H Johnstone & B Carter **Bred** John E Oldknow **Trained** Great Ness, Shropshire
■ Stewards' Enquiry : Jamie Spencer caution: used whip without giving gelding time to respond

FOCUS
This low-grade handicap was 0.6 seconds slower than the other division. The form looks fairly solid rated through the winner and third, although the fourth tempers confidence.
Risk Free Official explanation: jockey said gelding hung left in home straight

286 BETDIRECT FREEPHONE 0800 211 222 CLAIMING STKS 7f 32y(P)
3:20 (3:22) (Class 6) 3-Y-O £2,730 (£806; £403) Stalls High

Form RPR
-512 **1** **Inaminute (IRE)**[5] 241 3-8-8 55........................ PatCosgrave 9 61
(K R Burke) *sn w ldr: led 2f out: sn rdn: edgd lft 1f out: r.o wl* **11/10**[1]

00-3 **2** *2 ½* **Angelina Bankes**[18] 122 3-8-6 53........................ AdrianMcCarthy 5 53
(R A Harris) *led: rdn and hdd 2f out: one pce fnl f* **5/1**[3]

3 *3* **Glenargo (USA)** 3-8-0........................(t) RDEgan(7) 7 46
(P M Mooney, Ire) *s.i.s: hld up: hdwy on outside over 2f out: hung lft fr over 1f out: one pce* **22/1**

0-00 **4** *¾* **In The Fountain (IRE)**[11] 176 3-8-1 45 ow4.....(b[1]) RichardThomas(3) 2 41
(C A Dwyer) *prom: lost pl over 3f out: styd on ins fnl f: n.d* **33/1**

00-6 **5** *2 ½* **Bekoning (IRE)**[8] 199 3-8-6 54........................ RoryMoore(5) 1 42
(M Quinn) *wnt lft s: hld up and bhd: short-lived effrt over 2f out: btn whn nt clr run and swtchd rt ins fnl f* **18/1**

3-24 **6** *hd* **She Whispers (IRE)**[18] 122 3-8-6 54........................ RobertWinston 4 41+
(W M Brisbourne) *hld up: hdwy over 3f out: rdn 2f out: btn whn carried lft ins fnl f* **2/1**[2]

-520 **7** *2 ½* **Paris Power**[11] 176 3-8-10 45........................(v) DerekMcGaffin 3 33
(D Morris) *prom: rdn 3f out: wknd over 1f out: hmpd ins fnl f* **10/1**

0-00 **8** *15* **Blue Danielle (IRE)**[13] 165 3-7-9 40........................ DuranFentiman(5) 8 —
(A D Brown) *rdn virtually thrght: hdwy over 5f out: wknd 3f out* **66/1**

1m 30.42s (0.02) **Going Correction** -0.075s/f (Stan) 8 Ran SP% **120.8**
Speed ratings (Par 95):96,93,89,88,86 85,82,65
CSF £7.80 TOTE £2.10: £1.10, £1.60, £2.80; EX 7.60.
Owner Mrs Elaine M Burke **Bred** R Bailey **Trained** Middleham Moor, N Yorks
■ Stewards' Enquiry : Adrian McCarthy two-day ban: careless riding (Feb 14-15)
R D Egan two-day ban: careless riding (Feb 14-15)

FOCUS
A weak claimer and pretty straightforward form.

287 BE LUCKY @ LITTLEWOODSPOOLS.CO.UK H'CAP 5f 216y(P)
3:50 (3:51) (Class 6) (0-60,58) 3-Y-O £2,388 (£705; £352) Stalls Low

Form RPR
-022 **1** **Garstang**[6] 226 3-8-12 52........................(b) RobbieFitzpatrick 3 64
(Peter Grayson) *a.p: rdn over 2f out: led over 1f out: r.o wl* **5/2**[2]

5-60 **2** *1 ½* **Smile For Us**[16] 139 3-8-10 50........................(b[1]) TPQueally 4 57
(C Drew) *led: rdn whn hung rt and hdd over 1f out: hung lft ins fnl f: nt qckn* **50/1**

3-04 **3** *4* **Smart Ass (IRE)**[18] 120 3-8-10 50........................ FergalLynch 11 45
(J S Moore) *hld up and bhd: rdn and hdwy on outside over 2f out: kpt on ins fnl f* **7/1**[3]

5304 **4** *hd* **Twilight Avenger (IRE)**[7] 211 3-8-13 53........................(p) NCallan 5 47
(M J Polglase) *chsd ldr: rdn over 2f out: wknd ins fnl f* **8/1**

020- **5** *1 ¾* **Dora's Green**[132] 5465 3-9-0 54........................ FrancisNorton 12 43
(M Blanshard) *t.k.h in tch: edgd lft 4f out: rdn over 2f out: wknd over 1f out* **25/1**

0-6 **6** *nk* **Bella Fiorella (IRE)**[7] 211 3-8-7 54........................ JamesO'Reilly(7) 8 42
(T J Pitt) *mid-div: hdwy 4f out: rdn over 2f out: wknd over 1f out* **25/1**

406- **7** *2 ½* **Titus Wonder (IRE)**[190] 3886 3-8-11 58........................ KevinGhunowa(7) 2 39
(P A Blockley) *bhd: bmpd 4f out: nvr trbld ldrs* **40/1**

0-02 **8** *hd* **Mine The Balance (IRE)**[5] 239 3-8-10 50........................ SteveDrowne 9 30
(J R Best) *prom: rdn over 2f out: wknd wl over 1f out* **9/4**[1]

0-00 **9** *hd* **Jessica Wigmo**[18] 120 3-8-10 50........................ RobertWinston 6 30
(A W Carroll) *hld up in mid-div: hdwy whn nt clr run on ins over 3f out: sme prog whn n.m.r 1f out* **7/1**[3]

20-5 **10** *2* **Lasting Love**[4] 248 3-8-10 55........................ AndrewMullen(5) 7 29
(C R Dore) *s.i.s: a bhd* **50/1**

316- **11** *¾* **Suhezy (IRE)**[155] 4887 3-9-4 58........................ MickyFenton 10 29
(P T Midgley) *hld up towards rr: carried lft 4f out: a bhd* **25/1**

322- **12** *3 ½* **Song Huntress**[165] 4644 3-8-12 55........................ DNolan(3) 1 16
(D G Bridgwater) *sn bhd: hmpd on ins 4f out: sn struggling* **16/1**

1m 14.76s (-1.05) **Going Correction** -0.075s/f (Stan) 12 Ran SP% **119.2**
Speed ratings (Par 95):104,102,96,96,94 93,90,90,89,87 86,81
CSF £141.34 CT £805.91 TOTE £3.70: £1.40, £13.30, £2.30; EX 102.20 Trifecta £311.80 Part won. Pool: £439.28 - 0.50 winning tickets..
Owner The Foulrice Twenty **Bred** Mrs S E Barclay **Trained** Formby, Lancs
■ Stewards' Enquiry : Francis Norton one-day ban: careless riding (Feb 14)

FOCUS
This was won in the fastest time of the meeting comparatively and looks solid enough.
Mine The Balance(IRE) Official explanation: jockey said gelding lost its action going into bend and failed to travel thereafter

288 FREE £75 WITH LITTLEWOODSCASINO.COM H'CAP 5f 216y(P)
4:20 (4:22) (Class 6) (0-52,54) 4-Y-O+ £2,388 (£705; £352) Stalls Low

Form RPR
06-3 **1** **Desert Light (IRE)**[11] 178 5-8-7 47........................(v) RobertWinston 2 54
(D Shaw) *hld up and bhd: hdwy on ins wl over 1f out: squeezed through 1f out: rdn to ld wl ins fnl f: r.o* **9/2**[2]

1-04 **2** *nk* **Mind Alert**[8] 196 5-8-9 52........................(v) PatrickMathers(3) 3 58
(D Shaw) *hld up: smooth hdwy on ins over 2f out: rdn to ld briefly wl ins fnl f: r.o* **15/2**

406- **3** *nk* **Weakest Link**[113] 5854 5-8-6 46........................(p) JimmyQuinn 11 51
(E J Alston) *led: rdn wl over 1f out: hdd wl ins fnl f: nt qckn* **33/1**

0-50 **4** *½* **St Ivian**[24] 81 6-8-10 50........................ JamieSpencer 6 53
(Mrs N Macauley) *chsd ldrs: rdn over 1f out: nt qckn ins fnl f* **4/1**[1]

4-61 **5** *¾* **Lady Hopeful (IRE)**[7] 209 4-9-0 54 6ex........................(b) RobbieFitzpatrick 9 55
(Peter Grayson) *hld up and bhd: hdwy whn nt clr run over 1f out: nt rch ldrs* **16/1**

-252 **6** *shd* **Jalouhar**[11] 177 6-8-1 48........................ SoniaEaton(7) 5 49+
(B P J Baugh) *hld up and bhd: hdwy fnl f: nrst fin* **7/1**[3]

00-0 **7** *½* **Marshallspark (IRE)**[25] 67 7-8-12 52........................(p) PaulHanagan 10 51
(R A Fahey) *hld up: hdwy over 3f out: rdn over 2f out: one pce fnl f* **14/1**

06-2 **8** *1* **Davids Mark**[11] 178 6-8-9 49 ow1........................ NCallan 13 45
(J R Jenkins) *hld up in mid-div: hdwy whn hmpd jst over 1f out: nvr able to chal* **8/1**

500- **9** *¾* **Sapphire Dream**[34] 6696 4-8-7 47 ow1........................ DavidAllan 8 41
(A Bailey) *s.i.s: nvr nrr* **50/1**

-500 **10** *nk* **Party Princess (IRE)**[7] 212 5-8-0 47........................ KirstyMilczarek(7) 1 40
(S Parr) *prom: rdn whn hmpd on ins 1f out: wknd* **33/1**

4441 **11** *shd* **Mulberry Lad (IRE)**[2] 265 4-8-13 53 6ex........................ ChrisCatlin 4 46
(P W Hiatt) *prom: lost pl over 2f out: nt clr run jst over 1f out: n.d after* **15/2**

-002 **12** *1 ¼* **Chantelle's Dream**[2] 265 4-7-13 46 oh1........................(bt) JamesDoyle(7) 7 35
(Ms J S Doyle) *s.s: hdwy on outside over 2f out: wknd wl over 1f out* **9/1**

5-50 **13** *½* **Massey**[1] 274 10-8-7 52........................ AndrewMullen(5) 12 40
(C R Dore) *w ldr: rdn and ev ch over 2f out: wknd over 1f out* **40/1**

1m 15.34s (-0.47) **Going Correction** -0.075s/f (Stan) 13 Ran SP% **118.2**
Speed ratings (Par 101):100,99,99,98,97 97,96,95,94,94 93,92,91
CSF £36.79 CT £1033.19 TOTE £5.70: £1.70, £2.50, £7.70; EX 51.80.
Owner Danethorpe Racing Ltd **Bred** Anthony M Cahill **Trained** Danethorpe, Notts
■ Stewards' Enquiry : Robert Winston two-day ban: careless riding (Feb 14-15)

FOCUS
They went 4/1 the field in this open-looking low-grade affair. The form is slightly above previous solid bumper form.
Davids Mark Official explanation: jockey said gelding was denied a clear run

289 TEXT "BETDIRECT" TO 88600 MAIDEN STKS 1m 1f 103y(P)
4:50 (4:51) (Class 5) 4-Y-O+ £3,238 (£963; £481; £240) Stalls Low

Form RPR
-2 **1** **Custodian (IRE)**[20] 114 4-9-0........................ JamieSpencer 3 51+
(H R A Cecil) *hld up and bhd: hdwy over 3f out: led ins fnl f: readily* **4/11**[1]

2 *¾* **Steady Rain** 4-8-9........................ NCallan 4 45
(Lucinda Featherstone) *hld up and bhd: hdwy over 2f out: rdn over 1f out: kpt on ins fnl f* **33/1**

3 *nk* **Cuyamaca (IRE)** 4-8-9........................ TPQueally 6 44
(C F Wall) *t.k.h in mid-div: hdwy over 4f out: led 2f out: sn rdn: hdd and nt qckn ins fnl f* **20/1**

6 **4** *1 ¼* **Discord**[14] 162 5-9-0........................ PaulHanagan 7 47
(T H Caldwell) *chsd ldr tl rdn 3f out: outpcd 2f out: rallied ins fnl f* **50/1**

5 *2* **Bookman (IRE)**[137] 4-8-7........................(t) RDEgan(7) 8 43
(P M Mooney, Ire) *s.s and hmpd s: rdn over 2f out: hdwy fnl f: nt trble ldrs* **20/1**

0-0 **6** *¾* **Hometomammy**[6] 219 4-9-0........................ DarrenWilliams 2 42
(P W Hiatt) *led: rdn and hdd 2f out: wknd ins fnl f* **40/1**

6- **7** *¾* **Hilversum**[83] 6333 4-8-2........................ DawnRankin(7) 1 35
(Miss J A Camacho) *prom: rdn over 2f out: wknd jst over 1f out* **16/1**

8 *2* **Lord Raffles**[23] 4-9-0........................(v[1]) DaneO'Neill 12 37
(P R Webber) *hld up towards rr: hdwy 4f out: sn rdn: wknd 3f out* **20/1**

4/4- **9** *¾* **Hilltop Fantasy**[55] 6545 5-8-9........................ MatthewHenry 9 30
(V Smith) *sltly hmpd leaving stalls: prom: rdn over 3f out: wknd over 2f out* **14/1**[3]

10 *dist* **Royal Spell**[46] 4-8-9........................ RobbieFitzpatrick 5 —
(M Appleby) *bhd fnl 5f: t.o* **100/1**

04- **F** **Miss Inch**[83] 6333 4-8-9........................ SteveDrowne 11 —
(G Wragg) *fell leaving stalls* **7/1**[2]

2m 3.15s (0.53) **Going Correction** -0.075s/f (Stan) 11 Ran SP% **121.0**
Speed ratings (Par 103):94,93,93,91,90 89,88,87,86,— —
CSF £26.12 TOTE £1.30: £1.02, £11.20, £4.30; EX 24.20.
Owner Robert Lanigan & Mrs John Magnier **Bred** Tullamaine Castle Stud And Partners **Trained** Newmarket, Suffolk

FOCUS
This may not have been a great maiden and the time was moderate and the form looks suspect.

290 BETDIRECT.CO.UK H'CAP (DIV II) 1m 141y(P)
5:20 (5:21) (Class 6) (0-58,58) 4-Y-O+ £2,388 (£705; £352) Stalls Low

Form RPR
3-04 **1** **Bridgewater Boys**[14] 156 5-8-13 55........................(b) NCallan 9 63
(K A Ryan) *sn chsng ldr: rdn over 3f out: led wl ins fnl f: r.o* **4/1**[2]

1-22 **2** *shd* **New England**[14] 157 4-9-0 56........................ RobbieFitzpatrick 2 64+
(W M Brisbourne) *hld up towards rr: rdn and hdwy 2f out: r.o ins fnl f* **3/1**[1]

53-6 **3** *1 ¾* **Choristar**[14] 156 5-8-12 54........................ DaleGibson 12 58
(J Mackie) *hld up in mid-div: rdn and hdwy 3f out: kpt on ins fnl f* **16/1**

00-4 **4** *nk* **Spark Up**[6] 229 6-8-11 53........................(b) AdrianMcCarthy 5 56
(J W Unett) *a.p: rdn to ld wl over 1f out: hdd and no ex wl ins fnl f* **12/1**

3-30 **5** *2* **Super Dominion**[3] 258 9-8-5 47........................(p) AdrianTNicholls 4 46
(R Hollinshead) *hld up in tch: rdn over 3f out: swtchd lft 1f out: one pce* **20/1**

2-02 **6** *nk* **Pending (IRE)**[14] 156 5-9-2 58........................(p) PaulHanagan 6 56+
(R A Fahey) *plld hrd in rr: rdn and hdwy over 1f out: nvr trbld ldrs* **9/2**[3]

260- **7** *¾* **Fantasy Defender (IRE)**[38] 6667 4-8-8 50........................(v) LPKeniry 1 47
(Ernst Oertel) *broke wl: sn stdd into mid-div: rdn over 2f out: hdwy ins wl over 1f out: one pce fnl f* **28/1**

022- **8** *½* **Priorina (IRE)**[38] 6667 4-8-10 52........................(v) RobertHavlin 8 48
(D Haydn Jones) *led: rdn and hdd wl over 1f out: wknd ins fnl f* **14/1**

0-00 **9** *4* **Riska King**[10] 183 6-8-10 52 ow2........................ FergalLynch 3 39
(P A Blockley) *s.s: a bhd* **33/1**

00-0 **10** *3 ½* **Jun Fan (USA)**[8] 196 4-8-13 55........................ TomEaves 11 35
(B Ellison) *hld up: sn mid-div: rdn over 3f out: sn bhd* **50/1**

0-00 **11** *½* **Gallego**[5] 240 4-8-9 51........................ MatthewHenry 10 30
(R J Price) *a bhd* **20/1**

-055 **12** *3* **Savoy Chapel**[6] 232 4-8-11 53........................ RobertWinston 7 25
(A W Carroll) *hld up and bhd: short-lived effrt on outside over 2f out: eased whn btn jst over 1f out* **5/1**

000- **13** *5* **Mitchelland**[59] 6513 4-8-13 55........................ JimmyQuinn 13 17
(E J Alston) *prom: rdn 4f out: wknd 3f out* **14/1**

1m 49.95s (-1.81) **Going Correction** -0.075s/f (Stan) 13 Ran SP% **124.6**
Speed ratings (Par 101):105,104,103,103,101 101,100,99,96,93 92,90,85
CSF £16.05 CT £188.51 TOTE £7.60: £2.60, £1.80, £6.90; EX 22.40 Place 6 £134.49, Place 5 £55.22.
Owner Bishopthorpe Racing **Bred** Southill Stud **Trained** Hambleton, N Yorks

FOCUS
This modest handicap was 0.6 seconds faster than the first division and the form looks sound, rated through the winner.
T/Jkpt: £18,707.00 to a £1 stake. Pool: £26,348.00. 1.00 winning ticket. T/Plt: £168.80 to a £1 stake. Pool: £62,473.65. 270.05 winning tickets. T/Qpdt: £22.60 to a £1 stake. Pool: £5,490.70. 179.00 winning tickets. KH

^{262}LINGFIELD (L-H)

Saturday, February 4

OFFICIAL GOING: Standard

Wind: Nil Weather: Overcast

291 PLAY £1/4M SPOT THE BALL ON 0800 500 000 MAIDEN STKS (DIV I) 7f (P)

12:45 (12:46) (Class 5) 3-Y-0+ **£2,914** (£867; £433; £216) **Stalls** Low

Form RPR

40-5 **1** **Tamagin (USA)**^{7} [228] 3-8-9 63 ShaneKelly 2 54
(P D Evans) *taken down early: mde all: carried hd high but in command fr over 1f out: rdn out* **5/1**^{3}

06 **2** *1 1/4* **Coastal Breeze**^{14} [165] 3-8-9 MichaelHills 10 51
(J W Hills) *chsd ldrs: rdn over 2f out: styd on to take 2nd last 100yds: no real imp on wnr* **13/2**

00 **3** *3/4* **Busy Man (IRE)**^{7} [219] 7-9-12 FergalLynch 5 53
(J R Jenkins) *wl in rr on outer: rdn 1/2-way: styd on fnl 2f to take 3rd nr fin* **20/1**

0-00 **4** *1/2* **Megalala (IRE)**^{7} [217] 5-9-9 54 NeilChalmers$^{(3)}$ 1 52
(J J Bridger) *mostly chsd wnr: rdn to chal 3f out: no imp 2f out: wknd and lost 2 pls last 100yds* **33/1**

40-4 **5** *nk* **Tuckers Point (IRE)**^{9} [195] 3-8-4 62 EddieAhern 12 41
(J A Osborne) *chsd ldrs: rdn 3f out: no prog 2f out: styd on ins fnl f* **9/2**^{2}

640- **6** *1 3/4* **Boogie Magic**^{37} [6684] 6-9-4 40 AdamKirby$^{(3)}$ 6 42
(T T Clement) *towards rr: rdn over 2f out: kpt on same pce: n.d* **10/1**

050- **7** *1* **Good Article (IRE)**^{323} [650] 5-9-12 40 MickyFenton 11 44
(D K Ivory) *dwlt: towards rr on outer: prog to chse ldrs 3f out: hanging and wknd tamely over 1f out* **66/1**

0 **8** *1/2* **Iberian Light (USA)**^{32} [16] 3-8-2 SallyAdams$^{(7)}$ 3 38
(N A Callaghan) *s.s: hld up in last pair: pushed along over 2f out: one pce* **20/1**

9 *shd* **Boluisce (IRE)** 3-8-4 JoeFanning 9 33
(M H Tompkins) *a wl in rr: shkn up and no prog over 2f out* **33/1**

0 **10** *1/2* **Beauchamp Ultra**^{10} [191] 3-8-4 NickyMackay 8 31
(G A Butler) *taken down early: hld up in last pair: shuffled along 2f out: keeping on same pce whn n.m.r nr fin: nvr nr ldrs* **12/1**

04- **11** *hd* **Madame Constanze (IRE)**^{176} [4346] 3-8-4 MartinDwyer 4 31
(Miss Gay Kelleway) *chsd ldrs: u.p and struggling over 3f out: wknd 2f out* **7/2**^{1}

0 **12** *1/2* **Island Green (USA)**^{17} [138] 3-8-9 JamieSpencer 7 34
(B J Curley) *nt move wl to post: prom to over 2f out: wknd* **12/1**

1m 25.72s (-0.17) **Going Correction** -0.125s/f (Stan)
WFA 3 from 5yo+ 17lb 12 Ran SP% **111.8**
Speed ratings (Par 103):95,93,92,92,91 89,88,88,87,87 87,86
CSF £32.60 TOTE £5.10: £1.90, £2.00, £8.40; EX 51.40.

Owner Jordan E Lund **Bred** Stonehaven Farm Llc **Trained** Pandy, Abergavenny

FOCUS
A bad race, run in a time over half a second slower than the second division, and few got into it. The form is limited by the banded-class sixth and seventh.

Island Green(USA) Official explanation: jockey said gelding was hampered close home

292 TOM WINTERS "LIFETIME IN RACING" APPRENTICE H'CAP 7f (P)

1:20 (1:20) (Class 5) (0-70,68) 4-Y-0+ **£3,238** (£963; £481; £240) **Stalls** Low

Form RPR

-412 **1** **Glad Big (GER)**^{6} [236] 4-9-1 68 DerekNolan$^{(3)}$ 1 77
(J A Osborne) *trckd ldrs gng wl: effrt to ld jst over 1f out: sn clr: r.o wl* **5/2**^{1}

-030 **2** *2 1/2* **Greenwood**^{7} [225] 8-8-7 62 (t) JosephWalsh$^{(5)}$ 5 65
(P G Murphy) *stdd s: hld up wl in rr: prog on inner 2f out: eased out 1f out: hanging but styd on to take 2nd nr fin* **16/1**

00-1 **3** *3/4* **Arnie De Burgh**^{14} [170] 4-9-0 67 LiamJones$^{(3)}$ 10 68
(D J Daly) *led for 1f: pressed ldr: effrt on inner to chal again and w wnr jst over 1f out: wknd last 100yds* **9/2**^{2}

-021 **4** *shd* **Majestical (IRE)**^{7} [225] 4-9-3 67 (p) GregFairley 9 68
(J M Bradley) *dwlt: hld up wl in rr: prog 2f out: styd on fr over 1f out: nrst fin* **12/1**

000- **5** *3/4* **Go Garuda**^{151} [5034] 5-8-7 62 JamieHamblett$^{(5)}$ 6 61
(Miss Gay Kelleway) *hld up wl in rr: hmpd 2f out: bmpd along and styd on wl fr over 1f out: nrst fin* **16/1**

363- **6** *2 1/2* **Seneschal**^{46} [6631] 5-8-13 68 ThomasO'Brien$^{(5)}$ 2 60
(A B Haynes) *chsd ldrs: rdn over 2f out: wknd over 1f out* **6/1**^{3}

0-06 **7** *nk* **Amazin**^{7} [224] 4-9-0 67 (b) JamesDoyle$^{(3)}$ 3 59
(N P Littmoden) *dwlt: sn in midfield: rdn 3f out: no prog and btn wl over 1f out* **12/1**

3-55 **8** *hd* **Stylistic (IRE)**^{17} [137] 5-8-10 60 RoryMoore 11 51
(Patrick Morris, Ire) *racd freely: led after 1f to jst over 1f out: wknd rapidly* **25/1**

3-14 **9** *nk* **Kensington (IRE)**^{14} [169] 5-8-9 66 (p) FrankiePickard$^{(7)}$ 12 56
(P D Evans) *pressed ldrs tl wknd 2f out* **7/1**

516- **10** *1 3/4* **Vienna's Boy (IRE)**^{85} [6315] 5-9-4 68 StephenDonohoe 4 54
(W J Musson) *nvr on terms: struggling u.p fr 1/2-way* **9/1**

203- **11** *5* **Time N Time Again**^{145} [5188] 8-9-2 66 (p) DuranFentiman 7 39
(Peter Grayson) *hld up in rr: rdn 1/2-way: last and losing tch over 2f out* **50/1**

2-30 **12** *nk* **Hard To Catch (IRE)**^{7} [225] 8-8-10 65 LauraReynolds$^{(5)}$ 8 37
(D K Ivory) *racd wd: hld up: hanging and btn fr 3f out: wknd 2f out* **20/1**

1m 24.07s (-1.82) **Going Correction** -0.125s/f (Stan) 12 Ran SP% **121.3**
Speed ratings (Par 103):105,102,101,101,100 97,97,96,96,94 88,88
CSF £47.13 CT £180.68 TOTE £2.60: £1.20, £5.50, £2.20; EX 71.20.

Owner Mountgrange Stud **Bred** Gestut Auenquelle **Trained** Upper Lambourn, Berks

■ Stewards' Enquiry : Greg Fairley one-day ban: careless riding (Feb 21)

FOCUS
A decent pace and a very acceptable time for the grade, well over a second quicker than both divisions of the maiden. The form looks solid enough.

Amazin Official explanation: jockey said gelding hung right throughout

Stylistic(IRE) Official explanation: jockey said mare ran too free

293 PLAY £1/4M SPOT THE BALL ON 0800 500 000 MAIDEN STKS (DIV II) 7f (P)

1:55 (1:55) (Class 5) 3-Y-0+ **£2,914** (£867; £433; £108; £108) **Stalls** Low

Form RPR

22-2 **1** **Stonecrabstomorrow (IRE)**^{14} [165] 3-8-9 75 JoeFanning 5 63+
(P F I Cole) *chsd ldrs: prog to ld wl over 1f out: sn clr: 3l up ins fnl f: drvn out* **4/6**^{1}

06- **2** *1 1/4* **Princess Society (IRE)**^{156} [4895] 3-8-4 PaulHanagan 9 54+
(E A L Dunlop) *outpcd and pushed along wl in rr: prog u.p over 2f out : chsd wnr ins fnl f: clsng at fin* **9/2**^{2}

0-6 **3** *1 1/4* **Black Beauty**^{21} [112] 3-8-9 TPQueally 10 56+
(M G Quinlan) *pushed along in midfield 4f out: prog 2f out: styd on fr over 1f out: nvr able to chal* **6/1**^{3}

4 *5* **Tod Sloan (IRE)**^{65} [6037] 4-9-7 40 GregFairley$^{(5)}$ 7 48
(J M Bradley) *towards rr: outpcd and struggling 3f out: plugged on fnl f* **25/1**

05-5 **4** *dht* **Spanish Music**^{3} [266] 4-9-7 40 (t) ChrisCatlin 4 43
(R Ingram) *outpcd in last trio: styd on fnl 2f: no ch* **14/1**

6-30 **6** *1 1/2* **Salisbury World (IRE)**^{7} [219] 3-8-9 65 LPKeniry 11 39
(D R C Elsworth) *taken down early: led for 1f: outpcd on outer and nt looking keen fr 3f out: wknd fnl f* **10/1**

0-06 **7** *nk* **Chillin Out**^{7} [227] 4-9-12 45 PaulDoe 3 43
(W Jarvis) *chsd ldr after 1f: effrt to ld briefly 2f out: wknd rapidly fnl f* **25/1**

300- **8** *1 1/2* **Mister Aziz (IRE)**^{62} [6497] 4-9-12 45 (v^{1}) EddieAhern 2 39
(J R Jenkins) *racd freely: led after 1f to 2f out: wknd rapidly over 1f out* **33/1**

0 **9** *8* **Hello Molly**^{17} [138] 5-9-0 JamesMillman$^{(7)}$ 6 14
(E A Wheeler) *a wl in rr: bhd fnl 3f: t.o* **100/1**

10 *3 1/2* **Mayden Dream** 4-9-7 FergusSweeney 8 5
(D K Ivory) *a wl in rr: bhd fnl 3f: t.o* **66/1**

0- **11** *1 1/2* **Balfour House**^{44} [6653] 3-8-9 (b) AdrianMcCarthy 1 —
(R A Harris) *s.s: plld hrd and sn prom: wknd rapidly wl over 2f out: eased: t.o* **66/1**

1m 25.14s (-0.75) **Going Correction** -0.125s/f (Stan)
WFA 3 from 4yo+ 17lb 11 Ran SP% **122.8**
Speed ratings (Par 103):99,97,96,90,90 88,88,86,77,73 71
CSF £3.94 TOTE £1.70: £1.10, £1.80, £2.00; EX 6.00.

Owner Team Havana **Bred** P Dillon **Trained** Whatcombe, Oxon

FOCUS
Slightly stronger than the first division and the winning time was over half a second faster. The fourth sets a very ordinary standard.

Mister Aziz(IRE) Official explanation: jockey said gelding hung left

Balfour House Official explanation: jockey said gelding hung right throughout

294 PLAY NOW AT BETDIRECTCASINO.COM H'CAP 1m 2f (P)

2:30 (2:30) (Class 4) (0-85,81) 3-Y-0 **£6,477** (£1,927; £963; £481) **Stalls** Low

Form RPR

661- **1** **Royal Reservation**^{46} [6624] 3-9-0 77 EddieAhern 7 84+
(P W Chapple-Hyam) *hld up in last trio: prog 3f out: rdn to chse ldng pair 2f out: hung rt but styd on to ld last 100yds: hung lft nr fin* **3/1**^{3}

24-1 **2** *3/4* **Song Of Silence (USA)**^{6} [234] 3-8-7 70 6ex JohnEgan 3 76
(E A L Dunlop) *pressed ldr: led 3f out: drvn over 2l clr over 1f out: wknd and hdd last 100yds* **2/1**^{1}

-133 **3** *1/2* **Fusili (IRE)**^{15} [160] 3-8-8 78 JamesDoyle$^{(7)}$ 8 83
(N P Littmoden) *dwlt: hld up in last trio: rdn 3f out: prog u.p 2f out: r.o fnl f: gaining at fin* **16/1**

43-2 **4** *1 1/4* **Time For Life (USA)**^{24} [87] 3-9-4 81 (p) TQuinn 5 84
(H J Collingridge) *led and sn set decent pce: hdd 3f out: w ldr 2f out: wknd over 1f out* **11/1**

01-3 **5** *1 3/4* **Beauchamp Unique**^{10} [188] 3-8-4 67 oh2 NickyMackay 1 66
(G A Butler) *hld up in last trio: gng wl enough but last and outpcd 3f out: effrt 2f out: styd on fnl f: hopeless task* **16/1**

2-1 **6** *3* **Abstract Art (USA)**^{28} [62] 3-8-13 76 JamieSpencer 4 70
(N A Callaghan) *trckd ldrs: rdn 3f out: nt qckn over 2f out: btn after* **9/4**^{2}

01-1 **7** *3 1/2* **George's Flyer (IRE)**^{19} [123] 3-8-9 72 (b) PaulHanagan 2 59
(R A Fahey) *in tch: rdn over 4f out: struggling fr 3f out* **20/1**

2-45 **8** *9* **Outlook**^{17} [139] 3-8-12 75 (b) ChrisCatlin 6 45
(N P Littmoden) *trckd ldrs: pushed along 4f out: wknd wl over 2f out* **66/1**

2m 5.09s (-2.70) **Going Correction** -0.125s/f (Stan) 8 Ran SP% **115.5**
Speed ratings (Par 99):105,104,104,103,101 99,96,89
CSF £9.53 CT £79.06 TOTE £4.40: £1.10, £1.40, £3.40; EX 15.20.

Owner Colin Mercer **Bred** Mountgrange Stud Ltd **Trained** Newmarket, Suffolk

FOCUS
A decent little handicap run at a solid pace in a good time and the form should work out.

295 BETDIRECT.CO.UK H'CAP 5f (P)

3:00 (3:02) (Class 2) (0-100,102) 4-Y-0+

£12,464 (£3,732; £1,866; £934; £466; £234) **Stalls** High

Form RPR

01-1 **1** **Les Arcs (USA)**^{29} [54] 6-8-13 102 JamesO'Reilly$^{(7)}$ 4 113
(T J Pitt) *trckd ldng pair: rdn and effrt to ld narrowly ent fnl f: kpt on wl* **4/1**^{2}

21-1 **2** *1/2* **Fyodor (IRE)**^{34} [6] 5-9-0 96 JamieSpencer 7 105
(W J Haggas) *trckd ldrs: prog 2f out: effrt on inner to chal 1f out: nt qckn last 100yds* **7/4**^{1}

-060 **3** *shd* **One More Round (USA)**^{8} [213] 8-8-1 90 (b) JamesDoyle$^{(7)}$ 6 99
(N P Littmoden) *s.i.s: outpcd in last trio: prog over 1f out: r.o fnl f: nrst fin* **33/1**

102- **4** *1/2* **Fromsong (IRE)**^{49} [6602] 8-9-0 96 JohnEgan 8 103
(D K Ivory) *settled in midfield: rdn over 1f out: styd on ins fnl f: nvr able to chal* **9/2**^{3}

-316 **5** *nk* **Moayed**^{6} [238] 7-9-2 98 (bt) ChrisCatlin 9 104
(N P Littmoden) *dwlt: outpcd and last to 1/2-way: r.o fnl f: nrst fin* **10/1**

0-42 **6** *nk* **Dancing Mystery**^{9} [198] 12-8-12 94 (b) StephenCarson 2 99
(E A Wheeler) *led tl ent fnl f: wknd and lost several pls nr fin* **12/1**

00-5 **7** *1 1/2* **Zarzu**^{9} [198] 7-8-4 86 PaulHanagan 1 85
(C R Dore) *trckd ldrs: effrt on inner 2f out: wknd ins fnl f* **10/1**

440- **8** *1/2* **The Jobber (IRE)**^{63} [6489] 5-8-4 86 oh4 JimmyQuinn 3 84
(M Blanshard) *chsd ldr to over 1f out: wknd* **10/1**

14-3 **9** *shd* **Undeterred**^{8} [212] 10-8-4 86 oh11 JamieMackay 5 83?
(K J Burke) *reluctant to enter stalls: sn outpcd in last pair: detached last 2f out : kpt on last 150yds* **50/1**

58.25 secs (-1.53) **Going Correction** -0.125s/f (Stan) 9 Ran SP% **114.4**
Speed ratings (Par 109):107,106,106,105,104 104,101,101,100
CSF £11.25 CT £195.62 TOTE £3.50: £1.40, £1.10, £7.70; EX 17.20.

Owner Willie McKay **Bred** Elk Manor Farm **Trained** Bawtry, S Yorks

FOCUS

A solid pace for this quality sprint handicap even though several still held a big chance a furlong from home. The first two sets the level for the form.

NOTEBOOK

Les Arcs(USA), bidding for a hat-trick and down to the minimum trip for the very first time in his 30th race on the Flat, was always close to the pace and found plenty to get the better of the favourite in the run to the line. This was a fine effort off a 6lb higher mark, but opportunities for him on sand will be scarce once he is reassessed. However, there is a valuable conditions sprint here on Winter Derby day which would seem ideal. (op 7-2 tchd 3-1 and 9-2 in a place)

Fyodor(IRE), up another 7lb, had no excuses as an inviting gap opened up for him on the inside just when he needed it and the winner proved just the stronger. His only two defeats on sand have both been here and it may be this sharp five on a quicker surface does not suit him as well as Southwell or Wolverhampton. (tchd 2-1 and 9-4 in a place)

One More Round(USA) ◆ ran a remarkable race on this dramatic drop in trip, finishing like a train after being hopelessly outpaced until well past halfway. The Handicapper has given him a chance and he would be very interesting over six on Polytrack.

Fromsong(IRE) kept on down the outside from off the pace to reach his final position. He is now 11lb above his last winning mark, but although he has won over this trip he may prefer an extra furlong on this track when racing at this level. (op 5-1 tchd 13-2)

Moayed, like his stable companion, ran a remarkable race on this drop to the minimum trip. After giving away a lot of ground at the start, he was detached for the first half of the contest but he really motored in the home straight though he was never going to get there in time. This shows that he remains in good form. (op 9-1)

Dancing Mystery, a winner here in the past though possibly better suited by Fibresand these days, tried to make every yard. Although he was still in front a furlong out, the pack were closing in and he was swamped on both sides in the closing stages.

296 BETDIRECT FREEPHONE 0800 211 222 H'CAP — 1m 4f (P)

3:35 (3:36) (Class 2) (0-100,96) 4-Y-0+

£15,580 (£4,665; £2,332; £1,167; £582; £292) **Stalls** Low

Form | | | | RPR
015- **1** **Sri Diamond**[67] 6459 6-9-4 **96** ... JamieSpencer 6 — 107+
(S Kirk) *hld up in last trio: prog on inner over 2f out: led jst over 1f out: cruised clr* **4/1**[2]

006- **2** *3* **Zonergem**[67] 6459 8-8-10 **88** ... JoeFanning 9 — 93
(Lady Herries) *hld up in last pair: effrt over 2f out: urged along on inner and styd on fnl f to take 2nd nr fin* **10/1**

6-13 **3** *shd* **Polygonal (FR)**[7] 222 6-8-13 **91** ... EddieAhern 3 — 101+
(Ernst Oertel) *hld up in midfield: prog to trck ldng pair over 2f out: trapped bhd them tl swtchd rt 1f out: nt rcvr: snatched 3rd on line* **5/1**[3]

03-2 **4** *hd* **Rehearsal**[28] 65 5-9-1 **93** ... PaulHanagan 7 — 98
(L Lungo) *led at stdy pce: rdn 3f out: hdd jst over 1f out: lost 2 pls nr fin* **7/2**[1]

4-10 **5** *1* **Tiger Tiger (FR)**[7] 222 5-9-1 **93** ... JohnEgan 1 — 96
(Jamie Poulton) *trckd ldrs: rdn over 3f out: one pce and unable to chal fr over 1f out* **10/1**

01-5 **6** *1/2* **Wise Owl**[28] 65 4-8-1 **82** ... JimmyQuinn 8 — 85
(J Pearce) *t.k.h: trckd ldr: rdn to chal over 2f out: nt qckn and btn over 1f out* **4/1**[2]

11-2 **7** *3* **Kylkenny**[9] 194 11-8-7 **85** ... (t) ChrisCatlin 2 — 83
(H Morrison) *trckd ldrs: rdn over 3f out: btn 2f out* **20/1**

00-0 **8** *1/2* **Shahzan House (IRE)**[28] 65 7-8-12 **90** ... (p) MickyFenton 5 — 87
(Stef Liddiard) *hld up in last pair: last and struggling wl over 2f out: no prog* **50/1**

4112 **9** *1 1/2* **Willhego**[7] 222 5-8-7 **85** ... HayleyTurner 4 — 80
(J R Best) *racd on outer in midfield: wknd over 2f out* **7/1**

2m 29.99s (-4.40) **Going Correction** -0.125s/f (Stan)
WFA 4 from 5yo+ 3lb — **9** Ran SP% **116.3**
Speed ratings (Par 109):109,107,106,106,106 105,103,103,102
CSF £43.75 CT £204.75 TOTE £5.50: £1.70, £3.70, £2.10; EX 61.60.
Owner Ascot Brew Racing **Bred** B J And Mrs Crangle **Trained** Upper Lambourn, Berks

FOCUS

A hot handicap run at just an ordinary early pace, though eventually won in the sort of time you would expect for a race of its nature and the form should prove reliable.

NOTEBOOK

Sri Diamond is probably better suited by this trip than shorter now and the pace was just about solid enough for him. Travelling beautifully throughout, his rider was even able to take a pull round the home bend and he took full advantage when the leader drifted off the inside rail in the home straight before cantering away for a very impressive victory. The Handicapper will have his say, but even though he is not up to Winter Derby standard yet there should still be other opportunities. (op 5-1)

Zonergem, minus the cheekpieces, stayed on up the inside rail to snatch second place in a bunch finish. He is always capable of running well in decent races like this, but he is also a law unto himself and there is no guarantee he will repeat this. (op 12-1)

Polygonal(FR), back over a more suitable trip, travelled very well and looked sure to play a big part when poised to challenge behind the leading pair turning in, but he managed to get caught up behind them just as the winner was enjoying a charmed run against the inside rail and there was no way back. Given how easily the winner scored, he would have been pushed to have beaten him but he would have been very much closer. (tchd 11-2)

Rehearsal was allowed to dictate at his own pace before trying to wind things up from the front racing down the false straight, but although he battled hard and dug deep he was eventually run out of the places. He is always there to be shot at in races like this around here. (tchd 4-1)

Tiger Tiger(FR) seemed to have no excuses this time and is yet to win beyond ten furlongs. (tchd 9-1)

Wise Owl, possibly unlucky here last time, always had the leader in his sights but his prolonged and unsuccessful efforts to get on top of him eventually found him out. (op 7-2 tchd 9-2 in a place)

Kylkenny never looked happy and this is not his surface. (op 14-1)

Willhego is an admirable sort, but he may have been flattered by his effort in a similar grade race over shorter here the previous week and he was found out this time. (tchd 6-1)

297 OMAHA POKER AT LITTLEWOODSCASINO.COM (S) STKS — 1m (P)

4:10 (4:10) (Class 6) 4-Y-0+ — **£2,388** (£705; £352) **Stalls** High

Form | | | | RPR
4-14 **1** **Nisr**[4] 258 9-8-13 51 ... (t) JamieSpencer 3 — 56
(Miss Gay Kelleway) *hld up in midfield: nt clr run on inner over 2f out tl got through 1f out: rdn to ld last 75 yds* **5/1**[3]

-26U **2** *1/2* **Exit Smiling**[8] 210 4-8-13 52 ... ChrisCatlin 9 — 54
(G C H Chung) *trckd ldr: rdn to ld wl over 1f out: hdd and no ex last 75yds* **25/1**

06-5 **3** *1/2* **Supreme Salutation**[6] 240 10-8-6 50 ... LauraReynolds(7) 6 — 53
(D K Ivory) *prom: nt qckn 2f out: shkn up and styd on fnl f: nvr quite able to chal* **20/1**

02-3 **4** *shd* **Rowan Pursuit**[6] 235 5-8-8 50 ... (b) TQuinn 8 — 48
(J Akehurst) *hld up in rr: plld out and effrt wl over 1f out: r.o to press ldrs ins fnl f: nt qckn nr fin* **7/2**[2]

-224 **5** *3/4* **Samson Quest**[3] 268 4-8-13 60 ... (v) ShaneKelly 2 — 51+
(A W Carroll) *s.i.s: t.k.h in midfield: nt clr run over 1f out: n.d after: running on at fin* **13/8**[1]

3-00 **6** *shd* **Salinger (USA)**[3] 268 4-8-6 58 ... JamesDoyle(7) 7 — 51
(Mrs L J Mongan) *s.s: hld up: last to 1/2-way: plld v wd in st and hrd drvn: r.o wl last 150yds: no ch* **8/1**

05-0 **7** *3/4* **Wiltshire (IRE)**[29] 56 4-8-13 52 ... (v) FergalLynch 5 — 49
(P A Blockley) *trckd ldng pair to 1f out: fdd* **16/1**

200- **8** *1 1/2* **Frank's Quest (IRE)**[63] 6487 6-8-13 52 ... SamHitchcott 1 — 45+
(A B Haynes) *t.k.h: hld up in rr: nt clr run over 2f out to over 1f out: no ch after* **33/1**

010- **9** *1/2* **Writ (IRE)**[140] 5322 4-8-13 58 ... JohnEgan 12 — 44
(Ernst Oertel) *trckd ldrs: rdn over 2f out: wknd over 1f out* **20/1**

00-0 **10** *nk* **Edge Fund**[15] 157 4-8-10 55 ... (v[1]) AdamKirby(3) 4 — 44
(Miss Gay Kelleway) *racd freely: led at str pce: hdd wl over 1f out: wknd rapidly fnl f* **25/1**

40-3 **11** *3/4* **Welsh Wind (IRE)**[31] 35 10-8-13 57 ... (tp) JamieMackay 11 — 42
(M Wigham) *racd on outer: in tch tl wknd 2f out* **14/1**

0 **12** *1/2* **Jomelamin**[22] 107 4-8-8 ... JimmyQuinn 10 — 36
(R J Hodges) *a wl in rr: last and detached over 2f out* **100/1**

1m 38.0s (-1.43) **Going Correction** -0.125s/f (Stan) — **12** Ran SP% **121.8**
Speed ratings (Par 101):102,101,101,100,100 100,99,97,97,97 96,95
CSF £132.35 TOTE £5.60: £1.50, £6.40, £4.50; EX 165.70.The winner was bought in for 5,200gns
Owner W R B Racing 52 (wrbracing.com) **Bred** Downclose Stud **Trained** Exning, Suffolk

FOCUS

Probably a fair seller as the pace was strong and the time was more than acceptable, so the form should prove reliable.

Salinger(USA) ◆ Official explanation: jockey said gelding hung right

298 BET ON THE SIX NATIONS AT BETDIRECT.CO.UK MAIDEN STKS — 5f (P)

4:40 (4:41) (Class 5) 3-Y-0 — **£3,886** (£1,156; £577; £288) **Stalls** High

Form | | | | RPR
-220 **1** **Radiator Rooney (IRE)**[2] 275 3-9-0 68 ... (b) JamieSpencer 8 — 71
(Patrick Morris, Ire) *led for 1f: trckd ldr: effrt to ld ent fnl f: styd on wl* **7/4**[1]

0-56 **2** *1 3/4* **Hardy Norseman (IRE)**[26] 68 3-9-0 64 ... (b) SimonWhitworth 1 — 65
(W Jarvis) *led after 1f: urged along over 1f out: hdd and nt qckn ent fnl f* **9/2**[3]

30-0 **3** *3/4* **Grecianette (IRE)**[10] 190 3-8-9 65 ... JimmyQuinn 3 — 57
(J A R Toller) *chsd ldng pair: rdn and no imp fr over 1f out* **6/1**

425- **4** *nk* **Phinerine**[40] 6663 3-9-0 65 ... AdrianMcCarthy 4 — 61
(R A Harris) *awkward s: in tch in midfield: rdn 2f out: kpt on fnl f: n.d* **9/1**

-333 **5** *1 1/2* **Developer (IRE)**[3] 266 3-9-0 70 ... JoeFanning 6 — 56
(T G Mills) *chsd ldng trio: rdn over 2f out: wknd fnl f* **5/2**[2]

0-0 **6** *1 1/2* **Sir Mikeale**[30] 45 3-9-0 ... ChrisCatlin 2 — 50
(G Prodromou) *last of main gp: rdn over 2f out: no real prog* **66/1**

00- **7** *1* **Mon Petite Amour**[208] 3394 3-8-6 ... EdwardCreighton(3) 7 — 42
(D W P Arbuthnot) *dwlt: outpcd and detached in last: kpt on ins fnl f* **66/1**

00-0 **8** *nk* **Native Tiptoes**[6] 233 3-8-9 ... JohnEgan 5 — 41
(Miss Gay Kelleway) *in tch in rr: no prog 2f out: wknd fnl f* **20/1**

59.09 secs (-0.69) **Going Correction** -0.125s/f (Stan) — **8** Ran SP% **115.1**
Speed ratings (Par 97):100,97,96,95,93 90,89,88
CSF £10.07 TOTE £2.60: £1.10, £1.70, £2.30; EX 11.10 Place 6 £36.09, Place 5 £8.47.
Owner Hogs Syndicate **Bred** Barry Lyons **Trained** Ruanbeg, Co. Kildare

FOCUS

A moderate maiden, though the pace was decent and very few ever got into it. The easy winner can probably hold his own in handicap company, with the runner-up the guide to the level of the form.

T/Plt: £39.00 to a £1 stake. Pool: £41,273.15. 772.05 winning tickets. T/Qpdt: £8.20 to a £1 stake. Pool: £3,332.10. 297.90 winning tickets. JN

270 SOUTHWELL (L-H)

Sunday, February 5

OFFICIAL GOING: Standard

Wind: Light, across Weather: Overcast

299 WIN £2M AT LITTLEWOODSPOOLS.CO.UK BANDED STKS — 5f (F)

1:50 (1:50) (Class 7) 3-Y-0+ — **£1,365** (£403; £201) **Stalls** High

Form | | | | RPR
0-22 **1** **Byo (IRE)**[9] 212 8-9-5 50 ... TonyCulhane 4 — 55
(P Howling) *chsd ldrs: outpcd 1/2-way: rallied u.p over 1f out: led ins fnl f: r.o* **11/8**[1]

000- **2** *2 1/2* **Eternally**[122] 5702 4-9-0 35 ... (p) ShaneKelly 7 — 41
(R M H Cowell) *led: hdd over 3f out: rdn to ld and edgd lft 1f out: hdd and unable qck ins fnl f* **50/1**

-500 **3** *3/4* **Muktasb (USA)**[10] 195 5-8-13 47 ... (v) PatrickMathers(3) 6 — 40
(D Shaw) *s.i.s: outpcd: hdwy u.p over 1f out: r.o* **13/2**[3]

-004 **4** *hd* **Percy Douglas**[9] 216 6-8-7 45 ... (vt) AnnStokell(7) 2 — 38
(Miss A Stokell) *led over 3f out: rdn and hdd 1f out: no ex* **22/1**

40-3 **5** *1* **Town House**[9] 209 4-8-8 46 ... SoniaEaton(7) 3 — 35
(B P J Baugh) *chsd ldrs: rdn over 1f out: no ex ins fnl f* **12/1**

00-5 **6** *1 1/4* **Kashtanka (IRE)**[25] 90 4-8-11 40 ... (b) JasonEdmunds(3) 10 — 30
(J Balding) *hmpd s: sn prom: outpcd over 3f out: r.o ins fnl f* **20/1**

-000 **7** *3/4* **Lady Pekan**[9] 216 7-9-1 46 ... J-PGuillambert 9 — 29
(P Howling) *edgd rt s: sn chsng ldrs: rdn 1/2-way: wknd fnl f* **12/1**

00-0 **8** *1/2* **Baymist**[26] 81 4-9-0 48 ... (b[1]) PaulMulrennan(3) 8 — 29
(M W Easterby) *s.i.s: outpcd: styd on ins fnl f: nvr nrr* **33/1**

3-02 **9** *4* **Freshwinds**[12] 179 4-9-0 45 ... DarrenWilliams 14 — 12
(S L Keightley) *dwlt: hdwy over 3f out: rdn and hung lft over 1f out: sn wknd* **11/2**[2]

1-00 **10** *nk* **Lizzie Rocket**[17] 146 6-8-8 46 ... (v) JamesO'Reilly(7) 13 — 12
(J O'Reilly) *s.i.s: outpcd* **28/1**

000- **11** *1 1/4* **Danakim**[117] 5825 9-8-7 40 ... (be) JohnCavanagh(7) 12 — 7
(J R Weymes) *sn outpcd* **66/1**

5-06 **12** *1/2* **Hiamovi (IRE)**[17] 146 4-9-0 45 ... (b) EddieAhern 11 — —
(R M H Cowell) *trckd ldrs: rdn and hung lft over 1f out: sn wknd* **7/1**

120- **13** *1/2* **Mystery Pips**[104] 6076 6-9-3 48 ... (v) KimTinkler 5 — 7
(N Tinkler) *s.i.s: sn chsng ldrs: lost pl over 3f out: sn bhd* **11/1**

59.86 secs (-0.44) **Going Correction** -0.15s/f (Stan) — **13** Ran SP% **126.0**
Speed ratings (Par 97):97,93,91,91,89 87,86,85,79,79 77,76,75
CSF £120.37 TOTE £2.00: £1.10, £14.90, £2.50; EX 91.30.

Owner Mrs J P Howling **Bred** E Johnston **Trained** Newmarket, Suffolk

FOCUS
An ordinary banded contest which provided Byo with an ideal opportunity to get back on the winning trail. The placed horses indicate that the form is not strong.
Danakim Official explanation: jockey said gelding stumbled coming out of stalls
Hiamovi(IRE) Official explanation: jockey said gelding hung left-handed in final 2f

300 PLAY LITTLEWOODS POOLS ON 0800 500 000 BANDED STKS 7f (F)
2:25 (2:25) (Class 7) 4-Y-O+ **£1,365** (£403; £201) **Stalls** Low

Form RPR
0 **1** **Bahrain Gold (IRE)**[7] 242 6-9-0 48 (b) DaleGibson 2 57
(N P McCormack) *a.p: chsd ldr over 2f out: rdn to ld 1f out: r.o* **22/1**
-401 **2** *½* **Justcallmehandsome**[12] 180 4-8-4 45 (v) AnnStokell(7) 4 53
(D J S Ffrench Davis) *led: racd keenly: rdn and edgd lft over 2f out: hdd 1f out: r.o* **7/2**[3]
00-1 **3** *3* **Only If I Laugh**[12] 181 5-9-2 50 PatCosgrave 9 50
(M J Attwater) *hld up in tch: rdn and hung lft over 1f out: styd on same pce* **11/4**[1]
032 **4** *1 ¼* **Mount Royale (IRE)**[7] 247 8-8-13 47 (v) KimTinkler 3 44
(N Tinkler) *chsd ldr over 4f: styd on same pce appr fnl f* **10/3**[2]
0-63 **5** *1 ½* **Old Bailey (USA)**[5] 258 6-8-13 47 (b) AdrianMcCarthy 5 40
(G L Moore) *chsd ldrs: rdn over 4f out: wknd over 1f out* **4/1**
46-4 **6** *2* **Bronx Bomber**[12] 181 8-8-13 47 (b) MichaelTebbutt 1 35
(Dr J D Scargill) *hld up: rdn over 2f out: nvr trbld ldrs* **8/1**
03-6 **7** *4* **Polesworth**[17] 145 4-8-11 40 SamHitchcott 6 22
(C N Kellett) *sn pushed along in rr: n.d* **20/1**
050- **8** *20* **Sam The Sorcerer**[46] 6649 5-8-11 35 (p) MatthewHenry 8 —
(J R Norton) *chsd ldrs 4f* **50/1**
00-5 **9** *12* **Missin Margot**[17] 144 4-8-11 40 (v) GylesParkin 7 —
(P D Evans) *s.i.s and hmpd s: rdn 1/2-way: sn wknd: hung rt and virtually p.u fnl f* **40/1**

1m 30.28s (-0.52) **Going Correction** -0.10s/f (Stan) **9** Ran SP% **116.6**
Speed ratings (Par 97):98,97,94,92,90 88,84,61,47
CSF £95.77 TOTE £27.50: £6.10, £2.30, £1.10; EX 111.10.
Owner Mrs D McCormack **Bred** Mohammed Al Sulaum **Trained** Medomsley, Co Durham
■ The first Flat winner for Noel McCormack.

FOCUS
Not a bad performance from Bahrain Gold, as he beat two last-time-out winners into the places, giving the form a sound look, and is unexposed on this surface.

301 LITTLEWOODS POOLS BILLIONS WON BY MILLIONS MAIDEN CLAIMING STKS 1m 3f (F)
3:00 (3:00) (Class 7) 4-Y-O+ **£1,365** (£403; £201) **Stalls** Low

Form RPR
0-63 **1** **Shaheer (IRE)**[13] 173 4-8-11 50 TonyCulhane 6 43
(P Howling) *hld up: hdwy u.p over 4f out: hrd rdn fr over 1f out: led ins fnl f: styd on* **3/1**[2]
006- **2** *nk* **College Rebel**[46] 6650 5-8-9 35 ow1 MickyFenton 2 39
(J F Coupland) *chsd ldrs: rdn over 2f out: styd on u.p* **33/1**
0-30 **3** *hd* **Bamzooki**[8] 218 4-8-7 50 ow1 ShaneKelly 10 39
(D J Daly) *led: rdn over 1f out: hdd ins fnl f: styd on u.p* **11/4**[1]
0-55 **4** *6* **Noble Mind**[13] 173 5-8-12 50 (p) EddieAhern 7 32
(P G Murphy) *prom: rdn over 3f out: hung lft over 1f out: styd on same pce* **7/1**
-000 **5** *1 ¼* **The Plainsman**[12] 184 4-8-11 40 DarrenWilliams 4 31
(P W Hiatt) *s.i.s: plld hrd and sn prom: rdn over 3f out: styd on same pce fnl 2f* **33/1**
6-42 **6** *1 ¾* **Silsong (USA)**[5] 257 4-8-5 45 ow2 (v) AdamKirby(3) 9 25
(Miss Gay Kelleway) *hld up: rdn over 4f out: hdwy over 3f out: no imp fnl 2f* **7/2**[3]
000- **7** *8* **Courageous Dove**[73] 6079 5-8-13 35 SamHitchcott 14 15
(A Bailey) *chsd ldrs: rdn 1/2-way: wknd over 3f out* **66/1**
604- **8** *½* **Kristinor (FR)**[9] 6682 4-8-11 51 (b) J-PGuillambert 13 15
(G L Moore) *hld up: hdwy over 4f out: wknd over 2f out* **6/1**
050- **9** *5* **Lahob**[46] 6650 6-8-13 40 PatCosgrave 3 7
(P Howling) *chsd ldrs: lost pl over 7f out: wknd 5f out* **25/1**
10 *10* **Moffied (IRE)**[33] 6-8-8 GregFairley(5) 12 —
(J Barclay) *s.i.s: hld up: effrt over 5f out: sn rdn and wknd* **25/1**
0/0- **11** *5* **Nopleazinu**[46] 6649 6-8-8 40 DaleGibson 1 —
(Mrs N S Evans) *s.i.s: hld up: sme hdwy over 3f out: sn wknd* **33/1**
20/0 **12** *1 ½* **Shoof (USA)**[7] 240 7-8-8 53 FrancisFerris 5 —
(M J Gingell) *mid-div: rdn and n.m.r over 4f out: sn wknd* **33/1**
/00- **13** *25* **Maria Maria (IRE)**[263] 1808 5-8-6 35 HayleyTurner 11 —
(Mrs N Macauley) *prom to 1/2-way* **66/1**

2m 29.25s (0.35) **Going Correction** -0.10s/f (Stan)
WFA 4 from 5yo+ 2lb **13** Ran SP% **123.1**
Speed ratings (Par 97):94,93,93,89,88 87,81,80,77,70 66,65,47
CSF £108.82 TOTE £4.70: £1.90, £7.40, £1.80; EX 149.80.The winner was claimed by Mr J. Gallagher for £5,000. College Rebel was the subject of a friendly claim
Owner Paul Howling **Bred** David Crichton-Watt **Trained** Newmarket, Suffolk
■ Stewards' Enquiry : Tony Culhane four-day ban: used whip with excessive frequency (Feb 16-20)

FOCUS
A poor race unlikely to produce many future winners even at basement level.
Nopleazinu Official explanation: trainer said mare had a breathing problem

302 WIN £2M AT CLASSICVALUEPOOLS.COM BANDED STKS 1m 4f (F)
3:35 (3:35) (Class 7) 4-Y-O+ **£1,365** (£403; £201) **Stalls** Low

Form RPR
02-6 **1** **Bill Bennett (FR)**[33] 28 5-8-12 45 ShaneKelly 3 49
(J Jay) *hld up: hdwy over 3f out: rdn to ld 1f out: edgd lft: r.o u.p* **4/1**[2]
3-32 **2** *shd* **Liquid Lover (IRE)**[12] 182 4-8-9 45 EddieAhern 4 49
(W M Brisbourne) *mid-div: hdwy over 4f out: rdn and ev ch fr over 1f out : edgd rt: r.o* **8/13**[1]
04-5 **3** *6* **Dextrous**[33] 25 9-8-12 35 (p) MickyFenton 8 39
(P T Midgley) *chsd ldrs: rdn to ld 2f out: hdd 1f out: wknd ins fnl f* **20/1**
-000 **4** *3* **Simply The Guest (IRE)**[7] 243 7-8-12 45 (vt) KimTinkler 1 34
(N Tinkler) *hld up: hdwy on ins over 8f out: styd on same pce fnl 3f* **18/1**
0-00 **5** *4* **Son Of Sophie**[12] 180 4-8-9 35 (b) SamHitchcott 7 28
(C N Kellett) *led: rdn and hdd 2f out: sn hung rt and wknd* **66/1**
665/ **6** *3* **Sarenne**[478] 6182 5-8-12 45 NeilPollard 6 23
(John Berry) *chsd ldrs: rdn over 2f out: sn wknd* **18/1**
060- **7** *½* **Kuka**[39] 6678 5-8-12 40 TonyCulhane 2 22
(R Hollinshead) *prom: rdn over 3f out: wknd over 1f out* **20/1**
0-05 **8** *3 ½* **Heversham (IRE)**[5] 259 5-8-12 40 DaleGibson 5 17
(J Hetherton) *chsd ldrs: rdn 1/2-way: wknd 3f out* **12/1**[3]
0/0- **9** *4* **Grub Street**[45] 6658 10-8-7 35 MarkLawson(5) 9 10
(J Parkes) *hld up: wknd wl over 3f out* **50/1**
0-00 **10** *7* **Pharoah's Gold (IRE)**[7] 240 8-8-12 40 (e) AlanDaly 12 —
(Mrs N S Evans) *hld up: rdn over 5f out: a in rr* **33/1**
30-6 **11** *6* **Alqaayid**[12] 182 5-8-5 45 RussellKennemore(7) 10 —
(P W Hiatt) *chsd ldr over 6f: wknd over 2f out* **12/1**[3]
000- **12** *dist* **Gemini Lady**[33] 2838 6-8-7 35 AndrewMullen(5) 11 —
(Mrs J C McGregor) *hld up: rdn 7f out: sn wknd: virtually p.u fnl f* **40/1**

2m 41.74s (-0.35) **Going Correction** -0.10s/f (Stan)
WFA 4 from 5yo+ 3lb **12** Ran SP% **126.2**
Speed ratings (Par 97):97,96,92,90,88 86,85,83,80,76 72,—
CSF £6.79 TOTE £6.60: £1.80, £1.02, £6.00; EX 9.90.
Owner Mr & Mrs Jonathan Jay **Bred** J Jay **Trained** Newmarket, Suffolk
■ Stewards' Enquiry : Andrew Mullen one-day ban: used whip with excessive force and from above shoulder height (Feb 16)

FOCUS
The front two pulled clear in what was a fair race for the level, although they did not need to have improved to do so.
Gemini Lady Official explanation: trainer said mare had a breathing problem

303 LITTLEWOODS LOTTO4 0800 500 000 BANDED STKS 2m (F)
4:05 (4:05) (Class 7) 4-Y-O+ **£1,706** (£503; £252) **Stalls** Low

Form RPR
060- **1** **King's Envoy (USA)**[16] 3611 7-8-9 45 AndrewMullen(5) 3 46
(Mrs J C McGregor) *hld up in tch: rdn to ld over 1f out: hung lft ins fnl f: styd on: eased nr fin* **22/1**
0-62 **2** *1 ½* **Logger Rhythm (USA)**[5] 256 6-9-0 40 DaleGibson 6 44
(R Dickin) *hld up in tch: rdn to ld over 2f out: hdd over 1f out: styng on same pce whn nt clr run ins fnl f* **11/4**[2]
0-00 **3** *1* **Alexander Sapphire (IRE)**[3] 270 5-9-3 48 (bt[1]) JamieMackay 2 46
(N B King) *prom: rn in snatches: rdn 9f out: ev ch over 1f out: styd on same pce ins fnl f* **16/1**
204- **4** *8* **Esquillon**[26] 5294 4-8-5 45 DanielTudhope(3) 4 33
(S Parr) *led: rdn and hdd over 2f out: wknd and eased over 1f out* **4/1**[3]
65-4 **5** *4* **Maunby Reveller**[24] 28 4-8-8 45 LeeEnstone 7 28
(P C Haslam) *chsd ldrs: rdn over 3f out: wknd 2f out* **6/4**[1]
624- **6** *2* **Beauchamp Twist**[19] 4934 4-8-8 45 MickyFenton 5 26
(M R Hoad) *hld up: hdwy over 6f out: wknd 2f out* **6/1**
000- **7** *15* **Merryvale Man**[1] 3119 9-8-9 40 DerekNolan(5) 1 8
(Miss Kariana Key) *w ldr over 12f: sn wknd* **14/1**

3m 47.95s (3.41) **Going Correction** -0.10s/f (Stan)
WFA 4 from 5yo+ 6lb **7** Ran SP% **117.8**
Speed ratings (Par 97):87,86,85,81,79 78,71
CSF £85.39 TOTE £48.90: £11.30, £1.70; EX 216.40.
Owner Off And Running **Bred** Gainsborough Farm Llc **Trained** Milnathort, Perth & Kinross

FOCUS
A weak staying event run in a slow time, even for a banded contest and rated through the runner-up.

304 PLAY £1/4M SPOT THE BALL ON 0800 500 000 BANDED STKS 1m (F)
4:40 (4:41) (Class 7) 4-Y-O+ **£1,365** (£403; £201) **Stalls** Low

Form RPR
3-15 **1** **Latif (USA)**[2] 285 5-9-1 49 SamHitchcott 11 54
(Ms Deborah J Evans) *dwlt: hld up: hdwy over 3f out: led over 1f out: rdn out* **11/4**[1]
0-36 **2** *½* **It Must Be Speech**[5] 258 5-8-11 45 (v) AdrianMcCarthy 4 49
(S L Keightley) *chsd ldrs: rdn and ev ch ins fnl f: unable qck nr fin* **11/1**
200- **3** *3* **Starcross Maid**[62] 6512 4-8-11 45 MatthewHenry 8 43
(J F Coupland) *mid-div: hdwy over 1f out: nt rch ldrs* **16/1**
14-5 **4** *½* **Desert Fury**[25] 94 9-8-11 45 LeeEnstone 12 42
(R Bastiman) *hld up: hdwy over 4f out: led over 2f out: rdn and hdd over 1f out: no ex* **8/1**
05-2 **5** *¾* **To Be Fare (IRE)**[12] 184 6-8-11 45 (be[1]) MichaelTebbutt 13 41
(J Pearce) *trckd ldrs: racd keenly: led over 3f out: rdn and hdd over 2f out: wknd fnl f* **9/2**[3]
01-0 **6** *2* **Naughty Girl (IRE)**[25] 94 6-8-11 40 PaulEddery 7 37
(John A Harris) *hld up: hdwy u.p fnl 2f: nvr nrr* **25/1**
33-1 **7** *5* **Tacid**[12] 184 4-8-13 47 DaleGibson 9 29
(Dr J D Scargill) *w ldrs: rdn and ev ch over 2f out: wknd over 1f out* **7/2**[2]
033- **8** *1 ¾* **Tirailleur (IRE)**[49] 6609 6-8-11 45 PatCosgrave 6 23
(J R Boyle) *hld up: hdwy over 3f out: wkng whn swtchd rt over 1f out* **11/1**
000- **9** *½* **Buon Amici**[285] 1296 5-8-11 45 DavidMcCabe 10 22
(W J Musson) *hld up: rdn and c stands' side over 2f out: n.d* **20/1**
-500 **10** *½* **Flying Spud**[7] 247 5-8-11 40 AlanDaly 14 21
(A J Chamberlain) *s.i.s: sn outpcd* **40/1**
0363 **11** *9* **Crusoe (IRE)**[5] 261 9-8-11 45 (b) JamieMackay 1 3
(A Sadik) *s.i.s: sn pushed along in rr: hmpd over 4f out: sn wknd* **10/1**
044- **12** *4* **Grandma Ryta**[207] 3432 4-8-11 40 NeilPollard 3 —
(John Berry) *w ldrs: led over 4f out: hdd over 3f out: wknd over 2f out* **50/1**
600- **13** *5* **Printsmith (IRE)**[46] 6650 9-8-11 35 (v) GylesParkin 5 —
(J R Norton) *chsd ldrs: rdn 1/2-way: wknd 3f out* **33/1**
000/ **14** *2* **Dil**[454] 6593 11-8-8 35 JasonEdmunds(3) 2 —
(Mrs N Macauley) *led over 3f: wknd over 3f out* **80/1**

1m 43.71s (-0.89) **Going Correction** -0.10s/f (Stan) **14** Ran SP% **127.0**
Speed ratings (Par 97):100,99,96,96,95 93,88,86,86,85 76,72,67,65
CSF £34.60 TOTE £5.10: £2.50, £4.10, £4.10; EX 62.40 Place 6 £35.54, Place 5 £21.97.
Owner Paddy Mason **Bred** Shadwell Farm LLC **Trained** Lydiate, Merseyside

FOCUS
A weak heat, run at a fair pace, and the form is average for the class.
Crusoe(IRE) Official explanation: jockey said gelding hung right-handed round home bend

T/Plt: £110.90 to a £1 stake. Pool: £53,233.70. 350.10 winning tickets. T/Qpdt: £34.30 to a £1 stake. Pool: £4,315.60. 93.00 winning tickets. CR

ST MORITZ (R-H)

Sunday, February 5

OFFICIAL GOING: Frozen

305a GROSSER PREIS HANDELS & GEWERBEVEREIN ST MORITZ (SNOW) 5f 110y

11:45 (11:45) 4-Y-0+ **£4,248** (£1,699; £1,274; £850; £425)

RPR

1 **Sweet Venture (FR)**[85] 4-9-11 .... RobertHavlin 2 —
(M Weiss, Switzerland)

2 3 **Rascacio (GER)**[140] 4-9-4 .... ADeVries 1 —
(C Von Der Recke, Germany)

3 8 **Encanto (GER)**[819] 5964 6-9-4 .... GBocskai 7 —
(P Rau, Germany)

4 10 **Talcen Gwyn (IRE)**[18] 136 4-9-4 .... (b) EWehrel 3 —
(M F Harris) *slowly into stride, soon chasing leaders, could not handle turn and lost ground, no chance after* **51/10**[1]

5 10 **Gopura (USA)**[816] 5-8-11 .... SLadjadj 5 —
(G Martin,)

6 **Give Back Calais (IRE)**[728] 784 8-8-7 .... DMoffatt 4 —
(Miss A Casotti, Switzerland)

7 **Bischoff's Boy (GER)**[76] 6408 5-8-11 .... J-MBreux 8 —
(P Zollig)

8 **Mike Stone** 6-8-4 .... MKolb(5) 6 —
(F Fuhrmann)

61.50 secs **8** Ran SP% **16.4**

TOTE (Inc 10 Francs Stake): WIN 43; Pl 15, 17, 15; CSF 167.

Owner R & C Bertschi **Bred** S A R L Haras Du Taillis **Trained** Switzerland

NOTEBOOK

Talcen Gwyn(IRE) did not have a particularly happy experience in these unfamiliar conditions, but is likely to try his luck again here in a fortnight's time when he should be much more wiser.

306a GROSSER PREIS NOVOCAN (SNOW) 1m

1:15 (12:00) 4-Y-0+ **£3,186** (£1,274; £956; £637; £319)

RPR

1 **Dixigold (FR)**[28] 5-9-6 .... GBocskai 9 —
(Frau C Bocskai, Switzerland)

2 1 ½ **Carte Sauvage (USA)**[87] 4939 5-9-4 .... (b) ADeVries 7 —
(M F Harris) *led to 100yds out, ran on same pace* **33/10**[1]

3 7 **Rainstar (IRE)**[259] 1937 4-9-4 .... RobertHavlin 8 —
(M Weiss, Switzerland)

4 9 **Royal Fire (GER)**[350] 431 7-8-11 .... DMoffatt 5 —
(Miss A Casotti, Switzerland)

5 10 **Negrito (GER)** 7-7-12 .... MissRKlein(7) 4 —
(Dagmar Wernli)

6 **Indian Hall (IRE)**[151] 5-8-3 .... MKolb(4) 3 —
(U Muntwyler, Germany)

7 **All Theatrical (USA)**[494] 5883 6-8-1 .... FrauChantalZollet(7) 2 —
(C Hebeisen)

8 **Dusty Road (GER)**[364] 297 13-8-8 ow3.......... FrauNatalieFriberg 10 —
(Miss A Casotti, Switzerland)

9 **Weingeist (GER)**[364] 297 12-8-7 ow2.......... MsBeatWyss 6 —
(T Stauffer)

10 **Kerjouanno (FR)**[154] 4988 4-9-6 .... (b) EWehrel 1 —
(K Schafflutzel, Switzerland)

11 **Jeff Le Roi (FR)**[259] 1937 4-9-13 .... OPlacais 11 —
(K Schafflutzel, Switzerland)

1m 53.7s **11** Ran SP% **23.3**

TOTE (Inc 10 Francs Stake): WIN 30; Pl 13, 14, 14; CSF 47.

Owner M Hanni **Bred** A & Mme Ghislaine Head **Trained** Switzerland

NOTEBOOK

Carte Sauvage(USA) ran much better on the surface and will be out again like his stablemate in two weeks time. He is also expected to step up in trip which should be to his advantage.

291 LINGFIELD (L-H)

Monday, February 6

OFFICIAL GOING: Standard

Wind: Almost nil Weather: Overcast

307 CLASSICVALUEPOOLS.COM APPRENTICE BANDED STKS 6f (P)

2:10 (2:11) (Class 7) 4-Y-0+ **£1,365** (£403; £201) **Stalls** Low

Form RPR

63-0 1 **Zazous**[18] 146 5-8-6 49.......... DanielleMcCreery(5) 1 55
(J J Bridger) *trckd ldrs: effrt on inner over 1f out: narrow ld ins fnl f: pushed along and jst hld on* **8/1**

0-05 2 shd **Stagnite**[10] 210 6-8-7 50.......... (p) WilliamCarson(5) 2 55
(K McAuliffe) *racd freely: led: rdn and narrowly hdd 1f out: kpt on wl nr fin: jst failed* **9/2**[3]

-355 3 hd **Park Star**[7] 255 6-8-7 45.......... AndrewElliott 3 50
(D Shaw) *t.k.h: pressed ldr: rdn to ld narrowly 1f out: sn hdd and nt qckn* **3/1**[1]

4410 4 1 ¼ **Mulberry Lad (IRE)**[3] 288 4-8-8 45.......... JosephWalsh(5) 5 52
(P W Hiatt) *chsd ldrs: pushed along 1/2-way: struggling 2f out: kpt on again ins fnl f* **4/1**[2]

00-4 5 nk **Lauren Louise**[19] 138 4-8-9 47.......... NataliaGemelova 12 47
(T T Clement) *racd wd and wl in rr: effrt 2f out: kpt on same pce fnl f* **16/1**

04-6 6 nk **Beverley Beau**[33] 38 4-8-10 48.......... KristinStubbs 10 47
(Mrs L Stubbs) *trckd ldrs on outer: pushed along and nt qckn 2f out: one pce after* **10/1**

000- 7 hd **Noble Mount**[39] 6685 5-8-9 47.......... (p) DonnaCaldwell 4 46
(A B Haynes) *reminder after 1f: chsd ldrs: rdn 2f out: one pce and no real imp* **11/1**

-530 8 ½ **Mirasol Princess**[14] 177 5-8-5 48.......... LauraReynolds(5) 7 49+
(D K Ivory) *a towards rr: keeping on one pce and no ch whn nt clr run ins fnl f* **12/1**

64-0 9 shd **Radlett Lady**[18] 145 5-8-5 45 ow1.......... JamesMillman(3) 9 43
(D K Ivory) *a wl in rr: rdn and one pce fnl 2f* **33/1**

2-00 10 hd **Awarding**[10] 210 6-8-10 48.......... (vt) MichaelJStainton 6 44
(Dr J R J Naylor) *rrd s: mostly in last pair: nt clr run on inner 2f out: brief effrt over 1f out: no prog* **16/1**

51-0 11 hd **Rock Fever (IRE)**[10] 216 4-8-5 46.......... (b) RonanKeogh(3) 8 42
(Peter Grayson) *stdd s: a in rr: rdn and one pce fnl 2f* **14/1**

1m 12.61s (-0.20) **Going Correction** -0.125s/f (Stan) **11** Ran SP% **120.8**

Speed ratings (Par 97):96,95,95,93,93 93,92,92,92,91 91

CSF £45.16 TOTE £11.90: £2.60, £1.80, £1.50; EX 40.30.

Owner J J Bridger **Bred** Lordship Stud **Trained** Liphook, Hants

FOCUS

Typical form for the grade, straightforward to rate, and the first three came clear.

Beverley Beau Official explanation: vet said gelding had lost a shoe behind

308 BETDIRECT.CO.UK TRI-BANDED STKS 6f (P)

2:40 (2:44) (Class 7) 3-Y-0 **£1,365** (£403; £201) **Stalls** Low

Form RPR

0-02 1 **Berties Brother**[14] 176 3-8-10 45 ow1.......... DNolan(3) 2 46
(D G Bridgwater) *prom: chsd ldr 2f out: rdn to ld over 1f out: jst hld on* **11/4**[2]

-155 2 shd **My Reflection**[14] 176 3-8-12 45.......... RobertWinston 4 45+
(D Shaw) *settled in midfield: rdn and prog over 1f out: chsd wnr ins fnl f: jst failed* **2/1**[1]

0-20 3 ¾ **Chalice Welcome**[14] 176 3-8-12 45.......... (b[1]) FergalLynch 9 43
(J A Supple) *dwlt: wl in rr: rdn on outer over 2f out: prog over 1f out but hanging lft: styd on to take 3rd wl ins fnl f* **8/1**[3]

00-4 4 ½ **Sweet Cherokee**[24] 105 3-8-9 40 ow2.......... LPKeniry 11 38
(C N Kellett) *dwlt: wl in rr: throwing hd abt fr 1/2-way: styd on fnl f: nrst fin* **14/1**

0-00 5 1 **First Byte**[14] 176 3-8-8 40 ow1.......... (vt) OscarUrbina 1 34
(Miss D A McHale) *dwlt: sn midfield: effrt 2f out: kpt on same pce* **18/1**

000- 6 ½ **Royal Lass**[105] 6077 3-8-3 30 ow1.......... MartinDwyer 6 28
(Rae Guest) *wl in rr: shkn up 2f out: kpt on fnl f: n.d* **16/1**

000- 7 shd **Fashion Chic**[64] 6496 3-8-12 45.......... JimmyQuinn 10 36
(Stef Liddiard) *trckd ldrs: disp 2nd over 1f out: wknd tamely last 100yds* **16/1**

00-0 8 1 ¼ **Stoneacre Girl (IRE)**[24] 105 3-8-3 40 ow3.......... RonanKeogh(7) 3 30
(Peter Grayson) *s.s: hld up in last: rdn on inner 2f out: effrt over 1f out : wknd ins fnl f* **16/1**

05-0 9 nk **Left Nostril (IRE)**[24] 105 3-8-12 45.......... HayleyTurner 5 32
(P S McEntee) *led to over 1f out: wknd rapidly ins fnl f* **10/1**

05-0 10 2 ½ **Scherzo A La Russe (USA)**[14] 178 3-8-12 45.......... SimonWhitworth 7 24
(A G Newcombe) *mostly pressed ldr to 2f out: wknd rapidly* **12/1**

1m 13.32s (0.51) **Going Correction** -0.125s/f (Stan) **10** Ran SP% **117.5**

Speed ratings (Par 91):91,90,89,89,87 87,87,85,85,81

CSF £8.71 TOTE £3.50: £1.90, £1.10, £1.80; EX 7.20.

Owner R W Neale **Bred** R W And Mrs B D Neale **Trained** Icomb, Gloucs

FOCUS

A poor event, run at a sound pace, and the form looks fair for the class.

Stoneacre Girl(IRE) Official explanation: jockey said filly missed the break

309 FREE £25 WITH LITTLEWOODSPOKER.COM BANDED STKS 1m 5f (P)

3:10 (3:10) (Class 7) 4-Y-0+ **£1,365** (£403; £201) **Stalls** Low

Form RPR

500- 1 **Go Free**[159] 4866 5-8-10 48.......... StephenDonohoe(5) 1 55
(C J Down) *dwlt: keen early and hld up in last pair: stl plenty to do over 2f out: prog over 1f out: squeezed through and r.o to ld la* **9/1**[3]

000- 2 hd **Twentytwosilver (IRE)**[102] 5059 6-8-12 45.......... MichaelTebbutt 3 51
(D B Feek) *dwlt: keen early: hld up wl in rr: prog over 2f out: rdn to chal and upsides last 75yds: jst outpcd* **33/1**

540- 3 nk **Coppermalt (USA)**[40] 6678 8-8-12 45.......... LPKeniry 9 51
(R Curtis) *trckd ldrs: prog 3f out: rdn to join ldr over 1f out: upsides last 75yds: nt qckn* **20/1**

42-4 4 shd **Lysander's Quest (IRE)**[14] 174 8-8-13 46.......... (b) JamieSpencer 4 52
(R Ingram) *trckd ldrs: prog over 3f out: led 2f out: jnd over 1f out: kpt on u.p tl hdd and lost 3 pls nr fin* **4/1**[1]

3244 5 nk **Countback (FR)**[9] 231 7-9-3 50.......... RobertWinston 7 55
(A W Carroll) *dwlt: hld up wl in rr: n.m.r 4f out: prog over 2f out: styd on fr over 1f out: jst unable to chal* **9/2**[2]

5-52 6 ½ **Jadeeron**[9] 230 7-8-12 45.......... (v) OscarUrbina 5 50
(Miss D A McHale) *hld up in midfield: prog over 2f out: rdn and effrt over 1f out: cl up ins fnl f: no ex* **10/1**

01-0 7 3 **My Boo**[24] 109 4-8-6 46.......... (tp) AdamKirby(3) 14 47
(T Keddy) *wl in rr: drvn on outer 4f out: nt looking keen but plugged on fnl 2f: no ch* **20/1**

00-3 8 1 **Mujazaf**[19] 141 4-8-10 50.......... EdwardCreighton(3) 12 49
(Miss Sheena West) *settled midfield: rdn 4f out: no prog: nt clr run 2f out: taken to inner and no imp* **10/1**

000- 9 ¾ **Discomania**[156] 4169 4-8-9 46.......... (vp[1]) MatthewHenry 8 44
(V Smith) *dwlt: keen early: hld up wl in rr: rdn on outer 4f out: prog over 2f out: no hdwy fr over 1f out* **25/1**

3-02 10 nk **Mustang Ali (IRE)**[14] 174 5-9-2 49.......... (b) IanMongan 6 52+
(Dr J R J Naylor) *prom: led 4f out: rdn and hdd 2f out: heavily eased fnl f* **9/2**[2]

460- 11 2 ½ **Free Style (GER)**[49] 6612 6-8-13 46.......... DarrenWilliams 13 40
(Mrs H Sweeting) *a wl in rr: drvn 4f out: no prog* **9/1**[3]

6-00 12 6 **Karrnak**[14] 174 4-8-9 46.......... SimonWhitworth 11 32
(Miss J Feilden) *prom: btn whn bmpd wl over 1f out: wknd rapidly* **20/1**

506- 13 20 **Satin Rose**[35] 5377 4-8-8 45.......... MartinDwyer 10 3
(K J Burke) *led after 3f to 4f out: wkng rapidly whn n.m.r over 2f out: t.o* **20/1**

0- 14 10 **Nelson (POL)**[186] 4088 4-8-5 45.......... (bt[1]) StephaneBreux(3) 2 —
(Jean-Rene Auvray) *led to 10f out: wknd 4f out: t.o* **100/1**

2m 49.3s (1.00) **Going Correction** -0.125s/f (Stan)

WFA 4 from 5yo+ 4lb **14** Ran SP% **121.4**

Speed ratings (Par 97):91,90,90,90,90 90,88,87,87,87 85,81,69,63

CSF £282.30 TOTE £14.70: £4.50, £11.50, £3.50; EX 351.50.

Owner W R Baddiley **Bred** I H Stephenson **Trained** Mutterton, Devon

FOCUS

A modest time, even for a banded race, and the form looks fairly straightforward with the third running up to his recent best.

Mustang Ali(IRE) Official explanation: jockey said gelding hung right throughout

Free Style(GER) Official explanation: trainer said mare had bled from the nose

310 BETDIRECT FREEPHONE 0800 211 222 BANDED STKS 1m 2f (P)
3:40 (3:43) (Class 7) 4-Y-0+ £1,365 (£403; £201) Stalls Low

Form RPR

0-02 1 **Glendale**[14] [172] 5-9-3 50 JimmyQuinn 6 59
(D K Ivory) *trckd ldr for 4f: styd prom: effrt to ld 2f out: rdn and edgd rt fnl f: kpt on wl* **4/1**[2]

0-23 2 1 1/4 **Basinet**[14] [172] 8-9-3 50 (p) LPKeniry 4 57
(J J Quinn) *hld up in midfield: prog over 2f out: chsd wnr over 1f out: clsd ent fnl f: no imp last 100yds* **15/2**

342- 3 3 **Amnesty**[24] [1442] 7-9-0 47 (be) IanMongan 2 48
(G L Moore) *chsd ldrs: rdn over 3f out: styd on fr 2f out to take 3rd ins fnl f* **10/1**

6-10 4 3/4 **Opera Knight**[13] [181] 6-8-13 46 RobertWinston 11 46
(A W Carroll) *hld up wl in rr: effrt on inner 2f out: styd on fr over 1f out: no ch w ldrs* **16/1**

0-10 5 nk **Legacy (JPN)**[18] [143] 6-8-11 47 DNolan(3) 10 47+
(P D Evans) *settled towards rr: effrt on inner whn hmpd over 2f out: swtchd wd and styd on fnl f: no ch* **14/1**

220- 6 1 3/4 **Escobar (POL)**[224] [2992] 5-8-13 49 EdwardCreighton(3) 5 45
(Mrs P Townsley) *led to 2f out: wknd fnl f* **16/1**

610- 7 1/2 **Kinsman (IRE)**[39] [6683] 9-8-12 48 RobertMiles(3) 13 43
(T D McCarthy) *dwlt: hld up in last pair: detached 3f out: urged along on inner over 1f out: no ch* **20/1**

/06- 8 1 **Avenlea**[340] [548] 5-9-3 50 GeorgeBaker 12 43
(G L Moore) *hld up in midfield: rdn over 2f out: fnd nil over 1f out: wknd* **33/1**

-004 9 nk **Indigo Sky (IRE)**[8] [235] 5-9-3 50 HayleyTurner 9 43
(B G Powell) *hld up in rr: rdn over 4f out: no prog over 2f out* **16/1**

0-40 10 3/4 **Milk And Sultana**[17] [158] 6-8-12 45 OscarUrbina 8 36+
(G A Ham) *t.k.h: trckd ldrs: rdn whn carried v wd bnd 2f out: no ch after* **20/1**

001- 11 1 1/4 **Riviera Red (IRE)**[39] [6684] 6-9-0 47 (v) FergalLynch 7 36
(L Montague Hall) *hld up in last pair: detached last 3f out: rdn over 1f out: nvr a factor* **14/1**

101- 12 3 1/2 **Ndola**[24] [5965] 7-9-1 48 JamieSpencer 14 30
(B J Curley) *prom: trckd ldr 6f out to over 2f out: wknd* **9/2**[3]

02-3 P **Successor**[30] [63] 6-9-3 50 (t) MartinDwyer 3 —
(M D I Usher) *prom: effrt to chal over 2f out: broke down sn after and p.u: dead* **7/2**[1]

2m 7.25s (-0.54) **Going Correction** -0.125s/f (Stan) 13 Ran SP% **124.7**
Speed ratings (Par 97):97,96,93,93,92 91,90,90,89,89 88,85,—
CSF £34.99 TOTE £5.00: £1.40, £2.40, £3.50; EX 23.80.
Owner Mrs J A Cornwell **Bred** Mrs J A Cornwell **Trained** Radlett, Herts

FOCUS
A fair event for the class, run at a sound pace, and the form appears to make sense with the winner setting the standard.
Riviera Red(IRE) Official explanation: jockey said gelding ran too free
Ndola Official explanation: trainer had no explanation for the poor form shown

311 BETDIRECT ON SKYTEXT P371 BANDED STKS 1m 2f (P)
4:10 (4:10) (Class 7) 4-Y-0+ £1,365 (£403; £201) Stalls Low

Form RPR

00-6 1 **Ringarooma**[14] [175] 4-8-11 45 (t) MartinDwyer 2 51
(C N Allen) *dwlt: sn midfield on inner: prog 2f out: got through over 1f out: led ins fnl f: drvn out* **8/1**

04-6 2 3/4 **Larad (IRE)**[14] [172] 5-8-12 45 (b) JamieSpencer 12 50
(J S Moore) *hld up wl in rr: stl poorly plcd 2f out: hrd rdn and gd prog on wd outside fnl f: snatched 2nd on line* **9/2**[1]

0-00 3 shd **Dagola (IRE)**[14] [172] 5-8-12 45 OscarUrbina 6 50
(C A Dwyer) *t.k.h: hld up in last pair: stl poorly plcd 2f out: drvn and rapid prog fnl f: too much to do* **33/1**

25-0 4 nk **Tuscan Treaty**[33] [42] 6-8-9 45 (t) AdamKirby(3) 10 49
(P J McBride) *hld up wl in rr: prog on outer over 3f out: drvn to chal 1f out: nt qckn last 100yds* **7/1**[3]

4-00 5 shd **Glenviews Oldport (USA)**[14] [175] 4-8-4 45 (b) RonanKeogh(7) 14 49
(Peter Grayson) *hld up wl in rr: prog on outer over 2f out: cl up over 1f out: nt qckn and hld after* **20/1**

230- 6 nk **Belle Chanson**[126] [5655] 4-8-11 45 (v) HayleyTurner 1 48
(J R Boyle) *trckd ldrs: cl up and rdn over 1f out: one pce ins fnl f* **33/1**

06-3 7 1/2 **Diamond Dan (IRE)**[33] [42] 4-8-11 45 PaulFessey 8 47
(P D Evans) *trckd ldrs: prog over 2f out: drvn to ld over 1f out: hdd & wknd ins fnl f* **13/2**[2]

253- 8 nk **Lenwade**[109] [5998] 5-8-12 45 JimmyQuinn 3 47
(G G Margarson) *t.k.h: hld up towards rr: rdn 1/2-way: gng bttr 3f out: hmpd over 2f out: styd on fnl f: nt rch ldrs* **7/1**[3]

06-6 9 nk **Rasid (USA)**[17] [158] 8-8-7 45 GregFairley(5) 7 46
(C A Dwyer) *hld up wl in rr: stl wl in rr 2f out: effrt on outer over 1f out: styd on: nvr rchd ldrs* **8/1**

43-5 10 hd **Mutared (IRE)**[18] [143] 8-8-9 45 RichardThomas(3) 5 46
(N P Littmoden) *trckd ldrs: cl up over 1f out: one pce and lost several pls wl ins fnl f* **7/1**[3]

4-00 11 2 1/2 **Miss Monica (IRE)**[8] [240] 5-8-12 45 DarrenWilliams 9 41+
(P W Hiatt) *dwlt: t.k.h: hld up wl in rr: effrt on inner over 2f out: no imp on ldng gp fnl f* **20/1**

50-6 12 1 1/4 **Blaenavon**[33] [32] 4-8-11 45 SimonWhitworth 4 39
(D W P Arbuthnot) *ldng trio: jnd ldr 3f out: wknd rapidly over 1f out* **14/1**

3-60 13 1 1/4 **Level Par (IRE)**[14] [173] 6-8-12 45 (t) FergalLynch 13 38+
(J A Supple) *ldng trio: led over 3f out to over 1f out: wkng whn hmpd sn after* **25/1**

00-0 14 2 **Eskimo's Nest**[9] [231] 4-8-11 45 (v) RobertWinston 11 32
(D Shaw) *led to over 3f out: wkng whn hmpd on inner over 1f out* **33/1**

2m 7.40s (-0.39) **Going Correction** -0.125s/f (Stan)
WFA 4 from 5yo+ 1lb 39 Ran SP% **120.1**
Speed ratings (Par 97):96,95,95,95,95 94,94,94,93,93 91,90,89,88
CSF £39.72 TOTE £10.80: £4.00, £2.80, £10.40; EX 69.60.
Owner Mrs Henrietta Charlet **Bred** R B Burtt **Trained** Newmarket, Suffolk

FOCUS
A weak affair, run at a fair gallop, and the first ten home finished in a heap. The form looks pretty straightforward to rate.
Level Par(IRE) Official explanation: jockey said gelding had a breathing problem

312 FIRST PAST THE POST AT BETDIRECT BANDED STKS 1m (P)
4:40 (4:41) (Class 7) 4-Y-0+ £1,365 (£403; £201) Stalls High

Form RPR

0-34 1 **Young Kate**[14] [175] 5-8-11 45 RobertWinston 7 51
(J R Best) *trckd ldrs: effrt to chse ldng pair over 1f out: drvn and styd on fnl f: led last stride* **9/4**[1]

-056 2 shd **Dexileos (IRE)**[6] [260] 7-8-11 45 (t) HayleyTurner 8 51
(David Pinder) *pressed ldr: led narrowly 2f out: kpt on u.p fnl f: hdd last stride* **25/1**

03-3 3 1/2 **Mr Belvedere**[14] [175] 5-8-8 45 (p) RichardThomas(3) 10 50
(A J Lidderdale) *led to 2f out: styd w ldr: upsides ins fnl f: no ex nr fin* **10/3**[2]

01-0 4 3/4 **Soul Provider (IRE)**[34] [29] 5-8-11 45 JamieSpencer 3 48
(G Prodromou) *t.k.h: hld up in rr: plenty to do over 2f out: r.o fr over 1f out: nrst fin* **14/1**

300- 5 1/2 **Big Mystery (IRE)**[63] [6508] 5-8-11 45 (be[1]) MartinDwyer 2 47
(S C Williams) *trckd ldrs: rdn 2f out: nt qckn and no imp fnl f* **7/1**[3]

600- 6 1/2 **Maddox (POL)**[105] [6076] 4-8-8 45 EdwardCreighton(3) 11 46
(Mrs P Townsley) *t.k.h: hld up in midfield on outer: nt qckn over 2f out: kpt on fnl f* **25/1**

64-0 7 nk **Margaret's Dream (IRE)**[13] [184] 5-8-9 45 ow1 DNolan(3) 1 46
(D Carroll) *hld up in midfield: in tch on inner over 2f out: nt qckn and no imp over 1f out* **7/1**[3]

000- 8 hd **Coronado Forest (USA)**[39] [6684] 7-8-11 45 SimonWhitworth 4 45
(M R Hoad) *s.s: hld up in last: effrt 2f out: styd on: nvr on terms* **16/1**

5-63 9 2 **Paper Doll**[18] [148] 4-8-11 45 (p) JimmyQuinn 6 40
(B P J Baugh) *snatched up and lost pl over 6f out: outpcd over 2f out: btn after* **8/1**

-000 10 1/2 **Tally (IRE)**[6] [261] 6-8-11 45 PaulDoe 12 39
(D G Bridgwater) *pressed ldrs: rdn 3f out: wknd wl over 1f out* **25/1**

03-0 11 shd **Debs Broughton**[14] [173] 4-8-11 45 (t) LPKeniry 5 39
(W J Musson) *hld up in last pair: rdn and no prog 2f out* **25/1**

50-0 12 1/2 **La Musique**[14] [177] 4-8-8 45 AdamKirby(3) 9 38
(P J McBride) *t.k.h: hld up in rr: struggling on outer over 2f out* **25/1**

1m 39.14s (-0.29) **Going Correction** -0.125s/f (Stan) 38 Ran SP% **121.7**
Speed ratings (Par 97):96,95,95,94,94 93,93,93,91,90 90,90
CSF £72.70 TOTE £3.00: £1.10, £9.50, £1.60; EX 51.90 Place 6 £222.04, Place 5 £150.06.
Owner M F Kentish **Bred** M F Kentish **Trained** Hucking, Kent

FOCUS
A very poor event, which suited those racing handily, and the form looks sound for the class.
Paper Doll Official explanation: vet said filly was in season
La Musique Official explanation: jockey said gelding became unbalanced turning into straight
T/Plt: £853.50 to a £1 stake. Pool: £38,525.20. 32.95 winning tickets. T/Qpdt: £317.90 to a £1 stake. Pool: £2,620.90. 6.10 winning tickets. JN

[283]WOLVERHAMPTON (A.W) (L-H)
Monday, February 6

OFFICIAL GOING: Standard
Wind: Light, half-behind Weather: Fine

313 BETDIRECT FREEPHONE 0800 211 222 CLAIMING STKS 1m 141y(P)
1:50 (1:50) (Class 6) 4-Y-0+ £2,730 (£806; £403) Stalls Low

Form RPR

0033 1 **Risk Free**[3] [285] 9-8-7 56 ow2 (bt) ShaneKelly 1 57
(P D Evans) *hld up and bhd: hdwy on ins over 2f out: led over 1f out: r.o* **9/2**

0602 2 3/4 **Libre**[8] [235] 6-9-3 70 EddieAhern 6 66
(F Jordan) *a.p: rdn over 2f out: chsd wnr fnl f: kpt on* **9/4**[1]

-666 3 1 3/4 **Takes Tutu (USA)**[7] [251] 7-9-1 69 PatCosgrave 5 60
(K R Burke) *hld up towards rr: c wd st: hdwy on outside fnl f: nvr nrr* **9/1**

322- 4 shd **Linning Wine (IRE)**[319] [697] 10-8-12 80 KevinGhunowa(7) 2 64
(P A Blockley) *hld up in mid-div: hdwy on ins over 2f out: rdn over 1f out: one pce fnl f* **4/1**[3]

12-6 5 3/4 **Bijou Dan**[24] [106] 5-8-13 63 (b) TomEaves 9 56
(I Semple) *chsd ldr: rdn and ev ch wl over 1f out: no ex fnl f* **5/2**[2]

06-0 6 2 1/2 **Pearl Fisher (IRE)**[24] [104] 5-8-4 40 ow1 DanielTudhope(3) 4 45
(D Carroll) *led: rdn over 2f out: hdd over 1f out: wknd fnl f* **33/1**

0040 7 shd **Lakeside Guy (IRE)**[8] [247] 5-7-12 40 (vt) LiamJones(7) 3 43
(M Appleby) *hld up and bhd: hdwy on ins wl over 1f out: no imp fnl f* **50/1**

060- 8 5 **Xaloc Bay (IRE)**[264] [1812] 8-8-4 35 TolleyDean(7) 7 39
(R A Harris) *hld up in tch: rdn over 3f out: wknd 2f out* **33/1**

0-00 9 1 **Barzak (IRE)**[17] [163] 6-8-11 52 (bt) DeanMcKeown 10 36
(S R Bowring) *hld up in tch: rdn over 2f out: sn wknd* **20/1**

500/ 10 29 **Too Keen**[580] [3613] 5-8-2 35 PaulHanagan 8 —
(J M Jefferson) *hld up: sn bhd: pushed along 4f out: struggling 3f out: t.o* **100/1**

1m 49.38s (-2.38) **Going Correction** -0.125s/f (Stan) 10 Ran SP% **121.1**
Speed ratings (Par 101):105,104,102,102,102 99,99,95,94,68
CSF £15.15 TOTE £4.10: £1.40, £1.50, £2.00; EX 20.60.
Owner Miss S Howell **Bred** Roldvale Ltd **Trained** Pandy, Abergavenny

FOCUS
Just an ordinary claimer in which the pace appeared fair throughout.

314 OVER 60 GAMES AT LITTLEWOODSCASINO.COM MAIDEN STKS 1m 4f 50y(P)
2:20 (2:20) (Class 5) 4-Y-0+ £3,238 (£963; £481; £240) Stalls Low

Form RPR

/222 1 **Kirkstone (IRE)**[12] [185] 5-9-3 63 EddieAhern 12 66+
(J A Osborne) *a gng wl: led on bit wl over 1f out: comf* **8/13**[1]

460- 2 1 1/2 **Ganymede**[121] [3920] 5-9-3 71 FergusSweeney 2 59
(J G M O'Shea) *hld up: rdn and hdwy over 2f out: chsd wnr over 1f out: no imp* **7/2**[2]

3 1/2 **Dictator (IRE)**[33] [5323] 5-9-0 (t) NeilChalmers(3) 1 59
(D R Gandolfo) *hld up and bhd: hdwy on ins over 2f out: styd on ins fnl f* **9/1**[3]

6 4 6 **Real Chief (IRE)**[16] [166] 8-9-3 FrancisFerris 8 49
(Miss M E Rowland) *prom: rdn over 2f out: wknd over 1f out* **40/1**

00 5 3 **Rythm N Rhyme (IRE)**[16] [166] 7-9-3 PaulEddery 5 44
(John A Harris) *led: rdn over 2f out: hdd wl over 1f out: sn wknd* **66/1**

6 1 3/4 **Cappanrush (IRE)**[30] 6-9-3 J-PGuillambert 4 41
(A Ennis) *hld up and bhd: hdwy on outside 3f out: hung lft wl over 1f out: sn wknd* **20/1**

7 7 **Diafa (USA)**[221] 3069 4-8-9 65 RobertHavlin 11 25
(J G M O'Shea) *hld up: hdwy over 3f out: wkng whn n.m.r wl over 1f out* **12/1**
8 2 **Jose Bove**[9] 4-9-0 TonyCulhane 9 27
(R Dickin) *sn chsng ldr: rdn over 3f out: wknd wl over 1f out* **50/1**
0 9 ¾ **Pearl Oyster**[36] 2 4-9-0 SamHitchcott 7 26
(D J Wintle) *rdn 4f out: a towards rr* **25/1**
0 10 dist **Mr Jawbreaker (IRE)**[16] 166 7-9-3 MickyFenton 10 —
(J T Stimpson) *s.i.s: rdn and hdwy over 6f out: wknd 5f out: t.o* **16/1**

2m 40.61s (-1.81) **Going Correction** -0.125s/f (Stan)
WFA 4 from 5yo+ 3lb **10 Ran SP% 122.2**
Speed ratings (Par 103):101,100,99,95,93 92,87,86,86,—
CSF £2.95 TOTE £1.60: £1.10, £1.30, £1.80; EX 3.60.
Owner Mr & Mrs G Middlebrook **Bred** G And Mrs Middlebrook **Trained** Upper Lambourn, Berks

FOCUS
A modest, very uncompetitive maiden, but they went a reasonable enough pace throughout and Kirkstone basically outclassed his rivals. The race has been rated around the fourth and fifth.

315 HOTEL & CONFERENCING AT DUNSTALL PARK (S) STKS 7f 32y(P)
2:50 (2:51) (Class 6) 3-Y-0+ £2,388 (£705; £352) Stalls High

Form RPR
1324 1 **Magic Amour**[4] 271 8-9-6 64 (b) KevinGhunowa(7) 6 67
(P A Blockley) *sn chsng ldr: led 4f out: clr wl over 1f out: drvn out* **4/1**[2]
04-2 2 2 **Iced Diamond (IRE)**[9] 227 7-9-8 59 ShaneKelly 4 57
(W M Brisbourne) *hld up in tch: rdn to chse wnr over 2f out: kpt on same pce fnl f* **2/1**[1]
-665 3 1¼ **Musiotal**[13] 181 5-9-8 45 (p) PatCosgrave 8 54
(P A Blockley) *bhd tl hdwy on outside fnl f: nrst fin* **6/1**[3]
0-60 4 nk **Chickado (IRE)**[20] 127 5-9-8 49 RobertHavlin 2 53
(D Haydn Jones) *led early: prom: n.m.r and lost pl over 3f out: rdn and rallied over 2f out: kpt on one pce fnl f* **10/1**
-600 5 2½ **Piccolo Prince**[28] 67 5-9-1 52 JamesDoyle(7) 12 47
(E J Alston) *hld up: rdn and hdwy over 2f out: no imp fnl f* **12/1**
-020 6 1¼ **Aswan (IRE)**[4] 271 8-9-10 64 (t) AmirQuinn(3) 10 48
(S R Bowring) *hmpd sn after s: hdwy on outside after 1f: chsd wnr briefly 3f out: sn rdn: wknd wl over 1f out* **8/1**
0-00 7 3½ **Dematraf (IRE)**[7] 249 4-9-3 55 PhillipMakin 7 29
(Ms Deborah J Evans) *nvr nr ldrs* **25/1**
5-00 8 nk **Kiss The Rain**[7] 249 6-9-3 45 (b) TomEaves 9 28
(R Brotherton) *nvr nr ldrs* **25/1**
00-6 9 3 **Dundonald**[10] 210 7-9-8 45 (bt) DaneO'Neill 1 26
(M Appleby) *sn led: hdd 4f out: sn rdn: wknd wl over 2f out* **40/1**
000- 10 1 **Riquewihr**[156] 4959 6-9-3 54 TonyCulhane 5 18
(P Howling) *stdd sn after s: a bhd* **11/1**
0-50 11 ¾ **Missin Margot**[1] 300 4-9-3 40 (v) EddieAhern 3 16
(P D Evans) *prom 3f* **40/1**
5004 12 1¾ **Wilford Maverick (IRE)**[10] 210 4-9-8 45 PaulHanagan 11 16
(M J Attwater) *prom: rdn over 3f out: wknd 2f out* **10/1**

1m 29.63s (-0.77) **Going Correction** -0.125s/f (Stan) **12 Ran SP% 125.5**
Speed ratings (Par 101):99,96,95,94,92 90,86,86,82,81 80,78
CSF £12.74 TOTE £3.70: £1.60, £1.20, £2.70; EX 11.20.There was no bid for the winner.
Owner Joe McCarthy **Bred** Juddmonte Farms **Trained** Lambourn, Berks

FOCUS
This looked a competitive enough seller, albeit typically moderate, but nothing could go with Magic Amour when he kicked clear off the final bend. The winner has been rated a shade off his recent Southwell best.
Aswan(IRE) Official explanation: jockey said gelding suffered interference at the start

316 BET NOW AT BETDIRECT.CO.UK H'CAP 7f 32y(P)
3:20 (3:21) (Class 5) (0-75,75) 4-Y-0+ £3,238 (£963; £481; £240) Stalls High

Form RPR
30-4 1 **Bessemer (JPN)**[25] 100 5-9-0 73 (p) DanielTudhope(3) 1 84
(D Carroll) *led early: a.p: led over 1f out: r.o wl* **4/1**[1]
05-1 2 1½ **Raza Cab (IRE)**[12] 192 4-8-12 68 DaneO'Neill 8 75
(Karen George) *a.p: rdn and ev ch over 1f out: nt qckn ins fnl f* **5/1**[3]
-052 3 ¾ **Nautical**[7] 253 8-8-12 68 ShaneKelly 10 73
(A W Carroll) *t.k.h in rr: n.m.r after 1f: hdwy 2f out: rdn and r.o ins fnl f* **9/2**[2]
-140 4 1¾ **Kensington (IRE)**[2] 292 5-8-10 66 (p) EddieAhern 7 67
(P D Evans) *hld up and bhd: rdn 3f out: c wd st: hdwy fnl f: nrst fin* **9/1**
6201 5 ½ **Lincolneurocruiser**[7] 253 4-8-12 75 6ex RussellKennemore(7) 3 74
(Mrs N Macauley) *sn led: rdn over 2f out: hdd over 1f out: wknd ins fnl f* **8/1**
5215 6 nk **Blue Knight (IRE)**[9] 224 7-9-2 72 (v) AdrianTNicholls 4 70
(D Nicholls) *a.p: rdn over 2f out: one pce* **10/1**
00-0 7 shd **Mistral Sky**[7] 253 7-9-1 71 (v) MickyFenton 2 69
(Stef Liddiard) *hld up in mid-div: rdn and no hdwy fnl 2f* **33/1**
6-35 8 nk **Screwdriver**[12] 192 4-9-1 71 (b) PaulFitzsimons 5 68
(Miss J R Tooth) *nvr trbld ldrs* **6/1**
000- 9 1 **Linda's Colin (IRE)**[289] 1202 4-9-4 74 AdrianMcCarthy 12 71+
(R A Harris) *hld up and bhd: sme hdwy whn nt clr run ins fnl f* **16/1**
00-3 10 1¼ **Set Alight**[4] 276 5-8-9 65 (v) PhillipMakin 6 57
(Mrs C A Dunnett) *prom: ev ch over 2f out: sn rdn: wknd wl over 1f out* **12/1**
-006 11 nk **Queens Rhapsody**[8] 245 6-9-0 70 (p) SamHitchcott 9 61
(A Bailey) *hld up towards rr: short-lived effrt over 3f out* **10/1**
000- 12 6 **Exponential (IRE)**[58] 6544 4-9-0 70 J-PGuillambert 11 45
(S C Williams) *hdwy over 5f out: rdn over 2f out: c wd st: sn wknd* **40/1**

1m 29.24s (-1.16) **Going Correction** -0.125s/f (Stan) **12 Ran SP% 127.4**
Speed ratings (Par 103):101,99,98,96,95 95,95,95,93,92 92,85
CSF £25.76 CT £100.37 TOTE £4.40: £1.90, £2.40, £1.90; EX 29.20 Trifecta £243.10 Pool: £479.50 - 1.40 winning tickets..
Owner Mrs B Ramsden **Bred** Darley Stud **Trained** Warthill, N Yorks

FOCUS
Just a modest handicap and Bessemer did it in good style. The form has been rated through the runner-up, who appears to have run to about the level of his Lingfield win.
Nautical Official explanation: jockey said gelding suffered interference shortly after start

317 BET NOW ON 0800 211 222 H'CAP (DIV I) 5f 20y(P)
3:50 (3:51) (Class 6) (0-65,65) 4-Y-0+ £2,388 (£705; £352) Stalls Low

Form RPR
00-0 1 **Monte Major (IRE)**[10] 209 5-8-4 51 oh2 (v) FrancisNorton 2 59
(D Shaw) *a.p: led over 1f out: sn rdn: jst hld on* **33/1**
4-43 2 nk **Taboor (IRE)**[10] 216 8-8-5 52 EddieAhern 6 59
(R M H Cowell) *bhd tl hdwy on ins 2f out: r.o wl ins fnl f: jst failed* **4/1**[1]
-042 3 ¾ **Mind Alert**[3] 288 5-8-2 52 (v) PatrickMathers(3) 4 56
(D Shaw) *chsd ldrs: rdn over 1f out: kpt on ins fnl f* **4/1**[1]
0-06 4 ½ **Four Amigos (USA)**[4] 274 5-8-7 55 (v) SilvestreDeSousa(3) 1 60
(D Nicholls) *led: rdn over 2f out: hdd over 1f out: no ex towards fin* **14/1**
-261 5 ½ **Mambazo**[21] 126 4-9-2 63 (e) J-PGuillambert 13 64+
(S C Williams) *stdd s: hdwy on ins over 2f out: one pce fnl f* **5/1**[3]
03-1 6 nk **Blue Moon Hitman (IRE)**[10] 212 5-8-6 53 (b) PaulHanagan 3 53
(R Brotherton) *w ldr: ev ch over 2f out: sn rdn: no ex ins fnl f* **9/2**[2]
56-0 7 ½ **Alexia Rose (IRE)**[32] 47 4-9-1 62 TonyCulhane 10 60
(A Berry) *nrst fin* **20/1**
60-5 8 ¾ **Namir (IRE)**[34] 23 4-9-4 65 MickyFenton 9 60
(Stef Liddiard) *nvr nrr* **12/1**
50-0 9 1¼ **Count Cougar (USA)**[36] 1 6-8-8 55 DaleGibson 7 46
(S P Griffiths) *chsd ldrs tl wknd over 2f out* **33/1**
000- 10 nk **Vague Star (ITY)**[48] 6631 4-9-1 62 (b) RobertHavlin 11 52
(R Ingram) *a bhd* **33/1**
2-00 11 1¼ **Legal Set (IRE)**[10] 212 10-8-3 57 oh6 ow6 (bt) AnnStokell(7) 12 42
(Miss A Stokell) *chsd ldrs 2f* **66/1**
12-2 12 shd **Almaty Express**[21] 126 4-9-2 63 (b) JoeFanning 8 48
(J R Weymes) *prom: rdn over 2f out: wknd over 1f out* **15/2**
10-0 13 1 **Best Lead**[21] 126 7-8-8 58 (b) DanielTudhope(3) 5 39
(Ian Emmerson) *a bhd* **20/1**

61.91 secs (-0.91) **Going Correction** -0.125s/f (Stan) **13 Ran SP% 120.8**
Speed ratings (Par 101):102,101,100,99,98 98,97,96,94,93 91,91,90
CSF £154.64 CT £670.08 TOTE £63.40: £11.50, £1.50, £1.70; EX 276.50.
Owner Danethorpe Racing Ltd **Bred** B Kennedy **Trained** Danethorpe, Notts

FOCUS
A moderate sprint handicap in which Franny Norton and Monte Major gave a perfect example of how the majority of races seem to be won over this course and distance. The form has been rated through the runner-up and third.
Legal Set(IRE) Official explanation: jockey said gelding hung right throughout

318 HOLIDAY INN GARDEN COURT WOLVERHAMPTON H'CAP 1m 5f 194y(P)
4:20 (4:21) (Class 6) (0-65,64) 4-Y-0+ £2,388 (£705; £352) Stalls Low

Form RPR
12-1 1 **Sovereign Spirit (IRE)**[20] 131 4-9-7 64 (t) JoeFanning 9 74+
(W R Swinburn) *hld up in mid-div: hdwy over 6f out: led 3f out: rdn clr wl over 1f out: styd on* **2/1**[1]
R-30 2 ¾ **Keshya**[7] 251 5-9-3 62 JamesDoyle(7) 3 67
(N P Littmoden) *hld up towards rr: rdn and hdwy over 2f out: styd on ins fnl f: nt rch wnr* **20/1**
51-4 3 nk **I'll Do It Today**[16] 168 5-9-2 54 TomEaves 12 59
(J M Jefferson) *hld up towards rr: rdn and hdwy over 2f out: styd on ins fnl f* **7/2**[2]
50-0 4 4 **Smoothie (IRE)**[31] 52 8-9-1 53 (p) FergusSweeney 8 52
(Ian Williams) *hld up and bhd: hdwy on outside over 4f out: chsd wnr over 2f out tl wknd ins fnl f* **12/1**
-113 5 5 **Little Richard (IRE)**[16] 168 7-9-3 55 (p) AlanDaly 10 47
(M Wellings) *hld up in tch: rdn and hdwy over 3f out: wknd wl over 1f out* **8/1**
00P- 6 1¼ **Nakwa (IRE)**[237] 2569 8-9-7 59 DavidAllan 4 49
(E J Alston) *hld up in tch: n.m.r on ins bnd after 2f: hdwy on ins over 3f out: wknd over 1f out* **25/1**
061- 7 2 **Mungo Jerry (GER)**[49] 6620 5-9-3 55 MickyFenton 11 42
(B N Pollock) *s.i.s: hdwy on outside over 3f out: rdn over 2f out: sn wknd* **14/1**
6-00 8 3½ **Barking Mad (USA)**[9] 230 8-8-9 52 AndrewMullen(5) 1 35
(C R Dore) *led: hdd 3f out: wkng whn n.m.r on ins 2f out* **25/1**
44-0 9 1 **Medora Leigh (USA)**[9] 218 4-8-12 55 TonyCulhane 2 36
(J A R Toller) *a towards rr* **33/1**
06-2 10 3 **Dayoff (IRE)**[9] 166 5-9-3 55 (v[1]) ShaneKelly 13 32
(P D Evans) *prom: rdn 4f out: wknd over 2f out* **25/1**
/36- 11 19 **Aleron (IRE)**[12] 1502 8-9-10 62 (p) EddieAhern 5 12
(J J Quinn) *prom tl lost pl and eased over 3f out* **4/1**[3]
340- 12 ¾ **Hallucinate**[185] 4122 4-9-3 60 PaulHanagan 7 9
(R A Fahey) *broke wl: sn bhd: rdn 7f out: no rspnse* **25/1**
/0-0 13 ¾ **Daybreaking (IRE)**[9] 218 4-9-0 57 StephenCarson 6 5
(R F Johnson Houghton) *prom tl rdn and wknd 5f out* **50/1**

3m 3.92s (-3.45) **Going Correction** -0.125s/f (Stan)
WFA 4 from 5yo+ 5lb **13 Ran SP% 126.1**
Speed ratings (Par 101):104,103,103,101,98 97,96,94,93,92 81,80,80
CSF £52.82 CT £145.46 TOTE £3.40: £1.10, £7.90, £1.80; EX 65.40.
Owner Cunnane, Godfrey, Kirkland & Winter **Bred** Exors Of The Late Mrs I Morris **Trained** Aldbury, Herts

FOCUS
Only a moderate handicap, but reasonably competitive for the level and there was plenty of competition for the lead through the first couple of furlongs. The first three have all been rated as improving on their recent form.
Mungo Jerry(GER) Official explanation: trainer said gelding had a breathing problem
Aleron(IRE) Official explanation: jockey said gelding hung right-handed
Daybreaking(IRE) Official explanation: jockey said colt hung right-handed

319 LITTLEWOODSPOOLS.CO.UK H'CAP 1m 1f 103y(P)
4:50 (4:50) (Class 5) (0-70,69) 4-Y-0+ £3,238 (£963; £481; £240) Stalls Low

Form RPR
250- 1 **Parkview Love (USA)**[41] 6671 5-9-0 68 (v) PatrickMathers(3) 7 75
(D Shaw) *sn led: rdn over 2f out: jst hld on* **20/1**
1112 2 hd **Young Mick**[5] 263 4-8-5 63 (v) JamesDoyle(7) 1 72+
(G G Margarson) *hld up and bhd: swtchd rt wl over 1f out: gd hdwy fnl f: jst failed* **6/4**[1]
3-35 3 1¼ **Western Roots**[10] 214 5-9-4 69 MickyFenton 10 73
(M Appleby) *hld up and bhd: hdwy 2f out: r.o ins fnl f* **8/1**
3-00 4 hd **Corky (IRE)**[8] 236 5-9-1 66 PaulHanagan 11 70
(I W McInnes) *s.i.s: c wd st: hdwy fnl f: r.o* **16/1**
460- 5 1 **Low Cloud**[71] 3334 6-9-1 66 (v) EddieAhern 4 68
(J J Quinn) *hld up in mid-div: hdwy on ins 2f out: kpt on same pce fnl f* **22/1**
4-54 6 hd **Monte Mayor Boy**[8] 236 4-9-0 65 (p) RobertHavlin 9 66
(D Haydn Jones) *hld up in mid-div: hdwy on outside over 3f out: rdn over 2f out: one pce fnl f* **10/1**
6-20 7 nk **Midshipman**[24] 106 8-9-1 66 (vt) ShaneKelly 3 67
(A W Carroll) *dwlt: hdwy on outside fnl f: nvr nr to chal* **13/2**[3]
61-0 8 shd **Ronsard (IRE)**[23] 115 4-9-1 66 JohnEgan 5 67
(Heather Dalton) *prom: chsd wnr over 2f out tl wknd wl ins fnl f* **12/1**
33-3 9 ½ **Measured Response**[23] 114 4-9-1 66 FergusSweeney 2 66
(J G M O'Shea) *led early: prom: rdn over 2f out: wknd ins fnl f* **12/1**

-500 10 1 1/4 **Scottish River (USA)**[9] 223 7-9-2 67 ... DaneO'Neill 13 64
(M D I Usher) *dwlt: hld up: hdwy 3f out: rdn over 1f out: wknd fnl f* 12/1
0-06 11 2 1/2 **Flying Pass**[16] 171 4-8-7 65 ... LiamJones(7) 8 58
(D J S Ffrench Davis) *prom tl wknd 2f out* 20/1
40-0 12 1 **All A Dream**[24] 109 4-9-2 67 ... TomEaves 12 58
(Mrs L Williamson) *prom: rdn over 2f out: wknd over 1f out* 33/1
60-2 13 5 **Play Master (IRE)**[7] 251 5-8-11 62 ... PaulEddery 6 43
(B Smart) *t.k.h in tch: rdn and wknd over 2f out* 6/1[2]

2m 1.64s (-0.98) **Going Correction** -0.125s/f (Stan) 13 Ran SP% 133.6
Speed ratings (Par 103):99,98,97,97,96 96,96,96,95,94 92,91,87
CSF £53.78 CT £302.63 TOTE £34.40: £11.20, £1.10, £3.10; EX 92.90.
Owner Danethorpe Racing Ltd **Bred** Mark Johnston Racing Ltd **Trained** Danethorpe, Notts
■ Stewards' Enquiry : Patrick Mathers one-day ban: careless riding (Feb 17)

FOCUS
A modest but competitive enough handicap in which the favourite, rated the winner, looked particularly unlucky in defeat. The race has not been rated too positively through the third and fourth.

320 BET NOW ON 0800 211 222 H'CAP (DIV II) 5f 20y(P)
5:20 (5:20) (Class 6) (0-65,64) 4-Y-0+ **£2,388** (£705; £352) **Stalls** Low

Form RPR
0341 1 **Canadian Danehill (IRE)**[9] 227 4-9-3 63 ... (p) FergusSweeney 1 73
(R M H Cowell) *a.p: rdn over 1f out: led ins fnl f: r.o* 9/4[1]
/21- 2 nk **Hammer Of The Gods (IRE)**[322] 670 6-9-4 64 ... (bt) EddieAhern 4 73
(Lucinda Featherstone) *a.p: rdn over 1f out: ev ch ins fnl f: r.o* 9/2[2]
6-32 3 1 1/4 **Nova Tor (IRE)**[10] 216 4-8-6 52 ... (b) GylesParkin 9 57
(Peter Grayson) *s.i.s: hdwy whn swtchd rt and bmpd wl over 1f out: r.o ins fnl f* 7/1
41-6 4 1 3/4 **Tag Team (IRE)**[25] 96 5-9-2 62 ... PaulEddery 2 60
(John A Harris) *led: rdn wl over 1f out: hdd ins fnl f: wknd towards fin* 13/2[3]
62-0 5 1 **Blythe Spirit**[11] 196 7-8-6 52 ... (t) PaulHanagan 12 47
(R A Fahey) *bhd: rdn and hdwy jst over 1f out: nt rch ldrs* 13/2[3]
200- 6 1/2 **Ladies Knight**[292] 1138 6-8-4 53 ... (v) PatrickMathers(3) 5 46
(D Shaw) *s.i.s: hdwy over 1f out: nvr trbld ldrs* 16/1
0044 7 1/2 **Percy Douglas**[1] 299 6-8-3 56 oh5 ow6 ... (vt) AnnStokell(7) 3 47
(Miss A Stokell) *mid-div: hdwy on ins wl over 1f out: no imp fnl f* 20/1
5-06 8 1/2 **He's A Rocket (IRE)**[10] 212 5-8-9 55 ... (b) PatCosgrave 13 44
(K R Burke) *s.i.s: n.d* 25/1
3303 9 1 1/2 **Savile's Delight (IRE)**[9] 225 7-9-3 63 ... (b) TomEaves 7 47
(R Brotherton) *prom over 2f* 10/1
04-0 10 1/2 **Oceanico Dot Com (IRE)**[21] 126 4-9-0 60 ... FrancisNorton 8 42
(A Berry) *w ldrs: ev ch over 2f out: rdn whn bmpd wl over 1f out: sn wknd* 33/1
0-40 11 1/2 **Holly Springs**[7] 255 4-7-13 52 ... (b) KirstyMilczarek(7) 6 32
(Mrs C A Dunnett) *prom: bmpd wl over 1f out: sn wknd* 40/1
36-1 12 3 1/2 **Cashel Mead**[21] 119 6-8-12 58 ... (b) AdrianTNicholls 10 26
(J L Spearing) *prom: rdn over 3f out: wkng whn c wd and bmpd wl over 1f out* 12/1

62.00 secs (-0.82) **Going Correction** -0.125s/f (Stan) 12 Ran SP% 124.8
Speed ratings (Par 101):101,100,98,95,94 93,92,91,89,88 87,82
CSF £12.04 CT £66.07 TOTE £3.60: £1.20, £1.60, £5.10; EX 19.40 Place 6 £6.81, Place 5 £3.52.
Owner Blue Metropolis **Bred** Skymarc Farm Inc And Dr A J O'Reilly **Trained** Six Mile Bottom, Cambs

FOCUS
A similar sprint handicap to the first division, both in terms of quality and the way the race was run.
Ladies Knight Official explanation: jockey said gelding hung left
Percy Douglas Official explanation: jockey said horse had bled from the nose
T/Jkpt: Not won. T/Plt: £12.50 to a £1 stake. Pool: £45,720.90. 2,661.35 winning tickets. T/Qpdt: £6.20 to a £1 stake. Pool: £2,684.40. 317.50 winning tickets. KH

307 LINGFIELD (L-H)
Tuesday, February 7

OFFICIAL GOING: Standard
Wind: Moderate, half-behind

321 PLAY IN MONTE CARLO WITH LITTLEWOODSPOKER.COM CLAIMING STKS 7f (P)
1:30 (1:30) (Class 6) 4-Y-0+ **£2,388** (£705; £352) **Stalls** Low

Form RPR
-202 1 **Marko Jadeo (IRE)**[13] 192 8-9-3 76 ... DaneO'Neill 10 79+
(S Dow) *stdd s and held up in rr: hdwy whn swtchd rt over 1f out: str run to ld wl ins fnl f: won gng away* 5/2[1]
-121 2 1 1/4 **Mystic Man (FR)**[9] 235 8-9-3 77 ... (b) PaulHanagan 11 76
(I W McInnes) *b: t.k.h: mid-div: hdwy 2f out: rdn to ld ent fnl f: hdd wl ins* 7/1[3]
3-03 3 shd **Hadath (IRE)**[6] 262 9-8-6 60 ow1 ... (b) TQuinn 3 64
(B G Powell) *bhd tl hdwy over 1f out: rdn and r.o fnl f* 7/2[2]
-640 4 3 1/2 **Joy And Pain**[13] 192 5-9-4 65 ... GeorgeBaker 8 67
(J R Boyle) *s.i.s: sn mid-div: hdwy 2f out: ev ch ent fnl f: nt qckn ins* 8/1
-460 5 shd **Tregarron**[8] 251 5-8-2 56 ... StephaneBreux(3) 12 54
(R Hannon) *lw: hld up in rr: c wd into st: styd on wl fnl f* 14/1
000- 6 1 **Goldhill Prince**[121] 5754 4-8-5 53 ... (p) JohnEgan 1 52
(Ernst Oertel) *chsd ldrs: rdn wl over 1f out: kpt on one pce* 66/1
04-0 7 1 **Smokincanon**[6] 262 4-8-5 60 ow1 ... RobertMiles(3) 5 52
(W G M Turner) *chsd ldr fr 1/2-way tl wknd fnl f* 33/1
4-15 8 1/2 **Resplendent Prince**[26] 100 4-8-13 66 ... (v) IanMongan 9 56
(T G Mills) *lw: led tl rdn and hdd ent fnl f: wknd* 7/2[2]
05-5 9 nk **Sahara Prince (IRE)**[9] 235 6-8-10 68 ow1 ... (v[1]) TonyCulhane 2 52
(K A Morgan) *lw: chsd ldders tl rdn and wknd appr fnl f* 33/1
04-0 10 1 1/4 **Harbour House**[6] 262 7-8-3 40 ... ChrisCatlin 4 42
(J J Bridger) *trckd ldr to 1/2-way: rdn and wknd over 2f out* 66/1
20-0 11 shd **Rosiella**[11] 209 4-8-7 45 ow1 ... (b) FergusSweeney 6 45
(M Blanshard) *hld up: a in rr* 66/1
003- 12 1 3/4 **Silver Reign**[55] 6578 5-8-5 40 ... FrancisNorton 7 39
(J J Bridger) *mid-div: wknd over 2f out and eased whn beatern ins fnl f* 100/1

1m 24.17s (-1.72) **Going Correction** -0.175s/f (Stan) 12 Ran SP% 114.6
Speed ratings (Par 101):102,100,100,96,96 95,94,93,93,91 91,89
CSF £19.36 TOTE £2.80: £1.70, £2.40, £1.90; EX 14.90.Mystic Man was the subject of a friendly claim. Tregarron was claimed by P. A. Blockley for £6,000.
Owner J R May **Bred** P Casey **Trained** Epsom, Surrey
■ Stewards' Enquiry : Dane O'Neill six-day ban (inc four deferred days): used whip with excessive frequency and without giving time to respond (Feb 18, 20-24)

FOCUS
Not a bad claimer and the pace was strong, resulting in a finish fought out by hold-up performers.

322 $500K GUARANTEED WITH LITTLEWOODSPOKER.COM H'CAP 6f (P)
2:00 (2:00) (Class 6) (0-60,60) 3-Y-0 **£2,388** (£705; £352) **Stalls** Low

Form RPR
4-61 1 **Pauvic (IRE)**[10] 226 3-9-3 59 ... (v) TonyCulhane 5 71
(Mrs A Duffield) *lw: wnt lft s but led: clr over 2f out: drvn out fnl f and a in command* 2/1[1]
65-0 2 3 1/2 **Par Excellence**[9] 239 3-8-7 54 ... MarcHalford(5) 4 53
(W G M Turner) *hmpd s: rr whn n.m.r over 2f out: hdwy whn nt clr run over 1f out: r.o ins fnl f to go 2nd last strides* 20/1
00-0 3 hd **Spirit Of Coniston**[29] 68 3-9-0 56 ... DaneO'Neill 1 54
(M Wellings) *a in tch: rdn to chse wnr over 1f out: lost 2nd last strides* 6/1[3]
4-44 4 1 1/2 **Succeed (IRE)**[9] 239 3-9-3 59 ... GeorgeBaker 3 52
(Mrs H Sweeting) *hld up in tch: hdwy 2f out: r.o one pce fnl f* 11/4[2]
606- 5 1 3/4 **Otis B Driftwood**[129] 5627 3-9-4 60 ... (v) MickyFenton 6 47
(M Quinn) *bit bkwd: chsd wnr after 2f: sn rdn: wknd ent fnl f* 7/1
00-0 6 5 **Red Vixen (IRE)**[10] 226 3-8-8 50 ... MartinDwyer 7 19
(C N Allen) *racd wd thrght and lost tch wl over 1f out* 7/1
00-0 7 2 **Sea Of Serenity (IRE)**[17] 165 3-8-7 49 ... ChrisCatlin 2 10
(P A Blockley) *trckd wnr 2f: sn bhd* 14/1

1m 11.82s (-0.99) **Going Correction** -0.175s/f (Stan) 7 Ran SP% 110.7
Speed ratings (Par 95):99,94,94,92,89 83,80
CSF £39.00 CT £195.17 TOTE £2.20: £1.50, £11.00; EX 24.80.
Owner Middleham Park Racing XLV **Bred** Thomas Stacey **Trained** Constable Burton, N Yorks

FOCUS
An ordinary handicap made up mainly of plating-class performers.
Red Vixen(IRE) Official explanation: vet said filly returned lame

323 LITTLEWOODSPOKER.COM - THE TRUSTED NAME IN GAMING H'CAP 6f (P)
2:30 (2:31) (Class 5) (0-75,75) 4-Y-0+
£3,116 (£933; £466; £233; £116; £29) **Stalls** Low

Form RPR
106- 1 **Effective**[144] 5263 6-8-11 68 ow1 ... DarrenWilliams 4 77
(A P Jarvis) *mde all: drvn out fnl f* 9/1
350- 2 nk **Adantino**[120] 5802 7-8-13 70 ... (b) GeorgeBaker 9 78
(B R Millman) *hld up in rr: racd wd: gd hdwy over 1f out: r.o to go 2nd last stride* 14/1
060- 3 shd **Thurlestone Rock**[110] 5999 6-8-12 69 ... ChrisCatlin 6 77
(B J Meehan) *chsd wnr: hrd rdn fnl f: lost 2nd post* 6/1[3]
4-30 4 1 **Undeterred**[3] 295 10-9-4 75 ... JamieMackay 10 80
(K J Burke) *racd wd: rdn and kpt on fnl f: nvr nrr* 14/1
0214 5 1/2 **Majestical (IRE)**[3] 292 4-8-10 67 ... (p) TonyCulhane 2 70
(J M Bradley) *slowly away: hdwy over 1f out: n.d* 7/2[2]
-503 6 3/4 **Willheconquertoo**[10] 224 6-8-13 70 ... (v) PaulHanagan 8 71
(I W McInnes) *slowly away: a towards rr and nvr on terms* 10/1
0-20 6 dht **Cherokee Nation**[17] 169 5-8-9 66 ... (b[1]) TQuinn 1 67
(P W D'Arcy) *lw: trckd ldrs: rdn over 1f out: wknd ins fnl f* 9/1
455- 8 3/4 **Million Percent**[39] 6689 7-8-10 67 ... PatCosgrave 7 66
(K R Burke) *b: in tch on outside: effrt 2f out: wknd ins fnl f* 12/1
1-64 9 1 1/2 **Franksalot (IRE)**[10] 224 6-9-0 71 ... EddieAhern 5 65
(Miss B Sanders) *lw: prom: rdn 1/2-way: wknd 2f out* 3/1[1]
65-0 9 dht **Fizzlephut (IRE)**[28] 80 4-9-4 75 ... PaulFitzsimons 3 69
(Miss J R Tooth) *chsd ldrs: rdn 1/2-way: sn wknd* 25/1

1m 11.59s (-1.22) **Going Correction** -0.175s/f (Stan) 10 Ran SP% 115.5
Speed ratings (Par 103):101,100,100,99,98 97,97,96,94,94
CSF £125.61 CT £840.94 TOTE £7.20: £2.70, £4.40, £2.50; EX 243.80.
Owner Eurostrait Ltd **Bred** Peter Balding **Trained** Twyford, Bucks
■ Stewards' Enquiry : Darren Williams one-day ban: careless riding (Feb 18)

FOCUS
A competitive-looking handicap but the pace was only fair.

324 PLAY IN THE CARIBBEAN WITH LITTLEWOODSPOKER.COM H'CAP 1m 2f (P)
3:00 (3:01) (Class 6) (0-65,65) 4-Y-0+ **£3,238** (£963; £481; £240) **Stalls** Low

Form RPR
56-4 1 **Eloquent Knight (USA)**[10] 223 4-9-4 65 ... MartinDwyer 3 73
(W R Muir) *lw: chsd ldrs: rdn and responded wl to ld fnl 50yds* 9/2[1]
010 2 3/4 **Devil's Island**[9] 236 4-9-0 61 ... JamieMackay 6 68
(Sir Mark Prescott) *lw: in tch: prog to to go 2nd 3f out: led appr fnl f: no ex and hdd fnl 50yds* 6/1[3]
50-0 3 1 **King Of Knight (IRE)**[13] 186 5-9-0 60 ... TonyCulhane 8 65
(G Prodromou) *hld up in rr: hdwy on ins over 1f out: r.o: nvr nrr* 9/1
36-2 4 nk **Webbswood Lad (IRE)**[35] 18 5-9-0 60 ... (p) MickyFenton 2 64
(Stef Liddiard) *lw: t.k.h: hld up: hdwy on ins 2f out: styd on fnl f: nvr nrr* 14/1
-213 5 hd **Augustine**[9] 242 5-8-13 59 ... DarrenWilliams 1 63
(P W Hiatt) *led: rdn 2f out: hdd over 1f out: wknd ins fnl f* 5/1[2]
-136 6 hd **Barton Sands (IRE)**[13] 185 9-8-12 58 ... (t) J-PGuillambert 5 62
(Ernst Oertel) *bhd tl hdwy on ins over 1f out: r.o one pce* 8/1
1-25 7 1/2 **Competitor**[13] 185 5-8-12 58 ... (t) DaneO'Neill 12 61
(J Akehurst) *mid-divisision: effrt over 1f out: fadeed ins fnl f* 12/1
040- 8 7 **Eijaaz (IRE)**[181] 4272 5-8-8 61 ... KristinStubbs(7) 11 50
(Mrs L Stubbs) *slowly away: nvr on terms* 33/1
40-4 9 1/2 **Ramsgill (USA)**[13] 187 4-8-10 64 ... (b[1]) JamesDoyle(7) 4 52
(N P Littmoden) *trckd ldr to 3f out: sn btn* 9/1
6-13 10 5 **Bishops Finger**[13] 187 6-9-2 62 ... (b) JohnEgan 9 41
(Jamie Poulton) *b: mid-div: effrt over 3f out: wknd over 2f out* 12/1
0-00 11 nk **Baboosh (IRE)**[10] 223 5-9-4 64 ... MichaelTebbutt 14 42
(M Wigham) *hld up in rr: rdn over 2f out: a bhd* 100/1
200- 12 7 **Jubilee Dream**[52] 6596 4-9-2 63 ... IanMongan 7 28
(Mrs L J Mongan) *chsd ldrs: rdn 4f out: wknd 3f out* 20/1
04-0 13 1 3/4 **Contended (IRE)**[24] 114 4-8-13 60 ... HayleyTurner 13 22
(Mrs L C Jewell) *a bhd* 50/1
0-03 14 5 **Buscador (USA)**[10] 231 7-8-11 57 ... EddieAhern 10 9
(W M Brisbourne) *trckd ldrs tl wknd over 3f out* 12/1

2m 5.38s (-2.41) **Going Correction** -0.175s/f (Stan)
WFA 4 from 5yo+ 1lb 14 Ran SP% 120.6
Speed ratings (Par 101):102,101,100,100,100 100,99,94,93,89 89,83,82,78
CSF £30.09 CT £238.76 TOTE £5.70: £2.10, £2.90, £4.00; EX 43.80.

Owner M J Caddy **Bred** Eaglestone Farm Inc **Trained** Lambourn, Berks

FOCUS

Straightforward form to rate and sound enough for the grade judging by the performances of the third, sixth and seventh.

Bishops Finger Official explanation: jockey said gelding had no more to give

Buscador(USA) Official explanation: jockey said gelding hung right

325 GET TO THE WORLD SERIES @LITTLEWOODSPOKER.COM H'CAP — 1m 4f (P)

3:30 (3:30) (Class 4) (0-85,85) 4-Y-0+ — **£5,505** (£1,637; £818; £408) **Stalls** Low

Form — RPR

5-50 **1** **The Violin Player (USA)**[20] [135] 5-8-13 **80** .... TQuinn 9 — 85
(H J Collingridge) *hld up in rr: hdwy on outside over 1f out: rdn and r.o wl to ld cl home* **7/2**[2]

-203 **2** *shd* **Eastborough (IRE)**[9] [237] 7-8-8 **75** .... FergusSweeney 3 — 80
(B G Powell) *stdd s: hld up in rr: hdwy 2f out: stongly rdn to go 2nd post* **8/1**

2-32 **3** *hd* **Mad Carew (USA)**[24] [113] 7-8-8 **75** .... (e) MartinDwyer 6 — 80
(J R Boyle) *lw: a in tch: rdn to ld appr fnl f: rdn: hdd and lost 2nd nr fin* **13/2**

R1-3 **4** *½* **Champagne Shadow (IRE)**[27] [88] 5-8-12 **79** .... (b) GeorgeBaker 2 — 83
(G L Moore) *trckd ldrs: outpcd 3f out: rallied and r.o fnl f* **9/2**[3]

1-60 **5** *1* **Dower House**[10] [222] 11-9-4 **85** .... (t) ChrisCatlin 1 — 88
(Andrew Turnell) *hld up in rr: outpcd over 2f out: rallied and kpt on fnl f* **11/2**

056- **6** *5* **Wellington Hall (GER)**[53] [6592] 8-8-11 **78** .... EddieAhern 8 — 73
(P W Chapple-Hyam) *lw: trckd ldr tl rdn and wknd over 1f out* **3/1**[1]

120- **7** *9* **Habanero**[26] [5588] 5-9-4 **85** .... TonyCulhane 5 — 65
(Miss S J Wilton) *lw: set stdy pce: qcknd over 2f out: rdn and hdd over 1f out: eased whn btn ins fnl f* **25/1**

2m 35.11s (0.72) **Going Correction** -0.175s/f (Stan)
WFA 4 from 5yo+ 3lb — **7** Ran SP% **109.1**
Speed ratings (Par 105):90,89,89,89,88 85,79
CSF £27.88 CT £155.08 TOTE £7.10: £3.50, £3.10; EX 34.30 Trifecta £37.80 Pool: £645.20 - 12.10 winning tickets..

Owner Unicorn Free Spirit Partnership **Bred** Stephen D Peskoff **Trained** Exning, Suffolk

FOCUS

A slow early pace resulted in a sprint to the line and the winner came from last to first. The form is unreliable and the winning time was very moderate for a race of its class.

326 GET A £25 MONTHLY REWARD - LITTLEWOODSPOKER.COM FILLIES' (S) STKS — 1m (P)

4:00 (4:02) (Class 6) 3-Y-O — **£2,388** (£705; £352) **Stalls** High

Form — RPR

-424 **1** **Tafilah**[12] [197] 3-8-12 54 .... (v) JohnEgan 7 — 55
(P W D'Arcy) *settled in mid-div: hdwy 2f out: led 1f out: kpt up to work* **2/1**[1]

63-4 **2** *¾* **Franky'N'Jonny**[12] [193] 3-8-12 54 .... FergalLynch 8 — 53
(J Pearce) *lw: bhd tl hdwy on outside 2f out: drvn and r.o to go 2nd ins fnl f* **5/2**[2]

0-06 **3** *2* **Bahhmirage (IRE)**[15] [176] 3-8-12 45 .... (b) MickyFenton 11 — 49
(C N Kellett) *racd wd thrght: r.o to go 3rd wl ins fnl f* **33/1**

-540 **4** *1 ¼* **Miss Champagne (IRE)**[10] [226] 3-8-12 51 .... FrancisNorton 3 — 46
(M Quinn) *led after 2f: rdn and hdd 1f out: wknd ins fnl f* **17/2**

6405 **5** *shd* **In Hope**[9] [239] 3-8-5 52 .... JamesDoyle(7) 4 — 46
(Ernst Oertel) *b: hld up in tch: outpcd 2f out: kpt on but n.d fnl furloong* **14/1**

0- **6** *1 ¼* **Lillyella (IRE)**[103] [6122] 3-8-7 .... DerekNolan(5) 2 — 43
(M J Wallace) *chsd ldrs: rdn 3f out: one pce ins fnl 2f* **6/1**[3]

646- **7** *½* **Coffin Dodger**[224] [2995] 3-8-12 40 .... MartinDwyer 5 — 42
(C N Allen) *bhd: hdwy but little ch whn nt clr run over 1f out* **33/1**

-050 **8** *1* **Sounds Simla (IRE)**[20] [139] 3-9-4 65 .... ChrisCatlin 6 — 45
(Rae Guest) *leggy: prom: chsd ldr over 2f out tl wknd fnl f* **15/2**

9 *3 ½* **Bona Dea (GER)**[86] 3-8-7 .... RobynBrisland(5) 9 — 31
(G L Moore) *a in rr* **50/1**

06-0 **10** *8* **Carefree Girl**[22] [124] 3-8-12 45 .... (b[1]) StephenCarson 1 — 13
(E A Wheeler) *plld hrd: sn chsd ldrs: wknd over 2f out* **50/1**

06-0 **11** *5* **Honey Flame**[8] [248] 3-8-12 45 .... DarrenWilliams 10 — —
(A P Jarvis) *led for 2f: chsd ldr to 2f out: wknd qckly* **50/1**

00-0 **12** *29* **Amorada**[22] [122] 3-8-12 45 .... (v[1]) TonyCulhane 12 — —
(H Morrison) *racd wd: a bhd: and virtually p.u ins fnl 2f: t.o* **40/1**

1m 39.42s (-0.01) **Going Correction** -0.175s/f (Stan) — **12** Ran SP% **119.4**
Speed ratings (Par 92):93,92,90,89,88 87,87,86,82,74 69,40
CSF £6.68 TOTE £2.50: £1.20, £1.70, £8.80; EX 8.30.The winner was bought in for 5,200gns. Franky'n'jonny was claimed by John Purcell for £6,000.

Owner Mrs Jan Harris **Bred** Hellwood Stud Farm **Trained** Newmarket, Suffolk

FOCUS

An ordinary seller restricted to fillies, and the performance of the third limits the level of the form.

Miss Champagne(IRE) Official explanation: jockey said filly stumbled turning for home

327 BETDIRECT.CO.UK FILLIES' H'CAP — 1m (P)

4:30 (4:34) (Class 5) (0-70,69) 4-Y-0+ — **£3,238** (£963; £481; £240) **Stalls** High

Form — RPR

6/53 **1** **Luna Tacumana (IRE)**[9] [236] 6-8-12 **63** .... TPQueally 6 — 71+
(J J Lambe, Ire) *lw: trckd ldrs gng wl: led over 1f out: pushed out: comf* **3/1**[1]

-456 **2** *2* **Night Storm**[9] [236] 5-8-12 **63** .... JohnEgan 9 — 67
(S Dow) *hld up: hdwy over 1f out: r.o to go 2nd ins fnl f* **8/1**

3-00 **3** *1 ¼* **Tapa**[20] [137] 4-8-7 **58** .... FrancisNorton 4 — 59
(C A Dwyer) *a in tch: r.o but nt qckn ins fnl f* **66/1**

020- **4** *nk* **Meditation**[163] [4791] 4-8-11 **69** .... JamesDoyle(7) 2 — 69
(I A Wood) *led tl hdd over 1f out: no ex fnl f* **33/1**

434- **5** *1 ¼* **Full Of Zest**[101] [6160] 4-9-1 **66** .... IanMongan 11 — 63
(Mrs L J Mongan) *mid-div: rdn over 3f out: styd on one pce ins fnl 2f* **12/1**

0-51 **6** *½* **Madhavi**[8] [252] 4-8-9 **63** 6ex .... StephaneBreux(3) 1 — 59
(R Hannon) *lw: slowly away: bhd tl mde sme late hdwy* **13/2**[3]

3061 **7** *1 ½* **Danettie**[4] [285] 5-8-9 **60** 6ex .... ChrisCatlin 8 — 53
(W M Brisbourne) *lw: chsd ldrs: rdn and wknd over 1f out* **9/2**[2]

0-00 **8** *nk* **Sweet Namibia (IRE)**[17] [170] 4-8-6 **57** .... FrankieMcDonald 5 — 49
(J W Hills) *mid-div: effrt over 1f out: nvr on terms* **33/1**

0-04 **9** *½* **Taminoula (IRE)**[6] [265] 5-8-7 **58** .... EddieAhern 10 — 49
(P Mitchell) *hld up: a in rr* **8/1**

560- **10** *5* **Miss Madame (IRE)**[235] [2657] 5-8-11 **62** .... DaneO'Neill 3 — 41
(T G Mills) *trckd ldr to 2f out: wknd qckly* **7/1**

25-0 **11** *1 ½* **Ivory Lace**[35] [17] 5-8-11 **62** .... MartinDwyer 12 — 38
(S Woodman) *a bhd* **14/1**

06-0 **12** *6* **Littleton Zephir (USA)**[35] [17] 7-8-11 **65** .... EdwardCreighton(3) 7 — 27
(Mrs P Townsley) *slowly away: a bhd* **20/1**

1m 37.49s (-1.94) **Going Correction** -0.175s/f (Stan) — **12** Ran SP% **117.7**
Speed ratings (Par 100):102,100,98,98,97 96,95,94,94,89 87,81
CSF £26.16 CT £1330.68 TOTE £3.70: £1.90, £2.80, £13.30; EX 23.50 Place 6 £101.32, Place 5 £67.14.

Owner W Hitchen **Bred** Paul Starr **Trained** Dungannon, Co. Tyrone

FOCUS

A modest handicap in which the winner has been rated to her best form in Ireland.

Ivory Lace Official explanation: jockey said mare lost its action

T/Jkpt: Part won. £19,000.60 to a £1 stake. Pool: £26,761.50. 0.50 winning tickets. T/Plt: £342.30 to a £1 stake. Pool: £48,707.75. 103.85 winning tickets. T/Qpdt: £91.10 to a £1 stake. Pool: £2,954.80. 24.00 winning tickets. JS

[299]SOUTHWELL (L-H)

Tuesday, February 7

OFFICIAL GOING: Standard

The inside rail often rides deeper than the centre of the track in the straight, but that did not appear to be the case on this card and there was no obvious bias.

Wind: Moderate, across

328 DAILY OFFERS ON CH4 TEXT P613 AMATEUR RIDERS' H'CAP — 1m 3f (F)

1:10 (1:10) (Class 6) (0-55,53) 4-Y-0+ — **£2,307** (£709; £354) **Stalls** Low

Form — RPR

10-0 **1** **Three Ships**[29] [72] 5-11-1 **52** .... MrMatthewSmith(5) 4 — 58
(Miss J Feilden) *trckd ldrs: hdwy over 3f out: rdn and ev ch over 1f out: kpt on to ld nr fin* **11/4**[2]

04-0 **2** *hd* **Spitfire Bob (USA)**[9] [240] 7-10-13 **52** .... MissKSearby(7) 8 — 58
(M E Sowersby) *in tch: hdwy 3f out: rdn over 1f out: led ins last: hdd nr fin* **16/1**

050- **3** *nk* **Galley Law**[59] [6548] 6-11-5 **51** .... MrSWalker 2 — 56
(R Craggs) *led: rdn clr over 2f out: drvn and jnd over 1f out: hdd ins last: kpt on* **5/2**[1]

2445 **4** *5* **Countback (FR)**[1] [309] 7-10-13 **50** .... MrMJJSmith(5) 1 — 47
(A W Carroll) *s.i.s and bhd: hdwy 1/2-way: chsd ldrs 3f out: sn rdn and no imp* **5/2**[1]

/00- **5** *17* **Leyaaly**[57] [6556] 7-10-7 **44** oh4 .... (t) MissGDGracey-Davison(5) 6 — 14
(Miss Z C Davison) *in tch: hdwy 1/2-way: rdn along 4f out and sn outpcd* **40/1**

10-0 **6** *1 ¾* **Active Account (USA)**[18] [156] 9-11-2 **53** .... (b) ChrisGlenister(5) 7 — 20
(J R Holt) *a towards rr* **9/1**[3]

00-P **7** *½* **Cemgraft**[5] [270] 5-10-8 **47** .... (t) MissZoeLilly(7) 11 — 13
(A J Lidderdale) *prom: rdn along 5f out: sn wknd* **20/1**

0-00 **8** *10* **Acorazado (IRE)**[18] [156] 7-10-11 **50** .... (e) MissCGrime(7) 10 — —
(C P Morlock) *a towards rr* **66/1**

/0-0 **9** *7* **Rambo Blue**[7] [257] 6-10-6 **45** .... MrJGoss(7) 3 — —
(G J Smith) *prom: pushed along 6f out: sn wknd* **50/1**

00-0 **10** *6* **Vrubel (IRE)**[32] [52] 7-10-5 **44** oh4 .... MissJessicaHolt(7) 5 — —
(J R Holt) *a bhd* **50/1**

2m 30.96s (2.06) **Going Correction** +0.10s/f (Slow) — **10** Ran SP% **112.3**
Speed ratings (Par 101):96,95,95,92,79 78,78,70,65,61
CSF £39.84 CT £120.80 TOTE £3.90: £1.50, £2.60, £1.50; EX 36.10.

Owner Ocean Trailers Ltd **Bred** Juddmonte Farms **Trained** Exning, Suffolk

FOCUS

A moderate amateur riders' handicap and, despite the pace appearing to be very sensible for a race of this type, the front three came well clear of the fourth, who in turn, finished a long way ahead of the rest. The winner has been rated up to his banded form.

329 PLAY LITTLEWOODS POOLS ON 0800 500 000 MAIDEN H'CAP (DIV I) — 1m (F)

1:40 (1:41) (Class 6) (0-55,55) 3-Y-O — **£2,047** (£604; £302) **Stalls** Low

Form — RPR

00-3 **1** **Monte Mayor Junior**[12] [193] 3-8-12 **53** .... (v) RobertHavlin 12 — 58
(D Haydn Jones) *midfield: hdwy and in tch 1/2-way: led 2f out: sn rdn and hung lft: drvn ent last: kpt on* **4/1**[1]

4-00 **2** *nk* **Chookie Windsor**[12] [197] 3-9-0 **55** .... (p) TomEaves 5 — 59
(I Semple) *in tch: hdwy 1/2-way: rdn to chal over 1f out: evercy ch whn hung lft and drvn ins last: kpt on* **9/2**[2]

04-0 **3** *8* **Hillbilly Cat (USA)**[36] [14] 3-9-0 **55** .... PaulFessey 11 — 43
(T D Barron) *chsd ldrs: rdn over 2f out: drvn and styng on whn n.m.r ent last: swtchd rt and wknd* **16/1**

00-2 **4** *2* **Mykeyta**[27] [93] 3-8-5 **46** oh1 .... DaleGibson 10 — 30
(J G Given) *sn pushed along in midfield: hdwy 3f out: drvn 2f out and sn no imp* **12/1**

0-00 **5** *¾* **Drawn Out (IRE)**[12] [193] 3-8-8 **49** ow2 .... (b) LeeEnstone 2 — 32
(P C Haslam) *cl up: ev ch 2f out: sn rdn and wknd* **20/1**

00-0 **6** *5* **Mr Cheers**[22] [120] 3-8-9 **50** .... (b) RobertWinston 8 — 23
(Miss J A Camacho) *led: rdn along 3f out: hdd & wknd 2f out* **14/1**

00-6 **7** *½* **Ever Special (IRE)**[27] [93] 3-8-0 **46** oh1 .... AndrewMullen(5) 1 — 18
(P C Haslam) *in tch: rdn along after 2f: sn lost pl and bhd* **17/2**

00-0 **8** *1 ½* **Go Amwell**[24] [112] 3-8-9 **50** .... SimonWhitworth 9 — 19
(J R Jenkins) *dwlt: a rr* **12/1**

0-63 **9** *nk* **Three Feathers**[15] [176] 3-8-5 **46** oh1 .... AlanDaly 3 — 14
(M Salaman) *bhd fr 1/2-way* **8/1**

0-55 **10** *25* **Straight As A Die**[13] [189] 3-8-7 **48** .... JimmyQuinn 6 — —
(R J Hodges) *chsd ldrs 3f: sn lost pl and bhd* **28/1**

6-06 **11** *nk* **Jazz At The Sands (USA)**[10] [226] 3-8-4 **48** .... (be[1]) PatrickMathers(3) 4 — —
(D Shaw) *keen: hld up: a rr* **6/1**[3]

000- **12** *6* **Miss Lacey (IRE)**[125] [5696] 3-8-8 **49** .... ShaneKelly 7 — —
(J A Osborne) *sn outpcd and a bhd* **14/1**

1m 45.19s (0.59) **Going Correction** +0.10s/f (Slow) — **12** Ran SP% **116.9**
Speed ratings (Par 95):101,100,92,90,89 84,84,82,82,57 57,51
CSF £21.07 CT £264.14 TOTE £4.90: £2.10, £1.50, £4.30; EX 24.00.

Owner R Phillips **Bred** M R M Bloodstock **Trained** Efail Isaf, Rhondda C Taff

FOCUS

A predictably moderate handicap given it was restricted to maidens, but a handful of these were unexposed. The race has been rated around the runner-up, who has been considered to have run to the best view of his previous form.

Miss Lacey(IRE) Official explanation: jockey said filly resented kickback

330 BETDIRECT.CO.UK (S) STKS 7f (F)
2:10 (2:11) (Class 6) 3-Y-0+ £2,388 (£705; £352) Stalls Low

Form RPR

22-0 **1** **Priorina (IRE)**[4] 290 4-9-4 52 (v) RobertHavlin 8 53
(D Haydn Jones) *cl up: led wl over 2f out: rdn and hung lft 1f out: sn drvn and kpt on* **3/1**[2]

0-13 **2** *nk* **Vancouver Gold (IRE)**[11] 210 4-9-9 63 RobertWinston 1 57
(K R Burke) *hld up in rr: gd hdwy on inner 2f out: rdn to chal ins last and ev ch tl drvn and no ex nr fin* **11/4**[1]

0-05 **3** *½* **Far Note (USA)**[5] 271 8-9-11 55 (bt) AmirQuinn(3) 2 61
(S R Bowring) *hmpd s: trckd ldrs: n.m.r 3f out: hdwy 2f out: sn rdn: ev ch whn n.m.r and swtchd rt 1f out:kpt on* **20/1**

0-30 **4** *5* **King Forever**[8] 251 4-9-9 55 MichaelHills 5 43
(D E Cantillon) *racd wd and bhd tl styd on fnl 2f: nvr a factor* **7/2**[3]

000- **5** *6* **Panshir (FR)**[63] 6514 5-9-2 62 HarryPoulton(7) 3 27
(Julian Poulton) *wnt lft s: sn in tch: hdwy to chse ldrs 1/2-way: rdn wl over 2f out and sn wknd* **10/1**

5-06 **6** *1 ½* **Ballyrush (IRE)**[9] 240 6-9-7 45 (e) StephanieBancroft(7) 6 29
(Miss D A McHale) *led: rdn along 3f out: sn hdd and grad wknd* **40/1**

00-5 **7** *1 ¼* **Cleveland Way**[36] 11 6-9-6 40 (v) DanielTudhope(3) 7 20
(D Carroll) *cl up: rdn along 3f out: sn wknd* **50/1**

016- **8** *hd* **El Palmar**[256] 2059 5-9-9 58 DeanMcKeown 4 20
(J Pearce) *chsd ldrs: rdn 3f out: sn wknd* **4/1**

0- **9** *6* **Rectangle Blue**[54] 6583 4-9-9 ShaneKelly 9 4
(Micky Hammond) *bhd fr 1/2-way* **33/1**

1m 32.19s (1.39) **Going Correction** +0.10s/f (Slow) 9 Ran SP% **115.1**
Speed ratings (Par 101):96,95,95,89,82 80,79,79,72
CSF £11.23 TOTE £3.40: £1.10, £1.70, £3.90; EX 10.10.There was no bid for the winner. El Palmar was claimed by M. Attwater for £6,000.
Owner Joseph E Keeling **Bred** J Keeling **Trained** Efail Isaf, Rhondda C Taff

FOCUS
A typically moderate seller, rated through the third to his winter best.

331 BETDIRECT FREEPHONE 0800 211 222 MAIDEN STKS 6f (F)
2:40 (2:40) (Class 5) 3-Y-0+ £3,238 (£963; £481; £240) Stalls Low

Form RPR

-3 **1** **Crimson King (IRE)**[12] 195 5-9-9 AdamKirby(3) 4 74
(T T Clement) *hld up: wd strt: rdn and rn green wl over 1f out: styd on to ld ins last: sn clr* **7/4**[1]

0 **2** *5* **Ten Tenors (IRE)**[8] 254 3-8-7 ow1 ShaneKelly 7 51
(J A Osborne) *chsd ldrs: hdwy over 2f out: rdn to ld wl over 1f out: drvn: edgd lft and hdd ins last: one pce* **9/1**

3 *1 ¼* **Spinning** 3-8-11 PaulFessey 1 51
(T D Barron) *trckd ldrs: effrt over 2f out and sn rdn: kpt on same pce appr last* **4/1**[3]

600- **4** *3 ½* **Desert Dust**[43] 6661 3-8-11 60 RobertWinston 10 41
(R M H Cowell) *cl up: rdn to ld briefly 2f out: sn hdd: n.m.r and swtchd rt ent last: wknd* **11/4**[2]

40-0 **5** *1* **Canary Dancer**[14] 181 4-9-7 40 (b) AdrianMcCarthy 8 37
(Miss Z C Davison) *led: rdn along 2f out: hdd 2f out and grad wknd* **25/1**

6 *4* **Going Skint** 3-8-11 DavidAllan 3 26
(T D Easterby) *s.i.s and bhd tl sme late hdwy* **16/1**

030- **7** *¾* **Donya One**[126] 5687 4-9-7 57 NickyMackay 9 23
(John A Harris) *in tch: wd st: sn rdn along and wknd* **14/1**

0000 **8** *7* **Penway**[7] 257 5-9-12 30 (b) BrianReilly 5 7
(A Sadik) *a rr* **80/1**

0-60 **9** *5* **Lily On A Hill**[12] 197 3-8-6 30 PaulEddery 2 —
(B Smart) *in tch on inner: rdn along 3f out: sn wknd* **100/1**

/00- **10** *shd* **Value Plus (IRE)**[253] 2135 4-9-0 70 (t) MarkCoumbe(7) 6 —
(C J Teague) *in tch: rdn along 3f out: sn wknd* **25/1**

1m 16.23s (-0.67) **Going Correction** +0.10s/f (Slow)
WFA 3 from 4yo+ 15lb 10 Ran SP% **115.5**
Speed ratings (Par 103):108,101,99,95,93 88,87,78,71,71
CSF £18.18 TOTE £2.90: £1.60, £2.40, £1.80; EX 12.60.
Owner Rothmere Racing Limited **Bred** Hazel Kelly **Trained** Newmarket, Suffolk

FOCUS
As is to be expected for older horse sprint maidens, this was a pretty modest event, and not really that competitive, but the winning time was 1.29 seconds faster than the fillies' handicap over the same trip. It has been rated around the fifth to her recent banded form.

332 PLAY NOW AT BETDIRECTPOKER.COM FILLIES' H'CAP 6f (F)
3:10 (3:10) (Class 5) (0-70,67) 4-Y-0+ £3,238 (£963; £481; £240) Stalls Low

Form RPR

0-00 **1** **Missperon (IRE)**[8] 249 4-8-1 55 (b) AndrewMullen(5) 8 61
(K A Ryan) *a.p: effrt and ev ch 2f out: sn rdn: drvn and edgd lft ins last: styd on to ld post* **8/1**

060- **2** *shd* **Shifty Night (IRE)**[70] 6464 5-8-1 57 (v) KirstyMilczarek(7) 3 62
(Mrs C A Dunnett) *chsd ldrs: hdwy 2f out: sn rdn and edgd lft over 1f out: led ent last and sn drvn: ct on line* **14/1**

00-1 **3** *shd* **Dispol Isle (IRE)**[21] 133 4-8-11 60 PhillipMakin 2 65
(T D Barron) *dwlt: sn rdn along in rr: hdwy wl over 1f out: drvn and styd on ins last: jst failed* **10/3**[1]

-021 **4** *1 ½* **Sahara Silk (IRE)**[8] 249 5-9-0 66 6ex (v) PatrickMathers(3) 6 67
(D Shaw) *sn pushed along in rr: hdwy 2f out: drvn over 1f out: kpt on ins last: nrst fin* **4/1**[3]

420- **5** *1 ¼* **Witchelle**[249] 2267 5-8-12 61 PaulFessey 1 58
(R Craggs) *led: rdn along 2f out: drvn and hdd ent last: wknd* **9/1**

-006 **6** *nk* **Cerebus**[10] 225 4-9-1 64 (b) DeanMcKeown 7 60
(M J Polglase) *chsd ldrs: rdn 2f out: sn hung lft and wknd* **7/2**[2]

0-01 **7** *9* **Tuscarora (IRE)**[17] 171 7-9-4 67 RobertWinston 4 36
(A W Carroll) *dwlt: a rr* **7/1**

04-0 **8** *8* **Stargem**[27] 89 5-8-13 62 JimmyQuinn 5 7
(J Pearce) *chsd leaders: rdn along wl over 2f out: sn wknd* **12/1**

1m 17.52s (0.62) **Going Correction** +0.10s/f (Slow) 8 Ran SP% **113.3**
Speed ratings (Par 100):99,98,98,96,95 94,82,72
CSF £107.42 CT £446.66 TOTE £6.20: £1.40, £4.00, £1.80; EX 231.20.
Owner Mrs Angie Bailey **Bred** E O'Leary **Trained** Hambleton, N Yorks
■ Stewards' Enquiry : Andrew Mullen one-day ban: used whip with excessive frequency (Feb 18)

FOCUS
Just the eight runners and a modest sprint handicap for fillies and mares, but they went a fast pace from the start and there was next to nothing separating the front three at the line. The time was as one would expect for a race like this, despite being 1.29 seconds slower than the preceding maiden.

333 PLAY LITTLEWOODS POOLS ON 0800 500 000 MAIDEN H'CAP (DIV II) 1m (F)
3:40 (3:41) (Class 6) (0-55,55) 3-Y-0 £2,047 (£604; £302) Stalls Low

Form RPR

0-63 **1** **Katie Lawson (IRE)**[11] 211 3-8-13 54 (v) RobertHavlin 7 60
(D Haydn Jones) *trckd ldrs on inner: hdwy 2f out: rdn to ld 1f out: drvn and hld on wl towards fin* **6/1**

40-0 **2** *½* **Subsidise (IRE)**[22] 123 3-8-9 50 (b[1]) DaleGibson 6 55
(J G Given) *towards rr: hdwy and wd st: rdn and edgd lft 2f out: drvn and styng on whn hung lft ent last: kpt on wl* **14/1**

3-53 **3** *2* **Cool Isle**[12] 197 3-8-12 53 (b) RobertWinston 1 54
(K A Ryan) *trckd ldrs: hdwy over 2f out: sn rdn and kpt on same pce* **10/3**[1]

03-5 **4** *1 ¾* **Tirol Livit (IRE)**[12] 193 3-8-7 48 ShaneKelly 10 46
(N Wilson) *led after 1f: rdn clr over 2f out: drvn and hdd 1f out: wknd* **8/1**

00-0 **5** *¾* **Tesoro**[29] 70 3-8-0 48 KevinGhunowa(7) 3 44
(P A Blockley) *led 1f: prom tl rdn over 2f out and grad wknd* **25/1**

30-4 **6** *9* **Youralittlemiller**[33] 49 3-9-0 55 DavidKinsella 9 33
(P G Murphy) *chsd ldrs: rdn over 2f out: sn drvn and wknd* **5/1**[3]

0-00 **7** *7* **Sahara Secret (IRE)**[12] 199 3-8-2 46 oh16 (v) PatrickMathers(3) 12 10
(D Shaw) *a towards rr* **66/1**

00-0 **8** *2 ½* **Bright**[29] 69 3-8-6 47 oh1 ow1 SimonWhitworth 8 6
(Miss J Feilden) *chsd ldrs: rdn along 3f out: wknd 2f out* **14/1**

00-0 **9** *1 ¾* **Astronova**[11] 211 3-8-9 50 MichaelHills 4 6
(M H Tompkins) *chased ldrs to 1/2-way: sn wknd* **25/1**

0-44 **10** *¾* **Genoa Star**[15] 176 3-8-5 46 oh1 (b) NickyMackay 5 —
(T J Pitt) *v.s.a: a behind* **9/2**[2]

00-0 **11** *6* **Red Tsarina**[22] 124 3-8-0 48 oh16 ow2 TJHowell(7) 11 —
(V Smith) *chsd ldrs on outer: rdn along 1/2-way: sn wknd* **80/1**

00-4 **12** *¾* **Ayala Cove (USA)**[9] 241 3-8-1 47 (t) AndrewMullen(5) 2 —
(P C Haslam) *bhd fr 1/2-way* **12/1**

1m 47.02s (2.42) **Going Correction** +0.10s/f (Slow) 12 Ran SP% **114.8**
Speed ratings (Par 95):91,90,88,86,86 77,70,67,65,65 59,58
CSF £81.02 CT £330.23 TOTE £6.30: £1.70, £5.60, £1.20; EX 107.70.
Owner Monolithic Refractories Ltd **Bred** J Kilpatrick **Trained** Efail Isaf, Rhondda C Taff
■ A treble for trainer Derek Haydn Jones and jockey Robert Havlin, who had earlier won with Monte Mayor Junior and Priorina.

FOCUS
Like the first division, a moderate handicap restricted to maidens. The form looks sound but limited.

334 LITTLEWOODS BETDIRECT H'CAP 1m 3f (F)
4:10 (4:10) (Class 5) (0-70,68) 4-Y-0+ £3,238 (£963; £481; £240) Stalls Low

Form RPR

-333 **1** **Greenbelt**[21] 131 5-8-12 62 JoeFanning 6 77+
(G M Moore) *trckd ldng pair: smooth hdwy to ld 3f out: clr 2f out: comf* **9/4**[1]

-211 **2** *3 ½* **Sand Repeal (IRE)**[10] 231 4-8-12 64 SimonWhitworth 9 73
(Miss J Feilden) *in tch: hdwy to trck ldrs over 4f out: rdn to chse wnr over 2f out: sn drvn and no imp* **10/3**[2]

4-10 **3** *5* **Padre Nostro (IRE)**[9] 246 7-8-11 61 BrianReilly 4 62
(J R Holt) *hld up in rr: hdwy over 4f out: rdn along 3f out: kpt on same pce fnl 2f* **16/1**

00-5 **4** *½* **Kirkhammerton (IRE)**[10] 230 4-8-5 57 ow2 (v) DeanMcKeown 7 57
(M J Polglase) *cl up: rdn along 3f out: sn drvn and btn* **28/1**

3-60 **5** *1 ¾* **Simply St Lucia**[25] 109 4-8-1 58 (p) AndrewMullen(5) 2 55
(J R Weymes) *led: rdn along 4f out: hdd 3f out: sn drvn and wknd* **12/1**

53-4 **6** *nk* **Trew Style**[9] 246 4-9-2 68 MichaelHills 3 65
(M H Tompkins) *in tch: hdwy to chse ldrs over 4f out: sn rdn along and wknd over 2f out* **7/2**[3]

120- **7** *21* **Mandinka**[315] 794 6-8-10 67 AnnStokell(7) 1 30
(J F Coupland) *chsd ldrs: lost pl 1/2-way: sn bhd* **16/1**

05-0 **8** *3 ½* **Mi Odds**[9] 246 10-8-11 68 RussellKennemore(7) 10 26
(Mrs N Macauley) *stdd s: a bhd* **14/1**

03-5 **9** *1 ½* **Windy Prospect**[28] 75 4-8-8 60 RobertWinston 5 15
(C R Dore) *in tch: effrt over 4f out: sn rdn along: drvn 3f out and sn wknd* **7/1**

2m 26.12s (-2.78) **Going Correction** +0.10s/f (Slow)
WFA 4 from 5yo+ 2lb 9 Ran SP% **118.1**
Speed ratings (Par 103):114,111,107,107,106 105,90,88,87
CSF £10.01 CT £96.33 TOTE £3.70: £1.20, £1.60, £5.40; EX 9.30.
Owner Mrs A Roddis **Bred** Juddmonte Farms **Trained** Middleham Moor, N Yorks

FOCUS
An ordinary, uncompetitive middle-distance handicap, but the pace was good and Greenbelt pulled clear to record what was in fact a very smart winning time indeed. The race has been rated around the third's course and distance win last month.
Padre Nostro(IRE) Official explanation: jockey said gelding hung left in home straight

335 TEXT "BETDIRECT" TO 88600 H'CAP 5f (F)
4:40 (4:40) (Class 6) (0-60,60) 3-Y-0 £2,388 (£705; £352) Stalls High

Form RPR

26-1 **1** **Garlogs**[26] 102 3-9-4 60 RobertWinston 1 65
(A Bailey) *mde all: rdn clr 2f out: styd on strly* **7/4**[1]

3-12 **2** *2* **Diktalex (IRE)**[8] 248 3-8-11 60 (vt[1]) StacyRenwick(7) 4 58
(M J Attwater) *racd wd: chsd ldrs: rdn to chse wnr wl over 1f out: sn edgd lft and no imp* **7/1**

0-23 **3** *1 ¾* **Stoneacre Fred (IRE)**[9] 239 3-8-13 55 (b) RobbieFitzpatrick 6 47
(Peter Grayson) *s.i.s: hdwy to chse ldrs 1/2-way: rdn and hung lft wl over 1f out: sn no imp* **3/1**[2]

5-40 **4** *4* **No Inkling (IRE)**[22] 120 3-8-4 46 oh1 NickyMackay 2 24
(John A Harris) *chsd ldrs: rdn along over 2f out: sn one pce* **28/1**

001- **5** *2* **Tombalina**[51] 6605 3-8-9 58 MarkCoumbe(7) 5 30
(C J Teague) *cl up: rdn 1/2-way: wknd fnl 2f* **11/1**

2-00 **6** *2 ½* **Eeshee**[11] 212 3-8-12 54 AdrianMcCarthy 8 17
(S L Keightley) *in tch: rdn along 1/2-way and sn outpcd* **28/1**

5-10 **7** *¾* **Drink To Me Only**[11] 211 3-8-6 53 AndrewMullen(5) 9 14
(J R Weymes) *rdn along and outpcd fr 1/2-way* **7/1**

24-6 **8** *6* **Whipper In**[22] 120 3-8-8 50 (v[1]) LeeEnstone 7 —
(P C Haslam) *a rr: bhd fr 1/2-way* **13/2**[3]

00-0 **9** *11* **Wise Kid**[26] 102 3-8-4 46 oh16 (p) PaulFessey 10 —
(P T Midgley) *sn outpcd and wl bhd fr 1/2-way* **100/1**

59.11 secs (-1.19) **Going Correction** -0.35s/f (Stan) 9 Ran SP% **115.9**
Speed ratings (Par 95):95,91,89,82,79 75,74,64,47
CSF £14.70 CT £35.17 TOTE £2.60: £1.10, £2.30, £1.60; EX 8.10 Place 6 £23.03, Place 5 £14.26.

Owner Peter G Freeman **Bred** Peter Taplin **Trained** Cotebrook, Cheshire

FOCUS

A moderate, uncompetitive sprint handicap and, as is so often the case over this course and distance, those drawn low were at an advantage. It has been rated around the runner-up.
T/Plt: £17.40 to a £1 stake. Pool: £34,292.50. 1,434.20 winning tickets. T/Qpdt: £6.40 to a £1 stake. Pool: £2,629.50. 300.10 winning tickets. JR

[321]LINGFIELD (L-H)

Wednesday, February 8

OFFICIAL GOING: Standard

Wind: Moderate, half-against Weather: Fine but cloudy

336 WSOP QUALIFIERS WITH LITTLEWOODSPOKER.COM H'CAP (DIV I) 7f (P)

12:50 (12:54) (Class 6) (0-58,61) 4-Y-0+ **£2,047** (£604; £302) **Stalls** Low

Form RPR

33-1 **1** **Fajr (IRE)**[7] 268 4-9-5 **61** 6ex MickyFenton 14 71+
(N B King) *lw: pressed ldrs: wnt 2nd 2f out: rdn to ld 1f out: grad asserted* **2/1**[1]

000- **2** *1 ¼* **Grezie**[40] 6692 4-8-7 **52** RobertMiles(3) 3 58
(T D McCarthy) *b: b.hind: w ldr: led 5f out: rdn and edgd rt over 1f out: hdd 1f out: kpt on* **33/1**

-040 **3** *2* **Taminoula (IRE)**[1] 327 5-8-9 **58** JamesDoyle(7) 7 59
(P Mitchell) *pressed ldrs: pushed along 1/2-way: styd on u.p to chse ldng pair fnl f: no imp* **14/1**

000- **4** *1* **Secam (POL)**[43] 6671 7-8-12 **57** (b) EdwardCreighton(3) 8 55+
(Mrs P Townsley) *hld up on inner: nt clr run over 2f out: threaded through fr over 1f out: kpt on: nrst fin* **14/1**

3-35 **5** *nk* **Cayman Breeze**[11] 227 6-8-11 **53** ShaneKelly 1 50
(J M Bradley) *chsd ldrs: drvn fr 1/2-way: one pce and no real prog fnl 2f* **8/1**[2]

0-00 **6** *1* **Jennverse**[11] 227 4-8-12 **54** FergusSweeney 6 49
(D K Ivory) *towards rr: rdn 3f out: prog over 1f out: styd on same pce* **33/1**

600- **7** *½* **Even Hotter**[40] 6692 5-8-4 **46** oh1 ChrisCatlin 10 40
(D W P Arbuthnot) *wl in rr: kpt on fr over 1f out: no ch* **100/1**

0-33 **8** *nk* **Triple Zero (IRE)**[9] 255 4-9-2 **58** DarrenWilliams 13 51
(A P Jarvis) *led to 5f out: chsd ldr to 2f out: wknd over 1f out* **12/1**[3]

030- **9** *1* **Luciferous (USA)**[178] 4390 4-8-7 **52** ow1 AmirQuinn(3) 5 44+
(P G Murphy) *bit bkwd: w ldrs: rdn 1/2-way: btn 2f out: heavily eased fnl f* **66/1**

00-6 **10** *hd* **Siraj**[36] 21 7-8-12 **54** (p) MichaelTebbutt 12 44
(J Ryan) *hld up wl in rr: racd v wd: nvr a factor* **33/1**

0-00 **11** *½* **Marsad (IRE)**[18] 171 12-8-13 **55** PaulDoe 4 43
(J Akehurst) *dwlt: a in last trio: rdn and no prog over 2f out* **25/1**

04- **12** *1 ½* **Sunny Afternoon**[71] 6460 6-8-13 **55** (v) EddieAhern 2 47+
(Miss E C Lavelle) *trckd ldrs on inner: no prog 2f out: nt clr run 1f out and eased* **12/1**[3]

00-4 **13** *1* **Ernmoor**[35] 32 4-8-5 **47** HayleyTurner 9 29
(J R Best) *nvr beyond midfield: u.p 3f out: sn wknd* **20/1**

1m 24.64s (-1.25) **Going Correction** -0.20s/f (Stan) 13 Ran SP% **93.1**
Speed ratings (Par 101):99,97,95,94,93 92,92,91,90,90 89,88,86
CSF £51.33 CT £316.20 TOTE £2.00: £1.10, £10.20, £5.30; EX 58.80.
Owner C H Huggan **Bred** Shadwell Estate Company Limited **Trained** Newmarket, Suffolk
■ Stewards' Enquiry : Darren Williams one-day ban: careless riding (Feb 20)

FOCUS

A moderate contest but another decent performance by the progressive Fajr. The winning time was fractionally slower than the second division and the form does not look that strong.
Sunny Afternoon Official explanation: jockey said mare was denied a clear run

337 BETDIRECT.CO.UK MAIDEN STKS 1m 2f (P)

1:20 (1:22) (Class 5) 3-Y-O **£3,886** (£1,156; £577; £288) **Stalls** Low

Form RPR

53- **1** **Soho Square**[97] 6234 3-9-0 JoeFanning 12 71
(M Johnston) *mde virtually all and sn racd on inner: jnd 2f out: rdn and hung bdly rt ins fnl f: jst hld on* **3/1**[1]

660- **2** *hd* **Jebel Ali (IRE)**[145] 5271 3-9-0 67 ChrisCatlin 6 71
(B Gubby) *bit bkwd: hld up in midfield: prog on outer over 3f out: swtchd to inner and drvn over 1f out: jnd wnr nr fin: jst pipped* **16/1**

6 **3** *1* **Permanent Way (IRE)**[12] 215 3-9-0 MichaelTebbutt 5 69+
(B J Meehan) *w'like: hld up in midfield: prog over 3f out: jnd wnr 2f out: carried rt ins fnl f: nt qckn* **9/1**[3]

00- **4** *1 ¼* **Gus**[100] 6200 3-9-0 MichaelHills 2 66
(B W Hills) *w'like: snatched up on inner after 2f: swtchd to outer 1/2-way: prog and bmpd 3f out: pressed ldrs 2f out: one pce fnl f* **12/1**

5 *5* **Asarabacca (FR)** 3-8-9 ShaneKelly 3 52
(E A L Dunlop) *leggy: dwlt: hld up towards rr: sme prog 3f out but sn outpcd: nudged along and kpt on steadily* **25/1**

0-45 **6** *shd* **Questive**[14] 191 3-9-0 71 (t) PaulHanagan 11 57
(E A L Dunlop) *hld up in midfield: outpcd wl over 2f out: shuffled along and one pce fnl 2f* **3/1**[1]

-5 **7** *1* **Hazium (IRE)**[36] 16 3-8-9 LPKeniry 7 50
(Patrick Morris, Ire) *dwlt: t.k.h: hld up towards rr: outpcd 3f out: no real imp after* **25/1**

05- **8** *1* **Lord Laing (USA)**[65] 6502 3-9-0 JimmyQuinn 8 53
(H J Collingridge) *b: w ldrs: losing pl sltly whn snatched up on inner over 2f out: n.d after: shkn up and kpt on steadily* **10/1**

60- **9** *2* **Star Of Canterbury (IRE)**[141] 5390 3-9-0 DarrenWilliams 14 49
(A P Jarvis) *pressed wnr tl wknd over 2f out* **25/1**

0-5 **10** *shd* **Prince Darius**[11] 217 3-9-0 EddieAhern 1 49
(P W Chapple-Hyam) *hmpd on inner after 2f: a in rr after: brief effrt over 2f out: pushed along and no real prog* **7/2**[2]

00 **11** *nk* **King's College (USA)**[14] 191 3-8-7 (b[1]) JamieJones(7) 9 48
(G L Moore) *dwlt: a wl in rr: rdn and no prog 3f out* **100/1**

0-0 **12** *1* **Carpeting**[9] 254 3-9-0 DerekMcGaffin 4 46
(D Morris) *rn green: chsd ldrs tl wknd over 2f out* **100/1**

00 **13** *27* **Beginners Luck (IRE)**[22] 132 3-8-6 40 DanielTudhope(3) 13 —
(D Carroll) *t.k.h early: a wl in rr: t.o* **100/1**

-0 **14** *nk* **The Lady Ermyn**[14] 191 3-8-9 FrancisNorton 10 —
(T G Mills) *prom: wkng whn no room on inner 3f out: t.o* **66/1**

2m 8.01s (0.22) **Going Correction** -0.20s/f (Stan) 14 Ran SP% **120.9**
Speed ratings (Par 97):91,90,90,89,85 84,84,83,81,81 81,80,59,58
CSF £51.69 TOTE £3.00: £1.30, £5.70, £2.50; EX 92.80.
Owner Jumeirah Racing **Bred** Exors Of The Late Gerald W Leigh **Trained** Middleham Moor, N Yorks
■ Stewards' Enquiry : Michael Hills one-day ban: careless riding (Feb 20)
Jamie Jones one-day ban: used whip when out of contention (Feb 20)

FOCUS

A modest winning time, but the race should produce winners with the runner-up the best guide to the level.
Questive Official explanation: trainer's representative said colt had a breathing problem

338 BETDIRECT FREEPHONE 0800 211 222 CLAIMING STKS 1m 5f (P)

1:55 (1:55) (Class 6) 4-Y-0+ **£2,266** (£674; £337; £168) **Stalls** Low

Form RPR

0- **1** **Tignasse (FR)**[12] 6598 5-7-13 52 (be) RobynBrisland(5) 8 43
(G L Moore) *s.i.s: hld up in 6th: prog to chse clr ldng pair 3f out: clsd to ld 1f out: hung fire but rdn clr* **25/1**

-010 **2** *3* **Isa'Af (IRE)**[9] 250 7-8-10 69 JosephWalsh(7) 2 51
(P W Hiatt) *led: kicked on 4f out: hrd pressed 2f out: hdd 1f out: plugged on* **4/1**[2]

0-30 **3** *nk* **Mujazaf**[2] 309 4-8-4 50 EdwardCreighton(3) 5 45
(Miss Sheena West) *mostly chsd ldr: rdn to chal over 2f out: upsides 1f out: nt qckn* **7/1**

000- **4** *½* **Lewis Island (IRE)**[49] 6644 7-9-7 70 (e[1]) RobertWinston 3 54
(G L Moore) *s.v.s: hld up in last: sme prog 3f out but stl wl off the pce: styd on wl fron over 1f out: nvr nr ldrs* **5/1**[3]

-526 **5** *2* **Jadeeron**[2] 309 7-9-11 45 (v) OscarUrbina 1 56
(Miss D A McHale) *dwlt: hld up in rr: prog over 3f out but nt on terms w ldrs: one pce fnl 2f* **16/1**

000- **6** *2 ½* **Easter Ogil (IRE)**[81] 6377 11-9-4 56 AmirQuinn(3) 6 48
(P G Murphy) *dwlt: wl in rr: prog 3f out but nt on terms w ldrs: one pce fnl 2f* **12/1**

-362 **7** *1* **Khanjar (USA)**[6] 273 6-9-5 73 PatCosgrave 7 45
(K R Burke) *lw: chsd ldrs: outpcd 3f out: no ch after* **11/8**[1]

060- **8** *22* **Isabella Rossini**[56] 6577 4-8-4 35 ChrisCatlin 4 —
(A M Hales) *b. nr fore: chsd ldrs: wknd 3f out: t.o* **50/1**

06-0 **9** *6* **Satin Rose**[2] 309 4-9-2 45 JohnEgan 9 6
(K J Burke) *a in rr: wknd 3f out: t.o* **33/1**

000- **10** *dist* **Rhetorical**[80] 4934 5-8-13 35 LPKeniry 10 —
(P Butler) *prom tl wknd rapidly 5f out: wl t.o* **100/1**

2m 46.16s (-2.14) **Going Correction** -0.20s/f (Stan)
WFA 4 from 5yo+ 4lb 10 Ran SP% **114.6**
Speed ratings (Par 101):98,96,95,95,94 92,92,78,75,—
CSF £118.90 TOTE £40.10: £6.30, £1.40, £2.10; EX 158.00.
Owner The Ashden Partnership **Bred** Haras D'Ecouves And Ronald Reeves **Trained** Woodingdean, E Sussex

FOCUS

A moderate claimer in which those best in at the weights came to the fore, with the exception of disappointing favourite Khanjar. However, the proximity of the fifth tends to limit the form.
Easter Ogil(IRE) Official explanation: trainer said gelding had a breathing problem
Khanjar(USA) Official explanation: jockey said gelding was unsuited by being dropped in

339 WSOP QUALIFIERS WITH LITTLEWOODSPOKER.COM H'CAP (DIV II) 7f (P)

2:30 (2:30) (Class 6) (0-58,58) 4-Y-0+ **£2,047** (£604; £302) **Stalls** Low

Form RPR

32-3 **1** **White Bear (FR)**[10] 240 4-8-13 **55** (b[1]) RobertWinston 2 64
(C R Dore) *lw: trckd ldrs gng easily: smooth run on inner to ld jst over 1f out: sn in command* **7/1**

04-0 **2** *1 ½* **Bodden Bay**[22] 127 4-8-7 **52** DanielTudhope(3) 12 57
(D Carroll) *lw: w ldrs: rdn over 2f out: chal over 1f out: kpt on same pce* **13/2**[3]

-500 **3** *hd* **Pheckless**[5] 285 7-8-5 **47** JohnEgan 11 51
(J M Bradley) *b: t.k.h: hld up and sn last: stl wl in rr on inner 2f out: eased out over 1f out: r.o fnl f: snatched 3rd nr fin* **10/1**

6-22 **4** *hd* **Lowestoft Playboy**[7] 268 4-8-11 **58** GregFairley(5) 8 62
(J Jay) *led for 1f: pressed ldr: upsides and drvn 1f out: nt qckn* **4/1**[1]

0-21 **5** *¾* **Trouble Maker**[16] 177 5-8-11 **53** MartinDwyer 1 55
(A M Balding) *b.hind: hld up towards rr: effrt 2f out: styd on fr over 1f out: n.d* **5/1**[2]

3-01 **6** *1* **Zazous**[2] 307 5-8-7 **49** J-PGuillambert 7 48
(J J Bridger) *led after 1f: hdd jst over 1f out: wknd ins fnl f* **7/1**

-062 **7** *nk* **Taranaki**[11] 232 8-9-2 **58** SimonWhitworth 14 57
(P D Cundell) *chsd ldrs: rdn over 2f out: nt qckn and no prog over 1f out* **8/1**

0460 **8** *nk* **Captain Darling (IRE)**[7] 268 6-8-12 **57** EdwardCreighton(3) 13 55
(R W Price) *prog to press ldrs on outer 3f out: nt qckn 2f out: fdd* **16/1**

-003 **9** *1 ½* **Border Artist**[11] 227 7-8-12 **54** (p) TonyCulhane 9 48+
(B G Powell) *hld up wl in rr: effrt 2f out: nt clr run and hmpd over 1f out : nt rcvr* **16/1**

2-50 **10** *½* **I Wish**[21] 137 8-9-2 **58** PaulFitzsimons 4 51
(Miss J R Tooth) *chsd ldrs: pushed along 1/2-way: u.p and struggling 2f out* **16/1**

00-0 **11** *3* **Double M**[21] 137 9-8-10 **55** (v) RichardThomas(3) 5 40
(Mrs L Richards) *hld up in rr: no prog 2f out: wknd* **16/1**

0-00 **12** *5* **Agilete**[11] 225 4-9-0 **56** (bt[1]) JoeFanning 10 28
(J R Boyle) *s.v.s: rcvrd and in tch on outer 1/2-way: sn wknd* **33/1**

1m 24.39s (-1.50) **Going Correction** -0.20s/f (Stan) 12 Ran SP% **121.7**
Speed ratings (Par 101):100,98,98,97,96 95,95,95,93,92 89,83
CSF £53.52 CT £471.74 TOTE £5.40: £1.90, £3.20, £3.70; EX 97.70.
Owner Chris Marsh **Bred** J P Villey **Trained** West Pinchbeck, Lincs

FOCUS

The winning time was fractionally faster than the first division, but still only close to par for the grade. The form looks pretty sound with the principals running to form.
Border Artist Official explanation: jockey said gelding was denied a clear run

340 BETDIRECT FREEPHONE 0800 211 222 H'CAP 7f (P)

3:05 (3:05) (Class 4) (0-85,85) 4-Y-0+ **£6,477** (£1,927; £963; £481) **Stalls** Low

Form RPR

00-0 **1** **Mr Lambros**[33] 58 5-9-4 **85** MartinDwyer 8 101+
(A M Balding) *mde all and set gd pce: kicked clr 2f out: in n.d after: unchal* **10/1**

02-2 **2** *4* **Spring Goddess (IRE)**[11] 221 5-9-0 **81** DarrenWilliams 5 87
(A P Jarvis) *hld up in midfield: prog 2f out: styd on to take 2nd nr fin: no ch w wnr* **11/1**

0-21 **3** *½* **Farewell Gift**[11] 221 5-8-5 **75** (b) StephaneBreux(3) 1 79
(R Hannon) *prom: lost pl on inner over 2f out: renewed effrt and hanging lft 1f out: chsd wnr ins fnl f: no imp* **7/1**

2021 **4** ½ **Marko Jadeo (IRE)**[1] 321 8-9-1 **82** 6ex PaulFitzsimons 6 85
(S Dow) *lw: taken down early: s.i.s: t.k.h and hld up in last pair: styd on fr over 1f out: nvr nrr* **17/2**

-354 **5** nk **Katiypour (IRE)**[10] 238 9-9-1 **85** RichardThomas(3) 7 87
(Miss B Sanders) *lw: hld up in tch: outpcd over 2f out: kpt on same pce after* **11/2**[3]

4-02 **6** 1 **Outer Hebrides**[11] 220 5-9-3 **84** (vt) MickyFenton 4 84
(Stef Liddiard) *hld up in last pair: rdn over 2f out: kpt on fnl f: no ch* **25/1**

33-0 **7** hd **Pamir (IRE)**[10] 245 4-8-10 **77** IanMongan 3 76
(P R Chamings) *hld up in midfield: nt qckn over 2f out: n.d after* **25/1**

16/0 **8** nk **Polonius**[32] 64 5-9-4 **85** DaneO'Neill 2 83
(P R Webber) *settled in rr: rdn and no prog 2f out: one pce after* **4/1**[2]

1-40 **9** ¾ **Poker Player (IRE)**[10] 245 4-8-11 **78** MichaelHills 10 74
(G C Bravery) *lw: ldng trio tl wknd wl over 1f out* **33/1**

1/4- **10** 1 **Happy As Larry (USA)**[348] 493 4-9-4 **85** JohnEgan 9 79
(T J Pitt) *lw: mostly chsd wnr: rdn over 2f out: no imp: wknd rapidly ins fnl f* **3/1**[1]

1m 23.1s (-2.79) **Going Correction** -0.20s/f (Stan) **10** Ran SP% **111.5**
Speed ratings (Par 105):107,102,101,101,100 99,99,99,98,97
CSF £106.14 CT £822.32 TOTE £10.80: £2.20, £2.70, £3.00; EX 109.30.
Owner Winterbeck Manor Stud **Bred** Witney And Warren Enterprises Ltd **Trained** Kingsclere, Hants

FOCUS
This looked a reasonable handicap, but nothing could go with Mr Lambros, who got an easy lead and sustained a good pace from start to finish. The placed form looks sound enough with those in the frame behind the winner close to recent form.

341 BETDIRECT.CO.UK H'CAP 6f (P)
3:40 (3:41) (Class 4) (0-85,85) 3-Y-O **£6,477** (£1,927; £963; £481) **Stalls** Low

Form RPR

4-11 **1** **Kingsgate Prince (IRE)**[7] 269 3-9-0 **81** 6ex GeorgeBaker 4 93+
(J R Best) *lw: taken down early: settled bhd ldrs: smooth prog 2f out: led over 1f out: drew rt away fnl f* **4/6**[1]

361- **2** 3½ **Figaro Flyer (IRE)**[53] 6600 3-9-4 **85** TonyCulhane 5 86
(P Howling) *led: rdn 2f out: hdd over 1f out: kpt on but no ch w wnr* **16/1**

3-14 **3** 2 **Sands Crooner (IRE)**[14] 190 3-8-1 **71** (t) PatrickMathers(3) 7 66
(D Shaw) *lw: scrubbed along to stay in tch early: prog over 2f out: outpcd over 1f out: one pce after* **14/1**

103- **4** 1½ **Cavewarrior**[119] 5836 3-9-1 **82** ShaneKelly 1 73
(J Noseda) *pressed ldr 4f out: upsides fr 2f out tl wknd over 1f out* **3/1**[2]

200- **5** 1½ **Memphis Man**[133] 5557 3-9-3 **84** MichaelHills 3 70
(G C Bravery) *reluctant to go to post: stdd s: hld up in detached last: shkn up over 1f out: running on at fin* **33/1**

30-2 **6** ¾ **Diane's Choice**[10] 233 3-8-4 **71** ChrisCatlin 8 55
(J Akehurst) *reluctant to enter stalls: chsd ldr 5f out to 4f out: lost pl over 2f out: sn btn* **12/1**[3]

364- **7** 4 **Scooby Dude (IRE)**[44] 6662 3-8-10 **77** EddieAhern 6 49
(Ms Deborah J Evans) *t.k.h: pressed ldr for 1f: lost pl over 2f out: wknd* **14/1**

1m 11.3s (-1.51) **Going Correction** -0.20s/f (Stan) **7** Ran SP% **114.8**
Speed ratings (Par 99):102,97,94,92,90 89,84
CSF £14.34 CT £86.52 TOTE £1.60: £1.10, £3.90; EX 10.50.
Owner John Mayne **Bred** P G Lyons **Trained** Hucking, Kent

FOCUS
Not a very strong handicap for the grade and the improving Kingsgate Prince totally outclassed his six rivals. The runner-up is the best guide to the level.

342 CLASSICVALUEPOOLS.COM H'CAP 1m (P)
4:15 (4:15) (Class 5) (0-75,75) 3-Y-O **£3,238** (£963; £481; £240) **Stalls** High

Form RPR

4-12 **1** **Song Of Silence (USA)**[4] 294 3-8-13 **70** 6ex EddieAhern 9 82+
(E A L Dunlop) *led for 1f: trckd ldr: led over 2f out: sn clr: easily* **4/7**[1]

21-0 **2** 2½ **Isphahan**[25] 118 3-9-4 **75** MartinDwyer 7 76
(A M Balding) *lw: chsd ldrs: reminders over 4f out: effrt u.p over 2f out: wnt 2nd ins fnl f: no ch w wnr* **9/1**[3]

-452 **3** ½ **Scroll**[10] 234 3-8-13 **70** (v) J-PGuillambert 4 70
(P Howling) *hld up in rr: prog on outer 3f out: drvn to dispute 2nd ins fnl f: kpt on* **13/2**[2]

56-0 **4** 1 **Possessed**[14] 188 3-8-13 **73** RobertMiles(3) 3 71
(T D McCarthy) *plld hrd: hld up in last pair: prog on outer 2f out: coaxed along and styd on reluctantly ins fnl f* **16/1**

2366 **5** ½ **Ms Rainbow Runner**[10] 234 3-8-4 **61** oh1 JohnEgan 1 58
(P Butler) *chsd ldrs: rdn over 2f out: one pce and n.d fr over 1f out* **33/1**

-210 **6** nk **Bollywood (IRE)**[12] 211 3-9-1 **72** MatthewHenry 6 68
(M R Hoad) *t.k.h in ldng trio: drvn to chse wnr over 1f out to ins fnl f: fdd* **20/1**

-620 **7** nk **Simpsons Ross (IRE)**[10] 234 3-8-6 **63** JimmyQuinn 8 58
(R M Flower) *hld up towards rr: rdn over 2f out: no prog* **33/1**

-302 **8** ¾ **Lenoir (GER)**[14] 188 3-8-12 **69** (v) DaneO'Neill 2 69+
(V Smith) *dwlt: hld up towards rr: effrt over 2f out: styng on and ch of a pl whn nowhere to go on inner over 1f out* **9/1**[3]

00-0 **9** 6 **Galaxy Bound (IRE)**[14] 188 3-8-2 **62** (v[1]) PatrickMathers(3) 5 42
(D Shaw) *lw: s.s: plld hrd: hld up in last pair: wknd over 2f out* **33/1**

54-0 **10** 1¾ **Sharp Thrust (IRE)**[10] 233 3-8-13 **70** DarrenWilliams 10 46
(A P Jarvis) *t.k.h: led after 1f to over 2f out: wknd rapidly* **50/1**

1m 38.52s (-0.91) **Going Correction** -0.20s/f (Stan) **10** Ran SP% **118.4**
Speed ratings (Par 97):96,93,93,92,91 91,90,90,84,82
CSF £6.10 CT £21.05 TOTE £1.70: £1.10, £2.60, £1.50; EX 8.20.
Owner Gainsborough Stud **Bred** Gainsborough Farm Llc **Trained** Newmarket, Suffolk
■ Stewards' Enquiry : Eddie Ahern three-day ban: careless riding (Feb 20-22)

FOCUS
A modest handicap and not that competitive, but Song Of Silence was value for about double the winning margin and is clearly a fair bit better than her current mark would suggest.
Possessed Official explanation: jockey said filly hung left in straight
Lenoir(GER) Official explanation: jockey said colt suffered interference in running

343 LITTLEWOODS BETDIRECT H'CAP 1m (P)
4:45 (4:47) (Class 5) (0-70,70) 4-Y-O+ **£3,238** (£963; £481; £240) **Stalls** High

Form RPR

0-05 **1** **Star Magnitude (USA)**[10] 236 5-9-4 **70** JimmyQuinn 1 77
(S Dow) *lw: prom: lost pl 1/2-way: effrt again over 2f out: drvn to chse ldr ins fnl f: r.o wl to ld nr fin* **7/2**[2]

4121 **2** ½ **Glad Big (GER)**[4] 292 4-9-2 **68** EddieAhern 5 74
(J A Osborne) *cl up gng easily: prog to trck ldr 2f out: led over 1f out: r.o fnl f: hdd nr fin* **8/11**[1]

0/2- **3** 2 **Perez (IRE)**[60] 6545 4-8-11 **68** EmmettStack(5) 11 69
(Pat Eddery) *hld up in last trio and swtchd fr outside draw: plenty to do 3f out: prog on inner after: styd on to take 3rd nr fin* **20/1**

400- **4** ½ **Jilly Why (IRE)**[50] 6636 5-8-10 **62** SamHitchcott 8 62
(Ms Deborah J Evans) *t.k.h: hld up in midfield: effrt over 2f out: kpt on same pce: n.d* **33/1**

5-50 **5** ½ **State Dilemma (IRE)**[6] 274 5-8-4 **59** (v) PatrickMathers(3) 10 58
(D Shaw) *hld up in last pair: plenty to do 3f out: prog 2f out: cajoled along and carried hd high fr over 1f out: styd on* **33/1**

15-4 **6** nk **Night Wolf (IRE)**[28] 86 6-8-5 **57** oh4 ow1 PaulDoe 4 55
(Jamie Poulton) *pressed ldr: led wl over 2f out: hdd over 1f out: wknd ins fnl f* **16/1**

-031 **7** 2 **Height Of Spirits**[11] 217 4-8-9 **64** RobertMiles(3) 9 57
(T D McCarthy) *b: hld up in midfield: rdn and nt qckn over 2f out: one pce after* **20/1**

206- **8** nk **Moors Myth**[186] 4166 5-8-12 **64** MichaelHills 3 57
(B W Hills) *led at decent pce: hdd wl over 2f out: wknd rapidly fnl f* **9/1**[3]

0-00 **9** 2½ **Familiar Affair**[13] 200 5-8-6 **58** ChrisCatlin 6 45
(T D Barron) *chsd ldrs: drvn 3f out: wknd wl over 1f out* **50/1**

4-00 **10** 3 **Celtique**[11] 221 4-9-3 **69** JamieMackay 2 49
(M Wigham) *lw: s.s: a in last pair: rdn and wknd over 2f out* **33/1**

-100 **11** 7 **Border Edge**[11] 223 8-8-8 **60** (v) J-PGuillambert 12 24
(J J Bridger) *b: sn pressed ldrs: drvn over 3f out: sn wknd* **12/1**

1m 37.23s (-2.20) **Going Correction** -0.20s/f (Stan) **11** Ran SP% **124.0**
Speed ratings (Par 103):103,102,100,100,99 99,97,96,94,91 84
CSF £6.25 CT £48.49 TOTE £4.80: £1.40, £1.10, £4.20; EX 9.10 Place 6 £393.89, Place 5 £198.14.
Owner P McCarthy **Bred** Juddmonte Farms Inc **Trained** Epsom, Surrey

FOCUS
A modest handicap in which the odds-on favourite Glad Big could not take advantage of a mark 5lb lower than in future. The third sets the standard but the fourth and fifth represent less solid form.
T/Plt: £271.40 to a £1 stake. Pool: £40,362.50. 108.55 winning tickets. T/Qpdt: £88.90 to a £1 stake. Pool: £3,355.00. 27.90 winning tickets. JN

[328] SOUTHWELL (L-H)
Thursday, February 9

OFFICIAL GOING: Standard
For the second time this week, the gound against the inside rail did not seem to be as slow as it usually is.
Wind: Strong behind.

344 FOOTBALLPOOLS.COM H'CAP 5f (F)
1:30 (1:31) (Class 5) (0-75,74) 3-Y-O **£3,238** (£963; £481; £240) **Stalls** High

Form RPR

015- **1** **Stoneacre Lad (IRE)**[41] 6688 3-9-4 **74** (b[1]) RobbieFitzpatrick 2 83
(Peter Grayson) *cl up: pushed along 2f out: sn rdn and hung bdly lft over 1f out: led ent last and sn clr* **10/3**[2]

6-11 **2** 3 **Garlogs**[2] 335 3-8-10 **66** 6ex RobertWinston 3 65
(A Bailey) *led: pushed along 2f out: rdn and edgd lft over 1f out: drvn and hdd ent last: sn one pce* **10/11**[1]

210 **3** nk **Luloah**[15] 189 3-8-3 **66** DonnaCaldwell(7) 7 64
(P S McEntee) *cl up: ev ch 2f out: sn rdn and kpt on same pce ins last* **16/1**

-520 **4** 2½ **Money Mate (IRE)**[7] 275 3-8-9 **65** TomEaves 6 55
(C J Teague) *chsd ldrs: rdn along 2f out: sn drvn and no imp* **28/1**

400- **5** 1 **John Claude (IRE)**[56] 6581 3-8-11 **67** (t) PhillipMakin 1 53
(Ronald Thompson) *prom: rdn along 1/2-way: wknd 2f out* **66/1**

03-0 **6** 5 **Smooch**[26] 117 3-9-3 **73** ShaneKelly 4 42
(R M H Cowell) *sn rdn along in rr: a bhd* **14/1**

505- **7** ½ **The London Gang**[99] 6226 3-8-9 **72** FrankiePickard(7) 8 39
(P D Evans) *dwlt: rdn along and a rr* **20/1**

321 **8** 1 **Ockums Razor (IRE)**[10] 248 3-9-0 **70** 6ex DeanMcKeown 5 34
(M J Polglase) *dwlt: sn rdn along and outpcd: wl bhd after 2f* **6/1**[3]

58.45 secs (-1.85) **Going Correction** -0.425s/f (Stan) **8** Ran SP% **112.0**
Speed ratings (Par 97):97,92,91,87,86 78,77,75
CSF £6.38 CT £36.78 TOTE £4.10: £1.60, £1.10, £2.50; EX 9.20.
Owner Richard Teatum **Bred** Mrs Annie Hughes **Trained** Formby, Lancs

FOCUS
A fair handicap in which it paid to race close to the pace and the third sets the standard.
Smooch Official explanation: jockey said filly would not face kickback
Ockums Razor(IRE) Official explanation: jockey said colt never travelled

345 PLAY LITTLEWOODS POOLS ON 0800 500 000 CLAIMING STKS 6f (F)
2:00 (2:00) (Class 6) 4-Y-O+ **£2,388** (£705; £352) **Stalls** Low

Form RPR

/001 **1** **Winning Pleasure (IRE)**[7] 271 8-8-8 60 JasonEdmunds(3) 4 69
(J Balding) *trckd ldrs: hdwy 2f out: rdn to ld ins last: kpt on* **11/1**

330- **2** 1 **Up Tempo (IRE)**[219] 3210 8-8-10 69 (b) AndrewMullen(5) 7 70
(K A Ryan) *chsd ldrs: swtchd wd over 2f out: rdn and ev ch over 1f out: kpt on ins last* **9/1**

212- **3** ½ **Misaro (GER)**[114] 5956 5-9-3 68 (b) RobertWinston 2 71
(P D Evans) *cl up: led wl over 2f out: rdn wl over 1f out: hdd and no ex ins last* **7/2**[1]

-211 **4** ¾ **Shadow Jumper (IRE)**[14] 196 5-9-1 59 (v) RobbieFitzpatrick 3 66
(M J Attwater) *chsd ldng pair: hdwy 2f out: sn rdn and ev ch tl drvn and one pce ins last* **5/1**[3]

-202 **5** hd **Majik**[7] 271 7-8-5 70 (p) KevinGhunowa(7) 6 63
(P A Blockley) *outpcd and bhd: hdwy 2f out: sn rdn and kpt on ins last: nrst fin* **4/1**[2]

10-0 **6** 1 **Paso Doble**[28] 101 8-8-6 66 (p) JamesMillman(7) 5 61
(B R Millman) *bhd tl hdwy 2f out: n.m.r over 1f out: kpt on ins last: nrst fin* **14/1**

1244 **7** ¾ **Alpaga Le Jomage (IRE)**[12] 225 4-9-1 65 DeanMcKeown 1 60
(M J Polglase) *led: rdn along and hdd wl over 2f out: grad wknd* **18/1**

2244 **8** 4 **Soft Focus (IRE)**[8] 262 4-8-8 60 (b) ShaneKelly 9 41
(J A Osborne) *in tch: rdn along wl over 2f out: sn btn* **10/1**

1040 **9** ¾ **Owed**[7] 275 4-9-1 73 (t) HayleyTurner 8 46
(Robert Gray) *in tch: stirrup leather broke sn after s: bhd after 2f* **5/1**[3]

1m 16.28s (-0.62) **Going Correction** -0.075s/f (Stan) **9** Ran SP% **114.9**
Speed ratings (Par 101):101,99,99,98,97 96,95,90,89
CSF £104.52 TOTE £16.10: £3.50, £3.30, £1.50; EX 126.50.Misaro (GER) was claimed by Miss Gay Kelleway for £11,000. Shadow Jumper (IRE) was claimed by Mr J. T. Stimpson £10,000.

Owner R L Crowe **Bred** Mrs B A Headon **Trained** Scrooby, Notts

FOCUS
A fair claimer run at a reasonable pace and the form looks sound, rated through the fourth.

Owed Official explanation: jockey said gelding's stirrup leather snapped leaving stalls

346 LITTLEWOODS £2M FOOTBALL POOLS H'CAP 2m (F)
2:30 (2:30) (Class 6) (0-65,70) 4-Y-0+ **£2,388** (£705; £352) **Stalls** Low

Form				RPR
-505	1		**Victory Quest (IRE)**[11] [246] 6-9-10 **63**......................(v) RobertWinston 1 (Mrs S Lamyman) *led 1f: chsd ldr tl led 3f out: rdn 2f out: drvn over 1f out: styd on gamely* **9/1**	71
6626	2	1 ½	**High Frequency (IRE)**[12] [231] 5-8-11 **50**......................... PaulFessey 5 (T D Barron) *hld up: stdy hdwy to trck ldrs 5f out: rdn to chal 2f out and ev ch tl drvn and no ex ins last* **6/1**[3]	56
6-12	3	nk	**He's A Star**[11] [246] 4-9-4 **63**.. PaulHanagan 2 (Miss Gay Kelleway) *in tch: hdwy to chse ldrs 4f out: rdn 2f out and ch tl drvn and no ex ins last* **4/1**[2]	69
2232	4	4	**Blue Hills**[7] [270] 5-9-4 **57**...(v[1]) DarrenWilliams 8 (P W Hiatt) *cl up: led after 1f: rdn along 4f out: hdd 3f out: drvn 2f out and wknd appr last* **4/1**[2]	58
1131	5	5	**Cotton Eyed Joe (IRE)**[11] [246] 5-10-3 **70** 6ex........... DeanMcKeown 3 (G A Swinbank) *in tch: hdwy to trck ldrs 1/2-way: rdn along 3f out: drvn wl over 1f out: hung lft and sn wknd* **5/2**[1]	65
-365	6	dist	**Ice And Fire**[16] [182] 7-8-9 **48** ow3.................................(b) MickyFenton 7 (J T Stimpson) *hld up in rr: effrt and sme hdwy 6f out: rdn along 4f out and sn bhd* **22/1**	—
00-4	7	6	**Spectested (IRE)**[15] [55] 5-8-13 **52**...............................(p) ShaneKelly 6 (A W Carroll) *s.i.s: a bhd* **15/2**	—
5/3-	8	10	**Simlet**[56] [2968] 11-8-11 **50**...(t) TonyHamilton 9 (E W Tuer) *chsd ldrs: rdn along 1/2-way: sn lost pl and bhd* **40/1**	—

3m 44.22s (-0.32) **Going Correction** -0.075s/f (Stan)
WFA 4 from 5yo+ 6lb **8** Ran SP% **111.4**
Speed ratings (Par 101):97,96,96,94,91 —,—,—
CSF £58.40 CT £245.01 TOTE £11.60: £3.80, £3.80, £2.10; EX 73.30.
Owner P Lamyman **Bred** Miss Veronica Henley **Trained** Ruckland, Lincs

FOCUS
This moderate handicap was run at just a steady pace and the form is no better than average for the grade.

347 LITTLEWOODS POOLS BE LUCKY (S) STKS 7f (F)
3:00 (3:02) (Class 6) 3-Y-0 **£2,388** (£705; £352) **Stalls** Low

Form				RPR
-043	1		**Smart Ass (IRE)**[6] [287] 3-8-6 50.................................. RobertWinston 9 (J S Moore) *chsd ldrs: hdwy 2f out: rdn and slt ld over 1f out: drvn ins last and kpt on* **7/2**[2]	52
50	2	1	**Mind Out (USA)**[13] [215] 3-8-11 .... ShaneKelly 7 (J A Osborne) *led: rdn over 2f out: drvn and hdd over 1f out: rallied ins last: no ex towards fin* **11/1**	55
120-	3	1	**Psycho Cat**[52] [6617] 3-9-3 67...(p) FergalLynch 4 (P A Blockley) *keen: hld up: hdwy 2f out: rdn to chal over 1f out and ev ch tl drvn, wandered and wknd ent last* **9/4**[1]	58
3044	4	3 ½	**Twilight Avenger (IRE)**[6] [287] 3-8-11 52................... DeanMcKeown 3 (M J Polglase) *trckd ldrs: hdwy whn nt clr run wl over 1f out: sn rdn and no imp appr last* **20/1**	43
000-	5	1	**Wensleydale Star**[141] [5408] 3-8-11 61............................. PhillipMakin 10 (T D Barron) *chsd ldrs on outer: hdwy 2f out: sn rdn and edgd lft: drvn and wknd* **8/1**[3]	40
14-6	6	5	**Aysgarth Flyer (IRE)**[14] [197] 3-8-12 60.....................(b) GregFairley[(5)] 6 (I Semple) *towards rr and pushed along 1/2-way: sme hdwy u.p over 2f out: sn drvn and btn* **7/2**[2]	33
5-10	7	2 ½	**Crush On You**[14] [193] 3-8-12 57................................ GrahamGibbons 2 (R Hollinshead) *cl up on inner: rdn along wl over 2f out and sn wknd* **16/1**	22
3-06	8	3	**Musical City**[28] [99] 3-8-6 45...(p) PaulEddery 1 (B Smart) *in tch: rdn along on inner 3f out: sn wknd* **50/1**	8
00-0	9	3	**Dispol Valentine**[38] [10] 3-8-9 45 ow3.......................... MickyFenton 8 (P T Midgley) *cl up: rdn and hung lft over 2f out: sn wknd* **150/1**	3
060-	10	17	**Roman History (IRE)**[101] [6198] 3-8-11 58....................(p) HayleyTurner 5 (Robert Gray) *s.i.s: a bhd* **25/1**	—

1m 30.66s (-0.14) **Going Correction** -0.075s/f (Stan) **10** Ran SP% **111.8**
Speed ratings (Par 95):97,95,94,90,89 83,81,77,74,54
CSF £37.73 TOTE £4.00: £1.50, £2.20, £1.50; EX 49.90.The winner was bought in for 6,500 gns. Mind Out (USA) was claimed by Mr J. T. Stimpson for £6,000
Owner Bigwigs Bloodstock VII **Bred** M Ervine **Trained** Upper Lambourn, Berks
■ Stewards' Enquiry : Paul Eddery three-day ban: used whip with excessive frequency and when out of contention (Feb 20-22)

FOCUS
An ordinary seller rated through the fourth to course and distance form.

Mind Out(USA) Official explanation: jockey said gelding hung right-handed

348 LITTLEWOODS POOLS BILLIONS WON BY MILLIONS H'CAP 7f (F)
3:30 (3:32) (Class 2) (0-100,90) 4-Y-0+ **£12,954** (£3,854; £1,926; £962) **Stalls** Low

Form				RPR
1242	1		**Speed Dial Harry (IRE)**[7] [276] 4-7-11 **76** oh1........(v) AndrewElliott[(7)] 2 (K R Burke) *hld up in tch: gd hdwy on inner and swtchd lft over 1f out: rdn and hung rt ins last: styd on to ld last 100 yds* **6/1**[3]	87
1-52	2	½	**Wessex (USA)**[7] [275] 6-9-1 **87**................................... GrahamGibbons 9 (P A Blockley) *chsd ldrs on outer: pushed along and hdwy 2f out: rdn over 1f: drvn to ld ent last: hdd and no ex last 100 yds* **11/2**[2]	97
/121	3	hd	**Cummiskey (IRE)**[7] [275] 4-9-0 **86** 6ex...................... RobertWinston 11 (J A Osborne) *hld up towards rr: hdwy over 2f out: nt clr run over 1f out: sn rdn and ev ch ent last: nt qckn towards fin* **5/2**[1]	95
0-24	4	2 ½	**Rafferty (IRE)**[7] [275] 7-9-1 **87**.. PaulFessey 1 (T D Barron) *led: rdn along and hdd 2f out: drvn over 1f out: kpt on same pce* **20/1**	90
4445	5	nk	**Pawan (IRE)**[7] [275] 6-8-2 **81** ow1................................. AnnStokell[(7)] 10 (Miss A Stokell) *chsd ldrs: rdn along 2f out: kpt on same pce appr last* **25/1**	83
10-4	6	1 ¾	**Cardinal Venture (IRE)**[39] [7] 8-8-13 **90**...........(p) AndrewMullen[(5)] 8 (K A Ryan) *chsd ldrs: rdn along and hdwy to ld 2f out: drvn: hdd & wknd ent last* **8/1**	87
211-	7	1	**Rampage**[103] [6161] 5-8-0 **79**.. LiamJones[(7)] 3 (W J Haggas) *hld up in rr: gd hdwy on inner 3f out: chsd ldrs 2f out: sn rdn and btn* **8/1**	74
2500	8	1 ½	**Waterside (IRE)**[12] [221] 7-8-9 **81**.................................... HayleyTurner 7 (G L Moore) *in tch: rdn along 2f out: grad wknd* **16/1**	72
00-5	9	nk	**Te Quiero**[39] [7] 8-8-7 **79**...(bt) PaulHanagan 6 (Miss Gay Kelleway) *prom: rdn along over 2f out: grad wknd* **16/1**	69
6-25	10	¾	**Flint River**[7] [276] 8-8-4 **76** oh3... ChrisCatlin 4 (H Morrison) *chsd ldrs: rdn along 3f out: sn wknd* **16/1**	64
40-0	11	13	**Ali Bruce**[12] [220] 6-7-13 **78**...(p) JamesDoyle[(7)] 5 (G L Moore) *s.i.s: a rr* **14/1**	32

1m 28.69s (-2.11) **Going Correction** -0.075s/f (Stan) **11** Ran SP% **113.4**
Speed ratings (Par 109):109,108,108,105,105 103,101,100,99,98 84
CSF £37.48 CT £104.28 TOTE £7.30: £1.70, £1.80, £1.40; EX 45.50.
Owner Nigel Shields **Bred** Brendan Lavery **Trained** Middleham Moor, N Yorks
■ Owner Nigel Shields was well represented in this with five of the 11 runners including the winner, second and fourth.
■ Stewards' Enquiry : Andrew Elliott caution: careless riding

FOCUS
A fiercely competitive handicap run at a searching pace and the form looks reliable, with the runner-up the best guide to the form.

NOTEBOOK
Speed Dial Harry(IRE), in such great form here this winter though still 1lb out of the handicap, found the strong pace helping compensate for the shorter trip. Brought with his effort towards the far side, though still well away from the inside rail, he got up well inside the last furlong under a very competent ride. He has done nothing but improve in the last couple of months. (op 7-1)
Wessex(USA), back over a more suitable trip, was given every chance and looked the likely winner a furlong out, but he tended to edge to his left under pressure and was just worried out of it. He lost little in defeat and there will be other days. (op 6-1)
Cummiskey(IRE) ♦, trying this trip for the first time under his penalty, was produced with his effort in plenty of time but was done no favours by Wessex persistently hanging into him and was probably unlucky not to finish second at least. He certainly stayed and this consistent sort should gain compensation. (op 11-4)
Rafferty(IRE) managed to gain the early lead in a race in which there was always going to be plenty of pace and did not go down without a fight. He does like this surface, but remains 7lb above his last winning mark and does rather tend to blow hot and cold. (tchd 18-1)
Pawan(IRE) ran another creditable race, and even looked a possible winner when brought with his effort closest to the stands' rail halfway up the straight before his effort flattened out. He is consistent, in that he constantly misses the frame and this was the ninth consecutive race that he has finished fourth or fifth. Perhaps stronger handling could see him end what is becoming a lengthy losing run.
Cardinal Venture(IRE), 2lb lower than when winning this race last year, is at his best when able to dominate but he failed to get to the front until halfway up the home straight this time and his efforts to do so eventually told. (op 15-2)
Rampage, up another 6lb in only her fifth outing, was close enough turning for home but found these rivals much too tough. She has gone well fresh in the past, but perhaps lack a recent run was more telling at this level. (op 11-2)
Waterside(IRE) does not necessarily have to lead, but is yet to really prove that he is as effective on this surface.
Te Quiero was 20lb lower than when disappointing in this last year, but even that could not help him and he looks to have lost his way. (op 20-1)
Flint River has never won here and had a lot to do in this company from 3lb out of the handicap. (op 14-1)
Ali Bruce, still 5lb above his last winning mark, jumped in the air as the stalls opened and could ill-afford to do that in this company. Official explanation: jockey said gelding never travelled (op 12-1)

349 WIN £2M @ CLASSICVALUEPOOLS.COM H'CAP 1m 3f (F)
4:00 (4:00) (Class 5) (0-70,68) 3-Y-0 **£3,238** (£963; £481; £240) **Stalls** Low

Form				RPR
05-1	1		**La Via Ferrata (IRE)**[33] [61] 3-8-6 56................................ JoeFanning 3 (P F I Cole) *trckd ldrs: pushed along 2f out: rdn to chal ent last: hung rt: styd on to ld last 100 yds* **2/1**[1]	58
000-	2	nk	**Left Hand Drive**[129] [5665] 3-8-2 55........................(t) EdwardCreighton[(3)] 8 (B W Duke) *s.i.s and bhd: pushed along and sme hdwy 5f out: drvn and wd st: styd on u.p over 1f out: fin wl* **66/1**	56
02-2	3	hd	**Crazy Bear (IRE)**[23] [132] 3-8-13 68........................... AndrewMullen[(5)] 4 (K A Ryan) *trckd ldrs: hdwy to chal wl over 2f out: rdn to ld over 1f out: drvn ins last: hdd and no ex last 100 yds* **9/4**[2]	69
231-	4	3	**Mambo Sun**[51] [6634] 3-9-4 68.. FergalLynch 6 (P A Blockley) *a.p: effrt 3f out: rdn to ld wl over 1f out: sn drvn and hdd: wknd ins last* **6/1**[3]	64
300-	5	1 ¼	**Sahara Style**[52] [6617] 3-8-8 58...................................... GrahamGibbons 5 (R Hollinshead) *hld up: hdwy and in tch 4f out: sn rdn along and outpcd over 2f out: drvn and kpt on appr last: nt rch ldrs* **11/1**	52
000-	6	½	**Northerner (IRE)**[150] [5184] 3-8-7 57 ow1............................ ShaneKelly 7 (J R Norton) *led: rdn along 3f out: hdd wl over 1f out: drvn and wkng whn n.m.r and hmpd over 1f out: eased ins last* **25/1**	53+
-505	7	2 ½	**Duel In The Sands**[7] [272] 3-8-3 56.......................... PatrickMathers[(3)] 2 (D Shaw) *in tch on inner: rdn along 3f out: drvn 2f out and sn btn* **15/2**	45
402-	8	dist	**Stoneacre Lil (IRE)**[64] [6521] 3-8-5 55 oh5 ow1......(b) RobbieFitzpatrick 1 (Peter Grayson) *a rr: rdn along 1/2-way: sn wl bhd* **16/1**	—

2m 29.29s (0.39) **Going Correction** -0.075s/f (Stan) **8** Ran SP% **109.7**
Speed ratings (Par 97):95,94,94,92,91 91,89,—
CSF £103.24 CT £291.54 TOTE £2.40: £1.10, £4.90, £1.30; EX 87.80.
Owner P F I Cole Ltd **Bred** Roland H Alder **Trained** Whatcombe, Oxon

FOCUS
A real test of stamina for these three-year-olds and the ability to stay proved crucial. The form looks moderate though, especially given the proximity of the complete outsider in second.

Northerner(IRE) Official explanation: jockey said colt lost its action

350 TEXT "BETDIRECT" TO 88600 H'CAP 1m (F)
4:30 (4:30) (Class 6) (0-52,56) 4-Y-0+ **£2,388** (£705; £352) **Stalls** Low

Form				RPR
6-61	1		**Desert Lover (IRE)**[9] [261] 4-8-11 **51** 6ex........................... ShaneKelly 2 (R J Price) *trckd ldrs: hdwy to chse ldr 3f out: led wl over 1f out and sn rdn clr: styd on strly* **4/1**[3]	64
-005	2	5	**Sriology (IRE)**[11] [242] 5-8-12 **52**.. LPKeniry 1 (G Prodromou) *bhd: swtchd outside and rdn along after 2f: wd st: hdwy 2f out: sn rdn: styd on strly ins last: tk 2nd nr line* **14/1**	55
-420	3	nk	**Prince Of Gold**[6] [285] 6-8-12 **52**..............................(b) GrahamGibbons 3 (R Hollinshead) *rr and rdn along after 2f: hdwy on inner 3f out: sn rdn and kpt on appr last: nrst fin* **11/1**	54
0621	4	nk	**Lady Susanne (IRE)**[11] [240] 4-8-9 **56** 6ex............(b) JamesDoyle[(7)] 12 (M J Attwater) *sn led: rdn along over 2f out: drvn and hdd wl over 1f out: wknd appr last* **10/3**[1]	57
0-40	5	1 ¾	**Ming Vase**[11] [242] 4-8-11 **51**.. MickyFenton 4 (P T Midgley) *sn rdn along and outpcd in rr: hdwy u.p 2f out: nvr nr ldrs* **50/1**	49

0550 **6** 3/4 **Savoy Chapel**[6] 290 4-8-12 **52**....(vt) JimmyQuinn 7 48
(A W Carroll) *dwlt: sn in tch: hdwy to chse ldng pair over 2f out: sn rdn and wknd over 1f out* **25/1**
0-21 **7** 1 1/4 **Pearl Island (USA)**[9] 257 5-8-6 **46** 6ex.... ChrisCatlin 9 40
(D J Wintle) *midfield: rdn along and sme hdwy 3f out: sn drvn and wknd over 2f out* **4/1**[3]
0-66 **8** shd **Fiore Di Bosco (IRE)**[12] 229 5-8-10 **50**.... PhillipMakin 6 44
(T D Barron) *chsd ldrs: rdn along 3f out: drvn over 2f out and sn wknd* **7/2**[2]
000- **9** hd **Bob Baileys**[66] 6506 4-8-8 **48**.... StephenCarson 5 41
(P R Chamings) *a rr* **33/1**
0-60 **10** 6 **Opera Belle**[12] 231 4-8-10 **50**....(v) DarrenWilliams 11 31
(A P Jarvis) *cl up: rdn along 3f out: sn wknd* **22/1**
06-0 **11** 13 **Bint Royal (IRE)**[10] 249 8-8-9 **49**.... NeilPollard 10 4
(Miss V Haigh) *a towards rr: rdn along 1/2-way and sn bhd* **50/1**

1m 43.39s (-1.21) **Going Correction** -0.075s/f (Stan) **11** Ran SP% **115.4**
Speed ratings (Par 101):103,98,97,97,95 94,93,93,93,87 74
CSF £52.75 CT £435.58 TOTE £5.20: £1.30, £3.90, £3.10; EX 89.10 Place 6 £18.20, Place 5 £14.49.
Owner Multi Lines Partnership **Bred** Penfold Bloodstock And Mr D B Clark **Trained** Ullingswick, H'fords

FOCUS
A competitive little handicap, if short on quality, but the pace was solid and the winner was very impressive.
Lady Suesanne(IRE) Official explanation: jockey said filly lost its left front shoe
Bint Royal(IRE) Official explanation: trainer said mare was unsuited by the fibresand
T/Plt: £40.30 to a £1 stake. Pool: £49,920.45. 903.60 winning tickets. T/Qpdt: £10.50 to a £1 stake. Pool: £4,389.90. 307.20 winning tickets. JR

277 NAD AL SHEBA (L-H)
Thursday, February 9
OFFICIAL GOING: Dirt course - fast; turf course - good to firm

351a ACT ONE CAPE VERDI (LISTED RACE) (TURF) (F&M) 1m (T)
3:35 (3:35) 3-Y-0+ **£56,686** (£17,441; £8,720; £4,360)

RPR
1 **Clinet (IRE)**[21] 155 4-9-3 101.... EddieAhern 8 106
(J W Hills) *hld up in rr and wd: 2nd last ent st: rdn 2 1/2f out: prog to ld 1f out: r.o wl* **2/1**[1]
2 2 1/4 **Brindisi**[21] 155 5-9-3 96.... JMurtagh 1 101
(D Selvaratnam, UAE) *mid-div on rail: chal on rail 2f out: kpt on: no ch w wnr* **7/1**
3 3 1/4 **Shersha (IRE)**[14] 203 7-9-3 95.... PJSmullen 4 94
(Kevin F O'Donnell, Ire) *mid-div early: dropped to rr after trcking ldr in st: r.o wl* **12/1**
4 1 **Imperial Ice (SAF)**[14] 202 4-8-9 90.... KShea 7 83
(H J Brown, South Africa) *trckd ldr wd: ev ch 3f out: nt qckn but kpt on* **33/1**
5 1 3/4 **Kalaforte (SAF)**[194] 4-8-9 87.... MKhan 9 79
(H J Brown, South Africa) *hld up last: in rr of main gp: rail early st: n.m.r: r.o one pce* **33/1**
6 1 **Emerald Beauty (ARG)**[21] 155 6-9-3 100.... WCMarwing 5 85
(M F De Kock, South Africa) *trckd ldr centre: t.k.h: ev ch 3f out: wknd* **9/4**[2]
7 3/4 **Venus Arising (IND)**[21] 155 5-9-3 95....(t) TedDurcan 6 83
(V Gaekwad, India) *in rr of main gp gng wl: n.m.r 2f out and again 1f out: nt rcvr* **12/1**
8 1 1/2 **Quality Special (BRZ)**[21] 155 4-8-9 100.... MAlmeida 3 72
(C Morgado, Brazil) *led: chal 2f out: kpt on tl hdd 1 1/2f out: wknd* **5/1**[3]
9 2 3/4 **Cat Belling (IRE)**[7] 282 6-9-3 99....(t) PDillon 2 73
(R Bouresly, Kuwait) *trckd ldrs rail: disp ld 3f out: rdr dropped whip: wknd 2f out* **25/1**

1m 37.48s **Going Correction** +0.35s/f (Good) **9** Ran SP% **118.4**
Speed ratings: 110,107,104,103,101 100,100,98,95

Owner Wood Hall Stud Limited **Bred** Mrs J Costelloe **Trained** Upper Lambourn, Berks

FOCUS
A weak fillies' and mares' Listed race, but they went a good pace and Clinet followed up her recent handicap success in good style.

NOTEBOOK
Clinet(IRE) ◆, a narrow winner off a steady pace in a handicap (off a mark of 98) on her debut in Dubai three weeks previously, would have appreciated what was a noticeably stronger gallop on this step up to a mile and made light of the return to Listed company. She has taken really well to racing in this very different climate and could bid for further success in the Balanchine Stakes.
Brindisi ran creditably in second, but was beaten further by Clinet than in a handicap on her return to Dubai last time.
Shersha(IRE) picked up some black type but was still beaten a fair way and continues below the pick of her form.
Imperial Ice(SAF), returned to turf, ran better than on the dirt on her previous start but was still well held.
Kalaforte(SAF) was well held on her return from a 194-day break.
Emerald Beauty(ARG) was again well held and continues quite a way below her best.

352a BENGALI D'ALBRET CUP (H'CAP) (TURF) 6f 110y(T)
4:05 (4:05) (95-110,108) 4-Y-0+ **£45,348** (£13,953; £6,976; £3,488)

RPR
1 **Safe Structure (SAF)**[14] 203 6-9-0 **101**.... MKhan 7 104
(D Maroun, South Africa) *led then trckd ldr: rdn to chal 2f out: disp ld 1 1/2f out: led 1f out: r.o wl* **12/1**
2 1 1/4 **T-Bird (SAF)**[14] 201 5-9-6 **108**....(t) TPO'Shea 9 107
(E Charpy, UAE) *dropped to rr early: last ent st: rdn along: swtchd wd: last 1 1/2f out: r.o: nrst fin* **2/1**[1]
3 3/4 **Conceal**[14] 206 8-8-12 **100**.... PDillon 6 96
(R Bouresly, Kuwait) *mid-div: prog to trck wnr 3 1/2f out: ev ch 2 1/2f out: r.o wl* **20/1**
4 nk **Tiger Shark (SAF)**[278] 5-8-10 **98**.... KShea 8 94
(H J Brown, South Africa) *in rr early: 2nd last ent st: prog 1 1/2f out in centre: nrst fin* **14/1**
5 1 **Slip Dance (IRE)**[14] 201 4-8-12 **100**.... MCHussey 10 93
(Eamon Tyrrell, Ire) *mid-div: swtchd wd 3f out: ev ch: r.o one pce* **9/2**[3]
6 1 **Obe Gold**[14] 203 4-9-3 **105**.... TedDurcan 5 95
(M R Channon) *in rr of main gp: prog 2f out: ev ch: nt qckn* **4/1**[2]
7 1 **Candidato Roy (ARG)**[14] 206 5-9-5 **107**....(b[1]) WCMarwing 2 94
(M F De Kock, South Africa) *sn led: 2 l clr 3f out: disp ld 2f out: hdd 1f out: wknd* **13/2**
8 7 **Prince Charming**[14] 201 4-8-8 **96** ow1....(t) ASuborics 4 64
(R Bouresly, Kuwait) *in rr early: t.k.h on rail: wknd 2 1/2f out* **100/1**
9 shd **Three Graces (GER)**[14] 203 6-9-3 **105**....(vt) KerrinMcEvoy 1 78+
(I Mohammed, UAE) *trckd ldrs on rail: n.m.r 2 1/2f out: ev ch 1 1/2f out: wknd rapidly* **9/1**
10 shd **King Marju (IRE)**[21] 151 4-8-7 **95**.... RoystonFfrench 3 62
(K R Burke) *mid-div: trckd ldrs 3f out: nt qckn: wknd* **16/1**

1m 16.78s **Going Correction** +0.35s/f (Good) **10** Ran SP% **120.8**
Speed ratings: 115,113,112,112,111 110,108,100,100,100

Owner Y Khan & W Tollman **Bred** Maine Chance Farms Ltd **Trained** South Africa

FOCUS
Quite a competitive sprint handicap in which Safe Structure showed the benefit of his reappearance to deny the favourite T-Bird, who was forced to switch wide when making his effort from a long way off the pace.

NOTEBOOK
Safe Structure(SAF) never got involved after being hampered on the turn into the straight in a similar event over course and distance on his previous start, but he was said to have needed that run in any case. Sent to the front from the start this time, he was not allowed an easy lead and ended up tracking the pace, but he showed the right attitude when asked for his effort to ultimately win well. He could improve again and may go for a valuable sprint on Super Thursday.
T-Bird(SAF) could be considered unlucky not to have finished closer as he was forced to switch wide with his challenge having been positioned a long way off the pace. He clearly continues in good form and is one to keep on the right side of.
Conceal, given a rare run on turf on what was just his second run since returning from a long absence, ran well for a trainer who does well with this type of horse.
Tiger Shark(SAF) ◆, twice a winner in his native South Africa, got going too late and never looked like winning, but this was still a most encouraging return to action. He is open to improvement and could be one to look out for.
Slip Dance(IRE), second in a similar event off a 3lb lower mark on her previous start, came with a promising-looking run but could not sustain her effort and was a little bit below her best.
Obe Gold was below the form he showed to win over course and distance on his previous start, even allowing for a 5lb higher mark.
King Marju(IRE), without the visor this time, was again well beaten. He probably needs to drop a few pounds in the handicap.

353a HAAFHD STKS (H'CAP) (DIRT) 7f (D)
4:35 (4:36) (90-105,105) 4-Y-0+ **£41,569** (£12,790; £6,395; £3,197)

RPR
1 **Attilius (BRZ)**[103] 4-8-5 **90**.... ECruz 7 97
(P Nickel Filho, Brazil) *led after 1f: jnd 2f out: rdn clr: r.o wl* **33/1**
2 1 1/4 **Happy Pearl (AUS)**[14] 204 6-8-11 **96**....(b) MJKinane 14 100
(G Moore, Macau) *trckd ldr gng wl: rdn to chal 2f out: r.o wl but nt pce of wnr* **11/2**[1]
3 3 3/4 **Northern Rock (JPN)**[91] 8-8-10 **95**....(bt) TedDurcan 9 89
(A Laird, UAE) *trckd ldrs: rdn to chal 2f out: nt pce of wnr: kpt on* **10/1**
4 1 **Sea Hunter**[14] 204 4-8-10 **95**....(v) KerrinMcEvoy 13 87
(I Mohammed, UAE) *mid-div: rdn 4 1/2f out: wd into st: rdn to cl 3f out: nrst fin* **7/1**[3]
5 3/4 **Rockets 'n Rollers (IRE)**[14] 203 6-9-6 **105**.... WCMarwing 1 95
(M Al Muhairi, UAE) *trckd ldr on rail: rdn 4f out: nt qckn: one pce last 2f* **12/1**
6 3/4 **Marbush (IRE)**[14] 204 5-9-2 **100**....(bt) JMurtagh 15 89
(D Selvaratnam, UAE) *rr out wd: rdn to mid-div 3f out: 5th 1 1/2f out: nt qckn* **8/1**
7 nk **Kandidate**[7] 281 4-9-4 **102**.... EddieAhern 9 90
(C E Brittain) *mid-div: rdn 4f out: kpt on one pce: nvr a threat* **13/2**[2]
8 1 1/4 **Glad To Be Fast (IRE)**[14] 204 6-9-4 **102**....(b) AStarke 3 87
(Mario Hofer, Germany) *hld up in rr on rail: in last trio ent st: n.m.r 3f out: r.o fnl 2f: nrst fin* **12/1**
9 5 3/4 **Egyptian (USA)**[14] 204 7-8-12 **97**.... PDillon 5 66
(R Bouresly, Kuwait) *dropped to rr after 1f: n.d* **25/1**
10 1 1/4 **Aleutian**[14] 204 6-8-10 **95**.... WSupple 12 61
(Doug Watson, UAE) *sn in rr: sme late prog: nvr a factor* **14/1**
11 1 3/4 **Magnum Force (NZ)**[62] 7-8-9 **94**.... BVorster 4 55
(L Laxon, Singapore) *a in rr* **16/1**
12 3/4 **Secret Place**[138] 5460 5-8-10 **95**....(t) JAHeffernan 10 54
(M Al Muhairi, UAE) *mid-div: n.d* **33/1**
13 3 **Al Maali (IRE)**[71] 7-9-2 **100**.... RHills 2 52
(Doug Watson, UAE) *in rr on rail: rdn 3 1/2f out: clsd briefly tl wknd 1 1/2f out* **14/1**
14 2 1/4 **Master Robbie**[7] 7-8-6 **90**.... TPO'Shea 36
(R Bouresly, Kuwait) *s.i.s: a in rr* **33/1**
15 15 **Stetchworth Prince**[14] 201 4-9-3 **101**.... LDettori 11 8
(Saeed Bin Suroor) *mid-div: rdn 4f out: n.m.r 3 1/2f out: nvr a threat* **11/2**[1]
16 21 **Gypsy Johnny**[21] 152 4-8-10 **95**....(b) RichardMullen 16 —
(A Laird, UAE) *trckd ldr early stages: rdn 4f out: bdly hmpd 3 1/2f out: virtually p.u* **33/1**

1m 24.11s **Going Correction** +0.25s/f (Slow) **16** Ran SP% **127.0**
Speed ratings: 117,115,111,110,109 108,108,106,100,98 96,95,92,89,72 48

Owner Haras Xara & Haras Mineral Park **Bred** Haras Xara **Trained** Brazil

FOCUS
A good handicap and, with recent course and distance winner Happy Pearl giving the form a solid look in second, the Brazilian-trained Attilius showed himself a very useful sort on his debut in Dubai. As is so often the case on this dirt track, those drawn towards the inside seemed at a disadvantage.

NOTEBOOK
Attilius(BRZ), a multiple winner in his native Brazil, including over as short as four furlongs, was an unknown quantity on his debut in Dubai but showed himself to be very useful with a ready success over a pretty decent yardstick in Happy Pearl. Not badly drawn (far enough away from any possible trouble on the inside of the track), he broke well and, soon in a good rhythm up front, sustained his effort well in the straight when strongly challenged. There could be better to come and he is obviously not one to underestimate.
Happy Pearl(AUS) ran well off a 6lb higher mark than when winning over course and distance two weeks previously and basically just found one too good. He finished clear of the remainder and should continue to go well.
Northern Rock(JPN), quite a likeable, versatile type, ran well off the back of a three-month break.
Sea Hunter was just a length and a half behind today's runner-up when second in a course and distance handicap (representing Godolphin that day) on his previous start, but he was given too much to do this time. He was never too far away from the pace when gaining his four previous turf wins, and a return to more positive tactics should suit this surface ideally.

Rockets 'n Rollers(IRE) showed his ability to handle a fast dirt surface when winning at Jebal Ali last year and, returned to sand having been well held on turf on his reappearance, he ran a fine race from his unfavourable inside draw.
Marbush(IRE) again gave the impression he can do better when returned to further.
Kandidate, in good form on the turf out here recently, could not take advantage of his lower rating on dirt.
Glad To Be Fast(IRE), German trained, would have been quite a bit closer with a clearer run.
Stetchworth Prince did not enjoy that good a trip on this switch to dirt and finished up beaten a long way.
Gypsy Johnny had a good draw out wide and was going quite well until badly hampered inside the final four furlongs.

354a ACT ONE (H'CAP) (TURF) 1m 2f (T)
5:05 (5:11) (90-105,105) 4-Y-0+ **£41,569** (£12,790; £6,395; £3,197)

RPR

1 **Oracle West (SAF)**[14] [207] 5-9-2 **100** WCMarwing 10 105
(M F De Kock, South Africa) *racd alone in 4th: 2nd 3f out: rdn to cl 1 1/2f out: led wl ins fnl f: r.o wl* **5/2**[1]

2 1 3/4 **Alpacco (IRE)**[144] [5352] 4-9-0 **99** AStarke 5 101
(Mario Hofer, Germany) *racd alone in 5th: rdn to cl 3f out: ev ch: kpt on wl: nt qckn* **25/1**

3 nk **Earl's Court**[14] [207] 4-9-3 **102** (t) KerrinMcEvoy 12 103
(I Mohammed, UAE) *trckd ldrs: led 3 1/2f out: hdd wl ins fnl f: one pce* **7/2**[2]

4 4 1/4 **Billy Allen (IRE)**[21] [152] 5-9-6 **105** (t) SPasquier 9 97
(F Chappet, France) *mid-div: rdn to cl 3f out: nt qckn: kpt on one pce* **33/1**

5 nse **Cristoforo (IRE)**[33] [65] 9-8-10 **95** LDettori 6 87
(B J Curley) *mid-div: on rail 3f out: swtchd out 2 1/2f out: r.o: nrst fin* **4/1**[3]

6 1 1/4 **Festive Style (SAF)**[7] [282] 6-8-8 **93** MJKinane 2 82
(J Noseda) *settled in rr: disp last into st: sme hdwy wd in st: nrst fin* **20/1**

7 1/2 **Kestrel Cross (IRE)**[14] [208] 4-8-9 **95** TedDurcan 1 84
(V Smith) *broke awkwardly: in rr into st: mod prog: nvr involved* **20/1**

8 hd **Tipperary All Star (FR)**[14] [208] 6-8-11 **96** ow1 (t) JMurtagh 11 84
(M Halford, Ire) *settled in last: disp last into st: nrst fin* **33/1**

9 1/2 **Terfel**[14] [208] 7-9-1 **99** (t) JohnEgan 3 87
(Daniel J Murphy, Singapore) *in rr: rdn to cl 3f out: wd: n.d* **14/1**

10 2 1/4 **Mutafanen**[14] [208] 5-9-3 **101** RHills 4 85
(E Charpy, UAE) *in rr: on rail early st: gng wl: n.m.r 1 1/2f out: n.d* **6/1**

11 2 3/4 **Hippodrome (IRE)**[110] [6040] 4-8-10 **96** (b) PDillon 7 74
(H J Brown, South Africa) *trckd ldrs: rdn 4f out: sn wknd* **14/1**

12 16 **Kartago (GER)**[260] 4-9-3 **102** ASuborics 8 50
(R Suerland, Germany) *led: hdd 3f out: wknd* **11/1**

2m 3.75s **Going Correction** +0.35s/f (Good)
WFA 4 from 5yo+ 1lb 12 Ran SP% **126.0**
Speed ratings: 114,112,112,108,108 107,107,107,106,105 102,90

Owner A Geemooi **Bred** Langeberg Stud **Trained** South Africa

FOCUS
A high-class handicap but, with the pace good from the start, they were soon well strung out and it proved hard to make up significant amounts of ground from off the pace.

NOTEBOOK
Oracle West(SAF) was said by his trainer to have needed the run when winning by just a neck in a similar event over course and distance on his debut in Dubai two weeks previously, and duly improved to defy 5lb higher mark in clear-cut fashion. He should continue to progress and may be stepped up to Group company next time as connections try and find out if he will be good enough for the Sheema Classic on World Cup night. That race is over a mile and a half, but he is expected to stay.
Alpacco(IRE), a Listed winner in Germany, ran a fine race behind the progressive winner on his debut in Dubai. Given this was his first run in 144 days, he is obviously open to improvement.
Earl's Court, who represented Godolphin when a neck-second to today's winner on his previous start, had every chance but was beaten further this time and has clearly not progressed a great deal.
Billy Allen(IRE) has won on dirt in Yugoslavia, France, Germany and Sweden, but Nad Al Sheba's sand track did not appear to suit when he was well down the field on his previous start and, switched to turf, this was much better.
Cristoforo(IRE), a very useful, and possibly still improving handicapper in England, as well as a dual winner over hurdles, ran a fine race on his debut in Dubai. The way the race was run did not lend itself to making up a great deal of ground from off the pace, and he also just looked as though he would be sharper next time, so this can be considered a promising enough effort. (op 5/1)
Festive Style(SAF) is taking her time to hit top form for her new yard, but this was a creditable effort, especially considering how much ground she was given to make up. She would have an obvious chance if a fillies/mares' only race could be found for her.
Kestrel Cross(IRE) was soon out the back after starting slowly and would not have been suited by the way the race developed. (18/1)
Tipperary All Star(FR), just as on his debut out here, was well held, although he was given quite a bit to do.
Mutafanen, an unlucky second over course and distance two weeks previously, is much better than his finishing position would suggest as he again found trouble in running under Richard Hills. It is hard to say where he would have finished, but it would just be nice to see him get a clear run for once.

355a SAKHEE SH MAKTOUM BIN RASHID AL MAKTOUM CHALLENGE R2 (GROUP 3) (DIRT) 1m 1f (D)
5:35 (5:35) 4-Y-0+ **£75,581** (£23,255; £11,627; £5,813)

RPR

1 **Jack Sullivan (USA)**[103] [6169] 5-9-0 112 (t) EddieAhern 1 116
(G A Butler) *trckd ldr on rail: disp ld 2f out gng wl: led 1 1/2f out: tired fnl 100yds: hld on* **10/3**[2]

2 1 **Blatant**[21] [154] 7-9-0 120 (t) KerrinMcEvoy 3 114
(I Mohammed, UAE) *led on rail: length clear early st: jnd 2f out: kpt on wl and chal again* **4/5**[1]

3 nse **Eccentric**[75] [6439] 5-9-0 110 JMurtagh 2 114
(S Seemar, UAE) *mid-div on rail: rdn to cl 2f out: r.o wl: nrst fin* **14/1**

4 2 **Chiquitin (ARG)**[42] 6-9-0 112 (t) MJKinane 6 110
(I Jory, Saudi Arabia) *hmpd after 1f: dropped to last: rdn to cl 2f out: nt qckn* **10/1**

5 4 1/2 **Elmustanser**[21] [152] 5-9-0 104 (t) RHills 8 101
(Doug Watson, UAE) *mid-div: prog 4f out: prom 3 1/2f out: nt qckn* **33/1**

6 6 **Lundy's Liability (BRZ)**[21] [154] 6-9-0 113 (t) WCMarwing 5 89
(M F De Kock, South Africa) *mid-div: n.m.r 4 1/2f out: ev ch ent st: n.m.r: wknd* **9/2**[3]

7 1/2 **Baldaquin**[6] 9-9-0 100 PDillon 4 88
(R Bouresly, Kuwait) *trckd ldr early: wknd 4f out* **50/1**

8 7 1/4 **Ned Kelly (SAF)**[14] [201] 5-9-0 95 (bt) MKhan 9 74
(D Maroun, South Africa) *prom but wd: rdn 4 1/2f out: wknd* **100/1**

9 2 1/4 **Tableau (USA)**[6] 5-9-0 86 TPO'Shea 7 69
(R Bouresly, Kuwait) *sn in rr: nvr involved* **100/1**

1m 50.36s **Going Correction** +0.25s/f (Slow) 9 Ran SP% **119.5**
Speed ratings: 111,110,110,108,104 98,98,92,90

Owner The International Carnival Partnership **Bred** Hermitage Farm Llc **Trained** Blewbury, Oxon
■ Jack Sullivan landed this Group Three for the second year running, and provided Eddie Ahern with a double in the process.

FOCUS
A reasonable Group Three but, despite the confirmed front-runner Blatant being taken on for the lead, the pace was not noticeably strong.

NOTEBOOK
Jack Sullivan(USA), last year's Dubai World Cup fourth, had not been seen since finishing down the field in the Breeders' Cup Classic 103 days previously, but he was reported to have been training well and duly proved good enough to follow up last year's success in this very race. His effort is all the more creditable given he had the benefit of a prep before winning this last season. Stall one did not look ideal beforehand (he was drawn nine of nine in the previous year's renewal), but he did not find any trouble on the inside and got a lead off the confirmed front-runner Blatant. His jockey reported afterwards that in actual fact, he did not think the pace was strong enough, and he was travelling too well but, after cruising upsides about two out, he found enough to sustain his challenge despite understandably getting a little tired. He will apparently miss the World Cup this year, and go instead for the Godolphin Mile, but his aim before then is to try and repeat last year's win in the Burj Nahaar.
Blatant looked so impressive when winning in this grade over a mile on his debut for his current trainer three weeks previously, but he got a very easy lead that day and the form has been badly let down since, most notably when the runner-up Cherry Pickings could only finish sixth in a Listed race at Jebel Ali next time. Racing over a furlong further than he has ever won over, he did not go off that fast and, unsurprisingly taken on for the lead this time, could not run up to his very best. In his defence, this was still by no means a bad effort, and he should not be underestimated when likely to get his own way back over a mile. (op Evs)
Eccentric ◆, last year's Winter Derby winner, who also won a Group Three on turf, had not been seen since finishing tailed off in the Japan Cup Dirt and has since left Andrew Reid. While the winner was not inconvenienced by stall one, he soon got shuffled back from his similarly low draw and did extremely well to stay on for a close third. This was very promising effort and he must not be underestimated next time, especially if able to be ridden more positively from a wide draw.
Chiquitin(ARG), a length and a quarter second to Jack Sullivan in this race last year, ran well on his return to Dubai considering he was hampered early on and had to come from the back - his only success at last year's Carnival came from the front. (op 9/1)
Elmustanser was a little bit out of his depth.
Lundy's Liability(BRZ), beaten over 11 lengths into third behind Blatant in a similar event over a mile here on his previous start, did not get a very good trip and might have been a little closer with a clearer run. (op 4/1)

356a GREEN DESERT CUP (H'CAP) (TURF) 1m 2f (T)
6:05 (6:05) (90-105,104) 4-Y-0+ **£41,569** (£12,790; £6,395; £3,197)

RPR

1 **Falstaff (IRE)**[7] [282] 4-9-4 **102** WCMarwing 9 109
(M F De Kock, South Africa) *in rr main gp: last ent st: swtchd wd: 8th 1 1/2f out: r.o to ld nr line* **2/1**[1]

2 1 1/4 **Shanty Star (IRE)**[7] 6-9-4 **101** PDillon 2 106
(R Bouresly, Kuwait) *trckd ldrs: led 2f out: swtchd centre: kpt on wl* **14/1**

3 1 3/4 **The Carbon Unit (USA)**[14] [207] 4-8-10 **95** TPO'Shea 7 96
(E Charpy, UAE) *pushed along early: settled in rr: rdn to cl 3f out: disp 100yds out: nt qckn* **12/1**

4 3/4 **Jersey Bounce (IRE)**[14] [204] 5-8-11 **95** KShea 12 94
(H J Brown, South Africa) *broke awkwardly: racd wd: trckd ldrs: ev ch 2f out: r.o* **33/1**

5 1 1/2 **Evaluator (IRE)**[131] [5607] 5-9-3 **100** KerrinMcEvoy 6 97
(I Mohammed, UAE) *settled in rr rails: n.m.r 3f out: nvr a threat* **5/1**[3]

6 shd **Bianconi (SAF)**[14] [207] 7-9-6 **104** (bt) TedDurcan 10 100
(A Laird, UAE) *in rr main gp: mid-div 4f out gng wl: rdn cl 1 1/2f out: nt qckn* **9/2**[2]

7 1 3/4 **Whazzat**[79] [6416] 4-9-4 **102** (e^1) JMurtagh 4 96
(D Selvaratnam, UAE) *mid-div on rail: ev ch 3f out: one pce* **20/1**

8 5 **Realism (FR)**[14] [208] 6-9-0 **97** LDettori 3 81
(R A Fahey) *led: hdd 2f out: wknd* **7/1**

9 nk **Fallon (SAF)**[258] 6-8-9 **93** (t) WSupple 8 76
(S Seemar, UAE) *mid-div: wd into st: nvr a threat* **33/1**

10 1 3/4 **Courageous Duke (USA)**[14] [207] 7-9-2 **99** MJKinane 11 79
(J Noseda) *v s.i.s: disp last ent st: n.d* **6/1**

11 12 **Full Speed (IND)**[21] [153] 5-8-11 **95** EddieAhern 5 52
(Pesi Shroff, India) *trckd ldrs centre: rdn 4f: wknd* **40/1**

12 1/2 **Duijker (FR)**[6] 5-8-9 **93** (t) PJSmullen 1 49
(E Charpy, UAE) *trckd ldr on rail: ev ch 3f out: wknd* **33/1**

2m 3.76s **Going Correction** +0.35s/f (Good)
WFA 4 from 5yo+ 1lb 12 Ran SP% **125.4**
Speed ratings: 114,113,111,111,109 109,108,104,104,102 93,92

Owner L Nestadt & B Kantor **Bred** Gerard Callinan **Trained** South Africa
■ Flastaff was the second leg of a double for trainer Mike De Kock and jockey Weichong Marwing.

FOCUS
Another very good handicap and the form looks solid.

NOTEBOOK
Falstaff(IRE), a promising third on his debut for this yard over a mile here the previous week, improved on that form on this step up to a mile two to win decisively. He had a lot to do at the top of the straight, but enjoyed one continuous clear run when switched wide and there was a lot to like about the way in which he sustained his effort.
Shanty Star(IRE) has been running surprisingly well at this Carnival for a horse whose last success came over two miles and this was another terrific effort. He deserves to find a similar race, but is vulnerable to progressive types.
The Carbon Unit(USA) stepped up on the form he showed in a similar event over course and distance on his previous start with a creditable third.
Jersey Bounce(IRE), down the field in a seven-furlong handicap on the dirt course here on his previous start, would have appreciated the step back up in trip and return to turf, and ran well.
Evaluator(IRE), a progressive handicapper for Terry Mills last season who was second in the Cambridgeshire off a mark of 97 on his final start, could be considered a touch disappointing on his debut for a new trainer off the back of a 131-day break, although he did not get the clearest of runs. His trainer is not having a very good Carnival considering the horses he has at his disposal.
Bianconi(SAF) travelled well for much of the way, but was ultimately well held and did not improve on the form he showed on his reappearance.
Realism(FR) had every chance from the front but, just as on his debut in Dubai, was below the pick of his form.
Courageous Duke(USA) failed to build on the form he showed when fifth in a course and distance handicap on his previous start.

357a STORMING HOME TROPHY (H'CAP) (TURF) 7f 110y(D)

6:35 (6:35) (90-105,104) 4-Y-O+ **£41,569** (£12,790; £6,395; £3,197)

RPR

1 **Mandobi (IRE)**[21] 151 5-9-1 **98**.......................................(vt[1]) JMurtagh 2 101
(D Selvaratnam, UAE) *racd in rr: prog 3f out: n.m.r 1 1/2f out: r.o wl last 100yds: led last strides* **16/1**

2 *nk* **Parnassus (SAF)**[222] 4-8-5 **93**....................................... RichardMullen 9 95
(A Laird, UAE) *trckd ldr in centre: gng wl 3f out: disp 2f out: r.o wl: hdd last strides* **20/1**

3 *nk* **Millennium Force**[21] 149 8-8-9 **93**................................. JAHeffernan 7 94
(M R Channon) *mid-div: trckd ldrs 3f out: rdn to chal 1 1/2f out: disp 1f out: nt qckn* **7/1**

4 *nk* **Tajseed (IRE)**[21] 151 6-8-7 **90**... RHills 6 91
(A Manuel, UAE) *hld up in rr: n.m.r 3 1/2f out: swtchd wd: r.o nrst fin* **7/1**

5 *3* **Little Good Bay**[7] 282 6-8-9 **93**.....................................(b) TedDurcan 12 86
(A Laird, UAE) *in rr on rail: n.m.r 3 1/2f out: n.d* **5/1[3]**

6 *2* **Subpoena**[99] 6229 4-9-1 **98**...(vt) LDettori 11 87
(Saeed Bin Suroor) *led: v wd: disp top st: ev ch 3f out: one pce* **4/1[1]**

7 *½* **Mercury Chief (SAF)**[21] 151 5-8-7 **90**..................................... MKhan 5 77
(H J Brown, South Africa) *trckd ldr in centre: gng wl 3f out: disp 2f ent st: ev ch 2 1/2f out* **16/1**

8 *1 ¼* **Crimson Sun (USA)**[131] 5614 4-9-6 **104**.....................(t) KerrinMcEvoy 3 87
(I Mohammed, UAE) *mid-div on rail: n.m.r: 4f out: ev ch 3f out then disp ld briefly: wknd* **9/2[2]**

9 *2* **Waajeb (USA)**[20] 6-8-8 **91**...(t) RoystonFfrench 4 70
(A Al Raihe, UAE) *in rr on rail: n.m.r 3 1/2f out: n.d* **7/1**

10 *2* **Legal Approach**[7] 278 7-8-8 **91**... PDillon 10 65
(R Bouresly, Kuwait) *mid-div: wknd 3 1/2f out* **66/1**

11 *¾* **Party Boss**[21] 154 4-8-11 **95**...(t) EddieAhern 8 66
(C E Brittain) *mid-div: rdn along: 4f out: nvr a threat* **16/1**

12 *4* **Damachida (IRE)**[14] 201 7-9-2 **99**.................................(t) WCMarwing 1 61
(Eva Sundbye, Sweden) *s.i.s: last ent st on rail: n.m.r 2 1/2f out: nt rcvr* **20/1**

1m 30.76s **Going Correction** +0.35s/f (Good) **12 Ran SP% 121.0**
Speed ratings: 112,111,111,111,108 106,105,104,102,100 99,95

Owner Sheikh Ahmed Al Maktoum **Bred** High Bramley Grange Stud Ltd **Trained** United Arab Emirates

FOCUS
Another decent handicap, and very competitive.

NOTEBOOK
Mandobi(IRE) finished last in a similar event on his previous start, but had both a tongue-tie and blinkers fitted for the first time, and the booking of Johnny Murtagh was also a big positive. He appeared to be making hard work of it when meeting some trouble in running just over a furlong out, but his rider conjured a fine run out of him when switching to the inside and he got up almost on the line. It remains to be seen if he can repeat this next time, especially as the headgear and tongue-tie may not have the same effect again.
Parnassus(SAF) ◆, a winner over an extended nine furlongs when trained in South Africa, ran a fine race on his debut for a new trainer and first run in 222 days. His effort is all the more creditably given he was the stable second string, and even better can be expected in future.
Millennium Force ◆, 9lb lower than when winning at last year's Carnival, stepped up on the form he showed on his reappearance and was just held. It will be disappointing if he does not find a similar race.
Tajseed(IRE) confirmed the promise he showed in a similar event over course and distance on his previous start, and would have been even closer had he enjoyed a clearer run under Richard Hills.
Little Good Bay ran another solid race and may have been a little closer to the front four with a clearer run.
Subpoena is not the easiest to win with and was well held on debut in Dubai off the back of a 99-day break.
Party Boss, well beaten on the dirt on his previous start, failed to improve as one might have hoped for the return to turf, and the first-time tongue-tie did not seem to help much either.

313 WOLVERHAMPTON (A.W) (L-H)

Friday, February 10

OFFICIAL GOING: Standard to fast
Wind: Almost nil Weather: Fine and sunny

358 SPIN TO WIN @LITTLEWOODSCASINO.COM H'CAP (DIV I) 1m 1f 103y(P)

1:50 (1:50) (Class 6) (0-55,61) 4-Y-O+ **£2,047** (£604; £302) **Stalls Low**

Form RPR

/0-1 1 **Itcanbedone Again (IRE)**[37] 41 7-9-0 **55**.................... FrancisFerris 4 61
(Ian Williams) *led 1f: chsd ldrs: rdn to ld and edgd lft over 1f out: drvn out* **8/1**

-151 2 *nk* **Latif (USA)**[5] 304 5-9-0 **55** 6ex... SamHitchcott 9 61
(Ms Deborah J Evans) *hld up: hdwy over 2f out: rdn and edgd lft ins fnl f: r.o* **7/1**

-041 3 *nk* **Bridgewater Boys**[7] 290 5-9-1 **61** 6ex.................(b) AndrewMullen[(5)] 11 66
(K A Ryan) *a.p: chsd ldr 7f out: led over 2f out: rdn and hdd over 1f out: r.o* **9/2[2]**

-105 4 *2* **Legacy (JPN)**[4] 310 6-8-7 **48** ow1................................ RobertWinston 6 52+
(P D Evans) *s.i.s: hld up: nt clr run over 2f out: hdwy and nt clr run over 1f out: nt rch ldrs* **9/2[2]**

62-0 5 *2* **Hiawatha (IRE)**[7] 285 7-8-11 **52**.. ChrisCatlin 2 49
(A M Hales) *hld up in tch: nt clr run and lost pl over 2f out: r.o ins fnl f* **6/1[3]**

3-04 6 *4* **Bold Trump**[21] 162 5-8-9 **50**....................................... GrahamGibbons 1 40
(Mrs N S Evans) *prom: rdn over 3f out: wknd over 1f out* **20/1**

-000 7 *1* **Barzak (IRE)**[4] 313 6-8-11 **52**..(bt) JimmyQuinn 5 40
(S R Bowring) *chsd ldrs: rdn over 2f out: wknd over 1f out* **25/1**

8 *3 ½* **Atakama (GER)**[96] 6274 6-7-12 **46** oh6.................... DonnaCaldwell[(7)] 7 27
(A D Nolan, Ire) *s.s: hld up: a in rr* **25/1**

00 9 *nk* **Rose Thistle (UAE)**[20] 170 4-9-0 **55**............................(v[1]) ShaneKelly 8 36
(John A Quinn, Ire) *led over 8f out: rdn and hdd over 2f out: wknd over 1f out* **50/1**

0002 10 *¾* **Farnborough (USA)**[7] 285 5-8-3 **51**........................... JamesDoyle[(7)] 3 30
(R J Price) *hld up in tch: rdn over 3f out: wknd 2f out* **11/4[1]**

020- 11 *1* **Fortunes Favourite**[44] 6680 6-8-0 **46** oh1............ NataliaGemelova[(5)] 10 23
(J E Long) *hld up: wknd over 2f out* **66/1**

2m 0.48s (-2.14) **Going Correction** -0.175s/f (Stan) **11 Ran SP% 116.8**
Speed ratings (Par 101):102,101,101,99,97 94,93,90,90,89 88
CSF £58.63 CT £285.62 TOTE £8.20: £3.90, £2.10, £2.00; EX 88.80.
Owner Racing Shrews Syndicate Bayston Hill **Bred** R Hollinshead **Trained** Portway, Worcs
■ Stewards' Enquiry : Andrew Mullen one-day ban: used whip with excessive frequency (Feb 21)

FOCUS
The going was changed to standard to fast after this race, and there appeared more kickback than usual. A moderate handicap but a somewhat rough race producing a close finish. The form is not that strong.

359 SUPER JACKPOTS @LITTLEWOODSCASINO.COM H'CAP 5f 20y(P)

2:20 (2:21) (Class 6) (0-60,66) 3-Y-O **£2,388** (£705; £352) **Stalls Low**

Form RPR

12-3 1 **Angie And Liz (IRE)**[25] 120 3-8-13 **55**.................... RobbieFitzpatrick 6 59
(Peter Grayson) *chsd ldrs: rdn over 3f out: edgd lft ins fnl f: r.o to ld post* **9/2[3]**

-112 2 *shd* **Garlogs**[1] 344 3-9-10 **66** 6ex.. RobertWinston 4 70
(A Bailey) *sn drvn to ld: hdd post* **5/2[2]**

06-5 3 *1* **Otis B Driftwood**[3] 322 3-9-4 **60**..............................(b[1]) FrancisNorton 3 60
(M Quinn) *led early: chsd ldrs: rdn 1/2-way: edgd lft ins fnl f: styd on* **10/1**

0-51 4 *2* **Correct Time (IRE)**[12] 239 3-9-6 **62** 6ex........................ JimmyQuinn 1 55
(N P Littmoden) *sn outpcd: hung rt 1/2-way: hdwy 2f out: sn rdn and edgd lft: no ex fnl f* **6/5[1]**

010- 5 *2* **Soviet Legend (IRE)**[93] 6297 3-9-0 **59**.................(b) PatrickMathers[(3)] 2 45
(T J Etherington) *s.i.s: outpcd* **20/1**

0-50 6 *3* **Lasting Love**[7] 287 3-8-13 **55**.. TomEaves 5 30
(C R Dore) *chsd ldrs: rdn 1/2-way: wkng whn nt clr run over 1f out* **50/1**

62.55 secs (-0.27) **Going Correction** -0.175s/f (Stan) **6 Ran SP% 108.0**
Speed ratings (Par 95):95,94,93,90,86 82
CSF £14.87 TOTE £4.80: £2.00, £2.00; EX 15.40.
Owner R Teatum And Mrs S Grayson **Bred** John Perotta **Trained** Formby, Lancs

FOCUS
The first of three races over the distance on the day and the slowest time, despite being run at a frantic early pace. The race is rated through the winner, but could be a shade high.
Soviet Legend(IRE) Official explanation: jockey said colt missed the break

360 PLAY BEJEWELLED FOR £400K @LITTLEWOODSCASINO.COM (S) STKS 5f 20y(P)

2:50 (2:50) (Class 6) 3-Y-O+ **£2,388** (£705; £352) **Stalls Low**

Form RPR

20-1 1 **Henry Tun**[24] 130 8-9-9 52.....................................(b) JasonEdmunds[(3)] 1 63
(J Balding) *chsd ldrs: rdn to ld and edgd rt ins fnl f: r.o* **7/2[2]**

000- 2 *¾* **Obe Bold (IRE)**[67] 6511 5-9-2 40.................................... FrancisNorton 5 50
(A Berry) *son led: hung rt fr 1/2-way: rdn over 1f out: hdd ins fnl f: kpt on* **20/1**

34-4 3 *½* **Hello Roberto**[14] 212 5-9-2 40..............................(p) AdrianMcCarthy 10 48
(R A Harris) *sn chsng ldr: rdn and ev ch ins fnl f: unable qck towards fin* **9/2[3]**

-504 4 *¾* **St Ivian**[7] 288 6-9-2 50... DuranFentiman[(5)] 6 50
(Mrs N Macauley) *chsd ldrs: rdn 1/2-way: styd on* **3/1[1]**

00-0 5 *¾* **Piccleyes**[30] 90 5-9-7 40...(b) DeanMcKeown 7 48
(M J Polglase) *s.i.s: hld up: shkn up over 1f out: r.o: nvr nr to chal* **16/1**

00-5 6 *½* **Edged In Gold**[25] 119 4-9-2 55................................. FergusSweeney 12 41
(P J Makin) *chsd ldrs: rdn and hung rt over 1f out: hung lft and no ex ins fnl f* **11/2**

030- 7 *3 ½* **Dolce Maria (IRE)**[55] 6600 3-8-2 .... PaulHanagan 2 28
(K A Morgan) *s.i.s: hld up: nvr nrr* **10/1**

006- 8 *nk* **Hellbent**[221] 3179 7-9-7 50... JimmyQuinn 8 32
(M Appleby) *hld up: plld hrd: rdn over 1f out: n.d* **12/1**

00-0 9 *¾* **Winning Venture**[9] 265 9-9-7 55...........................(p) RobertWinston 11 29
(A W Carroll) *s.i.s: sn mid-div: rdn 1/2-way: wknd over 1f out* **14/1**

00-0 10 *1* **Bold Maggie**[17] 179 4-8-9 40........................... RussellKennemore[(7)] 9 21
(J A Pickering) *plld hrd and prom: rdn 1/2-way: sn wknd* **66/1**

00-0 11 *3* **Cayman Mischief**[11] 255 6-8-9 40................................ KatieHales[(7)] 3 10
(James Moffatt) *mid-div: rdn 1/2-way: sn wknd* **66/1**

000- 12 *1 ¾* **Turtle Magic (IRE)**[216] 3350 4-9-2 35.. AlanDaly 4 4
(Miss J S Davis) *s.s: a in rr* **66/1**

62.30 secs (-0.52) **Going Correction** -0.175s/f (Stan)
WFA 3 from 4yo+ 14lb **12 Ran SP% 119.4**
Speed ratings (Par 101):97,96,95,93,92 91,86,85,84,82 78,75
CSF £76.87 TOTE £3.70: £1.50, £4.20, £2.00; EX 89.50.There was no bid for the winner.
Owner Terry Reffell **Bred** T Tunstall **Trained** Scrooby, Notts
■ Stewards' Enquiry : Adrian McCarthy three-day ban: careless riding (Feb 21-23)

FOCUS
An ordinary seller run a quarter of a second faster than the previous race for three-year-olds and it paid to race close to the pace. The form is not that solid with the second the best guide to the level.
St Ivian Official explanation: jockey said gelding was struck into

361 SPIN TO WIN @LITTLEWOODSCASINO.COM CLAIMING STKS 1m 4f 50y(P)

3:25 (3:26) (Class 6) 4-Y-O+ **£2,730** (£806; £403) **Stalls Low**

Form RPR

/5-0 1 **Berkhamsted (IRE)**[14] 213 4-9-5 95................................... ShaneKelly 9 68+
(J A Osborne) *hld up in tch: edgd lft and led over 3f out: rdn clr fnl 2f* **3/1[2]**

-152 2 *3 ½* **Desperation (IRE)**[11] 250 4-9-5 73.............................. RobertWinston 7 59
(K R Burke) *hld up: hdwy and edgd lft fr over 3f out: rdn to chse wnr fnl 2f: no imp* **8/11[1]**

4654 3 *1* **York Cliff**[13] 230 8-8-3 50.. LiamJones[(7)] 10 46
(W M Brisbourne) *dwlt: hld up: nt clr run over 2f out: hdwy over 1f out: nt rch ldrs* **8/1[3]**

0/0- 4 *½* **Venetian Romance (IRE)**[32] 6381 5-7-11 35 ow1...(tp) JamesDoyle[(7)] 2 39
(D J S Ffrench Davis) *chsd ldrs: ev ch 3f out: styd on same pce fnl 2f* **80/1**

2-00 5 *2* **Danzolin**[9] 263 5-8-4 54 ow1.. MartinDwyer 5 36
(W R Muir) *hld up: hdwy over 3f out: sn rdn: styd on same pce fnl 2f* **16/1**

305 6 *6* **Mossmann Gorge**[13] 231 4-8-11 55..........................(b[1]) HayleyTurner 8 36
(M Wellings) *plld hrd and prom: hmpd over 3f out: sn wknd* **14/1**

60-4 7 *1 ¼* **Sungio**[23] 141 8-8-1 40..(b) SoniaEaton[(7)] 6 28
(B P J Baugh) *dwlt: hld up: a in rr* **22/1**

20-0 8 *½* **Legend Of Dance**[30] 91 4-8-9 40.............................. MarcHalford[(5)] 3 36
(J L Spearing) *led: hung rt over 4f out: hdd over 3f out: wknd over 2f out* **66/1**

00-0 9 *17* **Margarets Wish**[11] 55 6-8-7 35.................................. J-PGuillambert 4 —
(T Wall) *chsd ldrs: hmpd over 3f out: sn wknd* **50/1**

0/0- 10 *½* **April Shannon**[238] 2651 4-8-1 30........................ NataliaGemelova[(5)] 1 —
(J E Long) *chsd ldr over 7f: sn wknd* **100/1**

2m 40.61s (-1.81) **Going Correction** -0.175s/f (Stan)
WFA 4 from 5yo+ 3lb **10 Ran SP% 116.6**
Speed ratings (Par 101):99,96,96,95,94 90,89,89,77,77
CSF £5.38 TOTE £3.50: £1.40, £1.02, £2.70; EX 3.60.Berkhamsted (IRE) was claimed by M. Harris for £12,000; Desperation (IRE) was claimed by Barry Leavy for £12,000.

Owner Richard Leslie **Bred** E Lonergan **Trained** Upper Lambourn, Berks

FOCUS

An uncompetitive claimer in which only the first two had a serious chance on official ratings and they did not need to run to those marks. The form is not worth much.

Desperation(IRE) Official explanation: jockey said gelding hung left from 4f out

Legend Of Dance Official explanation: jockey said filly hung right throughout

362 "A £75 BONUS FOR NEW PLAYERS" @LITTLEWOODSCASINO.COM H'CAP 5f 20y(P)

4:00 (4:00) (Class 4) (0-85,81) 4-Y-0+ **£5,505** (£1,637; £818; £408) **Stalls** Low

Form RPR

1-11 **1** **Graze On**[12] [245] 4-9-2 **79** 6ex....................(b) AdrianMcCarthy 1 93+
(R A Harris) *trckd ldrs: nt clr run over 3f out: swtchd rt: rdn to ld 1f out: r.o wl* **11/8**[1]

033- **2** *2* **Countdown**[56] [6590] 4-9-1 **78**....................(b) TomEaves 3 85
(Miss J A Camacho) *mid-div: sn drvn along: hdwy 1/2-way: styd on* **7/1**[3]

0-50 **3** *1 3/4* **Gilded Cove**[12] [245] 6-8-10 **73**.................... GrahamGibbons 9 74+
(R Hollinshead) *sn outpcd: r.o ins fnl f: nrst fin* **7/1**[3]

5-00 **4** *3/4* **Fizzlephut (IRE)**[3] [323] 4-8-12 **75**.................... PaulFitzsimons 11 73
(Miss J R Tooth) *prom: rdn 1/2-way: styd on same pce appr fnl f* **80/1**

600- **5** *3/4* **Bonne De Fleur**[52] [6636] 5-9-3 **80**.................... DerekMcGaffin 6 75
(B Smart) *sn outpcd: hdwy and nt clr run over 1f out: nt rch ldrs* **33/1**

2010 **6** *nk* **Law Maker**[12] [244] 6-8-10 **80**....................(v) MichaelJStainton(7) 7 74
(A Bailey) *chsd ldrs: hmpd over 3f out: sn lost pl: n.d after* **12/1**

51-0 **7** *hd* **Harry Up**[31] [79] 5-8-8 **78**.................... CDTimmons(7) 4 72
(K A Ryan) *chsd ldrs: led over 2f out: rdn and hdd 1f out: sn wknd* **9/2**[2]

6050 **8** *1/2* **Cornus**[12] [238] 4-9-4 **81**.................... DeanMcKeown 10 73
(M J Polglase) *s.i.s: hld up: nvr nrr* **16/1**

01-0 **9** *1/2* **Ryedane (IRE)**[31] [79] 4-9-0 **77**....................(e) DavidAllan 5 67
(T D Easterby) *chsd ldrs over 3f* **12/1**

4-00 **10** *1* **Oceanico Dot Com (IRE)**[4] [320] 4-8-4 **67** oh7.......... FrancisNorton 2 53
(A Berry) *led: hdd over 3f out: rdn over 1f out: sn wknd* **80/1**

3-02 **11** *2* **Efistorm**[12] [244] 5-8-7 **70**.................... PaulFessey 8 49
(J Balding) *w ldrs: led over 3f out: hung rt and hdd 1/2-way: wknd over 1f out* **16/1**

61.19 secs (-1.63) **Going Correction** -0.175s/f (Stan) 11 Ran SP% **117.8**

Speed ratings (Par 105):106,102,100,98,97 97,96,96,95,93 90

CSF £11.38 CT £52.42 TOTE £2.10: £1.40, £2.00, £2.40; EX 12.50 Trifecta £69.40 Pool £1,812.17, 18.53 w/u.

Owner Tom Tuohy Paraic Gaffney **Bred** Mrs Sandra Cooper **Trained** Earlswood, Monmouths

FOCUS

A decent-quality sprint handicap run at a cracking pace in which the winning time was well over a second quicker than the two earlier races over the trip. The form looks reliable with the runner-up setting the standard.

Efistorm Official explanation: jockey said gelding hung right-handed

363 SPIN TO WIN @LITTLEWOODSCASINO.COM H'CAP (DIV II) 1m 1f 103y(P)

4:30 (4:30) (Class 6) (0-55,55) 4-Y-0+ **£2,047** (£604; £302) **Stalls** Low

Form RPR

0-62 **1** **Desert Hawk**[13] [231] 5-8-7 **48**....................(b) RobbieFitzpatrick 4 56
(W M Brisbourne) *chsd ldrs: led over 1f out: sn rdn: styd on: eased last strides* **7/2**[2]

0-02 **2** *1/2* **Friends Hope**[13] [229] 5-9-0 **55**.................... PatCosgrave 10 62
(P A Blockley) *hld up: hdwy over 2f out: rdn over 1f out: styd on* **10/3**[1]

031- **3** *nk* **Turner's Touch**[43] [6683] 4-8-13 **54** ow2....................(be) GeorgeBaker 2 60
(G L Moore) *hld up in tch: lost pl over 3f out: hung lft and hdwy u.p over 1f out: styd on reluctantly* **9/2**[3]

-300 **4** *1* **Wrenlane**[7] [285] 5-9-0 **55**....................(p) TonyHamilton 5 59
(R A Fahey) *w ldr tl led 5f out: rdn and hdd over 1f out: styd on same pce fnl f* **9/1**

-000 **5** *1 1/4* **Miss Monica (IRE)**[4] [311] 5-8-5 **46** oh1.................... AdrianTNicholls 6 48
(P W Hiatt) *hld up: hdwy over 2f out: styd on u.p* **40/1**

35-0 **6** *1* **Charnock Bates One (IRE)**[28] [109] 5-8-10 **51**.......(p) RobertWinston 7 51
(J J Quinn) *hld up in tch: rdn over 1f out: styd on same pce* **5/1**

51-0 **7** *5* **Sonntag Blue (IRE)**[30] [82] 4-8-13 **54**.................... ChrisCatlin 3 44
(Miss J Feilden) *led: hdd 5f out: rdn and wknd over 1f out* **11/2**

043- **8** *nk* **Princeable Lady (IRE)**[51] [6649] 4-8-2 **46** oh6....... EdwardCreighton(3) 1 36
(J A Pickering) *trckd ldrs: plld hrd: rdn and wknd over 1f out* **33/1**

505- **9** *2* **Summer Bounty**[43] [6683] 10-8-5 **46** oh6.................... JoeFanning 9 32
(F Jordan) *s.s: hld up: hdwy over 3f out: ev ch 2f out: sn hung lft and wknd* **25/1**

26-0 **10** *12* **Dara Mac**[12] [242] 7-8-11 **52**.................... MickyFenton 8 15
(L P Grassick) *chsd ldrs 7f* **40/1**

360/ **11** *29* **Prima Patrona**[1201] [5490] 6-9-0 **55**.................... RobertHavlin 11 —
(Mrs H Sweeting) *plld hrd and prom: wknd 4f out* **80/1**

2m 0.88s (-1.74) **Going Correction** -0.175s/f (Stan) 11 Ran SP% **118.4**

Speed ratings (Par 101):100,99,99,98,97 96,91,91,89,79 53

CSF £15.11 CT £53.79 TOTE £3.70: £1.80, £1.80, £2.20; EX 16.90.

Owner J Jones Racing Ltd **Bred** C J Mills **Trained** Great Ness, Shropshire

■ Stewards' Enquiry : George Baker three-day ban: used whip with excessive force (Feb 21-23)

FOCUS

The second division of this moderate handicap run 0.4sec slower that the first division and dominated by those at the head of the betting. The fourth sets the level for the form.

364 BIGGEST JACKPOT ON THE WEB @LITTLEWOODSCASINO.COM H'CAP 7f 32y(P)

5:00 (5:00) (Class 5) (0-70,74) 3-Y-0 **£3,886** (£1,156; £577; £288) **Stalls** High

Form RPR

3210 **1** **Ockums Razor (IRE)**[1] [344] 3-9-6 **70** 6ex.................... DeanMcKeown 6 77
(M J Polglase) *mde virtually all: rdn clr fnl f* **7/1**[3]

-062 **2** *2 1/2* **Royal Embrace**[14] [211] 3-8-4 **57**....................(v) PatrickMathers(3) 8 57
(D Shaw) *hld up: hdwy over 1f out: nt rch wnr* **8/1**

2-22 **3** *nk* **Canina**[32] [68] 3-9-1 **65**.................... J-PGuillambert 5 64
(Ms Deborah J Evans) *s.i.s: hld up: hdwy over 2f out: rdn over 1f out: styd on same pce* **7/1**[3]

6-41 **4** *nk* **Donna Giovanna**[11] [254] 3-9-3 **74** 6ex.................... JamesDoyle(7) 2 72
(J A Osborne) *hld up in tch: outpcd over 2f out: styd on u.p fnl f* **15/8**[1]

41-0 **5** *1 1/4* **Xpres Boy (IRE)**[32] [68] 3-8-12 **62**.................... PaulEddery 7 57
(S R Bowring) *chsd ldrs: rdn over 2f out: edgd lft over 1f out: no ex* **7/1**[3]

0-01 **6** *shd* **Tilen (IRE)**[18] [176] 3-7-11 **54** oh6....................(b) LiamJones(7) 3 49
(S Parr) *hld up: r.o ins fnl f: nrst fin* **12/1**

40-3 **7** *5* **Stoneacre Boy (IRE)**[13] [226] 3-9-3 **67**.................... RobbieFitzpatrick 10 49+
(Peter Grayson) *hld up in tch: plld hrd: chsd wnr 2f out: sn rdn: wknd fnl f* **9/2**[2]

04-0 **8** *1 1/4* **Jumanji (IRE)**[25] [124] 3-8-7 **57**.................... ChrisCatlin 1 36
(M J Attwater) *led early: chsd ldrs: hmpd and wknd over 2f out* **16/1**

050- **9** *11* **Under Fire (IRE)**[41] [6699] 3-8-9 **59**.................... ShaneKelly 9 9
(A W Carroll) *chsd wnr 6f out tl rdn over 2f out: sn wknd* **40/1**

1m 29.92s (-0.48) **Going Correction** -0.175s/f (Stan) 9 Ran SP% **117.6**

Speed ratings (Par 97):95,92,91,91,90 89,84,82,70

CSF £62.68 CT £410.72 TOTE £7.30: £2.70, £2.50, £2.80; EX 75.80.

Owner Paul J Dixon **Bred** Minch Bloodstock **Trained** Babworth, Notts

FOCUS

A fair little handicap run at a true pace, and although the form is strong it looks sound enough.

365 LITTLEWOODSCASINO.COM - THE TRUSTED NAME IN GAMING MAIDEN STKS 7f 32y(P)

5:30 (5:32) (Class 5) 3-Y-0+ **£3,238** (£963; £481; £240) **Stalls** High

Form RPR

54- **1** **Violent Velocity (IRE)**[101] [6213] 3-8-7.................... GrahamGibbons 2 79+
(J J Quinn) *a.p: chsd ldr 3f out: led on bit 1f out: comf* **11/2**[3]

4-2 **2** *1 1/2* **Siwa**[11] [254] 3-8-2.................... PaulHanagan 6 64
(E A L Dunlop) *sn led: rdn and hdd 1f out: unable qckn* **4/5**[1]

3 *1 1/4* **Pop Music (IRE)** 3-8-7.................... SimonWhitworth 12 66
(Miss J Feilden) *prom: outpcd over 2f out: rallied over 1f out: r.o* **80/1**

4 *nk* **Piano Player (IRE)** 3-8-7.................... ShaneKelly 4 65
(J A Osborne) *hld up: hdwy over 1f out: r.o* **20/1**

5-3 **5** *1 1/2* **The Rebound Kid**[13] [217] 4-9-3.................... DonnaCaldwell(7) 1 61
(G A Huffer) *hld up in tch: rdn over 2f out: styd on same pce fnl f* **16/1**

6 *4* **Sedgwick** 4-9-10.................... MickyFenton 10 51
(J G Given) *s.i.s: hld up: hdwy over 2f out: no imp fr over 1f out* **100/1**

6 **7** *nk* **Top Shot**[12] [233] 3-8-7.................... JoeFanning 5 50
(M H Tompkins) *chsd ldr 4f: wknd over 1f out* **50/1**

42-6 **8** *shd* **Kapellmeister (IRE)**[11] [254] 3-8-7.................... MartinDwyer 11 50
(C R Egerton) *chsd ldrs: rdn 1/2-way: wknd 2f out* **11/4**[2]

9 *1* **Alexian** 3-8-7.................... AdrianTNicholls 3 47
(R Hollinshead) *s.i.s: a in rr* **100/1**

3 **10** *hd* **Pretty Sister**[32] [70] 3-7-9.................... LiamJones(7) 8 41
(W J Haggas) *s.i.s: hld up: a in rr* **9/1**

11 *1/2* **Alucica** 3-8-3 ow4.................... PatrickMathers(3) 9 44
(D Shaw) *s.s: outpcd* **100/1**

12 *4* **Tapsalteerie** 3-8-2.................... ChrisCatlin 7 30
(M J Attwater) *s.i.s: a in rr* **100/1**

1m 29.84s (-0.56) **Going Correction** -0.175s/f (Stan)

WFA 3 from 4yo 17lb 12 Ran SP% **125.4**

Speed ratings (Par 103):96,94,92,92,90 86,85,85,84,84 83,79

CSF £10.80 TOTE £8.00: £1.90, £1.10, £21.70; EX 24.70 Place 6 £28.38, Place 5 £9.39.

Owner Mrs S Quinn **Bred** Miss Jill Finegan **Trained** Settrington, N Yorks

FOCUS

A modest maiden containing a number of unraced or inexperienced individuals in which they went 16/1 bar four. The race has been rated slightly negatively with the time modest.

T/Jkpt: £2,619.70 to a £1 stake. Pool: £11,069.50. 3.00 winning tickets. T/Plt: £11.00 to a £1 stake. Pool: £63,588.35. 4,188.05 winning tickets. T/Qpdt: £3.70 to a £1 stake. Pool: £6,032.60. 1,193.35 winning tickets. CR

[351]NAD AL SHEBA (L-H)

Friday, February 10

OFFICIAL GOING: Turf course - good to firm; dirt course - fast

366a DATEL TROPHY (H'CAP) (TURF) 6f 110y(T)

3:30 (3:30) (90-105,101) 4-Y-0+ **£41,569** (£12,790; £6,395; £3,197)

RPR

1 **Kodiac**[15] [203] 5-9-6 **101**....................(b) TPO'Shea 6 106
(E Charpy, UAE) *trckd ldrs gng wl: rdn to cl 2f out: hrd rdn 1f out: led nr line* **6/4**[1]

2 *1/2* **Royal Storm (IRE)**[165] [4837] 7-9-2 **97**.................... MJKinane 8 101
(Mrs A J Perrett) *trckd ldr: disp 2f out: led 1 1/2f out: hdd nr line* **12/1**

3 *1 3/4* **Lapwing (IRE)**[92] 8-8-9 **90**....................(t) RoystonFfrench 3 89
(Christian Wroe, UAE) *settled in rr: gng wl early st: chal 2 1/2f out: r.o: nrst fin* **33/1**

4 *3/4* **Wazir (USA)**[8] [282] 4-8-9 **90**.................... KerrinMcEvoy 1 87
(J H M Gosden) *trckd ldrs on rail: rdn 2 1/2 out: wknd* **6/1**[3]

5 *nk* **Hidden Dragon (USA)**[15] [204] 7-8-9 **90**.................... EddieAhern 5 86
(J Pearce) *settled in rr: prog on rail in st: n.m.r 2f out: kpt on* **6/1**[3]

6 *1 3/4* **Clod Ber Junior (BRZ)**[706] [974] 9-8-11 **93**....................(bt) JMurtagh 4 83
(A Selvaratnam, UAE) *led: clr 3f out: jnd 2f out: kpt on u.p* **40/1**

7 *hd* **Thajja (IRE)**[15] [206] 5-9-5 **100**....................(v) RHills 2 91
(Doug Watson, UAE) *settled in rr: n.d* **9/4**[2]

8 *5 1/4* **Prince Charming**[1] [352] 4-9-0 **95**....................(t) ASuborics 7 71
(R Bouresly, Kuwait) *s.i.s: a in rr* **40/1**

1m 17.46s **Going Correction** +0.45s/f (Yiel) 8 Ran SP% **114.9**

Speed ratings: 115,114,112,111,111 109,109,103

Owner Prince A A Faisal **Bred** Nawara Stud Co Ltd **Trained** United Arab Emirates

FOCUS

While this was a good class of handicap, there were just the eight runners and the likes of second-placed Royal Storm would face much stronger opposition for this sort of money back in England.

NOTEBOOK

Kodiac, a slightly unlucky second on his debut in Dubai just over two weeks previously, has clearly gone the right way since and was good enough to go one place better. He had the blinkers re-fitted this time, and did appear to need his mind making up for him, be his very much improving.

Royal Storm(IRE) struggled throughout 2005, but this was a fine effort on his debut in Dubai off the back of a 165-day break. There have been plenty of examples of horses being revitalised by the switch to Dubai, as well as benefiting from slightly less strength in opposition, and he looks another good example.

Lapwing(IRE), back on turf on his return from a three-month break, ran a fine race in third over a trip that could be considered a touch shorter than ideal. He has not won since 2001, but may do even better back over a little further.

Wazir(USA), unlucky in-running when down the field over a mile here on his debut in Dubai the previous week, ran better on this drop in trip but was still well held.

Hidden Dragon(USA) would have appreciated the return to turf and did not run badly, but he was unable to produce the sort of speed that he has been capable of in the past. He was third over seven and a half furlongs on his debut in Dubai and, on this evidence, he may benefit from a return to further.

367a DATEL STKS (H'CAP) (TURF) 6f 110y(T)

4:35 (4:37) (90-105,102) 4-Y-0+ **£41,569** (£12,790; £6,395; £3,197)

RPR

1 **Bahiano (IRE)**[8] 282 5-8-8 **90** RyanMoore 6 100
(C E Brittain) *trckd ldrs: rdn to cl 2 1/2f out: led 1 1/2f out: r.o strly* **7/1**[3]

2 2 3/4 **Compton's Eleven**[15] 201 5-9-6 **102** TedDurcan 3 104
(M R Channon) *trckd ldrs on rail: 2nd 4 1/2f out: led 2 1/2f out: hdd 2f out: kpt on* **6/5**[1]

3 1 3/4 **Protector (SAF)**[257] 5-8-8 **90** KShea 2 87
(H J Brown, South Africa) *mid-div on rail: bdly hmpd 4 1/2f out: last 3f out: r.o wl: nrst fin* **8/1**

4 nk **Talbot Avenue**[146] 5288 8-9-3 **99** EddieAhern 9 95
(M Mullineaux) *hld up early: racd on outside to ld 4f out: wd st: nt qckn* **11/2**[2]

5 nse **Sir Edwin Landseer (USA)**[50] 6-8-9 **95** (p) SaleemGolam(3) 1 90
(Christian Wroe, UAE) *settled last: hmpd 4 1/2f out: rdn 3 1/2f out: r.o: n.m.r wl ins fnl f out: one pce* **11/2**[2]

6 4 **Red Crescent (SAF)**[8] 278 9-8-8 **90** (bt) RichardMullen 8 75
(A Selvaratnam, UAE) *led: hdd 4f out: kpt on tl wknd 2 1/2f out* **14/1**

7 3/4 **In The Fan (USA)**[119] 5876 4-8-8 **90** RoystonFfrench 5 73
(A Al Raihe, UAE) *mid-div: n.m.r 4 1/2f out: rdn to cl 2 1/2f out: one pce* **28/1**

8 1 3/4 **Tahreeb (FR)**[22] 153 5-9-4 **100** (v1) JMurtagh 4 78
(D Selvaratnam, UAE) *v.s.a: nvr involved* **16/1**

1m 17.56s **Going Correction** +0.45s/f (Yiel) **8** Ran SP% **115.8**
Speed ratings: 114,110,108,108,108 103,103,101

Owner C E Brittain **Bred** Michael Henochsberg & Sunflower International **Trained** Newmarket, Suffolk

FOCUS
A decent enough sprint handicap, but perhaps not as competitive as one might expect for the prize money.

NOTEBOOK
Bahiano(IRE) would have been closer with a clearer run when fifth over a mile on his return to Dubai the previous week, and duly improved on that form to run out a most decisive winner on this drop in trip. He had not won since taking a Polytrack maiden back in February 2004, so this was very much overdue, but he will go up significantly in the weights and will struggled to follow up. (old market op 8/1; new market op 7/1)

Compton's Eleven, 4lb higher than when winning a similar race over course and distance on his return to Dubai two weeks previously, ran his race and was basically no match for the winner. He should continue to go well, but does look high enough in the weights now. (old market op 6/4; new market op 5/4)

Protector(SAF) ◆, a multiple sprint winner in his native South Africa, ran a fine race on his debut in Dubai off the back of a 257-day absence, considering he was badly hampered about four out. He did extremely well to recover from that to take third and, given he could be expected to improve for the run in any case, looks one to be with next time. (old market op 8/1; new market op 15/2)

Talbot Avenue, who ran some good races at the Carnival last year without managing to win, had not been seen since finishing ninth in the Ayr Gold Cup 146 days previously. This was a promising return to action and he should earn more prizemoney out here. (old market op 11/2)

Sir Edwin Landseer(USA), a winner on the dirt course here over five furlongs on his previous start, refused the enter the stalls on his first intended start at this year's Carnival. Consenting to race this time, he did not get a very good trip - he was hampered early on and did not enjoy a clear run in the straight - and is better than the bare form. (old market op 5/1; new market op 5/1)

368a DNRD UAE 2000 GUINEAS (GROUP 3) (DIRT) 1m (D)

5:10 (5:10) 3-Y-0 **£94,476** (£29,069; £14,534; £7,267)

RPR

1 **Gold For Sale (ARG)**[146] 4-9-4 108 (t) MJKinane 11 99
(I Jory, Saudi Arabia) *wd gng wl: hmpd 4f out: last ent st: fin fast and wd to ld cl home* **8/1**

2 1/2 **Where's That Tiger (USA)**[268] 1803 3-8-9 99 WCMarwing 15 102
(M F De Kock, South Africa) *wd: trckd ldrs into st: rdn to cl 2f out: led wl ins fnl f: hdd nr home* **5/1**[2]

3 1 3/4 **My Royal Captain (NZ)**[19] 4-9-4 85 JMurtagh 12 95
(L Laxon, Singapore) *trckd ldrs wd: disp 1 1/2f out: one pce* **66/1**

4 4 1/4 **Flashing Numbers (USA)**[90] 6338 3-8-9 106 AStarke 4 90
(Mario Hofer, Germany) *dropped to rr early: n.m.r 3 1/2f out: rdn to cl 3f out: r.o wl: nrst fin* **9/1**

5 1 1/2 **Azul Da Guanabara (BRZ)**[125] 4-9-4 95 EddieAhern 10 83
(Luis Singnoretti, Brazil) *trckd ldrs: ev ch 3f out: nt qckn* **20/1**

6 nk **Kilworth (IRE)**[111] 6019 3-8-9 107 KerrinMcEvoy 1 86
(I Mohammed, UAE) *rr on rail: swtchd wd 3f out: r.o: nrst fin* **11/1**

7 shd **Unification (CAN)**[123] 3-8-9 104 (t) RHills 5 86
(I Mohammed, UAE) *led: jnd 2f out: one pce: wknd fnl f* **8/1**

8 1/2 **Testimony (USA)**[22] 150 3-8-9 95 (t) LDettori 2 85
(Saeed Bin Suroor) *mid-div: trckd ldrs on rail 4f out: rdn 2 1/2f out: nt qckn* **13/2**[3]

9 7 1/4 **Well Armed (USA)**[22] 150 3-8-9 100 RyanMoore 3 71
(C E Brittain) *mid-div: nvr threatened* **5/2**[1]

10 nse **Nomoretaxes (BRZ)**[22] 150 4-9-4 93 KShea 14 67
(M F De Kock, South Africa) *mid-div wd: nvr a factor* **25/1**

11 4 1/4 **Golden Acer (IRE)**[22] 150 3-8-9 91 WSupple 7 62
(Doug Watson, UAE) *mid-div: prog to trck ldrs 3 1/2f out: wknd* **50/1**

12 3 3/4 **Wovoka (IRE)**[22] 150 3-8-9 95 JAHeffernan 13 55
(M R Channon) *trckd ldrs: wknd 4f out* **25/1**

13 2 3/4 **National Captain (SAF)**[22] 150 4-9-4 95 RichardMullen 6 45
(A Laird, UAE) *mid-div: n.d* **33/1**

14 3 1/4 **Renderoc (USA)**[22] 150 3-8-9 85 JohnEgan 9 43
(J S Moore) *nvr a threat* **66/1**

15 9 1/2 **Figjam**[22] 150 3-8-9 85 (b) PJSmullen 8 24
(S Seemar, UAE) *a in rr* **100/1**

1m 37.56s **Going Correction** +0.375s/f (Slow)
WFA 3 from 4yo 19lb **15** Ran SP% **120.5**
Speed ratings: 114,113,111,107,106 105,105,105,97,97 93,89,87,83,74

Owner Prince Sultan Mohammed Saud Al Kabeer **Bred** Haras Arroyo De Luna **Trained** Saudi Arabia

FOCUS
A typically competitive renewal of the UAE 2000 Guineas but, as is usually the case for this race, the bare form is nothing better than a Group Three. Once again on this dirt course, the draw played a huge part and four of the first five home had a double-figure stall.

NOTEBOOK
Gold For Sale(ARG), a multiple winner in South America and still unbeaten, had a advantageous draw away from the trouble on the inside, but was forced very wide on the turn into the straight and did well to retain his 100% record. Although not helped by having to forfeit so much ground on the final bend, it meant he enjoyed one continuous run in the straight and he sustained his challenge to get up close home. He will now go for the UAE Derby and will have an obvious chance there, although his chance will be helped if he can avoid an inside stall once more.

Where's That Tiger(USA), a very useful juvenile over five furlongs for Aidan O'Brien last season, who won a maiden before running well in Listed company, ran a fine race on his first start for new connections. He was stepping up fully three furlongs in trip and switching to dirt for the first time, but he is bred to be suited by these conditions - by Storm Cat out of a full-sister to Kentucky Derby winner Fusaichi Pegasus - and showed improved form. Although reeled in close home, he saw his race out well and deserves his chance over an extra furlong in the UAE Derby. One slight note of caution, however, is he clearly goes well fresh given he won first time out last season, and was not given a prep before this race, so it would be unwise to expect a lot improvement even though this was his first run in 268 days. (op 9/2)

My Royal Captain(NZ), a multiple winner over this trip on the turf in Singapore, belied his huge industry odds on his debut in Dubai to claim third. He admittedly had an advantageous draw, but still showed himself to be quite smart and is obviously one to respect on this surface.

Flashing Numbers(USA) ◆, a nine-furlong winner in Italy who was third of five in the ten-furlong Group One Criterium de Saint-Cloud in France when last seen three months previously, ran a fine race from his unfavourable low draw on his debut in Dubai and first run on dirt. Connections said after his last run that he was going to be aimed at the French Derby this year, and that may still be the case, but the decision to take him to Dubai in the meantime looks justified, and this performance should not be underestimated. He must be followed from now and, granted a better draw, could go very close in the UAE Derby. (op 8/1)

Azul Da Guanabara(BRZ), a six-furlong winner in his native Brazil who has also been placed over as far as ten furlongs, had a good draw and ran well on this debut in Dubai.

Kilworth(IRE), a Group-class juvenile on turf for Neville Callaghan last year, did not run badly on his debut for new connections and first start on dirt considering he found some trouble in-running from the lowest stall of all. He can also be expected to come on for the run given this was his first start in 111 days.

Unification(CAN), a dual winner in his native Canada, was able to get the lead from his low draw on his debut for new connections and can have few excuses.

Testimony(USA) would not have been helped by his inside stall and failed to build on the promise he showed on his debut for Godolphin over seven furlongs here on his previous start.

Well Armed(USA) was pretty impressive when winning on his debut in Dubai over seven furlongs here last time, but this was a much stronger race and he was not helped by a low draw (he was in stall nine of 16 when winning last time). He can be given another chance, but it was still disappointing he could not even confirm placings with Testimony, whom he beat three and a half lengths last time. (op 11/4)

Nomoretaxes(BRZ), a stablemate of the second, had a good draw but could not take advantage. (op 20/1)

Wovoka(IRE) did not run badly when fourth to Well Armed over seven furlongs here on his debut in Dubai, but this was a much tougher ask. (op20/1)

Renderoc(USA), well beaten behind Well Armed over seven furlongs on his debut in Dubai, again failed to prove his effectiveness on this surface.

369a DNRD CUP (H'CAP) (TURF) 1m (T)

5:40 (5:40) (95-110,110) 4-Y-0+ **£45,348** (£13,953; £6,976; £3,488)

RPR

1 **Sabirli (TUR)**[22] 151 5-9-0 **104** HKaratas 8 111
(C Kurt, Turkey) *s.i.s: hld up in rr: rdn to cl 2 1/2f out: in rr 1 1/2f out: fast fin: led cl home* **6/1**[3]

2 1/2 **Blue On Blues (ARG)**[8] 5-8-5 **95** (t) RyanMoore 2 101
(S Seemar, UAE) *racd in 3rd: chal 2 1/2f out: led 1f out: r.o wl: ct cl home* **10/1**

3 3 **Elliots World (IRE)**[154] 5091 4-9-1 **105** KerrinMcEvoy 1 104
(I Mohammed, UAE) *mid-div: chal 2f out: hmpd 1f out: nt rcvr* **7/2**[2]

4 1/2 **Key Of Destiny (SAF)**[8] 280 8-9-6 **110** (t) WCMarwing 5 108
(M F De Kock, South Africa) *broke awkwardly: hld up last: trckd wnr thrght: n.d* **10/1**

5 3/4 **Proudance (GER)**[103] 6190 4-9-3 **107** ASuborics 4 103
(R Suerland, Germany) *trckd ldrs: t.k.h: led 2 1/2f out: one pce* **8/1**

6 2 1/4 **Big Easy (NZ)**[19] 5-8-9 **99** (b) BVorster 3 90
(L Laxon, Singapore) *trckd ldrs on rail: rdn 3f out: nt qckn* **16/1**

7 1 1/2 **Desert Destiny**[8] 278 6-8-12 **102** (vt) LDettori 7 90
(Saeed Bin Suroor) *hld up in rr: n.d* **6/4**[1]

8 1/2 **Cat Belling (IRE)**[1] 351 6-8-9 **99** (t) PDillon 9 85
(R Bouresly, Kuwait) *in rr of main gp: n.d* **40/1**

9 1 3/4 **Hinterland (SAF)**[15] 201 8-8-10 **100** RichardMullen 6 82
(S Seemar, UAE) *led at stdy pce: qcknd 3 1/2f out: hdd 2 1/2f out: wknd* **20/1**

1m 37.84s **Going Correction** +0.45s/f (Yiel) **9** Ran SP% **118.9**
Speed ratings: 112,111,108,108,107 105,103,103,101

Owner Aydogan San **Bred** A San **Trained** Turkey

FOCUS
A high-class handicap, albeit not as competitive as some races of a similar type to be run at this year's Carnival. The pace through the first couple of furlongs was just steady, but they ultimately went a good gallop and few of these can have any excuses.

NOTEBOOK
Sabirli(TUR) ◆, an unlucky in-running fifth in a more competitive handicap over seven and a half furlongs here on his debut in Dubai three weeks previously, stepped up on that form - no less than 17lb according to RPR's - to get up close home. He did not have the assistance of Spencer this time and his jockey, despite having won on him in Turkey, did not really compare in terms of style, but he clearly knows how to get the best of him. Given he has won over an extended nine furlongs in his homeland, connections should have plenty of options and, progressing, he should remain competitive.

Blue On Blues(ARG), a winner on the dirt track over this trip towards the end of last season, was just held on his return to the turf. The eventual winner was probably not badly handicapped, and he finished clear of the remainder, so this must rate as a very good effort.

Elliots World(IRE), successful in a conditions race at Doncaster for Mark Johnston when last seen 154 days previously, ran a respectable race on his debut for new connections and first start in Dubai, and would have been closer with a clearer run.

Key Of Destiny(SAF) had no easy task off a mark of 110 but ran much better than on his two previous starts at this year's Carnival.

Proudance(GER), a multiple winner over a mile in his native Germany, was well held on his debut in Dubai off the back of a 103-day break.

Desert Destiny, a promising second in a very competitive handicap over course and distance on his return to Dubai last time, failed to build on that and was most disappointing. His attitude has looked questionable in the past, and he has plenty to prove now. (op 7/4)

370a DNRD TROPHY (H'CAP) (TURF) 1m 194y(T)

6:10 (6:10) (95-116,111) 4-Y-O+ **£66,133** (£20,348; £10,174; £2,543; £2,543)

RPR

1 **Tyson (SAF)**[15] 208 6-9-4 **109** WCMarwing 10 117
(M F De Kock, South Africa) *settled in rr: swtchd to ins 2 1/2f out to dispute w runner-up: r.o wl* **13/8**[1]

2 ¾ **Seihali (IRE)**[321] 737 7-9-6 **111** JMurtagh 1 117
(D Selvaratnam, UAE) *settled in rr: 2nd last ent st gng wl: prog w wnr 2 1/2f out: r.o wl* **11/1**

3 4 ¾ **Azarole (IRE)**[8] 278 5-9-1 **106** JohnEgan 8 103
(J S Moore) *t.k.h in 4th: ev ch 2f out: kpt on wl: no ch w ldrs* **9/1**

4 nk **Iqte Saab (USA)**[22] 153 5-9-1 **106** RHills 6 102
(Doug Watson, UAE) *mid-div on rail: n.m.r 2 1/2f out: r.o wl once clr: nrst fin* **9/2**[2]

4 dht **Colisay**[83] 6378 7-8-11 **102** KerrinMcEvoy 4 98
(Mrs A J Perrett) *racd in 3rd: rdn to chal 2 1/2f out: one pce* **20/1**

6 1 ¼ **Lundy's Lane (IRE)**[8] 278 6-8-11 **102** RyanMoore 9 95
(S Seemar, UAE) *settled in rr: n.d: sme prog 3 1/2f out* **6/1**

7 shd **Pentecost**[8] 282 7-9-0 **105** LDettori 5 98
(A M Balding) *s.i.s: hld up in last: stl last whn rdn 3 1/2f out: n.d* **5/1**[3]

8 1 ¾ **Bailador (IRE)**[15] 208 6-8-6 **97** RichardMullen 2 87
(A Laird, UAE) *led tl wknd rapidly 2f out* **50/1**

9 1 ¼ **Omikron (IRE)**[15] 205 5-9-0 **105** (t) MJKinane 7 92
(I Jory, Saudi Arabia) *mid-div: t.k.h: gng wl 3f out: clsd briefly: n.d* **25/1**

10 2 **Book Of Kings (USA)**[43] 5-9-5 **110** (bt) TedDurcan 3 93
(A Laird, UAE) *trckd ldrs: 2nd ent st whn rdn: dropped away 2 1/2f out* **16/1**

1m 50.24s **Going Correction** +0.45s/f (Yiel) **10** Ran SP% **122.0**
Speed ratings: 111,110,106,105,105 104,104,103,101,100

Owner M Naidoo, M De Kock, O Leibrandt, R Adair **Bred** M K Naidoo **Trained** South Africa

FOCUS
A very high-class handicap and the pace looked reasonable.

NOTEBOOK
Tyson(SAF) ◆, pretty impressive when winning over ten furlongs on his debut in Dubai two weeks previously, coped with the drop back in trip and defied a 7lb higher mark in good style. Both he and the runner-up got a dream run towards the inside the straight, but he always just looked the stronger. While he clearly has the speed to be effective at this sort of trip, the way he stayed on when in the clear suggests he can do even better back over further but, whatever the case, he deserves his chance in Group company. (op 11/4)
Seihali(IRE), tenth of 14 in the Group One Dubai Duty Free Stakes over course and distance when last seen 321 days previously, made a fine return to action under top weight. He got a lovely run up the inside early in the straight, but so did the favourite and that one, with the benefit of race fitness, was just too strong. He can be expected to improve on this. (op 9/1)
Azarole(IRE) was beaten far enough in third, but this has to rate as a very solid effort behind two high-class performers. He is holding his from well and earning plenty of prizemoney. (op 8/1)
Colisay, ninth in the Listed Churchill Stakes on Lingfield's Polytrack on his last start nearly three months previously, ran very creditably returned to turf on his debut in Dubai.
Iqte Saab(USA), 4lb higher than when winning over course and distance on his return from an absence three weeks previously, is not the first horse Hills has got into trouble at this year's Carnival and should have finished closer.
Pentecost, 4lb higher than when coming late to win over a mile here the previous week, could not repeat the tactics this time.

371a DATEL (H'CAP) (TURF) 1m 4f (T)

6:40 (6:41) (95-116,110) 4-Y-O+ **£66,133** (£20,348; £10,174; £5,087)

RPR

1 **Land 'n Stars**[15] 205 6-8-9 **99** JohnEgan 11 106
(Jamie Poulton) *in rr: gng wl: clsd 3f out: v wd: r.o wl: led cl home* **33/1**

2 ½ **Go For Gold (IRE)**[517] 5463 5-9-3 **107** TedDurcan 2 113
(A Laird, UAE) *mid-div: gng wl 4f out: rdn to chal 2 1/2f out: r.o* **10/1**

3 nk **Encinas (GER)**[15] 205 5-9-0 **104** WMongil 8 110
(P Schiergen, Germany) *mid-div: gng wl: n.m.r 3f out: swtchd v wd 2f out: r.o* **11/4**[2]

4 ¾ **Excalibur (IRE)**[15] 205 6-9-6 **110** (t) WCMarwing 3 114
(M F De Kock, South Africa) *trckd ldrs: gng wl 3f out: rdn to chal 2 1/2f out: nt qckn: then r.o wl* **11/8**[1]

5 nk **Corriolanus (GER)**[238] 2674 6-9-1 **105** RyanMoore 7 109
(S Seemar, UAE) *settled in rr: gng wl 3f out: rdn to cl 2 1/2f out: nrst fin* **12/1**

6 nk **Saintly Rachel (IRE)**[224] 3108 8-8-7 **97** MJKinane 5 100
(C F Swan, Ire) *hmpd s: settled in last and last ent st: rdn to cl 2 1/2f out: ev ch 1 1/2f out: one pce* **14/1**

7 7 **Ketter (BRZ)**[97] 5-8-10 **100** EddieAhern 4 92
(Luis Singnoretti, Brazil) *in rr on rail: rdn 3 1/2f out: rdn to cl on rail 2 1/2f out: one pce* **16/1**

8 3 ¼ **Mutasallil (USA)**[306] 6-8-11 **101** (t) RHills 9 88
(Doug Watson, UAE) *racd in 3rd: disp ld 3 1/2f out: chal 2f out: one pce* **13/2**[3]

9 3 ¼ **Oratory (SAF)**[15] 205 9-8-8 **98** RichardMullen 1 80
(A Laird, UAE) *racd in 4th: disp ld 3 1/2f out: wknd* **20/1**

10 15 **Baldaquin**[1] 355 9-8-10 **100** PDillon 10 58
(R Bouresly, Kuwait) *sn led: clr after 2f: jnd 3 /12f out: wknd* **50/1**

11 9 **Blue Corrig (IRE)**[15] 205 6-8-8 **98** (b) PJSmullen 6 41
(Joseph Crowley, Ire) *broke awkwardly: mid-div: n.d* **50/1**

2m 31.61s **Going Correction** +0.45s/f (Yiel) **11** Ran SP% **123.1**
Speed ratings: 113,112,112,111,111 111,106,104,102,92 86

Owner Paul Blows **Bred** C A Cyzer **Trained** Telscombe, E Sussex

FOCUS
A very good handicap. Despite the pace appearing strong from the start, any number of these were still in with a chance at the top of the straight and they spread out across the track to get clear runs through.

NOTEBOOK
Land 'n Stars is a thorough stayer (his last win came in a two-mile Listed race) and was well held over course and distance on his debut in Dubai two weeks previously, but the strong pace would have suited him well and he basically stayed on strongest. He ended up racing close to the stands'-side rail but, with the whole field spread out across the track, it had only a positive effect in allowing him one continuous run to the line. A rise in the weights will make things tougher and he could find it hard to follow up, but he cannot be totally dismissed when there is likely to be a decent gallop on. (op 28/1)
Go For Gold(IRE) ◆, although not quite a top notcher, was pretty decent when trained by Aidan O'Brien, as he showed when second in the Gordon Stakes and third in the Great Voltigeur in 2004. Not seen since running down the field in that year's St Leger, he showed he retains most, if not all of his ability with a fine effort off such a long absence. Just held by a rival who had the benefit of a recent run, he can be expected to improve and, providing he stands training, really should find success in the coming months. (op 9/1)
Encinas(GER) had Land 'n Stars well behind when winning over course and distance on his previous start, but that rival has clearly improved since and he could not confirm placings off a 3lb higher mark. He came very wide in the straight, but it surprisingly appeared to make little difference and he pretty much ran to form on a line through Excalibur, as he beat that rival half a length on his previous start. He should continue to go well.
Excalibur(IRE) could not reverse recent course and distance placings with Encinas and, although not running badly, he clearly failed to improve as much as one might have hoped. (op 15/8)
Corriolanus(GER) ◆ made a pleasing debut for his new connections off the back of a 238-day absence. He should go on from this.
Saintly Rachel(IRE) ran with plenty of promise off the back of a 224-day absence.
Blue Corrig(IRE) was again a long way below form. (op 40/1)

[336] LINGFIELD (L-H)

Saturday, February 11

OFFICIAL GOING: Standard
Wind: Light, half behind

372 BE LUCKY @ LITTLEWOODSPOOLS.CO.UK MAIDEN STKS (DIV I) 1m (P)

1:00 (1:02) (Class 5) 3-Y-O **£3,562** (£1,059; £529; £264) **Stalls** High

Form RPR

1 **Dame Hester (IRE)**[110] 6085 3-8-9 JamieSpencer 3 68+
(E J O'Neill) *trckd ldrs and gng wl: led over 1f out: stongly pressed ins fnl f: all out* **7/4**[2]

4- 2 nk **Rose Muwasim**[169] 4717 3-8-9 EddieAhern 4 65+
(E A L Dunlop) *t.k.h: hld up in tch: rdn to go 2nd ins fnl f: pressed wnr to line* **6/4**[1]

3 2 ½ **Fire Of Love** 3-8-9 TPQueally 2 59
(N P Littmoden) *trckd ldr for 2f: styd prom: no ex fnl f* **20/1**

00- 4 3 ½ **Kalantera (IRE)**[115] 5968 3-9-0 MartinDwyer 10 56
(A M Balding) *in tch: outpcd over 2f out: styd on fnl f* **14/1**

5 ½ **Simplified** 3-8-9 JimmyQuinn 9 50
(J Pearce) *racd on ins: kpt on one pce ins fnl 2f* **25/1**

0- 6 shd **Canyouwin**[121] 5850 3-8-9 RobertHavlin 6 50+
(J H M Gosden) *in rr whn hmpd on ins over 4f out: nvr on terms* **10/1**[3]

0- 7 ½ **Smokey Blue**[141] 5435 3-8-10 ow1 DerekNolan[(5)] 7 54
(M J Wallace) *a towards rr* **12/1**

0 8 ½ **Bobby Rose**[17] 191 3-9-0 MickyFenton 1 52
(D K Ivory) *led tl rdn and hdd over 1f out: wknd qckly* **50/1**

00 9 2 ½ **Iberian Light (USA)**[7] 291 3-8-7 SallyAdams[(7)] 5 47
(N A Callaghan) *sn in rr* **25/1**

0-0 10 ½ **Bold Pioneer (USA)**[28] 112 3-9-0 StephenCarson 11 45
(C P Morlock) *in rr: rdn over 2f out: nvr on terms* **66/1**

11 1 **Doctor David** 3-9-0 J-PGuillambert 8 43
(Ernst Oertel) *v.s.a: rapid hdwy to chse ldr after 2f: wknd qckly over 1f out* **40/1**

1m 40.0s (0.57) **Going Correction** -0.125s/f (Stan) **11** Ran SP% **118.2**
Speed ratings (Par 97):92,91,89,85,85 85,84,84,81,81 80
CSF £4.33 TOTE £2.40: £1.20, £1.10, £4.80; EX 5.60.
Owner Miss A H Marshall **Bred** Miss Honora Corridan **Trained** Averham Park, Notts

FOCUS
A modest winning time for the type of contest and 1.36 seconds slower than the second division. The form is limited by those outside the placings who were not beaten far.
Simplified Official explanation: jockey said filly had run too free
Canyouwin Official explanation: jockey said filly suffered interference in running

373 BETDIRECT 0800 211 222 MAIDEN STKS 5f (P)

1:30 (1:31) (Class 5) 3-Y-O+ **£3,886** (£1,156; £577; £288) **Stalls** High

Form RPR

1 **Mountain Pass (USA)**[127] 5723 4-9-7 (v[1]) JamieSpencer 5 70
(M J Wallace) *mde all: rdn out fnl f* **7/4**[1]

00- 2 1 ¾ **Hoh Wotanite**[173] 4636 3-8-7 LPKeniry 2 58
(A M Balding) *t.k.h: in tch: hdwy on ins to chse wnr fnl f* **5/1**[3]

00-4 3 ¾ **Desert Dust**[4] 331 3-8-7 **60** (p) EddieAhern 7 55
(R M H Cowell) *chsd wnr tl 1f out: kpt on one pce* **7/2**[2]

00- 4 1 ¾ **Edward (IRE)**[131] 5672 4-9-7 DarrenWilliams 9 55
(A P Jarvis) *sn prom on outside: rdn over 1f out: kpt on one pce* **14/1**

0020 5 hd **Chantelle's Dream**[8] 288 4-8-9 **47** (b) SophieDoyle[(7)] 1 49
(Ms J S Doyle) *slowly away: hdwy and swtchd rt ent fnl f: nvr nrr* **12/1**

00 6 1 ¼ **Billy Wizz (IRE)**[13] 233 3-8-7 MartinDwyer 3 44
(A M Balding) *in tch tl wknd appr fnl f* **8/1**

00-0 7 1 ¼ **Mon Petite Amour**[7] 298 3-8-0 **48** ow1 (v[1]) EdwardCreighton[(3)] 8 35
(D W P Arbuthnot) *a bhd* **33/1**

06- 8 3 ½ **Sendinpost**[47] 6661 3-8-2 HayleyTurner 6 21
(S C Williams) *a struggling in rr* **10/1**

59.60 secs (-0.18) **Going Correction** -0.125s/f (Stan)
WFA 3 from 4yo 14lb **8** Ran SP% **112.8**
Speed ratings (Par 103):96,93,92,89,88 86,84,79
CSF £10.39 TOTE £2.30: £1.10, £1.60, £1.70; EX 12.50.
Owner B Walsh **Bred** Marablue Farm **Trained** Newmarket, Suffolk

FOCUS
A moderate winning time for the class of contest but straightforward form with the fifth setting the standard, and it looks sound enough overall.

374 BE LUCKY @ LITTLEWOODSPOOLS.CO.UK MAIDEN STKS (DIV II) 1m (P)

2:00 (2:06) (Class 5) 3-Y-O **£3,562** (£1,059; £529; £264) **Stalls** High

Form RPR

1 **Lake Shabla (USA)** 3-8-9 PaulHanagan 9 79+
(E A L Dunlop) *slowly away and wl in rr: hdwy whn whn n.m.r over 1f out: r.o strly fnl f to ld post* **16/1**

2 2 shd **Just Logic (IRE)**[17] 191 3-9-0 ShaneKelly 7 77
(J Noseda) *led after 1f: shkn up appr fnl f: eased fnl strides: hdd post* **1/2**[1]

20-2 3 ¾ **Fiddlers Wood**[14] 219 3-9-0 **85** (v) ChrisCatlin 10 75
(V Smith) *trckd ldr after 3f: rdn and lost 2nd nr fin* **5/1**[2]

65- 4 3 **Eclipse Park**[91] 6319 3-9-0 JohnEgan 6 68
(M J McGrath) *hld up in rr: rdn and r.o fnl f: nvr nrr* **7/1**[3]

5 2½ **Plemont Bay** 3-8-7 .... LukeMorris(7) 2 62
(M L W Bell) *in tch: rdn and lost pl over 4f out: nvr on terms after* **50/1**

0 6 *nk* **Living On A Prayer**[12] [254] 3-8-9 .... JimmyQuinn 11 57
(J Pearce) *a towards rr* **25/1**

7 2½ **Wally Barge** 3-9-0 .... MickyFenton 3 56
(D K Ivory) *mid-div to 1/2-way: nvr on terms after* **50/1**

8 ½ **Macho Dancer (IRE)**[177] [4524] 3-8-6 .... NelsonDeSouza(3) 4 50
(R M Beckett) *led for 1f: rdn over 3f out: wknd wl over 1f out* **12/1**

-50 9 2 **Hazium (IRE)**[3] [337] 3-8-9 .... JamieSpencer 1 45
(Patrick Morris, Ire) *chsd ldrs: rdn 1/2-way: sn btn* **12/1**

00 10 11 **Batchworth Fleur**[13] [233] 3-8-9 .... StephenCarson 5 20
(E A Wheeler) *plld hrd: prom for 3f: sn wl bhd* **80/1**

1m 38.64s (-0.79) **Going Correction** -0.125s/f (Stan) **10** Ran SP% **126.1**
Speed ratings (Par 97):98,97,97,94,91 91,88,88,86,75
CSF £26.45 TOTE £16.30: £3.80, £1.10, £1.60; EX 54.80.
Owner Gainsborough Stud **Bred** Gainsborough Farm Llc **Trained** Newmarket, Suffolk
■ Stewards' Enquiry : Shane Kelly 10-day ban (reduced from 28 days on appeal): failed to take all reasonable and permissible measures to obtain best possible placing (Feb 22-Mar 3)

FOCUS
The winning time was 1.36 seconds faster than the first division and close to par for the grade. The form looks stronger and could rate higher.

375 BET ON THE SIX NATIONS AT BETDIRECT.CO.UK H'CAP 1m 2f (P)
2:30 (2:33) (Class 5) (0-75,75) 4-Y-0+ **£3,238** (£963; £481; £240) **Stalls** Low

Form RPR

-360 1 **Zalkani (IRE)**[8] [283] 6-8-13 **70** .... TQuinn 1 81
(B G Powell) *mid-div: hdwy and swtchd rt wl over 1f out: r.o wl to ld fnl 50yds* **12/1**

1-22 2 ½ **Red Birr (IRE)**[14] [223] 5-9-2 **73** .... DaneO'Neill 3 83
(P R Webber) *s.i.s: sn prom: led over 2f out: rdn and hdd fnl 50yds* **15/8**[1]

-220 3 1¼ **Holiday Cocktail**[14] [223] 4-8-8 **66** .... HayleyTurner 5 73
(S C Williams) *chsd ldrs: rdn over 1f out: nt qckn ins fnl f* **16/1**

340- 4 1¼ **Desert Reign**[196] [3937] 5-9-0 **71** .... JamieSpencer 10 76
(A P Jarvis) *in rr tl hdwy over 3f out: chsd ldr 2f out tl nt qckn fnl f* **15/2**[3]

-060 5 ½ **Flying Pass**[5] [319] 4-8-7 **65** .... JohnEgan 12 69
(D J S Ffrench Davis) *in rr tl rdn and hdwy over 1f out: r.o: nvr nrr* **66/1**

-420 6 1½ **Danger Zone**[17] [186] 4-8-12 **70** .... IanMongan 7 71
(Mrs A J Perrett) *t.k.h: racd wd: hdwy over 1f out: nvr nr to chal* **14/1**

-056 7 ½ **African Sahara (USA)**[12] [250] 7-8-7 **71** ow1......(t) ChrisCavanagh(7) 14 71
(Miss D Mountain) *bhd: styd on fnl f: nvr nr to chal* **20/1**

5-03 8 1 **Gingko**[24] [135] 9-9-4 **75** .... ChrisCatlin 13 73
(P R Webber) *slowly away: nvr nr to chal* **20/1**

0-00 9 1¼ **Northside Lodge (IRE)**[24] [140] 8-8-9 **71** ....(p) GregFairley(5) 4 67
(W R Swinburn) *prom: rdn over 3f out: wknd over 1f out* **20/1**

0/40 10 ¾ **Alekhine (IRE)**[15] [214] 5-9-4 **75** .... EddieAhern 6 70
(J R Boyle) *mid-div: tl dropped rr 3f out* **14/1**

0-41 11 5 **Alfridini**[28] [115] 5-9-0 **71** .... LPKeniry 2 56
(D R C Elsworth) *t.k.h: led for 3f: lost pl over 2f out: sn btn* **11/1**

50-3 12 2½ **Little Jimbob**[15] [214] 5-8-13 **70** .... PaulHanagan 8 50
(R A Fahey) *led 7f out tl rdn and hdd over 2f out: sn wknd* **5/1**[2]

001- 13 20 **Llamadas**[16] [6503] 4-9-0 **72** .... J-PGuillambert 9 14
(C Roberts) *racd wd: chsd ldrs tl rdn and wknd over 3f out* **33/1**

-123 14 5 **Port 'n Starboard**[14] [223] 5-8-5 **62** .... MartinDwyer 11 —
(C A Cyzer) *racd wd: in tch tl wknd over 2f out* **10/1**

2m 3.77s (-4.02) **Going Correction** -0.125s/f (Stan)
WFA 4 from 5yo+ 1lb **14** Ran SP% **126.3**
Speed ratings (Par 103):111,110,109,108,108 107,106,105,104,104 100,98,82,78
CSF £34.15 CT £395.34 TOTE £16.10: £3.30, £1.50, £4.70; EX 63.60.
Owner J W Mursell **Bred** His Highness The Aga Khan's Studs S C **Trained** Morestead, Hants

FOCUS
A fair contest and a very decent winning time for the grade, 0.69 seconds faster than the later Class 2 handicap. The form looks reliable with the four immediately behind the winner close to their marks.

376 BETDIRECT.CO.UK H'CAP 6f (P)
3:05 (3:06) (Class 4) (0-85,79) 4-Y-0+ **£6,477** (£1,927; £963; £481) **Stalls** Low

Form RPR

0-31 1 **Saviours Spirit**[14] [224] 5-9-1 **76** .... JoeFanning 2 84+
(T G Mills) *led for 1f: t.k.h and stdd: rdn to ld ins fnl f: r.o wl* **6/4**[1]

0-00 2 1 **Who's Winning (IRE)**[14] [220] 5-8-11 **79** .... JamesDoyle(7) 5 84
(B G Powell) *led after 1f: rdn and hdd ins fnl f* **5/1**[3]

113- 3 *nk* **Rezzago (USA)**[190] [4136] 6-9-3 **78** .... JamieSpencer 8 82+
(W R Swinburn) *t.k.h: sn trckd ldrs: wnt 2nd over 3f out: rdn and ev ch fnl f: no ex nr fin* **2/1**[2]

-124 4 1¼ **Ever Cheerful**[14] [220] 5-9-1 **76** .... GeorgeBaker 3 76
(G C H Chung) *stdd s: in rr tl r.o fnl f* **12/1**

40-0 5 ¾ **Depressed**[14] [224] 4-8-10 **71** ....(p) JohnEgan 4 69
(Ernst Oertel) *trckd ldr to over 3f out: rdn over 1f out: fdd ins fnl f* **40/1**

1-10 6 *nk* **Silent Storm**[14] [221] 6-9-3 **78** .... ChrisCatlin 1 75
(C A Cyzer) *outpcd and nvr on terms* **15/2**

1m 11.38s (-1.43) **Going Correction** -0.125s/f (Stan) **6** Ran SP% **111.9**
Speed ratings (Par 105):104,102,102,100,99 99
CSF £9.47 CT £14.23 TOTE £2.30: £1.20, £2.30; EX 13.10.
Owner J E Harley **Bred** Mrs S Shaw **Trained** Headley, Surrey

FOCUS
Just a fair handicap but run at a sound pace and the form is sound with the fifth the best guide.

377 BETDIRECT FREEPHONE 0800 211 222 H'CAP 1m 2f (P)
3:35 (3:36) (Class 2) (0-100,101) 4-Y-0+
£15,580 (£4,665; £2,332; £1,167; £582; £292) **Stalls** Low

Form RPR

/51- 1 **Arturius (IRE)**[242] [2565] 4-8-5 **88** .... EddieAhern 9 93
(P J Rothwell, Ire) *stdd s and swtchd to ins: hdwy on ins over 2f out: led over 1f out: wnt rt fnl f: r.o* **20/1**

16-2 2 1½ **Red Spell (IRE)**[13] [238] 5-9-5 **101** .... RichardHughes 4 104
(R Hannon) *in tch on ins: rdn and chsd wnr over 1f out: kpt on* **7/4**[1]

0-11 3 ¾ **Bravo Maestro (USA)**[14] [222] 5-8-1 **90** .... JamesDoyle(7) 5 94+
(N P Littmoden) *hld up in rr: hdwy over 1f out: r.o: nvr nrr* **7/2**[2]

1-25 4 2 **Boo**[14] [222] 4-8-7 **97** ....(v) AndrewElliott(7) 7 94
(K R Burke) *racd wd: hld up: hdwy over 4f out: outpcd 2f out: kpt on fnl f* **13/2**[3]

6663 5 *hd* **Takes Tutu (USA)**[5] [313] 7-8-4 **86** oh20........ FranciscoDaSilva 2 83?
(K R Burke) *led tl rdn and hdd over 1f out: one pce after* **66/1**

04- 6 1¼ **Gavroche (IRE)**[42] [6700] 5-8-11 **93** .... IanMongan 8 88
(J R Boyle) *hld up: hdwy over 4f out: wknd over 1f out* **9/1**

30-5 7 *hd* **Lygeton Lad**[13] [238] 8-8-10 **92** ....(t) MartinDwyer 1 86
(Miss Gay Kelleway) *trckd ldrs to 2f out: rdn and wknd appr fnl f* **14/1**

1120 8 5 **Willhego**[7] [296] 5-8-4 **86** oh1........ HayleyTurner 3 71
(J R Best) *trckd ldrs tl wknd 3f out* **10/1**

00-1 9 1½ **El Tiger (GER)**[24] [135] 5-8-8 **90** .... JamieSpencer 6 72
(B J Curley) *in tch to 1/2-way: sn bhd* **7/1**

2m 4.46s (-3.33) **Going Correction** -0.125s/f (Stan)
WFA 4 from 5yo+ 1lb **9** Ran SP% **116.4**
Speed ratings (Par 109):108,106,106,104,104 103,103,99,98
CSF £55.93 CT £161.14 TOTE £22.90: £3.70, £1.30, £1.60; EX 68.90.
Owner N O'Farrell **Bred** Floors Farming And London Thoroughbred Services Lt **Trained** Tinahely, Co. Wicklow

FOCUS
A decent handicap and, although the winning time was 0.69 seconds slower than the earlier Class 5 handicap, it was still close to par for the grade. The first three all came from off the pace but the proximity of the fifth tends to raise doubts about the form.

NOTEBOOK
Arturius(IRE), making his debut for the stable and having his first try on sand, had not been seen since winning a Carlisle maiden for Sir Michael Stoute last June. He travelled well in rear and got through on the inside of the runner-up on the run down to the straight, establishing an advantage that he never looked like relinquishing despite drifting right across the track under pressure. He does not look especially well handicapped, but can be expected to improve a little for the outing. (tchd 25-1)

Red Spell(IRE), stepping back up in trip, travelled well off the pace, but Hughes let the winner up his inside on the run to the straight, conceding an advantage that he was never able to reduce. His jockey has not exactly shone on him in his last two outings, but this trip is at the limit of his stamina, and a return to a mile may enable him to use his speed more effectively. (op 2-1 tchd 9-4)

Bravo Maestro(USA) likes this track and has been in good form for his new yard, but he was unable to dictate the pace with Takes Tutu in the line-up and so was settled at the back. He ran on in the closing stages but never looked like reaching the principals. He may be more effective settled just behind the leaders. Official explanation: jockey said gelding was denied a clear run early on (tchd 10-3)

Boo has been holding his form well in races here since winning twice at Wolverhampton at the turn of the year, and ran very close to recent form with today's third. He would still be of interest if another opportunity can be found for him back at the Midlands track. (op 6-1 tchd 7-1)

Takes Tutu(USA), who showed a return to form last time in a Wolverhamton claimer, was racing from 20lb out of the handicap and ran above himself. He has run some of his best races on this track, and could be interesting in lesser grade and a shorter trip around here. (op 50-1)

Gavroche(IRE), returning from a six-week break, was 9lb better off with today's fourth compared with their last meeting and was able to reduce the gap a little. (op 10-1)

Lygeton Lad has not won for 14 months but has dropped in the weights and showed last time that much of the ability is still there. This trip is beyond his optimum and a return to a mile will suit him better.

Willhego Official explanation: jockey said gelding finished lame

378 NO 5P RULE 4S AT BETDIRECT CLAIMING STKS 1m (P)
4:10 (4:10) (Class 5) 3-Y-0 **£3,886** (£1,156; £577; £288) **Stalls** High

Form RPR

-311 1 **Casablanca Minx (IRE)**[26] [122] 3-8-6 70 .... MartinDwyer 5 59+
(J R Boyle) *trckd ldng pair: led over 1f out: rdn clr: easily* **1/1**[1]

000- 2 5 **Danish Blues (IRE)**[110] [6072] 3-8-8 30 .... JimmyQuinn 2 49
(R M Flower) *hld up: hdwy over 1f out to chse easy wnr ins fnl f* **100/1**

5-24 3 1½ **Pab Special (IRE)**[14] [219] 3-9-5 71 .... PatCosgrave 4 57
(K R Burke) *trckd ldr tl rdn and fdd ins fnl f* **5/1**[3]

5-61 4 1¾ **Ohana**[13] [241] 3-8-8 71 .... JamesDoyle(7) 1 49
(N P Littmoden) *led tl hdd over 1f out: wknd qckly ins fnl f* **7/4**[2]

-306 5 9 **Salisbury World (IRE)**[7] [293] 3-8-12 62 .... LPKeniry 3 25
(D R C Elsworth) *fly-jmpd s and plld hrd: lost tch wl over 1f out* **12/1**

1m 38.55s (-0.88) **Going Correction** -0.125s/f (Stan) **5** Ran SP% **111.7**
Speed ratings (Par 97):99,94,92,90,81
CSF £47.87 TOTE £2.00: £1.30, £4.10; EX 39.30.The winner was claimed by Toby Brereton for £14,000. Danish Blues was claimed by Nigel Shields for £8,000.
Owner M Khan X2 **Bred** Airlie Stud And Widden Stud **Trained** Epsom, Surrey

FOCUS
Not strong form, although the race could be rated higher based on time.

379 PLAY MONTE CARLO WITH LITTLEWOODSPOKER.COM H'CAP 1m 4f (P)
4:40 (4:41) (Class 6) (0-60,58) 4-Y-0+ **£3,238** (£963; £481; £240) **Stalls** Low

Form RPR

0/05 1 **Ground Patrol**[10] [263] 5-9-1 **55** .... GeorgeBaker 14 64
(G L Moore) *hld up: hdwy over 2f out: led over 1f out: drvn out* **12/1**

001- 2 ½ **Soviet Sceptre (IRE)**[227] [3018] 5-8-8 **48** ....(t) TQuinn 13 56
(R T Phillips) *hld up in rr: hdwy over 2f out: hrd rdn to chse wnr over 1f out: kpt on* **14/1**

0-01 3 1¾ **Blue Hedges**[17] [185] 4-9-0 **57** .... JimmyQuinn 8 62+
(H J Collingridge) *slowly away: hdwy on ins over 2f out: kpt on u.p: nvr nrr* **11/2**[2]

50-3 4 *shd* **Champion Lion (IRE)**[22] [158] 7-8-12 **52** .... JamieSpencer 3 57
(J R Boyle) *hld up: hdwy over 1f out: styd on u.p* **12/1**

2-46 5 *nk* **Lady Pilot**[17] [187] 4-8-12 **58** .... RichardThomas(3) 4 63
(Dr J R J Naylor) *trckd ldrs:: rdn over 1f out: kpt on one pce* **20/1**

010- 6 ¾ **General Flumpa**[201] [3804] 5-8-11 **58** .... JonjoMilczarek(7) 7 61
(C F Wall) *hld up in mid-div: rdn over 1f out: nvr nr to chal* **16/1**

0-03 7 ½ **Birthday Star (IRE)**[10] [263] 4-8-10 **58** .... StephenDonohoe(5) 15 64+
(W J Musson) *in rr: rdn and mde sme late hdwy* **8/1**[3]

14-4 8 ¾ **Thebestisyettocome**[10] [263] 4-9-0 **57** .... IanMongan 2 58
(T G Mills) *sn tch: chsd ldrs tl wknd over 1f out* **9/4**[1]

0-05 9 1¼ **Postmaster**[14] [218] 4-9-0 **57** ....(t) MatthewHenry 16 56
(R Ingram) *in rr: nvr on terms* **25/1**

6-65 10 *hd* **Chocolate Boy (IRE)**[24] [141] 7-8-13 **53** ....(be) TPQueally 6 52
(G L Moore) *nvr bttr than mid-div* **20/1**

-436 11 3 **Jomus**[10] [263] 5-9-1 **55** ....(p) MartinDwyer 9 49
(L Montague Hall) *s.i.s: hdwy over 4f out: hdd & wknd qckly over 4f out* **10/1**

2-01 12 *shd* **Missie Baileys**[10] [263] 4-8-7 **57** .... JosephWalsh(7) 10 51
(Mrs L J Mongan) *trckd ldrs tl wknd over 3f out* **16/1**

-410 13 2½ **Night Warrior (IRE)**[10] [263] 6-8-6 **53** ....(b) JamesDoyle(7) 11 43
(N P Littmoden) *racd wd: rdn and wknd over 2f tou* **8/1**[3]

11-0 14 7 **Royal Axminster**[14] [230] 11-8-5 **52** .... AmyBaker(7) 1 31
(Mrs P N Dutfield) *led tl hdd over 4f out: sn bhd* **50/1**

0-05 15 5 **Pharaoh Prince**[14] [229] 5-8-11 **51** ....(b) J-PGuillambert 12 22
(G Prodromou) *t.k.h: racd wd: hdwy over 6f out: wknd qckly 2f out* **25/1**

051- **16** *10* **Picot De Say**[16] [5208] 4-9-1 **58**.. DaneO'Neill 5 13
(C Roberts) *trckd ldr tl rdn and wknd over 2f out* **25/1**
2m 31.59s (-2.80) **Going Correction** -0.125s/f (Stan)
WFA 4 from 5yo+ 3lb **16** Ran SP% **134.3**
Speed ratings (Par 101):104,103,102,102,102 101,101,100,100,99 97,97,96,91,88 81
CSF £171.14 CT £1061.23 TOTE £21.60: £2.90, £3.80, £2.20, £3.90; EX 285.40 Place 6 £4.96, Place 5 £4.06.
Owner D J Deer **Bred** D J And Mrs Deer **Trained** Woodingdean, E Sussex

FOCUS
A low-grade handicap but the pace was good and the form looks pretty sound.
T/Plt: £5.40 to a £1 stake. Pool: £52,447.55. 7,048.35 winning tickets. T/Qpdt: £4.30 to a £1 stake. Pool: £5,216.30. 878.00 winning tickets. JS

[358]WOLVERHAMPTON (A.W) (L-H)

Saturday, February 11

OFFICIAL GOING: Standard
Wind: Light becoming moderate, half-behind

380 FOOTBALLPOOLS.COM MAIDEN STKS 5f 216y(P)
7:00 (7:02) (Class 5) 3-Y-O **£3,238** (£963; £481; £240) **Stalls** Low

Form RPR
-223 **1** **Canina**[1] [364] 3-8-9 65.. EddieAhern 1 68
(Ms Deborah J Evans) *a.p: rdn over 2f out: led ins fnl f: r.o* **15/8**[1]
622- **2** *1 ½* **Rebellious Spirit**[88] [6351] 3-9-0 74........................ MickyFenton 5 69
(J G Given) *sn led: rdn wl over 1f out: hung rt and hdd ins fnl f: nt qckn* **9/4**[2]
5-5 **3** *1* **Miss Lopez (IRE)**[29] [110] 3-8-9 .... RobertWinston 2 61
(K R Burke) *led early: chsd ldr: rdn 2f out: one pce fnl f* **7/1**[3]
0-0 **4** *2* **Sorrel Point**[21] [165] 3-9-0 .... MichaelTebbutt 6 60+
(H J Collingridge) *t.k.h in mid-div: hdwy on ins 3f out: rdn and one pce fnl 2f* **100/1**
25-4 **5** *¾* **Phinerine**[7] [298] 3-9-0 63........................ AdrianMcCarthy 11 57
(R A Harris) *t.k.h: a.p: rdn 2f out: one pce* **12/1**
6 *2 ½* **Ransom Strip (USA)** 3-9-0 .... JoeFanning 3 50+
(M Johnston) *bhd tl hdwy over 1f out: nvr trbld ldrs* **7/1**[3]
00- **7** *2* **Noble Minstrel**[47] [6661] 3-9-0 .... RobbieFitzpatrick 9 44
(S C Williams) *nvr nr ldrs* **25/1**
0 **8** *4* **Beverley Bell**[21] [165] 3-8-9 .... TomEaves 8 27
(Miss J A Camacho) *s.i.s: hdwy on ins over 2f out: wknd fnl f* **50/1**
0-02 **9** *3* **Kings Cavalier (USA)**[17] [189] 3-9-0 62........................ PaulHanagan 10 23
(I W McInnes) *broke wl: sn lost pl: bhd fnl 3f* **12/1**
00 **10** *3 ½* **Maxemull**[15] [215] 3-8-9 .... FergusSweeney 4 7
(D J Wintle) *outpcd* **150/1**
00- **11** *13* **Grammaticus**[51] [6659] 3-9-0 .... AdrianTNicholls 7 —
(K A Ryan) *prom tl rdn and wknd over 2f out* **66/1**
1m 15.39s (-0.42) **Going Correction** -0.05s/f (Stan) 11 Ran SP% **114.9**
Speed ratings (Par 97):100,98,96,94,93 89,87,81,77,73 55
CSF £5.85 TOTE £2.70: £1.70, £1.50, £2.60; EX 7.30.
Owner Paul Green (Oaklea) **Bred** Exors Of The Late Lord Crawshaw **Trained** Lydiate, Merseyside

FOCUS
A very ordinary maiden and the form is pretty limited, rated through the first two.

381 BETDIRECT.CO.UK H'CAP 7f 32y(P)
7:30 (7:30) (Class 5) (0-70,70) 4-Y-0+ **£3,238** (£963; £481; £240) **Stalls** High

Form RPR
0-13 **1** **Arnie De Burgh**[7] [292] 4-9-1 **67**........................ ShaneKelly 3 77
(D J Daly) *mde all: rdn wl over 1f out: rdn out* **10/3**[1]
-114 **2** *1* **Samuel Charles**[9] [276] 8-9-4 **70**........................ RobertWinston 1 78+
(C R Dore) *s.i.s: bhd: rdn and hdwy on outside over 1f out: r.o wl towards fin: nt rch wnr* **4/1**[2]
00-0 **3** *nk* **Onlytime Will Tell**[12] [253] 8-8-13 **65**........................ JoeFanning 5 72
(D Nicholls) *a.p: chsd wnr over 2f out: rdn wl over 1f out: r.o one pce fnl f* **50/1**
1404 **4** *nk* **Kensington (IRE)**[5] [316] 5-8-10 **65**........................(p) DanielTudhope(3) 11 71
(P D Evans) *hld up towards rr: rdn and hdwy wl over 1f out: kpt on ins fnl f* **8/1**
230- **5** *2 ½* **Sling Back (IRE)**[71] [6483] 5-8-10 **62**........................ MCHussey 4 62
(Eamon Tyrrell, Ire) *hld up and bhd: swtchd lft and hdwy on ins over 1f out: one pce fnl f* **11/1**
00-6 **6** *2* **Soviet Threat (IRE)**[21] [169] 5-8-13 **65**........................ FergusSweeney 6 59
(A G Juckes) *hld up in mid-div: rdn over 2f out: hdwy over 1f out: nvr trbld ldrs* **16/1**
3-15 **7** *½* **Blue Empire (IRE)**[32] [77] 5-8-6 **63**........................ AndrewMullen(5) 8 56
(C R Dore) *w ldr tl rdn over 2f out: wknd over 1f out* **13/2**[3]
30-0 **8** *1* **Out For A Stroll**[10] [267] 7-9-0 **66**........................ HayleyTurner 7 56
(S C Williams) *nvr nr ldrs* **25/1**
1-20 **9** *2 ½* **Out Of India**[30] [100] 4-9-1 **67**........................ PaulEddery 12 51
(B Smart) *s.i.s: hld up: hdwy over 4f out: rdn over 2f out: wknd over 1f out* **16/1**
6-03 **10** *nk* **Merdiff**[21] [171] 7-8-10 **62**........................ EddieAhern 10 45
(W M Brisbourne) *prom: rdn over 3f out: wknd 1f out* **11/1**
00-3 **11** *¾* **Defi (IRE)**[12] [253] 4-9-4 **70**........................(bt) TomEaves 9 51
(I Semple) *hld up: sn mid-div: hdwy 3f out: sn rdn: wknd over 1f out* **7/1**
03-0 **12** *4* **Time N Time Again**[7] [292] 8-8-11 **63**........................(p) RobbieFitzpatrick 2 34
(Peter Grayson) *prom over 3f* **33/1**
1m 28.72s (-1.68) **Going Correction** -0.05s/f (Stan) 12 Ran SP% **117.2**
Speed ratings (Par 103):107,105,105,105,102 100,99,98,95,95 94,89
CSF £15.69 CT £560.12 TOTE £4.60: £1.40, £1.70, £7.00; EX 9.10.
Owner Gregory Way **Bred** Wyck Hall Stud Ltd **Trained** Newmarket, Suffolk

FOCUS
This modest handicap was run at a good pace and it was a fair winning time for the grade. The form looks sound rated through the placed horses.

382 NANTWICH VENEERS LTD (S) STKS 1m 1f 103y(P)
8:00 (8:00) (Class 6) 4-6-Y-O **£2,388** (£705; £352) **Stalls** Low

Form RPR
-400 **1** **Milk And Sultana**[5] [310] 6-8-8 45........................ AlanDaly 1 52
(G A Ham) *led early: hld up in tch: lost pl over 4f out: hdwy over 3f out: rdn over 2f out: led wl ins fnl f: r.o* **8/1**
-026 **2** *1* **Pending (IRE)**[8] [290] 5-8-13 57........................(p) PaulHanagan 8 55
(R A Fahey) *plld hrd in mid-div: hdwy over 3f out: rdn to ld 1f out: hdd and nt qckn wl ins fnl f* **3/1**[1]
3030 **3** *¾* **Sol Rojo**[12] [251] 4-8-13 53........................(b) RobbieFitzpatrick 10 54
(M J Attwater) *hld up and bhd: swtchd lft sn after s: rdn and hdwy wl over 1f out: r.o wl ins fnl f* **8/1**
-404 **4** *1* **Weet Yer Tern (IRE)**[11] [257] 4-8-13 45........................(p) RobertWinston 7 52
(P A Blockley) *t.k.h: led after 1f: rdn over 2f out: hdd 1f out: one pce* **14/1**
4430 **5** *½* **Look At The Stars (IRE)**[12] [251] 4-8-13 50........................(b) GrahamGibbons 4 51
(R Hollinshead) *hld up towards rr: rdn and hdwy over 2f out: one pce fnl f* **11/2**[3]
1-00 **6** *1* **Granary Girl**[10] [263] 4-9-0 53........................ JimmyQuinn 5 50
(J Pearce) *prom: rdn over 3f out: one pce fnl 2f* **7/2**[2]
5506 **7** *nk* **Savoy Chapel**[2] [350] 4-8-6 50........................(vt) JamesDoyle(7) 13 49
(A W Carroll) *hld up and bhd: hdwy on outside over 3f out: rdn over 2f out: no imp fnl f* **12/1**
0400 **8** *1 ¼* **Lakeside Guy (IRE)**[5] [313] 5-8-6 40........................(t) LiamJones(7) 2 46
(M Appleby) *bhd tl hdwy wl over 1f out: nvr trbld ldrs* **28/1**
0-25 **9** *10* **Colonel Bilko (IRE)**[36] [56] 4-8-13 49........................ ChrisCatlin 12 27
(Miss S J Wilton) *hld up: hdwy over 5f out: rdn and wknd over 2f out* **12/1**
-000 **10** *4* **Weet N Measures**[11] [260] 4-8-13 40........................ TonyCulhane 3 20
(T Wall) *sn led: hdd after 1f: wknd 4f out* **80/1**
11 *4* **Where's Sally**[29] 6-8-8 .... DaleGibson 6 7
(J Mackie) *a bhd* **33/1**
5000 **12** *16* **Flying Spud**[6] [304] 5-8-13 40........................ DeanMcKeown 11 —
(A J Chamberlain) *prom: rdn over 4f out: wknd over 3f out: t.o* **66/1**
2m 2.50s (-0.12) **Going Correction** -0.05s/f (Stan) 12 Ran SP% **116.0**
Speed ratings: 98,97,96,95,95 94,93,92,83,80 76,62
CSF £30.86 TOTE £13.40: £3.40, £1.50, £2.60; EX 50.20.Winner bought in for 4,250gns. Pending was claimed by Mustafa Khan for £6,000.
Owner Rose Farm Developments (UK) Ltd **Bred** D Malcolm Drury **Trained** Rooks Bridge, Somerset
■ Stewards' Enquiry : Paul Hanagan three-day ban: used whip with excessive frequency and without giving gelding time to respond (Feb 22-24)

FOCUS
A competitive if moderate seller and the form looks weak.

383 BE LUCKY ONLINE AT FOOTBALLPOOLS.COM H'CAP 1m 141y(P)
8:30 (8:30) (Class 6) (0-60,60) 4-Y-0+ **£2,388** (£705; £352) **Stalls** Low

Form RPR
-222 **1** **New England**[8] [290] 4-9-3 **59**........................ RobbieFitzpatrick 4 67+
(W M Brisbourne) *hld up and bhd: rdn and hdwy on ins wl over 1f out: squeezed through to ld cl home* **10/3**[1]
0-10 **2** *hd* **Cup Of Love (USA)**[17] [187] 4-9-2 **58**........................ ChrisCatlin 7 65
(Rae Guest) *a.p: rdn over 2f out: led 1f out: hdd cl home* **8/1**
-523 **3** *1 ¼* **Mister Benji**[25] [134] 7-9-3 **59**........................ DeanMcKeown 9 63
(B P J Baugh) *a.p: rdn over 2f out: ev ch whn carried lft jst ins fnl f: nt qckn* **16/1**
1-01 **4** *shd* **Lucius Verrus (USA)**[14] [232] 6-9-1 **60**........................(v) PatrickMathers(3) 3 64
(D Shaw) *hld up: rdn and hdwy over 1f out: r.o ins fnl f* **6/1**[3]
-254 **5** *¾* **Doctor's Cave**[9] [274] 4-9-3 **59**........................(b) AdrianTNicholls 13 61
(K O Cunningham-Brown) *sn led: rdn over 2f out: hdd and edgd lft 1f out: no ex* **16/1**
0-40 **6** *4* **My Pension (IRE)**[17] [187] 5-9-4 **60**........................ TonyCulhane 6 54
(P Howling) *hld up and bhd: rdn and hdwy over 1f out: n.d* **4/1**[2]
0/ **7** *3* **Hallings Overture (USA)**[527] [5252] 7-9-4 **60**........................ FergusSweeney 5 48
(C A Horgan) *nvr nr ldrs* **40/1**
3-15 **8** *shd* **Sonic Anthem (USA)**[25] [131] 4-8-13 **58**........................ SilvestreDeSousa(3) 11 46
(D Nicholls) *hld up: hdwy over 4f out: rdn over 2f out: wknd wl over 1f out* **6/1**[3]
44-0 **9** *½* **Atlantic Ace**[22] [157] 9-9-4 **60**........................(p) PaulEddery 1 51+
(B Smart) *hld up: n.m.r on ins bnd after 1f: rdn and hdwy on ins over 2f out: wknd over 1f out* **33/1**
0-60 **10** *4* **Dundonald**[5] [315] 7-7-11 **46** oh1........................(t) LiamJones(7) 12 24
(M Appleby) *a bhd* **66/1**
50-5 **11** *nk* **Triple Jump**[16] [200] 5-8-13 **60**........................ AndrewMullen(5) 2 37
(K A Ryan) *led early: hld up in tch: rdn over 2f out: wknd wl over 1f out* **9/1**
0-00 **12** *8* **Union Jack Jackson (IRE)**[16] [200] 4-8-13 **55**........................ MickyFenton 10 16
(J G Given) *hld up: hdwy over 4f out: rdn over 3f out: wknd over 2f out* **28/1**
1m 49.68s (-2.08) **Going Correction** -0.05s/f (Stan) 12 Ran SP% **114.8**
Speed ratings (Par 101):107,106,105,105,104 101,98,98,98,94 94,87
CSF £28.43 CT £371.55 TOTE £3.30: £1.70, £2.90, £2.90; EX 35.00.
Owner Stephen Walker **Bred** Darley **Trained** Great Ness, Shropshire

FOCUS
A moderate contest but a smart winning time for the grade, 2.7 seconds faster than the following Class 5 handicap over the same trip. The form looks sound and should prove reliable.

384 BETDIRECT FREEPHONE 0800 211 222 H'CAP 1m 141y(P)
9:00 (9:00) (Class 5) (0-75,75) 4-Y-0+ **£3,238** (£963; £481; £240) **Stalls** Low

Form RPR
/14- **1** **Compton Eclipse**[35] [5844] 6-8-8 **65**........................ EddieAhern 12 73
(J J Lambe, Ire) *a.p: rdn to ld ins fnl f: r.o wl* **11/2**[3]
0-15 **2** *1 ¼* **Burnley Al (IRE)**[22] [157] 4-8-5 **62**........................(v[1]) PaulHanagan 4 67
(R A Fahey) *set stdy pce: rdn over 1f out: hdd and nt qckn ins fnl f* **11/2**[3]
03-0 **3** *2* **Poppys Footprint (IRE)**[12] [252] 5-8-4 **66**........................(b[1]) AndrewMullen(5) 1 67
(K A Ryan) *hld up in mid-div: rdn and hdwy on ins 2f out: kpt on same pce fnl f* **10/1**
2015 **4** *shd* **Lincolneurocruiser**[5] [316] 4-9-0 **71**........................ RobertWinston 8 72
(Mrs N Macauley) *hld up in tch: rdn over 2f out: one pce fnl f* **7/1**
45-1 **5** *1* **Bazelle**[21] [167] 4-9-1 **75**........................ PatrickMathers(3) 7 73+
(D Shaw) *hld up in mid-div: hdwy over 2f out: rdn over 1f out: one pce* **9/2**[2]
002- **6** *shd* **Everest (IRE)**[99] [6245] 9-9-0 **71**........................ TomEaves 2 69
(B Ellison) *hld up: rdn and sme hdwy on ins over 1f out: n.d* **16/1**
050- **7** *1 ¾* **Following Flow (USA)**[42] [6698] 4-9-3 **74**........................ GrahamGibbons 11 69
(R Hollinshead) *hld up and bhd: effrt on outside 3f out: no real prog fnl 2f* **20/1**
/531 **8** *nk* **Luna Tacumana (IRE)**[4] [327] 6-8-12 **69** 6ex........................ TPQueally 3 63+
(J J Lambe, Ire) *nvr nrr* **11/4**[1]
33-0 **9** *hd* **Age Of Kings (USA)**[17] [192] 4-8-11 **68**........................ FergusSweeney 6 62
(A B Haynes) *n.d* **22/1**
000- **10** *nk* **Portacarron (IRE)**[57] [6593] 4-8-4 **61** oh1........................(b[1]) MCHussey 10 54
(Eamon Tyrrell, Ire) *hld up in tch: rdn over 2f out: wknd wl over 1f out* **66/1**
000- **11** *12* **Don Pasquale**[96] [6283] 4-8-6 **63**........................(v) RobbieFitzpatrick 13 31
(J T Stimpson) *s.v.s: a bhd* **66/1**

0/ 12 hd **Armanatta (IRE)**[216] [3382] 5-8-13 **70**................................ JimmyQuinn 5 37
(Mrs A M O'Shea, Ire) *prom: wkng whn n.m.r on ins over 2f out* **33/1**

1m 52.38s (0.62) **Going Correction** -0.05s/f (Stan) **12** Ran SP% **118.1**
Speed ratings (Par 103):95,93,92,92,91 91,89,89,89,88 78,77
CSF £33.80 CT £300.65 TOTE £10.40: £2.60, £1.60, £2.70; EX 74.10.
Owner Orchard County Syndicate **Bred** Grange Stud (uk) **Trained** Dungannon, Co. Tyrone

FOCUS
A modest time for the grade, 2.7 seconds slower than the preceding Class 6 handicap over the same trip, and a controversial result, with the favourite's well-backed stable companion winning. The first two set the standard but the form is far from solid.
Luna Tacumana(IRE) Official explanation: jockey said, regarding the running and riding, his orders were to get a nice position tracking leaders and to kick for home in straight, adding that race did not go to plan because filly was slow into her stride and he could not hold early position due to slow early pace, and furthermore he was blocked in; trainer added that mare seemed to run flat having had three close runs

385 97% PAYOUTS AT LITTLEWOODSCASINO.COM H'CAP 1m 4f 50y(P)
9:30 (9:31) (Class 5) (0-75,75) 4-Y-0+ **£3,238** (£963; £481; £240) **Stalls** Low

Form RPR
00-6 **1** **Cordier**[26] [125] 4-8-12 **72**................................ DaleGibson 3 78
(J Mackie) *plld hrd: set slow pce after 1f: rdn over 1f out: drvn out* **50/1**
31-2 **2** *1* **Tranquilizer**[29] [109] 4-8-10 **70**................................(t) EddieAhern 9 74
(D J Coakley) *hld up in tch: rdn wl over 1f out: chsd wnr fnl f: kpt on* **6/1**
20-0 **3** *1 1/4* **Torrid Kentavr (USA)**[16] [194] 9-9-2 **73**.................... RobertWinston 11 75
(B Ellison) *hld up and bhd: hdwy wl over 1f out: r.o ins fnl f* **16/1**
-623 **4** *1/2* **Dragon Slayer (IRE)**[12] [250] 4-8-12 **72**................ J-PGuillambert 10 73
(M J Attwater) *hld up and bhd: stdy hdwy over 5f out: rdn over 1f out: no ex ins fnl f* **9/2**[3]
10-4 **5** *1 3/4* **Top Spec (IRE)**[12] [250] 5-9-2 **73**................................ JimmyQuinn 7 71
(J Pearce) *s.s: hld up in rr: hdwy over 1f out: rdn and one pce fnl f* **4/1**[2]
3-51 **6** *shd* **Dovedon Hero**[10] [264] 6-9-0 **71**................................(b) TonyCulhane 4 69
(P J McBride) *hld up and bhd: hdwy on ins wl over 1f out: nt clr run and swtchd rt ins fnl f: nt rch ldrs* **11/2**
000- **7** *2* **Rashida**[7] [4347] 4-8-3 **70**................................(tp) LiamJones[(7)] 5 65
(M Appleby) *hld up: hdwy on ins 2f out: wknd ins fnl f* **100/1**
01 **8** *shd* **Stage Manager (IRE)**[14] [218] 4-8-7 **72** ow1................ DerekNolan[(5)] 2 67
(M J Wallace) *prom: chsd wnr wl over 1f out: sn rdn: wknd fnl f* **5/2**[1]
265- **9** *4* **Kavi (IRE)**[211] [3522] 6-8-13 **70**................................ ChrisCatlin 6 58
(Simon Earle) *hld up in mid-div: stdy hdwy over 5f out: wknd 3f out* **22/1**
00-0 **10** *1 3/4* **John Forbes**[12] [250] 4-8-7 **67** ow1................................ TomEaves 1 53
(B Ellison) *plld hrd: led 1f: chsd wnr tl rdn over 2f out: wknd wl over 1f out* **28/1**
020/ **11** *3* **Fort Churchill (IRE)**[386] [6143] 5-9-4 **75**.......................... MickyFenton 8 56
(B Ellison) *hld up in tch: rdn over 3f out: hmpd 2f out: sn wknd* **40/1**

2m 41.97s (-0.45) **Going Correction** -0.05s/f (Stan)
WFA 4 from 5yo+ 3lb **11** Ran SP% **115.5**
Speed ratings (Par 103):99,98,97,97,96 95,94,94,91,90 88
CSF £315.05 CT £5006.89 TOTE £31.40: £7.80, £1.70, £2.70; EX 302.80 Place 6 £204.64, Place 5 £162.31.
Owner F E And Mrs J J Brindley **Bred** Lord Halifax **Trained** Church Broughton , Derbys

FOCUS
A fair handicap but a tactical affair in which the winner dictated the pace and not an easy contest to rate.
T/Plt: £227.70 to a £1 stake. Pool: £62,404.30. 200.00 winning tickets. T/Qpdt: £81.70 to a £1 stake. Pool: £3,336.00. 30.20 winning tickets. KH

344 SOUTHWELL (L-H)
Sunday, February 12

OFFICIAL GOING: Standard
The rain made the surface ride 'a little more lively'.
Wind: Light, half behind Weather: Overcast with persistent light rain

386 PLAY LITTLEWOODS POOLS ON 0800 500 000 BANDED STKS 1m (F)
2:20 (2:21) (Class 7) 4-Y-0+ **£1,365** (£403; £201) **Stalls** Low

Form RPR
4-54 **1** **Desert Fury**[7] [304] 9-8-13 45................................(b) LeeEnstone 9 53
(R Bastiman) *s.i.s: hdwy on outside to trck ldrs over 3f out: shkn up to ld over 1f out: hld on towards fin* **10/1**
210- **2** *nk* **Bold Phoenix (IRE)**[90] [6347] 5-8-13 45.......................... JamieSpencer 8 52
(B J Curley) *trckd ldrs: effrt over 2f out: wnt 2nd jst ins last: hung lft and looked reluctant: jst hld nr line* **9/4**[1]
3630 **3** *3 1/2* **Crusoe (IRE)**[7] [304] 9-8-13 45................................(b) BrianReilly 4 45
(A Sadik) *led over 6f out tl over 1f out: kpt on same pce* **14/1**
-066 **4** *2* **Ballyrush (IRE)**[5] [330] 6-8-13 45................................ AlanDaly 5 41
(Miss D A McHale) *led over 1f: outpcd over 3f out: kpt on same pce fnl 2f* **33/1**
-040 **5** *1 1/2* **Kumakawa**[19] [184] 8-8-6 45................................ LauraReynolds[(7)] 3 38
(D K Ivory) *trckd ldrs: outpcd over 3f out: kpt on fnl 2f* **16/1**
6-00 **6** *nk* **Venetian Princess (IRE)**[19] [184] 4-8-13 45.................... ShaneKelly 11 37
(P Howling) *sn chsng ldrs: outpcd over 3f out: kpt on fnl f* **14/1**
265- **7** *2 1/2* **Tommytyler (IRE)**[82] [6413] 7-8-10 45.....................(t) DanielTudhope[(3)] 1 32
(D Carroll) *trckd ldrs: outpcd over 3f out: hdwy on inner over 2f out: wknd over 1f out* **7/1**[3]
00-3 **8** *5* **Starcross Maid**[7] [304] 4-8-13 45................................ MatthewHenry 6 22
(J F Coupland) *trckd ldrs: nt clr run and lost pl over 3f out: plld wd 2f out: no threat* **8/1**
330- **9** *6* **Silver Court**[155] [5129] 4-8-10 40.......................... RichardThomas[(3)] 10 10
(R A Harris) *w ldrs: lost pl over 2f out* **20/1**
-210 **10** *hd* **Pearl Island (USA)**[3] [350] 5-9-4 50................................(b) ChrisCatlin 7 15
(D J Wintle) *chsd ldrs: lost pl over 2f out* **11/4**[2]
500- **11** *hd* **Liability (IRE)**[134] [5622] 4-8-13 45.......................... RobbieFitzpatrick 2 10
(Miss S E Hall) *dwlt: sn trcking ldrs on inner: lost pl over 1f out* **80/1**

1m 43.55s (-1.05) **Going Correction** -0.075s/f (Stan) **11** Ran SP% **118.3**
Speed ratings (Par 97):102,101,98,96,94 94,91,86,80,80 80
CSF £32.47 TOTE £13.40: £3.50, £1.50, £2.00; EX 46.20.
Owner Robin Bastiman **Bred** Meon Valley Stud **Trained** Cowthorpe, N Yorks

FOCUS
Run-of-the-mill banded race, rated through the third.
Pearl Island(USA) Official explanation: trainer's representative had no explanation for the poor form shown
Liability(IRE) Official explanation: vet said filly bled from the nose

387 LITTLEWOODSPOOLS.CO.UK BANDED STKS 7f (F)
2:50 (2:50) (Class 7) 4-Y-0+ **£1,365** (£403; £201) **Stalls** Low

Form RPR
5045 **1** **Penel (IRE)**[12] [261] 5-8-11 45................................(p) LeeEnstone 5 51
(P T Midgley) *sn drvn along: reminders after 1f: hdwy over 2f out: edgd lft and led jst ins last: kpt on* **11/1**
0052 **2** *1* **Pawn In Life (IRE)**[12] [261] 8-8-11 45.......................(v) DeanMcKeown 8 49
(M J Polglase) *led: edgd lft bnd over 4f out: hdd jst ins last: no ex* **7/1**[3]
60-0 **3** *2 1/2* **Xaloc Bay (IRE)**[6] [313] 8-8-4 35................................ TolleyDean[(7)] 3 42
(R A Harris) *chsd ldrs: edgd lft and kpt on same pce fnl f* **40/1**
0-50 **4** *3/4* **Cleveland Way**[5] [330] 6-8-8 40.......................(v) DanielTudhope[(3)] 10 40
(D Carroll) *chsd ldrs on outer: chal over 2f out: one pce appr fnl f* **28/1**
-300 **5** *1 1/2* **Madame Guillotine**[17] [195] 4-8-9 40 ow1..........(b[1]) PaulMulrennan[(3)] 9 37
(P T Midgley) *trckd ldrs: outpcd over 2f out: kpt on fnl f* **25/1**
00-3 **6** *8* **Alzarma**[12] [257] 4-8-11 45................................(p) NCallan 6 15
(J Gallagher) *w ldr: hmpd bnd over 4f out: edgd lft and wknd over 1f out* **5/1**[2]
00-5 **7** *1/2* **In A Fit**[32] [84] 5-8-11 45................................ ShaneKelly 7 14
(P Howling) *sn drvn along on outer: nvr a threat* **7/1**[3]
004- **8** *6* **Miss Shontaine**[10] [6512] 4-8-11 35................................ HayleyTurner 4 —
(B G Powell) *hld up in rr: lost pl 3f out* **33/1**
4012 **9** *nk* **Justcallmehandsome**[7] [300] 4-8-4 45.................(v) DonnaCaldwell[(7)] 2 —+
(D J S Ffrench Davis) *sn trcking ldrs: hmpd bnd over 4f out: lost pl and stmbld over 3f out: n.d after: eased over 1f out* **11/10**[1]
040- **10** *3/4* **Doughty**[46] [6675] 4-8-11 40................................(b[1]) VinceSlattery 1 —
(D J Wintle) *s.i.s: a in rr: bhd fnl 3f* **20/1**

1m 30.92s (0.12) **Going Correction** -0.075s/f (Stan) **10** Ran SP% **115.1**
Speed ratings (Par 97):96,94,92,91,89 80,79,72,72,71
CSF £77.81 TOTE £16.20: £4.10, £2.00, £10.10; EX 83.80.
Owner M E Elsworthy **Bred** M Ervine **Trained** Westow, N Yorks
■ Stewards' Enquiry : Dean McKeown one-day ban: careless riding (Feb 23)
Lee Enstone three-day ban: careless riding (Feb 23-25)

FOCUS
With the favourite's misfortune it was a weak event but the first three ran to their marks.
In A Fit Official explanation: jockey said mare never travelled

388 LITTLEWOODS POOLS BILLIONS WON BY MILLIONS BANDED STKS 6f (F)
3:20 (3:20) (Class 7) 3-Y-0+ **£1,365** (£403; £201) **Stalls** Low

Form RPR
0-02 **1** **Blakeshall Quest**[12] [260] 6-9-0 45................................(b) TomEaves 2 57
(R Brotherton) *mde all: styd on strly to forge clr jst ins last* **7/1**
3561 **2** *5* **Christian Bendix**[12] [260] 4-9-3 48................................ ShaneKelly 7 45
(P Howling) *chsd ldrs: kpt on to take 2nd jst ins last: no ch w wnr* **13/8**[1]
4-00 **3** *1* **Radlett Lady**[6] [307] 5-9-0 45................................(p) JamieSpencer 1 39
(D K Ivory) *dwlt: sn chsng ldrs: kpt on same pce appr fnl f* **9/2**[2]
6-04 **4** *1/2* **Flying Dancer**[24] [144] 4-9-0 40................................ NCallan 9 38
(R A Harris) *chsd ldrs: reminder and outpcd over 3f out: styd on fnl f* **14/1**
0-56 **5** *shd* **Kashtanka (IRE)**[7] [299] 4-8-11 40.......................(b) JasonEdmunds[(3)] 3 37
(J Balding) *s.i.s: kpt on fnl 2f: nvr nr ldrs* **12/1**
5-05 **6** *1* **Polar Haze**[12] [260] 9-9-0 40................................(v) JimmyQuinn 11 34
(J Pearce) *swtchd lft after s: in rr tl kpt on fnl 2f* **16/1**
50-0 **7** *3/4* **Sergeant Slipper**[19] [179] 9-9-0 40.....................(v) RobbieFitzpatrick 6 32
(C Smith) *s.s: styd on fnl 2f: nvr on terms* **16/1**
2304 **8** *3/4* **Blue Power (IRE)**[12] [260] 5-9-0 45........................ FranciscoDaSilva 12 30
(K R Burke) *chsd ldrs: rdn over 2f out: sn btn* **6/1**[3]
0-05 **9** *1 1/4* **Canary Dancer**[5] [331] 4-9-0 40................................(b) AdrianMcCarthy 5 26
(Miss Z C Davison) *chsd ldrs: rdn and lost pl over 2f out* **25/1**
0000 **10** *3* **Cheeney Basin (IRE)**[19] [181] 8-9-0 35........................ BrianReilly 10 17
(M C Chapman) *chsd ldrs: outpcd over 2f out: sn btn* **80/1**
66-0 **11** *nk* **Mr Spliffy (IRE)**[12] [260] 7-8-7 40................................ AnnStokell[(7)] 8 16
(M C Chapman) *rr-div: sme hdwy on inner over 2f out: nvr a factor* **66/1**
0-00 **12** *13* **Katie Killane**[19] [179] 4-9-0 40................................(v) AlanDaly 4 —
(M Wellings) *s.i.s: bhd whn eased fnl f* **28/1**

1m 16.35s (-0.55) **Going Correction** -0.075s/f (Stan) **12** Ran SP% **119.2**
Speed ratings (Par 97):100,93,92,91,91 89,88,87,86,82 81,64
CSF £18.37 TOTE £8.00: £1.80, £1.20, £2.20; EX 15.50.
Owner Droitwich Jokers **Bred** M P Bishop **Trained** Elmley Castle, Worcs

FOCUS
An improved effort from the back-to-form winner and a good time too. The form looks reasonable for the grade.
Katie Killane Official explanation: trainer said filly was sore in shoulders

389 PLAY £1/4M SPOT THE BALL ON 0800 500 000 BANDED STKS 1m 6f (F)
3:50 (3:50) (Class 7) 4-Y-0+ **£1,706** (£503; £252) **Stalls** Low

Form RPR
-201 **1** **Jackie Kiely**[12] [259] 5-9-11 56................................ J-PGuillambert 6 60+
(P Howling) *hld up: trckd ldrs: led over 2f out: hung rt and drew clr 1f out: readily* **11/4**[3]
5513 **2** *2* **Makarim (IRE)**[10] [270] 10-9-5 50................................(p) AlanDaly 2 51
(M R Bosley) *hld up in last pl: t.k.h: effrt over 3f out: styd on to take 2nd jst ins last: no ch w wnr* **85/40**[1]
-223 **3** *2 1/2* **Bulberry Hill**[12] [259] 5-8-11 40........................ EdwardCreighton[(7)] 7 42
(R W Price) *t.k.h: in tch: hdwy to chse ldrs 6f out: effrt over 2f out: kpt on same pce* **6/1**
2212 **4** *1 1/2* **Moon Shot**[12] [259] 10-9-10 55................................ NCallan 5 50
(A G Juckes) *t.k.h: hdwy 3f out: kpt on same pce: nvr able chal* **9/4**[2]
10- **5** *3 1/2* **Next Flight (IRE)**[134] [5615] 7-9-1 46................................ TomEaves 1 36
(R E Barr) *dwlt: sn trcking ldrs: chal over 8f out: fdd over 1f out* **16/1**
60-0 **6** *nk* **Keltic Rainbow (IRE)**[41] [12] 5-9-0 40.....................(v) DavidKinsella 4 35
(D Haydn Jones) *set mod pce: qcknd over 3f out: hdd over 2f out: wknd over 1f out* **25/1**
60-0 **7** *18* **East Cape**[41] [12] 9-9-0 35................................ KimTinkler 3 9
(N Tinkler) *chsd ldrs: pushed along over 5f out: lost pl over 3f out: sn bhd* **66/1**

3m 9.23s (-0.37) **Going Correction** -0.075s/f (Stan) **7** Ran SP% **114.9**
Speed ratings (Par 97):98,96,95,94,92 92,82
CSF £9.15 TOTE £3.90: £1.70, £1.90; EX 9.00.
Owner P S J Croft **Bred** Mrs M Chaworth Musters **Trained** Newmarket, Suffolk

FOCUS
A steady pace until the home turn but a reasonable overall time. The winner seemed to steal a march on the runner-up.

390 LITTLEWOODS LOTTO3 0800 500 000 BANDED STKS 1m 3f (F)
4:20 (4:20) (Class 7) 4-Y-0+ £1,365 (£403; £201) **Stalls** Low

Form RPR
-621 **1** **Surdoue**[19] 182 6-8-13 45 J-PGuillambert 10 52
(P Howling) *trckd ldrs: t.k.h: led over 4f out: hld on towards fin* **11/8**[1]
5-25 **2** *nk* **To Be Fare (IRE)**[7] 304 6-8-13 45 DeanMcKeown 11 52
(J Pearce) *stdd s: stdy hdwy 4f out: wnt 2nd over 1f out: hung lft: kpt on towards fin* **8/1**[3]
000- **3** *2 1/2* **Mostakbel (USA)**[11] 5586 7-8-13 45 (v) HayleyTurner 12 48
(M D I Usher) *sn chsng ldrs: kpt on same pce fnl 2f* **40/1**
-322 **4** *shd* **Liquid Lover (IRE)**[7] 302 4-8-11 45 ShaneKelly 7 47
(W M Brisbourne) *sn chsng ldrs: wnt 2nd 3f out: one pce* **15/8**[2]
06-2 **5** *5* **College Rebel**[7] 301 5-8-13 35 RobbieFitzpatrick 4 39
(J F Coupland) *mid-div: outpcd over 3f out: hdwy on inner over 2f out: nvr trbld ldrs* **16/1**
0004 **6** *1/2* **Simply The Guest (IRE)**[7] 302 7-8-13 45 (vt) KimTinkler 5 39
(N Tinkler) *in rr: outpcd over 4f out: kpt on fnl 2f: nvr a threat* **20/1**
4-53 **7** *1* **Dextrous**[7] 302 9-8-13 35 (p) LeeEnstone 2 37
(P T Midgley) *hld up wl in tch: lost pl 5f out: hdwy on outer over 2f out: nvr a threat* **14/1**
304- **8** *1 3/4* **Danum**[70] 6494 6-8-13 35 GrahamGibbons 8 34
(R Hollinshead) *led 1f: chsd ldrs: lost pl over 1f out* **66/1**
5-50 **9** *1 1/4* **Donegal Shore (IRE)**[12] 258 7-8-13 45 (vt) AdrianTNicholls 3 32
(Jennie Candlish) *s.i.s: in rr: sme hdwy on outer over 2f out: nvr on terms* **14/1**
60-0 **10** *14* **Rock Concert**[20] 172 8-8-13 45 TomEaves 9 10
(I W McInnes) *led after 1f: hdd over 4f out: lost pl over 2f out: bhd whn eased fnl f* **28/1**
00-5 **11** *20* **Leyaaly**[5] 328 7-8-13 40 (t) AdrianMcCarthy 6 —
(Miss Z C Davison) *chsd ldrs: drvn over 4f out: lost pl over 3f out: bhd whn eased over 1f out* **80/1**

2m 27.25s (-1.65) **Going Correction** -0.075s/f (Stan)
WFA 4 from 5yo+ 2lb **11** Ran SP% **120.6**
Speed ratings (Par 97):103,102,100,100,97 96,96,94,93,83 69
CSF £13.37 TOTE £2.30: £1.10, £2.90, £13.70; EX 25.10.
Owner Les Amis Partners **Bred** R A G Robinson **Trained** Newmarket, Suffolk

FOCUS
Average banded form but it looks fairly reliable with the runner-up improving for the step up in trip.
Leyaaly Official explanation: jockey said mare had a breathing problem

391 LITTLEWOODS LOTTO4 0800 500 000 BANDED STKS 1m (F)
4:50 (4:50) (Class 7) 4-Y-0+ £1,365 (£403; £201) **Stalls** Low

Form RPR
1512 **1** **Latif (USA)**[2] 358 5-9-9 51 ChrisCatlin 6 68
(Ms Deborah J Evans) *s.s: nt clr run over 3f out: hdwy over 2f out: styd on to ld last 100yds* **11/8**[1]
0-13 **2** *1* **Golden Spectrum (IRE)**[14] 247 7-8-7 48 (b) WilliamCarson(7) 5 57
(R A Harris) *led after 1f: hdd and no ex ins last* **6/1**[3]
6-46 **3** *1 3/4* **High Swainston**[20] 177 5-8-12 46 PaulFessey 3 52
(R Craggs) *trckd ldrs: rdn and outpcd over 2f out: styd on fnl f* **16/1**
-604 **4** *1* **Chickado (IRE)**[6] 315 5-9-1 49 RobertHavlin 8 53
(D Haydn Jones) *trckd ldrs on outer: wnt 2nd 3f out: kpt on same pce fnl 2f* **14/1**
6-53 **5** *hd* **Supreme Salutation**[8] 297 10-8-12 53 LauraReynolds(7) 4 56
(D K Ivory) *t.k.h: trckd ldrs: n.m.r and lost pl bnd over 4f out: hdwy on wd outside over 2f out: nt rch ldrs* **12/1**
20-0 **6** *2* **Fillameena**[12] 259 6-8-8 45 (p) PaulMulrennan(3) 9 44
(P T Midgley) *racd on outer: hdwy and in tch over 4f out: outpcd 3f out: no threat after* **33/1**
0-13 **7** *1/2* **Only If I Laugh**[7] 300 5-9-2 50 GrahamGibbons 1 48
(M J Attwater) *led 1f: stdd: effrt over 3f out: sn chsng ldrs: wknd fnl f* **11/1**
-420 **8** *5* **Monkey Madge**[14] 247 4-9-2 50 GylesParkin 2 38
(B Smart) *trckd ldrs on inner: wknd 2f out* **25/1**
0-51 **9** *17* **Azreme**[19] 183 6-9-1 49 (b) ShaneKelly 7 3
(P Howling) *s.i.s: sn in tch: drvn and edgd lft bnd over 4f out: hung lft and lost pl over 2f out: sn bhd* **11/4**[2]

1m 43.06s (-1.54) **Going Correction** -0.075s/f (Stan) **9** Ran SP% **118.4**
Speed ratings (Par 97):104,103,101,100,100 98,97,92,75
CSF £10.61 TOTE £1.90: £1.10, £1.80, £4.80; EX 10.90 Place 6 £58.59, Place 5 £25.08.
Owner Paddy Mason **Bred** Shadwell Farm LLC **Trained** Lydiate, Merseyside

FOCUS
The winner is very tough and did well after a sluggish start. It was his fifth run in 12 days and his third success in that time, and he sets the standard.
Azreme Official explanation: jockey said horse never travelled after interference on back straight
T/Plt: £90.00 to a £1 stake. Pool: £43,057.35. 348.90 winning tickets. T/Qpdt: £5.90 to a £1 stake. Pool: £3,392.20. 418.80 winning tickets. WG

CAGNES-SUR-MER
Sunday, February 12

OFFICIAL GOING: Turf course - good to soft; all-weather - standard

392a PRIX DE LA CALIFORNIE (LISTED RACE) 7f 110y
2:35 (2:38) 3-Y-O £16,207 (£6,483; £4,862; £3,241; £1,621)

RPR
1 **Dream In Blue (FR)**[71] 6491 3-8-11 (b) JAuge 9 98
(Robert Collet, France)
2 *3/4* **Chief Commander (FR)**[15] 228 3-8-11 IMendizabal 10 96
(Jane Chapple-Hyam) *raced in 4th on outside, driven on wide outside* **straight, ran on from over 1f out, went 2nd inside final furlong, ran on** **15/2**[1]
3 *1 1/2* **Beau Monde**[15] 3-8-8 MAndrouin 1 90
(H-A Pantall, France)
4 *hd* **Salsalava (FR)**[92] 6338 3-9-2 DBoeuf 3 98
(P Demercastel, France)
5 *1* **Bertranicus (FR)**[15] 3-8-11 J-BEyquem 2 91
(L Urbano-Grajales, France)
6 *1 1/2* **Merlerault (USA)**[15] 3-8-11 SPasquier 8 88
(P Demercastel, France)
7 *2 1/2* **Miss Highjinks (USA)**[40] 16 3-8-8 RobertWinston 11 79
(E J O'Neill) *towards rear, 9th straight, effort over 1f out, one pace final stages* **24/1**[3]
8 *1 1/2* **Apamea**[75] 3-8-8 MBlancpain 4 76
(Mme C Head-Maarek, France)
9 *8* **Anais Filly (FR)**[101] 6240 3-8-8 GToupel 5 59
(H-A Pantall, France)
10 *1* **Grand Jour (IRE)**[23] 160 3-8-11 TonyCulhane 7 60
(K McAuliffe) *raced in 2nd, lost place briefly on turn but 2nd and ridden straight, one pace from over 1f out* **11/1**[2]
11 **Precious Bunny (FR)**[93] 3-9-2 (b) FGeroux 6 65
(R Chotard, France)

1m 31.4s **11** Ran SP% **24.1**
PARI-MUTUEL (Including 1 Euro stake): WIN 14.40; PL 3.70, 2.80, 2.20;DF 53.20.
Owner Mlle M Vidal **Bred** Sarl Classic Breeding & Eric Mimouni **Trained** Chantilly, France

NOTEBOOK
Chief Commander(FR) ran an excellent race and delighted connections. They plan to send him back to France for another Listed race when the Parisian tracks open next month.
Miss Highjinks(USA) flattered briefly with an effort entering the straight, but was unable to get competitive.
Grand Jour(IRE) raced prominently, but faded quickly in the final furlong and a half. Connections felt a faster surface would have been to his advantage.

393a GRAND PRIX DE LA RIVIERA COTE D'AZUR (LISTED RACE) (ALL-WEATHER) 1m 2f (D)
3:35 (3:42) 4-Y-0+ £20,690 (£8,276; £6,207; £4,138; £2,069)

RPR
1 **Howard Le Canard (FR)**[12] 5-8-9 F-XBertras 1 111
(F Rohaut, France)
2 *1/2* **Chopastair (FR)**[63] 6553 5-8-9 J-BEyquem 12 110
(D Soubagne, France)
3 *3/4* **Tigron (USA)**[12] 5-8-9 (b) FSpanu 2 109
(Mme C Barande-Barbe, France)
4 *1 1/2* **Cimyla (IRE)**[16] 213 5-8-9 SPasquier 13 106
(C F Wall) *towarss rear, progress 4f out, 9th straight, driven 2f out, went 4th 1f out, nearest at finish* **5/2**[1]
5 *3* **Menestrol (FR)**[148] 5336 4-8-9 TThulliez 4 102
(D Prod'Homme, France)
6 *1/2* **Limit Up (GR)**[48] 8-8-9 ADeVries 10 100
(Dr A Bolte, Germany)
7 *shd* **Bening (FR)**[273] 1736 6-8-9 IMendizabal 9 100
(O Pessi, Italy)
8 *1 1/2* **Pro Ken (FR)**[63] 6553 6-8-9 FBlondel 7 97
(Rod Collet, France)
9 *5* **Singapore Pearl (FR)**[119] 4-8-6 WIon 11 86
(S Wattel, France)
10 *1/2* **Cocodrail (IRE)**[66] 5-8-9 FBranca 6 87
(F Brogi, Italy)
0 **Too Nice (FR)**[114] 4-8-9 JAuge 5 —
(Robert Collet, France)
0 **Gandolfino (GER)**[91] 4-8-9 DBoeuf 3 —
(W Baltromei, Germany)
0 **Fianello (ITY)** 5-8-9 MPlanard 8 —
(Gianluca Bietolini, Italy)

2m 0.90s
WFA 4 from 5yo+ 1lb **13** Ran SP% **28.6**
PARI-MUTUEL: WIN 7.10; PL 2.50, 3.60, 3.70; DF 37.40.
Owner B Lalemant **Bred** Bsi Nv **Trained** Sauvagnon, France

NOTEBOOK
Howard Le Canard(FR) goes well on the all-weather and took this opening leg of the European All-Weather series. He heads to Neuss in Germany for the next leg on March, and depending on that run could well be seen in England for the Winter Derby.
Cimyla(IRE) was drawn 13 of 13 and this proved too difficult an obstacle to overcome. Most of his energy was spent getting competitive from that position, leaving little remaining for the final furlong.

372 LINGFIELD (L-H)
Monday, February 13

OFFICIAL GOING: Standard
Wind: Moderate, half-behind

394 "A £25 SIGN UP BONUS @ LITTLEWOODSPOKER.COM" BANDED STKS 1m 2f (P)
2:10 (2:10) (Class 7) 4-Y-0+ £1,365 (£403; £201) **Stalls** Low

Form RPR
04-4 **1** **Ten-Cents**[21] 172 4-9-2 50 GeorgeBaker 1 56
(C F Wall) *hld up in rr: hdwy 2f out: rdn to ld fnl 50yds* **5/2**[2]
-362 **2** *1* **It Must Be Speech**[8] 304 5-8-12 45 (v) AdrianMcCarthy 5 49
(S L Keightley) *trckd ldrs: rdn to ld briefly ins fnl f: kpt on* **6/1**[3]
-021 **3** *nk* **Glendale**[7] 310 5-9-9 50 JimmyQuinn 11 59
(D K Ivory) *trckd ldrs: led over 5f out: rdn and hdd ins fnl f: no ex nr fin* **9/4**[1]
10-0 **4** *nk* **Kinsman (IRE)**[7] 310 9-9-1 48 J-PGuillambert 8 51
(T D McCarthy) *stdd s: t.k.h: hdwy 1/2-way: r.o fnl f: nvr nrr* **12/1**
400- **5** *nk* **Double Ransom**[32] 6506 7-9-2 49 (b) TPQueally 2 51
(Mrs L Stubbs) *hld up: hdwy to chse ldrs over 2f out: rdn and ev ch tl nt qckn wl ins fnl f* **10/1**
4001 **6** *6* **Milk And Sultana**[2] 382 6-9-4 45 AlanDaly 9 43
(G A Ham) *sn trckd ldr: rdn over 2f out: wknd ent fnl f* **10/1**
42-3 **7** *7* **Amnesty**[7] 310 7-9-0 47 (be) IanMongan 7 26
(G L Moore) *in tch tl rdn and wknd over 2f out* **7/1**
8 *6* **Mia (POL)**[110] 5-9-0 47 (b[1]) DaneO'Neill 3 15
(Mrs P Townsley) *mid-div tl lost tch over 2f out* **20/1**
00-0 **9** *7* **Markusha**[40] 35 8-8-12 45 JohnEgan 6 1
(Jamie Poulton) *led tl hdd over 5f out: rdn and wknd over 3f out* **50/1**
-000 **10** *4* **Mujimac (IRE)**[13] 259 4-9-0 48 HayleyTurner 10 —
(P A Blockley) *bhd fr 1/2-way* **33/1**

2m 5.74s (-2.05) **Going Correction** +0.025s/f (Slow)
WFA 4 from 5yo+ 1lb **10** Ran SP% **121.7**
Speed ratings (Par 97):109,108,107,107,107 102,97,92,86,83
CSF £18.70 TOTE £4.20: £1.60, £2.40, £1.20; EX 27.00.

Owner A J Robinson **Bred** C A Cyzer **Trained** Newmarket, Suffolk

FOCUS
A reasonable enough race by banded standards and, despite the pace appearing just ordinary early on, the winning time was over four and a half seconds faster than the following race run over the same trip. There was little to separate the front five at the line but the form looks reliable with the first three close to their marks.

395 PLAY IN VEGAS WITH LITTLEWOODSPOKER.COM BANDED STKS 1m 2f (P)
2:40 (2:41) (Class 7) 4-Y-O+ £1,365 (£403; £201) Stalls Low

Form RPR
410- 1 **Revolve**[61] 6575 6-8-12 45....(p) IanMongan 13 51
(Mrs L J Mongan) *trckd ldr: led and rdn clr over 1f out: jst hld on u.p* 12/1
-003 2 shd **Dagola (IRE)**[7] 311 5-8-12 45.... JohnEgan 10 51
(C A Dwyer) *towards rr: hdwy on outside over 1f out: r.o strly fnl f: jst failed* 9/2[1]
5-04 3 3/4 **Tuscan Treaty**[7] 311 6-8-9 45....(tp) AdamKirby(3) 14 49
(P J McBride) *v.s.a: in rr tl hdwy on ins over 1f 1f out: r.o wl: nvr nrr* 8/1
30-6 4 1 **Belle Chanson**[7] 311 4-8-11 45....(v) HayleyTurner 2 48
(J R Boyle) *trckd ldrs: rdn over 1f out: nt qckn ins fnl f* 14/1
0-60 5 1 1/4 **Alqaayid**[8] 302 5-8-5 45.... RussellKennemore(7) 8 45
(P W Hiatt) *mid-div: rdn over 1f out: styd on fnl f* 25/1
32-0 6 shd **Prince Valentine**[13] 259 5-8-12 45....(be) TPQueally 6 45
(G L Moore) *chsd ldrs: rdn over 1f out: one pce after* 11/2[2]
-005 7 1 **Glenviews Oldport (USA)**[7] 311 4-8-11 45....(b) RobertWinston 4 43
(Peter Grayson) *mid-div: rdn and n.m.r ent fnl f: nt qckn* 6/1[3]
00-0 8 shd **Queue Up**[33] 92 4-8-11 45.... LPKeniry 5 43
(A G Newcombe) *led tl rdn and hdd over 1f out: sn wknd* 11/1
002- 9 1 3/4 **Halcyon Magic**[54] 6650 8-8-5 45....(b) StephanieBancroft(7) 3 40
(M Wigham) *trckd ldrs tl rdn and wknd 2f out* 12/1
00-0 10 2 **Piquet**[30] 113 8-8-12 45.... J-PGuillambert 7 37
(J J Bridger) *hld up: a in rr* 7/1
-305 11 shd **Super Dominion**[10] 290 9-8-12 45....(p) VinceSlattery 11 36
(R Hollinshead) *mid-div: wknd over 2f out* 12/1
6-60 12 3 1/2 **Rasid (USA)**[7] 311 8-8-12 45....(b[1]) SimonWhitworth 1 30
(C A Dwyer) *slowly away: racd wd: a in rr* 12/1
000- 13 2 1/2 **Little Gannet**[13] 5894 5-8-5 45.... JemmaMarshall(7) 9 26
(T D McCarthy) *racd wd: lost tch 4f out* 33/1

2m 9.29s (1.50) **Going Correction** +0.025s/f (Slow)
WFA 4 from 5yo+ 1lb 13 Ran SP% **124.0**
Speed ratings (Par 97):95,94,94,93,92 92,91,91,90,88 88,85,83
CSF £67.73 TOTE £11.10: £3.90, £1.90, £3.30; EX 93.50.
Owner Mrs P J Sheen **Bred** Wickfield Farm Partnership **Trained** Epsom, Surrey

FOCUS
A standard banded contest and a typically steady pace resulted in a winning time over four and a half seconds slower than the previous race. Despite that the form look solid enough on paper.

396 VISIT LITTLEWOODSPOKER.COM POKER SCHOOL MAIDEN CLAIMING STKS 6f (P)
3:10 (3:10) (Class 7) 3-Y-O+ £1,365 (£403; £201) Stalls Low

Form RPR
0-45 1 **Lauren Louise**[7] 307 4-9-2 47.... AdamKirby(3) 10 49+
(T T Clement) *hld up: gd hdwy over 1f out: r.o strly to ld ins fnl f* 3/1[1]
06-0 2 1 1/4 **Titus Wonder (IRE)**[10] 287 3-8-4 56.... JohnEgan 6 41
(P A Blockley) *stdd s: sn mid-div: hdwy to chse wnr wl ins fnl f: kpt on* 7/2[2]
05-0 3 1 1/2 **Cooleycall Star (IRE)**[20] 180 5-9-7 45....(p) J-PGuillambert 11 42
(A G Juckes) *bhd and racd wd: hdwy on outside turning into st: fin wl fnl f: nvr nrr* 9/1
005- 4 1/2 **Victoriana**[61] 6578 5-9-2 35....(p) NeilChalmers(3) 2 39
(H J Collingridge) *led tl rdn and hdd ins fnl f: no ex* 20/1
00-0 5 nk **Danethorpe Lady (IRE)**[14] 249 4-9-5 35.... FrankieMcDonald 1 38
(D Shaw) *in tch: chsd ldrs over 1f out: wknd ins fnl f* 66/1
0-44 6 1 1/2 **Sweet Cherokee**[7] 308 3-8-0 40 ow1.... EdwardCreighton(3) 12 29
(C N Kellett) *bhd tl mde sme late hdwy* 8/1[3]
030- 7 1 **Bennanabaa**[45] 6692 7-9-3 40....(tp) DonnaCaldwell(7) 8 36
(S C Burrough) *slowly away and wl in rr: effrt 2f out: nvr nr to chal* 10/1
03-0 8 nk **Silver Reign**[6] 321 5-9-10 40.... RobertWinston 3 35
(J J Bridger) *trckd ldr tl rdn and wknd ent fnl f* 8/1[3]
0-00 9 1 1/2 **Zambezi River**[31] 110 7-9-10 35.... GeorgeBaker 4 30
(J M Bradley) *t.k.h: hld up in tch: wknd ins fnl f* 25/1
0-00 10 3/4 **Caan**[18] 199 3-8-5 45.... JimmyQuinn 7 20
(D K Ivory) *mid-div: rdn and wknd over 1f out* 8/1[3]
3000 11 hd **Saxon Star (IRE)**[15] 239 3-8-9 45....(v) HayleyTurner 9 23
(M D I Usher) *racd wd: in tch tl wknd 2f out* 20/1
5-00 12 3 1/2 **Left Nostril (IRE)**[7] 308 3-8-4 45....(b[1]) AdrianMcCarthy 5 8
(P S McEntee) *prom tl rdn and wknd 2f out* 12/1

1m 13.13s (0.32) **Going Correction** +0.025s/f (Slow)
WFA 3 from 4yo+ 15lb 12 Ran SP% **122.2**
Speed ratings (Par 97):98,96,94,93,93 91,89,89,87,86 86,81
CSF £13.05 TOTE £3.90: £2.00, £1.20, £4.40; EX 10.70.
Owner John W Barnard **Bred** P D And Mrs Player **Trained** Newmarket, Suffolk

FOCUS
As is to be expected with maiden claimers, a very moderate race with the fifth limiting the form.

397 JOIN THE EPT WITH LITTLEWOODSPOKER.COM BANDED STKS 6f (P)
3:40 (3:40) (Class 7) 3-Y-O+ £1,365 (£403; £201) Stalls Low

Form RPR
-016 1 **Zazous**[5] 339 5-9-4 49.... J-PGuillambert 8 58
(J J Bridger) *trckd ldrs: rdn over 1f out: r.o wl to ld ins fnl f* 9/2[1]
5300 2 1/2 **Mirasol Princess**[7] 307 5-9-3 48.... DaneO'Neill 3 56
(D K Ivory) *wl in rr tl rdn and hdwy over 1f out: fin wl to chse wnr ins fnl f* 8/1
6-20 3 hd **Davids Mark**[10] 288 6-9-3 48.... JohnEgan 12 55
(J R Jenkins) *c over fr wd draw and sn ld rdn and hdd ins fnl f: no ex* 7/1
-301 4 1 **Shirley Oaks (IRE)**[12] 262 8-9-2 47.... AdrianMcCarthy 4 51
(Miss Z C Davison) *a in tch: r.o ins fnl f* 10/1
3553 5 3/4 **Park Star**[7] 307 6-9-0 45.... HayleyTurner 5 47
(D Shaw) *t.k.h: trckd ldr: fdd ins fnl f* 5/1[2]
00-0 6 nk **Noble Mount**[7] 307 5-9-2 47....(p) SamHitchcott 1 48
(A B Haynes) *a in tch: rdn and one pce fnl f* 16/1
54-0 7 hd **Dutch Key Card (IRE)**[34] 81 5-9-2 50.... RichardThomas(3) 7 50
(A W Carroll) *t.k.h: prom tl rdn appr fnl f* 6/1
4-66 8 1/2 **Beverley Beau**[7] 307 4-8-10 48.... KristinStubbs(7) 6 47
(Mrs L Stubbs) *a towards rr* 10/1
/0-0 9 hd **Chorus Beauty**[12] 268 5-9-2 50.... AdamKirby(3) 2 48
(N I M Rossiter) *a bhd* 33/1
-413 10 hd **Boanerges (IRE)**[13] 260 9-9-3 48.... RobertWinston 11 46
(J M Bradley) *in tch tl rdn and wknd appr fnl f* 11/2[3]
0-30 11 1 1/4 **Teyaar**[13] 260 10-9-0 45.... AlanDaly 10 39
(M Wellings) *racd wd: a bhd* 20/1
-060 12 5 **Jazz At The Sands (USA)**[6] 329 3-8-2 48....(v) FrankieMcDonald 9 27
(D Shaw) *plld hrd in rr: a bhd* 33/1

1m 12.79s (-0.02) **Going Correction** +0.025s/f (Slow)
WFA 3 from 4yo+ 15lb 12 Ran SP% **122.8**
Speed ratings (Par 97):101,100,100,98,97 97,97,96,96,95 94,87
CSF £41.30 TOTE £5.60: £2.00, £2.50, £2.80; EX 52.60.
Owner J J Bridger **Bred** Lordship Stud **Trained** Liphook, Hants

FOCUS
An ordinary banded sprint but the form looks solid enough.
Jazz At The Sands(USA) Official explanation: jockey said colt hung right-handed

398 JOIN THE WPT WITH LITTLEWOODSPOKER.COM BANDED STKS 7f (P)
4:10 (4:11) (Class 7) 4-Y-O+ £1,365 (£403; £201) Stalls Low

Form RPR
56-2 1 **Fulvio (USA)**[17] 210 6-9-1 49....(v) J-PGuillambert 8 57
(P Howling) *chsd ldrs: rdn to ld wl ins fnl f* 4/1[2]
0-55 2 1/2 **Cloann (IRE)**[12] 262 4-9-0 48....(b) StephenCarson 3 55
(E A Wheeler) *led on ins after 1f: drvn appr fnl f: hdd wl ins* 14/1
00-0 3 1 1/2 **Mister Aziz (IRE)**[9] 293 4-8-11 45....(v) RobertHavlin 14 48
(J R Jenkins) *hld up in rr: hdwy 2f out: kpt on one pce fnl f* 50/1
5-00 4 1 **Wiltshire (IRE)**[9] 297 4-9-2 50....(v) HayleyTurner 1 51
(P A Blockley) *bhd: reminders bef 1/2-way: picked up and mde hdwy to fin fast fnl f* 12/1
0-00 5 hd **Edge Fund**[9] 297 4-8-12 49....(v) AdamKirby(3) 6 49
(Miss Gay Kelleway) *chsd ldrs: rdn 2f out: one pce fnl f* 20/1
-550 6 hd **Temper Tantrum**[19] 187 8-8-10 49....(p) TravisBlock(5) 11 49
(J R Best) *hld up: effrt 2f out: one pce after* 12/1
5-20 7 1/2 **Aintnecessarilyso**[13] 261 8-8-11 45....(p) TPQueally 12 43
(J M Bradley) *plld hrd in rr: mde sme late hdwy* 33/1
5003 8 3/4 **Pheckless**[5] 339 7-8-12 46.... JohnEgan 9 42
(J M Bradley) *slowly away: hdwy 1/2-way: one pce ins fnl 2f* 2/1[1]
01-0 9 1/2 **Riviera Red (IRE)**[7] 310 6-8-13 47....(v) RobertWinston 7 42
(L Montague Hall) *in rr and nvr nr to chal* 12/1
44-6 10 1 **Tennessee Belle (IRE)**[14] 255 4-8-11 45....(e) OscarUrbina 2 38
(C N Allen) *mid-div tl lost pce 2f out and sn bhd* 25/1
00-5 11 1/2 **Big Mystery (IRE)**[7] 312 5-8-11 45....(be) NickyMackay 10 36
(S C Williams) *hdwy and rdn 2f out: sn btn* 14/1
20-6 12 2 1/2 **Escobar (POL)**[7] 310 5-9-1 49.... DaneO'Neill 4 34
(Mrs P Townsley) *led for 1f: rdn and wknd wl over 1f out* 11/2[3]
-635 13 1 1/4 **Old Bailey (USA)**[8] 300 6-9-0 48....(be) GeorgeBaker 5 30
(G L Moore) *trckd ldrs tl wknd qckly 2f out* 10/1
/10- 14 1/2 **Homebred Star**[61] 6574 5-8-8 47.... RobynBrisland(5) 13 28
(G P Enright) *hld up on outside: a bhd* 20/1

1m 25.2s (-0.69) **Going Correction** +0.025s/f (Slow) 14 Ran SP% **132.5**
Speed ratings (Par 97):104,103,101,100,100 100,99,98,98,96 96,93,92,91
CSF £61.54 TOTE £5.40: £2.10, £3.10, £16.80; EX 86.20.
Owner J L Guillambert **Bred** G G Campbell **Trained** Newmarket, Suffolk

FOCUS
A standard banded contest that should prove reliable enough.

399 LITTLEWOODSPOKER.COM - THE TRUSTED NAME IN GAMING BANDED STKS 1m (P)
4:40 (4:41) (Class 7) 4-Y-O+ £1,365 (£403; £201) Stalls High

Form RPR
3-33 1 **Mr Belvedere**[7] 312 5-8-8 45....(p) RichardThomas(3) 1 51
(A J Lidderdale) *mde all: rdn clr 1f out and in command after* 9/2[2]
0562 2 1 1/2 **Dexileos (IRE)**[7] 312 7-8-11 45....(t) HayleyTurner 12 48
(David Pinder) *chsd wnr thrght: no imp fnl f* 9/1
004- 3 shd **Majehar**[47] 6679 4-8-11 45.... DaneO'Neill 11 47
(A G Newcombe) *hld up: hdwy over 1f out: fin wl: nvr nrr* 5/1[3]
4 4 1/2 **Tod Sloan (IRE)**[9] 293 4-8-11 45.... RobertWinston 4 46
(J M Bradley) *a in tch: rdn over 1f out: kpt on fnl f* 7/1
-341 5 shd **Young Kate**[7] 312 5-9-3 45.... JimmyQuinn 8 52
(J R Best) *chsd ldrs: rdn 2f out: kpt on one pce fnl f* 5/1[3]
6653 6 1 **Musiotal**[7] 315 5-8-11 45....(p) JohnEgan 10 44
(P A Blockley) *in rr tl rdn and mde sme late hdwy* 3/1[1]
4-00 7 shd **Margaret's Dream (IRE)**[7] 312 5-8-11 45.... TPQueally 3 44
(D Carroll) *chsd ldrs rdn and wknd ins fnl f* 14/1
0-60 8 2 1/2 **Blaenavon**[7] 311 4-8-8 45.... EdwardCreighton(3) 2 38
(D W P Arbuthnot) *t.k.h in rr: nvr nr to chal* 33/1
5-54 9 1 3/4 **Spanish Music**[9] 293 4-8-11 45....(t) RobertHavlin 5 34
(R Ingram) *a in rr* 12/1
00-0 10 nk **Coronado Forest (USA)**[7] 312 7-8-11 45.... SimonWhitworth 6 34
(M R Hoad) *in rr whn hmpd over 4f out: nvr on terms after* 20/1
1-04 11 1 1/4 **Soul Provider (IRE)**[7] 312 5-8-11 45.... J-PGuillambert 9 31
(G Prodromou) *bhd tl hdwy over 3f out: sn rdn wknd over 1f out* 20/1
0-50 P **In A Fit**[1] 387 5-8-11 45.... OscarUrbina 7 —
(P Howling) *mid-div tl lost pce qckly 2f out: p.u over 1f out: lame* 20/1

1m 39.74s (0.31) **Going Correction** +0.025s/f (Slow) 12 Ran SP% **130.6**
Speed ratings (Par 97):99,97,97,96,96 95,95,93,91,91 89,—
CSF £47.15 TOTE £7.70: £1.70, £7.70, £1.90; EX 47.40 Place 6 £149.28, Place 5 £118.05.
Owner Entertainments Committee **Bred** Elaine Edwards And Mrs P Gulliver And Paddy O'Con **Trained** Eastbury, Berks

FOCUS
Just an ordinary banded contest with the first two up with the pace throughout.
T/Plt: £71.50 to a £1 stake. Pool: £40,316.90. 411.45 winning tickets. T/Qpdt: £36.80 to a £1 stake. Pool: £2,615.40. 52.50 winning tickets. JS

380 WOLVERHAMPTON (A.W) (L-H)
Monday, February 13

OFFICIAL GOING: Standard
Wind: Light, half-behind Weather: Overcast

400 PLAY LITTLEWOODS POOLS ON 0800 500 000 H'CAP (DIV I) 7f 32y(P)
1:50 (1:50) (Class 6) (0-52,54) 4-Y-O+ £2,047 (£604; £302) Stalls High

Form RPR
-611 1 **Desert Lover (IRE)**[4] 350 4-9-0 **54** 6ex.... ShaneKelly 6 64
(R J Price) *a.p: rdn to ld ins fnl f: r.o* 11/4[1]
10-0 2 1/2 **Joe Jo Star**[28] 121 4-8-7 **47** oh1 ow1....(p) RobbieFitzpatrick 7 56
(B P J Baugh) *a.p: rdn over 3f out: r.o ins fnl f* 28/1

22-1 **3** 1 **Beneking**[21] 178 6-8-12 **52**....(p) ChrisCatlin 8 58
(D Burchell) *sn chsng ldr: led 2f out: sn rdn: hdd and nt qckn ins fnl f* **11/4**[1]
3-00 **4** 1 ½ **Blushing Russian (IRE)**[25] 143 4-8-3 **48** ow1.... GregFairley(5) 9 51
(J M Bradley) *hld up in mid-div: hdwy over 3f out: rdn over 2f out: one pce fnl f* **12/1**
6-31 **5** nk **Desert Light (IRE)**[10] 288 5-8-8 **51**....(v) PatrickMathers(3) 10 53
(D Shaw) *hld up and bhd: rdn over 2f out: hdwy fnl f: nvr nrr* **9/1**[3]
4203 **6** shd **Prince Of Gold**[4] 350 6-8-12 **52**....(b) GrahamGibbons 4 54
(R Hollinshead) *s.i.s: bhd: rdn over 4f out: hdwy over 1f out: nt rch ldrs* **3/1**[2]
0-00 **7** ½ **Revien (IRE)**[28] 119 4-8-12 **52**.... PaulFitzsimons 1 52
(Miss J R Tooth) *led early: hld up in tch: rdn and no real prog fnl 2f* **25/1**
000- **8** 3 **Indian Gem**[135] 5618 5-8-6 **46** oh1.... DeanMcKeown 3 39
(A J Chamberlain) *sn led: rdn and hdd 2f out: wknd fnl f* **40/1**
210- **9** 3 **Colloseum**[91] 6346 5-8-8 **48**.... TomEaves 2 33
(T J Etherington) *rdn over 4f out: a bhd* **9/1**[3]
0/5- **10** 3 **Candy Anchor (FR)**[371] 309 7-8-6 **46** oh6.... AdrianTNicholls 5 24
(R E Peacock) *rdn 4f out: a bhd* **100/1**

1m 29.54s (-0.86) **Going Correction** -0.10s/f (Stan) **10** Ran SP% **116.7**
Speed ratings (Par 101):100,99,98,96,96 96,95,92,88,85
CSF £84.90 CT £233.33 TOTE £2.90: £1.10, £13.20, £1.30; EX 62.10.
Owner Multi Lines Partnership **Bred** Penfold Bloodstock And Mr D B Clark **Trained** Ullingswick, H'fords

FOCUS
A moderate handicap but the winner is on the upgrade and the form appears reasonable.

401 PLAY £1/4M SPOT THE BALL ON 0800 500 000 H'CAP 5f 20y(P)
2:20 (2:22) (Class 6) (0-58,58) 4-Y-0+ **£2,388** (£705; £352) **Stalls** Low

Form RPR
0-11 **1** **Henry Tun**[3] 360 8-9-2 **58** 6ex....(b) JasonEdmunds(3) 4 65
(J Balding) *a.p: rdn and edgd lft ins fnl f: led last strides* **10/1**
-221 **2** shd **Byo (IRE)**[8] 299 8-9-3 **56** 6ex.... TonyCulhane 5 63
(P Howling) *led early: a.p: rdn over 2f out: led jst over 1f out: hdd last strides* **10/1**
-432 **3** 1 **Taboor (IRE)**[7] 317 8-8-13 **52**.... EddieAhern 13 55
(R M H Cowell) *hld up and bhd: swtchd lft sn after s: hdwy fnl f: fin wl* **15/2**
2-05 **4** nk **Blythe Spirit**[7] 320 7-8-13 **52**....(t) PaulHanagan 1 54
(R A Fahey) *hld up in mid-div: rdn and hdwy on ins over 2f out: nt clr run over 1f out: kpt on towards fin* **4/1**[1]
0-56 **5** shd **Edged In Gold**[3] 360 4-9-2 **55**....(e[1]) FergusSweeney 7 57
(P J Makin) *t.k.h in tch: rdn wl over 1f out: kpt on ins fnl f* **20/1**
-060 **6** ½ **He's A Rocket (IRE)**[7] 320 5-9-2 **55**....(b) FrancisNorton 6 55
(K R Burke) *sn led: rdn and hdd jst over 1f out: no ex ins fnl f* **8/1**
0-00 **7** nk **Count Cougar (USA)**[7] 317 6-9-2 **55**.... DaleGibson 11 54
(S P Griffiths) *uns rdr and bolted bef s: prom: rdn over 2f out: no ex ins fnl f* **50/1**
-615 **8** nk **Lady Hopeful (IRE)**[10] 288 4-9-1 **54**....(b) RobbieFitzpatrick 3 52
(Peter Grayson) *hmpd s: hld up and bhd: hdwy over 2f out: kpt on ins fnl f* **7/1**[3]
40-0 **9** hd **Madrasee**[12] 265 8-8-13 **55**.... AmirQuinn(3) 8 52
(P G Murphy) *nvr nrr* **40/1**
3-16 **10** nk **Blue Moon Hitman (IRE)**[7] 317 5-9-0 **53**....(b) TomEaves 2 49
(R Brotherton) *hld up in mid-div: rdn 2f out: swtchd lft over 1f out: no hdwy* **11/2**[2]
-323 **11** 1 ½ **Nova Tor (IRE)**[7] 320 4-8-13 **52**....(b) GylesParkin 10 42
(Peter Grayson) *s.i.s: hld up and bhd: sn swtchd lft: no imp whn nt clr run on ins over 1f out* **9/1**
0-01 **12** ½ **Monte Major (IRE)**[7] 317 5-8-13 **55** 6ex....(v) PatrickMathers(3) 9 44
(D Shaw) *a bhd* **11/1**
60/0 **13** 12 **Galloway Boy (IRE)**[12] 262 9-9-2 **55**.... AdrianTNicholls 12 —
(J F Panvert) *chsd ldrs: rdn over 3f out: wknd over 2f out* **100/1**

62.30 secs (-0.52) **Going Correction** -0.10s/f (Stan) **13** Ran SP% **117.4**
Speed ratings (Par 101):100,99,98,97,97 96,96,95,95,95 92,91,72
CSF £101.69 CT £822.85 TOTE £15.80: £3.60, £2.50, £1.70; EX 31.10.
Owner Terry Reffell **Bred** T Tunstall **Trained** Scrooby, Notts
■ Stewards' Enquiry : Tom Eaves one-day ban: careless riding (Feb 24)

FOCUS
A moderate contest but the first two are in decent form at present and the form looks solid enough.
Blue Moon Hitman(IRE) Official explanation: jockey said gelding missed the break

402 LITTLEWOODS 3 JACKPOTS (S) STKS 5f 216y(P)
2:50 (2:52) (Class 6) 3-Y-0+ **£2,388** (£705; £352) **Stalls** Low

Form RPR
55-0 **1** **Million Percent**[6] 323 7-8-13 67.... AndrewElliott(7) 11 67
(K R Burke) *hld up in mid-div: hdwy on outside 3f out: rdn wl over 1f out: r.o to ld wl ins fnl f* **5/2**[2]
00-0 **2** ½ **Riquewihr**[7] 315 6-9-1 54.... TonyCulhane 3 61
(P Howling) *hld up in mid-div: hdwy on ins 2f out: sn rdn: ev ch whn n.m.r briefly ins fnl f: r.o* **18/1**
1-32 **3** hd **Tiviski (IRE)**[14] 255 4-9-6 57.... GrahamGibbons 13 65
(E J Alston) *a.p: rdn over 2f out: led ins fnl f: sn hdd: nt qckn* **8/1**
3241 **4** 1 ¼ **Magic Amour**[7] 315 8-9-4 64....(b) KevinGhunowa(7) 5 66
(P A Blockley) *a.p: led over 3f out: rdn over 1f out: hdd ins fnl f: no ex* **7/4**[1]
4-00 **5** 2 ½ **Smokincanon**[6] 321 4-9-1 57.... MarcHalford(5) 6 54
(W G M Turner) *hld up in mid-div: hdwy over 2f out: wknd jst over 1f out* **20/1**
00-6 **6** 2 **Ladies Knight**[7] 320 6-9-3 53.... PatrickMathers(3) 4 48
(D Shaw) *s.i.s: hdwy fnl f: nvr nrr* **12/1**
0-50 **7** 1 ¼ **Transaction (IRE)**[16] 232 4-9-6 52.... NCallan 10 44
(J M P Eustace) *bhd: rdn and hdwy over 2f out: wknd over 1f out* **6/1**[3]
-044 **8** hd **Flying Dancer**[1] 388 4-8-8 40.... TolleyDean(7) 8 38
(R A Harris) *bhd: reminder 4f out: hrd rdn 3f out: nvr nr ldrs* **40/1**
066- **9** 2 **Urban Calm**[61] 6580 5-9-1 40.... BrianReilly 7 32
(J W Unett) *chsd ldrs: lost pl over 3f out: short-lived effrt on outside over 2f out* **50/1**
5000 **10** 7 **Party Princess (IRE)**[10] 288 5-9-1 45.... DeanMcKeown 9 11
(S Parr) *broke wl: led over 2f: wknd wl over 1f out* **33/1**
-600 **11** 6 **King Marrakech (IRE)**[25] 145 4-9-11 40....(b[1]) RobbieFitzpatrick 2 3
(B P J Baugh) *bhd: nt clr run on ins over 2f out and wl over 1f out: sn eased* **66/1**
500- **12** 9 **Victimised (IRE)**[319] 809 4-9-6 40.... ShaneKelly 1 —
(R J Price) *prom tl rdn and wknd over 2f out: eased over 1f out* **33/1**

1m 15.35s (-0.46) **Going Correction** -0.10s/f (Stan)
WFA 3 from 4yo+ 15lb **12** Ran SP% **119.8**
Speed ratings (Par 101):99,98,98,96,93 90,88,88,85,76 68,56
CSF £43.01 TOTE £3.10: £1.10, £4.20, £2.10; EX 66.90.The winner was bought in for 6,500gns. Riquewihr was claimed by J. S. Wainwright for £6,000. Tiviski (IRE) was claimed by G. Margarson for £6,000
Owner Champagne Racing **Bred** D J And Mrs Deer **Trained** Middleham Moor, N Yorks
■ Stewards' Enquiry : Andrew Elliott caution: careless riding

FOCUS
This was run at a decent clip but the form is just average for the level.
King Marrakech(IRE) Official explanation: jockey said gelding suffered interference in running
Victimised(IRE) Official explanation: jockey said gelding hung right

403 PLAY LITTLEWOODS POOLS ON 0800 500 000 MAIDEN STKS 1m 4f 50y(P)
3:20 (3:21) (Class 5) 3-Y-0+ **£3,238** (£963; £481; £240) **Stalls** Low

Form RPR
1 **Magic Moth** 3-8-3.... JoeFanning 5 68+
(M Johnston) *rn green: sn led: hung rt bnd 7f out and bnd wl over 1f out: sn rdn: styd on wl* **15/8**[2]
6-30 **2** 1 **Opera Comica**[19] 188 3-7-12 66.... DaleGibson 2 59
(J H M Gosden) *hld up in mid-div: hdwy 4f out: rdn over 2f out: kpt on ins fnl f* **8/1**
64 **3** 1 ¼ **Discord**[10] 289 5-9-13.... PaulHanagan 1 63
(T H Caldwell) *chsd ldrs: rdn 3f out: nt qckn wl ins fnl f* **25/1**
2 **4** shd **Glentaisie (USA)**[17] 215 3-7-12.... JamieMackay 8 57
(J Noseda) *hld up in mid-div: hdwy over 4f out: rdn and ev ch over 2f out: nt qckn fnl f* **6/4**[1]
04-4 **5** 2 **Merchant Bankes**[19] 188 3-7-12 71.... MarcHalford(5) 11 59
(W G M Turner) *plld hrd towards rr: hdwy over 3f out: ev ch over 2f out: sn rdn: wknd over 1f out* **13/2**[3]
0-5 **6** 4 **Being There**[37] 62 3-8-1 ow1.... NelsonDeSouza(3) 12 54
(P F I Cole) *hld up and bhd: hdwy on outside over 3f out: no further prog fnl 2f* **20/1**
600- **7** 1 ½ **Mustakhlas (USA)**[54] 6650 5-9-6 35.... SoniaEaton(7) 6 52?
(B P J Baugh) *hld up in tch: wknd wl over 1f out* **125/1**
8 1 **Khadija**[83] 5-9-8.... TonyCulhane 10 45
(R Dickin) *dwlt: nvr nr ldrs* **66/1**
0-00 **9** 3 ½ **Legend Of Dance**[3] 361 4-8-12 40.... JamesDoyle(7) 3 40
(J L Spearing) *led early: lost pl after 2f: bhd fnl 6f* **66/1**
6-0 **10** 3 ½ **Hilversum**[10] 289 4-8-12.... DawnRankin(7) 7 35
(Miss J A Camacho) *a bhd* **66/1**
000 **11** 21 **Beginners Luck (IRE)**[5] 337 3-7-5 40....(v[1]) DanielleMcCreery(7) 4 —
(D Carroll) *hld up in mid-div: hdwy over 7f out: wknd 4f out: t.o* **100/1**
12 dist **Son Of Samson (IRE)**[23] 5-9-13....(t) ShaneKelly 9 —
(R J Price) *dwlt: hdwy to join wnr after 2f: wknd over 4f out: t.o* **66/1**

2m 41.4s (-1.02) **Going Correction** -0.10s/f (Stan)
WFA 3 from 4yo 24lb 4 from 5yo 3lb **12** Ran SP% **115.6**
Speed ratings (Par 103):99,98,97,97,96 93,92,91,89,87 73,—
CSF £15.80 TOTE £3.20: £1.40, £2.20, £3.20; EX 21.20.
Owner Mrs R J Jacobs **Bred** Newsells Park Stud Limited **Trained** Middleham Moor, N Yorks

FOCUS
A modest maiden but a promising performance from the winner although there was not much strength in depth.
Son Of Samson(IRE) Official explanation: jockey said gelding stopped quickly and he felt there was a problem

404 BE LUCKY AT LITTLEWOODS.CO.UK APPRENTICE H'CAP 1m 1f 103y(P)
3:50 (3:51) (Class 4) (0-85,85) 4-Y-0+ **£5,505** (£1,637; £818; £408) **Stalls** Low

Form RPR
-211 **1** **Newnham (IRE)**[14] 250 5-7-13 **71**.... WilliamCarson(5) 5 77
(J R Boyle) *hld up and bhd: hdwy on outside 2f out: r.o to ld wl ins fnl f* **9/4**[1]
/1-0 **2** ¾ **Ground Rules (USA)**[12] 267 4-8-2 **74**.... JosephWalsh(5) 1 79
(V Smith) *led: clr 6f out: rdn over 2f out: hdd and no ex wl ins fnl f* **20/1**
1112 **3** hd **Kindlelight Debut**[12] 267 6-8-6 **80**.... SophieDoyle(7) 6 85
(N P Littmoden) *hld up: hdwy over 2f out: nt qckn ins fnl f* **6/1**[3]
15-0 **4** 1 ¼ **St Savarin (FR)**[16] 221 5-8-9 **76**.... JamesMillman 4 78
(R A Fahey) *towards rr: rdn and edgd lft fr over 1f out: styd on ins fnl f* **12/1**
154- **5** 2 ½ **Zamboozle (IRE)**[204] 3772 4-8-7 **74** ow1.... RonanKeogh 2 72
(D R C Elsworth) *rrd and s.v.s: hld up in rr: nt clr run on ins over 2f out: nvr trbld ldrs* **7/2**[2]
-042 **6** 2 **Atlantic Quest (USA)**[24] 161 7-9-0 **84**....(p) TolleyDean(3) 7 78
(R A Harris) *a.p: chsd wnr 3f out: sn rdn: wknd fnl f* **7/2**[2]
043- **7** nk **Ermine Grey**[34] 3843 5-8-4 **78**.... JackDean(7) 8 71
(A W Carroll) *plld hrd: sn prom: rdn over 2f out: wknd over 1f out* **14/1**
20-0 **8** 4 **Habanero**[6] 325 5-9-4 **85**.... ThomasO'Brien 3 71
(Miss S J Wilton) *chsd ldr tl rdn 3f out: sn wknd* **20/1**

2m 1.18s (-1.44) **Going Correction** -0.10s/f (Stan) **8** Ran SP% **113.4**
Speed ratings (Par 105):102,101,101,100,97 96,95,92
CSF £48.91 CT £236.40 TOTE £2.80: £1.50, £3.10, £2.00; EX 37.30.
Owner M Khan X2 **Bred** Ballygallon Stud **Trained** Epsom, Surrey

FOCUS
This fair handicap was run at a good pace and the form should prove reliable enough.
Zamboozle(IRE) Official explanation: jockey said colt reared as the stalls opened and missed the break

405 WIN £2M AT CLASSICVALUEPOOLS.COM H'CAP 1m 1f 103y(P)
4:20 (4:20) (Class 6) (0-65,65) 4-Y-0+ **£2,388** (£705; £352) **Stalls** Low

Form RPR
201- **1** **Merrymadcap (IRE)**[140] 5506 4-9-1 **62**.... FrancisNorton 2 75+
(M Blanshard) *hld up and bhd: hdwy 2f out: rdn over 1f out: edgd lft and led wl ins fnl f: r.o wl* **16/1**
0-52 **2** 1 ¾ **Jakarmi**[18] 200 5-9-2 **63**.... FrancisFerris 10 73
(B Palling) *led: rdn over 2f out: edgd rt and hdd wl ins fnl f: no ex* **14/1**
-030 **3** hd **Buscador (USA)**[6] 324 7-8-3 **57**.... LiamJones(7) 11 67
(W M Brisbourne) *chsd ldr and wnt lft after 1f: rdn over 3f out: cl 3rd whn n.m.r wl ins fnl f: nt qckn* **25/1**
102 **4** 3 ½ **Devil's Island**[6] 324 4-8-13 **60**.... JamieMackay 4 63
(Sir Mark Prescott) *hld up in mid-div: hdwy on ins over 2f out: rdn and edgd lft 1f out: one pce* **15/8**[1]
2135 **5** ½ **Augustine**[6] 324 5-8-12 **59**.... JoeFanning 7 61
(P W Hiatt) *hmpd and lost pl after 1f: rdn and hdwy over 1f out: one pce fnl f* **4/1**[2]

05-0 **6** *nk* **Sorbiesharry (IRE)**42 15 7-8-8 **60**....................(p) DuranFentiman(5) 3 62
(Mrs N Macauley) *hld up towards rr: rdn and hdwy on ins over 1f out: no imp fnl f* **9/1**
-266 **7** *1* **Seattle Robber**10 285 4-8-11 **58**....................(v) FergalLynch 1 58
(P A Blockley) *nrst fin* **9/1**
4-30 **8** *3/4* **Iberus (GER)**19 187 8-8-13 **60**....................(p) NCallan 6 58
(S Gollings) *hld up towards rr: hdwy 3f out: rdn and wknd over 1f out* **20/1**
5-44 **9** *2* **Schinken Otto (IRE)**15 242 5-7-13 **51** oh6.............. AndrewMullen(5) 8 46
(J M Jefferson) *hld up in mid-div: rdn over 2f out: c wd st: sn bhd* **20/1**
0-54 **10** *1 1/4* **Kirkhammerton (IRE)**6 334 4-8-8 **55**....................(v) DeanMcKeown 13 47
(M J Polglase) *prom tl rdn and wknd over 2f out* **25/1**
-004 **11** *1/2* **Corky (IRE)**7 319 5-9-4 **65**.............................. PaulHanagan 9 57
(I W McInnes) *a bhd* **7/1**3
00P- **12** *1* **Cavan Gael (FR)**89 6372 4-8-13 **60**.............................. ShaneKelly 5 50
(P Howling) *prom: rdn over 2f out: wknd wl over 1f out* **66/1**
40-0 **13** *13* **Rock Haven (IRE)**24 162 4-8-11 **58**....................(p) DaleGibson 12 24
(J Mackie) *hld up in tch: wknd wl over 2f out* **40/1**

2m 0.31s (-2.31) **Going Correction** -0.10s/f (Stan) **13** Ran SP% **121.0**
Speed ratings (Par 101):106,104,104,101,100 100,99,98,97,96 95,94,83
CSF £203.62 CT £5491.02 TOTE £17.10: £7.10, £5.50, £11.70; EX 93.60.
Owner Mrs N L Young **Bred** Wickfield Farm Partnership **Trained** Upper Lambourn, Berks
■ Stewards' Enquiry : Liam Jones two-day ban: not riding to draw and careless riding (Feb 24-25)
Francis Ferris two-day ban: not riding to draw and careless riding (Feb 24-25); caution: further instance of careless riding

FOCUS
A modest contest but the runner-up set a decent pace and along with the third helps set a solid standard for the form.

406 WIN £2M WITH LITTLEWOODS POOLS H'CAP 1m 141y(P)
4:50 (4:50) (Class 5) (0-70,70) 3-Y-0 **£3,238** (£963; £481; £240) **Stalls** Low

Form RPR
002- **1** **Mystified (IRE)**56 6617 3-8-9 **64**....................(b) DNolan(3) 3 65
(R F Fisher) *led after 1f: rdn over 2f out: edgd rt ins fnl f: drvn out* **8/1**
060- **2** *1 1/2* **Hand Of Destiny (USA)**49 6661 3-7-12 **57**.............. JamesDoyle(7) 2 55
(N P Littmoden) *a.p: rdn 3f out: chsd wnr over 1f out: nt qckn ins fnl f* **10/1**
06-2 **3** *hd* **Princess Society (IRE)**9 293 3-9-1 **67**.............. PaulHanagan 7 64
(E A L Dunlop) *hld up: rdn and hdwy over 3f out: styd on towards fin* **5/4**1
40-3 **4** *1/2* **Stellenbosch (USA)**26 142 3-9-4 **70**.............. EddieAhern 6 66
(J W Hills) *hld up: rdn over 2f out: hdwy over 1f out: kpt on ins fnl f* **5/1**3
0-11 **5** *hd* **Petrichan (IRE)**18 193 3-9-0 **66**....................(p) NCallan 8 62
(K A Ryan) *led 1f: chsd wnr: rdn and ev ch 2f out: edgd rt 1f out: one pce* **7/2**2
0-00 **6** *6* **Galaxy Bound (IRE)**5 342 3-8-7 **62**.............. PatrickMathers(3) 1 45
(D Shaw) *hld up: nt clr run on ins over 2f out: nvr nr ldrs* **40/1**
132- **7** *2 1/2* **Solo Star**226 3114 3-8-6 **58** ow1.............................. TomEaves 5 36
(Miss J A Camacho) *prom: rdn and carried hd awkwardly over 3f out: sn wknd* **40/1**
063- **8** *9* **Divisive**94 6313 3-8-4 **56** oh2.............................. FrancisNorton 4 14
(M Blanshard) *pushed along over 5f out: a bhd* **25/1**

1m 51.18s (-0.58) **Going Correction** -0.10s/f (Stan) **8** Ran SP% **112.3**
Speed ratings (Par 97):98,96,96,96,95 90,88,80
CSF £78.15 CT £165.72 TOTE £6.70: £1.70, £1.90, £1.10; EX 113.40.
Owner A D Stoker **Bred** Denis And Mrs Teresa Bergin **Trained** Ulverston, Cumbria

FOCUS
A weak race and not strong form-wise.

407 PLAY LITTLEWOODS POOLS ON 0800 500 000 H'CAP (DIV II) 7f 32y(P)
5:20 (5:20) (Class 6) (0-52,52) 4-Y-0+ **£2,047** (£604; £302) **Stalls** High

Form RPR
0-44 **1** **Spark Up**10 290 6-8-12 **52**....................(b) ShaneKelly 10 61
(J W Unett) *hld up: hdwy over 4f out: rdn to ld wl over 1f out: drvn out* **9/4**1
4-02 **2** *1 1/4* **Bodden Bay**5 339 4-8-9 **52**.............. DanielTudhope(3) 7 58
(D Carroll) *a.p: rdn and edgd lft jst over 1f out: kpt on ins fnl f* **5/2**2
52-0 **3** *hd* **Blue Maeve**17 209 6-8-12 **52**.............. EddieAhern 9 57
(A D Brown) *a.p: led over 4f out: rdn and hdd wl over 1f out: nt qckn ins fnl f* **12/1**
2526 **4** *1 1/4* **Jalouhar**10 288 6-8-0 **47**.............. SoniaEaton(7) 1 50+
(B P J Baugh) *hmpd and lost pl on ins bnd after 1f: hld up: hdwy whn nt clr run on ins wl over 1f out: r.o ins fnl f* **10/3**3
4000 **5** *3/4* **Lakeside Guy (IRE)**2 382 5-7-13 **46** oh6....................(t) LiamJones(7) 6 46
(M Appleby) *s.i.s: hld up: hdwy over 3f out: ev ch over 2f out: rdn and edgd lft over 1f out: one pce* **12/1**
6-00 **6** *hd* **Bint Royal (IRE)**4 350 8-8-7 **47** ow1.............. RobbieFitzpatrick 2 47
(Miss V Haigh) *prom: lost pl 3f out: sn rdn: edgd lft 1f out: no imp* **16/1**
000- **7** *4* **Lord Conyers (IRE)**151 5246 7-8-6 **46** oh6.............. JamieMackay 4 36
(G Woodward) *led over 2f: prom tl wknd over 1f out* **20/1**
200- **8** *8* **Speedie Rossini (IRE)**245 2540 4-8-9 **49**....................(b) PaulFitzsimons 3 19
(Miss J R Tooth) *hld up in tch: lost pl over 3f out: sn bhd* **40/1**
0-00 **9** *5* **Eskimo's Nest**7 311 4-8-4 **47** oh1 ow1....................(v) PatrickMathers(3) 5 4
(D Shaw) *s.i.s: rdn over 2f out: a bhd* **20/1**

1m 29.76s (-0.64) **Going Correction** -0.10s/f (Stan) **36** Ran SP% **115.6**
Speed ratings (Par 101):99,97,97,95,95 94,90,81,75
CSF £7.84 CT £52.84 TOTE £3.70: £1.80, £1.40, £2.00; EX 8.90 Place 6 £2,039.35, Place 5 £1,159.20.
Owner Winning Formula Partnership **Bred** Cheveley Park Stud Ltd **Trained** Preston, Shropshire
■ Stewards' Enquiry : Jamie Mackay one-day ban: careless riding (Feb 24)

FOCUS
A moderate event but sound enough form.
T/Plt: £160.70 to a £1 stake. Pool: £40,276.55. 182.95 winning tickets. T/Qpdt: £62.70 to a £1 stake. Pool: £3,121.40. 36.80 winning tickets. KH

386SOUTHWELL (L-H)
Tuesday, February 14

OFFICIAL GOING: Standard
Wind: Light, across Weather: Overcast

408 BETDIRECT ON SKY ACTIVE H'CAP (DIV I) 6f (F)
1:30 (1:30) (Class 6) (0-55,55) 4-Y-0+ **£2,047** (£604; £302) **Stalls** Low

Form RPR
1025 **1** **Soba Jones**12 274 9-8-11 **55**.............. JasonEdmunds(3) 5 69
(J Balding) *chsd ldrs: led over 1f out: r.o* **9/2**
6005 **2** *1 3/4* **Piccolo Prince**8 315 5-8-4 **52**.............. JamesDoyle(7) 4 60
(E J Alston) *s.i.s: hdwy over 2f out: rdn and ev ch over 1f out: unable qck ins fnl f* **7/2**2
-100 **3** *1 3/4* **Straffan (IRE)**15 249 4-8-5 **46** oh1....................(b) DaleGibson 8 49
(J Hetherton) *w ldr: rdn and ev ch over 1f out: styd on same pce fnl f* **20/1**
-500 **4** *1* **Massey**11 288 10-8-2 **48**.............. AndrewMullen(5) 3 48
(C R Dore) *led over 4f: no ex ins fnl f* **50/1**
00-2 **5** *hd* **Imperium**35 81 5-8-13 **54**....................(p) EddieAhern 6 53
(Stef Liddiard) *hld up: rdn 1/2-way: edgd lft over 1f out: styd on ins fnl f: nrst fin* **10/3**1
-440 **6** *1 1/4* **A Teen**13 265 8-8-5 **46** oh6.............. AdrianTNicholls 1 42
(P Howling) *chsd ldrs: rdn and ev ch over 1f out: wknd fnl f* **40/1**
0-60 **7** *1* **Siraj**6 336 7-8-13 **54**....................(p) NCallan 11 47
(J Ryan) *prom over 4f* **4/1**3
0-00 **8** *3/4* **Marshallspark (IRE)**11 288 7-8-9 **50**....................(p) PaulHanagan 7 40
(R A Fahey) *prom over 3f* **18/1**
0423 **9** *nk* **Mind Alert**8 317 5-8-11 **55**....................(v) PatrickMathers(3) 10 45
(D Shaw) *s.i.s: sn trcking ldrs: rdn and wknd 2f out* **7/1**
-000 **10** *7* **Legal Set (IRE)**8 317 10-8-3 **51** oh1 ow5....................(bt) AnnStokell(7) 9 20
(Miss A Stokell) *prom: rdn and hung rt over 3f out: sn wknd* **50/1**

1m 16.76s (-0.14) **Going Correction** -0.175s/f (Stan) **10** Ran SP% **112.4**
Speed ratings (Par 101):93,90,88,87,86 85,83,82,82,73
CSF £19.16 CT £278.05 TOTE £6.40: £2.10, £1.70, £3.90; EX 32.50.
Owner R L Crowe **Bred** Mrs M J Hills **Trained** Scrooby, Notts

FOCUS
The winner continued the good form of trainer John Balding's horses. The runner-up had a smart 7lb claimer aboard and showed a return to form and the form shoudl prove reasonable.

409 HAPPY VALENTINES FROM BETDIRECT.CO.UK MAIDEN STKS 1m (F)
2:00 (2:02) (Class 5) 3-Y-0+ **£3,238** (£963; £481; £240) **Stalls** Low

Form RPR
25-0 **1** **Al Rayanah**41 30 3-8-2 56.............. ChrisCatlin 7 61
(G Prodromou) *dwlt: hdwy 6f out: rdn to ld ins fnl f: r.o* **66/1**
320- **2** *1 1/4* **Kintbury Cross**151 5274 4-9-12 77.............. JohnEgan 5 69
(P D Cundell) *sn pushed along in rr: hdwy u.p over 2f out: styd on* **4/1**2
6-50 **3** *3* **Drumroll (IRE)**25 157 4-9-12 56....................(p) SimonWhitworth 10 62
(Miss J Feilden) *chsd ldrs: led over 4f out: rdn over 2f out: hdd and no ex ins fnl f* **50/1**
32 **4** *3/4* **Airbound (USA)**12 272 3-8-7.............. JoeFanning 1 54
(M Johnston) *prom: jnd ldr over 4f out: rdn over 2f out: sn edgd lft: no ex ins fnl f* **1/3**1
54- **5** *11* **Young Scotton**262 2092 6-9-12.............. EddieAhern 8 36
(J Howard Johnson) *chsd ldrs over 4f* **20/1**
6 *shd* **Dinner Dance** 3-8-2.............. NickyMackay 9 25
(W J Haggas) *prom over 4f* **18/1**
20- **7** *19* **Mighty Kitchener (USA)**92 6342 3-8-7.............. ShaneKelly 3 —
(P Howling) *led: hdd over 4f out: wknd 3f out* **16/1**3
00- **8** *3* **Sealed Bid**239 2772 3-8-7 ow3.............. PaulMulrennan(3) 6 —
(M W Easterby) *s.i.s: a in rr* **125/1**
9 *21* **Bold Finch (FR)**62 4-9-12 59.............. AdrianTNicholls 4 —
(K O Cunningham-Brown) *chsd ldrs: lost pl 5f out: sn bhd* **200/1**

1m 43.1s (-1.50) **Going Correction** -0.175s/f (Stan)
WFA 3 from 4yo+ 19lb **9** Ran SP% **115.7**
Speed ratings (Par 103):100,98,95,95,84 83,64,61,40
CSF £311.15 TOTE £49.80: £14.60, £1.60, £25.60; EX 239.20.
Owner Faisal Al-Nassar **Bred** R P Kernohan **Trained** East Harling, Norfolk

FOCUS
With the odds-on favourite most disappointing this took little winning. The winner took full advantage of the weight-for-age allowance and faces a stiff rise, she was rated just 56 going into this.
Al Rayanah Official explanation: trainer's representative said, regarding the improved form shown, filly had probably benefited from a change in feeding regime and has been eating much better
Bold Finch(FR) Official explanation: jockey said gelding lost its action

410 BETDIRECT FREEPHONE 0800 211 222 (S) STKS 7f (F)
2:30 (2:31) (Class 6) 4-Y-0+ **£2,388** (£705; £352) **Stalls** Low

Form RPR
2-65 **1** **Bijou Dan**8 313 5-9-4 63....................(b) TomEaves 3 65
(I Semple) *dwlt: outpcd: hdwy u.p over 1f out: ld ins fnl f: styd on* **5/1**3
0324 **2** *1 3/4* **Mount Royale (IRE)**9 300 8-8-12 48....................(v) KimTinkler 6 55
(N Tinkler) *chsd ldrs: rdn to ld over 1f out: hdd and unable qck ins fnl f* **12/1**
6-30 **3** *1 1/2* **Mission Affirmed (USA)**12 276 5-8-12 73.............. TonyCulhane 4 51
(T P Tate) *s.s: outpcd: hdwy u.p over 1f out: nt rch ldrs* **2/1**1
5-20 **4** *2 1/2* **Musical Gift**11 285 6-8-5 50....................(v) KevinGhunowa(7) 2 45
(P A Blockley) *prom: outpcd 5f out: n.d after* **9/1**
-150 **5** *hd* **Resplendent Prince**7 321 4-9-4 66....................(v) IanMongan 5 50
(T G Mills) *chsd ldr: led wl over 1f out: sn rdn: edgd lft and hdd: wknd ins fnl f* **5/2**2
1-06 **6** *1/2* **Naughty Girl (IRE)**9 304 6-8-4 40.............. PatrickMathers(3) 8 38
(John A Harris) *prom: outpcd 5f out: n.d after* **40/1**
-053 **7** *1 1/2* **Far Note (USA)**7 330 8-9-1 53....................(bt) AmirQuinn(3) 7 45
(S R Bowring) *led: hung rt fr over 4f out: c stands' side over 2f out: hdd wl over 1f out: sn wknd* **20/1**
-641 **8** *11* **Distant Country (USA)**18 210 7-9-4 54....................(p) PatCosgrave 1 18
(K R Burke) *sn outpcd: effrt over 3f out: rdn and wknd over 2f out* **12/1**

1m 30.71s (-0.09) **Going Correction** -0.175s/f (Stan) **8** Ran SP% **111.2**
Speed ratings (Par 101):93,91,89,86,86 85,83,71
CSF £58.19 TOTE £5.30: £2.30, £3.00, £1.10; EX 42.00.There was no bid for the winner. Mission Affirmed was claimed by Ron Harris for £6,000. Resplendent Prince was claimed by Paul Howling for £6,000.
Owner Belstane Park Racing - Greens Committee **Bred** James Thom And Sons **Trained** Carluke, S Lanarks

FOCUS
Mission Affirmed, coughing afterwards, was again below form and long-time loser Mount Royale limits the form.
Mission Affirmed(USA) Official explanation: jockey said, regarding the running and riding, gelding dropped his head as gates opened, losing many lengths; vet said gelding was coughing post race
Resplendent Prince Official explanation: jockey said gelding lost its action and was eased in closing stages; vet said gelding was moving poorly post race
Far Note(USA) Official explanation: jockey said gelding hung right-handed throughout

411 BETDIRECT ON SKY ACTIVE H'CAP (DIV II) 6f (F)
3:00 (3:00) (Class 6) (0-55,55) 4-Y-0+ **£2,047** (£604; £302) **Stalls** Low

Form RPR
5612 1 **Christian Bendix**[2] 388 4-8-7 **48** ShaneKelly 10 56
(P Howling) *chsd ldrs: led over 1f out: rdn out* **7/2**[2]
-301 2 2 ½ **Ariesanne (IRE)**[26] 145 5-8-5 **46** AdrianTNicholls 5 47
(A C Whillans) *sn outpcd: hdwy u.p over 1f out: nt rch wnr* **8/1**
-064 3 hd **Four Amigos (USA)**[8] 317 5-8-11 **55** (v) SilvestreDeSousa(3) 9 55
(D Nicholls) *led 1f: chsd ldr: led over 2f out: sn rdn and edgd lft: hdd over 1f out: styd on same pce fnl f* **16/1**
5-53 4 2 **Orchestration (IRE)**[19] 196 5-8-13 **54** (v) RobbieFitzpatrick 8 48
(M J Attwater) *s.s: outpcd: styd on appr fnl f: nvr nrr* **3/1**[1]
0-40 5 1 ¼ **Larky's Lob**[18] 216 7-8-6 **54** ow2 (b[1]) JamesO'Reilly(7) 1 44
(J O'Reilly) *led 5f out: rdn and hdd over 2f out: wknd fnl f* **9/1**
5535 6 1 ¼ **Park Star**[1] 397 6-8-2 **46** oh1 PatrickMathers(3) 6 32
(D Shaw) *hld up: rdn over 3f out: n.d* **8/1**
1-00 7 3 **Boisdale (IRE)**[19] 196 8-8-12 **53** DarrenWilliams 7 30
(S L Keightley) *chsd ldrs: rdn over 2f out: wknd over 1f out* **12/1**
06-3 8 3 ½ **Weakest Link**[11] 288 5-8-7 **48** (p) GrahamGibbons 3 15
(E J Alston) *chsd ldrs: lost pl over 4f out: wknd over 3f out* **9/2**[3]

1m 16.85s (-0.05) **Going Correction** -0.175s/f (Stan) **8** Ran SP% **111.2**
Speed ratings (Par 101):93,89,89,86,85 83,79,74
CSF £29.51 CT £379.29 TOTE £4.70: £1.60, £1.90, £3.80; EX 32.50.
Owner Mrs A K Petersen **Bred** C B Petersen **Trained** Newmarket, Suffolk

FOCUS
A weak race in which the winner continued his good form in banded company, but he will not find things as easy in future.

412 PLAY LITTLEWOODS POOLS ON 0800 500 000 H'CAP 1m (F)
3:30 (3:30) (Class 4) (0-85,80) 4-Y-0+ **£6,477** (£1,927; £963; £481) **Stalls** Low

Form RPR
00-4 1 **Alfonso**[25] 161 5-8-13 **75** TomEaves 3 83
(I Semple) *led early: chsd ldrs: rdn to ld ins fnl f: r.o* **4/1**[3]
0-50 2 ½ **Te Quiero**[5] 348 8-9-3 **79** (bt) ShaneKelly 5 86
(Miss Gay Kelleway) *sn led: rdn and hdd ins fnl f: r.o* **12/1**
32-3 3 1 ¾ **Councellor (FR)**[16] 245 4-9-0 **76** PaulHanagan 4 79
(Stef Liddiard) *prom: plld hrd: stdd and lost pl 6f out: hdwy u.p over 2f out: sn edgd lft: styd on same pce ins fnl f* **7/2**[2]
000- 4 ¾ **Dispol Veleta**[120] 5940 5-8-4 **66** PaulFessey 8 67
(T D Barron) *hld up: hdwy over 3f out: sn rdn: styd on* **25/1**
0U-0 5 ¾ **Fiddlers Creek (IRE)**[13] 125 7-8-3 **70** (tp) AndrewMullen(5) 1 70
(R Allan) *chsd ldrs: outpcd over 2f out: styd on ins fnl f* **50/1**
2-31 6 ½ **Blue Patrick**[18] 214 6-9-0 **76** NCallan 9 75
(K A Ryan) *plld hrd and prom: chsd ldr 3f out: sn rdn: wknd ins fnl f* **7/4**[1]
000- 7 6 **Red Contact (USA)**[172] 4715 5-9-3 **79** (p) JohnEgan 6 64
(Lucinda Featherstone) *hld up: rdn over 3f out: nvr trbld ldrs* **7/1**
0/0- 8 8 **Buddy Brown**[251] 2391 4-9-4 **80** EddieAhern 7 48
(J Howard Johnson) *hld up: rdn over 3f out: a in rr* **40/1**
430- 9 ¾ **Imperialistic (IRE)**[10] 6253 5-9-1 **77** PatCosgrave 2 43
(K R Burke) *hld up: rdn over 3f out: sn wknd* **16/1**
01/ 10 21 **Snugfit Dubarry**[1298] 3372 6-8-4 **66** oh1 DaleGibson 10 —
(M W Easterby) *s.i.s: hdwy over 6f out: wknd over 3f out* **50/1**

1m 41.42s (-3.18) **Going Correction** -0.175s/f (Stan) **10** Ran SP% **114.9**
Speed ratings (Par 105):108,107,105,105,104 103,97,89,89,68
CSF £47.92 CT £181.55 TOTE £5.20: £1.50, £4.00, £1.50; EX 34.10.
Owner D Irvine **Bred** G Reed **Trained** Carluke, S Lanarks

FOCUS
Te Quiero had his own way out in front but in the end potentially leniently treated Alfonso proved more than a match. Overall the race could be rated a few pounds higher with the third the best guide to the level.
Buddy Brown Official explanation: jockey said colt hung right-handed round the bend

413 BETDIRECT.CO.UK H'CAP 6f (F)
4:00 (4:00) (Class 2) (0-100,97) 4-Y-0+ **£12,954** (£3,854; £1,926; £962) **Stalls** Low

Form RPR
-522 1 **Wessex (USA)**[5] 348 6-8-11 **87** GrahamGibbons 10 100
(P A Blockley) *s.i.s: hld up: hdwy to ld over 1f out: hung rt ins fnl f: r.o* **3/1**[2]
40-6 2 3 ½ **Glaramara**[19] 198 5-8-11 **87** SamHitchcott 7 90
(A Bailey) *chsd ldrs: rdn and ev ch whn hung lft over 1f out: styd on same pce fnl f* **8/1**
1213 3 nk **Cummiskey (IRE)**[5] 348 4-9-5 **95** EddieAhern 5 97
(J A Osborne) *trckd ldrs: ev ch whn edgd rt over 1f out: rdn and flashed tail ins fnl f: styd on same pce* **9/4**[1]
1-13 4 ¾ **Pinchbeck**[12] 275 7-8-8 **84** (p) MatthewHenry 8 83
(M A Jarvis) *chsd ldrs: rdn over 2f out: styd on* **9/2**[3]
0-00 5 1 ¼ **Qadar (IRE)**[12] 275 4-8-2 **85** JamesDoyle(7) 6 81
(N P Littmoden) *s.i.s: hld up: hdwy over 2f out: hmpd over 1f out: nt clr run ins fnl f: styd on same pce* **12/1**
4455 6 nk **Pawan (IRE)**[5] 348 6-8-2 **85** oh4 ow2 AnnStokell(7) 2 80
(Miss A Stokell) *chsd ldrs: rdn over 2f out: wknd ins fnl f* **20/1**
000- 7 4 **Bo McGinty (IRE)**[121] 5922 5-8-9 **85** PaulHanagan 9 68
(R A Fahey) *hld up: rdn 1/2-way: n.d* **12/1**
4001 8 nk **Zorn**[12] 274 7-8-7 **83** oh27 ShaneKelly 4 65
(P Howling) *led: hdd over 3f out: edgd lft and wknd over 1f out* **40/1**
2-00 9 1 **Quiet Times (IRE)**[39] 54 7-8-11 **87** (b) NCallan 3 66
(K A Ryan) *s.i.s: sn w ldr: led over 3f out: rdn: edgd lft and hdd over 1f out: sn wknd* **16/1**
3165 10 ½ **Moayed**[10] 295 7-9-7 **97** (bt) ChrisCatlin 1 74
(N P Littmoden) *s.i.s: outpcd* **12/1**

1m 14.59s (-2.31) **Going Correction** -0.175s/f (Stan) **10** Ran SP% **121.2**
Speed ratings (Par 109):108,103,102,101,100 99,94,94,92,92
CSF £28.79 CT £66.89 TOTE £4.00: £1.70, £2.10, £1.30; EX 43.90.
Owner Nigel Shields **Bred** Darley Stud Management, L L C **Trained** Lambourn, Berks

FOCUS
Solid form rated through the winner and the third.

NOTEBOOK
Wessex(USA), one of his owner's three runners, is in the form of his life and overcame the worst of the draw over a trip that is now his bare minimum. (op 7-2)
Glaramara, winner of just two of his previous 29 starts, was a lot sharper this time, his second outing after a break. He was rated 98 at one time on turf.
Cummiskey(IRE), closely matched with the winner, continues in fine form and his tail swishing may be unattractive to the eye but basically he does little wrong. (op 5-2)
Pinchbeck, closely matched with the winner and the third, continues in peak form. (op 6-1 tchd 7-1)
Qadar(IRE), having just his third start for this yard, met plenty of traffic problems and was unfortunate not to be more closely involved. He is worth bearing in mind. Official explanation: jockey said gelding suffered interference in running
Pawan(IRE), 4lb out of the handicap, probably ran right up to his best. (op 18-1)
Moayed Official explanation: jockey said gelding would not face the kickback

414 SOYUZ MEMORIAL H'CAP 1m 4f (F)
4:30 (4:31) (Class 6) (0-65,64) 4-Y-0+ **£2,388** (£705; £352) **Stalls** Low

Form RPR
2011 1 **Jackie Kiely**[2] 389 5-9-1 **61** 5ex TonyCulhane 9 67
(P Howling) *a.p: rdn to ld and edgd rt over 1f out: all out* **11/4**[1]
0-55 2 shd **Polish Power (GER)**[11] 283 6-8-4 **50** JohnEgan 12 55
(J S Moore) *hld up: hdwy 4f out: rdn over 1f out: r.o* **7/1**
0-21 3 nk **Hawkit (USA)**[16] 243 5-8-11 **64** (t) MichaelJStainton(7) 11 69
(A Bailey) *hld up: hdwy on outside over 3f out: rdn and ev ch whn edgd rt over 1f out: styd on* **13/2**[3]
-103 4 1 ¾ **Padre Nostro (IRE)**[7] 334 7-8-13 **59** BrianReilly 3 61
(J R Holt) *w ldr: rdn and ev ch whn hung lft over 1f out: no ex ins fnl f* **11/1**
50-3 5 1 **Galley Law**[7] 328 6-8-5 **51** PaulFessey 2 52
(R Craggs) *led: rdn and hdd over 1f out: no ex ins fnl f* **10/1**
0-15 6 8 **Beauchamp Star**[26] 147 5-8-6 **55** DanielTudhope(3) 4 44
(Mrs A Duffield) *chsd ldrs: rdn over 2f out: wknd over 1f out* **6/1**[2]
00-6 7 nk **High (IRE)**[42] 26 4-8-8 **57** SimonWhitworth 8 45
(W J Musson) *hld up: hmpd over 4f out: n.d* **33/1**
606- 8 8 **Acceleration (IRE)**[8] 978 6-8-10 **56** (t) TomEaves 5 32
(R Allan) *chsd ldrs over 8f* **40/1**
/5-0 9 1 **Bolshoi Ballet**[11] 283 8-8-11 **57** (b) TonyHamilton 6 32
(R A Fahey) *prom: hung lft and wknd over 4f out* **66/1**
106- 10 ½ **Efrhina (IRE)**[54] 6655 6-9-0 **60** EddieAhern 1 34
(Stef Liddiard) *chsd ldrs over 8f* **14/1**
305- 11 2 **Golden Measure**[54] 5789 6-8-4 **50** PaulHanagan 7 21
(G A Swinbank) *hld up: wknd over 4f out* **13/2**[3]
564- 12 2 **Caymans Gift**[95] 5568 6-8-7 **53** AdrianTNicholls 10 21
(A C Whillans) *chsd ldrs over 8f* **20/1**
200- 13 19 **Beauchamp Tiger**[97] 6298 4-9-1 **64** DeanMcKeown 13 4
(J Parkes) *hld up: wknd over 4f out* **25/1**

2m 38.75s (-3.34) **Going Correction** -0.175s/f (Stan)
WFA 4 from 5yo+ 3lb **13** Ran SP% **119.7**
Speed ratings (Par 101):104,103,103,102,101 96,96,91,90,90 88,87,74
CSF £20.44 CT £117.60 TOTE £4.80: £1.90, £2.40, £2.10; EX 45.30.
Owner P S J Croft **Bred** Mrs M Chaworth Musters **Trained** Newmarket, Suffolk

FOCUS
Modest form but a solid look about it with the winner adding to his two banded race wins and the third and fourth close to form.
Efrhina(IRE) Official explanation: jockey said mare had no more to give
Golden Measure Official explanation: jockey said gelding hung left throughout
Caymans Gift Official explanation: jockey said gelding had no more to give

415 TEXT "BETDIRECT" TO 88600 H'CAP 7f (F)
5:00 (5:02) (Class 6) (0-60,60) 3-Y-O **£2,388** (£705; £352) **Stalls** Low

Form RPR
0431 1 **Smart Ass (IRE)**[5] 347 3-8-11 **53** 4ex FergalLynch 10 68+
(J S Moore) *mid-div: hdwy over 3f out: rdn to ld and hung lft 2f out: drvn clr fnl f* **11/4**[1]
4-03 2 6 **Hillbilly Cat (USA)**[7] 329 3-8-13 **55** PaulFessey 6 55+
(T D Barron) *chsd ldr: rdn and ev ch whn hmpd 2f out: no ex fnl f* **10/1**
0-45 3 1 **Tuckers Point (IRE)**[10] 291 3-9-2 **58** EddieAhern 7 56
(J A Osborne) *chsd ldrs: rdn over 2f out: nt clr run over 1f out: styd on same pce* **8/1**
16-0 4 1 **Suhezy (IRE)**[11] 287 3-8-10 **52** PaulHanagan 12 47
(P T Midgley) *sn led: rdn and hdd 2f out: wknd fnl f* **50/1**
040- 5 5 **Appreciated**[56] 6628 3-9-3 **59** (b[1]) TonyCulhane 5 42
(W J Haggas) *s.s: hdwy over 3f out: hrd rdn and wknd 2f out* **11/2**[2]
0-05 6 1 ¼ **Tesoro**[7] 333 3-7-13 **48** KevinGhunowa(7) 9 27
(P A Blockley) *prom over 4f* **28/1**
00-0 7 1 ¾ **Bournonville**[29] 122 3-8-4 **46** oh1 ChrisCatlin 4 21
(J Ryan) *prom: sn drvn along: lost pl over 4f out: sn bhd* **16/1**
-631 8 ½ **Katie Lawson (IRE)**[7] 333 3-9-2 **58** 4ex (v) RobertHavlin 1 32
(D Haydn Jones) *dwlt: outpcd* **13/2**[3]
1552 9 3 **My Reflection**[8] 308 3-8-1 **46** oh1 PatrickMathers(3) 11 12
(D Shaw) *chsd ldrs over 4f* **11/1**
003- 10 1 ¼ **Mucho Loco (IRE)**[61] 6585 3-9-4 **60** J-PGuillambert 2 23
(J G Portman) *bhd fnl 4f* **33/1**
000- 11 1 **Yassooma (IRE)**[143] 5464 3-8-4 **53** JamesO'Reilly(7) 3 14
(T J Pitt) *chsd ldrs 4f* **18/1**

1m 29.29s (-1.51) **Going Correction** -0.175s/f (Stan) **11** Ran SP% **103.4**
Speed ratings (Par 95):101,94,93,91,86 84,82,82,78,77 76
CSF £23.82 CT £139.56 TOTE £4.40: £1.10, £2.90, £1.90; EX 41.80 Place 6 £162.23, Place 5 £64.16.
Owner Bigwigs Bloodstock VII **Bred** M Ervine **Trained** Upper Lambourn, Berks
■ Woodwee (6/1, vet's advice) was withdrawn. R4 applies, deduct 10p in the £.

FOCUS
Smart Ass followed up under her penalty pulling right away and is clearly much improved.
Katie Lawson(IRE) Official explanation: jockey said filly would not face the kickback
My Reflection Official explanation: jockey said saddle slipped
Mucho Loco(IRE) Official explanation: jockey said gelding hung badly right-handed throughout
T/Plt: £359.20 to a £1 stake. Pool: £38,921.55. 79.10 winning tickets. T/Qpdt: £10.70 to a £1 stake. Pool: £4,071.10. 280.00 winning tickets. CR

394 LINGFIELD (L-H)
Wednesday, February 15

OFFICIAL GOING: Standard
Wind: Strong, half-behind Weather: Fine but cloudy

416 PLAY FOR FREE AT LITTLEWOODSPOKER.COM H'CAP 1m (P)
1:50 (1:50) (Class 6) (0-65,65) 4-Y-0+ **£2,388** (£705; £352) **Stalls** High

Form RPR
1-13 1 **Hollow Jo**[25] 170 6-8-13 **60** EddieAhern 1 68
(J R Jenkins) *hw: hld up in midfield: gd prog on inner wl over 1f out: drvn and r.o wl to ld last strides* **7/1**
30-0 2 hd **Aggravation**[43] 17 4-9-1 **62** (t) JohnEgan 2 70
(D R C Elsworth) *t.k.h: trckd ldng pair: n.m.r on inner over 2f out: effrt over 1f out: r.o to ld last 100yds: collared fnl strides* **11/2**[3]

3-20 **3** 3/4 **Monashee Prince (IRE)**[17] 236 4-9-2 **63** NCallan 11 69
(J R Best) *lw: led: kicked 3l clr wl over 1f out: hdd last 100yds: kpt on* **5/1**[2]

-106 **4** nk **King Of Music (USA)**[14] 268 5-8-12 **59** (v) TonyCulhane 4 65
(G Prodromou) *dwlt: hld up in rr: plenty to do 3f out: prog 2f out: plld out and r.o fnl f: too much to do* **9/1**

00-5 **5** 1 **Go Garuda**[11] 292 5-9-1 **62** (t) JamieSpencer 12 65
(Miss Gay Kelleway) *lw: dwlt: mostly last and pushed along bef 1/2-way: prog over 1f out: styd on wl fnl f: nt rch ldrs* **4/1**[1]

00-4 **6** 3 **Secam (POL)**[7] 336 7-8-10 **57** (b) SteveDrowne 5 54
(Mrs P Townsley) *s.i.s: t.k.h and sn wl in tch: hrd rdn 2f out: no prog and sn btn* **5/1**[2]

006- **7** nk **Jazrawy**[50] 6671 4-9-1 **62** ShaneKelly 7 58
(Miss Gay Kelleway) *pressed ldr to over 2f out: wknd wl over 1f out* **14/1**

-003 **8** 1/2 **Tapa**[8] 327 4-8-11 **58** ChrisCatlin 9 53
(C A Dwyer) *chsd ldng pair: rdn over 3f out: wknd 2f out* **16/1**

6-00 **9** 1/2 **Littleton Zephir (USA)**[8] 327 7-9-4 **65** (t) DaneO'Neill 8 59
(Mrs P Townsley) *t.k.h: hld up in midfield on outer: rdn and no prog over 2f out: btn after* **33/1**

00-0 **10** shd **Qobtaan (USA)**[36] 77 7-8-8 **55** HayleyTurner 3 49
(M R Bosley) *dwlt: a in rr: rdn 3f out: no prog* **50/1**

-003 **11** shd **Physical (IRE)**[14] 268 4-8-10 **57** JoeFanning 10 51
(Mrs A J Perrett) *lw: hld up wl in rr: rdn over 3f out: no prog* **10/1**

1m 38.84s (-0.59) **Going Correction** -0.10s/f (Stan) **11** Ran SP% **117.8**
Speed ratings (Par 101):98,97,97,96,95 92,92,91,91,91 91
CSF £45.38 CT £216.06 TOTE £5.90: £1.50, £2.00, £2.00; EX 41.30.
Owner Jim McCarthy **Bred** K J Reddington **Trained** Royston, Herts

FOCUS
A modest handicap run at a steady early pace and reasonable form, rated through the runner-up.
Go Garuda Official explanation: jockey said gelding was never travelling

417 PLAYERS FROM ALL OVER THE WORLD @ LITTLEWOODSPOKER.COM CLAIMING STKS 1m (P)
2:20 (2:20) (Class 6) 4-Y-0+ **£2,388** (£705; £352) **Stalls** High

Form RPR

22-4 **1** **Lining Wine (IRE)**[9] 313 10-9-3 80 (p) NCallan 7 71+
(P A Blockley) *lw: hld up in last pair: rapid prog on outer fr 2f out to ld 1f out: shot clr* **9/4**[1]

-141 **2** 3 1/2 **Nisr**[11] 297 9-8-10 55 (t) JamieSpencer 5 56
(Miss Gay Kelleway) *lw: hld up towards rr: nt clr run 2f out to over 1f out: got through to take 2nd ins fnl f: no ch w wnr* **9/4**[1]

000- **3** 3/4 **Nuit Sombre (IRE)**[47] 5433 6-9-0 77 JamesDoyle(3) 2 65
(J G M O'Shea) *led after 1f: rdn 2f out: hdd and outpcd 1f out* **9/2**[2]

000- **4** 1/2 **Zinging**[92] 6361 7-8-3 40 PaulHanagan 9 46
(J J Bridger) *t.k.h: hld up in midfield: rdn and nt qckn 2f out: kpt on ins fnl f* **33/1**

065- **5** shd **Fayr Firenze (IRE)**[232] 2996 5-8-0 45 RichardThomas(3) 1 46
(M F Harris) *hld up in midfield: rdn and nt qckn over 2f out: kpt on fnl f* **40/1**

40-6 **6** hd **Boogie Magic**[11] 291 6-8-5 40 AdamKirby(3) 3 51
(T T Clement) *trckd ldrs: effrt over 2f out: cl up over 1f out: sn outpcd* **20/1**

-000 **7** 1 3/4 **Acorazado (IRE)**[8] 328 7-8-5 50 ow2 StephenCarson 8 44
(C P Morlock) *trckd ldrs: rdn and nt qckn wl over 1f out: wknd ins fnl f* **100/1**

26U2 **8** nk **Exit Smiling**[11] 297 4-8-5 54 ChrisCatlin 4 43
(G C H Chung) *led for 1f: pressed ldr to 2f out: wknd fnl f* **5/1**[3]

00 **9** 5 **Jomelamin**[11] 297 4-8-5 ow1 JohnEgan 10 32
(R J Hodges) *lw: hld up in last pair: pushed along 4f out: no prog whn bmpd wl over 1f out: eased fnl f* **100/1**

06/6 **10** 6 **Jewel Of India**[17] 235 7-9-1 69 JoeFanning 6 29
(Mrs A L M King) *v s.i.s: quick rcvry to trck ldrs: wknd rapidly 2f out* **12/1**

1m 38.14s (-1.29) **Going Correction** -0.10s/f (Stan) **10** Ran SP% **116.2**
Speed ratings (Par 101):102,98,97,97,97 96,95,94,89,83
CSF £6.83 TOTE £3.60: £1.10, £1.10, £1.80; EX 7.40.
Owner Nigel Shields **Bred** His Highness The Aga Khan's Studs S C **Trained** Lambourn, Berks

FOCUS
Just an ordinary claimer, but they went a good pace with the runner-up close to his mark, although the fifth limits the form.

418 FREE DAILY TOURNAMENTS @ LITTLEWOODSPOKER.COM MAIDEN STKS 7f (P)
2:50 (2:51) (Class 5) 3-Y-0 **£3,562** (£1,059; £529; £264) **Stalls** Low

Form RPR

1 **Ballet Pacifica (USA)** 3-8-9 ShaneKelly 6 68+
(J Noseda) *leggy: lw: trckd ldrs: pushed along 3f out: wd and green bnd 2f out: rdn and effrt over 1f out: led last 100yds: won gng aw* **2/1**[2]

333- **2** 1 1/2 **Rebellion**[105] 6227 3-9-0 76 JoeFanning 9 69
(M Johnston) *s.s: rcvrd to join ldrs after 1f: chsd ldr over 2f out: drvn to narrow ld over 1f out: hdd and outpcd last 100yds* **5/4**[1]

66 **3** nk **Blushing Thief (USA)**[21] 191 3-9-0 JamieSpencer 5 69
(W Jarvis) *lw: w ldr: led over 4f out: drvn 2f out: hdd over 1f out: kpt on same pce* **5/1**[3]

0444 **4** 5 **Twilight Avenger (IRE)**[6] 347 3-9-0 52 DeanMcKeown 3 56
(M J Polglase) *last of main gp: rdn 3f out: wl outpcd and nt looking keen 2f out: plugged on* **33/1**

5 1 1/2 **Musical Script (USA)** 3-9-0 ChrisCatlin 7 52
(Mrs A J Hamilton-Fairley) *strong: lengthy: scope: bkwd: led to over 4f out: chsd ldr to over 2f out: wknd over 1f out* **33/1**

0 **6** 1 1/4 **Miss Odd Sox**[14] 266 3-8-9 RobertHavlin 1 44
(R Ingram) *dwlt: chsd ldrs: pushed along over 4f out: wknd over 2f out* **100/1**

035- **7** 1 1/2 **Amygdala**[119] 5978 3-8-9 68 (t) OscarUrbina 2 40
(M Botti) *dwlt: chsd ldrs: rdn 3f out: wknd 2f out* **8/1**

8 2 **Tilsworth Charlie** 3-8-9 EddieAhern 4 35
(J R Jenkins) *neat: swtg: dwlt: sn wl detached in last pair: pushed along 4f out: no prog: eased fnl 2f but lost no more grnd* **33/1**

00 **9** 1/2 **King's Melody**[16] 254 3-8-7 JamesMillman(7) 8 39
(B R Millman) *sn wl detached in last pair and outpcd: nvr a factor* **100/1**

1m 25.01s (-0.88) **Going Correction** -0.10s/f (Stan) **9** Ran SP% **116.4**
Speed ratings (Par 97):101,99,98,93,91 90,88,86,85
CSF £4.78 TOTE £3.50: £1.10, £1.10, £1.40; EX 6.90.
Owner Budget Stable **Bred** Calumet Farm **Trained** Newmarket, Suffolk

FOCUS
A modest maiden in which fourth-placed Twilight Avenger, rated 52 and beaten several times in selling company, gives a good guide to the level of the form. The front three, though, did finish upwards of five lengths clear.
Blushing Thief(USA) Official explanation: jockey said colt hung right
King's Melody Official explanation: jockey said gelding hung right

419 £200K+ GUARANTEED WEEKLY @ LITTLEWOODSPOKER.COM MAIDEN STKS 1m 4f (P)
3:20 (3:21) (Class 5) 3-Y-0+ **£3,238** (£963; £481; £240) **Stalls** Low

Form RPR

00- **1** **Orvietan (IRE)**[119] 5970 3-8-3 JoeFanning 4 64
(M Johnston) *lw: led over 8f out: mde rest: drvn over 2f out: edgd rt to centre of the crse fnl f: kpt on* **8/1**

0-32 **2** 1 1/4 **Dubai Ace (USA)**[18] 218 5-9-10 63 EdwardCreighton(3) 11 66
(Miss Sheena West) *hld up: prog 1/2-way: chal 3f out: drvn and nt qckn over 2f out: styd wd ins st: kpt on same pce* **9/2**[3]

60-2 **3** 1/2 **Ganymede**[9] 314 5-9-13 71 FergusSweeney 1 65
(J G M O'Shea) *led to over 8f out: trckd ldrs after: effrt over 2f out: styd on inner fnl 2f: one pce fnl f* **11/1**

05-4 **4** hd **River Gypsy**[18] 218 5-9-13 63 JohnEgan 9 65
(D R C Elsworth) *lw: hld up: prog to trck ldrs 3f out gng wl: rdn and no rspnse 2f out: kpt on fnl f* **7/2**[2]

5 **5** nk **Fantastic Promise (USA)**[30] 124 3-7-12 DavidKinsella 2 56
(J H M Gosden) *trckd ldrs: rdn 3f out: sn outpcd: plugged on again fr over 1f out* **14/1**

420- **6** 4 **Pace Shot (IRE)**[45] 4783 4-9-10 72 GeorgeBaker 10 59
(G L Moore) *hld up: prog 1/2-way: rdn to chal 3f out: nt qckn and hld 2f out: fdd fnl f* **6/5**[1]

0- **7** 3 **Ashwell Rose**[92] 6355 4-9-5 SteveDrowne 5 49
(R T Phillips) *s.s: hld up in rr: struggling fr 3f out* **40/1**

000- **8** 1 **Health Spa**[60] 6600 3-8-2 48 ow4 (v[1]) FrankieMcDonald 8 48
(B R Johnson) *s.s: a wl in rr: struggling fnl 3f* **100/1**

0 **9** 1/2 **Lord Raffles**[12] 289 4-9-10 (v) DaneO'Neill 7 52
(P R Webber) *str reminders sn after s: in tch: drvn over 3f out: wknd 2f out* **50/1**

-00 **10** shd **Fantasy Legend (IRE)**[19] 215 3-7-10 JamesDoyle(7) 3 48
(N P Littmoden) *chsd ldrs tl wknd wl over 2f out* **50/1**

000/ **11** dist **Melmott**[940] 3465 6-9-6 40 JosephLoveridge(7) 6 —
(R Ingram) *bkwd: w ldrs to 1/2-way: wknd rapidly over 4f out: t.o* **100/1**

2m 34.48s (0.09) **Going Correction** -0.10s/f (Stan)
WFA 3 from 4yo 24lb 4 from 5yo+ 3lb **11** Ran SP% **120.3**
Speed ratings (Par 103):95,94,93,93,93 90,88,88,87,87 —
CSF £44.47 TOTE £16.00: £3.50, £2.10, £2.50; EX 66.80.
Owner Jumeirah Racing **Bred** King Bloodstock **Trained** Middleham Moor, N Yorks

FOCUS
A pretty moderate maiden with the runner-up and fourth limiting the form.
Melmott Official explanation: jockey said gelding had breathing problem

420 LITTLEWOODSPOKER.COM - THE TRUSTED NAME IN GAMING H'CAP 2m (P)
3:50 (3:50) (Class 4) (0-85,82) 4-Y-0+ **£6,477** (£1,927; £963; £481) **Stalls** Low

Form RPR

003/ **1** **Prins Willem (IRE)**[45] 6192 7-9-9 **82** (t) JamieSpencer 5 92
(J R Fanshawe) *lw: trckd ldrs: effrt and rdn over 2f out: chsd ldr fnl f : led last 100yds: r.o wl* **10/1**

4-00 **2** 1 1/4 **Nawow**[14] 264 6-8-9 **68** DaneO'Neill 8 77
(P D Cundell) *lw: prom: rdn to ld 2f out: hdd and no ex last 100yds* **12/1**

21-1 **3** 1 **Reggae Rhythm (IRE)**[17] 237 12-8-10 **72** RichardThomas(3) 1 79+
(A J Lidderdale) *dwlt: hld up in last trio: gd prog on inner whn nt clr run 3f out: hdwy and swtchd rt over 1f out: r.o: nvr nrr* **7/1**[2]

1-34 **4** nk **Champagne Shadow (IRE)**[8] 325 5-9-6 **79** (b) GeorgeBaker 11 86
(G L Moore) *lw: hld up wl in rr: prog on outer fr 3f out: drvn over 1f out: r.o ins fnl f: nrst fin* **12/1**

3-04 **5** 1 1/4 **Monte Cristo (FR)**[17] 237 8-8-8 **67** (v) ChrisCatlin 4 72
(Mrs L C Taylor) *led at fair pce: hrd pressed fr 3f out: hdd 2f out: one pce u.p* **16/1**

00B- **6** shd **Tender Trap (IRE)**[100] 6285 8-9-9 **82** IanMongan 3 87
(T G Mills) *hld up in midfield: prog to trck ldrs 3f out: drvn and cl up over 1f out: hanging and fnd nil* **25/1**

2032 **7** 1 **Eastborough (IRE)**[8] 325 7-9-2 **75** PaulHanagan 10 79
(B G Powell) *hld up in last: effrt 3f out: drvn and styd on fr wl over 1f out: nt rch ldrs* **14/1**

4115 **8** 1/2 **Moon Emperor**[17] 237 9-9-1 **74** (b) EddieAhern 6 78
(J R Jenkins) *lw: wl in tch in midfield: nt qckn over 2f out: wd bnd sn after: n.d fr over 1f out* **22/1**

664- **9** 2 **Screenplay**[80] 4570 5-8-9 **68** ow1 NCallan 2 69
(Miss Sheena West) *prom: rdn and cl up 2f out: btn 1f out: eased* **8/1**[3]

4-12 **10** 1/2 **Countrywide Luck**[12] 283 5-8-9 **75** JamesDoyle(7) 12 76
(N P Littmoden) *lw: pressed ldrs: rdn over 2f out: fdd fr over 1f out* **11/1**

1-12 **11** shd **Spitting Image (IRE)**[34] 98 6-9-3 **76** JoeFanning 9 76
(M Johnston) *pressed ldr to 3f out: losing pl whn squeezed out sn after: wknd* **10/1**

600- **12** 12 **Mesmeric (IRE)**[199] 3830 8-9-3 **76** TQuinn 7 62
(B G Powell) *towards rr: rdn over 4f out: wknd and bhd fr over 2f out* **25/1**

301- **13** 10 **Maystock**[97] 6308 6-8-11 **77** RonanKeogh(7) 14 51
(B G Powell) *hld up in rr: rdn 5f out: sn btn: t.o* **50/1**

51-3 **14** 14 **Fen Game (IRE)**[14] 264 4-8-5 **70** RobertHavlin 13 27
(J H M Gosden) *t.k.h: trckd ldrs: rdn over 4f out: sn wknd: t.o* **9/4**[1]

3m 23.79s (-5.00) **Going Correction** -0.10s/f (Stan)
WFA 4 from 5yo+ 6lb **14** Ran SP% **122.8**
Speed ratings (Par 105):108,107,106,106,106 106,105,105,104,104 104,98,93,86
CSF £121.99 CT £910.69 TOTE £9.30: £2.40, £3.70, £1.90; EX 186.10.
Owner Chris Van Hoorn **Bred** Mrs A Hughes **Trained** Newmarket, Suffolk

FOCUS
A good staying handicap for the grade and very competitive. The form looks sound rated through the runner-up.
Fen Game(IRE) Official explanation: jockey was unable to offer any explanation for poor form shown

421 TABLES FOR EVERYONE @ LITTLWOODSPOKER.COM H'CAP 1m 2f (P)
4:20 (4:20) (Class 5) (0-70,76) 4-Y-0+ **£3,238** (£963; £481; £240) **Stalls** Low

Form RPR

4206 **1** **Danger Zone**[4] 375 4-9-3 **70**....(p) IanMongan 9 77
(Mrs A J Perrett) *lw: trckd ldr: rdn to ld over 2f out: drvn 3l clr 1f out: kpt on* **10/1**

-051 **2** *1 1/4* **Star Magnitude (USA)**[7] 343 5-9-10 **76** 6ex.... JohnEgan 8 81
(S Dow) *lw: trckd ldrs: rdn over 3f out: prog over 1f out: chsd wnr ent fnl f and clsd: no real imp last 75yds* **5/1**[2]

3601 **3** *1 1/2* **Zalkani (IRE)**[4] 375 6-9-10 **76** 6ex.... TQuinn 7 78
(B G Powell) *hld up in rr: outpcd 3f out: effrt 2f out on outer 2f out: possible danger over 1f out: hanging and nt finding much fnl f* **6/1**[3]

-344 **4** *hd* **Captain Margaret**[14] 264 4-9-0 **67**.... EddieAhern 10 69
(J Pearce) *hld up in last pair: bdly outpcd 3f out: pushed along fnl 2f: styd on steadily: hopeless task* **10/1**

-21 **5** *shd* **Custodian (IRE)**[12] 289 4-9-3 **70**.... JamieSpencer 3 72
(H R A Cecil) *lw: trckd ldng pair: rdn 3f out: hanging and nt keen fnl 2f: no imp* **6/4**[1]

6-24 **6** *2* **Webbswood Lad (IRE)**[8] 324 5-8-8 **60**....(p) PaulHanagan 6 58
(Stef Liddiard) *t.k.h: hld up towards rr: outpcd 3f out: drvn and no prog after* **7/1**

060- **7** *3* **Carpet Ride**[140] 5549 4-8-7 **60**.... FergusSweeney 2 53
(B G Powell) *led: kicked on 3f out: hdd over 2f out: wknd rapidly fnl f* **80/1**

0560 **8** *shd* **African Sahara (USA)**[4] 375 7-8-11 **70**....(t) ChrisCavanagh(7) 4 63
(Miss D Mountain) *scratchy to post: hld up in last pair: bdly outpcd 3f out: styd on inner and no prog after* **14/1**

3-30 **9** *1 1/4* **Measured Response**[9] 319 4-8-13 **66**.... NCallan 1 56
(J G M O'Shea) *trckd ldng pair: rdn over 2f out: wknd rapidly jst over 1f out* **20/1**

2m 8.84s (1.05) **Going Correction** -0.10s/f (Stan)
WFA 4 from 5yo+ 1lb **9** Ran SP% **114.3**
Speed ratings (Par 103):91,90,88,88,88 86,84,84,83
CSF £58.68 CT £329.02 TOTE £11.30: £2.60, £1.60, £2.20; EX 106.70.
Owner The Masqueraders (jdrp) **Bred** Cheveley Park Stud Ltd **Trained** Pulborough, W Sussex

FOCUS
A fair handicap that was not run to suit most of these and the form looks ordinary, with the time limiting.
Measured Response Official explanation: jockey said gelding had no more to give

422 TEXT "BETDIRECT" TO 88600 H'CAP 1m 2f (P)
4:50 (4:50) (Class 5) (0-70,69) 3-Y-0 **£3,238** (£963; £481; £240) **Stalls** Low

Form RPR

-311 **1** **Prince Charlemagne (IRE)**[21] 188 3-8-10 **68**.... JamesDoyle(7) 7 75+
(N P Littmoden) *lw: wl plcd: clsd 3f out: led wl over 1f out: sn clr: comf* **4/6**[1]

04-6 **2** *3 1/2* **Gibbs Camp**[14] 269 3-9-0 **65**.... SteveDrowne 1 66
(E A L Dunlop) *trckd ldrs: rdn over 2f out: outpcd wl over 1f out: styd on to take 2nd ins fnl f: no ch w wnr* **9/1**[3]

006- **3** *3/4* **Coda Agency**[129] 5752 3-8-7 **58**.... EddieAhern 13 57
(D W P Arbuthnot) *chsd clr ldr: clsd to dispute ld 3f out to wl over 1f out: no ch w wnr after* **40/1**

3020 **4** *1/2* **Lenoir (GER)**[7] 342 3-9-4 **69**....(v) DaneO'Neill 11 67
(V Smith) *hld up wl in rr: prog whn nt clr run over 2f out: wd bnd sn after: rdn over 1f out: r.o: no ch* **7/1**[2]

3665 **5** *nk* **Ms Rainbow Runner**[7] 342 3-8-0 **58**.... AndrewElliott(7) 8 56
(P Butler) *trckd ldng pair over 7f out: clsd to dispute ld 3f out to wl over 1f out: one pce after* **12/1**

3-42 **6** *shd* **Franky'N'Jonny**[8] 326 3-8-4 **55** oh1.... ChrisCatlin 3 53
(I A Wood) *hld up wl in rr: effrt over 2f out: outpcd and no ch after: kpt on* **9/1**[3]

000- **7** *1 3/4* **Oasis Sun (IRE)**[121] 5946 3-8-4 **55** oh3.... HayleyTurner 4 50
(J R Best) *lw: settled in midfield: lost pl and rdn sn after 1/2-way: struggling over 3f out: kpt on fr over 1f out* **20/1**

0-5 **8** *1 3/4* **Earth Master (IRE)**[43] 19 3-9-3 **68**....(b) JamieSpencer 5 59
(S Kirk) *settled towards rr: rdn 3f out: effrt over 2f out: hanging and no imp over 1f out: wknd ins fnl f* **16/1**

0-05 **9** *5* **Flashing Floozie**[18] 219 3-8-3 **57**.... RichardThomas(3) 9 39
(M F Harris) *lw: towards rr: rdn over 3f out: no prog and btn over 2f out* **20/1**

020- **10** *2* **Captivate**[86] 6402 3-8-7 **58**.... DeanMcKeown 12 37
(M J Polglase) *led and sn clr: hdd 3f out: wkng whn hmpd over 2f out* **50/1**

11 *7* **Archidona (FR)**[82] 3-8-6 **62**.... RoryMoore(5) 6 28
(M Quinn) *hld up in last: rdn over 3f out: sn btn* **50/1**

6200 **12** *1 1/2* **Simpsons Ross (IRE)**[7] 342 3-8-12 **63**.... NCallan 14 27
(R M Flower) *t.k.h: racd wd: hld up in rr: rdn 3f out: wknd* **16/1**

2m 7.63s (-0.16) **Going Correction** -0.10s/f (Stan) **12** Ran SP% **127.8**
Speed ratings (Par 97):96,93,92,92,91 91,90,89,85,83 77,76
CSF £7.94 CT £158.69 TOTE £1.60: £1.10, £2.50, £16.50; EX 11.40 Place 6 £80.07, Place 5 £38.63.
Owner Neil Ryan **Bred** Michael O'Mahony **Trained** Newmarket, Suffolk

FOCUS
Just a modest handicap, but they went a good pace from the start and Prince Charlemagne continued his progression with a clear-cut success and the race should throw up future winners.
Simpsons Ross(IRE) Official explanation: jockey said gelding hung left
T/Plt: £55.60 to a £1 stake. Pool: £46,687.90. 612.80 winning tickets. T/Qpdt: £21.90 to a £1 stake. Pool: £3,407.00. 114.85 winning tickets. JN

408 SOUTHWELL (L-H)
Thursday, February 16

OFFICIAL GOING: Standard
Wind: Moderate, across

423 BET NOW ON 0800 211 222 APPRENTICE H'CAP 1m (F)
1:20 (1:21) (Class 6) (0-58,58) 4-Y-0+ **£2,388** (£705; £352) **Stalls** Low

Form RPR

0405 **1** **Kumakawa**[4] 386 8-8-1 **46** oh1.... TolleyDean(3) 3 54
(D K Ivory) *trckd ldrs: hdwy to ld wl over 1f out: rdn and edgd rt ent last: r.o* **22/1**

0-42 **2** *3/4* **Figurative (IRE)**[18] 242 4-8-12 **54**.... JamesMillman 5 60
(G A Swinbank) *trckd ldrs: effrt and nt clr run over 1f out: rdn to chse wnr ins last: kpt on same pce* **6/4**[1]

6303 **3** *3* **Crusoe (IRE)**[4] 386 9-8-1 **46** oh1....(b) AmyBaker(3) 9 46
(A Sadik) *led 2f: cl up: effrt and ev ch 2f out: sn rdn and kpt on same pce ent last* **14/1**

5-00 **4** *3/4* **Abbeygate**[27] 156 5-8-11 **53**.... RonanKeogh 11 52
(T Keddy) *hld up: hdwy on outer over 2f out: rdn to chse ldrs over 1f out: sn one pce* **7/1**[3]

030- **5** *3/4* **Nicozetto (FR)**[27] 2648 6-8-6 **48**....(p) KevinGhunowa 12 45
(N Wilson) *chsd ldrs on outer: pushed along over 2f out: rdn and hung lft over 1f out: sn btn* **33/1**

-261 **6** *nk* **Quiet Reading (USA)**[18] 242 9-8-11 **58**....(v) JosephWalsh(5) 7 54
(M R Bosley) *prom: effrt and ev ch over 2f out: sn rdn and wkng whn n.m.r over 1f out* **10/3**[2]

0-10 **7** *shd* **Favouring (IRE)**[14] 274 4-8-7 **52**.... RobbieMills(3) 4 48
(M C Chapman) *chsd ldrs: led after 2f: rdn along over 2f out: hdd wl over 1f out: wknd appr last* **9/1**

-535 **8** *2* **Supreme Salutation**[4] 391 10-8-6 **53**.... LauraReynolds(5) 10 45
(D K Ivory) *s.i.s and bhd: pushed along and hdwy on inner 2f out: rdn and in tch over 1f out: wknd ins last* **9/1**

0-06 **9** *1/2* **Active Account (USA)**[9] 328 9-8-8 **53**....(p) KirstyMilczarek(3) 8 44
(J R Holt) *sn outpcd and rdn along: a rr* **40/1**

000- **10** *dist* **Kalush**[261] 2147 5-8-4 **46** oh11.... SuzzanneFrance 1 —
(N Tinkler) *prom 2f: sn rdn along and lost pl: bhd fr 1/2-way* **50/1**

1m 44.39s (-0.21) **Going Correction** -0.075s/f (Stan) **10** Ran SP% **113.9**
Speed ratings (Par 101):98,97,94,93,92 92,92,90,89,—
CSF £53.14 CT £518.09 TOTE £23.80: £3.30, £1.70, £2.30; EX 71.10.
Owner R D Hartshorn **Bred** Carlton Consultants Ltd **Trained** Radlett, Herts

FOCUS
A moderate handicap and the form is little better than banded class with the winner and third setting the level.

424 LITTLEWOODS BETDIRECT H'CAP (DIV I) 5f (F)
1:50 (1:51) (Class 5) (0-70,70) 4-Y-0+ **£2,914** (£867; £433; £216) **Stalls** High

Form RPR

4030 **1** **Gone'N'Dunnett (IRE)**[14] 275 7-8-7 **66**....(v) KirstyMilczarek(7) 4 74
(Mrs C A Dunnett) *a cl up: rdn over 1f out: styd on u.p ins last to ld last 50 yds* **12/1**

3/0- **2** *1/2* **Nepro (IRE)**[32] 4-9-0 **69**....(t) EdwardCreighton(3) 6 75
(E J Creighton) *cl up: led 1/2-way: rdn and hdd ins last: kpt on wl towards fin* **20/1**

-020 **3** *nk* **Efistorm**[6] 362 5-9-1 **70**.... JasonEdmunds(3) 1 75
(J Balding) *cl up on outer: effrt over 1f out: rdn to ld ins last: hdd and no ex last 50 yds* **7/2**[1]

00-0 **4** *1* **Little Ridge (IRE)**[37] 79 5-9-4 **70**.... SteveDrowne 5 72
(H Morrison) *dwlt: hld up towards rr: hdwy 2f out: much room over 1f out: rdn and kpt on ins last* **14/1**

2212 **5** *hd* **Byo (IRE)**[3] 401 8-8-4 **56** 6ex.... AdrianTNicholls 8 57
(P Howling) *hld up in tch: hdwy over 1f out: sn rdn and kpt on ins last: nrst fin* **7/2**[1]

6-10 **6** *1 1/4* **Cashel Mead**[10] 320 6-8-6 **58**....(b) ChrisCatlin 7 54
(J L Spearing) *cl up: ev ch 2f out: sn rdn: edgd lft over 1f out: sn wknd* **12/1**

0214 **7** *nk* **Sahara Silk (IRE)**[9] 332 5-8-10 **65**....(v) PatrickMathers(3) 2 60
(D Shaw) *towards rr and pushed along after 1f: rdn wl over 1f out: kpt on ins last: nvr nr ldrs* **14/1**

410- **8** *2 1/2* **Muara**[213] 3584 4-8-4 **56**.... PaulHanagan 3 42
(D W Barker) *led to halfway: rdn along 2f out: wkng whn hmpd over 1f out* **10/1**

411- **9** *shd* **El Potro**[47] 6696 4-8-12 **64**.... GrahamGibbons 9 50
(E S McMahon) *dwlt: sn chsng ldrs: rdn over 1f out and sn wknd* **9/2**[2]

-534 **10** *3* **Orchestration (IRE)**[2] 411 5-8-5 **57** oh2 ow1....(v) RobbieFitzpatrick 10 32
(M J Attwater) *towards rr: rdn along 2f out: sn outpcd* **15/2**[3]

58.71 secs (-1.59) **Going Correction** -0.275s/f (Stan) **10** Ran SP% **117.0**
Speed ratings (Par 103):101,100,99,98,97 95,95,91,91,86
CSF £225.26 CT £1039.96 TOTE £21.70: £5.60, £4.60, £1.60; EX 290.70.
Owner Christine Dunnett Racing **Bred** Ocal Bloodstock **Trained** Hingham, Norfolk

FOCUS
A modest handicap but well contested, and the form looks pretty solid for the grade, rated through winner and third.

425 BETDIRECT.CO.UK CLAIMING STKS 1m 4f (F)
2:20 (2:20) (Class 6) 4-Y-0+ **£2,388** (£705; £352) **Stalls** Low

Form RPR

1-20 **1** **Kylkenny**[12] 296 11-9-5 85....(t) TravisBlock(5) 3 89
(H Morrison) *trckd ldrs: hdwy to ld 3f out: rdn over 1f out and styd on:* **4/7**[1]

5-00 **2** *2 1/2* **Mi Odds**[9] 334 10-8-12 67.... RobertWinston 1 73
(Mrs N Macauley) *hld up in tch: hdwy to chse ldrs 4f out: sn rdn along and outpcd wl over 2f out: kpt on u.p fnl f* **20/1**

6224 **3** *1/2* **Romil Star (GER)**[14] 273 9-8-3 65....(v) AndrewElliott(7) 6 71
(K R Burke) *prom: led over 5f out: rdn and hdd 3f out: drvn and one pce fnl 2f* **4/1**[2]

1-43 **4** *1/2* **Chater Knight (IRE)**[14] 273 5-7-13 59.... JamesDoyle(7) 4 66
(Micky Hammond) *cl up: rdn along to chse wnr over 2f out: sn drvn and one pce* **13/2**[3]

30-6 **5** *18* **Court Of Appeal**[13] 283 9-9-2 68....(tp) TomEaves 2 49
(B Ellison) *chsd ldrs: rdn along over 3f out: outpcd over 2f out* **7/1**

300- **6** *dist* **Form And Beauty (IRE)**[21] 3519 4-8-9 65....(p) ChrisCatlin 5 —
(C Roberts) *led: pushed along 1/2-way: sn hdd & wknd: bhd fnl 3f* **66/1**

2m 40.55s (-1.54) **Going Correction** -0.075s/f (Stan)
WFA 4 from 5yo+ 3lb **6** Ran SP% **115.7**
Speed ratings (Par 101):102,100,100,99,87 —
CSF £15.84 TOTE £1.80: £1.60, £4.40; EX 9.60.The winner was claimed by Diamond Racing Ltd for £14,000.
Owner W R B Racing 59 (wrbracing.com) **Bred** R M , P J And S R Payne **Trained** East Ilsley, Berks

FOCUS
The favourite won as he was entitled to, with more in hand than the margin of victory suggests. The third and fourth were close to form.
Court Of Appeal Official explanation: trainer's representative said gelding was suffering from a breathing problem

The Form Book, Raceform Ltd, Compton, RG20 6NL

426 LITTLEWOODS BETDIRECT H'CAP (DIV II) 5f (F)
2:50 (2:50) (Class 5) (0-70,70) 4-Y-0+ £2,914 (£867; £433; £216) Stalls High

Form RPR
-000 1 **Anfield Dream**[19] [224] 4-9-4 70 EddieAhern 1 87
(J R Jenkins) *trckd ldrs: smooth hdwy 2f out: led over 1f out and sn pushed clr* 7/2[1]
1-64 2 3 **Tag Team (IRE)**[10] [320] 5-8-11 63 ow1 NCallan 5 69
(John A Harris) *led: pushed along 2f out: rdn and hdd over 1f out: sn one pce* 7/2[1]
-111 3 1 ½ **Henry Tun**[3] [401] 8-8-3 58 6ex (b) JasonEdmunds(3) 10 59
(J Balding) *chsd ldrs: rdn wl over 1f out: kpt on same pce* 4/1[2]
6-00 4 ½ **Alexia Rose (IRE)**[10] [317] 4-8-10 62 TomEaves 3 61
(A Berry) *bmpd s: sn in tch: rdn 2f out and sn one pce* 8/1[3]
2440 5 1 ¼ **Alpaga Le Jomage (IRE)**[7] [345] 4-8-13 65 DeanMcKeown 6 60
(M J Polglase) *cl up: pushed along 1/2-way: rdn 2f out and sn btn* 11/1
-001 6 1 ¼ **Times Review (USA)**[20] [216] 5-8-1 60 (b) JamesDoyle(7) 8 50+
(C A Dwyer) *swtchd to stands side after 1f: sn rdn along in rr: nvr a factor* 8/1[3]
-010 7 hd **Monte Major (IRE)**[3] [401] 5-8-1 55 6ex (v) PatrickMathers(3) 4 45
(D Shaw) *bmpd s: sn rdn along in rr: a bhd* 11/1
2-20 8 1 ½ **Almaty Express**[10] [317] 4-8-11 63 (b) RobertWinston 2 47
(J R Weymes) *cl up: rdn along over 2f out: sn wknd* 8/1[3]
-030 9 1 **Orpen Wide (IRE)**[14] [276] 4-9-3 69 BrianReilly 9 49
(M C Chapman) *sn rdn along in rr: bhd fr 1/2-way* 20/1
58.72 secs (-1.58) **Going Correction** -0.275s/f (Stan) 9 Ran SP% 119.2
Speed ratings (Par 103):101,96,93,93,91 89,88,86,84
CSF £16.34 CT £51.93 TOTE £4.80: £2.00, £1.70, £1.50; EX 26.00.
Owner The Saints Partnership **Bred** Michael Ng **Trained** Royston, Herts
FOCUS
Run in almost an identical time to the first division, this looked another competitive handicap, but Anfield Dream ran out a comfortable winner. The race could be rated higher.
Alexia Rose(IRE) Official explanation: jockey said filly hung right

427 TEXT "BETDIRECT" TO 88600 (S) STKS 1m (F)
3:20 (3:20) (Class 6) 4-Y-0+ £2,388 (£705; £352) Stalls Low

Form RPR
-132 1 **Vancouver Gold (IRE)**[9] [330] 4-8-12 63 RobertWinston 7 57
(K R Burke) *trckd ldrs: hdwy to ld over 2f out: rdn and edgd lft over 1f out: styd on* 11/10[1]
-250 2 2 **Colonel Bilko (IRE)**[5] [382] 4-8-11 49 ChrisCatlin 4 52
(Miss S J Wilton) *in tch: hdwy to chse wnr over 2f out: rdn wl over 1f out and kpt on same pce* 12/1
00-6 3 5 **Elms Schoolboy**[23] [183] 4-9-3 45 FergalLynch 5 47
(P Howling) *in tch: hdwy 3f out: rdn over 2f out: drvn and no imp whn hung lft over 1f out* 10/1
-304 4 ¾ **King Forever**[9] [330] 4-8-11 55 EddieAhern 8 39
(D E Cantillon) *sn led: rdn along 3f out: hdd and hung rt over 2f out: sn drvn and btn* 6/1[3]
-006 5 ¾ **Venetian Princess (IRE)**[4] [386] 4-8-12 45 ShaneKelly 1 38
(P Howling) *cl up on inner: rdn along 3f out: sn drvn and wknd fnl 2f* 12/1
-650 6 1 ¾ **Scotty's Future (IRE)**[17] [251] 8-8-11 64 AdrianTNicholls 3 33
(D Nicholls) *sn rdn along in rr: hdwy and in tch on outer 1/2-way: wd st: sn rdn and btn over 2f out* 7/2[2]
00/ 7 9 **Jacobin (USA)**[8] [4554] 5-8-12 ow1 VinceSlattery 2 15
(M Scudamore) *a towards rr: rdn along and lost pl 1/2-way: sn bhd* 50/1
0 8 22 **Sandhill Dancer**[18] [243] 4-8-6 DeanMcKeown 6 —
(S Parr) *chsd ldrs: rdn along and lost pl 1/2-way: sn bhd* 66/1
1m 44.27s (-0.33) **Going Correction** -0.075s/f (Stan) 8 Ran SP% 112.1
Speed ratings (Par 101):98,96,91,90,89 87,78,56
CSF £15.70 TOTE £1.70: £1.10, £2.90, £2.90; EX 16.00.The winner was bought in for 6,000gns.
Owner Bigwigs Bloodstock II **Bred** Ballinacurra Stud **Trained** Middleham Moor, N Yorks
FOCUS
Moderate selling-grade form in which the winner only had run to recent form and just had to be pushed out to score.
Elms Schoolboy Official explanation: jockey said gelding hung left in home straight

428 CLASSICVALUEPOOLS.COM H'CAP 6f (F)
3:50 (3:51) (Class 6) (0-65,70) 4-Y-0+ £2,388 (£705; £352) Stalls Low

Form RPR
4-33 1 **Winthorpe (IRE)**[14] [274] 6-8-12 58 GrahamGibbons 7 67
(J J Quinn) *prom: hdwy to ld over 2f out: rdn wl over 1f out: drvn and edgd lft ins last: hld on wl* 11/2[1]
2114 2 ¾ **Shadow Jumper (IRE)**[7] [345] 5-8-13 59 (v) RobbieFitzpatrick 5 66
(J T Stimpson) *chsd ldrs on inner: rdn along over 2f out: hdwy over 1f out: sn drvn and ev ch ins last: kpt on* 8/1
0011 3 nk **Winning Pleasure (IRE)**[7] [345] 8-9-7 70 6ex JasonEdmunds(3) 11 76
(J Balding) *trckd ldrs: hdwy over 2f out: chsd wnr over 1f out: rdn: edgd lft and ev ch ins last: no ex towards fin* 12/1
60-2 4 1 ¼ **Shifty Night (IRE)**[9] [332] 5-8-4 57 (v) KirstyMilczarek(7) 3 59
(Mrs C A Dunnett) *bhd: rdn along 1/2-way: hdwy 2f out: drvn and hung lft over 1f out: nrst fin* 9/1
0010 5 1 **Zorn**[2] [413] 7-8-10 56 ShaneKelly 10 55
(P Howling) *prom on outer: rdn along over 2f out: sn drvn and wknd over 1f out* 13/2[3]
-210 6 shd **Ruman (IRE)**[14] [274] 4-8-13 59 ChrisCatlin 2 58
(M J Attwater) *dwlt and bhd: hdwy over 2f out: sn rdn and styd on ins last: nrst fin* 6/1[2]
-152 7 1 ½ **Doctor Dennis (IRE)**[14] [274] 9-8-13 59 (v) EddieAhern 4 53
(J Pearce) *towards rr: rdn along 1/2-way: nvr nr ldrs* 6/1[2]
3/00 8 3 ½ **Shannon Arms (USA)**[26] [171] 5-9-4 64 (p) NCallan 9 48
(K A Ryan) *sn led: rdn along and hdd over 2f out: sn drvn and wknd* 11/1
0-25 9 1 ½ **Imperium**[2] [408] 5-8-8 54 (p) PaulHanagan 8 33
(Stef Liddiard) *in tch: rdn along wl over 2f out: wknd and hld whn hmpd over 1f out* 11/2[1]
06-0 10 5 **Green Pirate**[14] [274] 4-8-11 57 PaulFessey 6 21
(R Craggs) *rrd s and slowly away: a bhd* 14/1
1m 16.31s (-0.59) **Going Correction** -0.075s/f (Stan) 10 Ran SP% 116.5
Speed ratings (Par 101):100,99,98,96,95 95,93,88,86,80
CSF £49.08 CT £520.10 TOTE £8.30: £2.50, £2.50, £3.80; EX 67.10.
Owner Green Roberts Savage Whittall Williams **Bred** M Conaghan **Trained** Settrington, N Yorks
■ Stewards' Enquiry : Graham Gibbons one-day ban: used whip with excessive force (Feb 27)
FOCUS
A competitive sprint handicap and sound enough form for the grade.
Shannon Arms(USA) Official explanation: jockey said gelding had no more to give

429 PLAY NOW AT BETDIRECTCASINO.COM H'CAP 7f (F)
4:20 (4:20) (Class 5) (0-70,66) 4-Y-0+ £3,238 (£963; £481; £240) Stalls Low

Form RPR
0-30 1 **Set Alight**[10] [316] 5-9-3 65 (v) AdrianTNicholls 10 74
(Mrs C A Dunnett) *cl up: led 2f out: rdn over 1f out: styd on strly ins last* 9/2[3]
-014 2 1 ¼ **Lucius Verrus (USA)**[5] [383] 6-8-9 60 (v) PatrickMathers(3) 9 66
(D Shaw) *hld up towards rr: hdwy on outer 2f out: rdn to chse wnr ins last: kpt on* 4/1[2]
1-60 3 1 **Preskani**[37] [77] 4-8-13 61 (p) RobertWinston 8 64
(Mrs N Macauley) *trckd ldrs: pushed along and sltly outpcd over 2f out: hdwy u.p over 1f out: kpt on same pce ins last* 10/1
0-13 4 nk **Dispol Isle (IRE)**[9] [332] 4-8-12 60 PhillipMakin 4 63
(T D Barron) *trckd ldrs: pushed along and sltly outpcd over 2f out: sn rdn and hdwy over 1f out: drvn and kpt on same pce ins last* 9/4[1]
3113 5 1 **Sierra**[23] [183] 5-8-8 56 PaulFessey 5 56
(A W Carroll) *towards rr: hdwy wl over 2f out: sn rdn and kpt on u.p appr last: nrst fin* 8/1
0-06 6 3 **Paso Doble**[7] [345] 8-8-11 66 (p) JamesMillman(7) 3 59
(B R Millman) *rr and rdn along 1/2-way: styd on u.p fnl 2f: nvr nr ldrs* 12/1
6-06 7 hd **Lord Links (IRE)**[21] [200] 5-9-0 62 VinceSlattery 6 54
(D J Daly) *dwlt and a towards rr* 25/1
6214 8 1 ¾ **Lady Suesanne (IRE)**[7] [350] 4-8-9 57 (b) RobbieFitzpatrick 1 45
(M J Attwater) *s.i.s: gd hdwy on inner to ld after 2f: rdn along and hdd 2f out: sn drvn and grad wknd* 11/1
0/00 9 1 ½ **Honest Injun**[26] [167] 5-9-4 66 (t) NCallan 2 50
(A G Juckes) *prom: effrt and ev ch over 2f out: sn rdn and wknd wl over 1f out* 28/1
-001 10 2 ½ **Missperon (IRE)**[9] [332] 4-8-3 58 6ex (b) CDTimmons(7) 7 36
(K A Ryan) *plld hrd: led 2f: cl up tl wknd qckly 3f out* 16/1
1m 29.58s (-1.22) **Going Correction** -0.075s/f (Stan) 10 Ran SP% 118.4
Speed ratings (Par 103):103,101,100,100,98 95,95,93,91,88
CSF £23.28 CT £153.47 TOTE £4.90: £2.40, £1.90, £2.90; EX 41.00.
Owner Nigel George **Bred** M V S And Mrs Aram **Trained** Hingham, Norfolk
■ Stewards' Enquiry : N Callan caution: careless riding
Robert Winston two-day ban: careless riding (27-28 Feb)
FOCUS
A modest handicap but a number of in-form horses in attendance, so the form should work out alright.

430 FREE £25 WITH LITTLEWOODSPOKER.COM H'CAP 1m (F)
4:50 (4:50) (Class 6) (0-65,61) 3-Y-0 £2,388 (£705; £352) Stalls Low

Form RPR
0-02 1 **Subsidise (IRE)**[9] [333] 3-8-7 50 (b) JoeFanning 9 61+
(J G Given) *rr and rdn along 1/2-way: gd hdwy on inner 2f out: styd on to ld wl over 1f out: sn rdn clr and styd on wl* 10/1
-533 2 4 **Cool Isle**[9] [333] 3-8-10 53 (b) NCallan 3 55
(K A Ryan) *sn led: rdn along over 2f out: drvn and hdd wl over 1f out: kpt on same pce* 12/1
60-4 3 1 ¾ **Chicherova (IRE)**[21] [199] 3-8-7 50 PaulFessey 1 48
(T D Barron) *trckd ldrs: effrt over 2f out: sn rdn and kpt on same pce* 20/1
06-1 4 1 **Hi Dancer**[21] [199] 3-8-11 54 LeeEnstone 8 50
(P C Haslam) *towards rr: hdwy on outer to chse ldrs 1/2-way: rdn 2f out: sn edgd lft and wknd* 11/4[1]
5121 5 5 **Inaminute (IRE)**[13] [286] 3-9-1 58 PatCosgrave 11 43
(K R Burke) *prom on outer: rdn along over 2f out: sn drvn and wknd* 11/2[2]
00-5 6 16 **Wensleydale Star**[7] [347] 3-9-4 61 PhillipMakin 10 11
(T D Barron) *chsd ldrs: rdn along 1/2-way: sn wknd* 25/1
60-1 7 2 ½ **Penang Cinta**[20] [211] 3-9-1 58 RobertWinston 4 2
(G A Butler) *in tch: pushed along over 3f out: rdn over 2f out and sn btn* 11/4[1]
6-02 8 ¾ **Perfect Order (USA)**[21] [193] 3-9-0 57 (p) SteveDrowne 2 —
(N A Callaghan) *cl up: rdn along over 3f out and sn wknd* 7/1[3]
5050 9 4 **Duel In The Sands**[7] [349] 3-8-10 56 PatrickMathers(3) 5 —
(D Shaw) *sn pushed along in rr: bhd fr 1/2-way* 16/1
1m 44.61s (0.01) **Going Correction** -0.075s/f (Stan) 9 Ran SP% 112.5
Speed ratings (Par 95):96,92,90,89,84 68,65,65,61
CSF £118.14 CT £2344.66 TOTE £8.70: £2.50, £2.60, £3.60; EX 41.70 Place 6 £34.06, Place 5 £16.97.
Owner J W Rowles **Bred** Limestone Stud **Trained** Willoughton, Lincs
FOCUS
Moderate handicap form but the winner looks an improver in the blinkers and the form is solid enough for the level.
Wensleydale Star Official explanation: jockey said gelding was hanging
Penang Cinta Official explanation: jockey said gelding was unsuited by the fibresand surface
Perfect Order(USA) Official explanation: jockey said filly was never travelling
T/Plt: £26.10 to a £1 stake. Pool: £39,845.15. 1,110.35 winning tickets. T/Qpdt: £5.20 to a £1 stake. Pool: £3,459.80. 488.80 winning tickets. JR

366 NAD AL SHEBA (L-H)
Thursday, February 16
OFFICIAL GOING: Turf course - firm; dirt course - fast

431a ENTERTAINMENT PLUS TROPHY (SPONSORED BY GULF NEWS) (H'CAP) (TURF) 6f (T)
2:55 (2:55) (90-105,105) 4-Y-0+ £41,569 (£12,790; £6,395; £3,197)

RPR
1 **Sir Edwin Landseer (USA)**[6] [367] 6-8-10 95 (p) RoystonFfrench 10 100
(Christian Wroe, UAE) *hld up in rr: last ent st: swtchd wd: rdn 2 1/2f out: chal 1 1/2f out: led last 50yds* 16/1
2 1 **Royal Storm (IRE)**[6] [366] 7-9-0 98 MJKinane 5 101
(Mrs A J Perrett) *wl away: led after 1f: rdn 2 1/2f out: kpt on wl: hdd last 50yds* 13/2[3]
3 2 ¼ **Obe Gold**[7] [352] 4-9-6 105 (v) RyanMoore 2 100
(M R Channon) *racd last: rdn 3 1/2f out: n.m.r on rail 3f out: r.o late: nrst fin* 8/1
4 nk **Protector (SAF)**[6] [367] 5-8-6 90 RichardMullen 13 85
(H J Brown, South Africa) *racd v wd: trckd ldrs ent st: clsd 2f out: ev ch: one pce* 8/1
5 1 ¾ **Mokabra (IRE)**[21] [203] 5-8-11 96 (v) JMurtagh 12 85
(D Selvaratnam, UAE) *prom early: trckd ldrs ent st: wknd* 33/1

6 ½ **Conceal**[7] 352 8-9-0 **98** .... PDillon 4 87
(R Bouresly, Kuwait) *trckd ldrs: ev ch 3f out: n.m.r 2 1/2f out: kpt on* **7/1**

7 shd **Sevillano**[21] 203 5-9-4 **102** .... (t) TedDurcan 6 90
(A Laird, UAE) *prom: keen: trckd ldrs 2 1/2f out: rdn 2f out: wknd* **7/2**[1]

8 ½ **Rosencrans (USA)**[216] 5-8-10 **95** .... (vt) LDettori 11 81
(Saeed Bin Suroor) *mid-div: t.k.h 4f out: trckd ldrs 3f out: prog wd 2f out: one pce* **6/1**[2]

9 1 ¼ **So Will I**[14] 281 5-9-5 **104** .... (t) RHills 9 86
(Doug Watson, UAE) *mid-div: n.m.r 4f out and 2 1/2f out: nt rcvr* **10/1**

10 ¾ **At Once (GER)**[21] 204 5-8-12 **97** .... PJSmullen 1 77
(Frau E Mader, Germany) *mid-div on rail: n.m.r 2 1/2f out: swtchd 1 1/2f out: n.m.r 1f out* **16/1**

11 ¾ **Howick Falls (USA)**[887] 4877 5-9-4 **102** .... (v) TPO'Shea 7 81
(E Charpy, UAE) *s.i.s: hld up in rr: gng wl 3f out: n.m.r: n.d* **12/1**

12 3 ¼ **Clod Ber Junior (BRZ)**[6] 366 9-8-8 **93** .... (bt) WayneSmith 3 61
(A Selvaratnam, UAE) *trckd ldr on rail: rdn 2 1/2f out: one pce* **40/1**

13 8 **Queleden Candela (ARG)**[28] 155 5-8-8 **93** .... (t) WSupple 8 37
(I Jory, Saudi Arabia) *prom wd: 3rd ent st: rdn 3f out: wknd* **22/1**

1m 12.0s **Going Correction** +0.475s/f (Yiel) **13** Ran SP% **122.8**
Speed ratings: 113,111,108,108,105 105,105,104,102,101 100,96,85

Owner Biz-Ability Old Master Syndicate **Bred** Mike Sloan **Trained** UAE

FOCUS
A good handicap, but perhaps just lacking in unexposed types.

NOTEBOOK
Sir Edwin Landseer(USA), better than the bare form when only fifth in a similar event over six and a half furlongs here last time, stepped up on that effort to run out a pretty decisive winner. He should continue to go well.

Royal Storm(IRE) pretty much ran to form he showed when second in a similar event over six and a half furlongs on his debut in Dubai, but is not an easy horse to win with and just found one too good.

Obe Gold, with the visor re-fitted, again failed to repeat the form he showed to win on his debut in Dubai and looks high in the weights.

Protector(SAF) ◆ had today's winner behind in fifth when an unlucky third over six and a half furlongs on his debut in Dubai, but he was stuck out very wide throughout from stall 13 and could not sustain his challenge. He has not had things go his way so far, but could find a similar race with a bit more luck.

Mokabra(IRE), with the visor re-fitted, ran a little better.

Sevillano failed to build on the promise he showed to win over six and a half furlongs here on his previous start and has to be considered a little disappointing.

Rosencrans(USA) was well held on his return from a 216-day break, but this should have set him up for a return to dirt.

433a TABLOID CUP (SPONSORED BY GULF NEWS) (H'CAP) (TURF) 6f (T)
3:55 (3:55) (90-105,105) 4-Y-0+ **£41,569** (£12,790; £6,395; £3,197)

RPR

1 **Montgomery's Arch (USA)**[21] 201 4-9-4 **102** .... (v[1]) MJKinane 7 110
(J Noseda) *hld up in last: swtchd wd: stl last 1 1/2f out: rdn to cl: fin fast: led last strides* **9/1**

2 ¾ **Bygone Days**[21] 203 5-9-4 **102** .... KerrinMcEvoy 1 108
(I Mohammed, UAE) *mid-div: gng strly on rail 3 1/2f out: rdn to cl 3f out: led 100yds out: hdd nr line* **5/2**[1]

3 hd **Bahiano (IRE)**[6] 367 5-8-12 **97** .... RyanMoore 8 101
(C E Brittain) *mid-div: rdn 4f out whn outpcd: qcknd 1 1/2f out: nrst fin* **8/1**

4 2 ¾ **Talbot Avenue**[6] 367 8-9-0 **98** .... PJSmullen 10 95
(M Mullineaux) *t.k.h: hld up in rr: gng wl 3f out: rdn 2 1/2f out: r.o: nrst fin* **11/1**

5 nk **Safe Structure (SAF)**[7] 352 6-9-6 **105** .... JBekker 6 100
(D Maroun, South Africa) *led main gp: rdn to chse ldr 2 1/2f out: wknd 1f out* **7/2**[2]

6 ½ **Gimasha**[146] 5438 4-8-10 **95** .... TPO'Shea 12 89
(E Charpy, UAE) *t.k.h and led: swtchd to rail after 200yds: clr 2 1/2f out: rdn 1 1/2f out: hdd 100yds out* **7/1**[3]

7 ½ **Karlo Guitar (BRZ)**[21] 206 6-9-0 **98** .... MAlmeida 11 91
(C Morgado, Brazil) *wd in mid -div: forced wd in st: n.d* **33/1**

8 nk **Harb (IRE)**[28] 149 6-8-8 **93** .... (t) RHills 9 84
(Doug Watson, UAE) *settled towards rr: rdn to cl on rail 2 1/2f out: n.m.r 2f out: nt qckn* **16/1**

9 1 ¾ **Baaridd**[14] 278 8-9-0 **98** .... JMurtagh 4 85
(D Selvaratnam, UAE) *s.i.s: mid-div on rail: gng wl 3 1/2f out: rdn 2f out: one pce* **16/1**

10 shd **Hidden Dragon (USA)**[6] 366 7-8-6 **90** .... TedDurcan 3 77
(J Pearce) *racd in rr of main gp: n.m.r 1 1/2f out: n.d* **12/1**

11 3 **Prince Charming**[6] 366 4-8-10 **95** .... (t) DDaniels 2 72
(R Bouresly, Kuwait) *trckd 2nd on rail: ev ch 3f out: wknd last 1 1/2f* **66/1**

12 9 **Treasure Cay**[150] 5369 5-8-11 **96** .... (t) JohnEgan 5 46
(P W D'Arcy) *mid-div: rdn 3f out: nt qckn: wknd* **16/1**

1m 12.37s **Going Correction** +0.475s/f (Yiel) **12** Ran SP% **122.5**
Speed ratings: 110,109,108,105,104 104,103,102,100,100 96,84

Owner Franconson Partners **Bred** Sycamore Hall Farm Llc **Trained** Newmarket, Suffolk

FOCUS
A high-class sprint handicap.

NOTEBOOK
Montgomery's Arch(USA) did not exactly shape like a future winner when only seventh over six and a half furlongs on his debut in Dubai but, 3lb lower this time and fitted with a visor for the first time, he showed the benefit of his reappearance to gain his first success since taking the Group Two Richmond Stakes as a juvenile. It remains to be seen if the headgear will work as well next time.

Bygone Days, third on his debut in Dubai in a similar event over six and a half furlongs, was produced with every chance and ran up to form in second. There could be a similar race in him, but his improvement may be levelling out.

Bahiano(IRE) ran well in defeat but was found out by a 7lb rise in the weights for his recent success over six and a half furlongs here.

Talbot Avenue ran his race in fourth but could not reverse form with Bahiano. He is a consistent sort, but not the easiest to win with.

Safe Structure(SAF) was below the form he showed to win a similar event over six and a half furlongs here on his previous start even allowing for a 4lb rise in the weights.

Hidden Dragon(USA) again gave the impression he may be better suited by further these days.

Treasure Cay, 8lb higher than when winning a handicap at Leicester when last seen 150 days previously, ran a shocker on his debut in Dubai.

434a AQUARIUS CUP (SPONSORED BY GULF NEWS) (H'CAP) (DIRT) 7f (D)
4:25 (4:25) (90-105,105) 4-Y-0+ **£41,569** (£12,790; £6,395; £3,197)

RPR

1 **Rock Music**[14] 277 4-8-12 **97** .... LDettori 16 92
(Saeed Bin Suroor) *a led: clr 3f out: hld on wl* **7/2**[1]

2 ½ **Thajja (IRE)**[6] 366 5-9-2 **100** .... (v) JMurtagh 2 95
(Doug Watson, UAE) *nt far away on rail: hrd rdn 2 1/2f out: r.o wl fnl 1f out: nrst fin* **14/1**

3 2 **Safsoof (USA)**[21] 206 4-8-6 **90** .... KerrinMcEvoy 8 80
(I Mohammed, UAE) *trckd ldr in centre: rdn 3 1/2f out: outpcd: swtchd wd: r.o last 1 1/2f: nrst fin* **9/2**[2]

4 2 ½ **Waajeb (USA)**[7] 357 6-8-7 **91** .... (t) RoystonFfrench 14 74
(A Al Raihe, UAE) *prom in centre: ev ch 3f out: rdn 2 1/2f out: kpt on wl* **14/1**

5 nk **Mukafeh (USA)**[13] 5-9-0 **98** .... WSupple 11 81
(E Charpy, UAE) *mid-div: rdn to cl 3f out: r.o nrst fin* **7/1**

6 1 ¾ **Delude (IRE)**[21] 204 8-8-6 **90** .... GHind 5 68
(A Laird, UAE) *swtchd to rail s: racd in last: sme prog in st: nrst fin* **33/1**

7 2 ½ **Northern Rock (JPN)**[7] 353 8-8-10 **95** .... (bt) TedDurcan 15 65
(A Laird, UAE) *trckd ldr: rdn to cl 3f out: nt qckn: kpt on* **8/1**

8 ½ **Egyptian (USA)**[7] 353 7-8-10 **95** .... PDillon 13 64
(R Bouresly, Kuwait) *towards rr: n.m.r after 2f: n.d* **40/1**

9 1 **Master Robbie**[7] 353 7-8-6 **90** .... DDaniels 9 58
(R Bouresly, Kuwait) *racd in rr: n.d* **66/1**

10 shd **Mogaamer (USA)**[13] 4-9-5 **104** .... (t) RHills 10 70
(S Seemar, UAE) *trckd ldrs centre: rdn 3f out: nt qckn* **11/2**[3]

11 3 ¼ **Damachida (IRE)**[7] 357 7-8-12 **97** .... (t) MJKinane 12 55
(Eva Sundbye, Sweden) *settled towards rr and wd: n.d* **25/1**

12 ½ **Sleeping Weapon (USA)**[13] 7-8-8 **93** .... (vt) TPO'Shea 3 50
(Doug Watson, UAE) *towards rr: n.d* **25/1**

13 shd **Naaddey**[69] 5-8-7 **91** .... PJSmullen 6 48
(D Selvaratnam, UAE) *in rr of mid-div: rdn 4f out: nvr a factor* **16/1**

14 2 ¾ **Hoy Soy Usted (BRZ)**[21] 204 5-8-6 **90** .... MAlmeida 7 40
(C Morgado, Brazil) *trckd ldrs: t.k.h: n.m.r 3f out: wknd* **40/1**

15 2 ¼ **Golden Stravinsky (USA)**[21] 203 4-8-12 **97** .... (t) PAragoni 1 40
(A Peraino, Italy) *mid-div: trckd ldrs 3f out: rdn: nt qckn: wknd* **25/1**

16 1 ¼ **Little Jim (ARG)**[14] 277 6-9-6 **105** .... (vt) RichardMullen 4 45
(A Laird, UAE) *s.i.s: prog to mid-div on rail: rdn 3f out: wknd* **9/1**

1m 24.22s **Going Correction** +0.225s/f (Slow) **16** Ran SP% **129.5**
Speed ratings: 115,114,112,109,108 106,104,103,102,102 98,97,97,94,92 90

Owner Godolphin **Bred** Mrs J Chandris **Trained** Newmarket, Suffolk

FOCUS
A good dirt handicap in which the progressive Rock Music followed up his recent course success with a good effort from the front.

NOTEBOOK
Rock Music ◆, 7lb higher than when winning a weaker race over a mile here last time, stepped up on the bare form of that success to follow up. Although a wide draw is often an advantage on this dirt course, he was forced to use a lot of energy up early on to get to the front and did extremely well to sustain his challenge. There should be more to come and it will be disappointing if he does not complete the hat-trick.

Thajja(IRE), below form on the turf last time, ran much better returned to his favoured surface from his unfavourable draw.

Safsoof(USA), a promising fourth on his debut for these connections over six furlongs here on his previous start, ran well on this step up in trip. On this evidence, he could progress again over another furlong.

Waajeb(USA) would have appreciated the return to dirt and ran well in fourth.

Mukafeh(USA), runner-up in a mile Listed race at Jebel Ali on his previous start, ran well returned to handicap company but just appeared found out by the drop back in trip.

435a FRIDAY STKS (SPONSORED BY GULF NEWS) (H'CAP) (TURF) 1m (T)
4:55 (4:55) (90-105,105) 4-Y-0+ **£41,569** (£12,790; £6,395; £3,197)

RPR

1 **Tiger Shark (SAF)**[7] 352 5-8-12 **97** .... KShea 2 102
(H J Brown, South Africa) *settled in rr: last of main gp 3f out: prog ins to chal 1f out: r.o wl* **4/1**[3]

2 ¾ **Blue On Blues (ARG)**[6] 369 5-9-0 **98** .... (t) RyanMoore 7 102
(S Seemar, UAE) *mid-div: prog wd 2 1/2f out: led 2f out: chal 1f out: kpt on wl* **10/3**[1]

3 2 ¼ **Spirit Of France (IRE)**[14] 282 4-8-10 **95** .... GBirrer 1 94
(Christian Wroe, UAE) *mid-div: swtchd off rail 3f out: rdn to cl 2f out: ev ch 1f out: nt qckn* **7/2**[2]

4 3 ¼ **Terra Verde (IRE)**[138] 5641 4-9-6 **105** .... KerrinMcEvoy 9 97
(I Mohammed, UAE) *disp 3rd on rail: n.m.r 3f out: rdn 2f out: kpt on* **7/1**

5 1 ¼ **Little Good Bay**[7] 357 6-8-7 **91** .... (b) TedDurcan 4 82
(A Laird, UAE) *s.i.s: racd in rr: n.m.r 2 1/2 out: swtchd centre 2f out: one pce* **7/1**

6 3 ¼ **In The Fan (USA)**[6] 367 4-8-6 **90** .... (bt[1]) RoystonFfrench 3 74
(A Al Raihe, UAE) *mid-div: rdn to chal 2f out: nt qckn* **33/1**

7 1 ½ **Documento Fiscal (BRZ)**[21] 207 4-8-5 **90** .... (p) MAlmeida 5 70
(C Morgado, Brazil) *settled in mid-div: n.m.r 4f out: hmpd 1 1/2f out: nt rcvr* **33/1**

8 1 ½ **Blue Corrig (IRE)**[6] 371 6-8-10 **95** .... (b) PJSmullen 13 72
(Joseph Crowley, Ire) *rushed to ld: clr 2 1/2f out: wknd qckly 2f out* **66/1**

9 3 **Ihla Grande (USA)**[158] 5162 5-9-2 **100** .... TPO'Shea 10 72
(E Charpy, UAE) *3rd in centre: ev ch 3f out: wknd qckly* **16/1**

10 3 ¼ **Walmooh**[14] 282 10-9-4 **102** .... (vt) JMurtagh 6 68
(D Selvaratnam, UAE) *settled towards rr: rdn wd 3f out: n.d* **14/1**

11 5 ¾ **State Shinto (USA)**[21] 208 10-8-8 **93** .... (bt) DDaniels 12 46
(R Bouresly, Kuwait) *led main gp: wknd 3f out: hmpd 1 1/2f out: wknd* **20/1**

12 nk **Country Rambler (USA)**[78] 4-8-6 **90** .... WSupple 11 43
(Doug Watson, UAE) *v.s.a: nvr involved* **25/1**

1m 38.88s **Going Correction** +0.475s/f (Yiel) **13** Ran SP% **118.8**
Speed ratings: 108,107,105,101,100 97,95,94,91,88 82,81

Owner R Plersch & D Scott **Bred** Scott Bros **Trained** South Africa

FOCUS
Another good handicap in which Tiger Shark built on the promise he showed on his debut in Dubai to deny a solid yardstick in Blue On Blues.

NOTEBOOK
Tiger Shark(SAF), upped in trip, confirmed the promise he showed on his debut in Dubai with a determined success. There should be more to come.

Blue On Blues(ARG), 3lb higher, ran to the sort of form that saw him finish second in a similar event over course and distance on his previous start.

Blue Corrig(IRE), dropped no less than half a mile in trip, ran a little better than of late and is clearly not without hope.

436a GULF NEWS UAE 1000 GUINEAS (SPONSORED BY GULF NEWS) (LISTED RACE) (FILLIES) (DIRT) 1m (D)

5:25 (5:25) 3-Y-O **£94,476** (£29,069; £14,534; £7,267)

RPR

1 **Vague (USA)**[21] [202] 3-8-9 106 MJKinane 5 104
(J Noseda) *trckd ldr in centre: prog to ld 2 1/2f out: kicked clr 2f out: easily* **13/8**[1]

2 5 ¼ **Imperial Ice (SAF)**[7] [351] 4-9-4 90 KShea 7 83
(H J Brown, South Africa) *mid-div: gng wl 3f out: rdn to cl: r.o wl: tk 2nd cl home but no ch w wnr* **33/1**

3 nk **Rock Opera (SAF)**[28] [155] 4-9-4 105 TedDurcan 10 82
(A Laird, UAE) *mid-div: clsd 4f out: prog to chal 3f out: nt pce of wnr: lost 2nd cl home* **9/4**[2]

4 4 **Give Me The Night (IRE)**[21] [202] 3-8-9 90 WSupple 6 84
(Doug Watson, UAE) *mid-div: n.d: kpt on last 2f* **22/1**

5 2 ¼ **Deveron (USA)**[137] [5649] 3-8-9 107 KerrinMcEvoy 1 80
(I Mohammed, UAE) *trckd ldr on rail: 4th ent st: rdn 3f out: nvr threatened* **10/3**[3]

6 1 ½ **Dont Dili Dali**[21] [202] 3-8-9 90 JohnEgan 11 77
(J S Moore) *mid-div: hrd rdn 3f out: kpt on but nvr a threat* **14/1**

7 ½ **Zeina Of Arabia**[21] [202] 3-8-9 TPO'Shea 9 76
(Doug Watson, UAE) *hld up in rr: n.d* **100/1**

8 nk **Lindus Atenor**[21] [202] 3-8-9 80 (t) WayneSmith 3 75
(M Al Muhairi, UAE) *racd in rr: mod prog 2f out: wknd 1f out* **50/1**

9 nk **Princess Woodman (BRZ)**[21] [202] 4-9-4 90 MAlmeida 4 65
(C Morgado, Brazil) *broke awkwardly: nvr involved* **66/1**

10 9 **Swan Maiden (USA)**[21] [202] 3-8-9 93 RichardMullen 8 57
(A Laird, UAE) *led after 2f tl 3f out: wknd* **12/1**

11 1 ½ **Donia Dubai (IRE)**[21] [202] 3-8-9 PDillon 2 54
(R Bouresly, Kuwait) *s.i.s: racd in rr: n.d* **100/1**

1m 37.83s **Going Correction** +0.225s/f (Slow)
WFA 3 from 4yo 19lb **11** Ran SP% **119.0**
Speed ratings: 106,100,100,96,94 92,92,91,91,82 81

Owner J Paul Reddam **Bred** Dr N M Cole And Christopher Kline **Trained** Newmarket, Suffolk

FOCUS
The Godolphin operation had won all five previous runnings of the UAE 1000 Guineas, so their absence significantly weakened the quality of this year's renewal and, with both Rock Opera and Deveron running below expectations, Vague had little to beat.

NOTEBOOK
Vague(USA), with no Godolphin challenger, only had Rock Opera and Deveron to beat on form and, with those two not running up to expectations, she came home alone. She was to be aimed at the UAE Oaks, but unfortunately sustained an injury that will keep her off the track until the middle of the year.
Imperial Ice(SAF), fourth in a Listed race on turf on her previous start, probably ran to a similar level of form on her return to turf.
Rock Opera(SAF), reportedly the most expensive filly ever sold out of South Africa, was third in a mile handicap on the turf off a mark of 105 on her debut in Dubai. Switched to dirt, she travelled as well as the eventual winner for much of the way, but fell apart when asked to sustain her challenge in the straight and was most disappointing. If she is persevered with on dirt, she may need a shorter trip.
Give Me The Night(IRE) had next to no chance of reversing form with Vague.
Deveron(USA), a smart juvenile for Clive Brittain on turf last season who was third behind Rumplestiltskin in the Group One Marcel Boussac when last seen 137 days previously, ran a long way below form on her debut on dirt and first start for new connections. Her trainer is having a poor Carnival.
Dont Dili Dali was beaten roughly double the distance by Vague than she was on her debut in Dubai over seven furlongs.

437a PROPERTY WEEKLY CUP (SPONSORED BY GULF NEWS) (H'CAP) (TURF) 1m 4f (T)

5:55 (5:55) (90-105,105) 4-Y-O+ **£41,569** (£12,790; £6,395; £3,197)

RPR

1 **Punch Punch (BRZ)**[21] [205] 5-8-10 95 (v) MAlmeida 4 103
(C Morgado, Brazil) *s.i.s: racd in rr: n.m.r 2 1/2f out: swtchd wd: r.o v strly to ld 100yds out: easily* **40/1**

2 2 **Bonecrusher**[312] 7-8-7 91 (t) WayneSmith 6 97
(M Al Muhairi, UAE) *racd in rr: hdwy 2f out to chal centre: led 1 1/2f out: hdd 100yds out: no ch w wnr* **25/1**

3 1 ¾ **Remaadd (USA)**[21] [205] 5-9-2 100 (t) JMurtagh 12 103
(D Selvaratnam, UAE) *prom on rail: rdn to ld 2f out: kpt on one pce* **6/1**[3]

4 1 **Corriolanus (GER)**[6] [371] 6-9-6 105 RyanMoore 10 106
(S Seemar, UAE) *settled towards rr: swtchd rail 2 1/2f out: n.m.r: r.o last 2f out: nrst fin* **9/2**[2]

5 nk **Realism (FR)**[7] [356] 6-8-10 95 KerrinMcEvoy 9 95
(R A Fahey) *led main gp: ev ch 3f out: nt qckn* **20/1**

6 nse **Attentive (IRE)**[13] 8-8-10 95 TedDurcan 8 95
(S Seemar, UAE) *towards rr main gp: mid-div 2 1/2f out: n.m.r swtchd rail 1 1/2f out: ev ch: nt qckn* **25/1**

7 3 **Shanty Star (IRE)**[7] [356] 6-9-5 104 PDillon 15 100
(R Bouresly, Kuwait) *trckd ldrs: rdn 3f out: nt qckn but kpt on one pce* **8/1**

8 hd **Velodrome (BRZ)**[21] [205] 7-9-2 100 (t) TPO'Shea 5 97
(E Charpy, UAE) *racd in rr: sme prog to mid-div after 3f: r.o past btn horses late on* **33/1**

9 shd **Zenato (GER)**[14] [279] 5-9-4 102 RoystonFfrench 13 98
(F Reuterskiold, Sweden) *mid-div: rdn 3f out: nt qckn* **33/1**

10 ½ **Zaajel (IRE)**[21] [205] 7-8-10 95 (t) RHills 3 90
(E Charpy, UAE) *mid-div on rail: swtchd centre 3f out: n.m.r 2 1/2f out: r.o one pce* **16/1**

11 ½ **Tipperary All Star (FR)**[7] [354] 6-8-8 93 (t) PJSmullen 2 87
(M Halford, Ire) *mid-div: trckd ldrs 3f out then rdn: nt qckn* **14/1**

12 1 ¼ **Cristoforo (IRE)**[7] [354] 9-8-8 93 LDettori 7 85
(B J Curley) *towards rr of main gp: rdn to cl 2 1/2f out: n.m.r on rail: nt rcvr* **11/4**[1]

13 nk **Saintly Rachel (IRE)**[6] [371] 8-8-12 97 MJKinane 14 89
(C F Swan, Ire) *settled towards rr: n.d* **8/1**

14 10 **Hippodrome (IRE)**[7] [354] 4-8-7 93 (b) RichardMullen 16 72
(H J Brown, South Africa) *nt far away: rdn 3f out: n.m.r: nt rcvr* **25/1**

15 nk **Amandus (USA)**[14] [282] 6-8-8 93 (be) WSupple 1 69
(Doug Watson, UAE) *mid-div: gng wl 3f out: n.m.r: nt rcvr* **28/1**

16 2 ¾ **Forty Hablador (ARG)**[14] [279] 5-8-7 91 (bt[1]) GHind 64
(S Seemar, UAE) *led: rdn 3f out: wknd* **20/1**

2m 33.58s **Going Correction** +0.475s/f (Yiel)
WFA 4 from 5yo+ 3lb **16** Ran SP% **126.7**
Speed ratings: 107,105,104,103,103 103,101,101,101,101 100,99,99,93,92 91

Owner Estrela Energia Stables **Bred** Haras Santa Rita Di Serra **Trained** Brazil

FOCUS
The form looks just ordinary for a race of this class, but Punch Punch won impressively.

NOTEBOOK
Punch Punch(BRZ), well beaten on his debut in Dubai, left that form well behind with a visor replacing blinkers and ran out a pretty impressive winner. He did not enjoy a clear run when originally looking to make his move, but showed a decent turn of foot when finally in the clear and won well.
Bonecrusher, winless since taking a conditions race for David Loder in 2003, ran a fine race on his return from a 312-day absence.
Remaadd(USA) ran creditably without really improving for the fitting of a tongue-tie.
Corriolanus(GER) failed to build on the promise he showed on his return to Dubai over course and distance.
Realism(FR), upped in trip, ran a little better than of late and offered hope.
Tipperary All Star(FR) continues to struggle.
Cristoforo(IRE) failed to build on the promise he showed on his debut in Dubai over this course and distance but was stopped in his run at a crucial point and is better than the bare form.
Saintly Rachel(IRE) shaped well on her debut in Dubai, but this was disappointing.

438a WHEELS TROPHY (SPONSORED BY GULF NEWS) (H'CAP) (TURF) 1m (T)

6:25 (6:26) (90-105,102) 4-Y-O+ **£41,569** (£12,790; £6,395; £3,197)

RPR

1 **Royal Prince**[138] [5607] 5-9-3 99 WSupple 3 104
(Doug Watson, UAE) *mid-div gng strly: rdn to cl 2f out: led 1f out: r.o wl* **9/2**[1]

2 1 ½ **Anani (USA)**[91] 6-8-8 90 RichardMullen 6 92
(A Laird, UAE) *hld up in rr: stl in rr on rail 3f out: swtchd centre 1 1/2f out: n.m.r: r.o wl once clr* **11/1**

3 ½ **Kestrel Cross (IRE)**[7] [354] 4-8-10 93 LDettori 5 93
(V Smith) *mid-div: rdn 3f out: r.o wl fnl 110yds: nrst fin* **10/1**

4 shd **Colisay**[6] [370] 7-9-6 102 RyanMoore 1 103
(Mrs A J Perrett) *mid-div on rail: trckd ldrs 3f out: led 1 1/2f out: hdd 1f out: nt qckn* **5/1**[2]

5 2 ¾ **Morshdi**[364] [412] 8-9-4 100 JMurtagh 12 95
(D Selvaratnam, UAE) *mid-div wd: rdn 3f out: nt qckn: r.o late: nrst fin* **25/1**

6 ¾ **Setembro Chove (BRZ)**[14] [282] 5-9-4 100 MJKinane 2 94
(P Nickel Filho, Brazil) *hld up in rr: n.d* **8/1**

7 1 ¼ **Persian Majesty (IRE)**[14] [278] 6-9-2 98 KShea 7 89
(H J Brown, South Africa) *trckd ldrs into st: prog to chal 2f out: led 1 1/2f out: wknd* **7/1**

8 1 ½ **Bold Demand**[14] [277] 12-8-9 91 DDaniels 11 79
(R Bouresly, Kuwait) *disp ld early: trckd ldr ent st: swtchd centre 1 1/2f out: n.m.r: r.o wl once clr* **33/1**

9 shd **One To Win (IRE)**[144] [5496] 4-8-8 90 TedDurcan 4 78
(J Noseda) *s.i.s: prog to r in mid-div 3f out: rdn 2f out: one pce* **6/1**

10 2 ½ **Berlioz (IND)**[28] [149] 5-8-12 95 (bt) KerrinMcEvoy 10 77
(S Padmanabhan, India) *led after 1f: hdd 2f out: wknd* **11/2**[3]

11 ¾ **Excellento (USA)**[14] [282] 6-8-12 95 (b) TPO'Shea 8 76
(E Charpy, UAE) *hld up in rr: nvr involved* **12/1**

12 3 ¾ **Eclipse West (ARG)**[6] 7-8-8 90 (t) PJSmullen 13 64
(S Seemar, UAE) *prom out wd: wd ent st: rdn 3f out: nt qckn* **50/1**

1m 38.96s **Going Correction** +0.475s/f (Yiel) **13** Ran SP% **122.0**
Speed ratings: 108,106,106,105,103 102,101,99,99,97 96,92

Owner Gainsborough Stud **Bred** Snailwell Stud Co Ltd **Trained** United Arab Emirates

FOCUS
Just an ordinary handicap for the grade.

NOTEBOOK
Royal Prince, 13th in the Cambridgeshire on his last start for James Fanshawe 138 days previously, made a successful debut for his new connections in decent enough style.
Anani(USA), dropped in trip and returned to turf off the back of a three-month break, can be considered unlucky not to have finished much closer as he got stopped in his run when looking to throw down a serious challenge.
Kestrel Cross(IRE) is finding his form now and ran with real credit in third on this drop back in trip.
Colisay ran another solid race in defeat and has clearly taken well to racing in Dubai.
Morshdi did not shape badly off the back of a near year-long absence.
One To Win(IRE), dropped half a mile in trip off the back of a 144-day break, proved disappointing and may do better back over a trip.

400 WOLVERHAMPTON (A.W) (L-H)

Friday, February 17

OFFICIAL GOING: Standard

Wind: Light behind becoming nil Weather: Sunny periods

439 FREE £75 WITH LITTLEWOODSCASINO.COM CLAIMING STKS 7f 32y(P)

2:10 (2:10) (Class 6) 3-Y-O **£2,730** (£806; £403) **Stalls High**

Form RPR

-013 1 **Prettilini**[18] [248] 3-7-12 68 JamesDoyle(7) 1 62
(A W Carroll) *a.p: led 2f out: rdn out* **9/2**[3]

0-03 2 1 ¼ **Mr Rigsby**[23] [189] 3-8-12 63 FergalLynch 3 66
(P Howling) *hld up and bhd: hdwy on ins over 2f out: rdn wl over 1f out: kpt on ins fnl f: nt trble wnr* **4/1**[2]

34-2 3 1 ¾ **Countrywide Belle**[42] [53] 3-8-5 59 (b) AdrianTNicholls 4 55
(K A Ryan) *led 1f: prom: led 3f out: rdn and hdd 2f out: one pce fnl f* **3/1**[1]

-125 4 2 ½ **Thoughtsofstardom**[20] [226] 3-8-12 71 BrianReilly 9 55
(P S McEntee) *hld up in rr: hdwy over 2f out: rdn and hung lft fr over 1f out: one pce* **7/1**

5-43 5 3 ½ **Woodwee**[22] [199] 3-8-10 58 ow3 DarryllHolland 8 45
(J R Weymes) *t.k.h: led after 1f to 3f out: sn rdn: wknd wl over 1f out* **7/1**

0-32 6 1 ¾ **Angelina Bankes**[14] [286] 3-8-3 51 AdrianMcCarthy 5 33
(R A Harris) *chsd ldrs: rdn 4f out: sn lost pl: fin lame* **16/1**

00-5 7 ¾ **Valentino Taffi**[39] [70] 3-8-12 65 J-PGuillambert 10 40
(S C Williams) *mid-div: hdwy on outside 4f out: rdn 3f out: sn wknd* **20/1**

-005 8 3 ½ **First Byte**[11] [308] 3-8-2 40 ow1 (vt) ChrisCatlin 7 22
(Miss D A McHale) *sn prom: rdn 3f out: sn wknd* **50/1**

-122 9 *dist* **Diktalex (IRE)**[10] 335 3-8-3 58.....................(v) PaulHanagan 6 —
(M J Attwater) *rel to r: a t.o* **6/1**
1m 30.59s (0.19) **Going Correction** -0.025s/f (Stan) **9** Ran SP% **115.1**
Speed ratings (Par 95):97,95,93,90,86 84,83,79,—
CSF £22.78 TOTE £5.50: £1.80, £1.40, £1.40; EX 25.00.The winner was subject to a friendly claim.
Owner David Shorthouse **Bred** G W Turner And Miss S J Turner **Trained** Cropthorne, Worcs
FOCUS
A moderate claimer. The winner, whose rider is extremely good value for his claim, did not need to be at her best to win.
Angelina Bankes Official explanation: vet said filly was lame on pulling up
Diktalex(IRE) Official explanation: jockey said filly was reluctant to race

440 HOLIDAY INN GARDEN COURT WOLVERHAMPTON H'CAP (DIV I) 7f 32y(P)
2:40 (2:40) (Class 6) (0-58,58) 4-Y-0+ £2,047 (£604; £302) Stalls High

Form RPR
24-2 1 **Scuba (IRE)**[47] 1 4-9-2 **58**.....................(v) SteveDrowne 3 68+
(H Morrison) *mde all: rdn over 1f out: r.o wl* **7/2**[1]
-445 2 *1* **Rowan Warning**[16] 268 4-9-1 **57**.....................(p) NCallan 2 64
(J R Boyle) *prom: hmpd and lost pl after 1f: rdn and hdwy on ins wl over 1f out: r.o ins fnl f: nt rch wnr* **9/2**[2]
3-31 3 *1 ¾* **Mister Elegant**[19] 247 4-8-12 **54**..................... AdrianTNicholls 6 57
(J L Spearing) *w wnr tl over 3f out: rdn over 2f out: wnt 2nd again wl over 1f out: sn edgd rt: one pce fnl f* **7/2**[1]
3033 4 *3 ½* **Crusoe (IRE)**[1] 423 9-8-6 **48** oh1 ow2.....................(b) EddieAhern 1 42
(A Sadik) *a.p: rdn over 2f out: one pce* **9/1**
453- 5 *1* **Just Bond (IRE)**[158] 5179 4-9-0 **56**..................... RobertWinston 10 47
(B Smart) *hld up: hdwy over 4f out: chsd wnr over 3f out tl wl over 1f out: wknd ent fnl f* **8/1**[3]
00-2 6 *1 ¾* **Grezie**[9] 336 4-8-10 **52**..................... DaneO'Neill 5 39
(T D McCarthy) *hld up in mid-div: lost pl over 3f out: n.d after* **9/1**
000- 7 *¾* **Motu (IRE)**[141] 5566 5-8-13 **55**.....................(v) TomEaves 8 40
(I W McInnes) *s.i.s: bhd tl rdn and hdwy on ins wl over 1f out: sn no imp* **25/1**
-000 8 *2* **Awarding**[11] 307 6-8-3 **48**.....................(vt) RichardThomas(3) 9 28
(Dr J R J Naylor) *a bhd* **20/1**
-006 9 *2* **Bint Royal (IRE)**[4] 407 8-8-5 **47** ow1..................... NeilPollard 7 22
(Miss V Haigh) *prom: rdn 3f out: sn wknd: fin lame* **16/1**
304- 10 *6* **First Rhapsody (IRE)**[184] 4470 4-8-9 **58**..................... KristinStubbs(7) 11 18
(T J Etherington) *s.i.s: a bhd* **66/1**
-004 11 *1 ½* **Blushing Russian (IRE)**[4] 400 4-8-5 **47**..................... PaulHanagan 4 3
(J M Bradley) *prom: rdn 3f out: sn wknd* **12/1**
1m 30.13s (-0.27) **Going Correction** -0.025s/f (Stan) **11** Ran SP% **117.4**
Speed ratings (Par 101):100,98,96,92,91 89,88,86,84,77 75
CSF £18.51 CT £59.21 TOTE £5.30: £1.70, £1.80, £2.00; EX 20.20.
Owner Graham Doyle and Applause PR **Bred** Mountarmstrong Stud **Trained** East Ilsley, Berks
FOCUS
This modest handicap was run in a time fractionally slower than the second division. The form does not look that strong.
Grezie Official explanation: jockey said filly struck its head on the stalls
Bint Royal(IRE) Official explanation: vet said mare finished lame

441 TEXT "BETDIRECT" TO 88600 H'CAP 5f 216y(P)
3:10 (3:11) (Class 4) (0-85,86) 4-Y-0+ £5,505 (£1,637; £818; £408) Stalls Low

Form RPR
-111 1 **Graze On**[7] 362 4-9-5 **86** 6ex.....................(b) AdrianMcCarthy 8 93+
(R A Harris) *mde all: clr 2f out: rdn over 1f out: sn edgd rt: drvn out* **11/10**[1]
0106 2 *1 ¼* **Law Maker**[7] 362 6-8-6 **80**.....................(v) MichaelJStainton(7) 1 83
(A Bailey) *chsd wnr: rdn over 1f out: r.o one pce fnl f* **14/1**
0-13 3 *2* **Chief Exec**[20] 220 4-9-3 **84**..................... MartinDwyer 3 81
(C A Cyzer) *chsd ldrs: rdn over 3f out: one pce fnl f* **11/2**[3]
50-2 4 *¾* **Adantino**[10] 323 7-8-4 **71** oh1.....................(b) ChrisCatlin 6 66
(B R Millman) *bhd: stmbld and swtchd rt over 4f out: hdwy over 2f out: kpt on same pce fnl f* **14/1**
33-2 5 *4* **Countdown**[7] 362 4-8-11 **78**.....................(b) TomEaves 5 61
(Miss J A Camacho) *hld up: hdwy 4f out: rdn 3f out: no further prog fnl 2f* **7/2**[2]
42-1 6 *nk* **Joyeaux**[43] 51 4-8-5 **72** oh1 ow1..................... EddieAhern 7 54
(J Hetherton) *broke wl: stdd into mid-div: lost pl 3f out: n.d after* **16/1**
5036 7 *nk* **Willheconquertoo**[10] 323 6-8-4 **71** oh1.....................(vt) PaulHanagan 2 52
(I W McInnes) *s.i.s: a bhd* **20/1**
0500 8 *½* **Cornus**[7] 362 4-9-0 **81**..................... DeanMcKeown 2 61
(M J Polglase) *s.i.s: sn chsng ldrs: rdn over 2f out: wknd 1f out* **16/1**
-040 9 *4* **Chateau Nicol**[19] 238 7-9-4 **85**.....................(v) TQuinn 9 53
(B G Powell) *a bhd* **12/1**
1m 14.54s (-1.27) **Going Correction** -0.025s/f (Stan) **9** Ran SP% **122.8**
Speed ratings (Par 105):107,105,102,101,96 95,95,94,89
CSF £21.52 CT £70.21 TOTE £1.90: £1.10, £3.50, £1.30; EX 31.00.
Owner Tom Tuohy Paraic Gaffney **Bred** Mrs Sandra Cooper **Trained** Earlswood, Monmouths
■ Stewards' Enquiry : Paul Hanagan two-day ban: careless riding (Feb 28-Mar 1)
FOCUS
The progressive Graze On continued on a roll and won in a respectable time. The form looks solid enough.
Chateau Nicol Official explanation: jockey said gelding was never travelling

442 WOLVERHAMPTON-RACECOURSE.CO.UK (S) STKS 1m 4f 50y(P)
3:40 (3:40) (Class 6) 4-Y-0+ £2,388 (£705; £352) Stalls Low

Form RPR
6543 1 **York Cliff**[7] 361 8-9-5 50..................... EddieAhern 7 54
(W M Brisbourne) *hld up in mid-div: hdwy on ins over 3f out: rdn to ld wl ins fnl f: r.o* **11/4**[1]
00-3 2 *shd* **Mostakbel (USA)**[5] 390 7-9-5 45.....................(v) HayleyTurner 4 54
(M D I Usher) *a.p: led over 2f out: hrd rdn and edgd lft over 1f out: hdd wl ins fnl f: r.o* **10/1**
0-24 3 *5* **Another Con (IRE)**[14] 284 5-9-0 45.....................(p) DaneO'Neill 6 41+
(A M Hales) *rrd s: hld up and bhd: hdwy over 3f out: rdn over 2f out: one pce* **6/1**
60-0 4 *hd* **Beaumont Girl (IRE)**[10] 147 4-8-11 45..................... RobertWinston 5 41
(Miss M E Rowland) *set slow pce: qcknd over 4f out: rdn and hdd over 2f out: swtchd rt jst over 1f out: wknd wl ins fnl f* **25/1**
-216 5 *nk* **Regency Red (IRE)**[20] 230 8-9-3 55..................... LiamJones(7) 1 51
(W M Brisbourne) *hld up towards rr: rdn over 2f out: hdwy over 1f out: styd on fnl f* **9/2**[2]
05-5 6 *nk* **Molly's Secret**[15] 273 8-9-0 45.....................(p) ChrisCatlin 12 40
(Miss S J Wilton) *hld up and bhd: rdn and hdwy on outside over 2f out: no further prog* **12/1**
056 7 *nk* **Mossmann Gorge**[7] 361 4-9-2 55.....................(v) DarryllHolland 10 45
(M Wellings) *hld up and bhd: hdwy over 2f out: rdn wl over 1f out: one pce* **5/1**[3]
000- 8 *6* **Weet Watchers**[9] 5516 6-9-0 40..................... StephanieHollinshead(5) 9 36
(T Wall) *t.k.h in mid-div: hdwy over 3f out: wknd over 1f out* **50/1**
-303 9 *4* **Mujazaf**[9] 338 4-8-13 50..................... EdwardCreighton(3) 11 30
(Miss Sheena West) *hld up in tch: wkng whn n.m.r briefly over 2f out* **5/1**[3]
00 10 *8* **Pearl Oyster**[11] 314 4-9-2..................... VinceSlattery 3 18
(D J Wintle) *hld up and mid-div: rdn and bhd fnl 4f* **28/1**
040- 11 *1 ½* **Cheeky Chi (IRE)**[61] 6609 5-9-0 40..................... FrancisFerris 2 10
(P S McEntee) *hld up in tch: rdn over 4f out: wknd over 3f out* **50/1**
0/00 12 *11* **Darling River (FR)**[17] 258 7-9-0 40..................... TomEaves 8 —
(R Brotherton) *chsd ldr tl rdn over 3f out: sn wknd* **50/1**
2m 43.7s (1.28) **Going Correction** -0.025s/f (Stan)
WFA 4 from 5yo+ 3lb **12** Ran SP% **122.4**
Speed ratings (Par 101):94,93,90,90,90 90,89,85,83,77 76,69
CSF £32.07 TOTE £3.60: £1.60, £4.50, £3.30; EX 41.60.There was no bid for the winner. Another Con was claimed by Paul Blockley for £6,000.
Owner P Wright-Bevans **Bred** F Hinojosa **Trained** Great Ness, Shropshire
FOCUS
A weak seller, and they went no pace. Hard to be sure what the form amounts to.
Another Con(IRE) Official explanation: jockey said mare reared as the stalls opened

443 WIN £2M AT LITTLEWOODSPOOLS.COM H'CAP 2m 119y(P)
4:10 (4:10) (Class 6) (0-65,64) 4-Y-0+ £2,388 (£705; £352) Stalls Low

Form RPR
2324 1 **Blue Hills**[8] 346 5-9-3 **57**..................... DarrenWilliams 7 64
(P W Hiatt) *a.p: rdn 4f out: styd on u.p to ld last strides* **9/1**
46-0 2 *hd* **Jamaar**[18] 250 4-9-0 **60**..................... MickyFenton 2 67
(C N Kellett) *set slow pce: qcknd over 6f out: rdn over 3f out: clr 2f out: ct last strides* **50/1**
4311 3 *nk* **Mister Completely (IRE)**[25] 174 5-8-13 **56**........ EdwardCreighton(3) 8 62
(Miss Sheena West) *hld up and bhd: hdwy over 5f out: rdn and outpcd over 3f out: rallied over 1f out: styd on ins fnl f* **9/2**[2]
0-60 4 *2* **Sandy's Legend (USA)**[16] 264 4-8-9 **55**.....................(p) PaulHanagan 1 59
(Mrs L Williamson) *hld up in mid-div: lost pl and bhd 4f out: styd on fnl f: nrst fin* **10/1**
-020 5 *nk* **Mustang Ali (IRE)**[11] 309 5-8-6 **49**.....................(b) RichardThomas(3) 11 53
(Dr J R J Naylor) *s.i.s: hld up and bhd: hdwy 4f out: nt clr run on ins over 2f out: sn rdn: one pce fnl f* **16/1**
100- 6 *½* **Vanishing Dancer (SWI)**[93] 6368 9-9-1 **55**.....................(t) DaneO'Neill 3 58
(B Ellison) *hld up in tch: rdn and lost pl 4f out: rallied on ins over 1f out: nvr trbld ldrs* **40/1**
6262 7 *1 ¼* **High Frequency (IRE)**[8] 346 5-8-10 **50**..................... PaulFessey 9 52
(T D Barron) *s.i.s: hld up and bhd: hdwy over 5f out: rdn over 3f out: one pce fnl 2f* **6/1**[3]
-605 8 *2* **Simply St Lucia**[10] 334 4-8-12 **58**..................... DarryllHolland 4 57
(J R Weymes) *prom: wnt 2nd over 3f out: rdn over 2f out: wknd over 1f out* **14/1**
54/0 9 *4* **Sono**[27] 168 9-9-6 **60**..................... TomEaves 6 54
(P D Niven) *hld up in tch: wknd over 4f out* **66/1**
504- 10 *¾* **Teorban (POL)**[36] 5502 7-9-10 **64**..................... TQuinn 12 57
(D J S Ffrench Davis) *hld up: stdy hdwy 8f out: wknd 3f out* **16/1**
230- 11 *nk* **Scott**[128] 5837 5-9-6 **60**..................... EddieAhern 13 53
(J Jay) *a bhd* **6/1**[3]
3-53 12 *¾* **Master'n Commander**[20] 218 4-9-3 **63**..................... JamieSpencer 10 55
(C A Cyzer) *chsd ldr tl rdn over 3f out: wknd wl over 1f out* **3/1**[1]
232- P **Chaka Zulu**[145] 5490 9-9-7 **61**..................... RobertWinston 5 —
(D W Thompson) *bhd tl p.u and collapsed over 1f out: dead* **9/1**
3m 48.12s (4.99) **Going Correction** -0.025s/f (Stan)
WFA 4 from 5yo+ 6lb **13** Ran SP% **125.2**
Speed ratings (Par 101):87,86,86,85,85 85,84,83,82,81 81,81,—
CSF £409.64 CT £2308.67 TOTE £11.40: £3.50, £17.10, £2.30; EX 541.80.
Owner Tom Pratt **Bred** Darley **Trained** Hook Norton, Oxon
FOCUS
A typically weak all-weather staying handicap,and the pace was funereal until early on the final circuit.
Sandy's Legend(USA) Official explanation: jockey said gelding was denied a clear run
Teorban(POL) Official explanation: jockey said gelding hung left-handed in the final 5f
Master'n Commander Official explanation: jockey said gelding had no more to give

444 BETDIRECT.CO.UK H'CAP 1m 141y(P)
4:40 (4:40) (Class 4) (0-85,84) 4-Y-0+
£5,297 (£1,586; £793; £396; £198; £99) Stalls Low

Form RPR
0426 1 **Atlantic Quest (USA)**[4] 404 7-8-13 **84**.....................(p) LiamTreadwell(5) 2 92
(R A Harris) *hld up in mid-div: hdwy on ins over 2f out:swtchd lft over 1f out: rdn to ld cl home* **12/1**
-206 2 *½* **Trifti**[20] 222 5-9-3 **83**..................... MartinDwyer 1 90
(C A Cyzer) *hld up in tch: rdn wl over 1f out: led ins fnl f: hdd cl home* **13/2**[3]
00-0 3 *1* **Baylaw Star**[21] 214 5-9-0 **80**..................... NCallan 8 85
(K A Ryan) *sn led: rdn over 2f out: hdd and nt qckn ins fnl f* **16/1**
50U- 4 *hd* **Dumaran (IRE)**[123] 5948 8-8-10 **76**..................... LPKeniry 5 81
(W J Musson) *led early: a.p: rdn over 2f out: r.o one pce fnl f* **33/1**
314- 5 *shd* **Obrigado (USA)**[70] 6533 6-9-0 **80**..................... DarryllHolland 7 84
(W J Haggas) *hld up in rr: rdn and hdwy on ins over 1f out: styd on towards fin* **7/2**[2]
-026 6 *1 ½* **Outer Hebrides**[9] 340 5-9-4 **84**.....................(vt) JamieSpencer 3 85
(Stef Liddiard) *hld up towards rr: rdn and hdwy over 1f out: one pce fnl f* **14/1**
212- 7 *1* **Mina A Salem**[90] 6373 4-8-13 **79**..................... EddieAhern 10 78
(C E Brittain) *prom tl rdn and wknd over 1f out* **3/1**[1]
-605 8 *hd* **Claret And Amber**[20] 221 4-8-10 **76**.....................(b) PaulHanagan 4 75
(R A Fahey) *hld up towards rr: hdwy over 3f out: rdn over 2f out: wknd over 1f out* **7/2**[2]
56-0 9 *2 ½* **Kabeer**[16] 267 8-8-10 **76**.....................(t) NeilPollard 9 69
(Lucinda Featherstone) *hld up in mid-div: bhd fnl 3f* **40/1**
360- 10 *1* **Commando Scott (IRE)**[104] 6248 5-8-5 **76**..................... GregFairley(5) 6 67
(I W McInnes) *hld up in tch: rdn and wknd over 2f out* **16/1**

440- **11** *21* **Anduril**132 [5743] 5-8-8 **74**..(b) RobertWinston 11 21
(I W McInnes) *a in rr: eased whn no ch over 1f out: t.o* **7/1**

1m 49.73s (-2.03) **Going Correction** -0.025s/f (Stan) **11** Ran SP% **126.8**
Speed ratings (Par 105):108,107,106,106,106 105,104,104,101,100 82
CSF £94.90 CT £1309.59 TOTE £19.00: £3.60, £1.60, £8.30; EX 58.10.
Owner Peter Warner **Bred** Bemark N V & Bon Marche **Trained** Earlswood, Monmouths
■ Stewards' Enquiry : Neil Pollard three-day ban: careless riding (Feb 28-Mar 2)

FOCUS
A tightly-knit handicap and the form looks okay, with the first two basically to form and the third looking ready to win if a suitable race can be found for him.
Obrigado(USA) Official explanation: jockey said gelding suffered interference
Mina A Salem Official explanation: jockey said colt had no more to give
Claret And Amber Official explanation: jockey said gelding hung right
Anduril Official explanation: jockey said gelding hung right

445 BETDIRECT ON CHANNEL 4 TEXT PAGE 613 MAIDEN STKS 1m 1f 103y(P)
5:10 (5:10) (Class 5) 3-Y-O **£3,886** (£1,156; £577; £288) **Stalls** Low

Form RPR
1 **Off Message (IRE)** 3-8-9 .... EddieAhern 3 74+
(E A L Dunlop) *hld up in mid-div: hdwy on ins over 3f out: led over 1f out: rdn out* **4/1**2

2 *nk* **Soapy Danger** 3-9-0 .... JoeFanning 11 78+
(M Johnston) *led after 1f: rdn over 2f out: hdd over 1f out: r.o* **10/11**1

600- **3** *10* **Manouche**59 [6634] 3-9-0 61..(p) NCallan 10 59
(K A Ryan) *w ldr: rdn and ev ch over 2f out: wknd over 1f out* **9/1**

60-6 **4** *3 ½* **Royal Moon (USA)**46 [10] 3-9-0 60.. PhillipMakin 2 53
(T D Barron) *led 1f: prom: rdn over 2f out: sn wknd* **7/1**3

5 *4* **Blanc Visage** 3-9-0 .... GeorgeBaker 8 45
(Mrs H Sweeting) *hld up and bhd: hdwy on outside 4f out: wknd over 2f out* **40/1**

30 **6** *¾* **Pretty Sister**7 [365] 3-8-9 .... NickyMackay 12 39
(W J Haggas) *s.i.s: nvr nr ldrs* **10/1**

0 **7** *shd* **Grand Assault**31 [132] 3-9-0 .... J-PGuillambert 7 44
(Lucinda Featherstone) *rrd and stmbld s: nvr nr ldrs* **50/1**

246- **8** *3 ½* **Eliminator**244 [2690] 3-9-0 71.. TomEaves 4 37
(I W McInnes) *hld up in mid-div: rdn over 4f out: wknd over 2f out* **20/1**

06- **9** *6* **Welcome Releaf**269 [1974] 3-9-0 .... NeilPollard 1 26
(Lucinda Featherstone) *a bhd* **20/1**

000- **10** *10* **Vehari**48 [6694] 3-9-0 45.. VinceSlattery 9 7
(M Scudamore) *s.i.s: a bhd* **100/1**

0 **11** *4* **Vi's Boy**18 [254] 3-9-0 .... ShaneKelly 5 —
(W M Brisbourne) *prom: rdn over 4f out: wknd over 3f out* **66/1**

12 *18* **Jay Jay Okocha** 3-9-0 .... MickyFenton 6 —
(James Moffatt) *prom tl wknd 4f out: t.o* **50/1**

2m 1.10s (-1.52) **Going Correction** -0.025s/f (Stan) **12** Ran SP% **122.3**
Speed ratings (Par 97):105,104,95,92,89 88,88,85,79,71 67,51
CSF £7.83 TOTE £7.50: £1.10, £1.10, £2.60; EX 15.10.
Owner Cliveden Stud **Bred** Cliveden Stud Ltd **Trained** Newmarket, Suffolk

FOCUS
A race dominated by two newcomers who came well clear in what could have been a fair maiden for the track.
Grand Assault Official explanation: jockey said gelding reared as stalls opened

446 HOLIDAY INN GARDEN COURT WOLVERHAMPTON H'CAP (DIV II) 7f 32y(P)
5:40 (5:40) (Class 6) (0-58,58) 4-Y-O+ **£2,047** (£604; £302) **Stalls** High

Form RPR
0-00 **1** **Winning Venture**7 [360] 9-8-3 **52**.. JamesDoyle(7) 1 57
(A W Carroll) *a.p: n.m.r on ins bnd after 1f: rdn over 2f out: edgd lft and led ins fnl f: r.o* **20/1**

-000 **2** *½* **Count Cougar (USA)**4 [401] 6-8-13 **55**.. AdrianTNicholls 10 59
(S P Griffiths) *a.p: rdn to ld over 2f out: hdd ins fnl f: kpt on* **16/1**

0-30 **3** *nk* **Wodhill Be**31 [134] 6-8-5 **47**.. AdrianMcCarthy 3 50
(D Morris) *mid-div: rdn over 4f out: hdwy on ins 3f out: ev ch ins fnl f: nt qckn cl home* **14/1**

-441 **4** *1 ¾* **Spark Up**4 [407] 6-9-2 **58** 6ex..(b) ShaneKelly 11 57
(J W Unett) *sn chsng ldrs: rdn and ev ch over 2f out: one pce fnl f* **9/4**1

0030 **5** *¾* **Pheckless**4 [398] 7-8-4 **46**.. PaulHanagan 8 43
(J M Bradley) *s.i.s: hdwy on ins 2f out: one pce fnl f* **11/2**3

000- **6** *5* **H Harrison (IRE)**124 [5923] 6-8-11 **58**.. NataliaGemelova(5) 2 42
(I W McInnes) *prom: led over 4f out tl over 2f out: wknd over 1f out* **10/1**

-054 **7** *hd* **Miskina**20 [232] 5-9-1 **57**.. EddieAhern 9 41
(W M Brisbourne) *chsd ldrs: rdn 3f out: wknd wl over 1f out* **5/2**2

10-0 **8** *10* **Colloseum**4 [400] 5-8-7 **49** ow1..(b) TomEaves 6 8
(T J Etherington) *s.v.s: a bhd* **25/1**

-000 **9** *5* **Revien (IRE)**4 [400] 4-8-10 **52**.. PaulFitzsimons 4 —
(Miss J R Tooth) *prom: rdn over 3f out: wknd over 2f out* **10/1**

0-06 **10** *1* **Miss Porcia**18 [249] 5-7-13 **46** oh6..(v1) DuranFentiman(5) 5 —
(S L Keightley) *led over 2f: rdn over 3f out: sn wknd* **16/1**

0/00 **11** *1 ½* **Vandal**27 [170] 6-8-13 **55**.. DaneO'Neill 7 —
(M Appleby) *a bhd* **33/1**

1m 29.99s (-0.41) **Going Correction** -0.025s/f (Stan) **11** Ran SP% **122.9**
Speed ratings (Par 101):101,100,100,98,97 91,91,79,74,73 71
CSF £311.62 CT £4647.81 TOTE £25.30: £6.10, £4.80, £3.20; EX 294.10 Place 6 £152.23, Place 5 £106.53.
Owner R G Owens **Bred** Woodsway Stud And Chao Racing And Bloodstock Ltd **Trained** Cropthorne, Worcs

FOCUS
This low grade handicap was run in a time marginally faster than the first division.
Colloseum Official explanation: jockey said gelding missed the break
Miss Porcia Official explanation: jockey said mare moved poorly throughout
T/Plt: £51.10 to a £1 stake. Pool: £54,476.55. 778.15 winning tickets. T/Qpdt: £18.00 to a £1 stake. Pool: £3,825.10. 156.90 winning tickets. KH

439WOLVERHAMPTON (A.W) (L-H)
Saturday, February 18

OFFICIAL GOING: Standard
Wind: Nil Weather: Fine

447 BETDIRECT.CO.UK CLAIMING STKS 1m 141y(P)
2:05 (2:05) (Class 5) 3-Y-O **£3,238** (£963; £481; £240) **Stalls** Low

Form RPR
-450 **1** **Outlook**14 [294] 3-8-12 73..(b) NCallan 9 71
(N P Littmoden) *w ldr: led wl over 2f out: rdn clr wl over 1f out: r.o* **4/1**3

3-0 **2** *1 ¼* **Kokila**31 [138] 3-8-3 .... HayleyTurner 2 59
(W J Haggas) *t.k.h: a.p: chsd wnr and edgd lft fr wl over 1f out: kpt on ins fnl f* **7/1**

-002 **3** *1 ¼* **Chookie Windsor**11 [329] 3-8-4 60..(p) PaulHanagan 8 58
(I Semple) *hld up: hdwy over 5f out: rdn over 3f out: one pce fnl f* **3/1**2

060- **4** *3 ½* **Aboyne (IRE)**91 [6386] 3-8-8 64.. TPQueally 3 54
(M G Quinlan) *hld up and bhd: rdn and effrt over 2f out: edgd lft over 1f out: nvr trbld ldrs* **12/1**

614 **5** *2 ½* **Ohana**7 [378] 3-9-3 71..(p) JamieSpencer 1 58
(N P Littmoden) *led: hdd wl over 2f out: sn rdn: wknd fnl f* **15/8**1

00- **6** *2 ½* **Polish Effigy**102 [6290] 3-8-2 ....(b1) EdwardCreighton(3) 5 41
(B W Duke) *prom: lost pl over 5f out: rdn over 3f out: sn bhd* **50/1**

00-5 **7** *1 ¼* **Sahara Style**9 [349] 3-8-9 55..(p) GrahamGibbons 6 42
(R Hollinshead) *s.i.s: hdwy whn nt clr run on ins over 5f out: rallied over 4f out: rdn and wknd 3f out* **10/1**

1m 52.34s (0.58) **Going Correction** -0.025s/f (Stan) **7** Ran SP% **111.0**
Speed ratings (Par 97):96,94,93,90,88 86,85
CSF £29.53 TOTE £5.50: £1.90, £3.40; EX 34.80.Chookie Windsor was claimed by Mr M. S. Saunders for £5,000
Owner Nigel Shields **Bred** W N Greig **Trained** Newmarket, Suffolk

FOCUS
Modest claiming form rated through the third.
Ohana Official explanation: trainer was unable to explain the poor run

448 PLAY ROULETTE AT LITTLEWOODSCASINO.COM H'CAP 1m 141y(P)
2:35 (2:35) (Class 4) (0-85,83) 3-Y-O **£5,505** (£1,637; £818; £408) **Stalls** Low

Form RPR
3111 **1** **Casablanca Minx (IRE)**7 [378] 3-7-13 **71**.. JamesDoyle(7) 4 78+
(N P Littmoden) *hld up: rdn over 3f out: hdwy on outside wl over 1f out: led ins fnl f: r.o wl* **6/1**3

3-24 **2** *1 ½* **Time For Life (USA)**14 [294] 3-9-2 **81**..(p) DarryllHolland 9 85
(H J Collingridge) *hld up: hdwy 5f out: rdn over 2f out: led over 1f out: sn edgd rt: hdd and nt qckn ins fnl f* **9/4**2

6-14 **3** *1 ½* **Keel (IRE)**21 [228] 3-8-11 **76**.. SteveDrowne 6 77
(J A Osborne) *hld up in rr: rdn 4f out: hdwy over 2f out: ev ch over 1f out: one pce fnl f* **7/1**

-121 **4** *1* **Song Of Silence (USA)**10 [342] 3-9-4 **83**.. EddieAhern 8 82+
(E A L Dunlop) *hld up: nt clr run on ins wl over 2f out: rdn and hdwy wl over 1f out: no ex ins fnl f* **15/8**1

301- **5** *1 ½* **Flylowflylong (IRE)**99 [6316] 3-8-5 **70**.. TomEaves 2 66
(I Semple) *chsd ldr tl n.m.r over 3f out: sn nt clr run and lost pl: rdn and hdwy over 1f out: wknd ins fnl f* **12/1**

21-0 **6** *11* **Bellsbank (IRE)**24 [190] 3-8-4 **69** oh1.. ChrisCatlin 5 42
(A Bailey) *led: clr over 6f out: rdn and hdd over 1f out: wknd fnl f* **33/1**

2-16 **7** *7* **Abstract Art (USA)**14 [294] 3-8-10 **75**..(v1) JamieSpencer 7 33
(N A Callaghan) *prom: rdn over 2f out: wknd wl over 1f out: sn eased* **6/1**3

1m 50.11s (-1.65) **Going Correction** -0.025s/f (Stan) **7** Ran SP% **117.3**
Speed ratings (Par 99):106,104,103,102,101 91,85
CSF £20.77 CT £98.39 TOTE £6.30: £2.80, £1.20; EX 24.80.
Owner Nigel Shields **Bred** Airlie Stud And Widden Stud **Trained** Newmarket, Suffolk
■ Apprentice James Doyle's allowance is reduced to 5lb following this win.

FOCUS
A decent handicap run at a good gallop and with the placed horses close to their marks the form looks sound enough.

449 PLAY LITTLEWOODS POOLS ON 0800 500 000 MAIDEN STKS 5f 216y(P)
3:10 (3:12) (Class 5) 3-Y-O+ **£3,238** (£963; £481; £240) **Stalls** Low

Form RPR
1 **Boldinor** 3-8-6 .... StephenCarson 12 67+
(W R Swinburn) *s.i.s: bhd tl hdwy and hung rt wl over 2f out: swtchd lft 1f out: led wl ins fnl f: drvn out* **33/1**

/5-0 **2** *½* **Oneiro Way (IRE)**21 [225] 4-9-7 65.. GeorgeBaker 1 69
(P R Chamings) *led early: hld up in tch: rdn over 2f out: led over 1f out: hdd wl ins fnl f: kpt on* **13/2**3

02- **3** *3* **Serevi (IRE)**259 [2301] 3-8-6 .... ShaneKelly 6 56
(J Noseda) *sn prom: wnt 2nd over 3f out: rdn and ev ch over 1f out: no ex ins fnl f* **8/15**1

6-2 **4** *5* **Creme Brulee**17 [266] 3-8-1 .... PaulHanagan 3 36
(C R Egerton) *t.k.h: prom: rdn whn nt clr run briefly 1f out: wknd ins fnl f* **9/2**2

00-0 **5** *1 ½* **Value Plus (IRE)**11 [331] 4-8-9 60.. MarkCoumbe(7) 4 36
(C J Teague) *s.s: hld up and bhd: hdwy on ins 3f out: no further prog fnl 2f* **66/1**

4-06 **6** *2* **Unprecedented (IRE)**17 [266] 5-9-7 45..(v) SamHitchcott 7 35
(T T Clement) *sn led: rdn over 2f out: hdd over 1f out: sn wknd* **100/1**

7 *2* **Enjoy The Magic** 4-9-2 .... PaulFitzsimons 8 24
(Miss J R Tooth) *s.s: nvr nr ldrs* **100/1**

502 **8** *9* **Mind Out (USA)**9 [347] 3-8-6 52.. GrahamGibbons 2 —
(J T Stimpson) *mid-div: rdn over 3f out: bmpd and carried wd wl over 2f out: sn bhd* **16/1**

000- **9** *hd* **Raven (IRE)**204 [3919] 4-8-11 50.. DuranFentiman(5) 9 —
(Mark Campion) *rdn over 3f out: carried wd wl over 2f out: a bhd* **150/1**

000- **10** *1 ¼* **Spectacular Dancer (IRE)**172 [4851] 4-9-7 35..(t) LPKeniry 5 —
(Heather Dalton) *rdn 4f out: a towards rr* **100/1**

000- **11** *5* **Danetime Lady (IRE)**167 [4982] 6-9-2 .... NCallan 10 —
(Adrian Sexton, Ire) *prom: rdn over 3f out: sn wknd* **33/1**

1m 15.21s (35.40) **Going Correction** -0.025s/f (Stan)
WFA 3 from 4yo+ 15lb **11** Ran SP% **113.6**
Speed ratings (Par 103):103,102,98,91,89 87,84,72,72,70 63
CSF £225.10 TOTE £33.70: £5.50, £2.00, £1.10; EX 178.20.
Owner Ron Collins **Bred** Ron Collins **Trained** Aldbury, Herts

FOCUS
A modest maiden run at a fair gallop but a surprise result. The runner-up is the best guide to the level.

450 BETDIRECT FREEPHONE 0800 211 222 H'CAP 5f 20y(P)
3:45 (3:46) (Class 2) (0-100,98) 4-Y-O+
£11,217 (£3,358; £1,679; £840; £419; £210) **Stalls** Low

Form RPR
1-12 **1** **Fyodor (IRE)**14 [295] 5-9-7 **98**.. GeorgeBaker 4 107
(W J Haggas) *hld up: hdwy on ins wl over 1f out: plld out 1f out: r.o to ld post* **10/11**1

-005 **2** *shd* **Qadar (IRE)**4 [413] 4-8-9 **86** ow1.. NCallan 5 95
(N P Littmoden) *a.p: wnt 2nd over 2f out: rdn to ld ins fnl f: hdd post* **8/1**3

060- **3** *1 ½* **Bayeux (USA)**176 [4722] 5-8-8 **85**.. NickyMackay 3 88
(G A Butler) *hld up in rr: rdn 3f: hdwy on outside fnl f: nrst fin* **16/1**

0-10 4 ½ **Maktavish**[23] 198 7-8-2 84 oh9 ....(b) GregFairley(5) 1 85
(I Semple) led: rdn wl over 1f out: hdd ins fnl f: no ex cl home 25/1
0603 5 2 **One More Round (USA)**[14] 295 8-8-7 91 ....(b) JamesDoyle(7) 2 85
(N P Littmoden) hld up and bhd: rdn wl over 1f out: nvr trbld ldrs 10/1
-426 6 1¼ **Dancing Mystery**[14] 295 12-9-2 93 ....(b) StephenCarson 7 83
(E A Wheeler) hld up in tch: rdn wl over 1f out: sn wknd 20/1
3316 7 1½ **Desperate Dan**[16] 275 5-9-0 91 ....(b) JamieSpencer 6 75
(J A Osborne) chsd ldr over 2f: wknd over 1f out 3/1[2]

61.04 secs (-1.78) **Going Correction** -0.025s/f (Stan) 7 Ran SP% **112.1**
Speed ratings (Par 109):113,112,110,109,106 104,102
CSF £8.77 TOTE £1.80: £1.40, £3.30; EX 9.60.
Owner The Fyodor Partnership **Bred** E J Banks And D I Scott **Trained** Newmarket, Suffolk

FOCUS
A good handicap run at a strong gallop with the progressive winner just getting up. The form looks fairly reliable.

NOTEBOOK
Fyodor(IRE) has been really progressive on sand this winter and gained his fourth win from six starts, during which time he has rised 25lb in the handicap. He only just made it though, having come from well back, and the Handicapper may now just about have his measure. (tchd Evens)
Qadar(IRE) ◆, making his debut on this track and over the shortest trip he has tackled to date, gave the winner a real fight and his rider's 1lb overweight may have been enough to make the difference. He seems more effective on Polytrack than Fibresand and could soon gain compensation off this mark. (op 15-2 tchd 13-2)
Bayeux(USA) ◆, making his sand debut, ran with plenty of promise doing his best work late over a trip way shorter than those he has been tackling on turf. He has not scored since his debut in May 2003, but he has dropped to a mark 27lb below his previous rating at the start of 2004, and looks potentially well handicapped. (op 18-1 tchd 20-1)
Maktavish ran well enough off his highest mark for a while, and a return to Southwell, where he is more effective, should be more in his favour. (tchd 33-1)
One More Round(USA) finished runner-up in Dubai last winter, but is now rated a stone lower and never really got involved on this occasion. (op 15-2 tchd 12-1)
Dancing Mystery, 9lb better off with today's winner compared with their meeting on New Year's Day, was beaten twice as far. To be fair, he is better over the straight five at Southwell. (op 14-1)
Desperate Dan, another whose best efforts have been at Southwell, also does not look that well treated now. (op 7-2 tchd 4-1 and 11-4)

451 FIRST PAST THE POST AT BETDIRECT H'CAP 7f 32y(P)
4:15 (4:16) (Class 5) (0-75,75) 4-Y-O+ **£3,238** (£963; £481; £240) **Stalls** High

Form RPR
242- 1 **Nice Tune**[91] 6376 4-9-4 75 .... J-PGuillambert 5 85
(C E Brittain) a.p: rdn to ld over 1f out: r.o wl 14/1
0154 2 2 **Lincolneurocruiser**[7] 384 4-9-1 72 .... RobertWinston 1 77+
(Mrs N Macauley) prom: n.m.r on ins and lost pl sn after s: hdwy over 2f out: rdn wl over 1f out: kpt on ins fnl f 13/2
16-0 3 ½ **Vienna's Boy (IRE)**[14] 292 5-8-10 67 .... SimonWhitworth 4 71
(W J Musson) hld up and bhd: hdwy and swtchd rt over 1f out: r.o ins fnl f 33/1
0-00 4 ½ **Mistral Sky**[12] 316 7-8-11 68 ....(v) JamieSpencer 3 71
(Stef Liddiard) led early: hld up in tch: rdn wl over 1f out: one pce fnl f 22/1
-131 5 2 **Arnie De Burgh**[7] 381 4-9-1 72 .... ShaneKelly 9 70
(D J Daly) a.p: rdn to ld 2f out: hdd over 1f out: wknd ins f 5/1[3]
1212 6 nk **Glad Big (GER)**[10] 343 4-9-2 73 .... EddieAhern 12 75+
(J A Osborne) hld up: hdwy over 5f out: rdn whn nt clr run fr over 1f out: nt rcvr 11/4[1]
-304 7 nk **Undeterred**[11] 323 10-9-4 75 .... NCallan 7 71
(K J Burke) hld up in mid-div: rdn over 3f out: nvr trbld ldrs 33/1
6234 8 hd **Dragon Slayer (IRE)**[7] 385 4-9-0 71 .... GrahamGibbons 8 67
(M J Attwater) sn led: rdn and hdd 2f out: wknd ins fnl f 7/1
5-12 9 ½ **Raza Cab (IRE)**[12] 316 4-8-13 70 .... ChrisCatlin 10 64
(Karen George) prom: rdn and ev ch 2f out: edgd lft over 1f out: wknd fnl f 12/1
-646 10 ¾ **Tanforan**[21] 221 4-8-13 70 .... SteveDrowne 2 62
(K McAuliffe) a bhd 7/2[2]
-010 11 2 **Tuscarora (IRE)**[11] 332 7-8-3 67 .... JamesDoyle(7) 6 54
(A W Carroll) c wd st: a bhd 14/1
0-00 12 9 **Selective**[17] 267 7-9-3 74 ....(t) MickyFenton 11 39
(A W Carroll) hld up towards rr: rdn and hdwy on outside over 3f out: wknd over 2f out 40/1

1m 28.94s (-1.46) **Going Correction** -0.025s/f (Stan) 12 Ran SP% **125.1**
Speed ratings (Par 103):107,104,104,103,101 100,100,100,99,98 96,86
CSF £104.50 CT £2995.60 TOTE £14.40: £4.50, £3.00, £7.70; EX 112.20.
Owner Saeed Manana **Bred** Bricklow Ltd **Trained** Newmarket, Suffolk

FOCUS
A fair handicap in which the exposed third is probably a good guide to the level of the form.
Mistral Sky Official explanation: jockey said gelding hung right-handed throughout
Glad Big(GER) Official explanation: jockey said gelding hung left-handed in the straight
Tanforan Official explanation: jockey said gelding had no more to give

452 BETDIRECT.CO.UK CONDITIONS STKS 1m 141y(P)
4:45 (4:45) (Class 2) 4-Y-O+ **£11,217** (£3,358; £1,260; £1,260; £419) **Stalls** Low

Form RPR
464- 1 **Nayyir**[144] 5527 8-8-13 115 .... EddieAhern 1 96+
(G A Butler) chsd ldr: led 1f out: rdn out 4/9[1]
2-43 2 1¾ **Appalachian Trail (IRE)**[22] 213 5-9-3 95 ....(b) TomEaves 3 96+
(I Semple) hld up: rdn and hdwy wl over 1f out: kpt on ins fnl f: nt trble wnr 4/1[2]
000- 3 nk **Impeller (IRE)**[119] 6025 7-9-3 98 .... MartinDwyer 4 96+
(W R Muir) hld up in rr: rdn and hdwy over 2f out: r.o wl towards fin 8/1[3]
00-4 3 dht **Always Esteemed (IRE)**[22] 213 6-9-3 90 ....(b) NCallan 2 96+
(K A Ryan) led: rdn over 2f out: hdd 1f out: one pce 16/1
4051 5 9 **Hurricane Coast**[19] 251 7-8-13 72 ....(b) JamieSpencer 5 78+
(K McAuliffe) hld up: short-lived effrt ins wl over 1f out: eased whn btn ins fnl f 25/1

1m 50.15s (-1.61) **Going Correction** -0.025s/f (Stan) 5 Ran SP% **110.1**
Speed ratings (Par 109):106,104,104,104,96
CSF £2.55 TOTE £1.40: £1.10, £2.30; EX 2.00.
Owner Abdulla Al Khalifa **Bred** Saeed Manana **Trained** Blewbury, Oxon

FOCUS
A decent contest on paper, and former Group Two winner Nayyir, who had plenty in his favour, took advantage of the drop in class. The form is limited however.

NOTEBOOK
Nayyir, with race conditions in his favour, made a successful debut on the All-Weather. He has endured a frustrating time of things over the past two years so hopefully this success in less-competitive company will do his confidence some good, but he certainly did not convince that he can hack it at the top level in the near future. He is apparently unlikely to go to Dubai so the Winter Derby could be his short-term target. (op 4-7 tchd 8-13)
Appalachian Trail(IRE) ran well considering he had to give 4lb to the winner, who is officially rated 20lb superior to him. It was probably a case of him running to his form and the winner being below his best, though. (op 7-2 tchd 10-3 and 9-2)
Always Esteemed(IRE), who has been rated as having run to his recent best, is a difficult horse to win with. He is likely to remain hard to place off his current mark. (op 10-1)
Impeller(IRE) is another whose rating makes him difficult to place. He rarely runs a bad race, though. (op 10-1)
Hurricane Coast was out of his depth in this grade. (tchd 22-1)

453 TEXT "BETDIRECT" TO 88600 MAIDEN STKS 1m 141y(P)
5:15 (5:16) (Class 5) 3-Y-O+ **£3,238** (£963; £481; £240) **Stalls** Low

Form RPR
6 1 **Ransom Strip (USA)**[7] 380 3-8-3 .... NickyMackay 9 60
(M Johnston) a.p: led over 2f out: drvn out 7/2[2]
00- 2 1½ **Kissi Kissi**[151] 5378 3-7-12 .... AdrianMcCarthy 8 51
(M J Attwater) s.i.s: hld up and bhd: hdwy on outside 3f out: ev ch 2f out: sn rdn: nt qckn fnl f 80/1
04-F 3 1½ **Miss Inch**[15] 289 4-9-5 .... SteveDrowne 7 54+
(G Wragg) hld up in tch: rdn and one pce fnl 2f 12/1
060- 4 nk **Stagecoach Emerald**[165] 5025 4-9-7 62 .... EdwardCreighton(3) 6 58
(R W Price) hld up and bhd: rdn and hdwy on ins over 1f out: kpt on ins fnl f 14/1
04- 5 2½ **Meadow Mischief (FR)**[169] 4922 3-8-3 .... PaulHanagan 3 47
(E A L Dunlop) led 1f: prom tl rdn and wknd 2f out 4/7[1]
5 6 ½ **Plemont Bay**[7] 374 3-8-3 .... HayleyTurner 4 46
(M L W Bell) hld up in tch: wknd 3f out 10/1[3]
7 5 **Silvertown Sky (IRE)** 3-7-5 .... NicolPolli(7) 11 30
(P L Gilligan) s.i.s: hld up and bhd: hdwy on outside 3f out: wknd 2f out 66/1
000- 8 5 **Dancing Moonlight (IRE)**[91] 6384 4-9-2 30 .... JasonEdmunds(3) 5 25
(Mrs N Macauley) plld hrd: set slow pce after 1f: rdn and hdd over 2f out: wknd wl over 1f out 66/1

1m 54.87s (3.11) **Going Correction** -0.025s/f (Stan)
WFA 3 from 4yo+ 21lb 8 Ran SP% **113.5**
Speed ratings (Par 103):85,83,82,82,79 79,74,70
CSF £200.41 TOTE £6.20: £1.10, £4.30, £2.30; EX 109.00.
Owner P Cutler & Mrs G Cutler **Bred** Gaines-Gentry Thoroughbreds **Trained** Middleham Moor, N Yorks

FOCUS
A modest maiden rated through the very poor eighth, but the winner and third look capable of better in handicaps.

454 PLAY NOW AT BETDIRECTPOKER.COM H'CAP 1m 4f 50y(P)
5:45 (5:45) (Class 4) (0-85,85) 4-Y-O+
£5,297 (£1,586; £793; £396; £198; £99) **Stalls** Low

Form RPR
2111 1 **Newnham (IRE)**[5] 404 5-8-4 71 .... MartinDwyer 3 77
(J R Boyle) led 1f: a.p: rdn over 1f out: led wl ins fnl f: r.o 5/2[1]
1522 2 nk **Desperation (IRE)**[8] 361 4-8-3 73 .... HayleyTurner 9 79
(B D Leavy) hld up in tch: rdn over 2f out: r.o towards fin 16/1
1/0- 3 hd **Modaffaa**[401] 106 6-8-13 80 .... FergusSweeney 1 85
(P R Webber) hld up in tch: rdn over 1f out: ev ch ins fnl f: r.o 10/1
15-4 4 nk **Graham Island**[22] 214 5-9-1 82 .... SteveDrowne 10 87
(G Wragg) set slow pce after 1f: qcknd over 3f out: rdn over 2f out: hdd wl ins fnl f: nt qckn 7/1
-501 5 ½ **The Violin Player (USA)**[11] 325 5-9-1 82 .... DarryllHolland 12 86
(H J Collingridge) hld up and bhd: rdn over 2f out: hdwy on outside fnl f: nrst fin 12/1
2-01 6 ½ **Pass The Port**[23] 194 5-8-12 79 .... EddieAhern 11 82
(D Haydn Jones) hld up and bhd: stdy hdwy 5f out: kpt on ins fnl f 13/2[3]
202- 7 ½ **Santando**[100] 6308 6-8-4 71 .... StephenCarson 8 74
(C E Brittain) a.p: rdn and ev ch over 2f out: one pce fnl f 16/1
0-03 8 nk **Torrid Kentavr (USA)**[7] 385 9-8-6 73 .... TomEaves 5 75
(B Ellison) t.k.h in rr: hdwy on ins wl over 1f out: no imp fnl f 20/1
1-64 9 ½ **Heathyards Pride**[23] 194 6-8-13 80 .... GrahamGibbons 4 81
(R Hollinshead) hld up in mid-div: rdn and hdwy over 2f out: eased whn btn cl home 7/2[2]
-605 10 4 **Dower House**[11] 325 11-9-4 85 ....(t) ChrisCatlin 7 80
(Andrew Turnell) hld up: rdn over 3f out: no rspnse 16/1
0-66 11 5 **Skidmark**[22] 214 5-8-11 78 .... LPKeniry 2 66
(Miss J R Tooth) plld hrd towards rr: hmpd 3f out: n.d after 20/1
320- 12 5 **Vicious Prince (IRE)**[133] 5744 7-8-5 72 .... DeanMcKeown 6 52
(R M Whitaker) hld up in tch: rdn 3f out: sn wknd 40/1

2m 42.46s (0.04) **Going Correction** -0.025s/f (Stan)
WFA 4 from 5yo+ 3lb 12 Ran SP% **123.0**
Speed ratings (Par 105):98,97,97,97,97 96,96,96,95,93 89,86
CSF £46.69 CT £361.24 TOTE £3.80: £1.80, £4.60, £6.70; EX 44.10 Place 6 £117.77, Place 5 £30.25.
Owner M Khan X2 **Bred** Ballygallon Stud **Trained** Epsom, Surrey

FOCUS
There was a slow early pace to this handicap and the form could be muddling as a result.
T/Plt: £165.60 to a £1 stake. Pool: £35,712.55. 157.40 winning tickets. T/Qpdt: £16.10 to a £1 stake. Pool: £2,321.80. 106.10 winning tickets. KH

305 ST MORITZ (R-H)
Sunday, February 19

OFFICIAL GOING: Frozen

455a GRAND PRIX CORPORATE EVENTS/NEWMARKET RACEOURSES (SNOW) 5f 110y
11:45 (11:50) 4-Y-O+ **£6,372** (£2,549; £1,912; £1,274; £637)

RPR
1 **Sweet Venture (FR)**[14] 305 4-9-6 .... RobertHavlin 5 —
(M Weiss, Switzerland)
2 1 **Rascacio (GER)**[14] 305 4-9-4 .... ADeVries 1 —
(C Von Der Recke, Germany)
3 6 **Encanto (GER)**[14] 305 6-9-6 .... GBocksai 3 —
(Carmen Bocskai, Switzerland)
4 hd **Sacho (GER)**[126] 5938 8-9-4 .... AHelfenbein 4 —
(W Kujath, Germany)
5 1¾ **Mike Stone**[14] 305 6-8-12 .... EWehrel 6 —
(F Fuhrmann)

6 *8* **Talcen Gwyn (IRE)**[14] [305] 4-9-2 (b) JoeFanning 2 —
(M F Harris) *always behind* **105/10**[1]
67.19 secs 6 Ran SP% **8.7**
(including 1SF stakes): WIN 1.60; PL 1.40, 2.30; SF 15.10.
Owner R & C Bertschi **Bred** S A R L Haras Du Taillis **Trained** Switzerland

NOTEBOOK
Talcen Gwyn(IRE) again was unable to handle the unusual conditions and made no show.

456a GRAND PRIX VON ST MORITZ (SNOW) 1m 2f
1:45 (1:55) 4-Y-0+ **£23,599** (£9,439; £7,080; £4,720; £2,360)

RPR

1 **Ianina (IRE)**[133] [5785] 6-8-8 DPorcu 6 98
(R Rohne, Germany)
2 *shd* **Collow (GER)**[856] [5629] 6-9-0 MKolb 3 104
(M Weiss, Switzerland)
3 *10* **Armand (GER)**[21] 5-9-9 WMongil 2 95
(P Schiergen, Germany)
4 *½* **Royal Island (IRE)**[36] [116] 4-9-5 JoeFanning 7 91
(M Johnston) *tracked leader to over 2f out, 3rd straight, kept on one pace, lost 3rd close home* **37/10**[1]
5 *4 ½* **Pauillac (GER)**[114] 5-9-0 SLadjadj 12 77
(U Suter, France)
6 *hd* **Shiraz (GER)**[364] [431] 6-9-4 RobertHavlin 4 81
(M Weiss, Switzerland)
7 *½* **Safin (GER)**[14] 6-9-4 DMoffatt 11 80
(Carmen Bocskai, Switzerland)
8 *2* **Quiron (IRE)** 5-9-4 GBocskai 13 76
(Carmen Bocskai, Switzerland)
9 *10* **Brother's Valcour (FR)**[665] [1655] 8-8-12 EWehrel 8 52
(K Schafflutzel, Switzerland)
10 *12* **Glavalcour (FR)**[541] 6-9-6 OPlacais 5 39
(K Schafflutzel, Switzerland)
11 *12* **Merioneth (IRE)**[42] 6-9-0 AHelfenbein 10 11
(W Kujath, Germany)
12 *12* **Flower Hill (FR)**[89] 8-8-12 SPasquier 9 —
(A Trybuhl, Germany)
13 *4* **Syrakus (GER)**[15] 8-9-6 ADeVries 1 —
(H Blume, Germany)
2m 13.41s
WFA 4 from 5yo+ 1lb 13 Ran SP% **21.3**
WIN 7.00; PL 2.40, 2.20, 1.90; SF 275.60.
Owner Erwin Haep **Bred** Erwin Haep **Trained** Germany

NOTEBOOK
Royal Island(IRE) ran well enough for his connections to be pleased with his effort, particularly as fresh snowfall made this more of a stamina test than was ideal.

416 LINGFIELD (L-H)
Monday, February 20

OFFICIAL GOING: Standard
Wind: Fresh, half-against

457 PLAY LITTLEWOODS POOLS ON 0800 500 000 AMATEUR RIDERS' H'CAP 1m 4f (P)
1:15 (1:16) (Class 6) (0-55,55) 4-Y-0+ **£2,307** (£709; £354) **Stalls** Low

Form RPR

-552 1 **Polish Power (GER)**[6] [414] 6-10-13 **50** MrsSMoore(3) 5 57
(J S Moore) *racd in tch: hdwy over 1f out: qcknd wl to ld ins fnl f: comf* **4/1**[1]
0-P0 2 *2* **Cemgraft**[13] [328] 5-10-5 **46** oh1 (tp) MissZoeLilly(7) 3 50
(A J Lidderdale) *hld up in rr: hdwy 2f out: styd on to go 2nd nr fin* **66/1**
66-0 3 *shd* **Lawaaheb (IRE)**[33] [141] 5-10-6 **47** (v) MissLBaldwin(7) 2 51
(B R Johnson) *led tl rdn and hdd ins fnl f: lost 2nd cl home* **7/1**[3]
-554 4 *2 ½* **Noble Mind**[15] [301] 5-10-7 **48** ow1 (p) MrJQuintin(7) 4 48
(P G Murphy) *trckd ldr: rdn 2f out: wknd ins fnl f* **20/1**
4-02 5 *3* **Spitfire Bob (USA)**[13] [328] 7-10-13 **54** MissKSearby(7) 8 50
(M E Sowersby) *in rr tl hdwy ins fnl 2f out: styd on: nvr nrr* **14/1**
44/0 6 *1* **Open Arms**[26] [186] 10-11-0 **55** MrHSkelton(7) 15 49
(Mrs A L M King) *towards rr tl hdwy over 3f out: rdn and fdd wl over 1f out* **25/1**
01-2 7 *2* **Soviet Sceptre (IRE)**[9] [379] 5-11-3 **51** (t) TJO'Brien 9 42
(R T Phillips) *hld up: nvr on terms* **9/2**[2]
64-2 8 *1 ¼* **Star Welcome**[42] [72] 5-11-3 **51** MrSDobson 12 40
(W J Musson) *in rr tl gd hdwy 1/2-way: wknd 2f out* **15/2**
1412 9 *hd* **Nisr**[5] [417] 9-11-0 **55** (t) MissNathalieNorgren(7) 6 44
(Miss Gay Kelleway) *bhd and nvr on terms* **10/1**
030- 10 *nk* **Hereditary**[17] [4683] 4-10-8 **52** MissKJewell(7) 16 40
(Mrs L C Jewell) *mid-div: bhd fnl 2f* **33/1**
062/ 11 *2 ½* **Tizi Ouzou (IRE)**[42] [5843] 5-11-0 **53** (v) MrSPearce(5) 10 38
(M C Pipe) *chsd ldrs tl rdn and wknd 3f out* **16/1**
26/0 12 *4* **Delta Force**[18] [270] 7-11-2 **53** MissFayeBramley(3) 11 32
(P A Blockley) *s.i.s: a bhd* **40/1**
0-1 13 *2* **Tignasse (FR)**[12] [338] 5-10-13 **52** (be) MissHayleyMoore(5) 14 28
(G L Moore) *rcd wd in mid-div: wknd 3f out* **8/1**
06-0 14 *8* **Whitsbury Common**[37] [114] 4-11-4 **55** MrSWalker 1 19
(D R C Elsworth) *in tch: rdn over 5f out: sn bhd* **14/1**
0-06 15 *28* **Hometomammy**[17] [289] 4-10-10 **52** MrsMarieKing(5) 13 —
(P W Hiatt) *in tch tl wknd qckly over 3f out: t.o* **25/1**
2m 36.65s (2.26) **Going Correction** +0.05s/f (Slow)
WFA 4 from 5yo+ 3lb 15 Ran SP% **121.2**
Speed ratings (Par 101):94,92,92,90,88 88,86,86,85,85 84,81,80,74,56
CSF £301.23 CT £1826.22 TOTE £4.30: £1.40, £27.30, £4.20; EX 449.40.
Owner Mrs Fitri Hay **Bred** Gestut Hofgut Mappen **Trained** Upper Lambourn, Berks
FOCUS
A moderate contest but they went a sensible pace early on against the strong headwind and the form looks reliable enough.
Nisr Official explanation: vet said gelding finished lame

458 LITTLEWOODS LOTTO3 0800 500 000 (S) STKS 1m (P)
1:45 (1:46) (Class 6) 3-Y-0+ **£2,388** (£705; £352) **Stalls** High

Form RPR

2245 1 **Samson Quest**[16] [297] 4-9-1 59 (v) JamesDoyle(7) 8 56
(A W Carroll) *hld up: hdwy over 3f out: rdn and r.o to ld nr fin* **2/1**[1]
0/06 2 *nk* **Christmas Truce (IRE)**[17] [284] 7-9-1 50 SophieDoyle(7) 12 55
(Ms J S Doyle) *trckd ldr: led 3f out: rdn over 1f out: hdd nr fin* **66/1**
000- 3 *1 ½* **Labelled With Love**[97] [6363] 6-9-5 55 (t) AmirQuinn(3) 2 52
(J R Boyle) *slowly away: t.k.h and sn trckd ldrs: rdn over 1f out: kpt on* **33/1**
-004 4 *nk* **Wiltshire (IRE)**[7] [398] 4-9-8 50 (v) NCallan 10 51
(P A Blockley) *t.k.h: hld up: hdwy to chsd ldrs 2f out: ev ch 1f out: nt qckn ins fnl f* **8/1**
2-34 5 *nk* **Rowan Pursuit**[16] [297] 5-9-3 48 (b) TQuinn 5 45
(J Akehurst) *in rr: rdn and r.o fr over 1f out: nvr nrr* **5/1**[3]
6U20 6 *hd* **Exit Smiling**[5] [417] 4-9-8 54 (b[1]) ChrisCatlin 1 50
(G C H Chung) *slowly away: in rr: hdwy over 1f out: r.o fnl f* **12/1**
06-0 7 *nk* **Moors Myth**[12] [343] 5-9-8 63 MartinDwyer 9 49
(B W Hills) *in tch: rdn over 2f out: nt qckn fnl f* **9/2**[2]
0-66 8 *shd* **Ladies Knight**[7] [402] 6-9-5 50 PatrickMathers(3) 6 49
(D Shaw) *bhd: rdn over 1f out: mde sme late hdwy* **33/1**
5-50 9 *½* **Sahara Prince (IRE)**[13] [321] 6-9-8 55 (v) SteveDrowne 3 48
(K A Morgan) *sn led: hdd 3f out: rdn 2f out: fdd ins fnl f* **14/1**
6410 10 *shd* **Distant Country (USA)**[6] [410] 7-9-7 54 (p) AndrewElliott(7) 11 54
(K R Burke) *in rr: hdwy on ins whn short of room over 1f out and no ch after* **10/1**
00-0 11 *1 ½* **Frank's Quest (IRE)**[16] [297] 6-9-8 52 SamHitchcott 4 44
(A B Haynes) *a bhd* **25/1**
0 12 *nk* **Mia (POL)**[7] [394] 5-9-9 47 (b) FergusSweeney 7 45
(Mrs P Townsley) *racd wd: effrt on outside over 2f out: btn over 1f out* **50/1**
1m 39.83s (0.40) **Going Correction** +0.05s/f (Slow) 12 Ran SP% **115.9**
Speed ratings (Par 101):100,99,98,97,97 97,97,97,96,96 94,94
CSF £192.94 TOTE £2.70: £1.80, £15.70, £6.80; EX 182.30.The winner was bought in for 5,600gns.
Owner A Sumner **Bred** A W J Perry **Trained** Cropthorne, Worcs
■ James Doyle on the winner snatched victory from a horse trained by his mother and ridden by his sister.
FOCUS
A run-of-the-mill seller in which they went no pace and finished in a bunch, so the form has been rated cautiously.
Sahara Prince(IRE) Official explanation: jockey said gelding was denied a clear run
Distant Country(USA) Official explanation: jockey said gelding was denied a clear run

459 BETDIRECT FREEPHONE 0800 211 222 MAIDEN STKS 7f (P)
2:15 (2:15) (Class 5) 3-Y-0+ **£3,238** (£963; £481; £240) **Stalls** Low

Form RPR

33-2 1 **Rebellion**[5] [418] 3-8-9 76 JoeFanning 1 71
(M Johnston) *mde all: kpt up to work ins fnl 2f: styd on wl* **7/4**[2]
22- 2 *½* **Shamila**[142] [5609] 3-8-4 NickyMackay 2 65
(G A Butler) *trckd ldrs: chsd wnr over 1f out: rdn: no imp fnl 100yds* **5/4**[1]
4523 3 *¾* **Scroll**[12] [342] 3-8-9 71 (v) ShaneKelly 4 68
(P Howling) *in tch: swtchd lft and hdwy on ins over 1f out: r.o fnl f* **10/1**
60 4 *½* **Top Shot**[10] [365] 3-8-6 SaleemGolam(3) 3 67
(M H Tompkins) *outpcd in rr tl rdn and hdwy over 1f out: styd on ins fnl f: nvr nrr* **50/1**
3- 5 *1 ¼* **Country Affair (USA)**[66] [6595] 3-8-9 ChrisCatlin 8 63
(P R Webber) *towards rr: sme late hdwy: nvr on terms* **7/1**[3]
-243 6 *1 ½* **Pab Special (IRE)**[9] [378] 3-8-2 71 (v[1]) AndrewElliott(7) 7 60
(K R Burke) *trckd wnr to over 1f out: no ex and wknd ins fnl f* **16/1**
-004 7 *3 ½* **Megalala (IRE)**[16] [291] 5-9-9 54 NeilChalmers(3) 6 56
(J J Bridger) *trckd ldrs: rdn 1/2-way: c wd into st: wknd appr fnl f* **66/1**
000- 8 *5* **Mephistos Kick**[63] [6611] 5-9-9 40 (t) StephaneBreux(3) 5 43
(Jean-Rene Auvray) *outpcd: a bhd* **150/1**
1m 25.31s (-0.58) **Going Correction** +0.05s/f (Slow)
WFA 3 from 5yo 17lb 8 Ran SP% **112.4**
Speed ratings (Par 103):105,104,103,103,101 99,95,90
CSF £4.09 TOTE £2.10: £1.10, £1.10, £2.60; EX 4.00.
Owner Jumeirah Racing **Bred** Darley **Trained** Middleham Moor, N Yorks
■ Stewards' Enquiry : Saleem Golam one-day ban: careless riding (Mar 3)
FOCUS
A two-horse race on paper but a good pace and with the placed horses close to their marks the form looks sound enough.
Pab Special(IRE) Official explanation: vet said gelding finished lame

460 LITTLEWOODS LOTTO4 0800 500 000 MAIDEN STKS 1m 2f (P)
2:50 (2:51) (Class 5) 3-Y-0+ **£3,238** (£963; £481; £240) **Stalls** Low

Form RPR

224- 1 **Ameeq (USA)**[80] [6028] 4-9-11 77 GeorgeBaker 1 69
(G L Moore) *trckd ldrs: rdn to ld ins fnl f: r.o wl* **3/1**[1]
00-4 2 *1 ¼* **Gus**[12] [337] 3-8-4 70 MartinDwyer 4 63
(B W Hills) *tracked ldr: rdn to ld wl over 1f out: hdd ins fnl f: no ex* **3/1**[1]
0-6 3 *2 ½* **Canyouwin**[9] [372] 3-7-13 PaulFessey 7 53
(J H M Gosden) *mid-div: rdn over 3f out: sn outpcd: r.o wl fnl f: nvr nrr* **16/1**
-456 4 *nk* **Questive**[12] [337] 3-8-4 70 (t) PaulHanagan 2 58
(E A L Dunlop) *led tl rdn and hdd wl over 1f out: one pce after* **8/1**[3]
0-56 5 *shd* **Grand Design**[23] [217] 4-9-6 53 NCallan 6 57
(C A Cyzer) *in tch: rdn over 2f out: no hdwy after* **25/1**
05- 6 *1 ½* **Christmas Player (USA)**[86] [6425] 3-7-13 DavidKinsella 5 50
(J H M Gosden) *trckd ldrs: rdn over 2f out: no hdwy after* **8/1**[3]
5 7 *½* **Bookman (IRE)**[17] [289] 4-9-11 (t) SteveDrowne 8 58
(P M Mooney, Ire) *in rr and nvr on terms* **16/1**
00- 8 *¾* **Archivist (IRE)**[205] [3946] 3-8-4 ChrisCatlin 12 53
(M Blanshard) *bhd: effrt over over 1f out: nvr nr to chal* **66/1**
9 *½* **Elated (IRE)** 4-9-11 DarryllHolland 13 56
(W J Haggas) *bhd: mde sme late hdwy* **25/1**
0-0 10 *nk* **Arthurs Legacy**[23] [217] 4-9-4 RonanKeogh(7) 11 55
(J A R Toller) *mid-div: rdn over 3f out: sn bhd* **100/1**
4 11 *1* **Western Sky**[19] [266] 3-7-13 NickyMackay 3 44
(J Noseda) *s.i.s: sn mid-div: rdn over 4f out: wknd over 2f out* **7/2**[2]
0-0 12 *1 ½* **Belrose (IRE)**[23] [219] 4-8-13 KirstyMilczarek(7) 10 46
(Mrs C A Dunnett) *racd wd: a towards rr* **100/1**
05/ 13 *5* **Hanazakari**[537] [5216] 5-9-12 PaulDoe 9 42
(J A R Toller) *a bhd* **100/1**
2m 6.54s (-1.25) **Going Correction** +0.05s/f (Slow)
WFA 3 from 4yo 22lb 4 from 5yo 1lb 13 Ran SP% **118.4**
Speed ratings (Par 103):107,106,104,103,103 102,102,101,101,100 100,98,94
CSF £11.33 TOTE £3.50: £2.10, £1.10, £4.40; EX 14.70.
Owner C E Stedman **Bred** Shadwell Farm LLC **Trained** Woodingdean, E Sussex
FOCUS
A weak maiden event anchored by the fifth.

Questive Official explanation: jockey said colt had a breathing problem
Western Sky Official explanation: jockey said filly hung badly right final furlong

461 WIN £2M AT CLASSICVALUEPOOLS.COM H'CAP (DIV I) 1m 2f (P)
3:20 (3:20) (Class 6) (0-60,60) 4-Y-O+ £2,047 (£604; £302) Stalls Low

Form RPR
-224 1 **Lowestoft Playboy**[12] 339 4-9-2 59 NCallan 4 68
(J Jay) *set stdy pce tl qcknd 2f out: sn in command and r.o wl* 6/1
-013 2 1 **Blue Hedges**[9] 379 4-8-7 57 JamesDoyle(7) 9 64
(H J Collingridge) *hld up in rr: hdwy over 2f out: rdn and r.o to go 2nd nr fin* 11/4[1]
04-4 3 ½ **Red Sail**[26] 185 5-8-10 52 (b) ShaneKelly 1 58
(Dr J D Scargill) *in tch on ins: chsd wnr fr over 2f out tl lost 2nd nr fin* 11/2[3]
-505 4 1 ½ **State Dilemma (IRE)**[12] 343 5-8-11 56 (v) PatrickMathers(3) 3 60
(D Shaw) *towards rr: hdwy on ins 2f out: r.o: nvr nrr* 16/1
4605 5 1 **Tregarron**[13] 321 5-8-12 54 ChrisCatlin 6 56
(P A Blockley) *racd wd towards rr: rdn over 2f out: r.o fnl f: nvr nrr* 11/1
1064 6 nk **King Of Music (USA)**[5] 416 5-8-10 59 (v) ChrisCavanagh(7) 7 60
(G Prodromou) *slowly away and bhd: hdwy on outside over 3f out: nvr nr to chal* 8/1
1/0- 7 shd **Graft**[411] 36 7-9-4 60 (p) SamHitchcott 10 61?
(Mrs P Townsley) *pulled hrd: in tch: outpcd over 2f out: sme late hdwy* 16/1
/051 8 3 **Ground Patrol**[9] 379 5-9-4 60 GeorgeBaker 5 56
(G L Moore) *prom on outside: rdn over 2f out: wknd over 1f out* 7/2[2]
06-0 9 ½ **Ready Teddy Go**[40] 94 4-7-12 47 oh7 MarcHalford(5) 8 41
(J Ryan) *trckd wnr to over 2f out: rdn and wknd over 1f out* 100/1
/00- 10 ¾ **Trew Flight (USA)**[66] 6594 4-9-0 60 SaleemGolam(3) 2 53
(M H Tompkins) *t.k.h: in tch tl wknd over 2f out* 25/1
2m 9.94s (2.15) **Going Correction** +0.05s/f (Slow)
WFA 4 from 5yo+ 1lb 10 Ran SP% 114.6
Speed ratings (Par 101):93,92,91,90,89 89,89,87,86,86
CSF £22.40 CT £95.96 TOTE £5.30: £2.10, £1.20, £1.90; EX 27.30.
Owner Play Boy Partnership II **Bred** Taylor Parker Associates Ltd **Trained** Newmarket, Suffolk
FOCUS
A very moderate winning time for a race like this and by far the slowest of the four races over the trip on the day, 3.54 seconds slower than the second division. The form looks reliable enough on paper but time suggests it is not the most solid.
Ground Patrol Official explanation: jockey said gelding was unsuited by the lack of pace

462 WIN £2M AT CLASSICVALUEPOOLS.COM H'CAP (DIV II) 1m 2f (P)
3:55 (3:55) (Class 6) (0-60,60) 4-Y-O+ £2,047 (£604; £302) Stalls Low

Form RPR
31-3 1 **Turner's Touch**[10] 363 4-8-10 53 (be) TPQueally 7 60
(G L Moore) *mid-div: hdwy whn short of room over 1f out: burst through gap u.p and r.o wl to ld post* 7/1
1355 2 shd **Augustine**[7] 405 5-9-3 59 JoeFanning 6 66+
(P W Hiatt) *trckd ldr: led 5f out: strly rdn appr fnl f: hdd post* 11/4[1]
0-30 3 1 ½ **Unrestricted**[19] 263 4-8-13 56 NCallan 3 60
(C F Wall) *trckd ldrs: ev ch ins fnl f: nt qckn fnl 100yds* 14/1
-406 4 shd **My Pension (IRE)**[9] 383 5-9-1 57 ShaneKelly 10 61
(P Howling) *mid-div: hdwy to chse ldrs 2f out: kpt on one pce fnl f* 7/1
4-40 5 ½ **Thebestisyettocome**[9] 379 4-9-0 57 (v[1]) IanMongan 8 60
(T G Mills) *t.k.h: in tch: wnt 2nd 3f out: tl rdn and nt qckn ins fnl f* 5/1[3]
0-03 6 ¾ **King Of Knight (IRE)**[13] 324 5-9-4 60 ChrisCatlin 5 62
(G Prodromou) *stdd s: bhd tl hdwy over 2f out: no ex fnl f* 4/1[2]
0-60 7 6 **Barachois Gaudy**[23] 217 4-7-10 40 oh6 JamesDoyle(7) 4 37
(Mrs N Smith) *hld up: a bhd* 66/1
362- 8 nk **Bauhinia**[70] 6567 4-8-8 51 PaulDoe 9 41
(J A R Toller) *towards rr: a bhd* 16/1
-000 9 5 **Baboosh (IRE)**[13] 324 5-9-4 60 JamieMackay 1 41
(M Wigham) *outpcd: a bhd* 66/1
20-3 10 24 **Mansiya**[21] 252 4-9-2 59 RichardHughes 2 —
(C E Brittain) *led to 5f out: wknd wl over 3f out* 8/1
2m 6.40s (-1.39) **Going Correction** +0.05s/f (Slow)
WFA 4 from 5yo 1lb 10 Ran SP% 115.0
Speed ratings (Par 101):107,106,105,105,105 104,99,99,95,76
CSF £26.15 CT £262.00 TOTE £9.90: £2.80, £1.50, £5.60; EX 29.10.
Owner The Wacko Partnership **Bred** Hedgeholme Stud **Trained** Woodingdean, E Sussex
FOCUS
A moderate but competitive handicap and a decent time for a race of its grade; 3.54 seconds faster than the first division. The placed horses give the form a solid appearance.
Unrestricted Official explanation: jockey said filly lost its off-fore shoe and hung right throughout
Mansiya Official explanation: jockey said filly did not feel right in straight

463 PLAY £1/4M SPOT BALL ON 0800 500 000 H'CAP 1m 2f (P)
4:30 (4:30) (Class 4) (0-85,82) 4-Y-O+ £6,477 (£1,927; £963; £481) Stalls Low

Form RPR
00/- 1 **Barry Island**[425] 6971 7-8-11 75 JamieMackay 4 82
(D R C Elsworth) *hld up in rr: hdwy on ins over 1f out: squeezed through to ld wl ins fnl f: drvn out* 20/1
-030 2 nk **Gingko**[9] 375 9-8-10 74 ChrisCatlin 10 81
(P R Webber) *hld up: rdn 3f out: r.o strly to go 2nd cl home* 20/1
21-3 3 1 **Bobby Charles**[33] 140 5-9-4 82 ShaneKelly 6 87
(Dr J D Scargill) *trckd ldr: rdn to ld appr fnl f: hdd ins: lost 2nd cl home* 11/4[1]
-652 4 nk **Just Fly**[24] 214 6-8-9 73 ow1 (v) NCallan 5 77
(Dr J R J Naylor) *a.p: rdn 2f out: r.o fnl f* 6/1[3]
/400 5 1 **Alekhine (IRE)**[9] 375 5-8-1 72 (e) JamesDoyle(7) 9 75
(J R Boyle) *hld up: hdwy on outside over 2f out: nt qckn fnl f* 14/1
1-56 6 nk **Wise Owl**[16] 296 4-9-3 82 DarryllHolland 3 84
(J Pearce) *led tl rdn and hdd appr fnl f: wknd ins* 7/2[2]
20-0 7 2 **Island Rapture**[23] 221 6-8-8 72 JoeFanning 1 71
(J A R Toller) *mid-div: outpcd 2f out: sn bhd* 12/1
5-15 8 ¾ **Bazelle**[9] 384 4-8-6 74 PatrickMathers(3) 7 71
(D Shaw) *trckd ldrs: rdn over 2f out: wknd over 1f out* 25/1
6013 9 ½ **Zalkani (IRE)**[5] 421 6-8-9 73 TQuinn 2 69+
(B G Powell) *plld hrd: prom on ins and frequently short of room: wknd over 1f out* 7/2[2]
2m 7.44s (-0.35) **Going Correction** +0.05s/f (Slow)
WFA 4 from 5yo+ 1lb 9 Ran SP% 113.1
Speed ratings (Par 105):103,102,101,101,100 100,99,98,98
CSF £335.99 CT £1442.72 TOTE £24.30: £4.90, £4.60, £1.20; EX 185.90 Trifecta £1105.90 Pool: £1,775.70 - 1.14 winning tickets..
Owner Matthew Green **Bred** The Lavington Stud **Trained** Newmarket, Suffolk
■ A first winner since moving from Whitsbury to Newmarket for trainer David Elsworth.
FOCUS
A very slow early pace meant that this developed into a sprint which did not suit a few, but despite the moderate pace the front pair came from well off the pace. The form is limited despite those in the frame behind the winner running close to their marks.
Zalkani(IRE) Official explanation: trainer said gelding ran flat

464 BE LUCKY @ LITTLEWOODSPOOLS.CO.UK H'CAP 5f (P)
5:05 (5:05) (Class 5) (0-70,70) 3-Y-O £3,238 (£963; £481; £240) Stalls High

Form RPR
-143 1 **Sands Crooner (IRE)**[12] 341 3-9-1 70 (v) PatrickMathers(3) 4 75
(D Shaw) *s.i.s: t.k.h: hdwy over 1f out: squeezeed through to ld nr fin* 8/1
-611 2 ½ **Pauvic (IRE)**[13] 322 3-9-2 68 (v) PaulFessey 2 71
(Mrs A Duffield) *led: rdn over 1f out: hdd nr fin* 3/1[2]
1-65 3 nk **Rapsgate (IRE)**[26] 190 3-9-1 67 (b) RichardHughes 9 69
(R Hannon) *bhd: rdn 2f out: edgd lft but r.o strly fnl f: nvr nrr* 12/1
-514 4 ½ **Correct Time (IRE)**[10] 359 3-8-10 62 NCallan 7 62
(N P Littmoden) *in rr: hdwy over 1f out: ev ch ins fnl f: nt qckn nr fin* 7/1
-020 5 ¾ **Mine The Balance (IRE)**[17] 287 3-7-11 56 oh3 JamesDoyle(7) 1 54
(J R Best) *bhd: rdn and hdwy on ins over 1f out: bmpd ins fnl f: no ex* 6/1[3]
2201 6 nk **Radiator Rooney (IRE)**[16] 298 3-9-4 70 (b) ShaneKelly 6 66
(Patrick Morris, Ire) *trckd ldrs on outside: no ex appr fnl f* 11/4[1]
3335 7 1 ¾ **Developer (IRE)**[16] 298 3-8-11 63 (p) JoeFanning 8 53
(T G Mills) *racd wd: nvr on terms* 12/1
14-4 8 1 ¼ **Glenviews Youngone (IRE)**[23] 226 3-8-7 66 (b[1]) RonanKeogh(7) 5 52
(Peter Grayson) *w ldr and ev ch tl started to edge lft ent fnl f: wknd qckly* 10/1
60.52 secs (0.74) **Going Correction** +0.05s/f (Slow) 8 Ran SP% 114.0
Speed ratings (Par 97):96,95,94,93,92 92,89,87
CSF £32.09 CT £290.94 TOTE £10.30: £4.30, £1.10, £4.90; EX 34.50 Place 6 £20.66, Place 5 £8.47.
Owner Danethorpe Racing Ltd **Bred** Peter Molony **Trained** Danethorpe, Notts
■ Stewards' Enquiry : Richard Hughes seven-day ban (inc five deferred days): careless riding (Mar 3-15)
FOCUS
A fair little sprint handicap but, despite there only being eight runners, this was a very rough race with two separate incidents inside the last furlong. The form is best rated through the placed horses.
Glenviews Youngone(IRE) Official explanation: jockey said filly hung left throughout
T/Jkpt: £3,550.00 to a £1 stake. Pool: £10,000.00. 2.00 winning tickets. T/Plt: £24.80 to a £1 stake. Pool: £50,020.60. 1,469.90 winning tickets. T/Qpdt: £4.80 to a £1 stake. Pool: £5,872.80. 900.90 winning tickets. JS

447 WOLVERHAMPTON (A.W) (L-H)
Monday, February 20

OFFICIAL GOING: Standard
Wind: Moderate, against Weather: Showers

465 PLAY BLACKJACKMANIA @ LITTLEWOODSCASINO.COM BANDED STKS 5f 20y(P)
2:25 (2:26) (Class 7) 3-Y-O+ £1,365 (£403; £201) Stalls Low

Form RPR
4-43 1 **Hello Roberto**[10] 360 5-8-12 45 (p) AdrianMcCarthy 9 53
(R A Harris) *led 1f: a.p: rdn to ld 1f out: drvn out* 6/1[3]
5003 2 shd **Muktasb (USA)**[15] 299 5-8-12 45 (v) TomEaves 10 53
(D Shaw) *hld up and bhd: hdwy over 1f out: hrd rdn and ev ch wl ins fnl f: r.o* 8/1
00-2 3 2 ½ **Obe Bold (IRE)**[10] 360 5-8-12 45 FergalLynch 5 47+
(A Berry) *n.m.r sn after s: bhd tl hdwy fnl f: nrst fin* 9/1
-300 4 ½ **Teyaar**[7] 397 10-8-12 45 AlanDaly 3 42+
(M Wellings) *hld up: hmpd and lost pl over 3f out: rdn and hdwy over 1f out: r.o ins fnl f* 18/1
052- 5 hd **Cark**[61] 6647 8-8-9 45 (p) JasonEdmunds(3) 1 44+
(J Balding) *chsd ldrs: rdn wl over 1f out: one pce fnl f* 9/2[1]
-020 6 shd **Freshwinds**[15] 299 4-8-12 45 MickyFenton 4 41
(S L Keightley) *bmpd s: plld hrd in rr: late hdwy on outside: nvr nrr* 11/2[2]
0000 7 ½ **Lady Pekan**[15] 299 7-8-12 45 (v) J-PGuillambert 11 39
(P Howling) *s.i.s: sn prom: led after 1f: rdn and hdd over 1f out: wknd wl ins fnl f* 25/1
30-0 8 ½ **Stephanie's Mind**[48] 22 4-8-12 45 (v) JamieSpencer 8 38
(M Quinn) *chsd ldrs: c wd st: wknd over 1f out* 13/2
0-05 9 1 **Carcinetto (IRE)**[21] 249 4-8-12 45 (v) FrancisFerris 6 34
(B Palling) *wnt lft s: prom: rdn over 2f out: wknd and eased wl ins fnl f* 33/1
0664 10 ¾ **Ballyrush (IRE)**[8] 386 6-8-12 45 (e) OscarUrbina 2 31
(Miss D A McHale) *bhd: sme hdwy on ins whn nt clr run and swtchd rt ins fnl f: n.d* 16/1
0440 11 hd **Percy Douglas**[14] 320 6-8-5 45 (vt) AnnStokell(7) 12 31
(Miss A Stokell) *jnd ldr after 1f: rdn and ev ch wl over 1f out: wknd ins fnl f* 28/1
060 12 ¾ **Hiamovi (IRE)**[15] 299 4-8-12 45 (b) RobertWinston 7 28
(R M H Cowell) *t.k.h in mid-div: btn whn n.m.r wl ins fnl f* 7/1
62.92 secs (0.10) **Going Correction** -0.05s/f (Stan)
WFA 3 from 4yo+ 14lb 12 Ran SP% 116.2
Speed ratings (Par 97):97,96,92,92,91 91,90,89,88,87 86,85
CSF £51.15 TOTE £8.10: £1.50, £4.00, £2.90; EX 60.70.
Owner Peter A Price **Bred** I B Barker **Trained** Earlswood, Monmouths
FOCUS
A competitive sprint for the grade which saw the first two come clear and the form looks reasonable.
Hiamovi(IRE) Official explanation: vet said gelding finished lame

466 WIN WITH RAGS2RICHES @ LITTLEWOODS CASINO MAIDEN CLAIMING STKS 7f 32y(P)
3:00 (3:00) (Class 7) 3-Y-O+ £1,365 (£403; £201) Stalls High

Form RPR
0-06 1 **Mr Cheers**[13] 329 3-8-9 47 (b) TomEaves 2 57
(Miss J A Camacho) *led early: prom: hmpd on ins over 3f out: rdn over 2f out: led ins fnl f: drvn out* 5/1[2]
5404 2 1 ½ **Miss Champagne (IRE)**[13] 326 3-7-13 51 RoryMoore(5) 3 48
(M Quinn) *sn led: rdn clr 2f out: edgd rt over 1f out: hdd ins fnl f: nt qckn* 7/2[1]

3 **3** 2 **Glenargo (USA)**[17] 286 3-8-2 (t) RDEgan(7) 9 48
(P M Mooney, Ire) *hld up: sn mid-div: lost pl 4f out: rdn and hdwy over 1f out: edgd lft wl ins fnl f: no ex* **8/1**

4055 **4** 2 **In Hope**[13] 326 3-8-0 48 HayleyTurner 4 34
(Ernst Oertel) *chsd ldrs: rdn over 2f out: wknd ins fnl f* **6/1**[3]

30-0 **5** 1/2 **Dolce Maria (IRE)**[10] 360 3-7-6 50 ow1 LiamJones(7) 5 32
(K A Morgan) *hld up in tch: rdn over 2f out: no hdwy* **6/1**[3]

2-00 **6** shd **Lady Palma Nova**[25] 197 3-7-11 55 AdeleRothery(7) 10 37
(M W Easterby) *s.i.s: rdn over 2f out: hdwy fnl f: n.d* **16/1**

60-0 **7** 2 **Mytass**[25] 197 3-8-2 50 (b) EdwardCreighton(3) 7 33
(J A Pickering) *hdwy after 1f: wknd over 2f out* **33/1**

50-4 **8** shd **Miss A Bargain (IRE)**[26] 189 3-8-4 48 FranciscoDaSilva 8 32
(K R Burke) *t.k.h: sn prom: hung lft over 3f out: chsd ldr over 2f out tl over 1f out: wknd fnl f* **14/1**

30-0 **9** 3/4 **Donya One**[13] 331 4-9-0 54 TomMessenger(7) 11 36
(John A Harris) *bhd: c wd st: nvr nrr* **25/1**

60- **10** 1 1/2 **Is**[145] 5541 3-8-4 FrancisFerris 6 26
(Rae Guest) *dwlt: rdn over 3f out: a bhd* **20/1**

6-40 **11** 1/2 **Teddy Monty (IRE)**[25] 193 3-8-8 48 ow1 MickyFenton 12 29
(M Quinn) *hdwy over 5f out: wknd over 3f out* **16/1**

-506 **12** 3/4 **Lasting Love**[10] 359 3-8-0 48 AdrianMcCarthy 1 19
(C R Dore) *chsd ldrs: n.m.r on ins and lost pl bnd after 1f: rdn over 2f out: sn bhd* **14/1**

1m 31.01s (0.61) **Going Correction** -0.05s/f (Stan)
WFA 3 from 4yo 17lb **12** Ran SP% **115.2**
Speed ratings (Par 97):94,92,90,87,87 87,84,84,83,82 81,80
CSF £21.49 TOTE £5.30: £1.20, £1.30, £2.50; EX 22.30.The winner was claimed by D. J. Simpson for £5,000. Glenargo was claimed by R. A. Harris for £5,000.
Owner David W Armstrong **Bred** B N And Mrs Toye **Trained** Norton, N Yorks

FOCUS
A very poor affair, but the form makes sense rated through the second and third.

467 WIN THE TREASURE OF ISIS @ LITTLEWOODSCASINO.COM BANDED STKS 1m 141y(P)
3:35 (3:37) (Class 7) 4-Y-O+ **£1,535** (£453; £226) **Stalls** Low

Form RPR

0-02 **1** **Joe Jo Star**[7] 400 4-8-11 45 (p) RobbieFitzpatrick 1 57
(B P J Baugh) *a.p: wnt 2nd over 2f out: sn rdn: led wl ins fnl f: r.o* **13/2**

-132 **2** nk **Golden Spectrum (IRE)**[8] 391 7-9-0 48 (b) AdrianMcCarthy 13 59
(R A Harris) *led: rdn wl over 1f out: hdd wl ins fnl f: r.o* **11/2**[3]

6536 **3** 7 **Musiotal**[7] 399 5-9-0 48 (p) GrahamGibbons 4 45
(P A Blockley) *hld up towards rr: rdn and hdwy on ins over 2f out: r.o one pce fnl f* **6/1**

044- **4** 1 1/4 **Summer Shades**[187] 4472 8-9-2 50 JamieSpencer 5 44
(W M Brisbourne) *hld up in mid-div: hdwy over 2f out: rdn over 1f out: one pce* **5/1**[2]

5622 **5** 3/4 **Dexileos (IRE)**[7] 399 7-8-11 45 (t) HayleyTurner 7 37
(David Pinder) *chsd ldrs tl wknd over 2f out* **7/1**

60-5 **6** 1 **Vizulize**[28] 172 7-9-1 49 MickyFenton 3 39
(A W Carroll) *hld up in tch: rdn over 3f out: wknd wl over 1f out* **20/1**

1054 **7** 1 1/2 **Legacy (JPN)**[10] 358 6-8-13 47 RobertWinston 9 34
(P D Evans) *no hdwy fnl 3f* **7/2**[1]

3-50 **8** shd **Mutared (IRE)**[14] 311 8-8-8 45 RichardThomas(3) 10 32
(N P Littmoden) *sn bhd: nvr nr ldrs* **12/1**

000- **9** 1/2 **Ruby Sunrise (IRE)**[119] 6078 4-8-6 47 SoniaEaton(7) 8 33
(B P J Baugh) *stdd s: a bhd* **66/1**

066- **10** 3/4 **Veneer (IRE)**[55] 6667 4-9-2 50 (b) TomEaves 11 34
(Miss Gay Kelleway) *prom: rdn over 3f out: wknd wl over 1f out* **20/1**

5-03 **11** nk **Cooleycall Star (IRE)**[7] 396 5-8-11 45 (p) J-PGuillambert 12 29
(A G Juckes) *stdd s: sn swtchd lft: a bhd* **33/1**

0005 **12** 16 **Lakeside Guy (IRE)**[7] 407 5-8-4 45 (bt[1]) LiamJones(7) 6 —
(M Appleby) *hld up and bhd: short-lived effrt over 3f out* **33/1**

1m 50.51s (-1.25) **Going Correction** -0.05s/f (Stan) **12** Ran SP% **119.0**
Speed ratings (Par 97):103,102,96,95,94 93,92,92,91,91 91,76
CSF £39.70 TOTE £9.20: £2.40, £2.20, £3.00; EX 43.10.
Owner Joe Singh **Bred** B J And Mrs Crangle **Trained** Audley, Staffs

FOCUS
A decent winning time for a banded contest and the form looks sound, although could be rated higher, with the first two coming well clear.
Mutared(IRE) Official explanation: jockey said gelding never travelled

468 BECOME MR RICH WITH LITTLEWOODSCASINO.COM BANDED STKS 1m 1f 103y(P)
4:10 (4:14) (Class 7) 4-Y-O+ **£1,365** (£403; £201) **Stalls** Low

Form RPR

10-2 **1** **Bold Phoenix (IRE)**[8] 386 5-8-11 45 (b) JamieSpencer 10 54
(B J Curley) *hld up and bhd: hdwy on ins 2f out: swtchd rt over 1f out: rdn to ld ins fnl f: sn edgd lft: r.o wl* **4/1**[2]

4-43 **2** 2 **Yashin (IRE)**[27] 182 5-8-11 45 LeeEnstone 1 50
(P A Blockley) *a.p: led 2f out: sn rdn: hdd ins fnl f: nt qckn* **9/2**[3]

4044 **3** 2 1/2 **Weet Yer Tern (IRE)**[9] 382 4-8-11 45 (p) GrahamGibbons 4 45
(P A Blockley) *led: hdd 2f out: rdn over 1f out: one pce fnl f* **10/1**

0005 **4** shd **Miss Monica (IRE)**[10] 363 5-8-11 45 AdrianTNicholls 13 45
(P W Hiatt) *hld up and bhd: plld out and hdwy over 1f out: r.o ins fnl f: nrst fin* **33/1**

-104 **5** hd **Opera Knight**[14] 310 6-8-11 45 MickyFenton 2 45
(A W Carroll) *hld up in mid-div: hdwy on ins over 2f out: rdn wl over 1f out: one pce fnl f* **9/1**

3622 **6** 1 **It Must Be Speech**[7] 394 5-8-11 45 (v) AdrianMcCarthy 9 43
(S L Keightley) *hld up in mid-div: hdwy 2f out: edgd lft fr over 1f out: one pce* **13/2**

3050 **7** 4 **Super Dominion**[7] 395 9-8-11 45 (p) VinceSlattery 8 35
(R Hollinshead) *hld up in mid-div: rdn over 3f out: hdwy over 2f out: wknd over 1f out* **25/1**

33-0 **8** hd **Tirailleur (IRE)**[15] 304 6-8-11 45 HayleyTurner 12 35
(J R Boyle) *nvr nr ldrs* **33/1**

0-06 **9** 1/2 **Fillameena**[8] 391 6-8-8 45 (p) PaulMulrennan(3) 11 34
(P T Midgley) *prom: rdn 5f out: wknd over 1f out* **25/1**

0032 **10** 3 **Dagola (IRE)**[7] 395 5-8-11 45 OscarUrbina 5 28
(C A Dwyer) *s.s: a bhd* **7/2**[1]

0-63 **11** 5 **Elms Schoolboy**[4] 427 4-8-11 45 FergalLynch 6 19
(P Howling) *chsd ldr: rdn and ev ch over 2f out: wknd wl over 1f out* **14/1**

341- **12** 12 **Wodhill Gold**[61] 6649 5-8-11 45 (v) DerekMcGaffin 7 —
(D Morris) *prom: rdn over 2f out: wknd wl over 1f out* **16/1**

2m 1.77s (-0.85) **Going Correction** -0.05s/f (Stan) **12** Ran SP% **119.0**
Speed ratings (Par 97):101,99,97,96,96 95,92,92,91,89 84,73
CSF £21.50 TOTE £4.60: £2.40, £2.50, £3.60; EX 23.20.
Owner Curley Leisure **Bred** Milton Park Stud Partnership **Trained** Newmarket, Suffolk

FOCUS
A fair time for the grade and 1.37 seconds faster than the following contest over the same trip. This was run at a solid pace and the form looks sound.
Dagola(IRE) Official explanation: jockey said gelding never travelled

469 LITTLEWOODSCASINO.COM - TRUSTED NAME BANDED STKS 1m 1f 103y(P)
4:45 (4:45) (Class 7) 4-Y-O+ **£1,365** (£403; £201) **Stalls** Low

Form RPR

-232 **1** **Basinet**[14] 310 8-9-2 50 (p) GrahamGibbons 5 57
(J J Quinn) *hld up in mid-div: hdwy over 2f out: rdn and edgd lft over 1f out: led ins fnl f: drvn out* **5/2**[1]

-000 **2** 3/4 **Gallego**[17] 290 4-8-12 46 OscarUrbina 12 52
(R J Price) *stdd s: hld up and bhd: hdwy 2f out: wnt 2nd wl ins fnl f: sn edgd lft: kpt on* **25/1**

-621 **3** 3/4 **Desert Hawk**[10] 363 5-9-2 50 (b) RobbieFitzpatrick 13 56+
(W M Brisbourne) *hld up in mid-div: nt clr run on ins over 2f out: hdwy wl over 1f out: cl 2nd whn nt clr run and swtchd rt ins fnl* **5/2**[1]

10-0 **4** 1 **Homebred Star**[7] 398 5-8-8 47 (p) RobynBrisland(5) 10 49
(G P Enright) *hld up in mid-div: hdwy whn nt clr run over 1f out: r.o ins fnl f* **50/1**

4024 **5** 1 1/2 **Spy Gun (USA)**[20] 261 6-8-11 45 J-PGuillambert 3 44
(T Wall) *led: hdd over 6f out: led over 3f out: rdn clr 2f out: hdd ins fnl f: wknd* **9/1**[3]

-440 **6** 2 1/2 **Schinken Otto (IRE)**[7] 405 5-8-11 45 TomEaves 4 40
(J M Jefferson) *w ldr: led over 6f out tl over 3f out: sn rdn: wknd over 1f out* **10/1**

0-0 **7** 6 **Settle (IRE)**[20] 259 7-8-11 40 (p) RobertWinston 2 28
(W M Brisbourne) *prom: rdn 6f out: wknd wl over 1f out* **12/1**

43-0 **8** nk **Princeable Lady (IRE)**[10] 363 4-8-8 40 EdwardCreighton(3) 6 28
(J A Pickering) *nvr nr ldrs* **33/1**

000/ **9** 1 **Mezereon**[674] 1479 6-8-13 50 DanielTudhope(3) 1 31
(D Carroll) *prom: rdn over 4f out: wknd over 2f out* **33/1**

01-0 **10** 1 **Ndola**[14] 310 7-8-13 47 (b[1]) JamieSpencer 11 26
(B J Curley) *w ldrs: rdn over 3f out: wknd over 1f out* **8/1**[2]

4305 **11** 2 1/2 **Look At The Stars (IRE)**[9] 382 4-8-9 50 (bt) RussellKennemore(7) 8 24
(R Hollinshead) *hld up towards rr: short-lived effrt over 2f out* **16/1**

0-64 **12** 5 **Belle Chanson**[7] 395 4-8-11 45 (v) HayleyTurner 7 10
(J R Boyle) *hld up in tch: rdn over 3f out: sn wknd* **22/1**

13 20 **One And Only (GER)**[33] 5-8-11 35 TonyHamilton 9 —
(D W Thompson) *hld up towards rr: rdn over 4f out: t.o fnl 2f* **50/1**

2m 3.14s (0.52) **Going Correction** -0.05s/f (Stan) **13** Ran SP% **118.9**
Speed ratings (Par 97):95,94,93,92,91 89,83,83,82,81 79,75,57
CSF £80.51 TOTE £3.40: £1.30, £6.60, £1.90; EX 81.30.
Owner Tara Leisure **Bred** Overbury Stud **Trained** Settrington, N Yorks
■ Stewards' Enquiry : J-P Guillambert one-day ban: careless riding (Mar 3)

FOCUS
An ordinary pace and the winning time was 1.37 seconds slower than the preceding contest over the same trip, despite which the form looks solid enough on paper.

470 GREAT JACKPOTS WAITING @ LITTLEWOODSCASINO.COM BANDED STKS 1m 4f 50y(P)
5:15 (5:15) (Class 7) 4-Y-O+ **£1,365** (£403; £201) **Stalls** Low

Form RPR

4/1- **1** **Debbie**[261] 515 7-9-0 45 RobbieFitzpatrick 2 51
(B D Leavy) *hld up: stdy hdwy over 5f out: led over 2f out: hrd rdn fnl f: jst hld on* **10/1**

-233 **2** shd **Zaffeu**[17] 284 5-9-3 48 J-PGuillambert 12 55+
(A G Juckes) *hld up: swtchd lft sn after s: hdwy and nt clr run 2f out: hmpd wl over 1f out: sn rdn: r.o ins fnl f: jst* **6/1**[2]

5265 **3** 1 **Jadeeron**[12] 338 7-9-5 50 (p) OscarUrbina 10 54
(Miss D A McHale) *hld up in mid-div: hdwy 2f out: rdn and edgd lft ins fnl f: r.o* **16/1**

505- **4** nk **Theatre Tinka (IRE)**[61] 5519 7-9-3 48 (p) GrahamGibbons 4 52
(R Hollinshead) *led early: a.p: hrd rdn and ev ch ins fnl f: nt qckn whn n.m.r on ins cl home* **14/1**

0/5- **5** nk **Valeureux**[56] 6534 8-9-3 48 MichaelTebbutt 1 51
(J Hetherton) *hld up in tch: lost pl 4f out: late hdwy on outside: nt rch ldrs* **16/1**

-631 **6** 3/4 **Shaheer (IRE)**[15] 301 4-9-2 50 JamieSpencer 11 52
(J Gallagher) *hld up in mid-div: rdn over 3f out: hdwy on ins 2f out: one pce fnl f* **9/1**

00-1 **7** hd **Go Free**[14] 309 5-9-0 50 StephenDonohoe(5) 5 52
(C J Down) *s.s: hld up in rr: rdn and hdwy on outside over 2f out: one pce fnl f* **6/1**[2]

5431 **8** 1 **York Cliff**[3] 442 8-9-4 50 LiamJones(7) 3 56
(W M Brisbourne) *s.i.s: hld up in rr: rdn over 2f out: sme hdwy fnl f: n.d* **7/1**[3]

551- **9** 1/2 **Saameq (IRE)**[82] 6475 5-9-5 50 RobertWinston 6 49
(D W Thompson) *plld hrd in rr: hdwy over 5f out: rdn 2f out: wknd ins fnl f* **5/2**[1]

-333 **10** 1/2 **Lake Wakatipu**[17] 283 4-9-2 50 DeanMcKeown 7 49
(M Mullineaux) *hld up in tch: bmpd wl over 1f out: wknd fnl f* **10/1**

/40- **11** 5 **Solipsist (IRE)**[227] 3294 5-9-2 50 AdamKirby(3) 9 41
(N I M Rossiter) *sn led: rdn over 3f out: hdd over 2f out: wknd wl over 1f out* **66/1**

-405 **12** 7 **Ming Vase**[11] 350 4-9-0 48 MickyFenton 8 29
(P T Midgley) *plld hrd: prom: rdn and ev ch over 2f out: sn wknd* **50/1**

2m 45.23s (2.81) **Going Correction** -0.05s/f (Stan)
WFA 4 from 5yo+ 3lb **12** Ran SP% **119.7**
Speed ratings (Par 97):88,87,87,87,86 86,86,85,85,84 81,76
CSF £69.62 TOTE £14.20: £3.60, £1.80, £8.70; EX 51.90 Place 6 £151.39, Place 5 £46.93.
Owner Bevan Holmes Underwood and Partners **Bred** Miss M E Gibbon **Trained** Forsbrook, Staffs

FOCUS
A complete mess of a race with a pedestrian early pace resulting in a sprint from the home bend. The winning time was very slow and the form should be treated with caution.

T/Plt: £122.40 to a £1 stake. Pool: £58,152.75. 346.75 winning tickets. T/Qpdt: £30.80 to a £1 stake. Pool: £5,873.40. 140.80 winning tickets. KH

[457]LINGFIELD (L-H)

Tuesday, February 21

OFFICIAL GOING: Standard

Wind: Moderate, against Weather: Cloudy

471 PLAY ROULETTE AT LITTLEWOODSCASINO.COM H'CAP (DIV I) 1m 2f (P)

1:40 (1:40) (Class 6) (0-52,56) 4-Y-0+ **£2,047** (£604; £302) **Stalls** Low

Form | RPR

06-6 **1** **Treetops Hotel (IRE)**[38] [113] 7-9-0 **52** FrankieMcDonald 4 57
(B R Johnson) hld up in midfield on ins rail: effrt over 1f out: qcknd to ld ins fnl f: rdn to hold on fnl 100 yds **8/1**

04-3 **2** *hd* **Majehar**[8] [399] 4-8-7 **46** oh1 SimonWhitworth 11 51
(A G Newcombe) lw: hld up in rr: effrt on outside 3f out: styd on to press wnr ins fnl f: jst hld **9/1**

4-41 **3** *½* **Ten-Cents**[8] [394] 4-9-3 **56** 6ex NCallan 7 60
(C F Wall) lw: hld up in rr: promising hdwy whn nt clr rn over 1f out: switched outside and r.o wl whn clr: clsng at fin **3/1**[1]

2-05 **4** *hd* **Hiawatha (IRE)**[11] [358] 7-8-5 **50** (p) JosephWalsh(7) 5 53
(A M Hales) chsd ldrs: rdn to dispute ld 1f out: nt qckn ins fnl f **7/1**[3]

0-00 **5** *½* **Piquet**[8] [395] 8-8-8 **46** oh1 PaulHanagan 6 48
(J J Bridger) mid-div: rdn to chse ldrs 2f out: styd on same pce **20/1**

14-0 **6** *nk* **So Elegant (IRE)**[43] [72] 4-8-13 **52** ChrisCatlin 2 54
(J Jay) towards rr: rdn 2f out: styd on fnl f: nvr nrr **8/1**

-040 **7** *¾* **J R Stevenson (USA)**[24] [231] 10-8-9 **47** (p) DarryllHolland 10 48
(Ernst Oertel) chsd ldr: led over 2f out tl ins fnl f: no ex **10/1**

0-40 **8** *2* **House Martin**[23] [242] 4-8-11 **50** RobertWinston 1 47
(C R Dore) lw: prom: losing pl whn n.m.r over 1f out: n.d after **8/1**

0052 **9** *1¼* **Sriology (IRE)**[12] [350] 5-9-0 **52** TonyCulhane 8 47
(G Prodromou) chsd ldrs on outside: rdn and lost pl over 2f out: sn struggling **6/1**[2]

100- **10** *2½* **Icannshift (IRE)**[54] [6683] 6-8-8 **46** oh6 FergusSweeney 3 36
(T M Jones) led tl over 2f out: wknd fnl f **25/1**

30-0 **11** *1½* **Luciferous (USA)**[13] [336] 4-8-8 **50** AmirQuinn(3) 9 38
(P G Murphy) dwlt: sn chsng ldrs: wknd 2f out **40/1**

2m 7.84s (0.05) **Going Correction** 0.0s/f (Stan)
WFA 4 from 5yo+ 1lb **11 Ran SP% 115.3**
Speed ratings (Par 101):99,98,98,98,97 97,97,95,94,92 91
CSF £74.44 CT £265.47 TOTE £10.00: £3.00, £2.80, £1.70; EX 108.50.
Owner Tann Racing **Bred** Miss Jill Finegan **Trained** Ashtead, Surrey
■ Stewards' Enquiry : N Callan one-day ban: careless riding (Mar 6)

FOCUS
A moderate handicap, little better than a banded race with the fifth the best guide to the level.

472 PLAY ROULETTE AT LITTLEWOODSCASINO.COM H'CAP (DIV II) 1m 2f (P)

2:10 (2:11) (Class 6) (0-52,52) 4-Y-0+ **£2,047** (£604; £302) **Stalls** Low

Form | RPR

4-20 **1** **Star Welcome**[1] [457] 5-8-8 **51** StephenDonohoe(5) 4 58
(W J Musson) lw: prom: drvn to ld ins fnl f: hld on wl **7/2**[1]

-605 **2** *¾* **Alqaayid**[8] [395] 5-8-3 **48** oh1 ow2 RussellKennemore(7) 6 54+
(P W Hiatt) lw: towards rr: gd hdwy to press ldrs on ins rail whn hmpd and snatched up 1f out: rallied and r.o wl fnl 100 yds: unlucky **16/1**

0040 **3** *nk* **Indigo Sky (IRE)**[15] [310] 5-8-9 **47** HayleyTurner 1 52
(B G Powell) chsd ldrs: hrd rdn and lost pl 3f out: rallied and styd on strly fnl f **16/1**

-050 **4** *hd* **Fortune Point (IRE)**[24] [229] 8-9-0 **52** (v) DarryllHolland 3 57
(A W Carroll) led 1f: chsd ldr after tl led over 2f out: hdd and one pce ins fnl f **8/1**

00-1 **5** *nk* **Whenwillitwin**[45] [63] 5-8-11 **49** (p) LPKeniry 11 53
(J S Moore) lw: hdwy to ld after 1f: hdd over 2f out: no ex fnl f **11/2**[2]

0-40 **6** *1¾* **Ernmoor**[13] [336] 4-8-8 **47** oh1 ow1 SteveDrowne 2 48
(J R Best) chsd ldrs: outpcd over 2f out: hld after **9/1**

-000 **7** *1¼* **Agilete**[13] [339] 4-8-13 **52** MartinDwyer 9 51
(J R Boyle) lw: s.s: sn in midfield and t.k.h: outpcd and dropped to rr 3f out: sme late hdwy **20/1**

0540 **8** *shd* **Legacy (JPN)**[1] [467] 6-8-9 **47** JamieSpencer 10 45
(P D Evans) stdd in rr s and plld hrd: rdn 3f out: nvr rchd ldrs **6/1**[3]

00-4 **9** *shd* **Zinging**[6] [417] 7-8-8 **46** oh6 PaulHanagan 8 44
(J J Bridger) towards rr: rdn and nt trble ldrs fnl 3f **25/1**

-006 **10** *1¼* **Granary Girl**[10] [382] 4-8-12 **51** DeanMcKeown 7 47
(J Pearce) hld up in rr: mod effrt and wd st: nt trble ldrs **8/1**

22-0 **11** *shd* **Hoh Bleu Dee**[24] [229] 5-9-0 **52** (p) J-PGuillambert 5 48
(T Keddy) in tch: rdn over 3f out: wknd ent st **15/2**

2m 7.61s (-0.18) **Going Correction** 0.0s/f (Stan)
WFA 4 from 5yo+ 1lb **11 Ran SP% 116.3**
Speed ratings (Par 101):100,99,99,99,98 97,96,96,95 95
CSF £62.39 CT £794.99 TOTE £4.00: £1.30, £5.90, £7.30; EX 74.80.
Owner The Runaway Partnership **Bred** Mrs N A Ward **Trained** Newmarket, Suffolk

FOCUS
Like the first division, a moderate handicap and the time was similar and the form looks weak.
Ernmoor Official explanation: jockey said gelding hung left throughout

473 BETLIVE IN-RUNNING AT BETDIRECT.CO.UK MAIDEN STKS 6f (P)

2:40 (2:41) (Class 5) 3-Y-0 **£3,886** (£1,156; £577; £288) **Stalls** Low

Form | RPR

1 **Lady Orpen (IRE)**[128] [5927] 3-8-9 JamieSpencer 5 75+
(Patrick Morris, Ire) w'like: lw: t.k.h: trckd ldrs: led over 1f out: rdn clr: comf **6/1**[3]

35 **2** *2½* **His Master's Voice (IRE)**[23] [233] 3-9-0 JoeFanning 12 68
(D W P Arbuthnot) mid-div on outside: hdwy over 2f out: wnt 2nd over 1f out: nt pce of wnr fnl f **6/1**[3]

5-45 **3** *nk* **Phinerine**[10] [380] 3-9-0 63 DarryllHolland 2 67
(R A Harris) mid-div on rail: rdn to chse ldrs over 1f out: one pce **16/1**

22-2 **4** *½* **Rebellious Spirit**[10] [380] 3-9-0 72 MickyFenton 4 66
(J G Given) wd: hld up towards rr: shkn up and r.o steadily fnl 2f: nvr nrr **6/1**[3]

3 **5** *1* **Arzaag**[23] [233] 3-9-0 LPKeniry 3 69+
(D M Simcock) lw: hld up towards rr: hdwy and in tch whn hmpd 1f out: rallied and r.o wl nr fin **5/2**[1]

02 **6** *nk* **Ten Tenors (IRE)**[14] [331] 3-8-9 ShaneKelly 8 57
(J A Osborne) prom: rdn to chal over 1f out: no ex fnl f **20/1**

04- **7** *nk* **Li Shih Chen**[195] [4254] 3-9-0 DarrenWilliams 7 61
(A P Jarvis) lw: chsd ldrs: no ex fnl f **33/1**

300- **8** *¾* **Just Down The Road (IRE)**[185] [4594] 3-8-9 70 NCallan 11 53
(R A Harris) led tl over 1f out: sn wknd **14/1**

560- **9** *½* **Cool Sting (IRE)**[206] [3936] 3-9-0 70 MartinDwyer 10 57
(A M Balding) lw: t.k.h towards rr: rdn over 2f out: nvr rchd ldrs **9/2**[2]

200- **10** *3½* **Reviving (IRE)**[141] [5668] 3-9-0 74 StephenCarson 9 46
(R F Johnson Houghton) prom tl wknd 2f out **20/1**

11 *½* **Datznyce (IRE)** 3-8-4 MarcHalford(5) 6 40
(D R C Elsworth) neat: s.s: a bhd: no ch whn rn wd home turn **25/1**

0-0 **12** *5* **Balfour House**[17] [293] 3-8-7 TolleyDean(7) 1 30
(R A Harris) s.s: rdn 3f out: a bhd **100/1**

1m 12.87s (0.06) **Going Correction** 0.0s/f (Stan) **12 Ran SP% 119.5**
Speed ratings (Par 97):99,95,95,94,93 92,92,91,90,86 85,78
CSF £39.49 TOTE £6.60: £2.60, £2.80, £4.30; EX 63.70.
Owner W J Crosbie **Bred** Pat Todd **Trained** Ruanbeg, Co. Kildare

FOCUS
Just an ordinary sprint maiden and third-placed Phinerine, rated 63, gives a good guide to the strength of the form.
Arzaag ◆ Official explanation: jockey said colt was denied a clear run in home straight
Just Down The Road(IRE) Official explanation: jockey said filly hung right

474 BETDIRECT FREEPHONE 0800 211 222 CLASSIFIED CLAIMING STKS 6f (P)

3:10 (3:10) (Class 6) 4-Y-0+ **£2,266** (£674; £337; £168) **Stalls** Low

Form | RPR

-003 **1** **Patternmaker (USA)**[19] [271] 4-8-13 60 ChrisCatlin 2 67
(A M Hales) mde all: rdn and qcknd 3l clr ent st: drvn to hold on fnl 100 yds **9/2**[2]

-033 **2** *nk* **Hadath (IRE)**[14] [321] 9-8-5 59 (b) JoeFanning 6 58
(B G Powell) towards rr: rdn 1/2-way: hdwy over 1f out: chsd wnr ins fnl f: clsng at fin: jst hld **9/4**[1]

-005 **3** *1½* **Smokincanon**[8] [402] 4-8-0 53 MarcHalford(5) 1 54
(W G M Turner) lw: prom: outpcd by wnr 2f out: kpt on fnl f **25/1**

-450 **4** *nk* **Sweet Pickle**[20] [265] 5-8-4 55 MartinDwyer 7 52
(J R Boyle) lw: t.k.h in midfield: towards rr whn hmpd on bnd 2f out: gd late hdwy **8/1**[3]

2440 **5** *¾* **Soft Focus (IRE)**[12] [345] 4-8-6 59 (b) ShaneKelly 11 51
(J A Osborne) dwlt: hld up towards rr: wd home turn: shkn up and r.o wl fnl f: nrst fin **8/1**[3]

0-00 **6** *shd* **Madrasee**[8] [401] 8-8-8 55 ow1 AmirQuinn(3) 10 56
(P G Murphy) rrd s: hld up in rr: rdn and hdwy over 1f out: kpt on **25/1**

04-0 **7** *nk* **Sunny Afternoon**[13] [336] 6-8-4 53 (v) HayleyTurner 4 48
(Miss E C Lavelle) lw: chsd ldrs 2f: rdn and no imp fr 1/2-way **20/1**

00-5 **8** *½* **Panshir (FR)**[14] [330] 5-8-9 55 NCallan 3 52
(Julian Poulton) chsd ldrs: outpcd fnl 2f **16/1**

-500 **9** *1½* **Transaction (IRE)**[8] [402] 4-8-0 52 RichardThomas(3) 5 41
(J M P Eustace) prom tl wknd 1f out **11/1**

0030 **10** *1¾* **Border Artist**[13] [339] 7-8-8 53 ow1 (p) MichaelHills 8 41
(B G Powell) sn chsng ldrs: wknd over 1f out **8/1**[3]

0-00 **11** *3½* **Bahamian Breeze**[20] [262] 5-7-12 58 (p) JosephWalsh(7) 12 28
(D M Simcock) wd and t.k.h: hdwy to chse ldrs 1/2-way: wknd 2f out **16/1**

1m 12.8s (-0.01) **Going Correction** 0.0s/f (Stan) **11 Ran SP% 114.8**
Speed ratings (Par 101):100,99,97,97,96 96,95,95,93,90 86
CSF £14.14 TOTE £5.30: £1.30, £1.30, £7.50; EX 20.90.
Owner Brick Farm Racing **Bred** D Ryan And Paul Saylor **Trained** Quainton, Bucks

FOCUS
A modest claimer, but competitive enough given there was just 9lb separating the entire field at the weights. The winner and third set a reasonable standard.

475 BETDIRECT FREEPHONE 0800 211 222 H'CAP 7f (P)

3:40 (3:40) (Class 5) (0-75,73) 3-Y-0 **£3,238** (£963; £481; £240) **Stalls** Low

Form | RPR

21-3 **1** **Orchard Supreme**[20] [269] 3-9-4 **73** RichardHughes 8 88
(R Hannon) lw: towards rr: hdwy 2f out: chsd ldr over 1f out: r.o to ld fnl 75 yds **9/4**[1]

-412 **2** *¾* **Didn't We (IRE)**[20] [269] 3-9-4 **73** (v) JoeFanning 12 87
(T G Mills) lw: racd freely: led and set str pce: rdn and hdd fnl 75 yds: kpt on **9/4**[1]

05-0 **3** *7* **The London Gang**[12] [344] 3-9-0 **69** JamieSpencer 9 65
(P D Evans) hld up and bhd: rdn and hdwy over 1f out: styd on to take mod 3rd ins fnl f **25/1**

31-4 **4** *1¼* **Mambo Sun**[12] [349] 3-8-13 **68** (p) PaulHanagan 10 61
(P A Blockley) sn outpcd towards rr: effrt and n.m.r ent st: styd on wl fnl f: nvr nrr **10/1**[3]

354- **5** *¾* **Endless Night**[98] [6351] 3-8-13 **68** SteveDrowne 2 59
(H Morrison) chsd ldrs tl wknd over 1f out **9/1**[2]

1254 **6** *shd* **Thoughtsofstardom**[4] [439] 3-9-2 **71** BrianReilly 1 62
(P S McEntee) chsd ldng pair at str pce: rdn and btn over 2f out **20/1**

60-0 **7** *2½* **Star Of Canterbury (IRE)**[13] [337] 3-8-10 **65** DarrenWilliams 6 50
(A P Jarvis) lw: keen early: chsd ldrs 2f: sn struggling to go pce: towards rr whn n.m.r 3f out: n.d **14/1**

6-04 **8** *shd* **Possessed**[13] [342] 3-9-3 **72** MartinDwyer 7 56
(T D McCarthy) mid-div: rdn and btn 2f out **10/1**[3]

3-30 **9** *hd* **Power Assisted**[20] [269] 3-9-3 **72** MickyFenton 3 56
(C F Wall) mid-div tl wknd wl over 1f out **14/1**

100- **10** *1½* **Peter Island (FR)**[157] [5318] 3-9-4 **73** (b) NCallan 13 53
(J Gallagher) lw: w ldr at str pce: lost 2nd pl over 1f out: wknd qckly **20/1**

00-0 **11** *½* **Rock Of Cloonavery (IRE)**[23] [234] 3-8-8 **66** SaleemGolam(3) 11 45
(S C Williams) sn outpcd: a bhd **33/1**

1m 25.35s (-0.54) **Going Correction** 0.0s/f (Stan) **11 Ran SP% 119.4**
Speed ratings (Par 97):103,102,94,92,91 91,88,88,88,86 86
CSF £6.20 CT £98.72 TOTE £3.60: £1.60, £1.20, £5.50; EX 6.40.
Owner Brian C Oakley **Bred** Mrs M H Goodrich **Trained** East Everleigh, Wilts

FOCUS
They went a strong pace throughout and the first two pulled clear of the remainder. Unsurprisingly, the winning time was good for a race of this type, only 0.36 seconds slower than the following higher-class handicap over the same trip for older horses. The form is solid and should work out .

476 LITTLEWOODS BETDIRECT H'CAP 7f (P)

4:10 (4:10) (Class 4) (0-85,85) 4-Y-0+ **£6,232** (£1,866; £933; £467; £233; £117) **Stalls** Low

Form | RPR

0214 **1** **Marko Jadeo (IRE)**[13] [340] 8-8-11 **78** PaulFitzsimons 4 88
(S Dow) lw: hld up towards rr: effrt and nt clr run early st: swtchd v wd: str run to ld nr fin **15/2**

2-22 **2** *¾* **Spring Goddess (IRE)**[13] [340] 5-9-0 **81** DarrenWilliams 9 89
(A P Jarvis) in tch: rdn to chal over 1f out: nt qckn fnl 50 yds **7/1**[3]

0-00 **3** nk **Ali Bruce**[12] [348] 6-8-2 **76** AndrewElliott(7) 14 83
(G L Moore) *wnt rt s and rdn early: mid-div after 2f: styd on wl fnl 2f: nrst fin* **14/1**

-010 **4** nk **Hayyani (IRE)**[22] [253] 4-8-10 **77** (e) JamieSpencer 11 84
(K McAuliffe) *led: hrd rdn and kpt on fnl 1f: hdd nr fin* **12/1**

0-02 **5** ½ **Lake Chini (IRE)**[24] [224] 4-8-9 **76** ow1 (b) NCallan 10 81
(M A Jarvis) *lw: towards rr: rdn and styd on fr over 1f out: nvr nrr* **10/1**

560- **6** ½ **Bobski (IRE)**[180] [4693] 4-9-1 **82** MartinDwyer 8 88+
(G A Huffer) *mid-div: effrt whn n.m.r over 1f out and ent fnl f: styd on* **13/2**[2]

2-33 **7** 1¼ **Councellor (FR)**[7] [412] 4-8-9 **76** MickyFenton 2 79+
(Stef Liddiard) *lw: s.i.s: sn in midfield: effrt over 1f out: n.m.r ins fnl f: no imp* **5/1**[1]

-133 **8** nk **Chief Exec**[4] [441] 4-9-3 **84** HayleyTurner 3 84
(C A Cyzer) *hld up in tch: smooth hdwy to press ldrs over 1f out: no ex fnl f* **7/1**[3]

0400 **9** ½ **Chateau Nicol**[4] [441] 7-9-4 **85** JoeFanning 6 84
(B G Powell) *chsd ldrs tl wknd 1f out* **16/1**

0-41 **10** ½ **Bessemer (JPN)**[15] [316] 5-8-9 **79** (p) DanielTudhope(3) 13 77
(D Carroll) *lw: midfield and wd: rdn and no imp fnl 2f* **10/1**

-002 **11** ½ **Who's Winning (IRE)**[10] [376] 5-8-13 **80** MichaelHills 1 76
(B G Powell) *t.k.h: prom tl wknd 1f out* **20/1**

-400 **12** shd **Poker Player (IRE)**[13] [340] 4-8-8 **75** (b) DarryllHolland 5 71
(G C Bravery) *prom tl wknd over 1f out* **25/1**

/4-0 **13** 1½ **Happy As Larry (USA)**[13] [340] 4-8-9 **83** JamesO'Reilly(7) 12 75
(T J Pitt) *rdn 3f out: a bhd* **16/1**

1m 24.99s (-0.90) **Going Correction** 0.0s/f (Stan) **13 Ran SP% 119.7**
Speed ratings (Par 105):105,104,103,103,102 102,100,100,99,99 98,98,97
CSF £59.34 CT £754.94 TOTE £7.70: £2.40, £1.90, £4.50; EX 48.00 Trifecta £496.20 Part won. Pool: £698.88 - 0.20 winning tickets..
Owner J R May **Bred** P Casey **Trained** Epsom, Surrey
■ Stewards' Enquiry : N Callan two-day ban: used whip with excessive force (Mar 7-8)

FOCUS
A good, competitive handicap and solid enough rated through the placed horses.

477 LITTLEWOODS LOTTO3 0800 500 000 (S) STKS 5f (P)
4:40 (4:41) (Class 6) 3-Y-O **£2,388** (£705; £352) **Stalls High**

Form RPR

0500 **1** **Sounds Simla (IRE)**[14] [326] 3-9-0 60 ChrisCatlin 6 55
(Rae Guest) *bhd: hdwy over 1f out: r.o u.str.p to ld on line* **8/1**

6-53 **2** shd **Otis B Driftwood**[11] [359] 3-9-5 59 (b) JamieSpencer 7 60
(M Quinn) *led 1f: chsd ldr after tl led jst ins fnl f: hrd rdn and kpt on: hdd on line* **9/2**[3]

0-03 **3** 1¾ **Grecianette (IRE)**[17] [298] 3-8-8 62 ow1 (b¹) DarryllHolland 3 43
(Miss Gay Kelleway) *lw: chsd ldrs: hrd rdn over 1f out: one pce* **15/8**[1]

103 **4** ½ **Luloah**[12] [344] 3-8-7 66 DonnaCaldwell(7) 8 47
(P S McEntee) *led after 1f tl jst ins fnl f: no ex* **11/4**[2]

0-00 **5** 2 **Stoneacre Girl (IRE)**[15] [308] 3-8-4 40 ow4 RonanKeogh(7) 2 37
(Peter Grayson) *s.i.s: 5th most of way: rdn and no hdwy fnl 2f* **33/1**

000- **6** 3½ **The Lady Caster**[135] [5755] 3-8-7 55 (p) ShaneKelly 5 20
(D Morris) *chsd ldrs over 3f* **6/1**

00-0 **7** 1¾ **Fashion Chic**[15] [308] 3-8-7 45 MickyFenton 4 14
(Stef Liddiard) *sn outpcd towards rr* **25/1**

60.69 secs (0.91) **Going Correction** 0.0s/f (Stan) **7 Ran SP% 111.8**
Speed ratings (Par 95):92,91,89,88,85 79,76
CSF £41.46 TOTE £9.20: £4.90, £2.50; EX 36.70.There was no bid for the winner. Grecianette was claimed by W. J. Musson for £6,000.
Owner D M Hill **Bred** A F O'Callaghan **Trained** Newmarket, Suffolk

FOCUS
Probably not that bad a race by selling standards and they went a strong pace, with the runner-up setting the standard.

478 PLAY NOW AT BETDIRECTPOKER.COM H'CAP 1m 4f (P)
5:10 (5:10) (Class 5) (0-70,70) 4-Y-O+ **£3,238** (£963; £481; £240) **Stalls Low**

Form RPR

123- **1** **Taxman (IRE)**[106] [6283] 4-8-8 **63** ow1 (p) DarryllHolland 14 69
(C E Brittain) *mid-div: rdn to chse ldrs 2f out: r.o to ld nr fin* **10/1**

3444 **2** nk **Captain Margaret**[6] [421] 4-8-12 **67** DeanMcKeown 7 73
(J Pearce) *lw: mid-div: rdn and hdwy over 1f out: chal wl ins fnl f: r.o* **7/1**[3]

6-41 **3** hd **Eloquent Knight (USA)**[14] [324] 4-8-13 **68** MartinDwyer 10 74
(W R Muir) *plld hrd: sn pressing ldr: led over 1f out: hrd rdn fnl f: hdd nr fin* **6/1**[2]

010 **4** shd **Stage Manager (IRE)**[10] [385] 4-8-10 **70** DerekNolan(5) 8 75
(M J Wallace) *lw: hld up towards rr: effrt and nt clr run over 1f out: swtchd rt: fin strly: unlucky* **14/1**

-516 **5** ½ **Dovedon Hero**[10] [385] 6-9-4 **70** (b) TonyCulhane 12 75
(P J McBride) *mid-div: effrt 2f out: styd on fnl f: nvr nrr* **11/1**

-030 **6** ½ **Birthday Star (IRE)**[10] [379] 4-8-2 **57** HayleyTurner 4 61
(W J Musson) *a.p: hld whn n.m.r ins fnl f* **12/1**

-322 **7** ½ **Dubai Ace (USA)**[6] [419] 5-8-8 **63** EdwardCreighton(3) 2 66
(Miss Sheena West) *led at modest pce: rdn and qcknd tempo 3f out: hdd over 1f out: wknd fnl f* **10/1**

3602 **8** hd **Blackmail (USA)**[20] [264] 8-8-12 **64** (b) JamieSpencer 5 67
(Miss B Sanders) *hld up towards rr: rdn 2f out: styd on wl fnl f* **9/2**[1]

0605 **9** shd **Flying Pass**[10] [375] 4-8-7 **62** ChrisCatlin 1 65
(D J S Ffrench Davis) *mid-div: rdn to chse ldrs 2f out: no ex fnl f* **20/1**

01-5 **10** ½ **Garibaldi (GER)**[36] [125] 4-9-1 **70** LPKeniry 6 72
(D R C Elsworth) *chsd ldrs: hld whn n.m.r over 1f out* **8/1**

005- **11** ½ **Street Life (IRE)**[21] [6247] 8-8-11 **68** StephenDonohoe(5) 9 69
(W J Musson) *hld up towards rr: shkn up over 1f out: nvr rchd chalng position* **8/1**

2221 **12** 1¼ **Kirkstone (IRE)**[15] [314] 5-9-4 **70** SteveDrowne 13 69
(J A Osborne) *prom tl wknd 1f out: eased whn btn* **7/1**[3]

00-0 **13** 6 **Afadan (IRE)**[36] [125] 8-9-1 **67** MickyFenton 11 56
(J R Jenkins) *s.s: t.k.h in rr: wd and n.d fnl 3f* **50/1**

2m 36.3s (1.91) **Going Correction** 0.0s/f (Stan)
WFA 4 from 5yo+ 3lb **13 Ran SP% 127.3**
Speed ratings (Par 103):93,92,92,92,92 91,91,91,91,91 90,89,85
CSF £83.65 CT £473.95 TOTE £16.30: £3.40, £2.80, £2.20; EX 142.00 Place 6 £166.59, Place 5 £72.88.
Owner C E Brittain **Bred** Darley **Trained** Newmarket, Suffolk

FOCUS
A modest handicap and a very steady early pace resulted in a moderate winning time for the grade. The form does not look worth a great deal.
T/Plt: £142.20 to a £1 stake. Pool: £43,014.80. 220.75 winning tickets. T/Qpdt: £17.90 to a £1 stake. Pool: £4,227.20. 174.20 winning tickets. LM

[471] LINGFIELD (L-H)
Wednesday, February 22

OFFICIAL GOING: Standard
Wind: Fresh, half-against

479 BETDIRECT.CO.UK MAIDEN STKS 1m (P)
1:40 (1:42) (Class 5) 3-Y-O **£3,886** (£1,156; £577; £288) **Stalls High**

Form RPR

06 **1** **Living On A Prayer**[11] [374] 3-8-9 NCallan 6 57
(J Pearce) *trckd ldr: rdn over 2f out: kpt up to work fnl f* **25/1**

2- **2** ½ **Tafiya**[141] [5692] 3-8-9 FrancisNorton 2 56
(G A Butler) *lw: t.k.h: a.p: wnt 2nd 2f out: rdn and nt qckn ins fnl f* **4/9**[1]

0-2 **3** 1¼ **Sky High Guy (IRE)**[46] [62] 3-9-0 FrankieMcDonald 4 63+
(S Kirk) *lw: t.k.h: hdwy on ins over 2f out: v short of room over 1f out: r.o wl whn clr run ins fnl f* **8/1**[2]

00 **4** ½ **Bobby Rose**[11] [372] 3-9-0 DarryllHolland 8 57
(D K Ivory) *t.k.h: hld up in rr: hdwy 3f out: r.o fnl f: nvr nrr* **40/1**

5 ¾ **Just Tilly** 3-8-9 StephenCarson 12 50
(P R Chamings) *small: hld up on wd outside: r.o fnl f: nvr nrr* **66/1**

000- **6** hd **Shannon House**[85] [6467] 3-9-0 56 JamieSpencer 11 55
(M J McGrath) *lw: bhd tl styd on fnl f: nvr nrr* **20/1**

0 **7** hd **Boluisce (IRE)**[18] [291] 3-8-6 SaleemGolam(3) 5 50
(M H Tompkins) *in tch on ins: rdn aand outpcd over 2f out: styd on fnl f* **50/1**

5 **8** 1¼ **Simplified**[11] [372] 3-8-9 TQuinn 1 47
(J Pearce) *prom tl rdn and wknd ent fnl f* **25/1**

0- **9** nk **Radical Attraction (USA)**[88] [6428] 3-8-6 StephaneBreux(3) 7 46+
(R Hannon) *slowly away: a bhd* **25/1**

-300 **10** 3½ **Zizou (IRE)**[28] [188] 3-9-0 60 J-PGuillambert 3 43
(J J Bridger) *led tl rdn and hdd 2f out: wknd rapidly fnl f* **16/1**

0 **11** ¾ **Wally Barge**[11] [374] 3-9-0 MickyFenton 10 42
(D K Ivory) *t.k.h: mid-div tl wknd over 2f out* **66/1**

12 3 **White Heather** 3-8-9 MartinDwyer 9 30
(A M Balding) *str: bkwd: prom on outside: rdn 3f out: wknd 2f out* **12/1**[3]

1m 41.96s (2.53) **Going Correction** +0.05s/f (Slow) **12 Ran SP% 117.6**
Speed ratings (Par 97):89,88,87,86,86 85,85,84,84,80 79,76
CSF £34.92 TOTE £33.60: £6.00, £1.10, £1.60; EX 96.10.
Owner F Butler **Bred** Beaumont Hall Bloodstock **Trained** Newmarket, Suffolk

FOCUS
A moderate time for a race of its type.
Sky High Guy(IRE) Official explanation: jockey said colt was denied a clear run
Simplified Official explanation: jockey said filly hung left
Zizou(IRE) Official explanation: jockey said gelding suffered interference

480 BETDIRECT FREEPHONE 0800 211 222 CLAIMING STKS 5f (P)
2:10 (2:10) (Class 6) 3-Y-O+ **£2,388** (£705; £352) **Stalls High**

Form RPR

-023 **1** **Native Title**[33] [159] 8-9-13 71 AdrianTNicholls 6 78+
(D Nicholls) *mid-div: rdn and gd hdwy to ld ent fnl f: won gng away* **10/3**[2]

-006 **2** 3½ **Madrasee**[1] [474] 8-9-1 55 AmirQuinn(3) 9 56
(P G Murphy) *in tch on outside: rdn and r.o to go 2nd ins fnl f* **12/1**

0-50 **3** nk **Namir (IRE)**[16] [317] 4-9-13 64 MickyFenton 8 64
(Stef Liddiard) *lw: t.k.h: racd wd in rr: r.o strly fnl f: nvr nrr* **8/1**

30-0 **4** hd **Goose Chase**[21] [267] 4-9-9 66 (b) FrankieMcDonald 7 60+
(C J Mann) *lw: slowly away: hdwy on ins over 1f out: r.o fnl f: nvr nrr* **33/1**

-565 **5** nk **Edged In Gold**[9] [401] 4-9-1 52 (e) FergusSweeney 5 51+
(P J Makin) *lw: hld up: n.m.r whn hdwy over 1f out: swtchd rt: r.o fnl f* **8/1**

040- **6** ¾ **Global Achiever**[54] [6693] 5-9-5 52 (p) OscarUrbina 4 52
(G C H Chung) *trckd ldrs: rdn over 1f out: one pce fnl f* **14/1**

/060 **7** nk **Lady Bahia (IRE)**[25] [225] 5-9-2 60 (b¹) RobbieFitzpatrick 1 48
(Peter Grayson) *led after 1f: rdn and hdd ent fnl f: wknd ins* **16/1**

6020 **8** 1¼ **Whitbarrow (IRE)**[25] [224] 7-9-8 74 (b) JamesDoyle(5) 10 54
(A W Carroll) *trckd ldrs tl rdn and wknd 1f out* **9/4**[1]

0606 **9** 1½ **He's A Rocket (IRE)**[9] [401] 5-9-7 52 (b) FrancisNorton 2 43
(K R Burke) *led for 1f: rdn 2f out: wknd fnl f* **11/2**[3]

10 6 **Pitton Justice** 4-9-1 MarcHalford(5) 3 20
(W G M Turner) *w'like: in tch tl wknd qckly 1/2-way* **50/1**

59.41 secs (-0.37) **Going Correction** +0.05s/f (Slow) **10 Ran SP% 116.6**
Speed ratings (Par 101):104,98,97,97,97 95,95,93,91,81
CSF £43.12 TOTE £3.60: £1.10, £4.50, £2.80; EX 54.50.
Owner C McKenna **Bred** Mrs W H Gibson Fleming **Trained** Sessay, N Yorks

FOCUS
The pace was strong from the outset and all of those who were close up eventually ended up well beaten.
Edged In Gold Official explanation: jockey said filly was denied a clear run

481 PLAY SLOTS AT LITTLEWOODSCASINO.COM H'CAP 6f (P)
2:40 (2:40) (Class 5) (0-70,70) 3-Y-O **£3,238** (£963; £481; £240) **Stalls Low**

Form RPR

6112 **1** **Pauvic (IRE)**[2] [464] 3-9-2 **68** (v) PaulFessey 2 73
(Mrs A Duffield) *lw: mde all: edgd lft ins fnl f: rdn out* **3/1**[1]

2016 **2** 1½ **Radiator Rooney (IRE)**[2] [464] 3-9-4 **70** (b) JamieSpencer 1 73+
(Patrick Morris, Ire) *lw: s.i.s: sn prom on ins: rdn and hmpd ent fnl f: pulled out: r.o but nt rcvr* **4/1**[2]

0205 **3** ½ **Mine The Balance (IRE)**[2] [464] 3-8-4 **56** oh3 MartinDwyer 12 55
(J R Best) *racd wd: hdwy 1/2-way to chse ldrs: rdn over 2f out: r.o fnl f* **15/2**

00-4 **4** nk **Patavium Prince (IRE)**[21] [269] 3-8-13 **65** NCallan 8 63
(J R Best) *trckd wnr: rdn 2f out: no ex fnl f* **7/1**

365- **5** nk **Gavarnie Beau (IRE)**[75] [6529] 3-9-2 **68** FrancisNorton 5 65+
(M Blanshard) *bhd tl str hdwy on ins over 1f out: fin wl: nvr nrr* **14/1**

5-02 **6** shd **Par Excellence**[15] [322] 3-7-13 **56** oh1 MarcHalford(5) 10 53
(W G M Turner) *bhd tl r.o fnl f: nvr nrr* **25/1**

0221 **7** shd **Garstang**[19] [287] 3-8-7 **59** (b) RobbieFitzpatrick 4 56+
(Peter Grayson) *mid-div: rdn 2f out: hdwy whn n.m.r ent fnl f: no hdwy after* **11/2**[3]

3-00 **8** ½ **African Concerto (IRE)**[24] [234] 3-8-12 **64** FrankieMcDonald 9 59
(S Kirk) *switche to ins fr wd draw sn after s: nvr on terms* **25/1**

305- **9** ½ **Almowj**[103] [6316] 3-8-13 **65** (p) RichardHughes 6 59
(C E Brittain) *hld up: a in rr* **16/1**

0-03 **10** 2½ **Spirit Of Coniston**[15] [322] 3-7-13 **56** oh1 JamesDoyle(5) 7 42
(M Wellings) *chsd ldrs tl wknd over 2f out* **25/1**

4-13 **11** *1¼* **Mister Incredible**[41] [102] 3-8-11 **63**..........(p) DarryllHolland 3 45
(C A Dwyer) *prom tl wknd over 2f out* **12/1**

1m 12.99s (0.18) **Going Correction** +0.05s/f (Slow) 11 Ran SP% **116.4**
Speed ratings (Par 97):100,98,97,96,96 96,96,95,94,91 89
CSF £14.01 CT £80.08 TOTE £4.20: £1.50, £2.30, £2.80; EX 15.70.
Owner Middleham Park Racing XLV **Bred** Thomas Stacey **Trained** Constable Burton, N Yorks
■ Stewards' Enquiry : Paul Fessey three-day ban: careless riding (Mar 6-8)

FOCUS
A very competitive handicap with plenty of in-form horses taking part. The early pace looked very modest.
Gavarnie Beau(IRE) Official explanation: jockey said gelding suffered interference on final bend

482 FOOTBALLPOOLS.COM H'CAP 2m (P)
3:10 (3:11) (Class 6) (0-60,58) 4-Y-0+ **£2,388** (£705; £352) **Stalls** Low

Form RPR
10-2 **1** **Tycheros**[47] [55] 4-8-6 **52**.......... SaleemGolam(3) 9 61
(S C Williams) *a front rnk: wnt 2nd over 2f out: led over 1f out: styd on wl* **11/2**[3]
1135 **2** *2* **Little Richard (IRE)**[16] [318] 7-9-4 **55**..........(p) AlanDaly 10 61
(M Wellings) *a in tch: rdn and styd on to go 2nd ins fnl f: nvr nrr* **14/1**
-465 **3** *½* **Lady Pilot**[11] [379] 4-8-12 **58**.......... RichardThomas(3) 2 63
(Dr J R J Naylor) *lw: trckd ldr to over 2f out: rdn and kpt on fnl f* **20/1**
246 **4** *1* **Sugitani (USA)**[25] [218] 4-9-0 **57**.......... MickyFenton 13 61
(N B King) *racd wd in mid-div: pushed along 5f out: styd on fnl f: nvr nrr* **8/1**
3113 **5** *2* **Mister Completely (IRE)**[5] [443] 5-9-2 **56**.......... EdwardCreighton(3) 4 57
(Miss Sheena West) *mid-div tl ost pl 3f out: styd onf fnl f* **10/3**[1]
046- **6** *1½* **Bravura**[277] [1150] 8-9-6 **57**.......... IanMongan 8 57
(G L Moore) *hld up: hdwy over 3f out: styd on fnl f* **25/1**
64-2 **7** *nk* **Three Boars**[19] [284] 4-8-12 **55**..........(b) NCallan 12 54
(S Gollings) *racd wd in tch: rdn 2f out: one pce after* **8/1**
4-30 **8** *2* **Olivino (GER)**[25] [231] 5-9-2 **53**.......... JamieSpencer 6 50
(S Dow) *led tl rdn and hdd over 1f out: wknd ins fnl f* **7/2**[2]
-050 **9** *4* **Postmaster**[11] [379] 4-8-12 **55**..........(t) MatthewHenry 11 46
(R Ingram) *lw: mid-div: hdwy on outside over 3f out: wknd 2f out* **16/1**
00-6 **10** *5* **Easter Ogil (IRE)**[14] [338] 11-9-2 **56**.......... AmirQuinn(3) 5 41
(P G Murphy) *hld up: a bhd* **40/1**
412- **11** *8* **Compton Eclaire (IRE)**[189] [4463] 6-9-3 **54**..........(b) TonyHamilton 14 28
(B Ellison) *hld up: rdn 5f out: nvr on terms* **10/1**
0-60 **12** *8* **Swell Lad**[28] [185] 4-8-5 **53**.......... JamesDoyle(5) 7 17
(S Gollings) *lw: mid-div: rdn 6f out: wknd 4f out* **50/1**
050- **13** *2* **Indian Chase**[141] [5683] 9-9-1 **52**.......... BrianReilly 1 13
(Dr J R J Naylor) *t.k.h: trckd ldrs tl rdn and wknd over 4f out* **40/1**
/06- **14** *30* **Imperial Dragon (USA)**[193] [4374] 6-8-11 **48**.......... FrancisNorton 3 —
(W A O'Gorman) *a bhd: virtually p.u ins fnl 2f: t.o* **66/1**

3m 27.46s (-1.33) **Going Correction** +0.05s/f (Slow)
WFA 4 from 5yo+ 6lb 14 Ran SP% **121.5**
Speed ratings (Par 101):105,104,103,103,102 101,101,100,98,95 91,87,86,71
CSF £75.27 CT £1453.55 TOTE £7.20: £2.30, £3.10, £6.60; EX 93.70.
Owner Stuart C Williams **Bred** London Thoroughbred Services Ltd **Trained** Newmarket, Suffolk

FOCUS
A weak staying handicap with many trying the trip for the first time.

483 BETDIRECT.CO.UK H'CAP 1m 2f (P)
3:40 (3:41) (Class 4) (0-85,79) 3-Y-O **£6,477** (£1,927; £963; £481) **Stalls** Low

Form RPR
3111 **1** **Prince Charlemagne (IRE)**[7] [422] 3-8-8 **74** 6ex.......... JamesDoyle(5) 4 80
(N P Littmoden) *hld up: racd wd: rdn and hdwy 2f out: r.o to ld nr fin* **5/4**[1]
60-2 **2** *½* **Jebel Ali (IRE)**[14] [337] 3-8-13 **74**.......... ChrisCatlin 7 79
(B Gubby) *a.p: rdn to ld ins fnl f: kpt on: hdd nr fin* **25/1**
31 **3** *1½* **Babcary**[28] [191] 3-8-13 **74**.......... RichardHughes 1 76
(M P Tregoning) *lw: led: t.k.h: rdn and hdd ins fnl f: no ex* **6/1**[2]
1333 **4** *shd* **Fusili (IRE)**[18] [294] 3-9-4 **79**.......... IanMongan 3 81+
(N P Littmoden) *trckd ldrs: nt qckn 2f out: r.o wl fnl f* **13/2**[3]
0-34 **5** *2* **Stellenbosch (USA)**[9] [406] 3-8-9 **70**.......... MichaelHills 2 68
(J W Hills) *lw: mid-div: outpcd 2f out: kpt on fnl f* **11/1**
1-02 **6** *¾* **Isphahan**[14] [342] 3-9-2 **77**.......... MartinDwyer 5 74
(A M Balding) *lw: sn trckd ldr: lost 2nd 2f out: wknd appr fnl f* **10/1**
1111 **7** *½* **Casablanca Minx (IRE)**[4] [448] 3-9-2 **77** 6ex.......... NCallan 8 73
(N P Littmoden) *hld up: rdn over 2f out: sn bhd* **8/1**
65-4 **8** *3* **Eclipse Park**[11] [374] 3-8-12 **73**.......... JamieSpencer 6 64
(M J McGrath) *lw: hld up: a bhd* **16/1**

2m 8.34s (0.55) **Going Correction** +0.05s/f (Slow) 8 Ran SP% **110.3**
Speed ratings (Par 99):99,98,97,97,95 95,94,92
CSF £34.43 CT £131.39 TOTE £1.90: £1.10, £2.70, £2.00; EX 31.40.
Owner Neil Ryan **Bred** Michael O'Mahony **Trained** Newmarket, Suffolk

FOCUS
A really strong handicap slightly devalued by a lack of pace.
Stellenbosch(USA) Official explanation: jockey said colt hung left

484 PLAY NOW AT BETDIRECTPOKER.COM (S) STKS 1m 2f (P)
4:10 (4:10) (Class 6) 4-Y-0+ **£2,388** (£705; £352) **Stalls** Low

Form RPR
0016 **1** **Milk And Sultana**[9] [394] 6-9-1 52.......... AlanDaly 13 48
(G A Ham) *slowly away: hld up: hdwy 2f out: strly rdn to ld post* **12/1**
6635 **2** *shd* **Takes Tutu (USA)**[11] [377] 7-9-1 66.......... PatCosgrave 8 48
(K R Burke) *lw: trckd ldrs: strly rdn to ld wl ins fnl f: hdd post* **2/1**[1]
6506 **3** *nk* **Scotty's Future(IRE)**[6] [427] 8-8-12 64.......... SilvestreDeSousa(3) 10 48
(D Nicholls) *lw: bhd: hdwy on ins whn swtchd rt over 1f out: raqn on strly: nvr nrr* **10/1**[3]
50-0 **4** *nk* **Good Article (IRE)**[18] [291] 5-9-1 40.......... MickyFenton 5 47
(D K Ivory) *trckd ldrs: rdn 2f out: hung lft over 1f out: r.o ins fnl f* **33/1**
0-40 **5** *shd* **Zinging**[1] [472] 7-9-1 40.......... FrancisNorton 6 47
(J J Bridger) *t.k.h: in tch: rdn and styd on fr over 1f out* **20/1**
-250 **6** *nk* **Competitor**[15] [324] 5-9-6 57..........(vt) TQuinn 7 51
(J Akehurst) *lw: led after 2f: rdn and hdd wl ins fnl f: no ex* **2/1**[1]
-650 **7** *1½* **Chocolate Boy (IRE)**[11] [379] 7-9-1 50..........(be) IanMongan 1 44
(G L Moore) *s.i.s: sn in tch: rdn 2f out: one pce fnl f* **13/2**[2]
4 **8** *1¾* **Ihuru**[42] [18] 4-9-0..........(p) NCallan 12 40
(J G Portman) *hdwy on outside over 3f out: sn rdn and no hdwy after* **14/1**
000- **9** *nk* **Esperance (IRE)**[8] [4653] 6-9-1 47..........(b) ChrisCatlin 4 40
(J Akehurst) *slowly away: hld up on outside: rdn over 2f out: sn btn* **25/1**
000- **10** *1* **Mr Strowger**[6] [683] 5-9-1 40.......... LPKeniry 2 38
(J C Fox) *lw: led for 2f: wknd over 1f out* **50/1**

60-0 **11** *1* **Isabella Rossini**[14] [338] 4-8-9 35..........(t) FrancisFerris 3 31
(A M Hales) *s.i.s: hld up: a bhd* **50/1**

2m 8.69s (0.90) **Going Correction** +0.05s/f (Slow)
WFA 4 from 5yo+ 1lb 11 Ran SP% **118.9**
Speed ratings (Par 101):98,97,97,97,97 97,95,94,94,93 92
CSF £35.18 TOTE £14.00: £2.80, £1.40, £2.70; EX 54.70.The winner was bought in for 5,600gns. Takes Tutu was claimed by C. R. Dore for £6,000.
Owner Rose Farm Developments (UK) Ltd **Bred** D Malcolm Drury **Trained** Rooks Bridge, Somerset

FOCUS
A moderate seller run in at a slow tempo.

485 BET NOW ON 0800 211 222 H'CAP (DIV I) 6f (P)
4:40 (4:40) (Class 6) (0-60,60) 4-Y-0+ **£2,047** (£604; £302) **Stalls** Low

Form RPR
4230 **1** **Mind Alert**[8] [408] 5-8-10 **55**..........(v) PatrickMathers(3) 5 62
(D Shaw) *hld up in rr: hdwy on ins over 1f out: strly rdn to ld ins fnl f* **16/1**
4-00 **2** *¾* **Sunny Afternoon**[1] [474] 6-8-11 **53**..........(v) MickyFenton 2 58
(Miss E C Lavelle) *hld up: rdn and hdwy over 1f out: sn ev ch: r.o wl* **25/1**
1-61 **3** *shd* **Segoria (IRE)**[23] [255] 4-9-4 **60**.......... ChrisCatlin 1 65
(A M Hales) *lw: hld up in rr: hdwy appr fnl f: r.o wl* **7/2**[1]
0332 **4** *shd* **Hadath (IRE)**[1] [474] 9-9-3 **59**..........(b) TQuinn 8 63
(B G Powell) *in rr: hdwy on outside over 1f out: r.o wl fnl f* **7/2**[1]
-330 **5** *shd* **Triple Zero (IRE)**[14] [336] 4-9-1 **57**.......... NCallan 11 61
(A P Jarvis) *prom: rdn and ev ch ins fnl f: no ex nr fin* **12/1**
0016 **6** *1½* **Times Review (USA)**[6] [426] 5-8-13 **60**..........(b) GregFairley(5) 10 60
(C A Dwyer) *led tl rdn and hdd ins fnl f: no ex* **16/1**
000- **7** *hd* **Music Teacher**[54] [6689] 4-8-10 **52**.......... SteveDrowne 4 51
(N A Callaghan) *mid-div: effrt appr fnl f: nt qckn* **8/1**[3]
-346 **8** *1¼* **Sir Sandrovitch (IRE)**[21] [262] 10-8-7 **52**..........(v) EdwardCreighton(3) 3 47
(R W Price) *lw: t.k.h: trckd ldr: wknd fnl f* **14/1**
50-6 **9** *½* **Kempsey**[39] [117] 4-9-4 **60**..........(v) J-PGuillambert 12 54
(J J Bridger) *trckd ldr tl rdn and wknd over 1f out* **8/1**[3]
3-33 **10** *nk* **Kitchen Sink (IRE)**[21] [265] 4-8-12 **54**..........(e) FergusSweeney 7 47
(P J Makin) *lw: racd wd: rdn 2f out: no hdwy after* **5/1**[2]
0643 **11** *3* **Four Amigos (USA)**[8] [411] 5-8-11 **56**..........(v) SilvestreDeSousa(3) 9 40
(D Nicholls) *prom on outside: rdn 2f out: wknd appr fnl f* **20/1**
0-00 **12** *2* **Oeuf A La Neige**[21] [262] 6-8-6 **55**..........(b[1]) DeanWilliams(7) 6 33
(G C H Chung) *v.s.a: a bhd* **66/1**

1m 12.67s (-0.14) **Going Correction** +0.05s/f (Slow) 12 Ran SP% **119.6**
Speed ratings (Par 101):102,101,100,100,100 98,98,96,96,95 91,88
CSF £367.67 CT £1724.14 TOTE £15.70: £4.10, £9.30, £2.20; EX 258.50.
Owner Simon Mapletoft Racing I **Bred** P T Tellwright **Trained** Danethorpe, Notts

FOCUS
The winning time was only par for the grade despite being 1.15 seconds faster than the second division.
Hadath(IRE) Official explanation: jockey said gelding hung right
Oeuf A La Neige Official explanation: jockey said gelding did not face the blinkers

486 BET NOW ON 0800 211 222 H'CAP (DIV II) 6f (P)
5:10 (5:11) (Class 6) (0-60,60) 4-Y-0+ **£2,047** (£604; £302) **Stalls** Low

Form RPR
-323 **1** **Tiviski (IRE)**[9] [402] 4-9-1 **57**.......... NCallan 7 65
(G G Margarson) *lw: trckd ldrs: rdn to ld wl ins fnl f: hld on* **6/1**
-645 **2** *hd* **Ashes (IRE)**[25] [225] 4-9-4 **60**.......... FrancisNorton 6 67
(K R Burke) *hld up in rr: hdwy over 1f out: drvn to go 2nd post* **12/1**
0-00 **3** *nk* **Clearing Sky (IRE)**[26] [216] 5-8-10 **55**.......... SaleemGolam(3) 4 62
(J R Boyle) *led tl rdn and hdd wl ins fnl f: lost 2nd post* **16/1**
2-13 **4** *hd* **Beneking**[9] [400] 6-8-10 **52**..........(p) ChrisCatlin 2 58
(D Burchell) *swtg: trckd ldrs on ins: short of room ent fnl f: swtchd rt: r.o cl home* **3/1**[1]
011- **4** *dht* **Edin Burgher (FR)**[63] [6646] 5-8-13 **55**.......... SamHitchcott 11 61
(T T Clement) *in tch: hrd rdn over 1f out: kpt on under continued pressure* **7/2**[2]
-006 **6** *1* **Jennverse**[14] [336] 4-8-10 **52**.......... FergusSweeney 8 55
(D K Ivory) *hld up in rr: hdwy on outside over 1f out but hung lft: no ex fnl 100yds* **25/1**
-032 **7** *shd* **Sweetest Revenge (IRE)**[23] [249] 5-9-4 **60**.......... HayleyTurner 3 63
(M D I Usher) *lw: hld up: effrt on ins over 1f out: no ex fnl f* **4/1**[3]
3-00 **8** *¾* **Time N Time Again**[11] [381] 8-9-4 **60**.......... RobbieFitzpatrick 10 60
(Peter Grayson) *swtchd lft to ins fr wd draw sn after s: nvr on terms* **33/1**
0-00 **9** *½* **Double M**[14] [339] 9-8-7 **52**..........(v) RichardThomas(3) 5 51
(Mrs L Richards) *lw: chsd ldrs tl nt qckn appr fnl f* **9/1**
-250 **10** *3½* **Imperium**[6] [428] 5-8-12 **54**..........(v[1]) MickyFenton 9 42
(Stef Liddiard) *trckd ldrs: rdn 2f out: wknd over 1f out* **16/1**

1m 13.82s (1.01) **Going Correction** +0.05s/f (Slow) 10 Ran SP% **117.8**
Speed ratings (Par 101):95,94,94,94,94 92,92,91,90,86
CSF £76.19 CT £1100.14 TOTE £7.20: £2.60, £3.40, £4.10; EX 72.70 Place 6 £58.67, Place 5 £49.75 .
Owner Miss Zora Fakirmohamed **Bred** Patrick J Fadden **Trained** Newmarket, Suffolk

FOCUS
The pace was not strong, producing a modest time for the grade, 1.15 seconds slower than the first division. Muddling form overall.
T/Plt: £49.70 to a £1 stake. Pool: £41,032.85. 602.10 winning tickets. T/Qpdt: £20.60 to a £1 stake. Pool: £3,028.30. 108.65 winning tickets. JS

[423]SOUTHWELL (L-H)
Thursday, February 23

OFFICIAL GOING: Standard to fast
Wind: Moderate, across

487 LITTLEWOODS POOLS BILLIONS WON BY MILLIONS MAIDEN STKS 5f (F)
1:40 (1:41) (Class 5) 3-Y-0+ **£3,238** (£963; £481; £240) **Stalls** High

Form RPR
0-30 **1** **Stoneacre Boy (IRE)**[13] [364] 3-8-12 67..........(b[1]) RobbieFitzpatrick 2 67+
(Peter Grayson) *cl up: led over 1f out: rdn clr ins last: comf* **13/8**[1]
-444 **2** *4* **Succeed (IRE)**[16] [322] 3-8-2 57.......... RichardKingscote(5) 5 46
(Mrs H Sweeting) *led: rdn 2f out: hdd over 1f out and sn one pce* **9/2**[3]
000- **3** *1* **Misty Princess**[71] [6580] 4-9-7 40.......... NCallan 7 48
(M J Attwater) *in tch: pushed along 2f out: sn rdn and styd on ins last* **25/1**
0032 **4** *nk* **Muktasb (USA)**[3] [465] 5-9-9 45..........(v) PatrickMathers(3) 8 52
(D Shaw) *trckd ldrs: hdwy 2f out: rdn over 1f out: drvn and btn ent last* **10/3**[2]

6 **5** 1 ¼ **Going Skint**[16] 331 3-8-12 .... DavidAllan 9 41
(T D Easterby) *dwlt and bhd: hdwy 1/2-way: rdn wl over 1f out: no imp* **14/1**

-050 **6** 1 ¼ **Canary Dancer**[11] 388 4-9-7 40..............................(p) DavidKinsella 1 38
(Miss Z C Davison) *in tch: rdn along over 2f out: sn btn* **33/1**

00 **7** 2 **Island Green (USA)**[19] 291 3-8-12 .... JamieSpencer 6 30
(B J Curley) *cl up: rdn along 1/2-way: sn wknd* **14/1**

030- **8** 4 **Signor Whippee**[106] 6297 3-8-12 55............................ FrancisNorton 3 15
(A Berry) *chsd ldrs: rdn along 1/2-way: sn wknd* **20/1**

0-0 **9** 1 ¾ **Safaah**[47] 62 3-8-12 .... ChrisCatlin 10 9
(G Prodromou) *sn outpcd: swtchd lft and a bhd* **33/1**

200- **10** nk **She Who Dares Wins**[135] 5825 6-9-7 45...................... HayleyTurner 4 9
(L R James) *cl up: rdn along after 2f: sn wknd* **40/1**

58.51 secs (-1.79) **Going Correction** -0.275s/f (Stan)
WFA 3 from 4yo+ 14lb **10** Ran SP% **109.6**
Speed ratings (Par 103):103,96,95,94,92 90,87,80,78,77
CSF £7.54 TOTE £2.40: £1.50, £1.90, £4.40; EX 10.20.
Owner Richard Teatum **Bred** Michael Dalton **Trained** Formby, Lancs

FOCUS
A poor maiden outside of the winner who was the clear pick of the weights and could hardly have won any easier. As usual those that raced down the middle of the track held sway.

488 PLAY LITTLEWOODS POOLS ON 0800 500 000 CLAIMING STKS 6f (F)
2:10 (2:11) (Class 6) 3-Y-O **£2,388** (£705; £352) **Stalls** Low

Form RPR

0131 **1** **Prettilini**[6] 439 3-8-7 68.................................... JamesDoyle(5) 1 71
(A W Carroll) *chsd ldrs: hdwy over 2f out: sn rdn: styd on to ent last: r.o wl* **9/4**[1]

1220 **2** 2 **Diktalex (IRE)**[6] 439 3-8-5 60 ow1.......................(t) RobbieFitzpatrick 8 58
(M J Attwater) *stdd and swtchd lft s: hdwy on inner 1/2-way: rdn to chse ldrs wl over 1f out: drvn and kpt on same pce ins last* **10/1**

20-3 **3** ¾ **Psycho Cat**[14] 347 3-8-11 65.................................(p) GrahamGibbons 7 62
(P A Blockley) *in rr on outer: hdwy over 2f out: sn rdn and hung bdly lft over 1f out: sn drvn: kpt on ins last* **11/4**[2]

034 **4** shd **Luloah**[2] 477 3-7-13 66.. DonnaCaldwell(7) 6 56
(P S McEntee) *cl up: led 1/2-way: rdn 2f out: hdd ent last: wknd* **12/1**

2-44 **5** ¾ **Amber Glory**[24] 248 3-8-10 66.....................................(p) NCallan 5 58
(K A Ryan) *led to 1/2-way: cl up: rdn over 2f out: drvn over 1f out and grad wknd* **8/1**

-435 **6** 3 **Woodwee**[6] 439 3-8-8 58.. DarryllHolland 3 47
(J R Weymes) *chsd ldrs: rdn along 1/2-way: sn wknd* **14/1**

4-66 **7** ½ **Aysgarth Flyer (IRE)**[14] 347 3-8-3 58........................(p) FrancisNorton 4 41
(I Semple) *pushed along 1/2-way: a rr* **7/1**[3]

1215 **8** 5 **Inaminute (IRE)**[7] 430 3-8-7 58 ow1............................ PatCosgrave 2 30
(K R Burke) *dwlt: sn pushed along and in tch: rdn wl over 2f out and sn wknd* **15/2**

6-6 **9** 9 **Sweet Rosella**[44] 76 3-8-2 .... ChrisCatlin 9 —
(G M Moore) *chsd ldrs to 1/2-way: sn wknd* **66/1**

1m 14.77s (-2.13) **Going Correction** -0.475s/f (Stan) **9** Ran SP% **117.8**
Speed ratings (Par 95):95,92,91,91,90 86,85,78,66
CSF £26.59 TOTE £3.00: £1.30, £3.30, £1.50; EX 28.00.The winner was claimed by Paul Howling for £12,000.
Owner David Shorthouse **Bred** G W Turner And Miss S J Turner **Trained** Cropthorne, Worcs

FOCUS
A routine claimer in which the early leaders may have gone off too quick and set the race up for the closers. The best effort yet from the winner, who was suited by the way the race panned out.
Psycho Cat Official explanation: jockey said gelding hung both ways

489 BE LUCKY AT LITTLEWOODSPOOLS.CO.UK H'CAP 6f (F)
2:40 (2:41) (Class 5) (0-75,75) 4-Y-0+ **£3,238** (£963; £481; £240) **Stalls** Low

Form RPR

-331 **1** **Winthorpe (IRE)**[7] 428 6-8-7 **64** 6ex.......................... GrahamGibbons 10 72
(J J Quinn) *trckd ldrs: hdwy 2f out: rdn to ld ins last: drvn out* **11/2**[2]

-004 **2** ½ **Alexia Rose (IRE)**[7] 426 4-8-4 **61** oh1.......................... FrancisNorton 9 68
(A Berry) *cl up: led 1/2-way: rdn wl over 1f out: drvn and hdd ins last: no ex towards fin* **33/1**

-250 **3** ½ **Flint River**[14] 348 8-9-1 **72**..(v[1]) SteveDrowne 1 77
(H Morrison) *towards rr: hdwy over 2f out: sn rdn and kpt on ins last nrst fin* **8/1**[3]

/0-2 **4** nk **Nepro (IRE)**[7] 424 4-8-9 **69**.................................(t) EdwardCreighton(3) 2 73
(E J Creighton) *chsd ldrs on inner: rdn along 2f out: drvn over 1f out: kpt on ins last* **8/1**[3]

61-1 **5** shd **Local Poet**[42] 100 5-9-4 **75**...(bt) TomEaves 8 79
(I Semple) *dwlt: sn in tch: hdwy and wd st: rdn to chse ldrs over 1f out: sn drvn and kpt on same pce ins last* **9/4**[1]

0105 **6** 4 **Zorn**[7] 428 7-8-4 **61** oh5.. JamieMackay 6 53
(P Howling) *prom: rdn along 1/2-way: sn wknd* **22/1**

0-24 **7** nk **Shifty Night (IRE)**[7] 428 5-8-4 **61**....................................(v) ChrisCatlin 4 52
(Mrs C A Dunnett) *led: rdn along and hdd 1/2-way: wknd 2f out* **9/1**

10-6 **8** ¾ **Middle Eastern**[21] 276 4-8-9 **66**... NCallan 5 55
(P A Blockley) *dwlt: a towards rr* **10/1**

0400 **9** ¾ **Owed**[14] 345 4-9-1 **72**...(t) HayleyTurner 7 58
(Robert Gray) *a rr* **20/1**

06-0 **10** 5 **Hit's Only Money (IRE)**[24] 253 6-8-11 **68**......................(t) FergalLynch 3 39+
(J Pearce) *v.s.i.s: a bhd* **12/1**

6121 **11** 5 **Christian Bendix**[9] 411 4-8-4 **61** 6ex oh1................. AdrianTNicholls 11 17
(P Howling) *in tch: hdwy on outer to chse ldrs 1/2-way: rdn over 2f out and sn wknd* **16/1**

1m 14.43s (-2.47) **Going Correction** -0.475s/f (Stan) **11** Ran SP% **113.1**
Speed ratings (Par 103):97,96,95,95,95 89,89,88,87,80 74
CSF £172.90 CT £1452.96 TOTE £9.80: £3.00, £5.50, £2.80; EX 193.20.
Owner Green Roberts Savage Whittall Williams **Bred** M Conaghan **Trained** Settrington, N Yorks

FOCUS
They did not seem to go that fast early and less than a length and a half covered the first five at the line. The winning time was only 0.34 seconds faster than the three-year-old claimer, which is modest for the grade. Sound enough form, the first three setting the standard.
Middle Eastern Official explanation: jockey said gelding had no more to give
Hit's Only Money(IRE) Official explanation: jockey said gelding threw its head up on leaving stalls, rendering him slowly away
Christian Bendix Official explanation: jockey said gelding had no more to give

490 LITTLEWOODS LOTTO3 0800 500 000 (S) STKS 1m 4f (F)
3:10 (3:10) (Class 6) 4-Y-0+ **£2,388** (£705; £352) **Stalls** Low

Form RPR

560 **1** **Mossmann Gorge**[6] 442 4-8-11 52...........................(v) DarryllHolland 3 53
(M Wellings) *trckd ldrs: hdwy over 2f out and sn cl up: swtchd rt and rdn ins last: led nr fin* **8/1**[3]

2243 **2** ½ **Romil Star (GER)**[7] 425 9-9-5 65...............................(v) PatCosgrave 1 57
(K R Burke) *chsd ldr: led 5f out: rdn along over 2f out: drvn and edgd lft ins last: hdd and no ex nr fin* **6/4**[2]

2124 **3** 1 ½ **Moon Shot**[11] 389 10-9-5 55.. NCallan 2 55
(A G Juckes) *hld up: hdwy over 3f out: rdn 2f out: styd on to chal ent last: sn drvn and no ex last 100 yds* **5/4**[1]

-530 **4** 1 ¾ **Dextrous**[11] 390 9-9-0 40...(p) MickyFenton 8 47
(P T Midgley) *hld up: hdwy to chse ldr 4f out: rdn 2f out: ev ch tl drvn and hld whn squeezed out ins last* **16/1**

000- **5** 12 **Tioga Gold (IRE)**[30] 3097 7-9-0 30...............................(p) ChrisCatlin 7 29
(L R James) *chsd ldrs: rdn along 4f out: wknd 3f out* **40/1**

0/0- **6** ¾ **Fleetfoot Mac**[42] 2187 5-8-7 63.........................(b) GemmaAnderson(7) 4 28
(B Storey) *led: hdd 5f out: sn wknd* **33/1**

05-0 **7** dist **Spanish Star**[30] 182 9-9-5 40...................................... RobertWinston 5 —
(Mrs N Macauley) *a rr: bhd and eased 2f out* **16/1**

2m 38.05s (-4.04) **Going Correction** -0.475s/f (Stan)
WFA 4 from 5yo+ 3lb **7** Ran SP% **112.7**
Speed ratings (Par 101):94,93,92,91,83 83,—
CSF £19.92 TOTE £7.50: £2.80, £1.80; EX 26.40.The winner was bought in for 6,500gns.
Owner Mrs Ruth M Serrell **Bred** R S Cockerill (farms) Ltd **Trained** Six Ashes, Shropshire
■ Stewards' Enquiry : N Callan caution: careless riding

FOCUS
The early pace was strong, but eventually it settled down and in the end the winning time was modest, even for a seller. The principals all came centre to stands' side in the home straight. Very weak form indeed.
Moon Shot Official explanation: jockey said gelding hung right-handed in straight

491 LITTLEWOODS LOTTO4 0800 500 000 H'CAP 1m 6f (F)
3:45 (3:45) (Class 5) (0-75,74) 4-Y-0+ **£3,238** (£963; £481; £240) **Stalls** Low

Form RPR

-123 **1** **He's A Star**[14] 346 4-8-9 **64**.. DarryllHolland 3 76
(Miss Gay Kelleway) *trckd ldrs: hdwy over 3f out: led wl over 1f out: sn rdn: drvn ins last and styd on wl* **6/1**

4-03 **2** nk **Trance (IRE)**[28] 194 6-9-10 **74**.. PhillipMakin 5 86
(T D Barron) *hld up: hdwy 4f out: rdn to chal over 1f out and ev ch tl drvn and no ex towards fin* **10/3**[2]

-130 **3** 8 **Oldenway**[22] 264 7-9-5 **69**... TonyHamilton 6 70
(R A Fahey) *led: rdn along 3f out: hdd wl over 1f out: grad wknd* **5/1**[3]

2-11 **4** ¾ **Sovereign Spirit (IRE)**[17] 318 4-8-12 **67**..........................(t) JoeFanning 2 67
(W R Swinburn) *trckd ldng pair: rdn along wl over 2f out: sn drvn and outpcd fr wl over 1f out* **11/4**[1]

3241 **5** 7 **Blue Hills**[6] 443 5-8-12 **62** 6ex...................................... DarrenWilliams 4 53
(P W Hiatt) *hld up: a rr* **7/1**

0111 **6** 2 **Jackie Kiely**[9] 414 5-8-12 **62** 6ex.................................... TonyCulhane 1 51
(P Howling) *hld up: pushed along in rr 6f out: a bhd* **8/1**

5051 **7** ¾ **Victory Quest (IRE)**[14] 346 6-9-2 **66**........................(v) RobertWinston 7 54
(Mrs S Lamyman) *trckd ldr: hdwy and cl up 4f out: rdn wl over 2f out and sn wknd* **12/1**

3m 3.50s (-6.10) **Going Correction** -0.475s/f (Stan)
WFA 4 from 5yo+ 5lb **7** Ran SP% **112.0**
Speed ratings (Par 103):98,97,93,92,88 87,87
CSF £25.12 TOTE £5.90: £2.50, £2.30; EX 24.70.
Owner Miss Gay Kelleway **Bred** Arnfin Lund And John James **Trained** Exning, Suffolk

FOCUS
Not a strong pace and the time was modest, but even so this took some getting and the front pair pulled a long way clear of the rest. Decent form for the grade, and it seems sound.

492 PLAY £1/4M SPOT THE BALL ON 0800 500 000 H'CAP 7f (F)
4:20 (4:20) (Class 6) (0-65,71) 4-Y-0+ **£3,238** (£963; £481; £240) **Stalls** Low

Form RPR

0522 **1** **Pawn In Life (IRE)**[11] 387 8-8-4 **51** oh6.....................(v) FrancisNorton 9 63
(M J Polglase) *midfield: hdwy 3f out: rdn to ld wl over 1f out: styd on strly ins last* **33/1**

5-00 **2** 2 **Dudley Docker (IRE)**[21] 276 4-8-11 **61**................ DanielTudhope(3) 13 68
(D Carroll) *s.i.s and bhd: hdwy 1/2-way: nt clr run over 2f out: rdn to chal and ev ch over 1f out: one pce ins last* **7/1**[3]

0310 **3** 1 ½ **Roman Empire**[21] 274 6-8-12 **59**..(b) NCallan 8 62
(K A Ryan) *cl up: led 3f out: rdn over 2f out: hdd wl over 1f out: kpt on same pce u.p ins last* **12/1**

00-0 **4** ½ **Elsie Hart (IRE)**[24] 252 4-9-2 **63**.. DavidAllan 6 65
(T D Easterby) *in tch: hdwy 3f out: rdn 2f out: kpt on ins last: nrst fin* **50/1**

4-21 **5** ½ **Scuba (IRE)**[6] 440 4-9-3 **64** 6ex....................................(v) SteveDrowne 7 65
(H Morrison) *prom: rdn along 2f out: drvn and one pce ent last* **10/3**[2]

-651 **6** hd **Bijou Dan**[9] 410 5-9-7 **68** 6ex..(b) TomEaves 5 68
(I Semple) *sn rdn along in rr: hdwy wl over 1f out: styd on strly ins last: nrst fin*

-301 **7** shd **Set Alight**[7] 429 5-9-10 **71** 6ex..................................(v) AdrianTNicholls 3 71
(Mrs C A Dunnett) *sn rdn along in rr: hdwy u.p on inner wl over 1f out: kpt on ins last: nrst fin* **11/4**[1]

1505 **8** hd **Resplendent Prince**[9] 410 4-9-4 **65**...........................(v) TonyCulhane 14 65
(P Howling) *chsd ldrs: wd st: rdn over 2f out: wknd appr last* **20/1**

0-05 **9** 3 **Shrine Mountain (USA)**[37] 127 4-7-12 **52**............ KirstyMilczarek(7) 1 44
(J R Holt) *chsd ldrs towards inner: rdn along over 2f out: grad wknd* **33/1**

2-14 **10** hd **Golden Square**[28] 200 4-8-8 **60**................................ JamesDoyle(5) 4 52
(A W Carroll) *hld up towards rr. effrt on inner wl over 2f out: sn rdn and nvr nr ldrs* **8/1**

-603 **11** shd **Preskani**[7] 429 4-9-0 **61**...(p) RobertWinston 12 52
(Mrs N Macauley) *towards rr: wd st: hdwy 2f out: rdn to chse ldrs over 1f out: wknd ent last* **12/1**

2414 **12** 1 ¼ **Magic Amour**[10] 402 8-8-10 **64**..................................(b) KevinGhunowa(7) 10 52
(P A Blockley) *prom: rdn along over 2f out: sn wknd* **20/1**

0030 **13** 5 **Penwell Hill (USA)**[21] 276 7-9-1 **62**.......................(b) RobbieFitzpatrick 2 38
(M J Attwater) *led: rdn along and hdd 3f out: sn drvn and wknd* **22/1**

000- **14** 2 ½ **Bogaz (IRE)**[79] 6513 4-8-10 **62**................................ RichardKingscote(5) 11 31
(Mrs H Sweeting) *midfield: rdn along 3f out: sn wknd* **66/1**

1m 27.22s (-3.58) **Going Correction** -0.475s/f (Stan) **14** Ran SP% **119.6**
Speed ratings (Par 101):101,98,97,96,95 95,95,95,91,91 91,90,84,81
CSF £236.06 CT £2961.00 TOTE £18.40: £4.80, £2.40, £3.40; EX 275.20.

Owner Geraldine Degville & Lawrence Degville **Bred** Lt-Col W L Newell **Trained** Babworth, Notts
■ Stewards' Enquiry : Adrian T Nicholls caution: used whip down the shoulder in the forehand position

FOCUS
A low-grade handicap, but very competitive and there were ten horses in a line across the track a furlong and a half from home. The winner had been well beaten of late, but otherwise this form is sound and it should work out.
Preskani Official explanation: jockey said gelding hung right-handed

493 LITTLEWOODS BETDIRECT H'CAP — 1m (F)
4:50 (4:51) (Class 6) (0-60,62) 4-Y-0+ — **£2,388** (£705; £352) **Stalls** Low

Form — RPR

3-10 **1** **Tacid**[18] 304 4-8-4 **46**........ FrancisNorton 5 — 54
(Dr J D Scargill) *hld up in tch: smooth hdwy on inner 3f out: rdn to ld over 1f out: drvn ins last: hld on wl* **10/1**[3]

5121 **2** *nk* **Latif (USA)**[11] 391 5-9-6 **62** 6ex........ SamHitchcott 12 — 69
(Ms Deborah J Evans) *s.i.s and bhd: gd hdwy 3f out: rdn to chal 1f out and ev ch tl drvn and no ex towards fin* **3/1**[1]

-503 **3** *1 ¾* **Drumroll (IRE)**[9] 409 4-9-0 **56**........(p) SimonWhitworth 9 — 59
(Miss J Feilden) *cl up: led 3f out: rdn wl over 1f out: hdd appr last: drvn and no ex ins fnl f* **12/1**

4 *1 ¼* **Ardea Brave (IRE)**[120] 6117 4-8-13 **58**........ SaleemGolam(3) 3 — 59
(M Botti) *chsd ldrs: rdn along and outpcd wl over 2f out: styd on u.p fnl f* **16/1**

0142 **5** *nk* **Lucius Verrus (USA)**[7] 429 6-9-1 **60**........(v) PatrickMathers(3) 11 — 60
(D Shaw) *chsd ldrs on outer: wd st: hdwy wl over 1f out: sn rdn and kpt on same pce* **9/2**[2]

0-00 **6** *1* **Diction (IRE)**[25] 247 4-8-1 **50**........(v¹) PatrickDonaghy(7) 2 — 48
(K R Burke) *dwlt: sn chsng ldrs: rdn 2f out: drvn and wknd appr last* **25/1**

5-06 **7** *3 ½* **Sorbiesharry (IRE)**[10] 405 7-9-4 **60**........(p) RobertWinston 4 — 50
(Mrs N Macauley) *in rr: rdn along 3f out: styd on u.p appr last: nt rch ldrs* **9/2**[2]

10-0 **8** *1* **Monkstown Road**[34] 157 4-9-2 **58**........(be) GrahamGibbons 14 — 46
(C N Kellett) *dwlt: sn chsng ldrs on outer: rdn along 3f out: wd st and wknd wl over 1f out* **14/1**

3-65 **9** *1* **Lord Of Dreams (IRE)**[34] 162 4-8-13 **58**........ EdwardCreighton(3) 6 — 44
(D W P Arbuthnot) *in tch: rdn along 3f out: sn wknd* **12/1**

16-0 **10** *2 ½* **El Palmar**[16] 330 5-8-13 **55**........ RobbieFitzpatrick 1 — 35
(M J Attwater) *led: rdn along and hdd 3f out: drvn 2f out and grad wknd* **18/1**

-660 **11** *10* **Fiore Di Bosco (IRE)**[14] 350 5-8-4 **46**........ PaulFessey 13 — 4
(T D Barron) *v.s.a: a bhd* **12/1**

00-0 **12** *9* **Speedie Rossini (IRE)**[10] 407 4-8-7 **49**........(b) PaulFitzsimons 8 — —
(Miss J R Tooth) *a rr: bhd fnl 2f* **66/1**

1m 41.21s (-3.39) **Going Correction** -0.475s/f (Stan) — **12** Ran SP% **116.7**
Speed ratings (Par 101):97,96,94,93,93 92,88,87,86,84 74,65
CSF £39.32 CT £377.15 TOTE £11.10: £3.00, £1.80, £2.80; EX 48.40 Place 6 £162.69, Place 5 £102.05.

Owner Derek W Johnson **Bred** J P T Partnership **Trained** Newmarket, Suffolk
■ Stewards' Enquiry : Sam Hitchcott caution: used whip down the shoulder in the forehand position

FOCUS
An ordinary handicap in which the pace was moderate. Again those that figured in the finish all came centre-to-stands' side in the home straight.
T/Plt: £511.00 to a £1 stake. Pool: £42,531.15. 60.75 winning tickets. T/Qpdt: £149.90 to a £1 stake. Pool: £3,445.90. 17.00 winning tickets. JR

[431]NAD AL SHEBA (L-H)
Thursday, February 23
OFFICIAL GOING: Dirt course - sloppy; turf course - good

494a AL ROSTAMANI GROUP TROPHY (H'CAP) (TURF) — 6f 110y(T)
3:50 (3:50) (95-110,110) 3-Y-0+ — **£45,348** (£13,953; £6,976; £3,488)

RPR

1 **Cartography (IRE)**[150] 5508 5-8-9 **99**........(t) RichardMullen 1 — 107
(E Charpy, UAE) *a.p: n.m.r 4f out: led 3f out: r.o wl to line: jst hld on* **18/1**

2 *hd* **Bahiano (IRE)**[7] 433 5-8-8 **98**........ RyanMoore 5 — 105
(C E Brittain) *settled in rr: rdn 3f out: prog 2f out: r.o wl: jst failed* **9/2**[3]

3 *3* **Al Maali (IRE)**[14] 353 7-8-10 **100**........ RHills 7 — 98
(Doug Watson, UAE) *racd in rr: rdn 2 1/2f out: n.m.r 1 1/2f out: swtchd and r.o nrst fin* **16/1**

4 *½* **Compton's Eleven**[13] 367 5-8-12 **102**........ JohnEgan 2 — 99
(M R Channon) *prom: rdn 3f out: ev ch 2f out: nt qckn* **4/1**[2]

5 *2 ½* **Starpix (FR)**[21] 281 4-9-6 **110**........(b) KShea 3 — 99
(H J Brown, South Africa) *v.s.a and sn rdn: last ent st: swtchd rail: hdwy 1 1/2f out: nt qckn* **16/1**

6 *1* **Kodiac**[13] 366 5-9-1 **105**........(b) TPO'Shea 12 — 91
(E Charpy, UAE) *mid-div wd: rdn 3f out: n.d* **4/1**[2]

7 *¾* **Talbot Avenue**[7] 433 8-8-8 **97** ow1........ PJSmullen 10 — 82
(M Mullineaux) *settled in rr: racd wd: hrd rdn 2f out: nvr involved* **9/1**

8 *hd* **Baaridd**[7] 433 8-8-5 **95**........ WSupple 4 — 78
(D Selvaratnam, UAE) *hld up in rr: prog to have ev ch 2 1/2f out: one pce after* **33/1**

9 *1* **Tahreeb (FR)**[13] 367 5-8-10 **100**........(v) JMurtagh 9 — 80
(D Selvaratnam, UAE) *s.i.s: settled in rr: prog to mid-div 4f out: trckd ldr 3f out: sn rdn: fnd little* **25/1**

10 *shd* **Commandocourageous (SAF)**[28] 206 5-8-5 **95**........ JBekker 11 — 75
(D Maroun, South Africa) *led tl 3f out: kpt on one pce: wknd 1 1/2f out* **10/1**

11 *shd* **Rock Opera (SAF)**[7] 436 4-8-8 **105**........ TedDurcan 8 — 78
(A Laird, UAE) *trckd ldr: rdn 3f out: fnd little: wknd 2f out: eased nr line* **10/3**[1]

1m 19.69s **Going Correction** +0.775s/f (Yiel) — **11** Ran SP% **124.2**
Speed ratings: 115,114,111,110,107 106,105,105,104,104 104

Owner Sheikh Ahmed Bin Mohammed Al Maktoum **Bred** Darley **Trained** United Arab Emirates

FOCUS
A good handicap, but again lacking in the unexposed types one would expect if this was run in England. With the ground riding on the easy side, all of the runners avoided the far-side rail in the straight.

NOTEBOOK
Cartography(IRE), with the tongue-tie re-fitted on his first run since leaving the Godolphin operation, defied a five-month absence to make a winning debut for his new connections. Although he is entitled to be sharper next time, everything went his way and he could be one to take on next time.
Bahiano(IRE) continues in tremendous form and did well to get so close to the winner as that one very much got the run of the race. He will go up in the weights for not winning, but is very much one to keep on the right side of.
Al Maali(IRE), returned to turf, proved no match for the front two but ran with credit and would have been a little closer had he enjoyed a clearer run - he was switched towards the inside the track as most of the others were going the other way.
Compton's Eleven seems at his best on a fast surface and was below the form he showed on his two previous runs at this Carnival Still, his proximity gives the form a solid enough look by Dubai standards.
Starpix(FR) would have been suited by the ground, but did not seem to take that well to the first-time blinkers.
Kodiac, 4lb higher, was below the form he showed to win over course and distance on his previous start and his record suggests he needs fast ground.
Talbot Avenue was not at his best and is another who seems to need decent ground.

495a AL ROSTAMANI GROUP PLATE (H'CAP) (DIRT) — 1m (D)
4:55 (4:56) (90-105,105) 3-Y-0+ — **£41,569** (£12,790; £6,395; £3,197)

RPR

1 **Marbush (IRE)**[14] 353 5-9-1 **99**........(e) JMurtagh 13 — 112
(D Selvaratnam, UAE) *trckd ldrs: prog to ld 2f: r.o wl: easily* **12/1**

2 *2 ¾* **Setembro Chove (BRZ)**[7] 438 5-8-12 **97**........ ECruz 7 — 104
(P Nickel Filho, Brazil) *slowly away: mid-div: forced switch wd 2 1/2f out: r.o wl: nrst fin* **20/1**

3 *3 ¾* **Happy Pearl (AUS)**[14] 353 6-9-2 **100**........(b) MJKinane 14 — 100
(G Moore, Macau) *sn led: chal 3f out: kpt on one pce: wknd last 100yds* **9/2**[1]

4 *3 ¼* **British Isles**[355] 565 4-8-6 **90**........(bt) RichardMullen 2 — 84
(A Laird, UAE) *trckd ldrs: ev ch 3f out: one pce* **10/1**

5 *nse* **Sea Hunter**[14] 353 4-8-10 **95**........(v) LDettori 12 — 87
(I Mohammed, UAE) *mid-div v wd: rdn 3f out: nvr a threat* **11/2**[3]

6 *3 ¼* **Gold History (USA)**[105] 5-8-6 **90**........(t) TPO'Shea 4 — 77
(A Laird, UAE) *sn struggling: n.d: nrst fin* **20/1**

7 *shd* **Safsoof (USA)**[7] 434 4-8-6 **90**........ KerrinMcEvoy 3 — 77
(I Mohammed, UAE) *racd in rr on rail: n.m.r 5f out: nt rcvr* **6/1**

8 *2 ¼* **Surbiton (USA)**[13] 6-8-8 **93**........(t) RoystonFfrench 10 — 74
(A Al Raihe, UAE) *a in rr: sme mod late prog* **16/1**

9 *¼* **Curule (USA)**[21] 277 9-8-10 **95**........(v) WSupple 11 — 76
(Doug Watson, UAE) *mid-div wd: rdn 4f out: nt qckn* **12/1**

10 *7 ¾* **Azul Da Guanabara (BRZ)**[13] 368 4-8-6 **95** ow1........ ADomingos 15 — 56
(Luis Singnoretti, Brazil) *trckd ldrs tl rdn 4 1/2f out: wknd* **20/1**

11 *2 ½* **Magnum Force (NZ)**[14] 353 7-8-8 **93**........ PJSmullen 6 — 53
(L Laxon, Singapore) *mid-div on rail: nvr competitive* **40/1**

12 *1 ¼* **Burnt Ember (USA)**[20] 7-9-2 **100**........ RyanMoore 8 — 59
(S Seemar, UAE) *prom early: sn wknd* **40/1**

13 *1 ¾* **Parole Board (USA)**[334] 734 4-9-6 **105**........(t) TedDurcan 16 — 59
(A Laird, UAE) *trckd ldrs: rdn 4f out: wknd* **5/1**[2]

14 *8 ½* **Wazir (USA)**[13] 366 4-8-6 **90**........ RHills 9 — 28
(J H M Gosden) *mid-div early: n.d* **14/1**

15 *dist* **Bold Demand**[7] 438 12-8-6 **90**........ SPasquier 1 — —
(R Bouresly, Kuwait) *racd in rr: nvr involved: t.o* **33/1**

1m 35.68s **Going Correction** +0.175s/f (Slow) — **15** Ran SP% **123.6**
Speed ratings: 115,112,108,105,105 101,101,99,99,91 89,87,86,77,—

Owner Sheikh Ahmed Al Maktoum **Bred** Stratford Place Stud & Watership Down Stud **Trained** United Arab Emirates

FOCUS
A decent handicap, and with the pace strong from the start they finished well strung out. As is so often the case on this dirt course, those drawn on the inside looked at a disadvantage.

NOTEBOOK
Marbush(IRE) had been running well over seven furlongs recently, but this sort of trip suits much better and he duly improved for the return to a mile. He stays even further and should remain very competitive.
Setembro Chove(BRZ), switched to dirt, ran to a very useful level of form in second and is clearly suited by this surface.
Happy Pearl(AUS) was 10lb higher than when winning over seven furlongs here two starts previously and did not appear to see out the mile.
British Isles ◆ ran well on his return from his unfavourable draw on his return from a near year-long absence and could be one to follow if going the right way from this.
Sea Hunter again gave the impression a return to more positive tactics will suit better.
Parole Board(USA), a very smart performer on this surface at last year's Carnival, was a long way below form on his return from a 334-day absence, but he was the stable's first choice on jockey booking and should not be written off just yet.
Wazir(USA), returned to a mile and switched to this dirt surface for the first time (he was second on Polytrack on his only previous try on sand), ran no sort race.

496a AL ROSTAMANI AL FAHIDI FORT (GROUP 2) (TURF) — 1m (T)
5:25 (5:28) 3-Y-0+ — **£94,476** (£29,069; £14,534; £7,267)

RPR

1 **Linngari (IRE)**[21] 280 4-9-4 113........ KShea 9 — 116
(H J Brown, South Africa) *led main gp: prog 2f out to chal: led 1 1/2f out: styd on wl* **5/2**[1]

2 *2 ¼* **Lord Admiral (USA)**[166] 5134 5-9-4 107........ JMurtagh 11 — 112
(Charles O'Brien, Ire) *mid-div: rdn to cl 3f out: hrd rdn 1f out: r.o nrst fin* **14/1**

3 *1 ¼* **Holiday Camp (USA)**[20] 4-9-4 98........ WayneSmith 1 — 109?
(M Al Muhairi, UAE) *disp on rail: clr ld 3f out: hdd 1 1/2f out: kpt on one pce* **33/1**

4 *shd* **King Jock (USA)**[21] 281 5-9-4 107........ PJSmullen 7 — 109
(E Charpy, UAE) *settled in rr: trckd ldrs 2 1/2f out gng wl: nt qckn* **10/1**

5 *½* **Near Dock (GER)**[21] 280 5-9-4 107........ ASuborics 10 — 108
(V Smith) *v.s.a: n.d after* **33/1**

6 *¾* **T-Bird (SAF)**[14] 352 5-9-4 108........(t) TPO'Shea 5 — 106
(E Charpy, UAE) *settled in rr: n.d* **10/1**

7 *nse* **Kandidate**[14] 353 4-9-4 110........(t) RyanMoore 12 — 106
(C E Brittain) *disp centre: rdn 3f out: kpt on all way to line* **12/1**

8 *2 ¼* **Elliots World (IRE)**[13] 369 4-9-4 104........ KerrinMcEvoy 3 — 102
(I Mohammed, UAE) *trckd ldrs: rdn 3f out: wknd* **11/1**

9 *shd* **Caesar Beware (IRE)**[21] 281 4-9-4 112........ TedDurcan 2 — 102
(A Laird, UAE) *mid-div on rail trcking wnr: ev ch 3f out: nt qckn fnl 2f* **11/4**[2]

The Form Book, Raceform Ltd, Compton, RG20 6NL

10 1 1/4 **Shersha (IRE)**[14] 351 7-9-0 95 .... MJKinane 8 95
(Kevin F O'Donnell, Ire) *a in rr: nvr involved* **20/1**

11 4 3/4 **Summoner**[35] 149 9-9-4 98 ....(bt) RoystonFfrench 6 90
(A Al Raihe, UAE) *mid-div: rdn 3f out: nvr involved* **33/1**

12 3/4 **Latino Magic (IRE)**[21] 280 6-9-4 110 .... LDettori 4 88
(R J Osborne, Ire) *settled in rr: rdn 3 1/2f out: n.d: virtually p.u* **6/1**[3]

1m 40.2s **Going Correction** +0.775s/f (Yiel) **12** Ran SP% **124.0**
Speed ratings: 114,111,110,110,109 109,109,106,106,105 100,100

Owner Jim Atkinson & P Walraninski **Bred** Hh Aga Khan's Stud **Trained** South Africa

FOCUS
The proximity of Lord Admiral and Holiday Camp in second and third respectively suggests this was not a very strong race by Group Two standards.

NOTEBOOK
Linngari(IRE), successful in a Group Three over an extended mile on his debut in Dubai, coped well with the easy ground to follow up. Although he was theoretically stepping up slightly in class, this did not turn out to be that strong a race by Group Two standards and he has been rated as having run to a run to a 3lb lower RPR than on his previous start. Just as he did last time, he very much got the run of the race. His trainer said afterwards that he had been working so well he would have been disappointed if he was beaten,and he will now aim him at the Group One Dubai Duty Free Stakes on World Cup night.

Lord Admiral(USA), making his debut in Dubai, ran a fine race for his Irish connections off the back of a 166-day break, but has never won above Listed company and his proximity casts doubt over the strength of the form.

Holiday Camp(USA), third in a Listed race on the dirt at Jebel Ali on his previous start, clearly ran a fine race to take third in this company, but he holds the form down as he had never previously run to an RPR above 96+.

King Jock(USA) promised to be competitive in Group company when winning a handicap off a mark of 102 at the beginning of this year's Carnival and ran well.

Near Dock(GER), unsuited by a steady pace in a Group Three on his previous start, would not have minded the easy ground and ran creditably.

T-Bird(SAF) was below form and did not appear suited by the return to a mile.

Kandidate, returned to turf with a tongue-tie fitted for the first time, was not at his best and seems better suited by fast ground.

Caesar Beware(IRE), so impressive when winning a seven and a half-furlong handicap off a mark of 105 on his first run in Dubai (King Jock and Kandidate behind), looked well worth his place in this sort of company, but the easing in the ground was totally against him and he could not produce anything like his best. He can be given another chance.

Shersha(IRE) continues to struggle.

Latino Magic(IRE) was just a length and a half behind today's winner on his previous start, but he was clearly nowhere near that form this time. Perhaps the easy ground did not suit.

497a AL ROSTAMANI GROUP (H'CAP) (TURF) 1m 194y(T)
5:55 (5:56) (95-110,110) 3-Y-O+ **£45,348** (£13,953; £6,976; £3,488)

RPR

1 **Evil Knievel (BRZ)**[21] 7-9-1 **105** .... WCMarwing 10 109
(M F De Kock, South Africa) *settled in rr: stl in rr 2 1/2f out: swtchd nr side 2f out: r.o to ld nr line* **11/2**[2]

2 nk **Le Prince Charmant (FR)**[159] 5-8-6 **96** .... RichardMullen 8 99
(E Charpy, UAE) *settled in rr: wd ent st: n.m.r 2 1/2f out: swtchd ins 1f out: r.o wl: jst failed* **20/1**

3 1 1/4 **Boule D'Or (IRE)**[21] 280 5-9-3 **107** .... MichaelHills 9 108
(J Akehurst) *settled in last gng wl: prog 2f out: swtchd ins: led 1f out: r.o wl* **12/1**

4 3 1/4 **Billy Allen (IRE)**[14] 354 5-8-12 **102** ....(t) SPasquier 7 97
(F Chappet, France) *mid-div: prog to dispute 2f out: kpt on: nt pce of first 3* **12/1**

5 3/4 **Organizer (NOR)**[130] 6-9-1 **105** .... TPO'Shea 11 98
(E Charpy, UAE) *mid-div wd: rdn 3f out whn outpcd: r.o wl fnl 1 1/2f: nrst fin* **25/1**

6 1 **Lundy's Lane(IRE)**[13] 370 6-8-10 **100** .... RyanMoore 4 92
(S Seemar, UAE) *trckd ldrs on rail: led 3f out: nt qckn* **9/1**

7 3/4 **Trademark (SAF)**[21] 280 10-9-4 **108** ....(bt) TedDurcan 1 98
(A Laird, UAE) *slowly away: t.k.h in rr: gng wl 3f out: nt qckn* **7/1**

8 3/4 **Shakis (IRE)**[21] 280 6-9-6 **110** ....(vt[1]) RHills 6 99
(Doug Watson, UAE) *trckd ldrs in centre: ev ch whn rdn 2f out: nt qckn* **4/1**[1]

9 3 1/4 **Baldaquin**[13] 371 9-8-10 **100** .... PDillon 3 82
(R Bouresly, Kuwait) *led: hdd 2 1/2f out: kpt on* **40/1**

10 4 1/4 **Mandobi (IRE)**[14] 357 5-8-12 **102** ....(vt) JMurtagh 5 76
(D Selvaratnam, UAE) *trckd front pair: ev ch in centre 2 1/2f out: nt qckn* **6/1**[3]

11 1 3/4 **Iqte Saab (USA)**[13] 370 5-9-1 **105** ....(t) WSupple 2 76
(Doug Watson, UAE) *hld up in rr: trckd ldrs far side 2f out gng wl: n.m.r 1 1/2f out: wknd* **6/1**[3]

12 15 **Eyjur (USA)**[284] 4-9-6 **110** .... MJKinane 12 53
(P Nickel Filho, Brazil) *trckd ldrs: ev ch 3f out: n.m.r 1 1/2f out: eased* **7/1**

1m 53.88s **Going Correction** +0.775s/f (Yiel) **12** Ran SP% **125.4**
Speed ratings: 107,106,105,102,102 101,100,99,96,93 91,78

Owner Stud Mega **Bred** Haras Louveira Ltda **Trained** South Africa

FOCUS
A good handicap, but the pace was just steady.

NOTEBOOK
Evil Knievel(BRZ) ◆, a beaten favourite on his debut in Dubai on the dirt, clearly appreciated the return to turf and just proved good enough. He took a long time to hit full stride and can do even better stepped back up in trip.

Le Prince Charmant(FR) ◆, a Listed winner over ten furlongs in France, would have been suited by the easy ground, but this trip looked short enough and he was just held after finding trouble in running. This was a promising debut for new connections and, like the winner, he can do even better back over further.

Boule D'Or(IRE), down in grade, looked the most likely winner when hitting the front, but may have got there too soon and his chance may also not have been helped by racing closest to the inside in the straight.

Billy Allen(IRE) could not sustain his challenge in the straight and was a touch disappointing, although a better pace might have suited.

Shakis(IRE) would not have minded the ground, but may not have taken to the first-time visor.

[465] WOLVERHAMPTON (A.W) (L-H)
Friday, February 24

OFFICIAL GOING: Standard
Wind: Fresh, against Weather: Overcast

498 BEST GAMES @ LITTLEWOODSPOKER.COM CLAIMING STKS 1m 141y(P)
1:50 (1:50) (Class 6) 4-Y-O+ **£2,388** (£705; £352) **Stalls** Low

Form RPR

/000 1 **Shannon Arms (USA)**[8] 428 5-8-6 64 ....(p) AndrewMullen(5) 4 70
(K A Ryan) *mde all: clr 6f out: rdn out* **16/1**

-604 2 1 1/2 **Cherished Number**[25] 251 7-8-5 58 ....(b) FrancisNorton 7 61
(I Semple) *s.s: hld up: hdwy over 2f out: nt rch wnr* **11/4**[2]

0-20 3 2 1/2 **Play Master (IRE)**[18] 319 5-9-1 63 .... PaulEddery 6 66
(B Smart) *s.i.s: hld up: hdwy over 2f out: rdn over 1f out: styd on same pce fnl f* **9/1**

-316 4 1 1/2 **Blue Patrick**[10] 412 6-9-5 76 .... NCallan 9 66
(K A Ryan) *prom: rdn to chse wnr over 2f out: no ex fnl f* **8/11**[1]

50-0 5 18 **Coronado's Gold (USA)**[30] 185 5-8-10 62 .... JoeFanning 5 20
(W R Swinburn) *chsd ldrs: rdn over 2f out: wknd over 1f out* **6/1**[3]

0000 6 4 **Acorazado (IRE)**[9] 417 7-8-5 47 ....(p) HayleyTurner 2 6
(C P Morlock) *prom: rdn 1/2-way: wknd 3f out* **33/1**

5/6- 7 8 **Mr Marucci (USA)**[9] 823 4-9-1 62 .... RobertWinston 11 —
(B Ellison) *hld up: hdwy over 3f out: wknd over 2f out* **28/1**

00 8 dist **Sandhill Dancer**[8] 427 4-8-2 ....(b[1]) MatthewHenry 3 —
(S Parr) *chsd ldrs to 1/2-way* **66/1**

1m 50.9s (-0.86) **Going Correction** 0.0s/f (Stan) **8** Ran SP% **122.6**
Speed ratings (Par 101):103,101,99,98,82 78,71,—
CSF £63.73 TOTE £16.60: £2.70, £1.20, £2.00; EX 50.10.Cherished Number was claimed by Gary P. Martin for £5,000.

Owner Mrs J Ryan **Bred** L Madere **Trained** Hambleton, N Yorks

FOCUS
An uncompetitive claiming stakes with likely favourite Linning Wine a non-runner, and the Ryan second string Shannon Arms caused something of a shock. He got a very soft lead and was helped by his stablemate being a stone below form. The second and third ran to their recent level.

Cherished Number Official explanation: jockey said gelding reared leaving stalls rendering it slowly away

Mr Marucci(USA) Official explanation: jockey said gelding hung left and lost its action

499 PLAY IN MONTE CARLO WITH LITTLEWOODSPOKER.COM (S) STKS 1m 141y(P)
2:25 (2:25) (Class 6) 3-Y-O **£2,388** (£705; £352) **Stalls** Low

Form RPR

4-23 1 **Countrywide Belle**[7] 439 3-8-9 59 ....(b) NCallan 2 55+
(K A Ryan) *mde all: rdn clr fnl 2f* **4/9**[1]

05-0 2 4 **Skin Sure Thing**[44] 93 3-8-3 35 ....(v[1]) AdrianMcCarthy 5 40
(A D Smith) *trckd ldrs: plld hrd: outpcd 3f out: styd on fnl f* **66/1**

0 3 shd **Archidona (FR)**[9] 422 3-8-9 62 .... MartinDwyer 7 46
(M Quinn) *hld up: styd on fnl f: nvr nrr* **14/1**

050- 4 shd **Count The Trees**[55] 6697 3-7-12 40 .... MarcHalford(5) 6 40
(W G M Turner) *hld up: nt clr run 2f out: swtchd lft and hdwy fnl f: n.d* **20/1**

600- 5 1 1/4 **The Jailer**[171] 5023 3-8-3 45 .... DavidKinsella 8 37
(J G M O'Shea) *prom: chsd wnr 5f out: rdn over 2f out: sn outpcd* **20/1**

0-65 6 8 **Bekoning (IRE)**[21] 286 3-8-8 48 .... FrancisNorton 1 24
(M Quinn) *prom: racd keenly: rdn over 3f out: wknd wl over 1f out* **8/1**[3]

-006 7 3 **Lady Palma Nova**[4] 466 3-8-3 55 .... DaleGibson 4 13
(M W Easterby) *chsd wnr over 3f: sn rdn: wknd over 2f out* **13/2**[2]

1m 53.87s (2.11) **Going Correction** 0.0s/f (Stan) **7** Ran SP% **111.4**
Speed ratings (Par 95):90,86,86,86,85 78,75
CSF £49.44 TOTE £1.40: £1.10, £15.50; EX 32.70.The winner was bought in for 6,500gns.

Owner Countrywide Racing **Bred** W G B Hungerford **Trained** Hambleton, N Yorks

FOCUS
A straightforward success for hot favourite Countrywide Belle in this dreadful seller. She did not need to run to her recent best to score.

Count The Trees Official explanation: jockey said filly hung right

500 PLAY IN THE CARIBBEAN WITH LITTLEWOODSPOKER.COM H'CAP 7f 32y(P)
3:00 (3:01) (Class 6) (0-65,63) 3-Y-O **£3,238** (£963; £481; £240) **Stalls** High

Form RPR

200- 1 **Grafton (IRE)**[144] 5659 3-9-1 **60** .... GrahamGibbons 1 65+
(J D Bethell) *mde all: rdn clr over 1f out* **9/1**

23-2 2 1 3/4 **Party Belle**[44] 85 3-9-4 **63** .... MartinDwyer 10 64
(C E Brittain) *hld up in tch: lost pl 3f out: hdwy over 1f out: nt rch wnr* **4/1**[2]

P4-4 3 1 1/4 **Next Ness (IRE)**[51] 31 3-8-12 **57** .... JoeFanning 7 55
(R F Fisher) *hld up: hdwy and hung lft over 1f out: nrst fin* **12/1**

-032 4 shd **Mr Rigsby**[7] 439 3-9-4 **63** .... TonyCulhane 9 60
(P Howling) *chsd ldrs: rdn 1/2-way: edgd lft and no ex ins fnl f* **7/2**[1]

4444 5 1 3/4 **Twilight Avenger (IRE)**[9] 418 3-8-7 **52** .... DeanMcKeown 2 45+
(M J Polglase) *chsd ldrs: n.m.r and lost pl 1/2-way: styd on ins fnl f* **13/2**

03-0 6 1 **Peephole**[51] 30 3-9-0 **59** ....(v) FergusSweeney 8 49
(P J Makin) *hld up in tch: rdn over 2f out: styng on same pce whn n.m.r ins fnl f* **16/1**

-100 7 1 **Drink To Me Only**[17] 335 3-8-9 **54** ow1 .... NCallan 4 42
(J R Weymes) *chsd ldrs: rdn and ev ch 2f out: wknd fnl f* **7/1**

46-0 8 1/2 **Tallyhobye**[22] 272 3-8-4 **54** .... JamesDoyle(5) 5 41
(J R Weymes) *hld up: effrt and edgd lft 1/2-way: wknd over 1f out* **28/1**

00-0 9 2 **Astorygoeswithit**[44] 85 3-9-1 **60** ....(b[1]) FrancisNorton 3 42
(Lucinda Featherstone) *chsd wnr: rdn and ev ch over 2f out: sn wknd* **28/1**

0-51 10 3 **Tamagin (USA)**[20] 291 3-9-4 **63** .... RobertWinston 6 37+
(P D Evans) *started slowly: hdwy 4f out: rdn and wknd over 2f out* **11/2**[3]

-006 11 9 **Galaxy Bound (IRE)**[11] 406 3-8-10 **58** .... PatrickMathers(3) 11 10
(D Shaw) *hld up: a in rr* **28/1**

1m 31.28s (0.88) **Going Correction** 0.0s/f (Stan) **11** Ran SP% **117.4**
Speed ratings (Par 95):94,92,90,90,88 87,86,85,83,79 69
CSF £43.95 CT £439.65 TOTE £8.00: £2.40, £1.90, £4.20; EX 62.90.

Owner D A West **Bred** Yeomanstown Stud **Trained** Middleham Moor, N Yorks

■ Stewards' Enquiry : James Doyle two-day ban: careless riding (Mar 7-8)

FOCUS
A modest handicap won in good style by the gambled-on Grafton. The level looks solid enough, with the second and third to form.

Next Ness(IRE) Official explanation: jockey said gelding hung as he entered home straight

Twilight Avenger(IRE) Official explanation: jockey said gelding was hampered going into bend

Drink To Me Only Official explanation: jockey said gelding had no more to give
Tallyhobye Official explanation: jockey said gelding was hanging both ways
Tamagin(USA) Official explanation: jockey said colt ran too freely in early stages
Galaxy Bound(IRE) Official explanation: jockey said gelding hung left

501 GET TO THE WORLD SERIES @ LITTLEWOODSPOKER.COM CLAIMING STKS (DIV I) — 5f 216y(P)

3:35 (3:35) (Class 5) 3-Y-0+ — £2,914 (£867; £433; £216) Stalls Low

Form — RPR

30-2 **1** **Up Tempo (IRE)**[15] [345] 8-9-13 67 .... (b) NCallan 1 — 64
(K A Ryan) *chsd ldrs: rdn and swtchd lft over 1f out: r.o to ld wl ins fnl f* 9/4[2]

2125 **2** *nk* **Byo (IRE)**[8] [424] 8-9-12 55 .... TonyCulhane 5 — 62
(P Howling) *chsd ldrs: rdn and edgd rt wl over 1f out: r.o* 9/1

/410 **3** *hd* **Miracle Ridge (IRE)**[31] [179] 11-9-7 45 .... (b) PatCosgrave 10 — 57
(Adrian McGuinness, Ire) *chsd ldr: led over 1f out: hdd wl ins fnl f* 33/1

3230 **4** *3/4* **Nova Tor (IRE)**[11] [401] 4-9-8 52 .... (b) RobbieFitzpatrick 3 — 55
(Peter Grayson) *led: hung rt fr over 3f out: rdn and hdd over 1f out: unable qck ins fnl f* 5/1[3]

0-05 **5** *3/4* **Piccleyes**[14] [360] 5-9-11 45 .... (b) DeanMcKeown 8 — 56
(M J Polglase) *s.i.s: hld up: hdwy over 2f out: rdn over 1f out: styd on same pce ins fnl f* 28/1

-030 **6** *3/4* **Merdiff**[13] [381] 7-9-10 61 .... FergalLynch 4 — 53
(W M Brisbourne) *hld up: plld hrd: rdn over 1f out: nt rch ldrs* 10/1

4-42 **7** *1/2* **Louphole**[34] [164] 4-9-10 66 .... FergusSweeney 2 — 51
(P J Makin) *s.s: hld up: effrt and nt clr run over 1f out: no imp ins fnl f* 7/4[1]

0-00 **8** *3 1/2* **Rosiella**[17] [321] 4-9-5 45 .... (b) FrancisNorton 6 — 36
(M Blanshard) *prom: rdn whn n.m.r over 1f out: sn btn* 33/1

00-0 **9** *1* **Game Flora**[26] [247] 5-8-13 35 .... (p) PatrickMathers(3) 7 — 30
(D Shaw) *prom over 3f* 100/1

00-0 **10** *2 1/2* **Lord Conyers (IRE)**[11] [407] 7-9-1 40 .... MickyFenton 9 — 21
(G Woodward) *mid-div: lost pl 4f out: sn bhd* 66/1

1m 15.73s (-0.08) **Going Correction** 0.0s/f (Stan) — 10 Ran SP% **114.7**
Speed ratings (Par 103):100,99,99,98,97 96,95,91,89,86
CSF £21.21 TOTE £2.80: £1.60, £2.60, £5.80; EX 17.90.
Owner Yorkshire Racing Club & Derek Blackhurst **Bred** T Burns **Trained** Hambleton, N Yorks

FOCUS
A tight race in which the field finished well-bunched at the line. A weakish claimer, the second and third setting the standard, and the winner is much better than these when on song.
Nova Tor(IRE) Official explanation: jockey said filly hung right
Lord Conyers(IRE) Official explanation: jockey said mare hung left

502 GET TO THE WORLD SERIES @ LITTLEWOODSPOKER.COM CLAIMING STKS (DIV II) — 5f 216y(P)

4:10 (4:11) (Class 5) 3-Y-0+ — £2,914 (£867; £433; £216) Stalls Low

Form — RPR

5264 **1** **Jalouhar**[11] [407] 6-9-3 47 .... SoniaEaton(7) 6 — 54
(B P J Baugh) *s.i.s: hdwy over 1f out: r.o to ld wl ins fnl f* 10/1

6404 **2** *3/4* **Joy And Pain**[17] [321] 5-9-12 64 .... (p) GeorgeBaker 8 — 54
(J R Boyle) *hld up: hdwy over 2f out: rdn and ev ch ins fnl f: kpt on* 4/1[2]

4405 **3** *3/4* **Alpaga Le Jomage (IRE)**[8] [426] 4-9-12 64 .... DeanMcKeown 3 — 52
(M J Polglase) *chsd ldrs: rdn to ld ins fnl f: sn hdd and unable qck* 15/2[3]

5044 **4** *shd* **St Ivian**[14] [360] 6-9-5 49 .... DuranFentiman(5) 11 — 49
(Mrs N Macauley) *sn outpcd: hdwy over 1f out: r.o* 16/1

4104 **5** *1* **Mulberry Lad (IRE)**[18] [307] 4-9-7 47 .... ChrisCatlin 5 — 43
(P W Hiatt) *chsd ldrs: rdn over 1f out: styd on same pce ins fnl f* 15/2[3]

-602 **6** *1* **Smile For Us**[28] [287] 3-8-8 53 .... (b) TPQueally 2 — 38
(C Drew) *chsd ldrs: rdn and nt mcuh room over 1f out: no ex fnl f* 8/1

-202 **7** *3* **Diamond Josh**[27] [225] 4-9-9 62 .... (v[1]) DanielTudhope(3) 9 — 36
(P D Evans) *chsd ldrs: rdn over 1f out: wknd fnl f* 4/1[2]

-352 **8** *shd* **Leah's Pride**[28] [209] 5-9-5 51 .... FergalLynch 1 — 29
(P Howling) *led: rdn over 1f out: hdd & wknd ins fnl f* 7/2[1]

05-0 **9** *hd* **Welsh Whisper**[27] [232] 7-8-10 40 .... NeilChalmers(3) 10 — 22
(S A Brookshaw) *dwlt: outpcd* 66/1

00-0 **10** *nk* **Danakim**[19] [299] 9-9-3 40 .... PaulMulrennan(3) 7 — 28
(J R Weymes) *hld up in tch: rdn over 2f out: btn over 1f out* 100/1

30-0 **11** *21* **Bennanabaa**[11] [396] 7-9-1 40 .... (tp) DonnaCaldwell(7) 4 — —
(S C Burrough) *dwlt: outpcd* 66/1

1m 15.5s (-0.31) **Going Correction** 0.0s/f (Stan)
WFA 3 from 4yo+ 15lb — 11 Ran SP% **115.8**
Speed ratings (Par 103):102,101,100,99,98 97,93,93,92,92 64
CSF £49.04 TOTE £12.60: £2.90, £1.90, £2.40; EX 71.50.Jalouhar was claimed by J. R. Best for £8,000.
Owner Miss S M Potts **Bred** Roy Matthews **Trained** Audley, Staffs

FOCUS
A weak event in which Jalouhar came through late to take the spoils. The winner is rated to his recent best.
Bennanabaa Official explanation: jockey said gelding lost its action

503 BETDIRECT.CO.UK MAIDEN STKS — 1m 4f 50y(P)

4:45 (4:46) (Class 5) 4-Y-0+ — £3,238 (£963; £481; £240) Stalls Low

Form — RPR

2- **1** **Lady Gregory (IRE)**[83] [6485] 4-8-6 .... ChrisCatlin 1 — 69+
(E J O'Neill) *chsd ldrs: led over 3f out: rdn over 1f out: all out* 1/1[1]

2 *shd* **Sweet Medicine**[27] 4-8-6 .... JoeFanning 8 — 69+
(P Howling) *a.p: chsd wnr over 2f out: sn rdn and ev ch: styd on* 28/1

3 *6* **Don And Gerry (IRE)**[50] 5-8-9 .... NCallan 9 — 60
(P D Evans) *chsd ldrs: rdn over 2f out: styd on same pce appr fnl f* 13/2[3]

000- **4** *3* **Brockhole (IRE)**[118] [6160] 4-8-11 65 .... TonyCulhane 6 — 60
(J G Given) *hld up: hdwy over 4f out: wknd over 1f out* 33/1

240- **5** *2 1/2* **Hue**[32] [6669] 5-9-0 70 .... RobertWinston 10 — 57
(B Ellison) *hld up: styd on fnl 2f: n.d* 8/1

643 **6** *7* **Discord**[11] [403] 5-8-9 .... GregFairley(5) 4 — 46
(T H Caldwell) *chsdv ldr 8f: weakend over 1f out* 14/1

530- **7** *4* **River Mist Image (USA)**[117] [6183] 4-8-6 64 .... MartinDwyer 11 — 35
(J R Fanshawe) *hld up in tch: wknd over 2f out* 8/1

2 **8** *7* **Steady Rain**[21] [289] 4-8-6 .... J-PGuillambert 7 — 25
(Lucinda Featherstone) *s.s: hld up: rdn over 3f out: a in rr* 18/1

0 **9** *shd* **Khadija**[11] [403] 5-8-9 .... MickyFenton 2 — 24
(R Dickin) *mid-div: lost pl 1/2-way: sn bhd* 16/1

64 **10** *1 1/2* **Real Chief (IRE)**[18] [314] 8-8-11 .... EdwardCreighton(3) 12 — 27
(Miss M E Rowland) *hld up in tch: rdn and wknd 3f out* 100/1

5-44 **11** *3 1/2* **River Gypsy**[9] [419] 5-9-0 63 .... LPKeniry 3 — 22
(D R C Elsworth) *led over 8f: sn rdn and wknd* 4/1[2]

620- **12** *15* **Royal Auditon**[135] [5837] 5-8-9 65 .... TPQueally 5 — —
(T T Clement) *s.s: rdn 8f out: a bhd* 25/1

2m 40.41s (-2.01) **Going Correction** 0.0s/f (Stan)
WFA 4 from 5yo+ 3lb — 12 Ran SP% **130.2**
Speed ratings (Par 103):106,105,101,99,98 93,90,86,86,85 82,72
CSF £48.78 TOTE £2.30: £1.20, £8.10, £1.40; EX 59.50.
Owner Miss A H Marshall **Bred** Frank Dunne **Trained** Averham Park, Notts

FOCUS
An ordinary maiden, but it was encouraging the front two pulled clear. This did not look a strong race of is type but it could have been rated up to 10lb higher.
River Mist Image(USA) Official explanation: vet said filly was moving poorly in its hind legs post-race
River Gypsy Official explanation: jockey said gelding hung right

504 $500K GUARANTEED WITH LITTLEWOODSPOKER.COM H'CAP — 1m 141y(P)

5:15 (5:17) (Class 5) (0-70,70) 4-Y-0+ — £3,886 (£1,156; £577; £288) Stalls Low

Form — RPR

0413 **1** **Bridgewater Boys**[14] [358] 5-8-9 61 .... (b) NCallan 12 — 69
(K A Ryan) *chsd ldr tl led 2f out: sn rdn: edgd lft 1f out: wnt rt towards fin: styd on* 11/2[2]

2221 **2** *nk* **New England**[13] [383] 4-8-10 62 .... RobbieFitzpatrick 1 — 69
(W M Brisbourne) *hld up in tch: rdn over 2f out: n.m.r over 1f out: r.o* 5/2[1]

/2-3 **3** *3/4* **Perez (IRE)**[16] [343] 4-8-10 67 .... EmmettStack(5) 6 — 73
(Pat Eddery) *hld up: hdwy over 1f out: r.o* 17/2

-060 **4** *nk* **Amazin**[20] [292] 4-8-7 64 .... (p) JamesDoyle(5) 3 — 69
(N P Littmoden) *s.i.s: hld up: r.o ins fnl f: nrst fin* 14/1

-400 **5** *shd* **Elrafa Mujahid**[25] [252] 4-8-13 68 .... (p) SaleemGolam(3) 9 — 73
(Ernst Oertel) *chsd ldrs: rdn and hung lft ins fnl f: styd on* 16/1

-152 **6** *1/2* **Burnley Al (IRE)**[13] [384] 4-8-13 65 .... (v) TonyHamilton 10 — 69
(R A Fahey) *chsd ldrs: rdn over 2f out: styng on same pce whn n.m.r ins fnl f* 16/1

1-41 **7** *hd* **Chicken Soup**[29] [200] 4-9-1 70 .... DanielTudhope(3) 7 — 73
(D Carroll) *hld up: hdwy over 3f out: rdn over 1f out: no ex ins fnl f* 11/2[2]

1-00 **8** *1* **Ronsard (IRE)**[18] [319] 4-8-13 65 .... GrahamGibbons 11 — 66
(Heather Dalton) *s.i.s: hld up: hdwy over 1f out: nt clr run ins fnl f: nt rch ldrs* 16/1

100- **9** *2* **Redwood Rocks (IRE)**[131] [5923] 5-9-2 68 .... DerekMcGaffin 8 — 65
(B Smart) *led: rdn and hdd 2f out: wkng whn n.m.r ins fnl f* 25/1

000- **10** *3* **Comeintothespace (IRE)**[69] [6598] 4-8-10 62 .... SamHitchcott 2 — 52
(A Bailey) *hld up: rdn over 2f out: n.d* 50/1

-350 **11** *1 1/2* **Screwdriver**[18] [316] 4-9-4 70 .... (b) PaulFitzsimons 5 — 57
(Miss J R Tooth) *s.i.s: hld up: a in rr* 15/2[3]

5-35 **12** *4* **The Rebound Kid**[14] [365] 4-9-1 67 .... MartinDwyer 4 — 45
(G A Huffer) *chsd ldrs: rdn over 3f out: sn wknd* 25/1

-546 **U** **Monte Mayor Boy**[18] [319] 4-8-12 64 .... (v) RobertHavlin 13 — —
(D Haydn Jones) *rrd and uns rdr s* 14/1

1m 50.55s (-1.21) **Going Correction** 0.0s/f (Stan) — 13 Ran SP% **122.3**
Speed ratings (Par 103):105,104,104,103,103 103,103,102,100,97 96,92,—
CSF £19.64 CT £124.78 TOTE £3.80: £1.10, £2.00, £3.50; EX 15.60 Trifecta £93.80 Pool: £956.08 - 7.23 winning units.
Owner Bishopthorpe Racing **Bred** Southill Stud **Trained** Hambleton, N Yorks

FOCUS
Modest form, but the race should produce the occasional winner at a similar level. Not the strongest form, with the first seven in a heap, and the winner should not be put up much for this.

505 LITTLEWOODSPOKER.COM - THE TRUSTED NAME IN GAMING H'CAP — 1m 1f 103y(P)

5:45 (5:46) (Class 5) (0-70,68) 4-Y-0+ — £3,238 (£963; £481; £240) Stalls Low

Form — RPR

01-1 **1** **Merrymadcap (IRE)**[11] [405] 4-9-4 68 6ex .... FrancisNorton 10 — 78
(M Blanshard) *hld up in tch: hmpd 2f out: styd on u.p to ld post* 7/2[1]

3552 **2** *shd* **Augustine**[4] [462] 5-8-9 59 .... ChrisCatlin 9 — 69
(P W Hiatt) *chsd ldrs: led over 2f out: rdn over 1f out: hdd post* 5/1[2]

-522 **3** *3/4* **Jakarmi**[11] [405] 5-8-13 63 .... TonyCulhane 6 — 73+
(B Palling) *chsd ldrs: hmpd and nt clr run 2f out: rdn and ev ch ins fnl f: unable qck nr fin* 11/2[3]

0-11 **4** *3 1/2* **Itcanbedone Again (IRE)**[14] [358] 7-8-4 59 ow1 .... GregFairley(5) 8 — 61
(Ian Williams) *chsd ldrs: rdn over 2f out: styd on same pce appr fnl f* 6/1

00-1 **5** *nk* **Orpendonna (IRE)**[35] [162] 4-8-11 61 .... (p) NCallan 7 — 62
(K A Ryan) *led 7f: hung lft over 1f out: no ex* 10/1

0020 **6** *nk* **Farnborough (USA)**[14] [358] 5-8-0 55 .... JamesDoyle(5) 3 — 56+
(R J Price) *hld up: rdn and nt clr run over 2f out: styd on ins fnl f: nvr nrr* 9/1

00-0 **7** *1* **Rashida**[13] [385] 4-9-4 68 .... (tp) GeorgeBaker 5 — 67
(M Appleby) *hld up: hdwy over 2f out: rdn and hung lft fr over 1f out: nt run on* 50/1

-060 **8** *shd* **Sorbiesharry (IRE)**[1] [493] 7-8-10 60 .... (p) RobertWinston 2 — 59
(Mrs N Macauley) *hld up: rdn over 3f out: hdwy over 1f out: nvr trbld ldrs* 7/1

065- **9** *1/2* **Nabir (FR)**[70] [6582] 6-8-12 65 .... PaulMulrennan(3) 12 — 63
(P D Niven) *chsd ldrs: rdn over 2f out: wknd over 1f out* 28/1

000- **10** *1/2* **Arabie**[163] [5233] 8-9-0 64 .... RobbieFitzpatrick 4 — 61
(Ian Williams) *dwlt: hld up: hdwy and hmpd over 1f out: nt rcvr* 16/1

4-00 **11** *9* **Carry On Doc**[26] [236] 5-8-13 66 .... SaleemGolam(3) 1 — 46
(Ernst Oertel) *hld up: a in rr* 25/1

0303 **12** *2* **Buscador (USA)**[11] [405] 7-8-2 57 .... DuranFentiman(5) 11 — 33
(W M Brisbourne) *chsd ldr: rdn whn hmpd 2f out: sn wknd* 16/1

2m 2.06s (-0.56) **Going Correction** 0.0s/f (Stan) — 12 Ran SP% **121.2**
Speed ratings (Par 103):102,101,101,98,97 97,96,96,96,95 87,85
CSF £20.50 CT £97.29 TOTE £6.40: £2.10, £1.70, £1.20; EX 30.00 Place 6 £119.75, Place 5 £45.21.
Owner Mrs N L Young **Bred** Wickfield Farm Partnership **Trained** Upper Lambourn, Berks

FOCUS
A tight race with several bang in-form runners on show and it was hat-trick-seeking Merrymadcap that came out on top. The form looks reliable, with the first three finishing clear.
Farnborough(USA) Official explanation: jockey said gelding was denied clear run
T/Plt: £144.70 to a £1 stake. Pool: £44,506.75. 224.50 winning tickets. T/Qpdt: £33.70 to a £1 stake. Pool: £4,500.90. 98.80 winning tickets. CR

[494]NAD AL SHEBA (L-H)

Friday, February 24

OFFICIAL GOING: Dirt course - sloppy; turf course - good to soft

506a ETISALAT ACADEMY CUP (H'CAP) (TURF) 6f (T)

3:05 (3:07) (95-110,109) 3-Y-0+ **£45,348** (£13,953; £6,976; £3,488)

RPR

1 **Obe Gold**[8] [431] 4-9-1 **104**.......(v) JohnEgan 10 109
(M R Channon) *settled in mid-div: last 3f out: askd to chal in centre: r.o wl to ld 1f out: comf* **13/2**[3]

2 1 **Sevillano**[8] [431] 5-9-0 **102**.......(t) TedDurcan 1 105
(A Laird, UAE) *t.k.h: mid-div on rail: trckd ldrs gng wl 2f out: n.m.r 1f out: wd: r.o wl* **9/1**

3 2 **Conceal**[8] [431] 8-8-8 **97**....... GHind 6 93
(R Bouresly, Kuwait) *s.i.s: trckd ldrs: disp 3f out: ev ch: kpt on: no ch w first two* **12/1**

4 shd **Royal Storm (IRE)**[8] [431] 7-8-11 **100**....... MJKinane 3 96
(Mrs A J Perrett) *led: jnd in front 3f out: rdn: kpt on wl for press* **5/1**[2]

5 1 1/4 **Candidato Roy (ARG)**[15] [352] 5-9-2 **105**.......(t) WCMarwing 5 97
(M F De Kock, South Africa) *settled last: prog to rail 3f out: trckd ldrs: n.m.r 2f out and 100yds out: eased* **11/1**

6 nk **Slip Dance (IRE)**[15] [352] 4-8-11 **100**....... MCHussey 2 91
(Eamon Tyrrell, Ire) *settled in rr: gng wl 3f out then n.m.r: one pce once clr* **8/1**

7 1/2 **Bygone Days**[8] [433] 5-9-2 **105**....... KerrinMcEvoy 4 95
(I Mohammed, UAE) *trckd ldrs: disp 3f out: nt qckn* **11/4**[1]

8 2 1/2 **National Icon (SAF)**[22] [281] 6-9-6 **109**....... JBekker 8 91
(D Maroun, South Africa) *s.i.s: settled in rr: rdn to cl 3f out: ev ch 2f out: one pce* **16/1**

9 6 1/2 **Hinterland (SAF)**[14] [369] 8-8-9 **98**....... RyanMoore 7 61
(S Seemar, UAE) *prom in centre: ev ch 3f out: nt qckn* **40/1**

1m 13.88s **Going Correction** +0.725s/f (Yiel) 9 Ran SP% **102.1**
Speed ratings: 110,108,106,105,104 103,103,99,91

Owner BDR Partnership **Bred** Mrs M Mason **Trained** West Ilsley, Berks

FOCUS
This did not look like a very strong handicap for the grade and the form wants treating with real caution.

NOTEBOOK
Obe Gold had been struggling a touch since winning over six and a half furlongs off a mark of 100 on his debut in Dubai, but this race lacked strength in depth and, handling the easy ground well, he returned to form with a decisive success.
Sevillano is proven on easy ground and returned to form with a creditable second. While he did not enjoy one continuous run, he was not unlucky.
Conceal has never won on turf and his proximity does not do a great deal for the form.
Royal Storm(IRE) looked to have every chance but was below form. His record suggests he needs better ground.
Candidato Roy(ARG), with blinkers left off and a tongue-tie fitted, would have been closer with a clearer run. He is going the right way, but this was a weak race for the grade. (op 10/1)
Slip Dance(IRE) did not enjoy a clear run and is a little better than the bare form. (op 9/1)
Bygone Days should not have minded the ground, but was quite a way below form. He has not totally convinced for his new connections and looks best watched for the time being.

507a AL SHAMIL (H'CAP) (TURF) 7f 110y(D)

3:40 (3:40) (90-105,105) 3-Y-0+ **£41,569** (£12,790; £6,395; £3,197)

RPR

1 **Winisk River (IRE)**[715] [1001] 6-9-6 **105**.......(t) TPO'Shea 9 111
(E Charpy, UAE) *s.i.s: settled in rr: rdn to mid-div 3f out: prog to chal over 1 1/2f out: led 1f out: r.o* **7/1**

2 2 1/4 **National Captain (SAF)**[14] [368] 4-8-6 **98**....... RichardMullen 12 90
(A Laird, UAE) *trckd ldrs: v wd ent st: rdn 2 1/2f out: ev ch 1 1/2f out: r.o wl: no ch w wnr* **7/1**

3 3 **King Marju (IRE)**[15] [352] 4-8-8 **93**.......(v) PJSmullen 5 84
(K R Burke) *restrained: settled last: t.k.h: stl last 3f out gng wl: rdn 2f out: r.o: nrst fin* **20/1**

4 1 1/2 **Damachida (IRE)**[8] [434] 7-8-12 **97**.......(t) JohnEgan 10 84
(Eva Sundbye, Sweden) *wl away: settled in rr: asked to cl 3f out: v wd: nvr a factor: nrst fin* **33/1**

5 1/2 **Spirit Of France (IRE)**[8] [435] 4-8-10 **95**....... RoystonFfrench 4 80
(Christian Wroe, UAE) *trckd ldrs: rdn 3f out: disp briefly: wknd* **10/3**[2]

6 shd **Parnassus (SAF)**[15] [357] 4-8-7 **100**....... TedDurcan 2 77
(A Laird, UAE) *nt far off pce: gng wl trcking ldrs 3f out: ev ch 2f out: nt qckn* **11/4**[1]

7 1 1/4 **Sapucai (ARG)**[14] 6-8-8 **93**.......(bt) RyanMoore 1 75
(S Seemar, UAE) *trckd ldrs on rail: chal 3f out on far side: ev ch 1f out: nt qckn* **16/1**

8 shd **Mukafeh (USA)**[8] [434] 5-9-4 **102**....... RHills 3 84
(E Charpy, UAE) *sn led on rail: hdd 1 1/2f out: nt qckn* **13/2**[3]

9 3/4 **Mokabra (IRE)**[8] [431] 5-8-10 **95**.......(v) JMurtagh 6 74
(D Selvaratnam, UAE) *prom in centre: rdn 3f out: ev ch: nt qckn* **10/1**

10 11 **Coral Gables (IND)**[22] [281] 6-8-10 **95**....... KerrinMcEvoy 11 43
(L D'Silva, India) *mid-div: dropped to rr 3f out: n.d* **40/1**

11 3/4 **Oriental Warrior**[125] [6017] 5-9-1 **99**....... GHind 7 46
(S Al Salloum, UAE) *puled hrd: trckd ldrs: dropped to mid-div 4f out: n.d after* **16/1**

1m 33.26s **Going Correction** +0.725s/f (Yiel) 11 Ran SP% **119.1**
Speed ratings: 114,111,108,107,106 106,105,105,104,93 92

Owner Sheikh Ahmed Bin Mohammed Al Maktoum **Bred** P H Betts **Trained** United Arab Emirates

FOCUS
Not a very strong race for the class, but a good effort from Winisk River to defy a near two-year absence.

NOTEBOOK
Winisk River(IRE), successful off a mark of 109 for Godolphin when last seen nearly two years previously, had been given a chance by the Handicapper and defied his absence to make a successful debut for new connections. This was not a great race for the grade, but he must be kept on the right side of if he stands training.
National Captain(SAF), down the field in the UAE 2000 Guineas on his previous start, ran much better returned to turf but was no match whatsoever for the winner.
King Marju(IRE), with the visor re-fitted, ran better than on his two previous starts out here and offered hope.
Damachida(IRE) returned to form in fourth but may have fared even better under a more positive ride.
Spirit Of France(IRE) had run well on his two previous starts in Dubai, but was not quite at his best this time.
Parnassus(SAF), a stablemate of the runner-up, failed to build on the promise he showed when second in a course and distance handicap on his debut in Dubai, and a 7lb higher mark would not have helped.

508a E-VISION (H'CAP) (DIRT) 7f (D)

4:15 (4:15) (95-110,108) 3-Y-0+ **£45,348** (£13,953; £6,976; £3,488)

RPR

1 **Tropical Star (IRE)**[29] [206] 6-9-6 **108**.......(vt) RoystonFfrench 8 114
(A Al Raihe, UAE) *nt far off pce wd: disp 3 1/2f out: led 2f out: r.o wl* **9/2**[3]

2 3 1/4 **Emerald Beauty (ARG)**[15] [351] 6-8-10 **98**.......(bt) WCMarwing 5 97
(M F De Kock, South Africa) *trckd ldrs: rdn through gap to chal 2f out: ev ch: kpt on but no ch w wnr* **7/2**[2]

3 1 1/2 **Glad To Be Fast (IRE)**[15] [353] 6-8-12 **100**.......(b) AStarke 4 96
(Mario Hofer, Germany) *settled in rr: rdn and swtchd wd 3f out: r.o wl wout threatening* **9/1**

4 3 1/4 **Sabbeeh (USA)**[22] [281] 5-9-4 **106**.......(t) LDettori 1 94
(Saeed Bin Suroor) *broke awkwardly: rdn to ld on rail: jnd in front 3 1/2f out: ev ch 3f out: nt qckn* **6/4**[1]

5 3 1/2 **Little Jim (ARG)**[8] [434] 6-9-3 **105**.......(t) TedDurcan 7 86
(A Laird, UAE) *prom in centre: ev ch 3f out: one pce* **7/1**

6 nse **Kill Cat (IRE)**[29] [204] 5-8-10 **98**.......(t) MJKinane 3 79
(A Peraino, Italy) *settled in rr: prog to mid-div on rail 4f out: rdn 3f out: nt qckn* **12/1**

7 3/4 **Secret Place**[15] [353] 5-8-7 **95**.......(t) WayneSmith 6 74
(M Al Muhairi, UAE) *trckd ldrs: prom 3f out and ev ch: sn wknd* **66/1**

8 14 **Party Boss**[15] [357] 4-9-2 **104**.......(t) RyanMoore 2 52
(C E Brittain) *n.d* **33/1**

1m 24.7s **Going Correction** +0.275s/f (Slow) 8 Ran SP% **115.0**
Speed ratings: 115,111,109,105,101 101,100,84

Owner Sheikh Mohammed Bin Maktoum Al Maktoum **Bred** Gainsborough Stud Management Ltd **Trained** UAE

FOCUS
Last year's Golden Shaheen runner-up, Tropical Star, returned to form to outclass his rivals in what was an ordinary handicap for the class.

NOTEBOOK
Tropical Star(IRE) was below form in a six-furlong Group Three on his previous start but, stepped back up in trip and eased in class, he returned to his best and totally outclassed his seven rivals. He will apparently be aimed at either the Golden Shaheen or Godolphin Mile on World Cup night.
Emerald Beauty(ARG), below form on both her previous starts at this year's Carnival, ran better switched to dirt but was basically no match for the classy winner. (op 4/1)
Glad To Be Fast(IRE) did not run badly and could do even better if ridden a little more positively. (op 8/1)
Sabbeeh(USA), a smart performer on turf, failed to prove his effectiveness on dirt, although stall one was hardly an ideal draw.
Party Boss does not act on this surface.

509a WASEL (H'CAP) (TURF) 1m 2f (T)

4:50 (4:50) (90-105,104) 3-Y-0+ **£41,569** (£12,790; £6,395; £3,197)

RPR

1 **Shanty Star (IRE)**[8] [437] 6-9-6 **104**....... GHind 6 109
(R Bouresly, Kuwait) *led: kicked clr 2 1/2f out: r.o wl: easily* **9/1**

2 5 **Craft Fair (IRE)**[22] [279] 4-9-1 **98**.......(vt1) LDettori 4 96
(Saeed Bin Suroor) *mid-div: hrd rdn 3f out: kpt on one pce* **4/1**[1]

3 nk **Clasp**[8] [432] 4-8-12 **96**.......(vt) TedDurcan 3 92
(A Laird, UAE) *trckd ldr centre: rdn to chal 3f out: kpt on wl but no ch w wnr* **11/2**[2]

4 3/4 **Mutafanen**[15] [354] 5-9-4 **101**....... RHills 12 96
(E Charpy, UAE) *settled in rr: last 3f out but gng wl: n.m.r 2 1/2f out: hrd rdn 2f out: nrst fin* **7/1**

5 1 1/4 **Terfel**[15] [354] 7-9-1 **98**.......(t) JohnEgan 5 91
(Daniel J Murphy, Singapore) *settled in last: swtchd wd 3f out: hrd rdn: kpt on: nrst fin* **12/1**

6 1/2 **Hallhoo (IRE)**[188] [4562] 4-8-11 **95**....... JMurtagh 10 87
(D Selvaratnam, UAE) *trckd ldrs: ev ch 3f out: rdn 2f out: one pce* **25/1**

7 nse **Little Good Bay**[8] [435] 6-8-7 **90**.......(b) RichardMullen 8 82
(A Laird, UAE) *s.i.s: settled in rr: gng wl 3f out: rdn 2f out: kpt on* **10/1**

8 4 **Kestrel Cross (IRE)**[8] [438] 4-8-9 **93**....... ASuborics 11 78
(V Smith) *mid-div: dropped to rr 3f out: rdn 2 1/2f out: nrst fin* **8/1**

9 2 1/2 **Amandus (USA)**[8] [437] 6-8-9 **93**.......(be) WSupple 9 72
(Doug Watson, UAE) *settled in rr on rail: gng wl 3f out whn n.m.r: n.d after* **33/1**

10 1 1/2 **Evaluator (IRE)**[15] [356] 5-9-3 **100**.......(t) KerrinMcEvoy 1 77
(I Mohammed, UAE) *mid-div on rail: rdn 2 1/2f out: ev ch 2f out on rail: nt qckn* **6/1**[3]

11 4 1/2 **The Carbon Unit (USA)**[15] [356] 4-8-11 **95**....... TPO'Shea 2 64
(E Charpy, UAE) *s.i.s: sn rdn into mid-div: trckd front gp 5f out: rdn: nt respond: wknd* **13/2**

12 1 **Sekula Pata (NZ)**[14] 7-8-7 **90**.......(b) RoystonFfrench 7 58
(Christian Wroe, UAE) *trckd ldrs wd: ev ch 3f out: wknd qckly* **66/1**

2m 7.86s **Going Correction** +0.725s/f (Yiel)
WFA 4 from 5yo+ 1lb 12 Ran SP% **121.7**
Speed ratings: 113,109,108,108,107 106,106,103,101,100 96,95

Owner Bouresly Racing Syndicate **Bred** Gainsborough Stud Management Ltd **Trained** Kuwait

FOCUS
Although running well, Shanty Star had been continually held in similar events at this year's Carnival, so his five-length success, albeit very much deserved, suggests the form is ordinary for a race of this class.

NOTEBOOK
Shanty Star(IRE), an admirable performer, got his own way in front and took advantage to end a losing run stretching back to his two-mile win in the 2003 Queen's Vase when trained by Mark Johnston. Easy ground was an unknown, but it helped bring his stamina into play. He deserved this, following some game efforts in defeat, and should continue to go well.
Craft Fair(IRE) had the ground to suit on his return to turf, but could not go with the winner, who had enjoyed an easy lead.
Clasp, given a rare outing on turf, handled the surface quite well and ran creditably.
Mutafanen was again denied a clear run under Richard Hills.
Kestrel Cross(IRE), back up in trip, lost his position at a crucial stage and never threatened. (op 15/2)

510a BALANCHINE (LISTED RACE) (F&M) (TURF) 1m 194y(T)
5:25 (5:25) 3-Y-0+ **£56,686** (£17,441; £8,720; £4,360)

RPR

1 **Irridescence (SAF)**[237] 5-9-11 102 .... WCMarwing 8 118
(M F De Kock, South Africa) *trckd ldr: led 2f out: rdn clr 1f out: r.o wl* **7/2**[2]

2 1 1/4 **Satwa Queen (FR)**[36] [155] 4-9-6 110 .... ELegrix 10 111
(J De Roualle, France) *racd in 3rd: wnt 2nd 2f out gng wl: rdn 1f out: nt able to catch wnr* **8/11**[1]

3 5 1/2 **Brindisi**[15] [351] 5-9-4 101 .... JMurtagh 1 99
(D Selvaratnam, UAE) *mid-div on rail: prog to trck ldrs 3f out: ev ch 2f out: no ch w first two* **8/1**[3]

4 5 1/4 **Shersha (IRE)**[1] [496] 7-9-4 95 .... PJSmullen 2 89
(Kevin F O'Donnell, Ire) *hld up in rr: last gng wl 3f out: trckd runner up 2f out: one pce* **14/1**

5 nk **Littletown Bridge (USA)**[351] [599] 4-9-4 96 .... (t) WSupple 6 88
(Doug Watson, UAE) *led at stdy pce: hdd 2f out: one pce* **16/1**

6 1 1/2 **Festive Style (SAF)**[15] [354] 6-9-4 91 .... KShea 5 85
(H J Brown, South Africa) *hld up in rr: rdn after 3f: n.d* **25/1**

7 2 3/4 **Kitara (GER)**[29] [208] 6-9-4 95 .... ASuborics 9 80
(P Vovcenko, Germany) *mid-div: nvr a factor* **25/1**

8 3 3/4 **Venus Arising (IND)**[15] [351] 5-9-4 95 .... (t) RyanMoore 11 73
(V Gaekwad, India) *hld up in rr: mid-div on rail 3f out: one pce* **25/1**

9 1 1/4 **Quality Special (BRZ)**[15] [351] 4-8-9 100 .... MAlmeida 4 61
(C Morgado, Brazil) *mid-div: nvr a threat* **16/1**

10 4 3/4 **Kalaforte (SAF)**[15] [351] 4-8-9 90 .... (b) TedDurcan 3 52
(H J Brown, South Africa) *led main gp: gng wl 3f out: nt qckn* **25/1**

1m 52.17s **Going Correction** +0.725s/f (Yiel) 10 Ran SP% **125.1**
Speed ratings: 113,111,107,102,102 100,98,94,93,89

Owner Team Valor **Bred** Mr & Mrs H Winterbach **Trained** South Africa

FOCUS
This fillies' and mares' Listed race lacked strength in depth but, in giving 5lb and a length-and-a-quarter beating to the smart Satwa Queen, Irridescence produced a high-class performance, and the pair finished upwards of five and a half lengths clear of the remainder.

NOTEBOOK
Irridescence(SAF) ◆, a high-class Grade One winner in her native South Africa, was said to be as fit as her trainer could get her without a run, and she produced a fine effort to give upwards of 5lb away all round. It remains to be seen how much improvement there is to come, and things will be tougher against the colts in the Dubai Duty Free Stakes, her next intended target, but this was a fine effort to give 5lb and a beating to Satwa Queen and she must be taken seriously.
Satwa Queen(FR), runner-up to subsequent Listed winner Clinet off a mark of 109 in a seven and a half-furlong handicap on her debut in Dubai, would have been suited by both the step up in trip and easier ground, but ran into a high-class rival. She may have been even closer had her rider got after her sooner, but she still finished clear of the remainder and emerges with plenty of credit. (op 10/11)
Brindisi picked up some more black type, but she is basically not as good as the front two. (op 7/1)
Shersha(IRE) was beaten a long way. (op 12/1)

511a E-COMPANY TROPHY (H'CAP) (TURF) 7f 110y(D)
5:55 (5:55) (90-105,105) 3-Y-0+ **£41,569** (£12,790; £6,395; £3,197)

RPR

1 **Stetchworth Prince**[15] [353] 4-9-0 98 .... LDettori 6 104
(Saeed Bin Suroor) *mid-div: v wd 3f out: rdn to cl 1 1/2f out: r.o wl nr rail: led 50yds out* **13/2**[3]

2 nk **Proudance (GER)**[14] [369] 4-9-6 105 .... ASuborics 1 109
(R Suerland, Germany) *racd in 3rd: gng wl 3f out: led 2f out: hdd: r.o wl: jst failed* **6/1**[2]

3 2 1/2 **Millbag (IRE)**[29] [201] 5-8-11 96 .... (v[1]) JMurtagh 12 94
(D Selvaratnam, UAE) *mid-div wd: rdn to chal 2f out: ev ch: r.o wl* **20/1**

4 3/4 **Blue On Blues (ARG)**[8] [435] 5-9-4 102 .... (t) RyanMoore 4 99
(S Seemar, UAE) *mid-div: trckd ldrs 2 1/2f out: rdn 2nd 1f out: one pce* **7/2**[1]

5 1 3/4 **Leicester Square (IRE)**[36] [151] 5-9-0 98 .... TPO'Shea 8 91
(E Charpy, UAE) *hld up last: sme late prog: nrst fin* **20/1**

6 2 1/4 **Bailador (IRE)**[14] [370] 6-8-10 95 .... RichardMullen 9 81
(A Laird, UAE) *s.i.s: gng wl in rr 3f out: n.m.r 2 1/2f out: one pce* **25/1**

7 hd **Millennium Force**[15] [357] 8-8-10 95 .... TedDurcan 10 80
(M R Channon) *settled in rr: rdn 3f out: one pce: n.d* **7/2**[1]

8 1 1/4 **Egyptian (USA)**[8] [434] 7-8-10 95 .... SPasquier 7 77
(R Bouresly, Kuwait) *trckd ldrs: rdn to dispute 2f out: hdd 1 1/2f out: one pce* **40/1**

9 4 1/4 **Ned Kelly (SAF)**[15] [355] 5-8-10 95 .... (b) JBekker 2 67
(D Maroun, South Africa) *hld up in rr: rdn 3f out: nt qckn* **17/2**

10 2 **Crimson Sun (USA)**[15] [357] 4-9-3 101 .... (t) KerrinMcEvoy 5 69
(I Mohammed, UAE) *led: rdn 4f out: hdd 2 1/2f out* **12/1**

11 9 1/2 **Ihla Grande (USA)**[8] [435] 5-8-12 97 .... PJSmullen 11 40
(E Charpy, UAE) *prom early: wd and t.k.h: rdn 3f out: wknd 2f out: virtually p.u* **33/1**

12 5 1/4 **Jalamid (IRE)**[22] [282] 4-9-1 99 .... (t) RHills 3 30
(J H M Gosden) *mid-div on rail: rdn 3f out: wknd: virtually p.u* **6/1**[2]

1m 33.52s **Going Correction** +0.725s/f (Yiel) 12 Ran SP% **123.3**
Speed ratings: 113,112,110,109,107 105,105,104,99,97 88,83

Owner Godolphin **Bred** Highclere Stud Ltd **Trained** Newmarket, Suffolk

FOCUS
A good quality handicap.

NOTEBOOK
Stetchworth Prince, returned to turf off the lowest mark he has ever raced off, just proved good enough. Things fell right for him in that he got one continuous run when switched towards the near-side rail in the straight, and things will be tougher in future.
Proudance(GER) stepped up on the form he showed on his debut in Dubai and was just held. On this evidence, there could be a similar race in him.
Millbag(IRE), with a visor fitted for the first time, ran better than of late but could not quite go with the front two.
Blue On Blues(ARG) has been running well out here and gives the form a solid look.
Millennium Force, 2lb higher, failed to build on the promise he showed when third in a similar event over course and distance on his previous start.
Jalamid(IRE), below form on his debut in Dubai, ran even worse this time and something is clearly not quite right.

512a ETISALAT GSM CUP (H'CAP) (TURF) 1m 4f (T)
6:25 (6:25) (95-110,110) 3-Y-0+ **£45,348** (£13,953; £6,976; £3,488)

RPR

1 **Jersey Bounce (IRE)**[15] [356] 5-8-5 95 .... RyanMoore 8 104
(H J Brown, South Africa) *trckd ldrs wd: led 3 1/2f out: wd ent st: r.o wl* **20/1**

2 4 **One Little David (GER)**[29] [205] 6-8-7 97 .... ASuborics 9 100
(P Vovcenko, Germany) *settled in rr: wd: prog to trck wnr 2 1/2f out: r.o wl: no ch w wnr* **25/1**

3 1 3/4 **Grand Ekinoks (TUR)**[29] [205] 8-9-4 108 .... (b) HKaratas 10 108
(C Kurt, Turkey) *hld up last: prog gng wl 4f out: taken far rail 3f out: r.o wl* **9/2**[2]

4 hd **Excalibur (IRE)**[14] [371] 6-9-6 110 .... (t) WCMarwing 6 110
(M F De Kock, South Africa) *trckd ldrs early: mid-div: rdn to chal 3f out: kpt on one pce* **7/2**[1]

5 2 3/4 **Land 'n Stars**[14] [371] 6-8-12 102 .... JohnEgan 4 98
(Jamie Poulton) *settled in rr: sn rdn: bk on bit: v wd ent st: nrst fin* **5/1**[3]

6 2 3/4 **Crosspeace (IRE)**[111] [6255] 4-9-3 109 .... KDarley 1 102
(M Johnston) *mid-div on rail: trckd ldr 3f out: rdn: nt qckn* **11/2**

7 3 1/4 **Remaadd (USA)**[8] [437] 5-8-10 100 .... (e[1]) JMurtagh 7 87
(D Selvaratnam, UAE) *mid-div: prog to trck ldrs 3f out and ev ch: one pce* **15/2**

8 14 **Kerashan (IRE)**[134] [5848] 4-8-7 99 .... KerrinMcEvoy 5 66
(I Mohammed, UAE) *settled in rr: rdn 4f out: wknd* **10/1**

9 11 **Velodrome (BRZ)**[8] [437] 7-8-10 100 .... (t) MAlmeida 2 49
(E Charpy, UAE) *rdn to ld v early: trckd ldrs on rail: rdn 4f out: wknd* **25/1**

10 19 **Mutasallil (USA)**[14] [371] 6-8-10 100 .... (t) RHills 3 21
(Doug Watson, UAE) *s.i.s: rdn to ld after 1f: hdd 3 1/2f out: wknd* **12/1**

11 6 **Book Of Kings (USA)**[14] [370] 5-9-1 105 .... (v) TedDurcan 11 17
(A Laird, UAE) *mid-div early: n.d: t.o* **25/1**

12 4 1/4 **Key Of Destiny (SAF)**[14] [369] 8-9-4 108 .... (t) KShea 12 14
(M F De Kock, South Africa) *settled in rr: nvr involved* **14/1**

2m 36.06s **Going Correction** +0.725s/f (Yiel)
WFA 4 from 5yo+ 3lb 12 Ran SP% **124.0**
Speed ratings: 109,106,105,105,103 101,99,89,82,69 65,63

Owner The Bayern Syndicate **Bred** Bsi N V **Trained** South Africa

FOCUS
A high-class handicap, although few of these were seen at their best on the easy ground. Jersey Bounce relished conditions and ran out an emphatic winner.

NOTEBOOK
Jersey Bounce(IRE), fourth in a good ten-furlong handicap on his previous start, improved for both the step up in trip and switch to easy ground, and ran out a pretty impressive winner. He is clearly one to have on your side when faced with these types of conditions.
One Little David(GER) would have been well suited by the easy ground and stepped up on the form he showed on his debut in Dubai.
Grand Ekinoks(TUR) confirmed the promise he showed when third on his debut in Dubai, but just lacked a change of pace on the easy ground.
Excalibur(IRE) reversed recent course and distance placings with Land 'n Stars, but was still not quite at his best.
Land 'n Stars should not really have minded the ground too much, but he was unable to defy a 3lb higher mark than when winning over course and distance on his previous start.
Crosspeace(IRE), successful in a mile and a half Listed race on heavy ground at Doncaster when last seen 111 days previously, was below form on his debut in Dubai.

513a ETISALAT CUP (H'CAP) (TURF) 1m 2f (T)
6:55 (6:55) (90-105,105) 4-Y-0+ **£41,569** (£12,790; £6,395; £3,197)

RPR

1 **Anani (USA)**[8] [438] 6-8-7 91 .... RichardMullen 8 94
(A Laird, UAE) *hld up last: prog to trck ldrs 2f out wd: swtchd ins fnl f out: led 100yds out* **8/1**

2 1 1/4 **Realism (FR)**[8] [437] 6-8-10 95 .... LDettori 12 95
(R A Fahey) *racd v wd: led: chal 2f out: hdd 1f out: kpt on wl* **5/1**[2]

3 1 1/4 **Ashkal Way (IRE)**[146] [5607] 4-9-1 99 .... KerrinMcEvoy 4 99
(I Mohammed, UAE) *settled in rr: gng wl 4f out: swtchd ins 3f out: rdn 2f out: ev ch 1f out* **6/1**[3]

4 1 1/4 **Aleutian**[15] [353] 6-8-8 93 .... WSupple 10 88
(Doug Watson, UAE) *mid-div: prog to trck ldrs 3f out: rdn 2f out: kpt on wl* **25/1**

5 nk **Morshdi**[8] [438] 8-9-0 98 .... JMurtagh 1 94
(D Selvaratnam, UAE) *settled in rr: prog to mid-div 4f out: rdn 3f out: kpt on: n.d: nrst fin* **14/1**

6 1 1/4 **Desert Anger**[29] [207] 5-8-8 93 .... (bt) RyanMoore 5 85
(S Seemar, UAE) *mid-div wd: rdn 3f out: n.d: nrst fin* **12/1**

7 nk **Alpacco (IRE)**[15] [354] 4-9-2 100 .... AStarke 6 94
(Mario Hofer, Germany) *trckd ldrs: chal 2 1/2f out: ev ch 2f out: wknd* **3/1**[1]

8 2 **Bianconi (SAF)**[15] [356] 7-9-4 102 .... (bt) TedDurcan 7 91
(A Laird, UAE) *trckd ldrs wd: chal 3f out: sn wknd* **5/1**[2]

9 1 3/4 **Big Easy (NZ)**[14] [369] 5-8-12 97 .... (b) PJSmullen 2 82
(L Laxon, Singapore) *mid-div: dropped in rr 3f out: rdn: nvr a factor* **22/1**

10 8 1/4 **John Falstaff (BRZ)**[36] [149] 5-8-6 90 .... ECruz 61
(C Morgado, Brazil) *prom rail for 4f: rdn 3f out: n.d after* **25/1**

11 shd **Excellento (USA)**[8] [438] 6-8-8 93 .... (b) TPO'Shea 3 63
(E Charpy, UAE) *hld up in rr: prog to trck ldrs 2f out: no qckn* **25/1**

12 18 **Thignon Boy (BRZ)**[364] [497] 6-9-6 105 .... MAlmeida 9 43
(C Morgado, Brazil) *mid-div on rail: n.m.r 3f out: wknd qckly* **12/1**

2m 8.16s **Going Correction** +0.725s/f (Yiel)
WFA 4 from 5yo+ 1lb 12 Ran SP% **121.7**
Speed ratings: 111,110,109,108,107 106,106,104,103,96 96,82

Owner Mohammed Jaber **Bred** Flaxman Holdings Ltd **Trained** United Arab Emirates

FOCUS
A good handicap.

NOTEBOOK
Anani(USA), unlucky on his return from a break over a mile here last time, was well suited by this step up in trip and gained compensation with a clear-cut success. This was his first success since September 2003, and should have provided a welcome confidence boost.
Realism(FR) has taken time to find his form at this year's Carnival, but he is running well now and took a creditable second.
Ashkal Way(IRE), below form when only mid-division in the Cambridgeshire on his final start for Brian Ellison 146 days previously, made a pleasing debut for new connections. It will be disappointing if he does not go on from this.
Aleutian, given another chance on turf, ran well enough.
Alpacco(IRE) should not have minded the ground, but he was unable to confirm the promise he showed when second on his debut in Dubai and was disappointig.

^{479}LINGFIELD (L-H)

Saturday, February 25

OFFICIAL GOING: Standard

Wind: Strong, half-against

514 PLAY £1/4M SPOT THE BALL ON 0800 500 000 H'CAP (DIV I) 7f (P)

1:30 (1:32) (Class 6) (0-60,66) 4-Y-O+ **£2,047** (£604; £302) **Stalls** Low

Form				RPR
2-31	1		**White Bear (FR)**^{17} [339] 4-9-4 **60**....(b) RobertWinston 8 (C R Dore) *a in tch: wnt 2nd over 1f out: rdn and styd on to ld nr fin* **5/1**^{1}	68
060	2	*shd*	**Hand Chime**^{24} [268] 9-8-11 **58**.... JamesDoyle$^{(5)}$ 12 (Ernst Oertel) *a.p: led wl over 1f out: rdn and hdd cl home* **12/1**	66
-215	3	*3 1/2*	**Trouble Maker**^{17} [339] 5-8-8 **53**.... NeilChalmers$^{(3)}$ 13 (A M Balding) *bhd tl hdwy 1/2-way: styd on ins fnl f: no ch w first 2* **5/1**^{1}	56+
-000	4	*1 1/2*	**Double M**^{3} [486] 9-8-7 **52**....(v) RichardThomas$^{(3)}$ 9 (Mrs L Richards) *hld up in rr: hdwy over 1f out: r.o: nvr nrr* **25/1**	47
062	5	*1 1/4*	**Christmas Truce (IRE)**^{5} [458] 7-8-1 **50**.... SophieDoyle$^{(7)}$ 4 (Ms J S Doyle) *s.i.s: in rr: styd on fnl f: nvr nrr* **20/1**	42
0540	6	*1 1/4*	**Miskina**^{8} [446] 5-9-0 **56**.... EddieAhern 6 (W M Brisbourne) *chsd ldrs: rdn over 1f out: one pce fnl f* **14/1**	45
6055	7	*3/4*	**Tregarron**^{5} [461] 5-8-12 **54**....(p) NCallan 2 (P A Blockley) *mid-div: rdn 1/2-way: wkng whn n.m.r ent fnl f* **9/1**	41
-002	8	*2 1/2*	**Sunny Afternoon**^{3} [485] 6-8-11 **53**....(v) SteveDrowne 10 (Miss E C Lavelle) *in front rnk tl wknd over 1f out* **9/1**	34
-022	9	*1/2*	**Bodden Bay**^{12} [407] 4-8-7 **52**.... DanielTudhope$^{(3)}$ 11 (D Carroll) *chsd ldrs: rdn to ld over 2f out: hdd wl over 1f out: wknd ins fnl f* **7/1**^{3}	32
0031	10	*1 1/4*	**Patternmaker (USA)**^{4} [474] 4-9-10 **66** 6ex.... ChrisCatlin 3 (A M Hales) *sn rdn in mid-div: nt clr run fr 1/2-way: wknd appr fnl f* **9/1**	43
2545	11	*2*	**Doctor's Cave**^{14} [383] 4-9-2 **58**....(b) DaneO'Neill 7 (K O Cunningham-Brown) *sn led: rdn and hdd over 2f out: wknd qckly* **13/2**^{2}	30
-000	12	*dist*	**Oeuf A La Neige**^{3} [485] 6-8-13 **55**.... FergusSweeney 1 (G C H Chung) *v.s.a: a bhd: t.o* **50/1**	—

1m 25.17s (-0.72) **Going Correction** -0.025s/f (Stan) 12 Ran SP% **114.1**

Speed ratings (Par 101):103,102,98,97,95 94,93,90,90,88 86,—

CSF £61.68 CT £318.51 TOTE £5.30: £2.20, £3.30, £2.00; EX 78.30.

Owner Page, Ward, Marsh **Bred** J P Villey **Trained** West Pinchbeck, Lincs

■ Stewards' Enquiry : Robert Winston one-day ban: used whip down the shoulder in the forehand position (Mar 8)

FOCUS

A moderate handicap, but run at a fair gallop. The first two came clear, and the form looks solid enough..

515 NO 5P RULE 4S AT BETDIRECT MAIDEN STKS 1m 4f (P)

2:00 (2:01) (Class 5) 3-Y-O **£3,886** (£1,156; £577; £288) **Stalls** Low

Form				RPR
63	1		**Permanent Way (IRE)**^{17} [337] 3-9-0.... MichaelTebbutt 4 (B J Meehan) *trckd ldrs and a gng wl: wnt over 3f out: led over 2f out: eased ins fnl f* **5/2**^{1}	81+
04-5	2	*7*	**Meadow Mischief (FR)**^{7} [453] 3-9-0 67....(b^{1}) EddieAhern 6 (E A L Dunlop) *hld up: in tch early: wl bhd 3f out: styd on strly 1f out to go 2nd ins fnl f: no ch w wnr* **9/2**	68
	3	*1 3/4*	**City Well** 3-9-0.... JoeFanning 3 (M Johnston) *bhd: rdn 7f out: mde late hdwy past btn horses* **11/4**^{2}	65
24	4	*3 1/2*	**Glentaisie (USA)**^{12} [403] 3-8-10 ow1.... NCallan 7 (J Noseda) *s.i.s: but led after 1f: hdd over 2f out: wknd ent fnl f* **7/2**^{3}	56
040-	5	*4*	**Beauchamp United**^{103} [6342] 3-8-11 65....(b^{1}) AdamKirby$^{(3)}$ 5 (G A Butler) *towards rr: rdn over 6f out: nvr on terms* **25/1**	54
06-3	6	*1/2*	**Coda Agency**^{10} [422] 3-9-0 58.... TQuinn 8 (D W P Arbuthnot) *trckd ldr to over 3f out: wknd qckly over 1f out* **12/1**	53
06-0	7	*3/4*	**Pocket Too**^{49} [61] 3-9-0 62.... J-PGuillambert 1 (Jean-Rene Auvray) *led for 1f: lost 2nd over 3f out: sn bhd* **20/1**	52
5	8	*shd*	**Asarabacca (FR)**^{17} [337] 3-8-9.... SteveDrowne 2 (E A L Dunlop) *hld up in tch: rdn and lost tch 3f out* **14/1**	47

2m 34.92s (0.53) **Going Correction** -0.025s/f (Stan) 8 Ran SP% **118.6**

Speed ratings (Par 97):97,92,91,88,86 85,85,85

CSF £14.88 TOTE £3.60: £1.50, £1.90, £1.40; EX 22.80.

Owner Dr T A Ryan **Bred** Dr T A Ryan **Trained** Manton, Wilts

FOCUS

A modest maiden, run at a solid pace. Permanent Way was in a different league, but it is debatable if he beat much.

City Well Official explanation: jockey said colt was denied a clear run

Coda Agency Official explanation: jockey said gelding ran flat

Asarabacca(FR) Official explanation: jockey said filly hung left

516 BETDIRECT FREEPHONE 0800 211 222 H'CAP 7f (P)

2:35 (2:36) (Class 2) (0-100,97) 4-Y-O+ **£12,464** (£3,732; £1,866; £934; £466; £234) **Stalls** Low

Form				RPR
100-	1		**Something (IRE)**^{133} [5900] 4-9-0 **90**.... IanMongan 4 (T G Mills) *racked keen early: trckd ldrs: wnt 2nd over 3f out: led appr fnl f: drvn clr* **9/4**^{1}	103+
1650	2	*3 1/2*	**Moayed**^{11} [413] 7-9-2 **97**....(bt) JamesDoyle$^{(5)}$ 8 (N P Littmoden) *stdd s: wl in rr: rdn and r.o fr over 1f out: wnt 2nd post* **10/1**	102
2133	3	*shd*	**Cummiskey (IRE)**^{11} [413] 4-9-3 **93**.... JamieSpencer 5 (J A Osborne) *mid-div: hdwy 2f out: r.o to dispute 2nd wl ins fnl f* **9/2**^{3}	97
24-2	4	*1/2*	**San Antonio**^{27} [238] 6-8-10 **89**....(b) EdwardCreighton$^{(3)}$ 2 (Mrs P Sly) *led: set str pce: rdn and hdd appr fnl f: no ex nr fin* **7/2**^{2}	92
3545	5	*3*	**Katiypour (IRE)**^{17} [340] 9-8-6 **85**.... RichardThomas$^{(3)}$ 3 (Miss B Sanders) *chsd ldrs tl rdn and wknd appr fnl f* **9/1**	81
0-50	6	*1*	**Lygeton Lad**^{14} [377] 8-9-2 **92**....(t) SteveDrowne 7 (Miss Gay Kelleway) *trckd ldr to over 3f out: sn wknd* **10/1**	85
040-	7	*nk*	**Uhoomagoo**^{121} [6125] 8-8-13 **89**....(b) NCallan 6 (K A Ryan) *hld up in rr: a bhd* **10/1**	81
004-	8	*1 3/4*	**Diktatorial**^{126} [6017] 4-9-5 **95**.... EddieAhern 1 (G A Butler) *a bhd: lost tch 3f out* **14/1**	83

1m 23.71s (-2.18) **Going Correction** -0.025s/f (Stan) 8 Ran SP% **115.1**

Speed ratings (Par 109):111,107,106,106,102 101,101,99

CSF £26.17 CT £95.25 TOTE £3.20: £1.40, £3.20, £1.70; EX 31.90.

Owner John Humphreys **Bred** Newlands House Stud **Trained** Headley, Surrey

FOCUS

San Antonio effectively set this up for the gambled-on Something, who was impressive. The second and third give the form a solid look.

NOTEBOOK

Something(IRE) ◆, who ran in Group races after last year's Newmarket maiden win, was very well backed on his return from a 133-day break and made an impressive handicap debut. Handy from the off, he could be named the winner turning for home, and was value for further. The Handicapper will no doubt have his say now, but he is lightly raced and there is better to come. (op 11-4)

Moayed, despite stepping back up another furlong, was again staying on all too late in the day and had no chance with the winner. He is capable of winning from this mark, and gives the form a solid look, but he has become very hard to predict of late. (op 8-1)

Cummiskey(IRE) ran his race in defeat and is another good yardstick for this form. He remains in decent form, but does look held by the Handicapper now. Official explanation: jockey said gelding was hampered at start (op 5-1 tchd 11-2)

San Antonio ultimately set the race up for the winner and was well held at the finish. He really deserves a change of fortune, and could be more effective from the front back over six furlongs, but he does look high enough in the weights.

Diktatorial, making his debut for new connections, posted a tame effort and was beaten from halfway.

517 BETDIRECT.CO.UK H'CAP 5f (P)

3:05 (3:05) (Class 4) (0-85,90) 4-Y-O+ **£6,477** (£1,927; £963; £481) **Stalls** High

Form				RPR
0052	1		**Qadar (IRE)**^{7} [450] 4-9-9 **90**.... NCallan 7 (N P Littmoden) *slowly away: hdwy on ins 2f out: drvn to ld fnl 100yds* **7/2**^{2}	96
0-50	2	*3/4*	**Zarzu**^{21} [295] 7-9-3 **84**.... RobertWinston 8 (C R Dore) *s.i.s: held up: hdwy whn swtchd rt ent fnl f: r.o to go 2nd nr fin* **14/1**	87
0-60	3	*shd*	**Kempsey**^{3} [485] 4-8-4 **74** oh11 ow3....(v) NeilChalmers$^{(3)}$ 4 (J J Bridger) *a.p: ev ch ent fnl f: kpt on ins* **20/1**	77?
6-32	4	*hd*	**Wicked Uncle**^{38} [136] 7-8-4 **71** oh1....(v) ChrisCatlin 2 (S Gollings) *hld up: rdn over 1f out: r.o wl fnl f* **8/1**	73
0-24	5	*1 1/2*	**Nepro (IRE)**^{2} [489] 4-8-1 **71** oh1....(t) EdwardCreighton$^{(3)}$ 3 (E J Creighton) *trckd ldr: rdn to ld appr fnl f: fdd fnl 100yds* **13/2**^{3}	68
546-	6	*hd*	**Intriguing Glimpse**^{128} [5999] 5-8-13 **85**.... JamesDoyle$^{(5)}$ 1 (Miss B Sanders) *mid-div: in tch: one pce ins fnl f* **15/2**	81
500-	7	*1 1/2*	**Silver Dane (IRE)**^{138} [5803] 4-8-0 **74** oh16 ow3...(v) KirstyMilczarek$^{(7)}$ 10 (Mrs C A Dunnett) *racd wd: in rr: nvr nr to chal* **66/1**	64
1062	8	*1/2*	**Law Maker**^{8} [441] 6-8-8 **82**....(v) MichaelJStainton$^{(7)}$ 9 (A Bailey) *racd wd: in tch tl rdn and wknd appr fnl f* **16/1**	71
-311	9	*1 3/4*	**Saviours Spirit**^{14} [376] 5-8-13 **80**.... JoeFanning 6 (T G Mills) *cl up tl rdn 2f out: sn wknd* **7/4**^{1}	62
56-0	10	*1/2*	**Tartatartufata**^{55} [6] 4-8-7 **77**....(v) PatrickMathers$^{(3)}$ 5 (D Shaw) *led tl rdn and hdd appr fnl f: wknd qckly* **33/1**	58

59.93 secs (0.15) **Going Correction** -0.025s/f (Stan) 10 Ran SP% **116.5**

Speed ratings (Par 105):97,95,95,95,92 92,90,89,86,85

CSF £50.14 CT £859.75 TOTE £5.00: £1.90, £3.00, £7.30; EX 61.50.

Owner Nigel Shields **Bred** Martin Francis **Trained** Newmarket, Suffolk

FOCUS

The pace was strong, but the form is not. It is clearly held down by the third and seventh.

518 BETDIRECT.CO.UK WINTER DERBY TRIAL CONDITIONS STKS 1m 2f (P)

3:40 (3:40) (Class 2) 4-Y-O+ **£15,580** (£4,665; £2,332; £1,167; £582; £292) **Stalls** Low

Form				RPR
44-6	1		**Grand Passion (IRE)**^{29} [213] 6-8-13 105.... SteveDrowne 4 (G Wragg) *hld up: hdwy 2f out: rdn to ld ins fnl f: drvn out* **11/2**	105
6-22	2	*1/2*	**Red Spell (IRE)**^{14} [377] 5-8-13 101.... RobertWinston 3 (R Hannon) *hld up: wl bhd 3f out: rdn and hdwy appoaching fnl f: r.o to go 2nd nr fin* **4/1**^{2}	104
240-	3	*3/4*	**Counsel's Opinion (IRE)**^{147} [5607] 9-9-4 101.... GeorgeBaker 6 (C F Wall) *slowly away: hdwy on outside over 2f out: wnt 2nd on ins fnl f tl cl home* **11/1**	108
/00-	4	*1/2*	**African Dream**^{318} [998] 5-8-13 108.... JamieSpencer 7 (J Noseda) *led for 2f: styd prom: rdn and nt qckn ins fnl f* **9/1**	102
001-	5	*1/2*	**Kew Green (USA)**^{98} [6378] 8-9-6 105.... DaneO'Neill 5 (P R Webber) *a.p: led over 1f out: led over 1f out: rdn and hdd ins: fade fnl 100yds* **11/4**^{1}	108
200-	6	*hd*	**Crow Wood**^{20} [4939] 7-8-13 98.... GrahamGibbons 8 (J J Quinn) *sn trckd ldr: led after 2f: rdn and hdd over 1f out: sn btn* **5/1**^{3}	100
332-	7	*nk*	**Compton Bolter (IRE)**^{49} [6592] 9-9-13 108.... EddieAhern 1 (G A Butler) *in tch: rdn and wknd wl over 1f out* **16/1**	114
-133	8	*5*	**Polygonal (FR)**^{21} [296] 6-8-13 92.... DarrylHolland 2 (Ernst Oertel) *trckd ldrs tl rdn and wknd 2f out* **10/1**	90

2m 4.46s (-3.33) **Going Correction** -0.025s/f (Stan) 8 Ran SP% **112.0**

Speed ratings (Par 109):112,111,111,110,110 110,109,105

CSF £26.56 TOTE £7.40: £2.70, £1.60, £3.50; EX 19.90.

Owner H H Morriss **Bred** And Mrs H H Morriss **Trained** Newmarket, Suffolk

FOCUS

A fair renewal of this event, run at a sound pace, and the form appears fairly straightforward. It is unlikely to prove all that informative for the Winter Derby, however, as the winner has twice been well beaten in that event.

NOTEBOOK

Grand Passion(IRE), a cosy winner of the corresponding race in 2004, showed the clear benefit of his recent seasonal comeback at Wolverhampton and got back to winning ways in ready fashion. He loves this venue, had the race run to suit, and appeared to have a little up his sleeve on passing the finish line. However, while he is fully entitled to have another crack in the Winter Derby next month, he has finished down the field in the last two runnings and needs to improve again to get involved. (tchd 5-1)

Red Spell(IRE) did all of his best work at the finish after being set plenty to do, but again managed to find one too good. He is capable of winning over this trip, and deserves a change of fortune, but his very best form is still at a mile and shorter. (op 9-2)

Counsel's Opinion(IRE) ◆, returning from a 147-day break, shaped encouragingly and should improve a deal for the outing. He enjoyed this sound surface. (op 12-1)

African Dream, making his debut for a new yard after a 318-day layoff, just flattened out in the final furlong after holding every chance. He should come on a deal for this outing and can better this in due course. (tchd 10-1)

Kew Green(USA), well backed ahead of this seasonal return, had every chance yet failed to sustain his effort when it really mattered. He is another who is entitled to improve for the outing. (tchd 3-1)

Crow Wood, reverting to the Flat after a career-best over hurdles at Musselburgh 20 days previously, failed to find all that much for pressure yet was not disgraced at the weights. He will now most likely go straight to Cheltenham for the Supreme Novices' Hurdle, with an each-way chance in that event. (op 4-1)

Polygonal(FR) Official explanation: jockey said gelding ran flat

519 BETLIVE IN-RUNNING AT BETDIRECT.CO.UK FILLIES' H'CAP 6f (P)
4:10 (4:11) (Class 5) (0-70,70) 4-Y-0+ £3,238 (£963; £481; £240) Stalls Low

Form				RPR
0320	1		**Sweetest Revenge (IRE)**[3] 486 5-8-8 60 HayleyTurner 11 (M D I Usher) *mid-div: hdwy and rdn over 1f out: r.o to ld ins fnl f* 10/1	70
5-00	2	3/4	**Ivory Lace**[18] 327 5-8-5 62 JamesDoyle(5) 3 (S Woodman) *in rr: rdn and str hdwy fnl f to go 2nd cl home* 16/1	70
6452	3	nk	**Ashes (IRE)**[3] 486 4-8-8 60 FrancisNorton 8 (K R Burke) *trckd ldrs: rdn and swtchd rt 1f out: wnt 2nd ins fnl f tl cl home* 5/1[2]	67
-240	4	1/2	**Shifty Night (IRE)**[2] 489 5-8-1 60 (v) KirstyMilczarek(7) 9 (Mrs C A Dunnett) *racd wd: bhd 1/2-way: hdwy whn edgd lft appr fnl f: r.o* 10/1	66
3231	5	nk	**Tiviski (IRE)**[3] 486 4-8-12 64 7ex NCallan 1 (G G Margarson) *mid-divison: rdn and r.o fnl f* 6/1[3]	69
2140	6	1/2	**Sahara Silk (IRE)**[9] 424 5-8-10 65 (v) PatrickMathers(3) 5 (D Shaw) *mid-div: rdn 1/2-way: effrt fnl f: nvr nr to chal* 25/1	68
6160	7	1	**Kallista's Pride**[31] 192 6-8-10 62 JamieSpencer 6 (J R Best) *slowly away: bhd tl rdn over 2f out: n.m.r whn hdwy on ins appr fnl f: no ch after* 9/2[1]	65+
-613	8	hd	**Segoria (IRE)**[3] 485 4-8-8 60 DaneO'Neill 7 (A M Hales) *hld up in rr: nvr on terms* 5/1[2]	60
0-05	9	3/4	**Depressed**[14] 376 4-9-3 69 (p) DarryllHolland 10 (Ernst Oertel) *led tl rdn: edgd lft and hdd ins fnl f: wknd qckly* 14/1	66
256-	10	nk	**Moon Bird**[220] 3639 4-8-12 64 ChrisCatlin 2 (C A Cyzer) *trckd ldr early: rdn over 2f out: wknd over 1f out* 16/1	60
4504	11	3	**Sweet Pickle**[4] 474 5-8-4 56 oh1 JoeFanning 4 (J R Boyle) *nvr on terms after hmpd over 4f out* 8/1	43+

1m 12.23s (-0.58) **Going Correction** -0.025s/f (Stan) 11 Ran SP% **117.4**
Speed ratings (Par 100):102,101,100,99,99 98,97,97,96,95 91
CSF £158.22 CT £916.53 TOTE £12.40: £2.30, £6.40, £2.00; EX 251.00.
Owner The Ridgeway Partnership **Bred** Joza Partnership **Trained** Upper Lambourn, Berks

FOCUS
A modest fillies' handicap, run at a sound pace. Very average form.

520 PLAY £1/4M SPOT THE BALL ON 0800 500 000 H'CAP (DIV II) 7f (P)
4:45 (4:46) (Class 6) (0-60,63) 4-Y-0+ £2,047 (£604; £302) Stalls Low

Form				RPR
0-02	1		**Riquewihr**[12] 402 6-8-8 50 (p) RobertWinston 11 (J S Wainwright) *hld up in rr: str hdwy to ld over 1f out: r.o to ld ins fnl f: won gng away* 8/1[3]	58+
0-26	2	1 1/2	**Grezie**[8] 440 4-8-12 54 JoeFanning 12 (T D McCarthy) *led tl rdn and hdd ins fnl f: nt pce of wnr* 10/1	58
1-00	3	2	**Sonntag Blue (IRE)**[15] 363 4-8-6 53 (v[1]) JamesDoyle(5) 6 (Miss J Feilden) *trckd ldrs: rdn and nt qckn ins fnl f* 11/2[2]	52
0030	4	nk	**Physical (IRE)**[10] 416 4-9-0 56 (p) IanMongan 4 (Mrs A J Perrett) *trckd ldrs: rdn and nt qckn ins fnl f* 11/1	54
0300	5	hd	**Border Artist**[4] 474 7-8-11 53 TQuinn 9 (B G Powell) *racd wd in mid-div: r.o one pce fnl fnl f* 14/1	51
/40-	6	3/4	**Elvina Hills (IRE)**[259] 2478 4-9-2 58 GeorgeBaker 2 (P Mitchell) *s.i.s and wl in rr: mde sme late prog* 33/1	54
4-00	7	nk	**Contended (IRE)**[18] 324 4-8-13 55 HayleyTurner 14 (Mrs L C Jewell) *in rr tl r.o fnl f: nvr nrr* 16/1	50
0066	8	3/4	**Jennverse**[3] 486 4-8-10 52 FergusSweeney 1 (D K Ivory) *hld up in mid-div: rdn 2f out: nvr nr to chal* 10/1	45
0-46	9	hd	**Secam (POL)**[10] 416 7-8-13 55 (b) SamHitchcott 13 (Mrs P Townsley) *s.i.s: hdwy over 4f out to chsd ldrs: edgd lft and wknd over 1f out* 8/1[3]	48
132-	10	1/2	**Humility**[80] 6525 5-8-8 50 ChrisCatlin 10 (C A Cyzer) *bhd: rdn over 1f out: nvr on terms* 5/1[1]	42
00-6	11	1 1/2	**Goldhill Prince**[18] 321 4-8-10 52 (p) DarryllHolland 7 (Ernst Oertel) *in tch: rdn and n.m.r over 1f out: sn btn* 16/1	40
4-22	12	1	**Iced Diamond (IRE)**[19] 315 7-9-3 59 JamieSpencer 5 (W M Brisbourne) *prom tl rdn and wknd over 1f out* 5/1[1]	44

1m 25.17s (-0.72) **Going Correction** -0.025s/f (Stan) 12 Ran SP% **118.8**
Speed ratings (Par 101):103,101,99,98,98 97,97,96,96,95 93,92
CSF £85.82 CT £490.14 TOTE £5.80: £2.50, £4.30, £2.50; EX 84.40.
Owner J S Wainwright **Bred** G B Partnership **Trained** Kennythorpe, N Yorks

FOCUS
A moderate handicap, but run at a solid pace. Average form.
Secam(POL) Official explanation: trainer said gelding pulled a muscle
Humility Official explanation: jockey said mare was denied a clear run
Iced Diamond(IRE) Official explanation: jockey said gelding had no more to give

521 PLAY IN MONTE CARLO WITH LITTLEWOODSPOKER.COM H'CAP 1m 5f (P)
5:15 (5:16) (Class 5) (0-75,74) 4-Y-0+ £3,238 (£963; £481; £240) Stalls Low

Form				RPR
01-0	1		**Llamadas**[14] 375 4-9-1 72 J-PGuillambert 10 (C Roberts) *a in tch: hdwy over 1f out: rdn and r.o to ld nr post* 33/1	78
024-	2	shd	**Montosari**[88] 6461 7-8-9 62 JoeFanning 6 (P Mitchell) *tracked ldr: led over 3f out: rdn over 1f out: hdd cl home* 10/1	68
B0-2	3	1 3/4	**Beauchamp Trump**[27] 237 4-8-10 67 (t) FrancisNorton 9 (G A Butler) *hld up in rr: hdwy over 1f out: r.o wl fnl f: nvr nrr* 7/1[3]	70
	4	1 1/4	**Eye Candy (IRE)**[13] 1611 5-9-7 74 NCallan 3 (Mrs Sandra McCarthy, Ire) *chsd ldrs: wnt 2nd over 2f out: rdn and wknd ins fnl f* 14/1	76
-120	5	shd	**Countrywide Luck**[10] 420 5-9-2 74 JamesDoyle(5) 2 (N P Littmoden) *t.k.h: hld up in tch: rdn over 1f out: nt qckn after* 6/1[2]	76
0104	6	1/2	**Stage Manager (IRE)**[4] 478 4-8-13 70 JamieSpencer 1 (M J Wallace) *hld up in rr: hdwy 2f out: one pce fnl f* 11/4[1]	71
6020	7	1 1/4	**Blackmail (USA)**[4] 478 8-8-10 63 (b) FrankieMcDonald 7 (Miss B Sanders) *racd wd towards rr: styd on fnl f: nvr nr to chal* 7/1[3]	62
02-0	8	3/4	**Santando**[7] 454 6-9-3 70 EddieAhern 8 (C E Brittain) *hld up: a towards rr* 6/1[2]	68
10-0	9	3/4	**Malibu (IRE)**[9] 88 5-9-2 69 DaneO'Neill 11 (S Dow) *trckd ldrs: rdn and wknd wl over 1f out* 33/1	66
00-6	10	7	**Summer Charm**[43] 109 4-8-11 68 AlanMunro 12 (W Jarvis) *racd wd: hld up in mid-div: wknd over 1f out* 8/1	55
520-	11	4	**Desert Secrets (IRE)**[21] 3532 4-8-8 65 RobertWinston 5 (J G Portman) *mid-div tl wknd over 2f out* 25/1	47

630-	12	2	**Son Of Greek Myth (USA)**[16] 5553 5-8-13 66 (be) IanMongan 13 (G L Moore) *led tl hdd over 3f out: wknd over 2f out* 50/1	45

2m 48.69s (0.39) **Going Correction** -0.025s/f (Stan)
WFA 4 from 5yo+ 4lb 12 Ran SP% **118.8**
Speed ratings (Par 103):97,96,95,95,95 94,93,93,93,88 86,85
CSF £326.82 CT £2590.37 TOTE £38.50: £6.30, £3.00, £2.50; EX 391.90 Place 6 £161.89, Place 5 £71.21.
Owner K Tyre **Bred** Burton Agnes Stud Co Ltd **Trained** Newport, Newport
■ Stewards' Enquiry : Jamie Spencer five-day ban: improper riding - tried to prevent a rival coming up on his inside (Mar 8,11,14-16)

FOCUS
A modest staying handicap, run at an uneven pace. The form looks fair.
T/Plt: £231.20 to a £1 stake. Pool: £49,392.60. 155.90 winning tickets. T/Qpdt: £50.40 to a £1 stake. Pool: £3,346.00. 49.10 winning tickets. JS

392 CAGNES-SUR-MER
Saturday, February 25

OFFICIAL GOING: Soft

522a PRIX POLICEMAN (LISTED RACE) 1m 2f 165y
2:20 (2:21) 3-Y-0 £16,207 (£6,483; £4,862; £3,241; £1,621)

			RPR
1		**Salsalava (FR)**[13] 392 3-9-2 DBoeuf 8 (P Demercastel, France)	105
2	1/2	**Papillon Rose (IRE)** 3-8-11 GToupel 4 (H-A Pantall, France)	100
3	2 1/2	**Milord Du Bourg (FR)**[191] 3-8-11 FSpanu 6 (J-L Pelletan, France)	95
4	nk	**Toorah Laura La (USA)** 3-8-8 TThulliez 1 (N Clement, France)	92
5	3/4	**Nice Applause (IRE)** 3-8-11 FBlondel 7 (Mme J Laurent-Joye Rossi, France)	93
6	4	**Mister Des Aigles (FR)**[98] 6392 3-8-11 (b) RMarchelli 5 (Mme C Barande-Barbe, France)	86
7	7	**Moi Aussi (USA)**[36] 160 3-8-8 (b) J-BEyquem 3 (Sir Mark Prescott) *prominent, close 3rd half-way, driven straight, one pace from over 1f out*	70

2m 25.2s 7 Ran
PARI-MUTUEL (Including 1 Euro stake): WIN 2.30; PL 1.50, 2.00; DF 4.40.
Owner B Chehboub **Bred** Bouzid & Kamel Chehboub **Trained** France

NOTEBOOK
Moi Aussi(USA) raced close to the pace until being readily outpaced entering the straight.

523a GRAND PRIX DU CONSEIL GENERAL DES ALPES MARITIMES (LISTED RACE) 1m 4f 110y
2:55 (2:56) 4-Y-0+ £25,862 (£10,345; £7,759; £5,172; £2,586)

			RPR
1		**Lord Du Sud (FR)**[76] 6553 5-8-12 IMendizabal 4 (J-C Rouget, France)	114
2	4	**Silver Cross (FR)**[167] 5158 4-8-9 TThulliez 7 (D Prod'Homme, France)	109
3	2 1/2	**Magadino (FR)**[99] 5-8-12 BrigitteRenk 2 (Brigitte Renk, Switzerland)	104
4	3/4	**Milongo (FR)**[11] 4-8-9 SPasquier 3 (Brigitte Renk, Switzerland)	104
5	2 1/2	**Billy The Kid (IRE)**[171] 5056 8-8-12 (b) SMaillot 6 (T Clout, France)	99
6	4	**Pro Ken (FR)**[13] 393 6-8-12 TGillet 1 (Rod Collet, France)	93
7	10	**Ascetic Silver (FR)**[14] 6-8-12 FBlondel 10 (D Prod'Homme, France)	78
8	1 1/2	**Corfu (IRE)**[257] 4-8-6 SRichardot 9 (K Borgel, France)	74
9	8	**Altamirano (GER)**[330] 830 7-8-12 DBoeuf 8 (W Baltromei, Germany)	64
10	7	**Kiswahili**[95] 6416 4-8-6 (b) J-BEyquem 5 (Sir Mark Prescott) *led to approaching straight, soon under pressure and weakened, eased from over 1f out*	52

2m 48.4s
WFA 4 from 5yo+ 3lb 10 Ran
PARI-MUTUEL: WIN 2.30; PL 1.30, 1.30, 1.90; DF 3.40.
Owner Mme B Hermelin **Bred** Alexandre Guerini **Trained** Pau, France

NOTEBOOK
Kiswahili set a good pace to the home turn, but was quickly beaten when headed.

487 SOUTHWELL (L-H)
Sunday, February 26

OFFICIAL GOING: Standard
Wind: Fresh, across Weather: Overcast

524 PLAY LITTLEWOODS POOLS ON 0800 500 000 BANDED STKS 5f (F)
2:30 (2:30) (Class 7) 3-Y-0+ £1,365 (£403; £201) Stalls High

Form				RPR
-431	1		**Hello Roberto**[6] 465 5-9-4 45 (p) AdrianMcCarthy 11 (R A Harris) *a.p: rdn and edgd lft 1f out: r.o to ld post* 8/1	58
4130	2	nk	**Boanerges (IRE)**[13] 397 9-9-1 48 RobertWinston 6 (J M Bradley) *chsd ldrs: rdn to ld 1f out: hdd post* 9/2[2]	54
0444	3	1 3/4	**St Ivian**[2] 502 6-8-11 49 DuranFentiman(5) 9 (Mrs N Macauley) *sn pushed along and prom: rdn over 1f out: styd on* 5/1[3]	49
20-0	4	1/2	**Mystery Pips**[21] 299 6-8-13 46 (v) KimTinkler 1 (N Tinkler) *led 4f: no ex ins fnl f* 25/1	44
00-0	5	1/2	**Sapphire Dream**[23] 288 4-8-5 45 MichaelJStainton(7) 10 (A Bailey) *dwlt: hdwy u.p over 1f out: styd on same pce towards fin* 25/1	41
4400	6	1/2	**Percy Douglas**[6] 465 6-8-5 45 (vt) AnnStokell(7) 7 (Miss A Stokell) *chsd ldrs: rdn and edgd lft over 1f out: no ex ins fnl f* 40/1	40
06-0	7	1 1/4	**Hellbent**[16] 360 7-8-12 47 ow1 DNolan(3) 8 (M Appleby) *hld up: rdn 2f out: no imp* 20/1	38

The Form Book, Raceform Ltd, Compton, RG20 6NL

0-00 **8** hd **Baymist**[21] 299 4-8-9 45 PaulMulrennan(3) 2 34
(M W Easterby) *chsd ldrs: rdn 1/2-way: wknd fnl f* **33/1**
-203 **9** 1 **Davids Mark**[13] 397 6-9-2 49 EddieAhern 13 35
(J R Jenkins) *s.i.s: hdwy u.p 2f out: edgd lft and wknd fnl f* **7/1**
4-00 **10** hd **Dutch Key Card (IRE)**[13] 397 5-9-1 48 (t) RobbieFitzpatrick 4 33
(A W Carroll) *prom to 1/2-way* **4/1**[1]
0000 **11** 2 **Lady Pekan**[6] 465 7-8-12 45 (v) J-PGuillambert 12 23
(P Howling) *mid-div: rdn 1/2-way: sn wknd* **14/1**
00-2 **12** 3 1/2 **Eternally**[21] 299 4-8-12 45 (p) JoeFanning 5 10
(R M H Cowell) *chsd ldrs: rdn whn hmpd over 1f out: sn wknd* **6/1**
05-0 **13** 5 **Boucheen**[48] 70 3-8-3 50 ChrisCatlin 14 —
(Ms Deborah J Evans) *dwlt: outpcd* **40/1**

59.68 secs (-0.62) **Going Correction** -0.175s/f (Stan)
WFA 3 from 4yo+ 14lb **13** Ran SP% **119.7**
Speed ratings (Par 97):97,96,93,92,92 91,89,89,87,87 83,78,70
CSF £40.48 TOTE £7.10: £2.20, £1.90, £2.00; EX 32.60.
Owner Peter A Price **Bred** I B Barker **Trained** Earlswood, Monmouths

FOCUS
A fair banded sprint dominated by in-form horses.

525 LITTLEWOODS POOLS BILLIONS WON BY MILLIONS BANDED STKS 1m 3f (F)
3:00 (3:00) (Class 7) 4-Y-0+ **£1,365** (£403; £201) **Stalls** Low

Form RPR
65-0 **1** **True To Yourself (USA)**[46] 91 5-8-13 40 (v) JoeFanning 2 53
(J G Given) *chsd ldrs: led over 2f out: edgd rt ins fnl f: rdn out* **18/1**
-252 **2** 2 **To Be Fare (IRE)**[14] 390 6-9-3 49 FergalLynch 6 54
(J Pearce) *hld up: rdn 1/2-way: hdwy over 2f out: edgd rt over 1f out: styd on* **3/1**[2]
6-25 **3** 1/2 **College Rebel**[14] 390 5-8-13 45 RobbieFitzpatrick 10 49
(J F Coupland) *hld up: hdwy over 3f out: rdn over 1f out: styd on same pce* **22/1**
3224 **4** 2 **Liquid Lover (IRE)**[14] 390 4-8-11 45 EddieAhern 3 46
(W M Brisbourne) *hld up in tch: rdn over 4f out: styd on* **5/2**[1]
5304 **5** shd **Dextrous**[3] 490 9-8-13 40 (p) MickyFenton 4 46
(P T Midgley) *s.s: hld up: hdwy over 3f out: rdn over 2f out: no ex fnl f* **14/1**
50-0 **6** hd **Kalishka (IRE)**[28] 242 5-8-13 45 TomEaves 12 46
(R Allan) *dwlt: sn prom: rdn over 2f out: no ex fnl f* **33/1**
6-06 **7** 5 **Pearl Fisher (IRE)**[20] 313 5-8-10 45 DanielTudhope(3) 9 38
(D Carroll) *led over 8f: wknd over 1f out* **33/1**
65/6 **8** 1 **Sarenne**[21] 302 5-8-8 45 StephenDonohoe(5) 5 36
(John Berry) *sn pushed along in rr: nvr nrr* **40/1**
2-61 **9** 5 **Bill Bennett (FR)**[21] 302 5-8-7 45 ow1 TJHowell(7) 14 29
(J Jay) *hld up: a bhd* **9/1**[3]
0005 **10** 3/4 **The Plainsman**[21] 301 4-8-11 40 DarrenWilliams 8 27
(P W Hiatt) *chsd ldr tl rdn over 3f out: sn wknd* **40/1**
000- **11** dist **Dishdasha (IRE)**[10] 4107 4-8-11 45 RobertWinston 13 —
(C R Dore) *s.s: hdwy 8f out: rdn and wknd 3f out: eased* **20/1**
6211 **12** 25 **Surdoue**[14] 390 6-9-5 51 J-PGuillambert 1 —
(P Howling) *chsd ldrs: rdn over 4f out: wknd over 3f out: eased* **3/1**[2]

2m 26.66s (-2.24) **Going Correction** -0.35s/f (Stan)
WFA 4 from 5yo+ 2lb **12** Ran SP% **120.4**
Speed ratings (Par 97):94,92,92,90,90 90,86,86,82,81 —,—
CSF £68.00 TOTE £22.40: £4.20, £1.80, £5.70; EX 139.00.
Owner Mike J Beadle **Bred** S D Plummer **Trained** Willoughton, Lincs

FOCUS
A moderate affair and a surprise result with one of the lower-rated horses prevailing. However, the form behind looks sound enough and average for the grade.
The Plainsman Official explanation: jockey said gelding had no more to give
Dishdasha(IRE) Official explanation: jockey said gelding stopped very quickly and had no more to give
Surdoue Official explanation: jockey said gelding hit head on stalls and was never travelling thereafter

526 WIN £2M WITH LITTLEWOODS POOLS BANDED STKS 1m (F)
3:30 (3:30) (Class 7) 4-Y-0+ **£1,706** (£503; £252) **Stalls** Low

Form RPR
1322 **1** **Golden Spectrum (IRE)**[6] 467 7-9-2 50 (p) AdrianMcCarthy 4 58
(R A Harris) *mde all: rdn over 1f out: styd on* **2/1**[1]
-463 **2** nk **High Swainston**[14] 391 5-8-12 46 (b[1]) RobertWinston 9 53
(R Craggs) *chsd wnr: rdn and ev ch fnl 2f: styd on* **7/1**[3]
6-21 **3** 1 **Fulvio (USA)**[13] 398 6-9-4 52 (v) J-PGuillambert 2 57
(P Howling) *chsd ldrs: rdn over 4f out: outpcd 3f out: hung rt over 1f out: styd on ins fnl f* **7/1**[3]
0-56 **4** nk **Zariano**[31] 196 6-9-0 48 PaulFessey 12 52
(T D Barron) *chsd ldrs: outpcd 3f out: nt clr run over 1f out: styd on* **13/2**[2]
-046 **5** 5 **Bold Trump**[16] 358 5-9-0 48 GrahamGibbons 7 41
(Mrs N S Evans) *prom: outpcd 1/2-way: styd on u.p appr fnl f* **33/1**
6226 **6** 1/2 **It Must Be Speech**[6] 468 5-8-11 45 (v) DarrenWilliams 3 37
(S L Keightley) *sn chsng ldrs: rdn over 3f out: sn outpcd* **9/1**
4050 **7** 2 **Ming Vase**[6] 470 4-9-0 48 MickyFenton 10 36
(P T Midgley) *nvr nrr* **50/1**
0451 **8** 1 1/2 **Penel (IRE)**[14] 387 5-8-13 47 (p) LeeEnstone 6 32
(P T Midgley) *prom over 4f* **14/1**
005 **9** 5 **Rythm N Rhyme (IRE)**[20] 314 7-9-2 50 PaulEddery 8 24
(John A Harris) *s.i.s: outpcd* **50/1**
46-1 **10** 1 3/4 **Wings Of Morning (IRE)**[54] 27 5-8-10 47 DanielTudhope(3) 13 17
(D Carroll) *bhd fr 1/2-way* **10/1**
-510 **11** 1 3/4 **Azreme**[14] 391 6-9-1 49 (p) TonyCulhane 5 15
(P Howling) *s.i.s: a in rr* **12/1**
-001 **12** 15 **Winning Venture**[9] 446 9-9-7 55 JoeFanning 11 —
(A W Carroll) *chsd ldrs over 4f* **11/1**
00-0 **13** 28 **Kalush**[10] 423 5-8-11 35 (vt[1]) TomEaves 14 —
(N Tinkler) *hld up in tch: wknd over 3f out* **100/1**

1m 42.6s (-2.00) **Going Correction** -0.35s/f (Stan) **13** Ran SP% **121.3**
Speed ratings (Par 97):96,95,94,94,89 88,86,85,80,78 76,61,33
CSF £15.84 TOTE £2.60: £1.40, £2.20, £2.30; EX 12.90.
Owner Peter A Price **Bred** Orpendale And Global Investments **Trained** Earlswood, Monmouths
■ Stewards' Enquiry : Adrian McCarthy one-day ban: used whip with excessive frequency (Mar 11)

FOCUS
A fair banded contest in which very few got involved from off the pace. The time was 0.56sec faster than the following contest over the same trip and the form looks solid.
Winning Venture Official explanation: jockey said gelding had no more to give

527 LITTLEWOODS POOLS BE LUCKY BANDED STKS 1m (F)
4:00 (4:01) (Class 7) 4-Y-0+ **£1,365** (£403; £201) **Stalls** Low

Form RPR
0334 **1** **Crusoe (IRE)**[9] 440 9-8-11 45 (b) BrianReilly 11 51
(A Sadik) *mid-div: hdwy 3f out: rdn to ld over 1f out: r.o* **12/1**
65-0 **2** 1 3/4 **Tommytyler (IRE)**[14] 386 7-8-8 45 (t) DanielTudhope(3) 12 47
(D Carroll) *s.i.s: hld up: hdwy over 2f out: rdn and ev ch over 1f out: hung rt fnl f: styd on* **16/1**
5221 **3** nk **Pawn In Life (IRE)**[3] 492 8-9-2 45 (v) JoeFanning 3 51
(M J Polglase) *chsd ldrs: rdn 1/2-way: styd on* **2/1**[1]
0-03 **4** nk **Xaloc Bay (IRE)**[14] 387 8-8-11 40 AdrianMcCarthy 10 46
(R A Harris) *chsd ldrs: rdn and ev ch over 1f out: no ex ins fnl f* **14/1**
0-30 **5** 1 1/4 **Starcross Maid**[14] 386 4-8-11 45 MatthewHenry 9 43
(J F Coupland) *hld up: hdwy u.p over 1f out: nvr nrr* **22/1**
00-0 **6** 2 **Bob Baileys**[17] 350 4-8-11 45 EddieAhern 5 39
(P R Chamings) *hld up: hdwy u.p over 1f out: nvr nrr* **20/1**
0-00 **7** 1/2 **Queue Up**[13] 395 4-8-11 45 MickyFenton 6 38
(A G Newcombe) *chsd ldrs: rdn over 3f out: styng on same pce whn hung lft over 1f out* **20/1**
4051 **8** 1 **Kumakawa**[10] 423 8-8-7 48 TolleyDean(7) 4 38
(D K Ivory) *s.i.s: hdwy 1/2-way: lost pl over 3f out: n.d after* **8/1**
-541 **9** nk **Desert Fury**[14] 386 9-9-0 48 (b) LeeEnstone 7 38
(R Bastiman) *s.i.s: hld up: rdn over 2f out: n.d* **11/2**[3]
-630 **10** 3 **Paper Doll**[20] 312 4-8-11 45 (p) TonyCulhane 14 28
(B P J Baugh) *s.i.s: rdn 1/2-way: a in rr* **12/1**
6640 **11** 1/2 **Ballyrush (IRE)**[6] 465 6-8-11 45 GrahamGibbons 13 27
(Miss D A McHale) *w ldrs: led and edgd lft over 3f out: sn clr: rdn: hdd & wknd over 1f out* **28/1**
44 **12** 1 1/2 **Tod Sloan (IRE)**[13] 399 4-8-11 45 RobertWinston 2 24
(J M Bradley) *mid-div: rdn and nt clr run over 3f out: sn wknd* **5/1**[2]
0-00 **13** 1 1/4 **Rock Concert**[14] 390 8-8-6 45 (v) NataliaGemelova(5) 8 21
(I W McInnes) *led: hdd over 6f out: chsd ldr: rdn over 3f out: wknd 2f out: hmpd over 1f out* **50/1**
-630 **14** 1 1/4 **Elms Schoolboy**[6] 468 4-8-11 45 (b) FergalLynch 1 18
(P Howling) *led over 6f out: hdd and hmpd over 3f out: sn wknd* **14/1**

1m 43.16s (-1.44) **Going Correction** -0.35s/f (Stan) **14** Ran SP% **130.4**
Speed ratings (Par 97):93,91,90,90,89 87,86,85,85,82 82,80,79,78
CSF £191.59 TOTE £12.60: £3.10, £6.60, £1.70; EX 292.80.
Owner A Sadik **Bred** John F Tuthill And Mrs A Whitehead **Trained** Wolverley, Worcs

FOCUS
An average standard contest for the grade run 0.56sec slower than the preceding event.
Kumakawa Official explanation: trainer said gelding bled from the nose

528 WIN £2M @ CLASSICVALUEPOOLS.COM TRI-BANDED STKS 7f (F)
4:30 (4:30) (Class 7) 3-Y-O **£1,365** (£403; £201) **Stalls** Low

Form RPR
00-0 **1** **Mid Valley**[41] 120 3-8-12 45 TonyCulhane 3 50
(J R Jenkins) *hld up in tch: rdn over 2f out: styd on u.p to ld wl ins fnl f* **11/2**[2]
0-00 **2** 2 **Midge's Girl (IRE)**[38] 145 3-8-7 40 (v[1]) PaulFessey 7 40
(Mrs A Duffield) *led 5f out: clr 1/2-way: rdn over 1f out: hdd wl ins fnl f* **12/1**
5200 **3** 3 1/2 **Paris Power**[23] 286 3-8-12 45 (b[1]) DerekMcGaffin 6 36
(D Morris) *s.i.s: sn chsng ldrs: rdn over 1f out: no ex* **9/2**[1]
-440 **4** 1 **Genoa Star**[19] 333 3-8-12 45 (b) RobbieFitzpatrick 5 34
(T J Pitt) *dwlt: hdwy u.p over 1f out: nrst fin* **6/1**[3]
004- **5** hd **Augustus Livius (IRE)**[117] 6212 3-8-7 40 RobertWinston 1 28
(W Storey) *s.i.s: sn prom: hmpd and lost pl over 4f out: styd on appr fnl f* **12/1**
00-0 **6** 2 1/2 **Lady Evi**[50] 62 3-8-7 40 ChrisCatlin 2 22
(D K Ivory) *led: hdd 5f out: rdn over 2f out: sn wknd* **16/1**
0000 **7** 1 1/4 **Beginners Luck (IRE)**[13] 403 3-8-5 40 ow1 DanielTudhope(3) 11 20
(D Carroll) *s.i.s: hld up: rdn and hung lft fr over 2f out: nvr trbld ldrs* **50/1**
000- **8** 3/4 **She's Dunnett**[222] 3614 3-8-12 45 AdrianTNicholls 12 22
(Mrs C A Dunnett) *s.i.s: nvr nrr* **14/1**
00-0 **9** 1 **Night Reveller (IRE)**[54] 29 3-8-2 35 AdrianMcCarthy 4 10
(M C Chapman) *chsd ldrs: rdn 1/2-way: wknd over 2f out* **50/1**
050- **10** 9 **Cora Pearl (IRE)**[155] 5464 3-8-12 45 EddieAhern 9 —
(M J Polglase) *prom to 1/2-way* **6/1**[3]
00-6 **11** 1 3/4 **Royal Lass**[20] 308 3-8-2 30 FrancisFerris 10 —
(Rae Guest) *chsd ldrs over 4f* **10/1**
-446 **12** nk **Sweet Cherokee**[13] 396 3-8-9 40 ow2 MickyFenton 8 —
(C N Kellett) *prom: lost pl 4f out: bhd fr 1/2-way* **11/2**[2]
000- **13** 9 **Lough Arrow (IRE)**[118] 6197 3-8-2 30 DaleGibson 13 —
(P S Felgate) *s.i.s: hld up: bhd fr 1/2-way* **40/1**

1m 30.35s (-0.45) **Going Correction** -0.35s/f (Stan) **13** Ran SP% **120.9**
Speed ratings (Par 91):88,85,81,80,80 77,76,75,74,63 61,61,51
CSF £70.33 TOTE £6.50: £1.80, £5.00, £2.30; EX 115.00.
Owner M Ng **Bred** Michael Ng **Trained** Royston, Herts
■ Stewards' Enquiry : Derek McGaffin one-day ban: used whip with excessive frequency (Mar 11)

FOCUS
A very moderate contest and the time was very ordinary.
Mid Valley Official explanation: trainer said, regarding the improved form shown, colt may have benefited from the drop in class

529 PLAY £1/4M SPOT THE BALL ON 0800 500 000 BANDED STKS 6f (F)
5:00 (5:01) (Class 7) 4-Y-0+ **£1,365** (£403; £201) **Stalls** Low

Form RPR
1003 **1** **Straffan (IRE)**[12] 408 4-8-6 45 (b) DaleGibson 2 52
(J Hetherton) *chsd ldr: led over 4f out: rdn and hdd whn edgd rt ins fnl f: rallied to ld nr fin* **7/1**[2]
4406 **2** shd **A Teen**[12] 408 8-8-6 40 AdrianTNicholls 1 52
(P Howling) *chsd ldrs: rdn to ld ins fnl f: hdd nr fin* **25/1**
0-00 **3** 2 **Sergeant Slipper**[14] 388 9-8-6 40 (v) RobbieFitzpatrick 7 46
(C Smith) *dwlt: outpcd: hdwy u.p over 1f out: r.o* **33/1**
552- **4** 1 3/4 **Dunnett Again (IRE)**[74] 6577 5-8-6 40 (b) ChrisCatlin 5 41
(Mrs C A Dunnett) *prom: outpcd 1/2-way: r.o ins fnl f* **15/2**[3]
0-03 **5** 1/2 **Mister Aziz (IRE)**[13] 398 4-8-6 45 (v) EddieAhern 6 39
(J R Jenkins) *s.i.s: hdwy over 3f out: sn outpcd: styd on fnl f* **8/1**
-200 **6** 1 1/4 **Aintnecessarilyso**[13] 398 8-8-6 45 (p) RobertWinston 9 36
(J M Bradley) *s.i.s: sme hdwy 1/2-way: n.d* **10/1**
-565 **7** nk **Kashtanka (IRE)**[14] 388 4-8-4 40 ow1 (b) JasonEdmunds(3) 4 36
(J Balding) *chsd ldrs: rdn over 2f out: sn outpcd* **16/1**
-021 **8** shd **Blakeshall Quest**[14] 388 6-8-13 52 (b) TomEaves 3 41
(R Brotherton) *led: hdd over 4f out: rdn over 2f out: wknd fnl f* **6/5**[1]

-400 **9** 1/2 **Ace Club**[26] 260 5-7-13 45..........(b) AdamCarter(7) 8 — 33
(J Hetherton) *chsd ldrs over 3f* **40/1**

-003 **10** 2 1/2 **Radlett Lady**[14] 388 5-8-9 45 ow3..........(p) MickyFenton 13 — 28
(D K Ivory) *sn bhd* **14/1**

-056 **11** 1/2 **Polar Haze**[14] 388 9-8-6 40..........(v) HayleyTurner 10 — 24
(J Pearce) *hld up: wknd 1/2-way* **22/1**

-504 **12** 1 **Cleveland Way**[14] 387 6-8-5 40 ow2..........(v) DanielTudhope(3) 11 — 23
(D Carroll) *prom: lost pl over 4f out: bhd fr 1/2-way* **33/1**

025- **13** 5 **Amber Nectar Two**[59] 6686 6-8-6 40..........(b) JoeFanning 12 — 6
(A G Newcombe) *sn outpcd* **16/1**

1m 15.77s (-1.13) **Going Correction** -0.35s/f (Stan) 13 Ran SP% **124.9**
Speed ratings (Par 97):93,92,90,87,87 85,85,85,84,81 80,79,72
CSF £182.17 TOTE £8.20: £2.70, £7.80, £8.50; EX 144.50 Place 6 £304.27, Place 5 £153.21 .
Owner K C West **Bred** Mountarmstrong Stud **Trained** Norton, N Yorks

FOCUS
A fairly competitive banded-class sprint rated through the the winner and third.
T/Plt: £978.10 to a £1 stake. Pool: £59,893.55. 44.70 winning tickets. T/Qpdt: £75.60 to a £1 stake. Pool: £4,382.90. 42.90 winning tickets. CR

[498]WOLVERHAMPTON (A.W) (L-H)
Monday, February 27

OFFICIAL GOING: Standard
Wind: Moderate, half-behind Weather: Showers after race 6 (4.35)

530 GREAT JACKPOTS WAITING @ LITTLEWOODSCASINO.COM APPRENTICE H'CAP 1m 1f 103y(P)
1:55 (1:55) (Class 5) (0-75,74) 4-Y-0+ **£3,238** (£963; £481; £240) **Stalls** Low

Form — RPR

1212 **1** **Latif (USA)**[4] 493 5-8-6 62.......... RichardKingscote 6 — 69
(Ms Deborah J Evans) *a.p: rdn over 1f out: led wl ins fnl f: r.o* **5/2**[1]

02-6 **2** nk **Everest (IRE)**[16] 384 9-9-0 70.......... StephenDonohoe 2 — 76
(B Ellison) *hld up: rdn over 2f out: hdwy jst over 1f out: r.o wl ins fnl f: nt rch wnr* **9/1**

3030 **3** 1/2 **Buscador (USA)**[3] 505 7-8-1 60 oh1.......... LiamJones(3) 1 — 65
(W M Brisbourne) *led: rdn over 2f out: hdd and nt qckn wl ins fnl f* **5/1**

40-0 **4** 2 **Eijaaz (IRE)**[20] 324 5-8-1 60.......... KristinStubbs(3) 3 — 62
(Mrs L Stubbs) *s.i.s: hld up and bhd: hdwy fnl f: r.o* **22/1**

3- **5** 1 1/4 **Smart Tiger (GER)**[120] 6183 4-8-10 69.......... JamesDoyle(3) 7 — 68
(N P Littmoden) *a.p: rdn over 2f out: wknd 1f out* **9/2**[3]

2061 **6** shd **Danger Zone**[12] 421 4-9-1 71..........(p) GregFairley 4 — 70
(Mrs A J Perrett) *chsd ldr: ev ch over 2f out: sn rdn: hung rt ent st: wknd ins fnl f* **7/2**[2]

40-0 **7** 7 **Anduril**[10] 444 5-9-4 74..........(b) AndrewMullen 5 — 60
(I W McInnes) *hld up towards rr: rdn over 2f out: no rspnse* **16/1**

5000 **8** 3/4 **Scottish River (USA)**[21] 319 7-8-2 65.......... FrankiePickard(7) 8 — 49
(M D I Usher) *s.v.s: hld up: hdwy over 3f out: wknd 2f out: hung lft fr over 1f out* **16/1**

600/ **9** 17 **Lyrical Girl (USA)**[542] 5257 5-8-1 60 oh6.......... DonnaCaldwell(3) 9 — 12
(H J Manners) *hld up in tch: wknd 5f out* **100/1**

2m 1.85s (-0.77) **Going Correction** 0.0s/f (Stan) 9 Ran SP% **112.7**
Speed ratings (Par 103):103,102,102,100,99 99,93,92,77
CSF £25.39 CT £103.11 TOTE £3.00: £1.10, £2.50, £2.20; EX 22.30.
Owner Paddy Mason **Bred** Shadwell Farm LLC **Trained** Lydiate, Merseyside

FOCUS
A modest but competitive handicap run at a fair pace and rated through the winner to recent form.

531 PLAY BEJEWELLED FOR £400K @ LITTLEWOODSCASINO.COM MEDIAN AUCTION MAIDEN STKS (DIV I) 1m 141y(P)
2:25 (2:26) (Class 5) 3-4-Y-0 **£2,914** (£867; £433; £216) **Stalls** Low

Form — RPR

2- **1** **John Charles (IRE)**[94] 6418 4-9-12.......... LPKeniry 2 — 66
(D R C Elsworth) *hld up towards rr: hdwy over 3f out: rdn to ld over 1f out: drvn out* **6/4**[1]

06-0 **2** 1 1/4 **Welcome Releaf**[10] 445 3-8-5 52.......... EddieAhern 4 — 57
(Lucinda Featherstone) *hld up in tch: rdn to ld 2f out: hdd over 1f out: kpt on ins fnl f* **25/1**

3 1 1/4 **Chart Oak** 3-8-5.......... JoeFanning 11 — 54
(P Howling) *hld up: hdwy 7f out: rdn and ev ch over 2f out: hung lft ins fnl f: nt qckn* **12/1**

3 **4** 1/2 **Cuyamaca (IRE)**[24] 289 4-9-7.......... TPQueally 12 — 48
(C F Wall) *hld up in mid-div: hdwy 4f out: rdn over 2f out: one pce fnl f* **7/1**[3]

6- **5** 1 1/2 **Supa Tramp**[94] 6417 3-8-3 ow1.......... SaleemGolam(3) 9 — 51
(J R Fanshawe) *hld up and bhd: rdn over 3f out: hdwy over 2f out: forced wd ent st: styd on towards fin* **10/1**

5 **6** 4 **Blanc Visage**[10] 445 3-8-5.......... SimonWhitworth 7 — 41
(Mrs H Sweeting) *t.k.h: in tch: n.m.r and lost pl 4f out: swtchd rt over 1f out: sme late prog* **28/1**

3 **7** 3 **Fire Of Love**[16] 372 3-8-1 ow1.......... ChrisCatlin 1 — 30
(N P Littmoden) *chsd ldr to 3f out: wknd wl over 1f out* **5/2**[2]

0- **8** 1/2 **Queen Tara**[238] 3196 4-9-7.......... AdrianTNicholls 6 — 34
(Mrs C A Dunnett) *a bhd* **66/1**

60-0 **9** 3 **Teenage Rampage**[27] 260 4-9-12 40.......... RobbieFitzpatrick 10 — 33
(W M Brisbourne) *led: rdn and hdd over 2f out: n.m.r ent st: sn wknd* **100/1**

650- **10** hd **Sharp Duo (IRE)**[141] 5753 3-8-5 62.......... FrancisNorton 3 — 26
(M S Saunders) *t.k.h in mid-div: sddle sn slipped: bhd fnl 6f* **10/1**

11 20 **Hollie Dellamore** 4-9-7.......... DarrenWilliams 8 — —
(A P Jarvis) *s.i.s: short-lived effrt on outside 4f out: t.o* **40/1**

1m 53.76s (2.00) **Going Correction** 0.0s/f (Stan)
WFA 3 from 4yo 21lb 11 Ran SP% **119.2**
Speed ratings (Par 103):91,89,88,88,87 83,80,80,77,77 59
CSF £50.69 TOTE £2.50: £1.20, £6.20, £4.00; EX 54.30.
Owner Mel Davies **Bred** M J Davies **Trained** Newmarket, Suffolk

FOCUS
A moderate contest but the runner-up looks a little better than her official rating of 52. The winning time was very moderate for a race of its type, 2.23 seconds slower than the second division.
Cuyamaca(IRE) Official explanation: vet said filly was lame off fore
Fire Of Love Official explanation: jockey said filly lost action in home straight
Teenage Rampage Official explanation: jockey said gelding hung right-handed on bend
Sharp Duo(IRE) Official explanation: jockey said saddle slipped
Hollie Dellamore Official explanation: jockey said filly hung right-handed throughout

532 MORE CHANCES TO WIN @ LITTLEWOODSCASINO.COM H'CAP 5f 20y(P)
2:55 (2:56) (Class 5) (0-75,72) 4-Y-0+ **£3,238** (£963; £481; £240) **Stalls** Low

Form — RPR

-200 **1** **Almaty Express**[11] 426 4-8-8 62 ow1..........(b) DarrylHolland 4 — 69
(J R Weymes) *mde all: rdn wl over 1f out: edgd lft ins fnl f: jst hld on* **14/1**

11-0 **2** shd **El Potro**[11] 424 4-8-10 64.......... FergalLynch 1 — 71
(E S McMahon) *a.p: wnt 2nd over 2f out: rdn over 1f out: r.o ins fnl f: jst failed* **9/2**[2]

2615 **3** hd **Mambazo**[21] 317 4-8-6 63..........(e) AdamKirby(3) 10 — 69+
(S C Williams) *hld up and bhd: c wd ent st: hdwy fnl f: fin wl* **8/1**

21-2 **4** nk **Hammer Of The Gods (IRE)**[21] 320 6-8-13 67..........(bt) EddieAhern 9 — 72
(Lucinda Featherstone) *mid-div: rdn over 2f out: swtchd lft and hdwy over 1f out: r.o ins fnl f* **11/2**[3]

-004 **5** 1 1/4 **Fizzlephut (IRE)**[17] 362 4-9-4 72.......... PaulFitzsimons 11 — 72
(Miss J R Tooth) *a.p: rdn over 2f out: one pce fnl f* **28/1**

0301 **6** 1/2 **Gone'N'Dunnett (IRE)**[11] 424 7-8-8 69..........(v) KirstyMilczarek(7) 12 — 68
(Mrs C A Dunnett) *hld up in mid-div: kpt on ins fnl f: nvr nr to chal* **22/1**

3411 **7** 1/2 **Canadian Danehill (IRE)**[21] 320 4-8-13 67..........(p) FergusSweeney 2 — 64
(R M H Cowell) *chsd ldrs: rdn over 2f out: wknd ins fnl f* **11/2**[3]

-503 **8** shd **Namir (IRE)**[5] 480 4-8-5 64.......... JamesDoyle(5) 5 — 60
(Stef Liddiard) *s.i.s: hdwy over 1f out: one pce fnl f* **4/1**[1]

1 **9** 1/2 **Mountain Pass (USA)**[16] 373 4-8-13 67..........(v) JamieSpencer 7 — 62
(M J Wallace) *mid-div: rdn whn n.m.r on ins over 2f out: hdwy wl over 1f out: wknd ins fnl f* **10/1**

030- **10** 1 1/4 **Domirati**[208] 4060 6-8-12 66..........(b) IanMongan 8 — 56
(J D Bethell) *s.i.s: a bhd* **16/1**

1-00 **11** 2 1/2 **Rock Fever (IRE)**[21] 307 4-8-5 59 oh13 ow1..........(b) RobbieFitzpatrick 6 — 40
(Peter Grayson) *w ldr: rdn over 2f out: wknd over 1f out* **66/1**

40-0 **12** 6 **Caustic Wit (IRE)**[53] 47 8-8-11 65.......... FrancisNorton 3 — 25
(M S Saunders) *a bhd* **28/1**

62.00 secs (-0.82) **Going Correction** 0.0s/f (Stan) 12 Ran SP% **114.4**
Speed ratings (Par 103):106,105,105,105,103 102,101,101,100,98 94,84
CSF £70.78 CT £553.76 TOTE £22.80: £4.00, £2.20, £2.90; EX 85.10.
Owner Sporting Occasions Racing No 5 **Bred** P G Airey **Trained** Middleham Moor, N Yorks

FOCUS
A decent sprint handicap for the class and predictably competitive. However, as is so often the case over this course and distance, those drawn low seemed at an advantage. The form looks solid with those in the frame close to their best or recent form.

533 BIGGEST JACKPOT ON WEB @ LITTLEWOODSCASINO.COM MAIDEN STKS 5f 216y(P)
3:30 (3:32) (Class 5) 3-Y-0+ **£3,238** (£963; £481; £240) **Stalls** Low

Form — RPR

1 **Sir Douglas** 3-8-11.......... JamieSpencer 1 — 77+
(J A Osborne) *s.i.s: swtchd rt and hdwy on outside 2f out: edgd lft and led wl ins fnl f: pushed out* **8/1**

323- **2** 1 **Best Double**[93] 6433 3-8-6 69.......... NickyMackay 7 — 69
(G A Butler) *a.p: rdn over 2f out: led 1f out: hdd and nt qckn wl ins fnl f* **4/1**[3]

35 **3** 2 **Arzaag**[6] 473 3-8-11.......... LPKeniry 11 — 68
(D M Simcock) *led early: clipped heels and lost pl 4f out: hdwy on outside over 2f out: nt qckn ins fnl f* **7/2**[2]

/0-0 **4** 2 1/2 **Rapid Flow**[31] 209 4-9-12 52.......... RobbieFitzpatrick 2 — 64
(J W Unett) *sn prom: led over 4f out: rdn over 2f out: hdd 1f out: wknd* **12/1**

4-22 **5** 2 **Siwa**[17] 365 3-8-6 71.......... EddieAhern 8 — 49
(E A L Dunlop) *bhd tl hdwy on ins and nt clr run 3f out: rdn wl over 1f out: no imp fnl f* **5/4**[1]

00- **6** 3 **Wolfman**[103] 6367 4-9-7.......... MarkLawson(5) 10 — 49
(D W Barker) *sn led: hdd over 4f out: rdn and ev ch over 2f out: wknd wl over 1f out* **50/1**

0-0 **7** 1 3/4 **Marron Flore**[51] 60 3-8-3.......... RichardThomas(3) 5 — 35
(A J Lidderdale) *prom: ev ch over 2f out: sn rdn: wknd over 1f out* **66/1**

8 4 **Silvanella (IRE)** 3-8-6.......... FrancisNorton 12 — 23
(M S Saunders) *prom early: sn bhd* **66/1**

0-05 **9** 1/2 **Value Plus (IRE)**[9] 449 4-9-0 55.......... MarkCoumbe(7) 3 — 25
(C J Teague) *prom: rdn 3f out: wknd 2f out* **40/1**

400- **10** 6 **Legal Call**[163] 5300 3-8-4 55.......... LiamJones(7) 9 — 8
(M Appleby) *prom 1f: sn bhd* **40/1**

00-0 **11** 1 **Dancing Moonlight (IRE)**[9] 453 4-9-4 30.......... SaleemGolam(3) 4 — —
(Mrs N Macauley) *a bhd* **200/1**

1m 15.28s (-0.53) **Going Correction** 0.0s/f (Stan)
WFA 3 from 4yo+ 15lb 11 Ran SP% **115.8**
Speed ratings (Par 103):103,101,99,95,93 89,86,81,80,72 71
CSF £38.63 TOTE £6.70: £2.20, £1.40, £1.20; EX 39.40.
Owner Richard Leslie **Bred** Overbury Partnership **Trained** Upper Lambourn, Berks

FOCUS
With the fourth home rated just 52, this was probably a pretty ordinary sprint maiden, but Sir Douglas created a good impression to overcome his inexperience and make a winning debut.
Siwa Official explanation: jockey said filly suffered interference in running

534 PLAY BEJEWELLED FOR £400K @ LITTLEWOODSCASINO.COM MEDIAN AUCTION MAIDEN STKS (DIV II) 1m 141y(P)
4:05 (4:06) (Class 5) 3-4-Y-0 **£2,914** (£867; £433; £216) **Stalls** Low

Form — RPR

0-23 **1** **Fiddlers Wood**[16] 374 3-8-5 80..........(v) ChrisCatlin 10 — 67
(V Smith) *a.p: rdn to ld 2f out: edgd lft 1f out: rdn out* **1/2**[1]

2 3 **Webbow (IRE)**[30] 4-9-12.......... DavidAllan 7 — 67
(T D Easterby) *led: rdn and hdd 2f out: edgd lft ins fnl f: one pce* **66/1**

3 **3** nk **Pop Music (IRE)**[17] 365 3-8-5.......... SimonWhitworth 9 — 60
(Miss J Feilden) *chsd ldrs: rdn over 2f out: hung lft wl over 1f out: swtchd rt wl ins fnl f: kpt on* **7/1**[3]

00- **4** 3 **Dickie's Dream (IRE)**[131] 5987 3-8-3 ow1.......... SaleemGolam(3) 4 — 55
(P J McBride) *prom: lost pl over 6f out: rdn over 3f out: no real prog fnl 2f* **6/1**[2]

00-2 **5** 1 **Danish Blues (IRE)**[16] 378 3-8-0 63.......... JamesDoyle(5) 6 — 52
(N P Littmoden) *t.k.h: prom: rdn over 2f out: sn wknd* **11/1**

-540 **6** 10 **Spanish Music**[14] 399 4-9-7 45..........(t) RobertHavlin 8 — 32
(R Ingram) *mid-div: rdn 4f out: sn struggling* **25/1**

7 14 **Sun Of The Glen (IRE)**[28] 4-9-7.......... MickyFenton 2 — —
(B D Leavy) *bhd fnl 4f: t.o* **80/1**

00-0 **8** 12 **Turtle Magic (IRE)**[17] 360 4-9-7 35.......... AlanDaly 3 — —
(Miss J S Davis) *s.i.s: t.k.h in rr: lost tch 3f out: t.o* **125/1**

00 **9** 5 **Vi's Boy**[10] 445 3-8-6 ow1.......... RobbieFitzpatrick 5 — —
(W M Brisbourne) *a bhd: lost tch 5f out: t.o* **100/1**

The Form Book, Raceform Ltd, Compton, RG20 6NL

0-0 **10** 3 **Silvabella (IRE)**[31] 215 3-8-0 ow3..................(v[1]) RichardThomas(3) 11 —
(D Haydn Jones) *a bhd: t.o fnl 5f* **66/1**

1m 51.53s (-0.23) **Going Correction** 0.0s/f (Stan)
WFA 3 from 4yo 21lb **10** Ran SP% **111.6**
Speed ratings (Par 103):101,98,98,95,94 85,73,62,58,55
CSF £66.03 TOTE £1.40: £1.02, £9.10, £2.00; EX 32.80.
Owner Stephen Dartnell **Bred** Minster Enterprises Ltd **Trained** Exning, Suffolk

FOCUS
A modest maiden that lacked any strength in depth. The winning time was 2.23 seconds faster than the first division, but still only ordinary for the grade.
Pop Music(IRE) Official explanation: jockey said gelding hung left up straight

535 97% PAYOUT @ LITTLEWOODSCASINO.COM H'CAP 1m 4f 50y(P)
4:35 (4:35) (Class 5) (0-75,74) 4-Y-0+ **£3,238** (£963; £481; £240) **Stalls** Low

Form RPR
5222 **1** **Desperation (IRE)**[9] 454 4-9-3 **74**.................. JamieSpencer 7 79
(B D Leavy) *led 1f: chsd ldr tl over 4f out: rdn and wnt 2nd again 2f out: r.o to ld post* **3/1**[2]
3331 **2** *shd* **Greenbelt**[20] 334 5-9-3 **71**.................. JoeFanning 4 76
(G M Moore) *led after 1f: rdn over 2f out: edgd rt ins fnl f: hdd post* **11/4**[1]
125- **3** ¾ **Amwell Brave**[79] 6540 5-8-6 **60**.................. EddieAhern 1 64
(J R Jenkins) *hld up and bhd: hdwy on ins 2f out: rdn over 1f out: ev ch ins fnl f: nt qckn cl home* **5/1**
-213 **4** 1½ **Hawkit (USA)**[13] 414 5-8-12 **66**..................(t) DarryllHolland 3 67
(A Bailey) *hld up in tch: rdn 3f out: swtchd lft 1f out: nt qckn* **4/1**[3]
0-40 **5** *nk* **Ramsgill (USA)**[11] 324 4-8-1 **63**.................. JamesDoyle(5) 8 64
(N P Littmoden) *hld up: rdn over 3f out: hdwy on outside 2f out: edgd lft ins fnl f: one pce* **5/1**
2653 **6** *shd* **Jadeeron**[7] 470 7-8-4 **58** oh8..................(v) AlanDaly 2 59?
(Miss D A McHale) *prom: lost pl over 3f out: sme hdwy on ins over 1f out: nvr able to chal* **20/1**
20/0 **7** 1¼ **Fort Churchill (IRE)**[16] 385 5-9-4 **72**..................(t) TomEaves 9 71
(B Ellison) *hld up and bhd: hdwy over 4f out: wknd wl over 1f out* **40/1**
400- **8** 2 **Border Tale**[12] 6566 6-9-0 **68**.................. MickyFenton 6 64
(James Moffatt) *hld up in tch: wnt 2nd over 4f out: rdn over 3f out: wknd wl over 1f out* **20/1**

2m 42.6s (0.18) **Going Correction** 0.0s/f (Stan)
WFA 4 from 5yo+ 3lb **8** Ran SP% **117.0**
Speed ratings (Par 103):99,98,98,97,97 97,96,95
CSF £11.71 CT £39.50 TOTE £3.30: £1.70, £1.60, £1.80; EX 11.30.
Owner Paul Ennis **Bred** Bernard Colclough **Trained** Forsbrook, Staffs

FOCUS
A decent enough handicap for the grade, that makes sense rated through the third and fourth, but the front two got the run of the race and it proved hard to make up significant amounts of ground from off the pace. Unsurprisingly, the winning time was modest for a race of this class.

536 LITTLEWOODSCASINO.COM - TRUSTED NAME IN GAMING MAIDEN STKS 1m 1f 103y(P)
5:05 (5:05) (Class 5) 3-Y-O **£3,886** (£1,156; £577; £288) **Stalls** Low

Form RPR
2 **1** **Soapy Danger**[10] 445 3-9-3.................. KDarley 6 76
(M Johnston) *a.p: led 5f out: rdn clr over 1f out: r.o wl* **2/11**[1]
40- **2** 3½ **Markington**[73] 6588 3-9-3.................. JamieSpencer 9 69
(J D Bethell) *s.i.s: sn swtchd lft: hld up: rdn over 2f out: hdwy over 1f out: edgd lft and r.o ins fnl f: no ch* **16/1**[2]
533- **3** 1½ **Genau (IRE)**[87] 6484 3-9-3 75.................. TomEaves 1 66
(Mrs L Stubbs) *t.k.h: a.p: rdn over 3f out: n.m.r on ins 2f out: one pce* **20/1**[3]
06 **4** 1¼ **Miss Odd Sox**[12] 418 3-8-12.................. RobertHavlin 2 59
(R Ingram) *hld up in mid-div: hdwy over 3f out: sn rdn: one pce fnl 2f* **66/1**
0-0 **5** 2 **Smokey Blue**[16] 372 3-8-12.................. DerekNolan(5) 5 60
(M J Wallace) *hld up: rdn and hdwy on ins over 2f out: swtchd rt jst over 1f out: wknd ins fnl f* **50/1**
000- **6** 8 **They All Laughed**[184] 4750 3-9-3 63.................. IanMongan 10 45
(T G Mills) *prom: jnd wnr over 3f out: sn rdn: wknd fnl f* **22/1**
0- **7** 4 **Zed Candy (FR)**[142] 5746 3-9-3.................. MickyFenton 8 37
(J T Stimpson) *s.s: t.k.h: a bhd* **33/1**
66 **8** 9 **Tip Top Style**[25] 272 3-9-3.................. DaleGibson 7 20
(J Mackie) *a bhd* **50/1**
06- **9** 10 **Mystic Queen (IRE)**[186] 4690 3-8-12.................. DarrenWilliams 4 —
(A P Jarvis) *t.k.h in tch: rdn over 3f out: sn wknd: t.o* **100/1**
0 **10** 24 **Tapsalteerie**[17] 365 3-8-12.................. ChrisCatlin 3 —
(M J Attwater) *led: hdd 5f out: rdn 4f out: sn wknd: t.o* **100/1**

2m 1.98s (-0.64) **Going Correction** 0.0s/f (Stan) **10** Ran SP% **109.9**
Speed ratings (Par 97):102,98,97,96,94 87,84,76,67,45
CSF £2.23 TOTE £1.10: £1.02, £2.10, £1.40; EX 4.30.
Owner Mrs R J Jacobs **Bred** Newsells Park Stud Limited **Trained** Middleham Moor, N Yorks

FOCUS
Not a very strong maiden, but Soapy Danger looks a nice type and there were one or two in behind who could be capable of a little better with the third to form.
Zed Candy(FR) Official explanation: jockey said gelding missed break
Mystic Queen(IRE) Official explanation: jockey said filly hung right throughout

537 BIGGEST JACKPOT ON WEB @ LITTLEWOODSCASINO.COM H'CAP 1m 141y(P)
5:35 (5:36) (Class 6) (0-60,65) 4-Y-0+ **£2,388** (£705; £352) **Stalls** Low

Form RPR
5233 **1** **Mister Benji**[16] 383 7-9-3 **59**.................. DarrenWilliams 5 67
(B P J Baugh) *hld up in tch: rdn over 1f out: led wl ins fnl f: r.o* **7/1**
2241 **2** *nk* **Lowestoft Playboy**[7] 461 4-9-9 **65** 6ex.................. EddieAhern 7 72
(J Jay) *hld up in mid-div: hdwy over 3f out: rdn to ld jst over 1f out: hdd wl ins fnl f: r.o* **13/2**
6111 **3** 1½ **Desert Lover (IRE)**[14] 400 4-9-4 **60**.................. JamieSpencer 3 64
(R J Price) *a.p: rdn and ev ch 1f out: nt qckn towards fin* **15/8**[1]
0646 **4** ½ **King Of Music (USA)**[7] 461 5-9-3 **59**.................. TonyCulhane 1 62
(G Prodromou) *hld up in mid-div: hdwy over 2f out: sn rdn: r.o one pce fnl f* **5/1**[2]
000- **5** *nk* **Ektishaaf**[152] 5549 4-9-4 **60**.................. GeorgeBaker 6 63
(C F Wall) *hld up and bhd: rdn and hdwy over 1f out: hung lft ins fnl f: one pce* **11/2**[3]
0600 **6** 1¼ **Sorbiesharry (IRE)**[3] 505 7-9-0 **59**..................(p) SaleemGolam(3) 2 59
(Mrs N Macauley) *hld up towards rr: hdwy 2f out: no imp fnl f* **8/1**
00-4 **7** 1 **Jilly Why (IRE)**[19] 343 5-9-4 **60**.................. SamHitchcott 8 58
(Ms Deborah J Evans) *nvr trbld ldrs* **25/1**
05-0 **8** *nk* **Danielle's Lad**[37] 169 10-9-4 **60**.................. FrancisFerris 13 57
(B Palling) *led: rdn over 2f out: hdd jst over 1f out: wknd ins fnl f* **50/1**
-252 **9** 1½ **Bavarica**[28] 252 4-8-13 **60**.................. JamesDoyle(5) 10 54
(Miss J Feilden) *hld up towards rr: hdwy whn nt clr run and swtchd rt over 2f out: n.d after* **16/1**
0P-6 **10** 3½ **Nakwa (IRE)**[21] 318 8-9-1 **57**.................. DavidAllan 9 44
(E J Alston) *chsd ldr: rdn over 2f out: wknd wl over 1f out* **50/1**
/3-0 **11** 12 **Duxford**[47] 84 5-9-4 **60**.................. DarryllHolland 4 21
(D K Ivory) *a bhd* **33/1**
400- **12** 2 **Worth Abbey**[215] 3844 4-8-12 **57**.................. DNolan(3) 12 14
(M Appleby) *rdn over 3f out: a bhd* **66/1**
00-0 **13** 22 **Don Pasquale**[16] 384 4-9-4 **60**.................. MickyFenton 11 —
(J T Stimpson) *s.i.s: hdwy after 1f: rdn over 3f out: wknd over 2f out: t.o* **100/1**

1m 50.7s (-1.06) **Going Correction** 0.0s/f (Stan) **13** Ran SP% **122.9**
Speed ratings (Par 101):104,103,102,101,101 100,99,99,98,94 84,82,62
CSF £51.60 CT £122.32 TOTE £8.30: £2.20, £2.40, £1.30; EX 85.60 Place 6 £44.26, Place 5 £21.95.
Owner J H Chrimes And Mr & Mrs G W Hannam **Bred** D J And Mrs K D Smart **Trained** Audley, Staffs
■ Stewards' Enquiry : Darren Williams one-day ban: used whip in the incorrect place (Mar 11)

FOCUS
A moderate but competitive handicap rated through the winner.
Bavarica Official explanation: jockey said filly hung right-handed throughout
T/Plt: £67.10 to a £1 stake. Pool: £45,877.90. 498.45 winning tickets. T/Qpdt: £13.90 to a £1 stake. Pool: £3,060.40. 162.70 winning tickets. KH

[514]LINGFIELD (L-H)
Tuesday, February 28

OFFICIAL GOING: Standard
Wind: Moderate, against Weather: Fine

538 BETDIRECT.CO.UK CLAIMING STKS 1m 2f (P)
1:30 (1:30) (Class 6) 3-Y-O **£2,730** (£806; £403) **Stalls** Low

Form RPR
0023 **1** **Chookie Windsor**[10] 447 3-8-7 60.................. FrancisNorton 7 56
(M S Saunders) *trckd ldrs: prog 3f out and sn cl up: effrt to ld over 1f out: in command fnl f: kpt on* **7/2**[2]
-426 **2** 2 **Franky'N'Jonny**[3] 422 3-8-1 54.................. JamesDoyle(5) 6 51
(I A Wood) *prom: trckd ldr over 3f out: rdn to ld 2f out: hdd and one pce over 1f out* **11/4**[1]
50-4 **3** *hd* **Count The Trees**[4] 499 3-7-11 40.................. MarcHalford(5) 10 47
(W G M Turner) *wl in rr: rdn over 4f out: hanging lft after but prog u.p over 2f out: styd on wl fnl f: nrst fin* **25/1**
040- **4** 2 **Bob's Your Uncle**[109] 6313 3-8-13 57.................. EddieAhern 12 54
(J G Portman) *dwlt: wl in rr: prog on outer 3f out: nt looking keen whn sltly impeded over 1f out: r.o last 150yds: n.d* **16/1**
60-4 **5** ½ **Aboyne (IRE)**[10] 447 3-8-9 60.................. TPQueally 8 49
(M G Quinlan) *settled midfield: effrt u.p over 2f out: kpt on one pce and nvr on terms w ldrs* **6/1**[3]
-063 **6** 3 **Bahhmirage (IRE)**[21] 326 3-8-0 50..................(b) AdrianMcCarthy 5 34
(C N Kellett) *led at str pce: 3 l clr over 3f out: hdd 2f out: wknd fnl f* **12/1**
0-46 **7** 1¼ **Youralittlemiller**[21] 333 3-8-2 55..................(p) DavidKinsella 2 34
(P G Murphy) *prom: chsd ldr 4f out to over 3f out: wknd 2f out* **10/1**
000- **8** 3½ **Ryhope Chief (IRE)**[137] 5878 3-8-11 52.................. JohnEgan 1 36
(M F Harris) *chsd ldrs: pushed along 6f out: no prog u.p 3f out: wknd wl over 1f out* **33/1**
63-0 **9** 1½ **Divisive**[15] 406 3-8-6 54.................. JimmyQuinn 14 28
(M Blanshard) *wl in rr: u.p and struggling over 4f out: sn detached* **20/1**
3000 **10** *shd* **Zizou (IRE)**[6] 479 3-8-11 60.................. J-PGuillambert 11 33
(J J Bridger) *a wl in rr: rdn over 4f out: sn bhd* **10/1**
0050 **11** 6 **First Byte**[11] 439 3-7-9 35..................(vt) DonnaCaldwell(7) 13 13
(Miss D A McHale) *s.v.s: a wl in rr: u.p and struggling over 4f out* **66/1**
0- **12** 3½ **Murts Magic (IRE)**[227] 3530 3-8-7.................. LPKeniry 9 11
(M J McGrath) *dwlt: sn midfield: rdn and no prog over 3f out: wknd rapidly fnl 2f* **100/1**
0-00 **13** *dist* **Bournonville**[14] 415 3-8-4 45.................. SaleemGolam(3) 3 —
(J Ryan) *chsd ldr to 4f out: wknd v rapidly and eased: t.o* **25/1**

2m 7.33s (-0.46) **Going Correction** -0.125s/f (Stan) **13** Ran SP% **112.8**
Speed ratings (Par 95):96,94,94,92,92 89,88,86,84,84 79,77,—
CSF £11.58 TOTE £3.20: £1.50, £1.30, £5.40; EX 10.80.Bahhmirage was claimed by Mrs Stef Liddiard for £5,000.
Owner A P Holland **Bred** D And J Raeburn **Trained** Green Ore, Somerset
■ Stewards' Enquiry : Marc Halford one-day ban: careless riding (Mar 11)

FOCUS
Just a moderate claimer and rated negatively, although they went a good pace from the start.
Youralittlemiller Official explanation: jockey said filly hung right throughout
Bournonville Official explanation: vet said gelding had a breathing problem

539 FOOTBALLPOOLS.COM MAIDEN STKS 7f (P)
2:00 (2:03) (Class 5) 3-Y-0+ **£3,886** (£1,156; £577; £288) **Stalls** Low

Form RPR
06-2 **1** **Trans Sonic**[52] 60 3-8-9 78.................. DarrenWilliams 3 78
(A P Jarvis) *mde all: drvn and in command 1f out: unchal after* **7/4**[1]
4-2 **2** 2½ **Rose Muwasim**[17] 372 3-8-5 ow1.................. EddieAhern 12 67
(E A L Dunlop) *trckd ldrs: prog to chse wnr 2f out: rdn and no imp over 1f out* **5/2**[2]
5233 **3** ¾ **Scroll**[8] 459 3-8-9 71..................(v) J-PGuillambert 10 69
(P Howling) *settled off the pce: prog 3f out: rdn to chse ldng pair over 1f out: one pce* **10/3**[3]
4 7 **Landela** 4-9-7.................. MatthewHenry 7 51
(M A Jarvis) *leggy: unf: taken down early: chsd wnr to 2f out: wd bnd sn after and rn green: wknd* **8/1**
00- **5** 3 **Light Of Day (IRE)**[74] 6595 3-8-5 ow4.................. AdamKirby(3) 13 41
(Miss Diana Weeden) *reluctant to enter stalls: dwlt: wl off the pce towards rr: nvr a factor* **80/1**
0 **6** 1½ **Jose Bove**[22] 314 4-9-12.................. TonyCulhane 4 44
(R Dickin) *w'like: stdd s: sn midfield: gng wl enough 3f out: sn outpcd: shuffled along and wknd over 1f out* **66/1**
7 ¾ **Wild Lass**[38] 5-9-7.................. LPKeniry 14 37
(J C Fox) *leggy: unf: a wl in rr: outpcd in last pair 4f out: no ch* **100/1**
0/ **8** 1 **The Stafford (IRE)**[40] 6222 5-9-9.................. EdwardCreighton(3) 9 39
(L Wells) *dwlt: a wl in rr: no ch fnl 3f* **100/1**

0 **9** ½ **Flyingwithoutwings**[31] 218 7-9-12 .... DavidKinsella 8 38
(A King) *chsd ldrs to 4f out: sn u.p and wknd* **33/1**
10 2 **Montanah Jet**[20] 4-9-12 .... SamHitchcott 2 33
(C N Kellett) *w'like: dwlt: sn prom on inner: wknd over 3f out* **100/1**
11 1 **Kilmeena Magic**[48] 4-9-7 .... MickyFenton 11 25
(J C Fox) *unf: dwlt: a toiling and wl in rr* **100/1**
1m 24.7s (-1.19) **Going Correction** -0.125s/f (Stan)
WFA 3 from 4yo+ 17lb 11 Ran SP% **108.8**
Speed ratings (Par 103):101,98,97,89,85 84,83,82,81,79 78
CSF £5.47 TOTE £2.30: £1.30, £1.30, £1.40; EX 6.30.
Owner Eurostrait Ltd **Bred** I A Balding **Trained** Twyford, Bucks

FOCUS
A pretty ordinary maiden that looks solid enough based on the time and the front three finished well clear.

540 FREE £75 WITH LITTLEWOODSCASINO.COM MAIDEN STKS 5f (P)
2:30 (2:32) (Class 5) 3-Y-O **£3,886** (£1,156; £577; £288) **Stalls** High

Form RPR
0-26 **1** **Diane's Choice**[20] 341 3-8-12 73 .... TQuinn 1 69
(J Akehurst) *disp ld tl def advantage wl over 1f out: clr ent fnl f: all out* **6/4**[1]
05- **2** hd **Total Impact**[218] 3799 3-9-3 .... ChrisCatlin 5 73
(C A Cyzer) *lw: hld up: prog 3f out: rdn 2f out: chsd wnr 1f out: clsd last 100yds: jst hld* **10/1**[3]
03-6 **3** 4 **Billy Bling (IRE)**[41] 138 3-9-0 65 .... StephaneBreux(3) 2 59
(R Hannon) *chsd ldng pair to over 3f out: lost pl and sn outpcd: rdn and plugged on to take 3rd nr fin* **5/1**[2]
0-44 **4** ½ **Patavium Prince (IRE)**[6] 481 3-9-3 65 .... NCallan 3 57
(J R Best) *disp ld to wl over 1f out: wknd fnl f* **6/4**[1]
5 nk **Kellys Dream (IRE)** 3-8-12 .... FrancisNorton 6 51
(M Quinn) *leggy: bit bkwd: chsd ldng pair over 3f out to 2f out: wknd fnl f* **33/1**
000 **6** 3 ½ **Batchworth Fleur**[17] 374 3-8-12 45 ....(b¹) StephenCarson 4 38
(E A Wheeler) *a last and struggling to stay in tch* **50/1**
59.18 secs (-0.60) **Going Correction** -0.125s/f (Stan) 6 Ran SP% **110.7**
Speed ratings (Par 97):99,98,92,91,91 85
CSF £17.80 TOTE £2.60: £1.60, £3.00; EX 18.20.
Owner The Grass Is Greener Partnership Ii **Bred** Green Pastures Farm **Trained** Epsom, Surrey

FOCUS
A poor turnout numerically and just a modest sprint maiden with the winner to her mark setting the level for the form.

541 PLAY NOW AT BETDIRECTPOKER.COM H'CAP 6f (P)
3:00 (3:02) (Class 4) (0-85,85) 3-Y-0+ **£6,477** (£1,927; £963; £481) **Stalls** Low

Form RPR
60-3 **1** **Bayeux (USA)**[10] 450 5-9-13 85 .... NickyMackay 4 93+
(G A Butler) *lw: settled in midfield: effrt 2f out: got through towards inner fnl f: r.o to ld last 75yds* **9/2**[2]
06-1 **2** ½ **Effective**[21] 323 6-8-7 72 .... AndrewElliott(7) 5 78
(A P Jarvis) *mde most at stdy pce: jnd over 1f out: hdd and no ex last 75yds* **8/1**[3]
0-24 **3** nk **Adantino**[11] 441 7-9-1 73 ....(b) AlanMunro 9 78
(B R Millman) *hld up towards rr: prog wl over 1f out: drvn and r.o fnl f to take 3rd nr fin* **10/1**
301- **4** ¾ **Roman Quintet (IRE)**[216] 3847 6-9-1 73 .... TQuinn 6 76
(D W P Arbuthnot) *trckd ldrs: effrt 2f out: rdn to chal 1f out: fnd little and hld whn hit over hd by rival's whip nr fin* **12/1**
13-3 **5** ¾ **Rezzago (USA)**[17] 376 6-9-6 78 .... JamieSpencer 3 79
(W R Swinburn) *lw: trckd ldrs: effrt to chal and upsides over 1f out: nt qckn fnl f* **7/4**[1]
2141 **6** hd **Marko Jadeo (IRE)**[7] 476 8-9-12 84 6ex .... PaulFitzsimons 11 84+
(S Dow) *lw: dwlt: hld up: 11th 2f out: stl same pl whn effrt on outer 1f out: checked sltly sn after: r.o wl last 100yds: hopeless* **8/1**[3]
60-3 **7** nk **Thurlestone Rock**[21] 323 6-9-0 72 .... ChrisCatlin 7 71
(B J Meehan) *prom: rdn over 2f out: nt qckn u.p over 1f out: one pce after* **16/1**
000- **8** ¾ **Steely Dan**[10] 2697 7-9-8 80 .... GeorgeBaker 10 77+
(J R Best) *settled midfield on outer: effrt and hanging over 2f out: one pce and no imp on ldrs* **50/1**
4000 **9** 2 **Chateau Nicol**[7] 476 7-9-6 83 .... JamesDoyle(5) 2 74
(B G Powell) *settled in rr: shkn up 2f out: no rspnse over 1f out: no prog* **16/1**
4556 **10** nk **Pawan (IRE)**[14] 413 6-8-13 78 .... AnnStokell(7) 1 68
(Miss A Stokell) *dwlt: sn midfield on inner: effrt 2f out: no prog over 1f out: wknd* **16/1**
-000 **11** 1 ¼ **Quiet Times (IRE)**[14] 413 7-9-13 85 ....(b) NCallan 12 71+
(K A Ryan) *w ldr to 2f out: losing pl whn queezed out jst ins fnl f: eased* **16/1**
4-00 **12** ¾ **Happy As Larry (USA)**[7] 476 4-9-4 83 .... JamesO'Reilly(7) 8 67
(T J Pitt) *s.s: mostly last: detached fr rest over 2f out: nudged along and no prog* **25/1**
1m 11.63s (-1.18) **Going Correction** -0.125s/f (Stan) 12 Ran SP% **122.9**
Speed ratings (Par 105):102,101,100,99,98 98,98,97,94,94 92,91
CSF £42.22 CT £356.73 TOTE £6.80: £2.30, £2.70, £3.10; EX 63.20.
Owner Beetle N Wedge Partnership **Bred** Darley **Trained** Blewbury, Oxon

FOCUS
A good, competitive sprint handicap, but Effective set just a steady pace and they predictably finished in a bunch. As a result, the well-handicapped and improving Bayeux looks better than the bare form, and a solid race with those in the frame behind running close to form.

542 BETDIRECT.CO.UK H'CAP 1m (P)
3:30 (3:32) (Class 3) (0-95,92) 4-Y-0+
£11,217 (£2,519; £2,519; £840; £419; £210) **Stalls** High

Form RPR
000- **1** **Capable Guest (IRE)**[148] 5660 4-9-1 89 .... TQuinn 11 97
(M R Channon) *wl in rr: rdn 1/2-way: u.p and no prog 2f out: rapid hdwy on outer 1f out: hanging but str run to ld last strides* **25/1**
14-5 **2** nk **Obrigado (USA)**[11] 444 6-8-6 80 .... JohnEgan 5 87
(W J Haggas) *lw: mde most: gng easily over 1f out: hrd pressed fnl f: hdd last strides* **9/2**[2]
340- **2** dht **Sew'N'So Character (IRE)**[137] 5876 5-8-13 87 .... TonyCulhane 12 94
(M Blanshard) *wl in rr: drvn over 2f out: gd prog on outer over 1f out: str run fnl f: jst outpcd by wnr* **10/1**
5000 **4** hd **Waterside (IRE)**[19] 348 7-8-6 80 .... HayleyTurner 2 87
(G L Moore) *taken down early: cl up: rdn to chal 1f out: almost upsides nr fin: jst outpcd* **12/1**
-131 **5** ¾ **Northern Desert (IRE)**[27] 267 7-8-11 85 .... ChrisCatlin 7 92+
(P W Hiatt) *hld up towards rr: prog 2f out: nowhere to go and hmpd fr over 1f out to ins fnl f: r.o nr fin: nt rcvr* **11/2**[3]
0266 **6** nk **Outer Hebrides**[11] 444 5-8-10 84 ow1 ....(vt) JamieSpencer 10 89+
(Stef Liddiard) *lw: settled wl in rr: nt wl plcd over 1f out: nt clr run sn after: shkn up and r.o nr fin: no ch* **25/1**
2062 **7** 1 ¾ **Trifti**[11] 444 5-8-11 85 .... EddieAhern 4 87+
(C A Cyzer) *hld up midfield: effrt over 2f out: rdn whn nt clr run over 1f out to ins fnl f: no ch after* **14/1**
4261 **8** shd **Atlantic Quest (USA)**[11] 444 7-9-0 88 ....(p) AdrianMcCarthy 8 88
(R A Harris) *hld up in midfield: prog on outer over 2f out: drvn to chal 1f out: fnd nil and sn lost pl* **16/1**
-113 **9** hd **Bravo Maestro (USA)**[17] 377 5-8-11 90 .... JamesDoyle(5) 6 90
(N P Littmoden) *prom: rdn to press ldr over 1f out: hanging and sn btn* **4/1**[1]
2421 **10** 1 ½ **Speed Dial Harry (IRE)**[19] 348 4-7-13 80 ....(v) AndrewElliott(7) 1 76
(K R Burke) *prom: cl up on inner wl over 1f out: steadily wknd* **6/1**
0-46 **11** 3 ½ **Cardinal Venture (IRE)**[19] 348 8-9-0 88 ....(p) NCallan 9 77+
(K A Ryan) *stmbld s: pressed ldr to wl over 1f out: wkng whn n.m.r fnl f* **33/1**
-506 **12** 12 **Lygeton Lad**[3] 516 8-9-4 92 ....(t) SteveDrowne 3 54
(Miss Gay Kelleway) *b: b.hind: taken down early: midfield tl wknd 3f out: t.o* **12/1**
1m 36.51s (-2.92) **Going Correction** -0.125s/f (Stan) 12 Ran SP% **115.5**
Speed ratings (Par 107):109,108,108,108,107 107,105,105,105,103 100,88
PL: SSC £3.10, OB £1.80; EX: SSC £86.20, OB £56.60; CSF: SSC £123.31, OB £64.48; TRICAST: SSC/OB £683.40; OB/SSC £622.82 TOTE £27.30: £6.60 Trifecta £246.80 Part won. Pool: £695.36 - 0.30 winning units..
Owner John Guest **Bred** Mountarmstrong Stud **Trained** West Ilsley, Berks

FOCUS
This was a good, competitive handicap, but as is so often the case round Lingfield they finished in a bunch and a few of these were unlucky. However, the time was decent and the second and fourth along with the fifth set a reasonable standard.

NOTEBOOK
Capable Guest(IRE) did not go on as expected after finishing third in the 2004 Coventry Stakes but, switched to Polytrack for the first time off the back of a 148-day break, he was racing off a career-low mark and took advantage. Given he was well off the pace and racing widest of all on the turn into the home straight, he probably did well to get up and it has to be hoped he can finally progress. His main aim is apparently the Lincoln (this year at Redcar), and a 5lb penalty should help his chances of getting into that race, but the Lincoln Trial at Wolverhampton looks the logical step before then.
Sew'N'So Character(IRE), back on a winning mark, ran a fine race off the back of a 137-day break. He is not easy to win with, but it will be disappointing if he does not confirm the promise of this effort in his next few runs. (op 9-1)
Obrigado(USA) appreciated the return to Lingfield and was just held. He is not that consistent, but is useful when things fall right. (op 9-1)
Waterside(IRE) has been eased in the handicap following some below-par runs recently and, only 2lb higher than when last winning, ran much better. (op 14-1)
Northern Desert(IRE), 5lb higher than when winning over course and distance on his previous start, would have gone very close indeed with a clear run when looking to make his challenge in the straight. He clearly remains in good form. Official explanation: jockey said gelding was denied a clear run (op 5-1 tchd 6-1 in a place)
Outer Hebrides, given another chance over a trip this far, is another who would have finished even closer with a clearer run. Official explanation: jockey said gelding was denied a clear run
Trifti does not exactly look well handicapped, but he got little luck in running and is better than the bare form.
Bravo Maestro(USA) has been in good form lately, but he has not always convinced with his attitude and did not look on a going day this time. He may be high enough in the weights now. (op 7-2)
Speed Dial Harry(IRE) put up a fine effort to win a really hot handicap at Southwell on his previous start, but he had a 4lb higher mark to contend with and this faster surface does appear to suit as well. (op 13-2)
Cardinal Venture(IRE) Official explanation: jockey said gelding stumbled leaving stalls
Lygeton Lad Official explanation: trainer said gelding bled from the nose

543 BETDIRECT FREEPHONE 0800 211 222 FILLIES' H'CAP (DIV I) 7f (P)
4:00 (4:01) (Class 6) (0-60,60) 3-Y-O **£2,388** (£705; £352) **Stalls** Low

Form RPR
015- **1** **Fateful Attraction**[105] 6359 3-8-13 60 .... JamesDoyle(5) 8 68+
(I A Wood) *mde virtually all: kicked 3l clr 2f out: styd on wl: unchal* **9/2**[2]
0554 **2** 3 **In Hope**[8] 466 3-8-6 48 .... HayleyTurner 5 48
(Ernst Oertel) *mostly chsd wnr: outpcd over 2f out: no imp after* **14/1**
00-0 **3** 1 ½ **Oasis Sun (IRE)**[13] 422 3-8-10 52 .... JamieSpencer 3 48
(J R Best) *hld up in last pair: outpcd fr 3f out: prog on inner 2f out: wnt 3rd jst ins fnl f: kpt on* **9/2**[2]
-050 **4** ¾ **Flashing Floozie**[13] 422 3-8-10 55 .... RichardThomas(3) 5 49
(M F Harris) *t.k.h: hld up in midfield: outpcd over 2f out: effrt over 1f out: kpt on same pce* **12/1**
4-45 **5** 1 **Attitude Annie**[27] 269 3-9-4 60 .... PaulDoe 10 52
(S Dow) *hld up towards rr: outpcd over 2f out: plugged on same pce fr over 1f out* **4/1**[1]
5332 **6** 1 **Cool Isle**[12] 430 3-8-13 55 ....(b) TonyCulhane 7 44
(P Howling) *sn lost pl and pushed along: last 3f out: no ch after: styd on fnl f* **5/1**[3]
0-00 **7** ¾ **Mon Petite Amour**[17] 373 3-8-1 46 oh1 ....(p) EdwardCreighton(3) 4 34
(D W P Arbuthnot) *hld up in last pair: outpcd 3f out: effrt on inner over 1f out: no real prog* **25/1**
050- **8** 1 ¾ **Cecchetti (IRE)**[91] 6467 3-8-8 55 .... RichardKingscote(5) 2 38
(Mrs H Sweeting) *plld hrd: trckd ldrs: rdn over 2f out: wknd over 1f out* **25/1**
6-02 **9** 1 ¾ **Titus Wonder (IRE)**[15] 396 3-8-8 50 .... JohnEgan 1 29
(P A Blockley) *chsd ldrs: rdn 3f out: wknd wl over 1f out* **7/1**
0-00 **10** ½ **Native Tiptoes**[24] 298 3-8-10 52 .... MickyFenton 9 30
(Miss Gay Kelleway) *ldng trio to wl over 1f out: wknd rapidly* **20/1**
1m 25.57s (-0.32) **Going Correction** -0.125s/f (Stan) 10 Ran SP% **112.3**
Speed ratings (Par 92):96,92,90,90,88 87,86,84,82,82
CSF £60.38 CT £301.64 TOTE £5.70: £1.80, £3.30, £2.40; EX 69.20.
Owner M I Forbes **Bred** Vidin Gate Stud **Trained** Upper Lambourn, Berks

FOCUS
Just a moderate fillies' handicap, but Fateful Attraction won well in a time was just over half a second faster than the second division and the form looks pretty solid.
Cool Isle Official explanation: trainer said filly was outpaced throughout
Cecchetti(IRE) Official explanation: jockey said filly had run too keenly early on

The Form Book, Raceform Ltd, Compton, RG20 6NL

544 BETDIRECT FREEPHONE 0800 211 222 FILLIES' H'CAP (DIV II) 7f (P)
4:30 (4:30) (Class 6) (0-60,60) 3-Y-O £2,388 (£705; £352) Stalls Low

Form RPR
4042 1 **Miss Champagne (IRE)**[8] 466 3-8-9 51 FrancisNorton 1 53
(M Quinn) *mde all: rdn 2f out: 2l clr 1f out: hld on wl* 13/2[3]
0-00 2 ¾ **Lady Zanzara (USA)**[30] 239 3-8-13 55 WandersonD'Avila 5 55
(J W Hills) *s.s: plld hrd: hld up in detached last: prog over 2f out : bmpd along furiously and r.o to take 2nd nr fin* 25/1
60-2 3 ¾ **Marachi Band (USA)**[33] 199 3-9-4 60 (b) JamieSpencer 7 58
(E J O'Neill) *lw: mostly chsd wnr: rdn and no imp wl over 1f out: kpt on ins fnl f: nvr able to chal* 13/8[1]
050- 4 shd **Miss Dagger (IRE)**[190] 4636 3-8-6 55 KylieManser(7) 8 53
(J R Best) *taken down early: t.k.h and hld up: sme prog but nt on terms 2f out: styd on fnl f: nrst fin* 12/1
-246 5 hd **She Whispers (IRE)**[25] 286 3-8-10 52 ChrisCatlin 9 49
(W M Brisbourne) *chsd ldrs: effrt 2f out: drvn to dispute 2nd 1f out: fdd nr fin* 10/1
6655 6 2 **Ms Rainbow Runner**[13] 422 3-9-1 57 EddieAhern 2 49
(P Butler) *prom: rdn on inner 2f out: wknd ins fnl f* 9/2[2]
006- 7 shd **Samsouma (IRE)**[105] 6359 3-8-13 55 J-PGuillambert 10 47
(C E Brittain) *dwlt: sn prom: rdn over 2f out: wknd over 1f out* 13/2[3]
00-0 8 3 **Kissimee**[29] 248 3-7-13 46 oh11 (t) JamesDoyle(5) 3 31
(N P Littmoden) *dwlt: a in rr: out of tch and struggling over 2f out* 33/1
500- 9 nk **Paddy's Place (IRE)**[113] 6281 3-8-5 47 JimmyQuinn 6 31
(M Blanshard) *bit bkwd: racd wd: nvr on terms: last and struggling over 2f out* 33/1
006- 10 nk **Musette (IRE)**[173] 5058 3-8-4 49 AdamKirby(3) 4 32
(C G Cox) *chsd ldrs: rdn 1/2-way: sn lost pl: no ch after* 12/1

1m 26.1s (0.21) **Going Correction** -0.125s/f (Stan) 10 Ran SP% 117.1
Speed ratings (Par 92):93,92,91,91,90 88,88,85,84,84
CSF £156.04 CT £390.12 TOTE £5.70: £1.70, £6.10, £1.10; EX 89.90.
Owner Mrs S G Davies **Bred** James Kavanagh **Trained** Newmarket, Suffolk

FOCUS
A moderate fillies' handicap and the winning time was just over half a second slower than the first division.
Ms Rainbow Runner Official explanation: jockey said filly hung right

545 FIRST PAST THE POST AT BETDIRECT APPRENTICE H'CAP 2m (P)
5:00 (5:00) (Class 5) (0-75,72) 4-Y-O+ £3,238 (£963; £481; £240) Stalls Low

Form RPR
0-21 1 **Tycheros**[6] 482 4-8-4 57 5ex SaleemGolam 4 63
(S C Williams) *sn prom: trckd ldr 1/2-way: rdn to ld 2f out: idled in front: drvn out* 11/10[1]
05-0 2 ¾ **High Point (IRE)**[14] 237 8-9-11 72 (v1) AmirQuinn 9 77
(G P Enright) *racd freely: led: rdn and hdd 2f out: kpt on and pressed wnr fnl f: nt qckn* 8/1
1150 3 shd **Moon Emperor**[13] 420 9-9-11 72 (b) AdamKirby 5 77
(J R Jenkins) *hld up in last pair: prog to trck ldrs 3f out: rdn and nt qckn 2f out: styd on fnl f: gaining at fin* 5/1[3]
44 4 2 **Candarli (IRE)**[12] 166 10-8-13 60 NeilChalmers 3 62
(D R Gandolfo) *hld up towards rr: prog to trck ldrs gng wl 3f out: rdn and nt qckn over 1f out: one pce after* 14/1
3220 5 1 ¼ **Dubai Ace (USA)**[7] 478 5-9-4 65 EdwardCreighton 6 66
(Miss Sheena West) *hld up in last trio: prog 5f out: rdn to chse ldrs over 2f out: one pce after* 4/1[2]
46-6 6 1 ¼ **Bravura**[6] 482 8-8-5 57 (b) JamieJones(5) 8 56
(G L Moore) *chsd ldr to 1/2-way: styd wl in tch: rdn 2f out: wknd fnl f* 12/1
000/ 7 8 **Honey's Gift**[11] 947 7-8-1 53 oh18 LiamJones(5) 10 42
(G G Margarson) *trckd ldrs: rdn and lost tch 3f out: n.d after* 20/1
000- 8 12 **Lord Of Adventure (IRE)**[25] 6231 4-8-2 60 (p) JamesDoyle(5) 2 33
(Mrs L C Jewell) *in tch: drvn and struggling 6f out: last 5f out: no ch after* 33/1
0S0- 9 1 ½ **Tilla**[50] 6448 6-8-10 62 (e1) TravisBlock(5) 1 33
(Mrs A J Hamilton-Fairley) *hld up towards rr: rdn and lost tch 3f out: sn bhd* 66/1
00-0 10 6 **Rhetorical**[20] 338 5-8-1 53 oh23 AndrewElliott(5) 7 16
(P Butler) *prom: lost pl 1/2-way: swtchd to outer and drvn 7f out: wknd 5f out* 100/1

3m 26.64s (-2.15) **Going Correction** -0.125s/f (Stan)
WFA 4 from 5yo+ 6lb 10 Ran SP% 119.9
Speed ratings (Par 103):100,99,99,98,97 97,93,87,86,83
CSF £11.15 CT £34.89 TOTE £1.80: £1.30, £2.10, £1.30; EX 13.20 Place 6 £60.03, Place 5 £41.73.
Owner Stuart C Williams **Bred** London Thoroughbred Services Ltd **Trained** Newmarket, Suffolk
■ Stewards' Enquiry : Neil Chalmers three-day ban: careless riding (Mar 11,14-15)

FOCUS
A reasonable enough staying handicap for the grade, but the pace was just steady. The runner-up is the best guide to the level of the form.
T/Jkpt: Not won. T/Plt: £181.10 to a £1 stake. Pool: £58,930.60. 237.50 winning tickets. T/Qpdt: £90.10 to a £1 stake. Pool: £4,154.90. 34.10 winning tickets. JN

[524]SOUTHWELL (L-H)
Wednesday, March 1

OFFICIAL GOING: Standard
Wind: Fresh, behind Weather: Sunny

546 WIN £2M @ FOOTBALLPOOLS.COM APPRENTICE H'CAP 1m (F)
1:50 (1:51) (Class 6) (0-58,58) 4-Y-O+ £2,388 (£705; £352) Stalls Low

Form RPR
40-P 1 **Pauline's Prince**[32] 227 4-8-10 58 HugoFellows(6) 1 64
(R Hollinshead) *hld up in tch: led and hung lft over 1f out: rdn out* 50/1
-050 2 ¾ **Shrine Mountain (USA)**[6] 492 4-8-10 52 KirstyMilczarek 8 56
(J R Holt) *chsd ldr: led wl over 2f out: rdn and hdd over 1f out: styd on* 40/1
4-32 3 ¾ **Majehar**[8] 471 4-8-0 46 oh1 JosephWalsh(4) 11 49
(A G Newcombe) *prom: lost pl 6f out: hdwy u.p over 1f out: hung lft : r.o* 9/2[2]
1045 4 2 ½ **Mulberry Lad (IRE)**[5] 502 4-8-2 48 ow1 WilliamCarson(4) 12 45
(P W Hiatt) *hld up: hdwy over 3f out: rdn and hung lft over 1f out: wknd ins fnl f* 11/1
2213 5 4 **Pawn In Life (IRE)**[3] 527 8-8-9 51 6ex (v) KevinGhunowa 2 39
(M J Polglase) *s.i.s: outpcd: rdn over 2f out: nvr nrr* 7/1
0520 6 nk **Sriology (IRE)**[8] 471 5-8-8 54 ow2 JBrennan(4) 9 42
(G Prodromou) *dwlt: outpcd: styd on ins fnl f: nvr nrr* 7/1
3221 7 ½ **Golden Spectrum (IRE)**[3] 526 7-8-10 56 6ex (p) TolleyDean(4) 5 43
(R A Harris) *sn led: rdn and hdd wl over 2f out: wknd over 1f out* 3/1[1]
-034 8 nk **Xaloc Bay (IRE)**[3] 527 8-8-4 46 oh6 (b) ThomasO'Brien 3 32
(R A Harris) *s.i.s: hdwy 6f out: rdn over 2f out: wknd over 1f out* 9/1
1321 9 1 ¼ **Vancouver Gold (IRE)**[13] 427 4-8-9 55 PatrickDonaghy(4) 13 38
(K R Burke) *prom over 5f* 5/1[3]
0050 10 dist **Glenviews Oldport (USA)**[16] 395 4-8-5 47 oh1 ow1 (b) RonanKeogh 6 —
(Peter Grayson) *chsd ldrs over 4f* 25/1
000/ 11 14 **Simnel (IRE)**[1219] 5534 7-8-2 48 oh16 ow2 MarkCoumbe(4) 7 —
(S L Keightley) *chsd ldrs to 1/2-way* 150/1

1m 45.06s (0.46) **Going Correction** -0.05s/f (Stan) 11 Ran SP% 112.1
Speed ratings (Par 101):95,94,93,91,87 86,86,85,84,—, —
CSF £1263.15 CT £10484.53 TOTE £40.70: £10.40, £13.90, £1.60; EX 1000.60.
Owner N Chapman **Bred** R Hollinshead **Trained** Upper Longdon, Staffs
■ The first career win for Hugo Fellows.

FOCUS
This did not look a great race beforehand and even less so afterwards as it proved a complete skinner for punters with a 50/1 shot beating a 40/1 shot The winning time was modest for the class and the first two are the best guides to the form.
Golden Spectrum(IRE) Official explanation: trainer said gelding finished distressed
Glenviews Oldport(USA) Official explanation: jockey said filly lost its action

547 DAVID ORTON'S 65TH BIRTHDAY CLAIMING STKS 5f (F)
2:25 (2:25) (Class 6) 4-Y-O+ £2,388 (£705; £352) Stalls High

Form RPR
-104 1 **Maktavish**[11] 450 7-9-0 82 (b) GregFairley(5) 2 74
(I Semple) *hmpd s: led and sn clr: pushed out* 8/15[1]
0600 2 1 ½ **Lady Bahia (IRE)**[7] 480 5-8-5 60 (b) RobbieFitzpatrick 5 55
(Peter Grayson) *sn outpcd: hdwy u.p over 1f out: r.o: no ch w wnr* 40/1
1252 3 1 ½ **Byo (IRE)**[5] 501 8-9-1 59 TonyCulhane 1 60
(P Howling) *wnt rt s: chsd wnr: rdn 3f out: no imp fnl f* 10/3[2]
6060 4 2 **He's A Rocket (IRE)**[7] 480 5-8-11 52 (b) FrancisNorton 4 48
(K R Burke) *chsd ldrs: rdn 1/2-way: wknd over 1f out* 9/1[3]
3460 5 1 ¾ **Sir Sandrovitch (IRE)**[7] 485 10-9-2 52 (p) EdwardCreighton(3) 3 50
(R W Price) *s.i.s: outpcd* 20/1
6-00 6 1 ½ **Hellbent**[3] 524 7-9-1 47 JimmyQuinn 6 41
(M Appleby) *sn outpcd* 66/1

59.22 secs (-1.08) **Going Correction** -0.175s/f (Stan) 6 Ran SP% 107.0
Speed ratings (Par 101):101,98,96,93,90 87
CSF £27.07 TOTE £1.60: £1.10, £5.40; EX 20.30.The winner was claimed by Declan Carroll for £12,000.
Owner D G Savala **Bred** V Robin Lawson **Trained** Carluke, S Lanarks

FOCUS
A moderate claimer in which the six runners finished in exactly the order adjusted official ratings suggested they should. The placed horses set the level for the form.

548 97% PAYOUTS AT LITTLEWOODSCASINO.COM H'CAP 1m 4f (F)
3:00 (3:00) (Class 5) (0-70,70) 3-Y-O £3,238 (£963; £481; £240) Stalls Low

Form RPR
644 1 **Bariloche**[33] 215 3-9-4 70 (be) DarryllHolland 7 77
(J R Boyle) *s.i.s and wnt lft s: sn drvn to chse ldrs: hung lft fr over 2f out: led over 1f out: styd on u.p* 10/1
00-1 2 5 **Orvietan (IRE)**[14] 419 3-9-4 70 JoeFanning 9 69
(M Johnston) *chsd ldr tl led 1/2-way: rdn: edgd lft and hdd over 1f out: styng on same pce whn hung rt ins fnl f* 7/2[1]
-260 3 8 **Night Groove (IRE)**[35] 188 3-8-8 60 ow1 (b1) NCallan 11 47
(N P Littmoden) *chsd ldrs: rdn over 3f out: hung lft and wknd over 2f out* 11/1
-021 4 2 **Subsidise (IRE)**[13] 430 3-8-8 60 (b) MickyFenton 4 44
(J G Given) *prom: lost pl 1/2-way: hdwy over 3f out: sn rdn: hung lft and wknd* 9/2[3]
20-0 5 12 **Captivate**[14] 422 3-8-4 56 oh3 (p) FrancisNorton 8 22
(M J Polglase) *prom: lost pl over 9f out: sn bhd* 25/1
00-6 6 1 ¾ **Northerner (IRE)**[20] 349 3-8-6 58 oh1 ow2 RobbieFitzpatrick 3 21
(J R Norton) *in rr: hdwy over 4f out: rdn and wknd over 3f out* 12/1
000- 7 3 ½ **Wise Choice**[155] 5536 3-7-13 56 JamesDoyle(5) 10 14
(N P Littmoden) *outpcd: sme hdwy over 3f out: sn wknd* 8/1
-020 8 2 ½ **Perfect Order (USA)**[13] 430 3-8-5 57 JohnEgan 2 11
(N A Callaghan) *led: racd keenly: hdd 1/2-way: wknd over 3f out* 12/1
6-60 9 23 **Ullah Pendragon (IRE)**[35] 188 3-8-4 56 oh5 (p) AdrianMcCarthy 1 —
(M J Polglase) *hld up in tch: rdn and wknd 1/2-way* 50/1
500- 10 10 **Sunderland Echo (IRE)**[133] 5976 3-8-8 60 TomEaves 6 —
(B Ellison) *hmpd s: in rr: effrt 1/2-way: sn wknd* 33/1
6-23 11 6 **Princess Society (IRE)**[16] 406 3-9-2 68 EddieAhern 5 —
(E A L Dunlop) *prom: rdn 5f out: wknd wl over 3f out* 4/1[2]

2m 42.88s (0.79) **Going Correction** -0.05s/f (Stan) 11 Ran SP% 113.1
Speed ratings (Par 98):95,91,86,85,77 75,73,71,56,49 45
CSF £42.51 CT £394.40 TOTE £10.80: £2.40, £1.60, £3.50; EX 46.20 Trifecta £706.70 Pool: £1,572.83 - 1.58 winning tickets..
Owner M Khan X2 **Bred** Meon Valley Stud **Trained** Epsom, Surrey

FOCUS
This was run at a decent early pace and it proved a real test of stamina. Only the front pair counted from some way out. Several in this line-up were stepping up in trip and some of them found it all too much and the extended distances exaggerate the superiority of the first two.
Wise Choice Official explanation: jockey said gelding was unsuited by the Southwell track
Princess Society(IRE) Official explanation: jockey said filly had no more to give

549 ANDY CLEMENTS OF TIBBY IS 40 TODAY H'CAP 1m 6f (F)
3:30 (3:30) (Class 6) (0-65,65) 4-Y-O+ £2,388 (£705; £352) Stalls Low

Form RPR
2464 1 **Sugitani (USA)**[7] 482 4-8-11 57 (b) MickyFenton 6 73+
(N B King) *m in snatches in rr: hdwy u.p over 2f out: led over 1f out: edgd rt ins fnl f: styd on wl* 11/2[2]
5521 2 6 **Polish Power (GER)**[9] 457 6-9-3 59 6ex JohnEgan 14 67
(J S Moore) *hld up: hdwy over 4f out: led 2f out: rdn: hung lft and hdd over 1f out: sn outpcd* 6/1[3]
2432 3 6 **Romil Star (GER)**[6] 490 9-9-8 64 (p) PatCosgrave 7 64
(K R Burke) *chsd ldr tl led over 5f out: rdn and hdd over 2f out: wknd over 1f out* 25/1
1116 4 ¾ **Jackie Kiely**[6] 491 5-9-8 64 TonyCulhane 13 63
(P Howling) *prom: chsd ldr over 4f out: led over 2f out: sn hdd & wknd* 11/1
14-6 5 nk **Blue Opal**[43] 131 4-8-4 50 JimmyQuinn 4 49
(Miss S E Hall) *trckd ldrs: rdn over 2f out: sn ev ch: wknd over 1f out* 14/1

2620 **6** ½ **High Frequency (IRE)**[12] 443 5-8-8 **50** .... PaulFessey 5 48
(T D Barron) *hld up in tch: rdn over 3f out: wknd over 2f out* **9/2**[1]
1034 **7** 5 **Padre Nostro (IRE)**[15] 414 7-9-2 **58** .... BrianReilly 1 50
(J R Holt) *hld up: plld hrd: hdwy over 5f out: wknd over 3f out* **20/1**
0-34 **8** nk **Sun Hill**[48] 98 6-9-4 **63** .... PaulMulrennan(3) 3 54
(C W Fairhurst) *mi-div: lost pl 1/2-way: rdn and nt clr run 3f out: n.d* **12/1**
5132 **9** 13 **Makarim (IRE)**[17] 389 10-8-8 **50** ....(p) AlanDaly 11 25
(M R Bosley) *hld up in tch: hmpd 4f out: hung rt and wknd over 3f out* **8/1**
/5-5 **10** 14 **Valeureux**[9] 470 8-8-6 **48** .... DaleGibson 9 4
(J Hetherton) *sn led: hdd over 5f out: rdn and wknd over 3f out* **11/1**
4100 **11** 11 **Night Warrior (IRE)**[18] 379 6-8-9 **51** ....(b) NCallan 12 —
(N P Littmoden) *hld up: plld hrd: wknd over 4f out* **8/1**
-002 **12** 27 **Mi Odds**[13] 425 10-9-9 **65** .... RobertWinston 8 —
(Mrs N Macauley) *in rr: hdwy 6f out: rdn and wknd 4f out* **20/1**
0/ **13** 8 **Mr Fast (ARG)**[187] 9-9-1 **57** .... LPKeniry 2 —
(J Gallagher) *s.i.s: hld up: plld hrd: rdn 1/2-way: sn wknd* **50/1**
206- **14** 7 **Mr Rein (IRE)**[345] 672 4-9-2 **62** .... TomEaves 10 —
(J Parkes) *prom: rdn 8f out: wknd over 6f out* **100/1**

3m 7.74s (-1.86) **Going Correction** -0.05s/f (Stan)
WFA 4 from 5yo+ 4lb **14** Ran SP% **117.4**
Speed ratings (Par 101):103,99,96,95,95 95,92,92,84,76 70,55,50,46
CSF £35.12 CT £765.77 TOTE £5.70: £2.00, £2.40, £5.30; EX 58.60.
Owner Martin Bailey **Bred** Jayeff 'B' Stables **Trained** Newmarket, Suffolk

FOCUS
Races over this trip on Fibresand are usually a proper test of stamina and that was again the case here. The first two set the standard and the form looks sound enough.
Valeureux Official explanation: trainer's representative said gelding had a breathing problem
Night Warrior(IRE) Official explanation: jockey said gelding hung left in the final 4f

550 TEXT "BETDIRECT" TO 88600 H'CAP — 7f (F)
4:05 (4:05) (Class 4) (0-85,80) 3-Y-O **£6,477** (£1,927; £963; £481) **Stalls** Low

Form RPR
22-3 **1** **Ludovico**[30] 254 3-8-12 **74** .... NCallan 6 87+
(K A Ryan) *w ldrs: racd keenly: led over 2f out: drvn clr fnl f* **3/1**[2]
2-21 **2** 3½ **Stonecrabstomorrow (IRE)**[25] 293 3-8-13 **75** .... JoeFanning 1 79
(P F I Cole) *a.p: rdn to chse wnr over 1f out: styd on same pce* **11/4**[1]
4501 **3** 1 **Outlook**[11] 447 3-8-11 **73** ....(b) GrahamGibbons 7 75
(N P Littmoden) *hld up: rdn over 4f out: hdwy u.p over 1f out: nt rch ldrs* **11/1**
102- **4** 2½ **Glenbuck (IRE)**[71] 6634 3-8-9 **71** ....(v) SamHitchcott 3 67
(A Bailey) *sn led: rdn and hdd over 2f out: wknd ins fnl f* **6/1**[3]
00-5 **5** 2 **Memphis Man**[21] 341 3-9-4 **80** .... MichaelHills 4 71
(G C Bravery) *s.i.s: hld up: effrt over 2f out: wknd fnl f* **12/1**
1311 **6** ¾ **Prettilini**[6] 488 3-8-12 **74** 6ex .... TonyCulhane 8 63
(P Howling) *chsd ldrs: rdn over 2f out: wknd fnl f* **12/1**
145 **7** 3½ **Ohana**[11] 447 3-8-4 **71** ....(b[1]) JamesDoyle(5) 2 51
(N P Littmoden) *s.i.s: outpcd* **12/1**
2101 **8** 3½ **Ockums Razor (IRE)**[19] 364 3-9-1 **77** .... EddieAhern 5 48
(M J Polglase) *chsd ldrs over 4f* **13/2**

1m 30.31s (-0.49) **Going Correction** -0.05s/f (Stan) **8** Ran SP% **110.7**
Speed ratings (Par 100):100,96,94,92,89 88,84,80
CSF £10.88 CT £72.20 TOTE £4.00: £1.80, £1.50, £2.90; EX 12.80.
Owner Pedro Rosas **Bred** M Grant And W Hawkings **Trained** Hambleton, N Yorks

FOCUS
With several of these having made the running in the past, there was always likely to be plenty of pace on. THe form looks reasonably solid and the winner scored decisively

551 PLAY NOW AT BETDIRECTPOKER.COM MAIDEN STKS — 6f (F)
4:40 (4:40) (Class 5) 3-Y-O **£3,238** (£963; £481; £240) **Stalls** Low

Form RPR
663 **1** **Blushing Thief (USA)**[14] 418 3-9-3 70 .... RobertWinston 2 81+
(W Jarvis) *s.i.s: sn chsng ldrs: led 1/2-way: rdn clr over 1f out* **13/8**[1]
5020 **2** 9 **Mind Out (USA)**[11] 449 3-9-3 52 .... MickyFenton 3 54
(J T Stimpson) *led to 1/2-way: outpcd over 1f out* **33/1**
05-2 **3** ¾ **Blue Beacon**[51] 70 3-8-12 69 .... NCallan 5 47
(K A Ryan) *chsd ldrs: rdn over 2f out: outpcd over 1f out* **6/1**[3]
60-5 **4** 1¼ **Tequila Rose (IRE)**[44] 120 3-8-12 46 .... SamHitchcott 6 43
(A Bailey) *hld up: plld hrd: effrt over 2f out: no imp* **66/1**
-453 **5** 1 **Phinerine**[8] 473 3-9-3 63 .... AdrianMcCarthy 4 45
(R A Harris) *prom: racd keenly: styd on same pce fnl 2f* **8/1**
322- **6** nk **Halfwaytoparadise**[133] 5985 3-8-12 72 .... HayleyTurner 7 39
(M L W Bell) *prom: outpcd wl over 2f out: no ch whn hung lft over 1f out* **9/4**[2]

1m 16.54s (-0.36) **Going Correction** -0.05s/f (Stan) **6** Ran SP% **98.7**
Speed ratings (Par 98):100,88,87,85,84 83
CSF £35.99 TOTE £2.30: £1.60, £4.70; EX 35.70.
Owner D Heath **Bred** I Cowan And Marjorie Cowan **Trained** Newmarket, Suffolk
■ Keelings Donabate was withdrawn on vet's advice (8/1). R4 applies, deduct 10p in the £.
■ Stewards' Enquiry : Adrian McCarthy two-day ban: used whip with excessive frequency (Mar 14-15)

FOCUS
What had looked an ordinary maiden beforehand was turned into a procession by the winner who completely routed his opponents after travelling well throughout. As the fields were finishing strung out all afternoon he could be flattered by the winning margin.

552 PLAY LITTLEWOODS POOLS ON 0800 500 000 H'CAP — 6f (F)
5:10 (5:10) (Class 6) (0-60,60) 4-Y-O+ **£2,388** (£705; £352) **Stalls** Low

Form RPR
5040 **1** **Sweet Pickle**[4] 519 5-8-10 **55** ....(e) AmirQuinn(3) 11 67
(J R Boyle) *s.i.s: hdwy over 4f out: led 2f out: rdn and hung lft over 1f out: r.o* **8/1**
1520 **2** 2 **Doctor Dennis (IRE)**[13] 428 9-9-3 **59** ....(v) JimmyQuinn 6 65
(J Pearce) *s.i.s: hld up: hdwy 1/2-way: rdn to chse wnr over 1f out: styd on* **13/2**[3]
1056 **3** 2 **Zorn**[6] 489 7-9-0 **56** .... J-PGuillambert 9 56
(P Howling) *led: hdd over 4f out: rdn over 2f out: styd on same pce fnl f* **7/1**
0042 **4** 1¼ **Alexia Rose (IRE)**[6] 489 4-9-3 **59** .... FrancisNorton 8 55
(A Berry) *chsd ldrs: rdn over 2f out: sn edgd lft: no ex fnl f* **11/2**[2]
1142 **5** shd **Shadow Jumper (IRE)**[13] 428 5-9-4 **60** ....(v) MickyFenton 5 56
(J T Stimpson) *w ldrs: led over 2f out: sn rdn and hdd: wknd fnl f* **4/1**[1]
10-0 **6** 6 **Muara**[13] 424 4-8-8 **55** .... MarkLawson(5) 13 33
(D W Barker) *sn pushed along in rr: nvr nrr* **33/1**
-000 **7** ½ **Time N Time Again**[7] 486 8-9-4 **60** .... RobbieFitzpatrick 2 36
(Peter Grayson) *s.i.s: hdwy 1/2-way: wknd 2f out* **18/1**
00-0 **8** ½ **Attorney**[59] 4 8-9-2 **58** .... RobertWinston 14 33
(P D Evans) *hld up: rdn over 3f out: n.d* **10/1**
0031 **9** nk **Straffan (IRE)**[3] 529 4-8-9 **51** 6ex ....(b) DaleGibson 4 25
(J Hetherton) *w ldrs: led over 4f out: rdn and hdd over 2f out: wknd over 1f out* **10/1**
00-0 **10** 3 **Trew Flight (USA)**[9] 461 4-9-1 **60** .... SaleemGolam(3) 7 25
(M H Tompkins) *dwlt: outpcd* **25/1**
1210 **11** 3 **Christian Bendix**[6] 489 4-8-13 **55** .... DarryllHolland 12 11
(P Howling) *mid-div: rdn over 3f out: wknd over 2f out* **8/1**

1m 16.37s (-0.53) **Going Correction** -0.05s/f (Stan) **11** Ran SP% **113.7**
Speed ratings (Par 101):101,98,95,94,93 85,85,84,84,80 76
CSF £57.17 CT £381.88 TOTE £10.10: £2.30, £2.10, £2.70; EX 89.20 Place 6 £110.03, Place 5 £18.97.
Owner M Khan X2 **Bred** C T Van Hoorn **Trained** Epsom, Surrey

FOCUS
A competitive if modest sprint handicap run at a decent pace with a three-way battle for the early lead. Those in the frame behind the winner give the form a strong and reliable appearance.
Sweet Pickle Official explanation: trainer said, regarding the improved form shown, mare had been hampered in running last time
Time N Time Again Official explanation: jockey said gelding hung right
T/Jkpt: Not won. T/Plt: £179.20 to a £1 stake. Pool: £91,145.10. 371.20 winning tickets. T/Qpdt: £21.70 to a £1 stake. Pool: £10,330.70. 351.50 winning tickets. CR

538 LINGFIELD (L-H)
Thursday, March 2

OFFICIAL GOING: Standard
Wind: Moderate, across

553 BETDIRECT ON CHANNEL 4 TEXT 613 MAIDEN STKS — 5f (P)
2:10 (2:10) (Class 5) 3-Y-O+ **£3,238** (£963; £481; £240) **Stalls** High

Form RPR
2/ **1** **Financial Times (USA)**[630] 2804 4-9-12 .... NCallan 7 78
(Stef Liddiard) *sn led: clr over 1f out: drvn out fnl f: jst hld on* **7/1**[3]
23-2 **2** shd **Best Double**[3] 533 3-8-8 69 .... NickyMackay 4 68
(G A Butler) *hld up in tch: rdn and hdwy over 1f out: r.o wl to go cl 2nd post* **5/4**[1]
60-0 **3** hd **Cool Sting (IRE)**[9] 473 3-8-13 70 .... DarryllHolland 5 72
(A M Balding) *chsd ldrs wnt 2nd 2f out: rdn and lost 2nd cl home* **7/1**[3]
02-3 **4** 3½ **Serevi (IRE)**[12] 449 3-8-13 75 .... JamieSpencer 8 60
(J Noseda) *in rr tl rdn and styd on ins fnl f: nvr nrr* **7/4**[2]
\- **5** 3½ **Peggys First** 4-9-12 .... PatCosgrave 1 52
(D E Cantillon) *v.s.a: a bhd* **40/1**
3-00 **6** 3 **Silver Reign**[17] 396 5-9-9 40 ....(p) NeilChalmers(3) 3 41
(J J Bridger) *broke wl: sn hdd: rdn and lost 2nd 2f out: wknd over 1f out* **50/1**
00-0 **7** 8 **War Dancer**[33] 219 4-9-12 47 .... VinceSlattery 2 12
(E A Wheeler) *slowly away and a outpcd* **100/1**

58.40 secs (-1.38) **Going Correction** -0.125s/f (Stan)
WFA 3 from 4yo+ 13lb **7** Ran SP% **111.2**
Speed ratings (Par 103):106,105,105,99,94 89,76
CSF £15.43 TOTE £6.70: £2.70, £1.10; EX 17.00.
Owner Mrs Stef Liddiard **Bred** Patricia Elia And Christopher Elia **Trained** Great Shefford, Berks

FOCUS
This modest maiden was run at a decent pace and the form looks reliable with the placed horses setting the standard..

554 BETDIRECT ON AT THE RACES INTERACTIVE CLAIMING STKS — 7f (P)
2:40 (2:40) (Class 6) 3-Y-O **£2,730** (£806; £403) **Stalls** Low

Form RPR
-061 **1** **Mr Cheers**[10] 466 3-8-6 47 ....(b) JohnEgan 1 55+
(C A Dwyer) *in tch: short of room fr 2f out tl fnd room and r.o to go 2nd cl home: fin 2nd, 1¼l: awrdd r* **5/1**[3]
1450 **2** 1¾ **Ohana**[1] 550 3-9-4 71 ....(b) NCallan 5 63
(N P Littmoden) *t.k.h: in tch: rdn to ld 1f out: hdd 50yds out and lost 2nd nr fin: fin 3rd, 1¼l & ½l: plcd 2nd* **5/1**[3]
0 **3** 4 **Macho Dancer (IRE)**[19] 374 3-8-8 .... NelsonDeSouza(7) 9 46
(R M Beckett) *in tch: hdwy 4f out: rdn and wknd appr fnl f: fin 4th,plcd 3rd* **16/1**
000- **4** hd **Sapphire Storm (IRE)**[106] 6366 3-7-8 50 ow2.....(tp) DonnaCaldwell(7) 3 35
(Miss D A McHale) *slowly away: nvr on terms: fin 5th, plcd 4th* **33/1**
4330 **5** ½ **Buzzin'Boyzee (IRE)**[33] 226 3-8-1 55 .... ChrisCatlin 10 34
(P D Evans) *racd wd: w ldrs tl wknd 2f out: fin 6th, plcd 5th* **11/1**
2106 **6** ½ **Bollywood (IRE)**[22] 342 3-9-8 70 .... MatthewHenry 4 54
(M R Hoad) *led tl rdn and hdd 1f out: wknd qckly: fin 7th, plcd 6th* **6/1**
6 **7** 4 **Dinner Dance**[16] 409 3-8-5 .... NickyMackay 11 27
(W J Haggas) *lost action over 4f out and a bhd after: fin 8th, plcd 7th* **11/1**
0324 **8** 1½ **Mr Rigsby**[6] 500 3-9-4 68 .... TonyCulhane 7 36
(P Howling) *w ldr: ev ch over 1f out: wknd rapidly: fin 9th, plcd 8th* **7/2**[1]
-000 **D** **African Concerto (IRE)**[8] 481 3-8-10 64 .... FrankieMcDonald 8 59
(S Kirk) *stdd s: hld up: rdn over 2f out: swtchd rt over 1f out: r.o strly to ld fnl 50yds: fin 1st, 1¼l: disq: prohibited substance (bute) in urine* **9/2**[2]

1m 26.13s (0.24) **Going Correction** -0.125s/f (Stan) **9** Ran SP% **113.5**
Speed ratings (Par 96):91,91,86,86,85 85,80,78,93
CSF £26.75 TOTE £6.10: £2.00, £2.10, £1.60; EX 35.10.African Concerto was claimed by Ernst Oertel for £8,000 (claim later annulled). Mr Cheers was claimed by Ron Harris for £6,000.
Owner D J Simpson **Bred** B N And Mrs Toye **Trained** Burrough Green, Cambs

FOCUS
There was no messing about in this with a four-horse battle for the lead from the start, which lasted until entering the home straight. However, it did not to them much good as none of the quartet made the frame and the front three all came from off the pace. The form looks reasonable rated around the first three.
Mr Cheers Official explanation: jockey said gelding was denied a clear run
Ohana Official explanation: trainer said colt bled from nose
Dinner Dance Official explanation: trainer said filly lost her action on bend

555 BETDIRECT FREEPHONE 0800 211 222 FILLIES' H'CAP — 7f (P)
3:10 (3:10) (Class 4) (0-85,81) 4-Y-O+ **£6,477** (£1,927; £963; £481) **Stalls** Low

Form RPR
1123 **1** **Kindlelight Debut**[17] 404 6-8-12 **80** .... JamesDoyle(5) 2 92
(N P Littmoden) *hld up in rr: swtchd rt over 1f out: r.o strly to ld cl home* **7/2**[2]
20-4 **2** hd **Meditation**[23] 327 4-8-5 **68** .... JoeFanning 6 80
(I A Wood) *led rdn and in command ent fnl f: kpt on but hdd by fast-finishing wnr cl home* **10/1**

15-6 **3** 2 1/2 **Perfect Story (IRE)**[33] 220 4-9-4 **81** OscarUrbina 8 86
(J A R Toller) *in tch: hdwy 1/2-wy: wnt 2nd 2f out tl rdn and fdd ins no ex ins fnl f* **7/2**[2]
42-1 **4** *shd* **Nice Tune**[12] 451 4-9-4 **81** J-PGuillambert 4 86
(C E Brittain) *t.k.h: trckd ldrs: rdn and no ex ins fnl f* **11/4**[1]
253- **5** *hd* **Enford Princess**[152] 5603 5-9-1 **78** NCallan 3 83
(Miss B Sanders) *hld up: rdn and r.o fnl f: nvr nr to chal* **9/2**[3]
1600 **6** 2 1/2 **Kallista's Pride**[5] 519 6-8-4 **67** oh5 HayleyTurner 7 65
(J R Best) *plld hrd: trckd ldr to 2f out: sn btn* **14/1**
-050 **7** *2* **Depressed**[5] 519 4-8-8 **71** ow2 (p) DarryllHolland 1 64
(Ernst Oertel) *trckd ldrs tl v short of room on ins over 1f out: nt rcvr* **25/1**
56-0 **8** *3* **Moon Bird**[5] 519 4-8-4 **67** oh3 ChrisCatlin 5 53
(C A Cyzer) *slowly away: a bhd* **25/1**

1m 24.01s (-1.88) **Going Correction** -0.125s/f (Stan) **8** Ran SP% **112.7**
Speed ratings (Par 102):105,104,101,101,101 98,96,93
CSF £36.64 CT £129.63 TOTE £3.90: £1.80, £2.30, £1.40; EX 29.60.
Owner Kindlelight Ltd **Bred** Cheveley Park Stud Ltd **Trained** Newmarket, Suffolk
FOCUS
A decent fillies' handicap in which the pace was sound and the form looks solid for the type of contest.

556 LITTLEWOODS BETDIRECT H'CAP 1m 4f (P)
3:40 (3:41) (Class 4) (0-85,84) 4-Y-0+ **£6,477** (£1,927; £963; £481) **Stalls** Low

Form RPR
54-5 **1** **Zamboozle (IRE)**[17] 404 4-8-5 **73** JohnEgan 7 84+
(D R C Elsworth) *hld up in rr: stdy hdwy on outside over 2f out: rdn and edgd lft but qcknd wl to ld ins fnl f* **4/1**[1]
5015 **2** 1 1/4 **The Violin Player (USA)**[12] 454 5-9-2 **82** DarryllHolland 8 90+
(H J Collingridge) *mid-div: hdwy and rdn to ld 1f out: nt pce of wnr and hdd ins fnl f* **4/1**[1]
0-25 **3** 1 3/4 **Tromp**[29] 264 5-8-7 **73** RobertWinston 1 79+
(D J Coakley) *trckd ldrs tl lost pl over 3f out: swtchd rt wl over 1f out: r.o fnl f* **9/2**[2]
05/ **4** *1* **High Hope (FR)**[550] 5152 8-7-13 **70** RobynBrisland(5) 9 73
(G L Moore) *hld up: hdwy 3f out: ev ch 2f out: one pce fnl f* **33/1**
0302 **5** 3/4 **Gingko**[10] 463 9-8-8 **74** TQuinn 5 76
(P R Webber) *hld up: hdwy 3f out: one pce ent fnl f* **6/1**
1111 **6** 3/4 **Newnham (IRE)**[12] 454 5-8-9 **75** JoeFanning 6 76
(J R Boyle) *slowly away: in rr: rdn over 2f out: nvr on terms* **5/1**[3]
6524 **7** 1 1/4 **Just Fly**[10] 463 6-8-3 **72** (v) RichardThomas(3) 10 71
(Dr J R J Naylor) *in tch: led over 2f out: rdn and hdd 1f out: wknd qckly* **12/1**
6050 **8** 1 3/4 **Dower House**[12] 454 11-9-4 **84** (t) ChrisCatlin 4 80
(Andrew Turnell) *in tch tl rdn and wknd over 2f out* **16/1**
025- **9** *5* **Flying Spirit (IRE)**[66] 5074 7-8-5 **71** PaulHanagan 3 60
(G L Moore) *trckd ldr: led over 4f out: hdd over 2f out: wknd qckly* **10/1**
610- **10** *dist* **Shakerattleandroll (IRE)**[71] 6644 5-8-7 **73** JimmyQuinn 2 —
(Mrs L Richards) *racd keenly: led to over 4f out: sn wknd: t.o* **50/1**

2m 32.25s (-2.14) **Going Correction** -0.125s/f (Stan)
WFA 4 from 5yo+ 2lb **10** Ran SP% **116.7**
Speed ratings (Par 105):102,101,100,99,98 98,97,96,93,—
CSF £19.92 CT £74.87 TOTE £5.00: £1.70, £1.90, £2.00; EX 28.10 Trifecta £85.30 Pool: £1,614.26 - 13.43 winning units..
Owner Raymond Tooth **Bred** E Duggan And D Churchman **Trained** Newmarket, Suffolk
FOCUS
A decent handicap, but a very modest early pace which inevitably resulted in traffic problems for a few later on. However, the form looks reasonable with the placed horses close to their marks.

557 BETDIRECT.CO.UK H'CAP 1m 2f (P)
4:10 (4:10) (Class 5) (0-70,69) 4-Y-0+ **£3,238** (£963; £481; £240) **Stalls** Low

Form RPR
4442 **1** **Captain Margaret**[9] 478 4-9-2 **67** JimmyQuinn 4 74
(J Pearce) *chsd ldrs: led over 3f out: drvn out fnl f: hld on* **5/2**[1]
-036 **2** *hd* **King Of Knight (IRE)**[10] 462 5-8-8 **59** OscarUrbina 3 66
(G Prodromou) *hld up in tch: rdn over 1f out and r.o to press wnr ins fnl f* **5/1**[2]
-530 **3** 1 1/2 **Master'n Commander**[13] 443 4-8-11 **62** ChrisCatlin 9 66
(C A Cyzer) *wl bhd: rdn and outpcd over 3f out: rdn and hdwy over 1f out: picked up fnl f: nvr nrr* **11/1**[3]
-516 **4** 3 1/2 **Madhavi**[23] 327 4-8-7 **61** StephaneBreux(3) 2 58
(R Hannon) *trckd ldrs tl rdn and hung lft appr fnl f: one one pce after* **11/1**[3]
2412 **5** 1/2 **Lowestoft Playboy**[3] 537 4-9-0 **65** 6ex NCallan 1 61
(J Jay) *led tl hdd over 3f out: wknd over 1f out* **5/2**[1]
-005 **6** 1 1/2 **Piquet**[9] 471 8-7-13 **55** oh10 MarcHalford(5) 8 48
(J J Bridger) *t.k.h: in tch on outside: rdn and wknd over 1f out* **50/1**
0040 **7** *1* **Megalala (IRE)**[10] 459 5-8-3 **57** oh1 ow2 NeilChalmers(3) 6 48
(J J Bridger) *hld up: a towards rr* **33/1**
-000 **8** *hd* **Celtique**[22] 343 4-9-0 **65** JamieMackay 5 56
(M Wigham) *v.s.a: a bhd* **33/1**
3-5 **9** *14* **Smart Tiger (GER)**[3] 530 4-9-4 **69** (p) JamieSpencer 10 33
(N P Littmoden) *sn trckd ldr tl rdn and wknd 2f out: eased appr fnl f* **5/1**[2]

2m 7.56s (-0.23) **Going Correction** -0.125s/f (Stan) **9** Ran SP% **115.0**
Speed ratings (Par 103):95,94,93,90,90 89,88,88,77
CSF £15.12 CT £114.84 TOTE £3.60: £1.10, £1.70, £3.40; EX 19.50.
Owner Mrs Margaret Baxter **Bred** J Wilson **Trained** Newmarket, Suffolk
■ Stewards' Enquiry : Jimmy Quinn one-day ban: used whip with excessive frequency (Mar 14)
FOCUS
They went a very steady pace until the winner stepped things up half a mile from home. A very moderate winning time for a race of its class but the form looks reasonable with the first two basically to form.
Smart Tiger(GER) Official explanation: jockey said gelding had no more to give

558 PLAY LITTLEWOODS POOLS ON 0800 500 000 H'CAP 1m (P)
4:40 (4:40) (Class 5) (0-75,79) 3-Y-0 **£3,238** (£963; £481; £240) **Stalls** High

Form RPR
1-31 **1** **Orchard Supreme**[9] 475 3-9-10 **79** 6ex RobertWinston 7 87+
(R Hannon) *hld up in rr: hdwy over 1f out rdn and r.o to ld wl ins fnl f* **2/1**[1]
-510 **2** *hd* **Tamagin (USA)**[6] 500 3-8-9 **64** ow1 (p) NCallan 3 68
(P D Evans) *t.k.h: led: clr over 3f out: rdn over 1f out: r.o but hdd wl ins fnl f* **25/1**
2333 **3** 1 1/4 **Scroll**[2] 539 3-9-2 **71** (v) J-PGuillambert 6 72
(P Howling) *hld up: hdwy on ins over 1f out: nt qckn ins fnl f* **7/1**
65-1 **4** 1/2 **Super Frank (IRE)**[57] 30 3-8-6 **64** AdamKirby(3) 5 64
(G A Butler) *s.i.s: hdwy on ins 2f out: one pce ins fnl f* **11/2**[3]
63-0 **5** 1 1/2 **Chia (IRE)**[32] 234 3-8-12 **67** RobertHavlin 1 64
(D Haydn Jones) *a.p: chsd ldr 3f out: wknd fnl f* **16/1**
05-0 **6** *6* **Almowj**[8] 481 3-8-10 **65** (p) DarryllHolland 9 48
(C E Brittain) *a in rr* **25/1**
000 **7** 2 1/2 **Iberian Light (USA)**[19] 372 3-7-11 **59** oh1 SallyAdams(7) 8 37
(N A Callaghan) *racd wd: a in rr* **33/1**
313 **8** *2* **Babcary**[8] 483 3-9-1 **70** SteveDrowne 4 44
(M P Tregoning) *mid-div: rdn 2f out: sn wknd* **9/4**[2]
0-50 **9** *5* **Earth Master (IRE)**[15] 422 3-8-11 **66** ow2 JamieSpencer 2 29
(S Kirk) *trckd ldr: rdn 1/2-way: sn wknd* **12/1**

1m 37.7s (-1.73) **Going Correction** -0.125s/f (Stan) **9** Ran SP% **116.2**
Speed ratings (Par 98):103,102,101,101,99 93,91,89,84
CSF £57.00 CT £304.86 TOTE £2.70: £1.30, £4.90, £1.60; EX 46.60.
Owner Brian C Oakley **Bred** Mrs M H Goodrich **Trained** East Everleigh, Wilts
FOCUS
A decent winning time for a race of its type and the form looks fair for the class, rated around the third and fourth.

559 FOOTBALLPOOLS.COM H'CAP 1m (P)
5:10 (5:11) (Class 5) (0-75,75) 4-Y-0+ **£3,412** (£1,007; £504) **Stalls** High

Form RPR
50-0 **1** **Habshan (USA)**[33] 221 6-9-3 **74** DarryllHolland 7 83
(C F Wall) *a in tch: rdn and edgd lft ins fnl f bef hdd nr fin* **6/1**
6-00 **2** 1/2 **Kabeer**[13] 444 8-8-11 **73** (t) StephenDonohoe(5) 3 80
(Lucinda Featherstone) *led: clr 3f out: rdn and edgd rt ins fnl f: hdd nr fin* **16/1**
412- **3** 1 1/4 **First Show**[125] 6134 4-9-2 **73** JamieSpencer 1 79+
(J Noseda) *trckd ldrs: wnt 2nd over 2f out: n.m.r whn rdr dropped reins ins fnl f and lost 2nd* **4/1**[2]
5-03 **4** 3/4 **Wavertree Warrior (IRE)**[29] 267 4-9-4 **75** NCallan 8 78
(N P Littmoden) *hld up in tch: rdn over 1f out: kpt on one pce* **11/4**[1]
40-1 **5** *hd* **Arctic Desert**[32] 236 6-9-3 **74** SteveDrowne 5 77
(A M Balding) *s.i.s: hld up: rdn and hdwy 2f out: nt qckn fnl f* **5/1**[3]
446- **6** 1 1/2 **Kew The Music**[90] 6483 6-8-8 **65** ChrisCatlin 9 64
(M R Channon) *in rr: outpcd over 2f out: mde sme late hdwy* **11/1**
-536 **7** *nk* **Quantum Leap**[29] 267 9-8-11 **68** (v) JimmyQuinn 11 67
(S Dow) *in rr: hdwy on outside 1/2-way: wknd fnl f* **14/1**
1212 **8** *nk* **Mystic Man (FR)**[23] 321 8-9-4 **75** (b) PaulHanagan 4 73
(I W McInnes) *t.k.h: hld up: hdwy whn swtchd rt over 1f out: no further prog* **14/1**
4005 **9** *6* **Alekhine (IRE)**[10] 463 5-8-12 **72** (e) AmirQuinn(3) 10 57
(J R Boyle) *swtchd lft fr outside draw s: sme hdwy 2f out: sn btn* **10/1**
3-00 **10** 1 1/2 **Pamir (IRE)**[22] 340 4-9-4 **75** GeorgeBaker 12 56
(P R Chamings) *trckd ldr to over 2f out: wknd qckly* **25/1**
-000 **11** *nk* **Carry On Doc**[6] 505 5-8-9 **66** J-PGuillambert 6 47
(Ernst Oertel) *v.s.a: a bhd* **100/1**

1m 37.16s (-2.27) **Going Correction** -0.125s/f (Stan) **11** Ran SP% **119.1**
Speed ratings (Par 103):106,105,104,103,103 101,101,101,95,93 93
CSF £98.79 CT £442.55 TOTE £7.50: £2.10, £5.00, £1.90; EX 191.00 Place 6 £32.79, Place 5 £18.35.
Owner Alan & Jill Smith **Bred** Darley Stud Management, L L C **Trained** Newmarket, Suffolk
FOCUS
An ordinary handicap though the pace was solid and rated around the principals.
Habshan(USA) ◆ Official explanation: jockey said gelding hung severely left
Carry On Doc Official explanation: jockey said gelding missed break
T/Jkpt: £37,946.10 to a £1 stake. Pool: £106,890.50. 2.00 winning tickets. T/Plt: £59.10 to a £1 stake. Pool: £96,415.30. 1,189.25 winning tickets. T/Qpdt: £16.10 to a £1 stake. Pool: £8,675.10. 397.85 winning tickets. JS

506 NAD AL SHEBA (L-H)
Thursday, March 2
OFFICIAL GOING: Dirt course - fast; turf course - good to firm
The times suggest that the dirt course was riding pretty fast.

560a DERRINSTOWN STUD BURJ NAHAAR (GROUP 3) (DIRT) 1m (D)
3:45 (3:50) 3-Y-0+ **£75,581** (£23,255; £11,627; £5,813)

RPR
1 **Marbush (IRE)**[7] 495 5-9-2 105 (e) JMurtagh 12 117
(D Selvaratnam, UAE) *trckd ldrs in centre: prog to dispute 3f out: led 2 1/2f out: clr 1f out: easily* **7/1**[3]
2 7 1/4 **Win River Win (USA)**[42] 152 7-9-2 107 HKaratas 9 103
(S Gokdemir, Turkey) *rdn early: settled in mid-div: rdn 4f out: 12th ent st: r.o fnl 2 1/2f: no ch w wnr* **11/2**[2]
3 2 1/4 **Opportunist (IRE)**[341] 733 7-9-2 108 (vt) WSupple 4 98
(Doug Watson, UAE) *mid-div on rail: prog to trck ldrs 4f out on rail: n.m.r 2 1/2f out: r.o wl* **14/1**
4 2 3/4 **Emerald Beauty (ARG)**[6] 508 6-8-11 96 (bt) WCMarwing 7 88
(M F De Kock, South Africa) *trckd ldrs: n.m.r 4 1/2f out: rdn 2 1/2f out: r.o but n.d* **10/1**
5 *3* **Thajja (IRE)**[14] 434 5-9-2 105 (v) RHills 15 87
(Doug Watson, UAE) *mid-div: prog to trck wnr 3f out: hrd rdn 2f out: kpt on one pce* **8/1**
6 1 3/4 **Rock Music**[14] 434 4-9-2 105 LDettori 8 83
(Saeed Bin Suroor) *disp centre: hdd 3f out: one pce* **5/2**[1]
7 3 1/2 **Happy Pearl (AUS)**[7] 495 6-9-2 100 (b) MJKinane 2 76
(G Moore, Macau) *disp on rail: led briefly 3f out: nt qckn* **14/1**
8 *nk* **Ned Kelly (SAF)**[6] 511 5-9-2 94 (be) JBekker 13 75
(D Maroun, South Africa) *racd towards rr: sme prog st: nrst fin* **100/1**
9 3 3/4 **Grand Emporium (SAF)**[260] 2602 6-9-6 113 (t) TPO'Shea 10 72
(A Laird, UAE) *trckd ldrs tl hrd rdn 4f out: wknd* **9/1**
10 2 3/4 **Checkit (IRE)**[357] 596 6-9-2 100 KDarley 14 62
(R Bouresly, Kuwait) *racd in rr: n.d* **33/1**
11 1 1/4 **Parole Board (USA)**[7] 495 4-9-2 102 (t) RichardMullen 6 60
(A Laird, UAE) *mid-div: rdn 4f out: nvr a threat* **16/1**
12 *11* **Berlioz (IND)**[14] 438 5-9-2 93 (bt) RyanMoore 1 38
(S Padmanabhan, India) *nvr threatened* **66/1**
13 3 1/2 **Princely Venture (IRE)**[914] 4606 7-9-2 102 GHind 3 31
(R Bouresly, Kuwait) *v.s.a: nvr a threat* **40/1**
14 1/2 **Sea Hunter**[7] 495 4-9-2 95 (v) KerrinMcEvoy 5 30
(I Mohammed, UAE) *towards rr of main gp: nvr a threat* **25/1**
15 *13* **Cherry Pickings (USA)**[27] 9-9-2 107 (t) TedDurcan 11 4
(A Laird, UAE) *sn outpcd: a in rr: virtually p.u* **8/1**

16 7¾ **Secret Place**[6] 508 5-9-2 95 ....(bt[1]) WayneSmith 16 —
(M Al Muhairi, UAE) *nvr involved* **66/1**

1m 35.79s **Going Correction** +0.225s/f (Slow) **16** Ran SP% **130.2**

Speed ratings: 117,109,107,104,101 100,96,96,92,89 88,77,73,73,60 52

Owner Sheikh Ahmed Al Maktoum **Bred** Stratford Place Stud & Watership Down Stud **Trained** United Arab Emirates

FOCUS

This looked a reasonable and pretty competitive Group Three, but Marbush thrashed his rivals in a smart time and has developed into a high-class performer.

NOTEBOOK

Marbush(IRE) ◆ improved for the return to a mile when winning a course and distance handicap off a mark of 99 on his previous start and stepped up on that effort to record by far his best effort yet. He has been a smart performer for some time now, but this performance marks him down as high class; a view backed up by the clock. His winning time would have been good enough to win five of the previous six Godolphin Miles, so he will obviously go very close in that race if able to repeat this level of form.

Win River Win(USA) ◆ really caught the eye when defying a low draw off a mark of 102 in a nine-furlong handicap for a different stable on his debut in Dubai, but Spencer was replaced in the saddle and that, combined with both the drop in trip and step up in class, appeared to find him found. He was having to be pushed along from some way out and did well to take second.

Opportunist(IRE) ran with a great deal of credit on his return from a 341-day absence and really should improve.

Emerald Beauty(ARG) had a bit to find in this company, but the form of her recent second received a significant boost when the winner of that race, Tropical Star, took the Group Three on this card, and she ran well.

Thajja(IRE), up in both trip and grade, had a little bit to find but ran well.

Rock Music has progressed well at this Carnival, but his last success came in a handicap off a mark of 97 and this was tougher.

Happy Pearl(AUS) has been running well in handicaps at this year's Carnival and to see him finish so far down the field helps give the form a solid look.

561a DERRINSTOWN STUD AL BASTIKIYA (DIRT) 1m 1f (D)

4:15 (4:20) 3-Y-O **£56,686** (£17,441; £8,720; £4,360)

RPR

1 **Simpatico Bribon (CHI)**[76] 4-9-11 105 ....(t) JMurtagh 8 109
(I Jory, Saudi Arabia) *trckd ldr ent st: disp 2f out gng wl: kicked clr: easily* **7/1**[3]

2 6 **Where's That Tiger (USA)**[20] 368 3-8-9 108 .... WCMarwing 4 102
(M F De Kock, South Africa) *trckd ldrs: n.m.r 2½f out: clr run 1½f out and r.o wl but no ch w wnr* **10/11**[1]

3 5¼ **Unification (CAN)**[20] 368 3-8-11 102 ....(t) LDettori 12 94
(I Mohammed, UAE) *trckd ldr wd: rdn to dispute 3f out: led briefly but outpcd by wnr: one pce* **11/1**

4 4 **Jackson (BRZ)**[7] 4-9-8 101 ....(b) MJKinane 10 77
(A Cintra, Brazil) *trckd ldrs: rdn to dispute 3f out: led 2 1/2f out: hrd rdn 2f out: wknd* **9/1**

5 1¼ **Kilworth (IRE)**[20] 368 3-8-9 102 .... KerrinMcEvoy 3 82
(I Mohammed, UAE) *racd in rr: gng wl in last 3f out: swtchd centre: n.d* **16/1**

6 2¾ **Flashing Numbers (USA)**[20] 368 3-8-9 104 .... AStarke 1 77
(Mario Hofer, Germany) *slowly away: hld up in rr: t.k.h: sn in mid-div then dropped to rr again: nvr a threat* **5/1**[2]

7 14 **Wovoka (IRE)**[20] 368 3-8-9 90 .... TedDurcan 6 50
(M R Channon) *mid-div: swtchd wd 3f out and rdn: n.d* **66/1**

8 5 **Nomoretaxes (BRZ)**[7] 4-9-4 100 .... KShea 7 30
(M F De Kock, South Africa) *led tl hdd 3f out: wknd: eased fnl f* **11/1**

1m 49.15s **Going Correction** +0.225s/f (Slow)
WFA 3 from 4yo 20lb **8** Ran SP% **115.6**

Speed ratings: 116,110,106,102,101 98,86,82

Owner Prince Sultan Mohammed Saud Al Kabeer **Bred** Haras Santa Olga **Trained** Saudi Arabia

FOCUS

A good trial for the UAE Derby in which Simpatico Bribon beat the UAE 2000 Guineas runner-up five and a half lengths further than his stablemate Gold For Sale managed in Dubai's first classic of the season.

NOTEBOOK

Simpatico Bribon(CHI) ◆'s stablemate Gold For Sale only had half a length to spare over Where's That Tiger when winning the UAE 2000 Guineas, so this has to rate as a high-class performance. A Group One winner in South America, he recorded a time that would have been good enough to win the last two runnings of the UAE Derby and must be a leading contender in that race. While the opposition in the Derby is likely to be stronger than he faced here, it will be disappointing if anything from the UAE 2000 Guineas beat him and he looks set to go very close indeed.

Where's That Tiger(USA), a half-length second to Gold For Sale in the UAE 2000 Guineas on his debut in Dubai, looked to run his race but was no match whatsoever for that one's stablemate. He can only really hope for a place at best in the UAE Derby.

Unification(CAN) was beaten a long way but stepped up on the form he showed in the UAE 2000 Guineas and reversed form with Kilworth and Flashing Numbers.

Kilworth(IRE) failed to improve on the form he showed in the UAE 2000 Guineas.

Flashing Numbers(USA) caught the eye when fourth in the UAE 2000 Guineas, and promised to be suited by this step up in trip, but he finished up well beaten after losing his position just as the race got serious. This was disappointing and represented a significant backward step.

Wovoka(IRE) had plenty to find but does not seem to be progressing any case. A return to turf may suit.

562a DERRINSTOWN STUD DUBAI CITY OF GOLD (GROUP 3) (TURF) 1m 4f (T)

4:45 (4:50) 4-Y-O+ **£75,581** (£23,255; £11,627; £5,813)

RPR

1 **Oracle West (SAF)**[21] 354 5-8-11 107 .... KShea 10 114
(M F De Kock, South Africa) *settled towards rr: mid-div 3f out: rdn 2f out: led 1f out: r.o wl* **6/1**[3]

2 1¾ **Alayan (IRE)**[28] 280 4-8-10 112 .... MJKinane 3 112
(John M Oxx, Ire) *trckd ldrs then led main gp: rdn 3f out: led briefly 1f out: r.o wl* **6/1**[3]

3 ¾ **Falstaff (IRE)**[21] 356 4-8-10 110 .... WCMarwing 6 111
(M F De Kock, South Africa) *hld up in last: stl last 2½f out: r.o wl: nrst fin* **5/2**[1]

4 3¼ **Encinas (GER)**[20] 371 5-8-11 105 .... WMongil 9 105
(P Schiergen, Germany) *hld up in rr: rail on rail 3f out: n.m.r: swtchd 1½f out: r.o: nrst fin* **14/1**

5 2½ **Shanty Star (IRE)**[6] 509 6-8-11 112 .... GHind 4 101
(R Bouresly, Kuwait) *rdn to ld early: qcknd 4f out: clr 2½f out: chal 2f out: kpt on* **12/1**

6 ½ **Collier Hill**[166] 5331 8-9-4 116 .... DeanMcKeown 7 107
(G A Swinbank) *broke wl to trck ldrs: rdn to cl 3f out: nt qckn: swtchd to rail 1½f out: one pce* **8/1**

7 ¾ **Cherry Mix (FR)**[81] 6549 5-9-4 115 ....(t) LDettori 5 106
(Saeed Bin Suroor) *mid-div: rdn to cl 3f out: nvr threatened* **7/2**[2]

8 2 **Corriolanus (GER)**[14] 437 6-8-11 105 .... RyanMoore 2 96
(S Seemar, UAE) *settled rr: gng wl on rail 3f out: rdn 2½f out: nvr a threat* **33/1**

9 8 **Crosspeace (IRE)**[6] 512 4-8-10 109 .... KDarley 8 84
(M Johnston) *mid-div: racd wd: rdn 6f out: sn btn* **11/1**

10 15 **Sights On Gold (IRE)**[341] 737 7-8-11 113 ....(t) KerrinMcEvoy 1 59
(Saeed Bin Suroor) *mid-div on rail: rdn to cl 2½f out: ev ch 2f out: nt qckn* **16/1**

2m 33.89s **Going Correction** +0.75s/f (Yiel)
WFA 4 from 5yo+ 2lb **10** Ran SP% **122.0**

Speed ratings: 117,115,115,113,111 111,110,109,104,94

Owner A Geemooi **Bred** Langeberg Stud **Trained** South Africa

FOCUS

A good Group Three that should provide a few clues to the Sheema Classic on World Cup night.

NOTEBOOK

Oracle West(SAF), successful in a couple of ten-furlong handicaps on his two previous starts at this year's Carnival off marks of 95 and 100 respectively, completed the hat-trick in pretty good style on this step up in class and trip. He will find things tougher in the Group One Sheema Classic on World Cup night, but deserves his chance and should go well.

Alayan(IRE), upped to a mile and a half for the first time, ran better than on his debut in Dubai when well held over an extended mile and found only the in-form winner too good.

Falstaff(IRE), successful in a ten-furlong handicap off a mark of 102 on his previous start, ran well behind his stablemate on this step up in class, but basically got going too late. He should be capable of better again.

Encinas(GER), upped in class, did not get a great run through when looking to make his move and is a better than he was able to show.

Shanty Star(IRE), successful in a ten-furlong handicap off a mark of 104 on his previous start, got his own way in front but could not repeat that level of form in this better company.

Collier Hill, a fine winner of the Irish St Leger when last seen 166 days previously, made a pleasing return to action under his Group One penalty and this should put him right for Sheema Classic on World Cup night - he was third in that race last year.

Cherry Mix(FR) lacks consistency and did not pick up after appearing to hold every chance.

Crosspeace(IRE) never really got involved and was below form.

Sights On Gold(IRE) offered nothing on his return from a near year-long absence.

563a DERRINSTOWN STUD MAHAB AL SHIMAAL (GROUP 3) (DIRT) 6f (D)

5:15 (5:20) 3-Y-O+ **£75,581** (£23,255; £11,627; £5,813)

RPR

1 **Tropical Star (IRE)**[6] 508 6-9-4 111 ....(vt) RoystonFfrench 4 108
(A Al Raihe, UAE) *slowly away: sn prom centre: rdn to ld 2f out: r.o wl* **11/4**[2]

2 2¼ **Azul Da Guanabara (BRZ)**[7] 495 4-9-0 95 ....(t) ADomingos 12 97
(Luis Singnoretti, Brazil) *nt far away nr side: rdn 3f out: ev ch 2f out: kpt on wl* **50/1**

3 ½ **Howick Falls (USA)**[14] 431 5-9-4 100 ....(v) TPO'Shea 11 100
(E Charpy, UAE) *mid-div: prog to chal 2f out: ev ch: nt pce of wnr* **14/1**

4 2¾ **Karlo Guitar (BRZ)**[14] 433 6-9-4 95 .... MAlmeida 10 91
(C Morgado, Brazil) *v.s.a: last 3½f out: u.p n.m.r 1½f out: r.o wl: nrst fin* **16/1**

5 ¾ **Conroy (USA)**[35] 206 8-9-4 110 .... JMurtagh 14 89
(A Selvaratnam, UAE) *wl away: led stands' side: rdn 3½f out: nt qckn* **9/4**[1]

6 3 **Conceal**[6] 506 8-9-4 102 .... GHind 7 80
(R Bouresly, Kuwait) *prom centre: ev ch 2½f out: one pce* **14/1**

7 1¼ **Glad To Be Fast (IRE)**[6] 508 6-9-4 97 ....(b) AStarke 9 76
(Mario Hofer, Germany) *n.d* **20/1**

8 hd **Rockets 'n Rollers (IRE)**[21] 353 6-9-4 105 .... WayneSmith 1 76
(M Al Muhairi, UAE) *wl away: prom early: ev ch 2f out: one pce* **20/1**

9 1¼ **At Once (GER)**[14] 431 5-9-0 95 .... WMongil 3 68
(Frau E Mader, Germany) *trckd ldrs centre: gng wl 2½f out: n.m.r: nt rcvr* **40/1**

10 nk **Botanical (USA)**[35] 206 5-9-4 107 ....(vt) KerrinMcEvoy 2 71
(I Mohammed, UAE) *prom in centre tl 2f out* **5/1**[3]

11 2¼ **Lindus Atenor**[14] 436 3-8-1 86 ....(t) JohnPanas 8 61
(M Al Muhairi, UAE) *prom early: sn wknd* **66/1**

12 ½ **In The Fan (USA)**[14] 435 4-9-4 90 ....(bt) RichardMullen 13 63
(A Al Raihe, UAE) *v.s.a: n.d* **100/1**

13 ¾ **Protector (SAF)**[14] 431 5-9-4 90 .... KShea 5 61
(H J Brown, South Africa) *mid-div early: nvr a threat* **33/1**

14 2½ **Safe Structure (SAF)**[14] 433 6-9-4 104 .... JBekker 6 53
(D Maroun, South Africa) *prom centre: wknd 2½f out* **7/1**

1m 10.92s **Going Correction** +0.225s/f (Slow)
WFA 3 from 4yo+ 14lb **14** Ran SP% **125.2**

Speed ratings: 106,103,102,98,97 93,92,91,90,89 86,86,85,81

Owner Sheikh Mohammed Bin Maktoum Al Maktoum **Bred** Gainsborough Stud Management Ltd **Trained** UAE

FOCUS

The sprinters in Dubai are just ordinary and Tropical Star took advantage to take this Group Three in good style.

NOTEBOOK

Tropical Star(IRE), back to form when winning a seven-furlong handicap from a mark of 108 on his previous start, followed up in good style on his return Group company. He will now try and better last season's surprise second in the Golden Shaheen but, from a neutral's point of view, it will be disappointing if he manages to do so.

Azul Da Guanabara(BRZ) improved for both the fitting of a tongue-tie and drop to sprinting, and ran a big race.

Howick Falls(USA), well beaten on the turf on his return from an absence, ran much better switched to dirt for the first time and clearly retains plenty of ability.

Karlo Guitar(BRZ) ◆ found trouble in-running after starting slowly and this was quite eye-catching.

Conroy(USA), three times a winner of this very race, was below form this time and could not make it four.

Botanical(USA) is not easy to catch right.

564a DERRINSTOWN STUD JEBEL HATTA (GROUP 2) (TURF) 1m 194y(T)

5:45 (5:50) 3-Y-O+ **£94,476** (£29,069; £14,534; £7,267)

RPR

1 **Touch Of Land (FR)**[81] 6552 6-9-4 115 .... C-PLemaire 3 116
(H-A Pantall, France) *settled towards rr: gng wl 2½f out: n.m.r 1½f out: r.o wl once clr 1f out* **8/1**

2 1¼ **Lord Admiral (USA)**[7] 496 5-9-4 109 .... MJKinane 113
(Charles O'Brien, Ire) *racd towards rr: rdn 3f out wd: in clr 1½f out: r.o wl* **14/1**

3 1 3/4 **Seihali (IRE)**[20] 370 7-9-4 113 .... JMurtagh 8 110
(D Selvaratnam, UAE) *hld up in last: racd on rail 3f out gng wl: n.m.r 2f out and 1 1/2f out: r.o once clr* **7/1**[3]

4 1/2 **Boule D'Or (IRE)**[7] 497 5-9-4 109 .... NigelDay 109
(J Akehurst) *slowly away: hld up towards rr: gng wl 3f out: r.o wl: nrst fin* **20/1**

5 1 1/4 **Tyson (SAF)**[20] 370 6-9-4 115 .... WCMarwing 1 107
(M F De Kock, South Africa) *mid-div on rail: rdn 2 1/2f out: wknd* **2/1**[1]

6 1/2 **Lundy's Liability(BRZ)**[21] 355 6-9-4 111 ....(t) KShea 5 106
(M F De Kock, South Africa) *mid-div: racd wd: rdn to cl 3f out: ev ch: one pce* **25/1**

7 hd **Valixir (IRE)**[124] 6166 5-9-11 122 .... LDettori 7 112
(Saeed Bin Suroor) *led tl hdd 4f out: led again 1f out: ev ch: nt qckn* **5/2**[2]

8 3/4 **Layman (USA)**[138] 5902 4-9-4 113 ....(t) KerrinMcEvoy 4 104
(I Mohammed, UAE) *trckd ldrs: ev ch 3f out: wknd* **10/1**

9 7 **Latino Magic (IRE)**[7] 496 6-9-4 110 ....(t) WayneSmith 9 91
(R J Osborne, Ire) *trckd ldrs: taken to ld 4f out: rdn clr 3f out: sn hdd* **33/1**

10 3 1/4 **Clinet (IRE)**[21] 351 4-9-0 107 .... EddieAhern 2 80
(J W Hills) *mid-div on rail: rdn 2 1/2f out: wknd* **10/1**

1m 52.05s **Going Correction** +0.75s/f (Yiel) 10 Ran SP% **121.9**
Speed ratings: 115,113,112,111,110 110,110,109,103,100

.

Owner Gary A Tanaka **Bred** Chevotel De La Hauquerie **Trained** France

FOCUS
Perhaps not quite as strong a Group Two as one might have hoped for, but this was still a fine effort from Touch Of Land considering his trainer reported afterwards he had left something to work on.

NOTEBOOK
Touch Of Land(FR), a multiple Group winner in France who was last seen finishing third in the Hong Kong Cup, ran out quite an impressive winner of his first start in Dubai. His trainer said afterwards that he expected him to run well, but had left something to work on and thinks he will improve for the run. That bodes well for his next intended target, presumably either Dubai Duty Free Stakes or Sheema Classic, but he has yet to win a Group One.

Lord Admiral(USA) has never won above Listed level, but he ran a fine race on his debut in Dubai when second in a similar race the previous week and, if anything, bettered that performance. He is clearly thriving under these conditions.

Seihali(IRE), second off a mark of 111 in a course and distance handicap on his return to action, confirmed that promise and would have been even closer with more luck in running.

Boule D'Or(IRE), returned to Group company, ran as well as he has ever done according to RPRs. He looks up to winning a Group race in Europe as some stage this year.

Tyson(SAF), chasing the hat-trick following a couple of wins in handicap company at this year's Carnival off mark of 102 and 109, ran a little bit below expectations. He might just be at his best over a touch further.

Valixir(IRE), a dual Group One winner when trained in France by Andre Fabre, had not been seen since running below form in the Breeders' Cup Mile and made a disappointing debut for Godolphin. He has not always looked straightforward and carried his head awkwardly when asked to go and win his race. His previous connections managed to squeeze the best out of him on a few occasions, but he had a hard enough season last year and has a bit to prove now.

Latino Magic(IRE) was again well below his best and did not really improve for the fitting of a tongue-tie.

Clinet(IRE) has been in fine form at this year's Carnival, winning a handicap and Listed race against fillies and mares but, while this would have been tougher, she was a long way below her best this time. Something may have been amiss.

565a SH MAKTOUM BIN RASHID AL MAKTOUM CHALLENGE (ROUND 3) (GROUP 2) (DIRT) 1m 2f (D)
6:15 (6:20) 3-Y-O+ **£113,372** (£34,883; £17,441; £8,720)

RPR

1 **Electrocutionist (USA)**[130] 6059 5-9-0 121 .... LDettori 8 123
(Saeed Bin Suroor) *trckd ldrs centre: rdn to chal 2f out: led 1 1/2f out: comf* **6/5**[1]

2 7 **Chiquitin (ARG)**[21] 355 6-9-0 112 ....(t) MJKinane 13 110
(I Jory, Saudi Arabia) *sn led: hdd 1 1/2f out: no ch w wnr but kpt on wl* **11/4**[2]

3 2 1/4 **Elmustanser**[21] 355 5-9-0 104 ....(vt[1]) RHills 2 106
(Doug Watson, UAE) *mid-div: clsd to trck ldrs 3f out: n.m.r 2 1/2f out: trckd ldrs: kpt on one pce* **20/1**

4 3 3/4 **Parasol (IRE)**[14] 432 7-9-0 106 ....(bt) RichardMullen 3 99
(Doug Watson, UAE) *settled towards rr: gng wl: prog in st: nvr a threat* **7/1**

5 2 **Ketter (BRZ)**[20] 371 5-9-0 97 .... ADomingos 9 96
(Luis Singnoretti, Brazil) *settled towards rr: n.d: sme prog st: nrst fin* **50/1**

6 2 1/4 **Surbiton (USA)**[7] 495 6-9-0 90 ....(t) RoystonFfrench 11 92
(A Al Raihe, UAE) *mid-div early: n.d* **66/1**

7 5 1/2 **Hippodrome (IRE)**[14] 437 4-9-0 91 .... JBekker 1 82
(H J Brown, South Africa) *n.d: sme late prog* **66/1**

8 1 1/2 **Mistongo (URU)**[7] 6-9-0 90 ....(t) KerrinMcEvoy 6 79
(S Seemar, UAE) *nvr involved* **66/1**

9 hd **Jader (IRE)**[14] 432 4-9-0 95 ....(b) RyanMoore 4 79
(S Seemar, UAE) *trckd ldrs on rail: rdn 3f out: sn wknd* **50/1**

10 4 1/2 **Eccentric**[21] 355 5-9-0 112 ....(t) JMurtagh 15 70
(S Seemar, UAE) *trckd ldrs: disp briefly 3f out: wknd* **9/2**[3]

11 6 **Attentive (IRE)**[7] 8-9-0 95 .... TPO'Shea 7 60
(S Seemar, UAE) *trckd ldrs wd early: wknd 4f out* **100/1**

12 5 3/4 **Bosra's Valentine (USA)**[434] 6-9-0 86 .... GHind 14 49
(R Bouresly, Kuwait) *s.i.s: n.d* **66/1**

13 6 1/2 **State Shinto (USA)**[14] 435 10-9-0 90 ....(bt) WSupple 12 38
(R Bouresly, Kuwait) *s.i.s: nvr involved* **100/1**

14 4 **Todman Avenue (USA)**[7] 4-9-0 87 .... WayneSmith 10 30
(A Al Raihe, UAE) *mid-div early: nvr a threat* **100/1**

2m 1.06s **Going Correction** +0.225s/f (Slow) 15 Ran SP% **120.4**
Speed ratings: 115,109,107,104,103 101,96,95,95,91 87,82,77,74

.

Owner Godolphin **Bred** Compagnia Generale **Trained** Newmarket, Suffolk

FOCUS
Not very much strength in depth for this Group Two, but Electrocutionist produced a terrific performance on his first start on dirt to thrash last year's winner Chiquitin. It must be worth noting that his stable saddled both Dubai Millennium and Street Cry to win this before going to Dubai World Cup Glory.

NOTEBOOK
Electrocutionist(USA) ◆, ex-Italian trained, won the International Stakes at York and was third in the Canadian International before being picked up by Godolphin. Switched to dirt for the first time so his new connections could find out whether or not he will a worthy Dubai World Cup contender, he gave them a pretty emphatic answer with as good as performance as they could possibly have hoped for. Settled just off the pacesetters, he raced a little more keenly than is really ideal for a high-class dirt racer and, perhaps as a result of that, got a bump off one of his rivals at about halfway. However, he was clearly enjoying this new experience and, coming right back on the bridle as if nothing had happened, he picked up quite impressively when moved into a challenging position at the top of the straight, despite showing an unorthodox action for the surface. Admittedly he was not faced with the sort of opposition he is used to racing against on turf, but he finished seven lengths clear of last year's winner and fourth-placed Parasol also helps give the form a solid look. While his time was a touch slower than is usually recorded by the winner of the World Cup when the track is riding similarly fast, it has only been bettered in the last six runnings of this race by same connections' brilliant Dubai Millennium (albeit significantly), and he should be able to improve on it with the benefit of this experience. Both the US and Japan are expected to bring over horses for the big one but, providing he recovers and progresses sufficiently in the three weeks or so leading up to the World Cup, it will take a very good one to beat him.

Chiquitin(ARG) did not have to face anything of Electrocutionist's class when winning this race last year. He looked to run his race and gives the form some substance.

Elmustanser showed improved form in the first-time visor, but could not reverse recent placings with Chiquitin.

Parasol(IRE), successful in a ten-furlong handicap off a mark of 101 on his previous start, was produced with every chance but is basically not good enough to produce high-class figures any more.

Eccentric shaped well when third on his debut in Dubai over nine furlongs and had Chiquitin two lengths behind that day, so this has to be considered most disappointing.

[530]WOLVERHAMPTON (A.W) (L-H)
Friday, March 3

OFFICIAL GOING: Standard
Wind: Almost nil Weather: Sunny but cold

566 FIRST PAST THE POST AT BETDIRECT MAIDEN STKS (DIV I) 1m 4f 50y(P)
1:50 (1:50) (Class 5) 3-Y-O+ **£2,914** (£867; £433; £216) **Stalls** Low

Form RPR

1 **Marmota (IRE)** 3-8-3 .... JoeFanning 7 66+
(M Johnston) *uns rdr bef s: mde all: rdn 3f out: edgd rt wl over 1f out: styd on* **9/2**[3]

0 2 2 **Elated (IRE)**[11] 460 4-9-10 .... DarryllHolland 9 69
(W J Haggas) *a.p: rdn 5f out: wnt 2nd over 2f out: swtchd lft wl over 1f out: nt qckn ins fnl f* **7/1**

3 5 **River City (IRE)**[300] 9-9-12 .... VinceSlattery 1 62
(Noel T Chance) *hld up in mid-div: rdn 4f out: hdwy on ins over 2f out: one pce fnl f* **8/1**

4-62 4 6 **Gibbs Camp**[16] 422 3-7-12 67 .... PaulHanagan 8 42
(E A L Dunlop) *t.k.h: mid-div: hdwy 4f out: sn rdn: wknd fnl f: dismntd after fin* **2/1**[1]

00-0 5 1 1/4 **Mustakhlas (USA)**[18] 403 5-9-5 45 .... SoniaEaton[(7)] 2 51
(B P J Baugh) *nvr nr ldrs* **100/1**

0-0 6 6 **Ashwell Rose**[16] 419 4-9-5 .... FergusSweeney 11 37
(R T Phillips) *hld up in mid-div: rdn and wknd 3f out* **100/1**

000/ 7 13 **Bowing**[616] 3281 6-9-12 45 .... LPKeniry 6 22
(J L Spearing) *plld hrd early: a bhd* **66/1**

0-50 8 23 **Sahara Style**[13] 447 3-8-3 53 .... ChrisCatlin 4 —
(R Hollinshead) *t.k.h in mid-div: lost pl 8f out: rdn over 6f out: t.o* **25/1**

9 13 **Pagan Game (IRE)** 4-9-5 .... NCallan 5 —
(David Marnane, Ire) *s.i.s: hdwy over 8f out: rdn over 5f out: wknd 4f out: t.o* **11/2**

3 10 28 **Don And Gerry (IRE)**[7] 503 5-9-7 .... RobertWinston 3 —
(P D Evans) *chsd wnr: rdn over 3f out: prom whn eased and virtually p.u over 2f out: t.o: dismntd after fin* **4/1**[2]

2m 43.84s (1.42) **Going Correction** +0.05s/f (Slow)
WFA 3 from 4yo 23lb 4 from 5yo+ 2lb 10 Ran SP% **117.8**
Speed ratings (Par 103):97,95,92,88,87 83,74,59,50,32
CSF £35.78 TOTE £4.50: £2.00, £2.50, £2.40; EX 48.50.
Owner Jumeirah Racing **Bred** Darley **Trained** Middleham Moor, N Yorks

FOCUS
This weak maiden was a second slower than the other division. The form is limited by the proximity of the fifth.
Gibbs Camp Official explanation: jockey said filly had lost her action
Bowing Official explanation: jockey said, regarding appearing to ease gelding turning in, in his opinion gelding is not very good and was having its first run for 616 days
Pagan Game(IRE) Official explanation: jockey said filly had not been moving well throughout
Don And Gerry(IRE) Official explanation: jockey said mare had lost her action

567 JASON FORREST 34TH BIRTHDAY H'CAP 1m 141y(P)
2:20 (2:20) (Class 5) (0-75,74) 4-Y-O+ **£3,238** (£963; £481; £240) **Stalls** Low

Form RPR

50-0 1 **Following Flow (USA)**[20] 384 4-9-2 72 .... GrahamGibbons 7 81
(R Hollinshead) *hld up towards rr: hdwy over 5f out: rdn to ld 2f out: edgd rt over 1f out: edgd lft ins fnl f: drvn out* **10/1**

3-03 2 1/2 **Poppys Footprint (IRE)**[20] 384 5-8-10 66 ....(b) NCallan 10 74
(K A Ryan) *hld up in mid-div: rdn and hdwy on outside 2f out: edgd lft over 1f out: r.o ins fnl f* **12/1**

2121 3 1 **Latif (USA)**[4] 530 5-8-6 62 .... ChrisCatlin 4 68
(Ms Deborah J Evans) *hld up in tch: rdn 2f out: kpt on ins fnl f* **3/1**[1]

50-1 4 2 1/2 **Parkview Love (USA)**[25] 319 5-8-12 71 ....(v) PatrickMathers[(3)] 6 72
(D Shaw) *sn led: hdd 7f out: prom: rdn and ev ch 2f out: one pce fnl f* **9/1**

14-1 5 hd **Compton Eclipse**[20] 384 6-9-1 71 .... EddieAhern 2 71
(J J Lambe, Ire) *led early: a.p: rdn 2f out: one pce fnl f* **7/1**[3]

0-00 6 1 1/2 **Out For A Stroll**[20] 381 7-8-8 64 .... HayleyTurner 5 61+
(S C Williams) *bhd: rdn over 4f out: nt clr run and forced wd over 2f out: nvr trbld ldrs* **16/1**

30-0 7 3 **Desert Lightning (IRE)**[41] 167 4-9-2 72 .... PatCosgrave 11 63
(K R Burke) *s.i.s: nvr nr ldrs* **100/1**

6/ 8 1 3/4 **Max Scal (IRE)**[16] 6186 5-9-2 72 .... TonyCulhane 1 59
(P J Rothwell, Ire) *led 7f out: rdn over 3f out: hdd 2f out: sn wknd* **16/1**

1542 9 nk **Lincolneurocruiser**[13] 451 4-9-3 73 .... RobertWinston 3 60+
(Mrs N Macauley) *hld up towards rr: rdn and hdwy wl over 1f out: eased whn btn jst ins fnl f* **7/1**[3]

1-02 10 1 **Ground Rules (USA)**[18] 404 4-9-4 74 .... DarryllHolland 8 58
(V Smith) *prom: rdn over 2f out: wknd wl over 1f out* **10/3**[2]

00-0 **11** *22* **Fair Shake (IRE)**[35] [214] 6-8-11 **67**..............................(v) PaulHanagan 9 5
(Karen McLintock) *s.i.s: reminders over 7f out: a bhd: t.o* **66/1**

1m 51.45s (-0.31) **Going Correction** +0.05s/f (Slow) **11** Ran SP% **114.1**
Speed ratings (Par 103):103,102,101,99,99 97,95,93,93,92 73
CSF £120.17 CT £455.64 TOTE £9.80: £2.10, £3.70, £1.90; EX 179.00.
Owner Tim Leadbeater **Bred** Villiers Syndicate **Trained** Upper Longdon, Staffs

FOCUS
A modest handicap run at a fair pace but the form looks reasonable rated around the first three.
Lincolneurocruiser Official explanation: jockey said gelding lost its action

568 BET LIVE IN-RUNNING AT BETDIRECT.CO.UK (S) STKS 1m 141y(P)
2:55 (2:55) (Class 6) 4-Y-0+ **£2,388** (£705; £352) **Stalls** Low

Form RPR
0303 **1** **Sol Rojo**[20] [382] 4-8-12 53..............................(b) RobbieFitzpatrick 6 60
(M J Attwater) *hld up in mid-div: rdn over 3f out: hdwy over 2f out: r.o to ld last stride* **9/1**
0001 **2** *hd* **Shannon Arms (USA)**[7] [498] 5-8-13 60................(p) AndrewMullen(5) 1 66
(K A Ryan) *led: rdn clr wl over 1f out: ct last stride* **8/1**[3]
4100 **3** *1 ¼* **Distant Country (USA)**[11] [458] 7-8-11 54..............(p) AndrewElliott(7) 5 63
(K R Burke) *hld up in mid-div: hdwy on ins over 2f out: rdn over 1f out: r.o ins fnl f* **20/1**
2451 **4** *1 ½* **Samson Quest**[11] [458] 4-8-13 59......................(v) JamesDoyle(5) 3 60
(A W Carroll) *hld up towards rr: rdn over 3f out: hdwy over 2f out: no ex towards fin* **4/1**[2]
6-03 **5** *3* **Lawaaheb (IRE)**[11] [457] 5-8-12 47........................(v) FrankieMcDonald 2 48
(B R Johnson) *a.p: rdn over 2f out: wknd 1f out* **8/1**[3]
2-00 **6** *1* **Hoh Bleu Dee**[10] [472] 5-8-12 52..(b) NCallan 9 45
(T Keddy) *hld up towards rr: rdn and hdwy on outside over 2f out: wknd over 1f out* **16/1**
/6-0 **7** *2* **Mr Marucci (USA)**[7] [498] 4-8-12 62..........................(b[1]) PatCosgrave 11 41
(B Ellison) *hmpd s: sn swtchd lft: nvr nr ldrs* **100/1**
6516 **8** *5* **Bijou Dan**[8] [492] 5-9-4 62..(b) RobertWinston 4 37
(I Semple) *a.p: rdn over 3f out: wknd qckly over 1f out* **6/4**[1]
005- **9** *2 ½* **Genuine Surprise (IRE)**[151] [5670] 4-8-5 45 ow1......... AdamKirby(3) 13 21
(A P Jarvis) *s.i.s: a bhd* **40/1**
-660 **10** *8* **Ladies Knight**[11] [458] 6-8-9 48................................ PatrickMathers(3) 12 9
(D Shaw) *rdn over 4f out: a bhd* **50/1**
00-0 **11** *1 ½* **Worth Abbey**[4] [537] 4-8-9 57.. DNolan(3) 7 6
(M Appleby) *hld up in tch: rdn over 4f out: wknd 3f out* **50/1**
5050 **12** *1 ¼* **Resplendent Prince**[8] [492] 4-9-4 62..........................(v) TonyCulhane 10 9
(P Howling) *hld up in tch: rdn over 3f out: wkng whn n.m.r over 2f out* **14/1**

1m 51.28s (-0.48) **Going Correction** +0.05s/f (Slow) **12** Ran SP% **116.9**
Speed ratings (Par 101):104,103,102,101,98 97,96,91,89,82 80,79
CSF £74.95 TOTE £9.10: £2.40, £2.20, £6.40; EX 82.80.The winner was sold to Jeff Pearce for 5,000gns. Shannon Arms was claimed by P.Howling for £6,000. Lawaheeb was claimed by M. Gingell for £6,000.
Owner Phones Direct Partnership **Bred** Mrs A Yearley **Trained** Wysall, Notts

FOCUS
An ordinary seller that is fairly solid but average for the grade.

569 BETDIRECT.CO.UK H'CAP 5f 216y(P)
3:30 (3:31) (Class 4) (0-80,80) 4-Y-0+ **£5,505** (£1,637; £818; £408) **Stalls** Low

Form RPR
330 **1** **Councellor (FR)**[10] [476] 4-9-0 **76**.................................... EddieAhern 11 84
(Stef Liddiard) *hld up in mid-div: rdn and hdwy 2f out: r.o to ld last strides* **11/2**[3]
00-4 **2** *shd* **Hits Only Cash**[57] [51] 4-8-7 **69**.. JimmyQuinn 5 77
(J Pearce) *hld up and bhd: rdn and hdwy wl over 1f out: r.o wl cl home* **6/1**
6-12 **3** *nk* **Effective**[3] [541] 6-8-10 **72**.. DarrenWilliams 3 79
(A P Jarvis) *led 1f: w ldr: rdn to ld over 1f out: hdd last strides* **3/1**[1]
0523 **4** *hd* **Nautical**[25] [316] 8-8-2 **69**.. JamesDoyle(5) 10 75
(A W Carroll) *t.k.h towards rr: hdwy wl over 1f out: sn rdn: r.o ins fnl f* **8/1**
-503 **5** *1 ½* **Gilded Cove**[21] [362] 6-8-9 **71**.. GrahamGibbons 2 73
(R Hollinshead) *hld up in mid-div: hdwy 2f out: ev ch ins fnl f: no ex towards fin* **5/1**[2]
4000 **6** *1* **Poker Player (IRE)**[10] [476] 4-8-13 **75**.......................(b) DarrylHolland 9 74
(G C Bravery) *led after 1f: rdn and hdd over 1f out: no ex wl ins fnl f* **25/1**
-640 **7** *1* **Franksalot (IRE)**[24] [323] 6-8-5 **70**.................................... RichardThomas(3) 6 66
(Miss B Sanders) *hld up in mid-div: hdwy 2f out: sn rdn: one pce fnl f* **33/1**
2-44 **8** *2* **General Feeling (IRE)**[32] [253] 5-9-0 **76** ow1............... GeorgeBaker 13 66
(M Mullineaux) *s.i.s: bhd: carried wd ent st: n.d* **20/1**
00-5 **9** *½* **Bonne De Fleur**[21] [362] 5-9-1 **77**................................... DerekMcGaffin 1 65
(B Smart) *prom: rdn 2f out: wknd 1f out* **22/1**
3-25 **10** *shd* **Countdown**[14] [441] 4-9-4 **80**...(v) PaulHanagan 8 68
(Miss J A Camacho) *chsd ldrs: lost pl and hmpd wl over 1f out: n.d after* **14/1**
5560 **11** *2* **Pawan (IRE)**[3] [541] 6-8-9 **78**... AnnStokell(7) 7 60
(Miss A Stokell) *s.s: a bhd* **25/1**
0-00 **12** *10* **Whinhill House**[36] [198] 6-9-4 **80**................................(p) RobertWinston 4 32
(D W Barker) *t.k.h: prom: rdn and wknd wl over 1f out* **20/1**
0360 **P** **Willheconquertoo**[14] [441] 6-8-4 **69**..................(vt) PatrickMathers(3) 12 —
(I W McInnes) *s.i.s: bhd: p.u lame 4f out* **66/1**

1m 15.03s (-0.78) **Going Correction** +0.05s/f (Slow) **13** Ran SP% **115.1**
Speed ratings (Par 105):107,106,106,106,104 102,101,98,98,98 95,82,—
CSF £33.07 CT £120.37 TOTE £7.50: £2.30, £2.80, £1.40; EX 50.40.
Owner D Gilbert **Bred** Janus Bloodstock & Pontchartrain Stud **Trained** Great Shefford, Berks

FOCUS
This typically competitive sprint handicap produced a tight finish and the fastest time of the day and the form looks solid enough.
Pawan(IRE) Official explanation: jockey said gelding missed the break

570 BETDIRECT FOOTBALL ON SKYTEXT PAGE 372 H'CAP 2m 119y(P)
4:05 (4:05) (Class 6) (0-65,63) 4-Y-0+ **£2,388** (£705; £352) **Stalls** Low

Form RPR
/00- **1** **Salut Saint Cloud**[13] [5760] 5-9-1 **55**......................(p) SimonWhitworth 10 63
(G L Moore) *hld up in tch: led over 4f out: rdn 2f out: drvn out* **12/1**
2415 **2** *1 ½* **Blue Hills**[8] [491] 5-9-5 **59**.. DarrenWilliams 6 65
(P W Hiatt) *hld up in tch: rdn over 2f out: styd on ins fnl f* **13/2**
1352 **3** *1* **Little Richard (IRE)**[9] [482] 7-9-1 **55**................................(p) AlanDaly 13 60
(M Wellings) *hld up and bhd: hdwy over 6f out: rdn over 2f out: nt qckn ins fnl f* **11/2**[2]
/0-4 **4** *nk* **Transit**[29] [270] 7-8-9 **49**...(p) PatCosgrave 5 54
(B Ellison) *hld up and bhd: hdwy over 3f out: rdn over 2f out: styd on ins fnl f* **33/1**
-604 **5** *¾* **Sandy's Legend (USA)**[14] [443] 4-8-10 **55**..............(p) RobertWinston 4 59
(Mrs L Williamson) *hld up and bhd: hdwy 5f out: rdn over 3f out: hung lft fr wl over 1f out: styd on* **6/1**[3]
1-43 **6** *2 ½* **I'll Do It Today**[25] [318] 5-9-2 **56**.. PaulHanagan 2 57
(J M Jefferson) *hld up in tch: bmpd 5f out: rdn over 2f out: wknd ins fnl f* **7/2**[1]
2-44 **7** *½* **Lysander's Quest (IRE)**[25] [309] 8-8-6 **46**..............(b) FergusSweeney 1 46
(R Ingram) *hld up in tch: rdn over 2f out: wknd fnl f* **9/1**
4-20 **8** *1 ¼* **Three Boars**[9] [482] 4-8-10 **55**...(b) NCallan 12 54
(S Gollings) *hld up towards rr: hdwy over 3f out: wknd wl over 1f out* **9/1**
6/0- **9** *dist* **Strident (USA)**[107] [4968] 5-9-8 **62**..................................(v[1]) EddieAhern 8 —
(J J Lambe, Ire) *prom: bmpd 5f out: sn rdn and lost pl: t.o* **14/1**
/0-6 **10** *20* **Fleetfoot Mac**[8] [490] 5-9-9 **63**..(b) TonyCulhane 7 —
(B Storey) *a bhd: rdn 10f out: t.o fnl 7f* **100/1**
11 *dist* **Relocation (IRE)**[212] [4077] 5-8-9 **49**.. TPQueally 9 —
(J J Lambe, Ire) *led 2f: prom: led 6f out: sn rdn: hdd over 4f out: wknd qckly: t.o* **33/1**
204- **12** *1* **Keepers Knight (IRE)**[259] [2665] 5-8-11 **51** ow1............ DarrylHolland 3 —
(Karen McLintock) *hld up in mid-div: wknd over 4f out: t.o* **10/1**
6/00 **13** *dist* **Delta Force**[11] [457] 7-8-13 **53**................................(p) GrahamGibbons 11 —
(P A Blockley) *led after 2f: hdd 6f out: n.m.r on ins 5f out: sn wknd: t.o* **50/1**

3m 42.77s (-0.36) **Going Correction** +0.05s/f (Slow)
WFA 4 from 5yo+ 5lb **13** Ran SP% **117.5**
Speed ratings (Par 101):102,101,100,100,100 99,98,98,—,— —,—,—
CSF £85.06 CT £485.33 TOTE £15.00: £5.10, £2.10, £2.00; EX 60.30.
Owner A Grinter **Bred** Mill House Stud **Trained** Woodingdean, E Sussex

FOCUS
They went a steady pace early on in this low-grade contest but the form appears solid enough rated around the runner-up and fifth.

571 WSOP QUALIFIERS WITH LITTLEWOODSPOKER.COM H'CAP 1m 141y(P)
4:35 (4:35) (Class 5) (0-70,70) 4-Y-0+ **£3,238** (£963; £481; £240) **Stalls** Low

Form RPR
5223 **1** **Jakarmi**[7] [505] 5-8-13 **65**... TonyCulhane 2 74
(B Palling) *a.p: rdn over 3f out: led jst ins fnl f: drvn out* **7/1**
2340 **2** *hd* **Dragon Slayer (IRE)**[13] [451] 4-9-4 **70**.............................. EddieAhern 7 78
(M J Attwater) *hld up in tch: rdn over 2f out: r.o ins fnl f* **11/2**[2]
2212 **3** *shd* **New England**[7] [504] 4-8-10 **62**................................ RobbieFitzpatrick 8 70
(W M Brisbourne) *hld up in mid-div: hdwy on ins over 3f out: rdn wl over 1f out: swtchd lft ent fnl f: sn ev ch: r.o* **7/2**[1]
0-30 **4** *2* **Defi (IRE)**[20] [381] 4-9-4 **70**..(b) RobertWinston 3 74
(I Semple) *led: rdn over 2f out: hdd jst ins fnl f: no ex towards fin* **20/1**
-353 **5** *nk* **Western Roots**[25] [319] 5-9-3 **69**.. GeorgeBaker 6 72
(M Appleby) *hld up and bhd: hdwy over 2f out: rdn over 1f out: one pce ins fnl f* **9/1**
2331 **6** *¾* **Mister Benji**[4] [537] 7-8-13 **65** 6ex............................ DarrenWilliams 4 67
(B P J Baugh) *hld up in tch: rdn over 2f out: one pce fnl f* **12/1**
4131 **7** *2* **Bridgewater Boys**[7] [504] 5-9-1 **67** 6ex..................................(b) NCallan 1 68+
(K A Ryan) *a.p: rdn over 3f out: cl up whn hmpd on ins ent fnl f: nt rcvr and eased* **7/1**
0604 **8** *1 ¼* **Amazin**[7] [504] 4-8-7 **64**..(p) JamesDoyle(5) 9 59
(N P Littmoden) *towards rr: rdn over 3f out: sltly hmpd on ins over 2f out: n.d* **13/2**[3]
-200 **9** *¾* **Midshipman**[25] [319] 8-8-6 **65**......................................(t) WilliamCarson(7) 11 58
(A W Carroll) *s.i.s: nvr nr ldrs* **33/1**
0040 **10** *3* **Corky (IRE)**[18] [405] 5-8-13 **65**.. HayleyTurner 5 52
(I W McInnes) *a bhd* **50/1**
-000 **11** *5* **Ronsard (IRE)**[7] [504] 4-8-13 **65**.................................. GrahamGibbons 12 41
(Heather Dalton) *rdn 4f out: a bhd* **25/1**
12 *1* **National Express (IRE)**[238] [3325] 4-8-13 **65**................. JimmyQuinn 10 39
(David Marnane, Ire) *hld up in mid-div: rdn over 2f out: sn struggling* **20/1**
064- **13** *dist* **Cordage (IRE)**[214] [3999] 4-8-13 **65**.................................... PaulHanagan 13 —
(Karen McLintock) *prom tl wknd over 4f out: t.o* **50/1**

1m 50.46s (-1.30) **Going Correction** +0.05s/f (Slow) **13** Ran SP% **113.9**
Speed ratings (Par 103):107,106,106,104,104 104,102,101,100,97 93,92,—
CSF £39.20 CT £162.19 TOTE £9.30: £3.20, £2.00, £1.30; EX 56.80.
Owner Bryn Palling **Bred** Llety Stud **Trained** Tredodridge, Vale Of Glamorgan
■ Stewards' Enquiry : Robbie Fitzpatrick three-day ban: careless riding (Mar 14-16)

FOCUS
A competitive handicap with a few coming into the race in good form and the race looks solid.

572 LITTLEWOODS BETDIRECT H'CAP 1m 4f 50y(P)
5:10 (5:11) (Class 2) (0-100,96) 4-Y-0+ **£11,658** (£3,468; £1,733; £865) **Stalls** Low

Form RPR
51-1 **1** **Arturius (IRE)**[20] [377] 4-9-4 **93**.. EddieAhern 1 103+
(P J Rothwell, Ire) *sn chsng ldr: led jst over 1f out: qcknd clr ins fnl f: easily* **11/4**[1]
006- **2** *4* **Dunaskin (IRE)**[155] [5565] 6-9-5 **92**.. NCallan 7 96
(Karen McLintock) *led: rdn 2f out: hdd jst over 1f out: one pce* **25/1**
04-6 **3** *½* **Gavroche (IRE)**[20] [377] 5-9-5 **92**.. GeorgeBaker 2 95
(J R Boyle) *dwlt: hld up in rr: c wd st: rdn over 1f out: hdwy and hung lft fnl f: r.o* **5/1**
0/0- **4** *shd* **Grooms Affection**[118] [6254] 6-8-2 **80** oh1...................... JamesDoyle(5) 6 83
(K A Morgan) *hld up: hdwy over 2f out: rdn wl over 1f out: one pce fnl f* **50/1**
31-4 **5** *hd* **Cold Turkey**[35] [65] 6-9-6 **93**.. SimonWhitworth 8 96
(G L Moore) *hld up: hdwy on ins over 2f out: rdn wl over 1f out: one pce fnl f* **9/2**[3]
-254 **6** *1 ¼* **Boo**[20] [377] 4-9-0 **96**..(v) AndrewElliott(7) 5 97
(K R Burke) *t.k.h: prom tl wknd 2f out* **5/1**
300- **7** *1* **Ringsider (IRE)**[161] [5436] 5-9-5 **92**...................................... NickyMackay 4 91
(G A Butler) *hld up: hdwy on ins wl over 1f out: wknd ins fnl f* **3/1**[2]

2m 44.6s (2.18) **Going Correction** +0.05s/f (Slow)
WFA 4 from 5yo+ 2lb **7** Ran SP% **109.0**
Speed ratings (Par 109):94,91,91,90,90 89,89
CSF £58.24 CT £292.92 TOTE £2.50: £1.60, £8.40; EX 40.10.
Owner N O'Farrell **Bred** Floors Farming And London Thoroughbred Services Lt **Trained** Tinahely, Co. Wicklow

FOCUS
This was run at a dawdle and the time was significantly slower than both divisions of the maiden. The form is not solid as a result but the winner looks a decent recruit.

NOTEBOOK
Arturius(IRE) ◆, a big drifter in the ring, showed a nice turn of foot off a slow pace and does look a useful performer on sand. However, this tells us little with regard to a possible tilt at the winter Derby. (op 15-8)
Dunaskin(IRE) set a slow pace and proved no match for the winner when it came to a sprint finish. He should come on for this first outing for five months. (op 22-1)
Gavroche(IRE) was 5lb better off than when beaten just under six lengths by the winner over a mile and a quarter at Lingfield. (op 15-2 tchd 8-1)
Grooms Affection, a dual ten-furlong winner for Peter Harris, was making his sand debut after trailing in on heavy in the November Handicap on his only start last year. (op 33-1)
Cold Turkey would have preferred a stronger gallop. (op 3-1 tchd 11-4)
Boo had finished just over four lengths behind the winner on 6lb better terms over ten furlongs at Lingfield. (op 11-2 tchd 13-2)

573 FIRST PAST THE POST AT BETDIRECT MAIDEN STKS (DIV II) 1m 4f 50y(P)
5:40 (5:40) (Class 5) 3-Y-O+ **£2,914** (£867; £433; £216) **Stalls** Low

Form RPR
3 **1** **City Well**[6] 515 3-8-3 .... JoeFanning 1 73+
(M Johnston) sn chsng ldr: led over 2f out: rdn clr wl over 1f out: eased ins fnl f **5/4**[1]
-302 **2** 5 **Opera Comica**[18] 403 3-7-12 65 .... DaleGibson 7 55
(J H M Gosden) a.p: rdn and wnt 2nd over 2f out: sn no ch w wnr **15/8**[2]
050- **3** 1 1/2 **Lynford Lady**[97] 6428 3-7-13 50 ow1 .... JimmyQuinn 11 54
(P W D'Arcy) hld up towards rr: rdn over 3f out: hdwy wl over 1f out: one pce fnl f **50/1**
4 5 **Belindas Dream (IRE)** 5-9-2 .... JerryO'Dwyer(5) 8 50
(Aidan Anthony Howard, Ire) s.i.s: hld up and bhd: rdn over 3f out: sme hdwy over 1f out: n.d **40/1**
5 1 **Fleur A Lay (USA)** 4-9-5 .... EddieAhern 6 49
(Mrs A J Perrett) hld up in tch: rdn over 3f out: wknd wl over 1f out **9/1**
00-0 **6** 5 **Discomania**[25] 309 4-9-10 45 .... (vp) MatthewHenry 10 46
(V Smith) hld up and bhd: hdwy over 4f out: wknd 2f out **50/1**
40-0 **7** 2 **Solipsist (IRE)**[11] 470 5-9-5 50 .... MarkCoumbe(7) 9 43
(N I M Rossiter) rdn over 4f out: a bhd **100/1**
6 **8** shd **Grey Report (IRE)**[48] 114 9-9-12 .... VinceSlattery 4 43
(R H Buckler) hld up: sn in tch: rdn and wknd over 3f out **7/1**[3]
0443 **9** 1 1/2 **Weet Yer Tern (IRE)**[11] 468 4-9-10 45 .... (p) GrahamGibbons 2 41
(P A Blockley) led: rdn and hdd over 2f out: wknd wl over 1f out **14/1**
/0-0 **10** dist **April Shannon**[21] 361 4-9-0 30 .... NataliaGemelova(5) 3 —
(J E Long) prom over 4f: t.o fnl 4f **150/1**

2m 42.85s (0.43) **Going Correction** +0.05s/f (Slow)
WFA 3 from 4yo 23lb 4 from 5yo+ 2lb **10** Ran SP% **116.4**
Speed ratings (Par 103):100,96,95,92,91 88,87,86,85,—
CSF £3.66 TOTE £2.80: £1.10, £1.10, £8.70; EX 4.40 Place 6 £276.58, Place 5 £89.35.
Owner Mrs R J Jacobs **Bred** Newsells Park Stud Limited **Trained** Middleham Moor, N Yorks

FOCUS
A modest maiden won in a time a second faster than the first division. The winner can rate higher but the third limits this form.
T/Plt: £287.70 to a £1 stake. Pool: £64,498.60. 163.60 winning tickets. T/Qpdt: £22.10 to a £1 stake. Pool: £7,387.60. 247.10 winning tickets. KH

553 LINGFIELD (L-H)
Saturday, March 4

OFFICIAL GOING: Standard
Wind: Light, against Weather: Sunny, cold

574 BETDIRECT.CO.UK H'CAP 1m 5f (P)
1:20 (1:20) (Class 6) (0-60,62) 4-Y-O+ **£2,388** (£705; £352) **Stalls** Low

Form RPR
5212 **1** **Polish Power (GER)**[3] 549 6-9-0 56 .... JohnEgan 13 67+
(J S Moore) hld up wl in rr: gd prog on inner fr over 3f out: trckd ldr over 2f out: led over 1f out: shkn up and sn clr **4/1**[1]
4641 **2** 2 1/2 **Sugitani (USA)**[3] 549 4-9-3 62 6ex .... (b) JamieMackay 9 69+
(N B King) dwlt: hld up in last trio: prog on wd outside fr 3f out: outpcd 2f out: r.o to take 2nd last 100yds: hopeless task **11/2**[2]
25-3 **3** nk **Amwell Brave**[5] 535 5-9-4 60 .... EddieAhern 10 67
(J R Jenkins) hld up wl in rr: prog on outer 3f out: outpcd 2f out: r.o over 1f out: tk 3rd last 100yds **11/2**[2]
-010 **4** 1 1/4 **Missie Baileys**[21] 379 4-8-12 57 .... IanMongan 8 62
(Mrs L J Mongan) pressed ldr: led over 5f out: hdd over 1f out but stl clr of rest : wknd ins fnl f **25/1**
60-0 **5** 2 1/2 **Free Style (GER)**[26] 309 6-8-5 47 ow1 .... SimonWhitworth 3 49
(Mrs H Sweeting) chsd ldrs: rdn over 3f out: outpcd 2f out: no imp after **16/1**
060- **6** 3/4 **Screen Test**[19] 4972 4-8-10 60 .... JamesDoyle(5) 2 61
(B G Powell) hld up in midfield: rdn 3f out: one pce and no imp ldrs fnl 2f **33/1**
235- **7** 3/4 **Rose Bien**[42] 6307 4-8-10 55 .... NickyMackay 7 55
(P J McBride) taken down early: hld up in midfield: n.m.r 3f out: lost pl and outpcd 2f out: nt clr run over 1f out: plugged on **10/1**
-220 **8** 1 **Robbie Can Can**[31] 131 7-8-10 59 .... WilliamCarson(7) 12 57
(A W Carroll) dwlt: hld up in last trio: struggling in last pair over 2f out: modest late prog **14/1**
06-0 **9** nk **Jazrawy**[17] 416 4-9-0 59 .... DarryllHolland 11 57
(Miss Gay Kelleway) racd freely: led to over 5f out: rdn over 3f out: wknd over 2f out **20/1**
10-6 **10** 3/4 **General Flumpa**[21] 379 5-8-9 58 .... JonjoMilczarek(7) 5 55+
(C F Wall) hld up in midfield: n.m.r and lost pl 4f out: nt clr run over 2f out: effrt wl over 1f out: sn wknd **8/1**[3]
00-0 **11** 1 **Esperance (IRE)**[10] 484 6-8-4 49 oh1 ow3 .... (b) NeilChalmers(3) 4 44
(J Akehurst) s.s: hld up in last pair: pushed along 5f out: struggling fnl 3f **66/1**
40-3 **12** 1 1/4 **Coppermalt (USA)**[26] 309 8-8-1 46 oh1 .... EdwardCreighton(3) 6 40
(R Curtis) trckd ldrs: effrt to dispute 2nd over 2f out: sn wknd **20/1**
0362 **13** 2 1/2 **King Of Knight (IRE)**[2] 557 5-9-2 58 .... OscarUrbina 14 48
(G Prodromou) hld up in rr: prog on outer over 3f out: wknd over 2f out **12/1**
060- **14** nk **Townsville (IRE)**[99] 6418 4-9-1 60 .... ChrisCatlin 1 50
(E J O'Neill) chsd ldrs: drvn over 5f out: wknd 3f out **12/1**

2m 45.76s (-2.54) **Going Correction** -0.15s/f (Stan)
WFA 4 from 5yo+ 3lb **14** Ran SP% **116.7**
Speed ratings (Par 101):101,99,99,98,96 96,96,95,95,94 94,93,91,91
CSF £22.08 CT £121.93 TOTE £6.40: £2.00, £3.10, £1.30; EX 21.80.
Owner Mrs Fitri Hay **Bred** Gestut Hofgut Mappen **Trained** Upper Lambourn, Berks

FOCUS
The pace was just fair and the in-form horses came to the fore but the winner had the rub of things against the inside rail and the third helps set the standard for the form.

575 BET DIRECT FREEPHONE 0800 211 222 H'CAP (DIV I) 7f (P)
1:50 (1:50) (Class 5) (0-70,68) 4-Y-O+ **£2,914** (£867; £324; £324) **Stalls** Low

Form RPR
0-55 **1** **Cool Sands (IRE)**[58] 47 4-8-11 61 .... (v) DaneO'Neill 7 68
(D Shaw) hld up towards rr: prog on inner wl over 1f out: drvn to ld jst ins fnl f: jst hld on **7/1**[3]
-311 **2** shd **White Bear (FR)**[7] 514 4-9-0 64 .... (b) DarryllHolland 11 71
(C R Dore) settled in last pair: pushed along over 2f out: prog and threaded through over 1f out: clsd on wnr nr fin: jst failed **11/2**[2]
602 **3** 3/4 **Hand Chime**[7] 514 9-8-6 61 .... JamesDoyle(5) 5 66
(Ernst Oertel) trckd ldrs: rdn to chal over 1f out: nt qckn: styd on ins fnl f **7/1**[3]
-203 **3** dht **Monashee Prince (IRE)**[17] 416 4-8-6 63 .... KylieManser(7) 4 68
(J R Best) led 6f out to 5f out: trckd ldr: rdn to ld over 1f out: hdd jst ins fnl f: kpt on **7/1**[3]
-131 **5** nk **Hollow Jo**[17] 416 6-8-13 63 .... EddieAhern 10 67+
(J R Jenkins) t.k.h and sn hld up: effrt on outer over 2f out: rdn and nt qckn over 1f out: kpt on **9/2**[1]
3324 **6** shd **Hadath (IRE)**[10] 485 9-8-9 59 .... (b) TQuinn 6 63
(B G Powell) t.k.h and hld up: rdn and nt qckn over 1f out: styd on ins fnl f **11/2**[2]
-345 **7** nk **Rowan Pursuit**[12] 458 5-8-4 54 oh7 .... (b) ChrisCatlin 3 57?
(J Akehurst) drvn in last over 3f out and looked reluctant: no prog tl brought wd and styd on fnl f: nrst fin **20/1**
6-03 **8** 2 1/2 **Vienna's Boy (IRE)**[14] 451 5-9-3 67 .... SimonWhitworth 2 64
(W J Musson) s.i.s: trckd ldrs: nt qckn wl over 1f out: wknd fnl f **7/1**[3]
-405 **9** nk **Zinging**[10] 484 7-8-4 54 oh9 .... (v) AdrianMcCarthy 8 50
(J J Bridger) hld up towards rr: rdn and no prog 2f out: n.d after **50/1**
00-5 **10** 2 1/2 **Storm Chase (USA)**[42] 169 4-8-11 61 .... DarrenWilliams 9 51
(A P Jarvis) led for 1f: restrained: chsd ldrs to 2f out: wknd **16/1**
506- **11** 1 **Mandarin Spirit (IRE)**[192] 4682 6-9-4 68 .... (b) OscarUrbina 1 55
(G C H Chung) dwlt: rcvrd to ld after 2f: hdd & wknd over 1f out **20/1**

1m 24.42s (-1.47) **Going Correction** -0.15s/f (Stan) **11** Ran SP% **116.3**
Speed ratings (Par 103):102,101,101,101,100 100,100,97,97,94 93
CSF £43.68 CT £143.74 TOTE £7.80: £2.60, £2.60; EX 70.30 Places: MP £1.30, HC £1.40; Tricast: CS/WB/MP £143.74, CS/WB/HC £143.74.
Owner Peter Swann **Bred** Rathasker Stud **Trained** Danethorpe, Notts
■ Stewards' Enquiry : Kylie Manser one-day ban: used whip with excessive frequency (Mar 15)

FOCUS
An open handicap run at an ordinary gallop and little to choose between the first seven home. The runner-up sets the standard.

576 BET DIRECT FREEPHONE 0800 211 222 H'CAP (DIV II) 7f (P)
2:25 (2:25) (Class 5) (0-70,68) 4-Y-O+ **£2,914** (£867; £433; £216) **Stalls** Low

Form RPR
0-42 **1** **Meditation**[2] 555 4-8-13 68 .... JamesDoyle(5) 2 77
(I A Wood) w ldrs: led 4f out: drew clr over 2f out: pushed out **7/4**[1]
6006 **2** 3 1/2 **Kallista's Pride**[2] 555 6-8-5 62 .... KylieManser(7) 7 62
(J R Best) led for 1f: trckd ldrs after: chsd wnr over 2f out: shuffled along and styd on: no imp **10/1**
0-55 **3** 1 3/4 **Go Garuda**[17] 416 5-8-11 61 .... (p) JohnEgan 3 62+
(Miss Gay Kelleway) s.i.s: hld up in midfield: rdn 3f out: lost pl over 2f out: nt clr run and stmbld wl over 1f out: r.o fnl f **9/2**[2]
06-6 **4** 3/4 **Louisiade (IRE)**[43] 159 5-8-11 61 .... DarryllHolland 11 55+
(K A Ryan) restrained s and hld up in last: effrt over 2f out: styd on fr over 1f out: no ch **11/2**[3]
4042 **5** 3 **Joy And Pain**[8] 502 5-8-13 63 .... DaneO'Neill 4 50
(J R Boyle) trckd ldrs: outpcd 2f out: chsd clr ldng pair briefly 1f out: wknd **11/2**[3]
003 **6** 1/2 **Busy Man (IRE)**[28] 291 7-8-5 55 .... EddieAhern 6 40
(J R Jenkins) dwlt: hld up in rr: rdn and c v wd bnd 2f out: one pce and no ch **10/1**
0/0- **7** 2 **A Woman In Love**[385] 366 7-8-7 60 .... RichardThomas(3) 9 40
(Miss B Sanders) taken down early: s.s: hld up in last pair: prog on inner 2f out: no ch w ldrs: wknd fnl f **20/1**
0-60 **8** 3 **Binnion Bay (IRE)**[31] 265 5-8-4 54 oh9 .... (v) AdrianMcCarthy 8 27
(J J Bridger) w ldrs: pushed along 1/2-way: wknd over 2f out **50/1**
000- **9** nk **Robin Sharp**[75] 6615 8-8-1 54 oh19 .... (p) EdwardCreighton(3) 10 26
(J Akehurst) led after 1f to 4f out: wknd over 2f out **125/1**
000- **10** hd **Simplify**[127] 6134 4-9-1 65 .... TQuinn 1 37
(T M Jones) chsd ldrs: rdn 1/2-way: brief effrt on inner wl over 1f out: sn wknd **12/1**

1m 23.63s (-2.26) **Going Correction** -0.15s/f (Stan) **10** Ran SP% **118.7**
Speed ratings (Par 103):106,102,100,99,95 95,92,89,89,88
CSF £21.44 CT £71.20 TOTE £2.80: £1.10, £3.50, £1.40; EX 21.80.
Owner Paddy Barrett **Bred** P E Barrett **Trained** Upper Lambourn, Berks

FOCUS
A better gallop than in the previous race and a convincing success from the in-form Meditation, who had the run of the race. The runner-up sets the standard.
A Woman In Love Official explanation: jockey said mare had bled from the nose

577 BETDIRECT.CO.UK H'CAP 6f (P)
3:00 (3:00) (Class 6) (0-65,65) 3-Y-O **£2,388** (£705; £352) **Stalls** Low

Form RPR
2210 **1** **Garstang**[10] 481 3-8-12 59 .... (b) RobbieFitzpatrick 8 68+
(Peter Grayson) trckd ldrs: prog on inner to chse ldr over 1f out: plld out and r.o to ld last 100yds: sn clr **9/4**[1]
00-5 **2** 1 1/2 **Danetime Lord (IRE)**[36] 211 3-8-4 51 .... (p) JohnEgan 5 56
(K A Ryan) disp ld tl def advantage 3f out: kicked on 2f out: flashed tail u.p fnl f: hdd and outpcd last 100yds **10/3**[2]
5144 **3** 1 1/4 **Correct Time (IRE)**[12] 464 3-8-10 62 .... JamesDoyle(5) 6 63
(N P Littmoden) trckd ldrs: effrt 2f out: hanging and nt keen over 1f out: kpt on to take 3rd ins fnl f **9/2**[3]
3-63 **4** 1 1/2 **Billy Bling (IRE)**[4] 540 3-9-1 65 .... StephaneBreux(3) 10 61
(R Hannon) disp ld to 3f out: nt qckn 2f out: wknd fnl f **11/1**
5520 **5** 1 3/4 **My Reflection**[18] 415 3-8-1 51 oh5 .... RichardThomas(3) 2 42
(D Shaw) off the pce in midfield: rdn and effrt over 2f out: one pce and no imp **16/1**
-030 **6** 1/2 **Spirit Of Coniston**[10] 481 3-8-9 56 ow2 .... DarryllHolland 3 46
(M Wellings) off the pce in midfield: rdn and effrt over 2f out: sn no prog **10/1**

50-0 7 hd **Cecchetti (IRE)**[4] 543 3-8-8 **55** SimonWhitworth 7 44
(Mrs H Sweeting) *dwlt: wl off the pce in last pair: rdn and kpt on one pce fnl 2f: no ch* **33/1**
4445 8 5 **Twilight Avenger (IRE)**[8] 500 3-8-8 **55** EddieAhern 1 29
(M J Polglase) *wl off the pce in last pair: struggling fr 3f out* **7/1**
0344 9 3 ½ **Luloah**[9] 488 3-8-10 **64** (b[1]) DonnaCaldwell(7) 9 27
(P S McEntee) *pushed up to join ldrs 5f out: wknd rapidly over 2f out* **14/1**
1m 11.46s (-1.35) **Going Correction** -0.15s/f (Stan) **9** Ran SP% **117.4**
Speed ratings (Par 96):103,101,99,97,95 94,94,87,82
CSF £9.88 CT £30.95 TOTE £3.50: £1.20, £1.80, £1.80; EX 16.30.
Owner The Foulrice Twenty **Bred** Mrs S E Barclay **Trained** Formby, Lancs

FOCUS
A decent gallop and a good time. Although the winner again did not look entirely straightforward, he continues to go in the right direction with the third and fourth close to form, and it should prove reliable.

578 BET DIRECT ON 0800 211 222 H'CAP 1m 2f (P)
3:30 (3:30) (Class 4) (0-85,85) 4-Y-0+ **£5,505** (£1,637; £818; £408) **Stalls** Low

Form RPR
12-0 1 **Mina A Salem**[15] 444 4-8-10 **77** DarryllHolland 8 86
(C E Brittain) *mde all at reasonable pce: kicked on wl over 2f out: clr over 1f out: unchal* **7/2**[2]
3025 2 2 **Gingko**[2] 556 9-8-8 **75** ChrisCatlin 5 80
(P R Webber) *chsd wnr: rdn 3f out: no imp and hld wl over 1f out: kpt on* **7/2**[2]
0-00 3 ¾ **Anduril**[5] 530 5-8-7 **74** (b) JohnEgan 1 78
(Miss M E Rowland) *hld up in last pair: outpcd whn nt clr run on inner over 2f out: prog over 1f out: kpt on: no ch* **25/1**
0130 4 nk **Zalkani (IRE)**[12] 463 6-8-6 **73** TQuinn 6 77
(B G Powell) *hld up in last pair: effrt on outer over 2f out: hanging lft and nt qckn over 1f out: one pce after* **7/2**[2]
10-2 5 ½ **Consonant (IRE)**[45] 135 9-8-11 **78** RobbieFitzpatrick 7 81
(D G Bridgwater) *trckd ldng trio: rdn and outpcd 2f out: kpt on same pce after* **11/4**[1]
0U-4 6 5 **Dumaran (IRE)**[15] 444 8-8-9 **76** SimonWhitworth 3 70
(W J Musson) *chsd ldng pair tl wknd 2f out* **10/1**
6/00 7 1 ½ **Polonius**[24] 340 5-9-1 **82** DaneO'Neill 2 73
(P R Webber) *hld up in tch: gng wl enough over 2f out: hanging lft and wknd rapidly over 1f out* **13/2**[3]
2m 5.16s (-2.63) **Going Correction** -0.15s/f (Stan) **7** Ran SP% **119.6**
Speed ratings (Par 105):104,102,101,101,101 97,95
CSF £17.26 CT £269.12 TOTE £3.40: £2.10, £2.20; EX 17.60.
Owner Saeed Manana **Bred** Darley **Trained** Newmarket, Suffolk

FOCUS
No progressive types and a race that should be treated with caution as the winner was given a peach of a ride from the front and ran to previous best with the runner-up close to his mark.

579 BET NOW AT BETDIRECT.CO.UK MAIDEN STKS 7f (P)
4:00 (4:00) (Class 5) 3-Y-0+ **£3,238** (£963; £481; £240) **Stalls** Low

Form RPR
04-0 1 **Li Shih Chen**[11] 473 3-8-9 69 DarrenWilliams 9 70
(A P Jarvis) *mde most: kicked 2l clr over 2f out: styd on steadily fr over 1f out* **12/1**
4- 2 1 **Lucky Token (IRE)**[128] 6122 3-8-5 ow1 EddieAhern 8 64
(E A L Dunlop) *chsd ldrs: rdn over 3f out: effrt to chse wnr over 1f out: kpt on but nvr able to chal* **9/4**[2]
352 3 1 **His Master's Voice (IRE)**[11] 473 3-8-9 75 DaneO'Neill 1 69+
(D W P Arbuthnot) *dwlt: hld up at rr of main gp: nt clr run fr 3f out to over 1f out: r.o fnl f: nt rcvr* **7/4**[1]
50 4 3 **Simplified**[10] 479 3-8-1 RichardThomas(3) 11 53
(J Pearce) *hld up wl in rr: effrt on outer over 2f out: hanging lft and shkn up over 1f out: styd on: nvr nr ldrs* **33/1**
5 ¾ **Rationale (IRE)** 3-8-9 J-PGuillambert 5 56
(S C Williams) *tall: strong: scope: s.v.s: detached in last to over 1f out: nudged along and r.o fnl f: nvr nrr: improve* **50/1**
20 6 nk **Stamford Street (IRE)**[35] 217 3-8-2 JosephWalsh(7) 2 55
(J S Moore) *dwlt: hld up in rr: prog over 2f out: no imp ldrs over 1f out: wknd ins fnl f* **33/1**
353- 7 nk **Precautionary**[73] 6640 3-8-4 68 NickyMackay 3 49
(Miss J Feilden) *hld up: n.m.r on inner over 5f out: shkn up over 2f out: one pce and no ch* **9/1**[3]
8 1 ½ **Lady Georgette (IRE)** 3-8-4 ChrisCatlin 7 45
(E J O'Neill) *chsd ldrs: rdn 1/2-way: lost pl and struggling over 2f out* **10/1**
0-66 9 hd **Boogie Magic**[17] 417 6-9-3 45 AdamKirby(3) 6 51
(T T Clement) *w wnr to 3f out: chsng after tl wknd over 1f out* **50/1**
0-25 10 ½ **Danish Blues (IRE)**[5] 534 3-8-4 63 JamesDoyle(5) 4 55
(N P Littmoden) *t.k.h: prom tl wknd wl over 1f out* **20/1**
00-6 11 9 **They All Laughed**[5] 536 3-8-9 63 (b[1]) JohnEgan 12 26
(T G Mills) *trckd ldrs tl wknd 2f out: eased whn btn fnl f* **10/1**
00 12 8 **Hello Molly**[28] 293 5-9-3 EdwardCreighton(3) 10 —
(E A Wheeler) *dwlt: effrt fr rr on outer over 3f out: sn wknd: t.o* **150/1**
1m 25.02s (-0.87) **Going Correction** -0.15s/f (Stan)
WFA 3 from 5yo+ 16lb **12** Ran SP% **118.2**
Speed ratings (Par 103):98,96,95,92,91 91,90,89,88,88 77,68
CSF £37.57 TOTE £12.20: £2.00, £2.00, £1.10; EX 62.40.
Owner Eurostrait Ltd **Bred** Jarvis Associates **Trained** Twyford, Bucks

FOCUS
A race lacking any real strength and a modest gallop suited those racing close to the pace. The fourth is the best guide to the level of the form.
Lucky Token(IRE) Official explanation: jockey said filly had been hanging left
Rationale(IRE) ◆ Official explanation: jockey said gelding was slowly into stride
Danish Blues(IRE) Official explanation: jockey said gelding had been hanging early on

580 NO 5P RULE 4S AT BETDIRECT H'CAP 5f (P)
4:35 (4:35) (Class 6) (0-60,60) 4-Y-0+ **£2,388** (£705; £352) **Stalls** High

Form RPR
6002 1 **Lady Bahia (IRE)**[3] 547 5-9-1 **57** (b) RobbieFitzpatrick 1 67
(Peter Grayson) *chsd ldrs: prog 2f out: rdn to ld 1f out: hld on wl nr fin* **10/1**
0166 2 nk **Times Review (USA)**[10] 485 5-9-3 **59** (b) JohnEgan 9 68
(C A Dwyer) *towards rr: prog on outer 2f out: drvn to chse wnr ins fnl f and looked dangerous: edgd lft and nt qckn nr fin* **9/1**
0100 3 1 ½ **Monte Major (IRE)**[16] 426 5-8-13 **55** (v) DaneO'Neill 6 59
(D Shaw) *hld up: last tl prog on inner wl over 1f out: styd on fnl f: nt pce to rch ldng pair* **20/1**
0062 4 ¾ **Madrasee**[10] 480 8-8-8 **53** AmirQuinn(3) 5 54
(P G Murphy) *wl in tch: rdn wl over 1f out: hanging lft and nt qckn: kpt on ins fnl f* **4/1**[2]
-003 5 ¾ **Clearing Sky (IRE)**[10] 486 5-8-13 **55** PatCosgrave 2 53
(J R Boyle) *mde most to 2f out: nt qckn over 1f out: one pce after* **6/1**[3]
600- 6 shd **Detonate**[95] 6462 4-8-3 **52** KirstyMilczarek(7) 3 53+
(Mrs C A Dunnett) *hld up in tch: hmpd and stmbld wl over 1f out: nt clr run 1f out: no ch after* **20/1**
00-4 7 ½ **Edward (IRE)**[21] 373 4-9-4 **60** DarrenWilliams 4 56
(A P Jarvis) *sn trckd ldrs: shkn up and nt qckn 2f out: struggling u.p over 1f out* **7/2**[1]
4311 8 nk **Hello Roberto**[6] 524 5-9-0 **56** 6ex (p) AdrianMcCarthy 10 51
(R A Harris) *w ldr: led 2f out to 1f out: wknd rapidly* **7/1**
6150 9 shd **Lady Hopeful (IRE)**[19] 401 4-8-11 **53** (b) ChrisCatlin 8 48
(Peter Grayson) *w ldng pair to 2f out: wknd over 1f out* **10/1**
5655 10 ½ **Edged In Gold**[10] 480 4-8-11 **53** (e) EddieAhern 7 46
(P J Makin) *snatched up after 100yds and in last pair: effrt whn hmpd jst over 1f out: nt rcvr* **13/2**
59.18 secs (-0.60) **Going Correction** -0.15s/f (Stan) **10** Ran SP% **120.0**
Speed ratings (Par 101):98,97,95,93,92 92,91,91,91,90
CSF £99.35 CT £1799.65 TOTE £15.10: £3.10, £3.20, £3.90; EX 135.00.
Owner Peter Grayson Racing Clubs Limited **Bred** Piercetown Stud **Trained** Formby, Lancs
■ Stewards' Enquiry : Amir Quinn two-day ban: careless riding (Mar 15-16)

FOCUS
A modest event in which the pace was sound and the winner got the rub of things against the inside rail. The runner-up sets the standard.
Times Review(USA) Official explanation: jockey said gelding had been hanging
Detonate Official explanation: jockey said gelding was denied a clear run
Edged In Gold Official explanation: jockey said filly was denied a clear run

566 WOLVERHAMPTON (A.W) (L-H)
Saturday, March 4

OFFICIAL GOING: Standard
Wind: Moderate, across Weather: Sunny, cold

581 £100 FIRST BET BONUS AT BETDIRECT.CO.UK (S) STKS 7f 32y(P)
1:30 (1:30) (Class 6) 3-Y-0+ **£2,388** (£705; £352) **Stalls** High

Form RPR
1003 1 **Distant Country (USA)**[1] 568 7-9-7 54 (p) AndrewElliott(7) 4 68
(K R Burke) *hld up in tch: hdwy over 1f out: edgd lft and rdn to ld cl home* **11/2**
3103 2 1 ¼ **Roman Empire**[9] 492 6-10-0 58 (b) NCallan 10 65
(K A Ryan) *a.p: rdn over 2f out: led jst over 1f out: sn hung lft: hdd cl home* **5/1**[3]
0044 3 4 **Wiltshire (IRE)**[12] 458 4-9-8 50 (v) GrahamGibbons 11 49
(P A Blockley) *s.s: bhd: rdn over 4f out: hdwy wl over 1f out: sn hung lft: kpt on ins fnl f* **8/1**
202- 4 1 **Quincannon (USA)**[96] 6449 5-9-8 57 GeorgeBaker 12 46
(W M Brisbourne) *hld up and bhd: hdwy over 2f out: rdn over 1f out: one pce fnl f* **9/2**[2]
0010 5 1 **Winning Venture**[6] 526 9-9-11 55 DNolan(3) 1 50
(A W Carroll) *a.p: rdn 2f out: swtchd rt jst ins fnl f: one pce* **16/1**
00-0 6 ¾ **Noul (USA)**[32] 258 7-9-8 45 (b) FrankieMcDonald 7 42
(J S Moore) *mid-div: rdn over 3f out: no imp whn hmpd ins fnl f* **16/1**
-220 7 1 ¼ **Iced Diamond (IRE)**[7] 520 7-9-8 57 ShaneKelly 6 39
(W M Brisbourne) *s.i.s: sn prom: led over 3f out: rdn over 2f out: hdd jst over 1f out: wknd ins fnl f* **7/2**[1]
0030 8 5 **Tapa**[17] 416 4-9-0 57 (b) SaleemGolam(3) 3 21
(C A Dwyer) *s.i.s: a bhd* **8/1**
010- 9 2 ½ **My Girl Pearl (IRE)**[66] 6676 6-9-9 50 FrancisNorton 2 21
(M S Saunders) *hld up in tch: wknd over 3f out* **14/1**
02-0 10 1 ¾ **Inescapable (USA)**[60] 27 5-9-1 45 JackDean(7) 5 16
(A W Carroll) *s.i.s: a towards rr* **50/1**
0-36 11 1 ½ **Alzarma**[20] 387 4-9-8 45 LPKeniry 9 12
(J Gallagher) *led: hdd over 3f out: sn rdn: wknd wl over 1f out* **33/1**
1m 30.17s (-0.23) **Going Correction** +0.025s/f (Slow) **11** Ran SP% **118.0**
Speed ratings (Par 101):102,100,96,94,93 92,91,85,82,80 79
CSF £33.30 TOTE £6.40: £1.80, £1.80, £2.60; EX 40.40.There was no bid for the winner. Roman Empire was claimed by Mr Joe McCarthy for £6,000
Owner Spigot Lodge Partnership **Bred** Audubon Farm And D L Martin **Trained** Middleham Moor, N Yorks

FOCUS
The front two pulled away in what was an average race for the grade run in a reasonable time.

582 BETLIVE IN-RUNNING AT BETDIRECT.CO.UK H'CAP (DIV I) 1m 1f 103y(P)
2:05 (2:06) (Class 6) (0-60,60) 4-Y-0+ **£2,047** (£604; £302) **Stalls** Low

Form RPR
0303 1 **Buscador (USA)**[5] 530 7-8-9 **58** LiamJones(7) 9 67
(W M Brisbourne) *sn led: rdn 3f out: clr wl over 1f out: rdn out* **9/2**[2]
-323 2 1 ¾ **Majehar**[3] 546 4-8-5 **47** LPKeniry 1 53
(A G Newcombe) *hld up in tch: rdn wl over 1f out: r.o ins fnl f: nt trble wnr* **7/2**[1]
5063 3 3 **Scotty's Future (IRE)**[10] 484 8-9-1 **60** SilvestreDeSousa(3) 11 60
(D Nicholls) *hld up and bhd: hdwy over 4f out: rdn over 2f out: one pce fnl f* **14/1**
0403 4 1 ¼ **Taminoula (IRE)**[24] 336 5-9-0 **56** MickyFenton 4 54
(J G Given) *hld up in tch: rdn to chse wnr 2f out: wknd ins fnl f* **9/1**
-043 5 2 **Tuscan Treaty**[19] 395 6-8-3 **48** oh1 ow2 (tp) SaleemGolam(3) 6 42
(P J McBride) *hld up and bhd: rdn and hdwy jst over 1f out: r.o* **10/1**
0-00 6 ¾ **Ballycroy Girl (IRE)**[31] 268 4-8-11 **53** (p) PaulHanagan 5 45
(A Bailey) *hld up in mid-div: kpt on same pce fnl f* **25/1**
3341 7 ½ **Crusoe (IRE)**[6] 527 9-8-10 **52** 6ex ow1 (b) BrianReilly 3 43
(A Sadik) *hld up: hdwy over 3f out: rdn over 2f out: wknd over 1f out* **16/1**
4064 8 ¾ **My Pension (IRE)**[12] 462 5-9-1 **57** ShaneKelly 8 47
(P Howling) *sn chsng wnr: rdn over 2f out: wknd fnl f* **9/2**[2]
0206 9 2 **Farnborough (USA)**[8] 505 5-8-12 **54** NCallan 10 40
(R J Price) *plld hrd early in rr: nt clr run 3f out: hdwy wl over 1f out: sn rdn: fnd nil* **6/1**[3]
0625 10 ¾ **Christmas Truce (IRE)**[7] 514 7-8-5 **54** SophieDoyle(7) 7 39
(Ms J S Doyle) *hmpd s: hld up towards rr: rdn 4f out: no rspnse* **25/1**
00-6 11 nk **Skelligs Rock (IRE)**[60] 18 6-8-13 **55** JimmyQuinn 12 39
(A W Carroll) *hld up in mid-div: rdn 4f out: wknd over 2f out* **50/1**
0-00 12 nk **Qobtaan (USA)**[17] 416 7-8-10 **52** HayleyTurner 13 36
(M R Bosley) *t.k.h: a bhd* **33/1**

460- **13** *10* **Didnt Tell My Wife**[67] [6674] 7-8-8 **50** NeilPollard 2 15
(Lucinda Featherstone) *led early: prom: rdn over 3f out: wknd over 2f out* **20/1**

2m 3.99s (1.37) **Going Correction** +0.025s/f (Slow) **13** Ran SP% **121.9**
Speed ratings (Par 101):94,92,89,88,86 86,85,85,83,82 82,82,73
CSF £19.70 CT £210.97 TOTE £6.90: £2.00, £1.70, £4.60; EX 27.90.
Owner David Robson And Sonia Nicholls **Bred** William H Floyd **Trained** Great Ness, Shropshire
■ Stewards' Enquiry : L P Keniry one-day ban: careless riding (Mar 15)

FOCUS
A modest winning time for the grade, almost a second slower than the other division rated through the runner-up to recent marks.
My Pension(IRE) Official explanation: vet said gelding pulled up lame
Farnborough(USA) Official explanation: jockey said gelding was denied a clear run
Didnt Tell My Wife Official explanation: jockey said gelding lost its action

583 NO 5P RULE 4'S AT BET DIRECT H'CAP 1m 141y(P)
2:35 (2:36) (Class 5) (0-75,75) 3-Y-O **£3,238** (£963; £481; £240) **Stalls** Low

Form RPR
5013 **1** **Outlook**[3] [550] 3-9-2 **73** (b) NCallan 9 76
(N P Littmoden) *a.p: led over 2f out: rdn clr over 1f out: hung rt ins fnl f: drvn out* **4/1**[2]
4311 **2** *shd* **Smart Ass (IRE)**[18] [415] 3-8-8 **65** RobertWinston 5 68
(J S Moore) *s.i.s: hld up: hdwy over 6f out: chsd wnr over 1f out: ev ch wl fnl f: r.o* **5/1**[3]
1-44 **3** *2* **Mambo Sun**[11] [475] 3-8-2 **66** (p) KevinGhunowa(7) 10 65
(P A Blockley) *hld up: hdwy over 3f out: sn rdn: kpt on ins fnl f* **15/2**
-160 **4** *½* **Abstract Art (USA)**[14] [448] 3-9-4 **75** JoeFanning 6 73
(N A Callaghan) *w ldr: rdn over 2f out: one pce* **10/1**
5102 **5** *1 ½* **Tamagin (USA)**[2] [558] 3-8-7 **64** ow1 (p) ShaneKelly 4 59
(P D Evans) *sn led: rdn and hdd over 2f out: one pce* **11/2**
604 **6** *hd* **Top Shot**[12] [459] 3-8-10 **70** SaleemGolam(3) 11 64
(M H Tompkins) *nvr trbld ldrs* **14/1**
005- **7** *5* **Pactolos Way**[126] [6148] 3-8-8 **65** StephenCarson 2 49
(P R Chamings) *nvr nr ldrs* **25/1**
061 **8** *1* **Living On A Prayer**[10] [479] 3-8-8 **65** JimmyQuinn 3 47
(J Pearce) *led early: chsd ldrs: rdn over 5f out: wknd over 4f out* **14/1**
61 **9** *18* **Ransom Strip (USA)**[14] [453] 3-8-13 **70** KDarley 1 14
(M Johnston) *broke wl: sn lost pl: nvr gng wl: bhd fnl 4f* **9/4**[1]
46-0 **10** *dist* **Eliminator**[15] [445] 3-8-9 **66** PaulHanagan 8 —
(I W McInnes) *a bhd: t.o* **50/1**

1m 52.35s (0.59) **Going Correction** +0.025s/f (Slow) **10** Ran SP% **122.8**
Speed ratings (Par 98):98,97,96,95,94 94,89,88,72,—
CSF £25.91 CT £149.66 TOTE £4.30: £1.80, £1.90, £2.30; EX 19.60.
Owner Nigel Shields **Bred** W N Greig **Trained** Newmarket, Suffolk

FOCUS
A modest handicap in which they went a decent gallop up front and it produced a cracking finish. The third sets the standard and the form looks solid enough.
Tamagin(USA) Official explanation: trainer said colt failed to get trip with fast early pace
Pactolos Way Official explanation: jockey said colt hung right early
Ransom Strip(USA) Official explanation: trainer had no explanation for the poor form shown

584 BETDIRECT.CO.UK MAIDEN STKS 1m 1f 103y(P)
3:10 (3:10) (Class 5) 3-4-Y-O **£3,238** (£963; £481; £240) **Stalls** Low

Form RPR
1 **Samurai Jack (IRE)**[133] [6036] 3-8-5 72 (t) JimmyQuinn 8 64+
(John A Quinn, Ire) *s.i.s: bhd: hdwy on outside whn bdly hmpd and carried wd ent st: sn edgd lft: rdn to ld wl ins* **11/2**[3]
00-3 **2** *½* **Manouche**[15] [445] 3-8-5 66 (p) FrancisNorton 4 61
(K A Ryan) *sn led: rdn and hdd 3f out: lft 2nd wl over 1f out: kpt on ins fnl f* **7/2**[1]
3 *¾* **Beowulf** 3-8-5 RobertWinston 10 60
(M Johnston) *chsd ldr: led 3f out: rdn whn lft clr wl over 1f out: hung lft and hdd wl ins fnl f: no ex* **7/2**[1]
20-0 **4** *1 ½* **Mighty Kitchener (USA)**[18] [409] 3-8-5 62 JoeFanning 3 59+
(P Howling) *hld up in mid-div: rdn over 3f out: hdwy over 2f out: bdly hmpd and carried wd ent st: sn edgd lft: kpt on one* **16/1**
00-0 **5** *4* **Wise Choice**[3] [548] 3-8-2 56 SaleemGolam(3) 1 49
(N P Littmoden) *hld up: sn mid-div: rdn over 3f out: no real prog fnl 2f* **13/2**
440 **6** *1* **Tod Sloan (IRE)**[6] [527] 4-9-6 45 GregFairley(5) 6 51?
(J M Bradley) *prom tl rdn and wknd over 1f out* **20/1**
4- **7** *½* **Bollin Michael**[329] [945] 4-9-11 NCallan 11 50+
(T D Easterby) *prom: rdn and wnt 2nd over 2f out: hung bdly rt and bmpd ent st: nt rcvr* **4/1**[2]
0 **8** *2* **Diafa (USA)**[26] [314] 4-9-6 60 RobertHavlin 2 42
(J G M O'Shea) *led early: prom: rdn 3f out: wknd 2f out* **25/1**
0 **9** *10* **Datznyce (IRE)**[11] [473] 3-7-9 MarcHalford(5) 7 19
(D R C Elsworth) *dwlt: rdn 4f out: a bhd* **16/1**
00-5 **10** *8* **Spasiba**[37] [199] 3-8-0 48 PaulHanagan 9 —
(Mrs L Williamson) *rdn 4f out: a bhd* **25/1**
00-0 **11** *hd* **Victimised (IRE)**[19] [402] 4-9-11 40 MickyFenton 5 12
(R J Price) *stdd s: a bhd* **66/1**

2m 3.39s (0.77) **Going Correction** +0.025s/f (Slow)
WFA 3 from 4yo 20lb **11** Ran SP% **118.9**
Speed ratings (Par 103):97,96,95,94,91 90,89,87,79,71 71
CSF £24.31 TOTE £6.90: £1.80, £1.60, £2.20; EX 29.40.
Owner D Buckley **Bred** Airlie Stud **Trained** Blackmiller Hill, Co. Kildare

FOCUS
A modest maiden but an eventful race with Bollin Michael hanging badly right off the final bend and hampering several of his opponents. The runner-up sets the standard for the form.
Bollin Michael Official explanation: jockey said he had steering problems turning into straight
Datznyce(IRE) Official explanation: jockey said filly hung right

585 BET DIRECT ON 0800 211 222 H'CAP 7f 32y(P)
3:40 (3:40) (Class 5) (0-75,75) 4-Y-O+ **£3,238** (£963; £481; £240) **Stalls** High

Form RPR
1-15 **1** **Local Poet**[9] [489] 5-9-4 **75** (bt) PaulHanagan 3 83
(I Semple) *hld up in tch: rdn over 2f out: led 1f out: drvn out* **11/4**[1]
-440 **2** *¾* **General Feeling (IRE)**[1] [569] 5-9-4 **75** GeorgeBaker 8 81
(M Mullineaux) *s.s: hld up and bhd: hdwy over 1f out: swtchd lft ins fnl f: r.o* **7/1**[3]
2120 **3** *nk* **Mystic Man (FR)**[2] [559] 8-9-4 **75** (b) JimmyQuinn 5 80
(I W McInnes) *hld up and bhd: hdwy 3f out: n.m.r briefly ent st: ev ch ins fnl f: sn edgd rt: nt qckn* **10/1**
-004 **4** *nk* **Mistral Sky**[14] [451] 7-8-10 **67** (v) MickyFenton 10 71
(Stef Liddiard) *hld up in mid-div: rdn and hdwy over 2f out: nt qckn ins fnl f* **10/1**
3311 **5** *hd* **Winthorpe (IRE)**[9] [489] 6-8-11 **68** GrahamGibbons 9 72
(J J Quinn) *t.k.h: sn prom: rdn and ev ch 1f out: one pce* **9/2**[2]
0-40 **6** *½* **True Night**[30] [276] 9-8-4 **68** ow1 VictoriaBehan(7) 1 71+
(D Nicholls) *led early: prom: rdn over 2f out: no hdwy fnl f* **25/1**
0-03 **7** *1 ¼* **Onlytime Will Tell**[21] [381] 8-8-9 **66** JoeFanning 4 65
(D Nicholls) *hld up towards rr: kpt on fnl f: nt rch ldr* **7/1**[3]
00-0 **8** *½* **Redwood Rocks (IRE)**[8] [504] 5-8-11 **68** PaulEddery 11 66
(B Smart) *sn led: rdn over 2f out: hdd 1f out: eased whn btn towards fin* **25/1**
1-35 **9** *hd* **Connotation**[33] [253] 4-9-0 **71** LPKeniry 6 69
(A G Newcombe) *hld up and bhd: short-lived effrt on outside over 1f out* **14/1**
0060 **10** *1* **Queens Rhapsody**[26] [316] 6-8-10 **67** ShaneKelly 7 62
(A Bailey) *hld up in mid-div: hdwy over 4f out: rdn over 2f out: wknd fnl f* **8/1**
0-00 **11** *2* **Desert Lightning (IRE)**[1] [567] 4-8-8 **72** AndrewElliott(7) 2 62
(K R Burke) *hld up in tch: lost pl over 3f out: bhd whn rdn and hung rt 1f out* **20/1**

1m 29.71s (-0.69) **Going Correction** +0.025s/f (Slow) **11** Ran SP% **118.3**
Speed ratings (Par 103):104,103,102,102,102 101,100,99,99,98 96
CSF £21.57 CT £169.01 TOTE £3.50: £1.80, £1.60, £3.50; EX 29.40.
Owner newkeylets **Bred** Richard Brunger **Trained** Carluke, S Lanarks

FOCUS
This fair handicap was run at a decent pace and it represents solid form for the grade.

586 BETLIVE IN-RUNNING AT BETDIRECT.CO.UK H'CAP (DIV II) 1m 1f 103y(P)
4:15 (4:15) (Class 6) (0-60,60) 4-Y-O+ **£2,047** (£604; £302) **Stalls** Low

Form RPR
0002 **1** **Gallego**[12] [469] 4-8-6 **48** MatthewHenry 9 55
(R J Price) *hld up and bhd: hdwy on outside 2f out: led over 1f out: edgd lft ins fnl f: r.o* **8/1**
2321 **2** *shd* **Basinet**[12] [469] 8-8-12 **54** (p) GrahamGibbons 12 61
(J J Quinn) *hld up and bhd: rdn over 3f out: swtchd lft and hdwy on ins over 1f out: r.o ins fnl f* **7/1**[3]
-021 **3** *nk* **Joe Jo Star**[12] [467] 4-8-9 **51** (p) MickyFenton 5 57
(B P J Baugh) *a.p: rdn and ev ch over 1f out: r.o* **8/1**
6052 **4** *1 ¼* **Alqaayid**[11] [472] 5-8-8 **50** PhillipMakin 1 54
(P W Hiatt) *hld up in tch: lost pl over 5f out: hdwy over 2f out: rdn over 1f out: no ex towards fin* **8/1**
6006 **5** *nk* **Sorbiesharry (IRE)**[5] [537] 7-9-1 **57** RobertWinston 2 60
(Mrs N Macauley) *hld up in mid-div: lost pl over 5f out: rdn 3f out: styd on ins fnl f: nrst fin* **5/1**[1]
6-61 **6** *½* **Treetops Hotel (IRE)**[11] [471] 7-8-12 **54** FrankieMcDonald 10 56
(B R Johnson) *hld up and bhd: hdwy on outside 2f out: hung lft 1f out: one pce* **13/2**[2]
-303 **7** *1 ¾* **Unrestricted**[12] [462] 4-9-0 **56** NCallan 6 55
(C F Wall) *hdwy 6f out: nt clr run over 2f out and over 1f out: no ex ins fnl f* **13/2**[2]
-400 **8** *2* **House Martin**[11] [471] 4-8-8 **50** PaulHanagan 13 45
(C R Dore) *nvr trbld ldrs* **25/1**
0550 **9** *2 ½* **Tregarron**[7] [514] 5-8-3 **52** KevinGhunowa(7) 11 42
(P A Blockley) *hdwy 6f out: rdn over 3f out: wknd 2f out* **25/1**
40-0 **10** *3* **Layed Back Rocky**[59] [38] 4-8-4 **46** oh1 JimmyQuinn 8 31
(M Mullineaux) *prom: led 6f out: rdn and hdd 2f out: wknd over 1f out* **40/1**
4414 **11** *1 ¼* **Spark Up**[15] [446] 6-8-8 **55** (v) RichardKingscote(5) 7 37
(J W Unett) *w ldr: rdn to ld 2f out: hdd over 1f out: eased whn btn fnl f* **7/1**[3]
3-00 **12** *2* **Lockstock (IRE)**[53] [77] 8-9-4 **60** FrancisNorton 3 38
(M S Saunders) *led: hdd 6f out: rdn over 3f out: wknd over 1f out: eased whn btn ins fnl f* **14/1**

2m 3.05s (0.43) **Going Correction** +0.025s/f (Slow) **12** Ran SP% **118.5**
Speed ratings (Par 101):99,98,98,97,97 96,95,93,91,88 87,85
CSF £61.77 CT £469.26 TOTE £10.80: £3.10, £2.80, £2.50; EX 81.90.
Owner My Left Foot Racing Syndicate **Bred** Mrs C C Regalado-Gonzalez **Trained** Ullingswick, H'fords

FOCUS
The winning time was almost a second quicker than the first division, but still only ordinary for the grade, and the form looks straightforward.
Spark Up Official explanation: jockey said mare hung right final bend

587 BET DIRECT CH4 TEXT P613 H'CAP (DIV I) 5f 216y(P)
4:50 (4:50) (Class 6) (0-65,65) 4-Y-O+ **£2,047** (£604; £302) **Stalls** Low

Form RPR
3201 **1** **Sweetest Revenge (IRE)**[7] [519] 5-9-3 **64** HayleyTurner 11 76
(M D I Usher) *led early: sn lost pl: hdwy on outside 2f out: led ins fnl f: r.o wl* **8/1**
4523 **2** *1 ½* **Ashes (IRE)**[7] [519] 4-9-0 **61** FrancisNorton 4 69+
(K R Burke) *s.i.s: sn mid-div: hdwy whn nt clr run and swtchd rt wl over 1f out: hrd rdn and r.o ins fnl furlong* **5/1**[2]
1406 **3** *hd* **Sahara Silk (IRE)**[7] [519] 5-9-3 **64** (v) PaulHanagan 6 71+
(D Shaw) *prom: n.m.r and lost pl sn after s: rdn and hdwy 2f out: ev ch ins fnl f: nt qckn* **16/1**
5450 **4** *¾* **Doctor's Cave**[7] [514] 4-8-10 **57** (b) LPKeniry 8 61
(K O Cunningham-Brown) *sn bhd: hdwy over 1f out: r.o ins fnl f* **14/1**
-055 **5** *1 ¾* **Piccleyes**[8] [501] 5-8-6 **53** (b) JoeFanning 10 52
(M J Polglase) *hld up and bhd: hdwy over 2f out: rdn to ld jst over 1f out: hdd ins fnl f: one pce* **18/1**
2301 **6** *1 ½* **Mind Alert**[10] [485] 5-8-4 **54** (v) PatrickMathers(3) 12 48+
(D Shaw) *hld up and bhd: sme hdwy whn hmpd ent st: nvr nrr* **9/1**
0000 **7** *¾* **Time N Time Again**[3] [552] 8-8-10 **57** RobertWinston 1 49
(Peter Grayson) *s.i.s: sn chsng ldr: rdn over 2f out: wknd ins fnl f* **7/1**
6430 **8** *1* **Four Amigos (USA)**[10] [485] 5-8-5 **55** (b[1]) SilvestreDeSousa(3) 7 44
(D Nicholls) *sn led: rdn and hdd jst over 1f out: wknd ins fnl f* **25/1**
2523 **9** *½* **Byo (IRE)**[3] [547] 8-8-12 **59** TonyCulhane 2 47
(P Howling) *prom: rdn over 2f out: wknd ins fnl f* **7/1**
0-00 **10** *½* **Caustic Wit (IRE)**[5] [532] 8-9-4 **65** FrankieMcDonald 3 51
(M S Saunders) *prom: lost pl over 3f out: n.d after* **25/1**
0-04 **11** *4* **Rapid Flow**[5] [533] 4-8-7 **54** ow2 ShaneKelly 9 28
(J W Unett) *chsd ldrs: rdn over 2f out: wknd wl over 1f out* **11/2**[3]

2315 **12** *1¾* **Tiviski (IRE)**[7] 519 4-9-1 **62**.......................... NCallan 5 31
(G G Margarson) *prom: rdn 3f out: sn wknd* **9/2**[1]

1m 15.46s (-0.35) **Going Correction** +0.025s/f (Slow) **12** Ran SP% **121.8**
Speed ratings (Par 101):103,101,100,99,97 95,94,93,92,91 86,84
CSF £49.14 CT £641.85 TOTE £10.90: £3.00, £2.50, £6.10; EX 53.70.
Owner The Ridgeway Partnership **Bred** Joza Partnership **Trained** Upper Lambourn, Berks

FOCUS
The winning time was marginally slower than the second division and the form looks average.
Tiviski(IRE) Official explanation: trainer had no explanation for the poor form shown

588 BET DIRECT CH4 TEXT P613 H'CAP (DIV II) 5f 216y(P)
5:20 (5:20) (Class 6) (0-65,64) 4-Y-0+ **£2,047** (£604; £302) **Stalls** Low

Form RPR

300- **1** **True Magic**[163] 5420 5-9-4 **64**.......................... GrahamGibbons 6 74
(J D Bethell) *hld up in tch: hrd rdn to ld wl ins fnl f: r.o* **9/1**

4053 **2** *1¼* **Alpaga Le Jomage (IRE)**[8] 502 4-9-2 **62**.......................... NCallan 4 68
(M J Polglase) *chsd ldr: rdn over 2f out: led 1f out: hdd and no ex wl ins fnl f* **5/1**[2]

-021 **3** *¾* **Riquewihr**[7] 520 6-8-11 **57**..........................(p) RobertWinston 9 61
(J S Wainwright) *towards rr: hdwy on outside over 2f out: carried wd ent st: hung lft and r.o fnl f* **2/1**[1]

3030 **4** *¾* **Savile's Delight (IRE)**[26] 320 7-9-2 **62**..........................(b) PaulHanagan 3 64
(R Brotherton) *led: rdn over 2f out: hdd 1f out: no ex towards fin* **7/1**[3]

020- **5** *shd* **Cyfrwys (IRE)**[95] 6455 5-8-9 **55**..........................(p) FrancisFerris 2 56
(B Palling) *chsd ldrs: rdn and one pce fnl 2f* **10/1**

00-6 **6** *nk* **H Harrison (IRE)**[15] 446 6-8-4 **57**.......................... AndrewElliott(7) 7 58
(I W McInnes) *a.p: ev ch over 2f out: sn rdn: one pce* **14/1**

0306 **7** *½* **Merdiff**[8] 501 7-9-0 **60**.......................... ShaneKelly 8 59
(W M Brisbourne) *mid-div: rdn over 2f out: hdwy and swtchd rt over 1f out: no further prog fnl f* **14/1**

-315 **8** *1¾* **Desert Light (IRE)**[19] 400 5-8-3 **52** ow1..........................(v) PatrickMathers(3) 11 46
(D Shaw) *sn outpcd: hdwy on ins over 1f out: no imp fnl f* **8/1**

5030 **9** *¾* **Namir (IRE)**[5] 532 4-9-3 **63**..........................(p) MickyFenton 13 55
(Stef Liddiard) *bhd: hdwy over 2f out: carried wd ent st: n.d after* **14/1**

-060 **10** *4* **Lord Links (IRE)**[16] 429 5-8-12 **58**.......................... VinceSlattery 10 38
(D J Daly) *sn outpcd* **18/1**

2304 **11** *2½* **Nova Tor (IRE)**[8] 501 4-8-6 **52**..........................(b) JoeFanning 5 24
(Peter Grayson) *t.k.h: prom: hung rt ent st: sn wknd* **15/2**

0-05 **12** *7* **Danethorpe Lady (IRE)**[19] 396 4-8-4 **50** oh10.......................... HayleyTurner 1 —
(D Shaw) *sn outpcd* **50/1**

1m 15.29s (-0.52) **Going Correction** +0.025s/f (Slow) **12** Ran SP% **131.7**
Speed ratings (Par 101):104,102,101,100,100 99,99,96,95,90 87,77
CSF £59.76 CT £134.00 TOTE £13.30: £3.70, £2.10, £1.60; EX 125.90 Place 6 £117.35, Place 5 £47.17..
Owner T R Lock **Bred** T R Lock **Trained** Middleham Moor, N Yorks

FOCUS
The winning time was 0.17 seconds faster than the first division and the form looks sound rated through the placed horses.
Nova Tor(IRE) Official explanation: jockey said filly lost its action turning into home straight
T/Plt: £46.80 to a £1 stake. Pool: £53,379.90. 831.80 winning tickets. T/Qpdt: £10.80 to a £1 stake. Pool: £3,656.50. 250.30 winning tickets. KH

574 LINGFIELD (L-H)
Monday, March 6

OFFICIAL GOING: Standard
Wind: Moderate against, becoming almost nil by race 6 Weather: Cloudy

589 GUINNESS DRAUGHT "BREWED IN DUBLIN" APPRENTICE H'CAP 2m (P)
2:00 (2:01) (Class 5) (0-75,74) 4-Y-0+ **£3,238** (£963; £481; £240) **Stalls** Low

Form RPR

-045 **1** **Monte Cristo (FR)**[19] 420 8-9-3 **67**..........................(v) NeilChalmers 7 73
(Mrs L C Taylor) *hld up towards rr: hdwy over 3f out: led and kicked for home over 2f out: drvn out* **17/2**

1-13 **2** *1½* **Reggae Rhythm (IRE)**[19] 420 12-9-3 **74**.......................... SophieDoyle(7) 9 79
(A J Lidderdale) *wd: hld up and bhd: hdwy on outside ent st: r.o to take 2nd fnl 75 yds* **13/2**[3]

4653 **3** *½* **Lady Pilot**[12] 482 4-8-4 **59** ow1.......................... AdamKirby 8 63
(Dr J R J Naylor) *prom: lost pl 7f out: rallied over 2f out: kpt on to take 3rd fnl 50 yds* **10/1**

24-2 **4** *¾* **Montosari**[9] 521 7-8-10 **65**.......................... JamesDoyle(5) 4 68
(P Mitchell) *t.k.h in tch: hdwy to go cl 2nd 10f out: outpcd by wnr 2f out: lost 2nd fnl 75 yds* **8/1**

-002 **5** *1½* **Nawow**[19] 420 6-9-1 **70**.......................... TravisBlock(5) 2 71
(P D Cundell) *prom: squeezed for room and lost pl over 5f out: renewed effrt on ins 2f out: no imp fnl f* **4/1**[2]

0/6- **6** *shd* **Stance**[30] 398 7-9-1 **70**.......................... JamieJones(5) 5 71
(G L Moore) *chsd ldrs: hrd rdn 3f out: no ex over 1f out* **8/1**

00-4 **7** *1½* **Lewis Island (IRE)**[8] 338 7-9-3 **70**.......................... CDHayes(3) 1 69
(G L Moore) *s.s: plld hrd and bhd: stdy hdwy and in tch 6f out: rdn and outpcd fnl 3f* **14/1**

616- **8** *1¼* **Aristi (IRE)**[123] 6239 5-8-5 **58**..........................(p) RoryMoore(3) 6 56
(M Quinn) *led and restrained in front: set modest pce: increased tempo 4f out: hdd over 2f out: wknd over 1f out* **20/1**

23-1 **9** *25* **Taxman (IRE)**[13] 478 4-8-2 **64**..........................(p) WilliamCarson(7) 10 32
(C E Brittain) *hld up in tch: eased across to ins rail after 4f: bdly hmpd 6f out and over 5f out: rdn and sn bhd: eased fnl f* **11/4**[1]

10 *dist* **Spy Game (IRE)**[554] 4204 6-8-10 **60**.......................... PaulMulrennan 3 —
(Jennie Candlish) *hld up and bhd: rdn and struggling fnl 5f: no ch whn virtually p.u over 1f out* **66/1**

3m 27.16s (-1.63) **Going Correction** -0.175s/f (Stan)
WFA 4 from 5yo+ 5lb **10** Ran SP% **114.8**
Speed ratings (Par 103):97,96,96,95,94 94,94,93,80,—
CSF £61.75 CT £562.56 TOTE £13.70: £3.60, £2.70, £2.60; EX 69.40.
Owner Mrs L C Taylor **Bred** C Cohen **Trained** Upper Lambourn, Berks
■ Stewards' Enquiry : William Carson two-day ban: careless riding (Mar 17-18)

FOCUS
A modest staying handicap run at a noticeably steady pace that did not increase significantly until about the final half mile. The race was restricted to apprentices and there were some promising young jockeys on show.
Monte Cristo(FR) Official explanation: trainer said, regarding the improved form shown, gelding was suited by the change of tactics
Taxman(IRE) Official explanation: jockey said gelding suffered interference in running

590 PLAY EPT EVENTS WITH LITTLEWOODSPOKER.COM MAIDEN STKS 7f (P)
2:30 (2:33) (Class 5) 3-Y-0 **£4,857** (£1,445; £722; £360) **Stalls** Low

Form RPR

4 **1** **Piano Player (IRE)**[24] 365 3-9-3.......................... SteveDrowne 10 65
(J A Osborne) *chsd ldrs: effrt 2f out: drvn to ld nr fin* **6/4**[1]

603- **2** *hd* **Ballybeg (IRE)**[115] 6309 3-9-0 63.......................... StephaneBreux(3) 4 64
(R Hannon) *prom: effrt and hung rt ent st: drvn to narrow ld 75 yds out: kpt on: hdd nr fin* **3/1**[2]

0- **3** *¾* **Royal Tavira Girl (IRE)**[182] 4989 3-8-12.......................... TPQueally 9 57
(M G Quinlan) *in tch: effrt over 2f out: drvn to chal fnl f: nt qckn nr fin* **25/1**

004 **4** *½* **Bobby Rose**[12] 479 3-9-3 65.......................... DarryllHolland 2 61
(D K Ivory) *prom: led over 2f out: hdd and no ex fnl 75 yds* **8/1**

0- **5** *¾* **Maximix**[150] 5708 3-9-3.......................... MichaelHills 3 59
(B W Hills) *t.k.h towards rr: hdwy and eased wd over 1f out: pushed along and r.o: nrst fin* **7/1**

6 *hd* **Abaconian (IRE)** 3-9-3.......................... JamieSpencer 5 59
(M J Wallace) *in tch: rdn and outpcd 3f out: rallied over 1f out: no imp fnl f* **9/2**[3]

7 *¾* **Pain In The Neck (IRE)** 3-8-12.......................... DerekNolan(5) 8 57
(M J Wallace) *hld up in midfield: effrt over 2f out: no imp over 1f out* **50/1**

00 **8** *hd* **Wally Barge**[12] 479 3-9-3.......................... MickyFenton 11 56
(D K Ivory) *sn outpcd and bhd: sme hdwy on ins ent st: nvr able to chal* **50/1**

56 **9** *1¾* **Plemont Bay**[16] 453 3-9-3.......................... HayleyTurner 1 52
(M L W Bell) *led tl over 2f out: wknd over 1f out* **20/1**

0- **10** *13* **Phills Pearl**[119] 6281 3-8-9..........................(t) AdamKirby(3) 7 14
(Miss Diana Weeden) *sn outpcd: a bhd: no ch fnl 3f* **100/1**

11 *3½* **Cortina** 3-8-12.......................... JohnEgan 6 6
(J Jay) *s.s: a bhd: no ch fnl 3f* **33/1**

1m 26.0s (0.11) **Going Correction** -0.175s/f (Stan) **11** Ran SP% **123.3**
Speed ratings (Par 98):92,91,90,90,89 89,88,86,71 67
CSF £6.00 TOTE £2.50: £1.10, £1.80, £12.40; EX 8.50.
Owner Mountgrange Stud **Bred** B W Hills And Mrs H Theodorou **Trained** Upper Lambourn, Berks

FOCUS
They seemed to go quite a good pace, but still finished in a bit of a bunch and this was probably a pretty ordinary maiden with the exposed runner-up setting the standard. The winning time was modest for the grade.
Maximix Official explanation: jockey said gelding hung right in straight

591 BETDIRECT FREEPHONE 0800 211 222 CLAIMING STKS 1m 4f (P)
3:00 (3:00) (Class 5) 4-Y-0+ **£3,238** (£963; £481; £240) **Stalls** Low

Form RPR

-344 **1** **Champagne Shadow (IRE)**[19] 420 5-9-5 80..........................(b) GeorgeBaker 2 67+
(G L Moore) *hld up in midfield: drvn to chse ldrs over 3f out: styd on to ld 1f out: rdn clr* **4/5**[1]

0320 **2** *2½* **Dagola (IRE)**[14] 468 5-8-7 45.......................... JohnEgan 8 51
(C A Dwyer) *hld up towards rr: stdy hdwy 3f out: nt clr run and swtchd rt over 1f out: r.o to take 2nd fnl 75 yds* **25/1**

00 **3** *1¼* **Lord Raffles**[19] 419 4-8-13.......................... DaneO'Neill 7 57
(P R Webber) *prom: led 6f out: hrd rdn and hdd 1f out: no ex* **50/1**

0-60 **4** *nk* **Easter Ogil (IRE)**[12] 482 11-8-12 54.......................... AmirQuinn(3) 9 57
(P G Murphy) *hld up in midfield: smooth hdwy to trck ldrs over 3f out: wd home turn and hung lft in st: nt qckn* **66/1**

-600 **5** *1½* **Rasid (USA)**[21] 395 8-8-3 45 ow1.......................... SaleemGolam(3) 4 45
(C A Dwyer) *hld up in rr: rdn 3f out: hdwy and swtchd lft ent st: styd on* **50/1**

0-00 **6** *1¼* **Shahzan House (IRE)**[30] 296 7-9-1 85..........................(v[1]) JamieSpencer 3 53
(Stef Liddiard) *led 1f: stdd to trck ldrs: chal over 1f out: shkn up and fnd nil: btn whn n.m.r ins fnl f* **2/1**[2]

00-2 **7** *1¼* **Twentytwosilver (IRE)**[28] 309 6-9-1 45.......................... MichaelTebbutt 6 51
(D B Feek) *stdd s: plld hrd in rr: mod effrt 3f out: no imp* **20/1**

0-00 **8** *nk* **Malibu (IRE)**[9] 521 5-8-11 67.......................... TQuinn 10 46
(S Dow) *w ldrs: 4th and rdn whn hmpd and snatched up early st: n.d after* **10/1**[3]

100/ **9** *8* **Global Challenge (IRE)**[38] 4862 7-9-7 85..........................(v) SteveDrowne 1 44
(P G Murphy) *towards rr: drvn along 1/2-way: sn no ch* **16/1**

00-0 **10** *3½* **Little Gannet**[21] 395 5-8-0 40.......................... HayleyTurner 11 18
(T D McCarthy) *prom tl wknd qckly over 3f out* **80/1**

005/ **11** *dist* **Hello Tiger**[592] 4069 5-8-5.......................... ChrisCatlin 5 —
(J A Supple) *led after 1f tl 6f out: wknd qckly 5f out: sn wl bhd* **100/1**

2m 32.45s (-1.94) **Going Correction** -0.175s/f (Stan)
WFA 4 from 5yo+ 2lb **11** Ran SP% **120.1**
Speed ratings (Par 103):99,97,96,96,95 94,93,93,88,85 —
CSF £32.37 TOTE £2.30: £1.10, £3.10, £9.30; EX 22.10.Shahzan House was claimed by P. G. Murphy for £10,000.
Owner D R Hunnisett **Bred** Mrs Kate Watson **Trained** Woodingdean, E Sussex

FOCUS
Just an moderate claimer in which Champagne Shadow did not have to be at his best to win.
Easter Ogil(IRE) Official explanation: jockey said gelding hung left

592 PLAY NOW AT BETDIRECTPOKER.COM H'CAP 1m 2f (P)
3:30 (3:31) (Class 4) (0-85,82) 3-Y-0 **£6,477** (£1,927; £963; £481) **Stalls** Low

Form RPR

3334 **1** **Fusili (IRE)**[12] 483 3-8-10 **79**.......................... JamesDoyle(5) 6 84
(N P Littmoden) *hld up in rr: rdn 3f out: swtchd wd and hdwy over 1f out: r.o u.p to ld on line* **7/2**[1]

5-1 **2** *hd* **Direct Debit (IRE)**[51] 112 3-9-4 **82**.......................... HayleyTurner 2 87
(M L W Bell) *trckd ldrs: qcknd to ld 1f out: hrd rdn and kpt on: hdd post* **11/2**[2]

4-1 **3** *2* **De La Rue (USA)**[49] 124 3-9-2 **80**.......................... TPQueally 8 81
(M G Quinlan) *hld up towards rr: hdwy to chse ldrs 3f out: nt qckn fnl f* **7/1**[3]

-143 **4** *¾* **Keel (IRE)**[16] 448 3-8-12 **76**.......................... SteveDrowne 1 75+
(J A Osborne) *towards rr: hmpd on rail 5f out: swtchd wd and effrt 3f out: styd on fnl 2f* **7/1**[3]

51- **5** *½* **Katies Tuitor**[91] 6502 3-8-12 **76**.......................... JamieSpencer 4 74
(B W Duke) *prom: led over 2f out tl 1f out: wknd fnl f* **10/1**

1010 **6** *6* **Ockums Razor (IRE)**[5] 550 3-8-13 **77**.......................... TQuinn 3 64
(M J Polglase) *led tl over 2f out: wknd over 1f out* **16/1**

0-22 **7** *shd* **Jebel Ali (IRE)**[12] 483 3-8-12 **76**.......................... ChrisCatlin 5 63
(B Gubby) *chsd ldrs tl rdn and btn 3f out* **7/2**[1]

8 9 **Lucky Lucioni (IRE)**[168] 5376 3-8-12 **81** .... CDHayes(5) 7 51
(Kevin Prendergast, Ire) *stdd s: plld hrd in midfield: n.m.r 5f out: wknd 4f out: sn bhd* **7/1**[3]

2m 4.99s (-2.80) **Going Correction** -0.175s/f (Stan) **8** Ran SP% **112.3**
Speed ratings (Par 100):104,103,102,101,101 96,96,89
CSF £21.91 CT £124.79 TOTE £7.80: £1.40, £2.30, £1.60; EX 27.70.
Owner Nigel Shields **Bred** Gestut Romerhof **Trained** Newmarket, Suffolk

FOCUS
A fair handicap featuring some unexposed types and they went a good pace from start to finish. The reliable winner sets the standard for the form.

593 PLAY NOW AT BETDIRECTCASINO.COM H'CAP 5f (P)
4:00 (4:00) (Class 4) (0-85,83) 3-Y-O **£6,477** (£1,927; £963; £481) **Stalls** High

Form RPR

1431 **1** **Sands Crooner (IRE)**[14] 464 3-8-6 **74** ....(v) PatrickMathers(3) 4 78
(D Shaw) *t.k.h: trckd ldrs: hung lft in st: led jst ins fnl f: rdn out* **11/4**[2]

1121 **2** ½ **Pauvic (IRE)**[12] 481 3-8-4 **72** ....(v) SaleemGolam(3) 6 74
(Mrs A Duffield) *in tch: effrt 2f out: rdn to chal fnl f: jst hld* **9/2**

15-1 **3** 1 ¼ **Stoneacre Lad (IRE)**[25] 344 3-9-4 **83** ....(b) RobbieFitzpatrick 5 81
(Peter Grayson) *led tl jst ins fnl f: no ex fnl 50 yds* **5/2**[1]

-653 **4** 1 **Rapsgate (IRE)**[14] 464 3-8-1 **69** oh2..................(b) StephaneBreux(3) 1 63
(R Hannon) *fair 5th tl outpcd and mod last over 2f out: rallied and r.o wl fnl f* **4/1**[3]

106- **5** 1 ¾ **Titus Maximus (IRE)**[130] 6124 3-8-2 **74** .... LiamJones(7) 3 62
(G A Butler) *s.i.s: in rr: mod effrt 2f out: nvr able to chal* **10/1**

-532 **6** ¾ **Otis B Driftwood**[13] 477 3-8-4 **69** oh7............................(b) ChrisCatlin 2 54
(M Quinn) *prom: hmpd over 2f out: sn lost pl* **11/1**

58.54 secs (-1.24) **Going Correction** -0.175s/f (Stan) **6** Ran SP% **110.8**
Speed ratings (Par 100):102,101,99,97,94 93
CSF £14.91 TOTE £3.40: £2.10, £2.00; EX 10.40.
Owner Danethorpe Racing Ltd **Bred** Peter Molony **Trained** Danethorpe, Notts

FOCUS
Only six horses turned out for this £10,000 sprint, which was a little disappointing, but it was still pretty competitive and with the placed horses close to their marks the form looks solid enough.

594 LITTLEWOODSPOOLS.CO.UK H'CAP (DIV I) 7f (P)
4:30 (4:32) (Class 6) (0-60,66) 3-Y-O **£2,388** (£705; £352) **Stalls** Low

Form RPR

50-4 **1** **Miss Dagger (IRE)**[6] 544 3-8-6 **55** .... KylieManser(7) 8 60
(J R Best) *s.s: plld hrd towards rr: eased outside and gd hdwy over 1f out: str run to ld on line* **14/1**

00-1 **2** shd **Welsh Dragon**[61] 31 3-9-2 **58** .... JamieSpencer 11 63
(A M Balding) *prom: led ent st: rdn and kpt on: ct post* **9/4**[1]

15-1 **3** 2 ½ **Fateful Attraction**[6] 543 3-9-5 **66** 6ex........................ JamesDoyle(5) 7 65+
(I A Wood) *mid-div: effrt 2f out: nt clr run and swtchd rt over 1f out: styd on wl fnl f* **11/4**[2]

5542 **4** 1 ¼ **In Hope**[6] 543 3-8-6 **48** .... HayleyTurner 1 43
(Ernst Oertel) *prom: hrd rdn over 1f out: one pce* **14/1**

0504 **5** 1 **Flashing Floozie**[6] 543 3-8-13 **55** .... SteveDrowne 5 48
(M F Harris) *trckd ldrs: rdn 2f out: btn whn hmpd over 1f out* **25/1**

0612 **6** nk **Mr Cheers**[4] 554 3-9-4 **60** ....(b) JohnEgan 4 52
(R A Harris) *chsd ldrs: n.m.r bnd after 2f: no ex fnl f* **7/2**[3]

-203 **7** 1 ¼ **Chalice Welcome**[28] 308 3-8-4 **46** oh1..........................(v[1]) ChrisCatlin 10 35
(J A Supple) *s.s: sn in mid-div: rdn 3f out: nvr able to chal* **20/1**

0060 **8** 1 ½ **Galaxy Bound (IRE)**[10] 500 3-8-7 **52**..................(v) PatrickMathers(3) 2 37
(D Shaw) *mid-div on rail: effrt over 2f out: no ex over 1f out* **40/1**

60-0 **9** ½ **Cape Latina**[61] 30 3-8-8 **50** .... TQuinn 6 34
(J R Best) *dwlt: plld hrd in rr: rdn over 2f out: nvr rchd ldrs* **25/1**

-400 **10** nk **Teddy Monty (IRE)**[14] 466 3-7-13 **46** oh1...................... RoryMoore(5) 3 29
(M Quinn) *led tl ent st: wknd 1f out* **33/1**

4450 **11** shd **Twilight Avenger (IRE)**[2] 577 3-8-13 **55**.................... DarryllHolland 12 38
(M J Polglase) *wd and towards rr: rdn over 2f out: n.d whn hmpd ent st* **10/1**

0-50 **12** 1 **Valentino Taffi**[17] 439 3-9-1 **60**.............................. AdamKirby(3) 13 41
(S C Williams) *s.s: a bhd* **33/1**

060- **13** 4 **Baytown Valentina**[175] 5171 3-8-11 **53** .... DaneO'Neill 9 24
(P Howling) *a bhd* **50/1**

1m 25.62s (-0.27) **Going Correction** -0.175s/f (Stan) **13** Ran SP% **124.8**
Speed ratings (Par 96):93,94,91,89,88 88,86,84,84,84 83,82,78
CSF £35.02 CT £96.41 TOTE £13.10: £1.60, £4.70, £1.40; EX 67.70.
Owner The Fruit Cake Partnership **Bred** P Holden **Trained** Hucking, Kent
■ This was Kylie Manser's first winner as a professional.

FOCUS
This looked like just a standard 46-60 handicap beforehand, but it could hardly have been more controversial. Miss Dagger and Welsh Dragon crossed the line pretty much as one, but the latter was announced the winner in ultra quick time given how close it looked and it turned out to be the wrong result. The placings were duly corrected, but for betting purposes Welsh Dragon remains the winner as the jockeys had already weighed in before the result was changed. The winning time was 0.4 seconds slower than the second division.

595 LITTLEWOODSPOOLS.CO.UK H'CAP (DIV II) 7f (P)
5:00 (5:03) (Class 6) (0-60,65) 3-Y-O **£2,388** (£705; £352) **Stalls** Low

Form RPR

2101 **1** **Garstang**[2] 577 3-9-9 **65** 6ex....................................(b) RobbieFitzpatrick 7 71
(Peter Grayson) *plld hrd: prom: drvn to ld ins fnl f* **15/8**[1]

2053 **2** 1 ¼ **Mine The Balance (IRE)**[12] 481 3-8-13 **55**............................ TQuinn 4 58
(J R Best) *mid-div: rdn and hdwy over 1f out: r.o to take 2nd fnl 50 yds* **5/2**[2]

500- **3** hd **George The Second**[86] 6539 3-8-6 **53**.............. RichardKingscote(5) 12 55
(Mrs H Sweeting) *disp ld: slt ld over 1f out: hdd and nt qckn ins fnl f* **14/1**

-000 **4** ¾ **Mon Petite Amour**[6] 543 3-8-4 **46** oh1.................. FrankieMcDonald 6 46
(D W P Arbuthnot) *mid-div: hdwy and swtchd rt over 1f out: styd on wl fnl f* **40/1**

-021 **5** 1 **Berties Brother**[28] 308 3-8-6 **48** .... JamieMackay 3 46
(D G Bridgwater) *disp ld tl over 1f out: no ex ins fnl f* **14/1**

-455 **6** ½ **Attitude Annie**[6] 543 3-9-4 **60**.. PaulDoe 1 56
(S Dow) *prom: hrd rdn over 1f out: wknd ins fnl f* **7/1**[3]

-033 **7** nk **Grecianette (IRE)**[13] 477 3-8-11 **60** .... AlanRutter(7) 11 56+
(W J Musson) *hld up in rr: plenty to do 2f out: rapid hdwy on ins over 1f out: 6th and hld whn nt clr run ins fnl f* **14/1**

006- **8** ½ **Fallal Parc**[135] 6030 3-8-1 **46** oh1 .... RichardThomas(3) 9 40
(M F Harris) *dwlt: bhd: rdn over 2f out: styd on wl fnl f* **66/1**

-026 **9** nk **Par Excellence**[12] 481 3-8-5 **54**... LiamJones(7) 5 48
(W G M Turner) *hld up towards rr: effrt on outside over 2f out: nvr able to chal* **10/1**

0-00 **10** nk **Smart Golden Boy (IRE)**[40] 188 3-8-13 **55**.................... DaneO'Neill 2 48
(Mrs L C Jewell) *mid-div: outpcd over 2f out: n.d after* **66/1**

000- **11** hd **Forces Sweetheart**[124] 6226 3-9-2 **58**............................ HayleyTurner 10 50
(M L W Bell) *prom tl wknd 2f out* **16/1**

406- **12** nk **Pertemps Heroine**[246] 3162 3-8-10 **52**...................... MichaelTebbutt 8 44
(A D Smith) *dwlt: a bhd* **66/1**

1m 25.22s (-0.67) **Going Correction** -0.175s/f (Stan) **36** Ran SP% **117.7**
Speed ratings (Par 96):96,94,94,93,92 91,91,90,90,90 89,89
CSF £6.26 CT £47.83 TOTE £2.10: £1.10, £1.30, £7.10; EX 6.10.
Owner The Foulrice Twenty **Bred** Mrs S E Barclay **Trained** Formby, Lancs

FOCUS
A moderate handicap and they finished in a bunch behind the decisive winner. The winning time was 0.4 seconds faster than the first division but the form looks reliable enough.
Grecianette(IRE) ◆ Official explanation: jockey said filly was denied a clear run

596 BETDIRECT.CO.UK H'CAP 1m (P)
5:30 (5:32) (Class 6) (0-65,65) 4-Y-0+ **£2,730** (£806; £403) **Stalls** High

Form RPR

0-02 **1** **Aggravation**[19] 416 4-9-3 **64**..(t) JohnEgan 4 72
(D R C Elsworth) *hld up in tch on ins rail: effrt and bmpd over 2f out: drvn to ld 1f out: sn clr* **13/8**[1]

063- **2** 1 ¾ **Burton Ash**[138] 5981 4-9-1 **62**..(v) MickyFenton 7 66
(J G Given) *prom: hrd rdn and nt qckn fnl f: kpt on to take 2nd nr fin* **10/1**

35-0 **3** hd **Storm Centre**[56] 71 4-9-1 **62** ....(b[1]) JamieSpencer 12 66
(A M Balding) *hld up towards rr: weaved through and smooth hdwy 3f out: styd on u.p to take 3rd nr fin* **12/1**

-150 **4** nk **Blue Empire (IRE)**[23] 381 5-8-9 **61**............................... TravisBlock(5) 6 64
(C R Dore) *led tl 1f out: lost 2nd under hand riding nr fin* **7/1**[3]

0310 **5** 1 ¼ **Height Of Spirits**[26] 343 4-8-13 **60**..................................... TQuinn 1 60
(T D McCarthy) *s.s: in rr tl rdn and styd on fnl 2f* **11/1**

6352 **6** 1 ¼ **Takes Tutu (USA)**[12] 484 7-9-2 **63**............................... DarryllHolland 5 61
(C R Dore) *mid-div: rdn over 3f out: n.m.r over 2f out: no prog st* **4/1**[2]

4 **7** 1 ¼ **Ardea Brave (IRE)**[11] 493 4-8-8 **58**.......................... SaleemGolam(3) 8 53
(M Botti) *hld up towards rr: rdn and sme hdwy over 1f out: nvr rchd ldrs* **14/1**

60-0 **8** 1 **Miss Madame (IRE)**[27] 327 5-9-1 **62**.............................. IanMongan 11 55
(T G Mills) *hld up towards rr: effrt on outside over 2f out: n.d* **25/1**

360- **9** ¾ **Meelup (IRE)**[201] 4472 6-9-1 **65**...................................(p) AmirQuinn(3) 3 56
(P G Murphy) *prom tl wknd over 1f out* **16/1**

4-F3 **10** nk **Miss Inch**[16] 453 4-8-11 **58** .... SteveDrowne 9 48
(G Wragg) *in tch on outside: wknd over 2f out* **14/1**

/0-0 **11** 5 **Graft**[14] 461 7-8-12 **59**...(p) HayleyTurner 10 38
(Mrs P Townsley) *wd: t.k.h in midfield: outpcd and n.d fnl 3f* **14/1**

120- **12** hd **Danzare**[46] 6626 4-8-11 **58**.. ChrisCatlin 2 37
(Mrs A J Hamilton-Fairley) *prom over 4f* **33/1**

1m 36.98s (-2.45) **Going Correction** -0.175s/f (Stan) **12** Ran SP% **128.4**
Speed ratings (Par 101):105,103,103,102,101 100,99,98,97,96 91,91
CSF £21.50 CT £169.10 TOTE £2.50: £1.30, £4.20, £2.80; EX 21.30 Place 6 £61.12, Place 5 £11.20.
Owner Perry, Vivian & Elsworth **Bred** John Khan **Trained** Newmarket, Suffolk

FOCUS
A moderate handicap but solid-enough form with the first three all close to their marks.
T/Plt: £40.60 to a £1 stake. Pool: £44,587.00. 801.00 winning tickets. T/Qpdt: £6.50 to a £1 stake. Pool: £3,436.70. 389.00 winning tickets. LM

581 WOLVERHAMPTON (A.W) (L-H)
Monday, March 6

OFFICIAL GOING: Standard
Wind: Moderate, half-against

597 LITTLEWOODS £2M POOLS ON 0800 500 000 AMATEUR RIDERS' H'CAP (DIV I) 1m 5f 194y(P)
1:50 (1:50) (Class 5) (0-70,69) 4-Y-0+ **£2,810** (£871; £435; £217) **Stalls** Low

Form RPR

6412 **1** **Sugitani (USA)**[2] 574 4-10-10 **61** 5ex..............................(b) MrSWalker 6 73+
(N B King) *bhd tl stdy hdwy 5f out: led over 2f out: sn clr: v easily* **5/2**[2]

4-62 **2** 7 **Larad (IRE)**[28] 311 5-10-2 **49** oh4.................................(b) MrsSMoore 1 51+
(J S Moore) *hld up in rr: hdwy over 2f out: styd on to go 2nd nr fin* **14/1**

00-0 **3** ½ **Border Tale**[7] 535 6-11-2 **68**.. MrMJJSmith(5) 3 70
(James Moffatt) *hld up: hdwy 4f out: chsd wnr appr fnl f tl lost 2nd nr fin* **22/1**

121- **4** 1 **Our Choice (IRE)**[119] 6280 4-11-4 **69**................... MrsEmmaLittmoden 2 69
(N P Littmoden) *in tch: rdn over 3f out: rdn and one pce appr fnl f* **9/4**[1]

40-5 **5** shd **Hue**[10] 503 5-11-1 **65** .... MissLEllison(3) 12 65
(B Ellison) *in tch: rdn to ld 4f out: hdd over 2f out: kpt on one pce after* **12/1**

500- **6** ¾ **High Country (IRE)**[99] 4058 6-9-12 **52**............................ MrsGHogg(7) 4 51
(Micky Hammond) *prom tl rdn and wknd over 1f out* **66/1**

0-10 **7** 9 **Tignasse (FR)**[14] 457 5-10-3 **50**................................ MissEJJones 10 36
(Karen George) *slowly away: nvr on terms* **28/1**

200- **8** 6 **Whitby Echo (IRE)**[127] 6184 4-10-2 **53**............................ MrSDobson 8 31
(R Hollinshead) *a towards rr* **12/1**

613- **9** 4 **Love You Always (USA)**[190] 4794 6-10-4 **58**................... MrRBirkett(7) 7 30
(Miss J Feilden) *led after 1f: clr 9f out: hdd 4f out: sn wknd* **25/1**

103- **10** 4 **Arctic Cove**[20] 5807 5-10-8 **62** ow1.......................... MrTWThompson(7) 13 29
(Micky Hammond) *rdr lost irons leaving stalls: recovered them after 3f and in tch tl wknd and no room over 3f out* **16/1**

0-00 **11** 12 **The Beduth Navi**[42] 174 6-9-12 **50** oh9 ow1.......... MrDanielChinn(5) 11 —
(D G Bridgwater) *led for 1f: trckd ldr tl wknd over 4f out* **100/1**

5-11 **U** **Bid For Fame (USA)**[31] 283 9-11-1 **67**........................ MrSPearce(5) 9 —
(J Pearce) *hld up in rr: bhd whn hmpd and uns rdr over 3f out* **13/2**[3]

3m 6.56s (-0.81) **Going Correction** -0.075s/f (Stan)
WFA 4 from 5yo+ 4lb **12** Ran SP% **114.7**
Speed ratings (Par 103):99,95,94,94,94 93,88,85,82,80 73,—
CSF £33.80 CT £626.81 TOTE £3.00: £1.10, £3.30, £7.70; EX 38.20.
Owner Martin Bailey **Bred** Jayeff 'B' Stables **Trained** Newmarket, Suffolk
■ Stewards' Enquiry : Miss L Ellison caution: careless riding

FOCUS
A modest event of its type, but the pace was decent thanks to Love You Always going off at a rate of knots and the winning time was 2.25 seconds faster than the second division. The winner is value for more than the official margin
Arctic Cove Official explanation: jockey said he lost his irons

598 WIN £2M AT LITTLEWOODSPOOLS.CO.UK (S) STKS 5f 216y(P)
2:20 (2:20) (Class 6) 3-Y-O £2,388 (£705; £352) Stalls Low

Form RPR
3306 1 Buzzin'Boyzee (IRE)[4] 554 3-9-0 55 JimmyFortune 2 60
(P D Evans) in rr tl rdn and hdwy 2f out: edgd lft u.p but r.o to ld wl ins fnl f 4/1[1]
6026 2 1 1/4 Smile For Us[10] 502 3-8-13 53 (b) BrianReilly 6 55
(C Drew) led tl rdn and hdd wl ins fnl f 9/2[2]
2465 3 1 She Whispers (IRE)[6] 544 3-9-0 52 EddieAhern 11 53
(W M Brisbourne) in rr tl hdwy over 2f out: rdn and kpt on fnl f 8/1
5001 4 1 Sounds Simla (IRE)[13] 477 3-9-0 60 TonyCulhane 1 50
(Rae Guest) chsd ldrs: riden 2f out: one pce after 4/1[1]
2202 5 1 1/2 Diktalex (IRE)[11] 488 3-9-0 60 (t) FrancisFerris 5 46
(M J Attwater) chsd ldrs: outpcd 1/2-way and nvr nr to chal after 11/2[3]
-020 6 2 Titus Wonder (IRE)[6] 543 3-8-8 50 (p) GrahamGibbons 4 34
(P A Blockley) trckd ldr tl edgd rt and wknd fnl f 14/1
00-5 7 9 Sapphire Storm (IRE)[4] 554 3-8-8 50 (t) AlanDaly 7 7
(Miss D A McHale) chsd ldrs tl rdn and wknd over 2f out 33/1
400- 8 1 Bowlander[170] 5300 3-8-13 40 J-PGuillambert 12 9
(Karen George) slowly away: c wd into st: nvr on terms 50/1
266- 9 nk Emily (FR)[161] 5501 3-8-8 66 (t) ShaneKelly 9 3
(Mrs L J Young) a in rr 8/1
0-40 10 nk Miss A Bargain (IRE)[14] 466 3-8-1 48 PatrickDonaghy(7) 3 2
(K R Burke) rdr lost irons s: a wl bhd 20/1
0 11 2 1/2 Jay Jay Okocha[17] 445 3-8-13 PaulHanagan 13 —
(James Moffatt) a outpcd in rr 66/1

1m 15.74s (-0.07) **Going Correction** -0.075s/f (Stan) 11 Ran SP% 113.6
Speed ratings (Par 96):97,95,94,92,90 88,76,74,74,73 70
CSF £20.36 TOTE £5.20: £2.00, £3.30, £1.30; EX 35.00.The winner was bought in for 6,500gns.
Owner P D Evans **Bred** Golden Vale Stud **Trained** Pandy, Abergavenny

FOCUS
A moderate event, run at a decent early pace, and the front three looked to run up to their respective best.
Bowlander Official explanation: jockey said gelding hung violently right coming round bend
Miss A Bargain(IRE) Official explanation: jockey said filly dived out of stalls causing him to lose irons

599 LITTLEWOODS £2M POOLS ON 0800 500 000 AMATEUR RIDERS' H'CAP (DIV II) 1m 5f 194y(P)
2:50 (2:50) (Class 5) (0-70,70) 4-Y-O+ £2,810 (£871; £435; £217) Stalls Low

Form RPR
0-50 1 Reminiscent (IRE)[36] 246 7-10-2 53 (p) JackMitchell(5) 6 59
(B P J Baugh) slowly away but sn in tch: hdwy whn c wd into st: r.o strly fnl f to ld post 14/1
5-50 2 hd Valeureux[5] 549 8-10-2 48 (t) MissADeniel 2 54
(J Hetherton) s.i.s: sn mid-div: hdwy over 2f out: edgd lft but led wl ins fnl f: hdd post 12/1
0102 3 2 Isa'Af (IRE)[26] 338 7-11-7 67 MissEJJones 9 70
(P W Hiatt) t.k.h: trckd ldr: led 5f out: rdn: edgd rt and hdd wl ins fnl f: no ex 6/1[2]
3 4 hd Dictator (IRE)[28] 314 5-11-5 65 (t) GerardTumelty 1 68
(D R Gandolfo) mid-div: rdn and hdwy 3f out: kpt on one pce fnl f 8/1
-253 5 1 College Rebel[8] 525 5-9-12 49 oh3 ow1 MrDanielChinn(5) 13 50
(J F Coupland) in tch: chsd ldr over 2f out to over 1f out: no ex 20/1
3330 6 3/4 Lake Wakatipu[14] 470 4-9-6 49 MissMMullineaux(7) 11 49
(M Mullineaux) v.s.a: in rr tl hdwy on ins over 1f out: running on whn n.m.r ins fnl f: nvr nrr 10/1
-025 7 hd Spitfire Bob (USA)[14] 457 7-9-13 52 MissKSearby(7) 4 52
(M E Sowersby) trckd ldrs: rdn 3f out: short of room and wknd ent fnl f 16/1
065- 8 3 William Tell (IRE)[27] 2669 4-10-8 65 ow1 MrTWThompson(7) 5 61
(Micky Hammond) mid-div: lost pl 5f out: n.d after 66/1
11-0 9 4 Piper General (IRE)[36] 246 4-11-1 70 MrStephenHarrison(5) 12 60
(J Mackie) t.k.h: trckd ldrs: rdn 3f out: wknd over 1f out 5/2[1]
6536 10 1 3/4 Jadeeron[7] 535 7-9-13 50 (p) MrHaythemEssaied(5) 7 38
(Miss D A McHale) a towards rr 11/1
250- 11 6 Neptune[296] 1315 10-9-11 48 oh8 MissSarah-JaneDurman(5) 8 27
(J C Fox) led tl hdd 5f out: wknd over 2f out 50/1
200- 12 hd Top Style (IRE)[13] 5185 8-10-6 57 (p) MissLStead(5) 10 36
(G A Harker) a bhd 16/1
0-23 13 2 Ganymede[9] 419 5-11-4 64 (v) MrSWalker 3 40
(J G M O'Shea) trckd ldrs tl rdn and wknd over 3f out 15/2[3]

3m 8.81s (1.44) **Going Correction** -0.075s/f (Stan)
WFA 4 from 5yo+ 4lb 42 Ran SP% 117.5
Speed ratings (Par 103):92,91,90,90,90 89,89,87,85,84 81,80,79
CSF £166.88 CT £1124.56 TOTE £27.60: £4.40, £7.10, £2.30; EX 209.80.
Owner F Burgess **Bred** Newtownbarry House Stud **Trained** Audley, Staffs

FOCUS
The pace did not look as strong as in the first division and the winning time was 2.25 seconds slower. However the form looks reasonable with the winner and third setting the standard.

600 LITTLEWOODS LOTTO3 0800 500 000 CLAIMING STKS 1m 1f 103y(P)
3:20 (3:21) (Class 6) 4-Y-O+ £2,730 (£806; £403) Stalls Low

Form RPR
-203 1 Play Master (IRE)[10] 498 5-8-11 63 PaulEddery 9 66
(B Smart) mid-div: hdwy to go 2nd over 3f out: led wl ins fnl f: all out 6/1
-460 2 shd Cardinal Venture (IRE)[6] 542 8-9-6 88 (p) AndrewMullen(5) 6 80
(K A Ryan) led: rdn and hdd wl ins fnl f: rallied gamely: jst failed 5/2[1]
000/ 3 1 3/4 Rapscallion (GER)[65] 6051 7-9-11 85 LPKeniry 1 76
(Heather Dalton) tracd ldr to over 2f out: rdn and swtchd rt over 1f out: r.o but no imp on first 2 10/1
4310 4 nk York Cliff[14] 470 8-8-7 50 EddieAhern 2 58
(W M Brisbourne) bhd tl hdwy over 1f out: r.o fnl f: nvr nrr 4/1[3]
402- 5 1/2 Scamperdale[77] 6619 4-8-2 56 EdwardCreighton(3) 3 55
(Karen George) chsd ldrs: outpcd over 2f out: styd on ins fnl f 10/1
-305 6 5 Starcross Maid[8] 527 4-8-4 45 MatthewHenry 10 44
(J F Coupland) hld up: rdn over 3f out: nvr nr to chal 50/1
2-41 7 1 1/4 Linning Wine (IRE)[19] 417 10-9-5 75 (p) GrahamGibbons 5 57
(P A Blockley) hld up: hdwy over 3f out: rdn and wknd over 1f out 11/4[2]
0-00 8 1 1/4 La Musique[28] 312 4-8-7 40 PaulHanagan 4 43
(P J McBride) hld up: effrt over 3f out: nvr on terms 66/1
-066 9 nk Paso Doble[18] 429 8-9-0 63 ow2 (p) JamesMillman(7) 13 56
(B R Millman) a bhd 16/1
65-6 10 1/2 Dane's Rock (IRE)[64] 3 4-8-5 45 FrancisNorton 11 39
(M S Saunders) trckd ldrs tl rdn and wknd over 2f out 25/1
00-0 11 3/4 Napapijri (FR)[54] 94 4-7-13 40 MarcHalford(5) 8 37
(W G M Turner) in tch tl rdn and wknd over 3f out 100/1
000- 12 dist Cabopino Lad (USA)[12] 6414 4-8-5 40 (p) AdrianMcCarthy 7 —
(Miss Tracy Waggott) a bhd: t.o 3f out 150/1

2m 1.96s (-0.66) **Going Correction** -0.075s/f (Stan) 12 Ran SP% 122.5
Speed ratings (Par 101):99,98,97,97,96 92,91,89,89,89 88,—
CSF £21.88 TOTE £7.70: £2.10, £1.60, £2.90; EX 35.80.The winner was claimed by R. A. Harris for £8,000. Scamperdale was claimed by B. P. J. Baugh for £5,000.
Owner P A Mason **Bred** R N Auld **Trained** Hambleton, N Yorks

FOCUS
A fair event of its type, run at a sound pace, and the form appears straightforward.

601 LITTLEWOODS LOTTO4 0800 500 000 H'CAP 5f 216y(P)
3:50 (3:50) (Class 5) (0-75,70) 3-Y-O £3,886 (£1,156; £577; £288) Stalls Low

Form RPR
1 1 Hypocrisy[44] 165 3-9-4 70 J-PGuillambert 6 85+
(S C Williams) s.i.s: in rr tl hdwy on ins over 2f out: r.o to ins fnl f: won gng away 8/1
-301 2 2 1/2 Stoneacre Boy (IRE)[11] 487 3-8-8 67 (b) RonanKeogh(7) 8 68
(Peter Grayson) led tl edgd rt and hdd ins fnl f: hld on for 2nd 11/2[2]
2231 3 hd Canina[23] 380 3-9-2 68 JimmyQuinn 2 68
(Ms Deborah J Evans) sn outpcd: rdn and hdwy on ins over 1f out: r.o fnl f: nvr nrr 15/2
330- 4 1/2 Highland Song (IRE)[66] 6688 3-9-4 70 FrancisNorton 5 69
(R F Fisher) in tch: rdn over 1f out: kpt on one pce fnl f 7/1[3]
00-0 5 3 Peter Island (FR)[13] 475 3-9-1 67 (b) TonyCulhane 3 57
(J Gallagher) chsd ldr: rdn over 1f out: wknd ins fnl f 12/1
5-03 6 shd The London Gang[13] 475 3-8-13 65 ShaneKelly 1 55
(P D Evans) v.s.a: hdwy on outside over 1f out: r.o fnl f: nvr nr to chal 7/1[3]
00-1 7 1 1/2 Grafton (IRE)[10] 500 3-9-0 66 GrahamGibbons 4 51
(J D Bethell) chsd ldrs tl no hdwy appr fnl f 9/2[1]
-341 8 3 Came Back (IRE)[33] 266 3-9-3 69 EddieAhern 7 45
(J A Osborne) mid-div: rdn over 2f out: sn btn 9/2[1]
1-06 9 5 Bellsbank (IRE)[16] 448 3-8-13 65 PaulHanagan 9 26
(A Bailey) in tch tl wknd over 2f out 20/1
5204 10 1/2 Money Mate (IRE)[25] 344 3-8-3 62 MarkCoumbe(7) 10 22
(C J Teague) trckd ldrs tl rdn and hung bdly rt over 2f out: wknd qckly 50/1

1m 15.1s (-0.71) **Going Correction** -0.075s/f (Stan) 10 Ran SP% 114.0
Speed ratings (Par 98):101,97,97,96,92 92,90,86,79,79
CSF £50.40 CT £352.16 TOTE £5.20: £3.90, £2.20, £2.70; EX 57.10.
Owner Fighttheban Partnership I **Bred** Hyperion Bloodstock **Trained** Newmarket, Suffolk

FOCUS
This solid handicap was run at a decent pace and the unbeaten winner looks a progressive sort.
The London Gang Official explanation: jockey said colt missed the break
Came Back(IRE) Official explanation: jockey said colt moved poorly throughout

602 CLASSICVALUEPOOLS.COM (S) STKS 5f 216y(P)
4:20 (4:20) (Class 6) 4-Y-O+ £2,388 (£705; £352) Stalls Low

Form RPR
2500 1 Imperium[12] 486 5-8-12 52 (p) NickyMackay 1 55
(Stef Liddiard) prom: lost pl over 3f out: rdn and hdwy over 1f out: led ins fnl f: rdn out 14/1
1032 2 1 Roman Empire[2] 581 6-9-3 58 (b) GrahamGibbons 5 57
(P A Blockley) in rr tl rdn and hdwy over 1f out: squeezed through to go 2nd ins fnl f 11/4[1]
6300 3 1 Elms Schoolboy[8] 527 4-9-3 45 (b) J-PGuillambert 8 54
(P Howling) trckd ldr tl hung lft and lost 2nd ins fnl f 66/1
3040 4 1 Undeterred[16] 451 10-8-12 75 EddieAhern 10 46
(K J Burke) bhd tl rdn and hdwy over 1f out: r.o: nvr nrr 4/1[2]
06-4 5 hd Desert Opal[60] 46 6-8-12 60 TonyCulhane 6 45
(D W Chapman) led tl rdn: edgd lft: hdd and fdd ins fnl f 10/1
0-00 6 hd Chorus Beauty[21] 397 5-8-7 47 JimmyQuinn 4 40
(N I M Rossiter) towards rr tl hdwy over 1f out: nt pce to chal 50/1
5-01 7 3/4 Million Percent[21] 402 7-8-10 64 AndrewElliott(7) 13 48
(K R Burke) chsd ldrs: edgd lft and bmpd 1f out: wknd ins fnl f 6/1
6044 8 nk Chickado (IRE)[22] 391 5-8-12 48 RobertHavlin 3 42
(D Haydn Jones) in tch tl rdn and wknd over 1f out 10/1
0053 9 shd Smokincanon[13] 474 4-8-7 50 MarcHalford(5) 2 41
(W G M Turner) chsd ldrs tl rdn and wknd fnl f 16/1
3060 10 1 1/4 Merdiff[2] 588 7-8-12 60 ShaneKelly 7 38
(W M Brisbourne) towards rr: effrt 2f out: sn btn 9/2[3]
60-4 11 2 1/2 Fizzy Lizzy[35] 249 6-8-0 45 JosephWalsh(7) 11 25
(H E Haynes) a outpcd in rr 40/1

1m 15.22s (-0.59) **Going Correction** -0.075s/f (Stan) 11 Ran SP% 115.8
Speed ratings (Par 101):100,98,97,96,95 95,94,94,93,92 88
CSF £51.40 TOTE £17.60: £4.20, £1.90, £8.20; EX 101.90.There was no bid for the winner.
Owner Mrs Stef Liddiard **Bred** Mrs H B Raw **Trained** Great Shefford, Berks

FOCUS
A weak affair, run at a sound early pace, and the form is held down by the proximity of the third-placed horse.
Elms Schoolboy Official explanation: jockey said gelding hung left

603 PLAY £1/4M SPOT THE BALL 0800 500 000 H'CAP 1m 4f 50y(P)
4:50 (4:50) (Class 5) (0-70,68) 4-Y-O+ £3,238 (£963; £481; £240) Stalls Low

Form RPR
1122 1 Young Mick[28] 319 4-9-0 66 (v) JimmyQuinn 10 76+
(G G Margarson) a in tch and gng wl: shkn up to ld ins fnl f: pushed out 11/4[1]
5522 2 1 Augustine[10] 505 5-8-12 62 DarrenWilliams 9 70
(P W Hiatt) chsd ldrs: wnt 2nd 3f out: led over 1f out: rdn: hdd ins fnl f: kpt on 7/1
00-0 3 1/2 Rare Coincidence[55] 75 5-8-4 54 oh1 (p) FrancisNorton 4 61
(R F Fisher) led tl rdn and hdd over 1f out: kpt on 12/1
134- 4 1 Easy Laughter (IRE)[22] 6432 5-9-3 67 (t) AlanDaly 8 73
(A King) bhd tl hdwy 2f out: kpt on one pce: nvr nrr 6/1
00-4 5 4 Brockhole (IRE)[10] 503 4-8-13 65 TonyCulhane 5 64
(J G Given) in rr tl rdn and styd on fnl f: nvr nr to chal 40/1
2660 6 1/2 Seattle Robber[21] 405 4-7-12 57 (v) KevinGhunowa(7) 6 55
(P A Blockley) in rr tl hdwy over 3f out: rdn 2f out: one pce after 33/1
2112 7 1 Sand Repeal (IRE)[27] 334 4-9-0 66 SimonWhitworth 12 63
(Miss J Feilden) mid-div: hdwy 4f out: rdn and wknd appr fnl f 4/1[2]
42-1 8 3/4 Millagros (IRE)[19] 109 6-9-4 68 PaulHanagan 11 64
(I Semple) hld up: mde som late hdwy: nvr on terms 9/1
0-04 9 1 Smoothie (IRE)[28] 318 8-7-12 55 oh2 ow1 (p) JosephWalsh(7) 1 49
(Ian Williams) hld up: a in rr 11/1

-246 **10** *hd* **Webbswood Lad (IRE)**[19] [421] 5-8-8 **58**......................(p) EddieAhern 3 52
(Stef Liddiard) *mid-div: wknd wl over 1f out* **11/2**[3]
60-4 **11** *1 ¾* **Stagecoach Emerald**[16] [453] 4-8-7 **62**................ EdwardCreighton(3) 2 53
(R W Price) *mid-div: rdn 3f out: sn wknd* **50/1**
-540 **12** *5* **Kirkhammerton (IRE)**[21] [405] 4-8-2 **54** oh4...........(v) AdrianMcCarthy 7 37
(M J Polglase) *trckd ldrs tl wknd over 2f out* **40/1**
2m 39.94s (-2.48) **Going Correction** -0.075s/f (Stan)
WFA 4 from 5yo+ 2lb 12 Ran SP% **124.6**
Speed ratings (Par 103):105,104,104,103,100 100,99,99,98,98 97,93
CSF £23.38 CT £210.06 TOTE £3.00: £1.40, £2.50, £6.60; EX 23.60 Trifecta £159.00 Pool: £1,068.71 - 4.77 winning tickets..
Owner M F Kentish **Bred** M F Kentish **Trained** Newmarket, Suffolk
FOCUS
They did not appear to go a great pace early, but certainly quickened things up over the last half-mile and the final time was very creditable. The form looks solid enough with those in the frame behind the winner giving it credence.

604 CLASSICVALUEPOOLS.COM H'CAP 1m 141y(P)
5:20 (5:20) (Class 6) (0-60,60) 3-Y-O **£2,730** (£806; £403) **Stalls** Low

Form RPR
201- **1** **Magical Music**[86] [6539] 3-9-3 **59**....................................... JimmyQuinn 2 71+
(J Pearce) *trckd ldrs: rdn to ld 1f out: edgd lft but r.o wl* **5/1**[2]
244- **2** *2 ½* **Mighty Dancer (IRE)**[86] [6539] 3-9-1 **57**........................ JimmyFortune 3 64
(S Kirk) *trckd ldr: ev ch wnt rt ent fnl f: kpt on* **2/1**[1]
4262 **3** *2 ½* **Franky'N'Jonny**[9] [538] 3-8-5 **54**.................................. AndrewElliott(7) 5 56
(I A Wood) *a in tch: rdn over 1f out: styd on one pce* **8/1**
00-2 **4** *1 ¼* **Mae Cigan (FR)**[49] [123] 3-9-4 **60**................................ FrancisNorton 13 59
(M Blanshard) *bhd tl rdn and hdwy over 1f out: styd on: nvr nrr* **17/2**
-231 **5** *½* **Countrywide Belle**[10] [499] 3-8-12 **59**...................(b) AndrewMullen(5) 1 57
(K A Ryan) *led tl rdn and hdd 1f out: wknd ins fnl f* **12/1**
304- **6** *1 ½* **Impeccable Guest (IRE)**[144] [5857] 3-8-11 **53**.................. LeeEnstone 4 48
(P C Haslam) *trckd ldrs rdn 2f out: sn struggling to hold pl* **16/1**
4-43 **7** *½* **Next Ness (IRE)**[10] [500] 3-9-1 **57**.................................. PaulHanagan 9 51
(R F Fisher) *wnt rt s: nvr on terms* **14/1**
000- **8** *2* **Lewis Lloyd (IRE)**[115] [6313] 3-8-12 **54**.......................... EddieAhern 12 44
(I A Wood) *a bhd* **25/1**
0-31 **9** *1* **Monte Mayor Junior**[27] [329] 3-9-3 **59**.........................(v) RobertHavlin 6 47
(D Haydn Jones) *mid-div: hdwy on outside over 3f out: wknd over 1f out* **7/1**[3]
-016 **10** *5* **Tilen (IRE)**[24] [364] 3-8-8 **50**.......................................(b) MatthewHenry 11 27
(S Parr) *in tch tl rdn and wknd over 2f out* **12/1**
004 **11** *2* **Rudry World (IRE)**[32] [272] 3-8-10 **59**..................... KevinGhunowa(7) 7 32
(P A Blockley) *a bhd* **33/1**
00-2 **12** *1* **Kissi Kissi**[16] [453] 3-9-4 **60**.. AdrianMcCarthy 10 31
(M J Attwater) *slowly away: a bhd* **33/1**
220- **13** *2 ½* **Enchanting Times (IRE)**[133] [6077] 3-9-4 **60**..................... PaulEddery 8 26
(D G Bridgwater) *racd wd: a bhd* **66/1**
1m 50.72s (-1.04) **Going Correction** -0.075s/f (Stan) 13 Ran SP% **123.3**
Speed ratings (Par 96):101,98,96,95,95 93,93,91,90,86 84,83,81
CSF £15.39 CT £83.26 TOTE £7.30: £2.10, £1.90, £2.10; EX 25.10 Place 6 £372.29, Place 5 £134.42.
Owner Killarney Glen & Mrs E M Clarke **Bred** Peter Taplin **Trained** Newmarket, Suffolk
FOCUS
A decent winning time for a race of its type and the form looks solid for the class.
Rudry World(IRE) Official explanation: jockey said gelding suffered interference on first bend
T/Jkpt: Not won. T/Plt: £248.10 to a £1 stake. Pool: £43,810.15. 128.90 winning tickets. T/Qpdt: £32.50 to a £1 stake. Pool: £3,316.50. 75.50 winning tickets. JS

546 SOUTHWELL (L-H)
Tuesday, March 7

OFFICIAL GOING: Standard
Wind: Light, across Weather: Raining

605 BIG CASH GAMES AT LITTLEWOODSPOKER.COM H'CAP 5f (F)
1:40 (1:40) (Class 5) (0-70,70) 3-Y-O+ **£3,238** (£963; £481; £240) **Stalls** High

Form RPR
0203 **1** **Efistorm**[19] [424] 5-9-4 **70**... AndrewElliott(7) 13 87
(J Balding) *chsd ldrs: rdn to ld over 1f out: r.o wl* **11/1**
3016 **2** *5* **Gone'N'Dunnett(IRE)**[8] [532] 7-9-3 **69**.................(v) KirstyMilczarek(7) 7 68
(Mrs C A Dunnett) *chsd ldrs: rdn over 1f out: styd on same pce* **10/1**
21-0 **3** *¾* **Aegean Dancer**[56] [80] 4-9-9 **68**................................ DerekMcGaffin 8 64
(B Smart) *dwlt: hdwy over 3f out: led 1/2-way: rdn: hung lft and hdd over 1f out: hung rt and wknd ins fnl f* **6/1**[3]
1-02 **4** *¾* **El Potro**[8] [532] 4-9-5 **64**... GrahamGibbons 1 58
(E S McMahon) *s.i.s: hdwy 1/2-way: rdn over 1f out: wknd ins fnl f* **4/1**[1]
00-0 **5** *shd* **Russian Rocket (IRE)**[63] [23] 4-9-10 **69**......................... HayleyTurner 6 62
(Mrs C A Dunnett) *sn outpcd: r.o ins fnl f: nt rch ldrs* **50/1**
0-04 **6** *1* **Little Ridge (IRE)**[19] [424] 5-9-9 **68**................................ SteveDrowne 3 58
(H Morrison) *chsd ldrs: rdn 1/2-way: wknd fnl f* **5/1**[2]
0110 **7** *3* **Amanda's Lad (IRE)**[33] [274] 6-8-11 **56** oh4............ AdrianMcCarthy 14 35
(M C Chapman) *sn outpcd: nvr nrr* **40/1**
01-5 **8** *2* **Tombalina**[28] [335] 3-7-13 **57** ow1................................ JimmyQuinn 12 29
(C J Teague) *sn outpcd: bhd whn hung lft 1/2-way* **66/1**
-642 **9** *hd* **Tag Team (IRE)**[19] [426] 5-9-3 **62**.................................... EddieAhern 9 33
(John A Harris) *chsd ldrs: led 3f out: sn rdn and hdd: wknd fnl f* **7/1**
4300 **10** *1 ¼* **Four Amigos (USA)**[3] [587] 5-8-11 **56** oh1.................(b) JoeFanning 2 22
(D Nicholls) *chsd ldrs: rdn 1/2-way: wknd over 1f out* **9/1**
056- **11** *3* **Oh Dara (USA)**[160] [5539] 4-9-5 **67**.......................... PatrickMathers(3) 11 23
(M J Attwater) *sn outpcd* **66/1**
0/20 **12** *½* **Borzoi Maestro**[38] [225] 5-8-12 **57**........................(p) DarryllHolland 10 11
(M Wellings) *chsd ldrs 3f* **33/1**
00-0 **13** *12* **Silver Dane (IRE)**[10] [517] 4-8-11 **56** oh1...............(v) AdrianTNicholls 5 —
(Mrs C A Dunnett) *led 2f: wknd 2f out: eased* **7/1**
61.23 secs (0.93) **Going Correction** +0.275s/f (Slow)
WFA 3 from 4yo+ 13lb 13 Ran SP% **113.7**
Speed ratings (Par 103):103,95,93,92,92 90,86,82,82,80 75,74,55
CSF £107.55 CT £746.33 TOTE £11.00: £3.20, £4.80, £2.00; EX 110.80.
Owner Mrs Jo Hardy **Bred** E Duggan And D Churchman **Trained** Scrooby, Notts
FOCUS
The wet weather seemed to have an affect on the way the track rode and the winning time was slow. Also the usual bias towards those drawn low was not as evident, but apart from the winner those drawn high were well beaten, suggesting the draw bias was nullified rather than reversed. The race has been rated negatively through the placed horses.
Russian Rocket(IRE) ◆ Official explanation: jockey said gelding was denied a clear run
Tag Team(IRE) Official explanation: jockey said gelding had no more to give
Silver Dane(IRE) Official explanation: jockey said gelding hung right

606 NO 5P RULE 4S AT BETDIRECT H'CAP (DIV I) 7f (F)
2:10 (2:10) (Class 6) (0-60,60) 4-Y-O+ **£2,047** (£604; £302) **Stalls** Low

Form RPR
0/1- **1** **Tyzack (IRE)**[174] [5236] 5-9-1 **57**...................................... MickyFenton 12 67
(Stef Liddiard) *hld up in tch: rdn to ld and hung lft ins fnl f: r.o* **5/1**[2]
-006 **2** *1 ¾* **Diction (IRE)**[12] [493] 4-8-6 **48**.....................................(v) FrancisNorton 7 54
(K R Burke) *chsd ldrs: rdn to ld 1f out: sn hdd and unable qckn* **16/1**
-313 **3** *1* **Mister Elegant**[18] [440] 4-8-12 **54**............................... AdrianTNicholls 9 57
(J L Spearing) *w ldr tl led over 4f out: rdn and hdd 1f out: no ex* **4/1**[1]
0262 **4** *nk* **Pending (IRE)**[24] [382] 5-8-13 **55**.............................(e[1]) DarryllHolland 10 57
(J R Boyle) *s.i.s: hld up: hdwy 4f out: styd on same pce ins fnl f* **4/1**[1]
545- **5** *1* **Sedge (USA)**[176] [5181] 6-8-10 **52**..................................... TonyCulhane 6 52
(P T Midgley) *sn outpcd: hdwy u.p and hung lft fr over 1f out: nt rch ldrs* **8/1**
3410 **6** *3* **Crusoe (IRE)**[3] [582] 9-8-9 **51** 6ex...............................(b) BrianReilly 5 43
(A Sadik) *chsd ldrs: rdn over 1f out: wknd ins fnl f* **12/1**
0-50 **7** *6* **Triple Jump**[24] [383] 5-8-8 **55**................................(tp) AndrewMullen(5) 4 32
(K A Ryan) *s.i.s: sn outpcd: nvr nrr* **16/1**
5-00 **8** *5* **Danielle's Lad**[8] [537] 10-8-11 **60**..................................(b) LiamJones(7) 2 25
(B Palling) *sn led: hdd over 4f out: rdn and wknd 2f out* **20/1**
6-00 **9** *5* **Moors Myth**[15] [458] 5-8-13 **55**.. MichaelHills 11 7
(B W Hills) *chsd ldrs: rdn 1/2-way: wknd over 2f out* **15/2**[3]
0300 **10** *¾* **Penwell Hill (USA)**[12] [492] 7-9-4 **60**...........................(v) HayleyTurner 3 11
(M J Attwater) *plld hrd and prom: n.m.r and lost pl 1/2-way: sn bhd* **16/1**
300- **11** *2 ½* **Kalani Star (IRE)**[144] [5884] 6-8-13 **55**...........................(vt) TomEaves 1 —
(I W McInnes) *s.i.s: effrt 1/2-way: sn wknd* **50/1**
000- **12** *nk* **Warlingham (IRE)**[195] [4671] 8-8-4 **46**.............................. JoeFanning 8 —
(P Howling) *plld hrd and prom: lost pl 5f out: wknd 1/2-way* **66/1**
1m 32.39s (1.59) **Going Correction** +0.275s/f (Slow) 12 Ran SP% **113.1**
Speed ratings (Par 101):101,99,97,97,96 92,86,80,74,73 70,70
CSF £76.70 CT £351.98 TOTE £7.50: £2.50, £5.50, £1.70; EX 117.00.
Owner Simon Mapletoft Racing I **Bred** Rabea Syndicate **Trained** Great Shefford, Berks
FOCUS
The testing surface seemed to take its toll on this field and they finished well spread out. The winning time was marginally slower than the second division and the placed horses set the standard.
Moors Myth Official explanation: jockey said gelding had no more to give

607 FOOTBALLPOOLS.COM CLAIMING STKS 1m 6f (F)
2:40 (2:40) (Class 6) 4-Y-O+ **£2,388** (£705; £352) **Stalls** Low

Form RPR
-340 **1** **Sun Hill**[6] [549] 6-8-9 63.. LeeEnstone 5 66
(C W Fairhurst) *a.p: chsd ldr 1/2-way: led over 3f out: sn rdn: edgd rt fnl f: styd on* **9/4**[1]
4323 **2** *2* **Romil Star (GER)**[6] [549] 9-8-11 61................................(p) PatCosgrave 2 65
(K R Burke) *led over 10f: sn rdn and stl w ev ch tl no ex wl ins fnl f* **5/2**[2]
-434 **3** *20* **Chater Knight (IRE)**[19] [425] 5-8-4 58..................... SaleemGolam(3) 4 35
(Micky Hammond) *chsd ldr to 1/2-way: rdn 4f out: wknd over 2f out* **3/1**[3]
26-6 **4** *17* **Ocean King (USA)**[45] [168] 5-8-13 56.................................. EddieAhern 1 19
(M G Quinlan) *hld up: rdn 5f out: sn wknd* **4/1**
50-0 **5** *dist* **Lahob**[27] [301] 6-8-9 40...(t) J-PGuillambert 3 —
(P Howling) *chsd ldrs: sn pushed along: wknd over 5f out* **40/1**
3m 14.2s (4.60) **Going Correction** +0.275s/f (Slow) 5 Ran SP% **106.8**
Speed ratings (Par 101):97,95,84,74,—
CSF £7.64 TOTE £2.90: £1.40, £1.50; EX 6.70.The winner was claimed by David Burchell for £6,000.
Owner William Hill **Bred** London Thoroughbred Services Ltd **Trained** Middleham Moor, N Yorks
FOCUS
A particularly poor race and a real test of stamina, but a decent finish between the front pair who were involved in a dour battle over the whole of the last half-mile. The winner sets the level for the form.

608 BETDIRECT FREEPHONE 0800 211 222 H'CAP 6f (F)
3:10 (3:12) (Class 6) (0-60,60) 4-Y-O+ **£2,388** (£705; £352) **Stalls** Low

Form RPR
0401 **1** **Sweet Pickle**[6] [552] 5-9-1 **60** 6ex...................................(e) AmirQuinn(3) 3 71
(J R Boyle) *dwlt: hld up: hdwy over 2f out: led and hung lft over 1f out: rdn out* **6/1**[3]
5202 **2** *nk* **Doctor Dennis (IRE)**[6] [552] 9-9-3 **59**............................(v) JimmyQuinn 4 69
(J Pearce) *s.i.s: hld up: hdwy and nt clr run over 2f out: rdn to chse wnr fnl f: r.o* **6/1**[3]
2404 **3** *5* **Shifty Night (IRE)**[10] [519] 5-9-4 **60**........................(v) DarryllHolland 12 55
(Mrs C A Dunnett) *chsd ldr: rdn to ld wl over 1f out: sn hung lft and hdd: wknd ins fnl f* **5/1**[1]
-106 **4** *2* **Cashel Mead**[19] [424] 6-9-1 **57**...................................... SteveDrowne 11 46
(J L Spearing) *chsd ldrs: rdn over 2f out: wknd fnl f* **14/1**
0002 **5** *1* **Count Cougar (USA)**[18] [446] 6-9-1 **57**...................... AdrianTNicholls 8 43
(S P Griffiths) *s.i.s: hdwy over 3f out: rdn over 2f out: wknd fnl f* **7/1**
0-00 **6** *½* **Attorney**[6] [552] 8-8-11 **58**..................................... StephenDonohoe(5) 14 43
(P D Evans) *hld up: rdn over 2f out: nvr trbld ldrs* **40/1**
1425 **7** *1* **Shadow Jumper (IRE)**[6] [552] 5-9-4 **60**...............(v) RobbieFitzpatrick 2 42
(J T Stimpson) *chsd ldrs: rdn and ev ch over 1f out: wknd fnl f* **11/2**[2]
0010 **8** *nk* **Missperon (IRE)**[19] [429] 4-8-12 **59**....................(b) AndrewMullen(5) 13 40
(K A Ryan) *chsd ldrs: rdn over 2f out: wknd over 1f out* **25/1**
20-5 **9** *1 ½* **Cyfrwys (IRE)**[3] [588] 5-8-13 **55**..............................(p) FrancisFerris 10 31
(B Palling) *chsd ldrs: rdn over 3f out: wknd over 1f out* **20/1**
000- **10** *nk* **George The Best (IRE)**[112] [6363] 5-8-8 **50**................. DeanMcKeown 7 25
(Micky Hammond) *s.i.s: outpcd* **40/1**
0210 **11** *5* **Blakeshall Quest**[9] [529] 6-8-10 **52**..................................(b) TomEaves 6 12
(R Brotherton) *led: rdn and hdd wl over 1f out: sn wknd* **12/1**
14-4 **12** *5* **Ardkeel Lass (IRE)**[63] [24] 5-8-7 **49**.............................. ShaneKelly 9 —
(P D Evans) *chsd ldrs over 4f* **8/1**
3150 **13** *nk* **Desert Light (IRE)**[3] [588] 5-8-6 **51**.....................(v) PatrickMathers(3) 5 —
(D Shaw) *mid-div: edgd lft wl over 4f out: rdn 1/2-way: sn wknd* **25/1**
000- **14** *11* **Imtalkinggibberish**[216] [4069] 5-9-2 **58**.............................. EddieAhern 1 —
(J R Jenkins) *hld up: hmpd wl over 4f out: sn bhd* **16/1**
1m 18.57s (1.67) **Going Correction** +0.275s/f (Slow) 14 Ran SP% **121.8**
Speed ratings (Par 101):99,98,91,89,87 87,85,85,83,83 76,69,69,54
CSF £39.74 CT £201.63 TOTE £8.00: £2.50, £1.80, £2.30; EX 20.00.
Owner M Khan X2 **Bred** C T Van Hoorn **Trained** Epsom, Surrey
FOCUS
Just an ordinary gallop for this handicap and again those that came centre to stands' side were favoured. This was a repeat of the handicap run here seven days earlier when Sweet Pickle beat Doctor Dennis and the order was maintained so the form could be rated a little higher.
Count Cougar(USA) Official explanation: jockey said gelding lost its action

Ardkeel Lass(IRE) Official explanation: trainer said mare was unable to dominate

609 BETDIRECT.CO.UK (S) STKS — 1m 3f (F)
3:40 (3:40) (Class 6) 3-6-Y-O — £2,388 (£705; £352) Stalls Low

Form / RPR

601 1 **Mossmann Gorge**[12] 490 4-10-0 54 (v) DarrylHolland 5 — 62
(M Wellings) *hld up: hdwy over 2f out: shkn up to ld ins fnl f: hung lft: r.o* **2/1**[2]

3253 2 2 **Noble Edge**[37] 241 3-8-7 59 (p) HayleyTurner 1 — 56
(Robert Gray) *chsd ldrs: rdn to ld over 2f out: hung lft over 1f out: hdd and unable qck ins fnl f* **11/1**

-156 3 3½ **Beauchamp Star**[21] 414 5-9-7 54 (p) DanielTudhope(3) 6 — 48
(Mrs A Duffield) *hld up: hdwy 3f out: rdn and ev ch over 1f out: wknd ins fnl f* **15/8**[1]

2502 4 5 **Colonel Bilko (IRE)**[19] 427 4-9-10 48 ChrisCatlin 4 — 41
(Miss S J Wilton) *plld hrd and prom: stdd and lost pl 9f out: hdwy over 2f out: wknd over 1f out* **12/1**

0-43 5 1½ **Count The Trees**[7] 538 3-7-5 45 LiamJones(7) 7 — 31
(W G M Turner) *hld up in tch: rdn over 3f out: wknd over 2f out* **12/1**

04-0 6 1½ **Trackattack**[18] 92 4-9-10 45 ShaneKelly 3 — 36
(P Howling) *sn led: rdn and hdd over 3f out: wknd over 1f out* **66/1**

32-0 7 ¾ **Solo Star**[22] 406 3-7-12 52 (e[1]) AdrianMcCarthy 8 — 27
(Miss J A Camacho) *trckd ldrs: led over 3f out: hung lft and hdd over 2f out: wknd over 1f out* **20/1**

/ 8 9 **Aqua**[38] 4-9-5 MickyFenton 9 — 16
(P T Midgley) *chsd ldrs over 8f* **66/1**

6316 9 4 **Shaheer (IRE)**[15] 470 4-10-0 49 TonyCulhane 10 — 18
(J Gallagher) *s.s: hdwy 8f out: rdn 5f out: wknd 3f out* **7/1**[3]

2m 33.28s (4.38) **Going Correction** +0.275s/f (Slow)
WFA 3 from 4yo 22lb 4 from 5yo 1lb — **9** Ran SP% **112.1**
Speed ratings: 95,93,91,87,86 85,84,78,75
CSF £23.00 TOTE £2.50: £1.10, £2.40, £1.50; EX 26.30.The winner was bought in for 8,000gns.
Owner Mrs Ruth M Serrell **Bred** R S Cockerill (farms) Ltd **Trained** Six Ashes, Shropshire

FOCUS
A very weak affair, run at an average pace and rated through the runner-up, with the winner value for slightly further.
Count The Trees Official explanation: jockey said saddle slipped

610 LITTLEWOODS BETDIRECT H'CAP — 1m 4f (F)
4:10 (4:10) (Class 4) (0-85,84) 4-Y-O+ — £6,477 (£1,927; £963; £481) Stalls Low

Form / RPR

-201 1 **Kylkenny**[19] 425 11-9-1 84 (t) DanielTudhope(3) 4 — 93
(D Carroll) *hld up: hdwy over 4f out: led over 2f out: rdn out* **8/1**

1231 2 1¾ **He's A Star**[12] 491 4-8-2 70 oh1 JimmyQuinn 5 — 76
(Miss Gay Kelleway) *a.p: chsd ldr over 4f out: rdn over 2f out: styd on* **5/1**[3]

0-61 3 5 **Cordier**[24] 385 4-8-10 78 DaleGibson 7 — 77
(J Mackie) *chsd ldr: led 9f out: rdn and hdd over 2f out: wknd fnl f* **14/1**

3312 4 ¾ **Greenbelt**[8] 535 5-8-5 71 JoeFanning 1 — 69
(G M Moore) *hld up: hdwy over 4f out: rdn and wknd over 2f out* **6/4**[1]

1-01 5 18 **Llamadas**[10] 521 4-8-7 75 J-PGuillambert 8 — 46
(C Roberts) *hld up in tch: rdn and wknd over 3f out* **14/1**

3-15 6 nk **Bethanys Boy (IRE)**[40] 194 5-8-7 78 GregFairley(5) 3 — 48
(B Ellison) *hld up: rdn over 4f out: sn wknd* **9/2**[2]

034- 7 2 **Kristensen**[209] 4244 7-8-8 74 EddieAhern 2 — 41
(Karen McLintock) *prom: riden 1/2-way: wknd over 4f out* **15/2**

2/0- 8 15 **Siena Star (IRE)**[21] 5759 8-8-4 70 (b[1]) HayleyTurner 6 — 15
(Robert Gray) *s.s: hdwy 1/2-way: wknd over 4f out* **66/1**

2m 42.73s (0.64) **Going Correction** +0.275s/f (Slow)
WFA 4 from 5yo+ 2lb — **8** Ran SP% **112.6**
Speed ratings (Par 105):108,106,103,103,91 90,89,79
CSF £45.98 CT £548.68 TOTE £9.80: £2.20, £1.30, £3.70; EX 30.60.
Owner Diamond Racing Ltd **Bred** R M , P J And S R Payne **Trained** Warthill, N Yorks

FOCUS
This was run at a solid pace in the testing conditions and the form appears solid for the class. The winner remains in grand form.
Greenbelt Official explanation: jockey said gelding hung right throughout

611 BET NOW AT BETDIRECT.CO.UK H'CAP — 1m (F)
4:40 (4:40) (Class 4) (0-85,82) 4-Y-O+ — £6,477 (£1,927; £963; £481) Stalls Low

Form / RPR

0004 1 **Waterside (IRE)**[7] 542 7-9-2 80 GrahamGibbons 11 — 90
(G L Moore) *chsd ldrs: rdn to ld over 1f out: r.o* **9/1**

-502 2 1¼ **Te Quiero**[21] 412 8-9-4 82 (vt[1]) ShaneKelly 9 — 89
(Miss Gay Kelleway) *led 1f: hed over 3f out: rdn and hdd over 1f out: styd on* **12/1**

4210 3 5 **Speed Dial Harry (IRE)**[7] 542 4-8-9 80 (v) AndrewElliott(7) 1 — 76
(K R Burke) *mid-div: rdn over 3f out: styd on fnl f: nt trble ldrs* **13/2**[2]

0-41 4 1¾ **Alfonso**[21] 412 5-9-2 80 TomEaves 8 — 72
(I Semple) *chsd ldrs: rdn 1/2-way: styd on same pce fnl 3f* **11/8**[1]

5420 5 hd **Lincolneurocruiser**[4] 567 4-8-6 73 SaleemGolam(3) 10 — 65
(Mrs N Macauley) *hld up in tch: rdn over 3f out: wknd over 1f out* **25/1**

200- 6 1¼ **Boundless Prospect (USA)**[95] 6482 7-8-8 72 MickyFenton 5 — 61
(Miss Gay Kelleway) *hld up: hdwy u.p over 1f out: nvr trbld ldrs* **33/1**

0-14 7 1¼ **Parkview Love (USA)**[4] 567 5-8-4 71 (v) PatrickMathers(3) 2 — 57
(D Shaw) *chsd ldrs: rdn over 3f out: wknd over 1f out* **25/1**

0-15 8 8 **Wahoo Sam (USA)**[46] 161 6-9-0 78 DarryllHolland 3 — 47
(K A Ryan) *led 7f out: rdn and hdd over 3f out: wknd over 1f out* **7/1**[3]

1142 9 4 **Samuel Charles**[24] 381 8-8-3 72 AndrewMullen(5) 4 — 32
(C R Dore) *dwlt: outpcd* **14/1**

4-65 10 3½ **Kingsmaite**[37] 245 5-8-10 77 (v[1]) AmirQuinn(3) 12 — 29
(S R Bowring) *racd wd: mid-div: dropped rr over 5f out: sn bhd* **14/1**

-003 11 16 **Ali Bruce**[14] 476 6-9-0 78 ow1 (p) GeorgeBaker 6 — —
(G L Moore) *s.i.s: hld up: rdn 1/2-way: sn wknd* **10/1**

000- 12 2½ **Tidy (IRE)**[122] 6248 6-8-7 71 DeanMcKeown 7 — —
(Micky Hammond) *bhd fr 1/2-way* **50/1**

1m 43.73s (-0.87) **Going Correction** +0.275s/f (Slow) — **12** Ran SP% **120.6**
Speed ratings (Par 105):115,113,108,107,106 105,104,96,92,88 72,70
CSF £109.58 CT £772.65 TOTE £10.50: £3.00, £2.80, £2.60; EX 108.40 Trifecta £512.50 Part won. Pool: £721.94 - 0.10 winning tickets..
Owner Nigel Shields **Bred** Yeomanstown Stud **Trained** Woodingdean, E Sussex

FOCUS
A competitive handicap for the grade and it produced an excellent winning time for a race of its type. The first two came clear and, although the form looks reasonable, confidence is restricted as the ground conditions appeared to have a bearing on the result.

612 NO 5P RULE 4S AT BETDIRECT H'CAP (DIV II) — 7f (F)
5:10 (5:11) (Class 6) (0-60,60) 4-Y-O+ — £2,047 (£604; £302) Stalls Low

Form / RPR

0563 1 **Zorn**[6] 552 7-9-0 56 ShaneKelly 4 — 65
(P Howling) *led: hdd over 4f out: rdn to ld and hung rt over 1f out: edgd lft ins fnl f: r.o* **9/2**[1]

6030 2 3 **Preskani**[12] 492 4-8-13 60 (p) DuranFentiman(5) 12 — 62
(Mrs N Macauley) *sn pushed along in rr: hdwy 1/2-way: rdn and hung rt fr over 2f out: styd on* **11/1**

1-00 3 1 **Gem Bien (USA)**[40] 200 8-9-2 58 (p) TonyCulhane 8 — 57
(D W Chapman) *chsd ldrs: rdn over 2f out: styd on same pce fnl f* **16/1**

4600 4 1¼ **Captain Darling (IRE)**[27] 339 6-8-10 55 EdwardCreighton(3) 7 — 51
(R W Price) *w ldr tl led over 4f out: rdn and hdd over 1f out: wknd ins fnl f* **5/1**[2]

-100 5 nk **Favouring (IRE)**[19] 423 4-8-8 50 AdrianMcCarthy 9 — 45
(M C Chapman) *chsd ldrs: rdn over 2f out: wknd over 1f out* **6/1**[3]

6-00 6 ½ **El Palmar**[12] 493 5-8-10 52 RobbieFitzpatrick 1 — 46
(M J Attwater) *chsd ldrs over 5f* **8/1**

2036 7 nk **Prince Of Gold**[22] 400 6-8-9 51 (b) VinceSlattery 6 — 44
(R Hollinshead) *hood removed late and s.s: hdwy over 2f out: wknd fnl f* **6/1**[3]

6000 8 9 **King Marrakech (IRE)**[22] 402 4-8-4 46 oh6 (be) JoeFanning 10 — 17
(B P J Baugh) *hld up: hdwy over 3f out: wknd over 2f out* **33/1**

0036 9 5 **Busy Man (IRE)**[3] 576 7-8-13 55 EddieAhern 2 — 13
(J R Jenkins) *in rr: rdn and hung lft over 3f out: sn wknd* **9/2**[1]

006- 10 2½ **Mccormack (IRE)**[46] 2617 4-8-13 55 DeanMcKeown 3 — 7
(Micky Hammond) *hld up: rdn 1/2-way: sn wknd* **50/1**

-050 11 3½ **Value Plus (IRE)**[8] 533 4-8-6 55 (t) MarkCoumbe(7) 5 — —
(C J Teague) *chsd ldrs to 1/2-way* **66/1**

6600 12 3 **Ladies Knight**[4] 568 6-8-3 48 (v) PatrickMathers(3) 11 — —
(D Shaw) *s.s: a bhd* **25/1**

1m 32.24s (1.44) **Going Correction** +0.275s/f (Slow) — **12** Ran SP% **117.2**
Speed ratings (Par 101):102,98,97,96,95 95,94,84,78,75 71,68
CSF £52.38 CT £741.07 TOTE £4.30: £1.40, £4.30, £3.70; EX 37.10 Place 6 £79.69, Place 5 £15.99.
Owner Mrs A K Petersen **Bred** C B Petersen **Trained** Newmarket, Suffolk
■ Stewards' Enquiry : Duran Fentiman three day ban: used whip with excessive force (Mar 18, 20-21)

FOCUS
A moderate heat, run at a sound pace, and the winner did the job nicely. the runner-up helps set the standard.
Ladies Knight Official explanation: jockey said due to difficulty removing blindfold, gelding was slow away
T/Jkpt: Not won. T/Plt: £93.60 to a £1 stake. Pool: £58,576.45. 456.60 winning tickets. T/Qpdt: £6.00 to a £1 stake. Pool: £4,997.20. 613.85 winning tickets. CR

605 SOUTHWELL (L-H)
Wednesday, March 8

OFFICIAL GOING: Standard
Wind: Light, across Weather: Early rain giving way to ovecast conditions

613 RACING POST - THE HORSES MOUTH BANDED STKS — 6f (F)
2:10 (2:16) (Class 7) 3-Y-O+ — £1,365 (£403; £201) Stalls Low

Form / RPR

3110 1 **Hello Roberto**[4] 580 5-9-9 50 (p) AdrianMcCarthy 6 — 67
(R A Harris) *a.p: led over 1f out: rdn out* **7/1**

4062 2 1½ **A Teen**[10] 529 8-8-12 40 DaleGibson 3 — 52
(P Howling) *a.p: rdn to chse wnr over 1f out: styd on* **13/2**[3]

4443 3 1¼ **St Ivian**[10] 524 6-8-12 48 JasonEdmunds(3) 4 — 51
(Mrs N Macauley) *hld up: hdwy over 2f out: rdn over 1f out: styd on same pce* **5/1**[1]

0454 4 ¾ **Mulberry Lad (IRE)**[7] 546 4-9-0 47 PaulDoe 7 — 48
(P W Hiatt) *chsd ldrs: rdn over 2f out: swtchd lft over 1f out: styd on same pce ins fnl f* **5/1**[1]

4605 5 ¾ **Sir Sandrovitch (IRE)**[7] 547 10-9-3 50 (b) SamHitchcott 12 — 49
(R W Price) *s.i.s: rdn over 1f out: r.o ins fnl f: nrst fin* **16/1**

0-05 6 1½ **Sapphire Dream**[10] 524 4-8-6 45 ow1 AnnStokell(7) 5 — 40
(A Bailey) *in rr: hdwy over 1f out: wknd ins fnl f* **28/1**

6-04 7 nk **Suhezy (IRE)**[22] 415 3-8-3 50 DavidKinsella 14 — 43
(P T Midgley) *hld up in tch: rdn over 2f out: wknd fnl f* **12/1**

0040 8 ¾ **Wilford Maverick (IRE)**[30] 315 4-8-12 45 (v[1]) FrancisFerris 10 — 36
(M J Attwater) *chsd ldr: rdn and ev ch over 1f out: wknd fnl f* **14/1**

04 9 ¾ **Teyaar**[16] 465 10-8-12 45 AlanDaly 13 — 34
(M Wellings) *prom over 4f* **20/1**

5004 10 1½ **Massey**[22] 408 10-8-13 46 LeeEnstone 2 — 30
(C R Dore) *led over 4f: wknd fnl f* **8/1**

3003 11 5 **Elms Schoolboy**[2] 602 4-8-12 45 (b) JamieMackay 11 — 14
(P Howling) *a in rr* **6/1**[2]

000- 12 3 **Goodbye Girl (IRE)**[124] 6244 3-8-3 50 (p) MatthewHenry 9 — 10
(Mrs C A Dunnett) *sn outpcd* **80/1**

000/ 13 1¼ **Mister Bell**[514] 6080 4-8-12 45 SimonWhitworth 1 — —
(J G M O'Shea) *s.i.s: plld hrd and sn prom: wknd over 2f out* **66/1**

-000 14 ¾ **Katie Killane**[24] 388 4-8-12 40 (v) PaulFitzsimons 8 — —
(M Wellings) *dwlt: sme hdwy over 3f out: sn wknd* **100/1**

1m 16.74s (-0.16) **Going Correction** -0.05s/f (Stan)
WFA 3 from 4yo+ 14lb — **14** Ran SP% **116.7**
Speed ratings (Par 97):99,97,95,94,93 91,90,89,88,86 80,76,74,73
CSF £48.59 TOTE £8.30: £2.40, £1.80, £1.70; EX 38.10.
Owner Peter A Price **Bred** I B Barker **Trained** Earlswood, Monmouths

FOCUS
There was a decent pace on and, as is the case with most meetings here, the centre of the track was the place to be. The form looks reliable with the placed horses setting the level.
Sir Sandrovitch(IRE) Official explanation: jockey said gelding hung left-handed
Elms Schoolboy Official explanation: jockey said gelding never travelled
Mister Bell Official explanation: jockey said gelding ran too free early and hung right-handed

614 RACING POST SELECT A STABLE BANDED STKS — 2m (F)
2:40 (2:45) (Class 7) 4-Y-O+ — £1,706 (£503; £252) Stalls Low

Form / RPR

50-0 1 **Indian Chase**[14] 482 9-9-2 50 RichardThomas(3) 8 — 53+
(Dr J R J Naylor) *s.i.s: hld up and bhd: hdwy over 6f out: chsd ldr over 4f out: led on bit over 1f out: nt extended* **10/3**[2]

The Form Book, Raceform Ltd, Compton, RG20 6NL

300- **2** 2 ½ **Scurra**150 5770 7-8-7 40 JosephWalsh(7) 7 43
(A C Whillans) *chsd ldrs: led 5f out: rdn and hdd over 1f out: no ch w wnr* **13/2**

-622 **3** 3 ½ **Logger Rhythm (USA)**8 303 6-9-0 45 DaleGibson 6 38
(R Dickin) *hld up in tch: rdn over 4f out: wknd over 2f out* **9/4**1

000/ **4** ½ **Flying Patriarch**10 2840 5-9-0 45 (e1) TPQueally 4 38
(G L Moore) *led 4f: chsd ldr: rdn 7f out: wknd over 3f out* **11/2**3

06-0 **5** 1 ¾ **Jamaican Flight (USA)**19 28 13-9-0 30 JimmyQuinn 1 36
(Mrs S Lamyman) *w ldr: led 12f out: rdn and hdd 5 out: wknd over 3f out* **25/1**

04-4 **6** 1 **Esquillon**31 303 4-8-9 45 (p) MickyFenton 5 34
(S Parr) *chsd ldrs: rdn over 4f out: wknd over 2f out* **16/1**

0-40 **7** 18 **Sungio**26 361 8-8-7 40 (be) SoniaEaton(7) 2 11
(B P J Baugh) *slowly into stride: a in rr: bhd fr 1/2-way* **8/1**

5/60 **8** 3 **Sarenne**10 525 5-8-9 45 (e1) StephenDonohoe(5) 3 7
(John Berry) *prom: rdn 5f out: sn wknd* **14/1**

0-56 **9** dist **Robbie Will**36 256 5-9-0 40 TonyCulhane 9 —
(F Jordan) *hld up: hdwy 9f out: rdn over 6f out: wknd and virtually p.u fnl 4f* **14/1**

3m 45.76s (1.22) **Going Correction** -0.05s/f (Stan)
WFA 4 from 5yo+ 5lb **9** Ran SP% **116.7**
Speed ratings (Par 97):94,92,91,90,89 89,80,78,—
CSF £25.69 TOTE £3.90: £1.40, £2.70, £1.20; EX 30.30.
Owner The Indian Chase Partnership **Bred** R T Crellin **Trained** Shrewton, Wilts
■ Stewards' Enquiry : Sonia Eaton seven-day ban: in breach of Rule 158 (Mar 20-26)

FOCUS
A test of stamina for these moderate horses, but even with Jamaican Flight in the field they did not go mad and the form is very limited.
Robbie Will Official explanation: jockey said gelding lost its action

615 WIN £100K IN THE RACING POST MAIDEN CLAIMING STKS 1m 4f (F)
3:10 (3:15) (Class 7) 4-Y-0+ **£1,365** (£403; £201) **Stalls** Low

Form RPR

3045 **1** **Dextrous**10 525 9-8-13 45 (p) MickyFenton 8 47
(P T Midgley) *hld up: hdwy 1/2-way: chsd ldr over 3f out: rdn to ld over 1f out: styd on* **7/2**2

-426 **2** 1 ¾ **Silsong (USA)**31 301 4-8-6 45 (v) JimmyQuinn 2 39
(Miss Gay Kelleway) *chsd ldrs: led 1/2-way: rdn and hdd over 1f out: styd on same pce* **4/1**3

0-60 **3** 2 ½ **High (IRE)**22 414 4-8-11 55 SimonWhitworth 3 41
(W J Musson) *mid-div: hdwy 8f out: outpcd over 4f out: hdwy over 3f out: styd on same pce fnl f* **15/8**1

40 **4** 14 **Ihuru**14 484 4-8-11 (b1) J-PGuillambert 7 20
(J G Portman) *mid-div: hdwy 1/2-way: rdn and wknd 3f out* **6/1**

0050 **5** 3 **The Plainsman**10 525 4-8-11 40 ChrisCatlin 1 15
(P W Hiatt) *prom: racd keenly: wknd 4f out* **16/1**

-005 **6** 7 **Son Of Sophie**31 302 4-8-11 35 (b) SamHitchcott 4 5
(C N Kellett) *led to 1/2-way: wknd 4f out* **25/1**

050- **7** 4 **Royal Lustre**191 4623 5-8-8 45 (p) GregFairley(5) 5 —
(Robert Gray) *chsd ldr to 1/2-way: wknd over 3f out* **8/1**

00-0 **8** 1 ¼ **Bodfari Dream**54 103 5-8-8 35 (b1) DeanMcKeown 9 —
(M Mullineaux) *s.i.s: hdwy 7f out: wknd 1/2-way* **40/1**

9 dist **Barney Bubble (IRE)**130 4374 5-8-10 45 VinceSlattery 10 —
(K J Burke) *sn pushed along in rr: hdwy 8f out: wknd 7f out* **33/1**

0/ **10** 2 **Peruvian Princess**480 6650 7-7-10 ow1 JosephWalsh(7) 6 —
(J T Stimpson) *prom to 1/2-way* **66/1**

2m 40.77s (-1.32) **Going Correction** -0.05s/f (Stan)
WFA 4 from 5yo+ 2lb **10** Ran SP% **119.0**
Speed ratings (Par 97):102,100,99,89,87 83,80,79,—,—
CSF £17.87 TOTE £3.90: £1.50, £1.90, £1.10; EX 20.10.
Owner O R Dukes **Bred** Newgate Stud Co **Trained** Westow, N Yorks

FOCUS
When a nine-year-old finally breaks his maiden tag after years of trying, you know it is a race to forget for future purposes.

616 RACING POST - OFFICIAL CHELTENHAM PAPER BANDED STKS 1m (F)
3:40 (3:45) (Class 7) 4-Y-0+ **£1,365** (£403; £201) **Stalls** Low

Form RPR

4106 **1** **Crusoe (IRE)**1 606 9-9-3 45 (b) BrianReilly 9 54
(A Sadik) *a.p: rdn to ld over 1f out: r.o* **5/1**2

-066 **2** 1 ½ **Naughty Girl (IRE)**22 410 6-8-8 40 PatrickMathers(3) 2 45+
(John A Harris) *chsd ldrs: outpcd over 4f out: hdwy and nt clr run 3f out: rdn over 1f out: styd on* **25/1**

6225 **3** 1 **Dexileos (IRE)**16 467 7-8-11 45 (t) HayleyTurner 13 43
(David Pinder) *chsd ldrs: led over 3f out: rdn and hdd over 1f out: styd on same pce* **8/1**

0-06 **4** ½ **Noul (USA)**4 581 7-8-11 45 (b) FrankieMcDonald 11 41
(J S Moore) *hld up: hdwy u.p over 1f out: nt rch ldrs* **11/2**3

5-02 **5** 5 **Tommytyler (IRE)**10 527 7-8-8 45 (t) DanielTudhope(3) 6 30+
(D Carroll) *hld up: swtchd rt over 2f out: rdn and hung rt ins fnl f: nvr nr to chal* **3/1**1

60/0 **6** ¾ **Inmom (IRE)**13 25 5-8-11 40 MichaelTebbutt 7 29+
(S R Bowring) *hld up: swtchd lft and hdwy over 1f out: nvr nrr* **100/1**

0-40 **7** ¾ **Fizzy Lizzy**2 602 6-8-4 45 JosephWalsh(7) 14 27
(H E Haynes) *hld up: hdwy over 4f out: rdn and wknd over 1f out* **25/1**

00-0 **8** 1 **Rocky Reppin**64 27 6-8-8 45 (b) JasonEdmunds(3) 8 25
(J Balding) *hld up: hdwy over 3f out: nt trble ldrs* **11/1**

0340 **9** 7 **Xaloc Bay (IRE)**7 546 8-8-11 40 (b) AdrianMcCarthy 12 10
(R A Harris) *prom: rdn over 2f out: wknd over 1f out* **15/2**

66-0 **10** 9 **Susiedil (IRE)**43 183 5-8-11 40 GylesParkin 5 —
(D Nicholls) *chsd ldrs: led 6f out: hdd over 3f out: wknd over 2f out* **20/1**

00-0 **11** nk **Raven (IRE)**18 449 4-8-11 45 MickyFenton 1 —
(Mark Campion) *led 2f: n.m.r and lost pl wl over 4f out: sn wknd* **66/1**

40-0 **12** 1 ¼ **Doughty**24 387 4-8-11 40 (t) VinceSlattery 4 —
(D J Wintle) *s.i.s and stmbld sn after s: hdwy over 6f out: rdn and wknd over 2f out* **40/1**

504- **13** 3 **Parisian Playboy**160 5566 6-8-6 45 DuranFentiman(5) 10 —
(A D Brown) *chsd ldrs over 5f* **10/1**

000- **14** 2 **Sinjaree**85 6573 8-8-11 40 (p) JimmyQuinn 3 —
(Mrs S Lamyman) *mid-div: rdn over 3f out: sn wknd* **66/1**

1m 43.89s (-0.71) **Going Correction** -0.05s/f (Stan) **14** Ran SP% **116.2**
Speed ratings (Par 97):101,99,98,98,93 92,91,90,83,74 74,72,69,67
CSF £127.95 TOTE £6.40: £2.60, £4.70, £2.60; EX 87.10.
Owner A Sadik **Bred** John F Tuthill And Mrs A Whitehead **Trained** Wolverley, Worcs

FOCUS
A weak race in which many of the horses who took part had not run well for some time and not a race to be positive about.

617 RACING POST SELECT A STABLE TRI-BANDED STKS 1m (F)
4:10 (4:15) (Class 7) 3-Y-O **£1,365** (£403; £201) **Stalls** Low

Form RPR

0-00 **1** **Hits Only Life (USA)**34 272 3-8-12 45 DeanMcKeown 6 54+
(J Pearce) *s.s: hdwy over 6f out: led and hung lft fr over 2f out: rdn clr over 1f out* **11/8**1

00-5 **2** 7 **The Jailer**12 499 3-8-12 45 DavidKinsella 2 39
(J G M O'Shea) *chsd ldrs: rdn over 2f out: sn outpcd* **25/1**

0-01 **3** ½ **Mid Valley**10 528 3-9-4 45 6ex TonyCulhane 7 44
(J R Jenkins) *hld up in tch: rdn 1/2-way: hung lft fnl 2f: no imp* **13/8**2

0-24 **4** ½ **Mykeyta**29 329 3-8-12 45 DaleGibson 5 36
(J G Given) *hld up: hdwy u.p over 3f out: r.o ins fnl f: nrst fin* **8/1**3

00-0 **5** 5 **Yassooma (IRE)**22 415 3-8-12 45 (b1) RobbieFitzpatrick 10 25
(T J Pitt) *chsd ldrs: rdn over 3f out: wknd over 1f out* **50/1**

000- **6** 2 **Mister Becks (IRE)**141 5958 3-8-2 30 AdrianMcCarthy 3 —
(M C Chapman) *led over 5f: wknd over 1f out* **100/1**

000- **7** 9 **Millbrook Star (IRE)**83 6585 3-8-2 35 JamieMackay 4 —
(M C Chapman) *chsd ldrs: rdn and lost pl 6f out: sn bhd* **66/1**

2003 **8** 1 ¼ **Paris Power**10 528 3-8-12 45 (b) DerekMcGaffin 1 —
(D Morris) *sn pushed along in rr: hdwy over 3f out: rdn and wknd over 2f out* **9/1**

000 **9** nk **Maxemull**25 380 3-8-1 35 ow2 EdwardCreighton(3) 9 —
(D J Wintle) *chsd ldrs: lost pl over 5f out: sn bhd* **50/1**

0-06 **10** 3 ½ **Lady Evi**10 528 3-8-7 40 ChrisCatlin 11 —
(D K Ivory) *mid-div: wknd over 4f out* **20/1**

1m 44.18s (-0.42) **Going Correction** -0.05s/f (Stan) **10** Ran SP% **116.3**
Speed ratings (Par 92):100,93,92,92,87 85,76,74,74,70
CSF £43.75 TOTE £2.40: £1.10, £4.00, £1.20; EX 41.30.
Owner Lynne Whiting & Judith Kell Stone **Bred** Phillips Racing Partnership **Trained** Newmarket, Suffolk

FOCUS
A one-horse race in the end and could be rated higher but the standard is weak.
Hits Only Life(USA) Official explanation: trainer said, regarding the improved form shown, gelding had benefited from the drop in class
Mid Valley Official explanation: jockey said, regarding the running and riding, his orders were to get immediate cover, as colt tends to run a bit free, and to track the favourite; this went to plan but approaching final bend the colt raced lazily, and had no chance with the winner, although he pushed all the way to the line for best possible placing
Paris Power Official explanation: jockey said gelding hung left back straight

618 RACING POST BANDED STKS 7f (F)
4:40 (4:45) (Class 7) 3-Y-0+ **£1,365** (£403; £201) **Stalls** Low

Form RPR

3242 **1** **Mount Royale (IRE)**22 410 8-9-3 48 (v) KimTinkler 6 52
(N Tinkler) *chsd ldrs: rdn to ld over 1f out: r.o* **4/1**1

4510 **2** nk **Penel (IRE)**10 526 5-9-2 47 (p) LeeEnstone 5 50+
(P T Midgley) *chsd ldrs: nt clr run and lost pl over 3f out: hdwy over 1f out: r.o* **14/1**

-035 **3** hd **Mister Aziz (IRE)**10 529 4-9-0 45 (b1) StephenCarson 3 48
(J R Jenkins) *s.i.s: hld up: hdwy over 2f out: r.o* **14/1**

0062 **4** 1 **Diction (IRE)**1 606 4-9-3 48 (v) PatCosgrave 2 48
(K R Burke) *s.s: outpcd: r.o ins fnl f: nt rch ldrs* **6/1**3

0000 **5** 1 **Barzak (IRE)**26 358 6-9-3 48 (bt) MichaelTebbutt 12 46
(S R Bowring) *hld up: hdwy over 2f out: rdn over 1f out: styd on* **16/1**

-000 **6** 3 ½ **Union Jack Jackson (IRE)**25 383 4-9-5 50 (b1) NeilPollard 8 39
(J G Given) *led 5f out: rdn and hdd over 1f out: wknd ins fnl f* **16/1**

-005 **7** 2 ½ **Edge Fund**23 398 4-9-2 47 (b) SimonWhitworth 9 30
(Miss Gay Kelleway) *s.s: hdwy over 2f out: edgd lft and wknd over 1f out* **16/1**

-266 **8** nk **The Job**38 247 5-9-5 50 (v) AdrianMcCarthy 7 32
(A D Smith) *chsd ldrs: rdn over 1f out: wknd fnl f* **4/1**1

3012 **9** nk **Ariesanne (IRE)**22 411 5-9-1 46 SamHitchcott 4 27
(A C Whillans) *chsd ldrs over 4f* **5/1**2

3005 **10** 1 ¼ **Madame Guillotine**24 387 4-9-0 40 (b) GylesParkin 13 23
(P T Midgley) *hld up: a in rr* **66/1**

4000 **11** hd **Ace Club**10 529 5-9-0 45 (b) DaleGibson 1 23
(J Hetherton) *led 2f: rdn and wknd over 2f out* **50/1**

52-4 **12** nk **Dunnett Again (IRE)**10 529 5-9-0 40 (b) MatthewHenry 11 22
(Mrs C A Dunnett) *chsd ldrs over 4f* **12/1**

0-00 **13** 4 **Donya One**16 466 4-9-5 50 PaulEddery 10 17
(John A Harris) *s.i.s: sn pushed along in rr: hdwy over 4f out: wknd 1/2-way* **28/1**

1m 30.05s (-0.75) **Going Correction** -0.05s/f (Stan) **13** Ran SP% **116.5**
Speed ratings (Par 97):102,101,101,100,99 95,92,91,91,90 89,89,85
CSF £59.79 TOTE £5.00: £1.30, £4.80, £7.30; EX 79.80 Place 6 £31.46, Place 5 £13.92.
Owner Langton Partnership **Bred** Joe Crowley And Mr And Mrs A P O'Brien **Trained** Langton, N Yorks
■ Race restricted to riders who rode fewer than 30 winners in 2005 and have ridden fewer than 30 so far this year.

FOCUS
Quite a rough race, run at a decent pace but the form is weak.
The Job Official explanation: vet said gelding bled from nose
T/Plt: £25.80 to a £1 stake. Pool: £60,222.95. 1,703.90 winning tickets. T/Qpdt: £15.20 to a £1 stake. Pool: £4,301.80. 209.00 winning tickets. CR

560 NAD AL SHEBA (L-H)
Thursday, March 9
OFFICIAL GOING: Turf course - good to firm; dirt course - fast

619a THE BVLGARI RACE (H'CAP) (TURF) 6f 110y(T)
3:00 (3:00) (100-112,108) 3-Y-0+ **£66,133** (£20,348; £10,174; £5,087)

RPR

1 **Candidato Roy (ARG)**13 506 5-9-3 105 (t) KShea 2 110
(M F De Kock, South Africa) *hld up in rr: gng wl 3f out: swtchd centre 2f out: r.o wl: led last 50yds* **10/1**

2 1 ½ **Bygone Days**13 506 5-9-3 105 KerrinMcEvoy 6 105
(I Mohammed, UAE) *mid-div: prog to ld over 1f out: r.o but no ch w wnr* **13/2**

3 ½ **T-Bird (SAF)**14 496 5-9-5 107 (bt1) TPO'Shea 1 106
(E Charpy, UAE) *hld up in rr: rdn 3f out: swtchd wd: nrst fin* **4/1**1

4 1 ¼ **Suggestive**35 281 8-9-6 108 (b) NickyMackay 5 104
(W J Haggas) *trckd ldrs on rail: rdn 2f out: ev ch 1f out: nt qckn* **7/1**

5 1 1/4 **National Icon (SAF)**[13] 506 6-9-6 **108** JBekker 3 100
(D Maroun, South Africa) *mid-div: gng wl on rail 2f out: n.m.r: nt rcvr* **25/1**
6 3/4 **Obe Gold**[13] 506 4-9-6 **108** (v) TedDurcan 7 98
(M R Channon) *trckd ldng pair: ev ch 3f out: one pce* **6/1**[3]
7 nk **Montgomery's Arch (USA)**[21] 433 4-9-6 **108** (v) MJKinane 4 97
(J Noseda) *settled towards rr: swtchd wd 3f out: prog but n.d* **5/1**[2]
8 2 **Cartography (IRE)**[14] 494 5-9-3 **105** (t) RichardMullen 9 88
(E Charpy, UAE) *disp then trckd ldrs: led 3f out: clr 2f out: hdd over 1f out: wknd* **7/1**
9 5 **Mogaamer (USA)**[21] 434 4-9-1 **102** (v) RHills 8 72
(S Seemar, UAE) *mid-div: wd 3f out: rdn but no rspnse* **16/1**
10 6 **Attilius (BRZ)**[28] 353 4-8-12 **105** LDettori 10 53
(I Mohammed, UAE) *disp then led tl 3f out: wknd* **7/1**
1m 18.8s **Going Correction** +0.575s/f (Yiel) **10** Ran SP% **120.6**
Speed ratings: 112,110,109,108,106 106,105,103,97,90

Owner Des Scott & Robert Muir **Bred** Vacacion **Trained** South Africa

FOCUS
An ordinary by Carnival standards considering the prize money on offer.

NOTEBOOK
Candidato Roy(ARG), unlucky not to have finished closer in a similar event over six furlongs here on his previous start, gained compensation with a clear-cut success. On this evidence he will have little problem getting seven furlongs.
Bygone Days had every chance and basically appeared to be outstayed by the winner.
T-Bird(SAF), with blinkers fitted, was dropping back from a mile and just got going too late. It may be that seven furlongs is his trip.
Suggestive, not seen since finishing second over a furlong further on his debut in Dubai 35 days previously, looked to have his chance. He seems better over slightly further.
National Icon(SAF) has not run to his best at this year's Carnival, although this was better.
Obe Gold was below the form he showed to win a six-furlong handicap from a 4lb lower mark on his previous start.
Montgomery's Arch(USA), 6lb higher, was quite a bit below the form he showed to win over six furlongs on his previous start and this visor clearly failed to have such a positive effect this time.

620a THE AREEJ TROPHY (DIRT) 1m (D)
3:35 (3:35) 3-Y-O **£11,337** (£3,488; £1,744; £872)

RPR
1 **Discreet Cat (USA)**[194] 3-8-9 105 LDettori 5 106+
(Saeed Bin Suroor) *hld up in rr: racd in mid-div 4f out: prog to ld 1 1/2f out: v easily* **2/7**[1]
2 4 **Golden Acer (IRE)**[27] 368 3-8-9 91 JMurtagh 2 92
(Doug Watson, UAE) *slowly away but sn led: clr 6f out: hdd 1 1/2f out: kpt on: no ch w wnr* **14/1**[3]
3 5 3/4 **Dynamic Saint (USA)**[20] 3-8-9 90 WSupple 4 80
(Doug Watson, UAE) *hld up in rr bef prog to trck ldr 4f out: rdn 3f out: nt qckn* **20/1**
4 1 1/2 **Jet Express (SAF)**[42] 203 4-9-5 90 KShea 7 69
(H J Brown, South Africa) *mid-div: rdn 3f out: nvr involved* **14/1**[3]
5 6 1/4 **Sand Cat**[14] 3-8-9 90 PatDobbs 1 65
(Doug Watson, UAE) *racd in rr: nvr involved* **28/1**
6 4 1/4 **Nomoretaxes (BRZ)**[7] 561 4-9-5 97 WayneSmith 6 48
(M F De Kock, South Africa) *racd in rr: n.d* **13/2**[2]
7 6 **Documento Fiscal (BRZ)**[21] 435 4-9-5 90 (p) MAlmeida 3 36
(C Morgado, Brazil) *led main gp: rdn 4f out: wknd* **50/1**
1m 35.91s **Going Correction** +0.30s/f (Slow)
WFA 3 from 4yo 18lb **7** Ran SP% **114.6**
Speed ratings: 119,115,109,107,101 97,91

Owner Godolphin **Bred** E Paul Robsham **Trained** Newmarket, Suffolk

FOCUS
Although he had little of real note to beat and the form is a long way short of what will be required in the Kentucky Derby, Discreet Cat still created a very good impression and recorded an incredibly fast time in the process.

NOTEBOOK
Discreet Cat(USA) ◆ had subsequent Breeders' Cup Juvenile fifth Superfly in second when making all in a six-furlong Saratoga maiden on his debut 194 days previously, and was subsequently bought privately by Godolphin. Upped two furlongs, he was dropped in this time to gain some experience of having horses around him but raced keenly under restraint despite the pace appearing very solid. He faced little serious opposition, though, and having made his way to the front in the straight without needing to be asked any sort of question he looked value for at least double the winning margin. Although it is easy to pick holes in the form, the time was significantly faster than all three of the previous UAE 2000 Guineas, and quicker than four of the previous six runnings of the Godolphin Mile. He seems quite highly strung and needs to settle better and prove his stamina if he is going to make it to the top, but there is no denying his potential. The UAE Derby should tell us if he is a genuine Kentucky Derby contender.
Golden Acer(IRE) had been well held in two runs since switching to Dubai, but was a smart sprinting juvenile on turf for Richard Hannon last year and returned to something like the pick of his form with a creditable second behind the classy winner, although he is flattered by his proximity as that one was value for at least double the winning margin.

621a LAND ROVER CUP (H'CAP) (TURF) 1m (T)
4:30 (4:30) (100-112,111) 3-Y-O+ **£66,133** (£20,348; £10,174; £5,087)

RPR
1 **Seihali (IRE)**[7] 564 7-9-6 **111** JMurtagh 3 118
(D Selvaratnam, UAE) *mid-div: swtchd wd 3f out gng wl: rdn to chal 1 1/2f out: led 1f out: easily* **5/2**[2]
2 1 3/4 **Brunel (IRE)**[35] 281 5-9-5 **110** (b) KerrinMcEvoy 7 113
(I Mohammed, UAE) *nt far off pce: rdn to dispute 1 1/2f out: r.o wl but no ch w wnr* **7/1**
3 1/2 **Near Dock (GER)**[14] 496 5-9-2 **107** ASuborics 9 109
(V Smith) *s.i.s: settled in rr: rdn to trck ldrs 2f out: hrd rdn 1f out: nrst fin* **14/1**
4 1 3/4 **Blue On Blues (ARG)**[13] 511 5-8-11 **102** (t) RyanMoore 5 101
(S Seemar, UAE) *mid-div: rdn 5f out: wd 3f out: n.d* **6/1**[3]
5 1 1/2 **Stetchworth Prince**[13] 511 4-8-11 **102** LDettori 4 98
(Saeed Bin Suroor) *settled in rr: rdn 3f out: nt qckn* **2/1**[1]
6 1/2 **Key Of Destiny (SAF)**[13] 512 8-9-3 **108** JBekker 6 103
(M F De Kock, South Africa) *settled in rr: last: gng wl 3f out: n.m.r 2f out: n.d* **10/1**
7 1 1/4 **Trademark (SAF)**[14] 497 10-9-2 **107** (bt) TedDurcan 2 99
(A Laird, UAE) *s.i.s: settled in rr: rn 3f out: nvr involved* **16/1**
8 2 1/2 **Eyjur (USA)**[14] 497 4-9-2 **107** MJKinane 8 94
(P Nickel Filho, Brazil) *led main gp: disp 2f out: wknd* **20/1**
9 1 **Checkit (IRE)**[7] 560 6-9-0 **105** GHind 10 90
(R Bouresly, Kuwait) *sn led: stl clr 2 1/2f out: wknd 1 1/2f out w no room on rail* **33/1**
10 1 3/4 **Kodiac**[14] 494 5-8-12 **104** (b) TPO'Shea 1 85
(E Charpy, UAE) *racd 3rd on rail: t.k.h: trckd ldrs 2f out: rdn: wknd* **18/1**
1m 39.11s **Going Correction** +0.575s/f (Yiel) **10** Ran SP% **123.3**
Speed ratings: 111,109,108,107,105 105,103,101,100,98

Owner Sheikh Ahmed Al Maktoum **Bred** Rathbarry Stud **Trained** United Arab Emirates
■ Seihali was providing both the winning trainer and jockey with a double on the night.

FOCUS
A high-class handicap - fourth-placed Blue On Blues gives the form a solid look - run in a time nearly two seconds faster than the mile handicap won by Azarole later on the card.

NOTEBOOK
Seihali(IRE), able to race off the same mark as when second in a similar event on his reappearance despite having subsequently finished third in a Group Two, took advantage with a decisive success.
Brunel(IRE) did not seem to mind being unable to dominate and was not far off his best.
Near Dock(GER), returned to handicap company, fared best of those to race well off the pace and emerges with plenty of credit. He should go well in pattern company in Europe this year.
Blue On Blues(ARG) seems quite a reliable yardstick and helps give the form a solid look.
Stetchworth Prince had things fall just right for him when winning an extended seven-furlong handicap on his previous start, but he had faster ground to contend with this time, as well as a 4lb higher mark, and could not follow up.

622a MASERATI TROPHY (H'CAP) (TURF) 1m 2f (T)
5:05 (5:05) (100-112,112) 3-Y-O+ **£66,133** (£20,348; £10,174; £5,087)

RPR
1 **Shakis (IRE)**[14] 497 6-9-4 **110** (vt) RHills 6 115
(Doug Watson, UAE) *mid-div: rdn to cl 2f out: led 1 1/2f out: r.o wl: comf* **12/1**
2 1 3/4 **Etesaal (USA)**[21] 432 6-9-4 **110** (t) KerrinMcEvoy 7 112
(I Mohammed, UAE) *mid-div: rdn to chal 2 1/2f out: ev ch but one pce* **10/1**
3 shd **Crosspeace (IRE)**[7] 562 4-9-1 **107** RoystonFfrench 8 109
(M Johnston) *led main gp: rdn 3f out: ev ch 2f out: nt qckn* **16/1**
4 1/2 **Boule D'Or (IRE)**[7] 564 5-9-3 **109** LDettori 9 110
(J Akehurst) *hld up last: gng wl on rail 3f out: swtchd centre: r.o last 2f: nrst fin* **7/2**[1]
5 2 **Evil Knievel (BRZ)**[14] 497 7-9-6 **112** JMurtagh 3 109
(M F De Kock, South Africa) *a in mid-div* **7/2**[1]
6 3 **Shanty Star (IRE)**[7] 562 6-9-6 **112** GHind 4 104
(R Bouresly, Kuwait) *trckd ldr: led 4f out: hdd 1 1/2f out: wknd* **8/1**
7 2 1/2 **Starpix (FR)**[14] 494 4-9-2 **108** KShea 2 95
(H J Brown, South Africa) *racd in rr: prog into mid-div 3f out: n.m.r 2f out: nvr a threat* **14/1**
8 shd **Hattan (IRE)**[180] 5109 4-9-3 **109** RyanMoore 5 96
(C E Brittain) *racd in rr: n.d* **14/1**
9 12 **Excalibur (IRE)**[13] 512 6-9-4 **110** JBekker 1 76
(M F De Kock, South Africa) *sn led: hdd 4f out: wknd 2f out: eased* **11/2**[2]
10 14 **Organizer (NOR)**[14] 497 6-8-10 **102** TPO'Shea 10 42
(E Charpy, UAE) *racd in rr: nvr involved: virtually p.u* **13/2**[3]
2m 6.33s **Going Correction** +0.575s/f (Yiel) **10** Ran SP% **120.3**
Speed ratings: 113,111,111,111,109 107,105,105,95,84

Owner Hamdan Al Maktoum **Bred** Shadwell Estate Co Ltd **Trained** United Arab Emirates

FOCUS
A very good handicap run at a strong pace from the start.

NOTEBOOK
Shakis(IRE) was well below form in an extended-mile handicap on his previous start, but the return to ten furlongs suited well and he came back to his best to run out a convincing winner.
Etesaal(USA) would have appreciated the return to turf and found only one too good. This looks to be about as good as he is these days.
Crosspeace(IRE), below form on both his previous starts at this year's Carnival, ran much better this time and emerges with plenty of credit.
Boule D'Or(IRE) had been running very creditably at this year's Carnival despite not always having the race run to suit, but they went a good pace form the start this time and he can have few excuses.
Evil Knievel(BRZ) looked as though he would improve for a return to this trip when winning over an extended mile on his debut in Dubai, but he was 7lb higher and finished well held in fifth.
Hattan(IRE) is pretty smart at his best - he was sixth behind Motivator in last year's Derby - but was well held on his debut in Dubai.
Excalibur(IRE) was ridden very forcefully and that may not have suited.

623a AL TAYER GROUP UAE OAKS (FILLIES) (LISTED RACE) (DIRT) 1m 1f (D)
5:35 (5:37) 3-Y-O **£94,476** (£29,069; £14,534; £7,267)

RPR
1 **Imperial Ice (SAF)**[21] 436 4-9-4 95 KShea 8 92
(H J Brown, South Africa) *trckd ldr wd: rdn to chal 2f out: led 100yds out: comf* **2/1**[1]
2 1 **Quality Special (BRZ)**[13] 510 4-9-4 100 MAlmeida 1 90
(C Morgado, Brazil) *sn led: disp 3f out: led again 2f out: hdd 100yds out* **11/2**[3]
3 2 1/4 **Dont Dili Dali**[21] 436 3-8-9 86 JohnEgan 3 97
(J S Moore) *mid-div: rdn 3f out: prog to trck ldrs 2f out: nt qckn* **13/2**
4 2 **Kalaforte (SAF)**[13] 510 4-9-4 90 RyanMoore 5 82
(H J Brown, South Africa) *trckd ldrs on rail: rdn 5f out: r.o one pce: styd on but nvr a threat* **15/2**
5 2 1/4 **Princess Woodman (BRZ)**[21] 436 4-9-4 85 ADomingos 7 78
(C Morgado, Brazil) *mid-div: rdn 4f out: wd: sme prog but n.d* **40/1**
6 2 1/4 **Give Me The Night (IRE)**[21] 436 3-8-9 90 WSupple 2 84
(Doug Watson, UAE) *nt far away on rail: trckd ldrs 3f out gng wl: led briefly but sn hdd and one pce* **11/1**
7 1 3/4 **Zeina Of Arabia**[21] 436 3-8-9 85 PatDobbs 6 81
(Doug Watson, UAE) *mid-div: n.d* **50/1**
8 5 1/2 **Donia Dubai (IRE)**[21] 436 3-8-9 75 GHind 9 71
(R Bouresly, Kuwait) *in rr: n.d* **100/1**
9 5 1/2 **Rock Opera (SAF)**[14] 494 4-9-4 102 TedDurcan 10 49
(A Laird, UAE) *settled in rr: nvr involved* **5/2**[2]
10 dist **Nawassi (CHI)**[42] 4-9-4 WayneSmith 4 —
(M Al Darmaki, Dubai) *v.s.a: nvr involved* **100/1**
1m 52.14s **Going Correction** +0.30s/f (Slow)
WFA 3 from 4yo 20lb **10** Ran SP% **117.1**
Speed ratings: 106,105,103,101,99 97,95,90,86,—

Owner Rupert Plersch & Robert Harrison **Bred** J Nash **Trained** South Africa
■ A double on the night for jockey Kevin Shea following Candidato Roy's success earlier on the card.

FOCUS
With the UAE 1000 Guineas winner Vague missing from the line up through injury, and Godolphin, who had won the previous four runnings not represented, this was a very weak renewal of the UAE Oaks.

NOTEBOOK
Imperial Ice(SAF), five and a quarter lengths second to Vague in the UAE 1000 Guineas on her previous start, had nothing of that one's class to contend with and stayed on best of all to land a very weak Classic.
Quality Special(BRZ), returned to dirt, had every chance and was basically just outstayed. (op 5/1)
Dont Dili Dali, although never really threatening the winner, stayed on to pinch some black type. She may now be aimed at the Irish 1000 Guineas and Italian Oaks, but a return to turf would need to bring around a significant about of improvement for her to have any chance at all in those types of races. (op 6/1)
Kalaforte(SAF), without the blinkers on her return to dirt, was well held in fourth. (tchd 7/1)
Rock Opera(SAF), reportedly the most expensive filly ever sold out of South Africa, did not stay and was never going to judged on her UAE 1000 Guineas running. She has still to prove she has trained on.

624a FERRARI CHALLENGE (H'CAP) (TURF) 1m 4f (T)
6:05 (6:05) (100-112,108) 3-Y-O+ **£66,133** (£20,348; £10,174; £5,087)

Pos	Dist	Horse	RPR
1		**Punch Punch (BRZ)**[21] [437] 5-9-3 **105**..........(v) MAlmeida 2 (C Morgado, Brazil) *sn pushed along: prog to mid-div 5f out: wd: chal 2f out: u.p: r.o wl* **8/1**	109
2	¾	**Corriolanus (GER)**[7] [562] 6-9-3 **105**.......... RyanMoore 6 (S Seemar, UAE) *mid-div: rdn 3f out: ev ch 2f out: one pce* **13/2**[3]	108
3	1 ¼	**Grand Ekinoks (TUR)**[13] [512] 8-9-6 **108**..........(b) HKaratas 10 (C Kurt, Turkey) *settled in rr: gng wl: rdn 3f out: fin wl: nrst fin* **11/2**[2]	109
4	1 ¾	**Encinas (GER)**[7] [562] 5-9-6 **108**.......... WMongil 3 (P Schiergen, Germany) *settled in rr gng wl: last and rdn 3f out: prog on rail 2f out: nrst fin* **5/1**[1]	106
5	2 ½	**Land 'n Stars**[13] [512] 6-9-1 **102**.......... JohnEgan 1 (Jamie Poulton) *nt far off pce: rdn along 4f out: n.d* **8/1**	98
6	¾	**Jersey Bounce (IRE)**[13] [512] 5-9-1 **102**.......... KShea 8 (H J Brown, South Africa) *disp ld on rail for 1 1/2f: trckd ldrs: gng wl 3f out: rdn 2f out: one pce* **5/1**[1]	97
7	nk	**Morshdi**[13] [513] 8-8-12 **100**.......... JMurtagh 7 (D Selvaratnam, UAE) *led main gp: trckd ldrs 6f out: led briefly 2 1/2f out: wknd* **8/1**	93
8	nse	**Velodrome (BRZ)**[13] [512] 7-8-12 **100**..........(t) TPO'Shea 5 (E Charpy, UAE) *hld up in rr: rdn 4f out: n.d* **33/1**	93
9	18	**Elmustanser**[7] [565] 5-9-3 **105**..........(vt) RHills 4 (Doug Watson, UAE) *nt far off pce: trckd ldrs 3f out: ev ch: wknd* **7/1**	71
10	22	**Fantastic Love (USA)**[42] [205] 6-9-1 **102**..........(vt) LDettori 9 (Saeed Bin Suroor) *disp ld for 1 1/2f then led: rdn 1 1/2f out: wknd: t.o* **8/1**	36

2m 34.2s **Going Correction** +0.575s/f (Yiel)
WFA 4 from 5yo+ 2lb **10** Ran SP% **121.9**
Speed ratings: 109,108,107,106,104 104,104,104,92,77

Owner Estrela Energia Stables **Bred** Haras Santa Rita Di Serra **Trained** Brazil

FOCUS
A good middle-distance handicap in which Punch Punch looked to win with a little more in hand than the official margin might suggest.

NOTEBOOK
Punch Punch(BRZ) ◆ defied a 10lb higher mark than when taking a similar event over course and distance on his previous start and looked to win with a little more in hand than the official margin might suggest, as he only seemed to be doing jusr enough to hold off Corriolanus when challenged. On this evidence, he must be kept on the right side of.
Corriolanus(GER) looked the most likely winner about a furlong out, but Punch Punch kept finding more when challenged.
Grand Ekinoks(TUR) just got going too late but continues to run with credit. His stable have had a successful Carnival and could be worth keeping in mind for next year.
Encinas(GER) was given plenty to do and finished well without managing to get there. He continues in good form.
Land 'n Stars again ran just a touch below the form he showed to win a similar event two starts previously, but this was by no means a bad run.
Jersey Bounce(IRE), 7lb higher, was the below the form he showed when winning a similar event on easy ground on his previous start.
Fantastic Love(USA), with a visor replacing blinkers, dropped out very tamely. He looks best watched for the time being.

625a THE LORO PIANA RACE (H'CAP) (TURF) 1m (T)
6:35 (6:40) (100-112,110) 3-Y-O+ **£66,133** (£20,348; £10,174; £5,087)

Pos	Dist	Horse	RPR
1		**Azarole (IRE)**[27] [370] 5-9-1 **105**.......... JohnEgan 5 (J S Moore) *led main gp: rdn to cl 2f out: led 1 1/2f out: kpt on wl* **13/2**	104
2	½	**Proudance (GER)**[13] [511] 4-9-3 **107**.......... ASuborics 8 (R Suerland, Germany) *trckd ldr: gng wl 2f out: led briefly 1 1/2f out: kpt on wl* **7/1**	105
3	shd	**Tiger Shark (SAF)**[21] [435] 5-9-0 **104**.......... KShea 9 (H J Brown, South Africa) *settled in rr: prog wd 2f out: ev ch: nrst fin* **5/1**[1]	102
4	1 ¼	**Billy Allen (IRE)**[14] [497] 5-8-11 **101**..........(t) SPasquier 10 (F Chappet, France) *settled in last: n.d but r.o wl fnl f: nrst fin* **14/1**	96
5	3	**King Jock (USA)**[14] [496] 5-9-3 **107**.......... PJSmullen 3 (E Charpy, UAE) *trckd ldrs: gng wl 2 1/2f out: n.m.r: r.o one pce* **11/2**[2]	96
6	3 ¼	**Caesar Beware (IRE)**[14] [496] 4-9-6 **110**.......... TedDurcan 4 (A Laird, UAE) *v.s.a: prog into mid-div on rail 3f out: n.m.r: nt qckn* **6/1**[3]	93
7	6	**Kandidate**[14] [496] 4-9-5 **109**..........(t) RyanMoore 2 (C E Brittain) *wl away: led: rdn 2 1/2f out: hdd 2f out: wknd rapidly* **14/1**	80

1m 41.08s **Going Correction** +0.575s/f (Yiel) **7** Ran SP% **85.5**
Speed ratings: 101,100,100,99,96 92,86

Owner Mrs Fitri Hay **Bred** Lord Vestey **Trained** Upper Lambourn, Berks

FOCUS
Only seven horses ended up taking part and this was an ordinary handicap for the class. They went a steady pace for much of the way so it was no surprise the winning time was nearly two seconds slower than the mile handicap won by Seihali earlier on the card.

NOTEBOOK
Azarole(IRE), although running well in his three previous starts at this year's Carnival, was continually held and looking pretty exposed, but he did not mind the steady pace and took advantage of what was probably an ordinary race for the grade. He may not be that easy to place back in England. (op 6/1)
Proudance(GER), second in a similar event over seven and a half furlongs on his previous start, ran his race once again and can have few excuses. (op 13/2)
Tiger Shark(SAF) would have preferred a much stronger pace and could not defy a 7lb higher mark than when winning over course and distance on his previous start. (op 11/2)
Billy Allen(IRE) is another who would have been better suited by a stronger gallop. (op 12/1)
King Jock(USA) would also have been unsuited by the way the race was run. (tchd 5/1)
Caesar Beware(IRE) was again below the form he showed when such an impressive winner on his debut in Dubai two starts previously. He would have appreciated the return to a decent surface having run below form on easy ground on his most recent start, but the steady pace was against him and he could not pick up when asked. He can do better when granted a strong pace on fast ground, but recent efforts suggest he is not one to keep following.
Kandidate dropped out very tamely and something may have been amiss.

597 WOLVERHAMPTON (A.W) (L-H)
Saturday, March 11

OFFICIAL GOING: Standard
Wind: Light, half-against Weather: Overcast

626 PLAY £1/4M SPOTTHEBALL ON 0800 500 000 CLAIMING STKS 5f 20y(P)
1:50 (1:51) (Class 6) 3-Y-O **£2,730** (£806; £403) Stalls Low

Form	Pos	Dist	Horse	RPR
244-	1		**City For Conquest (IRE)**[146] [5920] 3-8-12 81..........(v) FrancisNorton 9 (K R Burke) *mde all: rdn and edgd rt ins fnl f: r.o* **4/1**[2]	72
4535	2	nk	**Phinerine**[10] [551] 3-8-11 70..........(b) DarryllHolland 5 (R A Harris) *trckd ldrs: chsd wnr over 1f out: sn rdn: r.o* **7/2**[1]	70
4-40	3	3	**Glenviews Youngone (IRE)**[19] [464] 3-8-12 64...... RobbieFitzpatrick 8 (Peter Grayson) *mid-div: hdwy 1/2-way: rdn and hung lft fr over 1f out: styd on same pce* **9/2**[3]	60
5326	4	1	**Otis B Driftwood**[5] [593] 3-8-10 62..........(b) ShaneKelly 6 (M Quinn) *w wnr to 1/2-way: sn rdn: wknd fnl f* **11/2**	55
3440	5	1	**Luloah**[7] [577] 3-7-10 60.......... DonnaCaldwell(7) 4 (P S McEntee) *chsd ldrs: rdn 1/2-way: wknd over 1f out* **12/1**	44
306	6	¾	**Spirit Of Coniston**[7] [577] 3-8-12 52.......... DaneO'Neill 2 (M Wellings) *hld up in tch: rdn and wknd over 1f out* **14/1**	50
0014	7	nk	**Sounds Simla (IRE)**[5] [598] 3-8-5 60.......... ChrisCatlin 7 (Rae Guest) *s.i.s: nvr nrr* **6/1**	42
00-5	8	1 ¾	**John Claude (IRE)**[30] [344] 3-8-12 62..........(b[1]) PhillipMakin 3 (Ronald Thompson) *mid-div: effrt 1/2-way: wknd over 1f out* **16/1**	43
060-	9	¾	**Cuesta Canyon (IRE)**[110] [6403] 3-8-7 40.......... DeanMcKeown 1 (M J Polglase) *s.i.s: outpcd* **66/1**	35

62.17 secs (-0.65) **Going Correction** -0.125s/f (Stan) **9** Ran SP% **111.8**
Speed ratings (Par 96): 100,99,94,93,91 90,89,87,85
CSF £17.56 TOTE £4.20: £1.60, £1.60, £1.30; EX 14.80.
Owner F D C Partnership **Bred** Ballyhane Stud **Trained** Middleham Moor, N Yorks

FOCUS
Not a bad claimer, but City For Conquest had a little bit in hand at the weights and did not have to run up to her very best to make a winning return.

627 BETDIRECT.CO.UK H'CAP 5f 216y(P)
2:25 (2:26) (Class 2) (0-100,105) 4-Y-O+ **£11,658** (£3,468; £1,733; £865) Stalls Low

Form	Pos	Dist	Horse	RPR
0-31	1		**Bayeux (USA)**[11] [541] 5-8-8 **90**.......... NickyMackay 3 (G A Butler) *hld up: hdwy and hung rt over 2f out: led ins fnl f: rdn clr* **6/4**[1]	101
000-	2	3	**Quito (IRE)**[148] [5873] 9-9-9 **105**..........(b) TonyCulhane 7 (D W Chapman) *outpcd: hdwy over 1f out: no ch w wnr* **8/1**	107
130-	3	nk	**Indian Maiden (IRE)**[149] [5851] 6-9-9 **105**.......... FrancisNorton 1 (M S Saunders) *outpcd: r.o ins fnl f: nrst fin* **7/1**[3]	106
1-0	4	½	**Treasure Cay**[23] [433] 5-9-0 **96**.......... JohnEgan 6 (P W D'Arcy) *trckd ldrs: rdn and ev ch ins fnl f: sn outpcd* **20/1**	96
500-	5	½	**Roman Maze**[135] [6125] 6-8-8 **90**.......... DavidAllan 8 (W M Brisbourne) *led 1f: chsd ldr: led 2f out: sn rdn: hdd and no ex ins fnl f* **14/1**	88
540-	6	¾	**Josh**[162] [5593] 4-8-12 **94**.......... NCallan 9 (K A Ryan) *prom: rdn over 1f out: styd on same pce fnl f* **7/1**[3]	90
450-	7	½	**If Paradise**[126] [6252] 5-9-3 **99**.......... DaneO'Neill 5 (R Hannon) *chsd ldrs: rdn over 2f out: styd on same pce appr fnl f* **20/1**	93
6035	8	2	**One More Round (USA)**[21] [450] 8-8-4 **91**..........(b) JamesDoyle(5) 4 (N P Littmoden) *prom: chsd ldr over 1f out: sn rdn: wknd ins fnl f* **20/1**	79
006-	9	1 ¾	**Orientor**[149] [5853] 8-9-8 **104**.......... JimmyFortune 10 (J S Goldie) *hld up: rdn over 1f out: wknd fnl f* **25/1**	87
1111	10	7	**Graze On**[22] [441] 4-8-11 **93**..........(b) ShaneKelly 2 (R A Harris) *led 5f out: rdn and hdd 2f out: sn wknd: eased fnl f* **10/3**[2]	55

1m 13.87s (-1.94) **Going Correction** -0.125s/f (Stan) **10** Ran SP% **124.0**
Speed ratings (Par 109): 107,103,102,101,101 100,99,96,94,85
CSF £14.72 CT £72.94 TOTE £2.30: £1.30, £2.30, £2.50; EX 18.10.
Owner Beetle N Wedge Partnership **Bred** Darley **Trained** Blewbury, Oxon

FOCUS
A very good sprint handicap despite there being added prize money of just £18,000 on offer. They went a strong pace from the start and the first three home came from quite a way back.

NOTEBOOK
Bayeux(USA) ◆ defied a 5lb higher mark then when taking a competitive sprint at Lingfield on his previous start in some style. He was quite a way off the pace in the early stages, but the leaders had gone off very fast and he picked up pretty impressively when in the clear in the straight. He was Group placed on turf as a juvenile and looks up to contesting Pattern races once again. (op 7-4)
Quito(IRE), three times a Listed winner on turf since he was last seen on sand, would have been well suited by the strong pace and ran well, but the concession of 15lb to the smart Bayeux unsurprisingly proved too much. He looks set for another good season. (op 10-1 tchd 7-1)
Indian Maiden(IRE), 32lb higher than when she was last seen on sand having subsequently won four Listed races on turf and been placed in Group company, finished well from off the strong gallop. This was a pleasing return to action and she can be expected to have another good season. (tchd 12-1)
Treasure Cay ran no sort of race on the turf in Dubai on his previous start but, back in England and returned to Polytrack, this was not far off his very best form. (op 25-1)
Roman Maze, last year's Ayr Silver Cup runner-up, fared best of the pacesetters on his return from a 135-day break. This was a very promising return. (op 16-1)
Josh, dropped in trip and switched to Polytrack for the first time on his debut for a new trainer, ran respectably off the back of a 162-day break. (op 9-1 tchd 10-1)
Graze On, chasing a six-timer off a career-high mark having been raised 7lb for a recent course and distance success, could not sustain a very strong gallop and dropped out as if something was not quite right. The first two wins of his sequence came in claimers, suggesting previous connections did not mind losing him, so off the back of this effort he has a bit to prove. Official explanation: trainer had no explanation for the poor form shown (op 3-1 tchd 4-1)

628 TEXT "BETDIRECT" TO 88600 H'CAP — 2m 119y(P)

3:00 (3:00) (Class 4) (0-85,82) 4-Y-0+ £5,505 (£1,637; £818; £408) Stalls Low

Form			Horse	Jockey	RPR
-566	1		**Wise Owl**[19] 463 4-9-3 80 — (J Pearce) *hld up: hmpd over 3f out: hdwy over 2f out: hung rt and led 1f out: rdn out* **6/1**[3]	JimmyQuinn 11	90
1-22	2	1 ¼	**Tranquilizer**[28] 385 4-8-8 71 — (D J Coakley) *hld up: hdwy and hmpd over 3f out: led wl over 1f out: hung rt and hdd 1f out: styd on same pce* **14/1**	(t) EddieAhern 5	79
21-4	3	5	**Our Choice (IRE)**[5] 597 4-8-1 69 — (N P Littmoden) *hld up: hdwy 5f out: hung lft over 3f out: led wl over 2f out: ridde n and hdd wl over 1f out: nt clr run 1f out: sn wknd* **9/2**[2]	JamesDoyle(5) 3	71
/0-3	4	7	**Modaffaa**[21] 454 6-9-9 81 — (P R Webber) *hld up: hdwy and hmpd over 3f out: rdn: hung lft and wknd over 1f out* **4/1**[1]	DaneO'Neill 7	75
5-02	5	1	**High Point (IRE)**[11] 545 8-8-13 74 — (G P Enright) *chsd ldrs: rdn 1/2-way: hmpd over 3f out: wknd 2f out* **18/1**	(v) AmirQuinn(3) 2	66
2221	6	1 ½	**Desperation (IRE)**[12] 535 4-9-0 77 — (B D Leavy) *chsd ldrs: lost pl and hmpd over 3f out: hdwy over 2f out: sn rdn and wknd* **8/1**	RobbieFitzpatrick 1	68
0025	7	10	**Nawow**[5] 589 6-8-12 70 — (P D Cundell) *hld up in tch: led over 4f out: rdn and hdd wl over 2f out: wknd wl over 1f out* **6/1**[3]	DarryllHolland 10	49
4	8	10	**Eye Candy (IRE)**[14] 521 5-9-1 73 — (K A Ryan) *chsd ldrs: ev ch 3f out: hmpd and wknd over 2f out* **7/1**	(b1) NCallan 8	40
0-23	9	9	**Beauchamp Trump**[14] 521 4-8-4 67 — (G A Butler) *hld up: wknd over 3f out* **8/1**	(t) FrancisNorton 9	23
0510	10	dist	**Victory Quest (IRE)**[16] 491 6-8-8 66 — (Mrs S Lamyman) *sn led: hdd 14f out: chsd ldr tl rdn 5f out: wknd over 3f out* **66/1**	(v) ChrisCatlin 4	—
0B-6	P		**Tender Trap (IRE)**[24] 420 8-9-10 82 — (T G Mills) *led 14f out: rdn and hdd over 4f out: hmpd and wknd over 3f out: p.u and dismntd nr fin* **12/1**	IanMongan 6	—

3m 38.25s (-4.88) **Going Correction** -0.125s/f (Stan)
WFA 4 from 5yo+ 5lb — 11 Ran SP% **122.6**
Speed ratings (Par 105):106,105,103,99,99 98,93,89,84,—, —
CSF £90.64 CT £422.26 TOTE £6.70: £2.30, £3.60, £2.00; EX 60.10.
Owner S Birdseye **Bred** Darley **Trained** Newmarket, Suffolk
■ Stewards' Enquiry : James Doyle two-day ban: careless riding (Mar 22-23)

FOCUS
A reasonable staying handicap and the pace seemed fair.
Tender Trap(IRE) Official explanation: jockey said gelding lost its action

629 BETDIRECT.CO.UK LINCOLN TRIAL (HERITAGE H'CAP) — 1m 141y(P)

3:35 (3:36) (Class 2) (0-105,105) 4-Y-0+
£31,160 (£9,330; £4,665; £2,335; £1,165; £585) Stalls Low

Form			Horse	Jockey	RPR
1130	1		**Bravo Maestro (USA)**[11] 542 5-8-9 90 — (N P Littmoden) *hld up: hdwy over 1f out: led ins fnl f: rdn out* **12/1**	ChrisCatlin 6	101
230-	2	1 ¾	**Divine Gift**[254] 3045 5-8-11 92 — (K A Ryan) *chsd ldrs: swtchd rt over 1f out: r.o* **10/1**	DarryllHolland 2	100
0-43	3	nk	**Always Esteemed (IRE)**[21] 452 6-8-11 92 — (K A Ryan) *led: rdn over 1f out: hdd and unable qck ins fnl f* **6/1**[3]	(b) NCallan 1	99
/26-	4	hd	**Forgery (IRE)**[301] 1696 4-8-7 88 — (G A Butler) *mid-div: rdn over 3f out: nt clr run and lost pl over 1f out: r.o ins fnl f* **8/1**	NickyMackay 10	95
00-3	5	nk	**Impeller (IRE)**[21] 452 7-9-1 96 — (W R Muir) *hld up: r.o ins fnl f: nt rch ldrs* **16/1**	MartinDwyer 11	102
2546	6	hd	**Boo**[8] 572 4-8-10 96 — (K R Burke) *hld up: hdwy 1/2-way: rdn over 2f out: styd on* **14/1**	(v) AndrewElliott(5) 9	102
01-5	7	shd	**Kew Green (USA)**[14] 518 8-9-10 105 — (P R Webber) *chsd ldr: chal 2f out: sn rdn: no ex ins fnl f* **6/1**[3]	DaneO'Neill 5	110
013-	8	¾	**My Paris**[161] 5607 5-9-0 100 — (K A Ryan) *chsd ldrs: rdn over 3f out: edgd lft and no ex ins fnl f* **9/2**[1]	AndrewMullen(5) 3	104
4-34	9	shd	**Royal Island (IRE)**[20] 456 4-9-4 99 — (M Johnston) *chsd ldrs: rdn over 2f out: hmpd over 1f out: edgd lft and no ex fnl f* **11/2**[2]	JoeFanning 8	103
2610	10	1	**Atlantic Quest (USA)**[11] 542 7-8-7 88 — (R A Harris) *s.i.s: hld up: hdwy u.p over 1f out: no ex ins fnl f* **33/1**	(p) ShaneKelly 12	89
1333	11	hd	**Cummiskey (IRE)**[14] 516 4-8-12 93 — (J A Osborne) *hld up: hdwy over 1f out: rdn and n.m.r ins fnl f: no ex* **20/1**	EddieAhern 7	94
5221	12	¾	**Wessex (USA)**[25] 413 6-8-13 94 — (P A Blockley) *s.i.s: hld up: hdwy over 1f out: hmpd and no ex ins fnl f* **14/1**	GrahamGibbons 4	93
6502	13	½	**Moayed**[14] 516 7-8-11 97 — (N P Littmoden) *s.s: a in rr* **14/1**	(bt) JamesDoyle(5) 13	95

1m 49.51s (-2.25) **Going Correction** -0.125s/f (Stan) — 13 Ran SP% **123.6**
Speed ratings (Par 109):105,103,103,103,102 102,102,101,101,100 100,99,99
CSF £131.25 CT £808.23 TOTE £12.80: £2.70, £3.10, £2.90; EX 264.80 TRIFECTA Not won..
Owner Nigel Shields **Bred** Pacelco S A & Partners **Trained** Newmarket, Suffolk

FOCUS
A good, competitive renewal of the Lincoln Trial but, despite the pace appearing solid, they finished in a bunch behind the clear-cut winner.

NOTEBOOK
Bravo Maestro(USA) has not always looked straightforward and was disappointing when a beaten favourite at Lingfield on his most recent start, but he was only 2lb higher than when last winning and responded to a typically strong ride from Catlin to ultimately win very convincingly having been well off the pace as the race began to unfold. Connections hope this win will earn him a run in the Group Three Winter Derby, but he will have quite a bit to find in that company and would need everything to fall right.
Divine Gift ◆, off the track for 254 days, ran a blinder on his debut for the excellent Kevin Ryan team. Although he was seemingly not that easy to win with last season, he was rated 104 at one stage and could look on a very attractive mark in the Lincoln itself. This should have put him spot on and the 25/1 still available for that race looks well worth taking. (op 11-1 tchd 9-1)
Always Esteemed(IRE), a stablemate of the second, ran right up to his very best under a positive ride but is hard to win with. (op 8-1)
Forgery(IRE), who won his maiden over course and distance on his only previous start on this surface, ran a fine race off the back of a 301-day absence and would have been even closer with a clearer run. This was a very creditable effort and, if he stands training, there could well be more to come. (op 7-1)
Impeller(IRE), on a line through Always Esteemed, looked to run to a similar level of form than when third in a conditions race on his reappearance. (op 12-1)
Boo has done all of his racing over a little further this winter, and was most recently seen over a mile and a half, so this must rate as a very creditable effort.
Kew Green(USA), slightly disappointing when a beaten favourite in the Winter Derby Trial at Lingfield on his previous start, looked well placed on the turn into the straight, but could not sustain his challenge and was again below form. He is not in the Winter Derby and will have something to prove back on turf. (op 11-2 tchd 7-1)
My Paris, a stablemate of the second and third home, could not take advantage of a 5lb lower mark than when third in the Cambridgeshire on his last start 161 days previously. It may be that he is simply not as good on sand, or just that he needed the run, and he can be given another chance back on turf. (op 13-2)
Royal Island(IRE), fourth on the snow at St Moritz on his last start, was a little disappointing returned to less arctic-like conditions. He is better than this and holds entries in the Winter Derby and Lincoln. (op 7-1)
Cummiskey(IRE) Official explanation: jockey said gelding was denied a clear run

630 TEXT "BETDIRECT" TO 88600 MAIDEN STKS — 1m 141y(P)

4:10 (4:11) (Class 5) 3-Y-0 £3,886 (£1,156; £577; £288) Stalls Low

Form			Horse	Jockey	RPR
-	1		**Lucky Lark** 3-9-3 — (M Johnston) *chsd ldrs: rdn over 3f out: hung lft and r.o to ld wl ins fnl f* **5/2**[2]	KDarley 4	67
56	2	1	**Blanc Visage**[12] 531 3-9-3 — (Mrs H Sweeting) *led: rdn over 1f out: hdd wl ins fnl f* **80/1**	GeorgeBaker 6	65
33	3	1	**Pop Music (IRE)**[12] 534 3-9-3 — (Miss J Feilden) *hld up in tch: rdn and ev ch ins fnl f: styd on same pce* **14/1**	SimonWhitworth 1	63
22	4	¾	**Just Logic (IRE)**[28] 374 3-9-3 — (J Noseda) *s.i.s: hld up: hdwy 5f out: nt clr run and outpcd over 2f out: swtchd rt over 1f out: r.o: nt rch ldrs* **11/10**[1]	ShaneKelly 13	61
3333	5	shd	**Scroll**[9] 558 3-9-3 71 — (P Howling) *chsd ldrs: nt clr run over 2f out: rdn over 1f out: no ex ins fnl f* **6/1**[3]	(v) J-PGuillambert 5	61
0	6	1 ½	**Alexian**[29] 365 3-8-10 — (R Hollinshead) *hld up: hdwy u.p over 1f out: styd on same pce ins fnl f* **66/1**	RussellKennemore(7) 2	58
	7	6	**Marcello** 3-9-3 — (P F I Cole) *chsd ldrs: rdn over 2f out: wknd over 1f out* **9/1**	NCallan 9	45
5-6	8	4	**Shardia (IRE)**[61] 70 3-8-12 — (J Jay) *hld up: n.d* **66/1**	ChrisCatlin 8	32
	9	1	**Birbalini** 3-8-12 — (P J McBride) *s.s: a in rr* **80/1**	MartinDwyer 3	30
33	10	¾	**Glenargo (USA)**[19] 466 3-9-3 — (R A Harris) *chsd ldrs: rdn over 2f out: wknd fnl f* **28/1**	DarryllHolland 7	33
53-0	11	1 ¾	**Precautionary**[7] 579 3-8-7 66 — (Miss J Feilden) *prom over 6f* **40/1**	JamesDoyle(5) 12	25
	12	shd	**Prince Marju (IRE)** 3-9-5 ow2 — (P A Blockley) *hld up: wknd over 2f out* **66/1**	CraigCarver 11	32
	13	16	**Fashion Disaster** 3-8-12 — (A Crook) *s.i.s: a in rr* **80/1**	LeeEnstone 10	—

1m 51.37s (-0.39) **Going Correction** -0.125s/f (Stan) — 13 Ran SP% **121.2**
Speed ratings (Par 98):96,95,94,93,93 92,86,83,82,81 80,80,65
CSF £209.42 TOTE £3.40: £1.60, £14.00, £3.20; EX 181.70.
Owner Gainsborough Stud **Bred** Gainsborough Stud Management Ltd **Trained** Middleham Moor, N Yorks
■ Stewards' Enquiry : J-P Guillambert three-day ban: failed to ride out for fourth place (Mar 22-24)
K Darley caution: careless riding

FOCUS
With Just Logic disappointing, and the 80/1 Blanc Visage in second, this looked a pretty ordinary maiden.

631 BETDIRECT FREEPHONE 0800 211 222 CONDITIONS STKS — 7f 32y(P)

4:45 (4:46) (Class 2) 4-Y-0+ £11,217 (£3,358; £1,679; £840; £419) Stalls High

Form			Horse	Jockey	RPR
411-	1		**Border Music**[132] 6180 5-9-0 102 — (A M Balding) *sn led: qcknd clr over 1f out: eased nr fin* **8/11**[1]	(b) MartinDwyer 5	104+
061-	2	3 ½	**Kamanda Laugh**[167] 5497 5-9-0 95 — (K A Ryan) *led early: chsd wnr: rdn and ev ch over 2f out: sn outpcd* **10/3**[2]	NCallan 2	95
1231	3	2 ½	**Kindlelight Debut**[9] 555 6-8-9 80 — (N P Littmoden) *hld up: outpcd over 3f out: n.d* **9/1**	JamesDoyle 1	84
0521	4	3	**Qadar (IRE)**[14] 517 4-9-0 94 — (N P Littmoden) *chsd ldrs: rdn over 2f out: wknd over 1f out* **11/2**[3]	GeorgeBaker 4	81
0044	5	4	**Mistral Sky**[7] 585 7-9-4 67 — (Stef Liddiard) *hld up in tch: wknd over 2f out* **33/1**	(v) EddieAhern 3	75

1m 28.06s (-2.34) **Going Correction** -0.125s/f (Stan) — 5 Ran SP% **109.3**
Speed ratings (Par 109):108,104,101,97,93
CSF £3.36 TOTE £1.40: £1.10, £1.50; EX 3.70.
Owner Kingsclere Stud **Bred** Mrs I A Balding **Trained** Kingsclere, Hants

FOCUS
Just the five runners, but a very good conditions race and a hugely-impressive winner in Border Music.

NOTEBOOK
Border Music ◆, an impressive winner of his last three starts on Polytrack, defied a 132-day break with quite a taking success. He was entitled to win given he had upwards of 7lb in hand of his rivals at the weights, but this was still very impressive and he looked value for double the winning margin, if not more, as he did not have to be seriously asked to pull clear of the 95-rated Kamanda Laugh before easing down close home. His turf mark has been left on 79 but, while he is probably up to winning a race or two on that surface, sand racing looks to be his game and it would come as no surprise to see his ambitious trainer find suitable races for him abroad in the coming months - he placed a similar sort in Vanderlin (albeit on turf) to such good effect in the US and Canada last year. (tchd 4-6 and 4-5)
Kamanda Laugh, successful in a mile handicap off a mark of 92 on his final start for Barry Hills when last seen 167 days previously, ran well behind the very smart winner on his debut for new connections and time may show this was not a bad effort at all. (op 9-2)
Kindlelight Debut has been in great form this All-Weather season, but had it to do at the weights in this company, especially with her 5lb apprentice unable to claim his allowance, and ran about as well as could have been expected. However, if she can confirm her recent improvement back on turf, it is not out of the question that she could pick up some black types in fillies' and mares' only Listed company at some stage, as there is not always a great deal of strength in depth in such contests. (op 7-1 tchd 13-2)
Qadar(IRE) won his maiden over this trip when with Marcus Tregoning, but took a five-furlong handicap on his most recent start and did not appear suited by the jump back up in distance. (op 6-1 tchd 13-2)
Mistral Sky won this race last year, but could not repeat the feat against some quality animals. (op 22-1 tchd 20-1)

632 BETDIRECT FREEPHONE 0800 211 222 H'CAP 7f 32y(P)
5:15 (5:16) (Class 4) (0-85,85) 4-Y-0+ £5,505 (£1,637; £818; £408) Stalls High

Form RPR
1-51 1 **Byron Bay**[37] 276 4-9-0 81 TomEaves 10 91
(I Semple) *sn led: clr 5f out: rdn out* **17/2**
4205 2 2 **Lincolneurocruiser**[4] 611 4-8-2 72 SaleemGolam(3) 4 77
(Mrs N Macauley) *chsd ldrs: rdn over 1f out: wnt 2nd nr fin: nt rch wnr* **13/2**[3]
-025 3 hd **Lake Chini (IRE)**[18] 476 4-8-8 75 (p) MatthewHenry 5 80
(M A Jarvis) *chsd wnr: rdn over 2f out: styd on: lost 2nd nr fin* **8/1**
3301 4 2 **Councellor (FR)**[8] 569 4-8-12 79 EddieAhern 8 79
(Stef Liddiard) *hld up in tch: rdn and hung lft over 1f out: n.d* **9/4**[1]
1315 5 ½ **Northern Desert (IRE)**[11] 542 7-9-4 85 ChrisCatlin 11 83
(P W Hiatt) *hld up: r.o u.p fnl f: nvr nrr* **13/2**[3]
051- 6 nk **Dhaular Dhar (IRE)**[153] 5762 4-8-11 78 JimmyFortune 1 76
(J S Goldie) *prom: rdn over 2f out: no imp fr over 1f out* **9/2**[2]
300- 7 1½ **Play The Ball (USA)**[379] 493 4-8-8 75 NickyMackay 7 69
(G A Butler) *hld up: rdn over 2f out: n.d* **33/1**
0-00 8 ½ **Middleton Grey**[41] 238 8-9-4 85 (b) LPKeniry 12 78
(A G Newcombe) *hld up: nvr nr to chal* **20/1**
4402 9 1½ **General Feeling (IRE)**[7] 585 5-8-9 76 JimmyQuinn 6 65
(M Mullineaux) *hld up: nvr nr to chal* **12/1**
0/0- 10 5 **Sgt Pepper (IRE)**[80] 840 5-9-3 84 DaneO'Neill 9 60
(P L Gilligan) *s.s: a bhd* **25/1**
50L- R **High Dyke**[161] 5599 4-8-11 78 (p) NCallan 2 —
(K A Ryan) *ref to r* **16/1**

1m 28.42s (-1.98) **Going Correction** -0.125s/f (Stan) 11 Ran SP% **122.4**
Speed ratings (Par 105):106,103,103,101,100 100,98,98,96,90 —
CSF £63.99 CT £479.48 TOTE £13.40: £3.20, £2.80, £3.30; EX 91.20 Place 6 £70.04, Place 5 £49.76 .
Owner Ian Murray Tough **Bred** Ian Murray Tough **Trained** Carluke, S Lanarks

FOCUS
A decent handicap run at a sound gallop and the winner made all.
T/Plt: £348.60 to a £1 stake. Pool: £53,612.80. 112.25 winning tickets. T/Qpdt: £129.50 to a £1 stake. Pool: £3,046.10. 17.40 winning tickets. CR

613 SOUTHWELL (L-H)
Tuesday, March 14

OFFICIAL GOING: Standard
Wind: Light, across Weather: Overcast

633 LITTLEWOODS £2M POOLS ON 0800 500 000 BANDED STKS 5f (F)
2:25 (2:25) (Class 7) 4-Y-0+ £1,365 (£403; £201) Stalls High

Form RPR
0-04 1 **Mystery Pips**[16] 524 6-8-9 45 (v) KimTinkler 6 56
(N Tinkler) *led 2f: chsd ldr: led 2 out: rdn out* **9/2**[2]
4006 2 2 **Percy Douglas**[16] 524 6-8-4 45 ow2 (bt[1]) AnnStokell(7) 13 51
(Miss A Stokell) *chsd ldrs: rdn over 1f out: styd on* **25/1**
0-20 3 1¼ **Eternally**[16] 524 4-8-9 45 (p) PaulFitzsimons 2 45
(R M H Cowell) *chsd ldrs: rdn over 1f out: styd on same pce ins fnl f* **8/1**
00-3 4 shd **Misty Princess**[19] 487 4-8-9 45 FrancisFerris 9 45
(M J Attwater) *chsd ldrs: outpcd 3f out: r.o ins fnl f* **13/2**[3]
000- 5 1 **Prime Recreation**[122] 6326 9-8-9 45 PatCosgrave 8 41
(P S Felgate) *w ldr tl led 3f out: hdd 2f out: edgd rt and no ex fnl f* **20/1**
0000 6 1½ **Katie Killane**[6] 613 4-8-9 40 AlanDaly 1 36
(M Wellings) *chsd ldrs: rdn over 1f out: no ex* **100/1**
-320 7 shd **On The Trail**[54] 146 9-8-9 45 (p) MatthewHenry 3 36
(D W Chapman) *chsd ldrs: rdn 1/2-way: wknd over 1f out* **13/2**[3]
-056 8 ¾ **Comic Tales**[57] 126 5-8-9 40 SimonWhitworth 10 33
(M Mullineaux) *s.s: outpcd* **8/1**
6000 9 1¼ **Ladies Knight**[7] 612 6-8-9 45 JamieMackay 7 29
(D Shaw) *dwlt: outpcd* **12/1**
000/ 10 1 **Our Chelsea Blue (USA)**[694] 1497 8-8-9 40 StephenCarson 4 26
(J R Jenkins) *hld up in tch: wknd 2f out* **33/1**
52-5 11 1 **Cark**[22] 465 8-8-6 45 (p) JasonEdmunds(3) 14 22
(J Balding) *chsd ldrs over 3f* **8/1**
0622 12 3 **A Teen**[6] 613 8-8-9 45 DaleGibson 12 12
(P Howling) *chsd ldrs: n.m.r and lost pl over 4f out: sn bhd* **4/1**[1]
-006 13 13 **Hellbent**[13] 547 7-8-6 45 RichardThomas(3) 11 —
(M Appleby) *dwlt: outpcd* **25/1**

60.81 secs (0.51) **Going Correction** +0.05s/f (Slow) 13 Ran SP% **122.3**
Speed ratings (Par 97):97,93,91,91,90 87,87,86,84,82 81,76,55
CSF £122.62 TOTE £5.20: £2.10, £6.20, £2.80; EX 107.10.
Owner Paglia & Fieno Racing **Bred** Michael Worton **Trained** Langton, N Yorks

FOCUS
A routine banded contest in which those that came down the centre of the track and raced up with the pace throughout held the advantage, as is the case at most meetings here. The form is straightforward and average for the grade.
Our Chelsea Blue(USA) Official explanation: jockey said mare hung right-handed and lost its action
A Teen Official explanation: jockey said horse was hampered shortly after start

634 BETDIRECT.CO.UK MAIDEN CLAIMING STKS 1m (F)
3:05 (3:05) (Class 7) 4-Y-0+ £1,365 (£403; £201) Stalls Low

Form RPR
4262 1 **Silsong (USA)**[6] 615 4-8-11 45 (v) DarryllHolland 3 46
(Miss Gay Kelleway) *sn pushed along and prom: outpcd 5f out: hdwy u.p 2f out: led wl ins fnl f: eased nr fin* **11/8**[1]
2-50 2 1¼ **Faithisflying**[54] 144 4-8-13 40 (b) TonyCulhane 5 46
(D W Chapman) *led: rdn over 1f out: edgd rt and hdd wl ins fnl f: unable qckn* **11/1**
-000 3 1¾ **Donya One**[6] 618 4-8-10 50 NickyMackay 4 39
(John A Harris) *chsd wnr: rdn over 2f out: styd on same pce fnl f* **25/1**
300- 4 2½ **Heathyards Joy**[76] 6680 5-8-11 45 ow1 NCallan 2 35
(R Hollinshead) *chsd ldrs: rdn 1/2-way: styd on same pce appr fnl f* **6/1**[3]
04-0 5 1½ **Danum**[30] 390 6-8-8 35 HugoFellows(7) 13 36
(R Hollinshead) *s.s: hdwy over 3f out: hung lft and wknd over 1f out* **20/1**
-000 6 2½ **Queue Up**[16] 527 4-9-3 40 SimonWhitworth 1 33
(A G Newcombe) *outpcd: hdwy over 4f out: wknd over 2f out* **12/1**
0505 7 1¼ **The Plainsman**[6] 615 4-9-3 35 AdrianTNicholls 11 31
(P W Hiatt) *mid-div: lost pl 1/2-way: n.d after* **12/1**
0 8 3 **Where's Sally**[31] 382 6-8-10 DaleGibson 9 18
(J Mackie) *chsd ldrs over 5f* **33/1**
0 9 8 **Montanah Jet**[14] 539 4-8-12 (t) MarcHalford(5) 6 9
(C N Kellett) *outpcd* **50/1**
0 10 4 **Sun Of The Glen (IRE)**[15] 534 4-8-12 HayleyTurner 12 —
(B D Leavy) *chsd ldrs 5f* **50/1**
00-0 11 10 **Cabopino Lad (USA)**[8] 600 4-9-1 40 (b[1]) RobertWinston 7 —
(Miss Tracy Waggott) *outpcd whn hung rt over 6f out: a bhd* **50/1**
00-0 12 2½ **Silloth Spirit**[54] 144 6-8-6 30 (p) AnnStokell(7) 8 —
(Mrs A M Naughton) *dwlt: outpcd* **100/1**
-025 13 26 **Tommytyler (IRE)**[6] 616 7-8-11 45 (t) DanielTudhope(3) 10 —
(D Carroll) *s.i.s: hld up: wknd and eased over 3f out* **7/2**[2]

1m 45.49s (0.89) **Going Correction** 0.0s/f (Stan) 13 Ran SP% **120.8**
Speed ratings (Par 97):95,93,92,89,88 85,84,81,73,69 59,56,30
CSF £17.73 TOTE £2.30: £1.30, £2.50, £5.50; EX 14.90.
Owner Miss Gay Kelleway Miss Nicky Briggs **Bred** P Scanlon **Trained** Exning, Suffolk

FOCUS
A bad race, although the first three were roughly to form, especially with the second-favourite Tommytyler running so badly. The leaders probably went off too quick and set the race up for the favourite.
Tommytyler(IRE) Official explanation: vet said gelding returned lame

635 TEXT "BETDIRECT" TO 88600 BANDED STKS 1m 6f (F)
3:45 (3:45) (Class 7) 4-Y-0+ £1,365 (£403; £201) Stalls Low

Form RPR
054- 1 **Elaala (USA)**[20] 5892 4-8-10 45 RobertWinston 5 54
(B D Leavy) *chsd ldrs: rdn to ld over 1f out: r.o* **8/1**
4-65 2 3½ **Blue Opal**[13] 549 4-8-13 48 MickyFenton 7 52
(Miss S E Hall) *trckd ldrs: plld hrd: led over 2f out: rdn and hdd over 1f out: no ex ins fnl f* **5/1**
/00- 3 ½ **Step Perfect (USA)**[36] 4446 5-9-5 50 NCallan 1 53
(G M Moore) *led: rdn and hdd over 2f out: styd on same pce fnl f* **14/1**
1320 4 2½ **Makarim (IRE)**[13] 549 10-9-5 50 (p) GeorgeBaker 6 50
(M R Bosley) *s.i.s: hld up: hdwy over 3f out: sn rdn: styng on same pce whn hung rt ins fnl f* **4/1**[2]
0-01 5 ¾ **Indian Chase**[6] 614 9-9-8 50 RichardThomas(3) 2 55
(Dr J R J Naylor) *hld up in tch: rdn over 2f out: styd on same pce* **7/2**[1]
2233 6 nk **Bulberry Hill**[30] 389 5-8-11 45 EdwardCreighton(3) 3 43
(R W Price) *hld up: racd keenly: hdwy over 3f out: wknd fnl f* **4/1**[2]
2522 7 ¾ **To Be Fare (IRE)**[16] 525 6-9-4 49 DeanMcKeown 4 46
(J Pearce) *plld hrd and prom: lost pl 7f out: bhd and rdn 4f out: no ch whn hmpd ins fnl f* **9/2**[3]
50-0 8 2 **Royal Lustre**[6] 615 5-9-0 45 HayleyTurner 8 39
(Robert Gray) *chsd ldrs: rdn and ev ch over 2f out: wknd over 1f out* **66/1**

3m 11.99s (2.39) **Going Correction** 0.0s/f (Stan)
WFA 4 from 5yo+ 4lb 8 Ran SP% **116.3**
Speed ratings (Par 97):93,91,90,89,88 88,88,87
CSF £48.38 TOTE £9.20: £2.20, £2.00, £4.30; EX 57.30.
Owner Moorland Racing **Bred** Shadwell Farm LLC **Trained** Forsbrook, Staffs
■ Stewards' Enquiry : George Baker caution: careless riding

FOCUS
No great pace on early here, which did not make this the test of stamina it might have been and the form is not solid, though the winner is unexposed.

636 FREE £75 WITH LITTLEWOODSCASINO.COM BANDED STKS 1m 3f (F)
4:30 (4:30) (Class 7) 4-Y-0+ £1,706 (£503; £252) Stalls Low

Form RPR
1-00 1 **Royal Axminster**[31] 379 11-9-3 50 RobertHavlin 11 55
(Mrs P N Dutfield) *chsd ldr: led over 5f out: drvn out* **13/2**
0-00 2 ¾ **Eforetta (GER)**[42] 261 4-8-11 40 VinceSlattery 9 49
(D J Wintle) *sn pushed along in rr: hdwy u.p over 1f out: r.o* **33/1**
1061 3 3 **Crusoe (IRE)**[6] 616 9-9-8 49 (b) BrianReilly 3 54
(A Sadik) *a.p: rdn to chse wnr 3f out: no ex fnl f* **12/1**
5-01 4 3½ **True To Yourself (USA)**[16] 525 5-9-3 50 (v) JoeFanning 12 44
(J G Given) *mid-div: hdwy over 3f out: styd on same pce fnl 2f* **4/1**[2]
0-35 5 2 **Galley Law**[28] 414 6-8-12 50 AndrewMullen(5) 6 41
(R Craggs) *mid-div: hdwy over 3f out: sn rdn: styd on same pce fnl 2f* **11/4**[1]
0-50 6 2 **Shami**[42] 259 7-8-13 46 TonyCulhane 10 34
(D W Chapman) *sn pushed along in rr: hdwy over 3f out: wknd 2f out* **12/1**
02-0 7 5 **Halcyon Magic**[29] 395 8-8-12 45 (b) JamieMackay 14 26
(M Wigham) *hld up: n.d* **20/1**
0 8 nk **Atakama (GER)**[32] 358 6-8-5 40 DonnaCaldwell(7) 8 25
(A D Nolan, Ire) *led to 1/2-way: wknd 4f out* **20/1**
1-50 9 1¾ **Kentucky Bullet (USA)**[50] 172 10-8-13 46 SimonWhitworth 4 24
(A G Newcombe) *hld up in tch: rdn and wknd over 1f out* **8/1**
00-0 10 ¾ **Dishdasha (IRE)**[16] 525 4-8-11 45 RobertWinston 2 21
(C R Dore) *trckd ldrs: rdn over 2f out: wknd over 1f out* **25/1**
0-15 11 2 **Whenwillitwin**[21] 472 5-9-2 49 (p) LPKeniry 7 22
(J S Moore) *chsd ldrs over 8f* **11/2**[3]
4-06 12 dist **Trackattack**[7] 609 4-8-11 45 AdrianTNicholls 1 —
(P Howling) *chsd ldrs: rdn 8f out: wknd over 4f out* **50/1**
600/ 13 3½ **Look No More**[324] 6269 5-8-7 45 MarcHalford(5) 13 —
(W G M Turner) *s.i.s: rdn and wknd 1/2-way* **66/1**

2m 28.03s (-0.87) **Going Correction** 0.0s/f (Stan)
WFA 4 from 5yo+ 1lb 13 Ran SP% **121.6**
Speed ratings (Par 97):103,102,100,97,96 94,91,90,89,89 87,—,—
CSF £217.15 TOTE £7.30: £2.40, £19.50, £3.70; EX 271.70.
Owner Axminster Carpets Ltd **Bred** Meon Valley Stud **Trained** Axmouth, Devon

FOCUS
A fair event of its type and a very creditable winning time for a race like this. The first two give the form a sound look.
Kentucky Bullet(USA) Official explanation: jockey said gelding had no more to give

637 BET NOW AT BETDIRECT.CO.UK TRI-BANDED STKS 6f (F)
5:10 (5:11) (Class 7) 3-Y-0 £1,365 (£403; £201) Stalls Low

Form RPR
4000 1 **Teddy Monty (IRE)**[8] 594 3-8-12 45 (b[1]) NCallan 7 47
(M Quinn) *s.i.s: sn w ldrs: led over 2f out: edgd lft: rdn clr* **7/2**[2]
000- 2 3 **Silver Nun**[281] 2337 3-8-12 45 DavidAllan 9 38
(T D Easterby) *sn outpcd: hdwy u.p over 2f out: no ch w wnr* **16/1**
5060 3 hd **Lasting Love**[22] 466 3-8-12 45 (b[1]) DarryllHolland 3 37
(C R Dore) *chsd ldrs: rdn over 2f out: styd on same pce fnl f* **8/1**[3]
0-05 4 ¾ **Yassooma (IRE)**[6] 617 3-8-12 45 (b) JamieMackay 11 35
(T J Pitt) *s.i.s: outpcd: r.o ins fnl f: nrst fin* **16/1**
-002 5 ¾ **Midge's Girl (IRE)**[16] 528 3-8-12 45 (v) PaulFessey 10 33
(Mrs A Duffield) *outpcd: hdwy and hung lft over 1f out: nvr nrr* **7/2**[2]

06-0 **6** *1* **Musette (IRE)**[14] 544 3-8-9 45....................................(p) AdamKirby(3) 1 30
(C G Cox) *sn outpcd: rdn over 2f out: nvr nrr* **14/1**
0000 **7** *1 ½* **Beginners Luck (IRE)**[16] 528 3-7-9 35.............. DanielleMcCreery(7) 8 15
(D Carroll) *prom: lost pl over 4f out: n.d after* **40/1**
5205 **8** *3 ½* **My Reflection**[10] 577 3-8-9 45.. PatrickMathers(3) 6 15
(D Shaw) *hld up in tch: rdn and wknd over 1f out* **2/1**[1]
-005 **9** *5* **Stoneacre Girl (IRE)**[21] 477 3-8-9 40 ow2....................... GylesParkin 4 —
(Peter Grayson) *s.i.s: plld hrd and led 5f out: rdn and hdd over 2f out: wknd over 1f out* **11/1**
00-0 **10** *4* **Moraadi**[61] 102 3-8-2 30.. MatthewHenry 12 —
(D W Chapman) *prom over 3f* **66/1**
00-0 **11** *½* **Lough Arrow (IRE)**[16] 528 3-8-2 30................................ DaleGibson 5 —
(P S Felgate) *led 1f: chsd ldrs tl wknd wl over 1f out* **50/1**

1m 18.19s (1.29) **Going Correction** 0.0s/f (Stan) 11 Ran SP% **121.5**
Speed ratings (Par 92):91,87,86,85,84 83,81,76,70,64 64
CSF £59.88 TOTE £4.70: £1.50, £5.00, £2.20; EX 72.80.
Owner Paul Montgomery & Brian Morton **Bred** Mrs G W Robinson **Trained** Newmarket, Suffolk

FOCUS
Moderate fare but the winner was well supported and showed improvement to score.
Midge's Girl(IRE) Official explanation: jockey said filly hung left throughout
My Reflection Official explanation: trainer said gelding was unsuited by the fibresand
Stoneacre Girl(IRE) Official explanation: jockey said filly hung right-handed

638 BETDIRECT FREEPHONE 0800 211 222 BANDED STKS 7f (F)
5:40 (5:40) (Class 7) 3-Y-0+ £1,365 (£403; £201) Stalls Low

Form RPR
0400 **1** **Wilford Maverick (IRE)**[6] 613 4-9-0 45....................(v) FrancisFerris 11 52
(M J Attwater) *chsd ldrs: nt clr run and swtchd lft over 2f out: led 2f out: out: rdn and hung rt fnl f: eased nr fin* **14/1**
-000 **2** *¾* **La Musique**[8] 600 4-9-0 40... MatthewHenry 7 50
(P J McBride) *a.p: rdn to chse wnr over 1f out: edgd lft: styd on* **33/1**
0-00 **3** *1 ¼* **Rocky Reppin**[6] 616 6-8-11 45...........................(v) JasonEdmunds(3) 12 47
(J Balding) *s.i.s: hdwy 1/2-way: r.o ins fnl f: nt trble ldrs* **15/2**
0353 **4** *½* **Mister Aziz (IRE)**[6] 618 4-9-0 45...........................(b) StephenCarson 14 46
(J R Jenkins) *chsd ldrs: rdn adn edgd lft over 1f out: styd on same pce fnl f* **3/1**[1]
5-60 **5** *3* **Dane's Rock (IRE)**[8] 600 4-9-0 45.........................(p) SimonWhitworth 9 38
(M S Saunders) *mid-div: rdn over 2f out: nt trble ldrs* **10/1**
0-00 **6** *¾* **Sundried Tomato**[50] 178 7-9-0 45.............................(p) JamieMackay 2 36
(D W Chapman) *disp ld: ev ch 2f out: wknd ins fnl f* **12/1**
0030 **7** *2* **Elms Schoolboy**[6] 613 4-9-0 45..................................(b) DaleGibson 10 31
(P Howling) *s.i.s: rdn 1/2-way: n.d* **5/1**[2]
6400 **8** *½* **Ballyrush (IRE)**[16] 527 6-9-0 40.. AlanDaly 1 29
(Miss D A McHale) *led 5f: sn wknd* **16/1**
5040 **9** *5* **Cleveland Way**[16] 529 6-9-0 40...............................(v) LeeEnstone 4 16
(D Carroll) *s.i.s: hdwy over 4f out: rdn and wknd over 2f out* **33/1**
2-00 **10** *nk* **Inescapable (USA)**[10] 581 5-9-0 45................................. PaulFessey 5 15
(A W Carroll) *mid-div: effrt 1/2-way: wknd over 2f out* **40/1**
0065 **11** *1 ½* **Venetian Princess (IRE)**[26] 427 4-9-0 40...................... GylesParkin 6 12
(P Howling) *sn outpcd* **14/1**
0000 **12** *3* **Awarding**[25] 440 6-8-11 45................................(vt) RichardThomas(3) 13 4
(Dr J R J Naylor) *rrd s: a in rr* **12/1**
00-0 **13** *11* **Huxley (IRE)**[56] 127 7-9-0 45..(bt) VinceSlattery 8 —
(D J Wintle) *s.s: a bhd* **6/1**[3]
300- **14** *28* **Super Canyon**[126] 6291 8-9-0 35.............................(vt) MichaelTebbutt 3 —
(J Pearce) *s.i.s: sn outpcd* **20/1**

1m 30.83s (0.03) **Going Correction** 0.0s/f (Stan) 14 Ran SP% **124.5**
Speed ratings (Par 97):99,98,96,96,92 91,89,89,83,82 81,77,65,33
CSF £431.02 TOTE £27.30: £6.30, £6.60, £3.30; EX 684.20 Place 6 £5,244.98, Place 5 £1,480.26.
Owner Brooklands Racing **Bred** Gerard Burke **Trained** Wysall, Notts

FOCUS
Moderate form but the race was run at a fair pace and the form seems sound enough rated around the principals.
Elms Schoolboy Official explanation: jockey said gelding was slowly away
Super Canyon Official explanation: jockey said gelding lost its action
T/Plt: £8,771.50 to a £1 stake. Pool: £42,055.30. 3.50 winning tickets. T/Qpdt: £582.30 to a £1 stake. Pool: £4,092.50. 5.20 winning tickets. CR

626 WOLVERHAMPTON (A.W) (L-H)
Wednesday, March 15

OFFICIAL GOING: Standard
Wind: Fine Weather: Moderate against

639 BETDIRECT FREEPHONE 0800 211 222 H'CAP (DIV I) 7f 32y(P)
1:45 (1:46) (Class 5) (0-75,75) 4-Y-0+ £2,914 (£867; £433; £216) Stalls High

Form RPR
1203 **1** **Mystic Man (FR)**[11] 585 8-9-4 75................................(b) PaulHanagan 3 84
(I W McInnes) *a.p: rdn to ld 1f out: jst hld on* **9/1**
2126 **2** *nk* **Glad Big (GER)**[25] 451 4-9-2 73.................................... ShaneKelly 5 85+
(J A Osborne) *s.i.s: hld up and bhd: hdwy fnl f: fin wl: jst failed* **5/2**[1]
0031 **3** *1 ½* **Distant Country (USA)**[11] 581 7-8-4 61..................(p) FrancisNorton 4 65
(K R Burke) *hld up in mid-div: hdwy on ins over 2f out: rdn wl over 1f out: r.o one pce fnl f* **10/1**
2052 **4** *nk* **Lincolneurocruiser**[4] 632 4-8-12 72........................ SaleemGolam(3) 7 76
(Mrs N Macauley) *hld up: hdwy 2f out: rdn over 1f out: one pce fnl f* **4/1**[2]
46-6 **5** *½* **Kew The Music**[13] 559 6-8-6 63.................................... ChrisCatlin 10 65
(M R Channon) *s.i.s: bhd: rdn over 2f out: swtchd lft over 1f out: hdwy fnl f: nt rch ldrs* **13/2**[3]
6023 **6** *nk* **Hand Chime**[11] 575 9-7-13 61.................................. JamesDoyle(5) 8 62
(Ernst Oertel) *w ldr: rdn and ev ch 1f out: one pce* **12/1**
-000 **7** *¾* **Pamir (IRE)**[13] 559 4-9-2 73...(p) GeorgeBaker 2 73
(P R Chamings) *hld up and bhd: rdn and hdwy on outside over 1f out: no imp fnl f* **12/1**
0-21 **8** *½* **Up Tempo (IRE)**[19] 501 8-8-9 66.......................................(b) NCallan 11 64
(K A Ryan) *t.k.h: prom: rdn over 2f out: wknd ins fnl f* **13/2**[3]
0-40 **9** *½* **Tyrone Sam**[41] 276 4-8-8 65...(b) JohnEgan 1 62
(K A Ryan) *hld up towards rr: hdwy on ins over 1f out: nt clr run ins fnl f: n.d* **8/1**
51-0 **10** *1* **Forest Of Love**[62] 101 4-8-10 67..................................... DaleGibson 6 61
(M W Easterby) *led: rdn and hdd 1f out: wknd ins fnl f* **33/1**
2156 **11** *2* **Blue Knight (IRE)**[37] 316 7-9-0 71.......................... AdrianTNicholls 12 60
(D Nicholls) *hld up in mid-div: hdwy over 3f out: rdn and ev ch over 2f out: wknd over 1f out* **20/1**
0-00 **12** *1 ½* **Celtic Thunder**[46] 225 5-8-4 61 oh1.............................. NickyMackay 9 46
(T J Etherington) *hld up in tch: wknd wl over 1f out* **33/1**

1m 29.73s (-0.67) **Going Correction** 0.0s/f (Stan) 12 Ran SP% **131.5**
Speed ratings (Par 103):103,102,100,100,100 99,98,98,97,96 94,92
CSF £34.71 CT £248.25 TOTE £10.60: £3.20, £1.60, £4.00; EX 46.10.
Owner Dronsfield Mercedes Ltd **Bred** Gainsborough Stud Management Ltd **Trained** Catwick, E Yorks

FOCUS
An even pace to this ordinary handicap and the winning time was 0.27 seconds slower than the second division. The third and fourth help set the standard for the form.
Glad Big(GER) Official explanation: jockey said, regarding the running and riding, his orders were to cover gelding up and relax it as it can be keen, adding that this was his first ride on gelding who the trainer said is not straightforward and has a tendency to pull itself up when getting to the front; he said there was a slow early pace, he did not get the run of the race, and when the split eventually came he could not peg back the winner
Lincolneurocruiser Official explanation: trainer said gelding was struck into

640 PLAY NOW AT BETDIRECT.CO.UK CLAIMING STKS 1m 1f 103y(P)
2:15 (2:15) (Class 6) 4-Y-0+ £2,730 (£806; £403) Stalls Low

Form RPR
030- **1** **Vicious Knight**[179] 5285 8-9-7 86.................................. AdrianTNicholls 6 79
(D Nicholls) *set modest pce: rdn clr 2f out: r.o wl* **11/2**[3]
3164 **2** *3* **Blue Patrick**[19] 498 6-8-13 76.. NCallan 11 65
(K A Ryan) *plld hrd: in tch: rdn over 2f out: chsd wnr wl over 1f out: one pce* **1/1**[1]
-303 **3** *1 ¼* **Mission Affirmed (USA)**[29] 410 5-9-3 70.................... DarryllHolland 7 67
(R A Harris) *t.k.h: chsd wnr: rdn over 2f out: one pce* **5/1**[2]
0-05 **4** *nk* **Nimello (USA)**[44] 251 10-9-3 65................................ FergusSweeney 4 66
(A G Newcombe) *hld up: stdy hdwy over 5f out: rdn over 2f out: one pce* **10/1**
0633 **5** *4* **Scotty's Future (IRE)**[11] 582 8-9-0 58............... SilvestreDeSousa(3) 1 58
(D Nicholls) *hld up and bhd: rdn and hdwy wl over 1f out: nvr trbld ldrs* **16/1**
33-0 **6** *hd* **Weet A Head (IRE)**[69] 48 5-9-3 61......................... GrahamGibbons 3 58
(R Hollinshead) *hld up towards rr: rdn 4f out: hdwy over 1f out: nvr nr ldrs* **8/1**
4/0- **7** *5* **Annals**[38] 1699 4-8-8 76... JohnEgan 9 40
(R C Guest) *s.i.s: rdn over 3f out: sme hdwy on ins over 2f out: no further prog* **16/1**
6/60 **8** *3* **Jewel Of India**[28] 417 7-8-9 60.................................(b) RobertWinston 5 35
(Mrs A L M King) *hld up in tch: rdn over 2f out: wknd wl over 1f out* **25/1**
06-0 **9** *2 ½* **Mr Rein (IRE)**[14] 549 4-9-3 60....................................(t) DeanMcKeown 2 38
(J Parkes) *bhd fnl 4f* **33/1**
00-0 **10** *½* **Beauchamp Tiger**[29] 414 4-8-9 60..........................(t) FrancisNorton 10 29
(J Parkes) *plld hrd: sn in tch: rdn and wknd 3f out* **33/1**
0/ **11** *3 ½* **Kussharro**[536] 5803 5-8-7 ....(t) SimonWhitworth 13 20
(Mrs L J Young) *prom: rdn over 2f out: wknd wl over 1f out* **66/1**
0-00 **12** *2 ½* **Worth Abbey**[12] 568 4-8-7 52...(v) ChrisCatlin 8 16
(M Appleby) *rdn 4f out: a bhd* **33/1**

2m 3.81s (1.19) **Going Correction** 0.0s/f (Stan) 12 Ran SP% **128.2**
Speed ratings (Par 101):94,91,90,89,86 86,81,79,76,76 73,71
CSF £11.87 TOTE £8.80: £2.10, £1.10, £2.10; EX 14.60.Blue Patrick was claimed by Joe McCarthy for £8,000.
Owner The McCauley Boys **Bred** Limestone Stud **Trained** Sessay, N Yorks

FOCUS
A pedestrian early pace resulted in a moderate winning time. The winner was given a well-judged ride, but the form still looks suspect and very few ever got into it, so has been rated negatively around the fourth and fifth.

641 BETDIRECT ON 0800 211 222 H'CAP 1m 141y(P)
2:50 (2:50) (Class 5) (0-75,75) 4-Y-0+ £3,238 (£963; £481; £240) Stalls Low

Form RPR
1-11 **1** **Merrymadcap (IRE)**[19] 505 4-9-1 72........................... FrancisNorton 1 81
(M Blanshard) *hld up in mid-div: hdwy 2f out: rdn to ld ins fnl f: r.o* **3/1**[2]
4005 **2** *1* **Elrafa Mujahid**[19] 504 4-8-8 68...........................(p) SaleemGolam(3) 4 75
(Ernst Oertel) *a.p: rdn 2f out: ev ch ins fnl f: nt qckn* **14/1**
3402 **3** *½* **Dragon Slayer (IRE)**[12] 571 4-9-1 72.. NCallan 6 78
(M J Attwater) *hld up in mid-div: hdwy 2f out: rdn to ld and wandered 1f out: sn hdd: nt qckn* **5/1**[3]
6022 **4** *hd* **Libre**[37] 313 6-8-12 69.. JimmyFortune 8 75
(F Jordan) *hld up towards rr: rdn 3f out: hdwy on outside over 1f out: kpt on ins fnl f* **14/1**
-020 **5** *shd* **Ground Rules (USA)**[12] 567 4-8-10 74.................... JosephWalsh(7) 9 79
(V Smith) *w ldr: led after 1f: rdn and hdd 1f out: no ex* **25/1**
45S- **6** *nk* **Hatch A Plan (IRE)**[104] 5553 5-8-9 66............................. ChrisCatlin 5 71
(Mrs A J Hamilton-Fairley) *hld up and bhd: rdn and hdwy over 1f out: one pce fnl f* **50/1**
-003 **7** *1 ¾* **Anduril**[11] 578 5-9-2 73..(b) RobertWinston 10 74
(Miss M E Rowland) *stdd s: sn swtchd lft: hld up and bhd: rdn and hdwy over 1f out: swtchd lft jst ins fnl f: no imp* **16/1**
0515 **8** *hd* **Hurricane Coast**[25] 452 7-9-1 72............................(b) DarryllHolland 7 73
(K McAuliffe) *prom: ev ch over 2f out: sn rdn: wknd ins fnl f* **16/1**
12-3 **9** *¾* **First Show**[13] 559 4-9-4 75.. ShaneKelly 11 74
(J Noseda) *hld up towards rr: hdwy over 3f out: rdn over 2f out: wknd ins fnl f* **11/4**[1]
-406 **10** *8* **True Night**[11] 585 9-8-10 67.. AdrianTNicholls 2 49
(D Nicholls) *led 1f: prom: rdn over 3f out: wknd wl over 1f out* **20/1**
-350 **11** *6* **Connotation**[11] 585 4-9-0 71.................................... SimonWhitworth 13 41
(A G Newcombe) *rdn 3f out: a bhd* **25/1**
2-1 **12** *6* **John Charles (IRE)**[16] 531 4-8-13 70................................... JohnEgan 3 27
(D R C Elsworth) *s.i.s: hld up towards rr: rdn over 4f out: eased whn no ch fnl 2f* **6/1**

1m 50.43s (-1.33) **Going Correction** 0.0s/f (Stan) 12 Ran SP% **122.1**
Speed ratings (Par 103):105,104,103,103,103 103,101,101,100,93 88,82
CSF £44.09 CT £214.36 TOTE £3.60: £1.50, £6.60, £2.50; EX 78.80.
Owner Mrs N L Young **Bred** Wickfield Farm Partnership **Trained** Upper Lambourn, Berks

FOCUS
A solid pace for this handicap even though there was little covering the first six at the line. The form looks straightforward and sound rated through the placed horses.
Hurricane Coast Official explanation: jockey said gelding hung left-handed in the home straight
First Show Official explanation: jockey said gelding hung right-handed throughout
True Night Official explanation: jockey said gelding hung left-handed in home straight
John Charles(IRE) Official explanation: jockey said gelding hung left-handed down the back straight

642 FIRST PAST THE POST AT BETDIRECT (S) STKS 1m 141y(P)
3:30 (3:30) (Class 6) 3-Y-O £2,388 (£705; £352) Stalls Low

Form RPR

000- 1 **Royal Amnesty**[243] 3509 3-8-12 57 ... OscarUrbina 11 59
(G C H Chung) *hld up and bhd: hdwy 2f out: led wl ins fnl f: r.o wl* **8/1**

2315 2 1 1/2 **Countrywide Belle**[9] 604 3-8-13 59 ...(b) NCallan 2 57
(K A Ryan) *led: rdn 2f out: hdd and nt qckn wl ins fnl f* **10/11**[1]

4653 3 1 3/4 **She Whispers (IRE)**[9] 598 3-8-13 52 ... RobertWinston 7 53
(W M Brisbourne) *hld up and bhd: hdwy whn nt clr run and swtchd rt wl over 1f out: r.o ins fnl f* **9/2**[2]

0-00 4 nk **Rock Of Cloonavery (IRE)**[22] 475 3-8-12 61 ... J-PGuillambert 3 52
(S C Williams) *plld hrd: chsd ldr: ev ch over 2f out: sn rdn: one pce fnl f* **11/2**[3]

0004 5 1/2 **Mon Petite Amour**[9] 595 3-8-7 45 ... FrankieMcDonald 5 46
(D W P Arbuthnot) *s.i.s: hld up: hdwy whn swtchd lft and nt clr run on ins wl over 1f out: kpt on ins fnl f* **12/1**

60 6 3 **Dinner Dance**[13] 554 3-8-7 ...(b[1]) NickyMackay 1 39
(W J Haggas) *t.k.h: prom: rdn over 2f out: wknd over 1f out* **16/1**

5-02 7 3/4 **Skin Sure Thing**[19] 499 3-8-7 45 ...(v) MatthewHenry 6 38
(A D Smith) *hld up: sn in tch: rdn over 3f out: wknd over 1f out* **20/1**

0-50 8 1 1/2 **Sapphire Storm (IRE)**[9] 598 3-8-0 48 ...(tp) KirstyMilczarek[(7)] 8 35
(Miss D A McHale) *rdn over 3f out: a bhd* **40/1**

2-00 9 2 **Solo Star**[8] 609 3-8-13 52 ...(b[1]) TomEaves 4 36
(Miss J A Camacho) *t.k.h: in tch: wknd over 2f out* **25/1**

03 10 20 **Archidona (FR)**[19] 499 3-8-13 52 ...(v[1]) MartinDwyer 12 —
(M Quinn) *hld up: hdwy on outside over 4f out: wknd over 2f out: t.o* **16/1**

60-0 11 5 **Baytown Valentina**[9] 594 3-8-13 53 ... TonyCulhane 10 —
(P Howling) *prom tl wknd over 2f out: t.o* **33/1**

1m 52.97s (1.21) **Going Correction** 0.0s/f (Stan) 11 Ran SP% **130.5**
Speed ratings (Par 96):94,92,91,90,90 87,87,85,83,66 61
CSF £16.89 TOTE £11.60: £2.00, £1.20, £1.70; EX 34.70.The winner was bought in for 7,500gns. Countrywide Belle was claimed by J. L. Flint for £6,000.
Owner Willie Leung **Bred** Brick Kiln Stud, Mrs L Hicks And Partners **Trained** Newmarket, Suffolk

FOCUS
A run-of-the-mill seller and not a great pace on which caused a few to take a hold. However, the form looks sound enough with the third, fourth and fifth close to their marks.
Mon Petite Amour ◆ Official explanation: jockey said filly was unlucky in running

643 BETDIRECT.CO.UK H'CAP 2m 119y(P)
4:15 (4:15) (Class 6) (0-65,62) 4-Y-0+ £2,388 (£705; £352) Stalls Low

Form RPR

6533 1 **Lady Pilot**[9] 589 4-8-12 **58** ...(v[1]) RichardThomas[(3)] 3 66
(Dr J R J Naylor) *a.p: wnt 2nd 4f out: rdn to ld 2f out: hung lft over 1f out: styd on* **7/1**

0-03 2 1 1/4 **Rare Coincidence**[9] 603 5-8-12 **53** ...(p) DNolan[(3)] 11 60
(R F Fisher) *led: rdn and hdd 2f out: nt qckn ins fnl f* **9/1**

60-6 3 3/4 **Screen Test**[11] 574 4-8-10 **58** ... JamesDoyle[(5)] 9 64
(B G Powell) *hld up in mid-div: hdwy on outside over 3f out: styd on ins fnl f* **14/1**

200- 4 5 **Madiba**[154] 5837 7-9-8 **60** ... TonyCulhane 1 60
(P Howling) *hld up in mid-div: rdn over 3f out: hdwy over 1f out: nvr trbld ldrs* **20/1**

3104 5 nk **York Cliff**[9] 600 8-8-12 **50** ... RobertWinston 6 50
(W M Brisbourne) *hld up in mid-div: hdwy over 1f out: n.d* **6/1**[3]

3523 6 2 1/2 **Little Richard (IRE)**[12] 570 7-9-4 **56** ...(p) AlanDaly 5 53
(M Wellings) *hld up in mid-div: short-lived effrt 3f out* **5/1**[2]

0-10 7 nk **Cumbrian Knight (IRE)**[40] 283 8-9-10 **62** ... PaulHanagan 12 58
(J M Jefferson) *s.i.s: hld up and bhd: stdy hdwy 6f out: rdn over 3f out: wknd over 2f out* **6/1**[3]

16-0 8 2 **Aristi (IRE)**[9] 589 5-9-6 **58** ...(p) MartinDwyer 7 52
(M Quinn) *hld up in tch: rdn over 3f out: wknd over 2f out* **10/1**

/00- 9 shd **Mount Benger**[125] 5281 6-9-6 **58** ...(p) NCallan 4 52
(Mrs A J Hamilton-Fairley) *a bhd* **20/1**

60-0 10 1 3/4 **Townsville (IRE)**[11] 574 4-9-1 **58** ... ChrisCatlin 2 50
(E J O'Neill) *rdn 7f out: a towards rr* **20/1**

4152 11 7 **Blue Hills**[12] 570 5-9-8 **60** ... DarrenWilliams 10 43
(P W Hiatt) *hld up in tch: wknd 3f out* **7/2**[1]

S0-0 12 14 **Tilla**[15] 545 6-9-7 **59** ...(be) J-PGuillambert 13 25
(Mrs A J Hamilton-Fairley) *chsd ldr tl rdn 4f out: wknd 3f out* **50/1**

4/00 13 7 **Sono**[26] 443 9-9-3 **55** ...(p) TomEaves 8 13
(P D Niven) *hld up in tch: rdn 7f out: sn lost pl* **33/1**

3m 44.0s (0.87) **Going Correction** 0.0s/f (Stan)
WFA 4 from 5yo+ 5lb 13 Ran SP% **124.9**
Speed ratings (Par 101):97,96,96,93,93 92,92,91,91,90 87,80,77
CSF £66.75 CT £881.64 TOTE £8.20: £2.40, £3.40, £5.20; EX 73.20.
Owner W Wood **Bred** Genesis Green Stud Ltd **Trained** Shrewton, Wilts

FOCUS
A modest pace for this handicap and not the test of stamina that it might have been. The best place to be in a race like this was near the front and the first two home were in the leading trio throughout. Very few ever got into this.
Blue Hills Official explanation: trainer said, regarding the poor form show, gelding may have been feeling the effects of a long campaign

644 BETDIRECT FREEPHONE 0800 211 222 H'CAP (DIV II) 7f 32y(P)
4:55 (4:56) (Class 5) (0-75,75) 4-Y-0+ £2,914 (£867; £433; £216) Stalls High

Form RPR

06-0 1 **Mandarin Spirit (IRE)**[11] 575 6-8-10 **67** ...(b) OscarUrbina 10 77
(G C H Chung) *hld up and bhd: hdwy over 2f out: rdn to ld ins fnl f: drvn out* **20/1**

5-10 2 1 **Stoic Leader (IRE)**[70] 36 6-8-13 **70** ... FrancisNorton 4 77
(R F Fisher) *chsd ldr: led 2f out: sn rdn: hdd ins fnl f: nt qckn* **4/1**[2]

6-00 3 nk **Hit's Only Money (IRE)**[20] 489 6-8-8 **65** ...(t) DeanMcKeown 2 71
(J Pearce) *s.i.s: hdwy over 2f out: r.o ins fnl f* **7/1**

515- 4 2 **Ballyhurry (USA)**[28] 5491 9-8-4 **61** oh1 ... NickyMackay 5 62
(J S Goldie) *hld up: hdwy over 2f out: kpt on ins fnl f* **6/1**[3]

150- 5 1 1/4 **Nan Jan**[86] 6622 4-9-2 **73** ...(t) SimonWhitworth 8 71
(R Ingram) *bhd: hdwy fr over 1f out: nvr nrr* **12/1**

-030 6 hd **Onlytime Will Tell**[11] 585 8-8-9 **66** ... RobertWinston 11 63
(D Nicholls) *hld up: hdwy 2f out: rdn over 2f out: wknd wl ins fnl f* **12/1**

040- 7 3/4 **Lord Of The East**[152] 5874 7-9-1 **75** ... PatrickMathers[(3)] 3 70
(I W McInnes) *led: rdn and hdd 2f out: wknd ins fnl f* **13/2**

1315 8 2 **Arnie De Burgh**[25] 451 4-9-1 **72** ... ShaneKelly 1 62
(D J Daly) *prom: rdn over 2f out: wknd ins fnl f* **3/1**[1]

-000 9 5 **Desert Lightning (IRE)**[11] 585 4-8-9 **66** ...(v[1]) PatCosgrave 6 43
(K R Burke) *prom 4f* **25/1**

000- 10 3 **Grand Ideas**[280] 2385 7-8-4 **61** oh6 ... DaleGibson 9 30
(G J Smith) *bhd fnl 3f* **33/1**

0-15 11 7 **Orpendonna (IRE)**[19] 505 4-7-13 **61** ...(p) AndrewMullen[(5)] 7 12
(K A Ryan) *prom tl wknd over 2f out* **8/1**

1m 29.46s (-0.94) **Going Correction** 0.0s/f (Stan) 11 Ran SP% **123.2**
Speed ratings (Par 103):105,103,103,101,99 99,98,96,90,87 79
CSF £101.20 CT £653.25 TOTE £33.10: £5.40, £2.70, £2.20; EX 123.10.
Owner Peter Tsim **Bred** W Haggas And W Jarvis **Trained** Newmarket, Suffolk

FOCUS
A fair pace in this handicap and the winning time was 0.27 seconds faster than the first division. The form is not rock solid but could be alright, rated around the fourth and seventh.
Hit's Only Money(IRE) Official explanation: jockey said gelding missed the break

645 TEXT "BETDIRECT" TO 88600 MAIDEN STKS 5f 216y(P)
5:30 (5:32) (Class 5) 3-Y-O £3,886 (£1,156; £577; £288) Stalls Low

Form RPR

05-2 1 **Total Impact**[15] 540 3-9-3 76 ... DarrylHolland 2 74+
(C A Cyzer) *a.p: led jst over 1f out: pushed clr ins fnl f* **4/5**[1]

5 2 3 1/2 **Kellys Dream (IRE)**[15] 540 3-8-12 ... FrancisNorton 7 58
(M Quinn) *led: rdn an hdd jst over 1f out: one pce* **16/1**

35-0 3 1 3/4 **Amygdala**[28] 418 3-8-12 68 ... OscarUrbina 8 53
(M Botti) *hld up towards rr: hdwy 2f out: kpt on ins fnl f* **20/1**

5-4 4 1/2 **Keelings Donabate**[53] 165 3-9-3 ... PatCosgrave 3 57
(K R Burke) *hld up in mid-div: hdwy on ins 2f out: one pce fnl f* **9/1**[3]

4- 5 hd **Just Tallulah**[229] 3908 3-8-7 ... JamesDoyle[(5)] 11 51
(N P Littmoden) *a.p: rdn and one pce fnl 2f* **25/1**

6 3/4 **Lady Becks (IRE)** 3-8-5 ... TolleyDean[(7)] 10 49
(R A Harris) *t.k.h: chsd ldr: ev ch over 2f out: sn rdn: wknd wl ins fnl f* **33/1**

7 1 **Mandarin Lady** 3-8-12 ... TomEaves 4 46
(Miss J A Camacho) *s.s: nvr nr ldrs* **25/1**

8 shd **Electron Pulse** 3-8-12 ... NickyMackay 1 45
(J S Goldie) *n.d* **25/1**

9 nk **Danethorpe (IRE)** 3-9-0 ... PatrickMathers[(3)] 5 49
(D Shaw) *s.s: a bhd* **33/1**

42-0 10 hd **Radius**[67] 60 3-9-3 80 ... SteveDrowne 9 49
(H Morrison) *hld up in tch: rdn over 2f out: wknd wl over 1f out* **9/4**[2]

206 11 shd **Stamford Street (IRE)**[11] 579 3-8-10 62 ... JosephWalsh[(7)] 12 49
(J S Moore) *s.i.s: plld hrd: sn prom: wknd wl over 1f out* **33/1**

04- 12 8 **Inca Soldier (FR)**[139] 6121 3-9-3 ... JohnEgan 6 25
(R C Guest) *plld hrd: sn prom: wknd wl over 1f out* **11/1**

1m 16.25s (0.44) **Going Correction** 0.0s/f (Stan) 12 Ran SP% **135.7**
Speed ratings (Par 98):97,92,90,89,89 88,86,86,86,85 85,75
CSF £19.92 TOTE £1.90: £1.10, £3.80, £2.90; EX 29.00.
Owner Mrs Charles Cyzer **Bred** C A Cyzer **Trained** Maplehurst, W Sussex

FOCUS
A routine maiden run at just an ordinary pace and very few got into it. The form is far from solid and the winner is probably the best guide to the level.
Inca Soldier(FR) Official explanation: jockey said gelding ran too free early on

646 PLAY NOW AT BETDIRECTCASINO.COM H'CAP 5f 216y(P)
6:00 (6:00) (Class 6) (0-65,64) 3-Y-O £2,388 (£705; £352) Stalls Low

Form RPR

0-52 1 **Danetime Lord (IRE)**[11] 577 3-8-7 **53** ...(p) JohnEgan 2 72
(K A Ryan) *a.p: wnt 2nd 3f out: rdn to ld over 1f out: r.o* **2/1**[1]

0262 2 1 1/4 **Smile For Us**[9] 598 3-8-7 **53** ...(b) BrianReilly 9 68
(C Drew) *led: rdn and hdd over 1f out: nt qckn ins fnl f* **16/1**

061 3 4 **Buzzin'Boyzee (IRE)**[9] 598 3-8-10 **56** 6ex ... JimmyFortune 11 59
(P D Evans) *outpcd and bhd: hdwy on outside over 1f out: r.o ins fnl f* **15/2**[3]

06-5 4 nk **Musicmaestroplease (IRE)**[48] 195 3-8-9 **55** ... DeanMcKeown 12 57
(S Parr) *mid-div: hdwy over 1f out: kpt on ins fnl f* **33/1**

500- 5 1/2 **Arculinge**[149] 5945 3-8-12 **58** ... FrancisNorton 5 59+
(M Blanshard) *bhd tl sme hdwy over 2f out: kpt on ins fnl f* **8/1**

50-3 6 3/4 **Trombone Tom**[65] 68 3-9-3 **63** ... DarrenWilliams 3 61
(J R Norton) *prom tl rdn and wknd over 2f out* **4/1**[2]

-130 7 nk **Mister Incredible**[21] 481 3-9-3 **63** ...(p) DarrylHolland 6 60
(C A Dwyer) *chsd ldr 3f: sn wknd* **12/1**

2025 8 1 **Diktalex (IRE)**[9] 598 3-8-7 **60** ...(t) StacyRenwick[(7)] 1 54
(M J Attwater) *bhd: short-lived effrt over 2f out* **14/1**

006- 9 nk **Bold Love**[162] 5680 3-8-7 **53** ... GrahamGibbons 8 47
(J D Bethell) *prom over 2f* **12/1**

10-5 10 1/2 **Soviet Legend (IRE)**[33] 359 3-8-8 **57** ...(b) SaleemGolam[(3)] 10 49
(T J Etherington) *s.i.s: a bhd* **33/1**

026 11 nk **Ten Tenors (IRE)**[22] 473 3-9-0 **60** ... ShaneKelly 4 51
(J A Osborne) *s.i.s: a bhd* **9/1**

3240 12 5 **Mr Rigsby**[13] 554 3-9-4 **64** ... TonyCulhane 7 40
(P Howling) *mid-div: rdn over 3f out: sn bhd* **12/1**

1m 15.01s (-0.80) **Going Correction** 0.0s/f (Stan) 12 Ran SP% **127.7**
Speed ratings (Par 96):105,103,98,97,96 95,95,94,93,93 92,86
CSF £42.47 CT £220.14 TOTE £2.50: £1.60, £3.40, £1.90; EX 30.10 Place 6 £118.03, Place 5 £45.02.
Owner Bull & Bell Partnership **Bred** P J Murphy **Trained** Hambleton, N Yorks

FOCUS
A decent time for a race like this, 1.24 seconds faster than the preceding maiden, and the front pair pulled a long way clear of the rest. The form looks above average for the grade and should work out.
T/Plt: £156.00 to a £1 stake. Pool: £36,418.45. 170.35 winning tickets. T/Qpdt: £34.40 to a £1 stake. Pool: £2,524.50. 54.30 winning tickets. KH

633 SOUTHWELL (L-H)
Thursday, March 16

OFFICIAL GOING: Standard
Wind: Virtually nil.

647 $500K GUARANTEED WITH LITTLEWOODSPOKER.COM APPRENTICE H'CAP 1m 4f (F)
1:20 (1:20) (Class 6) (0-55,60) 4-Y-0+ £2,388 (£705; £352) Stalls Low

Form RPR

0-40 1 **Tiegs (IRE)**[44] 259 4-8-3 **44** oh4 ... MarcHalford 3 52
(P W Hiatt) *led: hdd over 5f out: rdn to ld again wl over 1f out: edgd rt and styd on fnl f* **10/1**

2060 **2** *4* **Farnborough (USA)**[12] [582] 5-8-12 **51**............................ JamesDoyle 5 53
(R J Price) *hld up in tch: hdwy over 3f out: rdn to chse ldng pair 2f out: kpt on same pce appr last* **5/1**[3]

0-34 **3** *nk* **Champion Lion (IRE)**[33] [379] 7-8-10 **52**...............(e[1]) AndrewElliott(3) 8 54
(J R Boyle) *prom: hdwy to ld over 5f out: rdn over 2f out: hdd wl over 1f out: sn hung rt and wknd ent last* **5/2**[2]

6011 **4** *3* **Mossmann Gorge**[9] [609] 4-9-0 **60** 6ex..................(v) JosephWalsh(5) 4 57
(M Wellings) *hld up and bhd: hdwy 3f out: rdn and kpt on fnl 2f: nvr nr ldrs* **15/8**[1]

2165 **5** *4* **Regency Red (IRE)**[27] [442] 8-8-11 **53**.............. RussellKennemore(3) 1 45
(W M Brisbourne) *hld up in tch: effrt and sme hdwy 4f out: sn rdn along and nvr a factor* **13/2**

0250 **6** *2 ½* **Spitfire Bob (USA)**[10] [599] 7-8-13 **52**.......................... AndrewMullen 2 40
(M E Sowersby) *chsd ldrs: rdn along over 4f out: outpcd over 3f out* **6/1**

00 **7** *16* **Diafa (USA)**[12] [584] 4-8-13 **54**.. JerryO'Dwyer 7 20
(J G M O'Shea) *cl up: rdn along over 4f out: sn wknd* **28/1**

300- **8** *5* **Temple Belle Xpres**[289] [2150] 4-8-0 **46** oh9 ow2..(b) ThomasO'Brien(5) 6 5
(S R Bowring) *chsd ldrs: rdn along 1/2-way: sn lost pl and bhd fnl 3f* **66/1**

2m 41.64s (-0.45) **Going Correction** -0.125s/f (Stan)
WFA 4 from 5yo+ 2lb **8** Ran SP% **121.7**
Speed ratings (Par 101):96,93,93,91,88 86,76,72
CSF £62.90 CT £168.40 TOTE £14.90: £3.60, £2.60, £1.10; EX 65.00.
Owner The Fox Inn Partnership **Bred** Paradime Ltd **Trained** Hook Norton, Oxon

FOCUS
A moderate affair run in a modest winning time, 4.41 seconds slower than the later handicap over the same trip. The form is weak and has been rated fairly negatively around the placed horses.
Tiegs(IRE) Official explanation: trainer said, regarding the improved form shown, filly has proved difficult to train but now appears to be going the right way

648 PLAY NOW AT BETDIRECTPOKER.COM CLASSIFIED CLAIMING STKS (DIV I) 1m (F)
1:50 (1:50) (Class 6) 3-Y-0+ **£2,047** (£604; £302) **Stalls** Low

Form RPR

0624 **1** **Diction (IRE)**[8] [618] 4-9-5 48.......................................(p) FrancisNorton 3 54
(K R Burke) *trckd ldrs: n.m.r 3f out: hdwy to chal over 1f out: rdn and edgd rt ins last: styd on to ld last 100 yds* **9/2**[2]

0613 **2** *¾* **Crusoe (IRE)**[2] [636] 9-9-9 49..(b) BrianReilly 10 56
(A Sadik) *cl up on outer: effrt over 2f out: rdn to ld over 1f out: drvn ins last: hdd and no ex last 100 yds* **7/2**[1]

2623 **3** *5* **Franky'N'Jonny**[10] [604] 3-8-2 54... ChrisCatlin 9 42
(I A Wood) *a cl up: effrt over 2f out: sn rdn and ev ch tl drvn ent last and grad wknd* **11/2**[3]

5-44 **4** *nk* **Legal Lover (IRE)**[51] [183] 4-9-1 46..................... RussellKennemore(7) 6 44
(R Hollinshead) *in tch: hdwy to chse ldrs over 2f out: sn rdn and kpt on same pce* **13/2**

0504 **5** *½* **Fortune Point (IRE)**[23] [472] 8-9-6 52.......................(v) JamesDoyle(5) 8 46
(A W Carroll) *cl up: led 1/2-way: rdn over 2f out: hdd wl over 1f out: sn drvn and wknd* **8/1**

2-01 **6** *2 ½* **Priorina (IRE)**[37] [330] 4-9-4 50...(v) RobertHavlin 1 34
(D Haydn Jones) *in tch: rdn along over 3f out: sn btn* **7/2**[1]

44-4 **7** *1 ¼* **Summer Shades**[24] [467] 8-9-3 49............................. PaulMulrennan(3) 7 34
(W M Brisbourne) *a towards rr* **14/1**

0662 **8** *3 ½* **Naughty Girl (IRE)**[8] [616] 6-9-0 40.......................... PatrickMathers(3) 2 24
(John A Harris) *in tch: pushed along 1/2-way: sn wknd* **12/1**

-200 **9** *18* **Castanza**[56] [148] 4-9-4 40.. DarryllHolland 4 —
(M Wellings) *led: pushed along and hdd 1/2-way: sn rdn and wknd over 2f out* **33/1**

1m 43.47s (-1.13) **Going Correction** -0.125s/f (Stan)
WFA 3 from 4yo+ 17lb **9** Ran SP% **119.8**
Speed ratings (Par 101):100,99,94,93,93 90,89,86,68
CSF £21.52 TOTE £5.50: £1.50, £1.50, £1.50; EX 26.40.
Owner J C S Wilson **Bred** Heatherwold Stud **Trained** Middleham Moor, N Yorks

FOCUS
The first two came nicely clear in this moderate heat, and set the level for the form, but the winning time was 0.45 seconds slower than the second division.

649 PLAY NOW AT BETDIRECTPOKER.COM CLASSIFIED CLAIMING STKS (DIV II) 1m (F)
2:25 (2:26) (Class 6) 3-Y-0+ **£2,047** (£604; £302) **Stalls** Low

Form RPR

3210 **1** **Vancouver Gold (IRE)**[15] [546] 4-9-6 55...................... RobertWinston 5 61
(K R Burke) *trckd ldrs: hdwy over 2f out: rdn to ld over 1f out: styd on* **7/2**[2]

-006 **2** *1 ¼* **El Palmar**[9] [612] 5-9-7 52... GrahamGibbons 6 60
(M J Attwater) *cl up: led over 2f out: rdn wl over 1f out: hdd appr last and kpt on u.p* **7/1**

2624 **3** *3* **Pending (IRE)**[9] [606] 5-9-8 55...................................(be[1]) DarryllHolland 2 55
(J R Boyle) *dwlt: sn cl up on inner: rdn along over 2f out and one pce appr last* **5/2**[1]

4632 **4** *1 ½* **High Swainston**[18] [526] 5-9-9 48.......................................(v[1]) PaulFessey 4 53
(R Craggs) *led: rdn along and hdd over 2f out: sn drvn and wknd* **11/2**[3]

2135 **5** *1* **Pawn In Life (IRE)**[15] [546] 8-9-6 55..........................(v) DeanMcKeown 8 48
(M J Polglase) *chsd ldrs: wd st: rdn 2f out and sn one pce* **11/2**[3]

2253 **6** *2 ½* **Dexileos (IRE)**[8] [616] 7-9-7 45..(t) HayleyTurner 3 44
(David Pinder) *t.k.h: chsd ldrs: rdn along over 3f out: sn wknd* **20/1**

02-4 **7** *1 ½* **Quincannon (USA)**[12] [581] 5-9-7 55.............................. ShaneKelly 7 41
(W M Brisbourne) *dwlt: a rr* **13/2**

00-0 **8** *20* **Kalani Star (IRE)**[9] [606] 6-9-7 55.....................................(vt) TomEaves 1 1
(I W McInnes) *dwlt: a rr* **33/1**

-000 **9** *7* **Inescapable (USA)**[2] [638] 5-9-0 45.............................. TolleyDean(7) 9 —
(A W Carroll) *in tch: pushed along 1/2-way: sn lost pl and bhd* **66/1**

1m 43.02s (-1.58) **Going Correction** -0.125s/f (Stan)
WFA 3 from 4yo+ 17lb **9** Ran SP% **116.6**
Speed ratings (Par 101):102,100,97,96,95 92,91,71,64
CSF £27.89 TOTE £3.60: £1.50, £2.50, £1.10; EX 33.70.
Owner Bigwigs Bloodstock II **Bred** Ballinacurra Stud **Trained** Middleham Moor, N Yorks

FOCUS
An ordinary claimer but the quicker of the two divisions by 0.45 seconds. The form makes sense rated around the first two.

650 BETDIRECT ON 0800 211 222 H'CAP 7f (F)
3:05 (3:05) (Class 6) (0-65,69) 4-Y-0+ **£2,388** (£705; £352) **Stalls** Low

Form RPR

/1-1 **1** **Tyzack (IRE)**[9] [606] 5-9-2 **63** 6ex.................................. MickyFenton 2 77
(Stef Liddiard) *trckd ldrs: hdwy 2f out: rdn to ld 1f out: styd on wl* **11/4**[1]

5631 **2** *2 ½* **Zorn**[9] [612] 7-9-0 **61** 6ex... ShaneKelly 13 68
(P Howling) *led: rdn 2f out: drvn and hdd 1f out: kpt on u.p ins last* **8/1**

0322 **3** *1* **Roman Empire**[10] [602] 6-8-11 **58**.......................................(b) NCallan 5 62
(P A Blockley) *chsd ldrs: hdwy 2f out: sn rdn and ev ch tl drvn and one pce ins last* **7/1**[3]

0302 **4** *¾* **Preskani**[9] [612] 4-8-10 **60**...(p) SaleemGolam(3) 1 62
(Mrs N Macauley) *towards rr: hdwy on inner 2f out: sn rdn and kpt on: nrst fin* **12/1**

1113 **5** *nk* **Desert Lover (IRE)**[17] [537] 4-8-13 **60**............................. PhillipMakin 3 62
(R J Price) *chsd ldrs: rdn along over 2f out: drvn and kpt on same pce appr last* **11/2**[2]

-003 **6** *1 ½* **Gem Bien (USA)**[9] [612] 8-8-11 **58**..............................(p) TonyCulhane 14 56
(D W Chapman) *chsd ldrs on outer: rdn along and outpcd 2f out: kpt on u.p ins last* **40/1**

1425 **7** *½* **Lucius Verrus (USA)**[21] [493] 6-8-11 **61**.............(v) PatrickMathers(3) 10 57
(D Shaw) *towards rr: hdwy 2f out: styd on ins last: nrst fin* **17/2**

3316 **8** *½* **Mister Benji**[13] [571] 7-9-1 **62**... DarrenWilliams 4 57
(B P J Baugh) *hld up: hdwy 3f out: rdn 2f out and sn no imp* **12/1**

0-P1 **9** *nk* **Pauline's Prince**[15] [546] 4-8-6 **60**................................ HugoFellows(7) 9 54
(R Hollinshead) *in tch: gd hdwy on outer 3f out: rdn to chal 2f out and ev ch tl drvn over 1f out and sn wknd* **25/1**

2031 **10** *1* **Play Master (IRE)**[10] [600] 5-9-3 **69** 6ex.................... LiamTreadwell(5) 8 61
(R A Harris) *midfield: rdn along 3f out: no hdwy* **10/1**

0012 **11** *½* **Shannon Arms (USA)**[13] [568] 5-9-4 **65**.................(p) J-PGuillambert 12 55
(P Howling) *dwlt: sn cl up: rdn over 2f out and ev ch tl wknd over 1f out* **18/1**

6464 **12** *1* **King Of Music (USA)**[17] [537] 5-8-11 **58**............................ ChrisCatlin 7 46
(G Prodromou) *s.i.s: a rr* **9/1**

2616 **13** *shd* **Quiet Reading (USA)**[28] [423] 9-8-11 **58**...................(v) HayleyTurner 11 46
(M R Bosley) *a towards rr* **16/1**

01/0 **14** *dist* **Snugfit Dubarry**[30] [412] 6-9-4 **65**.................................. DaleGibson 6 —
(M W Easterby) *a rr: lost tch and bhd fr 1/2-way* **66/1**

1m 28.68s (-2.12) **Going Correction** -0.125s/f (Stan) **14** Ran SP% **129.6**
Speed ratings (Par 101):107,104,103,102,101 100,99,98,98,97 96,95,95,—
CSF £26.54 CT £155.04 TOTE £3.10: £1.30, £3.00, £2.10; EX 18.20.
Owner Simon Mapletoft Racing I **Bred** Rabea Syndicate **Trained** Great Shefford, Berks

FOCUS
This looked fairly competitive and it produced a decent winning time for a race of its class. The form should work out.

651 LITTLEWOODS BETDIRECT (S) STKS 7f (F)
3:45 (3:45) (Class 6) 3-Y-O **£2,388** (£705; £352) **Stalls** Low

Form RPR

201- **1** **Tour D'Amour (IRE)**[86] [6635] 3-8-13 64.............................. PaulFessey 1 59
(R Craggs) *trckd ldrs: hdwy 2f out: rdn to ld ent last: edgd rt and kpt on* **4/1**[3]

0-33 **2** *¾* **Psycho Cat**[21] [488] 3-9-4 65..................................(p) GrahamGibbons 5 62
(P A Blockley) *in tch: hdwy 2f out: sn rdn: ev ch over 1f out: drvn and one pce ins last* **9/4**[1]

4356 **3** *shd* **Woodwee**[21] [488] 3-9-4 56... DarryllHolland 9 62
(J R Weymes) *led: rdn along 2f out: drvn and hdd ent last: sn no ex* **20/1**

0636 **4** *1* **Bahhmirage (IRE)**[16] [538] 3-8-8 50 ow1...................(b) MickyFenton 10 49
(Stef Liddiard) *cl up: rdn wl over 1f out: ev ch tl drvn and wknd ent last* **12/1**

04 **5** *2* **Macho Dancer (IRE)**[14] [554] 3-8-4 .... NelsonDeSouza(3) 4 43
(R M Beckett) *in tch: rdn along 2f out: sn wknd* **12/1**

330 **6** *6* **Glenargo (USA)**[5] [630] 3-8-5 .... TolleyDean(7) 2 33
(R A Harris) *keen: a.p: rdn and ev ch wl over 1f out: wknd appr last* **20/1**

6126 **7** *12* **Mr Cheers**[10] [594] 3-9-4 60...(b) FrancisNorton 11 7
(R A Harris) *sn outpcd and bhd fr 1/2-way* **6/1**

4503 **8** *4* **Ohana**[14] [554] 3-9-4 69...(b) NCallan 3 —
(N P Littmoden) *dwlt: swtchd rt in rr and rdn along after 1f: sn bhd and looked reluctant* **11/4**[2]

1m 29.94s (-0.86) **Going Correction** -0.125s/f (Stan) **8** Ran SP% **116.6**
Speed ratings (Par 96):99,98,98,96,94 87,74,69
CSF £13.75 TOTE £5.00: £1.50, £1.50, £3.90; EX 16.60.There was no bid for the winner.
Owner Ray Craggs **Bred** Peter McCutcheon **Trained** Sedgefield, Co Durham

FOCUS
An ordinary race of its type though made less competitive by the wretched runs of Mr Cheers and Ohana. The winner did not need to be at her best and those in the frame behind her set the level.
Mr Cheers Official explanation: jockey said gelding would not face the kickback
Ohana Official explanation: jockey said colt would not face the kickback

652 PLAY NOW AT BETDIRECTCASINO.COM H'CAP 1m 4f (F)
4:30 (4:30) (Class 5) (0-75,76) 4-Y-0+ **£3,238** (£963; £481; £240) **Stalls** Low

Form RPR

-413 **1** **Eloquent Knight (USA)**[23] [478] 4-8-11 **68**..................... MartinDwyer 2 77
(W R Muir) *trckd ldrs: smooth hdwy to ld 3f out: rdn wl over 1f out: drvn ins last and hld on wl* **11/4**[1]

5-33 **2** *hd* **Amwell Brave**[12] [574] 5-8-7 **62**.................................... RobertWinston 4 71
(J R Jenkins) *hld up: stdy hdwy over 4f out: chal 2f out: sn rdn and ev ch: drvn ins last: kpt on: jst hld* **14/1**

1164 **3** *7* **Jackie Kiely**[15] [549] 5-8-7 **62**... J-PGuillambert 5 61
(P Howling) *chsd ldrs: rdn along 3f out: drvn wl over 1f out and kpt on same pce* **16/1**

4121 **4** *1 ½* **Sugitani (USA)**[10] [597] 4-9-5 **76** 6ex..........................(b) MickyFenton 10 72
(N B King) *bhd and rdn along 1/2-way: hdwy on inner over 2f out: styd on appr last: nvr nr ldrs* **5/1**[2]

3232 **5** *¾* **Romil Star (GER)**[9] [607] 9-7-12 **60**.....................(p) PatrickDonaghy(7) 8 55
(K R Burke) *prom: rdn along over 4f out: wknd 3f out* **12/1**

-405 **6** *shd* **Ramsgill (USA)**[17] [535] 4-8-1 **63**................................ JamesDoyle(5) 7 58
(N P Littmoden) *hld up towards rr: gd hdwy 4f out: rdn to chse ldrs over 2f out: wknd over 1f out* **20/1**

6436 **7** *5* **Discord**[20] [503] 5-8-10 **65**.. PaulHanagan 1 52
(T H Caldwell) *trckd ldrs on inner: rdn along over 3f out: drvn and outpcd 2f out* **40/1**

2312 **8** *5* **He's A Star**[9] [610] 4-8-12 **69**... DarryllHolland 6 49
(Miss Gay Kelleway) *trckd ldrs on outer: pshd along over 5f out: rdn over 4f out and sn wknd* **11/4**[1]

5222 **9** *6* **Augustine**[10] [603] 5-8-7 **62**.. ChrisCatlin 9 33
(P W Hiatt) *racd wd: in tch tl rdn along over 4f out and sn wknd* **6/1**[3]

3620 **10** *19* **Khanjar (USA)**[36] [338] 6-9-4 **73**.....................................(p) PatCosgrave 3 15
(K R Burke) *led: rdn along 4f out: hdd 3f out and wknd qckly* **14/1**

2m 37.23s (-4.86) **Going Correction** -0.125s/f (Stan)
WFA 4 from 5yo+ 2lb **10** Ran SP% **118.4**
Speed ratings (Par 103):111,110,106,105,104 104,101,97,93,81
CSF £46.36 CT £531.16 TOTE £4.00: £1.60, £4.40, £4.00; EX 65.70.

Owner M J Caddy **Bred** Eaglestone Farm Inc **Trained** Lambourn, Berks
■ Stewards' Enquiry : Martin Dwyer three-day ban: used whip above shoulder height (Mar 27-29)

FOCUS
A decent pace and a very smart time for the grade, 4.41 seconds faster than the earlier apprentice handicap over the same trip. The form looks reliable rated around the principals.

He's A Star Official explanation: jockey said gelding is over the top

653 LITTLEWOODSPOOLS.CO.UK MAIDEN STKS 6f (F)
5:10 (5:10) (Class 5) 3-Y-0+ **£3,238** (£963; £481; £240) **Stalls** Low

Form RPR
5-53 **1** **Miss Lopez (IRE)**33 380 3-8-8 62 PatCosgrave 6 57
(K R Burke) *hld up in tch: hdwy over 2f out: rdn to ld over 1f out: hung rt ins last: drvn out* **11/4**2

42- **2** *2* **Generator**120 6367 4-9-12 ShaneKelly 3 61
(Dr J D Scargill) *cl up: effrt and ev ch 2f out tl rdn: hung rt and kpt on same pce fnl f* **5/6**1

65 **3** *hd* **Going Skint**21 487 3-8-13 DavidAllan 4 55
(T D Easterby) *cl up: led over 2f out: sn rdn: hdd over 1f out: sn drvn and kpt on fnl f* **25/1**

4-0 **4** *nk* **Bollin Michael**12 584 4-9-12 FergalLynch 7 60
(T D Easterby) *towards rr: wd st: gd hdwy wl over 1f out: swtchd lft ent last and styd on wl: nrst fin* **9/1**

030- **5** *1 3/4* **Coquin D'Alezan (IRE)**364 641 5-9-12 65 RobertWinston 2 54
(W Jarvis) *cl up on inner: rdn along 2f out: wknd appr last* **6/1**3

2-52 **6** *2 1/2* **Fir Tree**56 144 6-9-12 40 MichaelTebbutt 9 47
(S R Bowring) *midfield: hdwy 2f out: sn rdn and no imp* **20/1**

-250 **7** *nk* **Danish Blues (IRE)**12 579 3-8-13 65 NCallan 8 41
(N P Littmoden) *cl up: effrt and ev ch 2f out: sn rdn and wknd over 1f out* **20/1**

8 *3/4* **Scarlet Romance**22 4-9-4 PaulMulrennan(3) 11 39
(M W Easterby) *s.i.s: a bhd* **50/1**

606- **9** *20* **Jackie Francis (IRE)**213 4434 3-8-13 50 J-PGuillambert 12 —
(P Howling) *led: rdn along and hdd over 2f out: sn wknd* **40/1**

10 *2* **Shaika** 3-8-8 ChrisCatlin 1 —
(G Prodromou) *sn outpcd and a bhd* **40/1**

0/3- **11** *1* **Jabraan (USA)**286 2265 4-9-12 TonyCulhane 5 —
(D W Chapman) *sn outpcd and bhd fr 1/2-way* **10/1**

1m 17.24s (0.34) **Going Correction** -0.125s/f (Stan)
WFA 3 from 4yo+ 13lb **11** Ran SP% **134.8**
Speed ratings (Par 103):92,89,89,88,86 83,82,81,54,52 50
CSF £5.91 TOTE £4.40: £1.40, £1.30, £6.30; EX 10.20.

Owner Colin Bryce **Bred** J F Tuthill **Trained** Middleham Moor, N Yorks

FOCUS
This did not look a great race and the winning time was also modest for the class, 0.62 seconds slower than the following handicap. The form is not solid and is limited by the proximity of the sixth.

Bollin Michael ◆ Official explanation: jockey said colt was running green and hanging

654 FIRST PAST THE POST AT BETDIRECT H'CAP 6f (F)
5:40 (5:40) (Class 5) (0-70,70) 4-Y-0+ **£3,238** (£963; £481; £240) **Stalls** Low

Form RPR
0113 **1** **Winning Pleasure (IRE)**28 428 8-9-1 **70** JasonEdmunds(3) 4 82
(J Balding) *chsd ldrs: hdwy 2f out: swtchd lft and rdn over 1f out: led jst ins last: styd on wl* **7/1**

4043 **2** *2* **Shifty Night (IRE)**9 608 5-8-9 **61** ow1 (v) DarryllHolland 3 67
(Mrs C A Dunnett) *cl up: led 1/2-way: rdn 2f out: drvn and hung rt over 1f out: hdd ins last and one pce* **13/2**3

3115 **3** *3/4* **Winthorpe (IRE)**12 585 6-9-2 **68** GrahamGibbons 10 72
(J J Quinn) *a.p on outer: effrt 2f out: sn rdn: n.m.r and swtchd lft over 1f out: kpt on same pce* **4/1**2

2022 **4** *1/2* **Doctor Dennis (IRE)**9 608 9-8-7 **59** (v) HayleyTurner 8 63+
(J Pearce) *racd wd: bhd and rdn along 1/2-way: wd st: hdwy 2f out: styng on whn nt clr run over 1f out: kpt on ins last* **7/2**1

0532 **5** *2* **Alpaga Le Jomage (IRE)**12 588 4-8-12 **64** (p) DeanMcKeown 2 60
(M J Polglase) *led: pshd along and hdd 1/2-way: cl up and ev ch tl rdn and wknd over 1f out* **12/1**

4011 **6** *1 3/4* **Sweet Pickle**9 608 5-8-12 **67** 6ex (e) DanielTudhope(3) 1 58
(J R Boyle) *dwlt and towards rr: effrt and sme hdwy 2f out: sn rdn and no imp* **7/2**1

6-45 **7** *3/4* **Desert Opal**10 602 6-8-8 **60** PhillipMakin 7 49
(D W Chapman) *chsd ldrs: rdn over 2f out: grad wknd* **20/1**

12-3 **8** *1/2* **Misaro (GER)**35 345 5-8-9 **68** (b) TolleyDean(7) 5 55
(R A Harris) *wnt rt s: a rr* **4/1**2

000- **9** *1* **Bold Cheverak**153 5869 4-8-11 **63** ChrisCatlin 9 47
(Mrs C A Dunnett) *chsd ldrs on outer: rdn along wl over 2f: wknd wl over 1f out* **40/1**

006- **10** *16* **For Life (IRE)**164 5666 4-8-13 **65** DarrenWilliams 6 1
(A P Jarvis) *bmpd s: a rr* **33/1**

1m 16.62s (-0.28) **Going Correction** -0.125s/f (Stan) **10** Ran SP% **128.1**
Speed ratings (Par 103):96,93,92,91,89 86,85,85,83,62
CSF £56.26 CT £219.94 TOTE £12.70: £2.80, £2.00, £2.60; EX 90.00 Place 6 £36.47, Place 5 £12.72.

Owner R L Crowe **Bred** Mrs B A Headon **Trained** Scrooby, Notts

FOCUS
The winning time was moderate for a race like this, despite being 0.62 seconds quicker than the preceding maiden. The bulk of the field came over to the stands' side in the straight and they seemed to get bogged down in the slower ground, whilst the winner enjoyed a solo down the middle. The form looks straightforward rated around the placed horses.

Shifty Night(IRE) Official explanation: jockey said mare hung right

Doctor Dennis(IRE) Official explanation: jockey said gelding was denied a clear run in the final stages

T/Plt: £115.00 to a £1 stake. Pool: £44,459.45. 282.20 winning tickets. T/Qpdt: £19.20 to a £1 stake. Pool: £5,850.70. 224.40 winning tickets. JR

SAINT-CLOUD (L-H)
Wednesday, March 8

OFFICIAL GOING: Heavy

655a PRIX EXBURY (GROUP 3) 1m 2f
2:35 (2:34) 4-Y-0+ **£27,586** (£11,034; £8,276; £5,517; £2,759)

RPR
1 **Kendor Dine (FR)**146 5863 4-9-0 SPasquier 7 110
(Y De Nicolay, France) *led after 1f, pushed along and ran on 2f out, driven clear over 1f out, comfortably* **84/10**

2 *5* **Special Kaldoun (IRE)**129 6189 7-9-2 DBoeuf 1 107
(D Smaga, France) *in touch, 3rd straight, driven to chase leader 2f out, took 2nd easily but no impression on winner* **13/10**1

3 *6* **Gold Sound (FR)**172 5336 4-9-0 OPeslier 3 99
(C Laffon-Parias, France) *held up, 4th straight, stayed on final stages but never a threat* **56/10**3

4 *5* **Geordieland (FR)**178 5160 5-9-2 C-PLemaire 2 96
(J-M Beguigne, France) *led 1f and prominent, 2nd and came stands side straight, one pace from 1 1/2f out* **24/10**2

5 *4* **Petit Colibri (FR)**89 5-8-10 RMarchelli 4 86
(P Baudry, France) *towards rear, 5th straight, never a threat* **9/1**

6 *20* **Ianina (IRE)**17 456 6-8-6 DPorcu 6 62
(R Rohne, Germany) *disputed 4th early, niggled half-way, last and beaten straight* **78/10**

2m 15.6s **6** Ran SP% **120.0**
PARI-MUTUEL: WIN 9.40; PL 2.30, 2.10, 2.20; DF 20.00.
Owner D Kahn **Bred** E U R L Eskade **Trained** France

NOTEBOOK
Kendor Dine(FR) looked well and straight in the paddock and finally won his second Group race with plenty in hand. Asked to make all the running, he quickened halfway up the straight and passed the post on his own. He adores testing ground and will now go on to the Prix d'Harcourt at Longchamp.
Special Kaldoun(IRE) followed the winner throughout but could not quicken in the same fashion in the straight. This was a sound performance, though, as he was giving the winner a kilo, and the race will have brought him on. He will now be sent to Nad al Sheba for the Dubai Duty Free race.
Gold Sound(FR) raced away from the rail for much of this race but joined the main pack in the straight. He was well beaten a furlong and a half out but the outing will have done him some good.
Geordieland(FR) raced up the centre of the track down the back straight and was then the only horse to be brought over to the stands' rail. This tactic did not work out and he was finally well beaten in fourth.

589 LINGFIELD (L-H)
Friday, March 17

OFFICIAL GOING: Standard
Wind: Moderate; half against

656 BETDIRECT NO Q ON 08000 936693 MAIDEN STKS 1m 4f (P)
1:50 (1:50) (Class 5) 3-Y-0 **£3,886** (£1,156; £577; £288) **Stalls** Low

Form RPR
6 **1** **Lightning Strike (GER)**60 124 3-9-3 IanMongan 5 73+
(T G Mills) *trckd ldrs: led over 2f out: clr over 1f out: pushed out fnl f* **14/1**

0- **2** *2 1/2* **Raslan**154 5870 3-9-3 JoeFanning 4 69+
(M Johnston) *trckd ldr after 2f: led over 3f out: rdn and hdd over 2f out: kpt on but no ch w wnr fr over 1f out* **5/2**2

000- **3** *3* **Synonymy**160 5746 3-9-3 67 FrancisNorton 7 64
(M Blanshard) *led tl hdd over 3f out: one pce fnl 2f* **25/1**

434- **4** *1 3/4* **Crimson Flame (IRE)**152 5919 3-9-3 77 TQuinn 1 61
(M R Channon) *mid-div tl lst pl over 5f out: kpt on one pce fnl 2f* **3/1**3

0-04 **5** *3/4* **Mighty Kitchener (USA)**13 584 3-9-3 62 ShaneKelly 2 60
(P Howling) *trckd ldr for 2f: prom tl rdn 3f out: sn btn* **7/1**

64- **6** *1 1/2* **Special Moment (IRE)**174 5454 3-8-12 DarryllHolland 6 53
(B W Hills) *t.k.h: rdn over 3f out: nvr on terms* **7/4**1

2m 37.02s (2.63) **Going Correction** +0.05s/f (Slow) **6** Ran SP% **112.9**
Speed ratings (Par 98):93,91,89,88,87 86
CSF £49.52 TOTE £13.50: £4.00, £1.40; EX 46.00.
Owner T G Mills **Bred** Dr Chr Berglar **Trained** Headley, Surrey

FOCUS
A modest winning time for the class, but the first three home had been lightly-raced, so this moderate maiden may be a shade better than it looks. The third and fifth set the standard for the form.

657 BETDIRECT ON 0800 211 222 H'CAP 6f (P)
2:25 (2:25) (Class 4) (0-85,84) 4-Y-0+ **£5,505** (£1,637; £818; £408) **Stalls** Low

Form RPR
3110 **1** **Saviours Spirit**20 517 5-8-13 **79** JoeFanning 5 89
(T G Mills) *slowly away: hdwy on ins over 2f out: led 1f out: rdn out* **5/2**2

1-24 **2** *1/2* **Hammer Of The Gods (IRE)**18 532 6-8-5 **71** oh2 ow1(bt) EddieAhern 6 80+
(Lucinda Featherstone) *towards rr: hdwy hdwy whn short of room wl over 1f out: r.o wl to go 2nd ins fnl f* **2/1**1

020- **3** *1 1/2* **Plateau**189 5090 7-9-1 **81** AdrianTNicholls 7 85
(D Nicholls) *a in tch: rdn and outpcd over 2f out: r.o fnl f* **7/1**

5-63 **4** *hd* **Perfect Story (IRE)**15 555 4-8-7 **80** RonanKeogh(7) 3 84
(J A R Toller) *hld up: gd hdwy on ins 2f out: ld briefly appr fnl f: rdn and one pce ins* **5/1**3

2011 **5** *1/2* **Sweetest Revenge (IRE)**13 587 5-8-5 **71** HayleyTurner 2 73
(M D I Usher) *in tch tl rdn and outpcd 1/2-way: r.o on far rail ins fnl f* **8/1**

135- **6** *nk* **Blackheath (IRE)**187 5146 10-8-2 **71** SilvestreDeSousa(3) 1 72
(D Nicholls) *trckd ldr for 1f: prom tl rdn and wknd appr fnl f* **16/1**

0620 **7** *1 1/2* **Law Maker**20 517 6-9-2 **82** (v) JimmyFortune 4 79
(A Bailey) *trckd ldr after 1f: rdn and wkng whn hmpd on bnd wl over 1f out* **14/1**

000- **8** *nk* **Handsome Cross (IRE)**182 5262 5-8-11 **84** VictoriaBehan(7) 8 80
(D Nicholls) *led tl rdn and hdd over 1f out: wknd qckly* **20/1**

1m 12.49s (-0.32) **Going Correction** +0.05s/f (Slow) **8** Ran SP% **119.5**
Speed ratings (Par 105):104,103,101,101,100 100,98,97
CSF £8.38 CT £30.80 TOTE £4.50: £1.30, £1.50, £2.50; EX 10.90.

Owner J E Harley **Bred** Mrs S Shaw **Trained** Headley, Surrey

FOCUS

A decent sprint race, with several future winners in the field - though it may be summer before some of them are back to their peak.

Law Maker Official explanation: jockey said gelding did not handle final bend

658 BETDIRECT.CO.UK MAIDEN STKS — 7f (P)

3:05 (3:07) (Class 5) 3-Y-O — **£4,857** (£1,445; £722; £360) **Stalls** Low

Form — RPR

3335 **1** **Scroll**[6] 630 3-9-3 71 ....(v) J-PGuillambert 12 — 73
(P Howling) *hld up: hdwy on outside over 2f out: qcknd wl to ld ins fnl f* **7/1**

635- **2** *1 ½* **Lake Poet (IRE)**[147] 6002 3-9-3 85 .... RyanMoore 3 — 69
(C E Brittain) *in tch: outpcd over 2f out: r.o to go 2nd ins fnl f* **9/2**[2]

3 *¾* **Cape Of Storms** 3-9-3 .... TQuinn 11 — 67
(M R Channon) *trckd ldrs: led 2f out: rdn and hdd ins fnl f: nt qckn* **6/1**[3]

24 **4** *1 ¼* **Kasumi**[59] 132 3-8-12 .... SteveDrowne 7 — 58
(H Morrison) *a in tch: rdn over 1f out: kpt on one pce* **16/1**

00- **5** *2* **Roman Quest**[157] 5817 3-9-3 .... MickyFenton 8 — 58
(H Morrison) *bhd tl rdn and hdwy over 1f out: nvr nrr* **25/1**

460- **6** *shd* **Champagne Moment**[154] 5879 3-8-12 48 .... MichaelTebbutt 4 — 53
(V Smith) *prom: rdn over 2f out: one pce fnl f* **66/1**

7 *½* **Digger Boy** 3-9-3 .... MatthewHenry 1 — 57
(M A Jarvis) *v.s.a: sme late hdwy: nvr on terms* **8/1**

3 **8** *1 ½* **Beowulf**[13] 584 3-9-3 .... JoeFanning 9 — 53+
(M Johnston) *t.k.h: trckd ldr: led 3f out to 2f out: wknd appr fnl f* **6/4**[1]

0-00 **9** *½* **Star Of Canterbury (IRE)**[24] 475 3-9-3 62 .... DarrenWilliams 5 — 52+
(A P Jarvis) *led to 3f out: rdn and wknd 2f out* **33/1**

0-60 **10** *nk* **They All Laughed**[13] 579 3-9-3 57 .... IanMongan 10 — 51
(T G Mills) *s.i.s: a bhd* **16/1**

11 *24* **Solomans Prospect** 3-8-12 ....(v[1]) JamesDoyle(5) 6 — —
(Miss D A McHale) *v.s.a: outpcd: t.o* **100/1**

12 *11* **Loyal Friend (IRE)** 3-9-3 .... TPQueally 2 — —
(Niall Moran, Ire) *v.s.a: bhd: t.o* **16/1**

1m 25.68s (-0.21) **Going Correction** +0.05s/f (Slow) — 12 Ran SP% **123.0**

Speed ratings (Par 98):103,101,100,99,96 96,96,94,93,93 65,53

CSF £39.36 TOTE £9.80: £1.80, £1.70, £2.20; EX 41.00.

Owner J Hammond **Bred** Wyck Hall Stud Ltd **Trained** Newmarket, Suffolk

FOCUS

A fair winning time for a race like this, and - while nothing special on the face of it - several of the runners are likely to do better. The winner had previously failed to win his previous 20 races, but he is admirably consistent and that makes him a useful yardstick with the runner-up close to his mark.

Beowulf Official explanation: jockey said he thought colt was lame but it pulled up sound

They All Laughed Official explanation: jockey said gelding was hampered final bend

Solomans Prospect Official explanation: jockey said colt missed the break and ran green

659 TEXT "BETDIRECT" TO 88600 CLAIMING STKS — 1m (P)

3:45 (3:46) (Class 5) 4-6-Y-O — **£3,886** (£1,156; £577; £288) **Stalls** High

Form — RPR

-120 **1** **Raza Cab (IRE)**[27] 451 4-9-5 70 .... DarryllHolland 6 — 72
(Karen George) *hld up in tch: hdwy over 2f out: r.o wl to ld ins fnl f* **10/3**[2]

06-0 **2** *1 ¼* **Midnight Lace**[63] 106 4-8-3 63 .... JoeFanning 8 — 53
(J R Boyle) *hld up in in rr: hdwy over 2f out: led over 1f out: rdn and hdd wl ins fnl f: nt pce of wnr* **8/1**

0030 **3** *1 ¼* **Ali Bruce**[10] 611 6-9-7 77 .... RyanMoore 9 — 68
(G L Moore) *v.s.a: in rr tl hdwy on outside over 1f out: r.o wl fnl f: nvr nrr* **5/2**[1]

-213 **4** *hd* **Fulvio (USA)**[19] 526 6-8-11 52 ....(v) J-PGuillambert 7 — 58
(P Howling) *plld hrd: trckd ldrs: rdn over 2f out: one pce fnl f* **6/1**[3]

6040 **5** *½* **Amazin**[14] 571 4-8-13 63 ....(p) EddieAhern 12 — 59
(N P Littmoden) *bhd tl hdwy on ins over 1f out: r.o: nvr on terms* **13/2**

00-3 **6** *2 ½* **Nuit Sombre (IRE)**[30] 417 6-8-10 73 ....(p) JamesDoyle(5) 2 — 55
(J G M O'Shea) *led tl hdd and wknd over 1f out* **9/1**

44-0 **7** *1 ½* **Grandma Ryta**[40] 304 4-8-1 40 .... HayleyTurner 11 — 37
(John Berry) *racd wd: a bhd* **66/1**

00-3 **8** *2* **Labelled With Love**[25] 458 6-8-6 53 ....(t) FergusSweeney 4 — 38
(J R Boyle) *plld hrd: ev ch 2f out: wknd over 1f out* **20/1**

5-00 **9** *1 ¾* **Tricky Venture**[18] 111 6-8-9 52 .... RobertWinston 1 — 37
(Mrs L C Jewell) *a struggling in rr* **25/1**

0300 **10** *4* **Tapa**[13] 581 4-8-2 55 ....(b) FrancisNorton 10 — 21
(C A Dwyer) *v.s.a: a bhd* **25/1**

0000 **11** *9* **Desert Lightning (IRE)**[2] 644 4-9-2 66 ....(p) PatCosgrave 3 — 14
(K R Burke) *trckd ldr tl rdn and wknd qckly 3f out* **20/1**

1m 39.08s (-0.35) **Going Correction** +0.05s/f (Slow) — 11 Ran SP% **119.1**

Speed ratings: 103,101,100,100,99 97,95,93,92,88 79

CSF £28.09 TOTE £5.90: £2.10, £1.90, £1.60; EX 57.40.

Owner B R Phillips **Bred** Rathyork Stud **Trained** Higher Easington, Devon

FOCUS

A routine claimer contested largely by some unpredictable sorts with the fourth setting the standard.

Ali Bruce Official explanation: jockey said gelding missed break

660 BETDIRECT FILLIES' H'CAP — 1m 2f (P)

4:30 (4:30) (Class 4) (0-85,85) 4-Y-O+ — **£8,096** (£2,408; £1,203; £601) **Stalls** Low

Form — RPR

2-14 **1** **Nice Tune**[15] 555 4-9-2 80 .... RyanMoore 5 — 88
(C E Brittain) *a in tch: shkn up to ld over 1f out: r.o wl* **5/1**[3]

2313 **2** *1 ¼* **Kindlelight Debut**[6] 631 6-9-2 85 .... JamesDoyle(5) 6 — 91
(N P Littmoden) *hld up: hdwy over 2f out: rdn and r.o to chse wnr over 1f out* **7/2**[1]

0-00 **3** *3* **Island Rapture**[25] 463 6-8-7 71 oh1 .... EddieAhern 1 — 71
(J A R Toller) *in rr tl hdwy over 1f out: r.o: nvr nrr* **9/1**

206/ **4** *¾* **Aunty Euro (IRE)**[131] 6273 4-9-2 80 .... NCallan 7 — 79
(Patrick Morris, Ire) *slowly away: rdn and hdwy over 1f out: r.o: nvr nrr* **14/1**

40-0 **5** *¾* **Boot 'n Toot**[69] 65 5-9-0 78 .... JimmyFortune 3 — 75
(C A Cyzer) *trckd ldrs: wnt 2nd over 3f out tl rdn and wknd over 1f out* **4/1**[2]

141- **6** *½* **Noora (IRE)**[161] 5712 5-8-8 75 ....(v) AdamKirby(3) 8 — 72
(C G Cox) *racd wd: a towards rr and nvr on terms* **7/1**

240- **7** *4* **Uig**[190] 5075 5-8-7 71 oh1 .... DavidKinsella 10 — 60
(H S Howe) *led: clr over 4f out: rdn: wknd and hdd over 1f out* **25/1**

-032 **8** *2* **Poppys Footprint (IRE)**[14] 567 5-8-2 71 oh2 ....(b) AndrewMullen(5) 2 — 56
(K A Ryan) *chsd ldrs: rdn 3f out: wknd wl over 1f out* **6/1**

0/0- **9** *6* **Romanova (IRE)**[222] 4189 4-8-4 71 oh4 .... RichardThomas(3) 4 — 45
(Dr J R J Naylor) *plld ard: trckd ldr to 3f out: wknd 2f out* **66/1**

/00- **10** *20* **Cashbar**[22] 3508 5-8-7 71 oh1 .... RobertWinston 9 — 7
(J R Fanshawe) *hld up on outside: nvr gng wl: eased whn wl btn over 1f out: t.o* **6/1**

2m 6.40s (-26.26) **Going Correction** +0.05s/f (Slow) — **10** Ran SP% **122.0**

Speed ratings (Par 102):107,106,103,103,102 102,98,97,92,76

CSF £24.05 CT £158.69 TOTE £6.70: £2.10, £2.50, £2.50; EX 28.10.

Owner Saeed Manana **Bred** Bricklow Ltd **Trained** Newmarket, Suffolk

■ Stewards' Enquiry : Andrew Mullen one-day ban: used whip when out of contention and mare showing no response (Mar 28)

FOCUS

Hand timed. Just a fair fillies' handicap for the money rated through the first two, but not strong overall.

Cashbar Official explanation: jockey said mare moved poorly throughout

661 BETDIRECT.CO.UK H'CAP — 1m 5f (P)

5:10 (5:10) (Class 2) (0-100,93) 4-Y-O+

£12,464 (£3,732; £1,866; £934; £466; £234) **Stalls** Low

Form — RPR

1-45 **1** **Cold Turkey**[14] 572 6-9-7 93 .... RyanMoore 1 — 99
(G L Moore) *hld up: hdwy and shkn up appr fnl f: r.o to ld nr fin* **7/1**

126- **2** *hd* **Country Pursuit (USA)**[169] 5569 4-8-5 80 .... EddieAhern 2 — 86
(C E Brittain) *set slow pce: shkn up appr fnl f: hdd nr fin* **11/2**[2]

022- **3** *shd* **Nawamees (IRE)**[129] 6179 8-9-0 86 .... JimmyFortune 3 — 92
(G L Moore) *trckd ldr: rdn and ev ch ins fnl f: no ex cl home* **14/1**

0152 **4** *nk* **The Violin Player (USA)**[15] 556 5-8-12 84 .... DarryllHolland 4 — 89
(H J Collingridge) *trckd ldrs: ev ch whn n.m.r appr fnl f: r.o ins* **6/1**[3]

4-51 **5** *¾* **Zamboozle (IRE)**[15] 556 4-8-4 79 oh1 .... JohnEgan 7 — 83
(D R C Elsworth) *t.k.h: hld up: hdwy and c wd into home st: r.o fnl f: nvr nrr* **11/8**[1]

06-2 **6** *½* **Zonergem**[41] 296 8-9-3 89 .... JoeFanning 5 — 92
(Lady Herries) *trckd ldrs on outside: wkng wn hmpd ins fnl f* **8/1**

4-63 **7** *1 ½* **Gavroche (IRE)**[14] 572 5-9-6 92 .... GeorgeBaker 6 — 93
(J R Boyle) *hld up in tch: wknd over 1f out* **8/1**

2m 56.8s **Going Correction** +0.05s/f (Slow)

WFA 4 from 5yo+ 3lb — **7** Ran SP% **113.2**

Speed ratings (Par 109):75,74,74,74,74 73,72

CSF £43.53 TOTE £5.50: £2.10, £3.20; EX 44.60.

Owner A Grinter **Bred** Worksop Manor Stud **Trained** Woodingdean, E Sussex

■ Stewards' Enquiry : Ryan Moore caution: careless riding

FOCUS

Well contested, but a confusing, tactical race, and a pedestrian winning time.

NOTEBOOK

Cold Turkey is a smart performer round here on his day. Nicely ridden, everything dropped right for him and he quickened well to land his ninth win on sand. (op 5-1)

Country Pursuit(USA) tried to nick it, having dictated a weak tempo, and nearly pulled it off. He can be dangerous from the front - though he does not have to make to make the running - and this was a spirited first effort since September. (tchd 6-1)

Nawamees(IRE) has had a go at chasing, but still looks capable of winning decent races on the Flat. He ran over two miles last time, but is just effective at this trip. (op 12-1)

The Violin Player(USA) can never be ruled out, and again acquitted himself well in a hot little race. A stronger pace would have helped. Official explanation: jockey said gelding was denied a clear run on run to the line

Zamboozle(IRE) was unsuited by the dawdle, eventually failing to live up the promise of his previous run. He will bounce back. (op 13-8)

Zonergem did well considering the poor tempo, which would have been all against him. Though quirky, and without a win since 2002, he retains plenty of ability. (op 7-1)

Gavroche(IRE) is better when coming off a soundly-run ten furlongs.

662 BETDIRECT H'CAP — 7f (P)

5:40 (5:41) (Class 4) (0-80,78) 4-Y-O+ — **£6,477** (£1,927; £963; £481) **Stalls** Low

Form — RPR

5360 **1** **Quantum Leap**[15] 559 9-8-6 66 ....(v) JimmyQuinn 10 — 73
(S Dow) *hld up in rr: hdwy on outside 2f out: rdn and r.o to ld wl ins fnl f: sn in command* **9/1**

-421 **2** *1 ¼* **Meditation**[13] 576 4-8-13 73 .... JoeFanning 3 — 77
(I A Wood) *led tl hdd wl ins fnl f: jst hld on for 2nd* **3/1**[2]

-034 **3** *hd* **Wavertree Warrior (IRE)**[15] 559 4-8-10 75 .... JamesDoyle(5) 7 — 79
(N P Littmoden) *trckd ldrs: rdn and nt qckn ins fnl f* **10/3**[3]

4060 **4** *hd* **True Night**[2] 641 9-8-7 67 .... AdrianTNicholls 4 — 70
(D Nicholls) *mid-div: outpcd over 2f out: styd on ins fnl f: nvr nrr* **25/1**

3010 **5** *1* **Set Alight**[22] 492 5-8-9 69 ....(p) NCallan 5 — 69
(Mrs C A Dunnett) *trckd ldrs: n.m.r and lost pl 2f out: r.o ins fnl f* **14/1**

0313 **6** *½* **Distant Country (USA)**[2] 639 7-8-4 64 oh3 ....(p) FrancisNorton 8 — 63
(K R Burke) *bhd whn hmpd over 2f out: mde sme late hdwy* **6/1**

500- **7** *1 ¼* **Serieux**[182] 5266 7-9-0 77 .... SilvestreDeSousa(3) 2 — 73
(D Nicholls) *prom tl rdn and wknd ins fnl f* **20/1**

-021 **8** *½* **Aggravation**[11] 596 4-8-10 70 6ex ....(t) JohnEgan 1 — 65
(D R C Elsworth) *t.k.h: mid-div: hmpd 2f out: no ch after* **5/2**[1]

300- **9** *3 ½* **Acomb**[118] 6379 6-9-1 78 .... RichardThomas(3) 6 — 63
(Mrs L Richards) *slowly away: plld hrd: sn trckd ldrs: wknd over 1f out* **25/1**

550- **10** *8* **River Biscuit (USA)**[307] 1710 4-8-8 68 .... EddieAhern 9 — 33
(M J Polglase) *a bhd* **40/1**

1m 24.69s (-1.20) **Going Correction** +0.05s/f (Slow) — **10** Ran SP% **122.5**

Speed ratings (Par 105):108,106,106,106,104 104,102,102,98,89

CSF £36.63 CT £115.50 TOTE £15.70: £3.00, £1.70, £1.70; EX 60.00 Place 6 £89.66, Place 5 £32.74.

Owner Mrs M E O'Shea **Bred** L C And Mrs A E Sigsworth **Trained** Epsom, Surrey

FOCUS

A routine Lingfield handicap rated around the first two and the fourth.

True Night Official explanation: jockey said gelding hung left throughout

Aggravation Official explanation: jockey said gelding was denied a clear run

River Biscuit(USA) Official explanation: jockey said gelding had no more to give

T/Plt: £426.30 to a £1 stake. Pool: £38,548.40. 66.00 winning tickets. T/Qpdt: £28.50 to a £1 stake. Pool: £3,831.10. 99.30 winning tickets. JS

656 LINGFIELD (L-H)

Saturday, March 18

OFFICIAL GOING: Standard

Races 1, 2 and 5 were hand-timed.

663 PLAY NOW AT BETDIRECTCASINO.COM JUVENILE CONDITIONS STKS 5f (P)

1:35 (1:36) (Class 4) 2-Y-O

£12,464 (£3,732; £1,866; £934; £466; £234) **Stalls** High

Form RPR

1 **Love In May (IRE)** 2-8-7 MartinDwyer 4 72
(J S Moore) *wl grwn: bit bkwd: sn rdn in mid-div: wnt 2nd wl over 1f out: rdn to ld ins fnl f: drvn out* **8/1**

2 1 1/4 **Spoof Master (IRE)** 2-8-9 RobertMiles(3) 6 72
(W G M Turner) *tall: str: lw: led for 1f: led again 2f out: rdn and hdd ins fnl f: nt pce of wnr* **13/2**[3]

3 1 1/2 **Zafonical Storm (USA)** 2-8-12 JamieSpencer 2 66
(B W Duke) *leggy: trckd ldrs: sltly hmpd over 1f out: hung lft but kpt on fnl f* **9/1**

4 1 1/2 **Carlitos Spirit (IRE)** 2-8-12 AlanMunro 5 60
(B R Millman) *str: lw: pushed along fr s and towards rr: styd on fnl f: nvr nr to chal* **6/4**[1]

5 4 **It's No Problem (IRE)** 2-8-4 StephaneBreux(3) 1 39
(Jean-Rene Auvray) *tall: scope: s.i.s: bhd: styd on fnl f: nvr nr to chal* **25/1**

6 3/4 **Wrecking Crew (IRE)** 2-8-12 DaneO'Neill 8 41
(B R Millman) *cmpt: str: bkwd: prom: rdn 1/2-way: sn outpcd* **5/1**[2]

7 2 1/2 **Global Traffic** 2-8-12 JosedeSouza 3 31
(P F I Cole) *str: bit bkwd: sn outpcd and bhd* **10/1**

8 3/4 **Afric Star** 2-8-7 ShaneKelly 10 23
(P D Evans) *leggy: unf: a outpcd* **12/1**

9 1 3/4 **Banana Belle** 2-8-0 DonnaCaldwell(7) 7 16
(P S McEntee) *small: led after 1f out: hung rt and hdd 2f out: wkng qckly whn hmpd over 1f out* **66/1**

62.10 secs (2.32) **Going Correction** -0.025s/f (Stan) **9** Ran SP% **113.2**

Speed ratings (Par 94):80,78,75,73,66 65,61,60,57

CSF £57.77 TOTE £12.50: £2.30, £2.70, £2.10; EX 100.50 Trifecta £586.90 Part won. Pool: £826.69 - 0.35 winning units..

Owner A D Crook **Bred** Weathersfield Ltd **Trained** Upper Lambourn, Berks

■ The first two-year-old contest of the 2006 season.

FOCUS

A decent prize, but an impossible race to analyse form-wise. Not surprisingly some of these juveniles knew their job rather better than others and the front four pulled nicely clear of the rest.

NOTEBOOK

Love In May(IRE), a 3,000euros half-sister to two winners including one who scored as a juvenile, comes from a yard that can get them ready at the first time of asking. She certainly knew her job, especially in the second-half of the contest where she put her head down and battled on well to score. She will inevitably find things tough if turned out under a penalty in the coming weeks, but this was a nice prize to win at this stage of the season and her yard is eyeing up valuable sales races much later in the year. (op 11-1 tchd 12-1)

Spoof Master(IRE) ◆, also from a yard that does well with its early types, is bred to be speedy and was up with the pace the whole way. He did nothing wrong and never stopped trying, but the winner was too strong on the day. His experience will be a big asset in the next few weeks and he should go one better. (op 5-1)

Zafonical Storm(USA) ◆, out of a half-sister to the high-class Wharf, ran with credit but looked greener than the front pair in the home straight and should have learned something from this. (op 8-1)

Carlitos Spirit(IRE) ◆, a 33,000gns half-brother to three winners - two of them as juveniles - out of a juvenile winner, represented the trainer/jockey combination that took this race last year. However, their charge this time around had a problem going the early pace and when he did click into gear it was far too late. There was clear daylight back to the fifth horse though and he should be a different proposition next time. (tchd 13-8 and 7-4 in places)

It's No Problem(IRE) never really got into the race, but as she is out of a full-sister to Cold Turkey she may improve for a longer trip in time. (tchd 33-1)

Wrecking Crew(IRE), a 17,000euros yearling, showed up for a while but although he is bred for speed on the sire's side, there is enough stamina on the dam's side to suggest he may need further in time. (op 6-1)

Banana Belle, a cheap yearling, showed dazzling early speed, but did not handle the home bend very well and was already on the retreat when getting bumped about. She may not be an entirely lost cause on a more conventional track at a modest level. (op 50-1)

664 BETDIRECT.CO.UK SPRINT (CONDITIONS STKS) 5f (P)

2:05 (2:05) (Class 2) 4-Y-0+

£18,696 (£5,598; £2,799; £1,401; £699; £351) **Stalls** High

Form RPR

1-11 1 **Les Arcs (USA)**[42] 295 6-8-12 107 JohnEgan 8 105
(T J Pitt) *lw: a in tch: rdn to ld ins fnl f: all out* **5/2**[2]

-121 2 1/2 **Fyodor (IRE)**[28] 450 5-8-12 103 TonyCulhane 4 103
(W J Haggas) *lw: mid-div: hdwy whn hung rt over 1f out: squeezed through to go 2nd ins fnl f* **2/1**[1]

0350 3 1 **One More Round (USA)**[7] 627 8-8-12 91 (b) ChrisCatlin 3 99
(N P Littmoden) *s.i.s: outpcd tl picked up wl ent fnl f: r.o strly: nvr nrr* **40/1**

230- 4 1 3/4 **Peace Offering (IRE)**[182] 5288 6-8-12 94 VictoriaBehan 5 93
(D Nicholls) *t.k.h: in tch: n.m.r over 1f out: r.o again fnl f* **16/1**

003- 5 hd **Fire Up The Band**[167] 5647 7-9-6 109 AdrianTNicholls 6 100
(D Nicholls) *bit bkwd: trckd ldr: rdn and led appr fnl f: hdd & wknd ins* **7/2**[3]

50-0 6 1 **If Paradise**[7] 627 5-8-12 99 DaneO'Neill 10 89
(R Hannon) *racd wd towards rr: nvr on terms* **18/1**

5214 7 hd **Qadar (IRE)**[7] 631 4-8-12 94 NCallan 2 88
(N P Littmoden) *lw: trckd ldrs tl hmpd over 1f out: wknd ins fnl f* **7/1**

4266 8 1 1/4 **Dancing Mystery**[28] 450 12-9-3 92 (b) StephenCarson 1 89
(E A Wheeler) *led tl hdd appr fnl f: wknd qckly ins* **40/1**

-603 9 1 **Kempsey**[21] 517 4-8-12 75 (v) J-PGuillambert 9 80?
(J J Bridger) *slowly away: racd wd: a outpcd* **100/1**

450- 10 1 **No Time (IRE)**[308] 1713 6-8-12 80 EddieAhern 7 76
(M J Polglase) *racd wd: a bhd* **25/1**

58.70 secs (-1.08) **Going Correction** -0.025s/f (Stan) **10** Ran SP% **117.5**

Speed ratings (Par 109):107,106,104,101,101 99,99,97,95,94

CSF £7.79 TOTE £3.80: £1.50, £1.10, £8.30; EX 8.00 Trifecta £120.10 Pool: £1,126.97 - 6.66 winning units.

Owner Willie McKay **Bred** Elk Manor Farm **Trained** Bawtry, S Yorks

FOCUS

A decent line-up for this valuable conditions event and the pace was solid if not furious. The result was a carbon-copy of a handicap run over course and distance last month with the same one-two-three, albeit on very different terms. The time was nothing special, however, and the chances are that the third sets the standard and the first two were both a bit below their best.

NOTEBOOK

Les Arcs(USA) completed the four-timer and has become one of the revelations of the winter season. Still a longer price than Fyodor despite beating him half a length here last month and being 6lb better off, he had a different rider aboard this time as his usual apprentice could not claim. It made no difference though, as he confirmed his superiority with a battling victory, and it will be fascinating to see if he can transfer his improvement on to the grass. (op 9-4 tchd 11-4)

Fyodor(IRE) started favourite for this despite being 6lb worse off with Les Arcs compared to last month. Given a patient ride, he crept closer rounding the home bend and, although room was tight in the home straight, his momentum was never checked and he had no real excuses. He is a smart sprinter on sand, but the fact is that he has now raced here three times and been beaten each time. His trainer is looking forward to getting him back on a straight track. (tchd 9-4 in places tchd 85-40 in a place)

One More Round(USA), beaten less than a length into third behind Les Arcs and Fyodor in a handicap here last month, was 6lb worse off with the runner-up and 12lb worse off with the winner so he did wonderfully well to finish so close and was staying on very well at the death. The problem is that he has failed to win in three and a half years and this performance is not going to earn him any favours from the Handicapper. (op 33-1)

Peace Offering(IRE), off since finishing in the ruck in the Ayr Gold Cup last September and having his very first try on sand, ran with a great deal of credit and this was an especially decent effort considering he received quite a buffeting on reaching the straight and also his apprentice rider could not claim. Like the third horse, he has not won for three and a half years, but he has run some encouraging races since joining his current yard and he will be better off back in handicap company. (op 20-1 tchd 22-1)

Fire Up The Band won over seven furlongs here on his racecourse debut over four years ago, but his only appearance on sand since saw him finish seventh in this race two years ago. He ran with great credit and was in front a furlong out before lack of a recent run took its toll, but presumably the main aim was to put him straight before embarking on his turf campaign. (op 4-1 tchd 9-2)

If Paradise, seventh in this last year, improved a place but along with his effort at Wolverhampton the previous week this will also mean that he will start the turf season cherry-ripe. (op 16-1)

Qadar(IRE), who had a bit to do at the weights, showed up for a long way but was already beaten when getting hampered half a furlong from home. Official explanation: jockey said filly was denied a clear run in final furlong (op 9-1)

Dancing Mystery, winner of this race last year, tried to make all the running but did not get home. This looked a stronger renewal and obviously he is yet another year older.

Kempsey had no chance under these conditions.

No Time(IRE) has basically struggled since breaking the course record in winning this race two years ago.

665 BETDIRECT 0800 211 222 SPRING CUP (LISTED RACE) 7f (P)

2:40 (2:40) (Class 1) 3-Y-O

£42,585 (£16,140; £8,077; £4,027; £2,017; £1,012) **Stalls** Low

Form RPR

-111 1 **Kingsgate Prince (IRE)**[38] 341 3-8-11 97 TQuinn 3 105
(J R Best) *lw: hld up in tch: r.o to ld ins fnl f: won gng away* **7/2**[2]

200- 2 1 1/4 **Saabiq (USA)**[154] 5904 3-8-6 98 RyanMoore 8 97
(C E Brittain) *lw: racd wd: mid-div tl hdwy on outside over 2f out: led appr fnl f: hdd ins: nt pce of wnr* **10/1**

426- 3 1 1/2 **Rising Cross**[191] 5066 3-8-6 105 JohnEgan 4 93
(J R Best) *nt grwn: in rr: gd hdwy appr fnl f: r.o strly: nvr nrr* **10/1**

02-2 4 1 1/2 **Secret Night**[63] 117 3-8-6 84 JimmyQuinn 9 89
(J A R Toller) *in rr: hdwy whn swtchd rt appr fnl f: r.o* **20/1**

322- 5 1 1/4 **Campbeltown (IRE)**[175] 5484 3-8-11 100 ChrisCatlin 6 91
(E J O'Neill) *led for 1f: styd in tch: rdn over 1f out: one pce after* **10/1**

100- 6 1 1/2 **Cape Of Luck (IRE)**[128] 6304 3-8-11 86 EddieAhern 1 87
(P Mitchell) *in rr tl mde sme late hdwy* **33/1**

130- 7 1/2 **Art Market (CAN)**[182] 5308 3-8-11 102 JoeFanning 7 86
(P F I Cole) *h.d.w: bit bkwd: t.k.h: in tch: effrt 2f out: one pce appr fnl f* **7/1**[3]

-110 8 1/2 **Grand Jour (IRE)**[34] 392 3-8-11 87 DarryllHolland 13 84
(K McAuliffe) *led after 1f: rdn and hdd appr fnl f: wknd qckly* **20/1**

3-11 9 2 **Dingaan (IRE)**[52] 190 3-8-11 88 MartinDwyer 2 79
(A M Balding) *lw: mid-div: n.m.r over 2f out: nvr on terms* **7/1**[3]

000- 10 2 1/2 **Ooh Aah Camara (IRE)**[192] 5042 3-8-6 88 (t) KDarley 10 68
(T J Pitt) *s.i.s: a bhd* **40/1**

616- 11 nk **Humungous (IRE)**[154] 5901 3-8-11 103 SteveDrowne 12 72
(C R Egerton) *lw: prom tl rdn and wknd wl over 1f out* **3/1**[1]

0106 12 1 1/4 **Ockums Razor (IRE)**[12] 592 3-8-11 77 NCallan 5 69
(M J Polglase) *chsd ldr after 2f: wknd wl over 1f out* **100/1**

600- 13 9 **Danjet (IRE)**[183] 5261 3-8-7 82 ow1 ShaneKelly 11 41
(P D Evans) *racd wd: chsd ldrs tl wknd over 2f out* **100/1**

1m 24.1s (-1.79) **Going Correction** -0.025s/f (Stan) **13** Ran SP% **116.4**

Speed ratings (Par 106):109,107,105,104,102 101,100,99,97,94 94,92,82

CSF £34.51 TOTE £3.90: £2.00, £3.70, £3.80; EX 44.90 Trifecta £863.60 Part won. Pool: £1,216.46 - 0.80 winning units..

Owner John Mayne **Bred** P G Lyons **Trained** Hucking, Kent

FOCUS

A competitive contest, full of quality, and thankfully a decent pace to make it a real test. The form looks rock-solid, and the winner has been raised another 7lb.

NOTEBOOK

Kingsgate Prince(IRE) ◆ has done nothing but improve all winter and his official mark had been raised 16lb since his last start. Ridden with plenty of confidence, he was produced with precision timing to score and his rider never really had to get serious with him. It will be fascinating to see whether he can continue his progress on to the turf, but in the meantime possible targets could be a Listed race over a mile here in three weeks time - Party Boss completed the double last year - or the Easter Stakes on the new Kempton Polytrack a week earlier. (op 5-2)

Saabiq(USA), from the yard that won this last year, was making her sand debut. She was rushed around the field on the wide outside on the home bend and tried to steal the race at that point, but the race-fit winner always had her in his sights and his turn of foot proved superior. How much she will come on for this is anyone's guess, but she would probably have a better chance of winning a race like this against her own sex, so Kempton's Masaka Stakes in a fortnight's time would seem a likely target. (op 12-1)

Rising Cross, the best horse in the race on official ratings following her decent efforts in Group company at two, was doing all her best work late to make it a one-three for the stable. She is still tiny, but she appears to have trained on and the surface was no problem. She shapes as though an extra furlong would suit her better now, which makes the Masaka Stakes at Kempton in two weeks time an obvious target. (op 8-1)

Secret Night, trying this trip in her 13th race, was given a patient ride and travelled very well, but the gaps did not appear when she needed them and when she was finally in the clear it was too late. She is more exposed than most though and, bearing in mind her official rating compared with those around her, this was probably her only chance of making any impact at this level. Official explanation: jockey said filly was denied a clear run in final furlong

Campbeltown(IRE), already proven on this surface and placed three times in Listed company at two, had quite a busy campaign last term but ran with great credit on this first start in six months. This should have put him right, but he does not really possess that much scope and if he is to make an impact at this level it will probably need to be sooner rather than later.

Cape Of Luck(IRE) stayed on late, but never looked like landing a blow and probably found this company a bit too hot. (tchd 40-1)

Grand Jour(IRE) was given his usual attacking ride, but could not maintain it at this level.

Dingaan(IRE), trying an extra furlong in his hat-trick bid, has gained his two victories when ridden up with the pace, but he could never get to the front and did not look so effective as a result. Official explanation: jockey said colt was hampered on final bend (op 13-2)

Humungous(IRE), sixth in the Dewhurst when last seen and an impressive winner over course and distance before that, faded rather tamely from the home bend and it remains to be seen whether he has trained on. Official explanation: jockey said colt hung left (op 7-2 tchd 4-1)

666 BETDIRECT.CO.UK WINTER DERBY (3RD LEG OF THE EUROPEAN ALL WEATHER SERIES) (GROUP 3) 1m 2f (P)

3:15 (3:17) (Class 1) 4-Y-0+

£56,780 (£21,520; £10,770; £5,370; £2,690; £1,350) **Stalls** Low

Form				RPR
15-1	1		**Sri Diamond**[42] 296 6-8-12 105 ... JamieSpencer 14 (S Kirk) *lw: a in tch: rdn and led over 1f out: r.o u.p* **8/1**	110
4-61	2	½	**Grand Passion (IRE)**[21] 518 6-8-12 105 ... SteveDrowne 10 (G Wragg) *mid-div: hdwy 1/2-way: r.o to go 2nd ins fnl f* **9/1**	109
64-1	3	½	**Nayyir**[28] 452 8-8-12 115 ... JimmyFortune 11 (G A Butler) *bhd tl hdwy on ins 2f out: hmpd jst ins fnl f: r.o cl home* **13/2**[2]	111+
-222	4	hd	**Red Spell (IRE)**[21] 518 5-8-12 101 ... RichardHughes 9 (R Hannon) *lw: t.k.h: nvr far away: rdn and r.o ins fnl f* **7/1**[3]	108
1-14	5	shd	**Cimyla (IRE)**[34] 393 5-8-12 106 ... NCallan 7 (C F Wall) *bhd tl hdwy over 2f out: kpt on but nt qckn fnl f* **4/1**[1]	107
1301	6	hd	**Bravo Maestro (USA)**[7] 629 5-8-12 90 ... ChrisCatlin 12 (N P Littmoden) *lw: s.i.s: in rr tl hdwy on outside 2f out: rdn and r.o ins fnl f* **25/1**	107
40-3	7	hd	**Counsel's Opinion (IRE)**[21] 518 9-8-12 102 ... GeorgeBaker 2 (C F Wall) *lw: s.i.s: hld up in rr: hdwy whn short of room 1f out: nt qckn ins fnl f* **14/1**	107+
5466	8	3½	**Boo**[7] 629 4-8-12 96 ... (v) JohnEgan 4 (K R Burke) *hld up: in rr: mde sme late hdwy* **33/1**	100
0-44	9	1	**Colisay**[30] 438 7-8-12 ... RyanMoore 1 (Mrs A J Perrett) *in tch: rdn 3f out: wknd wl over 1f out* **40/1**	98
0-35	10	nk	**Impeller (IRE)**[7] 629 7-8-12 96 ... MartinDwyer 8 (W R Muir) *t.k.h: sn trckd ldrs: rdn and wknd wl over 1f out* **33/1**	98
00-4	11	nk	**African Dream**[21] 518 5-8-12 104 ... (v[1]) ShaneKelly 13 (J Noseda) *lw: trckd ldr: led 3f out: rdn: hung lft and hdd over 1f out: wknd qckly* **25/1**	97
1-11	12	2½	**Arturius (IRE)**[15] 572 4-8-12 ... EddieAhern 6 (P J Rothwell, Ire) *prom tl rdn and wknd over 1f out* **4/1**[1]	92
32-0	13	hd	**Compton Bolter (IRE)**[21] 518 9-9-1 108 ... DarryllHolland 3 (G A Butler) *led tl hdd 3f out: wknd 2f out* **16/1**	95
/20-	14	6	**Grantley**[13] 9-8-12 ... NRichter 5 (H Hesse, Germany) *a struggling in rr* **33/1**	81

2m 4.77s (-3.02) **Going Correction** -0.025s/f (Stan) 14 Ran SP% **118.4**

Speed ratings (Par 113):111,110,110,110,109 109,109,106,106,105 105,103,103,98

CSF £70.92 TOTE £11.60: £3.60, £3.80, £2.70; EX 137.00 Trifecta £1234.30 Pool: £1,912.33 - 1.10 winning units.

Owner Ascot Brew Racing **Bred** B J And Mrs Crangle **Trained** Upper Lambourn, Berks

■ The Winter Derby was being run as a Group Three for the first time.

■ Stewards' Enquiry : Jimmy Fortune three-day ban: careless riding (Mar 29-31)

FOCUS

A high-class line-up for the ninth Winter Derby, but the pace seemed to slow up a bit mid-race, causing the field to pack, and that was eventually to have an effect, with a few meeting trouble in running in the last couple furlongs and only a couple of lengths covering the first seven at the line.

NOTEBOOK

Sri Diamond, already a winner four times here, had the nightmare outside draw to overcome but thankfully for him he was able to edge across early without too much trouble and held a handy position throughout. Asked for his effort over a furlong from home whilst a few were getting into trouble behind, he found plenty and as he stays further he was never going to run out of gas. He may not have been the best horse in the race, but he certainly received the best ride. (op 9-1 tchd 10-1 in a place)

Grand Passion(IRE), like the winner, previously successful four times here - three of them over this trip - had finished ninth in the last two runnings of this race, but improved on that no end this time around. He seemed to have every chance and was produced at just the right time, but try as he might the winner was in no mood to give in. (op 15-2 tchd 7-1)

Nayyir, who had upwards of 7lb in hand of his rivals on official ratings, had made a successful racecourse debut on this track four years earlier so there were no doubts over the surface, but there remained a question mark over the trip. Switched off near the back, he tried to make his effort on the inside, which was always going to require some luck, and it ran out when he suffered serious interference in the process of trying for an audacious gap between African Dream and the inside rail a furlong out. He stayed on strongly once in the clear and would have gone very close with a clear run, but the fact is that he has not enjoyed the best of luck at various stages in his career. (op 7-1)

Red Spell(IRE) appeared to hold a very decent position throughout and ran right up to his best. There is no doubt that he is every bit as good over this trip as he is over shorter. (op 9-1)

Cimyla(IRE), deserted by George Baker in favour of Counsel's Opinion, had every chance and stayed on right to the line, but was just not quite good enough on the day. (op 9-2 tchd 5-1 in a place)

Bravo Maestro(USA), whose stamina for this was not totally guaranteed having only won a slowly-run race over course and distance earlier in the year, was ridden with plenty of patience. Making his effort widest of all in the home straight, he tended to look everywhere but in front of him yet still ran on without being able to land a blow. A strongly-run mile and being brought between horses may suit him better. (op 20-1)

Counsel's Opinion(IRE) ◆ switched right off early as usual, crept closer as the race progressed, but he did not get the gaps when he needed them and could never get there in time. He needs a stronger all-round pace, but still has the ability to make an impact in decent middle-distance handicaps back on grass this season.

Colisay Official explanation: jockey said gelding was denied a clear run in home straight

Arturius(IRE), bidding for an All-Weather hat-trick, held a good position until the home turn but then found it all too much. He may have been joint-favourite, but he had a lot to find with several of these on official ratings. (op 3-1)

Compton Bolter(IRE) made much of the running, but dropped out tamely once headed. He is finding life very tough on Polytrack these days. (op 14-1)

667 PLAY NOW AT BETDIRECTPOKER.COM H'CAP 7f (P)

3:50 (3:52) (Class 2) (0-100,99) 4-Y-0+

£15,580 (£4,665; £2,332; £1,167; £582; £292) **Stalls** Low

Form				RPR
00-1	1		**Something (IRE)**[21] 516 4-9-3 98 ... IanMongan 6 (T G Mills) *lw: trckd ldrs: wnt 2nd 3f out: rdn to ld ins fnl f: r.o wl* **1/1**[1]	108+
0-01	2	1¼	**Mr Lambros**[38] 340 5-8-12 93 ... MartinDwyer 4 (A M Balding) *led tl rdn and hdd ins fnl f: kpt on* **5/1**[2]	100+
-003	3	1¼	**King Marju (IRE)**[22] 507 4-8-8 89 ... (v) JohnEgan 5 (K R Burke) *a in tch: r.o but nt qckn fnl f* **25/1**	93
650-	4	nk	**Indian Steppes (FR)**[274] 2661 7-8-5 86 oh1 ow1 ... EddieAhern 7 (Lucinda Featherstone) *chsd ldrs: outpcd 1/2-way: rdn and r.o fnl f* **50/1**	89
500-	5	nk	**Marching Song**[155] 5874 4-8-12 93 ... RichardHughes 12 (R Hannon) *bhd tl hdwy over 1f out: r.o: nvr nrr* **25/1**	95
5020	6	¾	**Moayed**[7] 629 7-8-11 97 ... (bt) JamesDoyle(5) 1 (N P Littmoden) *slowly away: hdwy 1/2-way: nt qckn fnl f* **16/1**	97
40-0	7	2	**Uhoomagoo**[21] 516 8-8-7 88 ... (b) NCallan 13 (K A Ryan) *outpcd in rr: nvr nr to chal* **14/1**	83
000-	8	½	**Traytonic**[174] 5495 5-9-4 99 ... JimmyFortune 10 (D Nicholls) *bit bkwd: mid-div: outpcd over 2f out: nvr on terms after* **33/1**	93
0041	9	nk	**Waterside (IRE)**[11] 611 7-8-4 85 oh1 ... RyanMoore 2 (G L Moore) *mid-div: rdn 2f out: no hdwy after* **8/1**[3]	78
006-	10	2	**Thyolo (IRE)**[162] 5715 5-8-6 87 ... (b) PhilipRobinson 8 (C G Cox) *lw: trckd ldr to 3f out: wknd over 1f out* **14/1**	75
1416	11	¾	**Marko Jadeo (IRE)**[18] 541 8-8-4 85 oh3 ... PaulFitzsimons 3 (S Dow) *lw: hld up in rr: a bhd* **16/1**	71
1330	12	shd	**Chief Exec**[25] 476 4-8-4 85 oh2 ... AlanMunro 9 (C A Cyzer) *a in rr* **25/1**	71
0004	13	13	**Damachida (IRE)**[22] 507 7-9-0 95 ... (t) JamieSpencer 11 (Eva Sundbye, Sweden) *a in rr* **33/1**	47

1m 23.2s (-2.69) **Going Correction** -0.025s/f (Stan) **13** Ran SP% **122.3**

Speed ratings (Par 109):114,112,111,110,110 109,107,106,106,104 103,103,88

CSF £5.28 CT £83.83 TOTE £2.00: £1.20, £2.10, £5.60; EX 7.70 Trifecta £87.40 Pool: £1,384.30 - 11.24 winning units.

Owner John Humphreys **Bred** Newlands House Stud **Trained** Headley, Surrey

FOCUS

A competitive handicap and a furious pace resulting in a smart time for the grade. Very few ever got into it. Something impressed again and looks Listed class at least. The next three all ran close to their best.

NOTEBOOK

Something(IRE) ◆, so impressive on his sand debut here three weeks earlier, was always in the ideal position to strike and picked off the leader without too much bother. This was another smart effort off an 8lb higher mark and he looks the type to carry his decent current form back on to the turf, whilst given his liking for Polytrack perhaps the new and very valuable London Mile at Kempton in September would be an intriguing longer-term target. (op 11-10 tchd 6-5 and 5-4 in a place)

Mr Lambros ◆, raised 8lb for his impressive all-the-way-win over course and distance last month, tried the same tactics again, setting a furious gallop and succeeding in running the finish out of all bar the progressive winner. There was no disgrace in this defeat and there will be other days. (op 9-2)

King Marju(IRE) ◆ has not managed to win since his third start as a two-year-old, but there was the hint of a return to form in the most recent of his three outings in Dubai and he did well to keep on for third. He is better handicapped these days and is worth keeping in mind. (op 20-1)

Indian Steppes(FR) ◆, making her debut for her new trainer though still in the same yard, and racing for the first time in nine months, ran a blinder especially as with the 1lb overweight she was effectively 2lb wrong. She is more exposed than the trio that finished in front of her, but she is a versatile sort and if the break has rejuvenated her - the signs look encouraging judged on this performance - the stable should continue to have plenty of fun with her. (op 66-1)

Marching Song, on sand for the first time, made an encouraging return from a five-month break and seemed to see out the seventh furlong a bit better this time.

Moayed made some progress in the second half of the contest, but never looked like winning and does not seem to run two races alike these days. (op 14-1)

Waterside(IRE), raised 5lb for his Southwell win, is better when racing closer to the pace than he was able to do here. He has a good record on this track, but as he gets older he may prefer the slower Fibresand. (op 10-1)

668 TEXT "BETDIRECT" TO 88600 MAIDEN STKS 1m 2f (P)

4:20 (4:21) (Class 4) 3-Y-0 **£6,477** (£1,927; £963; £481) **Stalls** Low

Form				RPR
42-	1		**Pound Sign**[235] 3817 3-9-3 ... JamieSpencer 3 (M L W Bell) *h.d.w: scope: trckd ldrs: qcknd to ld 1f out: r.o strly* **9/4**[1]	84+
0-23	2	2	**Sky High Guy (IRE)**[24] 479 3-9-3 68 ... FrankieMcDonald 8 (S Kirk) *lw: racd wd tl swtchd to ins 2f out: r.o to chse wnr fnl f* **4/1**[3]	72
	3	2	**Bride To Be (USA)** 3-8-12 ... RyanMoore 4 (C E Brittain) *leggy: slowly away:: in rr: sme hdwy 4f out: styd on appr fnl f: r.o: nvr nrr* **33/1**	63
5-40	4	¾	**Eclipse Park**[24] 483 3-9-3 71 ... ShaneKelly 9 (M J McGrath) *towards rr: hdwy on outside 2f out: kpt on: nvr nr to chal* **20/1**	67
	5	1¼	**Calcutta Cup (UAE)** 3-9-3 ... KDarley 2 (M Johnston) *lengthy: scope: lw: trckd ldr tl rdn and fdd ins fnl f* **13/2**	65
0-42	6	1	**Gus**[26] 460 3-9-3 72 ... MichaelHills 1 (B W Hills) *lw: led tl hdd & wknd 1f out* **13/2**	63
2-2	7	1¼	**Tafiya**[24] 479 3-8-12 ... JimmyFortune 7 (G A Butler) *trckd ldrs tl wknd over 1f out* **7/2**[2]	55
000-	8	1¼	**It's Basil**[171] 5542 3-9-3 53 ... JimmyQuinn 5 (R M Flower) *a bhd* **100/1**	58?
	9	1	**Azurine (IRE)** 3-8-12 ... JoeFanning 6 (M Johnston) *neat: mid-div: rdn 4f out: wknd wl over 1f out* **33/1**	51
0-0	10	14	**Radical Attraction (USA)**[24] 479 3-8-12 ... RichardHughes 10 (R Hannon) *mid-div: lost tch over 2f out* **50/1**	25

2m 7.32s (-0.47) **Going Correction** -0.025s/f (Stan) **10** Ran SP% **113.3**

Speed ratings (Par 100):100,98,96,96,95 94,93,92,91,80

CSF £10.41 TOTE £3.10: £1.60, £1.80, £4.00; EX 16.80 Trifecta £162.40 Pool: £1,221.48 - 5.34 winning units.

Owner Fitzroy Thoroughbreds I **Bred** John And Susan Davis **Trained** Newmarket, Suffolk

■ Stewards' Enquiry : Frankie McDonald three-day ban: careless riding (Mar 29-31)

FOCUS

An ordinary maiden for the track and the pace was only fair, but the winner could hardly have been more impressive. He is the only one to take from the race.

669 **BETDIRECT 0800 211 222 MAIDEN STKS** **1m (P)**
4:50 (4:54) (Class 5) 3-Y-O+ **£4,857** (£1,445; £722; £360) **Stalls** High

Form RPR
0- **1** **Tommy Toogood (IRE)**[183] 5268 3-8-9 MichaelHills 5 77+
(B W Hills) *a in tch: shkn up to ld appr fnl f: sn clr: comf* **3/1**[2]
40- **2** *3* **Picture Show (USA)**[246] 3503 3-8-4 JimmyQuinn 11 65
(C E Brittain) *sn trckd ldr: ev ch appr fnl f: kpt but nt pce of wnr* **10/1**
2 **3** *2 1/2* **Sweet Medicine**[22] 503 4-9-7 TonyCulhane 10 65
(P Howling) *led after 1f: rdn and hdd appr fnl f: one pce after* **9/2**[3]
4 **4** *nk* **Landela**[18] 539 4-9-7 NCallan 9 64
(M A Jarvis) *in tch: rdn 2f out: r.o one pce fnl f* **15/2**
0-4 **5** *nk* **Henry Holmes**[70] 62 3-8-6 RichardThomas(3) 3 63
(Mrs L Richards) *led for 1f: in tch tl rdn and one pce fnl f* **20/1**
40- **6** *1 1/4* **Cool Customer (USA)**[155] 5870 3-8-9 EddieAhern 2 60
(E A L Dunlop) *lw: hld up: rdn over 1f out: nvr nr to chal* **2/1**[1]
7 *nk* **March Gold (IRE)** 3-8-4 JohnEgan 1 55
(H Morrison) *rangy: str: lw: towards rr: rdn and hdwy over 2f out but nvr pce to chal* **25/1**
0- **8** *2* **Gizmondo**[226] 4106 3-8-2 ChrisHough(7) 8 55
(M L W Bell) *t.k.h: racd wd in tch: wknd ent fnl f* **50/1**
30 **9** *1 1/4* **Fire Of Love**[19] 531 3-7-13 JamesDoyle(5) 7 47
(N P Littmoden) *mid-div: rdn 1/2-way: sn bhd* **16/1**
0- **10** *shd* **Eccollo (IRE)**[150] 5990 4-9-5 JamesO'Reilly(7) 12 57?
(T J Pitt) *a in rr and wl bhd fr 1/2-way* **25/1**
11 *10* **Medfae (KSA)** 3-8-9 JamieMackay 4 29
(C F Wall) *neat: a wl bhd* **33/1**

1m 38.97s (-0.46) **Going Correction** -0.025s/f (Stan)
WFA 3 from 4yo 17lb **11** Ran SP% **120.6**
Speed ratings (Par 103):101,98,95,95,94 93,93,91,90,90 80
CSF £31.43 TOTE £4.20: £2.00, £2.60, £2.30; EX 62.60 Trifecta £170.40 Pool: £1,226.62 - 5.11 winning units.
Owner Rick Barnes **Bred** Barronstown Stud And Orpendale **Trained** Lambourn, Berks

FOCUS
Not a particularly competitive maiden and the pace was ordinary, but the winner did it very nicely. Just modest form behind him, however.
Eccollo(IRE) Official explanation: jockey said, regarding running and riding, his orders were to jump out, get the gelding settled mid-division, and make the best of his way home, adding that he asked for an effort 3f out and the gelding stayed on; trainer said gelding is green and had problems with its feet in the past

670 **BETDIRECT NO Q ON 08000 936693 H'CAP** **1m (P)**
5:25 (5:26) (Class 4) (0-85,85) 4-Y-O+ **£6,477** (£1,927; £963; £481) **Stalls** High

Form RPR
00-0 **1** **Steely Dan**[18] 541 7-9-0 **78** GeorgeBaker 6 85
(J R Best) *lw: hld up in rr: swtchd rt and hdwy on outside over 1f out: drvn out to ld post* **14/1**
0620 **2** *shd* **Trifti**[18] 542 5-9-7 **85** MartinDwyer 8 92
(C A Cyzer) *hld up: hdwy over 1f out: rdn and ev ch wl ins fnl f: jst failed* **12/1**
-222 **3** *hd* **Spring Goddess (IRE)**[25] 476 5-9-4 **82** DarrenWilliams 9 89
(A P Jarvis) *lw: a in tch: rdn to ld jst ins fnl f: hdd by first 2 nr fin* **5/1**[2]
131- **4** *1 1/4* **Fasylitator (IRE)**[103] 6499 4-8-13 **77** EddieAhern 5 81
(D K Ivory) *trckd ldrs: led briefly appr fnl f: no ex ins* **6/1**[3]
3155 **5** *hd* **Northern Desert (IRE)**[7] 632 7-9-7 **85** ChrisCatlin 1 88
(P W Hiatt) *hld up: t.k.h: r.o fnl f but nt nr to chal* **5/1**[2]
4-52 **6** *nk* **Obrigado (USA)**[18] 542 6-9-2 **80** DarryllHolland 3 83
(W J Haggas) *lw: trckd ldrs: ev ch on ins appr fnl f: no ex* **10/3**[1]
560- **7** *1/2* **Prince Samos (IRE)**[155] 5876 4-9-6 **84** RyanMoore 10 85
(R Hannon) *in rr: sme hdwy over 1f out: nvr nr to chal* **12/1**
153- **8** *hd* **All Quiet**[172] 5525 5-9-0 **78** RichardHughes 2 79
(R Hannon) *hld up in tch: rdn over 1f out: one pce after* **9/1**
0104 **9** *2 1/2* **Hayyani (IRE)**[25] 476 4-8-13 **77**(e) JohnEgan 12 75+
(K McAuliffe) *trckd ldrs to 3f out: rdn and wknd fnl f* **20/1**
0-03 **10** *4* **Baylaw Star**[29] 444 5-9-2 **80** NCallan 4 66
(K A Ryan) *led tl rdn and hdd over 1f out: wknd qckly* **14/1**
650- **11** *4* **Winners Delight**[302] 1866 5-8-10 **77** AdamKirby(3) 11 54
(A P Jarvis) *slowly away: sme hdwy 1/2-way: wknd 2f out* **50/1**
/0-0 **12** *1 3/4* **Sgt Pepper (IRE)**[7] 632 5-9-0 **78** BrianReilly 7 51
(P L Gilligan) *slowly away: a bhd* **66/1**

1m 38.13s (-1.30) **Going Correction** -0.025s/f (Stan) **12** Ran SP% **117.6**
Speed ratings (Par 105):105,104,104,103,103 102,102,102,99,95 91,90
CSF £167.72 CT £964.91 TOTE £13.30: £3.60, £4.70, £2.10; EX 206.00 Trifecta £1039.30 Part won. Pool: £1,463.93 - 0.20 winning units. Place 6 £91.42, Place 5 £28.14.
Owner E A Condon **Bred** Mrs S E Barclay And L B Snowden **Trained** Hucking, Kent

FOCUS
A decent handicap run at a good clip and the front two both came from off the pace. The third offers the best guide to the form.
Hayyani(IRE) Official explanation: jockey said gelding ran too free
T/Plt: £207.10 to a £1 stake. Pool: £67,238.80. 236.95 winning tickets. T/Qpdt: £26.10 to a £1 stake. Pool: £5,827.70. 165.15 winning tickets. JS

647 SOUTHWELL (L-H)
Monday, March 20

OFFICIAL GOING: Standard
Wind: Moderate, half-against Weather: Overcast and cold.

673 **EXPERIENCE NOTTINGHAMSHIRE H'CAP** **5f (F)**
2:20 (2:20) (Class 5) (0-70,70) 3-Y-O **£3,238** (£963; £481; £240) **Stalls** High

Form RPR
3012 **1** **Stoneacre Boy (IRE)**[14] 601 3-9-2 **68**(b) RobbieFitzpatrick 4 83
(Peter Grayson) *chsd ldr: rdn to ld appr fnl f: r.o strly: readily* **6/4**[1]
1122 **2** *3* **Garlogs**[38] 359 3-9-2 **68** RobertWinston 1 73
(A Bailey) *led: hdd appr fnl f: no ex* **7/4**[2]
-445 **3** *6* **Amber Glory**[25] 488 3-8-9 **66**(b) AndrewMullen(5) 3 51
(K A Ryan) *chsd ldrs: outpcd fnl 2f* **18/1**
025- **4** *5* **Lucayos**[95] 6581 3-8-5 **62** RichardKingscote(5) 6 30
(Mrs H Sweeting) *hung lft thrght: sn outpcd and in rr: kpt on fnl f* **8/1**
2-24 **5** *2* **Rebellious Spirit**[27] 473 3-9-4 **70** MickyFenton 5 31
(J G Given) *sn drvn along to chse ldrs: lost pl 2f out* **15/2**[3]
560- **6** *4* **Coquet Island**[227] 4118 3-8-13 **68** BenSwarbrick(3) 2 15
(G M Moore) *chsd ldrs on outer: rdn and lost pl over 2f out* **50/1**
4405 **7** *8* **Luloah**[9] 626 3-8-8 **60** BrianReilly 7 —
(P S McEntee) *s.i.s: sn wl outpcd and bhd* **33/1**

60.24 secs (-0.06) **Going Correction** -0.05s/f (Stan) **7** Ran SP% **109.4**
Speed ratings (Par 98):98,93,83,75,72 66,53
CSF £3.91 TOTE £2.20: £1.60, £1.30; EX 4.10.
Owner Richard Teatum **Bred** Michael Dalton **Trained** Formby, Lancs

FOCUS
A modest sprint handicap with little strength in depth. The runner-up sets the standard but the form is not that solid.
Lucayos Official explanation: jockey said colt hung left-handed throughout

674 **BOOK TICKETS ON LINE CLAIMING STKS** **6f (F)**
2:50 (2:50) (Class 6) 4-Y-O+ **£2,388** (£705; £352) **Stalls** Low

Form RPR
0251 **1** **Soba Jones**[34] 408 9-8-12 62 JasonEdmunds(3) 3 71
(J Balding) *trckd ldr: led on bit 2f out: rdn out* **13/8**[2]
-210 **2** *1 3/4* **Up Tempo (IRE)**[5] 639 8-9-1 66(b) AdrianTNicholls 6 66
(K A Ryan) *reminders after s: sn drvn along: hdwy 3f out: wnt 2nd over 1f out: no real imp* **5/4**[1]
5230 **3** *6* **Byo (IRE)**[16] 587 8-9-1 59 TonyCulhane 5 48
(P Howling) *led early: chsd ldrs: wknd over 1f out* **8/1**[3]
300- **4** *3* **Government (IRE)**[84] 6497 5-8-5 45 BrianReilly 1 29
(M C Chapman) *in tch: rdn and outpcd over 3f out: sn lost pl* **50/1**
000- **5** *1 1/4* **Roko**[366] 666 4-8-2 35(b) MarcHalford(5) 4 27
(S R Bowring) *sn led: hdd 2f out: wknd appr fnl f* **50/1**
6055 **6** *9* **Sir Sandrovitch (IRE)**[12] 613 10-8-11 50(b) RobertWinston 2 4
(R W Price) *s.v.s: a detached in last* **10/1**

1m 16.19s (-0.71) **Going Correction** -0.075s/f (Stan) **6** Ran SP% **106.7**
Speed ratings (Par 101):101,98,90,86,85 73
CSF £3.52 TOTE £2.70: £1.40, £1.30; EX 5.70.
Owner R L Crowe **Bred** Mrs M J Hills **Trained** Scrooby, Notts

FOCUS
An uncompetitive claimer rated around the winner.

675 **DINE IN THE QUEEN MOTHER RESTAURANT H'CAP** **2m (F)**
3:20 (3:20) (Class 5) (0-75,75) 4-Y-O+ **£3,238** (£963; £481; £240) **Stalls** Low

Form RPR
1023 **1** **Isa'Af (IRE)**[14] 599 7-9-2 **67** PhillipMakin 8 76
(P W Hiatt) *trckd ldrs: led over 2f out: styd on u.p* **5/2**[1]
5100 **2** *2* **Victory Quest (IRE)**[9] 628 6-8-13 **64**(v) RobertWinston 5 71
(Mrs S Lamyman) *led tl over 2f out: kpt on same pce fnl f* **7/2**[3]
00-4 **3** *3* **Madiba**[5] 643 7-8-9 **60** J-PGuillambert 3 63
(P Howling) *chsd ldrs: sn pushed along: one pce fnl 2f* **5/1**
1503 **4** *6* **Moon Emperor**[20] 545 9-9-7 **72**(b) TonyCulhane 4 68
(J R Jenkins) *hld up in tch: drvn along 9f out: rdn and lost pl 6f out: kpt on fnl 2f* **3/1**[2]
-015 **5** *3/4* **Indian Chase**[6] 635 9-8-6 **60** RichardThomas(3) 1 55
(Dr J R J Naylor) *stdd s: hld up in tch: effrt 4f out: wknd 2f out* **7/1**
640 **6** *15* **Real Chief (IRE)**[24] 503 8-7-12 **56** oh4(b[1]) JosephWalsh(7) 6 33
(Miss M E Rowland) *hld up in tch: effrt 5f out: lost pl over 3f out: sn bhd* **40/1**

3m 42.93s (-1.61) **Going Correction** -0.075s/f (Stan)
WFA 4 from 6yo+ 5lb **6** Ran SP% **107.4**
Speed ratings (Par 103):101,100,98,95,95 87
CSF £10.44 CT £32.23 TOTE £3.10: £2.10, £2.30; EX 18.40 Trifecta £48.60 Pool: £861.50 - 12.56 winning tickets..
Owner Phil Kelly **Bred** T Monaghan **Trained** Hook Norton, Oxon
■ Stewards' Enquiry : Richard Thomas four-day ban: failed to ride out for fourth place (Mar 31-Apr 3)

FOCUS
This handicap took little winning and was run at just a steady gallop to the halfway mark. The third is the best guide to the level.
Moon Emperor Official explanation: trainer had no explanation for the poor form shown

676 **SOUTHWELL-RACECOURSE.CO.UK (S) H'CAP** **1m (F)**
3:50 (3:52) (Class 6) (0-60,55) 3-Y-O **£2,388** (£705; £352) **Stalls** Low

Form RPR
30-0 **1** **Secret Tender (IRE)**[70] 69 3-8-11 **48** RobertWinston 5 51
(J R Weymes) *chsd ldrs: hrd drvn 4f out: styd on to ld jst ins last: kpt on* **9/2**
0-43 **2** *3/4* **Chicherova (IRE)**[32] 430 3-8-12 **49** PaulFessey 2 50
(T D Barron) *chsd ldr: led over 5f out: hdd jst ins last: no ex* **15/8**[1]
04-5 **3** *4* **Assumption (IRE)**[76] 20 3-8-10 **47** J-PGuillambert 6 40
(S C Williams) *in tch: effrt over 2f out: edgd lft over 1f out: sn wknd* **4/1**[3]
3326 **4** *2* **Cool Isle**[20] 543 3-9-4 **55**(b) TonyCulhane 4 44
(P Howling) *in rr: sme drvn along: kpt on fnl 2f: nvr on terms* **7/2**[2]
0-00 **5** *5* **Cecchetti (IRE)**[16] 577 3-8-8 **50** RichardKingscote(5) 3 29
(Mrs H Sweeting) *sn chsng ldrs: hung rt over 3f out: lost pl over 1f out* **8/1**
0-00 **6** *29* **Baytown Valentina**[5] 642 3-8-13 **50**(v[1]) AdrianTNicholls 1 —
(P Howling) *led tl over 5f out: lost pl over 3f out: sn bhd and eased* **33/1**

1m 45.24s (0.64) **Going Correction** -0.075s/f (Stan) **6** Ran SP% **109.2**
Speed ratings (Par 96):93,92,88,86,81 52
CSF £12.65 TOTE £5.10: £3.30, £1.10; EX 14.50.There was no bid for the winner.
Owner J Weymes **Bred** E O'Leary **Trained** Middleham Moor, N Yorks

FOCUS
A poor seller rated around the first two.
Baytown Valentina Official explanation: jockey said filly had no more to give

677 **GOLF AND RACING AT SOUTHWELL MEDIAN AUCTION MAIDEN STKS** **7f (F)**
4:20 (4:22) (Class 6) 3-5-Y-O **£2,388** (£705; £352) **Stalls** Low

Form RPR
2 **1** **Webbow (IRE)**[21] 534 4-9-10 DavidAllan 4 69
(T D Easterby) *led: qcknd over 3f out: styd on wl fnl f* **4/1**[3]
-000 **2** *1 1/4* **Contented (IRE)**[23] 520 4-9-5 53(p) JamesDoyle(5) 7 66
(Mrs L C Jewell) *trckd ldrs on outer: wnt 2nd over 1f out: no ex ins last* **9/1**
3 *1 1/2* **Snowy Day (FR)** 3-8-9 TonyCulhane 2 57
(W J Haggas) *rangy: unf: scope: trckd ldrs: effrt 3f out: hung lft over 1f out: kpt on same pce* **7/2**[2]
63-2 **4** *nk* **Burton Ash**[14] 596 4-9-5 62(b[1]) MickyFenton 3 56
(J G Given) *chsd wnr: kpt on same pce appr fnl f* **11/4**[1]
562 **5** *5* **Blanc Visage**[9] 630 3-8-4 74 RichardKingscote(5) 6 43
(Mrs H Sweeting) *w ldrs: wknd 2f out* **7/2**[2]
6364 **6** *3* **Bahhmirage (IRE)**[4] 651 3-8-4 50(v[1]) NickyMackay 1 31
(Stef Liddiard) *s.i.s: rdn over 4f out: nvr on terms* **16/1**

7 3 **Galloping Gertie** 4-9-5 .... DaleGibson 5 28
(J Hetherton) *leggy: unf: s.i.s: nvr on terms* **50/1**
06-0 8 2 **Dangermouse**[63] 120 3-8-1 48 .... RichardThomas(3) 8 18
(A G Newcombe) *sn chsng ldrs: wknd over 2f out* **33/1**
1m 29.81s (-0.99) **Going Correction** -0.075s/f (Stan)
WFA 3 from 4yo 15lb 8 Ran SP% **111.9**
Speed ratings (Par 101):102,100,98,98,92 89,85,83
CSF £37.49 TOTE £4.70: £1.30, £3.00, £1.80; EX 50.90 Trifecta £182.30 Pool: £983.73 - 3.83 winning tickets..
Owner Wentdale Limited **Bred** Joe O'Callaghan **Trained** Great Habton, N Yorks
FOCUS
A weak maiden best measured through the runner-up and exposed 62-rated fourth.

678 SPONSOR A RACE AT SOUTHWELL FILLIES' H'CAP 1m (F)
4:50 (4:50) (Class 5) (0-70,65) 4-Y-0+ **£3,238** (£963; £481; £240) **Stalls** Low

Form RPR
2101 1 **Vancouver Gold (IRE)**[4] 649 4-9-0 **61** 6ex .... RobertWinston 3 67+
(K R Burke) *w ldr: led and qcknd 3f out: rdn clr over 1f out: eased towards fin* **9/4**[2]
6-02 2 6 **Midnight Lace**[3] 659 4-9-2 **63** .... (e[1]) PatCosgrave 4 56
(J R Boyle) *trckd ldrs: hrd drvn 4f out: wnt modest 2nd over 1f out: no ch w wnr* **5/1**
-101 3 ¾ **Tacid**[25] 493 4-8-4 **51** oh1 .... FrancisNorton 1 43
(Dr J D Scargill) *trckd ldrs: effrt 4f out: kpt on same pce* **2/1**[1]
00-4 4 ¾ **Dispol Veleta**[34] 412 5-9-4 **65** .... PhillipMakin 2 55
(T D Barron) *led tl 3f out: kpt on same pce* **11/4**[3]
1m 43.31s (-1.29) **Going Correction** -0.075s/f (Stan) 4 Ran SP% **107.4**
Speed ratings (Par 100):103,97,96,95
CSF £12.17 TOTE £2.90; EX 8.00 Place 6 £28.16, Place 5 £24.67.
Owner Bigwigs Bloodstock II **Bred** Ballinacurra Stud **Trained** Middleham Moor, N Yorks
FOCUS
A weak fillies' handicap and a one-horse race but not a contest to take at face value.
T/Plt: £30.40 to a £1 stake. Pool: £36,636.50. 879.35 winning tickets. T/Qpdt: £50.10 to a £1 stake. Pool: £2,080.10. 30.70 winning tickets. WG

639 WOLVERHAMPTON (A.W) (L-H)
Monday, March 20

OFFICIAL GOING: Standard
Wind: Light, against Weather: Overcast

679 ENJOY RACING FROM THE ZONGALERO RESTAURANT BANDED STKS 5f 20y(P)
2:00 (2:01) (Class 7) 4-Y-0+ **£1,365** (£403; £201) **Stalls** Low

Form RPR
0-06 1 **Red Sovereign**[62] 130 5-8-13 50 .... DNolan(3) 5 59
(D G Bridgwater) *mde all: rdn over 1f out: edgd rt ins fnl f: r.o* **20/1**
0324 2 ½ **Muktasb (USA)**[25] 487 5-9-1 49 .... (v) TomEaves 1 56
(D Shaw) *dwlt: nt clr run 1/2-way: hdwy over 1f out: rdn and edgd rt ins fnl f: r.o* **4/1**[1]
3520 3 1 ¾ **Leah's Pride**[24] 502 5-9-2 50 .... FergalLynch 12 51
(P Howling) *a.p: rdn to chse wnr and hung lft over 1f out: styd on same pce ins fnl f* **14/1**
2030 4 1 ¼ **Davids Mark**[22] 524 6-9-0 48 .... StephenCarson 6 44+
(J R Jenkins) *s.i.s: outpcd: nt clr run over 1f out: r.o ins fnl f* **9/1**
0-05 5 shd **Feminist (IRE)**[52] 212 4-8-11 40 .... ChrisCatlin 2 41
(J M Bradley) *chsd ldrs: rdn 1/2-way: eged rt fnl f: styd on same pce* **14/1**
40-6 6 shd **Global Achiever**[26] 480 5-9-2 50 .... (p) GeorgeBaker 10 46
(G C H Chung) *hld up: hdwy over 1f out: r.o* **8/1**
650- 7 shd **New Options**[101] 6527 9-8-9 50 .... (b) RonanKeogh(7) 3 45+
(Peter Grayson) *s.i.s: hdwy 1/2-way: nt clr run over 1f out: sn rdn : hung rt and styd on ins fnl f* **15/2**[3]
00-0 8 ½ **Music Teacher**[26] 485 4-9-2 50 .... SteveDrowne 13 44+
(N A Callaghan) *s.i.s: outpcd: nt clr run over 1f out: nt rch ldrs* **14/1**
-052 9 shd **Stagnite**[42] 307 6-9-2 50 .... (p) DarryllHolland 4 43
(K McAuliffe) *chsd ldrs: rdn 1/2-way: hung lft fr over 1f out: styd on same pce* **5/1**[2]
1302 10 ½ **Boanerges (IRE)**[22] 524 9-8-11 50 .... GregFairley(5) 11 41+
(J M Bradley) *chsd ldrs: nt clr run and lost pl wl over 1f out: hmpd 1f out: nvr able to chal* **9/1**
3200 11 5 **On The Trail**[6] 633 9-8-11 45 .... (p) DarrenWilliams 9 18
(D W Chapman) *chsd ldrs: rdn over 1f out: wknd fnl f* **25/1**
000- 12 3 **College Queen**[173] 5552 8-9-0 48 .... (b) IanMongan 7 11
(S Gollings) *s.s: outpcd* **25/1**
0-35 13 7 **Town House**[43] 299 4-8-11 45 .... JoeFanning 8 —
(B P J Baugh) *chsd ldrs over 3f* **40/1**
62.79 secs (-0.03) **Going Correction** -0.075s/f (Stan) 13 Ran SP% **114.4**
Speed ratings (Par 97):97,96,93,91,91 91,90,90,89,89 81,76,65
CSF £91.11 TOTE £30.90: £6.00, £1.50, £4.90; EX 133.50.
Owner M K F Seymour **Bred** Miss Jacqueline Goodearl **Trained** Icomb, Gloucs
FOCUS
A routine banded sprint in which the draw played its part and the inevitable problems in running for a couple. Despite that the form appears sound enough.

680 WOLVERHAMPTON-RACECOURSE.CO.UK BANDED STKS 5f 216y(P)
2:30 (2:31) (Class 7) 4-Y-0+ **£1,365** (£403; £201) **Stalls** Low

Form RPR
0-26 1 **Auentraum (GER)**[48] 261 6-8-11 45 .... (p) DarryllHolland 13 52
(K McAuliffe) *chsd ldr: led over 4f out: rdn out* **7/2**[1]
0-23 2 1 ½ **Obe Bold (IRE)**[28] 465 5-8-11 45 .... FrancisNorton 4 48
(A Berry) *led: hdd over 4f out: rdn over 2f out: styd on* **6/1**[3]
4001 3 hd **Wilford Maverick (IRE)**[6] 638 4-9-3 45 .... (v) FrancisFerris 3 53
(M J Attwater) *s.i.s: hld up: nt clr run over 2f out: hdwy over 1f out : styd on* **11/2**[2]
-000 4 1 ¼ **Headland (USA)**[53] 196 8-8-11 45 .... (be) DarrenWilliams 5 43
(D W Chapman) *plld hrd and prom: rdn over 2f out: no ex fnl f* **12/1**
32-0 5 1 **Strathclyde (IRE)**[52] 209 7-8-11 45 .... DaneO'Neill 10 40
(A M Hales) *stdd s: hld up: hdwy u.p over 1f out: no imp fnl f* **15/2**
0-00 6 ½ **Smirfys Party**[56] 175 8-8-8 45 .... PaulMulrennan(3) 9 39
(W M Brisbourne) *prom: rdn and hung rt over 2f out: styng on same pce whn hung lft fnl f* **14/1**
0-34 7 1 **Misty Princess**[6] 633 4-8-11 45 .... ChrisCatlin 6 36
(M J Attwater) *chsd ldrs: rdn and hung rt over 2f out: bmpd over 1f out: styd on same pce* **15/2**
0/0- 8 shd **Compton Earl**[83] 4882 6-8-6 45 .... EmmettStack(5) 7 35
(J J Lambe, Ire) *dwlt: hdwy u.p over 1f out: nvr nrr* **20/1**
060- 9 3 **Grand View**[153] 5966 10-8-11 45 .... (p) JoeFanning 12 26
(J R Weymes) *chsd ldrs over 4f* **14/1**
-056 10 3 ½ **Sapphire Dream**[12] 613 4-8-11 45 .... (v[1]) ShaneKelly 8 16
(A Bailey) *s.i.s: hdwy over 3f out: wkng whn n.m.r over 1f out* **16/1**
000- 11 ½ **Justenjoy Yourself**[162] 5754 4-8-11 45 .... SamHitchcott 1 14
(R W Price) *prom: rdn over 3f out: wknd over 1f out* **20/1**
000/ 12 9 **Pass Go**[274] 4128 5-8-11 45 .... (v[1]) PaulHanagan 2 —
(J J Lambe, Ire) *s.i.s: outpcd* **25/1**
060- 13 ½ **Compton Classic**[129] 6235 4-8-11 45 .... FergalLynch 11 —
(J S Goldie) *stdd s: hld up: rdn and wknd over 3f out* **25/1**
1m 15.75s (-0.06) **Going Correction** -0.075s/f (Stan) 13 Ran SP% **119.5**
Speed ratings (Par 97):97,95,94,93,91 91,89,89,85,80 80,68,67
CSF £22.01 TOTE £4.90: £2.10, £1.70, £1.80; EX 23.60.
Owner Nadeem Ahmad **Bred** Gestut Auenquelle **Trained** Fernham, Oxon
FOCUS
A modest banded event run at an even pace. Very few got into this and the front pair held those positions throughout, and the form looks average and sound enough, rated through the third..
Smirfys Party Official explanation: jockey said gelding hung right round bend
Compton Classic Official explanation: jockey said colt would not face kickback

681 WOLVERHAMPTON RACECOURSE ANY OCCASION ROOM HIRE BANDED STKS 7f 32y(P)
3:00 (3:01) (Class 7) 4-Y-0+ **£1,365** (£403; £201) **Stalls** High

Form RPR
-130 1 **Only If I Laugh**[36] 391 5-9-0 48 .... GrahamGibbons 7 56
(M J Attwater) *chsd ldrs: led over 1f out: edgd rt ins fnl f: drvn out* **4/1**[1]
2421 2 1 ½ **Mount Royale (IRE)**[12] 618 8-9-1 49 .... (v) KimTinkler 4 53
(N Tinkler) *a.p: chsd ldr 1/2-way tl 2f out: styd on u.p* **5/1**[2]
0360 3 hd **Prince Of Gold**[13] 612 6-9-2 50 .... VinceSlattery 9 54+
(R Hollinshead) *sn pushed along in rr: rdn and nt clr run over 2f out: hdwy and hmpd over 1f out: r.o ins fnl f* **8/1**
-552 4 nk **Cloann (IRE)**[35] 398 4-9-1 49 .... (b) StephenCarson 5 52
(E A Wheeler) *mid-div: hdwy over 1f out: sn rdn and edgd lft: styd on same pce ins fnl f* **15/2**
4-40 5 ½ **Ardkeel Lass (IRE)**[13] 608 5-8-13 47 .... (p) ShaneKelly 10 49
(P D Evans) *led: rdn and hdd over 1f out: no ex ins fnl f* **33/1**
32-0 6 hd **Humility**[23] 520 5-9-2 50 .... DarryllHolland 8 51
(C A Cyzer) *hld up: hdwy over 2f out: styd on same pce ins fnl f* **11/2**[3]
06-0 7 2 ½ **Avenlea**[42] 310 5-8-13 47 .... IanMongan 2 42
(G L Moore) *chsd ldrs: rdn over 2f out: edgd lft and no ex over 1f out* **7/1**
/00- 8 1 ½ **Geojimali**[252] 3392 4-9-2 50 .... FergalLynch 6 41
(J S Goldie) *chsd ldr tl rdn 1/2-way: nt clr run 2f out: sn btn* **33/1**
0-00 9 2 **Colloseum**[31] 446 5-8-13 47 .... TomEaves 11 33
(T J Etherington) *s.s: outpcd* **20/1**
-000 10 ½ **Qobtaan (USA)**[16] 582 7-9-0 48 .... (p) GeorgeBaker 1 32
(M R Bosley) *s.i.s: sn pushed along in rr: effrt over 2f out: sn wknd* **10/1**
/4-0 11 2 ½ **Hilltop Fantasy**[45] 289 5-8-13 47 .... (v[1]) MichaelTebbutt 3 25
(V Smith) *mid-div: sn pushed along: wknd over 2f out* **12/1**
0305 12 5 **Pheckless**[31] 446 7-8-13 47 .... PaulHanagan 12 12
(J M Bradley) *s.i.s: hld up: plld hrd: a in rr* **14/1**
1m 30.46s (0.06) **Going Correction** -0.075s/f (Stan) 12 Ran SP% **121.5**
Speed ratings (Par 97):96,94,94,93,93 92,90,88,86,85 82,76
CSF £23.52 TOTE £5.00: £2.00, £2.20, £3.30; EX 19.20.
Owner Phones Direct Partnership **Bred** The Lavington Stud **Trained** Wysall, Notts
■ Stewards' Enquiry : Graham Gibbons one-day ban: careless riding (Mar 31)
FOCUS
A fair pace for this ordinary banded event and the field spread right out across the track on reaching the straight, but there were still traffic problems. The form looks sound enough rated around those in the frame.

682 TO SPONSOR A RACE CALL 0870 220 2442 BANDED STKS 1m 1f 103y(P)
3:30 (3:30) (Class 7) 4-Y-0+ **£1,365** (£403; £201) **Stalls** Low

Form RPR
0520 1 **Indian Edge**[48] 261 5-8-11 45 .... FrancisFerris 10 54
(B Palling) *mde all: rdn over 1f out: hung rt ins fnl f: styd on* **7/1**[3]
-405 2 ½ **Miss Glory Be**[56] 175 8-8-11 45 .... (p) DarryllHolland 11 53
(Ernst Oertel) *a.p: chsd wnr 3f out: rdn over 1f out: styd on* **10/1**
0-00 3 2 ½ **Dishdasha (IRE)**[6] 636 4-8-11 45 .... PaulHanagan 4 48
(C R Dore) *s.i.s: hdwy over 2f out: sn rdn: edgd lft and styd on fnl f* **16/1**
0500 4 ¾ **Super Dominion**[28] 468 9-8-11 45 .... (p) VinceSlattery 7 47
(R Hollinshead) *chsd ldrs: rdn over 3f out: styng on same pce whn hung lft fnl f* **20/1**
3056 5 hd **Starcross Maid**[14] 600 4-8-11 45 .... JimmyQuinn 6 46
(J F Coupland) *hld up: hdwy over 1f out: nt rch ldrs* **14/1**
/0-0 6 ½ **String Serenade (IRE)**[51] 227 5-8-11 45 .... DManning 8 45
(V Smith) *hld up: hdwy over 3f out: rdn and hung lft fr over 1f out: styd on same pce* **25/1**
0-61 7 1 ¾ **Ringarooma**[42] 311 4-8-11 45 .... (t) MartinDwyer 1 42
(C N Allen) *hld up: hmpd over 3f out: hdwy u.p over 1f out: n.d* **2/1**[1]
1045 8 10 **Opera Knight**[28] 468 6-8-11 45 .... ShaneKelly 3 23
(A W Carroll) *hld up: rdn over 3f out: n.d* **10/3**[2]
240- 9 2 ½ **Danish Monarch**[163] 5740 5-8-11 45 .... FergusSweeney 9 18
(David Pinder) *chsd wnr over 6f: wknd over 1f out* **8/1**
000- 10 9 **Savernake Brave (IRE)**[103] 6525 5-8-11 45 .... ChrisCatlin 12 —
(Mrs H Sweeting) *s.i.s: sn mid-div: rdn and wknd over 2f out* **20/1**
4406 11 2 **Tod Sloan (IRE)**[16] 584 4-8-6 45 .... (b[1]) GregFairley(5) 5 —
(J M Bradley) *s.i.s: hld up: rdn and wknd over 2f out* **14/1**
450- 12 22 **Pick Of The Crop**[52] 3620 5-8-11 45 .... (v) StephenCarson 13 —
(J R Jenkins) *chsd ldrs over 5f* **25/1**
2m 2.22s (-0.40) **Going Correction** -0.075s/f (Stan) 12 Ran SP% **125.5**
Speed ratings (Par 97):98,97,95,94,94 94,92,83,81,73 71,52
CSF £75.26 TOTE £6.20: £2.00, £2.40, £4.20; EX 53.50.
Owner Nigel Thomas and Christopher Mason **Bred** Christopher J Mason **Trained** Tredodridge, Vale Of Glamorgan
FOCUS
A fair pace and the winning time was as you would expect for a race like this, despite being 1.26 seconds faster than the following contest. The form appears sound enough, rated around the runner-up.

683 RINGSIDE SUITE 700 THEATRE STYLE CONFERENCE BANDED STKS 1m 1f 103y(P)

4:00 (4:00) (Class 7) 4-Y-0+ £1,535 (£453; £226) Stalls Low

Form				RPR
0021	1		**Gallego**[16] 586 4-9-2 50 GeorgeBaker 9 (R J Price) *hld up: hdwy over 2f out: led ins fnl f: rdn out* 9/4[1]	58
-050	2	½	**Pharaoh Prince**[37] 379 5-9-0 48 ChrisCatlin 4 (G Prodromou) *chsd ldrs: rdn over 1f out: r.o* 14/1	55
0161	3	nk	**Milk And Sultana**[26] 484 6-9-2 50 AlanDaly 3 (G A Ham) *hld up: nt clr run over 2f out: hdwy over 1f out: sn rdn: rdr dropped whip ins fnl f: r.o* 9/1[3]	57+
-054	4	½	**Hiawatha (IRE)**[27] 471 7-9-2 50 DaneO'Neill 12 (A M Hales) *hld up: hdwy over 2f out: rdn over 1f out: styd on* 9/2[2]	55
0060	5	½	**Granary Girl**[27] 472 4-9-1 49 JimmyQuinn 2 (J Pearce) *chsd ldr: led 4f out: rdn over 1f out: edgd rt and hdd ins fnl f: no ex* 9/1[3]	53
3306	6	1¼	**Lake Wakatipu**[14] 599 4-8-8 49 LiamJones(7) 1 (M Mullineaux) *bhd: nt clr run over 1f out: styd on ins fnl f: nvr nrr* 10/1	51+
02-0	7	3	**Bond Millennium**[75] 41 8-8-13 47 PaulEddery 7 (B Smart) *prom: rdn over 2f out: edgd lft and styd on same pce appr fnl f* 16/1	43
0-04	8	1¼	**Homebred Star**[28] 469 5-8-8 47 GregFairley(5) 8 (G P Enright) *hld up: hdwy 1/2-way: ev ch over 2f out: edgd lft and wknd over 1f out* 12/1	41
-006	9	½	**Hoh Bleu Dee**[17] 568 5-9-0 48 (p) FrankieMcDonald 11 (T Keddy) *chsd ldrs: rdn over 3f out: hung lft and wknd over 1f out: hmpd ins fnl f* 25/1	41
3050	10	½	**Look At The Stars (IRE)**[28] 469 4-8-7 48 (b) RussellKennemore(7) 6 (R Hollinshead) *chsd ldrs: rdn over 2f out: hung lft and wknd over 1f out* 25/1	40
3415	11	2½	**Young Kate**[35] 399 5-9-1 49 SteveDrowne 13 (J R Best) *hld up in tch: lost pl 6f out: n.d after* 9/1[3]	36
-500	12	½	**Triple Jump**[13] 606 5-9-2 50 (tp) PaulHanagan 10 (K A Ryan) *hld up: rdn and wknd over 2f out* 33/1	36
-600	13	3½	**Swell Lad**[26] 482 4-9-2 50 (p) DarryllHolland 5 (S Gollings) *led over 5f: rdn and wknd over 2f out* 33/1	29

2m 3.48s (0.86) **Going Correction** -0.075s/f (Stan) 13 Ran SP% **128.0**
Speed ratings (Par 97):93,92,92,91,91 90,87,86,86,85 83,82,79
CSF £39.57 TOTE £2.00: £1.60, £5.40, £2.00; EX 53.10.

Owner My Left Foot Racing Syndicate **Bred** Mrs C C Regalado-Gonzalez **Trained** Ullingswick, H'fords

■ Stewards' Enquiry : Dane O'Neill two-day ban: (Mar 31-Apr 1)

FOCUS
A moderate contest rated around the runner-up and fourth. No pace on at all early here and the tempo did not increase until well past halfway. As a result the winning time was modest, even for a banded race, and 1.26 seconds slower than the preceding event over the same trip.

Granary Girl Official explanation: jockey said filly hung right-handed under pressure

Lake Wakatipu Official explanation: jockey said filly suffered interference in running

684 REMEMBER FAMILY FUN DAYS AT WOLVERHAMPTON BANDED STKS 1m 4f 50y(P)

4:30 (4:30) (Class 7) 4-Y-0+ £1,365 (£403; £201) Stalls Low

Form				RPR
0-05	1		**Mustakhlas (USA)**[17] 566 5-9-0 45 JoeFanning 5 (B P J Baugh) *chsd ldrs: led ins fnl f: styd on* 16/1	54
0-20	2	1¾	**Twentytwosilver (IRE)**[14] 591 6-9-0 45 MichaelTebbutt 1 (D B Feek) *hld up in tch: racd keenly: led on bit 2f out: sn edgd lft: hdd and unable qck ins fnl f* 8/1	51
2535	3	1	**College Rebel**[14] 599 5-9-0 45 DarryllHolland 12 (J F Coupland) *led: rdn and hdd 2f out: styd on same pce fnl f* 11/1	50
2244	4	nk	**Liquid Lover (IRE)**[22] 525 4-8-12 45 ShaneKelly 4 (W M Brisbourne) *w ldr: rdn over 3f out: styd on same pce fnl f* 11/2[3]	49
2-00	5	7	**Halcyon Magic**[6] 636 8-9-0 45 (b) JamieMackay 2 (M Wigham) *hld up: n.m.r 8f out: styd on appr fnl f: nvr nrr* 16/1	38
-243	6	1	**Another Con (IRE)**[31] 442 5-8-7 45 KevinGhunowa(7) 3 (P A Blockley) *hld up: styd on ins fnl f: nvr nrr* 7/1	36
1-00	7	2½	**My Boo**[42] 309 4-8-9 45 (tp) AdamKirby(3) 8 (T Keddy) *hld up: rdn 1/2-way: n.d* 14/1	32
6-30	8	¾	**Diamond Dan (IRE)**[42] 311 4-8-9 45 (p) DanielTudhope(3) 9 (P D Evans) *hld up: rdn over 3f out: n.d* 16/1	31
	9	15	**Galantos (GER)**[65] 5-9-0 45 IanMongan 7 (G L Moore) *chsd ldrs: rdn 4f out: wknd over 2f out: eased over 1f out* 4/1[1]	7
0-05	10	7	**Free Style (GER)**[16] 574 6-9-0 45 GeorgeBaker 10 (Mrs H Sweeting) *hld up: rdn over 2f out: n.d* 5/1[2]	—
24-4	11	¾	**Melograno (IRE)**[55] 182 6-8-13 45 ow2 DNolan(3) 11 (Mark Campion) *prom over 9f* 12/1	—
0-00	12	3½	**Layed Back Rocky**[16] 586 4-8-12 45 JimmyQuinn 6 (M Mullineaux) *hld up: rdn over 3f out: sn wknd* 40/1	—

2m 41.9s (-0.52) **Going Correction** -0.075s/f (Stan)
WFA 4 from 5yo+ 2lb 12 Ran SP% **118.4**
Speed ratings (Par 97):98,96,96,95,91 90,88,88,78,73 73,70
CSF £138.46 TOTE £23.60: £6.80, £2.00, £4.00; EX 274.40 Place 6 £452.97, Place 5 £151.77.

Owner Miss S M Potts **Bred** Shadwell Estate Company Limited **Trained** Audley, Staffs

FOCUS
A solid pace for this race and very few ever got into it. The front quartet pulled miles clear of the others and the form looks average, rated around the placed horses to recent marks.

Mustakhlas(USA) Official explanation: trainer's representative said, regarding the improved form shown, gelding had been suffering from a kidney problem and seems to have only just got over it

Galantos(GER) Official explanation: jockey said gelding moved poorly throughout

Free Style(GER) Official explanation: jockey said mare never travelled and pulled up short

Layed Back Rocky Official explanation: vet said colt bled from the nose

T/Plt: £1,090.00 to a £1 stake. Pool: £39,870.25. 26.70 winning tickets. T/Qpdt: £189.90 to a £1 stake. Pool: £3,054.30. 11.90 winning tickets. CR

[673] SOUTHWELL (L-H)

Tuesday, March 21

OFFICIAL GOING: Standard

Wind: Light, across Weather: Overcast

686 WAYNE & SALLY 25TH WEDDING ANNIVERSARY BANDED STKS 5f (F)

2:30 (2:34) (Class 7) 4-Y-0+ £1,365 (£403; £201) Stalls High

Form				RPR
0062	1		**Percy Douglas**[7] 633 6-8-5 45 ow1 (bt) AnnStokell(7) 1 (Miss A Stokell) *w ldr tl rdn to ld ins fnl f: r.o* 15/2[3]	51
-041	2	hd	**Mystery Pips**[7] 633 6-9-3 45 (v) KimTinkler 4 (N Tinkler) *mde most tl ins fnl f: r.o* 11/4[1]	55
-203	3	3	**Eternally**[7] 633 4-8-11 45 (p) ShaneKelly 5 (R M H Cowell) *uns rdr to post: chsd ldrs: rdn 1/2-way: styd on same pce fnl f* 8/1	39
0006	4	nk	**Katie Killane**[7] 633 4-8-11 35 AlanDaly 3 (M Wellings) *s.i.s: sn chsng ldrs: rdn over 1f out: styd on same pce* 66/1	38
4344	5	1½	**Beamsley Beacon**[56] 179 5-8-11 45 (b) PhillipMakin 7 (M Dods) *mid-div: rdn 1/2-way: nvr trbld ldrs* 4/1[2]	33
040	6	½	**Blue Power (IRE)**[37] 388 5-8-11 45 NeilPollard 6 (K R Burke) *mid-div: rdn 1/2-way: nvr trbld ldrs* 4/1[2]	31
000-	7	2	**Laurel Dawn**[113] 6441 8-8-11 35 SamHitchcott 2 (C N Kellett) *dwlt: sn prom: rdn over 3f out: hung rt and wknd 1/2-way* 40/1	25
0560	8	nk	**Comic Tales**[7] 633 5-8-11 40 AdrianTNicholls 9 (M Mullineaux) *s.s: outpcd* 11/1	23
00/0	9	nk	**Our Chelsea Blue (USA)**[7] 633 8-8-11 40 StephenCarson 12 (J R Jenkins) *chsd ldrs over 3f* 66/1	22
030-	10	1¼	**Jahia (NZ)**[168] 5684 7-8-11 45 MickyFenton 10 (P T Midgley) *dwlt: outpcd* 14/1	18
0-00	11	5	**Game Flora**[25] 501 5-8-11 35 (p) HayleyTurner 11 (D Shaw) *sn outpcd* 50/1	1
20-0	12	shd	**Torrent**[69] 90 11-8-11 45 (b) TonyCulhane 13 (D W Chapman) *sn outpcd* 20/1	1
0-00	13	2	**Danakim**[25] 502 9-8-11 35 (b) DarryllHolland 8 (J R Weymes) *sn outpcd* 20/1	—

59.99 secs (-0.31) **Going Correction** -0.125s/f (Stan) 13 Ran SP% **121.5**
Speed ratings (Par 97):97,96,91,91,89 88,85,84,84,82 74,73,70
CSF £27.28 TOTE £8.70: £2.20, £1.50, £2.70; EX 31.40 Trifecta £75.80 Pool £638.02, 5.97 w/u.

Owner Ms Caron Stokell **Bred** Qualitair Stud Ltd **Trained** Brompton-on-Swale, N Yorks

FOCUS
A typical banded sprint and the form is average for the grade.

Comic Tales Official explanation: jockey said gelding missed break

687 RACING AGAIN ON THE 24TH MAIDEN CLAIMING STKS 6f (F)

3:00 (3:02) (Class 7) 3-Y-0+ £1,365 (£403; £201) Stalls Low

Form				RPR
-656	1		**Bekoning (IRE)**[25] 499 3-8-12 45 ShaneKelly 10 (M Quinn) *chsd ldrs: led over 2f out: rdn and hung lft fr over 1f out: all out* 22/1	47
-502	2	shd	**Faithisflying**[7] 634 4-9-7 40 (p) TonyCulhane 11 (D W Chapman) *sn pushed along and prom: rdn to chse wnr over 1f out: edgd lft: r.o* 9/2[2]	47
5650	3	3½	**Kashtanka (IRE)**[23] 529 4-9-8 40 (b) JasonEdmunds(3) 7 (J Balding) *chsd ldrs: rdn over 2f out: styd on* 7/1	41
-526	4	4	**Fir Tree**[5] 653 6-9-11 40 MichaelTebbutt 3 (S R Bowring) *sn led: rdn and hdd over 2f out: wknd fnl f* 11/4[1]	29
0	5	¾	**Silvertown Sky (IRE)**[31] 453 3-8-8 ow1 BrianReilly 13 (P L Gilligan) *prom: rdn 1/2-way: wknd 2f out* 40/1	18
-5	6	hd	**Peggys First**[19] 553 4-9-11 PatCosgrave 14 (D E Cantillon) *sn pushed along in rr: rdn and hung lft fr over 2f out: n.d* 11/1	26
0-66	7	5	**Bella Fiorella (IRE)**[46] 287 3-8-2 50 JamieMackay 1 (T J Pitt) *wnt rt s: sn chsng ldrs: lost pl over 3f out: sn bhd* 6/1[3]	—
-030	8	shd	**Cooleycall Star (IRE)**[29] 467 5-9-7 45 (p) DarryllHolland 4 (A G Juckes) *s.s: outpcd* 7/1	6
-000	9	1	**Native Tiptoes**[21] 543 3-8-8 48 ow1 (p) MickyFenton 12 (Miss Gay Kelleway) *chsd ldr: rdn over 3f out: wknd 2f out* 16/1	—
-006	10	1½	**Eeshee**[42] 335 3-8-5 45 AdrianMcCarthy 5 (S L Keightley) *chsd ldrs over 3f* 16/1	—
0-00	11	1½	**Victimised (IRE)**[17] 584 4-9-11 40 PhillipMakin 2 (R J Price) *s.i.s: a in rr* 66/1	—
0-00	12	2	**Safaah**[26] 487 3-8-12 LPKeniry 8 (G Prodromou) *hld up: rdn and wknd 1/2-way* 80/1	—
60-0	13	½	**Is**[29] 466 3-8-7 52 ChrisCatlin 9 (Rae Guest) *s.i.s: outpcd* 28/1	—

1m 16.8s (-0.10) **Going Correction** -0.125s/f (Stan)
WFA 3 from 4yo+ 13lb 13 Ran SP% **117.2**
Speed ratings (Par 97):95,94,90,84,83 83,76,76,75,73 71,68,68
CSF £113.44 TOTE £10.00: £1.70, £2.10, £3.00; EX 114.40 Trifecta £222.70 Part won. Pool £313.67 - 0.10 winning units..Bella Fiorella was claimed by Miss V Haigh for £2,500

Owner Mrs S G Davies **Bred** Mrs Eileen Moran **Trained** Newmarket, Suffolk

FOCUS
Pretty much the lowest grade of all but the form should prove sound enough with the first three running to form.

Cooleycall Star(IRE) Official explanation: jockey said gelding would not face kickback

688 BOOK TICKETS ON-LINE BANDED STKS 2m (F)

3:30 (3:30) (Class 7) 4-Y-0+ £1,365 (£403; £201) Stalls Low

Form				RPR
353-	1		**Trebello**[26] 6099 5-9-0 40 (e[1]) PatCosgrave 6 (J R Boyle) *s.i.s and hmpd s: hdwy 11f out: rdn over 4f out: led over 2f out: edgd rt: styd on u.p* 9/2[2]	51
00-3	2	2½	**Step Perfect (USA)**[7] 635 5-9-5 50 (p) ShaneKelly 5 (G M Moore) *led 2f: led again 13f out: rdn and hdd over 2f out: ev ch over 1f out: no ex ins fnl f* 6/1[3]	53
6206	3	shd	**High Frequency (IRE)**[20] 549 5-9-3 48 PaulFessey 3 (T D Barron) *prom: chsd ldr 1/2-way: rdn over 3f out: edgd rt 2f out: no ex fnl f* 9/4[1]	51
6223	4	2½	**Logger Rhythm (USA)**[13] 614 6-9-0 45 DaleGibson 11 (R Dickin) *hld up: hdwy 6f out: sn rdn: styd on same pce fnl 3f* 7/1	45

05/0 **5** 9 **Hanazakari**[29] 460 5-9-0 45................(v[1]) TPQueally 7 34
(J A R Toller) *prom over 12f* **50/1**

6-05 **6** 8 **Jamaican Flight (USA)**[13] 614 13-9-0 30.................. RobertWinston 1 24
(Mrs S Lamyman) *rdn to ld after 2f: hdd 13f out: remained handy tl wknd 6f out* **20/1**

020- **7** 1 1/4 **Midnight Creek**[83] 6678 8-9-4 49.................. BrianReilly 2 27
(A Sadik) *prom: rdn: lost pl and dropped rr after 3f: n.d after* **9/1**

00-2 **8** 1 1/2 **Scurra**[13] 614 7-8-7 45.................. JosephWalsh(7) 4 21
(A C Whillans) *hld up: rdn 1/2-way: wknd 6f out* **7/1**

5-45 **9** 2 **Maunby Reveller**[44] 303 4-8-9 45..................(vt[1]) LeeEnstone 9 19
(P C Haslam) *hld up: plld hrd: hdwy over 6f out: wknd 5f out* **14/1**

/0-0 **10** dist **Grub Street**[44] 302 10-8-9 35..................(t) MarkLawson(5) 8 —
(J Parkes) *trckd ldrs: racd keenly: wknd over 4f out* **100/1**

11 nk **Boulevin (IRE)**[124] 3605 6-9-0 40.................. PhillipMakin 10 —
(R J Price) *hld up: plld hrd: wknd over 6f out* **20/1**

3m 44.16s (-0.38) **Going Correction** -0.125s/f (Stan)
WFA 4 from 5yo+ 5lb 11 Ran SP% **117.4**
Speed ratings (Par 97):95,93,93,92,87 83,83,82,81,— —
CSF £30.41 TOTE £5.30: £2.10, £2.40, £1.50; EX 44.10 Trifecta £123.60 Pool £349.95 - 2.01 winning units..
Owner John Hopkins (t/a South Hatch Racing) **Bred** Mrs W H Gibson Fleming **Trained** Epsom, Surrey

FOCUS
A standard staying contest for the level rated around the first two.
Midnight Creek Official explanation: jockey said gelding was never travelling

689 BETDIRECT.CO.UK BANDED STKS 1m (F)
4:00 (4:01) (Class 7) 4-Y-0+ **£1,706** (£503; £252) **Stalls** Low

Form RPR

0062 **1** **El Palmar**[5] 649 5-9-1 49.................. GrahamGibbons 12 58
(M J Attwater) *led 1f: remained handy: led over 3f out: rdn out* **2/1**[1]

5410 **2** 2 **Desert Fury**[23] 527 9-9-0 48..................(b) RobertWinston 7 53
(R Bastiman) *hld up: hdwy over 3f out: rdn over 1f out: styd on* **5/1**[2]

-003 **3** 1 **Rocky Reppin**[7] 638 6-8-8 40..................(v) JasonEdmunds(3) 8 48
(J Balding) *s.i.s: hdwy 6f out: chsd wnr 2f out: sn rdn and rdr dropped reins: hung lft ins fnl f: nt run on* **10/1**

3-00 **4** 2 1/2 **Tirailleur (IRE)**[29] 468 6-8-12 45 ow1..................(v[1]) FergalLynch 9 44
(J R Boyle) *chsd ldrs: rdn over 2f out: styd on same pce appr fnl f* **33/1**

-564 **5** 1 1/2 **Zariano**[23] 526 6-9-0 48.................. PaulFessey 5 43
(T D Barron) *chsd ldrs: outpcd wl over 3f out: styd on appr fnl f* **5/1**[2]

5206 **6** 4 **Sriology (IRE)**[20] 546 5-9-2 50.................. LPKeniry 4 37
(G Prodromou) *prom: lost pl and dropped rr over 5f out: rdn 1/2-way: n.d after* **8/1**

5024 **7** nk **Colonel Bilko (IRE)**[14] 609 4-9-0 48.................. ChrisCatlin 3 34
(Miss S J Wilton) *mid-div: lost pl over 3f out: n.d after* **16/1**

300- **8** 1 1/2 **Mexican (USA)**[10] 6444 7-8-11 40..................(b) PaulHanagan 2 28
(Micky Hammond) *chsd ldrs: led 5f out: hdd over 3f out: wknd over 1f out* **50/1**

0-06 **9** 1/2 **Discomania**[18] 573 4-8-11 45..................(vp) MichaelTebbutt 14 27
(V Smith) *hld up: rdn 1/2-way: sn wknd* **50/1**

4000 **10** shd **Ballyrush (IRE)**[7] 638 6-8-11 40.................. AlanDaly 6 27
(Miss D A McHale) *chsd ldrs over 5f* **50/1**

5350 **11** 5 **Supreme Salutation**[33] 423 10-8-9 50.................. LauraReynolds(7) 1 22
(D K Ivory) *led 7f out: hdd 5f out: wknd over 3f out* **25/1**

2266 **12** hd **It Must Be Speech**[23] 526 5-8-11 45..................(v) AdrianMcCarthy 11 17
(S L Keightley) *bhd fr 1/2-way* **15/2**[3]

1m 43.44s (-1.16) **Going Correction** -0.125s/f (Stan) 12 Ran SP% **117.2**
Speed ratings (Par 97):100,98,97,94,93 89,88,87,86,86 81,81
CSF £10.89 TOTE £2.40: £1.50, £2.60, £3.70; EX 15.20 Trifecta £92.70 Pool £581.44, 4.45 w/u.

Owner Phones Direct Partnership **Bred** A C M Spalding **Trained** Wysall, Notts

FOCUS
An average banded contest and not that competitive rated around the placed horses to recent form.

690 BETDIRECT.CO.UK TRI-BANDED STKS 7f (F)
4:30 (4:31) (Class 7) 3-Y-0 **£1,365** (£403; £201) **Stalls** Low

Form RPR

0025 **1** **Midge's Girl (IRE)**[7] 637 3-9-0 45..................(v) PaulFessey 5 46
(Mrs A Duffield) *prom: lost pl and dropped rr over 5f out: hdwy over 2f out: rdn to ld and hung lft over 1f out: jst hld on* **6/1**[2]

0000 **2** hd **Beginners Luck (IRE)**[7] 637 3-8-4 35.................. AdrianMcCarthy 6 35
(D Carroll) *sn outpcd: hdwy to chse wnr fnl f: r.o: jst failed* **80/1**

00-2 **3** 3 1/2 **Silver Nun**[7] 637 3-9-0 45..................(b[1]) DavidAllan 4 36
(T D Easterby) *unruly on way to post: s.s: rel to r: swtchd rt over 2f out: hdwy u.p over 1f out: hung lft: styd on* **10/1**

0-54 **4** 1 3/4 **Tequila Rose (IRE)**[20] 551 3-9-0 45.................. SamHitchcott 1 31+
(A Bailey) *trckd ldrs: plld hrd: led 2f out: sn rdn and hdd: wknd ins fnl f* **15/2**[3]

0603 **5** 1/2 **Lasting Love**[7] 637 3-9-0 45..................(b) DarryllHolland 7 30
(C R Dore) *led: rdn and hdd 2f out: wknd fnl f* **12/1**

0-00 **6** 1 1/4 **Moraadi**[7] 637 3-8-4 30..................(p) DaleGibson 2 17
(D W Chapman) *chsd ldrs: rdn over 2f out: wknd fnl f* **100/1**

000- **7** 5 **Alarm Call**[258] 3224 3-9-0 45..................(b[1]) FergalLynch 10 14
(T D Easterby) *chsd ldrs over 5f* **25/1**

04-5 **8** 1/2 **Augustus Livius (IRE)**[23] 528 3-8-9 40.................. RobertWinston 8 8
(W Storey) *s.i.s: sn prom: rdn 1/2-way: wknd 2f out* **6/1**[2]

000- **9** hd **Xaar Breeze**[212] 4602 3-8-9 40.................. ChrisCatlin 11 7
(Rae Guest) *s.i.s: sn chsng ldrs: rdn over 2f out: sn wknd* **12/1**

0001 **10** 3 1/2 **Teddy Monty (IRE)**[7] 637 3-9-6 45 6ex..................(b) ShaneKelly 9 9
(M Quinn) *w ldr: rdn and ev ch 2f out: sn wknd* **6/4**[1]

-054 **11** dist **Yassooma (IRE)**[7] 637 3-8-9 40..................(b) JamieMackay 3 —
(T J Pitt) *sn outpcd: virtually p.u fnl 2f* **8/1**

1m 31.96s (1.16) **Going Correction** -0.125s/f (Stan) 11 Ran SP% **122.0**
Speed ratings (Par 92):88,87,83,81,81 79,74,73,73,69 —
CSF £419.28 TOTE £8.00: £2.00, £20.80, £2.30; EX 423.10 TRIFECTA Not won..
Owner Mrs B Midgley,Ann Duffield & Les Shears **Bred** Razza Pallorsi **Trained** Constable Burton, N Yorks

FOCUS
An ordinary event featuring a field made up mostly of fillies and rated around the principals. It was run in a modest time, even for a race like this and the form is not solid.
Silver Nun Official explanation: jockey said filly missed break
Lasting Love Official explanation: vet said filly was lame on right fore
Yassooma(IRE) Official explanation: jockey said gelding lost action

691 EXPERIENCE NOTTINGHAMSHIRE BANDED STKS 6f (F)
5:00 (5:00) (Class 7) 4-Y-0+ **£1,365** (£403; £201) **Stalls** Low

Form RPR

-006 **1** **Sundried Tomato**[7] 638 7-8-11 45..................(p) TonyCulhane 10 55
(D W Chapman) *chsd ldrs: led over 3f out: edgd rt over 1f out: rdn out* **14/1**

0006 **2** 1 **Union Jack Jackson (IRE)**[13] 618 4-8-11 45..................(b) MickyFenton 4 52+
(J G Given) *s.i.s and hmpd s: hdwy u.p over 1f out: r.o* **8/1**

3534 **3** 2 1/2 **Mister Aziz (IRE)**[7] 638 4-8-11 45..................(b) DarryllHolland 14 45
(J R Jenkins) *wnt lft s: hld up in tch: rdn and edgd lft over 1f out: styd on same pce fnl f* **4/1**[1]

3400 **4** 1 3/4 **Xaloc Bay (IRE)**[13] 616 8-8-11 45..................(p) AdrianMcCarthy 11 39
(R A Harris) *prom: outpcd over 3f out: hdwy over 1f out: styd on* **20/1**

020- **5** shd **Aboustar**[171] 5619 6-8-8 45..................(b) DanielTudhope(3) 12 39
(M Brittain) *chsd ldrs: rdn over 2f out: styd on same pce appr fnl f* **16/1**

0000 **6** 1/2 **Ace Club**[13] 618 5-8-4 40..................(b) AdamCarter(7) 5 37
(J Hetherton) *wnt lft s: hld up: hung lft thrght: hdwy over 1f out: nt trble ldrs* **66/1**

000- **7** 3 **Sound That Alarm**[90] 6646 4-9-0 48.................. RobertWinston 1 31
(P D Evans) *chsd ldrs: rdn over 3f out: wknd over 1f out* **25/1**

405 **8** 1/2 **Ardkeel Lass (IRE)**[1] 681 5-8-13 47..................(p) ShaneKelly 7 29
(P D Evans) *led: hdd over 3f out: wknd over 1f out* **13/2**[3]

0310 **9** 3/4 **Straffan (IRE)**[20] 552 4-8-12 46..................(b) DaleGibson 13 26
(J Hetherton) *s.i.s and hmpd s: hdwy over 3f out: rdn and wknd over 1f out* **8/1**

-000 **10** 3/4 **Boisdale (IRE)**[35] 411 8-8-9 50.................. KellyHarrison(7) 8 27
(S L Keightley) *chsd ldrs 4f* **22/1**

0560 **11** 1/2 **Sapphire Dream**[1] 680 4-8-11 45..................(v) DavidAllan 3 21
(A Bailey) *hmpd s: sn outpcd* **22/1**

00-0 **12** 2 **George The Best (IRE)**[14] 608 5-8-11 45.................. PaulHanagan 6 15
(Micky Hammond) *hld up: bhd fr 1/2-way* **15/2**

0660 **13** 3/4 **Jennverse**[24] 520 4-9-2 50.................. FergusSweeney 2 18
(D K Ivory) *hmpd s: outpcd* **12/1**

0120 **14** 1 3/4 **Ariesanne (IRE)**[13] 618 5-8-12 46.................. AdrianTNicholls 9 8
(A C Whillans) *chsd ldrs over 3f* **6/1**[2]

1m 16.27s (-0.63) **Going Correction** -0.125s/f (Stan) 14 Ran SP% **120.6**
Speed ratings (Par 97):99,97,94,92,91 91,87,86,85,84 83,81,80,77
CSF £113.91 TOTE £12.90: £4.50, £3.00, £1.70; EX 106.10 Trifecta £262.50 Part won. Pool £369.72 - 0.20 winning units. Place 6 £153.61, Place 5 £72.05.
Owner Clive Roberts **Bred** Butts Enterprises Limited **Trained** Stillington, N Yorks

FOCUS
An average banded sprint but a welcome return to the winners' enclosure for All-Weather favourite Sundried Tomato. The first two were better than this in the past and the form could rate higher through the third.
Union Jack Jackson(IRE) Official explanation: jockey said gelding was hampered on leaving stalls
Straffan(IRE) Official explanation: jockey said filly was slowly away from stalls
T/Plt: £111.10 to a £1 stake. Pool: £47,849.60. 314.40 winning tickets. T/Qpdt: £35.70 to a £1 stake. Pool: £3,983.50. 82.50 winning tickets. CR

663 LINGFIELD (L-H)
Wednesday, March 22

OFFICIAL GOING: Standard
Wind: Light across Weather: Fine but cloudy

692 DHL CITISPEED MEDIAN AUCTION MAIDEN STKS 7f (P)
1:30 (1:35) (Class 6) 3-4-Y-0 **£2,730** (£806; £403) **Stalls** Low

Form RPR

600- **1** **Miss Patricia**[189] 5227 4-9-7 72.................. DarryllHolland 5 73
(J G Portman) *t.k.h: trckd ldng pair: effrt to ld over 1f out: sn drew clr* **3/1**[2]

225- **2** 1 1/2 **Danawi (IRE)**[127] 6349 3-8-11 75.................. RichardHughes 4 69
(R Hannon) *hld up midfield: trckd ldrs gng wl 2f out: effrt over 1f out: sn rdn and fnd nil: kpt on to take 2nd ins fnl f* **8/11**[1]

50- **3** 3/4 **Aurora Jane (FR)**[198] 5005 3-8-6.................. MichaelHills 8 62
(B W Hills) *pressed ldr: led 2f out: hdd over 1f out: outpcd* **9/1**[3]

4 2 **Lisathedaddy** 4-9-7.................. HayleyTurner 6 62
(B G Powell) *neat: s.s: hld up in last: stl wl in rr but gng wl enough 2f out: shkn up over 1f out: r.o fnl f: decent debut* **20/1**

450- **5** hd **Tuscany Queen (IRE)**[222] 4329 3-8-3 53.................. StephaneBreux(3) 1 56
(R Hannon) *settled in midfield: prog 2f out: chsd ldrs over 1f out: wknd ins fnl f* **20/1**

6 1 **Riolo (IRE)**[29] 4-9-9.................. AdamKirby(3) 10 63
(K F Clutterbuck) *led to 2f out: wknd fnl f* **66/1**

00- **7** 2 **Muckle**[176] 5531 3-8-6.................. MartinDwyer 2 48
(S C Williams) *dwlt: wl in rr: rdn 3f out: nvr on terms* **25/1**

8 2 1/2 **Very Clear** 4-9-7.................. ShaneKelly 9 47
(R M H Cowell) *w'like: s.s: rcvrd after 1f: rdn and green 4f out: losing tch whn bmpd over 2f out* **14/1**

500- **9** hd **Charles Street Lad (IRE)**[187] 5276 3-8-11 62..................(t) AlanDaly 7 46
(M R Bosley) *h.d.w: uns rdr and bolted bef s: hld up in rr: wnt rt over 2f out: no real prog* **33/1**

P- **10** 3 **Mind That Fox**[245] 3636 4-9-5.................. SladeO'Hara(7) 3 43
(T Wall) *chsd ldrs tl wknd 2f out* **100/1**

0 **11** 17 **Bold Finch (FR)**[36] 409 4-9-12 59.................. ChrisCatlin 11 —
(K O Cunningham-Brown) *prom to 1/2-way: wknd: t.o* **100/1**

1m 27.31s (1.42) **Going Correction** -0.075s/f (Stan)
WFA 3 from 4yo 15lb 11 Ran SP% **119.4**
Speed ratings (Par 101):88,86,85,83,82 81,79,76,76,72 53
CSF £5.23 TOTE £4.00: £1.10, £1.10, £2.10; EX 6.90 Trifecta £30.60 Pool: £703.78 - 16.26 winning units.
Owner Mrs J Edwards-Heathcote **Bred** Mrs R Pease **Trained** Compton, Berks

FOCUS
This was a weak maiden, run at an average pace in a slow time, and the form is ordinary. The first two did not need to be at their best.
Charles Street Lad(IRE) Official explanation: jockey said gelding hung right

693 DHL GLOBAL MAIL CHALLENGE H'CAP 7f (P)
2:00 (2:02) (Class 6) (0-60,60) 4-Y-0+ **£2,590** (£770; £385; £192) **Stalls** Low

Form RPR

0213 **1** **Riquewihr**[18] 588 6-9-1 57..................(p) AlanMunro 8 64
(J S Wainwright) *hld up in midfield: prog on outer fr over 2f out: rdn to chal fnl f: led nr fin* **3/1**[1]

5406 **2** *nk* **Miskina**[25] 514 5-8-13 **55** RobbieFitzpatrick 10 61
(W M Brisbourne) *trckd ldng pair: effrt 2f out: rdn to ld ins fnl f: hdd nr fin* **16/1**

2200 **3** *1/2* **Iced Diamond (IRE)**[18] 581 7-8-13 **55** ShaneKelly 9 60
(W M Brisbourne) *lw: settled in rr: effrt over 2f out: hrd rdn over 1f out: styd on ins fnl f: nrst fin* **33/1**

0002 **4** *shd* **Contented (IRE)**[2] 677 4-8-11 **53** (p) DaneO'Neill 5 60+
(Mrs L C Jewell) *lw: settled wl in rr: prog over 2f out: nt clr run over 1f out: swtchd to inner and r.o fnl f: nvr nrr* **8/1**

-553 **5** *nk* **Go Garuda**[18] 576 5-9-4 **60** (v[1]) DarryllHolland 3 64
(Miss Gay Kelleway) *lw: chsd ldrs: u.p over 2f out: kpt on one pce fr over 1f out* **4/1**[2]

-460 **6** *nk* **Secam (POL)**[25] 520 7-8-11 **53** (b) SamHitchcott 11 56
(Mrs P Townsley) *wl in rr: sme prog on wd outside over 2f out: hrd rdn and styd on fnl f: nvr rchd ldrs* **14/1**

-262 **7** *nk* **Grezie**[25] 520 4-8-13 **55** JoeFanning 6 57
(T D McCarthy) *led for 1f: chsd ldr: led again 2f out: drvn and hdd ins fnl f: wknd last 75yds* **8/1**

00-0 **8** *1/2* **Imtalkinggibberish**[15] 608 5-8-12 **54** MickyFenton 12 55
(J R Jenkins) *hld up wl in rr: n.m.r wl over 1f out: styd on fnl f: no ch* **25/1**

-003 **9** *nk* **Sonntag Blue (IRE)**[25] 520 4-8-4 **53** (v) DonnaCaldwell(7) 4 53+
(Miss J Feilden) *chsd ldrs: lost pl wl over 2f out: nt clr run over 1f out: running on at fin: no ch* **16/1**

3246 **10** *1/2* **Hadath (IRE)**[18] 575 9-9-3 **59** (b) TQuinn 14 58
(B G Powell) *last and drvn 5f out: sme prog on outer 2f out: keeping on whn no room ins fnl f* **11/2**[3]

-000 **11** *3/4* **Caustic Wit (IRE)**[18] 587 8-9-4 **60** FrancisNorton 7 57
(M S Saunders) *trckd ldrs: lost pl 2f out: shuffled along over 1f out: n.m.r sn after: eased last 100yds* **66/1**

50-0 **12** *nk* **Balerno**[60] 170 7-9-4 **60** PaulEddery 13 56
(R Ingram) *stdd s: hld up wl in rr: prog on outer 3f out: drvn over 2f out: no imp fnl f: fdd* **66/1**

0-50 **13** *7* **Storm Chase (USA)**[18] 575 4-9-0 **59** (v) AdamKirby(3) 1 37
(A P Jarvis) *led after 1f and set str pce: hdd 2f out: sn wknd* **20/1**

0-30 **14** *28* **Mansiya**[30] 462 4-9-3 **59** SebSanders 2 —
(C E Brittain) *lw: nvr gng wl: bhd fnl 3f: t.o* **14/1**

1m 25.42s (-0.47) **Going Correction** -0.075s/f (Stan) **14** Ran SP% **122.2**
Speed ratings (Par 101):99,98,98,97,97 97,96,96,96,95 94,94,86,54
CSF £52.46 CT £1356.38 TOTE £3.90: £1.40, £8.40, £5.40; EX 101.30 TRIFECTA Not won..
Owner J S Wainwright **Bred** G B Partnership **Trained** Kennythorpe, N Yorks
■ Stewards' Enquiry : Alan Munro caution: used whip without giving mare time to respond

FOCUS
A moderate handicap, and though it was run at a fair gallop, they were closely bunched at the finish. Pretty average form.
Iced Diamond(IRE) Official explanation: jockey said gelding missed break
Imtalkinggibberish Official explanation: jockey said gelding was denied a clear run in final furlong
Hadath(IRE) Official explanation: jockey said gelding was denied clear run in final furlong

694 NICHOLAS HALL (S) STKS 1m 4f (P)
2:35 (2:35) (Class 6) 4-Y-0+ **£2,388** (£705; £352) **Stalls** Low

Form RPR

2506 **1** **Competitor**[28] 484 5-9-9 55 (bt) TQuinn 11 62
(J Akehurst) *lw: trckd ldrs: brought wd in st: pushed into ld over 1f out: sn clr* **9/2**[3]

3030 **2** *5* **Mujazaf**[33] 442 4-8-13 50 (p) NeilChalmers(3) 2 49
(Miss Sheena West) *pressed ldr: led over 3f out: drvn and hdd over 1f out: no ch w wnr* **7/1**

020/ **3** *shd* **Bhutan (IRE)**[597] 4398 11-9-4 SteveDrowne 9 49
(Jim Best) *trckd ldrs: gng wl 2f out: rdn and nt qckn over 1f out: kpt on same pce* **12/1**

3202 **4** *3* **Dagola (IRE)**[16] 591 5-9-4 47 FrancisNorton 10 44
(C A Dwyer) *lw: settled midfield: rdn over 3f out: effrt 2f out: one pce* **4/1**[2]

-000 **5** *hd* **Malibu (IRE)**[16] 591 5-9-4 65 (p) DarryllHolland 8 44
(S Dow) *lw: led to over 3f out: sn rdn: wknd over 1f out* **7/2**[1]

6005 **6** *1/2* **Rasid (USA)**[16] 591 8-9-1 45 SaleemGolam(3) 4 43
(C A Dwyer) *settled in rr: brief effrt over 3f out: sn rdn and no imp* **16/1**

043/ **7** *2 1/2* **One Alone**[27] 4600 5-8-10 40 (b) StephaneBreux(3) 3 34
(Jean-Rene Auvray) *a in rr: wl outpcd whn nt clr run on inner over 2f out* **66/1**

1243 **8** *shd* **Moon Shot**[27] 490 10-9-9 55 VinceSlattery 1 44
(A G Juckes) *t.k.h early: trckd ldrs: rdn over 2f out: wknd wl over 1f out* **9/2**[3]

-400 **9** *1 1/4* **Sungio**[14] 614 8-9-4 40 (b) JoeFanning 7 37
(B P J Baugh) *dwlt: a in rr: rdn and struggling over 3f out* **16/1**

040/ **10** *dist* **Breuddwyd Lyn**[92] 639 8-9-4 ChrisCatlin 5 —
(D Burchell) *dwlt: a last: t.o 3f out: walking last 2f* **40/1**

2m 34.26s (-0.13) **Going Correction** -0.075s/f (Stan)
WFA 4 from 5yo+ 2lb **10** Ran SP% **114.5**
Speed ratings (Par 101):97,93,93,91,91 91,89,89,88,—
CSF £35.35 TOTE £6.90: £2.00, £2.60, £3.20; EX 45.50 Trifecta £510.60 Part won. Pool: £719.17 - 0.45 winning units..There was no bid for the winner. Mujazaf was claimed by David Burchell for £6,000.
Owner Who Cares Who Wins **Bred** Cheveley Park Stud Ltd **Trained** Epsom, Surrey

FOCUS
A dire event which was run at a steady early pace.
Breuddwyd Lyn Official explanation: vet said gelding bled from nose

695 EES LIGHTNING H'CAP 1m 4f (P)
3:05 (3:06) (Class 5) (0-75,75) 3-Y-0 **£3,238** (£963; £481; £240) **Stalls** Low

Form RPR

1604 **1** **Abstract Art (USA)**[18] 583 3-9-2 **73** JimmyFortune 8 76
(N A Callaghan) *lw: hld up: trckd ldrs gng easily 3f out: swtchd rt over 2f out: hrd rdn to ld last 150yds: kpt on* **9/2**[3]

4-52 **2** *1* **Meadow Mischief (FR)**[25] 515 3-8-13 **70** (b) ShaneKelly 2 71
(E A L Dunlop) *led: kpt on wl whn pressed fr 3f out: hdd and one pce last 150yds* **5/1**

5-60 **3** *1 1/4* **Archimboldo (USA)**[54] 213 3-9-4 **75** SebSanders 5 74
(T Wall) *lw: hld up in last: prog 5f out to chse ldr over 3f out: carried hd v awkwardly u.p: lost 2nd over 2f out: kpt on reluctant* **20/1**

0-05 **4** *hd* **Wise Choice**[18] 584 3-8-4 **61** oh6 ChrisCatlin 6 60?
(N P Littmoden) *trckd ldrs: rdn to chse ldr over 2f out to over 1f out: one pce u.p* **16/1**

3022 **5** *6* **Opera Comica**[19] 573 3-8-5 **62** DavidKinsella 3 51
(J H M Gosden) *in tch: rdn and struggling in last pair over 4f out: no ch after* **9/1**

400- **6** *1 3/4* **Gigs Magic (USA)**[187] 5276 3-8-13 **70** KDarley 1 56
(M Johnston) *lw: mostly chsd ldr to over 3f out: wknd over 2f out* **7/1**

1434 **7** *7* **Keel (IRE)**[16] 592 3-9-4 **75** SteveDrowne 7 56+
(J A Osborne) *lw: prom: rdn over 4f out: losing pl whn squeezed out over 2f out: wknd* **5/2**[1]

0231 **8** *18* **Chookie Windsor**[22] 538 3-8-4 **61** oh1 FrancisNorton 4 7
(M S Saunders) *prom to 1/2-way: struggling in last pair over 4f out: eased: t.o* **4/1**[2]

2m 34.14s (-0.25) **Going Correction** -0.075s/f (Stan) **8** Ran SP% **116.6**
Speed ratings (Par 98):97,96,95,95,91 90,85,73
CSF £27.79 CT £409.39 TOTE £6.40: £1.50, £2.20, £7.70; EX 29.00 Trifecta £350.10 Pool: £1,173.86 - 2.38 winning units.
Owner Matthew Green **Bred** Ms J L Mills **Trained** Newmarket, Suffolk

FOCUS
This was a fair handicap, run at a sound enough pace, and the first four came clear.
Archimboldo(USA) Official explanation: jockey said gelding hung left
Keel(IRE) Official explanation: trainer was unable to offer any explanation for poor form shown
Chookie Windsor Official explanation: jockey said gelding hung left

696 CHURCHILL INSURANCE H'CAP (DIV I) 1m 2f (P)
3:40 (3:40) (Class 6) (0-60,60) 4-Y-0+ **£2,388** (£705; £352) **Stalls** Low

Form RPR

1-31 **1** **Turner's Touch**[30] 462 4-9-1 **57** (be) GeorgeBaker 7 68
(G L Moore) *hld up wl in rr: prog to trck ldrs over 2f out: hanging and reluctant fr over 1f out: forced ahd last strides* **5/2**[1]

0213 **2** *hd* **Glendale**[37] 394 5-8-13 **55** JimmyQuinn 3 66
(D K Ivory) *lw: wl plcd: effrt to chse ldr over 3f out: drvn 2f out: chal and upsides fnl f: jst pipped* **7/2**[2]

40 **3** *shd* **Ardea Brave (IRE)**[16] 596 4-9-0 **56** NickyMackay 11 67
(M Botti) *lw: led after 2f: kicked on wl over 2f out: kpt on wl whn chal fnl f: hdd last strides* **14/1**

3620 **4** *5* **King Of Knight (IRE)**[18] 574 5-9-4 **60** OscarUrbina 9 61
(G Prodromou) *dwlt: hld up wl in rr: nt clr run 3f out: rdn 2f out: styd on fnl f: no ch of rching ldrs* **7/1**

200 **5** *nk* **Three Boars**[19] 570 4-8-11 **53** (b) DarryllHolland 4 54
(S Gollings) *prog into midfield 7f out: chsd ldrs 3f out: rdn and nt qckn: one pce after* **8/1**

000- **6** *shd* **Star Rising**[154] 5980 4-8-10 **52** LPKeniry 14 53
(W J Musson) *hld up wl in rr: sme prog 3f out: outpcd 2f out: shkn up and kpt on: no ch* **25/1**

1230 **7** *shd* **Port 'n Starboard**[39] 375 5-9-4 **60** MartinDwyer 12 60
(C A Cyzer) *trckd ldrs: rdn and effrt 4f out: disp 2nd over 3f out: wknd over 1f out* **6/1**[3]

0-00 **8** *1 3/4* **Miss Madame (IRE)**[16] 596 5-9-3 **59** IanMongan 13 56
(T G Mills) *dwlt: hld up in last: gng wl enough but plenty to do over 2f out: rdn and nt qckn sn after: one pce* **20/1**

0-00 **9** *1/2* **Arthurs Legacy**[30] 460 4-8-9 **58** RonanKeogh(7) 8 54
(J A R Toller) *lw: trckd ldrs: cl enough 3f out: drvn and outpcd 2f out: wknd on inner over 1f out* **50/1**

0502 **10** *2 1/2* **Shrine Mountain (USA)**[21] 546 4-8-3 **52** KirstyMilczarek(7) 2 43
(J R Holt) *t.k.h: prom to 3f out: sn lost pl and btn* **25/1**

000- **11** *shd* **War Feather**[127] 6355 4-8-3 **48** EdwardCreighton(3) 10 39
(T D McCarthy) *dwlt: wl in rr: rdn 5f out: brief effrt on outer over 3f out: sn wknd* **100/1**

5164 **12** *4* **Madhavi**[20] 557 4-9-4 **60** (v[1]) RichardHughes 5 44
(R Hannon) *hld up towards rr: pushed along and sme prog over 3f out: wknd tamely 2f out* **12/1**

2110 **13** *24* **Surdoue**[24] 525 6-8-9 **51** ShaneKelly 1 —
(P Howling) *led for 2f: chsd ldr to over 3f out: wknd rapidly: t.o* **20/1**

2m 5.25s (-2.54) **Going Correction** -0.075s/f (Stan) **13** Ran SP% **123.2**
Speed ratings (Par 101):107,106,106,102,102 102,102,100,100,98 98,95,76
CSF £10.27 CT £106.62 TOTE £3.70: £1.90, £2.40, £4.20; EX 15.20 Trifecta £141.20 Pool: £819.80 - 4.12 winning units.
Owner The Wacko Partnership **Bred** Hedgeholme Stud **Trained** Woodingdean, E Sussex

FOCUS
This modest handicap was run at a strong pace, which saw the field strung out from an early stage, and the first three came nicely clear. Modest form, nevertheless.
Three Boars Official explanation: jockey said gelding hung right
Port 'n Starboard Official explanation: jockey said gelding hung right

697 CHURCHILL INSURANCE H'CAP (DIV II) 1m 2f (P)
4:15 (4:15) (Class 6) (0-60,60) 4-Y-0+ **£2,388** (£705; £352) **Stalls** Low

Form RPR

2520 **1** **Bavarica**[23] 537 4-8-10 **59** SladeO'Hara(7) 7 66
(Miss J Feilden) *hld up in midfield on inner: prog 2f out: rdn to ld jst ins fnl f: kpt on wl* **12/1**

6042 **2** *3/4* **Cherished Number**[26] 498 7-9-1 **57** (b) DaneO'Neill 3 63
(A M Hales) *hld up in cl tch: prog over 2f out: effrt to chal 1f out: a jst hld ins fnl f* **10/1**

120- **3** *1/2* **Nina Fontenail (FR)**[208] 4729 5-9-4 **60** RobertHavlin 8 65+
(B R Millman) *dwlt: sn in tch: lost pl 3f out: effrt again wl over 1f out: r.o fnl f: nt quite rch ldrs* **10/1**

1366 **4** *shd* **Barton Sands (IRE)**[43] 324 9-9-2 **58** (t) DarryllHolland 10 63+
(Ernst Oertel) *hld up wl in rr: delayed effrt tl jst over 1f out whn stl only 9th: flew up fnl f: hopeless task* **9/2**[2]

0104 **5** *1/2* **Missie Baileys**[18] 574 4-9-0 **56** IanMongan 1 60
(Mrs L J Mongan) *prog to ld 7f out: jnd 2f out: hdd jst ins fnl f: wknd nr fin* **4/1**[1]

-004 **6** *3/4* **Abbeygate**[34] 423 5-8-10 **52** (p) MickyFenton 12 54
(T Keddy) *lw: hld up in rr: prog on outer fr over 2f out: drvn over 1f out: nt qckn and nvr able to chal* **20/1**

0213 **7** *3/4* **Joe Jo Star**[18] 586 4-8-10 **52** RobbieFitzpatrick 5 53
(B P J Baugh) *lw: t.k.h early: trckd ldrs: effrt over 2f: pressed ldrs over 1f out: one pce* **5/1**[3]

60-0 **8** *3 1/2* **Didnt Tell My Wife**[18] 582 7-8-5 **47** MartinDwyer 14 41
(Lucinda Featherstone) *hld up in last: shkn up over 1f out: kpt on: nvr nr ldrs* **20/1**

0524 **9** *hd* **Alqaayid**[18] 586 5-8-2 **51** ow2 RussellKennemore(7) 4 45
(P W Hiatt) *lw: ldng trio: rdn to chal and upsides 2f out: wknd rapidly jst over 1f out* **13/2**

056- **10** *3/4* **Aberdeen Park**[55] 6468 4-8-5 **52** RichardKingscote(5) 9 45
(Mrs H Sweeting) *trckd ldrs: rdn and nt qckn over 2f out: wknd over 1f out* **20/1**

620- **11** *hd* **Primeshade Promise**[46] 4497 5-8-12 **54** ChrisCatlin 13 46
(D Burchell) *mostly in last pair: pushed along and nt clr run on inner 2f out: no prog* **20/1**

12 1½ **Silvo (NZ)**^{539} 7-9-4 **60** .... SteveDrowne 6 49
(M F Harris) *bit bkwd: wl in rr: rdn and sme prog 3f out: no imp over 2f out: wknd* **50/1**

-000 13 2½ **Lockstock (IRE)**^{18} [586] 8-9-1 **57** ....(p) FrancisNorton 2 47+
(M S Saunders) *led at stdy pce to 7f out: styd in ldng trio: lost pl rapidly 3f out though stl gng wl enough: heavily eased fnl f* **25/1**

2m 6.97s (-0.82) **Going Correction** -0.075s/f (Stan) **13** Ran SP% **118.9**
Speed ratings (Par 101):100,99,99,98,98 97,97,94,94,93 93,92,90
CSF £111.75 CT £1256.21 TOTE £15.10: £7.30, £4.40, £4.80; EX 114.00 Trifecta £386.30 Part won. Pool: £544.11 - 0.35 winning units..

Owner Mr & Mrs M Jenner, E Jenner **Bred** Juddmonte Farms **Trained** Exning, Suffolk

FOCUS
This second division of the ten-furlong handicap looked slightly the weaker of the pair and was run at a slower pace.
Barton Sands(IRE) Official explanation: jockey said gelding was denied clear run turning for home

698 CRYSTAL PALACE CENTENARY H'CAP 1m (P)
4:50 (4:51) (Class 6) (0-65,65) 4-Y-0+ **£2,730** (£806; £403) **Stalls** High

Form RPR

324- 1 **Oakley Absolute**^{70} [6596] 4-9-4 65 .... RichardHughes 11 74
(R Hannon) *lw: trckd ldrs: rdn to chal over 1f out: led jst ins fnl f: hld on nr fin* **8/1**

0304 2 nk **Physical (IRE)**^{25} [520] 4-8-8 55 ....(p) NickyMackay 10 63
(Mrs A J Perrett) *lw: prog to press ldr over 6f out: chal 2f out: led briefly 1f out: pressed wnr after: jst hld* **11/1**

1315 3 shd **Hollow Jo**^{18} [575] 6-9-2 63 .... MickyFenton 7 71
(J R Jenkins) *hld up in rr: prog over 1f out: r.o wl fnl f: gaining at fin* **7/2**^{1}

0236 4 1 **Hand Chime**^{7} [639] 9-9-0 61 .... SebSanders 2 66
(Ernst Oertel) *trckd ldrs: rdn wl over 1f out: styd on ins fnl f: nvr able to chal* **11/1**

0-04 5 ½ **Goose Chase**^{28} [480] 4-9-4 65 .... DaneO'Neill 4 69
(A M Hales) *lw: prom: rdn on inner over 1f out: kpt on same pce* **20/1**

3-00 6 ½ **Duxford**^{23} [537] 5-8-13 60 .... JimmyQuinn 1 63
(D K Ivory) *dwlt: hld up wl in rr: effrt over 1f out: styd on ins fnl f: nt rch ldrs* **100/1**

00-0 7 nk **Simplify**^{18} [576] 4-8-13 60 .... FergusSweeney 6 62
(T M Jones) *hld up in rr: nt clr run over 1f out: styd on fnl f: no ch* **50/1**

1526 8 shd **Burnley Al (IRE)**^{26} [504] 4-9-4 65 ....(v) PaulHanagan 5 67
(R A Fahey) *led: hrd pressed 2f out: hdd & wknd 1f out* **9/2**^{2}

2033 9 nk **Monashee Prince (IRE)**^{18} [575] 4-8-9 63 .... KylieManser$^{(7)}$ 8 65
(J R Best) *trckd ldrs: shkn up and hanging over 1f out: sn btn* **11/2**

360- 10 hd **The Bonus King**^{158} [5893] 6-9-0 61 .... ChrisCatlin 3 62
(J Jay) *hld up in rr: effrt on inner over 1f out: no ch whn nt clr run wl ins fnl f: kpt on* **10/1**

0000 11 2 **Celtique**^{20} [557] 4-8-13 60 .... JamieMackay 12 57
(M Wigham) *reminders to enter stalls: s.i.s: a in last pair: rdn and no rspnse over 2f out* **25/1**

00-5 12 shd **Ektishaaf**^{23} [537] 4-8-13 60 .... TQuinn 9 56
(C F Wall) *lw: racd wd: in tch: reminders 2f out: no prog: wknd over 1f out* **5/1**^{3}

1m 38.1s (-1.33) **Going Correction** -0.075s/f (Stan) **12** Ran SP% **120.9**
Speed ratings (Par 101):103,102,102,101,101 100,100,100,99,99 97,97
CSF £91.43 CT £369.80 TOTE £10.00: £2.30, £3.60, £1.60; EX 73.40 Trifecta £569.50 Part won. Pool: £802.15 - 0.75 winning units..

Owner Brian C Oakley **Bred** B C Oakley **Trained** East Everleigh, Wilts

FOCUS
Another moderate handicap, but the pace was fair and the form looks sound enough for the class.

699 THE SPORTSMAN OUT TODAY H'CAP 5f (P)
5:20 (5:20) (Class 5) (0-75,75) 4-Y-0+ **£3,886** (£1,156; £577; £288) **Stalls** High

Form RPR

6153 1 **Mambazo**^{23} [532] 4-8-5 **65** ....(e) AdamKirby$^{(3)}$ 2 73
(S C Williams) *lw: taken down early: hld up in detached last: effrt on inner 2f out: r.o wl fnl f: edgd rt but led nr fin* **5/2**^{1}

4110 2 nk **Canadian Danehill (IRE)**^{23} [532] 4-8-10 **67** .... ShaneKelly 3 74
(R M H Cowell) *pressed ldrs: led on inner 2f out: edgd rt fnl f: hdd nr fin* **12/1**

6030 3 1¼ **Kempsey**^{4} [664] 4-9-1 **75** ....(v) NeilChalmers$^{(3)}$ 9 78
(J J Bridger) *pressed ldrs: rdn over 2f out: nt qckn over 1f out: kpt on again fnl f* **14/1**

-324 4 nk **Wicked Uncle**^{25} [517] 7-8-13 **70** ....(v) DarryllHolland 1 71
(S Gollings) *pushed along in rr 3f out: prog u.p 2f out: styd on fnl f* **7/2**^{2}

111- 5 shd **Holbeck Ghyll (IRE)**^{194} [5093] 4-9-2 **73** .... MartinDwyer 7 74
(A M Balding) *lw: pressed ldrs: effrt 2f out: chal and upsides 1f out: one pce* **7/2**^{2}

0115 6 1½ **Sweetest Revenge (IRE)**^{5} [657] 5-9-0 **71** .... HayleyTurner 4 73+
(M D I Usher) *sn pushed along in rr: effrt 2f out: running on whn hmpd last 150yds: nt rcvr* **9/1**^{3}

0006 7 1¾ **Poker Player (IRE)**^{19} [569] 4-9-1 **72** ....(b) SebSanders 6 61
(G C Bravery) *a towards rr: rdn bef 1/2-way: no real prog* **9/1**^{3}

6-00 8 hd **Tartatartufata**^{25} [517] 4-9-3 **74** ....(v) DaneO'Neill 5 63
(D Shaw) *mde most to 2f out: wknd ins fnl f* **25/1**

620- 9 4 **Wise Wager (IRE)**^{189} [5225] 4-8-13 **70** .... AdrianMcCarthy 8 44
(Miss Z C Davison) *lw: pressed ldrs for 2f: wknd over 2f out* **66/1**

-046 10 1½ **Little Ridge (IRE)**^{15} [605] 5-8-5 **67** .... TravisBlock$^{(5)}$ 10 36
(H Morrison) *racd wd: rdn and struggling 3f out: wknd 2f out* **14/1**

59.00 secs (-0.78) **Going Correction** -0.075s/f (Stan) **10** Ran SP% **119.4**
Speed ratings (Par 103):103,102,100,100,99 97,94,94,87,85
CSF £35.75 CT £367.62 TOTE £4.10: £1.10, £6.30, £4.90; EX 51.30 Trifecta £233.80 Pool: £490.82 - 1.49 winning units. Place 6 £312.27, Place 5 £284.84.

Owner D G Burge **Bred** Barry Taylor **Trained** Newmarket, Suffolk

FOCUS
An open-looking sprint, but the form is not totally convincing, with those racing prominently going very quick and stopping, and the race possibly set up for a finisher like the winner.
Sweetest Revenge(IRE) Official explanation: jockey said mare was denied clear run at furlong marker
Tartatartufata Official explanation: jockey said filly hung right

T/Jkpt: Not won. T/Plt: £550.70 to a £1 stake. Pool: £46,284.55. 61.35 winning tickets. T/Qpdt: £113.00 to a £1 stake. Pool: £3,619.60. 23.70 winning tickets. JN

692 LINGFIELD (L-H)
Thursday, March 23

OFFICIAL GOING: Standard
Meeting switched from Doncaster and, although run on sand, counted for statistical purposes as the first day of the Flat turf season.
Wind: Light, behind Weather: Fine

700 FURLONGS & FAIRWAYS APPRENTICE H'CAP 1m 4f (P)
1:50 (1:50) (Class 5) (0-70,70) 4-Y-0+ **£3,238** (£963; £481; £240) **Stalls** Low

Form RPR

6/ 1 **Shaunas Vision (IRE)**^{155} [5676] 7-8-12 **64** .... RobertMiles 3 74+
(D K Ivory) *hld up towards rr: prog on wd outside fr over 3f out to ld over 2f out: 3 l clr fnl f: heavily eased nr fin* **14/1**

0-45 2 ½ **Brockhole (IRE)**^{17} [603] 4-8-9 **63** .... DanielTudhope 6 67
(J G Given) *trckd ldng trio over 7f out: rdn over 2f out: prog to chse wnr ins fnl f: r.o but flattered by proximity* **8/1**^{3}

-405 3 2 **Swainson (USA)**^{57} [186] 5-8-10 **62** .... AdamKirby 1 63
(P Mitchell) *led at slow pce for 4f: trckd ldr: rdn to chal 3f out: outpcd by wnr wl over 1f out: one pce after* **3/1**^{1}

1213 4 3½ **Latif (USA)**^{20} [567] 5-8-10 **65** .... RichardKingscote$^{(3)}$ 7 60+
(Ms Deborah J Evans) *plld hrd: led after 4f and qcknd: hdd and outpcd over 2f out* **9/2**^{2}

5165 5 1¾ **Dovedon Hero**^{30} [478] 6-9-3 **69** ....(b) SaleemGolam 2 62
(P J McBride) *plld hrd: trckd ldrs: lost pl 4f out: outpcd over 2f out: brief effrt over 1f out: sn btn* **3/1**^{1}

0-04 6 3 **Eijaaz (IRE)**^{24} [530] 5-8-1 **58** .... KristinStubbs$^{(5)}$ 5 46
(Mrs L Stubbs) *s.s: hld up in last pair: outpcd over 2f out: bmpd along and no prog after* **8/1**^{3}

/00- 7 1¼ **Redi (ITY)**^{70} [5074] 5-9-4 **70** ....(t) NeilChalmers 4 56
(A M Balding) *trckd ldr for 4f: styd prom: rdn over 3f out: wknd 2f out* **10/1**

0-00 8 ¾ **Afadan (IRE)**^{30} [478] 8-8-13 **65** ....(t) PaulMulrennan 8 50
(J R Jenkins) *s.s: a last: outpcd wl over 2f out* **25/1**

2m 36.24s (1.85) **Going Correction** -0.05s/f (Stan)
WFA 4 from 5yo+ 2lb **8** Ran SP% **110.0**
Speed ratings (Par 103):91,90,89,87,85 83,83,82
CSF £110.41 CT £402.46 TOTE £11.50: £2.70, £2.50, £1.40; EX 107.40 Trifecta £535.00 Pool: £783.72 - 1.04 winning tickets..

Owner John F Connolly **Bred** Ruairi O'Coileain **Trained** Radlett, Herts
■ For statistical purposes the first race of the new turf season, even though it was run on Polytrack.

FOCUS
Very little early pace led to this mile and a half handicap turning into something of a sprint. The form is far from solid.
Latif(USA) Official explanation: jockey said gelding ran too free
Afadan(IRE) Official explanation: jockey said gelding hung right

701 NEWCHAPEL MAIDEN AUCTION STKS 5f (P)
2:20 (2:20) (Class 5) 2-Y-0 **£3,886** (£1,156; £577; £288) **Stalls** High

Form RPR

1 **Hephaestus** 2-8-11 .... TQuinn 10 72
(M R Channon) *s.s: rcvrd and in tch after 2f: prog to chse ldr wl over 1f out: hanging lft but kpt on wl to ld nr fin* **13/2**^{3}

2 nk **Fast Freddie** 2-8-12 .... JohnEgan 1 72
(T J Pitt) *fast away: led: pressed fnl f: worn down nr fin* **11/10**^{1}

3 1½ **Satulagi (USA)** 2-8-4 .... MartinDwyer 6 58
(J S Moore) *s.s: sn rcvrd and cl up: rdn to chse ldr briefly 2f out: styd on same pce* **11/2**^{2}

4 1 **Our Blessing (IRE)** 2-8-10 .... DarrenWilliams 8 60
(A P Jarvis) *s.s: last to 3f out: prog to chse ldng trio over 1f out: kpt on but no imp* **8/1**

5 5 **Weyba Downs (IRE)** 2-8-12 .... SteveDrowne 5 42
(J R Best) *prom for 1f: sn outpcd and struggling: last and outpcd 1/2-way: sme prog 2f out: no ch* **14/1**

6 ¾ **Beckenham's Secret** 2-8-10 .... AlanMunro 7 37
(B R Millman) *racd wd and hanging rt: outpcd after 2f: n.d fnl 2f* **9/1**

7 1¼ **Ivorys Song** 2-8-4 .... FrancisNorton 9 26
(D K Ivory) *sn wl in rr: outpcd fr 1/2-way: no ch after* **33/1**

8 ½ **Fasuby (IRE)** 2-8-5 .... GrahamGibbons 3 25
(P D Evans) *chsd ldr for 1f: wknd over 2f out* **25/1**

9 2 **Auctioneerscouk (IRE)** 2-8-9 .... ShaneKelly 2 21
(P D Evans) *dwlt: rcvrd to chse ldr after 1f to 2f out: wknd* **25/1**

10 1 **Catweasel** 2-8-8 ow1 .... RobertMiles$^{(3)}$ 4 19
(W G M Turner) *racd wd: in tch for 2f: sn struggling* **16/1**

60.60 secs (0.82) **Going Correction** -0.05s/f (Stan) **10** Ran SP% **120.6**
Speed ratings (Par 92):91,90,88,86,78 77,75,74,71,69
CSF £14.25 TOTE £7.60: £2.00, £1.30, £1.60; EX 24.40 Trifecta £71.10 Pool: £382.00 - 3.81 winning tickets..

Owner Box 41 **Bred** M F Kentish **Trained** West Ilsley, Berks

FOCUS
Impossible to gauge the level of the form, given this was only the second two-year-old race of the season, but there were some nice types on show for the time of year and the race should produce winners. For what it's worth, the winning time was 1.5 second faster than the first juvenile race of the season won by Love In May.

NOTEBOOK
Hephaestus, a 17,000gns first foal of a middle-distance maiden, benefited from a good ride from Quinn to make a winning debut. Settled in a good position just off the fast pace, he had to come a little wide into the straight, but kept responding to sympathetic handling and wore down the far more vigorously-ridden runner-up near the line. He looks up to holding his own in winners' company. (op 6-1 tchd 7-1)
Fast Freddie, a 35,000gns first foal of the triple five/six-furlong juvenile winner Bella Chica, was really well backed on his racecourse debut and was clearly expected to go in at the first time of asking, but he just failed. Well away and soon in front, he knew his job but could not get away in the straight and received a much harder ride than the eventual winner to try and justify his short price. As a result, it remains to be seen which way he will go from this and he is not one to take a short price about next time. (op 6-5 tchd 5-4 in places)
Satulagi(USA), a half-sister to six-furlong juvenile winner Mister Saif and dual mile winner September Harvest, out of a nine-furlong two-year-old winner, was representing the stable who won the first juvenile race of the year. She did not help her chance with a slow start, but kept on for pressure and can probably be placed to effect in the coming weeks. (op 5-1)

Our Blessing(IRE) ◆, a 13,000gns half-brother the useful Berenica, a five/six-furlong winner at two and three, and multiple five-furlong scorer Gaelic Princess, was really well backed but blew his chance with a very slow start. He did, though, stay on nicely in the latter stages to take an eye-catching fourth and looks capable of improving quite significantly with the benefit of this experience. (op 33-1)
Weyba Downs(IRE), a 25,000gns yearling, has a mix of speed and stamina in his pedigree, as he is a half-brother to Ash Moon, a dual sprint winner at two, as well as a half-brother to a multiple winner over hurdles. This was a satisfactory introduction and he can be expected to improve. (op 12-1)
Beckenham's Secret, a 9,000gns yearling, out of a full-sister to a smart winner over a mile six, should be capable of quite a bit better with the benefit of this experience. He gave himself no chance by coming widest of all and hanging right on the final bend, but he did not drop away in the straight and clearly possesses ability. (op 7-1)

702 MARSH GREEN H'CAP — 7f (P)
2:55 (2:57) (Class 4) (0-85,85) 3-Y-O — **£5,505** (£1,637; £818; £408) **Stalls** Low

Form — RPR
3-21 **1** **Rebellion**[31] [459] 3-8-8 **75** .... JoeFanning 9 — 77
(M Johnston) *mde all: set stdy pce tl kicked on 2f out: drvn and in command fnl f* **7/2**[2]
4122 **2** *1 ½* **Didn't We (IRE)**[30] [475] 3-8-12 **79** .... IanMongan 10 — 77
(T G Mills) *plld hrd early: pressed wnr: rdn and nt qckn wl over 1f out: kpt on but no imp fnl f* **7/4**[1]
512- **3** *hd* **Broken Spur (FR)**[133] [6304] 3-8-8 **75** .... MichaelHills 4 — 73+
(B W Hills) *dwlt: hld up towards rr: plenty to do whn effrt on inner over 1f out: r.o fnl f: nvr nrr* **7/1**
3351 **4** *½* **Scroll**[6] [658] 3-8-10 **77** 6ex .... (v) ShaneKelly 1 — 73
(P Howling) *trckd ldrs: rdn and nt qckn wl over 1f out: one pce after* **14/1**
061- **5** *¾* **Sands Of Barra (IRE)**[108] [6501] 3-8-6 **73** .... JohnEgan 6 — 67
(N A Callaghan) *sn in last trio: prog 3f out: rdn wl over 1f out: kpt on same pce: n.d* **13/2**[3]
540- **6** *shd* **Sgt Schultz (IRE)**[174] [5582] 3-8-5 **72** .... RobertWinston 7 — 66
(J S Moore) *prom: rdn to press ldng pair 2f out: outpcd sn after* **20/1**
4-01 **7** *nk* **Li Shih Chen**[19] [579] 3-8-9 **76** ow1 .... DarrenWilliams 5 — 69
(A P Jarvis) *settled in rr: shkn up over 2f out: styd on fnl f: no ch w ldrs* **14/1**
3523 **8** *shd* **His Master's Voice (IRE)**[19] [579] 3-8-7 **74** .... TQuinn 8 — 67
(D W P Arbuthnot) *chsd ldrs: rdn and nt qckn 2f out: one pce after* **10/1**
2313 **9** *5* **Canina**[17] [601] 3-8-2 **72** oh3 ow1 .... EdwardCreighton(3) 2 — 52
(Ms Deborah J Evans) *dwlt: a in last pair: lost tch w main gp over 2f out* **33/1**
15- **10** *13* **Bucharest**[176] [5556] 3-9-4 **85** .... JamieMackay 3 — 31
(M Wigham) *restrained s: plld hrd and hld up in last: wknd 3f out: t.o* **33/1**

1m 26.08s (0.19) **Going Correction** -0.05s/f (Stan) **10** Ran SP% **117.5**
Speed ratings (Par 100):96,94,94,93,92 92,92,92,86,71
CSF £9.86 CT £39.85 TOTE £4.60: £1.50, £1.20, £2.50; EX 10.80 Trifecta £49.20 Pool: £945.13 - 13.62 winning tickets..
Owner Jumeirah Racing **Bred** Darley **Trained** Middleham Moor, N Yorks

FOCUS
A good handicap for the grade, but there was no pace and several ran too keen behind the winner, who was favoured by being allowed the run of the race. Not form to take too literally.
Broken Spur(FR) ◆ Official explanation: jockey said colt was denied a clear run on run to line

703 EDENBRIDGE MAIDEN STKS — 1m (P)
3:25 (3:28) (Class 5) 3-Y-O — **£3,886** (£1,156; £577; £288) **Stalls** High

Form — RPR
222- **1** **Kalankari (IRE)**[177] [5524] 3-9-3 75 .... MartinDwyer 6 — 75
(A M Balding) *mde all: gng much bttr than only chalr fr over 2f out: drvn fnl f: edgd rt but kpt on* **4/9**[1]
6 **2** *1 ¼* **Abaconian (IRE)**[17] [590] 3-9-3 .... (t) JimmyFortune 7 — 72
(M J Wallace) *pressed wnr: rdn 3f out: chal u.p 1f out: no ex* **11/2**[2]
3 *2 ½* **Evident Pride (USA)** 3-9-3 .... DaneO'Neill 3 — 66
(B R Johnson) *reluctant to enter stalls: s.v.s: in tch in last pair 5f out: prog over 2f out: rdn and kpt on fr over 1f out* **33/1**
004- **4** *1 ½* **Gattuso**[87] [6663] 3-9-3 63 .... SamHitchcott 8 — 63
(Ms Deborah J Evans) *hld up and immediately detached: in tch in last pair 5f out: rdn and prog over 2f out: kpt on* **16/1**
0-00 **5** *2 ½* **Titus Lumpus (IRE)**[71] [85] 3-9-3 55 .... JoeFanning 5 — 57
(R M Flower) *chsd ldng pair: outpcd wl over 2f out: wknd over 1f out* **25/1**
6 *5* **Karijini (IRE)** 3-8-12 .... ShaneKelly 2 — 41
(E A L Dunlop) *in tch tl wknd wl over 2f out* **11/1**[3]
0 **7** *½* **Tilsworth Charlie**[36] [418] 3-8-12 .... RobertWinston 4 — 39
(J R Jenkins) *trckd ldrs tl wknd rapidly over 2f out* **50/1**

1m 38.92s (-0.51) **Going Correction** -0.05s/f (Stan) **7** Ran SP% **107.6**
Speed ratings (Par 98):100,98,96,94,92 87,86
CSF £2.67 TOTE £1.20: £1.10, £2.00; EX 2.90 Trifecta £36.10 Pool: £549.00 - 10.79 winning tickets..
Owner Dubai Thoroughbred Racing **Bred** B Kennedy **Trained** Kingsclere, Hants
■ Maud's Cat (7/1) was withdrawn (refused to enter stalls). R4 applies, deduct 10p in the £.

FOCUS
An uncompetitive maiden, and the favourite did not need to be at his best. The modest fifth looks the best guide to the form.

704 DONCASTER MILE (LISTED RACE) — 1m (P)
4:00 (4:01) (Class 1) 4-Y-O+ — **£11,435** (£11,435; £3,136; £1,568) **Stalls** High

Form — RPR
424- **1** **Vanderlin**[151] [6057] 7-9-5 .... MartinDwyer 6 — 113
(A M Balding) *trckd ldr: clr of rest wl over 1f out: sustained chal fnl f: forced dead-heat last stride* **8/1**
6000 **1** *dht* **Kandidate**[14] [625] 4-8-12 .... (t) SebSanders 5 — 106
(C E Brittain) *mde all: set stdy pce tl qcknd over 2f out: hrd pressed fnl f: kpt on wl: jnd on line* **7/1**[3]
2331 **3** *1 ½* **Azarole (IRE)**[14] [625] 5-8-12 .... JohnEgan 4 — 103
(J S Moore) *hld up: outpcd and trapped bhd horses over 2f out: chsd clr ldng pair over 1f out: r.o: no ch* **2/1**[2]
0206 **4** *shd* **Moayed**[5] [667] 7-8-12 97 .... (b) IanMongan 2 — 102
(N P Littmoden) *s.s: hld up: last and outpcd over 2f out: r.o wl fr jst over 1f out: no ch of rching ldng pair* **14/1**
3016 **5** *3 ½* **Bravo Maestro (USA)**[5] [666] 5-8-12 96 .... ChrisCatlin 7 — 94
(N P Littmoden) *hld up: prog over 2f out: sn outpcd: hanging lft and btn wl over 1f out* **15/8**[1]
3132 **6** *1 ½* **Kindlelight Debut**[6] [660] 6-8-7 85 .... TQuinn 1 — 86
(N P Littmoden) *trckd ldng pair to 5f out: outpcd over 2f out: no imp after* **16/1**
030- **7** *5* **Lord Mayor**[124] [6378] 5-8-12 100 .... ShaneKelly 3 — 79+
(R M H Cowell) *chsd ldng pair 5f out to 2f out: btn whn squeezed out shortly after* **10/1**

1m 38.88s (-0.55) **Going Correction** -0.05s/f (Stan) **7** Ran SP% **113.4**
Speed ratings (Par 111):100,100,98,98,94 93,88
WIN: Vanderlin £3.50, Kandidate £3.60. PL: Vanderlin £2.50, Kandidate £3.90. EX: Van/Kan £19.50, Kan/Van £19.90. CSF: Van/Kan £30.02, Kan/ Van £29.33..
Owner J C, J R And S R Hitchins **Bred** Ellway Breeding **Trained** Kingsclere, Hants
Owner A J Richards **Bred** Proton Partnership **Trained** Newmarket, Suffolk
■ Stewards' Enquiry : John Egan three-day ban: careless riding (Apr 3-5)
Seb Sanders two-day ban: used whip down shoulder with whip in forehand position and with excessive frequency (Apr 3-4)

FOCUS
Not a very strong Listed race and the lack of pace meant it was hard to come from off the pace. The dead-heaters were dominant throughout.

NOTEBOOK
Vanderlin, really well placed to pick up tremendous amounts of prize money in Canada and the US towards the end of last season, showed himself as good as ever under his Group winner's penalty on his return from a 151-day break. Connections were understandably pleased and will now aim him at the Betfred Mile before sending him on his travels once more. (op 6-1 tchd 15-2)
Kandidate was well below form on the last of his five runs in Dubai (he won the first of them) but, switched to Polytrack on his return to England, he got the run of the race in front and just proved up to the task. This was a soft enough option for a Listed race, and he was getting 7lb from a reappearing Vanderlin, so connections will do well to find as good an opportunity next time. (op 6-1 tchd 15-2)
Azarole(IRE), successful in a handicap off a mark of 105 at Nad Al Sheba on his previous start, ran well back in England and stepped up to Listed company considering he found himself in an unpromising position on the turn into the straight. (op 7-4)
Moayed, back up to a mile, could have done with a stronger pace and never looked like winning, but kept on and ran close to his best in fourth. He is rated lower on turf and could get competitive in a valuable handicap or two. (op 11-1)
Bravo Maestro(USA), successful in the Lincoln Trial at Wolverhampton before running sixth in the Winter Derby, was unsuited by the way the race was run and could not produce his best. (op 11-4)
Kindlelight Debut did not have the race run to suit and was well held, but will be worth another try in Listed company in fillies and mares only company. (tchd 20-1)
Lord Mayor Official explanation: jockey said gelding suffered interference in running

705 LINGFIELD-RACECOURSE.CO.UK STKS (H'CAP) — 5f (P)
4:35 (4:38) (Class 2) (0-100,96) 4-Y-O+
£11,217 (£3,358; £1,679; £840; £419; £210) **Stalls** High

Form — RPR
2140 **1** **Qadar (IRE)**[5] [664] 4-9-2 **94** .... IanMongan 9 — 106
(N P Littmoden) *hld up in last pair: gd prog on outer wl over 1f out: str run to ld last 75yds: won gng away* **6/1**[3]
02-4 **2** *1 ¼* **Fromsong (IRE)**[47] [295] 8-9-4 **96** .... JohnEgan 6 — 103
(D K Ivory) *trckd ldrs: outpcd 2f out: effrt over 1f out: styd on but nt pce of wnr* **4/1**[2]
3503 **3** *hd* **One More Round (USA)**[5] [664] 8-8-12 **90** .... (b) ChrisCatlin 5 — 96
(N P Littmoden) *hld up in last pair: effrt on inner over 1f out: styd on: nt pce of wnr* **6/1**[3]
400- **4** *½* **Merlin's Dancer**[187] [5288] 6-8-12 **90** .... AdrianTNicholls 4 — 94
(D Nicholls) *trckd ldrs: prog to ld over 2f out: idled in front over 1f out: hdd and btn last 75yds* **12/1**
2660 **5** *½* **Dancing Mystery**[5] [664] 12-9-0 **92** .... (b) StephenCarson 3 — 95
(E A Wheeler) *trckd ldrs: n.m.r 2f out: one pce over 1f out* **25/1**
044- **6** *shd* **Green Manalishi**[96] [6602] 5-9-4 **96** .... TQuinn 7 — 105+
(D W P Arbuthnot) *trckd ldrs: hmpd over 2f out and lost all ch: r.o again ins fnl f* **7/2**[1]
235- **7** *hd* **Malapropism**[152] [6021] 6-8-1 **82** .... EdwardCreighton(3) 1 — 84
(M R Channon) *led to over 2f out: pressed ldr over 1f out tl no ex ins fnl f* **14/1**
240- **8** *3* **Cape Royal**[152] [6021] 6-9-4 **96** .... (t) KDarley 2 — 87
(J M Bradley) *trckd ldrs: rdn whn hmpd over 2f out: nt rcvr* **8/1**

58.50 secs (-1.28) **Going Correction** -0.05s/f (Stan) **8** Ran SP% **100.1**
Speed ratings (Par 109):108,106,105,104,104 103,103,98
CSF £21.82 CT £79.81 TOTE £6.00: £1.60, £1.50, £1.70; EX 30.00 Trifecta £119.80 Pool: £548.77 - 3.25 winning tickets..
Owner Nigel Shields **Bred** Martin Francis **Trained** Newmarket, Suffolk

FOCUS
A competitive sprint handicap and solid form for the grade. The form has been rated through the runner-up, with Qadar raised another 7lb.

NOTEBOOK
Qadar(IRE), who appreciates a good gallop off which to challenge, stayed on strongly from off the pace to win quite comfortably in the end. He has had a good winter on the All-Weather for his new stable and it will be interesting to see if he can continue progressing back on turf, with races like the Stewards' Cup on the agenda later on in the season. (tchd 13-2)
Fromsong(IRE) is currently on a mark 11lb higher than for his last win and ran a solid race in defeat. His performance is a good guide to the level of the form. (op 9-2)
One More Round(USA) ran a good race at the weights behind Les Arcs last time, but he has failed to get his head in front in his last 36 starts and once again found a couple too good. (op 5-1)
Merlin's Dancer, making his All-Weather debut, won on his seasonal reappearance last season. He was denied an easy lead this time, though, and having had to work too hard to get it he paid the price in the closing stages, losing three places inside the final half furlong. (op 14-1)
Dancing Mystery has lost some of the speed he once had, which is not surprising given his age, and he looks like he needs some help from the Handicapper now.
Green Manalishi ◆ deserves rating better than his finishing position as he was hampered just as the race was getting serious and his challenge was badly delayed. He should be fit for the start of the turf campaign now, though, and has the ability to win off this sort of mark. (op 9-2)

706 LINGFIELD PARK RACECOURSE LADY RIDERS' H'CAP — 1m 2f (P)
5:05 (5:05) (Class 5) (0-70,64) 4-Y-O+ — **£3,123** (£968; £484; £242) **Stalls** Low

Form — RPR
2121 **1** **Polish Power (GER)**[19] [574] 6-10-4 **61** .... MrsSMoore 10 — 78
(J S Moore) *prom in chsng gp: clsd to dispute ld wl over 2f out: gained upper hand nr fin* **3/1**[1]
2220 **2** *nk* **Augustine**[7] [652] 5-10-0 **62** .... MrsMarieKing(5) 5 — 78
(P W Hiatt) *prom: chsd clr ldr over 5f out: clsd to dispute ld wl over 2f out: hdd and no ex nr fin* **3/1**[1]
4056 **3** *9* **Ramsgill (USA)**[7] [652] 4-10-6 **63** .... MrsEmmaLittmoden 1 — 62
(N P Littmoden) *hld up wl in rr: prog over 3f out: outpcd over 2f out: kpt on to take modest 3rd fnl f* **7/2**[2]
0000 **4** *2 ½* **Scottish River (USA)**[24] [530] 7-10-3 **63** .... MissEALalor(3) 9 — 58
(M D I Usher) *s.v.s: sn in tch: prog to chse ldng pair over 2f out: no imp: lost 3rd fnl f* **6/1**[3]

50-0 **5** 3 **Neptune**[17] [599] 10-9-2 **50** oh10 .... MissSarah-JaneDurman(5) 4 39
(J C Fox) *hld up and sn last: sme prog whn rn v wd bnd 2f out: kpt on fnl f: no ch* **66/1**

0-00 **6** nk **Monkstown Road**[28] [493] 4-9-13 **56** .... (b) MissEJJones 13 44
(C N Kellett) *in tch in chsng gp: wl outpcd 3f out: plugged on fr over 1f out* **25/1**

13-0 **7** ½ **Love You Always (USA)**[17] [597] 6-9-12 **55** .... MrsACooke 7 42
(Miss J Feilden) *prom in chsng gp: outpcd wl over 2f out: n.d after* **9/1**

660- **8** nk **Spring Time Girl**[175] [5564] 4-9-4 **50** oh2 .... (p) MissLEllison(3) 3 37
(B Ellison) *nvr beyond midfield: effrt on inner and n.m.r over 2f out: no prog after* **25/1**

000- **9** 2 ½ **Just A Fluke (IRE)**[207] [4794] 5-9-13 **56** .... (t) MrsSBosley 2 38
(M R Bosley) *hld up in last trio: bhd 3f out: modest late prog* **40/1**

0-00 **10** 2 **Graft**[17] [596] 7-9-7 **55** .... (b) MrsCThompson(5) 11 33
(Mrs P Townsley) *s.v.s: sn in tch: brief effrt on outer 3f out: sn btn* **16/1**

34-5 **11** 12 **Full Of Zest**[44] [327] 4-10-0 **64** .... MissLauraGray(7) 8 19
(Mrs L J Mongan) *chsd clr ldr to over 5f out: sn lost pl and btn* **16/1**

000- **12** 11 **Beau Jazz**[315] [1648] 5-9-2 **50** oh5 .... MrsIDeBest(5) 6 —
(W De Best-Turner) *tore off in clr ld: hdd & wknd rapidly wl over 2f out: t.o* **100/1**

2m 5.93s (-1.86) **Going Correction** -0.05s/f (Stan) **12** Ran SP% **120.9**
Speed ratings (Par 103):105,104,97,95,93 92,92,92,90,88 79,70
CSF £11.74 CT £33.49 TOTE £4.20: £1.20, £2.40, £2.10; EX 15.00 Trifecta £41.90 Pool: £521.71 - 8.83 winning tickets. Place 6 £52.19, Place 5 £20.01.
Owner Mrs Fitri Hay **Bred** Gestut Hofgut Mappen **Trained** Upper Lambourn, Berks

FOCUS
A modest handicap which concerned only the joint-favourites from the turn into the straight.
T/Jkpt: Not won. T/Plt: £58.00 to a £1 stake. Pool: £50,064.35. 629.85 winning tickets. T/Qpdt: £11.50 to a £1 stake. Pool: £4,147.90. 266.75 winning tickets. JN

700 LINGFIELD (L-H)
Friday, March 24

OFFICIAL GOING: Standard
Wind: Light, behind Weather: Overcast

707 LINGFIELD-RACECOURSE.CO.UK MAIDEN AUCTION STKS 5f (P)
2:10 (2:12) (Class 6) 2-Y-O **£2,590** (£770; £385; £192) **Stalls High**

Form RPR

1 **Bazroy (IRE)** 2-8-9 .... ShaneKelly 9 89
(P D Evans) *mde all: set stdy pce tl qcknd away wl over 1f out: shkn up and r.o wl fnl f* **11/2**[3]

2 5 **Urban Warrior** 2-8-9 .... AlanMunro 3 69
(J R Best) *chsd ldrs: shkn up and outpcd wl over 1f out: r.o fnl f to take 2nd last 75yds* **5/1**[2]

3 1 ½ **Pernomente (IRE)** 2-8-11 .... JohnEgan 6 65
(J S Moore) *chsd wnr after 1f: outpcd wl over 1f out: no ch after: lost 2nd last 75yds* **4/1**[1]

4 ½ **Hucking Hill (IRE)** 2-8-13 .... TQuinn 4 65
(J R Best) *chsd ldrs: shkn up and outpcd wl over 1f out: kpt on same pce fnl f* **4/1**[1]

5 1 **Right Option (IRE)** 2-8-11 .... DarrenWilliams 5 59
(A P Jarvis) *dwlt: off the pce in last trio: shkn up 2f out: sme prog over 1f out: n.d* **8/1**

6 hd **Sad Times (IRE)** 2-7-11 .... LiamJones(7) 2 51
(W G M Turner) *chsd wnr for 1f: prom tl wknd on inner over 1f out* **12/1**

7 1 **Emergency Services** 2-8-6 .... JamesDoyle(5) 10 54
(Tom Dascombe) *mounted on crse: racd wd: in tch to 1/2-way: no ch over 1f out* **13/2**

8 4 **Alittleriskie (IRE)** 2-8-4 .... MartinDwyer 7 31
(J S Moore) *s.s: rn green in last pair and a bhd* **8/1**

9 1 ¾ **Bathwick Princess** 2-8-4 .... StephenCarson 1 24
(P D Evans) *s.i.s: sn outpcd in last pair: nvr a factor* **33/1**

60.40 secs (0.62) **Going Correction** -0.125s/f (Stan) **9** Ran SP% **118.2**
Speed ratings (Par 90):90,82,79,78,77 76,75,68,66
CSF £34.00 TOTE £8.10: £3.10, £2.70, £1.50; EX 43.00.
Owner Barry McCabe **Bred** P D Savill **Trained** Pandy, Abergavenny

FOCUS
A race run at a muddling gallop but an impressive winner, who showed a fine turn of foot to power clear off the home turn and appeals strongly as the type to win more races.

NOTEBOOK
Bazroy(IRE) ◆, who has plenty of speed in his pedigree, was allowed to set his own pace in what was almost certainly an ordinary race but showed a fine turn of foot to burst clear. He looks well up to winning again in the early months. (op 9-2)
Urban Warrior, out of a mile and a quarter winner, showed ability on this racecourse debut and left the strong impression (backed up by pedigree) that the step up to six furlongs would be in his favour in due course. (tchd 11-2)
Pernomente(IRE), from a stable that has already been on the mark with a juvenile at this course this year, showed ability on this racecourse debut and is entitled to improve for the experience. (op 9-2 tchd 7-2)
Hucking Hill(IRE) ◆, a half-brother to fair juvenile Chiselled, shaped with a fair degree of promise on this racecourse debut, despite his apparent greenness, and he appeals as the type to win races in the near future. (tchd 9-2)
Right Option(IRE), who attracted a bit of support on this racecourse debut, hinted at ability after a tardy start. He should be better for this experience and is capable of better, especially over further in due course. (op 14-1)
Sad Times(IRE), the first foal of a poor dam, had the run of the race against the inside rail and wasn't totally disgraced. She may do better but is likely to remain vulnerable in this type of event.

708 LINGFIELD LEISURE CLUB CLAIMING STKS 7f (P)
2:45 (2:45) (Class 6) 3-Y-O+ **£2,730** (£806; £403) **Stalls Low**

Form RPR

000- **1** **Banjo Bay (IRE)**[191] [5222] 8-9-7 62 .... FrancisNorton 8 64
(D Nicholls) *hld up: prog on outer fr 1/2-way: effrt and r.o to ld last 150yds: rdn out* **14/1**

0604 **2** 1 **True Night**[7] [662] 9-9-11 67 .... (v[1]) RobertWinston 2 66
(D Nicholls) *trckd ldrs: rdn 2f out: effrt on inner over 1f out: r.o to take 2nd nr fin: nt rch wnr* **3/1**[1]

3305 **3** ½ **Triple Zero (IRE)**[30] [485] 4-9-4 57 .... DarrenWilliams 10 58
(A P Jarvis) *trckd ldr: led 3f out: drvn 2f out: hdd and one pce last 150yds* **8/1**[3]

2460 **4** ¾ **Hadath (IRE)**[2] [693] 9-9-5 59 .... (v) TQuinn 1 57
(B G Powell) *hld up in midfield: effrt 2f out: drvn and styd on fnl f: nt rch ldrs* **3/1**[1]

0-30 **5** shd **Labelled With Love**[7] [659] 6-9-1 53 .... AmirQuinn(3) 4 55+
(J R Boyle) *dwlt: plld hrd and hld up in last trio: stl pulling over 2f out: rdn over 1f out: r.o fnl f: too much to do* **16/1**

-016 **6** ½ **Priorina (IRE)**[8] [648] 4-9-0 50 .... (p) RobertHavlin 3 50
(D Haydn Jones) *prom: rdn 1/2-way: outpcd and lost pl over 2f out: kpt on again fnl f* **9/1**

0660 **7** 1 ¼ **Paso Doble**[18] [600] 8-9-1 62 .... (b[1]) JamesMillman(7) 6 55
(B R Millman) *settled wl in rr: rdn over 2f out: styd on fnl f: n.d* **20/1**

3450 **8** ¾ **Rowan Pursuit**[20] [575] 5-8-13 50 .... (b) DaneO'Neill 11 44
(J Akehurst) *hld up in rr: rdn wl over 2f out: plugged on but no imp on ldrs* **15/2**[2]

3005 **9** ¾ **Border Artist**[27] [520] 7-9-7 51 .... (p) HayleyTurner 12 53+
(B G Powell) *restrained fr outside draw and hld up in last pair: stl last whn nt clr run 1f out: gng on at fin* **33/1**

3014 **10** nk **Shirley Oaks (IRE)**[39] [397] 8-9-2 47 .... AdrianMcCarthy 5 44
(Miss Z C Davison) *led to 3f out: wknd wl over 1f out* **20/1**

65-5 **11** ½ **Fayr Firenze (IRE)**[11] [417] 5-9-5 45 .... (v) JohnEgan 7 46
(M F Harris) *hld up in midfield: pushed along 3f out and 2f out: reminder over 1f out: nt clr run ins fnl f and eased* **50/1**

4544 **12** nk **Mulberry Lad (IRE)**[16] [613] 4-9-4 46 .... MickyFenton 9 44
(P W Hiatt) *prom: drvn to press ldr over 2f out: wknd v rapidly fnl f* **12/1**

1m 25.09s (-0.80) **Going Correction** -0.125s/f (Stan) **12** Ran SP% **117.5**
Speed ratings (Par 101):99,97,97,96,96 95,94,93,92,92 91,91
CSF £53.13 TOTE £20.50: £5.10, £1.60, £3.10; EX 52.70.
Owner Middleham Park Racing Xxiii **Bred** Yeomanstown Stud **Trained** Sessay, N Yorks

FOCUS
An ordinary claimer in which the pace was just fair. The principals were not at their best and the level of the form is limited, if sound enough.
Border Artist Official explanation: jockey said gelding was denied clear run

709 BRIAN WILKINS "BEEN & GONE & WENT" H'CAP 7f (P)
3:20 (3:20) (Class 5) (0-70,70) 3-Y-O **£3,238** (£963; £481; £240) **Stalls Low**

Form RPR

03-2 **1** **Ballybeg (IRE)**[18] [590] 3-9-2 **68** .... RichardHughes 4 72
(R Hannon) *trckd ldng pair: rdn and effrt over 1f out: styd on to ld last 75yds* **7/1**

65-5 **2** ½ **Gavarnie Beau (IRE)**[30] [481] 3-9-2 **68** .... FrancisNorton 11 71
(M Blanshard) *chsd ldrs: rdn wl over 2f out: r.o fnl f to press wnr nr fin: a hld* **6/1**[3]

0-11 **3** ¾ **Welsh Dragon**[18] [594] 3-8-11 **63** .... MartinDwyer 2 64
(A M Balding) *mde most but nvr allowed uncontested ld: rdn over 2f out: hdd and no ex last 75yds* **4/1**[1]

0001 **4** nk **African Concerto (IRE)**[22] [554] 3-8-13 **65** .... SebSanders 3 65
(Ernst Oertel) *trckd ldng pair: drvn and effrt on inner over 1f out: kpt on but nvr quite rchd ldrs* **9/1**

1011 **5** nk **Garstang**[18] [595] 3-9-4 **70** .... (b) RobbieFitzpatrick 13 69
(Peter Grayson) *w ldr: drvn and stl upsides ins fnl f: wknd nr fin* **11/2**[2]

045- **6** shd **Cheveley Flyer**[140] [6244] 3-8-6 **58** .... JimmyQuinn 14 57
(J Pearce) *dwlt: settled towards rr: rdn over 2f out: styd on fr over 1f out : nrst fin* **7/1**

-036 **7** hd **The London Gang**[18] [601] 3-8-13 **65** .... ShaneKelly 10 64
(P D Evans) *dwlt: wl in rr: sme prog over 2f out: drvn and styd on fnl f: nrst fin* **20/1**

0330 **8** ½ **Grecianette (IRE)**[18] [595] 3-8-6 **58** .... LPKeniry 7 55
(W J Musson) *trckd ldrs: rdn and nt qckn wl over 1f out: one pce after* **16/1**

3130 **9** 3 **Canina**[1] [702] 3-8-13 **68** .... EdwardCreighton(3) 5 58
(Ms Deborah J Evans) *in tch in midfield on inner: rdn over 2f out: cl up but no imp over 1f out: wknd ins fnl f* **20/1**

040- **10** 2 ½ **Sparkbridge (IRE)**[157] [5953] 3-8-5 **57** .... JohnEgan 8 40
(R F Fisher) *last early: nvr on terms w ldrs: lost tch 2f out* **33/1**

000- **11** 5 **Leo McGarry (IRE)**[200] [4996] 3-8-8 **60** .... HayleyTurner 12 30
(S C Williams) *racd wd in rr: rdn 4f out: struggling wl over 2f out* **33/1**

504 **12** 1 **Simplified**[20] [579] 3-8-9 **61** ow1 .... DaneO'Neill 9 28
(J Pearce) *a towards rr: bhd fnl 2f* **33/1**

0-42 **R** **Miss Dagger (IRE)**[18] [594] 3-8-3 **62** ow1 .... KylieManser(7) 1 —
(J R Best) *ref to r: tk no part* **10/1**

1m 25.1s (-0.79) **Going Correction** -0.125s/f (Stan) **13** Ran SP% **118.0**
Speed ratings (Par 98):99,98,97,97,96 96,96,95,92,89 83,82,—
CSF £44.62 CT £194.44 TOTE £6.00: £2.10, £2.50, £1.60; EX 67.40.
Owner Des Kavanagh & Partners **Bred** Rathasker Stud **Trained** East Everleigh, Wilts

FOCUS
An ordinary handicap in which the pace was fair. The form looks sound enough.
Welsh Dragon Official explanation: jockey said colt hung right
Cheveley Flyer Official explanation: jockey said colt missed break
The London Gang Official explanation: jockey said colt ran too free
Simplified Official explanation: trainer said filly ran flat

710 LINGFIELD-RACECOURSE.CO.UK MAIDEN STKS 1m (P)
3:55 (3:55) (Class 5) 3-Y-O **£3,412** (£1,007; £504) **Stalls High**

Form RPR

1 **Wagtail** 3-8-12 .... ShaneKelly 4 65+
(E A L Dunlop) *s.s: sn in tch: prog over 3f out: shkn up to ld over 1f out: clr fnl f: readily* **7/1**[3]

0 **2** 4 **Marcello**[13] [630] 3-9-3 .... RichardHughes 3 61+
(P F I Cole) *led: jnd over 2f out: hdd over 1f out: kpt on but no ch w wnr* **9/2**[2]

00- **3** hd **Davidia (IRE)**[251] [3530] 3-9-3 .... JimmyFortune 5 61+
(S Kirk) *chsd ldrs: rdn over 2f out: styd on wl u.p fnl f* **9/2**[2]

0- **4** hd **Gnillah**[168] [5711] 3-8-12 .... MichaelHills 7 55+
(B W Hills) *trckd ldr after 2f: rdn to chal over 2f out: nt qckn over 1f out: one pce after* **11/10**[1]

506- **5** 4 **Blue Army (IRE)**[298] [2118] 3-9-3 45 .... AdrianMcCarthy 1 51?
(Jane Southcombe) *chsd ldr for 2f: styd prom on inner tl wknd wl over 1f out* **66/1**

0 **6** ½ **Postage (USA)**[53] [254] 3-8-12 .... JamesDoyle(5) 6 50
(K A Morgan) *chsd ldrs: rdn over 2f out: green and wknd wl over 1f out* **25/1**

7 1 **Yeoman Spirit (IRE)** 3-9-3 .... MartinDwyer 9 48
(A M Balding) *s.i.s: rn green in last pair: nvr a factor* **10/1**

8 ½ **Musical Chimes** 3-8-12 .... DarryllHolland 2 41
(C A Cyzer) *chsd ldrs: pushed along over 3f out: sn struggling* **25/1**

5 **9** 1 ½ **Just Tilly**[30] [479] 3-8-12 .... StephenCarson 8 38
(P R Chamings) *rn green and a in last pair: struggling over 2f out* **14/1**

1m 38.79s (-0.64) **Going Correction** -0.125s/f (Stan) **9** Ran SP% **121.4**
Speed ratings (Par 98):98,94,93,93,89 89,88,87,86
CSF £39.93 TOTE £8.30: £2.40, £1.80, £1.40; EX 35.40.

Owner Hesmonds Stud **Bred** Jeremy Gompertz **Trained** Newmarket, Suffolk

FOCUS

A race lacking strength and the proximity of the 45-rated fifth confirms this bare form is nothing special. However the winner won well on her debut and may do better.

711 LINGFIELD GOLF CLUB H'CAP — 1m (P)

4:30 (4:31) (Class 5) (0-70,70) 4-Y-0+ — **£3,238** (£963; £361; £361) **Stalls** High

Form — RPR

3042 **1** — **Physical (IRE)**[2] 698 4-7-13 **56** oh1............(p) JamesDoyle(5) 4 — 63
(Mrs A J Perrett) *trckd ldrs: rdn over 2f out: effrt on outer over 1f out: led jst ins fnl f: styd on wl* **5/1**[3]

0210 **2** ¾ **Aggravation**[7] 662 4-9-3 **69**............ JohnEgan 1 — 74
(D R C Elsworth) *hld up in midfield: trckd ldrs gng wl 2f out: swtchd to inner to chal fnl f: styd on but a hld* **4/1**[2]

042- **3** ½ **Torquemada (IRE)**[185] 5380 5-8-8 **63**............ AdamKirby(3) 10 — 67
(W Jarvis) *awkward s: hld up in last trio: nowhere to go 3f out: swtchd rt jst over 1f out: r.o fnl f: nrst fin* **9/1**

00-5 **3** *dht* **Luis Melendez (USA)**[51] 267 4-8-13 **65**............(t) RobertHavlin 7 — 69
(Tom Dascombe) *hld up on outer in midfield: rdn over 2f out: no prog tl r.o ins fnl f: nrst fin* **7/1**

-102 **5** ½ **Stoic Leader (IRE)**[9] 644 6-9-4 **70**............(p) FrancisNorton 9 — 73
(R F Fisher) *prom: rdn to chse ldr briefly over 1f out: one pce fnl f* **7/1**

2-33 **6** 2½ **Perez (IRE)**[28] 504 4-9-2 **68**............ DarryllHolland 5 — 65
(Pat Eddery) *dwlt: keen early and hld up towards rr: rn in snatches fr 1/2-way: outpcd 2f out: n.d after* **5/2**[1]

0000 **7** *nk* **Carry On Doc**[22] 559 5-8-11 **63**............ SebSanders 8 — 60
(Ernst Oertel) *hld up in last pair: hmpd on inner 5f out: no prog over 2f out: kpt on fnl f: no ch* **66/1**

0062 **8** ½ **Kallista's Pride**[20] 576 6-8-3 **62** ow1............ KylieManser(7) 6 — 57
(J R Best) *led at decent pce: hdd & wknd jst ins fnl f* **20/1**

201- **9** ½ **Another Faux Pas (IRE)**[221] 4431 5-9-3 **69**............ TQuinn 3 — 63
(B G Powell) *chsd ldr to over 1f out: wknd rapidly ins fnl f* **14/1**

536- **10** ½ **Laugh 'n Cry**[297] 2166 5-9-3 **69**............ MartinDwyer 2 — 62
(C A Cyzer) *trckd ldrs on inner: cl up 2f out: btn whn n.m.r ins fnl f* **25/1**

3150 **11** 3 **Tiviski (IRE)**[20] 587 4-8-10 **62**............(p) JimmyQuinn 11 — 48
(G G Margarson) *plld hrd on outer early: rdn over 2f out: a in rr* **33/1**

1m 37.73s (-1.70) **Going Correction** -0.125s/f (Stan) — **11** Ran SP% **119.9**

Speed ratings (Par 103):103,102,101,101,101 98,98,97,97,96 93

WIN: Physical £7.20. PL: Physical £2.40, Aggravation £1.30, Luis Melendez £1.40, Torquemada £1.00. TRIC: P/A/LM £73.13, P/A/T £91.40. CSF £24.92; EX 32.10.

Owner Fred And Sacha Cotton **Bred** Knocklong House Stud **Trained** Pulborough, W Sussex

FOCUS

Mainly exposed handicappers and the pace was ordinary. Ordinary form too.

Torquemada(IRE) Official explanation: jockey said gelding was denied a clear run

Carry On Doc Official explanation: jockey said gelding hung right up straight

712 LUNCH IN THE TRACKSIDE CARVERY H'CAP — 1m (P)

5:00 (5:01) (Class 5) (0-70,70) 3-Y-O — **£3,238** (£963; £481; £240) **Stalls** High

Form — RPR

1025 **1** — **Tamagin (USA)**[20] 583 3-8-10 **67**............(p) StephenDonohoe(5) 2 — 73
(P D Evans) *mde all: clr bef 1/2-way: rdn and looked vulnerable 2f out: sn drvn clr again: unchal after* **6/1**[3]

050- **2** 1½ **Emotive**[129] 6357 3-8-1 **56** oh5............(b[1]) RichardThomas(3) 4 — 58
(I A Wood) *hld up in last pair: nt clr run wl over 2f out: effrt and hmpd wl over 1f out: r.o wl to take 2nd last 100yds: nt rch wnr* **50/1**

560- **3** 1½ **Cantabilly (IRE)**[177] 5555 3-9-4 **70**............ TQuinn 6 — 69
(M R Channon) *sn prom: chsd wnr over 3f out: clsd 2f out: sn outpcd and no imp: lost 2nd last 100yds* **12/1**

3-05 **4** ½ **Chia (IRE)**[22] 558 3-8-13 **65**............ RobertHavlin 1 — 63+
(D Haydn Jones) *hld up towards rr: hmpd over 2f out: effrt and hmpd wl over 1f out: kpt on fnl f: nt rcvr* **12/1**

04-4 **5** 1¾ **Gattuso**[1] 703 3-8-11 **63**............ SamHitchcott 10 — 57+
(Ms Deborah J Evans) *settled in last: rdn whn hmpd over 2f out and again wl over 1f out: kpt on fnl f: nt rcvr* **25/1**

01-1 **6** *shd* **Magical Music**[18] 604 3-9-1 **67**............ JimmyQuinn 7 — 61
(J Pearce) *hld up in midfield: rdn on outer over 2f out: one pce and no imp over 1f out* **11/4**[1]

000- **7** *shd* **Sweet Boulangere**[165] 5795 3-9-2 **68**............ RichardHughes 11 — 61
(R Hannon) *sn hld up in last trio: hrd rdn on outer over 1f out: kpt on: no ch* **25/1**

0532 **8** ½ **Mine The Balance (IRE)**[18] 595 3-8-4 **56**............ MartinDwyer 3 — 48+
(J R Best) *hld up in midfield: hmpd over 2f out and wl over 1f out: no ch whn nt clr run 1f out* **5/1**[2]

02-1 **9** 1 **Mystified (IRE)**[39] 406 3-9-2 **68**............(b) JohnEgan 8 — 58
(R F Fisher) *chsd wnr to over 3f out: styd prom but outpcd wl over 1f out: wknd fnl f* **15/2**

5-13 **10** 3 **Fateful Attraction**[18] 594 3-8-11 **68**............ JamesDoyle(5) 9 — 51
(I A Wood) *racd on outer and keen early: rdn 3f out: wknd 2f out* **5/1**[2]

00-6 **11** 2 **Shannon House**[30] 479 3-8-10 **62**............ ShaneKelly 5 — 40
(M J McGrath) *chsd ldrs: rdn and no prog 2f out: wkng whn nowhere to go ent fnl f* **33/1**

1m 38.11s (-1.32) **Going Correction** -0.125s/f (Stan) — **11** Ran SP% **114.0**

Speed ratings (Par 98):101,99,98,97,95 95,95,95,94,91 89

CSF £277.59 CT £3427.43 TOTE £9.00: £3.10, £13.90, £3.60; EX 312.60.

Owner Jordan E Lund **Bred** Stonehaven Farm Llc **Trained** Pandy, Abergavenny

FOCUS

A decent gallop set by the winner who won unchallenged. There was some trouble in behind but the level of the form does not look too far out.

Chia(IRE) Official explanation: jockey said filly was denied a clear run

Gattuso Official explanation: jockey said gelding was denied a clear run

Mystified(IRE) Official explanation: jockey said gelding hung badly right

Fateful Attraction Official explanation: jockey said filly was never travelling

713 SPONSOR A RACE AT LINGFIELD H'CAP — 1m 4f (P)

5:30 (5:30) (Class 5) (0-70,70) 4-Y-0+ — **£3,238** (£963; £481; £240) **Stalls** Low

Form — RPR

2134 **1** — **Latif (USA)**[1] 700 5-8-13 **65**............ SamHitchcott 5 — 72
(Ms Deborah J Evans) *dwlt: hld up in last: prog on outer 3f out: urged into ld wl over 1f out: in command fnl f* **5/1**[3]

3-10 **2** 1½ **Taxman (IRE)**[18] 589 4-8-10 **64**............(p) DarryllHolland 4 — 69
(C E Brittain) *hld up in tch: pushed along over 3f out: outpcd 2f out: drvn and styd on to take 2nd ins fnl f* **13/8**[1]

5303 **3** ½ **Master'n Commander**[22] 557 4-8-8 **62**............ MartinDwyer 6 — 66
(C A Cyzer) *trckd ldr: effrt to ld over 2f out: hdd wl over 1f out: one pce after* **9/2**[2]

000- **4** *nk* **Rio De Janeiro (IRE)**[285] 1655 5-9-4 **70**............ AlanMunro 2 — 74
(Miss E C Lavelle) *settled in rr: outpcd in last over 3f out: swtchd rt and rdn 1f out: r.o wl nr fin* **20/1**

34-4 **5** ¾ **Easy Laughter (IRE)**[18] 603 5-9-1 **67**............(t) AlanDaly 7 — 70
(A King) *trckd ldrs: rdn and effrt to try to chal over 2f out: one pce fr over 1f out* **6/1**

5/4 **6** 2 **High Hope (FR)**[22] 556 8-9-4 **70**............ GeorgeBaker 3 — 69
(G L Moore) *trckd ldng pair: rdn over 2f out: nt qckn and btn over 1f out: wknd ins fnl f* **9/2**[2]

10-0 **7** 15 **Shakerattleandroll (IRE)**[22] 556 5-8-10 **65**............ RichardThomas(3) 1 — 40
(Mrs L Richards) *racd freely: led to over 2f out: wkng whn n.m.r wl over 1f out: eased* **50/1**

2m 33.36s (-1.03) **Going Correction** -0.125s/f (Stan)

WFA 4 from 5yo+ 2lb — **7** Ran SP% **112.1**

Speed ratings (Par 103):98,97,96,96,95 94,84

CSF £13.03 TOTE £5.30: £3.10, £2.20; EX 19.30 Place 6 £197.26, Place 5 £107.44 .

Owner Paddy Mason **Bred** Shadwell Farm LLC **Trained** Lydiate, Merseyside

FOCUS

A very ordinary handicap in which the pace was only fair.

Taxman(IRE) Official explanation: jockey said gelding hung left

T/Plt: £203.70 to a £1 stake. Pool: £48,963.85. 175.45 winning tickets. T/Qpdt: £63.20 to a £1 stake. Pool: £3,565.40. 41.70 winning tickets. JN

686 SOUTHWELL (L-H)

Friday, March 24

OFFICIAL GOING: Heavy

Switched from Doncaster. The first turf card on the Flat in 2006, but the previous day's AW meeting at Lingfield counts as the season's opener.

Wind: Virtually nil

714 BETFRED CONDITIONS STKS — 1m 4f

2:20 (2:20) (Class 3) 4-Y-0+ — **£7,790** (£2,332; £1,166; £583) **Stalls** Low

Form — RPR

356- **1** — **Into The Shadows**[104] 6130 6-8-8 81............ PaulHanagan 1 — 89
(K G Reveley) *hld up in tch: pushed along 1/2-way: smooth hdwy 4f out: cl up on bit over 2f out: shkn up to ld appr last: sn clr* **10/1**[2]

320- **2** 7 **Shalapour (IRE)**[188] 5331 4-9-1............ JoeFanning 2 — 88+
(M Johnston) *led: pushed along and jnd 1/2-way: rdn over 2f out: drvn and hdd appr last: sn btn* **1/6**[1]

010/ **3** 12 **Mudawin (IRE)**[645] 2999 5-8-13............ TonyCulhane 4 — 67
(Jane Chapple-Hyam) *cl up: hdwy to join ldr 1/2-way: pushed along 4f out: rdn 3f out and wknd fnl 2f* **28/1**

424/ **4** 7 **Double Obsession**[579] 4983 6-8-13 102............ AdrianTNicholls 3 — 58
(D Nicholls) *chsd ldr to 1/2-way: rdn along over 4f out: outpcd fr 3f out* **16/1**[3]

2m 56.29s (15.99) **Going Correction** +1.30s/f (Soft)

WFA 4 from 5yo+ 2lb — **4** Ran SP% **104.1**

Speed ratings (Par 107):98,93,85,80

CSF £12.08 TOTE £8.90; EX 10.80.

Owner R C Mayall **Bred** Mrs Linda Corbett And Mrs Mary Mayall **Trained** Lingdale, Redcar & Cleveland

FOCUS

Very testing ground and clearly form to be dubious about with the odds-on favourite running well below his best.

NOTEBOOK

Into The Shadows, last seen running over hurdles in December, had a stiff task strictly at the weights, but she handles testing conditions well and was always travelling smoothly, in contrast to the odds-on favourite. She looks to have run right up to her best here, but it is doubtful that the same can be said of the opposition. Her next outing could well be back over timber at Aintree. (op 11-1 tchd 12-1)

Shalapour(IRE), third in the Irish Derby for John Oxx last season, was without his usual tongue tie on this debut for the Johnston yard and never travelled with any fluency in these desperate conditions. He ran way below his best form, but it is too early to write him off, and he might well bounce back on a better surface with the tongue tie re-fitted. Official explanation: trainer was unable to offer any explanation for poor form shown (tchd 2-11, 1-5 in places)

Mudawin(IRE), off the track since Royal Ascot 2004, has since changed stables twice. These were gruelling conditions in which to make his reappearance and he should not be judged too harshly. (op 25-1)

Double Obsession, another who has changed stables twice since his last outing, has run his best races on faster ground. He was fully entitled to need this reappearance run. (op 12-1)

715 BETFREDPOKER.COM (S) STKS — 1m 3f

2:55 (2:55) (Class 5) 4-Y-0+ — **£3,238** (£963; £481; £240) **Stalls** Low

Form — RPR

-343 **1** — **Champion Lion (IRE)**[8] 647 7-8-13 55............ NCallan 5 — 59+
(J R Boyle) *trckd ldrs: smooth hdwy 3f out: sn cl up on bit: led over 1f out: pushed clr ins last* **4/6**[1]

0- **2** 7 **Soviet Joy (IRE)**[11] 702 5-8-13............ GrahamGibbons 6 — 49
(J J Quinn) *led: rdn along 3f out: drvn and hdd over 1f out: kpt on same pce* **9/2**[3]

5-56 **3** 5 **Molly's Secret**[35] 442 8-8-8 40............(p) ChrisCatlin 4 — 37
(Miss S J Wilton) *hld up in rr: hdwy to chse ldrs 5f out: rdn along 3f out: drvn and outpcd fnl 2f* **16/1**

6335 **4** 3 **Scotty's Future (IRE)**[9] 640 8-8-13 58............ AdrianTNicholls 3 — 38
(D Nicholls) *hld up in rr: hdwy to c hase ldrs 4f out: rdn along over 2f out and sn btn* **4/1**[2]

00 **5** *dist* **Montanah Jet**[10] 634 4-8-7............(b[1]) MarcHalford(5) 1 — —
(C N Kellett) *chsd ldr: rdn along over 3f out: sn wknd* **100/1**

004- **6** *dist* **Fayrz Please (IRE)**[87] 6672 5-8-7 35 ow1............ RobbieMills(7) 2 — —
(M C Chapman) *chsd ldng pair: rdn along over 4f out and sn wknd* **40/1**

2m 43.84s

WFA 4 from 5yo+ 1lb — **6** Ran SP% **107.5**

CSF £3.60 TOTE £1.80: £1.10, £2.30; EX 4.50.There was no bid for the winner.

Owner M Khan X2 **Bred** Biddestone Stud **Trained** Epsom, Surrey

FOCUS

An uncompetitive seller and weak form.

Montanah Jet Official explanation: jockey said gelding was unsuited by heavy ground

Fayrz Please(IRE) Official explanation: jockey said gelding was unsuited by heavy ground

716 BETFRED MAIDEN STKS — 7f

3:30 (3:30) (Class 5) 3-Y-O — **£3,886** (£1,156; £577; £288) **Stalls** Low

Form — RPR

1 **Braddock (IRE)** 3-9-3 ... PaulFessey 3 — 60+
(T D Barron) *a.p: led 3f out: rdn over 1f out: drvn and styd on wl fnl f* **14/1**

2 *3 ½* **Trumpita** 3-9-3 ... DavidAllan 4 — 52
(T D Easterby) *in tch: gd hdwy over 2f out: rdn to chal wl over 1f out and ev ch tl drvn and one pce ins last* **25/1**

6- **3** *¾* **Choreography**[250] [3562] 3-9-0 ... SilvestreDeSousa(3) 9 — 50
(D Nicholls) *in tch: rdn along 3f out: drvn to chse ldrs 2f out: kpt on u.p fnl f* **25/1**

3-54 **4** *shd* **Tirol Livit (IRE)**[45] [333] 3-9-0 48 ... DNolan(3) 7 — 50
(N Wilson) *bhd and rdn along 1/2-way: hdwy wl over 1f out: styd on u.p ins last: nrst fin* **66/1**

024- **5** *8* **Street Warrior (IRE)**[168] [5708] 3-9-3 75 ... JoeFanning 1 — 31+
(M Johnston) *dwlt: sn chsng ldrs: rdn along over 2f out: drvn wl over 1f out: sn wknd* **8/11**[1]

00-6 **6** *4* **Mister Becks (IRE)**[16] [617] 3-8-12 30 ... EmmettStack(5) 8 — 21
(M C Chapman) *chsd ldrs: rdn along 3f out: sn outpcd* **100/1**

3 **7** *8* **Cape Of Storms**[7] [658] 3-9-3 ... TonyCulhane 2 — —+
(M R Channon) *led: pushed along and hdd 3f out: sn rdn and wknd wl over 1f out* **9/4**[2]

045- **8** *dist* **Final Tune (IRE)**[210] [4733] 3-9-3 68 ... AdrianTNicholls 5 — —+
(D Nicholls) *chsd ldrs on outer: rdn along 3f out: sn wknd* **10/1**[3]

9 *22* **Rainbow Prince** 3-9-3 ... PaulHanagan 6 — —
(A Dickman) *a rr: bhd fr 1/2-way* **33/1**

1m 40.54s (11.34) **Going Correction** +1.30s/f (Soft) — **9** Ran SP% **117.5**
Speed ratings (Par 98):87,83,82,82,72 68,59,—,—
CSF £279.75 TOTE £18.80: £2.60, £3.20, £3.20; EX 234.30 TRIFECTA Not won..
Owner James M Egan **Bred** Corduff Stud And J Corcoran **Trained** Maunby, N Yorks

FOCUS
A modest maiden, highlighted by the proximity of the 48-rated fourth.
Street Warrior(IRE) Official explanation: trainer was unable to offer any explanation for poor form shown
Final Tune(IRE) Official explanation: jockey said gelding had no more to give

717 BETFREDCASINO.COM CONDITIONS STKS — 7f

4:05 (4:05) (Class 3) 3-Y-O — **£9,067** (£2,697; £1,348; £673) **Stalls** Low

Form — RPR

135- **1** **South Cape**[153] [6020] 3-8-13 100 ... TonyCulhane 3 — 86
(M R Channon) *trckd ldng pair: pushed along over 2f out: swtchd rt and rdn over 1f out: styd on wl to ld last 100 yds* **15/8**[2]

655- **2** *1 ½* **Charlton**[161] [5871] 3-8-13 90 ... IanMongan 5 — 82
(T G Mills) *hld up: wd st: pushed along and outpcd 2f out: sn rdn: kpt on wl u.p ins last* **13/8**[1]

10- **3** *nk* **Marriage Value (IRE)**[280] [2671] 3-8-8 ... SteveDrowne 2 — 77
(J A Osborne) *hld up: gd hdwy over 2f out: chal over 1f out: rdn to ld ins last: hdd and no ex last 100 yds* **3/1**[3]

601- **4** *½* **Bathwick Emma (IRE)**[156] [5985] 3-8-6 77 ... GrahamGibbons 1 — 74
(P D Evans) *led: rdn along 2f out: drvn over 1f out: hdd ins last: no ex* **16/1**

655- **5** *9* **Spectacular Show (IRE)**[150] [6098] 3-8-8 75 ... PaulFessey 4 — 62+
(M Quinn) *chsd ldr: rdn along 2f out and ev ch tl drvn and wknd appr last: eased* **20/1**

1m 39.63s (10.43) **Going Correction** +1.30s/f (Soft) — **5** Ran SP% **108.5**
Speed ratings (Par 102):92,90,89,89,79
CSF £5.14 TOTE £2.50: £1.30, £1.70; EX 5.80.
Owner Heart Of The South Racing **Bred** John And Mrs Caroline Penny **Trained** West Ilsley, Berks

FOCUS
The race was won in a time less than a second quicker than the preceding maiden, suggesting the first two did not run to their best. It has been rated through the fourth.

NOTEBOOK
South Cape did not run too badly in a Listed contest in heavy ground last backend and that experience helped him deal with these gruelling conditions. He came home well and should not struggle to get a mile this season. (op 13-8 tchd 5-2)
Charlton was gelded over the winter and was missing the visor he wore on his final two starts last season. He was never going that well but stayed on from off the pace, and connections will now be hoping that the Handicapper does not bump him up for finishing quite close to the winner, who is officially rated 10lb higher than him. (op 2-1 tchd 6-4)
Marriage Value(IRE), last seen disappointing on fast ground in the Albany Stakes at Royal Ascot at York, appreciated these softer conditions on her seasonal return. She will be of more interest when racing against her own sex. (op 7-2 tchd 11-4)
Bathwick Emma(IRE), by far the most experienced in the line-up, is probably the best guide to the level of the form. She handles soft ground but is rated only 77, and her proximity suggests that the first two ran a fair way below their official marks. (op 12-1)
Spectacular Show(IRE), a winner of a maiden in soft ground, is bred to get this trip but she did not get home on this seasonal reappearance. Perhaps she needed the run. (tchd 16-1)

718 BETFRED THE BONUS KING STKS (H'CAP) — 6f

4:40 (4:41) (Class 2) (0-100,96) 4-Y-O+
£12,464 (£3,732; £1,866; £934; £466; £234) **Stalls** Low

Form — RPR

000- **1** **Philharmonic**[188] [5288] 5-9-4 96 ... PaulHanagan 8 — 104
(R A Fahey) *hld up in tch: smooth hdwy 2f out: rdn over 1f out: led ins last: styd on* **10/1**

500- **2** *1 ¾* **Coleorton Dancer**[188] [5288] 4-9-3 95 ... NCallan 9 — 102+
(K A Ryan) *hld up in tch: hdwy and n.m.r 2f out and again over 1f out: swtchd lft and rdn ent last: swtchd rt and styd on* **4/1**[2]

412- **3** *½* **King's Gait**[53] [6021] 4-9-1 93 ... (b) DavidAllan 2 — 94
(T D Easterby) *hld up in tch: gd hdwy over 2f out: rdn to ld wl over 1f out drvn and hdd ins last: one pce* **5/2**[1]

220- **4** *1 ¼* **Pieter Brueghel (USA)**[188] [5288] 7-9-0 92 ... JoeFanning 5 — 90
(D Nicholls) *led: rdn along and wd st: hdd wl over 1f out: kpt on same pce* **10/1**

500- **5** *5* **Idle Power (IRE)**[119] [6421] 8-8-8 86 ... PatCosgrave 7 — 69
(J R Boyle) *cl up: rdn along 2f out: sn drvn and edgd lft: wknd appr last* **20/1**

0-62 **6** *2* **Glaramara**[38] [413] 5-8-4 82 ... ChrisCatlin 11 — 59
(A Bailey) *cl up on outer: rdn along 2f out: sn drvn and wknd* **6/1**[3]

310- **7** *4* **Inter Vision (USA)**[223] [4377] 6-8-5 88 ... MarcHalford(5) 10 — 53
(A Dickman) *in tch: rdn along 2f out: sn wknd* **40/1**

20-3 **8** *shd* **Plateau**[7] [657] 7-8-4 82 oh1 ... AdrianTNicholls 3 — 46
(D Nicholls) *prom: effrt and cl up over 2f out: sn rdn and wknd over 1f out* **12/1**

-030 **9** *¾* **Millennium Force**[28] [511] 8-9-2 94 ... TonyCulhane 1 — 56
(M R Channon) *s.i.s and bhd: wd st and gd hdwy 2f out: sn rdn and wknd appr last: eased* **9/1**

300- **10** *3 ½* **Johnston's Diamond (IRE)**[146] [6157] 8-8-4 82 ... NickyMackay 6 — 33
(E J Alston) *cl up: rdn over 2f out: ev ch tl drvn: edgd lft and wknd wl over 1f out* **14/1**

210/ **11** *30* **Big Hassle (IRE)**[583] [4857] 4-8-2 87 ow2 ... VictoriaBehan(7) 4 — —
(D Nicholls) *a rr* **33/1**

1m 22.55s (6.45) **Going Correction** +1.30s/f (Soft) — **11** Ran SP% **115.5**
Speed ratings (Par 109):109,106,106,104,97 95,89,89,88,83 43
CSF £47.97 CT £134.65 TOTE £10.70: £3.50, £2.10, £1.70; EX 62.80 Trifecta £321.80 Pool: £1,192.30 - 2.63 winning tickets..
Owner R Cowie **Bred** Raymond Cowie **Trained** Musley Bank, N Yorks

FOCUS
A decent handicap fought out by three horses proven in testing conditions.

NOTEBOOK
Philharmonic, only narrowly denied on his seasonal reappearance last year, goes well fresh and he had run with credit on soft ground in the past. He saw his race out strongly and has clearly returned in top form. (op 5-1)

Coleorton Dancer, denied a clear run in the latter stages, would have probably gone close with a smoother passage. He has always reserved his best for when he can get his toe in and, having dropped in the weights since last summer, he is handicapped to win a race of this nature. (op 9-2)

King's Gait, well drawn and proven in testing conditions, was a well-backed favourite but he did have a stamina question to answer over this trip in bad ground, and he appeared to fail the test. He remains open to further improvement back over the minimum trip. (op 9-2)

Pieter Brueghel(USA) seems to go on all sorts of ground and once again made a bold bid from the front. He tends to need a run or two before he hits peak fitness, though, so is entitled to come on for this outing. (op 9-1)

Idle Power(IRE) has had the usual cheekpieces left off on his seasonal return for the past three years now and, interestingly, when they have been slapped back on, he has won one of his next two starts in each of the past two seasons. Expect the headgear to be back on next time out. (op 22-1 tchd 25-1)

Glaramara has been sent off at single figures for 11 separate races so far in his career, but has only won one of them, an uncompetitive conditions event on Fibresand. It goes without saying that he is a difficult horse to win with. (op 8-1 tchd 11-2)

Plateau, a market drifter, failed to get home over a trip which is further than ideal in ground more testing than he would have liked. Official explanation: trainer said gelding was unsuited by heavy ground (op 11-1)

Big Hassle(IRE) Official explanation: trainer said colt bled from nose

719 BETFRED MILLION H'CAP — 7f

5:10 (5:12) (Class 4) (0-85,85) 4-Y-O+ — **£6,477** (£1,927; £963; £481) **Stalls** Low

Form — RPR

003- **1** **Dancing Lyra**[151] [6073] 5-8-6 73 ... PaulHanagan 8 — 86
(R A Fahey) *hld up towards rr: hdwy on outer 3f out and wd st: rdn over 1f out: styd on to ld wl ins the last: sn clr* **6/1**[2]

230- **2** *4* **Lucayan Dancer**[222] [4389] 6-8-2 76 ... KellyHarrison(7) 7 — 79
(D Nicholls) *hld up in midfield: gd hdwy 2rf out: rdn to ld briefly ins last: sn hdd and one pce* **25/1**

006- **3** *1* **Digital**[167] [5735] 9-8-4 71 oh1 ... ChrisCatlin 5 — 72
(M R Channon) *hld up in rr: gd hdwy 3f out: rdn to ld over 1f out: drvn and hdd ins last: one pce* **9/1**

00-0 **4** *3* **Serieux**[7] [662] 7-8-7 77 ... (v) SilvestreDeSousa(3) 10 — 71
(D Nicholls) *led 1f: cl up tl led again 4f out: rdn 2f out: hdd over 1f out and grad wknd* **33/1**

-244 **5** *5* **Rafferty (IRE)**[43] [348] 7-8-9 76 ... GrahamGibbons 12 — 58
(T D Barron) *chsd ldrs: rdn along 2f out: wknd appr last* **8/1**[3]

00-0 **6** *14* **Bo McGinty (IRE)**[38] [413] 5-9-4 85 ... TonyHamilton 11 — 33
(R A Fahey) *in tch: rdn along 2f out and sn wknd* **33/1**

-030 **7** *2 ½* **Baylaw Star**[6] [670] 5-9-2 83 ... NCallan 13 — 25
(K A Ryan) *s.i.s: rapid hdwy to ld after 1f: hdd 4f out: rdn over 2f out: sn drvn and wknd* **9/1**

310- **8** *2* **Royal Dignitary (USA)**[189] [5266] 6-8-9 76 ... JoeFanning 1 — 13
(D Nicholls) *chsd ldrs on inner: hdwy over 2f out: rdn and wknd wl over 1f out* **33/1**

006- **9** *½* **Rain Stops Play (IRE)**[153] [6022] 4-8-11 78 ... PaulFessey 3 — 14
(M Quinn) *towards rr: sme headway on inner 3f out: rdn over 2f out and sn wknd* **14/1**

1560 **10** *1 ½* **Blue Knight (IRE)**[9] [639] 7-8-4 71 ... (v) PaulQuinn 6 — 4
(D Nicholls) *a rr* **50/1**

-151 **11** *3* **Local Poet**[20] [585] 5-8-6 73 ... (bt) TomEaves 2 — —
(I Semple) *in tch: hdwy to chse ldrs over 2f out: sn rdn and btn* **15/8**[1]

0- **12** *¾* **Betsen (IRE)**[188] [5329] 4-8-8 82 ... VictoriaBehan(7) 4 — 6
(D Nicholls) *prom: rdn along over 2f out and sn wknd* **66/1**

5/ **13** *13* **Night Prayers (IRE)**[515] [6408] 4-9-4 85 ... AdrianTNicholls 9 — —
(D Nicholls) *a rr* **20/1**

555- **U** **Flying Bantam (IRE)**[146] [6149] 5-8-1 75 ... NSLawes(7) 14 — —
(R A Fahey) *jinked and uns rdr shortly after s* **9/1**

1m 37.29s (8.09) **Going Correction** +1.30s/f (Soft) — **14** Ran SP% **117.7**
Speed ratings (Par 105):105,100,99,95,90 74,71,69,68,66 63,62,47,—
CSF £151.34 CT £1344.72 TOTE £7.40: £2.60, £7.10, £3.30; EX 125.40 Trifecta £693.80 Part won. Pool: £977.30 - 0.50 winning tickets. Place 6 £1,783.75, Place 5 £147.13.

Owner Aidan J Ryan Racing **Bred** Shadwell Estate Company Limited **Trained** Musley Bank, N Yorks

FOCUS
A fair handicap in which a change of scenery and drop in trip worked the oracle for Dancing Lyra. The form is not the most solid, however.

Rain Stops Play(IRE) Official explanation: jockey said gelding had no more to give

Local Poet Official explanation: jockey said gelding was unsuited by heavy ground

T/Plt: £7,753.30 to a £1 stake. Pool: £38,766.65. 3.65 winning tickets. T/Qpdt: £165.00 to a £1 stake. Pool: £4,550.50. 20.40 winning tickets. JR

KEMPTON (A.W) (R-H)

Saturday, March 25

OFFICIAL GOING: Standard

The first meeting on the new RH Polytrack. 5f & 10f races use inner course, 6f, 7f, 1m, 11f, 12f & 2m races use outer course & separate home turn.

Wind: Slight, behind Weather: Mild and cloudy

720 JYSKE BANK PRIVATE BANKING COPENHAGEN MAIDEN STKS 1m (P)

2:30 (2:55) (Class 4) 3-Y-0+ £5,505 (£1,637; £818; £408) Stalls Low

Form				RPR
063-	1		**Akona Matata (USA)**[249] 3619 4-10-0 75 .... JimmyFortune 12 (C E Brittain) *led for 2f: chsd ldrs: rdn to ld wl over 1f out: drvn out* **5/1**	85
65-	2	1 3/4	**Scot Love (IRE)**[140] 6251 3-8-11 .... TPQueally 3 (J Noseda) *prom: led after 2f: rdn and hdd wl over 1f out: kpt on* **10/1**	76
342-	3	3/4	**Feu D'Artifice (USA)**[198] 5058 3-8-11 77 .... RichardHughes 4 (R Hannon) *chsd ldrs: rdn 3f out: styd on fnl f* **11/4**[1]	74
	4	4	**Star Of The Desert (IRE)** 3-8-8 .... AdamKirby(3) 10 (C G Cox) *mid div: rdn 3f out: styd on fnl f* **16/1**	65
333	5	3/4	**Pop Music (IRE)**[14] 630 3-8-11 72 .... SimonWhitworth 8 (Miss J Feilden) *prom for 2f: lost pl and dropped rr 5f out: styd on again fr 2f out* **15/2**	63
0	6	shd	**Doctor David**[42] 372 3-8-11 .... J-PGuillambert 6 (Ernst Oertel) *chsd ldrs: rdn over 2f out: one pce after* **66/1**	63
	7	hd	**Warne's Way (IRE)** 3-8-11 .... PatDobbs 11 (R Hannon) *drvn along 4f out: nvr bttr than mid div* **25/1**	63
	8	1 1/2	**Muscari** 4-9-9 .... DarrenWilliams 13 (A P Jarvis) *s.i.s: bhd: sme late hdwy: nvr trbld ldrs* **50/1**	59
443-	9	8	**Power Broker**[261] 3273 3-8-11 78 .... SteveDrowne 1 (P F I Cole) *w ldr tl 3f out: sn rdn: wkng whn drifted lft over 1f out* **7/2**[2]	41
00	10	6	**Flyingwithoutwings**[25] 539 7-10-0 .... DavidKinsella 5 (A King) *chsd ldrs tl lost pl 5f out* **50/1**	32
06	11	1 3/4	**Jose Bove**[25] 539 4-10-0 .... DaneO'Neill 9 (R Dickin) *a towards rr* **100/1**	28
0-5	12	3 1/2	**Maximix**[19] 590 3-8-11 .... MichaelHills 7 (B W Hills) *a towards rr* **9/2**[3]	15
06-5	13	9	**Blue Army (IRE)**[1] 710 3-8-11 45 .... AdrianMcCarthy 2 (Jane Southcombe) *w ldrs tl wknd 3f out* **100/1**	—

1m 41.98s **Going Correction** +0.425s/f (Slow)
WFA 3 from 4yo+ 17lb 13 Ran SP% **121.7**
Speed ratings (Par 105):111,109,108,104,103 103,103,101,93,87 86,82,73
CSF £53.54 TOTE £6.30: £2.10, £3.70, £2.30; EX 57.20.
Owner Sheikh Hamdan Bin Mohammed Al Maktoum **Bred** Jayeff 'B' Stables **Trained** Newmarket, Suffolk

FOCUS
This first race on Kempton's new course was delayed by 25 minutes after several stones were found on the track. Riders described the surface as 'slowish'. A fair maiden, featuring some lightly-raced runners who can improve with racing. It was run at a modest tempo and favoured the prominent runners.
Blue Army(IRE) Official explanation: jockey said gelding ran flat

721 JBPB.COM H'CAP 7f (P)

3:00 (3:26) (Class 4) (0-80,80) 4-Y-0+ £5,505 (£1,637; £818; £408) Stalls High

Form				RPR
3-00	1		**Binanti**[56] 220 6-9-4 80 .... GeorgeBaker 13 (P R Chamings) *chsd ldrs: rdn to ld jst ins fnl f: sn edgd lft: all out* **12/1**	89
6460	2	hd	**Tanforan**[35] 451 4-8-0 69 .... SophieDoyle(7) 11 (K McAuliffe) *led: edgd lft 2f out: pushed along and narrowly hdd jst ins fnl f: rallied gamely but edgd lft cl home* **14/1**	77
1262	3	nk	**Glad Big (GER)**[10] 639 4-9-0 76 .... SteveDrowne 2 (J A Osborne) *hld up towards rr: hdwy over 2f out: rdn over 1f out: styd on to go 3rd ins fnl f* **10/3**[1]	84
3601	4	2	**Quantum Leap**[8] 662 9-8-8 70 ....(v) JimmyQuinn 8 (S Dow) *mid div: rdn and hdwy 2f out: kpt on same pce fnl f* **10/1**	73
231-	5	nk	**Conjuror**[183] 5439 5-9-1 77 ....(t) MartinDwyer 3 (A M Balding) *prom: rdn and ev ch over 2f out: kpt on same pce* **9/2**[2]	79
-106	6	hd	**Silent Storm**[42] 376 6-9-1 77 .... MichaelHills 7 (C A Cyzer) *wnt lft s: in tch: rdn 3f out: kpt on same pce fnl 2f* **16/1**	78
01-4	7	1 1/2	**Roman Quintet (IRE)**[25] 541 6-8-11 73 .... JimmyFortune 1 (D W P Arbuthnot) *chsd ldrs: rdn and ev ch over 1f out: wknd ins fnl f* **11/2**[3]	70
1420	8	1 1/4	**Samuel Charles**[18] 611 8-8-10 72 .... RobbieFitzpatrick 9 (C R Dore) *towards rr: sme late hdwy: n.d* **11/1**	66
6-01	9	3/4	**Mandarin Spirit (IRE)**[10] 644 6-8-9 71 ....(b) OscarUrbina 4 (G C H Chung) *t.k.h in tch: hdwy on outer 4f out: grad fdd fr 2f out* **10/1**	63
0000	10	1 1/2	**Pamir (IRE)**[10] 639 4-8-9 71 ....(p) StephenCarson 10 (P R Chamings) *chsd ldrs tl 2f out* **14/1**	59
50-5	11	6	**Nan Jan**[10] 644 4-8-10 72 ....(t) SimonWhitworth 5 (R Ingram) *mid div: rdn 3f out: sn wknd* **16/1**	45
000-	12	5	**Aastral Magic**[176] 5585 4-8-9 74 .... StephaneBreux(3) 6 (R Hannon) *hmpd s: a in rr* **25/1**	34
0105	13	4	**Set Alight**[8] 662 5-8-7 69 ....(v) HayleyTurner 12 (Mrs C A Dunnett) *mid div for 4f* **16/1**	18

1m 28.26s **Going Correction** +0.425s/f (Slow) 13 Ran SP% **125.7**
Speed ratings (Par 105):108,107,107,105,104 104,102,101,100,98 92,86,81
CSF £178.25 CT £719.65 TOTE £16.80: £3.80, £4.90, £2.10; EX 245.00.
Owner Mrs J E L Wright **Bred** Wheelersland Stud **Trained** Baughurst, Hants

FOCUS
A fair handicap, featuring mainly exposed types, run at a medium tempo.
Binanti Official explanation: jockey said gelding hung left in latter stages
Pamir(IRE) Official explanation: jockey said gelding hung right in early stages

722 JYSKE BANK PRIVATE BANKING INVEST LOAN MAIDEN STKS 6f (P)

3:35 (3:55) (Class 4) 3-Y-0 £5,505 (£1,637; £818; £408) Stalls High

Form				RPR
	1		**Swiper Hill (IRE)** 3-9-3 .... DaneO'Neill 6 (B Ellison) *s.i.s: bhd: nt clr run over 2f out: gd hdwy and hung lft wl over 1f out: kpt on wl to ld cl home* **5/1**[3]	71+
	2	nk	**Royal Bandit** 3-8-10 .... SallyAdams(7) 4 (N A Callaghan) *led: rdn and narrowly hdd 2f out: rallied gamely and ev ch ins fnl f: no ex cl home* **16/1**	71
	3	1/2	**Pititana (IRE)** 3-8-12 .... RichardHughes 9 (R Hannon) *travelled wl: prom: tk narrow advantage 2f out: sn rdn: no ex whn hdd cl home* **7/4**[1]	64
	4	2 1/2	**Crafty Fox** 3-9-3 .... DarrenWilliams 2 (A P Jarvis) *chsd ldrs: rdn and effrt 3f out: kpt on same pce fnl 2f* **12/1**	62
3-00	5	1 1/2	**Precautionary**[14] 630 3-8-5 62 .... SladeO'Hara(7) 5 (Miss J Feilden) *hld up: rdn and hdwy over 2f out: kpt on same pce fnl f* **11/1**	52
02-	6	3/4	**Bellabelini (IRE)**[106] 6528 3-8-12 .... JimmyFortune 8 (S Kirk) *racd keenly early: trckd ldrs: rdn over 2f out: wknd fnl f* **3/1**[2]	50
00-	7	5	**Meddle**[194] 5170 3-8-7 .... GregFairley(5) 3 (J Jay) *towards rr: hdwy on outer 4f out: rdn 3f out: sn btn* **33/1**	35
000-	8	nk	**Atticus Trophies (IRE)**[134] 6316 3-8-12 64 .... JamesDoyle(5) 1 (K McAuliffe) *slowly away: towards rr: hdwy on outer 4f out: rdn 3f out: sn btn* **12/1**	39
0	9	nk	**Danethorpe (IRE)**[10] 645 3-9-0 .... PatrickMathers(3) 7 (D Shaw) *in tch tl wknd 2f out* **25/1**	38

1m 16.27s **Going Correction** +0.425s/f (Slow) 9 Ran SP% **114.4**
Speed ratings (Par 100):99,98,97,94,92 91,84,84,84
CSF £79.32 TOTE £7.90: £1.70, £3.10, £1.30; EX 129.70.
Owner Swiper Hill **Bred** Richard O' Hara **Trained** Norton, N Yorks

FOCUS
An interesting maiden, with several promising debutants in the line-up. None of the first four had raced before, so the form is hardly rock solid, but there is a suspicion the form will prove above average.

723 JYSKE BANK PRIVATE BANKING PORTFOLIO MANAGEMENT H'CAP 1m 4f (P)

4:10 (4:25) (Class 5) (0-75,75) 4-Y-0+ £3,238 (£963; £481; £240) Stalls Low

Form				RPR
1221	1		**Young Mick**[19] 603 4-8-10 69 ....(v) JimmyQuinn 11 (G G Margarson) *a travelling wl: hld up in tch: qcknd up wl to ld jst over 1f out: r.o wl: readily* **11/4**[1]	80+
1304	2	3 1/2	**Zalkani (IRE)**[21] 578 6-9-1 72 .... GeorgeBaker 8 (B G Powell) *hld up towards rr: hdwy over 2f out: rdn over 1f out: sn hung lft: styd on to go 2nd fnl strides: no ch w wnr* **7/1**[2]	77
4-60	3	nk	**Duelling Banjos**[59] 186 7-8-9 66 .... MartinDwyer 12 (J Akehurst) *led at stdy pce: rdn to qckn pce 3f out: hdd jst over 1f out: nt pce of wnr: lost 2nd fnl strides* **14/1**	71
0320	4	1	**Eastborough (IRE)**[38] 420 7-8-13 75 .... JamesDoyle(5) 5 (B G Powell) *s.i.s: bhd: styd on fr over 1f out: nvr trbld ldrs* **12/1**	78
05-0	5	hd	**Street Life (IRE)**[32] 478 8-8-11 68 .... LPKeniry 9 (W J Musson) *hld up towards rr: styd on fr over 1f out: n.d* **16/1**	71
302-	6	1/2	**Mister Right (IRE)**[220] 4467 5-9-1 72 .... RichardHughes 1 (D J S Ffrench Davis) *restrained s: plld hrd early: mid div: hdwy over 2f out: kpt on same pce* **15/2**[3]	74
-332	7	1 1/4	**Amwell Brave**[9] 652 5-8-8 65 .... StephenCarson 10 (J R Jenkins) *in tch: rdn over 2f out: one pce after* **9/1**	65
1120	8	1/2	**Sand Repeal (IRE)**[19] 603 4-8-7 66 .... SimonWhitworth 7 (Miss J Feilden) *chsd ldrs: rdn 3f out: wknd fnl f* **9/1**	65
050-	9	3/4	**The Composer**[72] 5433 4-8-10 69 .... FergusSweeney 4 (M Blanshard) *prom: rdn and ev ch over 2f out: wknd fnl f* **8/1**	67
0/00	10	1 1/2	**Fort Churchill (IRE)**[26] 535 5-8-13 70 ....(t) DaneO'Neill 2 (B Ellison) *hld up: hdwy 5f out: rdn over 2f out: wknd over 1f out* **20/1**	66
425-	11	2 1/2	**Love Angel (USA)**[8] 5792 4-8-7 71 .... GregFairley(5) 3 (J J Bridger) *chsd ldrs: rdn and effrt over 2f out: wknd over 1f out* **14/1**	63
3535	12	1 1/4	**Western Roots**[22] 571 5-8-11 68 .... RobbieFitzpatrick 6 (M Appleby) *a bhd* **14/1**	58

2m 43.07s **Going Correction** +0.425s/f (Slow)
WFA 4 from 5yo+ 2lb 12 Ran SP% **120.4**
Speed ratings (Par 103):96,93,93,92,92 92,91,91,90,89 88,87
CSF £21.41 CT £236.13 TOTE £2.40: £1.80, £2.50, £3.20; EX 20.20.
Owner M F Kentish **Bred** M F Kentish **Trained** Newmarket, Suffolk

FOCUS
A modest handicap, but with a progressive winner. It was run at a weak tempo, but hold-up horses still got involved and so it should work out.

724 JYSKE BANK PRIVATE BANKING NO 1 ACCOUNT H'CAP 1m (P)

4:45 (4:54) (Class 4) (0-85,85) 3-Y-0 £5,505 (£1,637; £818; £408) Stalls Low

Form				RPR
222-	1		**Porters (USA)**[89] 6663 3-9-4 85 .... RichardHughes 2 (R Hannon) *hld up bhd ldrs: shkn up to ld 1f out: hung bdly lft fnl 50yds: rdn out* **3/1**[2]	89
103-	2	1	**Kaveri (USA)**[135] 6304 3-9-2 83 .... JimmyFortune 3 (C E Brittain) *hld up: rdn and ev ch over 1f out: kpt on cl home* **9/2**	85
101-	3	hd	**Celebration Song (IRE)**[196] 5102 3-9-3 84 .... StephenCarson 1 (W R Swinburn) *hld up in cl 5th: hdwy 2f out: sn rdn: kpt on fnl f* **7/2**[3]	86
001-	4	1 1/4	**Silver Chariot**[145] 6199 3-8-7 74 .... MichaelHills 4 (B W Hills) *sn led: rdn and hung lft 2f out: hdd 1f out: no ex* **4/1**	73
1110	5	11	**Casablanca Minx (IRE)**[31] 483 3-8-4 76 .... JamesDoyle(5) 5 (N P Littmoden) *trckd ldrs: n.m.r on rails and lost pl 4f out: wknd over 1f out* **11/4**[1]	49+

1m 46.52s **Going Correction** +0.425s/f (Slow) 5 Ran SP% **112.1**
Speed ratings (Par 100):88,87,86,85,74
CSF £16.48 TOTE £4.50: £1.70, £2.40; EX 20.90.
Owner Mrs Perle O'Rourke **Bred** John T L Jones Jr & Robert S Folsom **Trained** East Everleigh, Wilts

FOCUS
Tight betting for a decent little handicap, with several relatively unexposed types on display, but no pace and a bunch finish, so the form is not at all solid.
Casablanca Minx(IRE) Official explanation: jockey said filly suffered interference in running

725 JYSKE BANK PRIVATE BANKING 08000 517257 H'CAP 6f (P)

5:15 (5:23) (Class 4) (0-85,84) 3-Y-0 £5,505 (£1,637; £818; £408) Stalls High

Form				RPR
6631	1		**Blushing Thief (USA)**[24] 551 3-8-10 76 .... MartinDwyer 6 (W Jarvis) *hld up but in tch: rdn over 2f out: styd on wl u.p to ld ins fnl f: drvn out* **3/1**[2]	82
415-	2	nk	**Scarlet Knight**[130] 6352 3-9-4 84 .... JimmyFortune 3 (P Mitchell) *trckd ldr: hrd rdn to press ldr fr 2f out: ev ch ins fnl f: no ex cl home* **8/1**	89
004-	3	2	**Phantom Whisper**[215] 4638 3-9-3 83 .... DaneO'Neill 4 (B R Millman) *led: rdn and hrd pressed fr 2f out: hdd ins fnl f: no ex* **12/1**	82
11	4	1 1/2	**Hypocrisy**[19] 601 3-8-12 78 .... J-PGuillambert 5 (S C Williams) *plld hrd: trckd ldr: rdn and effrt 2f out: kpt on same pce* **13/8**[1]	73

1 **5** *hd* **Boldinor**[35] 449 3-8-9 **75**........ StephenCarson 1 69
(W R Swinburn) *hld up bhd ldrs: rdn and hung lft 2f out: kpt on same pce fnl f* **7/1**
1 **6** *2 ½* **Sir Douglas**[26] 533 3-9-0 **80**........ SteveDrowne 2 66
(J A Osborne) *restrained s: hld up: rdn and short lived effrt 2f out* **4/1**[3]
1m 15.76s **Going Correction** +0.425s/f (Slow) **6** Ran SP% **114.4**
Speed ratings (Par 100):103,102,99,97,97 94
CSF £26.58 TOTE £6.00: £1.70, £3.10; EX 42.50 Place 6 £136.45, Place 5 £63.09.
Owner D Heath **Bred** I Cowan And Marjorie Cowan **Trained** Newmarket, Suffolk
FOCUS
A decent little race, with several unexposed and progressive types in the field, and four of the runners having won last time out. However, it was run at a modest tempo.
T/Plt: £208.70 to a £1 stake. Pool: £40,737.60. 142.45 winning tickets. T/Qpdt: £34.50 to a £1 stake. Pool: £2,106.40. 45.10 winning tickets.

REDCAR (L-H)
Saturday, March 25

OFFICIAL GOING: Soft
The meeting was transferred from Doncaster, which is being redeveloped. The going was described as 'very testing, bordering on heavy'.
Wind: Moderate, half behind Weather: Overcast

726 WILLIAM HILL SPRING MILE (H'CAP) 1m
2:10 (2:19) (Class 2) 4-Y-0+
£15,580 (£4,665; £2,332; £1,167; £582; £292) **Stalls** Centre

Form RPR
354- **1** **Mezuzah**[168] 5743 6-8-5 **70**........ PaulMulrennan(3) 2 84
(M W Easterby) *trckd ldrs: hdwy over 3f out: led over 2f out: rdn clr over 1f out: drvn ins last and kpt on wl* **14/1**
130- **2** *4* **Granston (IRE)**[147] 6147 5-9-10 **86**........ GrahamGibbons 20 92
(J D Bethell) *hld up: hdwy 3f out: rdn and edgd lft over 1f out: styd on ins last* **16/1**
020- **3** *¾* **Harvest Warrior**[147] 6147 4-9-7 **83**........ DavidAllan 10 88
(T D Easterby) *bmpd s and towards rr: pushed along and hdwy over 3f out: rdn along over 2f out: drvn and edgd lft ins last: styd on* **25/1**
60-0 **4** *1 ½* **Commando Scott (IRE)**[36] 444 5-9-4 **80**........ SebSanders 3 82
(I W McInnes) *hld up: hdwy on outer 3f out: rdn to chse ldrs wl over 1f out: kpt on u.p fnl f* **25/1**
00-6 **5** *3* **Boundless Prospect (USA)**[18] 611 7-9-4 **80**........ MickyFenton 17 76
(Miss Gay Kelleway) *bhd: hdwy on stands side 3f out: sn rdn and edgd rt: styd on u.p: nt rch ldrs* **20/1**
2-62 **6** *nk* **Everest (IRE)**[26] 530 9-8-13 **80**........ CDHayes(5) 12 75
(B Ellison) *towards rr: hdwy 3f out: rdnd along 2f out: edgd lft and styd on appr last: nrst fin* **9/1**
140- **7** *4* **Davenport (IRE)**[119] 6437 4-9-4 **80**........ AlanMunro 15 67
(B R Millman) *midfield: rdn along and outpcd wl over 2f out: styd on ins last: n.d* **7/1**[2]
605- **8** *4* **Freeloader (IRE)**[168] 5730 6-9-6 **82**........ PaulHanagan 8 61
(R A Fahey) *in tch: hdwy and ev ch 2f out: sn rdn and wknd over 1f out* **14/1**
5234 **9** *shd* **Nautical**[22] 569 8-8-8 **70**........ ShaneKelly 19 49
(A W Carroll) *bhd tls tayed on fnl 2f: nvr a factor* **40/1**
-414 **10** *nk* **Alfonso**[18] 611 5-9-0 **76**........(b[1]) TomEaves 21 54
(I Semple) *in touych: hdwy to chse ldrs 3f out: rdn along 2f out and sn no imp* **8/1**[3]
0343 **11** *2* **Wavertree Warrior (IRE)**[8] 662 4-9-3 **79**........ ChrisCatlin 16 53
(N P Littmoden) *a towards rr* **14/1**
-433 **12** *9* **Always Esteemed (IRE)**[14] 629 6-9-3 **79**........(b) NCallan 7 35
(K A Ryan) *cl up: led over 3f out: rdn and hdd over 2f out: gradsually wknd* **12/1**
100- **13** *3* **Barathea Dreams (IRE)**[168] 5730 5-9-4 **80**........ DarryllHolland 9 30
(J S Moore) *wnt lft s: sn eld: pushed alonga nd hdd over 3f out: rdn over 2f out and sn wknd* **13/2**[1]
2666 **14** *1 ½* **Outer Hebrides**[25] 542 5-9-6 **82**........(vt) RobertWinston 5 29
(Stef Liddiard) *midfield: rdn along over 3f out: sn wknd* **18/1**
004- **15** *3* **Yakimov (USA)**[140] 6248 7-9-2 **78**........ VinceSlattery 1 19
(D J Wintle) *in tch on outer: rdn along over 3f out: sn wknd* **20/1**
001- **16** *6* **Wing Commander**[202] 4970 7-9-5 **81**........ GylesParkin 23 10
(I W McInnes) *cl up: rdn along bef 1/2-way and sn wknd* **66/1**
50-0 **17** *¾* **River Biscuit (USA)**[8] 662 4-8-2 **64**........ FrankieMcDonald 13 —
(M J Polglase) *cl up: rdn along over 3f out: sn wknd* **100/1**
51-6 **18** *1* **Dhaular Dhar (IRE)**[14] 632 4-9-2 **78**........ FergalLynch 24 4
(J S Goldie) *prom: rdn along 1/2-way: sn wknd* **50/1**
050- **19** *shd* **Middlemarch (IRE)**[166] 5792 6-8-10 **72**........ DaleGibson 6 —
(J S Goldie) *a bhd* **50/1**
000- **20** *9* **Aperitif**[234] 4055 5-8-5 **67**........ FrancisNorton 11 —
(D Nicholls) *trckd ldrs: effrt 3f out: sn rdn along and wknd qckly 2f out* **16/1**
0404 **21** *½* **Undeterred**[19] 602 10-8-12 **79**........ EmmettStack(5) 22 —
(K J Burke) *bhd fr 1/2-way* **100/1**
0L-R **R** **High Dyke**[14] 632 4-9-2 **78**........(p) KDarley 4 —
(K A Ryan) *ref to r* **66/1**
1m 44.78s (6.98) **Going Correction** +1.05s/f (Soft) **22** Ran SP% **120.2**
Speed ratings (Par 109):107,103,102,100,97 97,93,89,89,89 87,78,75,73,70 64,63,62,62,53 53,—
CSF £191.31 CT £5530.26 TOTE £18.10: £3.90, £6.50, £9.50, £6.00; EX 466.30 TRIFECTA Not won..
Owner Woodford Group Plc **Bred** Mrs Rebecca Philipps **Trained** Sheriff Hutton, N Yorks
■ After a false start due to one set of stalls opening late, two horses, Ermine Grey and Lincolneurocruiser, had to be withdrawn.
■ Stewards' Enquiry : Graham Gibbons caution: careless riding
FOCUS
The winner had a going day and with conditions against the runner-up, it does not look strong form at all.
NOTEBOOK
Mezuzah, whose honesty has been questioned in the past, is a proven mudlark. He had this won in a matter of strides when sent on, but will shoot up in the ratings as a result.
Granston(IRE), who has not shone on soft ground in the past, ran a stormer on his return and career win number six is surely in the pipeline.
Harvest Warrior, out of sorts at three, did well to finish where he did after meeting trouble leaving ths stalls. He has certainly slipped to a winning mark.
Commando Scott(IRE) travelled strongly but a mile stretches his stamina to the very limit. He can surely find an opening in his new quarters.
Boundless Prospect(USA), suited by a straight mile, came off a straight line and ended up against the stands' side rail.
Everest(IRE) likes a straight track but, now a veteran, he has lost some of his speed and an uphill finish suits him better. (tchd 17-2)
Davenport(IRE), staying on in good style when it was all over, was found to have suffered an over-reach. Official explanation: jockey said gelding suffered an over reach (tchd 15-2)
Barathea Dreams(IRE), backward in his coat, took this at Doncaster last year from a 6lb lower mark. He was not in the same sort of form this time though. (op 15-2)

727 WILLIAMHILLPOKER.COM BROCKLESBY CONDITIONS STKS 5f
2:40 (2:45) (Class 4) 2-Y-0
£6,855 (£2,052; £1,026; £513; £256; £128) **Stalls** Centre

Form RPR
2 **1** **Spoof Master (IRE)**[7] 663 2-8-8........ RobertMiles(3) 2 86
(W G M Turner) *mde all:r idden 2f out: styd on strly fnl f* **5/2**[2]
2 *4* **Rouen (IRE)** 2-8-11........ TQuinn 8 71
(M R Channon) *w'like; cmpt: dwlt: sn travcking ldrs: hdwy to chse wnr 2f out: sn rdn and kpt ons ame pce fnl f* **9/4**[1]
3 *2 ½* **Everyman** 2-8-11........ ShaneKelly 7 62+
(P D Evans) *tall: unf: s.i.s: hdwy to chse ldrs 1/2-way: rdn 2f out and kpt on same pce appr last* **4/1**[3]
4 *3* **Elizabeth Garrett** 2-8-6........ AlanMunro 6 45
(R M H Cowell) *neat: chsd ldrs on outer: rdn along over 2f out: sn one pce* **9/1**
5 *8* **Flying Lion** 2-8-3........ EdwardCreighton(3) 3 15
(M R Channon) *cmpt: s.i.s: a bhd* **12/1**
6 *3 ½* **Wiseton Dancer (IRE)** 2-8-11........ NeilPollard 5 7
(Miss V Haigh) *leggy: unf: scope: cl up: rdn along 1/2-way: wknd 2f out* **20/1**
7 *2 ½* **Jojesse** 2-8-11........ MickyFenton 1 —
(S Parr) *cmpt: in tch: rdn along over 2f out: sn wknd* **11/1**
8 *26* **Citoyen (IRE)** 2-8-11........ RobertWinston 4 —
(Ronald Thompson) *leggy: unf: dwlt: sn rdn along: rn green and wandered: a rr* **16/1**
63.68 secs (4.98) **Going Correction** +1.05s/f (Soft) **8** Ran SP% **116.0**
Speed ratings (Par 94):102,95,91,86,74 68,64,22
CSF £8.72 TOTE £3.30: £1.40, £1.80, £1.50; EX 8.00 Trifecta £36.40 Pool: £302.60 - 5.90 winning units..
Owner Bill Hinge & Gary Smallbone **Bred** Chris McHale And Oghill House Stud **Trained** Sigwells, Somerset
FOCUS
The winner's experience was decisive. There was little strength outside the first three in what was just an average renewal.
NOTEBOOK
Spoof Master(IRE), still backward in his coat, was very professional and never really looked like being pegged back. He should enjoy further success. (op 9-4)
Rouen(IRE), a March foal, is well made and was on his toes beforehand. He missed a beat at the start and when sent in pursuit of the winner he never really threatened to close the gap. A mature type, he will soon go one better. (op 7-4)
Everyman ◆, a February foal, is very much up in the air. After a tardy start, he kept on well to finish clear third best and he can soon find a race. (op 7-1)
Elizabeth Garrett, a March foal, is not very big. Very green to post, she tired badly after chasing the winner to past halfway. (op 11-1 tchd 8-1)
Flying Lion, a slip of a thing, will probably be seen in a seller soon. (op 14-1)

728 WILLIAM HILL LINCOLN HERITAGE H'CAP 1m
3:15 (3:18) (Class 2) 4-Y-0+
£62,320 (£18,660; £9,330; £4,670; £2,330; £1,170) **Stalls** Centre

Form RPR
300- **1** **Blythe Knight (IRE)**[162] 5876 6-8-10 **95**........ GrahamGibbons 9 106
(J J Quinn) *lw: mid-div: smooth hdwy 3 f out: led appr fnl f: hld on towards fin* **22/1**
-340 **2** *¾* **Royal Island (IRE)**[14] 629 4-9-0 **99**........ JoeFanning 7 109
(M Johnston) *chsd ldrs: outpcd over 3f out: hdwy over 1f out: wnt 2nd ins last: styd on towards fin* **25/1**
00-1 **3** *3 ½* **Capable Guest (IRE)**[25] 542 4-8-9 **94** 5ex........ TQuinn 14 97
(M R Channon) *mid-div: hdwy over 3f out: styd on wl fnl f* **25/1**
531- **4** *nk* **Zero Tolerance (IRE)**[147] 6147 6-9-4 **103**........ PhillipMakin 4 105
(T D Barron) *led: edgd lft and hdd appr fnl f: wknd ins last* **14/1**
004- **5** *nk* **Audience**[147] 6147 6-8-4 **89**........(p) PaulDoe 22 90
(J Akehurst) *chsd ldrs: outpcd over 2f out: styd on ins last* **33/1**
405- **6** *3* **Babodana**[147] 6146 6-9-4 **106**........ SaleemGolam(3) 21 101
(M H Tompkins) *lw: in rr: hdwy over 2f out: styd on wl ins last* **16/1**
/12- **7** *hd* **King's Majesty (IRE)**[181] 5497 4-8-3 **88**........ RobertWinston 27 83
(Sir Michael Stoute) *lw: swtchd lft s: rr-div: effrt over 2f out: hung lft and kpt on fnl f* **8/1**[2]
000- **8** *3 ½* **Mine (IRE)**[175] 5614 8-9-7 **106**........(v) AlanMunro 1 94
(J D Bethell) *lw: mid-div on outer: effrt 3f out: nvr rchd ldrs* **50/1**
552- **9** *nk* **Dansili Dancer**[199] 5052 4-8-5 **90**........ PhilipRobinson 13 77
(C G Cox) *trckd ldrs: effrt over 2f out: wknd over 1f out* **16/1**
40-2 **10** *3 ½* **Sew'N'So Character (IRE)**[25] 542 5-8-1 **89** ow2 EdwardCreighton(3) 15 69
(M Blanshard) *rr-div: kpt on fnl 3f: nvr nr ldrs* **20/1**
046- **11** *nk* **Zomerlust**[162] 5874 4-7-12 **88**........ CDHayes(5) 25 68
(J J Quinn) *mid-div: hdwy over 3f out: wknd fnl 2f* **50/1**
113- **12** *1 ½* **Cesare**[239] 3896 5-8-10 **95** ow1........ SebSanders 6 83+
(J R Fanshawe) *mid-div: effrt 3f out: wknd over 1f out: eased ins last* **7/2**[1]
300- **13** *2 ½* **Blue Spinnaker (IRE)**[169] 5717 7-8-4 **92**........ PaulMulrennan(3) 24 64
(M W Easterby) *swtchd lft s: bhd: sme hdwy over 2f out: nvr on terms* **25/1**
006- **14** *½* **Shot To Fame (USA)**[162] 5876 7-8-10 **95**........ AdrianTNicholls 8 66
(D Nicholls) *trckd ldrs: t.k.h: lost pl over 2f out* **50/1**
13-0 **15** *hd* **My Paris**[14] 629 5-9-1 **105**........ AndrewMullen(5) 3 75
(K A Ryan) *chsd ldrs: sn drvn along: lost pl over 2f out* **20/1**
003- **16** *¾* **Nero's Return (IRE)**[147] 6138 5-8-3 **88**........ NickyMackay 20 57
(M Johnston) *in rr: edgd rt and nt much room after 2f* **50/1**
100- **17** *1* **Common World (USA)**[139] 6270 7-9-8 **107**........ FMBerry 29 74
(T Hogan, Ire) *rr-div: sme hdwy over 3f out: nvr on terms* **16/1**
1330 **18** *1* **Polygonal (FR)**[28] 518 6-8-7 **92** ow1........ DarryllHolland 19 57
(Ernst Oertel) *swtg: s.i.s: nvr on terms* **66/1**
040- **19** *½* **Coup D'Etat**[176] 5588 4-8-3 **88**........ JamieMackay 11 52
(J L Dunlop) *mid-div: effrt over 3f out: sn btn* **66/1**
4602 **20** *1* **Cardinal Venture (IRE)**[19] 600 8-8-8 **93**........(p) FergalLynch 26 55
(K A Ryan) *chsd ldrs stands' side: lost pl 3f out* **100/1**

1/11 **21** *2 ½* **Gentleman's Deal (IRE)**[71] 108 5-8-9 **94**...................... DaleGibson 30 51
(M W Easterby) *swtchd lft s: in rr: effrt over 3f out: hung lft: nvr a factor* **10/1**[3]

40-6 **22** *1 ½* **Josh**[14] 627 4-8-9 **94**...................... KDarley 18 48
(K A Ryan) *w ldrs: lost pl 3f out* **66/1**

/44- **23** *3* **Fiefdom (IRE)**[308] 1892 4-8-9 **94**...................... TomEaves 23 42
(I W McInnes) *chsd ldrs: lost pl over 3f out* **100/1**

000- **24** *5* **Primus Inter Pares (IRE)**[182] 5452 5-8-7 **92**................ FrancisNorton 5 30
(D Nicholls) *a in rr* **100/1**

61-2 **25** *1* **Kamanda Laugh**[14] 631 5-8-10 **95**...................... NCallan 17 31
(K A Ryan) *prom: effrt over 3f out: sn btn* **10/1**[3]

631- **26** *1* **Chrysander**[143] 6229 4-9-10 **109**...................... TonyCulhane 16 43
(M R Channon) *a in rr* **33/1**

052- **27** *½* **Postgraduate (IRE)**[173] 5660 4-8-5 **90**...................... ChrisCatlin 10 23
(W J Knight) *mid-div: effrt over 3f out: sn btn* **40/1**

405- **28** *1* **Kings Quay**[167] 5767 4-8-10 **98**...................... DNolan(3) 12 29
(J J Quinn) *mid-div: effrt over 3f out: sn wknd* **80/1**

0052 **29** *22* **Realism (FR)**[29] 513 6-9-0 **99**......................(t) PaulHanagan 2 —
(R A Fahey) *swtg: mid-div: lost pl over 2f out: sn bhd and heavily eased* **40/1**

124- **P** **Benedict**[154] 6025 4-8-10 **95**...................... ShaneKelly 28 —
(John Berry) *in rr: hmpd after 2f: last whn p.u 4f out: dead* **16/1**

1m 44.33s (6.53) **Going Correction** +1.05s/f (Soft) **30** Ran SP% **134.4**
Speed ratings (Par 109):109,108,104,104,104 101,100,97,97,93 93,91,89,88,88 87,86,85,85,84 81,80,77,72,71 70,69,68,46
CSF £496.85 CT £13065.12 TOTE £35.00: £7.10, £7.10, £5.00, £3.70; EX 959.80 Trifecta £11146.70 Part won. Pool: £15,699.58 - 0.10 winning units..
Owner Maxilead Limited **Bred** Gainsborough Stud Management Ltd **Trained** Settrington, N Yorks
■ Stewards' Enquiry : Graham Gibbons one-day ban: used whip wth excessive force (Apr 5)

FOCUS
The temporary transfer of the Lincoln to Redcar brought at least one major benefit in that we did not have the usual Doncaster scenario of separate races up either side of the track. Blythe Knight had an obvious chance at the weights if at his best and ran to last year's best. The runner-up turned in another improved effort, but overall the form is nothing out of the ordinary.

NOTEBOOK
Blythe Knight(IRE), gelded since being sold out of Ed Dunlop's yard, looked to have done plenty of work. He took it up travelling easily best but, having got there plenty soon enough, he had to be vigorously rousted along near the line. His rating will shoot back up and he may have to try his hand in Listed races once more. (op 25-1)
Royal Island(IRE), already a winner in heavy ground, stuck on strongly after getting tapped for toe. His rating will go up as a result and he may now be ready for a try over a bit further.
Capable Guest(IRE), under a 5lb penalty, ran a sound race but these days he seems happier on the All-Weather.
Zero Tolerance(IRE), racing from a career-high mark, tried to run them ragged and deserves plenty of credit for this.
Audience, who has slipped to a lenient mark, does not like being crowded but with the field well spread out, he took it into his head to stay on in good style late on.
Babodana, who took this at Doncaster two years ago, looked in fine fettle and made a pleasing return.
King's Majesty(IRE) ◆, who looked bright and well, was switched to overcome his high draw. He hung in the ground but deserves credit for the way he kept on all the way to the line. Still unexposed and from a stable that excels with older horses, he must be kept on the right side in less testing conditions. (op 7-1)
Mine(IRE), who has never won before May, looked in good trim but does not really appreciate ground as testing as this.
Cesare, still hanging on to his winter coat, was making hard work of this some way out and never really threatened. In the end his rider gave up, but he will bounce back in due course. Official explanation: jockey said gelding had no more to give (op 9-2)
Polygonal(FR) Official explanation: jockey said gelding was unsuited by soft going and lost a front shoe

729 WILLIAMHILL.CO.UK CAMMIDGE TROPHY (LISTED RACE) 6f
3:50 (3:53) (Class 1) 3-Y-0+ **£17,781** (£6,723; £3,360; £1,680) **Stalls** Centre

Form RPR

-111 **1** **Les Arcs (USA)**[7] 664 6-9-2 107...................... NCallan 1 116
(T J Pitt) *trckd ldrs on outer: smooth hdwy over 2f out: led wl over 1f out: rdn and edgd rt ins last: styd on* **15/2**

00-2 **2** *¾* **Quito (IRE)**[14] 627 9-9-5 110......................(b) TonyCulhane 11 117
(D W Chapman) *in tch: rdn along halfway: hdwy 2f out: drvn and styng on whn n.m.r ins last: kpt on towards fin* **9/2**[1]

111- **3** *shd* **Reverence**[154] 6021 5-9-2 95...................... KDarley 13 113
(E J Alston) *a.p: effrt and led briefly 2f out: sn rdn and hdd wl over 1f out: drvn and edgd rt ins last: no ex* **5/1**[2]

330- **4** *4* **Pivotal Flame**[161] 5900 4-9-2 105......................(v¹) DarryllHolland 4 101
(E S McMahon) *lw: bmpd s and hld up in rr: smooth hdwy over 2f out: rdn and ev ch over 1f out: drvn: sltly hmpd and wknd inslast* **9/2**[1]

050- **5** *nk* **Steenberg (IRE)**[161] 5906 7-9-2 108...................... SaleemGolam 12 101
(M H Tompkins) *trckd ldrs: rdn along and sltly outpcd 2f out: kpt on ins last* **9/1**

06-0 **6** *2 ½* **Orientor**[14] 627 8-9-2 103...................... ChrisCatlin 2 93
(J S Goldie) *chsd ldrs: rdn along 2f out: sn one pce* **16/1**

03-5 **7** *nk* **Fire Up The Band**[7] 664 7-9-7 109...................... AdrianTNicholls 14 97
(D Nicholls) *sn led: rdn along and hdd 2f out: grad wknd* **12/1**

500- **8** *3 ½* **The Kiddykid (IRE)**[162] 5873 6-9-2 106...................... ShaneKelly 8 82
(P D Evans) *cl up: rdn along over 2f out: sn wknd* **7/1**[3]

105- **9** *2* **Coconut Squeak**[140] 6252 4-9-0 101...................... MickyFenton 9 74
(Stef Liddiard) *n.d* **25/1**

046- **10** *2* **Tom Tun**[140] 6252 11-9-2 88......................(b) JoeFanning 5 70
(J Balding) *hmpd s and bhd: swtchd rt and gd hdwy over 2f out: rdn to chse ldrs wl over 1f out: sn wknd* **40/1**

6316 **11** *5* **Obe Gold**[16] 619 4-9-2 ....(v) TQuinn 6 55
(M R Channon) *hmpd s: sn rdn along towards rr: bhd fr 1/2-way* **10/1**

300- **12** *3 ½* **Continent**[168] 5745 9-9-2 93...................... SilvestreDeSousa 7 44
(D Nicholls) *cl up: rdn along over 2f out and sn wknd* **66/1**

/00- **13** *16* **Captain Hurricane**[280] 2722 4-9-2 .... AlanMunro 3 —
(P W Chapple-Hyam) *wnt rt s: a rr* **25/1**

1m 16.36s (4.66) **Going Correction** +1.05s/f (Soft) **13** Ran SP% **121.6**
Speed ratings (Par 111):110,109,108,103,103 99,99,94,92,89 82,78,56
CSF £40.71 TOTE £10.10: £3.60, £2.00, £2.20; EX 29.10 Trifecta £112.20 Pool: £727.16 - 4.60 winning units..
Owner Willie McKay **Bred** Elk Manor Farm **Trained** Bawtry, S Yorks

FOCUS
Decent form for the grade, well up to Listed standard. Les Arcs, much improved on the All-Weather, carried it over to turf. While Quito was not at his very best, Reverence ran way above his official rating and will be even better over five.

NOTEBOOK
Les Arcs(USA), who has improved by leaps and bounds on the All-Weather, allayed fears about his ability to handle soft ground and gave his first-season trainer a big boost. (op 7-1 tchd 9-1)
Quito(IRE), who took three similar events last year, was tightened up slightly inside the last but in truth he was never quite going to pull it off. He should continue to give a good account of himself at various levels.
Reverence ◆, who has twice injured his pelvis, made great strides in just six outings last year, his first season on a racetrack. Looking fit, he just missed out in the end after taking charge. Considered better over five furlongs, he must be kept on the right side even though his rating will shoot up as a result of this. (op 11-2 tchd 9-2)
Pivotal Flame looked exceptionally well. Tried in a visor and over a trip a furlong short of his best, he gave his rider problems by wanting to hang left throughout. His lengthy losing run must be a cause for concern. Official explanation: jockey said colt hung left-handed (op 7-1)
Steenberg(IRE), tried over a fair bit further last year, was best in on official figures but he is an infrequent winner and he was struggling to keep up soon after the halfway mark. (op 8-1)
Orientor, placed three times in this at Doncaster, was trying to make it fifth time lucky but he has lost some of his edge. (op 14-1)
Fire Up The Band took them along, but he is not fully fit yet and five is his trip now.
Captain Hurricane Official explanation: jockey said colt was unsuited by soft ground

730 WILLIAMHILLCASINO.COM MARCH H'CAP 1m 2f
4:25 (4:25) (Class 4) (0-80,78) 3-Y-0 **£6,477** (£1,927; £963; £481) **Stalls** Low

Form RPR

100- **1** **Gracechurch (IRE)**[155] 6005 3-9-1 **75**...................... TonyCulhane 3 80
(M R Channon) *chsd ldrs: effrt 4f out: styd on to ld over 1f out: edgd rt and hrd rdn: jst hld on* **5/1**[3]

516- **2** *nk* **Gee Dee Nen**[155] 6005 3-8-13 **76**...................... SaleemGolam(3) 7 80+
(M H Tompkins) *hld up: last 4f out: hdwy over 2f out: styd on wl: no ex nr fin* **7/2**[2]

520- **3** *hd* **Bedouin Blue (IRE)**[147] 6158 3-8-8 **68**...................... LeeEnstone 5 72
(P C Haslam) *trckd ldrs: led over 2f out: hdd and bmpd over 1f out: no ex ins last* **16/1**

200- **4** *2 ½* **Stainley (IRE)**[140] 6249 3-8-8 **68**...................... GrahamGibbons 10 68
(J D Bethell) *swtchd lft after s: led tl over 2f out: one pce appr fnl f* **11/1**

5-01 **5** *1 ¾* **Al Rayanah**[39] 409 3-8-7 **67**...................... ChrisCatlin 4 64
(G Prodromou) *s.i.s: hdwy 5f out: kpt on fnl 3f: nvr rchd ldrs* **16/1**

546- **6** *13* **Marronnier (IRE)**[204] 4917 3-8-11 **71**...................... DavidAllan 8 46
(T D Easterby) *hld up in rr: effrt 4f out: hung rt: lost pl and eased fnl f* **18/1**

-1 **7** *9* **Lucky Lark**[14] 630 3-9-4 **78**...................... KDarley 2 37+
(M Johnston) *swtg: sn trcking ldrs: hmpd after 150 yds: drvn over 4f out: btn whn n.m.r 3f out: sn lost pl* **6/4**[1]

440- **8** *5* **Grand Cherokee (IRE)**[181] 5489 3-8-7 **67**...................... TomEaves 6 18
(B Ellison) *hld up in rr: effrt 4f out: sn btn* **14/1**

33-5 **9** *19* **Rosthwaite (IRE)**[74] 76 3-8-12 **72**...................... MickyFenton 1 —
(Ronald Thompson) *mid-div: rdn and lost pl over 3f out* **25/1**

006- **10** *dist* **Obscene**[147] 6144 3-8-5 **65**...................... PaulHanagan 9 —
(M J Polglase) *trckd ldrs: lost pl over 5f out: bhd fnl 3f: virtually p.u: tained off: btn total of 42 l* **25/1**

2m 18.68s (11.88) **Going Correction** +1.25s/f (Soft) **10** Ran SP% **118.6**
Speed ratings (Par 100):102,101,101,99,98 87,80,76,61,—
CSF £23.30 CT £259.16 TOTE £6.50: £2.10, £1.80, £3.00; EX 24.70.
Owner Gracechurch Racing Syndicate **Bred** Major K R Thompson **Trained** West Ilsley, Berks
■ Stewards' Enquiry : Graham Gibbons three-day ban: careless riding (Apr 6-8)
Tony Culhane two-day ban: careless riding (Apr 5,6)

FOCUS
A messy affair not run at a strong pace and the form looks dubious.

731 WILLIAM HILL 0800 444040 MEDIAN AUCTION MAIDEN STKS 1m 1f
4:55 (4:57) (Class 5) 3-Y-0 **£3,886** (£1,156; £577; £288) **Stalls** Low

Form RPR

32- **1** **Estiqraar (IRE)**[204] 4922 3-9-3 .... SebSanders 8 81+
(J L Dunlop) *trckd ldrs: shkn up over 4f out: rdn to ld 2f out: styd on wl: readily* **10/11**[1]

403- **2** *4* **Chronomatic**[159] 5944 3-9-0 78...................... SaleemGolam(3) 7 69
(M H Tompkins) *trckd ldrs: led over 3f out tl 2f out: kpt on same pce* **3/1**[2]

0-0 **3** *1 ½* **Zed Candy (FR)**[26] 536 3-9-3 .... MickyFenton 2 66
(J T Stimpson) *sn trcking ldrs: t.k.h: outpcd over 2f out: styd on ins last* **50/1**

40-2 **4** *shd* **Markington**[26] 536 3-9-3 73...................... GrahamGibbons 1 66
(J D Bethell) *s.i.s: sn trcking ldrs: one pce fnl 2f* **10/1**

6-00 **5** *11* **Eliminator**[21] 583 3-9-3 70...................... PaulHanagan 4 44
(I W McInnes) *sn chsng ldrs: rdn 4f out: lost pl over 2f out* **33/1**

6 *14* **Every Inch (IRE)** 3-9-3 .... FergalLynch 5 16
(T D Easterby) *rangy: scope: in rr: lost pl over 5f out: sn bhd* **16/1**

045- **7** *5* **Methusaleh (IRE)**[173] 5658 3-9-3 74...................... DavidAllan 6 6
(T D Easterby) *led: hdd over 3f out: sn lost pl: bhd whn heavily eased ins last* **5/1**[3]

8 *dist* **Celtic Jig (IRE)** 3-8-12 .... DuranFentiman(5) 3 —
(T D Easterby) *rangY; unf: scope: s.i.s: detached in last 6f out: t.o: btn total 68 l* **25/1**

2m 5.76s (12.36) **Going Correction** +1.25s/f (Soft) **8** Ran SP% **117.8**
Speed ratings (Par 98):95,91,90,90,80 67,63,—
CSF £3.87 TOTE £1.90: £1.10, £1.60, £6.00; EX 4.00 Place 6 £292.65, Place 5 £46.89.
Owner Hamdan Al Maktoum **Bred** Shadwell Estate Company Limited **Trained** Arundel, W Sussex

FOCUS
A slow time and an ordinary early season maiden rated through the fourth for the time being. The winner might struggle in handicaps if, as seems likely, he is given a rating in the mid 80s.
T/Jkpt: Not won. T/Plt: £579.00 to a £1 stake. Pool: £101,060.40. 127.40 winning tickets. T/Qpdt: £54.00 to a £1 stake. Pool: £7,316.20. 100.10 winning tickets. JR

679 WOLVERHAMPTON (A.W) (L-H)
Saturday, March 25

OFFICIAL GOING: Standard
Wind: Moderate behind

732 WOLVERHAMPTON-RACECOURSE.CO.UK CLAIMING STKS 5f 216y(P)
7:00 (7:00) (Class 6) 4-Y-0+ **£2,730** (£806; £403) **Stalls** Low

Form RPR

5035 **1** **Gilded Cove**[22] 569 6-8-12 70...................... RussellKennemore(7) 3 75
(R Hollinshead) *hld up: hdwy over 2f out: rdn and r.o to ld ins fnl f* **3/1**[1]

2102 **2** *½* **Up Tempo (IRE)**[5] 674 8-9-1 65......................(b) RobertWinston 4 69
(K A Ryan) *trckd ldrs: rdn and ev ch 1f out: r.o to go 2nd* **7/2**[2]

3033 **3** *¾* **Mission Affirmed (USA)**[10] 640 5-9-1 68..............(b) AdrianMcCarthy 8 67
(R A Harris) *mid-div: rdn and hdwy on outside over 1f out: r.o wl fnl f* **8/1**

0116 **4** *1* **Sweet Pickle**[9] [654] 5-8-11 65 .... AmirQuinn(3) 2 63
(J R Boyle) *a in tch: rdn and ev ch appr fnl f: kpt on one pce* **6/1**[3]
2020 **5** *½* **Diamond Josh**[29] [502] 4-8-7 62 .... DanielTudhope(3) 7 58
(P D Evans) *led tl rdn and hdd ins fnl f: no ex* **13/2**
5001 **6** *nk* **Imperium**[19] [602] 5-8-11 52 .... (p) NickyMackay 1 58
(Stef Liddiard) *towards rr and sn rdn: hdwy wl over 1f out: nvr nr to chal* **10/1**
56-0 **7** *5* **Oh Dara (USA)**[18] [605] 4-8-10 62 .... PaulEddery 6 42
(M J Attwater) *plld hrd: trckd ldr tl wknd appr fnl f* **33/1**
010 **8** *1 ¼* **Million Percent**[19] [602] 7-8-6 61 .... AndrewElliott(5) 10 39
(K R Burke) *trckd ldrs c wd into st: sn btn* **16/1**
5325 **9** *2* **Alpaga Le Jomage (IRE)**[9] [654] 4-8-13 63 .... HayleyTurner 9 35
(M J Polglase) *prom tl wknd 2f out* **12/1**
0000 **10** *¾* **Time N Time Again**[21] [587] 8-8-9 55 .... (b) DaleGibson 12 29
(Peter Grayson) *slowly away: a bhd* **25/1**
0- **11** *1* **Auburn Lodge (IRE)**[77] [4885] 5-8-10 40 .... TPQueally 11 27
(J J Lambe, Ire) *hld up in rr: rdn 2f out: sn wl bhd* **66/1**
600- **12** *2* **Pays D'Amour (IRE)**[180] [5508] 9-8-11 40 ow2 .... (t) DerekMcGaffin 5 22
(D A Nolan) *slowly away: a bhd* **100/1**
630- **13** *14* **Ruby Muja**[268] [3064] 4-8-2 50 .... DavidKinsella 13 —
(T G McCourt, Ire) *racd wd: lost tch 1/2-way* **50/1**

1m 15.55s (-0.26) **Going Correction** -0.05s/f (Stan) **13** Ran SP% **119.8**
Speed ratings (Par 101):99,98,97,96,95 94,88,86,83,82 81,78,60
CSF £12.86 TOTE £3.90: £1.60, £1.30, £2.40; EX 9.80.The winner was the subject of a friendly claim
Owner M Johnson **Bred** R Hollinshead And M Johnson **Trained** Upper Longdon, Staffs

FOCUS
A modest event, run at a decent pace, and the form looks solid for the class.
Time N Time Again Official explanation: jockey said gelding lost its action inside final furlong
Ruby Muja Official explanation: jockey said filly hung right-handed throughout

733 ENTERTAINMENT AFTER RACING - A WOLVERHAMPTON SPECIALITY H'CAP 1m 4f 50y(P)
7:30 (7:30) (Class 6) (0-60,60) 4-Y-0+ **£2,388** (£705; £352) **Stalls** Low

Form RPR
0306 **1** **Birthday Star (IRE)**[32] [478] 4-8-7 **56** .... StephenDonohoe(5) 2 66
(W J Musson) *w.w in mid-div: hdwy to ld wl over 1f out: kpt up to work fnl f* **4/1**[2]
3-50 **2** *¾* **Lady Taverner**[52] [263] 5-8-9 **56** .... NataliaGemelova(5) 5 65
(J E Long) *hld up in tch: rdn and hdwy to chse wnr ins fnl f: no ex nr fin* **10/1**
-032 **3** *1 ¾* **Rare Coincidence**[10] [643] 5-8-10 **55** .... (p) DNolan(3) 1 61
(R F Fisher) *led tl rdn and hdd wl over 1f out: one pce fnl f* **7/2**[1]
-501 **4** *2* **Reminiscent (IRE)**[19] [599] 7-8-13 **55** .... (p) PaulEddery 3 58
(B P J Baugh) *s.i.s: hld up: rdn and hdwy over 2f out: nvr nrr* **14/1**
0/0- **5** *1 ¼* **Lefonic**[409] [325] 4-8-9 **53** .... RobertWinston 4 54
(G C H Chung) *trckd ldrs: wnt 2nd over 3f out to 2f out: rdn and fdd ent fnl f* **20/1**
-040 **6** *9* **Smoothie (IRE)**[19] [603] 8-8-9 **51** .... (p) FergusSweeney 11 38
(Ian Williams) *hld up: effrt on outside 3f out: no hdwy ins fnl 2f* **10/1**
5236 **7** *shd* **Little Richard (IRE)**[10] [643] 7-8-13 **55** .... (p) AlanDaly 10 41
(M Wellings) *in rr: hdwy over 1f out: nvr nr to chal* **7/1**
35-0 **8** *3 ½* **Rose Bien**[21] [574] 4-8-9 **53** .... TPQueally 9 34
(P J McBride) *trckd ldrs tl rdn over 3f out: wknd qckly* **14/1**
020- **9** *dist* **Be Wise Girl**[293] [2315] 5-8-13 **55** .... ShaneKelly 12 —
(A W Carroll) *flashed tail s: sn trckd ldr: lost 2nd over 3f out and sn wknd: t.o* **16/1**
0602 **10** *nk* **Farnborough (USA)**[9] [647] 5-8-9 **51** .... RobbieFitzpatrick 7 —
(R J Price) *prom tl wknd over 3f out: t.o* **11/2**[3]
/0-0 **11** *nk* **Strident (USA)**[22] [570] 5-9-4 **60** .... HayleyTurner 6 —
(J J Lambe, Ire) *towards rr whn completely lost pl over 7f out: t.o* **50/1**
420- **12** *26* **Dizzy Future**[148] [5959] 4-8-9 **53** .... (b[1]) RobertHavlin 8 —
(B J Llewellyn) *hld up: a trailing in rr: t.o* **40/1**

2m 40.69s (-1.73) **Going Correction** -0.05s/f (Stan)
WFA 4 from 5yo+ 2lb **12** Ran SP% **116.7**
Speed ratings (Par 101):103,102,101,100,99 93,93,90,—,— —,—
CSF £42.28 CT £153.86 TOTE £5.20: £2.00, £3.10, £1.30; EX 68.70.
Owner F Al Tamimi **Bred** Woodhouse Syndicate **Trained** Newmarket, Suffolk

FOCUS
A moderate handicap, run at a fair gallop, and the form looks sound enough.
Lefonic Official explanation: jockey said colt hung left
Smoothie(IRE) Official explanation: jockey said gelding had no more to give
Be Wise Girl Official explanation: jockey said mare had no more to give

734 TO SPONSOR A RACE CALL 0870 220 2442 (S) STKS 1m 141y(P)
8:00 (8:00) (Class 6) 4-Y-0+ **£2,388** (£705; £352) **Stalls** Low

Form RPR
0600 **1** **Merdiff**[19] [602] 7-8-12 55 .... ShaneKelly 10 53
(W M Brisbourne) *in tch: led over 3f out: clr whn hng rt ent fnl f: hung on wl* **13/2**
0-00 **2** *nk* **Frank's Quest (IRE)**[33] [458] 6-8-12 47 .... SamHitchcott 3 52
(A B Haynes) *in rr tl hdwy 4f out: hrd rdn and r.o strly fnl f to go 2nd nr fin* **20/1**
3136 **3** *hd* **Distant Country (USA)**[8] [662] 7-8-13 61 .... (p) AndrewElliott(5) 2 58
(K R Burke) *mid-div tl lost pl 6f out: n.m.r over 3f out: hdwy on ins over 1f out: rdn and r.o wl fnl f* **13/8**[1]
-605 **4** *nk* **Dane's Rock (IRE)**[11] [638] 4-8-7 45 .... RichardKingscote(5) 9 51
(M S Saunders) *in tch tl lost pl over 4f out: hdwy over 1f out: rdn and r.o wl fnl f* **16/1**
6243 **5** *1 ½* **Pending (IRE)**[9] [649] 5-8-9 54 .... (p) AmirQuinn(3) 8 48
(J R Boyle) *in tch: hdwy to go 2nd 3f out: rdn and wknd fnl f* **4/1**[2]
4-00 **6** *10* **Atlantic Ace**[42] [383] 9-8-12 58 .... (p) PaulEddery 6 27
(B Smart) *slowly away: sme hdwy over 2f out: nvr on terms* **11/1**
00/0 **7** *10* **Bowing**[22] [566] 6-8-12 45 .... LPKeniry 5 6
(J L Spearing) *chsd ldrs to 1/2-way: sn bhd* **33/1**
500- **8** *½* **Lucky Largo (IRE)**[61] [6236] 6-8-12 30 .... (b) DerekMcGaffin 1 5
(D A Nolan) *led: early: trckd ldr to over 3f out: sn wknd* **100/1**
0-00 **9** *6* **Teenage Rampage**[26] [531] 4-8-12 40 .... RobbieFitzpatrick 4 —
(W M Brisbourne) *sn led: hdd over 3f out: wknd qckly* **50/1**
5160 **10** *1* **Bijou Dan**[22] [568] 5-9-4 63 .... (b) TomEaves 7 —
(W G Harrison) *towards rr: c wd into st: wknd qckly* **9/2**[3]

1m 51.29s (-0.47) **Going Correction** -0.05s/f (Stan) **10** Ran SP% **114.5**
Speed ratings (Par 101):100,99,99,99,97 89,80,79,74,73
CSF £124.52 TOTE £6.40: £1.40, £3.60, £1.10; EX 107.30.There was no bid for the winner
Owner J F Thomas **Bred** Sheikh Ahmed Bin Rashid Al Maktoum **Trained** Great Ness, Shropshire
■ Stewards' Enquiry : Derek McGaffin three-day ban: weighed in 3.5lb heavier than weighing out (Apr 5-7)
Richard Kingscote one-day ban: failed to keep straight from stalls (Apr 5)

FOCUS
A poor affair, run at a decent clip, and the first four were closely covered at the finish. The form should be treated with caution.

735 HOOLEY WITH THE HOOKEY BAND MAIDEN STKS 1m 1f 103y(P)
8:30 (8:32) (Class 5) 3-Y-O **£3,238** (£963; £481; £240) **Stalls** Low

Form RPR
05-6 **1** **Christmas Player (USA)**[33] [460] 3-8-12 67 .... RobertHavlin 1 73
(J H M Gosden) *hld up in tch: wnt 2nd 3f out: led wl over 1f out: in command fnl f* **7/1**[3]
00-4 **2** *2 ½* **Dickie's Dream (IRE)**[26] [534] 3-9-3 65 .... TPQueally 9 73
(P J McBride) *outpcd 1/2-way: kpt up to work in rr: hdwy over 1f out: r.o wl fnl f to go 2nd nr fin* **16/1**
-232 **3** *nk* **Sky High Guy (IRE)**[7] [668] 3-9-3 75 .... FrankieMcDonald 2 72
(S Kirk) *prom: rdn whn n.m.r 3f out: swtchd rt: hung lft over 1f out: chsd wnr sn after tl lost 2nd cl home* **10/11**[1]
2-23 **4** *1 ¾* **Crazy Bear (IRE)**[44] [349] 3-8-12 69 .... RobertWinston 5 64
(K A Ryan) *trckd ldr: led over 3f out: hdd wl over 1f out: wknd ent fnl f* **9/4**[2]
6-02 **5** *22* **Welcome Releaf**[26] [531] 3-8-12 65 .... StephenDonohoe(5) 4 27
(Lucinda Featherstone) *led tl hdd over 3f out: wknd wl over 1f out* **14/1**
00- **6** *7* **October Sun**[141] [6246] 3-9-3 .... MichaelTebbutt 6 14
(Miss D Mountain) *sn trckd ldrs: rtidden and wknd over 3f out* **100/1**
0 **7** *7* **Solomans Prospect**[8] [658] 3-9-3 .... RobbieFitzpatrick 7 —
(Miss D A McHale) *a bhd* **200/1**
0 **8** *23* **Prince Marju (IRE)**[14] [630] 3-8-10 .... KevinGhunowa(7) 3 —
(P A Blockley) *plld hrd in mid-div: bhd fr 1/2-way* **100/1**

2m 1.99s (-0.63) **Going Correction** -0.05s/f (Stan) **8** Ran SP% **113.1**
Speed ratings (Par 98):100,97,97,95,76 70,63,43
CSF £96.77 TOTE £9.90: £1.60, £2.00, £1.10; EX 106.70.
Owner Edward P Evans **Bred** E P Evans **Trained** Newmarket, Suffolk
■ John Gosden's first winner since moving from Manton to Clarehaven Stables in Newmarket.

FOCUS
A moderate maiden, run at a fair gallop, and the form looks suspect.
Prince Marju(IRE) Official explanation: trainer said gelding had breathing problem

736 ENJOY RACING FROM THE ZONGALERO RESTAURANT H'CAP 1m 141y(P)
9:00 (9:00) (Class 5) (0-70,70) 4-Y-0+ **£3,238** (£963; £481; £240) **Stalls** Low

Form RPR
-P10 **1** **Pauline's Prince**[9] [650] 4-8-8 **60** .... LPKeniry 2 68
(R Hollinshead) *mid-div: rdn to go 2nd wl over 1f out: kpt on to ld ins fnl f: won gng away* **33/1**
2231 **2** *3* **Jakarmi**[22] [571] 5-9-2 **68** .... TonyCulhane 4 70
(B Palling) *chsd ldr: led over 2f out: edgd lft bef hdd ins fnl f: sn no ch w wnr* **11/4**[1]
-114 **3** *2 ½* **Itcanbedone Again (IRE)**[29] [505] 7-8-6 **58** .... FrancisFerris 9 54
(Ian Williams) *led tl hdd over 2f out: hmpd and snatched up ent fnl f: nt rcvr* **8/1**
3160 **4** *1 ½* **Mister Benji**[9] [650] 7-8-10 **62** .... DarrenWilliams 6 55
(B P J Baugh) *towards rr: styd on ins fnl 2f: nvr nr to chal* **16/1**
400- **5** *2* **Arran Scout (IRE)**[23] [6208] 5-9-2 **68** .... ShaneKelly 5 57
(T G McCourt, Ire) *slowly away: sn mid-div: rdn over 2f out: sn wknd* **20/1**
0-00 **6** *1 ¾* **Redwood Rocks (IRE)**[21] [585] 5-9-0 **66** .... DerekMcGaffin 3 51
(B Smart) *chsd ldrs tl rdn and wknd 3f out* **16/1**
0211 **7** *2* **Gallego**[5] [683] 4-8-6 **58** 6ex ow2 .... RobbieFitzpatrick 1 39
(R J Price) *hld up: rdn over 3f out: wknd wl over 1f out* **9/2**[3]
1310 **8** *7* **Bridgewater Boys**[22] [571] 5-8-12 **64** .... (b) RobertWinston 10 31
(K A Ryan) *prom: rdn 1/2-way: wknd over 2f out* **7/2**[2]
4-15 **9** *5* **Compton Eclipse**[22] [567] 6-8-13 **70** .... JamesDoyle(5) 8 26
(J J Lambe, Ire) *mid-div: lost pl over 5f out: wknd over 2f out* **7/1**
3-00 **10** *15* **Age Of Kings (USA)**[42] [384] 4-9-0 **66** .... SteveDrowne 7 —
(A B Haynes) *sn outpcd: a wl in rr* **20/1**

1m 50.25s (-1.51) **Going Correction** -0.05s/f (Stan) **10** Ran SP% **114.9**
Speed ratings (Par 103):104,101,99,97,96 94,92,86,82,68
CSF £118.47 CT £843.05 TOTE £31.70: £4.10, £1.90, £1.90; EX 278.60.
Owner N Chapman **Bred** R Hollinshead **Trained** Upper Longdon, Staffs

FOCUS
A modest handicap that saw the field finish strung out behind the ready winner.
Pauline's Prince Official explanation: trainer's representative said, regarding the improved form shown, colt was better suited by today's longer trip
Arran Scout(IRE) Official explanation: jockey said gelding hung left on final turn

737 CRAIC IS MIGHTY ON IRISH NIGHT H'CAP 7f 32y(P)
9:30 (9:30) (Class 5) (0-70,72) 4-Y-0+ **£3,886** (£1,156; £577; £288) **Stalls** High

Form RPR
1135 **1** **Desert Lover (IRE)**[9] [650] 4-8-8 **60** .... ShaneKelly 1 68
(R J Price) *a.p: rdn to ld ins fnl f: all out* **9/2**[2]
-002 **2** *nk* **Dudley Docker (IRE)**[30] [492] 4-8-7 **62** .... DanielTudhope(3) 4 69
(D Carroll) *bhd: tl hdwy on wd outside over 2f out: edgd lft u.p fnl f but r.o to go 2nd nr fin* **10/1**
0445 **3** *1* **Mistral Sky**[14] [631] 7-9-1 **67** .... (p) RobertWinston 3 71
(Stef Liddiard) *mid-division: hdwy on outside over 1f out: keeping on whn short of room cl home* **11/2**[3]
1025 **4** *1* **Stoic Leader (IRE)**[1] [711] 6-9-3 **72** .... (p) DNolan(3) 10 74
(R F Fisher) *chsd ldr: led 2f out: rdn and hdd ins fnl f: no ex* **9/1**
0120 **5** *2* **Shannon Arms (USA)**[9] [650] 5-8-12 **64** .... (p) J-PGuillambert 5 61
(P Howling) *led tl hdd 2f out: rdn and wknd fnl f* **12/1**
521- **6** *½* **Imperial Rule (IRE)**[167] [5766] 4-9-2 **68** .... SteveDrowne 12 63
(W J Knight) *in tch: rdn and edgd lft appr fnl f: wknd ins* **15/8**[1]
-400 **7** *¾* **Tyrone Sam**[10] [639] 4-8-12 **64** .... (b) TonyCulhane 7 57
(K A Ryan) *mid-div: effrt over 2f out: nvr on terms* **14/1**
2-16 **8** *6* **Joyeaux**[36] [441] 4-9-4 **70** .... DerekMcGaffin 9 48
(J Hetherton) *a bhd* **40/1**
006 **9** *1 ¼* **Out For A Stroll**[22] [567] 7-8-10 **62** .... RobbieFitzpatrick 2 37
(S C Williams) *bhd fr s: nvr on terms* **12/1**
1-00 **10** *2 ½* **Forest Of Love**[10] [639] 4-8-13 **65** .... DaleGibson 8 33
(M W Easterby) *a bhd* **33/1**
4000 **11** *4* **Owed**[30] [489] 4-9-4 **70** .... (t) HayleyTurner 6 28
(B Ellison) *in tch tl rdn and wknd 1/2-way* **25/1**

1m 29.96s (-0.44) **Going Correction** -0.05s/f (Stan) **11** Ran SP% **118.7**
Speed ratings (Par 103):100,99,98,97,95 94,93,86,85,82 77
CSF £48.58 CT £215.38 TOTE £6.00: £1.70, £2.30, £2.10; EX 36.10 Place 6 £28.21, Place 5 £18.14.

Owner Multi Lines Partnership **Bred** Penfold Bloodstock And Mr D B Clark **Trained** Ullingswick, H'fords

FOCUS

A moderate handicap, run at an average pace, and the form appears sound enough.

Imperial Rule(IRE) Official explanation: jockey said, regarding the running and riding, his orders were to pop gelding out and be handy from the poor draw, adding that being unable to get any cover in the back straight he allowed gelding to make ground before making his effort early in the home straight but gelding failed to stay 7f; having ridden gelding at Windsor last season he believed it ran up to its best here; trainer said gelding has a history of muscle problems but was fit to run here

Joyeaux Official explanation: jockey said filly did not face kick-back

T/Plt: £29.40 to a £1 stake. Pool: £52,474.40. 1,301.80 winning tickets. T/Qpdt: £10.10 to a £1 stake. Pool: £2,916.90. 213.20 winning tickets. JS

619 NAD AL SHEBA (L-H)

Saturday, March 25

OFFICIAL GOING: Dirt course - fast; turf course - good to firm

738a GODOLPHIN MILE (SPONSORED BY JEBEL ALI INTERNATIONAL HOTELS) (GROUP 2) (DIRT) 1m (D)

1:40 (1:40) 4-Y-O+

£348,837 (£116,279; £58,139; £29,069; £17,441; £11,627)

			RPR
1		**Utopia (JPN)**[34] 6-9-0 ....(b) YTake 1 (K Hashiguchi, Japan) *sn led on rail: a gng wl: wnt clr: easily* **13/2**	120
2	4	**Win River Win (USA)**[23] [560] 7-9-0 107.... HKaratas 4 (C Kurt, Turkey) *sn rdn: racd in rr: last 4f out: r.o wl: nrest at fin* **25/1**	112
3	*nk*	**Jack Sullivan (USA)**[44] [355] 5-9-0 115....(t) EddieAhern 8 (G A Butler) *trckd front trio: hrd rdn 3f out: kpt on wl: nrest at fin but no ch w wnr* **9/4**[1]	111
4	*hd*	**Marbush (IRE)**[23] [560] 5-9-0 113....(e) JMurtagh 6 (D Selvaratnam, UAE) *trckd ldr: ev ch 4f out: hrd rdn 2 1/2f out: kpt on: lost 2nd cl home* **7/2**[2]	111
5	2 1/4	**Shamoan (IRE)**[70] 4-9-0 ....(t) JRVelazquez 5 (E G Harty, U.S.A) *trckd ldrs: ev ch 4f out: wknd* **25/1**	107
6	3 1/2	**Court Masterpiece**[104] [6551] 6-9-0 .... MJKinane 3 (E A L Dunlop) *settled last: rdn 4f out: n.d* **9/2**[3]	100
7	2 3/4	**Island Fashion (USA)**[104] 6-8-9 ....(bt) MPedroza 9 (J Canani, U.S.A) *racd in rr: hrd rdn 4f out: nvr involved* **16/1**	89
8	5 3/4	**Blatant**[44] [355] 7-9-0 118....(t) KerrinMcEvoy 10 (I Mohammed, UAE) *mid-div: rdn 5f out: wd 4f out: nvr a factor* **11/2**	83
9	3/4	**Lundy's Liability(BRZ)**[23] [564] 6-9-0 108....(e[1]) WCMarwing 7 (M F De Kock, South Africa) *sn rdn in mid-div: hrd rdn 4f out: nvr a factor* **16/1**	81
10	*hd*	**Holiday Camp (USA)**[30] [496] 4-9-0 107....(b[1]) WayneSmith 2 (M Al Muhairi, UAE) *mid-div on rail: rdn 4f out: nvr involved* **33/1**	81

1m 35.88s **Going Correction** +0.25s/f (Slow) 10 Ran SP% **122.3**

Speed ratings: 117,113,112,112,110 106,104,98,97,97

Owner Makoto Kaneko **Bred** Northern Farm **Trained** Japan

FOCUS

Not a strong renewal of the Godolphin Mile, but the Japanese-trained Utopia ran out an impressive winner.

NOTEBOOK

Utopia(JPN), third in a Grade One over a mile on a fast dirt surface in his native Japan on his most recent start, found this a suitable opportunity on his first run outside of his homeland and won impressively, overcoming an unfavourable draw in the process.

Win River Win(USA) had over seven lengths to find with Marbush on his running in a Group Three over course and distance on his previous start, but reversed placings with that rival and took a most creditable second. He did not have the speed to pose a threat to the winner and should be suited by a return to further (he has won over 11 furlongs in Turkey).

Jack Sullivan(USA), last year's World Cup fourth, came here off the back of a successful reappearance, but he failed to produce his best. His trainer said afterwards that he had a "blip" in training the week before the race and he is better than he showed. (op 5/2)

Marbush(IRE) had today's runner-up Win River Win over seven lengths away in second when winning a course and distance Group Three on his previous start, so this has to be considered a little disappointing. (op 4/1)

Shamoan(IRE) had a little bit to find in this company and did not run badly. (op 28/1)

Court Masterpiece escaped a penalty for his success in last season's Group One Prix de la Foret, and finished second on Polytrack on his only previous start on sand, but he failed to prove himself as effective on this particular dirt surface and was well held. He will now return to Europe for a turf campaign.

Blatant has not progressed since winning on his reappearance.

739a UAE DERBY (SPONSORED BY S & M AL NABOODAH GROUP) (GROUP 2) (DIRT) 1m 1f (D)

2:15 (2:16) 3-Y-O

£697,674 (£232,558; £116,279; £58,139; £34,883; £23,255)

			RPR
1		**Discreet Cat (USA)**[16] [620] 3-8-9 110.... LDettori 9 (Saeed Bin Suroor) *racd in 4th: rdn to chal 3f out: led 2f out: easily* **2/1**[2]	114+
2	6	**Testimony (USA)**[43] [368] 3-8-9 95....(t) GKGomez 7 (Saeed Bin Suroor) *settled in rr: rdn 4f out: prog on rail 2f out: r.o: nrest at fin* **66/1**	95
3	*nk*	**Flamme De Passion (JPN)**[34] 3-8-9 .... YTake 1 (Katsuhiko Sumii, Japan) *settled in rr on rail: gng wl 4f out: prog: trckd ldrs 3f out: n.m.r: no ch w wnr* **16/1**	95
4	3/4	**Invasor (ARG)**[132] 4-9-4 .... RHills 2 (K McLaughlin, U.S.A) *mid-div on rail: rdn 5f out: kpt on wl in st: nrst fin* **16/1**	83
5	3 3/4	**Dominguin (PER)**[287] 4-9-4 ....(t) JRVelazquez 5 (D Zanelli, U.S.A) *trckd ldrs: rdn to cl 3 1/2f out: one pce* **40/1**	76
6	1 1/2	**Simpatico Bribon (CHI)**[23] [561] 4-9-4 120....(t) JMurtagh 12 (I Jory, Saudi Arabia) *prom early: dropped to mid-div after 1f: rdn 4f out: nvr a factor* **13/8**[1]	73
7	1 3/4	**Gaburin (AUS)**[90] 4-9-4 .... OPeslier 3 (Hideyuki Mori, Japan) *sn led: ev ch 3f out: nt qckn* **33/1**	70
8	3 1/4	**Where's That Tiger (USA)**[23] [561] 3-8-9 108.... WCMarwing 10 (M F De Kock, South Africa) *settled in rr: n.d* **20/1**	74
9	1 1/2	**My Royal Captain (NZ)**[43] [368] 4-9-4 105.... EddieAhern 6 (L Laxon, Singapore) *led main gp: rdn 4f out: wknd* **40/1**	61
10	3 3/4	**Gold For Sale (ARG)**[43] [368] 4-9-4 110....(t) MJKinane 4 (I Jory, Saudi Arabia) *racd in last early: sn rdn: nvr involved* **9/2**[3]	54
11	3 1/2	**Well Armed (USA)**[43] [368] 3-8-9 100.... RyanMoore 11 (C E Brittain) *settled in rr: nvr involved* **33/1**	57
12	10	**Jackson (BRZ)**[23] [561] 4-9-4 101....(b) MAlmeida 13 (A Cintra, Brazil) *sn rdn along: n.d* **66/1**	28
13	5 3/4	**Unification (CAN)**[23] [561] 3-8-9 102....(t) KerrinMcEvoy 8 (I Mohammed, UAE) *mid-div: rdn 4f out: n.d* **66/1**	27

1m 48.59s **Going Correction** +0.25s/f (Slow)

WFA 3 from 4yo 19lb 13 Ran SP% **121.4**

Speed ratings: 119,113,113,112,109 108,106,103,102,98 95,86,81

Owner Godolphin **Bred** E Paul Robsham **Trained** Newmarket, Suffolk

FOCUS

This promised to be a fascinating renewal of the UAE Derby, but the form is seriously devalued by the failure of the highly talented Ian Jory pair Simpatico Bribon and Gold For Sale to run their races, besides which the third, fourth and fifth are all unknown quantities whose success has come in Japan and South America. Nevertheless, the highly-promising Discreet Cat made it three from three with another imoressive success, and he again recorded a very good time.

NOTEBOOK

Discreet Cat(USA), successful in a minor race over a mile on his debut for Godolphin, followed up with similar ease in what was supposed to be a much tougher test. However, with the highly-promising Simpatico Bribon and UAE 2000 Guineas winner Gold For Sale both well below their best, his task was made much easier. He settled better this time off what was a noticeably decent pace and never looked in any danger. He will now continue his career in the US and his connections have every reason to hope he will develop into a top-class performer. The Kentucky Derby is a possibility, but a prep run has already been ruled out and it would take a remarkable performance to win arguably the toughest Classic in the calendar off a preparation that has hardly seen him come off the bridle against vastly inferior opposition. Another option is to wait for the Preakness Stakes, but wherever he goes it will be fascinating to watch his progress. (tchd 15/8)

Testimony(USA), second to Well Armed on his debut for Godolphin before running down the field from a poor draw in the UAE 2000 Guineas, improved for the step up in trip and seemed to run his best race yet behind his impressive stablemate. His connections will now have the option of bringing him to Europe or continuing his career in the US.

Flamme De Passion(JPN), a Listed winner over a mile on the dirt in his native Japan on his most recent start, would have found this tougher but took advantage of the Jory pair running below form to grab a place. This was a good effort from his inside draw.

Invasor(ARG), a multiple winner and successful in Group One company over a mile and a half in Uruguay, had a moderate draw and was unsurprisingly doing his best work late on. He will now continue his career in the US. (op 20/1)

Dominguin(PER), a Group Three winner in Peru, ran creditably on his debut in Dubai.

Simpatico Bribon(CHI), who was apparently being considered for the Dubai World Cup after running out a very impressive winner of a minor race over course and distance on his debut in Dubai, ran well below form. There was no obvious excuse, but he is much better than this and can be given another chance to fulfil his potential.

Gold For Sale(ARG), the UAE 2000 Guineas winner on his debut in Dubai, like his stablemate Simpatico Bribon ran well below form. His inside draw would not have been ideal, but he should still have fared better.

Well Armed(USA) beat Testimony into second when winning on his debut in Dubai, but he has since run down the field in the UAE 2000 Guineas and was again disappointing.

740a DUBAI GOLDEN SHAHEEN (SPONSORED BY GULF NEWS) (GROUP 1) (DIRT) 6f (D)

2:55 (2:55) 3-Y-O+

£697,674 (£232,558; £116,279; £58,139; £34,883; £23,255)

			RPR
1		**Proud Tower Too (USA)**[34] 4-9-0 ....(bt) DCohen 2 (S Gonzalez, U.S.A) *a.p: rdn 2f out: a holding runner-up: comf* **5/1**[2]	117
2	1 1/4	**Thor's Echo (USA)**[34] 4-9-0 ....(bt) CNakatani 12 (Doug O'Neill, U.S.A) *trckd ldr: rdn to chal 2f out: kpt on wl* **33/1**	113
3	3/4	**Jet West (USA)**[35] 5-9-0 ....(t) GKGomez 10 (Ted H West, U.S.A) *racd alone centre: hrd rdn 2f out: 8th 1f out: fin v fast: nrest at fin* **10/1**	111
4	1/2	**Captain Squire (USA)**[56] 7-9-0 116....(t) VEspinoza 13 (Jeff Mullins, U.S.A) *chsd ldrs for 4f: nvr able to chal* **9/1**	109
5	1 1/4	**Gaff (USA)**[77] 4-9-0 ....(t) SBridgmohan 9 (S Asmussen, U.S.A) *trckd ldrs: ev ch 2f out: kpt on one pce* **7/1**[3]	106
6	1	**Agnes Jedi (JPN)**[55] 4-9-0 ....(b) HYoshihara 8 (Hideyuki Mori, Japan) *in rr far side: rdn 3f out: r.o fnl f: nrest at fin* **16/1**	103
7	*shd*	**Tropical Star (IRE)**[23] [563] 6-9-0 111....(vt) RoystonFfrench 4 (A Al Raihe, UAE) *trckd ldng gp: hrd rdn 3f out: kpt on one pce* **8/1**	102
8	7 3/4	**Perfectly Ready (AUS)**[35] 4-8-10 ....(b) TedDurcan 1 (Mick Price, Australia) *sn rdn along: trckd ldrs for 2f: nt qckn* **20/1**	75
9	3/4	**Azul Da Guanabara (BRZ)**[23] [563] 4-8-10 105....(t) ADomingos 15 (Luis Singnoretti, Brazil) *nvr involved: racd nr side* **33/1**	73
10	3 1/4	**Thajja (IRE)**[23] [560] 5-9-0 105....(v) RHills 11 (Doug Watson, UAE) *racd nr side: n.d* **50/1**	67
11	5	**Heart Alone (BRZ)**[58] [206] 5-9-0 115.... KerrinMcEvoy 5 (I Mohammed, UAE) *nvr involved* **5/2**[1]	52
12	1/2	**The Lord (ARG)**[105] 6-9-0 105....(t) RyanMoore 14 (S Seemar, UAE) *racd nr side: nvr involved* **33/1**	50
13	3/4	**Howick Falls (USA)**[23] [563] 5-9-0 104....(v) TPO'Shea 7 (E Charpy, UAE) *slowly away: n.d* **33/1**	48
14	6 3/4	**Conroy (USA)**[23] [563] 8-9-0 104....(e[1]) LDettori 6 (A Selvaratnam, UAE) *trckd ldrs for 2f: rdn 4f out: one pce* **33/1**	28
15	1 3/4	**Raging Creek (USA)**[8] 7-9-0 100....(t) JMurtagh 3 (D Selvaratnam, UAE) *prom far side tl 3f out: wknd* **66/1**	23

69.86 secs **Going Correction** +0.25s/f (Slow) 15 Ran SP% **116.7**

Speed ratings: 114,112,111,110,109 107,107,97,96,91 85,84,83,74,72

Owner Tricar Stables Inc **Bred** Tricar Stables Inc **Trained** USA

FOCUS

A pretty ordinary sprint by Grade One standards and easy pickings for the Americans whose five runners were the first five home. The field were spread out all over the track and those towards the far side looked to be at an advantage.

NOTEBOOK

Proud Tower Too(USA), a Grade One winner in the US, had a reasonable draw given the way the race developed and ran out a decisive winner. It would be no surprise to see his campaign geared towards a tilt at the Breeders' Cup Sprint.

Thor's Echo(USA) had a bit to find on US form but ran a huge race to take second. He is likely to find things harder back in his homeland.

Jet West(USA), Graded-placed in the US, ran a fine race switched to Dubai given he raced more towards the centre of the track than some of his main rivals. He finished as well as any.

Captain Squire(USA), a Grade One winner in the States since his third in this race back in 2003, ran a creditable enough race in fourth behind his compatriots.

Gaff(USA) has progressed well since returning to the US after a spell in Ireland with Dermot Weld, and this was a respectable performance.

Tropical Star(IRE), last year's runner-up, has been in good form with two wins at this year's Carnival, but he was not at his best this time and posed no threat to the Americans.
Heart Alone(BRZ), an ex-Brazilian who impressed in a course and distance Group Three on his debut in Dubai, has since switched stables, but his new yard has endured a Carnival to forget and he was beaten a long way. (op 11/4)

741a DUBAI SHEEMA CLASSIC (SPONSORED BY NAKHEEL) (GROUP 1) (TURF) 1m 4f (T)

3:50 (3:52) 4-Y-0+

£1,744,186 (£581,395; £290,697; £145,348; £87,209; £58,139)

			RPR
1		**Heart's Cry (JPN)**[90] 5-8-11 .... C-PLemaire 13 (K Hashiguchi, Japan) *wd: sn led: chal 2 1/2f out: qckd away: comf* **11/4**[2]	125+
2	4 1/4	**Collier Hill**[23] [562] 8-8-11 116........ DeanMcKeown 3 (G A Swinbank) *trckd front pair: rdn to chal 3f out: kpt on wl: no ch w wnr* **22/1**	117
3	1 1/4	**Falstaff (IRE)**[23] [562] 4-8-11 113........(b) JMurtagh 2 (M F De Kock, South Africa) *settled in mid-div: gng wl 2 1/2f out: r.o but no ch w first two* **25/1**	117
4	3 1/2	**Ouija Board**[104] [6549] 5-8-7 .... KFallon 8 (E A L Dunlop) *mid-div: n.m.r 4f out: wd 3f out: r.o: nvr nrr* **9/4**[1]	106+
5	5 3/4	**Alexander Goldrun (IRE)**[104] [6552] 5-8-7 116........ KJManning 7 (J S Bolger, Ire) *settled rr: last 4f out: nvr involved: nrst fin* **10/1**	97+
6	2 1/4	**Alayan (IRE)**[23] [562] 4-8-11 113........ MJKinane 12 (John M Oxx, Ire) *trckd ldrs tl 4f out: wknd* **20/1**	100
7	1/2	**Layman (USA)**[23] [564] 4-8-11 111........(t) KerrinMcEvoy 1 (I Mohammed, UAE) *nt far away: rdn 3f out: no rspnse* **50/1**	99
8	3/4	**Norse Dancer (IRE)**[104] [6549] 6-8-11 .... JohnEgan 10 (D R C Elsworth) *racd rr: 2nd last 3f out: hrd rdn: n.d* **25/1**	96
9	3 3/4	**Mustanfar (USA)**[28] 5-8-11 ....(v) RHills 5 (K McLaughlin, U.S.A) *mid-div: rdn 3f out: kpt on one pce* **50/1**	90
10	1/2	**Punch Punch (BRZ)**[16] [624] 5-8-11 110........(v) MAlmeida 6 (C Morgado, Brazil) *s.i.s: racd in last: v wd 4f out: n.d after* **40/1**	89
11	2 3/4	**Oracle West (SAF)**[23] [562] 5-8-11 116........ KShea 4 (M F De Kock, South Africa) *mid-div: dropped to rr 4f out whn n.m.r: nt rcvr* **12/1**	85
12	2 1/2	**Relaxed Gesture (IRE)**[153] [6059] 5-8-11 ....(t) CNakatani 14 (Christophe Clement, U.S.A) *nt far off pce: disp 4f out: ev ch: nt qckn* **7/1**[3]	81
13	3 1/4	**Greys Inn (USA)**[51] [280] 6-8-11 115........ WCMarwing 9 (M F De Kock, South Africa) *settled rr: forced wd 3f out: n.d* **15/2**	77
14	dist	**Shanty Star (IRE)**[16] [622] 6-8-11 110........ GAvranche 11 (R Bouresly, Kuwait) *s.i.s: mid-div early: n.d* **66/1**	—

2m 31.89s **Going Correction** +0.55s/f (Yiel)
WFA 4 from 5yo+ 2lb 14 Ran SP% **123.1**
Speed ratings: 116,113,112,110,106 104,104,103,101,101 99,97,95,—

Owner Shadai Race Horse Co Ltd **Bred** Shadai Farm **Trained** Japan
■ A double for Japanese trainer Kojiro Hashiguchi, following the earlier success of Utopia in the Godolphin Mile.

FOCUS
This looked like a reasonable renewal of the Sheema Classic beforehand, but Heart's Cry was allowed to dictate at a steady gallop and took full advantage in a race nothing could get into from off the pace.

NOTEBOOK
Heart's Cry(JPN), second to Alkaased (Ouija Board fifth) in the Japan Cup before beating the previously undefeated and high-class Deep Impact in a Grade One at Nakayama, was left alone up front and, after dictating at just a steady pace, pulled well clear in the straight. He may now be aimed at the King George at Ascot in July. (tchd 3/1)
Collier Hill, successful in a Group Two in Germany and winner of the Irish St Leger since his third in this race last year, was always well placed given the way the race was run and stepped up on the form he showed over course and distance on his reappearance to take a most creditable second. He would appear to be every bit as good as he was and should have another good year.
Falstaff(IRE) was well enough positioned, given the steady pace, and he ran a huge race to take third. He is evidently still improving, but looks a little flattered all the same.
Ouija Board, last seen winning the Hong Kong Vase 104 days previously, had previously finished about two lengths behind Heart's Cry when fifth in the Japan Cup. Held up here, while the winner dictated just a steady pace before quickening away in the straight, she could never pose a threat, but this is best forgotten. Connections reckon she hardly had a race and so are tempted to target major spring targets in Hong Kong and Singapore before bringing her back for an autumn campaign in Europe and then the Breeders' Cup.
Alexander Goldrun(IRE), eighth in the Hong Kong Cup on her last start 104 days previously, had never previously tried a mile and a half and was unable to show her best off the steady pace.
Alayan(IRE) finished in front of Falstaff in a course and distance Group Three on his previous start, but could not confirm the form in this muddling contest. He can show himself better than this when he returns to Europe.
Norse Dancer(IRE), still in search of that elusive Group One, had little chance getting involved given how far off the steady pace he was in the early stages. He is much better than this.

742a DUBAI DUTY FREE (SPONSORED BY DUBAI DUTY FREE) (GROUP 1) (TURF) 1m 194y(T)

4:30 (4:31) 4-Y-0+

£1,744,186 (£581,395; £290,697; £145,348; £87,209; £58,139)

			RPR
1		**David Junior (USA)**[161] [5902] 4-9-0 .... JamieSpencer 1 (B J Meehan) *mid-div: prog 3f out: stl on bridle 1 1/2f out: rdn to ld: easily* **9/2**[1]	127+
2	3 1/2	**The Tin Man (USA)**[62] 8-9-0 .... VEspinoza 2 (Richard E Mandella, U.S.A) *sn led: stl gng wl 1 1/2f out: kpt on wl but no ch w wnr* **14/1**	119
3	1 1/4	**Seihali (IRE)**[16] [621] 7-9-0 115........ JMurtagh 5 (D Selvaratnam, UAE) *mid-div: gng wl 4f out: n.m.r 2 1/2f out: swtchd to trck wnr: kpt on: nrest at fin* **25/1**	117
4	1 3/4	**Host (CHI)**[42] 6-9-0 .... JRVelazquez 7 (T Pletcher, U.S.A) *settled in rr on rail: hrd rdn 3 1/2f out: n.d* **20/1**	113
5	nk	**Bullish Luck (USA)**[27] 7-9-0 ....(b) CSoumillon 15 (A S Cruz, Hong Kong) *settled in rr: prog mid-div on rail 3f out: n.m.r 2 1/2f out: swtchd rdr: r.o: nrst fin* **12/1**	112
6	nk	**Perfect Promise (SAF)**[21] 7-8-9 .... KerrinMcEvoy 8 (Lee Freedman, Australia) *mid-div: nvr nr to chal* **22/1**	107
7	nk	**Fields Of Omagh (AUS)**[21] 9-9-0 ....(p) StevenKing 3 (D Hayes, Australia) *trckd eventual runner-up: ev ch 2 1/2f out: one pce* **16/1**	111
8	1 1/2	**Touch Of Land (FR)**[23] [564] 6-9-0 115........ C-PLemaire 10 (H-A Pantall, France) *mid-div: swtchd rail 3f out: n.m.r 2 1/2f out: one pce once clr* **6/1**[2]	108
9	2 1/4	**Russian Pearl (NZ)**[27] 6-9-0 ....(t) FCoetzee 16 (A S Cruz, Hong Kong) *mid-div: nvr nr to chal* **18/1**	104
10	3/4	**Tyson (SAF)**[23] [564] 6-9-0 113........ MJKinane 14 (M F De Kock, South Africa) *settled last: nvr involved* **22/1**	102
11	1/2	**Whilly (IRE)**[62] 5-9-0 110........(t) FFMartinez 11 (Doug O'Neill, U.S.A) *trckd ldrs wd: ev ch whn rdn 3f out: one pce* **20/1**	101
12	3/4	**Hat Trick (JPN)**[27] 5-9-0 .... OPeslier 13 (Katsuhiko Sumii, Japan) *s.i.s: settled in rr: rdn 3f out: n.d* **6/1**[2]	100
13	2 3/4	**Linngari (IRE)**[30] [496] 4-9-0 115........ KShea 4 (H J Brown, South Africa) *trckd ldng gp: rdn 3f out: one pce* **10/1**[3]	94
14	8 1/2	**Valixir (IRE)**[23] [564] 5-9-0 122........ LDettori 12 (Saeed Bin Suroor) *mid-div wd: n.d* **6/1**[2]	77
15	14	**Asakusa Den'En**[104] [6551] 7-9-0 ....(p) YTake 9 (Michifumi Kono, Japan) *trckd ldr tl 4f out: wknd qckly* **12/1**	49

1m 49.65s **Going Correction** +0.55s/f (Yiel) 15 Ran SP% **125.4**
Speed ratings: 117,113,112,111,110 110,110,109,107,106 105,105,102,95,82

Owner Roldvale Ltd & Gold Group International **Bred** A I Appleton **Trained** Manton, Wilts
■ The biggest prize ever won by a British-trained horse, and Brian Meehan's first runner from his new base at Manton.

FOCUS
By no means a strong renewal of the Dubai Duty Free Stakes. David Junior was very impressive, but he did not need to better last year's Champion Stakes form.

NOTEBOOK
David Junior(USA) ◆, last seen winning the Champion Stakes at Newmarket in October, returned to action as good as ever and won impressively. Always travelling strongly, he showed a smart change of pace when asked for his effort in the straight and had this won well before the line. He is likely to face tougher opposition when he returns to Europe, but is sure to be a leading contender in many of the top races from a mile to ten furlongs again. He will now be aimed at the Prince Of Wales's Stakes at Royal Ascot, but in the longer term his main aim is said to be the Breeders' Cup Classic at Churchill Downs. (old market 11/2)
The Tin Man(USA), the winner of his last two starts in the US, including in a Grade Two on his most recent start when he had Milk It Mick a length away in second, ran well behind the comfortable winner on his return to the highest level. He has returned form an absence pretty much as good as ever. (old market 16/1)
Seihali(IRE), tenth in this race last year, came into this off the back of a success off a mark of a 111 in a mile handicap and acquitted himself well. He would have been even closer with a clearer run and would appear to still be improving. (old market 25/1)
Host(CHI), seventh in last year's Breeders' Cup Mile, had conditions to suit and took a respectable fourth. (old market 20/1)
Bullish Luck(USA), a high-class miler to ten-furlong performer in Hong Kong, did not get a clear run and could not produce his best on his first start in Dubai. (old market 14/1)
Perfect Promise(SAF), a Group One winner in Australia, did not run badly on his first start in Dubai. (old market 25/1)
Touch Of Land(FR) was an impressive winner of a course and distance Group Two on his reappearance, but was disappointing on this return to Group One company and remains winless at the highest level. (old market 7/1, new market op 7/1)
Hat Trick(JPN), last year's Hong Kong Mile winner, never featured after starting slowly and was disappointing. (old market 7/1)
Linngari(IRE) has progressed well since switching to Dubai, but ran well below the form he showed when winning a Group Three and a Group Two earlier at the Carnival. (old market 12/1)
Valixir(IRE) put in a mulish display when only seventh in a course and distance Group Two behind Touch Of Land on his reappearance and fared even worse this time. He has plenty to prove now, but may be suited by a return to racing in Europe. (old market 7/1)

743a DUBAI WORLD CUP (SPONSORED BY EMIRATES AIRLINE) (GROUP 1) (DIRT) 1m 2f (D)

5:20 (5:20) 4-Y-0+

£2,093,023 (£697,674; £348,837; £174,418; £104,651; £69,767)

			RPR
1		**Electrocutionist (USA)**[23] [565] 5-9-0 121........ LDettori 1 (Saeed Bin Suroor) *rdn early strides: racd mid-div: rdn 4f out: swtchd wd: rdn 1 1/2f out: r.o wl* **5/4**[1]	126
2	4½	**Wilko (USA)**[21] 4-9-0 .... GKGomez 9 (J Noseda) *trckd ldrs: rdn 3 1/2f out: r.o wl: led briefly 1f out: wknd wl ins fnl f: fin 3rd, 1½l & 3l: plcd 2nd* **33/1**	118
3	2 3/4	**Magna Graduate (USA)**[49] 4-9-0 ....(b) JRVelazquez 8 (T Pletcher, U.S.A) *disp on rail: led 3 1/2f out: hdd 2f out: one pce: plcd 3rd* **12/1**	113
4	2 3/4	**Kane Hekili (JPN)**[34] 4-9-0 .... YTake 3 (Katsuhiko Sumii, Japan) *trckd ldrs on rail: gng v wl 3f out: rdn 2f out: nt qckn: fin 5th, plcd 4th* **7/2**[2]	108
5	1 1/2	**Chiquitin (ARG)**[23] [565] 6-9-0 110........(t) MJKinane 5 (I Jory, Saudi Arabia) *sn outpcd: n.d: fin 6th, plcd 5th* **50/1**	105
6	3 1/2	**Maraahel (IRE)**[104] [6552] 5-9-0 115........(v) RHills 6 (Sir Michael Stoute) *mid-div: wd: nvr involved: fin 7th, plcd 6th* **9/1**	99
7	nk	**Star King Man (USA)**[34] 7-9-0 .... OPeslier 10 (Hideyuki Mori, Japan) *racd in rr: n.d: fin 8th, plcd 7th* **40/1**	99
8	1 3/4	**Super Frolic (USA)**[49] 6-9-0 ....(t) CNakatani 11 (V Cerin, U.S.A) *disp centre: rdn 3 1/2f out: wknd: fin 9th, plcd 8th* **16/1**	95
9	nk	**Choctaw Nation (USA)**[43] 6-9-0 113........(vt) VEspinoza 4 (Jeff Mullins, U.S.A) *dropped to rr early: nvr involved: fin 10th, plcd 9th* **16/1**	95
10	4 3/4	**Shakis (IRE)**[16] [622] 6-9-0 113........(vt) WSupple 2 (Doug Watson, UAE) *a in rr: fin 11th, plcd 10th* **66/1**	86
D		**Brass Hat (USA)**[49] 5-9-0 ....(bt) WillieMartinez 7 (W Bradley, U.S.A) *mid-div wd: rdn to chal 2 1/2f out: ev ch 2f out: r.o: led 100yds out: hdd cl home: fin 2nd, 1½l: disq* **11/2**[3]	123

2m 1.32s **Going Correction** +0.25s/f (Slow) 11 Ran SP% **120.3**
Speed ratings: 115,111,109,107,105 103,102,101,101,97 113

Owner Godolphin **Bred** Compagnia Generale **Trained** Newmarket, Suffolk
■ A fifth winner of the Dubai World Cup for Godolphin, and a third for Frankie Dettori.

FOCUS
As is often the case with the Dubai World Cup, a race that lacked real strength in depth and one would expect a better turnout for the 'world's richest race'. However, this was still a tremendous effort from Electrocutionist to overcome his inside stall and reel in the progressive American-trained performer Brass Hat, who was subsequently disq. for failing a drugs test. He has been rated on RPRs as bettering last year's International Stakes success by 2lb.

NOTEBOOK

Electrocutionist(USA), an impressive winner of a trial over course and distance on his Godolphin and dirt debut, ran right up to, and possibly even bettered, the pick of his turf form to overcome the inside stall. The plan was to avoid any possible trouble from his low draw by racing handy from the start but, taking time to get into his stride, he was soon stuck in behind the leaders and being faced with their kickback. However, Frankie Dettori managed to switch him towards the outside and, benefitting from the long straight, he battled on most gamely when asked to go and reel in Brass Hat. He took a little while to get into full stride and pass Brass Hat, but he stays well and was going away at the finish. He may lack the basic speed of a typical high-class middle-distance dirt horse, but he can run to a very high level indeed and will deserve his chance in the Breeders' Cup Classic later in the year. In the meantime his first target could be the Prince Of Wales's Stakes, where he may clash with Dubai Duty Free winner David Junior.

Wilko(USA) failed to win for Craig Dollase after transferring from Jeremy Noseda following his success in the 2004 Breeders' Cup Juvenile but, back with his original trainer, he ran a fine race in defeat. He will stay in the care of Noseda for the time being and return to Newmarket. Connections have not ruled out targeting a big prize in Europe, but think he is a better horse on dirt and nominated either the Metropolitan at Belmont Park at the end of May, or the Stephen Foster at Churchill Downs in mid-June as his most likely next target.

Magna Graduate(USA), beaten over nine lengths into fourth behind Brass Hat in the Donn Handicap over nine furlongs at Gulfstream Park on his most recent start, got closer to that rival this time and emerges with plenty of credit.

Kane Hekili(JPN), who had subsequent Godolphin Mile winner Utopia behind when winning both the Japan Cup Dirt over an extended ten furlongs and the Grade One February Stakes over a mile on his most recent start, failed to produce his best and was disappointing.

Chiquitin(ARG) was beaten further by Electrocutionist than he was in a trial for this over course and distance on his previous start, but still bettered last year's performance, when he could finish only eleventh of 12.

Maraahel(IRE), beaten just a neck and a head by today's winner in the International Stakes at York last season, failed to produce his best on his first start on dirt. He can do better back on turf in Europe.

Brass Hat(USA), a progressive, high-class dirt performer in the US who won the Grade One Donn Handicap at Gulfstream Park over nine furlongs on his most recent start, ran a terrific race on his first start outside of the States and only gave way late on to the strong-staying winner. There could well be more to come and it would be no surprise to see him line up in the Breeders' Cup Classic towards the end of the season, when he could face a re-match with Electrocutionist.

BRIGHTON (L-H)

Sunday, March 26

744 Meeting Abandoned - Fog

750 - 752a (Foreign Racing) - See Raceform Interactive

CURRAGH (R-H)

Sunday, March 26

OFFICIAL GOING: Round course - soft to heavy; straight course - heavy

753a PARK EXPRESS EUROPEAN BREEDERS FUND STKS (GROUP 3) (F&M) — 1m

3:30 (3:32) 3-Y-0+ **£44,896** (£13,172; £6,275; £2,137)

RPR

1 — **Danehill Music (IRE)**[140] 6271 3-8-7 93 ... WMLordan 6 — 99
(David Wachman, Ire) *hld up: 8th 1/2-way: 7th and prog 3f out: chal and led under 1f out: styd on wl* **10/1**[3]

2 — 2 — **Utterly Heaven (IRE)**[197] 5135 4-9-9 106 ... PJSmullen 9 — 99
(D K Weld, Ire) *trckd ldrs: 4th 1/2-way: 5th 3f out: rdn under 2f out: mod 3rd ins fnl f: kpt on* **6/1**[2]

3 — nk — **Gemini Gold (IRE)**[154] 6044 3-8-7 ... NGMcCullagh 7 — 94
(M J Grassick, Ire) *disp ld: led bef 1/2-way: hdd over 3f out: regained ld 2f out: strly pressed 1 1/2f out: hdd under 1f out: no ex cl home* **20/1**

4 — 1 1/2 — **Chenchikova (IRE)**[192] 5258 3-8-7 ... KFallon 1 — 91
(A P O'Brien, Ire) *trckd ldrs: cl 5th 1/2-way: 3rd 3f out: cl 2nd and chal over 1f out: sn no ex* **11/10**[1]

5 — 2 1/2 — **Yaria (IRE)**[203] 4978 4-9-9 96 ... DPMcDonogh 8 — 90
(Kevin Prendergast, Ire) *hld up in tch: 6th after 1/2-way: 4th 2f out: sn rdn and no imp* **12/1**

6 — 9 — **Shersha (IRE)**[30] 510 7-9-9 ... WSupple 10 — 72
(Kevin F O'Donnell, Ire) *hld up towards rr: kpt on same pce fr over 2f out* **25/1**

7 — 6 — **Pout (IRE)**[81] 4-9-9 92 ... DMGrant 3 — 60
(John Joseph Murphy, Ire) *hld up in tch: no imp fr 3f out* **33/1**

8 — 5 — **Saintly Rachel (IRE)**[38] 437 8-9-9 97 ... JamieSpencer 5 — 50
(C F Swan, Ire) *trckd ldrs: impr into 2nd 1/2-way: led over 3f out: hdd 2f out: sn wknd: eased ins fnl f* **14/1**

9 — 2 — **Bahia Breeze**[270] 3032 4-9-9 ... TQuinn 4 — 46
(Rae Guest) *disp ld early: 3rd after 1/2-way: 4th and rdn 3f out: sn wknd: eased under 2f out* **6/1**[2]

10 — 10 — **Sandie (IRE)**[197] 5139 3-8-7 103 ... DJMoran 2 — 22
(J S Bolger, Ire) *hld up in tch: 7th 1/2-way: rdn and wknd 3f out* **6/1**[2]

2m 5.60s **Going Correction** +2.50s/f (Heavy)
WFA 3 from 4yo+ 17lb — **10** Ran SP% **125.5**
Speed ratings: 82,80,79,78,75 66,60,55,53,43
CSF £72.50 TOTE £9.90: £2.00, £2.10, £3.80; DF 70.70.
Owner Jack Of Trumps Racing Club **Bred** Patrick J Connolly **Trained** Goolds Cross, Co Tipperary

NOTEBOOK

Danehill Music(IRE) was successful in nurseries last season off 80 & 85 before running second to Wovoka in a Listed race at Leopardstown. She handled the ground well and got on top inside the last furlong.

Utterly Heaven(IRE) was fit but still needed to be nursed home in the bad ground. Fourth in last season's Irish 1000 Guineas, she has never reproduced that form. (op 5/1)

Gemini Gold(IRE), another whose best form is on soft ground, was in the front rank throughout before weakening inside the last. The German 1000 was mooted as an option for her. (op 16/1)

Chenchikova(IRE) was certainly fit enough and flattered over a furlong out, but her effort petered out in the ground. She has to be given another chance but does not look a Classic filly. (op 5/4 tchd 6/4)

Yaria(IRE)was not able to make any headway over the last furlong and a half.

Shersha(IRE) stayed on at the one pace.

Bahia Breeze disputed and went with the pace but was flying distress signals two and a half furlongs out and was eased right down in the last furlong.

755a UNICORN HOMES MADRID H'CAP — 7f

5:00 (5:00) 3-Y-0 **£15,713** (£4,610; £2,196; £748) **Stalls** Far side

RPR

1 — **Spring Snowdrop (IRE)**[155] 6036 3-8-9 80 ... (b[1]) PJSmullen 9 — 87
(D K Weld, Ire) *led: hdd after 2f: rdn to dispute ld 1 1/2f out: slt advantage 150 yds out: kpt on u.p: all out* **14/1**

2 — shd — **Misskinta (IRE)**[153] 6084 3-8-4 75 ... NGMcCullagh 3 — 82
(M J Grassick, Ire) *trckd ldrs: prog under 2f out: 4th over 1f out: 2nd and chal wl ins fnl f: jst failed* **8/1**

3 — 5 — **Chiado (IRE)**[175] 5643 3-9-10 95 ... DPMcDonogh 11 — 90
(Kevin Prendergast, Ire) *trckd ldrs: brought to stand's rail under 2f out: 5th 1 1/2f out: kpt on u.p* **12/1**

4 — 1/2 — **Rockie**[162] 5912 3-8-9 80 ... WSupple 8 — 74
(T Hogan, Ire) *hld up towards rr: smooth hdwy over 2f out: disp ld 1 1/2f out: rdn and hdd 150 yds out: no ex* **33/1**

5 — 1 1/2 — **Moone Cross (IRE)**[161] 5926 3-8-9 80 ... TPO'Shea 1 — 70
(Mrs John Harrington, Ire) *hld up: kpt on same pce fr over 2f out* **10/1**

6 — 3 — **Taqseem (IRE)**[140] 6269 3-9-5 95 ... PBBeggy[(5)] 2 — 78
(Kevin Prendergast, Ire) *trckd ldrs on far side: 4th and effrt 2f out: sn no ex* **10/1**

7 — 5 — **Alocin (IRE)**[140] 6269 3-8-6 77 ... CatherineGannon 5 — 48
(John A Quinn, Ire) *led after 2f: hdd 1 1/2f out: sn no ex* **5/1**[2]

8 — 11 — **Set Fire (IRE)**[161] 5927 3-8-10 84 ... (p) RPCleary[(3)] 7 — 28
(M Halford, Ire) *hld up in tch: no imp fr 2f out* **14/1**

9 — 13 — **Monthly Medal**[140] 6269 3-9-1 86 ... FMBerry 10 — —
(Charles O'Brien, Ire) *in tch: 5th and drvn along over 2f out: sn no ex* **11/2**[3]

10 — 1 1/2 — **Celtic Warrior (IRE)**[140] 6269 3-9-2 87 ... MJKinane 6 — —
(Liam Roche, Ire) *prom: 5th appr 1/2-way: sn rdn: wknd over 2f out: eased fnl f* **9/2**[1]

11 — 1 1/2 — **Basra (IRE)**[161] 5927 3-8-12 88 ... (t) DJMoran[(5)] 4 — —
(J S Bolger, Ire) *nvr a factor: wknd 2f out: eased ins fnl f* **12/1**

12 — dist — **Salute Him (IRE)**[156] 6005 3-9-2 87 ... TQuinn 12 — —
(M R Channon) *chsd ldrs early: wknd over 3f out: virtually p.u over 1f out* **5/1**[2]

1m 46.5s **Going Correction** +2.70s/f (Heavy) — **12** Ran SP% **127.9**
Speed ratings: 99,98,93,92,90 87,81,69,54,52 50,—
CSF £131.14 CT £1440.04 TOTE £17.70: £7.00, £2.40, £5.00; DF 108.30.
Owner Dr R Lambe **Bred** Sean M Collins **Trained** The Curragh, Co Kildare

NOTEBOOK

Celtic Warrior(IRE) Official explanation: vet said colt was blowing hard post race

Salute Him(IRE) ran up with the pace till halfway but then dropped right away and finished completely tailed off, being almost pulled up. (op 9/2)

754 - 756a (Foreign Racing) - See Raceform Interactive

TURFWAY PARK

Saturday, March 25

OFFICIAL GOING: Fast

757a LANE'S END STKS (GRADE 2) (POLYTRACK) — 1m 1f

10:45 (10:47) 3-Y-0

£174,419 (£58,140; £29,070; £14,535; £8,721; £5,814)

RPR

1 — **With A City (USA)** 3-8-9 ... (b) BBlanc 2 — 110
(Michael J Maker, U.S.A) **488/10**

2 — 1 1/4 — **Seaside Retreat (USA)**[35] 3-8-9 ... PHusbands 7 — 107
(M Casse, Canada) **112/10**

3 — 1 1/2 — **Malameeze (USA)** 3-8-9 ... (b) JohnMcKee 1 — 104
(B Barnett, U.S.A) **152/10**

4 — 3 — **More Than Regal (USA)** 3-8-9 ... (b) DFlores 10 — 99
(S Asmussen, U.S.A) **103/10**

5 — hd — **Superfly (USA)**[147] 6163 3-8-9 ... JRose 3 — 98
(N Zito, U.S.A) **42/10**[2]

6 — 2 3/4 — **Hemingway's Key (USA)**[21] 3-8-9 ... (b) EPrado 8 — 93
(N Zito, U.S.A) **52/10**[3]

7 — 1/2 — **Pair Of Kings (USA)** 3-8-9 ... (b) RBracho 11 — 92
(W Bradley, U.S.A) **113/10**

8 — 2 1/4 — **Sharp Attack (USA)**[28] 3-8-9 ... (b) JGarcia 6 — 88
(D Wayne Lukas, U.S.A) **26/1**

9 — 8 3/4 — **Tahoe Warrior (USA)**[238] 3-8-9 ... CDeCarlo 5 — 71
(T Pletcher, U.S.A) **62/10**

10 — nk — **Laity (USA)**[168] 5783 3-8-9 ... (b) CLanerie 9 — 71
(F Brothers, U.S.A) **72/10**

11 — 2 3/4 — **Silent Times (IRE)**[197] 5088 3-8-9 ... RAlbarado 12 — 65
(E J O'Neill) *s.i.s on outside, gradually made ground to disp 6th after 3f, wknd qckly 3f out, last str* **36/10**[1]

12 — 3 1/4 — **Starspangled Gator (USA)** 3-8-9 ... CWoodsJr 4 — 59
(W G Gowan, U.S.A) **162/10**

1m 51.11s — **12** Ran SP% **126.1**
PARI-MUTUEL (including $2 stakes): WIN 99.60; PL (1-2) 38.20, 11.20;SHOW (1-2-3) 17.00, 7.80, 11.40; SF 930.20.
Owner equirace.com LLC **Bred** Carl Bowling **Trained** USA

NOTEBOOK

Silent Times(IRE), sent off favourite, but was sluggish from the gate. He seemed to use up his energy in an attempt to get a good position in the first half of the race.

PISA (R-H)

Sunday, March 26

OFFICIAL GOING: Good

758a PREMIO PISA (LISTED RACE) — 7f 110y

4:50 (4:59) 3-Y-0 **£27,931** (£12,290; £6,703; £3,352)

RPR

1 — **Magic Box (ITY)** 3-9-2 ... FBranca 5 — 101
(F Brogi, Italy)

2 — 9 — **Sgiaff**[105] 3-9-2 ... EBotti 7 — 83
(A & G Botti, Italy)

3 4 ¾ **My Pension (FR)** 3-8-13 .... DVargiu 4 71
(B Grizzetti, Italy)
4 1 ¾ **Romanae Memento (ITY)** 3-9-2 .... SLandi 6 70
(F & L Camici, Italy)
5 2 ½ **Wovoka (IRE)**[24] [561] 3-9-2 .... MMonteriso 2 65
(M R Channon) *held up towards rear, never a factor* **282/100**[1]
6 ½ **Fresh Bread (USA)** 3-8-13 .... CFiocchi 1 61
(R Meichetti, Italy)
7 5 **Pressing (IRE)**[154] [6052] 3-9-2 .... MTellini 9 54
(R Feligioni, Italy)
8 ½ **Villa Sciarra (IRE)**[31] 3-9-2 .... CColombi 10 53
(A Peraino, Italy)
9 2 ½ **Windhuk (GER)**[105] 3-8-13 .... AMuzzi 11 45
(P Giannotti, Italy)
10 8 **L'Ombrone (ITY)** 3-9-2 .... PAgus 8 32
(A Calderone, Italy)
11 ¾ **Enda Bu Bu** 3-9-2 .... LManiezzi 3 31
(G Wildgen)

1m 27.4s **11** Ran SP% **26.2**
WIN 4.22 (coupled with Villa Sciarra); PL 1.96, 1.41, 2.84; DF 9.02.
Owner Allevamento La Nuova Sbarra **Bred** Patrizia Brogi **Trained** Italy

NOTEBOOK
Wovoka(IRE) was settled towards the rear and never got competitive as front runners fared much the best.

[720]KEMPTON (A.W) (R-H)
Monday, March 27

OFFICIAL GOING: Standard

760 PANORAMIC BAR AND RESTAURANT MAIDEN AUCTION STKS 5f (P)
2:10 (2:10) (Class 5) 2-Y-O **£3,238** (£963; £481; £240) **Stalls** High

Form RPR
1 **Il Palio (IRE)** 2-8-8 .... AlanMunro 2 69
(B R Millman) *tall: str: lw: mde all: drvn fnl f: jst hld on* **8/1**[3]
2 2 shd **Urban Warrior**[3] [707] 2-8-7 .... TQuinn 8 68
(J R Best) *chsd ldrs 1/2-way:rdn 2f out: kpt on strly fr over 1f out: fin wl: jst failed* **10/11**[1]
3 4 **Diminuto** 2-8-2 .... HayleyTurner 3 47
(M D I Usher) *neat: chsd ldrs: drvn along 1/2-way: kpt on fnl f but nvr a danger* **28/1**
4 ¾ **Gilded (IRE)** 2-8-6 .... RyanMoore 5 48
(R Hannon) *rangy: lw: slowly int stride: bhd: sn pushed along: kpt on fr over 1f out: nt rch ldrs* **5/1**[2]
5 3 **Granny Peel (IRE)** 2-8-5 .... AdrianTNicholls 7 35
(K A Ryan) *neat: in tch: rdn 1/2-way: kpt on fr over 1f out but nvr gng pce to rch ldrs* **8/1**[3]
6 6 4 **Sad Times (IRE)**[3] [707] 2-7-9 .... LiamJones(7) 6 16
(W G M Turner) *s.i.s: sn drvn along: a outpcd* **8/1**[3]
7 7 **Piccolo Prezzo** 2-8-3 .... JimmyQuinn 1 —
(Stef Liddiard) *cmpt: v.s.a: a outpcd* **50/1**
8 1 ¾ **All Talk** 2-8-3 ow1 .... JohnEgan 4 —
(I A Wood) *leggy: chsd ldr to 1/2-way: sn wknd* **25/1**

63.98 secs **Going Correction** +0.40s/f (Slow) **8** Ran SP% **111.6**
Speed ratings (Par 92):87,86,80,79,74 68,56,54
CSF £15.01 TOTE £10.30: £1.90, £1.10, £5.50; EX 14.30.
Owner Mrs L S Millman **Bred** Blue Bloodstock Limited **Trained** Kentisbeare, Devon
■ Stewards' Enquiry : Alan Munro caution: used whip without allowing sufficient time for response

FOCUS
A weak-looking maiden which saw the first two come clear.

NOTEBOOK
Il Palio(IRE), a half-brother to modest sprinter Efistorm, showed excellent early speed to get across from his low draw and just did enough to hold on near the line and get his career off to a perfect start. He is entitled to improve for this experience, but this looked as far as he wants to go and he lacks scope, so could be hard to place now.
Urban Warrior, runner-up on his debut at Lingfield three days earlier, lacked the early pace to really take advantage of his decent draw and, despite hitting top gear in the final furlong, he could not quite peg back the winner. As on his debut, he did not handle the bends too well, and again suggested another furlong ought to be right up his street in due course. (op 5-6 tchd Evens)
Diminuto, bred to make her mark as a juvenile, was doing all of her best work at the finish and looks sure to be sharper on her next assignment. (op 25-1)
Gilded(IRE), a half-sister to six-furlong winner Jasmine Pearl and out of a multiple winning sprinter, lost all chance with a tardy start yet shaped with ability and ought to be all the wiser for this debut experience. (tchd 11-2)
Granny Peel(IRE), whose dam was a seven-furlong winner at two, ran green through the first half of the race and was not given a hard time in the final two furlongs. (op 10-1)

761 KEMPTON.CO.UK H'CAP 5f (P)
2:40 (2:40) (Class 4) (0-85,85) 4-Y-O+
£7,790 (£2,332; £1,166; £583; £291; £146) **Stalls** High

Form RPR
0231 1 **Native Title**[33] [480] 8-8-6 **73** .... AdrianTNicholls 4 84
(D Nicholls) *lw: s.i.s: bhd: hdwy over 1f out: str run between horses ins last to ld nr fin* **9/2**[2]
500- 2 ½ **Lindbergh**[100] [6602] 4-8-13 **80** .... RichardHughes 5 89
(R Hannon) *lw: s.i.s: sn in tch: rdn 2f out: r.o strly to chal wl ins last: no ex cl home* **14/1**
600- 3 ¾ **Desert Lord**[163] [5891] 6-9-2 **83** .... NCallan 12 89
(K A Ryan) *led: rdn over 1f out: hdd and no ex nr fin* **9/2**[2]
2031 4 ¾ **Efistorm**[20] [605] 5-8-9 **79** .... JasonEdmunds(3) 9 83
(J Balding) *chsd ldrs: rdn and kpt on wl fnl f but nt pce to chal* **13/2**[3]
-123 5 1 ¼ **Effective**[24] [569] 6-8-4 **74** .... AdamKirby(3) 7 73
(A P Jarvis) *bhd: hdwy over 1f out: kpt on ins last but nvr gng pce to rch ldrs* **4/1**[1]
-502 6 ½ **Zarzu**[30] [517] 7-9-4 **85** .... RobertWinston 1 82
(C R Dore) *behind: hdwy over 1f out: fin wl but nt rch ldrs* **10/1**
1156 7 nk **Sweetest Revenge (IRE)**[5] [699] 5-8-4 **71** .... HayleyTurner 6 67
(M D I Usher) *lw: bhd: rdn 1/2-way: kpt on fnl f but nvr in contention* **12/1**
-666 8 hd **Magic Glade**[57] [244] 7-8-8 **75** .... PaulHanagan 10 70
(R Brotherton) *chsd ldr: rdn to chal 2f out: wknd fnl f* **10/1**
50-0 9 1 ¼ **No Time (IRE)**[9] [664] 6-8-13 **80** .... EddieAhern 2 71
(M J Polglase) *outpcd in rr: sme hdwy fnl f* **50/1**
0303 10 nk **Kempsey**[5] [699] 4-8-5 **75** .... (v) NeilChalmers(3) 11 65
(J J Bridger) *chsd ldrs: rdn 1/2-way: wknd over 1f out* **9/1**
00-0 11 1 ½ **Handsome Cross (IRE)**[10] [657] 5-8-9 **83** .... VictoriaBehan(7) 3 67
(D Nicholls) *chsd ldrs: rdn 1/2-way: wknd over 1f out* **40/1**
02R- R **Piccled**[111] [6518] 8-9-2 **83** .... DavidAllan 8 —
(E J Alston) *ref to r* **25/1**

61.73 secs **Going Correction** +0.40s/f (Slow) **12** Ran SP% **120.5**
Speed ratings (Par 105):105,104,103,101,99 99,98,98,96,95 93,—
CSF £66.19 CT £309.44 TOTE £7.20: £1.70, £6.00, £1.80; EX 102.20.
Owner C McKenna **Bred** Mrs W H Gibson Fleming **Trained** Sessay, N Yorks

FOCUS
A fair sprint which saw the first four finish nicely clear. The form is not convincing overall but there is a chance this was above-average for the grade.

762 DAY TIME, NIGHT TIME, GREAT TIME MAIDEN STKS 1m 2f (P)
3:10 (3:10) (Class 4) 3-Y-O **£5,505** (£1,637; £818; £408) **Stalls** High

Form RPR
52- 1 **Awatuki (IRE)**[227] [4338] 3-9-3 .... TPQueally 11 78+
(A P Jarvis) *h.d.w: trckd ldrs: led appr 2f out: c clr fnl f: easily* **7/2**[2]
2 5 **Virgin Islands (IRE)** 3-8-12 .... PhilipRobinson 7 64+
(M A Jarvis) *lengthy: scope: lw: s.i.s: bhd: gd hdwy 3f out: chsd ldrs 2f out: kpt on fnl f but no ch w wnr* **4/1**[3]
0- 3 1 ¼ **Dragon Dancer**[167] [5823] 3-9-3 .... DarryllHolland 2 66+
(G Wragg) *lw: bhd: hdwy whn bdly hmpd bnd 2f out: swtchd lft and r.o wl fnl f but nt trble ldrs* **9/4**[1]
0- 4 2 **Newport Boy (IRE)**[284] [2619] 3-9-3 .... RyanMoore 5 62+
(S Kirk) *lw: s.i.s: bhd: hdwy whn nt clr run bnd 2f out: swtchd lft and r.o fr over 1f out: fin wl: nt a danger* **20/1**
6-36 5 ½ **Coda Agency**[30] [515] 3-9-3 58 .... EddieAhern 8 61
(D W P Arbuthnot) *chsd ldrs: led briefly over 2f out: sn rdn: wknd fnl f* **25/1**
006- 6 1 ¼ **Gaelic Games (UAE)**[135] [6334] 3-9-3 60 .... SteveDrowne 10 59
(P G Murphy) *chsd ldrs: rdn over 2f out: wknd fnl f* **25/1**
04- 7 5 **Mirth**[174] [5688] 3-8-12 .... RichardHughes 1 45
(R Hannon) *in tch: rdn 3f out: one pce and hld whn bmpd bnd 2f out: sn wknd* **9/2**
0 8 3 ½ **Azurine (IRE)**[9] [668] 3-8-12 .... JoeFanning 3 38+
(M Johnston) *t.k.h: trckd ldr: led over 5f out: hdd over 2f out and sn wknd* **14/1**
00-5 9 nk **Light Of Day (IRE)**[27] [539] 3-8-9 45 .... AdamKirby(3) 4 37
(Miss Diana Weeden) *bhd: rapid hdwy to chse ldrs 3f out: wknd ins fnl 2f* **100/1**
0-0 10 6 **Murts Magic (IRE)**[27] [538] 3-9-3 .... JohnEgan 6 31
(M J McGrath) *led tl hdd over 5f out: wknd over 2f out* **100/1**
00- 11 dist **Erhgent Sea**[191] [5316] 3-9-0 .... NeilChalmers(3) 9 —
(T M Jones) *bit bkwd: s.i.s: a bhd: t.o* **100/1**

2m 12.47s **Going Correction** +0.40s/f (Slow) **11** Ran SP% **113.3**
Speed ratings (Par 100):102,98,97,95,95 94,90,87,86,82 —
CSF £16.10 TOTE £3.00: £1.10, £2.10, £1.50; EX 21.20.
Owner Allen B Pope, Andrew J King **Bred** Yeomanstown Stud **Trained** Twyford, Bucks

FOCUS
A fair maiden, run at just an ordinary pace, and the winner can be rated value for a bit further. The first two could well prove better than the bare form, which is held down by the fifth and sixth.
Mirth Official explanation: jockey said filly ran green
Murts Magic(IRE) Official explanation: jockey said colt ran green

763 HYDE H'CAP 1m 2f (P)
3:40 (3:41) (Class 3) (0-90,90) 4-Y-O+
£7,790 (£2,332; £1,166; £583; £291; £146) **Stalls** High

Form RPR
24-1 1 **Ameeq (USA)**[35] [460] 4-8-5 **77** .... RyanMoore 4 84
(G L Moore) *lw: prom: rdn to chse ldr over 2f out: led 1f out: hld on all out* **9/2**[2]
200- 2 ¾ **Danehill Willy (IRE)**[177] [5608] 4-9-4 **90** .... LDettori 6 96
(N A Callaghan) *lw: sn led: drvn 2f ot: hdd 1f out: styd chalng tl no ex nr fin* **9/4**[1]
5-04 3 1 ¼ **St Savarin (FR)**[42] [404] 5-8-4 **76** .... PaulHanagan 2 80
(R A Fahey) *rr: hdwy and rdn 3f out: r.o u.p fr over 1f out but nvr gng pce to rch ldrs* **11/2**[3]
00-0 4 1 **Red Contact (USA)**[41] [412] 5-8-4 **76** .... (p) AlanMunro 3 78
(Lucinda Featherstone) *chsd ldr: rdn over 3f out: lost 2nd 2f out: styd on same pce* **40/1**
0512 5 1 **Star Magnitude (USA)**[40] [421] 5-8-4 **76** oh1 .... JimmyQuinn 8 76
(S Dow) *rr but in tch: drvn and hdwy 3f out: chsd ldrs u.p 2f out: one pce fnl f* **13/2**
0-25 6 1 ¾ **Consonant (IRE)**[23] [578] 9-8-6 **78** ow1 .... MickyFenton 1 75
(D G Bridgwater) *bhd: rdn and hung rt ins fnl 2f: kpt on fnl f but nvr in contention* **14/1**
0/-1 7 2 ½ **Barry Island**[35] [463] 7-8-6 **78** .... JamieMackay 5 70
(D R C Elsworth) *hld up in rr: pushed along and sme hdwy ins fnl 2f: nvr in contention* **13/2**
0-01 8 3 **Steely Dan**[9] [670] 7-8-9 **81** .... TQuinn 7 67
(J R Best) *rr but in tch: hdwy to chse ldrs 3f out: wknd ins fnl 2f* **8/1**
116- 9 25 **Celticello (IRE)**[252] [3581] 4-9-1 **87** .... (p) LPKeniry 9 26
(Heather Dalton) *chsd ldrs: rdn 5f out: wknd qckly over 3f out* **14/1**

2m 10.64s **Going Correction** +0.40s/f (Slow) **9** Ran SP% **117.9**
Speed ratings (Par 107):109,108,107,106,105 104,102,100,80
CSF £15.39 CT £57.45 TOTE £7.20: £2.30, £1.50, £1.60; EX 18.10.
Owner C E Stedman **Bred** Shadwell Farm LLC **Trained** Woodingdean, E Sussex

FOCUS
A fair handicap, run at a strong pace, but the form is only ordinary, rated through the third, and not entirely convincing.

NOTEBOOK
Ameeq(USA) gamely followed-up his Lingfield maiden success under a strong ride from Moore. He is clearly going the right way now, proved well suited by the strong gallop over this trip, and appeals as one to follow on this surface. (tchd 5-1)
Danehill Willy(IRE), returning from a 177-da absence, posted a solid effort from the front under top weight and has clearly resumed life this term in decent fettle. (op 11-4)
St Savarin(FR) was again staying on all too late, but he is on good terms with himself at present, and the return to a longer trip ought to see him get closer in this grade. He is also well suited by cut in the ground, so the switch to turf should prove more to his liking in the coming weeks.
Red Contact(USA) showed his best form to date for current connections, but failed to see out the longer trip all that well, and can build on this when reverting to a mile.

The Form Book, Raceform Ltd, Compton, RG20 6NL

764 KEMPTON FOR WEDDINGS H'CAP 1m (P)

4:10 (4:11) (Class 5) (0-75,75) 4-Y-0+ **£3,238** (£963; £481; £240) **Stalls** Low

Form RPR

1201 **1** **Raza Cab (IRE)**[10] 659 4-8-13 **70**................................ DarryllHolland 12 81
(Karen George) *lw: trckd ldrs: drvn and str run to ld jst ins last: styd on wl: readily* **9/2**[1]

3-11 **2** *1 ½* **Fajr (IRE)**[47] 336 4-8-11 **68**................................ MickyFenton 10 76
(Miss Gay Kelleway) *lw: chsd ldrs:edgd lft 2f out: led wl over 1f out: hdd jst ins last: one pce u.p* **9/2**[1]

0-15 **3** *1 ¼* **Arctic Desert**[25] 559 6-9-3 **74**................................ RichardHughes 9 79
(A M Balding) *in tch: hdwy over 2f out: chsd ldrs and rdn over 1f out: one pce ins last* **5/1**[2]

-140 **4** *¾* **Parkview Love (USA)**[20] 611 5-8-10 **70**.............(v) PatrickMathers(3) 1 73
(D Shaw) *bhd: hdwy on outside 3f out: kpt on u.p ins last but nt rch ldrs* **25/1**

-213 **5** *shd* **Farewell Gift**[47] 340 5-9-1 **75**................................(b) StephaneBreux(3) 3 78
(R Hannon) *hld up in rr: hdwy whn n.m.r 2f out: kpt on wl u.p fnl f but nt pce to rch ldrs* **8/1**[3]

310- **6** *1 ½* **Sawwaah (IRE)**[177] 5612 9-9-2 **73**................................ AdrianTNicholls 8 73
(D Nicholls) *bhd: hdwy on ins fr 2f out: kpt on fnl f but nvr gng pce to rch ldrs* **16/1**

050- **7** *1* **Whitgift Rock**[242] 3871 5-8-12 **69**................................ JohnEgan 2 66
(S Dow) *chsd ldrs: rdn whn n.m.r 2f out: wknd fnl f* **25/1**

000- **8** *hd* **Pianoforte (USA)**[159] 5981 4-8-10 **67**................................ DavidAllan 6 64
(E J Alston) *lw: bhd: rdn over 2f out: kpt on fr over 1f out: nvr gng pce to rch ldrs* **50/1**

5240 **9** *1 ½* **Just Fly**[25] 556 6-9-1 **72**................................(v) NCallan 4 65
(Dr J R J Naylor) *in tch: chsd ldrs and pushed along 2f out: wknd fnl f* **12/1**

1504 **10** *4* **Blue Empire (IRE)**[21] 596 5-8-4 **61**................................ PaulHanagan 7 45
(C R Dore) *lw: chsd ldr: chal and rdn 3f out to 2f out: sn wknd* **12/1**

000- **11** *shd* **Phluke**[181] 5526 5-9-1 **72**................................ StephenCarson 11 56
(R F Johnson Houghton) *slt ld tl hdd jst ins fnl 3f: wknd fr 2f out: no chance whn n.m.r 1f out* **12/1**

215- **12** *nk* **Burhaan (IRE)**[135] 6336 4-8-9 **69**................................(t) AmirQuinn(3) 5 52
(J R Boyle) *chsd ldrs: led ins fnl 3f: hdd & wknd wl over 1f out* **14/1**

-040 **13** *dist* **Admiral Compton**[58] 223 5-8-13 **70**................................(b) SteveDrowne 13 —
(J R Boyle) *bhd fr 1/2-way: t.o* **14/1**

1m 41.74s (-0.24) **Going Correction** +0.40s/f (Slow) **13** Ran SP% **116.1**

Speed ratings (Par 103):111,109,108,107,107 105,104,104,103,99 99,98,—

CSF £22.72 CT £98.06 TOTE £5.40: £1.80, £1.40, £3.00; EX 17.40.

Owner B R Phillips **Bred** Rathyork Stud **Trained** Higher Easington, Devon

■ Stewards' Enquiry : Micky Fenton two-day ban: careless riding (Apr 7-8)

FOCUS

A modest handicap, run at a fair pace, and the form looks sound enough for the grade with the third setting the standard. High numbers came out on top.

765 KEMPTON FOR EXHIBITIONS H'CAP 2m (P)

4:40 (4:40) (Class 3) (0-95,95) 4-Y-0+

£7,790 (£2,332; £1,166; £583; £291; £146) **Stalls** High

Form RPR

-015 **1** **Llamadas**[20] 610 4-7-6 **77** oh2 ow1................................ LukeMorris(7) 2 83
(C Roberts) *chsd ldrs: led ins fnl 3f: drvn 6l clr over 1f out: readily* **20/1**

5661 **2** *4* **Wise Owl**[16] 628 4-8-7 **85**................................ JimmyQuinn 3 87
(J Pearce) *rr: hdwy to cl on ldrs 4f out: rdn and outpcd over 2f out: kpt on again ins last to take 2nd nr fin but no ch w wnr* **15/8**[1]

242- **3** *½* **Spear Thistle**[41] 6239 4-8-8 **86**................................ TQuinn 5 87
(Mrs N Smith) *mde most tl hdd ins fnl 3f: kpt on u.p fnl 2f but nvr any ch w wnr and lost 2nd nr fin* **11/2**[3]

22-3 **4** *½* **Nawamees (IRE)**[10] 661 8-8-13 **86**................................(p) RyanMoore 6 86
(G L Moore) *lw: chsd ldrs: wnt 2nd over 5f out: drvn to chal 3f out: styd on same pce fnl 2f* **9/2**[2]

60/- **5** *½* **Lunar Exit (IRE)**[293] 5919 5-8-11 **84**................................(p) LDettori 4 84
(Lady Herries) *chsd ldrs: rdn 4f out: styd on same pce fr over 2f out* **15/2**

00/0 **6** *6* **Global Challenge (IRE)**[21] 591 7-8-3 **76** oh1................ DavidKinsella 1 69
(P G Murphy) *bhd: pushed along fr 7f out: nvr gng pce to rch ldrs but mod prog fnl 2f* **66/1**

1524 **7** *2 ½* **The Violin Player (USA)**[10] 661 5-8-12 **85**................ DarryllHolland 8 75
(H J Collingridge) *swtg: s.i.s: bhd: rdn and no imp on ldrs fr over 3f out* **7/1**

/0-4 **8** *9* **Grooms Affection**[24] 572 6-8-1 **79**................................ JamesDoyle(5) 7 58
(K A Morgan) *lw: slowly away: sn in tch: chsd ldrs after 3f: rdn 4f out: wknd 3f out* **10/1**

/00- **9** *dist* **Lights Out (DEN)**[118] 6459 6-9-8 **95**................................(t) EddieAhern 9 —
(C A Horgan) *lw: chsd ldr: chal 7f out: wknd fr 6f out: t.o fnl 2f* **20/1**

3m 37.32s **Going Correction** +0.40s/f (Slow)

WFA 4 from 5yo+ 5lb **9** Ran SP% **112.7**

Speed ratings (Par 107):101,99,98,98,98 95,94,89,—

CSF £55.50 CT £243.83 TOTE £32.30: £4.50, £1.20, £2.00; EX 79.90 Place 6 £9.61, Place 5 £6.01.

Owner K Tyre **Bred** Burton Agnes Stud Co Ltd **Trained** Newport, Newport

FOCUS

A decent enough handicap for the grade, run at an average early pace, but the form is not that solid and should be treated with caution.

NOTEBOOK

Llamadas, 2lb out of the handicap, put the race to bed when scooting clear nearing the final furlong and got back to winning ways in great fashion. He stayed this longer trip well enough, and this must rate a career-best effort, but his ability to get home over this far off a true pace must still be taken on trust.

Wise Owl, raised 5lb for winning at Wolverhampton last time, got going too late and would have no doubt been seen in a better light granted a stronger early pace. He is worthy of another chance over this trip. (tchd 7-4 and 2-1 in places)

Spear Thistle, reverting from a recent spell over hurdles, had very much the run of the race from the front and posted a pleasing return to this sphere. He is probably slightly happier over a shorter trip. Official explanation: jockey said gelding hung left (op 6-1)

Nawamees(IRE) found just the one pace when it mattered and ran to his recent level in defeat. He is a very hard horse to win with. (op 11-2)

Lunar Exit(IRE), returning from a 293-day layoff and having his first spin on the Flat since 2004, ran as though the race was needed and ought to be of more interest with this outing under his belt. (op 8-1 tchd 7-1)

The Violin Player(USA), having his first outing over the trip, was ridden conservatively yet failed to make an impression. He is better than he showed this time. Official explanation: jockey said gelding hung right (op 5-1)

T/Jkpt: Not won. T/Plt: £15.50 to a £1 stake. Pool: £48,905.85. 2,294.85 winning tickets. T/Qpdt: £5.60 to a £1 stake. Pool: £3,103.50. 405.80 winning tickets. ST

732 WOLVERHAMPTON (A.W) (L-H)

Monday, March 27

OFFICIAL GOING: Standard

Wind: Strong, behind Weather: Cloudy

766 WOLVERHAMPTON-RACECOURSE.CO.UK TO BOOK ONLINE BANDED STKS 5f 216y(P)

2:30 (2:30) (Class 7) 4-Y-0+ **£1,365** (£403; £201) **Stalls** Low

Form RPR

-261 **1** **Auentraum (GER)**[7] 680 6-9-3 45................................(p) JamieSpencer 1 57+
(K McAuliffe) *a.p: led 1f out: pushed out* **5/4**[1]

-340 **2** *1* **Misty Princess**[7] 680 4-8-11 45................................ RobbieFitzpatrick 13 48
(M J Attwater) *chsd ldrs: rdn 3f out: r.o ins fnl f* **20/1**

60-0 **3** *½* **Grand View**[7] 680 10-8-8 45................................(p) PaulMulrennan(3) 7 47
(J R Weymes) *sn outpcd: hdwy on ins over 1f out: r.o ins fnl f* **33/1**

5343 **4** *nk* **Mister Aziz (IRE)**[6] 691 4-8-11 45................................(b) RobertHavlin 12 46
(J R Jenkins) *hld up: sltly hmpd after 1f: hdwy over 2f out: edgd lft over 1f out: kpt on ins fnl f* **10/1**

-050 **5** *nk* **Carcinetto (IRE)**[35] 465 4-8-11 45................................(p) DaneO'Neill 9 45
(B Palling) *hld up: rdn and hdwy on outside over 2f out: flashed tail fr over 1f out: kpt on* **20/1**

6220 **6** *shd* **A Teen**[13] 633 8-8-11 45................................ ShaneKelly 11 44
(P Howling) *led early: w ldr: edgd lft after 1f: rdn 3f out: led over 1f out: sn hdd: no ex towards fin* **14/1**

040 **7** *¾* **Teyaar**[19] 613 10-8-11 45................................ AlanDaly 3 42
(M Wellings) *hld upin mid-diviison: hdwy on ins over 2f out: swtchd rt over 1f out: one pce* **20/1**

0-00 **8** *5* **Princess Arwen**[62] 181 4-8-11 45................................(p) FrankieMcDonald 10 27
(Mrs Barbara Waring) *prom: hmpd after 1f: sn lost pl and bhd: rdn over 3f out: n.d after* **66/1**

0061 **9** *nk* **Sundried Tomato**[6] 691 7-9-3 45................................(p) TonyCulhane 5 32
(D W Chapman) *sn led: rdn and hdd over 1f out: wknd ins fnl f* **6/1**[3]

-060 **10** *1 ¼* **Chillin Out**[51] 293 4-8-11 45................................ PaulDoe 4 23
(W Jarvis) *prom 4f* **9/2**[2]

0000 **11** *1 ¾* **King Marrakech (IRE)**[20] 612 4-8-11 40................................(b) PaulEddery 2 17
(B P J Baugh) *sn outpcd* **22/1**

000- **12** *2* **Danescourt (IRE)**[170] 5736 4-8-6 40................................(b) GregFairley(5) 6 11
(J M Bradley) *chsd ldrs: rdn over 3f out: wknd over 2f out* **50/1**

0060 **13** *3 ½* **Enjoy The Buzz**[55] 260 7-8-11 45................................ PaulFitzsimons 8 1
(J M Bradley) *prom: bdly hmpd after 1f: sn bhd* **25/1**

1m 16.06s (0.25) **Going Correction** -0.075s/f (Stan) **13** Ran SP% **121.5**

Speed ratings (Par 97):95,93,93,92,92 92,91,84,84,82 80,77,72

CSF £35.95 TOTE £2.10: £1.20, £6.20, £8.80; EX 43.30 TRIFECTA Not won..

Owner Nadeem Ahmad **Bred** Gestut Auenquelle **Trained** Fernham, Oxon

FOCUS

A reasonable banded sprint overall, with an above-average effort from the winner.

767 ZONGALERO RESTAURANT OVERLOOKS THE RACETRACK BANDED STKS 1m 5f 194y(P)

3:00 (3:02) (Class 7) 4-Y-0+ **£1,876** (£554; £277) **Stalls** Low

Form RPR

3656 **1** **Ice And Fire**[46] 346 7-8-8 45 ow1................................(b) AshleyHamblett(7) 5 54
(J T Stimpson) *hld up towards rr: hdwy on outside and edgd lft over 1f out: edgd rt and styd on to ld wl ins fnl f* **33/1**

-622 **2** *1 ½* **Larad (IRE)**[21] 597 5-9-2 47................................(b) NickyMackay 8 53
(J S Moore) *hld up in mid-div: hdwy over 3f out: rdn over 1f out: led ins fnl f: sn hdd: nt qckn* **11/2**[3]

-202 **3** *1 ½* **Twentytwosilver (IRE)**[7] 684 6-9-0 45................................ MichaelTebbutt 11 49
(D B Feek) *hld up and bhd: hdwy over 5f out: rdn wl over 1f out: styd on ins fnl f* **15/2**

51-0 **4** *hd* **Saameq (IRE)**[35] 470 5-9-4 49................................ GeorgeBaker 6 53
(D W Thompson) *stdd s: hld up and bhd: hdwy on ins over 2f out: rdn over 1f out: kpt on ins fnl f* **5/1**[2]

/1-1 **5** *shd* **Debbie**[35] 470 7-9-2 47................................ ShaneKelly 9 50
(B D Leavy) *led after 1f: clr whn rdn over 2f out: hdd and no ex ins fnl f* **11/2**[3]

3066 **6** *nk* **Lake Wakatipu**[7] 683 4-9-0 49................................ JamieSpencer 7 52
(M Mullineaux) *hld up and bhd: rdn and hdwy on outside over 2f out: sltly bmpd over 1f out: one pce fnl f* **9/2**[1]

450/ **7** *3 ½* **Heathers Girl**[51] 6751 7-9-0 45................................ TonyCulhane 2 43
(R Dickin) *a.p: rdn to chse ldr over 3f out: wknd ins fnl f* **50/1**

344- **8** *½* **Royal Melbourne (IRE)**[144] 6236 6-9-3 48................................ TomEaves 12 45
(Miss J A Camacho) *t.k.h in rr: hdwy 3f out: sn rdn and swtchd rt: wknd ins fnl f* **9/2**[1]

6-00 **9** *2 ½* **Ready Teddy Go**[35] 461 4-8-10 40................................ PaulDoe 3 39
(J Ryan) *prom: lost pl after 2f: hld up in mid-div: rdn over 2f out: sn bhd* **66/1**

350- **10** *7* **Quest On Air**[15] 6571 7-9-0 40................................(v) RobertHavlin 4 29
(J R Jenkins) *hld up in tch: rdn over 3f out: wknd over 2f out* **25/1**

530- **11** *7* **Make My Hay**[37] 6472 7-9-0 45................................(b) ChrisCatlin 13 19
(J Gallagher) *sn led: hdd after 1f: chsd ldr tl rdn over 3f out: wknd over 2f out* **14/1**

003- **12** *dist* **Garple Burn**[303] 2090 4-8-13 48................................(b) SebSanders 10 —
(Jim Best) *led early: stdd into mid-div: hdwy over 5f out: rdn over 3f out: wknd qckly: t.o* **20/1**

3m 6.84s (-0.53) **Going Correction** -0.075s/f (Stan)

WFA 4 from 5yo+ 4lb **12** Ran SP% **117.2**

Speed ratings (Par 97):98,97,96,96,96 95,93,93,92,88 84,—

CSF £197.27 TOTE £40.60: £6.40, £1.80, £2.90; EX 327.20 Trifecta £217.10 Part won. Pool: £305.85 - 0.10 winning tickets..

Owner J T Stimpson & B Trubshaw **Bred** Abdullah Saeed Bul Hab **Trained** Newcastle-Under-Lyme, Staffs

FOCUS

Not a bad race by banded standards. The winner's record is hardly convincing, but the placed horses were close to their recent form.

768 RACING IS FOR EVERYONE AT WOLVERHAMPTON BANDED STKS 7f 32y(P)

3:30 (3:30) (Class 7) 4-Y-0+ **£1,365** (£403; £201) **Stalls** High

Form RPR

-400 **1** **Fizzy Lizzy**[19] 616 6-8-11 45................................ RobbieFitzpatrick 4 50
(H E Haynes) *mid div: rdn over 3f out: swtchd rt and hdwy over 1f out: led ins fnl f: r.o wl* **16/1**

-000 **2** *1* **Margaret's Dream (IRE)**[42] 399 5-8-8 45............. DanielTudhope(3) 7 47
(D Carroll) *s.i.s: hld up: rdn and hdwy 2f out: led 1f out: hdd and nt qckn ins fnl f* **11/2**
0004 **3** *2 1/2* **Headland (USA)**[7] 680 8-8-11 45............................(be) TonyCulhane 5 41
(D W Chapman) *a.p: rdn 3f out: one pce fnl f* **9/2**[2]
4004 **4** *hd* **Xaloc Bay (IRE)**[6] 691 8-8-11 45............................. AdrianMcCarthy 2 40
(R A Harris) *a.p: rdn over 3f out: led over 1f out: sn hdd: no ex ins fnl f* **5/1**[3]
-006 **5** *1/2* **Smirfys Party**[7] 680 8-8-8 45.................................. PaulMulrennan(3) 6 39
(W M Brisbourne) *hld up and bhd: hdwy on ins and nt clr run over 2f out: rdn whn struck by rival jockey's whip 1f out: one pce* **14/1**
6300 **6** *nk* **Paper Doll**[29] 527 4-8-11 45...(b1) PaulEddery 1 38
(B P J Baugh) *sn bhd: hdwy fnl f: nvr trbld ldrs* **10/1**
00-0 **7** *1 1/4* **Indian Gem**[42] 400 5-8-11 45....................................... DeanMcKeown 8 35
(A J Chamberlain) *hld up in mid-div: hdwy 3f out: rdn 2f out: wknd ins fnl f* **16/1**
-000 **8** *6* **Teenage Rampage**[2] 734 4-8-11 40.................................. TomEaves 3 19
(W M Brisbourne) *carried hd high: led: rdn over 2f out: hdd over 1f out: edgd rt jst ins fnl f: wknd qckly* **33/1**
0002 **9** *5* **La Musique**[13] 638 4-8-11 45... ChrisCatlin 9 6
(P J McBride) *sn chsng ldr: rdn over 2f out: wknd wl over 1f out* **7/2**[1]
00-0 **10** *hd* **Warlingham (IRE)**[20] 606 8-8-11 45.............................. ShaneKelly 11 6
(P Howling) *hld up in mid-div: hdwy 3f out: wknd 2f out: eased whn no ch fnl f* **20/1**
-006 **11** *15* **Chorus Beauty**[21] 602 5-8-11 45................................ JamieSpencer 10 —
(N I M Rossiter) *bhd: rdn and short-lived effrt on outside over 2f out: eased whn btn over 1f out* **12/1**

1m 30.98s (0.58) **Going Correction** -0.075s/f (Stan) **11** Ran SP% **115.4**
Speed ratings (Par 97):93,91,89,88,88 87,86,79,73,73 56
CSF £99.79 TOTE £12.10: £3.00, £2.50, £1.80; EX 67.60 Trifecta £179.90 Part won. Pool: £253.52 - 0.50 winning tickets..
Owner Mrs H E Haynes **Bred** J Johnson **Trained** Highworth, Wilts

FOCUS
A moderate race even by banded standards and the winning time was not great, even though the pace seemed fair. The winner is exposed and the runner-up ran to recent form.
Warlingham(IRE) Official explanation: jockey said gelding hung right-handed throughout
Chorus Beauty Official explanation: trainer said mare was in season

769 TO SPONSOR A RACE CALL 0870 220 2442 BANDED STKS 1m 141y(P)
4:00 (4:00) (Class 7) 4-Y-0+ **£1,365** (£403; £201) **Stalls** Low

Form RPR
2-00 **1** **Wanna Shout**[55] 258 8-8-12 45.............................. TonyCulhane 5 54
(R Dickin) *hld up: rdn and hdwy over 3f out: led wl over 1f out: sn edgd rt: drvn out* **16/1**
0-04 **2** *1 1/2* **Good Article (IRE)**[33] 484 5-8-12 45.......................... JamieSpencer 1 51
(D K Ivory) *led: hdd and edgd rt wl over 1f out: rdn and jinked rt jst ins fnl f: nt run on* **9/2**[3]
4052 **3** *1 3/4* **Miss Glory Be**[7] 682 8-8-12 45......................................(p) TomEaves 9 47
(Ernst Oertel) *chsd ldr: rdn over 3f out: one pce fnl f* **6/4**[1]
5-00 **4** *1* **Welsh Whisper**[31] 502 7-8-12 40.............................. SamHitchcott 2 45
(S A Brookshaw) *hld up and bhd: rdn and hdwy over 2f out: one pce fnl f* **50/1**
4430 **5** *4* **Weet Yer Tern (IRE)**[24] 573 4-8-12 45..........................(t) ShaneKelly 4 37
(W M Brisbourne) *hld up in tch: rdn over 2f out: wknd wl over 1f out* **5/2**[2]
5-50 **6** *3 1/2* **Fayr Firenze (IRE)**[3] 708 5-8-9 45......................(v) RichardThomas(3) 8 29
(M F Harris) *a bhd* **14/1**
500/ **7** *2 1/2* **Double Helix**[573] 4730 7-8-12 45.............................. RobbieFitzpatrick 6 24
(B P J Baugh) *hld up: hdwy over 3f out: sn rdn: wknd 2f out* **5/1**
00-0 **8** *2 1/2* **Temple Belle Xpres**[11] 647 4-8-12 35..........................(b) PaulEddery 3 19
(S R Bowring) *prom: rdn over 3f out: wknd over 2f out* **100/1**

1m 51.23s (-0.53) **Going Correction** -0.075s/f (Stan) **8** Ran SP% **118.9**
Speed ratings (Par 97):99,97,96,95,91 88,86,84
CSF £89.61 TOTE £14.70: £3.00, £1.50, £1.20; EX 49.40 Trifecta £151.50 Pool: £657.33 - 3.08 winning tickets..
Owner E R C Beech & B Wilkinson **Bred** C C Bromley And Son **Trained** Atherstone on Stour, Warwicks

FOCUS
A weak event, the form limited by the proximity of the fourth.

770 MOORCROFT RACEHORSE WELFARE CENTRE BANDED STKS 1m 1f 103y(P)
4:30 (4:30) (Class 7) 4-Y-0+ **£1,876** (£554; £277) **Stalls** Low

Form RPR
00-0 **1** **Ballare (IRE)**[63] 175 7-8-11 40.................................(v) FergusSweeney 6 52
(P J Makin) *hld up: rdn and hdwy over 2f out: led ins fnl f: drvn out* **33/1**
00-0 **2** *1 1/2* **Whitby Echo (IRE)**[21] 597 4-8-9 50................... RussellKennemore(7) 2 54
(R Hollinshead) *led: rdn over 2f out: hdd and edgd rt ins fnl f: nt qckn* **6/1**
5400 **3** *1* **Legacy (JPN)**[34] 472 6-8-13 47..................................(b1) JamieSpencer 8 49
(P D Evans) *swtchd lft sn after s: hld up in rr: rdn over 1f out: hdwy fnl f: r.o* **4/1**[3]
4 *shd* **At The Helm (IRE)**[206] 4929 4-9-2 50.............................. ChrisCatlin 1 52
(W J Knight) *t.k.h in tch: rdn over 2f out: one pce fnl f* **14/1**
6250 **5** *hd* **Christmas Truce (IRE)**[23] 582 7-9-2 50......................... DaneO'Neill 4 52
(Ms J S Doyle) *w ldr: rdn over 2f out: no ex ins fnl f* **10/1**
1613 **6** *1/2* **Milk And Sultana**[7] 683 6-9-2 50.................................. ShaneKelly 3 51
(G A Ham) *hld up: rdn and outpcd over 2f out: c wd st: kpt on ins fnl f* **5/2**[2]
-432 **7** *1 1/4* **Yashin (IRE)**[35] 468 5-8-12 46...................................... LeeEnstone 7 44
(P A Blockley) *prom tl rdn and wknd 2f out* **9/4**[1]

2m 3.21s (0.59) **Going Correction** -0.075s/f (Stan) **7** Ran SP% **112.3**
Speed ratings (Par 97):94,92,91,91,91 91,89
CSF £206.74 TOTE £36.90: £9.50, £4.20; EX 116.00 Trifecta £446.10 Part won. Pool: £628.32 - 0.69 winning tickets..
Owner D M Ahier **Bred** Oyster Farm **Trained** Ogbourne Maisey, Wilts

FOCUS
A competitive banded race and not a bad standard for the grade, but the form is not all that convincing.
Yashin(IRE) Official explanation: trainer was unable to offer any explanation for poor form shown

771 STAY AT WOLVERH'TON HOLIDAY INN BANDED STKS 1m 1f 103y(P)
5:00 (5:01) (Class 7) 4-Y-0+ **£1,365** (£403; £201) **Stalls** Low

Form RPR
-300 **1** **Diamond Dan (IRE)**[7] 684 4-8-8 45......................... DanielTudhope(3) 12 53
(P D Evans) *stdd s: hld up: hdwy 3f out: rdn 2f out: led wl ins fnl f: r.o* **4/1**[2]
5201 **2** *1* **Indian Edge**[7] 682 5-9-3 45.. FrancisFerris 2 57
(B Palling) *led: rdn clr 2f out: hung rt ins fnl f: sn hdd: nt qckn* **6/4**[1]
3 *1 1/2* **Ivorbella (IRE)**[154] 6090 4-8-11 40..........................(t) NickyMackay 8 48
(M Botti) *chsd ldr: rdn over 2f out: cl 3rd whn hmpd ins fnl f: nt qckn* **14/1**[3]
0435 **4** *6* **Tuscan Treaty**[23] 582 6-8-11 45...................................(tp) ChrisCatlin 4 37
(P J McBride) *hld up in mid-div: stdy hdwy over 5f out: rdn over 2f out: wknd fnl f* **4/1**[2]
0500 **5** *hd* **Glenviews Oldport (USA)**[26] 546 4-8-11 45......(b) RobbieFitzpatrick 5 36
(Peter Grayson) *s.i.s: hld up and bhd: hdwy on ins over 3f out: rdn over 2f out: wknd fnl f* **14/1**[3]
0/0- **6** *7* **Jack Durrance (IRE)**[163] 2347 6-8-11 35.......................... ShaneKelly 3 23
(G A Ham) *hld up in mid-div: rdn and hdwy over 3f out: wknd 2f out* **14/1**[3]
/5-0 **7** *3* **Candy Anchor (FR)**[42] 400 7-8-11 40.......................(b) PhillipMakin 10 17
(R E Peacock) *t.k.h in tch: rdn over 3f out: wknd over 2f out* **66/1**
6-00 **8** *4* **Hilversum**[42] 403 4-8-11 45.. TomEaves 11 10
(Miss J A Camacho) *stdd s: nvr nr ldrs* **14/1**[3]
0/06 **9** *1* **Inmom (IRE)**[19] 616 5-8-11 40................................... MichaelTebbutt 6 8
(S R Bowring) *plld hrd early: sn bhd* **20/1**
00-0 **10** *5* **Showtime Faye**[51] 182 4-8-11 40...................................(v1) LeeEnstone 1 —
(A Bailey) *prom over 3f* **66/1**
20-0 **11** *2 1/2* **Danger Bird (IRE)**[62] 184 6-8-5 40 ow1.................(p) HugoFellows(7) 7 —
(R Hollinshead) *stdd s: sn mid-div: hdwy over 6f out: wknd over 3f out* **20/1**
/05- **12** *13* **Breeder's Folly**[300] 2150 4-8-11 40.............................. JamieSpencer 9 —
(T J Fitzgerald) *hld up in mid-div: hdwy over 5f out: rdn over 3f out: sn wknd* **16/1**

2m 2.19s (-0.43) **Going Correction** -0.075s/f (Stan) **12** Ran SP% **125.1**
Speed ratings (Par 97):98,97,95,90,90 84,81,77,76,72 70,58
CSF £10.60 TOTE £5.80: £1.90, £1.40, £5.40; EX 19.70 Trifecta £139.10 Pool: £495.72 - 2.53 winning tickets..
Owner Diamond Racing Ltd **Bred** Golden Vale Stud **Trained** Pandy, Abergavenny
■ Stewards' Enquiry : Francis Ferris one-day ban: careless riding (Apr 7)

FOCUS
The winning time was as you would expect for a banded race, despite being just over a second quicker than the preceding contest over the same trip. This looks sound form, the first three finishing clear.

772 RINGSIDE SUITE 700 THEATRE STYLE CONFERENCE BANDED STKS 5f 216y(P)
5:30 (5:31) (Class 7) 4-Y-0+ **£1,876** (£554; £277) **Stalls** Low

Form RPR
1500 **1** **Desert Light (IRE)**[20] 608 5-9-2 50..............................(v) DaneO'Neill 2 59
(D Shaw) *hld up and bhd: swtchd rt and hdwy over 1f out: edgd lft ins fnl f: r.o to ld cl home* **11/2**[2]
-660 **2** *1* **Beverley Beau**[42] 397 4-8-5 46.................................. KristinStubbs(7) 7 52
(Mrs L Stubbs) *chsd ldr: rdn 2f out: led jst ins fnl f: hdd and nt qckn cl home* **40/1**
2641 **3** *shd* **Jalouhar**[31] 502 6-9-2 50.. GeorgeBaker 4 56
(J R Best) *hld up and bhd: hdwy over 2f out: rdn over 1f out: ev ch ins fnl f: nt qckn* **6/4**[1]
3020 **4** *2* **Boanerges (IRE)**[7] 679 9-9-2 50................................. RobertWinston 3 50
(J M Bradley) *hld up in tch: rdn over 2f out: swtchd rt over 1f out: one pce fnl f* **7/1**
0- **5** *hd* **Glenviews Babalou (USA)**[184] 5473 4-9-2 50.....(b) RobbieFitzpatrick 9 49
(Peter Grayson) *bhd: rdn and hdwy on ins over 1f out: no ex ins fnl f* **33/1**
-006 **6** *1/2* **Gaudalpin (IRE)**[54] 265 4-8-13 47...............................(t) TomEaves 1 45
(Ernst Oertel) *hld up: sn in tch: rdn over 2f out: one pce fnl f* **12/1**
0520 **7** *1* **Stagnite**[7] 679 6-9-2 50..(b) JamieSpencer 12 45
(K McAuliffe) *sn led: rdn wl over 1f out: sn edgd rt: hdd jst ins fnl f: wknd* **12/1**
0304 **8** *2 1/2* **Davids Mark**[7] 679 6-9-0 48... RobertHavlin 6 35
(J R Jenkins) *hld up in tch: rdn over 2f out: wknd ins fnl f* **11/1**
4433 **9** *1/2* **St Ivian**[19] 613 6-8-7 46.. DuranFentiman(5) 11 32
(Mrs N Macauley) *led early: prom: rdn over 2f out: wknd wl over 1f out* **12/1**
662- **10** *10* **Stamford Blue**[167] 5819 5-8-13 47..........................(b) AdrianMcCarthy 8 3
(R A Harris) *hld up in tch: rdn and wknd 2f out* **13/2**[3]
000- **11** *3 1/2* **Mister Regent**[205] 4936 5-8-11 35.................................... ShaneKelly 5 —
(W M Brisbourne) *hld up towards rr: rdn 3f out: sn struggling* **40/1**
25-0 **12** *7* **Amber Nectar Two**[29] 529 6-8-11 40................(b) SimonWhitworth 10 —
(A G Newcombe) *a bhd* **33/1**

1m 15.75s (-0.06) **Going Correction** -0.075s/f (Stan) **12** Ran SP% **123.4**
Speed ratings (Par 97):97,95,95,92,92 91,90,87,86,73 68,59
CSF £221.49 TOTE £7.20: £2.40, £11.70, £1.10; EX 207.80 Place 6 £712.46, Place 5 £357.71 .
Owner Danethorpe Racing Ltd **Bred** Anthony M Cahill **Trained** Danethorpe, Notts

FOCUS
A reasonable banded contest, and sound form.
T/Plt: £3,194.90 to a £1 stake. Pool: £40,921.10. 9.35 winning tickets. T/Qpdt: £145.40 to a £1 stake. Pool: £3,636.80. 18.50 winning tickets. KH

671 SAINT-CLOUD (L-H)
Monday, March 27

OFFICIAL GOING: Heavy

773a PRIX LA CAMARGO (LISTED RACE) (FILLIES) 1m
1:50 (1:52) 3-Y-O **£17,241** (£6,897; £5,172; £3,448; £1,724)

RPR
1 **On A Cloud (USA)**[176] 5649 3-9-0 .... CSoumillon 3 102
(A Fabre, France)
2 *3/4* **Danzon (USA)**[128] 6392 3-9-0 .... IMendizabal 6 100
(J-C Rouget, France)
3 *2 1/2* **Sirene Doloise (FR)**[176] 5649 3-9-0 .... SPasquier 1 95
(A Bonin, France)
4 *3* **Folle Biche (FR)**[11] 3-9-0 .... RCampos 7 89
(Mme N Rossio, France)
5 *4* **Indian Fun**[13] 3-9-0 .... OPeslier 5 81
(F Head, France)
6 *1 1/2* **Blue Blue Sky (IRE)**[176] 5649 3-9-0 .... C-PLemaire 2 78
(Y De Nicolay, France)

7 *8* **Manbala (FR)**[169] [5787] 3-9-0 .... TThulliez 4 62
(J L Dunlop) *led to half-way, 2nd and pushed along straight, beaten 1 1/2f out, eased* **9/1**[1]

1m 53.1s 7 Ran SP% **10.0**
PARI-MUTUEL: WIN 3.90; PL 1.90, 2.20; SF 11.60.
Owner J Wigan **Bred** J Wigan **Trained** Chantilly, France

NOTEBOOK
Manbala(FR), smartly away, was one of the leaders from the start but was never really travelling well. Niggled rounding the final turn, she was a beaten force early in the straight and eventually dropped out last. She was not the same filly who won a Group Three at San Siro last autumn and it is now a case of back to the drawing board.

FOLKESTONE (R-H)
Tuesday, March 28

OFFICIAL GOING: Soft (heavy in places)
Wind: Very strong, behind Weather: Fine

775 EUROPEAN BREEDERS FUND TENTERDEN MAIDEN STKS 5f
2:10 (2:15) (Class 5) 2-Y-O **£3,886** (£1,156; £577; £288) **Stalls** Low

Form RPR
3 **1** **Zafonical Storm (USA)**[10] [663] 2-9-3 .... JamieSpencer 1 66
(B W Duke) *pressed ldrs: hrd rdn against nr side rail over 1f out: kpt on to ld nr fin* **4/6**[1]
2 *nk* **Racing Stripes (IRE)** 2-9-3 .... PatDobbs 3 65
(A B Haynes) *reluctant to enter stalls and restless in them: led: hung rt across crse fr 2f out and ended on far rail: wknd and hdd nr f* **16/1**
3 *2* **Goose Green (IRE)** 2-9-3 .... TedDurcan 5 58
(M R Channon) *dwlt: sn pressed ldr: carried rt 2f out and swtchd lft: shkn up over 1f out: one pce* **5/2**[2]
4 *16* **Alice Who (IRE)** 2-8-12 .... JohnEgan 2 —
(J S Moore) *outpcd and sn rdn: a bhd* **8/1**[3]

65.82 secs (5.02) **Going Correction** +0.70s/f (Yiel) **4** Ran SP% **105.6**
Speed ratings (Par 92):87,86,83,57
CSF £10.09 TOTE £1.40; EX 11.40.
Owner Briton International **Bred** Millsec, Ltd **Trained** Lambourn, Berks
■ River Prince (10/1, unruly at s) was withdrawn. R4 applies, deduct 5p in the £.

FOCUS
Hard to know what to make of the form with outsider Racing Stripes throwing the race away by hanging badly to his right and ending up on the far rail, before being claimed close home by the favourite.

NOTEBOOK
Zafonical Storm(USA), who shaped well when third on his debut at Lingfield, a place behind the subsequent Brocklesby winner Spoof Master, held strong claims with the stands' rail to race against, but he made hard work of it in the ground and only just collared Racing Stripes, who had veered across to the far rail. Better ground will suit the son of Aljabr and he rates a little bit better than the bare form, but he is not the scopiest and may begin to find life hard in conditions events. (tchd 8-13)
Racing Stripes(IRE), who is bred for speed, gave plenty of trouble down at the start, but he was very quickly into his stride and would have won had he not veered right across to the far rail. He was nabbed close home by the winner as he began to get tired, but compensation awaits assuming he goes the right way from this, and better ground may well suit. (op 14-1 tchd 20-1)
Goose Green(IRE), who is bred to appreciate further, comes from a stable who have made a bright start to the season and he made a highly pleasing debut, simply lacking the pace of the front two. He looked well in the paddock beforehand and can probably find a race over this distance, but six furlongs plus is ultimately going to suit. (op 7-2 tchd 9-2)
Alice Who(IRE), whose stable trained the first juvenile winner of the season, was struggling from an early stage and looks in need of more time/a rise in distance. (op 10-1)

776 BARHAM MEDIAN AUCTION MAIDEN STKS 6f
2:40 (2:42) (Class 5) 3-Y-O **£3,238** (£963; £481; £240) **Stalls** Low

Form RPR
1 **Mango Music** 3-8-12 .... TQuinn 3 75+
(M R Channon) *hld up nr side: prog to ld wl over 1f out: shkn up and styd on wl: readily* **7/2**[3]
622- **2** *2 ½* **Cloud Atlas (IRE)**[150] [6156] 3-9-3 75 .... JamieSpencer 6 72+
(S Kirk) *racd virtually alone far side: overall ldr to over 1f out: kpt on u.p* **9/4**[2]
00- **3** *1 ¼* **Proud Killer**[160] [5984] 3-9-3 .... JohnEgan 4 68
(J R Jenkins) *reluctant to enter stalls: dwlt: led nr side gp to wl over 1f out: wknd wl ins f* **16/1**
036- **4** *1 ½* **La Fanciulla**[166] [5852] 3-8-12 71 .... RichardHughes 1 59
(R Hannon) *trckd nr side ldrs: rdn 2f out: one pce and btn fnl f* **7/4**[1]
0-3 **5** *5* **Royal Tavira Girl (IRE)**[22] [590] 3-8-12 .... TPQueally 2 44
(M G Quinlan) *chsd nr side ldr: effrt to chal 2f out: wknd over 1f out* **7/1**
00- **6** *dist* **Marvin Gardens**[100] [6605] 3-8-10 .... DonnaCaldwell(7) 5 —
(P S McEntee) *uns rdr in paddock: rrd s: taken to far side but sn lft bhd by ldr: t.o whn virtually p.u 2f out* **66/1**

1m 17.63s (4.03) **Going Correction** +0.70s/f (Yiel) **6** Ran SP% **109.2**
Speed ratings (Par 98):101,97,96,94,87 —
CSF £11.13 TOTE £5.50: £2.70, £1.50; EX 14.70.
Owner M Channon **Bred** A G Antoniades **Trained** West Ilsley, Berks
■ Stewards' Enquiry : Jamie Spencer one-day ban: failed to ride to draw (Apr 8)

FOCUS
Modest maiden form and it was newcomer Mango Music who ran out a ready winner.
Marvin Gardens Official explanation: jockey said gelding was unsuited by the soft (heavy in places) ground

777 CHARLIE GOLDUP MEMORIAL H'CAP 7f (S)
3:10 (3:12) (Class 5) (0-75,74) 4-Y-O+ **£3,238** (£963; £481; £240) **Stalls** Low

Form RPR
3-45 **1** **Hail The Chief**[60] [213] 9-8-10 66 .... RichardHughes 6 76
(R Hannon) *trckd far side ldrs: effrt over 2f out: pressed ldr over 1f out: drvn to ld last 100yds* **11/2**[1]
0400 **2** *¾* **Corky (IRE)**[25] [571] 5-9-0 70 .... SebSanders 8 78
(I W McInnes) *dwlt: chsd far side ldrs: prog to ld 2f out: drvn over 1f out : hanging and hdd last 100yds* **7/1**[3]
310- **3** *1 ¼* **Resplendent Nova**[179] [5585] 4-8-13 69 .... IanMongan 1 74+
(T G Mills) *led nr side: clr of other pair over 1f out: styd on wl but nvr quite on terms* **12/1**
6-65 **4** *3* **Kew The Music**[13] [639] 6-8-4 60 oh1 .... ChrisCatlin 12 57
(M R Channon) *dwlt: racd far side: last early and wl bhd: rdn and prog 3f out: chsd ldng pair fnl f: no imp after* **6/1**[2]
000- **5** *5* **Marker**[162] [5951] 6-8-13 72 .... RichardThomas(3) 2 57+
(J A Geake) *chsd nr side ldr: outpcd over 1f out: wknd fnl f* **20/1**
63-6 **6** *1* **Seneschal**[52] [292] 5-8-10 66 .... SamHitchcott 3 48+
(A B Haynes) *dwlt: chsd nr side ldr: outpcd over 1f out: wknd fnl f* **8/1**
536- **7** *½* **Linda Green**[150] [6139] 5-8-4 63 .... EdwardCreighton(3) 5 44
(M R Channon) *rr of far side gp: effrt 3f out: rdn to chse ldrs 2f out: wknd over 1f out* **14/1**
006- **8** *1 ¾* **Dr Synn**[154] [6103] 5-8-7 66 .... AdamKirby(3) 4 43
(J Akehurst) *wl in rr far side: rdn and effrt 3f out: no imp 2f out: wknd over 1f out* **16/1**
0620 **9** *2 ½* **Taranaki**[48] [339] 8-8-8 64 .... LPKeniry 9 35
(P D Cundell) *prom far side: rdn to chal over 2f out: wknd rapidly over 1f out* **16/1**
0052 **10** *11* **Elrafa Mujahid**[13] [641] 4-8-13 69 .... (p) NCallan 10 12
(Ernst Oertel) *led far side to 2f out: wknd v rapidly* **8/1**
0205 **11** *17* **Ground Rules (USA)**[13] [641] 4-9-4 74 .... (v[1]) DarryllHolland 7 —
(V Smith) *w far side ldr for 3f: wknd rapidly 1/2-way: t.o* **12/1**
5-03 **P** **Storm Centre**[22] [596] 4-8-10 66 ow2 .... (b) JamieSpencer 11 —
(A M Balding) *t.k.h: pressed far side ldrs early: lost pl and p.u 1/2-way: dismntd* **6/1**[2]

1m 30.9s (3.00) **Going Correction** +0.70s/f (Yiel) **12** Ran SP% **117.3**
Speed ratings (Par 103):110,109,107,104,98 97,96,94,92,79 60,—
CSF £42.72 CT £453.20 TOTE £6.70: £2.30, £2.60, £3.50; EX 54.30 Trifecta £645.30 Part won. Pool: £908.97 - 0.10 winning tickets..
Owner Peter M Crane **Bred** Green Meadow Stud And P Crane **Trained** East Everleigh, Wilts

FOCUS
A decent winning time for the grade in the conditions, much the best of the three races over the trip, but the form is not easy to assess. The race has been rated through the runner-up.
Storm Centre Official explanation: trainer said gelding finished distressed

778 HOLLINGBOURNE REMEMBERS CHARLIE MAIDEN STKS 7f (S)
3:40 (3:41) (Class 5) 3-Y-O+ **£3,562** (£1,059; £529; £264) **Stalls** Low

Form RPR
33- **1** **My Obsession (IRE)**[196] [5210] 4-9-10 .... TedDurcan 2 60
(John Berry) *trckd ldrs: effrt to ld 2f out: green fnl f but styd on wl* **5/2**[1]
5 **2** *1 ½* **Musical Script (USA)**[41] [418] 3-8-9 .... TPQueally 10 51
(Mrs A J Hamilton-Fairley) *trckd ldrs: effrt over 2f out: pressed wnr wl over 1f out: hld ins fnl f* **7/1**[3]
3 *2* **Days Of My Life (IRE)** 3-8-9 .... SteveDrowne 9 46+
(R Charlton) *dwlt: wl in rr: effrt over 2f out: rdn and styd on fr over 1f out: nvr able to chal* **4/1**[2]
-600 **4** *1 ¼* **Barachois Gaudy**[36] [462] 4-9-0 45 .... JamesDoyle(5) 7 43
(Mrs N Smith) *chsd ldrs: effrt over 2f out: kpt on one pce fr over 1f out* **33/1**
5 **5** *1 ½* **Rationale (IRE)**[24] [579] 3-8-9 .... J-PGuillambert 11 39
(S C Williams) *wl in rr and racd against rail: swtchd lft 2f out and again 1f out: nvr nr ldrs* **5/2**[1]
6 *½* **Red Raptor**[40] 5-9-7 .... (t) RichardThomas(3) 4 43+
(J A Geake) *s.v.s: sn in tch: last of main gp 3f out: outpcd over 2f out: styd on fr over 1f out* **14/1**
00- **7** *8* **In Fashion**[306] [2028] 3-8-4 .... AlanMunro 5 13
(R J Hodges) *t.k.h: w ldr: led 3f out to 2f out: wknd* **20/1**
4-00 **8** *9* **Hilltop Fantasy**[8] [681] 5-9-5 47 .... MichaelTebbutt 1 —
(V Smith) *swtchd to far side after 1f: chsd ldrs tl wknd over 2f out* **16/1**
000- **9** *1 ½* **Dancing Beauty (IRE)**[88] [6687] 4-9-5 35 .... NCallan 8 —
(T T Clement) *dwlt: a in rr: wknd over 2f out* **66/1**
0/0 **10** *1 ½* **The Stafford (IRE)**[28] [539] 5-9-10 .... LPKeniry 6 —
(L Wells) *racd against far side rail: led to 3f out: wknd rapidly 2f out* **66/1**
11 *12* **Maya's Prince**[43] 4-9-10 .... HayleyTurner 3 —
(M D I Usher) *in tch to 1/2-way: wknd u.p: t.o* **66/1**

1m 34.11s (6.21) **Going Correction** +0.70s/f (Yiel)
WFA 3 from 4yo+ 15lb **11** Ran SP% **114.4**
Speed ratings (Par 103):92,90,88,86,84 84,75,64,63,61 47
CSF £19.53 TOTE £3.60: £1.30, £1.60, £2.00; EX 23.80 Trifecta £76.30 Pool: £407.61 - 3.79 winning tickets..
Owner J Berry And D Huelin **Bred** John Brady **Trained** Newmarket, Suffolk

FOCUS
A very moderate time for the grade, slower even than the following three-year-old seller over the same trip. They all raced down the far side. The bare form is poor, anchored by the fourth.

779 COME RACING IN KENT (S) H'CAP 7f (S)
4:10 (4:10) (Class 6) (0-60,60) 3-Y-O **£2,730** (£806; £403) **Stalls** Low

Form RPR
4-53 **1** **Assumption (IRE)**[8] [676] 3-7-12 47 .... LiamJones(7) 2 54
(S C Williams) *mde most nr side: clr of rival over 2f out: wl clr over 1f out: unchal* **11/2**[3]
006- **2** *8* **Safari**[231] [4236] 3-8-4 46 oh1 .... AlanMunro 1 33
(R J Hodges) *racd nr side: on terms w wnr to 3f out: sn btn but hld on for overall 2nd* **11/1**
3646 **3** *3 ½* **Bahhmirage (IRE)**[8] [677] 3-8-10 52 .... (b) JamieSpencer 8 30
(Stef Liddiard) *pressed far side ldrs: rdn over 2f out: led gp over 1f out: all out and no ch w nr side pair* **9/2**[2]
-630 **4** *1 ¼* **Three Feathers**[49] [329] 3-8-1 46 oh1 .... SaleemGolam(3) 6 21
(M Salaman) *chsd far side ldrs: rdn over 2f out: plugged on to chse ldr ins fnl f: no ch* **4/1**[1]
0000 **5** *1 ½* **Saxon Star (IRE)**[43] [396] 3-8-4 46 oh6 .... (v) HayleyTurner 7 17
(M D I Usher) *led far side gp to over 2f out: wknd fnl f* **9/1**
00-5 **6** *3* **Sarah's Art (IRE)**[83] [39] 3-7-13 46 oh1 .... JamesDoyle(5) 3 10+
(N A Callaghan) *pressed far side ldr: led gp over 2f out: hung all over the pl in front: lost ld over 1f out: wknd rapidly fnl f* **4/1**[1]
2060 **7** *7* **Stamford Street (IRE)**[13] [645] 3-8-11 60 .... JosephWalsh(7) 4 6
(J S Moore) *dwlt: racd far side: a in rr of gp: wknd over 1f out* **9/2**[2]

1m 33.4s (5.50) **Going Correction** +0.70s/f (Yiel) **7** Ran SP% **110.1**
Speed ratings (Par 96):96,86,82,81,79 76,68
CSF £56.58 CT £274.65 TOTE £4.80: £3.10, £4.30; EX 49.50 Trifecta £117.60 Pool: £399.21 - 2.41 winning tickets..There was no bid for the winner.
Owner P McCutcheon **Bred** Peter McCutcheon **Trained** Newmarket, Suffolk

FOCUS
Hand-timed. Assumption turned this into a procession, seemingly relishing the ground. The first two were the only ones to race on the stands' side. Not an easy race to assess, although it could have been rated higher.

780 WEATHERBYS BANK FILLIES' H'CAP 1m 4f
4:40 (4:40) (Class 5) (0-70,70) 4-Y-0+ £3,238 (£963; £481; £240) Stalls Low

Form RPR
6/1 1 **Shaunas Vision (IRE)**5 [700] 7-9-0 **64** SebSanders 7 71+
(D K Ivory) *sn trckd ldr: led 4f out: clr over 2f out: pushed out ins fnl f* 8/13 1
400- 2 3 **Sabbiosa (IRE)**149 [6183] 4-8-11 **63** TQuinn 2 65
(J L Dunlop) *in tch: outpcd 3f out: drvn and styd on to chse wnr over 1f out : clsd grad but no real threat* 6/1 2
050- 3 5 **Iamback**99 [6612] 6-7-11 **54** oh9 (t) LiamJones(7) 6 49
(Miss D A McHale) *hld up in last: outpcd and rdn over 3f out: plugged on reluctantly to take 3rd ins fnl f* 20/1
100- 4 1 3/4 **Sovietta (IRE)**33 [6582] 5-8-9 **59** (t) DaneO'Neill 1 51
(A G Newcombe) *in tch: chsd wnr over 3f out: brushed aside over 2f out: wknd over 1f out* 10/1 3
354- 5 13 **Ma'Am (USA)**127 [6405] 4-9-4 **70** (b) NCallan 3 44
(I A Wood) *led for 1f: trckd ldrs: outpcd 3f out: shkn up over 2f out: sn wknd* 10/1 3
4-50 6 9 **Full Of Zest**5 [706] 4-8-12 **64** (p) IanMongan 5 26
(Mrs L J Mongan) *chsd ldrs: hrd rdn over 3f out: wknd rapidly over 2f out* 12/1
0056 7 20 **Piquet**26 [557] 8-8-4 **54** oh9 AlanMunro 4 —
(J J Bridger) *racd freely: led after 1f to 4f out: wknd rapidly: t.o* 40/1

2m 56.87s (16.37) **Going Correction** +1.525s/f (Heav)
WFA 4 from 5yo+ 2lb 7 Ran SP% **109.3**
Speed ratings (Par 100):106,104,100,99,90 84,71
CSF £4.14 CT £28.93 TOTE £1.20: £1.10, £2.00; EX 4.90 Trifecta £35.90 Pool: £554.72 - 10.95 winning tickets..
Owner John F Connolly **Bred** Ruairi O'Coileain **Trained** Radlett, Herts

FOCUS
A decent time for the type of contest in the conditions. This took little winning, though, and is basically weak form.

781 THE SUGARLOAVES REMEMBERS CHARLIE H'CAP 1m 1f 149y
5:10 (5:10) (Class 5) (0-70,70) 3-Y-0 £3,238 (£963; £481; £240) Stalls Low

Form RPR
4564 1 **Questive**36 [460] 3-9-1 **67** (t) JamieSpencer 2 72
(E A L Dunlop) *hld up in last trio: stdy prog fr 4f out: hrd rdn over 1f out: led last 150yds: styd on* 13/2 3
41- 2 1 1/4 **Juniper Girl (IRE)**195 [5223] 3-9-1 **67** HayleyTurner 12 71+
(M L W Bell) *led to 8f out: trckd ldrs: rdn and effrt over 2f out: n.m.r briefly ins fnl f: styd on to take 2nd last 75yds* 5/2 1
0-24 3 1 **Mae Cigan (FR)**22 [604] 3-8-8 **60** TedDurcan 9 61
(M Blanshard) *settled in midfield: prog over 4f out to chse ldr 3f out: rdn to ld wl over 1f out: hdd and no ex last 150yds* 7/1
0-63 4 2 1/2 **Black Beauty**52 [293] 3-9-0 **66** TPQueally 11 63+
(M G Quinlan) *hld up in rr: pushed along over 4f out: prog to chse ldrs over 2f out: one pce u.p fnl 2f* 7/2 2
0000 5 3/4 **Zizou (IRE)**28 [538] 3-8-4 **56** oh1 (t) AlanMunro 14 51
(J J Bridger) *settled in midfield: n.m.r on inner and snatched up 4f out: no prog after tl r.o fr over 1f out* 25/1
-404 6 6 **Norman Beckett**69 [142] 3-8-9 **68** ThomasO'Brien(7) 8 52
(M R Channon) *s.i.s: t.k.h: hld up in last: sme prog on inner fr 3f out: nvr on terms w ldrs* 25/1
520- 7 4 **Miss Wedge**169 [5795] 3-9-4 **70** IanMongan 7 47
(T G Mills) *t.k.h: prom: effrt to ld 3f out: hdd wl over 1f out: wknd rapidly* 10/1
0610 8 nk **Living On A Prayer**24 [583] 3-8-13 **65** JimmyQuinn 5 42
(J Pearce) *t.k.h: hld up bhd ldrs: rdn and struggling 3f out* 33/1
000- 9 6 **Brabazon (IRE)**150 [6142] 3-9-1 **67** SteveDrowne 4 33
(R Charlton) *led 8f out to 3f out: wknd rapidly* 7/1
000 10 1 3/4 **King's College (USA)**48 [337] 3-7-12 **57** (b) JamieJones(7) 13 20
(G L Moore) *a towards rr: rdn and wknd over 3f out* 33/1
00-0 11 3 **Lewis Lloyd (IRE)**22 [604] 3-7-13 **56** oh5 JamesDoyle(5) 10 13
(I A Wood) *racd wd in midfield: wknd 3f out* 20/1
00-2 12 1 3/4 **Left Hand Drive**47 [349] 3-8-5 **57** StephenCarson 6 11
(B W Duke) *prog to trck ldr 7f out: wknd rapidly over 3f out* 12/1

2m 21.7s (16.47) **Going Correction** +1.525s/f (Heav) 12 Ran SP% **124.2**
Speed ratings (Par 98):95,94,93,91,90 85,82,82,77,76 73,72
CSF £22.76 CT £122.30 TOTE £8.00: £2.10, £1.40, £2.40; EX 43.70 Trifecta £492.50 Pool: £1,380.54 - 1.99 winning tickets. Place 6 £208.35, Place 5 £123.65.
Owner Gainsborough Stud **Bred** Gainsborough Stud Management Ltd **Trained** Newmarket, Suffolk

FOCUS
A modest three-year-old handicap run at a steady gallop. The race has been rated through the third and there is a chance the principals will go on from here.
Lewis Lloyd(IRE) Official explanation: jockey said gelding was unsuited by the soft (heavy in places) ground
T/Plt: £46.10 to a £1 stake. Pool: £43,738.00. 691.70 winning tickets. T/Qpdt: £12.70 to a £1 stake. Pool: £3,838.10. 222.90 winning tickets. JN

714 SOUTHWELL (L-H)
Tuesday, March 28

OFFICIAL GOING: Standard
Wind: Fresh, across Weather: Cloudy with sunny spells

782 SOUTHWELL-RACECOURSE.CO.UK BANDED STKS 5f (F)
2:20 (2:20) (Class 7) 4-Y-0+ £1,876 (£554; £277) Stalls High

Form RPR
044- 1 **Bahamian Bay**150 [6155] 4-8-8 45 DanielTudhope(3) 4 51
(M Brittain) *w ldr: rdn to ld 1f out: edgd lft: r.o* 8/1
0204 2 1 1/4 **Boanerges (IRE)**1 [772] 9-9-2 50 RyanMoore 12 52
(J M Bradley) *sn outpcd: hdwy over 1f out: rdn and hung lft ins fnl f: r.o* 6/1 3
0621 3 3/4 **Percy Douglas**7 [686] 6-8-10 45 (bt) AnnStokell(7) 3 50
(Miss A Stokell) *led: rdn and hdd 1f out: styd on same pce* 9/1
6-00 4 nk **Mr Spliffy (IRE)**44 [388] 7-8-6 35 (b) EmmettStack(5) 2 43
(M C Chapman) *s.i.s: sn chsng ldrs: rdn over 1f out: no ex ins fnl f* 66/1
00-0 5 nk **Laurel Dawn**7 [686] 8-8-11 35 (b) MickyFenton 5 42
(C N Kellett) *dwlt: hdwy over 3f out: hung lft and outpcd 1/2-way: r.o ins fnl f* 80/1
0412 6 3 **Mystery Pips**7 [686] 6-9-2 50 (v) KimTinkler 1 37
(N Tinkler) *s.i.s: sn prom: rdn and wknd fnl f* 5/1 1
502- 7 2 **Fox Covert (IRE)**143 [6256] 5-8-11 45 (p) RobertWinston 10 25
(D W Barker) *chsd ldrs: rdn 1/2-way: hung lft over 1f out: wknd fnl f* 11/2 2
-000 8 1 **Dutch Key Card (IRE)**30 [524] 5-8-12 46 (b1) GylesParkin 6 23
(C Smith) *chsd ldrs over 3f* 14/1
0-00 9 hd **Music Teacher**8 [679] 4-9-2 50 FergalLynch 11 26
(N A Callaghan) *s.i.s: outpcd* 8/1
50-0 10 6 **New Options**8 [679] 9-9-2 50 (b) RobbieFitzpatrick 8 6
(Peter Grayson) *s.s: outpcd* 5/1 1
000- 11 1 3/4 **Shamrock Tea**330 [1418] 5-8-11 45 TomEaves 7 —
(M E Sowersby) *s.s: outpcd* 28/1

59.74 secs (-0.56) **Going Correction** -0.175s/f (Stan) 11 Ran SP% **108.1**
Speed ratings (Par 97):97,95,93,93,92 88,84,83,82,73 70
CSF £49.46 TOTE £10.60: £2.40, £2.10, £2.50; EX 106.60.
Owner Mel Brittain **Bred** The National Stud **Trained** Warthill, N Yorks

FOCUS
A poor contest and the usual draw bias was in operation with the five lowest-drawn runners finishing in the first six. The winner is less exposed than most of these.
Dutch Key Card(IRE) Official explanation: jockey said gelding would not face the kickback
New Options Official explanation: jockey said gelding would not face the kickback

783 DINE IN THE QUEEN MOTHER RESTAURANT MAIDEN CLAIMING STKS 7f (F)
2:50 (2:50) (Class 7) 4-Y-0+ £1,365 (£403; £201) Stalls Low

Form RPR
00-4 1 **Government (IRE)**8 [674] 5-8-8 45 StephenDonohoe(5) 4 53
(M C Chapman) *mde all: clr 1/2-way: rdn over 1f out: edgd rt ins fnl f: styd on* 20/1
0250 2 3 **Tommytyler (IRE)**14 [634] 7-8-12 45 (t) DanielTudhope(3) 9 47
(D Carroll) *hld up: hdwy 1/2-way: chsd wnr over 1f out: styd on u.p* 5/1 2
5022 3 2 **Faithisflying**7 [687] 4-8-10 40 (p) TonyCulhane 8 37
(D W Chapman) *sn pushed along and prom: rdn to chse wnr 1/2-way to over 1f out: no ex* 9/4 1
6503 4 3 **Kashtanka (IRE)**7 [687] 4-8-12 40 (b) JasonEdmunds(3) 3 34
(J Balding) *prom: pushed along 1/2-way: wknd over 2f out* 5/1 2
00-0 5 5 **Mister Regent**1 [772] 5-8-11 35 ShaneKelly 11 17
(W M Brisbourne) *chsd ldrs over 4f* 40/1
04-6 6 3 1/2 **Fayrz Please (IRE)**4 [715] 5-8-10 35 EmmettStack(5) 5 12
(M C Chapman) *chsd ldrs: rdn 1/2-way: wknd over 2 out* 33/1
0-00 7 2 1/2 **Mad Marty Wildcard**68 [144] 4-9-1 35 TomEaves 7 5
(R Brotherton) *chsd ldrs 4f* 40/1
-360 8 4 **Alzarma**24 [581] 4-8-11 45 (b1) DeanMcKeown 2 —
(J Gallagher) *s.i.s: hdwy over 4f out: wknd 1/2-way* 25/1
400- 9 nk **Compton Bay**178 [5623] 6-8-13 40 DavidAllan 6 —
(M Brittain) *chsd ldrs to 1/2-way* 14/1
0003 10 1 1/4 **Donya One**14 [634] 4-8-8 40 EddieAhern 1 —
(John A Harris) *hld up: effrt 1/2-way: sn wknd* 11/1
34-0 11 14 **Nebraska City**11 [173] 5-9-1 45 RobertWinston 10 —
(D W Thompson) *in rr: rdn 1/2-way: virtually p.u fnl 3f* 11/2 3
12 1/2 **Red Ruth Lady** 4-8-10 FrancisFerris 12 —
(D L Williams) *dwlt: outpcd* 66/1

1m 31.06s (0.26) **Going Correction** -0.10s/f (Stan) 12 Ran SP% **112.4**
Speed ratings (Par 97):94,90,88,84,79 75,72,67,67,65 49,49
CSF £106.24 TOTE £21.00: £4.70, £1.90, £1.40; EX 187.20.
Owner Peter Taylor **Bred** C H Wacker Iii **Trained** Market Rasen, Lincs

FOCUS
Not a race that will live long in the memory. The route taken by the winner suggested that racing towards the inside of the track was not the handicap it usually is. Poor form.
Nebraska City Official explanation: jockey said gelding hung left and felt amiss

784 BUY TICKETS ON LINE BANDED STKS 7f (F)
3:20 (3:20) (Class 7) 4-Y-0+ £1,876 (£554; £277) Stalls Low

Form RPR
1005 1 **Favouring (IRE)**21 [612] 4-9-0 48 (v) AdrianMcCarthy 9 58
(M C Chapman) *hld up: hdwy 1/2-way: rdn to ld over 1f out: r.o* 13/2 2
1301 2 3/4 **Only If I Laugh**8 [681] 5-9-6 48 GrahamGibbons 3 62
(M J Attwater) *chsd ldrs: led wl over 1f out: sn rdn: hung lft and hdd: unable qck towards fin* 11/2 1
4212 3 2 1/2 **Mount Royale (IRE)**8 [681] 8-9-1 49 (v) KimTinkler 11 51
(N Tinkler) *chsd ldrs: rdn and ev ch 2f out: styd on same pce appr fnl f* 11/2 1
6-10 4 2 **Wings Of Morning (IRE)**30 [526] 5-8-10 47 (v) DanielTudhope(3) 4 43
(D Carroll) *s.i.s: plld hrd and sn prom: rdn over 2f out: styd on same pce* 16/1
0013 5 3/4 **Wilford Maverick (IRE)**8 [680] 4-8-13 47 (v) FrancisFerris 7 41
(M J Attwater) *chsd ldrs: rdn over 2f out: sn ev ch: wknd fnl f* 7/1 3
3603 6 1 **Prince Of Gold**8 [681] 6-9-2 50 VinceSlattery 8 42
(R Hollinshead) *s.i.s: rdn 1/2-way: nvr nrr* 11/2 1
0040 7 5 **Massey**20 [613] 10-8-11 45 RobertWinston 10 24
(C R Dore) *w ldr tl led 1/2-way: rdn and hdd wl over 1f out: sn wknd* 25/1
20-5 8 2 1/2 **Aboustar**7 [691] 6-8-11 45 (b) DavidAllan 6 17
(M Brittain) *led to 1/2-way: wknd over 1f out* 20/1
0120 9 10 **Justcallmehandsome**44 [387] 4-9-1 49 (v) EddieAhern 1 —
(D J S Ffrench Davis) *hld up: bhd fnl 4f* 8/1
5102 10 3 **Penel (IRE)**20 [618] 5-8-13 47 (p) LeeEnstone 2 —
(P T Midgley) *chsd ldrs: sn pushed along: lost pl over 4f out: wknd over 2f out* 13/2 2

1m 29.92s (-0.88) **Going Correction** -0.10s/f (Stan) 10 Ran SP% **110.9**
Speed ratings (Par 97):101,100,97,95,94 93,87,84,73,69
CSF £39.70 TOTE £9.60: £3.50, £2.50, £2.10; EX 79.60.
Owner Eric Knowles **Bred** Christopher John Strain **Trained** Market Rasen, Lincs

FOCUS
Plenty of pace on here and a fair time for a banded race, 1.14 seconds faster than the preceding maiden claimer. Above-average form from the first two.
Justcallmehandsome Official explanation: jockey said gelding never travelled

785 SPONSOR A RACE AT SOUTHWELL BANDED STKS 1m 4f (F)
3:50 (3:50) (Class 7) 4-Y-0+ £1,876 (£554; £277) Stalls Low

Form RPR
1045 1 **York Cliff**13 [643] 8-9-4 50 EddieAhern 3 58+
(W M Brisbourne) *hld up: hdwy over 8f out: chsd ldr over 3f out: led on bit over 1f out: nt extended* 7/2 2
2063 2 3/4 **High Frequency (IRE)**7 [688] 5-9-2 48 (b) PaulFessey 5 51
(T D Barron) *led: rdn over 2f out: hdd over 1f out: edgd rt ins fnl f: no ch w wnr* 6/4 1
500- 3 14 **Scott's Mill**147 [6215] 4-8-8 45 StanleyChin(3) 2 28
(M Johnston) *chsd ldrs: rdn and lost pl over 8f out: outpcd fnl 4f* 9/2 3

-401 **4** 2 **Tiegs (IRE)**12 647 4-8-11 50 MarcHalford(5) 6 31
(P W Hiatt) *chsd ldr over 8f: wknd over 2f out* **7/2**2

0-00 **5** 21 **Solipsist (IRE)**25 573 5-8-9 48 MarkCoumbe(7) 1 —
(N I M Rossiter) *hld up: rdn and wknd over 4f out* **20/1**

2m 43.25s (1.16) **Going Correction** -0.10s/f (Stan)
WFA 4 from 5yo+ 2lb **5** Ran SP% **107.4**
Speed ratings (Par 97):92,91,82,80,66
CSF £8.74 TOTE £4.10: £2.10, £1.20; EX 7.00.
Owner P Wright-Bevans **Bred** F Hinojosa **Trained** Great Ness, Shropshire

FOCUS
A poor contest that became a match from some way out. A very moderate winning time too, even for a race like this.
Solipsist(IRE) Official explanation: trainer said gelding bled from the nose

786 HOSPITALITY PACKAGES AVAILABLE TRI-BANDED STKS 1m (F)
4:20 (4:20) (Class 7) 3-Y-O **£1,876** (£554; £277) **Stalls** Low

Form RPR

6-00 **1** **Dylan (IRE)**70 132 3-9-0 45 KimTinkler 6 48
(N Tinkler) *chsd ldrs: led over 4f out: rdn and hung lft fr over 1f out: styd on* **3/1**2

60-0 **2** 2 1/2 **Cuesta Canyon (IRE)**17 626 3-8-9 40 RobertWinston 5 38
(M J Polglase) *hld up in tch: plld hrd: rdn to chse wnr fnl 2f: sn edgd lft: styng on same pce whn nt clr run ins fnl f* **9/2**3

0002 **3** 4 **Beginners Luck (IRE)**7 690 3-8-4 30 AdrianMcCarthy 3 25
(D Carroll) *s.s: sn prom: rdn over 4f out: styd on same pce fnl 2f* **9/4**1

00-0 **4** nk **Xaar Breeze**7 690 3-8-10 40 ow1 TonyCulhane 4 30
(Rae Guest) *broke wl: plld hrd: stdd and lost pl 7f out: chsd ldr over 3f out: sn rdn: wknd over 1f out* **3/1**2

605- **5** 8 **Zastra's Pride**194 5251 3-7-13 35 (t) MarcHalford(5) 1 8
(W G M Turner) *chsd ldrs over 4f* **13/2**

-006 **6** 7 **Moraadi**7 690 3-8-4 30 (p) DaleGibson 2 —
(D W Chapman) *plld hrd: sn led: hdd over 4f out: rdn and wknd over 2f out* **20/1**

1m 47.4s (2.80) **Going Correction** -0.10s/f (Stan) **6** Ran SP% **117.0**
Speed ratings (Par 92):82,79,75,75,67 60
CSF £17.60 TOTE £4.60: £1.60, £2.40; EX 23.60.
Owner G T S Macdonald & West Wing Racing **Bred** Brian Williamson **Trained** Langton, N Yorks

FOCUS
A poor heat run at a slow early gallop, resulting in a pedestrian winning time, even for a race like this, 3.61 seconds slower than the following contest for older horses.
Beginners Luck(IRE) Official explanation: jockey said filly missed the break

787 EXPERIENCE NOTTINGHAMSHIRE BANDED STKS 1m (F)
4:50 (4:50) (Class 7) 4-Y-O+ **£1,876** (£554; £277) **Stalls** Low

Form RPR

4102 **1** **Desert Fury**7 689 9-9-0 48 (b) RobertWinston 6 55
(R Bastiman) *s.i.s: hdwy over 3f out: ev ch fr over 2f out: styd on u.p to ld towards fin* **9/4**1

230- **2** nk **King Zafeen (IRE)**204 5001 4-9-2 50 DaleGibson 4 56
(M W Easterby) *hld up in tch: plld hrd: led over 2f out: rdn and hdd towards fin* **9/4**1

6324 **3** 9 **High Swainston**12 649 5-9-0 48 PaulFessey 2 36
(R Craggs) *led over 5f: rdn and wknd over 1f out* **10/3**2

540- **4** 3 1/2 **Wood Fern (UAE)**143 6262 6-9-1 49 ShaneKelly 3 30
(W M Brisbourne) *prom over 5f* **12/1**

0-06 **5** 2 1/2 **Bob Baileys**30 527 4-8-11 40 (p) EddieAhern 7 21
(P R Chamings) *chsd ldrs 6f* **15/2**3

00/0 **6** 19 **Simnel (IRE)**27 546 7-8-4 30 MarkCoumbe(7) 5 —
(S L Keightley) *chsd ldrs over 5f* **125/1**

7 dist **Queen Meabh (IRE)**509 3891 6-8-8 35 DanielTudhope(3) 1 —
(P J Rothwell, Ire) *prom: rdn and lost pl over 4f out: sn bhd* **25/1**

1m 43.79s (-0.81) **Going Correction** -0.10s/f (Stan) **7** Ran SP% **108.7**
Speed ratings (Par 97):100,99,90,87,84 65,—
CSF £6.61 TOTE £2.90: £1.40, £2.00; EX 3.40.
Owner Robin Bastiman **Bred** Meon Valley Stud **Trained** Cowthorpe, N Yorks

FOCUS
Moderate form but the first two came clear and the form looks solid for the grade.

788 TURF RACING ON 3RD APRIL BANDED STKS 1m 3f (F)
5:20 (5:20) (Class 7) 4-Y-O+ **£1,876** (£554; £277) **Stalls** Low

Form RPR

0451 **1** **Dextrous**20 615 9-8-12 45 (p) MickyFenton 4 49
(P T Midgley) *a.p: racd keenly: led ins fnl f: rdn clr* **9/2**2

-500 **2** 5 **Kentucky Bullet (USA)**14 636 10-8-12 45 SimonWhitworth 9 40
(A G Newcombe) *hld up: hdwy over 6f out: led over 1f out: hdd and no ex ins fnl f* **6/1**

0046 **3** shd **Simply The Guest (IRE)**44 390 7-8-12 40 (vt) KimTinkler 6 40
(N Tinkler) *hld up: hdwy u.p over 1f out: nrst fin* **8/1**

000- **4** 1 1/2 **Sudden Impulse**90 6680 5-8-7 35 (p) DuranFentiman(5) 2 37
(A D Brown) *chsd ldr tl led over 3f out: rdn and hdd over 1f out: wknd fnl f* **12/1**

00-0 **5** 2 1/2 **Mr Strowger**34 484 5-8-12 40 FergusSweeney 5 33
(J C Fox) *hld up: effrt over 2f out: n.d* **40/1**

2444 **6** shd **Liquid Lover (IRE)**8 684 4-8-11 45 EddieAhern 7 33
(W M Brisbourne) *chsd ldrs: rdn over 3f out: nt much over 2f out: nt run on* **5/2**1

0/4- **7** 1/2 **A Bit Of Fun**15 321 5-8-12 40 DaleGibson 8 32
(J T Stimpson) *hld up: rdn over 2f out: n.d* **11/2**3

566- **8** 10 **Gran Dana (IRE)**77 5855 6-8-12 40 (v1) TonyCulhane 1 16
(G Prodromou) *led over 7f: wknd over 2f out* **8/1**

9 dist **Holding Hands (IRE)**312 1875 5-8-9 40 DanielTudhope(3) 3 —
(Patrick Morris, Ire) *chsd ldrs over 7f* **16/1**

2m 27.15s (-1.75) **Going Correction** -0.10s/f (Stan)
WFA 4 from 5yo+ 1lb **9** Ran SP% **114.7**
Speed ratings (Par 97):102,98,98,97,95 95,94,87,—
CSF £31.39 TOTE £4.60: £1.60, £1.60, £3.20; EX 33.70 Place 6 £55.54, Place 5 £10.45 .
Owner O R Dukes **Bred** Newgate Stud Co **Trained** Westow, N Yorks

FOCUS
An ordinary banded affair which did not take a great deal of winning but which produced a fair time for the grade.
T/Plt: £90.40 to a £1 stake. Pool: £39,474.55. 318.75 winning tickets. T/Qpdt: £14.00 to a £1 stake. Pool: £3,663.80. 192.70 winning tickets. CR

766 WOLVERHAMPTON (A.W) (L-H)
Wednesday, March 29

OFFICIAL GOING: Standard
Wind: Moderate, behind Weather: Heavy shower after race 2 (3.00)

789 NAME A RACE TO ENHANCE YOUR BRAND BANDED STKS 5f 20y(P)
2:30 (2:30) (Class 7) 4-Y-O+ **£1,706** (£503; £252) **Stalls** Low

Form RPR

6213 **1** **Percy Douglas**1 782 6-8-10 45 (bt) AnnStokell(7) 5 53
(Miss A Stokell) *s.s: hdwy on ins over 2f out: led wl ins fnl f: r.o* **11/2**3

00-5 **2** 3/4 **Prime Recreation**15 633 9-8-11 45 RobertWinston 11 44
(P S Felgate) *swtchd lft and led after 1f: hdd wl over 1f out: led ins fnl f: sn hdd: nt qckn* **14/1**

-055 **3** nk **Feminist (IRE)**9 679 4-8-11 40 (p) NCallan 1 43
(J M Bradley) *led 1f: w ldr: led wl over 1f out tl ins fnl f: nt qckn* **9/2**2

035- **4** 1/2 **So Sober (IRE)**375 666 8-8-8 40 PatrickMathers(3) 3 41
(D Shaw) *chsd ldrs: rdn over 2f out: ev ch wl ins fnl f: no ex* **16/1**

2033 **5** nk **Eternally**8 686 4-8-11 45 (p) ShaneKelly 2 40
(R M H Cowell) *a.p: rdn over 2f out: one pce fnl f* **7/1**

406- **6** 1/2 **Petana**98 6647 6-8-11 45 (p) RobbieFitzpatrick 9 39
(Peter Grayson) *bhd: rdn and hdwy on ins over 1f out: r.o one pce fnl f* **12/1**

-232 **7** nk **Obe Bold (IRE)**9 680 5-8-11 45 (v) FergalLynch 4 37
(A Berry) *chsd ldrs: rdn over 2f out: kpt on towards fin* **4/1**1

0064 **8** 1 1/4 **Katie Killane**8 686 4-8-11 35 AlanDaly 6 33
(M Wellings) *hld up: n.m.r over 3f out: sn bhd: rdn and hdwy over 1f out: n.d* **25/1**

400 **9** 3/4 **Teyaar**2 766 10-8-11 45 J-PGuillambert 7 30
(M Wellings) *nvr trbld ldrs* **8/1**

-350 **10** 3/4 **Town House**9 679 4-8-4 45 SoniaEaton(7) 12 28
(B P J Baugh) *t.k.h: sn chsng ldrs: rdn over 1f out: wknd fnl f* **25/1**

-000 **11** 1 **Rock Fever (IRE)**30 532 4-8-5 45 ow1 (b) RonanKeogh(7) 8 25
(Peter Grayson) *a bhd* **14/1**

00/0 **12** 8 **Mister Bell**21 613 4-8-8 40 (p) BenSwarbrick(3) 10 —
(J G M O'Shea) *chsd ldrs tl c wd and wknd over 2f out* **40/1**

060- **13** 7 **Mickledo**292 2446 4-8-11 35 SamHitchcott 13 —
(A Bailey) *a bhd* **66/1**

62.82 secs **Going Correction** -0.05s/f (Stan) **13** Ran SP% **115.7**
Speed ratings (Par 97):98,96,96,95,95 94,93,91,90,89 87,74,63
CSF £74.55 TOTE £7.40: £2.20, £5.10, £1.60; EX 107.10.
Owner Ms Caron Stokell **Bred** Qualitair Stud Ltd **Trained** Brompton-on-Swale, N Yorks

FOCUS
The usual suspects for a race like this and the draw played its part with four of the first five home coming from the five inside stalls. Average form for the grade, but probably sound enough.

790 REMEMBER FAMILY FUN DAYS AT WOLVERHAMPTON TRI-BANDED STKS 5f 216y(P)
3:00 (3:00) (Class 7) 3-Y-O **£1,876** (£554; £277) **Stalls** Low

Form RPR

000- **1** **Joking John**147 6224 3-7-9 35 LeanneKershaw(7) 5 41
(C W Fairhurst) *sn led: hdd over 3f out: rdn 2f out: led jst ins fnl f: rdn and r.o wl* **16/1**

000- **2** 1 1/2 **Bertie Bear**124 6424 3-8-7 40 (vt1) NCallan 2 42
(G G Margarson) *bhd: rdn and hdwy on ins over 2f out: r.o ins fnl f* **7/1**

0215 **3** 1 1/4 **Berties Brother**23 595 3-8-11 45 ow2 DNolan(3) 10 45
(D G Bridgwater) *led early: a.p: rdn over 2f out: kpt on ins fnl f* **10/3**2

0050 **4** 1/2 **Stoneacre Girl (IRE)**15 637 3-8-8 40 ow1 RobbieFitzpatrick 3 38
(Peter Grayson) *prom: led over 3f out: rdn and edgd rt over 1f out: hdd jst ins fnl f: no ex towards fin* **7/1**

0-00 **5** shd **Marron Flore**30 533 3-8-9 45 RichardThomas(3) 12 41
(A J Lidderdale) *chsd ldrs: rdn wl over 1f out: one pce fnl f* **25/1**

0-00 **6** nk **Cape Latina**23 594 3-8-12 45 SteveDrowne 7 40
(J R Best) *bhd: rdn and hdwy over 1f out: nvr trbld ldrs* **6/1**

6561 **7** nk **Bekoning (IRE)**8 687 3-9-4 45 6ex ShaneKelly 1 45
(M Quinn) *sn prom: rdn over 2f out: no ex ins fnl f* **3/1**1

0-40 **8** 1 **Sanders Boy**65 176 3-8-12 45 DarrenWilliams 4 39+
(J R Norton) *prom: rdn over 2f out: one pce whn nt clr run and eased wl ins fnl f* **7/1**

4460 **9** hd **Sweet Cherokee**31 528 3-8-2 40 MarcHalford(5) 9 31
(C N Kellett) *prom: lost pl after 1f: n.d after* **25/1**

-544 **10** 1 1/2 **Tequila Rose (IRE)**8 690 3-8-12 45 SamHitchcott 8 31
(A Bailey) *t.k.h towards rr: short-lived effrt on outside over 2f out* **5/1**3

040- **11** nk **Stanley Wolfe (IRE)**198 5175 3-8-12 45 RoystonFfrench 13 30
(James Moffatt) *chsd ldrs tl rdn and wknd over 2f out* **40/1**

000- **12** 1/2 **Royal Song**301 2183 3-8-9 45 PatrickMathers(3) 6 29
(D Shaw) *hld up in tch: rdn and wknd over 2f out* **14/1**

1m 17.4s (1.59) **Going Correction** -0.05s/f (Stan) **12** Ran SP% **139.2**
Speed ratings (Par 92):87,85,83,82,82 82,81,80,80,78 77,77
CSF £142.70 TOTE £34.00: £9.80, £3.00, £1.30; EX 357.70.
Owner North Cheshire Trading & Storage Ltd **Bred** North Cheshire Trading And Storage Ltd **Trained** Middleham Moor, N Yorks

FOCUS
This looked as though it might be quite a competitive event beforehand as a few were well backed, but it was won in a modest winning time, even for a race like this. Poor form, and probably none-too-reliable.
Stoneacre Girl(IRE) Official explanation: jockey said filly hung right-handed home straight

791 HIRE WOLVERHAMPTON RACECOURSE 4 ANY OCCASION MAIDEN CLAIMING STKS 1m 1f 103y(P)
3:30 (3:36) (Class 7) 4-Y-O+ **£1,365** (£403; £201) **Stalls** Low

Form RPR

6-0 **1** **Hillfield Flyer (IRE)**64 183 6-8-7 45 DanielTudhope(3) 1 43
(Samuel Murphy, Ire) *a.p: rdn over 3f out: led wl over 1f out: r.o* **7/1**

4-05 **2** 1 3/4 **Danum**15 634 6-8-6 35 (p) RussellKennemore(7) 2 43
(R Hollinshead) *led: hdd over 4f out: rdn to ld over 2f out: hdd wl over 1f out: nt qckn ins fnl f* **6/1**2

00-4 **3** 1/2 **Heathyards Joy**15 634 5-8-8 40 (p) NCallan 3 37
(R Hollinshead) *hld up: rdn and hdwy over 2f out: kpt on towards fin* **7/2**1

0006 **4** nk **Queue Up**15 634 4-9-1 40 SimonWhitworth 7 43
(A G Newcombe) *hld up towards rr: hdwy on ins over 2f out: sn rdn: kpt on towards fin* **13/2**3

05-0 **5** *3* **Viscount Rossini**[65] 174 4-8-12 40 RichardThomas(3) 9 38
(A W Carroll) *hld up in mid-div: rdn over 2f out: hung lft and sme hdwy over 1f out: one pce fnl f* **8/1**

00 **6** *1 ¾* **Where's Sally**[15] 634 6-8-8 RobertWinston 4 27
(J Mackie) *prom tl rdn and wknd 2f out* **10/1**

-600 **7** *1 ¼* **Level Par (IRE)**[51] 311 6-8-11 45 (t) FergalLynch 12 28
(J A Supple) *prom: led over 4f out tl over 2f out: sn rdn: wknd over 1f out* **7/1**

0-00 **8** *shd* **Doughty**[9] 616 4-8-9 35 (t) VinceSlattery 8 26
(D J Wintle) *uns rdr and bolted bef s: nvr trbld ldrs* **20/1**

0050 **9** *1 ¾* **Rythm N Rhyme (IRE)**[31] 526 7-9-1 45 PaulEddery 10 29
(John A Harris) *w ldrs: rdn over 3f out: wknd 2f out* **8/1**

/000 **10** *4* **Darling River (FR)**[40] 442 7-8-10 35 TomEaves 5 16
(R Brotherton) *hld up in tch: rdn over 3f out: wknd over 2f out* **50/1**

0000 **11** *3* **Teenage Rampage**[2] 768 4-8-13 40 RobbieFitzpatrick 6 13
(W M Brisbourne) *s.i.s: t.k.h: a bhd* **25/1**

00-0 **12** *15* **Taylor Maid**[16] 148 4-8-10 40 (v) ShaneKelly 11 —
(G A Ham) *rrd s: hld up: hdwy and hung rt 4f out: sn rdn and wknd: eased whn no ch over 1f out* **6/1**[2]

2m 2.53s (-0.09) **Going Correction** -0.05s/f (Stan) **12** Ran SP% **131.0**
Speed ratings (Par 97):98,96,96,95,93 91,90,90,88,85 82,69
CSF £53.17 TOTE £9.20: £2.80, £2.80, £1.70; EX 107.00.
Owner Sam Murphy **Bred** Sam Murphy **Trained** Monasterevin,Co Kildare
■ A first ever winner for Curragh trainer Sam Murphy, with the only horse he has in training.

FOCUS
By its very nature this was a moderate contest, but the pace was fair and the time was almost identical to the following banded contest over the same trip. Poor form, but sound enough.
Taylor Maid Official explanation: jockey said filly jumped awkwardly out of stalls and hung right

792 THEMED RACE NIGHTS AT WOLVERHAMPTON BANDED STKS 1m 1f 103y(P)
4:00 (4:01) (Class 7) 4-Y-0+ **£1,706** (£503; £252) **Stalls** Low

Form RPR

6600 **1** **Fiore Di Bosco (IRE)**[34] 493 5-8-11 45 PhillipMakin 11 49
(T D Barron) *s.i.s: t.k.h: hdwy over 2f out: rdn to ld jst over 1f out: r.o* **10/1**

0245 **2** *1 ¼* **Spy Gun (USA)**[37] 469 6-8-11 45 J-PGuillambert 4 47
(T Wall) *hld up and bhd: hdwy on ins over 2f out: rdn and ev ch 1f out: nt qckn* **6/1**[2]

0-01 **3** *1* **Ballare (IRE)**[2] 770 7-9-3 40 (v) FergusSweeney 6 51
(P J Makin) *t.k.h: in tch: rdn over 2f out: ev ch 1f out: kpt on ins fnl f* **6/1**[2]

400- **4** *shd* **Emperor Cat (IRE)**[309] 1986 5-8-11 40 GrahamGibbons 2 45
(Mrs N S Evans) *a.p: rdn over 2f out: ev ch over 1f out: nt qckn* **20/1**

-004 **5** *¾* **Welsh Whisper**[2] 769 7-8-8 40 NeilChalmers(3) 9 44
(S A Brookshaw) *s.i.s: hld up and bhd: hdwy over 3f out: rdn wl over 1f out: r.o one pce fnl f* **25/1**

04-0 **6** *1 ¾* **Parisian Playboy**[21] 616 6-8-6 40 DuranFentiman(5) 12 40
(A D Brown) *s.i.s: hld up: rdn over 2f out: hdwy over 1f out: one pce fnl f* **25/1**

526- **7** *5* **Come On**[245] 3849 7-8-11 45 MichaelTebbutt 13 31
(J Hetherton) *sn chsng ldr: led 6f out: rdn and hdd jst over 1f out: wknd fnl f* **12/1**

000- **8** *¾* **Tonight (IRE)**[170] 5790 4-8-11 45 (bt) ShaneKelly 1 29
(W M Brisbourne) *led: hdd 6f out: w ldr: rdn over 2f out: wknd over 1f out* **25/1**

540- **9** *2 ½* **Wind Chime (IRE)**[98] 6651 9-8-9 45 ow1 (p) RobertMiles(3) 7 26
(A G Newcombe) *hld up in tch: hdwy 4f out: wknd wl over 1f out* **9/1**[3]

53-0 **10** *2 ½* **Lenwade**[51] 311 5-8-11 45 (p) NCallan 10 20
(G G Margarson) *hld up in tch: rdn over 3f out: wknd over 2f out* **4/1**[1]

0-00 **11** *¾* **Huxley (IRE)**[15] 638 7-8-4 40 (t) JosephWalsh(7) 5 18
(D J Wintle) *s.i.s: plld hrd: a bhd* **14/1**

5004 **12** *3* **Super Dominion**[9] 682 9-8-11 45 (p) VinceSlattery 8 13
(R Hollinshead) *hld up in tch: hdwy over 5f out: rdn 3f out: sn wknd* **10/1**

-406 **13** *2* **Ernmoor**[36] 472 4-8-11 45 SteveDrowne 3 9
(J R Best) *t.k.h in tch: hung lft and lost pl over 5f out* **4/1**[1]

2m 2.52s (-0.10) **Going Correction** -0.05s/f (Stan) **13** Ran SP% **127.4**
Speed ratings (Par 97):98,96,96,95,95 93,89,88,86,84 83,80,79
CSF £70.22 TOTE £15.40: £4.80, £2.30, £3.20; EX 150.50.
Owner Miss Pauline Laycock **Bred** Rathbarry Stud **Trained** Maunby, N Yorks

FOCUS
A fair race of its type, run at a solid pace, and there were still five in a line across the track passing the furlong pole. Average form, the fifth helping set the standard.
Ernmoor Official explanation: jockey said gelding hung badly left-handed throughout

793 STAY AT THE WOLVERHAMPTON HOLIDAY INN BANDED STKS 7f 32y(P)
4:30 (4:31) (Class 7) 4-Y-0+ **£1,706** (£503; £252) **Stalls** High

Form RPR

0300 **1** **Elms Schoolboy**[15] 638 4-8-11 45 (b) J-PGuillambert 5 52
(P Howling) *bhd: rdn and hdwy over 2f out: hung lft over 1f out: r.o to ld cl home* **8/1**[3]

2536 **2** *½* **Dexileos (IRE)**[13] 649 7-8-11 45 (t) FergusSweeney 3 51
(David Pinder) *a.p: rdn over 3f out: hung lft and led over 1f out: hdd cl home* **6/1**[2]

0-5 **3** *½* **Midmaar (IRE)**[77] 95 5-8-11 45 (p) JamieMackay 2 50
(M Wigham) *led early: a.p: rdn over 3f out: ev ch fnl f: r.o* **7/4**[1]

00-0 **4** *½* **Sabo Prince**[61] 210 4-8-11 40 (p) NCallan 9 48
(J M Bradley) *hld up in mid-div: hdwy over 3f out: rdn over 2f out: ev ch ins fnl f: no ex towards fin* **20/1**

-000 **5** *1 ½* **Mytton's Dream**[57] 261 4-8-11 40 (b[1]) TomEaves 1 45
(R Brotherton) *s.i.s: hld up in mid-div: hdwy on ins over 2f out: one pce fnl f* **33/1**

4305 **6** *2 ½* **Weet Yer Tern (IRE)**[2] 769 4-8-11 45 ShaneKelly 12 38
(W M Brisbourne) *sn led: rdn over 2f out: hdd over 1f out: wknd in side fnl f* **10/1**

4001 **7** *2* **Fizzy Lizzy**[2] 768 6-9-3 45 RobbieFitzpatrick 10 39
(H E Haynes) *sn chsng ldrs: rdn over 3f out: wknd over 2f out* **8/1**[3]

0-06 **8** *1* **Noble Mount**[44] 397 5-8-11 45 SamHitchcott 11 30
(A B Haynes) *s.i.s: nvr trbld ldrs* **14/1**

0065 **9** *nk* **Smirfys Party**[2] 768 8-8-8 45 (v) PaulMulrennan(3) 4 29
(W M Brisbourne) *plld hrd: prom: rdn over 2f out: wknd wl over 1f out* **6/1**[2]

0000 **10** *nk* **Tally (IRE)**[51] 312 6-8-11 40 ow3 DNolan(3) 8 32
(D G Bridgwater) *n.m.r sn after s: a bhd* **20/1**

00-0 **11** *nk* **Ruby Sunrise (IRE)**[37] 467 4-8-4 45 SoniaEaton(7) 6 28
(B P J Baugh) *s.s: a bhd* **25/1**

4-60 **12** *1 ½* **Tennessee Belle (IRE)**[44] 398 4-8-7 45 ow1 (e) StephenDonohoe(5) 7 25
(C N Allen) *bhd fnl 4f* **14/1**

1m 30.09s (-0.31) **Going Correction** -0.05s/f (Stan) **12** Ran SP% **125.9**
Speed ratings (Par 97):99,98,97,97,95 92,90,89,88,88 88,86
CSF £56.18 TOTE £6.30: £3.00, £2.10, £1.20; EX 17.10.
Owner Paul Howling **Bred** L A C Ashby **Trained** Newmarket, Suffolk
■ Stewards' Enquiry : Robbie Fitzpatrick one-day ban: careless riding (Apr 10)

FOCUS
A decent pace in this and although there was little covering the first four at the line, the form does look solid for the grade.
Smirfys Party Official explanation: jockey said gelding hung right

794 BOOK ONLINE AT WOLVERHAMPTON-RACECOURSE.CO.UK BANDED STKS 1m 4f 50y(P)
5:00 (5:00) (Class 7) 4-Y-0+ **£1,876** (£554; £277) **Stalls** Low

Form RPR

-603 **1** **High (IRE)**[21] 615 4-8-10 45 NCallan 3 52
(W J Musson) *hld up in tch: rdn over 2f out: r.o to ld nr fin* **5/2**[1]

060/ **2** *½* **King's Crest**[427] 3810 8-8-12 45 GrahamGibbons 10 51
(J J Quinn) *w ldr: led 2f out: sn rdn: clr 1f out: ct nr fin* **7/2**[2]

-002 **3** *2 ½* **Eforetta (GER)**[15] 636 4-8-10 45 VinceSlattery 6 47
(D J Wintle) *led: rdn and hdd 2f out: one pce* **12/1**

-563 **4** *½* **Molly's Secret**[6] 715 8-8-12 40 (p) FergusSweeney 5 46
(Miss S J Wilton) *hld up: rdn and hdwy over 2f out: one pce fnl f* **12/1**

05-0 **5** *1* **Summer Bounty**[47] 363 10-8-9 40 RobertMiles(3) 1 45
(F Jordan) *s.s: hld up in rr: hdwy over 2f out: swtchd lft wl over 1f out: styd on ins fnl f* **14/1**

556- **6** *2 ½* **Ulshaw**[137] 6329 9-8-12 35 SteveDrowne 2 41
(J M Bradley) *hld up and bhd: rdn and hdwy on ins over 2f out: wknd over 1f out* **8/1**

4446 **7** *½* **Liquid Lover (IRE)**[1] 788 4-8-10 45 ShaneKelly 11 40
(W M Brisbourne) *hld up in tch: rdn 3f out: sn wknd* **11/2**

43/0 **8** *9* **One Alone**[7] 694 5-8-9 40 (v) StephaneBreux(3) 7 25
(Jean-Rene Auvray) *s.i.s: hld up: rdn over 3f out: sn struggling* **33/1**

-051 **9** *1 ½* **Mustakhlas (USA)**[9] 684 5-9-4 45 RobbieFitzpatrick 12 29
(B P J Baugh) *hld up in tch: rdn 3f out: sn wknd* **9/2**[3]

-005 **10** *dist* **Halcyon Magic**[9] 684 8-8-12 40 (b) DarrenWilliams 9 —
(M Wigham) *hld up: rdn over 3f out: sn struggling: eased whn no ch wl over 1f out* **20/1**

2m 43.86s (1.44) **Going Correction** -0.05s/f (Stan)
WFA 4 from 5yo+ 2lb **10** Ran SP% **125.2**
Speed ratings (Par 97):93,92,91,90,90 88,88,82,81,—
CSF £12.16 TOTE £2.80: £1.70, £2.10, £3.50; EX 25.20 Place 6 £91.77, Place 5 £42.35.
Owner I Johnson **Bred** Gerard Phelan And Liam Phelan **Trained** Newmarket, Suffolk

FOCUS
Not much pace on here and it turned into a bit of a sprint from the home bend, which would not have suited a few. Average for the grade.
Summer Bounty Official explanation: jockey said gelding was denied a clear run
T/Plt: £132.40 to a £1 stake. Pool: £41,710.10. 229.85 winning tickets. T/Qpdt: £14.70 to a £1 stake. Pool: £3,571.40. 178.90 winning tickets. KH

YARMOUTH (L-H)
Wednesday, March 29

OFFICIAL GOING: Firm (good to firm in places)
Wind: Light, across Weather: Sunshine and showers

795 LETHEBY & CHRISTOPHER MEDIAN AUCTION MAIDEN STKS 7f 3y
2:20 (2:21) (Class 6) 3-Y-0 **£3,238** (£963; £481; £240) **Stalls** High

Form RPR

0- **1** **Red Evie (IRE)**[190] 5391 3-8-12 JamieSpencer 6 81
(M L W Bell) *racd centre: mid-div: hdwy over 2f out: led over 1f out: r.o: eased nr fin* **8/1**

2 *1 ¾* **River Kirov (IRE)** 3-9-3 AlanMunro 9 81
(P W Chapple-Hyam) *racd centre: a.p: rdn over 2f out: chsd wnr over 1f out: no imp* **5/4**[1]

3 *6* **Five Two** 3-9-3 TedDurcan 1 66
(M R Channon) *s.i.s: racd centre and sn prom: rdn over 2f out: styd on same pce appr fnl f* **9/2**[2]

50- **4** *3 ½* **Penny Glitters**[238] 4053 3-8-12 DeanMcKeown 2 52
(S Parr) *led centre over 5f: wknd fnl f* **20/1**

2436 **5** *2 ½* **Pab Special (IRE)**[37] 459 3-9-3 71 PatCosgrave 3 50
(K R Burke) *dwlt: racd centre: hld up: hdwy u.p over 1f out: nvr nrr* **12/1**

00- **6** *1 ¼* **Shore Thing (IRE)**[151] 6142 3-9-0 SaleemGolam(3) 11 47+
(M H Tompkins) *swtchd to r alone stands' side over 5f out: chsd ldrs: rdn out : sn wknd* **16/1**

6- **7** *5* **Captain Torrance (IRE)**[226] 4426 3-9-3 AdrianMcCarthy 12 34
(P W Chapple-Hyam) *racd centre: chsd ldr 5f: sn wknd* **25/1**

0- **8** *½* **Glitterati**[159] 6011 3-8-12 RichardHughes 8 28
(R Charlton) *racd centre: chsd ldrs 5f* **6/1**[3]

0 **9** *3* **Shaika**[13] 653 3-8-12 AdrianTNicholls 7 20
(G Prodromou) *s.i.s: racd centre: a in rr* **150/1**

00- **10** *7* **Master Malarkey**[117] 6477 3-9-3 JimmyQuinn 10 7
(Mrs C A Dunnett) *dwlt: racd centre: a in rr* **150/1**

000- **11** *3 ½* **Southborough Lad**[196] 5231 3-9-3 30 JohnEgan 4 —
(Mrs C A Dunnett) *racd centre: chsd ldrs to 1/2-way* **150/1**

5-0 **12** *3* **Boss Mak (IRE)**[60] 217 3-9-3 SebSanders 5 —
(V Smith) *swtchd to r alone far side over 5f out: bhd fr 1/2-way* **40/1**

1m 26.01s (-0.59) **Going Correction** +0.10s/f (Good) **12** Ran SP% **114.6**
Speed ratings (Par 96):107,105,98,94,91 89,84,83,80,72 68,64
CSF £17.18 TOTE £13.30: £2.90, £1.10, £1.90; EX 32.20 Trifecta £167.70 Pool: £595.45 - 2.52 winning tickets..
Owner Terry Neill **Bred** Dermot Cantillon And Forenaghts Stud **Trained** Newmarket, Suffolk

FOCUS
An ordinary maiden but the winner recorded a decent winning time for a race like this, more than a second quicker than the following handicap over the same trip. The first two pulled clear and are above average, although it is doubtful many of the others showed their form on the firm ground.
Master Malarkey Official explanation: jockey said gelding was unsuited by the firm (good to firm places) ground
Boss Mak(IRE) Official explanation: jockey said gelding was not suited by the firm (good to firm places) ground

The Form Book, Raceform Ltd, Compton, RG20 6NL

796 RACECOURSE VIDEO SERVICES H'CAP — 7f 3y
2:50 (2:51) (Class 6) (0-65,65) 3-Y-O — £3,238 (£963; £481; £240) Stalls High

Form — RPR

6-54 **1** **Musicmaestroplease (IRE)**[14] 646 3-8-5 **52** DeanMcKeown 5 — 62
(S Parr) *chsd ldrs: led 2f out: rdn out* **13/2**[2]

00-0 **2** 3 **She's Dunnett**[31] 528 3-8-4 **51** oh6 JohnEgan 4 — 53
(Mrs C A Dunnett) *led 6f out: hdd 2f out: styd on same pce fnl f* **100/1**

0044 **3** 3 1/2 **Bobby Rose**[23] 590 3-9-4 **65** DarryllHolland 7 — 58
(D K Ivory) *wnt rt s: hld up: plld hrd: hdwy over 2f out: styng on same pce whn edgd rt ins fnl f* **15/2**

060- **4** 1/2 **Scuzme (IRE)**[188] 5422 3-8-5 **52** PaulHanagan 13 — 44+
(B Ellison) *wnt lft s: hld up: hdwy u.p over 1f out: edgd lft: nt trble ldrs* **7/1**[3]

5-06 **5** 1 1/4 **Almowj**[27] 558 3-9-4 **65** (b) RyanMoore 9 — 53
(C E Brittain) *chsd ldrs: rdn over 2f out: wkng whn hung lft ins fnl f* **9/1**

5320 **6** 1 1/2 **Mine The Balance (IRE)**[5] 712 3-8-4 **58** ow2 KylieManser(7) 14 — 43
(J R Best) *chsd ldrs over 5f* **13/2**[2]

006- **7** 1 3/4 **Valhar**[98] 6640 3-8-10 **57** EddieAhern 1 — 37
(J R Jenkins) *chsd ldrs over 5f* **28/1**

0421 **8** 1 1/2 **Miss Champagne (IRE)**[29] 544 3-8-8 **55** FrancisNorton 6 — 31
(M Quinn) *led 1f: chsd ldr: rdn and ev ch over 2f out: wknd over 1f out* **6/1**[1]

0160 **9** nk **Tilen (IRE)**[23] 604 3-8-4 **51** oh1 (b) DaleGibson 2 — 26
(S Parr) *hld up: nvr nrr* **14/1**

060- **10** 1/2 **Woolfall King (IRE)**[145] 6244 3-8-4 **51** oh1 NickyMackay 8 — 25
(G G Margarson) *s.i.s and hmpd s: sn rdn along: a in rr* **25/1**

000- **11** 5 **Distant Mind (IRE)**[175] 5694 3-7-11 **51** oh4 KirstyMilczarek(7) 15 — 12
(Mrs C A Dunnett) *chsd ldrs 5f* **40/1**

0-06 **12** 1 1/2 **Red Vixen (IRE)**[50] 322 3-8-4 **51** oh1 HayleyTurner 10 — 8
(C N Allen) *hld up: rdn and wknd over 2f out* **16/1**

60-6 **13** 5 **Champagne Moment**[12] 658 3-8-11 **58** MatthewHenry 16 — —
(V Smith) *hld up: effrt over 2f out: sn wknd* **16/1**

006- **14** 27 **Bold Tiger (IRE)**[133] 6366 3-8-11 **58** AdrianTNicholls 12 — —
(D Nicholls) *chsd ldrs 4f* **9/1**

1m 27.03s (0.43) **Going Correction** +0.10s/f (Good) **14** Ran SP% **114.4**
Speed ratings (Par 96):101,97,93,93,91 89,87,86,85,85 79,77,72,41
CSF £556.30 CT £4868.83 TOTE £8.90: £2.60, £7.20, £2.50; EX 313.40 TRIFECTA Not won..
Owner The Another Fine Mess Partnership **Bred** A Class Racing Ltd **Trained** Carburton, Notts

FOCUS
Modest handicap form, but the race should produce the odd winner at a similar level. An improvement of 7lb from the winner.
Bold Tiger(IRE) Official explanation: jockey said gelding hung right throughout

797 WIN MORE AT BRECKLAND BINGO THETFORD H'CAP — 1m 3y
3:20 (3:23) (Class 6) (0-65,65) 3-Y-O — £3,238 (£963; £481; £240) Stalls High

Form — RPR

300- **1** **Malech (IRE)**[165] 5887 3-9-1 **62** JamieSpencer 16 — 73+
(M L W Bell) *hld up: racd centre: swtchd to stands' side over 3f out: hdwy over 2f out: led on bit over 1f out: comf* **8/1**[3]

066- **2** 1 1/4 **Woolly Bully**[147] 6227 3-9-4 **65** FrancisNorton 14 — 70+
(G A Huffer) *racd centre: prom: swtchd to chse ldr stands' side 1/2-way: led over 2f out: rdn: edgd lft and hdd over 1f out: no ch w wnr* **15/8**[1]

036- **3** 4 **Winds Of Change**[170] 5788 3-9-4 **65** JoeFanning 6 — 61+
(M Johnston) *led centre: hdd over 5f out: rdn and ev ch over 1f out: styd on same pce* **10/1**

0200 **4** nk **Perfect Order (USA)**[28] 548 3-8-10 **57** (p) RyanMoore 12 — 52
(N A Callaghan) *s.i.s: racd centre: hld up: r.o ins fnl f: nt trble ldrs* **14/1**

0-60 **5** 3/4 **Shannon House**[5] 712 3-9-4 **65** JohnEgan 4 — 58
(M J McGrath) *hld up: racd centre: hdwy over 2f out: rdn over 1f out: styd on same pce* **50/1**

460- **6** 1 **Noble Nova**[160] 5994 3-8-2 **56** ThomasO'Brien(7) 9 — 47
(M R Channon) *racd centre: chsd ldrs: rdn over 2f out: no ex fnl f* **33/1**

-001 **7** 1/2 **Hits Only Life (USA)**[21] 617 3-8-6 **53** DeanMcKeown 13 — 43
(J Pearce) *hld up: racd centre: nt clr run over 2f out: swtchd lft over 1f out: n.m.r ins fnl f: nvr nr to chal* **11/2**[2]

00-0 **8** 1/2 **Sunderland Echo (IRE)**[28] 548 3-8-10 **57** PaulHanagan 1 — 46
(B Ellison) *hld upin tch: racd centre: rdn over 1f out: no ex* **80/1**

0-03 **9** 2 1/2 **Oasis Sun (IRE)**[29] 543 3-7-13 **51** JamesDoyle(5) 2 — 34
(J R Best) *racd centre: chsd ldrs: rdn over 2f out: wknd fnl f* **8/1**[3]

000 **10** 1 **Wally Barge**[23] 590 3-8-13 **60** MickyFenton 3 — 41
(D K Ivory) *hld up: racd centre: hdwy over 2f out: sn rdn: wknd fnl f* **25/1**

0-00 **11** 5 **Go Amwell**[50] 329 3-8-5 **52** oh1 ow1 (v[1]) EddieAhern 10 — 21
(J R Jenkins) *racd centre: prom: swtchd to stands' side 1/2-way: wknd over 1f out* **50/1**

500- **12** 1 **Red Pride (IRE)**[158] 6024 3-8-6 **53** BrianReilly 5 — 20
(Miss J Feilden) *racd centre: chsd ldrs over 6f* **50/1**

1-50 **13** 4 **Cragganmore Creek**[72] 123 3-8-12 **59** DerekMcGaffin 8 — 17
(D Morris) *racd centre: mid-div: rdn 1/2-way: wknd over 1f out* **16/1**

0-00 **14** 3 **Astorygoeswithit**[33] 500 3-8-8 **55** (p) AlanMunro 11 — 6
(Lucinda Featherstone) *racd centre: prom: rdn and c stands' side 1/2-way: wknd wl over 1f out* **50/1**

04-0 **15** 10 **Madame Constanze (IRE)**[53] 291 3-8-11 **58** ow1 SebSanders 15 — —
(Miss Gay Kelleway) *racd alone stands' side and overall ldr: hdd & wknd over 2f out* **33/1**

325- **16** 1/2 **Glendening**[185] 5489 3-8-10 **57** AdrianTNicholls 7 — —
(D Nicholls) *s.i.s: racd centre: plld hrd and hdwy to ld that gp over 5f out: hdd & wknd over 2f out* **14/1**

1m 42.63s (2.73) **Going Correction** +0.10s/f (Good) **16** Ran SP% **119.5**
Speed ratings (Par 96):90,88,84,84,83 82,82,81,79,78 73,72,68,65,55 54
CSF £21.42 CT £164.67 TOTE £10.50: £1.90, £1.10, £2.40, £3.20; EX 35.30 TRIFECTA Not won..
Owner Lord Blyth **Bred** Roger Macnair **Trained** Newmarket, Suffolk

FOCUS
A moderate winning time for the grade, but there were one or two pleasing performances with the first three all looking improvers. The race should produce winners.
Hits Only Life(USA) Official explanation: jockey said gelding was denied a clear run
Wally Barge Official explanation: jockey said colt ran too free
Cragganmore Creek Official explanation: jockey said gelding was unsuited by the firm (good to firm places) ground
Glendening Official explanation: jockey said gelding ran too free early stages

798 PEGGY FARLEY MEMORIAL H'CAP — 6f 3y
3:50 (3:51) (Class 4) (0-85,82) 4-Y-O+
£7,790 (£2,332; £1,166; £583; £291; £146) Stalls High

Form — RPR

0-00 **1** **Silver Dane (IRE)**[22] 605 4-8-4 **68** oh14 (v) JohnEgan 7 — 78
(Mrs C A Dunnett) *hld up: hdwy over 1f out: rdn to ld ins fnl f: r.o* **33/1**

1102 **2** 1 1/2 **Canadian Danehill (IRE)**[7] 699 4-8-5 **69** oh1 ow1 EddieAhern 1 — 74
(R M H Cowell) *led: rdn and hdd ins fnl f: unable qck* **5/1**[2]

60-6 **3** nk **Bobski (IRE)**[36] 476 4-9-4 **82** OscarUrbina 2 — 86
(G A Huffer) *hld up: hdwy over 2f out: rdn over 1f out: nt run on* **5/2**[1]

050- **4** 3 **Hiccups**[214] 4767 6-8-7 **74** SilvestreDeSousa(3) 5 — 69
(D Nicholls) *chsd ldrs: rdn over 2f out: wknd ins fnl f* **20/1**

0-30 **5** nk **Plateau**[5] 718 7-9-3 **81** AdrianTNicholls 9 — 75
(D Nicholls) *chsd ldrs: n.m.r over 4f out: rdn over 2f out: wknd fnl f* **5/1**[2]

540- **6** 3/4 **Bold Marc (IRE)**[150] 6182 4-9-4 **82** FrancisNorton 3 — 74
(K R Burke) *prom: rdn over 2f out: wknd fnl f* **7/1**

000- **7** 1 1/2 **Yorkshire Lad (IRE)**[92] 6668 4-7-13 **68** oh10 JamesDoyle(5) 10 — 55
(Miss Gay Kelleway) *hld up: rdn and nt clr run over 1f out: nvr trbld ldrs* **28/1**

0162 **8** nk **Gone'N'Dunnett (IRE)**[22] 605 7-7-11 **68** (v) KirstyMilczarek(7) 11 — 55
(Mrs C A Dunnett) *prom: hmpd and dropped rr over 4f out: nt rcvr* **6/1**[3]

00-0 **9** 3 1/2 **Bold Cheverak**[13] 654 4-8-1 **68** oh10 EdwardCreighton(3) 6 — 44
(Mrs C A Dunnett) *unruly in stalls: chsd ldrs: rdn over 2f out: wknd fnl f* **33/1**

0432 **10** 1 **Shifty Night (IRE)**[13] 654 5-8-4 **68** oh19 (v) HayleyTurner 8 — 41
(Mrs C A Dunnett) *prom over 4f* **20/1**

300- **11** 7 **Trick Cyclist**[137] 6335 5-8-4 **68** DaleGibson 4 — 20
(M W Easterby) *s.s: outpcd* **16/1**

1m 14.32s (0.62) **Going Correction** +0.10s/f (Good) **11** Ran SP% **113.4**
Speed ratings (Par 105):99,97,96,92,92 91,89,88,84,82 73
CSF £175.39 CT £580.08 TOTE £53.80: £9.10, £1.90, £1.50; EX 329.90 Trifecta £695.10 Part won. Pool: £979.09 - 0.10 winning tickets..
Owner Mrs Christine Dunnett **Bred** Tally-Ho Stud **Trained** Hingham, Norfolk
■ Stewards' Enquiry : Eddie Ahern 18-day ban (3 days deferred, takes into account previous offences): careless riding (Apr 15-29)

FOCUS
A moderate winning time for a race of its type and Silver Dane caused a minor shock in winning from 14lb out of the handicap. Unconvincing form as a result.
Trick Cyclist Official explanation: jockey said gelding was upset by horse in next stall and was slowly away

799 WEATHERBYS PRINTING H'CAP — 1m 3f 101y
4:20 (4:20) (Class 3) (0-90,84) 4-Y-O+
£11,217 (£3,358; £1,679; £840; £419; £210) Stalls Low

Form — RPR

2211 **1** **Young Mick**[4] 723 4-8-8 **75** 6ex (v) JimmyQuinn 9 — 87+
(G G Margarson) *a.p: led over 1f out: r.o wl* **2/1**[1]

411- **2** 5 **Caribbean Pearl (USA)**[152] 6130 4-8-8 **75** FrancisNorton 1 — 77
(C E Brittain) *chsd ldrs: rdn and ev ch over 1f out: sn outpcd* **11/4**[2]

210- **3** 1 1/2 **Sirce (IRE)**[144] 6254 4-9-3 **84** (v) SebSanders 3 — 84
(D J Coakley) *dwlt: hld up: hdwy over 3f out: rdn and ev ch 2f out: styd on same pce appr fnl f* **11/2**

200- **4** hd **Annambo**[117] 6482 6-8-9 **75** TedDurcan 7 — 74
(D Morris) *chsd ldr tl led over 3f out: rdn and hdd over 1f out: no ex* **16/1**

000- **5** 1 **Top Seed (IRE)**[258] 3461 5-8-7 **76** EdwardCreighton(3) 8 — 74
(M R Channon) *trckd ldrs: plld hrd: rdn and ev ch over 2f out: styd on same pce appr fnl f* **12/1**

401- **6** 6 **Magic Amigo**[17] 6247 5-8-8 **74** EddieAhern 2 — 62
(J R Jenkins) *led over 7f: wknd over 1f out* **25/1**

250- **7** 1 3/4 **Ski Jump (USA)**[172] 5744 6-9-4 **84** (v) PaulHanagan 6 — 69
(R A Fahey) *hld up: rdn over 3f out: sn wknd* **5/1**[3]

2m 28.52s (1.02) **Going Correction** +0.35s/f (Good)
WFA 4 from 5yo+ 1lb **7** Ran SP% **109.5**
Speed ratings (Par 107):110,106,105,105,104 100,98
CSF £6.91 CT £21.46 TOTE £1.90: £1.50, £1.90; EX 8.10 Trifecta £28.10 Pool: £1,012.20 - 25.50 winning tickets..
Owner M F Kentish **Bred** M F Kentish **Trained** Newmarket, Suffolk

FOCUS
Not a bad handicap but the early pace was not frantic by any means. The winner impressed and could rate higher still. The race has been rated through the runner-up.

NOTEBOOK
Young Mick, in such good form on the All-Weather this year, scoring five times, won easily. Despite racing keenly, he was still full of running in the straight and, when asked to take the race, bounded clear in great style. His trainer fancies aiming the gelding at the Ebor, and he may well have the improvement in him to be considered for that valuable handicap. (tchd 15-8)
Caribbean Pearl(USA) also travelled well and looked a danger until the winner swept clear approaching the final furlong. There was no disgrace in finishing second on her seasonal reappearance to a rival fit from the All-Weather and clearly on the upgrade, and she could well go one better next time. (op 7-2)
Sirce(IRE), who had a successful season last year, is on a pretty stiff mark now, but she is a consistent type and once again ran her race. She looks a versatile sort with regard to ground conditions but all her wins to date have come with some cut. (op 9-2)
Annambo is now back down to the mark off which he won a handicap at Newmarket last summer over an extended mile and three-quarters. This was not a bad effort but staying trips are probably more his thing these days. (op 25-1)
Top Seed(IRE) has cost his supporters plenty over the years and, despite continuing to fall in the handicap, he remains difficult to win with.
Ski Jump(USA) has won first time out in the past and his stable has kicked off this season in good form, but he ran as though this run will bring him on. (op 7-2)

800 VAUXHALL HOLIDAY PARKS H'CAP — 1m 2f 21y
4:50 (4:50) (Class 4) (0-80,80) 4-Y-O+
£7,790 (£2,332; £1,166; £583; £291; £146) Stalls Low

Form — RPR

4023 **1** **Dragon Slayer (IRE)**[14] 641 4-8-10 **72** EddieAhern 7 — 78
(M J Attwater) *trckd ldrs: r.o to ld wl ins fnl f* **6/1**

400- **2** 1/2 **Namroc (IRE)**[212] 4820 5-9-4 **80** JamieSpencer 6 — 85
(N A Callaghan) *led: qcknd over 3f out: hdd 1f out: r.o* **11/2**[3]

4421 **3** 3/4 **Captain Margaret**[27] 557 4-8-8 **70** JimmyQuinn 3 — 74
(J Pearce) *chsd ldr tl led 1f out: hdd and unable qck wl ins fnl f* **11/2**[3]

/00- **4** 1 1/2 **Haatmey**[319] 1696 4-8-13 **75** TedDurcan 8 — 76
(M R Channon) *hld up: nt clr run over 2f out: hdwy over 1f out: nt trble ldrs* **10/1**

0-65 **5** 1/2 **Boundless Prospect (USA)**[4] 726 7-9-4 **80**................ MickyFenton 2 80
(Miss Gay Kelleway) *chsd ldrs: rdn over 2f out: styd on same pce fnl f* **9/2**[2]

/0-0 **6** 1 1/2 **Fame**[70] 140 6-8-10 **72**.. AlanMunro 9 69
(W Jarvis) *dwlt: hld up: rdn over 2f out: nvr trbld ldrs* **22/1**

000- **7** *nk* **Tata Naka**[137] 6323 6-8-4 **66** oh20.................................... HayleyTurner 4 63?
(Mrs C A Dunnett) *chsd ldrs: rdn over 2f out: wknd fnl f* **16/1**

30-2 **8** *shd* **Lucayan Dancer**[5] 719 6-9-0 **76**................................ AdrianTNicholls 1 73
(D Nicholls) *hld up: rdn over 2f out: n.d* **4/1**[1]

356- **9** 2 **Active Asset (IRE)**[159] 6003 4-8-10 **75**................ EdwardCreighton(3) 5 68
(M R Channon) *hld up: hdwy over 2f out: wknd fnl f* **10/1**

2m 11.03s (2.93) **Going Correction** +0.35s/f (Good) **9** Ran SP% **111.6**
Speed ratings (Par 105):102,101,101,99,99 98,97,97,96
CSF £37.07 CT £187.48 TOTE £5.00: £2.20, £2.10, £1.80; EX 61.40 Trifecta £315.40 Pool: £1,488.55 - 3.35 winning tickets. Place 6 £33.63, Place 5 £25.85.
Owner Carl Would **Bred** Arandora Star Syndicate **Trained** Wysall, Notts

FOCUS
A fair handicap which looked pretty competitive. The winner did not need to improve but the form looks solid enough despite the disappointing effort of the favourite.
T/Jkpt: Not won. T/Plt: £58.40 to a £1 stake. Pool: £49,714.65. 621.30 winning tickets. T/Qpdt: £9.70 to a £1 stake. Pool: £3,884.10. 294.90 winning tickets. CR

707 LINGFIELD (L-H)
Thursday, March 30

OFFICIAL GOING: Standard
Wind: Strong, behind Weather: Overcast

801 NEXT MEETING APRIL 1ST MEDIAN AUCTION MAIDEN STKS 5f (P)
2:30 (2:30) (Class 5) 3-Y-O **£3,886** (£1,156; £577; £288) **Stalls** High

Form RPR

00- **1** **Devine Dancer**[99] 6641 3-8-12 .... DaneO'Neill 4 58
(H Candy) *lw: led after 1f: mde rest: rdn 2 l clr 1f out: hld on: all out* **33/1**

0-03 **2** 3/4 **Cool Sting (IRE)**[28] 553 3-9-3 73.. DarryllHolland 1 61
(A M Balding) *swtg: chsd ldrs: hanging fr 3f out: effrt over 1f out: chsd wnr ins fnl f: styd on* **2/1**[1]

2500 **3** 1/2 **Danish Blues (IRE)**[14] 653 3-9-3 60...................................(p) NCallan 6 59
(N P Littmoden) *taken down early: chsd ldrs: rdn 2f out: kpt on fnl f to take 3rd nr fin* **20/1**

2 **4** *nk* **Royal Bandit**[5] 722 3-9-3 .... JamieSpencer 3 58+
(N A Callaghan) *lw: hld up: rdn and hanging over 2f out: brought wd in st: r.o fnl f: nrst fin* **2/1**[1]

20-5 **5** 1/2 **Dora's Green**[55] 287 3-8-12 48.. TedDurcan 9 51
(M Blanshard) *prom: chsd wnr 3f out: upsides 2f out: nt qckn over 1f out: fdd ins fnl f* **50/1**

05- **6** 1/2 **Burning Incense (IRE)**[171] 5801 3-8-12 .... RichardKingscote(5) 7 67+
(R Charlton) *h.d.w: w'like: scope: stdd s: hld up last: prog & reminder 1f out: gng strly whn rn up bhd 2 rivals 100yds out: nt rcvr: im* **4/1**[2]

4-5 **7** 1 1/2 **Just Tallulah**[15] 645 3-8-7 .... JamesDoyle(5) 8 44
(N P Littmoden) *a in last trio: rdn and brief effrt over 1f out: sn no prog* **33/1**

52 **8** 3 1/2 **Kellys Dream (IRE)**[15] 645 3-8-12 .... FrancisNorton 5 31
(M Quinn) *led for 1f: rdn 1/2-way: wknd rapidly fnl f* **10/1**[3]

00- **9** *hd* **Hogan's Heroes**[216] 4724 3-9-3 .... NickyMackay 2 35
(G A Butler) *dwlt: hld up in last pair: n.m.r briefly over 2f out: shuffled along and wknd over 1f out* **50/1**

59.12 secs (-0.66) **Going Correction** -0.15s/f (Stan) **9** Ran SP% **110.3**
Speed ratings (Par 98):99,97,97,96,95 94,92,86,86
CSF £92.38 TOTE £49.10: £5.30, £1.10, £3.60; EX 129.10 Trifecta £513.80 Part won. Pool: £723.78 - 0.35 winning tickets..
Owner John Simms **Bred** J Simms **Trained** Kingston Warren, Oxon

FOCUS
A modest maiden in which the 48-rated Dora's Green anchors the form. The unlucky sixth has been rated the winner.
Royal Bandit Official explanation: jockey said colt hung right
Burning Incense(IRE) ◆ Official explanation: jockey said colt was denied clear run

802 ARENALEISUREPLC.COM MAIDEN STKS 1m (P)
3:05 (3:05) (Class 5) 3-Y-O **£4,210** (£1,252; £625; £312) **Stalls** High

Form RPR

62 **1** **Abaconian (IRE)**[7] 703 3-9-3 ....(t) JamieSpencer 3 71
(M J Wallace) *lw: led for 1f: trckd ldr: led gng easily over 2f out: hrd drvn over 1f out: kpt on* **5/4**[1]

0 **2** 1 1/2 **Digger Boy**[13] 658 3-9-3 .... PhilipRobinson 2 67
(M A Jarvis) *lw: led after 1f: clr w wnr 3f out: hdd over 2f out: kpt on same pce* **4/1**[3]

400- **3** *shd* **Prince Ary**[182] 5570 3-9-3 71.. MichaelHills 5 67
(B W Hills) *lw: hld up in last: outpcd and rdn over 3f out: prog to chse clr ldng pair over 2f out: styd on: nvr able to chal* **9/4**[2]

4 5 **Darker Than Blue** 3-8-12 .... AlanMunro 4 51
(B J Meehan) *w'like: bit bkwd: hld up: outpcd and rdn 3f out: n.d after* **20/1**

05- **5** 2 1/2 **Coltchester (IRE)**[111] 6528 3-9-3 .... RobbieFitzpatrick 1 50+
(Peter Grayson) *w'like: bit bkwd: dwlt: in tch: rdn 5f out: detached last and btn over 3f out* **14/1**

0-0 **6** 5 **Gizmondo**[12] 669 3-9-3 .... HayleyTurner 6 38
(M L W Bell) *b: t.k.h: hld up: outpcd 3f out: wknd wl over 1f out* **16/1**

1m 39.58s (0.15) **Going Correction** -0.15s/f (Stan) **6** Ran SP% **112.5**
Speed ratings (Par 98):93,91,91,86,83 78
CSF £6.75 TOTE £1.80: £1.30, £2.30; EX 6.20.
Owner Miss L Magnier **Bred** Quay Bloodstock, Peter Magnier And Dr M Wallace **Trained** Newmarket, Suffolk

FOCUS
Only two counted from a long way out and this looks modest maiden form., rated through the third.

803 LINGFIELD-RACECOURSE.CO.UK H'CAP 7f (P)
3:35 (3:35) (Class 4) (0-80,79) 3-Y-O **£6,477** (£1,927; £963; £481) **Stalls** Low

Form RPR

455- **1** **Go Figure (IRE)**[172] 5761 3-8-7 **68**.................................... ChrisCatlin 4 79
(B J Meehan) *sn restrained bhd ldrs: rdn 3f out: sustained prog over 2f out to ld jst ins fnl f: styd on wl* **7/2**[2]

0251 **2** 1 1/2 **Tamagin (USA)**[6] 712 3-8-7 **73** 6ex..................(p) StephenDonohoe(5) 7 80
(P D Evans) *sn led and clr: drvn over 2f out: hdd and one pce jst ins fnl f* **4/1**[3]

0115 **3** 3 **Garstang**[6] 709 3-8-9 **70**...(b) RobbieFitzpatrick 6 69
(Peter Grayson) *prom: chsd ldr briefly over 2f out: one pce u.p after* **8/1**

61-5 **4** 1/2 **Sands Of Barra (IRE)**[7] 702 3-8-7 **73**......................... JamesDoyle(5) 2 71
(N A Callaghan) *hld up in last pair: effrt over 2f out: sn drvn: plugged on fr over 1f out: nt rch ldrs* **11/4**[1]

622- **5** 9 **Hits Only Jude (IRE)**[118] 6479 3-9-2 **77**...................... DeanMcKeown 3 52
(J Pearce) *prom early: u.p and wkng 3f out: sn bhd* **13/2**

300- **6** 1 1/4 **Musical Guest (IRE)**[145] 6249 3-9-4 **79**.................................. NCallan 5 50
(G G Margarson) *hld up in last pair: drvn 3f out: sn struggling and bhd* **14/1**

0261 **7** 3 1/2 **Sigismundus (IRE)**[61] 228 3-8-11 **72**............................ PatCosgrave 1 34
(J R Boyle) *chsd ldr 5f out to over 2f out: wknd rapidly* **8/1**

1m 24.06s (-1.83) **Going Correction** -0.15s/f (Stan) **7** Ran SP% **111.1**
Speed ratings (Par 100):104,102,98,98,88 86,82
CSF £16.78 TOTE £3.60: £2.10, £2.20; EX 27.20.
Owner O'Donnell And Associates **Bred** Irish National Stud **Trained** Manton, Wilts

FOCUS
Just the seven runners but four of them were previous course and distance winners and this looked pretty competitive. The level of the form is not rock solid but it could rate a bit higher.

804 ARENA LEISURE PLC H'CAP 1m 2f (P)
4:10 (4:10) (Class 4) (0-80,76) 3-Y-O **£6,477** (£1,927; £963; £481) **Stalls** Low

Form RPR

-220 **1** **Jebel Ali (IRE)**[24] 592 3-8-13 **76**................................. JamesDoyle(5) 1 81+
(B Gubby) *trckd ldr: led 3f out: hanging but qcknd clr over 2f out: rdn out: unchal* **5/1**

-234 **2** 2 1/2 **Katchit (IRE)**[69] 160 3-9-4 **76**.. TQuinn 2 75
(M R Channon) *lw: hld up bhd ldrs: outpcd and trapped bhd rivals over 2f out: no ch after: styd on to take 2nd last 150yds* **11/4**[3]

454- **3** 1 **Deutschland (USA)**[162] 5977 3-9-0 **72**......................... PhilipRobinson 3 69
(M A Jarvis) *hld up bhd ldng pair: effrt 3f out: sn outpcd: chsd wnr over 1f out to last 150yds: one pce* **9/4**[2]

0-12 **4** 2 1/2 **Orvietan (IRE)**[29] 548 3-8-12 **70**.. JoeFanning 5 62
(M Johnston) *led at stdy pce: rdn and hdd 3f out: fdd over 1f out* **2/1**[1]

2m 7.54s (-0.25) **Going Correction** -0.15s/f (Stan) **4** Ran SP% **107.4**
Speed ratings (Par 100):95,93,92,90
CSF £17.76 TOTE £4.50; EX 16.30.
Owner Brian Gubby **Bred** C A Jennings And S G Collen **Trained** Bagshot, Surrey

FOCUS
A disappointing turnout numerically and the top weight was rated 4lb below the ceiling of 80, but still quite an interesting race. Unsurprisingly given there were just four runners, the pace was pretty ordinary for much of the way and the form may not prove too strong.

805 FURLONGS & FAIRWAYS H'CAP 1m 4f (P)
4:45 (4:45) (Class 4) (0-85,83) 3-Y-O **£8,096** (£2,408; £1,203; £601) **Stalls** Low

Form RPR

61 **1** **Lightning Strike (GER)**[13] 656 3-8-10 **75**........................ IanMongan 6 82+
(T G Mills) *lw: t.k.h: trckd ldrs: disp ld 5f out tl led over 3f out : forged 2 l clr 2f out: drvn out* **2/1**[1]

3341 **2** 1 1/4 **Fusili (IRE)**[24] 592 3-9-4 **83**... NCallan 5 86
(N P Littmoden) *dwlt: hld up in last pair: effrt 4f out: rdn 3f out: kpt on to take 2nd over 1f out: no real imp on wnr* **3/1**[2]

53-1 **3** 3/4 **Soho Square**[50] 337 3-8-12 **77**... JoeFanning 4 79
(M Johnston) *lw: led for 2f: disp ld again 5f out to over 3f out: sn drvn: kpt on u.p but lost 2nd over 1f out* **7/2**[3]

6041 **4** 11 **Abstract Art (USA)**[8] 695 3-8-9 **79** 6ex.................... JamesDoyle(5) 3 63
(N A Callaghan) *t.k.h: hld up in last pair: effrt 4f out: sn rdn: cl up 2f out: wknd sn after* **5/1**

-231 **5** 9 **Fiddlers Wood**[31] 534 3-9-1 **80**......................................(v) ChrisCatlin 2 50
(V Smith) *trckd ldrs: n.m.r 5f out: sn bdly outpcd and bhd* **14/1**

6441 **6** 20 **Bariloche**[29] 548 3-8-13 **78**...(b) DarryllHolland 1 16
(J R Boyle) *racd freely: led after 2f: hdd and rdn whn n.m.r 5f out: sn bhd: t.o* **12/1**

2m 32.44s (-1.95) **Going Correction** -0.15s/f (Stan) **6** Ran SP% **111.6**
Speed ratings (Par 100):100,99,98,91,85 72
CSF £8.12 TOTE £2.70: £1.60, £1.90; EX 10.00.
Owner T G Mills **Bred** Dr Chr Berglar **Trained** Headley, Surrey

FOCUS
It could be considered disappointing only six turned out for the richest race on the card, but a case could be made for all of them beforehand (they had all won on their previous start) and this was a very good contest for the grade. However, rather disappointingly, the pace was muddling with nobody keen to set a good gallop. The winner is likely to rate a lot higher and the first three finished clear.

806 GOLF & RACING AT LINGFIELD PARK H'CAP 6f (P)
5:15 (5:16) (Class 6) (0-65,64) 4-Y-O+ **£3,238** (£963; £481; £240) **Stalls** Low

Form RPR

0-66 **1** **H Harrison (IRE)**[26] 588 6-8-4 **55**......................... NataliaGemelova(5) 9 62
(I W McInnes) *w ldrs: drvn to ld narrowly ins fnl f: hld on* **11/1**

0161 **2** *nk* **Zazous**[45] 397 5-8-6 **52**.. J-PGuillambert 3 58
(J J Bridger) *w ldrs for over 2f: sn rdn: effrt u.p on inner over 1f out: jnd wnr last 100yds: nt qckn nr fin* **13/2**[3]

0330 **3** *nk* **Monashee Prince (IRE)**[8] 698 4-9-3 **63**................(v[1]) GeorgeBaker 12 68
(J R Best) *sn w ldrs fr wd draw: rdn and nt qckn 2f out: styd on again ins fnl f* **8/1**

3040 **4** *shd* **Nova Tor (IRE)**[26] 588 4-8-6 **52**.........................(b) RobbieFitzpatrick 2 57
(Peter Grayson) *t.k.h: hld up in midfield: n.m.r 4f out: drvn 2f out: styd on fnl f: nvr able to chal* **11/1**

30-5 **5** *shd* **Coquin D'Alezan (IRE)**[14] 653 5-8-10 **63**.................. BRoper(7) 10 68
(W Jarvis) *hld up in detached last: c wdst of all bnd 2f out: bmpd along and r.o wl fnl f: hopeless task* **20/1**

0624 **6** 3/4 **Madrasee**[26] 580 8-8-7 **53**.. RobertHavlin 11 55
(P G Murphy) *settled towards rr: rdn over 2f out: styd on fr over 1f out: nt rch ldrs* **16/1**

0620 **7** *shd* **Kallista's Pride**[6] 711 6-8-8 **61**...................................... KylieManser(7) 7 63
(J R Best) *hld up bhd ldrs: effrt 2f out: nt qckn over 1f out: one pce after* **6/1**[2]

300- **8** *shd* **African Gift**[152] 6140 4-9-4 **64**.. TonyCulhane 8 66
(J G Given) *settled wl in rr: drvn 2f out: kpt on fr over 1f out: n.d* **5/1**[1]

0310 **9** 3/4 **Patternmaker (USA)**[33] 514 4-9-3 **63**................................ ChrisCatlin 6 62
(A M Hales) *settled in last trio: effrt 2f out: kpt on: no ch w ldrs* **7/1**

00-6 **10** 1/2 **Detonate**[26] 580 4-8-6 **52**.. AlanMunro 4 50
(Mrs C A Dunnett) *mde most tl hdd & wknd ins fnl f* **15/2**

1500 **11** 1/2 **Tiviski (IRE)**[6] 711 4-9-2 **62**..(p) NCallan 1 67+
(G G Margarson) *chsd ldrs: drvn 3f out: styng on wl whn nowhere to go and snatched up 1f out: nt clr run and eased nr fin* **10/1**

221/ **12** *17* **Ex Mill Lady**[631] [3635] 5-8-11 **60** SaleemGolam(3) 5 5
(W De Best-Turner) *drvn in midfield over 3f out: sn wknd: t.o* **50/1**

1m 11.76s (-1.05) **Going Correction** -0.15s/f (Stan) **12** Ran SP% **118.0**
Speed ratings (Par 101):101,100,100,100,99 98,98,98,97,97 96,73
CSF £80.48 CT £622.00 TOTE £11.90: £2.90, £1.90, £3.50; EX 102.10 Trifecta £570.20 Part won. Pool: £803.23 - 0.10 winning tickets..
Owner David Lees **Bred** Margaret Conlon **Trained** Catwick, E Yorks

FOCUS
Just a modest handicap but any number of these looked to have chances beforehand and this was very competitive - they predictably finished in a bunch. Modest form, and far from solid given the messy nature of the race.
Tiviski(IRE) ◆ Official explanation: jockey said filly was denied clear run

807 LINGFIELD PARK LEISURE CLUB H'CAP 6f (P)
5:45 (5:45) (Class 5) (0-70,74) 3-Y-O **£3,886** (£1,156; £577; £288) **Stalls** Low

Form RPR
0121 **1** **Stoneacre Boy (IRE)**[10] [673] 3-9-10 **74** 6ex (b) RobbieFitzpatrick 3 85+
(Peter Grayson) *prom: trckd ldr over 2f out: led over 1f out: sn in command: pushed out* **9/4**[1]

25-4 **2** *1* **Lucayos**[10] [673] 3-8-7 **62** (b[1]) RichardKingscote(5) 2 66+
(Mrs H Sweeting) *s.i.s: hmpd over 5f out and dropped to last pair: plenty to do over 1f out: str run fnl f: fin fast* **16/1**

440- **3** *hd* **Piccostar**[177] [5682] 3-8-12 **65** RichardSmith(3) 12 68
(A B Haynes) *chsd ldrs: rdn over 2f out: effrt to chse wnr ins fnl f: no imp: lost 2nd last stride* **40/1**

0-05 **4** *3/4* **Peter Island (FR)**[24] [601] 3-9-0 **64** NCallan 9 65
(J Gallagher) *chsd ldrs: drvn over 2f out: styd on fr over 1f out: nt pce to chal* **14/1**

-42R **5** *1/2* **Miss Dagger (IRE)**[6] [709] 3-8-4 **61** KylieManser(7) 10 61
(J R Best) *hld up in midfield: effrt over 1f out: sn bmpd along and nt qckn* **20/1**

300- **6** *1* **Bathwick Prince**[160] [6004] 3-9-0 **64** (b) AlanMunro 8 61
(B R Millman) *mostly pressed ldr to over 2f out: one pce over 1f out* **16/1**

4050 **7** *nk* **Luloah**[10] [673] 3-8-3 **60** DonnaCaldwell(7) 11 56
(P S McEntee) *led and sn crossed to inner: kicked 2 l clr 2f out: hdd and fdd over 1f out* **40/1**

0360 **8** *3/4* **The London Gang**[6] [709] 3-9-1 **65** (p) ShaneKelly 7 59
(P D Evans) *s.s: rdn in last pair 1/2-way: no prog tl styd on ins fnl f* **6/1**[3]

0014 **9** *1* **African Concerto (IRE)**[6] [709] 3-8-13 **63** EddieAhern 4 54
(Ernst Oertel) *trckd ldrs on inner: effrt 2f out: sn no prog and btn* **4/1**[2]

2546 **10** *1* **Thoughtsofstardom**[37] [475] 3-9-2 **66** BrianReilly 6 54
(P S McEntee) *a wl in rr: struggling over 2f out* **10/1**

400- **11** *1* **Peak Seasons (IRE)**[145] [6249] 3-8-11 **64** SaleemGolam(3) 1 49
(W De Best-Turner) *nvr on terms w ldrs: struggling over 2f out* **20/1**

000- **12** *1* **Berti Bertolini**[153] [6128] 3-8-11 **61** IanMongan 5 43
(T G Mills) *hmpd over 5f out and dropped to rr: no prog and btn over 2f out* **9/1**

1m 11.67s (-1.14) **Going Correction** -0.15s/f (Stan) **12** Ran SP% **117.0**
Speed ratings (Par 98):101,99,99,98,97 96,96,95,93,92 91,89
CSF £39.24 CT £1137.32 TOTE £2.50: £1.40, £4.90, £9.70; EX 30.60 Trifecta £460.80 Part won. Pool: £649.06 - 0.10 winning tickets. Place 6 £273.38, Place 5 £112.44..
Owner Richard Teatum **Bred** Michael Dalton **Trained** Formby, Lancs
■ Stewards' Enquiry : Donna Caldwell three-day ban: careless riding (Apr 10-12)

FOCUS
A modest sprint, but the winning time was faster than the previous race, an older-horse handicap over the same trip. Improved form from the winner.
Berti Bertolini Official explanation: jockey said gelding had to check after a furlong
T/Plt: £286.20 to a £1 stake. Pool: £58,878.80. 150.15 winning tickets. T/Qpdt: £63.60 to a £1 stake. Pool: £5,344.80. 62.10 winning tickets. JN

811 - 812a (Foreign Racing) - See Raceform Interactive

MUSSELBURGH (R-H)
Friday, March 31

OFFICIAL GOING: Heavy (soft in places)
Wind: Virtually nil

813 WALLYFORD FILLIES' H'CAP 5f
2:10 (2:10) (Class 5) (0-70,68) 3-Y-O+ **£3,886** (£1,156; £577; £288) **Stalls** High

Form RPR
000- **1** **Dorn Dancer (IRE)**[196] [5277] 4-9-3 **57** RobertWinston 3 66
(D W Barker) *dwlt: pushed along in rr 1/2-way: hdwy and n.m.r wl over 1f out:switched lft and rdn to ld ins last: styd on* **7/1**

5232 **2** *2* **Ashes (IRE)**[27] [587] 4-9-11 **65** PatCosgrave 7 67
(K R Burke) *cl up: led wl over 1f out: sn rdn: hdd and kpt on same pce ins last* **11/2**[3]

300- **3** *1* **Champagne Cracker**[197] [5243] 5-9-12 **66** TonyHamilton 2 65
(I Semple) *prom on outer: effrt to chal over 2f out and ev ch tl rdn and hld whn n.m.r ent last* **12/1**

0-06 **4** *1/2* **Muara**[30] [552] 4-8-9 **54** oh2 MarkLawson(5) 8 51+
(D W Barker) *led: rdn along over 2f out: hdd wl over 1f out and kpt on same pce* **14/1**

121- **5** *shd* **Brave Bear**[186] [5507] 4-9-9 **63** (b) DavidAllan 5 60+
(T D Easterby) *s.i.s: sn chsng ldrs: rdn and ev ch 2f out tl drvn and wknd ins last* **9/2**[2]

033- **6** *1/2* **Angelofthenorth**[148] [6235] 4-9-11 **65** AlanMunro 4 60
(J D Bethell) *chsd ldrs: rdn along 2f out: sn one pce* **13/8**[1]

000- **7** *6* **Rancho Cucamonga (IRE)**[163] [5986] 4-9-11 **68** BenSwarbrick(3) 6 43
(T D Barron) *sn rdn along in rr: nvr a factor* **25/1**

-000 **8** *1 3/4* **Oceanico Dot Com (IRE)**[49] [362] 4-9-11 **65** FrancisNorton 9 34
(A Berry) *cl up on inner: rdn along over 2f out: sn wknd* **16/1**

/0-0 **9** *9* **Annals**[16] [640] 4-9-6 **60** JohnEgan 1 —
(R C Guest) *in tch: rdn along 1/2-way: sn wknd* **33/1**

66.00 secs (5.50) **Going Correction** +0.80s/f (Soft) **9** Ran SP% **111.2**
Speed ratings (Par 100):88,84,83,82,82 81,71,69,54
CSF £42.72 CT £443.22 TOTE £8.20: £2.00, £1.70, £3.60; EX 62.10.
Owner The Ebor Partnership **Bred** Timothy Coughlan **Trained** Scorton, N Yorks

FOCUS
Untrustworthy heavy-ground form and the time was slow even allowing for the conditions, but there were one or two promising performances. The race has been rated through the winner to last year's best soft-ground form.

814 CALEDONIAN PRODUCE DOUG'S LEAVING DO MAIDEN AUCTION STKS 5f
2:40 (2:40) (Class 5) 2-Y-O **£3,238** (£963; £481; £240) **Stalls** High

Form RPR
1 **Ingleby Image** 2-8-6 PaulFessey 7 73
(T D Barron) *mde all: swtchd lft and rdn clr over 1f out: styd on strly* **6/1**

2 *3* **My Mirasol** 2-8-10 NCallan 5 66
(K A Ryan) *chsd ldrs: pushed along and outpcd after 2f: styd on appr last: nrst fin* **4/1**[2]

3 *1 1/4* **Stir Crazy (IRE)** 2-8-13 TedDurcan 4 65
(M R Channon) *cl up: ev ch 2f out: sn rdn and one pce appr last* **3/1**[1]

4 *1 3/4* **Joseph Locke (IRE)** 2-8-13 FergalLynch 6 58
(M Dods) *trckd ldrs on inner: effrt 2f out: sn rdn and one pce* **9/2**[3]

5 *4* **Tokyo Jo (IRE)** 2-8-5 ow1 RobertWinston 1 36
(K R Burke) *chsd ldrs: rdn along 2f out: sn wknd* **9/2**[3]

6 *4* **Our Toy Soldier** 2-8-13 PaulEddery 3 30
(B Smart) *dwlt: a rr* **10/1**

7 *6* **Minimum Fuss (IRE)** 2-7-11 AdeleRothery(7) 2 —
(M W Easterby) *s.i.s: rapid hdwy to join ldrs after 1f: rdn over 2f out and sn wknd* **50/1**

66.77 secs (6.27) **Going Correction** +0.80s/f (Soft) **7** Ran SP% **106.7**
Speed ratings (Par 92):81,76,74,71,65 58,49
CSF £25.99 TOTE £7.50: £3.00, £2.60; EX 41.20.
Owner Dave Scott **Bred** N C D Horn **Trained** Maunby, N Yorks

FOCUS
Another slow time even with conditions taken into account, but the race is likely to produce winners.

NOTEBOOK
Ingleby Image, by smart sprinter Averti, knew her job and she was soon in the lead, travelling well. She led them across towards the stands' rail and never looked in any danger, edging clear from over a furlong out. The testing conditions clearly posed her no problems and she may be a useful type for the time of year. Connections are now planning to run her in a fillies' novice event at Thirsk in a couple of weeks time. (op 8-1 tchd 9-1)
My Mirasol, a half-sister to Distinctly Game, who scored over this trip at two, shaped well in second, keeping on well in the closing stages, and it is safe to assume that she is going to come on for the run. An ordinary contest should be hers for the taking. (op 10-3 tchd 3-1)
Stir Crazy(IRE), a first two-year-old runner for smart six to seven-furlong performer Fath, has already been gelded, and the negative vibes for him in the market beforehand pretty much told the story. He held every chance, but lacked the speed of the front pair and he may be better suited to a faster surface. He too can find a race. (op 9-4)
Joseph Locke(IRE), whose stable is hardly renowned for its juvenile success, ran well to a point and was a few lengths ahead of the fifth. He is another for whom better ground may help, as will a sixth furlong in time. (op 7-1 tchd 8-1)
Tokyo Jo(IRE), a cheap purchase, played up beforehand, unseating her rider and having to be led down past the enclosures, and it was no surprise to see her disappoint. She may yet be capable of a little better and deserves another chance. (tchd 5-1, 6-1 in a place)
Our Toy Soldier, whose dam was best at a mile and ten furlongs, simply lacked the pace to get involved, but he is a nice looking sort who is going to appreciate the step up to six furlongs on better ground in time. (op 7-1)
Minimum Fuss(IRE), whose dam was a middle-distance performer, ran away with her rider after a slow start and came through to join the leaders, but the effort took its toll in the ground and she ultimately weakened out of it. She did not look devoid of ability and deserves another chance. (op 40-1)

815 DM HALL H'CAP 1m
3:10 (3:10) (Class 4) (0-85,82) 4-Y-O+ **£6,477** (£1,927; £963; £481) **Stalls** Low

Form RPR
03-1 **1** **Dancing Lyra**[7] [719] 5-9-1 **79** 6ex PaulHanagan 7 88
(R A Fahey) *trckd ldrs: hdwy to chal wl over 1f out: rdn to ld and edgd lft ins last: sn hdd: drvn and rallied to ld nr line* **5/6**[1]

335- **2** *hd* **Emerald Bay (IRE)**[233] [4251] 4-9-4 **82** TomEaves 3 91
(I Semple) *trckd ldr: effrt 2f out: rdn and styd on to ld ins last: sn drvn: hdd and no ex nr line* **9/1**[3]

216- **3** *8* **Dakota Rain (IRE)**[174] [5730] 4-9-0 **78** JohnEgan 1 71
(R C Guest) *led: rdn along 2f out: drvn and hdd ins last: sn wknd* **9/1**[3]

140/ **4** *3 1/2* **Cita Verda (FR)**[13] [5537] 8-8-4 **68** oh3 PaulFessey 6 54
(P Monteith) *chsd ldrs: rdn along 3f out: outpcd fnl 2f* **20/1**

400- **5** *2* **Kirkby's Treasure**[150] [6216] 8-8-11 **75** ow2 FergalLynch 4 57
(A Berry) *a rr* **14/1**

006- **6** *20* **Flighty Fellow (IRE)**[237] [4152] 6-9-4 **82** RobertWinston 5 24
(Miss J A Camacho) *chsd ldrs: rdn along wl over 2f out: sn wknd* **16/1**

/65- **7** *12* **Amongst Amigos (IRE)**[152] [6186] 5-8-2 **69** RPCleary(3) 2 —
(Barry Potts, Ire) *trckd ldrs: pushed along over 3f out: sn rdn and wknd* **9/2**[2]

1m 49.09s (6.59) **Going Correction** +1.05s/f (Soft) **7** Ran SP% **110.0**
Speed ratings (Par 105):109,108,100,97,95 75,63
CSF £8.40 TOTE £1.70: £1.10, £3.50; EX 10.40.
Owner Aidan J Ryan Racing **Bred** Shadwell Estate Company Limited **Trained** Musley Bank, N Yorks

FOCUS
A fair time given the ground and the first two came clear. The winner has been rated to last year's best form.
Amongst Amigos(IRE) Official explanation: trainer had no explanation for the poor form shown

816 LOTHIAN H'CAP 2m
3:40 (3:41) (Class 4) (0-85,80) 4-Y-O+ **£6,477** (£1,927; £963; £481) **Stalls** High

Form RPR
0-00 **1** **John Forbes**[38] [385] 4-8-12 **69** PatCosgrave 7 69
(B Ellison) *mde virtually all: rdn clr over 2f out: styd far rail and r.o strly* **16/1**

631- **2** *8* **Hernando's Boy**[113] [6218] 5-9-2 **68** PaulHanagan 9 60
(K G Reveley) *trckd ldrs gng wl: smooth hdwy to chse wnr over 2f out: swtchd lft wl over 1f out: sn rdn and no imp* **5/2**[1]

163- **3** *1/2* **Gone Too Far**[44] [6239] 8-8-9 **61** oh1 (v) KDarley 5 52
(P Monteith) *a.p: effrt to chse wnr 3f out: sn rdn along and kpt on same pce u.p fnl 2f* **12/1**

350/ **4** *6* **Sconced (USA)**[44] [3391] 11-8-9 **61** oh26 JohnEgan 11 46
(R C Guest) *bhd tl styd on fnl 3f: nvr nr ldrs* **33/1**

0323 **5** *3/4* **Rare Coincidence**[6] [733] 5-8-9 **61** oh6 (p) FrancisNorton 6 45
(R F Fisher) *prom: rdn along 3f out. drvn and outpcd fnl 2f* **10/1**

34-0 **6** *17* **Kristensen**[24] [610] 7-9-7 **73** AlanMunro 10 40
(Karen McLintock) *hld up: a rr* **16/1**

20-0 **7** *1 3/4* **Vicious Prince (IRE)**[41] [454] 7-9-6 **72** DeanMcKeown 1 38
(R M Whitaker) *midfield: effrt 5f out: sn rdn along and nvr a factor* **10/1**

-032 **8** *10* **Trance (IRE)**[36] 491 6-9-12 **78** .... NCallan 3 34
(T D Barron) *hld up: effrt and sme hdwy 3f out: sn rdn and nvr a factor* **7/2**[2]

310/ **9** *14* **Zoltano (GER)**[99] 1615 8-8-13 **65** .... TomEaves 8 7
(M Todhunter) *chsd ldrs: rdn along over 5f out: sn wknd* **7/1**[3]

-004 **10** *2 ½* **Golden Boot**[56] 283 7-9-1 **67** .... RobertWinston 4 6
(A Bailey) *hld up: hdwy over 4f out: rdn along over 3f out and sn wknd* **11/1**

660/ **11** *dist* **Bernardon (GER)**[51] 4973 10-9-11 **80** .... RPCleary(3) 2 —
(Barry Potts, Ire) *chsd ldrs: rdn along 1/2-way: sn wknd* **66/1**

3m 50.11s (16.21) **Going Correction** +1.05s/f (Soft)
WFA 4 from 5yo+ 5lb 11 Ran SP% **113.7**
Speed ratings (Par 105):101,97,96,93,93 84,84,79,72,70 —
CSF £54.08 CT £510.29 TOTE £22.90: £5.20, £1.50, £3.30; EX 103.90.
Owner Mrs Claire Ellison & Ray Wagner **Bred** Northmore Stud **Trained** Norton, N Yorks

FOCUS
A modest handicap, featuring largely dual-purpose performers, which was run at an uneven gallop. The form looks suspect.
Trance(IRE) Official explanation: jockey said gelding had no more to give

817 JOCK WHITELAW MAIDEN STKS 1m 1f
4:10 (4:10) (Class 5) 3-Y-0+ **£3,238** (£963; £481; £240) **Stalls** Low

Form RPR

0-32 **1** **Manouche**[27] 584 3-8-7 67 .... (p) NCallan 1 71
(K A Ryan) *mde all: rdn 2f out: jnd and drvn ent last: styd on gamely* **10/1**[3]

603- **2** *½* **Historic Appeal (USA)**[161] 6013 3-8-7 79 .... TedDurcan 7 70
(M R Channon) *prom: chsd wnr fr 1/2-way: rdn over 2f out: drvn to chal 1f out and ev ch tl no ex towards fin* **8/11**[1]

30- **3** *1* **Sunbolt (IRE)**[212] 4871 3-8-7 .... PaulFessey 8 68
(T D Barron) *chsd ldng pair: rdn along and sltly outpcd 2f out: styd on wl fnl f* **16/1**

40-0 **4** *6* **Sparkbridge (IRE)**[7] 709 3-8-4 62 .... PaulMulrennan(3) 9 56
(R F Fisher) *midfield: hdwy to chse leading pair 2f out: sn rdn and wknd appr last* **100/1**

6-00 **5** *5* **Tallyhobye**[35] 500 3-8-7 57 .... RobertWinston 5 46
(J R Weymes) *bhd tl styd on fnl 3f: nvr nr ldrs* **66/1**

6 *21* **Luck In Running (USA)** 3-8-7 .... JoeFanning 4 4
(M Johnston) *chsd ldrs: pushed along 4f out: rdn 3f out and sn wknd* **5/2**[2]

7 *2* **Keisha Kayleigh (IRE)** 3-8-2 .... PaulHanagan 3 —
(B Ellison) *s.i.s: a rr* **25/1**

8 *11* **Megalo Maniac** 3-8-7 .... DeanMcKeown 6 —
(K G Reveley) *s.i.s: a rr* **25/1**

0 **9** *dist* **Scarlet Romance**[15] 653 4-9-0 .... AdeleRothery(7) 2 —
(M W Easterby) *s.i.s: a rr* **100/1**

2m 4.38s (8.38) **Going Correction** +1.05s/f (Soft)
WFA 3 from 4yo 19lb 9 Ran SP% **112.6**
Speed ratings (Par 103):104,103,102,97,92 74,72,62,—
CSF £17.20 TOTE £5.50: £1.80, £1.10, £2.20; EX 16.20.
Owner Centaur Racing Ltd **Bred** Chess Racing Ab **Trained** Hambleton, N Yorks

FOCUS
A weak maiden, run at a fair pace, and the first three came clear. The form looks far from solid.

818 RECTANGLE GROUP H'CAP 7f 30y
4:40 (4:40) (Class 6) (0-65,64) 4-Y-0+ **£3,238** (£963; £481; £240) **Stalls** Low

Form RPR

610- **1** **Attacca**[186] 5520 5-8-4 **50** .... JoeFanning 8 58
(J R Weymes) *trckd ldrs: hdwy 2f out: rdn to ld over 1f out: drvn ins last and styd on wl* **16/1**

050- **2** *nk* **Insubordinate**[32] 2883 5-8-8 **54** .... TedDurcan 10 61
(J S Goldie) *hld up in rr: hdwy on inner over 2f out: rdn to chal ins last and ev ch tl drvn and no ex towards fin* **14/1**

1011 **3** *2 ½* **Vancouver Gold (IRE)**[11] 678 4-9-4 **64** 7ex .... RobertWinston 5 65
(K R Burke) *sn led: pushed along and hdd over 3f out: rdn and ev ch wl over 1f out tl wknd ins last* **8/11**[1]

04-0 **4** *2 ½* **First Rhapsody (IRE)**[42] 440 4-8-11 **57** .... KDarley 11 52
(T J Etherington) *chsd ldrs: rdn along over 2f out: kpt on same pce appr last* **25/1**

-134 **5** *½* **Dispol Isle (IRE)**[43] 429 4-9-3 **63** .... PhillipMakin 1 57
(T D Barron) *cl up: led over 3f out: rdn along 2f out: drvn and hdd over 1f out: sn wknd* **8/1**[2]

400- **6** *7* **Flaxby**[218] 4700 4-8-7 **53** .... AlanMunro 7 30
(J D Bethell) *in tch: effrt over 2f out: sn rdn and no imp* **10/1**[3]

220- **7** *½* **Montara (IRE)**[143] 5321 7-8-6 **55** .... RPCleary(3) 6 31
(Barry Potts, Ire) *midfield: rdn along 3f out: sn no imp* **16/1**

000/ **8** *2 ½* **Haulage Man**[535] 6144 8-8-4 **50** .... PaulHanagan 4 20
(Karen McLintock) *towards rr: hdwy 3f out: rdn along 2f out: sn wknd* **25/1**

410- **9** *2 ½* **Wayward Shot (IRE)**[163] 5981 4-9-1 **64** .... PaulMulrennan(3) 3 28
(M W Easterby) *prom: rdn along 3f out: sn wknd* **16/1**

000- **10** *4* **Cashema (IRE)**[32] 2763 5-8-4 **50** oh10 .... PaulEddery 9 4
(D R MacLeod) *a rr* **100/1**

500- **11** *10* **Yorkshire Blue**[153] 6140 7-9-4 **64** .... FergalLynch 2 —
(J S Goldie) *a rr* **20/1**

1m 37.33s (7.39) **Going Correction** +1.05s/f (Soft) 11 Ran SP% **115.9**
Speed ratings (Par 101):99,98,95,92,92 84,83,80,78,73 62
CSF £206.51 CT £382.60 TOTE £19.10: £3.40, £3.50, £1.30; EX 169.20.
Owner High Moor Racing 2 **Bred** Pigeon House Stud **Trained** Middleham Moor, N Yorks

FOCUS
A moderate handicap run at an average pace, but the form looks sound enough for the grade with the first two coming clear.

819 BALCARRES H'CAP 5f
5:10 (5:11) (Class 6) (0-65,65) 3-Y-0 **£3,412** (£1,007; £504) **Stalls** High

Form RPR

1222 **1** **Garlogs**[11] 673 3-8-13 **60** .... RobertWinston 1 70
(A Bailey) *mde all: rdn wl over 1f out: edgd lft and drvn ins last: styd on strly* **11/8**[1]

-521 **2** *2* **Danetime Lord (IRE)**[16] 646 3-9-0 **61** .... (p) NCallan 3 64
(K A Ryan) *chsd wnr: hdwy to chal wl over 1f out: sn rdn and ev ch tl kpt on same pce ins last* **11/4**[2]

3563 **3** *5* **Woodwee**[15] 651 3-8-13 **60** .... KDarley 4 46
(J R Weymes) *chsd ldng pair: rdn along 2f out: sn drvn and wknd* **7/1**[3]

000- **4** *1 ¼* **Mormeatmic**[179] 5659 3-8-8 **58** .... PaulMulrennan(3) 7 40
(M W Easterby) *chsd ldrs: rdn along 1/2-way: sn outpcd* **18/1**

054- **5** *1 ½* **Superior Star**[201] 5145 3-9-4 **65** .... (b) PaulHanagan 5 42
(R A Fahey) *in tch: rdn along 1/2-way: sn outpcd* **7/1**[3]

100- **6** *1 ¼* **Beverley Polo (IRE)**[258] 3523 3-9-1 **62** .... DaleGibson 2 35
(M W Easterby) *dwlt: a outpcd and bhd* **22/1**

63.92 secs (3.42) **Going Correction** +0.80s/f (Soft) 6 Ran SP% **103.4**
Speed ratings (Par 96):104,100,92,90,88 86
CSF £4.28 CT £11.12 TOTE £2.10: £1.50, £1.60; EX 4.10 Place 6 £58.42, Place 5 £14.29.
Owner Peter G Freeman **Bred** Peter Taplin **Trained** Cotebrook, Cheshire

FOCUS
A very decent winning time in the conditions, especially in comparison to the two earlier races over the same trip, and the form looks sound for the grade.
T/Jkpt: Not won. T/Plt: £55.10 to a £1 stake. Pool: £63,228.80. 837.10 winning tickets. T/Qpdt: £3.10 to a £1 stake. Pool: £5,854.40. 1,381.55 winning tickets. JR

789 WOLVERHAMPTON (A.W) (L-H)
Friday, March 31

OFFICIAL GOING: Standard
Wind: Moderate, behind Weather: Showers

820 WATCH OUT FOR THEMED DAYS AT WOLVERHAMPTON H'CAP 1m 1f 103y(P)
2:30 (2:30) (Class 6) (0-60,60) 4-Y-0+ **£2,388** (£705; £352) **Stalls** Low

Form RPR

-650 **1** **Lord Of Dreams (IRE)**[36] 493 4-8-13 **55** .... EddieAhern 8 65
(D W P Arbuthnot) *a.p: rdn to ld over 2f out: clr over 1f out: jst hld on* **16/1**

2300 **2** *hd* **Port 'n Starboard**[9] 696 5-9-4 **60** .... MartinDwyer 5 70
(C A Cyzer) *led early: hld up in tch: rdn over 2f out: chsd wnr wl over 1f out: r.o ins fnl f: jst failed* **8/1**[3]

2132 **3** *3* **Glendale**[9] 696 5-8-13 **55** .... JimmyQuinn 7 59
(D K Ivory) *hld up in tch: rdn over 2f out: kpt on one pce fnl f* **7/2**[1]

02-5 **4** *shd* **Scamperdale**[25] 600 4-8-6 **55** .... SoniaEaton(7) 3 59
(B P J Baugh) *hld up in tch: rdn over 1f out: kpt on same pce fnl f* **25/1**

6204 **5** *1 ½* **King Of Knight (IRE)**[9] 696 5-9-4 **60** .... OscarUrbina 9 61
(G Prodromou) *s.i.s: hld up and bhd: rdn over 3f out: hdwy and hung lft over 1f out: nvr trbld ldrs* **9/1**

-046 **6** *shd* **Eijaaz (IRE)**[8] 700 5-8-9 **58** .... KristinStubbs(7) 4 59
(Mrs L Stubbs) *s.i.s: sn mid-div: pushed along 4f out: hdwy on ins wl over 1f out: wknd ent fnl f* **14/1**

-343 **7** *nk* **Lord Chamberlain**[77] 106 13-9-4 **60** .... (b) RyanMoore 1 60
(J M Bradley) *bhd: hdwy on outside fnl f: n.d* **8/1**[3]

0065 **8** *shd* **Sorbiesharry (IRE)**[27] 586 7-8-11 **56** .... (p) SaleemGolam(3) 6 56
(Mrs N Macauley) *sn led: rdn and hdd over 2f out: wknd ins fnl f* **9/1**

514 **9** *2 ½* **Samson Quest**[28] 568 4-8-12 **59** .... JamesDoyle(5) 13 54
(A W Carroll) *dwlt: a bhd* **12/1**

3031 **10** *nk* **Sol Rojo**[28] 568 4-9-3 **59** .... SebSanders 10 54
(J Pearce) *mid-div: rdn over 3f out: wknd over 1f out* **6/1**[2]

3-06 **11** *1* **Weet A Head (IRE)**[16] 640 5-9-4 **60** .... SteveDrowne 12 53
(R Hollinshead) *wnt rt s: sn prom: rdn and ev ch over 2f out: wknd over 1f out* **20/1**

06-0 **12** *½* **Futoo (IRE)**[23] 131 5-9-2 **58** .... (p) TonyCulhane 2 50
(D W Chapman) *mid-div: rdn 3f out: sn bhd* **10/1**

2m 0.77s (-1.85) **Going Correction** -0.05s/f (Stan) 12 Ran SP% **116.7**
Speed ratings (Par 101):106,105,103,103,101 101,101,101,99,98 97,97
CSF £136.43 CT £557.35 TOTE £21.30: £4.60, £3.80, £1.80; EX 290.80.
Owner N Cronin & P Banfield **Bred** B Ryan **Trained** Upper Lambourn, Berks
■ Stewards' Enquiry : Martin Dwyer caution: careless riding

FOCUS
Modest stuff to say the least, but the time was good. It has been rated around the runner-up and fourth.

821 REMEMBER FAMILY FUN DAYS AT WOLVERHAMPTON (S) STKS 5f 216y(P)
3:00 (3:00) (Class 6) 4-Y-0+ **£2,388** (£705; £352) **Stalls** Low

Form RPR

000- **1** **Magical Mimi**[347] 1100 5-8-7 45 .... (t) ChrisCatlin 6 55
(K G Wingrove) *s.i.s: hdwy on ins over 2f out: rdn to ld jst ins fnl f: r.o wl* **40/1**

5200 **2** *2* **Stagnite**[4] 772 6-8-12 50 .... (b) DarryllHolland 8 54
(K McAuliffe) *led: rdn wl over 1f out: hdd jst ins fnl f: nt qckn* **4/1**[3]

0-66 **3** *3 ½* **Global Achiever**[11] 679 5-8-12 50 .... (p) OscarUrbina 7 44
(G C H Chung) *hld up and bhd: rdn and hdwy over 1f out: one pce fnl f* **11/4**[2]

0105 **4** *2* **Winning Venture**[27] 581 9-9-3 55 .... RyanMoore 1 43
(A W Carroll) *prom: rdn over 2f out: wkng whn edgd lft 1f out* **5/1**

40-0 **5** *½* **Cheeky Chi (IRE)**[42] 442 5-8-0 35 .... (b) DonnaCaldwell(7) 3 31
(P S McEntee) *chsd ldrs: rdn over 2f out: wknd jst over 1f out* **50/1**

0000 **6** *2* **King Marrakech (IRE)**[4] 766 4-8-5 40 .... (p) SoniaEaton(7) 5 30
(B P J Baugh) *prom: lost pl after 2f: carried wd over 2f out: sn bhd* **16/1**

0016 **7** *½* **Imperium**[6] 732 5-9-3 52 .... (p) SebSanders 4 34
(Stef Liddiard) *prom: rdn over 3f out: wknd wl over 1f out* **13/8**[1]

1m 15.97s (0.16) **Going Correction** -0.05s/f (Stan) 7 Ran SP% **111.7**
Speed ratings (Par 101):96,93,88,86,85 82,82
CSF £183.03 TOTE £26.80: £6.20, £2.90; EX 103.20 Trifecta £403.50.There was no bid for the winner.
Owner M M Foulger **Bred** Mrs M J Tipson And K F Tipson **Trained** Highley, Shropshire
■ Trainer Ken Wingrove's first winner for nearly four years.

FOCUS
Quite a shock here with Magical Mimi making a winning reappearance at 40/1. The time was also modest, even for a seller, and the form has been rated around the runner-up.

822 RACE SPONSORSHIP - A GREAT PROMOTIONAL TOOL H'CAP 1m 141y(P)
3:30 (3:31) (Class 5) (0-75,74) 3-Y-0 **£3,238** (£963; £481; £240) **Stalls** Low

Form RPR

00-1 **1** **Royal Amnesty**[16] 642 3-8-4 **60** oh1 .... ChrisCatlin 2 66
(G C H Chung) *a.p: rdn to ld over 1f out: edgd lft towards fin: r.o* **12/1**

1-16 **2** *¾* **Magical Music**[7] 712 3-8-11 **67** .... JimmyQuinn 3 71
(J Pearce) *hld up in tch: rdn 2f out: ev ch ins fnl f: nt qckn* **9/4**[2]

-115 **3** *2* **Petrichan (IRE)**[46] 406 3-8-10 **66** .... (p) DarryllHolland 8 66
(K A Ryan) *led: rdn over 2f out: edgd rt and hdd over 1f out: edgd lft ins fnl f: one pce* **9/1**

1 **4** *3 ½* **Samurai Jack (IRE)**[27] 584 3-9-2 **72** .... (t) EddieAhern 5 64
(John A Quinn, Ire) *hld up: rdn 2f out: nvr trbld ldrs* **13/8**[1]

5-03 **5** *1* **Amygdala**[16] 645 3-8-10 **66** .... OscarUrbina 4 56
(M Botti) *hld up: rdn over 1f out: nvr nr ldrs* **12/1**

The Form Book, Raceform Ltd, Compton, RG20 6NL

3-02 **6** *shd* **Kokila**[41] 447 3-8-5 **61** NickyMackay 7 51
(W J Haggas) *sn chsng ldr: rdn over 2f out: wknd over 1f out* **7/1**[3]

5230 **7** *shd* **His Master's Voice (IRE)**[8] 702 3-9-4 **74** RyanMoore 6 64
(D W P Arbuthnot) *hld up: stdy hdwy over 4f out: rdn over 3f out: wknd over 1f out* **8/1**

1m 51.26s (-0.50) **Going Correction** -0.05s/f (Stan) **7** Ran SP% **117.9**
Speed ratings (Par 98):100,99,97,94,93 93,93
CSF £41.12 CT £265.80 TOTE £9.70: £3.90, £1.60; EX 43.90 Trifecta £231.60.
Owner G C H Chung **Bred** Brick Kiln Stud, Mrs L Hicks And Partners **Trained** Newmarket, Suffolk

FOCUS
The pace was steady for the first half of the contest, but things quickened up considerably in the second half and the winning time was perfectly acceptable. The race has been rated around the runner-up.

823 BOOK ONLINE AT WOLVERHAMPTON-RACECOURSE.CO.UK MAIDEN STKS 1m 141y(P)
4:00 (4:04) (Class 5) 3-Y-O **£3,238** (£963; £361; £361) **Stalls** Low

Form RPR

4-2 **1** **Lucky Token (IRE)**[27] 579 3-8-12 EddieAhern 4 72+
(E A L Dunlop) *chsd ldr: led on bit over 2f out: sn clr: swvd rt 1f out: easily* **4/11**[1]

5625 **2** *2* **Blanc Visage**[11] 677 3-9-3 74 GeorgeBaker 7 60
(Mrs H Sweeting) *led: rdn and hdd over 2f out: r.o one pce* **9/2**[2]

06 **3** *1* **Alexian**[20] 630 3-8-10 RussellKennemore(7) 2 58
(R Hollinshead) *hld up in rr: rdn 3f out: hdwy over 1f out: one pce fnl f* **12/1**[3]

3 *dht* **Soldiers Romance** 3-8-12 DuranFentiman(5) 1 58
(T D Easterby) *chsd ldrs: rdn 3f out: one pce fnl 2f* **20/1**

4-00 **5** *¾* **Jumanji (IRE)**[49] 364 3-8-12 54 AdrianMcCarthy 6 51
(M J Attwater) *hld up: hdwy on ins over 3f out: rdn over 2f out: one pce* **22/1**

0- **6** *1 ¼* **Dzhani**[163] 5988 3-9-3 MickyFenton 3 53
(Jedd O'Keeffe) *chsd ldrs: rdn 3f out: wknd over 1f out* **20/1**

1m 52.68s (0.92) **Going Correction** -0.05s/f (Stan) **6** Ran SP% **113.1**
Speed ratings (Par 98):93,91,90,90,89 88
CSF £2.25 TOTE £1.50: £1.10, £1.70; EX 2.50.
Owner Gainsborough Stud **Bred** Gainsborough Stud Management Ltd **Trained** Newmarket, Suffolk

FOCUS
This was run at a very steady pace and the winning time was modest for a race of its type. The form is hardly solid.

824 ENJOY RACING FROM THE ZONGALERO RESTAURANT H'CAP 5f 20y(P)
4:30 (4:31) (Class 6) (0-65,65) 4-Y-O+ **£2,730** (£806; £403) **Stalls** Low

Form RPR

-450 **1** **Desert Opal**[15] 654 6-8-10 **57** TonyCulhane 8 65
(D W Chapman) *chsd ldrs: rdn over 1f out: edgd lft and led wl ins fnl f: r.o* **20/1**

4063 **2** *½* **Sahara Silk (IRE)**[27] 587 5-9-1 **65** (v) PatrickMathers(3) 4 71+
(D Shaw) *towards rr: rdn over 3f out: hdwy over 1f out: swtchd rt ins fnl f: r.o wl* **8/1**

2001 **3** *nk* **Almaty Express**[32] 532 4-9-4 **65** (b) DarryllHolland 6 70
(J R Weymes) *sn led: rdn over 1f out: edgd lft and hdd wl ins fnl f: nt qckn* **11/2**[1]

1101 **4** *nk* **Hello Roberto**[23] 613 5-9-1 **62** (p) AdrianMcCarthy 3 67+
(R A Harris) *led early: hld up in tch: rdn wl over 1f out: nt clr run on ins and swtchd rt wl ins fnl f: r.o* **15/2**

1064 **5** *1 ¼* **Cashel Mead**[24] 608 6-8-8 **55** SteveDrowne 10 55
(J L Spearing) *s.i.s: hdwy over 3f out: sn rdn: r.o one pce fnl f* **11/1**

1662 **6** *¾* **Times Review (USA)**[27] 580 5-8-10 **62** (b) GregFairley(5) 9 59
(C A Dwyer) *a.p: rdn over 2f out: c wd st: one pce fnl f* **8/1**

0300 **7** *2* **Namir (IRE)**[27] 588 4-9-1 **62** (v) RyanMoore 13 52
(Stef Liddiard) *s.i.s: hdwy over 2f out: no further prog* **20/1**

1003 **8** *¾* **Monte Major (IRE)**[27] 580 5-8-8 **55** (v) EddieAhern 12 42
(D Shaw) *nvr nr ldrs* **16/1**

1113 **9** *1 ½* **Henry Tun**[43] 426 8-8-12 **62** (v) JasonEdmunds(3) 1 44
(J Balding) *a towards rr* **6/1**[2]

00-4 **10** *¾* **Salon Prive**[87] 23 6-9-4 **65** (b) MartinDwyer 11 44
(C A Cyzer) *chsd ldr tl rdn 2f out: sn wknd* **8/1**

4250 **11** *nk* **Shadow Jumper (IRE)**[24] 608 5-8-12 **59** (v) MickyFenton 2 37
(J T Stimpson) *bhd fnl 2f* **7/1**[3]

0021 **12** *2* **Lady Bahia (IRE)**[27] 580 5-9-1 **62** (b) RobbieFitzpatrick 5 33
(Peter Grayson) *s.i.s: a bhd* **9/1**

61.96 secs (-0.86) **Going Correction** -0.05s/f (Stan) **12** Ran SP% **121.0**
Speed ratings (Par 101):104,103,102,102,100 99,95,94,92,91 90,87
CSF £175.52 CT £1012.92 TOTE £19.00: £4.50, £4.20, £1.70; EX 239.20 Trifecta £580.20.
Owner Miss N F Thesiger **Bred** Juddmonte Farms **Trained** Stillington, N Yorks

FOCUS
A competitive if modest sprint handicap run at a sound pace. The form looks solid rated around the third and fourth.
Times Review(USA) Official explanation: jockey said gelding hung right
Salon Prive Official explanation: jockey said gelding hung left after start
Lady Bahia(IRE) Official explanation: jockey said mare missed the break

825 HOTEL AND CONFERENCING AT DUNSTALL PARK APPRENTICE H'CAP 1m 5f 194y(P)
5:00 (5:01) (Class 5) (0-75,73) 4-Y-O+ **£4,095** (£1,209; £604) **Stalls** Low

Form RPR

-436 **1** **I'll Do It Today**[28] 570 5-8-5 **55** AndrewMullen 6 61
(J M Jefferson) *hld up in tch: rdn to ld 3f out: clr over 1f out: r.o wl* **3/1**[1]

-502 **2** *4* **Valeureux**[25] 599 8-8-4 **54** oh4 (t) MarcHalford 7 54
(J Hetherton) *hld up: hdwy over 3f out: rdn over 2f out: chsd wnr fnl f: no imp* **14/1**

1- **3** *½* **Will He Rock (IRE)**[208] 4976 5-9-9 **73** JerryO'Dwyer 2 72
(John A Quinn, Ire) *hld up in mid-div: hdwy 5f out: rdn over 2f out: one pce fnl f* **7/2**[2]

/62- **4** *1 ¼* **Shingle Street (IRE)**[10] 2854 4-8-9 **66** (b) JamesDoyle(3) 3 64
(Miss Venetia Williams) *sn chsng ldr: lost 2nd and n.m.r 3f out: sn rdn: edgd lft over 1f out: one pce* **10/1**

400- **5** *½* **Mary Gray**[150] 6218 4-8-3 **57** oh1 GregFairley 4 54
(M Johnston) *led: hdd 3f out: sn rdn: wknd ins fnl f* **11/2**[3]

1341 **6** *3 ½* **Latif (USA)**[7] 713 5-9-7 **71** 6ex RichardKingscote 5 63
(Ms Deborah J Evans) *s.i.s: a bhd* **7/2**[2]

502/ **7** *2 ½* **Slalom (IRE)**[189] 6395 6-8-10 **65** JosephWalsh(5) 1 53
(D Burchell) *prom: rdn 4f out: sn wknd* **20/1**

6561 **8** *8* **Ice And Fire**[4] 767 7-8-0 **61** 6ex oh3 ow1 (b) JemmaMarshall(5) 8 32
(J T Stimpson) *hld up: bhd most of way* **12/1**

3m 6.24s (-1.13) **Going Correction** -0.05s/f (Stan)
WFA 4 from 5yo+ 4lb **8** Ran SP% **113.0**
Speed ratings (Par 103):101,98,98,97,97 95,94,89
CSF £44.17 CT £151.31 TOTE £4.60: £1.80, £2.80, £2.10; EX 32.40 Trifecta £375.60 Place 6 £187.95, Place 5 £77.94.
Owner Mr & Mrs J M Davenport **Bred** Mrs D W Davenport **Trained** Norton, N Yorks

FOCUS
They went a very steady pace for much of the way and the race developed into a four-furlong sprint. Far from convincing form, rated around the runner-up.
Shingle Street(IRE) Official explanation: jockey said gelding was denied a clear run
Latif(USA) Official explanation: jockey said gelding ran flat
T/Plt: £332.20 to a £1 stake. Pool: £68,914.05. 151.40 winning tickets. T/Qpdt: £26.70 to a £1 stake. Pool: £6,589.70. 182.15 winning tickets. KH

760 KEMPTON (A.W) (R-H)
Saturday, April 1

OFFICIAL GOING: Standard
Wind: Half across Weather: Fine

826 INTERCASINO.CO.UK LONDON MILE QUALIFIER H'CAP 1m (P)
2:10 (2:10) (Class 4) (0-80,82) 4-Y-O+ **£5,505** (£1,637; £818; £408) **Stalls** High

Form RPR

2623 **1** **Glad Big (GER)**[7] 721 4-9-1 **77** SteveDrowne 9 88
(J A Osborne) *hld up rr: hdwy over 1f out: qcknd to ld jst ins fnl f: drvn out* **13/2**[3]

63-1 **2** *1 ½* **Akona Matata (USA)**[7] 720 4-9-6 **82** JimmyFortune 8 89
(C E Brittain) *lw: hld up mid-div: hdwy 3f out: led ins fnl 2f: hdd jst ins fnl f :kpt on same pce* **6/1**[2]

2102 **3** *shd* **Aggravation**[8] 711 4-8-8 **70** JohnEgan 2 77
(D R C Elsworth) *bhd: hdwy on outside over 3f out: kpt on wl fnl f:nt pce to rch wnr* **14/1**

31-4 **4** *1* **Fasylitator (IRE)**[14] 670 4-9-1 **77** EddieAhern 6 82
(D K Ivory) *lw: mid-div: hdwy 3f out: kpt on fnl f but nt pce to rch ldrs* **7/1**

53-0 **5** *4* **All Quiet**[14] 670 5-9-2 **78** RichardHughes 7 74
(R Hannon) *hld up in rr: hdwy fr 2f out: kpt on fnl f: one pce ins last* **14/1**

0-04 **6** *hd* **Serieux**[8] 719 7-8-10 **75** (v) SilvestreDeSousa(3) 3 70
(D Nicholls) *t.k.h: bhd: hdwy 4f out: led over 2f out: hdd ins fnl quarter m: wknd fnl f* **20/1**

-111 **7** *hd* **Merrymadcap (IRE)**[17] 641 4-9-1 **77** FrancisNorton 15 72+
(M Blanshard) *in tch: n.m.r over 2f out: sn no imp* **11/2**[1]

524 **8** *½* **Lincolneurocruiser**[17] 639 4-8-7 **72** SaleemGolam(3) 14 73+
(Mrs N Macauley) *lw: in tch: hdwy on ins 2f out: nt much room and stmbld appr fnl f: nt rcvr* **14/1**

251- **9** *1* **Parnassian**[150] 6230 6-8-12 **74** StephenCarson 4 65
(J A Geake) *bit bkwd: s.i.s: bhd: sme hdwy fnl 2f* **25/1**

0/P- **10** *¾* **Surwaki (USA)**[352] 1004 4-9-4 **80** PhilipRobinson 11 69
(C G Cox) *bit bkwd: chsd ldrs tl grad lost pl fr over 1f out* **25/1**

4020 **11** *1 ½* **General Feeling (IRE)**[21] 632 5-9-0 **76** TPQueally 17 62
(M Mullineaux) *s.i.s: bhd: kpt on fnl f* **25/1**

2031 **12** *3* **Mystic Man (FR)**[17] 639 8-9-3 **79** (b) PaulHanagan 12 58
(I W McInnes) *chsd ldrs 6f* **16/1**

2103 **13** *shd* **Speed Dial Harry (IRE)**[25] 611 4-8-13 **80** (v) AndrewElliott(5) 5 59
(K R Burke) *chsd ldrs: led 3f out: hdd over 2f out: wknd fnl f* **10/1**

60-0 **14** *5* **Meelup (IRE)**[26] 596 6-8-4 **66** oh3 MartinDwyer 10 33
(P G Murphy) *nvr bttr than mid-div: wknd 2f out* **50/1**

0-01 **15** *14* **Following Flow (USA)**[29] 567 4-9-0 **76** (p) GrahamGibbons 16 11
(R Hollinshead) *chsd ldrs to 1/2-way* **16/1**

2050 **16** *2 ½* **Ground Rules (USA)**[4] 777 4-8-5 **74** JosephWalsh(7) 13 —
(V Smith) *sn drvn to ld: hdd 3f out: sn wknd* **22/1**

1m 41.05s (-0.93) **Going Correction** +0.20s/f (Slow) **16** Ran SP% **119.0**
Speed ratings (Par 105):106,104,104,103,99 99,99,98,97,96 95,92,92,87,73 70
CSF £39.51 CT £557.33 TOTE £9.20: £1.90, £1.60, £2.60, £1.80; EX 48.40.
Owner Mountgrange Stud **Bred** Gestut Auenquelle **Trained** Upper Lambourn, Berks
■ Stewards' Enquiry : Silvestre De Sousa one-day ban: careless riding (Apr 12)

FOCUS
A fiercely competitive handicap run at a solid pace, though the winning time was slower than both three-year-old Listed contests. The first four came well clear of the others so the form looks sound, and the draw did not have the impact that might have been expected, with no double-figure stall making the first six.
Merrymadcap(IRE) Official explanation: jockey said gelding lost a shoe
Mystic Man(FR) Official explanation: jockey said gelding was struck into behind

827 INTERCASINO.CO.UK MASAKA STKS (LISTED RACE) (FILLIES) 1m (P)
2:45 (2:47) (Class 1) 3-Y-O
£15,898 (£6,025; £3,015; £1,503; £753; £378) **Stalls** High

Form RPR

-563 **1** **Dont Dili Dali**[23] 623 3-8-10 92 JohnEgan 3 97
(J S Moore) *lw: bhd: stl last appr fnl 2f: str run fr over 1f out to ld fnl 50yds: kpt on strly* **12/1**

1214 **2** *2* **Song Of Silence (USA)**[42] 448 3-8-10 82 LDettori 11 92
(E A L Dunlop) *sn led: 3l clr over 1f out: sn drvn: hdd and no ex fnl 50yds* **7/1**[3]

61- **3** *nk* **Nyarhini**[137] 6349 3-8-10 79 SteveDrowne 4 92
(G Wragg) *bit bkwd: in tch: drvn and hdwy 2f out: styd on fnl f but nt pce to chal* **10/1**

145- **4** *1 ½* **Suzy Bliss**[182] 5605 3-8-10 100 StephenCarson 1 88
(W R Swinburn) *lw: rr but in tch: hdwy on outside 2f out: sn rdn: kpt on same pce ins last* **12/1**

315- **5** *shd* **Cross Channel (USA)**[189] 5459 3-8-10 98 JamieSpencer 6 88
(E A L Dunlop) *chsd ldrs: rdn over 2f out: wknd fnl f* **9/2**[1]

26-3 **6** *½* **Rising Cross**[14] 665 3-8-10 100 TQuinn 2 87
(J R Best) *s.i.s: bhd: rdn 3f out: edgd rt over 1f out: kpt on fnl f and fin wl: nt a danger* **11/2**[2]

214- **7** *1* **Choosy (IRE)**[161] 6027 3-8-10 95 RichardHughes 8 85
(R Hannon) *hld up in rr: rdn and hdwy over 2f out: nvr gng pce to trouble ldrs: wknd ins last* **16/1**

411- **8** *¾* **Rajeem**[154] 6145 3-8-13 96 SebSanders 10 86
(C E Brittain) *s.i.s: hdwy whn hmpd after 1f: sme hdwy and n.m.r over 2f out: wknd over 1f out* **9/2**[1]

3-10 **9** *1* **Miss Highjinks (USA)**[48] 392 3-8-10 82 EddieAhern 7 81
(E J O'Neill) *chsd ldrs: rdn over 2f out: wknd over 1f out* **33/1**

610- **10** *6* **Sleeping Storm (IRE)**[206] 5043 3-8-10 83 .... JimmyFortune 9 67
(B J Meehan) *bit bkwd: chsd ldrs: rdn over 2f out: wknd 2f out* **7/1**[3]

00-0 **11** *10* **Ooh Aah Camara (IRE)**[14] 665 3-8-10 88 .... TedDurcan 5 44
(T J Pitt) *chsd ldrs 6f* **40/1**

1m 40.61s (-1.37) **Going Correction** +0.20s/f (Slow) **11** Ran SP% **112.5**
Speed ratings (Par 103):108,106,105,104,104 103,102,101,100,94 84
CSF £89.46 TOTE £14.60: £2.90, £2.00, £3.90; EX 110.00.
Owner Peter Webb & Peter Lay **Bred** G Russell **Trained** Upper Lambourn, Berks
■ The first running of this established Classic trial on Polytrack.

FOCUS
This looked to be a tactical affair at first glance, but the winning time was faster than both the opening handicap for older horses and the Easter Stakes, so the form may not be at all bad, although probably a fair way off regular Classic trial standard.

NOTEBOOK
Dont Dili Dali, third in the UAE Oaks on her previous start, deserves a lot of credit for this victory as she had to come from right out the back, yet the turn of foot she showed to mow down the leader was extremely impressive. Quite how the form will work out is uncertain, and she is hardly unexposed - this was her 14th race - but she has obviously trained on and the Italian Oaks looks a likely target. Her dam and grandam were both placed in the race.
Song Of Silence(USA), the stable's second string according to the market, was given a canny front-running ride by Dettori and for much of the home straight it seemed that he had judged things to perfection, but he reckoned without the winner's dazzling turn of speed and there was little the filly could do about it. This was a decent effort to make the frame at this level considering only one filly in this race had a lower BHB rating than her. (op 8-1)
Nyarhini ◆, absent since winning a Lingfield maiden in November, stayed on down the home straight and nearly got up for second. She would have been getting weight from all her rivals had this been a handicap, but she does have scope and her stable does well with progressive three-year-old fillies, such as her half-sister Rebecca Sharp. Her breeding and style of racing suggests she will get further, so perhaps one of the Oaks Trials could be on the agenda.
Suzy Bliss, racing for the first time since October, had shown enough in her last two outings in Pattern company as a juvenile to suggest that she was capable of running well here, and she did just that, though her effort down the outside never really looked like succeeding. Her half-brothers Mad Carew and Cutting Crew both won at up to 12 furlongs and she shapes as though she now needs further as well. (tchd 11-1)
Cross Channel(USA), last seen finishing fifth in last season's Fillies' Mile at Newmarket, was the stable's number one according to the market, but was making hard work of getting to her stable-companion from a long way out and it may be that she also needs a stiffer test now. (op 10-3)
Rising Cross, held up right at the back, was given a bit to do but so was the eventual winner and she was unable to make anything like the same impression. This looks about as good as she is. Official explanation: jockey said filly never travelled (op 5-1)
Rajeem, not seen since winning a Newmarket Listed race last October, did not enjoy the clearest of runs at various stages of the contest, but in reality she lacked the tactical speed to get herself out of trouble. A return to soft ground on turf may see her in a better light. (op 6-1)

828 PLAY BLACKJACK AT INTERCASINO.CO.UK H'CAP 7f (P)
3:20 (3:20) (Class 2) (0-100,98) 4-Y-0+

£11,217 (£3,358; £1,679; £840; £419; £210) **Stalls** High

Form RPR

050- **1** **Visionist (IRE)**[169] 5874 4-8-11 **91** .... DarryllHolland 8 103+
(Pat Eddery) *lw: hld up mid-div: gng wl and squeezed through to ld 1f out: pushed clr: comf* **9/1**

010- **2** *2 ½* **Presumptive (IRE)**[270] 3201 6-8-7 **87** .... SteveDrowne 12 92
(R Charlton) *lw: sn prom: chsd ldrs fr 3f out: rdn and str chal over 1f out: kpt on but no ch w wnr ins last* **12/1**

-001 **3** *½* **Binanti**[7] 721 6-8-4 **84** oh1 .... FrancisNorton 7 88
(P R Chamings) *bhd: hdwy on outside over 2f out: kpt on ins last but nt rch ldrs* **10/1**

132- **4** *1* **Desert Dreamer (IRE)**[182] 5603 5-8-4 **84** oh2 .... AlanMunro 11 85
(P R Chamings) *rr: hdwy 3f out: kpt on fr over 1f out but nvr gng pce rch ldrs* **10/1**

3300 **5** *nk* **Chief Exec**[14] 667 4-8-1 **84** oh2 .... EdwardCreighton(3) 2 84
(C A Cyzer) *lw: chsd ldrs: chal over 1f out: wknd last half f* **50/1**

2064 **6** *hd* **Moayed**[9] 704 7-8-13 **98** ....(b) JamesDoyle(5) 13 98
(N P Littmoden) *s.i.s: bhd: hrd drvn 3f out: kpt on ins fnl f: gng on cl home* **10/1**

6202 **7** *1 ¾* **Trifti**[14] 670 5-8-6 **86** .... MartinDwyer 10 81+
(C A Cyzer) *bhd: hdwy fr 2f out: r.o ins last but n.d* **8/1**[3]

420- **8** *1* **King's Caprice**[126] 6431 5-8-8 **88** ....(t) StephenCarson 6 81
(J A Geake) *t.k.h:chsd ldrs: led ins fnl 3f: rdn over 2f out: hdd 1f out: sn wknd* **14/1**

-134 **9** *¾* **Pinchbeck**[46] 413 7-8-4 **84** oh1 ....(p) PhilipRobinson 3 75
(M A Jarvis) *towards rr: hdwy whn n.m.r and bumped appr fnl 2f: kpt on again ins last but nvr a danger* **12/1**

10 *½* **Marajaa (IRE)**[173] 4-8-8 **88** .... LPKeniry 1 83+
(W J Musson) *cmpt: bit bkwd: bhd: gd hdwy fr 2f out: styng on wl whn swtchd rt to rail and hmpd appr fnl f: nt rcvr* **66/1**

140- **11** *4* **Prince Of Thebes (IRE)**[183] 5593 5-8-12 **92** .... PaulDoe 14 71
(J Akehurst) *chsd ldrs: rdn over 2f out: wknd over 1f out* **5/1**[1]

200- **12** *½* **Cool Panic (IRE)**[217] 4764 4-9-2 **96** .... JamieSpencer 4 74
(M L W Bell) *lw: sn led: hdd ins fnl 3f: stl ev ch over 1f out: sn wknd* **7/1**[2]

204- **13** *1 ¼* **Moonlight Man**[224] 4568 5-9-3 **97** .... RichardHughes 9 71
(R Hannon) *bit bkwd: chsd ldrs: rdn 3f out: wknd qckly appr fnl f* **8/1**[3]

14 *3* **Major League (USA)**[23] 4-9-0 **94** .... TedDurcan 5 61
(K Bishop) *lw: a in rr* **100/1**

004- **15** *11* **Asharon**[251] 3782 4-8-5 **85** ....(b) EddieAhern 15 23+
(C E Brittain) *lw: mid-div: hdwy on ins whn hmpd over 2f out: sn wknd* **25/1**

1m 27.02s (-1.24) **Going Correction** +0.20s/f (Slow) **15** Ran SP% **119.0**
Speed ratings (Par 109):106,103,102,101,101 100,98,97,96,96 91,91,89,86,73
CSF £108.72 CT £1109.39 TOTE £10.10: £3.10, £4.20, £4.00; EX 197.70.
Owner Pat Eddery Racing (Alvaro) **Bred** Frank Barry **Trained** Nether Winchendon, Bucks
■ A first winner as a trainer for 11-time champion jockey Pat Eddery.

FOCUS
An extemely competitive handicap, run at a true pace, and the time was 1.76 seconds quicker than the three-year-old handicap over the same trip later in the afternoon. It was something of a rough race too, with a few in behind meeting trouble in running. Visionist, who was Group-placed at two, impressed and is one to keep on the right side of.

NOTEBOOK
Visionist(IRE) ◆, returning from a six-month break and making his debut for the yard, could be seen cruising behind the leaders from a long way out and the only question was whether he would get the gap when he needed it. Once he found one, he was quickly through it and showed a smart turn of foot to leave his rivals behind. He obviously relished this first try on sand and he looks better than ever. (op 10-1 tchd 11-1)
Presumptive(IRE) ◆, returning from a nine-month break and racing on sand for the first time, ran a blinder. Switched over to the inside rail after the false rail ended, he kept on really well but the winner was different gear. This is definitely his trip and this effort bodes well for future. (op 10-1)
Binanti, raised 4lb for his course-and-distance victory the previous week, was forced to make his challenge down the outside, unlike last time, and kept on to the line. Even though he had the benefit of race-fitness on the front pair, there is no reason to believe he did not run his race. He has taken very well to this track.
Desert Dreamer(IRE), reappearing from a six-month break, was 5lb higher than when winning over this trip on the Lingfield Polytrack last autumn. Making his effort widest of all in the home straight, he lacked the finishing pace of the principals but at least this should have put him right. (op 14-1)
Chief Exec, who has been on the go all winter, was never far away and had every chance, but he was always being held out towards the outside from his low draw and in the end he had nothing left. (op 66-1)
Moayed, an habitual slow starter, which would have negated any advantage he had with the draw, gave himself a lot to do and, although he was coming home strongly, he never had a hope of getting there in time. He is talented, but sometimes frustrating. (op 9-1 tchd 11-1)
Trifti, stayed on well once switched to the inside rail over a furlong out, but this trip is probably too sharp for him now. (op 9-1)
King's Caprice did far too much too early and ultimately paid the penalty. (tchd 16-1)
Pinchbeck, who is yet to win beyond six, got rather messed about on the outside soon after turning for home, but it is doubtful that he would have been involved in the finish even with a clear run. Official explanation: jockey said gelding was hampered
Marajaa(IRE) ◆, a French import making his debut for the yard following a six-month break, was held up early from the outside stall but was coming with a promising-looking run when running into a brick wall over a furlong out and his chance ended there and then. He has obviously retained the ability that saw him win twice on turf in France last year and he is worth making a note of, especially for when the money is down. Official explanation: jockey said colt was denied a clear run (op 50-1)
Prince Of Thebes(IRE), returning from a seven-month break, had every chance but faded tamely over the last couple of furlongs. He has won after a year's absence before now, so fitness ought not to have been a problem.
Cool Panic(IRE) Official explanation: jockey said colt had no more to give

829 INTERCASINO.CO.UK EASTER STKS (LISTED RACE) (C&G) 1m (P)
3:55 (3:55) (Class 1) 3-Y-0

£15,898 (£6,025; £3,015; £1,503; £753; £378) **Stalls** High

Form RPR

413- **1** **Asset (IRE)**[224] 4585 3-8-10 102 .... RichardHughes 3 106+
(R Hannon) *lw: s.i.s: sn rcvrd to chse ldr 2f: styd in 3rd: qcknd between horses to ld over 1f out: sn clr: easily* **6/4**[1]

322- **2** *3 ½* **Royal Power (IRE)**[203] 5139 3-8-10 96 .... TedDurcan 7 95
(M R Channon) *bit bkwd: rr but in tch: rdn: hdwy and hung rt 2f out: kpt on fr over 1f out to chse wnr cl home but no ch* **7/1**[2]

510- **3** *1* **Dubai Typhoon (USA)**[210] 4946 3-8-10 95 .... SebSanders 1 93
(C E Brittain) *lw: chsd ldr after 2f: rdn 3f out: led 2f out: hdd 1f out: wknd and lost 2nd cl home* **14/1**[3]

1111 **4** *1 ½* **Kingsgate Prince (IRE)**[14] 665 3-8-13 102 .... TQuinn 6 93
(J R Best) *lw: plld hrd in rr but in tch: rdn over 2f out: styd on fnl f but nvr gng pce to trble ldrs* **6/4**[1]

410- **5** *4* **Luberon**[193] 5393 3-8-10 97 .... JoeFanning 5 80
(M Johnston) *led: rdn 3f out: hdd 2 out: sn btn* **14/1**[3]

22-5 **6** *2 ½* **Campbeltown (IRE)**[14] 665 3-8-10 95 .... RichardMullen 2 75
(E J O'Neill) *chsd ldrs: rdn 3f out: wknd 2f out* **20/1**

1m 40.87s (-1.11) **Going Correction** +0.20s/f (Slow) **6** Ran SP% **110.6**
Speed ratings (Par 106):107,103,102,101,97 94
CSF £12.73 TOTE £2.20: £1.50, £2.40; EX 13.40.
Owner Highclere Thoroughbred Racing XXVI **Bred** Peter Gibbons And Dermot Forde **Trained** East Everleigh, Wilts
■ The first running of the Easter Stakes on Polytrack, and a new date for it and the Masaka Stakes.

FOCUS
A small but select field. The early pace was not strong and the race developed into something of a sprint, so it was no surprise that the winning time was slightly slower than the Masaka, but still faster than the earlier handicap for older horses. The overall form is not that strong, rated through the runner-up and third, but the winner is highly regarded and open to improvement.

NOTEBOOK
Asset(IRE) ◆, last seen finishing third in the Solario on soft ground at Sandown eight months ago, could hardly have been more impressive. Although not best away, the early pace was modest which enabled him to take a handy position, and when his rider could still be seen sitting motionless over a furlong from home, there was only ever going to be one result. The turn of foot he showed to settle matters was impressive and although quotes of 25-1 for the Guineas do not look generous, he looks more than capable of winning in Group company. Connections regard a sound surface as essential on turf. (op 11-8 tchd 5-4)
Royal Power(IRE), reappearing from a seven-month break, came from off the pace to win the separate race for second. He was inclined to throw his head about in the home straight, which considering his busy juvenile campaign could hardly be through greenness. He may not prove easy to place for the rest of this season. (op 11-1)
Dubai Typhoon(USA), returning from a seven-month break, seemed to travel well enough but was eventually left choking on the winner's dust. Nonetheless he has probably done well to make the frame in a race like this. (tchd 16-1)
Kingsgate Prince(IRE), bidding for a five-timer, tended to take a keen grip out the back and, when an effort was asked for in the home straight, it proved somewhat laboured. He was of course taking on a classy sort in the winner, almost certainly a better horse than he has faced before, but it may be that he is just not as effective here over a mile as he is at Lingfield over shorter. (tchd 13-8 and 7-4 in places)
Luberon, well beaten in a Newmarket nursery when last seen seven months ago, was allowed to set his own pace but was easily brushed aside and is not up to this level. (op 20-1)
Campbeltown(IRE) could never make any impression and is beginning to look exposed, but interestingly he was beaten only a length further by Kingsgate Prince than he was in the Spring Cup at Lingfield last month, which suggests this race was much stronger. (op 18-1 tchd 16-1)

830 INTERCASINO.CO.UK CONDITIONS STKS 6f (P)
4:25 (4:25) (Class 3) 3-Y-0+

£7,790 (£2,332; £1,166; £583; £291; £146) **Stalls** High

Form RPR

11-1 **1** **Border Music**[21] 631 5-9-10 102 ....(b) MartinDwyer 5 109+
(A M Balding) *sn trcking ldr: drvn to ld appr fnl f: hrd rdn ins last: hld on all out* **1/1**[1]

111- **2** *nk* **Presto Shinko (IRE)**[147] 6252 5-9-10 108 .... RichardHughes 1 108
(R Hannon) *lw: hld up in rr: stl last over 1f out: rapid hdwy to chse wnr ins last: fin strly: nt quite get up* **4/1**[2]

30-4 **3** *¾* **Peace Offering (IRE)**[14] 664 6-9-3 94 .... AdrianTNicholls 3 99
(D Nicholls) *led: rdn over 2f out: hdd appr fnl f: kpt on same pce ins last* **12/1**

-124 **4** *¾* **Compton's Eleven**[37] 494 5-9-3 .... TedDurcan 2 97
(M R Channon) *chsd ldrs: rdn over 2f out: kpt on u.p ins last but nver gng pce to chal* **4/1**[2]

3160 **5** ¾ **Obe Gold**[7] 729 4-9-6 SamHitchcott 6 98
(M R Channon) *lw: rr but in tch: hdwy on ins and rdn to chse ldrs 3f out: wknd ins fnl f* **16/1**

160- **6** 1¼ **Indian Trail**[189] 5452 6-9-3 96 JoeFanning 4 91
(D Nicholls) *chsd ldrs: pushed along 1/2-way: grad fdd fr over 1f out* **10/1**[3]

1m 13.7s (-2.57) **Going Correction** +0.20s/f (Slow) **6** Ran SP% **112.7**
Speed ratings (Par 107):108,107,106,105,104 102
CSF £5.35 TOTE £1.70: £1.20, £1.60; EX 3.90.
Owner Kingsclere Stud **Bred** Mrs I A Balding **Trained** Kingsclere, Hants
■ Stewards' Enquiry : Martin Dwyer caution: used whip with whip arm above shoulder height

FOCUS
A small field, but decent quality in this conditions event and there was not much covering the six runners at the line. The race has been rated around the third.

NOTEBOOK
Border Music, winner of his last four starts on Polytrack, got a nice tow from the leader for most of the way, but had to work hard to get on top of him and then had precious little to spare at the line. To be fair, he is probably better over seven these days and would have been better off with all his rivals in a handicap, which puts the performance into better context. He is rated 23lb lower on turf and would be a handicap snip if able to translate his sand ability onto grass, but he is still yet to win on it. (op 11-10 tchd 5-4 and 6-5 in places)
Presto Shinko(IRE), bidding for a five-timer on this return from a five-month break, has won twice at Lingfield so the surface was unlikely to be a problem. Given a patient ride, he came with a strong late run that only just failed to get him there but this should still have put him cherry-ripe. (op 3-1 tchd 9-2)
Peace Offering(IRE) made a bold bid to make all and did not go down without a fight. He is running well enough to end his very long losing run. (op 9-1 tchd 14-1 in a place)
Compton's Eleven had every chance, but he may find this trip on the sharp side for him now. He is not proving easy to place these days and his two wins since the summer of 2004 have both been in Dubai. (op 7-1)
Obe Gold, winner of this race last year when it was run on turf, never looked like following up and does not appear to have returned from Dubai at the top of his game. (op 14-1)
Indian Trail, returning from a seven-month break and making his debut for the yard, ran as though the outing was needed and much better can be expected once connections have learned a bit more about him. (tchd 9-1)

831 INTERCASINO.CO.UK H'CAP 7f (P)
4:55 (4:56) (Class 4) (0-85,88) 3-Y-0 £5,505 (£1,637; £818; £408) Stalls High

Form RPR

2-31 **1** **Ludovico**[31] 550 3-9-3 **84** NCallan 1 90
(K A Ryan) *lw: chsd ldrs: edgd rt appr fnl 2f: sn hrd drvn: led ins fnl quarter m: hrd rdn ins last: all out* **5/2**[2]

22-1 **2** *hd* **Porters (USA)**[7] 724 3-9-7 **88** RichardHughes 4 93+
(R Hannon) *swtg: trckd ldrs: n.m.r and one pce 2f out: hdwy over 1f out: swtchd rt and str run ins last: fin wl: nt quite get up* **11/4**[3]

0-55 **3** 2½ **Memphis Man**[31] 550 3-8-10 **77** MichaelHills 2 76
(G C Bravery) *s.i.s: rr but in tch: outpcd 2f out: kpt on again fnl f but nvr gng pce to rch ldrs* **14/1**

122- **4** ½ **Creative Mind (IRE)**[200] 5209 3-8-11 **78** RichardMullen 5 75
(E J O'Neill) *lw: chsd ldrs: n.m.r and one pce 2f out: kpt on again fnl f but nvr a danger* **6/1**

-211 **5** *shd* **Rebellion**[9] 702 3-8-13 **80** JoeFanning 6 77
(M Johnston) *lw: disp ld tl slt advantage 3f out: hdd ins fnl 2f: wknd ins last* **9/4**[1]

15-0 **6** *17* **Bucharest**[9] 702 3-9-2 **83** JamieMackay 3 36
(M Wigham) *disp ld: stl upsides and rdn 3f out: wkng whn hmpd appr fnl 2f: eased whn no ch* **33/1**

1m 28.78s (0.52) **Going Correction** +0.20s/f (Slow) **6** Ran SP% **109.9**
Speed ratings (Par 100):96,95,92,92,92 72
CSF £9.35 TOTE £3.70: £1.40, £2.50; EX 13.60.
Owner Pedro Rosas **Bred** M Grant And W Hawkings **Trained** Hambleton, N Yorks

FOCUS
Just a fair pace and the winning time was 1.76 seconds slower than the earlier handicap, but considering that race was for older horses and had a much bigger field, the margin is understandable. The form looks sound and the winner can rate higher.

832 PLAY ROULETTE AT INTERCASINO.CO.UK H'CAP 2m (P)
5:25 (5:25) (Class 4) (0-80,80) 4-Y-0+ £5,505 (£1,637; £818; £408) Stalls High

Form RPR

304- **1** **Establishment**[155] 6133 9-8-12 **68** LDettori 2 81
(C A Cyzer) *in tch: hdwy 7f out: drvn and str run fr 2f out to ld appr fnl f: sn clr: comf* **8/1**

-211 **2** 5 **Tycheros**[32] 545 4-7-7 **60** LiamJones[(7)] 7 67
(S C Williams) *lw: t.k.h early: chsd ldrs: wnt 2nd over 5f out: chal 4f out: led over 2f out: hdd appr fnl f: sn outpcd* **6/1**

0-00 **3** *hd* **Salute (IRE)**[22] 237 7-9-2 **72** RobertHavlin 9 79
(P G Murphy) *chsd ldrs: led 7f out: hdd over 2f out: rallied to chal over 1f out: sn outpcd* **25/1**

-640 **4** 2½ **Heathyards Pride**[42] 454 6-9-9 **79** GrahamGibbons 5 83+
(R Hollinshead) *lw: hmpd in rr after 7f: rdn and hdwy over 2f out: kpt on fr over 1f out: fin wl but n.d* **14/1**

-222 **5** *1* **Tranquilizer**[21] 628 4-9-0 **74** (t) EddieAhern 6 77
(D J Coakley) *lw: hld up in tch: hdwy 3f out: nvr gng pce to trble ldrs: one pce fnl 2f* **11/2**[3]

1-43 **6** 1½ **Our Choice (IRE)**[21] 628 4-8-3 **68** JamesDoyle[(5)] 4 69
(N P Littmoden) *lw: bhd: hmpd bnd after 7f: kpt on fnl 2f: nvr nr ldrs* **5/1**[2]

5034 **7** *5* **Moon Emperor**[12] 675 9-9-1 **71** (b) JimmyFortune 11 66
(J R Jenkins) *chsd ldrs: rdn over 3f out: wknd 2f out* **16/1**

0151 **8** 1½ **Llamadas**[5] 765 4-8-13 **80** 6ex LukeMorris[(7)] 12 73
(C Roberts) *chsd ldrs: rdn 4f out: wknd over 2f out* **9/2**[1]

105/ **9** *9* **Fiddlers Ford (IRE)**[473] 6891 5-9-0 **70** TedDurcan 3 52
(T Keddy) *bkwd: hld up rr: edgd rt bnd after 7f: sme hdwy 4f out: nvr in contention* **40/1**

-025 **10** *nk* **High Point (IRE)**[21] 628 8-8-13 **72** (v) AmirQuinn[(3)] 8 54
(G P Enright) *sn led: hdd 7f out: wknd fr 3f out* **20/1**

04-0 **11** *3* **Teorban (POL)**[43] 443 7-8-6 **62** (p) MartinDwyer 1 40
(D J S Ffrench Davis) *s.i.s: sn drvn to chse ldrs: rdn 6f out: wknd over 3f out* **66/1**

3204 **12** *8* **Eastborough (IRE)**[7] 723 7-9-4 **74** JamieSpencer 10 43
(B G Powell) *lw: a in rr* **7/1**

3m 34.32s **Going Correction** +0.20s/f (Slow)
WFA 4 from 5yo+ 4lb **12** Ran SP% **113.2**
Speed ratings (Par 105):100,97,97,96,95 94,92,91,87,87 85,81
CSF £50.79 CT £1140.39 TOTE £8.60: £2.30, £3.10, £7.70; EX 65.50 Place 6 £276.17, Place 5 £132.15.
Owner Mrs Charles Cyzer **Bred** C A And R M Cyzer **Trained** Maplehurst, W Sussex

FOCUS
A competitive staying handicap, but the gallop looked only fair and not that many got into it. The front trio raced close to the pace the whole way.
T/Jkpt: £22,864.10 to a £1 stake. Pool: £32,203.00. 1.00 winning ticket. T/Plt: £306.60 to a £1 stake. Pool: £99,613.70. 237.15 winning tickets. T/Qpdt: £20.50 to a £1 stake. Pool: £6,344.00. 228.80 winning tickets. ST

801 LINGFIELD (L-H)
Saturday, April 1

OFFICIAL GOING: Standard
Wind: Strong behind Weather: Fine

833 INTERCASINO.CO.UK CLAIMING STKS 1m 2f (P)
1:55 (1:55) (Class 6) 4-Y-0+ £2,388 (£705; £352) Stalls Low

Form RPR

3042 **1** **Zalkani (IRE)**[7] 723 6-9-7 72 GeorgeBaker 8 70
(B G Powell) *lw: stdd s: hld up in last: gd prog to trck ldng pair 2f out : hanging but urged into ld last 150yds* **1/1**[1]

0563 **2** 1¼ **Ramsgill (USA)**[9] 706 4-8-13 60 JamesDoyle[(5)] 9 65
(N P Littmoden) *trckd ldr: led 4f out: kicked on over 2f out: hrd rdn and hdd last 150yds: kpt on* **15/2**[3]

5061 **3** 1¼ **Competitor**[10] 694 5-9-0 60 (vt) AdamKirby[(3)] 4 62
(J Akehurst) *cl up: chsd ldr wl over 3f out: rdn and nt qckn 2f out: kpt on same pce* **8/1**

-610 **4** ¾ **Ringarooma**[12] 682 4-8-11 45 (t) RyanMoore 6 54
(C N Allen) *dwlt: hld up in last trio: rdn and nt qckn over 2f out: styd on fr over 1f out* **16/1**

0422 **5** ½ **Cherished Number**[10] 697 7-9-5 57 (b) ChrisCatlin 7 61
(A M Hales) *trckd ldrs: rdn over 2f out: one pce and no real prog* **14/1**

-410 **6** *2* **Linning Wine (IRE)**[26] 600 10-9-7 73 (p) NCallan 5 59
(P A Blockley) *dwlt: hld up in last pair: rdn and no rspnse wl over 2f out: plugged on same pce after* **5/1**[2]

-604 **7** 1¾ **Easter Ogil (IRE)**[26] 591 11-9-2 53 AmirQuinn[(3)] 3 54
(P G Murphy) *dwlt: sn midfield: rdn whn n.m.r over 2f out: no prog* **33/1**

6042 **8** 1½ **True Night**[8] 708 9-9-7 67 AdrianTNicholls 2 53
(D Nicholls) *led to 4f out: rdn and losing pl whn bmpd over 2f out* **10/1**

-000 **9** *5* **Tricky Venture**[15] 659 6-9-2 49 (p) ShaneKelly 1 39+
(Mrs L C Jewell) *trckd ldng pair: rdn and losing pl whn hmpd twice over 2f out: no ch after* **25/1**

2m 7.12s (-0.67) **Going Correction** -0.025s/f (Stan) **9** Ran SP% **118.0**
Speed ratings (Par 101):101,100,99,98,98 96,95,93,89
CSF £9.51 TOTE £2.20: £1.60, £1.80, £2.50; EX 13.10 Trifecta £97.30 Pool: £677.09 - 4.94 winning tickets.Ramsgill (USA) claimed by Jeff Pearce £9,000. Zalkani (IRE) claimed J. R. Boyle £12,000.
Owner J W Mursell **Bred** His Highness The Aga Khan's Studs S C **Trained** Morestead, Hants

FOCUS
A modest claimer run at a steady early pace. The proximity of the 45-rated fourth holds down the value of the form and the winner was a stone off his best.
Competitor Official explanation: jockey said horse had been struck into

834 PLAY BLACKJACK AT INTERCASINO.CO.UK H'CAP 1m 4f (P)
2:30 (2:30) (Class 4) (0-85,83) 4-Y-0+ £6,477 (£1,927; £963; £481) Stalls Low

Form RPR

26-2 **1** **Country Pursuit (USA)**[15] 661 4-9-1 **80** RyanMoore 5 91+
(C E Brittain) *lw: led to 7f out: pushed along to chse ldng pair over 3f out: drvn to ld over 1f out: styd on wl* **11/2**[3]

2111 **2** *2* **Young Mick**[3] 799 4-9-4 **83** 6ex (v) JimmyQuinn 8 91
(G G Margarson) *lw: hld up in last pair: prog to trck ldng trio over 2f out: rdn over 1f out: r.o to take 2nd last 100yds: no imp on wnr* **13/8**[1]

411- **3** 1¼ **Prime Contender**[57] 6183 4-8-6 **71** MichaelHills 6 77
(B W Hills) *lw: prom: led over 4f out: jnd over 2f out: hdd and one pce over 1f out* **12/1**

034- **4** ¾ **Flotta**[171] 5274 7-9-4 **82** GeorgeBaker 7 87
(B G Powell) *cl up: effrt to join ldr over 2f out: drvn and nt qckn over 1f out: one pce after* **25/1**

0-34 **5** *5* **Modaffaa**[21] 628 6-9-2 **80** ChrisCatlin 3 77
(P R Webber) *hld up in last pair: pushed along over 4f out: outpcd fr 3f out: no ch after* **14/1**

1- **6** ¾ **I Have Dreamed (IRE)**[223] 4606 4-9-1 **80** IanMongan 1 76+
(T G Mills) *unf: tall: lw: restless stalls and rrd s: chsd ldrs: pushed along over 4f out: outpcd wl over 2f out: n.d after* **2/1**[2]

623- **7** *12* **Spinning Coin**[182] 5610 4-9-1 **80** PatCosgrave 2 56
(J G Portman) *chsd ldrs: rdn over 4f out: wknd over 3f out: sn bhd* **16/1**

40 **8** *dist* **Eye Candy (IRE)**[21] 628 5-8-8 **72** (b) NCallan 4 —
(K A Ryan) *t.k.h: trckd ldr: led 7f out to over 4f out: sn wknd: t.o whn virtually p.u fnl 2f* **28/1**

2m 30.1s (-4.29) **Going Correction** -0.025s/f (Stan)
WFA 4 from 5yo+ 1lb **8** Ran SP% **114.3**
Speed ratings (Par 105):113,111,110,110,107 106,98,—
CSF £14.86 CT £102.16 TOTE £6.40: £1.90, £1.10, £2.90; EX 9.80 Trifecta £58.30 Pool: £1,073.83 - 13.06 winning tickets.
Owner Sheikh Hamdan Bin Mohammed Al Maktoum **Bred** Allen E Paulson Living Trust **Trained** Newmarket, Suffolk

FOCUS
A decent handicap run in a very smart winning time indeed for a race of its class. Solid form.

835 INTERCASINO.CO.UK MAIDEN FILLIES' STKS 7f (P)
3:05 (3:05) (Class 5) 3-Y-0 £3,238 (£963; £481; £240) Stalls Low

Form RPR

460- **1** **My Amalie (IRE)**[205] 5066 3-9-0 95 RyanMoore 6 64+
(C E Brittain) *trckd ldr: rdn 2f out: led over 1f out: steadily drew clr* **2/7**[1]

2 *3* **Catherine Medici** 3-9-0 RobertWinston 1 56
(R M H Cowell) *leggy: unf: dwlt: in tch: taken wd and rdn 3f out: styd on fr over 1f out to take 2nd last 50yds* **14/1**[3]

456- **3** ¾ **Discotheque (USA)**[171] 5836 3-9-0 66 ShaneKelly 2 54
(P Howling) *lw: led: jnd over 3f out: drvn and hdd over 1f out: no ch w wnr after: lost 2nd last 50yds* **6/1**[2]

00 **4** ½ **Tilsworth Charlie**[9] 703 3-9-0 NCallan 5 53
(J R Jenkins) *trckd ldng pair: drvn and flashed tail repeatedly fr over 2f out: fnd nil* **33/1**

0- **5** *10* **Eldori**[255] 3637 3-9-0 MickyFenton 4 27
(M S Saunders) *s.s: sn in tch and t.k.h: wknd over 2f out* **33/1**

6 **6** *5* **Lady Becks (IRE)**[17] 645 3-8-7 .... TolleyDean(7) 3 14
(R A Harris) *w'like: plld hrd early: hld up: lost tch fr 1/2-way: sn wl bhd* **14/1**[3]

1m 26.43s (0.54) **Going Correction** -0.025s/f (Stan) **6** Ran SP% **111.3**
Speed ratings (Par 95):95,91,90,90,78 73
CSF £5.70 TOTE £1.20: £1.10, £4.00; EX 6.10.
Owner Saeed Manana **Bred** John T L Jones, W McMinn And Live Foal Inc **Trained** Newmarket, Suffolk

FOCUS
An uncompetitive maiden won in workmanlike style by the heavy odds-on favourite who did not need to be anywhere near her best.

836 PLAY ROULETTE AT INTERCASINO.CO.UK H'CAP 6f (P)
3:35 (3:35) (Class 2) (0-100,100) 4-Y-0+
£12,464 (£3,732; £1,866; £934; £466; £234) **Stalls** Low

Form RPR

010- **1** **Mutamared (USA)**[175] 5745 6-8-8 **90** .... NCallan 3 97
(K A Ryan) *trckd ldrs: effrt to ld wl over 1f out: edgd lft ent fnl f: drvn and jst hld on* **5/1**[3]

1101 **2** *hd* **Saviours Spirit**[15] 657 5-8-5 **87** oh2 ow1 .... KDarley 1 94
(T G Mills) *lw: chsd ldrs: effrt and rdn 2f out: chsd wnr ins fnl f: clsng fin: jst hld* **9/2**[2]

1401 **3** *hd* **Qadar (IRE)**[9] 705 4-9-4 **100** .... IanMongan 2 106
(N P Littmoden) *chsd ldrs: effrt and wd bnd 2f out: r.o fnl f: jst hld* **4/1**[1]

3330 **4** *1 1/4* **Cummiskey (IRE)**[21] 629 4-8-11 **93** ....(b[1]) ShaneKelly 8 95
(J A Osborne) *s.s: in tch in last pair: rdn 2f out: styd on fnl f: nvr able to chal* **8/1**

2-42 **5** *1 1/4* **Fromsong (IRE)**[9] 705 8-8-12 **97** .... RobertMiles(3) 4 98+
(D K Ivory) *lw: led after 1f to wl over 1f out: btn whn n.m.r jst ins fnl f: wknd* **6/1**

20-4 **6** *1 1/4* **Pieter Brueghel (USA)**[8] 718 7-8-10 **92** .... RobertWinston 5 87
(D Nicholls) *sltly missed break and unable to ld: chsd ldrs: effrt 2f out: nt qckn over 1f out: wknd* **11/2**

5033 **7** *4* **One More Round (USA)**[9] 705 8-9-2 **98** ....(b) RyanMoore 6 81
(N P Littmoden) *a in last pair: struggling 2f out: sn no ch* **8/1**

400- **8** *8* **Hornpipe**[190] 5438 4-8-9 **91** .... MickyFenton 7 50
(M S Saunders) *led for 1f: chsd ldr to 2f out: wknd rapidly* **18/1**

1m 11.03s (-1.78) **Going Correction** -0.025s/f (Stan) **8** Ran SP% **112.0**
Speed ratings (Par 109):110,109,109,107,106 104,99,88
CSF £26.51 CT £92.44 TOTE £5.60: £2.00, £1.50, £1.40; EX 35.40 Trifecta £325.90 Pool: £1,009.91 - 2.20 winning tickets.
Owner Errigal Racing **Bred** E J Hudson Jr, Irrevocable Trust & Kilroy T'Bred **Trained** Hambleton, N Yorks

FOCUS
A decent sprint handicap, rated around the third, in which the winning time was 1.26 seconds faster than the following race over the same trip, but still around par for the grade of contest. Sound form.

NOTEBOOK
Mutamared(USA) held a good position just behind the leader for much of the race and, when switched entering the straight, found another gear to grab a lead he held to the line. He won only once in eight starts for his previous trainers but since joining Kevin Ryan and being dropped back to sprinting, he has won three times from five starts. The big sprint handicaps on turf are his targets this season. (op 11-2 tchd 6-1 and 9-2)
Saviours Spirit, whose rider put up 1lb overweight and who was running from 2lb out of the handicap, had won his last three starts over this course and distance and only just failed to make it four. He has improved over the winter and is rated only 77 on turf, so he should be well handicapped when he goes back on grass, but his winning form so far is all on the sand. (tchd 5-1)
Qadar(IRE), who came wide into the straight and finished well, confirmed recent five-furlong form around here with Fromsong and One More Round. This was a sound effort off a career-high mark and he probably ran to a similar level as last time.
Cummiskey(IRE) continues to look held by the Handicapper off his current mark and the first-time blinkers made little difference. (op 9-1 tchd 15-2)
Fromsong(IRE) is another who now looks held off his current mark. (op 4-1)
Pieter Brueghel(USA) runs his best races from the front but he was unable to get the lead on this All-Weather debut. Connections will be hoping the Handicapper drops him a few pounds too, as his last win came off a mark of 86. (op 5-1 tchd 6-1)
One More Round(USA) was surprisingly raised 8lb in the handicap for his third place in a conditions race around here last month. (op 10-1)
Hornpipe, somewhat frustrating for Sir Michael Stoute last season, was having his first outing for his new yard. He starts the year on a stiff mark and he will be of more interest when his mark has fallen back to a more realistic level. (op 20-1 tchd 16-1)

837 PLAY POKER AT INTERCASINO.CO.UK H'CAP 6f (P)
4:10 (4:10) (Class 6) (0-60,61) 4-Y-0+ **£2,730** (£806; £403) **Stalls** Low

Form RPR

-661 **1** **H Harrison (IRE)**[2] 806 6-9-2 **61** 6ex.......................... AndrewElliott(5) 8 71
(I W McInnes) *trckd ldr: led over 3f out: kicked on over 2f out: hrd rdn fnl f: kpt on* **11/2**[2]

1612 **2** *1* **Zazous**[2] 806 5-8-12 **52** .... J-PGuillambert 9 59
(J J Bridger) *prom: chsd wnr over 2f out: sn drvn: kpt on fr over 1f out but a readily hld* **4/1**[1]

4323 **3** *hd* **Taboor (IRE)**[47] 401 8-9-1 **55** .... RyanMoore 5 61
(R M H Cowell) *hld up bhd ldrs: gng easily over 2f out: rdn and nt qckn wl over 1f out: styd on ins fnl f* **13/2**

5001 **4** *nk* **Desert Light (IRE)**[5] 772 5-9-2 **56** 6ex....................(v) RobertWinston 7 62
(D Shaw) *hld up in rr: prog over 2f out: drvn and effrt over 1f out: hanging and nt qckn fnl f* **6/1**[3]

0-50 **5** *1 3/4* **Ektishaaf**[10] 698 4-9-4 **58** .... GeorgeBaker 6 58
(C F Wall) *stdd s: hld up in last trio: plenty to do whn hrd rdn over 1f out: styd on: no ch* **8/1**

4604 **6** *3* **Hadath (IRE)**[8] 708 9-9-3 **57** ....(b) KDarley 10 48
(B G Powell) *settled in last trio: pushed along 1/2-way: no imp fnl 2f* **8/1**

0600 **7** *3/4* **Lord Links (IRE)**[28] 588 5-9-0 **54** .... VinceSlattery 3 43
(D J Daly) *led to over 3f out: chsd wnr to over 2f out: wknd over 1f out* **18/1**

-500 **8** *1/2* **I Wish**[52] 339 8-9-2 **56** .... PaulFitzsimons 1 44
(Miss J R Tooth) *dwlt: sn chsd ldrs: rdn over 2f out: wknd wl over 1f out* **16/1**

6246 **9** *1/2* **Madrasee**[2] 806 8-8-10 **53** .... AmirQuinn(3) 4 39
(P G Murphy) *prom: rdn over 2f out: wknd wl over 1f out* **7/1**

3016 **10** *nk* **Mind Alert**[28] 587 5-8-12 **55** ....(v) PatrickMathers(3) 11 40
(D Shaw) *dwlt: t.k.h and hld up in last pair: rdn and no prog over 2f out* **12/1**

1m 12.29s (-0.52) **Going Correction** -0.025s/f (Stan) **10** Ran SP% **116.6**
Speed ratings (Par 101):102,100,100,100,97 93,92,92,91,90
CSF £27.78 CT £147.28 TOTE £5.90: £2.20, £1.70, £3.60; EX 20.40 Trifecta £111.80 Pool: £553.11 - 3.51 winning tickets.
Owner David Lees **Bred** Margaret Conlon **Trained** Catwick, E Yorks

FOCUS
A competitive, if moderate, handicap in which the winning time was 1.26 seconds slower than the previous contest, but still perfectly acceptable considering the difference in class. The winner improved on his win the previous day and basically ran to his All-Weather best, while the placed form is sound enough.
Desert Light(IRE) Official explanation: jockey said gelding hung left-handed
Madrasee Official explanation: jockey said mare ran flat

838 PLAY BACCARAT AT INTERCASINO.CO.UK H'CAP 2m (P)
4:40 (4:45) (Class 5) (0-70,70) 4-Y-0+ **£3,238** (£963; £481; £240) **Stalls** Low

Form RPR

4-24 **1** **Montosari**[26] 589 7-9-3 **64** .... GeorgeBaker 2 71
(P Mitchell) *lw: trckd ldr: led over 3f out and gng much bttr than rest: clr over 2f out: pushed out fnl f* **10/3**[2]

0451 **2** *2* **Monte Cristo (FR)**[26] 589 8-9-6 **70** ....(v) NeilChalmers(3) 4 75+
(Mrs L C Taylor) *in tch: rdn over 4f out: effrt u.p to chse wnr over 1f out: styd on but nvr able to chal* **4/1**[3]

-102 **3** *1 1/4* **Taxman (IRE)**[8] 713 4-9-0 **65** ....(p) RyanMoore 8 69
(C E Brittain) *trckd ldng pair: rdn over 4f out: chsd wnr 2f out to over 1f out: one pce* **2/1**[1]

030- **4** *shd* **Arch Folly**[164] 5973 4-8-4 **55** .... PaulHanagan 7 58
(J G Portman) *hld up: sme prog on outer 5f out: rdn 4f out: kpt on same pce fr over 2f out* **15/2**

5331 **5** *3* **Lady Pilot**[17] 643 4-8-8 **62** ....(v) AdamKirby(3) 1 62
(Dr J R J Naylor) *led to over 3f out: no ch w wnr after: wknd over 1f out* **6/1**

050- **6** *2 1/2* **Mac Han (IRE)**[93] 5980 7-8-11 **58** .... MCHussey 5 55
(Eamon Tyrrell, Ire) *hld up in last: nt clr run wl over 3f out and sn outpcd: no ch after* **20/1**

00-0 **7** *3 1/2* **Jubilee Dream**[29] 324 4-8-9 **60** ....(b[1]) J-PGuillambert 3 53
(Mrs L J Mongan) *dwlt: chsd ldrs: rdn over 4f out: wknd 3f out* **33/1**

3m 28.34s (-0.45) **Going Correction** -0.025s/f (Stan)
WFA 4 from 7yo+ 4lb **7** Ran SP% **110.2**
Speed ratings (Par 103):100,99,98,98,96 95,93
CSF £15.71 CT £29.78 TOTE £4.90: £2.00, £3.00; EX 11.70 Trifecta £37.90 Pool: £692.73 - 12.96 winning tickets.
Owner Caterham Racing (jdrp) **Bred** S Gollogly **Trained** Epsom, Surrey

FOCUS
There was not much pace on in the first half of this staying handicap so the form might not be totally reliable.

839 INTERCASINO.CO.UK H'CAP 1m (P)
5:10 (5:15) (Class 5) (0-70,70) 3-Y-O **£3,238** (£963; £481; £240) **Stalls** High

Form RPR

41 **1** **Piano Player (IRE)**[26] 590 3-9-4 **70** .... SteveDrowne 7 71+
(J A Osborne) *hld up: prog to chse ldng pair over 2f out: drvn and r.o to ld last 100yds* **1/1**[1]

030- **2** *1/2* **Ellesappelle**[168] 5887 3-9-1 **67** ....(v) RobertWinston 5 67
(K R Burke) *dwlt: t.k.h: hld up in last pair: effrt over 2f out: r.o wl fnl f: tk 2nd nr fin* **12/1**

-113 **3** *1/2* **Welsh Dragon**[8] 709 3-8-8 **63** ....(p) NeilChalmers(3) 4 62
(A M Balding) *lw: led: set stdy pce to 1/2-way: drvn and hrd pressed over 1f out: hdd and one pce last 100yds* **3/1**[2]

4 *shd* **Pep In Her Step (IRE)**[198] 5258 3-8-13 **65** .... MCHussey 8 64
(Eamon Tyrrell, Ire) *unf: angular: t.k.h: mostly pressed ldr: rdn 3f out: chal and upsides over 1f out tl no ex last 75yds* **10/1**[3]

5045 **5** *2 1/2* **Flashing Floozie**[26] 594 3-8-4 **56** oh4 .... JohnEgan 3 49
(M F Harris) *t.k.h: hld up bhd ldrs: rdn 3f out: no prog and btn wl over 1f out* **22/1**

003- **6** *nk* **Grand Sefton**[165] 5958 3-8-13 **65** .... PaulHanagan 6 57
(J G Portman) *bit bkwd: s.s: t.k.h and hld up in last: outpcd over 2f out: pushed along and plugged on fr over 1f out* **14/1**

1060 **7** *4* **Bollywood (IRE)**[30] 554 3-9-4 **70** .... DarryllHolland 1 53
(J J Bridger) *hld up in tch: rdn 3f out: sn struggling* **11/1**

1260 **8** *6* **Mr Cheers**[16] 651 3-8-6 **58** ....(b) AdrianMcCarthy 2 27
(R A Harris) *prom tl wknd rapidly 2f out* **25/1**

1m 41.14s (1.71) **Going Correction** -0.025s/f (Stan) **8** Ran SP% **115.0**
Speed ratings (Par 98):90,89,89,88,86 86,82,76
CSF £15.27 CT £29.28 TOTE £1.80: £1.02, £2.60, £1.60; EX 15.20 Trifecta £42.40 Pool: £1,041.19 - 17.43 winning tickets. Place 6 £9.39, Place 5 £6.37.
Owner Mountgrange Stud **Bred** B W Hills And Mrs H Theodorou **Trained** Upper Lambourn, Berks

FOCUS
A modest, steadily-run handicap run in a very slow winning time for a race of its type. It has been rated through the third.
T/Plt: £15.30 to a £1 stake. Pool £62,324.25. 2960.20 winning tickets. T/Qpdt: £8.70 to a £1 stake. Pool £4,147.70. 350.35 winning tickets. JN

773 SAINT-CLOUD (L-H)
Saturday, April 1

OFFICIAL GOING: Heavy

841a PRIX EDMOND BLANC (GROUP 3) 1m
2:20 (2:19) 4-Y-0+ **£27,586** (£11,034; £8,276; £5,517; £2,759)

RPR

1 **Svedov (FR)**[16] 685 5-8-12 .... SPasquier 2 111
(E Lellouche, France) *hld up, disp 5th between Art Master & Krataios ent str, edged out wl over 1f out, qckned to ld 150y out, sn clr, driven out* **196/10**

2 *1 1/2* **Art Master (USA)**[314] 1941 5-9-0 .... CSoumillon 7 110
(A Fabre, France) *hld up in rr, disp 5th on outside str, carried rt & slightly hmpd wl over 1f out, ran on ins fnl f but too late to worry wn* **7/5**[1]

3 *1 1/2* **Helios Quercus (FR)**[153] 6189 4-8-12 .... OPeslier 4 105
(C Diard, France) *hdwy on outside to go 2nd at half-way, slight ld over 2f out, pushed clr wl over 1f out, hdd 150y out, one pace* **8/1**

4 hd **Ghair (IRE)**[300] 2328 4-8-12 .... TGillet 6 105
(J E Hammond, France) *plld early, sn wnt up to disp 2nd, cl 4th str, effort & went 2nd jst ins fnl f, kpt on same pace* **33/10**[2]

5 shd **Krataios (FR)**[16] 685 6-8-12 .... MBlancpain 1 104
(C Laffon-Parias, France) *hld up, disp 5th on ins str, not clr run over 1f out, edged out ins fnl f, fin wl* **4/1**[3]

6 1 **Rageman**[153] 6189 6-9-0 .... DBoeuf 3 104
(M Cheno, France) *disp 2nd, 3rd str, one pace fr wl over 1f out* **64/10**

7 shd **Ysoldina (FR)**[16] 685 4-8-9 .... C-PLemaire 5 99
(A De Royer-Dupre, France) *led to over 2f out, one pace* **12/1**

1m 52.0s **Going Correction** +0.95s/f (Soft) 7 Ran SP% **122.1**
Speed ratings: 115,113,112,111,111 110,110
PARI-MUTUEL: WIN 19.60; PL 4.60, 2.10; SF 19.30.
Owner C Cohen **Bred** Claude Cohen **Trained** Lamorlaye, France

NOTEBOOK
Svedov(FR), a soft-ground specialist, landed his first Group race in style. Held up for the early part of the race, he was extracted a furlong and a half out and made contact with the runner-up (a Stewards' enquiry left the result unchanged) before taking control of the race at the furlong marker and running on strongly. If the ground is soft, he will run in the Prix du Muguet.
Art Master(USA) was held up in last place in what was a slowly-run race and was slightly hampered when starting his effort a furlong and a half out. He ran on again in the final stages, but never looked like catching the winner. This was his first race for nearly 11 months, though, and he will be much fitter in the Muguet.
Helios Quercus(FR) moved up to challenge early in the straight and led until the furlong marker. He then battled on well to the line, and the plan is now to head for the Prix d'Ispahan via the Muguet.
Gharir(IRE) pulled early on in what was a slowly-run race and was given every chance. He was still there halfway up the straight but then gradually dropped out of contention for a major place. This was a decent effort for a colt who had not been out since last June, and a Group event looks sure to come his way this season.

826 KEMPTON (A.W) (R-H)
Sunday, April 2

OFFICIAL GOING: Standard
Wind: Fresh across Weather: Fine after early showers

843 INTERCASINO.CO.UK H'CAP 1m 2f (P)
2:30 (2:47) (Class 4) (0-85,85) 4-Y-0+
£7,790 (£2,332; £1,166; £583; £291; £146)

Form RPR

-526 1 **Obrigado (USA)**[15] 670 6-8-13 **80** .... DarryllHolland 1 96+
(W J Haggas) *lw: hld up in rr: rapid hdwy over 2f out: led over 1f out: rdn clr* **15/2**[3]

-141 2 5 **Nice Tune**[16] 660 4-9-4 **85** .... RyanMoore 10 91
(C E Brittain) *lw: hld up: hdwy over 2f out: r.o to chse wnr fnl f* **3/1**[1]

100- 3 3 **South O'The Border**[102] 6645 4-8-9 **76** .... IanMongan 3 76
(T G Mills) *swtg: mde most tl rdn and hdd over 1f out: nt pce of first 2* **5/1**[2]

0252 4 1 1/4 **Gingko**[29] 578 9-8-9 **76** ow1 .... DaneO'Neill 11 74
(P R Webber) *hld up: rdn and styd on fnl 2f: nvr nr to chal* **8/1**

350- 5 1/2 **Secretary General (IRE)**[163] 6015 5-8-7 **74** oh1 ow3 .... ShaneKelly 9 71+
(P F I Cole) *lw: chsd ldrs tl bdly hmpd wl over 2f out: nt rcvr* **5/1**[2]

00-0 6 5 **Bentley Brook (IRE)**[71] 167 4-8-6 **73** .... GrahamGibbons 12 60
(P A Blockley) *mid-div tl hdwy over 2f out: sn btn* **50/1**

1555 7 5 **Northern Desert (IRE)**[15] 670 7-9-4 **85** .... ChrisCatlin 5 63
(P W Hiatt) *hld up towards rr: nvr on terms* **8/1**

503- 8 4 **Pevensey (IRE)**[165] 5989 4-9-4 **85** .... SteveDrowne 6 55
(M A Buckley) *lw: mid-div tl wknd over 2f out* **12/1**

1040 9 5 **Hayyani (IRE)**[15] 670 4-8-10 **77** ....(e) JamieSpencer 8 38
(K McAuliffe) *hld up: a bhd* **9/1**

2101 10 15 **Danelor (IRE)**[59] 273 8-8-8 **78** ....(v[1]) PatrickMathers(3) 7 10
(D Shaw) *swtg: t.k.h: chsd ldrs tl wknd over 2f out: bbv* **16/1**

-660 11 1/2 **Skidmark**[43] 454 5-8-8 **75** ....(b[1]) PaulFitzsimons 4 6
(Miss J R Tooth) *lw: plld v hrd: w ldr tl wknd rapidly over 2f out* **20/1**

2m 6.90s **Going Correction** +0.125s/f (Slow) 11 Ran SP% **122.6**
Speed ratings (Par 105):113,109,106,105,105 101,97,94,90,78 77
CSF £31.59 CT £129.07 TOTE £9.00: £2.60, £1.40, £2.40; EX 42.10.
Owner B Haggas **Bred** Bradyleigh Farms Inc **Trained** Newmarket, Suffolk

FOCUS
Hand-timed. This looked like a reasonable handicap beforehand but, with a damaged valve in the hydraulic system putting the stalls out of action, a flip start was required. The runners had to be recalled after about a furlong and a half when they were first let go as, ironically, the eventual winner Obrigado had been left. They got underway at the second attempt and, with the pace soon pretty strong, they quickly became well strung out. Needless to say, the form is best treated with caution.
Secretary General(IRE) Official explanation: jockey said gelding suffered interference in running
Hayyani(IRE) Official explanation: jockey said gelding ran flat
Danelor(IRE) Official explanation: jockey said gelding bled from the nose

844 PLAY BLACKJACK AT INTERCASINO.CO.UK MAIDEN STKS 7f (P)
3:00 (3:20) (Class 4) 3-Y-0+ **£5,505** (£1,637; £818; £408) **Stalls** High

Form RPR

03- 1 **Dream Theme**[195] 5361 3-8-11 .... RichardHughes 2 80+
(B W Hills) *h.d.w: gd sort: hmpd s: hld up in mid-div: rdn and gd hdwy to ld 1f out: won gng away* **5/2**[2]

4- 2 5 **Red Diadem**[172] 5833 3-8-6 .... MichaelHills 11 62
(W J Haggas) *lw: led tl rdn and hdd 1f out: nt pce of wnr* **5/4**[1]

3 nk **Magic Rush** 4-9-11 .... JohnEgan 3 71
(Mrs Norma Pook) *tall: str: scope: wnt lft leaving stalls: chsd ldr 3f out: ev ch whn hung lft appr fnl f: no ex ins fnl f* **20/1**

4 5 **Eagle Eye** 3-8-11 .... SteveDrowne 1 53+
(G Wragg) *str: slowly away and bmpd s: hdwy over 1f out: r.o: nvr nrr* **13/2**[3]

5 2 1/2 **Lady Ambitious** 3-8-6 .... ChrisCatlin 12 42
(D K Ivory) *w/like: sn bhd: rdn 2f out and mde late hdwy* **14/1**

4- 6 3/4 **Ocean Valentine**[259] 3561 3-8-11 .... AlanMunro 4 45
(B R Millman) *bkwd: t.k.h: trckd ldr to 3f out: wknd over 1f out* **9/1**

06- 7 1 3/4 **Hahns Peak**[248] 3865 3-8-11 .... JimmyQuinn 10 40
(Mrs A L M King) *t.k.h: prom tl rdn and wknd wl over 1f out* **100/1**

-000 8 shd **Zambezi River**[48] 396 7-9-11 35 .... DaneO'Neill 9 45?
(J M Bradley) *bhd whn hmpd over 4f out: nvr on terms after* **100/1**

6 9 1/2 **Riolo (IRE)**[11] 692 4-9-8 .... AdamKirby(3) 8 44
(K F Clutterbuck) *prom: rdn 3f out: wknd wl over 1f out* **100/1**

10 1 1/4 **Two Acres (IRE)** 3-8-11 .... LPKeniry 6 35
(A G Newcombe) *neat: a bhd* **33/1**

0 11 2 1/2 **Enjoy The Magic**[43] 449 4-9-6 ....(p) PaulFitzsimons 7 29
(Miss J R Tooth) *mid-div tl wknd 3f out* **100/1**

0- 12 1 3/4 **Kris Spring**[354] 1001 4-9-6 .... ShaneKelly 5 29
(R M H Cowell) *a struggling in rr* **25/1**

1m 27.58s (-0.68) **Going Correction** +0.125s/f (Slow)
WFA 3 from 4yo+ 14lb 12 Ran SP% **118.5**
Speed ratings (Par 105):100,94,93,88,85 84,82,82,81,80 77,75
CSF £5.69 TOTE £2.80: £1.40, £1.40, £7.20; EX 7.00.
Owner K Abdulla **Bred** Juddmonte Farms Ltd **Trained** Lambourn, Berks

FOCUS
A weakish maiden, the poor eighth finishing closer than desirable, but the first two are promising.
Magic Rush Official explanation: jockey said gelding hung left

845 PLAY BLACKJACK AT INTERCASINO.CO.UK H'CAP 7f (P)
3:30 (3:50) (Class 6) (0-65,65) 4-Y-0+ **£3,238** (£963; £481; £240) **Stalls** High

Form RPR

-045 1 **Goose Chase**[11] 698 4-9-3 **64** .... DaneO'Neill 1 73
(A M Hales) *lw: hld up: rdn and gd hdwy over 1f out: led nr fin* **33/1**

405- 2 nk **Red Rudy**[167] 5950 4-8-13 **60** .... JimmyFortune 6 68
(A W Carroll) *lw: hld up: hdwy on outside to ld appr fnl f: r.o: hdd nr fin* **13/2**[1]

-654 3 1 **Kew The Music**[5] 777 6-9-1 **62** ....(v) ChrisCatlin 3 67
(M R Channon) *lw: slowly away: hdwy fr over 1f out: r.o strly: nvr nrr* **8/1**[3]

3153 4 1 **Hollow Jo**[11] 698 6-9-4 **65** .... MickyFenton 7 68
(J R Jenkins) *lw: a in tch: rdn to ld 2f out: edgd lft and hdd appr fnl f: no ex ins* **7/1**[2]

2364 5 nk **Hand Chime**[11] 698 9-8-9 **61** .... JamesDoyle(5) 9 63
(Ernst Oertel) *a.p: rdn and ev ch appr fnl f: wknd wl ins fnl f* **16/1**

000- 6 shd **Jools**[167] 5948 8-8-6 **60** .... LauraReynolds(7) 10 62
(D K Ivory) *mid-div: hdwy on outside over 1f out: kpt on fnl f* **25/1**

4250 7 1 3/4 **Lucius Verrus (USA)**[17] 650 6-8-10 **60** ....(v) PatrickMathers(3) 2 57
(D Shaw) *a towards rr* **16/1**

0302 8 shd **Greenwood**[57] 292 8-9-1 **62** ....(t) SteveDrowne 12 59
(P G Murphy) *mid-div: hdwy to hold ev ch appr fnl f: wknd ins fnl f* **10/1**

000- 9 1 3/4 **Peruvian Style (IRE)**[209] 4995 5-9-2 **63** .... RyanMoore 5 55
(J M Bradley) *hld up: gd hdwy and ev ch 2f out: wknd appr fnl f* **40/1**

00-1 10 hd **Banjo Bay (IRE)**[9] 708 8-9-3 **64** .... AdrianTNicholls 11 56
(D Nicholls) *trckd ldrs tl rdn and wknd appr fnl f* **10/1**

6312 11 1/2 **Zorn**[17] 650 7-9-1 **62** .... ShaneKelly 8 53
(P Howling) *trckd ldr: led briefly 2f out: wknd 1f out* **10/1**

6-64 12 1 3/4 **Louisiade (IRE)**[29] 576 5-8-13 **60** .... NCallan 4 46
(K A Ryan) *racd on outside: rdn 1/2-way: nvr on terms* **13/2**[1]

6611 13 13 **H Harrison (IRE)**[1] 837 6-8-9 **61** 6ex .... NataliaGemelova(5) 13 13
(I W McInnes) *led tl hdd over 2f out: sn wknd* **7/1**[2]

1m 27.4s (-0.86) **Going Correction** +0.125s/f (Slow) 13 Ran SP% **111.0**
Speed ratings (Par 101):101,100,99,98,98 97,95,95,93,93 93,91,76
CSF £196.91 CT £1423.34 TOTE £32.70: £7.00, £3.50, £2.30; EX 437.10.
Owner Brick Farm Racing **Bred** Sir Thomas Pilkington **Trained** Quainton, Bucks
■ Go Garuda was withdrawn (8/1, unruly in stalls). R4 applies, deduct 10p in the £.

FOCUS
A modest but competitive handicap. Sound enough form.

846 PLAY ROULETTE AT INTERCASINO.CO.UK H'CAP 6f (P)
4:00 (4:16) (Class 3) (0-90,90) 4-Y-0+
£7,790 (£2,332; £1,166; £583; £291; £146) **Stalls** High

Form RPR

200- 1 **Fantaisiste**[134] 6376 4-8-5 **80** .... NelsonDeSouza(3) 5 94+
(P F I Cole) *slowly away: in rr whn short of room and swtchd lft over 1f out: fin fast to ld nr fin* **14/1**

350- 2 3/4 **Golden Dixie (USA)**[163] 6014 7-8-11 **83** .... AdrianMcCarthy 13 91
(R A Harris) *chsd ldrs: rdn to ld 1f out: r.o: hdd nr fin* **10/1**

021- 3 2 **Fullandby (IRE)**[156] 6132 4-9-2 **88** .... KDarley 2 90+
(T J Etherington) *a.p: r.o fnl f* **13/2**[3]

00-2 4 nk **Lindbergh**[6] 761 4-8-8 **80** .... RichardHughes 6 81
(R Hannon) *lw: in tch: chsd ldrs over 1f out: one pce ins fnl f* **13/2**[3]

012- 5 nk **Machinist (IRE)**[176] 5745 6-9-4 **90** .... AdrianTNicholls 4 90
(D Nicholls) *bhd tl hdwy over 1f out: r.o: nvr nrr* **7/1**

3014 6 shd **Councellor (FR)**[22] 632 4-8-8 **80** ow1 .... JamieSpencer 7 80
(Stef Liddiard) *lw: in rr tl mde sme late hdwy* **6/1**[2]

000- 7 nk **Funfair Wane**[197] 5288 7-9-1 **90** .... SilvestreDeSousa(3) 8 89
(D Nicholls) *chsd ldr: led 2f out: hdd 1f out: wknd ins fnl f* **33/1**

062/ 8 shd **First Order**[564] 5564 5-9-2 **88** .... DarryllHolland 9 89+
(Ernst Oertel) *bkwd: bhd whn hmpd after 1f: nt clr run 2f out tl r.o fnl f* **33/1**

-000 9 1 3/4 **Middleton Grey**[22] 632 8-8-10 **82** ....(b) FergusSweeney 1 75
(A G Newcombe) *slowly away: hld up in rr: nvr nr to chal* **25/1**

030- 10 1/2 **Night Prospector**[154] 6180 6-8-13 **85** .... RyanMoore 3 77
(G L Moore) *led tl hdd 2f out: wknd qckly* **16/1**

0-06 11 nk **Bo McGinty (IRE)**[9] 719 5-8-10 **82** .... PaulHanagan 11 73
(R A Fahey) *chsd ldrs tl wknd over 1f out* **9/1**

00-0 12 shd **Acomb**[16] 662 6-8-4 **76** .... AlanDaly 12 67
(Mrs L Richards) *a in rr* **50/1**

000- 13 1 1/2 **Royal Orissa**[170] 5874 4-8-11 **83** .... LDettori 14 69
(D Haydn Jones) *plld hrd: hld up: bhd fnl 2f* **5/1**[1]

1m 13.57s (-2.70) **Going Correction** +0.125s/f (Slow) 13 Ran SP% **113.4**
Speed ratings (Par 107):105,104,101,100,100 100,100,99,97,96 96,96,94
CSF £135.14 CT £1033.14 TOTE £16.20: £4.30, £4.20, £2.50; EX 186.20 Trifecta £586.70 Part won. Pool: £826.42 - 0.10 winning units. £743.77 carried over to Saturday..
Owner Miss Alfiya Shaykhutdinova **Bred** Miss K Rausing **Trained** Whatcombe, Oxon

FOCUS
A very good sprint handicap for the grade that should produce winners in the coming months. Sound form, rated through the runner-up, with the winner value for extra.

NOTEBOOK
Fantaisiste ◆, in foal to Cadeaux Genereux, was dropping back two furlongs in trip on her return from a 134-day break. With her rider slow to remove the blindfold, she took time to find her stride and, soon well off the pace, she had to be switched with her run inside the final third before flying down the outside to get up near the line. She did remarkably well to get up and win and looks to have improved for both her winter break and going in foal. She looks capable of rating quite a bit higher and must be kept on the right side. (tchd 16-1)
Golden Dixie(USA), three times a winner on Wolverhampton's Polytrack, ran a fine race off the back of a 163-day break and was just caught by the improved winner. He finished clear of the remainder and it will be disappointing if he does not find a similar race. (op 11-1)
Fullandby(IRE) looked as though this first run in five months would bring him on and emerges with plenty of credit. He should progress. (tchd 6-1)

Lindbergh, second off this mark over five furlongs here on his previous start, looked to run his race and gives the form a solid look. (op 6-1)
Machinist(IRE) ◆, who won his maiden round Lingfield on his only previous start on Polytrack, would have been closer with a better trip and this was a very pleasing reappearance. He should go on from this. (op 13-2)
Councellor(FR) ◆, back a furlong in trip, caught the eye running on when it was all too late. A return to seven furlongs should suit. (op 5-1)
Funfair Wane ◆ showed he retains plenty of dash and should improve given this was his first run since the Ayr Gold Cup, a race he has won twice in the past. (op 40-1)
First Order, ex-Sir Mark Prescott, ran well on his belated debut for new connections off the back of a 564-day absence, especially as he enjoyed a far from ideal trip. He was hampered soon after the start approaching the bend and did not enjoy a clear passage when looking to make his move in the straight. If he stands training, he could be one to keep on the right side of. (op 40-1)
Royal Orissa dropped out tamely after racing keenly on his Polytrack debut off the back of a 170-day break. (op 9-2)

847 £600 FREE AT INTERCASINO.CO.UK H'CAP — 1m 4f (P)

4:30 (4:46) (Class 5) (0-75,79) 4-Y-0+ — **£5,505** (£1,637; £818; £408) **Stalls** Low

Form — RPR

1211 **1** **Polish Power (GER)**[10] 706 6-8-11 **65** .... JohnEgan 10 — 76
(J S Moore) *lw: trckd ldrs: led over 2f out: pushed clr 1f out: eased nr fin* **2/1**[1]

6/11 **2** *3 ½* **Shaunas Vision (IRE)**[5] 780 7-9-11 **79** 6ex .... SebSanders 1 — 84
(D K Ivory) *a in tch: chsd wnr over 2f out: no imp fnl f* **7/2**[2]

1655 **3** *2* **Dovedon Hero**[10] 700 6-9-0 **68** .... (b) JimmyFortune 9 — 70
(P J McBride) *hld up: hdwy 4f out: swtchd lft over 2f out: styd on fnl f: nvr nrr* **8/1**

2-00 **4** *¾* **Santando**[36] 521 6-9-0 **68** .... RyanMoore 11 — 69
(C E Brittain) *led tl rdn and hdd over 2f out: kpt on one pce* **11/2**[3]

00-4 **5** *1 ¾* **Rio De Janeiro (IRE)**[9] 713 5-9-2 **70** .... AlanMunro 8 — 68
(Miss E C Lavelle) *lw: trckd ldrs: one pce fnl 2f* **9/1**

500/ **6** *1 ¼* **Bukit Fraser (IRE)**[557] 5728 5-9-0 **68** .... LDettori 4 — 64
(P F I Cole) *trckd ldr to over 2f out: wknd over 1f out* **8/1**

0/0- **7** *3* **Salisbury Plain**[143] 6305 5-8-11 **65** .... JimmyQuinn 5 — 56
(N I M Rossiter) *lw: prom: rdn 4f out: wknd 2f out* **66/1**

-000 **8** *2 ½* **Afadan (IRE)**[10] 700 8-8-8 **62** .... RobertWinston 2 — 49
(J R Jenkins) *slowly away: a bhd* **33/1**

010/ **9** *½* **Worcester Lodge**[592] 4849 5-8-11 **65** .... AlanDaly 3 — 51
(Mrs L Richards) *a bhd* **40/1**

0-00 **10** *shd* **Sgt Pepper (IRE)**[15] 670 5-9-2 **70** .... (e[1]) ChrisCatlin 7 — 56
(P L Gilligan) *hld up in rr: a bhd* **40/1**

2m 37.73s (-5.27) **Going Correction** +0.125s/f (Slow) — **10** Ran SP% **112.5**
Speed ratings (Par 103):102,99,98,97,96 95,93,92,91,91
CSF £8.21 CT £43.26 TOTE £2.60: £1.30, £1.70, £2.10; EX 10.20.
Owner Mrs Fitri Hay **Bred** Gestut Hofgut Mappen **Trained** Upper Lambourn, Berks

FOCUS
Quite a good handicap for the grade dominated by two in-form improvers. The pace was only modest which suited those racing prominently.

848 WIN AT INTERCASINO.CO.UK H'CAP — 1m (P)

5:00 (5:16) (Class 4) (0-80,79) 3-Y-0
£7,790 (£2,332; £1,166; £583; £291; £146) **Stalls** High

Form — RPR

6-21 **1** **Trans Sonic**[33] 539 3-9-3 **78** .... DarrenWilliams 7 — 83
(A P Jarvis) *lw: mde all: rdn over 1f out: hld on gamely whn chal ins fnl f* **2/1**[1]

511- **2** *½* **Namid Reprobate (IRE)**[152] 6214 3-9-4 **79** .... ShaneKelly 6 — 83
(P F I Cole) *h.d.w: lw: chsd wnr thrght: chal ins fnl f: no imp cl home* **9/1**

35-2 **3** *2* **Lake Poet (IRE)**[16] 658 3-9-0 **75** .... RyanMoore 5 — 74
(C E Brittain) *mid-div: hdwy to go 3rd 2f out: kpt on one pce fnl f* **5/1**

350- **4** *1 ¾* **Hill Of Almhuim (IRE)**[162] 6016 3-9-1 **76** .... (v) FrancisNorton 1 — 71
(K R Burke) *in rr: rdn 1/2-way: styd on ins fnl 2f: nvr nr to chal* **8/1**

6-20 **5** *3* **Fangorn Forest (IRE)**[74] 139 3-8-10 **71** .... (p) AdrianMcCarthy 2 — 59
(R A Harris) *bhd and nvr on terms* **25/1**

11- **6** *20* **Suits Me**[219] 4712 3-9-0 **75** .... GrahamGibbons 8 — 17
(J J Quinn) *lw: t.k.h: trckd ldrs tl wknd over 2f out* **9/2**[3]

3-21 **7** *3 ½* **Ballybeg (IRE)**[9] 709 3-8-11 **72** .... RichardHughes 3 — 6
(R Hannon) *lw: in tch: rdn oer 3f out: sn btn* **7/2**[2]

1m 41.53s (-0.45) **Going Correction** +0.125s/f (Slow) — **7** Ran SP% **115.4**
Speed ratings (Par 100):101,100,98,96,93 73,70
CSF £21.50 CT £79.89 TOTE £3.00: £2.00, £4.00; EX 22.10 Place 6 £61.96, Place 5 £35.18.
Owner Eurostrait Ltd **Bred** I A Balding **Trained** Twyford, Bucks

FOCUS
A reasonable-looking handicap, but the first two were in the first two throughout. The winner could rate a bit better than the bare form.
Ballybeg(IRE) Official explanation: jockey said gelding never travelled
T/Jkpt: Not won. T/Plt: £86.20 to a £1 stake. Pool: £109,262.65. 925.10 winning tickets. T/Qpdt: £41.20 to a £1 stake. Pool: £6,742.60. 121.00 winning tickets. JS

[833] LINGFIELD (L-H)

Monday, April 3

OFFICIAL GOING: Standard
Wind: Moderate, half-against Weather: Fine

849 LINGFIELD-RACECOURSE.CO.UK MEDIAN AUCTION MAIDEN STKS — 5f (P)

2:40 (2:40) (Class 6) 2-Y-0 — **£2,388** (£705; £352) **Stalls** High

Form — RPR

1 **Lord Charles** 2-8-11 .... AmirQuinn[(3)] 1 — 72+
(W G M Turner) *s.i.s: outpcd and wl bhd: stl plenty to do whn swtchd rt over 1f out: str run fnl f to ld last stride* **25/1**

3 **2** *hd* **Pernomente (IRE)**[10] 707 2-9-0 .... MartinDwyer 4 — 71
(J S Moore) *pressed ldr: rdn to ld over 1f out: tired ins fnl f: hdd last stride* **7/1**

2 **3** *½* **Fast Freddie**[11] 701 2-8-12 ow5 .... JamesO'Reilly[(7)] 8 — 74
(T J Pitt) *fast away and set str pce: rdn and hdd over 1f out: pressed ldr tl no ex nr fin* **5/2**[2]

4 *1* **Miss Kool Kat (USA)** 2-8-9 .... NCallan 2 — 60
(K A Ryan) *chsd ldng trio: rdn 1/2-way: no real imp 2f out: kpt on nr fin* **4/1**[3]

3 **5** *3* **Everyman**[9] 727 2-9-0 .... ShaneKelly 3 — 53+
(P D Evans) *restless stalls and v.s.a: wl bhd and nvr any ch: wd and hanging bnd 2f out: r.o fnl f* **9/4**[1]

6 *nk* **She Wont Wait** 2-8-9 .... FergusSweeney 7 — 47
(T M Jones) *s.i.s: outpcd and wl bhd: kpt on fr over 1f out: no ch* **50/1**

7 *¾* **Peppin's Gold (IRE)** 2-8-9 .... DaneO'Neill 6 — 44
(B R Millman) *chsd clr ldng quartet: no imp whn hung rt bnd 2f out: n.d after* **33/1**

8 *shd* **Bertie Swift** 2-9-0 .... JamieSpencer 9 — 48
(J Gallagher) *s.i.s: outpcd and wl bhd: hung rt and wd bnd 2f out: plugged on* **12/1**

9 *3* **Circle Of Truth** 2-8-11 .... RobertMiles[(3)] 5 — 36
(W G M Turner) *w ldrs to 1/2-way: wknd wl over 1f out: eased whn no ch* **50/1**

10 *1* **Elle's Angel (IRE)** 2-8-9 .... AlanMunro 10 — 27
(B R Millman) *outpcd and a wl bhd* **16/1**

60.62 secs (0.84) **Going Correction** -0.05s/f (Stan) — **10** Ran SP% **116.1**
Speed ratings (Par 90):91,90,89,88,83 83,81,81,76,75
CSF £185.52 TOTE £26.10: £4.80, £1.70, £1.30; EX 227.80.
Owner Mrs M S Teversham **Bred** Mrs M S Teversham **Trained** Sigwells, Somerset

FOCUS
A moderate event, run at a decent clip, and the form should be treated with a degree of caution.

NOTEBOOK
Lord Charles, a half-brother to three winners at up to seven furlongs, came from an impossible looking position at the top of the straight to mow down his rivals and just do enough to get his career off to a perfect start. Considering he lost ground at the start and ran green through the early stages, there was a lot to like about this effort, and while the form may not amount to much, he should only improve for the experience. Another furlong should also be well within his compass.
Pernomente(IRE), third over course and distance on his recent debut, looked the most likely winner entering the final furlong yet proved powerless to the winner's late thrust. This must rate an improved effort, with his previous experience proving a distinct advantage, and he deserves to go one better. (op 9-1)
Fast Freddie, very well backed when just denied on his recent debut over course and distance, showed decent early dash from his unfavourable draw and, considering his rider carried 5lb overweight, he must emerge with credit. However, he has now had two fairly hard races, and his stamina for even this trip is not yet fully assured. (op 2-1 tchd 3-1)
Miss Kool Kat(USA), a 17,000gns purchase related to winners in the US, proved very popular in the betting ring ahead of this debut. However, she failed to rate a serious threat, and should be sharper with this outing under her belt. (op 8-1)
Everyman, slow to break when third in the Brocklesby on debut nine days previously, lost any chance at the start and did fairly well to finish as close as he did. He clearly has issues with the starting gates, but also possesses an engine, and has a future providing his trainer can get him to break on terms. Official explanation: jockey said colt missed the break (tchd 2-1)

850 ENTERTAIN AT LINGFIELD PARK MAIDEN STKS — 1m 2f (P)

3:10 (3:12) (Class 5) 3-Y-0 — **£3,238** (£963; £481; £240) **Stalls** Low

Form — RPR

1 **Leningrad (IRE)** 3-9-3 .... JamieSpencer 7 — 86+
(M L W Bell) *dwlt: sn wl in tch: eased out over 2f out: trckd ldr over 1f out: led last 150yds: carried hd high but won easily* **10/11**[1]

2 *1 ¼* **Alcyon (IRE)** 3-9-3 .... ShaneKelly 8 — 78
(E A L Dunlop) *dwlt: hld up: prog on outer over 4f out to trck ldrs: rdn to ld 2f out: hdd last 150yds: styd on but no ch w wnr* **12/1**

662- **3** *1 ½* **Dyanita**[173] 5833 3-8-12 74 .... MichaelHills 2 — 70
(B W Hills) *trckd ldrs: cl up over 2f out: n.m.r sn after: rdn and kpt on same pce fr over 1f out* **7/1**[3]

4 *¾* **Scotland Yard (UAE)** 3-9-3 .... KDarley 6 — 74
(M Johnston) *hld up in rr: effrt and sme prog over 2f out: shkn up and kpt on fnl f* **12/1**

5 *hd* **Congestion Charge** 3-8-12 .... TedDurcan 9 — 68+
(E A L Dunlop) *hld up in rr: prog on wd outside fr 3f out: green and hanging lft over 1f out: kpt on same pce* **25/1**

00- **6** *hd* **Telegonus**[156] 6148 3-9-3 .... SteveDrowne 10 — 73
(G Wragg) *hld up towards rr: sme prog over 2f out: bmpd over 1f out: kpt on fnl f* **33/1**

7 *4* **In On The Act (IRE)** 3-8-12 .... EddieAhern 11 — 60+
(Jamie Poulton) *dwlt: hld up: last tl effrt wl over 2f out: pushed along and nvr on terms w ldrs fnl 2f* **10/1**

40-2 **8** *¾* **Picture Show (USA)**[16] 669 3-8-12 67 .... RyanMoore 1 — 59
(C E Brittain) *led for 2f: rdn to ld over 3f out: hdd & wknd 2f out* **5/1**[2]

0-0 **9** *5* **Kinetic Power (IRE)**[90] 16 3-9-3 .... LPKeniry 3 — 54+
(D R C Elsworth) *chsd ldrs: rdn 4f out: wkng whn n.m.r 2f out* **100/1**

0 **10** *2 ½* **Lady Georgette (IRE)**[30] 579 3-8-12 .... RichardMullen 12 — 45
(E J O'Neill) *in tch: wkng whn squeezed out over 2f out* **50/1**

06- **11** *3 ½* **Queen Of Diamonds (IRE)**[150] 6246 3-8-12 .... RobertHavlin 4 — 38
(Mrs P N Dutfield) *prom tl wknd wl over 2f out* **100/1**

6-0 **12** *20* **Skye Boat Song**[60] 272 3-9-3 .... NCallan 5 — 5
(J Jay) *led after 2f to over 3f out: wknd rapidly: t.o* **100/1**

2m 7.29s (-0.50) **Going Correction** -0.05s/f (Stan) — **12** Ran SP% **117.7**
Speed ratings (Par 98):100,99,97,97,97 96,93,93,89,87 84,68
CSF £13.04 TOTE £1.90: £1.10, £3.20, £2.20; EX 13.60.
Owner Philip Green & M Tabor **Bred** Kilcarn Stud **Trained** Newmarket, Suffolk

FOCUS
An above-average maiden for the track, run at a fair pace, and the winner is value for further.
Skye Boat Song Official explanation: jockey said colt hung right throughout

851 LINGFIELD PARK GOLF CLUB H'CAP — 6f (P)

3:40 (3:40) (Class 5) (0-75,75) 3-Y-0 — **£3,238** (£963; £481; £240) **Stalls** Low

Form — RPR

-634 **1** **Billy Bling (IRE)**[30] 577 3-8-7 **64** .... RichardHughes 5 — 66
(R Hannon) *dwlt: sn wl in tch: trckd ldng pair 3f out: effrt on inner over 1f out: drvn and styd on to ld wl ins fnl f* **7/1**

100- **2** *nk* **Dasheena**[196] 5370 3-8-5 **62** .... MartinDwyer 1 — 63
(M J Polglase) *pressed ldr after 2f: upsides ent fnl f: nt qckn last 75yds* **16/1**

5-52 **3** *shd* **Gavarnie Beau (IRE)**[10] 709 3-8-13 **70** .... FrancisNorton 4 — 71
(M Blanshard) *t.k.h: chsd ldr for 2f: sltly outpcd and rdn 1/2-way: effrt again over 1f out: styd on ins fnl f* **3/1**[1]

164- **4** *hd* **Bathwick Alice**[163] 6024 3-9-2 **73** .... AlanMunro 3 — 73
(B R Millman) *mde most: set stdy pce tl qcknd over 3f out: hdd wl ins fnl f: wknd nr fin* **9/2**[2]

-261 **5** *1 ¼* **Diane's Choice**[34] 540 3-9-1 **72** .... TQuinn 6 — 68
(J Akehurst) *chsd ldrs: wnt rt 4f out: sltly outpcd and rdn 3f out: kpt on again fr over 1f out: nvr able to chal* **5/1**[3]

55-5 **6** ¾ **Spectacular Show (IRE)**[10] 717 3-9-4 **75**........................ RyanMoore 2 69
(M Quinn) *lost pl over 4f out and in rr after: swtchd rt jst over 1f out: shkn up and kpt on: nvr nr ldrs* **16/1**

3600 **7** ½ **The London Gang**[4] 807 3-8-8 **65**.................................... ShaneKelly 8 58
(P D Evans) *s.s: wl in rr: drvn and outpcd 1/2-way: effrt on wd outside over 1f out: no imp whn siwtched lft last 100yds* **7/1**

000- **8** 1 ½ **Catherines Cafe (IRE)**[164] 6010 3-8-13 **70**.................... RobertHavlin 9 58
(Mrs P N Dutfield) *dwlt: t.k.h and hld up in rr: outpcd 1/2-way: no imp after* **14/1**

034- **9** ¾ **Bouzouki (USA)**[122] 6484 3-9-3 **74**.............................. StephenCarson 7 60
(W R Swinburn) *dwlt: plld hrd early and hld up: outpcd 1/2-way: effrt on inner over 1f out: sn wknd* **7/1**

1m 13.71s (0.90) **Going Correction** -0.05s/f (Stan) **9** Ran SP% **115.8**
Speed ratings (Par 98):92,91,91,91,89 88,87,85,84
CSF £110.43 CT £410.84 TOTE £9.60: £2.00, £4.70, £1.60; EX 115.30.
Owner Ms V O'Sullivan **Bred** Brian Killeen **Trained** East Everleigh, Wilts

FOCUS
A moderate winning time for a race of its type and the form looks ordinary.
Diane's Choice Official explanation: jockey said filly suffered interference and never travelled after

852 HBLB LINGFIELD PARK LEISURE CLUB H'CAP 7f (P)
4:10 (4:10) (Class 4) (0-80,80) 3-Y-O **£5,505** (£1,637; £818; £408) **Stalls** Low

Form RPR

1- **1** **Easy Air**[139] 6351 3-9-1 **77**.. JamieSpencer 7 92+
(E A L Dunlop) *s.s: hld up in last pair: prog 2f out: shkn up to ld 1f out: rdn to assert wl ins fnl f* **10/11**[1]

120- **2** 1 ¼ **Grimes Faith**[142] 6320 3-9-4 **80**...................................... RichardHughes 1 83
(R Hannon) *hld up in tch: trckd ldrs over 2f out: effrt on inner to chal 1f out: readily outpcd by wnr last 100yds* **20/1**

41- **3** 2 **Sant Elena**[166] 5984 3-9-0 **76**.. SteveDrowne 6 74+
(G Wragg) *racd wd: hld up in tch: outpcd and wd bnd 2f out: styd on wl fnl f to take 3rd nr fin* **7/1**

-41 **4** ¾ **Westport**[60] 272 3-8-9 **71**.. NCallan 3 67
(K A Ryan) *trckd ldr: rdn to chal over 2f out: led briefly over 1f out: wknd fnl f* **13/2**[3]

12-3 **5** 1 ¾ **Broken Spur (FR)**[11] 702 3-8-13 **75**.............................. MichaelHills 4 66
(B W Hills) *chsd ldrs: rdn over 2f out: one pce and no imp after* **10/3**[2]

12-0 **6** ½ **Littledodayno (IRE)**[68] 190 3-9-3 **79**........................... JamieMackay 2 69
(M Wigham) *s.i.s: a in last pair: outpcd over 2f out: n.d after* **40/1**

045- **7** 4 **Lyrical Blues (IRE)**[129] 6423 3-8-12 **74**.......................... AlanMunro 5 54
(B R Millman) *racd freely: led: pressed over 2f out: hdd over 1f out: wknd rapidly* **20/1**

1m 25.85s (-0.04) **Going Correction** -0.05s/f (Stan) **7** Ran SP% **113.3**
Speed ratings (Par 100):98,96,94,93,91 90,86
CSF £23.99 TOTE £1.80: £1.60, £3.50; EX 15.80.
Owner Gainsborough Stud **Bred** Gainsborough Stud Management Ltd **Trained** Newmarket, Suffolk

FOCUS
A decent three-year-old handicap for the class, run at just an average pace, and the progressive winner is value for further.

853 COME RACING AT LINGFIELD PARK (S) STKS 1m (P)
4:40 (4:41) (Class 6) 3-Y-O+ **£2,388** (£705; £352) **Stalls** High

Form RPR

2505 **1** **Christmas Truce (IRE)**[7] 770 7-8-13 50.................(v) SophieDoyle(7) 6 60
(Ms J S Doyle) *mde all: clr fr 3f out: pushed along fnl 2f: unchal* **12/1**

-005 **2** 4 **Titus Lumpus (IRE)**[11] 703 3-8-5 55................................ EddieAhern 7 47
(R M Flower) *prom: rdn to chse wnr over 3f out: no imp: jst hld on for 2nd* **6/1**[2]

0-60 **3** ½ **Escobar (POL)**[49] 398 5-9-6 45..................................... SamHitchcott 1 50
(Mrs P Townsley) *hld up: hmpd on inner over 5f out: taken to outer and prog over 2f out: hrd rdn to go 3rd 1f out: plugged on* **10/1**

6600 **4** ¾ **Paso Doble**[10] 708 8-9-5 62.................................(b) JamesMillman(7) 8 54
(B R Millman) *chsd ldrs: outpcd over 3f out: kpt on one pce u.p fnl 2f* **15/2**[3]

4500 **5** 1 **Rowan Pursuit**[10] 708 5-9-7 48..(b) TQuinn 11 47
(J Akehurst) *hld up and sn last: wl adrift 3f out: styd on fnl 2f: no ch* **6/1**[2]

6054 **6** hd **Dane's Rock (IRE)**[9] 734 4-9-7 48.................... RichardKingscote(5) 10 52
(M S Saunders) *chsd ldrs: u.p bef 1/2-way: sn outpcd: no imp fnl 3f* **9/1**

0000 **7** 2 **Inescapable (USA)**[18] 649 5-9-6 40................................ MartinDwyer 12 41
(A W Carroll) *chsd wnr to over 3f out: wknd wl over 1f out* **40/1**

-022 **8** hd **Midnight Lace**[14] 678 4-9-7 63.. NCallan 4 43+
(J R Boyle) *chsd ldrs: outpcd and u.p over 3f out: n.d after* **9/4**[1]

0-00 **9** 8 **Warlingham (IRE)**[7] 768 8-9-12 45.................................. J-PGuillambert 9 28
(P Howling) *restrained s: hld up: prog on wd outside 5f out: rdn and struggling over 3f out: bhd fnl 2f* **20/1**

0-00 **10** 1 ¼ **Coronado Forest (USA)**[49] 399 7-9-12 40...................... DaneO'Neill 3 25
(M R Hoad) *settled in rr: outpcd fr 1/2-way: wl bhd fnl 2f* **12/1**

0/0 **11** ¾ **Kussharro**[19] 640 5-9-6 40.......................................(t) SimonWhitworth 2 17
(Mrs L J Young) *hmpd on inner over 5f out: wl bhd fr over 2f out* **50/1**

66-0 **12** 1 ¾ **Emily (FR)**[28] 598 3-8-1 60 ow4...............................(t) EdwardCreighton(3) 5 8
(Mrs L J Young) *hld up: a wl in rr: last and wl bhd over 2f out* **25/1**

1m 38.99s (-0.44) **Going Correction** -0.05s/f (Stan)
WFA 3 from 4yo+ 15lb **12** Ran SP% **118.6**
Speed ratings (Par 101):100,96,95,94,93 93,91,91,83,82 81,79
CSF £79.45 TOTE £14.30: £3.30, £2.10, £4.80; EX 106.30.There was no bid for the winner.
Owner Gayler William Chambers **Bred** John McDonnell **Trained** Upper Lambourn, Berks
■ A first winner for 19-year-old Sophie Doyle, daughter of Jacqui and sister of James.

FOCUS
A weak affair, run at a decent pace, and the winner did the job nicely from the front.

854 GOLF AND RACING DAYS OUT H'CAP 1m (P)
5:10 (5:11) (Class 6) (0-65,65) 4-Y-O+ **£2,388** (£705; £176; £176) **Stalls** High

Form RPR

625- **1** **Molem**[155] 6183 4-9-4 **65**..(tp) JamieSpencer 4 72
(Lady Herries) *chsd ldng pair: wnt 2nd over 2f out: urged along and styd on to ld ins fnl f: in command after* **7/2**[2]

-134 **2** 1 ¾ **Beneking**[40] 486 6-8-2 **52**..................................(p) EdwardCreighton(3) 10 55
(D Burchell) *led: clr 1/2-way: drvn and hdd ins fnl f: jst hld on for 2nd* **12/1**

4606 **3** hd **Secam (POL)**[12] 693 7-8-6 **53**..(b) SamHitchcott 11 56
(Mrs P Townsley) *hld up early: prog over 4f out: chsd ldng pair 2f out: kpt on same pce: nvr able to chal* **14/1**

3105 **3** dht **Height Of Spirits**[28] 596 4-8-8 **58**.................................. RobertMiles(3) 12 61
(T D McCarthy) *hld up wl in rr and swtchd to inner: prog over 2f out: drvn and kpt on fnl f: nvr able to chal* **8/1**

0421 **5** shd **Physical (IRE)**[10] 711 4-8-7 **59**.................................(p) JamesDoyle(5) 8 62
(Mrs A J Perrett) *forced to r wd thrght: hld up: prog over 2f out: kpt on same pce fr over 1f out* **3/1**[1]

010- **6** shd **Mad**[94] 6693 5-8-4 **51** oh1.. AlanMunro 9 54
(Ernst Oertel) *hld up and racd wd: wl in rr and rdn 3f out: no prog tl r.o fnl f* **20/1**

-006 **7** 1 ¾ **Duxford**[12] 698 5-8-12 **59**...(p) JimmyFortune 2 58
(D K Ivory) *chsd ldrs: u.p 3f out: no imp over 1f out* **16/1**

2153 **8** ¾ **Trouble Maker**[37] 514 5-8-5 **52**...................................(b[1]) MartinDwyer 6 49
(A M Balding) *t.k.h early: hld up: no prog over 2f out: plugged on* **6/1**[3]

326- **9** nk **Ile Michel**[249] 3871 9-9-1 **62**... KDarley 1 58
(Lady Herries) *chsd ldr to over 2f out: wknd over 1f out* **8/1**

0-00 **10** ½ **Simplify**[12] 698 4-8-12 **59**.. TQuinn 5 54
(T M Jones) *hld up wl in rr: hmpd wl over 2f out: nt clr run after: swtchd to inner over 1f out: no ch* **12/1**

0-06 **11** ½ **String Serenade (IRE)**[14] 682 5-8-4 **51** oh6................ JamieMackay 7 45
(V Smith) *racd wd: wl in rr: brief effrt over 2f out: wknd wl over 1f out* **50/1**

/0-0 **12** 4 **Romanova (IRE)**[17] 660 4-8-11 **65**............................ SladeO'Hara(7) 3 50
(Dr J R J Naylor) *racd towards outer: nvr on terms w ldrs: wknd rapidly fnl f* **50/1**

1m 38.89s (-0.54) **Going Correction** -0.05s/f (Stan) **12** Ran SP% **120.3**
Speed ratings (Par 101):100,98,98,98,97 97,96,95,95,94 94,90
WIN: £3.90. PL: £1.50, £2.60, Height Of Spirits £2.10, Secam £2.10. TRIC: Molem/Beneking/Height Of Spirits £161.98, Molem/Beneking/Secam £269.71. CSF £45.41; EX 58.40.
Owner Seymour Racing Partnership **Bred** Shadwell Estate Company Limited **Trained** Patching, W Sussex

FOCUS
A moderate handicap, run at an average pace, and the winner is value for slightly further.
Simplify Official explanation: jockey said gelding was denied a clear run

855 DINE IN THE TRACKSIDE CARVERY H'CAP 1m (P)
5:40 (5:41) (Class 5) (0-75,75) 3-Y-O **£3,238** (£963; £481; £240) **Stalls** High

Form RPR

2512 **1** **Tamagin (USA)**[4] 803 3-8-10 **72**.......................(p) StephenDonohoe(5) 4 86
(P D Evans) *mde all and set decent pce: kicked on again over 2f out: drvn and hld on gamely fnl f* **4/1**[3]

22-1 **2** nk **Kalankari (IRE)**[11] 703 3-9-4 **75**.. MartinDwyer 5 88
(A M Balding) *prom: chsd wnr over 3f out: drvn fr 2f out: clsd fnl f: jst hld* **7/2**[2]

55-1 **3** 1 ¾ **Go Figure (IRE)**[4] 803 3-9-3 **74** 6ex................................ JimmyFortune 2 83
(B J Meehan) *trckd ldrs: effrt over 2f out: tried to cl 1f out: no imp last 100yds* **9/4**[1]

035- **4** 5 **Fann (USA)**[184] 5604 3-8-13 **70**... RyanMoore 3 68
(C E Brittain) *dwlt: off the pce in last trio: rdn over 3f out: no prog tl styd on fnl f* **12/1**

4-22 **5** 1 ¾ **Rose Muwasim**[34] 539 3-8-12 **69**.................................. JamieSpencer 1 62
(E A L Dunlop) *hld up off the pce: trckd ldng trio and gng wl enough 3f out: hanging and fnd nil over 1f out: wknd* **7/2**[2]

3514 **6** 11 **Scroll**[11] 702 3-9-4 **75**...(v) J-PGuillambert 8 43
(P Howling) *off the pce in last trio: rdn bef 1/2-way: no prog: t.o* **20/1**

152 **7** 1 ¼ **Ten Shun**[67] 197 3-8-9 **66**.. ShaneKelly 7 31
(P D Evans) *off the pce in last trio: rdn and no prog over 3f out: t.o* **28/1**

-040 **8** 3 ½ **Possessed**[41] 475 3-8-10 **70**...................................(v[1]) RobertMiles(3) 6 27
(T D McCarthy) *t.k.h: chsd wnr to over 3f out: wknd rapidly: t.o* **20/1**

1m 36.89s (-2.54) **Going Correction** -0.05s/f (Stan) **8** Ran SP% **115.9**
Speed ratings (Par 98):110,109,107,102,101 90,88,85
CSF £18.12 CT £38.46 TOTE £6.30: £1.60, £1.50, £1.30; EX 21.10 Place 6 £125.28, Place 5 £45.08.
Owner Jordan E Lund **Bred** Stonehaven Farm Llc **Trained** Pandy, Abergavenny

FOCUS
A very smart winning time indeed for a race of its type, exactly two seconds faster than the preceding handicap for older horses over the same trip, and the form looks solid rated through the penalised third horse.
T/Plt: £174.20 to a £1 stake. Pool: £44,162.70. 185.05 winning tickets. T/Qpdt: £52.30 to a £1 stake. Pool: £3,369.90. 47.60 winning tickets. JN

782 SOUTHWELL (L-H)
Monday, April 3

OFFICIAL GOING: Standard
Wind: Fresh, behind Weather: Sunshine with light cloud

856 GOLF AND RACING AT SOUTHWELL MAIDEN AUCTION STKS 5f (F)
2:30 (2:30) (Class 6) 2-Y-O **£2,730** (£806; £403) **Stalls** High

Form RPR

1 **Chief Editor** 2-8-10 ow3.. DerekNolan(5) 6 76
(M J Wallace) *s.i.s: hdwy 1/2-way: led over 1f out: rdn out* **10/1**[3]

22 **2** hd **Urban Warrior**[7] 760 2-8-9... LDettori 4 69
(J R Best) *chsd ldr tl led 1/2-way: rdn and hdd over 1f out: edgd lft: styd on* **30/100**[1]

3 **3** 5 **Diminuto**[7] 760 2-8-4 .... HayleyTurner 7 44
(M D I Usher) *chsd ldrs: rdn over 1f out: sn wknd* **9/1**[2]

0 **4** 5 **Banana Belle**[16] 663 2-7-11 .... DonnaCaldwell(7) 1 24
(P S McEntee) *led: rdn and hdd 1/2-way: sn hung lft: wknd over 1f out* **50/1**

5 nk **Readyforone** 2-8-9 .... RobertWinston 2 28
(P D Evans) *s.i.s: hdwy over 3f out: wknd 2f out* **12/1**

6 1 ¼ **Baytown Rosie (IRE)** 2-8-4 .... FrancisFerris 3 18
(P S McEntee) *chsd ldrs 3f* **40/1**

7 1 **Baytown Paikea** 2-8-4 .... RoystonFfrench 5 14
(P S McEntee) *s.i.s: hdwy over 3f out: wknd wl over 1f out* **50/1**

59.36 secs (-0.94) **Going Correction** -0.375s/f (Stan) **7** Ran SP% **110.1**
Speed ratings (Par 90):92,91,83,75,75 73,71
CSF £12.66 TOTE £12.90: £3.10, £1.20; EX 20.70.
Owner Mrs P Good **Bred** J R And Mrs P Good **Trained** Newmarket, Suffolk

FOCUS
Just a modest maiden, but Chief Editor was giving weight away all round and has some scope.

NOTEBOOK
Chief Editor, a 9,000gns full-brother to seven-furlong juvenile winner Chief Scout, missed the break but was soon travelling well behind the leaders and found plenty when asked for his effort to deny the more experienced Urban Warrior. This was just a modest race, but he is open to improvement. (op 8-1 tchd 11-1)
Urban Warrior, a promising second on his debut before narrowly failing to justify favouritism at Kempton, again found one too good. He looks genuine enough and is not doing a great deal wrong, but he lacks size and appeals as one to keep opposing. (op 4-11 tchd 2-5 in a place)

Diminuto, four lengths behind today's runner-up on her debut at Kempton a week previously, would not appeared to have progressed much. (op 8-1)
Banana Belle, just as she did on her debut, showed plenty of early pace but did not get home. She looks to be a short-runner and could need dropping into selling company. (op 33-1)
Readyforone, a 3,000gns half-brother a moderate seven-furlong juvenile winner, out of a multiple sprint scorer, never really featured after starting slowly and should do better with the benefit of this experience. (op 8-1)

857 BOOK TICKETS ON-LINE AMATEUR RIDERS' CLAIMING STKS 1m 4f (F)
3:00 (3:00) (Class 6) 4-Y-0+ **£2,307** (£709; £354) **Stalls** Low

Form RPR
2325 **1** **Romil Star (GER)**[18] 652 9-10-6 59 (v) MissKellyBurke(5) 1 64
(K R Burke) *chsd ldrs: led over 3f out: hdd over 1f out: styd on to ld nr fin* **10/3**[2]
60- **2** *hd* **Mr Wong (IRE)**[343] 1266 10-10-2 60 MrLRPayter(5) 4 60
(M Sheppard) *mid-div: hdwy 1/2-way: led over 1f out: rdn and hdd nr fin* **20/1**
0310 **3** *3 ½* **Sol Rojo**[3] 820 4-10-9 59 (v[1]) MrSPearce(5) 9 62
(J Pearce) *hld up: hdwy over 1f out: nt rch ldrs* **8/1**[3]
3431 **4** *3* **Champion Lion (IRE)**[10] 715 7-10-8 52 (e) MrSWalker 13 51
(J R Boyle) *hld up: hdwy over 4f out: rdn over 2f out: wknd over 1f out* **15/8**[1]
5353 **5** *½* **College Rebel**[14] 684 5-10-3 45 MissFayeBramley(3) 6 48
(J F Coupland) *prom over 9f* **9/1**
2506 **6** *2* **Spitfire Bob (USA)**[18] 647 7-10-6 50 MissKSearby(7) 8 52
(M E Sowersby) *mid-div: hdwy over 3f out: rdn and wknd over 1f out* **18/1**
5634 **7** *1* **Molly's Secret**[5] 794 8-9-9 40 (p) MissAlexWells(7) 5 40
(Miss S J Wilton) *hld up: hdwy 1/2-way: wknd over 2f out* **14/1**
0-00 **8** *5* **Royal Lustre**[20] 635 5-10-7 40 MissSBrotherton 2 37
(Robert Gray) *chsd ldr: led over 4f out: hdd over 3f out: wknd over 2f out* **25/1**
0-05 **9** *¾* **Neptune**[11] 706 10-10-2 40 MissSarah-JaneDurman(5) 14 36
(J C Fox) *s.i.s: hdwy 1/2-way: wknd over 4f out* **28/1**
060/ **10** *23* **Impero**[22] 2579 8-10-2 35 (p) MrDanielChinn(5) 11 —
(G F Bridgwater) *prom to 1/2-way* **66/1**
11 *1 ¾* **King Of Scots**[8] 5-10-2 MrMPrice(7) 3 —
(R J Price) *bhd fnl 7f* **66/1**
-006 **12** *5* **Monkstown Road**[11] 706 4-10-12 54 (b) MrSDobson 12 —
(C N Kellett) *hld up: hdwy 8f out: wknd wl over 3f out* **22/1**
66-0 **13** *17* **Veneer (IRE)**[42] 467 4-10-9 46 (b) MissNathalieNorgren(7) 10 —
(Miss Gay Kelleway) *plld hrd: led and sn clr: hdd & wknd over 4f out* **33/1**
005/ **14** *dist* **Redouble**[252] 3238 10-10-2 30 MissCScott(7) 7 —
(N B King) *bhd fnl 8f* **100/1**

2m 42.89s (0.80) **Going Correction** -0.125s/f (Stan)
WFA 4 from 5yo+ 1lb **14** Ran SP% **114.2**
Speed ratings (Par 101):92,91,89,87,87 85,85,81,81,66 64,61,50,—
CSF £72.28 TOTE £4.50: £1.60, £8.40, £2.40; EX 107.30 TRIFECTA Not won..Champion Lion claimed by D. J. Moffatt for £5,500.
Owner Mrs Elaine M Burke **Bred** J H A Baggen **Trained** Middleham Moor, N Yorks

FOCUS
A moderate claimer won by course specialist Romil Star.
Redouble Official explanation: jockey said gelding lost its action at end of back straight

858 EXPERIENCE NOTTINGHAMSHIRE H'CAP 5f (F)
3:30 (3:30) (Class 6) (0-60,60) 4-Y-0+ **£2,730** (£806; £403) **Stalls** High

Form RPR
0025 **1** **Count Cougar (USA)**[27] 608 6-9-1 **57** AdrianTNicholls 8 68
(S P Griffiths) *s.i.s: sn chsng ldrs: rdn over 3f out: led and hung lft ins fnl f: r.o* **10/1**
5340 **2** *1* **Orchestration (IRE)**[46] 424 5-8-11 **53** (v) RobbieFitzpatrick 4 61
(M J Attwater) *chsd ldrs: rdn and hung lft 1/2-way: led 1f out: sn hdd: styd on same pce* **11/2**[2]
00-0 **3** *¾* **Vague Star (ITY)**[56] 317 4-9-2 **58** (b) LDettori 1 63
(R Ingram) *outpcd: hdwy over 1f out: r.o* **8/1**[3]
0645 **4** *½* **Cashel Mead**[3] 824 6-8-13 **55** RobertWinston 5 59
(J L Spearing) *dwlt: hdwy 1/2-way: nt clr run over 1f out: styd on* **5/1**[1]
2131 **5** *1 ¼* **Percy Douglas**[5] 789 6-8-5 **54** 6ex (bt) AnnStokell(7) 10 54
(Miss A Stokell) *led over 3f: styd on same pce* **14/1**
0-60 **6** *nk* **Detonate**[4] 806 4-8-10 **52** (p) ChrisCatlin 6 50
(Mrs C A Dunnett) *w ldr tl led over 1f out: sn hdd: wknd ins fnl f* **11/1**
6420 **7** *1 ½* **Tag Team (IRE)**[27] 605 5-9-4 **60** DarryllHolland 7 53
(John A Harris) *chsd ldrs: rdn 1/2-way: wknd fnl f* **11/2**[2]
2100 **8** *2 ½* **Blakeshall Quest**[27] 608 6-8-10 **52** (v) TomEaves 12 37
(R Brotherton) *s.i.s: outpcd* **28/1**
1100 **9** *1* **Amanda's Lad (IRE)**[27] 605 6-8-5 **52** EmmettStack(5) 3 33
(M C Chapman) *sn outpcd* **10/1**
600- **10** *hd* **Valiant Romeo**[184] 5616 6-8-7 **49** RoystonFfrench 2 30
(R Bastiman) *chsd ldrs: rdn over 3f out: sn lost pl* **25/1**
0140 **11** *2 ½* **Shirley Oaks (IRE)**[10] 708 8-8-5 **47** AdrianMcCarthy 11 19
(Miss Z C Davison) *sn outpcd* **25/1**
0-40 **12** *dist* **Edward (IRE)**[30] 580 4-9-2 **58** DarrenWilliams 9 —
(A P Jarvis) *s.i.s: hdwy over 3f out: sn rdn: wknd 1/2-way: eased fnl f* **8/1**[3]

58.56 secs (-1.74) **Going Correction** -0.375s/f (Stan) **12** Ran SP% **114.0**
Speed ratings (Par 101):98,96,95,94,92 91,89,85,83,83 79,—
CSF £60.17 CT £471.61 TOTE £12.80: £3.50, £2.20, £4.80; EX 82.80 Trifecta £578.50 Part won. Pool: £814.92 - 0.10 winning tickets..
Owner M Grant **Bred** Angus Glen Farm (1996) Ltd **Trained** Easingwold, N Yorks

FOCUS
A moderate sprint handicap.
Edward(IRE) Official explanation: trainer said gelding bled from the nose

859 DINE IN THE QUEEN MOTHER RESTAURANT H'CAP 1m 3f (F)
4:00 (4:00) (Class 6) (0-60,60) 3-Y-0 **£2,730** (£806; £403) **Stalls** Low

Form RPR
-000 **1** **Star Of Canterbury (IRE)**[17] 658 3-9-3 59 (v[1]) DarrenWilliams 10 65
(A P Jarvis) *mde all: sn clr: rdn over 2f out: sn edgd lft: styd on* **14/1**
000- **2** *nk* **Bollin Derek**[203] 5184 3-8-4 46 oh1 DavidAllan 7 52+
(T D Easterby) *hld up: rdn 1/2-way: hdwy over 3f out: chsd wnr over 1f out: styd on wl* **12/1**
053- **3** *5* **At The Money**[150] 6244 3-9-2 58 HayleyTurner 1 56
(J M P Eustace) *chsd ldrs: rdn over 3f out: styd on same pce appr fnl f* **5/1**[1]
000- **4** *nk* **El Dee (IRE)**[166] 5987 3-8-6 51 ow1 DanielTudhope(3) 11 49
(D Carroll) *hld up: hdwy over 3f out: sn rdn: hung lft over 1f out: nt rch ldrs* **40/1**
2532 **5** *10* **Noble Edge**[27] 609 3-8-12 59 (p) GregFairley(5) 3 46+
(Robert Gray) *chsd ldrs: rdn over 2f out: wknd over 1f out* **8/1**[3]
-500 **6** *9* **Sahara Style**[31] 566 3-8-8 50 (v[1]) GrahamGibbons 5 17
(R Hollinshead) *s.i.s: hdwy over 8f out: wknd 4f out* **11/1**
06-0 **7** *5* **Samsouma (IRE)**[34] 544 3-8-10 52 LDettori 8 11
(C E Brittain) *hld up: nt clr run over 4f out: n.d* **5/1**[1]
0-23 **8** *15* **Marachi Band (USA)**[34] 544 3-9-4 60 ChrisCatlin 2 —
(E J O'Neill) *chsd ldrs: rdn 5f out: wknd over 3f out* **8/1**[3]
40-4 **9** *1 ¼* **Bob's Your Uncle**[34] 538 3-9-1 57 PaulHanagan 12 —
(J G Portman) *s.i.s: hld up: rdn and wknd 4f out* **15/2**[2]
005- **10** *1* **Follow My Trail (IRE)**[203] 5177 3-9-0 56 PaulEddery 6 —
(B Smart) *plld hrd: prom over 7f* **20/1**
3264 **11** *8* **Cool Isle**[14] 676 3-8-11 53 (b) TonyCulhane 9 —
(P Howling) *chsd ldrs over 7f* **14/1**
000- **12** *dist* **Veneto (IRE)**[239] 4185 3-8-13 55 (t) RobertWinston 4 —
(K G Reveley) *prom: lost pl over 6f out: virtually p.u fnl 3f* **10/1**

2m 26.63s (-2.27) **Going Correction** -0.125s/f (Stan) **12** Ran SP% **113.0**
Speed ratings (Par 96):103,102,99,98,91 85,81,70,69,68 63,—
CSF £163.89 CT £957.25 TOTE £15.30: £8.30, £4.60, £1.80; EX 254.00 Trifecta £247.10 Part won. Pool: £348.06 - 0.35 winning tickets..
Owner Eurostrait Ltd **Bred** Tally-Ho Stud **Trained** Twyford, Bucks

FOCUS
A moderate handicap in which Star Of Canterbury set a good pace from the start and had just enough left in the straight.
Samsouma(IRE) Official explanation: jockey said filly had a breathing problem
Marachi Band(USA) Official explanation: trainer had no explanation for the poor form shown
Cool Isle Official explanation: jockey said filly moved poorly throughout

860 BRIGG WINN 60TH BIRTHDAY H'CAP 7f (F)
4:30 (4:32) (Class 5) (0-70,70) 4-Y-0+ **£3,562** (£1,059; £529; £264) **Stalls** Low

Form RPR
1-11 **1** **Tyzack (IRE)**[18] 650 5-9-4 70 MickyFenton 6 84+
(Stef Liddiard) *s.i.s and hmpd s: sn prom: n.m.r over 4f out: nt clr run 1/2-way: styd on u.p to ld nr fin* **11/8**[1]
000- **2** *nk* **Sir Bond (IRE)**[205] 5121 5-8-6 58 RobertWinston 1 71
(B Smart) *s.s: hdwy over 2f out: led over 1f out: hdd nr fin* **9/1**
1050 **3** *4* **Set Alight**[9] 721 5-9-2 68 (v) LDettori 7 71
(Mrs C A Dunnett) *wnt lft s: chsd ldrs: lost pl over 5f out: hdwy 1/2-way: rdn and hung lft over 1f out: no ex* **5/1**[2]
0621 **4** *½* **El Palmar**[13] 689 5-8-4 56 oh1 PaulHanagan 5 58
(M J Attwater) *chsd ldrs: led 2f out: sn rdn and hdd: styd on same pce fnl f* **7/1**[3]
3024 **5** *8* **Preskani**[18] 650 4-8-3 60 (p) DuranFentiman(5) 13 41
(Mrs N Macauley) *prom: led 3f out: sn rdn and hung rt: hdd 2f out: sn wknd* **20/1**
1355 **6** *2* **Pawn In Life (IRE)**[18] 649 8-8-4 56 oh3 (v) JoeFanning 8 32
(M J Polglase) *chsd ldrs over 4f* **18/1**
000- **7** *shd* **Downland (IRE)**[211] 4971 10-9-1 67 KimTinkler 9 42
(N Tinkler) *racd keenly: prom: rdn and ev ch over 2f out: sn wknd* **33/1**
1351 **8** *3 ½* **Desert Lover (IRE)**[9] 737 4-8-11 63 PhillipMakin 2 29
(R J Price) *started slowly: outpcd* **9/1**
6132 **9** *5* **Crusoe (IRE)**[18] 648 9-8-6 58 oh2 ow2 (b) BrianReilly 3 11
(A Sadik) *in rr whn hmpd over 4f out: sn wl bhd* **20/1**
400- **10** *5* **Circuit Dancer (IRE)**[170] 5893 6-9-1 67 AdrianTNicholls 4 7
(D Nicholls) *hld up: edgd lft over 4f out: wknd 3f out* **16/1**
00-0 **11** *5* **Pianoforte (USA)**[7] 764 4-9-1 67 (b[1]) JimmyQuinn 12 —
(E J Alston) *chsd ldrs: rdn over 2f out: sn wknd* **14/1**
00-0 **12** *12* **Newsround**[92] 6 4-9-4 70 (b) TonyCulhane 11 —
(D W Chapman) *led 4f: sn wknd* **50/1**

1m 29.28s (-1.52) **Going Correction** -0.125s/f (Stan) **12** Ran SP% **123.5**
Speed ratings (Par 103):103,102,98,97,88 86,85,81,76,70 64,51
CSF £14.65 CT £55.32 TOTE £1.90: £1.30, £2.00, £2.10; EX 27.40 Trifecta £267.30 Pool: £1,332.82 - 3.54 winning tickets..
Owner Simon Mapletoft Racing I **Bred** Rabea Syndicate **Trained** Great Shefford, Berks

FOCUS
A competitive little handicap run at a solid pace, but there were some decent margins separating the 12 runners, especially between the front four and the rest.
Desert Lover(IRE) Official explanation: jockey said gelding hung left-handed from end of back straight
Newsround Official explanation: jockey said gelding lost its action

861 RACING HERE TOMORROW H'CAP 6f (F)
5:00 (5:01) (Class 6) (0-60,60) 3-Y-0 **£2,730** (£806; £403) **Stalls** Low

Form RPR
0250 **1** **Diktalex (IRE)**[19] 646 3-9-4 60 (t) RobbieFitzpatrick 1 66
(M J Attwater) *chsd ldrs: led over 1f out: rdn out* **12/1**
2622 **2** *¾* **Smile For Us**[19] 646 3-9-2 58 (b) BrianReilly 5 62
(C Drew) *led: hdd over 4f out: led 2f out: sn rdn and hdd: styd on* **6/1**[2]
613 **3** *hd* **Buzzin'Boyzee (IRE)**[19] 646 3-9-1 57 RobertWinston 6 60
(P D Evans) *hld up: hdwy over 2f out: rdn over 1f out: styd on* **7/1**[3]
1300 **4** *5* **Mister Incredible**[19] 646 3-9-4 60 (v[1]) DarryllHolland 3 48
(C A Dwyer) *s.i.s: sn chsng ldrs: led over 4f out: rdn and hdd 2f out: wknd fnl f* **6/1**[2]
005- **5** *¾* **Alwariah**[147] 6282 3-9-2 58 LDettori 2 44
(C E Brittain) *chsd ldrs: rdn over 2f out: hung lft and wknd over 1f out* **5/1**[1]
660- **6** *½* **Dancing Storm**[144] 6304 3-9-2 58 ChrisCatlin 9 42
(W S Kittow) *hld up: rdn over 3f out: n.d* **18/1**
06-0 **7** *¾* **Bold Love**[19] 646 3-8-8 50 GrahamGibbons 13 32
(J D Bethell) *mid-div: rdn over 3f out: wknd over 2f out* **12/1**
-040 **8** *¾* **Suhezy (IRE)**[26] 613 3-8-5 47 PaulHanagan 7 27
(P T Midgley) *prom: rdn 1/2-way: wknd 2f out* **14/1**
000- **9** *4* **Asmaradana**[196] 5361 3-8-10 55 NelsonDeSouza(3) 12 23
(P F I Cole) *prom to 1/2-way: no ch whn rdn and hung lft 2f out* **12/1**
000- **10** *1 ½* **Seesawmilu (IRE)**[269] 3301 3-8-7 49 JimmyQuinn 14 12
(E J Alston) *s.i.s: hld up: a in rr* **28/1**
000- **11** *3* **Cape Sydney (IRE)**[219] 4766 3-8-7 49 NeilPollard 10 3
(D W Barker) *a in rr* **20/1**
0600 **12** *1* **Galaxy Bound (IRE)**[28] 594 3-8-3 48 ow1 (v) PatrickMathers(3) 8 —
(D Shaw) *rrd s: outpcd* **33/1**
004- **13** *nk* **Casonova (IRE)**[220] 4732 3-8-11 58 DuranFentiman(5) 11 8
(T D Easterby) *chsd ldrs over 3f* **20/1**
000- **14** *½* **Moonlight Fantasy (IRE)**[176] 5769 3-8-13 55 TonyCulhane 4 4
(N Tinkler) *chsd ldrs over 3f* **9/1**

1m 16.28s (-0.62) **Going Correction** -0.125s/f (Stan) **14** Ran SP% **118.7**
Speed ratings (Par 96):99,98,97,91,90 89,88,87,82,80 76,74,74,73
CSF £77.17 CT £553.41 TOTE £13.00: £3.70, £2.00, £1.80; EX 68.60 Trifecta £136.50 Pool: £286.54 - 1.49 winning tickets..

Owner Brooklands Racing **Bred** G B Turnbull Ltd **Trained** Wysall, Notts

FOCUS

A modest handicap run at an average pace, but very few got into it and the first three pulled well clear. There was a definite bias towards those drawn low with the front five coming from the six lowest stalls.

Diktalex(IRE) Official explanation: trainer said, regarding the improved form shown, filly had benefited from more positive tactics

862 ON THE TURF ON THE 25TH H'CAP — 6f (F)

5:30 (5:30) (Class 6) (0-60,63) 4-Y-0+ **£2,730** (£806; £403) **Stalls** Low

Form RPR

0555 **1** **Piccleyes**[30] 587 5-8-10 52 (b) DeanMcKeown 8 — 57
(M J Polglase) *chsd ldrs: nt clr run over 1f out: led 1f out: rdn out* **20/1**

0024 **2** *1* **Contented (IRE)**[12] 693 4-9-1 57 (p) HayleyTurner 9 — 59
(Mrs L C Jewell) *s.i.s: hdwy u.p over 2f out: ev ch 1f out : styd on* **12/1**

000- **3** *hd* **Mill By The Stream**[196] 5360 4-9-2 58 (p) MickyFenton 4 — 59
(P T Midgley) *chsd ldrs: rdn 1/2-way: ev ch 1f out: styd on u.p* **66/1**

01 **4** *nk* **Bahrain Gold (IRE)**[57] 300 6-8-11 53 (b) DaleGibson 2 — 53
(N P McCormack) *hld up: hdwy over 2f out: rdn and ev ch whn n.m.r 1f out: styd on* **9/1**

424- **5** *hd* **Val De Maal (IRE)**[191] 5469 6-9-4 60 (v) TomEaves 6 — 60
(Miss J A Camacho) *led: rdn: edgd lft and hdd 1f out: styd on same pce* **8/1**

4501 **6** *2 1/2* **Desert Opal**[3] 824 6-9-7 63 6ex TonyCulhane 3 — 55
(D W Chapman) *mid-div: hdwy over 2f out: rdn and ev ch 1f out: no ex ins fnl f* **6/1[3]**

4320 **7** *nk* **Shifty Night (IRE)**[5] 798 5-9-4 60 (v) DarryllHolland 7 — 51
(Mrs C A Dunnett) *chsd ldr: rdn and ev ch whn edgd lft 1f out: no ex* **5/1[2]**

0224 **8** *1/2* **Doctor Dennis (IRE)**[18] 654 9-9-4 60 (v) JimmyQuinn 1 — 50
(J Pearce) *s.s: hld up: n.d* **9/2[1]**

000- **9** *3/4* **Waggledance (IRE)**[232] 4398 4-8-8 53 DanielTudhope(3) 5 — 40
(D Carroll) *chsd ldrs: rdn whn hmpd over 1f out: sn wknd* **20/1**

2435 **10** *1/2* **Pending (IRE)**[9] 734 5-8-10 52 (e) LDettori 11 — 38
(J R Boyle) *s.s: hld up: n.d* **5/1[2]**

-006 **11** *1 1/2* **Attorney**[27] 608 8-8-13 55 RobertWinston 12 — 36
(P D Evans) *sn pushed along: a in rr* **14/1**

500- **12** *1/2* **Drum Dance (IRE)**[171] 5880 4-8-11 53 KimTinkler 10 — 33
(N Tinkler) *dwlt: outpcd* **20/1**

1m 16.66s (-0.24) **Going Correction** -0.125s/f (Stan) **12** Ran SP% **117.0**

Speed ratings (Par 101):96,94,94,94,93 90,90,89,88,87 85,85

CSF £229.07 CT £14702.63 TOTE £19.20: £4.40, £2.80, £12.90; EX 294.70 TRIFECTA Not won. Place 6 £98.62, Place 5 £85.11.

Owner Paul J Dixon **Bred** Mrs M Gutkin **Trained** Babworth, Notts

■ Stewards' Enquiry : Tony Culhane one-day ban: careless riding (Apr 15)

FOCUS

This looked a poor race and there were seven in a line across the track passing the furlong pole. The winning time was also modest, 0.38 seconds slower than the preceding same-class handicap over the same trip restricted to three-year-olds.

Drum Dance(IRE) Official explanation: jockey said gelding did not face kickback

T/Jkpt: Not won. T/Plt: £111.10 to a £1 stake. Pool: £40,964.65. 269.15 winning tickets. T/Qpdt: £34.00 to a £1 stake. Pool: £2,844.70. 61.80 winning tickets. CR

PONTEFRACT (L-H)

Tuesday, April 4

OFFICIAL GOING: Heavy

Wind: Moderate, across

863 YORKSHIRE RACING CLUB MEDIAN AUCTION MAIDEN STKS — 1m 2f 6y

2:20 (2:21) (Class 5) 3-Y-0 **£3,886** (£1,156; £577; £288)

Form RPR

1 **Hero Worship (IRE)** 3-9-3 PhilipRobinson 4 — 76
(M A Jarvis) *a.p: effrt to ld over 2f out: rdn over 1f out: styd on wl* **17/2[3]**

2 *2* **Hernando Royal** 3-9-3 SteveDrowne 5 — 73
(H Morrison) *trckd ldrs: pushed along 4f out: hdwy wl over 2f out: rdn to chal over 1f out: kpt on same pce fnl f* **14/1**

36-4 **3** *8* **Disco Lights**[87] 61 3-8-12 75 LDettori 6 — 54
(D J Daly) *hld up in tch: hdwy to trck ldrs 4f out: effrt and ch wl over 1f out: sn rdn and wknd appr last* **11/4[2]**

0-03 **4** *1* **Zed Candy (FR)**[10] 731 3-9-3 71 MickyFenton 2 — 58
(J T Stimpson) *trckd ldrs on inner: pushed along and outpcd 3f out: styd on u.p appr last* **12/1**

5 *1 1/4* **King Of Rhythm (IRE)** 3-9-0 DanielTudhope(3) 7 — 56
(D Carroll) *trckd ldrs on outer: hdwy and clsoe up over 3f out: rdn along 2f out and sn wknd* **25/1**

0-2 **6** *8* **Raslan**[18] 656 3-9-3 KDarley 1 — 42
(M Johnston) *led: rdn along 3f out: sn hdd & wknd* **10/11[1]**

0- **7** *shd* **The Preacher**[153] 6228 3-9-3 NeilPollard 3 — 42
(J G Given) *a rr* **33/1**

2m 27.4s (13.32) **Going Correction** +1.025s/f (Soft) **7** Ran SP% **110.7**

Speed ratings (Par 98):87,85,79,78,77 70,70

CSF £104.79 TOTE £8.70: £3.30, £5.40; EX 69.70.

Owner Jumeirah Racing **Bred** Duncan A McGregor **Trained** Newmarket, Suffolk

FOCUS

Han-timed. Just the seven runners and these inexperienced maidens had pretty testing ground to contend with. The time was very slow, even allowing for these conditions, but still a race that should produce some winners. A flip start was used to get them underway.

Raslan Official explanation: trainer had no explanation for the poor form shown

864 TERENCE GRADY 70TH BIRTHDAY H'CAP — 6f

2:50 (2:50) (Class 6) (0-65,65) 4-Y-0+ **£3,238** (£963; £481; £240) **Stalls** Low

Form RPR

0052 **1** **Piccolo Prince**[49] 408 5-8-6 53 KDarley 10 — 66
(E J Alston) *in tch: pushed along 1/2-way: hdwy 2f out: rdn to chse ldr and hung bdly lft ins last: kpt on to ld nr fin* **11/2[1]**

05-0 **2** *nk* **Mynd**[82] 96 6-8-6 53 DeanMcKeown 6 — 65
(R M Whitaker) *sn led: rdn clr wl over 1f out: drvn ins last: hdd and no ex nr fin* **16/1**

003- **3** *3* **Word Perfect**[157] 6139 4-9-4 65 DaleGibson 17 — 68+
(M W Easterby) *stdd s and towards rr: hdwy over 2f out: rdn over 1f out: kpt on ins last: nrst fin* **10/1[3]**

000- **4** *1 1/2* **Obe One**[195] 4461 6-8-7 57 SilvestreDeSousa(3) 1 — 56
(D Nicholls) *hld up towards rr: hdwy on inner 2f out: styd on ins last: nrst fin* **28/1**

3000 **5** *2 1/2* **Four Amigos (USA)**[28] 605 5-8-5 52 AdrianTNicholls 16 — 43
(D Nicholls) *chsd ldrs: rideden along 2f out: drvn and kpt on same pce appr last* **10/1[3]**

20-5 **6** *3/4* **Witchelle**[56] 332 5-8-12 59 PaulFessey 8 — 48
(R Craggs) *promiennt: hdwy to chse ldr 2f out: sn rdn and grad wknd fnl f* **25/1**

500- **7** *2 1/2* **Hula Ballew**[177] 5773 6-9-0 61 PhillipMakin 11 — 42+
(M Dods) *dwlt and bhd tl styd on fnl 2f: nrst fin* **16/1**

1022 **8** *2* **Up Tempo (IRE)**[10] 732 8-9-3 64 (b) JamieSpencer 15 — 39
(K A Ryan) *dwlt: towards rr: rdn along and hdwy over 2f out: sn drvn and no imp appr last* **6/1[2]**

00-0 **9** *1 3/4* **Exponential (IRE)**[57] 316 4-9-3 64 (e[1]) SteveDrowne 5 — 34
(S C Williams) *bhd tl styd on fnl 2f* **25/1**

600- **10** *hd* **Hamaasy**[223] 4679 5-7-13 53 KellyHarrison(7) 2 — 22
(D Nicholls) *chsd ldrs on inner: rdn along over 2f out: grad wknd* **33/1**

003- **11** *4* **Bundy**[293] 2590 10-8-10 57 TomEaves 4 — 14
(M Dods) *chsd ldrs: rdn along over 2f out: sn wknd* **12/1**

200- **12** *3* **Tagula Bay (IRE)**[157] 6140 4-9-3 64 DavidAllan 18 — 12
(T D Easterby) *towards rr: hdwy and wd st: rdn wl over 1f out and sn wknd* **16/1**

005- **13** *3/4* **Estoille**[269] 3353 5-8-5 52 (t) PaulHanagan 12 — —
(Mrs S Lamyman) *midfield: pushed along 1/2-way: sn wknd* **25/1**

1205 **14** *2* **Shannon Arms (USA)**[10] 737 5-9-1 62 (p) JoeFanning 3 — 2
(P Howling) *prom: rdn along 1/2-way: sn wknd* **10/1[3]**

320- **15** *1* **King Of Meze (IRE)**[151] 6243 5-8-4 54 PaulMulrennan(3) 7 — —
(J S Wainwright) *a rr* **14/1**

004- **16** *dist* **Maromito (IRE)**[279] 3011 9-8-9 56 RoystonFfrench 14 — —
(R Bastiman) *bhd fr 1/2-way* **50/1**

0424 **17** *1 3/4* **Alexia Rose (IRE)**[34] 552 4-9-2 63 FrancisNorton 9 — —
(A Berry) *chsd ldrs: rdn along over 2f out: sn wknd* **12/1**

1m 23.38s (5.98) **Going Correction** +1.025s/f (Soft) **17** Ran SP% **116.5**

Speed ratings (Par 101):101,100,96,94,91 90,86,84,81,81 76,72,71,68,67 —,—

CSF £79.48 CT £888.71 TOTE £6.20: £1.70, £3.20, £3.20, £3.90; EX 91.80.

Owner The Burlington Partnership **Bred** Theobalds Stud **Trained** Longton, Lancs

FOCUS

A typical early-season sprint handicap and the bare form is likely to be worth little when the ground dries out.

Maromito(IRE) Official explanation: jockey said gelding had no more to give

Alexia Rose(IRE) Official explanation: jockey said filly hung right-handed throughout

865 PONTEFRACT PARK H'CAP — 1m 4y

3:20 (3:21) (Class 3) (0-95,95) 4-Y-0+

£11,217 (£3,358; £1,679; £840; £419; £210) **Stalls** Low

Form RPR

2/1- **1** **Fortunate Isle (USA)**[325] 1700 4-8-7 84 MichaelHills 2 — 95
(B W Hills) *in tch: hdwy on inner 3f out: chsd ldr wl over 1f out: swtchd rt and rdn ent last: kpt on to ld last 100 yds* **10/1**

-511 **2** *2 1/2* **Byron Bay**[24] 632 4-8-5 82 oh4 ow1 TomEaves 3 — 88
(I Semple) *cl up: led 3f out: rdn clr wl over 1f out: edgd lft ins last hdd and no ex last 100 yds* **6/1[3]**

00-0 **3** *2 1/2* **Blue Spinnaker (IRE)**[10] 728 7-8-10 90 PaulMulrennan(3) 5 — 91
(M W Easterby) *hld up towards rr: stdy hdwy on inner over 2f out: styd on ins last: nrst fin* **12/1**

4-24 **4** *shd* **San Antonio**[38] 516 6-8-8 85 (b) MickyFenton 8 — 86
(Mrs P Sly) *cl up: rdn along wl over 2f out: kpt on same pce* **11/2[2]**

210- **5** *3* **Wigwam Willie (IRE)**[150] 6248 4-8-0 84 HelenGarner(7) 10 — 79
(K A Ryan) *chsd ldrs: rdn along wl over 2f out: sn one pce* **20/1**

05-0 **6** *1 3/4* **Freeloader (IRE)**[10] 726 6-8-5 82 PaulHanagan 11 — 73
(R A Fahey) *midfield: hdwy to trck ldrs 3f out: rdn 2f out and sn btn* **12/1**

1/1- **7** *1 1/2* **Focus Group (USA)**[186] 5588 5-8-12 89 GrahamGibbons 6 — 77
(J J Quinn) *chsd ldrs: rdn along wl over 2f out and sn wknd* **6/1[3]**

03-0 **8** *7* **Nero's Return (IRE)**[10] 728 5-8-11 88 JoeFanning 12 — 62
(M Johnston) *a towards rr* **8/1**

042- **9** *1 1/2* **Thunderwing (IRE)**[150] 6248 4-8-8 85 FrancisNorton 1 — 56
(K R Burke) *chsd ldrs: pushed along 1/2-way: sn wknd* **5/1[1]**

00-0 **10** *2* **Primus Inter Pares (IRE)**[10] 728 5-8-6 90 VictoriaBehan(7) 4 — 57
(D Nicholls) *dwlt: a rr* **66/1**

606- **11** *3* **King's Thought**[18] 4821 7-8-13 90 DarryllHolland 9 — 51
(S Gollings) *led: rdn along over 3f out: sn hdd & wknd* **16/1**

641- **12** *5* **El Coto**[311] 2075 6-9-1 95 BenSwarbrick(3) 7 — 46
(E S McMahon) *a rr* **25/1**

1m 51.54s (5.84) **Going Correction** +1.025s/f (Soft) **12** Ran SP% **112.2**

Speed ratings (Par 107):111,108,106,105,102 101,99,92,91,89 86,81

CSF £63.76 CT £726.07 TOTE £11.40: £2.80, £2.30, £4.80; EX 66.10.

Owner Gainsborough Stud **Bred** Gainsborough Stud Management Ltd **Trained** Lambourn, Berks

FOCUS

A reasonable handicap for the grade and they went quite a good pace. The time was fair time for the grade given the conditions.

NOTEBOOK

Fortunate Isle(USA), runner-up to the Group-class Rob Roy on his sole start in 2004 before winning a firm ground maiden at Newbury on his only outing last season, handled the testing ground well enough and defied his 325-day absence to run out a clear-cut winner. He has presumably had some training problems, but is progressive and will be one to have on your side if he stands up to racing. (op 11-1)

Byron Bay, who progressed well to win three of his four starts on sand over the winter, was 4lb out of the handicap on his return to turf (and his rider put up 1lb overweight) but still only 1lb higher than when winning at Wolverhampton on his most recent outing. He would not have minded the ground and looked to have every chance, but was unable to resist the potentially well-handicapped winner's strong challenge, despite having a fitness edge. He has developed into a useful handicapper, and may still be improving, but he will go up in the weights despite having not won. (op 8-1)

Blue Spinnaker(IRE) ◆ stepped up on the form he showed when 13th of 30 in the Lincoln on his reappearance over a trip short of his best. His effort is all the more creditable given he has never won on ground worse than good and, 8lb lower than when last winning, he could be one to keep in mind when stepped back up in trip with conditions to suit. (op 10-1)

San Antonio, in good form on the sand recently, was a little bit below his best returned to turf. He seems best with some cut in the ground, but perhaps this surface was too testing. (op 9-2)

Wigwam Willie(IRE) had the ground in his favour, but may have needed this first run in 150 days. (op 16-1)

Freeloader(IRE) ◆ travelled strongly but did not find as much as had looked likely in the straight and basically needs better ground. He could be worth supporting when conditions come in his favour.

Focus Group(USA), twice a winner for Henry Cecil, was 10lb higher than when gaining the last of those successes on easy ground at Newmarket 186 days previously. Making his debut for a new trainer having been sold at the Horses In Training Sale at Newmarket for 35,000gns, he never featured but may have needed the run and this ground could have been soft enough. (op 5-1)

Thunderwing(IRE) had the ground to suit but never featured on his return from a 150-day break. (op 6-1)

866 JAMAICAN FLIGHT H'CAP — 2m 1f 216y
3:50 (3:50) (Class 5) (0-75,72) 4-Y-0+ **£3,886** (£1,156; £577; £288)

Form				RPR
/0-0	1		**Great As Gold (IRE)**[17] 52 7-9-2 **60** ....(p) TomEaves 6	67
			(B Ellison) *hld up in tch: hdwy over 4f out: led over 2f out: sn rdn and styd on wl* **11/2**[3]	
0/4-	2	3 ½	**Turtle Soup (IRE)**[20] 1851 10-10-0 **72** .... JamieSpencer 8	76
			(T R George) *hld up in tch: hdwy 5f out: led 3f out: sn rdn and hdd over 2f out: drvn and kpt on same pce appr last* **7/2**[1]	
/55-	3	¾	**Ocean Tide**[7] 6239 9-9-6 **64** ....(v) PaulHanagan 9	67
			(R Ford) *led 7f: cl up tl lost pl 3f out: swtchd rt and rdn over 2f out: styd on ins last* **6/1**	
0/4-	4	1 ¼	**Robbo**[17] 5943 12-8-11 **55** .... KDarley 1	57
			(K G Reveley) *in tch: pushed along and outpac ed 5f out: hdwy over 2f out: plugged on u.p appr last* **7/1**	
/22-	5	1	**Totally Scottish**[17] 1299 10-8-2 **53** oh4 .... JamesReveley(7) 7	54
			(K G Reveley) *hld up in rr: hdwy 3f out: rdn and kpt on same pce fnl 2f* **6/1**	
-056	6	30	**Jamaican Flight (USA)**[14] 688 13-8-9 **53** oh23 .... RoystonFfrench 3	24
			(Mrs S Lamyman) *chsd ldrs: lost pl and bhd fnl 6f* **66/1**	
0-32	7	shd	**Step Perfect (USA)**[14] 688 5-8-9 **53** oh4 ....(p) JoeFanning 5	23
			(G M Moore) *prom: effrt to ld briefly and hung lft over 3f out: sn rdn along and wknd* **11/1**	
2112	8	¾	**Tycheros**[3] 832 4-8-8 **60** .... SaleemGolam(3) 4	30
			(S C Williams) *keen: trckd ldng pair tl led after 7f: rdn along and hdd over 3f out: sn wknd* **5/1**[2]	
/02-	9	4	**Farne Isle**[52] 2866 7-9-4 **65** .... PaulMulrennan(3) 2	31
			(G A Harker) *a rr* **16/1**	

4m 27.0s (24.00) **Going Correction** +1.15s/f (Soft)
WFA 4 from 5yo+ 5lb **9** Ran SP% **111.1**
Speed ratings (Par 103):92,90,90,89,89 75,75,75,73
CSF £23.60 CT £113.68 TOTE £7.40: £2.00, £2.10, £1.80; EX 30.40.
Owner Keith Middleton **Bred** Rathasker Stud **Trained** Norton, N Yorks

FOCUS
Hand-timed. A pretty ordinary staying handicap and, with the pace steady owing to the bad ground, the winning time was very moderate. A flip start was used to get them going.
Step Perfect(USA) Official explanation: jockey said gelding hung left in final 4f

867 HIGH-RISE H'CAP — 1m 2f 6y
4:20 (4:20) (Class 3) (0-95,90) 3-Y-0+
£9,348 (£2,799; £1,399; £700; £349; £175)

Form				RPR
122-	1		**London Express (IRE)**[150] 6249 3-8-4 **85** .... RoystonFfrench 6	99
			(M Johnston) *a.p: led 3f out: rdn clr wl over 1f out: styd on strly* **13/2**[3]	
135-	2	8	**Shape Up (IRE)**[373] 740 6-9-3 **79** ....(b) PaulFessey 2	83
			(R Craggs) *in tch: hdwy top chse wnr 2f oyut: sn rdn and no imp* **40/1**	
042-	3	¾	**Dance To My Tune**[164] 6029 5-8-11 **76** oh1 .... PaulMulrennan(3) 3	79
			(M W Easterby) *hld up: hdwy on inner to chse eladers over 2f out: sn rdn and kpt on same pce appr last* **7/1**	
20-3	4	3 ½	**Harvest Warrior**[10] 726 4-9-7 **83** .... DavidAllan 5	80
			(T D Easterby) *trckd ldrs: effrt 3f out: sn rdn and kpt on same pce* **11/2**[2]	
040-	5	7	**Go Tech**[126] 6459 6-10-0 **90** .... GrahamGibbons 9	75
			(T D Easterby) *led to 1/2-way: sn pushed along and wknd over 3f out* **25/1**	
00-2	6	½	**Danehill Willy (IRE)**[8] 763 4-10-0 **90** .... LDettori 4	74
			(N A Callaghan) *hld up towards rr: sme hdwy on outer 2f out: sn rdn and no further prog* **11/2**[2]	
1-33	7	nk	**Bobby Charles**[43] 463 5-9-5 **81** .... JamieSpencer 10	65
			(Dr J D Scargill) *plld hrd: hld up in rr: sme hdwy over 2f out: sn rdn and nvr a factor* **7/2**[1]	
412-	8	6	**Toldo (IRE)**[150] 6250 4-9-10 **86** .... DarryllHolland 1	59
			(G M Moore) *in tch: pushed along over 4f out: sn wknd* **7/1**	
062-	9	22	**Instructor**[179] 5715 5-9-6 **82** .... PaulHanagan 7	18
			(R A Fahey) *keen: cl up tl eld 1/2-way: rdn along and hdd 3f out: sn wknd* **20/1**	
162-	10	12	**Magic Sting**[198] 5339 5-9-5 **81** .... HayleyTurner 8	—
			(M L W Bell) *prom: rdn along 4f out: wknd over 2f out* **10/1**	

2m 23.5s (9.42) **Going Correction** +1.15s/f (Soft)
WFA 3 from 4yo+ 19lb **10** Ran SP% **111.5**
Speed ratings (Par 107):108,101,101,98,92 92,91,87,69,59
CSF £233.72 CT £1818.78 TOTE £8.10: £3.00, £9.40, £2.30; EX 325.20.
Owner Leung Kai Fai & Vincent Leung **Bred** Denis McDonnell **Trained** Middleham Moor, N Yorks
■ Stewards' Enquiry : Jamie Spencer one-day ban: failed to line up in draw order (Apr 15)

FOCUS
Hand-timed. Several of these were making their reappearance, and a few did not seem to act on the heavy ground, so perhaps not that strong a race for the grade, but still a very impressive performance from the only three-year-old in the line up London Express. The third and final race on the card in which a flip start was used to get them underway.

NOTEBOOK
London Express(IRE) ◆, who showed useful form at both seven furlongs and a mile at two, got this longer trip well and showed himself to be on a very fair mark with an impressive success on his return from a 150-day break. While distances can be exaggerated in ground this testing, this was still a smart effort from the only three-year-old in the line up and he looks very useful. (op 6-1)
Shape Up(IRE) ran well over a trip that is perhaps short of his best on his return from a 373-day absence and is open to improvement.
Dance To My Tune, the only mare in the line up, had the ground to suit on her return from a 164-day break and ran with promise. (op 9-1)
Harvest Warrior had never previously raced beyond a mile and lacked a change of pace. (op 6-1)
Go Tech was well held on his return from a 126-day break and probably wants better ground.
Danehill Willy(IRE) failed to run anywhere near the form he showed when second on the Polytrack at Kempton on his reappearance and was disappointing, especially considering he won on soft ground as a juvenile. (op 9-2)
Bobby Charles's form figures on ground soft or worse going into this were 1121, and he had been in good form on the sand recently, so this has to be considered most disappointing. (op 10-3 tchd 4-1 in a place)

868 TOM PAWSON'S BIRTHDAY MAIDEN FILLIES' STKS — 6f
4:50 (4:51) (Class 5) 3-Y-0 **£4,533** (£1,348; £674; £336) Stalls Low

Form				RPR
0-	1		**Apply Dapply**[169] 5945 3-9-0 .... SteveDrowne 2	76
			(H Morrison) *chsd ldrs: rdn along over 1f out: styd on wl u.p ins last to ld nr fin* **7/2**[2]	
0-00	2	nk	**Sunderland Echo (IRE)**[6] 797 3-9-0 57 .... TomEaves 5	75
			(B Ellison) *led: hdd over 2f out and sn rdn: rallied to ld to ld ins last: sn drvn: hdd and no ex nr fin* **16/1**	
240-	3	1 ¾	**Shes Minnie**[263] 3516 3-9-0 69 .... FergusSweeney 4	70
			(J G M O'Shea) *cl up: led over 2f out:. sn rdn: drvn and hdd ins last: one pce* **7/1**[3]	
40-	4	2	**Lisfannon**[148] 6282 3-9-0 .... MichaelHills 8	64
			(B W Hills) *trckd ldrs: effrt and hung lft wl over 1f out: kpt on same pce* **10/3**[1]	
22-6	5	5	**Halfwaytoparadise**[34] 551 3-9-0 72 ....(v[1]) JamieSpencer 7	49
			(M L W Bell) *chsd ldrs: rdn wl over 1f out and sn btn* **10/3**[1]	
	6	6	**Cordelia** 3-8-7 .... SladeO'Hara(7) 9	31
			(B W Hills) *s.i.s: a rr* **9/1**	
000-	7	shd	**Jenny Soba**[191] 5489 3-8-7 60 .... MichaelJStainton(7) 3	31
			(R M Whitaker) *bhd fr 1/2-way* **8/1**	
00-	8	13	**Whistleupthewind**[251] 3846 3-9-0 .... JoeFanning 1	—
			(J M P Eustace) *a rr: bhd fr 1/2-way* **33/1**	

1m 23.62s (6.22) **Going Correction** +1.15s/f (Soft) **8** Ran SP% **110.8**
Speed ratings (Par 95):104,103,101,98,91 83,83,66
CSF £52.43 TOTE £4.70: £1.50, £3.40, £2.20; EX 58.20.
Owner L A Garfield **Bred** N R Shields And K R Burke **Trained** East Ilsley, Berks

FOCUS
The runner-up had an official rating of just 57, but was unexposed over this trip and may have improved, although this was still a modest maiden. The winning time, though, was very decent for a race of its type given the ground.

869 BETFAIR.COM APPRENTICE SERIES (ROUND ONE) H'CAP — 1m 4f 8y
5:20 (5:20) (Class 5) (0-75,72) 4-Y-0+ **£3,886** (£1,156; £577; £288) Stalls Low

Form				RPR
0231	1		**Isa'Af (IRE)**[15] 675 7-9-1 **71** .... TolleyDean(3) 3	78
			(P W Hiatt) *trckd ldrs: hdwy on inner to ld over 2f out: rdn clr over 1f out: styd on* **9/2**[1]	
600/	2	2	**Middlethorpe**[17] 6047 9-8-2 **60** ....(b) AdeleRothery(5) 4	64
			(M W Easterby) *hld up: hdwy on inenr 4f out: rdn to chse wnr over 1f out: kpt on* **16/1**	
3124	3	5	**Greenbelt**[28] 610 5-9-5 **72** .... ThomasO'Brien 6	69
			(G M Moore) *hld up in tch: hdwy over 2f out: rdn and egded lft over 1f out: kpt on same pce under preessure ins last* **6/1**[3]	
600-	4	2 ½	**Mceldowney**[179] 5720 4-8-13 **72** .... WilliamCarson(5) 8	66
			(M Johnston) *trckd ldrs: effrt over 2f out and ev ch: sn rdn and wknd over 1f out* **11/2**[2]	
650-	5	1 ½	**Just Waz (USA)**[139] 6368 4-7-12 **59** oh3 ow1 .... DeanHeslop(7) 2	51
			(R M Whitaker) *cl up: led 1/2-way: rdn along and hdd over 2f out: drvn and wknd over 1f out* **11/2**[2]	
100-	6	3 ½	**Platinum Charmer (IRE)**[123] 6478 6-8-5 **63** .... PatrickDonaghy(5) 7	50
			(K R Burke) *hld up in rr: hdwy and in tch 4f out: rdn wl over 2f out and no imp* **10/1**	
000-	7	5	**Melodian**[185] 5620 11-8-3 **63** oh3 ow5 ....(b) ShaunBushby(7) 1	50+
			(M Brittain) *led to 1/2-way: cl up tl rdn and wknd 2f out* **20/1**	
253-	8	7	**Ego Trip**[154] 6218 5-8-8 **61** ....(b) RonanKeogh 5	31
			(M W Easterby) *chsd ldrs: rdn along over 2f out: sn wknd* **6/1**[3]	
/00-	9	1	**October Mist (IRE)**[32] 2261 12-8-12 **68** .... JamesReveley(3) 10	37
			(K G Reveley) *chsd ldrs 4f: sn lost pl and bhd fr 1/2-way* **10/1**	
550-	10	dist	**Pont Neuf (IRE)**[46] 5890 6-8-5 **58** oh3 ....(t) KevinGhunowa 9	—
			(A Crook) *chsd ldrs 4f: sn lost pl and bhd fr 1/2-way* **12/1**	

2m 53.67s (13.37) **Going Correction** +1.15s/f (Soft)
WFA 4 from 5yo+ 1lb **10** Ran SP% **114.0**
Speed ratings (Par 103):101,99,96,94,93 91,88,83,82,—
CSF £75.72 CT £433.35 TOTE £4.70: £1.60, £4.40, £1.90; EX 81.30 Place 6 £3,087.44, Place 5 £213.49.
Owner Phil Kelly **Bred** T Monaghan **Trained** Hook Norton, Oxon

FOCUS
A fair apprentice handicap in which Tolley Dean was seen to good effect in guiding home Isa'Af.
Pont Neuf(IRE) Official explanation: jockey said mare was never travelling
T/Plt: £2,026.70 to a £1 stake. Pool: £48,032.30. 17.30 winning tickets. T/Qpdt: £134.70 to a £1 stake. Pool: £5,497.90. 30.20 winning tickets. JR

856 SOUTHWELL (L-H)
Tuesday, April 4

OFFICIAL GOING: Standard
Wind: Moderate, half-behind Weather: Overcast, wintry showers race 4 onwards

870 GOLF AND RACING MAIDEN CLAIMING STKS — 5f (F)
2:30 (2:30) (Class 7) 3-Y-0+ **£1,365** (£403; £201) Stalls High

Form				RPR
404-	1		**Axis Shield (IRE)**[112] 6569 3-8-8 50 .... J-PGuillambert 4	42
			(J G Portman) *chsd ldr: led over 1f out: pushed along: readily* **9/2**[1]	
0005	2	1 ¼	**Saxon Star (IRE)**[7] 779 3-8-10 40 ....(v) HayleyTurner 3	40
			(M D I Usher) *chsd ldrs: outpcd over 3f out: hrd rdn and hdwy over 1f out: edgd lft: no imp* **5/1**[2]	
0640	3	nk	**Katie Killane**[6] 789 4-9-3 40 .... AlanDaly 9	40
			(M Wellings) *hld up: hdwy over 2f out: sn chsng ldrs: kpt on same pce fnl f* **9/2**[1]	
0060	4	1 ¾	**Eeshee**[14] 687 3-8-5 45 ....(v[1]) EddieAhern 2	28
			(S L Keightley) *led tl over 1f out: wknd ins last* **6/1**[3]	
4-66	5	1 ¼	**Fayrz Please (IRE)**[7] 783 5-9-5 35 .... StephenDonohoe(5) 6	37
			(M C Chapman) *chsd ldrs: outpcd over 3f out: kpt on fnl f* **15/2**	
0-00	6	6	**Temple Belle Xpres**[8] 769 4-9-5 35 ....(b) PaulEddery 7	11
			(S R Bowring) *dwlt: sn detached in rr stands' side: sme late hdwy: nvr on terms* **25/1**	
0066	7	2	**Moraadi**[7] 786 3-8-3 35 ....(b[1]) MatthewHenry 8	—
			(D W Chapman) *chsd ldrs: outpcd over 2f out: sn lost pl* **33/1**	
420-	8	6	**True Valentine**[273] 3208 3-8-8 49 .... RobertWinston 5	—
			(A Berry) *chsd ldrs: lost pl over 3f out: sn bhd* **6/1**[3]	
000-	9	½	**Dispol Lady**[215] 4886 3-8-8 49 .... LeeEnstone 1	—
			(P T Midgley) *chsd ldrs: hung lft over 3f out: sn lost pl* **8/1**	

59.86 secs (-0.44) **Going Correction** -0.175s/f (Stan)
WFA 3 from 4yo+ 11lb **9** Ran SP% **111.3**
Speed ratings (Par 97):96,94,93,90,88 79,75,66,65
CSF £25.43 TOTE £5.80: £1.10, £2.80, £1.30; EX 23.20 Trifecta £55.60 Pool: £328.34 - 4.19 winning tickets..The winner was claimed by M. C. Chapman for £5,000.
Owner Steve Evans **Bred** Mrs P Grubb **Trained** Compton, Berks

FOCUS
A bad race even by maiden claiming standards, but the winner has some untapped potential.
Dispol Lady Official explanation: jockey said filly bled from the nose

871 DINE IN THE QUEEN MOTHER RESTAURANT BANDED STKS 1m 3f (F)
3:00 (3:00) (Class 7) 4-Y-0+ £1,876 (£554; £277) Stalls Low

Form RPR

30-5 **1** **Nicozetto (FR)**[27] 423 6-8-10 46 ow1 (b[1]) DNolan(3) 4 53
(N Wilson) *t.k.h: smooth hdwy to go 2nd over 2f out: shkn up to ld jst ins last: sn clr* **15/2**

000- **2** *4* **Trysting Grove (IRE)**[185] 5620 5-8-11 45 DarrenWilliams 10 45
(E G Bevan) *tk str hold: trckd ldrs: wnt 2nd 7f out: led over 3f out: hdd jst ins last: no ch w wnr* **16/1**

0463 **3** *1 1/4* **Simply The Guest (IRE)**[7] 788 7-8-11 40 (vt) KimTinkler 3 43
(N Tinkler) *chsd ldrs: hrd drvn 5f out: one pce fnl 2f* **6/1[3]**

0451 **4** *1/2* **York Cliff**[7] 785 8-9-8 50 EddieAhern 9 53
(W M Brisbourne) *in rr: hrd drvn over 4f out: sn outpcd: styd on fnl 2f* **9/4[1]**

0565 **5** *2* **Starcross Maid**[15] 682 4-8-11 45 TonyCulhane 7 39
(J F Coupland) *chsd ldrs: one pce fnl 3f* **8/1**

4511 **6** *hd* **Dextrous**[7] 788 9-9-3 45 (p) LeeEnstone 1 45
(P T Midgley) *led: qcknd 5f out: hdd over 3f out: wknd over 1f out* **7/2[2]**

-06 **7** *1/2* **Kalishka (IRE)**[16] 525 5-8-11 45 (t) RobertWinston 5 38+
(R Allan) *hld up: effrt over 3f out: sn outpcd: kpt on fnl 2f* **6/1[3]**

400- **8** *23* **Money Hills**[183] 5652 4-8-4 35 KirstyMilczarek(7) 6 1
(Mrs C A Dunnett) *chsd ldrs: lost pl over 4f out: sn bhd: t.o* **80/1**

2m 27.65s (-1.25) **Going Correction** -0.225s/f (Stan) 8 Ran SP% **111.6**
Speed ratings (Par 97):95,92,91,90,89 89,88,72
CSF £109.31 TOTE £7.20: £2.40, £5.80, £3.00; EX 381.00 TRIFECTA Not won..
Owner Malcom Wilson **Bred** Classic Breeding S R L **Trained** Upper Helmsley, N Yorks

FOCUS
No pace for the first three-quarters of a mile. An ordinary banded race rated through the third.

872 BOOK TICKETS ON LINE BANDED STKS 5f (F)
3:30 (3:30) (Class 7) 4-Y-0+ £1,876 (£554; £277) Stalls High

Form RPR

000- **1** **Sharp Hat**[248] 3959 12-8-11 45 TonyCulhane 5 47
(D W Chapman) *trckd ldrs: effrt 2f out: r.o to ld last 75yds* **16/1**

1315 **2** *1/2* **Percy Douglas**[1] 858 6-8-13 48 (bt) AnnStokell(7) 7 54
(Miss A Stokell) *led: hdd and no ex wl ins last* **5/1[2]**

1400 **3** *1* **Shirley Oaks (IRE)**[1] 858 8-8-6 47 JemmaMarshall(7) 1 44
(Miss Z C Davison) *chsd ldrs on wd outside: outpcd over 3f out: styd on wl appr fnl f* **16/1**

0335 **4** *1/2* **Eternally**[6] 789 4-8-11 45 (p) EddieAhern 9 40
(R M H Cowell) *chsd ldrs: shkn up over 2f out: kpt on fnl f* **8/1[3]**

2042 **5** *1 1/4* **Boanerges (IRE)**[7] 782 9-9-2 50 RobertWinston 3 41
(J M Bradley) *in tch: sn drvn along: outpcd over 2f out: swtchd rt over 1f out: kpt on* **1/1[1]**

5-60 **6** *1* **Off Hire**[63] 260 10-8-11 40 (b[1]) RobbieFitzpatrick 4 32
(C Smith) *sn drvn along: sn chsng ldrs: one pce fnl 2f* **33/1**

0/0- **7** *3/4* **Sowerby**[203] 5207 4-8-13 50 DNolan(3) 6 35
(M Brittain) *s.i.s: kpt on fnl 2f: nvr nr ldrs* **11/1**

35-4 **8** *1* **So Sober (IRE)**[6] 789 8-8-8 40 PatrickMathers(3) 2 26
(D Shaw) *chsd ldrs on outer: outpcd over 3f out: n.d after* **14/1**

-004 **9** *3 1/2* **Mr Spliffy (IRE)**[7] 782 7-8-6 35 (b) StephenDonohoe(5) 8 14
(M C Chapman) *s.s: edgd lft and a detached in last* **14/1**

59.68 secs (-0.62) **Going Correction** -0.175s/f (Stan) 9 Ran SP% **114.2**
Speed ratings (Par 97):97,96,94,93,91 90,89,87,81
CSF £92.88 TOTE £27.50: £5.10, £1.80, £3.30; EX 141.70 TRIFECTA Not won..
Owner Miss N F Thesiger **Bred** Littleton Stud **Trained** Stillington, N Yorks

FOCUS
The winner was back to something like his best after an absence, the runner-up ran to form for the second day running.
Mr Spliffy(IRE) Official explanation: jockey said gelding anticipated the start and hit the gates

873 EXPERIENCE NOTTINGHAMSHIRE BANDED STKS 6f (F)
4:00 (4:01) (Class 7) 4-Y-0+ £1,215 (£1,215; £277) Stalls Low

Form RPR

1020 **1** **Penel (IRE)**[7] 784 5-8-13 47 (p) LeeEnstone 7 52
(P T Midgley) *w ldr: hung lft and led over 2f out: hrd rdn and jnd on line* **8/1**

44-1 **1** *dht* **Bahamian Bay**[7] 782 4-9-0 45 DanielTudhope(3) 6 56+
(M Brittain) *stdd s: sn trcking ldrs: effrt on outside over 2f out: r.o fnl f to force dead heat on line* **7/2[1]**

2123 **3** *hd* **Mount Royale (IRE)**[7] 784 8-9-1 49 (v) KimTinkler 5 53
(N Tinkler) *chsd ldrs: hrd rdn and upsides fnl f: no ex nr line* **4/1[2]**

0006 **4** *1/2* **Ace Club**[14] 691 5-8-11 40 (b) TonyHamilton 4 48
(J Hetherton) *led tl over 2f out: hrd rdn and no ex ins last* **11/1**

0-03 **5** *3* **Grand View**[8] 766 10-8-11 40 (p) RobertWinston 3 39
(J R Weymes) *trckd ldrs: outpcd over 2f out: kpt on fnl f* **11/2[3]**

00-6 **6** *1 1/2* **Wolfman**[36] 533 4-8-11 50 (p) MarkLawson(5) 9 39
(D W Barker) *w ldrs: effrt over 3f out: wknd over 1f out* **8/1**

3100 **7** *5* **Straffan (IRE)**[14] 691 4-8-7 46 (b) MarcHalford(5) 1 20
(J Hetherton) *swvd rt s: in tch: rdn over 2f out: sn btn* **9/1**

0-00 **8** *nk* **Indian Gem**[8] 768 5-8-6 45 ow2 AnnStokell(7) 10 21
(A J Chamberlain) *rrd s: hld up: effrt over 3f out: sn outpcd* **25/1**

0-46 **9** *3 1/2* **Karashino (IRE)**[66] 232 4-9-0 48 (p) RobbieFitzpatrick 2 11
(Mrs L Williamson) *s.i.s and hmpd s: a detached in last* **8/1**

1m 15.75s (-1.15) **Going Correction** -0.225s/f (Stan) 9 Ran SP% **113.1**
Speed ratings (Par 97): **98,98,97,97,93 91,84,84,79**WIN: Bahamian Bay £2.50, Penel £3.70. PL: Bahamian Bay £1.80, Penel £1.60, Mount Royale £1.10. EX: BB/P £43.90, P/BB £30.50. CSF: BB/P £15.53, P/BB £17.69. TRIF: BB/P/MR £71.20 - 2.34 winning tickets, P/BB/MR £101.00 - 1.65 winning tickets. Pool: £469.66.27
Owner M E Elsworthy **Bred** M Ervine **Trained** Westow, N Yorks.
Owner Mel Brittain **Bred** The National Stud **Trained** Warthill, N Yorks
■ Stewards' Enquiry : Tony Hamilton four-day ban: used whip with excessive force (Apr 15-18)

FOCUS
A strong gallop and the form looks sound.
Penel(IRE) Official explanation: trainer said, regarding the improved form shown, gelding is a temperamental type who consented to show his best form today
Indian Gem Official explanation: jockey said mare missed the break

874 HOSPITALITY PACKAGES AVAILABLE TRI-BANDED STKS 7f (F)
4:30 (4:36) (Class 7) 3-Y-0 £1,876 (£554; £277) Stalls Low

Form RPR

0023 **1** **Beginners Luck (IRE)**[7] 786 3-8-6 40 DanielTudhope(3) 3 40
(D Carroll) *t.k.h in raer: effrt over 3f out: styd on to ld last 50yds: all out* **6/1[3]**

-001 **2** *hd* **Dylan (IRE)**[7] 786 3-9-6 45 KimTinkler 11 50
(N Tinkler) *trckd ldrs: effrt 3f out: slt ld 1f out: hdd and no ex wl ins last* **7/2[1]**

0-23 **3** *1/2* **Silver Nun**[14] 690 3-8-9 45 DuranFentiman(5) 5 43
(T D Easterby) *drvn along thrght: w ldrs: kpt on to r upsides ins last: no ex* **7/1**

00-6 **4** *2* **October Sun**[10] 735 3-8-5 35 ow1 (p) BrianReilly 1 29
(Miss D Mountain) *reluctant and sn wl detached in last: hdwy 2f out: styd on ins last* **16/1**

4600 **5** *nk* **Sweet Cherokee**[6] 790 3-8-4 40 (be[1]) MarcHalford(5) 10 32
(C N Kellett) *t.k.h: led on outer: hrd rdn and hung lft over 2f out: hdd 1f out: fdd* **40/1**

00-0 **6** *1* **Royal Song**[6] 790 3-8-11 45 PatrickMathers(3) 9 34
(D Shaw) *swtchd lft after s: outpcd and drvn over 4f out: kpt on fnl 2f* **28/1**

00-0 **7** *nk* **Alarm Call**[14] 690 3-9-0 45 FergalLynch 6 33
(T D Easterby) *trckd ldrs: wknd appr fnl f* **40/1**

00-2 **8** *1 1/4* **Bertie Bear**[6] 790 3-8-9 40 (vt) EddieAhern 4 25
(G G Margarson) *trckd ldrs: drvn over 4f out:m edgd rt over 1f out: sn btn* **4/1[2]**

0-50 **9** *2 1/2* **Spasiba**[31] 584 3-9-0 45 (v[1]) RobbieFitzpatrick 2 24
(Mrs L Williamson) *drvn along to chse ldrs: wknd over 1f out* **9/1**

0-02 **10** *1/2* **Cuesta Canyon (IRE)**[7] 786 3-8-9 40 RobertWinston 8 17
(M J Polglase) *t.k.h: trckd ldrs: effrt on outside over 2f out: lost pl over 1f out* **4/1[2]**

1m 31.53s (0.73) **Going Correction** -0.225s/f (Stan) 10 Ran SP% **113.2**
Speed ratings (Par 92):86,85,85,82,82 81,81,79,76,76
CSF £26.05 TOTE £9.00: £1.80, £1.20, £3.10; EX 33.90 Trifecta £97.70 Pool: £501.13 - 3.64 winning tickets..
Owner Leslie Laverty **Bred** Eamon D Delany **Trained** Warthill, N Yorks
■ Stewards' Enquiry : Duran Fentiman three-day ban: used whip with excessive frequency (Apr 15-17)
Brian Reilly three-day ban: weighed in 3lb heavier than he weighed out (Apr 15-17)
Marc Halford three-day ban: used whip with excessive frequency and down the shoulder in the forehand position (Apr 15-17)

FOCUS
A moderate time, even for a race like this. Poor stuff rated through the runner-up.

875 SPONSOR A RACE AT SOUTHWELL BANDED STKS 1m (F)
5:00 (5:01) (Class 7) 4-Y-0+ £1,876 (£554; £277) Stalls Low

Form RPR

-444 **1** **Legal Lover (IRE)**[19] 648 4-8-4 45 RussellKennemore(7) 3 53
(R Hollinshead) *led after 1f: styd on wl u.p fnl 2f: hld on wl* **5/1[1]**

0500 **2** *1* **Ming Vase**[37] 526 4-8-11 45 LeeEnstone 9 51
(P T Midgley) *trckd ldrs: rdn and hung lft over 1f out: no ex ins last* **16/1**

0020 **3** *1* **La Musique**[8] 768 4-8-11 45 TonyCulhane 12 49
(P J McBride) *trckd ldrs on outer: effrt 2f out: nt qckn fnl f* **11/1**

5362 **4** *hd* **Dexileos (IRE)**[6] 793 7-8-8 45 (t) NeilChalmers(3) 8 49
(David Pinder) *trckd ldrs: styd far side: edgd rt and kpt on same pce fnl f* **11/2[2]**

3001 **5** *5* **Elms Schoolboy**[6] 793 4-9-3 45 (b) J-PGuillambert 5 45
(P Howling) *s.s: sn chsng ldrs on outer: edgd lft and wknd over 1f out* **7/1[3]**

005- **6** *1* **Cottingham (IRE)**[48] 5381 5-8-6 45 StephenDonohoe(5) 11 37
(M C Chapman) *s.s: hdwy over 2f out: nvr nr ldrs* **5/1[1]**

-004 **7** *shd* **Tirailleur (IRE)**[14] 689 6-8-11 45 (v) FergalLynch 2 36
(J R Boyle) *s.i.s: sme hdwy over 2f out: wknd fnl f* **8/1**

2-40 **8** *6* **Dunnett Again (IRE)**[27] 618 5-8-11 40 (b) BrianReilly 10 24
(Mrs C A Dunnett) *led 1f: chsd ldrs: rdn over 4f out: lost pl over 1f out* **25/1**

206- **9** *5* **Ginger Cookie**[112] 6572 4-8-11 40 PaulEddery 6 14
(B Smart) *sn drvn along: chsd ldrs: lost pl over 3f out* **16/1**

0-04 **10** *8* **Sabo Prince**[6] 793 4-8-11 40 (b[1]) RobertWinston 1 —
(J M Bradley) *s.i.s: hdwy and in tch over 4f out: lost pl over 2f out* **10/1**

0/0- **11** *28* **Last Chapter (IRE)**[333] 1514 4-8-11 45 EddieAhern 4 —
(C A Dwyer) *rr-div: t.o 3f out* **16/1**

00-0 **12** *3* **Shamrock Tea**[7] 782 5-8-11 45 TonyHamilton 7 —
(M E Sowersby) *in tch on outer: lost pl over 4f out: t.o 3f out* **66/1**

1m 42.83s (-1.77) **Going Correction** -0.225s/f (Stan) 12 Ran SP% **112.7**
Speed ratings (Par 97):99,98,97,96,91 90,90,84,79,71 43,40
CSF £80.78 TOTE £6.40: £2.90, £9.60, £4.00; EX 76.80 TRIFECTA Not won..
Owner Tim Leadbeater **Bred** Ballyhane Stud **Trained** Upper Longdon, Staffs
■ Stewards' Enquiry : Russell Kennemore three-day ban: used whip with excessive frequency (Apr 15-17)

FOCUS
An ordinary gallop but the form, rated through the first three, looks sound.
Elms Schoolboy Official explanation: jockey said gelding lost a shoe and hung left-handed
Tirailleur(IRE) Official explanation: jockey said mare was never travelling
Sabo Prince Official explanation: jockey said gelding hung left-handed
Last Chapter(IRE) Official explanation: jockey said gelding had no more to give

876 SEE YOU ON THE 7TH BANDED STKS 6f (F)
5:30 (5:32) (Class 7) 4-Y-0+ £1,876 (£554; £277) Stalls Low

Form RPR

3402 **1** **Misty Princess**[8] 766 4-8-11 45 RobbieFitzpatrick 9 47
(M J Attwater) *in rr: hdwy on wd outside 2f out: styd on wl ins last: led nr fin* **11/2[2]**

0062 **2** *nk* **Union Jack Jackson (IRE)**[14] 691 4-8-11 45 (b) MickyFenton 6 46+
(J G Given) *trckd ldrs: led 2f out: hung fire ins last: hrd rdn and hdd nr fin* **5/2[1]**

-003 **3** *nk* **Sergeant Slipper**[37] 529 9-8-11 40 (v) EddieAhern 10 46
(C Smith) *s.s: hdwy over 2f out: styd on strly ins last* **8/1**

0400 **4** *1/2* **Cleveland Way**[21] 638 6-8-8 40 (v) DanielTudhope(3) 11 44
(D Carroll) *led: hdd 2f out: kpt on ins last* **18/1**

2206 **5** *1/2* **A Teen**[8] 766 8-8-11 45 J-PGuillambert 12 43
(P Howling) *in tch on outer: effrt over 2f out: hung lft over 1f out: kpt on ins last* **14/1**

2320 **6** *1 3/4* **Obe Bold (IRE)**[6] 789 5-8-11 45 RobertWinston 2 37
(A Berry) *chsd ldrs: one pce fnl 2f* **13/2[3]**

000 **7** *1 3/4* **Princess Arwen**[8] 766 4-8-11 45 (p) FrankieMcDonald 5 32
(Mrs Barbara Waring) *in rr: kpt on fnl 2f: nvr nr ldrs* **40/1**

02-0 **8** *2 1/2* **Fox Covert (IRE)**[7] 782 5-8-11 45 (p) FergalLynch 7 25
(D W Barker) *w ldr: edgd lft over 4f out: wknd over 1f out* **14/1**

0400 **9** *nk* **Massey**[7] 784 10-8-6 45 DuranFentiman(5) 8 24
(C R Dore) *in rr: effrt on outside over 2f out: nvr nr ldrs* **16/1**

0000 **10** *1 1/4* **Cheeney Basin (IRE)**[51] 388 8-8-6 35 StephenDonohoe(5) 3 20
(M C Chapman) *s.i.s: nvr on terms* **66/1**

0-05 **11** ½ **Laurel Dawn**[7] [782] 8-8-11 35 (b) PaulEddery 4 18
(C N Kellett) *trckd ldrs: t.k.h: lost pl over 4f out: n.d after* **33/1**
640- **12** *shd* **Tiny Tim (IRE)**[106] [6613] 8-8-4 40 (b) JamesRogers(7) 14 18
(A M Balding) *racd wd: a in rr* **33/1**
00-5 **13** 1 ½ **Roko**[15] [674] 4-8-6 35 (b) MarcHalford(5) 1 14
(S R Bowring) *chsd ldrs: hmpd over 4f out: lost pl over 2f out* **50/1**
0043 **14** 2 ½ **Headland (USA)**[8] [768] 8-8-11 45 (be) TonyCulhane 13 6
(D W Chapman) *racd wd: a towards rr* **8/1**
1m 16.31s (-0.59) **Going Correction** -0.225s/f (Stan) **14** Ran SP% **115.8**
Speed ratings (Par 97):94,93,93,92,91 89,87,83,83,81 81,81,79,75
CSF £18.02 TOTE £7.10: £1.80, £1.10, £3.30; EX 25.20 Trifecta £47.00 Pool: £314.37 - 4.74 winning tickets. Place 6 £257.01, Place 5 £173.88 .
Owner Mrs M Tanner **Bred** G L And Mrs Tanner **Trained** Wysall, Notts
■ Stewards' Enquiry : Fergal Lynch four-day ban: careless riding (Apr 15-18)

FOCUS
The first five were stacked up at the line. The form looks weak and the race has been rated around the winner.
T/Plt: £1,141.70 to a £1 stake. Pool: £43,716.85. 27.95 winning tickets. T/Qpdt: £37.00 to a £1 stake. Pool: £4,372.50. 87.30 winning tickets. WG

WARWICK (L-H)

Tuesday, April 4

OFFICIAL GOING: Good to soft (soft in places)
Wind: Light, against Weather: Fine

877 RACING UK (S) STKS 5f
2:10 (2:11) (Class 6) 2-Y-O **£3,238** (£963; £481; £240) **Stalls** Low

Form RPR
0 **1** **Alittleriskie (IRE)**[11] [707] 2-8-6 LPKeniry 2 50
(J S Moore) *s.i.s: sn chsng ldrs: rdn over 2f out: lft in ld ins fnl f: jst hld on* **6/1**[3]
66 **2** *shd* **Sad Times (IRE)**[8] [760] 2-7-13 LiamJones(7) 3 50
(W G M Turner) *sn outpcd: rdn 3f out: hdwy over 1f out: r.o wl and edgd lft ins fnl f: jst failed* **7/1**
0 **3** ¾ **Afric Star**[17] [663] 2-8-7 ow1 ShaneKelly 7 48
(P D Evans) *chsd ldrs: rdn 3f out: kpt on ins fnl f* **4/1**[2]
5 **4** 1 **Granny Peel (IRE)**[8] [760] 2-8-6 NCallan 1 43+
(K A Ryan) *led to post: led: rdn over 2f out: 3 l clr whn hung bdly rt jst over 1f out: swvd bdly rt and hdd ins fnl f: nt rcvr* **10/3**[1]
0 **5** 1 **All Talk**[8] [760] 2-8-6 ChrisCatlin 6 39
(I A Wood) *w ldr: rdn over 2f out: ev ch jst ins fnl f: sn edgd rt: nt qckn* **25/1**
5 **6** 2 **Flying Lion**[10] [727] 2-8-6 TQuinn 4 35+
(M R Channon) *tried to unseat rdr and wnt rt sn after s: rdn and hdwy over 2f out: swvd bdly rt ins fnl f: nt rcvr* **4/1**[2]
7 *nk* **Sardis Road** 2-8-8 RobertMiles(3) 5 34+
(W G M Turner) *s.s: sn carried rt: rdn and hdwy over 2f out: edgd rt over 1f out: eased whn btn ins fnl f* **9/1**
8 2 **Mamalini** 2-8-6 MartinDwyer 8 21
(J Gallagher) *wnt rt s: a bhd* **16/1**
66.62 secs (6.42) **Going Correction** +0.725s/f (Yiel) **8** Ran SP% **109.6**
Speed ratings (Par 90):77,76,75,74,72 69,68,65
CSF £43.11 TOTE £6.90: £1.80, £2.70, £2.00; EX 35.90.There was no bid for the winner.
Owner Miss Karen Theobald **Bred** Stanley Moore Bloodstock **Trained** Upper Lambourn, Berks
■ Stewards' Enquiry : L P Keniry three-day ban: used whip with excessive frequency (Apr 15-17)

FOCUS
A bad race and a very dramatic one with several of these youngsters either swerving or hanging badly at various stages of the contest. The winning time was very moderate, even for a race like this, 1.9 seconds slower than the following fillies' maiden.

NOTEBOOK
Alittleriskie(IRE) was dropping in class and managed to land the gamble, but only by the skin of her teeth and the antics of several of her rivals would have made things a whole lot easier. She will do extremely well to add to this in the foreseeable future. (op 12-1 tchd 11-2)
Sad Times(IRE), another with previous experience dropping in grade, had finished in front of Alittleriskie on their respective debuts and very nearly got up to deprive her old rival. She looks to need further already, but even so this is pretty poor form. (tchd 6-1)
Afric Star, taking a big step down in class, was brought over to race more towards the stands' side of the track in the home straight and stayed on without managing to land a blow. She will need to improve again on this to win a race. (op 5-1)
Granny Peel(IRE), green on her debut and down in class here, tried to make every yard. Kept closer to the inside rail than her rivals in the home straight, she looked likely to score when suddenly making a beeline across the track towards the section of the stands' rail where she had exited the paddock on to the course before the race. That cost her all chance and although she has the ability to win a race like this, she cannot be backed with confidence until she shows a bit more maturity. (op 11-4)
All Talk, behind a couple of these on her Kempton debut, showed up for a while but ultimately finished behind her two old rivals again, if a little closer to them. A sharper track and faster ground may help her, but she is obviously of very limited ability. (op 28-1 tchd 33-1)
Flying Lion, beaten a long way in the Brocklesby, was all over the place right from the very start including when trying to copy the antics of Granny Peel inside the last furlong. Her future depends entirely on whether her quirks can be ironed out. (op 11-4)
Sardis Road, out of a winner over a mile in France, was hampered by Flying Lion exiting the stalls and came right over to the stands' rail in the home straight, but could never get on terms. He does have the excuse that he was conceding previous experience to the six fillies that finished ahead of him. (op 8-1 tchd 10-1)

878 EUROPEAN BREEDERS FUND MAIDEN FILLIES' STKS 5f
2:40 (2:42) (Class 5) 2-Y-O **£4,210** (£1,252; £625; £312) **Stalls** Low

Form RPR
4 **1** **Gilded (IRE)**[8] [760] 2-9-0 RyanMoore 6 78
(R Hannon) *a.p: rdn to ld jst over 1f out: edgd rt ins fnl f: r.o* **11/10**[1]
2 1 ¾ **Gradetime (IRE)** 2-8-9 DerekNolan(5) 11 71
(M J Wallace) *a.p: rdn wl over 1f out: ev ch whn edgd lft ins fnl f: nt qckn* **8/1**[3]
3 1 ¾ **Queen Of Narnia** 2-9-0 TedDurcan 8 64
(M R Channon) *a.p: rdn to ld 2f out: hdd jst over 1f out: no ex wl ins fnl f* **8/1**[3]
4 *shd* **Miss Ippolita** 2-9-0 JimmyFortune 9 64
(J R Jenkins) *s.i.s: sn mid-div: rdn and hdwy over 2f out: edgd lft over 1f out: kpt on towards fin* **16/1**
5 1 ¾ **Our Susie (IRE)** 2-9-0 MartinDwyer 10 57
(M D I Usher) *sn outpcd: hdwy over 1f out: nt rchd ldrs* **20/1**
0 **6** ½ **Fasuby (IRE)**[12] [701] 2-9-0 ShaneKelly 2 55
(P D Evans) *sn outpcd: hdwy over 1f out: nvr trbld ldrs* **14/1**
5 **7** *shd* **It's No Problem (IRE)**[17] [663] 2-8-11 StephaneBreux(3) 7 54
(Jean-Rene Auvray) *mid-div: rdn and outpcd 3f out: hdwy and edgd lft over 1f out: no imp fnl f* **7/1**[2]
8 4 **Three Mates** 2-8-11 RobertMiles(3) 4 38
(W G M Turner) *led: rdn and hdd 2f out: wknd over 1f out* **16/1**
9 10 **Charlies Girl (IRE)** 2-9-0 FrancisFerris 3 —
(M J Attwater) *s.i.s: outpcd* **18/1**
10 1 ¼ **Bathwick Style** 2-9-0 AlanMunro 5 —
(B R Millman) *dwlt: outpcd* **14/1**
11 5 **Sainara (IRE)** 2-9-0 NCallan 1 —
(J M Bradley) *s.i.s: sn prom: rdn over 2f out: wknd over 1f out* **50/1**
64.72 secs (4.52) **Going Correction** +0.725s/f (Yiel) **11** Ran SP% **119.4**
Speed ratings (Par 89):92,89,86,86,83 82,82,76,60,58 50
CSF £10.54 TOTE £2.00: £1.10, £2.60, £2.50; EX 12.70.
Owner Mrs J Wood **Bred** Tally-Ho Stud **Trained** East Everleigh, Wilts

FOCUS
They were a little more organised in this race than they were in the seller and the time was 1.9 seconds faster. The front three were up with the pace throughout.

NOTEBOOK
Gilded(IRE), well backed, seemed to have learned a bit from her debut and was always in a good position. After taking over in front on the nearside halfway up the home straight, she did hang to her right passing the furlong pole but was always going to score. She still looked a little green so there may be a bit more to come from her. (op 6-4 tchd 13-8 and 7-4 in places)
Gradetime(IRE), a half-sister to two winners including the useful March Star, was fairly weak in the market but showed up for a long way and only the experienced winner was able to get the better of her. She should come on for this and is bred to get a bit further in time. (op 6-1 tchd 5-1)
Queen Of Narnia, a full-sister to Garlogs and half-sister to three other winners, was always up with the pace and did little wrong on this debut. There should be a small race in her before long. (tchd 9-1)
Miss Ippolita, a half-sister to the Fibresand winner Mid Valley, did best of those that tried to come from off the pace. There is plenty of stamina in her pedigree so she ought to be suited by a stiffer test in time. (op 14-1)
Our Susie(IRE), who cost just 3,000euros at a yearling, showed a bit of ability as the race progressed and should come on for it.
Fasuby(IRE) had shown early pace on Polytrack on her debut, but she seemed to struggle to go the early pace on this different surface. Her half-brother won over seven furlongs as a juvenile and it looks as though she is going to need that sort of trip too.
Sainara(IRE) Official explanation: jockey said filly had no more to give

879 BRENDA WHITING H'CAP 7f 26y
3:10 (3:11) (Class 6) (0-60,60) 3-Y-O **£2,730** (£806; £403) **Stalls** Low

Form RPR
400- **1** **Leamington Lad (IRE)**[180] [5703] 3-8-10 **55** RichardThomas(3) 5 64+
(J A Geake) *t.k.h in tch: rdn 2f out: led wl ins fnl f: drvn out* **28/1**
00-3 **2** 1 ¼ **George The Second**[29] [595] 3-8-6 **53** RichardKingscote(5) 4 59
(Mrs H Sweeting) *led: rdn and edgd rt jst over 1f out: hdd and nt qckn wl ins fnl f* **15/2**[2]
6233 **3** 1 **Franky'N'Jonny**[19] [648] 3-8-6 **53** (p) JamesDoyle(5) 9 56
(I A Wood) *hld up in mid-div: rdn over 2f out: hdwy whn nt clr run briefly over 1f out: r.o ins fnl f* **7/1**[1]
-100 **4** ¾ **Crush On You**[54] [347] 3-8-10 **52** LPKeniry 3 53
(R Hollinshead) *hld up in mid-div: rdn and hdwy over 2f out: kpt on ins fnl f* **25/1**
6533 **5** ¾ **She Whispers (IRE)**[20] [642] 3-8-4 **53** LiamJones(7) 6 53
(W M Brisbourne) *hld up and bhd: hdwy 2f out: rdn and swtchd lft over 1f out: nt rchd ldrs* **11/1**
000- **6** *nk* **Haiti Dancer**[157] [6145] 3-9-1 **60** AdamKirby(3) 7 59
(C G Cox) *chsd ldr: rdn over 2f out: swtchd rt over 1f out: wknd ins fnl f* **8/1**[3]
2004 **7** *shd* **Perfect Order (USA)**[6] [797] 3-8-13 **55** (p) RyanMoore 1 53+
(N A Callaghan) *s.s: hdwy over 1f out: nvr trbld ldrs* **7/1**[1]
000- **8** ½ **Wizby**[140] [6357] 3-8-12 **54** ShaneKelly 2 51
(P D Evans) *prom: rdn over 2f out: wknd ins fnl f* **9/1**
064- **9** ½ **Moody Tunes**[157] [6136] 3-9-3 **59** PatCosgrave 8 55
(K R Burke) *hld up and bhd: sme hdwy fnl f: n.d* **8/1**[3]
064- **10** 2 **Black Sea Pearl**[99] [6661] 3-9-3 **59** JimmyQuinn 14 50
(P W D'Arcy) *stmbld s: a bhd* **12/1**
06-0 **11** *shd* **Valhar**[6] [796] 3-9-1 **57** JimmyFortune 10 47
(J R Jenkins) *prom: rdn over 2f out: carried rt over 1f out: sn wknd* **22/1**
0005 **12** 3 **Zizou (IRE)**[7] [781] 3-8-13 **55** (t) ChrisCatlin 12 38
(J J Bridger) *hld up in mid-div: rdn 3f out: wknd 2f out* **8/1**[3]
000 **13** ½ **King's Melody**[48] [418] 3-8-10 **52** AlanMunro 13 33
(B R Millman) *a bhd* **18/1**
560- **14** 1 ¼ **The Grey One (IRE)**[217] [4847] 3-8-12 **54** NCallan 11 32
(J M Bradley) *s.i.s: hld up towards rr: hdwy over 2f out: wknd 1f out* **16/1**
1m 28.0s (3.00) **Going Correction** +0.425s/f (Yiel) **14** Ran SP% **118.9**
Speed ratings (Par 96):99,97,96,95,94 94,94,93,93,90 90,87,86,85
CSF £219.84 CT £1657.22 TOTE £35.80: £14.60, £3.20, £2.20; EX 268.20.
Owner Three Off The Tee Partnership **Bred** Daniel Galavan **Trained** Kimpton, Hants

FOCUS
A modest handicap, but they went a decent pace in the conditions. The draw played its part too with all the single draws beating all the double-figure stalls.
Black Sea Pearl Official explanation: jockey said filly stumbled leaving the stalls

880 WEATHERBYS BANK MAIDEN STKS 1m 22y
3:40 (3:46) (Class 5) 3-Y-O **£3,238** (£963; £481; £240) **Stalls** Low

Form RPR
1 **Ivy Creek (USA)** 3-9-3 NCallan 8 81+
(G Wragg) *hld up in mid-div: hdwy and swtchd rt 2f out: swtchd lft and led jst over 1f out: rdn and r.o wl* **9/1**
5-0 **2** 3 ½ **Airbuss (IRE)**[91] [16] 3-9-3 TedDurcan 6 68+
(M R Channon) *hld up in mid-div: rdn and hdwy 3f out: wnt 2nd jst ins fnl f: one pce* **16/1**
4- **3** 3 **Conservation (FR)**[158] [6128] 3-9-3 AlanMunro 9 62+
(P W Chapple-Hyam) *s.i.s: rdn and hdwy on ins over 2f out: one pce fnl f* **11/2**[3]
650- **4** ½ **Bellini Star**[140] [6359] 3-9-3 57 (v) ShaneKelly 11 61
(P D Evans) *w ldr: rdn to ld 2f out: hdd and edgd rt jst over 1f out: hung lft and wknd ins fnl f* **50/1**
24- **5** 1 ½ **Luckylover**[172] [5864] 3-9-3 TPQueally 3 58
(M G Quinlan) *a.p: rdn and carried lft over 1f out: wknd fnl f* **20/1**
003- **6** ¾ **Capistrano**[148] [6281] 3-9-3 71 SamHitchcott 12 56
(B W Hills) *sn mid-div: rdn and hdwy on ins 2f out: one pce fnl f* **14/1**
0- **7** 3 **Electric Warrior (IRE)**[257] [3662] 3-9-3 PatCosgrave 7 50+
(K R Burke) *hld up in tch: rdn and lost pl 3f out: n.d after* **50/1**

336- **8** *hd* **Zamala**[192] 5454 3-8-12 78 ... RHills 15 45
(J L Dunlop) *chsd ldrs: lost pl 3f out: n.d after* **9/2**[2]
9 *4* **Jiggy Spriggy (IRE)** 3-8-12 ... MichaelTebbutt 10 36
(V Smith) *s.i.s: nvr nr ldrs* **50/1**
030- **10** *nk* **Croft (IRE)**[162] 6072 3-9-3 71 ... FrankieMcDonald 17 41
(J W Hills) *towards rr: sme hdwy on ins 2f out: n.d* **40/1**
42-3 **11** *hd* **Feu D'Artifice(USA)**[10] 720 3-9-3 77 ... RichardHughes 1 47+
(R Hannon) *prom: rdn over 3f out: wknd over 1f out* **7/2**[1]
032- **12** *1 1/4* **Ollie George (IRE)**[248] 3946 3-9-3 79 ... MartinDwyer 2 37
(A M Balding) *s.i.s: a bhd* **13/2**
0- **13** *1 1/4* **Travolta**[167] 5970 3-9-0 ... AdamKirby(3) 14 35
(C G Cox) *a towards rr* **10/1**
30 **14** *3/4* **Beowulf**[18] 658 3-8-12 ... GregFairley(5) 4 33
(M Johnston) *led: rdn and hdd 2f out: hung lft and wknd over 1f out* **14/1**
0006 **15** *3* **Batchworth Fleur**[35] 540 3-8-12 45 ... StephenCarson 16 22
(E A Wheeler) *sn bhd* **125/1**
6-0 **16** *6* **Captain Torrance (IRE)**[6] 795 3-9-3 ... AdrianMcCarthy 13 14+
(P W Chapple-Hyam) *prom tl rdn and wknd over 2f out* **66/1**
17 *dist* **Ronaldo** 3-9-3 ... TQuinn 5 —
(W R Muir) *s.i.s: a bhd: t.o fnl 3f* **50/1**

1m 44.19s (4.59) **Going Correction** +0.425s/f (Yiel) **17** Ran SP% **124.8**
Speed ratings (Par 98):94,90,87,87,85 84,81,81,77,77 77,75,74,73,70 64,—
CSF £140.50 TOTE £10.90: £3.30, £3.50, £2.70; EX 258.30.
Owner Mollers Racing **Bred** Eleanor Drake Rose Trust Et Al **Trained** Newmarket, Suffolk

FOCUS
A modest maiden, run at a fair pace, which saw the field come home fairly strung out behind the ready winner.
Feu D'Artifice(USA) Official explanation: jockey said colt had no more to give
Batchworth Fleur Official explanation: jockey said filly bled from the nose
Ronaldo Official explanation: jockey said colt was slowly away and never travelling

881 WEATHERBYS INSURANCE H'CAP 1m 6f 213y
4:10 (4:10) (Class 5) (0-75,75) 4-Y-0+ **£4,210** (£1,252; £625; £312) **Stalls** Low

Form RPR
240- **1** **Precious Mystery (IRE)**[42] 6490 6-9-2 **65** ... (v) DaneO'Neill 9 75
(A King) *wnt rt s: prom: rdn to ld wl over 1f out: sn edgd lft: r.o wl* **11/4**[1]
0-63 **2** *3 1/2* **Screen Test**[20] 643 4-8-7 **59** ... RyanMoore 2 64
(B G Powell) *a.p: rdn over 3f out: wnt 2nd ins fnl f: one pce* **11/2**[2]
400- **3** *1* **My Legal Eagle (IRE)**[190] 5518 12-8-0 **56** oh11 ... LiamJones(7) 3 60?
(E G Bevan) *hld up and bhd: rdn over 2f out: hdwy fnl f: r.o* **10/1**
6-00 **4** *3/4* **Aristi (IRE)**[20] 643 5-8-7 **56** oh1 ... (p) ShaneKelly 8 59
(M Quinn) *led: rdn 3f out: hdd wl over 1f out: no ex ins fnl f* **9/1**
000- **5** *1 3/4* **Kaluana Court**[169] 5943 10-8-2 **56** oh6 ... JamesDoyle(5) 6 57
(R J Price) *hld up in tch: rdn 3f out: wknd ins fnl f* **14/1**
200- **6** *nk* **Mythical King (IRE)**[17] 4841 9-8-7 **56** oh5 ... AlanMunro 5 56
(R Lee) *hld up: hdwy over 5f out: no real prog fnl 3f* **6/1**[3]
1214 **7** *14* **Sugitani (USA)**[19] 652 4-8-9 **61** ... (b) JamieMackay 1 43
(N B King) *hld up in tch: pushed along over 6f out: lost pl over 3f out: eased whn btn fnl f* **11/4**[1]
400/ **8** *11* **Business Traveller (IRE)**[20] 5205 6-8-2 **56** oh16..(bt) EmmettStack(5) 4 24
(R J Price) *t.k.h: prom: lost pl after 2f: rdn over 5f out: bhd fnl 4f* **20/1**

3m 32.33s (16.43) **Going Correction** +0.575s/f (Yiel)
WFA 4 from 5yo+ 3lb **8** Ran SP% **113.5**
Speed ratings (Par 103):79,77,76,76,75 75,67,61
CSF £17.89 CT £129.10 TOTE £3.40: £1.30, £1.50, £2.80; EX 15.90.
Owner The Dunnkirk Partnership **Bred** Miss Wendy Fox **Trained** Barbury Castle, Wilts

FOCUS
A pedestrian winning time and, while the winner readily repeated her success in this event last year, the form looks ordinary.
Sugitani(USA) Official explanation: trainer had no explanation for the poor form shown

882 RACING UK H'CAP 1m 2f 188y
4:40 (4:40) (Class 6) (0-60,60) 4-Y-0+ **£2,730** (£806; £403) **Stalls** Low

Form RPR
5-05 **1** **Summer Bounty**[6] 794 10-9-4 **60** ... NCallan 15 69
(F Jordan) *hld up in mid-div: hdwy over 2f out: rdn over 1f out: led ins fnl f: sn edgd lft: r.o* **8/1**
130- **2** *2* **Dove Cottage (IRE)**[167] 5980 4-9-4 **60** ... ChrisCatlin 2 66
(W S Kittow) *led: rdn 2f out: hdd and nt qckn ins fnl f* **11/1**
500- **3** *2 1/2* **Tagula Blue (IRE)**[63] 3691 6-9-4 **60** ... SimonWhitworth 3 62
(Ian Williams) *s.v.s: hdwy over 3f out: hung lft fr over 1f out: one pce* **15/2**[3]
1-20 **4** *hd* **Soviet Sceptre (IRE)**[43] 457 5-8-13 **55** ... (t) TQuinn 9 56
(R T Phillips) *prom: chsd ldr over 4f out tl rdn over 1f out: one pce* **12/1**
526- **5** *3/4* **Darghan (IRE)**[171] 5892 6-8-9 **58** ... AlanRutter(7) 11 58
(W J Musson) *stdd s: sn mid-div: hdwy over 2f out: one pce fnl f* **20/1**
000- **6** *1* **Count Boris**[11] 5983 5-8-10 **55** ... RichardThomas(3) 5 58+
(J A Geake) *hld up towards rr: nt clr run on ins and stmbld over 3f out: hdwy over 1f out: nt rchd ldrs* **6/1**[2]
2000 **7** *2 1/2* **Midshipman**[32] 571 8-9-1 **57** ... (vt) JimmyFortune 6 51
(A W Carroll) *s.i.s: hld up and bhd: hdwy over 1f out: nvr trbld ldrs* **8/1**
434- **8** *1 1/4* **Icecap**[243] 4081 6-8-9 **51** ... JimmyQuinn 7 43
(W G M Turner) *t.k.h in tch: nt clr run over 2f out: wknd over 1f out* **25/1**
456- **9** *nk* **Acuzio**[243] 4110 5-8-10 **52** ... ShaneKelly 4 44
(W M Brisbourne) *hld up in tch: rdn over 2f out: wknd over 1f out* **16/1**
-610 **10** *1 1/4* **Bill Bennett (FR)**[37] 525 5-9-4 **60** ... GeorgeBaker 17 49
(J Jay) *bhd tl hdwy over 1f out: n.d* **12/1**
0-40 **11** *1 3/4* **Stagecoach Emerald**[29] 603 4-9-4 **60** ... SamHitchcott 12 46
(R W Price) *prom: rdn over 3f out: wknd over 1f out* **50/1**
000 **12** *1 3/4* **Diafa (USA)**[19] 647 4-8-10 **52** ... RobertHavlin 14 35
(J G M O'Shea) *nvr nr ldrs* **66/1**
-452 **13** *3* **Brockhole (IRE)**[12] 700 4-9-2 **58** ... RyanMoore 13 36
(J G Given) *hld up in tch: rdn and wknd 3f out* **11/2**[1]
002/ **14** *2* **Three Welshmen**[462] 3684 5-8-10 **52** ... MichaelTebbutt 16 27
(D Burchell) *bhd fnl 4f* **16/1**
2110 **15** *2* **Gallego**[10] 736 4-8-13 **55** ... MatthewHenry 10 27
(R J Price) *stdd s: a bhd* **14/1**
00-0 **16** *6* **Bogaz (IRE)**[40] 492 4-8-11 **58** ... RichardKingscote(5) 1 19
(Mrs H Sweeting) *chsd ldr tl over 4f out: rdn over 2f out: wknd qckly wl over 1f out* **50/1**
/50- **17** *18* **Cultured**[40] 6626 5-9-1 **57** ... TedDurcan 8 —
(Mrs A J Bowlby) *hld up in mid-div: rdn over 4f out: lost pl over 3f out* **66/1**

2m 25.81s (6.41) **Going Correction** +0.575s/f (Yiel) **17** Ran SP% **121.3**
Speed ratings (Par 101):99,97,95,95,95 94,92,91,91,90 89,87,85,84,82 78,65
CSF £87.10 CT £695.58 TOTE £8.70: £2.50, £2.40, £2.30, £3.30; EX 139.80 Place 6 £155.03, Place 5 £60.75.

Owner Tim Powell **Bred** Berkshire Equestrian Services Ltd **Trained** Adstone, Northants

FOCUS
A moderate handicap, run at a decent pace, and the form looks fair.
Count Boris Official explanation: jockey said gelding was denied a clear run on the home bend
T/Jkpt: Not won. T/Plt: £472.40 to a £1 stake. Pool: £44,045.25. 68.05 winning tickets. T/Qpdt: £143.40 to a £1 stake. Pool: £4,148.60. 21.40 winning tickets. KH

MAISONS-LAFFITTE (R-H)
Tuesday, April 4

OFFICIAL GOING: Heavy

885a PRIX COR DE CHASSE (LISTED RACE) (STRAIGHT) 5f 110y
2:50 (3:00) 3-Y-0+ **£17,241** (£6,897; £5,172; £3,448; £1,724)

RPR
1 **Matrix (GER)**[134] 6408 5-9-6 ... DBoeuf 5 108
(W Baltromei, Germany)
2 *3/4* **Indian Maiden (IRE)**[24] 627 6-9-6 ... OPeslier 2 106
(M S Saunders) *in touch, 6th half-way, stayed on from 1 1/2f out and went 2nd, ridden final f, nearest at finish*
3 *1 1/2* **Donatello (GER)**[134] 6408 5-9-9 ... JVictoire 7 104
(W Baltromei, Germany)
4 *3* **Ricine (IRE)**[240] 4-9-6 ... F-XBertras 4 91
(F Rohaut, France)
5 *2* **Campo Bueno (FR)**[26] 4-9-6 ... GBenoist 1 84
(X Nakkachdji, France) **11/4**[1]
6 *5* **Omasheriff (IRE)**[219] 4804 4-9-13 ... SPasquier 3 75
(Bruce Hellier, Germany)
7 *2 1/2* **Satchmo Bay (FR)**[19] 685 5-9-6 ... (b) CSoumillon 6 59
(C Boutin, France)
8 *3/4* **Carmelixia (IRE)**[26] 4-9-3 ... C-PLemaire 8 54
(R Pritchard-Gordon, France)

68.50 secs **8** Ran SP% **26.7**
PARI-MUTUEL: WIN 6.70; PL 2.50, 2.20, 4.70; DF 15.20.
Owner Stall Lindenfeld **Bred** I Markides **Trained** Germany

NOTEBOOK
Indian Maiden(IRE), slowly into her stride, raced in second last during the early part of this sprint. She still had plenty to do when things quickened up a furlong and a half out and she ran on really well late on. Her next targets looks like being the Abernant Stakes at Newmarket and the Landsdown Fillies Stakes at Bath.

843 KEMPTON (A.W) (R-H)
Wednesday, April 5

OFFICIAL GOING: Standard
Wind: Light, half-against

886 INTERCASINO.CO.UK BANDED STKS 5f (P)
2:20 (2:21) (Class 7) 4-Y-0+ **£2,388** (£705; £352) **Stalls** High

Form RPR
0-52 **1** **Prime Recreation**[7] 789 9-8-11 45 ... RobertWinston 3 53
(P S Felgate) *mde all: sn crossed to inner and clr: rdn and wkng fnl f but won unchal* **12/1**
501- **2** *1* **Forest Dane**[184] 5657 6-9-0 48 ... OscarUrbina 5 52
(Mrs N Smith) *outpcd and wl in rr: swtchd to inner and prog 2f out: chsd wnr wl ins fnl f: clsd fin but unable to chal* **8/1**
0004 **3** *3/4* **Double M**[39] 514 9-8-13 50 ... (v) RichardThomas(3) 11 51
(Mrs L Richards) *chsd clr ldrs: rdn 2f out: styd on fr over 1f out: nrst fin* **9/1**
6602 **4** *hd* **Beverley Beau**[9] 772 4-8-5 46 ... KristinStubbs(7) 9 47
(Mrs L Stubbs) *chsd clr ldng pair: bmpd along 2f out: kpt on same pce* **8/1**
5203 **5** *nk* **Leah's Pride**[16] 679 5-9-1 49 ... JamieSpencer 8 49
(Miss D A McHale) *chsd wnr: rdn and no imp fr 2f out: one pce and lost 3rd pl wl ins fnl f* **9/2**[1]
3040 **6** *1/2* **Davids Mark**[9] 772 6-8-13 47 ... (vt) PaulHanagan 6 47+
(J R Jenkins) *outpcd and wl in rr: prog over 1f out: styng on whn rn out of room nr fin* **8/1**
0-60 **7** *nk* **Goldhill Prince**[39] 520 4-8-10 49 ... (p) JamesDoyle(5) 12 46
(Ernst Oertel) *chsd ldrs: rdn 1/2-way: no imp after: one pce* **10/1**
0205 **8** *3/4* **Chantelle's Dream**[53] 373 4-8-12 49 ... (b) AdamKirby(3) 1 43
(Ms J S Doyle) *unruly preliminaries: s.s: nvr any ch in last pair: sme prog on outer fnl f* **25/1**
3242 **9** *3/4* **Muktasb (USA)**[16] 679 5-8-13 50 ... (v) PatrickMathers(3) 2 41
(D Shaw) *forced to r wd thrght: nvr beyond midfield: no prog fnl 2f* **11/2**[2]
600- **10** *1/2* **Renegade (IRE)**[105] 6646 5-9-1 49 ... IanMongan 10 38+
(Mrs L J Mongan) *squeezed out sn after s: rdn in midfield 1/2-way: struggling after* **7/1**[3]
600- **11** *2 1/2* **Princess Kai (IRE)**[105] 6647 5-8-11 45 ... (b) RobertHavlin 4 25+
(R Ingram) *hmpd s: a in last trio: nvr a factor* **66/1**
00-0 **12** *1 1/2* **College Queen**[16] 679 8-8-12 46 ... (t) NCallan 7 21+
(S Gollings) *hmpd sn after s and stmbld bdly: rcvrd to midfield after 2f: wknd 2f out* **25/1**

60.66 secs **Going Correction** +0.05s/f (Slow) **12** Ran SP% **115.4**
Speed ratings (Par 97):99,97,96,95,95 94,94,92,91,90 86,84
CSF £100.15 TOTE £13.90: £3.50, £3.20, £3.40; EX 113.70.
Owner Michael Heywood **Bred** Alan Gibson **Trained** Grimston, Leics
■ Stewards' Enquiry : Robert Winston five-day ban: careless riding (Apr 16-20)

FOCUS
A competitive race by banded standard but nothing could get to Prime Recreation, who set a strong pace from the start. The form looks sound enough.
Prime Recreation Official explanation: jockey said gelding hung right from start
Double M Official explanation: jockey said gelding was hampered shortly after start

887 INTERCASINO.CO.UK TRI-BANDED STKS 1m 2f (P)
2:50 (2:50) (Class 7) 3-Y-0 **£2,388** (£705; £352) **Stalls** High

Form RPR
000- **1** **Carlton Scroop (FR)**[29] 6228 3-8-9 40 ... (b[1]) ShaneKelly 4 51+
(J Jay) *dwlt: hld up midfield: prog over 2f out: nt clr run over 1f out and swtchd lft: led last 150yds: r.o wl and sn clr* **20/1**

000- **2** 3 1/2 **Monte Major (GER)**[189] 5548 3-9-0 45 JamieSpencer 9 46
(D J Daly) *trckd ldrs: effrt over 2f out: hrd rdn to ld over 1f out: hdd and outpcd last 150yds* **9/2**[1]

0-52 **3** 1/2 **The Jailer**[28] 617 3-9-0 45 DavidKinsella 8 45
(J G M O'Shea) *hld up towards rr: prog on outer 2f out: clsd on ldrs 1f out: fnd nil fnl f* **13/2**

46-0 **4** 1 **Coffin Dodger**[57] 326 3-9-0 45 RyanMoore 2 43
(C N Allen) *pressed ldr: led after 3f: hrd rdn and hdd over 1f out: wknd last 100yds* **13/2**

-006 **5** 3 1/2 **Cape Latina**[7] 790 3-9-0 45 SteveDrowne 3 36
(J R Best) *t.k.h: hld up in last: rdn and prog whn hmpd wl over 1f out: kpt on fnl f but no ch* **6/1**[3]

-244 **6** 2 **Mykeyta**[28] 617 3-9-0 45 DaleGibson 5 33
(J G Given) *chsd ldrs: rdn over 4f out: fdd fnl 2f* **11/2**[2]

00-0 **7** 3/4 **The Great Delaney**[66] 241 3-8-9 40 DarryllHolland 1 26
(K McAuliffe) *chsd ldrs: rdn over 5f out: tried to chal u.p over 2f out: wknd over 1f out* **16/1**

4404 **8** 3/4 **Genoa Star**[38] 528 3-9-0 45 (v) RobbieFitzpatrick 7 30
(T J Pitt) *dwlt: settled towards rr: rdn 1/2-way: struggling after* **6/1**[3]

-000 **9** 9 **Safaah**[15] 687 3-8-9 40 ChrisCatlin 10 8
(G Prodromou) *hld up in last pair: wknd over 2f out* **20/1**

000- **10** 26 **Sunny Disposition (IRE)**[144] 6334 3-9-0 45 (v[1]) NCallan 6 —
(E F Vaughan) *led for 3f: pressed ldr tl wknd and eased over 2f out: t.o* **9/1**

2m 10.47s **Going Correction** +0.05s/f (Slow) **10** Ran SP% **114.2**
Speed ratings (Par 92):96,93,92,92,89 87,87,86,79,58
CSF £105.75 TOTE £27.30: £5.80, £2.10, £1.40; EX 148.40.
Owner David Fremel and Mrs Sylvia Jay **Bred** J Jay **Trained** Newmarket, Suffolk

FOCUS
A moderate event that is unlikely to produce that many winners. The third and fourth set the standard.
Sunny Disposition(IRE) Official explanation: jockey said colt had no more to give

888 PLAY BLACKJACK AT INTERCASINO.CO.UK BANDED STKS 1m 2f (P)
3:20 (3:21) (Class 7) 4-Y-0+ **£2,388** (£705; £352) **Stalls** High

Form RPR

1200 **1** **Justcallmehandsome**[8] 784 4-8-8 49 (v) DonnaCaldwell(7) 12 53
(D J S Ffrench Davis) *mde all: pushed along over 3f out: edgd lft over 1f out: hld on wl: bbv* **50/1**

-042 **2** 1/2 **Good Article (IRE)**[9] 769 5-9-0 48 DarryllHolland 3 51
(D K Ivory) *dwlt and squeezed out s: rcvrd to trck wnr after 2f: rdn to chal over 1f out: edgd lft and nt qckn fnl f* **10/1**

0360 **3** shd **Busy Man (IRE)**[29] 612 7-9-2 50 NCallan 9 56+
(J R Jenkins) *t.k.h: hld up in last trio: stl only 12th over 1f out: rapid prog and twice checked fnl f: fin wl: too much to do* **14/1**

0544 **4** 1 **Hiawatha (IRE)**[16] 683 7-9-2 50 DaneO'Neill 11 51
(A M Hales) *hld up in midfield: effrt on outer over 2f out: drvn and kpt on same pce fr over 1f out* **15/2**[3]

0403 **5** nk **Indigo Sky (IRE)**[43] 472 5-8-13 47 HayleyTurner 2 47
(B G Powell) *restrained into midfield after 1f: sn pushed along: prog to chse ldrs 1/2-way: rdn and kpt on same pce fnl 2f* **12/1**

0502 **6** 1/2 **Pharaoh Prince**[16] 683 5-9-1 49 ChrisCatlin 14 48
(G Prodromou) *trckd ldrs on inner: no prog fr 2f out: one pce* **13/2**[2]

6500 **7** 1/2 **Chocolate Boy (IRE)**[42] 484 7-9-0 48 (be) RyanMoore 10 46
(G L Moore) *settled towards rr: brought to wd outside over 2f out: rdn and fnd nil over 1f out: one pce after* **10/1**

00-5 **8** 1/2 **Double Ransom**[51] 394 7-9-0 48 (b) TPQueally 4 45
(Mrs L Stubbs) *trckd ldrs: hrd rdn and one pce fnl 2f* **9/1**

4354 **9** 1/2 **Tuscan Treaty**[9] 771 6-8-8 45 (t) SaleemGolam(3) 7 42
(P J McBride) *dwlt: hld up in last trio: effrt over 2f out: no imp on ldrs* **20/1**

3232 **10** 3/4 **Majehar**[32] 582 4-8-8 47 StephenDonohoe(5) 6 42
(A G Newcombe) *settled in midfield: rdn and no prog over 2f out* **4/1**[1]

5240 **11** 1/2 **Alqaayid**[14] 697 5-8-11 48 SColas(3) 8 42
(P W Hiatt) *hld up towards rr: rdn and no prog 2f out* **14/1**

0523 **12** 3 **Miss Glory Be**[9] 769 8-8-6 45 (p) JamesDoyle(5) 1 33
(Ernst Oertel) *t.k.h: sn pressed ldng pair: wknd over 1f out* **12/1**

20-0 **13** 2 **Fortunes Favourite**[54] 358 6-8-6 45 NataliaGemelova(5) 5 30
(J E Long) *nvr bttr than midfield: lost pl 1/2-way: wknd 2f out* **33/1**

0-00 **14** 29 **Belrose (IRE)**[44] 460 4-9-2 50 JamieSpencer 13 —
(Mrs C A Dunnett) *dwlt: t.k.h: hld up in last: wd and wknd bnd over 2f out: eased and t.o* **16/1**

2m 10.56s **Going Correction** +0.05s/f (Slow) **14** Ran SP% **117.5**
Speed ratings (Par 97):95,94,94,93,93 93,92,92,91,91 90,88,86,63
CSF £480.30 TOTE £48.20: £13.70, £3.10, £6.20; EX 349.30.
Owner Mrs J E Taylor **Bred** Mrs J E Taylor **Trained** Lambourn, Berks
■ Stewards' Enquiry : N Callan two-day ban: careless riding (Apr 16-17)

FOCUS
Just an ordinary banded contest and the time, very similar to the previous race for three-year-olds, was not great.
Miss Glory Be Official explanation: trainer said mare bled from the nose

889 PLAY ROULETTE AT INTERCASINO.CO.UK BANDED STKS 7f (P)
3:50 (3:51) (Class 7) 4-Y-0+ **£2,388** (£705; £352) **Stalls** High

Form RPR

2611 **1** **Auentraum (GER)**[9] 766 6-9-6 48 (p) DarryllHolland 12 64
(K McAuliffe) *trckd ldng trio gng easily: effrt 2f out: led jst over 1f out: shkn up and kpt on wl* **6/1**[3]

0443 **2** hd **Wiltshire (IRE)**[32] 581 4-9-2 50 (v) NCallan 7 59
(P A Blockley) *hld up in last trio: prog on inner over 2f out: drvn to press wnr fnl f: a jst hld* **9/1**

0-00 **3** 2 1/2 **Luciferous (USA)**[43] 471 4-8-11 48 (v[1]) AmirQuinn(3) 1 51
(P G Murphy) *s.i.s: rcvrd on outer to chse ldrs: rdn over 3f out: nt qckn over 2f out: kpt on again fr over 1f out* **66/1**

0066 **4** 3/4 **Gaudalpin (IRE)**[9] 772 4-8-13 47 (t) J-PGuillambert 4 48
(Ernst Oertel) *pressed ldng pair: rdn to ld 2f out to jst over 1f out: wknd ins fnl f* **33/1**

0046 **5** hd **Abbeygate**[14] 697 5-9-2 50 (p) MickyFenton 2 50
(T Keddy) *hld up in last trio: plenty to do and hanging bnd 3f out: styd on fr over 1f out: nrst fin* **16/1**

6036 **6** 1 **Prince Of Gold**[8] 784 6-9-2 50 (p) VinceSlattery 9 47
(R Hollinshead) *sn rdn in midfield: kpt on u.p fnl 2f but nvr a threat* **10/1**

-303 **7** nk **Wodhill Be**[47] 446 6-9-0 48 AdrianMcCarthy 11 45
(D Morris) *hld up in last: no prog tl styd on fnl 2f: no ch* **25/1**

30-2 **8** shd **King Zafeen (IRE)**[8] 787 4-9-2 50 JamieSpencer 5 46
(M W Easterby) *hld up towards rr: effrt over 2f out: nt clr run wl over 1f out: wknd last 100yds* **3/1**[1]

6600 **9** 1 1/2 **Jennverse**[15] 691 4-9-0 48 FergusSweeney 14 40
(D K Ivory) *hld up towards rr: prog on inner over 2f out: chsd ldrs over 1f out: wknd fnl f* **20/1**

0166 **10** hd **Priorina (IRE)**[12] 708 4-9-2 50 (p) RobertHavlin 3 42
(D Haydn Jones) *t.k.h: hld up in midfield: no prog 2f out: fdd* **14/1**

5051 **11** 2 1/2 **Christmas Truce (IRE)**[2] 853 7-9-1 50 (v) SophieDoyle(7) 8 41
(Ms J S Doyle) *pushed up to press ldr: led briefly over 2f out: wknd rapidly fnl f* **10/1**

6413 **12** 2 **Jalouhar**[9] 772 6-9-2 50 (p) GeorgeBaker 13 30
(J R Best) *dwlt: hld up wl in rr: no prog fnl 2f* **11/2**[2]

5524 **13** 2 **Cloann (IRE)**[16] 681 4-9-1 49 (b) StephenCarson 10 24
(E A Wheeler) *drvn to ld and set str pce: hdd over 2f out: wknd rapidly over 1f out* **16/1**

4050 **14** 10 **Zinging**[32] 575 7-9-0 48 (v) PaulHanagan 6 —+
(J J Bridger) *t.k.h: trckd ldrs: wkng whn stmbld bdly over 1f out: eased* **25/1**

1m 27.2s (-1.06) **Going Correction** +0.05s/f (Slow) **14** Ran SP% **118.2**
Speed ratings (Par 97):99,98,95,95,94 93,93,93,91,91 88,86,83,72
CSF £54.23 TOTE £5.60: £2.40, £2.30, £14.60; EX 65.90.
Owner Nadeem Ahmad **Bred** Gestut Auenquelle **Trained** Fernham, Oxon

FOCUS
This looks fair form for the class and the first two came clear. The form, rated through the the runner-up, should be reliable enough, although the third and fourth do not totally convince.
Zinging Official explanation: jockey said gelding lost its action

890 INTERCASINO.CO.UK MAIDEN CLAIMING STKS 6f (P)
4:20 (4:23) (Class 7) 3-Y-0+ **£2,388** (£705; £352) **Stalls** High

Form RPR

6-00 **1** **Avenlea**[16] 681 5-9-7 45 RyanMoore 7 53
(G L Moore) *in tch in chsng gp: rdn over 2f out: styd on fr over 1f out to ld last 100yds* **13/2**[3]

-56 **2** 3/4 **Peggys First**[15] 687 4-9-7 PatCosgrave 8 51
(D E Cantillon) *in tch in chsng gp: rdn 1/2-way: styd on fnl f to take 2nd last strides* **40/1**

5424 **3** nk **In Hope**[30] 594 3-8-0 50 HayleyTurner 13 38
(Ernst Oertel) *prom in chsng gp: drvn to try to cl fr 2f out: kpt on fnl f* **7/1**

5406 **4** hd **Spanish Music**[37] 534 4-9-2 45 RobertHavlin 11 46+
(R Ingram) *outpcd in rr and drvn: nt clr run 2f out: gd prog fnl f: styng on whn nowhere to go last 50yds* **16/1**

0206 **5** hd **Titus Wonder (IRE)**[30] 598 3-7-13 45 ow2 KevinGhunowa(7) 3 43+
(P A Blockley) *disp ld at furious pce: wknd and hdd last 100yds* **25/1**

6463 **6** shd **Bahhmirage (IRE)**[8] 779 3-8-4 52 (b) JimmyQuinn 5 41
(Stef Liddiard) *outpcd and off the pce in rr: styd on fr over 1f out: nrst fin* **12/1**

-245 **7** hd **Rebellious Spirit**[16] 673 3-8-5 68 NeilPollard 2 41+
(J G Given) *disp ld at furious pce: wknd last 100yds* **2/1**[1]

6304 **8** 1 1/4 **Three Feathers**[8] 779 3-8-6 45 SaleemGolam(3) 10 41
(M Salaman) *off the pce towards rr: kpt on fr over 1f out: n.d* **20/1**

0540 **9** hd **Yassooma (IRE)**[15] 690 3-8-6 45 (v[1]) RobbieFitzpatrick 9 38
(T J Pitt) *n.m.r s: outpcd and wl bhd: effrt on inner 2f out: keeping on but no ch whn rn out of room last 50yds* **50/1**

3434 **10** 5 **Mister Aziz (IRE)**[9] 766 4-9-7 45 (b) NCallan 12 29
(J R Jenkins) *chsd clr ldrs: wknd over 1f out* **7/2**[2]

0 **11** 2 1/2 **Red Ruth Lady**[8] 783 4-8-13 NelsonDeSouza(3) 1 16
(D L Williams) *s.i.s: outpcd and a bhd* **100/1**

-006 **12** shd **Silver Reign**[34] 553 5-9-4 40 NeilChalmers(3) 14 21
(J J Bridger) *chsd clr ldng pair tl wknd rapidly over 2f out* **33/1**

-600 **13** dist **They All Laughed**[19] 658 3-8-9 57 DarryllHolland 4 —
(Karen George) *off the pce towards rr: hanging fr 3f out: virtually p.u over 1f out* **12/1**

1m 15.1s (-1.17) **Going Correction** +0.05s/f (Slow)
WFA 3 from 4yo+ 12lb **13** Ran SP% **119.6**
Speed ratings (Par 97):92,91,90,90,90 89,89,88,87,81 77,77,—
CSF £256.51 TOTE £6.40: £1.90, £9.40; EX 269.30.Rebellious Spirit was claimed by P. W. Hiatt for £3,000. They All Laughed was claimed by P. W. Hiatt for £5,000.
Owner D J Deer **Bred** D J Deer **Trained** Woodingdean, E Sussex
■ Stewards' Enquiry : Kevin Ghunowa one-day ban: failed to ride to draw (Apr 16)
Robert Havlin one-day ban: careless riding (Apr 16)

FOCUS
A weak affair, run at a very strong early pace, and those coming from off the pace were at a distinct advantage. The form looks far from solid.
They All Laughed Official explanation: jockey said gelding cocked his jaw and hung left

891 WIN AT INTERCASINO.CO.UK BANDED STKS 1m 4f (P)
4:50 (4:50) (Class 7) 4-Y-0+ **£2,388** (£705; £352) **Stalls** Low

Form RPR

243- **1** **Shekan Star**[126] 6475 4-8-11 45 PaulHanagan 9 51
(K G Reveley) *dwlt: hld up towards rr: prog over 2f out: led narrowly over 1f out : drvn out* **7/2**[1]

-440 **2** 1/2 **Lysander's Quest (IRE)**[33] 570 8-8-12 45 DaneO'Neill 6 50
(R Ingram) *trckd ldrs: rdn to chal wl over 1f out: pressed wnr after : jst hld* **13/2**[3]

2023 **3** 3/4 **Twentytwosilver (IRE)**[9] 767 6-9-0 47 MichaelTebbutt 10 51
(D B Feek) *v.s.i.s: hld up and racd wd: prog on outer over 2f out: pressed ldrs 1f out: nt qckn* **10/1**

0- **4** 3/4 **Nobelmann (GER)**[81] 5859 7-8-12 45 MickyFenton 13 48
(A W Carroll) *hld up wl in rr: rapid prog fr 2f out to press ldrs 1f out: kpt on same pce* **50/1**

64-0 **5** shd **Gaelic Roulette (IRE)**[24] 174 6-9-1 48 ShaneKelly 8 51
(J Jay) *hld up in midfield: nt qckn 2f out: kpt on again fnl f* **16/1**

352- **6** nk **Equilibria (USA)**[79] 5998 4-9-2 50 RyanMoore 4 52
(G L Moore) *settled wl in rr: rdn over 2f out: styd on fr over 1f out: nt rch ldrs* **4/1**[2]

5544 **7** shd **Noble Mind**[44] 457 5-9-0 47 (p) SteveDrowne 1 49
(P G Murphy) *pressed ldr: upsides 2f out: sn nt qckn: one pce after* **14/1**

-003 **8** 1 **Dishdasha (IRE)**[16] 682 4-8-11 45 RobertWinston 12 45
(C R Dore) *trckd ldrs: gng wl 2f out: rousted along and effrt over 1f out: ch whn hmpd jst ins fnl f: wknd* **16/1**

00-0 **9** 3/4 **War Feather**[14] 696 4-8-11 45 RobertHavlin 3 44
(T D McCarthy) *wl in tch: effrt to press ldrs on outer over 2f out: one pce and btn over 1f out* **50/1**

2024 **10** hd **Dagola (IRE)**[14] 694 5-8-13 46 NCallan 14 45
(C A Dwyer) *stdd s: t.k.h: hld up in last: effrt over 2f out: kpt on but no ch* **11/1**

0-02 **11** *1 1/4* **Whitby Echo (IRE)**[9] 770 4-8-9 50.................... RussellKennemore(7) 2 47
(R Hollinshead) *led: set stdy pce: rdn over 2f out: hdd & wknd over 1f out* **10/1**

-100 **12** *1* **Tignasse (FR)**[30] 597 5-9-1 48.................................... DarrylHolland 11 43
(Karen George) *hld up in midfield: effrt on inner 2f out: no prog over 1f out* **16/1**

50-3 **13** *3 1/2* **Iamback**[8] 780 6-8-12 45..(t) JamieMackay 5 35
(Miss D A McHale) *trckd ldng pair: rdn and effrt on inner over 2f out: wknd over 1f out* **12/1**

020- **14** *3 1/2* **Terraquin (IRE)**[141] 6361 6-8-12 45....................................(v) AlanDaly 7 29
(J J Bridger) *dwlt: t.k.h: hld up in midfield: wknd 2f out: lame* **33/1**

2m 39.99s (-3.01) **Going Correction** +0.05s/f (Slow)
WFA 4 from 5yo+ 1lb **14** Ran SP% **120.9**
Speed ratings (Par 97):91,90,90,89,89 89,89,88,88,88 87,86,84,81
CSF £25.80 TOTE £5.80: £2.20, £2.20, £3.20; EX 37.10 Place 6 £3,703.45, Place 5 £697.18.
Owner Star Alliance **Bred** The Welcome Alliance **Trained** Lingdale, Redcar & Cleveland
■ Stewards' Enquiry : Dane O'Neill two-day ban: careless riding (Apr 16-17)

FOCUS
They went very steady in this moderate event and it effectively turned into a two-furlong sprint. The first seven were closely covered at the finish but the form looks sound for the grade.
Terraquin(IRE) Official explanation: vet said gelding finished lame
T/Plt: £1,477.00 to a £1 stake. Pool: £41,479.30. 20.50 winning tickets. T/Qpdt: £238.70 to a £1 stake. Pool: £3,581.60. 11.10 winning tickets. JN

LEICESTER (R-H)
Thursday, April 6

OFFICIAL GOING: Good to soft (good in places)
Wind: Half behind

892 LADBROKES.COM MEDIAN AUCTION MAIDEN STKS 5f 2y
2:10 (2:10) (Class 6) 2-Y-O **£3,238** (£963; £481; £240) **Stalls** Low

Form RPR

1 **Hellvelyn** 2-9-3 .... TedDurcan 5 89+
(B Smart) *a.p: rdn to ld over 1f out: r.o* **3/1**[1]

2 *1 1/4* **Dimboola** 2-9-3 .... MichaelHills 6 84+
(B W Hills) *slowly away and rn green in rr: hdwy 1/2-way: r.o wl fnl f: bttr for r* **5/1**[3]

3 *shd* **Cassiara** 2-8-12 .... JimmyQuinn 4 79+
(J Pearce) *t.k.h: in tch: kpt on fnl f to press for 2nd* **9/1**

4 *4* **Fool Me (IRE)** 2-9-3 .... RichardMullen 10 68
(E S McMahon) *in rr and sn rdn: swtchd lft over 1f out: r.o fnl f: nvr nr to chal* **7/1**

5 *3/4* **Precocious Star (IRE)** 2-8-12 .... PatCosgrave 8 60
(K R Burke) *s.i.s and outpcd: styd on fnl f: nvr nearer* **12/1**

6 **6** *1 1/2* **Wrecking Crew (IRE)**[19] 663 2-9-3 .... AlanMunro 7 59
(B R Millman) *prom: ev ch 2f out: wknd appr fnl f* **5/1**[3]

3 **7** *1 3/4* **Goose Green (IRE)**[9] 775 2-9-3 .... TQuinn 2 52
(M R Channon) *prom tl rdn and wknd over 1f out* **9/2**[2]

8 *6* **Tom Paris** 2-9-3 .... MartinDwyer 1 28
(W R Muir) *a outpcd in rr* **16/1**

9 *6* **Bentley** 2-9-0 .... PatrickMathers(3) 3 —
(D Shaw) *sn in rr and nvr on terms* **50/1**

0 **10** *7* **Auctioneerscouk (IRE)**[14] 701 2-9-3 ....(v1) JamieSpencer 9 —
(P D Evans) *led tl rdn and hdd 2f out: wknd qckly* **16/1**

62.61 secs (1.71) **Going Correction** +0.175s/f (Good) **10** Ran SP% **120.4**
Speed ratings (Par 90):93,91,90,84,83 80,78,68,58,47
CSF £18.61 TOTE £4.10: £1.20, £2.40, £3.70; EX 21.70.
Owner H E Sheikh Rashid Bin Mohammed **Bred** N E and Mrs Poole and Trickledown Stud **Trained** Hambleton, N Yorks

FOCUS
This could prove a fair event of it's type for the time of year and the first three came clear.

NOTEBOOK
Hellvelyn, a 100,000gns half-brother to several sprint winners, got his career off to a perfect start in workmanlike fashion. He took time to find his stride, but duly quickened when asked to win his race, and looks assured to improve for the experience. Clearly a nice sprinting prospect for connections, it will be interesting to see where he is pitched in next, but he was easily the most expensive purchase in this line-up, and it would have been disappointing had he not done the business. (op 2-1 tchd 10-3, 7-2 in a place)
Dimboola ◆, speedily-bred, made a promising debut and may well have given the winner more to think about without making a sluggish start. He was not given a hard time late on and it will take a sharp juvenile to stop him going one better next time. (tchd 11-2)
Cassiara, whose dam was a multiple winner over this trip, travelled nicely in midfield for most of the race until ultimately finding just the same pace under pressure. She was nicely clear of the rest and looks to have a future. (op 11-1)
Fool Me(IRE), a 34,000gns half-brother to two winners at up to seven furlongs, was doing his best work at the finish after running distinctly green through the early parts. (op 12-1)
Precocious Star(IRE), whose dam is a half-sister to multiple winner Kindlelight Debut, lost all chance at the start and shaped as through the experience was very much needed. (op 11-1)
Wrecking Crew(IRE) had his chance, yet failed to improve on his recent debut at Lingfield. (op 8-1)
Goose Green(IRE) proved disappointing and ran well below the form of his recent Folkestone debut. (op 5-1)

893 LADBROKES.COM (S) STKS 5f 218y
2:45 (2:45) (Class 5) 3-Y-O **£3,238** (£963; £481; £240) **Stalls** Low

Form RPR

20-0 **1** **Taras Tornado**[73] 177 3-8-9 52..................................... JamieSpencer 5 56
(J J Quinn) *a.p: rdn to ld 1f out: kpt up to work* **7/2**[1]

-332 **2** *1 1/4* **Psycho Cat**[21] 651 3-9-5 62...(b1) NCallan 1 62
(P A Blockley) *in tch: led on stands' side 1/2-way: rdn and hdd 1f out: kpt on* **9/2**[3]

5633 **3** *3* **Woodwee**[6] 819 3-9-5 60... DarrylHolland 3 53
(J R Weymes) *led to 1/2-way: rdn and kpt on one pce fnl f* **9/2**[3]

030- **4** *1 1/4* **Coalite (IRE)**[234] 4420 3-9-0 74.. DaneO'Neill 9 45
(B Palling) *a.p on outside: rdn over 1f out: no ex* **4/1**[2]

-000 **5** *3* **Lucys Lady**[66] 248 3-8-9 55... AndrewElliott(5) 2 36
(K R Burke) *s.i.s: in rr tl sme late hdwy* **10/1**

4210 **6** *5* **Miss Champagne (IRE)**[8] 796 3-9-0 55...................... FrancisNorton 8 21
(M Quinn) *in front rnk tl rdn over 2f out: wknd over 1f out* **7/1**

00-0 **7** *1/2* **Southborough Lad**[8] 795 3-9-0 30...................................... JohnEgan 6 19
(Mrs C A Dunnett) *outpcd thrght* **25/1**

-400 **8** *1 1/4* **Sanders Boy**[8] 790 3-9-0 45... DarrenWilliams 7 15
(J R Norton) *outpcd thrght* **50/1**

0010 **9** *10* **Teddy Monty (IRE)**[16] 690 3-9-5 52...............................(b) RyanMoore 4 —
(M Quinn) *sn prom: rdn over 3f out: wknd over 2f out* **9/1**

1m 15.56s (2.36) **Going Correction** +0.175s/f (Good) **9** Ran SP% **116.0**
Speed ratings (Par 98):91,89,85,83,79 73,72,70,57
CSF £19.49 TOTE £3.70: £1.30, £1.40, £1.90; EX 19.50 Trifecta £138.80 Pool: £467.61 - 2.40 winning units.The winner was bought in for 8,500gns. Coalite (IRE) was claimed by Mr R. G. Fell for £6,000. Psycho Cat was the subject of a friendly claim.
Owner Tara Leisure **Bred** T J Cooper **Trained** Settrington, N Yorks

FOCUS
A weak affair, run at a sound pace, and the form looks fair for the class.
Sanders Boy Official explanation: jockey said gelding was unsuited by ground

894 LADBROKESCASINO.COM MAIDEN STKS 1m 3f 183y
3:20 (3:23) (Class 5) 3-4-Y-O **£5,181** (£1,541; £770; £384) **Stalls** High

Form RPR

40-6 **1** **Cool Customer (USA)**[19] 669 3-8-8 74 ow2.............. JamieSpencer 4 72
(E A L Dunlop) *towards rr: short of room fr over 4f out but hdwy on ins whn swtchd rt and qcknd to ld over 1f out: sn clr* **11/2**[2]

00-0 **2** *3* **Vehari**[48] 445 3-8-3 40... EdwardCreighton(3) 13 66
(M Scudamore) *led tl rdn and hdd over 1f out: nt pce of wnr* **150/1**

3 *3/4* **Som Tala** 3-8-6 .... TedDurcan 11 64
(M R Channon) *trckd ldrs: lost place 4f out: hung rt 2f out: r.o and gd hdwy fnl f* **10/1**

0-4 **4** *1 1/2* **Newport Boy (IRE)**[10] 762 3-8-6 .... RyanMoore 2 62
(S Kirk) *hld up in rr: hdwy whn hung lft and c over to stands' rail over 2f out: r.o fnl fnl f* **7/1**[3]

00- **5** *3/4* **Dawn's Last Shot (IRE)**[248] 4006 4-9-12 .... IanMongan 3 64
(J L Dunlop) *hld up towards rr: styd on fnl 2f: nvr nr to chal* **16/1**

40- **6** *1 1/2* **Tayman (IRE)**[353] 1096 4-9-12 .... SteveDrowne 12 61
(G Wragg) *hld up in mid-div: kpt on one pce fnl 3f* **9/1**

7 *2 1/2* **To Dubai** 3-8-1 .... MatthewHenry 7 49
(M A Jarvis) *prom: rdn over 3f out: one pce after* **7/1**[3]

5 **8** *2* **Calcutta Cup (UAE)**[19] 668 3-8-6 .... KDarley 9 51
(M Johnston) *trckd ldr: rdn and ev ch 3f out tl weakened over 1f out* **5/1**[1]

234- **9** *11* **Lady Diktat**[227] 4643 4-9-7 69... NCallan 1 32
(Mrs A J Hamilton-Fairley) *t.k.h: in tch: rdn and wknd over 1f out* **8/1**

0-0 **10** *3/4* **Queen Tara**[38] 531 4-9-0 .... KirstyMilczarek(7) 8 30
(Mrs C A Dunnett) *mid-divisision: hung lft over 5f out: sn bhd* **66/1**

11 *nk* **Good Intentions** 4-9-7 .... ChrisCatlin 5 30
(P W Hiatt) *v.s.aa: a bhd* **50/1**

02 **12** *7* **Elated (IRE)**[34] 566 4-9-12 .... DarrylHolland 10 24
(W J Haggas) *trckd ldrs: rdn over 3f out: sn bhd* **5/1**[1]

30-0 **13** *3 1/2* **Silver Court**[53] 386 4-9-7 40.. JamesDoyle(5) 6 18
(A W Carroll) *pulle hrd in rr: hdwy on outside whn bumpered over 5f out: sn bhd* **66/1**

2m 40.83s (6.33) **Going Correction** +0.65s/f (Yiel)
WFA 3 from 4yo 21lb **13** Ran SP% **115.4**
Speed ratings (Par 103):104,102,101,100,100 99,97,96,88,88 87,83,80
CSF £663.95 TOTE £3.80: £2.00, £31.10, £3.20; EX 303.20.
Owner Gainsborough Stud **Bred** Dell Ridge Farm **Trained** Newmarket, Suffolk
■ Stewards' Enquiry : Ted Durcan one-day ban: careless riding (Apr 17)

FOCUS
A modest maiden, full of late-maturing types, and the form looks suspect.
Lady Diktat Official explanation: jockey said filly had no more to give
Silver Court Official explanation: jockey said gelding ran too free

895 LADBROKES.COM KIBWORTH H'CAP 1m 1f 218y
3:55 (3:57) (Class 3) (0-95,85) 3-Y-O
£7,790 (£2,332; £1,166; £583; £291; £146) **Stalls** High

Form RPR

021- **1** **High Command**[247] 4027 3-9-5 **83**.................................. JamieSpencer 2 90
(E A L Dunlop) *hld up in rr: hung rt fr over 3f out but r.o to ld wl ins fnl f* **10/3**[2]

21 **2** *nk* **Soapy Danger**[38] 536 3-9-2 **80**.. KDarley 1 86
(M Johnston) *led: rdn 2f out: hdd wl ins fnl f* **9/2**

41-2 **3** *1 1/4* **Juniper Girl (IRE)**[9] 781 3-8-3 **67**................................... HayleyTurner 4 71
(M L W Bell) *t.k.h: a in tch: rdn and hdwy 2f out: carried rt by wnr ins fnl f and no ex* **4/1**[3]

001- **4** *4* **Twill (IRE)**[136] 6402 3-9-4 **82**.. SteveDrowne 6 78+
(H Morrison) *mid-div: hdwy 2f out: held whn short of room ins fnl f* **10/1**

303- **5** *3* **Ocean Pride (IRE)**[152] 6249 3-9-7 **85**........................... RichardHughes 5 76
(R Hannon) *t.k.h: hld up in rr: effrt 2f out: sn btn* **7/1**

32-1 **6** *2* **Estiqraar (IRE)**[12] 731 3-9-6 **84**.. RHills 3 71
(J L Dunlop) *trckd ldr tl rdn and wknd over 1f out* **5/2**[1]

2m 13.98s (5.68) **Going Correction** +0.65s/f (Yiel) **6** Ran SP% **111.4**
Speed ratings (Par 102):103,102,101,98,96 94
CSF £18.10 TOTE £5.20: £2.20, £2.20; EX 22.10.
Owner Mohammed Jaber **Bred** Whitsbury Manor Stud And Tower Bloodstock **Trained** Newmarket, Suffolk
■ Stewards' Enquiry : Jamie Spencer caution: careless riding; two-day ban: used whip with excessive force (Apr 17-18)

FOCUS
A fair handicap for three-year-olds, run at an average pace, and the first two came clear.

NOTEBOOK
High Command, last seen getting off the mark at Catterick 247 days previously, followed-up to make a winning three-year-old debut despite not looking the easiest of rides. Being by Galileo, it was little surprise that he relished the step up to this longer trip, and he is clearly open to further improvement this term. Official explanation: jockey said colt was hanging right (op 7-2)
Soapy Danger, off the mark at the second time of asking on the All-Weather last term, stepped-up on that form with a brave effort and only just lost out. He looked suited by the ground, has developed a likeable attitude, and may be ready to tackle slightly further now. (op 5-1)
Juniper Girl(IRE), runner-up on her recent return to action at Folkestone nine days previously, was not done many favours by the winner late on, yet looked held at the time and eventually paid for refusing to settle though the early parts. She may face a rise in the weights now. (op 11-4)
Twill(IRE), off the mark at the third attempt on his final outing last season, emerged to have his chance around two out and was already on the retreat when slightly hampered late on. He is entitled to improve for the run, but still has to prove he is up to his current mark. (op 9-1 tchd 11-1)
Estiqraar(IRE), easily off the mark on his recent comeback at Redcar, faded disappointingly when it mattered and is not going to prove easy to place now. Official explanation: trainer was unable to offer any explanation for poor form shown (op 3-1)

896 LADBROKES.COM CONDITIONS STKS 5f 218y
4:30 (4:30) (Class 4) 3-Y-O

£6,232 (£1,866; £933; £467; £233; £117) Stalls Low

Form RPR
343- 1 **Angus Newz**[160] 6129 3-8-5 90 ....(v) FrancisNorton 6 93
(M Quinn) *mde all: rdn out fnl f* 11/2[3]
266- 2 1 ¾ **Gamble In Gold (IRE)**[264] 3537 3-8-7 90 .... RichardHughes 2 90
(R Hannon) *bhd tl hdwy over 2f out: wnt 2nd over 1f out: no imp on wnr fnl f* 11/8[1]
656- 3 1 **Puskas (IRE)**[180] 5742 3-9-0 100 .... TQuinn 4 94
(M R Channon) *trckd ldr: chsd wnr over 2f out to over 1f out: kpt on one pce* 11/4[2]
245- 4 5 **Charles Darwin (IRE)**[180] 5742 3-8-10 91 .... FergusSweeney 1 75
(M Blanshard) *hld up in rr: effrt 2f out: wknd appr fnl f* 11/2[3]
01-4 5 5 **Bathwick Emma (IRE)**[13] 717 3-8-5 77 .... RichardMullen 5 55
(P D Evans) *trckd wnr to over 2f out: rdn and sn btn* 14/1
430- 6 3 ½ **Dune Melody (IRE)**[166] 6027 3-8-7 79 .... JohnEgan 3 47
(J S Moore) *in tch: rdn 1/2-way: sn bhd* 20/1

1m 13.6s (0.40) **Going Correction** +0.175s/f (Good) **6** Ran SP% **111.0**
Speed ratings (Par 100):104,101,100,93,87 82
CSF £13.26 TOTE £2.70: £1.80, £2.00; EX 15.80.
Owner J G Dooley M Quinn **Bred** Henry And Mrs Rosemary Moszkowicz **Trained** Newmarket, Suffolk
FOCUS
A decent little conditions event and the form looks sound with the first three coming clear.

897 LADBROKES.COM MAIDEN STKS 1m 1f 218y
5:05 (5:06) (Class 5) 3-Y-O+ £5,181 (£1,541; £770; £384) Stalls High

Form RPR
1 **Faversham** 3-8-7 .... PhilipRobinson 5 69+
(M A Jarvis) *racd wd: hdwy to trck ldrs over 5f out: hung lft but led over 1f out: rdn out* 5/1[3]
2 2 **Souffleur** 3-8-8 ow1 .... JamieSpencer 3 66+
(M L W Bell) *a.p on outside: kpt on fnl f* 11/2
56- 3 1 ¼ **Strategic Mount**[167] 6013 3-8-7 .... TQuinn 15 63+
(P F I Cole) *trckd ldr: led over 3f out: rdn and hdd over 1f out: kpt on one pce* 7/2[1]
0- 4 hd **Swan Queen**[159] 6143 3-8-2 .... JimmyQuinn 13 57
(J L Dunlop) *a int tch: rdn over 3f out: lost pl 2f out: styd on again wl fnl f* 18/1
4- 5 2 ½ **Altenburg (FR)**[10] 4833 4-9-7 .... JamesDoyle(5) 9 62
(Mrs N Smith) *in rr tl hdwy 2f out: r.o on fnl f: nvr nrr* 25/1
-350 6 ¾ **The Rebound Kid**[41] 504 4-9-12 63 .... MartinDwyer 2 61
(G A Huffer) *prom on outside: ev ch 2f out: wknd appr fnl f* 25/1
7 ¾ **Ghallab** 3-8-7 .... RHills 17 55
(E A L Dunlop) *plld hrd: in tch tl no hdwy appr fnl f* 9/2[2]
8 ½ **Kathleen Kennet**[56] 6-9-7 .... GeorgeBaker 1 54
(Mrs H Sweeting) *slowly away: in rr tl mde sme late hdwy* 25/1
9 ¾ **La Estrella (USA)** 3-8-7 .... MickyFenton 10 52
(J G Given) *mid-div: wknd 2f out* 20/1
0 10 ¾ **Must Be Keen**[84] 97 7-9-12 .... AlanMunro 4 56
(Ernst Oertel) *plld hrd: mid-div: hdwy over 2f out: wknd over 1f out* 100/1
00- 11 nk **Soufah (IRE)**[265] 3507 4-9-12 .... SebSanders 8 55
(J L Dunlop) *mid-div: no hdwy ins fnl 3f* 16/1
0- 12 1 ½ **Call Me George**[202] 5279 3-8-7 .... JoeFanning 12 47
(M Johnston) *mid-div: rdn 1/2-way: nvr on terms* 20/1
5 13 20 **Fleur A Lay (USA)**[34] 573 4-9-7 .... RyanMoore 16 9
(Mrs A J Perrett) *led tl hdd over 3f out: wknd qckly and eased over 1f out* 14/1
14 8 **Lets Be Lucky (IRE)** 4-9-12 .... PaulFitzsimons 7 —
(F Jordan) *in tch: hdwy 6f out: wknd over 3f out* 66/1
0-0 15 5 **Eccollo (IRE)**[19] 669 4-9-12 .... JohnEgan 14 —
(T J Pitt) *hld up in rr: a wl bhd* 40/1
16 nk **Asleep At The Back (IRE)** 3-8-7 .... NeilPollard 11 —
(J G Given) *mid-div: wl bhd fnl 4f* 33/1
17 18 **Kentuckian** 4-9-12 .... StephenCarson 6 —
(P W Hiatt) *slowly away: sn wl bhd: t.o* 50/1

2m 12.96s (4.66) **Going Correction** +0.65s/f (Yiel)
WFA 3 from 4yo+ 19lb **17** Ran SP% **121.2**
Speed ratings (Par 103):107,105,104,104,102 101,101,100,100,99 99,98,82,75,71 71,56
CSF £28.35 TOTE £5.40: £2.30, £2.50, £1.40; EX 28.50 Trifecta £85.70 Pool: £187.14 - 1.55 winning units.
Owner Jumeirah Racing **Bred** Darley **Trained** Newmarket, Suffolk
FOCUS
A fair maiden, run at a sound pace, and the form should work out.
Eccollo(IRE) Official explanation: jockey said gelding had a breathing problem
Asleep At The Back(IRE) Official explanation: trainer said gelding had a breathing problem

898 LEVY BOARD H'CAP 7f 9y
5:40 (5:42) (Class 4) (0-85,83) 4-Y-O+ **£6,309** (£1,888; £944; £472; £235) Stalls Low

Form RPR
-451 1 **Hail The Chief**[9] 777 9-8-6 71 5ex .... RyanMoore 8 85
(R Hannon) *rdn and hdwy 2f out: led ent fnl f: drvn clr* 7/1[3]
0-04 2 2 ½ **Commando Scott (IRE)**[12] 726 5-9-0 79 .... SebSanders 4 86
(I W McInnes) *hld up: hdwy over 2f out: rdn to chse wnr fnl f* 11/2[2]
442- 3 3 **Dabbers Ridge (IRE)**[159] 6149 4-9-2 81 .... MichaelHills 16 80
(B W Hills) *led 1/2-way tl hdd ent fnl f: nt qckn ins* 2/1[1]
-153 4 1 **Arctic Desert**[10] 764 6-8-9 74 .... RichardHughes 12 71
(A M Balding) *hld up: hdwy over 1f out: r.o: nvr nrr* 11/1
/10- 5 ½ **Puya**[181] 5713 4-9-4 83 .... DaneO'Neill 13 78
(H Candy) *a.p: rdn and one pce fr over 1f out* 9/1
10-3 6 3 **Resplendent Nova**[9] 777 4-8-4 69 .... JoeFanning 11 57
(T G Mills) *prom: chsd ldr over 2f out tl wknd appr fnl f* 7/1[3]
000- 7 2 **Distant Times**[249] 3968 5-8-4 69 .... AlanMunro 14 51
(T D Easterby) *mid-vision and nvr nr to chal* 66/1
55-U 8 ¾ **Flying Bantam (IRE)**[13] 719 5-8-10 75 .... PaulHanagan 6 55
(R A Fahey) *mid-div: rdn and no hdwy fnl 2f* 14/1
020- 9 ¾ **Burley Flame**[159] 6149 5-8-10 75 .... (v) MickyFenton 2 53
(J G Given) *chsd ldrs tl rdn and wknd over 2f out* 20/1
0520 10 1 ¾ **Elrafa Mujahid**[9] 777 4-8-1 69 .... (p) SaleemGolam(3) 10 43
(Ernst Oertel) *prom tl wknd over 2f out* 66/1
306- 11 9 **Saxon Lil (IRE)**[195] 5440 4-8-10 75 .... SteveDrowne 7 25
(J L Spearing) *a towards rr* 25/1
06-0 12 1 ¼ **Rain Stops Play (IRE)**[13] 719 4-8-12 77 .... FrancisNorton 15 24
(M Quinn) *hld up: a bhd* 33/1
400- 13 1 **Ginger Spice (IRE)**[178] 5806 4-8-12 77 .... JamieSpencer 1 22
(W J Haggas) *prom on stands' side tl wknd over 2f out* 14/1
000- 14 5 **Sabrina Brown**[105] 6657 5-9-0 79 .... (t) StephenCarson 3 11
(J A Geake) *led to 1/2-way: wknd qckly* 33/1
030- 15 5 **Paris Bell**[152] 6248 4-8-10 75 .... PaulQuinn 5 —
(T D Easterby) *slowly away: a bhd* 25/1
02P- 16 1 ¾ **Grizedale (IRE)**[159] 6149 7-8-12 77 .... (t) PaulDoe 9 —
(J Akehurst) *in tch to 1/2-way* 40/1

1m 26.86s (0.76) **Going Correction** +0.175s/f (Good) **16** Ran SP% **129.1**
Speed ratings (Par 105):102,99,95,94,94 90,88,87,86,84 74,72,71,66,60 58
CSF £44.43 CT £113.71 TOTE £9.70: £2.40, £2.30, £1.60, £3.20; EX 58.30 Trifecta £79.30 Pool: £335.38 - 3 winning units. Place 6 £70.95, Place 5 £39.29.
Owner Peter M Crane **Bred** Green Meadow Stud And P Crane **Trained** East Everleigh, Wilts
FOCUS
A fair handicap, run at a decent early pace, and the form looks solid enough.
Ginger Spice(IRE) Official explanation: jockey said filly hung right
T/Plt: £58.40 to a £1 stake. Pool: £36,586.60. 457.10 winning tickets. T/Qpdt: £12.90 to a £1 stake. Pool: £2,764.60. 157.60 winning tickets. JS

849 LINGFIELD (L-H)
Friday, April 7

OFFICIAL GOING: Standard
Wind: Strong, behind

900 LINGFIELD PARK GOLF CLUB MEDIAN AUCTION MAIDEN STKS 1m (P)
2:10 (2:11) (Class 6) 3-4-Y-O £2,730 (£806; £403) Stalls High

Form RPR
3- 1 **Herring (IRE)**[170] 5968 3-8-9 .... JamieSpencer 5 65
(D J Coakley) *trckd ldrs: jnd ldr 4f out: rdn to ld over 1f out: jst hld on* 3/1[2]
2-2 2 hd **Dream Champion**[63] 112 3-8-9 .... TonyCulhane 6 64
(M R Channon) *chsd ldrs: sltly outpcd over 2f out: styd on strly ins fnl f: jst failed* 5/4[1]
0- 3 nk **Greenwich Village**[217] 4916 3-8-9 .... EddieAhern 1 63
(W J Knight) *s.i.s: sn rcvrd in mid div: hdwy over 2f out: sn rdn: styd on ins fnl f* 14/1
4 4 hd **Lisathedaddy**[16] 692 4-9-5 .... HayleyTurner 8 62
(B G Powell) *hld up: hdwy over 2f out: sn rdn: styd on wl fnl f* 14/1
02 5 nk **Marcello**[14] 710 3-8-9 .... RichardHughes 4 62
(P F I Cole) *led: rdn and hdd over 1f out: wknd cl home* 8/1
0P- 6 6 **Ferrando**[335] 1552 4-9-10 .... TPQueally 9 53
(D J Daly) *restrained s: t.k.h early: hld up: sme late prog but nvr a danger* 66/1
000- 7 7 **Iceni Warrior**[202] 5302 4-9-10 45 .... J-PGuillambert 10 36
(P Howling) *in tch tl wknd 2f out* 100/1
0 8 ½ **Maya's Prince**[10] 778 4-9-10 .... RobbieFitzpatrick 7 35
(M D I Usher) *a towards rr* 100/1
036- 9 2 ½ **Squadron Leader (IRE)**[133] 6423 3-8-9 71 .... RyanMoore 2 26
(R Hannon) *chsd ldrs: rdn 3f out: wknd over 1f out* 6/1[3]
50 10 ¾ **Just Tilly**[14] 710 3-8-4 .... ChrisCatlin 3 19
(P R Chamings) *in tch: rdn 3f out: sn btn* 33/1

1m 39.17s (-0.26) **Going Correction** -0.10s/f (Stan)
WFA 3 from 4yo 15lb **10** Ran SP% **114.6**
Speed ratings (Par 101):97,96,96,96,96 90,83,82,80,79
CSF £6.90 TOTE £5.10: £1.80, £1.02, £4.50; EX 9.80 Trifecta £86.40 Pool: £564.07 - 4.63 winning tickets..
Owner Bolam Hurley Ross **Bred** J Fisher **Trained** West Ilsley, Berks
FOCUS
This looked just an average maiden run at only a steady pace in the early stages. Modest form; the first two were probably not at their best but the next four ran close enough to their previous form.

901 WEATHERBYS BANK MAIDEN STKS 5f (P)
2:45 (2:47) (Class 5) 3-Y-O+ £3,238 (£963; £481; £240) Stalls High

Form RPR
0- 1 **Ripples Maid**[172] 5946 3-8-6 .... RichardThomas(3) 3 68
(J A Geake) *prom: led after 1f: rdn and drifted off rails ins fnl f: drvn out* 10/1
3 2 ¾ **Pititana (IRE)**[13] 722 3-8-9 .... RichardHughes 2 65
(R Hannon) *led for over 1f: chsd wnr: nt clr run on rails 2f out tl 1f out: r.o* 5/2[2]
0- 3 shd **Pride Of Joy**[326] 1756 3-8-9 .... MartinDwyer 8 65
(D K Ivory) *hld up: hdwy 2f out: sn rdn: r.o to go 3rd ins fnl f* 66/1
3- 4 ¾ **Hang Loose**[179] 5796 3-9-0 .... DaneO'Neill 7 67
(R Charlton) *chsd ldrs: rdn 2f out: kpt on same pce fnl f* 2/1[1]
5352 5 nk **Phinerine**[27] 626 3-9-0 72 .... (b) AdrianMcCarthy 1 66
(R A Harris) *trckd ldrs: snatched up briefly over 2f out: nt clr run and swtchd rt over 1f out: kpt on* 8/1
3-22 6 ½ **Best Double**[36] 553 3-8-9 69 .... NickyMackay 5 59
(G A Butler) *s.i.s: bhd: hdwy over 2f out: rn wd into st: kpt on same pce fnl f* 4/1[3]
5003 7 ¾ **Danish Blues (IRE)**[8] 801 3-8-9 60 .... (p) JamesDoyle(5) 4 61
(N P Littmoden) *in tch: effrt 2f out: wknd ins fnl f* 16/1
000- 8 2 ½ **Double Valentine**[146] 6320 3-8-9 55 .... SteveDrowne 6 47
(R Ingram) *chsd ldrs: rdn whn forced wd on bnd 2f out: no ch after* 66/1
00-0 9 ¾ **Just Down The Road (IRE)**[45] 473 3-8-9 67 .... EddieAhern 9 45
(R A Harris) *a towards rr* 25/1
00 10 3 ½ **Danethorpe (IRE)**[13] 722 3-8-11 .... PatrickMathers(3) 10 37
(D Shaw) *sn outpcd in rr* 100/1

59.15 secs (-0.63) **Going Correction** -0.10s/f (Stan) **10** Ran SP% **115.8**
Speed ratings (Par 103):101,99,99,98,97 97,95,91,90,85
CSF £34.74 TOTE £12.50: £2.30, £1.50, £14.70; EX 47.70 Trifecta £517.60 Part won. Pool: £729.04 - 0.70 winning tickets..
Owner Rex L Mead **Bred** Compton Down Stud **Trained** Kimpton, Hants
FOCUS
A modest maiden and, quite ridiculously for a sprint, they went no pace in the early stages.

902 VIZARDS WYETH SOLICITORS FILLIES' H'CAP 7f (P)
3:20 (3:21) (Class 5) (0-70,69) 3-Y-O+ £3,238 (£963; £481; £240) Stalls Low

Form RPR
1- 1 **Redeye Special**[206] 5213 4-9-2 57 .... JamieSpencer 10 68+
(M L W Bell) *in tch: rdn and hdwy fr over 2f out: r.o ins fnl f: led fnl strides* 11/8[1]
-002 2 nk **Ivory Lace**[41] 519 5-9-4 64 .... JamesDoyle(5) 13 74
(S Woodman) *hld up: swtchd to outer 2f out: rdn and hung lft over 1f out: r.o strly ins fnl f: tk 2nd fnl stride* 8/1[3]

2131 **3** *shd* **Riquewihr**[16] [693] 6-9-6 **61**..........(p) RobertWinston 4 71
(J S Wainwright) *in tch: rdn to ld 1f out: kpt on but no ex whn ct fnl strides* **7/1**[2]

4062 **4** *1 ½* **Miskina**[16] [693] 5-9-2 **57**.......... EddieAhern 1 63
(W M Brisbourne) *led: rdn and hdd 1f out: kpt on* **12/1**

600- **5** *½* **Blue Line**[181] [5734] 4-9-4 **59**.......... GeorgeBaker 5 64
(M Madgwick) *hld up: rdn over 2f out: styd on fr over 1f out: nrst fin* **33/1**

6200 **6** *1 ¾* **Kallista's Pride**[8] [806] 6-8-13 **61**.......... KylieManser(7) 3 61
(J R Best) *mid div: rdn over 1f out: kpt on same pce* **18/1**

3053 **7** *shd* **Triple Zero (IRE)**[14] [708] 4-8-13 **57**.......... AdamKirby(3) 9 57
(A P Jarvis) *chsd ldrs: rdn 2f out: ono pce fnl f* **14/1**

400- **8** *1 ¼* **Pippa's Dancer (IRE)**[174] [5893] 4-9-12 **67**.......... RichardHughes 8 64
(W R Muir) *in tch: rdn 2f out: wknd fnl f* **40/1**

-005 **9** *1 ¾* **Precautionary**[13] [722] 3-8-2 **60**.......... EdwardCreighton(3) 2 52
(Miss J Feilden) *hld up: sme hdwy over 1f out: no further imp ins fnl f* **66/1**

6-00 **10** *1 ¼* **Moon Bird**[36] [555] 4-9-5 **60**.......... DarryllHolland 6 49
(C A Cyzer) *chsd ldrs: rdn 3f out: wknd 1f out* **33/1**

-225 **11** *5* **Siwa**[39] [533] 3-9-0 **69**.......... SteveDrowne 14 45
(E A L Dunlop) *in tch: rdn over 2f out: wkng whn forced wd on bnd wl over 1f out* **10/1**

330- **12** *1* **Pink Bay**[170] [5981] 4-9-11 **66**.......... FergusSweeney 7 39
(W S Kittow) *chsd ldrs: rdn 3f out: sn wknd* **25/1**

4556 **13** *nk* **Attitude Annie**[32] [595] 3-8-2 **57**.......... ChrisCatlin 11 29
(S Dow) *a bhd* **50/1**

42R5 **R** **Miss Dagger (IRE)**[8] [807] 3-8-6 **61**.......... MartinDwyer 12 —
(J R Best) *ref to r: tk no part* **8/1**[3]

1m 24.7s (-1.19) **Going Correction** -0.10s/f (Stan)
WFA 3 from 4yo+ 14lb **14** Ran SP% **121.2**
Speed ratings (Par 100):102,101,101,99,99 97,97,95,93,92 86,85,85,—
CSF £11.72 CT £63.90 TOTE £2.00: £1.40, £3.40, £1.70; EX 17.80 Trifecta £88.70 Pool: £453.99 - 3.83 winning tickets..
Owner R L W Frisby **Bred** Sentinel Bloodstock **Trained** Newmarket, Suffolk

FOCUS
A modest fillies' handicap, run at a decent pace, and the form appears solid for the class.
Pippa's Dancer(IRE) Official explanation: jockey said, regarding the running and riding, his orders were to get filly settled and make the best of his way home at it was filly's first run over 7f, adding that filly settled well but probably failed to stay
Siwa Official explanation: jockey said filly hung right throughout

903 LINGFIELD PARK LEISURE CLUB H'CAP — 6f (P)
3:55 (3:56) (Class 6) (0-60,60) 4-Y-0+ **£2,730** (£806; £403) **Stalls** Low

Form RPR

0014 **1** **Desert Light (IRE)**[6] [837] 5-9-1 **57** 7ex..........(v) DaneO'Neill 1 66
(D Shaw) *s.i.s: sn rcvrd into mid div: hdwy over 2f out: swtchd lft 1f out: r.o wl to ld ins fnl f: rdn out* **10/1**

1342 **2** *nk* **Beneking**[4] [854] 6-8-10 **52**..........(p) ChrisCatlin 7 60
(D Burchell) *sn drvn along to chse ldrs: led over 2f out: no ex whn hdd ins fnl f* **10/3**[2]

5000 **3** *½* **Tiviski (IRE)**[8] [806] 4-9-4 **60**..........(p) JamieSpencer 2 67
(G G Margarson) *chsd ldrs: rdn over 2f out: kpt on ins fianl f* **6/1**[3]

2620 **4** *1* **Grezie**[16] [693] 4-8-12 **54**.......... EddieAhern 4 58
(T D McCarthy) *prom: lft in ld over 4f out: rdn and hdd 2f out: kpt on same pce* **10/1**

0-00 **5** *hd* **Imtalkinggibberish**[16] [693] 5-8-12 **54**.......... RobertWinston 6 57
(J R Jenkins) *in tch: rdn 2f out: kpt on same pce* **8/1**

0160 **6** *¾* **Mind Alert**[6] [837] 5-8-10 **55**..........(v) PatrickMathers(3) 9 56
(D Shaw) *s.i.s: bhd: hdwy on inner wl over 1f out: no further imp ins fnl f* **16/1**

6046 **7** *shd* **Hadath (IRE)**[6] [837] 9-9-1 **57**..........(p) TQuinn 3 57
(B G Powell) *towards rr: drvn along over 4f out: styd on fnl f: nvr trbld ldrs* **8/1**

6111 **8** *hd* **Auentraum (GER)**[2] [889] 6-8-13 **55** 7ex..........(p) DarryllHolland 5 55
(K McAuliffe) *s.i.s: bhd: styd on fnl f: n.d* **3/1**[1]

-355 **9** *1* **Charlie Bear**[79] [138] 5-8-13 **55**.......... AdrianMcCarthy 12 52
(Miss Z C Davison) *chsd ldrs: rdn 2f out: wknd fnl f* **20/1**

236- **10** *15* **Pro Tempore**[209] [5119] 4-8-10 **52**.......... FergusSweeney 11 4+
(David Pinder) *w ldr tl carried wd appr bnd over 4f out: no ch after: virtually p.u* **33/1**

005- **11** *24* **Drumming Party (USA)**[185] [5693] 4-9-1 **57**.......... MartinDwyer 8 —+
(A M Balding) *led tl rn wd appr bnd over 4f out: no ch after and virtually p.u* **20/1**

1m 11.86s (-0.95) **Going Correction** -0.10s/f (Stan) **11** Ran SP% **121.1**
Speed ratings (Par 101):102,101,100,99,99 98,98,97,96,76 44
CSF £43.61 CT £231.61 TOTE £12.90: £3.40, £1.50, £1.70; EX 56.40 Trifecta £122.20 Pool: £361.50 - 2.10 winning tickets..
Owner Danethorpe Racing Ltd **Bred** Anthony M Cahill **Trained** Danethorpe, Notts

FOCUS
A moderate handicap run at just a fair pace and a dramatic race with the leader Drumming Party virtually running out on the top bend and carrying out Pro Tempore as he did so. Despite that the form appears sound enough.
Auentraum(GER) Official explanation: jockey said gelding reared as stalls opened
Pro Tempore Official explanation: jockey said filly was hampered approaching 4f marker
Drumming Party(USA) Official explanation: jockey said gelding cocked its jaw and ran out approaching the 4f marker

904 LINGFIELD-RACECOURSE.CO.UK (S) STKS — 1m 2f (P)
4:30 (4:31) (Class 6) 3-Y-0+ **£2,388** (£705; £352) **Stalls** Low

Form RPR

0613 **1** **Competitor**[6] [833] 5-9-13 60..........(vt) TQuinn 2 63
(J Akehurst) *towards rr: hdwy over 2f out: styd on strly to ld wl ins fnl f* **2/1**[2]

3664 **2** *nk* **Barton Sands (IRE)**[16] [697] 9-9-13 59..........(t) J-PGuillambert 3 62
(Ernst Oertel) *mid div: gd hdwy to ld wl over 1f out: sn rdn: no ex whn hdd ins wl ins fnl f* **7/4**[1]

6004 **3** *1 ¼* **Paso Doble**[4] [853] 8-9-6 62.......... JamesMillman(7) 1 60
(B R Millman) *hld up towards rr: hdwy over 2f out: nt clr run twice over 1f out: styd on to go 3rd cl home* **9/1**[3]

4 *¾* **Tullochrome**[73] 3-8-0 56 ow1.......... ChrisCatlin 5 51
(E J O'Neill) *chsd ldrs: rdn and ev ch over 1f out: no ex* **11/1**

20/3 **5** *3* **Bhutan (IRE)**[16] [694] 11-9-9 48.......... SteveDrowne 4 49
(Jim Best) *mid div: hdwy over 2f out: rdn and effrt over 1f out: one pce fnl f* **11/1**

0560 **6** *½* **Piquet**[10] [780] 8-9-4 45.......... TPQueally 7 43
(J J Bridger) *chsd ldrs: rdn over 2f out: sn one pce* **16/1**

03-0 **7** *2 ½* **Garple Burn**[11] [767] 4-9-6 48..........(p) AmirQuinn(3) 9 43
(Jim Best) *trckd ldr: jnd ldr over 4f out: led 3f out tl over 1f out: sn wknd* **33/1**

00 **8** *½* **Beauchamp Ultra**[62] [291] 3-7-13.......... NickyMackay 11 37
(G A Butler) *a towards rr* **16/1**

40-0 **9** *15* **Danish Monarch**[18] [682] 5-9-9 40.......... FergusSweeney 8 14
(David Pinder) *sn led: rdn and hdd 3f out: sn wknd* **33/1**

000- **10** *2 ½* **Miss Cue**[216] [4934] 4-9-4 30.......... TonyCulhane 6 4
(J Pearce) *a bhd* **66/1**

0000 **11** *2* **Tally (IRE)**[9] [793] 6-9-9 40.......... RobbieFitzpatrick 10 5
(D G Bridgwater) *in tch: rdn over 4f out: sn btn* **25/1**

2m 7.40s (-0.39) **Going Correction** -0.10s/f (Stan)
WFA 3 from 4yo+ 19lb **11** Ran SP% **119.3**
Speed ratings (Par 101):97,96,95,95,92 92,90,89,77,75 74
CSF £5.77 TOTE £2.80: £1.10, £1.10, £3.00; EX 6.40 Trifecta £38.50 Pool: £530.43 - 9.76 winning tickets..There was no bid for the winner.
Owner Who Cares Who Wins **Bred** Cheveley Park Stud Ltd **Trained** Epsom, Surrey
■ Stewards' Enquiry : J-P Guillambert two-day ban: careless riding (Apr 18-19)

FOCUS
The leading duo on form fought out the finish, with Competitor coming late to deny the favourite and the form appears reliable.

905 COME RACING TOMORROW APPRENTICE H'CAP — 1m 2f (P)
5:05 (5:05) (Class 5) (0-75,75) 4-Y-0+ **£3,238** (£963; £481; £240) **Stalls** Low

Form RPR

5125 **1** **Star Magnitude (USA)**[11] [763] 5-9-4 **75**.......... DeanWilliams 9 85
(S Dow) *s.i.s: bhd: gd hdwy 2f out: sn rdn: r.o wl to ld fnl 20yds* **7/1**

2202 **2** *1* **Augustine**[15] [706] 5-8-3 **65**.......... TolleyDean(5) 5 73
(P W Hiatt) *chsd ldrs: rdn over 1f out: led wl ins fnl f: no ex whn hdd fnl 20yds* **13/8**[1]

632- **3** *1* **Compton Court**[180] [5762] 4-8-6 **68**.......... JosephWalsh(5) 7 74
(A M Balding) *chsd ldrs: led 4f out: rdn over 1f out: hdd wl ins fnl f: kpt on* **13/2**[3]

5201 **4** *2* **Bavarica**[16] [697] 4-8-4 **61**.......... SladeO'Hara 3 63
(Miss J Feilden) *hld up in tch: rdn and effrt 2f out: kpt on same pce* **10/1**

0310 **5** *1* **Play Master (IRE)**[22] [650] 5-8-3 **63**.......... KevinGhunowa(3) 1 63
(R A Harris) *plld hrd: prom for 6f: chsd ldrs: rdn over 2f out: one pce fnl f* **16/1**

40-4 **6** *3 ½* **Desert Reign**[55] [375] 5-9-0 **71**.......... AndrewElliott 2 65
(A P Jarvis) *led tl 4f out: sn rdn: one pce fr 2f out* **11/4**[2]

300- **7** *3 ½* **Asaateel (IRE)**[97] [5764] 4-8-10 **67**..........(be) JamieJones 4 54
(G L Moore) *trckd ldrs: rdn 3f out: wknd over 1f out* **16/1**

020- **8** *4* **The Gaikwar (IRE)**[158] [6201] 7-8-4 **68**.......... JasonLetherby(7) 6 48
(R A Harris) *restrained s and a bhd* **18/1**

000- **9** *5* **Viable**[177] [4834] 4-8-6 **66**.......... AshleyHamblett(3) 8 36
(Mrs P Sly) *a bhd* **50/1**

2m 5.56s (-2.23) **Going Correction** -0.10s/f (Stan) **9** Ran SP% **118.7**
Speed ratings (Par 103):104,103,102,100,100 97,94,91,87
CSF £19.33 CT £80.82 TOTE £8.20: £2.10, £1.10, £2.40; EX 26.80 Trifecta £104.80 Pool: £353.04 - 2.39 winning tickets. Place 6 £19.34, Place 5 £14.35..
Owner P McCarthy **Bred** Juddmonte Farms Inc **Trained** Epsom, Surrey

FOCUS
Modest form for the grade but it should be reliable enough. They went a decent pace in the early parts.
T/Plt: £13.90 to a £1 stake. Pool: £39,817.35. 2,082.20 winning tickets. T/Qpdt: £4.70 to a £1 stake. Pool: £2,849.40. 443.25 winning tickets. TM

870 SOUTHWELL (L-H)
Friday, April 7

OFFICIAL GOING: Standard
Wind: Light, across

906 FIRST EVENING ON 27TH AMATEUR RIDERS' H'CAP — 1m (F)
2:20 (2:20) (Class 6) (0-60,59) 4-Y-0+ **£2,637** (£811; £405) **Stalls** Low

Form RPR

U206 **1** **Exit Smiling**[46] [458] 4-10-13 **51**.......... MrSWalker 8 69+
(P T Midgley) *trckd ldrs: led 3f out: sn clr: eased ins fnl f* **11/1**

6160 **2** *9* **Quiet Reading (USA)**[22] [650] 9-11-5 **57**..........(v) MrsSBosley 14 51
(M R Bosley) *prom on outside tl outpcd 3f out: styd on to go 2nd ins fnl f: no ch w wnr* **12/1**

3556 **3** *2* **Pawn In Life (IRE)**[4] [860] 8-10-12 **53**..........(v) MissFayeBramley(3) 6 43
(M J Polglase) *w ldr: lost 2nd whn wl hld ins fnl f* **14/1**

1320 **4** *¾* **Crusoe (IRE)**[4] [860] 9-11-2 **54**..........(b) MissEJJones 11 43
(A Sadik) *prom: outpcd over 3f out: plugged on past btn horses after* **9/1**

3-63 **5** *1 ¼* **Choristar**[63] [290] 5-10-11 **54**.......... MrStephenHarrison(5) 13 40
(J Mackie) *mid-div: sme hdwy 3f out: n.d* **13/2**[2]

4/4- **6** *2* **Dubonai (IRE)**[30] [1068] 6-11-0 **52**..........(t) MrSDobson 7 34
(G M Moore) *bhd and nvr nr to chal* **12/1**

140 **7** *1 ½* **Samson Quest**[7] [820] 4-11-2 **59**..........(v) MrMJJSmith(5) 9 38
(A W Carroll) *slowly away: a bhd* **14/1**

0000 **8** *1 ½* **Lockstock (IRE)**[16] [697] 8-10-13 **56**..........(b) MrPCollington(5) 5 32
(M S Saunders) *awkward leaving stalls: sn led: hdd 3f out: wknd over 1f out* **11/1**

6214 **9** *5* **El Palmar**[4] [860] 5-11-3 **55**.......... MrWHogg 12 21
(M J Attwater) *prom: effrt over 3f out: wknd over 2f out* **7/2**[1]

2130 **10** *shd* **Joe Jo Star**[16] [697] 4-10-9 **52**.......... JackMitchell(5) 2 18
(B P J Baugh) *hld up in mid-div: rdn and wknd over 2f out* **11/1**

3-00 **11** *6* **Love You Always (USA)**[15] [706] 6-10-7 **52**.......... MrRBirkett(7) 3 6
(Miss J Feilden) *a struggling in rr* **18/1**

0 **12** *7* **Lyrical Girl (USA)**[39] [530] 5-10-9 **54**.......... MissJJenner(7) 1 —
(H J Manners) *a bhd* **100/1**

1021 **13** *¾* **Desert Fury**[10] [787] 9-10-11 **54** 6ex..........(b) MissRBastiman(5) 10 —
(R Bastiman) *v.s.a: nvr got into r* **15/2**[3]

1m 44.07s (-0.53) **Going Correction** -0.125s/f (Stan) **13** Ran SP% **117.3**
Speed ratings (Par 101):97,88,86,85,84 82,80,79,74,73 67,60,60
CSF £134.06 CT £1917.85 TOTE £14.00: £3.50, £4.10, £2.80; EX 141.00.
Owner Peter Mee **Bred** Mrs D O Joly **Trained** Westow, N Yorks

FOCUS
A change of scenery brought about a return to his best from Exit Smiling, value for a greater margin of victory, but he beat a poor bunch and the placed form is not strong.
Desert Fury Official explanation: jockey said gelding was reluctant to race

907 GOLF AND RACING AT SOUTHWELL (S) STKS 6f (F)
2:55 (2:56) (Class 6) 3-Y-O+ £2,388 (£705; £352) Stalls Low

Form				RPR
0440	1		**Chickado (IRE)**[32] 602 5-9-8 46 (p) RobertHavlin 1 (D Haydn Jones) *in rr: rdn and hdwy over 2f out: styd on to ld ins fnl f* **7/1**[3]	56
2501	2	2 ½	**Diktalex (IRE)**[4] 861 3-8-3 60 (t) StacyRenwick(7) 5 (M J Attwater) *trckd ldr: led over 2f out: drvn and hdd ins fnl f: no ex* **1/1**[1]	44
0033	3	1 ¼	**Sergeant Slipper**[3] 876 9-9-9 40 (v) JoeFanning 9 (C Smith) *hld up: styd on ins fnl f: nvr nr to chal* **5/1**[2]	46
2065	4	2	**A Teen**[3] 876 8-9-9 45 ShaneKelly 2 (P Howling) *led tl hdd over 2f out: sn one pce* **8/1**	40
000	5	4	**Teyaar**[9] 789 10-9-9 45 AlanDaly 7 (M Wellings) *racd wd: prom on outside to 1/2-way* **20/1**	28
	6	4	**Agnes Pearl** 3-8-6 PaulEddery 4 (B Smart) *slowly away: a bhd* **16/1**	11
0-05	7	dist	**Cheeky Chi (IRE)**[7] 821 5-9-4 35 (bt) NCallan 6 (P S McEntee) *prom tl wknd rapidly 1/2-way:: eased wl over 1f out: t.o* **14/1**	—

1m 16.67s (-0.23) **Going Correction** -0.125s/f (Stan)
WFA 3 from 5yo+ 12lb 7 Ran SP% **107.6**
Speed ratings (Par 101):96,92,91,88,83 77,—
CSF £12.76 TOTE £8.70: £2.30, £1.20; EX 27.10.There was no bid for the winner. Diktalex was claimed by C.Teague for £6,000.
Owner Monolithic Refractories Ltd **Bred** M Channon **Trained** Efail Isaf, Rhondda C Taff
FOCUS
A weak seller in which the favourite ran at least a stone off her best form.
Cheeky Chi(IRE) Official explanation: jockey said mare had no more to give

908 SOUTHWELL-RACECOURSE.CO.UK MAIDEN AUCTION FILLIES' STKS 5f (F)
3:30 (3:31) (Class 6) 2-Y-O £2,730 (£806; £403) Stalls High

Form				RPR
2	1		**Gradetime (IRE)**[3] 878 2-8-8 NCallan 3 (M J Wallace) *mde all: clr over 1f out: comf* **8/11**[1]	65+
33	2	3 ½	**Diminuto**[4] 856 2-8-4 JamieMackay 10 (M D I Usher) *chsd wnr: hung lft ins fnl f: no hdwy* **7/1**[2]	47
0	3	1 ¾	**Piccolo Prezzo**[11] 760 2-8-4 FrancisNorton 2 (Stef Liddiard) *chsd ldrs: rdn 1/2-way: no hdwy fnl f* **20/1**	40
0	4	1	**Minimum Fuss (IRE)**[7] 814 2-8-4 DaleGibson 1 (M W Easterby) *trckd ldrs: rdn 1/2-way: no prog after* **25/1**	36
0	5	nk	**Ivorys Song**[15] 701 2-8-6 JohnEgan 5 (D K Ivory) *chsd ldrs tl wknd over 1f out* **28/1**	37
	6	1	**Foxxy** 2-8-6 JoeFanning 8 (K A Ryan) *slowly away: nvr on terms* **8/1**[3]	33
	7	nk	**Angeletta** 2-8-4 JimmyQuinn 9 (E S McMahon) *chsd ldrs to 1/2-way* **16/1**	30
	8	shd	**Emma Told Lies** 2-8-5 ow2 PaulMulrennan(3) 6 (M W Easterby) *outpcd: hung lft fr over 1f out* **33/1**	33
	9	1 ¾	**Ensign's Trick** 2-8-4 RichardMullen 7 (W M Brisbourne) *wnt lft s: a bhd* **14/1**	22
	10	nk	**Inflagranti** 2-8-11 PaulHanagan 4 (J G Portman) *sn outpcd and a bhd* **16/1**	28
	11	½	**Saxenberg** 2-8-7 ow3 AlanDaly 11 (Miss J R Gibney) *slowly away: a bhd* **100/1**	22

59.55 secs (-0.75) **Going Correction** -0.375s/f (Stan) 11 Ran SP% **115.9**
Speed ratings (Par 87):91,85,82,81,80 78,78,78,75,75 74
CSF £5.31 TOTE £1.60: £1.10, £1.20, £3.50; EX 5.50.
Owner Mrs E O'Leary **Bred** Noel O'Callaghan **Trained** Newmarket, Suffolk
FOCUS
A modest fillies' maiden dominated by those with previous experience. The winner won well but it was not a strong race overall.
NOTEBOOK
Gradetime(IRE), runner-up at Warwick three days earlier, put her experience to good use and made every yard for a comfortable success. Her yard is in good form with its juveniles and, while this race probably did not take much winning, she did it nicely enough and could have improvement in her. (op 4-6 tchd 4-5 in places)
Diminuto, who finished in the frame for the third time in as many starts, will appreciate dropping into selling company to get off the mark.
Piccolo Prezzo, slowly away on her debut, knew a bit more about the game this time. Her dam was a dual winner over seven furlongs and is from the family of 1,000 Guineas winner and influential broodmare Glad Rags. (tchd 18-1 and 25-1)
Minimum Fuss(IRE), who is not really bred to be sharp, was another to record a better result on this second start. (tchd 33-1)
Ivorys Song, out of a mare who was placed over a mile at two, should stay further than this in time. (op 25-1 tchd 33-1)
Foxxy, whose dam was a nine-furlong winner, did best of those without the benefit of previous racecourse experience. (op 15-2 tchd 13-2)
Emma Told Lies Official explanation: jockey said filly hung left throughout

909 DINE IN THE QUEEN MOTHER RESTAURANT MAIDEN STKS 1m 4f (F)
4:05 (4:05) (Class 5) 3-Y-O+ £3,238 (£963; £481; £240) Stalls Low

Form				RPR
-522	1		**Meadow Mischief (FR)**[16] 695 3-8-5 72 (b) RichardMullen 1 (E A L Dunlop) *led for 1f: led again over 5f out: drvn clr over 1f out: easily* **5/2**[1]	78
54-3	2	3 ½	**Deutschland (USA)**[8] 804 3-8-5 72 PhilipRobinson 7 (M A Jarvis) *led after 1f: hdd over 5f out: rallied over 1f out: one pce after* **5/2**[1]	72
	3	8	**Dubai Sunday (JPN)**[23] 5-9-12 LDettori 4 (P S McEntee) *slowly away: hld up: hdwy over 2f out: nvr on terms* **4/1**[2]	56
	4	16	**The Grey Man**[352] 5-9-12 SebSanders 5 (E S McMahon) *trckd leaers tl wknd over 2f out* **8/1**	31
0-	5	10	**Lord Adonis (IRE)**[156] 6228 3-8-5 JohnEgan 2 (M J Attwater) *chsd ldrs tl lost pl ovr 2f out* **25/1**	18
	6	15	**Impress** 3-8-5 KDarley 6 (M Johnston) *s.i.s: wl bhd fr 1/2-way* **5/1**[3]	—
0-00	7	28	**Don Pasquale**[39] 537 4-9-8 53 (b[1]) JasonEdmunds(3) 3 (J T Stimpson) *pulle hrds: prom tl weqkened over 4f out* **33/1**	—

2m 37.62s (-4.47) **Going Correction** -0.125s/f (Stan)
WFA 3 from 4yo 21lb 4 from 5yo 1lb 7 Ran SP% **111.7**
Speed ratings (Par 103):109,106,101,90,84 74,55
CSF £8.34 TOTE £3.30: £2.50, £1.30; EX 7.20.
Owner Gainsborough Stud **Bred** Gainsborough Stud Management Ltd **Trained** Newmarket, Suffolk
FOCUS
An uncompetitive maiden that did not take a great deal of winning. The first two are fairly exposed.

910 BOOK TICKETS ON LINE H'CAP 5f (F)
4:40 (4:41) (Class 6) (0-60,60) 3-Y-O £2,730 (£806; £403) Stalls High

Form				RPR
5-42	1		**Lucayos**[8] 807 3-8-13 60 (b) RichardKingscote(5) 6 (Mrs H Sweeting) *a.p: led 1/2-way: hung rt fnl f but kpt on wl* **4/1**[2]	66
3004	2	1 ¼	**Mister Incredible**[4] 861 3-9-4 60 (v) SebSanders 3 (C A Dwyer) *a.p: ev ch appr fnl f but nt pce of wnr* **5/1**[3]	62
3264	3	3	**Otis B Driftwood**[27] 626 3-9-4 60 (b) ShaneKelly 4 (M Quinn) *chsd ldrs: wnt lft over 1f out and sn btn* **15/2**	52
0600	4	2	**Jazz At The Sands (USA)**[53] 397 3-8-4 46 oh1 (v) FrancisNorton 8 (D Shaw) *outpcd: styd on fnl f: nvr nr to chal* **20/1**	31
6222	5	1 ¼	**Smile For Us**[4] 861 3-9-2 58 (b) BrianReilly 9 (C Drew) *sn outpcd: nvr nr to chal* **7/2**[1]	39
650-	6	½	**Bahamian Duke**[191] 5547 3-8-12 54 PatCosgrave 7 (K R Burke) *chsd ldrs tl wknd over 1f out* **16/1**	33
1-50	7	1 ¼	**Tombalina**[31] 605 3-8-5 54 MarkCoumbe(7) 11 (C J Teague) *led to 1/2-way: rdn and sn wknd* **28/1**	29
0500	8	1 ½	**Luloah**[8] 807 3-9-1 57 LDettori 2 (P S McEntee) *prom tl rdn and wknd over 1f out* **13/2**	26
05-2	9	5	**Tatstheticket**[84] 105 3-8-5 50 ow1 (bt) JasonEdmunds(3) 1 (J Balding) *slowly away: a bhd* **8/1**	2
0-50	10	3	**John Claude (IRE)**[27] 626 3-9-2 58 PhillipMakin 10 (Ronald Thompson) *a struggling in rr* **33/1**	—
300-	11	5	**Chisom**[183] 5703 3-9-1 57 DaleGibson 5 (M W Easterby) *a bhd* **20/1**	—

58.94 secs (-1.36) **Going Correction** -0.375s/f (Stan) 11 Ran SP% **116.9**
Speed ratings (Par 96):95,93,88,85,83 82,80,77,69,65 57
CSF £22.83 CT £145.00 TOTE £3.60: £1.30, £1.80, £2.10; EX 39.30.
Owner Alex Sweeting **Bred** P Sweeting **Trained** Lockeridge, Wilts
FOCUS
Ordinary stuff, but Lucayos is heading the right way in the blinkers. Sound enough form.
Smile For Us Official explanation: jockey said gelding would not face kickback
Tatstheticket Official explanation: jockey said gelding never travelled

911 EXPERIENCE NOTTINGHAMSHIRE H'CAP 1m 6f (F)
5:15 (5:16) (Class 6) (0-65,65) 4-Y-O+ £2,730 (£806; £403) Stalls Low

Form				RPR
1200	1		**Sand Repeal (IRE)**[13] 723 4-9-12 65 NCallan 5 (Miss J Feilden) *trckd ldrs: led over 2f out: in command after* **4/1**[2]	76
4514	2	2	**York Cliff**[3] 871 8-8-13 56 6ex LiamJones(7) 10 (W M Brisbourne) *in tch: wnt 2nd over 1f out: kpt on but no imp on wnr* **4/1**[2]	64
0-43	3	5	**Madiba**[18] 675 7-9-8 58 ShaneKelly 3 (P Howling) *a.p: trckd ldr 1/2-way: lost 2nd over 1f out: one pce* **5/1**[3]	59
-001	4	3 ½	**Royal Axminster**[24] 636 11-9-2 52 RobertHavlin 4 (Mrs P N Dutfield) *led tl hdd over 2f out: wknd over 1f out* **15/2**	48
0-06	5	9	**Keltic Rainbow (IRE)**[54] 389 5-8-7 43 oh3 (v) FrancisNorton 8 (D Haydn Jones) *hld up in rr: nvr on terms* **12/1**	27
006/	6	½	**Show No Fear**[128] 2361 5-9-7 60 (t) BenSwarbrick(3) 2 (G M Moore) *mid-div: wknd over 3f out* **25/1**	43
00-3	7	shd	**Scott's Mill**[10] 785 4-8-3 45 StanleyChin(3) 1 (M Johnston) *sn bhd* **16/1**	28
20-0	8	12	**Midnight Creek**[17] 688 8-8-11 47 (b[1]) BrianReilly 7 (A Sadik) *bhd: lost tch 1/2-way* **16/1**	13
220-	9	12	**Kiama**[180] 5765 4-9-11 64 JoeFanning 6 (M Johnston) *trckd ldr tl wknd over 4f out* **3/1**[1]	13
400/	10	dist	**San Marco (IRE)**[616] 812 8-8-7 43 oh3 (b) DaleGibson 9 (M Sheppard) *hld up: lost tch 1/2-way: eased over 2f out: t.o* **20/1**	—

3m 6.38s (-3.22) **Going Correction** -0.125s/f (Stan)
WFA 4 from 5yo+ 3lb 10 Ran SP% **121.5**
Speed ratings (Par 101):104,102,100,98,92 92,92,85,78,—
CSF £21.43 CT £84.03 TOTE £3.60: £3.10, £1.60, £1.20; EX 33.90 Place 6 £57.81, Place 5 £7.71..
Owner The Sultans of Speed **Bred** Don Commins **Trained** Exning, Suffolk
FOCUS
A decent gallop on here and the runners finished strung out. Very ordinary form but sound for the level.
Kiama Official explanation: jockey said filly had no more to give
T/Plt: £73.30 to a £1 stake. Pool: £35,180.95. 350.20 winning tickets. T/Qpdt: £5.10 to a £1 stake. Pool: £3,078.70. 438.30 winning tickets. JS

900 LINGFIELD (L-H)
Saturday, April 8

OFFICIAL GOING: Standard
Wind: Strong, across

912 BETDIRECT.CO.UK MAIDEN AUCTION STKS 5f (P)
1:40 (1:40) (Class 5) 2-Y-O £3,238 (£963; £481; £240) Stalls High

Form				RPR
3	1		**Stir Crazy (IRE)**[8] 814 2-8-8 EdwardCreighton(3) 4 (M R Channon) *trckd ldrs: rdn to join ldrs on outer 2f out: sn rdn: r.o wl to ld fnl 30yds* **7/2**[3]	71
4	2	½	**Hucking Hill (IRE)**[15] 707 2-8-11 TQuinn 3 (J R Best) *broke wl: led for 1f: w ldr: rdn over 1f out: ev ch ins fnl f: no ex cl home* **6/4**[1]	69
	3	¾	**Hart Of Gold** 2-8-9 NCallan 2 (M J Wallace) *led after 1f: narrow advantage and rdn over 1f out: no ex whn hdd fnl 30yds* **5/2**[2]	64
5	4	3	**Weyba Downs (IRE)**[16] 701 2-9-2 SteveDrowne 5 (J R Best) *chsd ldrs: rdn 2f out: kpt on same pae* **7/1**	59
	5	nk	**Mrs Crossy (IRE)** 2-8-3 RichardSmith(3) 1 (R Hannon) *s.i.s: sn pushed along to chse ldrs: rdn 2f out: no imp* **10/1**	48

60.16 secs (0.38) **Going Correction** -0.125s/f (Stan) 5 Ran SP% **112.4**
Speed ratings (Par 92):91,90,89,84,83
CSF £9.45 TOTE £3.70: £1.80, £1.50; EX 7.50.
Owner Miss F V Cove & Mrs V Beech **Bred** Paddy Kennedy **Trained** West Ilsley, Berks
■ The first winner to be sired by the stallion Fath.
FOCUS
Just an ordinary juvenile maiden that was fought out by two of those with previous experience. The runner-up is the best guide to the level at this stage.
NOTEBOOK
Stir Crazy(IRE), a beaten favourite on heavy ground on his debut, found these conditions much more to his liking and picked up well late on to score. He is engaged at Folkestone next week and it would be no surprise to see him turn out again if conditions are in his favour. (op 10-3)

Hucking Hill(IRE) was beaten over course and distance on his debut, but clearly has shown ability as he was again made favourite. He appeared to have every chance and, although he could not hold off the winner, he looks capable of getting off the mark before long. (op 7-4 tchd 2-1)
Hart Of Gold, a half-brother to the modest but speedy sorts Maunby Rocker and Keresforth by the sprinter Foxhound, knew his job on this debut and broke well, but was unable to the resist the challenges of the more experienced pair in the straight. He should not be long in getting off the mark. (op 11-4 tchd 3-1 in a place)
Weyba Downs(IRE), a stable companion of the favourite, was beaten a fair way on his debut and despite finishing closer never really figured. He may need more time. (op 8-1 tchd 13-2)
Mrs Crossy(IRE), despite being from a powerful yard, was unfancied in the market and after missing the break never got involved. She did suggest that the run will bring her on a fair amount and she can be expected to do better in time. (op 9-1 tchd 17-2)

913 PLAY NOW AT BETDIRECTPOKER.COM CONDITIONS STKS 7f (P)
2:10 (2:10) (Class 4) 4-Y-0+ **£5,297** (£1,586; £793; £396) **Stalls** Low

Form RPR
-012 **1** **Mr Lambros**[21] [667] 5-8-12 95 MartinDwyer 1 98+
(A M Balding) *mde all: qcknd clr over 1f out: readily* **2/9**[1]
3005 **2** *6* **Chief Exec**[7] [828] 4-8-12 82 DarrylIHolland 2 82
(C A Cyzer) *chsd wnr thrght: rdn 2f out: sn edgd rt and nt pce of wnr* **7/1**[2]
6660 **3** *¾* **Outer Hebrides**[14] [726] 5-8-12 82 (vt) EddieAhern 4 80
(Stef Liddiard) *chsd ldng pair: rdn to chal for 2nd over 1f out: kpt on same pce* **7/1**[2]
0- **4** *1 ¼* **Zarakash (IRE)**[219] [4899] 6-8-12 DaneO'Neill 3 77?
(Jonjo O'Neill) *chsd ldng trio: outpcd 4f out: styd on again fnl f* **40/1**[3]
1m 23.65s (-2.24) **Going Correction** -0.125s/f (Stan) **4** Ran SP% **109.3**
Speed ratings (Par 105):107,100,99,97
CSF £2.42 TOTE £1.20; EX 2.30.
Owner Winterbeck Manor Stud **Bred** Witney And Warren Enterprises Ltd **Trained** Kingsclere, Hants
FOCUS
An uncompetitive conditions event that panned out as the market suggested.

914 BETDIRECT.CO.UK INTERNATIONAL TRIAL STKS (LISTED RACE) 1m (P)
2:45 (2:45) (Class 1) 3-Y-O **£23,708** (£8,964; £4,480; £2,240) **Stalls** High

Form RPR
610- **1** **Close To You (IRE)**[175] [5901] 3-9-3 113 IanMongan 7 108
(T G Mills) *trckd ldrs on outer: led wl over 1f out: sn rdn: kpt on wl fnl 50yds* **1/1**[1]
1114 **2** *¾* **Kingsgate Prince (IRE)**[7] [829] 3-9-0 102 GeorgeBaker 4 104
(J R Best) *hld up bhd: smooth prog 2f out: rdn to chse wnr over 1f out: kpt on but hld fnl 50yds* **5/2**[2]
153- **3** *2* **Zato (IRE)**[203] [5335] 3-9-0 103 TQuinn 3 99
(M R Channon) *t.k.h trcking ldrs: rdn 2f out: kpt on same pce* **7/1**[3]
2-24 **4** *3* **Secret Night**[21] [665] 3-8-9 88 JimmyQuinn 5 87
(J A R Toller) *sn restrained bhd ldrs: hdwy on rails wl over 1f out: sn rdn: no further imp fr 1f out* **25/1**
6-36 **5** *½* **Rising Cross**[7] [827] 3-8-9 100 SteveDrowne 2 86
(J R Best) *w ldr: rdn over 2f out: wknd ins fnl f* **10/1**
-122 **6** *3* **Chief Commander (FR)**[55] [392] 3-9-0 98 JohnEgan 6 84
(Jane Chapple-Hyam) *chsd ldrs tl 3f out: sn rdn: wknd over 1f out* **12/1**
1100 **7** *nk* **Grand Jour (IRE)**[21] [665] 3-9-0 87 DarrylIHolland 1 83
(K McAuliffe) *sn led: rdn and hdd wl over 1f out: sn wknd* **25/1**
1m 38.01s (-1.42) **Going Correction** -0.125s/f (Stan) **7** Ran SP% **115.5**
Speed ratings (Par 106):102,101,99,96,95 92,92
CSF £3.73 TOTE £2.00: £1.40, £1.60; EX 4.20.
Owner Miss J A Leighs **Bred** Kevin B Lynch **Trained** Headley, Surrey
FOCUS
A decent Listed race with the winner scoring well enough on his return to action and the form looks sound rated through the runner-up and fourth.
NOTEBOOK
Close To You(IRE), joint winner of the Champagne Stakes and seventh in the Dewhurst in his last two outings of last season, looked to have an outstanding chance in this if he had trained on. A course and distance winner last summer, the surface held no fears for him and he picked up well in the straight having had to race wide in the early stages. Connections are likely to go direct to Newmarket for the 2000 Guineas in four weeks' time, for which he is currently a 50/1 shot, although there is the temptation to take in the Premio Parioli beforehand. (tchd 10-11, 11-10, 6-5 and 5-4 in places)
Kingsgate Prince(IRE), who has been a real standard-bearer for his yard around here this winter, looked much happier back on this course than he had at Kempton and gave the winner a race. He is probably the best guide to the level of the form and, with options on this track dwindling, he may be due for a break. (op 3-1 tchd 10-3)
Zato(IRE), who was a consistent juvenile last year at a similar level, was making his All-Weather debut. He was pretty keen early on, but stuck to his task in the straight without troubling the principals. Hopefully, he can go on from this and, effective on any ground, could pick up a Group contest this season. (op 6-1 tchd 11-2)
Secret Night, who had a difficult task judged on official ratings and trying her longest trip to date, ran close to previous course and distance form with Kingsgate Prince. She has twice now just missed out on picking up black type, so presumably connections will be looking for a similar contest against her own sex to achieve that goal now. (op 20-1)
Rising Cross, third to the runner-up here last month, was beaten twice as far this time and this diminutive filly is not going to find things easy from now on, but she has already earned black type for breeding purposes. (tchd 11-1)
Chief Commander(FR), placed in a Listed contest at Cagnes-Sur-Mer in February, has previously looked no more than a handicapper on this surface and that was born out by this effort. He may well prove better back on turf if his French effort can be taken at face value. Official explanation: jockey said colt did not handle the track (tchd 16-1)
Grand Jour(IRE), with a lot to find on official ratings, set the pace and ran fairly close to previous course form with the runner-up. However, he will not find things easy in handicaps off his current mark. (op 28-1 tchd 33-1)

915 BETDIRECT 0800 211 222 H'CAP 1m (P)
3:15 (3:15) (Class 5) (0-70,72) 4-Y-O+ **£3,238** (£963; £481; £240) **Stalls** High

Form RPR
-112 **1** **Fajr (IRE)**[12] [764] 4-9-4 70 LDettori 1 82+
(Miss Gay Kelleway) *hld up mid-div on rails: smooth hdwy over 1f out: r.o wl to ld ins fnl f: pushed out* **15/8**[1]
641- **2** *¾* **Cursum Perficio**[292] [2770] 4-9-4 70 MartinDwyer 10 81+
(W R Muir) *sn led: narrowly hdd over 4f out: led 2f out: sn rdn: no ex whn hdd ins fnl f* **10/1**
4215 **3** *2* **Physical (IRE)**[5] [854] 4-8-2 59 (p) JamesDoyle[(5)] 6 65
(Mrs A J Perrett) *in tch: chsd ldrs after 4f: rdn over 2f out: ev ch over 1f out: kpt on* **7/1**
-003 **4** *nk* **Island Rapture**[22] [660] 6-9-3 69 EddieAhern 9 74
(J A R Toller) *hld up towards rr: swtchd rt wl over 1f out: styd on wl fnl f: nt rch ldrs* **12/1**
24-1 **5** *1* **Oakley Absolute**[17] [698] 4-9-3 69 RichardHughes 2 72
(R Hannon) *chsd ldrs: rdn 2f out: edgd rt over 1f out: kpt on same pce* **6/1**[3]
50-0 **6** *½* **Whitgift Rock**[12] [764] 5-9-2 68 DarrylIHolland 4 70
(S Dow) *hld up towards rr: c wd into st: styd on fnl f: nvr trbld ldrs* **33/1**
1023 **7** *1* **Aggravation**[7] [826] 4-9-6 72 JohnEgan 5 72
(D R C Elsworth) *mid div: rdn and effrt wl over 1f out: kpt on same pce* **5/1**[2]
660- **8** *½* **Voice Mail**[171] [5974] 7-8-12 67 NeilChalmers[(3)] 3 65
(A M Balding) *prom: led over 4f out tl 2f out: sn rdn: wknd ins fnl f* **50/1**
504- **9** *4* **Mr Velocity (IRE)**[297] [2597] 6-8-13 65 NCallan 7 54
(E F Vaughan) *s.i.s: sn drvn along to chse ldrs: wknd 1f out* **9/1**
0-53 **10** *1 ½* **Luis Melendez (USA)**[15] [711] 4-8-13 65 (t) SteveDrowne 8 51
(Tom Dascombe) *broke wl: chsd ldrs for 4f: grad fdd* **12/1**
1m 37.94s (-1.49) **Going Correction** -0.125s/f (Stan) **10** Ran SP% **117.6**
Speed ratings (Par 103):102,101,99,98,97 97,96,95,91,90
CSF £22.49 CT £114.37 TOTE £2.30: £1.20, £2.60, £2.20; EX 28.70 Trifecta £364.60 Part won. Pool £513.61. 0.89 winning units..
Owner The New Dawn Partnership **Bred** Shadwell Estate Company Limited **Trained** Exning, Suffolk
FOCUS
A modest handicap but won in cosy fashion by a progressive gelding, who will rate higher. The third sets the standard for the form.
Aggravation Official explanation: jockey said gelding had no more to give

916 PLAY NOW AT BETDIRECTCASINO.COM MAIDEN STKS 6f (P)
3:50 (3:50) (Class 5) 3-Y-O **£3,562** (£1,059; £529; £264) **Stalls** Low

Form RPR
-032 **1** **Cool Sting (IRE)**[9] [801] 3-9-3 73 DarrylIHolland 2 70
(A M Balding) *chsd ldr: rdn to ld over 1f out: drifted sltly rt ins fnl f: kpt on wl: drvn out* **7/2**[2]
3- **2** *1* **Macademy Royal (USA)**[149] [6303] 3-9-3 SteveDrowne 6 67
(H Morrison) *chsd ldrs: rdn and ev ch over 1f out: kpt on* **3/1**[1]
0- **3** *shd* **Dream Forest (IRE)**[331] [1642] 3-9-3 JohnEgan 1 67
(Mrs P N Dutfield) *s.i.s: outpcd in rr early: styd on wl fnl f: wnt 3rd fnl stride* **33/1**
243- **4** *shd* **Aristofilia**[203] [5315] 3-8-9 78 NelsonDeSouza[(3)] 3 61
(P F I Cole) *chsd ldrs: rdn and effrt 2f out: kpt on ins fnl f* **7/2**[2]
00- **5** *hd* **Bold Argument (IRE)**[180] [5796] 3-9-3 RobertHavlin 4 66
(Mrs P N Dutfield) *slowly away: bhd: hdwy on rails over 1f out: styd on* **25/1**
24 **6** *1* **Royal Bandit**[9] [801] 3-9-3 NCallan 5 63
(N A Callaghan) *led: rdn and hdd over 1f out: ev ch ins fnl f: wknd fnl 30yds* **3/1**[1]
30 **7** *shd* **Cape Of Storms**[15] [716] 3-9-3 TedDurcan 7 63
(M R Channon) *in tch: rdn over 2f out: kpt on same pce fnl f* **11/2**[3]
1m 12.42s (-0.39) **Going Correction** -0.125s/f (Stan) **7** Ran SP% **116.6**
Speed ratings (Par 98):97,95,95,95,95 93,93
CSF £14.98 TOTE £4.40: £2.30, £2.00; EX 17.70.
Owner The Toucan Syndicate **Bred** John Foley **Trained** Kingsclere, Hants
FOCUS
An ordinary maiden in which the field finished in a heap, with just over two lengths between them at the line. The winner offers the best guide to the level.
Royal Bandit Official explanation: jockey said colt hung badly right

917 TEXT "BETDIRECT" TO 88600 FILLIES' H'CAP 1m (P)
4:30 (4:38) (Class 6) (0-60,60) 3-Y-O+ **£2,730** (£806; £403) **Stalls** High

Form RPR
2-06 **1** **Humility**[19] [681] 5-9-2 49 DarrylIHolland 10 56
(C A Cyzer) *in tch: hdwy over 3f out: rdn into narrow advantage wl over 1f out: jst hld on* **8/1**
4 **2** *shd* **At The Helm (IRE)**[12] [770] 4-9-3 50 EddieAhern 6 57
(W J Knight) *mid-div: hdwy 4f out: edgd lft u.p 2f out: styd on strly fnl f: jst failed* **12/1**
10-6 **3** *1 ¼* **Mad**[5] [854] 5-9-3 50 AlanMunro 8 54
(Ernst Oertel) *towards rr: hdwy on outer 2f out: styd on strly: wnt 3rd fnl stride* **11/2**[3]
00-0 **4** *shd* **Overjoy Way**[66] [268] 4-9-5 52 (b[1]) IanMongan 4 56
(P R Chamings) *mid div: rdn and hdwy 2f out: kpt on: lost 3rd fnl stride* **50/1**
6104 **5** *¾* **Ringarooma**[7] [833] 4-9-3 50 (t) OscarUrbina 7 52
(C N Allen) *s.i.s: towards rr: prog into midfield after 4f: rdn 2f out: kpt on same pce* **10/1**
3-24 **6** *¾* **Burton Ash**[19] [677] 4-9-13 60 (b) SebSanders 1 60
(J G Given) *led: rdn and narrowly hdd wl over 1f out: wknd wl ins fnl f* **6/1**
506- **7** *5* **Tamora**[247] [4107] 4-9-1 48 DarrenWilliams 12 37
(A P Jarvis) *chsd ldrs: rdn and effrt 2f out: wknd fnl f* **33/1**
4034 **8** *¾* **Taminoula (IRE)**[35] [582] 5-9-7 54 TQuinn 5 41
(J G Given) *chsd ldrs: pushes along 4f out: short of room 2f out: wknd 1f out* **8/1**
1013 **9** *4* **Tacid**[19] [678] 4-9-3 50 LDettori 9 28
(Dr J D Scargill) *nvr travelling and a towards rr* **3/1**[1]
6-00 **10** *5* **Whitsbury Common**[47] [457] 4-9-5 52 (b[1]) LPKeniry 2 18
(D R C Elsworth) *w ldr: rdn over 3f out: wkng whn n.m.r 2f out* **50/1**
40-6 **11** *hd* **Elvina Hills (IRE)**[42] [520] 4-9-9 56 GeorgeBaker 3 22
(P Mitchell) *mid-div: rdn to hold pl whn hmpd 2f out: nt rcvr* **5/1**[2]
41-0 **P** **Ragasah**[70] [232] 8-8-8 46 (p) JamesDoyle[(5)] 11 —
(Ernst Oertel) *hld up towards rr: p.u over 3f out (lame)* **25/1**
1m 39.13s (-0.30) **Going Correction** -0.125s/f (Stan) **12** Ran SP% **121.1**
Speed ratings (Par 98):96,95,94,94,93 93,88,87,83,78 78,—
CSF £99.02 CT £579.24 TOTE £12.60: £2.80, £3.30, £1.90; EX 109.90 TRIFECTA Not won..
Owner Mrs Charles Cyzer **Bred** C A Cyzer **Trained** Maplehurst, W Sussex
FOCUS
A very moderate fillies' handicap, little better than banded class and rated around the winner and third.
Tacid Official explanation: jockey said filly hung right
Ragasah Official explanation: jockey said mare pulled up lame behind

918 BETDIRECT.CO.UK H'CAP 1m 2f (P)
5:10 (5:10) (Class 6) (0-65,65) 3-Y-O **£2,388** (£705; £352) **Stalls** Low

Form RPR
-230 **1** **Marachi Band (USA)**[5] [859] 3-8-13 60 (b) ChrisCatlin 1 65
(E J O'Neill) *mid-div: hdwy to chse ldrs 4f out: rdn and swtchd rt 1f out: r.o strly to ld fnl 20yds* **14/1**
004- **2** *¾* **Dark Planet**[198] [5422] 3-8-13 60 RyanMoore 2 64
(C E Brittain) *chsd ldr: led 2f out: sn hrd rdn: kpt on but no ex whn hdd fnl 20yds* **10/1**

-365 **3** *nk* **Coda Agency**[12] 762 3-8-11 **58** EddieAhern 3 61
(D W P Arbuthnot) *led tl 2f out: sn rdn: ev ch 1f out: sn drifted rt: kpt on* **10/1**

000- **4** *½* **Rahy's Crown (USA)**[169] 6013 3-9-0 **61** RichardHughes 11 63
(R Hannon) *hld up towards rr: hdwy on rails wl over 1f out: kpt on ins fnl f* **10/1**

000- **5** *nk* **Life Peer**[281] 3084 3-9-1 **62** J-PGuillambert 9 63
(J G Portman) *hld up towards rr: hdwy into mid div 6f out: rdn over 2f out: styd on* **66/1**

06-0 **6** *shd* **Raise The Heights (IRE)**[70] 219 3-8-11 **58** DaneO'Neill 8 59
(C Tinkler) *s.i.s: towards rr: hdwy over 3f out: rdn 2f out: styd on but nvr trbld ldrs* **16/1**

00-3 **7** *3* **Davidia (IRE)**[15] 710 3-9-3 **64** TQuinn 14 60
(S Kirk) *chsd ldrs: rdn and effrt wl over 1f out: wknd ins fnl f* **3/1**[1]

064 **8** *hd* **Miss Odd Sox**[40] 536 3-9-0 **61** RobertHavlin 4 56
(R Ingram) *towards rr: sme late hdwy: nvr a factor* **16/1**

00-0 **9** *1 ¼* **It's Basil**[21] 668 3-8-9 **56** JimmyQuinn 5 49
(R M Flower) *nvr bttr than mid div* **25/1**

50-2 **10** *nk* **Emotive**[15] 712 3-8-11 **58** (b) SebSanders 10 50
(I A Wood) *mid-div: hdwy to chse ldrs 4f out: rdn over 2f out: wknd over 1f out* **6/1**[3]

36-3 **11** *1 ¼* **Winds Of Change**[10] 797 3-8-11 **63** GregFairley(5) 12 53
(M Johnston) *mid div tl lost pl 4f out* **9/2**[2]

6556 **12** *½* **Ms Rainbow Runner**[39] 544 3-8-3 **55** JamesDoyle(5) 6 44
(P Butler) *hld up towards rr: sme hdwy 2f out: sn hung bdly rt: nvr a danger* **9/1**

00-4 **13** *3 ½* **Kalantera (IRE)**[56] 372 3-9-1 **62** MartinDwyer 7 44
(A M Balding) *in tch tl dropped rr over 4f out* **12/1**

0-45 **14** *3 ½* **Henry Holmes**[21] 669 3-9-1 **65** RichardThomas(3) 13 41
(Mrs L Richards) *chsd ldrs: rdn over 2f out: sn wknd* **20/1**

2m 8.12s (0.33) **Going Correction** -0.125s/f (Stan) 14 Ran SP% **131.0**
Speed ratings (Par 96):93,92,92,91,91 91,89,88,87,87 86,86,83,80
CSF £157.45 CT £1503.26 TOTE £23.60: £5.80, £3.70, £3.50; EX 146.40 Trifecta £253.70 Part won. Pool £357.40. 0.35 winning units. Place 6 £19.79, Place 5 £11.90.
Owner Jerry Jamgotchian **Bred** Gainsborough Farm Llc **Trained** Averham Park, Notts

FOCUS
A modest handicap run at a steady pace and producing a typically close finish.
Winds Of Change Official explanation: jockey said filly did not appreciate kickback and hung left
Ms Rainbow Runner Official explanation: jockey said filly hung right
T/Plt: £25.10 to a £1 stake. Pool: £43,819.25. 1,270.60 winning tickets. T/Qpdt: £20.90 to a £1 stake. Pool: £3,137.50. 111.00 winning tickets. TM

NEWCASTLE (L-H)
Saturday, April 8
919 Meeting Abandoned - Waterlogged

DUSSELDORF (R-H)
Saturday, April 8
OFFICIAL GOING: Soft

925a HENKEL TRIAL DUSSELDORFER STUTENPREIS (LISTED RACE) 1m
4:00 (4:01) 3-Y-O **£8,276** (£3,034; £1,655; £828)

RPR

1 **Lolita (GER)**[181] 3-8-13 AHelfenbein 6 100
(Andreas Lowe, Germany) **4/1**

2 *nse* **Mrs Snow**[167] 6054 3-8-13 J-PCarvalho 7 100
(Mario Hofer, Germany) **69/10**

3 *2 ½* **Tech Engine (GER)**[167] 6051 3-8-13 WMongil 1 95
(P Schiergen, Germany) **37/10**[3]

4 *3 ½* **Manda Honor (GER)**[159] 3-8-13 AStarke 2 88
(Mario Hofer, Germany) **21/10**[1]

5 *3 ½* **Big Bunny (GER)** 3-9-1 FilipMinarik 4 83
(M Weiss, Switzerland) **71/10**

6 *4* **Creative Mind (IRE)**[7] 831 3-8-13 RichardMullen 5 73
(E J O'Neill) *disputed 4th on outside for 5f, 6th straight, soon ridden & beaten* **23/10**[2]

7 *12* **Star Of India (GER)**[251] 3-8-7 (b) NRichter 3 43
(R Rohne, Germany) **26/1**

1m 45.42s 7 Ran SP% **132.5**
(including ten euro stakes): WIN 50; PL 20, 20, 19: SF 437.
Owner Stall Le Rastaquouere **Bred** Wilhelm Jackson **Trained** Germany

NOTEBOOK
Creative Mind(IRE), only two tenths of a point off starting favourite, gave little hint of being worthy of the support. She shared fourth place until beginning the turn into the straight, but lost her place so quickly that the soft ground cannot be blamed for the below-par effort.

750 CURRAGH (R-H)
Sunday, April 9
OFFICIAL GOING: Straight course - heavy; round course - yielding to soft

928a OAK LODGE SIRES LOUGHBROWN STKS (LISTED RACE) 7f
3:15 (3:17) 3-Y-O **£22,448** (£6,586; £3,137; £1,068)

RPR

1 **Decado (IRE)**[154] 6268 3-9-1 DPMcDonogh 5 111
(Kevin Prendergast, Ire) *hld up: 6th and smooth hdwy over 2f out: rdn to ld over 1f out: styd on strly* **7/1**[3]

2 *4* **Queen Cleopatra (IRE)**[169] 6027 3-8-12 101 KFallon 2 98
(A P O'Brien, Ire) *trckd ldrs: 5th 1/2-way: led 2 1/2f out: strly pressed 1 1/2f out: hdd over 1f out: kpt on same pce* **11/2**[2]

3 *4* **Danehill Music (IRE)**[14] 753 3-9-1 105 WMLordan 1 91
(David Wachman, Ire) *chsd ldrs: 6th and rdn 1/2-way: styd on fr 1 1/2f out* **5/4**[1]

4 *2* **Jioconda (IRE)**[160] 6205 3-8-12 99 JMurtagh 6 84
(Edward Lynam, Ire) *led: hdd 2 1/2f out: rallied u.p 1 1/2f out: no ex ins fnl f* **11/2**[2]

5 *6* **Ardbrae Lady**[173] 5967 3-8-12 105 FMBerry 8 69
(Joseph G Murphy, Ire) *trckd ldrs: 4th 1/2-way: 3rd travelling wl 2f out: sn chal: no ex fr over 1f out* **12/1**

6 *1 ½* **Celtic Furrow (IRE)**[14] 752 3-9-1 KJManning 4 69
(J S Bolger, Ire) *a bhd: rdn and no imp fr 1/2-way* **33/1**

7 *2* **Royal Intrigue (IRE)**[154] 6271 3-9-1 100 (b[1]) PJSmullen 3 64
(D K Weld, Ire) *prom: 2nd 1/2-way: 4th and no ex over 2f out: wknd* **7/1**[3]

8 *25* **An Tadh (IRE)**[203] 5348 3-9-1 102 TPO'Shea 7 4
(G M Lyons, Ire) *prom: 3rd 1/2-way: rdn and wknd over 2f out: eased fnl f* **9/1**

1m 36.3s **Going Correction** +1.55s/f (Heav) 8 Ran SP% **120.8**
Speed ratings: 111,106,101,99,92 91,88,60
CSF £47.68 TOTE £5.70: £1.70, £2.00, £1.10; DF 78.00.
Owner Mrs Catherine O'Flynn **Bred** Stonehorn Stud Farms Ltd **Trained** Friarstown, Co Kildare

NOTEBOOK
Decado(IRE) has done well and came from off the pace to clinch this with fully a furlong to race. He will take his chance in the Irish 2,000 here on May 27th and will certainly come on for this run. (op 7/1 tchd 8/1)
Queen Cleopatra(IRE) is still a maiden after three runs in varying company in Britain last season. She looked to have stolen the race when going on with over two furlongs to race, but was effortlessly reeled in by the winner. She ought to improve a good deal from this. (op 5/1 tchd 6/1)
Danehill Music(IRE) never travelled comfortably and was ridden at halfway. She was doing her best work inside the last and looked as though she would prefer to be going further. (op 5/4 tchd 11/8)
Jioconda(IRE) went off in front, and she appeared to blow up when headed, but stayed on again under pressure. She is better than she showed this time. (op 5/1)
Royal Intrigue(IRE), blinkered for the first time, went with them until weakening two furlongs out. (op 9/2)

930a CASTLEMARTIN & LA LOUVIERE STUDS GLADNESS STKS (GROUP 3) 7f
4:15 (4:17) 4-Y-O+ **£31,379** (£9,172; £4,344; £1,448)

RPR

1 **Common World (USA)**[15] 728 7-9-3 107 FMBerry 5 114
(T Hogan, Ire) *led: hdd 1/2-way: sn rdn: regained ld 2f out: styd on strly to draw clr fnl f* **25/1**

2 *6* **Mustameet (USA)**[160] 6210 5-9-3 109 DPMcDonogh 6 103
(Kevin Prendergast, Ire) *slowly away: prog into 5th 3f out: 4th 2f out: 2nd and no imp fnl f* **11/4**[1]

3 *3* **Turnkey**[154] 6270 4-9-0 TonyCulhane 8 95
(M R Channon) *cl up: led 1/2-way: rdn 3f out: hdd 2f out: 5th 1f out: kpt on same pce* **8/1**[3]

4 *¾* **Indesatchel (IRE)**[189] 5644 4-9-3 116 WMLordan 2 96
(David Wachman, Ire) *hld up in tch: 6th travelling wl 1/2-way: 4th under 3f out: 3rd 2f out: kpt on same pce fr over 1f out* **11/4**[1]

5 *1* **Steenberg (IRE)**[15] 729 7-9-0 MichaelHills 1 92
(M H Tompkins) *prom: 3rd 1/2-way: 2nd and chal over 2f out: no ex fr over 1f out* **9/1**

6 *20* **Ad Valorem (USA)**[162] 6166 4-9-0 116 KFallon 4 56
(A P O'Brien, Ire) *chsd ldrs in 5th: wknd fr 3f out* **3/1**[2]

7 *5* **Deerpark (IRE)**[14] 754 4-9-0 95 CDHayes 3 47
(John F Gleeson, Ire) *a towards rr: wknd fr 3f out* **50/1**

8 *¾* **Johnny Jumpup (IRE)**[162] 6146 4-9-0 SebSanders 7 45
(R M Beckett) *prom: 4th 1/2-way: sn rdn: wknd over 2 1/2f out* **14/1**

1m 35.9s **Going Correction** +1.55s/f (Heav) 8 Ran SP% **111.9**
Speed ratings: 114,107,103,102,101 78,73,72
CSF £89.37 TOTE £17.10: £3.00, £1.50, £2.00; DF 45.80.
Owner Ms Teresa Costello **Bred** Denoli Stud & S D Brille Lp **Trained** Nenagh, Co. Tipperary

NOTEBOOK
Common World(USA) had his mind made up for him at the start and was not given a chance to loiter. Never out of the first three, he went on again with over a furlong and a half to race and stretched right away. He has two ways of running, but this must nearly be a career-best display.
Mustameet(USA) won this race last year when rated 98. He missed the break and, although running on in second place from over a furlong out, he was never on terms with the winner. (op 7/2)
Turnkey ran prominently and got his nose in front at halfway, but he was readily outpaced by the winner and again is going to prove difficult to win with at this level. (op 7/1)
Indesatchel(IRE) was the bridle horse at halfway, but failed to raise his effort over the last quarter mile. The majority of his trainer's runners on the Flat are seemingly in need of their first run at present and he is not one to write off on the back of this below-par effort. (op 7/4)
Steenberg(IRE), runner-up in this event for the last two seasons, was able to flatter briefly two furlongs out but weakened gradually from over a furlong out. (op 8/1)
Ad Valorem(USA) looked in need of the run and, weak in the market, dropped right away over two furlongs out. He needs better ground, but still has a bit to prove now. (op 5/2)
Johnny Jumpup(IRE) was ridden along at halfway and dropped himself right out over the last two furlongs. (op 12/1)

932a ALLEGED STKS (LISTED RACE) 1m 2f
5:15 (5:15) 4-Y-O+ **£22,448** (£6,586; £3,137; £1,068)

RPR

1 **Arch Rebel (USA)**[23] 5781 5-9-1 100 JMurtagh 3 111
(Noel Meade, Ire) *hld up in rr: hdwy ent st: rdn to ld 2f out: sn clr: styd on wl* **9/1**

2 *4 ½* **Tolpuddle (IRE)**[14] 754 6-9-4 108 WMLordan 6 109
(T Stack, Ire) *settled 4th: 3rd travelling wl ent st: impr to chal 2f out: sn rdn: kpt on fnl f* **9/4**[1]

3 *7* **Kalderon (GER)**[14] 754 6-9-4 103 FMBerry 5 102
(T Hogan, Ire) *prom: 2nd bef 1/2-way: rdn ent st: 4th 2f out: kpt on same pce* **4/1**[3]

4 *7* **Cairdeas (IRE)**[160] 6210 5-9-6 110 (b[1]) PJSmullen 1 97
(D K Weld, Ire) *led: rdn and hdd 2f out: sn no ex* **10/3**[2]

5 *9* **Media Puzzle (USA)**[512] 6652 9-9-1 DPMcDonogh 4 83
(D K Weld, Ire) *hld up: 7th 1/2-way: kpt on same pce st* **20/1**

6 *3 ½* **Gift Range (IRE)**[127] 6492 4-8-12 101 MJKinane 2 77
(John M Oxx, Ire) *prom: 3rd and pushed along 1/2-way: 4th into st: sn no ex* **9/2**

7 *9* **Imperial Rose (IRE)**[154] 6275 4-8-12 92 CDHayes 7 68
(H Rogers, Ire) *hld up: 6th 1/2-way: effrt ent st: sn no ex* **33/1**

8 *dist* **Redstone Dancer (IRE)**[167] 6090 4-8-12 KJManning 8 —
(Miss S Collins, Ire) *settled 5th: rdn after 1/2-way: no ex st: virtually p.u fnl f* **12/1**

2m 26.0s **Going Correction** +1.775s/f (Heavy) 8 Ran SP% **117.4**
Speed ratings: 104,100,94,89,82 79,72,—
CSF £30.51 TOTE £10.70: £1.70, £1.90, £1.30; DF 46.60.

Owner P Garvey **Bred** Hargus Sexton & Sandra Sexton **Trained** Castletown, Co Meath

NOTEBOOK

Arch Rebel(USA) was very fit from his hurdling stint and came from the rear of the pack to lead two furlongs down. Soon clear, he won without being extended, and will reportedly be kept to the Flat now.

Tolpuddle(IRE) is a hardy customer and dwarfed some of these. He travelled well enough but has little in the way of a turn of foot these days. However, he still finished well clear of a strung-out field, and will have his turn somewhere in due course.

Kalderon(GER) could not confirm Lincoln form with Tolpuddle on these terms. He could be a better horse on good ground. (op 7/2)

Cairdeas(IRE) took them along until headed by the winner. He will come on greatly for this. (op 3/1)

Media Puzzle(USA), the 2002 Melbourne Cup winner, was not disgraced on his racecourse return, over 500 days since he broke down after finishing third in a Group Two in Australia in November 2004.

Gift Range(IRE) was never really travelling and it remains to be seen if she has trained on. (op 4/1)

929 - 933a (Foreign Racing) - See Raceform Interactive

899 LONGCHAMP (R-H)

Sunday, April 9

OFFICIAL GOING: Good to soft

934a PRIX D'HARCOURT (GROUP 2) 1m 2f

2:20 (2:22) 4-Y-0+ **£51,103** (£19,724; £9,414; £6,276; £3,138)

RPR

1 **Manduro (GER)**154 [6278] 4-8-12 SPasquier 4 115
(A Fabre, France) *in touch in 5th, disputing 5th straight, headway 2f out, driven and ran on well to lead over 1f out, driven out* **32/10**1

2 ½ **Corre Caminos (FR)**190 [5641] 4-8-12 TJarnet 11 114
(M Delzangles, France) *held up in 9th, 11th straight, ran on from over 2f out through field, wnet 2nd 100 yards out, nearest at finish* **13/1**

3 ¾ **Archange D'Or (IRE)**217 [4984] 4-9-1 CSoumillon 2 116
(A Fabre, France) *disputed 6th, 4th straight, stayed on from 2f out, went 2nd briefly 100 yards out, stayed on* **44/10**3

4 1½ **Kendor Dine (FR)**32 [655] 4-8-12 C-PLemaire 3 110
(Y De Nicolay, France) *disputed 2nd, 2nd straight, driven to chase leader over 1 1/2f out, kept on* **72/10**

5 nk **Gold Sound (FR)**32 [655] 4-8-12 OPeslier 9 109
(C Laffon-Parias, France) *held up in 8th, 7th straight, stayed on final stages, nearest at finsh* **24/1**

6 ½ **Enforcer**176 [5906] 4-8-12 MartinDwyer 7 109
(W R Muir) *held up in 11th, 8th straight, stayed on final 1 1/2f through field, nearest at finish* **20/1**

7 ½ **Geordieland (FR)**32 [655] 5-9-1 (b) J-BEyquem 5 111
(J-M Beguigne, France) *led, ridden 2f out, ran on til headed over 1f out, no extra* **21/1**

8 ½ **Ruwi**161 [6189] 4-9-1 IMendizabal 1 110
(J-C Rouget, France) *held up in 10th, effort and disputing 5th straight, no extra final 1 1/2f* **47/10**

9 hd **Walk In The Park (IRE)**287 [2961] 4-8-12 TGillet 10 106
(J E Hammond, France) *disputed 6th, 10th straight, pushed along over 2f out, no impression* **43/10**2

10 2½ **Corso Palladio (IRE)**128 4-8-12 SMaillot 12 102
(J E Hammond, France) *raced in 4th on outside, driven 4f out, 9th straight, soon beaten* **43/10**2

11 3 **Alost (FR)**190 6-8-12 FSpanu 8 97
(A Spanu, France) *raced in last, never a factor* **37/1**

12 1½ **Delfos (IRE)**154 [6278] 5-9-1 MBlancpain 6 97
(C Laffon-Parias, France) *disputed 2nd, 3rd straight, weakened over 1f out* **18/1**

2m 1.40s **12** Ran SP% **138.1**
PARI-MUTUEL: WIN 4.20; PL 1.80, 3.50, 1.90; DF 40.50.
Owner Baron G Von Ullmann **Bred** Rolf Brunner **Trained** Chantilly, France

NOTEBOOK

Manduro(GER) put up a very impressive performance. In mid-division early, he produced an outstanding turn of foot from a furlong and a half out. He then idled soon after hitting the front but still set a course record. Since coming to France he has improved out of all proportions, and he now goes for the Prix Ganay. He will be a force to be reckoned with throughout the season.

Corre Caminos(FR), last early on, had only two behind him at the entrance to the straight. After slaloming through the field, he still had five lengths to make up at the furlong marker, but he was slightly flattered as the winner lost concentration in the final 50 metres. He also goes for the Ganay.

Archange D'Or(IRE) was given every possible chance. He was slightly hampered halfway up the straight and then stayed on in good style. He is sure to come on for the outing and another Group race certainly looks within his grasp.

Kendor Dine(FR) ran a brave race and was always well placed. He battled gamely to the line but conditions were not so much on his side on this occasion.

Enforcer put up a satisfactory seasonal debut, which augurs well for the future. He was towards the tail of the field and made his run in the straight up the rail. He was running on at the end and will now be aimed at races like the Presidente della Republica and the Brigadier Gerard Stakes.

906 SOUTHWELL (L-H)

Monday, April 10

OFFICIAL GOING: Standard

Wind: Virtually nil

936 BOOK TICKETS ON LINE TRI-BANDED STKS 5f (F)

1:50 (1:50) (Class 7) 3-Y-O **£1,467** (£433; £216) **Stalls** High

Form RPR

2065 1 **Titus Wonder (IRE)**5 [890] 3-8-7 45 KevinGhunowa(7) 8 45
(P A Blockley) *cl up: effrt to chal wl over 1f out: sn rdn: drvn and edgd lft ins last: led nr line* **7/2**2

00-0 2 hd **In Fashion**13 [778] 3-9-0 45 JimCrowley 3 44
(R J Hodges) *wnt rt s: sn led: rdn over 1f out: drvn ins last: hdd and nt qckn nr fin* **9/1**

0-66 3 1 **Mister Becks (IRE)**17 [716] 3-7-13 35 EmmettStack(5) 1 31
(M C Chapman) *cl up on outer: rdn along 2f out: drvn and wknd ent last* **12/1**

6004 4 2½ **Jazz At The Sands (USA)**3 [910] 3-8-11 45 (v) BenSwarbrick(3) 9 32
(D Shaw) *dwlt: sn chsd along towards rr: rdn and hdwy 2f out: edgd lft and kpt on ins last* **5/1**3

0504 5 ¾ **Stoneacre Girl (IRE)**12 [790] 3-8-9 40 (b1) TonyHamilton 5 25
(Peter Grayson) *dwlt: sn chasing ldrs: rdn 2f out and sn one pce* **15/2**

0052 6 ½ **Saxon Star (IRE)**6 [870] 3-8-9 40 (v) RobertHavlin 4 23
(M D I Usher) *bmpd and dwlt s: sn rdn along in rr: styd on fnl 2f* **3/1**1

0660 7 3 **Moraadi**6 [870] 3-8-4 30 (b) MatthewHenry 6 8
(D W Chapman) *prom: rdn along 1/2-way: sn wknd* **50/1**

600- 8 2 **Nimble Star**268 [3549] 3-9-0 45 LeeEnstone 2 11
(C W Fairhurst) *cl up: rdn along 1/2-way: wknd over 2f out* **9/1**

6005 9 ½ **Sweet Cherokee**6 [874] 3-8-9 40 (b) JimmyQuinn 7 4
(C N Kellett) *in tch to 1/2-way: sn wknd* **10/1**

59.58 secs (-0.72) **Going Correction** -0.30s/f (Stan) 9 Ran SP% **114.4**
Speed ratings (Par 92):93,92,91,87,85 85,80,77,76
CSF £34.57 TOTE £4.20: £1.40, £6.70, £11.50; EX 74.60.
Owner Mrs Joanna Hughes **Bred** Newlands House Stud **Trained** Lambourn, Berks

FOCUS
A typically weak sprint for the class and the first three came clear. The winner ran to this year's form.

937 EXPERIENCE NOTTINGHAMSHIRE MAIDEN CLAIMING STKS 1m (F)

2:20 (2:22) (Class 7) 4-Y-0+ **£1,365** (£403; £201) **Stalls** Low

Form RPR

0223 1 **Faithisflying**13 [783] 4-8-10 40 (p) PhillipMakin 7 47
(D W Chapman) *cl up: led after 2f: rdn and hdd 3f out: rallied to ld 1f out: drvn and styd on* **4/1**2

2502 2 2½ **Tommytyler (IRE)**13 [783] 7-8-11 45 (t) DNolan(3) 6 46
(D Carroll) *trckd ldrs: smooth hdwy to ld 3f out: rdn 2f out: drvn and hdd 1f out: kpt on same pce* **7/2**1

-065 3 2 **Bob Baileys**13 [787] 4-8-9 40 (b1) AmirQuinn(3) 10 40
(P R Chamings) *in tch: hdwy over 2f out: sn rdn and no imp appr last* **5/1**

0064 4 6 **Queue Up**12 [791] 4-9-0 45 FergusSweeney 4 30
(A G Newcombe) *in tch: hdwy 1/2-way: sn rdn along and no imp fnl 2f* **9/2**3

00 5 6 **Scarlet Romance**10 [817] 4-8-6 PaulMulrennan(3) 3 13
(M W Easterby) *cl up on inner: rdn along 3f out: grad wknd* **20/1**

-000 6 3½ **Doughty**12 [791] 4-8-8 35 (t) JimmyQuinn 1 5
(D J Wintle) *stmbld s: hdwy and in tch over 3f out: sn rdn and btn* **8/1**

7 1 **Tofta Tilly**47 6-8-9 TonyHamilton 8 4
(L R James) *s.i.s: a rr* **100/1**

0 8 1½ **King Of Scots**7 [857] 5-8-11 BenSwarbrick(3) 2 6
(R J Price) *s.i.s: a rr* **50/1**

000- 9 5 **Russian Cafe (IRE)**283 [3078] 5-8-11 45 ow2 (t) FergalLynch 9 —
(N Tinkler) *cl up on outer: rdn along 1/2-way: sn wknd* **9/1**

00-6 P **Catheriniski (IRE)**76 [180] 4-7-12 35 KevinGhunowa(7) 5 —
(P A Blockley) *led 2f: lost action, wknd qckly & p.u bef halfway* **20/1**

1m 42.93s (-1.67) **Going Correction** -0.375s/f (Stan) **10** Ran SP% **110.7**
Speed ratings (Par 97):93,90,88,82,76 73,72,70,65,—
CSF £16.62 TOTE £5.10: £1.20, £1.10, £2.20; EX 7.50.
Owner David W Chapman **Bred** Mrs H T Jones **Trained** Stillington, N Yorks

FOCUS
Typically weak form for the class and the field came home fairly strung out.
Doughty Official explanation: jockey said gelding stumbled leaving stalls
King Of Scots Official explanation: jockey said gelding had no more to give
Russian Cafe(IRE) Official explanation: jockey said mare had no more to give

938 ON THE TURF ON THE 25TH BANDED STKS 1m 6f (F)

2:50 (2:51) (Class 7) 4-Y-0+ **£1,467** (£433; £216) **Stalls** Low

Form RPR

0 1 **Galantos (GER)**21 [684] 5-9-0 45 GeorgeBaker 10 56+
(G L Moore) *trckd ldrs: smooth hdwy 3f out: led 2f out: sn rdn and edgd lft: drvn and styd on fnl f* **7/1**

00-1 2 3 **Smart Boy Prince (IRE)**65 [28] 5-8-8 46 RussellKennemore(7) 2 53
(C Smith) *led: rdn along 3f out: hdd 2f out: drvn and one pce fnl f* **10/3**1

3204 3 3 **Makarim (IRE)**27 [635] 10-9-4 49 (p) FergusSweeney 5 52
(M R Bosley) *hld up in tch: hdwy over 5f out: rdn along over 2f out: kpt on same pce* **5/1**2

5610 4 1¼ **Ice And Fire**10 [825] 7-8-10 48 (b) JosephWalsh(7) 7 49
(J T Stimpson) *plld hrd: in tch: n.m.r 3f out: swtchd wd and hdwy 2f out: sn rdn and no imp appr last* **9/1**

-060 5 1 **Discomania**20 [689] 4-8-11 45 (v) MatthewHenry 6 45
(V Smith) *towards rr: hdwy 4f out: rdn 3f out: no imp fnl 2f* **18/1**

60-1 6 shd **King's Envoy (USA)**18 [303] 7-9-0 45 RoystonFfrench 8 45
(Mrs J C McGregor) *prom: effrt 3f out: sn rdn and wknd 2f out* **6/1**

3535 7 2½ **College Rebel**7 [857] 5-9-0 45 JimmyQuinn 1 42+
(J F Coupland) *chsd ldr: rdn along 3f out: wknd 2f out* **11/2**3

000- 8 6 **Birdwatch**15 [3126] 8-9-0 30 (b) JimCrowley 4 33
(K G Reveley) *s.i.s and sn rdn along: hdwy and i n tch after 3f: rdn along over 4f out and sn wknd* **13/2**

000/ 9 shd **That's Racing**63 [5129] 6-9-0 36 MichaelTebbutt 9 33
(J Hetherton) *i n tch: pushed along over 4f out: sn wknd* **16/1**

3m 7.03s (-2.57) **Going Correction** -0.375s/f (Stan)
WFA 4 from 5yo+ 3lb **9** Ran SP% **116.4**
Speed ratings (Par 97):92,90,88,87,87 87,85,82,82
CSF £30.86 TOTE £5.10: £3.70, £2.00, £2.20; EX 56.70.
Owner David Allen **Bred** R Zimmer **Trained** Woodingdean, E Sussex

FOCUS
A fair event for the class, which produced a modest winning time, due to the steady early pace. The form seems sound.
Makarim(IRE) Official explanation: jockey said gelding hung right in straight
Ice And Fire Official explanation: jockey said gelding hung right throughout

939 SOUTHWELL-RACECOURSE.CO.UK BANDED STKS 1m 3f (F)

3:20 (3:21) (Class 7) 4-Y-0+ **£1,467** (£433; £216) **Stalls** Low

Form RPR

50/0 1 **Heathers Girl**14 [767] 7-8-11 45 JimmyQuinn 10 51
(R Dickin) *trckd ldrs: led over 4f out: rdn clr 2f out: styd on wl* **25/1**

4633 2 1¾ **Simply The Guest (IRE)**6 [871] 7-8-11 40 (vt) KimTinkler 9 48
(N Tinkler) *in tch: hdwy to chse ldrs 4f out: rdn over 2f out: drvn and styd on appr last* **16/1**

0-51 3 2 **Nicozetto (FR)**6 [871] 6-9-1 46 (b) DNolan(3) 2 52
(N Wilson) *hld up in tch: hdwy on inner over 3f out: rdn 2f out: drvn and kpt on same pce appr last* **4/1**1

5655 **4** ½ **Starcross Maid**^{6} [871] 4-8-11 45 .... MatthewHenry 12 44
(J F Coupland) *in tch on outer: hdwy to chse ldrs 3f out: rdn 2f out: kpt on same pce appr last* **33/1**

0465 **5** 1½ **Bold Trump**^{35} [526] 5-8-9 46 .... EdwardCreighton$^{(3)}$ 6 43
(Mrs N S Evans) *towards rr: hdwy over 4f out: rdn along 3f out: styd on u.p fnl 2f: nrst fin* **33/1**

-355 **6** 1¾ **Galley Law**^{27} [636] 6-9-0 48 .... PaulFessey 13 42
(R Craggs) *chsd ldrs: rdn along 3f out: drvn 2f out and sn one pce* **5/1**^{2}

-652 **7** ½ **Blue Opal**^{27} [635] 4-9-0 48 .... PaulEddery 7 43+
(Miss S E Hall) *hld up in toch: hdwy 4f out: rdn wl over 2f out and sn btn* **11/2**^{3}

005- **8** nk **Flaming Weapon**^{14} [3138] 4-8-13 47 .... GeorgeBaker 1 40
(G L Moore) *midfield: effrt and sme hdwy over 4f out: rdn along over 3f out: sn wknd* **4/1**^{1}

0/0- **9** ½ **Dance Party (IRE)**^{23} [528] 6-8-8 45 .... PaulMulrennan$^{(3)}$ 3 37
(M W Easterby) *a towards rr* **16/1**

0023 **10** ½ **Eforetta (GER)**^{12} [794] 4-8-4 45 .... JosephWalsh$^{(7)}$ 4 36
(D J Wintle) *s.i.s and bhd tl styd on fnl 2f: nvr a factor* **8/1**

0040 **11** 4 **Tirailleur (IRE)**^{6} [875] 6-8-11 45 ....(v) FergalLynch 8 30
(J R Boyle) *led: pushed along and hdd over 4f out: rdn wl over 2f out and grad wknd* **20/1**

5002 **12** 14 **Kentucky Bullet (USA)**^{13} [788] 10-8-11 45 .... FergusSweeney 11 7
(A G Newcombe) *a rr* **8/1**

550- **13** dist **Safe Shot**^{156} [5924] 7-8-11 40 ....(p) RoystonFfrench 14 —
(Mrs J C McGregor) *in tch: rdn along and wknd qckly 5f out: t.o fnl 3f* **40/1**

2m 24.8s (-4.10) **Going Correction** -0.375s/f (Stan) 13 Ran SP% **123.0**
Speed ratings (Par 97):99,97,96,95,94 93,93,92,92,92 89,79,—
CSF £370.23 TOTE £16.50: £4.00, £7.60, £1.60; EX 159.90.
Owner Trio Racing **Bred** Barry Adams **Trained** Atherstone on Stour, Warwicks

FOCUS
Another poor event, but it was run at a fair pace and the form looks sound enough.

940 DINE IN THE QUEEN MOTHER RESTAURANT BANDED STKS 1m (F)
3:50 (3:55) (Class 7) 4-Y-0+ **£1,569** (£463; £231) **Stalls** Low

Form RPR

0-21 **1** **Bold Phoenix (IRE)**^{49} [468] 5-9-2 50 ....(b) TPQueally 3 61+
(B J Curley) *stdd s and hld up towards rr: smooth hdwy on outer 3f out: led on bit over 1f out: qcknd clr ins last: easily* **9/4**^{1}

0051 **2** 2½ **Favouring (IRE)**^{13} [784] 4-8-11 50 ....(v) EmmettStack$^{(5)}$ 5 51+
(M C Chapman) *hld up on inner: hdwy over 2f out: rdn wl over 1f out: styd on ins last* **7/2**^{2}

2100 **3** 1½ **Pearl Island (USA)**^{35} [386] 5-8-12 49 ....(b) EdwardCreighton$^{(3)}$ 4 47
(D J Wintle) *chsd ldrs: hdwy 3f out: rdn to chal 2f out and ev ch tl drvn and one pce ent last* **20/1**

5020 **4** 1¼ **Shrine Mountain (USA)**^{19} [696] 4-9-2 50 .... J-PGuillambert 8 46
(J R Holt) *cl up: effrt and ev ch 2f out: sn rdn and one pce appr last* **4/1**^{3}

500- **5** 4 **Extemporise (IRE)**^{126} [6508] 6-8-13 47 .... PhillipMakin 2 35
(T T Clement) *led: rdn along wl over 2f out: drvn over 1f out: sn hdd & wknd ent last* **14/1**

245- **6** 1½ **Pepper Road**^{168} [6082] 7-9-1 49 .... RoystonFfrench 9 34
(R Bastiman) *towards rr: hdwy wl over 2f out: sn rdn and kpt on appr last* **16/1**

0135 **7** 2½ **Wilford Maverick (IRE)**^{13} [784] 4-8-7 48 ....(v) StacyRenwick$^{(7)}$ 13 28
(M J Attwater) *chsd ldrs: rdn along over 2f out: sn wknd* **20/1**

3243 **8** 2½ **High Swainston**^{13} [787] 5-9-0 48 ....(b) PaulFessey 7 23
(R Craggs) *cl up: rdn along over 2f out: grad wknd* **16/1**

00-4 **9** 1 **King Nicholas (USA)**^{99} [3] 7-9-2 50 ....(tp) TonyCulhane 6 23
(J Parkes) *a midfield* **16/1**

26-0 **10** 1½ **Come On**^{12} [792] 7-8-11 45 .... MichaelTebbutt 11 15
(J Hetherton) *chsd ldrs: rdn along wl over 2f out: sn wknd* **66/1**

200- **11** 3½ **Apache Point (IRE)**^{178} [5884] 9-9-0 48 .... KimTinkler 14 11
(N Tinkler) *a towards rr* **18/1**

510- **12** 7 **Louve Heureuse (IRE)**^{116} [6587] 5-8-13 50 ....(e^{1}) AmirQuinn$^{(3)}$ 12 —
(J R Boyle) *s.i.s: a bhd* **12/1**

000- **13** 6 **Baileys Honour**^{233} [4583] 4-9-2 50 .... FergusSweeney 10 —
(A G Newcombe) *s.i.s: a rr* **33/1**

1m 41.68s (-2.92) **Going Correction** -0.375s/f (Stan) 13 Ran SP% **124.2**
Speed ratings (Par 97):99,96,95,93,89 88,85,83,82,80 77,70,64
CSF £9.61 TOTE £3.40: £1.60, £1.90, £8.40; EX 12.40.
Owner Curley Leisure **Bred** Milton Park Stud Partnership **Trained** Newmarket, Suffolk

FOCUS
A race run at a decent pace, but what had looked a fairly competitive event of its type beforehand was turned into a cakewalk by the favourite who won with embarrassing ease. However, what he actually beat is open to debate.
High Swainston Official explanation: jockey said gelding ran flat
Louve Heureuse(IRE) Official explanation: jockey said mare was hampered at start

941 GOLF AND RACING BANDED STKS 7f (F)
4:20 (4:23) (Class 7) 4-Y-0+ **£1,467** (£433; £216) **Stalls** Low

Form RPR

0203 **1** **La Musique**^{6} [875] 4-8-11 45 .... TonyCulhane 7 49+
(P J McBride) *mde all: pushed clr 2f out: rdn and kpt on strly ins last* **15/8**^{1}

0033 **2** 3 **Rocky Reppin**^{20} [689] 6-8-11 45 ....(b) DavidAllan 1 41
(J Balding) *in tch and sn pushed along: hdwy on outer wl over 2f out: sn rdn: kpt on to chse wnr ins last: no imp* **2/1**^{2}

00-4 **3** ½ **Emperor Cat (IRE)**^{12} [792] 5-8-4 45 .... FrankiePickard$^{(7)}$ 3 40+
(Mrs N S Evans) *chsd wnr: rdn along wl over 2f out: drvn and one pce fr wl over 1f out* **11/1**

000/ **4** 1¼ **Chiracahua (IRE)**^{529} [6448] 4-8-11 45 .... PaulEddery 5 37
(B Smart) *keen: chsd ldrs: rdn along 3f out: drvn 2f out and sn wknd* **9/1**

550- **5** 1 **Adalar (IRE)**^{197} [5127] 6-8-11 40 ....(t) RoystonFfrench 6 34
(P W D'Arcy) *chsd ldrs: rdn along 3f out: wknd 2f out* **13/2**^{3}

0060 **6** 10 **Chorus Beauty**^{14} [768] 5-8-11 45 .... JimmyQuinn 2 8
(N I M Rossiter) *chsd ldrs on inner: rdn along 1/2-way: sn wknd* **12/1**

05/0 **7** 5 **Hello Tiger**^{24} [591] 5-8-11 30 .... FergalLynch 4 —
(J A Supple) *dwlt: a rr* **66/1**

1m 29.5s (-1.30) **Going Correction** -0.375s/f (Stan) 7 Ran SP% **109.0**
Speed ratings (Par 97):92,88,88,86,85 74,68
CSF £5.27 TOTE £1.70: £1.20, £2.10; EX 3.60.
Owner P J McBride **Bred** Llety Stud **Trained** Newmarket, Suffolk

FOCUS
This was a two-horse race according to the market and they finished one-two. A poor race even of its type and a modest winning time to boot. The winner ran to his recent form.
Hello Tiger Official explanation: jockey said gelding missed break

942 SOUTHWELL BANDED STKS 6f (F)
4:50 (4:50) (Class 7) 4-Y-0+ **£1,467** (£433; £216) **Stalls** Low

Form RPR

0622 **1** **Union Jack Jackson (IRE)**^{6} [876] 4-8-11 45 ....(b) FergalLynch 8 52+
(J G Given) *stdd s and hld up in rr: hdwy over 2f out: shkn up to chse ldr ins last: rdn and qcknd to ld nr fin* **11/10**^{1}

0654 **2** ½ **A Teen**^{3} [907] 8-8-11 45 .... J-PGuillambert 3 50
(P Howling) *chsd ldrs: hdwy over 2f out: led wl over 1f out: rdn ins last: hdd and no ex nr fin* **7/1**^{3}

0064 **3** 3 **Ace Club**^{6} [873] 5-8-11 40 ....(b) TonyHamilton 5 41
(J Hetherton) *cl up: rdn along over 2f out: kpt on same pce appr last* **10/1**

4021 **4** 1½ **Misty Princess**^{6} [876] 4-9-3 45 .... JimmyQuinn 9 43
(M J Attwater) *rr and pushed along 1/2-way: hdwy over 2f out: styd on ins last: nrst fin* **4/1**^{2}

-606 **5** ½ **Off Hire**^{6} [872] 10-8-4 40 ....(v) RussellKennemore$^{(7)}$ 7 35
(C Smith) *cl up: rdn to ld 2f out: sn hdd & wknd over 1f out* **25/1**

0-50 **6** 3 **Aboustar**^{13} [784] 6-8-11 40 ....(b) DavidAllan 6 26
(M Brittain) *chsd ldrs on outer: rdn over 2f out: grad wknd* **20/1**

4004 **7** nk **Cleveland Way**^{6} [876] 6-8-10 40 ow2 ....(v) DNolan$^{(3)}$ 2 27
(D Carroll) *led: rdn along over 2f out: sn hdd & wknd wl over 1f out* **8/1**

/00- **8** 2 **Zap Attack**^{179} [5859] 6-8-11 45 ....(p) TonyCulhane 1 19
(J Parkes) *chsd ldrs on inner: rdn wl over 1f out and sn wknd* **20/1**

-000 **9** 8 **Victimised (IRE)**^{20} [687] 4-8-8 40 .... BenSwarbrick$^{(3)}$ 4 —
(R J Price) *a rr* **80/1**

1m 15.71s (-1.19) **Going Correction** -0.375s/f (Stan) 9 Ran SP% **114.9**
Speed ratings (Par 97):92,91,87,85,84 80,80,77,66
CSF £8.76 TOTE £3.90: £1.10, £1.90, £4.10; EX 8.30.
Owner Andy Clarke **Bred** Tom Foley **Trained** Willoughton, Lincs

FOCUS
Another moderate contest, but an intriguing one nonetheless with the winner's previous antics in mind. A modest winning time, even for a race like this.
Off Hire Official explanation: jockey said gelding hung right from 3f out
Victimised(IRE) Official explanation: jockey said gelding had no more to give

943 EVENING RACING ON THE 27TH BANDED STKS 5f (F)
5:20 (5:20) (Class 7) 4-Y-0+ **£1,467** (£433; £216) **Stalls** High

Form RPR

-050 **1** **Laurel Dawn**^{6} [876] 8-8-11 45 ....(b) JimmyQuinn 1 53
(C N Kellett) *cl up on outer: rdn to ld over 1f out: c lear ins last* **9/1**

5600 **2** 5 **Comic Tales**^{20} [686] 5-8-11 40 .... TPQueally 3 36
(M Mullineaux) *dwlt: in tch: swtchd rt to stands rail and hdwy 2f out: sn rdn: styd on ins last* **5/1**^{3}

04-0 **3** ½ **Maromito (IRE)**^{6} [864] 9-8-11 45 .... RoystonFfrench 6 34
(R Bastiman) *led 11/2f: cl up tl rdn and one pce fr over 1f out* **11/2**

-050 **4** 1¼ **Secret Vision (USA)**^{70} [255] 5-8-11 45 ....(p) FergusSweeney 7 30
(R M H Cowell) *cl up: led after 11/2f: rdn along 2f out: hdd over 1f out and sn wknd* **9/4**^{1}

00-6 **5** 2 **Keresforth**^{53} [90] 4-8-11 40 ....(p) PaulEddery 2 23
(Mrs L C Jewell) *prom: rdn along 1/2-way: outpcd fnl 2f* **12/1**

0-50 **6** 3 **Roko**^{6} [876] 4-8-11 35 ....(b) MichaelTebbutt 4 13
(S R Bowring) *chsd ldrs: rdn along 1/2-way: sn wknd* **25/1**

2000 **7** 1¼ **On The Trail**^{21} [679] 9-8-11 45 ....(p) TonyCulhane 5 9
(D W Chapman) *s.i.s: a bhd* **3/1**^{2}

59.18 secs (-1.12) **Going Correction** -0.30s/f (Stan) 7 Ran SP% **109.4**
Speed ratings (Par 97):96,88,87,85,82 77,75
CSF £48.20 TOTE £11.60: £4.00, £6.80; EX 46.40 Place 6 £37.51, Place 5 £9.47.
Owner The JJP Partnership **Bred** Mrs J M Berry **Trained** Woodlane, Staffs

FOCUS
A dire contest and the form probably amounts to little.
Comic Tales Official explanation: jockey said gelding missed break
On The Trail Official explanation: jockey said gelding tried to break out under stalls immediately before start
T/Plt: £33.20 to a £1 stake. Pool: £31,450.90. 690.25 winning tickets. T/Qpdt: £4.80 to a £1 stake. Pool: £2,865.30. 435.00 winning tickets. JR

WINDSOR (R-H)
Monday, April 10
OFFICIAL GOING: Good (good to soft in places)
Wind: Virtually nil

944 GOLDRING SECURITY MAIDEN STKS 5f 10y
2:30 (2:30) (Class 5) 2-Y-0 **£3,238** (£963; £481; £240) **Stalls** High

Form RPR

1 **Espartano** 2-9-3 .... JamieSpencer 1 84+
(M J Wallace) *trckd ldrs: qcknd to ld appr fnl f: readily* **4/1**^{2}

2 2½ **Camissa** 2-8-12 .... DaneO'Neill 7 69
(D K Ivory) *rr but in tch: drvn 1/2-way: hdwy over 1f out: styd on wl to take 2nd last strides but no ch w wnr* **50/1**

3 shd **Oi Vay Joe (IRE)** 2-9-3 .... RobertWinston 6 74
(W Jarvis) *slt advantage on rail tl hdd appr fnl f: kpt on same pce and lost 2nd last strides* **8/1**

2 **4** 1¼ **Rouen (IRE)**^{16} [727] 2-9-3 .... TQuinn 5 69
(M R Channon) *w ldr: rdn and hung lft 2f out: wknd fnl f* **10/11**^{1}

4 **5** 1¼ **Carlitos Spirit (IRE)**^{23} [663] 2-9-3 .... AlanMunro 2 64
(B R Millman) *pressed ldrs: rdn and carried hd high 2f out: sn hung rt: hung lft and eased ins fnl f* **11/2**^{3}

6 5 **Lord Blue Boy** 2-9-0 .... RobertMiles$^{(3)}$ 8 44
(W G M Turner) *s.i.s: bhd: swtchd lft and hdwy 1/2-way but nvr gng pce to rch ldrs* **25/1**

7 7 **Chip Leader** 2-9-3 .... RichardHughes 3 16
(R Hannon) *chsd ldrs early: bhd fr 1/2-way* **14/1**

8 18 **Lenard Frank (IRE)** 2-9-3 .... MartinDwyer 4 —
(M D I Usher) *slowly away: a wl bhd* **40/1**

62.97 secs (1.87) **Going Correction** +0.225s/f (Good) 8 Ran SP% **113.8**
Speed ratings (Par 92):94,90,89,87,85 77,66,37
CSF £171.45 TOTE £5.40: £1.10, £7.40, £3.10; EX 188.70.
Owner Pedro Rosas **Bred** Barton Stud Partnership **Trained** Newmarket, Suffolk

FOCUS
A fair juvenile contest in which Brocklesby runner-up Rouen could only manage fourth. An impressive winner, and the form looks sound enough.

NOTEBOOK
Espartano, whose stable have made a bright start to the season with their juveniles, knew his job and proved good enough to overcome stall one, quickening smartly to win going away. This was Wallace's third winner from four runners in the juvenile division in April and Spencer reported afterwards that the colt could develop into a Royal Ascot contender. (op 7-2 tchd 9-2)
Camissa, the sole filly in the line-up, was unsure what was required of her early and she ran too green to win, but her efforts in the latter part of the race were most encouraging and she kept on nicely to snatch second. She should know a good deal more next time and it will be surprising if she cannot pick up a small race.
Oi Vay Joe(IRE), a 20,000gns Namid colt, was quickly into stride and led on the favoured rail, but he was unable to match the winner, who quickened well, and Camissa just ran him out of second. There was plenty of encouragement to be taken from this and it is unlikely his trainer would have had him fully wound up for this. (op 6-1)
Rouen(IRE), who shaped well when runner-up in the Brocklesby on debut, was expected to be helped by this slightly better ground, but having raced up there early he began to hang and failed to see his race out. This was disappointing. (op 6-5 tchd 5-4 in places)
Carlitos Spirit(IRE) failed to build on his promising Lingfield fourth - the form has otherwise worked out well - and he looked a tricky ride, hanging and carrying his head high. Official explanation: jockey said colt hung right-handed (tchd 6-1)

945 AT THE RACES CLAIMING STKS — 1m 2f 7y
3:00 (3:00) (Class 5) 3-Y-O — **£3,238** (£963; £481; £240) **Stalls** Low

Form — RPR
0-40 **1** **Bob's Your Uncle**[7] [859] 3-8-12 57 ... RyanMoore 6 — 60
(J G Portman) *rr but in tch: pushed along 4f out: hdwy 3f out: led ins fnl 2f:rdn clr ins last* **8/1**
2603 **2** *2 ½* **Night Groove (IRE)**[40] [548] 3-9-1 56 ... (b) JamesDoyle(5) 1 — 63
(N P Littmoden) *chsd ldrs: drvn to chal ins fnl 2f: kpt on fnl f but nt pce of wnr* **10/1**
-210 **3** *4* **Ballybeg (IRE)**[8] [848] 3-9-3 72 ... RichardHughes 10 — 52
(R Hannon) *t.k.h: chsd ldrs: rdn 2f out: styd on same pce fnl f* **10/3**[2]
030 **4** *½* **Archidona (FR)**[26] [642] 3-8-1 50 ... RoryMoore(5) 2 — 40
(M Quinn) *in tch: rdn and effrt over 2f out: nvr gng pce to trble ldrs and sn one pce* **22/1**
340- **5** *¾* **Zabeel Tower**[157] [6244] 3-9-3 71 ... TQuinn 8 — 50
(M R Channon) *disp ld tl def advantage 4f out: rdn 3f out: hdd ins fnl 2f: wknd qckly fnl f* **3/1**[1]
-523 **6** *2 ½* **The Jailer**[5] [887] 3-8-5 45 ... DavidKinsella 11 — 33
(J G M O'Shea) *chsd ldrs: rdn 3f out: wknd fnl f* **11/2**[3]
0-00 **7** *½* **Lewis Lloyd (IRE)**[13] [781] 3-8-12 51 ... (t) NCallan 5 — 39
(I A Wood) *rr early: chsd ldrs after 2f: rdn 3f out: wknd 2f out* **50/1**
0-45 **8** *2* **Aboyne (IRE)**[41] [538] 3-8-9 67 ... ShaneKelly 4 — 33
(M G Quinlan) *sn bhd: rdn and sme hdwy over 2f out: n.d* **13/2**
0000 **9** *1 ½* **King's Melody**[6] [879] 3-8-13 52 ... JamesMillman(7) 7 — 41
(B R Millman) *s.i.s: bhd most of way* **33/1**
00-0 **10** *shd* **Ryhope Chief (IRE)**[41] [538] 3-8-10 49 ... JohnEgan 3 — 30
(M F Harris) *bhd most of way* **33/1**
000- **11** *17* **Mullzima (IRE)**[124] [6521] 3-8-3 50 ... MartinDwyer 9 — —
(P D Evans) *disp ld tl def advantage 5f out: hdd 4f out: wknd 3f out: eased whn no ch fnl f* **33/1**

2m 11.19s (2.89) **Going Correction** +0.10s/f (Good) — 11 Ran SP% **112.1**
Speed ratings (Par 98):92,90,86,86,85 83,83,81,80,80 66
CSF £75.44 TOTE £11.40: £2.90, £3.30, £1.50; EX 96.30.
Owner A S B Portman **Bred** Wheelersland Stud **Trained** Compton, Berks

FOCUS
A race in which two stood out at the weights, Ballybeg and Zabeel Tower, but neither ran to form and Bob's Your Uncle ran out a comfy winner of this modest event.
Bob's Your Uncle Official explanation: trainer said had no explanation for the improved form shown
Night Groove(IRE) Official explanation: jockey said gelding hung right-handed
The Jailer Official explanation: jockey said filly hung right-handed under pressure
Aboyne(IRE) Official explanation: jockey said colt was never travelling

946 CRIMESTOPPERS H'CAP — 1m 67y
3:30 (3:30) (Class 4) (0-85,85) 4-Y-O+ — **£6,477** (£1,927; £963; £481) **Stalls** High

Form — RPR
3430 **1** **Wavertree Warrior (IRE)**[16] [726] 4-8-5 77 ... JamesDoyle(5) 1 — 86
(N P Littmoden) *trckd ldrs: led ins fnl 2f: rdn ins last: hld on wl* **14/1**
2-30 **2** *nk* **First Show**[26] [641] 4-8-7 74 ow1 ... ShaneKelly 9 — 82
(J Noseda) *chsd ldrs: slt ld 3f out: sn rdn: hdd ins fnl 2f: styd pressing ldr and rallied cl home but a hld* **11/2**[1]
040- **3** *1 ¾* **Blue Trojan (IRE)**[121] [6547] 6-8-12 79 ... FrankieMcDonald 7 — 83
(S Kirk) *chsd ldrs: rdn 3f out: kpt on u.p fnl f but nvr gng pce to chal* **25/1**
0146 **4** *nk* **Councellor (FR)**[8] [846] 4-8-12 79 ... JamieSpencer 13 — 83
(Stef Liddiard) *rr but in tch: rdn 4f out: edgd rt 2f out: kpt on ins last but nvr gng pce to rch ldrs* **6/1**[2]
60-0 **5** *nk* **Prince Samos (IRE)**[23] [670] 4-9-3 84 ... RichardHughes 10 — 87
(R Hannon) *bhd: rdn over 3f out: hdwy 2f out: kpt on ins last but nvr gng pce to rch ldrs* **11/2**[1]
130- **6** *½* **Trafalgar Square**[170] [6022] 4-8-11 81 ... AdamKirby(3) 4 — 83
(J Akehurst) *s.i.s: sn rcvrd and in tch: drvn to chse ldrs over 2f out: kpt on same pce ins last* **16/1**
6231 **7** *1* **Glad Big (GER)**[9] [826] 4-9-1 82 ... SteveDrowne 14 — 81
(J A Osborne) *chsd ldrs: pushed along over 2f out: kpt on same pce fnl 2f* **11/2**[1]
5-01 **8** *1 ¾* **Berkhamsted (IRE)**[15] [361] 4-9-4 85 ... (v[1]) RobertWinston 6 — 80
(M F Harris) *chsd ldrs: drvn to chal fr 3f out: wknd fnl f* **28/1**
10-6 **9** *1 ½* **Sawwaah (IRE)**[14] [764] 9-8-5 72 ... (v) AdrianTNicholls 5 — 64
(D Nicholls) *bhd: hdwy 3f out: sooin pushed along: nvr gng pce to rch ldrs* **14/1**
420- **10** *3 ½* **Bold Diktator**[173] [5974] 4-8-4 71 ... MartinDwyer 3 — 55
(W R Muir) *rr but in tch: rdn and sme hdwy 3f out: nvr gng pce to trble ldrs* **18/1**
0U0- **11** *6* **Wujood**[149] [6325] 4-8-4 71 ... ChrisCatlin 12 — 41
(H Morrison) *sn led: hdd after 2f: styd chsng ldr tl wknd ins fnl 3f* **20/1**
600- **12** *6* **Giocoso (USA)**[184] [5743] 6-8-11 78 ... JohnEgan 11 — 34
(B Palling) *led after 2f: hdd 3f out: sn wknd* **7/1**[3]
160- **13** *8* **Blue Train (IRE)**[269] [3506] 4-9-4 85 ... KFallon 8 — 23
(Jonjo O'Neill) *s.i.s: a bhd* **14/1**
6- **14** *24* **Quasimodo (IRE)**[38] [3303] 4-8-5 72 ... (v) AlanMunro 2 — —
(A W Carroll) *sn wl bhd* **40/1**

1m 44.69s (-0.91) **Going Correction** +0.10s/f (Good) — 14 Ran SP% **118.6**
Speed ratings (Par 105):108,107,105,105,105 104,103,102,100,97 91,85,77,53
CSF £84.16 CT £1977.77 TOTE £16.10: £5.60, £2.00, £9.80; EX 128.10.
Owner Wavertree Racing Partnership C **Bred** Liam Queally **Trained** Newmarket, Suffolk

FOCUS
A decent gallop on here thanks to Giocoso and Wavertree Warrior stuck his neck out gamely under a fine ride from Doyle. Sound form.
Wavertree Warrior(IRE) Official explanation: trainer said, regarding the improved form shown, gelding had been affected by the false start at Redcar last time out
Glad Big(GER) Official explanation: jockey said gelding was unsuited by good (good to soft in places) going

947 FELTONS CHARTERED ACCOUNTANTS TAX NO H'CAP — 5f 10y
4:00 (4:02) (Class 4) (0-80,80) 4-Y-O+ — **£6,477** (£1,927; £963; £481) **Stalls** High

Form — RPR
050- **1** **Auwitesweetheart**[194] [5558] 4-9-4 80 ... AlanMunro 2 — 87
(B R Millman) *trckd ldrs: rdn over 1f out: str run to ld wl ins last: hld on all out* **12/1**
110- **2** *hd* **Fisberry**[225] [4787] 4-9-4 80 ... NCallan 3 — 87
(M S Saunders) *s.i.s: bhd: rdn and hdwy over 1f out: str run ins last: fin strly: nt quite get up* **10/1**
430- **3** *hd* **Devon Flame**[226] [4746] 7-9-0 76 ... RichardHughes 5 — 82
(R J Hodges) *chsd ldrs: rdn and str run ins last: fin wl but nt quite get up* **15/2**
2311 **4** *nk* **Native Title**[14] [761] 8-9-4 80 ... AdrianTNicholls 8 — 85
(D Nicholls) *behund: plenty to do 2f out: sn rdn rapid hdwy fnl f: fin wl but nt rch ldrs* **7/2**[1]
230- **5** *½* **Quality Street**[232] [4605] 4-9-0 76 ... RobertWinston 1 — 79
(P Butler) *chsd ldr: led 2f out: sn rdn: hdd and no ex wl ins last* **20/1**
35-0 **6** *½* **Malapropism**[18] [705] 6-9-4 80 ... SamHitchcott 6 — 81
(M R Channon) *behimd: n.m.r and swtchd lft 1/2-way:rdn and hdwy over 1f out: kpt on u.p fnl f but nvr gng pce of ldrs* **13/2**[3]
6605 **7** *shd* **Dancing Mystery**[18] [705] 12-8-10 72 ... (b) StephenCarson 14 — 73
(E A Wheeler) *led tl hdd 2f out: styd pressing ldrs tl outpcd ins last* **6/1**[2]
3030 **8** *1* **Kempsey**[14] [761] 4-8-7 74 ... (v) RichardKingscote(5) 9 — 71
(J J Bridger) *chsd ldrs: rdn 1/2-way: outpcd ins fnl f* **12/1**
0045 **9** *¾* **Fizzlephut (IRE)**[42] [532] 4-8-13 75 ... PaulFitzsimons 11 — 70
(Miss J R Tooth) *chsd ldrs: rdn 1/2-way: wknd ins fnl f* **14/1**
000- **10** *6* **Whistler**[100] [6698] 9-8-13 75 ... (p) DaneO'Neill 10 — 48
(Miss J R Tooth) *a outpcd and nvr in contention* **16/1**
10 **11** *1 ¼* **Mountain Pass (USA)**[42] [532] 4-8-5 67 ... (v) ChrisCatlin 4 — 36
(M J Wallace) *bhd: sme hdwy: over 2f out: nvr in contention and sn wknd* **16/1**
330- **12** *9* **Danzig River (IRE)**[226] [4767] 5-9-3 79 ... JoeFanning 12 — 15
(D Nicholls) *unruly as stalls opened and rdr lost irons: nvr rcvrd and a bhd* **7/1**

61.54 secs (0.44) **Going Correction** +0.225s/f (Good) — 12 Ran SP% **121.8**
Speed ratings (Par 105):105,104,104,103,103 102,102,100,99,89 87,73
CSF £130.10 CT £977.31 TOTE £17.90: £4.40, £4.70, £3.00; EX 95.60.
Owner D R Windebank **Bred** D R Windebank **Trained** Kentisbeare, Devon

FOCUS
The action developed down the centre of the track, with the low-drawn runners who took a wider course coming out on top. Sound form.
Danzig River(IRE) Official explanation: jockey said he lost his irons as gates opened

948 ARENA LEISURE MAIDEN STKS — 1m 2f 7y
4:30 (4:31) (Class 5) 3-Y-O — **£3,238** (£963; £481; £240) **Stalls** Low

Form — RPR
5- **1** **The Last Drop (IRE)**[205] [5311] 3-9-3 ... MichaelHills 12 — 80+
(B W Hills) *in tch: n.m.r on rail over 5f out:drvn and styd on wl fr over 1f out: led wl ins last: readily* **10/3**[1]
0- **2** *1 ¼* **Summer's Eve**[188] [5688] 3-8-12 ... DaneO'Neill 5 — 73
(H Candy) *led 1f: styd chsng ldrs: led again 2f out: rdn over 1f out: hdd and one pce wl ins last* **5/1**[3]
\- **3** *2* **Just Devine (IRE)** 3-8-12 ... JohnEgan 10 — 69
(B Palling) *s.i.s: bhd: rdn over 3f out: swtchd lft sn after and styd on to chse ldrs over 1f out: one pce ins last* **100/1**
4 *½* **Belanak (IRE)** 3-9-3 ... RobertWinston 9 — 73+
(Sir Michael Stoute) *in tch: pushed along over 3f out: kpt on ins fnl f but nvr gng pce to rch ldrs* **7/1**
0- **5** *hd* **Impostor (IRE)**[168] [6068] 3-9-3 ... JamieSpencer 8 — 73
(J R Fanshawe) *chsd ldrs: rdn over 2f out: styd on same pce appr fnl f* **25/1**
6 *1 ¾* **Dream Prize (IRE)** 3-9-3 ... KFallon 15 — 73+
(Sir Michael Stoute) *s.i.s and reminders in rr: hdwy 4f out: chsd ldrs and rdn over 2f out: wknd fnl f* **9/2**[2]
0- **7** *6* **Counting House (IRE)**[240] [4361] 3-9-3 ... SteveDrowne 2 — 58
(R Charlton) *bhd: hdwy 4f out: chsd ldrs and pushed along 3f out: wknd ins fnl 2f* **7/1**
040- **8** *nk* **Hoh Bla Daa**[175] [5949] 3-9-3 71 ... MartinDwyer 13 — 58
(S Kirk) *bhd: pushed along over 3f out: kpt on ins fnl f but nvr in contention* **33/1**
0- **9** *1 ¼* **Oporto (UAE)**[188] [5692] 3-8-12 ... PhilipRobinson 7 — 50
(M A Jarvis) *sn w ldr: slt advantage fr 5f out: hdd 2f out: sn wknd* **12/1**
10 *1 ¼* **Jack Absolute (IRE)** 3-9-3 ... AlanMunro 6 — 53
(B J Meehan) *bhd: pushed along and stl plenty to do 2f out: kpt on ins last but nvr in contention* **18/1**
30- **11** *½* **On Air (USA)**[198] [5454] 3-8-12 ... JoeFanning 4 — 47
(M Johnston) *chsd ldrs tl rdn and wknd fr 3f out* **16/1**
0 **12** *2* **Warne's Way (IRE)**[16] [720] 3-9-3 ... RyanMoore 11 — 48
(R Hannon) *s.i.s: rdn into mid-div 5f out: wknd 3f out* **25/1**
00- **13** *1 ¾* **Girardii**[194] [5555] 3-9-3 ... RichardHughes 1 — 45
(R Charlton) *chsd ldrs: chal 4f out: wknd fr 3f out* **25/1**
000- **14** *½* **Master Mark**[246] [4185] 3-9-3 57 ... ShaneKelly 14 — 44
(P D Evans) *led after 1f: hdd 5f out: wknd over 3f out* **100/1**

2m 11.29s (2.99) **Going Correction** +0.10s/f (Good) — 14 Ran SP% **118.2**
Speed ratings (Par 98):92,91,89,89,88 87,82,82,81,80 80,78,77,76
CSF £17.78 TOTE £3.90: £1.60, £2.60, £11.90; EX 16.00.
Owner J Hanson, Cavendish Inv Ltd, A Patrick **Bred** Sunderland Holdings **Trained** Lambourn, Berks

FOCUS
A decent maiden in which the first half-dozen finished clear. The form is not particularly strong or solid but winners should come out of it.
Master Mark Official explanation: jockey said gelding ran too free

949 **COME RACING EVERY MONDAY THIS SUMMER H'CAP** 6f
5:00 (5:00) (Class 5) (0-75,75) 4-Y-O+ **£3,238** (£963; £481; £240) **Stalls** High

Form RPR
2340 **1** **Nautical**[16] 726 8-8-7 **69** JamesDoyle(5) 6 77+
(A W Carroll) *hld up rr: racd towards centre crse: stdy hdwy over 1f out: drvn: edgd lft and qcknd to ld cl home: readily* **20/1**
0253 **2** ½ **Lake Chini (IRE)**[30] 632 4-9-4 **75** (p) PhilipRobinson 9 81
(M A Jarvis) *racd far side: chsd ldrs: rdn 2f out: styd on to ld wl ins last: ct cl home* **14/1**
1620 **3** ¾ **Gone'N'Dunnett (IRE)**[12] 798 7-8-4 **68** (v) KirstyMilczarek(7) 1 72
(Mrs C A Dunnett) *racd far side: chse ldrs: rdn over 2f out: led 1f out: hdd and outpcd wl ins last* **25/1**
3020 **4** *shd* **Greenwood**[8] 845 8-8-13 **70** (t) SteveDrowne 2 73
(P G Murphy) *racd centre crse: chsd ldrs: rdn over 2f out: kpt on ins last but nt pce to chal* **20/1**
06-3 **5** *1* **Digital**[17] 719 9-8-13 **70** ChrisCatlin 5 70
(M R Channon) *bhd: racd centre crse: rdn: hdwy and swtchd lft 2f out: kpt on ins last but nvr gng pce to chal* **16/1**
1-40 **6** 1¼ **Roman Quintet (IRE)**[16] 721 6-9-1 **72** TQuinn 12 69
(D W P Arbuthnot) *t.k.h: chsd ldrs in centre crse: rdn 2f out: kpt on same pce fnl f* **17/2**[3]
030- **7** ¾ **Chinalea (IRE)**[175] 5951 4-8-13 **73** (t) AdamKirby(3) 7 67
(C G Cox) *racd centre crse: chsd ldrs: rdn 1/2-way: one pce fnl 2f* **20/1**
-243 **8** ½ **Adantino**[41] 541 7-8-11 **68** (b) AlanMunro 15 61
(B R Millman) *racd centre but towards stands side: bhd: hdwy fnl f: kpt on but nvr in contention* **6/1**[2]
21- **9** *hd* **Zidane**[178] 5883 4-9-2 **73** JamieSpencer 11 65
(J R Fanshawe) *hld up mid-div and racd centre crse: hrd rdn and no prog ins fnl 2f* **10/11**[1]
0000 **10** ½ **Pamir (IRE)**[16] 721 4-8-12 **69** IanMongan 14 60
(P R Chamings) *chsd ldrs in centre crse: rdn over 2f out: wknd fnl f* **28/1**
5600 **11** ¾ **Blue Knight (IRE)**[17] 719 7-8-11 **68** (v) AdrianTNicholls 10 57
(D Nicholls) *racd centre crse: outpcd: kpt on fnl f but nvr in contention* **50/1**
0060 **12** ½ **Poker Player (IRE)**[19] 699 4-8-13 **70** (b) MichaelHills 4 57
(G C Bravery) *chsd ldrs far side over 4f* **40/1**
010- **13** *3* **Extremely Rare (IRE)**[163] 6157 5-9-3 **74** MickyFenton 8 52
(M S Saunders) *racd far side and led: rdn 2f out: hdd 1f out and sn wknd* **16/1**
100- **14** ½ **Prince Cyrano**[163] 6157 7-8-10 **72** StephenDonohoe(5) 3 49
(W J Musson) *racd far side: bhd fr 1/2-way* **50/1**
445/ **15** *16* **Grand Place**[555] 5932 4-8-13 **70** RyanMoore 16 —
(R Hannon) *racd alone stands side: spd tl wknd fr 2f out* **40/1**

1m 14.43s (0.76) **Going Correction** +0.225s/f (Good) **15** Ran SP% **126.0**
Speed ratings (Par 103):103,102,101,101,99 98,97,96,96,95 94,93,89,89,67
CSF £259.83 CT £7009.30 TOTE £26.60: £5.40, £3.40, £7.50; EX 305.70 Place 6 £5,286.34, Place 5 £1,466.06.
Owner Gary J Roberts **Bred** Sheikh Mohammed Bin Rashid Al Maktoum **Trained** Cropthorne, Worcs

FOCUS
The field fanned out across the course once in line for home. The winner comprehensively beat the remainder of those who raced down the centre. Ordinary form, but sound.
Nautical Official explanation: trainer said, regarding improved form shown, gelding was affected by false start on previous run
T/Jkpt: Not won. T/Plt: £12,840.40 to a £1 stake. Pool: £52,769.15. 3.00 winning tickets. T/Qpdt: £676.00 to a £1 stake. Pool: £5,664.00. 6.20 winning tickets. ST

820 WOLVERHAMPTON (A.W) (L-H)
Monday, April 10

OFFICIAL GOING: Standard changing to standard to fast after race 2 (2.40)
Wind: Moderate, behind Weather: Fine

950 **WOLVERHAMPTON-RACECOURSE.CO.UK H'CAP** 7f 32y(P)
2:10 (2:10) (Class 6) (0-60,63) 4-Y-O+ **£2,730** (£806; £403) **Stalls** High

Form RPR
3430 **1** **Lord Chamberlain**[10] 820 13-9-3 **59** (b) TomEaves 2 69
(J M Bradley) *hld up: hdwy on ins over 2f out: rdn to ld over 1f out: rdn out* **12/1**
00-2 **2** *2* **Sir Bond (IRE)**[7] 860 5-9-2 **58** TonyCulhane 12 68+
(B Smart) *bhd: hdwy over 3f out: rdn over 2f out: nt clr run wl over 1f out: sn swtchd lft: r.o ins fnl f: nt rch wnr* **5/1**[1]
60-0 **3** ¾ **The Bonus King**[19] 698 6-9-4 **60** KDarley 3 63
(J Jay) *chsd ldrs: rdn over 3f out: ev ch over 1f out: nt qckn ins fnl f* **11/2**[2]
203- **4** 2½ **Crystal Mystic (IRE)**[224] 4813 4-9-2 **58** FrancisFerris 5 54
(B Palling) *led: rdn 3f out: hdd over 1f out: wknd fnl f* **14/1**
400- **5** *nk* **Joshua's Gold (IRE)**[149] 6336 5-8-13 **58** DanielTudhope(3) 10 54
(D Carroll) *hld up: hdwy on outside 4f out: rdn and ev ch over 1f out: wknd ins fnl f* **8/1**
0-40 **6** *1* **Jilly Why (IRE)**[42] 537 5-9-3 **59** DarryllHolland 1 52
(Ms Deborah J Evans) *w ldr: rdn and ev ch over 2f out: edgd rt over 1f out: wknd ins fnl f* **7/1**[3]
0245 **7** 1¼ **Preskani**[7] 860 4-9-4 **60** (p) SebSanders 9 50
(Mrs N Macauley) *chsd ldrs: rdn and lost pl over 3f out: rallied over 1f out: no imp fnl f* **25/1**
0251 **8** *hd* **Count Cougar (USA)**[7] 858 6-9-4 **63** 6ex NeilChalmers(3) 4 52
(S P Griffiths) *prom: rdn 3f out: ev ch over 1f out: wknd ins fnl f* **10/1**
2500 **9** *3* **Lucius Verrus (USA)**[8] 845 6-9-4 **60** (v) PaulHanagan 7 41
(D Shaw) *hld up: sn mid-div: lost pl over 5f out: nt clr run over 3f out: n.d after* **9/1**
00-6 **10** *3* **Jools**[8] 845 8-9-4 **60** EddieAhern 11 34
(D K Ivory) *chsd ldrs: rdn over 3f out: wknd wl over 1f out* **14/1**
0425 **11** *8* **Joy And Pain**[37] 576 5-9-4 **60** GrahamGibbons 8 13
(M J Attwater) *hld up: rdn over 3f out: bhd fnl 2f* **8/1**
0/0 **12** *8* **Hallings Overture (USA)**[58] 383 7-9-3 **59** JimmyFortune 6 —
(C A Horgan) *s.i.s: hld up and bhd: bdly hmpd over 3f out: nt rcvr* **14/1**

1m 28.36s (-2.04) **Going Correction** -0.20s/f (Stan) **12** Ran SP% **117.4**
Speed ratings (Par 101):103,100,99,97,96 95,94,93,90,87 77,68
CSF £70.30 CT £379.78 TOTE £17.80: £5.10, £1.40, £1.90; EX 84.40 Trifecta £201.70 Part won. Pool: £284.10 - 0.10 winning tickets..
Owner W C Harries **Bred** Dragon's Stud **Trained** Sedbury, Gloucs

FOCUS
A moderate handicap but the pace was strong from the start and the form is solid.

951 **ZONGALERO RESTAURANT OVERLOOKS THE RACETRACK (S) STKS** 5f 20y(P)
2:40 (2:41) (Class 6) 3-Y-O+ **£2,388** (£705; £352) **Stalls** Low

Form RPR
1130 **1** **Henry Tun**[10] 824 8-9-8 60 (b) JasonEdmunds(3) 7 64
(J Balding) *chsd ldrs: rdn over 3f out: hung lft over 1f out: led wl ins fnl f: r.o* **6/1**[2]
0604 **2** *1* **He's A Rocket (IRE)**[40] 547 5-9-11 52 (b) FrancisNorton 1 60
(K R Burke) *led over 1f: led over 2f out: rdn wl over 1f out: sn edgd rt: hdd wl ins fnl f* **15/2**[3]
-061 **3** ¾ **Red Sovereign**[21] 679 5-8-13 54 AshleyHamblett(7) 3 53
(D G Bridgwater) *chsd ldrs: rdn wl over 1f out: nt qckn ins fnl f* **9/2**[1]
-000 **4** ½ **Bahamian Breeze**[48] 474 5-9-6 55 LPKeniry 5 51
(D M Simcock) *outpcd and bhd: hdwy and edgd rt over 1f out: swtchd rt ins fnl f: kpt on* **9/1**
6550 **5** *1* **Edged In Gold**[37] 580 4-9-1 52 (e) SebSanders 11 42
(P J Makin) *racd wd: chsd ldr: rdn wl over 1f out: hung lft ins fnl f: one pce* **8/1**
-000 **6** ½ **Indian Gem**[6] 873 5-9-1 40 FrancisFerris 9 41
(A J Chamberlain) *s.i.s: swtchd lft after 1f: hdwy on ins 2f out: sn swtchd lft: rdn and one pce fnl f* **50/1**
06-6 **7** ½ **Petana**[12] 789 6-9-1 45 HayleyTurner 8 39
(Peter Grayson) *bhd: swtchd lft after 1f: sme late hdwy: nvr nrr* **25/1**
00-0 **8** *hd* **Danescourt (IRE)**[14] 766 4-9-1 40 (b) GregFairley(5) 6 43
(J M Bradley) *mid-div: rdn 3f out: sn lost pl: sme late prog* **66/1**
-160 **9** 2½ **Blue Moon Hitman (IRE)**[56] 401 5-9-11 52 (b) TomEaves 12 39
(R Brotherton) *racd wd: led over 3f out: rdn and hdd over 2f out: wknd jst over 1f out* **16/1**
0553 **10** *1* **Feminist (IRE)**[12] 789 4-9-1 45 (p) JimmyFortune 2 25
(J M Bradley) *w ldrs: rdn over 2f out: wknd wl over 1f out* **8/1**
/200 **11** *7* **Borzoi Maestro**[34] 605 5-9-6 52 (p) DarryllHolland 10 5
(M Wellings) *w ldrs over 2f: sn wknd* **20/1**
2R-R **12** *17* **Piccled**[14] 761 8-9-6 83 WSupple 4 —
(E J Alston) *v rel to r: a t.o* **9/2**[1]

62.24 secs (-0.58) **Going Correction** -0.20s/f (Stan) **12** Ran SP% **112.6**
Speed ratings (Par 101):96,94,93,92,90 90,89,88,84,83 72,44
CSF £45.94 TOTE £6.50: £2.00, £3.20, £2.40; EX 34.20 Trifecta £112.10 Pool: £290.65 - 1.84 winning tickets..There was no bid for the winner. Red Sovereign was the subject of a friendly claim.
Owner Terry Reffell **Bred** T Tunstall **Trained** Scrooby, Notts

FOCUS
A fair seller in which Piccled had upwards of 26lb in hand of his rivals at the weights, but he had refused to race on his last two starts and did not fancy it this time either. That left the race wide-open but the winning time was still modest.

952 **CONSTRUCTION DAY IS COMING ON JUNE 2ND MAIDEN STKS** 1m 141y(P)
3:10 (3:11) (Class 5) 3-Y-O **£3,238** (£963; £481; £240) **Stalls** Low

Form RPR
045- **1** **Tempsford Flyer (IRE)**[194] 5555 3-9-3 78 EddieAhern 6 81+
(J W Hills) *hld up and bhd: hdwy 3f out: swtchd lft over 1f out: led ins fnl f: r.o wl* **20/1**
323- **2** 1½ **Just Observing**[225] 4777 3-9-3 77 SebSanders 2 78
(E A L Dunlop) *led: hdd over 6f out: led over 3f out: rdn and edgd rt over 1f out: hdd ins fnl f: nt qckn* **5/2**[2]
50- **3** *2* **Hunting Party (IRE)**[248] 4131 3-9-3 PaulHanagan 1 74
(B W Hills) *hld up in tch: rdn over 3f out: one pce fnl f* **6/1**[3]
4 **4** *nk* **Scotland Yard (UAE)**[7] 850 3-9-3 KDarley 9 73
(M Johnston) *stmbld s: hld up: hdwy over 5f out: ev ch over 2f out: sn rdn: c wd st: styd on same pce fnl f* **9/1**
0- **5** 1¾ **Italian Romance**[255] 3901 3-9-3 HayleyTurner 5 69
(M L W Bell) *hld up in tch: rdn over 3f out: hung rt over 1f out: one pce* **9/1**
0-0 **6** ¾ **Electric Warrior (IRE)**[6] 880 3-9-3 PatCosgrave 13 68+
(K R Burke) *bhd: hdwy wl over 1f out: nt clr run and swtchd lft ent fnl f: nvr nrr* **100/1**
3-5 **7** *1* **Country Affair (USA)**[49] 459 3-9-3 79 DarryllHolland 7 66
(P R Webber) *mid-div: rdn over 3f out: no hdwy fnl 2f* **12/1**
3- **8** *6* **Star Crowned (USA)**[135] 6435 3-9-3 (t) JimmyFortune 3 53+
(B J Meehan) *chsd ldrs: lost pl over 6f out: n.d after* **2/1**[1]
33-3 **9** *1* **Genau (IRE)**[42] 536 3-9-3 72 TomEaves 11 51
(Mrs L Stubbs) *hld up in mid-div: rdn over 2f out: sn bhd* **40/1**
00- **10** 1¾ **Bauer (IRE)**[208] 5231 3-9-3 NickyMackay 4 47
(L M Cumani) *rdn over 3f out: a bhd* **66/1**
222- **11** *3* **Queen's Composer (IRE)**[140] 6402 3-9-3 74 DerekMcGaffin 12 41+
(B Smart) *prom: rdn and ev ch over 2f out: wknd over 1f out: sn eased* **16/1**
340- **12** *5* **Is It Me (USA)**[140] 6402 3-9-3 65 GrahamGibbons 8 31
(P A Blockley) *chsd ldrs: rdn 4f out: sn lost pl* **100/1**
4 **13** *12* **Darker Than Blue**[11] 802 3-8-5 KMay(7) 10 —
(B J Meehan) *prom: sddle slipped and led over 6f out: hdd over 3f out: wknd over 2f out* **100/1**

1m 49.91s (-1.85) **Going Correction** -0.20s/f (Stan) **13** Ran SP% **121.4**
Speed ratings (Par 98):100,98,96,96,95 94,93,88,87,85 83,78,67
CSF £70.12 TOTE £35.80: £5.30, £1.70, £2.10; EX 90.40 TRIFECTA Not won..
Owner Mrs Brian Kingham **Bred** P Connolly **Trained** Upper Lambourn, Berks

FOCUS
An above-average maiden for the track and it really ought to produce a few winners. The runner-up sets the standard.
Scotland Yard(UAE) Official explanation: jockey said colt stumbled on leaving stalls
Star Crowned(USA) Official explanation: jockey said colt was never travelling
Queen's Composer(IRE) Official explanation: jockey said colt lost his action

953 **PARADE RESTAURANT APPRENTICE CLAIMING STKS** 1m 141y(P)
3:40 (3:40) (Class 6) 4-Y-O+ **£2,730** (£806; £403) **Stalls** Low

Form RPR
1363 **1** **Distant Country (USA)**[16] 734 7-8-4 61 (p) PatrickDonaghy(7) 1 60+
(K R Burke) *hld up in mid-div: hdwy 2f out: n.m.r over 1f out: rdn to ld wl ins fnl f: r.o* **7/1**
0113 **2** *nk* **Vancouver Gold (IRE)**[10] 818 4-8-5 70 AndrewElliott(5) 6 59
(K R Burke) *led after 1f: rdn over 1f out: hung rt and hdd wl ins fnl f: r.o* **7/2**[1]
2210 **3** ¾ **Golden Spectrum (IRE)**[40] 546 7-8-6 53 (p) TolleyDean(5) 8 58
(R A Harris) *hld up in mid-div: hdwy 3f out: rdn over 1f out: kpt on ins fnl f* **13/2**[3]

-054 **4** *nk* **Nimello (USA)**[26] [640] 10-9-1 65 NeilChalmers 2 61
(A G Newcombe) *hld up and bhd: rdn and hdwy on ins over 2f out: r.o one pce fnl f* **8/1**

0420 **5** *3/4* **True Night**[9] [833] 9-8-12 65 VictoriaBehan(7) 5 64+
(D Nicholls) *t.k.h: in tch: lost pl 6f out: nt clr run on ins over 3f out: rallied over 1f out: one pce fnl f* **11/1**

540- **6** *3/4* **Angel River**[126] [6511] 4-8-1 40 MarcHalford(3) 7 47
(J Ryan) *led 1f: prom: rdn over 2f out: wknd ins fnl f* **100/1**

6001 **7** *nk* **Merdiff**[16] [734] 7-8-4 55 LiamJones(5) 11 52
(W M Brisbourne) *t.k.h: prom: rdn and ev ch over 2f out: wknd ins fnl f* **14/1**

4003 **8** *1 1/4* **Legacy (JPN)**[14] [770] 6-8-7 45 (b) DanielTudhope 9 47
(P D Evans) *dwlt: bhd tl sme hdwy fnl f: n.d* **16/1**

4350 **9** *nk* **Pending (IRE)**[7] [862] 5-8-5 52 (p) SaleemGolam 3 44
(J R Boyle) *s.i.s: plld hrd: hdwy 6f out: rdn over 2f out: edgd lft over 1f out: sn wknd* **9/1**

4106 **10** *2 1/2* **Linning Wine (IRE)**[9] [833] 10-8-6 70 (b[1]) GregFairley(3) 12 43
(P A Blockley) *s.s and wnt rt: sn mid-div: rdn 3f out: wknd wl over 1f out* **6/1[2]**

4-00 **11** *1 1/4* **Grandma Ryta**[24] [659] 4-7-11 40 DuranFentiman(3) 4 31
(John Berry) *sn bhd* **40/1**

2-54 **12** *7* **Scamperdale**[10] [820] 4-8-8 54 SoniaEaton(7) 10 32
(B P J Baugh) *prom tl wknd over 3f out* **25/1**

1m 51.12s (-0.64) **Going Correction** -0.20s/f (Stan) **12** Ran SP% **111.6**
Speed ratings (Par 101):94,93,93,92,92 91,91,90,89,87 86,80
CSF £29.28 TOTE £5.20: £1.80, £1.60, £2.50; EX 27.80 Trifecta £68.40 Pool: £294.20 - 3.05 winning tickets..
Owner Spigot Lodge Partnership **Bred** Audubon Farm And D L Martin **Trained** Middleham Moor, N Yorks

FOCUS
A modest but competitive claimer in which they went just a steady gallop for much of the way. The winning time was moderate, 1.21 seconds slower than the preceding three-year-old maiden. The form looks shaky.

954 WEATHERBYS BANK FILLIES' H'CAP 5f 20y(P)
4:10 (4:10) (Class 5) (0-75,74) 3-Y-0+ **£5,181** (£1,541; £770; £384) **Stalls** Low

Form RPR

2322 **1** **Ashes (IRE)**[10] [813] 4-8-11 **62** PatCosgrave 2 69
(K R Burke) *w ldrs: led on bit over 2f out: rdn over 1f out: drvn out* **9/4[1]**

0632 **2** *3/4* **Sahara Silk (IRE)**[10] [824] 5-9-2 **67** (v) PaulHanagan 7 71
(D Shaw) *chsd ldrs: rdn 2f out: r.o fnl f* **11/2[3]**

1014 **3** *shd* **Hello Roberto**[10] [824] 5-8-11 **62** (p) AdrianMcCarthy 8 66
(R A Harris) *chsd ldrs: edgd lft 1f out: r.o towards fin* **6/1**

00-1 **4** *shd* **True Magic**[37] [588] 5-9-6 **71** GrahamGibbons 1 74
(J D Bethell) *chsd ldrs: rdn over 2f out: kpt on fnl f* **5/1[2]**

0-50 **5** *1* **Bonne De Fleur**[38] [569] 5-9-4 **74** (b[1]) GregFairley(5) 10 74
(B Smart) *w ldrs: ev ch 2f out: sn rdn: edgd lft ent fnl f: nt qckn* **9/1**

40-3 **6** *1 1/4* **Piccostar**[11] [807] 3-8-3 **68** ow1 RichardSmith(3) 6 63
(A B Haynes) *dwlt: hdwy fnl f: nvr nrr* **20/1**

36-0 **7** *1* **Pro Tempore**[3] [903] 4-8-2 **60** oh8 LiamJones(7) 5 52
(David Pinder) *hld up in mid-div: rdn wl over 1f out: no hdwy* **40/1**

1300 **8** *1 1/4* **Canina**[17] [709] 3-8-5 **67** FrancisNorton 9 54
(Ms Deborah J Evans) *n.d* **25/1**

3-06 **9** *1 1/4* **Smooch**[60] [344] 3-8-8 **70** EddieAhern 11 53
(R M H Cowell) *a bhd* **20/1**

600- **10** *1 1/2* **Ruby's Dream**[188] [5686] 4-8-9 **60** oh6 (p) TomEaves 3 37
(J M Bradley) *led: rdn and hdd over 2f out: wknd wl over 1f out* **25/1**

0210 **11** *hd* **Lady Bahia (IRE)**[10] [824] 5-8-11 **62** (b) GylesParkin 4 38
(Peter Grayson) *s.i.s: a bhd* **16/1**

61.67 secs (-1.15) **Going Correction** -0.20s/f (Stan)
WFA 3 from 4yo+ 11lb **11** Ran SP% **112.6**
Speed ratings (Par 100):101,99,99,99,97 95,94,92,90,87 87
CSF £12.24 CT £64.46 TOTE £2.30: £1.20, £1.60, £2.20; EX 8.70 Trifecta £52.80 Pool: £321.82 - 4.32 winning tickets..
Owner Bryce, Dower, Morgan **Bred** E Campion **Trained** Middleham Moor, N Yorks

FOCUS
A modest sprint handicap for fillies. Sound but ordinary form.
Smooch Official explanation: jockey said filly would not face kickback.

955 STAY AT THE WOLVERHAMPTON HOLIDAY INN H'CAP 1m 1f 103y(P)
4:40 (4:40) (Class 6) (0-65,65) 4-Y-0+ **£2,730** (£806; £403) **Stalls** Low

Form RPR

6501 **1** **Lord Of Dreams (IRE)**[10] [820] 4-8-12 **59** EddieAhern 9 70
(D W P Arbuthnot) *hld up and bhd: hdwy on ins 3f out: squeezed through 2f out: hung lft and led over 1f out: r.o wl* **5/1[1]**

0004 **2** *2 1/2* **Scottish River (USA)**[18] [706] 7-8-13 **60** HayleyTurner 5 67
(M D I Usher) *s.i.s: hld up: sn mid-div: hdwy over 3f out: rdn over 2f out: ev ch over 1f out: sn edgd lft: nt qckn* **8/1**

6606 **3** *nk* **Seattle Robber**[35] [603] 4-8-8 **55** (p) GrahamGibbons 3 61
(P A Blockley) *hld up in mid-div: hdwy over 3f out: sn rdn: edgd lft 1f out: kpt on* **5/1[1]**

560- **4** *2* **Archirondel**[191] [5615] 8-8-6 **56** ow2 DanielTudhope(3) 6 58
(N Wilson) *chsd ldrs: rdn over 2f out: wknd ins fnl f* **6/1[2]**

3031 **5** *1/2* **Buscador (USA)**[37] [582] 7-8-8 **62** LiamJones(7) 7 63
(W M Brisbourne) *led 1f: w ldr: led over 5f out: rdn over 2f out: hdd over 1f out: wknd ins fnl f* **13/2[3]**

/21- **6** *1 1/4* **Kings Topic (USA)**[318] [2060] 6-9-0 **61** PatDobbs 8 60
(A B Haynes) *hld up in tch: rdn and no hdwy fnl 3f* **5/1[1]**

5260 **7** *hd* **Burnley Al (IRE)**[19] [698] 4-9-3 **64** (v) PaulHanagan 12 62
(R A Fahey) *led after 1f: hdd over 5f out: rdn and ev ch over 2f out: wknd 1f out* **11/1**

0650 **8** *2* **Sorbiesharry (IRE)**[10] [820] 7-8-5 **55** (p) JasonEdmunds(3) 13 50
(Mrs N Macauley) *nvr nr ldrs* **10/1**

200/ **9** *hd* **Travelling Band (IRE)**[400] [6081] 8-8-10 **57** DaleGibson 2 54+
(J Mackie) *hld up in tch: rdn 3f out: wkng whn n.m.r 2f out* **25/1**

002- **10** *3* **Inn For The Dancer**[47] [3350] 4-8-6 **53** LPKeniry 4 42
(J C Fox) *s.i.s: a bhd* **20/1**

11 *7* **Khetaab (IRE)**[318] [2067] 4-9-3 **64** WSupple 10 39
(E J Alston) *in tch: lost pl over 6f out: n.d after* **14/1**

060- **12** *dist* **Mcqueen (IRE)**[20] [6029] 6-9-4 **65** SebSanders 11 —
(Heather Dalton) *a bhd: rdn 4f out: t.o fnl 2f* **20/1**

00-0 **13** *dist* **Grand Ideas**[26] [644] 7-8-3 **55** MarcHalford(5) 1 —
(G J Smith) *stmbld and rdr lost irons s: a bhd: t.o fnl 2f* **50/1**

2m 0.25s (-2.37) **Going Correction** -0.20s/f (Stan) **13** Ran SP% **128.2**
Speed ratings (Par 101):102,99,99,97,97 96,96,94,94,91 85,—,—
CSF £46.42 CT £220.56 TOTE £5.40: £1.60, £3.10, £2.60; EX 44.90 Trifecta £139.80 Pool: £214.68 - 1.09 winning tickets. Place 6 £32.94, Place 5 £15.20.
Owner N Cronin & P Banfield **Bred** B Ryan **Trained** Upper Lambourn, Berks

FOCUS
Just a moderate handicap, not all that strongly-run. Fair form for the grade.
Scottish River(USA) Official explanation: jockey said gelding hung left
T/Plt: £26.60 to a £1 stake. Pool: £40,317.05. 1,102.90 winning tickets. T/Qpdt: £8.30 to a £1 stake. Pool: £3,258.60. 287.40 winning tickets. KH

840 SAINT-CLOUD (L-H)
Monday, April 10

OFFICIAL GOING: Good to soft

959a PRIX PENELOPE (GROUP 3) (FILLIES) 1m 2f 110y
2:20 (2:30) 3-Y-0 **£27,856** (£11,034; £8,276; £5,517; £2,759)

RPR

1 **Germance (USA)**[26] 3-9-0 IMendizabal 3 109
(J-C Rouget, France) *racd in 4th, disp last str, hdwy on outside 1 1/2f out, chal 150y out, led 100y out, pushed out* **22/10[2]**

2 *1* **Sanaya (IRE)**[174] [5967] 3-9-0 CSoumillon 4 107
(A De Royer-Dupre, France) *raced in 2nd, pushed along to press leader 1 1/2f out but unable to pass her, stayed on, took 2nd close home* **14/10[1]**

3 *1/2* **Alix Road (FR)**[33] 3-9-0 TThulliez 2 106
(Mme M Bollack-Badel, France) *led, ran on from 1 1/2f out when pressed, headed 100 yards out, no extra close home* **9/1**

4 *1 1/2* **Fauvelia (FR)**[23] [671] 3-9-0 SPasquier 1 103
(Y De Nicolay, France) *raced in 3rd, driven 1 1/2f out, no extra under pressure final furlong* **42/10**

5 *1/2* **Sister Trouble (FR)**[23] [671] 3-9-0 DBonilla 5 103
(F Head, France) *raced in last, disputing last straight, pushed along 1 1/2f out, one pace* **39/10[3]**

2m 20.1s **5** Ran SP% **122.6**
PARI-MUTUEL: WIN 3.20; PL 1.50, 1.40; SF 8.00.
Owner N Radwan **Bred** Edmund J Loder **Trained** Pau, France

NOTEBOOK
Germance(USA), switched off towards the tail of the field in what was just a slowly run race, basically just produced the best finishing speed. This was her first win at a major Parisian track and she is now unbeaten in three races. She could go directly for the Prix de Diane and looks likely to stay even further.
Sanaya(IRE) did not appear suited by the lack of early pace and should do better off a stronger gallop.
Alix Road(FR) led at just a moderate pace and stuck on when headed She may not be up to Group standard, but a decent Listed race could come her way.
Fauvelia(FR) was another unsuited by the falsely-run race.

BATH (L-H)
Tuesday, April 11

OFFICIAL GOING: Good to soft changing to soft after race 5 (4.10)
As conditions worsened through the afternoon, visibility was moderate for race 5 and poor for race 6.
Wind: Strong, against Weather: Raining

961 SHONE BUILDING RACECOURSE CONTRACTOR MAIDEN STKS 5f 11y
2:10 (2:12) (Class 5) 2-Y-0 **£3,562** (£1,059; £529; £264) **Stalls** Low

Form RPR

1 **Carson's Spirit (USA)** 2-9-3 ChrisCatlin 9 78
(W S Kittow) *mid-div: rdn over 3f out: hdwy 2f out: edgd lft and r.o to ld cl home* **20/1**

2 *1* **Alternative** 2-9-3 SebSanders 10 74
(R M Beckett) *mid-div: hdwy over 2f out: rdn to ld jst over 1f out: hdd cl home* **6/1[3]**

3 *2* **Tune Up The Band** 2-9-3 RichardHughes 7 66
(R J Hodges) *w ldrs: led 2f out: rdn and hdd jst over 1f out: one pce* **9/1**

4 *1* **Eager Lover (USA)** 2-9-3 MichaelHills 5 62
(B W Hills) *dwlt: hdwy over 1f out: r.o ins fnl f* **7/1**

32 **5** *1 1/2* **Pernomente (IRE)**[8] [849] 2-9-3 MartinDwyer 4 56
(J S Moore) *led: rdn and hdd 3f out: wknd ins fnl f* **7/2[1]**

6 *1* **Mac Gille Eoin** 2-9-3 NCallan 8 52
(J Gallagher) *chsd ldrs: rdn 2f out: wknd ins fnl f* **40/1**

7 *1/2* **Just Dust** 2-9-0 RobertMiles(3) 12 50
(W G M Turner) *s.s: outpcd: hdwy fnl f: nrst fin* **33/1**

35 **8** *3/4* **Everyman**[8] [849] 2-9-3 ShaneKelly 13 47
(P D Evans) *prom: rdn over 2f out: wknd over 1f out* **5/1[2]**

9 *1 3/4* **Stunningjo** 2-8-12 RobertWinston 3 35
(J L Spearing) *dwlt: n.d* **25/1**

10 *nk* **Private Peachey (IRE)** 2-9-3 DaneO'Neill 11 39
(B R Millman) *s.i.s: a bhd* **16/1**

11 *7* **Tom Tower (IRE)** 2-9-3 TQuinn 6 11
(M R Channon) *chsd ldrs: rdn over 2f out: wknd wl over 1f out* **5/1[2]**

12 *hd* **Tagula Music (IRE)** 2-8-12 JohnEgan 1 —
(B Palling) *s.s: outpcd* **25/1**

13 *1/2* **Topsy Maite** 2-8-12 LPKeniry 2 —
(R Curtis) *s.i.s: sn mid-div: rdn over 3f out: sn struggling* **66/1**

65.00 secs (2.50) **Going Correction** +0.30s/f (Good) **13** Ran SP% **117.6**
Speed ratings (Par 92):92,90,87,85,83 81,80,79,76,76 65,64,64
CSF £126.66 TOTE £22.00: £7.90, £3.00, £2.90; EX 124.50.
Owner K B Hodges **Bred** Pontchartrain Stud **Trained** Blackborough, Devon

FOCUS
Just a fair two-year-old contest, but it should produce winners.

NOTEBOOK
Carson's Spirit(USA), whose dam was related to hurdles winners, hardly comes from a stable renowned for their juvenile success, but he ran out quite a taking winner on this racecourse debut, getting going late on to win going away. He clearly has the speed to be effective at this distance, but six furlongs is going to suit in future and he looks capable of winning a novice stakes before the better juveniles begin to emerge. (op 25-1)
Alternative ◆, another bred to improve for a bit further, comes from a stable who largely do well with their juveniles and, having made headway, he looked the likeliest winner when going on over a furlong out. Carson's Spirit proved too strong in the end however and he was reeled in deep inside the final furlong. There was plenty of promise to be taken from this and it will be both disappointing and surprising if he cannot pick up a maiden in the near future. (tchd 11-2 and 13-2)

Tune Up The Band, a very cheap purchase, was nibbled at in the market and he shaped extremely well back in third having been up there throughout. It transpired he had broken down however and it remains to be seen how he goes on from this. Official explanation: vet said colt was lame behind (op 12-1)
Eager Lover(USA) is bred for speed, but he was done no favours by a tardy start and was unable to make an impact. He made some nice late headway however, not being given a hard time, and should come on appreciably for the outing. (tchd 15-2)
Pernomente(IRE), the most experienced in the line-up, led early and had every chance, but he was readily brushed aside and is likely to continue to struggle to find a maiden. (op 9-2 tchd 5-1)
Mac Gille Eoin showed up well early before fading out of it in the closing stages, but there was plenty of promise to be gleamed from this and he is likely to come on for the outing. (tchd 50-1)
Just Dust comes from a stable who traditionally do well with their juveniles, but he shaped as though the experience was needed first time up and did not get going until the race was all but over. He should benefit from the outing.
Everyman has not built on his Brocklesby third and may be one for nurseries later in the season. (tchd 9-2)
Tom Tower(IRE), a 110,000gns son of Cape Cross, appeared to know his job, as you would expect of a Channon juvenile, but he found little under pressure and faded right out of it. This was disappointing, but he deserves another chance to show what he can do. (op 7-2)

962 P.J.M. MECHANICAL SERVICES (S) STKS 5f 11y
2:40 (2:44) (Class 6) 2-Y-O **£2,266** (£674; £337; £168) **Stalls** Low

Form RPR
1 **No Worries Yet (IRE)** 2-8-6 .... RobertWinston 7 63
(J L Spearing) *w ldr: led over 2f out: sn rdn: drvn out* **7/2**[1]
0 2 1 **Sardis Road**[7] [877] 2-8-8 .... RobertMiles(3) 8 64
(W G M Turner) *a.p: rdn and ev ch 2f out: edgd rt fnl f: r.o* **15/2**
3 1 ½ **Auction Time** 2-8-6 .... JohnEgan 3 54
(B Palling) *s.i.s: sn chsng ldrs: hmpd and lost pl over 3f out: rdn and hdwy over 2f out: r.o ins fnl f* **8/1**
662 4 3 **Sad Times (IRE)**[7] [877] 2-7-13 .... LiamJones(7) 10 43
(W G M Turner) *s.i.s: outpcd: hdwy on outside over 1f out: nt rchd ldrs* **4/1**[2]
03 5 ¾ **Afric Star**[7] [877] 2-8-7 ow1 .... ShaneKelly 4 41
(P D Evans) *a.p: rdn over 2f out: no hdwy* **6/1**
0 6 hd **Circle Of Truth**[8] [849] 2-8-6 .... MarcHalford(5) 9 45
(W G M Turner) *hld up in tch: rdn 2f out: wknd ins fnl f* **14/1**
7 nk **Mr Mini Scule** 2-8-8 .... RichardSmith(3) 2 44
(A B Haynes) *led: hdd over 2f out: sn rdn: wknd fnl f* **18/1**
56 8 6 **Flying Lion**[7] [877] 2-8-6 .... TQuinn 6 17
(M R Channon) *chsd ldrs: rdn and wknd over 2f out* **9/2**[3]
0 9 4 **Bathwick Princess**[18] [707] 2-8-6 .... GrahamGibbons 1 —
(P D Evans) *wnt lft s: sn chsng ldrs: rdn over 3f out: wknd over 2f out* **33/1**
4 10 9 **Alice Who (IRE)**[14] [775] 2-7-13 .... JosephWalsh(7) 5 —
(J S Moore) *s.i.s: outpcd* **25/1**

65.15 secs (2.65) **Going Correction** +0.30s/f (Good) **10** Ran SP% **116.3**
Speed ratings (Par 90):90,88,86,81,80 79,79,69,63,48
CSF £30.09 TOTE £3.60: £1.40, £2.80, £2.60; EX 39.30.Winner bought in 4,800gns. Auction Time claimed by Diamond Racing Ltd £6,000. Sardis Road claimed by Claes Bjorling £6,000.
Owner J Spearing **Bred** Mark Donohoe **Trained** Kinnersley, Worcs

FOCUS
Not a bad seller, with the front three possibly capable of going on to nurseries.

NOTEBOOK
No Worries Yet(IRE), supported in the market beforehand, knew her job on this racecourse debut and, unlike the runner-up, she was able to run straight under pressure. That ultimately made the difference, but there is no reason why she cannot score again at this sort of level. (op 5-1)
Sardis Road, who ran green and wandered on his debut at Warwick, was well supported in the market and he had every chance inside the final quarter mile, but he continually edged to his right under pressure and it may have cost him the race. Compensation awaits at a similar level. (op 12-1)
Auction Time comes from a stable who do well with their juveniles at this sort of level and she too may have been an unfortunate loser. She may have more to offer and it will be disappointing if she cannot find a race at this level. (op 9-1)
Sad Times(IRE) surprisingly missed the break, considering it was her fourth outing, and she was always struggling to get on terms. (tchd 7-2)
Afric Star was unable to build on a fair recent third at Warwick and it may be she requires a sounder surface. (op 5-1 tchd 13-2)
Circle Of Truth did not shape without promise on this first turf start and he may have a small race in him with some further experience. (op 12-1 tchd 16-1)

963 CLIFFORD CONSTRUCTION MAIDEN STKS (DIV I) 1m 5y
3:10 (3:11) (Class 5) 3-Y-O+ **£3,238** (£963; £481; £240) **Stalls** Low

Form RPR
642- 1 **Acrobatic (USA)**[174] [5970] 3-8-11 79 .... RichardHughes 1 74+
(R Charlton) *sn led: shkn up over 1f out: sn clr: comf* **4/7**[1]
065- 2 5 **Follow The Colours (IRE)**[169] [6068] 3-8-11 68 .... EddieAhern 10 63
(J W Hills) *hld up towards rr: hdwy 3f out: styng on whn edgd lft wl ins fnl f: tk 2nd nr post* **11/1**
52 3 hd **Musical Script (USA)**[14] [778] 3-8-11 .... NCallan 7 63
(Mrs A J Hamilton-Fairley) *led early: chsd wnr tl over 4f out: rdn and wnt 2nd again whn hung rt 2f out: one pce* **8/1**[3]
5- 4 1 ¼ **Emilion**[201] [5418] 3-8-6 .... TQuinn 9 55+
(W J Haggas) *s.i.s: hld up and bhd: pushed along over 2f out: swtchd lft over 1f out: styd on ins fnl f: nvr nr to chal* **10/1**
5 1 **Smemi An Nada**[241] 4-9-12 .... RobertWinston 2 62
(P Bowen) *s.s: gd hdwy on outside over 3f out: sn rdn: btn whn sltly hmpd wl ins fnl f* **50/1**
00- 6 1 ¾ **Haneen (USA)**[172] [6007] 3-8-6 .... RHills 4 49
(J L Dunlop) *hld up in mid-div: rdn over 2f out: no hdwy* **7/1**[2]
00- 7 hd **Precious Dancer**[110] [6659] 3-8-11 .... SamHitchcott 8 54
(W R Muir) *hld up in mid-div: hdwy 4f out: rdn whn bmpd 2f out: sn wknd* **66/1**
8 ½ **Lol Draper** 3-8-7 ow1 .... ShaneKelly 3 49?
(P D Evans) *s.i.s: bhd: rdn over 2f out: n.d* **66/1**
0 9 6 **Wild Lass**[42] [539] 5-9-7 .... LPKeniry 6 39
(J C Fox) *hld up in tch: wnt 2nd over 4f out: ev ch 3f out: sn rdn and wknd* **150/1**
0 10 8 **White Heather**[48] [479] 3-8-6 .... MartinDwyer 5 18
(A M Balding) *hld up in tch: wknd over 2f out* **50/1**

1m 46.0s (4.90) **Going Correction** +0.525s/f (Yiel)
WFA 3 from 4yo+ 15lb **10** Ran SP% **112.3**
Speed ratings (Par 103):96,91,90,89,88 86,86,86,80,72
CSF £7.39 TOTE £1.50: £1.10, £2.20, £1.90; EX 8.00.
Owner K Abdulla **Bred** Juddmonte Farms Inc **Trained** Beckhampton, Wilts

FOCUS
A smooth display by hot favourite Acrobatic, but the form is held down by the close proximity of the fifth. It has been rated 18lb inferior to the second division.

964 CLIFFORD CONSTRUCTION MAIDEN STKS (DIV II) 1m 5y
3:40 (3:41) (Class 5) 3-Y-O+ **£3,238** (£963; £481; £240) **Stalls** Low

Form RPR
0- 1 **Teach To Preach (USA)**[193] [5592] 3-8-11 .... MichaelHills 6 71
(B W Hills) *w ldr: rdn to ld over 1f out: edgd rt cl home: r.o* **7/2**[2]
0 2 nk **Yeoman Spirit (IRE)**[18] [710] 3-8-11 .... MartinDwyer 10 71
(A M Balding) *led: hdd over 1f out: hrd rdn and r.o ins fnl f* **14/1**
533- 3 1 ¾ **Multakka (IRE)**[174] [5970] 3-8-11 85 .... RHills 9 67
(M P Tregoning) *a.p: rdn and ev ch over 1f out: nt qckn* **1/2**[1]
6-50 4 3 **Blue Army (IRE)**[17] [720] 3-8-11 50 .... AdrianMcCarthy 3 61?
(Jane Southcombe) *hld up in mid-div: rdn over 3f out: hdwy over 2f out: one pce fnl f* **100/1**
5 1 ½ **Gelder** 3-8-6 .... RyanMoore 8 53
(H Morrison) *prom: flashed tail over 3f out: rdn 2f out: wkng whn flashed tailed ins fnl f* **16/1**
6 1 **Celtic Spirit (IRE)** 3-8-11 .... SebSanders 4 55
(R M Beckett) *s.s: bhd tl hdwy fnl f: nrst fin* **10/1**[3]
7 13 **Levin (IRE)** 3-8-11 .... TQuinn 7 28
(J L Dunlop) *a towards rr* **16/1**
0 8 ½ **Kilmeena Magic**[42] [539] 4-9-7 .... MickyFenton 1 26
(J C Fox) *t.k.h: a bhd* **200/1**
0 9 8 **Ronaldo**[7] [880] 3-8-11 .... SamHitchcott 5 10
(W R Muir) *a bhd* **100/1**
000 10 17 **Hello Molly**[38] [579] 5-9-7 35 .... StephenCarson 2 —
(E A Wheeler) *hld up in mid-div: rdn over 3f out: sn struggling: t.o* **200/1**

1m 44.7s (3.60) **Going Correction** +0.525s/f (Yiel)
WFA 3 from 4yo+ 15lb **44** Ran SP% **119.4**
Speed ratings (Par 103):103,102,100,97,96 95,82,81,73,56
CSF £52.04 TOTE £4.00: £1.20, £1.70, £1.10; EX 63.30.
Owner Gainsborough Stud **Bred** Mrs J G Jones Snr **Trained** Lambourn, Berks

FOCUS
An ordinary maiden, but Blue Army finishing fourth somewhat holds down the form. Not solid.

965 BRADLEY JAMES FLOORING CONTRACTORS H'CAP 1m 2f 46y
4:10 (4:13) (Class 6) (0-65,66) 4-Y-O+ **£2,590** (£770; £385; £192) **Stalls** Low

Form RPR
2022 1 **Augustine**[4] [905] 5-9-4 65 .... RobertWinston 8 72
(P W Hiatt) *a.p: nt clr run on ins wl ins fnl f: swtchd rt and led cl home* **15/2**
3-04 2 1 **Gramada (IRE)**[71] [252] 4-8-12 59 .... GrahamGibbons 15 65
(P A Blockley) *w ldr: rdn over 2f out: led jst ins fnl f: hdd cl home* **28/1**
2312 3 2 **Jakarmi**[17] [736] 5-8-12 62 .... RobertMiles(3) 12 64
(B Palling) *led: rdn whn rdr dropped whip over 1f out: hdd jst ins fnl f: no ex* **13/2**[2]
-051 4 nk **Summer Bounty**[7] [882] 10-9-5 66 6ex .... NCallan 3 67
(F Jordan) *hld up and bhd: hdwy over 2f out: one pce fnl f* **12/1**
-440 5 6 **River Gypsy**[46] [503] 5-9-4 65 .... JohnEgan 9 56
(D R C Elsworth) *mid-div: styd on same pce fnl 2f* **16/1**
-311 6 2 ½ **Turner's Touch**[20] [696] 4-9-2 63 ....(b) RyanMoore 6 49
(G L Moore) *mid-div: rdn 4f out: no hdwy fnl 3f* **7/1**[3]
-000 7 ¾ **Age Of Kings (USA)**[17] [736] 4-8-12 62 .... RichardSmith(3) 11 47
(A B Haynes) *prom tl wknd over 2f out* **25/1**
/10- 8 nk **Gambling Spirit**[160] [6230] 4-9-1 62 .... DaneO'Neill 5 46
(H Candy) *prom tl wknd over 2f out* **7/1**[3]
0-00 9 1 **Meelup (IRE)**[10] [826] 6-9-3 64 ....(p) RobertHavlin 13 46
(P G Murphy) *mid-div: rdn over 3f out: sn struggling* **80/1**
4-45 10 ½ **Easy Laughter (IRE)**[18] [713] 5-9-2 63 ....(vt[1]) AlanDaly 10 45
(A King) *hld up in mid-div: rdn over 4f out: no rspnse* **10/1**
6050 11 2 **Flying Pass**[49] [478] 4-8-13 60 .... TQuinn 16 38
(D J S Ffrench Davis) *nvr nr ldrs* **22/1**
-300 12 nk **Measured Response**[55] [421] 4-9-3 64 .... MartinDwyer 4 41
(J G M O'Shea) *a towards rr* **33/1**
2524 13 nk **Gingko**[9] [843] 9-9-1 62 .... ChrisCatlin 14 39
(P R Webber) *a towards rr* **14/1**
236- 14 ½ **Thorny Mandate**[176] [5940] 4-9-1 62 .... StephenCarson 2 38
(R F Johnson Houghton) *mid-div: wknd 3f out* **16/1**
/01- 15 3 ½ **Cleaver**[174] [5980] 5-9-4 65 .... SebSanders 7 35
(Lady Herries) *a bhd* **10/3**[1]
0000 16 shd **Ronsard (IRE)**[39] [571] 4-9-1 62 .... MickyFenton 1 32
(Heather Dalton) *t.k.h: sn in tch: lost pl over 4f out: sn bhd* **40/1**

2m 14.75s (3.75) **Going Correction** +0.525s/f (Yiel) **16** Ran SP% **126.6**
Speed ratings (Par 101):106,105,103,103,98 96,95,95,94,94 92,92,92,92,89 89
CSF £219.74 CT £1464.96 TOTE £9.70: £2.60, £6.70, £2.10, £3.10; EX 337.20.
Owner Phil Kelly **Bred** Darley **Trained** Hook Norton, Oxon

FOCUS
The visibility had worsened by this stage of the day and it seemed to pay to race prominently here. Not solif form. The first four finished clear.
Flying Pass Official explanation: jockey said gelding was never travelling
Cleaver Official explanation: trainer had no explanation for the poor form shown
Ronsard(IRE) Official explanation: jockey said gelding lost its action

966 SHONE BUILDING RACECOURSE CONTRACTOR H'CAP 2m 1f 34y
4:40 (4:41) (Class 5) (0-75,75) 4-Y-O+ **£3,562** (£1,059; £529; £264) **Stalls** Low

Form RPR
406- 1 **Kayf Aramis**[176] [5943] 4-8-4 55 oh10 .... PaulQuinn 1 63
(J L Spearing) *mde virtually all: rdn over 4f out: hld on wl* **28/1**
2 1 ½ **Irish Wolf (FR)**[117] 6-9-13 74 ....(p) RobertWinston 5 80
(P Bowen) *mid-div: 5th st: styd on ins fnl f* **14/1**
304- 3 1 ¾ **Tavalu (USA)**[192] [5615] 4-8-9 60 .... RyanMoore 7 65
(G L Moore) *hld up in tch: rdn 4f out: 4th st: chsd wnr over 2f out: styd on one pce* **5/1**[3]
40-1 4 2 ½ **Precious Mystery (IRE)**[7] [881] 6-9-10 71 6ex ....(v) DaneO'Neill 12 73
(A King) *hld up in tch: 3rd st: c stands' side: rdn over 2f out: one pce* **7/2**[1]
4512 5 shd **Monte Cristo (FR)**[10] [838] 8-9-7 68 ....(v) ChrisCatlin 13 69
(Mrs L C Taylor) *mid-div: 6th st: rdn over 2f out: no hdwy* **9/2**[2]
62-4 6 3 **Shingle Street (IRE)**[11] [825] 4-9-1 66 ....(b) RichardHughes 6 65
(Miss Venetia Williams) *chsd wnr: c wd st: rdn over 2f out: wknd over 1f out* **9/1**
2040 7 2 ½ **Eastborough (IRE)**[10] [832] 7-9-11 72 .... GeorgeBaker 2 68
(B G Powell) *hld up and bhd: improving gng wl and 7th st: rdn over 2f out: wknd over 1f out* **8/1**

0155 **8** ½ **Indian Chase**[22] 675 9-8-6 **56** oh10 RichardThomas(3) 4 — 51
(Dr J R J Naylor) *mid-div: no hdwy fnl 3f* **16/1**

005- **9** shd **Harlestone Linn**[196] 5530 4-8-4 **55** oh3 JamieMackay 14 — 51
(J L Dunlop) *mid-div: no real prog fnl 3f* **7/1**

00/0 **10** 2 **Business Traveller (IRE)**[7] 881 6-8-4 **56** oh16..(vt[1]) EmmettStack(5) 3 — 49?
(R J Price) *n.d* **40/1**

P20/ **11** ½ **Lowe Go**[19] 4639 6-8-13 **60** AlanDaly 8 — 53
(Miss J S Davis) *a bhd* **40/1**

0/ **12** 1¼ **Lets Try Again (IRE)**[35] 1733 9-8-9 **56** oh1 RobertHavlin 9 — 48
(R A Farrant) *hld up in mid-div: rdn and 8th st: wknd over 2f out* **33/1**

/01- **13** 16 **Garhoud**[29] 1086 4-8-5 **56** ow1 (p) EddieAhern 15 — 33
(Karen George) *prom early* **25/1**

6/0- **14** 3½ **Argonaut**[456] 76 6-10-0 **75** VinceSlattery 10 — 47
(P Bowen) *bhd most of way* **20/1**

4m 4.44s (14.84) **Going Correction** +0.90s/f (Soft)
WFA 4 from 6yo+ 4lb — **14** Ran SP% **123.1**
Speed ratings (Par 103):103,102,101,100,100 99,97,97,97,96 96,96,88,87
CSF £363.67 CT £2297.83 TOTE £41.50: £11.10, £5.60, £2.10; EX 638.10.
Owner Mrs Isobel Phipps Coltman **Bred** Mrs Isobel Phipps Coltman **Trained** Kinnersley, Worcs

FOCUS
Dubious form with the winner scoring from 10lb out of the handicap. The pace was moderate in a race run in poor visibility.

967 BET365 CALL 08000 322 365 H'CAP — 5f 11y
5:10 (5:13) (Class 5) (0-75,75) 3-Y-O+ — **£3,886** (£1,156; £577; £288) **Stalls** Low

Form — RPR

161- **1** **Jimmy The Guesser**[116] 6591 3-8-13 **74** RichardThomas(3) 9 — 78+
(N P Littmoden) *mid-div: hdwy 2f out: sn rdn: r.o to ld last strides* **10/1**

2-40 **2** hd **Willhewiz**[72] 244 6-9-12 **73** JohnEgan 1 — 81
(M S Saunders) *led: rdn over 1f out: hdd last strides* **14/1**

532- **3** 1¼ **Don't Tell Sue**[153] 6296 3-8-13 **71** MichaelHills 5 — 70
(B W Hills) *hmpd sn after s: bhd tl hdwy over 1f out: kpt on ins fnl f* **11/2**[2]

1153 **4** ½ **Winthorpe (IRE)**[26] 654 6-9-7 **68** GrahamGibbons 11 — 70
(J J Quinn) *bhd: rdn 3f out: hdwy over 1f out: kpt on ins fnl f* **4/1**[1]

506- **5** 1¾ **Seven No Trumps**[161] 6217 9-9-2 **63** NCallan 7 — 59
(J M Bradley) *a.p: rdn 2f out: one pce fnl f* **11/2**[2]

41-2 **6** nk **After The Show**[91] 79 5-9-12 **73** ChrisCatlin 12 — 68
(Rae Guest) *bhd tl hdwy over 1f out: no ex ins fnl f* **6/1**[3]

1022 **7** 1 **Canadian Danehill (IRE)**[13] 798 4-9-9 **70** EddieAhern 10 — 62
(R M H Cowell) *chsd ldrs: no hdwy fnl 2f* **7/1**

6200 **8** shd **Law Maker**[25] 657 6-8-12 **66** (v) MichaelJStainton(7) 3 — 57
(A Bailey) *mid-div: rdn over 2f out: no imp* **16/1**

1-04 **9** 1¾ **Clipper Hoy**[83] 136 4-9-6 **67** GeorgeBaker 2 — 52
(Mrs H Sweeting) *chsd ldr: hung rt over 1f out: wknd ins fnl f* **16/1**

600- **10** 12 **Bluebok**[234] 4571 5-10-0 **75** (t) RyanMoore 4 — 20
(J M Bradley) *chsd ldrs: rdn over 2f out: edgd rt and wknd over 1f out: sn eased* **25/1**

330- **11** 5 **Redwood Star**[202] 5406 6-9-8 **69** (e) SebSanders 8 — —
(P L Gilligan) *bmpd s: a bhd* **16/1**

0460 **12** 1 **Little Ridge (IRE)**[20] 699 5-9-3 **64** (v[1]) MickyFenton 6 — —
(H Morrison) *prom tl wknd over 2f out* **18/1**

66.45 secs (3.95) **Going Correction** +0.875s/f (Soft)
WFA 3 from 4yo+ 11lb — **12** Ran SP% **120.1**
Speed ratings (Par 103):103,102,100,99,97 96,95,94,92,72 64,63
CSF £143.88 CT £869.70 TOTE £11.10: £3.20, £3.90, £2.10; EX 136.60 Place 6 £214.26, Place 5 £42.95.
Owner Miss Vanessa Church **Bred** Mrs P Lewis **Trained** Newmarket, Suffolk

FOCUS
The cloud lifted just before this event. Not a bad sprint handicap and the three-year-olds Jimmy The Guesser and Don't Tell Sue were a little unlucky not to land a one-two. Ordinary form, but sound enough.
Clipper Hoy Official explanation: jockey said gelding was hanging right in final 2f
Redwood Star Official explanation: jockey said mare was never travelling
T/Plt: £456.60 to a £1 stake. Pool: £42,257.80. 67.55 winning tickets. T/Qpdt: £55.20 to a £1 stake. Pool: £4,207.30. 56.40 winning tickets. KH

[775]FOLKESTONE (R-H)
Tuesday, April 11

OFFICIAL GOING: Good to soft (soft in places)
Wind: Strong, half-behind Weather: Rain from race 3 (3.20) onwards

968 INVICTA MOTORS MEDIAN AUCTION MAIDEN STKS — 5f
2:20 (2:21) (Class 6) 2-Y-O — **£2,730** (£806; £403) **Stalls** Low

Form — RPR

222 **1** **Urban Warrior**[8] 856 2-9-3 LDettori 4 — 69
(J R Best) *mde all: clr 2f out: rdn and hanging rt fnl f: hld on* **7/4**[1]

2 1 **Rippling River** 2-9-3 AlanMunro 1 — 65
(W Jarvis) *racd against nr side rail: chsd wnr: rdn and no imp 2f out: kpt on ins fnl f* **9/2**[3]

30 **3** 1¼ **Goose Green (IRE)**[5] 892 2-9-0 EdwardCreighton(3) 6 — 60
(M R Channon) *in tch: rdn and effrt 2f out: chsd ldng pair fnl f: kpt on* **12/1**

4 ½ **Princely Royal** 2-9-3 TPQueally 3 — 58
(J J Bridger) *dwlt: in tch in rr: rdn 2f out: styd on fnl f: nrst fin* **50/1**

3 **5** 1 **Queen Of Narnia**[7] 878 2-8-12 TedDurcan 5 — 49
(M R Channon) *dwlt: sn chsd ldng pair: wknd jst over 1f out* **11/4**[2]

6 1¾ **Temtation (IRE)** 2-8-9 AmirQuinn(3) 7 — 42
(J R Boyle) *wnt rt s: racd on outer: in tch: no imp 2f out: hanging and fdd over 1f out* **20/1**

7 12 **Lansdown** 2-8-12 FergusSweeney 2 — —
(M Meade) *dwlt: outpcd and a bhd* **50/1**

8 hd **Mr Klick (IRE)** 2-8-12 DerekNolan(5) 8 — —
(M J Wallace) *dwlt: racd on wd outside: in tch 1/2-way: sn rdn and wknd* **13/2**

61.64 secs (0.84) **Going Correction** +0.025s/f (Good) — **8** Ran SP% **110.9**
Speed ratings (Par 90):94,92,90,89,88 85,66,65
CSF £9.24 TOTE £2.20: £1.10, £1.60, £2.90; EX 10.20 Trifecta £77.40 Pool: £671.61 - 6.16 winning tickets..
Owner A Morris **Bred** White Horse Bloodstock Ltd **Trained** Hucking, Kent

FOCUS
A modest juvenile maiden, run at an average pace, and the form should be treated with a degree of caution.

NOTEBOOK
Urban Warrior, runner-up on all his previous three career outings, gained a deserved success under a forceful ride from Dettori on this turf debut. He is a game sort, yet while he should relish the chance to race over another furlong in due course, he lacks scope and it remains to be seen how much he will progress after this. (op 6-4)
Rippling River, a 14,000gns purchase bred to be effective at a mile plus, showed decent early speed and clearly knew his job ahead of this debut. He ran green when it mattered, but was coming back at the winner in the final furlong, and would have obvious claims of reversing this form in the future. (op 6-1)
Goose Green(IRE) was doing his best work at the finish and posted his best display to date. He now becomes eligible for a nursery mark. (op 10-1 tchd 9-1)
Princely Royal, whose dam was a triple sprint winner at five, stayed on to post an eye-catching debut and looks sure to improve a deal for this outing. He has a race of this nature within his compass.
Queen Of Narnia was none too quick into her stride and, getting no cover on the outside of the pack, her fate was sealed with two to run. She has it to prove now. (op 5-2)
Mr Klick(IRE), who cost 40,000 euros as a foal, was always playing catch-up after a sluggish start and never figured. He was nibbled at in the betting ring and is surely capable of better. (op 9-1 tchd 10-1 in places)

969 VISIT PORT LYMPNE & HOWLETTS H'CAP — 6f
2:50 (2:52) (Class 5) (0-70,70) 3-Y-O — **£3,238** (£963; £481; £240) **Stalls** Low

Form — RPR

00-5 **1** **Roman Quest**[25] 658 3-8-11 **63** SteveDrowne 8 — 69+
(H Morrison) *chsd ldrs: plld out and drvn wl over 1f out: r.o to ld last 150yds: styd on wl* **6/1**[2]

-523 **2** ¾ **Gavarnie Beau (IRE)**[8] 851 3-9-4 **70** FrancisNorton 9 — 74
(M Blanshard) *settled in midfield: plld out wd and effrt over 1f out: hung lft but r.o to chse wnr wl ins fnl f* **7/1**[3]

61- **3** 1 **Guilded Warrior**[192] 5626 3-9-3 **69** FergusSweeney 10 — 70
(W S Kittow) *trckd ldrs: effrt 2f out: chal and upsides ent fnl f: one pce* **9/1**

0443 **4** 1 **Bobby Rose**[13] 796 3-8-12 **64** DarrylIHolland 7 — 62
(D K Ivory) *racd freely: w ldr: led 1/2-way: hrd pressed over 1f out: hdd & wknd last 150yds* **10/1**

050- **5** 2½ **Deep Sleep**[175] 5955 3-8-12 **67** SaleemGolam(3) 2 — 58+
(M H Tompkins) *sn swtchd to far side and racd in last trio: plld wd and effrt 2f out: kpt on: no ch* **12/1**

066- **6** 1 **Mr Cellophane**[174] 5985 3-8-10 **62** JamieSpencer 3 — 50+
(J R Jenkins) *restrained s: hld up in last trio and sn swtchd to far side: nt clr run 2f out and over 1f out: pushed along and r.o: nvr n* **14/1**

0600 **7** hd **Bollywood (IRE)**[10] 839 3-9-1 **67** TPQueally 12 — 54
(J J Bridger) *racd against far side rail: led to 1/2-way: wknd rapidly over 1f out* **33/1**

3322 **8** 1 **Psycho Cat**[5] 893 3-8-10 **62** (b) AlanMunro 14 — 46
(P A Blockley) *prom: rdn 1/2-way: wknd u.p 2f out* **5/1**[1]

553- **9** hd **One Night In Paris (IRE)**[184] 5761 3-9-0 **66** HayleyTurner 6 — 49
(M J Wallace) *hld up in midfield: effrt over 2f out: no prog over 1f out: fdd* **12/1**

02-6 **10** ½ **Bellabelini (IRE)**[17] 722 3-8-12 **64** JimmyFortune 5 — 46
(S Kirk) *swtchd to far side and prom: wknd wl over 1f out* **7/1**[3]

440- **11** 1 **Sunset Ridge (IRE)**[189] 5682 3-8-8 **60** FrancisFerris 1 — 39
(Rae Guest) *sn swtchd to far side and racd in last trio: nvr a factor* **33/1**

0-05 **12** shd **Deserted Prince (IRE)**[72] 234 3-8-11 **63** TedDurcan 13 — 42
(M J Wallace) *nvr beyond midfield: rdn and struggling 2f out* **20/1**

053- **13** ¾ **Arkadia Honey**[193] 5581 3-8-10 **62** AdrianTNicholls 4 — 38
(J L Spearing) *nvr beyond midfield: no prog 2f out: wknd* **12/1**

000- **14** 1 **Mamichor**[172] 6011 3-9-2 **68** IanMongan 11 — 41
(J R Boyle) *a wl in rr: no ch fnl 2f* **16/1**

1m 14.23s (0.63) **Going Correction** +0.025s/f (Good) — **14** Ran SP% **121.3**
Speed ratings (Par 98):96,95,93,92,89 87,87,86,85,85 83,83,82,81
CSF £47.05 CT £380.40 TOTE £8.20: £2.50, £2.40, £3.10; EX 59.90 Trifecta £185.60 Part won. Pool: £261.45 - 0.85 winning tickets..
Owner Scott-Barrett,Bryant,Dibb,Eavis,Morrison **Bred** Theakston Stud **Trained** East Ilsley, Berks

FOCUS
A modest three-year-old handicap, run at a fair pace, and the form looks sound enough.
Gavarnie Beau(IRE) Official explanation: jockey said gelding hung left
Mr Cellophane Official explanation: jockey said gelding was denied a clear run

970 EGG CUP H'CAP — 6f
3:20 (3:21) (Class 4) (0-85,85) 4-Y-O+ — **£5,505** (£1,637; £818; £408) **Stalls** Low

Form — RPR

00-5 **1** **Idle Power (IRE)**[18] 718 8-9-1 **85** AmirQuinn(3) 5 — 98
(J R Boyle) *racd nr side: mde all: shkn up and clr 1f out: rdn out* **16/1**

200- **2** 3 **Exmoor**[227] 4755 4-8-10 **77** SteveDrowne 3 — 81
(R Charlton) *racd nr side: mostly chsd wnr: rdn over 2f out: kpt on same pce* **6/1**[3]

050- **3** shd **Bird Over**[193] 5585 4-8-12 **82** NelsonDeSouza(3) 9 — 86
(R M Beckett) *racd on outer of nr side gp: prom: disp 2nd over 1f out: kpt on* **16/1**

231- **4** hd **Swinbrook (USA)**[174] 5986 5-8-13 **80** (v) AlanMunro 13 — 83+
(J A R Toller) *mde all on far side: edgd lft fr over 1f out: clr of rivals fnl f but no ch w wnr* **10/1**

000- **5** 1 **Capricho (IRE)**[164] 6149 9-8-12 **79** PaulDoe 4 — 79
(J Akehurst) *dwlt: wl in rr nr side: shkn up and styd on fr over 1f out: n.d* **20/1**

1340 **6** ¾ **Pinchbeck**[10] 828 7-9-0 **81** (p) PhilipRobinson 1 — 79
(M A Jarvis) *chsd nr side ldrs: rdn 1/2-way: outpcd fr over 1f out* **17/2**

0020 **7** shd **Who's Winning (IRE)**[49] 476 5-8-12 **79** JimmyFortune 6 — 77
(B G Powell) *racd nr side: nvr beyond midfield: rdn and one pce fnl 2f* **16/1**

1012 **8** shd **Saviours Spirit**[10] 836 5-8-13 **80** KDarley 7 — 77
(T G Mills) *prom nr side: effrt to dispute 2nd over 2f out: wknd fnl f* **4/1**[1]

000- **9** 1 **Guildenstern (IRE)**[186] 5713 4-8-8 **80** (t) TravisBlock(5) 12 — 74+
(H Morrison) *racd freely on far side: pressed ldr to over 1f out: edgd lft and fdd* **11/2**[2]

040- **10** nk **Royal Challenge**[164] 6149 5-8-9 **76** DarrylIHolland 2 — 69
(M H Tompkins) *hld up in last pair nr side: nt clr run over 1f out: nvr on terms* **16/1**

012- **11** 6 **Pure Imagination (IRE)**[177] 5923 5-8-7 **79** GregFairley(5) 8 — 54
(J M Bradley) *reluctant to go on to crse: restless stalls: rrd s: in tch to 2f out on nr side: wknd* **12/1**

0-42 **12** nk **Hits Only Cash**[39] 569 4-8-4 **71** DeanMcKeown 14 — 45+
(J Pearce) *pressed far side ldrs over 3f: wandered and wknd rapidly* **6/1**[3]

5-30 **13** *16* **Sir Desmond**72 245 8-8-9 **76**....(p) JamieSpencer 11 —
(Rae Guest) *outpcd far side: effrt u.p over 2f out: sn wknd: eased over 1f out* **11/1**
1m 12.9s (-0.70) **Going Correction** +0.025s/f (Good) **13** Ran SP% **127.9**
Speed ratings (Par 105):105,101,100,100,99 98,98,98,96,96 88,87,66
CSF £116.79 CT £1662.33 TOTE £17.90: £5.50, £2.60, £6.70; EX 197.50 TRIFECTA Not won..
Owner The Idle B's **Bred** Mountarmstrong Stud **Trained** Epsom, Surrey
FOCUS
A fair sprint, which saw those racing on the stands' side at a distinct advantage. Most of the principals were making their seasonal bows but the form looks sound enough.
Royal Challenge Official explanation: jockey said gelding was denied a clear run
Hits Only Cash Official explanation: jockey said gelding lost its action
Sir Desmond Official explanation: jockey said gelding was never travelling

971 KENTISH EXPRESS FUN CLUB MAIDEN FILLIES' STKS 1m 1f 149y
3:50 (3:52) (Class 5) 3-Y-O **£3,562** (£1,059; £529; £264) **Stalls** Low

Form RPR
003- **1** **Time On**172 6007 3-9-0 75.... LDettori 8 81+
(J L Dunlop) *mde all: shkn up and drew clr 2f out: 4 l up fnl f: eased nr fin* **5/2**2
2 **2** *2* **Virgin Islands (IRE)**15 762 3-9-0 .... PhilipRobinson 10 74+
(M A Jarvis) *prom: chsd wnr wl over 2f out: sn rdn and no imp: styd on* **11/8**1
3 *13* **Capriolla** 3-8-11 .... NelsonDeSouza(3) 11 49
(P F I Cole) *rn green: lost pl after 2f and sn in last pair: wl bhd over 2f out: r.o wl fr over 1f out: snatched 3rd nr fin* **16/1**
4 *1* **Star Jasmine** 3-9-0 .... JamieSpencer 4 47
(M L W Bell) *hld up in midfield: effrt 4f out: chsd ldng pair over 2f out: sn wl outpcd: wknd and lost modest 3rd nr fin* **8/1**
0 **5** *½* **March Gold (IRE)**24 669 3-9-0 .... SteveDrowne 5 46
(H Morrison) *chsd ldrs: pushed along 4f out: wl outpcd fr over 2f out: no ch after* **14/1**
00 **6** *1¼* **Shaika**13 795 3-9-0 .... AdrianTNicholls 1 44
(G Prodromou) *dwlt: hld up in rr: effrt and sme prog on outer over 3f out: sn wl outpcd and btn* **100/1**
0- **7** *2½* **Maidford (IRE)**293 2825 3-9-0 .... FergusSweeney 6 39
(M Meade) *hld up towards rr: effrt 4f out: no prog 3f out: outpcd and wl btn sn after* **100/1**
8 *4* **Shawl** 3-9-0 .... MichaelTebbutt 2 32
(B J Meehan) *rn v green in last pair and sn pushed along: nvr a factor* **33/1**
3- **9** *9* **Puteri Sas (IRE)**285 3049 3-9-0 .... JimmyFortune 7 15
(P F I Cole) *chsd wnr to wl over 2f out: wd bnd sn after and wknd rapidly* **5/1**3
00-0 **10** *2½* **Health Spa**55 419 3-9-0 48....(v) JimmyQuinn 9 10
(B R Johnson) *dwlt: hld up wl in rr: wl bhd fnl 3f* **66/1**
0 **11** *2* **Musical Chimes**18 710 3-9-0 .... DarryllHolland 3 6
(C A Cyzer) *t.k.h early: hld up in midfield: pushed along 1/2-way: wknd over 3f out* **50/1**
2m 11.55s (6.12) **Going Correction** +0.875s/f (Soft) **11** Ran SP% **119.4**
Speed ratings (Par 95):109,107,97,96,95 94,92,89,82,80 78
CSF £6.33 TOTE £3.70: £1.40, £1.10, £3.50; EX 9.30 Trifecta £90.90 Pool: £744.43 - 5.81 winning tickets..
Owner R Barnett **Bred** W And R Barnett Ltd **Trained** Arundel, W Sussex
FOCUS
Perhaps not a competitive maiden, but the first two came well clear and, given her pedigree, it would not be a surprise to see the winner soon pitched in at Pattern level. The winning time was 2.2 seconds faster than the following handicap.
Star Jasmine Official explanation: jockey said filly hung left

972 EASTWELL MANOR H'CAP 1m 1f 149y
4:20 (4:23) (Class 6) (0-60,60) 4-Y-O+ **£3,238** (£963; £481; £240) **Stalls** Low

Form RPR
01-0 **1** **Le Soleil (GER)**99 12 5-8-13 **55**.... JamieSpencer 9 63
(B J Curley) *hld up in midfield: lost pl on inner over 3f out and wl in rr: rdn and gd prog 2f out: led jst ins fnl f: r.o* **9/4**1
-502 **2** *¾* **Lady Taverner**17 733 5-8-12 **59**.... NataliaGemelova(5) 11 66
(J E Long) *hld up wl in rr: gd prog on outer fr 2f out: r.o to chse wnr nr fin: a hld* **7/1**
05-2 **3** *1* **Red Rudy**9 845 4-9-4 **60**.... JimmyFortune 3 65
(A W Carroll) *trckd ldrs: effrt 2f out: drvn to ld jst over 1f out: hdd and one pce jst ins fnl f* **13/2**3
2-30 **4** *nk* **Amnesty**29 394 7-9-1 **57**....(be) IanMongan 10 62
(G L Moore) *rousted along in last early: stl last and u.p over 2f out: weaved through fr over 1f out: nrst fin* **12/1**
0132 **5** *1* **Blue Hedges**50 461 4-9-2 **58**.... JimmyQuinn 12 61
(H J Collingridge) *hld up wl in rr: gd prog on inner fr 2f out: chal 1f out: nt qckn* **6/1**2
6-00 **6** *2½* **Veneer (IRE)**8 857 4-8-13 **58**....(b) AdamKirby(3) 5 56
(Miss Gay Kelleway) *sn led: drvn over 2f out: hdd & wknd jst over 1f out* **22/1**
403 **7** *1¾* **Ardea Brave (IRE)**20 696 4-9-4 **60**.... LDettori 1 55
(M Botti) *prom: chsd ldr 3f out to over 1f out: wknd* **7/1**
-000 **8** *2½* **Simplify**8 854 4-9-3 **59**.... FergusSweeney 7 49
(T M Jones) *hld up towards rr: rdn over 2f out: no prog: wknd over 1f out* **22/1**
060- **9** *shd* **Polish Index**158 6247 4-9-4 **60**....(p) DarryllHolland 13 50
(J R Jenkins) *pressed ldrs: rdn over 2f out: wknd rapidly jst over 1f out* **18/1**
40-6 **10** *¾* **Magic Warrior**90 82 6-8-7 **52**.... EdwardCreighton(3) 4 40
(J C Fox) *t.k.h: hld up in tch: wknd 2f out* **33/1**
0060 **11** *2* **Duxford**8 854 5-9-3 **59**.... PhilipRobinson 14 43
(D K Ivory) *hld up bhd ldrs: effrt on inner 2f out: wknd rapidly jst over 1f out* **12/1**
0242 **12** *2½* **Contented (IRE)**8 862 4-9-1 **57**.... HayleyTurner 6 37
(Mrs L C Jewell) *trckd ldng gp: pushed along 3f out: wknd 2f out* **25/1**
540- **13** *½* **Play Up Pompey**165 6134 4-8-12 **54**.... SteveDrowne 2 33
(J J Bridger) *dwlt: sn rushed up to trck ldr: wknd 3f out* **28/1**
4640 **14** *2* **King Of Music (USA)**26 650 5-9-2 **58**.... AdrianTNicholls 8 33
(G Prodromou) *hld up wl in rr: prog on wd outside over 4f out to chse ldrs 3f out: wknd rapidly sn after* **20/1**
2m 13.75s (8.52) **Going Correction** +0.875s/f (Soft) **14** Ran SP% **127.7**
Speed ratings (Par 101):100,99,98,98,97 95,94,92,92,91 89,87,87,85
CSF £16.96 CT £97.85 TOTE £3.20: £1.70, £2.70, £2.10; EX 36.40 Trifecta £200.70 Part won. Pool: £282.69 - 0.40 winning tickets..
Owner Curley Leisure **Bred** Gestut Wittekindshof **Trained** Newmarket, Suffolk
FOCUS
A moderate handicap run at a fair gallop, which suited those who were held up. Far from solid form.
Veneer(IRE) Official explanation: jockey said gelding hung left throughout

973 STOWTING APPRENTICE H'CAP 1m 4f
4:50 (4:50) (Class 6) (0-60,60) 4-Y-O+ **£2,730** (£806; £403) **Stalls** Low

Form RPR
6100 **1** **Bill Bennett (FR)**7 882 5-9-2 **60**.... GregFairley(3) 2 70
(J Jay) *pressed ldr and clr in ldng trio: rdn over 3f out: led wl over 1f out: edgd lft and kpt on* **9/1**
2200 **2** *2* **Robbie Can Can**38 574 7-8-4 **55**.... JackDean(10) 10 62
(A W Carroll) *settled in last pair: sme prog over 3f out but stl wl bhd: gd hdwy over 1f out: bmpd along and r.o to take 2nd nr fin* **8/1**
0-60 **3** *nk* **General Flumpa**38 574 5-8-6 **57**.... JonjoMilczarek(10) 8 63
(C F Wall) *pressed ldr and sn clr in ldng trio: rdn and nt qckn 3f out: kpt on u.str.p fr over 1f out* **8/1**
0-30 **4** *2* **Iamback**6 891 6-8-2 **46** oh1....(t) JamesDoyle(3) 1 49
(Miss D A McHale) *hld up off the pce in midfield: clsd on ldrs fr 3f out: rdn and nt qckn over 1f out* **16/1**
3320 **5** *1¼* **Amwell Brave**17 723 5-8-9 **55**.... DerekNolan(5) 13 56
(J R Jenkins) *hld up bhd ldrs: effrt 3f out: plugged on fnl 2f: nvr able to chal* **6/1**3
00-0 **6** *shd* **Icannshift (IRE)**49 471 6-8-9 **50**.... NeilChalmers 3 51
(T M Jones) *racd freely: led and set str pce: hdd wl over 1f out: wknd fnl f* **25/1**
224- **7** *¾* **Figaro's Quest (IRE)**173 5998 4-8-5 **50**.... NelsonDeSouza(3) 4 50
(P F I Cole) *hld up in midfield and off the pce: pushed along 5f out: sn struggling: styd on again fnl 2f: n.d* **5/1**2
061/ **8** *8* **Jolizero**535 6357 5-9-5 **60**.... SaleemGolam 11 47
(John Berry) *hld up bhd ldrs: rdn and no imp over 3f out: wl btn fnl 2f* **8/1**
123- **9** *1½* **Dark Parade (ARG)**58 5-8-8 **54**.... JamieJones(5) 6 38
(G L Moore) *dwlt: sn chsd clr ldrs: rdn and no prog 3f out: wknd* **9/2**1
0-00 **10** *2* **Tilla**27 643 6-8-10 **56**....(be) TravisBlock(5) 14 37
(Mrs A J Hamilton-Fairley) *dwlt and reluctant early: wl adrift in last pair: nvr a factor* **40/1**
00/ **11** *6* **Batswing**17 305 11-9-5 **60**.... AdamKirby 5 32
(G L Moore) *dwlt: wl in rr and hrd rdn over 6f out: no prog* **16/1**
6040 **12** *7* **Easter Ogil (IRE)**10 833 11-8-9 **50**.... AmirQuinn 9 10
(P G Murphy) *dwlt: hld up wl in rr: no prog 4f out: eased whn no ch wl over 1f out* **25/1**
-005 **13** *nk* **Solipsist (IRE)**14 785 5-8-0 **48**.... MarkCoumbe(7) 12 8
(N I M Rossiter) *nvr beyond midfield: rdn and struggling 5f out* **40/1**
3315 **14** *11* **Lady Pilot**10 838 4-8-5 **52** ow1....(v) SladeO'Hara(5) 7 —
(Dr J R J Naylor) *prom whn squeezed out and snatched up bnd over 9f out: wknd over 4f out: t.o* **10/1**
2m 50.41s (9.91) **Going Correction** +0.875s/f (Soft)
WFA 4 from 5yo+ 1lb **14** Ran SP% **125.9**
Speed ratings (Par 101):101,99,99,98,97 97,96,91,90,89 85,80,80,72
CSF £80.31 CT £615.36 TOTE £13.50: £4.60, £2.70, £4.00; EX 96.90 TRIFECTA Not won. Place 6 £167.91, Place 5 £102.75.
Owner Mr & Mrs Jonathan Jay **Bred** J Jay **Trained** Newmarket, Suffolk
FOCUS
A moderate handicap run at a good pace and sound, albeit weak, form.
T/Plt: £366.80 to a £1 stake. Pool: £49,429.60. 98.35 winning tickets. T/Qpdt: £88.00 to a £1 stake. Pool: £3,853.20. 32.40 winning tickets. JN

CATTERICK (L-H)
Wednesday, April 12

OFFICIAL GOING: Good to soft
The going was described as 'dead, with a poor cover of grass due to the late spring'.
Wind: Moderate, half-against Weather: Overcast and blustery

974 GO RACING AT REDCAR ON EASTER MONDAY (S) STKS 7f
2:20 (2:20) (Class 6) 3-Y-O+ **£2,730** (£806; £403) **Stalls** Low

Form RPR
630- **1** **Donna's Double**162 6218 11-9-5 49....(p) TonyHamilton 5 56
(Karen McLintock) *mid-div: hdwy over 3f out: nt clr run 2f out: styd on to ld nr fin* **8/1**3
0000 **2** *¾* **Desert Lightning (IRE)**26 659 4-9-11 58.... NeilPollard 3 60
(K R Burke) *chsd ldrs: styd on to ld 100yds out: no ex and hdd nr fin* **10/1**
0306 **3** *1¼* **Onlytime Will Tell**28 644 8-9-11 78....(v1) RobertWinston 14 57
(D Nicholls) *chsd ldrs: led over 3f out: hdd and no ex ins last* **2/1**1
4-50 **4** *1½* **Augustus Livius (IRE)**22 690 3-8-5 40.... PaulFessey 11 42
(W Storey) *chsd ldrs: one pce appr fnl f* **50/1**
45-0 **5** *1¾* **Tinian**57 147 8-9-2 49....(p) BenSwarbrick(3) 2 42
(Miss Tracy Waggott) *bhd: hdwy 2f out: styd on ins last* **25/1**
650- **6** *1½* **Airedale Lad (IRE)**141 6414 5-9-5 40.... DeanMcKeown 10 38
(R M Whitaker) *prom: outpcd over 3f out: hdwy 2f out: edgd lft: nvr a threat* **9/1**
2-00 **7** *1¼* **Fox Covert (IRE)**8 876 5-9-0 45.... MarkLawson(5) 9 35
(D W Barker) *led: hdd over 3f out: hmpd over 2f out: wknd fnl f* **12/1**
5400 **8** *1½* **Yassooma (IRE)**7 890 3-8-5 45....(v) RobbieFitzpatrick 12 26
(T J Pitt) *mid-div: hdwy on ins 2f out: nvr trbld ldrs* **25/1**
0-00 **9** *¾* **Annals**12 813 4-9-0 55....(b1) FergalLynch 6 24
(R C Guest) *s.i.s: hdwy 2f out: kpt on ins last* **16/1**
4-00 **10** *5* **Nebraska City**15 783 5-9-2 45.... PaulMulrennan(3) 8 16
(D W Thompson) *chsd ldrs: wkng whn hmpd 2f out* **25/1**
000- **11** *3* **Make Us Flush**127 6515 4-9-0 45.... FrancisNorton 17 4
(A Berry) *a in rr* **25/1**
000- **12** *nk* **Kristalchen**235 4565 4-8-9 55.... GregFairley(5) 15 3
(D W Thompson) *sn bhd* **28/1**
034- **13** *1* **Luke After Me (IRE)**170 6082 6-9-5 50.... PhillipMakin 4 5
(Miss Tracy Waggott) *s.i.s: n.m.r over 4f out: nvr on terms* **9/1**
-665 **14** *shd* **Fayrz Please (IRE)**8 870 5-9-0 35.... EmmettStack(5) 7 5
(M C Chapman) *chsd ldrs: lost pl over 3f out* **40/1**
00-0 **15** *8* **Pays D'Amour (IRE)**18 732 9-9-5 40....(t) DerekMcGaffin 1 —
(D A Nolan) *dwlt: sn prom: lost pl over 2f out: bhd whn eased ins last* **100/1**

520- **16** *9* **Pax**[199] 5488 9-9-5 71 .... AdrianTNicholls 16 —
(D Nicholls) *chsd ldrs: lost pl over 1f out: bhd whn heavily eased ins last* **6/1**[2]

1m 30.79s (3.43) **Going Correction** +0.50s/f (Yiel)
WFA 3 from 4yo+ 14lb **16** Ran SP% **125.6**
Speed ratings (Par 101):100,99,97,96,94 92,90,89,88,82 79,78,77,77,68 58
CSF £80.94 TOTE £12.00: £3.10, £3.80, £1.20; EX 114.60.There was no bid for the winner.
Owner J R Adams (Newcastle) Limited **Bred** Aston Park Stud **Trained** Ingoe, Northumberland
■ Stewards' Enquiry : Mark Lawson caution: careless riding

FOCUS
A poor seller won by a horse who stays almost twice as far as seven furlongs. The form looks suspect although the time suggests otherwise.
Annals Official explanation: jockey said filly was denied a clear run
Pax Official explanation: jockey said gelding bled from nose

975 "TUESDAY 9TH MAY IS LADIES NIGHT" H'CAP — 1m 7f 177y
2:50 (2:51) (Class 6) (0-65,65) 4-Y-0+ **£2,730** (£806; £403) **Stalls** Low

Form RPR

105- **1** **Liberty Seeker (FR)**[26] 4628 7-9-10 **62** .... RobertWinston 7 73
(G A Swinbank) *hld up towards rr: smooth hdwy 1/2-way: trckd ldrs over 3f out: rdn to ld over 1f out: sn clr* **8/1**

422- **2** *4* **Pee Jay's Dream**[184] 5789 4-9-1 **57** .... DaleGibson 2 63
(M W Easterby) *in tch: hdwy over 2f out: cl up 3f out: rdn to ld 2f out: drvn and hdd over 1f out: kpt on same pce* **5/1**[1]

3235 **3** *shd* **Rare Coincidence**[12] 816 5-9-0 **55** ....(p) DNolan(3) 13 61
(R F Fisher) *led after 1f: pushed along 4f out: rdn 3f out: hdd 2f out: sn drvn and outpcd: styd on u.p ins last* **15/2**[3]

22-5 **4** *2* **Totally Scottish**[8] 866 10-8-11 **49** .... TonyCulhane 12 52
(K G Reveley) *hld up towards rr: hdwy 1/2-way: effrt and in tch over 3f out: sn rdn and kpt on same pce fnl 2f* **13/2**[2]

600- **5** *1 3/4* **Siegfrieds Night (IRE)**[86] 5244 5-8-10 **53** .... EmmettStack(5) 11 54
(M C Chapman) *chsd ldrs: rdn along 3f out: drvn and one pce fnl 2f* **20/1**

4314 **6** *8* **Champion Lion (IRE)**[9] 857 7-9-3 **55** .... RobbieFitzpatrick 4 47
(James Moffatt) *hld up: stdy hdwy over 4f out: rdn along over 2f out: sn no imp* **16/1**

12-0 **7** *2 1/2* **Compton Eclaire (IRE)**[49] 482 6-9-1 **53** ....(b) PatCosgrave 3 42
(B Ellison) *a towards rr* **14/1**

540- **8** *3/4* **Villago (GER)**[46] 5943 6-9-8 **60** .... MickyFenton 6 48
(E W Tuer) *a rr* **9/1**

00-5 **9** *nk* **Kaluana Court**[8] 881 10-8-7 **50** .... JamesDoyle(5) 10 38
(R J Price) *hld up in rr: hdwy over 6f out: rdn along and in tch 3f out: sn wknd* **9/1**

02-0 **10** *1/2* **Farne Isle**[8] 866 7-9-6 **65** ....(t) PJMcDonald(7) 5 52
(G A Harker) *hld up and bhd: stdy hdwy 1/2-way: in tch over 3f out: sn rdn along and wknd fnl 2f* **25/1**

3251 **11** *hd* **Romil Star (GER)**[9] 857 9-8-8 **51** 6ex ....(v) AndrewElliott(5) 14 38
(K R Burke) *a rr* **10/1**

000- **12** *7* **Minivet**[96] 4395 11-8-9 **50** .... DanielTudhope(3) 9 28
(R Allan) *in tch: rdn along 6f out: sn wknd* **33/1**

04-0 **13** *19* **Keepers Knight (IRE)**[40] 570 5-8-13 **51** ....(p) TonyHamilton 16 6
(Karen McLintock) *chsd ldrs: rdn along 6f out: sn wknd* **20/1**

-320 **14** *12* **Step Perfect (USA)**[8] 866 5-8-8 **49** ....(p) BenSwarbrick(3) 17 —
(G M Moore) *prom: chsd ldr after 6f tl rdn along and wknd over 4f out* **33/1**

15 *12* **Durba (AUS)**[96] 6-9-13 **65** .... FergalLynch 15 —
(R C Guest) *led 1f: cl up tl rdn along over 7f out and sn wknd* **40/1**

00-0 **16** *3/4* **Top Style (IRE)**[37] 599 8-9-0 **55** ....(p) PaulMulrennan(3) 1 —
(G A Harker) *in tch: rdn along 1/2-way and sn wknd* **16/1**

/06- **17** *dist* **Starmix**[309] 2368 5-8-7 **50** .... GregFairley(5) 8 —
(G A Harker) *a rr: t.o fnl 3f* **50/1**

3m 38.91s (7.51) **Going Correction** +0.50s/f (Yiel)
WFA 4 from 5yo+ 4lb **17** Ran SP% **124.1**
Speed ratings (Par 101):101,99,98,97,97 93,91,91,91,91 90,87,77,71,65 65,—
CSF £44.25 CT £323.87 TOTE £8.80: £2.40, £1.80, £2.80, £1.80; EX 66.40.
Owner M Sawers **Bred** Aylesfield Farms Stud Ltd **Trained** Melsonby, N Yorks

FOCUS
A low-grade staying race contested by quite a few horses that run over obstacles. The early pace did not look very quick and the form is ordinary.

976 CATTERICKBRIDGE.CO.UK H'CAP — 1m 5f 175y
3:20 (3:21) (Class 4) (0-85,84) 4-Y-0+ **£6,477** (£1,927; £963; £481) **Stalls** Low

Form RPR

61S- **1** **Maneki Neko (IRE)**[17] 5511 4-8-7 **68** .... RobertWinston 5 79
(E W Tuer) *hld up in mid-field: hdwy to trck ldrs 7f out: led over 1f out: styd on wl* **9/1**

364- **2** *2* **Charlotte Vale**[97] 6218 5-8-12 **70** .... DeanMcKeown 13 78
(Micky Hammond) *hld up in mid-div: hdwy on wd outside over 4f out: led over 2f out: hdd over 1f out: no ex* **16/1**

124- **3** *5* **Numero Due**[173] 6006 4-9-2 **77** .... DavidAllan 6 78
(G M Moore) *s.i.s: bhd and drvn 7f out: hdwy over 2f out: styd on fnl f* **15/2**[3]

013- **4** *2* **Tcherina (IRE)**[166] 6130 4-9-5 **80** .... FergalLynch 8 78
(T D Easterby) *hld up towards rr: hdwy 7f out: wnt 2nd 2f out: wknd fnl f* **16/1**

34- **5** *1 1/2* **Tilt**[197] 5533 4-8-13 **74** .... FrancisNorton 7 70
(B Ellison) *hld up in rr: effrt and n.m.r 2f out: styd on fnl f* **11/1**

060- **6** *1 1/2* **Nessen Dorma (IRE)**[158] 6254 5-9-10 **82** ....(v) MickyFenton 4 76
(J G Given) *led tl over 2f out: wknd and eased ins last* **16/1**

-436 **7** *1 1/4* **Our Choice (IRE)**[11] 832 4-8-0 **68** oh2 .... JamesDoyle(5) 2 58
(N P Littmoden) *trckd ldrs: effrt 3f out: one pce* **5/1**[1]

00-4 **8** *shd* **Mceldowney**[8] 869 4-8-6 **72** .... GregFairley(5) 10 64
(M Johnston) *chsd ldrs: wknd appr fnl f* **8/1**

0-55 **9** *1 3/4* **Hue**[26] 597 5-8-12 **70** .... PatCosgrave 12 60
(B Ellison) *hld up in rr: hdwy 6f out: kpt on fnl f* **20/1**

2311 **10** *nk* **Isa'Af (IRE)**[8] 869 7-8-13 **71** .... PhillipMakin 11 60
(P W Hiatt) *mid-div: hdwy to trck ldrs 8f out: effrt over 3f out: fdd over 1f out* **11/2**[2]

144- **11** *3 1/2* **Sporting Gesture**[187] 5720 9-9-12 **84** .... DaleGibson 1 68
(M W Easterby) *mid-div: effrt 6f out: nvr nr ldrs* **25/1**

400- **12** *3 1/2* **Prairie Sun (GER)**[172] 5296 5-8-8 **66** .... PaulFessey 9 45
(Mrs A Duffield) *prom: outpcd over 3f out: n.d after* **12/1**

50-0 **13** *9* **Ski Jump (USA)**[14] 799 6-9-10 **82** ....(v) TonyHamilton 14 49
(R A Fahey) *a in rr: t.o 3f out* **16/1**

1243 **14** *2 1/2* **Greenbelt**[8] 869 5-8-11 **72** .... BenSwarbrick(3) 15 35
(G M Moore) *chsd ldrs: lost pl over 3f out* **16/1**

00- **15** *3 1/2* **Tiger King (GER)**[33] 5433 5-8-9 **70** .... PaulMulrennan(3) 3 28
(P Monteith) *chsd ldrs: drvn along over 6f out: lost pl over 5f out: t.o 3f out* **100/1**

3m 9.25s (4.75) **Going Correction** +0.50s/f (Yiel)
WFA 4 from 5yo+ 3lb **15** Ran SP% **120.0**
Speed ratings (Par 105):106,104,102,100,100 99,98,98,97,97 95,93,88,86,84
CSF £141.12 CT £1143.12 TOTE £14.20: £4.50, £3.80, £3.00; EX 200.00.
Owner E Tuer **Bred** Miss Orlagh Sherry **Trained** Great Smeaton, N Yorks

FOCUS
A weak staying event won by an improver over hurdles during the winter and rated through the exposed runner-up. A couple in behind suggested they were capable of winning in the near future.
Tilt ◆ Official explanation: jockey said gelding was denied a clear run
Isa'Af(IRE) Official explanation: jockey said gelding was unsuited by track

977 GODS SOLUTION H'CAP — 7f
3:50 (3:51) (Class 5) (0-75,75) 4-Y-0+ **£3,886** (£1,156; £577; £288) **Stalls** Low

Form RPR

4205 **1** **True Night**[2] 953 9-8-8 **65** .... PaulFessey 8 75
(D Nicholls) *trckd ldrs: hdwy over 2f out: rdn to chal and edgd lft over 1f out: styd on to ld and hung lft ins last: kpt on* **14/1**

50-4 **2** *2 1/2* **Hiccups**[14] 798 6-9-3 **74** .... RobertWinston 1 77
(D Nicholls) *dwlt: sn trcking ldrs on inner: hdwy over 2f out: rdn to ld over 1f out: drvn and hdd ins last: one pce* **11/1**

-046 **3** *2 1/2* **Serieux**[11] 826 7-9-2 **73** ....(v) AdrianTNicholls 2 70
(D Nicholls) *sn led: rdn 2f out: drvn and hdd over 1f out: kpt on same pce* **6/1**[1]

3510 **4** *shd* **Desert Lover (IRE)**[9] 860 4-8-1 **63** .... JamesDoyle(5) 15 59
(R J Price) *cl up: rdn along over 2f out: drvn and edgd lft wl over 1f out: kpt on same pce* **14/1**

240- **5** *1 1/2* **Zhitomir**[151] 6336 8-8-12 **69** .... PhillipMakin 4 61
(M Dods) *chsd ldr: rdn along over 2f out: sn one pce* **14/1**

-551 **6** *shd* **Cool Sands (IRE)**[39] 575 4-8-5 **62** ....(v) FrancisNorton 5 54
(D Shaw) *midfield: hdwy on inner to chse ldrs 3f out: rdn 2f out and sn one pce* **14/1**

0-00 **7** *1* **Wistman (UAE)**[82] 161 5-8-8 **65** .... PaulQuinn 16 54
(D Nicholls) *midfield: hdwy on outer to chse ldrs over 2f out: sn rdn: edgd lft and no imp* **80/1**

-003 **8** *1 1/4* **Hit's Only Money (IRE)**[28] 644 6-8-8 **65** ....(t) DeanMcKeown 13 51
(J Pearce) *in tch: pushed along 1/2-way: nvr rch ldrs* **8/1**[3]

0405 **9** *1 1/2* **Amazin**[26] 659 4-8-4 **61** oh1 ....(p) NickyMackay 12 43
(N P Littmoden) *nvr bttr than midfield* **8/1**[3]

4-04 **10** *1* **Bollin Michael**[27] 653 4-8-8 **65** .... DavidAllan 3 45
(T D Easterby) *s.i.s and bhd tl styd on fnl 2f* **7/1**[2]

03-3 **11** *3/4* **Word Perfect**[8] 864 4-8-8 **65** .... DaleGibson 10 43
(M W Easterby) *in tch tl pushed alonga nd outpcd 3f out* **7/1**[2]

06-0 **12** *hd* **Saxon Lil (IRE)**[6] 898 4-9-4 **75** .... RobbieFitzpatrick 14 52
(J L Spearing) *dwlt: a rr* **25/1**

13 *6* **Spirit Guide (FR)**[299] 4-8-11 **68** ow2 .... FergalLynch 6 30
(R C Guest) *s.i.s: a rr* **100/1**

-160 **14** *3/4* **Joyeaux**[18] 737 4-8-12 **69** .... DerekMcGaffin 11 29
(J Hetherton) *a rr* **50/1**

440- **15** *3 1/2* **Ask The Clerk (IRE)**[194] 5593 5-9-1 **72** .... MickyFenton 7 23
(Mrs P Sly) *towards rr: sme hdwy 3f out: sn rdn and wknd* **8/1**[3]

100- **16** *5* **Geordie Dancer (IRE)**[180] 5880 4-7-13 **61** oh2 .... DuranFentiman(5) 9 —
(A Berry) *chsd ldrs: pushed along 1/2-way: sn wknd* **66/1**

1m 30.56s (3.20) **Going Correction** +0.50s/f (Yiel) **16** Ran SP% **117.1**
Speed ratings (Par 103):101,98,95,95,93 93,92,90,89,87 87,86,79,79,75 69
CSF £150.68 CT £1073.15 TOTE £16.90: £3.20, £3.30, £2.40, £3.30; EX 168.40.
Owner Mrs L Scaife, Mrs S Radford **Bred** Crichel Farms Ltd **Trained** Sessay, N Yorks

FOCUS
An ordinary handicap that provided Dandy Nicholls with a one-two-three from his four runners. The time was modest and the form, rated through the second, does not look strong.
Word Perfect Official explanation: trainer was unable to offer any explanation for poor form shown

978 TOYTOP MAIDEN STKS — 5f 212y
4:20 (4:21) (Class 5) 3-Y-0+ **£3,886** (£1,156; £577; £288) **Stalls** Low

Form RPR

664- **1** **Mulligan's Gold (IRE)**[201] 5429 3-8-13 69 .... FergalLynch 7 70
(T D Easterby) *mde all: styd on fnl f* **16/1**

000- **2** *1 3/4* **Angaric (IRE)**[193] 5613 3-8-13 67 .... TonyCulhane 9 65
(B Smart) *trckd ldrs: outpcd over 2f out:m styd on to take 2nd nr line* **8/1**[2]

3- **3** *hd* **Esoterica (IRE)**[214] 5120 3-8-13 .... PaulFessey 8 64
(T D Barron) *mid-div: hdwy over 2f out: styd on wl ins last* **12/1**[3]

300 **4** *1/2* **Beowulf**[8] 880 3-8-8 .... GregFairley(5) 4 63
(M Johnston) *chsd ldrs: wnt 2nd 3f out: ev ch tl wknd and lost 2nd ins last* **14/1**

6- **5** *3 1/2* **Madaares (USA)**[228] 4766 3-8-13 .... RHills 5 52
(M Johnston) *s.i.s: sn drvn along: hdwy 2f out: sn swtchd rt: kpt on: nvr nr ldrs* **4/6**[1]

6 *1* **Chateau (IRE)**[136] 4-9-11 .... DeanMcKeown 10 54
(G A Swinbank) *hld up towards rr: styd on fnl 2f: nt rch ldrs* **66/1**

06- **7** *1 1/4* **Silk Merchant (IRE)**[179] 5888 3-8-13 .... RobertWinston 3 46
(J Howard Johnson) *chsd ldrs: outpcd over 2f out: n.d after* **16/1**

550- **8** *1 1/4* **Chiselled (IRE)**[203] 5411 4-9-11 65 .... PatCosgrave 1 47
(K R Burke) *chsd ldrs: n.m.r on ins 4f out: wknd fnl f* **12/1**[3]

00- **9** *3/4* **Eurana**[184] 5801 3-8-8 .... MickyFenton 12 35
(Jedd O'Keeffe) *chsd ldrs on outside: lost pl after 1f: sme hdwy 2f out: nvr a threat* **100/1**

2 **10** *11* **Trumpita**[19] 716 3-8-13 .... DavidAllan 11 7
(T D Easterby) *s.i.s: a in rr* **14/1**

11 *5* **Wee Ziggy** 3-8-13 .... AdrianTNicholls 6 —
(D Nicholls) *uns rdr and led to post: s.i.s: a bhd* **33/1**

0 **12** *3* **Fashion Disaster**[32] 630 3-8-9 ow1 .... LeeEnstone 2 —
(A Crook) *s.s: a bhd* **100/1**

1m 18.04s (4.04) **Going Correction** +0.70s/f (Yiel)
WFA 3 from 4yo 12lb **12** Ran SP% **118.0**
Speed ratings (Par 103):101,98,98,97,93 91,90,88,87,72 66,62
CSF £136.73 TOTE £18.70: £3.90, £2.70, £2.00; EX 219.60.
Owner C H Stevens **Bred** Mrs H D McCalmont **Trained** Great Habton, N Yorks

FOCUS
A low-grade maiden that should proe sound rated through the third and fourth, and could produce a few winners in the future.

979 YARM H'CAP — 1m 3f 214y
4:50 (4:50) (Class 5) (0-70,70) 3-Y-O — **£3,886** (£1,156; £577; £288) **Stalls** Low

Form — RPR

505- **1** **Unique Moment**[202] [5419] 3-8-13 **70** .... GregFairley(5) 4 — 79+
(M Johnston) *cl up: led 1/2-way: rdn clr 3f out: drvn 2f out: styd on wl* **7/1**

5325 **2** *5* **Noble Edge**[9] [859] 3-8-5 **60** .... (p) DanielTudhope(3) 5 — 61
(Robert Gray) *trckd ldrs: hdwy to chse wnr over 3f out: rdn to chal over 2f out: drvn and one pce fr over 1f out* **9/1**

00-3 **3** *6* **Synonymy**[26] [656] 3-9-1 **67** .... FrancisNorton 3 — 58
(M Blanshard) *in tch: hdwy 1/2-way: rdn along to chse ldng pair whn outpcd over 3f out: drvn and kpt on fnl 2f* **6/1**[3]

-054 **4** *1/2* **Wise Choice**[21] [695] 3-8-1 **58** .... JamesDoyle(5) 6 — 49
(N P Littmoden) *hld up in rr: hdwy over 3f out: sn rdn: drvn and kpt on fnl 2f: nrst fin* **3/1**[1]

0-34 **5** *5* **King's Fable (USA)**[86] [123] 3-8-5 **60** .... StanleyChin(3) 7 — 43
(M Johnston) *a towards rr* **13/2**

500- **6** *8* **William John**[197] [5536] 3-7-11 **56** oh1 .... KristinStubbs(7) 9 — 26
(B Ellison) *midfield: hdwy and in tch over 4f out: wd st and sn bhd* **8/1**

-230 **7** *11* **Princess Society (IRE)**[42] [548] 3-9-2 **68** .... RobertWinston 8 — 20
(E A L Dunlop) *a rr* **5/1**[2]

0-05 **8** *6* **Captivate**[42] [548] 3-8-4 **56** oh5 .... FrankieMcDonald 2 — —
(M J Polglase) *led: hdd 1/2-way: sn lost pl and bhd* **25/1**

0-64 **9** *20* **Royal Moon (USA)**[54] [445] 3-8-3 **58** .... BenSwarbrick(3) 10 — —
(T D Barron) *plld hrd: prom tl rdn along and lost pl 4f out: sn bhd* **11/1**

2m 47.32s (8.32) **Going Correction** +0.70s/f (Yiel) — **9** Ran SP% **115.1**
Speed ratings (Par 98):100,96,92,92,89 83,76,72,59
CSF £67.63 CT £400.94 TOTE £6.30: £2.10, £3.80, £1.80; EX 98.20.
Owner J Shack **Bred** The Lavington Stud **Trained** Middleham Moor, N Yorks

FOCUS
A moderate handicap run in testing ground, and it proved far too much of a test for most of these three-year-olds. As a result it has not been rated positively, witrh the runner-up the best guide.
William John Official explanation: jockey said colt hung right-handed
Princess Society(IRE) Official explanation: jockey said filly appeared not to stay

980 TOTESPORT BIG SCREEN IS HERE EVERY DAY H'CAP — 5f
5:20 (5:20) (Class 6) (0-65,64) 3-Y-O — **£2,730** (£806; £403) **Stalls** Low

Form — RPR

00-4 **1** **Mormeatmic**[12] [819] 3-8-6 **55** .... PaulMulrennan(3) 4 — 61
(M W Easterby) *chsd ldrs on inner: effrt 2f out: sn rdn: styd on to ld ins last: kpt on* **16/1**

530- **2** *1 1/2* **Toy Top (USA)**[163] [6196] 3-8-13 **59** .... (b) PhillipMakin 12 — 60
(M Dods) *in tch: hdwy on outer 2f out: rdn and ev ch over 1f out tl drvn and nt qckn wl ins last* **28/1**

454- **3** *nk* **Northern Chorus (IRE)**[190] [5680] 3-9-4 **64** .... DavidAllan 8 — 64
(A Dickman) *in tch: hdwy 2f out: rdn to chal over 1f out and ev ch tl drvn and nt qckn wl ins last* **12/1**[3]

0400 **4** *1* **Suhezy (IRE)**[9] [861] 3-8-6 **55** .... DanielTudhope(3) 13 — 51
(P T Midgley) *dwlt and bmpd s: towards rr tl hdwy 2f out: rdn and ch over 1f out: kpt on same pce fnl f* **12/1**[3]

-500 **5** *hd* **Tombalina**[5] [910] 3-8-1 **54** .... MarkCoumbe(7) 7 — 50
(C J Teague) *led: rdn 2f out: drvn over 1f out: hdd & wknd ins last* **20/1**

2040 **6** *3 1/2* **Money Mate (IRE)**[37] [601] 3-8-8 **59** .... (p) GregFairley(5) 1 — 42
(C J Teague) *chsd ldrs: rdn wl over 1f out: grad wknd* **14/1**

000- **7** *hd* **Sweetly Sharp (IRE)**[226] [4829] 3-8-4 **50** oh1 .... AdrianTNicholls 6 — 32
(A Berry) *outpcd and bhd 1/2-way: hdwy wl over 1f out: kpt on ins last: nrst fin* **33/1**

1153 **8** *nk* **Garstang**[13] [803] 3-9-4 **64** .... (b) RobbieFitzpatrick 11 — 45
(Peter Grayson) *cl up: rdn along wl over 1f out: grad wknd* **13/8**[1]

40-0 **9** *shd* **Stanley Wolfe (IRE)**[14] [790] 3-8-0 **53** oh5 ow3 .... GemmaAnderson(7) 2 — 34
(James Moffatt) *wnt lft s: sn chsng ldrs: rdn along 2f out and wknd over 1f out* **66/1**

400- **10** *2 1/2* **Jellytot (USA)**[203] [5408] 3-8-10 **63** .... HelenGarner(7) 3 — 35
(K A Ryan) *a rr* **20/1**

000- **11** *1* **Boy Dancer (IRE)**[175] [5977] 3-8-8 **54** .... RobertWinston 5 — 22
(D W Barker) *dwlt: sn in tch: rdn along 2f out and sn wknd* **10/3**[2]

100- **12** *2 1/2* **One Trick Pony**[212] [5183] 3-9-4 **64** .... TonyHamilton 14 — 23
(Karen McLintock) *cl up: rdn along over 2f out and sn wknd* **14/1**

0-55 **13** *1* **Dora's Green**[13] [801] 3-9-0 **60** .... FrancisNorton 9 — 16
(M Blanshard) *chsd ldrs to 1/2-way: snw eakened* **16/1**

60-6 **14** *4* **Coquet Island**[23] [673] 3-9-0 **63** .... BenSwarbrick(3) 10 — 4
(G M Moore) *outpcd and bhd fr 1/2-way* **40/1**

63.23 secs (2.63) **Going Correction** +0.45s/f (Yiel) — **14** Ran SP% **121.5**
Speed ratings (Par 96):96,93,93,91,91 85,85,84,84,80 79,75,73,67
CSF £416.64 CT £5591.03 TOTE £20.40: £2.90, £6.40, £3.20; EX 343.00 Place 6 £453.77, Place 5 £273.34.
Owner M Broad & Mrs M E Attwood **Bred** A C Birkle **Trained** Sheriff Hutton, N Yorks

FOCUS
A moderate sprint handicap notable for a failed gamble on Boy Dancer. The form looks sound enough with the first five close to form.
Boy Dancer(IRE) Official explanation: jockey said colt hung right from halfway
Dora's Green Official explanation: jockey said filly had no more to give
T/Plt: £460.40 to a £1 stake. Pool: £40,364.80. 64.00 winning tickets. T/Qpdt: £332.90 to a £1 stake. Pool: £2,879.20. 6.40 winning tickets. JR

912 LINGFIELD (L-H)
Wednesday, April 12

OFFICIAL GOING: Standard
Wind: Fresh, across Weather: Sunny spells

981 LINGFIELD-RACECOURSE.CO.UK MAIDEN STKS — 7f (P)
2:30 (2:33) (Class 5) 3-Y-O — **£3,238** (£963; £481; £240) **Stalls** Low

Form — RPR

2- **1** **Mary Delaney (USA)**[201] [5435] 3-8-12 .... TedDurcan 11 — 68
(M J Wallace) *bit bkwd: led after 1f: qcknd over 2f out: drvn to hold on fnl f: gamely* **5/1**[3]

60- **2** *nk* **Burnbank (IRE)**[183] [5821] 3-9-3 .... MartinDwyer 2 — 72
(W Jarvis) *bit bkwd: in tch: effrt over 2f out: drvn to press wnr ins fnl f: r.o: jst hld* **25/1**

026- **3** *shd* **Areyoutalkingtome**[199] [5494] 3-9-3 100 .... DarryllHolland 5 — 72+
(C A Cyzer) *lw: in tch: effrt over 2f out: hung rt over 1f out: styd on wl nr fin* **10/11**[1]

0- **4** *1* **Captain Xaar (FR)**[181] [5850] 3-9-3 .... OscarUrbina 8 — 69+
(J R Fanshawe) *hld up in midfield: effrt and carried rt over 1f out: styd on fnl f* **20/1**

305- **5** *2* **Elusive Warrior (USA)**[167] [6123] 3-9-3 70 .... JimCrowley 10 — 64
(Mrs A J Perrett) *led 1f: pressed wnr after tl hrd rdn and no ex ins fnl f* **25/1**

0- **6** *shd* **Velvet Valley (USA)**[298] [2704] 3-9-3 .... RichardHughes 1 — 64+
(Sir Michael Stoute) *lw: s.s: t.k.h towards rr: pushed along and styd on steadily fnl 2f: nt rch ldrs* **7/2**[2]

7 *1* **Panic Stations** 3-8-12 .... HayleyTurner 7 — 56+
(M L W Bell) *w'like: bit bkwd: prom: rdn and n.m.r over 1f out: no ex* **25/1**

8 *1* **Debord (FR)** 3-9-3 .... JohnEgan 9 — 59
(Jamie Poulton) *w'like: towards rr: mod effrt on outside 3f out: nvr able to chal* **14/1**

55 **9** *1/2* **Laheen (IRE)**[72] [254] 3-8-12 .... MichaelHills 12 — 52
(M H Tompkins) *prom on outside: rn wd and btn ent st* **66/1**

00- **10** *1* **Madam Mac (IRE)**[259] [3840] 3-8-12 .... JimmyFortune 6 — 50
(B J Meehan) *t.k.h in rr: outpcd and drvn along 3f out: n.d* **40/1**

11 *3/4* **Transponder** 3-9-3 .... SamHitchcott 3 — 53
(W R Muir) *unf: scope: bit bkwd: s.s: drvn along 3f out: a bhd* **66/1**

1m 25.63s (-0.26) **Going Correction** -0.125s/f (Stan) — **11** Ran SP% **119.7**
Speed ratings (Par 98):96,95,95,94,92 92,90,89,89,88 87
CSF £121.75 TOTE £5.60: £2.00, £5.70, £1.10; EX 62.80 Trifecta £194.00 Pool: £475.60 - 1.74 winning tickets..
Owner B Walsh **Bred** M A Parris And Ashford Stud **Trained** Newmarket, Suffolk

FOCUS
Most of the interest in this maiden surrounded last season's Royal Lodge sixth Areyoutalkingtome, but he could not cope with the winner who looks a nice prospect. The form is rated around the first two, but a modest time tempers enthusiasm.
Areyoutalkingtome Official explanation: jockey said colt hung right

982 LINGFIELD PARK GOLF CLUB (S) STKS — 6f (P)
3:00 (3:03) (Class 6) 3-Y-O+ — **£2,388** (£705; £352) **Stalls** Low

Form — RPR

2050 **1** **Chantelle's Dream**[7] [886] 4-9-0 49 .... AdamKirby(3) 2 — 54
(Ms J S Doyle) *trckd ldng pair: led 1f out: drvn clr* **12/1**

0050 **2** *1 3/4* **Border Artist**[19] [708] 7-9-8 51 .... MichaelHills 11 — 54
(B G Powell) *outpcd towards rr: gd hdwy on outside ent st: kpt on fnl f* **14/1**

-600 **3** *shd* **Goldhill Prince**[7] [886] 4-9-8 49 .... (p) JohnEgan 1 — 54
(Ernst Oertel) *in tch: effrt over 2f out: styd on fnl f* **12/1**

0460 **4** *hd* **Hadath (IRE)**[5] [903] 9-9-13 56 .... (b) GeorgeBaker 6 — 58
(B G Powell) *sn outpcd and wl bhd: rapid hdwy fr over 1f out: fin fast* **5/2**[1]

-305 **5** *1/2* **Labelled With Love**[19] [708] 6-9-5 53 .... (t) AmirQuinn(3) 9 — 52
(J R Boyle) *s.s: outpcd and bhd: hdwy over 1f out: kpt on fnl f* **9/2**[2]

-663 **6** *1/2* **Global Achiever**[12] [821] 5-9-8 46 .... (b) OscarUrbina 8 — 50
(G C H Chung) *led and set str pce: hdd and no ex 1f out* **7/1**[3]

2035 **7** *3/4* **Leah's Pride**[7] [886] 5-9-1 49 .... KirstyMilczarek(7) 10 — 48
(Miss D A McHale) *pressed ldr at str pce: no ex fnl f* **11/1**

300- **8** *1/2* **Jasmine Pearl (IRE)**[104] [6686] 5-9-3 45 .... FergusSweeney 7 — 41
(T M Jones) *mid-div: rdn to chse ldng gp ent st: no ex fnl f* **33/1**

2-05 **9** *3/4* **Strathclyde (IRE)**[23] [680] 7-9-8 45 .... ChrisCatlin 5 — 44
(A M Hales) *mid-div: pushed along over 3f out: n.d after* **8/1**

-040 **10** *3/4* **Sabo Prince**[8] [875] 4-9-8 45 .... (p) LPKeniry 4 — 42
(J M Bradley) *chsd ldrs tl wknd 1f out* **33/1**

0600 **11** *1 1/2* **Stamford Street (IRE)**[15] [779] 3-8-3 58 .... JosephWalsh(7) 3 — 32
(J S Moore) *hmpd s: sn in midfield: wknd 2f out* **8/1**

12 *5* **Numidas (POL)**[119] 4-9-8 .... JimmyQuinn 12 — 22
(Mrs A L M King) *s.s: a wl bhd* **25/1**

1m 12.11s (-0.70) **Going Correction** -0.125s/f (Stan)
WFA 3 from 4yo+ 12lb — **12** Ran SP% **121.6**
Speed ratings (Par 101):99,96,96,96,95 94,93,93,92,91 89,82
CSF £169.70 TOTE £13.40: £3.80, £3.70, £5.60; EX 81.60 Trifecta £321.50 Part won. Pool: £452.89 - 0.55 winning tickets..There was no bid for the winner.
Owner Ms J S Doyle **Bred** Martin Blandford **Trained** Upper Lambourn, Berks

FOCUS
A routine seller full of the usual suspects, but notable for a rapid early pace with Global Achiever and Leah's Pride taking each other on. The form should prove sound enough.
Sabo Prince Official explanation: trainer's representative said gelding bled from nose
Numidas(POL) Official explanation: jockey said colt missed break

983 DAVE HILL 65TH BIRTHDAY H'CAP — 1m 4f (P)
3:30 (3:30) (Class 5) (0-75,75) 4-Y-0+ — **£3,238** (£963; £481; £240) **Stalls** Low

Form — RPR

/112 **1** **Shaunas Vision (IRE)**[10] [847] 7-9-4 **73** .... SebSanders 1 — 82
(D K Ivory) *lw: led 1f: prom: led ins fnl f: drvn out* **4/1**[3]

4131 **2** *1/2* **Eloquent Knight (USA)**[27] [652] 4-9-2 **72** .... MartinDwyer 7 — 80
(W R Muir) *stdd s: hdwy to ld after 1f and set modest pce: qckrnd 1/2-way: hdd 1f out: r.o* **7/2**[2]

4213 **3** *nk* **Captain Margaret**[14] [800] 4-9-0 **70** .... (p) JimmyQuinn 4 — 78
(J Pearce) *chsd ldrs: drvn to narrow ld 1f out: sn hdd: kpt on* **9/1**

2111 **4** *1 3/4* **Polish Power (GER)**[10] [847] 6-9-2 **71** 6ex .... JohnEgan 6 — 76+
(J S Moore) *lw: towards rr: rdn 1/2-way: hdwy over 1f out: kpt on fnl f* **5/2**[1]

-603 **5** *nk* **Duelling Banjos**[18] [723] 7-8-11 **66** .... ChrisCatlin 10 — 70
(J Akehurst) *prom: rdn 5f out: styd on same pce fnl 3f* **16/1**

6-05 **6** *1 3/4* **Burgundy**[84] [135] 9-9-3 **72** .... (b) TPQueally 5 — 73
(P Mitchell) *bhd: rdn 1/2-way: effrt on outside over 1f out: nt pce to chal* **25/1**

00-4 **7** *1/2* **Haatmey**[14] [800] 4-9-5 **75** .... TedDurcan 3 — 76
(M R Channon) *mid-div: n.m.r and lost pl over 3f out: rallied on rail ent st: sn hld* **7/1**

0421 **8** *2* **Zalkani (IRE)**[11] [833] 6-9-3 **72** .... GeorgeBaker 2 — 69
(J R Boyle) *hld up in rr: hdwy on outside over 3f out: wknd over 1f out* **12/1**

0050 **9** *5* **Alekhine (IRE)**[41] [559] 5-8-11 **69** .... (p) AmirQuinn(3) 9 — 58
(J R Boyle) *stdd s: plld hrd in rr: hdwy to press ldr 1/2-way: wknd over 1f out* **40/1**

10 *2 1/2* **White On Black (GER)**[21] 5-9-0 **74** .... RobynBrisland(5) 8 — 59
(G L Moore) *mid-div: wknd over 3f out: sn bhd* **25/1**

2m 36.01s (1.62) **Going Correction** -0.125s/f (Stan)
WFA 4 from 5yo+ 1lb — **10** Ran SP% **117.0**
Speed ratings (Par 103):89,88,88,87,87 85,85,84,80,79
CSF £18.11 CT £119.18 TOTE £4.00: £1.40, £1.40, £2.30; EX 23.90 Trifecta £79.90 Pool: £526.99 - 4.66 winning tickets..

Owner John F Connolly **Bred** Ruairi O'Coileain **Trained** Radlett, Herts
FOCUS
No pace on at all in the early stages of this handicap and it developed into something of a sprint. As a result a very slow winning time for a race of its class, althjough the form makes sense on paper.

984 LINGFIELD PARK LEISURE CLUB H'CAP — 1m (P)
4:00 (4:01) (Class 6) (0-60,60) 3-Y-O — **£2,730** (£806; £403) **Stalls** High

Form — RPR
0052 **1** **Titus Lumpus (IRE)**[9] [853] 3-8-13 **55** .... FergusSweeney 6 — 62
(R M Flower) *led after 1f tl 6f out: led 3f out: qcknd clr ent st: rdn out: readily* **12/1**
44-2 **2** *2* **Mighty Dancer (IRE)**[37] [604] 3-9-4 **60** .... JimmyFortune 2 — 62
(S Kirk) *chsd ldrs: drvn to chse wnr over 1f out: no imp* **7/4**[1]
3-06 **3** *2 1/2* **Peephole**[47] [500] 3-9-1 **57** ....(v) SebSanders 3 — 53
(P J Makin) *w ldrs: led 6f out tl 3f out: hrd rdn and outpcd by wnr 2f out: lost 2nd over 1f out* **10/1**[3]
3300 **4** *nk* **Grecianette (IRE)**[19] [709] 3-9-0 **56** .... LPKeniry 1 — 52
(W J Musson) *patiently rdn in midfield to rr: shkn up and hdwy over 1f out: kpt on fnl f* **10/1**[3]
45-6 **5** *nk* **Cheveley Flyer**[19] [709] 3-9-2 **58** .... JimmyQuinn 12 — 53
(J Pearce) *lw: sn outpcd in rr: hrd rdn 2f out: nrst fin* **4/1**[2]
-004 **6** *hd* **Rock Of Cloonavery (IRE)**[28] [642] 3-9-1 **57** .... J-PGuillambert 9 — 51
(S C Williams) *mid-div: rdn to chse ldrs 2f out: one pce* **16/1**
-065 **7** *nk* **Almowj**[14] [796] 3-9-4 **60** ....(b) TedDurcan 4 — 54
(C E Brittain) *chsd ldrs: rdn over 2f out: sn btn* **12/1**
-002 **8** *1 1/4* **Lady Zanzara (USA)**[43] [544] 3-9-1 **57** .... WandersonD'Avila 7 — 48
(J W Hills) *t.k.h: hld up and bhd: rdn and sme hdwy on outside over 1f out: edgd lft: nt rch ldrs* **12/1**
006 **9** *2* **Billy Wizz (IRE)**[60] [373] 3-8-13 **55** ....(v[1]) MartinDwyer 11 — 41
(A M Balding) *hld up in midfield: effrt over 2f out: no imp* **16/1**
05-0 **10** *3/4* **Pactolos Way**[39] [583] 3-9-4 **60** .... GeorgeBaker 8 — 45
(P R Chamings) *led 1f: prom tl wknd ent st* **11/1**
05-5 **11** *7* **Coltchester (IRE)**[13] [802] 3-9-4 **60** ....(b[1]) GylesParkin 10 — 28
(Peter Grayson) *stdd towards rr and plld hrd early: rdn 5f out: hrd drvn over 3f out: no rspnse* **33/1**
00-0 **12** *7* **Meddle**[18] [722] 3-9-1 **57** .... ChrisCatlin 5 — 9
(J Jay) *rdn 1/2-way: a bhd* **25/1**
1m 38.16s (-1.27) **Going Correction** -0.125s/f (Stan) **12** Ran SP% **124.5**
Speed ratings (Par 96):101,99,96,96,95 95,95,94,92,91 84,77
CSF £34.87 CT £238.20 TOTE £21.70: £5.70, £1.30, £3.20; EX 46.30 TRIFECTA Not won..
Owner Richard Chew **Bred** Aston Mullins Stud And D J Erwin **Trained** Jevington, E Sussex
FOCUS
A moderate three-year-old handicap containing a few making their handicap debuts. The third is the best guide to the form.

985 GOLF & GAMBLE AT LINGFIELD PARK H'CAP — 7f (P)
4:30 (4:33) (Class 5) (0-70,71) 4-Y-O+ — **£3,238** (£963; £481; £240) **Stalls** Low

Form — RPR
-505 **1** **Ektishaaf**[11] [837] 4-8-4 **56** .... JamieMackay 5 — 63
(C F Wall) *hld up in midfield: hdwy to press ldrs 2f out: led fnl 100 yds: all out* **16/1**
00-0 **2** *nk* **Aastral Magic**[18] [721] 4-9-4 **70** .... RichardHughes 6 — 76
(R Hannon) *chsd ldr: led over 2f out: hrd rdn and hdd fnl 100 yds: rallied wl* **33/1**
3112 **3** *shd* **White Bear (FR)**[39] [575] 4-9-0 **66** ....(b) LDettori 8 — 72
(C R Dore) *lw: mid-div: hdwy on ins 2f out: drvn to press ldng pair fnl f: r.o* **15/8**[1]
6014 **4** *1/2* **Quantum Leap**[18] [721] 9-9-4 **70** ....(v) JimmyQuinn 7 — 75
(S Dow) *lw: mid-div: rdn and styd on wl fnl 2f: nvr nrr* **15/2**[3]
500- **5** *1/2* **Regal Dream (IRE)**[186] [5735] 4-9-3 **69** .... MichaelHills 9 — 72
(J W Hills) *towards rr: effrt and wd st: gd hdwy over 1f out: nrst fin* **9/1**
4453 **6** *hd* **Mistral Sky**[18] [737] 7-9-1 **67** ....(v) JimmyFortune 1 — 70
(Stef Liddiard) *dwlt: sn prom: hrd rdn and one pce fnl f* **16/1**
4044 **7** *1/2* **Kensington (IRE)**[60] [381] 5-8-8 **65** ....(p) StephenDonohoe[(5)] 10 — 67
(P D Evans) *prom: hrd rdn and no ex fnl f* **7/1**[2]
3645 **8** *nk* **Hand Chime**[10] [845] 9-8-9 **61** .... JohnEgan 4 — 62
(Ernst Oertel) *t.k.h: sn stdd bk into midfield: drvn to chse ldrs over 1f out: one pce* **25/1**
1534 **9** *1/2* **Hollow Jo**[10] [845] 6-8-13 **65** .... DarryllHolland 3 — 70+
(J R Jenkins) *chsd ldrs: rdn and lost pl over 2f out: hld but styng on whn nt clr run and eased ins fnl f* **15/2**[3]
0-55 **10** *1* **Coquin D'Alezan (IRE)**[13] [806] 5-8-4 **63** .... BRoper[(7)] 11 — 60+
(W Jarvis) *lw: hld up in midfield: lost pl over 2f out: kpt on fnl f* **8/1**
5040 **11** *hd* **Blue Empire (IRE)**[16] [764] 5-8-9 **61** .... DavidKinsella 2 — 57
(C R Dore) *led tl over 2f out: hrd rdn over 1f out: wknd fnl f* **50/1**
0451 **12** *1* **Goose Chase**[10] [845] 4-9-2 **71** 7ex........ AdamKirby[(3)] 13 — 65
(A M Hales) *hld up in rr: mod effrt ent st: nt trble ldrs* **16/1**
223- **13** *18* **Tipsy Lad**[127] [6516] 4-8-4 **56** oh1........(t) MartinDwyer 12 — 3
(D J S Ffrench Davis) *a bhd: lost tch 3f out* **16/1**
1m 24.65s (-1.24) **Going Correction** -0.125s/f (Stan) **13** Ran SP% **124.2**
Speed ratings (Par 103):102,101,101,100,100 100,99,99,98,97 97,96,75
CSF £478.08 CT £1461.92 TOTE £24.10: £5.60, £8.60, £1.60; EX 653.30 TRIFECTA Not won..
Owner T S M S Riley-Smith **Bred** Lark Copse Ltd **Trained** Newmarket, Suffolk
FOCUS
A competitive handicap run at a decent pace, and the form is ordinary but sound.
Quantum Leap Official explanation: vet said gelding was struck into
Hollow Jo Official explanation: jockey said gelding was denied clear run in closing stages

986 FURLONGS & FAIRWAYS H'CAP — 5f (P)
5:00 (5:02) (Class 5) (0-70,70) 4-Y-O+ — **£3,238** (£963; £481; £240) **Stalls** High

Form — RPR
3244 **1** **Wicked Uncle**[21] [699] 7-9-4 **70** ....(v) JimmyFortune 2 — 77
(S Gollings) *chsd ldng pair: wnt 2nd over 1f out: led ins fnl f: drvn out* **6/1**[2]
6626 **2** *nk* **Times Review (USA)**[12] [824] 5-8-10 **62** ....(b) JohnEgan 3 — 68
(C A Dwyer) *sn led: hrd rdn and hdd ins fnl f: r.o* **15/2**
0013 **3** *1 1/2* **Almaty Express**[12] [824] 4-9-0 **66** ....(b) DarryllHolland 4 — 67
(J R Weymes) *lw: chsd ldr tl over 1f out: kpt on same pce* **11/4**[1]
0-40 **4** *1 1/4* **Salon Prive**[12] [824] 6-8-11 **63** .... MartinDwyer 10 — 59
(C A Cyzer) *broke wl: chsd ldrs: hrd rdn over 1f out: one pce* **10/1**
3000 **5** *nk* **Namir (IRE)**[12] [824] 4-8-7 **59** ....(v) TPQueally 1 — 54
(Stef Liddiard) *dwlt: towards rr: hdwy on rail ent st: no imp* **8/1**
2100 **6** *1* **Lady Bahia (IRE)**[2] [954] 5-8-10 **62** ....(b) GylesParkin 7 — 53
(Peter Grayson) *mid-div: sn pushed along: no imp whn edgd lft over 1f out* **20/1**
3233 **7** *nk* **Taboor (IRE)**[11] [837] 8-8-4 **56** .... HayleyTurner 5 — 51+
(R M H Cowell) *s.s: rdn along and bhd: sme hdwy whn squeezed and swtchd rt ins fnl f: gng on at fin* **6/1**[2]
310- **8** *1/2* **Cosmic Destiny (IRE)**[203] [5406] 4-8-8 **60** .... RichardMullen 8 — 49+
(E F Vaughan) *rrd s: towards rr: hmpd over 2f out: nt trble ldrs* **10/1**
0-00 **9** *shd* **Bold Cheverak**[14] [798] 4-8-6 **58** .... ChrisCatlin 6 — 46
(Mrs C A Dunnett) *in tch: hrd rdn over 1f out: no ex* **14/1**
2145 **10** *1 3/4* **Majestical (IRE)**[64] [323] 4-9-1 **67** ....(p) GeorgeBaker 9 — 49
(J M Bradley) *hld up in midfield on outside: outpcd and btn 2f out* **13/2**[3]
58.42 secs (-1.36) **Going Correction** -0.125s/f (Stan) **10** Ran SP% **121.1**
Speed ratings (Par 103):105,104,102,100,99 98,97,96,96,93
CSF £52.55 CT £144.25 TOTE £7.20: £2.30, £3.20, £1.20; EX 58.50 Trifecta £340.70 Pool: £494.37 - 1.03 winning tickets. Place 6 £146.19, Place 5 £102.60.
Owner Roy G Gibney, P & Mrs A Allen **Bred** Lady Jennifer Green **Trained** Scamblesby, Lincs
■ Stewards' Enquiry : Jimmy Fortune caution: careless riding
Gyles Parkin two-day ban: careless riding (Apr 23-24)
FOCUS
Very few got into this sprint and the first three home were up with the pace throughout. The draw also played its part with the front trio coming from the four lowest stalls. Despite that the form appears solid enough.
Taboor(IRE) Official explanation: jockey said gelding missed break
T/Plt: £176.50 to a £1 stake. Pool: £45,953.55. 190.05 winning tickets. T/Qpdt: £6.00 to a £1 stake. Pool: £4,567.90. 557.00 winning tickets. LM

NOTTINGHAM (L-H)
Wednesday, April 12

OFFICIAL GOING: Soft (good to soft in places)
Wind: Light, across Weather: Overcast

987 EUROPEAN BREEDERS FUND MAIDEN STKS — 5f 13y
2:10 (2:10) (Class 5) 2-Y-O — **£3,886** (£1,156; £577; £288) **Stalls** High

Form — RPR
1 **Chjimes (IRE)** 2-9-3 .... PaulHanagan 6 — 71+
(K R Burke) *sn pushed along in rr: hdwy 2f out: nt clr run over 1f out: led ins fnl f: r.o wl* **25/1**
2 *2* **Fractured Foxy** 2-8-12 .... GrahamGibbons 8 — 59
(J J Quinn) *s.i.s: in rr whn n.m.r over 4f out: hdwy and hung lft over 1f out: r.o: nt trble wnr* **16/1**
3 *1* **Castano** 2-9-3 .... AlanMunro 2 — 60
(B R Millman) *chsd ldr: led over 1f out: hdd ins fnl f: styd on same pce* **9/4**[2]
3 **4** *2 1/2* **Hart Of Gold**[4] [912] 2-9-3 .... JamieSpencer 5 — 51
(M J Wallace) *chsd ldrs: rdn 1/2-way: no ex fnl f* **1/1**[1]
5 *3/4* **Little Tommy Fella** 2-9-3 .... SteveDrowne 3 — 49
(S C Williams) *dwlt: sn pushed along in rr: n.d* **25/1**
0 **6** *7* **Bentley**[6] [892] 2-9-3 .... DaneO'Neill 9 — 23
(D Shaw) *dwlt: sn pushed along in rr: wknd 1/2-way* **50/1**
7 *6* **Emefdream** 2-9-3 .... NCallan 1 — —
(K A Ryan) *s.i.s and wnt lft s: sn w ldr: rdn 1/2-way: ev ch over 1f out: sn wknd* **10/1**[3]
8 *2 1/2* **Baileys Hilight (IRE)** 2-9-3 .... KDarley 7 — —
(M Johnston) *mde most over 3f: sn n.m.r and wknd* **10/1**[3]
66.02 secs (4.22) **Going Correction** +0.575s/f (Yiel) **8** Ran SP% **114.5**
Speed ratings (Par 92):89,85,84,80,79 67,58,54
CSF £351.03 TOTE £34.70: £8.00, £3.30, £1.10; EX 274.40.
Owner Philip Richards **Bred** Morgan O'Flaherty **Trained** Middleham Moor, N Yorks
FOCUS
This juvenile maiden was run at a strong early pace, suiting those racing from behind, and while the bare form looks ordinary, the winner may go on to better things.
NOTEBOOK
Chjimes(IRE), related to winners from five to ten furlongs, struggled to go the strong early pace, but responded positively to his rider's urgings at halfway and ultimately finished strongly to win this going away. On this evidence, he looks an above-average juvenile for the time of year, and the step up to a sixth furlong in due course should see him in an even better light. (op 20-1)
Fractured Foxy, a 4,000gns purchase related to winning sprinters, was slow to break and ran green early on, but the strong pace played into her hands and she finished her race in fair style. The easy ground was in her favour and she should be a lot sharper with this debut experience under her belt. (op 12-1)
Castano ◆, who cost 12,500gns and is a half-brother to winning sprinters Maddie's A Jem and Imtalkinggibberish, is an April foal and was well backed ahead of this racecourse debut. He travelled well enough until halway, before making what appeared to be a decisive challenge, but ultimately he was betrayed by his lack of experience. This outing should ensure he improves a deal and he looks a likely candidate to win a maiden in the coming weeks. (op 5-2 tchd 11-4)
Hart Of Gold, third on his recent debut at Lingfield, failed to improve for the switch to this more demanding surface and was beaten at halfway. He again left the impression this experience would not be lost on him, however, and he is not one to write off. Official explanation: jockey said colt hung left (op 6-5 tchd 5-4 in places)
Little Tommy Fella, whose dam was a twelve-furlong winner, was not surprisingly all at sea through the early parts, but the penny started to drop in the final two furlongs and he did more than enough to suggest he has a future.
Emefdream Official explanation: jockey said colt hung
Baileys Hilight(IRE), the first juvenile runner of the season from his powerful yard, was very smart to break yet ultimately paid for his early exertions and was well beaten. (op 9-1)

988 WELCOME BACK TO NOTTINGHAM FOR 2006 H'CAP — 5f 13y
2:40 (2:40) (Class 5) (0-70,70) 3-Y-O — **£3,238** (£963; £481; £240) **Stalls** High

Form — RPR
645- **1** **Miltons Choice**[225] [4847] 3-8-5 **57** .... KDarley 5 — 64
(J M Bradley) *s.i.s: sn chsng ldrs: rdn over 1f out: edgd rt and styd on to ld wl ins fnl f* **14/1**
064- **2** *1 1/2* **Mannikko (IRE)**[159] [6242] 3-9-2 **68** .... SteveDrowne 4 — 70
(G Wragg) *mid-div: sn pushed along: hdwy over 1f out: styd on* **2/1**[2]
2221 **3** *1 1/4* **Garlogs**[12] [819] 3-9-2 **68** .... PaulHanagan 7 — 66
(A Bailey) *chsd ldr: rdn to ld ins fnl f: wkng whn hdd and hmpd wl ins fnl f* **13/8**[1]
5460 **4** *1/2* **Thoughtsofstardom**[13] [807] 3-8-11 **63** ....(v[1]) JamieSpencer 8 — 59
(P S McEntee) *sn pushed along in rr: swtchd lft over 1f out: r.o ins fnl f: nrst fin* **10/1**
4453 **5** *1/2* **Amber Glory**[23] [673] 3-9-0 **66** ....(b) NCallan 1 — 60
(K A Ryan) *led: clr 1/2-way: rdn hdd & wknd ins fnl f* **8/1**[3]
002- **6** *2* **Immaculate Red**[188] [5703] 3-9-1 **67** .... RoystonFfrench 6 — 54
(R Bastiman) *s.i.s: sn prom: rdn 1/2-way: wknd over 1f out* **33/1**
3000 **7** *2 1/2* **Canina**[2] [954] 3-9-4 **70** .... EddieAhern 2 — 49
(Ms Deborah J Evans) *sn pushed along: a in rr* **12/1**

645- **8** *2* **Quaker Boy**230 4697 3-8-11 **63** .... TomEaves 3 35
(M Dods) *sn outpcd* **20/1**
64.83 secs (3.03) **Going Correction** +0.575s/f (Yiel) **8** Ran SP% **113.7**
Speed ratings (Par 98):98,95,93,92,92 88,84,81
CSF £41.96 CT £72.07 TOTE £17.20: £2.50, £1.80, £1.10; EX 61.00.
Owner racingshares.co.uk **Bred** G C Neate **Trained** Sedbury, Gloucs

FOCUS
A modest sprint, run at a decent pace, and the form looks sound enough ated around the runner-up.

989 APRIL CONDITIONS STKS 5f 13y
3:10 (3:10) (Class 4) 3-Y-O+ **£6,477** (£1,927; £963; £481) **Stalls** High

Form RPR
11-3 **1** **Reverence**18 729 5-9-4 107 .... KDarley 3 114
(E J Alston) *racd stands' side: chsd ldrs: led that gp 1/2-way: overall ldr over 1f out: r.o* **1/2**1
640- **2** *1 3/4* **Bahamian Pirate (USA)**199 5495 11-9-1 103 .... EddieAhern 7 105
(D Nicholls) *racd stands' side: hld up: hdwy u.p over 1f out: nt rch wnr* **12/1**
0-06 **3** *2* **If Paradise**25 664 5-9-1 99 .... DaneO'Neill 4 98
(R Hannon) *racd stands' side: chsd ldrs: rdn over 1f out: styd on same pce* **9/1**3
0-10 **4** *hd* **The Lord**76 198 6-8-12 93 .... RobertMiles(3) 5 97
(W G M Turner) *dwlt: racd stands' side: hdwy over 3f out: rdn: hung lft and ev ch over 1f out: no ex ins fnl f* **33/1**
40-0 **5** *2 1/2* **Cape Royal**20 705 6-9-1 95 .... (t) RyanMoore 1 89
(J M Bradley) *racd alone centre: overall ldr over 3f: wknd ins fnl f* **14/1**
44-6 **6** *1 3/4* **Green Manalishi**20 705 5-9-1 95 .... TQuinn 2 83
(D W P Arbuthnot) *chsd ldrs stands' side over 3f* **8/1**2
040/ **7** *5* **Next Time Around (IRE)**550 6068 4-9-1 95 .... TomEaves 9 66
(Mrs L Stubbs) *racd stands' side: sn outpcd* **100/1**
214- **8** *5* **Neverletme Go (IRE)**267 3612 4-8-13 84 .... SteveDrowne 10 47
(G Wragg) *racd stands' side: chsd ldrs to 1/2-way* **18/1**
6660 **9** *2* **Magic Glade**16 761 7-9-1 82 .... PaulHanagan 8 42
(R Brotherton) *led stands' side to 1/2-way: wknd wl over 1f out* **100/1**
63.31 secs (1.51) **Going Correction** +0.575s/f (Yiel)
WFA 3 from 4yo+ 11lb **9** Ran SP% **112.3**
Speed ratings (Par 105):110,107,104,103,99 96,88,80,77
CSF £7.33 TOTE £1.50: £1.20, £2.50, £1.60; EX 9.50.
Owner Mr & Mrs G Middlebrook **Bred** G And Mrs Middlebrook **Trained** Longton, Lancs

FOCUS
A decent sprint won by a progressive sprinter who should rate higher. The form looks solid, and the winning time was decent for a Class 4 contest, though some very smart performers took part in this.
Magic Glade Official explanation: jockey said gelding bled from nose

990 ABBA 70'S NIGHT ON SATURDAY 22 APRIL H'CAP 1m 6f 15y
3:40 (3:40) (Class 5) (0-70,70) 4-Y-O+ **£5,181** (£1,541; £770; £384) **Stalls** Low

Form RPR
4-00 **1** **Sphinx (FR)**88 111 8-9-5 **63** .... (b1) SteveDrowne 8 73
(Jamie Poulton) *a.p: led 1f out: styd on wl* **50/1**
550- **2** *2 1/2* **Dhehdaah**26 6029 5-9-0 **58** .... AlanMunro 16 65
(Mrs P Sly) *hld up: hdwy over 3f out: rdn over 1f out: styd on* **7/1**2
6/0- **3** *1* **Patrixprial**29 5661 5-9-9 **70** .... (b1) SaleemGolam(3) 15 76
(M H Tompkins) *hld up: hdwy over 2f out: styd on* **25/1**
5022 **4** *shd* **Valeureux**12 825 8-8-10 **54** .... MichaelTebbutt 17 60
(J Hetherton) *a.p: led wl over 1f out: rdn and hdd 1f out: styng on same pce whn eased nr fin* **28/1**
054- **5** *1/2* **Bollin Thomas**24 6239 8-9-9 **67** .... EddieAhern 7 72
(R Allan) *a.p: rdn over 2f out: styd on* **11/1**
00-2 **6** *nk* **Sabbiosa (IRE)**15 780 4-9-4 **65** .... TQuinn 3 70
(J L Dunlop) *trckd ldrs: rdn and ev ch over 1f out: no ex ins fnl f* **9/1**
00-6 **7** *1 3/4* **Count Boris**8 882 5-8-8 **55** .... RichardThomas(3) 11 57
(J A Geake) *hld up in tch: hmpd and lost pl over 3f out: styd on ins fnl f* **8/1**3
5-05 **8** *1 1/4* **Street Life (IRE)**18 723 8-9-11 **69** .... NCallan 12 70
(W J Musson) *s.i.s: hld up: hdwy over 2f out: nt clr run over 1f out : wknd ins fnl f* **10/1**
00/2 **9** *2* **Middlethorpe**8 869 9-9-2 **60** .... (b) JoeFanning 14 58
(M W Easterby) *hld up: hdwy u.p and edgd lft over 3f out: wknd wl over 1f out* **7/1**2
00-5 **10** *1 3/4* **Mary Gray**12 825 4-8-9 **56** .... KDarley 5 52
(M Johnston) *racd keenly: led 1f: chsd ldr: led over 3f out: rdn and hdd wl over 1f out: wknd fnl f* **20/1**
/000 **11** *5* **Fort Churchill (IRE)**18 723 5-9-10 **68** .... (p) DaneO'Neill 4 57
(B Ellison) *led after 1f: rdn and hdd over 3f out: wknd wl over 1f out* **13/2**1
-060 **12** *3* **Weet A Head (IRE)**12 820 5-9-3 **61** .... GrahamGibbons 6 46
(R Hollinshead) *mid-div: rdn and wknd over 2f out* **40/1**
010- **13** *3/4* **Treason Trial**173 6006 5-9-8 **66** .... JamieSpencer 2 50
(Stef Liddiard) *hld up: a in rr* **13/2**1
450- **14** *nk* **Nobbler**175 5973 4-8-8 **55** .... RyanMoore 1 39
(N A Callaghan) *hld up: rdn over 2f out: a in rr* **14/1**
400/ **15** *1 3/4* **Lawood (IRE)**447 2895 6-9-10 **68** .... VinceSlattery 9 50
(L P Grassick) *hld up: a in rr* **66/1**
114- **16** *4* **Celtic Carisma**196 5550 4-8-5 **54** oh2 .... PaulHanagan 10 29
(K G Reveley) *hld up: hdwy over 3f out: rdn and wknd over 2f out* **8/1**3
3m 15.69s (8.59) **Going Correction** +0.70s/f (Yiel)
WFA 4 from 5yo+ 3lb **16** Ran SP% **125.9**
Speed ratings (Par 103):103,101,101,100,100 100,99,98,97,96 93,92,91,91,90 88
CSF £369.40 CT £8805.64 TOTE £54.60: £16.50, £1.70, £6.40, £4.10; EX 755.10.
Owner R W Huggins **Bred** M Arbib **Trained** Telscombe, E Sussex

FOCUS
A modest staying handicap, run at an average pace, and the form looks fair for the class rated around the first two.
Valeureux Official explanation: jockey said, regarding the apparent tender ride approaching the line, having contested the lead throughout the home straight gelding had no more to give having become very tired; gelding was not fitted with usual tongue-strap and appeared to be struggling for breath in final furlong, so he held him together rather than exert further pressure
Count Boris Official explanation: jockey said gelding hung left
Celtic Carisma Official explanation: jockey said filly hung right

991 WEATHERBYS BANK "FURTHER FLIGHT" STKS (LISTED RACE) 1m 6f 15y
4:10 (4:10) (Class 1) 4-Y-O+
£15,898 (£6,025; £3,015; £1,503; £753; £378) **Stalls** Low

Form RPR
453- **1** **Frank Sonata**151 6339 5-9-0 102 .... RyanMoore 4 107
(M G Quinlan) *s.i.s: hld up: hdwy over 3f out: led over 2f out: rdn out* **10/3**2
544- **2** *3 1/2* **Dancing Bay**28 6237 9-9-0 105 .... TQuinn 7 102
(N J Henderson) *hld up: hdwy and hmpd over 3f out: sn rdn: styd on* **6/1**
610- **3** *2* **Shabernak (IRE)**258 3879 7-9-3 106 .... JamieSpencer 1 102
(M L W Bell) *led 1f: chsd ldr: led 10f out: rdn and hdd over 2f out: no ex fnl f* **6/1**
332- **4** *1 1/2* **Larkwing (IRE)**200 5458 5-9-0 102 .... SteveDrowne 3 97
(G Wragg) *hld up: hdwy and hung lft over 3f out: sn rdn: styd on same pce fnl 2f* **5/1**3
-603 **5** *shd* **Crosspeace (IRE)**34 622 4-9-0 .... JoeFanning 8 100
(M Johnston) *trckd ldrs: racd keenly: swtchd lft over 3f out: sn rdn: styd on same pce fnl 2f* **11/4**1
56-1 **6** *1/2* **Into The Shadows**19 714 6-8-9 87 .... PaulHanagan 9 92?
(K G Reveley) *hld up: hdwy over 2f out: nt trble ldrs* **16/1**
014- **7** *2 1/2* **Casual Glance**169 6100 4-8-6 82 .... NeilChalmers 2 88?
(A M Balding) *hld up: hdwy over 5f out: hmpd over 3f out: sn outpcd: styd on ins fnl f* **33/1**
5- **8** *13* **Sworn In (USA)**298 2725 5-9-0 .... NCallan 6 77?
(N I M Rossiter) *plld hrd: led after 1f: hdd 10f out: rdn and wkng whn hmpd over 3f out* **66/1**
442- **9** *7* **Fuerta Ventura (IRE)**164 6192 4-8-6 .... EddieAhern 5 62
(K J Condon, Ire) *prom: chsd ldr 6f out: rdn and edgd lft over 3f out: sn wknd* **11/1**
3m 12.8s (5.70) **Going Correction** +0.70s/f (Yiel)
WFA 4 from 5yo+ 3lb **9** Ran SP% **113.6**
Speed ratings (Par 111):111,109,107,107,106 106,105,97,93
CSF £23.28 TOTE £4.30: £1.90, £1.30, £2.20; EX 24.30.
Owner W P Flynn **Bred** Bishop Wilton Stud **Trained** Newmarket, Suffolk

FOCUS
A fair Listed contest with last year's second and third finishing first and third on this occasion.

NOTEBOOK
Frank Sonata ◆, whose last success came in Listed company at Haydock back in July 2004, has run some good races in defeat since then, notably in this last season, and he looked in really good shape on this seasonal reappearance, having reportedly strengthened over the winter. He came through with quarter of a mile to run before powering clear to win in good style and may now take in the Group Three John Porter at Newbury, in which he was second last term, before a possible venture to Baden-Baden for a two-mile Group Three later in the season. He must have soft ground, but is always likely to get that abroad and there may well be more to come. (op 4-1)
Dancing Bay, who ran a fair race in the Coral Cup at Cheltenham last month, is another who is at his best when the mud is flying and he came through to represent the winner's only danger. He will again not find winning easy this season, but is sure to amass some good place money. (op 5-1)
Shabernak(IRE), fourth in this last season, showed improved form subsequently and was expected to go well, despite the penalty, on this seasonal reappearance with Spencer a significant booking. However, with the ground far from ideal, he could find no more under pressure once past, but still held on for a highly creditable third. He is one to keep on side this season when the ground is quick. (op 13-2 tchd 7-1)
Larkwing(IRE) often ran well without winning last season and, whilst this reappearance was mildly pleasing, it did not suggest he has improved. (op 11-2)
Crosspeace(IRE), whose stable are having winners wthout suggesting they are in top form, had a bit to prove on this rise in distance considering he was contesting a six-furlong handicap this time last year and, having raced keenly, he was unable to see his race out as strongly as some. He still gives the impression he has not done improving yet, and the four-year-old may have more to offer back at shorter. (op 3-1 tchd 10-3 in a place)
Into The Shadows, who took advantage of a massively below-par performance from Irish Derby-placed Shalapour when winning in atrocious ground at Southwell on the first day of the turf season, was not disgraced considering she had plenty to find at the weights, but any further winning she does this season is likely to come at handicap level. (op 14-1)
Casual Glance, who appeared to run above herself when finishing fourth in a Listed race at Yarmouth towards the backend of last season, was another who ran better than could have been expected considering this would have been a much stronger contest than at Yarmouth. She could be up to winning at this sort of level against her own sex if progressing.
Sworn In(USA) was out of his grade on this second Flat start and it was surprising he was not beaten further. Official explanation: jockey said horse hung left (op 100-1)
Fuerta Ventura(IRE), a useful Irish filly who likes soft ground, showed up well early but dropped away disappointingly and there may well have been a problem. (op 9-1 tchd 12-1)

992 BUY YOUR TICKETS ON-LINE AT NOTTINGHAMRACECOURSE.CO.UK H'CAP 1m 54y
4:40 (4:40) (Class 5) (0-75,76) 4-Y-O+ **£3,238** (£963; £481; £240) **Stalls** Centre

Form RPR
4511 **1** **Hail The Chief**6 898 9-9-5 **76** 6ex .... RyanMoore 11 86
(R Hannon) *mid-div: hdwy over 3f out: led over 1f out: rdn out* **9/4**1
100- **2** *3* **Firesong**186 5730 4-9-4 **75** .... ShaneKelly 2 79+
(Pat Eddery) *hld up: racd keenly: hdwy over 2f out: nt clr run over 1f out: swtchd rt ins fnl f: r.o: no ch w wnr* **7/1**2
21 **3** *nk* **Webbow (IRE)**23 677 4-9-1 **72** .... JamieSpencer 1 75
(T D Easterby) *led: hdd over 6f out: chsd ldr tl led 3f out: rdn: edgd rt and hdd over 1f out: styd on same pce* **10/1**
0224 **4** *hd* **Libre**28 641 6-8-12 **69** .... EddieAhern 8 72+
(F Jordan) *chsd ldrs: rdn over 1f out: styd on same pce* **17/2**3
43-0 **5** *3* **Ermine Grey**58 404 5-8-10 **67** .... KDarley 7 64
(A W Carroll) *led over 6f out: hdd 3f out: rdn and ev ch over 1f out: wkng whn hmpd ins fnl f* **11/1**
1-44 **6** *nk* **Fasylitator (IRE)**11 826 4-8-13 **70** .... SteveDrowne 15 66+
(D K Ivory) *chsd ldrs: rdn and ev ch over 1f out: wkng whn hmpd ins fnl f* **14/1**
030- **7** *2 1/2* **Barataria**350 1310 4-8-11 **68** .... RoystonFfrench 9 59
(R Bastiman) *s.i.s: hld up: styd on ins fnl f: nvr nrr* **33/1**
514- **8** *1 1/2* **Little Bob**161 6230 5-8-12 **69** .... (b) GrahamGibbons 6 57
(J D Bethell) *hld up: hdwy u.p over 2f out: no imp whn nt clr run ins fnl f* **10/1**
2-00 **9** *1/2* **Monash Lad (IRE)**64 114 4-8-5 **69** .... PatrickHills(7) 16 56
(M H Tompkins) *chsd ldrs over 5f* **33/1**
4002 **10** *6* **Corky (IRE)**15 777 5-9-1 **72** .... NCallan 10 47+
(I W McInnes) *s.s: hld up: hdwy over 2f out: sn rdn: styng on whn hmpd ins fnl f: eased* **7/1**2
000- **11** *5* **Final Promise**166 6134 4-8-11 **68** .... StephenCarson 17 33
(J A Geake) *prom over 5f* **50/1**

The Form Book, Raceform Ltd, Compton, RG20 6NL

450- **12** *nk* **Celtic Spa (IRE)**[196] 5553 4-9-0 **71** .... RobertHavlin 12 36
(Mrs P N Dutfield) *hld up: n.d* **33/1**
400- **13** *3* **Elkhorn**[177] 5951 4-9-0 **71** .... TomEaves 3 30
(Miss J A Camacho) *chsd ldrs over 5f* **10/1**
230- **14** *½* **Sun Bian**[233] 4646 4-8-13 **70** .... VinceSlattery 4 28
(L P Grassick) *mid-div: lost pl whn hmpd over 5f out* **66/1**
230- **15** *2½* **Bolton Hall (IRE)**[191] 5662 4-9-1 **72** .... PaulHanagan 13 25
(R A Fahey) *hld up: a in rr* **20/1**

1m 48.74s (2.34) **Going Correction** +0.375s/f (Good) 15 Ran SP% **125.6**
Speed ratings (Par 103):103,100,99,99,96 96,93,92,91,85 80,80,77,76,74
CSF £16.89 CT £144.91 TOTE £3.10: £1.80, £3.00, £2.60; EX 31.90.
Owner Peter M Crane **Bred** Green Meadow Stud And P Crane **Trained** East Everleigh, Wilts
FOCUS
A modest handicap won in taking fashion by the evergreen Hail The Chief. The pace was sound and the form looks solid.

993 NOTTINGHAM RACECOURSE CONFERENCE CENTRE H'CAP 1m 54y
5:10 (5:12) (Class 5) (0-70,70) 3-Y-O **£3,238** (£963; £481; £240) **Stalls** Centre

Form RPR
6046 **1** **Top Shot**[39] 583 3-8-12 **67** .... SaleemGolam(3) 4 78
(M H Tompkins) *a.p: rdn to ld 2f out: r.o* **6/1**[1]
154- **2** *3½* **European Dream (IRE)**[214] 5111 3-9-2 **68** .... ShaneKelly 13 72
(R C Guest) *hld up: hdwy over 2f out: rdn to chse wnr fnl f: no imp* **15/2**[3]
60-3 **3** *1* **Cantabilly (IRE)**[19] 712 3-9-3 **69** .... TQuinn 7 71
(M R Channon) *hld up in tch: outpcd over 2f out: styd on ins fnl f* **9/1**
030- **4** *2* **Mocha Java**[152] 6309 3-9-1 **67** .... JosedeSouza 16 65
(P F I Cole) *chsd ldrs: rdn over 2f out: sn ev ch: wknd ins fnl f* **33/1**
54-5 **5** *nk* **Endless Night**[50] 475 3-9-2 **68** .... SteveDrowne 5 65
(H Morrison) *trckd ldrs: rdn over 2f out: wknd over 1f out* **10/1**
000- **6** *3½* **Wannabe Posh (IRE)**[190] 5692 3-8-11 **63** .... EddieAhern 11 53
(J L Dunlop) *bhd: rdn over 2f out: styd on ins fnl f: nvr nrr* **7/1**[2]
050- **7** *nk* **Floodlight Fantasy**[187] 5711 3-9-2 **68** .... GrahamGibbons 2 58
(E S McMahon) *prom: rdn over 4f out: wknd over 1f out* **12/1**
610- **8** *3½* **Penny Whisper (IRE)**[229] 4719 3-8-13 **65** .... RoystonFfrench 1 48
(I W McInnes) *prom: racd keenly: rdn and wknd over 2f out* **14/1**
00-6 **9** *nk* **Gigs Magic (USA)**[21] 695 3-8-13 **65** .... KDarley 9 47
(M Johnston) *hld up: hdwy over 3f out: wknd over 2f out* **16/1**
066- **10** *1¾* **Swayze (IRE)**[124] 6532 3-8-13 **65** .... RyanMoore 10 44
(N P Littmoden) *hld up: n.d* **8/1**
02-4 **11** *½* **Glenbuck (IRE)**[42] 550 3-8-11 **70** ....(v) MichaelJStainton(7) 17 48
(A Bailey) *chsd ldrs over 5f* **14/1**
220- **12** *1½* **Little Miss Daisy**[186] 5733 3-9-2 **68** .... DaneO'Neill 12 43
(A B Haynes) *hld up: a in rr* **16/1**
006- **13** *1½* **Kick And Prance**[173] 6009 3-8-12 **64** .... StephenCarson 14 36
(J A Geake) *prom over 5f* **20/1**
410- **14** *3* **Feelin Irie (IRE)**[203] 5408 3-8-13 **65** .... KimTinkler 3 31
(N Tinkler) *sn led: hdd & wknd 2f out* **25/1**
0204 **15** *shd* **Lenoir (GER)**[56] 422 3-8-11 **70** ....(v) TJHowell(7) 6 36
(V Smith) *s.i.s: hdwy over 4f out: wknd over 2f out* **16/1**
-005 **16** *2* **Eliminator**[18] 731 3-8-13 **65** ....(p) TomEaves 8 27
(I W McInnes) *hld up: rdn over 4f out: wknd over 3f out* **16/1**
0-05 **17** *5* **Smokey Blue**[44] 536 3-8-7 **64** .... DerekNolan(5) 15 16
(M J Wallace) *hld up: a in rr* **10/1**

1m 49.97s (3.57) **Going Correction** +0.375s/f (Good) 17 Ran SP% **133.9**
Speed ratings (Par 98):97,93,92,90,90 86,86,82,82,80 80,78,77,74,74 72,67
CSF £52.44 CT £440.86 TOTE £6.90: £1.90, £1.70, £2.10, £7.10; EX 81.20 Place 6 £116.94, Place 5 £40.02.
Owner J H Ellis **Bred** M P Bowring **Trained** Newmarket, Suffolk
FOCUS
Modest three-year-old handicap form, but the race should still produce winners at a similar level.
European Dream(IRE) Official explanation: jockey said gelding suffered interference immediately after start
T/Jkpt: Not won. T/Plt: £151.20 to a £1 stake. Pool: £45,926.10. 221.60 winning tickets. T/Qpdt: £29.00 to a £1 stake. Pool: £4,300.50. 109.40 winning tickets. CR

998 - 1000a (Foreign Racing) - See Raceform Interactive

950 WOLVERHAMPTON (A.W) (L-H)
Thursday, April 13

OFFICIAL GOING: Standard
Wind: Fresh, behind Weather: Cloudy with sunny spells

1001 WOLVERHAMPTON-RACECOURSE.CO.UK AMATEUR RIDERS' CLAIMING STKS 1m 141y(P)
2:40 (2:40) (Class 6) 4-Y-0+ **£2,637** (£811; £405) **Stalls** Low

Form RPR
4040 **1** **Undeterred**[19] 726 10-10-4 71 .... MrMatthewSmith(3) 4 67
(K J Burke) *hld up: hdwy over 2f out: led ins fnl f: edgd lft: rdn out* **12/1**
4301 **2** *1½* **Lord Chamberlain**[3] 950 13-10-4 59 ....(b) MissSBradley(7) 5 68
(J M Bradley) *mid-div: hdwy over 2f out: hung lft over 1f out: styd on* **7/1**[3]
3631 **3** *nk* **Distant Country (USA)**[3] 953 7-10-6 61 ....(p) MissKellyBurke(5) 1 67
(K R Burke) *s.i.s: hld up: hdwy over 2f out: hmpd over 1f out: styd on* **10/3**[1]
00-0 **4** *2* **Fraternity**[77] 200 9-10-4 60 .... MissKJames(7) 7 63
(J A Pickering) *led: pushed along over 1f out: unbalanced and hdd ins fnl f: no ex* **33/1**
1132 **5** *1¼* **Vancouver Gold (IRE)**[3] 953 4-11-0 70 .... MrWHogg 3 64
(K R Burke) *chsd ldr: rdn and ev ch over 1f out: wknd ins fnl f* **4/1**[2]
-640 **6** *1¾* **Louisiade (IRE)**[11] 845 5-11-0 60 .... MissARyan(5) 6 65
(K A Ryan) *chsd ldrs: rdn over 2f out: wknd over 1f out* **12/1**
0010 **7** *2½* **Merdiff**[3] 953 7-10-4 55 .... MrBenBrisbourne(7) 2 52
(W M Brisbourne) *prom 7f* **12/1**
1060 **8** *½* **Linning Wine (IRE)**[3] 953 10-10-9 70 ....(p) MrSWalker 8 49
(P A Blockley) *mid-div: hdwy over 2f out: rdn and hung lft over 1f out: nt run on* **8/1**
6-00 **9** *hd* **Mr Marucci (USA)**[41] 568 4-10-2 50 ....(b) MissLEllison(3) 12 44
(B Ellison) *a in rr* **66/1**
10 *3½* **Gawrosz (POL)**[159] 7-10-0 53 ....[1] MrJGoss(7) 13 39
(G J Smith) *a in rr* **50/1**
0544 **11** *¾* **Nimello (USA)**[3] 953 10-11-1 65 .... MissCHannaford 9 45
(A G Newcombe) *hld up: a in rr* **9/1**
4225 **12** *nk* **Cherished Number**[12] 833 7-11-1 57 .... MrSDobson 11 45
(A M Hales) *s.i.s: hld up: a in rr* **12/1**
/000 **13** *15* **Vandal**[55] 446 6-10-0 50 .... MrsDButler(7) 10 5
(M Appleby) *a in rr: bhd fnl 3f* **100/1**

1m 51.73s (-0.03) **Going Correction** -0.15s/f (Stan) 13 Ran SP% **114.8**
Speed ratings (Par 101):94,92,92,90,89 87,85,85,85,82 81,81,67
CSF £88.92 TOTE £13.30: £4.80, £2.70, £1.50; EX 95.90 Trifecta £257.00 Pool: £557.63 - 1.54 winning tickets..Distant Country was claimed by Barry Leavy for £8,000.
Owner Peter Valentine **Bred** Deerfield Farm **Trained** Bourton-on-the-Water, Gloucs
FOCUS
A poor race, but a decent early gallop thanks to Fraternity which eventually played into the hands of those that came from off the pace.
Cherished Number Official explanation: jockey said gelding reared leaving stalls

1002 ENJOY RACING FROM THE ZONGALERO RESTAURANT H'CAP 1m 141y(P)
3:10 (3:13) (Class 5) (0-70,69) 4-Y-0+ **£3,238** (£963; £481; £240) **Stalls** Low

Form RPR
0-22 **1** **Sir Bond (IRE)**[3] 950 5-8-7 **58** .... RobertWinston 11 70
(B Smart) *dwlt: hld up: hdwy over 3f out: bmpd wl over 1f out: rdn to ld ins fnl f: swished tail: all out* **9/4**[1]
-336 **2** *nk* **Perez (IRE)**[20] 711 4-8-12 **68** ....(b) EmmettStack(5) 3 79
(Pat Eddery) *a.p: rdn and edgd rt over 1f out: ev ch ins fnl f: kpt on* **11/2**[3]
3100 **3** *2½* **Bridgewater Boys**[19] 736 5-8-13 **64** ....(b) NCallan 12 70
(K A Ryan) *led: rdn over 1f out: hdd and no ex ins fnl f* **12/1**
00-0 **4** *4* **Comeintothespace (IRE)**[48] 504 4-8-9 **60** .... ShaneKelly 4 58
(J A Osborne) *chsd ldrs: rdn over 3f out: bmpd wl over 1f out: styd on same pce* **25/1**
0333 **5** *½* **Mission Affirmed (USA)**[19] 732 5-9-1 **66** ....(p) AdrianMcCarthy 8 63
(R A Harris) *s.i.s: hld up: hdwy u.p over 1f out: nvr nrr* **16/1**
0022 **6** *½* **Dudley Docker (IRE)**[19] 737 4-8-10 **64** .... DanielTudhope(3) 5 60
(D Carroll) *chsd ldrs: rdn over 2f out: wknd over 1f out* **9/2**[2]
P101 **7** *shd* **Pauline's Prince**[19] 736 4-8-9 **67** .... RussellKennemore(7) 7 62
(R Hollinshead) *trckd ldr: racd keenly: chal 3f out: wknd fnl f* **8/1**
2-10 **8** *½* **John Charles (IRE)**[29] 641 4-9-3 **68** .... LPKeniry 10 62
(D R C Elsworth) *hld up: nvr nrr* **20/1**
1604 **9** *¾* **Mister Benji**[19] 736 7-8-10 **61** .... DeanMcKeown 2 54
(B P J Baugh) *hld up in tch: rdn over 3f out: wknd over 2f out* **28/1**
6063 **10** *nk* **Secam (POL)**[10] 854 7-8-4 **55** oh2 ....(b) FrancisNorton 9 47
(Mrs P Townsley) *hld up: a in rr* **25/1**
2400 **11** *shd* **Just Fly**[17] 764 6-9-1 **69** ....(v) RichardThomas(3) 6 61
(Dr J R J Naylor) *hld up in tch: rdn and wknd over 2f out* **12/1**
546U **12** *1½* **Monte Mayor Boy**[48] 504 4-8-13 **64** ....(v) RobertHavlin 13 53
(D Haydn Jones) *s.s: hld up: hdwy over 3f out: rdn and wknd over 1f out* **28/1**
410- **13** *17* **Ferrara Flame (IRE)**[270] 3299 4-8-8 **59** .... PaulHanagan 1 12
(R Brotherton) *bhd fr 1/2-way* **66/1**

1m 49.88s (-1.88) **Going Correction** -0.15s/f (Stan) 13 Ran SP% **117.6**
Speed ratings (Par 103):102,101,99,95,95 95,94,94,93,93 93,92,77
CSF £12.39 CT £126.97 TOTE £2.90: £1.40, £2.20, £3.50; EX 19.00 Trifecta £109.40 Pool: £635.17 - 4.12 winning tickets..
Owner R C Bond **Bred** Seamus Phelan **Trained** Hambleton, N Yorks
■ Stewards' Enquiry : N Callan two-day ban: careless riding (Apr 24-25)
FOCUS
They did not seem to go a great pace here, despite the winning time being almost two seconds quicker than the opening amateur riders' event, and the race developed into something of a sprint from the home bend. Even so, not that many got into it.
Secam(POL) Official explanation: jockey said gelding was denied a clear run in home straight

1003 NAME A RACE TO ENHANCE YOUR BRAND (S) STKS 5f 20y(P)
3:40 (3:40) (Class 6) 3-Y-O **£2,388** (£705; £352) **Stalls** Low

Form RPR
030- **1** **Twinned (IRE)**[138] 6433 3-8-12 65 ....(p) JohnEgan 2 65
(J S Moore) *chsd ldr: led over 3f out: rdn clr over 1f out: jst hld on* **9/4**[1]
5012 **2** *nk* **Diktalex (IRE)**[6] 907 3-8-6 60 ....(t) MarkCoumbe(7) 1 65
(C J Teague) *sn outpcd: hdwy u.p over 1f out: r.o wl* **11/2**[3]
066 **3** *1¾* **Spirit Of Coniston**[33] 626 3-8-12 52 ....(p) DarryllHolland 4 58
(M Wellings) *led: hdd over 3f out: outpcd over 1f out: edgd lft and styd on ins fnl f* **7/1**
400- **4** *5* **Penny Thoughts**[138] 6433 3-8-7 52 .... RichardMullen 7 35
(E S McMahon) *s.i.s: hdwy over 3f out: rdn and wknd over 1f out* **12/1**
0651 **5** *hd* **Titus Wonder (IRE)**[3] 936 3-8-6 45 .... KevinGhunowa(7) 6 40
(P A Blockley) *chsd ldrs over 3f* **13/2**
5000 **6** *hd* **Luloah**[6] 910 3-8-6 57 .... DonnaCaldwell(7) 3 40
(P S McEntee) *prom over 3f* **16/1**
2643 **7** *7* **Otis B Driftwood**[6] 910 3-9-4 60 ....(p) FrancisNorton 5 19
(M Quinn) *chsd ldrs: rdn 1/2-way: wknd over 1f out* **4/1**[2]
000- **8** *½* **Wizard Prince**[130] 6496 3-8-12 50 ....(b) AdrianMcCarthy 9 12
(R A Harris) *sn outpcd* **20/1**

62.60 secs (-0.22) **Going Correction** -0.15s/f (Stan) 8 Ran SP% **108.5**
Speed ratings (Par 96):95,94,91,83,83 83,71,71
CSF £13.14 TOTE £3.20: £1.10, £1.60, £2.40; EX 10.40 Trifecta £43.60 Pool: £702.74 - 11.43 winning tickets..There was no bid for the winner. Spirit of Coniston was claimed by P. M. Grayson for £6,000.
Owner A D Crook **Bred** Philip Hore Jnr **Trained** Upper Lambourn, Berks
FOCUS
An ordinary seller, dominated by the pair that were best in at the weights and who started from the two inside stalls, though that does not tell the whole story.
Spirit Of Coniston Official explanation: jockey said colt hung left

1004 STAY AT THE WOLVERHAMPTON HOLIDAY INN H'CAP 7f 32y(P)
4:10 (4:10) (Class 5) (0-75,75) 3-Y-O **£3,238** (£963; £481; £240) **Stalls** High

Form RPR
5212 **1** **Danetime Lord (IRE)**[13] 819 3-8-6 **63** ow1 ....(p) NCallan 1 79
(K A Ryan) *chsd ldrs: led over 1f out: r.o wl* **5/2**[1]
355- **2** *5* **Cape Diamond (IRE)**[229] 4750 3-9-2 **73** .... SebSanders 5 76
(W R Swinburn) *s.i.s: hld up: hdwy over 2f out: nt clr run over 1f out : styd on: no ch w wnr* **11/2**[2]
00-2 **3** *¾* **Dasheena**[10] 851 3-8-5 **62** .... MartinDwyer 2 63
(M J Polglase) *led: rdn: edgd rt and hdd over 1f out: sn outpcd* **16/1**
635- **4** *3½* **Orange Dancer (IRE)**[176] 5969 3-8-13 **70** .... SteveDrowne 3 62
(H Morrison) *chsd ldrs: rdn over 2f out: wknd over 1f out* **6/1**[3]
020- **5** *1* **Musical Romance (IRE)**[139] 6420 3-8-10 **67** .... MichaelTebbutt 4 56
(B J Meehan) *hld up: hdwy over 2f out: rdn and wknd over 1f out* **25/1**
40-6 **6** *¾* **Sgt Schultz (IRE)**[21] 702 3-8-13 **70** .... RobertWinston 11 57
(J S Moore) *s.s: bhd: hung lft over 1f out: styd on ins fnl f: nvr nrr* **12/1**
53-0 **7** *nk* **Bacharach (IRE)**[100] 19 3-8-11 **68** .... FrancisNorton 6 55
(R F Fisher) *prom: chsd ldr 1/2-way: rdn and wknd over 1f out* **33/1**

-054 **8** *nk* **Peter Island (FR)**[14] [807] 3-8-9 **66** ow2 .... DarryllHolland 8 52
(J Gallagher) *prom: rdn over 2f out: wknd over 1f out* **9/1**

1 **9** *¾* **Swiper Hill (IRE)**[19] [722] 3-9-4 **75** .... DaneO'Neill 7 59
(B Ellison) *hld up: rdn over 2f out: n.d* **6/1**[3]

3116 **10** *5* **Prettilini**[43] [550] 3-9-1 **72** .... TonyCulhane 10 43
(P Howling) *a in rr* **25/1**

150- **11** *dist* **Il Castagno (IRE)**[153] [6309] 3-9-1 **72** .... KDarley 12 —
(B Smart) *chsd ldr to 1/2-way: wknd and eased over 2f out* **11/1**

1m 30.02s (-0.38) **Going Correction** -0.15s/f (Stan) 11 Ran SP% **115.1**
Speed ratings (Par 98):96,90,89,85,84 83,83,82,81,76 —
CSF £14.82 CT £179.56 TOTE £3.00: £1.20, £2.80, £4.00; EX 22.70 Trifecta £146.70 Pool: £553.81 - 2.68 winning tickets..
Owner Bull & Bell Partnership **Bred** P J Murphy **Trained** Hambleton, N Yorks

FOCUS
This looked like quite a fair handicap for the grade but Danetime Lord, having just his second run over seven furlongs, showed improved form to win well.
Sgt Schultz(IRE) Official explanation: jockey said gelding missed break and lost a shoe

1005 TO SPONSOR A RACE CALL 0870 220 2442 H'CAP 1m 1f 103y(P)
4:40 (4:40) (Class 5) (0-75,75) 3-Y-O **£3,238** (£963; £481; £240) **Stalls** Low

Form RPR

0-11 **1** **Royal Amnesty**[13] [822] 3-8-8 **65** .... OscarUrbina 3 68
(G C H Chung) *hld up: hdwy over 2f out: nt clr run over 1f out: rdn and edgd lft ins fnl f: r.o to ld nr fin* **9/2**[2]

5-13 **2** *hd* **Go Figure (IRE)**[10] [855] 3-9-3 **74** .... ChrisCatlin 4 77
(B J Meehan) *chsd ldrs: rdn to ld wl ins fnl f: hdd nr fin* **9/2**[2]

-443 **3** *¾* **Mambo Sun**[40] [583] 3-8-8 **65** .... PaulHanagan 1 67
(P A Blockley) *hld up: hdwy over 2f out: rdn to ld 1f out: hdd wl ins fnl f* **6/1**[3]

0-24 **4** *½* **Markington**[19] [731] 3-9-2 **73** .... GrahamGibbons 2 74
(J D Bethell) *hld up: hdwy and nt clr run over 1f out: r.o: nt rch ldrs* **12/1**

-321 **5** *½* **Manouche**[13] [817] 3-8-8 **65** ....(p) NCallan 8 65
(K A Ryan) *chsd ldrs: led 2f out: rdn and hdd 1f out: styng on same pce whn hmpd wl ins fnl f* **4/1**[1]

104- **6** *shd* **Truly Fruitful (IRE)**[236] [4579] 3-9-1 **72** .... PatCosgrave 9 71
(K R Burke) *chsd ldrs: rdn and hung lft over 1f out: sn ev ch: styng on same pce whn hmpd wl ins fnl f* **20/1**

-162 **7** *3* **Magical Music**[13] [822] 3-8-13 **70** .... JimmyQuinn 11 64
(J Pearce) *hld up: hdwy 1/2-way: rdn and wknd fnl f* **10/1**

6252 **8** *3* **Blanc Visage**[13] [823] 3-8-8 **70** .... RichardKingscote(5) 7 58
(Mrs H Sweeting) *led over 7f: wknd fnl f* **33/1**

010- **9** *2½* **Razed**[159] [6249] 3-9-4 **75** .... JoeFanning 5 58
(M Johnston) *trckd ldrs: rdn over 2f out: wknd wl over 1f out* **8/1**

2-10 **10** *5* **Mystified (IRE)**[20] [712] 3-8-9 **69** ow1 ....(b) DNolan(3) 10 43
(R F Fisher) *hld up: rdn and wknd over 2f out* **33/1**

40-0 **11** *5* **Grand Cherokee (IRE)**[19] [730] 3-8-7 **64** ....(p) TomEaves 6 28
(B Ellison) *prom: rdn and lost pl 4f out: wknd over 2f out* **100/1**

-243 **12** *6* **Mae Cigan (FR)**[16] [781] 3-8-4 **61** oh1 .... FrancisNorton 12 14
(M Blanshard) *hld up: rdn 1/2-way: wknd over 2f out* **12/1**

2m 1.39s (-1.23) **Going Correction** -0.15s/f (Stan) 12 Ran SP% **117.9**
Speed ratings (Par 98):99,98,98,97,97 97,94,91,89,85 80,75
CSF £24.08 CT £123.79 TOTE £4.70: £1.70, £2.70, £2.20; EX 32.20 Trifecta £314.40 Pool: £571.28 - 1.29 winning tickets..
Owner G C H Chung **Bred** Brick Kiln Stud, Mrs L Hicks And Partners **Trained** Newmarket, Suffolk
■ Stewards' Enquiry : Oscar Urbina two-day ban: careless riding (Apr 24-25)

FOCUS
A fair handicap.

1006 RINGSIDE SUITE 700 THEATRE STYLE CONFERENCE MAIDEN STKS 1m 4f 50y(P)
5:10 (5:11) (Class 5) 3-Y-O+ **£3,238** (£963; £481; £240) **Stalls** Low

Form RPR

/52- **1** **Arbella**[220] [4993] 4-9-7 80 .... SebSanders 2 84
(W R Swinburn) *led 1f: chsd ldr tl led over 3f out: clr 2f out: styd on wl* **11/4**[2]

2- **2** *6* **Fyvie**[152] [6318] 3-8-1 .... MartinDwyer 3 72
(E A L Dunlop) *hld up in tch: rdn over 2f out: styd on same pce fnl 2f* **15/8**[1]

23 **3** *hd* **Sweet Medicine**[26] [669] 4-9-7 .... TonyCulhane 1 74
(P Howling) *prom: chsd wnr over 3f out: sn rdn: styd on same pce fnl 2f* **11/2**

0-26 **4** *nk* **Raslan**[9] [863] 3-8-6 .... JoeFanning 11 77
(M Johnston) *hld up: effrt over 3f out: outpcd over 2f out: styd on ins fnl f* **5/1**[3]

/42- **5** *12* **My Putra (USA)**[326] [1921] 4-9-12 79 .... NCallan 7 59
(P F I Cole) *hld up: hdwy over 3f out: rdn and wknd 2f out* **10/1**

6 *6* **Dreams Jewel**[140] 6-9-13 .... CraigCarver 8 50
(C Roberts) *s.s: hdwy over 3f out: wknd over 2f out* **125/1**

5-3 **7** *10* **Tara King**[82] [166] 4-9-7 .... SamHitchcott 4 29
(A B Haynes) *led after 1f: rdn and hdd over 3f out: wknd over 2f out* **40/1**

00 **8** *8* **Khadija**[48] [503] 5-9-1 .... JohnPritchard(7) 5 16
(R Dickin) *hld up: a in rr* **125/1**

00 **9** *hd* **Datznyce (IRE)**[40] [584] 3-7-10 .... MarcHalford(5) 10 14
(D R C Elsworth) *hld up: bhd fnl 7f* **66/1**

10 *3* **Sheikh Shakey** 5-9-13 .... DaneO'Neill 12 16
(R Hannon) *hld up: rdn 7f out: hdwy and hung rt over 4f out: wknd over 3f out* **50/1**

3 **11** *2½* **Dubai Sunday (JPN)**[6] [909] 5-9-13 .... RobertWinston 9 12
(P S McEntee) *chsd ldrs 9f* **16/1**

12 *dist* **Terrys Alfie** 3-8-1 .... JamesDoyle(5) 6 —
(N P Littmoden) *chsd ldrs over 7f* **33/1**

2m 37.99s (-4.43) **Going Correction** -0.15s/f (Stan)
WFA 3 from 4yo 21lb 4 from 5yo+ 1lb 12 Ran SP% **118.9**
Speed ratings (Par 103):108,104,103,103,95 91,85,79,79,77 75,—
CSF £8.16 TOTE £5.10: £1.30, £1.30, £2.60; EX 10.40 Trifecta £69.70 Pool: £478.12 - 4.87 winning tickets. Place 6 £15.44, Place 5 £7.24.
Owner Mrs P W Harris **Bred** Pendley Farm **Trained** Aldbury, Herts

FOCUS
Not a bad maiden in which the once 98-rated Arbella finally got off the mark. She recorded a decent time for a race of this class in the process.
Datznyce(IRE) Official explanation: jockey said filly hung right
Sheikh Shakey Official explanation: jockey said gelding hung
Dubai Sunday(JPN) Official explanation: jockey said gelding stopped very quickly 3f out
T/Plt: £18.10 to a £1 stake. Pool: £53,879.00. 2,164.45 winning tickets. T/Qpdt: £6.00 to a £1 stake. Pool: £4,374.10. 534.90 winning tickets. CR

1007 - 1013a (Foreign Racing) - See Raceform Interactive

BREMEN
Friday, April 14

OFFICIAL GOING: Soft

1014a ALBERS GERMAN TURF OPEN 2006 - GROSSER PREIS DER BREMER WIRTSCHAFT (GROUP 3) 1m 3f
4:15 (4:21) 4-Y-O+ **£22,069** (£6,897; £3,448; £2,069)

RPR

1 **Birkspiel (GER)**[173] [6050] 5-8-11 .... DarryllHolland 5 106
(S Dow) *raced in 3rd, led 4f out to over 3f out, 2nd straight, led again approaching final f, ridden out* **38/10**[2]

2 *2½* **Bailamos (GER)**[173] [6050] 6-8-11 .... FilipMinarik 4 102
(P Schiergen, Germany) *held up, close 6th straight, stayed on steadily to take 2nd isnide final f* **116/10**

3 *1½* **Laredo Sound (IRE)**[230] 4-8-9 .... J-PCarvalho 3 98
(Mario Hofer, Germany) *close up in 4th, led over 3f out to over 2f out, dropped back to 4th, rallied to regain 3rd well inside final f* **58/10**[3]

4 *nk* **Near Honor (GER)**[173] [6050] 8-8-11 .... APietsch 8 99
(P Vovcenko, Germany) *midfield, 4th straight, 5th 1f out, stayed on under pressure to regain 4th close home* **156/10**

5 *1½* **Soldier Hollow**[159] [6278] 6-9-4 .... WMongil 7 104
(P Schiergen, Germany) *held up, hdwy to go 3rd straight, led narrowly travelling strongly over 2f out, hdd appr fnl f, wknd* **7/10**[1]

6 *7* **One Little David (GER)**[49] [512] 6-8-9 .... ASuborics 1 84
(P Vovcenko, Germany) *held up, 5th straight, soon ridden and beaten* **61/10**

7 *3* **Palais Tiff (GER)**[202] [5482] 7-8-9 .... JPalik 10 79
(Frau M Fechner, Germany) *pushed along from outside draw to lead after 1f, set strong pace, headed 4f out, weakened* **323/10**

8 *dist* **Mick Jerome (IRE)**[131] 5-8-9 .... AHelfenbein 6 —
(Rune Haugen, Norway) *always in rear, tailed off final 3f* **364/10**

9 *13* **Alpino Chileno (ARG)**[215] [5164] 7-9-0 ....(b) CLopez 2 —
(Rune Haugen, Norway) *raced in 2nd til weakened rapidly over 4f out, soon tailed off* **313/10**

2m 30.51s 9 Ran SP% **131.2**
WIN (including 10 Euro stake): 48; PL 19, 26, 26; SF 421.
Owner Miss Helen Chamberlain **Bred** Dr F Feldmann **Trained** Epsom, Surrey

NOTEBOOK
Birkspiel(GER), who was previously trained by Andreas Wohler, made a successful debut for his new stable, and can take plenty of credit for regaining the lead after being headed.

886 KEMPTON (A.W) (R-H)
Saturday, April 15

OFFICIAL GOING: Standard
Wind: Fresh, half behind Weather: Overcast

1015 THE SPORTSMAN FILLIES' STKS (REGISTERED AS THE SNOWDROP FILLIES' STAKES) (LISTED RACE) 1m (P)
2:10 (2:11) (Class 1) 4-Y-O+
£15,898 (£6,025; £3,015; £1,503; £753; £378) **Stalls** High

Form RPR

023- **1** **Royal Alchemist**[161] [6253] 4-8-12 103 .... MartinDwyer 8 98
(M D I Usher) *prom: led 1f out: drvn out* **9/2**[2]

202- **2** *½* **Violet Park**[168] [6146] 5-8-12 88 .... RichardHughes 6 97
(B J Meehan) *s.i.s: hld up and bhd: rdn and gd hdwy fnl 2f: nt rch wnr* **13/2**

1412 **3** *1¼* **Nice Tune**[13] [843] 4-8-12 85 .... RyanMoore 2 94
(C E Brittain) *sn towards rr: rdn and hdwy over 2f out: kpt on fnl f* **7/1**

124- **4** *hd* **Three Wrens (IRE)**[119] [6601] 4-8-12 84 .... ShaneKelly 1 94
(D J Daly) *lw: trckd ldrs: led 2f out tl 1f out: one pce* **13/2**

100- **5** *3½* **Salamanca**[167] [6181] 4-9-1 96 .... JimmyFortune 10 88
(S Kirk) *bit bkwd: hld up towards rr: swtchd to ins and hdwy 2f out: one pce* **10/1**

054- **6** *hd* **Heat Of The Night**[267] [3688] 4-8-12 88 .... AlanMunro 7 85
(P W Chapple-Hyam) *mid-div: effrt over 2f out: btn over 1f out* **14/1**

1326 **7** *1½* **Kindlelight Debut**[23] [704] 6-8-12 86 .... JamesDoyle 5 82
(N P Littmoden) *hld up in rr: rdn over 2f out: n.d* **25/1**

520- **8** *1½* **Bon Nuit (IRE)**[209] [5347] 4-9-1 102 .... SteveDrowne 9 81
(G Wragg) *b.hind: bit bkwd: prom early: settled in tch: outpcd fnl 2f* **4/1**[1]

5200 **9** *5* **Elrafa Mujahid**[9] [898] 4-8-12 69 ....(b) SaleemGolam 3 67
(Ernst Oertel) *b: prom: chsd ldr after 3f tl over 2f out: wknd wl over 1f out* **66/1**

202- **10** *7* **Quadrupa (GER)**[188] [5785] 4-8-12 .... LDettori 4 51
(C Von Der Recke, Germany) *angular: led tl wknd rapidly 2f out* **11/2**[3]

1m 38.77s (-3.21) **Going Correction** +0.075s/f (Slow) 10 Ran SP% **113.8**
Speed ratings (Par 108):113,112,111,111,107 107,105,104,99,92
CSF £33.00 TOTE £5.90: £1.60, £2.80, £2.50; EX 44.70.
Owner The Ridgeway Partnership **Bred** B Minty **Trained** Upper Lambourn, Berks

FOCUS
By no means strong Listed form, and Royal Alchemist did not need to reproduce her three-year-old form in order to win.

NOTEBOOK
Royal Alchemist, who looked fit for this reappearance and goes well fresh, won for the first time in two years but had every right to do so, since she had the highest official rating in the field. She got first run on Violet Park, but for which the result might have been different, but it confirmed that she goes well when fresh. (op 5-1 tchd 11-2 in a place)
Violet Park, under a patient ride, ran on really well but had been set just a bit too much to do. She ended last season on a high note, and this encouraging seasonal debut suggests she has trained on well enough to expect a fourth success before long. (tchd 7-1)
Nice Tune made a creditable step up to Listed company. She is in fine form at present, but did have a fitness advantage over many of here rivals here. (op 9-1)
Three Wrens(IRE) did well in handicaps last season and looked completely at home in this higher grade, even appearing set to win the race at one stage. She seems likely to have a good season and is worth another crack at Listed company. (op 7-1)
Salamanca proved she was up to winning in Listed company last season, albeit in a handicap. That gave her a 3lb penalty here, but the extra weight was not the difference between victory and defeat.

Heat Of The Night, on her toes beforehand, had a stone to find at the weights, so just about ran her race. She needs to improve a bit more to make the step from good handicap performer to Listed winner.
Kindlelight Debut was a shade outclassed, and looks set for return to handicaps. (tchd 28-1)
Bon Nuit(IRE) was well below her best. From a stable which has been doing reasonably well in recent weeks, she was running for the first time on Polytrack and still needs to prove herself on the surface.
Elrafa Mujahid Official explanation: trainer said filly bled from the nose
Quadrupa(GER), second in last year's German 1000 Guineas, looked fit and is happiest in front, but she overdid it and folded quickly when headed. Official explanation: vet said filly returned lame behind (op 7-2)

1016 THE SPORTSMAN LONDON MILE QUALIFIER H'CAP 1m (P)

2:45 (2:46) (Class 3) (0-90,90) 3-Y-O

£11,217 (£3,358; £1,679; £840; £419; £210) **Stalls** High

Form RPR

115- **1** **Archerfield Links (USA)**[184] 5852 3-8-13 **85** .... LDettori 3 93
(N A Callaghan) *hld up in rr: gd hdwy 2f out: qcknd wl to ld ins fnl f: readily* **11/1**

65-2 **2** ¾ **Scot Love (IRE)**[21] 720 3-8-7 **79** ow1 .... ShaneKelly 14 85
(J Noseda) *t.k.h: chsd ldrs: rdn 3f out: kpt on fnl f* **8/1**[2]

321- **3** ½ **Bomber Command (USA)**[159] 6284 3-8-9 **81** .... MichaelHills 6 86
(J W Hills) *hld up in rr: hdwy over 2f out: swtchd rt over 1f out: styd on* **9/1**[3]

11-2 **4** nk **Namid Reprobate (IRE)**[13] 848 3-8-7 **82** .... NelsonDeSouza(3) 12 86
(P F I Cole) *lw: led 1f: w ldrs after: nt qckn fnl f* **9/1**[3]

315- **5** 3 **Call My Number (IRE)**[224] 4942 3-8-9 **81** .... TedDurcan 15 78
(M R Channon) *bit bkwd: prom: led on far rail over 1f out: hdd and no ex ins fnl f* **16/1**

221- **6** nk **Yarqus**[183] 5864 3-8-13 **85** .... RyanMoore 9 81
(C E Brittain) *bit bkwd: sn pushed along towards rr: styd on fnl 2f: nvr nrr* **10/1**

104- **7** 1½ **Ans Bach**[199] 5557 3-9-4 **90** ....(p) PhilipRobinson 1 83
(M A Jarvis) *led after 1f tl wknd over 1f out* **20/1**

601- **8** nk **Participation**[190] 5711 3-9-0 **86** ....(vt[1]) JimmyFortune 10 78
(M J Wallace) *in rr tl hrd rdn and styd on fnl 2f* **12/1**

213- **9** ¾ **Mutamarres**[182] 5887 3-8-12 **84** .... RHills 5 75
(Sir Michael Stoute) *hld up in rr of midfield: rdn and hdwy 2f out: no imp* **8/1**[2]

-311 **10** 2 **Ludovico**[14] 831 3-9-2 **88** .... NCallan 4 74
(K A Ryan) *chsd ldrs tl rdn and outpcd fnl 2f* **8/1**[2]

-211 **11** 2½ **Trans Sonic**[13] 848 3-8-10 **82** .... DarrenWilliams 8 62
(A P Jarvis) *t.k.h in rr of midfield: hmpd and dropped to rr ent st: n.d after* **7/1**[1]

250- **12** shd **Mujood**[198] 5570 3-8-10 **82** .... StephenCarson 2 62
(R F Johnson Houghton) *stdd s: hld up in rr: rdn and nt trble ldrs fnl 2f* **66/1**

03-5 **13** ¾ **Ocean Pride (IRE)**[9] 895 3-8-13 **85** .... RichardHughes 11 63
(R Hannon) *mid-div: effrt over 2f out: sn outpcd* **14/1**

1000 **14** nk **Grand Jour (IRE)**[7] 914 3-9-1 **87** .... DarrylHolland 7 65
(K McAuliffe) *t.k.h: in tch tl wknd 3f out* **25/1**

55-2 **15** 1¼ **Charlton**[22] 717 3-9-4 **90** .... IanMongan 13 65
(T G Mills) *lw: chsd ldrs: rdn 1/2-way: wknd over 2f out* **14/1**

510- **16** nk **Scarlet Flyer (USA)**[183] 5871 3-8-7 **79** .... TPQueally 16 53
(G L Moore) *b. nr hind: in tch tl wknd 2f out* **33/1**

1m 39.61s (-2.37) **Going Correction** +0.075s/f (Slow) **16** Ran SP% **123.2**
Speed ratings (Par 102):108,107,106,106,103 103,101,101,100,98 96,96,95,94,93 93
CSF £93.75 CT £877.80 TOTE £11.80: £3.10, £2.40, £2.70, £2.70; EX 175.70 TRIFECTA Not won..
Owner Team Havana **Bred** Ben Sangster **Trained** Newmarket, Suffolk

FOCUS
A hot handicap with several progressive types, most notably the impressive winner. The first four, all of whom remain open to further improvement, made their efforts in the centre of the track and finished clear of the rest. The first home on the inside rail was Call My Number.

NOTEBOOK
Archerfield Links(USA) ◆ has the ability to quicken devastatingly off a good pace, the hallmark of a smart performer. He could head for the Britannia Stakes at Ascot, where his chance should not be underestimated, with a step up in grade on the cards in due course for this exciting youngster. (op 12-1)
Scot Love(IRE) ran a fine race in a competitive heat. Running for only the fourth time here, after being runner-up in maiden company in his previous race, he is capable of winning in decent handicap grade as he matures. (op 9-1)
Bomber Command(USA), who looked as though he would be better for run, arrived from the rear of the field along with the winner, and got the longer trip really well. He looks a handy handicapper in the making.
Namid Reprobate(IRE) did well, having been up with the pace all the way. Unlike several of his rivals, he had had a recent outing, but he looks a reliable sort and has started the season in very good shape. (tchd 10-1)
Call My Number(IRE) was having having only his fourth outing and this was a promising start to the season. He needs to improve a bit to have a winning chance in this kind of company, but - having been lightly raced to date - is probably capable of finding a bit.
Yarqus, from a stable in fine form, was carrying his fair share of weight considering his only success was in a Brighton maiden. Never quite laying up with any comfort, he gave the impression that ten furlongs would suit. (op 9-1)
Ans Bach bowled along in first-time cheekpieces but merely set the race up for the others. He showed he can win from the front last season, and there will be easier opportunities where he is able to dictate a more suitable tempo for himself. (op 16-1)
Participation was going on reasonably well at the finish, and should come on for the run. Official explanation: jockey said colt suffered interference on leaving stalls (op 16-1)
Ludovico found this competitive handicap a bit tougher than his previous two races, particularly from a 4lb higher mark. Forced to use his pace early from a wide draw, that was the final straw. (op 7-1)
Trans Sonic, with different tactics this time, looked as if he would be happier attempting to make all for the third time running and was already in trouble when being squeezed out turning for home. This run is best ignored. Official explanation: trainer had no explanation for the poor form shown (op 6-1)

1017 CORAL ROSEBERY STKS (HERITAGE H'CAP) 1m 2f (P)

3:15 (3:17) (Class 2) (0-105,105) 4-Y-O+

£31,160 (£9,330; £4,665; £2,335; £1,165; £585) **Stalls** High

Form RPR

0001 **1** **Kandidate**[23] 704 4-9-10 **105** ....(t) SebSanders 15 115
(C E Brittain) *lw: trckd ldng pair: led wl over 1f out: rdn out* **20/1**

114- **2** 1 **Rohaani (USA)**[210] 5309 4-9-2 **97** .... RHills 14 105
(Sir Michael Stoute) *rrd s: sn in tch: rdn over 2f out: kpt on to take 2nd nr fin* **7/2**[1]

1112 **3** nk **Young Mick**[14] 834 4-8-8 **89** ....(v) JimmyQuinn 9 97
(G G Margarson) *t.k.h in midfield: gd hdwy on ins rail to chse wnr over 1f out: nt qckn fnl 75 yds* **9/1**

0165 **4** ½ **Bravo Maestro (USA)**[23] 704 5-9-3 **103** .... JamesDoyle(5) 13 110
(N P Littmoden) *dwlt: hld up towards rr: rdn and r.o fnl 2f: nvr nrr* **20/1**

5261 **5** shd **Obrigado (USA)**[13] 843 6-8-7 **88** ow1 .... DarrylHolland 1 94
(W J Haggas) *lw: b.hind: stdd s: hld up and wl bhd: shkn up and sltly unbalanced ent st: gd late hdwy* **8/1**

316- **6** shd **Red Racketeer (USA)**[196] 5608 4-8-12 **93** .... LDettori 12 99
(E A L Dunlop) *bit bkwd: in tch: rdn over 2f out: kpt on fnl f* **9/2**[2]

4660 **7** ¾ **Boo**[28] 666 4-9-1 **96** ....(v) JohnEgan 6 101
(K R Burke) *towards rr: rdn 1/2-way: hdwy 2f out: one pce fnl f* **25/1**

600- **8** 2 **Profit's Reality (IRE)**[203] 5467 4-8-10 **91** ....(t) GrahamGibbons 5 92
(P A Blockley) *w ldr: led after 2f tl wknd wl over 1f out* **25/1**

0520 **9** nk **Realism (FR)**[21] 728 6-9-2 **97** .... PaulHanagan 10 97
(R A Fahey) *swtg: in tch: rdn and no hdwy fnl 2f* **25/1**

200/ **10** ¾ **Blue Sky Thinking (IRE)**[501] 6777 7-8-12 **93** .... PatCosgrave 8 92
(K R Burke) *warm: hld up towards rr: rdn 3f out: nt pce to chal* **66/1**

3402 **11** 3 **Royal Island (IRE)**[21] 728 4-9-4 **99** .... JoeFanning 11 92
(M Johnston) *chsd ldrs tl wknd 2f out* **7/1**[3]

100- **12** ½ **Artistic Style**[161] 6254 6-8-11 **92** .... TomEaves 2 84
(B Ellison) *fit: in tch: rdn 1/2-way: wknd over 2f out* **66/1**

30-2 **13** 7 **Divine Gift**[35] 629 5-8-12 **93** .... NCallan 7 72
(K A Ryan) *chsd ldrs tl wknd 3f out* **15/2**

006/ **14** 8 **Cherub (GER)**[90] 6-8-11 **92** ....(t) DaneO'Neill 4 56
(Jonjo O'Neill) *lw: a bhd* **66/1**

06-2 **15** 14 **Dunaskin (IRE)**[29] 572 6-8-11 **92** .... KDarley 16 29
(Karen McLintock) *lw: led 2f: pressed ldr after tl wknd qckly 4f out: eased whn wl btn over 2f out* **16/1**

00-0 **16** hd **Ringsider (IRE)**[43] 572 5-8-11 **92** ....(tp) NickyMackay 3 29
(G A Butler) *stood in stalls and lost 15 l: a t.o* **66/1**

2m 5.73s **Going Correction** +0.075s/f (Slow) **16** Ran SP% **118.7**
Speed ratings (Par 109):116,115,114,114,114 114,113,112,111,111 108,108,102,96,85 85
CSF £80.58 CT £689.81 TOTE £21.70: £3.20, £1.80, £1.90, £5.50; EX 113.50 Trifecta £1055.00 Part won. Pool £1486.00 - 0.70 winning units..
Owner A J Richards **Bred** Proton Partnership **Trained** Newmarket, Suffolk
■ The first running of this famous event on Polytrack.

FOCUS
A decent handicap, run at a good pace, in which high-drawn horses did particularly well. Solid form.

NOTEBOOK
Kandidate sat behind the two front-runners, always travelling comfortably, and finished the job off readily in the home straight. Unproven over this trip beforehand, he got it really well and can happily be campaigned at ten furlongs from now on.
Rohaani(USA) ◆, who has developed into a really powerful, rangy sort, got a bit warm beforehand and reared leaving the stalls, probably through a little over-enthusiasm, but he settled okay and came home well enough too. He still looks to be capable of winning off this kind of mark, and should have a good season. (op 3-1)
Young Mick continues in great nick, showing a fine burst of speed to get into contention before flattening a out a little near the finish. Upped in class here, he would not be out of place in similar events. (op 12-1)
Bravo Maestro(USA) is still doing well despite undergoing a steady rise in the handicap. He looks really at home over this trip nowadays, and stayed on well enough to suggest he might stay even farther.
Obrigado(USA) ◆ had the worst of the draw and did not appear ideally suited by the sharp nature of the track, but he also appeared to be given a lot to do. He can be rated significantly better than this, and would be one to consider closely next time. (tchd 9-1)
Red Racketeer(USA), after taking a little time to pick up early in the straight, was coming again near the finish, giving the impression that he would be sharper for the outing. He had a good time of it in 2006 and is capable of resuming the winning thread before long. (op 5-1 tchd 11-2 in places)
Boo defied his odds with a big effort, only just being run out of fourth place. He is running much better than his recent form figures seem to indicate. (op 33-1)
Profit's Reality(IRE) ran respectably on this seasonal debut despite helping to set a stiff early tempo.
Ringsider(IRE) threw away what chance he had by taking an age to exit the stalls. Official explanation: jockey said gelding missed the break

1018 THE SPORTSMAN MAGNOLIA STKS (LISTED RACE) 1m 2f (P)

3:45 (3:45) (Class 1) 4-Y-O+

£15,898 (£6,025; £3,015; £1,503; £753; £378) **Stalls** High

Form RPR

006- **1** **Simple Exchange (IRE)**[147] 6378 5-8-13 .... RobertWinston 3 109
(D K Weld, Ire) *trckd ldr: led 2f out: drvn out* **3/1**[2]

1-50 **2** ½ **Kew Green (USA)**[35] 629 8-9-2 105 .... DaneO'Neill 1 111
(P R Webber) *hld up in 4th: rdn to chse wnr 1f out: r.o: jst hld* **7/1**[3]

0053 **3** ¾ **Near Dock (GER)**[37] 621 5-8-13 .... JohnEgan 4 107
(K R Burke) *edgy: t.k.h in 5th: effrt 2f out: r.o to take 3rd ins fnl f* **16/1**

4-13 **4** 1 **Nayyir**[28] 666 8-8-13 107 .... LDettori 2 105
(G A Butler) *b.hind: lw: stdd s: hld up in rr: rdn 3f out: styd on appr fnl f: nt pce to chal* **1/1**[1]

0-40 **5** ½ **African Dream**[28] 666 5-8-13 100 .... JimmyQuinn 6 104
(J Noseda) *chsd ldng pair: rdn 2f out: one pce appr fnl f* **16/1**

500- **6** nk **Wunderwood (USA)**[161] 6254 7-8-13 105 .... SebSanders 5 103
(Lady Herries) *led tl 2f out: lost 2nd and no ex 1f out* **9/1**

2m 8.35s **Going Correction** +0.075s/f (Slow) **6** Ran SP% **109.3**
Speed ratings (Par 111):105,104,104,103,102 102
CSF £22.01 TOTE £4.50: £1.70, £3.00; EX 21.70.
Owner Sir Michael Smurfit **Bred** Moyglare Stud Farm Ltd **Trained** The Curragh, Co Kildare

FOCUS
In theory, well up to Listed standard, but the runners are not known for their consistency and the time was slow, so it remains to be seen how reliable the form With Nayyir frustrating yet again, Simple Exchange did not need to be at his best.

NOTEBOOK
Simple Exchange(IRE), who returned with pulled muscles when a gambled-on disappointment at York last June, got a nice tow along and was in the ideal position to strike when the leader finally gave way. However, it remains to be seen just how well this race will stand up as the season progresses. (op 7-2 tchd 11-4)
Kew Green(USA) made a brave attempt to concede the weight. He retains his form well despite advancing years. (op 4-1)
Near Dock(GER), who looked fit but was on his toes, took to the surface well and saw his race out creditably despite being too headstrong early on. (op 20-1)

Nayyir was a flop, failing to reproduce his unlucky effort in the Winter Derby or any number of high-class efforts in Group company over the years. A stronger pace would have helped, despite this trip being at the top end of his range. (op 11-10 tchd 6-5 in places)
African Dream ran as well as could have been expected, but this was a muddling race and the form is hard to be dogmatic about. (tchd 20-1)
Wunderwood(USA) is normally sharper for his first outing of the season, so this was a fair effort even though he eventually brought up the rear. (op 10-1 tchd 8-1)

1019 EUROPEAN BREEDERS FUND MAIDEN STKS 5f (P)
4:15 (4:16) (Class 4) 2-Y-O **£5,181** (£1,541; £770; £384) **Stalls** High

Form				RPR
6	**1**		**Beckenham's Secret**[23] 701 2-9-3 AlanMunro 1 (B R Millman) *lw: t.k.h: trckd ldr: led over 1f out: pushed out* **11/2**[3]	71
	2	½	**Suhayl Star (IRE)** 2-9-3 TedDurcan 3 (M R Channon) *w'like: leggy: lw: dwlt: hld up in rr: effrt and wd st: hung rt: r.o to take 2nd fnl 50 yds: green* **7/1**	69+
	3	½	**Monkey Glas (IRE)** 2-9-3 PatCosgrave 6 (K R Burke) *unf: scope: chsd ldrs: rdn 2f out: kpt on fnl f* **2/1**[1]	67+
	4	hd	**Riverside Dancer (USA)** 2-8-12 NCallan 4 (K A Ryan) *unf: s.s: hld up in 5th: hdwy on ins 2f out: wnt 2nd ins fnl f: one pce* **9/4**[2]	61+
	5	1	**Dear One (IRE)** 2-8-12 GrahamGibbons 5 (P A Blockley) *w'like: bit bkwd: t.k.h: in tch: rdn and rn green over 1f out: one pce* **12/1**	57
0	**6**	2	**Chip Leader**[5] 944 2-9-3 RichardHughes 2 (R Hannon) *w'like: bit bkwd: led tl over 1f out: no ex fnl f* **13/2**	54

63.10 secs **Going Correction** +0.075s/f (Slow) **6** Ran SP% **113.0**
Speed ratings (Par 94):81,80,79,79,77 74
CSF £41.90 TOTE £7.10: £2.20, £2.90; EX 27.00.
Owner The Club Beckenham Partnership **Bred** Mrs D Brown And Mrs P Barclay **Trained** Kentisbeare, Devon

FOCUS
Not much to go on here, but a suspicion that the form is ordinary.

NOTEBOOK
Beckenham's Secret knew more about the game this time, winning with a little in hand. As he learns to settle better, he should improve, and more success is on the cards. (op 9-2)
Suhayl Star(IRE) ◆, a 54,000euros yearling, was all at sea on the home turn - a tough test for a first-time-out juvenile. There is plenty more to come, and victory at the second time of asking would be no surprise following this unlucky debut. (op 13-2 tchd 15-2)
Monkey Glas(IRE), a son of Mull of Kintyre, shaped with credit on this debut. He is capable of winning a similar event. (op 9-4 tchd 5-2 in places)
Riverside Dancer(USA)who looked fit but slightly dull in her coat, has a speedy pedigree but was ridden with restraint on this debut. She should soon be adding to the long list of family successes. (op 5-2 tchd 11-4)
Dear One(IRE) ran respectably considering she is likely to improve over longer trips in due course. Like her sire, the great middle-distance performer Montjeu, she tended to carry her head a shade high but that may just be an inherited characteristic. Official explanation: jockey said filly's bit slipped (tchd 14-1)
Chip Leader showed even more early speed than he had on his debut, and was not knocked about when beaten. He is not quite getting home at present, but may be one for nurseries as he matures. (tchd 7-1)

1020 DAY TIME, NIGHT TIME, GREAT TIME H'CAP 5f (P)
4:50 (5:00) (Class 2) (0-105,99) 3-Y-O
£11,217 (£3,358; £1,679; £840; £419; £210) **Stalls** High

Form				RPR
5-21	**1**		**Total Impact**[31] 645 3-8-4 82 MartinDwyer 4 (C A Cyzer) *lw: mde all: hrd rdn fnl f: hld on wl* **7/1**[3]	91
312-	**2**	hd	**Prince Tamino**[173] 6071 3-8-3 81 JoeFanning 1 (H Morrison) *wd: in tch: effrt 2f out: r.o to press wnr fnl 100 yds: jst hld* **11/2**[2]	90
5-13	**3**	1	**Stoneacre Lad (IRE)**[40] 593 3-8-5 83 (b) RobertWinston 3 (Peter Grayson) *w ldr: rn v wd home turn and c to stands' rail: remained prom: kpt on fnl f* **12/1**	88
116-	**4**	nk	**Come Out Fighting**[175] 6020 3-8-13 91 GrahamGibbons 10 (P A Blockley) *lw: a.p: nt qckn fnl f* **9/2**[1]	95
1211	**5**	1 ¼	**Stoneacre Boy (IRE)**[16] 807 3-8-4 82 (b) RobbieFitzpatrick 12 (Peter Grayson) *pressed ldrs tl no ex fnl f* **9/2**[1]	81
04-3	**6**	1 ½	**Phantom Whisper**[21] 725 3-8-4 82 AlanMunro 9 (B R Millman) *t.k.h in rr: rdn and styd on fnl 2f: nt rch ldrs* **8/1**	76
022-	**7**	shd	**Brandywell Boy (IRE)**[154] 6320 3-8-9 87 TQuinn 11 (D J S Ffrench Davis) *towards rr: hdwy and in tch 2f out: no ex fnl f* **10/1**	81
456-	**8**	½	**Clare Hills (IRE)**[210] 5286 3-9-7 99 PatCosgrave 5 (K R Burke) *swtg: mid-div: effrt and hung rt over 1f out: no imp* **12/1**	91
312-	**9**	shd	**Grantley Adams**[199] 5557 3-8-13 94 EdwardCreighton(3) 7 (M R Channon) *s.s: bhd: shkn up 2f out: nvr rchd ldrs* **11/1**	86
220-	**10**	1 ½	**Azygous**[154] 6320 3-8-7 85 JimmyQuinn 6 (J Akehurst) *lw: prom 3f* **16/1**	71
000-	**11**	1 ½	**Supercast (IRE)**[189] 5732 3-8-7 85 JohnEgan 8 (J S Moore) *bit bkwd: chsd ldrs over 3f* **16/1**	66
300-	**12**	1 ¾	**Waterline Twenty (IRE)**[189] 5732 3-8-5 83 PaulHanagan 2 (P D Evans) *sn outpcd and bhd* **33/1**	57

59.78 secs **Going Correction** +0.075s/f (Slow) **12** Ran SP% **122.9**
Speed ratings (Par 104):107,106,105,104,102 100,100,99,99,96 94,91
CSF £47.07 CT £360.92 TOTE £10.20: £3.00, £2.70, £2.40; EX 61.20.
Owner Mrs Charles Cyzer **Bred** C A Cyzer **Trained** Maplehurst, W Sussex

FOCUS
A competitive handicap with a number of future winners in the line-up. A race worth taking a positive view of.

NOTEBOOK
Total Impact made a successful step up to handicap company. Though only just scrambling home, he was less experienced than most of his rivals and probably has a bit more improvement in him. (op 8-1)
Prince Tamino ◆ ran a blinder, particularly considering the terrible draw and the fact that he was not as hard ridden as the winner. Compensation awaits, either over this trip or an extra furlong, and this progressive sort is one to follow. (tchd 5-1 and 6-1)
Stoneacre Lad(IRE) ◆'s steering went haywire on the home turn, with his rider unable to stop him hanging wildly across the track. In the circumstances, it was a remarkable performance, and he will merit serious consideration when returning to one of the three left-handed all-weather courses. Official explanation: jockey said colt hung badly left (op 16-1 tchd 20-1 in a place)
Come Out Fighting, on his toes beforehand, made a solid seasonal debut. He has obviously trained on and should pay his way in decent handicaps. (op 11-2)
Stoneacre Boy(IRE) used his good draw to good effect, only to be run out of it late on. He continues in top form, but things will become more difficult for him from now on. (tchd 5-1)
Phantom Whisper has now run quite well in both his races this season, apparently recapturing some of his early two-year-old form. (tchd 9-1)
Brandywell Boy(IRE) had a useful pipe-opener and can be more competitive with the run behind him. (op 11-1)
Clare Hills(IRE) had a stiff task at the weights thanks to some high-class juvenile form last season. Even so, she was a bit disappointing and started to hang when attempting a forward move. (op 11-1)
Grantley Adams did not handle the turn out the back straight too well, maybe in part because he was a bit short of room. Though never looking like achieving a challenging position, he did give the impression that there is much better to come with this seasonal debut behind him. (op 12-1)

1021 QUEEN'S PRIZE (H'CAP) 2m (P)
5:25 (5:28) (Class 2) (0-105,100) 4-Y-O+
£11,217 (£3,358; £1,679; £840; £419; £210) **Stalls** High

Form				RPR
-451	**1**		**Cold Turkey**[29] 661 6-9-3 94 RyanMoore 8 (G L Moore) *hld up in rr: smooth hdwy 2f out: led 1f out: qcknd wl: comf* **5/2**[1]	97+
106-	**2**	1 ¾	**Valance (IRE)**[177] 4330 6-8-5 82 AlanMunro 6 (C R Egerton) *hdwy to chse ldrs after 5f: slt ld over 1f out: sn hdd and nt pce of wnr* **14/1**	83
3441	**3**	hd	**Champagne Shadow (IRE)**[40] 591 5-8-4 81 oh1 (b) PaulHanagan 7 (G L Moore) *hld up towards rr: gd hdwy to press ldrs 1f out: nt qckn fnl f* **12/1**	82
04-1	**4**	1 ½	**Establishment**[14] 832 9-8-4 81 oh5 MartinDwyer 9 (C A Cyzer) *trckd ldrs: rdn to join ldrs over 1f out: no ex fnl f* **6/1**[3]	80
0250	**5**	½	**High Point (IRE)**[14] 832 8-7-13 81 oh11 RobynBrisland(5) 4 (G P Enright) *in tch: effrt over 2f out: one pce appr fnl f* **33/1**	80
202-	**6**	5	**Hiddensee (USA)**[203] 5451 4-8-12 93 KDarley 2 (M Johnston) *bit bkwd: prom: wnt 2nd 1/2-way: wknd over 1f out: eased whn btn ins fnl f* **4/1**[2]	86
453/	**7**	½	**Akritas**[631] 4075 5-8-7 84 RichardHughes 11 (P F I Cole) *b.hind: hld up towards rr: shkn up over 2f out: nvr rchd ldrs* **12/1**	76
/21-	**8**	1 ¾	**Michabo (IRE)**[317] 2240 5-8-8 85 SteveDrowne 3 (H Morrison) *led and racd freely: restrained in front and dictated modest pce: hdd & wknd over 1f out* **9/1**	75
400/	**9**	4	**Savannah Bay**[193] 3076 7-9-9 100 TomEaves 10 (B Ellison) *mid-div: rdn along 5f out: n.d fnl 3f* **33/1**	85
402-	**10**	1 ¼	**Fortune Island (IRE)**[133] 6133 7-9-2 93 (vt) JimmyFortune 5 (M C Pipe) *hld up in rr: hdwy on outside 6f out: wknd over 3f out* **10/1**	77
42-3	**11**	1 ¾	**Spear Thistle**[19] 765 4-8-0 86 JamesDoyle(5) 1 (Mrs N Smith) *prom: drvn along fr 1/2-way: rdr lost whip 3f out: wknd 2f out* **10/1**	68

3m 31.02s **Going Correction** +0.075s/f (Slow)
WFA 4 from 5yo+ 4lb **11** Ran SP% **119.0**
Speed ratings (Par 109):103,102,102,101,101 98,98,97,95,94 93
CSF £40.98 CT £357.74 TOTE £2.80: £1.20, £4.30, £3.60; EX 53.50 Place 6 £788.58, Place 5 £311.05.
Owner A Grinter **Bred** Worksop Manor Stud **Trained** Woodingdean, E Sussex
■ The first running on sand of a race dating back to 1891.

FOCUS
A routine handicap for the money, run at a modest tempo, and won by Cold Turkey for the second year running - this time on Polytrack. The fourth and fifth were both racing from well out of the handicap, which limits the form.

NOTEBOOK
Cold Turkey was beautifully ridden to win this event for the second year running - though last year it was on turf. With the race going nicely to plan, and the gaps all opening at the right time, he scored stylishly. (op 3-1)
Valance(IRE), recent winner over fences at Ludlow, gave a reminder that he is also capable of winning on the Flat. Being beaten only by an impressive in-form rival must go down as a good performance. (op 12-1)
Champagne Shadow(IRE)'s stable has been in fine shape of late, and he kept up the good work with a sound effort in this decent handicap following his success in claiming company last time out. (op 14-1)
Establishment had been raised 8lb for his recent course-and-distance victory and was out of the proper handicap, and that more or less sealed his fate. However, he has started the season in good form.
High Point(IRE) had the headgear left off this time and was a long way out of the proper handicap. He did not run badly, though falling just a bit short of what was required in this company.
Hiddensee(USA) ran really well for a long way, and can do even better when his stable returns to form. Though unproven at this trip, he stayed a mile-and-three-quarters well last year, and a drop back to that distance is always an option. (op 7-2)
Akritas, given a quiet ride from the back, had been off the track since July 2004. He can build on this kind re-introduction if coming out of it in good shape. (op 14-1)
Michabo(IRE) should have been suited by being allowed a soft lead, so his sudden capitulation in the straight was disappointing. He ought to be capable of much better if allowed to have his own way again.
Fortune Island(IRE) was stuck wide all the way, and can do better as the season progresses. (op 9-1)
T/Plt: £506.00 to a £1 stake. Pool: £88,116.80. 127.10 winning tickets. T/Qpdt: £64.10 to a £1 stake. Pool: £4,877.85. 56.25 winning tickets. LM

1022 - (Foreign Racing) - See Raceform Interactive

LEOPARDSTOWN (L-H)
Saturday, April 15
OFFICIAL GOING: Yielding to soft

1023a DIMITROVA 1,000 GUINEAS TRIAL STKS (FILLIES) (GROUP 3) 7f
2:50 (2:50) 3-Y-O **£35,917** (£10,537; £5,020; £1,710)

			RPR
1		**Kamarinskaya (USA)**[181] 5926 3-9-0 103 JAHeffernan 6 (A P O'Brien, Ire) *mde virtually all: rdn st: clr fnl f: comf* **8/1**	105
2	2	**Beauty Bright (IRE)**[182] 5904 3-9-0 106 KFallon 1 (A P O'Brien, Ire) *hld up in tch: 6th appr st: 4th and hdwy 2f out: mod 2nd fnl f: kpt on u.p* **5/4**[1]	100
3	shd	**Ugo Fire (IRE)**[196] 5633 3-9-0 110 DPMcDonogh 2 (Kevin Prendergast, Ire) *trckd ldrs: 5th 1/2-way: prog on outer early st: 3rd over 1f out: kpt on same pce* **2/1**[2]	100
4	hd	**Mrs Snaffles (IRE)**[226] 4898 3-9-0 92 JMurtagh 4 (Francis Ennis, Ire) *settled 4th: 5th and rdn early st: kpt on ins fnl f* **9/1**	99?
5	¾	**Asaawir**[175] 6027 3-9-0 ChrisCatlin 7 (M R Channon) *dwlt: hld up: last and outpcd ent st: 5th over 1f out: r.o* **7/1**[3]	98

6 4 1/2 **Gist (IRE)**[267] 3719 3-9-0 ....(b[1]) NGMcCullagh 5 86?
(W J Martin, Ire) *sn cl up: 2nd 1/2-way: rdn to chal ent st: wknd under 2f out* **33/1**
7 3 **Chennai (IRE)**[238] 4594 3-9-0 83....................(t) KJManning 3 78
(J S Bolger, Ire) *hld up early: impr into 3rd 1/2-way: wknd u.p early st* **33/1**

1m 32.1s **Going Correction** +0.15s/f (Good) **7** Ran SP% **117.3**
Speed ratings: 106,103,103,103,102 97,93
CSF £19.30 TOTE £13.40: £4.40, £1.10; DF 13.30.
Owner M Tabor & Mrs John Magnier **Bred** Pacelco S A **Trained** Ballydoyle, Co Tipperary

NOTEBOOK
Kamarinskaya(USA), a half-sister to Fasliyev, was soon in front on settling down and proceeded to make all. She had them all stretched early in the straight and was still strong at the end. She has all the Guineas options and another furlong will not trouble her. (op 6/1)
Beauty Bright(IRE), stable companion of the winner and heavily supported, was held up. When she finally got her run over a furlong out the winner had flown. Her trainer suggested fast ground will suit better and the French 1,000 is the target. (op 9/4)
Ugo Fire(IRE) had the best juvenile form but was a market drifter. She kept on throughout the last furlong but never looked like collaring the winner. She will come on fair bit from this. (op 5/4)
Mrs Snaffles(IRE) put up her best effort on ground that did not really suit. (op 8/1)
Asaawir gave ground away at the start and was a bit outpaced. She stayed on when switched out inside the last. (op 6/1)
Gist(IRE) Official explanation: trainer said filly scoped abnormally post race

1025a LEOPARDSTOWN 2,000 GUINEAS TRIAL STKS (C & G) (GROUP 3) 1m
3:50 (3:50) 3-Y-O **£31,427** (£9,220; £4,393; £1,496)

RPR
1 **Yasoodd**[175] 6023 3-9-0 .... ChrisCatlin 2 109+
(M R Channon) *hld up in rr: rdn and no imp early st: hdwy over 1f out: 4th and swtchd to chal under 1f out: r.o wl to ld cl home* **8/1**
2 nk **Heliostatic (IRE)**[272] 3570 3-9-0 ....(t) KJManning 4 108
(J S Bolger, Ire) *trckd ldr in 2nd: rdn 3f out: 3rd early st: rallied 1f out: sn ev ch: kpt on wl* **9/4**[1]
3 hd **Rekaab (IRE)**[188] 5779 3-9-0 107.................... DPMcDonogh 3 108
(Kevin Prendergast, Ire) *hld up in tch: prog into 3rd 1/2-way: 2nd early st: chal over 1f out: led ins fnl f: hdd and no ex cl home* **3/1**[2]
4 2 **James Joyce (IRE)**[166] 6206 3-9-0 .... KFallon 5 104
(A P O'Brien, Ire) *led: rdn and edgd clr early st: strly pressed over 1f out: hdd and no ex ins fnl f* **10/3**[3]
5 5 **Caribbean**[174] 6047 3-9-0 .... MJKinane 1 94
(John M Oxx, Ire) *settled 3rd: 4th 1/2-way: effrt early st: wknd fr 2f out* **9/2**

1m 45.6s **Going Correction** +0.35s/f (Good) **5** Ran SP% **108.1**
Speed ratings: 108,107,107,105,100
CSF £25.21 TOTE £8.40: £3.00, £1.50; DF 22.30.
Owner Sheikh Ahmed Al Maktoum **Bred** Mrs Jd Railton & Miss R Dobson **Trained** West Ilsley, Berks
■ Stewards' Enquiry : K J Manning caution: used whip with excessive frequency and without giving colt time to respond

NOTEBOOK
Yasoodd ran last throughout until switched out under pressure to deliver a sustained run inside the last that saw him ahead close home. He had the form to win this but there appeared to be little fancy for him and it was Catlin's tactical expertise that won it.
Heliostatic(IRE) is a very taking colt but looked pretty one-paced here. He appeared to be struggling early in the straight but kept coming back for more under strong pressure. He had a hard enough race but might be seen to better effect over further and on better ground. He is flattered by his new 107 rating. (op 5/2 tchd 2/1)
Rekaab(IRE) had his chance on the outer from over a furlong out and poked his nose in front inside the last but he could not sustain the effort. He was not as forward as some of his stable's other runners have been.
James Joyce(IRE) was very much in need of this, went off in front and tried to slip his field early in the straight, but he never got away and was headed inside the last and tired. He will progress, but to what extent remains the question. (op 5/2)
Caribbean needed the run and blew up in the straight. (op 9/2 tchd 4/1)

1026a ENNISTOWN STUD EUROPEAN BREEDERS FUND SALSABIL STKS (FILLIES) (LISTED RACE) 1m 2f
4:20 (4:20) 3-Y-O+ **£33,672** (£9,879; £4,706; £1,603)

RPR
1 **Perfect Hedge**[172] 6104 4-10-0 107.................... MJKinane 6 96+
(John M Oxx, Ire) *settled 4th: 2nd and chal early st: kpt on wl u.p fnl f to ld cl home* **11/4**[2]
2 1 **Sina Cova (IRE)**[20] 754 4-9-11 88....................(b) JAHeffernan 7 91
(Peter Casey, Ire) *attempted to make all: rdn st: strly pressed fr over 1f out: hdd cl home* **33/1**
3 3/4 **Kushnarenkovo**[173] 6086 3-8-8 ow1.................... KFallon 9 92
(A P O'Brien, Ire) *hld up: 8th and hdwy appr st: 3rd over 1f out: kpt on* **8/1**
4 1/2 **Saintly Rachel (IRE)**[20] 753 8-9-11 97.................... JMurtagh 4 89
(C F Swan, Ire) *hld up in rr: 9th into st: swtchd rt over 1f out: 4th and r.o ins fnl f* **9/1**
5 3 1/2 **Million Waves (IRE)**[174] 6044 3-8-7 94.................... DPMcDonogh 8 84
(Kevin Prendergast, Ire) *hld up in tch: 7th 1/2-way: kpt on same pce st* **9/1**
6 nk **Utterly Heaven (IRE)**[20] 753 4-9-11 106.................... PJSmullen 5 82
(D K Weld, Ire) *mid-div: 6th 3f out: rdn and no imp st* **5/2**[1]
7 1 1/2 **Requested Pleasure (IRE)**[272] 3573 4-9-11 94.................... KJManning 10 79
(J S Bolger, Ire) *chsd ldrs in 5th: rdn and no imp st* **10/1**
8 3/4 **Subtle Affair (IRE)**[144] 6416 4-9-11 72.................... WMLordan 1 78
(P F Cashman, Ire) *trckd ldrs in 3rd: wknd ent st* **50/1**
9 1 1/2 **Gemini Gold (IRE)**[20] 753 3-8-7 98.................... NGMcCullagh 2 76
(M J Grassick, Ire) *chsd ldr in 2nd: rdn ent st: wknd under 2f out* **9/2**[3]
10 3 1/2 **Imperial Rose (IRE)**[6] 932 4-9-11 92.................... WSupple 3 69
(H Rogers, Ire) *a towards rr: no ex early st* **50/1**

2m 13.9s **Going Correction** +0.35s/f (Good)
WFA 3 from 4yo+ 19lb **10** Ran SP% **120.5**
Speed ratings: 100,99,98,98,95 95,93,93,92,89
CSF £94.15 TOTE £4.00: £1.70, £11.80, £2.50; DF 223.90.
Owner S Hanson **Bred** H P Bloodstock Ltd **Trained** Currabeg, Co Kildare
■ This race was transferred from the abandoned meeting at Navan on April 8th.

NOTEBOOK
Perfect Hedge had too much stamina and pace for the runner-up inside the last and was value for further. Ex-French, she can be placed to win again in better class. (op 7/2)
Sina Cova(IRE) got a bit of black type after a gutsy front-running effort and goes up 11lb to 99.
Kushnarenkovo did best of the three-year-olds and showed plenty of stamina with her late effort. (op 7/1)
Saintly Rachel(IRE) had only one behind her turning for home and had to be switched for a run. She will get her turn but is a luckless mare at this stage. (op 10/1)
Million Waves(IRE) was outpaced before the straight but kept on well enough over the last furlong and a half. (op 7/1)
Utterly Heaven(IRE) might not have been as comfortable over this trip but certainly did not build on her previous Curragh run. She was never travelling with any style. (op 9/4)
Gemini Gold(IRE) was another who failed to improve on her Curragh run behind Danehill Music. (op 4/1 tchd 5/1)

1027 - 1029a (Foreign Racing) - See Raceform Interactive

[813]MUSSELBURGH (R-H)
Sunday, April 16

OFFICIAL GOING: Straight course - good; round course - good to firm (good in places)
Wind: Slight across

1030 TOTEJACKPOT MAIDEN STKS 5f
2:20 (2:20) (Class 5) 2-Y-O **£3,886** (£1,156; £577; £288) **Stalls** High

Form RPR
1 **Stolt (IRE)** 2-9-0 .... DNolan[(3)] 5 72
(N Wilson) *qckly away and led: rdn wl over 1f out: wandered ins last: hdd last 50yds: rallied to ld on line* **12/1**
2 2 shd **My Mirasol**[16] 814 2-8-12 .... JamieSpencer 6 67
(K A Ryan) *chsd ldrs: hdwy 2f out: rdn over 1f out: styd on u.p to ld last 50 yds: hdd on line* **11/10**[1]
3 1 3/4 **Jack Rackham** 2-9-3 .... PaulEddery 8 65
(B Smart) *in tch: hdwy 2f out: sn rdn and kpt on ins last: nrst fin* **12/1**
4 shd **The Nifty Fox** 2-9-3 .... DavidAllan 2 65+
(T D Easterby) *prom: effrt 2f out and ev ch tl rdn and one pce appr last* **6/1**[3]
5 3 **Stepaside (IRE)** 2-9-3 .... KDarley 7 53+
(M Johnston) *cl up: rdn along 2f out: sn wknd* **5/1**[2]
6 2 1/2 **Top Tier** 2-8-12 .... TomEaves 1 38
(I Semple) *s.i.s: a rr* **20/1**
0 7 2 1/2 **Just Dust**[5] 961 2-9-0 .... RobertMiles[(3)] 3 33
(W G M Turner) *chsd ldrs: rdn along over 2f out and sn wknd* **15/2**
8 7 **Makeusabuck** 2-8-12 .... TedDurcan 4 —
(A Berry) *dwlt: sn outpcd and bhd* **33/1**

63.53 secs (3.03) **Going Correction** +0.425s/f (Yiel) **8** Ran SP% **113.4**
Speed ratings (Par 92): 92,91,89,88,84 80,76,64
CSF £25.35 TOTE £16.70: £3.40, £1.10, £2.60; EX 43.30.
Owner Dixon, McIntyre, Tobin **Bred** Seamus Phelan **Trained** Upper Helmsley, N Yorks

FOCUS
Riders in this reported the ground to be 'dead'. The runner-up is the best guide to the form.

NOTEBOOK
Stolt(IRE), a 20,000gns yearling, is a brother to multiple sprint winner Aahgowangowan. He made just about all the running and, after being joined close home, got his nose back in front on the line to give his trainer his first ever juvenile winner. There might well be a bit more to come from him. (op 10-1)
My Mirasol, whose debut over course and distance was on heavy ground, put her head narrowly in front close home but lost the race on the nod. An ordinary race should come her way. (op 11-8)
Jack Rackham is a half-brother to a couple of useful sprint juveniles in Mary Read, from the Smart yard, and Tiana, out of a half-sister to Middle Park Stakes winner Stalker. He ran a little green on this debut but was keeping on at the end. (op 9-1)
The Nifty Fox, sprint bred out of a mare who won twice over this course and distance, showed a bit of pace and like most of his stable's youngsters he will benefit from the experience. (op 8-1)
Stepaside(IRE), a half-brother to useful 2004 juvenile Bunditten out of a Listed two-year-old scorer in France, had two handlers in the paddock. He showed pace on this debut and should improve for the outing. (op 4-1)
Top Tier, a cheap buy, is out of a winning sprint juvenile. She unshipped her rider in the paddock and was green in the early stages, but she was grasping what was required late on. (tchd 16-1)

1031 TOTEPOOL "A BETTER WAY TO BET" H'CAP 5f
2:50 (2:50) (Class 4) (0-85,85) 3-Y-O+ **£6,477** (£1,927; £963; £481) **Stalls** High

Form RPR
00-3 1 **Desert Lord**[20] 761 6-10-0 85....................(b) JamieSpencer 4 98
(K A Ryan) *cl up: led after 1f: swtchd lft 1/2-way: clr over 1f out: rdn out* **9/4**[1]
005- 2 2 **Highland Warrior**[169] 6140 7-9-8 79.................... TonyCulhane 10 85
(J S Goldie) *dwlt: hdwy 2f out: styd on to chse wnr ent last: kpt on* **14/1**
200- 3 3 **Wanchai Lad**[176] 6021 5-9-13 84.................... PaulQuinn 1 79
(D Nicholls) *chsd ldrs stands rail: hdwy 2f out: sn rdn: kpt on ins last* **12/1**[3]
000- 4 nk **Westbrook Blue**[176] 6021 4-9-10 84.................... RobertMiles[(3)] 5 78
(W G M Turner) *midfield: hdwy 2f out: sn rdn and kpt on ins last: nrst fin* **16/1**
-000 5 2 **Whinhill House**[44] 569 6-9-1 77....................(p) MarkLawson[(5)] 11 64
(D W Barker) *chsd ldrs centre: rdn along 2f out: sn one pce* **12/1**[3]
600- 6 1 **Bond Boy**[182] 5922 9-9-11 82.................... KDarley 6 65
(B Smart) *chsd wnr: rdn along 2f out: grad wknd* **14/1**
134- 7 1 3/4 **Grigorovitch (IRE)**[182] 5922 4-10-0 85.................... TomEaves 2 62
(I Semple) *s.i.s and towards rr: gd headway to chse ldrs 2f out: sn rdn and wknd* **5/1**[2]
3114 8 nk **Native Title**[6] 947 8-9-9 80.................... AdrianTNicholls 8 56
(D Nicholls) *s.i.s: hdwy and in tch 1/2-way: rdn to chse ldrs 2f out:d riven and wknd 1f out* **5/1**[2]
000- 9 nk **Jadan (IRE)**[199] 5567 5-9-0 71 oh1.................... GrahamGibbons 7 46
(E J Alston) *a rr* **20/1**
002- 10 2 **The Leather Wedge (IRE)**[180] 5954 7-9-0 71 oh2.......... PaulEddery 12 38
(R Johnson) *led on far side for 1f: swtchd lft 1/2-way: sn rdn and wknd* **16/1**
00-3 11 2 **Champagne Cracker**[16] 813 5-9-0 71 oh6.................... RoystonFfrench 9 31
(I Semple) *chsd ldrs centre: rdn along 1/2-way: sn wknd* **16/1**
000- 12 14 **Mister Marmaduke**[262] 3888 5-9-0 71 oh14..........(p) DerekMcGaffin 3 —
(D A Nolan) *chsd ldrs towards stands side: rdn along 1/2-way: wknd fnl 2f* **100/1**

63.28 secs (2.78) **Going Correction** +0.425s/f (Yiel) **12** Ran SP% **116.2**
Speed ratings (Par 105): 94,90,86,85,82 80,77,77,76,73 70,48
CSF £36.18 CT £319.63 TOTE £2.50: £1.30, £4.90, £2.80; EX 47.10.
Owner Bull & Bell Partnership **Bred** Cheveley Park Stud Ltd **Trained** Hambleton, N Yorks

FOCUS
A very moderate winning time for a race of its class, just a quarter of a second faster than the two-year-old maiden and over half a second slower than the later Class 5 three-year-old handicap. The winner brought the field to race over on the stands' side. This was not that competitive and has been rated through the winner.

Native Title Official explanation: jockey said gelding hung right-handed throughout
The Leather Wedge(IRE) Official explanation: jockey said gelding hung left-handed in the final furlong

1032 TOTEQUADPOT MAIDEN STKS — 7f 30y
3:20 (3:24) (Class 5) 3-Y-0+ **£3,886** (£1,156; £577; £288) **Stalls** Low

Form RPR

55- **1** **King Of The Moors (USA)**[183] 5886 3-8-11 .... PhillipMakin 8 — 72
(T D Barron) *led to 1/2-way: led again wl over 1f out: rdn ent last and styd on wl* **20/1**

2 *1 1/4* **Hams (USA)** 3-8-6 .... RHills 14 — 64
(M Johnston) *s.i.s: sn in midfield: swtchd outside 3f out: gd hdwy 2f out: rdn and ch whn edgd rt ent fnl f: kpt on* **4/1**[2]

364- **3** *1 3/4* **Sunrise Safari (IRE)**[181] 5946 3-8-11 85 .... TomEaves 1 — 64
(I Semple) *in tch: headway to chse ldrs 3f out: rdn 2f out: drvn and kpt on same pce ent last* **3/1**[1]

0- **4** *1 1/4* **Torgiano (IRE)**[312] 2392 5-9-7 .... PaulMulrennan(3) 12 — 66
(P Monteith) *rr: hdwy over 2f out: sn rdn and styd on wl fnl f: nrst fin* **100/1**

042- **5** *hd* **Grey Outlook**[164] 6234 3-8-6 69 .... RoystonFfrench 10 — 55
(Miss L A Perratt) *towards rr: gd hdwy 3f out: rdn to chse ldrs over 1f out: kpt on same pce fnl f* **13/2**

6 *1 1/4* **For No One (IRE)** 3-8-11 .... JoeFanning 4 — 57
(M Johnston) *sn outpcd and bhd tl styd on fnl 2f: nvr rch ldrs* **14/1**

0 **7** *shd* **Electron Pulse**[32] 645 3-8-6 .... NickyMackay 11 — 52
(J S Goldie) *bhd: gd hdwy over 2f out: styd on wl fnl f: nrst fin* **40/1**

340- **8** *2* **Glasshoughton**[204] 5466 3-8-8 75 .... BenSwarbrick(3) 7 — 52
(M Dods) *cl up: led 1/2-way: rdn over 2f out: hdd wl over 1f out: drvn and wknd ent last* **12/1**

/0 **9** *2 1/2* **Aqua**[40] 609 4-9-5 .... MickyFenton 3 — 45
(P T Midgley) *bhd tl sme late hdwy* **100/1**

05- **10** *hd* **Malakiya (IRE)**[128] 6532 3-8-11 .... SebSanders 2 — 45
(G A Butler) *s.i.s: a rr* **6/1**

424/ **11** *1/2* **Tamatave (IRE)**[544] 6283 4-9-10 75 .... JamieSpencer 9 — 48
(K A Ryan) *cl up on inner: rdn along wl over 2f out: wknd over 1f out* **9/2**[3]

0 **12** *3* **Megalo Maniac**[16] 817 3-8-11 .... DeanMcKeown 13 — 36
(K G Reveley) *chsd ldrs: rdn along over 3f out: sn wknd* **66/1**

13 *14* **Frank Cartwright (IRE)** 3-8-11 .... TedDurcan 5 — —
(A Berry) *s.i.s: a bhd* **66/1**

1m 32.2s (2.26) **Going Correction** +0.35s/f (Good)
WFA 3 from 4yo+ 13lb — 13 Ran SP% **117.3**
Speed ratings (Par 103):101,99,97,96,95 94,94,92,89,89 88,85,69
CSF £95.26 TOTE £19.80: £4.20, £2.00, £1.60; EX 143.80.
Owner G Fawcett **Bred** F Brown, Hedberg Hall & Keith Hernandez **Trained** Maunby, N Yorks

FOCUS
Not a strong maiden. The bare form is a little shaky and the fourth will set the standard in time.
Tamatave(IRE) Official explanation: jockey said gelding had no more to give

1033 TOTESPORT.COM MUSSELBURGH GOLD CUP (H'CAP) — 1m 6f
3:50 (3:50) (Class 4) (0-85,82) 4-Y-0+ **£16,192** (£4,817; £2,407; £1,202) **Stalls** High

Form RPR

406- **1** **Reluctant Suitor**[200] 5550 4-8-3 63 .... NickyMackay 11 — 73+
(J S Goldie) *trckd ldrs on inner: effrt 3f out and sn rdn along: led 2f out: drvn: hung lft & hdd ent last: sn ld again: styd on wl* **16/1**

0320 **2** *3/4* **Trance (IRE)**[16] 816 6-9-3 75 .... PaulFessey 7 — 84
(T D Barron) *hld up in rr: gd hdwy on wd outside whn bmpd 2f out: rdn: hung rt and led briefly ent last: sn hdd: drvn and one pce* **9/1**

4-06 **3** *1 1/4* **Kristensen**[16] 816 7-8-13 71 ....(v[1]) SebSanders 1 — 78
(Karen McLintock) *hld up in midfield: hdwy on inner over 5f out: swtchd rt 3f out: rdn and ev ch whn hung lft 2f out: sn drvn and one pce* **16/1**

022- **4** *6* **Calatagan (IRE)**[70] 5685 7-8-10 68 .... PaulHanagan 3 — 67
(J M Jefferson) *hld up: hdwy on outer over 4f out: rdn to chse ldrs 2f out: sn drvn and no imp* **16/1**

001- **5** *2 1/2* **Rooftop Protest (IRE)**[7] 931 9-9-9 81 ....(tp) JamieSpencer 5 — 76
(T Hogan, Ire) *a.p: effrt to chal 3f out: ev ch 2f out and sn rdn: drvn and wknd over 1f out* **7/2**[1]

-001 **6** *1 3/4* **John Forbes**[16] 816 4-9-2 76 .... PatCosgrave 12 — 69
(B Ellison) *led: rdn along 3f out: drvn and hdd 2f out: sn wknd* **8/1**

0040 **7** *11* **Golden Boot**[16] 816 7-8-7 65 .... KDarley 10 — 42
(A Bailey) *hld up: a rr* **20/1**

54-5 **8** *1 1/4* **Bollin Thomas**[4] 990 8-8-9 67 ....(p) DavidAllan 8 — 43
(R Allan) *chsd ldrs: rdn along after 6f: sn lost pl and bhd* **9/1**

140- **9** *3/4* **Rule For Ever**[181] 5943 4-8-11 71 .... JoeFanning 9 — 46
(M Johnston) *cl up: rdn along 4f out: sn wknd* **13/2**[3]

0/0- **10** *5* **Protective**[85] 6254 5-9-10 82 .... MickyFenton 4 — 50
(J G Given) *a rr: bhd fr 1/2-way* **33/1**

00-4 **11** *1/2* **Annambo**[18] 799 6-9-3 75 .... TedDurcan 6 — 42
(D Morris) *trckd ldrs: hdwy over 4f out: rdn 3f out: sn btn* **6/1**[2]

02-6 **12** *1 1/4* **Mister Right (IRE)**[22] 723 5-9-0 72 .... JohnEgan 2 — 37
(D J S Ffrench Davis) *inm tch: effrt to chse ldrs 4f out: rdn 3f out and sn wknd* **9/1**

3m 6.08s (0.38) **Going Correction** +0.35s/f (Good)
WFA 4 from 5yo+ 2lb — 12 Ran SP% **116.3**
Speed ratings (Par 105):112,111,110,107,106 105,98,98,97,94 94,93
CSF £150.17 CT £2342.89 TOTE £26.50: £7.50, £3.40, £4.20; EX 500.10.
Owner The Reluctant Suitor's **Bred** Chippenham Lodge Stud Ltd **Trained** Uplawmoor, E Renfrews
■ Stewards' Enquiry : Paul Fessey caution: careless riding

FOCUS
A decent pace, and a smart winning time for a race of its class. The first three finished clear and the form looks sound.
Mister Right(IRE) Official explanation: jockey said gelding had no more to give

1034 TOTESPORT 0800 221 221 MAIDEN STKS — 1m 4f
4:20 (4:20) (Class 5) 3-Y-0+ **£3,886** (£1,156; £577; £288) **Stalls** High

Form RPR

03- **1** **Remember Ramon (USA)**[141] 6425 3-8-8 ow1 .... JamieSpencer 9 — 71+
(M J Wallace) *t.k.h: trckd ldrs: swtchd lft and hdwy on bit 2f out: sn led: cheekily* **4/9**[1]

0- **2** *1/2* **Trinity Rose**[164] 6234 3-8-2 .... JoeFanning 11 — 64
(M Johnston) *led: rdn along and jnd 3f out: drvn 2f out: sn hdd: kpt on: no ch w wnr* **25/1**

4-45 **3** *1 1/4* **Merchant Bankes**[62] 403 3-8-8 70 ow1 .... TonyCulhane 4 — 68
(W G M Turner) *plld hrd: cl up: rdn along over 3f out: drvn 2f out: kpt on same pce* **16/1**[3]

4 *3* **Accordello (IRE)**[57] 5-9-1 .... JamesReveley(7) 12 — 60
(K G Reveley) *hld up towards rr: hdwy 4f out: styd on fnl 2f: nrst fin* **20/1**

005- **5** *1 1/2* **Cool Ebony**[216] 5184 3-8-7 73 .... PhillipMakin 2 — 60
(M Dods) *in tch: rdn along over 3f out: sn drvn and one pce* **33/1**

003- **6** *2 1/2* **Boquilobo**[182] 5919 3-8-7 76 .... KDarley 3 — 56
(M Johnston) *trckd ldng pair: hdwy 4f out: chal 3f out: sn rdn and ev ch tl drvn and wknd wl over 1f out* **3/1**[2]

0/5- **7** *5* **Royal Glen (IRE)**[105] 5771 8-9-8 45 .... PatCosgrave 5 — 46
(W S Coltherd) *midfield: effrt and sme hdwy 3f out: sn rdn along and no imp fnl 2f* **100/1**

003- **8** *3 1/2* **Scarrabus (IRE)**[39] 4994 5-9-13 55 .... MickyFenton 7 — 45
(A Crook) *chsd ldrs: rdn along over 4f out: sn wknd* **66/1**

9 *5* **Now Tell Me This** 3-8-7 .... TomEaves 10 — 34
(I Semple) *a bhd* **66/1**

10 *hd* **Final Esteem** 3-8-5 ow5 .... StephenCairns(7) 8 — 39
(I Semple) *a bhd* **66/1**

46-0 **11** *2 1/2* **Power Strike (USA)**[86] 40 5-9-13 45 .... PaulHanagan 1 — 33
(Mrs L B Normile) *a bhd* **100/1**

000/ **12** *dist* **Opal's Helmsman (USA)**[61] 3483 7-9-10 30 .... PaulMulrennan(3) 6 — —
(W S Coltherd) *chsd ldrs to 1/2-way: sn lost pl and bhd* **100/1**

2m 43.63s (6.73) **Going Correction** +0.35s/f (Good)
WFA 3 from 5yo+ 20lb — 12 Ran SP% **119.1**
Speed ratings (Par 103):91,90,89,87,86 85,81,79,76,76 74,—
CSF £22.80 TOTE £1.50: £1.10, £4.30, £2.30; EX 25.10.
Owner Mrs M Findlay **Bred** B T Hundley **Trained** Newmarket, Suffolk

FOCUS
A very moderate winning time for the grade. A modest maiden, the third setting the standard, but the easy winner is capable of better.

1035 TOTETRIFECTA H'CAP — 7f 30y
4:50 (4:51) (Class 4) (0-85,83) 4-Y-0+ **£6,477** (£1,927; £963; £481) **Stalls** Low

Form RPR

0300 **1** **Baylaw Star**[23] 719 5-9-3 82 .... JoeFanning 7 — 93
(K A Ryan) *sn led and set stdy pce: qcknd clr 2f out: pushed out* **12/1**

0-60 **2** *2 1/2* **Sawwaah (IRE)**[6] 946 9-8-7 72 ....(v) AdrianTNicholls 10 — 77
(D Nicholls) *hld up in rr: hdwy over 2f out: rdn to chse wnr over 1f out: sn no imp* **13/2**[2]

4140 **3** *2* **Alfonso**[22] 726 5-8-11 76 ....(b) TomEaves 13 — 75
(I Semple) *trckd ldrs: hdwy to chse wnr wl over 2f out: sn rdn and kpt on same pce* **7/1**[3]

15-4 **4** *2 1/2* **Ballyhurry (USA)**[32] 644 9-8-5 70 .... NickyMackay 3 — 63
(J S Goldie) *bhd: hdwy over 2f out: swtchd rt and rdn over 1f out: kpt on: nrst fin* **12/1**

645- **5** *1/2* **Dispol Katie**[225] 4953 5-9-4 83 .... PhillipMakin 12 — 75
(T D Barron) *hld up in midfield: hdwy 3f out: nt clr run 2f out: sn rdn and no imp* **8/1**

420- **6** *nk* **Jordans Elect**[189] 5772 6-8-4 69 .... PaulFessey 9 — 60
(P Monteith) *chsd wnr: rdn along 3f out: drvn 2f out: grad wknd* **14/1**

005- **7** *1/2* **Regent's Secret (USA)**[169] 6137 6-8-12 77 .... TonyCulhane 2 — 66
(J S Goldie) *hld up in rr: hdwy over 2f out: nt clr run over 1f out: kpt on ins last* **25/1**

660- **8** *7* **Sea Storm (IRE)**[128] 6533 8-8-10 78 .... DNolan(3) 6 — 49
(D R MacLeod) *hld up: effrt and sme hdwy on outer over 2f out: sn rdn and wknd* **20/1**

0254 **9** *2* **Stoic Leader (IRE)**[22] 737 6-9-3 82 .... JohnEgan 4 — 48
(R F Fisher) *hld up: hdwy on outer 3f out: rdn 2f out and sn wknd* **11/2**[1]

-006 **10** *6* **Redwood Rocks (IRE)**[22] 736 5-8-6 71 .... PaulEddery 5 — 21
(B Smart) *prom: rdn along 3f out: sn wknd* **14/1**

6110 **11** *12* **H Harrison (IRE)**[14] 845 6-9-0 79 .... RoystonFfrench 8 — —
(I W McInnes) *in tch: effrt to chse ldrs over 3f out: sn rdn and wknd over 2f out* **13/2**[2]

060- **12** *4* **Throw The Dice**[217] 5146 4-9-2 81 .... JamieSpencer 11 — —
(D W Barker) *hld up: hdwy on inner 3f out: shkn up over 2f out: sn wknd and eased.* **15/2**

1m 31.3s (1.36) **Going Correction** +0.35s/f (Good) — 12 Ran SP% **114.8**
Speed ratings (Par 105):106,103,100,98,97 97,96,88,86,79 65,61
CSF £85.16 CT £600.68 TOTE £12.90: £3.70, £2.70, £2.90; EX 117.30 Trifecta £379.10 Part won. Pool: £534.04 - 0.10 winning units..
Owner T C Racing Partnership **Bred** John Wilkinson Bloodstock **Trained** Hambleton, N Yorks

FOCUS
A modest handicap in which the winner was able to dictate. He did not have to improve and the remainder were probably not seen to best advantage.
Regent's Secret(USA) Official explanation: jockey said gelding was continually denied a run
Stoic Leader(IRE) Official explanation: jockey said gelding lost its action
H Harrison(IRE) Official explanation: jockey said gelding was unsuited by the good going
Throw The Dice Official explanation: jockey said saddle slipped and gelding hung left-handed throughout

1036 TOTESPORTCASINO.COM H'CAP — 5f
5:20 (5:20) (Class 5) (0-75,74) 3-Y-O **£3,886** (£1,156; £577; £288) **Stalls** High

Form RPR

500- **1** **Sandwith**[135] 6479 3-8-11 67 .... PaulHanagan 4 — 72
(I Semple) *trckd ldrs: hdwy 2f out: rdn to ld and edgd lft over 1f out: kpt on u.p ins last* **8/1**

530- **2** *1* **Imperial Sword**[204] 5466 3-9-3 73 .... PaulFessey 6 — 74
(T D Barron) *hld up: hdwy on stands rail over 1f out: rdn and kpt on wl fnl f* **10/1**

30-4 **3** *shd* **Highland Song (IRE)**[41] 601 3-8-9 65 .... JohnEgan 10 — 66
(R F Fisher) *bmpd s: hdwy on outer 1/2-way: rdn and ch over 1f out: drvn and nt qckn ins last* **6/1**[3]

000- **4** *3* **Welcome Approach**[177] 6004 3-8-11 67 .... PhillipMakin 2 — 57
(J R Weymes) *trckd ldrs: effrt and nt clr run over 1f out: swtchd rt and rdn ent last: no imp* **6/1**[3]

162- **5** *1 1/4* **Blazing Heights**[182] 5920 3-9-3 73 .... TedDurcan 3 — 58
(J S Goldie) *chsd ldr: rdn wl over 1f out: sn drvn and wknd* **11/2**[2]

000- **6** *2* **Howards Prince**[216] 5178 3-9-1 71 ....(p) TomEaves 1 — 49
(I Semple) *chsd ldr: rdn along 2f out: drvn and wknd over 1f out* **12/1**

000- **7** *2 1/2* **Mytton's Pride**[158] 6297 3-9-0 70 .... MickyFenton 8 — 39
(A Bailey) *led: rdn along 2f out: hdd & wknd over 1f out* **25/1**

300- **8** *3/4* **Active Audience (IRE)**[169] 6136 3-8-5 61 oh1 ow1.... AdrianTNicholls 7 — 27
(A Berry) *bhd tl sme late hdwy* **33/1**

020 **9** *2 1/2* **Kings Casualty (USA)**[64] 380 3-9-2 72 ....(v) RoystonFfrench 9 — 29
(I W McInnes) *sn outpcd and bhd fr 1/2-way* **20/1**

06-5 **10** *1 1/2* **Titus Maximus (IRE)**[41] 593 3-9-4 74 ....(t) SebSanders 5 — 26
(G A Butler) *chsd ldrs on outer: rdn along 2f out: sn wknd* **9/2**[1]

021- 11 1 1/4 **Rothesay Dancer**[194] [5680] 3-9-3 73 TonyCulhane 11 21
(J S Goldie) *in tch: rdn along 1/2-way: sn wknd* 6/1[3]

62.76 secs (2.26) **Going Correction** +0.425s/f (Yiel) 11 Ran SP% **115.9**
Speed ratings (Par 98):98,96,96,91,89 86,82,81,77,74 72
CSF £81.76 CT £525.12 TOTE £10.70: £3.40, £3.90, £2.00; EX 193.30 Place 6 £174.69, Place 5 £101.85.
Owner M Sawers **Bred** R R Whitton **Trained** Carluke, S Lanarks

FOCUS
A run-of-the-mill handicap. The first two have been rated to their early juvenile form in a race lacking progressive types. The field came over to the stands' rail again.
T/Jkpt: Not won. T/Plt: £442.70 to a £1 stake. Pool: £50,853.40. 83.85 winning tickets. T/Qpdt: £118.00 to a £1 stake. Pool: £2,791.50. 17.50 winning tickets. JR

1037 - 1039a (Foreign Racing) - See Raceform Interactive

726 REDCAR (L-H)
Monday, April 17

OFFICIAL GOING: Good to firm (good in places)
There was a definite high-draw bias on the straight course on the day.
Wind: Strong across

1040 NATIONALRAIL.COM FOR OYSTER CARDS MAIDEN (S) STKS 5f
2:15 (2:15) (Class 6) 2-Y-O **£2,730** (£806; £403) **Stalls** Centre

Form RPR
54 1 **Granny Peel (IRE)**[13] [877] 2-8-12 PaulHanagan 8 60
(K A Ryan) *cl up effrt 2f out: rdn to ld ins last: edgd lft and hld on wl towards fin* 7/2[3]
5 2 hd **Tokyo Jo (IRE)**[17] [814] 2-8-12 PatCosgrave 5 59
(K R Burke) *cl up: rdn to ld over 1f out: hdd ins last: rallied wl towards fin* 5/2[2]
3 nk **Picture Frame** 2-9-3 JoeFanning 2 63
(N Tinkler) *clsd up: rn green and outpcd 1/2-way: hdwy over 1f out: rdn and ev ch ins last: kpt on wl* 10/1
4 shd **Jord (IRE)** 2-8-12 TonyCulhane 4 58
(M R Channon) *cl up: effrt 2f out: sn rdn and ev ch: drvn ins last and no ex nr fin* 2/1[1]
5 5 3/4 **Readyforone**[14] [856] 2-9-3 (b[1]) GrahamGibbons 6 60
(P D Evans) *chsd ldrs: pushed along: hung rt and outpcd 1/2-way: sn rdn and styd on wl u.p fnl f: nrst fin* 25/1
0 6 3/4 **Emma Told Lies**[10] [908] 2-8-9 PaulMulrennan(3) 3 52
(M W Easterby) *chsd ldrs: rdn along over 2f out: kpt on same pce* 20/1
0 7 4 **Three Mates**[13] [878] 2-8-9 RobertMiles(3) 1 36
(W G M Turner) *wnt lft s: sn led: rdn along 2f out: hdd over 1f out and sn wknd* 9/1
8 6 **Milly Beat** 2-8-12 TomEaves 7 12
(C Grant) *wnt rt s: s.i.s and a bhd* 66/1

60.85 secs (2.15) **Going Correction** +0.125s/f (Good) 8 Ran SP% **113.3**
Speed ratings (Par 90):87,86,86,86,84 83,77,67
CSF £12.31 TOTE £4.10: £1.60, £1.10, £2.20; EX 17.10.There was no bid for the winner. Jord (IRE) was claimed by C. A. Dwyer £6,000. Tokyo Jo (IRE) was the subject of a friendly claim
Owner J Hopkinson and R Peel **Bred** Tally-Ho Stud **Trained** Hambleton, N Yorks

FOCUS
An ordinary juvenile seller where experience proved the decisive factor and the form is average for the grade.

NOTEBOOK
Granny Peel(IRE), who threw away her chance in a similar race at Warwick when swerving across the track, showed no sign of doing that on this occasion and put her previous experience to good use to get home in a blanket finish. There was no bid for her at the auction. (tchd 4-1)
Tokyo Jo(IRE), who played up before being well beaten on her debut on much softer ground, showed the benefit of that experience and was only just run out of it. She looks capable of winning a similar contest. (op 3-1)
Picture Frame ◆, related to several winners at up to a mile, was a relatively cheap purchase and has already been gelded. He ran well despite looking in need of the experience and having to race on the least favoured side of the track. It would be no surprise to see him improve past those that beat him here. (op 14-1 tchd 16-1)
Jord(IRE), a half-sister to a couple of fair winners at around seven furlongs, was another to run well on this debut and, claimed for £6,000, can improve with this experience under her belt. (op 15-8)
Readyforone, fitted with blinkers having been slowly away and well beaten on his debut, came closest to the stands' rail and was doing his best work late on to finish on the heels of those in the frame. Official explanation: jockey said gelding hung right-handed final 2f
Emma Told Lieschased the leaders all the way but could never make an impression. (op 16-1)

1041 MAYOR'S CHARITY DAY H'CAP 7f
2:50 (2:50) (Class 5) (0-70,70) 4-Y-O+ **£3,238** (£963; £481; £240) **Stalls** Centre

Form RPR
1345 1 **Dispol Isle (IRE)**[17] [818] 4-8-7 62 BenSwarbrick(3) 18 69
(T D Barron) *in tch: hdwy over 2f out: rdn to ld jst over 1f out: drvn ins last and jst hld on* 22/1
000- 2 shd **Grande Terre (IRE)**[210] [5359] 5-8-4 56 oh1 PaulHanagan 13 68+
(R A Fahey) *bhd and pushed along 1/2-way: swtchd rt to wd outside 2f out: hdwy over 1f out: rdn and styd on strly ins last: jst failed* 11/1
500- 3 1 1/2 **Sake (IRE)**[214] [5242] 4-8-8 60 KimTinkler 14 63
(N Tinkler) *dwlt: sn chsng ldrs: rdn wl over 1f out: kpt on u.p ins last* 14/1
00-0 4 nk **Aperitif**[23] [726] 5-8-12 64 SamHitchcott 16 66
(D Nicholls) *trckd ldrs: swtchd lft and hdwy 2f out: rdn and ch over 1f out: kpt on same pce ins last* 40/1
50-2 5 1/2 **Insubordinate**[17] [818] 5-8-5 57 JoeFanning 3 58
(J S Goldie) *s.i.s and bhd: hdwy on outer 1/2-way: rdn to chse ldrs over 1f out: kpt on same pce ins last* 8/1[2]
10-0 6 1/2 **Wayward Shot (IRE)**[17] [818] 4-8-8 63 PaulMulrennan(3) 10 62
(M W Easterby) *led: rdn along over 2f out: drvn and hdd jst over 1f out: wknd ins last* 33/1
3/0- 7 1 **Bond Playboy**[345] [1554] 6-8-11 63 TomEaves 11 60
(G R Oldroyd) *midfield: hdwy 2f out: styd on wl fnl f: nrst fin* 20/1
000- 8 1/2 **Queen's Echo**[190] [5773] 5-8-10 62 PhillipMakin 12 58
(M Dods) *dwlt and bhd tl styd on fnl 2f: nrst fin* 28/1
6-35 9 1 1/4 **Digital**[7] [949] 9-9-4 70 TonyCulhane 5 62
(M R Channon) *in tch: effrt to chse ldrs over 2f out: sn rdn and no imp appr last* 8/1[2]
050- 10 1/2 **Tiber Tiger (IRE)**[169] [6177] 6-8-7 64 (b) JamesDoyle(5) 9 55
(N P Littmoden) *in tch: hdwy 2f out: swtchd lft and rdn to chse ldrs over 1f out: drvn and wknd ins last* 5/1[1]
6406 11 1 3/4 **Louisiade (IRE)**[4] [1001] 5-8-0 57 (p) AndrewMullen(5) 1 43
(K A Ryan) *midfield: effrt and rdn along 3f out: sn no imp* 8/1[2]
33-1 12 hd **My Obsession (IRE)**[20] [778] 4-8-13 65 GrahamGibbons 17 51
(John Berry) *trckd ldrs: hdwy and ev ch 2f out tl rdn and wknd appr last* 8/1[2]
362- 13 1/2 **Borodinsky**[224] [4999] 5-8-4 56 oh1 RoystonFfrench 15 41
(R E Barr) *prom: rdn along wl over 2f out: sn wknd* 20/1
000- 14 2 1/2 **Kaymich Perfecto**[156] [6325] 6-8-8 67 MichaelJStainton(7) 6 45
(R M Whitaker) *hld up in midfield: swtchd lft and hdwy over 2f out: sn rdn and wknd over 1f out* 25/1
-223 15 9 **Art Elegant**[79] [219] 4-8-12 64 AdrianTNicholls 2 19
(G A Swinbank) *stdd s: a bhd* 10/1[3]
000- 16 8 **Etijahaat (IRE)**[198] [5625] 4-9-2 68 LeeEnstone 4 2
(C W Fairhurst) *a rr* 50/1
000- 17 1 1/4 **Fardi (IRE)**[212] [5297] 4-8-11 63 PatCosgrave 8 —
(K W Hogg) *cl up: rdn along 1/2-way: sn lost pl and bhd* 100/1
3-03 18 nk **Second Reef**[98] [71] 4-8-9 61 PaulQuinn 7 —
(E J Alston) *cl up: rdn along 1/2-way: sn lost pl and bhd fnl 2f* 11/1

1m 25.12s (0.22) **Going Correction** +0.125s/f (Good) 18 Ran SP% **123.0**
Speed ratings (Par 103):103,102,101,100,100 99,98,97,96,95 93,93,93,90,80 70,69,69
CSF £226.07 CT £2001.34 TOTE £29.60: £4.20, £3.80, £4.20, £13.40; EX 380.00.
Owner W B Imison **Bred** Mrs I A Balding **Trained** Maunby, N Yorks

FOCUS
A modest handicap producing a close finish, were those drawn high or racing on the stands' side seemed to have an advantage. The form looks reliable rated around the winner and fourth.
Second Reef Official explanation: jockey said gelding was unsuited by the good to firm (good in places) ground

1042 EASTER BUNNY H'CAP 6f
3:25 (3:26) (Class 4) (0-85,85) 4-Y-O+ **£6,477** (£1,927; £963; £481) **Stalls** Centre

Form RPR
30-0 1 **Paris Bell**[11] [898] 4-8-6 73 PaulQuinn 16 82
(T D Easterby) *s.i.s and bhd: gd hdwy over 2f out: swtchd lft and rdn over 1f out: led jst ins last and kpt on wl* 20/1
4602 2 nk **Tanforan**[23] [721] 4-8-3 75 (b) JamesDoyle(5) 17 83
(K McAuliffe) *towards rr: gd hdwy over 2f out: hmpd over 1f out: sn rdn and kpt on strly ins last* 6/1[1]
460- 3 1 **Titinius (IRE)**[184] [5893] 6-8-5 72 oh4 ow1 DeanMcKeown 13 77
(Micky Hammond) *hld up towards rr: gd hdwy whn nt clr run and hmpd over 1f out: styd on wl fnl f* 40/1
041- 4 nk **Raymond's Pride**[170] [6140] 6-8-11 83 (b) AndrewMullen(5) 11 87+
(K A Ryan) *chsd ldrs: ev ch and rdn whn hung bdly rt over 1f out: kpt on ins last* 14/1
102- 5 shd **Sir Nod**[170] [6157] 4-8-11 78 TomEaves 2 82+
(Miss J A Camacho) *in tch: hdwy 2f out: rdn to ld briefly 1f out: sn hdd and nt qckn* 8/1[2]
002- 6 1/2 **Trojan Flight**[167] [6216] 5-8-8 75 TonyCulhane 6 77+
(D W Chapman) *hld up in tch: hdwy whn nt clr run 2f out and again wl over 1f out: styd on ins last: nrst fin* 8/1[2]
30-0 7 3/4 **Danzig River (IRE)**[7] [947] 5-8-12 79 AdrianTNicholls 15 79
(D Nicholls) *in tch on outer: hdwy to chse ldrs and ch over 1f out: sn rdn and nt qckn* 10/1
203- 8 hd **Mr Wolf**[184] [5891] 5-8-13 85 MarkLawson(5) 9 84
(D W Barker) *led: rdn along 2f out: hdd & wknd 1f out* 9/1[3]
-060 9 1 1/4 **Bo McGinty (IRE)**[15] [846] 5-9-3 84 PaulHanagan 10 80
(R A Fahey) *chsd ldrs: rdn along wl over 1f out: sn one pce* 12/1
000- 10 1/2 **High Voltage**[170] [6140] 5-8-0 72 (t) AndrewElliott(5) 5 66
(K R Burke) *cl up: rdn along over 2f out: grad wknd* 9/1[3]
000- 11 1/2 **Ellens Academy (IRE)**[213] [5262] 11-8-13 80 DavidAllan 8 73
(E J Alston) *a midfield* 18/1
300- 12 1/2 **Steel Blue**[163] [6248] 6-8-7 81 MichaelJStainton(7) 3 72
(R M Whitaker) *cl up: rdn along over 2f out and sn wknd* 9/1[3]
160- 13 nk **Brigadore**[165] [6238] 7-8-6 73 NeilPollard 12 63
(J G Given) *midfield: gd hdwy to chse ldrs whn carried rt and bdly hmpd over 1f out: nt rcvr* 25/1
000- 14 shd **Apex**[163] [6248] 5-8-10 77 KimTinkler 7 67
(N Tinkler) *n.d* 25/1
000- 15 13 **Briannsta (IRE)**[169] [6180] 4-9-4 85 SamHitchcott 1 36
(M R Channon) *midfield: effrt 1/2-way: sn rdn along and wknd 2f out* 10/1
000- 16 6 **Katie Boo (IRE)**[203] [5508] 4-8-6 73 JoeFanning 14 6+
(A Berry) *chsd ldrs: rdn along and wkng whn hmpd over 1f out and bhd after* 25/1
0-00 17 9 **Newsround**[14] [860] 4-8-4 71 oh1 (b) DaleGibson 4 —
(D W Chapman) *s.i.s: a bhd* 50/1

1m 11.62s (-0.08) **Going Correction** +0.125s/f (Good) 17 Ran SP% **125.0**
Speed ratings (Par 105):105,104,103,102,102 102,101,100,99,98 97,97,96,96,79 71,59
CSF £130.18 CT £2872.73 TOTE £28.80: £5.10, £1.70, £8.90, £2.60; EX 208.70.
Owner Ryedale Partners No 8 **Bred** M H Easterby **Trained** Great Habton, N Yorks
■ Stewards' Enquiry : Mark Lawson one-day ban: careless riding (Apr 28)

FOCUS
A fair handicap producing another close finish and another race where it paid to be drawn high. There are questions over the form but the time suggests it will work out.
Titinius(IRE) ◆ Official explanation: jockey said gelding suffered interference in running
Raymond's Pride Official explanation: jockey said gelding hung right-handed
Katie Boo(IRE) Official explanation: jockey said filly suffered interference in running
Newsround Official explanation: jockey said gelding hung right-handed throughout

1043 JOHN SMITH'S REDCAR STRAIGHT-MILE CHAMPIONSHIP STKS (H'CAP) (QUALIFIER) 1m
4:00 (4:08) (Class 3) (0-90,90) 4-Y-O+
£8,724 (£2,612; £1,306; £653; £326; £163) **Stalls** Centre

Form RPR
014- 1 **Rio Riva**[170] [6159] 4-9-2 88 TonyCulhane 18 102+
(Miss J A Camacho) *hld up and bhd: stdy hdwy 3f out: swtchd rt and rdn over 1f out: led ins last: rdn out* 9/1
00-2 2 1 3/4 **Namroc (IRE)**[19] [800] 5-8-7 82 DanielTudhope(3) 9 92
(N A Callaghan) *uns rdr and bolted bef s: in tch: hdwy to ld 2f out: sn rdn: drvn and hdd ins last: one pce* 7/1[2]
100- 3 4 **Jubilee Street (IRE)**[167] [6216] 7-8-5 77 RoystonFfrench 13 78
(Mrs A Duffield) *chsd ldrs: rdn along 2f out: drvn and kpt on same pce fnl f* 16/1
0-34 4 3/4 **Harvest Warrior**[13] [867] 4-8-11 83 (b[1]) DavidAllan 10 82
(T D Easterby) *hld up: gd hdwy on outer 3f out: rdn and ev ch over 2f out: drvn and one pce over 1f out* 14/1
40-3 5 1/2 **Blue Trojan (IRE)**[7] [946] 6-8-7 79 FrankieMcDonald 11 77
(S Kirk) *hld up: hdwy over 2f out: sn rdn and kpt on ins last: nrst fin* 8/1[3]

3-00 **6** 1 1/2 **Nero's Return (IRE)**[13] 865 5-9-0 **86** .... JoeFanning 15 80
(M Johnston) bhd: hdwy 3f out: rdn wl over 1f out: styd on ins last: nrst fin **10/1**

023- **7** 1 1/2 **Flipando (IRE)**[192] 5717 5-9-3 **89** .... PhillipMakin 14 80+
(T D Barron) cl up: rdn along over 2f out: grad wknd fr wl over 1f out **6/1**[1]

0-00 **8** 1 **Lake Andre (IRE)**[78] 238 5-8-11 **88** .... AndrewMullen(5) 16 77
(K A Ryan) led: rdn along over 2f out: sn hdd and gradully wknd **33/1**

160- **9** 3/4 **Hypnotic**[196] 5662 4-8-5 **77** .... AdrianTNicholls 17 64
(D Nicholls) hld up towards rr: hdwy over 2f out: rdn over 1f out and no imp fnl f **28/1**

01-0 **10** 1/2 **Wing Commander**[23] 726 7-8-2 **79** .... AndrewElliott(5) 7 65
(I W McInnes) midfield: swtchd outside and hdwy over 2f out: sn rdn and btn **25/1**

346- **11** 3/4 **Go Solo**[198] 5612 5-8-5 **77** .... DeanMcKeown 6 61
(G A Swinbank) bhd tl sme hdwy fnl 2f: nvr a factor **14/1**

54-1 **12** 3/4 **Mezuzah**[23] 726 6-8-4 **79** ow1 .... PaulMulrennan(3) 4 61
(M W Easterby) chsd ldrs: rdn along wl over 2f out: sn wknd **8/1**[3]

010- **13** 1/2 **Dark Charm (FR)**[228] 4889 7-8-5 **77** .... PaulHanagan 12 58
(R A Fahey) chsd ldrs: rdn along wl over 2f out: sn wknd **18/1**

62-0 **14** 1/2 **Instructor**[13] 867 5-8-2 **81** .... NSLawes(7) 8 61
(R A Fahey) in tch: rdn along over 2f out: sn wknd **40/1**

35-2 **15** hd **Emerald Bay (IRE)**[17] 815 4-8-12 **84** .... TomEaves 2 64
(I Semple) chsd ldrs on outer: rdn along 3f out: wknd over 2f out **6/1**[1]

6- **16** 2 1/2 **Indian's Feather (IRE)**[162] 6270 5-9-4 **90** ....(b) KimTinkler 3 64
(N Tinkler) in tch: rdn along 3f out: sn wknd **33/1**

006- **17** 1 **Society Music (IRE)**[196] 5662 4-8-3 **78** .... BenSwarbrick(3) 5 50
(M Dods) cl up: rdn along 3f out: sn wknd **50/1**

42-0 **18** 11 **Thunderwing (IRE)**[13] 865 4-8-10 **82** .... PatCosgrave 1 28
(K R Burke) a rr: pushed along and bhd fr 1/2-way **33/1**

1m 36.58s (-1.22) **Going Correction** +0.125s/f (Good) **18** Ran SP% **127.4**
Speed ratings (Par 107):111,109,105,104,104 102,101,100,99,98 98,97,96,96,96 93,92,81
CSF £68.45 CT £1053.91 TOTE £10.70: £2.40, £2.90, £3.90, £3.00; EX 86.30.
Owner Rio Riva Partnership **Bred** Mrs S Camacho **Trained** Norton, N Yorks

FOCUS
A decent handicap for the track and a fair winning time for the grade. The first two came clear in the closing stages and the form looks solid.

NOTEBOOK
Rio Riva ◆, a pretty consistent colt with not many miles on the clock, returned to action with a decisive victory in what looked a competitive handicap. Although the draw again played its part, the first two came clear and with the second having had a run, this looks the performance of an improved colt. He is worth keeping on the right side. (op 10-1)
Namroc(IRE), who got loose before the start, can be given credit for being the only one to get near the winner. He had shown his wellbeing with a good effort over ten furlongs recently, and he looks capable of adding to his sole previous success, gained on his racecourse debut.
Jubilee Street(IRE), well suited by fast ground, put up a decent effort on this return to action, but was left behind by the principals in the closing stages.
Harvest Warrior, whose seasonal debut was over ten furlongs on much softer ground, ran better back at this trip with the blinkers on for the first time but has not won since his juvenile days and has something to prove now.
Blue Trojan(IRE), who ran well on his return to action last time, should have been helped by this faster ground but could never land a blow having been held up. He is pretty well handicapped at present so can be given another chance. (op 7-1)
Nero's Return(IRE), who has been racing on testing ground so far this season, found this going more to his liking but was never in contention. He was however, keeping on quite nicely in the latter stages. (op 11-1)
Flipando(IRE) went close in tougher handicaps than this at the end of last season, and ran as if this outing was needed. He looks the sort who could pick up a decent race this term, but probably needs to drop a few pounds in the handicap. (op 7-1)
Emerald Bay(IRE), narrowly beaten on his seasonal return on heavy, was disappointing this time but may have bounced or not fully recovered from the effects of that hard race. Official explanation: trainer had no explanation for the poor form shown (op 5-1)
Thunderwing(IRE) Official explanation: jockey said gelding finished distressed

1044 MICHELLE & RICHARD GUDGEON WEDDING H'CAP 1m 2f
4:35 (4:37) (Class 5) (0-70,70) 3-Y-O **£3,238** (£963; £481; £240) **Stalls** Low

Form RPR

20-3 **1** **Bedouin Blue (IRE)**[23] 730 3-8-11 **70** .... LeanneKershaw(7) 9 77
(P C Haslam) in tch: hdwy on outer 4f out: effrt to chse ldrs over 2f out: styd on to ld ins last **4/1**[2]

6032 **2** 3/4 **Night Groove (IRE)**[7] 945 3-7-13 **56** ....(b) JamesDoyle(5) 6 62
(N P Littmoden) trckd ldng pair: hdwy to ld over 2f out: sn rdn: drvn over 1f out: hdd and no ex ins last **5/2**[1]

610 **3** 2 **Ransom Strip (USA)**[44] 583 3-9-4 **70** .... JoeFanning 7 72
(M Johnston) led: rdn along over 3f out: hdd over 2f out: drvn and kpt on same pce ent last **7/1**

00-4 **4** 1/2 **Stainley (IRE)**[23] 730 3-9-2 **68** .... GrahamGibbons 4 69
(J D Bethell) keen: prom: effrt 3f out: rdn along wl over 1f out and kpt on same pce **6/1**[3]

030- **5** 1 **Carr Hall (IRE)**[182] 5939 3-8-10 **62** .... DavidAllan 1 61
(T D Easterby) chsd ldrs: rdn along and sltly outpcd over 2f out: styd on ins last **14/1**

660- **6** 2 **Dubai Around (IRE)**[182] 5944 3-8-5 **57** .... DeanMcKeown 3 53
(Micky Hammond) a rr **16/1**

004- **7** 1 **Nimrana Fort**[178] 6002 3-9-2 **68** .... TomEaves 5 62
(I Semple) chsd ldrs: rdn along 3f out: drvn 2f out: sn wknd **13/2**

0214 **8** 18 **Subsidise (IRE)**[47] 548 3-8-8 **60** ....(b) PaulHanagan 2 19
(F P Murtagh) dwlt: hld up towards rr: effrt and sme hdwy 4f out: sn rdn along and wknd: bhd fnl 2f **14/1**

60-0 **9** dist **Guideline**[81] 199 3-8-4 **56** oh1 .... DaleGibson 8 —
(M W Easterby) a rr: t.o fnl 3f **16/1**

2m 9.70s (2.90) **Going Correction** +0.40s/f (Good) **9** Ran SP% **113.8**
Speed ratings (Par 98):104,103,101,101,100 99,98,83,—
CSF £14.17 CT £66.13 TOTE £4.40: £2.00, £1.40, £3.30; EX 14.40.
Owner Blue Lion Racing VI **Bred** John Weld **Trained** Middleham Moor, N Yorks

FOCUS
A modest handicap but run at a sound gallop and the form appears solid enough with those just outside the places running to form.
Subsidise(IRE) Official explanation: trainer said gelding would not face the blinkers

1045 "GET YOUR REDCAR ANNUAL-BADGE TODAY!" H'CAP 1m 3f
5:10 (5:10) (Class 6) (0-65,65) 4-Y-0+ **£2,730** (£806; £403) **Stalls** Low

Form RPR

0-60 **1** **Summer Charm**[51] 521 4-9-4 **65** .... PaulHanagan 6 71
(W Jarvis) hld up in rr: gd hdwy 3f out: swtchd lft over 1f out: rdn and qcknd to ld ins last: edgd rt nr fin **6/1**[1]

00-6 **2** hd **Platinum Charmer (IRE)**[13] 869 6-8-7 **61** .... PatrickDonaghy(7) 4 67
(K R Burke) dwlt: sn in tch: hdwy on outer 3f out: rdn to chal over 1f out and ev ch tl hung lft ins last: no ex nr fin **9/1**

424- **3** 1 1/4 **Charlie Tango (IRE)**[55] 5884 5-8-11 **58** .... JoeFanning 14 63+
(D W Thompson) trckd ldr: hdwy to ld over 2f out: rdn over 1f out: drvn and hdd ins last: hld whn n.m.r nr fin **13/2**[2]

400- **4** 1 1/2 **Mr Majestic**[165] 6236 4-8-4 **58** .... MichaelJStainton(7) 2 60
(R M Whitaker) hld up: hdwy on inner over 4f out: swtchd rt and effrt over 2f out: sn rdn and kpt on same pce **33/1**

00-0 **5** shd **Apache Point (IRE)**[7] 940 9-8-11 **58** .... KimTinkler 13 59
(N Tinkler) led: rdn along 3f out: hdd over 2f out: sn drvn and grad wknd **16/1**

266- **6** 1 1/2 **San Deng**[190] 5759 4-9-2 **63** .... DarrenWilliams 11 62
(Micky Hammond) in tch: hdwy to chse ldrs 4f out: rdn along 3f out: drvn over 2f out and sn wknd **9/1**

0-44 **7** 1/2 **Dispol Veleta**[28] 678 5-9-2 **63** .... PaulFessey 3 61
(T D Barron) trckd ldrs: hdwy 4f out: rdn along over 2f out and sn one pce **10/1**

60/2 **8** 2 **King's Crest**[19] 794 8-8-12 **59** .... GrahamGibbons 9 54
(J J Quinn) trckd ldrs: effrt over 3f out: sn rdn along and wknd over 2f out **7/1**[3]

0/0- **9** shd **Perfect Punch**[112] 5983 7-8-8 **62** .... JamesReveley(7) 8 57
(K G Reveley) hld up and towards rr tl sme late hdwy **25/1**

005- **10** 2 **Trouble Mountain (USA)**[166] 6230 9-9-0 **61** ....(t) DaleGibson 15 53
(M W Easterby) stdd s: hld up: a rr **12/1**

600- **11** shd **Son Of Thunder (IRE)**[185] 5884 5-8-10 **57** .... TomEaves 7 49
(M Dods) a rr **9/1**

65-0 **12** 8 **William Tell (IRE)**[30] 599 4-8-12 **62** .... PaulMulrennan(3) 5 41
(Micky Hammond) chsd ldrs: rdn along over 3f out and sn wknd **33/1**

600- **13** 1 **Toss The Caber (IRE)**[157] 4834 4-8-10 **57** ....(t) TonyCulhane 16 34
(K G Reveley) a bhd **15/2**

50-0 **14** 15 **Pont Neuf (IRE)**[13] 869 6-8-8 **55** ....(t) AdrianTNicholls 10 8
(A Crook) a bhd **25/1**

2m 26.88s (5.88) **Going Correction** +0.40s/f (Good) **14** Ran SP% **118.1**
Speed ratings (Par 101):94,93,92,91,91 90,90,88,88,87 87,81,80,69
CSF £55.35 CT £362.41 TOTE £5.70: £2.60, £3.10, £2.40; EX 35.00 Place 6 £349.16, Place 5 £181.29.
Owner William Jarvis **Bred** Blackdown Stud **Trained** Newmarket, Suffolk
■ Stewards' Enquiry : Patrick Donaghy three-day ban: careless riding (Apr 28-30)

FOCUS
A modest handicap and a moderate winning time for the class. The form is ordinary and is limited by the third.
Dispol Veleta Official explanation: jockey said mare was unsuited by the good to firm (good in places) ground
T/Jkpt: Not won. T/Plt: £865.20 to a £1 stake. Pool: £45,394.20. 38.30 winning tickets. T/Qpdt: £34.90 to a £1 stake. Pool: £2,514.20. 53.30 winning tickets. JR

877 WARWICK (L-H)
Monday, April 17

OFFICIAL GOING: Good (good to firm in places)
Wind: Moderate, half-behind Weather: Fine

1046 BETFRED MILLION MAIDEN FILLIES' STKS 5f
2:10 (2:11) (Class 5) 2-Y-O **£3,238** (£963; £481; £240) **Stalls** Low

Form RPR

1 **Just Joey** 2-9-0 .... JimmyFortune 4 64
(J R Weymes) hmpd s: a.p: rdn over 1f out: led ins fnl f: r.o **14/1**

0 **2** 1 **Peppin's Gold (IRE)**[14] 849 2-9-0 .... AlanMunro 6 60+
(B R Millman) chsd ldrs: rdn over 1f out: hung bdly rt and rdr lost iron ins fnl f: r.o to take 2nd on stand rail towards fin **14/1**

5 **3** 3/4 **Our Susie (IRE)**[13] 878 2-9-0 .... HayleyTurner 3 57
(M D I Usher) wnt rt s: led: rdn over 1f out: hdd ins fnl f: nt qckn towards fin **6/1**[2]

6 **4** 2 **She Wont Wait**[14] 849 2-9-0 .... FergusSweeney 2 49
(T M Jones) prom: rdn over 1f out: no ex wl ins fnl f **25/1**

5 hd **Caj (IRE)** 2-9-0 .... RobertHavlin 13 48+
(M Quinn) chsd ldrs: rdn wl over 1f out: hung lft ins fnl f: styd on same pce **14/1**

6 1 **La Roca (IRE)** 2-9-0 .... SebSanders 1 44
(R M Beckett) midfield: pushed along 1/2-way: kpt on fnl f: nvr trbld ldrs: improve **5/1**[1]

5 **7** 1 **Mrs Crossy (IRE)**[9] 912 2-8-11 .... RichardSmith(3) 10 40
(R Hannon) chsd ldrs: rdn 1/2-way: one pce fr over 1f out **10/1**

8 1/2 **Cotswold Traveller** 2-9-0 .... SteveDrowne 12 38
(Tom Dascombe) s.s and sltly hmpd s: outpcd: styd on fnl f **28/1**

9 3/4 **Splendidio** 2-9-0 .... TQuinn 9 35
(M R Channon) midfield: rdn 2f out: nvr on terms **15/2**

10 1/2 **Almora Guru** 2-9-0 .... MartinDwyer 15 33
(W M Brisbourne) s.i.s: outpcd: nvr on terms **33/1**

11 1/2 **Cadi May** 2-9-0 .... RichardMullen 5 31
(W M Brisbourne) s.s: a in rr div **40/1**

12 hd **Springtime Parkes** 2-9-0 .... KDarley 14 30
(K A Ryan) midfield: rdn 1/2-way: sn wknd **6/1**[2]

13 nk **Cavort (IRE)** 2-8-9 .... EmmettStack(5) 11 29+
(Pat Eddery) s.s: a outpcd **7/1**[3]

14 5 **Vizionary** 2-9-0 .... MickyFenton 8 9
(Mrs P Sly) s.s: a pushed along and outpcd **20/1**

0 **15** 15 **Sainara (IRE)**[13] 878 2-8-9 .... GregFairley(5) 16 —
(J M Bradley) wnt rt s: midfield on outside: hung rt 1/2-way: sn bhd **66/1**

60.57 secs (0.37) **Going Correction** -0.175s/f (Firm) **15** Ran SP% **117.5**
Speed ratings (Par 89):90,88,87,84,83 82,80,79,78,77 76,76,76,68,44
CSF £176.56 TOTE £20.40: £6.10, £4.80, £2.70; EX 183.70.
Owner Rosemary's Racing **Bred** Mrs D O Joly **Trained** Middleham Moor, N Yorks

FOCUS
There was little strength in depth to this juvenile event and the form is hard to assess.

NOTEBOOK
Just Joey, a half-sister to fair mile winner Whitgift Rock, did well to overcome a troubled start and showed a decent attitude when it mattered to make a winning debut. Entitled to improve for the experience, she may only prove modest, yet her pedigree suggests a stiffer test should prove to her liking before the end of the year. (op 16-1)
Peppin's Gold(IRE), who looked tricky when seventh on her recent debut at Lingfield, again displayed her quirks and would have most likely prevailed but for hanging under pressure. She is talented enough to win a race of this nature, but her attitude is now under close scrutiny.
Our Susie(IRE), fifth over course and distance on debut 13 days previously, put her experience to good use early on yet ultimately proved a sitting duck for the first two. She is going the right way. (op 13-2 tchd 7-1 and 11-2 in a place)

She Wont Wait had her chance yet failed to sustain her effort in the final furlong. She helps to set the level of this form. (op 20-1)
La Roca(IRE) ◆, the highest-priced runner in this line-up and related to winners from six to 14 furlongs, shaped very much as though she would improve plenty for this debut experience and ought to get much closer next time. (op 13-2)
Cavort(IRE), whose dam was a mile winner at two, was never in contention after a sluggish start and should really only be of more interest when faced with a stiffer test in due course. (op 5-1)

1047 BETFREDPOKER.COM H'CAP 5f
2:45 (2:46) (Class 5) (0-75,76) 4-Y-0+ **£3,238** (£963; £481; £240) **Stalls Low**

Form RPR
000- **1** **Spanish Ace**227 [4915] 5-9-4 **75** RyanMoore 2 86
(J M Bradley) *wnt rt s: mde all: shkn up over 1f out: r.o wl* **13/2**2
560- **2** 2 **Cesar Manrique (IRE)**248 [4333] 4-8-9 **66** MichaelHills 7 70+
(B W Hills) *in rr: hdwy over 1f out: r.o strly ins fnl f: nrst fin* **15/2**3
0450 **3** ½ **Fizzlephut (IRE)**7 [947] 4-9-4 **75** PaulFitzsimons 13 77
(Miss J R Tooth) *midfield: pushed along 1/2-way: hdwy over 1f out: r.o ins fnl f* **9/1**
00-0 **4** nk **Bluebok**6 [967] 5-8-13 **75** (t) GregFairley(5) 17 76+
(J M Bradley) *upset in stalls: chsd ldrs: rdn to chse wnr over 1f out: hung lft ins fnl f: no ex and lost 2nd towards fin* **28/1**
0133 **5** 1¼ **Almaty Express**5 [986] 4-8-9 **66** (b) KDarley 6 62
(J R Weymes) *w wnr tl rdn and hung rt over 1f out: nt qckn ins fnl f* **15/2**3
0300 **6** 1 **Kempsey**7 [947] 4-9-0 **74** (v) NeilChalmers(3) 16 67
(J J Bridger) *carried rt s: chsd ldrs after 1f: rdn and hung rt over 1f out: kpt on same pce fnl f* **25/1**
000- **7** nk **Dunn Deal (IRE)**200 [5567] 6-8-10 **67** MartinDwyer 12 59
(W M Brisbourne) *in tch: rdn over 1f out: kpt on same pce fnl f* **9/1**
-040 **8** ¾ **Clipper Hoy**6 [967] 4-8-5 **67** RichardKingscote(5) 3 56
(Mrs H Sweeting) *carried rt s: chsd ldrs: rdn 1f out: sn fdd* **12/1**
2441 **9** nk **Wicked Uncle**5 [986] 7-9-5 **76** 6ex (v) JimmyFortune 11 64
(S Gollings) *midfield: rdn over 1f out: nt pce to trble ldrs* **9/1**
00-0 **10** ½ **Whistler**7 [947] 9-9-1 **75** (p) DNolan(3) 1 61
(Miss J R Tooth) *in tch: rdn over 1f out: sn outpcd* **20/1**
363- **11** nk **Cerulean Rose**189 [5802] 7-8-12 **69** MickyFenton 9 54
(A W Carroll) *bhd: mod hdwy ins fnl f: nvr trbld ldrs* **20/1**
200- **12** 1 **My Only Sunshine**182 [5951] 7-8-11 **68** HayleyTurner 4 49
(M J Wallace) *hmpd s: a towards rr* **6/1**1
440- **13** 2½ **Starduster**189 [5802] 4-8-9 **66** AlanMunro 5 38
(B R Millman) *hmpd and squeezed out s: sn in midfield: wknd 2f out* **9/1**
30-0 **14** 6 **Domirati**49 [532] 6-8-6 **63** (b) JamieMackay 10 14
(J D Bethell) *s.s and bmpd s: a bhd* **25/1**
0-00 **15** 9 **No Time (IRE)**21 [761] 6-9-2 **73** TQuinn 14 —
(M J Polglase) *wnt rt s: a in rr div* **20/1**
58.69 secs (-1.51) **Going Correction** -0.175s/f (Firm) **15** Ran SP% **124.3**
Speed ratings (Par 103):105,101,101,100,98 96,96,95,94,93 93,91,87,78,63
CSF £49.84 CT £462.53 TOTE £8.00: £2.70, £3.20, £3.30; EX 82.20.
Owner The Farleigh Court Racing Partnership **Bred** Farleigh Court Racing Partnership **Trained** Sedbury, Gloucs

FOCUS
A modest sprint which saw a ready winner who can rate higher for his new yard.
Clipper Hoy Official explanation: jockey said gelding didn't handle the track
My Only Sunshine Official explanation: jockey said gelding suffered interference leaving stalls
No Time(IRE) Official explanation: jockey said horse slipped leaving stalls

1048 BETFRED.COM MAIDEN STKS (DIV I) 7f 26y
3:20 (3:22) (Class 5) 3-Y-0 **£3,562** (£1,059; £529; £264) **Stalls Low**

Form RPR
0- **1** **Portland**178 [6002] 3-9-3 RichardHughes 12 84+
(B W Hills) *w ldr: rdn to ld over 1f out: r.o* **40/1**
24-5 **2** ½ **Street Warrior (IRE)**24 [716] 3-9-3 75 KDarley 3 83
(M Johnston) *led: rdn and hdd over 1f out: styd on* **14/1**
3 1 **Mumaathel (IRE)** 3-9-3 RHills 2 80
(M P Tregoning) *trckd ldrs: rdn over 1f out: edgd rt ins fnl f: styd on* **5/1**3
66- **4** 1 **Jihaaz (IRE)**209 [5392] 3-9-3 MartinDwyer 11 78
(B W Hills) *chsd ldrs: rdn and edgd rt over 1f out: nt qckn fnl f* **33/1**
2 **5** shd **River Kirov (IRE)**19 [795] 3-9-3 AlanMunro 10 78
(P W Chapple-Hyam) *midfield: hdwy over 2f out: rdn over 1f out: kpt on ins fnl f: nt pce to trble ldrs* **5/4**1
030- **6** 2½ **King's Revenge**153 [6352] 3-9-3 79 TQuinn 4 71
(T D Easterby) *in tch: rdn 2f out: btn over 1f out* **16/1**
434- **7** ½ **Ingratitude (IRE)**182 [5944] 3-9-3 76 SebSanders 5 70
(R M Beckett) *midfield: rdn over 2f out: no hdwy* **12/1**
0 **8** 7 **Jiggy Spriggy (IRE)**13 [880] 3-8-12 MichaelTebbutt 1 47
(V Smith) *bhd: swtchd rt ins fnl f: kpt on: nvr on terms w ldrs* **100/1**
502- **9** nk **High Octave (IRE)**217 [5171] 3-9-3 72 GeorgeBaker 7 51
(B G Powell) *hld up: pushed along over 2f out: nvr trbld ldrs* **33/1**
10 nk **Ashford Castle (IRE)** 3-9-3 JimmyFortune 8 50
(B J Meehan) *s.s: hld up: n.m.r after 1f: rdn over 2f out: no imp* **9/2**2
30-0 **11** 2 **Croft (IRE)**13 [880] 3-9-3 69 WandersonD'Avila 9 45
(J W Hills) *a bhd* **100/1**
0- **12** hd **North Fleet**315 [2332] 3-8-12 GregFairley(5) 14 44
(J M Bradley) *wnt rt s: a bhd* **100/1**
0- **13** 13 **Ferroli**318 [2263] 3-9-0 (b1) JasonEdmunds(3) 13 10
(J Balding) *midfield: rdn and hung rt over 3f out: sn wknd* **100/1**
220- **14** 14 **Woolfall Blue (IRE)**240 [4598] 3-9-3 82 JamieMackay 6 —
(G G Margarson) *racd keenly: midfield: n.m.r after 1f and again over 3f out: sn lost pl: eased whn bhd fnl 2f* **14/1**
1m 23.2s (-1.80) **Going Correction** -0.30s/f (Firm) **14** Ran SP% **118.5**
Speed ratings (Par 98):98,97,96,95,95 92,91,83,83,82 80,80,65,49
CSF £511.51 TOTE £55.10: £8.10, £3.50, £1.80; EX 325.20.
Owner K Abdulla **Bred** Juddmonte Farms Ltd **Trained** Lambourn, Berks

FOCUS
The winning time was 2.4 seconds quicker than the second division, but still only par for a race like this, and the form should work out.
Ashford Castle(IRE) Official explanation: jockey said gelding panicked in stalls
Woolfall Blue(IRE) Official explanation: jockey said colt lost its action

1049 BETFRED.COM MAIDEN STKS (DIV II) 7f 26y
3:55 (4:01) (Class 5) 3-Y-0 **£3,562** (£1,059; £529; £264) **Stalls Low**

Form RPR
42- **1** **Baskerville**186 [5850] 3-9-3 AlanMunro 10 69
(P W Chapple-Hyam) *trckd ldrs: rdn 2f out: sn chalng: edgd rt and rdr lost iron ins fnl f: r.o to ld post* **11/8**1
35- **2** shd **Marmooq**180 [5977] 3-9-3 RHills 6 69
(M Johnston) *w ldr: hung rt on bnd over 3f out: led wl over 1f out: hdd post* **4/1**3
3 **3** ¾ **Days Of My Life (IRE)**20 [778] 3-9-3 SteveDrowne 11 67+
(R Charlton) *hld up: hdwy 2f out: r.o ins fnl f: nrst fin* **7/2**2
4 2 **Over Ice** 3-8-12 SebSanders 3 56
(Karen George) *midfield: rdn and hdwy over 2f out: kpt on same pce ins fnl f* **20/1**
00 **5** 2½ **Ronaldo**6 [964] 3-9-3 MartinDwyer 2 55
(W R Muir) *in tch: rdn over 3f out: one pce fr over 1f out* **66/1**
04- **6** ¾ **Miss Redactive**218 [5155] 3-8-12 HayleyTurner 5 48
(M D I Usher) *trckd ldrs: rdn over 3f out: outpcd over 1f out* **25/1**
45 **7** hd **Russian Mist (IRE)**80 [215] 3-9-3 JimmyFortune 7 52
(M J Wallace) *in rr: hdwy 3f out: rdn 2f out: nvr trbld ldrs* **16/1**
0 **8** 2½ **Lol Draper**6 [963] 3-8-12 RobertHavlin 4 41
(P D Evans) *led: rdn 2f out: sn hdd: wknd fnl f* **50/1**
00- **9** 2½ **Foreign Envoy (IRE)**172 [6121] 3-9-3 MichaelHills 9 39
(B W Hills) *swtchd lft s: bhd: kpt on fnl f: nvr trbld ldrs* **16/1**
10 ½ **Haughton Hope** 3-9-0 JasonEdmunds(3) 1 38
(J Balding) *racd keenly: midfield: rdn over 1f out: sn wknd* **66/1**
224- **11** 1½ **Bold Cross (IRE)**178 [6005] 3-9-3 70 MichaelTebbutt 13 34
(E G Bevan) *hld up: n.d* **8/1**
00- **12** nk **Freeze The Flame (GER)**153 [6351] 3-9-3 MickyFenton 14 34
(C R Egerton) *midfield: wknd 3f out* **40/1**
00 **13** 1¾ **Prince Marju (IRE)**23 [735] 3-9-3 CraigCarver 8 29
(P A Blockley) *hld up: rdn over 2f out: nvr on terms* **80/1**
1m 25.6s (0.60) **Going Correction** -0.30s/f (Firm) **52** Ran SP% **124.4**
Speed ratings (Par 98):84,83,83,80,77 77,76,73,71,70 68,68,66
CSF £6.79 TOTE £2.50: £1.20, £1.90, £1.80; EX 9.40.
Owner Hintlesham Racing **Bred** Mrs J A Prescott **Trained** Newmarket, Suffolk

FOCUS
The winning time was 2.4 seconds slower than the first division, which is pedestrian for a race of its type, and the first three came clear. The form does not look that reliable.
Marmooq Official explanation: jockey said colt tried to run out
Foreign Envoy(IRE) Official explanation: jockey said, regarding the running and riding, his orders were to keep gelding in mid-division and teach it about racing in the last couple of furlongs, adding that he was unable to carry out orders as gelding jumped slowly from stalls and, not wishing to run wide, he felt it prudent to track towards the inner; trainer added that gelding is very difficult to train at home being inclined to run away, and they were conerned about it settling in its races
Bold Cross(IRE) Official explanation: jockey said, regarding the running and riding, his orders were to drop in on gelding, a big free-running animal, ride from there and get it to finish, adding that it appeared to be running on its nerves early on and found very little when asked for an effort in the home straight; trainer added that gelding had been held up for two hours in heavy traffic travelling to course and so was very buzzy and dripping in sweat on arrival; vet said gelding had a high heart rate when examined half an hour after race
Freeze The Flame(GER) Official explanation: jockey said gelding hung left-handed

1050 BETFRED MILLION CONDITIONS STKS 7f 26y
4:30 (4:31) (Class 4) 4-Y-0+ **£6,477** (£1,927; £963; £481) **Stalls Low**

Form RPR
600- **1** **Etlaala**184 [5900] 4-8-8 110 RHills 6 113+
(B W Hills) *mde all: clr over 1f out: r.o wl* **7/4**1
056- **2** 5 **Mac Love**213 [5269] 5-8-8 107 SteveDrowne 7 100
(R Charlton) *hld up: hdwy 2f out: wnt 2nd wl over 1f out: no ch w wnr* **15/8**2
456- **3** 1½ **Jedburgh**198 [5614] 5-8-8 103 (b) TQuinn 5 96
(J L Dunlop) *hld up: pushed along over 2f out: hdwy over 1f out: one pce fnl f* **10/3**3
00-5 **4** 7 **Roman Maze**37 [627] 6-8-8 89 MartinDwyer 2 78
(W M Brisbourne) *prom tl rdn and wknd over 1f out* **9/1**
5563 **5** 7 **Pawn In Life (IRE)**10 [906] 8-8-8 40 (v) FrancisNorton 3 60?
(M J Polglase) *trckd ldrs: lost pl over 4f out: bhd after* **50/1**
4504 **6** 1¼ **Doctor's Cave**44 [587] 4-8-8 56 (b) FergusSweeney 4 56
(K O Cunningham-Brown) *prom: rdn 2f out: sn wknd* **100/1**
1m 20.7s (-4.30) **Going Correction** -0.30s/f (Firm) course record **6** Ran SP% **107.2**
Speed ratings (Par 105):112,106,104,96,88 87
CSF £4.80 TOTE £2.70: £1.60, £1.60; EX 5.40.
Owner Hamdan Al Maktoum **Bred** Matthews Breeding And Racing Ltd **Trained** Lambourn, Berks

FOCUS
The winning time was not surprisingly much faster than both divisions of the three-year-old maiden, but still a smart one for a race of its class, and the winner bounced back to near his best.

1051 BETFREDPOKER.COM H'CAP 1m 2f 188y
5:05 (5:07) (Class 4) (0-85,85) 4-Y-0+ **£6,477** (£1,927; £963; £481) **Stalls Low**

Form RPR
04-0 **1** **Yakimov (USA)**23 [726] 7-8-6 **76** EdwardCreighton(3) 1 89
(D J Wintle) *trckd ldrs: led over 1f out: r.o wl* **25/1**
500- **2** 5 **Snowed Under**182 [5948] 5-8-6 **73** TQuinn 15 78
(J D Bethell) *trckd ldrs: rdn and ev ch over 1f out: nt pce of wnr fnl f* **14/1**
210- **3** 1 **Balance Of Power**242 [4514] 4-9-0 **81** RichardHughes 2 84+
(R Charlton) *hld up: rdn and hdwy 2f out: kpt on ins fnl f* **9/4**1
206- **4** nk **Gringo**174 [6101] 4-8-8 **75** MichaelHills 5 77+
(B W Hills) *hld up: rdn and hdwy over 1f out whn carried lft: swtchd lft ent fnl f: styd on wl towards fin* **9/2**2
020- **5** ½ **Hawridge Star (IRE)**208 [5404] 4-8-7 **74** AlanMunro 17 75
(W S Kittow) *prom: rdn and ev ch over 1f out: one pce ins fnl f* **20/1**
-222 **6** 1 **Red Birr (IRE)**65 [375] 5-8-9 **76** ow1 SebSanders 12 76
(P R Webber) *hld up: hdwy over 2f out: rdn and hung lft over 1f out: one pce ins fnl f* **9/2**2
51-0 **7** 2½ **Parnassian**16 [826] 6-8-4 **74** RichardThomas(3) 9 69
(J A Geake) *midfield: rdn over 1f out: nvr able to chal* **14/1**
00-0 **8** ½ **Rawaabet (IRE)**52 [223] 4-8-4 **71** oh4 FrancisFerris 8 66
(P W Hiatt) *led: rdn and hdd over 1f out: wknd fnl f* **50/1**
62-0 **9** hd **Magic Sting**13 [867] 5-8-13 **80** HayleyTurner 4 74+
(M L W Bell) *hld up: rdn and swtchd lft wl over 1f out: no imp* **10/1**
63- **10** 4 **Diamond Diggins (GER)**248 [4348] 4-8-8 **75** MichaelTebbutt 13 63
(V Smith) *in rr: rdn 2f out: sn wknd* **33/1**
25-0 **11** 6 **Love Angel (USA)**23 [723] 4-8-4 **71** (v) FrancisNorton 3 48
(J J Bridger) *s.s: a bhd* **33/1**
-256 **12** 1¼ **Consonant (IRE)**21 [763] 9-8-8 **75** MickyFenton 14 50
(D G Bridgwater) *midfield: rdn and hdwy over 3f out: wknd 2f out: btn whn hmpd over 1f out* **20/1**
230- **13** 2 **Terminate (GER)**206 [5433] 4-8-8 **75** RyanMoore 7 47
(N P Littmoden) *racd keenly: midfield: rdn over 2f out: wknd over 1f out* **7/1**3

1642 **14** *13* **Blue Patrick**[33] 640 6-8-1 **75**.................................. KevinGhunowa(7) 11 25
(P A Blockley) *s.s: a bhd* **16/1**

2m 18.03s (-1.37) **Going Correction** +0.10s/f (Good) **14** Ran SP% **129.2**
Speed ratings (Par 105):108,104,103,103,103 102,100,100,100,97 92,91,90,80
CSF £339.08 CT £1124.07 TOTE £36.40: £8.90, £5.30, £1.60; EX 631.00.
Owner B E T Partnership **Bred** Jane & Jeff Wooder **Trained** Naunton, Gloucs

FOCUS
A fair handicap, run at a solid pace, and the winner did the job nicely. The runner-up sets the standard.
Terminate(GER) Official explanation: jockey said gelding was unsuited by the uneven ground
Blue Patrick Official explanation: trainer said gelding was unsuited by good (good to firm in places) ground

1052 BETFRED MILLION H'CAP 1m 2f 188y
5:40 (5:40) (Class 5) (0-70,69) 3-Y-O **£3,238** (£963; £481; £240) **Stalls** Low

Form RPR
00-4 **1** **Rahy's Crown (USA)**[9] 918 3-8-10 **61**..................... RichardHughes 14 67
(R Hannon) *midfield: hdwy over 4f out: led over 1f out: edgd rt ins fnl f: drvn out* **6/1**
4433 **2** *1* **Mambo Sun**[4] 1005 3-8-7 **65**...................................... KevinGhunowa(7) 8 69
(P A Blockley) *in tch: rdn 2f out: ev ch whn hung lft 1f out: r.o* **11/2[3]**
063 **3** *nk* **Alexian**[17] 823 3-9-2 **67**.. GeorgeBaker 11 70
(R Hollinshead) *hld up: hdwy over 4f out: nt clr run 2f out: rdn and cl up whn nt clr run ent fnl f: sn swtchd lft: r.o* **16/1**
60-0 **4** *1 ½* **Asbury Park**[91] 123 3-9-0 **65**... RichardMullen 9 66
(E S McMahon) *t.k.h: in tch: effrt whn hung rt on bnd 3f out: styd on ins fnl f* **4/1[1]**
050- **5** *4* **Citelle (IRE)**[182] 5939 3-8-6 **60**.................................(t) RichardThomas(3) 2 54
(Mrs P N Dutfield) *midfield: outpcd 3f out: rdn and edgd lft over 1f out: kpt on ins fnl f* **20/1**
-124 **6** *nk* **Orvietan (IRE)**[18] 804 3-9-3 **68**.. KDarley 4 62
(M Johnston) *trckd ldrs: lost pl after 3f: nt clr run and hmpd over 2f out: hung rt 1f out: kpt on same pce* **5/1[2]**
025 **7** *hd* **Marcello**[10] 900 3-9-3 **68**... JimmyFortune 10 61
(P F I Cole) *trckd ldrs: led over 2f out: rdn and hdd over 1f out: wknd ins fnl f* **7/1**
00-5 **8** *1 ½* **Life Peer**[9] 918 3-8-11 **62**.. TQuinn 13 53
(J G Portman) *hld up: kpt on fnl f: nvr nr to chal* **25/1**
100- **9** *2* **Generous Lad (IRE)**[202] 5536 3-9-1 **66**................................ AlanDaly 6 53
(Miss J S Davis) *racd keenly: led: hdd after 2f: remained cl up: rdn and wknd 2f out* **11/1**
066- **10** *6* **Rebelling (IRE)**[180] 5970 3-9-4 **69**.............................. StephenCarson 17 46
(R F Johnson Houghton) *in tch: rdn and wknd over 4f out* **16/1**
40-0 **11** *nk* **Is It Me (USA)**[7] 952 3-9-4 **69**.. CraigCarver 7 46
(P A Blockley) *prom: led after 2f: rdn and hdd over 2f out: wknd over 1f out* **33/1**
050- **12** *12* **Royal Premier (IRE)**[164] 6244 3-8-8 **59**.............................. AlanMunro 1 15
(H J Collingridge) *a bhd* **14/1**
-310 **13** *2 ½* **Monte Mayor Junior**[42] 604 3-8-8 **59**...............................(v) RobertHavlin 12 11
(D Haydn Jones) *in tch: rdn and wknd over 3f out* **20/1**
650- **14** *7* **Azime (IRE)**[208] 5401 3-8-13 **64**.. RyanMoore 16 4
(C E Brittain) *racd wd: prom tl wknd over 3f out* **12/1**

2m 21.69s (2.29) **Going Correction** +0.10s/f (Good) **14** Ran SP% **129.6**
Speed ratings (Par 98):95,94,94,92,90 89,89,88,87,82 82,73,72,66
CSF £40.18 CT £529.36 TOTE £6.70: £2.90, £2.90, £4.80; EX 48.90 Place 6 £145.24, Place 5 £40.15.
Owner Jaber Abdullah **Bred** Gainsborough Stud Management Llc **Trained** East Everleigh, Wilts

FOCUS
A modest handicap, run at an average pace, and the form looks fair.
Life Peer Official explanation: jockey said gelding was never travelling
Monte Mayor Junior Official explanation: jockey said gelding wouldn't let himself down
T/Plt: £306.20 to a £1 stake. Pool: £32,198.35. 76.75 winning tickets. T/Qpdt: £25.50 to a £1 stake. Pool: £2,241.70. 64.85 winning tickets. DO

795 YARMOUTH (L-H)
Monday, April 17

OFFICIAL GOING: Good to firm
Wind: Fresh, across Weather: Cloudy with sunny spells

1053 BANHAM POULTRY MAIDEN AUCTION STKS 5f 43y
2:25 (2:25) (Class 6) 2-Y-O **£2,590** (£770; £385; £192) **Stalls** High

Form RPR
3 **1** **Satulagi (USA)**[25] 701 2-8-5 .... JohnEgan 1 65
(J S Moore) *s.i.s: sn chsng ldrs: rdn and hung lft 1/2-way: r.o u.p to ld towards fin* **6/4[1]**
42 **2** *nk* **Hucking Hill (IRE)**[9] 912 2-8-13 .... LDettori 3 72
(J R Best) *led: rdn over 1f out: hdd towards fin* **6/4[1]**
3 *¾* **Kompete** 2-8-4 .... MatthewHenry 4 60
(V Smith) *a.p: rdn over 1f out: styd on* **12/1[3]**
4 *2 ½* **Amber Valley** 2-8-7 .... DarryllHolland 5 54
(K A Ryan) *dwlt: hld up: effrt and hung lft over 1f out: styd on same pce ins fnl f* **13/2[2]**
5 *2 ½* **Juan Bol (IRE)** 2-8-9 .... ChrisCatlin 2 46
(V Smith) *hld up in tch: racd keenly: rdn over 1f out: wknd fnl f* **25/1**
0 **6** *1* **Jojesse**[23] 727 2-8-11 .... J-PGuillambert 6 44
(S Parr) *w ldr tl rdn 1/2-way: hung lft and wknd over 1f out* **14/1**

64.21 secs (1.41) **Going Correction** +0.175s/f (Good) **6** Ran SP% **111.5**
Speed ratings (Par 90):95,94,93,89,85 83
CSF £3.72 TOTE £2.60: £1.10, £1.90; EX 4.70.
Owner Mrs Fitri Hay **Bred** Lantern Hill Farm Llc **Trained** Upper Lambourn, Berks
■ Stewards' Enquiry : J-P Guillambert one-day ban: failed to keep straight from stalls (Apr 28)

FOCUS
An ordinary maiden in which previous experience proved the key and the runner-up sets the level.

NOTEBOOK
Satulagi(USA), whose debut third at Kempton was given a boost by the subsequent victory of the sixth, battled on really well to get the better of the other joint-favourite, but she still showed a few signs of greenness so may progress a bit further as she gains experience. (tchd 11-8 and 13-8 in places)
Hucking Hill(IRE), the most experienced in the line-up, tried to make it count by making the running but was unable to cope with the winner. Whilst his experience is an asset at present, races like this are not going to get any easier and he may need to drop in grade in order to get off the mark in the coming weeks. (tchd 2-1)
Kompete ◆, who cost just 2,500gns as a yearling, ran with plenty of promise to finish right on the heels of two rivals who had both already shown ability. She should get a bit further and, being by Komaite, may appreciate easier ground or even Fibresand. (op 10-1 tchd 9-1, 16-1 and 14-1 in a place)
Amber Valley, resold for 9,500gns as a yearling, is a half-sister to six winners including the smart Golden Nun. She was always playing catch-up after missing the break, but did show some ability as the race progressed and, with this outing under her belt, there should be better to come from her. (op 8-1 tchd 6-1)
Juan Bol(IRE), a 2,000gns yearling, did not help his chance by taking a good hold early and had nothing left in the latter stages. Although by a very speedy performer, there is plenty of stamina on the dam's side so he may need more time and eventually a longer trip. (op 20-1)
Jojesse, beaten miles in the Brocklesby on his debut, fared little better here despite the faster ground and looks to be of very limited ability. (tchd 16-1)

1054 AGGBAG LIMITED CLAIMING STKS 6f 3y
3:00 (3:00) (Class 6) 3-Y-O+ **£2,331** (£693; £346; £173) **Stalls** High

Form RPR
0220 **1** **Up Tempo (IRE)**[13] 864 8-9-11 63.............................(b) DarryllHolland 1 68
(K A Ryan) *chsd ldrs: lost pl 4f out: hdwy over 1f out: r.o to ld wl ins fnl f* **5/1[1]**
0-10 **2** *¾* **Banjo Bay (IRE)**[15] 845 8-9-6 63.......................... SilvestreDeSousa(3) 4 64
(D Nicholls) *chsd ldrs: led over 1f out: hdd wl ins fnl f* **5/1[1]**
5006 **3** *hd* **Norcroft**[77] 253 4-9-4 66... KirstyMilczarek(7) 8 65
(Mrs C A Dunnett) *s.i.s: swtchd lft and hdwy over 1f out: hung lft ins fnl f: r.o* **7/1**
0160 **4** *2 ½* **Imperium**[17] 821 5-9-8 51..(p) JohnEgan 11 55
(Stef Liddiard) *sn pushed along in rr: rdn 1/2-way: hung lft and r.o ins fnl f: nrst fin* **16/1**
-200 **5** *1 ¼* **Feast Of Romance**[76] 261 9-9-2 45.............................(b) DerekNolan(5) 3 50
(G A Huffer) *chsd ldrs: rdn and ev ch 2f out: no ex fnl f* **40/1**
5551 **6** *shd* **Piccleyes**[14] 862 5-9-13 55..(b) LDettori 2 56
(M J Polglase) *hld up: hdwy over 1f out: no ex fnl f* **6/1[3]**
0006 **7** *1 ¼* **Indian Gem**[7] 951 5-9-1 40... J-PGuillambert 7 40
(A J Chamberlain) *mid-div: pushed along 1/2-way: nvr trbld ldrs* **33/1**
1000 **8** *nk* **Straffan (IRE)**[13] 873 4-9-4 45...(b) ChrisCatlin 14 42
(J Hetherton) *chsd ldr: led over 3f out: rdn and hdd over 1f out: wknd fnl f* **14/1**
3402 **9** *4* **Orchestration (IRE)**[14] 858 5-9-11 48................(v) RobbieFitzpatrick 12 37
(M J Attwater) *prom: rdn over 2f out: wknd wl over 1f out* **10/1**
-562 **10** *¾* **Peggys First**[12] 890 4-9-8 50.. ShaneKelly 13 32
(D E Cantillon) *s.i.s: a in rr* **9/1**
00-0 **11** *nk* **Yorkshire Lad (IRE)**[19] 798 4-9-13 58...................................... KFallon 6 36
(Miss Gay Kelleway) *mid-div: rdn over 2f out: hung lft and wknd over 1f out* **11/2[2]**
00-0 **12** *1* **Shopfitter**[103] 39 3-8-12 40...(v[1]) OscarUrbina 5 29
(Mrs C A Dunnett) *led: hdd over 3f out: wknd wl over 1f out* **40/1**
0643 **13** *1* **Ace Club**[7] 942 5-9-6 45..(b) JimmyQuinn 10 23
(J Hetherton) *chsd ldrs: lost pl wl over 3f out: sn bhd* **25/1**
0333 **14** *1 ½* **Sergeant Slipper**[10] 907 9-9-0 45..........................(v) JosephWalsh(7) 9 19
(C Smith) *s.s: outpcd* **20/1**

1m 14.8s (1.10) **Going Correction** +0.175s/f (Good)
WFA 3 from 4yo+ 11lb **14** Ran SP% **123.6**
Speed ratings (Par 101):99,98,97,94,92 92,90,90,85,84 83,82,81,79
CSF £28.46 TOTE £6.30: £3.00, £2.60, £2.20; EX 23.00 Trifecta £208.20 Part won. Pool: £293.35 - 0.95 winning tickets..
Owner Yorkshire Racing Club & Derek Blackhurst **Bred** T Burns **Trained** Hambleton, N Yorks
■ Stewards' Enquiry : Kirsty Milczarek one-day ban: used whip with excessive frequency (Apr 28)

FOCUS
A modest claimer in which each of the 14 runners had been kept busy on sand during the winter and the first three placings were filled by the trio best in at the weights and the form should prove sound enough. The action unfolded centre to far side and those drawn high tended to struggle.

1055 GREAT YARMOUTH GLASS MAIDEN STKS 1m 3y
3:35 (3:36) (Class 5) 3-Y-O+ **£3,497** (£1,040; £520; £259) **Stalls** High

Form RPR
0- **1** **Pearly King (USA)**[209] 5392 3-8-11 .... KFallon 2 84+
(Sir Michael Stoute) *chsd ldrs: led 2f out: r.o wl* **7/2[1]**
04- **2** *3* **My Lovely Lady (IRE)**[202] 5535 3-7-13 .... ChrisHough(7) 6 70
(M L W Bell) *hld up: hdwy over 2f out: rdn over 1f out: no ex fnl f* **25/1**
3 *1 ½* **Country Escape** 3-8-11 .... TPQueally 10 72+
(C F Wall) *s.s: hdwy over 3f out: shkn up over 1f out: nt trble ldrs* **33/1**
4-3 **4** *1 ¾* **Conservation (FR)**[13] 880 3-8-11 .... AdrianMcCarthy 9 68
(P W Chapple-Hyam) *chsd ldrs: led 3f out: hdd 2f out: styd on same pce appr fnl f* **11/2[3]**
0- **5** *2* **Sea Of Calm (USA)**[209] 5391 3-8-6 .... OscarUrbina 11 58
(E A L Dunlop) *hld up: hdwy over 2f out: shkn up over 1f out: nvr nr to chal* **4/1[2]**
3335 **6** *1 ¼* **Pop Music (IRE)**[23] 720 3-8-4 72................................... SladeO'Hara(7) 8 60
(Miss J Feilden) *w ldrs: rdn 1/2-way: hung lft over 2f out: wknd over 1f out* **16/1**
7 *½* **Nassar (IRE)** 3-8-11 .... ChrisCatlin 3 59
(G Prodromou) *prom: rdn over 2f out: sn wknd* **40/1**
06- **8** *1 ¾* **Bramcote Lorne**[163] 6251 3-8-11 .... J-PGuillambert 14 55
(S Parr) *prom: rdn over 2f out: sn edgd lft and wknd* **66/1**
9 *6* **Florimund** 3-8-11 .... StephenDavies 4 41
(Sir Michael Stoute) *s.s: nvr nrr* **6/1**
10 *½* **Kapiolani (USA)** 3-8-6 .... JimmyQuinn 5 35
(J M P Eustace) *s.s: a in rr* **66/1**
0- **11** *1 ½* **Lennoxtown (IRE)**[170] 6148 3-8-11 .... PhilipRobinson 1 36
(M A Jarvis) *chsd ldrs: rdn over 2f out: sn wknd* **11/1**
4 **12** *1 ¾* **Eagle Eye**[15] 844 3-8-11 .... JohnEgan 12 32
(G Wragg) *hld up: rdn 1/2-way: wknd wl over 2f out* **8/1**
00- **13** *5* **Spaceman**[170] 6148 3-8-4 .... AshleyHamblett(7) 13 21
(L M Cumani) *hld up: rdn 1/2-way: a in rr* **33/1**
-005 **14** *11* **Jumanji (IRE)**[17] 823 3-8-6 54.................................. RobbieFitzpatrick 7 —
(M J Attwater) *plld hrd: led 5f: sn wknd* **66/1**
053- **15** *8* **Chanteuse Noire (USA)**[224] 4996 3-8-7 69 ow1............. ShaneKelly 15 —
(J Noseda) *s.i.s: hld up: hdwy 1/2-way: wknd 3f out* **7/1**

1m 40.65s (0.75) **Going Correction** +0.175s/f (Good) **15** Ran SP% **126.4**
Speed ratings (Par 103):103,100,98,96,94 93,93,91,85,84 83,81,76,65,57
CSF £101.87 TOTE £4.10: £2.30, £7.60, £9.80; EX 87.80 Trifecta £184.10 Part won. Pool: £259.31 - 0.35 winning tickets..
Owner Gainsborough Stud **Bred** Swettenham Stud **Trained** Newmarket, Suffolk

FOCUS
Probably a fair maiden despite its fair share of dead wood and the winner looks a progressive sort. The second and fourth set the standard.
Eagle Eye Official explanation: jockey said colt had no more to give

Jumanji(IRE) Official explanation: jockey said filly lost its action

1056 BOS MAGAZINE 25TH ANNIVERSARY FILLIES' H'CAP — 1m 3y
4:10 (4:12) (Class 4) (0-85,83) 3-Y-O+ — £5,505 (£1,637; £818; £408) Stalls High

Form — RPR

0-1 **1** — **Red Evie (IRE)**[19] [795] 3-8-12 **77** ... KFallon 6 — 86+
(M L W Bell) *hmpd s: sn chsng ldrs: led over 2f out: rdn out* **2/1**[1]

03-2 **2** 2 **Kaveri (USA)**[23] [724] 3-9-4 **83** ... PhilipRobinson 5 — 87
(C E Brittain) *wnt rt s: led: rdn and hdd over 2f out: styd on same pce fnl f* **9/1**

41-3 **3** 2½ **Sant Elena**[14] [852] 3-8-11 **76** ... JohnEgan 8 — 74
(G Wragg) *chsd ldrs: rdn and swtchd lft over 2f out: no ex fnl f* **5/2**[2]

310- **4** 5 **My Princess (IRE)**[233] [4753] 4-10-0 **79** ... LDettori 7 — 70
(N A Callaghan) *prom: rdn and edgd lft over 2f out: wknd over 1f out* **3/1**[3]

-015 **5** 1½ **Al Rayanah**[23] [730] 3-8-2 **67** ... ChrisCatlin 2 — 50
(G Prodromou) *s.i.s: sn prom: rdn over 3f out: wknd wl over 1f out* **25/1**

314- **6** 2 **Rakata (USA)**[177] [6022] 4-9-2 **70** ... NelsonDeSouza(3) 4 — 53
(P F I Cole) *trckd ldrs: plld hrd: rdn and wknd wl over 1f out* **10/1**

526- **7** 10 **Life's A Whirl**[202] [5537] 4-9-8 **73** ... DarryllHolland 1 — 33
(Mrs C A Dunnett) *chsd ldrs over 4f* **14/1**

-000 **8** 5 **Belrose (IRE)**[12] [888] 4-8-7 **65** oh17 ... KirstyMilczarek(7) 3 — 13
(Mrs C A Dunnett) *s.i.s: sn prom: wknd 3f out* **66/1**

1m 40.69s (0.79) **Going Correction** +0.175s/f (Good)
WFA 3 from 4yo 14lb — **8** Ran SP% **118.0**
Speed ratings (Par 102):103,101,98,93,92 90,80,75
CSF £22.10 CT £47.67 TOTE £2.10: £1.40, £1.90, £1.40; EX 22.80 Trifecta £28.80 Pool: £401.04 - 9.87 winning tickets..
Owner Terry Neill **Bred** Dermot Cantillon And Forenaghts Stud **Trained** Newmarket, Suffolk

FOCUS
For the first time in the afternoon, the field raced centre to stands' side. Although the eight runners were virtually in a line passing the three-furlong pole, the front three eventually pulled well clear of the others. The winning time was virtually identical to the preceding maiden and the form looks solid.

1057 EXPRESS CAFES H'CAP — 7f 3y
4:45 (4:46) (Class 6) (0-65,65) 4-Y-O+ — £2,914 (£867; £433; £216) Stalls High

Form — RPR

3550 **1** — **Charlie Bear**[10] [903] 5-8-6 **53** ... AdrianMcCarthy 6 — 63
(Miss Z C Davison) *s.i.s: hld up: swtchd rt and hdwy over 2f out: rdn to ld ins fnl f: r.o* **25/1**

4212 **2** 1½ **Meditation**[31] [662] 4-9-1 **62** ... LDettori 7 — 68
(I A Wood) *led over 5f: styd on same pce* **2/1**[1]

4536 **3** shd **Mistral Sky**[5] [985] 7-9-3 **64** ... (v) JohnEgan 11 — 70
(Stef Liddiard) *hld up: hdwy over 2f out: led over 1f out: sn rdn: hdd and nt qckn ins fnl f* **10/1**

6543 **4** ½ **Kew The Music**[15] [845] 6-8-11 **58** ... (v) ChrisCatlin 10 — 62
(M R Channon) *dwlt: sn drvn along in rr: hdwy 1/2-way: nt clr run over 2f out: r.o u.p ins fnl f* **6/1**[2]

3012 **5** 2 **Only If I Laugh**[20] [784] 5-8-7 **54** ... RobbieFitzpatrick 5 — 53
(M J Attwater) *chsd ldrs: rdn over 2f out: edgd rt over 1f out: styd on same pce fnl f* **13/2**[3]

0503 **6** 2½ **Set Alight**[14] [860] 5-9-4 **65** ... (v) DarryllHolland 2 — 58
(Mrs C A Dunnett) *chsd ldrs: rdn over 1f out: wknd ins fnl f* **9/1**

11-4 **7** 1 **Edin Burgher (FR)**[54] [486] 5-8-5 **55** ... AdamKirby(3) 15 — 45
(T T Clement) *outpcd: styd on ins fnl f: nrst fin* **9/1**

00-0 **8** hd **Motu (IRE)**[59] [440] 5-8-0 **52** ... (v) NataliaGemelova(5) 12 — 42
(I W McInnes) *hld up: rdn over 4f out: sme hdwy 2f out: edgd lft and wknd fnl f* **25/1**

0030 **9** ½ **Sonntag Blue (IRE)**[26] [693] 4-8-2 **56** ow4 ... (v) SladeO'Hara(7) 1 — 44
(Miss J Feilden) *chsd ldrs: rdn 1/2-way: wknd over 1f out* **25/1**

2050 **10** 2½ **Shannon Arms (USA)**[13] [864] 5-8-13 **60** ... (p) J-PGuillambert 9 — 42
(P Howling) *w ldrs: rdn and ev ch 2f out: sn wknd* **33/1**

3506 **11** 1¾ **The Rebound Kid**[11] [897] 4-8-11 **63** ... DerekNolan(5) 4 — 40
(G A Huffer) *chsd ldrs over 5f* **25/1**

010- **12** 1 **Piddies Pride (IRE)**[255] [4127] 4-9-3 **64** ... (p) JimmyQuinn 8 — 39
(Miss Gay Kelleway) *prom: rdn over 2f out: wknd over 1f out* **33/1**

2003 **13** 5 **Iced Diamond (IRE)**[26] [693] 7-8-7 **54** oh2 ow3 ... ShaneKelly 3 — 16
(W M Brisbourne) *hld up in tch: rdn over 2f out: sn wknd* **14/1**

-000 **14** 3½ **Wistman (UAE)**[5] [977] 5-9-1 **65** ... SilvestreDeSousa(3) 16 — 18
(D Nicholls) *hld up: plld hrd: a in rr* **25/1**

0060 **15** 5 **Out For A Stroll**[23] [737] 7-9-4 **65** ... OscarUrbina 13 — 5
(S C Williams) *sn pushed along: a in rr* **16/1**

40-6 **16** 5 **Angel River**[7] [953] 4-8-4 **51** oh11 ... MatthewHenry 14 — —
(J Ryan) *a in rr* **66/1**

1m 27.14s (0.54) **Going Correction** +0.175s/f (Good) — **16** Ran SP% **129.2**
Speed ratings (Par 101):103,101,101,100,98 95,94,94,93,90 88,87,81,77,72 66
CSF £73.94 CT £591.45 TOTE £32.80: £3.80, £1.60, £2.00, £1.30; EX 191.80 TRIFECTA Not won..
Owner Mervyn Merwood **Bred** Old Road Securities Plc **Trained** Hammerwood, E Sussex

FOCUS
A competitive little handicap and the field reverted to the style of earlier in the afternoon by racing centre to far side. Those drawn very high really struggled and never looked like getting into it. The form is ordinary rated through the third.
Edin Burgher(FR) ◆ Official explanation: jockey said gelding never travelled
Piddies Pride(IRE) Official explanation: jockey said filly had no more to give

1058 RACECOURSE VIDEO SERVICES H'CAP — 1m 3f 101y
5:20 (5:21) (Class 6) (0-60,60) 4-Y-O+ — £2,914 (£867; £433; £216) Stalls Low

Form — RPR

200- **1** — **High Treason (USA)**[164] [6247] 4-9-1 **57** ... PhilipRobinson 16 — 73
(W J Musson) *hld up in tch: led over 2f out: rdn clr fnl f: eased nr fin* **8/1**

066- **2** 3½ **Dinner Date**[128] [6548] 4-8-13 **55** ... ShaneKelly 14 — 65
(T Keddy) *s.i.s: hld up: hdwy over 2f out: rdn over 1f out: styd on same pce fnl f* **14/1**

3103 **3** 1 **Sol Rojo**[14] [857] 4-8-8 **50** ... (v) JimmyQuinn 6 — 58
(J Pearce) *hld up in tch: rdn over 2f out: no ex fnl f* **8/1**

1-00 **4** 2½ **La Gessa**[21] [252] 4-8-8 **55** ... DerekNolan(5) 8 — 59
(John Berry) *a.p: rdn over 2f out: no ex fnl f* **16/1**

5-00 **5** 4 **Rose Bien**[23] [733] 4-8-8 **50** ... KFallon 5 — 48
(P J McBride) *mid-div: effrt over 2f out: wknd over 1f out* **13/2**[2]

0-00 **6** 1 **Trew Flight (USA)**[47] [552] 4-8-10 **55** ... SaleemGolam(3) 13 — 51
(M H Tompkins) *chsd ldr: led over 8f out: rdn and hdd over 2f out: sn wknd* **22/1**

0-50 **7** shd **Panshir (FR)**[55] [474] 5-8-11 **53** ... ChrisCatlin 15 — 49
(Mrs C A Dunnett) *hld up: hdwy over 1f out: n.d* **18/1**

-300 **8** 1¼ **Yenaled**[10] [186] 9-8-11 **60** ... DonnaCaldwell(7) 7 — 54
(P S McEntee) *hld up: rdn over 3f out: n.d* **14/1**

0060 **9** 2½ **Monkstown Road**[14] [857] 4-8-11 **60** ... (b) SladeO'Hara(7) 11 — 50
(C N Kellett) *prom: chsd ldr 5f out: rdn over 3f out: wknd over 2f out* **50/1**

2045 **10** 2 **King Of Knight (IRE)**[17] [820] 5-8-10 **52** ... (t) OscarUrbina 1 — 39
(G Prodromou) *hld up: hdwy over 2f out: sn rdn and wknd* **7/1**[3]

0466 **11** hd **Eijaaz (IRE)**[17] [820] 5-8-3 **52** ... KristinStubbs(7) 10 — 39
(Mrs L Stubbs) *dwlt: hld up: a in rr* **16/1**

00-0 **12** 1½ **Tata Naka**[19] [800] 6-8-10 **55** ... AdamKirby(3) 4 — 39
(Mrs C A Dunnett) *chsd ldrs over 8f* **10/1**

0-00 **13** ½ **River Biscuit (USA)**[23] [726] 4-9-4 **60** ... JohnEgan 9 — 44
(M J Polglase) *hld up: n.d* **33/1**

323- **14** 8 **Trials 'n Tribs**[119] [6612] 4-8-8 **50** ... TPQueally 3 — 21
(C A Cyzer) *hld up: nt clr run 3f out: n.d* **13/2**[2]

1643 **15** 5 **Jackie Kiely**[32] [652] 5-9-4 **60** ... J-PGuillambert 2 — 23
(P Howling) *chsd ldrs 9f* **4/1**[1]

6-00 **16** 1½ **Jazrawy**[44] [574] 4-9-0 **56** ... (e[1]) DarryllHolland 12 — 16
(Miss Gay Kelleway) *led 3f: rdn and wknd 3f out* **16/1**

2m 30.11s (2.61) **Going Correction** +0.275s/f (Good) — **16** Ran SP% **136.0**
Speed ratings (Par 101):101,98,97,95,93 92,92,91,89,88 87,86,86,80,76 75
CSF £127.02 CT £964.83 TOTE £10.90: £2.80, £4.90, £2.50, £3.20; EX 269.30 TRIFECTA Not won. Place 6 £41.53, Place 5 £36.75.
Owner S Rudolf **Bred** Helmut Von Finck **Trained** Newmarket, Suffolk

FOCUS
A modest if competitive handicap in which the pace was ordinary, but the front four still pulled nicely clear of the others and the form looks moderate but sound.
Trew Flight(USA) Official explanation: jockey said gelding hung right throughout
River Biscuit(USA) Official explanation: jockey said gelding had no more to give
Jackie Kiely Official explanation: jockey said gelding lost its action
T/Plt: £110.60 to a £1 stake. Pool: £40,190.50. 265.10 winning tickets. T/Qpdt: £68.30 to a £1 stake. Pool: £2,049.70. 22.20 winning tickets. CR

1059 - 1063a (Foreign Racing) - See Raceform Interactive

934 LONGCHAMP (R-H)
Monday, April 17

OFFICIAL GOING: Good

1064a PRIX NOAILLES (GROUP 2) (C&F) — 1m 2f 110y
2:50 (2:49) 3-Y-O — £51,103 (£19,724; £9,414; £6,276; £3,138)

RPR

1 — **Gentlewave (IRE)**[30] [672] 3-9-2 ... OPeslier 2 — 107
(A Fabre, France) *hld up in 5th, last str, outpcd & reminder 2f out, switched outside 1f out, strong run under driving to ld last stride* **23/10**[2]

2 shd **Bremen**[18] 3-9-2 ... SPasquier 5 — 106
(A Fabre, France) *raced in close 4th to straight, ridden to lead approaching final f, caught on line* **59/10**

3 nk **Grand Couturier**[28] 3-9-2 ... IMendizabal 1 — 106
(J-C Rouget, France) *disputed 2nd, 3rd on inside straight, not clear run on rail over 1f out, got through 1f out, kept on under pressure* **34/10**[3]

4 ½ **Linda's Lad**[156] [6338] 3-9-2 ... CSoumillon 6 — 105
(A Fabre, France) *led, ridden & headed approaching final f, one pace last 100y* **8/5**[1]

5 ½ **Salsalava (FR)**[21] [774] 3-9-2 ... DBoeuf 3 — 104
(P Demercastel, France) *held up in rear, went 5th appraoching straight, headway on outside & 4th over 1f out, kept on same pace final f* **13/1**

6 6 **Hello Sunday (FR)**[135] [6491] 3-9-2 ... RonanThomas 4 — 93
(Mme C Head-Maarek, France) *raced in 2nd, went up to press leader approaching straight, ridden & weakened over 1f out* **10/1**

2m 11.0s — **6** Ran SP% **122.2**
PARI-MUTUEL: WIN 3.30; PL 1.70, 2.80; SF 13.10.
Owner Gary A Tanaka **Bred** Haras De La Perelle **Trained** Chantilly, France

NOTEBOOK
Gentlewave(IRE) looked to have a hopeless task halfway up the straight and still had five lengths to make up at the furlong marker, but he suddenly slipped into top gear and fairly flew the last 100 yards to get up on the line. Unraced at two, he is now unbeaten in three races but is still on the green side. He certainly looks as if he will stay a longer trip and further progress can be expected.
Bremen settled well in fourth place running down the hill before the straight and quickened well from two out to lead at the furlong marker. He ran on in good style but could not quicken in the same way as the winner.
Grand Couturier, a provincially-trained colt, settled in second place and had to wait a little before making his challenge halfway up the straight. Making up ground up the far rail, he was running on well at the finish.
Linda's Lad did not appear to act at Longchamp on this occasion and was hanging left for much of the race. Asked to go from pillar to post, he was put under pressure at the furlong and half marker but battled on well given that he was the only horse in the first four not to have had a previous outing this year. A tilt at the Epsom Derby is on hold for the moment.

NEWMARKET (ROWLEY) (R-H)
Tuesday, April 18

OFFICIAL GOING: Good (good to firm in places)
Wind: Fresh, half-behind Weather: Cloudy with sunny spells

1065 ALEX SCOTT MAIDEN STKS (C&G) — 7f
1:30 (1:31) (Class 5) 3-Y-O — £5,181 (£1,541; £770; £384) Stalls High

Form — RPR

2- **1** — **Aeroplane**[265] [3842] 3-9-0 ... AlanMunro 11 — 97+
(P W Chapple-Hyam) *hld up in tch: rdn to ld 1f out: r.o wl* **5/1**[3]

3-0 **2** 3½ **Star Crowned (USA)**[8] [952] 3-9-0 ... (bt[1]) JimmyFortune 4 — 88
(B J Meehan) *chsd ldr: led over 4f out: rdn and hdd over 1f out: styd on same pce ins fnl f* **33/1**

622- **3** ½ **Alhaitham (USA)**[200] [5592] 3-9-0 86 ... RHills 1 — 87
(J L Dunlop) *dwlt: sn chsng ldrs: rdn to ld over 1f out: sn hdd: no ex ins fnl f* **11/4**[1]

02- **4** 1¾ **Muzher (IRE)**[193] [5718] 3-9-0 ... MartinDwyer 8 — 83
(B W Hills) *led: hdd over 4f out: rdn over 2f out: edgd lft and no ex fnl f* **9/2**[2]

302- **5** 1¼ **Loyal Royal (IRE)**[179] [6011] 3-9-0 84 ... JohnEgan 7 — 79
(D R C Elsworth) *lw: plld hrd and prom: rdn over 1f out: styd on same pce appr fnl f* **6/1**

2-34 **6** 1¼ **Serevi (IRE)**[47] [553] 3-9-0 80 ... ShaneKelly 5 — 76
(J Noseda) *hld up: hdwy 1/2-way: wknd over 1f out* **50/1**

0- 7 1 3/4 **Nefski Alexander (USA)**[270] 3689 3-9-0 .... RyanMoore 3 71
(P F I Cole) *lw: chsd ldrs 5f* **25/1**
8 1 3/4 **Pescatorio (USA)** 3-9-0 .... KFallon 6 67
(A P O'Brien, Ire) *w'like: scope: bit bkwd: s.s: sn prom: lost pl 5f out: n.d after* **9/2**[2]
9 1 **Bordello** 3-9-0 .... MichaelHills 12 64
(B W Hills) *gd sort: stdd s: hld up: nvr trbld ldrs* **25/1**
0- 10 nk **Prince Zafonic**[171] 6142 3-9-0 .... DarryllHolland 2 64
(W Jarvis) *bkwd: s.s: a in rr* **28/1**
11 1/2 **Regal Raider (IRE)** 3-9-0 .... TomEaves 10 62
(I Semple) *w'like: scope: s.s: a in rr* **66/1**
12 19 **Special Place** 3-8-7 .... RonanKeogh(7) 9 13
(J A R Toller) *cmpt: bkwd: prom: rdn 1/2-way: wknd over 2f out* **100/1**

1m 24.32s (-2.18) **Going Correction** -0.20s/f (Firm) 12 Ran SP% **112.5**
Speed ratings (Par 98):104,100,99,97,96 94,92,90,89,89 88,66
CSF £156.73 TOTE £6.00: £2.10, £6.80, £1.50; EX 158.30.
Owner Saleh Al Homaizi & Imad Al Sagar **Bred** C R Mason **Trained** Newmarket, Suffolk

FOCUS
Traditionally a decent maiden, and a very taking performance from Aeroplane, who showed a smart turn of foot to settle matters. It is questionable whether he beat much quality, though.

1066 NGK SPARK PLUGS CONDITIONS STKS 5f
2:00 (2:01) (Class 3) 2-Y-O **£7,124** (£2,119; £1,059; £529) **Stalls** High

Form RPR
41 1 **Gilded (IRE)**[14] 878 2-8-13 .... RyanMoore 6 89
(R Hannon) *chsd ldrs: outpcd over 3f out: hdwy 2f out: rdn to ld ins fnl f: r.o wl* **5/1**[2]
1 2 2 **Lord Charles**[15] 849 2-8-9 .... AmirQuinn(3) 7 80
(W G M Turner) *lw: s.i.s: sn chsng ldrs: lft in ld 2f out: sn rdn and hdd: styd on same pce ins fnl f* **10/1**
1 3 nk **Chief Editor**[15] 856 2-8-7 .... DerekNolan(5) 8 79
(M J Wallace) *lw: s.i.s: sn chsng ldrs: led over 1f out: sn rdn: hdd and unable qck ins fnl f* **4/1**[1]
4 1 1/2 **Deadshot Keen (IRE)** 2-8-9 .... JimmyFortune 2 70+
(B J Meehan) *w'like: s.s: nt clr run 2f out: swtchd rt: hdwy and n.m.r over 1f out: nt rch ldrs* **20/1**
2221 5 1 1/2 **Urban Warrior**[7] 968 2-8-12 .... KFallon 10 67+
(J R Best) *chsd ldrs: outpcd 3f out: nt clr run over 1f out: swtchd lft and styd on ins fnl f* **11/2**[3]
6 1/2 **Resignation (IRE)** 2-8-9 .... RichardHughes 5 62+
(R Hannon) *leggy: scope: lw: s.s: hdwy 1/2-way: swtchd rt over 1f out: wknd ins fnl f* **5/1**[2]
1 7 1/2 **Il Palio (IRE)**[22] 760 2-8-9 .... JamesMillman(7) 1 67
(B R Millman) *led: hung lft and hdd 2f out: wknd fnl f* **12/1**
31 8 2 **Stir Crazy (IRE)**[10] 912 2-8-13 .... EdwardCreighton(3) 9 59
(M R Channon) *chsd ldrs: rdn over 1f out: wknd fnl f* **10/1**
1 9 1 1/2 **Love In May (IRE)**[31] 663 2-8-13 .... MartinDwyer 3 50
(J S Moore) *s.i.s: sn pushed along in rr: effrt 1/2-way: wknd over 1f out* **7/1**

59.46 secs (-1.01) **Going Correction** -0.20s/f (Firm) 9 Ran SP% **111.9**
Speed ratings (Par 96):100,96,96,93,91 90,89,86,84
CSF £51.36 TOTE £6.70: £2.10, £3.20, £1.70; EX 64.20.
Owner Mrs J Wood **Bred** Tally-Ho Stud **Trained** East Everleigh, Wilts

FOCUS
The best two-year-old race of the season so far and sound form rated around the fifth.

NOTEBOOK
Gilded(IRE), one of only two fillies in the race, has improved with every run and she saw this stiff five furlongs out strongly, coming from the back of the field to mow down the leaders up the hill. Six furlongs is likely to suit her in time, and she could be up to running in the Queen Mary. (op 4-1 tchd 11-2 in a place)
Lord Charles was not as slowly away this time and stepped up on his debut effort, keeping on well at the finish. His stable sent out The Lord to finish third in this race four years ago prior to going and winning the Lily Agnes at Chester, and it would not be a great surprise to see this colt take a similar route.
Chief Editor, a narrow winner over Urban Warrior on his debut, had no trouble confirming that form and ran a solid race in defeat. Given that his debut success was on Fibresand and his pedigree is all about a preference for soft ground, it will be a surprise if he does not go on to show his best form on turf with more cut. (op 9-2)
Deadshot Keen(IRE) ◆, a half-brother to Play Master, a triple winner around eight to nine furlongs, was one of only two in the race making their racecourse bows, and he was sent off the complete outsider of the field. He shaped with plenty of promise, though, especially as he did not get the best of runs, and with his stable's juveniles invariably improving for their debuts, a maiden should be a formality. (tchd 25-1 in a place)
Urban Warrior, the most exposed runner in the line-up, did not achieve much when successful at the fourth attempt at Folkestone last time and it was slightly surprising to see him so short in the betting for this much stronger heat. He probably ran close to his best in finishing where he did. (tchd 6-1)
Resignation(IRE), bred for speed as a half-brother to five-furlong juvenile winners Joyce's Choice, Laurel Dawn and Telepathic, overcame a slow start to show pace to a furlong out. The market suggested he was quite well fancied and he should know more next time. (op 11-2 tchd 6-1)
Il Palio(IRE) failed to build on his debut success at Kempton, hanging badly and proving very difficult to stear. He lacks scope as is likely to continue to struggle. Official explanation: jockey said colt hung left (op 14-1)
Love In May(IRE) Official explanation: jockey said filly hung left

1067 NEWMARKETRACECOURSES.CO.UK H'CAP 7f
2:35 (2:38) (Class 3) (0-95,92) 3-Y-O **£9,067** (£2,697; £1,348; £673) **Stalls** High

Form RPR
421- 1 **Levera**[265] 3842 3-8-8 **82** .... JDSmith 17 97
(A King) *racd far side: mde all: rdn over 1f out: r.o: 1st home that side* **9/2**[1]
1- 2 2 **Obe Brave**[193] 5718 3-9-2 **90** .... TonyCulhane 4 100
(M R Channon) *lw: racd stands' side: chsd ldr: rdn and edgd rt over 1f out: led that gp ins fnl f: r.o: 1st home that side* **12/1**
61- 3 nk **Giganticus (USA)**[227] 4941 3-9-3 **91** .... MichaelHills 2 100+
(B W Hills) *racd stands' side: prom: led that gp and hung rt fr over 2f out: hdd and unable qck ins fnl f: 2nd home that side* **5/1**[2]
1 4 3/4 **Dame Hester (IRE)**[66] 372 3-8-6 **80** .... ChrisCatlin 13 87
(E J O'Neill) *racd far side: hld up: hdwy over 1f out: r.o to chse wnr that side ins fnl f: 2nd of that gp* **33/1**
034- 5 1 **Layazaal (IRE)**[189] 5818 3-9-2 **90** .... RHills 10 95
(J L Dunlop) *racd far side: hld up in tch: rdn over 2f out: styd on same pce appraoching fnl f: 3rd of that gp* **25/1**
152- 6 nk **The Snatcher (IRE)**[172] 6132 3-9-2 **90** .... RichardHughes 11 94
(R Hannon) *lw: racd far side: chsd wnr: rdn and hung lft fr over 1f out: no ex: fin 3rd of stands' side gp* **16/1**
440- 7 3/4 **Glenmuir (IRE)**[201] 5570 3-8-7 **81** .... AlanMunro 8 83
(B R Millman) *racd stands' side: hld up: hdwy and hung rt over 1f out: nt rch ldrs: 4th of stands' side gp* **50/1**
101- 8 1 3/4 **John Keats**[197] 5659 3-8-7 **81** .... TomEaves 3 79
(I Semple) *led stands' side over 4f: sn hung rt: wknd over 1f out: 5th of that gp* **20/1**
315- 9 nk **Collateral Damage (IRE)**[164] 6249 3-8-7 **81** .... DavidAllan 12 78
(T D Easterby) *bit bkwd: racd far side: hld up: rdn over 2f out: styd on ins fnl f: nvr nrr: 4th of that gp* **25/1**
10- 10 nk **Regal Royale**[245] 4455 3-9-4 **92** .... MJKinane 7 88
(Sir Michael Stoute) *racd stands' side: prom over 5f: 6th of that gp* **10/1**
341- 11 1/2 **Savernake Blue**[185] 5889 3-8-10 **84** .... TedDurcan 14 79
(M R Channon) *lw: racd far side s.s: rdn 1/2-way: nvr nrr: 5th of that gp* **12/1**
615- 12 1/2 **Sivivatu (USA)**[234] 4752 3-8-8 **82** .... DarryllHolland 18 75
(J Noseda) *racd far side: prom: rdn over 2f out: wknd over 1f out: 6th of that gp* **9/1**[3]
5-23 13 1 3/4 **Lake Poet (IRE)**[16] 848 3-8-10 **84** .... RyanMoore 16 73
(C E Brittain) *lw: racd far side: hld up: hdwy over 3f out: wknd over 1f out: 7th of that gp* **20/1**
101- 14 1 3/4 **Rubenstar (IRE)**[191] 5761 3-8-7 **81** .... NickyMackay 15 65
(M H Tompkins) *bkwd: racd far side: prom: rdn over 2f out: sn edgd rt and wknd: 8th of that gp* **16/1**
10-3 15 3 **Marriage Value (IRE)**[25] 717 3-8-11 **85** .... SteveDrowne 6 61
(J A Osborne) *racd stands' side: hld up: n.d: 7th of that gp* **25/1**
00-6 16 14 **Cape Of Luck (IRE)**[31] 665 3-9-0 **88** .... JimmyFortune 5 28
(P Mitchell) *lw: racd stands' side: hld up in tch: rdn and wknd over 2f out: 8th of that gp* **50/1**
612- 17 9 **Red Cape (FR)**[122] 6599 3-8-12 **86** .... KFallon 1 —
(N A Callaghan) *unruly stalls: racd stands' side: hld up: wknd 3f out: 9th and last of that gp* **12/1**

1m 24.08s (-2.42) **Going Correction** -0.20s/f (Firm) 17 Ran SP% **116.7**
Speed ratings (Par 102):105,102,102,101,100 100,99,97,96,96 95,95,93,91,87 71,61
CSF £47.93 CT £288.01 TOTE £5.90: £1.80, £3.20, £1.70, £4.70; EX 68.60 Trifecta £116.60 Pool: £722.82 - 4.40 winning tickets..
Owner Four Mile Racing **Bred** Cheveley Park Stud Ltd **Trained** Barbury Castle, Wilts

FOCUS
A competitive handicap run at a good pace and the field split into two equally-sized groups. The far-side group provided the winner, but any advantage looked minimal. The winning time was about as you would expect, sitting neatly between the opening maiden and the Nell Gwyn. The seventh looks the best guide to the form, which should prove strong.

NOTEBOOK
Levera ◆, whose Leicester victory last summer was boosted by the victory of the runner-up Aeroplane in the opener, was returning from a nine-month break and stepping up a furlong, but the market suggested he was ready. He was not ridden as though fitness was going to be an issue either, making every yard against the far rail and never looking likely to be caught. A progressive sort, he should enjoy plenty more success this season. (op 4-1 tchd 5-1 in a place)
Obe Brave ◆, winner of his sole outing last term, was always prominent in the stands'-side group and battled on well to win the race on that side, but the winner on the other flank had gone beyond recall. He is still open to plenty of improvement and should go one better before too long.
Giganticus(USA) ◆, returning from a seven-month break, came through to hold every chance on the stands' side passing the quarter-mile pole, but was inclined to lug to his right up the final climb and was never quite getting there. This should have put him right. (op 4-1)
Dame Hester(IRE) ran a decent race over in the far-side group and only the winner was able to beat her on that side. She has already proved that she stays further than this and there will be other opportunities for her.
Layazaal(IRE) ran with credit in the far-side group on this reappearance and should come on for it.
The Snatcher(IRE), well beaten in his only previous try over this trip, albeit in Listed company, was never far away in the far-side group but he hung so badly left up the final climb that he ended up alongside those in the nearside group and had nothing more to offer. He is entitled to come on for this, but he had a very busy juvenile campaign so may lack the scope of a few of these. (tchd 20-1 in a place)
Glenmuir(IRE) was noted staying on nicely in the closing stages without offering a threat. He failed to win again in eight attempts after making a successful racecourse debut last season, so it remains to be seen whether he can step up on this.
Savernake Blue basically blew all chance leaving the stalls, so should be given another chance.
Cape Of Luck(IRE) Official explanation: jockey said colt moved poorly throughout
Red Cape(FR) Official explanation: jockey said colt hit its head on stalls prior to race

1068 SHADWELL NELL GWYN STKS (GROUP 3) (FILLIES) 7f
3:10 (3:10) (Class 1) 3-Y-O
£28,390 (£10,760; £5,385; £2,685; £1,345; £675) **Stalls** High

Form RPR
131- 1 **Speciosa (IRE)**[185] 5904 3-9-1 **109** .... MickyFenton 8 107+
(Mrs P Sly) *mde all: hung lft fr 2f out: rdn out* **9/1**
406- 2 1 **Spinning Queen**[185] 5904 3-8-12 **102** .... MichaelHills 7 101
(B W Hills) *b.hind: hld up: hdwy 2f out: rdn 1f out: r.o* **9/1**
226- 3 3/4 **Salut D'Amour (IRE)**[206] 5459 3-8-12 **105** .... KFallon 1 99
(J Noseda) *s.i.s: swtchd rt 6f out: hdwy 1/2-way: rdn over 1f out: styd on* **9/2**[2]
22- 4 nk **Sweet Travel (IRE)**[200] 5595 3-8-12 .... OPeslier 9 98+
(A Fabre, France) *lt-f: unf: chsd ldrs: rdn over 1f out: styd on* **10/3**[1]
311- 5 1 1/4 **Mostaqeleh (USA)**[214] 5272 3-8-12 **96** .... MartinDwyer 4 95
(J L Dunlop) *plld hrd and prom: outpcd over 2f out: rallied over 1f out: no ex towards fin* **5/1**[3]
00-2 6 1 3/4 **Saabiq (USA)**[31] 665 3-8-12 **98** .... RyanMoore 2 90
(C E Brittain) *chsd ldr: rdn over 1f out: styd on same pce* **10/1**
3- 7 nk **Wasseema (USA)**[228] 4923 3-8-12 .... RHills 5 90
(Sir Michael Stoute) *s.i.s: hld up: rdn over 1f out: nvr trbld ldrs* **6/1**
000- 8 3 1/2 **Dizzy Dreamer (IRE)**[201] 5571 3-8-12 **96** .... AlanMunro 6 81
(P W Chapple-Hyam) *lw: chsd ldrs over 5f* **16/1**
021- 9 3/4 **I'm In Love (USA)**[157] 6318 3-8-12 **85** .... SteveDrowne 3 79
(M A Magnusson) *h.d.w: s.i.s: hdwy 4f out: wknd over 1f out* **25/1**

1m 23.45s (-3.05) **Going Correction** -0.20s/f (Firm) 9 Ran SP% **111.0**
Speed ratings (Par 105):109,107,107,106,105 103,102,98,98
CSF £81.73 TOTE £9.90: £2.80, £3.10, £2.20; EX 71.00.
Owner Michael H Sly Dr T Davies Mrs Pam Sly **Bred** K And Mrs Cullen **Trained** Thorney, Cambs

FOCUS
An average renewal rated around the second and third, but a decent performance from the winner under her penalty. The winning time was perfectly commendable for a race like this and the form looks sound.

NOTEBOOK

Speciosa(IRE), last year's Rockfel winner, was thought likely to just need the run according to her trainer, but she was bounced out in front and, in a race lacking in early pace, she was in the right position throughout. She hung right over to the stands' side from two furlongs out and some punters who shunted her out to big prices in-running thought she had thrown the race away, but she was actually never headed in the race. She is probably value for a bit further than the winning margin as a result of her antics, and this was a good effort to defy a penalty, but she still has a fair bit to find to trouble the the main contenders in the 1000 Guineas. (op 7-1)

Spinning Queen made her run up the far rail and had every chance. She had been unlucky in running in the Rockfel behind Speciosa but had no such excuse this time, especially given that she was in receipt of 3lb from that rival and surely benefited from her hanging across to the other side of the track. (tchd 8-1)

Salut D'Amour(IRE), who finished a neck in front of Spinning Queen in the Cherry Hinton last year, again finished close up to that rival. She was generally held in good company last season and might be difficult to place this time around, too. (op 5-1)

Sweet Travel(IRE), runner-up in a Group Three race on her final start at two, was the only runner in the line-up not entered for a Guineas, and it looked like merely a black-type hunting misson to bring her over for this Classic trial. Quite a light-framed type, she was presumably trained to the minute for this and may struggle to improve on it. (op 3-1 tchd 7-2 in a place)

Mostaqeleh(USA) was the owner's second string on jockey bookings but had the better form in the book and was well supported as a result. A little keen in the early stages, she struggled when the pace quickened but was staying on again at the finish. A stronger run race may have suited her better, but she did not totally impress with her head carriage. (op 6-1 tchd 9-2)

Saabiq(USA) was the only runner in the race with the benefit of a previous outing this season and her trainer was at his most optimistic beforehand, but she was beaten with a quarter mile to run. A drop back to sprinting may be the answer. (op 12-1 tchd 14-1)

Wasseema(USA) had been backed into as short as 14-1 for the 1000 Guineas over the past few weeks, presumably on the back of impressive work on the gallops, and Richard Hills had chosen her over the far more experienced Mostaqeleh, but she was weak in the market for this reappearance outing and failed to live up to the hype. Although fully entitled to come on for the run, it is impossible to believe that she will improve sufficiently in the coming fortnight to land a blow in the first fillies' Classic. (op 5-1)

1069 BLANDFORD BLOODSTOCK ABERNANT STKS (LISTED RACE) 6f

3:45 (3:46) (Class 1) 3-Y-0+

£15,898 (£6,025; £3,015; £1,503; £753; £378) **Stalls** High

Form					RPR
014-	**1**		**Paradise Isle**^{187} [5851] 5-8-13 102 ... KDarley 16 (C F Wall) *mde all far side: rdn over 1f out: all out*	**14/1**	106
1111	**2**	*shd*	**Les Arcs (USA)**^{24} [729] 6-9-8 109 ... JohnEgan 18 (T J Pitt) *chsd wnr far side: rdn over 1f out: r.o: 2nd of 4 that side*	**6/1**^{1}	114
030-	**3**	*½*	**Beckermet (IRE)**^{213} [5310] 4-9-8 107 ... MartinDwyer 2 (R F Fisher) *racd stands' side: led: rdn and hung rt ins fnl f: r.o : 1st of 13 in gp*	**33/1**	113
30-4	**4**	*1 ¼*	**Pivotal Flame**^{24} [729] 4-9-4 105 ...(p) DarryllHolland 15 (E S McMahon) *bit bkwd: racd far side: chsd ldrs: rdn over 1f out: styd on: 3rd of 4 that side*	**14/1**	105
-224	**5**	*1*	**Royal Storm (IRE)**^{53} [506] 7-9-4 ... MJKinane 1 (Mrs A J Perrett) *lw: chsd ldr stands' side: rdn over 1f out: styd on same pce: 2nd of 13 that side*	**25/1**	102
023-	**6**	*¾*	**One Putra (IRE)**^{164} [6252] 4-9-4 101 ... PhilipRobinson 9 (M A Jarvis) *lw: chsd ldrs stands' side: rdn over 1f out: styd on same pce: 3rd of 13 that side*	**20/1**	100
0-22	**7**	*½*	**Quito (IRE)**^{24} [729] 9-9-8 110 ...(b) TonyCulhane 10 (D W Chapman) *b: racd stands: side: rdn over 1f out: styng on whn hmpd ins fnl f: nvr trbld ldrs: 4th of 13 that side*	**10/1**	102+
542-	**8**	*½*	**Baltic King**^{186} [5873] 6-9-4 107 ...(t) SteveDrowne 12 (H Morrison) *bkwd: racd stands' side: hld up in tch: rdn over 1f out: styd on same pce: 5th of 13 that side*	**13/2**^{2}	97
310-	**9**	*½*	**Ashdown Express (IRE)**^{205} [5495] 7-9-8 111 ... SebSanders 7 (C F Wall) *racd stands' side: hld up: swtchd lft and hdwy over 1f out: sn nt clr run: nvr trbld ldrs: 6th of 13 that side*	**10/1**	99+
11-2	**10**	*½*	**Presto Shinko (IRE)**^{17} [830] 5-9-8 108 ... RichardHughes 8 (R Hannon) *lw: racd stands' side: hld up in tch: effrt over 1f out: nt trble ldrs: 7th of 13 that side*	**8/1**	98
406-	**11**	*1*	**Royal Millennium (IRE)**^{233} [4804] 8-9-4 105 ... TedDurcan 5 (M R Channon) *racd stands' side: hld up: rdn whn n.m.r over 1f out: n.d: 8th of 13 that side*	**33/1**	91
210-	**12**	*nk*	**Out After Dark**^{213} [5288] 5-9-4 104 ...(p) AdamKirby 17 (C G Cox) *dwlt: hld up: rdn over 2f out: n.d: 4th of 4 that side*	**25/1**	90
165-	**13**	*½*	**The Tatling (IRE)**^{186} [5873] 9-9-10 114 ... RyanMoore 14 (J M Bradley) *lw: racd stands' side: hld up: effrt and nt clr run over 1f out: n.d: 9th of 13 that side*	**20/1**	94
130-	**14**	*¾*	**River Thames**^{213} [5308] 3-8-7 100 ... TPQueally 3 (J A R Toller) *racd stands' side: s.i.s: hld up: n.d: 10th of 13 that side*	**100/1**	86
546-	**15**	*nk*	**Cape Columbine**^{287} [3204] 4-8-13 105 ... TQuinn 11 (D R C Elsworth) *racd stands' side: chsd ldrs: wkng whn n.m.r 1f out: 11th of 13 that side*	**15/2**^{3}	80+
0-32	**16**	*shd*	**Indian Maiden (IRE)**^{14} [885] 6-9-3 105 ... OPeslier 4 (M S Saunders) *racd stands' side: hld up: swtchd rt over 1f out: n.d: 12th of 13 that side*	**14/1**	84
3-50	**17**	*1 ¾*	**Fire Up The Band**^{24} [729] 7-9-10 108 ... AdrianTNicholls 13 (D Nicholls) *racd stands' side: hld up in tch: effrt over 2f out: wknd over 1f out: 13th of 13 that side*	**33/1**	86

1m 10.5s (-2.60) **Going Correction** -0.20s/f (Firm)

WFA 3 from 4yo+ 11lb **17** Ran SP% **115.7**

Speed ratings (Par 111):109,108,108,106,105 104,103,102,102,101 100,99,99,98,97 97,95

CSF £80.71 TOTE £21.20: £5.20, £2.40, £12.80; EX 190.60.

Owner The Equema Partnership **Bred** Jeremy Green And Sons **Trained** Newmarket, Suffolk

FOCUS

A strange race in many ways, with the pace not looking that strong for a race of its quality and only four of the 17 runners deciding to stay far side despite the stalls being there. They had the last laugh though, as three of the first four home came from that side, including the front pair. The winning time was only ordinary for a Listed contest and the fourth limits the form.

NOTEBOOK

Paradise Isle decided to stay on the far side from her high draw, whilst the bulk of the field came over to the stands' side, and she made every yard of the running though she had nothing to spare at the line. The way this race was run does raise question marks over the form and she had come up short in six previous attempts at this level, but it is not unusual for mares to keep on progressing as they get older so it may be worth giving her the benefit of the doubt.

Les Arcs(USA), bidding for a six-timer, also wisely decided to stay far side from the inside stall. He put in a strong finish, but the mare kept on finding a bit more and he failed by a whisker to get up. He hardly deserved to lose and has been a real credit to connections in recent months. (tchd 13-2)

Beckermet(IRE) ran a cracker on this return to action, leading the stands'-side group throughout but unfortunately the pair on the far side just had his measure. This is his level and it is only when he goes up into Group company that he really struggles.

Pivotal Flame, now tried in cheekpieces, was 4lb better off with Les Arcs for a five-length beating in the Cammidge Trophy and at least he managed to narrow the gap having stayed in the far-side quartet along with his old rival. He ideally needs more cut in the ground than he got here. (op 16-1)

Royal Storm(IRE), fit from racing in Dubai, ran with credit in the nearside group considering he was badly in at the weights, but he seems to have become the archetypal 'twilight' horse. (op 33-1 tchd 40-1)

One Putra(IRE) ran with plenty of credit on this return to action, but whether he is up to this level remains to be seen and it may be significant that he has gained both his victories when able to make all the running. (tchd 22-1)

Quito(IRE), winner of this race last year, needs the gaps to appear at the right time, but that never really happened for him here and he was unable to produce his trademark whirlwind finish as a result. His style of running does require some luck. Official explanation: jockey said rig was denied clear run closing stages (op 15-2)

Ashdown Express(IRE), runner-up in this last year, was trying to stay on when running out of room entering the last furlong though he would not been placed even with a clear run. (op 11-1)

Presto Shinko(IRE) was rather disappointing following his eye-catching return to action at Kempton. (op 15-2 tchd 7-1 and 9-1 in places)

Cape Columbine Official explanation: jockey said filly was hampered when weakening closing stages

1070 MUSEUM MAIDEN STKS 1m 2f

4:20 (4:22) (Class 5) 3-Y-0 **£5,181** (£1,541; £770; £384) **Stalls** High

Form					RPR
64-	**1**		**Markovitch**^{201} [5574] 3-9-3 ... AlanMunro 9 (P W Chapple-Hyam) *led: rdn and hdd over 1f out: rallied to ld wl ins fnl f: styd on*	**25/1**	92+
02-	**2**	*¾*	**Degas Art (IRE)**^{171} [6148] 3-9-3 ... JohnEgan 4 (D R C Elsworth) *h.d.w: hld up: plld hrd: hdwy over 2f out: rdn to ld ins fnl f: sn hung rt and hdd: kpt on*	**14/1**	91
62-	**3**	*½*	**Mashaahed**^{201} [5574] 3-9-3 ... RHills 2 (B W Hills) *lw: hld up in tch: led and edgd rt over 1f out: hdd ins fnl f: styng on whn hmpd sn after*	**5/4**^{1}	91+
54-	**4**	*shd*	**Senor Dali (IRE)**^{179} [6013] 3-9-3 ... TQuinn 11 (J L Dunlop) *plld hrd and prom: outpcd over 1f out: r.o wl towards fin*	**16/1**	90+
0	**5**	*6*	**La Estrella (USA)**^{12} [897] 3-9-3 ... MickyFenton 6 (J G Given) *b.off hind: chsd ldr tl rdn over 2f out: edgd lft and wknd over 1f out*	**100/1**	78
	6	*¾*	**Sixties Icon** 3-9-3 ... ShaneKelly 7 (J Noseda) *gd sort: bit bkwd: hld up: rdn over 3f out: edgd lft over 1f out: n.d*	**20/1**	77
	7	*½*	**Seeking Straight (IRE)** 3-9-3 ... NickyMackay 5 (Sir Michael Stoute) *leggy: scope: s.i.s: hld up: rdn over 4f out: lost pl over 3f out: n.d after*	**50/1**	76+
	8	*hd*	**Hasayaz (IRE)** 3-9-3 ... RyanMoore 1 (Sir Michael Stoute) *gd sort: s.s: hld up: rdn over 4f out: n.d*	**33/1**	76
00-	**9**	*2 ½*	**Paradise Street (IRE)**^{179} [6007] 3-8-12 ... JMurtagh 3 (J R Fanshawe) *prom tl rdn and wknd over 1f out*	**100/1**	66
	10	*17*	**Brideshead (IRE)** 3-9-3 ... KFallon 12 (A P O'Brien, Ire) *gd sort: bkwd: prom over 7f*	**10/1**^{3}	39
	11	*1 ¾*	**Flamingo Guitar (USA)** 3-8-12 ... WMLordan 8 (David Wachman, Ire) *w'like: s.s: hld up: hdwy over 4f out: wknd over 2f out*	**6/1**^{2}	30
	12	*15*	**Dipped Wings (IRE)** 3-8-12 ... IanMongan 10 (J L Dunlop) *w'like: sn outpcd and bhd*	**100/1**	2

2m 4.60s (-1.11) **Going Correction** -0.20s/f (Firm) **12** Ran SP% **96.9**

Speed ratings (Par 98):96,95,95,94,90 89,89,88,86,73 71,59

CSF £207.40 TOTE £26.20: £3.60, £3.30, £1.10; EX 229.10.

Owner K Panos, Miss C Spurrier, C J Jones **Bred** Theobalds Stud **Trained** Newmarket, Suffolk

■ Galactic Star (4/1, bolted bef s) was withdrawn. R4 applies, deduct 20p in the £.

FOCUS

Another maiden which traditionally throws up plenty of winners but perhaps not the strongest of renewals. The early pace was steady and the first four finished nicely clear.

1071 BABRAHAM H'CAP 1m 4f

4:55 (4:58) (Class 3) (0-95,95) 4-Y-0+ **£9,067** (£2,697; £1,348; £673) **Stalls** High

Form					RPR
241-	**1**		**Mikao (IRE)**^{213} [5320] 5-8-3 **82** ... SaleemGolam(3) 6 (M H Tompkins) *hld up in tch: led over 1f out: sn rdn: jst hld on*	**8/1**^{3}	91
2-34	**2**	*shd*	**Nawamees (IRE)**^{22} [765] 8-8-9 **85** ...(p) RyanMoore 7 (G L Moore) *hld up: hdwy over 3f out: rdn over 1f out: edgd lft ins fnl f: styd on u.p*	**10/1**	94
240-	**3**	*3*	**Wingman (IRE)**^{150} [6377] 4-8-10 **87** ... KFallon 9 (J W Hills) *hld up: hdwy over 2f out: swtchd lft over 1f out: styd on*	**15/2**^{2}	91
310-	**4**	*nk*	**Ebtikaar (IRE)**^{164} [6254] 4-9-2 **93** ... RHills 4 (J L Dunlop) *hld up: rdn over 1f out: r.o ins fnl f: too much to do*	**6/1**^{1}	102+
121-	**5**	*¾*	**Bulwark (IRE)**^{203} [5533] 4-9-1 **92** ...(be) JMurtagh 11 (Mrs A J Perrett) *hld up in tch: rdn over 1f out: edgd rt and no ex ins fnl f*	**9/1**	95
106-	**6**	*hd*	**Lets Roll**^{164} [6254] 5-8-13 **89** ... DeanMcKeown 13 (C W Thornton) *chsd ldrs: rdn and ev ch 2f out: no ex ins fnl f*	**12/1**	91
0-26	**7**	*1 ¼*	**Danehill Willy (IRE)**^{14} [867] 4-8-13 **90** ...(p) NCallan 2 (N A Callaghan) *hld up: hdwy and swtchd rt over 1f out: nt trble ldrs*	**20/1**	90
050-	**8**	*nk*	**Le Corvee (IRE)**^{35} [5767] 4-8-10 **87** ... RichardHughes 5 (A King) *chsd ldr: led over 5f out: rdn and hdd over 1f out: wknd ins fnl f*	**33/1**	88+
/50-	**9**	*1 ½*	**Hawridge Prince**^{339} [1694] 6-9-5 **95** ... AlanMunro 15 (B R Millman) *hld up: nt clr run and lost pl over 4f out: styd on ins fnl f: nt trble ldrs*	**20/1**	92
050-	**10**	*¾*	**Jeepstar**^{164} [6254] 6-8-10 **86** ... SteveDrowne 14 (S C Williams) *led: edgd lft over 8f out: hdd over 5f out: wknd and eased fnl f*	**16/1**	82
103-	**11**	*4*	**Inchnadamph**^{185} [5903] 6-8-9 **85** ...(t) MickyFenton 1 (T J Fitzgerald) *hld up: rdn and hung rt over 1f out: n.d*	**16/1**	75
210-	**12**	*5*	**Fairmile**^{178} [6018] 4-8-11 **88** ... SebSanders 3 (W R Swinburn) *hld up: hdwy 4f out: rdn and wknd over 1f out*	**10/1**	70
-515	**13**	*¾*	**Zamboozle (IRE)**^{32} [661] 4-8-4 **81** oh2 ... JohnEgan 16 (D R C Elsworth) *h.d.w: hld up: hdwy over 3f out: wknd and eased over 1f out*	**9/1**	62+
510-	**14**	*shd*	**Rawdon (IRE)**^{164} [6254] 5-8-11 **87** ... HayleyTurner 12 (M L W Bell) *prom: rdn over 3f out: wknd over 2f out*	**14/1**	67
110-	**15**	*1 ½*	**Baddam**^{185} [5903] 4-9-1 **92** ... IanMongan 8 (M R Channon) *lw: prom: rdn 1/2-way: wknd wl over 1f out*	**16/1**	70

24/4 **16** *16* **Double Obsession**[25] 714 6-9-5 **95** .... AdrianTNicholls 10 47
(D Nicholls) *lw: chsd ldrs over 9f* **66/1**

2m 28.95s (-4.55) **Going Correction** -0.20s/f (Firm)
WFA 4 from 5yo+ 1lb **16** Ran SP% **121.3**
Speed ratings (Par 107):107,106,104,104,104 104,103,103,102,101 98,95,95,94 83
CSF £81.59 CT £635.31 TOTE £10.50: £2.20, £2.50, £2.10, £1.90; EX 97.50 Place 6 £101.22, Place 5 £46.76.
Owner Ben Allen **Bred** Kildaragh Stud **Trained** Newmarket, Suffolk

FOCUS
A competitive handicap in which the pace was fair, but the hold-up horses were still favoured as things turned out. THe form looks ordinary for the grade, rated around those in the frame behind the winner.

NOTEBOOK
Mikao(IRE) ◆, 3lb higher than when winning over two miles on his final outing last season, appreciated this galloping track and showed plenty of guts to hold off the runner-up. He looks a versatile type and should be set for a good season. (op 10-1 tchd 9-1 in a place)
Nawamees(IRE), fit from the sand, is another who stays further than this and, after being held up for most of the race, stayed on to all but snatch the race out of the fire. He deserves to go one better, but despite some smart efforts on the Flat and plenty of success over obstacles in the meantime, he is without a victory on the level since scoring in the French Provinces in the summer of 2001. (tchd 11-1)
Wingman(IRE) finished in good style, but the front pair had already gone beyond recall. He may be worth a try over a bit further, but remains without a win since his third outing as a two-year-old. (tchd 8-1 in a place)
Ebtikaar(IRE) ◆ was given a very patient ride, too patient as it turned out, and when he did eventually engage the afterburner it was way too late. Losses are only lent. (op 13-2)
Bulwark(IRE), did not run badly on this return to action in terms of his finishing position, but he showed a particularly ugly head carriage over the last couple of furlongs and a tendency to roll all over the track. Aside from his quirks, he also finds himself 8lb higher than when winning on his final outing of last season and it remains to be seen whether he can be competitive off this sort of mark. (op 10-1)
Lets Roll showed up for a long way on this reappearance, but is still 7lb higher than for his last win. (op 8-1)
Le Corvee(IRE) Official explanation: jockey said colt hung left
Inchnadamph needs further than this and could never land a blow. He is currently 11lb above his last winning mark, but he did look a progressive sort last year and this should at least have blown the cobwebs away.
Zamboozle(IRE), fit from the sand, made a promising effort from off the pace inside the last half-mile but it came to little and he dropped rather tamely away. This was disappointing. Official explanation: jockey said colt ran too free closing stages and had no more to give (op 10-1)
Rawdon(IRE) seemed to find this trip on a galloping track finding him out. (op 16-1)
T/Jkpt: Not won. T/Plt: £176.80 to a £1 stake. Pool: £73,618.75. 303.80 winning tickets. T/Qpdt: £38.60 to a £1 stake. Pool: £5,142.30. 98.40 winning tickets. CR

BEVERLEY (R-H)
Wednesday, April 19

OFFICIAL GOING: Good to soft (good in places)
After heavy rain at first, the ground was on the easy side for the first race but it soon became good to soft.
Wind: Moderate, across (first 4 races) becoming almost nil Weather: Heavy rain race 1, then changeable.

1073 WELCOME BACK TO BEVERLEY (S) STKS 1m 100y
2:10 (2:10) (Class 5) 3-Y-O+ **£3,400** (£1,011; £505; £252) **Stalls** High

Form RPR
3354 **1** **Scotty's Future (IRE)**[26] 715 8-9-6 54 .... PaulQuinn 10 63
(D Nicholls) *squeezed out s and bhd: gd hdwy over 2f out: rdn to ld 1f out: styd on wl* **8/1**[3]
400- **2** *1 3/4* **Bond Diamond**[134] 6514 9-9-6 63 .... MickyFenton 11 60+
(P T Midgley) *hld up towards rr: effrt 3f out: swtchd rt 2f out: rdn over 1f out: styd on ins last* **9/1**
0-00 **3** *5* **Motu (IRE)**[2] 1057 5-9-9 52 ....(v) PatrickMathers(3) 9 55
(I W McInnes) *hld up in rr: hdwy on inner over 2f out: rdn over 1f out: styd on ins last: nrst fin* **16/1**
-006 **4** *1/2* **Veneer (IRE)**[8] 972 4-9-12 57 ....(b) KDarley 8 54
(Miss Gay Kelleway) *sn chsng ldr: led 2f out: sn rdn and hdd 1f out: wknd* **12/1**
4441 **5** *1* **Legal Lover (IRE)**[15] 875 4-9-5 50 .... RussellKennemore(7) 7 52
(R Hollinshead) *led: pushed along 3f out and sn hung bdly lft: hdd 2f out: rdn: edgd rt and kpt on over 1f out* **7/1**[2]
0-00 **6** *2* **Kalani Star (IRE)**[34] 649 6-9-6 50 ....(vt) TomEaves 14 42
(I W McInnes) *in tch: effrt 3f out: sn rdn and kpt on same pce fnl 2f* **20/1**
62-0 **7** *3/4* **Stamford Blue**[23] 772 5-9-7 62 ....(b) LiamTreadwell(5) 15 46
(R A Harris) *chsd ldrs: rdn along 3f out: drvn and wknd appr last* **10/1**
4 **8** *2* **Tullochrome**[12] 904 3-8-1 52 .... JamieMackay 2 31
(E J O'Neill) *bhd tl styd on fnl 2f: nvr nr ldrs* **14/1**
0-2 **9** *1 3/4* **Soviet Joy (IRE)**[26] 715 5-9-6 .... GrahamGibbons 12 32
(J J Quinn) *bhd tl styd on fnl 2f: nvr a factor* **6/1**[1]
60-0 **10** *nk* **Roman History (IRE)**[69] 347 3-8-3 63 .... BenSwarbrick(3) 3 32
(Miss Tracy Waggott) *bhd: wd st: kpt on fnl 2f: nvr a factor* **28/1**
0204 **11** *3/4* **Shrine Mountain (USA)**[9] 940 4-9-6 50 .... SamHitchcott 1 30
(J R Holt) *s.i.s: a rr* **25/1**
5-05 **12** *3* **Tinian**[7] 974 8-9-6 49 ....(p) PhillipMakin 6 24
(Miss Tracy Waggott) *a rr* **28/1**
0050 **13** *1/2* **Edge Fund**[42] 618 4-9-7 55 ....(b) JamesDoyle(5) 13 29
(Miss Gay Kelleway) *midfield: effrt 3f out: snr idden and wknd* **10/1**
05-0 **14** *1 1/2* **Follow My Trail (IRE)**[16] 859 3-8-6 55 .... GylesParkin 5 19
(B Smart) *chsd ldrs: rdn along 3f out: sn wknd* **28/1**
000- **15** *18* **Countess Carmine**[219] 5183 3-7-8 60 .... LeanneKershaw(7) 16 —
(P C Haslam) *chsd ldrs to 1/2-way: sn rdn along and wknd* **11/1**
16 *1 3/4* **Senor Mac** 3-8-6 .... JoeFanning 4 —
(B J Meehan) *dwlt and towards rr: sme hdwy 1/2-way: sn rdn along and wknd* **16/1**

1m 48.79s (1.39) **Going Correction** +0.125s/f (Good)
WFA 3 from 4yo+ 14lb **16** Ran SP% **119.5**
Speed ratings (Par 103):98,96,91,90,89 87,87,85,83,82 82,79,78,77,59 57
CSF £70.84 TOTE £8.20: £3.20, £3.30, £6.80; EX 71.90.There was no bid for the winner.
Owner J Higginson **Bred** William J Hamilton **Trained** Sessay, N Yorks

FOCUS
An ordinary seller but it was run at a good pace which suited those who were held up.

1074 BEVERLEY-RACECOURSE.CO.UK MAIDEN AUCTION STKS (DIV I) 5f
2:45 (2:47) (Class 5) 2-Y-O **£3,238** (£963; £481; £240) **Stalls** High

Form RPR
1 **Prospect Place** 2-9-2 .... PhillipMakin 9 74+
(M Dods) *w'like: leggy: chsd ldrs: styd on to ld last 100yds* **4/1**[2]
2 *2* **Hill Of Lujain** 2-8-9 .... DaleGibson 3 59
(M W Easterby) *cmpt: swvd lft s: bhd tl hdwy 2f out: styd on wl ins last: tk 2nd nr fin* **16/1**
6 **3** *1/2* **Our Toy Soldier**[19] 814 2-8-11 .... PaulEddery 6 59
(B Smart) *led: hdd ins last: no ex* **13/2**
4 *shd* **Smirfy's Silver** 2-8-11 .... FergalLynch 8 59
(W M Brisbourne) *neat: t.k.h: lost pl over 3f out: hdwy over 1f out: nt clr run and swtchd ins jst ins last: r.o* **9/1**
5 *nk* **Burlington Fayr (IRE)** 2-8-4 .... KimTinkler 10 50
(N Tinkler) *neat: chsd ldrs: rdn and hung lft 2f out: kpt on ins last* **12/1**
6 *3* **Esprit D'Amour (IRE)** 2-8-8 .... DavidAllan 11 42
(T D Easterby) *leggy: unf: dwlt: sn in tch: hdwy to chse ldrs 1f out: sn wknd* **7/2**[1]
7 *1/2* **Mystery World** 2-8-11 .... JoeFanning 2 43
(M Johnston) *neat: s.s: hdwy over 2f out: edgd rt over 1f out: fdd jst ins last* **11/2**[3]
8 *1/2* **Homes By Woodford** 2-8-6 .... PaulMulrennan(3) 7 39
(M W Easterby) *leggy: s.i.s: sn in rr: sme hdwy over 1f out: nvr on terms* **10/1**
9 *1* **Soundasapound** 2-8-1 .... PatrickMathers(3) 1 30
(I W McInnes) *leggy: uns rdr and led to s: s.s: a bhd* **33/1**
0 **10** *1 3/4* **Citoyen (IRE)**[25] 727 2-8-9 .... MickyFenton 4 28
(Ronald Thompson) *prom on outer: lost pl 2f out* **20/1**
11 *4* **Fath And Furiouth (IRE)** 2-8-11 .... LeeEnstone 5 14
(P C Haslam) *cmpt: chsd ldrs: wknd over 1f out: sn bhd* **14/1**

65.74 secs (1.74) **Going Correction** +0.125s/f (Good) **11** Ran SP% **118.0**
Speed ratings (Par 92):91,87,87,86,86 81,80,79,78,75 69
CSF £66.64 TOTE £5.40: £2.20, £5.10, £2.30; EX 83.00.
Owner A Mallen **Bred** Dragon's Stud **Trained** Denton, Co Durham

FOCUS
The winning time was just over half a second slower than the second division and the race is probably only just above selling-race standard but the winner , the pick of the paddock, will improve.

NOTEBOOK
Prospect Place, a February foal, has more size and substance than most in the line-up. He really knuckled down to get on top inside the last and should build on this. (op 7-2)
Hill Of Lujain, a late April foal, is a close-coupled type. Ducking left at the start he stayed on to some purpose to grab second spot near the line. He looks as though a sixth furlong already will not come amiss.
Our Toy Soldier, with the benefit of a previous outing, took them along and poached a useful lead soon after halfway but he could not last out on this stiff track on easy ground. (op 6-1)
Smirfy's Silver, a March foal, is a lip of a thing and was very green to post. Taking a fierce grip early on, he met trouble and had to switch inside. He was staying on in good style at the finish and this was an encouraging first effort. (op 12-1)
Burlington Fayr(IRE), a March foal, is not that big. She gave her rider problems hanging left but did enought o suggest she can win in a lesser grade. (op 14-1 tchd 16-1)
Esprit D'Amour(IRE), a March foal, is on the leg and narrow. After a tardy start she improved to chase the leader a furlong out only to weaken soon after. The stable's youngsters generally improve for an outing. (op 9-2)
Mystery World, a May foal, missed the break but moved up travelling nicely only to come off a straight line and fail to get home. He may need a little more time yet. (op 6-1)

1075 RAPID LAD STKS (H'CAP) 1m 1f 207y
3:20 (3:20) (Class 5) (0-70,73) 4-Y-O+ **£3,562** (£1,059; £529; £264) **Stalls** High

Form RPR
0221 **1** **Augustine**[8] 965 5-9-7 73 6ex .... DarrenWilliams 10 82
(P W Hiatt) *keen: trckd ldrs: swtchd rt and hdwy to ld over 1f out: kpt on ins last* **11/2**[2]
044- **2** *1/2* **Saif Sareea**[11] 5980 6-8-7 59 .... TonyHamilton 9 69+
(R A Fahey) *midfield: pushed along 1/2-way: gd hdwy over 2f out: effrt and nt clr run over 1f out: swtchd lft and rdn: fin wl* **2/1**[1]
3416 **3** *1/2* **Latif (USA)**[19] 825 5-9-4 70 .... SamHitchcott 11 77
(Ms Deborah J Evans) *hld up in midfield: hdwy over 2f out: effrt and n.m.r over 1f out: rdn and styd on wl fnl f* **20/1**
040- **4** *1/2* **Silverhay**[180] 6008 5-9-2 68 .... PhillipMakin 12 74
(T D Barron) *in tch: hdwy on outer over 2f out: rdn and edgd rt over 1f out: drvn and kpt on same pce ins last* **9/1**
400- **5** *nk* **Foolish Groom**[216] 5250 5-8-9 61 .... GrahamGibbons 17 66
(R Hollinshead) *trckd ldrs on inner: effrt over 2f out: sn rdn and kpt on same pce fnl f* **16/1**
2134 **6** *nk* **Hawkit (USA)**[51] 535 5-9-0 66 .... MickyFenton 13 71
(A Bailey) *towards rr: hdwy on outer 2f out: sn rdn and kpt on ins last: nrst fin* **14/1**
00-0 **7** *2* **Asaateel (IRE)**[12] 905 4-8-13 65 ....(b) TPQueally 7 66
(G L Moore) *in tch: hdwy 3f out: rdn to chse ldrs wl over 1f out: drvn: edgd rt and wknd ins last* **20/1**
213- **8** *2* **Qualitair Wings**[158] 6324 7-8-11 63 .... DerekMcGaffin 15 60
(J Hetherton) *hld up: hdwy 3f out: rdn to chse ldrs whn hung rt over 1f out: sn drvn and one pce* **16/1**
203- **9** *shd* **Bright Sun (IRE)**[192] 5772 5-9-2 68 ....(t) KimTinkler 14 65
(N Tinkler) *plld hrd: chsd ldr: led 3f out: rdn 2f out: hdd & wknd wl over 1f out* **14/1**
13-0 **10** *shd* **Rotuma (IRE)**[81] 229 7-8-6 58 ....(b) TomEaves 4 55
(M Dods) *bhd tl sme late hdwy* **25/1**
0-06 **11** *1 1/2* **Fame**[21] 800 6-9-4 70 .... KDarley 2 64
(W Jarvis) *cl up on outer: effrt 3f out and ev ch tl rdn and wkng whn hmpd over 1f out* **14/1**
3526 **12** *12* **Takes Tutu (USA)**[44] 596 7-8-12 64 .... PatCosgrave 3 35
(C R Dore) *a rr* **28/1**
00-0 **13** *1* **Fardi (IRE)**[2] 1041 4-8-11 63 .... NeilPollard 6 32
(K W Hogg) *a rr* **100/1**
50-5 **14** *1* **Just Waz (USA)**[15] 869 4-8-4 56 oh2 .... HayleyTurner 16 23
(R M Whitaker) *led: rdn along and hdd 3f out: sn wknd* **17/2**[3]
262- **P** **Royal Master**[135] 5359 4-7-13 58 ....(p) LeanneKershaw(7) 8 —
(P C Haslam) *plld hrd: sddle slipped after 1f: sn bhd and p.u over 2f out* **20/1**

2m 8.48s (1.18) **Going Correction** +0.125s/f (Good) **15** Ran SP% **123.6**
Speed ratings (Par 103):100,99,99,98,98 98,96,95,95,94 93,84,83,82,—
CSF £15.45 CT £217.02 TOTE £5.00: £1.50, £1.50, £6.90; EX 20.90.
Owner Phil Kelly **Bred** Darley **Trained** Hook Norton, Oxon
■ Stewards' Enquiry : Graham Gibbons caution: careless riding

FOCUS
An ordinary handicap run at a modest pace and the inevitable traffic problems for a few.
Royal Master Official explanation: jockey said saddle slipped

1076 FLYING FIVE H'CAP — 5f
3:55 (3:57) (Class 3) (0-95,93) 4-Y-0+ **£9,067** (£2,697; £1,348; £673) **Stalls** High

Form — RPR

3500 **1** **Trinculo (IRE)**[80] 244 9-8-10 **85** PaulFessey 7 — 93
(D Nicholls) *mde all: edgd lft fnl f: jst hld on* **20/1**

12-3 **2** *shd* **King's Gait**[26] 718 4-9-4 **93** (b) DavidAllan 6 — 101
(T D Easterby) *chsd wnr: kpt on wl ins fnl f: jst failed* **5/1**[2]

303/ **3** *½* **Crimson Silk**[618] 4614 6-9-0 **89** PaulEddery 9 — 95
(B Smart) *mid-div: hdwy on ins over 1f out: kpt on wl ins last* **16/1**

120- **4** *hd* **Golden Asha**[167] 6238 4-8-5 **80** RichardMullen 3 — 85+
(N A Callaghan) *in rr on outer: hdwy over 1f out: styd on strly ins last* **9/1**

000- **5** *nk* **Melalchrist**[186] 5891 4-8-5 **80** GrahamGibbons 11 — 84
(J J Quinn) *chsd ldrs: sn drvn along: styd on fnl f* **9/2**[1]

000- **6** *½* **Fast Heart**[179] 6021 5-8-12 **87** (t) JoeFanning 10 — 89+
(B J Meehan) *rrd s: hdwy and nt clr run over 1f out: kpt on fnl f* **7/1**

00-4 **7** *1* **Westbrook Blue**[3] 1031 4-8-7 **85** ow1 RobertMiles(3) 2 — 84
(W G M Turner) *sn outpcd in rr on outer: kpt on fnl 2f: nvr nr to chal* **25/1**

50-2 **8** *1 ½* **Golden Dixie (USA)**[17] 846 7-8-10 **85** AdrianMcCarthy 8 — 78
(R A Harris) *mid-div: nt clr run over 1f out: edgd rt and kpt on* **7/1**

000- **9** *1* **Folga**[188] 5851 4-8-12 **87** MickyFenton 4 — 77
(J G Given) *s.i.s: kpt on fnl 2f: nvr on terms* **25/1**

5-06 **10** *hd* **Malapropism**[9] 947 6-8-5 **80** SamHitchcott 12 — 69
(M R Channon) *chsd ldrs: wknd appr fnl f* **6/1**[3]

000- **11** *1 ½* **Right Answer**[245] 4482 4-8-13 **88** FergalLynch 1 — 72
(T D Easterby) *stl had blindfold on whn stalls opened: swvd lft s: sme hdwy and nt clr run over 2f out: nvr on terms* **66/1**

006- **12** *5* **Loaderfun (IRE)**[242] 4587 4-8-10 **88** DNolan(3) 13 — 54
(N Wilson) *chsd ldrs on inner: hmpd after 1f: no threat after* **17/2**

050- **13** *2* **Artie**[235] 4767 7-8-8 **83** KDarley 5 — 41
(T D Easterby) *chsd ldrs: lost pl over 1f out* **16/1**

63.55 secs (-0.45) **Going Correction** +0.125s/f (Good) **13** Ran SP% **120.4**
Speed ratings (Par 107):108,107,107,106,106 105,103,101,99,99 97,89,85
CSF £114.53 CT £1677.83 TOTE £26.80: £5.90, £1.90, £6.20; EX 163.80.
Owner Nigel Shields **Bred** Humphrey Okeke **Trained** Sessay, N Yorks

FOCUS
On the easy ground the high drawn horses did not enjoy the usual advantage.

NOTEBOOK
Trinculo(IRE), absent since January, was taken to post early. Bursting out of the stalls he overcame his middle draw but it was a close call in the end. (op 16-1)
King's Gait, suited by the rain, went in pursuit of the winner from start to finish but needed one more stride. A stiff five or easy six is ideal. (tchd 11-2)
Crimson Silk, on the comeback trail for his new stable, stuck on really well. He last tasted success over three years ago and he prefers much quicker ground than he encountered here.
Golden Asha ◆, a mover on the morning line, did well from her outside draw and should enjoy further success this year. (op 8-1)
Melalchrist, back on a winning mark, was flat out from start to finish and may need six furlongs now. (op 6-1)
Fast Heart, on a long losing run, as usual gave away ground at the start and was then tightened up when trying to improve. With him he needs everything to fall just right. (op 15-2 tchd 8-1)
Westbrook Blue was always truggling from his outside draw.

1077 LEVY BOARD H'CAP — 1m 4f 16y
4:30 (4:31) (Class 4) (0-85,83) 3-Y-0 **£6,477** (£1,927; £963; £481) **Stalls** High

Form — RPR

212 **1** **Soapy Danger**[13] 895 3-9-4 **83** KDarley 3 — 91+
(M Johnston) *trckd ldr: led over 3f out: rdn wl over 1f out: styd on strly* **4/5**[1]

3412 **2** *1 ¾* **Fusili (IRE)**[20] 805 3-8-10 **80** JamesDoyle(5) 6 — 86
(N P Littmoden) *trckd ldrs: hdwy to chse wnr over 2f out: sn rdn: drvn and no imp fnl f* **4/1**[2]

0-42 **3** *1* **Dickie's Dream (IRE)**[25] 735 3-8-5 **70** JoeFanning 2 — 74
(P J McBride) *hld up in tch: hdwy on outer over 2f out:sn rdn and kpt on same pce appr last* **9/1**

0414 **4** *15* **Abstract Art (USA)**[20] 805 3-8-12 **77** RichardMullen 5 — 57
(N A Callaghan) *hld up: effrt 3f out: sn rdn and nvr nr ldrs* **12/1**

-603 **5** *7* **Archimboldo (USA)**[28] 695 3-9-1 **80** JamieMackay 7 — 49
(T Wall) *hld up: a rr* **33/1**

03-2 **6** *2 ½* **Historic Appeal (USA)**[19] 817 3-8-9 **74** SamHitchcott 1 — 50+
(M R Channon) *chsd ldng pair: rdn along over 4f out: drvn 3f out and sn wknd* **6/1**[3]

023- **7** *24* **Sinner Or Saint (IRE)**[207] 5463 3-8-9 **74** FergalLynch 4 — —
(T D Easterby) *led: rdn along 4f out: sn hdd & wknd* **16/1**

2m 39.42s (-0.79) **Going Correction** +0.125s/f (Good) **7** Ran SP% **116.4**
Speed ratings (Par 100):107,105,105,95,90 88,72
CSF £4.48 TOTE £1.80: £1.30, £2.20; EX 4.30.
Owner Mrs R J Jacobs **Bred** Newsells Park Stud Limited **Trained** Middleham Moor, N Yorks
■ Stewards' Enquiry : Sam Hitchcott caution: allowed gelding to coast home with no assistance from saddle

FOCUS
Despite the smallish field the pace was generous and it resulted in a decent winning time for a race like this. The front three pulled miles clear of the others.
Historic Appeal(USA) Official explanation: jockey said gelding had no more to give
Sinner Or Saint(IRE) Official explanation: jockey said colt ran too free

1078 THE COMMITMENTS PLAY HERE ON 22 JUNE STKS (H'CAP) — 7f 100y
5:05 (5:05) (Class 5) (0-70,70) 3-Y-0 **£3,562** (£1,059; £529; £264) **Stalls** High

Form — RPR

000- **1** **Viva Volta**[180] 6004 3-9-0 **66** DavidAllan 3 — 72
(T D Easterby) *hdw: w ldrs: led over 2f out: narrowly hdd jst ins last: kpt on wl to ld last strides* **25/1**

304- **2** *hd* **Deira (USA)**[181] 5994 3-9-2 **68** JoeFanning 14 — 73
(C E Brittain) *t.k.h: trckd ldrs: hung lft and slt ld jst ins last: hdd nr fin* **8/1**

01-1 **3** *shd* **Tour D'Amour (IRE)**[34] 651 3-8-12 **64** TomEaves 4 — 69
(R Craggs) *t.k.h: sn trcking ldrs on outer: kpt on wl ins last: no ex towards fin* **12/1**

40-4 **4** *1* **Lisfannon**[15] 868 3-8-11 **63** OscarUrbina 9 — 65
(B W Hills) *mid-div: hdwy u.p over 2f out: swtchd rt ins last: no ex* **15/2**[3]

00-1 **5** *½* **Leamington Lad (IRE)**[15] 879 3-8-5 **60** RichardThomas(3) 5 — 61+
(J A Geake) *hld up in rr: hdwy on outer over 3f out: edgd rt and styd on wl fnl f* **9/2**[2]

2121 **6** *2 ½* **Danetime Lord (IRE)**[6] 1004 3-8-11 **68** 6ex (p) AndrewMullen(5) 10 — 63
(K A Ryan) *lw: in rr: effrt over 2f out: kpt on: nvr rchd ldrs* **13/8**[1]

4-45 **7** *½* **Gattuso**[26] 712 3-8-10 **62** SamHitchcott 11 — 56
(Ms Deborah J Evans) *s.i.s: t.k.h: hdwy over 4f out: one pce fnl 2f* **14/1**

0-10 **8** *5* **Grafton (IRE)**[44] 601 3-9-0 **66** GrahamGibbons 7 — 48
(J D Bethell) *chsd ldrs: wknd appr fnl f* **14/1**

2-40 **9** *½* **Glenbuck (IRE)**[7] 993 3-9-4 **70** MickyFenton 2 — 51
(A Bailey) *sn bhd: kpt on fnl 2f: nvr on terms* **25/1**

400- **10** *2 ½* **English City (IRE)**[230] 4887 3-8-8 **60** PaulEddery 12 — 35
(B Smart) *s.i.s: sn chsng ldrs: lost pl over 3f out* **20/1**

00-6 **11** *shd* **Beverley Polo (IRE)**[19] 819 3-8-5 **60** PaulMulrennan(3) 16 — 35
(M W Easterby) *led tl over 2f out: lost pl over 1f out* **25/1**

000- **12** *7* **Surf City**[128] 6562 3-8-8 **60** (b) AdrianMcCarthy 8 — 18
(R A Harris) *in rr: effrt on outer over 2f out: sn lost pl* **33/1**

1m 35.03s (0.72) **Going Correction** +0.125s/f (Good) **12** Ran SP% **119.4**
Speed ratings (Par 98):100,99,99,98,97 95,94,88,88,85 85,77
CSF £202.92 CT £2586.31 TOTE £23.50: £6.00, £2.30, £2.50; EX 208.10.
Owner Mrs Jennifer E Pallister **Bred** T W H And Mrs Dancer **Trained** Great Habton, N Yorks

FOCUS
The gallop was not strong and it was hard to make ground from off the pace.
Grafton(IRE) Official explanation: jockey said gelding had no more to give

1079 RACING HERE AGAIN NEXT THURSDAY STKS (FILLIES' H'CAP) — 1m 4f 16y
5:35 (5:35) (Class 5) (0-70,76) 3-Y-0 **£3,562** (£1,059; £529; £264) **Stalls** High

Form — RPR

2301 **1** **Marachi Band (USA)**[11] 918 3-8-11 **63** (b) RichardMullen 7 — 70
(E J O'Neill) *trckd ldrs: hdwy 4f out: chal over 2f out: rdn to ld wl over 1f out: styd on strly* **11/1**

1-23 **2** *3* **Juniper Girl (IRE)**[13] 895 3-9-3 **69** HayleyTurner 5 — 71
(M L W Bell) *chsd ldrs: hdwy 4f out: rdn over 2f out: drvn and kpt on same pce appr last* **2/1**[1]

64-6 **3** *1 ½* **Special Moment (IRE)**[33] 656 3-9-1 **67** OscarUrbina 8 — 67
(B W Hills) *in tch: hdwy 4f out: rdn over 2f out: kpt on same pce* **12/1**

05-1 **4** *1 ¾* **Unique Moment**[7] 979 3-9-5 **76** 6ex GregFairley(5) 3 — 73
(M Johnston) *trckd ldrs: hdwy over 4f out: led 3f out: sn rdn: drvn and hdd wl over 1f out: grad wknd appr last* **9/4**[2]

300- **5** *hd* **Squirtle (IRE)**[201] 5583 3-8-10 **62** RobbieFitzpatrick 4 — 58
(W M Brisbourne) *hld up towards rr: hdwy on outer 4f out: rdn to chse ldrs 2f out: sn drvn and no imp* **20/1**

645- **6** *1 ½* **Spring Dream (IRE)**[191] 5788 3-9-0 **66** SamHitchcott 12 — 60
(M R Channon) *in tch: hdwy to chse ldrs 3f out: rdn over 2f out and sn btn* **16/1**

50-3 **7** *1 ½* **Lynford Lady**[47] 573 3-8-6 **58** JimmyQuinn 11 — 50
(P W D'Arcy) *midfield: pushed along and outpcd 5f out: styd on u.p fnl 2f* **16/1**

06-0 **8** *shd* **Queen Of Diamonds (IRE)**[16] 850 3-8-1 **56** oh7. RichardThomas(3) 1 — 48
(Mrs P N Dutfield) *bhd tl styd on fnl 2f* **66/1**

000- **9** *2* **Ebony Lady**[167] 6234 3-8-5 **57** oh7 ow1 DeanMcKeown 6 — 45
(R M Whitaker) *a towards rr* **66/1**

303- **10** *19* **Eskimo Nell**[326] 2093 3-8-6 **58** DavidAllan 2 — 16
(T D Easterby) *a towards rr* **20/1**

626- **11** *10* **Teide Lady**[204] 5535 3-8-13 **65** KDarley 9 — 7
(Rae Guest) *chsd ldr: led 5f out: rdn along and hdd 3f out: sn wknd* **10/1**[3]

04-0 **12** *10* **Mirth**[23] 762 3-9-1 **67** PatDobbs 10 — —
(R Hannon) *led: pushed along and hdd 5f out: wknd over 3f out* **14/1**

2m 43.12s (2.91) **Going Correction** +0.125s/f (Good) **12** Ran SP% **120.2**
Speed ratings (Par 95):95,93,92,90,90 89,88,88,87,74 67,61
CSF £32.65 CT £282.07 TOTE £8.70: £2.70, £1.50, £3.60; EX 45.30.
Owner Jerry Jamgotchian **Bred** Gainsborough Farm Llc **Trained** Averham Park, Notts

FOCUS
A modest handicap restricted to three-year-old fillies, but the early pace was fair.
Teide Lady Official explanation: jockey said filly ran too free

1080 BEVERLEY-RACECOURSE.CO.UK MAIDEN AUCTION STKS (DIV II) — 5f
6:05 (6:06) (Class 5) 2-Y-0 **£3,238** (£963; £481; £240) **Stalls** High

Form — RPR

1 **Everymanforhimself (IRE)** 2-8-9 MickyFenton 7 — 71
(J G Given) *w'like: str: scope: w ldrs: rn green and hung rt over 3f out: led over 1f out: jst hld on* **4/1**[2]

2 *½* **Mind The Style** 2-8-6 RobertMiles(3) 5 — 69
(W G M Turner) *rangy: unf: sn outpcd: hdwy and hung rt over 1f out: styd on strly ins last: fin wl* **12/1**

3 *¾* **Argentine (IRE)** 2-8-13 JoeFanning 1 — 70+
(M Johnston) *lengthy: unf: s.s: hdwy gng wl to join ldr over 3f out: kpt on same pce fnl f: will improve* **13/2**[3]

4 **4** *1 ¾* **Miss Kool Kat (USA)**[16] 849 2-8-8 JimmyQuinn 2 — 58
(K A Ryan) *trckd ldrs: led over 3f out tl over 1f out: wknd ins last* **7/4**[1]

5 *2 ½* **Bowl Em Over** 2-8-4 NeilPollard 8 — 44
(M E Sowersby) *lengthy: trckd ldrs: one pce fnl 2f* **16/1**

6 *1 ½* **Major Third (IRE)** 2-8-11 FergalLynch 4 — 45
(T D Easterby) *w'like: rangy: scope: hmpd and swvd lft s: bhd: styd on fnl 2f: nvr nr ldrs* **12/1**

7 *nk* **Mr Wall Street** 2-8-13 TomEaves 9 — 46
(Mrs L Williamson) *w'like: sn outpceed and in rr: kpt on fnl 2f* **12/1**

8 *1 ¾* **Mum's Memories** 2-8-11 TPQueally 10 — 37
(Jedd O'Keeffe) *neat: led over 1f: wknd over 2f out* **7/1**

9 *shd* **Flamestone** 2-8-9 GrahamGibbons 6 — 34
(J D Bethell) *w'like: scope: chsd ldrs: lost pl 2f out* **9/1**

10 *8* **Marryl** 2-8-6 PaulMulrennan(3) 3 — 2
(M W Easterby) *cmpt: s.s: a bhd* **25/1**

65.16 secs (1.16) **Going Correction** +0.125s/f (Good) **10** Ran SP% **125.0**
Speed ratings (Par 92):95,94,93,90,86 83,83,80,80,67
CSF £55.38 TOTE £5.10: £1.60, £4.00, £3.20; EX 69.60 Place 6 £509.04, Place 5 £139.40.
Owner Pickering Properties Ltd **Bred** Denis McDonnell **Trained** Willoughton, Lincs

FOCUS
The winning time was just over half a second quicker than the first division. Almost certainly the better half and the winner looks well bought at just 4,000gns.

NOTEBOOK
Everymanforhimself(IRE), a January foal, is well developed and a typical sprinter. He knew his job going down but tended to hang right at the junction of the round course. He did just enough in the end but will improve and will be suited by less testing conditions. (op 11-2)
Mind The Style, a March foal, stands over plenty of ground. Struggling to keep up and hanging when called on for a real effort, in the end he was just held at bay. (op 11-1 tchd 10-1)
Argentine(IRE) ◆, an April foal, is long in the back. After missing the break, he came there on the bridle and looks a big improver especially on better ground. (op 9-2)
Miss Kool Kat(USA), on her toes in the pre-parade ring, went on before halfway but didn't get home. She doesn't look to have much improvement in her. (tchd 9-4)
Bowl Em Over, an immature January foal, made a satisfactory bow but will appreciate a little more time.

Major Third(IRE), a february foal, has bags of size and scope. backward in his coast, after losing ground at the start he stayed on in his own time and will improve a fair bit in time. (op 14-1 tchd 16-1)
Mr Wall Street, a March foal, was clueless but stayed on when it was all over. (op 14-1 tchd 11-1)
Mum's Memories, a March foal, lacks size and scope and merely showed speed to the halfway mark. (op 12-1)
T/Plt: £1,348.80 to a £1 stake. Pool: £39,634.20. 21.45 winning tickets. T/Qpdt: £101.40 to a £1 stake. Pool: £3,974.70. 29.00 winning tickets. JR

1065
NEWMARKET (ROWLEY) (R-H)
Wednesday, April 19
OFFICIAL GOING: Good to firm
Wind: Fresh, half-behind Weather: Overcast

1081 SPACEWORKS FURNITURE HIRE MAIDEN STKS 1m 4f
1:30 (1:34) (Class 5) 3-Y-O **£5,181** (£1,541; £770; £384) **Stalls** High

Form RPR
0- **1** **Galient (IRE)**[180] 6013 3-9-3 .... PhilipRobinson 5 98
(M A Jarvis) *lw: mde all: rdn over 1f out: hung lft ins fnl f: sn lft clr* **5/1**
2 6 **Cougar Bay (IRE)**[175] 6115 3-9-3 .... MJKinane 2 88
(David Wachman, Ire) *w'like: hld up: hdwy over 2f out: sn rdn: edgd rt over 1f out: styd on same pce: lft 2nd wl ins fnl f* **9/2**[3]
0- **3** 1 ¾ **Alhaajes (USA)**[180] 6001 3-9-3 .... RHills 4 96+
(B W Hills) *prom: chsd wnr over 1f out: sn edgd lft: rdn and hung rt 1f out: sn hmpd and rdr lost iron: nt rcvr* **7/1**
2 **4** 3 **Souffleur**[13] 897 3-9-3 .... JamieSpencer 6 83+
(M L W Bell) *w'like: chsd wnr: rdn over 2f out: wknd over 1f out* **7/4**[1]
4- **5** 2 ½ **Profitable**[158] 6318 3-8-12 .... MichaelHills 3 71
(B W Hills) *lw: chsd ldrs over 9f* **7/2**[2]
0-0 **6** 9 **Startengo (IRE)**[106] 16 3-9-3 .... JohnEgan 7 62
(D R C Elsworth) *hld up: rdn and wknd over 3f out* **33/1**
2m 29.66s (-3.84) **Going Correction** -0.15s/f (Firm) **6** Ran SP% **108.9**
Speed ratings (Par 98):106,102,100,98,97 91
CSF £25.44 TOTE £6.60: £2.90, £2.20; EX 37.90.
Owner Mr & Mrs Kevan Watts **Bred** Cliveden Stud Ltd **Trained** Newmarket, Suffolk
FOCUS
A decent winning time for a race of its type, and while the overall form should be treated with a degree of caution, the winner could rate higher in due course.
Startengo(IRE) Official explanation: jockey said gelding moved badly

1082 WYCK HALL STUD MAIDEN FILLIES' STKS 5f
2:00 (2:02) (Class 4) 2-Y-O **£4,533** (£1,348; £674; £336) **Stalls** High

Form RPR
1 **Silk Blossom (IRE)** 2-9-0 .... MichaelHills 6 86+
(B W Hills) *w'like: s.i.s: hdwy 1/2-way: r.o to ld wl ins fnl f* **7/1**
2 1 ¼ **Tarkamara (IRE)** 2-9-0 .... RyanMoore 3 81+
(P F I Cole) *led: rdn over 1f out: hdd wl ins fnl f* **9/1**
3 1 ¾ **Isobel Rose (IRE)** 2-9-0 .... JamieSpencer 8 74
(E A L Dunlop) *trckd ldrs: rdn over 1f out: styd on same pce ins fnl f* **11/2**[1]
4 hd **Fairfield Princess** 2-9-0 .... DaneO'Neill 7 73+
(N A Callaghan) *w'like: dwlt: outpcd: hdwy over 1f out: r.o: nt rch ldrs* **8/1**
5 1 ½ **Top Royelle** 2-9-0 .... RichardHughes 10 67
(R Hannon) *s.i.s: outpcd: hdwy over 1f out: wknd towards fin* **6/1**[2]
6 1 ½ **Cosmopolitan Lady** 2-9-0 .... MartinDwyer 12 61
(D M Simcock) *mid-div: rdn 1/2-way: wknd fnl f* **13/2**[3]
7 nk **Fontana Amorosa** 2-9-0 .... NCallan 2 60
(K A Ryan) *dwlt: rn green in rr: outpcd 1/2-way: r.o ins fnl f* **12/1**
8 nk **Frisky Talk (IRE)** 2-9-0 .... RHills 1 59
(B W Hills) *disp ld 3f: wknd fnl f* **14/1**
9 1 ½ **Happy Love** 2-9-0 .... RoystonFfrench 4 53
(M Johnston) *prom over 3f* **14/1**
10 1 ¼ **Bridge It Jo** 2-8-7 .... SladeO'Hara(7) 9 48
(Miss J Feilden) *w'like: bit bkwd: chsd ldrs: lost pl over 3f out: sn bhd: hung bdly lft fr over 1f out* **40/1**
4 **11** nk **Elizabeth Garrett**[25] 727 2-9-0 .... AlanMunro 5 47
(R M H Cowell) *chsd ldrs over 3f* **8/1**
12 22 **Bonny Scotland (IRE)** 2-9-0 .... DarryllHolland 11 —
(Miss V Haigh) *w'like: s.s: outpcd* **25/1**
60.15 secs (-0.32) **Going Correction** -0.15s/f (Firm) **12** Ran SP% **115.0**
Speed ratings (Par 91):96,94,91,90,88 86,85,85,82,80 80,45
CSF £66.53 TOTE £7.80: £2.90, £3.10, £2.00; EX 89.10.
Owner E D Kessly **Bred** Richard F Barnes **Trained** Lambourn, Berks
FOCUS
An above-average maiden for the time of year and the winning time was fair.
NOTEBOOK
Silk Blossom(IRE) ◆, a 50,000euros first foal of Lovely Blossom, who was placed once as a three-year-old in France, made the ideal start to her career. Having taken the best part of a furlong to find her stride, she moved nicely in the middle stages and cleared away when asked for her effort. She looks above average for the time of year and must be respected in better company. She may have one more run before being aimed at the Queen Mary. (op 6-1)
Tarkamara(IRE), a half-sister to several winners, notably 12-furlong winner Taraka, out of a nine-furlong scorer, made a pleasing debut. It may be there are a few others open to more improvement, but she really should win her maiden. (op 10-1)
Isobel Rose(IRE), out of a smart performer at around six furlongs, made quite a pleasing debut in third. She should have little bother in winning a maiden.
Fairfield Princess ◆, a 75,000gns first foal of a triple sprint winner at two, really caught eye on her racecourse debut. She never looked likely to win, but stayed on really nicely in the closing stages without being given a hard time. She can be backed with confidence to win her maiden. (op 17-2)
Top Royelle, a 17,000gns half-sister to a three-year-old winner in Yugoslavia, out of a triple winner in France, made a respectable and should be better for the experience. (tchd 13-2 in a place)
Cosmopolitan Lady, a 19,000gns half-sister to a dual seven-furlong/mile winner, shaped promisingly and should do better. (op 9-1)
Fontana Amorosa, a 13,000gns purchase, is bred to appreciate quite a bit further than this, but she is sharp enough and showed ability on her debut. This run should bring her on significantly and she ought to progress.
Bridge It Jo Official explanation: jockey said filly hung badly left
Elizabeth Garrett, fourth in a disappointing renewal of the Brocklesby on her debut, failed to build on that. (op 7-1)
Bonny Scotland(IRE) Official explanation: jockey said filly missed break

1083 BANSHAHOUSESTABLES.COM EUROPEAN FREE H'CAP (LISTED RACE) 7f
2:35 (2:40) (Class 1) 3-Y-O
£15,898 (£6,025; £3,015; £1,503; £753; £378) **Stalls** High

Form RPR
101- **1** **Misu Bond (IRE)**[200] 5613 3-8-13 **100** .... TonyCulhane 9 109
(B Smart) *lw: hld up: hdwy 1/2-way: led 2f out: drvn out* **5/2**[1]
212- **2** nk **Jeremy (USA)**[179] 6020 3-8-13 **100** .... MJKinane 8 108+
(Sir Michael Stoute) *lw: hld up: plld hrd: hdwy over 1f out: r.o u.p* **4/1**[2]
010- **3** 1 ¾ **Advanced**[193] 5742 3-8-13 **100** .... DaneO'Neill 4 104
(R Charlton) *hld up: plld hrd: hdwy over 1f out: r.o* **8/1**
212- **4** 3 ½ **Johannes (IRE)**[233] 4832 3-9-3 **104** .... KFallon 6 99
(D Nicholls) *bit bkwd: chsd ldrs: rdn and ev ch 2f out: styd on same pce fnl f* **9/2**[3]
116- **5** 1 ¼ **Manston (IRE)**[169] 6220 3-9-5 **106** .... LDettori 5 97
(B J Meehan) *lw: led 5f: sn rdn: wknd ins fnl f* **13/2**
221- **6** ¾ **Baan (USA)**[200] 5597 3-9-0 **101** .... RHills 7 90
(M Johnston) *chsd ldrs: rdn over 2f out: wknd over 1f out* **15/2**
400- **7** 8 **Ba Foxtrot**[169] 6220 3-9-4 **105** .... ChrisCatlin 3 74
(M R Channon) *chsd ldrs over 4f* **33/1**
221- **8** 1 ¾ **Strike Up The Band**[267] 3826 3-9-7 **108** .... AdrianTNicholls 1 72
(D Nicholls) *bit bkwd: plld hrd and prom: rdn and wknd over 1f out* **14/1**
1m 24.11s (-2.39) **Going Correction** -0.15s/f (Firm) **8** Ran SP% **112.6**
Speed ratings (Par 106):107,106,104,100,99 98,89,87
CSF £12.05 CT £67.37 TOTE £3.50: £1.50, £1.40, £3.40; EX 10.00 Trifecta £258.70 Pool: £510.24 - 1.40 winning tickets..
Owner R C Bond **Bred** Mary Rose Hayes **Trained** Hambleton, N Yorks
FOCUS
A fair renewal of this event, which produced a perfectly acceptable winning time for a race of its stature, and the form looks sound with the first two coming clear.
NOTEBOOK
Misu Bond(IRE), who signed off his juvenile campaign by landing the Two-Year-Old-Trophy at Redcar and the only runner in this field holding an entry in the 2000 Guineas, got his new season off to a perfect start with a dogged display. His success is made all the more meritorious considering he twice lost a shoe before the race and he would have ideally preferred a stronger early pace. Whether he will really appreciate the extra furlong in the Guineas must be of some doubt on this evidence, but he is clearly still improving, and does look up to finding a Group race this term. (op 9-4 tchd 11-4 in places)
Jeremy(USA), a runner-up in Listed company in testing ground on his final outing last season, did not help his cause by running freely through the early stages, yet finished his race with gusto and was eventually only just denied. He is headstrong, but this must rate as by far his best effort to date, and he should win a race or two this term. (op 9-2 tchd 5-1)
Advanced, who was reported to have a suffered a breathing problem when disappointing on his final start last year, ran too freely through the early stages on this return to action, yet finished his race in encouraging style once finding his full stride. This faster ground was much to his liking and he should do better with this outing under his belt. (op 11-1)
Johannes(IRE), just denied in Lisedt company on his final start as a juvenile, turned in a pleasing return from a 233-day break and only tired out of contention inside the final furlong. His pedigree suggests a mix of speed and stamina, but on this evidence he may well prove happier back at six furlongs, and it is unlikely we have seen the best of him yet. (op 4-1 tchd 5-1)
Manston(IRE), who showed progressive form at two and denied Jeremy in Listed event at Doncaster on his penultimate start, showed his customary early speed before tamely fading out of contention nearing the final furlong. He will need to improve a deal for this if he is to justify his official rating this term. (op 6-1 tchd 7-1)
Baan(USA), dropped in trip for this seasonal return, not that surprisingly failed to sustain his effort when it really mattered and shaped as though he is crying out for the return to further. (op 8-1 tchd 17-2 and 9-1 in a place)
Ba Foxtrot, whose decent early season form tailed off towards the end of the year, did not show a great deal on this three-year-old bow and still has to prove he has fully trained-on.
Strike Up The Band, who showed high-class form as a sprinter last year including a success in the Molecomb Stakes at Goodwood, proved too keen on this return to action and did little to convince that he stays this trip. He has plenty to prove this year from his current rating, but is certainly not one to be writing off on the back of this display. Official explanation: jockey said colt ran too freely in early stages, and as a result had no more to give (op 12-1)

1084 WEATHERBYS EARL OF SEFTON STKS (GROUP 3) 1m 1f
3:10 (3:11) (Class 1) 4-Y-O+
£28,390 (£10,760; £5,385; £2,685; £1,345; £675) **Stalls** High

Form RPR
021- **1** **Notnowcato**[187] 5876 4-8-12 101 .... MJKinane 5 116
(Sir Michael Stoute) *lw: hld up in tch: racd keenly: rdn over 1f out: r.o to ld wl ins fnl f* **5/2**[2]
-502 **2** 1 ¼ **Kew Green (USA)**[4] 1018 8-8-12 105 .... DaneO'Neill 9 113
(P R Webber) *trckd ldrs: led over 1f out: sn rdn and edgd rt: hdd wl ins fnl f* **7/1**[3]
60-2 **3** 3 ½ **Tolpuddle (IRE)**[10] 932 6-8-12 .... (t) WMLordan 6 106
(T Stack, Ire) *trckd ldrs: racd keenly: rdn over 2f out: styd ons ame pce fnl f* **12/1**
516- **4** 2 **Kings Point (IRE)**[204] 5527 5-8-12 105 .... (p) PaulHanagan 1 102
(R A Fahey) *led: rdn and hdd over 1f out: wknd ins fnl f* **25/1**
000- **5** 1 ¾ **Tucker**[220] 5153 4-8-12 105 .... TQuinn 2 99
(D R C Elsworth) *lw: hld up: plld hrd: rdn over 2f out: nvr trbld ldrs* **7/1**[3]
443- **6** 5 **Rocamadour**[290] 3171 4-8-12 112 .... TedDurcan 7 89
(M R Channon) *bit bkwd: trckd ldr: rdn over 2f out: wknd and eased fnl f* **9/4**[1]
040- **7** 1 ½ **Spanish Don**[146] 5607 8-8-12 97 .... LPKeniry 3 86
(D R C Elsworth) *bit bkwd: chsd ldrs: rdn over 2f out: hung rt and wknd over 1f out* **16/1**
235- **8** 2 **Calcutta**[206] 5497 10-8-12 92 .... MichaelHills 10 82
(B W Hills) *bit bkwd: hld up in tch: rdn and wknd over 1f out* **40/1**
500- **9** 10 **Bahar Shumaal (IRE)**[186] 5906 4-8-12 105 .... RyanMoore 4 62
(C E Brittain) *s.i.s: hld up: hdwy over 3f out: wknd over 2f out* **16/1**
1m 49.21s (-2.74) **Going Correction** -0.15s/f (Firm) **9** Ran SP% **110.1**
Speed ratings (Par 113):106,104,101,100,98 94,92,90,82
CSF £18.84 TOTE £3.80: £1.30, £2.20, £2.80; EX 22.00.
Owner Anthony & David de Rothschild **Bred** Southcourt Stud **Trained** Newmarket, Suffolk
FOCUS
Notnowcato would appear to have improved considerably for his winter break, but the form of this year's Earl Of Sefton looks little better than Listed class. The time was modest for the grade.
NOTEBOOK
Notnowcato, back up in trip, improved considerably on the form he showed when winning a mile-handicap here off a mark of 96 on his final start last year. Given this was his first run in 187 days, there could well be better to come, but this did not look a strong race and it may pay to take him on again tougher opposition. (op 11-4 tchd 3-1)

Kew Green(USA), back to form when second in a Listed race on the Polytrack at Kempton on his previous start, ran right up to form on his return to turf.
Tolpuddle(IRE), second in a ten-furlong Listed race at the Curragh on his latest start, had never previously raced on ground this fast and ran well in the circumstances.
Kings Point(IRE), back up in trip on his return from a 204-day break, looked to get tired late on and can be expected to come on for the outing.
Tucker did not help his chance by racing keenly and was well held on his return from a 220-day break. (op 6-1)
Rocamadour, last year's French Derby third who was also placed in a Group One on his final start in France 290 days previously, looked to have a good opportunity to make a winning return in this company but was a major disappointment. Official explanation: trainer was unable to offer any explanation for poor form shown (op 2-1 tchd 5-2 in a place and 13-8 in a place)

1085 ROSSDALES MAIDEN FILLIES' STKS — 7f
3:45 (3:46) (Class 5) 3-Y-O — **£5,181** (£1,541; £770; £384) **Stalls** High

Form — RPR

5- **1** **Illuminise (IRE)**^{197} [5688] 3-9-0 .... LDettori 17 — 82
(E A L Dunlop) *lw: racd far side: hld up in tch: rdn to ld nr fin* **5/1**^{2}

32- **2** ½ **Edaara (IRE)**^{187} [5872] 3-9-0 .... RHills 9 — 81
(W J Haggas) *lw: racd far side: led 1f: chsd ldr: rdn to ld over 1f out: hdd nr fin: 2nd of 13 that side* **6/5**^{1}

04- **3** ¾ **Pirouetting**^{200} [5609] 3-9-0 .... MichaelHills 2 — 79
(B W Hills) *led stands' side: rdn over 1f out: r.o: 1st of 6 that side* **10/1**

4 ¾ **Adventuress** 3-9-0 .... KFallon 15 — 77
(B J Meehan) *w'like: racd far side: dwlt: hdwy over 4f out: rdn over 1f out: r.o: 3rd of 13 that side* **20/1**

224- **5** 1 ¼ **You Call That Art (USA)**^{173} [6129] 3-9-0 89 .... RichardHughes 11 — 74
(R Hannon) *racd far side: led 6f out: rdn and hdd over 1f out: no ex ins fnl f: 4th of 13 that side* **8/1**^{3}

6 ¾ **Uno** 3-9-0 .... MartinDwyer 4 — 72+
(B W Hills) *racd stands' side: dwlt: hld up: rdn over 2f out: r.o ins fnl f: nrst fin: 2nd of 6 that side* **66/1**

0- **7** hd **Princess Lavinia**^{188} [5850] 3-9-0 .... JohnEgan 6 — 72
(G Wragg) *racd stands' side: chsd ldrs: riddden over 1f out: styd on: 3rd of 6 that side* **66/1**

8 2 ½ **Double Bay (USA)** 3-9-0 .... JamieSpencer 10 — 65
(Jane Chapple-Hyam) *racd far side: chsd ldrs: rdn over 2f out: edgd rt and wknd over 1f out: 5th of 13 that side* **50/1**

9 nk **Musical Magic** 3-9-0 .... MJKinane 7 — 64+
(J Noseda) *racd far side: s.i.s: hld up: r.o ins fnl f: nrst fin: 6th of 13 that side* **33/1**

10 1 **Rose Briar (IRE)** 3-9-0 .... SteveDrowne 5 — 62
(R Charlton) *racd stands' side: hld up: nvr trbld ldrs: 4th of 6 that side* **33/1**

11 nk **Sujana (USA)** 3-9-0 .... JimmyFortune 3 — 61
(B J Meehan) *racd stands' side: chsd ldrs over 5f: 5th of 6 that side* **16/1**

50- **12** ¾ **Me**^{235} [4766] 3-9-0 .... (t) AlanMunro 13 — 59
(P W Chapple-Hyam) *lw: racd far side: chsd ldrs 5f: 7th of 13 that side* **14/1**

13 ¾ **Mozie Cat (IRE)** 3-9-0 .... ShaneKelly 18 — 57
(D J Daly) *racd far side: hld up: plld hrd: n.d: 8th of 13 that side* **100/1**

234- **14** ½ **Dream Rose (IRE)**^{225} [5022] 3-9-0 78 .... TedDurcan 14 — 56
(M R Channon) *racd far side: hld up: hrd rdn over 2f out: n.d: 9th of 13 that side* **16/1**

0- **15** 1 ½ **Goodwood March**^{293} [3048] 3-9-0 .... SebSanders 12 — 52
(J L Dunlop) *racd far side: prom: rdn over 2f out: wknd over 1f out: 10th of 13 that side* **33/1**

50-4 **16** 1 ¾ **Penny Glitters**^{21} [795] 3-9-0 65 .... DarryllHolland 1 — 47
(S Parr) *racd stands' side: chsd ldrs over 5f: last of 6 that side* **80/1**

17 2 ½ **Convallaria (FR)** 3-9-0 .... NCallan 16 — 41
(G Wragg) *w'like: bit bkwd: racd far side: sn pushed along: a in rr: 11th of 13 that side* **50/1**

0- **18** 3 ½ **Polish Welcome**^{165} [6251] 3-9-0 .... PaulHanagan 8 — 32
(S C Williams) *racd far side: hld up: a in rr: 12th of 13 that side* **100/1**

19 1 ½ **Reeling N' Rocking (IRE)** 3-8-7 .... SladeO'Hara$^{(7)}$ 19 — 28
(B W Hills) *bit bkwd: w'like: racd far side: s.s: outpcd: last of 13 that side* **66/1**

1m 25.47s (-1.03) **Going Correction** -0.15s/f (Firm) **19** Ran SP% **125.0**
Speed ratings (Par 95):99,98,97,96,95 94,94,91,91,89 89,88,87,87,85 83,80,76,74
CSF £10.51 TOTE £6.50: £2.20, £1.30, £3.30; EX 14.80.
Owner Ballygallon Stud Ltd **Bred** Ballygallon Stud **Trained** Newmarket, Suffolk

Princess Lavinia Official explanation: jockey said filly hung left

1086 THE CURRAGH "HOME OF THE IRISH CLASSICS" H'CAP — 7f
4:20 (4:20) (Class 2) (0-105,100) 4-Y-O+
£11,217 (£3,358; £1,679; £840; £419; £210) **Stalls** High

Form — RPR

20-0 **1** **King's Caprice**^{18} [828] 5-8-5 87 .... (t) StephenCarson 14 — 95
(J A Geake) *disp ld far side tl hdd over 2f out: rallied to ld over 1f out: r.o* **20/1**

40-0 **2** ½ **Prince Of Thebes (IRE)**^{18} [828] 5-8-9 91 .... PaulDoe 13 — 98
(J Akehurst) *racd far side: diputed ld tl led over 2f out: rdn and hdd over 1f out: r.o: 2nd of 8 that side* **16/1**

116- **3** nk **Game Lad**^{165} [6248] 4-8-9 91 .... JamieSpencer 5 — 97
(T D Easterby) *racd stands' side: chsd ldr tl rdn to ld over 1f out: r.o: 1st of 6 that side* **9/1**^{2}

603- **4** ¾ **Zohar (USA)**^{291} [3151] 4-8-8 90 .... RHills 16 — 94
(B J Meehan) *racd far side: hld up: rdn over 2f out: r.o ins fnl f: nrst fin: 3rd of 8 that side* **16/1**

221- **5** nk **All Ivory**^{207} [5460] 4-8-13 95 .... RichardHughes 3 — 98+
(R Charlton) *lw: racd stands' side: hld up: r.o ins fnl f: nrst fin: 2nd of 6 that side* **6/1**^{1}

00-1 **6** ½ **Fantaisiste**^{17} [846] 4-8-1 86 .... NelsonDeSouza$^{(3)}$ 8 — 88
(P F I Cole) *lw: racd far side: hld up: hdwy over 1f out: nt rch ldrs: 4th of 8 that side* **6/1**^{1}

/11- **7** shd **River Royale**^{370} [1004] 4-8-10 92 .... AlanMunro 9 — 94
(P W Chapple-Hyam) *lw: racd far side: plld hrd and prom: rdn over 2f out: outpcd over 1f out: styd on ins fnl f: 5th of 8 that side* **6/1**^{1}

0-60 **8** shd **Josh**^{25} [728] 4-8-10 92 .... NCallan 10 — 94
(K A Ryan) *racd far side: prom: rdn over 2f out: styd on same pce appr fnl f: 6th of 8 that side* **20/1**

60-6 **9** ¾ **Indian Trail**^{18} [830] 6-8-13 95 .... AdrianTNicholls 2 — 95
(D Nicholls) *racd stands' side: chsd ldrs: rdn over 2f out: no ex fnl f: 3rd of 6 that side* **16/1**

000- **10** 1 ½ **Partners In Jazz (USA)**^{207} [5460] 5-8-13 95 .... JimmyFortune 15 — 91
(T D Barron) *racd far side: s.s: hld up: effrt over 2f out: n.d: 7th of 8 that side* **11/1**^{3}

134- **11** 1 **Paper Talk (USA)**^{207} [5460] 4-8-11 93 .... MichaelHills 1 — 86
(B W Hills) *racd stands' side: led: rdn and hdd over 1f out: wknd ins fnl f: 4th of 6 that side* **6/1**^{1}

04-0 **12** 3 **Moonlight Man**^{18} [828] 5-9-0 96 .... RyanMoore 11 — 86+
(R Hannon) *racd far side: prom over 5f: last of 8 that side* **18/1**

1244 **13** 13 **Compton's Eleven**^{18} [830] 5-9-4 100 .... TedDurcan 6 — 52+
(M R Channon) *racd stands' side: prom over 4f: eased: 5th of 6 that side* **22/1**

0300 **14** 8 **Millennium Force**^{26} [718] 8-8-10 92 .... ChrisCatlin 7 — 23+
(M R Channon) *racd stands' side: a in rr: wknd over 2f out: eased: last of 6 that side* **28/1**

1m 23.55s (-2.95) **Going Correction** -0.15s/f (Firm) **14** Ran SP% **115.7**
Speed ratings (Par 109):110,109,109,108,107 107,107,107,106,104 103,99,85,75
CSF £285.60 CT £3145.52 TOTE £25.40: £6.80, £5.60, £3.70; EX 187.00.
Owner Miss B Swire **Bred** Miss B Swire **Trained** Kimpton, Hants

FOCUS
A good, competitive handicap. The field split into two groups and those on the far side appeared at a slight advantage.

NOTEBOOK
King's Caprice, back on turf, went to post early and proved good enough to end a losing run stretching back to August 2004. His overall record suggests he could be one to take on when reassessed.
Prince Of Thebes(IRE), well down the field when favourite at Kempton on the Polytrack on his reappearance, appreciated the return to turf and was just held. On this evidence he could find a race off his current sort of mark.
Game Lad, returning from a 165-day break, looked fit and won the race of those on the stands' side. This must rate as a very pleasing return and he looks capable of progressing again this season. (tchd 10-1)
Zohar(USA), not seen since finishing third off this mark at Sandown last July, made a pleasing reappearance. He is lightly raced and open to improvement. (tchd 20-1)
All Ivory, 5lb higher than when winning over course and distance on his final start last year, ran well to finish second of those who raced near side. There should be more to come. (op 13-2)
Fantaisiste, 6lb higher than when coming from well off the pace to win over six furlongs at Kempton (Polytrack) on her previous start, could not quite match that level of form, but she would not have been suited by the field splitting into two groups. She can be given another chance in a bigger field when the pace is strong throughout. (tchd 13-2)
River Royale, not seen since winning over course and distance off a 4lb lower mark at this meeting last year, raced keenly and was perhaps a bit fresh. He should do better. (op 9-2)
Partners In Jazz(USA) Official explanation: jockey said gelding missed break and was slowly away from stalls
Paper Talk(USA), returning from a 207-day break, looked fit enough but only managed to beat two home on his side and was disappointing. (tchd 11-2)

1087 BASIC BLOODSTOCK INSURANCE WOOD DITTON STKS (DIV I) — 1m
4:55 (4:59) (Class 4) UNRACED 3-Y-O — **£6,153** (£1,830; £914; £456) **Stalls** High

Form — RPR

1 **Secret World (IRE)** 3-9-3 .... ShaneKelly 4 — 95+
(J Noseda) *unf: scope: lw: rangy: hld up: hdwy over 2f out: led ins fnl f: r.o wl* **11/4**^{1}

2 1 ¼ **Mosharref (IRE)** 3-9-3 .... RHills 2 — 88
(B W Hills) *w'like: athletic: dwlt: hdwy over 6f out: led over 2f out: rdn and hdd ins fnl f: r.o* **3/1**^{2}

3 5 **Red Somerset (USA)** 3-9-3 .... RyanMoore 1 — 77+
(R Hannon) *w'like: scope: s.s: hld up: hdwy over 2f out: rdn over 1f out: wknd ins fnl f* **6/1**^{3}

4 ½ **Archiestown (USA)** 3-9-3 .... TQuinn 3 — 75
(J L Dunlop) *w'like: hld up: outpcd 1/2-way: r.o ins fnl f* **20/1**

5 ½ **Dixie Storm (USA)** 3-9-3 .... LDettori 8 — 74
(A M Balding) *w'like: chsd ldrs: led 3f out: sn rdn and hdd: wknd fnl f* **20/1**

6 ½ **Invention (USA)** 3-9-3 .... RichardHughes 6 — 73
(J H M Gosden) *cmpt: hld up in tch: rdn over 2f out: wknd over 1f out* **8/1**

7 1 ¾ **Great Hawk (USA)** 3-9-3 .... MJKinane 11 — 69
(Sir Michael Stoute) *w'like: bit bkwd: scope: hld up: rdn over 2f out: no ch whn hung lft ins fnl f* **8/1**

8 3 **Shangazi (USA)** 3-8-12 .... MichaelHills 12 — 57
(B W Hills) *s.s: hdwy over 5f out: rdn and wknd over 1f out* **25/1**

9 nk **Marajel (IRE)** 3-9-3 .... AlanMunro 5 — 61
(P W Chapple-Hyam) *prom: racd keenly: rdn over 3f out: wknd over 1f out* **16/1**

10 7 **Stroll In The Park (IRE)** 3-9-3 .... KFallon 9 — 45
(D R C Elsworth) *w'like: scope: bit bkwd: s.s: sn prom: jnd ldr 1/2-way: rdn and wknd wl over 1f out* **16/1**

11 2 ½ **Wabra (USA)** 3-8-12 .... TedDurcan 10 — 35
(C E Brittain) *w'like: led: plld hrd: hdd 3f out: wknd 2f out* **33/1**

1m 39.29s (-0.08) **Going Correction** -0.15s/f (Firm) **11** Ran SP% **116.3**
Speed ratings (Par 100):94,92,87,87,86 86,84,81,81,74 71
CSF £10.18 TOTE £3.60: £1.50, £1.60, £2.20; EX 12.90.
Owner Mrs Susan Roy **Bred** Lodge Park Stud **Trained** Newmarket, Suffolk

FOCUS
Unraced horses, but still strictly a moderate winning time for a Class 4 contest in the conditions and nearly half a second slower than the second division. It still produced an impressive looking winner, however.
Red Somerset(USA) Official explanation: jockey said colt was slowly away from stalls

1088 BASIC BLOODSTOCK INSURANCE WOOD DITTON STKS (DIV II) — 1m
5:25 (5:27) (Class 4) UNRACED 3-Y-O — **£6,153** (£1,830; £914; £456) **Stalls** High

Form — RPR

1 **Petrovich (USA)** 3-9-3 .... KFallon 6 — 84+
(J Noseda) *str: athletic: lw: awkward leaving stalls: hld up in tch: edgd lft over 1f out: rdn to ld towards fin: comf* **8/11**^{1}

2 ½ **Minister Of State** 3-9-3 .... PhilipRobinson 1 — 83
(M A Jarvis) *w'like: str: bit bkwd: led: rdn and edgd lft over 1f out: hdd towards fin* **9/1**^{3}

3 1 **Ask** 3-9-3 .... MJKinane 2 — 81
(Sir Michael Stoute) *w'like: chsd ldrs: outpcd over 1f out: r.o ins fnl f* **10/1**

4 1 ½ **Valverde (IRE)** 3-9-3 .... SebSanders 7 — 77
(J L Dunlop) *w'like: hld up: hdwy over 2f out: rdn and edgd lft 1f out: styd on same pce* **16/1**

5 2 **Motaraqeb** 3-9-3 .... RHills 10 — 73
(Sir Michael Stoute) *w'like: scope: bit bkwd: hld up in tch: rdn over 1f out: wknd ins fnl f* **8/1**^{2}

6 2 ½ **Tropical Climate (USA)** 3-8-12 .... RichardHughes 9 62
(B W Hills) *unf: scope: lw: hld up: outpcd over 2f out: styd on ins fnl f: nvr nrr* **14/1**

7 1 ½ **Evening** 3-8-12 .... MichaelHills 5 58
(B W Hills) *hld up: hdwy 3f out: sn nt clr run and lost pl: n.d after* **25/1**

8 1 ½ **Poseidon's Secret (IRE)** 3-9-3 .... JimmyFortune 3 60
(Pat Eddery) *chsd ldrs: rdn over 3f out: edgd lft over 2f out: wknd over 1f out* **25/1**

9 1 **King's Spear (IRE)** 3-9-3 .... AlanMunro 8 58
(P W Chapple-Hyam) *s.i.s: hld up: hdwy over 2f out: nt mcuh room and wknd over 1f out* **16/1**

10 ½ **Mookerr (IRE)** 3-9-3 ....(b[1]) MartinDwyer 11 56
(M P Tregoning) *unf: scope: chsd ldr: rdn over 2f out: sn wknd* **25/1**

1m 38.87s (-0.50) **Going Correction** -0.15s/f (Firm) **10** Ran SP% **118.1**
Speed ratings (Par 100):96,95,94,93,91 88,87,85,84,84
CSF £7.85 TOTE £1.60: £1.10, £2.70, £2.50; EX 8.10 Place 6 £255.83, Place 5 £67.14.
Owner Michael Tabor **Bred** Allen E Paulson Living Trust Et Al **Trained** Newmarket, Suffolk

FOCUS
The Wood Ditton does not always produce as many winners as one might think at the time, but there were a few nice types on show in this division, not least the winner. The winning time was almost half a second faster than the first division, but still strictly modest for a race of its class.
T/Plt: £483.00 to a £1 stake. Pool: £59,162.15. 89.40 winning tickets. T/Qpdt: £60.80 to a £1 stake. Pool: £5,276.20. 64.20 winning tickets. CR

1081
NEWMARKET (ROWLEY) (R-H)
Thursday, April 20

OFFICIAL GOING: Good to firm
Wind: Fresh, across Weather: Overcast

1089 FEDERATION OF BLOODSTOCK AGENTS MAIDEN STKS 6f
1:30 (1:31) (Class 5) 3-Y-O **£5,181** (£1,541; £770; £384) **Stalls** Low

Form RPR

1 **Pearly Wey** 3-9-0 .... AdamKirby(3) 1 86
(C G Cox) *neat: trckd ldrs: racd keenly: rdn and swtchd rt over 1f out: led and edgd lft ins fnl f: r.o* **40/1**

224- 2 1 ¼ **Mr Sandicliffe**[212] [5394] 3-9-3 95................................(p) JamieSpencer 5 82
(B W Hills) *lw: w ldr tl led 1/2-way: rdn and hdd over 1f out: ev ch ins fnl f: nt qckn* **13/8**[1]

32 3 ¾ **Pititana (IRE)**[13] [901] 3-8-12 .... RichardHughes 4 75
(R Hannon) *led to 1/2-way: rdn to ld over 1f out: hdd and unable qck ins fnl f* **10/1**

3- 4 1 **Music By Mozart**[156] [6349] 3-9-3 .... AlanMunro 6 77+
(P W Chapple-Hyam) *s.i.s: hld up: plld hrd: rdn over 1f out: styd on: nt trble ldrs* **9/4**[2]

3- 5 2 ½ **Starlight Gazer**[216] [5268] 3-9-0 .... RichardThomas(3) 2 70
(J A Geake) *plld hrd and prom: rdn over 2f out: wknd over 1f out* **5/1**[3]

353 6 hd **Arzaag**[52] [533] 3-9-3 72................................ MartinDwyer 7 69
(D M Simcock) *chsd ldrs: rdn over 2f out: hung lft and wknd fnl f* **14/1**

044- 7 6 **Diktatorship (IRE)**[182] [5993] 3-9-3 70................................ JimmyQuinn 3 51
(Miss Gay Kelleway) *bkwd: hld up: rdn 1/2-way: wknd 2f out* **25/1**

1m 13.7s (0.60) **Going Correction** +0.05s/f (Good) **7** Ran SP% **107.6**
Speed ratings (Par 98):98,96,95,94,90 90,82
CSF £93.76 TOTE £29.40: £6.60, £1.50; EX 123.80.
Owner Dennis Shaw **Bred** Leydens Farm Stud **Trained** Lambourn, Berks

FOCUS
With Mr Sandicliffe such an unreliable yardstick this is not the easiest form to assess, but a decent debut by Pearly Wey nevertheless.

1090 EUROPEAN BREEDERS FUND MAIDEN STKS (C&G) 5f
2:00 (2:00) (Class 4) 2-Y-O **£4,533** (£1,348; £674; £336) **Stalls** Low

Form RPR

1 **Excellent Art** 2-9-0 .... LDettori 5 91+
(N A Callaghan) *w'like: scope: trckd ldrs: swtchd rt 3f out: led ins fnl f: r.o wl* **9/4**[2]

2 2 1 ¼ **Dimboola**[14] [892] 2-9-0 .... MichaelHills 4 86
(B W Hills) *lw: led: rdn over 1f out: hdd and unable qck ins fnl f* **10/11**[1]

3 ½ **Captain Marvelous (IRE)** 2-9-0 .... RHills 1 84+
(B W Hills) *neat: s.i.s: hld up: swtchd rt and hdwy over 1f out: styd on* **14/1**

4 2 **King's Bastion (IRE)** 2-9-0 .... JamieSpencer 3 76
(M L W Bell) *cmpt: bit bkwd: chsd ldr: rdn over 1f out: no ex* **13/2**[3]

5 1 **As One Does** 2-9-0 .... NCallan 2 72
(K A Ryan) *cmpt: s.i.s: sn pushed along and prom: rdn over 1f out: wknd ins fnl f* **33/1**

6 5 **Pietersen (IRE)** 2-9-0 .... PaulFessey 6 52
(T D Barron) *w'like: scope: lw: swvd rt leaving stalls: sn chsng ldrs: rdn and wknd over 1f out* **20/1**

61.19 secs (0.72) **Going Correction** +0.05s/f (Good) **6** Ran SP% **110.9**
Speed ratings (Par 94):96,94,93,90,88 80
CSF £4.51 TOTE £3.30: £1.60, £1.20; EX 5.40.
Owner Matthew Green **Bred** Cheveley Park Stud Ltd **Trained** Newmarket, Suffolk

FOCUS
Just the six runners, but the runner-up Dimboola gives the form a solid look and it looks quite a strong little race.

NOTEBOOK
Excellent Art ◆, a 76,000gns half-brother to Double Obsession, who won from seven furlongs to a mile and a half, out of six-furlong juvenile scorer, won well on his debut. The favourite Dimboola set a reasonable standard and this has to rate as a useful performance. He unshipped his jockey soon after the line, but he basically just seemed to jink at the crossing and little should be read into that. Connections hope he can develop into a Coventry Stakes horse. (op 3-1 tchd 7-2 in a place)
Dimboola, who showed a fair level of form when second on his debut at Leicester, just found one too good again. He should win a maiden before much longer, but it remains to be seen how much improvement there is to come in the long run. (op 5-6 tchd Evens and 11-10 in a place)
Captain Marvelous(IRE) ◆, a 100,000euros half-brother to ten-furlong winner Hero Worship, was not given a very hard time at all in third and was a real eye catcher. He should show improvement next time. (tchd 12-1)
King's Bastion(IRE), a 72,000gns first foal of a five-furlong juvenile winner who is a half-sister to Attraction, made a satisfactory debut. He looked a touch backward and can be expected to improve for the run. (op 6-1)
As One Does, a 20,000gns half-brother to Mrs Seek, a triple ten-furlong winner in Italy, was the rank outsider but offered promise. Kevin Ryan tends to place his horses quite well, so the fact he thought this one good enough to run at Newmarket is probably worth keeping in mind.
Pietersen(IRE), a 25,000gns half-brother to several winners, including the useful five-furlong scorer Sharp Phrase, appeared to need this experience. He has scope and can do better. (op 16-1)

1091 EXNING STKS (H'CAP) 6f
2:35 (2:37) (Class 2) (0-100,97) 3-Y-O **£11,658** (£3,468; £1,733; £865) **Stalls** Low

Form RPR

304- 1 **Ingleby Arch (USA)**[185] [5942] 3-8-11 **87**................................ PaulFessey 14 101+
(T D Barron) *racd centre: hld up: outpcd 1/2-way: hdwy to ld overall over 1f out: hung lft: rdn clr* **11/1**

43-1 2 3 **Angus Newz**[14] [896] 3-9-3 **93**................................(v) FrancisNorton 2 98
(M Quinn) *racd stands' side: disp ld tl led that gp over 1f out: styd on same pce fnl f* **12/1**

20-2 3 ¾ **Grimes Faith**[17] [852] 3-8-7 **83**................................ RichardHughes 1 86
(R Hannon) *lw: racd stands' side: trckd ldrs: nt clr run over 1f out: swtchd rt and r.o ins fnl f* **20/1**

300- 4 ½ **Louie Louie (IRE)**[180] [6016] 3-8-10 **86**................................ KFallon 15 88
(N A Callaghan) *mde most centre over 4f: sn rdn and edgd lft: styd on same pce* **9/1**[3]

140- 5 1 ¼ **Adeje Park (IRE)**[307] [2671] 3-8-9 **85**................................ AlanMunro 10 83
(P W Chapple-Hyam) *b.hind: lw: racd centre: hld up: hdwy u.p and edgd lft over 1f out: styd on* **16/1**

15-2 6 shd **Scarlet Knight**[26] [725] 3-8-11 **87**................................ JimmyFortune 4 84
(P Mitchell) *racd stands' side: hld up: rdn over 1f out: r.o ins fnl f: nt rch ldrs* **33/1**

460- 7 nk **High Curragh**[170] [6214] 3-8-6 **82**................................ NCallan 6 79
(K A Ryan) *disp ld stands' side over 4f: wknd ins fnl f* **10/1**

14- 8 ½ **Hogmaneigh (IRE)**[142] [6456] 3-8-11 **87**................................ J-PGuillambert 8 82
(S C Williams) *racd stands' side: mid-div: hdwy and hung rt over 2f out: sn rdn: wknd ins fnl f* **33/1**

56-3 9 nk **Puskas (IRE)**[14] [896] 3-9-7 **97**................................ TQuinn 17 91
(M R Channon) *racd centre: chsd ldrs: rdn and hung lft over 1f out: wknd fnl f* **16/1**

10-0 10 hd **Sleeping Storm (IRE)**[19] [827] 3-8-7 **83**................................ RyanMoore 16 77+
(B J Meehan) *sn w ldrs in centre: rdn and wkng whn n.m.r 1f out* **14/1**

1222 11 ½ **Didn't We (IRE)**[28] [702] 3-8-3 **79**................................ JoeFanning 3 71
(T G Mills) *racd stands' side: chsd ldrs: rdn over 2f out: wknd over 1f out* **7/1**[1]

310- 12 1 ¼ **Qusoor (IRE)**[174] [6129] 3-8-12 **88**................................ RHills 11 82+
(J L Dunlop) *racd centre: hld up: hdwy u.p 2f out: wknd over 1f out* **20/1**

423- 13 1 **Categorical**[222] [5111] 3-8-2 **81**................................ SaleemGolam(3) 9 66
(J A R Toller) *s.i.s: racd stands' side: sn outpcd* **33/1**

54-1 14 ¾ **Violent Velocity (IRE)**[69] [365] 3-8-4 **80**................................ GrahamGibbons 7 63
(J J Quinn) *racd stands' side: hld up in tch: rdn and wknd over 1f out* **11/1**

6311 15 5 **Blushing Thief (USA)**[26] [725] 3-8-4 **80**................................ MartinDwyer 13 48
(W Jarvis) *racd centre: prom over 3f* **8/1**[2]

160- 16 12 **Calypso King**[215] [5308] 3-9-0 **90**................................ MichaelHills 5 22
(J W Hills) *lw: racd stands' side: hld up: plld hrd: wknd over 2f out* **25/1**

1m 12.4s (-0.70) **Going Correction** +0.05s/f (Good) **16** Ran SP% **107.7**
Speed ratings (Par 104):106,102,101,100,98 98,98,97,97,96 96,94,93,92,85 69
CSF £97.42 CT £1945.05 TOTE £12.10: £2.80, £2.90, £3.20, £2.60; EX 176.00.
Owner Dave Scott **Bred** Alexander-Groves Thoroughbreds **Trained** Maunby, N Yorks
■ Trafalgar Bay (6/1 fav) was withdrawn after bolting before the start. Rule 4 applies, deduct 10p in the pound.

FOCUS
A competitive handicap in which the field split into two. One group of nine raced against the stands' rail whilst the other seven raced down the centre. The two groups had merged before they reached the furlong pole and though the winner came down the middle, there did not seem to be a great advantage. Solid form.

NOTEBOOK
Ingleby Arch(USA) ◆, last seen finishing fourth in a one-mile Listed race on his final start as a juvenile, has matured and was well supported in the market. Racing in the centre group, he made his effort furthest from the stands' rail and showed an impressive turn of foot to bury his rivals. This looked a decent race and he looks a nice prospect for this season. (op 16-1)
Angus Newz, already a winner on turf this term, was given another positive ride against the stands' rail, but in no way did she enjoy an uncontested lead this time so deserves credit for battling on to win the separate race for second.
Grimes Faith, fit from his Polytrack return, did not have a lot of room to play with against the stands' rail from about a furlong out, but stayed on in pleasing style once switched. He still looks more than capable off this sort of mark and should find another opportunity on a decent surface.
Louie Louie(IRE) ◆ made much of the running in the centre group and kept on going to the line. He is entitled to come on for this first run in six months and should not be long in winning provided the ground remains on top. (op 8-1)
Adeje Park(IRE) ◆, last seen finishing tailed off in the Albany Stakes at Royal Ascot at York, made an eye-catching return to action and should come on a good deal for this first run in ten months. She shapes as though an extra furlong would not come amiss either.
Scarlet Knight ran with credit, but he has been busy on the sand during the winter so did hold a fitness advantage over several of these.
Puskas(IRE) Official explanation: jockey said gelding hung left
Sleeping Storm(IRE) Official explanation: jockey said filly was denied a clear run
Didn't We(IRE), who started favourite following the withdrawal of Trafalgar Bay, did not reproduce his Polytrack form on this return to turf and the way he faded did not suggest the drop in trip could be blamed. (tchd 13-2)
Categorical Official explanation: jockey said gelding was unsuited by the good to firm ground
Blushing Thief(USA), up another 4lb, failed in his hat-trick bid after two wins on sand and perhaps he does not want the ground as quick as this. (tchd 9-1)
Calypso King was free to post and gave himself no chance in the race. He has plenty of ability but needs to settle. (op 33-1)

1092 UNICORN ASSET MANAGEMENT CRAVEN STKS (GROUP 3) (C&G) 1m
3:10 (3:10) (Class 1) 3-Y-O
£28,390 (£10,760; £5,385; £2,685; £1,345; £675) **Stalls** Low

Form RPR

132- 1 **Killybegs (IRE)**[203] [5572] 3-8-12 110................................ MichaelHills 8 111+
(B W Hills) *lw: chsd ldrs: led wl over 1f out: eged lft: rdn clr* **9/2**[2]

315- 2 3 ½ **Metropolitan Man**[203] [5572] 3-8-12 108................................ RyanMoore 2 103
(D M Simcock) *chsd ldrs: rdn and swtchd rt over 1f out: hung rt ins fnl f: styd on* **16/1**

11- 3 nk **Gin Jockey (FR)**[253] [4281] 3-8-12 96................................ RichardHughes 1 102
(R Hannon) *led: rdn and hdd wl over 1f out: bmpd jst over 1f out: styd on same pce* **11/2**[3]

26-3 4 nk **Areyoutalkingtome**[8] [981] 3-8-12 100................................ LDettori 4 102
(C A Cyzer) *lw: chsd ldr 6f: rdn and edgd lft over 1f out: styd on same pce fnl f* **25/1**

22- 5 1 **Cousteau**[173] [6142] 3-8-12 .... AlanMunro 3 99
(P W Chapple-Hyam) *h.d.w: plld hrd and prom: rdn over 1f out: styd on same pce fnl f* **16/1**

111- **6** *nk* **Mulaqat**[191] 5818 3-8-12 92 MartinDwyer 7 99+
(M P Tregoning) *hld up: rdn over 2f out: styd on ins fnl f: nrst fin* **11/1**

512- **7** *shd* **Sir Xaar (IRE)**[215] 5308 3-8-12 109 JamieSpencer 6 98
(B Smart) *s.i.s: hld up: rdn over 2f out: styd on ins fnl f: nvr trbld ldrs* **11/1**

114- **8** *nk* **City Of Troy**[207] 5494 3-8-12 102 KFallon 5 98
(Sir Michael Stoute) *lw: hld up in tch: rdn over 1f out: wknd ins fnl f* **11/8**[1]

1- **9** *11* **It's A Dream (FR)**[121] 6628 3-8-12 LPKeniry 9 72
(D R C Elsworth) *b.hind: lw: s.s: hld up: rdn and wknd over 2f out* **16/1**

1m 38.79s (-0.58) **Going Correction** +0.05s/f (Good) 9 Ran SP% **113.8**
Speed ratings (Par 108):104,100,100,99,98 98,98,98,87
CSF £71.41 TOTE £5.80: £1.90, £4.30, £2.00; EX 84.40.
Owner John C Grant & D M James **Bred** E O'Leary **Trained** Lambourn, Berks
■ Stewards' Enquiry : Ryan Moore one-day ban: careless riding (May 1)

FOCUS
The pace looked ordinary and as a result this was a somewhat messy contest in which horses racing prominently, and towards the stands' rail, appeared to be favoured. The winning time was also modest for a race like this, and while Killybegs won in style he will need to improve significantly again if he is to get into the shake-up in the 2,000 Guineas.

NOTEBOOK
Killybegs(IRE), who had the highest official rating in the field following his solid efforts in Group company in his last two outings last season, was always in a good position in a race run at an average pace and produced by far the best turn of foot where it mattered. He doubled his advantage over Metropolitan Man compared to their meeting in the Somerville Tattersall Stakes here last September, which does suggest he has improved, but this is still well short of Guineas form. (op 7-2)
Metropolitan Man stayed on to win the separate race for second, but finished further behind Killybegs than he did in his final outing here last season. He still does not look quite the finished article and, with a little more experience, he could be capable of picking up a Listed race. Connections are eyeing Goodwood's Heron Stakes.
Gin Jockey(FR) ◆, unbeaten in two outings as a juvenile, set an ordinary pace against the stands' rail but was inclined to carry his head to one side, which suggests he still lacks a bit of experience. When it came down to a test of speed over the last couple of furlongs, he was just found wanting but he still looks capable of further improvement. He will be suited by a bit further and connections have a Group 3 in Frankfurt in mind next. (tchd 6-1)
Areyoutalkingtome, disappointing in a Polytrack maiden on his return, was always up with the pace and, although done for foot where it mattered, this was more like the sort of form that saw him finish an unlucky-in-running sixth in the Royal Lodge. Even so, it is hard to see him winning in Pattern company and he may not be an easy horse to place. (op 33-1)
Cousteau ran with credit, but got caught for pace at the business end. His half-brother Ti Adora came into his own when tacking middle distances and it may be the same with him. (op 20-1)
Mulaqat, who ended last season on a real high, was not suited by the way the race was run and his final position was as close as he got. This was a big step up in class, but he did not get the chance to show his true mettle here and should be given another chance. (op 12-1)
Sir Xaar(IRE), runner-up in the Group Two Mill Reef Stakes when last seen, seemed to be ridden to get the trip but this was a race in which it proved difficult to come from off the pace. As a result this performance told us little about his stamina limitations. (op 12-1)
City Of Troy, from a yard with a great record in this race, had every chance but found disappointingly little off the bridle and has it all to prove now. (tchd 6-4 and 13-8 in a place)
It's A Dream(FR) was taking a massive step up in class after impressing in a Polytrack maiden on his only previous appearance. He was never competitive, but he should not be condemned. (op 25-1)

1093 CONNAUGHT ACCESS FLOORING FEILDEN STKS (LISTED RACE) 1m 1f
3:45 (3:47) (Class 1) 3-Y-O

£15,898 (£6,025; £3,015; £1,503; £753; £378) **Stalls** Low

Form RPR

15- **1** **Atlantic Waves (IRE)**[194] 5731 3-8-13 96 JoeFanning 4 100+
(M Johnston) *lw: led: rdn and hdd over 1f out: rallied to ld nr fin* **3/1**[1]

321- **2** *shd* **Olympian Odyssey**[173] 6148 3-8-13 90 JamieSpencer 3 102+
(B W Hills) *lw: trckd ldrs: n.m.r after s: nt clr run fr over 2f out: n.m.r ins fnl f: r.o wl* **3/1**[1]

140- **3** *nk* **Silver Blue (IRE)**[194] 5731 3-8-13 95 RyanMoore 2 99
(R Hannon) *lw: hld up: rdn over 2f out: r.o wl ins fnl f* **40/1**

5631 **4** *shd* **Dont Dili Dali**[19] 827 3-8-11 103 JohnEgan 6 97
(J S Moore) *hld up: hdwy over 2f out: rdn to ld and edgd lft over 1f out: hdd nr fin* **5/1**[2]

11-0 **5** *nk* **Rajeem**[19] 827 3-8-11 96 RichardHughes 1 96
(C E Brittain) *hld up in tch: rdn and swtchd rt over 1f out: r.o* **25/1**

1- **6** *1* **Morghim (IRE)**[237] 4720 3-8-13 RHills 5 97+
(J L Dunlop) *hld up: hdwy over 1f out: styng on same pce whn n.m.r nr fin* **8/1**[3]

21- **7** *1 ½* **Judge (USA)**[204] 5555 3-8-13 97 LDettori 8 93
(B J Meehan) *lw: chsd ldrs: rdn and ev ch over 1f out: no ex ins fnl f* **3/1**[1]

1- **8** *3* **Salt Man**[172] 6178 3-8-13 MartinDwyer 7 87
(M P Tregoning) *trckd ldr: racd keenly: rdn over 2f out: wknd fnl f* **25/1**

1m 53.35s (1.40) **Going Correction** +0.05s/f (Good) 8 Ran SP% **112.9**
Speed ratings (Par 106):95,94,94,94,94 93,92,89
CSF £11.55 TOTE £4.10: £1.50, £1.50, £5.80; EX 14.90.
Owner Jaber Abdullah **Bred** Premier Bloodstock **Trained** Middleham Moor, N Yorks

FOCUS
No pace at all in this race, resulting in a messy contest and a blanket finish, so very dubious form. Not surprisingly the time was very moderate for a Listed race.

NOTEBOOK
Atlantic Waves(IRE) ◆ was in the ideal position in a moderately run race - out in front. Despite facing serious challenges on either side, he dug deep to regain the advantage after being headed and just managed to hold on to win with nothing to spare. He was undoubtedly fortunate to win this, but the way the race was run may not have suited him either and he still has the scope to go on to better things, especially as he will be suited by further and there is every likelihood he will appreciate more give in the ground. (op 5-2 tchd 7-2)
Olympian Odyssey ◆ was soon tucked in behind the leaders against the stands' rail, but his position always made him a captive to fortune and he never had a gap present itself that was big enough without running the risk of causing interference. An audacious late effort against the stands' rail all but succeeded and with a clear run he would have won comfortably. He has obviously trained on, and he will hopefully gain compensation before too long. (op 7-2)
Silver Blue(IRE) came from off the pace and finished in good style out towards the centre of the track, but too late. He was one of the more exposed in this line-up and certainly does not possess the scope of the front pair. (tchd 50-1)
Dont Dili Dali, the most experienced in the field, was also race fit. Making her effort from off the pace, she hit the front a furlong out but did not appear to see out the longer trip and was swamped close home. Official explanation: jockey said filly hung left (op 11-2 tchd 6-1)
Rajeem came from off the pace and was one of several with a chance inside the last furlong, but she found an extra spurt beyond her. She will no doubt continue to campaign in Pattern company throughout the season in the hope of nicking another one to add to her juvenile Listed success.
Morghim(IRE) looked fit enough for his return from a 237-day break and had every chance, but was already booked for sixth when getting hampered near the line. This was only his second outing, so improvement is likely.
Judge(USA), who has grown into a fine big three-year-old and looked well, showed up for a long way until appearing to blow up. This run will not be lost on him. (tchd 10-3 and 7-2)
Salt Man, winner of a Polytrack maiden on his only previous start, did himself no favours by pulling too hard and eventually paid the penalty. (op 20-1)

1094 OUSDEN CONDITIONS STKS 7f
4:20 (4:20) (Class 4) 3-Y-O

£6,232 (£1,866; £933; £467; £233; £117) **Stalls** Low

Form RPR

620- **1** **Saville Road**[246] 4477 3-8-12 96 ShaneKelly 2 97
(D J Daly) *lw: hld up in tch: rdn and swtchd rt over 2f out: stmbld and outpcd wl over 1f out: swtchd lft: r.o wl to ld nr fin* **4/1**[3]

143- **2** *¾* **Dark Islander (IRE)**[218] 5226 3-8-12 92 MichaelHills 1 95
(J W Hills) *chsd ldr: rdn to ld 1f out: hdd nr fin* **9/2**

1- **3** *2 ½* **King Orchisios (IRE)**[320] 2301 3-9-2 95 NCallan 7 93+
(K A Ryan) *lw: led 6f: no ex* **5/2**[1]

240- **4** *1 ½* **Upper Hand**[203] 5570 3-8-12 105 TQuinn 6 85
(M R Channon) *bit bkwd: chsd ldrs: rdn over 2f out: wknd fnl f* **7/1**

1- **5** *¾* **Bouboulina**[175] 6120 3-8-11 90 JamieSpencer 4 82
(E A L Dunlop) *lw: prom: rdn over 1f out: wknd ins fnl f* **11/4**[2]

00- **6** *1 ¼* **Madame Medusa (IRE)**[173] 6145 3-8-7 AlanMunro 3 74
(J A R Toller) *bit bkwd: s.i.s: outpcd* **28/1**

0- **7** *dist* **Misterbianco (IRE)**[145] 6427 3-8-12 LDettori 5 —
(B J Meehan) *bit bkwd: s.i.s: hld up: wknd over 2f out* **20/1**

1m 25.23s (-1.27) **Going Correction** +0.05s/f (Good) 7 Ran SP% **114.1**
Speed ratings (Par 100):109,108,105,103,102 101,—
CSF £22.11 TOTE £5.40: £2.40, £3.10; EX 40.60.
Owner F Deely **Bred** Dachel Stud **Trained** Newmarket, Suffolk

FOCUS
A good conditions event, but it's not easy to assess as Saville Road got up to win having appeared to be struggling about a furlong and a half out and sectional times provided by TurfTrax show that Dark Islander and King Orchisios simply slowed down at a much quicker rate than he did. Still, the overall race time was very smart for a race of this type.

Upper Hand Official explanation: jockey said colt hung right
Misterbianco(IRE) Official explanation: trainer said colt was unsuited by the good to firm ground

1095 NEWMARKETEXPERIENCE.CO.UK H'CAP 1m 2f
4:55 (4:56) (Class 3) (0-95,88) 3-Y-O **£9,067** (£2,697; £1,348; £673) **Stalls** Low

Form RPR

421- **1** **Papal Bull**[191] 5817 3-9-4 **88** KFallon 2 101+
(Sir Michael Stoute) *lw: dwlt: hld up: hdwy 1/2-way: led ins fnl f: r.o* **5/1**[2]

041- **2** *1 ¼* **Linas Selection**[225] 5051 3-8-13 **83** JoeFanning 10 92+
(M Johnston) *sn led: rdn over 1f out: hdd and unable qck ins fnl f* **14/1**

231- **3** *4* **Dunelight (IRE)**[212] 5390 3-9-4 **88** PhilipRobinson 1 89
(C G Cox) *bit bkwd: chsd ldr 6f: swtchd rt and rdn 2f out: wknd ins fnl f* **6/1**[3]

2315 **4** *1 ½* **Fiddlers Wood**[21] 805 3-9-4 **88** (v) NCallan 8 86
(V Smith) *prom: chsd ldr 4f out: rdn 2f out: wknd fnl f* **50/1**

035- **5** *1 ¾* **Zabeel House**[212] 5393 3-9-2 **86** JamieSpencer 3 81
(E A L Dunlop) *hld up: hdwy over 3f out: rdn 2f out: btn whn nt clr run over 1f out* **10/1**

060- **6** *1 ¾* **Quince (IRE)**[142] 6457 3-8-12 **82** JimmyQuinn 5 74
(J Pearce) *hld up: rdn over 1f out: n.d* **33/1**

61-1 **7** *2* **Royal Reservation**[75] 294 3-8-12 **82** AlanMunro 7 70
(P W Chapple-Hyam) *lw: chsd ldrs: rdn whn bmpd 2f out: sn wknd* **5/2**[1]

510- **8** *1 ¼* **Rayhani (USA)**[189] 5852 3-8-12 **82** MartinDwyer 4 67
(M P Tregoning) *bit bkwd: hld up in tch: lost pl 1/2-way: n.d after* **10/1**

631 **9** *shd* **Permanent Way (IRE)**[54] 515 3-9-2 **86** LDettori 9 71
(B J Meehan) *swtg: hld up: hdwy over 3f out: wknd over 1f out* **5/1**[2]

422- **10** *1* **Aamaaq**[210] 5422 3-9-4 **88** RHills 6 71
(J L Dunlop) *hld up: plld hrd: wknd 2f out* **10/1**

2m 5.86s (0.15) **Going Correction** +0.05s/f (Good) 10 Ran SP% **115.0**
Speed ratings (Par 102):101,100,96,95,94 92,91,90,90,89
CSF £71.35 CT £428.73 TOTE £4.90: £2.30, £3.80, £2.10; EX 78.00 Place 6 £107.35, Place 5 £50.11.
Owner Mrs J Magnier, D Smith & M Tabor **Bred** B H And C F D Simpson **Trained** Newmarket, Suffolk

FOCUS
A very good handicap, with progressive sorts taking the first three places. A race that looks sure to produce winners.

NOTEBOOK
Papal Bull ◆, off the mark at the third attempt over in a seven-furlong maiden at Leicester when last seen 191 days previously, stepped up on the bare form of that success to create quite a good impression on his return. An Irish Derby entry, he has a long way to go to reach that level but does have the potential to develop into a pattern-class performer in time. (op 10-3 tchd 11-2)
Linas Selection ◆, last seen winning an extended-mile maiden at Epsom 225 day previously, looked fit enough for his return and ran well. This was a hot race and he should be able to exploit his current sort of mark in the coming weeks. (op 16-1 tchd 12-1)
Dunelight(IRE) ◆, off the mark in a mile maiden on his last start 212 days previously, ran well on his return to action. A nice type, he should progress throughout the season and is one to follow. (op 7-1)
Fiddlers Wood was very disappointing in a mile and a half handicap on the Polytrack on his most recent start, but his career-best performance came when second in the Zetland Stakes over this course and distance, and he again showed his liking for the place.
Zabeel House, upped in trip off the back of a 212-day break, looked as though this run would bring him on. (op 14-1)
Quince(IRE) ran with credit on his return from a 142-day break.
Royal Reservation, chasing the hat-trick following a couple of wins on Polytrack, was well below his best returned to turf. This was disappointing but surely he can do better. (op 9-4)
Permanent Way(IRE) would have found this a very different test to the mile and a half maiden he landed at Lingfield on his previous start, but still has to be considered disappointing. (op 13-2)
Aamaaq Official explanation: jockey said colt pulled too hard early stages

T/Plt: £209.70 to a £1 stake. Pool: £58,839.80. 204.80 winning tickets. T/Qpdt: £90.70 to a £1 stake. Pool: £4,523.60. 36.90 winning tickets. CR

RIPON (R-H)

Thursday, April 20

OFFICIAL GOING: Soft (good to soft in places)

The rail on the home turn had been moved out by 3m. The ground was described as 'soft side of good, softer than that in places'.

Wind: Virtually nil Weather: Overcast

1096 E B F SHAROW MAIDEN STKS 5f

2:10 (2:12) (Class 5) 2-Y-O **£4,533** (£1,348; £674; £336) **Stalls** Low

Form RPR

1 **Kerry's Dream** 2-8-12 .... DavidAllan 5 70
(T D Easterby) *lengthy: unf: scope: sn trcking ldrs: hdwy and swtchd rt over 1f out: rdn and styd on ins last to ld last 100 yds* **10/1**

4 2 ½ **Joseph Locke (IRE)**[20] 814 2-9-3 .... FergalLynch 4 73
(M Dods) *led 1f: cl up tl eld again 1/2-way: rdn wl over 1f out: hdd and no ex last 100 yds* **7/2**[2]

3 3½ **Josr's Magic (IRE)** 2-9-3 .... TonyCulhane 3 59+
(Mrs A Duffield) *w'like: cmpt: dwlt: sn outpcd in rr: hdwy 1/2-way: swtchd rt and hdwy over 1f out: styd on strly ins last: nrst fin* **6/1**[3]

2 4 hd **Fractured Foxy**[8] 987 2-8-12 .... PaulHanagan 1 53
(J J Quinn) *chsd ldrs: rdn along 2f out: kpt on same pce* **13/8**[1]

0 5 1¼ **Baileys Hilight (IRE)**[8] 987 2-9-3 .... KDarley 9 53
(M Johnston) *cl up: led after 1f: hdd 1/2-way: sn rdn along and wknd appr last* **11/1**

0 6 1¾ **Mr Klick (IRE)**[9] 968 2-9-3 .... TedDurcan 2 46
(M J Wallace) *dwlt: sn in tch: rdn along 2f out and sn no imp* **13/2**

7 3½ **Disco Queen (IRE)** 2-8-12 .... LeeEnstone 6 27
(P C Haslam) *lengthy: unf: a towards rr* **20/1**

8 nk **Abdu** 2-9-0 .... PaulMulrennan(3) 10 31
(M W Easterby) *leggy: unf: chsd ldrs on outer: rdn along ½-wy: sn wknd* **33/1**

9 4 **Micky Mac (IRE)** 2-9-3 .... RoystonFfrench 7 15
(I W McInnes) *s.i.s and wnt rt s: a bhd* **40/1**

62.80 secs (2.60) **Going Correction** +0.275s/f (Good) **9** Ran SP% **115.5**

Speed ratings (Par 92):90,89,83,83,81 78,72,72,66

CSF £44.18 TOTE £11.70: £3.00, £1.30, £1.70; EX 58.70 Trifecta £299.00 Part won. Pool: £421.14 - 0.69 winning tickets..

Owner Salifix **Bred** Beechgrove Stud **Trained** Great Habton, N Yorks

FOCUS

A modest juvenile maiden, run at a decent pace, and the first two came clear. The form is difficult to assess and could be a few pounds out either way.

NOTEBOOK

Kerry's Dream, a half-sister to numerous winners from six to 12 furlongs, defied greeness to make a winning debut under a strong ride. She enjoyed the easy ground, shaped as though she would get another furlong, and is entitled to improve for the experience. (op 8-1)

Joseph Locke(IRE), fourth at Musselburgh on his recent debut, held every chance yet could not cope with the winner's late burst. He acts well on this sort of ground, finished clear of the rest, and can find a race of this nature in the coming weeks. (op 3-1)

Josr's Magic(IRE) ◆, the first foal of a moderate five-furlong winner, was always playing catch-up after losing ground at the start and never seriously threatened. He finished his race in taking style, however, and looks the one to take out of the race with the short-term future in mind. (op 12-1)

Fractured Foxy, runner-up on similar ground on her debut last time, was never travelling all that well and failed to put her previous experience to advantage. This confirms her limitations. Official explanation: jockey said filly ran green and became unbalanced on undulations (op 15-8 tchd 2-1)

Baileys Hilight(IRE) again showed decent early dash and managed to finish a lot closer to Fractured Foxy than had been the case at Nottingham on his recent debut. He has yet to quite reach his second birthday and is more likely to come into his own at a later date. (op 12-1)

Mr Klick(IRE), as on his recent debut at Folkestone, was never really on terms after a sluggish start and was not given too hard a time of things. (tchd 7-1)

1097 COPT HEWICK H'CAP 6f

2:45 (2:47) (Class 4) (0-85,82) 3-Y-O **£6,309** (£1,888; £944; £472; £235) **Stalls** Low

Form RPR

231- 1 **Antica (IRE)**[194] 5737 3-9-7 **82** .... DarryllHolland 12 90
(M H Tompkins) *trckd ldrs far side: switrchd lft and hdwy over 1f out: rdn to ld jst ins last: styd on wl* **11/1**

1- 2 1¼ **Bentong (IRE)**[132] 6532 3-9-6 **81** .... SteveDrowne 9 85+
(P F I Cole) *trckd ldr stands side: hdwy 2f out: rdn to ld that gp ent last: kpt on* **7/2**[1]

130- 3 1 **Ryedale Ovation (IRE)**[203] 5570 3-9-7 **82** .... DavidAllan 13 83
(T D Easterby) *hdw: trckd ldrs far side: effrt over 1f out: sn rdn and kpt on ins last* **9/1**

014- 4 ¾ **Rochdale**[233] 4856 3-9-3 **78** .... PhilipRobinson 7 77+
(M A Jarvis) *led stands side gp: rdn along wl over 1f out: one pce fnl f* **4/1**[2]

1212 5 hd **Pauvic (IRE)**[45] 593 3-8-8 **69** ....(v) StephenCarson 11 67
(Mrs A Duffield) *overall ldr far side: rdn along 2f out:d riven and hdd jst ins last: wknd* **16/1**

1 6 nk **Mango Music**[23] 776 3-9-1 **76** .... TonyCulhane 5 74+
(M R Channon) *chsd ldrs stands side: rdn along wl over 1f out: kpt on same pce* **8/1**[3]

650- 7 ¾ **Soto**[170] 6214 3-9-1 **76** .... DaleGibson 15 71
(M W Easterby) *chsd ldng pair far side: rdn along 2f out: sn one pce fnl f* **9/1**

001- 8 1¼ **The History Man (IRE)**[173] 6136 3-8-11 **75** ....(b) PaulMulrennan(3) 4 67+
(M W Easterby) *cl up stands side: rdn along 2f out: grad wknd* **18/1**

410- 9 1¾ **The Thrifty Bear**[216] 5261 3-8-12 **73** .... LeeEnstone 16 59
(C W Fairhurst) *prom far side: rdn along 2f out: sn wknd* **33/1**

033- 10 2½ **Twindego**[301] 2850 3-8-11 **72** .... PhillipMakin 2 51+
(T D Barron) *in tch stands side: rdn along 2f out: no hdwy* **16/1**

604- 11 ¾ **Ochre Bay**[125] 6591 3-8-10 **78** .... RussellKennemore(7) 6 55+
(R Hollinshead) *in tch stands side: rdn along 2f out: sn btn* **66/1**

2-06 12 1½ **Littledodayno (IRE)**[17] 852 3-9-2 **77** .... NickyMackay 17 49
(M Wigham) *racd far side: a towards rr* **33/1**

010- 13 3 **Making Music**[216] 5265 3-8-9 **70** .... FergalLynch 14 33
(T D Easterby) *a towards rr far side* **40/1**

013- 14 4 **North Walk (IRE)**[180] 6016 3-9-6 **81** .... DO'Donohoe 10 32
(K A Ryan) *chsd ldrs stands side: rdn along over 2f out and sn wknd* **14/1**

11-6 15 hd **Suits Me**[18] 848 3-9-0 **75** .... PaulHanagan 3 25
(J J Quinn) *a rr stands side* **25/1**

5-06 16 10 **Bucharest**[19] 831 3-9-4 **79** .... JamieMackay 8 —
(M Wigham) *a rr stands side: bhd fr 1/2-way* **66/1**

403- 17 2½ **Surely Truly (IRE)**[178] 6071 3-9-4 **79** .... PatCosgrave 1 —
(K R Burke) *a towards rr stands side: bhd fr 1/2-way* **14/1**

1m 14.78s (1.78) **Going Correction** +0.275s/f (Good) **17** Ran SP% **120.1**

Speed ratings (Par 100):99,97,96,95,94 94,93,91,89,86 85,83,79,73,73 60,56

CSF £45.54 CT £372.21 TOTE £15.10: £3.30, £1.70, £2.30, £2.00; EX 70.20 Trifecta £147.40 Part won. Pool: £207.74 - 0.50 winning tickets..

Owner Phil Green and Partners **Bred** Ardrums House Stud **Trained** Newmarket, Suffolk

■ Stewards' Enquiry : Stephen Carson one-day ban: failed to ride to draw (May 1)

FOCUS

A fair handicap, run at a sound pace, and the form should work out.

Making Music Official explanation: jockey said filly was unsuited by the track

Surely Truly(IRE) Official explanation: trainer said filly lost a shoe during the race

1098 RIPON SILVER BOWL CONDITIONS STKS 1m 1f 170y

3:20 (3:21) (Class 3) 4-Y-O+

£7,790 (£2,332; £1,166; £583; £291; £146) **Stalls** High

Form RPR

00-0 1 **Profit's Reality (IRE)**[5] 1017 4-9-0 91 ....(t) RobbieFitzpatrick 5 106
(P A Blockley) *hld up: hdwy over 2f out: swtchd lft over 1f out and rdn to chal whn bmpd ins last: drvn and styd on to ld nr line* **20/1**

421- 2 shd **Blue Monday**[201] 5607 5-9-0 108 .... SteveDrowne 7 106
(R Charlton) *trckd ldrs: hdwy over 3f out: pushed along over 2f out: rdn to ld jst over 1f out: drvn and edgd lft ins last: hdd nr line* **4/9**[1]

31-0 3 4 **Chrysander**[26] 728 4-9-6 107 .... TedDurcan 4 105
(M R Channon) *hld up: hdwy on outer 3f out: rdn to chal wl over 1f out: drvn and one pce ins last* **14/1**[3]

-612 4 4 **Grand Passion (IRE)**[33] 666 6-9-7 105 .... SebSanders 1 99
(G Wragg) *hld up: hdwy over 2f out: n.m.r wl over 1f out: sn rdn and btn* **5/1**[2]

30-0 5 3 **Lord Mayor**[28] 704 5-9-0 102 .... DarryllHolland 2 87
(R M H Cowell) *sn led: rdn along over 2f out: drvn and hdd jst over 1f out: wknd* **16/1**

10/3 6 1¾ **Mudawin (IRE)**[27] 714 5-9-0 92 .... TonyCulhane 3 84?
(Jane Chapple-Hyam) *chsd ldng pair: rdn along over 3f out: sn wknd* **33/1**

00-0 7 3½ **Traytonic**[33] 667 5-9-5 97 .... AdrianTNicholls 6 83?
(D Nicholls) *chsd ldr: rdn along 3f out: sn wknd* **25/1**

2m 6.14s (1.14) **Going Correction** +0.275s/f (Good) **7** Ran SP% **110.0**

Speed ratings (Par 107):106,105,102,99,97 95,92

CSF £27.62 TOTE £24.40: £5.50, £1.10; EX 46.30.

Owner Phones Direct Partnership **Bred** Michael Munnelly **Trained** Lambourn, Berks

FOCUS

A decent conditions event, run at just an average early pace, and the form looks suspect with the lowest rated runner in the field prevailing. The third is the best guide to the level.

NOTEBOOK

Profit's Reality(IRE), reverting to more patient tactics after running too freely in the Rosebery at Kempton last time, did well to overcome a troubled passage after entering the final furlong and mow on down the runner-up to get up near the line. This has to rate as just about his best effort to date, especially considering he looked to face a very stiff task at the weights on the softest ground he has encountered to date. While he is open to further improvement this season, a significant hike in the weights is now inevitable, and he will no doubt struggle in handicaps as a result. (tchd 25-1)

Blue Monday, who looked backward in his coat for this seasonal return, proved very popular in the betting to follow up his success in the Cambridgeshire. Despite having every chance after hitting the front entering the final furlong, he found just the same pace when it mattered, and always looked like being reeled in the eventual winner. Considering he would have been giving that rival 17lb in a handicap, this has to rate as disappointing and, although his yard is not in the best of form at present, he is likely to find life hard from his current rating this year. (op 4-6 tchd 8-11 in a place)

Chrysander, well beaten in the Lincoln on his seasonal debut 26 days previously, showed the benefit of that outing and turned in an improved effort. He was in-turn clear of the rest in third but, like the runner-up, he is going to find life tricky from his current official mark. (op 12-1)

Grand Passion(IRE), reverting to turf after an excellent second in the Winter Derby last time, was not totally disgraced considering he would have been better suited by a stronger early pace and less-taxing ground. (op 4-1)

Lord Mayor set the tempo until weakening tamely nearing the final furlong. He looks regressive. (op 8-1)

Traytonic Official explanation: jockey said gelding ran too free early stages

1099 RIPON "COCK O' THE NORTH" H'CAP 1m

3:55 (3:56) (Class 3) (0-90,82) 3-Y-O

£9,348 (£2,799; £1,399; £700; £349; £175) **Stalls** High

Form RPR

415- 1 **Kinsya**[185] 5949 3-8-11 **75** .... DarryllHolland 6 82
(M H Tompkins) *trckd ldrs: swtchd lft and hdwy 2f out: rdn to ld ent last: edgd rt and styd on wl* **4/1**[1]

10- 2 2½ **Top Jaro (FR)**[181] 6005 3-8-11 **75** .... TonyCulhane 10 77
(T P Tate) *sn led: pushed along and jnd 3f out: rdn 2f out: drvn and hdd ent last: kpt on same pce* **9/1**

16- 3 3 **Jaad**[181] 6010 3-9-3 **81** .... KDarley 9 77
(M Johnston) *keen: prom: effrt to dispute ld over 2f out and ev ch tl rdn and wknd appr last* **9/2**[2]

100- 4 nk **Damelza (IRE)**[180] 6016 3-9-4 **82** .... DavidAllan 7 77
(T D Easterby) *dwlt: hld up: hdwy 3f out: rdn wl over 1f out: sn no imp* **16/1**

50-4 5 1 **Hill Of Almhuim (IRE)**[18] 848 3-8-11 **75** ....(v) PatCosgrave 3 68
(K R Burke) *in tch: effrt on inner over 3f out: sn rdn and wknd fnl 2f* **15/2**[3]

000- 6 4 **Chris Corsa**[181] 6010 3-8-10 **74** .... HayleyTurner 2 59
(M L W Bell) *a rr* **9/1**

10- 7 13 **Coalpark (IRE)**[181] 6010 3-9-1 **79** .... RoystonFfrench 8 38
(M Johnston) *chsd ldrs: rdn along 4f out: sn wknd* **12/1**

422- 8 2½ **Zaharath Al Bustan**[221] 5148 3-8-12 **76** .... TedDurcan 5 30
(M R Channon) *hld up: hdwy on outer and in tch over 3f out: sn rdn and wknd* **12/1**

1m 42.14s (1.04) **Going Correction** +0.275s/f (Good) **8** Ran SP% **91.2**

Speed ratings (Par 102):105,102,99,99,98 94,81,78

CSF £24.49 CT £80.71 TOTE £3.80: £1.80, £2.40, £1.90; EX 31.40 Trifecta £51.90 Pool: £73.13 - 1.00 winning ticket..

Owner Roalco Limited **Bred** Whitsbury Manor Stud And Clarendon Farms **Trained** Newmarket, Suffolk

■ Nawaqees (7/2 fav) was withdrawn after spreading a plate at the start. Rule 4 applies, deduct 20p in the pound.

FOCUS

A fair three-year-old handicap, run at a sound pace, and the field came home fairly strung out behind the ready winner and the race has been rated positively.

NOTEBOOK
Kinsya, returning from a 185-day break, came right away in the final furlong for a comfortable success. He took time to find his full stride, but responded to his rider's urgings, and showed a fair turn of foot on this deep ground to settle the issue. He looks sure to improve again and would have to be of obvious interest if turned out under a penalty.
Top Jaro(FR) ◆, who won on debut over course and distance last year, showed his true colours with a sound effort from the front and was nicely clear of the rest at the finish. He handled the easy ground well enough and, while he looks a long-term hurdling prospect, it would be a surprise were he not to find a race or two this term. The step-up to a slightly stiffer test should also suit. (op 10-1)
Jaad, beaten in a nursery on his second and final outing last term, ultimately paid for running too freely through the early stages and had no more to offer inside the final furlong. He may want better ground, and possibly this trip is as far as he wants to go, but he still has to prove he is worthy of his current mark. (tchd 5-1)
Damelza(IRE), who took a nursery from a 1lb lower mark last year, was not disgraced on this seasonal return under top weight. She needs faster ground and can better this in due course. (op 12-1)
Hill Of Almhuim(IRE) Official explanation: trainer said gelding lost a shoe during the race
Zaharath Al Bustan Official explanation: jockey said filly had no more to give

1100 SKELTON MAIDEN STKS (DIV I) 1m
4:30 (4:32) (Class 5) 3-Y-O £3,562 (£1,059; £529; £264) Stalls High

Form				RPR
023-	1		**Conkering (USA)**[212] 5390 3-9-3 85 ... OscarUrbina 9 (J R Fanshawe) *lw: trckd ldrs: hdwy 3f out: rdn over 1f out: styd on to ld ins last* **5/2**[2]	80+
330-	2	¾	**Angel Voices (IRE)**[203] 5570 3-8-12 82 ... PatCosgrave 12 (K R Burke) *trckd ldrs: hdwy on inner 4f out: led 21/2f out: rdn over 1f out: hdd and no ex ins last* **15/8**[1]	73
54-	3	1	**Forroger (CAN)**[177] 6102 3-9-3 ... ChrisCatlin 2 (V Smith) *midfield: hdwy over 3f out: rdn wl over 1f out: styd on ins last: nrst fin* **9/2**[3]	76
00	4	5	**Lady Georgette (IRE)**[17] 850 3-8-12 ... RichardMullen 11 (E J O'Neill) *led: rdn along 3f out: sn hdd and grad wknd* **20/1**	61
46-	5	6	**English Archer**[213] 5356 3-9-3 ... PhillipMakin 3 (J R Weymes) *prom: rdn along 4f out: wknd 3f out* **50/1**	54
25-	6	shd	**Baileys Polka**[146] 6417 3-8-12 ... MickyFenton 10 (J G Given) *a midfield* **11/1**	49+
0-	7	3	**Baltic Princess (FR)**[226] 5022 3-8-12 ... KDarley 1 (M Johnston) *in tch: rdn along 4f out: sn outpcd* **8/1**	43
0-6	8	1 ¼	**Dzhani**[20] 823 3-9-0 ... PaulMulrennan[(3)] 4 (Jedd O'Keeffe) *chsd ldrs: rdn along 4f out: sn wknd* **66/1**	45
0	9	20	**Rainbow Prince**[27] 716 3-9-3 ... DavidAllan 8 (A Dickman) *a rr* **80/1**	5
	10	2 ½	**Delamead (IRE)** 3-9-3 ... TomEaves 6 (B Ellison) *tall: a rr* **50/1**	—
	11	3	**Mister Pete (IRE)** 3-9-3 ... FergalLynch 5 (D W Barker) *bkwd: dwlt: a rr* **50/1**	—
00-0	12	¾	**Master Malarkey**[22] 795 3-9-3 35 ... SebSanders 7 (Mrs C A Dunnett) *a rr* **100/1**	—

1m 43.23s (2.13) **Going Correction** +0.275s/f (Good) **12** Ran SP% **115.3**
Speed ratings (Par 98):100,99,98,93,87 87,84,82,62,60 57,56
CSF £7.02 TOTE £3.60: £1.20, £1.40, £2.30; EX 10.30 Trifecta £14.70 Pool: £584.97 - 28.18 winning tickets..
Owner Mrs B Oppenheimer **Bred** B D Oppenheimer **Trained** Newmarket, Suffolk

FOCUS
A fair maiden, run at a sound pace, and the form looks solid. The winning time was 0.67 seconds faster than the second division.
Baileys Polka Official explanation: jockey said filly became unbalanced on undulations

1101 SKELTON MAIDEN STKS (DIV II) 1m
5:05 (5:16) (Class 5) 3-Y-O £3,562 (£1,059; £529; £264) Stalls High

Form				RPR
33-	1		**Peppertree Lane (IRE)**[264] 3935 3-9-3 ... KDarley 7 (M Johnston) *lw: trckd ldr: hdwy to ld over 2f out: rdn over 1f out: drvn ins last and styd on wl* **15/8**[2]	88+
5-	2	nk	**Font**[188] 5870 3-9-3 ... SebSanders 10 (J R Fanshawe) *trckd ldrs: hdwy 3f out: rdn to chal and rn green over 1f out: drvn and ev ch ins last: no ex nr fin* **7/4**[1]	87+
2-	3	5	**O'Tara (IRE)**[183] 5977 3-9-3 ... DarryllHolland 11 (M H Tompkins) *trckd ldrs on inner: hdwy 3f out: swtchd lft and rdn over 1f out: kpt on same pce* **5/2**[3]	77+
220-	4	3	**Fire Two**[194] 5746 3-9-3 81 ... TedDurcan 8 (M R Channon) *led: rdn along 3f out: hdd over 2f out: sn drvn and grad wknd* **12/1**	71
	5	2 ½	**Prince Egor (IRE)** 3-9-3 ... PhillipMakin 1 (M Dods) *rangy: s.i.s and bhd tl styd on fnl 2f: nrst fin* **100/1**	66
0-	6	5	**Orpen's Astaire (IRE)**[181] 6002 3-9-0 ... PaulMulrennan[(3)] 6 (Jedd O'Keeffe) *chsd ldrs: rdn along 3f out: wknd over 2f out* **100/1**	56
	7	nk	**Prophet Preacher (IRE)** 3-8-12 ... RobbieFitzpatrick 2 (M J Attwater) *unf: scope: s.i.s: a rr* **100/1**	50
	8	6	**Little Lily Morgan** 3-8-12 ... RoystonFfrench 3 (R Bastiman) *cmpt: unf: s.i.s: a rr* **100/1**	38
	9	¾	**Mister Jingles** 3-8-10 ... MichaelJStainton[(7)] 4 (R M Whitaker) *rangy: bkwd: a rr* **100/1**	42
00-0	10	2	**Distant Mind (IRE)**[22] 796 3-8-12 45 ... ChrisCatlin 5 (Mrs C A Dunnett) *in tch: effrt to chse ldrs on outer over 3f out: sn rdn and wknd over 2f out* **100/1**	33

1m 43.9s (2.80) **Going Correction** +0.275s/f (Good) **10** Ran SP% **113.4**
Speed ratings (Par 98):97,96,91,88,86 81,80,74,74,72
CSF £5.43 TOTE £3.50: £1.10, £1.10, £1.50; EX 6.80 Trifecta £12.30 Pool: £501.79 - 28.86 winning tickets..
Owner P D Savill **Bred** Gestut Wittekindshof **Trained** Middleham Moor, N Yorks
■ Soldiers Romance (25/1) was withdrawn after getting loose at the start with the blindfold still on

FOCUS
The winning time was 0.67 seconds slower than the first division, but the first two came clear, and both can rate higher in due course.

1102 NEWBY APPRENTICE H'CAP 5f
5:35 (5:42) (Class 5) (0-70,70) 4-Y-O+ £3,238 (£963; £481; £240) Stalls Low

Form				RPR
554-	1		**Our Little Secret (IRE)**[170] 6217 4-8-4 56 oh1 ... KevinGhunowa 7 (A Berry) *overall ldr stands side: rdn clr wl over 1f out: kpt on wl* **33/1**	69
00-1	2	2 ½	**Dorn Dancer (IRE)**[20] 813 4-8-12 64 ... TolleyDean 11 (D W Barker) *outpcd and towards rr far side: hdwy over 2f out: styd on strly ins last: nt rch wnr* **10/1**	68
5-02	3	1 ½	**Mynd**[16] 864 6-8-0 57 ... PatrickDonaghy[(5)] 13 (R M Whitaker) *chsd ldrs far side: hdwy over 2f out: sn rdn and kpt on same pce fnl f* **9/4**[1]	56
200-	4	1	**Desertina (IRE)**[129] 6559 4-7-13 56 oh10 ... LauraReynolds[(5)] 18 (R M Whitaker) *led far side gp: rdn along and hdd 2f out: kpt on same pce fnl f* **80/1**	52
0-00	5	1 ½	**George The Best (IRE)**[30] 691 5-8-4 56 oh8 ... ThomasO'Brien 20 (Micky Hammond) *cl up far side: effrt to ld that gp 2f out: sn rdn and wknd fnl f* **14/1**	46
33-6	6	½	**Angelofthenorth**[20] 813 4-8-7 67 ow4 ... (b) JohnCavanagh[(8)] 6 (J D Bethell) *chsd ldrs stands side: rdn along 2f out: kpt on same pce* **10/1**	56
6203	7	nk	**Gone'N'Dunnett (IRE)**[10] 949 7-8-13 68 ... (v) KirstyMilczarek[(3)] 15 (Mrs C A Dunnett) *in tch far side: hdwy to chse ldrs over 2f out: sn rdn and no imp* **9/1**[3]	56
400-	8	1 ¼	**Harrington Bates**[196] 5705 5-7-13 56 oh8 ... LukeMorris[(5)] 9 (R M Whitaker) *chsd ldrs far side: rdn along over 2f out: grad wknd* **66/1**	39
35-6	9	nk	**Blackheath (IRE)**[34] 657 10-8-12 70 ... VictoriaBehan[(6)] 3 (D Nicholls) *rrd s: sn in tch stands side: rdn 2f out and sn btn* **14/1**	52
-000	10	nk	**Marshallspark (IRE)**[65] 408 7-8-0 60 ... (p) NSLawes[(8)] 8 (R A Fahey) *in tch stands side: rdn along 1/2-way: sn one pce* **33/1**	41
446-	11	½	**Unlimited**[168] 6235 4-8-13 65 ... RonanKeogh 16 (Mrs A Duffield) *cl up far side: rdn along 2f out: sn wknd* **5/1**[2]	45
00-0	12	nk	**Rancho Cucamonga (IRE)**[20] 813 4-8-3 65 ... DeanHeslop[(10)] 14 (T D Barron) *bhd centre tl styd on appr last: nvr a factor* **25/1**	44
3152	13	½	**Percy Douglas**[16] 872 6-8-4 56 oh2 ... (bt) StacyRenwick 2 (Miss A Stokell) *cl up stands side: rdr lost iron after 1f: rdn along 1/2-way and sn wknd* **20/1**	33
2025	14	hd	**Majik**[70] 345 7-7-13 56 oh8 ... (v) SophieDoyle[(5)] 5 (P A Blockley) *s.i.s: a rr stands side* **16/1**	32
564-	15	½	**Diamond Katie (IRE)**[220] 5172 4-9-1 70 ... RobbieMills[(3)] 4 (N Tinkler) *chsd ldrs stands side: rdn along 1/2-way: sn wknd* **25/1**	45
0000	16	shd	**Legal Set (IRE)**[65] 408 10-7-13 56 oh11 ... (t) MarkCoumbe[(5)] 1 (Miss A Stokell) *chsd ldrs stands side: rdn along and edgd rt 1/2-way: sn wknd* **50/1**	30
0-00	17	8	**Bennanabaa**[55] 502 7-8-1 56 oh16 ... (tp) JemmaMarshall[(3)] 12 (S C Burrough) *s.i.s: a rr centre* **100/1**	3
00-0	18	16	**Trick Cyclist**[22] 798 5-8-8 68 ... AdeleRothery[(8)] 19 (M W Easterby) *v.s.a: a wl bhd* **25/1**	—

61.22 secs (1.02) **Going Correction** +0.275s/f (Good) **18** Ran SP% **122.7**
Speed ratings (Par 103):102,98,95,94,91 90,90,88,87,87 86,86,85,84,84 84,71,45
CSF £313.58 CT £1065.47 TOTE £38.20: £7.70, £2.70, £1.50, £9.60; EX 529.60 Trifecta £295.30 Part won. Pool: £415.95 - 0.89 winning tickets. Place 6 £5.69, Place 5 £2.04.
Owner J Berry **Bred** Camogue Stud Ltd **Trained** Cockerham, Lancs
■ Stewards' Enquiry : Luke Morris one-day ban: failed to ride to draw (May 1)
Tolley Dean one-day ban: failed to ride to draw (May 1)

FOCUS
A moderate sprint, which saw the field split into two groups with no obvious bias, and the winner won readily. The runner-up and fourth set the standard which is sound but ordinary.
Blackheath(IRE) Official explanation: jockey said gelding missed the break
Percy Douglas Official explanation: jockey said she lost her irons as gates opened
Trick Cyclist Official explanation: jockey said gelding missed the break
T/Plt: £12.50 to a £1 stake. Pool: £48,613.50. 2,834.25 winning tickets. T/Qpdt: £2.30 to a £1 stake. Pool: £3,963.30. 1,229.50 winning tickets. JR

1103 - 1106a (Foreign Racing) - See Raceform Interactive

1015 KEMPTON (A.W) (R-H)
Friday, April 21

OFFICIAL GOING: Standard
The first ever Kempton meeting to be staged under floodlights.
Wind: Light across Weather: Overcast

1107 HAPPY BIRTHDAY TO HER MAJESTY THE QUEEN MAIDEN AUCTION STKS 5f (P)
7:00 (7:02) (Class 5) 2-Y-O £3,238 (£963; £481; £240) Stalls High

Form				RPR
422	1		**Hucking Hill (IRE)**[4] 1053 2-8-11 ... TQuinn 1 (J R Best) *prom: rdn to chse ldr wl over 1f out: styd on to ld ins fnl f: in command nr fin* **11/4**[2]	74
2	2	1 ¼	**Rippling River**[10] 968 2-8-11 ... AlanMunro 9 (W Jarvis) *racd freely: led: rdn over 1f out: hdd and no ex ins fnl f* **5/4**[1]	69
	3	2 ½	**Mogok Ruby** 2-8-13 ... RobertWinston 5 (L Montague Hall) *racd freely: chsd ldng pair: hung bdly lft fr over 1f out: one pce* **20/1**	61
6	4	hd	**Mac Gille Eoin**[10] 961 2-8-7 ... TedDurcan 2 (J Gallagher) *outpcd in midfield: effrt 2f out: styd on fnl f: n.d* **28/1**	54
332	5	¾	**Diminuto**[14] 908 2-8-2 ... HayleyTurner 8 (M D I Usher) *racd freely: chsd ldr to wl over 1f out: fdd* **10/1**[3]	46
	6	2 ½	**Down The Brick (IRE)** 2-8-8 ... DaneO'Neill 10 (B R Millman) *s.s: wl bhd in last pair: pushed along and kpt on fnl f: nrst fin* **14/1**	42
	7	1 ¼	**Emma Jean Lad (IRE)** 2-8-8 ... LPKeniry 6 (J S Moore) *dwlt: outpcd and bhd: effrt 1/2-way: no prog fnl 2f* **16/1**	37
	8	¾	**Gibsons** 2-8-7 ... RobertHavlin 4 (Mrs P N Dutfield) *s.v.s: hanging lft and a wl bhd* **33/1**	33
0	9	2	**Emefdream**[9] 987 2-9-0 ... NCallan 7 (K A Ryan) *chsd ldrs for 2f: wknd* **10/1**[3]	44+

61.54 secs **Going Correction** +0.025s/f (Slow) **9** Ran SP% **113.0**
Speed ratings (Par 92):91,89,85,84,83 79,77,76,73
CSF £6.17 TOTE £3.40: £1.20, £1.20, £4.50; EX 6.30.
Owner Hucking Horses **Bred** Ballyhane Stud **Trained** Hucking, Kent

FOCUS
A two-horse race according to the market and so it proved. Nothing else ever got into it and the form looks sound but average.

NOTEBOOK
Hucking Hill(IRE), already streetwise compared with most of these, tracked the favourite before delivering a race-winning challenge down the centre of the track. He will not be easy to place now, at least until the nurseries start. (op 9-4 tchd 3-1 in places)
Rippling River had his own way out in front, but could do nothing to hold the winner in the closing stages. He did not appear to step up from his debut, but has shown enough to suggest he can still find an ordinary early-season maiden. (op 11-8)
Mogok Ruby, a £20,000 colt out of a winning half-sister to several winners, was conceding experience to the front pair and it showed, especially late on. Normal improvement should see him win a race.

Mac Gille Eoin struggled to go the pace on this switch to sand before making some late progress. He cost very little and has shown enough to suggest he will more than repay his purchase price. (op 33-1)
Diminuto has plenty of experience on sand, but after showing up for a while she was unable to maintain it. She is not progressing at all. (op 14-1)
Gibsons Official explanation: jockey said gelding missed break
Emefdream Official explanation: jockey said colt had no more to give

1108 ABACUS LIGHTING H'CAP 1m 2f (P)
7:28 (7:28) (Class 4) (0-85,85) 3-Y-O

£7,790 (£2,332; £1,166; £583; £291; £146) **Stalls** High

Form RPR

032- **1** **Stage Gift (IRE)**[228] 5004 3-8-9 **76** ... RobertWinston 1 — 82+
(Sir Michael Stoute) *dwlt: sn trckd ldrs: effrt to ld wl over 1f out: shkn up and styd on wl fnl f* **9/4**[1]

010- **2** 1 **Giving**[202] 5605 3-9-0 **81** ... SteveDrowne 2 — 85+
(G Wragg) *pressed ldr: effrt to chal 2f out: pressed wnr after: styd on but a hld fnl f* **16/1**

52-1 **3** 1 ¼ **Awatuki (IRE)**[25] 762 3-8-13 **80** ... KFallon 3 — 81+
(A P Jarvis) *dwlt: t.k.h and hld up in last trio: effrt over 2f out: rdn and kpt on to take 3rd ins fnl f* **9/4**[1]

35-4 **4** ¾ **Fann (USA)**[18] 855 3-8-4 **71** oh1 ... AlanMunro 8 — 71
(C E Brittain) *racd freely: led: rdn and hdd wl over 1f out: nt qckn* **20/1**

033- **5** nk **Tumbleweed Glory (IRE)**[200] 5667 3-8-10 **77** ... JimmyFortune 5 — 76
(B J Meehan) *t.k.h: trckd ldrs: effrt 2f out: stl cl up over 1f out: nt qckn* **20/1**

2201 **6** 1 **Jebel Ali (IRE)**[22] 804 3-8-8 **80** ... JamesDoyle(5) 9 — 78
(B Gubby) *trckd ldrs: rdn 2f out: sn outpcd: kpt on fnl f* **12/1**[3]

42-1 **7** ½ **Pound Sign**[34] 668 3-9-4 **85** ... JamieSpencer 4 — 82
(M L W Bell) *hld up in last pair: hanging lft 2f out: pushed along and kpt on same pce* **3/1**[2]

430- **8** hd **Nesno (USA)**[182] 6005 3-8-9 **76** ... TQuinn 6 — 72
(J D Bethell) *hld up in last pair: shkn up over 2f out: one pce after* **20/1**

605- **9** hd **Apt To Run (USA)**[176] 6121 3-8-5 **72** ... RichardMullen 7 — 68
(E A L Dunlop) *hld up in midfield: effrt on inner 2f out: no imp over 1f out: fdd* **50/1**

2m 9.38s **Going Correction** +0.025s/f (Slow) **9** Ran SP% **116.4**
Speed ratings (Par 100):99,98,97,96,96 95,95,95,94
CSF £37.42 CT £90.46 TOTE £4.30: £1.70, £2.50, £1.40; EX 31.50.
Owner Ballymacoll Stud **Bred** Ballymacoll Stud Farm Ltd **Trained** Newmarket, Suffolk

FOCUS
A fair little handicap and a few of these are capable of further improvement. The third is the best guide to the level, although the fourth and fifth limit the form.

1109 THE SPORTSMAN H'CAP 6f (P)
7:56 (7:56) (Class 6) (0-65,69) 3-Y-O **£3,238** (£963; £481; £240) **Stalls** High

Form RPR

0540 **1** **Peter Island (FR)**[8] 1004 3-9-3 **64** ... NCallan 2 — 78
(J Gallagher) *w ldr: rdn to ld 2f out: drvn and r.o wl fnl f* **7/1**[3]

-403 **2** 3 **Glenviews Youngone (IRE)**[41] 626 3-9-3 **64** ... RobbieFitzpatrick 4 — 69
(Peter Grayson) *led to 2f out: pressed wnr after tl outpcd u.p ins fnl f* **16/1**

56-3 **3** 1 ¾ **Discotheque (USA)**[20] 835 3-9-4 **65** ... KFallon 6 — 65+
(P Howling) *hld up in midfield: hrd rdn over 1f out: kpt on to take 3rd wl ins fnl f* **7/1**[3]

0-51 **4** ½ **Roman Quest**[10] 969 3-9-8 **69** 6ex ... SteveDrowne 12 — 68
(H Morrison) *dwlt: sn trckd ldrs on inner: rdn and nt qckn 2f out: fdd ins fnl f* **15/8**[1]

064- **5** nk **Light Mozart**[165] 6284 3-9-1 **62** ... RyanMoore 8 — 60
(C E Brittain) *t.k.h: prom: snatched up over 4f out: rdn and outpcd fr over 1f out* **14/1**

-421 **6** 1 ½ **Lucayos**[14] 910 3-8-13 **65** ... (b) RichardKingscote(5) 7 — 58
(Mrs H Sweeting) *prom and racd v freely: awkward bnd over 4f out: w ldng pair 1/2-way: sn hrd rdn: btn 2f out* **5/1**[2]

0122 **7** 1 **Diktalex (IRE)**[8] 1003 3-8-10 **64** ... (t) MarkCoumbe(7) 5 — 54
(C J Teague) *settled in midfield: bmpd along and wknd fr over 1f out* **14/1**

0-00 **8** ½ **Just Down The Road (IRE)**[14] 901 3-9-3 **64** ... AdrianMcCarthy 3 — 53
(R A Harris) *t.k.h: hld up: last 1/2-way: shuffled along over 1f out: kpt on but nvr nr ldrs* **50/1**

6000 **9** 3 **The London Gang**[18] 851 3-9-2 **63** ... ShaneKelly 10 — 43
(P D Evans) *s.s and drvn early: brief effrt on inner over 2f out: sn no prog* **8/1**

050- **10** 1 ¼ **Double Carpet (IRE)**[217] 5275 3-9-1 **62** ... FergusSweeney 11 — 38
(G Woodward) *dwlt: a in rr: rdn and no prog 2f out* **33/1**

500- **11** 1 ½ **Sprouston (FR)**[182] 6011 3-9-2 **63** ... JohnEgan 1 — 34
(J S Moore) *forced wd bnd over 4f out: struggling in rr over 2f out* **16/1**

1m 13.65s (-2.62) **Going Correction** +0.025s/f (Slow) **11** Ran SP% **117.6**
Speed ratings (Par 96):101,97,94,94,93 91,90,89,85,83 81
CSF £112.86 CT £817.37 TOTE £8.40: £2.10, £4.10, £2.70; EX 187.60.
Owner C R Marks (banbury) **Bred** E A R L Elevage De La Source **Trained** Chastleton, Oxon
■ Peter Island became the first horse to win under the Kempton floodlights.
■ Stewards' Enquiry : N Callan one-day ban: not riding to draw (May 2)

FOCUS
A decent and competitive little sprint handicap in which the winning time was fractionally faster than the following handicap over the same trip. The front pair were up with the pace the whole way and the race is rated positively, with the third and fifth the best guides to the form.
Lucayos Official explanation: jockey said colt suffered interference in running
Double Carpet(IRE) Official explanation: jockey said colt failed to handle first bend

1110 BETBROKERS OPEN AN ACCOUNT ON 0844 8552111 MAIDEN FILLIES' STKS 6f (P)
8:24 (8:25) (Class 5) 3-Y-O+ **£3,238** (£963; £481; £240) **Stalls** High

Form RPR

40-3 **1** **Shes Minnie**[17] 868 3-8-12 65 ... RobertWinston 7 — 70
(J G M O'Shea) *chsd ldng gp: rdn and prog over 2f out: drvn and styd on to ld ins fnl f: hld on* **5/1**[2]

65- **2** nk **Spirit Of Arosa (IRE)**[196] 5710 3-8-12 ... TQuinn 5 — 69
(J Akehurst) *hld up in midfield: rdn 2f out: prog over 1f out: r.o to press wnr nr fin: jst hld* **11/2**[3]

335- **3** ¾ **Rubber (IRE)**[251] 4362 3-8-9 87 ... StephaneBreux(3) 12 — 67
(R Hannon) *led: rdn and wandered 2f out: hdd and nt qckn ins fnl f* **15/8**[1]

0-3 **4** 1 ½ **Pride Of Joy**[14] 901 3-8-12 ... MartinDwyer 10 — 62
(D K Ivory) *plld hrd: trckd ldrs: effrt to press ldr over 2f out: upsides ent fnl f: fdd* **8/1**

0- **5** 1 ½ **Palais Polaire**[200] 5666 4-9-9 ... StephenCarson 2 — 61
(J A Geake) *dwlt: hld up in midfield: outpcd over 2f out: rn green but kpt on fr over 1f out: nt pce to rch ldrs* **33/1**

0- **6** 1 ½ **Free Silver (IRE)**[196] 5710 3-8-12 ... PaulDoe 8 — 53
(Miss K B Boutflower) *dwlt and n.m.r s: wl in rr: pushed along 1/2-way: kpt on fnl 2f: n.d* **66/1**

00 **7** 2 **Musical Chimes**[10] 971 3-8-12 ... NCallan 6 — 47
(C A Cyzer) *trckd ldrs: rdn over 2f out: steadily fdd* **28/1**

8 nk **Lady Duxyana** 3-8-12 ... HayleyTurner 9 — 46
(M D I Usher) *dwlt: hld up towards rr: outpcd and struggling over 2f out: no real imp after* **20/1**

264- **9** nk **Divine White**[151] 6395 3-8-12 60 ... RyanMoore 1 — 45
(Mrs A J Perrett) *prom: rdn and nt qckn wl over 2f: btn after: wknd fnl f* **11/2**[3]

0 **10** ½ **Very Clear**[30] 692 4-9-9 ... AlanMunro 3 — 47
(R M H Cowell) *dwlt: a wl in rr: nvr a factor* **33/1**

520 **11** 2 **Kellys Dream (IRE)**[22] 801 3-8-12 65 ... FrancisNorton 4 — 38
(M Quinn) *plld hrd: chsd ldr tl wknd rapidly over 2f out* **16/1**

0-0 **12** 7 **Kris Spring**[19] 844 4-9-9 ... TedDurcan 11 — 20
(R M H Cowell) *dwlt: a wl bhd* **40/1**

1m 13.8s (-2.47) **Going Correction** +0.025s/f (Slow)
WFA 3 from 4yo 11lb **12** Ran SP% **117.2**
Speed ratings (Par 100):100,99,98,96,94 92,89,89,89,88 85,76
CSF £29.85 TOTE £6.40: £1.70, £2.30, £1.40; EX 39.30.
Owner Alan Purvis **Bred** S Martin And Alan Purvis **Trained** Elton, Gloucs

FOCUS
An ordinary maiden and the winning time was 0.15 seconds slower than the preceding handicap, and the form looks modest.

1111 THE SPORTSMAN LONDON MILE QUALIFIER H'CAP 1m (P)
8:52 (8:54) (Class 3) (0-95,94) 4-Y-O+

£11,217 (£3,358; £1,679; £840; £419; £210) **Stalls** High

Form RPR

5111 **1** **Hail The Chief**[9] 992 9-9-8 **94** 6ex ... RyanMoore 5 — 102
(R Hannon) *w ldr: rdn 2f out: led over 1f out: r.o gamely fnl f* **9/2**[1]

30-2 **2** ¾ **Granston (IRE)**[27] 726 5-9-1 **87** ... TQuinn 10 — 93
(J D Bethell) *trckd ldng pair: rdn 2f out: nt qckn over 1f out: styd on fnl f to take 2nd last strides* **9/2**[1]

0013 **3** nk **Binanti**[20] 828 6-8-12 **84** ... FrancisNorton 14 — 89
(P R Chamings) *trckd ldng pair: swtchd lft and effrt over 1f out: styd on same pce fnl f* **10/1**

0410 **4** ¾ **Waterside (IRE)**[34] 667 7-8-12 **84** ... IanMongan 11 — 88
(G L Moore) *mde most: drvn and hdd over 1f out: one pce* **12/1**

0-00 **5** hd **Uhoomagoo**[34] 667 8-9-0 **86** ... (b) NCallan 4 — 89+
(K A Ryan) *hld up wl in rr: drvn and effrt over 2f out: styd on: nt rch ldrs* **9/1**[3]

0-20 **6** nk **Sew'N'So Character (IRE)**[27] 728 5-9-1 **87** ... TedDurcan 8 — 89
(M Blanshard) *hld up in midfield: rdn and nt qckn 2f out: kpt on fnl f: nvr able to chal* **13/2**[2]

52-0 **7** nk **Postgraduate (IRE)**[27] 728 4-9-4 **90** ... SteveDrowne 3 — 92
(W J Knight) *trckd ldrs: rdn over 2f out: one pce and no imp* **10/1**

51- **8** 1 ½ **Kelucia (IRE)**[244] 4581 5-8-8 **83** ... NelsonDeSouza(3) 13 — 81+
(R M Beckett) *fractious in preliminaries: hld up wl in rr: swtchd to wd outside over 2f out: kpt on one pce: no ch* **14/1**

6100 **9** nk **Atlantic Quest (USA)**[41] 629 7-9-1 **87** ... (p) AdrianMcCarthy 2 — 85
(R A Harris) *hld up in midfield: rdn and no prog 2f out: n.d after* **33/1**

460- **10** 1 **Landucci**[223] 5114 5-8-11 **83** ... MichaelHills 6 — 78
(J W Hills) *hld up wl in rr: prog on wd outside 3f out: no imp over 1f out: fdd* **12/1**

2020 **11** shd **Trifti**[20] 828 5-8-13 **85** ... MartinDwyer 7 — 80
(C A Cyzer) *dwlt: sn in midfield: rdn over 2f out: wknd over 1f out* **10/1**

3260 **12** ½ **Kindlelight Debut**[6] 1015 6-8-9 **86** ... JamesDoyle(5) 12 — 80
(N P Littmoden) *hld up in midfield: rdn and no prog 2f out: wknd fnl f* **25/1**

001- **13** 2 ½ **Krugerrand (USA)**[195] 5743 7-8-13 **85** ... LPKeniry 9 — 73
(W J Musson) *hld up in last pair: shuffled along and no rspnse over 2f out* **14/1**

04-0 **14** 2 ½ **Diktatorial**[55] 516 4-9-4 **90** ... (t) NickyMackay 1 — 72
(G A Butler) *hld up and sn detached in last: rdn and no prog wl over 2f out* **40/1**

1m 39.67s (-2.31) **Going Correction** +0.025s/f (Slow) **14** Ran SP% **124.9**
Speed ratings (Par 107):106,105,104,104,104 103,103,101,101,100 100,100,97,95
CSF £23.37 CT £206.41 TOTE £4.60: £1.90, £2.00, £3.30; EX 17.60.
Owner Peter M Crane **Bred** Green Meadow Stud And P Crane **Trained** East Everleigh, Wilts

FOCUS
A very competitive handicap with about three lengths covering the first seven home. The pace was decent, but not that many managed to get into it and those that raced handily were favoured. The form looks solid.

NOTEBOOK
Hail The Chief, bidding for a four-timer, including his penalty was racing off an 18lb higher mark than when winning at Nottingham last time and 5lb higher than for his last handicap on sand. Considering he was unable to establish an uncontested lead and had to battle hard to gain the verdict, this was a cracking effort. He obviously took very well to this surface and remains a credit to the yard. (op 5-1 tchd 4-1)
Granston(IRE) ◆, making his sand debut, was never far away and kept on battling right to the line but the winner just knew too much. It should not take him long to go one better on this surface. (op 5-1 tchd 6-1)
Binanti was always in a good position to strike, but he did not find quite as much as had looked likely when switched but still recorded another decent effort on this surface. On balance, he may be slightly better over seven. (op 11-1)
Waterside(IRE) was given a positive ride, but with Hail The Chief in opposition it was unlikely he would be given much peace and so it proved. Despite that, he never gave in and ran right up to his best.
Uhoomagoo is not the easiest to predict but, given a strong pace to run at, he is always capable of running well and he finished in good style on this occasion. He stays this trip, but does most of his winning over seven. (op 8-1)
Sew'N'So Character(IRE) is another who needs a strong pace and stayed on well without ever quite looking likely to get there. (op 7-1 tchd 8-1)
Kindlelight Debut never got into it and may have had enough for the time being. Official explanation: jockey said mare ran flat

1112 BETBROKERS BETTING JUST GOT BETTER H'CAP 7f (P)
9:20 (9:22) (Class 4) (0-85,85) 4-Y-O+

£7,790 (£2,332; £1,166; £583; £291; £146) **Stalls** High

Form RPR

001- **1** **Into The Breeze (IRE)**[246] 4503 6-8-13 **80** ... MichaelHills 13 — 90
(J W Hills) *hld up in midfield: swtchd to inner over 2f out: prog to ld jst over 1f out: hung lft but kpt on wl* **9/1**

6603 **2** ¾ **Outer Hebrides**[13] [913] 5-9-0 **81**............(vt) NCallan 5 89
(Stef Liddiard) *hld up in last trio: prog over 2f out: hrd rdn and r.o fr over 1f out: tk 2nd last strides* **14/1**

041- **3** *nk* **Will He Wish**[126] [6590] 10-9-4 **85**............ JohnEgan 6 93
(S Gollings) *taken down early: hld up in midfield: rdn and effrt 2f out: chal over 1f out: hld by wnr ins fnl f: lost 2nd last strides* **12/1**

/25- **4** 1 ¾ **Dry Ice (IRE)**[286] [3359] 4-8-13 **80**............ DaneO'Neill 3 83
(H Candy) *hld up wl in rr: rdn over 2f out: styd on fr over 1f out: nrst fin* **10/1**

2223 **5** *shd* **Spring Goddess (IRE)**[34] [670] 5-9-1 **82**............ KFallon 2 85
(A P Jarvis) *hld up in midfield: effrt 2f out: hrd rdn and kpt on same pce fr over 1f out* **4/1**[1]

0200 **6** 1 ½ **Who's Winning (IRE)**[10] [970] 5-8-12 **79**............ TQuinn 12 78
(B G Powell) *hld up wl in rr: effrt and swtchd to inner 2f out: kpt on: nt rch ldrs* **16/1**

210- **7** *hd* **Top Mark**[181] [6022] 4-8-11 **78**............ SteveDrowne 7 76
(H Morrison) *chsd ldr to over 1f out: fdd fnl f* **6/1**[2]

0/0 **8** *hd* **Purus (IRE)**[82] [238] 4-9-4 **85**............ RyanMoore 9 83
(P Mitchell) *led at str pce: hdd & wknd jst over 1f out* **16/1**

-010 **9** 1 **Berkhamsted (IRE)**[11] [946] 4-9-4 **85**............(v) RobertWinston 4 80
(M F Harris) *hld up wl in rr: prog over 2f out: chsd ldrs over 1f out: hld whn squeezed out jst ins fnl f* **20/1**

32-4 **10** 2 **Desert Dreamer (IRE)**[20] [828] 5-9-1 **82**............ IanMongan 1 72
(P R Chamings) *taken down early: racd wd towards rr: effrt over 2f out: no prog over 1f out* **8/1**[3]

0052 **11** 1 ¼ **Chief Exec**[13] [913] 4-9-1 **82**............ MartinDwyer 10 69
(C A Cyzer) *prom tl wknd rapidly over 1f out* **8/1**[3]

04-0 **12** 7 **Asharon**[20] [828] 4-9-2 **83**............(b) TedDurcan 14 52
(C E Brittain) *a struggling in rr: wknd and wl bhd fnl 2f* **33/1**

400- **13** 7 **Bow Wave**[193] [5806] 4-8-6 **78**............ AurelioMedeiros(5) 11 28
(H Candy) *chsd ldrs on inner: hit rail 4f out: wknd rapidly over 2f out* **25/1**

5022 **14** 1 **Te Quiero**[45] [611] 8-9-2 **83**............(b) ShaneKelly 8 31
(Miss Gay Kelleway) *prom to 1/2-way: sn wknd* **12/1**

1m 25.65s (-2.61) **Going Correction** +0.025s/f (Slow) 14 Ran SP% **121.0**
Speed ratings (Par 105):107,106,105,103,103 101,101,101,100,98 96,88,80,79
CSF £126.51 CT £1570.00 TOTE £9.50: £2.50, £5.20, £2.90; EX 507.70 Place 6 £92.36, Place 5 £69.47.
Owner Eric Whitehouse And Partners **Bred** Janus Bloodstock Inc **Trained** Upper Lambourn, Berks

FOCUS
Another competitive handicap, but the leaders may have gone off too quick as the race was eventually dominated by those that were held up. The form looks solid rated through those in the frame behind the winner.

Desert Dreamer(IRE) Official explanation: jockey said gelding hung left

T/Plt: £44.60 to a £1 stake. Pool: £51,915.85. 849.65 winning tickets. T/Qpdt: £34.20 to a £1 stake. Pool: £2,672.50. 57.70 winning tickets. JN

NEWBURY (L-H)
Friday, April 21

OFFICIAL GOING: Good (good to soft in back straight)
Wind: Slight behind

1113 BGC EUROPEAN BREEDERS FUND MAIDEN STKS 5f 34y
1:40 (1:41) (Class 4) 2-Y-O £5,829 (£1,734; £866; £432) **Stalls** Centre

Form RPR

1 **Cav Okay (IRE)** 2-9-3............ RichardHughes 5 96+
(R Hannon) *w'like: str: mde all: sn clr pushed along and edgd lft ins last: easily* **3/1**[1]

2 5 **See In The Dark (IRE)** 2-9-3............ JimmyFortune 4 76
(B J Meehan) *unf: bit bkwd: chsd ldrs: wnt 2nd 2f out: kpt on but nvr any ch w easy wnr* **7/1**

3 6 **Make Me An Offer (IRE)** 2-9-3............ MichaelHills 6 52
(B W Hills) *str: bit bkwd: mid-div but nvr nr to sn clr and easy wnr: one pce fnl 2f* **7/2**[3]

4 1 ¼ **Callisto Moon** 2-9-3............ DaneO'Neill 1 47
(R Curtis) *leggy: bhd: mod hdwy fr over 1f out: nvr in contention* **50/1**

2 **5** 1 **Suhayl Star (IRE)**[6] [1019] 2-9-3............ TedDurcan 2 43
(M R Channon) *lw: chsd easy wnr 3f: sn wknd* **10/3**[2]

6 2 ½ **The Illies (IRE)** 2-9-3............ RHills 3 33
(B W Hills) *unf: scope: v.s.a: a in rr* **9/2**

7 7 **Dories Dream** 2-8-12............ AdrianMcCarthy 7 —
(Jane Southcombe) *leggy: unf: bit bkwd: s.i.s: a in rr* **16/1**

61.18 secs (-1.38) **Going Correction** -0.20s/f (Firm) 7 Ran SP% **108.8**
Speed ratings (Par 94):103,95,85,83,81 77,66
CSF £21.77 TOTE £3.20: £1.80, £3.90; EX 23.90.
Owner Mrs John Lee **Bred** Patrick M Ryan **Trained** East Everleigh, Wilts

FOCUS
A splendid performance on the clock by Cav Okay, who recorded a time just 0.89sec slower than that taken by Green Manalishi over the same trip in a high-class handicap later on the card. He is obvious Royal Ascot material.

NOTEBOOK
Cav Okay(IRE) ◆, a half-brother to Distinctly Chic, who won over this trip at two, was supported into favouritism on his racecourse debut. Bursting out of the gates, he had built up a clear lead within seconds and, when asked to pick up towards the end of the race, he responded immediately. It was an impressive debut and the clock confirmed that he had put up a smart performance. The Norfolk Stakes looks the obvious target as he is all speed and will surely be kept to the minimum distance. The biggest worry would be that, following such a big effort, he bounces next time. (op 11-4)

See In The Dark(IRE), whose dam is well related, was the only gelding in the field. He could not hold a candle to the impressive winner but he kept on to finish a clear second. His stable's juveniles always come on for their debut outings so he should be sharper next time. (op 11-2)

Make Me An Offer(IRE), whose dam was a ten-furlong winner, is a half-brother to Rajam, a dual 12-furlong winner in France. The speed in his pedigree comes from his sire Fasliyev, but this trip looked on the sharp side for him, especially with the winner setting such a scorching pace. (op 9-2)

Callisto Moon, a cheap purchase from a yard not known for sending out juvenile winners, merely stayed on without ever posing a threat. He is likely to need much further in time.

Suhayl Star(IRE) was sharper away this time and tried his best to keep tabs on the winner, but the effort took its toll on him in the second half of the race and he dropped right out. He is proabably better than his finishing position suggests. (tchd 3-1 and 7-2)

The Illies(IRE), a half-brother to three winners in Craiova, Nephetriti Way and Macvel, missed the break badly and, with the favourite pinging the gates and soon clear, he was always struggling to get into any sort of contention. He should know more next time. (tchd 5-1)

1114 ROBERT SANGSTER MEMORIAL MAIDEN FILLIES' STKS (DIV I) 1m 2f 6y
2:10 (2:10) (Class 4) 3-Y-O £6,153 (£1,830; £914; £456) **Stalls** Centre

Form RPR

0- **1** **Cortesia (IRE)**[174] [6143] 3-9-0............ AlanMunro 1 75
(P W Chapple-Hyam) *str: bit bkwd: chsd ldrs: pushed along over 2f out: slt ld ins fnl 2f: narrowly hdd 1f out: rallied u.p to ld last strides* **10/1**[3]

3- **2** *shd* **Safqa**[190] [5850] 3-9-0............ RHills 10 75+
(B W Hills) *t.k.h in rr and stl keen 5f out: smooth hdwy on outside 3f out: qcknd to ld 1f out: rdn ins last: ct last strides* **11/10**[1]

3 1 ½ **Red Countess** 3-9-0............ RyanMoore 6 72
(Mrs A J Perrett) *w'like: scope: bit bkwd: lengthy: chsd ldrs: rdn to chal fr over 1f out: kpt on same pce ins last* **11/1**

4 ¾ **Shout (IRE)** 3-9-0............ SteveDrowne 3 71+
(R Charlton) *w'like: scope: lengthy: bhd: hdwy fr 3f out n.m.r and green 2f out: edgd lft and kpt on ins last but nt pce of ldrs* **12/1**

00- **5** 3 **Temperance (IRE)**[205] [5555] 3-9-0............ DaneO'Neill 2 65
(S Kirk) *chsd ldrs: rdn 3f out: outpcd fnl 2f* **16/1**

0- **6** *nk* **Green Room (FR)**[174] [6143] 3-9-0............ TQuinn 7 64
(J L Dunlop) *bit bkwd: bhd: pushed along over 3f out: kpt on fnl 2f but nvr gng pce to get in contention* **10/1**[3]

3 **7** *nk* **Capriolla**[10] [971] 3-9-0............ RichardHughes 8 64
(P F I Cole) *sn chsng ldr: slt ld fr over 3f out: rdn over 2f out: hdd ins fnl 2f: wknd over 1f out* **15/2**[2]

8 6 **Blessings Count (USA)** 3-9-0............ JamieSpencer 9 52
(E A L Dunlop) *w'like: str: bit bkwd: bhd: pushed along 3f out: nvr gng pce to get competitive and no ch fnl 2f* **10/1**[3]

00- **9** 1 ¼ **Arsad (IRE)**[213] [5391] 3-9-0............ PhilipRobinson 4 50
(C E Brittain) *bit bkwd: chsd ldrs: rdn over 3f out: wknd over 2f out* **40/1**

05 **10** 11 **March Gold (IRE)**[10] [971] 3-9-0............ RobertHavlin 5 29
(H Morrison) *led tl hdd over 3f out: wknd qckly appr fnl 2f* **33/1**

2m 9.86s (1.15) **Going Correction** +0.075s/f (Good) 10 Ran SP% **113.9**
Speed ratings (Par 97):98,97,96,96,93 93,93,88,87,78
CSF £20.83 TOTE £10.80: £3.10, £1.10, £3.10; EX 28.00.
Owner Hintlesham Racing **Bred** Islanmore Stud **Trained** Newmarket, Suffolk

FOCUS
Fractionally the slower of the two divisions, and not the strongest of fillies' maidens.

1115 DUBAI DUTY FREE FINEST SURPRISE H'CAP 1m (S)
2:45 (2:46) (Class 3) (0-95,90) 3-Y-O
£9,971 (£2,985; £1,492; £747; £372; £187) **Stalls** Centre

Form RPR

631- **1** **Night Crescendo (USA)**[179] [6068] 3-8-13 **85**............ RyanMoore 6 98+
(Mrs A J Perrett) *h.d.w: hld up in rr: gd hdwy 2f out: drvn to ld ins fnl f: r.o strly u.p* **5/1**[2]

321- **2** *nk* **Acheekyone (IRE)**[176] [6123] 3-8-8 **80**............ JimmyFortune 7 89
(B J Meehan) *swtg: bhd: hdwy over 2f out: drvn to ld over 1f out: hdd ins last: kpt on u.p but nt pce of wnr cl home* **5/1**[2]

-026 **3** 3 **Isphahan**[58] [483] 3-8-5 **77**............(v[1]) HayleyTurner 3 79
(A M Balding) *led: rdn over 2f out: hdd over 1f out: one pce ins last* **25/1**

114- **4** 1 ¾ **Bonnie Prince Blue**[202] [5613] 3-9-3 **89**............ MichaelHills 4 87
(B W Hills) *s.i.s: bhd: pushed along and styd on fr over 2f out: no imp on ldrs ins last* **9/2**[1]

230- **5** *nk* **Hill Spirit**[190] [5852] 3-8-5 **77**............ JohnEgan 8 74
(D R C Elsworth) *hld up in rr: smooth hdwy to trck ldrs 2f out: sn rdn: one pce ins fnl f* **14/1**

20-0 **6** *nk* **Salute Him (IRE)**[26] [755] 3-9-1 **87**............ TedDurcan 10 84
(M R Channon) *s.i.s: bhd: sme hdwy fr 2f out: sn rdn and nvr gng pce to trble ldrs* **16/1**

104- **7** 1 ¾ **Envision**[189] [5872] 3-9-4 **90**............ PatDobbs 11 83
(R Hannon) *bit bkwd: bhd: sme hdwy fr 3f out: nvr rchd ldrs: and one pce fnl f* **33/1**

2110 **8** *shd* **Trans Sonic**[6] [1016] 3-8-10 **82**............ KFallon 5 74
(A P Jarvis) *chsd ldrs: rdn 3f out: wknd over 1f out* **6/1**

014- **9** 5 **Cape Presto (IRE)**[195] [5733] 3-9-3 **89**............ RichardHughes 2 70
(R Hannon) *chsd ldr over 4f: wknd over 2f out* **10/1**

150- **10** 2 **Mister Benedictine**[230] [4942] 3-8-11 **83**............ MartinDwyer 1 59
(W R Muir) *chsd ldrs: rdn 1/2-way: wknd 2f out* **25/1**

531- **11** 2 **Cote D'Argent**[169] [6233] 3-8-13 **85**............ KDarley 9 57
(M Johnston) *lw: chsd ldrs: rdn over 3f out: wknd over 2f out* **11/2**[3]

1m 37.67s (-2.95) **Going Correction** -0.20s/f (Firm) 11 Ran SP% **113.5**
Speed ratings (Par 102):106,105,102,100,100 100,98,98,93,91 89
CSF £28.35 CT £562.70 TOTE £6.50: £2.30, £1.90, £4.60; EX 34.10.
Owner John Connolly **Bred** Audley Farm Inc **Trained** Pulborough, W Sussex

FOCUS
Traditionally a strong handicap, and no reason to think this latest renewal was an exception.The two who hold Group 1 entries pulled nicely clear at the finish, and the form of the third to fifth looks solid enough.

NOTEBOOK
Night Crescendo(USA) ◆, a Derby entry, had shaped with plenty of promise when successful on the All-Weather last backend, and he always looked the type to improve at three. He saw this trip out strongly and looks the type to progress again, especially when stepped up in distance. (op 9-2)

Acheekyone(IRE) ◆, another who won a maiden on the All-Weather last autumn, has an Irish 2000 Guineas entry. He only went down narrowly and pulled nicely clear of the third, so he will be difficult to beat in similar company next time. (tchd 11-2)

Isphahan, visored for the first time, was settled well in front by Hayley Turner, but he proved unable to cope with a pair of well-handicapped rivals who could well prove themselves quite a bit better than this grade. He still recorded by far the best placing of those who were up with the pace, though, and he could well find a race off this sort of mark. (tchd 28-1)

Bonnie Prince Blue, fourth in the Redcar Two-Year-Old Trophy on his final start as a juvenile, was slowly away but stayed on fairly well in the closing stages. He is by Tipsy Creek but got this trip well enough. (op 5-1)

Hill Spirit, whose stable has not had a winner yet this turf season, ran as though needing this seasonal reappearance. (op 16-1)

Salute Him(IRE), race-fit after a run in Ireland last month, has done his winning on easier ground than this, and he could not muster the pace to get involved. (op 12-1)

Trans Sonic, fit from the All-Weather, did not look badly handicapped on his return to turf racing, but his two wins to date have come when he has made all, and he was denied the lead by Isphahan here. (op 9-2)

1116 DUBAI DUTY FREE FULL OF SURPRISES H'CAP 5f 34y

3:15 (3:17) (Class 2) (0-110,109) 4-Y-0+

£12,464 (£3,732; £1,866; £934; £466; £234) **Stalls** Centre

Form RPR

4-66 **1** **Green Manalishi**[9] 989 5-8-4 **95** PhilipRobinson 10 106
(D W P Arbuthnot) *trckd ldrs: led appr fnl f: drvn out ins last* **7/1**[3]

523- **2** 1 ½ **Corridor Creeper (FR)**[190] 5853 9-9-3 **108** (p) JamieSpencer 8 114
(J M Bradley) *lw: w ldr tl def advantage over 2f out: hdd appr fnl f: one pce ins last but hld on wl for 2nd* **11/1**

-04 **3** shd **Treasure Cay**[41] 627 5-8-4 **95** (t) JohnEgan 13 101
(P W D'Arcy) *chsd ldrs: rdn and kpt on fr over 1f out to press for 2nd cl home but no imp on wnr* **14/1**

6-06 **4** hd **Orientor**[27] 729 8-8-9 **100** KFallon 1 105
(J S Goldie) *sn in tch: rdn over 2f out: styd on u.p ins last but nvr gng pce to rch wnr* **10/1**

-425 **5** nk **Fromsong (IRE)**[20] 836 8-8-8 **99** ow2 DaneO'Neill 11 103
(D K Ivory) *racd along stand side and slt ld tl narrowly hdd over 2f out: kpt on same pce ins last* **33/1**

-063 **6** ½ **If Paradise**[9] 989 5-8-5 **99** RichardSmith(3) 9 101
(R Hannon) *chsd ldrs: rdn and effrt 2f out: kpt on but nvr gng pce to chal* **8/1**

0330 **7** shd **One More Round (USA)**[20] 836 8-8-0 **96** (b) JamesDoyle(5) 6 98
(N P Littmoden) *swtg: bhd: rdn 3f out: kpt on ins last: fin wl but nt rch ldrs* **20/1**

-104 **8** nk **The Lord**[9] 989 6-8-4 **95** oh2 MartinDwyer 12 96
(W G M Turner) *s.i.s: sn rdn in rr: hdwy 2f out: kpt on fnl f but nvr gng pce to rch ldrs* **20/1**

440- **9** ½ **Tournedos (IRE)**[216] 5310 4-9-0 **105** SteveDrowne 7 104
(R Charlton) *bit bkwd: bhd: hdwy 2f out: trckd ldrs 1f out: one pce ins last* **10/1**

0-05 **10** 1 ½ **Cape Royal**[9] 989 6-8-5 **96** ow1 (t) RyanMoore 3 89
(J M Bradley) *chsd ldrs: rdn to chal over 1f out: wknd ins last* **12/1**

4013 **11** 2 **Qadar (IRE)**[20] 836 4-8-9 **100** NCallan 5 86
(N P Littmoden) *in tch: rdn 1/2-way: wknd over 1f out* **11/1**

110- **12** 1 ¼ **Nota Bene**[325] 2168 4-9-4 **109** LPKeniry 2 91
(D R C Elsworth) *bit bkwd: pressed ldrs: ev ch over 1f out: sn wknd* **6/1**[2]

1212 **13** nk **Fyodor (IRE)**[34] 664 5-8-12 **103** TonyCulhane 4 84
(W J Haggas) *lw: chsd ldrs: rdn 2f out: wknd over 1f out* **9/2**[1]

60.29 secs (-2.27) **Going Correction** -0.20s/f (Firm) **13** Ran SP% **117.8**
Speed ratings (Par 109):110,107,107,107,106 105,105,105,104,102 98,96,96
CSF £78.31 CT £1054.36 TOTE £9.00: £2.70, £2.90, £4.60; EX 69.50.
Owner Derrick C Broomfield **Bred** E Aldridge **Trained** Upper Lambourn, Berks

FOCUS
This decent sprint handicap was contested by mostly exposed performers and the time was less than a second quicker than that taken by Cav Okay in the opening juvenile maiden. The form makes sense, though.

NOTEBOOK
Green Manalishi had a good season on turf last year and, having found the ground too soft and the weights against him last time in a conditions race at Nottingham, the return to handicap company on better ground saw him return to winning ways. He was a clear winner in fact, and is now two from two at this track. Chester is the next stop. (op 15-2)
Corridor Creeper(FR), a consistent performer in top handicap company for the past two seasons, ran a super race on his reappearance. He has gone well fresh in the past, though, so his performance should not have been a shock to anyone. (op 8-1 tchd 12-1)
Treasure Cay had the tounge tie back on and ran a solid race off what looked a pretty stiff mark - 7lb higher than for his last success at Leicester back in September. (op 16-1)
Orientor is a difficult horse to place and wins only rarely, but he ran one his better races this time. He had no excuse, though, and is likely to continue finding one or two too good. (op 8-1)
Fromsong(IRE), fit from the All-Weather but on a stiff mark at present, did not look particularly advantaged by racing on his own next to the stands' rail.
If Paradise, who won this race last year off the same mark, could not confirm Nottingham form with Green Manalishi on 4lb worse terms and with the ground riding quicker this time. (op 10-1 tchd 11-1)
One More Round(USA) stayed on without being a serious threat and looks impossible to win with.
Nota Bene looked a promising sort when winning a couple of races last spring, but he burst a blood vessel when beaten at Sandown in May and was not seen again after that. He still looked an exciting type for this year, but this was a very disappointing reappearance. Runners from his stable have generally been needing an outing, but he has a question mark over him now. (op 11-2)
Fyodor(IRE) made brilliant progress on the All-Weather over the winter and spring, winning four times, but that improvement meant that he was reappearing off a 38lb higher mark than when scoring on turf at Redcar in October. On this evidence he is going to struggle on turf now. Official explanation: trainer's representative said gelding ran flat (op 5-1)

1117 DUBAI DUTY FREE GOLF WORLD CUP CONDITIONS STKS 1m 2f 6y

3:45 (3:53) (Class 4) 3-Y-0 **£7,478** (£2,239; £1,119; £560) **Stalls** Centre

Form RPR

251- **1** **Hazeymm (IRE)**[196] 5709 3-8-11 107 TedDurcan 4 97
(M R Channon) *t.k.h: trckd ldr and settled after 3f: slt ld ins fnl 4f: drvn over 1f out: hld on gamely ins last* **13/8**[1]

2 nk **Rumsfeld (ITY)**[174] 3-8-11 92 KFallon 3 96
(M Botti) *w'like: lw: hld up in cl 3rd: pushed along fr over 3f out: trckd wnr over 2f out: drvn and str run fnl f: kpt on but a jst* **4/1**[3]

210- **3** 1 ¾ **Criminal Act (USA)**[195] 5731 3-8-11 91 MichaelHills 1 93
(B W Hills) *t.k.h: hld up in cl 4th: hdwy 3f out: trckd ldrs and drvn 2f out: outpcd fnl f* **9/2**

10-5 **4** 23 **Luberon**[20] 829 3-8-11 94 KDarley 2 81+
(M Johnston) *led tl hdd ins fnl 4f: wknd wl over 2f out: eased whn no ch* **5/2**[2]

2m 8.77s (0.06) **Going Correction** +0.075s/f (Good) **4** Ran SP% **104.8**
Speed ratings (Par 100):102,101,100,81
CSF £7.56 TOTE £2.20; EX 6.00.
Owner Sheikh Ahmed Al Maktoum **Bred** Darley **Trained** West Ilsley, Berks

FOCUS
The form of this small-field conditions event is not sound and the second and third could be flattered by their proximity to the winner, who was officially rated over a stone higher than both of them coming into the race.

1118 ROBERT SANGSTER MEMORIAL MAIDEN FILLIES' STKS (DIV II) 1m 2f 6y

4:20 (4:21) (Class 4) 3-Y-0 **£6,153** (£1,830; £914; £456) **Stalls** Centre

Form RPR

- **1** **Divine River** 3-9-0 KFallon 4 79
(A P Jarvis) *w'like: lengthy: trckd ldrs: pushed along to go 2nd 2f out: strly drvn and kpt on ins last to ld fnl 100yds: readily* **11/1**

340- **2** ½ **Distinctive Look (IRE)**[182] 6007 3-9-0 81 JimmyFortune 3 78
(B J Meehan) *lw: sn chsng ldr: led over 2f out: hrd rdn fnl f: hdd and no ex fnl 100yds* **5/2**[1]

3 1 ½ **Garafena** 3-9-0 RyanMoore 9 75
(Pat Eddery) *w'like: str: bit bkwd: bhd: hdwy over 2f out: kpt on ins last: nt pce of ldrs cl home* **16/1**

40- **4** ½ **Fantastisch (IRE)**[182] 6007 3-9-0 TedDurcan 8 74
(H R A Cecil) *unf: chsd ldrs: rdn along fr 3f out: one pce fnl 2f* **11/2**[2]

5 1 **Fondness** 3-9-0 SteveDrowne 6 72+
(R Charlton) *w'like: bit bkwd: in tch: drvn and hdwy to chse ldrs over 2f out: nvr gng pce to chal: outpcd fnl f* **6/1**[3]

-3 **6** 6 **Just Devine (IRE)**[11] 948 3-8-11 AdamKirby(3) 10 61
(B Palling) *b.off hind: t.k.h: sn led: hdd over 2f out: wknd qckly over 1f out* **13/2**

00- **7** ½ **Spanish Rainbow (IRE)**[206] 5535 3-9-0 IanMongan 7 60
(J L Dunlop) *bhd: sme hdwy on outside to cl on ldrs 3f out: nvr a danger: wknd fnl 2f* **15/2**

8 ¾ **Farafran (IRE)** 3-9-0 RichardMullen 2 59
(E A L Dunlop) *leggy: bit bkwd: bhd: rdn and sme hdwy 3f out: nvr in contention and sn wknd* **9/1**

00- **9** 13 **Sara Mana Mou**[209] 5464 3-9-0 J-PGuillambert 1 34
(J G Portman) *bit bkwd: rdn 5f out: a in rr* **66/1**

3-0 **10** 1 **Puteri Sas (IRE)**[10] 971 3-9-0 RichardHughes 5 32
(P F I Cole) *chsd ldrs: rdn over 3f out: wknd over 2f out* **12/1**

2m 9.74s (1.03) **Going Correction** +0.075s/f (Good) **10** Ran SP% **116.7**
Speed ratings (Par 97):98,97,96,96,95 90,90,89,79,78
CSF £38.76 TOTE £12.70: £3.00, £1.50, £4.30; EX 58.70.
Owner Mrs Ann Jarvis **Bred** Mrs D Brown And Mrs P Barclay **Trained** Twyford, Bucks

FOCUS
Marginally the quicker of the two divisions, and the form has been rated a little more positively. With the favourite, rated 81, appearing to run her race in second, it is pretty straightforward to rate.

1119 BRIDGET MAIDEN FILLIES' STKS 7f (S)

4:50 (4:56) (Class 5) 3-Y-0 **£5,181** (£1,541; £770; £384) **Stalls** Centre

Form RPR

1 **Silver Touch (IRE)** 3-9-0 TedDurcan 10 86+
(M R Channon) *unf: scope: angular: trckd ldrs: drvn to ld jst ins fnl f: r.o strly cl home: readily* **5/4**[1]

2 2 ½ **Ghost Story (JPN)** 3-9-0 PhilipRobinson 2 80
(M A Jarvis) *unf: bit bkwd: chsd ldrs: rdn over 2f out: kpt on ins last and tk 2nd cl home but nvr any ch w wnr* **10/1**[3]

3 nk **Rydal Mount (IRE)** 3-9-0 FergusSweeney 6 79
(W S Kittow) *w'like: led: rdn over 2f out: hdd jst ins fnl f: kpt on but ct for 2nd cl home* **100/1**

4 3 ½ **Greek Easter (IRE)** 3-9-0 JimmyFortune 12 70
(B J Meehan) *w'like: leggy: bit bkwd: bhd: hdwy over 2f out: kpt on fnl f but nvr gng pce to trble ldrs* **20/1**

5 shd **Regent's Park** 3-9-0 DaneO'Neill 7 70+
(R Charlton) *unf: scope: bit bkwd: s.i.s: bhd: hdwy 3f out: kpt on fr over 1f out but nvr gng pce to rch ldrs* **20/1**

6 hd **Tawaajud (USA)** 3-9-0 RHills 4 79+
(B W Hills) *unf: scope: bit bkwd: chsd ldrs: n.m.r and lost position ins fnl 2f: kpt on again fnl f: gng on cl home* **11/4**[2]

7 1 ¾ **Lilac Star** 3-9-0 PaulEddery 13 65+
(Pat Eddery) *w'like: bit bkwd: s.i.s: bhd: hdwy 3f out: hung lft u.p 2f out: nvr gng pce to rch ldrs and sn one pce* **33/1**

8 2 ½ **Miswadah (IRE)** 3-9-0 MartinDwyer 14 58
(E A L Dunlop) *w'like: leggy: bhd: drvn along 1/2-way: hdwy over 2f out: styd on fnl f but nvr gng pce to trble ldrs* **20/1**

9 2 ½ **Rada (IRE)** 3-9-0 RyanMoore 3 52
(R Hannon) *w'like: bit bkwd: chsd ldrs: rdn 1/2-way: sn outpcd: n.d after* **33/1**

10 1 **Evolve (USA)** 3-9-0 RichardHughes 1 49+
(B W Hills) *w'like: scope: bit bkwd: lengthy: chsd ldrs: rdn and one pce whn hmpd 2f out: sn btn* **16/1**

11 1 ¼ **Good Turn** 3-9-0 PatDobbs 8 46
(R Hannon) *w'like: chsd ldrs: rdn 3f out: wknd 2f out* **40/1**

12 2 ½ **Salvia** 3-9-0 SteveDrowne 5 39
(R Charlton) *w'like: bit bkwd: in tch: rdn 3f out: wknd over 2f out* **28/1**

13 2 ½ **Serene Dancer** 3-9-0 RobertHavlin 11 33
(Mrs P N Dutfield) *w'like: bkwd: s.i.s: bhd and nvr in contention* **100/1**

14 19 **Extraordinary (IRE)** 3-9-0 AlanMunro 9 —
(P W Chapple-Hyam) *leggy: bit bkwd: b: stdd rr: a bhd* **18/1**

1m 25.76s (-1.24) **Going Correction** -0.20s/f (Firm) **14** Ran SP% **119.4**
Speed ratings (Par 95):99,96,95,91,91 91,89,86,83,82 81,78,75,53
CSF £12.82 TOTE £2.30: £1.10, £2.70, £16.30; EX 20.00.
Owner Jaber Abdullah **Bred** Kildaragh Stud **Trained** West Ilsley, Berks
■ Stewards' Enquiry : Paul Eddery one-day ban: careless riding (May 2)

FOCUS
A fillies' maiden for newcomers and it was won in style by Guineas entry Silver Touch. The 100-1 third puts a question mark over the value of the form, but the winner looks a good prospect and the race should throw up a few winners.

1120 PETER SMITH MEMORIAL MAIDEN STKS 1m 3f 5y

5:25 (5:25) (Class 5) 3-Y-0 **£5,181** (£1,541; £770; £384) **Stalls** Centre

Form RPR

1 **Hala Bek (IRE)** 3-9-3 PhilipRobinson 9 97+
(M A Jarvis) *gd sort: lw: trckd ldrs: led wl over 1f out: pushed clr ins last: comfortably* **6/5**[1]

0-3 **2** 1 ¼ **Dragon Dancer**[25] 762 3-9-3 DarryllHolland 13 90+
(G Wragg) *sn chsd ldrs: led wl over 3f out: sn pushed along: hdd wl over 1f out: no ch w wnr ins last but kpt on wl for clr 2nd* **7/1**[3]

44- **3** 6 **Snoqualmie Boy**[122] 6628 3-9-3 JohnEgan 2 80
(D R C Elsworth) *bhd: hdwy 3f out: rdn over 2f out: styd on to take 3rd appr fnl but nvr nr ldrs* **15/2**

3 **4** 4 **Som Tala**[15] 894 3-9-3 TedDurcan 6 74
(M R Channon) *bhd: hdwy 3f out: sn rdn: kpt on fnl 2f but nvr in contention* **20/1**

0- **5** ¾ **Moohimm (IRE)**[290] 3205 3-9-3 MartinDwyer 5 73
(M P Tregoning) *chsd ldrs: rdn 3f out: wknd ins fnl 2f* **50/1**

6 1 **Mount Kilimanjaro (IRE)** 3-9-3 MJKinane 4 71+
(J L Dunlop) *w'like: scope: lw: bhd: pushed along over 4f out: hdwy on outside fnl 2f but nvr nr ldrs* **12/1**

7 hd **Alqaab (USA)** 3-9-3 RHills 8 71+
(M P Tregoning) *str: scope: bit bkwd: s.i.s: bhd: rdn 3f out: kpt on fr over 1f out but nvr in contention* **33/1**

4- **8** 1 ½ **King Of Argos**[271] 3774 3-9-3 .... JamieSpencer 11 68
(E A L Dunlop) *plld hrd in rr: hdwy on outside over 2f out: but nvr nr ldrs* **11/2**[2]
00 **9** hd **Warne's Way (IRE)**[11] 948 3-9-3 .... PatDobbs 3 68
(R Hannon) *chsd ldrs: rdn 4f out: wknd 3f out* **100/1**
0- **10** ½ **El Faro (FR)**[184] 5988 3-9-3 .... SamHitchcott 10 67
(M R Channon) *bit bkwd: sn led: rdn 4f out: hdd wl over 3f out: wknd qckly 2f out* **66/1**
0 **11** 2 ½ **Jack Absolute (IRE)**[11] 948 3-9-3 .... MichaelTebbutt 1 63
(B J Meehan) *chsd ldrs tl wknd over 2f out* **100/1**
12 nk **Moon Melody (GER)** 3-9-3 .... HayleyTurner 7 63
(M L W Bell) *w'like: leggy: bit bkwd: chsd ldrs: rdn 3f out: wknd over 2f out* **33/1**
13 17 **Border News** 3-9-3 .... RichardHughes 12 36
(H R A Cecil) *w'like: chsd ldrs: rdn 3f out: wknd over 2f out* **22/1**

2m 21.23s (-1.04) **Going Correction** +0.075s/f (Good) **13** Ran SP% **113.2**
Speed ratings (Par 98):106,105,100,97,97 96,96,95,95,94 92,92,80
CSF £8.08 TOTE £1.90: £1.30, £2.40, £2.00; EX 15.40 Place 6 £202.26, Place 5 £72.52.
Owner Sheikh Ahmed Al Maktoum **Bred** Cliveden Stud Ltd **Trained** Newmarket, Suffolk

FOCUS
Plenty of potential on show here and probably quite a decent maiden. Certainly a race to treat positively for the time being.
King Of Argos Official explanation: jockey said colt ran too free early on
T/Plt: £247.80 to a £1 stake. Pool: £45,986.25. 135.45 winning tickets. T/Qpdt: £76.90 to a £1 stake. Pool: £3,694.90. 35.55 winning tickets. ST

THIRSK (L-H)
Friday, April 21

OFFICIAL GOING: Good to soft
Wind: Virtually nil.

1121 E B F CARPENTERS ARMS FELIXKIRK NOVICE STKS 5f
2:30 (2:30) (Class 3) 2-Y-O **£7,772** (£2,312; £1,155; £577) **Stalls High**

Form RPR
1 **Lovelace** 2-8-12 .... JoeFanning 4 79
(M Johnston) *cl up: rdn to ld over 1f out: sn hung bdly lft: kpt on* **11/2**[2]
21 **2** 1 **Spoof Master (IRE)**[27] 727 2-9-2 .... RobertMiles(3) 7 82
(W G M Turner) *led: rdn along 2f out: drvn and hdd over 1f out: kpt on u.p ins last* **8/11**[1]
3 nk **Diamond Hurricane (IRE)** 2-8-9 .... JohnMcAuley(3) 3 74
(P D Evans) *chsd ldrs: pushed along over 2f out: sn rdn: drvn and kpt on ins last* **20/1**
4 3 ½ **Fly So Free (IRE)** 2-8-7 .... AdrianTNicholls 6 55
(D Nicholls) *s.i.s: sn in tch: hdwy 2f out: sn rdn and rn green: kpt on same pce* **9/1**[3]
5 hd **Perlachy** 2-8-12 .... DavidAllan 2 59
(T D Easterby) *sn pushed along towards rr: hdwy to trck ldrs 1/2-way: sn rdn and wknd over 1f out* **16/1**
6 1 ¼ **Avertuoso** 2-8-12 .... DerekMcGaffin 1 54
(B Smart) *s.i.s: pushed along and in tch whn hung bdly lft fr 1/2-way* **11/2**[2]
7 8 **Rose Court** 2-8-7 .... PaulHanagan 5 17
(K G Reveley) *s.i.s: a outpcd and bhd* **50/1**

62.56 secs (2.66) **Going Correction** +0.50s/f (Yiel) **7** Ran SP% **111.3**
Speed ratings (Par 96):98,96,95,90,90 88,75
CSF £9.36 TOTE £7.00: £2.00, £1.10; EX 14.70.
Owner Hamad Suhail **Bred** Mrs Mary Taylor **Trained** Middleham Moor, N Yorks

FOCUS
The level of the form is not easy to be too confident about, although the time was reasonable.

NOTEBOOK
Lovelace, the highest priced of these at the yearling sales at 76,000gns, is out of a mare who won over a mile. He took command despite drifting badly to his left once in front and ending up on the far side, and is capable of improvement. (op 5-1)
Spoof Master(IRE), whose Brocklesby form has taken a few knocks, was attempting to give away 7lb and more. He knew his job and had the rail to help, but found one too strong at the weights. (tchd 4-5 and 5-6 in places)
Diamond Hurricane(IRE) is a half-brother to three winners out of a sister to high-class sprinter Hever Golf Rose. He was keeping on at the end and this was a fair introduction. (op 25-1)
Fly So Free(IRE), a half-sister to a couple of winning sprinters, was green to post and in the race, but was keeping on at the end and should improve for the run. (op 7-1)
Perlachy should be sharper for the run and by need a bit further, as though he is by a sprinter he is out of a mare who ran over middle distances. (op 28-1 tchd 33-1)
Avertuoso, whose dam won four times over sprint distances at two, was somewhat green and hung to his left from halfway, although not to the same extent as the winner. Official explanation: jockey said colt hung left throughout (op 13-2)

1122 CHRISTA ACKROYD LAUNCHES YORKSHIRE'S LADIES' DAYS H'CAP 1m
3:05 (3:07) (Class 5) (0-75,75) 3-Y-O **£5,181** (£1,541; £770; £384) **Stalls Low**

Form RPR
0461 **1** **Top Shot**[9] 993 3-8-13 **73** 6ex.......... SaleemGolam(3) 9 80+
(M H Tompkins) *hld up towards rr: stdy hdwy 3f out: trckd ldrs 2f out: sn swtchd rt and rdn to ld ins last: kpt on wl* **15/8**[1]
03-6 **2** hd **Bin Rahy (IRE)**[86] 188 3-9-2 **73** .... ChrisCatlin 10 80
(M R Channon) *chsd ldng pair: hdwy to led 2f out: sn rdn: drvn and hdd ins last: kpt on wl* **16/1**
45-0 **3** 1 ¼ **Methusaleh (IRE)**[27] 731 3-9-2 **73** .... DavidAllan 13 77
(T D Easterby) *bhd: gd hdwy over 2f out: rdn over 1f out: styd on wl fnl f: nrst fin* **20/1**
30-2 **4** 1 **Ellesappelle**[20] 839 3-8-11 **68** .... (v) PaulHanagan 7 70
(K R Burke) *hld up towards rr: hdwy on inner over 2f out: sn rdn and kpt on ins last: nrst fin* **11/1**
5121 **5** 1 **Tamagin (USA)**[18] 855 3-8-13 **75** .... (p) StephenDonohoe(5) 3 76+
(P D Evans) *plld hrd: led after 1f: rdn along and hdd 2f out: grad wknd* **7/1**[3]
243- **6** ¾ **Abbey Cat (IRE)**[216] 5295 3-8-12 **69** .... DeanMcKeown 14 67+
(G A Swinbank) *midfield: hdwy on outer to chse ldrs over 2f out: sn rdn and kpt on same pce* **20/1**
360- **7** 5 **Rainbow's Classic**[216] 5289 3-9-1 **72** .... DO'Donohoe 11 60
(K A Ryan) *in tch: hdwy 3f out: rdn and ch 2f out: bmpd wl over 1f out and sn wknd* **25/1**
00-0 **8** nk **Goodbye Girl (IRE)**[44] 613 3-8-4 **61** oh16.......... (p) AdrianTNicholls 5 48?
(Mrs C A Dunnett) *led 1f: chsd ldr tl rdn along 3f out and sn wknd* **100/1**
15 **9** nk **Boldinor**[27] 725 3-9-1 **72** .... SebSanders 8 60+
(W R Swinburn) *chsd ldrs: hdwy 3f out: rdn and ev ch 2f out: sn drvn: hung rt and wknd* **10/1**
540- **10** hd **Dancing Flame**[186] 5939 3-8-4 **61** oh2.......... PaulQuinn 6 47
(E J Alston) *s.i.s: a rr* **25/1**
205- **11** ½ **Golden Alchemist**[182] 6010 3-9-4 **75** .... DavidKinsella 4 60
(M D I Usher) *a rr* **16/1**
14- **12** 7 **Hearthstead Dancer (USA)**[181] 6016 3-9-4 **75** .... JoeFanning 2 45
(M Johnston) *towards rr: effrt on inner 1/2-way: sn rdn along and nvr a factor* **7/2**[2]
3-50 **13** nk **Rosthwaite (IRE)**[27] 730 3-9-1 **72** .... MickyFenton 12 42
(Ronald Thompson) *a rr* **66/1**
000- **14** 9 **Mycenean Prince (USA)**[212] 5407 3-8-1 **61** oh9....... JohnMcAuley(3) 1 12
(R C Guest) *chsd ldrs: rdn along over 3f out and sn wknd* **66/1**

1m 43.3s (3.60) **Going Correction** +0.50s/f (Yiel) **14** Ran SP% **119.9**
Speed ratings (Par 98):102,101,100,99,98 97,92,92,92,92 91,84,84,75
CSF £32.82 CT £480.59 TOTE £2.90: £1.40, £3.90, £5.30; EX 49.20.
Owner J H Ellis **Bred** M P Bowring **Trained** Newmarket, Suffolk

FOCUS
This was run at a fair pace. The first six finished clear and the form looks pretty sound, with the third and fourth setting the standard.
Tamagin(USA) Official explanation: jockey said colt lost its action
Golden Alchemist Official explanation: jockey said gelding was unsuited by good to soft ground

1123 HYGI-TACK H'CAP 1m
3:35 (3:37) (Class 5) (0-70,65) 3-Y-O+ **£3,886** (£1,156; £577; £288) **Stalls Low**

Form RPR
020- **1** **Commitment Lecture**[174] 6139 6-9-11 **62**.......... (t) PhillipMakin 9 74
(M Dods) *hld up in midfield: gd hdwy over 2f out: rdn to ld over 1f out styd on strly* **14/1**
241- **2** 1 ¼ **Time To Regret**[170] 6231 6-9-2 **53** .... TonyHamilton 11 62
(J S Wainwright) *chsd ldrs: hdwy to ld over 2f out: sn rdn: drvn and hdd over 1f out: kpt on u.p ins last* **25/1**
1404 **3** ¾ **Parkview Love (USA)**[25] 764 5-9-11 **65**.......... (v) PatrickMathers(3) 14 72
(D Shaw) *hld up in tch: smooth hdwy 3f out: effrt wl over 1f out and ev ch tl rdn and nt qckn ent last* **11/1**
210- **4** ½ **Dium Mac**[182] 6008 5-9-3 **61** .... SuzzanneFrance(7) 15 67
(N Bycroft) *towards rr: hdwy on outer 3f out: rdn and edgd lft over 1f out: kpt on ins last: nrst fin* **22/1**
110- **5** hd **Shifty**[330] 2026 7-9-9 **63** .... DanielTudhope(3) 7 69
(D Carroll) *midfield: hdwy on inner 3f out: rdn along wl over 1f out: kpt on ins last: nrst fin* **10/1**[3]
565- **6** 1 **Major Magpie (IRE)**[253] 4299 4-9-13 **64** .... FergalLynch 18 73+
(M Dods) *stdd s and bhd: hdwy wl over 2f out: shkn up and trckd ldrs over 1f out: eased ins last* **20/1**
045- **7** 1 ¼ **Champain Sands (IRE)**[207] 5509 7-9-1 **52** .... JimmyQuinn 17 53+
(E J Alston) *hld up in rr: stdy hdwy 3f out: rdn to chse ldrs over 1f out wknd ins last* **16/1**
3-05 **8** ½ **Sforzando**[81] 252 5-9-7 **65** .... KristinStubbs(7) 1 65
(Mrs L Stubbs) *s.i.s and bhd: pushed along 1/2-way: rdn and kpt on fnl 2f: nrst fin* **20/1**
5002 **9** 3 **Ming Vase**[17] 875 4-9-0 **51** oh4.......... LeeEnstone 10 45
(P T Midgley) *sn led: rdn along 3f out: hdd over 2f out and sn wknd* **33/1**
-150 **10** ½ **Sonic Anthem (USA)**[69] 383 4-8-12 **52**.......... SilvestreDeSousa(3) 16 45
(D Nicholls) *keen: in tch on outer: hdsway 3f out: rdn to chse ldrs whn bmpd wl over 1f out: sn wknd* **20/1**
54-5 **11** shd **Young Scotton**[66] 409 6-9-8 **62** .... PaulMulrennan(3) 12 55
(J Howard Johnson) *cl up: rdn along over 3f out:sn wknd* **16/1**
0300 **12** ½ **Orpen Wide (IRE)**[26] 426 4-10-0 **65** .... BrianReilly 8 57
(M C Chapman) *chsd ldrs: rdn along over 3f out: sn wknd* **16/1**
22-0 **13** nk **Grande Roche (IRE)**[83] 231 4-9-5 **56** .... DeanMcKeown 5 47
(G A Swinbank) *midfield: effrt on inner over 3f out: rdn along over 2f out and sn no imp* **15/2**[2]
/00- **14** shd **Grandos (IRE)**[220] 5207 4-9-7 **58** .... SebSanders 3 49
(T D Easterby) *a towards rr* **20/1**
00-2 **15** 1 **Grande Terre (IRE)**[4] 1041 5-9-4 **55** .... PaulHanagan 4 44+
(R A Fahey) *hld up towards rr: pushed along over 3f out: sn rdn and nvr a factor* **3/1**[1]
330- **16** ½ **Royal Pardon**[232] 4882 4-9-3 **54** .... JoeFanning 2 42
(R C Guest) *a rr* **33/1**
0000 **17** 3 ½ **Wistman (UAE)**[4] 1057 5-10-0 **65** .... (v[1]) AdrianTNicholls 13 45
(D Nicholls) *s.i.s: a rr* **33/1**
000- **18** 12 **Young Mr Grace (IRE)**[171] 6216 6-10-0 **65** .... DavidAllan 6 20
(T D Easterby) *cl up: rdn along over 3f out and sn wknd* **12/1**

1m 43.23s (3.53) **Going Correction** +0.50s/f (Yiel) **18** Ran SP% **122.3**
Speed ratings (Par 103):102,100,100,99,99 98,97,96,93,93 92,92,92,92,91 90,87,75
CSF £329.91 CT £3936.32 TOTE £14.50: £3.10, £3.70, £2.90, £7.50; EX 397.90.
Owner Mrs B Riddell **Bred** Mrs Ian Pilkington **Trained** Denton, Co Durham
■ Stewards' Enquiry : Suzzanne France one-day ban: careless riding (May 2)

FOCUS
Modest form, but more solid than most.
Major Magpie(IRE) Official explanation: jockey said gelding was denied clear run
Grandos(IRE) Official explanation: jockey said gelding was denied clear run
Grande Terre(IRE) Official explanation: jockey said mare was never travelling
Royal Pardon Official explanation: jockey said filly was denied clear run
Wistman(UAE) Official explanation: jockey said gelding hung right down straight

1124 HAWNBY H'CAP 7f
4:10 (4:11) (Class 5) (0-70,71) 3-Y-O+ **£3,886** (£1,156; £577; £288) **Stalls Low**

Form RPR
212- **1** **Stellite**[160] 6336 6-9-4 **63** .... DanielTudhope(3) 8 75
(J S Goldie) *hld up towards rr: stdy hdwy on outer 3f out: rdn to chal and edgd lft over 1f out: styd on to ld ins last* **13/2**[2]
0-04 **2** nk **Aperitif**[4] 1041 5-9-8 **64** .... AdrianTNicholls 16 75
(D Nicholls) *chsd ldrs on outer: hdwy 3f out: rdn to ld over 1f out: hdd and no ex ins last* **8/1**
00-0 **3** ¾ **Hula Ballew**[17] 864 6-9-3 **59** .... PhillipMakin 4 68
(M Dods) *hld up in rr: hdwy over 2f out: rdn wl over 1f out: styd on ins last: nrst fin* **10/1**
1313 **4** ½ **Riquewihr**[14] 902 6-9-10 **66** .... (p) SebSanders 3 74
(J S Wainwright) *hld up towards rr: hdwy 3f out: rdn to chse ldrs and n.m.r ent last: kpt on* **7/1**[3]
60-3 **5** 1 ¼ **Titinius (IRE)**[4] 1042 6-9-11 **67** .... PaulHanagan 11 72
(Micky Hammond) *hld up: hdwy 3f out: rdn to chse ldrs over 1f out: n.m.r ent last: wknd* **13/2**[2]

2051 **6** *1* **True Night**[9] 977 9-9-10 **71** 6ex................................ LiamTreadwell(5) 2 73
(D Nicholls) *chsd ldrs: rdn along over 2f out: drvn and n.m.r over 1f out: sn one pce* **7/1**[3]

102- **7** *½* **Hewaraat (IRE)**[221] 5172 4-9-11 **67**........................... DeanMcKeown 10 68
(G A Swinbank) *chsd ldrs: effrt over 2f out: sn rdn and no imp appr last* **9/2**[1]

0 **8** *3* **Khetaab (IRE)**[11] 955 4-9-8 **64**.. DavidAllan 15 57
(E J Alston) *led to 1/2-way: cl up tl rdn to ld again over 2f out: hdd over 1f out and wkng whn n.m.r ent last* **33/1**

325- **9** *5* **Billy One Punch**[301] 2874 4-9-11 **67**............................ JimmyQuinn 12 47
(G G Margarson) *midfield: hdwy on outer 3f out: rdn along to chse ldrs 2f out: wknd over 1f out* **16/1**

00-0 **10** *1¾* **Downland (IRE)**[18] 860 10-9-4 **60**..................................... KimTinkler 7 36
(N Tinkler) *cl up: led 1/2-way: rdn and hdd over 2f out: grad wknd* **66/1**

010- **11** *2½* **Kabis Amigos**[218] 5242 4-10-0 **70**.................................... JoeFanning 14 39
(D Nicholls) *a rr* **20/1**

300- **12** *1* **Compton Plume**[188] 5893 6-9-13 **69**................................ DaleGibson 6 35
(M W Easterby) *cl up: rdn along 3f out and sn wknd* **40/1**

5516 **13** *1* **Cool Sands (IRE)**[9] 977 4-9-3 **62**........................(v) PatrickMathers(3) 1 26
(D Shaw) *chsd ldrs: rdn along over 3f out: sn wknd* **20/1**

000- **14** *hd* **Moon Forest (IRE)**[195] 5735 4-10-0 **70**............................ TomEaves 13 33
(J M Bradley) *chsd ldrs: rdn along over 3f out: sn wknd* **25/1**

00-0 **15** *¾* **Yorkshire Blue**[21] 818 7-9-6 **62**...................................... FergalLynch 9 23
(J S Goldie) *s.i.s: a rr* **20/1**

1m 29.72s (2.62) **Going Correction** +0.50s/f (Yiel) **15** Ran SP% **120.9**
Speed ratings (Par 103):105,104,103,103,101 100,100,96,90,88 86,84,83,83,82
CSF £52.35 CT £537.80 TOTE £8.90: £2.50, £3.40, £3.50; EX 82.40.
Owner S Bruce **Bred** Cheveley Park Stud Ltd **Trained** Uplawmoor, E Renfrews
■ Stewards' Enquiry : Daniel Tudhope caution: careless riding

FOCUS
An ordinary handicap, run at a sound pace. Straightforward form.
Titinius(IRE) Official explanation: jockey said gelding hung left

1125 SWAINBY H'CAP 5f
4:40 (4:41) (Class 4) (0-80,80) 3-Y-O+ **£6,477** (£1,927; £963; £481) **Stalls** High

Form RPR

461/ **1** **Desert Commander (IRE)**[618] 4649 4-9-6 **78**................ DO'Donohoe 5 101+
(K A Ryan) *trckd ldrs far side: hdwy to ld and overall ldr wl over 1f out: sn clr* **20/1**

-250 **2** *3* **Countdown**[49] 569 4-9-6 **78**...(b) TomEaves 2 85
(Miss J A Camacho) *in tch far side: hdwy 2f out: sn rdn and styd on ins last: no ch w wnr* **14/1**

40-6 **3** *1½* **Bold Marc (IRE)**[23] 798 4-9-2 **79**.............................. AndrewElliott(5) 11 81
(K R Burke) *trckd ldrs far side: hdwy to ld that gp 2f out: sn rdn and hdd: kpt on same pce appr last* **11/1**

-505 **4** *shd* **Bonne De Fleur**[11] 954 5-9-2 **74**.............................(b) DerekMcGaffin 4 75
(B Smart) *led far side: rdn along over 2f out: sn hdd and kpt on same pce* **20/1**

0314 **5** *nk* **Efistorm**[25] 761 5-9-4 **79**... JasonEdmunds(3) 10 79
(J Balding) *chsd ldrs stands side: hdwy to ld that gp over wl over 1f out: sn rdn and one pce ins last* **8/1**[1]

300- **6** *¾* **Pomfret Lad**[202] 5603 8-9-3 **75**................................ GrahamGibbons 18 72
(J J Quinn) *hld up stand side: hdwy 2f out: sn rdn and kpt on ins last: nrst fin* **12/1**

030- **7** *shd* **Peopleton Brook**[160] 6321 4-9-7 **79**............................... MickyFenton 17 76
(J M Bradley) *bmpd s: sn chsng ldrs stands side: rdn along over 2f out and sn one pce* **10/1**[3]

10/0 **8** *½* **Big Hassle (IRE)**[28] 718 4-9-8 **80**............................. AdrianTNicholls 8 75
(D Nicholls) *chsd ldrs stands side: rdn along over 2f out: grad wknd* **33/1**

000- **9** *shd* **Catch The Cat (IRE)**[171] 6217 7-8-10 **68**....................... JimmyQuinn 13 63
(Robert Gray) *chsd ldrs stands side: rdn over 2f out: grad wknd* **20/1**

0005 **10** *½* **Whinhill House**[5] 1031 6-9-0 **77**..............................(p) MarkLawson(5) 14 70
(D W Barker) *cl up stands side: overall ldr 1/2-way: rdn and hdd wl over 1f out: sn wknd* **9/1**[2]

304- **11** *hd* **Divine Spirit**[160] 6335 5-8-9 **67** ow1.............................. FergalLynch 15 59+
(M Dods) *hld up and bhd stands side: hdwy over 2f out: swtchd rt over 1f out: eased ins last* **8/1**[1]

001 **12** *½* **Silver Dane (IRE)**[23] 798 4-9-1 **73**.............................(v) SebSanders 6 64
(Mrs C A Dunnett) *chsd ldr far side: rdn along over 2f out: sn wknd* **8/1**[1]

540- **13** *nk* **Henry Hall (IRE)**[224] 5090 10-8-13 **71**........................... KimTinkler 20 61
(N Tinkler) *chsd ldrs stands side: rdn along over 2f out: sn wknd* **16/1**

306- **14** *nk* **Prince Namid**[169] 6238 4-9-2 **77**.............................. SaleemGolam(3) 3 65
(Mrs A Duffield) *a rr far side* **9/1**[2]

026/ **15** *½* **Shank On Fourteen (IRE)**[916] 5630 5-9-8 **80**................ PatCosgrave 7 67
(K R Burke) *chsd ldrs far side: rdn along over 2f out and sn wknd* **33/1**

0-00 **16** *½* **Handsome Cross (IRE)**[25] 761 5-9-1 **80**............. VictoriaBehan(7) 19 65
(D Nicholls) *overall ldr stands side: hdd 1/2-way: sn wknd* **14/1**

261- **17** *¾* **Further Outlook (USA)**[219] 5225 12-8-12 **77**..... DanielleMcCreery(7) 16 59
(D Carroll) *cl up stands side: rdn along 1/2-way: sn wknd* **20/1**

1-00 **18** *1¼* **Ryedane (IRE)**[70] 362 4-9-4 **76**..(e) DavidAllan 9 54
(T D Easterby) *in tch far side: rdn along 1/2-way: sn wknd* **25/1**

61.32 secs (1.42) **Going Correction** +0.50s/f (Yiel) **18** Ran SP% **126.4**
Speed ratings (Par 105):108,103,100,100,100 98,98,98,97,97 96,95,95,94,94 93,92,90
CSF £262.56 CT £3328.71 TOTE £34.20: £5.00, £4.70, £3.30, £4.70; EX 400.80.
Owner R J H Limited **Bred** Gainsborough Stud Management Ltd **Trained** Hambleton, N Yorks
■ A comeback winner for Daragh O'Donohoe who has been based abroad in the last three years.

FOCUS
The field divided into two groups of nine, with the far side coming out on top. Ordinary form, but solid enough, with the winner looking the type to go in again.
Divine Spirit Official explanation: jockey said gelding was denied clear run

1126 HABTON MEDIAN AUCTION MAIDEN STKS (DIV I) 6f
5:10 (5:12) (Class 5) 3-4-Y-O **£3,562** (£1,059; £529; £264) **Stalls** High

Form RPR

2- **1** **Buachaill Dona (IRE)**[341] 1723 3-9-0 .... AdrianTNicholls 7 65+
(D Nicholls) *trckd ldrs: n.m.r and swtchd lft wl over 1f out: rdn to ld ent last: 2l up whn fly-leapt on line* **8/15**[1]

0-02 **2** *1* **She's Dunnett**[23] 796 3-8-9 **51**.. ChrisCatlin 6 53
(Mrs C A Dunnett) *chsd ldrs: rdn along and hdwy on inner 2f out: drvn and ch ent last: sn one pce* **15/2**[2]

3 *1* **Diamond Winnie** 3-8-6 .... JohnMcAuley(3) 2 50
(Mrs A Duffield) *sn pushed along in rr: hdwy over 2f out: rdn over 1f out: kpt on ins last* **20/1**

500- **4** *4* **The Salwick Flyer (IRE)**[171] 6213 3-9-0 **54**.................. FergalLynch 10 43
(A Berry) *led: rdn along 2f out: drvn and hdd ent last: edgd lft and wknd* **14/1**

5 *1½* **Ailsa**[106] 4-9-6 .... DeanMcKeown 3 37
(C W Thornton) *s.i.s and bhd tl styd on fnl 2f* **25/1**

00- **6** *8* **Networker**[288] 3285 3-8-7 .... JamesReveley(7) 8 15
(K G Reveley) *cl up: ev ch 2f out: sn rdn and wknd* **100/1**

20 **7** *6* **Trumpita**[9] 978 3-9-0 .... DavidAllan 5 —
(T D Easterby) *chsd ldrs on outer: rdn along wl over 2f out and sn wknd* **10/1**[3]

000- **8** *5* **Look Here's May**[242] 4646 4-8-13 **40**.................. RussellKennemore(7) 4 —
(R Hollinshead) *a rr* **50/1**

9 *1¾* **Azerley (IRE)** 3-8-9 .... SebSanders 1 —
(J D Bethell) *sn rdn along: a bhd* **14/1**

00 **10** *2½* **Beverley Bell**[69] 380 3-8-9 ....(p) TomEaves 11 —
(Miss J A Camacho) *prom: pushed along after 2f: sn lost pl and bhd fr over 2f out* **25/1**

1m 16.41s (3.91) **Going Correction** +0.50s/f (Yiel)
WFA 3 from 4yo 11lb **10** Ran SP% **114.8**
Speed ratings (Par 103):93,91,90,85,83 72,64,57,55,52
CSF £4.28 TOTE £1.50: £1.10, £2.00, £4.80; EX 4.80.
Owner Mike Browne **Bred** John O Browne **Trained** Sessay, N Yorks

FOCUS
A weak race, run in the same time as the second division, in which the 51-rated runner-up limits the form. The first five finished clear.

1127 HABTON MEDIAN AUCTION MAIDEN STKS (DIV II) 6f
5:40 (5:43) (Class 5) 3-4-Y-O **£3,562** (£1,059; £529; £264) **Stalls** High

Form RPR

4- **1** **Rondo**[324] 2183 3-9-0 .... PhillipMakin 3 72+
(T D Barron) *chsd ldrs: hdwy 2f out: rdn to ld ent last: kpt on* **10/3**[2]

225- **2** *1¾* **Lucksin (IRE)**[202] 5626 3-9-0 **79**.. JoeFanning 2 69+
(N Tinkler) *cl up: led 1/2-way: rdn over 1f out: hdd ent last: kpt on* **10/3**[2]

360- **3** *2½* **Primarily**[174] 6140 4-9-11 **64**.. PaulHanagan 4 63
(A Berry) *chsd ldrs: effrt 2f out: sn rdn and kpt on same pce* **9/2**[3]

4 *7* **Forestelle (IRE)** 3-8-6 .... BenSwarbrick(3) 8 34
(M Dods) *towards rr: hdwy on outer over 2f out: sn rdn and kpt on: nvr nr ldrs* **16/1**

5- **5** *2* **Mujeak (IRE)**[358] 1321 3-9-0 .... GrahamGibbons 7 33
(J J Quinn) *s.i.s and bhd tl sme late hdwy* **3/1**[1]

0-00 **6** *1½* **Shopfitter**[4] 1054 3-9-0 **40**..(v) ChrisCatlin 9 28
(Mrs C A Dunnett) *cl up: rdn along 1/2-way: sn wknd* **33/1**

/06- **7** *½* **Diamond Heritage**[402] 628 4-9-11 **45**......................... DeanMcKeown 5 30
(S Parr) *a rr* **33/1**

400- **8** *½* **Graceful Flight**[214] 5360 4-9-6 **40**..................................... MickyFenton 1 23
(P T Midgley) *wnt bdly rt s: racd wd: a rr* **50/1**

00- **9** *20* **Maison Dieu**[205] 5547 3-8-11 .... PaulMulrennan(3) 10 —
(J Howard Johnson) *led: rdn along and hdd 1/2-way: sn wknd* **12/1**

1m 16.41s (3.91) **Going Correction** +0.50s/f (Yiel)
WFA 3 from 4yo 11lb **9** Ran SP% **110.8**
Speed ratings (Par 103):93,90,87,78,75 73,72,72,45
CSF £13.81 TOTE £4.00: £1.60, £1.60, £1.60; EX 10.90 Place 6 £241.00, Place 5 £188.50.
Owner Mrs J Hazell **Bred** Wyck Hall Stud Ltd **Trained** Maunby, N Yorks

FOCUS
This was run in the same time as division one, but the form looks better. The first three finished clear.
Mujeak(IRE) Official explanation: jockey said gelding became upset in stalls and missed break
T/Plt: £462.40 to a £1 stake. Pool: £38,267.10. 60.40 winning tickets. T/Qpdt: £189.00 to a £1 stake. Pool: £2,694.90. 10.55 winning tickets. JR

1113 NEWBURY (L-H)
Saturday, April 22

OFFICIAL GOING: Good (good to soft in back straight)
Wind: Virtually nil

1128 DUBAI TENNIS CHAMPIONSHIPS STKS (REGISTERED AS THE JOHN PORTER STAKES) (GROUP 3) 1m 4f 5y
2:10 (2:11) (Class 1) 4-Y-O+
£28,390 (£10,760; £5,385; £2,685; £1,345; £675) **Stalls** Centre

Form RPR

104- **1** **Mubtaker (USA)**[182] 6026 9-9-1 **115**............................. MartinDwyer 11 119
(M P Tregoning) *sn trcking ldr: qckd to chal 4 out: slt ld 3f out: hrd drvn fnl f: hld on gamely* **9/1**

113- **2** *nk* **Munsef**[182] 6026 4-8-11 **107**... TQuinn 5 116+
(J L Dunlop) *hld up in rr: pushed along 3 out: hdwy over 2f out: chsd wnr fnl f: kpt on u.p ins last but a jst hld* **4/1**[2]

33-0 **3** *½* **Maraahel (IRE)**[28] 743 5-8-12 **120**..................................... RHills 4 115
(Sir Michael Stoute) *lw: hld up in rr: hdwy over 2f out: rdn and qcknd over 1f out: chsd ldrs ins last but hung lft: styd on but a hld cl home* **3/1**[1]

121- **4** *2½* **Sergeant Cecil**[189] 5903 7-8-12 **112**............................... AlanMunro 10 111
(B R Millman) *bit bkwd: hld up in rr: swtchd to outside 3f out: rdn and kpt on wl fnl 2f but nvr gng pce to rch ldrs* **9/1**

320- **5** *½* **The Whistling Teal**[181] 6055 10-8-12 **115**.................... SteveDrowne 1 110
(G Wragg) *bit bkwd: in tch: rdn and outpcd 3f out: styd on again fr over 1f out: gng on cl home* **16/1**

53-1 **6** *nk* **Frank Sonata**[10] 991 5-8-12 **102**................................... RyanMoore 9 109
(M G Quinlan) *lw: chsd ldrs: rdn 3f out: one pce fnl 2f* **6/1**[3]

261- **7** *2* **Allexina**[195] 5781 4-8-8 .... MJKinane 8 103
(John M Oxx, Ire) *angular: sn led: rdn and narrowly hdd 3f out:wknd qckly fnl f* **15/2**

2-00 **8** *11* **Compton Bolter (IRE)**[35] 666 9-9-1 **110**.......................... CSoumillon 6 105+
(G A Butler) *in tch: chsd ldrs over 4f out: sn rdn: wknd over 2f out: eased whn no ch fnl f* **28/1**

010- **9** *½* **Swift Sailor**[189] 5903 5-8-12 **100**................................ JimmyFortune 7 88
(G L Moore) *chsd ldrs: rdn over 3f out: sn btn* **50/1**

/23- **10** *16* **Gulf (IRE)**[301] 2934 7-8-12 **105**...................................... JohnEgan 2 62
(D R C Elsworth) *s.i.s: t.k.h in rr: lost tch fnl 3f* **50/1**

5-11 **11** *16* **Sri Diamond**[35] 666 6-9-1 **98**.................................... JamieSpencer 3 40
(S Kirk) *chsd ldrs: rdn 3f out: sn wknd: eased whn no ch over 1f out* **10/1**

2m 33.18s (-2.81) **Going Correction** -0.025s/f (Good)
WFA 4 from 5yo+ 1lb **11** Ran SP% **113.4**
Speed ratings (Par 113):108,107,107,105,105 105,103,96,96,85 74
CSF £42.75 TOTE £8.60: £2.80, £1.90, £1.50; EX 43.30.
Owner Hamdan Al Maktoum **Bred** Warren W Rosenthal **Trained** Lambourn, Berks
■ A first Group winner for Martin Dwyer in his new role as second jockey for Sheikh Hamdan, who owned the first three home.

■ Stewards' Enquiry : T Quinn caution: used whip with excessive frequency and without giving horse time to respond

FOCUS

A competitive renewal of the John Porter, but the pace was just ordinary and Mubtaker, well placed throughout, took advantage to extend his impressive Newbury record, despite looking in the paddock as though this run would bring him on. The first two set the level for the form.

NOTEBOOK

Mubtaker(USA), returning from a 182-day break for his eighth straight season on the track, looked as though this run would bring him on, but both he and eventual seventh Allexina did not have to expend much energy to build up a three-to-four length lead over their pursuers in the straight, and he ran on gamely when strongly challenged. His form figures at Newbury now read 1211110241 but, while he will probably be back here later in the year for races like the Geoffrey Freer and St Simon Stakes, he is fully effective elsewhere and his next target is the Jockey Club Stakes at Newmarket. (op 7-1)

Munsef, who won his maiden, a handicap off 88 and then a Listed race last season, had Mubtaker a short head behind for his final start when stepped up to Group company in the St Simon Stakes but, despite looking very fit for his first run in 182 days, he could not quite confirm form. There may not be much room for improvement fitness wise, but he appears capable of continuing the significant progression he showed last year. (op 9-2)

Maraahel(IRE), down the field and apparently unsuited by dirt in the Dubai World Cup on his previous start, was the highest rated of these on official figures but did not run to his mark of 120 with the visor left off this time. While he has won in Group company over this trip, he has a very high cruising speed and seems to be getting faster as he gets older; that would certainly appear to be the case if last season's efforts are any guide. This was a creditable effort, but he should be capable of running to a significantly higher figure when returned to shorter. (tchd 10-3)

Sergeant Cecil ◆, who progressed terrifically well to become the first horse ever to complete the Northumberland Plate, Ebor, Cesarewitch treble in the same season last year, ran a fine race on his start since gaining the last of those success'. This effort is all the more creditable given he still looked a little backward and was racing over a trip that is surely short of his optimum. He should have no trouble making the grade at Group level now and heads to York for the Yorkshire Cup.

The Whistling Teal showed he still capable of running to a high level of form when second in the Irish St Leger last season and this must rate as a creditable return, especially as he is another who still looked a bit backward. (op 14-1)

Frank Sonata, successful in a Listed race over a mile six at Nottingham on his reappearance, would have found this tougher and seems better on softer ground. (tchd 13-2)

Allexina, an Irish raider returning from a 195-break, looked plenty fit enough and had the run of the race, along with Mubtaker. Her last three wins have come in Listed company and she did not look good enough. (tchd 8-1 in places and 9-1 in a place)

Swift Sailor, having his first start since leaving Mark Johnston's yard, looked very fit but had a stiff task and needs further. (op 66-1)

Sri Diamond is much improved on Polytrack but faced a very stiff task judged on his turf form. (op 12-1)

1129 BLOOR HOMES SPRING CUP (HERITAGE H'CAP) 1m (S)

2:40 (2:44) (Class 2) 4-Y-0+

£28,044 (£8,397; £4,198; £2,101; £1,048; £526) **Stalls** Centre

Form				RPR
26-4	**1**		**Forgery (IRE)**[42] 629 4-8-6 **88** .... NickyMackay 13 (G A Butler) *bhd: rdn and hdwy 2f out: str run to ld ins fnl f: drvn out* **12/1**	99+
-440	**2**	½	**Colisay**[35] 666 7-9-6 **102** .... OPeslier 16 (Mrs A J Perrett) *chsd ldrs: rdn to ld over 1f out: hdd ins last: kpt on wl for 2nd but nt pce of wnr* **20/1**	112
2224	**3**	nk	**Red Spell (IRE)**[35] 666 5-8-9 **91** .... RichardHughes 9 (R Hannon) *mid-divison: hdwy 2f out: r.o strly fnl f: nt quite pce to chal wl ins last* **8/1**[2]	100
100-	**4**	1 ¼	**Another Bottle (IRE)**[203] 5607 5-9-2 **98** .... SteveDrowne 22 (R Charlton) *lw: hld up in rr: stdy hdwy 2f out: qcknd to chse ldrs 1f out: one pce last half f* **15/2**[1]	104+
040-	**5**	nk	**Eden Rock (IRE)**[224] 5116 5-8-12 **94** .... PaulEddery 18 (Pat Eddery) *bit bkwd: hld up in rr: hdwy fr 2f out: shkn up: qcknd but edgd lft ins last: gng on cl home* **12/1**	100+
1-20	**6**	¾	**Kamanda Laugh**[28] 728 5-8-13 **95** .... NCallan 24 (K A Ryan) *swtg: pressed ldrs: rdn over 2f out: nt qckn u.p fnl f* **10/1**[3]	99
0-13	**7**	nk	**Capable Guest (IRE)**[28] 728 4-8-12 **94** .... TQuinn 6 (M R Channon) *racd far side: chsd ldrs and led that gp fnl f but a hld by stands side* **12/1**	97
305-	**8**	nk	**Sky Crusader**[177] 6125 4-8-6 **88** .... JohnEgan 11 (R Ingram) *in tch: chsd ldrs 3f out: dtiven to chal 2f out: one pce ins fnl f* **25/1**	91
050-	**9**	½	**Wise Dennis**[218] 5269 4-9-4 **100** .... KFallon 20 (A P Jarvis) *bit bkwd: bhd: hdwy 2f out: r.o ins fnl f but nvr gng pce to chal* **10/1**[3]	101
06-0	**10**	shd	**Shot To Fame (USA)**[28] 728 7-8-11 **93** .... SamHitchcott 21 (D Nicholls) *overall ldr: rdn 3f out: hdd over 1f out: wknd ins fnl f* **33/1**	94
00-1	**11**	hd	**Blythe Knight (IRE)**[28] 728 6-9-5 **101** .... GrahamGibbons 14 (J J Quinn) *chsd ldrs: rdn over 2f out: styd on same pce ins last* **12/1**	102
35-0	**12**	¾	**Calcutta**[3] 1084 10-8-10 **92** .... MichaelHills 17 (B W Hills) *bhd: hdwy fr 2f out: kpt on ins last but nvr gng pce to rch ldrs* **40/1**	91
04-5	**13**	hd	**Audience**[28] 728 6-8-7 **89** ....(p) PaulDoe 5 (J Akehurst) *lw: racd far side and led that gp over 3f out but a hld by main group: hdd far side 1f out: sn wknd* **16/1**	88
40-0	**14**	nk	**Coup D'Etat**[28] 728 4-8-5 **87** .... JamieMackay 25 (J L Dunlop) *fly j. stalls: bhd: hdwy 2f out: kpt on fnl f but n.d* **33/1**	85
502-	**15**	½	**Skidrow**[211] 5432 4-8-7 **89** .... HayleyTurner 23 (M L W Bell) *bit bkwd: bhd: hdwy over 1f out: r.o ins last: nvr gng pce to rch ldrs* **16/1**	86
03-0	**16**	½	**Pevensey (IRE)**[20] 843 4-8-3 **85** .... RichardMullen 15 (M A Buckley) *bhd: hdwy over 1f out: nvr in contention* **100/1**	81
105-	**17**	½	**Ace Of Hearts**[203] 5607 7-9-6 **102** .... SebSanders 3 (C F Wall) *racd far side: chsd ldrs tl wknd over 1f out* **16/1**	96
010-	**18**	1	**Prime Number (IRE)**[195] 5767 4-8-4 **89** ow1 ....(t) AdamKirby(3) 19 (G A Butler) *bhd tl r.o wl fnl f: nvr in contention* **20/1**	81
060-	**19**	shd	**Diamonds And Dust**[203] 5599 4-8-3 **88** .... SaleemGolam(3) 12 (M H Tompkins) *in tch: rdn 3f out: sn one pce* **33/1**	80
5132	**20**	3 ½	**Bahiano (IRE)**[58] 494 5-9-6 **102** .... RyanMoore 8 (C E Brittain) *bhd: hdwy to chse ldrs 2f out: wknd fnl f* **33/1**	86
41-0	**21**	6	**El Coto**[18] 865 6-8-13 **95** .... MickyFenton 10 (E S McMahon) *chsd ldrs: rdn 3f out: wknd ins fnl 2f* **33/1**	65
05-0	**22**	hd	**Kings Quay**[28] 728 4-9-0 **96** .... LPKeniry 4 (J J Quinn) *racd far side: chsd ldrs over 5f* **50/1**	66
00-0	**23**	1 ¼	**Mine (IRE)**[28] 728 8-9-10 **106** ....(v) AlanMunro 7 (J D Bethell) *in tch: rdn over 2f out: sn wknd* **33/1**	73
52-0	**24**	12	**Dansili Dancer**[28] 728 4-8-7 **89** .... PhilipRobinson 1 (C G Cox) *led far side tl hdd over 3f out: wknd over 2f out* **14/1**	28
300-	**25**	23	**Desert Fantasy (IRE)**[245] 4568 7-9-6 **102** ....(bt) MartinDwyer 2 (M Meade) *racd far side: sn bhd* **100/1**	—

1m 37.35s (-3.27) **Going Correction** -0.10s/f (Good) **25** Ran SP% **133.5**

Speed ratings (Par 109):112,111,111,109,109 108,108,108,107,107 107,106,106,106,105 105,104,103,103,100 94,93,92,80,57

CSF £244.98 CT £2091.90 TOTE £15.70: £3.90, £5.60, £2.40, £3.00; EX 537.80 TRIFECTA Not won..

Owner Highclere Thoroughbred Racing XXIII **Bred** Mount Coote Stud **Trained** Blewbury, Oxon

FOCUS

A typically competitive renewal of the Spring Cup although the form does not look outstanding. The field split into two groups and, although they began to merge in the closing stages, those who had raced near side from the start were at an advantage.

NOTEBOOK

Forgery(IRE), a promising fourth on his return from an absence in the Lincoln Trial on Polytrack at Wolverhampton, showed improved form to take this valuable handicap. He still had plenty to do when having to switched to the centre of the track, but he found plenty to get up near the line. He has already been placed over ten furlongs and, on this evidence, will improve for a return to that sort of trip. His main target is the John Smith's Cup at York and he must have a serious chance there if things go well in the meantime. (op 11-1)

Colisay, who ran well in Dubai before finishing down the field in the Winter Derby, had every chance on his return to turf and ran a huge race. He is clearly in good enough form to end a losing run stretching back to September 2004, but will go up in the weights for this and that will make things tougher.

Red Spell(IRE) ◆, who showed improved form on Polytrack over the winter to break both the seven- and eight-furlong course records at Lingfield, was last seen finishing fourth in the Winter Derby. Returned to turf off a 12lb lower mark, he produced a very pleasing performance and looks well up to exploiting his current mark. (op 9-1)

Another Bottle(IRE), down the field in the Cambridgeshire on his last start 203 days previously, has since joined Roger Charlton and ran creditably. He can be expected to improve for the run. (op 8-1)

Eden Rock(IRE) ◆, returning from a 224-day break and having his first start since leaving Michael Stoute's yard, still looked a bit backward, so this has to rate as a pleasing performance. There should be better to come. (op 9-1)

Kamanda Laugh, who got pretty warm beforehand, ran much better than in the Lincoln on his previous start and offered hope. (op 11-1)

Capable Guest(IRE), third in the Lincoln on his previous start, finished best of those on the far side but had no chance with the others. He is holding his form well.

Wise Dennis, returning from a 218-day break, looked as though this run would do him good. (op 9-1)

1130 DUBAI DUTY FREE STKS (REGISTERED AS THE FRED DARLING STAKES) (GROUP 3) (FILLIES) 7f (S)

3:15 (3:16) (Class 1) 3-Y-0

£28,390 (£10,760; £5,385; £2,685; £1,345; £675) **Stalls** Centre

Form				RPR
113-	**1**		**Nasheej (USA)**[210] 5459 3-9-0 107 .... RyanMoore 6 (R Hannon) *trckd ldrs: chsd ldr over 1f out: led jst ins last: hrd rdn: hld on all out* **6/4**[1]	99
022-	**2**	shd	**Cantabria**[182] 6027 3-9-0 99 .... KFallon 1 (Sir Michael Stoute) *bhd: pushed along 3f out: str run fr 2f out to chse wnr ins last: str chal fnl 100yds: no ex last strides* **5/1**[2]	99
141-	**3**	1 ½	**Short Dance (USA)**[182] 6027 3-9-0 100 .... RichardHughes 4 (B W Hills) *led: rdn 2f out: hdd ins last and kpt on same pce* **11/2**[3]	95
143-	**4**	½	**Strut**[217] 5286 3-9-0 101 .... SteveDrowne 11 (R Charlton) *bit bkwd: stdd s and hld up in rr: hdwy 2f out: r.o wl fnl f but nt pce to rch ldrs nr fin* **11/1**	94
1-	**5**	¾	**After You**[161] 6332 3-9-0 82 .... MichaelHills 9 (B W Hills) *w'like: sn chsng ldr: rdn over 2f out: outpcd ins fnl f* **28/1**	92
1-	**6**	½	**Dictatrix**[169] 6242 3-9-0 73 .... NCallan 8 (J M P Eustace) *w'like: s.i.s: hld up in rr: pushed along over 2f out: r.o wl fnl f but nvr gng pce to rch ldrs* **50/1**	91
021-	**7**	shd	**Culture Queen**[218] 5275 3-9-0 85 .... MartinDwyer 10 (M P Tregoning) *rr but in tch: rdn and styd on 2f out: nt pce to rch ldrs and sn one pce u.p* **33/1**	90
60-1	**8**	½	**My Amalie (IRE)**[21] 835 3-9-0 95 .... SebSanders 5 (C E Brittain) *in tch: rdn to chse ldrs 3f out: wknd ins fnl f* **33/1**	89
410-	**9**	¾	**In The Fashion (IRE)**[258] 4206 3-9-0 91 .... CSoumillon 7 (J Noseda) *chsd ldrs: rdn 3f out: no imp on ldrs over 2f out: wknd ins last* **28/1**	87
	10	½	**Arrivee (FR)**[33] 3-9-0 .... OPeslier 2 (A Fabre, France) *w'like: scope: hld up rr: effrt and nt clr run over 2f out: nvr gng pce to rch ldrs after* **7/1**	86
2142	**11**	19	**Song Of Silence (USA)**[21] 827 3-9-0 99 .... JamieSpencer 3 (E A L Dunlop) *lw: chsd ldrs tl rdn and lost action jst ins fnl 2f: nt rcvr and eased* **16/1**	36

1m 24.61s (-2.39) **Going Correction** -0.10s/f (Good) **11** Ran SP% **113.5**

Speed ratings (Par 105):109,108,107,106,105 105,105,104,103,103 81

CSF £7.81 TOTE £2.30: £1.10, £1.80, £2.00; EX 10.60.

Owner Malih L Al Basti **Bred** D Henderson **Trained** East Everleigh, Wilts

■ Stewards' Enquiry : Ryan Moore caution: used whip with excessive frequency

FOCUS

Although the winning time was very creditable - just over a second quicker than the colts in the Greenham - the likes of After You, Dictatrix and Culture Queen hold the form down, and Nasheej did not need to reproduce her juvenile best to win. She will be suited by a return to a mile, but will have to improve to get in the shake up in the 1,000 Guineas.

NOTEBOOK

Nasheej(USA), winner of the Sweet Solera and May Hill before running third in the Fillies' Mile, looked fit for her return, although Richard Hannon felt she had not quite come in her coat. Always going well enough, close to the pace, she was made to work pretty hard, but kept finding under pressure and showed a very likable attitude. She will now be aimed at the 1,000 Guineas but, while Ryan Moore thinks she will be suited by the return to a mile, her trainer has admitted to not knowing if she will be good enough. It will be a little surprising if she does not find at least a couple better than her. (op 7-4)

Cantabria, second in a nursery off a mark of 88 before going down narrowly in a course and distance Listed event on her last start 182 days previously, looked fit enough for her return but had not quite come in her coat and was just held. She looks capable of progressing and could have a good season in fillies/mares company. (op 6-1)

Short Dance(USA), who had Cantabria a short-head away in second when winning a course and distance Listed event on her final start last season, was another who looked fit enough for her reappearance, although she had not quite come in her coat. This was a promising return and she is open to improvement. (op 9-2)

Strut, a very useful sprinting juvenile, still looked a bit backward for her reappearance. Upped to seven furlongs for the first time, she ran well without ever really looking likely to win. In the longer term, it would be no surprise to see her revert to shorter distances. (op 14-1)

After You would have found this much tougher than the Wolverhampton maiden she won on her only previous start 161 days ago and ran extremely well. In fact her proximity could be used to hold the form down, so it will be interesting to see if she can confirm this in future. (op 25-1)
Dictatrix, who looked potentially useful when winning a six-furlong maiden on heavy ground at Yarmouth on her only previous start 169 days previously, fell out of the stalls and still looked in need of further experience. In the circumstances she did well to finish so close, and it will be interesting to see if she can confirm this. (op 40-1 tchd 33-1)
Culture Queen seemed to step up on the form she showed when winning a six-furlong Nottingham maiden on her final start last season. (op 25-1)
In The Fashion(IRE) was on her toes beforehand and was well held. (op 33-1)
Arrivee(FR), a French raider who won a minor race over this trip on soft ground on her most recent start, looked a nice type and travelled quite well, but something happened to her about 2f out and she finished up well beaten. Her trainer presumably thinks she is capable of better and it would be unwise to dismiss her if she comes over to England again. (op 6-1)

1131 LANE'S END GREENHAM STKS (GROUP 3) (C&G) 7f (S)

3:50 (3:52) (Class 1) 3-Y-O **£28,390** (£10,760; £5,385; £2,685; £1,345) **Stalls** Centre

Form				RPR
224-	1		**Red Clubs (IRE)**[189] 5901 3-9-0 **117** MichaelHills 2 *(B W Hills) led 2f: styd pressing ldr tl led again 2f out: drvn 3l clr ins fnl f: comf* **6/4**[1]	114+
524-	2	1 3/4	**Marcus Andronicus (USA)**[182] 6020 3-9-0 KFallon 5 *(A P O'Brien, Ire) lw: hld up rr but in tch: hdwy 2f out: qcknd to dispute 2nd appr fnl f but nvr nr wnr: tk clr 2nd cl home* **5/1**	106
163-	3	nk	**Assertive**[248] 4477 3-9-0 **106** RichardHughes 4 *(R Hannon) lw: chsd ldrs: hdwy to dispute 2nd appr fnl f: outpcd close home* **4/1**[3]	105
	4	1 1/4	**Reve Lunaire (USA)**[33] 3-9-0 CSoumillon 1 *(A Fabre, France) w'like: lw: chsd ldrs: drvn along over 2f out: no imp on ldrs and styd on same pce ins last* **10/3**[2]	102
53-3	5	1 1/4	**Zato (IRE)**[14] 914 3-9-0 **103** TQuinn 3 *(M R Channon) trckd wnr: led after 2f: rdn and hdd 2f out: lost 2nd appr fnl f: sn btn* **12/1**	99

1m 25.69s (-1.31) **Going Correction** -0.10s/f (Good) 5 Ran SP% **107.4**
Speed ratings (Par 108):103,101,100,99,97
CSF £8.76 TOTE £1.90: £1.30, £2.30; EX 7.40.
Owner R J Arculli **Bred** J Fike **Trained** Lambourn, Berks

FOCUS
The smallest field since 1983 and a disappointing renewal. Although taken on for the lead at about half way by Zato, Red Clubs very much had the run of things in a race run at a steady pace and he won in the manner he was entitled to, eased down close home and value for more like three lengths. Unsurprisingly the winning time was modest, just over a second slower than the fillies in the Fred Darling.

NOTEBOOK
Red Clubs(IRE) ran some fine races in defeat after winning last season's Coventry Stakes, but it soon became apparent he wasn't quite up to winning at the top level. Fit for his first run since finishing fourth in the Dewhurst, he was allowed an easy time of things towards the front end, and when Zato began to weaken he came clear without having had to do a great deal. He was eased near the line and was probably value for more like three lengths. Michael Hills said he saw the seven furlongs out very well and that he will find it hard to choose between him and Craven winner Killybegs for the 2,000 Guineas mount, but it would be a bit of a shock if he did not pick the latter. The French Guineas is an alternative option and Red Clubs might have more chance there, as it is unlikely to test his stamina to such a degree. (op 11-8 tchd 13-8)
Marcus Andronicus(USA), disappointing in a couple of Listed races after finishing fifth to Red Clubs in the Coventry last season, did not appear to be given a very inspired ride as he was doing all of his best work late on in a race in which the favourite had things more or less his own way throughout. He looked well beforehand, but was still carrying come condition and should be able to improve. (tchd 11-2 in places)
Assertive, a smart sprinting juvenile, made an unspectacular reappearance on his first run over seven furlongs. However, Richard Hannon says he is the type to only just do enough on the gallops, and expects him to improve a bundle for this. (op 7-2)
Reve Lunaire(USA), beaten at odds on in a minor race on his reappearance, was well held on his British debut. (op 9-2)
Zato(IRE) was below the form he showed when third in the International Trial Stakes at Lingfield on his previous start and was a little disappointing. (tchd 10-1)

1132 PERTEMPS H'CAP 2m

4:20 (4:22) (Class 4) (0-80,80) 4-Y-O+ **£7,772** (£2,312; £1,155; £577) **Stalls** High

Form				RPR
3202	1		**Trance (IRE)**[6] 1033 6-9-8 **75** (p) NCallan 13 *(T D Barron) lw: bhd: hrd drvn 3f out: stil plenty to do over 2f out: str run fr over 1f out: led wl ins last and r.o strly* **6/1**[1]	83
106-	2	1/2	**Gandalf**[232] 4919 4-9-4 **75** JamieSpencer 4 *(J R Fanshawe) bit bkwd: mid-div: hdwy to trck ldrs over 3f out: rdn to ld appr fnl f: hdd and one pce wl ins last* **9/1**	82
206-	3	1 1/2	**Dundry**[183] 6006 5-9-8 **75** (p) RyanMoore 8 *(G L Moore) bhd: hdwy 3f out: styd on to chse ldrs 1f out: one pce ins last* **14/1**	80
510-	4	nk	**Queen Of Iceni**[176] 6133 4-9-1 **72** TQuinn 9 *(J L Dunlop) bhd: gd hdwy on outside 4f out: trckd ldrs 3 out: rdn to chal 1f out: no ex ins last* **16/1**	77
-001	5	5	**Sphinx (FR)**[10] 990 8-9-2 **69** (b) JohnEgan 3 *(Jamie Poulton) b: hld up mid-div: hdwy 5f out: led 3f out: rdn 2f out: hdd appr fnl f: sn btn* **14/1**	68
0400	6	hd	**Eastborough (IRE)**[11] 966 7-9-3 **70** GeorgeBaker 1 *(B G Powell) stdd rr and bhd: rdn 3f out: hdwy fr 2f out: kpt on fnl f but nvr gng pce to rch ldrs* **25/1**	69
435-	7	2	**Estrelle (GER)**[176] 6130 4-9-3 **74** AlanMunro 6 *(H R A Cecil) t.k.h: chsd ldrs: rdn 3f out: wknd over 2f out* **14/1**	70
23-0	8	6	**Spinning Coin**[21] 834 4-9-4 **80** JamesDoyle(5) 12 *(J G Portman) chsd ldr to 6f out: styd front rnk: rdn 3f out: wknd appr fnl 2f* **33/1**	69
/0-3	9	5	**Patrixprial**[10] 990 5-9-3 **70** (b) RHills 14 *(M H Tompkins) chsd ldrs: chal fr 6f out tl led over 4f out: hdd 3f out: wknd over 2f out* **8/1**	53
022-	10	2 1/2	**Spanish Ridge (IRE)**[185] 5973 4-9-4 **75** OPeslier 5 *(J L Dunlop) chsd ldrs tl steadily lost pl fnl 3f* **10/1**	55
035-	11	2 1/2	**Aylmer Road (IRE)**[207] 5533 4-8-10 **67** KFallon 7 *(P F I Cole) lw: sn led: jnd 6f out: hdd over 4f out: wknd 3f out* **8/1**	44
50-0	12	1 1/4	**The Composer**[16] 723 4-8-10 **67** SteveDrowne 10 *(M Blanshard) mid-div: hdwy to trck ldrs 6f out: wknd qckly over 3f out* **25/1**	43
11-3	13	1/2	**Prime Contender**[21] 834 4-9-0 **71** MichaelHills 11 *(B W Hills) mid-div 10f: bhd fnl 3f* **13/2**[2]	46
061-	14	dist	**Gifted Musician**[172] 6215 4-8-13 **70** JimmyFortune 2 *(J L Dunlop) bit bkwd: chsd ldrs tl wknd 3f out: eased whn no ch fnl f: t.o* **7/1**[3]	—

3m 33.61s (-2.54) **Going Correction** -0.025s/f (Good)
WFA 4 from 5yo+ 4lb 14 Ran SP% **117.9**
Speed ratings (Par 105):105,104,104,103,101 101,100,97,94,93 92,91,91,—
CSF £56.25 CT £730.49 TOTE £5.50: £2.20, £2.80, £4.60; EX 33.60.
Owner Nigel Shields **Bred** Forenaghts Stud Co Ltd **Trained** Maunby, N Yorks

FOCUS
A fair staying handicap in which the fitness of Trance proved the difference between winning and losing, as Gandalf, who came through to lead a furlong out, was making his seasonal debut and was unable to hold off the winner's late thrust. The form looks ordinary, rated around the winner and fourth.

1133 DUBAI DUTY FREE MILLENNIUM MILLIONAIRE H'CAP 1m 2f 6y

4:50 (4:51) (Class 4) (0-85,85) 4-Y-O+ **£6,477** (£1,927; £963; £481) **Stalls** Centre

Form				RPR
0-05	1		**Prince Samos (IRE)**[12] 946 4-9-2 **83** RichardHughes 9 *(R Hannon) mid-div: hdwy 3f out: hrd drvn to ld ins fnl 2f: hld on all out* **15/2**[3]	92
1/2-	2	nk	**River Alhaarth (IRE)**[355] 1416 4-9-1 **82** AlanMunro 5 *(P W Chapple-Hyam) lw: chsd ldrs: rdn to ld jst over 1f out: hdd ins last: kpt on u.p but no ex last strides* **6/1**[1]	91
431-	3	shd	**Chantaco (USA)**[183] 6003 4-9-4 **85** MartinDwyer 13 *(A M Balding) b.hind: bhd: hdwy 4f out: pushed along and n.m.r over 2f out: rdn and str run appr fnl f: fin wl: nt quite get up* **16/1**	93
600-	4	1 1/4	**Transvestite (IRE)**[187] 5948 4-8-9 **76** MichaelHills 14 *(J W Hills) hld up in rr: plenty to do whn swtchd rt to outside over 2f out: str run appr fnl f: fin wl: nt rch ldrs* **25/1**	82
220-	5	1/2	**Ionian Spring (IRE)**[175] 6159 11-9-0 **81** NCallan 12 *(C G Cox) bhd: rdn and hdwy over 2f out: kpt un fnl f but nvr gng pce to chal* **9/1**	86
4-11	6	1 1/2	**Ameeq (USA)**[26] 763 4-9-0 **81** RyanMoore 2 *(G L Moore) lw: mid-div: pushed along 3f out: styng on whn n.m.r over 2f out: keeping on again whn nt clr rin ins last: nt rcvr* **15/2**[3]	87+
06-0	7	1/2	**Thyolo (IRE)**[35] 667 5-9-1 **85** (v[1]) AdamKirby(3) 8 *(C G Cox) swtg: chsd ldrs: led wl over 1f out: hdd jst over 1f out: wknd ins last* **12/1**	86
060-	8	hd	**Liakoura (GER)**[190] 5876 4-9-4 **85** OPeslier 15 *(Mrs A J Perrett) t.k.h: hld up in rr: stdy hdwy on outside over 2f out: sn rdn and fnd no ex* **12/1**	86
00-3	9	3/4	**South O'The Border**[20] 843 4-8-8 **75** IanMongan 10 *(T G Mills) chsd ldrs: slt ld 3f out: sn rdn: hdd wl over 1f out: sn wknd* **16/1**	74
140-	10	3/4	**Cool Hunter**[199] 5698 5-8-12 **79** JamieSpencer 7 *(W R Swinburn) bit bkwd: t.k.h: chsd ldrs: rdn ins fnl 3f: wknd ins fnl 2f* **10/1**	77
1251	11	3/4	**Star Magnitude (USA)**[15] 905 5-8-13 **80** TQuinn 16 *(S Dow) lw: bhd: sme hdwy fr 3f out: nvr gng pce to trble ldrs* **16/1**	77
/-10	12	1	**Barry Island**[26] 763 7-8-11 **78** JamieMackay 11 *(D R C Elsworth) t.k.h in rr: nvr in contention* **25/1**	73
100-	13	hd	**Given A Choice (IRE)**[227] 5048 4-9-3 **84** MickyFenton 1 *(J G Given) t.k.h: in tch: rdn over 2f out: sn wknd* **33/1**	78
2-01	14	nk	**Mina A Salem**[49] 578 4-8-10 **77** JimmyFortune 3 *(C E Brittain) led tl hdd 3f out: sn wknd* **12/1**	71
311-	15	19	**Strawberry Leaf**[269] 3839 4-9-2 **83** SteveDrowne 6 *(R Charlton) chsd ldrs: rdn over 3f out: sn wknd* **7/1**[2]	41

2m 7.16s (-1.55) **Going Correction** -0.025s/f (Good) 15 Ran SP% **120.8**
Speed ratings (Par 105):105,104,104,103,103 102,101,101,100,100 99,98,98,98,83
CSF £50.63 CT £713.75 TOTE £5.50: £2.20, £2.80, £4.60; EX 33.60.
Owner Mrs Suzanne Costello-Haloute **Bred** Rathasker Stud **Trained** East Everleigh, Wilts

FOCUS
A good handicap for the grade and the form looks quite strong.

1134 DUBAI INTERNATIONAL AIRPORT MAIDEN STKS (DIV I) 1m (S)

5:25 (5:37) (Class 5) 3-Y-O **£4,857** (£1,445; £722; £360) **Stalls** Centre

Form				RPR
3-	1		**Makderah (IRE)**[200] 5692 3-8-12 RHills 5 *(M P Tregoning) h.d.w: t.k.h early: led travelling wl: shkn up fnl f: edgd lft cl home but a in command* **11/4**[1]	88+
04-	2	3/4	**Rodeo**[175] 6142 3-9-3 MichaelHills 1 *(B W Hills) bit bkwd: bhd: hdwy fr 3f out: styd on wl fr over 1f out to chse wnr ins last: clsng nr fin but a hld* **12/1**	83
4-	3	1	**Incidentally (IRE)**[273] 3729 3-9-3 RyanMoore 8 *(R Hannon) lw: bhd: rdn 1/2-way: hdwy 2f out: edgd lft over 1f out: kpt on ins last but nvr gng pce to trble wnr* **7/1**[3]	81
62-	4	shd	**Numeric (GER)**[169] 6246 3-9-3 JimmyFortune 13 *(J H M Gosden) bit bkwd: bhd: pushed along 3f out: hdwy ins fnl 2f: kpt on ins last: one pce cl home* **7/1**[3]	80
	5	2	**His Honour (IRE)** 3-9-3 SteveDrowne 11 *(R Charlton) w'like: str: scope: bit bkwd: bhd: rdn and hdwy fr 1/2-way: chsd ldrs ins fnl 2f: one pce fnl f* **25/1**	76+
	6	1	**Balanced Budget** 3-9-3 ShaneKelly 2 *(J Noseda) w'like: bit bkwd: chsd wnr: rdn over 2f out: wknd fnl f* **9/1**	74
0-	7	5	**Jamaahir (USA)**[183] 6001 3-9-3 IanMongan 6 *(J L Dunlop) t.k.h early: chsd ldrs: rdn over 2f out: sn btn* **20/1**	62
30-	8	3	**Time Out (IRE)**[183] 6009 3-9-3 LPKeniry 4 *(A M Balding) bit bkwd: chsd ldrs: rdn over 2f out: wknd wl over 1f out* **20/1**	55
	9	1 1/2	**Free Speech** 3-9-3 RichardHughes 7 *(Sir Michael Stoute) bhd and sn drvn: hrd rdn over 3f out: little rspnse* **9/1**	52
0	10	1/2	**Ashford Castle (IRE)**[5] 1048 3-8-10 KMay(7) 12 *(B J Meehan) tall: chsd ldrs over 5f* **33/1**	51
02-	11	1 3/4	**Zaif (IRE)**[183] 6009 3-9-3 TQuinn 3 *(D R C Elsworth) s.i.s: plld hrd in rr: hdwy over 3f out: wknd qckly over 2f out* **5/1**[2]	47
	12	1 1/4	**Even Bolder** 3-9-3 JamieSpencer 9 *(S Kirk) unf: scope: bit bkwd: stdd s: plld hrd in rr: rdn and hung lft 2f out: a bhd* **40/1**	44
	13	9	**Mukaaber** 3-9-3 MartinDwyer 10 *(M P Tregoning) w'like: scope: rangy: bit bkwd: chsd ldrs: rdn 1/2-way: wknd 3f out* **14/1**	23

1m 40.55s (-0.07) **Going Correction** -0.10s/f (Good) 13 Ran SP% **121.4**
Speed ratings (Par 98):96,95,94,94,92 91,86,83,81,81 79,78,69
CSF £35.64 TOTE £3.30: £1.50, £3.70, £2.80; EX 52.10.

Owner Hamdan Al Maktoum **Bred** Shadwell Estate Company Limited **Trained** Lambourn, Berks
FOCUS
This looked like a reasonable enough maiden and there was plenty to like about Makderah's performance. It is probably not worth dwelling on the false start, because the winner looked as inconvenienced as any of 13 runners.

1135 DUBAI INTERNATIONAL AIRPORT MAIDEN STKS (DIV II) 1m (S)
5:55 (6:13) (Class 5) 3-Y-O £4,857 (£1,445; £722; £360) Stalls Centre

Form RPR
1 **Purple Moon (IRE)** 3-9-3 ... JimmyFortune 8 89+
(Sir Michael Stoute) *w/like: in tch: drvn: rn green and hung lft 2f out: stl green but kpt on strly fnl f to ld fnl 100yds: won gng away* **13/8**[1]
05- 2 1½ **Royal Envoy (IRE)**[183] [6011] 3-9-3 ... MichaelHills 10 79
(B W Hills) *chsd ldrs: led ins fnl 2f: drvn ins last: hdd and outpcd fnl 100yds* **14/1**
4- 3 nk **Mahrajaan (USA)**[183] [6009] 3-9-3 ... RHills 3 78+
(J H M Gosden) *b: chsd ldrs: rdn and kpt on fr over 1f out but nvr gng pce to chal* **15/2**[3]
4 4 2 **Star Of The Desert (IRE)**[28] [720] 3-9-0 ... AdamKirby(3) 9 74
(C G Cox) *w/like: bit bkwd: chsd ldrs: outpcd 2f out and sn n.m.r: kpt on again ins last* **25/1**
3 5 nk **Five Two**[24] [795] 3-9-3 ... TQuinn 6 73
(M R Channon) *bit bkwd: led tl hdd ins fnl 2f: wknd fnl f* **25/1**
46- 6 ¾ **Nawaadi**[190] [5870] 3-9-3 ... MartinDwyer 13 71
(M P Tregoning) *in tch: rdn 3f out: sn edgd lft u.p and n.d after* **16/1**
7 hd **Masterofthecourt (USA)** 3-9-3 ... SteveDrowne 12 71+
(H Morrison) *w/like: scope: bit bkwd: s.i.s: sn in tch: hdwy 3f out: nvr toubled ldrs and sn one pce* **10/1**
8 3 **Soar With Eagles (USA)** 3-9-3 ... KFallon 2 64
(A P O'Brien, Ire) *w/like: wnt lft s: sn trcking ldrs: rdn and effrt over 2f out: wknd qckly appr fnl f* **11/2**[2]
9 3 **Collusion (FR)** 3-9-3 ... RyanMoore 4 57
(Pat Eddery) *tall: w/like: s.i.s: in tch 1/2-way: no ch fnl 3f* **33/1**
10 dist **Double Agent (FR)** 3-9-3 ... IanMongan 11 —
(J L Dunlop) *w/like: bit bkwd: a bhd: lost tch 1/2-way: t.o fnl 2f* **50/1**
1m 40.28s (-0.34) **Going Correction** -0.10s/f (Good) **10** Ran SP% **99.5**
Speed ratings (Par 98):97,95,95,93,92 92,91,88,85,—
CSF £18.26 TOTE £2.30: £1.30, £3.30, £1.80; EX 22.30 Place 6 £38.27, Place 5 £23.74.Smart Enough and Wizards Dream were withdrawn. Respective prices at time of withdrawal were 13-2 and 50-1. Rule 4 applies to all bets, deduction 10p in the pound
Owner M Tabor, D Smith & Mrs John Magnier **Bred** Gestut Shohrenhof **Trained** Newmarket, Suffolk
FOCUS
A decent-looking maiden in which Purple Moon overcame greenness to make a winning debut. The runner-up is the best guide to the form.
Nawaadi Official explanation: jockey said gelding was hanging badly left-handed
Double Agent(FR) Official explanation: jockey said gelding was never travelling
T/Jkpt: Not won. T/Plt: £34.10 to a £1 stake. Pool: £97,375.75. 2,079.20 winning tickets. T/Qpdt: £9.90 to a £1 stake. Pool: £3,905.20. 291.90 winning tickets. ST

987 NOTTINGHAM (L-H)
Saturday, April 22

OFFICIAL GOING: Soft (good to soft in places)
Wind: Light, across Weather: Overcast

1136 BETFREDPOKER.COM MAIDEN STKS 5f 13y
5:10 (5:16) (Class 5) 2-Y-O £3,238 (£963; £481; £240) Stalls High

Form RPR
1 **La Neige** 2-9-3 ... TedDurcan 3 74+
(M R Channon) *s.s: outpcd: hdwy over 1f out: led ins fnl f: r.o* **11/4**[2]
2 2½ **Karayel (IRE)** 2-9-3 ... PatDobbs 4 64
(R Hannon) *chsd ldrs: led over 1f out: hdd and no ex ins fnl f* **6/4**[1]
3 1¼ **Calloff The Search** 2-8-12 ... MarcHalford(5) 6 59
(W G M Turner) *chsd ldrs: rdn over 1f out: styd on same pce fnl f* **16/1**
4 2½ **River Prince** 2-8-10 ... RichardGordon(7) 8 49
(W G M Turner) *uns rdr and rn loose bef s: sn led: hdd over 1f out: edgd lft and wknd ins fnl f* **28/1**
5 ¾ **Avoncreek** 2-9-3 ... JoeFanning 5 46
(B P J Baugh) *s.s: hdwy over 3f out: wknd over 1f out* **16/1**
6 ½ **Me And Mine (USA)** 2-9-3 ... PaulFessey 2 44+
(T D Barron) *chsd ldrs: rdn edgd lft and ev ch over 1f out: wknd fnl f* **11/2**[3]
7 1½ **For Eileen** 2-8-9 ... EdwardCreighton(3) 1 33
(D Burchell) *s.s and wnt lft s: outpcd* **33/1**
8 10 **Shes Millie** 2-8-12 ... RobertWinston 7 —
(J G M O'Shea) *s.s: sn prom: wknd 1/2-way* **8/1**
64.74 secs (2.94) **Going Correction** +0.30s/f (Good) **8** Ran SP% **111.3**
Speed ratings (Par 92):88,84,82,78,76 76,73,57
CSF £6.81 TOTE £2.80: £1.40, £1.10, £3.40; EX 4.50.
Owner Ridgeway Downs Racing **Bred** The Duchess Of Sutherland **Trained** West Ilsley, Berks
FOCUS
An ordinary looking maiden run at a fair pace which is difficut to rate but set at around average.
NOTEBOOK
La Neige is a half-brother to three-year-old mile winner Ten Shun out of a sister to top-class juvenile Bahamian Bounty. Slowly away and outpaced in the early stages, he really picked up in the second half of the race and saw the trip out strongly. He did it the hard way and could be a bit better than the bare form suggests. (tchd 7-2)
Karayel(IRE) looked the likeliest winner when hitting the front going well, but he could not hold off the strong late challenge of his main market rival. A half-brother to Methusaleh, placed once over seven furlongs at two out of a mare who won over ten furlongs, he should be found a similar contest, perhaps on better ground. (op 2-1)
Calloff The Search, whose dam was a multiple winner over seven furlongs to a mile, was staying on at the finish and made a pleasing enough debut. (op 12-1)
River Prince, who is by Rooster Booster's sire out of a mare who won a six-furlong seller (later disqualified) at two, played up before the start but ran with credit in the race itself, showing good speed. (op 25-1)
Avoncreek is bred to be sharp as he is by a high-class sprinter out of a juvenile five-furlong winner, and he is a half-brother to Town House, also a winner over the minimum trip at two. He might be better suited by quicker ground. (tchd 12-1)
Me And Mine(USA), whose dam is related to several winners, is a January foal. Representing a stable already on the scoresheet from two previous runners, he had his chance before weakening. (op 4-1 tchd 6-1)

1137 BETFRED MILLION FILLIES' H'CAP 5f 13y
5:45 (5:45) (Class 5) (0-70,70) 3-Y-O £3,238 (£963; £481; £240) Stalls High

Form RPR
6534 1 **Rapsgate (IRE)**[47] [593] 3-9-1 67 ...(b) PatDobbs 4 73
(R Hannon) *s.i.s: outpcd: hdwy over 1f out: rdn and hung rt ins fnl f: r.o to ld nr fin* **4/1**[1]
30-2 2 ¾ **Toy Top (USA)**[10] [980] 3-8-8 60 ...(b) JimmyQuinn 1 63
(M Dods) *w ldr: led 1/2-way: rdn and edgd rt ins fnl f: hdd nr fin* **8/1**
146- 3 2½ **Fayr Sky (IRE)**[200] [5681] 3-9-3 69 ... JoeFanning 6 64
(J J Quinn) *s.i.s: outpcd: nt clr run over 1f out: r.o ins fnl f: nrst fin* **9/2**[2]
0-02 4 2 **In Fashion**[12] [936] 3-8-4 56 oh10 ... FrankieMcDonald 7 44
(R J Hodges) *s.i.s: sn chsng ldrs: rdn 1/2-way: hung lft over 1f out: wknd ins fnl f* **16/1**
210- 5 1¼ **Quadrophenia**[194] [5791] 3-8-10 62 ... DaleGibson 5 46
(J G Given) *sn pushed along and prom: rdn 1/2-way: wknd fnl f* **11/2**
025- 6 1½ **Myths And Verses**[215] [5370] 3-8-11 63 ... RobertWinston 3 42
(T D Easterby) *mid-div: hdwy 2f out: wknd fnl f* **5/1**[3]
5005 7 2½ **Tombalina**[10] [980] 3-7-13 58 oh4 ow2 ... MarkCoumbe(7) 2 28
(C J Teague) *sn led: hdd 1/2-way: wknd over 1f out* **14/1**
00P- 8 2½ **Colourpoint (USA)**[162] [6312] 3-9-4 70 ...(b) TedDurcan 9 32
(C E Brittain) *mid-div: sn pushed along: hdwy 1/2-way: rdn: hung lft and wknd wl over 1f out* **33/1**
00-1 9 1½ **Devine Dancer**[23] [801] 3-9-4 70 ... DaneO'Neill 8 27
(H Candy) *chsd ldrs: rdn over 1f out: sn wknd* **5/1**[3]
63.41 secs (1.61) **Going Correction** +0.30s/f (Good) **9** Ran SP% **113.5**
Speed ratings (Par 95):99,97,93,90,88 86,82,78,75
CSF £35.57 CT £149.13 TOTE £6.40: £1.80, £1.60, £1.80; EX 55.40.
Owner Team Havana **Bred** J F O'Malley **Trained** East Everleigh, Wilts
FOCUS
A modest fillies' handicap in which the leaders appeared to go off a bit too quick. The runner-up and fourth set the level.

1138 BETFREDPOKER.COM H'CAP 1m 6f 15y
6:15 (6:16) (Class 6) (0-65,65) 4-Y-O+ £2,730 (£806; £403) Stalls Low

Form RPR
050- 1 **Duroob**[185] [5973] 4-9-3 64 ... AndrewElliott(5) 3 73
(K R Burke) *a.p: rdn to ld over 1f out: styd on* **22/1**
2002 2 1¼ **Robbie Can Can**[11] [973] 7-8-8 55 ... JackDean(7) 8 62
(A W Carroll) *s.i.s: hld up: hdwy over 2f out: rdn over 1f out: edgd lft ins fnl f: styd on* **10/1**[3]
61/0 3 ¾ **Jolizero**[11] [973] 5-9-3 57 ... TedDurcan 6 63
(John Berry) *a.p: rdn over 2f out: styd on* **25/1**
00-3 4 nk **My Legal Eagle (IRE)**[18] [881] 12-8-10 50 ... AdrianMcCarthy 10 56
(E G Bevan) *hld up: hdwy over 4f out: rdn over 1f out: styng on whn n.m.r wl ins fnl f* **12/1**
1001 5 1½ **Bill Bennett (FR)**[11] [973] 5-9-6 65 ... GregFairley(5) 9 69
(J Jay) *hld up in tch: outpcd 3f out: rallied over 1f out: styng on same pce whn n.m.r wl ins fnl f* **8/1**[2]
22-2 6 ½ **Pee Jay's Dream**[10] [975] 4-9-1 57 ... DaleGibson 15 60
(M W Easterby) *hld up: hdwy over 5f out: nt clr run over 2f out: sn rdn: no ex ins fnl f* **8/1**[2]
306- 7 2 **Whoopsie**[194] [5789] 4-8-10 52 ... J-PGuillambert 4 53
(S Parr) *chsd ldrs: led over 3f out: rdn and hdd over 1f out: wknd ins fnl f* **12/1**
00-5 8 nk **Dawn's Last Shot (IRE)**[16] [894] 4-9-6 62 ... SebSanders 7 62+
(J L Dunlop) *hld up in tch: rdn and nt clr run over 2f out: wknd fnl f* **13/2**[1]
310/ 9 nk **Only For Sue**[689] [2590] 7-9-0 54 ... FergusSweeney 2 54
(W S Kittow) *chsd ldr: rdn over 2f out: wknd fnl f* **20/1**
26-5 10 3½ **Darghan (IRE)**[18] [882] 6-9-3 57 ... PhilipRobinson 14 52
(W J Musson) *hld up: hdwy over 3f out: nt clr run over 2f out: nt trble ldrs* **13/2**[1]
0400 11 2½ **Golden Boot**[6] [1033] 7-9-11 65 ...(p) DarrenWilliams 12 57
(A Bailey) *s.s: hld up: rdn over 2f out: n.d* **33/1**
6020 12 12 **Farnborough (USA)**[28] [733] 5-8-4 49 ... MarcHalford(5) 16 26
(R J Price) *dwlt: hld up: plld hrd: n.d* **40/1**
3061 13 7 **Birthday Star (IRE)**[28] [733] 4-8-9 56 ... StephenDonohoe(5) 11 23
(W J Musson) *hld up: rdn over 4f out: sn wknd* **8/1**[2]
0-50 14 6 **Mary Gray**[10] [990] 4-8-11 53 ... JoeFanning 1 13
(M Johnston) *led over 10f: wknd over 2f out* **12/1**
/0-5 15 ¾ **Lefonic**[28] [733] 4-8-4 53 ... DeanWilliams(7) 17 12
(G C H Chung) *hld up: bhd fnl 8f* **33/1**
/0-0 16 5 **Perfect Punch**[5] [1045] 7-9-8 62 ... RobertWinston 5 14
(K G Reveley) *prom: rdn over 4f out: wknd over 2f out* **14/1**
000/ 17 11 **Kaparolo (USA)**[13] [6084] 7-9-6 60 ...(t) DaneO'Neill 13 —
(John A Harris) *hld up: wknd over 4f out* **80/1**
3m 11.23s (4.13) **Going Correction** +0.30s/f (Good)
WFA 4 from 5yo+ 2lb **17** Ran SP% **121.3**
Speed ratings (Par 101):100,99,98,98,97 97,96,96,96,94 92,85,81,78,77 75,68
CSF £214.21 CT £5479.13 TOTE £29.10: £7.50, £2.50, £6.70, £2.60; EX 280.60.
Owner Mrs M Gittins **Bred** Shadwell Estate Company Limited **Trained** Middleham Moor, N Yorks
FOCUS
A modest staying contest run at a fair pace. The runner-up and fifth set an ordinary standard.
Golden Boot Official explanation: jockey said gelding hung right in straight
Lefonic Official explanation: jockey said colt hung left throughout

1139 BETFRED MILLION MEDIAN AUCTION MAIDEN STKS 1m 1f 213y
6:45 (6:47) (Class 6) 3-Y-O £2,730 (£806; £403) Stalls Low

Form RPR
624- 1 **Kyoto Summit**[196] [5748] 3-9-3 86 ... NickyMackay 10 85+
(L M Cumani) *hld up in tch: racd keenly: led over 1f out: edgd lft over 1f out: pushed clr* **4/1**[3]
0- 2 5 **Kerriemuir Lass (IRE)**[214] [5390] 3-8-12 ... PhilipRobinson 4 74+
(M A Jarvis) *chsd ldrs: led 2f out: rdn: hung lft and hdd over 1f out: eased whn btn ins fnl f* **5/2**[2]
02 3 1½ **Yeoman Spirit (IRE)**[11] [964] 3-9-3 ... FergusSweeney 7 74
(A M Balding) *chsd ldr tl led over 2f out: sn hdd: styd on same pce appr fnl f* **12/1**
0- 4 2 **Bamboo Banks (IRE)**[261] [4093] 3-9-3 ... SebSanders 2 71+
(J L Dunlop) *mid-div: hdwy 6f out: rdn over 2f out: edgd lft and wknd over 1f out* **66/1**
6- 5 ½ **Alasoun (IRE)**[185] [5988] 3-9-3 ... RobertWinston 13 70+
(Sir Michael Stoute) *hld up: hdwy over 3f out: edgd lft and wknd over 1f out* **11/8**[1]
236- 6 2½ **Nelsons Column (IRE)**[201] [5658] 3-9-3 74 ... J-PGuillambert 9 65
(G M Moore) *hld up: hdwy over 2f out: rdn and wknd over 1f out* **14/1**

7 3 ½ **Garrulous (UAE)** 3-9-3 .... JoeFanning 3 60
(M Johnston) *chsd ldrs over 7f* **28/1**

-034 8 ¾ **Zed Candy (FR)**[18] [863] 3-9-3 70 .... DaleGibson 1 58
(J T Stimpson) *sn drvn to ld: hdd over 2f out: wknd wl over 1f out* **40/1**

9 9 **Virginia Plain** 3-8-12 .... DaneO'Neill 8 38
(Miss Diana Weeden) *s.i.s: a in rr* **100/1**

0-0 10 7 **Travolta**[18] [880] 3-9-3 .... AlanDaly 12 31
(C G Cox) *chsd ldrs: pushed along 1/2-way: wknd over 3f out* **25/1**

0-0 11 11 **The Preacher**[18] [863] 3-9-3 .... NeilPollard 6 12
(J G Given) *mid-div: rdn 1/2-way: wknd 4f out* **100/1**

40 12 8 **Darker Than Blue**[12] [952] 3-8-12 .... MichaelTebbutt 11 —
(B J Meehan) *hld up: bhd fr 1/2-way* **66/1**

2m 13.12s (3.42) **Going Correction** +0.30s/f (Good) 12 Ran SP% **119.7**
Speed ratings (Par 96):98,94,92,91,90 88,86,85,78,72 63,57
CSF £14.11 TOTE £5.90: £2.00, £1.50, £4.10; EX 22.90.
Owner Castle Down Racing **Bred** Meon Valley Stud **Trained** Newmarket, Suffolk

FOCUS
Quite a decent maiden but only three could be seriously fancied. The form looks sound enough despite the steady pace.
Darker Than Blue Official explanation: jockey said filly hung to the right

1140 BETFREDCASINO.COM H'CAP 1m 1f 213y
7:15 (7:16) (Class 6) (0-60,61) 3-Y-O £2,730 (£806; £403) Stalls Low

Form RPR

6-06 1 **Raise The Heights (IRE)**[14] [918] 3-9-2 58 .... JoeFanning 14 61
(C Tinkler) *chsd ldrs: led 2f out: rdn out* **13/2**[3]

0010 2 1 ¼ **Hits Only Life (USA)**[24] [797] 3-8-11 53 .... DeanMcKeown 9 54
(J Pearce) *hld up: hung lft fnl 4f: hdwy over 2f out: nt rch wnr* **7/2**[1]

5-60 3 1 ¼ **Shardia (IRE)**[42] [630] 3-8-5 52 .... GregFairley(5) 4 51
(J Jay) *a.p: rdn over 1f out: styd on same pce fnl f* **25/1**

000- 4 1 ¾ **Changiz**[185] [5970] 3-8-13 55 .... DavidKinsella 6 51
(J A Geake) *chsd ldr: led 6f out: hdd over 2f out: no ex* **40/1**

060- 5 nk **Persian Conqueror (IRE)**[206] [5554] 3-8-9 51 .... JimmyQuinn 10 47
(J L Dunlop) *hld up: nt clr run over 3f out: hdwy u.p over 1f out: nt rch ldrs* **20/1**

05-5 6 2 ½ **Alwariah**[19] [861] 3-9-0 56 .... TedDurcan 2 47
(C E Brittain) *chsd ldrs: led over 2f out: sn rdn and hdd: wknd fnl f* **16/1**

000- 7 1 ¼ **Vice Admiral**[168] [6249] 3-8-12 57 .... PaulMulrennan(3) 13 46
(M W Easterby) *hld up: hdwy and edgd lft over 1f out: nvr nr to chal* **40/1**

4-22 8 ¾ **Mighty Dancer (IRE)**[10] [984] 3-9-5 61 .... FrankieMcDonald 7 49
(S Kirk) *sn led: hdd 6f out: rdn and ev ch over 2f out: wknd over 1f out* **9/2**[2]

000- 9 6 **Hope's Eternal**[224] [5113] 3-9-4 60 .... SebSanders 5 38
(J L Dunlop) *hld up: hdwy u.p 3f out: wknd 2f out* **8/1**

000- 10 nk **Great Composer (IRE)**[122] [6642] 3-8-13 55 .... JimCrowley 3 32
(Mrs A J Perrett) *plld hrd and prom: rdn and wknd 2f out* **9/1**

000- 11 3 ½ **King Of Chav's (IRE)**[161] [6334] 3-8-13 55 .... VinceSlattery 11 26
(A Bailey) *hld up: a in rr* **66/1**

000- 12 5 **Sarwin (USA)**[197] [5718] 3-9-1 57 .... PhilipRobinson 16 20
(W J Musson) *hld up: hdwy 1/2-way: wknd 3f out* **12/1**

-500 13 7 **Valentino Taffi**[47] [594] 3-8-8 50 ....(b[1]) J-PGuillambert 12 —
(S C Williams) *plld hrd and prom: rdn and hung lft 4f out: sn wknd* **28/1**

1-05 14 3 ½ **Xpres Boy (IRE)**[71] [364] 3-9-3 59 .... PaulEddery 15 4
(S R Bowring) *chsd ldrs over 7f* **22/1**

000- 15 1 ½ **Move On (IRE)**[213] [5407] 3-8-10 52 .... DaneO'Neill 8 —
(B Ellison) *hld up: a in rr* **22/1**

600- 16 11 **Flying Penne**[159] [6342] 3-8-12 54 .... RobertWinston 1 —
(M R Channon) *hld up: hdwy over 4f out: wknd over 2f out* **25/1**

2m 16.16s (6.46) **Going Correction** +0.30s/f (Good) 16 Ran SP% **119.4**
Speed ratings (Par 96):86,85,84,82,82 80,79,78,73,73 70,66,61,58,57 48
CSF £24.85 CT £546.17 TOTE £8.30: £1.60, £1.60, £7.70, £12.40; EX 22.10.
Owner George Ward **Bred** Deep Water Blues Syndicate **Trained** Compton, Berks

FOCUS
A moderate handicap run in a very moderate winning time, more than three seconds slower than the preceding maiden over the same trip. The third, fourth and fifth set the level for the form.
Hits Only Life(USA) Official explanation: jockey said gelding was unsuited by soft, good to soft in places ground
Changiz Official explanation: jockey said gelding hung right throughout

1141 BETFRED 570 SHOPS NATIONWIDE H'CAP 1m 54y
7:45 (7:46) (Class 6) (0-65,65) 3-Y-O £2,730 (£806; £403) Stalls Centre

Form RPR

1 1 **Braddock (IRE)**[29] [716] 3-9-4 65 .... PaulFessey 1 71+
(T D Barron) *led 1f: chsd clr ldr: led over 2f out: drvn out* **7/2**[1]

2450 2 ½ **Rebellious Spirit**[17] [890] 3-9-4 65 .... DarrenWilliams 6 70
(P W Hiatt) *hld up: hdwy over 3f out: rdn over 1f out: hung lft ins fnl f: styd on* **14/1**

000- 3 ¾ **Lester Leaps In (USA)**[214] [5392] 3-9-2 63 .... PatDobbs 12 66+
(R Hannon) *dwlt: hld up: hdwy u.p over 2f out: nt rch ldrs* **16/1**

050- 4 1 **Air Biscuit (IRE)**[192] [5833] 3-9-4 65 .... GeorgeBaker 5 66+
(C F Wall) *chsd ldrs: rdn over 2f out: styd on same pce fnl f* **12/1**

0-30 5 nk **Davidia (IRE)**[14] [918] 3-9-1 62 .... FrankieMcDonald 16 62
(S Kirk) *prom: rdn over 2f out: no ex fnl f* **15/2**[3]

400- 6 3 **Dancing Melody**[195] [5761] 3-8-11 61 .... RichardThomas(3) 9 55
(J A Geake) *hld up: rdn over 4f out: hung lft over 1f out: nrst fin* **16/1**

00-6 7 shd **Haiti Dancer**[18] [879] 3-8-11 58 .... PhilipRobinson 13 52
(C G Cox) *hld up: rdn over 3f out: sn outpcd: styd on ins fnl f* **4/1**[2]

00-0 8 1 **Master Mark**[12] [948] 3-8-10 57 .... RobertWinston 10 49
(P D Evans) *hld up: nvr nrr* **66/1**

000- 9 1 **Constant Cheers (IRE)**[228] [5027] 3-9-1 62 .... TedDurcan 14 52+
(W R Swinburn) *s.s: hld up: hdwy over 3f out: sn lost pl: styd on ins fnl f* **20/1**

055- 10 4 **Captain Bolsh**[200] [5682] 3-9-0 61 .... JimmyQuinn 8 43
(J Pearce) *chsd ldrs 6f* **18/1**

000- 11 ½ **Dynamite Deano**[206] [5542] 3-8-8 55 .... StephenCarson 3 36
(D K Ivory) *prom over 5f* **40/1**

0046 12 3 ½ **Rock Of Cloonavery (IRE)**[10] [984] 3-8-11 58 .... DaneO'Neill 4 32
(S C Williams) *s.i.s: hld up: hdwy over 3f out: wknd wl over 1f out* **11/1**

003- 13 ½ **Punjabi**[159] [6342] 3-9-0 61 .... J-PGuillambert 7 34
(Mrs G S Rees) *hld up: a in rr* **33/1**

665- 14 shd **Waiting For Mary (IRE)**[200] [5681] 3-9-2 63 .... FergusSweeney 2 36
(J G M O'Shea) *hld up: hdwy over 3f out: wknd over 1f out* **22/1**

10-0 15 5 **Feelin Irie (IRE)**[10] [993] 3-9-2 63 .... KimTinkler 11 26
(N Tinkler) *led after 1f: clr 5f out: hdd & wknd over 2f out* **33/1**

500- 16 2 **Sirbrit**[168] [6251] 3-8-9 56 .... TPQueally 17 15
(W J Musson) *s.i.s: a in rr* **25/1**

650- 17 9 **Paddy Moon**[171] [6225] 3-9-1 62 .... SebSanders 15 —
(J G Given) *hld up: effrt over 4f out: wknd 3f out* **20/1**

1m 48.72s (2.32) **Going Correction** +0.30s/f (Good) 17 Ran SP% **121.2**
Speed ratings (Par 96):100,99,98,97,97 94,94,93,92,88 87,84,83,83,78 76,67
CSF £46.21 CT £732.19 TOTE £3.30: £1.40, £4.30, £2.30, £2.30; EX 110.70 Place 6 £141.98, Place 5 £103.45.
Owner James M Egan **Bred** Corduff Stud And J Corcoran **Trained** Maunby, N Yorks

FOCUS
Modest handicap form but the winner is unexposed and could be capable of better than the bare form suggests.
T/Plt: £151.30 to a £1 stake. Pool: £26,127.00. 126.05 winning tickets. T/Qpdt: £72.00 to a £1 stake. Pool: £2,347.60. 24.10 winning tickets. CR

[1121]THIRSK (L-H)
Saturday, April 22

OFFICIAL GOING: Good
The ground had dried out overnight but was still described as 'on the easy side of good'.
Wind: Moderate, half-behind Weather: Fine

1142 SQUIRE FREDERICK BELL CLAIMING STKS 5f
2:30 (2:30) (Class 5) 2-Y-O £3,886 (£1,156; £577; £288) Stalls High

Form RPR

3 1 **Auction Time**[11] [962] 2-8-3 .... DanielTudhope(3) 9 60
(D Carroll) *chsd ldrs: effrt on ins to ld appr fnl f: hung bdly lft: kpt on wl* **2/1**[1]

2 2 **Go On Jessica (IRE)** 2-8-8 .... PaulHanagan 10 54+
(P D Evans) *dwlt: hdwy 2f out: edgd lft and styd on wl fnl f to take 2nd on line* **12/1**

541 3 shd **Granny Peel (IRE)**[5] [1040] 2-8-12 .... DO'Donohoe 2 58
(K A Ryan) *chsd ldrs: kpt on same pce fnl f* **3/1**[2]

4 1 ¼ **Onenightinlisbon (IRE)** 2-8-8 .... LeeEnstone 4 49
(P T Midgley) *s.i.s: hung lft and kpt on fnl 2f* **66/1**

6 5 1 ¾ **Lord Blue Boy**[12] [944] 2-9-0 .... RobertMiles(3) 6 51
(W G M Turner) *w ldr: led over 2f out: hdd appr fnl f: sn wknd* **6/1**[3]

04 6 2 **Minimum Fuss (IRE)**[15] [908] 2-8-6 .... DaleGibson 11 32
(M W Easterby) *led tl 2f out: sn wknd* **9/1**

01 7 2 **Alittleriskie (IRE)**[18] [877] 2-8-1 .... JosephWalsh(7) 5 26
(J S Moore) *plld hrd early: sn bhd: nvr on terms* **8/1**

8 ¾ **Poniard (IRE)** 2-9-1 .... NeilPollard 7 30
(D W Barker) *sn chsng ldrs: lost pl over 1f out* **20/1**

9 1 **Minnie Magician** 2-8-2 .... RoystonFfrench 8 13
(C Grant) *dwlt: a outpcd and bhd* **50/1**

10 7 **Job Done** 2-8-4 ow1 .... PaulMulrennan(3) 1 —
(M W Easterby) *swvd bdly lft s: a bhd* **28/1**

11 2 **Mister Cricket (IRE)** 2-8-11 .... TomEaves 3 —
(M E Sowersby) *outpcd and bhd after 2f* **33/1**

62.40 secs (2.50) **Going Correction** +0.275s/f (Good) 11 Ran SP% **116.0**
Speed ratings (Par 92):91,87,87,85,82 79,76,75,73,62 59
CSF £25.81 TOTE £3.10: £1.30, £2.60, £1.50; EX 37.80.Auction Time was claimed by J Spearing for £7,000; Go On Jessica (IRE) was claimed by D Nicholls for £8,000
Owner Diamond Racing Ltd **Bred** Mrs M M Palling **Trained** Warthill, N Yorks

FOCUS
A modest event but the form appears sound.

NOTEBOOK
Auction Time gave her new connections a quick return despite hanging right across the track once she hit the front. She changed hands yet again and now joins John Spearing. (op 11-4)
Go On Jessica(IRE), a February foal, recovered from a tardy start and some solid work in the final furlong saw her snatch second spot on the line. It was enough for David Nicholls to claim her. (op 11-1)
Granny Peel(IRE), making a quick return, found this step up to claiming company from a seller too tough. (op 11-4)
Onenightinlisbon(IRE), an April foal, has more size than most of these. After a tardy start her inexperience showed but this should have taught her a fair bit. (op 50-1)
Lord Blue Boy went on at halfway but his chance had gone when the winner went across him just inside the last. (tchd 11-2 and 13-2)
Minimum Fuss(IRE), having her third outing, took them along for three furlongs before folding. (op 11-1)

1143 OLD BYLAND H'CAP 7f
3:05 (3:07) (Class 3) (0-90,88) 3-Y-O+ £11,658 (£3,468; £1,733; £865) Stalls Low

Form RPR

42-3 1 **Dabbers Ridge (IRE)**[16] [898] 4-9-7 81 .... TonyCulhane 11 98
(B W Hills) *chsd ldrs: led 2f out: hld on wl ins last* **11/4**[1]

430- 2 1 **Malcheek (IRE)**[201] [5660] 4-9-3 77 .... DavidAllan 6 91
(T D Easterby) *trckd ldrs: wnt 2nd over 1f out: kpt on wl ins last* **8/1**[3]

1030 3 5 **Speed Dial Harry (IRE)**[21] [826] 4-9-0 79 ....(v) AndrewElliott(5) 4 80
(K R Burke) *chsd ldrs: rdn on same pce fnl 2f* **40/1**

0-00 4 nk **Danzig River (IRE)**[5] [1042] 5-9-5 79 .... AdrianTNicholls 7 79
(D Nicholls) *trckd ldrs: effrt 2f out: kpt on same pce* **20/1**

1-60 5 ½ **Dhaular Dhar (IRE)**[28] [726] 4-9-4 78 .... FergalLynch 5 77
(J S Goldie) *in rr: effrt on inner 2f out: swtchd outside: r.o fnl f* **14/1**

315- 6 ½ **Isidore Bonheur (IRE)**[197] [5715] 5-9-10 84 .... DeanMcKeown 15 82
(G A Swinbank) *sn bhd: swtchd outside 2f out: styd on steadily* **16/1**

500- 7 1 **Tagula Sunrise (IRE)**[190] [5874] 4-9-10 84 .... PaulHanagan 2 79+
(R A Fahey) *mid-div: kpt on fnl 2f: nvr nr ldrs* **16/1**

10-5 8 ¾ **Wigwam Willie (IRE)**[18] [865] 4-9-10 84 .... DO'Donohoe 3 77+
(K A Ryan) *s.i.s: hdwy on inner and n.m.r over 2f out: nvr nr ldrs* **7/1**[2]

062- 9 2 **Top Dirham**[266] [3960] 8-9-5 79 .... DaleGibson 16 67+
(M W Easterby) *mid-div: nvr nr ldrs* **14/1**

10-0 10 1 **Inter Vision (USA)**[29] [718] 6-9-11 88 .... DanielTudhope(3) 10 73
(A Dickman) *hld up in mid-div: nvr a threat* **33/1**

000- 11 nk **King Harson**[172] [6216] 7-9-3 77 ....(v) KDarley 9 61+
(J D Bethell) *led after 1f. hdd 2f out: edgd rt and sn lost pl* **11/1**

060- 12 3 **Primo Way**[190] [5874] 5-9-11 85 ....(b) TomEaves 8 62
(I Semple) *stl had blind on whn stalls opened: s.i.s: sme hdwy and n.m.r over 2f out: nvr on terms* **10/1**

2-40 13 hd **Prince Tum Tum (USA)**[84] [220] 6-9-6 85 .... MarkLawson(5) 1 61
(D W Barker) *reluctant to go to post. t.k.h in mid-field: nvr a threat* **16/1**

10-0 14 2 **Royal Dignitary (USA)**[29] [719] 6-8-9 76 .... KellyHarrison(7) 13 47
(D Nicholls) *t.k.h: in tch: rdn and lost pl over 2f out* **40/1**

40-0 15 2 **Lord Of The East**[38] [644] 7-9-11 88 .... PatrickMathers(3) 12 54+
(I W McInnes) *led 1f: chsd ldrs: lost pl over 2f out* **20/1**

043- 16 1 1/4 **Inside Story (IRE)**[183] 6003 4-9-1 78 .... PaulMulrennan(3) 14 41
(M W Easterby) *swtchd lft s: sn detached in rr* **20/1**

1m 27.35s (0.25) **Going Correction** +0.275s/f (Good) **16** Ran SP% **124.2**
Speed ratings (Par 107):109,107,102,101,101 100,99,98,96,95 94,91,91,88,86 85
CSF £21.63 CT £324.71 TOTE £3.20: £1.10, £1.90, £4.10, £3.50; EX 27.00.
Owner Maurice Mogg **Bred** Franco Castelfranci **Trained** Lambourn, Berks

FOCUS
A good handicap for the grade run at a strong gallop but it was difficult to make ground from off the pace. The form looks solid and the first two should rate higher.

NOTEBOOK
Dabbers Ridge(IRE) was always in the right position. He had first run and under strong pressure was always doing just enough. (op 3-1 tchd 10-3)
Malcheek(IRE), who wears a device to prevent him putting his head down in the stalls, went in pursuit. He was gradually closing the gap all the way to the line but in truth was never going to quite get there. He prefers slightly quicker ground. (op 11-1 tchd 12-1 in a place)
Speed Dial Harry(IRE), a stone higher than when last seen on turf, has three All-Weather wins to his credit already this year.
Danzig River(IRE), who has not won since he was a juvenile, was making a quick return with the headgear again left off. Whether he is as effective over seven as he is over six remains to be seen. (tchd 16-1)
Dhaular Dhar(IRE), very wintry, stayed on when switched wide and much prefers a mile. Official explanation: jockey said colt was denied a clear run (op 16-1 tchd 18-1)
Isidore Bonheur(IRE) ◆ made a highly satisfactory return over a trip short of his best. He is well worth keeping an eye on.
Inside Story(IRE) Official explanation: jockey said colt was slow away and never travelling

1144 SPRING H'CAP 1m 4f
3:40 (3:41) (Class 5) (0-75,75) 4-Y-0+ **£3,886** (£1,156; £577; £288) **Stalls** Low

Form RPR
511- 1 **Greenwich Meantime**[235] 4858 6-9-5 74 .... PaulHanagan 8 84
(R A Fahey) *hld up towards rr: hdwy over 3f out: led 1f out: r.o* **11/1**
64-2 2 1 1/4 **Charlotte Vale**[10] 976 5-8-13 73 .... GregFairley(5) 5 81
(Micky Hammond) *trckd ldrs: led and edgd lft over 1f out: sn hdd and no ex* **9/2**[1]
53-0 3 3 **Ego Trip**[18] 869 5-8-5 60 ....(b) DO'Donohoe 12 63
(M W Easterby) *t.k.h: trckd ldrs: led 8f out tl over 2f out: one pce* **14/1**
040- 4 shd **Rocket Force (USA)**[194] 5792 6-8-12 70 .... DNolan(3) 11 73
(N Wilson) *w ldrs: led over 2f out tl over 1f out: one pce* **25/1**
1S-1 5 1 3/4 **Maneki Neko (IRE)**[10] 976 4-9-2 75 .... DanielTudhope(3) 13 75
(E W Tuer) *hld up in rr: hdwy over 3f out: rdn and hung lft over 1f out: nvr rchd ldrs* **5/1**[2]
1315 6 3 1/2 **Cotton Eyed Joe (IRE)**[72] 346 5-9-3 72 .... DeanMcKeown 9 67
(G A Swinbank) *hld up in rr: styd on fnl 2f: nvr nr to chal* **10/1**
-050 7 1 **Street Life (IRE)**[10] 990 8-8-11 66 .... TPQueally 10 59
(W J Musson) *swtchd lft s: hld up in rr: kpt on fnl 2f: nvr nrr* **13/2**[3]
0-65 8 nk **Court Of Appeal**[65] 425 9-8-13 68 .... TomEaves 3 61
(B Ellison) *set modest pce: hdd 8f out: wknd fnl 2f* **20/1**
2-00 9 1 3/4 **Farne Isle**[10] 975 7-8-4 62 ....(t) PaulMulrennan(3) 6 52
(G A Harker) *in tch: drvn over 4f out: sn outpcd* **25/1**
0-00 10 3 **Pianoforte (USA)**[19] 860 4-8-7 63 .... DavidAllan 7 48
(E J Alston) *plld hrd in mid-field: effrt 3f out: wknd fnl 2f* **40/1**
131- 11 1 **Melvino**[194] 5797 4-8-11 67 .... PhillipMakin 4 50
(T D Barron) *plld hrd: detached in rr: nvr on terms* **15/2**
0/20 12 1/2 **Middlethorpe**[10] 990 9-8-6 61 ow1 ....(b) KDarley 1 44
(M W Easterby) *mid-div: drvn and lost pl over 4f out: sn bhd* **16/1**
0-40 13 10 **Haatmey**[10] 983 4-9-3 73 .... TonyCulhane 2 40
(M R Channon) *chsd ldrs: hrd drvn 5f out: sn lost pl and bhd: eased* **15/2**

2m 40.26s (5.06) **Going Correction** +0.275s/f (Good)
WFA 4 from 5yo+ 1lb **13** Ran SP% **116.6**
Speed ratings (Par 103):94,93,91,91,89 87,86,86,85,83 82,82,75
CSF £55.76 CT £708.06 TOTE £12.70: £4.20, £2.10, £5.00; EX 59.40.
Owner R A Fahey **Bred** Juddmonte Farms **Trained** Musley Bank, N Yorks

FOCUS
An ordinary handicap and just a steady pace for the first half mile, so the time was slow. The fourth and fifth set the standard and the form is modest.

1145 MICHAEL FOSTER MEMORIAL CONDITIONS STKS 6f
4:15 (4:16) (Class 3) 3-Y-0+
£11,217 (£3,358; £1,679; £840; £419; £210) **Stalls** High

Form RPR
012- 1 **Welsh Emperor (IRE)**[172] 6221 7-9-13 110 .... TonyCulhane 3 114
(T P Tate) *sltly hmpd s: bhd and pushed along: swtchd outside and hdwy over 2f out: str run on inner to ld ins last: r.o wl* **6/1**
000- 2 2 1/2 **River Falcon**[182] 6021 6-9-1 92 .... DanielTudhope(3) 1 98
(J S Goldie) *trckd ldrs: led 2f out: hdd and no ex ins last* **14/1**
210- 3 1 1/2 **Eisteddfod**[202] 5647 5-9-8 112 .... KDarley 5 97
(P F I Cole) *chsd ldrs: rdn end edgd lft over 1f out: kpt on same pce* **15/8**[1]
202- 4 3 1/2 **Lafi (IRE)**[238] 4751 7-9-1 108 .... AdrianTNicholls 4 80
(D Nicholls) *swvd lft s: t.k.h: trckd ldrs: effrt over 2f out: sn btn* **11/4**[2]
5600 5 1 **Pawan (IRE)**[50] 569 6-8-8 75 .... AnnStokell(7) 6 77
(Miss A Stokell) *sn pushed along: outpcd after 2f: edgd lft and kpt on fnl 2f* **80/1**
30-3 6 7 **Beckermet (IRE)**[4] 1069 4-9-8 107 .... PaulHanagan 2 63+
(R F Fisher) *led tl 2f out: wkng whn hmpd over 1f out: eased* **7/2**[3]
46-0 7 7 **Tom Tun**[28] 729 11-9-6 88 ....(b) DeanMcKeown 7 40
(J Balding) *w ldrs: lost pl over 1f out: eased* **25/1**

1m 13.35s (-10.10) **Going Correction** +0.275s/f (Good) **7** Ran SP% **109.7**
Speed ratings (Par 107):105,101,99,95,93 84,75
CSF £73.93 TOTE £7.30: £3.40, £3.90; EX 54.20.
Owner Mrs Sylvia Clegg **Bred** Times Of Wigan Ltd **Trained** Tadcaster, N Yorks

FOCUS
A decent conditions race rated through the winner, but several will improve for the run.

NOTEBOOK
Welsh Emperor(IRE), who took this two years ago, had a big penalty to overcome this time. Full of beans beforehand, the hood was very late coming off and he collected a bump leaving the stalls. He came from last to first and, making his final effort on the inside of the leader, in the end he won going right away. He seems happier without the headgear and does not need conditions testing now. Better than ever, he will now take in the Duke Of York Stakes at York next month. (op 5-1)
River Falcon, looking wintry, had plenty to find on official ratings. He went on travelling easily but in the end found the winner much too good. In the past he has needed an outing or two to come to hand. (op 12-1 tchd 10-1)
Eisteddfod, who looked fit, ran a bit rustily and will improve on this with some sun on his back. (tchd 9-4)
Lafi(IRE), absent since August, looked to be carrying plenty of condition. He was too keen for his own good early and tired soon after halfway. A fast-ground specialist, no doubt he will bounce back in the big handicaps in due course. (op 3-1)
Pawan(IRE), totally out of his depth, picked up appearance money and fifth place prizemoney. (op 66-1)
Beckermet(IRE), making a quick return, was well below his best even taking into account the easy ground. No doubt he will soon bounce back. (op 10-3 tchd 4-1)
Tom Tun took a weaker renewal a year ago. He had plenty on his plate this time but at least showed all his old speed. (tchd 20-1 and 33-1)

1146 THOMAS LORD STKS (H'CAP) 5f
4:45 (4:46) (Class 3) (0-90,90) 3-Y-0 **£11,658** (£3,468; £1,733; £865) **Stalls** High

Form
212- 1 **Guto**[183] 6004 3-9-2 88 .... DO'Donohoe 4 95
(K A Ryan) *mde all: hld on wl* **6/1**[2]
64-0 2 1/2 **Scooby Dude (IRE)**[73] 341 3-8-1 76 oh3 .... NelsonDeSouza(3) 1 81
(Ms Deborah J Evans) *w ldrs: no ex wl ins last* **16/1**
311- 3 1 1/4 **Indigo Nights (IRE)**[301] 2905 3-8-12 84 .... TPQueally 2 85+
(Mrs A Duffield) *hld up: effrt and nt clr run over 2f out: n.m.r over 1f out: styd on wl ins last* **8/1**
560- 4 shd **Overstayed (IRE)**[203] 5613 3-9-4 90 .... CraigCarver 10 90
(P A Blockley) *w ldrs: hung lft over 1f out: kpt on ins last* **20/1**
61-1 5 shd **Jimmy The Guesser**[11] 967 3-8-4 79 ....(b) RichardThomas(3) 11 79
(N P Littmoden) *chsd ldrs: effrt and swtchd lft over 1f out: kpt on same pce* **7/2**[1]
600- 6 1/2 **Cheap N Chic**[161] 6320 3-8-8 80 .... FergalLynch 9 78
(T D Easterby) *sn outpcd: hdwy over 1f out: styd on ins last* **14/1**
61-2 7 3/4 **Figaro Flyer (IRE)**[73] 341 3-9-4 90 .... TonyCulhane 5 85
(P Howling) *mid-div: kpt on fnl f* **14/1**
44-1 8 1 **City For Conquest (IRE)**[42] 626 3-8-7 79 ....(v) FrancisNorton 8 71
(K R Burke) *in tch: edgd rt and kpt on same pce fnl f* **16/1**
00-0 9 1 3/4 **Danjet (IRE)**[35] 665 3-8-8 80 .... PaulHanagan 6 65
(P D Evans) *in tch: effrt 2f out: nvr really threatened* **33/1**
4311 10 nk **Sands Crooner (IRE)**[47] 593 3-8-3 78 ....(v) PatrickMathers(3) 7 62
(D Shaw) *dwlt: kpt on fnl 2f: nvr nr ldrs* **9/1**
00-0 11 3 1/2 **Supercast (IRE)**[7] 1020 3-8-11 83 .... DeanMcKeown 12 55
(J S Moore) *rrd s: nvr a factor* **25/1**
31- 12 1 **Night In (IRE)**[220] 5219 3-8-7 79 .... KimTinkler 14 47
(N Tinkler) *chsd ldrs: lost pl over 1f out* **20/1**
2115 13 3 **Stoneacre Boy (IRE)**[7] 1020 3-8-7 79 ....(b) RobbieFitzpatrick 3 36
(Peter Grayson) *unruly in stalls: chsd ldrs: lost pl over 1f out: eased* **7/1**[3]
120- 14 26 **Choysia**[217] 5286 3-9-1 87 .... KDarley 13 —
(D W Barker) *s.s: a detached in last: virtually p.u* **7/1**[3]

61.08 secs (1.18) **Going Correction** +0.275s/f (Good) **14** Ran SP% **124.0**
Speed ratings (Par 102):101,100,98,98,97 97,95,94,91,91 85,83,79,37
CSF £96.05 CT £568.10 TOTE £7.30: £3.40, £3.90; EX 54.20.
Owner H B Hughes **Bred** H B Hughes **Trained** Hambleton, N Yorks
■ Stewards' Enquiry : Paul Hanagan one-day ban: not riding to draw (May 3)

FOCUS
A tight-knit sprint handicap with the first seven stacked up at the line. The first three were drawn low but the form appears sound enough.

NOTEBOOK
Guto is all speed and stuck on in most willing fashion. (op 8-1)
Scooby Dude(IRE), worst drawn, hassled the winner all the way and went down fighting. 3lb out of the handicap here, his rating will rise as a result. (op 20-1)
Indigo Nights(IRE) ◆, absent since making it two from two at Chester in June, met all sorts of traffic problems before staying on in willing fashion to snatch third on the line. She can certainly win off this sort of mark. (op 11-1)
Overstayed(IRE), who proved himself tough at two, looks to have returned as good as ever. (op 22-1)
Jimmy The Guesser, a big sort, had the headgear back on. He did not seem totally at home on this track and a sixth furlong will not come amiss. (op 4-1 tchd 9-2)
Cheap N Chic, who won over six at Brighton on fast ground at two, stayed on in fine style when it was all over and should more than pay her way when upped again in trip. (op 16-1)
Sands Crooner(IRE) Official explanation: jockey said colt was unsuited by good ground
Stoneacre Boy(IRE) became upset in the stalls. (op 11-2)
Choysia, who had two handlers, gave away several lengths at the start and trailed home detached in last. Official explanation: trainer was unable to offer any explanation for poor form shown

1147 COXWOLD MAIDEN STKS 5f
5:15 (5:15) (Class 5) 3-Y-0 **£5,181** (£1,541; £770; £384) **Stalls** High

Form RPR
40- 1 **Borehan**[205] 5570 3-9-3 .... KDarley 8 79
(M A Jarvis) *chsd ldrs: effrt over 2f out: styd on to ld ins last: all out* **8/11**[1]
054- 2 1/2 **Sea Salt**[229] 4996 3-9-3 68 .... PhillipMakin 10 77
(T D Barron) *led: edgd lft 2f out: hdd and no ex ins last* **13/2**[2]
3- 3 3/4 **Monashee Brave (IRE)**[199] 5696 3-9-0 .... DNolan(3) 11 75
(J J Quinn) *chsd ldrs: carried hd high and kpt on ins last* **8/1**[3]
4 5 **Dragon Flame (IRE)** 3-9-3 .... FrancisNorton 12 57
(M Quinn) *dwlt: sn bhd: styd on fnl 2f* **16/1**
5 1 **Artie's Son (IRE)** 3-9-3 .... FergalLynch 3 53
(T D Easterby) *s.s: bhd tl kpt on wl fnl 2f* **33/1**
4- 6 3/4 **Targer Place**[162] 6311 3-9-3 .... TPQueally 6 50
(T T Clement) *mid-div: keeping on one pce whn nt clr run and swtchd lft ins last* **33/1**
-663 7 nk **Mister Becks (IRE)**[12] 936 3-8-12 35 .... EmmettStack(5) 13 49
(M C Chapman) *sn outpcd and in rr: kpt on fnl 2f: nvr on terms* **66/1**
0- 8 1 1/4 **Steel City Boy (IRE)**[230] 4974 3-9-0 .... DanielTudhope(3) 4 45
(D Carroll) *rrd s: sn w ldrs: wknd over 1f out* **20/1**
30-4 9 3 1/2 **Coalite (IRE)**[16] 893 3-9-3 69 .... TonyCulhane 9 32
(A D Brown) *sn outpcd and in rr: nvr on terms* **25/1**
200- 10 nk **Moorhouse Lad**[227] 5043 3-9-3 82 .... PaulHanagan 5 31
(G Woodward) *bdly bmpd s: nvr on terms* **8/1**[3]
0- 11 1 3/4 **Missouri (USA)**[280] 3530 3-9-3 .... DavidAllan 7 25
(G M Moore) *prom: lost pl over 2f out* **40/1**
00 12 2 **Fashion Disaster**[10] 978 3-8-5 .... AshleyHamblett(7) 1 13
(A Crook) *prom on outer: lost pl over 2f out* **100/1**

61.34 secs (1.44) **Going Correction** +0.275s/f (Good) **12** Ran SP% **118.8**
Speed ratings (Par 98):99,98,97,89,87 86,85,83,78,77 74,71
CSF £5.15 TOTE £1.70: £1.10, £1.70, £2.00; EX 7.40 Place 6 £311.05, Place 5 £77.54.
Owner Sheikh Ahmed Al Maktoum **Bred** Stratford Place Stud **Trained** Newmarket, Suffolk

FOCUS
A weak sprint maiden and Kevin Darley had to be at his most forceful. The winner was nowhere near his best but the form behind looks solid and reliable.
Moorhouse Lad Official explanation: jockey said colt had no more to give
T/Plt: £165.40 to a £1 stake. Pool: £39,350.10. 173.60 winning tickets. T/Qpdt: £86.00 to a £1 stake. Pool: £1,883.10. 16.20 winning tickets. WG

1001 WOLVERHAMPTON (A.W) (L-H)

Saturday, April 22

OFFICIAL GOING: Standard
Wind: Light behind

1148 ASHBY LONDON FINANCIAL SERVICES APPRENTICE H'CAP 1m 141y(P)
7:00 (7:00) (Class 5) (0-70,68) 4-Y-0+ **£3,886** (£1,156; £577; £288) **Stalls** Low

Form RPR
4163 **1** **Latif (USA)**[3] 1075 5-9-1 **68**.............. DerekNolan(3) 8 79
(Ms Deborah J Evans) *hld up in mid-div: swtchd rt and hdwy to ld 1f out: r.o wl* 3/1[2]
1600 **2** *1 ½* **Bijou Dan**[28] 734 5-8-11 **61**..............(b) DuranFentiman 1 69
(W G Harrison) *a.p: rdn over 2f out: kpt on one pce fnl f* 14/1
3123 **3** *1 ½* **Jakarmi**[11] 965 5-9-4 **68**.............. JamesDoyle 9 73
(B Palling) *trckd ldr: ev ch tl edgd rt appr fnl f: fdd ins* 5/2[1]
0036 **4** *3* **Gem Bien (USA)**[37] 650 8-8-4 **57**..............(p) KellyHarrison(3) 7 55
(D W Chapman) *in tch: kpt on one pce ins fnl 2f* 12/1
5363 **5** *½* **Musiotal**[61] 467 5-7-13 **54** oh9..............(v) KevinGhunowa(5) 6 51
(P A Blockley) *bhd whn hung lft over 1f out but styd on ins* 12/1
20-0 **6** *½* **The Gaikwar (IRE)**[15] 905 7-8-12 **67**..............(b) TolleyDean(5) 2 63
(R A Harris) *led tl rdn and hdd 1f out: sn wknd* 10/1
7 *¾* **Kickahead (USA)**[57] 4-8-10 **65**.............. StuartHaddon(5) 10 60
(Ian Williams) *chsd ldrs: rdn 3f out: wknd appr fnl f* 16/1
6313 **8** *nk* **Distant Country (USA)**[9] 1001 7-8-6 **61**..............(p) PatrickDonaghy(5) 11 55
(B D Leavy) *bhd: rdn 2f out: nvr on terms* 8/1
1010 **9** *5* **Pauline's Prince**[9] 1002 4-9-0 **67**.............. RussellKennemore(3) 3 51
(R Hollinshead) *bhd: rdn 2f out: nvr on terms* 7/1[3]
0 **10** *5* **Spirit Guide (FR)**[10] 977 4-8-9 **64**.............. RobbieMills(5) 4 37
(R C Guest) *hmpd s: t.k.h: hld up: wknd 3f out* 50/1
-204 **U** **Musical Gift**[67] 410 6-7-13 **54** oh6..............(v) SophieDoyle(5) 5 —
(P A Blockley) *wnt lft and rdr hit stalls s and was uns* 20/1

1m 50.72s (-1.04) **Going Correction** -0.075s/f (Stan) 11 Ran SP% **120.9**
Speed ratings (Par 103):101,99,98,95,95 94,94,93,89,84 —
CSF £46.54 CT £124.65 TOTE £4.40: £1.80, £3.30, £1.70; EX 34.90.
Owner Paddy Mason **Bred** Shadwell Farm LLC **Trained** Lydiate, Merseyside

FOCUS
Just a modest handicap restricted to apprentice riders but no fewer than seven of the 11 runners were previous course and distance winners and it was certainly competitive enough. The form appears sound enough rated around the first three.
Bijou Dan Official explanation: jockey said gelding hung sharply right when hitting front

1149 SOUL SENSATION (S) STKS 7f 32y(P)
7:30 (7:30) (Class 6) 3-Y-0 **£2,388** (£705; £352) **Stalls** High

Form RPR
2150 **1** **Inaminute (IRE)**[58] 488 3-8-12 58.............. PatCosgrave 1 66
(K R Burke) *mde all: clr 2f out: unchal* 3/1[1]
2106 **2** *5* **Miss Champagne (IRE)**[16] 893 3-8-12 55.............. NCallan 4 53
(M Quinn) *trckd wnr thrght: kpt on but hld fnl 2f* 5/1[3]
4636 **3** *1* **Bahhmirage (IRE)**[17] 890 3-8-7 48..............(b) JohnEgan 2 45
(Stef Liddiard) *a.p: nt clr run over 2f out: kpt on but little ch after* 5/1[3]
5335 **4** *nk* **She Whispers (IRE)**[18] 879 3-8-5 52.............. LiamJones(7) 5 50
(W M Brisbourne) *towards rr tl hdwy 1/2-way: styd on fnl f but n.d* 9/2[2]
-640 **5** *1* **Royal Moon (USA)**[10] 979 3-8-9 56.............. BenSwarbrick(3) 6 47
(T D Barron) *mid-div: rdn 1/2-way: sme hdwy over 1f out but nvr on terms* 7/1
-005 **6** *1 ¾* **Cecchetti (IRE)**[33] 676 3-8-4 45.............. EdwardCreighton(3) 7 37
(Mrs H Sweeting) *slowly away: a towards rr* 16/1
04- **7** *2 ½* **Making Moves**[134] 6532 3-8-7.............. TomEaves 11 31
(Miss J A Camacho) *towards rr: rdn and no hdwy fr over 2f out* 8/1
0-0 **8** *nk* **Ferroli**[5] 1048 3-8-9..............(p) JasonEdmunds(3) 8 35
(J Balding) *mid-div: rdn 1/2-way: nvr on terms* 40/1
06-0 **9** *6* **Fallal Parc**[47] 595 3-8-12 40.............. MickyFenton 10 20
(M F Harris) *slowly away: a wl in rr* 20/1
0060 **10** *1* **Billy Wizz (IRE)**[10] 984 3-8-12 53..............(v) ChrisCatlin 9 17
(A M Balding) *trckd ldrs: rdn 4f out: sn wknd* 16/1

1m 30.56s (0.16) **Going Correction** -0.075s/f (Stan) 10 Ran SP% **119.1**
Speed ratings (Par 96):96,90,89,88,87 85,82,82,75,74
CSF £18.36 TOTE £3.90: £2.00, £1.90, £2.70; EX 16.70.The winner was bought in for 7,200gns
Owner Ray Bailey **Bred** R Bailey **Trained** Middleham Moor, N Yorks

FOCUS
As is to be expected in a seller, moderate stuff, and only three of the ten runners could boast winning form. The form is weak rated around the winner and third.
Cecchetti(IRE) Official explanation: jockey said filly was unlucky in running

1150 STEVE BULL 20TH ANNIVERSARY YEAR CLAIMING STKS 5f 20y(P)
8:00 (8:00) (Class 6) 3-Y-0+ **£2,730** (£806; £403) **Stalls** Low

Form RPR
0425 **1** **Boanerges (IRE)**[18] 872 9-9-2 50.............. TomEaves 2 58
(J M Bradley) *chsd ldrs: rdn to ld ins fnl f: drvn out* 12/1
6042 **2** *1* **He's A Rocket (IRE)**[12] 951 5-9-2 54..............(b) FrancisNorton 1 54
(K R Burke) *a.p: led over 1f out: rdn and hdd ins fnl f: kpt on* 3/1[1]
3525 **3** *shd* **Phinerine**[15] 901 3-8-7 72..............(b) TolleyDean(7) 10 58
(R A Harris) *hld up: hdwy on ins over 2f out: n.m.r appr fnl f: swtchd rt: r.o* 14/1
1500 **4** *½* **Lady Hopeful (IRE)**[49] 580 4-8-13 52..............(b) GylesParkin 9 49
(Peter Grayson) *slowly away and swtchd to ins after s: hdwy over 1f out: r.o wl fnl f* 33/1
1301 **5** *1 ¼* **Henry Tun**[12] 951 8-9-5 60..............(b) JasonEdmunds(3) 12 54
(J Balding) *towards rr: styd on fnl f: nvr nrr* 10/1
404 **6** *½* **Nova Tor (IRE)**[23] 806 4-9-1 52..............(b) RobbieFitzpatrick 6 45
(Peter Grayson) *led tl rdn and hdd over 1f out: wknd ins fnl f* 9/2[3]
P-0 **7** *nk* **Mind That Fox**[31] 692 4-9-6.............. MickyFenton 3 49?
(T Wall) *mid-div: kpt on one pce ins fnl 2f* 66/1
0350 **8** *¾* **Leah's Pride**[10] 982 5-8-4 47..............(t) KirstyMilczarek(7) 8 37
(Miss D A McHale) *trckd ldr tl wknd over 1f out* 20/1
-102 **9** *½* **Banjo Bay (IRE)**[5] 1054 8-9-6 63.............. AdrianTNicholls 5 44
(D Nicholls) *in tch tl rdn and wknd 1/2-way* 10/3[2]
00-4 **10** *1* **Penny Thoughts**[9] 1003 3-8-3 49.............. ChrisCatlin 4 30
(E S McMahon) *slowly away: a bhd* 25/1
2460 **11** *shd* **Madrasee**[21] 837 8-9-0 51.............. AmirQuinn(3) 11 37
(P G Murphy) *bhd: rdn 1/2-way: nvr on terms* 33/1
006- **12** *5* **Arisea (IRE)**[236] 4823 3-8-6 45 ow1.............. JohnEgan 13 14
(R C Guest) *a bhd* 66/1
1041 **13** *5* **Maktavish**[52] 547 7-9-11 82..............(b) DanielTudhope(3) 7 12
(D Carroll) *slowly away: a bhd* 5/1

63.22 secs (0.40) **Going Correction** -0.075s/f (Stan)
WFA 3 from 4yo+ 10lb 13 Ran SP% **123.9**
Speed ratings (Par 101):93,91,91,90,88 87,87,85,85,83 83,75,67
CSF £47.15 TOTE £15.30: £5.40, £1.70, £4.70; EX 36.10.Maktavish claimed by Roy Brotherton for £12,000. Phinerine was subject to a friendly claim.
Owner E A Hayward **Bred** Clare Dore Ltd **Trained** Sedbury, Gloucs

FOCUS
Just an ordinary sprint claimer and, with the best off at the weights Maktavish running well below form, it was not that solid.
Maktavish Official explanation: jockey said gelding missed break; jockey said, regarding running and riding, his orders were to jump out and try to make the running, but gelding dwelt in stalls and was slowly away, subsequently not coming off the bridle at any stage despite being asked for an effort 4f out; trainer said he was disappointed and thought gelding had a good chance in claiming race; vet said gelding was blowing quite hard and exhibited a heart rate that was slow relative to respiratory rate

1151 JOAN CHALK MEMORIAL H'CAP 5f 216y(P)
8:30 (8:30) (Class 5) (0-70,70) 4-Y-0+ **£3,886** (£1,156; £577; £288) **Stalls** Low

Form RPR
0063 **1** **Norcroft**[5] 1054 4-8-9 **66**..............(p) JamesDoyle(5) 5 75
(Mrs C A Dunnett) *mid-div: rdn and hdwy 2f out: r.o to ld ins fnl f* 7/1
1534 **2** *1 ½* **Winthorpe (IRE)**[11] 967 6-9-2 **68**.............. GrahamGibbons 1 73
(J J Quinn) *a.p: led over 2f out: rdn and hdd ins fnl f: r.o* 11/2[2]
2-30 **3** *1 ½* **Misaro (GER)**[37] 654 5-9-1 **67**..............(b) AdrianMcCarthy 12 67
(R A Harris) *trckd ldrs: ev ch 2f out: hung lft over 1f out: one pce ins fnl f* 22/1
5363 **4** *hd* **Mistral Sky**[5] 1057 7-9-0 **66**..............(v) JohnEgan 2 65
(Stef Liddiard) *chsd ldrs: rdn 2f out: one pce fnl f* 9/2[1]
3-66 **5** *1 ½* **Seneschal**[25] 777 5-8-12 **64**.............. SamHitchcott 8 59
(A B Haynes) *slowly away: in rr: r.o wl fnl f: nvr nrr* 7/1
0351 **6** *nk* **Gilded Cove**[28] 732 6-8-11 **70**.............. RussellKennemore(7) 11 64
(R Hollinshead) *racd wd: effrt over 1f out: nvr nr to chal* 13/2[3]
00-0 **7** *hd* **African Gift**[23] 806 4-8-11 **63**.............. MickyFenton 13 56
(J G Given) *racd wd: nvr bttr than mid-div* 20/1
2030 **8** *nk* **Gone'N'Dunnett (IRE)**[2] 1102 7-9-2 **68**..............(v) ChrisCatlin 6 61
(Mrs C A Dunnett) *led to over 2f out: rdn and wknd appr fnl f* 8/1
6000 **9** *¾* **Blue Knight (IRE)**[12] 949 7-9-4 **70**..............(v) AdrianTNicholls 7 60
(D Nicholls) *a towards rr* 14/1
/00- **10** *1 ¼* **Treasure House (IRE)**[324] 2231 5-9-4 **70**.............. FrancisNorton 4 57
(M Blanshard) *in tch tl rdn and wknd 2f out* 12/1
1450 **11** *hd* **Majestical (IRE)**[10] 986 4-8-13 **65**..............(p) ShaneKelly 10 51
(J M Bradley) *a in rr* 25/1
000/ **12** *hd* **Smirfys Systems**[525] 6649 7-9-3 **69**.............. RobbieFitzpatrick 3 54
(W M Brisbourne) *s.i.s: sn in tch: rdn 2f out: wknd over 1f out* 33/1
-024 **13** *1 ¾* **El Potro**[46] 605 4-9-0 **66**.............. NCallan 9 46
(E S McMahon) *in tch tl rdn and wknd 2f out* 7/1

1m 14.74s (-1.07) **Going Correction** -0.075s/f (Stan) 13 Ran SP% **125.8**
Speed ratings (Par 103):104,102,100,99,97 97,97,96,95,94 93,93,91
CSF £45.58 CT £860.68 TOTE £9.20: £1.90, £2.70, £9.50; EX 60.90.
Owner John Purcell **Bred** Norcroft Park Stud **Trained** Hingham, Norfolk

FOCUS
The form of this sprint handicap is just modest, but it was competitive enough with the whole field rated within 7lb of each other, and seven of the 13 runners having previously been successful over course and distance and appears sound.
El Potro Official explanation: jockey said colt was hanging right-handed in home straight

1152 STEVEBULLEVENTS.COM H'CAP 1m 1f 103y(P)
8:55 (8:55) (Class 6) (0-60,60) 4-Y-0+ **£2,730** (£806; £403) **Stalls** Low

Form RPR
0042 **1** **Scottish River (USA)**[12] 955 7-9-4 **60**.............. HayleyTurner 2 68
(M D I Usher) *a in tch on ins: rdn to ld ins fnl f: hld on wl* 5/1[2]
1323 **2** *nk* **Glendale**[22] 820 5-8-11 **56**.............. SaleemGolam(3) 3 64
(D K Ivory) *a.p: wnt 2nd over 3f out: hung rt and hdd ins fnl f: rallied cl home* 9/2[1]
6063 **3** *nk* **Seattle Robber**[12] 955 4-8-13 **55**..............(v) CraigCarver 7 62
(P A Blockley) *a in tch: rdn whn carried rt ins fnl f* 12/1
4030 **4** *1 ¼* **Ardea Brave (IRE)**[11] 972 4-9-2 **58**..............(p) NickyMackay 9 63
(M Botti) *chsd ldrs: outpcd 2f out: styd on wl fnl f* 11/1
3223 **5** *nk* **Roman Empire**[37] 650 6-9-1 **57**..............(b) NCallan 4 61
(P A Blockley) *mid-div: hdwy 3f out: rdn 2f out: one pce fnl f* 8/1
026- **6** *¾* **Abstract Folly (IRE)**[157] 6365 4-9-4 **60**..............(b) GrahamGibbons 12 63
(J D Bethell) *towards rr: mde sme late hdwy* 14/1
1100 **7** *¾* **Gallego**[18] 882 4-8-6 **53**.............. JamesDoyle(5) 13 54
(R J Price) *slowly away: sme late hdwy but nvr on terms* 20/1
6-00 **8** *1* **Futoo (IRE)**[22] 820 5-8-12 **54**..............(p) PaulQuinn 1 53
(D W Chapman) *trckd ldrs: rdn 3f out: wknd fnl f* 50/1
030- **9** *3* **Golo Gal**[113] 6687 4-9-3 **59**.............. IanMongan 11 53
(Mrs L J Mongan) *a bhd* 25/1
1143 **10** *3* **Itcanbedone Again (IRE)**[28] 736 7-9-1 **57**.............. FrancisFerris 8 45
(Ian Williams) *led tl hdd 2f out: wknd qckly* 6/1[3]
0-04 **11** *2 ½* **Comeintothespace (IRE)**[9] 1002 4-9-2 **58**.............. ShaneKelly 5 41
(J A Osborne) *v.s.a: a bhd* 6/1[3]
400- **12** *12* **Factual Lad**[236] 4820 8-9-0 **56**.............. RobertHavlin 10 16
(B R Millman) *in tch: rdn 4f out: sn wknd* 20/1
444- **13** *dist* **Seldemosa**[121] 6660 5-8-9 **54**.............. RobertMiles(3) 6 —
(M S Saunders) *trckd ldr tl wknd over 3f out: sn wl bhd* 8/1

2m 1.60s (-1.02) **Going Correction** -0.075s/f (Stan) 13 Ran SP% **123.7**
Speed ratings (Par 101):101,100,100,99,99 98,97,96,94,91 89,78,—
CSF £27.45 CT £266.30 TOTE £5.60: £1.80, £2.40, £2.50; EX 17.60.
Owner M D I Usher **Bred** The Thoroughbred Corporation **Trained** Upper Lambourn, Berks

FOCUS
A moderate handicap but just 7lb separated the entire field at the weights and the form looks solid for the level.
Gallego Official explanation: jockey said gelding jinked leaving stalls and pulled up lame
Seldemosa Official explanation: jockey said mare stopped very quickly

1153 306 GOALS MAIDEN STKS 1m 141y(P)
9:20 (9:21) (Class 5) 3-Y-0+ **£3,238** (£963; £481; £240) **Stalls** Low

Form RPR
02- **1** **Reem Three**[148] 6424 3-8-6.............. NickyMackay 3 75+
(L M Cumani) *trckd ldrs: nt clr run over 2f out: shkn up over 1f out: r.o to ld wl ins fnl f* 9/2[2]
43- **2** *¾* **Le Colombier (IRE)**[236] 4810 3-8-11.............. MichaelHills 1 78
(J W Hills) *a in tch: led over 2f out: rdn and hdd wl ins fnl f* 8/11[1]

The Form Book, Raceform Ltd, Compton, RG20 6NL

0- **3** *3* **Blacktoft (USA)**[205] 5574 3-8-11 ShaneKelly 2 72
(E A L Dunlop) *bhd tl hdwy over 3f out: fdd ins fnl f* **9/1**[3]

0-3 **4** *½* **Greenwich Village**[15] 900 3-8-11 ChrisCatlin 5 71
(W J Knight) *outpcd and in rr: styd on ins fnl 2f* **10/1**

0- **5** *3½* **Tabulate**[171] 6228 3-7-13 NicolPolli(7) 4 58
(P L Gilligan) *led tl hdd over 2f out: sn wknd* **66/1**

2520 **6** *3½* **Blanc Visage**[9] 1005 3-8-6 68 RichardKingscote(5) 6 56
(Mrs H Sweeting) *trckd ldr tl wknd over 2f out* **10/1**

0- **7** *7* **Osolomio (IRE)**[221] 5203 3-8-11 MickyFenton 7 41
(J G Given) *bhd fr 1/2-way* **40/1**

8 *17* **Fikri**[189] 5912 3-8-11 JohnEgan 9 6
(T J Pitt) *mid-div tl lost tch over 3f out* **18/1**

9 *16* **Hippolyte (USA)** 3-8-6 NeilPollard 8 —
(J G Given) *in tch: rdn 4f out: sn wl bhd* **40/1**

1m 50.13s (-1.63) **Going Correction** -0.075s/f (Stan) **9** Ran SP% **115.9**
Speed ratings (Par 103):104,103,100,100,97 94,87,72,58
CSF £8.07 TOTE £4.60: £2.10, £1.02, £3.00; EX 6.10 Place 6 £39.43, Place 5 £25.15.
Owner Sheikh Mohammed Obaid Al Maktoum **Bred** Darley **Trained** Newmarket, Suffolk
■ A treble for Nicky Mackay spread over three different racecourses, following earlier wins at Newbury and Nottingham.

FOCUS
Just an ordinary maiden but the time was decent.
Fikri Official explanation: jockey said gelding had no more to give
T/Plt: £27.00 to a £1 stake. Pool: £48,071.95. 1,298.40 winning tickets. T/Qpdt: £14.40 to a £1 stake. Pool: £3,256.90. 166.60 winning tickets. JS

1154 - 1155a (Foreign Racing) - See Raceform Interactive

NAAS (L-H)
Saturday, April 22

OFFICIAL GOING: Yielding to soft

1156a SUMMER BARBEQUE EVENINGS H'CAP 7f
3:30 (3:32) (60-100,98) 3-Y-0+ **£11,224** (£3,293; £1,568; £534)

RPR

1 **Rockazar**[27] 754 5-8-11 81 TPO'Shea 16 89+
(G M Lyons, Ire) *hld up: hdwy on outer 2f out: rdn to ld 1f out: kpt on wl u.p* **12/1**

2 *½* **Bay Boy**[7] 1029 4-8-8 78 DPMcDonogh 11 85+
(Andrew Oliver, Ire) *mid-div: rdn 2f out: 3rd over 1f out: kpt on u.p* **10/1**

3 *hd* **Master Marvel (IRE)**[6] 1038 5-8-2 79 MACleere(7) 8 85+
(T J O'Mara, Ire) *towards rr: last and swtchd to outer 2f out: styd on wl fr over 1f out* **7/1**[3]

4 *nk* **Shayrazan (IRE)**[7] 1029 5-8-6 76 (t) MCHussey 12 81
(James Leavy, Ire) *hld up: rdn 2f out: styd on wl fnl f* **5/1**[2]

5 *3* **Spainnash (IRE)**[7] 1029 6-8-5 80 SMGorey(5) 9 78
(Mrs Valerie Keatley, Ire) *mid-div: 6th on inner early st: 5th 1f out: sn no ex* **16/1**

6 *¾* **Fields Of Joy (GER)**[7] 1029 5-8-13 83 WSupple 14 79
(H Rogers, Ire) *hld up: hdwy on outer early st: 5th over 1f out: kpt on same pce* **16/1**

7 *1½* **Cheddar Island (IRE)**[13] 927 4-9-7 96 PBBeggy(5) 3 88
(Kevin Prendergast, Ire) *trckd ldrs: 5th appr st: 4th and rdn 2f out: no ex ins fnl f* **4/1**[1]

8 *1* **Oversighted (GER)**[7] 1029 5-9-0 84 (b) PJSmullen 1 73
(D K Weld, Ire) *disp ld: slt advantage 2f out: hdd 1f out: sn wknd* **12/1**

9 *1* **Striking Force (IRE)**[212] 5425 4-8-1 74 CDHayes(3) 13 61
(D Broad, Ire) *hld up: kpt on fr 1 1/2f out* **16/1**

10 *1½* **Vicious Knight**[38] 640 8-9-2 86 (b[1]) WMLordan 2 69
(D Nicholls) *disp ld: hdd 2f out: sn wknd* **12/1**

11 *2* **Manor Law (IRE)**[197] 5724 4-7-13 76 (t) ElizabethSheehan(7) 5 53
(C Collins, Ire) *prom: 4th 1/2-way: no ex early st* **14/1**

12 *½* **Zarandja (IRE)**[189] 5908 4-8-7 77 (t) NGMcCullagh 10 53
(Patrick Martin, Ire) *chsd ldrs: 6th 1/2-way: wknd st* **20/1**

13 *¾* **Delphie Queen (IRE)**[210] 5462 5-9-4 88 JMurtagh 15 62
(M Halford, Ire) *chsd ldrs: 3rd and rdn ent st: wknd 2f out: eased* **10/1**

14 *1½* **King's Jester (IRE)**[63] 4-9-0 84 FMBerry 6 54
(A J Martin, Ire) *a towards rr* **10/1**

15 *shd* **Alone He Stands (IRE)**[13] 927 6-10-0 98 KJManning 7 68
(J C Hayden, Ire) *hld up towards rr: effrt early st: no ex whn eased fnl f* **8/1**

16 *1½* **Aqualung**[17] 1915 5-8-10 83 (t) WJLee(3) 4 49
(D Broad, Ire) *chsd ldrs early: bhd st* **33/1**

1m 27.6s **16** Ran SP% **142.6**
CSF £148.13 CT £982.52 TOTE £18.40: £2.70, £5.80, £1.50, £2.00; DF 229.80.
Owner Cathair Na Mart Syndicate **Bred** Mrs Marigold West **Trained** Dunsany, Co. Meath

NOTEBOOK
Vicious Knight led and disputed but fell away quite tamely when headed two furlongs out.

1158a WOODLANDS STKS (LISTED RACE) 5f
4:30 (4:30) 3-Y-0+ **£22,448** (£6,586; £3,137; £1,068)

RPR

1 **Moon Unit (IRE)**[202] 5644 5-9-9 106 WSupple 11 112
(H Rogers, Ire) *s.i.s and hld up in rr: hdwy under 2f out: chal 1f out: sn led: styd on wl* **9/1**[3]

2 *1* **Dandy Man (IRE)**[216] 5348 3-9-2 106 NGMcCullagh 10 107
(C Collins, Ire) *trckd ldrs on stand's side: impr to ld over 1f out: hdd ins fnl f: kpt on* **10/1**

3 *2* **Kingsdale Ocean (IRE)**[27] 751 3-8-13 94 TPO'Shea 8 97
(W M Roper, Ire) *prom: chal 2f out: led briefly 1 1/2f out: 3rd and kpt on ins fnl f* **9/1**[3]

4 *shd* **Peace Offering (IRE)**[21] 830 6-9-9 JMurtagh 12 101
(D Nicholls) *chsd ldrs: 5th and rdn 1 1/2f out: kpt on fnl f* **10/1**

5 *¾* **Senor Benny (USA)**[5] 1062 7-9-9 95 JAHeffernan 5 99
(M McDonagh, Ire) *hld up: 7th after 1/2-way: kpt on fnl f* **10/1**

6 *2* **Majestic Times (IRE)**[189] 5910 6-9-12 103 VRDeSouza 7 95
(Liam McAteer, Ire) *chsd ldrs: 4th and rdn after 1/2-way: lost pl 1 1/2f out: kpt on same pce fnl f* **9/2**[1]

7 *2* **Belleinga (IRE)**[5] 1062 5-9-6 86 (p) PJSmullen 6 82
(T F Lacy, Ire) *hld up in tch: no imp fr 1 1/2f out* **25/1**

8 *nk* **Bahamian Pirate (USA)**[10] 989 11-9-9 WMLordan 1 83
(D Nicholls) *s.i.s and hld up towards rr: sme prog whn nt clr run over 1f out: kpt on same pce* **5/1**[2]

9 *2* **Mother's Day**[180] 6085 3-8-10 74 FranciscoDaSilva 3 68
(Martin Browne, Ire) *trckd ldrs on far side: no ex fr under 2f out* **66/1**

10 *3* **Kay Two (IRE)**[13] 927 4-9-9 98 DPMcDonogh 4 66
(Ms F M Crowley, Ire) *disp ld: led briefly over 1 1/2f out: no ex whn eased fnl f* **16/1**

11 *½* **Osterhase (IRE)**[189] 5910 7-9-12 111 (b) FMBerry 2 67
(J E Mulhern, Ire) *disp ld: hdd over 1 1/2f out: eased fnl f* **5/1**[2]

12 *5* **Blue Dakota (IRE)**[268] 3878 4-9-9 102 KJManning 9 47
(J S Bolger, Ire) *trckd ldrs on outer: wknd fr 1 1/2f out* **11/1**

60.50 secs
WFA 3 from 4yo+ 10lb **12** Ran SP% **118.3**
CSF £95.75 TOTE £10.70: £2.80, £3.80, £2.50; DF 101.30.
Owner Mrs Paula Davison **Bred** Ivan W Allan **Trained** Ardee, Co. Louth
■ Stewards' Enquiry : J A Heffernan one-day ban: carelss riding (May 1)

NOTEBOOK
Moon Unit(IRE), in foal to Rock Of Gibraltar and a course and distance winner, came from well off the pace, showing a neat turn of foot to lead well inside the last. She should be able to add to this, although she is not the most consistent of performers. She will be kept busy, with a repeat win in the Group Three Greenlands Stakes next month the immediate target. (op 8/1)
Dandy Man(IRE), a fast colt, ran well, coming up the stands' side to take over with a furlong to run. He failed to match the winner's burst but it was a pleasing reappearance under a 3lb penalty.
Kingsdale Ocean(IRE) was in the front rank throughout and, although unable to quicken a second time, is better than a handicapper. (op 7/1)
Peace Offering(IRE) was going on again inside the last furlong after racing up with the pace throughout.
Senor Benny(USA) kept on without ever looking a possibility.
Majestic Times(IRE) lost his place with under two furlongs to race and then appeared to get his second wind. This was not too bad a reappearance. (op 6/1)
Belleinga(IRE) was a bit out of her depth.
Bahamian Pirate(USA) lost ground at the start and met with a bit of trouble with over a furlong to run. He just kept on at the one pace. (op 4/1)
Osterhase(IRE) was a big drifter in the market. He ran up front until headed a furlong and a half out and was eased. Official explanation: vet said gelding finished lame near fore (op 3/1)

1157 - 1160a (Foreign Racing) - See Raceform Interactive

1107 KEMPTON (A.W) (R-H)
Sunday, April 23

OFFICIAL GOING: Standard
Wind: Virtually nil

1161 DAY TIME, NIGHT TIME, GREAT TIME H'CAP 5f (P)
2:10 (2:11) (Class 4) (0-85,85) 3-Y-0+
£7,790 (£2,332; £1,166; £583; £291; £146) **Stalls** High

Form RPR

010 **1** **Silver Dane (IRE)**[2] 1125 4-9-0 71 oh1 (v) JohnEgan 8 80
(Mrs C A Dunnett) *chsd ldrs: drvn and str run fnl f to ld fnl 100yds* **17/2**

0-20 **2** *hd* **Golden Dixie (USA)**[4] 1076 7-10-0 **85** AdrianMcCarthy 4 93
(R A Harris) *hld up in rr: rapid hdwy over 1fout: chal betwen horses and led ins last: ct and no ex fnl 100yds* **5/1**[3]

0-24 **3** *1½* **Lindbergh**[21] 846 4-9-13 **84** RichardHughes 5 87
(R Hannon) *lw: s.i.s: sn trcking ldrs: drvn to take slt ld 1f out: hdd ins last: sn one pce* **5/2**[1]

1531 **4** *hd* **Mambazo**[32] 699 4-8-11 71 oh1 (e) AdamKirby(3) 6 73
(S C Williams) *lw: in tch: hdwy over 1f out: kpt on wl fnl f but nvr gng pce to chal* **7/1**

-000 **5** *½* **No Time (IRE)**[6] 1047 6-9-7 **78** MartinDwyer 7 78
(M J Polglase) *disp ld to 2f out: stl ev ch fr wl over 1f out: wknd ins last* **33/1**

605- **6** *½* **Salviati (USA)**[198] 5719 9-9-0 **71** RobertWinston 3 70
(J M Bradley) *s.i.s: rdn 2f out: hdwy over 1f out: kpt on ins last but nvr gng pce to trble ldrs* **20/1**

30-0 **7** *1* **Night Prospector**[21] 846 6-9-12 **83** RyanMoore 10 78
(G L Moore) *lw: disp ld tl slt but def advantage 2f out: hdd 1f out and sn wknd* **10/3**[2]

6322 **8** *½* **Sahara Silk (IRE)**[13] 954 5-8-11 71 oh4 (v) PatrickMathers(3) 2 64
(D Shaw) *lw: a outpcd but sme hdwy fnl f* **16/1**

0400 **9** *¾* **Clipper Hoy**[6] 1047 4-8-9 71 oh6 RichardKingscote(5) 1 62
(Mrs H Sweeting) *lw: dispute ld to 1/2-way: wknd over 1f out* **20/1**

000/ **10** *nk* **Silver Prelude**[570] 5893 5-9-6 **77** DaneO'Neill 9 67
(D K Ivory) *bkwd: outpced most of way* **66/1**

60.12 secs **Going Correction** +0.05s/f (Slow) **10** Ran SP% **111.2**
Speed ratings (Par 105):104,103,101,100,100 99,97,96,95,95
CSF £45.97 CT £133.42 TOTE £12.10: £3.10, £2.00, £1.30; EX 102.00.
Owner Mrs Christine Dunnett **Bred** Tally-Ho Stud **Trained** Hingham, Norfolk

FOCUS
A competitive handicap run at a good pace. Sound form.

1162 KEMPTON PARK PUNTERS CLUB FILLIES' H'CAP 1m 2f (P)
2:40 (2:40) (Class 4) (0-80,78) 3-Y-0+
£7,790 (£2,332; £1,166; £583; £291; £146) **Stalls** High

Form RPR

341- **1** **Let Slip**[204] 5602 4-9-5 **69** AlanMunro 5 78
(W Jarvis) *lw: keen early: sn trcking ldrs: chal fr 2f out tl slt ld 1f out: drvn and kpt on strly ins last* **15/2**

3011 **2** *1* **Marachi Band (USA)**[4] 1079 3-8-2 **69** 6ex (b) RichardMullen 3 73
(E J O'Neill) *sn chsng ldr: slt ld 2f out: sn rdn: narrowly hdd 1f out: kpt on same pce nr fin* **5/1**[3]

0-05 **3** *2* **Boot 'n Toot**[37] 660 5-9-12 **76** MartinDwyer 7 79
(C A Cyzer) *in tch: hdwy fr 3f out: rdn and effrt over 1f out: nvr gng pce to rch ldrs but kpt on wl for 3rd* **9/2**[2]

01-0 **4** *1¼* **Another Faux Pas (IRE)**[30] 711 5-9-3 **67** RyanMoore 2 68
(B G Powell) *bhd: rdn over 2f out: styd on u.p ins last but nvr gng pce to rch ldrs* **12/1**

40-0 **5** *1* **Uig**[37] 660 5-9-5 **69** DaneO'Neill 8 68
(H S Howe) *sn led: rdn 3f out: narrowly hdd 2f out: wknd fnl f* **16/1**

150- **6** *hd* **Danehill Dazzler (IRE)**[205] 5585 4-10-0 **78** ChrisCatlin 10 77
(Ian Williams) *lw: hld up in rr: drvn along over 2f oput: styd on u.p ins last but nvr in contention* **33/1**

502- **7** *hd* **Spectral Star**[235] 4864 4-9-10 **74** JamieSpencer 4 72+
(J R Fanshawe) *lw: t.k.h: chsd ldrs: rdn 2f out: nt pce to rch ldrs: wknd fnl f* **7/2**[1]

1- **8** *shd* **Quizzical Question (IRE)**[260] 4155 4-9-12 **76** NickyMackay 6 74
(L M Cumani) *b.bkwd: hld up in rr: t.k.h 1/2-way: drvn and sme hdwy fr 2f out: nt rch ldrs and wknd ins last* **9/2**[2]

150- **9** *2 ½* **Crystal Air (IRE)**[204] 5604 3-8-3 **75** .... JamesDoyle(5) 1 65
(Miss J Feilden) *bhd: sme hdwy over 3f out: nvr gng pce to rch ldrs: wknd over 1f out* **50/1**

0-00 **10** *1* **Tata Naka**[6] 1058 6-9-0 **64** oh18 .... HayleyTurner 11 56
(Mrs C A Dunnett) *bhd most of way* **50/1**

0-0 **11** *2* **Sweet Boulangere**[30] 712 3-7-13 **69** ow3 .... StephaneBreux(3) 9 54
(R Hannon) *chsd ldrs: rdn along 5f out: styd chsng ldrs tl wknd appr fnl f* **16/1**

2m 9.47s **Going Correction** +0.05s/f (Slow)
WFA 3 from 4yo+ 17lb 11 Ran SP% **113.3**
Speed ratings (Par 102):100,99,97,96,95 95,95,95,93,92 91
CSF £42.68 CT £187.20 TOTE £8.30: £2.50, £1.50, £2.10; EX 56.30.
Owner William Jarvis **Bred** John And Susan Davis **Trained** Newmarket, Suffolk

FOCUS
An interesting fillies' handicap featuring a few interesting, unexposed sorts.

1163 BOOK NOW FOR WEDNESDAY APRIL 26TH H'CAP 1m 4f (P)
3:10 (3:11) (Class 6) (0-65,64) 4-Y-0+ **£3,238** (£963; £481; £240) **Stalls** Low

Form RPR

3116 **1** **Turner's Touch**[12] 965 4-9-1 **60** ....(be) RyanMoore 11 69+
(G L Moore) *hld up in rr: stdy hdwy over 2f out: led over 1f out: hrd drvn and hung lft ins last: styd on* **5/1**[2]

00-1 **2** *1 ¾* **High Treason (USA)**[6] 1058 4-9-5 **64** 6ex .... PhilipRobinson 10 70
(W J Musson) *lw: bhd: hdwy and c wd to stands rail over 2f out: styd on to chse wnr ins last but a hld* **9/2**[1]

6131 **3** *2* **Competitor**[16] 904 5-9-2 **60** ....(v) TQuinn 13 63
(J Akehurst) *chsd ldr: chal 3f out: sn slt ld: rdn 2f out: hdd over 1f out: wknd and lost 2nd ins last* **9/1**

-506 **4** *nk* **Full Of Zest**[26] 780 4-9-2 **61** ....(b) IanMongan 3 64
(Mrs L J Mongan) *mid-div: rdn and outpcd over 2f out: kpt on again u.p fnl f but nvr gng pce to rch ldrs* **66/1**

3205 **5** *nk* **Amwell Brave**[12] 973 5-9-5 **63** .... RobertWinston 2 65
(J R Jenkins) *bhd: pushed along and hdwy 3f out: kpt on u.p fnl 2f but nvr gng pce to rch ldrs* **8/1**

000- **6** *3 ½* **Bullseye**[269] 3868 4-8-11 **56** .... DarrenWilliams 5 52
(A P Jarvis) *bit bkwd: chsd ldrs: rdn nd effrt 2f out: nvr gng pce to chal: wknd ins fnl f* **11/2**[3]

020- **7** *2* **Distant Cousin**[205] 5587 9-8-9 **58** ....(v) RichardKingscote(5) 4 51
(M A Buckley) *bhd: pushed along and hdwy on rails 3f out: nvr gng pce to rch ldrs: sayed on same pce fr over 1f out* **25/1**

3150 **8** *1 ¼* **Lady Pilot**[12] 973 4-8-12 **60** ....(v) RichardThomas(3) 1 51
(Dr J R J Naylor) *lw: t.k.h: in tch: rdn 3f out: wknd over 2f out* **50/1**

600- **9** *nk* **Rafelite**[159] 6356 4-9-1 **60** .... SebSanders 8 51
(Lady Herries) *lw: chsd ldrs: rdn to chal 4f out: wknd fr 2f out* **20/1**

0 **10** *shd* **Silvo (NZ)**[32] 697 7-8-13 **57** .... JohnEgan 12 48
(M F Harris) *chsd ldrs to 3f out: wknd ins fnl 2f* **100/1**

300- **11** *1* **Perfidious (USA)**[138] 6519 8-9-1 **62** ....(v) AmirQuinn(3) 14 51
(J R Boyle) *drvn to ld: narrowly hdd ins fnl 3f: wknd 2f out* **20/1**

441- **12** *2 ½* **Pleasant**[272] 3804 5-9-1 **59** .... JamieSpencer 6 44
(D P Keane) *nvr bttr than mid-div: nvr in contention* **12/1**

3033 **13** *19* **Master'n Commander**[30] 713 4-9-1 **60** .... MartinDwyer 9 15
(C A Cyzer) *nvr in contention and towards rr most of way* **5/1**[2]

-230 **14** *dist* **Ganymede**[48] 599 5-9-4 **62** .... FergusSweeney 7 —
(J G M O'Shea) *a bhd: lost tch fnl 4f* **25/1**

2m 34.76s (-8.24) **Going Correction** +0.05s/f (Slow)
WFA 4 from 5yo+ 1lb 14 Ran SP% **117.4**
Speed ratings (Par 101):109,107,106,106,106 103,102,101,101,101 100,99,86,—
CSF £24.87 CT £198.92 TOTE £5.70: £2.10, £2.00, £3.30; EX 25.20.
Owner The Wacko Partnership **Bred** Hedgeholme Stud **Trained** Woodingdean, E Sussex

FOCUS
A modest handicap dominated by in-form performers.
Rafelite Official explanation: jockey said filly made a noise
Perfidious(USA) Official explanation: jockey said gelding had no more to give
Pleasant Official explanation: jockey said mare hung right throughout
Master'n Commander Official explanation: jockey said gelding pulled hard early on
Ganymede Official explanation: jockey said gelding suffered interference early on and was never travelling

1164 R.H.T. H'CAP 1m (P)
3:40 (3:42) (Class 5) (0-70,70) 4-Y-0+ **£5,505** (£1,637; £818; £408) **Stalls** High

Form RPR

54-5 **1** **Ma'Am (USA)**[26] 780 4-9-2 **68** .... RyanMoore 12 76
(I A Wood) *hld up in rr: stl plenty to do over 2f out: rdn and qcknd smartly appr fnl f: led fnl 75yds: r.o strly* **25/1**

122- **2** *½* **Cross The Line (IRE)**[181] 6075 4-9-4 **70** .... JamieSpencer 5 79+
(A P Jarvis) *h.d.w: lw: t.k.h: hdwy 3f out: chal and edgd rt ins fnl 2f: sn led: hrd rdn and hdd fnl 75yds* **10/3**[1]

1123 **3** *1 ¼* **White Bear (FR)**[11] 985 4-9-1 **67** ....(b) RobertWinston 13 71
(C R Dore) *chsd ldrs: rdn and kpt on wl thrght fnl f but nvr gng pce to chal* **5/1**[3]

0000 **4** *nk* **Midshipman**[19] 882 8-8-8 **60** ....(vt) MartinDwyer 4 64
(A W Carroll) *lw: hld up in rr: gd hdwy on outside fr 2f out: fnished wl but nt rch ldrs* **14/1**

0600 **5** *nk* **Out For A Stroll**[6] 1057 7-8-8 **60** .... HayleyTurner 6 63
(S C Williams) *lw: bhd: pushed aong 4 out: hdwy on rails over 2f out: n.m.r over 1f out: kpt on ins last but nt rch ldrs* **40/1**

42-3 **6** *¾* **Torquemada (IRE)**[30] 711 5-8-8 **63** .... AdamKirby(3) 11 64
(W Jarvis) *mid-div: hdwy on rails over 2f out and sn ev ch: one pce ins fnl f* **9/2**[2]

0-60 **7** *1 ½* **Jools**[13] 950 8-8-6 **58** .... TQuinn 1 56
(D K Ivory) *bhd: hday fr 2f out but nvr in contention* **14/1**

6642 **8** *nk* **Barton Sands (IRE)**[16] 904 9-8-7 **59** ....(t) J-PGuillambert 2 56
(Ernst Oertel) *bhd: rdn and hdwy over 3f out: chsd ldrs 2f out and sn one pce* **10/1**

0-00 **9** *1 ¾* **Rawaabet (IRE)**[6] 1051 4-9-1 **67** .... ChrisCatlin 3 60
(P W Hiatt) *chsd ldrs: chal 3f out tl over 2f out: sn wknd* **16/1**

000- **10** *5* **Finished Article (IRE)**[188] 5948 9-9-4 **70** .... LPKeniry 10 52
(W J Musson) *s.i.s: nvr in contention* **25/1**

15-0 **11** *4* **Burhaan (IRE)**[27] 764 4-8-13 **68** ....(t) AmirQuinn(3) 7 40+
(J R Boyle) *chsd ldrs: slt ld ins fnl 3f: hdd ins fnl 2f and sn wknd* **14/1**

626- **12** *3* **Catskill**[232] 4944 4-9-1 **67** .... RichardMullen 8 33
(E F Vaughan) *chsd ldrs: rdn 3f out: wknd over 2f out* **10/1**

2000 **13** *1 ¾* **Elrafa Mujahid**[8] 1015 4-9-0 **69** ....(b) SaleemGolam(3) 14 30
(Ernst Oertel) *led: hdd ins fnl 3f: wkng whn hung rt and hmpd over 2f out* **33/1**

1m 39.68s (-2.30) **Going Correction** +0.05s/f (Slow) 13 Ran SP% **115.1**
Speed ratings (Par 103):107,106,105,104,104 103,102,102,100,95 91,88,86
CSF £100.29 CT £514.76 TOTE £33.00: £7.10, £1.70, £1.50; EX 113.20.
Owner Neardown Stables **Bred** Belgrave Bloodstock **Trained** Upper Lambourn, Berks

FOCUS
A modest heat run at a strong early gallop, which played into the hands of the winner, who gets much further than a mile.

1165 KEMPTON FOR WEDDINGS MAIDEN STKS (DIV I) 7f (P)
4:10 (4:11) (Class 4) 3-Y-0+ **£5,181** (£1,541; £770; £384) **Stalls** High

Form RPR

1 **Massaro Pape (IRE)** 4-9-11 .... NickyMackay 5 74+
(L M Cumani) *wl grwn: lw: hld up in rr: gd hdwy over 2f out to ld appr fnl f: kpt on wl* **9/2**[2]

2 *1 ½* **Reballo (IRE)** 3-8-12 .... JamieSpencer 9 65+
(J R Fanshawe) *cmpt: strong: b.bkwd: s.i.s: bhd: smooth hdwy whn n.m.r 2f out: qckdn ins last to take 2nd cl home but nt rch wnr: improve* **2/1**[1]

44 **3** *½* **Lisathedaddy**[16] 900 4-9-6 .... HayleyTurner 11 64
(B G Powell) *chsd ldrs: led jst ins fnl 2f: hdd appr fnl f: sn outpcd by wnr: lost 2nd cl home* **6/1**[3]

505- **4** *5* **Arian's Lad**[186] 5975 5-9-11 53 .... FrancisFerris 6 56
(B Palling) *chsd ldr: chal 3f out: led over 2f out:hdd jst ins fnl quarter m: wknd ins last* **16/1**

06- **5** *nk* **Spanish Story**[172] 6228 3-8-7 .... RyanMoore 8 45
(A M Balding) *bhd: gd hdwy over 3f out: trckd ldrs 2f out: shkn up and one pce ins last* **11/1**

00- **6** *nk* **Dado Mush**[176] 6156 3-8-12 .... SamHitchcott 14 49
(T T Clement) *chsd ldrs: rdn 3f out: wknd fnl f* **66/1**

7 *4* **Press The Button (GER)** 3-8-12 .... PatCosgrave 10 39+
(J R Boyle) *leggy: scope: chsd ldrs: rdn 3f out: wknd fr 2f out* **33/1**

00- **8** *1* **Moonlight (GER)**[237] 4809 3-8-4 .... RichardThomas(3) 1 31
(Dr J R J Naylor) *bhd: pushed along over 2f out: styd on fr over 1f out but nvr in contention* **100/1**

05- **9** *1 ½* **Gateland**[196] 5753 3-8-12 .... TQuinn 3 33
(W R Swinburn) *bhd: racd on outside and nvr in contention* **6/1**[3]

00- **10** *shd* **Mystic Storm**[193] 5832 3-8-12 .... SebSanders 4 32
(Lady Herries) *lw: a in rr and nvr in contention* **20/1**

4064 **11** *½* **Spanish Music**[18] 890 4-9-6 45 .... RobertHavlin 12 31
(R Ingram) *chsd ldrs: rdn 3f out: sn btn* **25/1**

003- **12** *4* **Pyramid**[207] 5543 4-9-11 54 .... JohnEgan 7 26
(P L Gilligan) *rr: drvn and effrt on outside 3f out: nt rch ldrs: fdd fnl 2f* **16/1**

0000 **13** *hd* **Zambezi River**[21] 844 7-9-11 35 .... MickyFenton 13 25
(J M Bradley) *slt ld tl hdd ins fnl 2f: sn wknd* **100/1**

14 *2* **Grand Palace (IRE)** 3-8-9 .... PatrickMathers(3) 2 15
(D Shaw) *strong: b.bkwd: a in rr* **20/1**

1m 26.36s (-1.90) **Going Correction** +0.05s/f (Slow)
WFA 3 from 4yo+ 13lb 14 Ran SP% **120.0**
Speed ratings (Par 105):104,102,101,96,95 95,90,89,87,87 87,82,82,80
CSF £12.87 TOTE £5.50: £2.80, £1.30, £1.90; EX 14.90.
Owner Equibreed S.R.L. **Bred** Franco Giacopalli **Trained** Newmarket, Suffolk

FOCUS
A maiden lacking strength in depth and the slower of the two divisions by 0.53sec. While the first two are likely to rate higher in future, the bare form is ordinary.
Pyramid Official explanation: jockey said gelding had no more to give

1166 KEMPTON FOR WEDDINGS MAIDEN STKS (DIV II) 7f (P)
4:40 (4:43) (Class 4) 3-Y-0+ **£5,181** (£1,541; £770; £384) **Stalls** High

Form RPR

42- **1** **Deepwater Bay (USA)**[196] 5752 3-8-12 .... MartinDwyer 14 82
(A M Balding) *lw: chsd ldrs: wnt 2nd 2f out: drvn to ld jst ins fnl f: kpt on strly cl home* **13/2**[3]

3- **2** *1* **Escape Clause (USA)**[176] 6142 3-8-12 .... RyanMoore 6 79+
(Sir Michael Stoute) *lw: trckd ldrs: gng wl whn led ins fnl 2f: shkn up and hdd jst ins last: kpt on but nt a hld cl home* **4/9**[1]

3 *7* **Titian Dancer** 3-8-12 .... TQuinn 12 61+
(W R Swinburn) *rangy: lw: in tch: hdwy 2f out: but edgd lft and rn green: stl green but styd on wl for 3rd fnl f but no ch w 1st two* **5/1**[2]

4 *3* **Neardown Queen** 3-8-2 .... JamesDoyle(5) 11 48
(I A Wood) *unf: in tch: rdn snd styd on same pce fnl 2f* **66/1**

50 **5** *¾* **Fleur A Lay (USA)**[17] 897 4-9-6 .... KDarley 3 51
(Mrs A J Perrett) *lw: in tch: chsd ldrs and pushed aloing 3f out: one pce and no ch fnl 2f* **50/1**

00 **6** *nk* **Must Be Keen**[17] 897 7-9-11 .... JohnEgan 7 55
(Ernst Oertel) *led after 1f: hdd ins fnl 2f: sn wknd* **100/1**

55- **7** *1 ½* **Southport Star (IRE)**[194] 5817 3-8-12 .... JamieSpencer 4 46
(J R Fanshawe) *hld up in rr: styd on fnl 2f: nvr in contention* **14/1**

5 **8** *1 ¾* **Lady Ambitious**[21] 844 3-8-7 .... ChrisCatlin 1 37
(D K Ivory) *slowly away: bhd: styd on fnl 2f: nvr in contention* **40/1**

4 **9** *½* **Crafty Fox**[29] 722 3-8-12 .... DarrenWilliams 10 40
(A P Jarvis) *lw: bhd: styd on fnl 2f: nvr in contention* **20/1**

00 **10** *nk* **Maya's Prince**[16] 900 4-9-11 .... HayleyTurner 5 45
(M D I Usher) *bhd: styd on fnl 2f: nvr in contention* **100/1**

00-0 **11** *½* **Peak Seasons (IRE)**[24] 807 3-8-12 60 .... MickyFenton 9 38
(W De Best-Turner) *led 1f: styd chsng ldr to 3f out: sn wknd* **66/1**

500- **12** *¾* **Compton Flyer**[240] 4725 3-8-12 54 .... DaneO'Neill 8 36
(J M Bradley) *ken hold in rr: a bhd* **66/1**

0P-6 **13** *¾* **Ferrando**[16] 900 4-9-11 .... TPQueally 13 39
(D J Daly) *chsd ldrs early: grad lost pl fnl 3f* **66/1**

60 **14** *shd* **Riolo (IRE)**[21] 844 4-9-8 .... AdamKirby(3) 2 39
(K F Clutterbuck) *a in rr* **100/1**

1m 25.83s (-2.43) **Going Correction** +0.05s/f (Slow)
WFA 3 from 4yo+ 13lb 14 Ran SP% **124.0**
Speed ratings (Par 105):107,105,97,94,93 93,91,89,88,88 88,87,86,86
CSF £9.77 TOTE £7.10: £1.50, £1.10, £2.20; EX 11.30.
Owner E N Kronfeld **Bred** Justice Farm, Greg Justice & Steve Justice **Trained** Kingsclere, Hants

FOCUS
Few could be fancied for this maiden. It was the quicker of the two divisions and the first two pulled nicely clear.
Must Be Keen Official explanation: jockey said gelding had no more to give

1167 KEMPTON.CO.UK H'CAP — 2m (P)

5:10 (5:11) (Class 3) (0-95,92) 4-Y-O+

£7,790 (£2,332; £1,166; £583; £291; £146) **Stalls** High

Form — RPR

10-3 **1** **Sirce (IRE)**[25] [799] 4-9-5 **84**............(v) JimmyQuinn 4 — 94+
(D J Coakley) *lw: hld up rr and confidently rdn: smooth hdwy fr 3f out: qcknd to ld appr fnl f: kpt on wl: readily* — **8/1**

11P- **2** 3 ½ **The Nawab (IRE)**[169] [6250] 4-9-10 **89**............IanMongan 1 — 95+
(J L Dunlop) *lw: hld up rr but in tch: pushed along and styd on wl fr 2f out to chse wnr ins last but no imp* — **8/1**

1510 **3** 2 ½ **Llamadas**[22] [832] 4-8-8 **80**............LukeMorris(7) 2 — 83
(C Roberts) *t.k.h: chsd ldrs: drvn to ld over 2f out: hdd appr fnl f: sn no ch w wnr and lost 2nd ins last* — **8/1**

-241 **4** 1 ½ **Montosari**[22] [838] 7-8-8 **69**............JamieSpencer 6 — 70
(P Mitchell) *lw: chsd ldr: led 9f out: hdd over 2f out: sn outpcd* — **9/2**[3]

4413 **5** 3 **Champagne Shadow (IRE)**[8] [1021] 5-9-6 **81**............(b) RyanMoore 3 — 79
(G L Moore) *bhd: pushed along and outpcd 1/2-way: nvr gng pce to rch ldrs fnl 4f* — **10/3**[2]

02-6 **6** ½ **Hiddensee (USA)**[8] [1021] 4-9-13 **92**............KDarley 5 — 89
(M Johnston) *sn led: hdd 9f out: sn drvn along: chal 6f out to 5f out: wknd fnl 2f* — **5/2**[1]

205/ **7** shd **North Lodge (GER)**[10] 6-9-5 **80**............RichardHughes 7 — 77
(A King) *lw: chsd ldrs: stl wl there 2f out: wknd fnl f* — **10/1**

3m 36.55s **Going Correction** +0.05s/f (Slow)
WFA 4 from 5yo+ 4lb — **7** Ran SP% **112.3**
Speed ratings (Par 107): 89,87,86,85,83 83,83
CSF £65.43 TOTE £8.80: £4.00, £2.00; EX 47.80 Place 6 £12.83, Place 5 £7.70.
Owner Dorothy & Ivan Topley **Bred** W P Churchward, D J Bloodstock And C Hue-Will **Trained** West Ilsley, Berks

FOCUS
A fairly decent handicap rated through the third. They went a good gallop.

NOTEBOOK
Sirce(IRE), suited by the decent gallop, travelled well off the pace and picked up in style to win fairly impressively. This was her first attempt at a staying distance and she is open to further improvement at the trip, but to be seen at her best she may well be reliant on others going off too quick. (op 7-1 tchd 9-1)
The Nawab(IRE), running on the All-Weather for the first time, stayed on well in the closing stages and, although currently on a career-high mark, he looks capable of further progress this season. (op 7-1)
Llamadas, more exposed than the first two, ran close to his best in third and will have to find some improvement from somewhere to defy his current career-high mark. (op 10-1)
Montosari, up in grade, is another about whom the Handicapper knows plenty. He was up with the decent gallop throughout and was not disgraced in the circumstances. (tchd 4-1)
Champagne Shadow(IRE), who ran well in the Queen's Prize over this course and distance last time, failed to land a blow. (op 3-1 tchd 7-2)
Hiddensee(USA) again ran as though finding two miles a bit too far. His best form on turf last season was with some cut in the ground. (op 3-1)
North Lodge(GER), an ex-German Flat performer, was fit from hurdling and only dropped out of things inside the final furlong. He is not one to give up on. (op 15-2 tchd 11-1)
T/Plt: £12.50 to a £1 stake. Pool: £48,918.70. 2,844.80 winning tickets. T/Qpdt: £3.20 to a £1 stake. Pool: £2,877.60. 654.80 winning tickets. ST

1168 - 1170a (Foreign Racing) - See Raceform Interactive

[1022]LEOPARDSTOWN (L-H)

Sunday, April 23

OFFICIAL GOING: Good to firm

1171a HERITAGE STKS (LISTED RACE) (C&G) — 1m

4:15 (4:15) 4-Y-O+ — **£22,448** (£6,586; £3,137; £1,068)

RPR

1 **Mustameet (USA)**[14] [930] 5-9-5 109............DPMcDonogh 4 — 113
(Kevin Prendergast, Ire) *in tch: 4th 1/2-way: 2nd and hdwy ent st: led 1f out: kpt on wl u.p* — **9/4**[1]

2 ½ **Hard Rock City (USA)**[168] [6270] 6-9-0 106............NGMcCullagh 9 — 107
(M J Grassick, Ire) *hld up in rr: hdwy ent st: 3rd over 1f out: 2nd and chal ins fnl f: kpt on wl* — **7/2**[2]

3 ¾ **Democratic Deficit (IRE)**[80] [281] 4-9-5 109............(t) KJManning 1 — 111
(J S Bolger, Ire) *hld up towards rr: 6th and hdwy 1 1/2f out: 3rd and kpt on wl cl home* — **6/1**

4 1 **Bawaader (IRE)**[6] [1963] 4-9-0 103............(b) PJSmullen 5 — 104
(D K Weld, Ire) *cl 3rd: led appr 1/2-way: strly pressed st: hdd 1f out: sn no ex* — **5/1**[3]

5 1 ½ **Bobs Pride (IRE)**[28] [754] 4-9-5 101............TPO'Shea 3 — 106
(D K Weld, Ire) *chsd ldrs in 5th: 3rd and effrt ent st: no ex fr 1 1/2f out* — **16/1**

6 4 ½ **Indesatchel (IRE)**[14] [930] 4-9-5 112............WMLordan 6 — 97
(David Wachman, Ire) *trckd ldrs: 5th 1/2-way: 4th into st: wknd fr 1 1/2f out* — **7/1**

7 4 **Fit The Cove (IRE)**[28] [754] 6-9-0 102............WSupple 2 — 84
(H Rogers, Ire) *led and disp: hdd appr 1/2-way: wknd st* — **20/1**

8 12 **Bective Ranger (IRE)**[212] [5443] 4-9-0 93............JAHeffernan 7 — 60
(Peter Casey, Ire) *led and disp: hdd appr 1/2-way: wknd appr st* — **25/1**

1m 39.1s **Going Correction** -0.45s/f (Firm) — **9** Ran SP% **110.9**
Speed ratings: 108,107,106,105,104 99,95,83
CSF £9.42 TOTE £3.00: £1.40, £1.80, £1.50; DF 7.60.
Owner Hamdan Al Maktoum **Bred** Shadwell Farm LLC **Trained** Friarstown, Co Kildare

NOTEBOOK
Mustameet(USA), purported to have lost a couple of teeth when banging his head leaving the stalls in the Gladness Stakes, appreciated this fast ground and got first run when quickening to lead a furlong out. (op 2/1)
Hard Rock City(USA) had every chance after exaggerated waiting tactics looked to have given him a bit too much to do. He ran on strongly but was not able to match the winner. (op 3/1)
Democratic Deficit(IRE), who was also held up in the rear, ran on strongly but all too late. (op 7/1)
Bawaader(IRE), fresh from two handicap wins and 19lb higher, continued his rate of improvement. In front before halfway, he was cut down by the winner's turn of foot but kept on well.
Bobs Pride(IRE), last season's Ballysax winner, showed a return to form on only his second Flat start since the Irish 2000 Guineas. He wore blinkers in the Lincoln, but not here. (op 16/1 tchd 20/1)
Indesatchel(IRE) ran with the pace to the straight but weakened from two furlongs out. He would not have appreciated this changed ground but remains disappointing. (op 6/1)

1172a P.W. MCGRATH MEMORIAL BALLYSAX STKS (GROUP 3) — 1m 2f

4:45 (4:45) 3-Y-O — **£31,427** (£9,220; £4,393; £1,496)

RPR

1 **Rhythm'n Roots (IRE)**[168] [6271] 3-9-1 103............(t) KJManning 6 — 107+
(J S Bolger, Ire) *chsd ldr in 2nd: chal early st: led 1 1/2f out: sn strly pressed: kpt on wl u.p fnl f: all out* — **10/1**

2 nk **Golden Arrow (IRE)**[217] [5346] 3-9-1 111............PJSmullen 1 — 106+
(D K Weld, Ire) *mod 3rd: drvn along and hdwy 3f out: cl 2nd and chal over 1f out: ev ch: jst failed* — **11/4**[2]

3 1 ½ **Altius (IRE)**[196] [5779] 3-9-1 103............WMLordan 4 — 103+
(A P O'Brien, Ire) *led: clr 1/2-way: strly pressed ent st: hdd 1 1/2f out: 3rd and no ex fnl f* — **10/3**[3]

4 1 ½ **Mountain (IRE)**[168] [6271] 3-9-1 93............JAHeffernan 3 — 101
(A P O'Brien, Ire) *hld up in rr: 5th and prog 3f out: 4th and kpt on fr over 1f out* — **9/4**[1]

5 3 ½ **Chiado (IRE)**[28] [755] 3-9-1 95............DPMcDonogh 5 — 94
(Kevin Prendergast, Ire) *mod 4th: rdn and no imp 3f out: wknd fr 1 1/2f out* — **8/1**

6 1 ½ **Jioconda (IRE)**[14] [928] 3-8-12 99............JMurtagh 2 — 89
(Edward Lynam, Ire) *hld up in 5th: wknd appr st* — **14/1**

2m 5.90s **Going Correction** -0.25s/f (Firm) — **6** Ran SP% **107.4**
Speed ratings: 108,107,106,105,102 101
CSF £34.28 TOTE £11.00: £2.70, £1.70; DF 13.50.
Owner Val Joyce **Bred** D H W Dobson **Trained** Coolcullen, Co Carlow

NOTEBOOK
Rhythm'n Roots(IRE) ran second until getting on top a furlong and a half down. He responded well to pressure and just managed to hold on. Despite seven runs last season, including two nursery defeats, he is not easy to assess. Ground seems to make little difference to him but he certainly seems to appreciate distance. (op 12/1)
Golden Arrow(IRE) has not grown much but he is tough. Ridden to get into a challenging position in the straight, he put in a sustained effort throughout the last furlong but could not manage to get on top. (op 2/1)
Altius(IRE) boasted the better public form of the Ballydoyle pair and went off in front. Still clear before the straight, he was headed over a furlong and a half out and kept on to the end despite an inability to quicken. (op 7/2 tchd 3/1)
Mountain(IRE), the other Ballydoyle runner, started a surprise favourite. Held up in the rear and well off the pace, he made a forward move well before the straight but it was not carrying him anywhere and he was a one-paced fourth over the last furlong. (op 11/4 tchd 3/1)

1173 - 1174a (Foreign Racing) - See Raceform Interactive

CAPANNELLE (R-H)

Sunday, April 23

OFFICIAL GOING: Good to soft

1175a PREMIO PARIOLI ABN AMRO BANK (GROUP 2) (ENTIRE COLTS) — 1m

3:45 (4:00) 3-Y-O — **£86,762** (£42,353; £24,328; £12,164)

RPR

1 **Rattle And Hum (ITY)** 3-9-2............SLandi 5 — 109
(L Camici, Italy) *raced in 4th to straight, tracked leader over 2f out, led over 1f out, ran on well* — **19/10**[2]

2 1 ¼ **Royal Power (IRE)**[22] [829] 3-9-2............TedDurcan 9 — 106
(M R Channon) *held up, 8th straight, moved outside, stayed on well final f, nearest at finish* — **31/10**[3]

3 2 **Adorabile Fong**[182] [6052] 3-9-2............FSpanu 6 — 102
(M Guarnieri, Italy) *held up in rear, 7th straight, switched outside, stayed on final 2f, nearest at finish* — **56/10**

4 2 ½ **Sgiaff**[28] [758] 3-9-2............MMonteriso 3 — 97
(A & G Botti, Italy) *held up, headway over 3f out, moved outside 2f out, stayed on to take 4th last stride* — **22/1**

5 nse **Magic Box (ITY)**[28] [758] 3-9-2............MDemuro 1 — 97
(F & L Brogi, Italy) *raced keenly, set good pace, led to over 1f out, weakened final furlong* — **8/5**[1]

6 nse **Re Barolo (IRE)** 3-9-2............EBotti 11 — 97
(A & G Botti, Italy) *last early, some progress final 2f, never nearer* — **34/1**

7 1 **Margine Rosso (IRE)** 3-9-2............(b) MPasquale 2 — 95
(R Brogi, Italy) *raced in 3rd to straight, 4th 2 1/2f out, weakened 2f out* — **10/1**

8 2 **Carlomagno (IRE)**[182] [6052] 3-9-2............SMulas 7 — 91
(B Grizzetti, Italy) *5th straight, soon beaten* — **96/1**

9 2 **Mr Hicks (IRE)** 3-9-2............FBranca 10 — 87
(F & L Brogi, Italy) *always towards rear* — **8/5**[1]

10 1 ½ **Great Uncle Ted (USA)**[309] [2733] 3-9-2............DVargiu 8 — 84
(B Grizzetti, Italy) *hampered after 3f, 6th straight, beaten over 2f out* — **11/1**

11 4 **Thinking Robins (IRE)** 3-9-2............(b) PAragoni 4 — 76
(P Martometti, Italy) *tracked leader to straight, weakening when hampered 2f out* — **146/10**

1m 36.9s — **11** Ran SP% **183.0**
(including 1 euro stake): WIN 2.90; PL 1.45, 1.67, 1.82; DF 8.30.
Owner Scuderia San Valentino **Bred** Azienda Agricola Loreto Luciani **Trained** Italy

NOTEBOOK
Rattle And Hum(ITY), always going well, moved up behind the leader two and a half furlongs from home and took over inside the final 300 yards. He stayed on well and is clearly the leading home candidate for the Derby Italiano on May 21.
Royal Power(IRE), held up towards the rear while Magic Box set a strong pace, was moved to the outside early in the straight. He stayed on in good style in the closing stages but never looked likely to worry the winner.
Adorabile Fong, who made fair progress from the back, will take on the winner again in the Derby. Although there is stamina on the dam's side, he has never looked the type for 12 furlongs.

KREFELD (R-H)

Sunday, April 23

OFFICIAL GOING: Good

1176a PREIS DER WIRTSCHAFTSFORDERUNGSGESELLSCHAFT KREFELD MBH - DR BUSCH-MEMORIAL (GROUP 3) 1m 110y

3:05 (3:18) 3-Y-O **£22,069** (£6,897; £3,448; £2,069)

				RPR
1		**Aspectus (IRE)**[189] 5931 3-9-2 ... ADeVries 3 (H Blume, Germany) *raced in 3rd to straight, led over 1f out, pushed out*	**6/5**[1]	104
2	3/4	**Lord Of England (GER)**[189] 5935 3-9-2 ... ASuborics 7 (Mario Hofer, Germany) *held up in rear early, 5th straight, switched outside 2f out, stayed on under strong pressure, nearest at finish*	**19/2**	102
3	hd	**Oriental Tiger (GER)**[189] 5931 3-9-2 ...(b) ABoschert 1 (U Ostmann, Germany) *held up, 6th straight, stayed on from over 1f out, nearest at finish*	**28/10**[2]	102
4	1 1/2	**Mannico (GER)**[189] 5931 3-9-2 ... AStarke 5 (Mario Hofer, Germany) *tracked leader, led 2f out to over 1f out, one pace*	**4/1**[3]	99
5	5	**World's Mission (GER)**[189] 5931 3-9-2 ... AHelfenbein 2 (Mario Hofer, Germany) *mid-division to half-way, 3rd straight, some progress final f*	**81/10**	89
6	shd	**Mharadono (GER)**[202] 5679 3-9-2 ... TMundry 4 (P Hirschberger, Germany) *led to 2f out*	**20/1**	89
7	shd	**Naxon (GER)**[224] 5165 3-9-2 ... EPedroza 6 (W Baltromei, Germany) *close up 5f, last straight*	**104/10**	89
8	4 1/2	**Silex (GER)**[171] 6240 3-9-2 ... WMongil 8 (P Schiergen, Germany) *7th straight, always in rear*	**13/1**	89

1m 47.97s **8** Ran SP% **133.0**

(including 10 euro stakes): WIN 22.00; PL 11.00, 18.00, 14.00;SF 147.00.

Owner Gestut Rottgen **Bred** Gestut Roettgen **Trained** Germany

NOTEBOOK

Aspectus(IRE) was always going best in the straight and should handle his two closest pursuers again when they reoppose in the Mehl Mulhens Rennen-German 2000 on May 14. His first Group One target is the Prix du Jockey-Club.

1064 LONGCHAMP (R-H)

Sunday, April 23

OFFICIAL GOING: Good

1177a PRIX DE LA GROTTE (GROUP 3) (FILLIES) 1m

2:20 (2:21) 3-Y-O **£27,586** (£11,034; £8,276; £5,517; £2,759)

				RPR
1		**Daltaya (FR)**[17] 3-9-0 ... CSoumillon 4 (A De Royer-Dupre, France) *broke well, led for 1 1/2f, led again entering straight, hard ridden over 1f out, driven out*	**34/10**[2]	109
2	3/4	**Quiet Royal (USA)**[173] 6219 3-9-0 ... OPeslier 2 (Mme C Head-Maarek, France) *held up behind leaders, 4th straight, switched left approaching final f, ran on to take 2nd close home*	**4/5**[1]	108+
3	1/2	**Price Tag**[223] 5193 3-9-0 ... TThulliez 6 (P Bary, France) *raced in 3rd to straight, soon chasing winner, one pace final f & lost 2nd close home*	**10/1**	107
4	nk	**Queen Cleopatra (IRE)**[14] 928 3-9-0 ... KFallon 1 (A P O'Brien, Ire) *raced in 6th to straight, went 4th on inside over 1f out, one pace final f*	**10/1**	106
5	snk	**Galma (FR)**[26] 3-9-0 ... SPasquier 8 (E Lellouche, France) *raced in 7th to straight, headway on outside to dispute 4th over 1f out, one pace final f*	**17/2**	106
6	3/4	**On A Cloud (USA)**[27] 773 3-9-0 ... TJarnet 3 (A Fabre, France) *raced in 5th to straight, never able to challenge*	**73/10**[3]	104
7	3	**Ikra (FR)**[17] 3-9-0 ... RonanThomas 9 (X Guigand, France) *held up in rear, last straight, hard ridden over 1f out, never a factor*	**54/1**	98
8	8	**Beau Monde**[70] 392 3-9-0 ... C-PLemaire 5 (H-A Pantall, France) *raced in 8th to straight, soon ridden & beaten*	**21/1**	82
9	20	**Ring Hill**[224] 3-9-0 ... OPlacais 7 (Mme C Head-Maarek, France) *ridden to lead over 6f out, headed entering straight, eased*	**4/5**[1]	42

1m 38.3s **9** Ran SP% **181.0**

PARI-MUTUEL: WIN 4.40; PL 1.20, 1.10, 2.00; DF 4.10.

Owner H H Aga Khan **Bred** S A Aga Khan **Trained** Chantilly, France

NOTEBOOK

Daltaya(FR) looked much straighter on this occasion and won staying on at the end. She took the lead early in the straight and kept up the gallop until the line, lengthening her stride rather than accelerating, and is certainly a filly going the right way. Connections will look at the Pouliches but will also take the longer Prix Saint-Alary into consideration.

Quiet Royal(USA) finished best of all, having looked to have a hopeless task halfway up the straight. After one slap from her jockey, she quickened impressively inside the final furlong and this race will certainly have taken her to a peak for the Pouliches. This was an excellent trial and she has certainly trained on.

Price Tag, who had not been out since a disappointing run seven months previously, put up a decent performance. Always well up, she stayed on well in the straight before losing second place in the last 50 yards. She is sure to improve for this outing and is another to have been marked down for the Pouliches.

Queen Cleopatra(IRE) was putting her best work in at the end. She was outpaced a little in the straight before coming with a run up the far rail and certainly looks like a filly who will stay further than a mile.

1178a PRIX DE FONTAINEBLEAU (GROUP 3) (COLTS) 1m

2:50 (2:52) 3-Y-O **£27,586** (£11,034; £8,276; £5,517; £2,759)

				RPR
1		**Stormy River (FR)**[19] 884 3-9-2 ... TThulliez 8 (N Clement, France) *tracked leader to straight, led 2f out, pushed clear over 1f out, ran on strongly*	**10/1**	113+
2	4	**Light Of Joy (FR)**[34] 3-9-2 ... DBonilla 9 (R Pritchard-Gordon, France) *soon led, raced keenly to half-way, headed 2f out, kept on one pace under pressure final f*	**60/1**	105
3	nk	**Dream In Blue (FR)**[27] 774 3-9-2 ... JAuge 5 (Robert Collet, France) *mid-division, 6th on inside straight, went 3rd approaching final f, kept on same pace*	**38/1**	104
4	3/4	**Spirito Del Vento (FR)**[203] 5650 3-9-2 ... OPeslier 7 (J-M Beguigne, France) *last to half-way, 7th straight, stayed on at one pace on outside final 2f*	**29/1**	103
5	3/4	**Aussie Rules (USA)**[206] 5572 3-9-2 ... KFallon 10 (A P O'Brien, Ire) *held-up, last straight, headway on outside from over 1f out, nearest at finish*	**5/1**[2]	101
6	snk	**Carlotamix (FR)**[175] 6188 3-9-2 ... CSoumillon 6 (A Fabre, France) *soon well in touch on outside, 3rd straight, soon one pace*	**1/2**[1]	101
7	nk	**Porto Santo (FR)**[27] 774 3-9-2 ... SPasquier 3 (P Demercastel, France) *pulled early, raced in 5th, 4th straight, kept on one pace final 2f*	**53/10**[3]	101
8	1 1/2	**Ivan Denisovich (IRE)**[176] 6163 3-9-2 ... CO'Donoghue 1 (A P O'Brien, Ire) *held up, 9th straight, never a factor*	**5/1**[2]	98
9	nk	**Royal Mirage (FR)**[172] 3-9-2 ... C-PLemaire 2 (P Bary, France) *first to show, held up in 3rd, 5th straight, 3rd approaching final f, gradually weakened*	**17/1**	97
10	snk	**Major Grace (FR)**[40] 3-9-2 ... FBlondel 4 (Mme J Laurent-Joye Rossi, France) *pulled early, restrained towards rear, 8th straight, never a factor*	**48/1**	97

1m 38.2s **10** Ran SP% **140.1**

PARI-MUTUEL: WIN 11.30; PL 3.20, 11.60, 7.50; DF 204.50.

Owner Ecurie Mister Ess A S **Bred** J & Mlle Marie-Laure Collet **Trained** Chantilly, France

NOTEBOOK

Stormy River(FR) put up an excellent performance and has trained on to become a top-class three-year-old. He was never far from the lead and always travelling easily. At the head of affairs soon after entering the straight, he surged clear of his rivals to win on his own. He has now proved he can act on any ground and will be aimed at the Poulains.

Light Of Joy(FR) ran here in preference to a handicap at Newmarket the previous Thursday. For a long time he was at the head of affairs and ran quite freely, and the lead was taken off him soon after entering the straight, but he ran on very courageously to the line. The Poulains is not being considered for him.

Dream In Blue(FR), a consistent individual, won a couple of races at Cagnes earlier in the season. He was held up for much of this race and ran on well up the far rail from a furlong and a half out.

Spirito Del Vento(FR), who was given permission not to parade in the paddock and went to the post on his own, was slowly into his stride. He came with a progressive run from a furlong and a half out, was slightly hampered towards the end of this race, and was promoted to fourth as a result. The outing will have done him good.

Aussie Rules(USA) was well behind early on and came with a late run up the centre of the track. He was demoted for hanging slightly right and causing minor interference to the fifth.

Carlotamix(FR), who has not grown much, proved very disappointing, looking very one-paced in the straight.

1179a PRIX LA FORCE (GROUP 3) 1m 2f

3:20 (3:23) 3-Y-O **£27,586** (£11,034; £6,897; £6,897; £2,759)

				RPR
1		**Barastraight**[39] 3-9-2 ... IMendizabal 4 (J-C Rouget, France) *raced in 5th to straight, ridden over 1f out, driven to lead close home*	**64/10**	105
2	nk	**Echoes Rock (GER)**[17] 3-9-2 ... TJarnet 5 (A Fabre, France) *soon tracking leader, 2nd straight, led 1f out til caught close home*	**23/10**[2]	104
3	1/2	**Irish Wells (FR)**[36] 672 3-9-2 ... DBoeuf 1 (F Rohaut, France) *led to 1f out, kept on under pressure*	**21/1**	103
4	shd	**Gravitas**[22] 840 3-9-2 ... CSoumillon 2 (A Fabre, France) *always close up, 3rd straight, hard ridden over 1f out, every chance inside final f, one pace closing stages*	**8/5**[1]	103
4	dht	**Moon Prospect (IRE)**[14] 935 3-9-2 ... OPeslier 7 (F Head, France) *held-up, 6th straight on outside, kept on under pressure from over 1f out, never able to challenge*	**71/10**	103
6	3/4	**Zatonic (FR)**[14] 935 3-9-2 ... SPasquier 8 (P Demercastel, France) *held-up, last straight, headway to be 5th 1f out, not clear run inside final f & accepted position in last 100y*	**11/1**	104+
7	nk	**Septimus (IRE)**[183] 6019 3-9-2 ... KFallon 9 (A P O'Brien, Ire) *held up, 8th straight, switched out & stayed on at one pace*	**11/4**[3]	101
8	1/2	**Pegase Jem (FR)**[22] 3-9-2 ... C-PLemaire 3 (P Bary, France) *7th straight, disputing 4th on rails when not much room over 1f out, kept on same pace*	**18/1**	100
9	3	**Poseidon Adventure (IRE)**[175] 6188 3-9-2 ... CO'Donoghue 6 (A P O'Brien, Ire) *4th straight, weakened well over 1f out*	**11/4**[3]	95

2m 4.40s **9** Ran SP% **166.1**

PARI-MUTUEL: WIN 7.40; PL 3.00, 3.00, 4.50; DF 26.60.

Owner S Boucheron **Bred** S Boucheron **Trained** Pau, France

NOTEBOOK

Barastraight, having his first run at a major Paris track, found a gap a furlong and a half out and quickened late on to take the lead 50 yards from the post. He has a decent turn of foot and is certainly going the right way. Now unbeaten in three races, he will probably be supplemented into the Prix du Jockey-Club.

Echoes Rock(GER), who only started racing this year, put up a game effort. He battled on very gamely to the line and was only run out of things at the very end of the race. There are no plans for him at the moment.

Irish Wells(FR) made most of the running and was then passed by the winner just after the two-furlong post. He stayed on gamely on the far rail to keep third place by a close margin.

Gravitas, tucked in behind the leaders, was asked to make his effort soon after entering the straight. He buttoned down to the task and was only run out of a better place as the race came to an end.

Zatonic(FR) picked up well from the back of the field when the ear plugs were pulled out approaching the straight, but he ran out of room in the final furlong and the situation was accepted.

Septimus(IRE), whose stable's colts have been slow to come to hand this spring, stayed on well enough but looked rather one-paced. He will have to show more next time to warrant consideration for the Derby.

SHA TIN (R-H)

Sunday, April 23

OFFICIAL GOING: Good to firm

1180a AUDEMARS PIGUET QUEEN ELIZABETH II CUP (GROUP 1) 1m 2f

9:30 (9:31) 3-Y-0+

£601,052 (£225,394; £112,697; £60,105; £33,809; £18,783)

RPR

1 **Irridescence (SAF)**[58] 510 5-8-10 ... WCMarwing 6 118
(M F De Kock, South Africa) *led to 2f out, led again 1f out, driven out* **5/1**[3]

2 *hd* **Best Gift (NZ)**[56] 5-9-0 ... ESaint-Martin 10 121
(J Moore, Hong Kong) *raced in 4th, 5th straight, strong run from distance, ran on well under pressure, just failed* **12/1**

3 *shd* **Ouija Board**[29] 741 5-8-10 ... LDettori 8 117
(E A L Dunlop) *broke awkwardly, 10th straight, switched out & headway from 2f out, ran on strongly final f, just failed* **5/2**[1]

4 *1 1/2* **Super Kid (NZ)**[56] 7-9-0 ... SDye 2 118
(J Moore, Hong Kong) *raced in 3rd, 2nd straight, led 2f out to 1f out, no extra last 100y* **9/1**

5 *1 3/4* **Bullish Luck (USA)**[29] 742 7-9-0 ...(b) BPrebble 5 115
(A S Cruz, Hong Kong) *held up, 9th half-way, 6th on inside straight, headway to go 3rd over 1f out, one pace final f* **10/1**

6 *1 1/4* **Viva Pataca**[28] 4-9-0 ... GMosse 12 113
(J Moore, Hong Kong) *drawn wide & raced on outside towards rear, 7th straight on outside, stayed on from over 1f out, never nearer* **9/2**[2]

7 *1 1/4* **Bowman's Crossing (IRE)**[35] 7-9-0 ... DDunn 3 111
(C Fownes, Hong Kong) *mid-division, 8th straight, headway 2f out, 5th approaching final f, one pace* **22/1**

8 *nk* **Green Treasure (AUS)**[22] 5-9-0 ... YTCheng 4 110
(D Cruz, Hong Kong) *mid-division, 9th straight, no headway* **33/1**

9 *1 1/4* **Russian Pearl (NZ)**[29] 742 6-9-0 ... FCoetzee 13 108
(A S Cruz, Hong Kong) *reared start, last straight, never a factor* **14/1**

10 *shd* **River Dancer (IRE)**[22] 7-9-0 ... GSchofield 7 108
(J Size, Hong Kong) *tracked winner to over 2f out, 3rd straight, soon beaten* **66/1**

11 *6* **Falstaff (IRE)**[29] 741 4-9-0 ...(b) DWhyte 11 97
(M F De Kock, South Africa) *12th straight, always behind* **16/1**

12 *1 1/2* **Laverock (IRE)**[192] 5863 4-9-0 ... MBlancpain 1 94
(C Laffon-Parias, France) *raced in 5th, 4th on inside straight, went 3rd 2f out, soon weakened* **25/1**

13 *7 3/4* **Norse Dancer (IRE)**[29] 741 6-9-0 ... DarryllHolland 9 80
(D R C Elsworth) *slowly into stride, 11th straight, no real progress, eased in final f* **20/1**

2m 2.00s **13** Ran SP% **120.1**
(including $HK10 stakes): WIN 58.50; PL 22.50, 24.50, 14.50;DF 405.00.
Owner Team Valor **Bred** Mr & Mrs H Winterbach **Trained** South Africa

NOTEBOOK

Irridescence(SAF) was quickly away and given an enterprising ride, and having regained the advantage at the furlong marker she had just enough in hand to hold on gamely in a cracking finish. She is likely to join John Hammond in France for a European campaign after serving quarantine in Dubai.

Best Gift(NZ) stayed on gamely. His trainer, who said that the horse needs at least an extra furlong, is now considering opportunities in Australia at the Melbourne Spring Carnival.

Ouija Board broke awkwardly and gave her rider an uncomfortable first few strides before he could get her balanced. She only had three or four behind her entering the short straight, but when switched to the wide outside for her run she made such rapid progress that she would have won in another stride or two. The fact that she was on the outside exaggerated the extent of her task, and Dettori was about right when he said that she had four lengths to make up, for she ran the last two furlongs 0.56 seconds faster than the winner. At least she has returned in far better form than last year, and she appears set for a good season. The Coronation Cup at Epsom was nominated as her likely next target.

Laverock(IRE) was able to slip through on the inside to reach third with two furlongs to run but he found absolutely nothing when asked.

Norse Dancer(IRE) missed the break and was always among the backmarkers. He returned jarred up and will be rested at his owner's stud.

863 PONTEFRACT (L-H)

Monday, April 24

OFFICIAL GOING: Good (good to soft in places)

The ground was described as 'on the easy side of good'.

Wind: Light, half-behind Weather: Fine

1181 WENT EDGE MEDIAN AUCTION MAIDEN FILLIES' STKS 5f

2:10 (2:13) (Class 5) 2-Y-O **£3,886** (£1,156; £577; £288) **Stalls** Low

Form RPR

1 **Eloquent Rose (IRE)** 2-9-0 ... PaulFessey 11 69+
(Mrs A Duffield) *tall: chsd ldrs: led jst ins last: hld on wl* **12/1**

2 *3/4* **Voodoo Moon** 2-9-0 ... KDarley 5 66
(M Johnston) *leggy: unf: scope: led tl over 2f out: kpt on wl ins last* **11/2**[3]

3 *1* **Startolini** 2-9-0 ... PaulEddery 2 62+
(B Smart) *cmpt: unf: sn outpcd and drvn along: hdwy 2f out: styd on fnl f* **15/2**

0 4 *1 1/2* **Angeletta**[17] 908 2-9-0 ... WSupple 7 56
(E S McMahon) *chsd ldrs: outpcd 2f out: styd on ins last* **33/1**

5 *nk* **Stormburst (IRE)** 2-9-0 ... TomEaves 3 55
(M Dods) *leggy: w ldrs: hmpd and lost pl 2f out: swtchd rt and styd on ins last* **5/2**[1]

6 *1/2* **Reflective Glory (IRE)** 2-9-0 ... GrahamGibbons 9 53
(J J Quinn) *rangy: unf: s.i.s: kpt on fnl 2f: nt rch ldrs* **20/1**

7 *1/2* **The Italian Job** 2-9-0 ... DavidAllan 6 51+
(T D Easterby) *cmpt: w ldrs: led over 2f out: hdd jst ins last: wknd towards fin* **7/1**

8 *2 1/2* **Absent Love** 2-9-0 ... SebSanders 1 41
(G G Margarson) *leggy: scope: sn outpcd and in rr: sme hdwy over 1f out: nvr on terms* **16/1**

5 9 *2* **Caj (IRE)**[7] 1046 2-9-0 ... FrancisNorton 8 33
(M Quinn) *w ldrs: lost pl over 1f out* **5/1**[2]

10 *1* **Suntan Lady (IRE)** 2-9-0 ... NeilPollard 12 29
(Miss V Haigh) *unf: swvd rt s: sn chsng ldrs: wknd over 1f out* **66/1**

0 11 *8* **Stunningjo**[13] 961 2-9-0 ... RobertWinston 10 —
(J L Spearing) *s.i.s: bhd fnl 2f* **16/1**

12 *15* **The Dandy Fox** 2-9-0 ... AdrianTNicholls 4 —
(D Nicholls) *leggy: sn outpcd and bhd: eased ins last* **16/1**

67.16 secs (3.36) **Going Correction** +0.35s/f (Good) **12** Ran SP% **119.4**
Speed ratings (Par 89):87,85,84,81,81 80,79,75,72,70 58,34
CSF £76.09 TOTE £16.20: £3.90, £2.10, £3.10; EX 117.00.
Owner Mrs D Addison and Mr & Mrs P Addison **Bred** Colin Kennedy **Trained** Constable Burton, N Yorks

FOCUS

Just a modest fillies' maiden and not much previous form to go on.

NOTEBOOK

Eloquent Rose(IRE), a 10,000gns half-sister to multiple sprint winner Who's Winning, proved good enough to make a successful debut. Quite a big filly, her connections think she already needs six furlongs and will leave her alone for the time being. (tchd 11-1)

Voodoo Moon, an 8,500gns half-sister to ten-furlong winner Moonfleet, out of a winner over a mile six, showed good pace and found only one too good. She should be able to progress as the season goes on. (op 9-2 tchd 6-1)

Startolini, a 15,500gns half-sister to My Raggedy Man, a triple seven-furlong winner from two to three, out of a dual mile scorer, looked as though this experience would do her good and ran well in the circumstances. She should show improved form next time. (op 7-1 tchd 8-1)

Angeletta stepped up on the form she showed on her debut on Southwell's Fibresand and would appear better suited by turf. (op 25-1)

Stormburst(IRE), a 21,000gns half-sister to several winners, including useful six- to eight-furlong Italian winner Sonda, and multiple sprint scorer Type One, was well backed for the stable that had trained the last two winners of this race. Just unable to hold her position early on, tight against the rail, she soon had horses coming across her and was short of room on the final bend. That effectively did for her chance of winning, but there was plenty to like about the way she stayed on and she looks well worth taking from the race. Likely to be all the better of this experience, she could be worth a bet in similar company next time, possibly over another furlong. (op 10-3 tchd 7-2)

Reflective Glory(IRE), a half-sister to several winners, including a triple five-furlong juvenile winner in Italy, should do better in time. (op 16-1)

The Italian Job, a 12,000gns yearling, out of a multiple six-furlong winner, attracted some market support but finished up well held. (op 14-1)

Caj(IRE) failed to build on the promise she showed on her debut in a five-furlong maiden at Warwick. (op 7-2)

1182 CORNMARKET H'CAP 1m 4f 8y

2:40 (2:43) (Class 5) (0-70,70) 3-Y-O **£4,533** (£1,348; £674; £336) **Stalls** Low

Form RPR

-232 1 **Juniper Girl (IRE)**[5] 1079 3-8-9 **68** ... LukeMorris(7) 2 76
(M L W Bell) *sn trcking ldrs: effrt over 2f out:wnt 2nd over 1f out: rdr dropped reign and led ins last: r.o* **5/1**[2]

0-66 2 *1/2* **Northerner (IRE)**[54] 548 3-8-4 **56** oh3 ... PaulHanagan 8 63
(J R Norton) *led: qcknd over 5f out: hdd and no ex ins last* **25/1**

003- 3 *3/4* **Karlani (IRE)**[173] 6228 3-9-1 **67** ... RobertWinston 3 73+
(Sir Michael Stoute) *hld up in rr: shkn up and hdwy over 4f out: styd on wl ins last* **2/1**[1]

000- 4 *7* **Alf Tupper**[192] 5870 3-8-12 **67** ... SaleemGolam(3) 7 62
(M H Tompkins) *trckd ldr: t.k.h: wknd fnl f* **6/1**[3]

604- 5 *5* **Pukka Tique**[189] 5939 3-9-4 **70** ... GrahamGibbons 6 57
(R Hollinshead) *in tch: sn pushed along: lost pl over 1f out* **8/1**

50-0 6 *2 1/2* **Cora Pearl (IRE)**[57] 528 3-8-4 **56** oh11 ... FrancisNorton 1 39
(M J Polglase) *t.k.h: trckd ldrs: lost pl over 4f out* **100/1**

1 7 *5* **Marmota (IRE)**[52] 566 3-9-4 **70** ... KDarley 4 45
(M Johnston) *trckd ldrs: drvn along 5f out: lost pl over 1f out* **5/1**[2]

46-6 8 *16* **Marronnier (IRE)**[30] 730 3-9-3 **69** ... DavidAllan 5 18
(T D Easterby) *hld up in rr: drvn along 5f out: lost pl over 3f out: sn bhd* **16/1**

3-30 9 *1 3/4* **Genau (IRE)**[14] 952 3-9-4 **70** ... TomEaves 9 16
(Mrs L Stubbs) *hld up in rr: bhd fnl 3f* **25/1**

2m 44.5s (4.20) **Going Correction** +0.35s/f (Good) **9** Ran SP% **106.6**
Speed ratings (Par 98):100,99,99,94,91 89,86,75,74
CSF £105.90 CT £274.96 TOTE £4.90: £1.40, £4.50, £1.10; EX 143.30.
Owner M B Hawtin **Bred** Mrs E Kent **Trained** Newmarket, Suffolk

FOCUS

The likes of Karlani, Alf Tupper and Marmota were unexposed and looked quite interesting, but they were all well held and the bare form is just modest. One of the outsiders, Northerner, had the run of the race at just a steady gallop and a few of these were caught out when he increased the pace.

1183 FRYSTON H'CAP 6f

3:10 (3:11) (Class 3) (0-90,90) 3-Y-O+

£11,217 (£3,358; £1,679; £840; £419; £210) **Stalls** Low

Form RPR

46-0 1 **Zomerlust**[30] 728 4-9-12 **88** ... GrahamGibbons 15 101
(J J Quinn) *in rr: effrt on inner 2f out: styd on wl to ld 1f out: r.o wl* **16/1**

-042 2 *2 1/2* **Commando Scott (IRE)**[18] 898 5-9-5 **81** ... SebSanders 10 86
(I W McInnes) *in rr: hdwy on outer over 1f out: styd on to take 2nd nr fin* **9/2**[1]

40-0 3 *nk* **Royal Challenge**[13] 970 5-8-11 **76** ... SaleemGolam(3) 7 80
(M H Tompkins) *sn chsng ldrs: kpt on same pce fnl f* **16/1**

510- 4 *1* **Ice Planet**[220] 5262 5-9-13 **89** ... PaulHanagan 9 90
(D Nicholls) *in rr: hdwy on outer 2f out: styd on: nvr rchd ldrs* **12/1**

00-0 5 *1 1/2* **Johnston's Diamond (IRE)**[31] 718 8-9-4 **80** ... DavidAllan 5 77
(E J Alston) *chsd ldr: led 2f out tl 1f out: wknd ins last* **25/1**

-244 6 *1 1/4* **San Antonio**[20] 865 6-9-9 **85** ...(b) MickyFenton 11 78
(Mrs P Sly) *chsd ldrs: sn pushed along: one pce fnl 2f* **17/2**

060- 7 *nk* **Gifted Gamble**[240] 4764 4-10-0 **90** ... DO'Donohoe 3 82
(K A Ryan) *rr-div: hdwy on inner over 1f out: nvr nr ldrs* **25/1**

3406 8 *3 1/2* **Pinchbeck**[13] 970 7-9-3 **79** ...(p) MatthewHenry 12 60+
(M A Jarvis) *in rr: hmpd over 4f out: kpt on fnl 2f: nvr on terms* **20/1**

12-5 9 *nk* **Machinist (IRE)**[22] 846 6-10-0 **90** ... AdrianTNicholls 8 71
(D Nicholls) *mid-div: sn drvn along: nvr nr ldrs* **15/2**

350- 10 *1 1/4* **Rising Shadow (IRE)**[185] 6014 5-10-0 **90** ... PaulFessey 13 91+
(T D Barron) *s.i.s: swtchd lft after s: hdwy whn nt clr run pver 1f out: styd on ins last* **9/1**

030- 11 *2 1/2* **Fun To Ride**[189] 5941 5-8-11 **76** oh2 ... PaulMulrennan(3) 6 45
(M W Easterby) *chsd ldrs: lost pl over 1f out* **50/1**

00-2 12 *hd* **Exmoor**[13] 970 4-9-1 **77** ... SteveDrowne 1 46
(R Charlton) *sn trcking ldrs: rdn 2f out: btn whn nt clr run over 1f out* **5/1**[2]

03-0 13 *2* **Mr Wolf**[7] 1042 5-9-9 **85** ...(p) RobertWinston 2 48
(D W Barker) *led tl 2f out: wknd appr fnl f* **7/1**[3]

22-5 14 *20* **Hits Only Jude (IRE)**[25] 803 3-8-4 **77** ... FrancisNorton 14 —
(J Pearce) *in rr: eased appr fnl f* **50/1**

030- **15** *2* **Highland Cascade**[186] [5999] 4-9-3 **79** .... KDarley 4 —
(J M P Eustace) *chsd ldrs: lost pl and eased over 1f out* **40/1**

1m 17.78s (0.38) **Going Correction** +0.35s/f (Good)
WFA 3 from 4yo+ 11lb **15** Ran SP% **117.9**
Speed ratings (Par 107):111,107,107,105,103 102,101,97,96,95 91,91,88,62,59
CSF £78.50 CT £1215.99 TOTE £19.90: £6.00, £2.30, £4.50; EX 142.90.
Owner P J Carr **Bred** The Lavington Stud **Trained** Settrington, N Yorks

FOCUS
A good handicap for the grade run at a very strong pace. Solid form.

NOTEBOOK
Zomerlust looked in peak condition following his eleventh in the Lincoln on his reappearance and proved well suited by this drop in trip. He had plenty to do at halfway, but the leaders had gone off very fast and he finished stronger than anything. He may now step back up in trip for the seven-furlong Victoria Cup.
Commando Scott(IRE), second over seven furlongs at Leicester on his previous start, ran well dropped in trip but was no match for the winner.
Royal Challenge hails from a yard in good form and stepped up on the form he showed on his reappearance.
Ice Planet was starting the season off a career-high mark and did not run badly at all. (op 16-1)
Johnston's Diamond(IRE) did a lot of work early and probably did well to finish so close.
San Antonio started slowly and met trouble when beginning to make up the lost ground. An encouraging effort and he is one to look out for. (op 9-1)
Rising Shadow(IRE) Official explanation: jockey said gelding was denied a clear run
Exmoor shaped well when second at Folkestone on his reappearance, but failed to build on that. (tchd 9-2 in places)
Mr Wolf showed good speed but stopped very quickly and is not quite there yet. He is one to keep in mind for when his stable hit form.

1184 PONTEFRACT MARATHON H'CAP — 2m 5f 122y
3:40 (3:40) (Class 5) (0-75,71) 4-Y-0+ **£5,181** (£1,541; £770; £384) **Stalls** Low

Form — RPR

40-0 **1** **Villago (GER)**[12] [975] 6-9-1 **58** .... RobertWinston 3 — 65
(E W Tuer) *hld up in rr: shkn up and hd over 5f out: styd on to ld jst ins last: kpt on wl* **7/1**
06-1 **2** *1 3/4* **Kayf Aramis**[13] [966] 4-8-9 **58** .... PaulQuinn 12 — 63
(J L Spearing) *fly-jmpd s: hld up in rr: pushed along and hdwy 6f out: led 3f out tl jst ins last: kpt on same pce* **6/1**[3]
0-01 **3** *1 1/2* **Great As Gold (IRE)**[20] [866] 7-9-8 **65** .... (p) TomEaves 1 — 69
(B Ellison) *bhd: pushed along and hdwy 6f out: styd on fnl 2f: nvr able chal* **9/2**[1]
2-54 **4** *3* **Totally Scottish**[12] [975] 10-8-5 **53** oh4 ow1 .... GregFairley(5) 11 — 54
(K G Reveley) *hld up in rr: hdwy 6f out: one pce fnl 2f* **10/1**
-063 **5** *2 1/2* **Kristensen**[8] [1033] 7-10-0 **71** .... (v) KDarley 9 — 69
(Karen McLintock) *mid-div: hdwy to trck ldrs 6f out: wknd ins last* **12/1**
55-3 **6** *8* **Ocean Tide**[20] [866] 9-9-6 **63** .... (b) PaulHanagan 8 — 53
(R Ford) *chsd ldrs: jnd ldrs after 6f: wknd appr fnl f* **15/2**
304- **7** *8* **Habitual Dancer**[16] [5789] 5-9-3 **60** .... MickyFenton 4 — 42
(Jedd O'Keeffe) *led after 1f: drvn along 7f out: hdd 3f out: wknd over 1f out* **5/1**[2]
00-0 **8** *24* **Prairie Sun (GER)**[12] [976] 5-9-7 **64** .... WSupple 5 — 22
(Mrs A Duffield) *trckd ldrs: wknd over 2f out: eased ins last* **10/1**
-004 **9** *5* **Aristi (IRE)**[20] [881] 5-8-11 **54** .... (p) FrancisNorton 6 — 7
(M Quinn) *trckd ldrs: wkng whn n.m.r over 2f out: sn bhd* **12/1**
000/ **10** *23* **Lake 'O' Gold**[566] [6005] 7-8-9 **52** oh7 .... PaulEddery 7 —
(D W Thompson) *mid-div: lost pl over 4f out: t.o 3f out* **100/1**
200- **11** *dist* **Sovereign State (IRE)**[15] [5892] 9-8-6 **52** oh2 ......(p) PaulMulrennan(3) 10 —
(D W Thompson) *t.k.h: hdwy to trck ldrs 10f out: lost pl 4f out: sn t.o* **40/1**
160- **P** **Solomon's Mine (USA)**[347] [1654] 7-9-6 **66** .... SaleemGolam(3) 2 —
(M J Polglase) *led 1f: lost pl 6f out: sn hopelessly t.o: p.u over 2f out* **25/1**

5m 3.34s (2.54) **Going Correction** +0.35s/f (Good)
WFA 4 from 5yo+ 6lb **12** Ran SP% **114.2**
Speed ratings (Par 103):109,108,107,106,105 102,100,91,89,81 —,—
CSF £46.23 CT £209.83 TOTE £8.30: £3.00, £2.80, £1.40; EX 75.50.
Owner E Tuer **Bred** Gestut Hof Ittlingen **Trained** Great Smeaton, N Yorks

FOCUS
Quite a unique distance, and the form may not be worth that much back in normal staying events.

1185 LADY BALK MAIDEN STKS — 6f
4:10 (4:13) (Class 5) 3-Y-0+ **£3,886** (£1,156; £577; £288) **Stalls** Low

Form — RPR

-002 **1** **Sunderland Echo (IRE)**[20] [868] 3-8-9 65 .... TomEaves 8 — 56
(B Ellison) *mde virtually all: hld on wl* **10/1**
046- **2** *3/4* **Briery Lane (IRE)**[146] [6462] 5-9-6 50 .... GregFairley(5) 4 — 62
(Mrs K Walton) *chsd ldrs: kpt on fnl 2f: no ex ins last* **28/1**
4-52 **3** *1 1/4* **Street Warrior (IRE)**[7] [1048] 3-9-0 75 .... KDarley 2 — 55
(M Johnston) *w ldrs: rdn over 1f out: kpt on same pce* **4/5**[1]
4 *1/2* **Eternal Legacy (IRE)** 4-9-6 .... MickyFenton 7 — 52+
(J Parkes) *lengthy: s.s: stdy hdwy 2f out: styd on ins last* **100/1**
5 *1* **Josarty** 3-9-0 .... GrahamGibbons 5 — 51
(J J Quinn) *rangy: scope: s.s: hdwy over 2f out: nvr rchd ldrs* **14/1**
30- **6** *1 1/4* **Royal Composer (IRE)**[254] [4379] 3-9-0 .... DavidAllan 3 — 47
(T D Easterby) *sn in rr: kpt on fnl f* **7/1**[3]
50 **7** *1/2* **Bookman (IRE)**[63] [460] 4-9-11 .... (t) LeeEnstone 1 — 49
(P C Haslam) *chsd ldrs: wknd over 1f out* **25/1**
06-0 **8** *hd* **Obscene**[30] [730] 3-8-11 60 .... SaleemGolam(3) 10 — 45
(M J Polglase) *hld up in rr: effrt over 2f out: nvr nr ldrs* **33/1**
3-3 **9** *hd* **Esoterica (IRE)**[12] [978] 3-9-0 .... PaulFessey 11 — 44
(T D Barron) *chsd ldrs: outpcd over 2f out: no threat after* **11/2**[2]
030- **10** *27* **Warren Place**[397] [693] 6-9-6 45 .... DuranFentiman(5) 9 —
(A D Brown) *prom: lost pl over 3f out: sn bhd: t.o* **100/1**
00- **11** *1/2* **Steel Grey**[266] [4000] 5-9-11 .... RobertWinston 6 —
(M Brittain) *chsd ldrs: lost pl over 2f out: sn bhd: t.o* **66/1**

1m 20.16s (2.76) **Going Correction** +0.35s/f (Good)
WFA 3 from 4yo+ 11lb **11** Ran SP% **112.9**
Speed ratings (Par 103):95,94,92,91,90 88,88,87,87,51 50
CSF £246.71 TOTE £9.80: £2.60, £5.60, £1.10; EX 264.10.
Owner Black and White Diamond Partnership **Bred** Ms Audrey Barlow **Trained** Norton, N Yorks

FOCUS
A moderate sprint maiden, as the proximity of the 50-rated runner-up would suggest. The time was modest too.
Esoterica(IRE) Official explanation: jockey said gelding hung right throughout

1186 CATTERICK RACES ON 26TH APRIL H'CAP — 1m 4y
4:40 (4:40) (Class 5) (0-75,75) 4-Y-0+ **£4,533** (£1,348; £674; £336) **Stalls** Low

Form — RPR

65-6 **1** **Major Magpie (IRE)**[3] [1123] 4-8-7 **64** .... PaulFessey 11 — 78+
(M Dods) *hld up: hdwy on ins over 2f out: nt clr run and swtchd outside over 1f out: r.o strly to ld ins last: fin wl* **5/1**[2]
305- **2** *1 1/4* **Topatoo**[198] [5743] 4-9-0 **74** .... SaleemGolam(3) 5 — 80
(M H Tompkins) *too t.k.h in mid-field: hdwy and nt clr run over 1f out: led ins last: sn hdd and no ex* **11/2**[3]
40-0 **3** *2* **Ask The Clerk (IRE)**[12] [977] 5-8-13 **70** .... MickyFenton 1 — 71
(Mrs P Sly) *trckd ldrs: kpt on same pce fnl f* **20/1**
-042 **4** *1 1/4* **Aperitif**[3] [1124] 5-8-7 **64** .... AdrianTNicholls 8 — 63
(D Nicholls) *sn trcking ldr: led over 1f out: hdd and no ex ins last* **7/2**[1]
0-03 **5** *2* **The Bonus King**[14] [950] 6-8-7 **64** .... KDarley 9 — 58
(J Jay) *trckd ldrs on outer: effrt over 2f out: kpt on same pce appr fnl f* **9/1**
2600 **6** *shd* **Burnley Al (IRE)**[14] [955] 4-8-4 **61** .... (v) PaulHanagan 2 — 55
(R A Fahey) *led: hdd over 1f out: wknd jst ins last* **14/1**
6-00 **7** *1* **Rain Stops Play (IRE)**[18] [898] 4-9-4 **75** .... FrancisNorton 3 — 66
(M Quinn) *trckd ldrs: wknd appr fnl f* **50/1**
213 **8** *1* **Webbow (IRE)**[12] [992] 4-9-1 **72** .... DavidAllan 4 — 61
(T D Easterby) *trckd ldrs: outpcd over 2f out: no threat after* **5/1**[2]
/32- **9** *3* **Phoebe Woodstock (IRE)**[301] [2979] 4-9-4 **75** .... RobertWinston 10 — 57
(W R Swinburn) *mid-div: effrt on outer over 2f out: nvr trbld ldrs* **7/1**
30-0 **10** *2 1/2* **Bolton Hall (IRE)**[12] [992] 4-8-13 **70** .... TonyHamilton 7 — 46
(R A Fahey) *hld up in rr: nvr on terms* **33/1**
/00- **11** *nk* **Ariodante**[346] [1677] 4-9-3 **74** .... GrahamGibbons 6 — 50
(J M P Eustace) *in rr: drvn over 3f out: nvr on terms* **66/1**
0020 **12** *25* **Corky (IRE)**[12] [992] 5-9-1 **72** .... TomEaves 12 —
(I W McInnes) *s.v.s: a detached in last* **20/1**

1m 47.85s (2.15) **Going Correction** +0.35s/f (Good) **12** Ran SP% **116.0**
Speed ratings (Par 103):103,101,99,98,96 96,95,94,91,88 88,63
CSF £29.95 CT £513.90 TOTE £6.20: £2.40, £1.90, £4.70; EX 39.70.
Owner Mrs Patsy Monk **Bred** J Hutchinson **Trained** Denton, Co Durham

FOCUS
A fair handicap and the form looks good for the grade. The first two were less exposed than most.
Phoebe Woodstock(IRE) Official explanation: jockey said filly had no more to give

1187 BETFAIR.COM APPRENTICE SERIES ROUND 2 H'CAP — 1m 2f 6y
5:10 (5:13) (Class 5) (0-70,76) 4-Y-0+ **£3,886** (£1,156; £577; £288) **Stalls** Low

Form — RPR

00-3 **1** **Tagula Blue (IRE)**[20] [882] 6-8-5 **60** .... NeilBrown(3) 9 — 70+
(Ian Williams) *s.s: hld up in rr: stdy hdwy 4f out: led 2f out: shkn up and wnt clr 1f out: readily* **6/1**[3]
500- **2** *4* **Archie Babe (IRE)**[42] [1448] 10-8-4 **56** oh5 .... ThomasO'Brien 8 — 58
(J J Quinn) *hld up in rr: drvn along 4f out: hdwy over 2f out: styd on to take 2nd jst ins last: no ch w wnr* **14/1**
2211 **3** *8* **Augustine**[5] [1075] 5-9-10 **76** 6ex .... TolleyDean 6 — 63
(P W Hiatt) *t.k.h: sn w ldr: led over 5f out: hdd 2f out: wknd jst ins last* **15/8**[1]
000- **4** *5* **Fair Spin**[37] [6141] 6-8-4 **56** oh6 .... (b) RonanKeogh 4 — 33
(Micky Hammond) *trckd ldrs: chal over 3f out: wknd over 1f out* **33/1**
30-1 **5** *1 1/4* **Donna's Double**[12] [974] 11-7-13 **56** oh3 .... (p) JamieHamblett(5) 7 — 31
(Karen McLintock) *trckd ldrs: wknd over 1f out* **10/1**
000- **6** *nk* **Mixing**[185] [6015] 4-8-8 **67** .... BRoper(7) 5 — 41
(W Jarvis) *s.i.s: hdwy and swtchd outside over 5f out: lost pl over 2f out* **14/1**
-000 **7** *shd* **Monash Lad (IRE)**[12] [992] 4-8-8 **67** .... PatrickHills(7) 3 — 41
(M H Tompkins) *t.k.h: trckd ldrs: lost pl 3f out* **11/1**
24-3 **8** *1* **Charlie Tango (IRE)**[7] [1045] 5-8-6 **58** .... KevinGhunowa 2 — 30
(D W Thompson) *trckd ldrs: outpcd rt 2f out: sn wknd* **5/1**[2]
00-0 **9** *3 1/2* **Melodian**[20] [869] 11-8-5 **64** oh1 ow8 .... (b) ShaunBushby(7) 1 — 30
(M Brittain) *reluctant ldr: tk str hold: hdd over 5f out: lost pl 3f out* **33/1**
-156 **10** *17* **Bethanys Boy (IRE)**[48] [610] 5-8-5 **62** .... NSLawes(5) 10 —
(B Ellison) *s.i.s: t.k.h on outer: hdwy 6f out: lost pl over 3f out: sn bhd: t.o* **7/1**

2m 17.58s (3.50) **Going Correction** +0.35s/f (Good) **10** Ran SP% **114.9**
Speed ratings (Par 103):100,96,90,86,85 85,85,84,81,67
CSF £84.79 CT £213.97 TOTE £7.50: £2.50, £3.10, £1.20; EX 81.60 Place 6 £122.97, Place 5 £27.10.
Owner Boston R S Ian Bennett **Bred** Michael Conlon **Trained** Portway, Worcs

FOCUS
A modest and uncompetitive apprentice handicap, run at a moderate pace, but Tagula Blue looked better than his current mark and had them well strung out.
Charlie Tango(IRE) Official explanation: jockey said gelding ran too free
T/Jkpt: Not won. T/Plt: £171.30 to a £1 stake. Pool: £49,474.10. 210.75 winning tickets. T/Qpdt: £32.80 to a £1 stake. Pool: £3,095.70. 69.80 winning tickets. WG

944 WINDSOR (R-H)
Monday, April 24

OFFICIAL GOING: Good
Wind: Nil Weather: Fine but cloudy

1188 READING EVENING POST APPRENTICE H'CAP — 6f
5:30 (5:31) (Class 5) (0-75,74) 4-Y-0+ **£3,238** (£963; £481; £240) **Stalls** High

Form — RPR

2430 **1** **Adantino**[14] [949] 7-8-6 **67** .... (b) JamesMillman(5) 3 — 76+
(B R Millman) *hld up in last pair: prog on outer 2f out: nt clr run jst over 1f out: r.o wl to ld last strides* **12/1**
0-36 **2** *shd* **Resplendent Nova**[18] [898] 4-8-7 **68** .... RobbieMills(5) 14 — 75+
(T G Mills) *w ldng pair: led 2f out: bmpd along furiously fnl f: hdd last stride* **4/1**[1]
3401 **3** *nk* **Nautical**[14] [949] 8-9-3 **73** .... JamesDoyle 4 — 79
(A W Carroll) *dwlt: hld up in last pair: gd prog 2f out: hanging lft over 1f out: r.o ins fnl f: gaining at fin* **7/1**[2]
3150 **4** *1/2* **Arnie De Burgh**[40] [644] 4-8-6 **67** .... DerekNolan(3) 1 — 72
(D J Daly) *hld up wl in rr: prog over 2f out: chal fnl f: no ex nr fin* **14/1**
00-5 **5** *hd* **Marker**[27] [777] 6-8-11 **70** .... TravisBlock(3) 2 — 74
(J A Geake) *hld up in midfield: prog 2f out: cl up ent fnl f: hld whn n.m.r nr fin* **14/1**
426- **6** *1/2* **Rosapenna (IRE)**[224] [5172] 4-9-0 **73** .... SladeO'Hara(3) 6 — 75
(C F Wall) *towards rr: prog 2f out: rdn and hanging lft over 1f out: kpt on fnl f: nt pce to chal* **16/1**

06-0 **7** ½ **Dr Synn**[27] 777 5-8-9 **65** RoryMoore 9 66
(J Akehurst) *settled midfield: rdn and effrt 2f out: kpt on: nvr able to chal* **16/1**

0440 **8** ½ **Kensington (IRE)**[12] 985 5-8-5 **64** MichaelJStainton(3) 5 63
(P D Evans) *wl in rr: swtchd lft 2f out: kpt on fr over 1f out: nt rch ldrs* **11/1**

10-0 **9** 3 ½ **Extremely Rare (IRE)**[14] 949 5-9-3 **73** RichardKingscote 8 62
(M S Saunders) *taken down early: w ldr: led over 3f out to 2f out: w ldr jst over 1f out: wknd rapidly ins fnl f* **12/1**

5150 **10** hd **Hurricane Coast**[33] 641 7-8-11 **72** (b) SophieDoyle(5) 11 60
(K McAuliffe) *pressed ldrs tl wknd jst over 1f out* **20/1**

000- **11** ½ **Cree**[189] 5951 4-8-11 **67** MarcHalford 15 54
(W R Muir) *pressed ldrs: wknd u.p over 1f out* **16/1**

0204 **12** hd **Greenwood**[14] 949 8-8-9 **70** JosephWalsh(5) 10 56
(P G Murphy) *settled off the pce nr side: effrt 2f out: no prog and btn 1f out* **8/1**[3]

0000 **13** 7 **Caustic Wit (IRE)**[33] 693 8-8-4 **65** (p) WilliamCarson(5) 16 30
(M S Saunders) *taken down early: racd nr side: led to over 3f out: wknd rapidly 2f out* **9/1**

564- **14** 2 ½ **Full Spate**[238] 4817 11-8-5 **64** AndrewElliott(3) 12 22
(J M Bradley) *chsd ldrs: bmpd after 2f: wknd rapidly 2f out* **16/1**

040- **15** 7 **Elgin Marbles**[317] 2486 4-8-13 **74** MarkCoumbe(5) 13 11
(A B Haynes) *chsd ldrs: bmpd after 2f: wknd rapidly over 2f out* **33/1**

1m 12.85s (-0.82) **Going Correction** -0.075s/f (Good) **15** Ran SP% **121.9**
Speed ratings (Par 103):102,101,101,100,100 99,99,98,93,93 92,92,83,80,70
CSF £59.57 CT £383.34 TOTE £16.50: £5.00, £2.40, £2.60; EX 72.40.
Owner Tarka Two Racing **Bred** S D Bevan **Trained** Kentisbeare, Devon

FOCUS
13mm of rain since the last meeting two weeks ago ensured there was no sting. After a rapid pace, horses who enjoy some juice in the ground dominated, and three of the first four came from the back. Essentially ordinary form.
Dr Synn Official explanation: jockey said gelding was denied a clear run
Extremely Rare(IRE) Official explanation: jockey said mare had no more to give
Elgin Marbles Official explanation: jockey said saddle slipped

1189 ARENA LEISURE PLC MAIDEN STKS 5f 10y
6:00 (6:01) (Class 5) 2-Y-O **£3,886** (£1,156; £577; £288) **Stalls** High

Form RPR

1 **Elhamri** 2-9-3 DPMcDonogh 2 84
(S Kirk) *mde virtually all: hrd rdn over 1f out: hld on wl nr fin* **16/1**

2 nk **Hoh Mike (IRE)** 2-9-3 JamieSpencer 7 83+
(M L W Bell) *s.s: rcvrd and in tch after 2f: prog on outer 2f out: rdn to chse wnr over 1f out: chal last 75yds: jst hld* **10/3**[2]

3 ¾ **Benchmark** 2-9-3 RichardHughes 8 80+
(R Hannon) *w wnr over 1f: lost pl and rdn 1/2-way: swtchd lft ins fnl f: r.o last 100yds* **13/8**[1]

4 ¾ **Longquan (IRE)** 2-9-3 SebSanders 3 77
(P J Makin) *prom: chsd wnr 3f out to over 1f out: one pce* **11/1**

2 **5** shd **Camissa**[14] 944 2-8-12 DaneO'Neill 1 71
(D K Ivory) *prom: chsd wnr 3f out to over 1f out: one pce fnl f* **7/1**[3]

6 2 **Nina Blini** 2-8-12 JimmyFortune 9 63
(B J Meehan) *chsd ldrs: shkn up over 1f out: no imp ent fnl f: wkng nr fin* **10/1**

7 7 **Stagehand (IRE)** 2-9-3 AlanMunro 6 40
(B R Millman) *outpcd after 1f and sn drvn: nvr on terms* **10/1**

4 **8** ½ **Princely Royal**[13] 968 2-9-3 MartinDwyer 4 38
(J J Bridger) *rrd in stalls bef s: chsd ldng gp tl wknd rapidly over 1f out* **16/1**

9 5 **Beatani** 2-8-12 ShaneKelly 10 13
(P D Evans) *s.s: outpcd and a wl bhd* **40/1**

10 10 **Yve Sam La Champ** 2-9-3 TPQueally 5 —
(A W Carroll) *s.s: sn t.o* **66/1**

61.64 secs (0.54) **Going Correction** -0.075s/f (Good) **10** Ran SP% **115.9**
Speed ratings (Par 92):92,91,90,89,88 85,74,73,65,49
CSF £68.52 TOTE £22.80: £5.20, £1.10, £1.30; EX 104.90.
Owner Norman Ormiston **Bred** Highfield Stud Ltd **Trained** Upper Lambourn, Berks

FOCUS
The ground was surprisingly changed to good after this race failed to get anywhere near standard time but that was hardly surprising as plenty ran around under pressure. Not an easy race to assess, it has been rated through the fifth but could turn out to have been a decent event.

NOTEBOOK
Elhamri was the first juvenile runner of the season for Kirk, who described him as "a little speedball". Fast away to overcome his low draw, he soon got the rail and found that little bit more when needed to hold the challenge of the runner-up. He is not very big, but he can run and, out of a seven-furlong winner, he should get another furlong or two in time. (op 20-1)
Hoh Mike(IRE) ◆ is a half-brother to a couple of winning two-year-olds. He soon sat comfortably off the fast pace and, despite running green, laid down a strong challenge going inside the final furlong which was just repelled. Likely to stay further, he has plenty of size and substance and should have no problem winning his maiden. (op 4-1 tchd 9-2 in a place)
Benchmark, a half-brother to the smart Enforcer, broke well but could not match the winner's early pace, which saw him stuck in a pocket into the final two furlongs. When extricated, switching left around his two main rivals, he started to pick up but he was not given a hard time when held. He can certainly build on the bare form. (op 2-1 tchd 9-4 in places)
Longquan(IRE), his trainer's first turf runner of the season, is a half-brother to several winners, mainly at three. Looking fit and well, he showed speed before running green under pressure, coming together with the eventual fifth which ended what chance he had. He should make the grade. (op 12-1)
Camissa, who had the benefit of a previous run but wanted to hang right under pressure, ran well enough in what looked an above-average contest. (op 9-2)
Nina Blini was outpaced mid-race and had to switch sharply left to get running room. She was not given a hard time in the last half-furlong when well held and can improve considerably on the bare form. (op 8-1)
Stagehand(IRE) is a half-brother to the smart 2004 juvenile filly Salsa Brava. He looked the part but, after showing speed, was slightly squeezed out and looked after himself. He can improve on the bare form if learning from the experience. (op 8-1 tchd 7-1)
Princely Royal showed good speed but, considering he was still on the tails of the main group going to the final furlong, he weakened alarmingly quickly.

1190 ATTHERACES.COM H'CAP 1m 67y
6:30 (6:30) (Class 4) (0-85,80) 3-Y-O **£6,477** (£1,927; £963; £481) **Stalls** High

Form RPR

100- **1** **Polliwilline (IRE)**[178] 6129 3-9-1 **77** RyanMoore 7 82
(R Hannon) *settled in midfield: prog over 2f out: rdn to ld over 1f out: r.o wl* **10/1**

0-1 **2** 1 ½ **Tommy Toogood (IRE)**[37] 669 3-9-4 **80** MichaelHills 11 84+
(B W Hills) *trckd ldrs: shkn up over 2f out: hanging lft but prog to chse wnr ent fnl f: nt qckn and no imp* **5/2**[1]

103- **3** ¾ **Robustian**[216] 5395 3-9-1 **77** StephenCarson 2 77
(R F Johnson Houghton) *hld up in midfield: effrt on outer and bmpd over 2f out: rdn and styd on same pce fnl 2f* **16/1**

34-4 **4** ¾ **Crimson Flame (IRE)**[38] 656 3-8-13 **75** TQuinn 10 73
(M R Channon) *hld up in rr: plenty to do whn effrt jst over 2f out: styd on fr over 1f out: nt rch ldrs* **20/1**

42-1 **5** 1 **Acrobatic (USA)**[13] 963 3-9-3 **79** RichardHughes 5 75
(R Charlton) *prom: hrd rdn and nt qckn 2f out: sn lost pl: one pce after* **4/1**[2]

240- **6** ¾ **Urban Tiger (GER)**[185] 6010 3-9-2 **78** DaneO'Neill 8 72
(A King) *dwlt: hld up in last pair: effrt on wd outside over 2f out: nt qckn and no prog over 1f out* **8/1**

361- **7** hd **Kings Heir (IRE)**[191] 5886 3-9-3 **79** MartinDwyer 1 73
(R M Beckett) *led at gd pce: hanging lft fr 1/2-way: hung lft and hdd over 1f out: wknd* **25/1**

030- **8** 1 ½ **Mystic Roll**[179] 6121 3-8-13 **75** JimmyFortune 6 65
(B J Meehan) *mostly chsd ldr to over 2f out: wknd* **16/1**

01- **9** 3 ½ **Snark (IRE)**[149] 6427 3-9-2 **78** SebSanders 9 60
(P J Makin) *a towards rr and nvr gng that wl: pushed along 1/2-way: struggling over 2f out* **5/1**[3]

-205 **10** ¾ **Fangorn Forest (IRE)**[22] 848 3-8-13 **75** (p) AdrianMcCarthy 3 55
(R A Harris) *prom: rdn 3f out: wknd 2f out* **50/1**

1105 **11** nk **Casablanca Minx (IRE)**[30] 724 3-8-9 **76** JamesDoyle(5) 4 56
(N P Littmoden) *a in last pair: rdn halfway: no prog* **20/1**

1m 43.29s (-2.31) **Going Correction** -0.20s/f (Firm) **11** Ran SP% **112.5**
Speed ratings (Par 100):103,101,100,100,99 98,98,96,93,92 92
CSF £32.03 CT £407.37 TOTE £14.00: £4.10, £1.10, £4.30; EX 46.50.
Owner de La Warr Racing **Bred** John And Bill Dwan **Trained** East Everleigh, Wilts

FOCUS
This was notable for a decent pace and consequently a good time, although with the top-weight rated just 80 in an 85-ceiling handicap, this was not the strongest race of its class. Solid form, however.
Crimson Flame(IRE) Official explanation: jockey said gelding suffered interference in running
Kings Heir(IRE) Official explanation: jockey said colt hung left

1191 NEIL HOWARD'S 50TH BIRTHDAY CELEBRATION COURTESY OF LADBROKES MAIDEN FILLIES' STKS 1m 67y
7:00 (7:03) (Class 5) 3-Y-O **£3,886** (£1,156; £577; £288) **Stalls** High

Form RPR

03- **1** **Heaven Sent**[231] 5005 3-9-0 LDettori 6 78+
(Sir Michael Stoute) *mde all: shkn up and in command 2f out: pushed out fnl f* **9/4**[1]

0- **2** 1 ½ **Otelcaliforni (USA)**[230] 5032 3-9-0 ShaneKelly 8 74+
(J Noseda) *prom: disp 2nd 1/2-way: pushed along and lost pl over 2f out: styd on again to take 2nd last 100yds* **33/1**

02- **3** nk **Fluorescent**[181] 6097 3-9-0 NickyMackay 13 73+
(L M Cumani) *prom: mostly chsd wnr fr 1/2-way: rdn and no imp fr over 2f out: lost 2nd last 100yds* **5/1**[3]

2- **4** 1 ½ **Dama'A (IRE)**[255] 4329 3-9-0 JimmyFortune 2 70+
(J H M Gosden) *dwlt: rcvrd to chse ldrs: effrt to dispute 2nd over 2f out: kpt on same pce* **11/4**[2]

5 **5** ¾ **Gelder**[13] 964 3-9-0 SteveDrowne 11 68
(H Morrison) *sn chsd ldrs w much tail swishing: cl up over 2f out: one pce over 1f out* **50/1**

6 5 **Scylla Cadeaux (IRE)** 3-9-0 RyanMoore 1 57+
(Sir Michael Stoute) *dwlt: settled in last trio: shuffled along 3f out: kpt on steadily: nvr nr ldrs* **33/1**

3- **7** ½ **Servillia (IRE)**[140] 6502 3-9-0 TedDurcan 4 56
(W R Swinburn) *hld up in midfield: pushed along and no prog over 3f out: outpcd over 2f out: one pce after* **16/1**

8 shd **Dunlin** 3-9-0 SebSanders 10 55
(H Morrison) *wl in rr: shkn up and struggling 1/2-way: kpt on over 1f out: n.d* **66/1**

9 1 ½ **Consuelita** 3-9-0 RichardHughes 7 52
(B J Meehan) *dwlt: wl in rr: pushed along 1/2-way: nvr on terms* **50/1**

4-2 **10** shd **Nikki Bea (IRE)**[86] 217 3-9-0 JohnEgan 12 52?
(Jamie Poulton) *chsd ldrs: shkn up and hanging lft fr 3f out: eased over 1f out* **50/1**

3- **11** 1 ½ **Chasing A Dream**[163] 6332 3-9-0 MichaelHills 5 48
(B W Hills) *prom for 3f: hanging lft and losing pl over 3f out* **10/1**

12 1 **Little Miss Verity** 3-8-11 RichardThomas(3) 14 46
(J A Geake) *plld hrd: chsd wnr 4f: sn lost pl: wknd 2f out* **66/1**

13 ¾ **Boreana** 3-9-0 AlanMunro 9 44
(P W Chapple-Hyam) *s.i.s: a wl in rr: shkn up and no prog 4f out* **13/2**

14 2 ½ **Aitch (IRE)** 3-9-0 TPQueally 3 38
(J Noseda) *a in last pair: rdn and struggling 1/2-way* **66/1**

1m 43.96s (-1.64) **Going Correction** -0.20s/f (Firm) **14** Ran SP% **118.7**
Speed ratings (Par 95):100,98,98,96,95 90,90,90,88,88 87,86,85,83
CSF £89.65 TOTE £3.40: £1.40, £7.60, £2.30; EX 139.30.
Owner Cheveley Park Stud **Bred** Cheveley Park Stud Ltd **Trained** Newmarket, Suffolk

FOCUS
Not a lot of strength in depth with the first five finishing well clear. The principals are all likely to rate better than the bare form.

1192 REED AND MACKAY MAIDEN STKS 1m 2f 7y
7:30 (7:32) (Class 5) 3-Y-O **£3,238** (£963; £481; £240) **Stalls** Low

Form RPR

032- **1** **Red Rocks (IRE)**[192] 5872 3-9-3 **92** LDettori 8 104+
(B J Meehan) *mde most: hung rght bnd 1/2-way: drew away over 2f out: at least 6 l up fnl f: heavily eased* **10/11**[1]

0- **2** 3 **Duty (IRE)**[143] 6477 3-9-3 JimmyFortune 13 88+
(Sir Michael Stoute) *dwlt: rr of main gp after 4f: rdn and prog over 3f out: hrd drvn and r.o to take 2nd ins fnl f: no ch w wnr* **16/1**

3 2 ½ **Montpellier (IRE)** 3-9-3 RichardMullen 7 83
(E A L Dunlop) *dwlt and wnt lft s: pushed up to chse ldrs: effrt over 2f out: shkn up to chse wnr over 1f out: no ch: lost 2nd ins fnl f* **20/1**

2342 **4** 2 ½ **Katchit (IRE)**[25] 804 3-9-3 **77** TQuinn 9 78
(M R Channon) *prom: chsd wnr 1/2-way to over 1f out: one pce* **8/1**[3]

0- **5** ½ **New Guinea**[195] 5821 3-9-3 PhilipRobinson 10 77
(M A Jarvis) *hld up wl in rr: wl off the pce 4f out: nudged along and styd on steadily fr over 2f out: nvr nr ldrs* **20/1**

6 nk **Soulard (USA)** 3-9-3 ShaneKelly 3 76
(J Noseda) *t.k.h: sn chsd ldrs: shkn up and wl outpcd over 2f out: n.d after* **16/1**

05- **7** 2½ **Kalatime (IRE)**[203] 5667 3-8-12 .... MartinDwyer 15 67
(A M Balding) *hld up wl in rr and off the pce: pushed along 3f out: styd on after : shkn up over 1f out: nvr nrr* **50/1**

5- **8** 3½ **Rhinebird**[278] 3637 3-9-3 .... JamieSpencer 6 65
(J R Fanshawe) *prom: outpcd fr 3f out: wknd wl over 1f out* **7/1**[2]

0-0 **9** *nk* **Counting House (IRE)**[14] 948 3-9-3 .... SteveDrowne 14 65+
(R Charlton) *settled wl in rr and wl off the pce: shuffled along fr 3f out: no ch* **33/1**

10 *hd* **Project Sunshine (GER)** 3-9-3 .... DaneO'Neill 16 64
(J A Osborne) *dwlt: wl in rr: shkn up 3f out: kpt on same pce: nvr on terms* **66/1**

0- **11** 3 **Scrummage**[185] 6002 3-9-3 .... RyanMoore 12 58
(Sir Michael Stoute) *stmbld s: chsd wnr to 1/2-way: wknd over 2f out* **10/1**

0-00 **12** 1½ **Kinetic Power (IRE)**[21] 850 3-9-3 58.............................. JohnEgan 11 56
(D R C Elsworth) *chsd ldng gp: n.m.r 4f out: sn rdn and struggling* **66/1**

324- **13** *hd* **Cabourg (IRE)**[217] 5356 3-9-3 80...................................(b[1]) AlanMunro 2 55
(C R Egerton) *plld hrd and prom: wknd 3f out* **12/1**

14 1¼ **Mika's Fable (FR)** 3-8-12 .... FergusSweeney 5 48
(M Meade) *s.s: a wl bhd* **100/1**

15 2½ **Travelling Fox** 3-8-12 .... TravisBlock[(5)] 4 48
(H Morrison) *plld hrd: prom to 1/2-way: sn wknd and bhd* **100/1**

0- **16** 11 **Star Of Erhaab**[133] 6557 3-9-3 .... StephenCarson 1 27
(E A Wheeler) *sn last: wl bhd 1/2-way: t.o* **100/1**

2m 5.66s (-2.64) **Going Correction** -0.20s/f (Firm) **16** Ran SP% **124.9**
Speed ratings (Par 98):102,99,97,95,95 94,92,90,89,89 87,86,86,85,83 74
CSF £17.35 TOTE £2.00: £1.20, £4.40, £4.50; EX 28.60.
Owner J Paul Reddam **Bred** Ballylinch Stud **Trained** Manton, Wilts

FOCUS
The gallop was a sound one although these inexperienced maidens took things easily around the bottom bend. Red Rocks impressed and is a well above-average maiden winner. The fourth sets the standard and the race should throw up winners.
New Guinea Official explanation: jockey said colt ran too keen early on
Kinetic Power(IRE) Official explanation: jockey said gelding was hampered on bend
Cabourg(IRE) Official explanation: jockey said gelding ran too free

1193 COME RACING AGAIN BANK HOLIDAY MONDAY H'CAP 1m 3f 135y
8:00 (8:03) (Class 5) (0-75,75) 3-Y-0 **£3,238** (£963; £481; £240) **Stalls** Low

Form RPR

424- **1** **Island Odyssey**[276] 3693 3-9-1 **72**.................................... LDettori 5 81
(E A L Dunlop) *mde all: qcknd 4f out and sn clr w 3 rivals: hrd rdn 2f out : kpt on wl* **9/1**

00-0 **2** 1¼ **Brabazon (IRE)**[27] 781 3-8-9 **66**.. SteveDrowne 2 73
(R Charlton) *mostly chsd wnr: rdn 4f out: kpt on u.p fr over 2f out but nvr really able to chal* **16/1**

400- **3** *shd* **Ritsi**[196] 5795 3-8-11 **68**.. RyanMoore 4 75
(Mrs A J Perrett) *hld up in rr: bdly outpcd 4f out: drvn and prog fr 3f out: styd on fnl 2f: nrst fin* **8/1**

56-3 **4** 1¾ **Strategic Mount**[18] 897 3-9-1 **72**..(b[1]) TQuinn 11 76
(P F I Cole) *sn prom: rdn 4f out: no imp on wnr over 2f out: one pce* **9/2**[2]

2103 **5** 5 **Ballybeg (IRE)**[14] 945 3-8-13 **70**.. RichardHughes 10 66
(R Hannon) *hld up in midfield: bdly outpcd 4f out: drvn and tried to cl 3f out: wknd fnl f* **12/1**

044- **6** 2½ **Tower Hill (IRE)**[149] 6428 3-9-3 **74**.................................. PhilipRobinson 8 66
(M A Jarvis) *reluctant to enter stalls: hld up in midfield: bdly outpcd 4f out: shkn up and brief effrt over 2f out: no ch after* **5/2**[1]

6-43 **7** ¾ **Disco Lights**[20] 863 3-8-13 **70**.. ShaneKelly 3 61
(D J Daly) *prom: disp 2nd and pushed along 4f out: wknd 2f out* **25/1**

501- **8** 3 **Risk Runner (IRE)**[171] 6244 3-9-3 **74**................................... JDSmith 1 60
(A King) *dwlt: hld up in rr: bdly outpcd 4f out: sme prog 3f out: pushed along and no hdwy over 2f out* **17/2**

50-5 **9** 3½ **Citelle (IRE)**[7] 1052 3-8-1 **61** oh1.............................(t) RichardThomas[(3)] 7 41
(Mrs P N Dutfield) *a in rr: bdly outpcd 4f out: no ch after* **20/1**

060- **10** 1 **Recalcitrant**[185] 6009 3-8-4 **61** oh1.. JohnEgan 6 40
(S Dow) *plld hrd: prom to 1/2-way: outpcd and btn 4f out: wknd* **25/1**

6-00 **11** 10 **Pocket Too**[58] 515 3-8-5 **62** oh1 ow1....................(b[1]) StephenCarson 12 25
(Jean-Rene Auvray) *chsd ldrs: awkward bnd over 5f out: bdly outpcd 4f out: wknd* **66/1**

51-5 **12** ¾ **Katies Tuitor**[49] 592 3-9-4 **75**.. JamieSpencer 9 37
(B W Duke) *t.k.h: hld up in last pair: bdly outpcd 4f out: hrd rdn 3f out: lost action and eased over 1f out* **6/1**[3]

2m 28.9s (-1.20) **Going Correction** -0.20s/f (Firm) **12** Ran SP% **120.2**
Speed ratings (Par 98):96,95,95,93,90 88,88,86,84,83 76,76
CSF £138.62 CT £1210.50 TOTE £7.10: £3.10, £4.10, £2.90; EX 109.50 Place 6 £67.64, Place 5 £36.18.
Owner Mrs Janice Quy **Bred** Catridge Farm Stud Ltd **Trained** Newmarket, Suffolk

FOCUS
Another race run at a solid pace and again few got into the argument. The race was run in a fair time and has been rated around that with little solid form to go on.
Katies Tuitor Official explanation: jockey said gelding hung right throughout
T/Plt: £52.10 to a £1 stake. Pool: £52,630.60. 736.90 winning tickets. T/Qpdt: £23.50 to a £1 stake. Pool: £4,032.50. 126.50 winning tickets. JN

1148 WOLVERHAMPTON (A.W) (L-H)
Monday, April 24

OFFICIAL GOING: Standard
Wind: Almost nil Weather: Overcast

1194 BETFRED BANDED STKS 1m 141y(P)
1:50 (1:50) (Class 7) 4-Y-0+ **£1,365** (£403; £201) **Stalls** Low

Form RPR

204U **1** **Musical Gift**[2] 1148 6-9-1 48....................................(p) RobbieFitzpatrick 6 55
(P A Blockley) *chsd ldrs: n.m.r over 3f out: rdn to ld and edgd lft 1f out: jst hld on* **12/1**

0-60 **2** *shd* **Magic Warrior**[13] 972 6-9-3 50.. PatDobbs 5 57
(J C Fox) *hld up in tch: rdn over 1f out: edgd lft: r.o* **10/1**

-013 **3** ¾ **Ballare (IRE)**[26] 792 7-9-1 48....................................(v) FergusSweeney 2 53
(P J Makin) *hld up: hdwy over 2f out: swtchd lft ins fnl f: r.o* **7/2**[1]

416- **4** *nk* **Merlins Profit**[235] 4883 6-9-2 49.. DeanMcKeown 11 53
(G A Swinbank) *hld up: hdwy 1/2-way: rdn over 2f out: r.o* **7/2**[1]

56-0 **5** 1¼ **Acuzio**[20] 882 5-9-3 50... ShaneKelly 9 52
(W M Brisbourne) *chsd ldrs: led over 2f out: rdn and hdd 1f out: n.m.r ins fnl f: styd on same pce* **17/2**[3]

0020 **6** ½ **Ming Vase**[3] 1123 4-8-11 47...................................... StanleyChin[(3)] 4 48
(P T Midgley) *led: rdn and hdd over 2f out: styng on same pce whn n.m.r ins fnl f* **12/1**

56-0 **7** *shd* **Aberdeen Park**[33] 697 4-9-3 50...............................(b) GeorgeBaker 1 50
(Mrs H Sweeting) *hld up: hdwy and swtchd lft over 1f out: nt rch ldrs* **12/1**

34-0 **8** *nk* **Icecap**[20] 882 6-9-3 50.. JimmyQuinn 3 50
(W G M Turner) *trckd ldrs: racd keenly: rdn over 1f out: styng on same pce whn hmpd nr fin* **15/2**[2]

-001 **9** 1¼ **Wanna Shout**[28] 769 8-9-2 49.. TonyCulhane 12 46
(R Dickin) *hld up: rdn over 3f out: n.d* **9/1**

-003 **10** 3½ **Luciferous (USA)**[19] 889 4-8-11 47...........................(v) AmirQuinn[(3)] 10 37
(P G Murphy) *s.i.s: hdwy 6f out: rdn and wknd over 2f out* **33/1**

0000 **11** 2½ **Belrose (IRE)**[7] 1056 4-9-1 48.. BrianReilly 7 33
(Mrs C A Dunnett) *mid-div: rdn over 2f out: sn wknd* **50/1**

-000 **12** *hd* **Don Pasquale**[5] 909 4-8-13 49.............................. JasonEdmunds[(3)] 8 33
(J T Stimpson) *sn pushed along in rr: hdwy over 2f out: sn rdn and wknd* **33/1**

5620 **13** 12 **Peggys First**[7] 1054 4-9-3 50...(p) PatCosgrave 13 9
(D E Cantillon) *trckd ldr: racd keenly: rdn and wknd over 2f out* **16/1**

1m 50.83s (-0.93) **Going Correction** -0.15s/f (Stan) **13** Ran SP% **122.6**
Speed ratings (Par 97):98,97,97,96,95 95,95,95,93,90 88,88,77
CSF £128.58 TOTE £14.00: £4.20, £3.40, £1.60; EX 168.80 Trifecta £140.40 Pool: £197.76. 1.00 winning ticket.
Owner S H Thorne **Bred** Benedikt Fabbender **Trained** Lambourn, Berks

FOCUS
A reasonable contest of its type, run at a decent pace, and the time was over a second quicker than the later race over the same trip. The form should prove reliable.
Acuzio Official explanation: jockey said gelding had no more to give
Luciferous(USA) Official explanation: trainer's rep said filly was unsuited by the track

1195 BETFRED MILLION BANDED STKS 5f 20y(P)
2:20 (2:20) (Class 7) 4-Y-0+ **£1,365** (£403; £201) **Stalls** Low

Form RPR

2420 **1** **Muktasb (USA)**[19] 886 5-8-13 49.........................(v) PatrickMathers[(3)] 2 59
(D Shaw) *hld up: hdwy 1/2-way: rdn to ld wl ins fnl f* **10/3**[1]

0-00 **2** 1 **New Options**[27] 782 9-9-0 47...............................(b) RobbieFitzpatrick 9 53
(Peter Grayson) *s.i.s: outpcd: hdwy over 1f out: r.o* **14/1**

130- **3** *shd* **Rowanberry**[237] 4852 4-9-0 47.. ShaneKelly 13 53+
(R M H Cowell) *hld up: hdwy over 1f out: sn rdn and hung lft: r.o* **22/1**

5505 **4** *nk* **Edged In Gold**[14] 951 4-9-3 50.................................(e) DarryllHolland 1 55
(P J Makin) *chsd ldrs: rdn to ld and edgd lft 1f out: hdd wl ins fnl f* **4/1**[2]

3500 **5** *hd* **Leah's Pride**[2] 1150 5-9-0 47... PhillipMakin 4 51
(Miss D A McHale) *s.i.s: sn drvn to chse ldrs: led over 3f out: rdn and hdd 1f out: unable qck ins fnl f* **8/1**

-000 **6** 3½ **Music Teacher**[27] 782 4-8-13 46.. JohnEgan 7 37
(N A Callaghan) *prom: rdn over 1f out: no ex* **8/1**

05-0 **7** *nk* **Estoille**[20] 864 5-9-1 48..(t) JimmyQuinn 10 38
(Mrs S Lamyman) *prom over 3f* **25/1**

00-1 **8** *nk* **Sharp Hat**[20] 872 12-9-0 47... TonyCulhane 12 36
(D W Chapman) *chsd ldrs: lost pl 3f out: n.d after* **14/1**

00-0 **9** 5 **Valiant Romeo**[21] 858 6-9-0 47.............................(v) DarrenWilliams 5 18
(R Bastiman) *chsd ldrs: rdn 1/2-way: wknd over 1f out* **9/1**

0-00 **10** 1¼ **College Queen**[19] 886 8-8-12 45.. IanMongan 6 12
(S Gollings) *led: hdd over 3f out: rdn and wknd over 1f out* **33/1**

1600 **11** ¾ **Blue Moon Hitman (IRE)**[14] 951 5-9-3 50...................(b) ChrisCatlin 11 14
(R Brotherton) *chsd ldrs: rdn 1/2-way: sn wknd* **14/1**

-521 **12** ½ **Prime Recreation**[19] 886 9-9-3 50...................................... DaleGibson 3 12
(P S Felgate) *s.s: hld up: wknd 2f out* **15/2**[3]

62.48 secs (-0.34) **Going Correction** -0.15s/f (Stan) **12** Ran SP% **118.2**
Speed ratings (Par 97):96,94,94,93,93 87,87,86,78,76 75,74
CSF £50.10 TOTE £5.20: £1.30, £4.40, £5.20; EX 103.60.
Owner Simon Mapletoft Racing I **Bred** Shadwell Farm LLC **Trained** Danethorpe, Notts

FOCUS
A routine banded sprint in which the front five finished in a heap. Straightforward and reliable form.
Rowanberry Official explanation: jockey said filly hung left in straight
Prime Recreation Official explanation: jockey said he had problems removing blindfold at start rendering gelding slowly away

1196 BETFREDPOKER.COM BANDED STKS 5f 216y(P)
2:50 (2:50) (Class 7) 4-Y-0+ **£1,365** (£403; £201) **Stalls** Low

Form RPR

0214 **1** **Misty Princess**[14] 942 4-8-13 46.................................... FrancisFerris 6 53
(M J Attwater) *chasd ldrs: rdn to ld ins fnl f: jst hld on* **11/2**[2]

00-0 **2** *shd* **Geojimali**[35] 681 4-9-3 50.. LPKeniry 3 57+
(J S Goldie) *dwlt: hdwy over 1f out: sn rdn: r.o* **33/1**

0502 **3** 1¼ **Border Artist**[12] 982 7-9-3 50.................................(b) DarryllHolland 10 53
(B G Powell) *hld up: hdwau over 1f out: sn rdn and hung lft: r.o* **8/1**[3]

0501 **4** *nk* **Laurel Dawn**[14] 943 8-9-0 47..(b) JimmyQuinn 1 49
(C N Kellett) *sn led: rdn over 1f out: hdd and unable qck ins fnl f* **14/1**

6221 **5** ¾ **Union Jack Jackson (IRE)**[14] 942 4-9-2 49...............(b) FergalLynch 7 56+
(J G Given) *hld up: hdwy and nt clr run over 1f out: rdn and edgd lft ins fnl f: r.o* **3/1**[1]

00-1 **6** ¾ **Magical Mimi**[24] 821 5-9-0 47...(t) ChrisCatlin 12 45
(K G Wingrove) *s.i.s: outpcd: hdwy over 1f out: styd on* **12/1**

030- **7** ½ **Haroldini (IRE)**[248] 4558 4-9-0 50........................(p) JasonEdmunds[(3)] 5 46
(J Balding) *mid-divsion: rdn over 2f out: swtchd rt over 1f out: styd on same pce* **12/1**

6024 **8** ½ **Beverley Beau**[19] 886 4-8-6 46.................................. KristinStubbs[(7)] 9 41
(Mrs L Stubbs) *led early: chsd ldrs: rdn over 2f out: styd on same pce appr fnl f* **10/1**

0000 **9** ¾ **Time N Time Again**[30] 732 8-9-3 50..................(b) RobbieFitzpatrick 2 42
(Peter Grayson) *mid-div: effrt and nt clr run over 1f out: n.d* **8/1**[3]

00-0 **10** 1 **Waggledance (IRE)**[21] 862 4-9-0 50..................... DanielTudhope[(3)] 13 39
(D Carroll) *chsd ldrs: rdn over 2f out: wkng whn hmpd ins fnl f* **20/1**

000- **11** ½ **Mostanad**[187] 5975 4-9-3 50.. ShaneKelly 4 38
(J M Bradley) *prom over 4f* **10/1**

0610 **12** 2½ **Sundried Tomato**[28] 766 7-9-0 47..............................(p) TonyCulhane 8 27
(D W Chapman) *hld up in tch: rdn over 2f out: wknd over 1f out* **12/1**

106- **13** *shd* **Tuscan Flyer**[182] 6076 8-9-1 48...................................... DarrenWilliams 11 28
(R Bastiman) *mid-div: hdwy u.p over 2f out: wknd over 1f out* **18/1**

1m 15.62s (-0.19) **Going Correction** -0.15s/f (Stan) **13** Ran SP% **123.5**
Speed ratings (Par 97):95,94,93,92,91 90,90,89,88,87 86,83,83
CSF £177.93 TOTE £6.20: £1.90, £7.70, £3.00; EX 170.00.
Owner Mrs M Tanner **Bred** G L And Mrs Tanner **Trained** Wysall, Notts

FOCUS
A very ordinary banded contest run at an even pace. The winner is rated back to her best.
Union Jack Jackson(IRE) Official explanation: jockey said gelding was denied a clear run

Sundried Tomato Official explanation: trainer's rep said gelding lost a front plate

1197 BETFREDCASINO.COM BANDED STKS 1m 141y(P)
3:20 (3:20) (Class 7) 4-Y-0+ £1,365 (£403; £201) Stalls Low

Form RPR
0653 1 **Bob Baileys**[14] [937] 4-8-12 40..........(b) JimmyQuinn 4 48
(P R Chamings) *chsd ldrs: rdn to ld over 1f out: all out* 10/1
3540 2 hd **Tuscan Treaty**[19] [888] 6-8-12 45..........(tp) DarryllHolland 10 48
(P J McBride) *hld up: hdwy u.p and hung lft over 1f out: r.o* 11/2[2]
06-0 3 nk **Tamora**[16] [917] 4-8-12 45.......... DarrenWilliams 1 47
(A P Jarvis) *led: hung rt sn after s: rdn and hdd over 1f out: r.o* 5/1[1]
0-43 4 ½ **Heathyards Joy**[26] [791] 5-8-5 40..........(p) RussellKennemore(7) 6 46
(R Hollinshead) *hld up: hdwy over 3f out: rdn 2f out: r.o* 12/1
0045 5 hd **Welsh Whisper**[26] [792] 7-8-9 45.......... NeilChalmers(3) 13 46
(S A Brookshaw) *dwlt: hld up: hdwy over 1f out: r.o* 16/1
-000 6 1 ½ **Annals**[12] [974] 4-8-12 45..........(p) JohnEgan 7 43
(R C Guest) *prom: rdn over 1f out: no ex ins fnl f* 10/1
0040 7 shd **Super Dominion**[26] [792] 9-8-12 45.......... VinceSlattery 11 43
(R Hollinshead) *hld up: rdn over 2f out: r.o ins fnl f: nvr nrr* 16/1
3006 8 nk **Paper Doll**[28] [768] 4-8-5 45..........(p) SoniaEaton(7) 9 42
(B P J Baugh) *prom: nt clr run over 2f out: sn lost pl: styd on ins fnl f* 16/1
0005 9 ¾ **Mytton's Dream**[26] [793] 4-8-12 45..........(b) ChrisCatlin 2 40
(R Brotherton) *stmbld sn after s: mid-div: hdwy over 2f out: sn rdn: styd on same pce fnl f* 12/1
000 10 1 ½ **Qobtaan (USA)**[35] [681] 7-8-12 45.......... IanMongan 5 37
(M R Bosley) *hld up: effrt over 1f out: nt trble ldrs* 8/1[3]
2231 11 ½ **Faithisflying**[14] [937] 4-8-12 45..........(p) TonyCulhane 3 36
(D W Chapman) *hld up: rdn over 2f out: nt clr run over 1f out: n.d* 11/2[2]
000- 12 1 ¾ **Mazindar (USA)**[205] [5618] 4-8-9 45.......... DanielTudhope(3) 8 32
(P T Midgley) *chsd ldrs: rdn over 1f out: wknd fnl f* 16/1
00-0 13 7 **Tonight (IRE)**[26] [792] 4-8-12 45..........(bt) ShaneKelly 12 18
(W M Brisbourne) *chsd ldrs: rdn over 3f out: wknd wl over 1f out* 20/1

1m 51.95s (0.19) **Going Correction** -0.15s/f (Stan) 13 Ran SP% 120.4
Speed ratings (Par 97):93,92,92,92,91 90,90,90,89,88 87,86,80
CSF £64.63 TOTE £11.80: £3.50, £1.80, £1.90; EX 98.40.
Owner Mrs J E L Wright **Bred** Wheelersland Stud **Trained** Baughurst, Hants

FOCUS
A moderate race and the pace was ordinary resulting in a time over a second slower than the earlier race over the same trip. There were five virtually in a line across the track passing the post. Modest form even for the grade.
Faithisflying Official explanation: jockey said gelding was hampered at the start
Mazindar(USA) Official explanation: trainer said gelding failed to stay 1m4f

1198 BETFRED "THE BONUS KING" BANDED STKS 1m 1f 103y(P)
3:50 (3:50) (Class 7) 4-Y-0+ £1,365 (£403; £201) Stalls Low

Form RPR
5230 1 **Miss Glory Be**[19] [888] 8-8-12 45..........(p) DarryllHolland 3 51
(Ernst Oertel) *hld up in tch: chsd ldr over 1f out: r.o to ld wl ins fnl f* 6/1[3]
-052 2 1 **Danum**[26] [791] 6-8-5 45..........(p) RussellKennemore(7) 8 49
(R Hollinshead) *led: rdn clr over 1f out: hdd wl ins fnl f* 14/1
-040 3 shd **Homebred Star**[35] [683] 5-8-7 45.......... RobynBrisland(5) 1 49+
(G P Enright) *hld up: hdwy over 1f out: edgd lft: r.o* 7/1
2452 4 shd **Spy Gun (USA)**[26] [792] 6-8-12 45.......... J-PGuillambert 4 49
(T Wall) *s.i.s: hld up: hdwy over 1f out: r.o* 5/1[2]
0450 5 1 ¼ **Opera Knight**[35] [682] 6-8-12 45.......... TonyCulhane 13 46
(A W Carroll) *hld up: rdn over 3f out: hdwy over 1f out: r.o* 15/2
50-0 6 1 ¼ **Longing For Cindy (USA)**[95] [147] 4-8-5 45..........(v) LiamJones(7) 11 44
(W M Brisbourne) *prom: rdn over 2f out: hung lft over 1f out: styd on same pce* 16/1
331- 7 ½ **Komreyev Star**[177] [6141] 4-8-12 45.......... JimmyQuinn 6 43
(M Mullineaux) *prom: rdn to chse ldr over 2f out: wknd fnl f* 4/1[1]
006- 8 3 ½ **Gravardlax**[127] [6606] 5-8-12 45..........(t) JamieMackay 9 36
(Miss D A McHale) *hld up: rdn over 2f out: n.d* 33/1
005- 9 ½ **Fit To Fly (IRE)**[205] [5621] 5-8-12 45..........(p) JohnEgan 12 35
(R C Guest) *mid-div: rdn over 2f out: sn wknd* 10/1
0-60 10 ½ **Angel River**[7] [1057] 4-8-5 45..........(p) DonnaCaldwell(7) 2 34
(J Ryan) *hld up: n.d* 25/1
000- 11 1 ½ **Rainbow Treasure (IRE)**[207] [5564] 4-8-9 45.......... NelsonDeSouza(3) 5 32
(R M Beckett) *prom: rdn 1/2-way: wknd over 3f* 16/1
005- 12 hd **Senor Eduardo**[115] [6691] 9-8-12 45..........(p) IanMongan 7 31
(S Gollings) *chsd ldr 7f: wknd over 1f out* 16/1
0-00 13 9 **Fortunes Favourite**[19] [888] 6-8-7 45.......... NataliaGemelova(5) 10 14
(J E Long) *s.i.s: a in rr* 33/1

2m 2.19s (-0.43) **Going Correction** -0.15s/f (Stan) 13 Ran SP% 118.4
Speed ratings (Par 97):95,94,94,93,92 91,91,88,87,87 85,85,77
CSF £84.64 TOTE £6.00: £2.80, £4.30, £2.30; EX 62.00 Trifecta £106.30 - part won..
Owner Winning Colours Racing Club **Bred** Khalid Al Ghurair **Trained** Newmarket, Suffolk
■ Ernst Oertel's first winner from his new base at Mill Hill in London, where Andrew Reid was previously the licence holder.

FOCUS
A routine banded contest and the winning time was fractionally slower than the later contest over the same trip. Sound enough form.
Homebred Star Official explanation: jockey said, regarding the running and riding, his orders were to hold gelding up and make his run as late as possible to ensure gelding stayed the trip; trainer added that gelding must be delivered to challenge very late to show its best form
Fit To Fly(IRE) Official explanation: trainer's rep said gelding had a breathing problem
Fortunes Favourite Official explanation: jockey said mare had lost her action

1199 BETFRED 570 SHOPS NATIONWIDE BANDED STKS 2m 119y(P)
4:20 (4:20) (Class 7) 4-Y-0+ £1,365 (£403; £201) Stalls Low

Form RPR
0666 1 **Lake Wakatipu**[28] [767] 4-9-0 47.......... JimmyQuinn 11 58
(M Mullineaux) *hld up: hdwy over 3f out: rdn over 1f out: styd on to ld post* 16/1
-005 2 shd **Rose Bien**[7] [1058] 4-9-3 50..........(p) TonyCulhane 6 61
(P J McBride) *hld up: hdwy 7f out: rdn to ld 1f out: hdd post* 12/1
6222 3 5 **Larad (IRE)**[28] [767] 5-9-4 47..........(b) JohnEgan 3 52
(J S Moore) *hld up: hdwy over 5f out: rdn and ev ch over 1f out: sn wknd* 4/1[1]
6104 4 nk **Ice And Fire**[14] [938] 7-8-10 46.......... AshleyHamblett(7) 8 51
(J T Stimpson) *s.i.s: hld up: hdwy over 2f out: sn rdn: styd on same pce* 16/1
-204 5 ¾ **Soviet Sceptre (IRE)**[20] [882] 5-9-7 50..........(t) FergusSweeney 10 54
(R T Phillips) *hld up in tch: led 5f out: hdd & wknd 1f out* 9/1
-P02 6 nk **Cemgraft**[42] [457] 5-9-2 48..........(tp) RichardThomas(3) 7 52+
(A J Lidderdale) *hld up: hdwy 5f out: nt clr run and lost pl over 2f out: styd on ins fnl f* 11/1
1-04 7 6 **Saameq (IRE)**[28] [767] 5-9-2 48.......... DanielTudhope(3) 9 44
(D W Thompson) *s.i.s: hld up: hdwy over 3f out: wknd 2f out* 6/1[3]
310- 8 2 ½ **Michaels Dream (IRE)**[133] [6563] 7-8-13 45..........(b) DNolan(3) 1 38
(N Wilson) *w ldr over 2f: remained handy tl rdn and wknd 2f out* 16/1
0-30 9 20 **Scott's Mill**[17] [911] 4-8-9 45.......... StanleyChin(3) 2 14
(M Johnston) *rdn to ld sn after s: hdd 10f out: lost pl 6f out: sn bhd* 16/1
6031 10 6 **High (IRE)**[26] [794] 4-9-3 50.......... LPKeniry 12 12
(W J Musson) *hld up: hdwy 6f out: rdn and wknd over 2f out* 11/2[2]
5440 11 7 **Noble Mind**[19] [891] 5-9-4 47..........(p) RobertHavlin 5 —
(P G Murphy) *prom over 12f* 50/1
0632 12 1 ¼ **High Frequency (IRE)**[27] [785] 5-9-1 47..........(b) BenSwarbrick(3) 4 —
(T D Barron) *trckd ldrs: racd keenly: led 6f out: rdn and hdd 5f out: wknd over 3f out* 6/1[3]
320- 13 21 **Gabor**[169] [6081] 7-9-2 45..........(e) DarryllHolland 13 —
(D W Thompson) *trckd ldrs: racd keenly: led 10f out: hdd 6f out: wknd 4f out* 18/1

3m 41.17s (-1.96) **Going Correction** -0.15s/f (Stan)
WFA 4 from 5yo+ 4lb 13 Ran SP% 120.7
Speed ratings (Par 97):98,97,95,95,95 94,92,90,81,78 75,74,64
CSF £197.69 TOTE £25.80: £4.60, £4.50, £1.60; EX 215.20 TRIFECTA Not won..
Owner Esprit De Corps Racing **Bred** T S And Mrs Wallace **Trained** Alpraham, Cheshire

FOCUS
A fair pace for this modest race and the ability to see out the trip was of paramount importance. The front two pulled well clear and the form is slightly above average for the grade.

1200 BETFRED TRI-BANDED STKS 5f 216y(P)
4:50 (4:51) (Class 7) 3-Y-O £1,365 (£403; £201) Stalls Low

Form RPR
-060 1 **Red Vixen (IRE)**[26] [796] 3-8-7 45.......... KirstyMilczarek(7) 4 56
(C N Allen) *hld up: hdwy over 2f out: led over 1f out: rdn clr* 16/1
0-50 2 2 ½ **Light Of Day (IRE)**[28] [762] 3-8-7 45.......... KylieManser(7) 7 48
(J R Best) *s.i.s: outpcd: r.o ins fnl f: nrst fin* 14/1
2153 3 1 ¾ **Berties Brother**[26] [790] 3-8-11 45.......... DNolan(3) 1 43
(D G Bridgwater) *led: rdn and hdd over 1f out: no ex* 5/1[2]
-233 4 1 **Silver Nun**[20] [874] 3-9-0 45.......... FergalLynch 8 40
(T D Easterby) *trckd ldrs: nt clr run over 2f out: styd on same pce appr fnl f* 6/1[3]
0044 5 ¾ **Jazz At The Sands (USA)**[14] [936] 3-9-0 45..........(v) RobbieFitzpatrick 2 38
(D Shaw) *prom: rdn over 2f out: styd on same pce appr fnl f* 8/1
0-20 6 ½ **Bertie Bear**[20] [874] 3-8-9 40..........(bt[1]) JimmyQuinn 3 31
(G G Margarson) *hld up: rdn 1/2-way: styd on ins fnl f: nrst fin* 8/1
00-0 7 hd **Whistleupthewind**[20] [868] 3-8-9 40..........(b[1]) TonyCulhane 12 31
(J M P Eustace) *chsd ldrs: rdn and ev ch 2f out: wknd fnl f* 16/1
00-1 8 2 **Joking John**[26] [790] 3-8-4 40.......... LeanneKershaw(5) 5 25
(C W Fairhurst) *prom: hmpd and lost pl 5f out: hdwy 2f out: wknd over 1f out* 4/1[1]
2050 9 hd **My Reflection**[41] [637] 3-8-11 45..........(v) PatrickMathers(3) 6 29
(D Shaw) *hld up: hdwy over 2f out: rdn and wknd over 1f out* 15/2
0526 10 2 **Saxon Star (IRE)**[14] [936] 3-9-0 45..........(v) HayleyTurner 9 23
(M D I Usher) *rrd in stalls: chsd ldr: rdn over 2f out: wknd over 1f out* 16/1
000- 11 3 **Cape Courier (IRE)**[187] [5977] 3-9-0 45..........(p) PatCosgrave 10 14
(I W McInnes) *prom: rdn over 3f out: wknd over 2f out* 33/1
6035 12 dist **Lasting Love**[34] [690] 3-9-0 45..........(b) DarryllHolland 11 —
(C R Dore) *rrd in stalls: dwlt: outpcd* 20/1

1m 16.02s (0.21) **Going Correction** -0.15s/f (Stan) 12 Ran SP% 117.0
Speed ratings (Par 92):92,88,86,85,84 83,83,80,80,77 73,—
CSF £219.62 TOTE £26.20: £6.10, £4.70, £2.60; EX 448.90 TRIFECTA Not won..
Owner Red Vixen Partnership **Bred** Darley **Trained** Newmarket, Suffolk

FOCUS
A poor race, but a convincing winner.
Joking John Official explanation: jockey said gelding was hampered shortly after start
Lasting Love Official explanation: jockey said filly hung right-handed throughout

1201 BETFRED PAY DOUBLE RESULT BANDED STKS 1m 1f 103y(P)
5:20 (5:20) (Class 7) 4-Y-0+ £1,535 (£453; £226) Stalls Low

Form RPR
0465 1 **Abbeygate**[19] [889] 5-9-1 48..........(p) J-PGuillambert 10 54
(T Keddy) *hld up: hdwy over 1f out: r.o u.p to ld nr fin* 12/1
2 ½ **Hillhall (IRE)**[238] [4845] 4-8-8 48.......... LiamJones(7) 1 53
(W M Brisbourne) *led: rdn over 1f out: hdd nr fin* 25/1
6001 3 shd **Fiore Di Bosco (IRE)**[26] [792] 5-9-1 48.......... PhillipMakin 9 53
(T D Barron) *s.s: hld up: nt clr run over 2f out: hdwy over 1f out: r.o* 6/1[1]
0/01 4 nk **Heathers Girl**[14] [939] 7-9-0 47.......... TonyCulhane 2 51
(R Dickin) *a.p: rdn to chse ldr 2f out: styd on* 6/1[1]
3001 5 ½ **Diamond Dan (IRE)**[28] [771] 4-8-13 49.......... DanielTudhope(3) 12 55+
(P D Evans) *hld up: nt clr run over 2f out: r.o ins fnl f: nrst fin* 6/1[1]
0200 6 1 ¼ **Farnborough (USA)**[2] [1138] 5-9-2 49.......... GeorgeBaker 13 50+
(R J Price) *hld up: hdwy u.p over 1f out: nt rch ldrs* 10/1[3]
5026 7 ¾ **Pharaoh Prince**[19] [888] 5-9-1 48.......... ChrisCatlin 5 48
(G Prodromou) *hld up: nt clr run over 2f out: styd on ins fnl f: nvr nrr* 13/2[2]
0422 8 1 ½ **Good Article (IRE)**[19] [888] 5-9-3 50.......... DarryllHolland 6 47
(D K Ivory) *chsd ldr over 7f: sn rdn: styd on same pce* 13/2[2]
360- 9 ½ **Kyle Of Lochalsh**[164] [5892] 6-9-3 50.......... FergalLynch 3 46
(J S Goldie) *mid-div: rdn over 2f out: hdwy over 1f out: wknd ins fnl f* 10/1[3]
-006 10 5 **Ballycroy Girl (IRE)**[51] [582] 4-9-3 50..........(p) SamHitchcott 4 36
(A Bailey) *hld up: rdn over 3f out: wknd over 2f out* 16/1
5500 11 1 **Tregarron**[51] [586] 5-9-2 49.......... CraigCarver 8 33
(P A Blockley) *hld up in tch: rdn and wknd over 2f out* 16/1
0000 12 hd **Agilete**[62] [472] 4-9-3 50.......... PatCosgrave 11 34
(R A Harris) *chsd ldrs: rdn over 2f out: sn wknd* 12/1
-150 13 7 **Whenwillitwin**[41] [636] 5-9-1 48..........(b[1]) LPKeniry 7 19
(J S Moore) *chsd ldrs 7f* 11/1

2m 1.98s (-0.64) **Going Correction** -0.15s/f (Stan) 13 Ran SP% 127.0
Speed ratings (Par 97):96,95,95,95,94 93,92,91,91,86 85,85,79
CSF £295.58 TOTE £17.80: £5.00, £6.90, £3.60; EX 287.70 TRIFECTA Not won. Place 6 £492.19, Place 5 £170.98.
Owner Mrs H Keddy **Bred** I A Southcott **Trained** Newmarket, Suffolk

FOCUS
Not a bad race for the grade but only ordinary form and the winning time was slightly slower than the earlier race over the same trip won by Miss Glory Be.
Fiore Di Bosco(IRE) Official explanation: jockey said mare was slowly away from stalls
T/Plt: £355.70 to a £1 stake. Pool: £30,310.65. 62.20 winning tickets. T/Qpdt: £40.90 to a £1 stake. Pool: £2,624.20. 47.40 winning tickets. CR

961 BATH (L-H)
Tuesday, April 25

OFFICIAL GOING: Good
Wind: Slight, ahead

1203 TONY SMALLWOOD RETIREMENT AND SMALLWOOD CARPENTRY MAIDEN AUCTION STKS 5f 11y
5:10 (5:12) (Class 4) 2-Y-O £4,533 (£1,348; £674; £336) Stalls Low

Form RPR
2 1 **Alternative**[14] [961] 2-8-11 SebSanders 7 85
(R M Beckett) *trckd ldrs: led jst ins fnl f: drvn out* 2/1[1]
2 2½ **Mood Music** 2-8-13 RichardMullen 6 77+
(E J O'Neill) *s.i.s: bhd: rdn over 2f out: hdwy over 1f out: r.o strly to take 2nd nr fin but no ch w wnr* 15/2
3 nk **Grand Prix** 2-8-11 RichardHughes 2 74
(R Hannon) *sn slt advantage on rail: rdn 2f out: hdd jst ins last: sn one pce: ct for 2nd cl home* 4/1[2]
4 1¾ **Tencendur (IRE)** 2-8-11 KDarley 4 67
(M Johnston) *bhd and sn pushed along: swtchd to outside and hdwy fr 2f out: r.o fnl f but nt rch ldrs* 13/2[3]
06 5 1¾ **Chip Leader**[10] [1019] 2-8-13 PatDobbs 3 62
(R Hannon) *w ldr: rdn over 2f out: wknd fnl f* 33/1
6 nk **Bahamian Love** 2-8-4 TQuinn 10 52
(B W Hills) *in tch tl n.m.r and lost position 2f out: kpt on again fnl f* 12/1
7 nk **Cesc** 2-8-9 JimmyFortune 5 55
(P J Makin) *t.k.h early: chsd ldrs: rdn 2f out: wknd fnl f* 8/1
8 1 **Benllech** 2-8-9 DarryllHolland 11 51
(S Kirk) *s.i.s: sn rcvrd to chse ldrs and c wd bnd 3f out: rdn 2f out: wknd fnl f* 16/1
06 9 2½ **Fasuby (IRE)**[21] [878] 2-8-6 JohnEgan 9 38
(P D Evans) *pressed ldrs: rdn 3f out: wknd appr fnl f* 40/1
10 ¾ **Star Strider** 2-8-11 FergusSweeney 1 40
(A M Balding) *sn in tch: rdn 1/2-way: wknd ins fnl 2f* 14/1
11 hd **Montemayorprincess (IRE)** 2-8-1 RichardThomas(3) 12 33
(D Haydn Jones) *prssed ldrs: v green whn rdn 1/2-way: wknd and hung bdly lft ins fnl 2f* 66/1
12 8 **High Bullen** 2-8-6 ChrisCatlin 8 —
(M Meade) *bhd: lost tch fr 1/2-way* 100/1

64.37 secs (1.87) **Going Correction** +0.20s/f (Good) 12 Ran SP% **117.6**
Speed ratings (Par 94):93,89,88,85,82 82,81,80,76,75 74,62
CSF £17.09 TOTE £2.50: £1.30, £3.00, £1.70; EX 18.60.
Owner Thurloe Thoroughbreds XVIII **Bred** R Haim **Trained** Whitsbury, Hants
■ A first winner for Ralph Beckett from his new base at Whitsbury.

FOCUS
An ordinary maiden run at a fair pace. The winner won it well but the level of the form is far from solid.

NOTEBOOK
Alternative made his previous experience count, quickening clear of his rivals when the gap finally opened. He looks a fair early-season sort and will presumably head to a novice event next time. (op 9-4 tchd 15-8)
Mood Music, by first-season sire Kyllachy, took a while to get the hang of things but stayed on strongly to grab second. With normal improvement, he should go very close next time. (op 5-1 tchd 8-1)
Grand Prix, a half-brother to six-furlong winners, showed some speed on his debut but did not get home as well as the front two. It was a promising enough debut, and it will be a surprise if his trainer is not able to get a win out of his charge as a juvenile. (op 5-1)
Tencendur(IRE), who was a late foal, was fairly clueless on his debut and should derive plenty of improvement for the run. (op 11-2 tchd 7-1)
Chip Leader, who had run twice before, had every chance but did not see the trip out as well as others. He will need an ease in grade to be fully competitive in the short-term. (op 28-1)
Bahamian Love shaped with some promise and will know more next time. Official explanation: jockey said filly was denied a clear run 2f out (op 10-1)
Cesc was really well supported in the market prior to the race but did not get home after taking a strong grip early on. Evidently well thought of, he is one to watch out for next time if tried in similar company. (op 25-1)
Montemayorprincess(IRE) Official explanation: jockey said filly hung left-handed

1204 32RED ONLINE CASINO H'CAP 1m 2f 46y
5:40 (5:43) (Class 6) (0-65,65) 4-Y-0+ £3,238 (£963; £481; £240) Stalls Low

Form RPR
1233 1 **Jakarmi**[3] [1148] 5-9-1 62 TonyCulhane 12 75
(B Palling) *mde all: drvn 4l clr over 2f out: kpt on strly: unchal* 5/1[1]
20-3 2 5 **Nina Fontenail (FR)**[34] [697] 5-8-13 60 RobertHavlin 15 63
(B R Millman) *chsd ldrs: rdn and kpt on fr over 2f out: styd ins last to take 2nd cl home but nvr nr unchal wnr* 15/2
640- 3 ¾ **Kathryn Janeway (IRE)**[295] [3177] 4-9-2 63 SebSanders 4 65
(W R Muir) *chsd ldrs: rdn to chse clr ldr and subsequent unchal wnr over 2f out: nvr a danger: lost 2nd nr fin* 25/1
000- 4 nk **Ruling Reef**[206] [5629] 4-8-5 52 ow1 RobertWinston 5 53
(M D I Usher) *chsd ldrs: rdn 3f out: kpt on same pce fnl 2f* 25/1
000 5 ¾ **Flyingwithoutwings**[31] [720] 7-8-2 52 RichardThomas(3) 7 52
(A King) *behind: rdn and hdwy over 2f out: kpt on wl fr over 1f out but nvr in contention* 22/1
0406 6 hd **Smoothie (IRE)**[31] [733] 8-8-4 51 oh1 ChrisCatlin 18 51
(Ian Williams) *bhd: hdwy on outside fr 3f out: kpt on fr over 1f out but nvr in contention* 12/1
0514 7 1¼ **Summer Bounty**[14] [965] 10-9-3 64 JimmyFortune 11 61
(F Jordan) *in tch: riddne and hdwy over 2f out: kpt on same pce ins last* 8/1
02/0 8 1¼ **Three Welshmen**[21] [882] 5-8-4 51 oh1 NickyMackay 6 46
(D Burchell) *bhd: rdn 3f out: kpt on fnl 2f but nvr rchd ldrs* 40/1
030- 9 1¼ **Arthurs Dream (IRE)**[170] [5866] 4-8-6 58 JamesDoyle(5) 2 51
(A W Carroll) *s.i.s: bhd: pushed along over 3f out: kpt on fnl 2f and styd on cl home but nvr in contention* 33/1
-000 10 4 **Meelup (IRE)**[14] [965] 6-8-10 60 (p) AmirQuinn(3) 16 45
(P G Murphy) *chsd ldrs: rdn 3f out: edgd lft over 2f out: wknd over 1f out* 40/1
02-0 11 shd **Inn For The Dancer**[15] [955] 4-8-6 53 ow2 FergusSweeney 13 38
(J C Fox) *sn in rr: nvr in contention* 28/1
166/ 12 1¼ **Garston Star**[572] [5889] 5-8-9 56 DarryllHolland 10 38
(J S Moore) *chsd ldrs tl wknd ins fnl 3f* 14/1
20-0 13 nk **Primeshade Promise**[34] [697] 5-8-7 57 EdwardCreighton(3) 8 39
(D Burchell) *bhd most of way* 33/1
0000 14 1 **Lockstock (IRE)**[18] [906] 8-9-0 64 (p) RobertMiles(3) 14 44
(M S Saunders) *wd bnd 3f out: a in rr* 33/1
5011 15 3 **Lord Of Dreams (IRE)**[15] [955] 4-9-4 65 TQuinn 9 39
(D W P Arbuthnot) *mid-div: effrt over 3f out: wknd over 2f out* 13/2[2]
0500 16 26 **Postmaster**[62] [482] 4-8-6 53 JohnEgan 17 —
(R Ingram) *pressed ldr: 5f: wknd ins fnl 3f: eased whn no ch fnl f* 11/1
030- 17 12 **Xacobeo (IRE)**[166] [6307] 4-8-8 55 RichardHughes 3 —
(R Hannon) *in tch early: bhd fnl 3f and eased whn no ch* 7/1[3]

2m 11.92s (0.92) **Going Correction** +0.20s/f (Good) 17 Ran SP% **117.3**
Speed ratings (Par 101):104,100,99,99,98 98,97,96,95,92 92,91,90,90,87 66,57
CSF £33.82 CT £849.85 TOTE £5.00: £1.40, £1.90, £6.60, £7.50; EX 28.70.
Owner Bryn Palling **Bred** Llety Stud **Trained** Tredodridge, Vale Of Glamorgan

FOCUS
A very moderate event in which the winner dictated. The form looks fairly sound.
Lord Of Dreams(IRE) Official explanation: jockey said colt lost its action
Xacobeo(IRE) Official explanation: jockey said colt hung badly left-handed

1205 32 RED ONLINE POKER ROOM H'CAP 1m 2f 46y
6:10 (6:12) (Class 4) (0-85,84) 3-Y-O £7,886 (£2,360; £1,180; £590; £293) Stalls Low

Form RPR
00-1 1 **Gracechurch (IRE)**[31] [730] 3-8-13 79 TonyCulhane 3 82
(M R Channon) *trckd ldrs: wnt 2nd over 2f out: hrd rdn and r.o gamely fnl f to ld last stride* 11/2[3]
-132 2 shd **Go Figure (IRE)**[12] [1005] 3-8-9 75 (t) JimmyFortune 5 78
(B J Meehan) *led: hrd rdn and kpt on fnl f: ct last stride* 10/3[1]
005- 3 ¾ **Ogee**[164] [6334] 3-8-5 71 ow1 RobertWinston 4 72
(Sir Michael Stoute) *chsd ldrs: nt handle bnd and pushed along 5f out: sn rcvrd: rdn and outpcd over 2f out:kpt on again fnl f gng on fin* 7/1
1111 4 1½ **Prince Charlemagne (IRE)**[62] [483] 3-8-11 82 JamesDoyle(5) 8 81
(N P Littmoden) *hld up rr: swtchd rt to outer and hdwy fr 2f out: kpt on same pce u.p ins last* 13/2
01- 5 shd **Zilcash**[261] [4188] 3-8-12 78 JDSmith 1 76
(A King) *rr but in tch: hdwy on rails to chse ldrs ins fnl 3f: rdn 2f out and sn outpcd* 16/1
51- 6 1 **All The Good (IRE)**[150] [6428] 3-9-4 84 KDarley 9 80
(G A Butler) *hld up in rr: hday on outside fr 5f out to chse ldrs 3f out: rdn and effrt 2f out: hung lft and wknd wl over 1f out* 9/2[2]
650- 7 3½ **Fear To Tread (USA)**[206] [5604] 3-8-7 73 TQuinn 6 63
(J L Dunlop) *in tch: rdn to chse ldrs 3f out: wknd over 2f out* 8/1
01-4 8 6 **Silver Chariot**[31] [724] 3-8-8 74 MichaelHills 7 52
(B W Hills) *sn chsng ldr: rdn 3f out: wknd over 2f out* 12/1
-100 9 ½ **Miss Highjinks (USA)**[24] [827] 3-9-2 82 ChrisCatlin 2 59
(E J O'Neill) *a in rr: wknd ins fnl 3f* 20/1

2m 12.84s (1.84) **Going Correction** +0.20s/f (Good) 9 Ran SP% **111.9**
Speed ratings (Par 100):100,99,99,98,98 97,94,89,89
CSF £23.13 CT £127.26 TOTE £6.60: £2.10, £1.60, £2.30; EX 25.20.
Owner Gracechurch Racing Syndicate **Bred** Major K R Thompson **Trained** West Ilsley, Berks
■ Stewards' Enquiry : Tony Culhane caution: used whip without giving gelding time to respond

FOCUS
A decent little handicap that looks sure to throw up some winners.

1206 GET £100 FREE AT 32RED H'CAP 1m 3f 144y
6:40 (6:41) (Class 4) (0-85,85) 4-Y-O-£7,886 (£2,360; £1,180; £590; £293) Stalls Low

Form RPR
00-5 1 **Top Seed (IRE)**[27] [799] 5-8-7 73 SamHitchcott 4 85
(M R Channon) *hld up in rr: rdn and hdwy on outside over 2f out: led appr fnl f: drvn clr ins last* 14/1
142- 2 3 **Prince Vector**[190] [5948] 4-9-1 82 SebSanders 7 89
(A King) *chsd ldrs on rail: hdwy over 2f out: chsd wnr ins last but no imp* 11/2[3]
-345 3 ¾ **Modaffaa**[24] [834] 6-8-12 78 JimmyFortune 11 84
(P R Webber) *in tch: rdn and outpcd appr fnl 2f: kpt on again u.p ins last: kpt on cl home* 10/1
040- 4 hd **Solo Flight**[185] [6025] 9-9-5 85 TonyCulhane 2 90+
(H Morrison) *t.k.h:hld up in tch: hdwy and hmpd appr fnl f: nt clr run again ins last: fin strly cl home* 28/1
006- 5 1¼ **Jack Of Trumps (IRE)**[185] [6025] 6-9-3 83 FrancisNorton 9 86+
(G Wragg) *rr: n.m.r and swtchd towards outside 3f out: hdwy whn hmpd appr fnl f: r.o ins last: nt a danger* 7/1
4-01 6 shd **Yakimov (USA)**[8] [1051] 7-8-12 81 5ex EdwardCreighton(3) 5 84
(D J Wintle) *bhd: hdwy on outside 3f out: drvn to ld ins fnl 2f: hdd appr fnl f: sn wknd* 10/1
10-3 7 ½ **Balance Of Power**[8] [1051] 4-9-0 81 RichardHughes 1 84
(R Charlton) *trckd ldrs: led 9f out: rdn 3f out: hdd ins fnl 2f: wknd fnl f* 11/4[1]
053- 8 3 **Tribe**[358] [1413] 4-8-5 72 oh1 ow1 RobertWinston 10 70
(Sir Michael Stoute) *led tl hdd 9f out: chsd ldrs: rdn 3f out: no imp: wknd fr 2f out* 4/1[2]
210- 9 nk **Karlu (GER)**[206] [5610] 4-9-1 82 PaulEddery 8 79
(Pat Eddery) *chsd ldrs: rdn ins fnl 3f: wknd ins fnl 2f* 10/1
130- 10 2½ **Takafu (USA)**[206] [5610] 4-8-11 78 FergusSweeney 12 71
(W S Kittow) *chsd ldrs: rdn 3f out: wknd 2f out* 40/1
3/0- 11 1¼ **Eldorado**[339] [1909] 5-8-7 73 DarryllHolland 3 64
(S Kirk) *bhd most of way* 66/1
650- 12 3 **Love Always**[230] [5053] 4-8-12 79 PatDobbs 6 65
(S Dow) *w ldr 1m out to 3f out: wknd qckly appr fnl 2f* 100/1

2m 31.64s (1.34) **Going Correction** +0.20s/f (Good)
WFA 4 from 5yo+ 1lb 12 Ran SP% **116.9**
Speed ratings (Par 105):103,101,100,100,99 99,99,97,96,95 94,92
CSF £86.67 CT £817.61 TOTE £19.10: £4.00, £2.20, £3.00; EX 181.40.
Owner John Livock Bloodstock Limited **Bred** Hugo Merry And Jack Dorrian **Trained** West Ilsley, Berks

FOCUS
A fair handicap run at only a modest tempo. The winner has become well handicapped and this form looks sound enough.
Solo Flight ◆ Official explanation: jockey said gelding was unlucky in running closing stages

1207 32RED.COM H'CAP 1m 5y
7:10 (7:10) (Class 4) (0-85,82) 4-Y-O-£7,886 (£2,360; £1,180; £590; £293) Stalls Low

Form RPR
221- 1 **Pride Of Nation (IRE)**[210] [5537] 4-8-12 76 NickyMackay 8 102+
(L M Cumani) *t.k.h: trckd ldrs: led ins fnl 2f: pushed clr fnl f: easily* 2/1[1]
4301 2 5 **Wavertree Warrior (IRE)**[15] [946] 4-8-10 79 JamesDoyle(5) 10 86
(N P Littmoden) *hld up towards rr: hdwy fr 2f out: drvn and styd on to chse wnr fnl f but nvr any ch* 5/1[2]

1110 **3** *1* **Merrymadcap (IRE)**[24] [826] 4-8-6 **70** FrancisNorton 4 — 75
(M Blanshard) *chsd ldrs: rdn and kpt on fr 2f out: disp 2nd ins last: no ch w wnr and sn one pce* **10/1**[3]

40-0 **4** *3/4* **Davenport (IRE)**[31] [726] 4-9-2 **80** AlanMunro 7 — 83
(B R Millman) *hld up in rr: hdwy on outside 2f out: kpt on u.p fnl f but a danger* **10/1**[3]

060- **5** *2* **Desert Cristal (IRE)**[147] [6459] 5-9-1 **82** AmirQuinn(3) 13 — 80
(J R Boyle) *chsd ldrs: rdn over 2f out: styd on same pce* **25/1**

650- **6** *1/2* **Lizarazu (GER)**[141] [6503] 7-8-4 **75** TolleyDean(7) 3 — 72
(R A Harris) *chsd ldrs: rdn over 2f out: wknd appr fnl f* **50/1**

60-0 **7** *hd* **Voice Mail**[17] [915] 7-8-7 **71** (b) LPKeniry 11 — 68
(A M Balding) *hld up towards rr: pushed along over 2f out: kpt on fnl f but nvr in contention* **16/1**

022- **8** *1/2* **Fabrian**[218] [5372] 8-8-6 **73** RobertMiles(3) 14 — 69
(R J Price) *chsd ldrs: chal over 2f out: wknd over 1f out* **40/1**

50-0 **9** *nk* **Celtic Spa (IRE)**[13] [992] 4-8-2 **69** RichardThomas(3) 5 — 64
(Mrs P N Dutfield) *bhd: n.m.r ins fnl 3f: swtchd to outside and kpt on fr over 1f out but nvr a danger* **20/1**

2135 **10** *2 1/2* **Farewell Gift**[29] [764] 5-8-11 **75** (b) RichardHughes 1 — 64
(R Hannon) *chsd ldr: n.m.r on rails 2f out and lost pl: n.d after* **11/1**

021- **11** *nk* **Pillars Of Wisdom**[193] [5868] 4-9-0 **78** TQuinn 2 — 67
(J L Dunlop) *t.k.h: led tl hdd ins fnl 2f: sn wknd* **11/1**

41-2 **12** *1/2* **Cursum Perficio**[17] [915] 4-8-10 **74** SteveDrowne 9 — 61
(W R Muir) *sn chsng ldrs: rdn 3f out: wknd 2f out* **10/1**[3]

145- **13** *hd* **Della Salute**[210] [5525] 4-8-11 **75** SebSanders 15 — 62
(Miss E C Lavelle) *s.i.s: bhd: sme hdwy whn nt clr run over 1f out: nvr in contention* **20/1**

140/ **14** *1 1/4* **Personify**[557] [6188] 4-8-10 **77** AdamKirby(3) 6 — 61
(C G Cox) *mid-div: drvn over 3f out: wknd 2f out* **50/1**

6420 **15** *14* **Blue Patrick**[8] [1051] 6-8-11 **75** JohnEgan 12 — 27
(P A Blockley) *behimd: sme hdwy 4f out: rdn 3f out: sn wknd* **50/1**

1m 41.51s (0.41) **Going Correction** +0.20s/f (Good) **15** Ran SP% **121.5**
Speed ratings (Par 105):100,99,98,96 95,95,95,94,92 91,91,91,90,76
CSF £9.87 CT £83.64 TOTE £2.50: £1.40, £2.30, £3.60; EX 11.60.

Owner Equibreed S.R.L. **Bred** Deni S R L **Trained** Newmarket, Suffolk

FOCUS
A case of the winner first, the rest nowhere. However, the first four are all capable of going close next time. The race has been rated through the fourth's best form on this type of ground.

Cursum Perficio Official explanation: jockey said gelding was unsuited by the good ground; vet said gelding lost a front shoe

Della Salute Official explanation: jockey said filly was denied clear run home straight

1208 32REDPOKER.COM H'CAP — 5f 161y

7:40 (7:44) (Class 5) (0-75,75) 3-Y-O — **£5,505** (£1,637; £818; £408) **Stalls** Low

Form — RPR

0-1 **1** **Ripples Maid**[18] [901] 3-8-13 **73** RichardThomas(3) 8 — 87+
(J A Geake) *bmpd s and bhd: stl plenty to do 1/2-way: gd hdwy fr 2f out: drvn to press wnr ins last: styd on to ld cl home* **16/1**

5232 **2** *nk* **Gavarnie Beau (IRE)**[14] [969] 3-9-1 **72** FrancisNorton 6 — 85
(M Blanshard) *pressed ldrs: slt ld 2f out: sn hdd: slt advantage again 1f out: hdd and no ex cl home* **16/1**

150- **3** *2* **Tous Les Deux**[293] [3237] 3-9-4 **75** StephenCarson 14 — 82
(R F Johnson Houghton) *chsd ldrs: led ins fnl 2f: hdd 1f out: wknd ins last* **11/1**[3]

444- **4** *3 1/2* **Waddon (IRE)**[211] [5501] 3-8-12 **72** (p) AdamKirby(3) 17 — 68+
(C G Cox) *bhd: hrd rdn 1/2-way: swtchd to outside and r.o under presusre fnl f: gng on cl home but nt a danger* **20/1**

01- **5** *3/4* **Blue Aura (IRE)**[197] [5796] 3-9-4 **75** SteveDrowne 7 — 69
(R Charlton) *rr: hdwy 3f out: chsd ldrs: 2f out: styd on same pce* **6/1**[2]

5253 **6** *2* **Phinerine**[3] [1150] 3-8-1 **65** TolleyDean(7) 5 — 52
(R A Harris) *in tch: rdn 1/2-way: sn one pce* **16/1**

610- **7** *1/2* **Xaluna Bay (IRE)**[164] [6320] 3-9-4 **75** SebSanders 10 — 61
(W R Muir) *in tch: rdn and one pce fnl 2f* **100/1**

0321 **8** *2* **Cool Sting (IRE)**[17] [916] 3-9-4 **75** DarryllHolland 9 — 54
(A M Balding) *bhd: rdn 3f out: styd on fr over 1f out: n.d* **16/1**

000- **9** *nk* **Montzando**[198] [5755] 3-8-12 **69** AlanMunro 12 — 47
(B R Millman) *chsd ldrs: rdn 1/2-way: wknd fr 2f out* **20/1**

024- **10** *2 1/2* **Gwilym (GER)**[202] [5695] 3-9-4 **75** RobertHavlin 16 — 46
(D Haydn Jones) *pressed ldrs 3f: wknd ins fnl 2f* **40/1**

45-1 **11** *1* **Miltons Choice**[13] [988] 3-8-6 **63** KDarley 2 — 30
(J M Bradley) *chsd ldrs on ins rdn over 2f out: sn wknd* **14/1**

2-00 **12** *1/2* **Radius**[41] [645] 3-9-4 **75** (vt) JimmyFortune 11 — 41
(H Morrison) *bhd: rdn and swtchd rt to outside over 2f out: little rspnse* **66/1**

64-4 **13** *shd* **Bathwick Alice**[22] [851] 3-9-2 **73** ChrisCatlin 4 — 39
(B R Millman) *slt ld tl hdd 2f out: sn wknd* **33/1**

6341 **14** *1 1/4* **Billy Bling (IRE)**[22] [851] 3-8-9 **66** RichardHughes 15 — 28
(R Hannon) *sn outpcd* **14/1**

2-1 **15** *hd* **Mary Delaney (USA)**[13] [981] 3-8-11 **68** TedDurcan 3 — 29+
(M J Wallace) *s.i.s: stmbld over 3f out: a outpcd* **11/4**[1]

32-3 **16** *3 1/2* **Don't Tell Sue**[14] [967] 3-9-1 **72** MichaelHills 1 — 22
(B W Hills) *plld hrd: stdd rr: n.d* **6/1**[2]

461- **17** *1 3/4* **Valentino Swing (IRE)**[221] [5276] 3-9-3 **74** LPKeniry 13 — 18
(J L Spearing) *pressed ldrs 3f* **20/1**

1m 12.42s (1.22) **Going Correction** +0.20s/f (Good) **17** Ran SP% **122.6**
Speed ratings (Par 98):99,98,95,91,90 87,86,84,83,80 79,78,78,76,76 71,69
CSF £233.78 CT £3029.90 TOTE £25.50: £3.70, £2.90, £2.90, £5.30; EX 601.90 Place 6 £135.99, Place 5 £91.22.

Owner Rex L Mead **Bred** Compton Down Stud **Trained** Kimpton, Hants

FOCUS
A decent little contest won by a horse from a stable in good form. An improved run from the winner, although the fairly exposed runner-up holds down the form slightly. That said, the first three were clear and the form ought to work out.

Billy Bling(IRE) Official explanation: jockey said gelding was denied a clear run

Don't Tell Sue Official explanation: jockey said colt ran too free

T/Plt: £356.50 to a £1 stake. Pool: £40,028.30. 81.95 winning tickets. T/Qpdt: £91.80 to a £1 stake. Pool: £3,623.00. 29.20 winning tickets. ST

[968] FOLKESTONE (R-H)

Tuesday, April 25

OFFICIAL GOING: Good to firm (good in places)
Wind: Light, across Weather: Overcast and drizzly

1209 BETDAQXPRESS.CO.UK APPRENTICE H'CAP — 6f

2:10 (2:10) (Class 6) (0-60,63) 4-Y-0+ — **£2,730** (£806; £403) **Stalls** Low

Form — RPR

-303 **1** **Misaro (GER)**[3] [1151] 5-9-4 **60** (b) JamieHamblett 7 — 75
(R A Harris) *racd nr side: mde all: clr 1/2-way: pushed along and kpt on wl fnl f* **5/1**[1]

522- **2** *2* **Mina**[198] [5766] 4-9-0 **59** RobbieMills(3) 8 — 68
(Rae Guest) *chsd nr side ldrs: effrt over 2f out: chsd wnr jst ins fnl f: kpt on but no imp* **6/1**[2]

6200 **3** *1 3/4* **Taranaki**[28] [777] 8-9-4 **60** HugoFellows 2 — 64
(P D Cundell) *racd nr side: chsd wnr: bmpd along and no imp 2f out: one pce after* **9/1**

00-0 **4** *2* **Peruvian Style (IRE)**[23] [845] 5-9-1 **57** LukeMorris 11 — 55+
(J M Bradley) *chsd far side ldr: edgd to nr side 2f out and chsng ldrs there : kpt on same pce* **12/1**

0003 **5** *1 1/2* **Tiviski (IRE)**[18] [903] 4-8-13 **63** ow5 (p) NathanHitchcock(8) 3 — 56
(G G Margarson) *prom nr side: fdd fr over 1f out* **10/1**

0504 **6** *1 1/2* **Secret Vision (USA)**[15] [943] 5-8-4 **46** oh1 MarkWaite 13 — 35+
(R M H Cowell) *led far side gp: edgd to centre fr 1/2-way: nt on terms fnl 2f* **20/1**

0600 **7** *hd* **Enjoy The Buzz**[29] [766] 7-8-10 **52** VictoriaBehan 10 — 40+
(J M Bradley) *restless stalls: racd on outer of nr side gp: chsd ldrs 4f: n.d after* **20/1**

0406 **8** *shd* **Davids Mark**[20] [886] 6-8-4 **46** oh1 (vt) JemmaMarshall 9 — 34+
(J R Jenkins) *racd on outer of far side gp: edgd across to nr side fr 1/2-way: nvr on terms* **10/1**

2100 **9** *shd* **Christian Bendix**[55] [552] 4-8-13 **55** ChrisCavanagh 4 — 43
(P Howling) *restless stalls: racd nr side: a off the pce: nvr a factor* **25/1**

5314 **10** *nk* **Mambazo**[2] [1161] 4-9-1 **57** (e) RichardGordon 5 — 44
(S C Williams) *taken down early: restless stalls: s.s: racd nr side: in tch to 1/2-way: sn struggling* **5/1**[1]

0-00 **11** *6* **Yorkshire Lad (IRE)**[8] [1054] 4-9-2 **58** WilliamCarson 1 — 27
(Miss Gay Kelleway) *taken down early: racd nr side: chsd ldrs tl wknd rapidly 2f out* **12/1**

6122 **12** *1 1/4* **Zazous**[24] [837] 5-8-11 **61** ow8 AshleyBird(8) 12 — 26
(J J Bridger) *s.s: racd far side: nvr on terms: edgd to far rail and wl bhd fnl 2f* **8/1**[3]

300- **13** *25* **Gavioli (IRE)**[197] [5803] 4-8-9 **56** ChrisHough(5) 14 — —
(J M Bradley) *taken down early and bolted to post: racd far side: a bhd: t.o whn hung violently lft fr 2f out* **25/1**

1m 11.6s (-2.00) **Going Correction** -0.40s/f (Firm) **13** Ran SP% **119.5**
Speed ratings (Par 101):97,94,92,89,87 85,85,84,84,84 76,74,41
CSF £31.96 CT £263.03 TOTE £6.30: £2.20, £1.70, £3.90; EX 34.10 Trifecta £114.60 Part won. Pool £161.47. - 0.80 winning tickets..

Owner C Waters **Bred** Wilhelm Fasching **Trained** Earlswood, Monmouths

FOCUS
Hand-timed. Five of the field went far side, two of them edging across to the main group at halfway. A moderate sprint, which saw those drawn low at an advantage, and the form looks pretty reliable.

1210 BETDAQ.CO.UK CLAIMING STKS — 5f

2:40 (2:40) (Class 6) 3-Y-O — **£2,730** (£806; £403) **Stalls** Low

Form — RPR

0663 **1** **Spirit Of Coniston**[12] [1003] 3-8-8 62 (v[1]) JoeFanning 3 — 61
(Peter Grayson) *mde all: clr over 1f out: pushed out: comf* **11/4**[1]

6430 **2** *3 1/2* **Otis B Driftwood**[12] [1003] 3-8-5 56 (b) RyanMoore 2 — 45
(M Quinn) *pressed wnr: drvn and nt qckn 2f out and lost pl: kpt on again to take 2nd last 75yds* **4/1**[3]

4604 **3** *3/4* **Thoughtsofstardom**[13] [988] 3-9-1 61 (v) JamieSpencer 1 — 53
(P S McEntee) *trckd ldng pair: chsd wnr 2f out: no imp: fdd ins fnl f* **3/1**[2]

060- **4** *shd* **Danny The Dip**[207] [5583] 3-8-12 57 NeilChalmers(3) 6 — 52
(J J Bridger) *racd on outer: chsd ldrs but nt on terms: effrt 2f out to dispute 2nd over 1f out: one pce* **10/1**

6-00 **5** *1* **Valhar**[21] [879] 3-8-8 54 ow3 (v[1]) DeanCorby(3) 5 — 45
(J R Jenkins) *nvr on terms: outpcd and rdn 1/2-way: kpt on fnl f* **16/1**

-035 **6** *1 3/4* **Amygdala**[25] [822] 3-9-0 64 AlanMunro 7 — 41
(M Botti) *outpcd in last and sn struggling: plugged on u.p fr over 1f out* **9/2**

0604 **7** *8* **Eeshee**[21] [870] 3-7-10 45 ow3 (v) DonnaCaldwell(7) 4 — 2
(Miss Diana Weeden) *chsd ldrs 2f: wknd u.p* **20/1**

59.54 secs (-1.26) **Going Correction** -0.40s/f (Firm) **7** Ran SP% **109.6**
Speed ratings (Par 96):94,88,87,87,85 82,69
CSF £12.80 TOTE £3.50: £2.30, £2.80; EX 18.60.Spirit of Coniston was the subject of a friendly claim.

Owner Richard Teatum **Bred** Green Square Racing **Trained** Formby, Lancs

FOCUS
A weak event and the form looks slightly suspect. The winner is back to his best on turf if this can be believed.

1211 BETDAQ.CO.UK H'CAP — 5f

3:10 (3:10) (Class 5) (0-75,81) 4-Y-0+ — **£3,886** (£1,156; £577; £288) **Stalls** Low

Form — RPR

00-1 **1** **Spanish Ace**[8] [1047] 5-9-10 **81** 6ex RyanMoore 4 — 89
(J M Bradley) *w ldr: rdn to ld wl over 1f out: kpt on wl fnl f* **1/1**[1]

0220 **2** *3/4* **Canadian Danehill (IRE)**[14] [967] 4-8-13 **70** AlanMunro 5 — 75
(R M H Cowell) *hld up bhd ldrs: rdn 2f out: r.o to take 2nd wl ins fnl f: a hld* **6/1**[2]

06-5 **3** *nk* **Seven No Trumps**[14] [967] 9-8-4 **61** JoeFanning 3 — 65
(J M Bradley) *hld up bhd ldrs: shuffled along 2f out: hanging but styd on steadily fnl f: nvr nrr* **14/1**

103- **4** *hd* **Matsunosuke**[225] [5172] 4-8-8 **72** LukeMorris(7) 10 — 75
(A B Coogan) *cl up on outer: rdn to chse wnr over 1f out: no imp ent fnl f: one pce* **16/1**

6050 **5** *1* **Dancing Mystery**[15] [947] 12-8-13 **70** (b) StephenCarson 2 — 70
(E A Wheeler) *led to wl over 1f out: one pce* **8/1**[3]

3006 **6** *hd* **Kempsey**[8] [1047] 4-8-12 **72** (v) NeilChalmers(3) 6 — 71
(J J Bridger) *in tch in rr: rdn 1/2-way: kpt on ins fnl f: nt pce to rch ldrs.* **33/1**

4503 **7** ½ **Fizzlephut (IRE)**[8] [1047] 4-9-2 **73**................................(p) PaulFitzsimons 8 70
(Miss J R Tooth) *s.i.s: racd on outer: effrt 1/2-way: kpt on but no imp fnl f* **9/1**

0-05 **8** 1 **Russian Rocket (IRE)**[49] [605] 4-8-9 **66**........................... DaneO'Neill 9 59
(Mrs C A Dunnett) *pressed ldrs: nt qckn 2f out: wknd ins fnl f* **14/1**

100 **9** 15 **Mountain Pass (USA)**[15] [947] 4-8-8 **65**........................ JamieSpencer 1 4
(M J Wallace) *dwlt: outpcd and a bhd: eased whn no ch over 1f out* **10/1**

58.56 secs (-2.24) **Going Correction** -0.40s/f (Firm) course record **9** Ran SP% **116.6**
Speed ratings (Par 103):101,99,99,99,97 97,96,94,70
CSF £7.35 CT £53.85 TOTE £1.90: £1.10, £2.00, £2.90; EX 10.00 Trifecta £27.10 Pool £386.67. - 10.12 winning units..
Owner The Farleigh Court Racing Partnership **Bred** Farleigh Court Racing Partnership **Trained** Sedbury, Gloucs

FOCUS
A fair sprint, which saw the first four quite closely covered at the finish, and the in-form winner broke the track record. Solid enough form.

1212 BETDAQ TELEBET @ 0870 178 1221 MAIDEN STKS 7f (S)
3:40 (3:42) (Class 5) 3-Y-O+ **£3,562** (£1,059; £529; £264) **Stalls** Low

Form RPR

33 **1** **Days Of My Life (IRE)**[8] [1049] 3-8-13 .... SteveDrowne 11 76+
(R Charlton) *trckd ldrs gng wl: effrt to ld over 1f out: shkn up and styd on wl* **9/4**[2]

3- **2** ½ **Compromiznotension (IRE)**[179] [6128] 3-8-13 .... PhilipRobinson 14 74+
(M A Jarvis) *led against far side rail: rdn and hdd over 1f out: styd on but hld fnl f* **11/10**[1]

3 **3** 2 **Evident Pride (USA)**[33] [703] 3-8-13 .... RyanMoore 7 69
(B R Johnson) *w ldrs: upsides 2f out: edgd lft fr over 1f out: nt qckn* **6/1**[3]

0-5 **4** 3½ **Palais Polaire**[4] [1110] 4-9-7 .... StephenCarson 12 60
(J A Geake) *s.i.s: hld up in midfield: prog over 2f out: outpcd wl over 1f out: carried hd awkwardly but kpt on* **25/1**

00- **5** 1 **Sanctity**[190] [5945] 3-8-8 .... JamieSpencer 13 52
(J R Fanshawe) *trckd ldrs: pushed along 2f out: sn outpcd and btn* **12/1**

-605 **6** 2 **Shannon House**[27] [797] 3-8-13 62........................ FrankieMcDonald 8 52
(M J McGrath) *chsd ldrs: rdn 3f out: fdd fnl 2f* **66/1**

6 **7** shd **Red Raptor**[28] [778] 5-9-12 ....(t) AlanDaly 4 57
(J A Geake) *s.s: hld up in midfield: outpcd over 2f out: plugged on* **40/1**

5 **8** 1 **Smemi An Nada**[14] [963] 4-9-12 .... JimmyQuinn 2 54
(P Bowen) *hld up towards rr: wl outpcd fr over 2f out: kpt on: no ch* **33/1**

0 **9** 2½ **Levin (IRE)**[14] [964] 3-8-13 .... DaneO'Neill 3 43+
(J L Dunlop) *hld up wl in rr: sme prog into midfield 3f out: sn outpcd: shuffled along and no ch after* **40/1**

000- **10** 14 **African Star**[166] [5448] 5-9-9 45.................................... SaleemGolam(3) 10 11
(J M Bradley) *w ldrs tl wknd rapidly over 2f out* **100/1**

00 **11** 8 **Enjoy The Magic**[23] [844] 4-9-7 .... PaulFitzsimons 6 —
(Miss J R Tooth) *a wl in rr: bhd over 2f out* **100/1**

0- **12** hd **Club Captain (USA)**[293] [3246] 3-8-13 .... FJohansson 5 —
(G A Butler) *racd on outer: nvr beyond midfield: wknd over 2f out* **20/1**

13 5 **Stock Exchange (IRE)**[259] 4-9-9 .... NeilChalmers(3) 9 —
(P Bowen) *dwlt: sn in midfield: wknd over 2f out* **100/1**

14 1½ **Zumrah (IRE)**[201] 5-9-12 .... JoeFanning 1 —
(P Bowen) *s.s: racd on outer: a wl in rr: wl bhd fnl 2f* **33/1**

1m 26.25s (-1.65) **Going Correction** -0.40s/f (Firm)
WFA 3 from 4yo+ 13lb **14** Ran SP% **124.2**
Speed ratings (Par 103):93,92,90,86,85 82,82,81,78,62 53,53,47,45
CSF £4.83 TOTE £3.70: £1.70, £1.10, £1.90; EX 7.50 Trifecta £18.90 Pool £310.39. - 11.63 winning units..
Owner Mountgrange Stud **Bred** Sir E J Loder **Trained** Beckhampton, Wilts

FOCUS
A fair maiden, run at a sound pace, and the form looks solid. The first two look capable of better.
Levin(IRE) Official explanation: jockey said gelding hung right

1213 BETDAQ - BETTING EXCHANGE H'CAP 1m 7f 92y
4:10 (4:10) (Class 5) (0-75,73) 4-Y-O+ **£3,238** (£963; £481; £240) **Stalls** Low

Form RPR

3-46 **1** **Trew Style**[77] [334] 4-9-0 **67**.. SaleemGolam(3) 11 80
(M H Tompkins) *led after 2f and sn clr w one rival: wl clr over 3f out: hrd rdn over 1f out: unchal* **9/2**[1]

0-50 **2** 6 **Linden Lime**[83] [264] 4-8-5 **55**... PaulDoe 8 61
(Jamie Poulton) *plld hrd early and hld up wl in rr: effrt over 3f out: r.o to take 2nd last 100yds: hopeless task* **12/1**

4053 **3** 1½ **Swainson (USA)**[33] [700] 5-9-3 **64**...............................(p) RyanMoore 10 68
(P Mitchell) *t.k.h: led chsng gp to 3f out: sn drvn: kpt on to go 2nd over 1f out to last 100yds: nvr able to chal* **6/1**[3]

233 **4** 2½ **Sweet Medicine**[12] [1006] 4-9-9 **73**................................. JamieSpencer 4 74
(P Howling) *prom in chsng gp: effrt to chse clr wnr 3f out: no imp: fdd over 1f out* **5/1**[2]

5 hd **Megaton**[48] 5-9-9 **70**... JimmyQuinn 7 71
(P Bowen) *prom in chsng gp: rdn 4f out: one pce and n.d fr over 2f out* **16/1**

-230 **6** 1½ **Beauchamp Trump**[45] [628] 4-9-2 **66**.........................(bt) FJohansson 2 65
(G A Butler) *hld up wl in rr: rdn 4f out: plugged on one pce: nvr on terms* **10/1**

0/06 **7** 6 **Global Challenge (IRE)**[29] [765] 7-9-12 **73**..................... DaneO'Neill 1 65
(P G Murphy) *hld up wl in rr: rdn and no prog 4f out: no ch* **14/1**

/40- **8** ½ **Blue Away (IRE)**[198] [5780] 8-9-11 **72**..................... FrankieMcDonald 6 63
(S Kirk) *hld up in last pair: nvr on terms: rdn and wl btn 4f out* **13/2**

0340 **9** hd **Moon Emperor**[24] [832] 9-8-9 **59**..................................(p) DeanCorby(3) 3 50
(J R Jenkins) *hld up wl in rr: no prog and no ch fnl 3f* **6/1**[3]

0-00 **10** 22 **Shakerattleandroll (IRE)**[32] [713] 5-9-9 **70**....................... AlanDaly 5 35
(Mrs L Richards) *dwlt: hld up in last: a wl bhd: t.o 3f out* **25/1**

20-0 **11** 1 **Kiama**[18] [911] 4-8-12 **62**... JoeFanning 9 25
(M Johnston) *t.k.h: led for 2f: chsd clr wnr and wl clr of rest tl wknd rapidly 3f out: t.o* **9/1**

3m 23.87s (-3.33) **Going Correction** -0.125s/f (Firm)
WFA 4 from 5yo+ 3lb **11** Ran SP% **119.9**
Speed ratings (Par 103):103,99,99,97,97 96,93,93,93,81 80
CSF £60.23 CT £332.57 TOTE £5.60: £1.90, £4.60, £2.10; EX 105.80 Trifecta £139.40 Part won. Pool: £196.41. - 0.10 winning tickets..
Owner Russell Trew Ltd **Bred** P And Mrs Venner **Trained** Newmarket, Suffolk

FOCUS
A modest handicap, run at an uneven pace, with the winner making the most of an easy lead. The form has been rated at face value and should be treated with a degree of caution.
Kiama Official explanation: jockey said filly had no more to give

1214 BETDAQXPRESS.CO.UK MAIDEN FILLIES' STKS 1m 4f
4:40 (4:40) (Class 5) 3-Y-O+ **£3,562** (£1,059; £529; £264) **Stalls** Low

Form RPR

0-4 **1** **Swan Queen**[19] [897] 3-8-6 .... JimmyQuinn 10 72+
(J L Dunlop) *trckd ldrs: rdn to chse ldr over 1f out: checked ins fnl f: r.o nr fin: jst failed: fin 2nd, shd: awrdd r* **15/2**

0-2 **2** shd **Summer's Eve**[15] [948] 3-8-6 .... DaneO'Neill 3 72+
(H Candy) *awkward bnd over 9f out: sn trckd ldr: led over 2f out: rdn and hanging lft fr over 1f out: jst hld on: fin 1st, shd: disq* **10/11**[1]

03- **3** 2½ **Italic**[187] [5995] 3-8-6 .... RyanMoore 2 68
(Mrs A J Perrett) *trckd ldrs: effrt over 2f out: rdn and styd on same pce fr over 1f out* **14/1**

0-2 **4** ½ **Trinity Rose**[9] [1034] 3-8-6 .... JoeFanning 9 67
(M Johnston) *led after 2f: rdn and hdd over 2f out: one pce* **5/1**[2]

0 **5** 2½ **To Dubai**[19] [894] 3-8-6 .... PhilipRobinson 5 63
(M A Jarvis) *hld up towards rr: outpcd 3f out: shkn up 2f out: one pce and no imp* **12/1**

0-00 **6** 3½ **Romanova (IRE)**[22] [854] 4-9-4 60.................................. SladeO'Hara(7) 4 59?
(Dr J R J Naylor) *chsd ldrs: rdn 3f out: wknd wl over 1f out* **100/1**

62-3 **7** 8 **Dyanita**[22] [850] 3-8-6 74... RHills 7 45+
(B W Hills) *t.k.h: rn wd bnd over 9f out: wl in rr after: no ch fnl 2f* **7/1**[3]

000- **8** 1¾ **Plain Champagne (IRE)**[188] [5971] 4-9-11 35..................... AlanDaly 6 44?
(Dr J R J Naylor) *hld up: carried wd bnd over 9f out: wl in rr whn shkn up over 2f out: no prog* **100/1**

0 **9** 9 **Shawl**[14] [971] 3-8-8 ow2.. JamieSpencer 8 29
(B J Meehan) *led for 2f: chsd ldrs: rdn 3f out: wknd and eased wl over 1f out* **33/1**

10 nk **Gran Amor** 3-8-3 .... NelsonDeSouza(3) 1 27
(P D Cundell) *dwlt: carried wd bnd over 9f out: a in rr after: rdn and no prog 3f out* **66/1**

2m 39.63s (-0.87) **Going Correction** -0.125s/f (Firm)
WFA 3 from 4yo 20lb **10** Ran SP% **114.1**
Speed ratings (Par 100):96,97,95,94,93 90,85,84,78,78
CSF £14.34 TOTE £9.20: £2.20, £1.10, £3.20; EX 27.40 Trifecta £144.30 Pool £422.77.- 2.08 winning units..
Owner Sir Thomas Pilkington **Bred** Sir Thomas Pilkington **Trained** Arundel, W Sussex

FOCUS
A fair fillies' maiden, run at an average pace, and the form looks sound enough despite the intitial placings of the first two later being reversed in the Stewards' room. The race has been rated through the fourth and both the first two are capable of considerably better than the bare form.
Dyanita Official explanation: jockey said filly hung left throughout

1215 BETDAQ FOR MULTIPLES H'CAP 1m 1f 149y
5:15 (5:15) (Class 5) (0-70,70) 3-Y-O **£3,238** (£963; £481; £240) **Stalls** Low

Form RPR

-634 **1** **Black Beauty**[28] [781] 3-8-13 **65**.. RyanMoore 11 68+
(M G Quinlan) *mistimed s: trckd ldrs: nt clr run 2f out: got through to ld jst over 1f out: hung lft: drvn out* **15/8**[1]

-220 **2** 1¼ **Mighty Dancer (IRE)**[3] [1140] 3-8-9 **61**..................... FrankieMcDonald 9 61
(S Kirk) *t.k.h: hld up in midfield: effrt whn nt clr run 2f out tl swtchd lft 1f out: r.o to chse wnr last 75yds: a hld* **11/2**[2]

640- **3** 1¼ **Salvestro**[141] [6501] 3-8-13 **65**.. JimmyQuinn 7 63
(Mrs A J Perrett) *hld up in tch: rdn over 2f out: effrt on outer over 1f out: styd on fnl f* **17/2**

220- **4** ½ **Sapienza**[183] [6068] 3-9-4 **70**.. RHills 10 67+
(C E Brittain) *snatched up after 1f and dropped to last: tried to cl on inner 2f out: nt qckn over 1f out: r.o last 100yds* **14/1**

-013 **5** hd **Mid Valley**[48] [617] 3-8-1 **56** oh2............................ NelsonDeSouza(3) 4 53
(J R Jenkins) *trckd ldrs: rdn to chal and upsides over 1f out: fdd ins fnl f* **16/1**

0050 **6** nk **Zizou (IRE)**[21] [879] 3-8-5 **60** oh4 ow4........................(t) NeilChalmers(3) 5 56?
(J J Bridger) *pressed ldr: led over 2f out to over 1f out: fdd* **16/1**

0-60 **7** 9 **Gigs Magic (USA)**[13] [993] 3-8-10 **62**................................ JoeFanning 8 41
(M Johnston) *led to over 2f out: wkng whn squeezed out over 1f out* **10/1**

-624 **8** 3 **Gibbs Camp**[53] [566] 3-9-1 **67**.. JamieSpencer 2 55+
(E A L Dunlop) *trckd ldrs: effrt on inner to ld briefly over 1f out: lost action and heavily eased fnl f* **10/1**

040- **9** 4 **Henchman**[195] [5832] 3-9-2 **68**.. PhilipRobinson 3 34
(Lady Herries) *hld up in last pair: lost tch w ldng gp over 3f out: shuffled along and nvr on terms after: eased fnl f* **8/1**[3]

5-14 **10** dist **Super Frank (IRE)**[54] [558] 3-8-12 **64**............................(b) FJohansson 1 —
(G A Butler) *t.k.h: hld up: hmpd 5f out: bhd after: t.o* **12/1**

06-6 **P** **Gaelic Games (UAE)**[29] [762] 3-8-8 **60**............................ DaneO'Neill 6 —
(P G Murphy) *trckd ldr tl broke down and p.u 5f out* **33/1**

2m 4.32s (-0.91) **Going Correction** -0.125s/f (Firm) **11** Ran SP% **119.1**
Speed ratings (Par 98):98,97,96,95,95 95,88,85,82,— —
CSF £11.78 CT £72.69 TOTE £2.40: £1.60, £2.90, £3.10; EX 17.60 TRIFECTA Not won. Place 6 £9.00, Place 5 £4.45.
Owner Anglo Irish Racing **Bred** N E Poole And Paul Trickey **Trained** Newmarket, Suffolk

FOCUS
A modest handicap, and a messy race, though the winner is value for further.
Sapienza Official explanation: jockey said filly suffered interference in running
Gibbs Camp Official explanation: jockey said filly had no more to give
Henchman Official explanation: jockey said gelding was unsuited by the good to firm (good in places) ground
T/Plt: £18.70 to a £1 stake. Pool: £35,444.30. 1,376.75 winning tickets. T/Qpdt: £5.10 to a £1 stake. Pool: £2,632.00. 377.10 winning tickets. JN

936 SOUTHWELL (L-H)
Tuesday, April 25

OFFICIAL GOING: Good (good to soft in places)
The ground was described as 'good, good to soft in places and patchy.
Wind: Moderate, half-behind Weather: Fine

1216 BETFRED MILLION MEDIAN AUCTION MAIDEN STKS 1m 3f
2:00 (2:01) (Class 6) 3-Y-O **£2,730** (£806; £403) **Stalls** Low

Form RPR

450- **1** **Free To Air**[204] [5658] 3-9-3 74.. PaulHanagan 5 71
(A M Balding) *sn trcking ldrs: effrt over 4f out: styd on to ld jst ins last: hld on wl* **11/4**[2]

2-22 **2** ½ **Dream Champion**[18] [900] 3-9-3 79................................... TedDurcan 4 71
(M R Channon) *trckd ldrs: rdn to ld 2f out: hdd jst ins last: kpt on* **5/2**[1]

 The Form Book, Raceform Ltd, Compton, RG20 6NL

6-5 **3** *7* **Supa Tramp**^{57} [531] 3-9-3 .... LDettori 10 61+
(J R Fanshawe) *sn trcking ldr: led over 2f out: sn hdd: one pce* **4/1**^{3}
5 **4** *shd* **King Of Rhythm (IRE)**^{21} [863] 3-9-0 .... DanielTudhope$^{(3)}$ 6 59
(D Carroll) *hld up in rr: hdwy over 4f out: one pce fnl 2f* **16/1**
030- **5** *5* **Patavium (IRE)**^{217} [5393] 3-9-3 73..................... RichardMullen 8 51
(E J O'Neill) *hld up in mid-div: rdn over 3f out: one pce* **5/1**
5006 **6** *shd* **Sahara Style**^{22} [859] 3-9-3 48..................... (v) GrahamGibbons 9 51?
(R Hollinshead) *s.s: hdwy to ld after 1f: hdd over 2f out: wknd over 1f out* **40/1**
00- **7** *11* **Enthusius**^{188} [5987] 3-9-3 .... MickyFenton 3 33
(M L W Bell) *s.i.s: in rr and drvn over 4f out: sn lost tch* **14/1**
5-06 **8** *5* **Master Ben (IRE)**^{89} [193] 3-9-3 50..................... DeanMcKeown 1 25
(S R Bowring) *sn in rr: bhd fnl 3f* **50/1**
00-0 **9** *12* **Millbrook Star (IRE)**^{48} [617] 3-8-12 30..................... EmmettStack$^{(5)}$ 2 6
(M C Chapman) *led: reminders and hdd after 1f: rdn 5f out: lost pl over 3f out: sn bhd* **200/1**
-060 **10** *19* **Lady Evi**^{48} [617] 3-8-12 35..................... AdrianTNicholls 7 —
(D K Ivory) *trckd ldrs: rdn and lost pl over 5f out: sn bhd: t.o* **150/1**
2m 27.84s **10** Ran SP% **110.0**
CSF £9.17 TOTE £4.50: £1.20, £1.10, £1.70; EX 12.50.
Owner Miss Clare Balding **Bred** Robert Charles Key **Trained** Kingsclere, Hants

FOCUS
Just a handful of these had shown better than modest form, but several were open to improvement for the step up in trip, although they did not go a great pace. The way the first two pulled well clear and confirmed they are both probably fair three-year-olds. The sixth does limit the form.
Enthusius Official explanation: jockey said colt had a breathing problem

1217 BETFRED MILLION (S) STKS 7f
2:30 (2:31) (Class 6) 3-Y-O+ **£2,388** (£705; £352) **Stalls** Low

Form RPR
3063 **1** **Onlytime Will Tell**^{13} [974] 8-9-7 68..................... AdrianTNicholls 10 64
(D Nicholls) *prom: hdwy on ins to ld over 1f out: drvn out* **9/2**^{1}
0002 **2** *1* **Desert Lightning (IRE)**^{13} [974] 4-9-7 57..................... NeilPollard 2 61
(K R Burke) *trckd ldrs: nt clr run and swtchd rt 2f out: wnt 2nd 1f out: kpt on same pce* **15/2**
300- **3** *1 1/4* **Aventura (IRE)**^{328} [2187] 6-9-2 61..................... StephenDonohoe$^{(5)}$ 8 58
(S R Bowring) *w ldrs: led over 2f out tl over 1f out: no ex* **10/1**
-000 **4** *nk* **Riska King**^{81} [290] 6-9-7 47..................... PaulHanagan 14 57
(P A Blockley) *s.i.s: bhd to styd on fnl 2f: gng on strly at fin* **10/1**
3541 **5** *nk* **Scotty's Future (IRE)**^{6} [1073] 8-9-12 54..................... PaulQuinn 12 61
(D Nicholls) *rel to r and sn detached in last: hdwy 2f out: styd on strly ins last* **6/1**^{3}
0064 **6** *shd* **Veneer (IRE)**^{6} [1073] 4-9-7 55..................... (b) LDettori 9 56
(Miss Gay Kelleway) *chsd ldrs: kpt on same pce fnl 2f* **5/1**^{2}
2-00 **7** *shd* **Stamford Blue**^{6} [1073] 5-9-7 62..................... (b) AdrianMcCarthy 3 56
(R A Harris) *chsd ldrs: one pce fnl 2f* **8/1**
00-0 **8** *5* **Zap Attack**^{15} [942] 6-9-4 45..................... (tp) DanielTudhope$^{(3)}$ 5 43
(J Parkes) *s.i.s: sme hdwy 2f out: nvr on terms* **50/1**
00- **9** *nk* **Lucky Lil**^{160} [6367] 4-8-9 .... MichaelJStainton$^{(7)}$ 7 37
(R M Whitaker) *in rr: sme hdwy on wd outside over 2f out: nvr on terms* **100/1**
2000 **10** *3 1/2* **Castanza**^{40} [648] 4-9-2 53..................... (v^{1}) MickyFenton 13 28
(M Wellings) *racd wd: prom: drvn over 4f out: lost pl over 2f out* **66/1**
0500 **11** *1 3/4* **Resplendent Prince**^{53} [568] 4-9-9 56..................... (v) JohnMcAuley$^{(3)}$ 4 33
(P Howling) *led: hrd rdn and hdd over 2f out: sn wknd* **14/1**
5-00 **12** *1 1/4* **Follow My Trail (IRE)**^{6} [1073] 3-8-8 55..................... GylesParkin 1 20
(B Smart) *sn outpcd and bhd* **50/1**
-500 **13** *nk* **Sahara Prince (IRE)**^{64} [458] 6-9-7 51..................... DO'Donohoe 11 24
(K A Morgan) *hld up in rr: nvr a factor* **10/1**
0050 **14** *1/2* **Jumanji (IRE)**^{8} [1055] 3-8-3 54..................... FrancisFerris 6 13
(M J Attwater) *sn chsng ldrs: lost pl over 2f out* **25/1**
1m 30.38s (1.18) **Going Correction** +0.10s/f (Good)
WFA 3 from 4yo+ 13lb **14** Ran SP% **116.2**
Speed ratings (Par 101):97,95,94,94,93 93,93,87,87,83 81,80,79,79
CSF £35.52 TOTE £6.30: £2.20, £3.80, £3.70; EX 20.40.There was no bid for the winner. Desert Lightning (IRE) was the subject of a friendly claim. Scotty's Future (IRE) was claimed by Mr E. Nisbet for £6,000
Owner Mrs E G Faulkner **Bred** L C And Mrs A E Sigsworth **Trained** Sessay, N Yorks

FOCUS
A modest seller contested by several disappointing or out-of-form performers. The form is sound enough but very limited.
Scotty's Future(IRE) Official explanation: trainer's representative had no explanation for the poor form shown
Jumanji(IRE) Official explanation: vet said filly returned injured

1218 BETFRED MILLION MAIDEN STKS 6f
3:00 (3:03) (Class 5) 3-Y-O **£3,238** (£963; £481; £240) **Stalls** Low

Form RPR
320- **1** **Spiritual Peace (IRE)**^{224} [5203] 3-9-3 82..................... DO'Donohoe 14 79
(K A Ryan) *swtchd lft after s: mde all: kpt on u.p fnl 2f: all out* **7/2**^{2}
05-6 **2** *1* **Burning Incense (IRE)**^{26} [801] 3-9-3 74..................... LDettori 1 76
(R Charlton) *w ldrs: rdn over 2f out: kpt on same pce ins fnl last* **4/5**^{1}
043- **3** *shd* **Bel Cantor**^{124} [6659] 3-8-12 70..................... RichardKingscote$^{(5)}$ 13 76
(W J H Ratcliffe) *chsd ldrs: effrt over 2f out: styd on fnl f* **11/1**
424- **4** *5* **Rainbow Bay**^{219} [5340] 3-9-3 73..................... PaulHanagan 2 61+
(R A Fahey) *mid-div: kpt on fnl 2f: nvr a threat* **8/1**^{3}
55 **5** *1/2* **Rationale (IRE)**^{28} [778] 3-9-3 .... MickyFenton 12 60+
(S C Williams) *s.i.s: sn bhd: hdwy 2f out: styd on wl ins last* **20/1**
00- **6** *6* **Black Jade**^{248} [4572] 3-9-3 .... MatthewHenry 9 42
(M A Jarvis) *mid-div: kpt on fnl 2f: nvr on terms* **25/1**
7 *1/2* **Bee Magic** 3-9-3 .... GeorgeBaker 7 40
(C N Kellett) *rrd s: bhd tl sme hdwy fnl 2f* **66/1**
0 **8** *nk* **Grand Palace (IRE)**^{2} [1165] 3-9-3 .... TomEaves 8 39
(D Shaw) *sn bhd: sme hdwy 2f out: nvr a factor* **66/1**
9 *1/2* **Centreofattention** 3-8-12 .... PaulFessey 4 33
(Mrs A Duffield) *in rr: and uns rdr bef s: s.s: nvr on terms* **33/1**
6630 **10** *1 3/4* **Mister Becks (IRE)**^{3} [1147] 3-8-12 35..................... EmmettStack$^{(5)}$ 11 32
(M C Chapman) *chsd ldrs: sn drvn along: lost pl 3f out* **66/1**
00- **11** *3/4* **Saint Bernadette**^{293} [3229] 3-8-9 .... PaulMulrennan$^{(3)}$ 5 25
(P T Midgley) *sn bhd* **100/1**
0 **12** *2* **Two Acres (IRE)**^{23} [844] 3-9-3 .... AdrianTNicholls 6 24
(A G Newcombe) *chsd ldrs: lost pl over 2f out* **100/1**
00- **13** *1/2* **Maxolini**^{287} [3412] 3-9-3 .... GrahamGibbons 3 23
(J J Quinn) *chsd ldrs: lost pl over 2f out* **50/1**
66 **14** *11* **Lady Becks (IRE)**^{24} [835] 3-8-12 .... AdrianMcCarthy 10 —
(R A Harris) *a bhd: eased ins last* **50/1**
1m 15.66s (-0.44) **Going Correction** +0.10s/f (Good) **14** Ran SP% **119.2**
Speed ratings (Par 98):106,104,104,97,97 89,88,88,87,85 84,81,80,66
CSF £6.10 TOTE £4.30: £1.80, £1.10, £2.20; EX 7.90.
Owner M P Burke **Bred** M P B Bloodstock Ltd **Trained** Hambleton, N Yorks

FOCUS
A decent winning time for a race like this but the overall form looks moderate, limited by the third. The first two should rate higher, though.
Bee Magic Official explanation: jockey said gelding missed the break
Centreofattention Official explanation: jockey said filly hung right-handed throughout

1219 BETFRED MILLION H'CAP 2m
3:30 (3:35) (Class 6) (0-65,61) 4-Y-O+ **£2,730** (£806; £403) **Stalls** Low

Form RPR
14-0 **1** **Celtic Carisma**^{13} [990] 4-9-3 **51**..................... TomEaves 13 63+
(K G Reveley) *hld up in tch: effrt over 2f out: str run to ld 1f out: drvn clr* **12/1**
1/03 **2** *3 1/2* **Jolizero**^{3} [1138] 5-9-13 **57**..................... TedDurcan 3 65
(John Berry) *trckd ldrs: kpt on fnl f: tk 2nd on line* **5/1**^{1}
000- **3** *shd* **Senor Set (GER)**^{82} [6368] 5-9-1 **45**..................... DavidAllan 5 53
(J Pearce) *in tch: hdwy over 5f out: led over 2f out: hdd and no ex 1f out* **16/1**
005- **4** *1 3/4* **Cava Bien**^{31} [5629] 4-8-10 **49**..................... StephenDonohoe$^{(5)}$ 14 56+
(B J Llewellyn) *a handy: one pce appr fnl f* **7/1**
30-4 **5** *8* **Arch Folly**^{24} [838] 4-9-7 **55**..................... PaulHanagan 7 51
(J G Portman) *s.i.s: hld up in rr: hdwy 6f out: sn chsng ldrs: wknd 2f out* **6/1**^{3}
044- **6** *shd* **Woodford Consult**^{45} [6637] 4-9-3 **54**..................... PaulMulrennan$^{(3)}$ 4 50
(M W Easterby) *chsd ldrs: rdn to ld over 3f out: hdd over 2f out: wknd over 1f out* **16/1**
01 **7** *15* **Galantos (GER)**^{15} [938] 5-9-6 **50**..................... GeorgeBaker 2 28
(G L Moore) *in rr: shkn up after 5f: hdwy to chse ldrs over 4f out: lost pl over 2f out* **11/2**^{2}
0 **8** *8* **Gawrosz (POL)**^{12} [1001] 7-8-13 **50**..................... AshleyHamblett$^{(7)}$ 8 19
(G J Smith) *hld up in rr: hdwy 6f out: sn in tch: wknd over 2f out* **100/1**
-060 **9** *3 1/2* **Pearl Fisher (IRE)**^{8} [525] 5-8-7 **40**..................... DanielTudhope$^{(3)}$ 12 4
(D Carroll) *led: clr after 4f: hdd over 3f out: sn lost pl* **33/1**
-433 **10** *10* **Madiba**^{18} [911] 7-9-0 **47**..................... JohnMcAuley$^{(3)}$ 11 —
(P Howling) *mid-div: drvn along 8f out: lost pl over 4f out: sn bhd* **10/1**
6-02 **11** *19* **Jamaar**^{67} [443] 4-9-13 **61**..................... MickyFenton 10 —
(C N Kellett) *chsd ldrs: sn pushed along: lost pl over 4f out: t.o 3f out* **20/1**
066- **12** *26* **Water Pistol**^{8} [4748] 4-9-3 **56**..................... EmmettStack$^{(5)}$ 1 —
(M C Chapman) *bhd: t.o over 5f out: virtually p.u* **33/1**
412- **13** *6* **Dan's Heir**^{10} [2177] 4-9-11 **59**..................... (p) LDettori 6 —
(P C Haslam) *last: nvr threatened to improve: t.o 3f out* **5/1**^{1}
0-06 **14** *dist* **Ashwell Rose**^{53} [566] 4-8-11 **45**..................... DaleGibson 9 —
(R T Phillips) *mid-div: lost pl 8f out: sn wl t.o: virtually p.u* **20/1**
3m 38.6s (-2.90) **Going Correction** +0.10s/f (Good)
WFA 4 from 5yo+ 4lb **14** Ran SP% **120.4**
Speed ratings (Par 101):101,99,99,98,94 94,86,82,81,76 66,53,50,—
CSF £67.22 CT £985.87 TOTE £14.00: £3.70, £2.40, £5.60; EX 136.90.
Owner Bill Brown **Bred** H G W Brown **Trained** Lingdale, Redcar & Cleveland

FOCUS
A moderate handicap in which the first four came clear. The winner did not need to improve but should be capable of better.
Galantos(GER) Official explanation: jockey said gelding was unsuited by the good (good to soft places), ground
Madiba Official explanation: jockey said gelding lost its action
Dan's Heir Official explanation: jockey said gelding never travelled

1220 BETFREDPOKER.COM H'CAP 7f
4:00 (4:02) (Class 4) (0-80,79) 4-Y-O+ **£6,477** (£1,927; £963; £481) **Stalls** Low

Form RPR
00-0 **1** **Phluke**^{29} [764] 5-8-10 **71**..................... JamieMackay 1 79
(R F Johnson Houghton) *w ldr: led over 4f out: hld on gamely* **22/1**
-000 **2** *nk* **Selective**^{66} [451] 7-8-9 **70**..................... DaleGibson 9 78
(A W Carroll) *w ldrs: t.k.h: chal 1f out: no ex ins last* **16/1**
400- **3** *3/4* **Breaking Shadow (IRE)**^{171} [6248] 4-8-12 **76**..................... BenSwarbrick$^{(3)}$ 3 82+
(T D Barron) *hld up in mid-div: nt clr run and swtchd outside over 1f out: fin wl* **9/1**^{2}
-410 **4** *1* **Bessemer (JPN)**^{63} [476] 5-9-1 **79**..................... (p) DanielTudhope$^{(3)}$ 8 82
(D Carroll) *in tch: effrt over 2f out: hung lft: kpt on same pce fnl f* **14/1**
500- **5** *1/2* **Tough Love**^{206} [5612] 7-8-11 **72**..................... DavidAllan 2 74
(T D Easterby) *trckd ldrs: one pce appr fnl f* **14/1**
1-11 **6** *nk* **Border Music**^{24} [830] 5-9-4 **79**..................... (b) LDettori 14 80
(A M Balding) *trckd ldrs on outer: effrt and n.m.r over 2f out: fdd ins last* **10/11**^{1}
0-20 **7** *1 1/2* **Lucayan Dancer**^{27} [800] 6-8-8 **76**..................... KellyHarrison$^{(7)}$ 12 73
(D Nicholls) *hld up in rr: kpt on fnl f* **16/1**
-602 **8** *1/2* **Sawwaah (IRE)**^{9} [1035] 9-8-9 **70**..................... (v) AdrianTNicholls 13 66
(D Nicholls) *in tch on outer: t.k.h: effrt over 2f out: nvr rchd ldrs* **11/1**^{3}
/0-0 **9** *1* **Bond Playboy**^{8} [1041] 6-8-4 **65** oh2..................... PaulHanagan 7 58
(G R Oldroyd) *led tl over 4f out: lost pl over 1f out* **20/1**
6005 **10** *nk* **Pawan (IRE)**^{3} [1145] 6-8-7 **75**..................... (p) AnnStokell$^{(7)}$ 10 67
(Miss A Stokell) *hld up in rr: kpt on fnl 2f: nvr nr ldrs* **25/1**
4200 **11** *1/2* **Samuel Charles**^{31} [721] 8-8-4 **70**..................... AndrewMullen$^{(5)}$ 4 61
(C R Dore) *rr-div: hdwy on inner over 2f out: put hd in air and hung lft: nvr on terms* **20/1**
000- **12** *1 3/4* **Riley Boys (IRE)**^{171} [6248] 5-9-1 **76**..................... MickyFenton 5 62
(J G Given) *s.i.s: nvr on terms* **16/1**
3500 **13** *3 1/2* **Connotation**^{41} [641] 4-8-9 **70**..................... BrianReilly 6 47
(A G Newcombe) *chsd ldrs: lost pl over 2f out* **50/1**
0000 **14** *10* **Middleton Grey**^{23} [846] 8-8-8 **76**..................... (b) JamesMillman$^{(7)}$ 11 27
(A G Newcombe) *s.s: a bhd* **25/1**
1m 29.75s (0.55) **Going Correction** +0.10s/f (Good) **14** Ran SP% **125.2**
Speed ratings (Par 105):100,99,98,97,97 96,95,94,93,92 92,90,86,74
CSF £323.14 CT £3477.79 TOTE £19.10: £3.10, £3.40, £2.30; EX 272.50.
Owner Mrs R F Johnson Houghton **Bred** Mrs R F Johnson Houghton **Trained** Blewbury, Oxon

FOCUS
An uncompetitive race on paper with Border Music seemingly thrown in for this return to turf, but he failed to shine from a wide berth and two of the outsiders were left to fight out the finish. Breaking Shadow was the moral winner as he would have won had he got into the clear sooner. The winner ran to his mark and the form makes sense on paper.
Border Music Official explanation: jockey said gelding was unsuited by the good (good to soft places) ground

Bond Playboy Official explanation: jockey said gelding hung left-handed throughout
Riley Boys(IRE) Official explanation: jockey said gelding missed the break

1221 BETFREDCASINO.COM H'CAP 1m 3f
4:30 (4:31) (Class 6) (0-60,59) 3-Y-O £2,730 (£806; £403) **Stalls** Low

Form RPR
00-2 **1** **Bollin Derek**^{22} [859] 3-8-9 **50** .... DavidAllan 2 64+
(T D Easterby) *mde all: drvn clr over 1f out: heavily eased ins last* **9/2**^{1}
53-3 **2** *2 ½* **At The Money**^{22} [859] 3-9-3 **58** .... PaulHanagan 11 62
(J M P Eustace) *chsd ldrs: kpt on fnl 2f: tk 2nd nr line: no ch w wnr* **6/1**^{3}
00-1 **3** *½* **Carlton Scroop (FR)**^{20} [887] 3-8-4 **50** ....(b) GregFairley$^{(5)}$ 1 53
(J Jay) *chsd ldrs: wnt 2nd 4f out: kpt on same pce fnl 2f* **9/1**
-401 **4** *6* **Bob's Your Uncle**^{15} [945] 3-9-3 **58** .... LDettori 13 52+
(J G Portman) *hld up towards rr: effrt over 3f out: nt clr run and swtchd outside over 2f out: kpt on: nvr nr ldrs* **5/1**^{2}
00-4 **5** *hd* **El Dee (IRE)**^{22} [859] 3-8-6 **50** .... DanielTudhope$^{(3)}$ 14 43
(D Carroll) *stdd s: hdwy over 5f out: sn chsng ldrs: one pce fnl 2f* **16/1**
3252 **6** *½* **Noble Edge**^{13} [979] 3-9-4 **59** ....(p) DO'Donohoe 9 51
(Robert Gray) *mid-div: effrt and hung lft over 2f out: nvr nr ldrs* **8/1**
0-30 **7** *4* **Lynford Lady**^{6} [1079] 3-9-3 **58** .... MickyFenton 7 44
(P W D'Arcy) *in tch: effrt 3f out: sn wknd* **14/1**
00-0 **8** *1 ¼* **Ebony Lady**^{6} [1079] 3-8-5 **49** .... StanleyChin$^{(3)}$ 4 33
(R M Whitaker) *chsd ldrs: hmpd bnd after 2f: wknd over 2f out* **33/1**
0-00 **9** *½* **Mytass**^{64} [466] 3-7-13 **47** ....(b) JosephWalsh$^{(7)}$ 3 30+
(J A Pickering) *hld up: hmpd bnd after 2f: effrt on inner whn hmpd bnd 3f out: nvr a factor* **40/1**
-544 **10** *shd* **Tirol Livit (IRE)**^{32} [716] 3-8-9 **50** .... GrahamGibbons 8 33
(N Wilson) *mid-div: effrt over 3f out: sn btn* **14/1**
-026 **11** *1 ¾* **Kokila**^{25} [822] 3-8-11 **59** .... LiamJones$^{(7)}$ 5 39
(W J Haggas) *in tch: lost pl over 3f out* **12/1**
U00- **12** *dist* **Tay Bridge (IRE)**^{198} [5768] 3-8-9 **50** .... JamieMackay 10 —+
(M L W Bell) *t.k.h: chsd ldrs: wknd 4f out: bhd whn eased fnl f: virtually p.u: t.o* **13/2**
000- **13** *dist* **Silver Bank**^{254} [4393] 3-8-6 **47** .... DaleGibson 6 —
(M W Easterby) *stdd s: sn detached in last: hopelessly t.o 3f out: virtually p.u* **40/1**

2m 27.84s **13** Ran SP% **118.3**
CSF £30.19 CT £233.43 TOTE £4.80: £1.10, £3.40, £4.80; EX 28.40.
Owner Sir Neil Westbrook **Bred** Sir Neil And Lady Westbrook **Trained** Great Habton, N Yorks

FOCUS
A moderate handicap, but the form looks solid for the class with the first three coming clear, and the winner is value for plenty further than his winning margin.
Mytass Official explanation: jockey said gelding suffered interference in running

1222 TELETEXT RACING "HANDS AND HEELS" APPRENTICE H'CAP 1m 4f
5:00 (5:00) (Class 5) (0-70,70) 4-Y-O+ £3,238 (£963; £481; £240) **Stalls** Low

Form RPR
000- **1** **Migration**^{67} [4217] 10-8-5 **58** oh20 ow3.......... JohnCavanagh$^{(3)}$ 6 64
(Mrs S Lamyman) *s.i.s: hld up in rr: gd hdwy on outer 2f out: led appr fnl f: hld on wl* **40/1**
0-62 **2** *1 ½* **Platinum Charmer (IRE)**^{8} [1045] 6-8-8 **61** ....(p) PatrickDonaghy$^{(3)}$ 8 65
(K R Burke) *hld up in tch: hdwy to ld over 2f out: hdd appr fnl f: kpt on same pce* **11/4**^{1}
00-4 **3** *5* **Sovietta (IRE)**^{28} [780] 5-8-4 **57** ....(t) JosephWalsh$^{(3)}$ 4 53
(A G Newcombe) *hld up off the pce: hdwy over 2f out: styd on to take 3rd nr line* **10/1**
0315 **4** *1* **Buscador (USA)**^{15} [955] 7-8-5 **55** oh3.......... KevinGhunowa 7 49
(W M Brisbourne) *led: hdd over 2f out: fdd fnl f* **7/1**
2001 **5** *2 ½* **Sand Repeal (IRE)**^{18} [911] 4-9-5 **70** .... RonanKeogh 2 60
(Miss J Feilden) *trckd ldrs: effrt over 2f out: wknd appr fnl f* **10/3**^{2}
1303 **6** *¾* **Oldenway**^{61} [491] 7-9-0 **67** .... NSLawes$^{(3)}$ 5 56
(R A Fahey) *trckd ldrs: effrt over 2f out: wknd over 1f out* **7/2**^{3}
223- **7** *11* **Optimum (IRE)**^{194} [545] 4-9-0 **65** .... AshleyHamblett 1 37
(J T Stimpson) *chsd ldr: chal 3f out: lost pl over 1f out* **12/1**
34-0 **8** *1 ½* **Lady Diktat**^{19} [894] 4-9-0 **65** .... JamesMillman 3 34
(Mrs A J Hamilton-Fairley) *in rr: bhd fnl 3f* **14/1**
0-00 **9** *1 ½* **Queen Tara**^{19} [894] 4-8-4 **55** oh15.......... KirstyMilczarek 9 22
(Mrs C A Dunnett) *sn chsng ldrs on outer: lost pl over 3f out: sn bhd* **33/1**

2m 41.7s (1.40) **Going Correction** +0.10s/f (Good)
WFA 4 from 5yo+ 1lb **9** Ran SP% **113.3**
Speed ratings (Par 103):99,98,94,94,92 91,84,83,82
CSF £145.75 CT £1224.06 TOTE £53.70: £13.40, £1.60, £2.90; EX 283.50 Place 6 £ 92.48, Place 5 £75.94.
Owner Rosehill Racing Club **Bred** Juddmonte Farms **Trained** Ruckland, Lincs

FOCUS
A shock result with rank outsider Migration coming through to topple favourite Platinum Charmer. They went no pace and this is very suspect form.
Lady Diktat Official explanation: jockey said filly lost a front shoe
T/Jkpt: Part won. £60,485.90 to a £1 stake. Pool: £85,191.50. 0.50 winning tickets. T/Plt: £149.50 to a £1 stake. Pool: £41,530.55. 202.75 winning tickets. T/Qpdt: £141.70 to a £1 stake. Pool: £2,107.40. 11.00 winning tickets. WG

1194 WOLVERHAMPTON (A.W) (L-H)
Tuesday, April 25

OFFICIAL GOING: Standard
Wind: Moderate behind Weather: Fine

1223 BETFRED MILLION MAIDEN AUCTION STKS 5f 20y(P)
2:20 (2:20) (Class 7) 2-Y-O £1,467 (£433; £216) **Stalls** Low

Form RPR
1 **Ask Don't Tell (IRE)** 2-8-8 .... JohnEgan 2 59
(Tom Dascombe) *chsd ldrs: rdn over 2f out: led ins fnl f: edgd lft: r.o wl* **7/1**^{3}
2 *1 ¾* **Hucking Hot** 2-8-8 .... LPKeniry 3 52+
(J R Best) *s.i.s: sn rdn and outpcd: hdwy on ins 2f out: swtchd rt ins fnl f: fin wl* **7/1**^{3}
53 **3** *nk* **Our Susie (IRE)**^{8} [1046] 2-8-6 .... HayleyTurner 6 49
(M D I Usher) *a.p: rdn to ld and edgd rt jst over 1f out: hdd ins fnl f: nt qckn* **2/1**^{1}
4 *1 ½* **Dotty's Daughter** 2-8-5 .... WSupple 10 42
(Mrs A Duffield) *chsd ldrs: rdn 2f out: kpt on same pce fnl f* **5/1**^{2}
0 **5** *¾* **Mr Mini Scule**^{14} [962] 2-8-10 .... RichardSmith$^{(3)}$ 1 47
(A B Haynes) *chsd ldr: rdn and ev ch over 1f out: wknd ins fnl f* **10/1**
6 *3* **Generist** 2-8-6 .... RobbieFitzpatrick 5 28
(M J Attwater) *s.i.s: outpcd: nvr nrr* **14/1**
7 *1 ¼* **Crystal Ice (IRE)** 2-8-1 .... PatrickMathers$^{(3)}$ 11 21
(Mrs L Williamson) *led: rdn and hdd jst over 1f out: wknd fnl f* **20/1**
55 **8** *5* **Readyforone**^{8} [1040] 2-8-11 ....(b) ShaneKelly 7 8
(P D Evans) *mid-div: n.m.r over 3f out: sn rdn and bhd* **17/2**
9 *½* **Only A Grand** 2-8-4 .... RoystonFfrench 4 —
(R Bastiman) *outpcd* **16/1**
10 *1 ¾* **Sunstroke (IRE)** 2-8-7 ow3.......... TPQueally 9 —
(M G Quinlan) *outpcd* **9/1**
0 **11** *1 ¾* **Lenard Frank (IRE)**^{15} [944] 2-8-11 .... DavidKinsella 8 —
(M D I Usher) *s.i.s: outpcd* **33/1**

63.05 secs (0.23) **Going Correction** -0.25s/f (Stan) **11** Ran SP% **124.9**
Speed ratings (Par 86):88,85,84,82,81 76,74,66,65,62 59
CSF £59.02 TOTE £8.30: £2.30, £3.20, £1.20; EX 49.20.
Owner Sideways Racing V **Bred** Tally-Ho Stud **Trained** Lambourn, Berks

FOCUS
The only race on the card with any semblance of quality but it is very difficult to set the level of the form with confidence.

NOTEBOOK
Ask Don't Tell(IRE), a sister to fair sprinter Fizzlephut, made a pleasing debut. Always up with the pace, she led before edging left inside the final furlong but was already in command. Connections fancy a tilt at the Chester May meeting with her. (op 9-1)
Hucking Hot, a cheap yearling, missed the break and was in the rear before making headway coming into the home straight. Only sixth passing the furlong pole, she had to be switched right to the outer but finished well.
Our Susie(IRE), more experienced than most, was slowly away but was soon in touch. However, after showing ahead she did not help her chance by hanging right and she was also caught for second on the line. (op 10-3)
Dotty's Daughter, who is bred to be sharp, looked one-paced when push came to shove (op 7-2)
Mr Mini Scule improved on the form of his debut seventh on easy ground at Bath. (op 9-1)
Crystal Ice(IRE) has a pedigree that suggests she needs further, but she showed plenty of pace to grab the lead despite her outside draw and was only done for inside the last.
Lenard Frank(IRE) Official explanation: jockey said gelding hung left

1224 BETFREDPOKER.COM BANDED STKS 1m 4f 50y(P)
2:50 (2:50) (Class 7) 4-Y-O+ £1,365 (£403; £201) **Stalls** Low

Form RPR
40-4 **1** **Wood Fern (UAE)**^{28} [787] 6-8-13 45.......... ShaneKelly 2 54
(W M Brisbourne) *hld up in mid-div: swtchd rt and hdwy to chse ldr 8f out: led 3f out: rdn out* **3/1**^{1}
00-4 **2** *1 ¼* **Sudden Impulse**^{28} [788] 5-8-13 35.......... PaulEddery 4 52
(A D Brown) *hld up in mid-div: hdwy over 5f out: rdn to chse wnr over 2f out: kpt on ins fnl f* **8/1**
0-4 **3** *6* **Nobelmann (GER)**^{20} [891] 7-8-13 45.......... WSupple 9 42
(A W Carroll) *hld up and bhd: stdy hdwy over 6f out: rdn over 3f out: wknd 2f out* **9/2**^{3}
0644 **4** *¾* **Queue Up**^{15} [937] 4-8-12 40.......... LPKeniry 5 41
(A G Newcombe) *hld up and bhd: stdy hdwy over 5f out: rdn over 4f out: wknd 2f out* **9/1**
-000 **5** *3 ½* **Ready Teddy Go**^{29} [767] 4-8-12 40..........(v^{1}) MichaelTebbutt 10 36
(J Ryan) *led: rdn and hdd 3f out: wknd 2f out* **14/1**
600- **6** *18* **Pitsi Kahtoh**^{199} [5741] 4-8-12 40.......... DarrenWilliams 1 7
(P W Hiatt) *a bhd* **14/1**
/0-4 **7** *1 ¼* **Venetian Romance (IRE)**^{20} [361] 5-8-13 40..........(tp) HayleyTurner 12 5
(M R Bosley) *s.i.s: sn rdn into mid-div: nvr gng wl: wl bhd fnl 3f* **9/1**
000- **8** *½* **Yeldham Lady**^{382} [927] 4-8-12 45.......... VinceSlattery 6 4
(A J Chamberlain) *a towards rr* **20/1**
305- **9** *nk* **Zeena**^{117} [6681] 4-8-12 45.......... JohnEgan 3 4
(C A Horgan) *prom: wknd 3f out: sn eased* **10/3**^{2}
000/ **10** *16* **Lasser Light (IRE)**^{526} [6654] 6-8-10 35.......... DNolan$^{(3)}$ 11 —
(D G Bridgwater) *chsd ldr 6f: rdn and wknd 5f out: t.o* **33/1**
000- **11** *dist* **Glowette (IRE)**^{171} [6260] 4-8-7 35.......... NataliaGemelova$^{(5)}$ 7 —
(I W McInnes) *prom 6f: t.o* **40/1**

2m 41.14s (-1.28) **Going Correction** -0.25s/f (Stan)
WFA 4 from 5yo+ 1lb **11** Ran SP% **120.8**
Speed ratings (Par 97):94,93,89,88,86 74,73,73,72,62 —
CSF £27.94 TOTE £3.40: £1.70, £2.70, £2.30; EX 26.60.
Owner The Generals Men Racing Club **Bred** Darley Dubai **Trained** Great Ness, Shropshire

FOCUS
This was run at only a steady pace. The first five finished a long way clear but this is ordinary form at best.
Zeena Official explanation: jockey said filly stopped quickly three furlong mark
Lasser Light(IRE) Official explanation: jockey said gelding hung left-handed
Glowette(IRE) Official explanation: jockey said filly lost her action

1225 BETFREDCASINO.COM BANDED STKS 1m 141y(P)
3:20 (3:22) (Class 7) 4-Y-O+ £1,365 (£403; £201) **Stalls** Low

Form RPR
0455 **1** **Welsh Whisper**^{1} [1197] 7-8-12 45.......... SamHitchcott 4 47
(S A Brookshaw) *s.i.s: sn wl bhd: hdwy on ins over 2f out: rdn over 1f out: led wl ins fnl f: r.o* **13/2**
3624 **2** *nk* **Dexileos (IRE)**^{21} [875] 7-8-12 45..........(t) HayleyTurner 1 46
(David Pinder) *led: rdn over 2f out: hdd wl ins fnl f: r.o* **5/2**^{1}
00-0 **3** *1 ½* **Iceni Warrior**^{18} [900] 4-8-12 45.......... J-PGuillambert 6 43
(P Howling) *hld up in mid-div: hdwy on ins 2f out: rdn and swtchd rt over 1f out: kpt on ins fnl f* **40/1**
5-05 **4** *1 ¼* **Viscount Rossini**^{27} [791] 4-8-12 40.......... RobbieFitzpatrick 10 40
(A W Carroll) *hld up in mid-div: rdn over 2f out: hdwy on outside over 1f out: styd on ins fnl f* **12/1**
0-43 **5** *1 ½* **Emperor Cat (IRE)**^{15} [941] 5-8-12 45.......... VinceSlattery 3 37
(Mrs N S Evans) *chsd ldr: rdn 3f out: wknd ins fnl f* **9/1**
0000 **6** *¾* **Qobtaan (USA)**^{1} [1197] 7-8-12 45.......... LPKeniry 5 36
(M R Bosley) *hld up towards rr: rdn and hdwy over 1f out: nvr trbld ldrs* **11/1**
2310 **7** *1 ¾* **Faithisflying**^{1} [1197] 4-8-12 45..........(p) PhillipMakin 13 32
(D W Chapman) *prom tl rdn and wknd 2f out* **5/1**^{2}
0-00 **8** *nk* **Silver Court**^{19} [894] 4-8-12 40.......... FrancisNorton 11 31
(A W Carroll) *hld up in mid-div: hdwy over 4f out: rdn over 3f out: wknd over 1f out* **12/1**
00/4 **9** *1* **Chiracahua (IRE)**^{15} [941] 4-8-12 45.......... PaulEddery 7 29
(B Smart) *plld hrd early: prom: rdn over 2f out: hung rt over 1f out: sn wknd* **16/1**
0-00 **10** *7* **Ruby Sunrise (IRE)**^{27} [793] 4-8-5 40.......... SoniaEaton$^{(7)}$ 9 15
(B P J Baugh) *s.i.s: a bhd* **25/1**

400- 11 hd **Miracle Baby**[199] 5736 4-8-12 40 MichaelTebbutt 2 14
(A J Chamberlain) *sn wl bhd* **16/1**
0332 12 2 **Rocky Reppin**[15] 941 6-8-9 45 (b) JasonEdmunds(3) 8 10
(J Balding) *s.i.s: hdwy over 4f out: rdn over 3f out: sn wknd* **11/2**[3]
0-00 13 2 **Tonight (IRE)**[1] 1197 4-8-12 45 (bt) ShaneKelly 12 6
(W M Brisbourne) *s.i.s: a bhd* **33/1**
1m 50.62s (-1.14) **Going Correction** -0.25s/f (Stan) 13 Ran SP% **128.7**
Speed ratings (Par 97):95,94,93,92,90 90,88,88,87,81 81,79,77
CSF £24.51 TOTE £7.80: £2.30, £1.80, £10.40; EX 38.90.
Owner S A Brookshaw **Bred** Lloyd Bros **Trained** Wollerton, Shropshire
FOCUS
The pace steadied at halfway. This is weak form, with the winner not having to improve.
Miracle Baby Official explanation: jockey said filly hung right-handed

1226 BETFRED "THE BONUS KING" TRI-BANDED STKS 1m 141y(P)
3:50 (3:51) (Class 7) 3-Y-O £1,365 (£403; £201) Stalls Low

Form RPR
000- 1 **Indigo Dancer**[196] 5823 3-8-12 45 TPQueally 11 42
(C F Wall) *hld up towards rr: rdn and hdwy over 2f out: edgd lft over 1f out: r.o to ld nr fin* **7/2**[1]
5236 2 ½ **The Jailer**[15] 945 3-8-12 45 (p) DavidKinsella 13 41
(J G M O'Shea) *sn led: rdn clr wl over 1f out: ct nr fin* **15/2**[3]
6-00 3 ½ **Skye Boat Song**[22] 850 3-8-12 45 (t) DerekMcGaffin 1 40
(J Jay) *chsd ldrs: rdn over 2f out: wnt 2nd over 1f out: kpt on ins fnl f* **40/1**
000- 4 shd **Joy In The Guild (IRE)**[197] 5796 3-8-12 45 LPKeniry 6 40
(W S Kittow) *bhd: rdn and hdwy whn edgd lft jst over 1f out: r.o* **16/1**
-020 5 2 **Skin Sure Thing**[41] 642 3-8-7 45 (v) MarcHalford(5) 9 35
(A D Smith) *bhd tl hdwy and edgd lft fnl f: nvr nrr* **20/1**
5-00 6 1¼ **Boucheen**[58] 524 3-8-12 45 SamHitchcott 5 33
(Ms Deborah J Evans) *stdd s: hdwy whn nt clr run and swtchd rt jst over 1f out: styng on whn nt clr run wl ins fnl f* **12/1**
0231 7 nk **Beginners Luck (IRE)**[21] 874 3-8-9 45 DNolan(3) 2 32
(D Carroll) *mid-div: hdwy and swtchd rt over 1f out: nvr trbld ldrs* **6/1**[2]
6-04 8 nk **Coffin Dodger**[20] 887 3-8-12 45 ShaneKelly 7 32
(C N Allen) *hld up towards rr: stdy hdwy over 6f out: wknd over 2f out* **7/2**[1]
00-0 9 ¾ **Seesawmilu (IRE)**[22] 861 3-8-7 45 DerekNolan(5) 4 30
(E J Alston) *led early: chsd ldr: rdn and ev ch over 2f out: wknd over 1f out* **14/1**
0065 10 ¾ **Cape Latina**[20] 887 3-8-5 45 KylieManser(7) 12 28
(J R Best) *hld up in mid-div: rdn over 3f out: hdwy on ins wl over 1f out: wknd fnl f* **12/1**
06-2 11 2 **Safari**[28] 779 3-8-7 45 TravisBlock(5) 8 24
(R J Hodges) *prom: rdn over 3f out: wknd wl over 1f out* **12/1**
000- 12 25 **Follingworth (IRE)**[174] 6228 3-8-7 45 DuranFentiman(5) 3 —
(A D Brown) *a bhd: t.o fnl 2f* **50/1**
063- 13 1¼ **Ten Commandments (IRE)**[242] 4713 3-8-9 45(b[1]) JasonEdmunds(3) 10 —
(J Balding) *t.k.h: chsd ldrs: rdn 4f out: sn wknd: t.o fnl 2f* **8/1**
1m 51.93s (0.17) **Going Correction** -0.25s/f (Stan) 13 Ran SP% **126.4**
Speed ratings (Par 92):89,88,88,88,86 85,84,84,83,83 81,59,58
CSF £31.30 TOTE £3.00: £2.20, £3.50, £13.80; EX 51.80.
Owner Induna Racing Partners Two **Bred** Stourbank Stud **Trained** Newmarket, Suffolk
FOCUS
Poor fare, the winner only needing to reproduce the form of his twelfth in a Yarmouth maiden last September to take this.

1227 BETFRED 570 SHOPS NATIONWIDE BANDED STKS 7f 32y(P)
4:20 (4:20) (Class 7) 4-Y-O+ £1,706 (£503; £252) Stalls High

Form RPR
16-4 1 **Merlins Profit**[1] 1194 6-9-2 49 DeanMcKeown 4 60
(G A Swinbank) *a.p: rdn over 2f out: led jst over 1f out: hld on wl* **5/2**[1]
0-02 2 ½ **Geojimali**[1] 1196 4-9-3 50 FergalLynch 11 60
(J S Goldie) *hld up in rr: hdwy on ins over 2f out: rdn wl over 1f out: r.o ins fnl f* **13/2**[3]
20-0 3 1½ **King Of Meze (IRE)**[21] 864 5-9-1 48 (p) TonyHamilton 1 54
(J S Wainwright) *led over 1f: led over 3f out: rdn and hdd jst over 1f out: nt qckn ins fnl f* **9/1**
45-6 4 3½ **Pepper Road**[15] 940 7-9-0 47 RoystonFfrench 3 44
(R Bastiman) *hld up in tch: rdn over 2f out: wknd fnl f* **10/1**
0015 5 1¼ **Elms Schoolboy**[21] 875 4-9-0 47 (b) J-PGuillambert 6 41
(P Howling) *mid-div: rdn and swtchd rt over 2f out: hdwy over 1f out: no imp fnl f* **6/1**[2]
1233 6 2 **Mount Royale (IRE)**[21] 873 8-9-3 50 (v) KimTinkler 12 38
(N Tinkler) *prom: rdn over 2f out: sn wknd* **15/2**
000- 7 nk **Bakke**[220] 5303 4-9-0 47 (bt[1]) LPKeniry 8 35
(B I Case) *hld up in tch: hmpd and lost pl over 2f out: n.d after* **20/1**
3500 8 2 **Supreme Salutation**[35] 689 10-8-9 47 DerekNolan(5) 7 29
(D K Ivory) *s.i.s: nvr nr ldrs* **7/1**
3030 9 3½ **Wodhill Be**[20] 889 6-9-0 47 DerekMcGaffin 10 20
(D Morris) *swtchd lft sn after s: a bhd* **16/1**
0-5 10 5 **Glenviews Babalou (USA)**[29] 772 4-9-1 48 RobbieFitzpatrick 9 8
(Peter Grayson) *w ldr: led over 5f out tl over 3f out: sn rdn: wknd 2f out* **11/1**
0-56 11 1½ **Vizulize**[64] 467 7-9-0 47 ShaneKelly 5 3
(A W Carroll) *a bhd* **14/1**
1m 28.89s (-1.51) **Going Correction** -0.25s/f (Stan) 11 Ran SP% **125.2**
Speed ratings (Par 97):98,97,95,91,90 88,87,85,81,75 73
CSF £19.91 TOTE £3.30: £1.50, £2.70, £3.40; EX 14.90.
Owner William A Powrie **Bred** Helshaw Grange Stud Ltd **Trained** Melsonby, N Yorks
FOCUS
The finish was fought out by two horses who ran close here the previous day, albeit in separate races, and both posted above-average efforts here. It was run at a fair pace and produced much the best time on the card.
Elms Schoolboy Official explanation: jockey said gelding hung left
Vizulize Official explanation: jockey said mare was slowly away and hung right

1228 BETFRED MILLION BANDED STKS 5f 20y(P)
4:50 (4:50) (Class 7) 4-Y-O+ £1,365 (£403; £201) Stalls Low

Form RPR
60-0 1 **Compton Classic**[36] 680 4-8-12 45 (p) FergalLynch 5 52
(J S Goldie) *hld up and bhd: hdwy on ins wl over 1f out: rdn to ld ins fnl f: r.o* **12/1**
6002 2 1¼ **Comic Tales**[15] 943 5-8-12 40 (b) DarrenWilliams 1 48
(M Mullineaux) *hld up and bhd: hdwy over 2f out: sn rdn: r.o ins fnl f* **9/2**[2]
6542 3 2 **A Teen**[15] 942 8-8-12 45 J-PGuillambert 11 40+
(P Howling) *bhd: swtchd rt and hdwy over 1f out: kpt on ins fnl f* **7/1**[3]
4-03 4 hd **Maromito (IRE)**[15] 943 9-8-12 45 RoystonFfrench 4 40
(R Bastiman) *led: rdn over 1f out: hdd and no ex ins fnl f* **9/1**
000- 5 shd **King Egbert (FR)**[199] 5736 5-8-12 45 ShaneKelly 3 39
(A W Carroll) *chsd ldrs: rdn and wnt 2nd wl over 1f out: one pce* **4/1**[1]
3500 6 ¾ **Town House**[27] 789 4-8-5 45 SoniaEaton(7) 13 37
(B P J Baugh) *rrd and s.s: hdwy and swtchd lft 1f out: nt rch ldrs* **33/1**
0-00 7 nk **Torrent**[35] 686 11-8-12 45 (b) PaulQuinn 12 35
(D W Chapman) *racd wd: prom: rdn over 2f out: edgd lft over 1f out: wknd fnl f* **16/1**
0000 8 shd **Dutch Key Card (IRE)**[28] 782 5-8-12 45 (b) RobbieFitzpatrick 10 35
(C Smith) *no hdwy fnl 2f* **8/1**
-060 9 1¼ **Noble Mount**[27] 793 5-8-9 45 (p) RichardSmith(3) 7 31
(A B Haynes) *dropped rr 3f out: c wd st: n.d after* **12/1**
6-60 10 nk **Petana**[15] 951 6-8-12 45 TonyHamilton 6 30
(Peter Grayson) *chsd ldr: rdn over 2f out: wknd over 1f out* **16/1**
3354 11 2 **Eternally**[21] 872 4-8-12 45 (p) TPQueally 8 22
(R M H Cowell) *prom: rdn over 2f out: wknd over 1f out* **10/1**
0/00 12 ½ **Our Chelsea Blue (USA)**[35] 686 8-8-12 40 VinceSlattery 9 21
(J R Jenkins) *prom: btn whn sltly hmpd over 1f out* **40/1**
05-4 13 6 **Victoriana**[71] 396 5-8-12 40 (p) MichaelTebbutt 2 —
(H J Collingridge) *a bhd* **8/1**
62.38 secs (-0.44) **Going Correction** -0.25s/f (Stan) 13 Ran SP% **124.5**
Speed ratings (Par 97):93,91,87,87,87 86,85,85,83,83 79,79,69
CSF £68.01 TOTE £12.60: £5.60, £1.90, £2.50; EX 90.10 Place 6 £53.66, Place 5 £34.14.
Owner J S Goldie **Bred** James Thom And Sons And Peter Orr **Trained** Uplawmoor, E Renfrews
FOCUS
An ordinary event. The winner ran to something like his turf form of the latter part of last season.
Town House Official explanation: jockey said filly reared up in stalls and missed break
T/Plt: £188.60 to a £1 stake. Pool: £29,557.70. 114.35 winning tickets. T/Qpdt: £77.20 to a £1 stake. Pool: £1,795.70. 17.20 winning tickets. KH

[974]CATTERICK (L-H)
Wednesday, April 26

OFFICIAL GOING: Firm
Wind: Light across

1229 WOT-IF-WE (S) STKS 5f
2:05 (2:07) (Class 6) 2-Y-O £2,730 (£806; £403) Stalls Low

Form RPR
00 1 **Just Dust**[10] 1030 2-8-8 (p) RobertMiles(3) 3 59
(W G M Turner) *chsd ldrs: rdn along and outpcd after 2f: swtchd rt and hdwy 2f out: rdn over 1f out: styd on to ld post* **6/1**[3]
5413 2 shd **Granny Peel (IRE)**[4] 1142 2-8-12 (p) DO'Donohoe 4 60
(K A Ryan) *led: rdn wl over 1f out: hdd on line* **11/10**[1]
0 3 3 **Minnie Magician**[4] 1142 2-8-6 TonyHamilton 5 42
(C Grant) *dwlt: sn chsng ldrs: rdn along 2f out: kpt on same pce fnl f* **33/1**
4 1¾ **Argent Danseur** 2-8-11 PaulHanagan 8 40
(B S Rothwell) *wnt bdly rt s and outpcd: hdwy on outer 1/2-way: rdn to chse ldrs and hung lft over 1f out: no imp* **16/1**
0 5 1¾ **Baytown Paikea**[23] 856 2-8-6 FrancisFerris 7 28
(P S McEntee) *cl up: rdn 2f out and ev ch tl drvn and wknd appr fnl f* **25/1**
035 6 hd **Afric Star**[15] 962 2-8-6 GrahamGibbons 6 27
(P D Evans) *cl up: rdn along 2f out: sn wknd* **6/1**[3]
6624 7 ½ **Sad Times (IRE)**[15] 962 2-7-13 LiamJones(7) 1 25
(W G M Turner) *sn outpcd and a rr* **10/3**[2]
60.91 secs (0.31) **Going Correction** -0.20s/f (Firm) 7 Ran SP% **111.9**
Speed ratings (Par 90):89,88,84,81,78 78,77
CSF £12.50 TOTE £7.90: £3.80, £1.20; EX 17.30.There was no bid for the winner.
Owner T.O.C.S. Ltd **Bred** T O C S Ltd And W G M Turner **Trained** Sigwells, Somerset
FOCUS
An average-looking juvenile seller, rated around the runner-up.
NOTEBOOK
Just Dust, who gave plenty of trouble at the start, took a long time to get going and only just got there on the line. This is probably his level and a sixth furlong is within his scope. (op 7-1)
Granny Peel(IRE), already a winner in selling company, led everywhere bar the line and was a little bit unlucky not to hold on. She should remain a force at this level. (tchd Evens and 6-5 and 5-4 in a place)
Minnie Magician got much closer to Granny Peel than she had done on worse terms on her debut, but is clearly pretty moderate. (tchd 40-1)
Argent Danseur made a really bad start but still managed to have a chance of sorts a furlong out. Clearly very green, he is entitled to come on for the race but may have his quirks. (op 14-1)
Baytown Paikea had every chance but was left wanting, even in this company. (op 20-1)
Afric Star managed to reverse recent placings with Sad Times, but that was only because that rival made a really bad start.
Sad Times(IRE) was slowly away and never got into the race. (op 7-2 tchd 4-1)

1230 PRINCE OF MY HEART MAIDEN STKS 7f
2:40 (2:42) (Class 5) 3-Y-O £3,886 (£1,156; £577; £288) Stalls Low

Form RPR
636- 1 **Stonehaugh (IRE)**[210] 5548 3-9-3 73 (t) RobertWinston 7 74
(J Howard Johnson) *led 2f. cl up: rdn over 1f out: led ins last and styd on wl* **7/1**[3]
2 2 1 **Hams (USA)**[10] 1032 3-8-12 RHills 4 66
(M Johnston) *cl up: led after 2f: rdn along wl over 1f out: hdd and no ex ins last* **5/6**[1]
430- 3 2 **Elegant Times (IRE)**[219] 5355 3-8-12 76 FergalLynch 5 61
(T D Easterby) *chsd ldrs: rdn along 2f out: kpt on same pce appr last* **13/2**[2]
6- 4 1¼ **Bolckow**[243] 4735 3-9-3 DO'Donohoe 2 63
(K A Ryan) *in tch: hdwy on inner over 2f out: rdn to chse ldrs over 1f out: sn one pce* **14/1**
6-3 5 1½ **Choreography**[33] 716 3-9-3 FrancisNorton 1 59
(D Nicholls) *hld up in rr: hdwy 3rf out: pushed along to chse ldrs 2f out: sn one pce* **7/1**[3]
00- 6 2½ **Princess Cocoa (IRE)**[249] 4559 3-8-12 PaulHanagan 3 48
(R A Fahey) *bhd tl sme hdwy fnl 2f: nvr a factor* **40/1**
7 nk **Light Sentence** 3-9-3 DeanMcKeown 6 52
(G A Swinbank) *s.i.s and bhd tl sme late hdwy* **16/1**
000- 8 2 **Red Iris (IRE)**[257] 4317 3-8-12 30 DaleGibson 9 42?
(G A Swinbank) *a rr* **100/1**

440- **9** 3/4 **Chilsdown**[188] [5994] 3-9-3 72 PhillipMakin 10 45
(Ronald Thompson) *chsd ldrs: rdn along over 2f out: sn drvn and wknd* **20/1**

0 **10** 1 1/2 **Wee Ziggy**[14] [978] 3-9-3 PaulQuinn 11 41
(D Nicholls) *in tch: rdn along to chse ldrs 1/2-way: wknd over 2f out* **33/1**

1m 25.91s (-1.45) **Going Correction** -0.20s/f (Firm) **10** Ran SP% **116.6**
Speed ratings (Par 98):100,98,96,95,93 90,90,87,87,85
CSF £12.88 TOTE £6.80: £1.90, £1.10, £2.00; EX 18.90.
Owner Transcend Bloodstock LLP **Bred** Yakup Demir Tokdemir **Trained** Billy Row, Co Durham

FOCUS
A modest maiden that featured a few horses that were having their third starts and the first two are the best guides to the level, but the form is limited by the fourth, fifth and sixth.
Princess Cocoa(IRE) Official explanation: jockey said filly was unsuited by the track

1231 RICHMOND CONDITIONS STKS 1m 3f 214y
3:15 (3:16) (Class 4) 3-Y-O **£6,232** (£1,866; £933) **Stalls** Low

Form RPR
031- **1** **Youmzain (IRE)**[242] [4745] 3-9-1 88 TonyCulhane 4 101+
(M R Channon) *trckd ldr: hdwy over 1f out: shkn up and qckd wl to ld ins last: cleverly* **5/4[2]**

22-1 **2** 1/2 **London Express (IRE)**[22] [867] 3-9-1 97 StanleyChin(3) 6 99
(M Johnston) *set stdy pce: qckd 1/2-way: shkn up and qckd 2f out: rdn over 1f out: hdd and nopt qckn ins last* **4/6[1]**

3 *dist* **Dawn Spirit** 3-8-4 JoeFanning 2 —
(J R Weymes) *trckd ldrs: hdwy and cl up 1/2-way: rdn along over 2f out and sn wknd* **33/1[3]**

2m 40.38s (1.38) **Going Correction** -0.20s/f (Firm) **3** Ran SP% **107.4**
Speed ratings (Par 100):87,86,—
CSF £2.48 TOTE £2.30; EX 2.20.
Owner Jaber Abdullah **Bred** Frank Dunne **Trained** West Ilsley, Berks

FOCUS
A very slow time and only two counted. It is impossible to know the value of the form at this stage.

1232 9TH MAY IS LADIES NIGHT H'CAP 7f
3:50 (3:50) (Class 6) (0-60,60) 3-Y-O **£2,730** (£806; £403) **Stalls** Low

Form RPR
6133 **1** **Buzzin'Boyzee (IRE)**[23] [861] 3-8-6 53 StephenDonohoe(5) 6 60
(P D Evans) *dwlt: hld up towards rr: swtchd rt and hdwy 2f out: rdn over 1f out: styd on to ld ins last* **11/2[2]**

-541 **2** 1 **Musicmaestroplease (IRE)**[28] [796] 3-9-3 59 DeanMcKeown 5 63
(S Parr) *in tch: hdwy 3f out: rdn to chse ldrs over 1f out: drvn and kpt on ins last* **2/1[1]**

00-0 **3** 2 1/2 **Hogan's Heroes**[27] [801] 3-8-13 55 RobertWinston 3 53
(G A Butler) *dwlt and bhd: hdwy 3f out: rdn wl over 1f out: kpt on ins last: nrst fin* **7/1[3]**

00-0 **4** *shd* **Moonlight Fantasy (IRE)**[23] [861] 3-8-10 52 JoeFanning 14 49
(N Tinkler) *chsd ldrs: hdwy over 2f out: rdn to ld and hung bdly lft over 1f out: hdd ins last: wknd* **33/1**

400- **5** 1 1/4 **River Logic (IRE)**[227] [5145] 3-8-9 54 PaulMulrennan(3) 10 48
(J Howard Johnson) *chsd ldrs: rdn along over 2f out: drvn whn n.m.r over 1f out: kpt on same pce* **16/1**

0-01 **6** 1 1/2 **Taras Tornado**[20] [893] 3-8-12 54 GrahamGibbons 2 44
(J J Quinn) *midfield: hdwy to chse ldrs over 2f out: rdn and n.m.r over 1f out: sn one pce* **7/1[3]**

04-0 **7** 1 **Casonova (IRE)**[23] [861] 3-8-13 55 DavidAllan 9 42
(T D Easterby) *cl up: led 4f out: rdn along over 2f out: drvn: hdd and n.m.r over 1f out: sn one pce* **16/1**

00-0 **8** *nk* **King Of Chav's (IRE)**[4] [1140] 3-8-13 55 JosedeSouza 11 42
(A Bailey) *towards rr tl sme late hdwy* **33/1**

45-0 **9** 1 **Quaker Boy**[14] [988] 3-9-4 60 (p) TomEaves 4 44+
(M Dods) *chsd ldrs: rdn along 2f out: keeping on along inner whn bdly hmpd over 1f out and no ch after* **12/1**

0-60 **10** 1/2 **Nilsatisoptimum (USA)**[103] [104] 3-9-2 58 TPQueally 8 41
(M Mullineaux) *led 3f: cl up tl rdn along 2f out: drvn and wkng whn hmpd over 1f out: sn wknd* **16/1**

0-56 **11** 1 **Wensleydale Star**[69] [430] 3-8-13 55 (p) PaulFessey 7 35
(T D Barron) *a rr* **12/1**

000- **12** *hd* **Pontefract Glory**[199] [5769] 3-8-11 53 PhillipMakin 16 33
(M Dods) *midfield: rdn along and wd st: sn bhd* **25/1**

000- **13** *dist* **Be Like A Lion**[190] [5955] 3-8-13 55 FrancisFerris 17 —
(B Palling) *a rr: bhd fnl 2f* **20/1**

00-0 **14** 21 **Worldly Pursuit**[89] [211] 3-8-13 55 TonyCulhane 1 —
(B Smart) *s.i.s: a bhd: t.o fnl 3f* **16/1**

1m 25.61s (-1.75) **Going Correction** -0.20s/f (Firm) **14** Ran SP% **127.1**
Speed ratings (Par 96):102,100,98,97,96 94,93,93,92,91 90,90,—,—
CSF £17.03 CT £83.03 TOTE £6.90: £1.90, £1.30, £2.40; EX 17.40.
Owner P D Evans **Bred** Golden Vale Stud **Trained** Pandy, Abergavenny
■ Stewards' Enquiry : Joe Fanning one-day ban: careless riding (May 8)

FOCUS
A moderate handicap but the right horses dominated the finish and the form looks sound for the grade. It was run in a decent time for a race like this.
Pontefract Glory Official explanation: jockey said gelding hung right on bend into home straight

1233 MOONAX H'CAP 1m 3f 214y
4:25 (4:25) (Class 5) (0-70,70) 4-Y-O+ **£5,181** (£1,541; £770; £384) **Stalls** Low

Form RPR
44-2 **1** **Saif Sareea**[7] [1075] 6-8-8 59 PaulHanagan 16 73+
(R A Fahey) *plld hrd and rapid hdwy to ld after 4f: qckd clr over 2f out easily* **4/5[1]**

0-40 **2** 3 1/2 **Mceldowney**[14] [976] 4-8-11 68 GregFairley(5) 15 72
(M Johnston) *trckd ldrs: hdwy 3f out: rdn along 2f out: styd on ins last: no ch w wnr* **5/1[2]**

246- **3** *hd* **Zarova (IRE)**[170] [6286] 4-7-11 56 oh1 AdeleRothery(7) 13 60
(M W Easterby) *hld up: hdwy over 3f out: rdn to chse wnr wl over 1f out: eased ins last: lost 2nd nr fin* **12/1[3]**

0-00 **4** 2 **Fardi (IRE)**[7] [1075] 4-8-8 63 DanielTudhope(3) 6 63
(K W Hogg) *midfield: hdwy to chse ldrs over 2f out: sn rdn and kpt on ins last* **66/1**

660- **5** 1/2 **Hugs Destiny (IRE)**[138] [4095] 5-8-5 56 oh3 DeanMcKeown 5 56
(M A Barnes) *led over 3f: chsd wnr tl rdn along 3f out: drvn and one pce fnl 2f* **20/1**

554- **6** *nk* **Royal Flynn**[215] [5431] 4-8-11 63 PhillipMakin 12 62
(M Dods) *towards rr: hdwy wl over 2f out: sn rdn and kpt on: nt rch ldrs* **12/1[3]**

000- **7** 3/4 **Loves Travelling (IRE)**[221] [5296] 6-9-2 70 DNolan(3) 7 68
(N Wilson) *hld up and bhd: hdwy 4f out: rdn along over 2f out: sn drvn and no imp* **20/1**

03-0 **8** 2 **Scarrabus (IRE)**[10] [1034] 5-8-3 57 oh1 ow1 SaleemGolam(3) 9 52
(A Crook) *nvr nr ldrs* **25/1**

000- **9** 1 **Bramantino (IRE)**[143] [5890] 6-9-0 65 FergalLynch 1 58
(T A K Cuthbert) *a towards rr* **25/1**

/00- **10** 1/2 **Tiger Frog (USA)**[104] [4001] 7-8-9 60 (p) DaleGibson 8 52
(J Mackie) *a towards rr* **16/1**

000- **11** 3/4 **Celtic Shadow (IRE)**[322] [2383] 4-8-4 56 oh1 DavidAllan 14 47
(K G Reveley) *prom: rdn along over 4f out: drvn over 2f out and sn wknd* **25/1**

00-0 **12** 16 **Etijahaat (IRE)**[9] [1041] 4-9-2 68 LeeEnstone 11 34
(C W Fairhurst) *midfield: hdwy and cl up 7f out: rdn along 4f out: sn wknd* **50/1**

2m 36.62s (-2.38) **Going Correction** -0.20s/f (Firm)
WFA 4 from 5yo+ 1lb **12** Ran SP% **118.0**
Speed ratings (Par 103):99,96,96,95,94 94,94,92,92,91 91,80
CSF £3.95 CT £28.83 TOTE £1.70: £1.10, £2.10, £2.70; EX 6.40.
Owner The Ipso Facto Syndicate **Bred** Mrs M Beddis **Trained** Musley Bank, N Yorks
■ Stewards' Enquiry : Adele Rothery 10-day ban: dropped hands and lost 2nd place (May 7, 9-13, 15-18); further one-day ban: careless riding (May 8)

FOCUS
A modest handicap in which the winner was value for much more than the winning distance after travelling powerfully throughout. The placed form is not that solid, however.

1234 WHITE MUZZLE H'CAP 5f
4:55 (4:55) (Class 6) (0-60,60) 3-Y-O **£3,412** (£1,007; £504) **Stalls** Low

Form RPR
0-22 **1** **Toy Top (USA)**[4] [1137] 3-9-4 60 (b) PhillipMakin 11 68
(M Dods) *chsd ldrs on outer: led 1/2-way: clr fr wl over 1f out* **11/8[1]**

0-50 **2** 3 **Soviet Legend (IRE)**[42] [646] 3-8-7 52 (v[1]) SaleemGolam(3) 10 49
(T J Etherington) *in tch: hdwy 2f out: sn ridde: styd on ins last: no ch w wnr* **11/1**

0-00 **3** 1/2 **Stanley Wolfe (IRE)**[14] [980] 3-8-4 46 oh1 RoystonFfrench 8 41
(James Moffatt) *s.i.s: gd hdwy 1/2-way: rdn to chse wnr ent last: kpt on same pce* **20/1**

50-6 **4** 1/2 **Bahamian Duke**[19] [910] 3-8-10 52 PatCosgrave 1 45
(K R Burke) *prom on inner: rdn along 2f out: sn drvn and kpt on same pce* **7/1[3]**

4004 **5** 3/4 **Suhezy (IRE)**[14] [980] 3-8-11 53 PaulHanagan 7 51+
(P T Midgley) *in tch: hdwy and nt clr run 2f out: swtchd lft and rdn over 1f out: kpt on ins last* **13/2[2]**

000- **6** 3 **First Among Equals**[135] [6562] 3-9-2 58 (p) PaulFitzsimons 5 38
(Miss J R Tooth) *led to 1/2-way: sn rdn and one pce fr wl over 1f out* **20/1**

500- **7** *hd* **Maayafushi**[193] [5889] 3-8-10 52 DeanMcKeown 2 31
(Micky Hammond) *sn outpcd and bhd tl sme late hdwy* **20/1**

25- **8** 1 3/4 **Queens Bounty**[232] [5016] 3-8-8 50 TomEaves 9 23
(B Ellison) *chsd ldrs: rdn 2f out: sn drvna nd wknd* **10/1**

060- **9** 1 **Pensata**[223] [5237] 3-8-4 46 oh1 PaulFessey 6 15
(Miss L A Perratt) *cl up: rdn along 1/2-way: sn wknd* **25/1**

0050 **10** *nk* **Tombalina**[4] [1137] 3-8-3 52 MarkCoumbe(7) 3 20
(C J Teague) *prom: rdn along halfway: sn wknd* **10/1**

60.31 secs (-0.29) **Going Correction** -0.20s/f (Firm) **10** Ran SP% **112.6**
Speed ratings (Par 96):94,89,88,87,86 81,81,78,76,76
CSF £15.28 CT £197.77 TOTE £1.70: £1.10, £4.70, £7.30; EX 20.60.
Owner D Vic Roper **Bred** L Kengye **Trained** Denton, Co Durham

FOCUS
A moderate sprint handicap won in decisive fashion, but there was little to get excited about in behind. The runner-up sets the standard but the form is limited.

1235 IVAN LUIS APPRENTICE H'CAP 5f 212y
5:25 (5:25) (Class 6) (0-65,65) 4-Y-O+ **£2,730** (£806; £403) **Stalls** Low

Form RPR
00-0 **1** **Circuit Dancer (IRE)**[23] [860] 6-9-4 65 SilvestreDeSousa 5 76
(D Nicholls) *trckd ldrs: hdwy 2f out: rdn to ld appr last: styd on* **9/1**

2330 **2** 1/2 **Taboor (IRE)**[14] [986] 8-8-8 55 SaleemGolam 12 64
(R M H Cowell) *bhd: gd hdwy on outer 2f out: rdn and styd on strly ins last* **7/1[3]**

0100 **3** 1 1/2 **Million Percent**[32] [732] 7-8-8 60 AndrewElliott(5) 1 65
(K R Burke) *trckd ldrs: hdwy 2f out: rdn and ch over 1f out: drvn and one pce ins last* **6/1[2]**

6-00 **4** 1 1/2 **Green Pirate**[69] [428] 4-8-6 53 PaulMulrennan 3 53
(R Craggs) *cl up: rdn along 2f out: drvn and one pce ent last* **20/1**

0521 **5** 1 1/4 **Piccolo Prince**[22] [864] 5-8-12 59 DanielTudhope 11 55
(E J Alston) *hld up: hdwy on outer whn hung lft 2f out: sn rdn and btn* **9/2[1]**

-064 **6** *nk* **Muara**[26] [813] 4-8-2 52 AndrewMullen(3) 9 47
(D W Barker) *led: rdn along 2f out: drvn and hdd appr last: sn wknd* **7/1[3]**

03-4 **7** 1 1/4 **Crystal Mystic (IRE)**[16] [950] 4-8-10 57 BenSwarbrick 4 49
(B Palling) *chsd ldrs: rdn 2f out: wkng whn n.m.r over 1f out* **7/1[3]**

2-03 **8** 1 3/4 **Blue Maeve**[72] [407] 6-8-2 52 DuranFentiman(3) 7 38
(A D Brown) *in tch: rdn along over 2f out and sn btn* **6/1[2]**

330- **9** 1 **Montana**[148] [6462] 6-8-1 53 LeanneKershaw(5) 2 36
(C W Fairhurst) *a towards rr* **11/1**

-040 **10** *hd* **Rapid Flow**[53] [587] 4-8-7 57 StephenDonohoe(3) 10 40
(P D Evans) *a towards rr* **28/1**

1m 11.97s (-2.03) **Going Correction** -0.20s/f (Firm) **10** Ran SP% **110.8**
Speed ratings (Par 101):105,104,102,100,98 98,96,94,92,92
CSF £66.48 CT £402.22 TOTE £9.80: £3.40, £2.50, £1.90; EX 88.70 Place 6 £10.08, Place 5 £6.33.
Owner David Fish **Bred** Michael Staunton **Trained** Sessay, N Yorks

FOCUS
A modest sprint handicap but sound enough, rated through the runner-up. The winner is very well handicapped on his old form and just the type his trainer does well with.
T/Plt: £8.40 to a £1 stake. Pool: £30,183.80. 2,618.10 winning tickets. T/Qpdt: £6.40 to a £1 stake. Pool: £1,668.80. 191.85 winning tickets. JR

EPSOM (L-H)

Wednesday, April 26

OFFICIAL GOING: Sprint course - good to firm (good in places); remainder - good (good to firm in places)

Wind: Light; half against Weather: Fine

1236 WORLD CUP CASHBACK @ BLUE SQUARE STKS (H'CAP) 5f

1:50 (1:51) (Class 3) (0-95,94) 4-Y-0+

£9,348 (£2,799; £1,399; £700; £349; £175) **Stalls** High

Form				RPR
010-	**1**		**Zowington**[178] 6182 4-9-1 **88** GeorgeBaker 2 (C F Wall) *b.bkwd: trckd ldrs: effrt to ld over 1f out: rdn out and in command last 150yds* **11/1**	98
-050	**2**	¾	**Cape Royal**[5] 1116 6-9-7 **94** (t) RyanMoore 8 (J M Bradley) *s.s: wl off the pce in last trio: prog 1/2-way: chsd wnr ins fnl f: styd on but no imp* **4/1**[1]	101
000-	**3**	*hd*	**High Reach**[261] 4222 6-9-4 **91** MartinDwyer 6 (W R Muir) *lw: outpcd towards rr: rdn bef 1/2-way: styd on fnl f: gaining at fin* **8/1**	97
/30-	**4**	½	**Rare Cross (IRE)**[312] 2703 4-9-0 **87** SebSanders 4 (Miss B Sanders) *b.bkwd: led: rdn and hdd over 1f out: kpt on same pce* **20/1**	91
040-	**5**	*shd*	**Jayanjay**[142] 6504 7-9-1 **91** RichardThomas(3) 5 (Miss B Sanders) *swtg: sn outpcd in last trio: prog and swtchd lft wl over 1f out: tried to cl ent fnl f: one pce last 100yds* **10/1**	95
-305	**6**	*nk*	**Plateau**[28] 798 7-8-7 **80** MichaelHills 3 (D Nicholls) *pressed ldrs: lost pl and n.m.r wl over 1f out: kpt on again nr fin* **5/1**[2]	83
0-31	**7**	*nk*	**Desert Lord**[10] 1031 6-8-11 **91** 6ex (p) HelenGarner(7) 1 (K A Ryan) *b: s.i.s: racd on outer and nvr on terms: shuffled along and no prog 2f out* **13/2**	93
300-	**8**	5	**Polish Emperor (USA)**[130] 6602 6-8-12 **85** (p) TedDurcan 9 (W R Swinburn) *sn outpcd: a struggling* **7/1**	69
00-3	**9**	1	**Wanchai Lad**[10] 1031 5-8-11 **84** KDarley 7 (D Nicholls) *lw: pressed ldr to 2f out: hanging lft and wknd* **11/2**[3]	64

55.92 secs (0.24) **Going Correction** +0.225s/f (Good) 9 Ran SP% **111.2**

Speed ratings (Par 107):107,105,105,104,104 104,103,95,93

CSF £51.77 CT £365.31 TOTE £14.40: £3.10, £1.90, £2.90; EX 68.20.

Owner O Pointing **Bred** O Pointing **Trained** Newmarket, Suffolk

FOCUS

Despite the official going description, the runners in this opening contest seemed to be making a good print on the stands' side part of the track at least. A decent handicap and the form looks straightforward, rated through the runner-up, fourth and fifth.

NOTEBOOK

Zowington made light of his six-month break with a clear-cut victory, despite fears that this quick five furlongs would be too sharp. He is still relatively unexposed and there is probably more to come. (op 12-1)

Cape Royal, who has a decent record here, was drawn one off the stands' rail yet had to come around the field and make his effort wide, and was never quite able to get there. He does not win as often as he should and is still 7lb above his last winning mark. (op 7-2 tchd 9-2)

High Reach, making his debut for the yard, was returning from an eight-month break, but has gone well fresh before and offered encouragement with a staying-on third. (op 9-1)

Rare Cross(IRE) made much of the running and kept in quite well. She was making her debut for her third different trainer in only her eighth start, and this was a positive performance following a ten-month break. (op 25-1)

Jayanjay, a four-time winner here, stayed on out in the middle of the track without managing to land a blow.

Plateau was briefly short of room but it probably made little difference to his finishing position.

Desert Lord always seemed to be struggling from the outside stall. (op 6-1)

Wanchai Lad dropped away rather tamely after racing up with the pace for much of the way.

1237 WEATHERBYS BANK BLUE RIBAND TRIAL STKS (CONDITIONS RACE) 1m 2f 18y

2:20 (2:23) (Class 2) 3-Y-O **£12,464** (£3,732; £1,866) **Stalls** Low

Form				RPR
1-21	**1**		**Before You Go (IRE)**[105] 87 3-9-1 88 IanMongan 2 (T G Mills) *lw: dwlt: hld up in last: rdn wl over 2f out: clsd grad to ld ent fnl f: styd on* **8/13**[1]	103+
550-	**2**	1¼	**Hanoona (IRE)**[241] 4786 3-8-10 103 TedDurcan 3 (M R Channon) *led at slow pce for over 1f: trckd ldr: rdn to ld narrowly wl over 1f out: hdd ent fnl f: one pce* **5/2**[2]	90
010-	**3**	1¼	**Sienna Storm (IRE)**[191] 5942 3-9-1 80 DarrylHolland 1 (M H Tompkins) *lw: led over 8f out and set stdy pce: rdn over 2f out: narrowly hdd wl over 1f out: one pce fnl f* **5/1**[3]	93

2m 14.02s (4.98) **Going Correction** +0.40s/f (Good) 3 Ran SP% **107.2**

Speed ratings (Par 104):96,95,94

CSF £2.40 TOTE £1.50; EX 1.90.

Owner Mrs Tina Smith **Bred** The Niarchos Family **Trained** Headley, Surrey

FOCUS

Not a race that has thrown up many clues to the Derby itself in recent years and once again a small field went to post, reduced further by the absence of London Express. The pace was inevitably slow and the winning time was almost two seconds slower than the City And Suburban, and the runnerup looks the best guide to the level.

NOTEBOOK

Before You Go(IRE) was happy to sit last of the trio in this moderately run race and produced the best turn of foot to record his third win from just five starts, but his first on turf. He may go for the Lingfield Derby Trial en-route to the Derby itself, but wherever he goes his trainer is hoping for cut in the ground. (op 5-6 tchd 10-11)

Hanoona(IRE), from the stable that took this last year, had 20lb in hand of the winner on adjusted official ratings, but found nothing like the same turn of foot on this step up in trip. Perhaps she needed this after eight months off, but her Oaks entry does now look very optimistic. (op 7-4 tchd 11-4)

Sienna Storm(IRE) was given a soft lead and tried to quicken from the front, but found his two rivals much too strong. To be fair he had no chance at the weights in any case. (op 11-2 tchd 6-1)

1238 BET @ BLUE SQUARE GREAT METROPOLITAN STKS (H'CAP) 1m 4f 10y

2:55 (2:56) (Class 3) (0-95,93) 4-Y-0+

£11,217 (£3,358; £1,679; £840; £419; £210) **Stalls** Centre

Form				RPR
155/	**1**		**Vengeance**[38] 4163 6-9-3 90 PatDobbs 1 (S Dow) *trckd ldng pair: wnt 2nd 3f out: rdn to ld over 1f out: pushed out and in command fnl f* **11/2**	100
16-6	**2**	1	**Red Racketeer (USA)**[11] 1017 4-9-5 93 LDettori 7 (E A L Dunlop) *lw: sn led: shkn up and pressed over 2f out whn clr w wnr: hdd over 1f out: readily hld ins fnl f* **6/4**[1]	101
44-0	**3**	5	**Sporting Gesture**[14] 976 9-8-10 83 JimmyQuinn 5 (M W Easterby) *hld up: 5th st: outpcd wl over 2f out: plugged on to take modest 3rd fnl f* **20/1**	83
/10-	**4**	1½	**Tender Falcon**[326] 2296 6-9-0 87 MartinDwyer 4 (R J Hodges) *trckd ldrs: 4th st: outpcd wl over 2f out: n.d after* **5/1**[3]	85
000-	**5**	½	**Quizzene (USA)**[243] 4722 4-8-12 86 KDarley 6 (M Johnston) *b.bkwd: trckd ldr to 3f out: sn u.p and btn: hanging lft 2f out* **4/1**[2]	83
635/	**6**	*hd*	**Kalambari (IRE)**[179] 5276 7-8-9 82 MickyFenton 2 (S Dow) *dwlt: in tch: 6th and pushed along st: sn struggling* **40/1**	78?
600-	**7**	1	**Nordwind (IRE)**[255] 4394 5-9-1 88 TedDurcan 3 (W R Swinburn) *hld up in last: plenty to do ent st: pushed along and no handling trck: no prog* **9/1**	83

2m 42.52s (3.79) **Going Correction** +0.40s/f (Good)

WFA 4 from 5yo+ 1lb 7 Ran SP% **109.3**

Speed ratings (Par 107):103,102,99,98,97 97,96

CSF £12.91 TOTE £7.10: £2.70, £1.40; EX 14.60.

Owner T Staplehurst **Bred** T Staplehurst **Trained** Epsom, Surrey

FOCUS

Another race run at an ordinary pace. The winner sets the standard but the form looks somewhat shaky.

NOTEBOOK

Vengeance, warm prior to the race, battled on well to come out best in what eventually became a match between himself and the favourite over the last couple of furlongs. A winner over hurdles at Fontwell last month, he is a true dual-purpose performer but the plan is to keep him on the Flat for the time being and contest more handicaps like this. (op 7-1)

Red Racketeer(USA) was allowed to set his own pace and tried to steal this from the front but, although he did little wrong and pulled clear of the others, the winner had the legs of him where it mattered. He still stepped up on his reappearance effort in the Rosebery and has proved that he does stay this trip. (op 11-10 tchd 13-8 in a place)

Sporting Gesture may be getting on a bit, but even though he was well adrift of the front pair he still posted a decent effort off a 3lb higher mark than for his last win. (op 18-1)

Tender Falcon was off a 5lb higher mark than when taking this last year, but could never land a blow. He was returning from a break when winning this last year, but was coming back from a ten-month layoff this time around and perhaps this was needed. (op 11-2)

Quizzene(USA) raced handily for much of the way, but faded rather tamely in the home straight and has not started this season off as well as he did last. (op 9-2)

Kalambari(IRE), who at least managed to start this time, was reportedly unsuited by the track. Official explanation: jockey said gelding had been unsuited by the track (op 25-1)

Nordwind(IRE) never managed to get himself into contention and hung badly on the camber. Official explanation: jockey said gelding hung left down the camber (op 12-1)

1239 BET @ BLUE SQUARE CITY AND SUBURBAN STKS (H'CAP) 1m 2f 18y

3:30 (3:31) (Class 2) (0-105,102) 4-Y-0+

£18,696 (£5,598; £2,799; £1,401; £699; £351) **Stalls** Low

Form				RPR
110-	**1**		**All That And More (IRE)**[207] 5608 4-8-7 88 MichaelHills 1 (B W Hills) *mde all: pushed clr over 1f out: r.o wl: readily* **9/2**[1]	100+
-350	**2**	2½	**Impeller (IRE)**[39] 666 7-8-12 93 MartinDwyer 9 (W R Muir) *hld up: 6th st: prog on outer over 2f out: chsd wnr over 1f out: styd on but no imp* **11/2**[2]	100
0-20	**3**	1¾	**Divine Gift**[11] 1017 5-8-12 93 NCallan 2 (K A Ryan) *mostly chsd wnr to over 1f out: one pce u.p* **7/1**	97
0-01	**4**	*hd*	**Profit's Reality (IRE)**[6] 1098 4-9-1 96 5ex (t) RobbieFitzpatrick 7 (P A Blockley) *lw: trckd ldrs: 5th st: rdn and nt qckn over 2f out: n.d after: kpt on again ins fnl f* **9/2**[1]	99
0-30	**5**	¾	**Counsel's Opinion (IRE)**[39] 666 9-9-7 102 GeorgeBaker 5 (C F Wall) *lw: dwlt: hld up: 8th st: effrt on outer over 2f out: one pce and no real prog* **9/2**[1]	104
/3P-	**6**	*hd*	**Diego Cao (IRE)**[164] 6018 5-8-7 88 RyanMoore 6 (Mrs N Smith) *settled towards rr: 7th st: effrt on inner over 2f out: one pce and no imp* **16/1**	89
210-	**7**	1¼	**Ofaraby**[186] 6025 6-9-4 99 PhilipRobinson 4 (M A Jarvis) *v s.i.s: hld up in last: outpcd 3f out: pushed along over 2f out: nvr a factor* **6/1**[3]	98
-006	**8**	2½	**Shahzan House (IRE)**[51] 591 7-8-9 93 ow3 (p) AmirQuinn(3) 8 (P G Murphy) *prom: disp 2nd 4f out to 3f out: sn rdn and fnd nil: wknd 2f out* **20/1**	87?
0-05	**9**	½	**Lord Mayor**[6] 1098 5-9-7 102 DarrylHolland 3 (R M H Cowell) *s.i.s: sn trckd ldrs: awkward downhill 5f out: 5th st: wknd 2f out* **16/1**	95

2m 12.27s (3.23) **Going Correction** +0.40s/f (Good) 9 Ran SP% **113.2**

Speed ratings (Par 109):103,101,99,99,98 98,97,95,95

CSF £28.50 CT £168.82 TOTE £4.40: £1.90, £2.00, £2.20; EX 30.90 Trifecta £147.10 Pool: £1,243.10 - 6 winning units.

Owner Gainsborough Stud **Bred** Gainsborough Stud Management Ltd **Trained** Lambourn, Berks

FOCUS

Once again they seemed to go no more than an ordinary pace in this, but even so the winning time was still nearly two seconds quicker than the moderately-run Blue Riband Trial, though that is still modest for the class. The form looks sound, rated through those in the frame behind the progressive winner.

NOTEBOOK

All That And More(IRE) ◆, who looked very fit for his first run of the season, had not been intended to lead, but once under way his rider decided to be positive and he basically ground his rivals into submission. After winning his first three starts last term, he then disappointed on soft ground but enjoyed this faster surface and connections believe he will get a bit further. (op 5-1 tchd 6-1)

Impeller(IRE), fit from a few spins on Polytrack, ran on to finish a clear second and obviously likes this track with his only two wins in recent seasons coming here, but perhaps he does not win as often as he should these days.

Divine Gift kept on for third having been close to the pace the whole way and his new yard should find an opportunity for him.

Profit's Reality(IRE) ran a fair race under his penalty, but it does seem as though his Ripon conditions race victory the previous week flattered him. He is due to go up another 6lb so things are not going to get any easier. (op 4-1)

Counsel's Opinion(IRE) needs a strongly-run race to show his best, but did not get that here and there will be other days.

Diego Cao(IRE) looked fit for his first run after a long absence. (op 14-1 tchd 20-1)

Ofaraby was a bit disappointing, but he needed his first couple of outings last term and might have needed this after six months off. Official explanation: jockey said gelding missed the break (op 7-1)

1240 TROY O'CONNOR MEMORIAL MAIDEN STKS 1m 114y
4:05 (4:09) (Class 5) 3-Y-0+ £5,181 (£1,541; £770; £384) Stalls Low

Form RPR
0- 1 Gandor (IRE)[197] 5823 3-8-11 JimmyFortune 3 89+
(J H M Gosden) mde virtually all: shkn up and forged clr fr 2f out: r.o wl 3/1[2]
0- 2 5 Zaafran[179] 6143 3-8-6 PhilipRobinson 6 74
(M A Jarvis) trckd ldrs: keen and awkward downhill: 3rd st: effrt over 2f out: kpt on to take 2nd ins fnl f: no ch w wnr 11/4[1]
020- 3 2 First Approval[211] 5531 3-8-6 77 MichaelHills 4 69
(B W Hills) b.bkwd: w wnr to 2f out: sn rdn and outpcd: fdd and lost 2nd ins fnl f 5/1
2-30 4 3 Feu D'Artifice (USA)[22] 880 3-8-11 75 RichardHughes 10 68
(R Hannon) wl in tch: 6th st: rdn over 2f out: sn outpcd: plugged on 7/2[3]
00-0 5 3 ½ Foreign Envoy (IRE)[9] 1049 3-8-11 SamHitchcott 7 61
(B W Hills) lw: wl in tch: 7th st: rdn on inner over 2f out: sn struggling 22/1
50- 6 nk Ennobling[142] 6502 3-8-6 RichardMullen 1 55
(E F Vaughan) trckd ldrs: 5th st: rdn and btn over 2f out: wknd fnl f 25/1
7 6 Grave Matters (USA) 3-8-11 KDarley 9 47
(M Johnston) b.bkwd: unf: sn last: lost tch 5f out: t.o st: r.o fnl f 12/1
0 8 1 ¼ Debord (FR)[14] 981 3-8-11 JohnEgan 2 54+
(Jamie Poulton) lw: dwlt: wl in rr: 8th and lost tch st: brief effrt over 2f out: eased over 1f out 20/1
00/0 9 14 Melmott[70] 419 6-9-12 30 RobertHavlin 8 15
(R Ingram) prom: cl 4th and rdn st: sn wknd rapidly: t.o 100/1
10 1 Berylune (GER)[271] 4-9-7 DaneO'Neill 5 8
(S Dow) s.s: a in last pair: lost tch over 4f out: 9th st: t.o 50/1

1m 46.59s (0.85) **Going Correction** +0.40s/f (Good)
WFA 3 from 4yo+ 15lb 10 Ran SP% 114.2
Speed ratings (Par 103):112,107,105,103,100 99,94,93,80,79
CSF £10.68 TOTE £3.70: £1.40, £1.30, £1.80; EX 11.20.
Owner H R H Princess Haya Of Jordan **Bred** Barouche Stud Ireland Ltd **Trained** Newmarket, Suffolk

FOCUS
A modest maiden in which few could be fancied, though the winner could hardly have been more impressive. Once again the place to be was near the front and not many got into it. The winning time was very smart for a race like this, 0.75 seconds quicker than the following handicap, and the form looks above average.

Foreign Envoy(IRE) Official explanation: jockey said gelding was unsuited by the track
Debord(FR) Official explanation: jockey said colt was unsuited by the track

1241 MICHAEL CHURCH STKS (H'CAP) 1m 114y
4:35 (4:40) (Class 5) (0-75,75) 3-Y-0 £5,181 (£1,541; £770; £384) Stalls Low

Form RPR
5-02 1 Airbuss (IRE)[22] 880 3-9-1 72 TedDurcan 3 79
(M R Channon) rousted along in rr early: 9th st: gd prog on outer over 2f out: led jst over 1f out: styd on wl 9/2[2]
60-2 2 1 ¾ Burnbank (IRE)[14] 981 3-9-1 72 MartinDwyer 4 75
(W Jarvis) lw: in tch: 8th st: drvn over 2f out: prog wl over 1f out: styd on to take 2nd nr fin 7/1
65-2 3 nk Follow The Colours (IRE)[15] 963 3-8-11 68 LDettori 12 71
(J W Hills) prom: 3rd st: sn pressed ldr: drvn to ld wl over 1f out: edgd lft and hdd jst over 1f out: one pce 4/1[1]
20-0 4 3 ½ Miss Wedge[29] 781 3-8-11 68 IanMongan 10 63
(T G Mills) chsd ldrs: 5th st: drvn wl over 2f out: kpt on same pce: nvr able to chal 20/1
206- 5 ¾ Fratt'n Park (IRE)[180] 6129 3-8-11 68 J-PGuillambert 1 62+
(J J Bridger) t.k.h: prom: stl keen and cl 4th st: rdn whn nt clr run and swtchd lft 2f out: no prog and btn after 33/1
0-20 6 1 Emotive[18] 918 3-7-13 61 oh6 (b) JamesDoyle(5) 2 53
(I A Wood) wl in rr: 10th and rdn st: styd on fr 2f out: swtchd sharply rt wl ins fnl f: nrst fin 9/1
2040 7 hd Lenoir (GER)[14] 993 3-8-10 67 (v) ChrisCatlin 9 58
(V Smith) wl in rr: 11th and struggling st: kpt on u.p fr 2f out: rdr dropped whip 1f out: bmpd twice nr fin: nvr nrr 16/1
100- 8 shd Catspraddle (USA)[186] 6024 3-9-1 72 RichardHughes 5 63
(R Hannon) racd freely: led: drvn and hdd wl over 1f out: wknd 12/1
05-5 9 3 Elusive Warrior (USA)[14] 981 3-9-1 72 JimCrowley 8 57
(Mrs A J Perrett) chsd ldng gp: 7th st: rdn and effrt over 2f out: sn no prog: fdd fnl f 16/1
650- 10 3 ½ Benbrook[172] 6249 3-8-5 62 PhilipRobinson 11 39
(J L Dunlop) detached in last pair after 3f: t.o in 12th st: kpt on fnl 2f: no ch 10/1
550 11 4 Laheen (IRE)[14] 981 3-8-4 61 oh1 NickyMackay 13 30
(M H Tompkins) swtchd fr outside draw and sn last: detached 5f out: t.o st: plugged on 20/1
106- 12 3 Lyrical Sound (IRE)[209] 5570 3-9-4 75 MichaelHills 7 38
(B W Hills) pressed ldr tl wknd rapidly 3f out 5/1[3]
00-0 13 5 Mamichor[15] 969 3-8-8 65 NCallan 6 17
(J R Boyle) chsd ldrs: 6th and rdn st: wknd rapidly over 2f out 25/1

1m 47.34s (1.60) **Going Correction** +0.40s/f (Good) 13 Ran SP% 122.2
Speed ratings (Par 98):108,106,106,103,102 101,101,101,98,95 91,89,84
CSF £35.02 CT £144.47 TOTE £4.40: £2.10, £2.40, £2.10; EX 27.10 Place 6 £22.59, Place 5 £7.86.
Owner Sheikh Ahmed Al Maktoum **Bred** Roger Charlton And Floors Farming **Trained** West Ilsley, Berks

FOCUS
Probably the most competitive race on the card and a decent winning time for the grade despite being 0.75 seconds slower than the preceding maiden. The winner should rate higher.

Emotive Official explanation: jockey said colt was unsuited by the track
Benbrook Official explanation: jockey said colt was unsuited by the track
Mamichor Official explanation: jockey said gelding had been hanging left

T/Jkpt: Not won. T/Plt: £26.20 to a £1 stake. Pool: £53,503.45. 1,487.75 winning tickets. T/Qpdt: £5.20 to a £1 stake. Pool: £3,782.80. 534.00 winning tickets. JN

[1161]KEMPTON (A.W) (R-H)
Wednesday, April 26

OFFICIAL GOING: Standard
Wind: Nil

1242 KEMPTON PARK E B F MAIDEN FILLIES' STKS 5f (P)
7:00 (7:01) (Class 5) 2-Y-0 £3,886 (£1,156; £577; £288) Stalls High

Form RPR
4 1 Fairfield Princess[7] 1082 2-9-0 DaneO'Neill 3 78
(N A Callaghan) mde virtually all: qcknd clr appr fnl f: pushed out 4/6[1]
2 1 ¼ Crystal Gazer (FR) 2-9-0 RichardHughes 4 73+
(R Hannon) rrd s: sn rcvrd to trck ldrs: wnt 2nd wl over 1f out: sn rdn: kpt on 2/1[2]
3 2 ½ Three Decades (IRE) 2-9-0 LDettori 1 63
(C A Cyzer) chsd ldrs: rdn over 2f out: kpt on same pce 10/1[3]
4 4 Autumn Storm 2-9-0 RobertHavlin 5 47
(R Ingram) w wnr: rdn over 2f out: wknd over 1f out 33/1
5 hd Little Hotpotch 2-8-11 DeanCorby(3) 2 46
(J R Jenkins) sn outpcd: rdn 3f out: no imp fnl 2f 50/1

61.76 secs (0.76) **Going Correction** -0.025s/f (Stan) 5 Ran SP% 107.3
Speed ratings (Par 89):88,86,82,75,75
CSF £2.05 TOTE £1.40: £1.02, £3.60; EX 2.50.
Owner J S May **Bred** Lady Fairhaven **Trained** Newmarket, Suffolk

FOCUS
A decent juvenile event rated through the winner, in which the front three look worth following.

NOTEBOOK
Fairfield Princess, who shaped most pleasingly on her debut at Newmarket last week, was soon in the lead, making plenty of use of her experience, and she found what was required to run out a ready winner from the Hannon debutant in second. Connections believe five furlongs is her trip for the time being, but admitted that she would probably prefer getting a toe of something in future. With further improvement expected, it is not hard to see her picking up another race before going in search of some black type later in the season. (tchd 8-11)
Crystal Gazer(FR) ◆, a big, scopey filly, looked green in the paddock beforehand and did herself no favours in rearing at the start. She was soon on the heels of the leaders though and held every chance in the straight, but her lack of previous experience told and she was unable to get near the winner. This was a highly pleasing debut and it is likely she can progress into a useful filly, with further expected to suit in time. Official explanation: jockey said filly missed the break (op 15-8)
Three Decades(IRE) ◆, a speedily-bred juvenile from a yard hardly renowned for their success for two-year-olds, was never far off the pace and kept on nicely in third without being given a hard time. She looks a fine, big horse and it will be disappointing if she does not step up on this. (tchd 12-1)
Autumn Storm appeared to know her job, but she lacked the quality of the front three and was left trailing in the straight. She is likely to prove more of a nursery prospect.
Little Hotpotch was always struggling to go the gallop, but her stable's runners usually come on for a run and better can be expected once she tackles a greater distance. (op 66-1 tchd 80-1 in a palce)

1243 WEDNESDAY NIGHT IS RACE NIGHT H'CAP 5f (P)
7:28 (7:29) (Class 6) (0-65,65) 4-Y-0+ £3,238 (£963; £481; £240) Stalls High

Form RPR
6454 1 Cashel Mead[23] 858 6-8-7 54 SteveDrowne 11 60+
(J L Spearing) chsd ldrs: nt clr run over 1f out tl ins fnl f: r.o wl to ld nr fin 4/1[2]
5046 2 ½ Doctor's Cave[9] 1050 4-8-9 56 (b) SebSanders 6 60
(K O Cunningham-Brown) chsd ldrs: rdn and ev ch over 1f out: kpt on 13/2[3]
1006 3 shd Lady Bahia (IRE)[14] 986 5-8-13 60 (b) RobbieFitzpatrick 8 64
(Peter Grayson) s.i.s: towards rr: r.o wl fnl f f to take 3rd fnl strides: nrst fin 10/1
100- 4 shd Campeon (IRE)[145] 6480 4-9-3 64 JamieSpencer 1 68
(J M Bradley) led: rdn over 1f out: no ex whn hdd nr fin 12/1
-606 5 nk Detonate[23] 858 4-7-13 51 oh1 JamesDoyle(5) 12 54
(Mrs C A Dunnett) chsd ldrs: rdn and hung rt fr 2f out: nt clr run briefly 1f out: kpt on 13/2[3]
4000 6 nk Clipper Hoy[3] 1161 4-8-13 65 RichardKingscote(5) 3 66
(Mrs H Sweeting) in tch: rdn and effrt 2f out: sn hung rt: kpt on fnl f 10/1
00-0 7 1 ¾ Ruby's Dream[16] 954 4-8-7 54 (p) NCallan 7 49
(J M Bradley) a mid div 33/1
1520 8 1 ½ Percy Douglas[6] 1102 6-8-4 58 ow4 (bt) AnnStokell(7) 5 48
(Miss A Stokell) s.i.s: towards rr: swtchd to outer over 3f out: nvr trbld ldrs 11/1
6262 9 nk Times Review (USA)[14] 986 5-9-4 65 (b) JohnEgan 10 54
(C A Dwyer) mid div: rdn over 2f out: one pce after 7/2[1]
4600 10 1 ¼ Madrasee[4] 1150 8-8-5 52 ow1 RobertHavlin 2 36
(P G Murphy) carried wd on bnd over 3f out: a towards rr 20/1
050- 11 2 ½ Italian Mist (FR)[372] 1104 7-8-9 56 AlanMunro 4 31
(R M H Cowell) bmpd on bnd over 3f out: a towards rr 20/1

60.57 secs (-0.43) **Going Correction** -0.025s/f (Stan) 11 Ran SP% 115.6
Speed ratings (Par 101):97,96,96,95,95 94,92,89,89,87 83
CSF £28.77 CT £242.50 TOTE £4.10: £1.90, £4.20, £2.80; EX 43.70.
Owner Masonaires **Bred** D R Tucker **Trained** Kinnersley, Worcs

FOCUS
A tight handicap and runners finished well-bunched at the line. The third, fourth and fifth suggest the form is modest.

Detonate Official explanation: jockey said gelding was denied a clear run final furlong
Percy Douglas Official explanation: jockey said horse missed break and failed to handle bend
Italian Mist(FR) Official explanation: jockey said gelding was carried wide on final bend

1244 SPONSOR AT KEMPTON H'CAP 1m 2f (P)
7:56 (7:57) (Class 6) (0-65,65) 4-Y-0+ £3,238 (£963; £481; £240) Stalls High

Form RPR
3002 1 Port 'n Starboard[26] 820 5-9-2 63 MartinDwyer 5 70
(C A Cyzer) chsd ldr: led jst ins 2f out: sn rdn: all out 9/2[1]
0500 2 hd Flying Pass[15] 965 4-8-11 58 (t) LDettori 3 65
(D J S Ffrench Davis) hld up bhd: hdwy 2f out: styd on strly ins fnl f: jst failed 5/1[2]
10-0 3 nk Gambling Spirit[15] 965 4-9-2 63 DaneO'Neill 12 69
(H Candy) chsd ldrs: rdn 2f out: kpt on wl cl home 5/1[2]
30-2 4 nk Dove Cottage (IRE)[22] 882 4-8-13 60 ChrisCatlin 8 65
(W S Kittow) led tl jst ins 2f out: sn rdn: kpt on but drifted lft ins fnl f 15/2[3]
40-0 5 shd Play Up Pompey[15] 972 4-8-6 56 ow4 NeilChalmers(3) 10 61
(J J Bridger) chsd ldrs: lost pl 3f out: sn rdn: styd on again ins fnl f 33/1

-616 **6** ½ **Treetops Hotel (IRE)**[53] [586] 7-8-7 **54**..................... FrankieMcDonald 6 58
(B R Johnson) *hld up bhd: styd on fr 2f out: nrst fin* **16/1**
-000 **7** *nk* **Jazrawy**[9] [1058] 4-8-4 **56**.................................. JamesDoyle(5) 11 60
(Miss Gay Kelleway) *mid div: hdwy 2f out: sn rdn: kpt on same pce fnl f* **20/1**
3603 **8** ¾ **Busy Man (IRE)**[21] [888] 7-8-6 **53**.. NCallan 13 55+
(J R Jenkins) *hld up towards rr: swtchd lft 2f out: styng on whn nt clr run 1f out: no further imp* **9/1**
0-06 **9** *nk* **Whitgift Rock**[18] [915] 5-9-4 **65**....................................... DarryllHolland 4 67
(S Dow) *chsd ldrs: rdn over 2f out: one pce fnl f* **10/1**
-000 **10** *hd* **Graft**[34] [706] 7-8-5 **52**...(p) SamHitchcott 7 53
(Mrs P Townsley) *mid div: hdwy 4f out: rdn over 2f out: one pce fr 1f out* **25/1**
530- **11** ½ **Aimee Vibert**[217] [5410] 4-9-4 **65**... TedDurcan 1 68+
(W R Swinburn) *hld up towards rr: hdwy on rails over 2f out: nt clr run over 1f out: no ch after* **8/1**
6500 **12** ½ **Sorbiesharry (IRE)**[16] [955] 7-8-0 **52**............................. MarcHalford(5) 9 51
(Mrs N Macauley) *mid div: brief effrt 3f out* **16/1**
000- **13** *8* **Fortiszamo**[170] [6287] 4-8-7 **54** ow1.................................. MickyFenton 14 38
(A W Carroll) *mid div tl 3f out* **100/1**
2m 9.08s (-1.92) **Going Correction** -0.025s/f (Stan) **13** Ran SP% **117.8**
Speed ratings (Par 101):98,97,97,97,97 96,96,96,95,95 95,94,88
CSF £25.00 CT £117.85 TOTE £4.70: £1.50, £7.00, £3.00; EX 33.00.
Owner Mrs Charles Cyzer **Bred** C A Cyzer **Trained** Maplehurst, W Sussex
■ Stewards' Enquiry : Martin Dwyer caution: used whip with whip arm above shoulder height

FOCUS
With the first 12 home covered by around four lengths, it is safe to assume the form needs treating with caution, that said the first three were all fancied runners.
Busy Man(IRE) Official explanation: jockey said gelding was denied a clear run

1245 RACING UK H'CAP 1m (P)
8:24 (8:25) (Class 6) (0-65,63) 4-Y-0+ **£3,238** (£963; £481; £240) **Stalls** High

Form RPR
2012 **1** **Indian Edge**[30] [771] 5-8-7 **52**...................................... FergusSweeney 14 60
(B Palling) *led: rdn 2f out: narrowly hdd 1f out: rallied gamely u.p: led fnl stride* **16/1**
5-23 **2** *shd* **Red Rudy**[15] [972] 4-9-4 **63**.. JimmyFortune 9 71
(A W Carroll) *mid div: rdn and hdwy over 2f out: led 1f out: hrd rdn and no ex whn ct fnl stride* **4/1**[2]
1-1 **3** *hd* **Redeye Special**[19] [902] 4-9-2 **61**.................................... JamieSpencer 5 73+
(M L W Bell) *hld up towards rr: hdwy and weaved her way through field fr over 2f out: r.o ins fnl f: nrst fin* **6/4**[1]
3012 **4** 2½ **Lord Chamberlain**[13] [1001] 13-9-4 **63**...........................(b) RyanMoore 12 65
(J M Bradley) *mid div tl dropped rr after 2f: hdwy 2f out: styd on fnl f* **14/1**
0-63 **5** ¾ **Mad**[18] [917] 5-8-5 **50**... JohnEgan 10 50
(Ernst Oertel) *chsd ldrs: rdn over 3f out: wknd ins fnl f* **16/1**
23-0 **6** 2½ **Tipsy Lad**[14] [985] 4-8-10 **55**..(tp) LDettori 4 49
(D J S Ffrench Davis) *in tch: rdn and effrt over 2f out: one pce fnl f* **25/1**
1053 **7** *hd* **Height Of Spirits**[23] [854] 4-8-10 **58**............................. RobertMiles(3) 1 52
(T D McCarthy) *nvr bttr than mid div on outer* **25/1**
-061 **8** *hd* **Humility**[18] [917] 5-8-7 **52**.. DarryllHolland 7 45+
(C A Cyzer) *broke wl: sn restrained in tch: nt clr run 2f out: no imp fnl f: nt rcvr* **12/1**
-005 **9** ¾ **Imtalkinggibberish**[19] [903] 5-8-8 **53**.............................. MickyFenton 8 45
(J R Jenkins) *s.i.s: bhd: styd on and wandered u.p fr 2f out: nvr a danger* **40/1**
3133 **10** ½ **Mister Elegant**[50] [606] 4-8-8 **53**...................................... SteveDrowne 6 44
(J L Spearing) *plld hrd: sn trcking ldr: rdn over 2f out: wknd 1f out* **8/1**[3]
0630 **11** 1½ **Secam (POL)**[13] [1002] 7-8-8 **53**.....................................(b) SamHitchcott 2 40
(Mrs P Townsley) *mid-div: rdn and effrt over 2f out: wknd over 1f out* **40/1**
0-00 **12** *5* **Hey Presto**[87] [236] 6-9-3 **62**.. PaulDoe 3 38
(R Rowe) *a towards rr* **66/1**
2153 **13** *3* **Physical (IRE)**[18] [915] 4-8-9 **59**...............................(p) JamesDoyle(5) 11 28
(Mrs A J Perrett) *chsd ldrs: rdn and n.m.r on rails over 3f out: wknd 2f out* **12/1**
0510 **14** *shd* **Christmas Truce (IRE)**[21] [889] 7-8-4 **56**.................. SophieDoyle(7) 13 24
(Ms J S Doyle) *chsd ldrs for 3f: grad fdd* **40/1**
1m 39.81s (-2.17) **Going Correction** -0.025s/f (Stan) **14** Ran SP% **121.4**
Speed ratings (Par 101):103,102,102,100,99 96,96,96,95,95 93,88,85,85
CSF £75.80 CT £163.28 TOTE £23.80: £8.90, £1.70, £2.00; EX 248.30.
Owner Nigel Thomas and Christopher Mason **Bred** Christopher J Mason **Trained** Tredodridge, Vale Of Glamorgan

FOCUS
Ordinary stuff with the first two pretty exposed, but the race should produce the odd winner.
Imtalkinggibberish Official explanation: jockey said gelding hung right
Mister Elegant Official explanation: jockey said colt ran too free

1246 KEMPTON FOR CONFERENCES H'CAP 6f (P)
8:52 (8:52) (Class 3) (0-95,95) 4-Y-0+
£11,217 (£3,358; £1,679; £840; £419; £210) **Stalls** High

Form RPR
0-16 **1** **Fantaisiste**[7] [1086] 4-8-6 **86**...................................... NelsonDeSouza(3) 11 102+
(P F I Cole) *chsd ldrs: rdn to ld 1f out: r.o: rdn out* **9/2**[2]
0-51 **2** 1¾ **Idle Power (IRE)**[15] [970] 8-8-5 **82**.................................... MartinDwyer 7 91
(J R Boyle) *led for 1f: chsd ldr: rdn and ev ch over 1f out: kpt on but nt pce of wnr* **11/2**[3]
163- **3** *1* **Beaver Patrol (IRE)**[187] [6014] 4-8-13 **90**................................ LDettori 9 96
(R F Johnson Houghton) *chsd ldrs: outpcd 4f out: hdwy and checked over 2f out: kpt on* **4/1**[1]
0120 **4** 1¼ **Saviours Spirit**[15] [970] 5-8-11 **88**...................................... IanMongan 12 90
(T G Mills) *s.i.s: sn rcvrd to chse ldrs: rdn over 2f out: kpt on same pce fnl f* **12/1**
300- **5** ½ **Viking Spirit**[242] [4764] 4-9-4 **95**... TQuinn 4 96
(W R Swinburn) *mid div: rdn and hdwy over 2f out: one pce fnl f* **8/1**
2210 **6** *nk* **Wessex (USA)**[46] [629] 6-9-3 **94**... NCallan 8 94
(P A Blockley) *mid-div: rdn and hdwy 2f out: one pce fnl f* **10/1**
1110 **7** *nk* **Graze On**[46] [627] 4-9-1 **92**..(b) AdrianMcCarthy 1 91
(R A Harris) *chsd ldr: led after 1f: rdn and hdd 1f out: wknd* **20/1**
62/0 **8** *shd* **First Order**[24] [846] 5-8-11 **88**.. JohnEgan 6 87
(Ernst Oertel) *mid-div: hdwy wl over 2f out: sn rdn: one pce fr over 1f out* **28/1**
1-33 **9** ¾ **Hits Only Heaven (IRE)**[96] [161] 4-8-5 **82**....................(e) JimmyQuinn 2 78
(D Nicholls) *bmpd s: towards rr: sme hdwy over 2f out: no further imp fr over 1f out* **10/1**
00-6 **10** ¾ **Fast Heart**[7] [1076] 5-8-10 **87**..(t) ChrisCatlin 10 81
(B J Meehan) *a bhd* **8/1**

0520 **11** *6* **Chief Exec**[5] [1112] 4-8-5 **82**......................................(v[1]) RobbieFitzpatrick 3 58
(C A Cyzer) *bdly bmpd s: nvr rcvrd and a in rr* **25/1**
12 *13* **Pachello (IRE)**[252] 4-9-1 **92**.. RyanMoore 5 29
(J M Bradley) *mid div tl wknd over 3f out* **50/1**
1m 11.66s (-4.61) **Going Correction** -0.025s/f (Stan) **12** Ran SP% **115.7**
Speed ratings (Par 107):112,109,108,106,106 105,105,105,104,103 95,77
CSF £27.34 CT £106.90 TOTE £10.80: £1.90, £3.00, £2.00; EX 17.50.
Owner Miss Alfiya Shaykhutdinova **Bred** Miss K Rausing **Trained** Whatcombe, Oxon

FOCUS
A decent handicap that went the way of the sole filly in the field. The form looks reliable with the placed horses to form.

NOTEBOOK
Fantaisiste, who came from a mile back to win here on her penultimate outing, was not as effective back on turf over seven furlongs last week. However, she was able to return to her best here, staying on strongly to win without something in hand. Currently in-foal to Cadeux Generaux, she has not finished improving yet and it will be interesting to see where connections head next. (op 11-2)
Idle Power(IRE) was given a positive ride by Dwyer and he beat everything else well enough, but lacked the winner's turn of pace. He continues in good form. (op 9-2)
Beaver Patrol(IRE) will no doubt have pleased connections with this All-Weather debut, and the likelihood is he would have been closer had he not been checked in his run. (op 9-2)
Saviours Spirit bounced back from a disappointing effort at Folkestone and definitely seems more at home on Polytrack. (op 14-1 tchd 16-1)
Viking Spirit made a pleasing reappearance for his stable who have made a slow start to the season and the gelding remains capable of further progression this term. (op 7-1)

1247 KEMPTON.CO.UK H'CAP 2m (P)
9:20 (9:21) (Class 4) (0-85,84) 4-Y-0+
£7,790 (£2,332; £1,166; £583; £291; £146) **Stalls** High

Form RPR
332- **1** **Velvet Heights (IRE)**[187] [6006] 4-9-2 **77**.................................. KDarley 11 91+
(J L Dunlop) *hld up towards rr: gd hdwy on outer fr 4f out: rdn 2f out: led jst over 1f out: styd on strly* **6/1**[3]
0/0- **2** 2½ **Archduke Ferdinand (FR)**[139] [2240] 8-9-9 **80**.................. DaneO'Neill 1 87
(A King) *hld up towards rr: stdy hdwy fr 5f out: rdn to ld over 2f out: hdd jst over 1f out: kpt on* **14/1**
2505 **3** *1* **High Point (IRE)**[11] [1021] 8-8-11 **73**........................... RobynBrisland(5) 6 79
(G P Enright) *mid-div: hdwy 5f out: led over 3f out: rdn and hdd over 2f out: kpt on same pce* **11/1**
4-14 **4** *2* **Establishment**[11] [1021] 9-9-8 **79**... LDettori 3 82
(C A Cyzer) *hld up mid-div: hdwy 4f out: sn rdn: styd on* **9/4**[1]
5125 **5** ½ **Monte Cristo (FR)**[15] [966] 8-9-0 **71**.........................(v) ChrisCatlin 12 74
(Mrs L C Taylor) *in tch: slty outpcd over 3f out: styd on fr over 1f out* **10/1**
0/0- **6** *6* **Halland**[373] [1088] 8-9-4 **75**...(e[1]) MickyFenton 14 71
(T J Fitzgerald) *hld up bhd: swtchd lft wl over 2f out: sn rdn: styd on past btn horses fr over 1f out: n.d* **25/1**
01-0 **7** *1* **Maystock**[70] [420] 6-9-6 **77**.. TedDurcan 7 71
(B G Powell) *chsd ldrs: rdn over 3f out: wknd over 1f out* **25/1**
-003 **8** 1½ **Salute (IRE)**[25] [832] 7-9-2 **73**... RobertHavlin 10 66
(P G Murphy) *chsd ldrs: rdn over 3f out: wknd over 1f out* **10/1**
05/0 **9** *nk* **Fiddlers Ford (IRE)**[25] [832] 5-8-10 **67**......................... J-PGuillambert 5 59
(T Keddy) *hld up towards rr: short lived effrt over 3f out* **40/1**
5/46 **10** *14* **High Hope (FR)**[15] [713] 8-8-11 **68**.................................(b) RyanMoore 4 43
(G L Moore) *a towards rr* **5/1**[2]
3110 **11** *nk* **Isa'Af (IRE)**[14] [976] 7-8-12 **76**..................................... TolleyDean(7) 9 51
(P W Hiatt) *in tch: rdn over 4f out: sn wknd* **25/1**
0/-5 **12** *2* **Lunar Exit (IRE)**[30] [765] 5-9-13 **84**................................(p) SebSanders 8 57
(Lady Herries) *chsd ldrs: led briefly 4f out: wknd over 2f out* **14/1**
53/0 **13** *28* **Akritas**[11] [1021] 5-9-11 **82**...(t) RichardHughes 2 21
(P F I Cole) *sn led: hdd 4f out: wknd rapidly over 2f out: eased fnl f* **16/1**
065- **14** *22* **Wait For The Will (USA)**[167] [6308] 10-9-1 **72**............... GeorgeBaker 13 —
(G L Moore) *a bhd: t.o fnl 3f* **20/1**
3m 27.49s (-15.51) **Going Correction** -0.025s/f (Stan)
WFA 4 from 5yo+ 4lb **14** Ran SP% **126.2**
Speed ratings (Par 105):108,106,106,105,105 102,101,100,100,93 93,92,78,67
CSF £85.17 CT £927.65 TOTE £9.20: £3.30, £6.10, £2.70; EX 110.80 Place 6 £27.64, Place 5 £26.32.
Owner Windflower Overseas Holdings Inc **Bred** Windflower Overseas **Trained** Arundel, W Sussex

FOCUS
A fair handicap best rated through the third and fourth likely to produce winners.
High Hope(FR) Official explanation: jockey said gelding hung right
Akritas Official explanation: jockey said gelding lost its action
T/Plt: £22.00 to a £1 stake. Pool: £41,569.50. 1,375.10 winning tickets. T/Qpdt: £10.20 to a £1 stake. Pool: £3,086.55. 222.95 winning tickets. TM

1073 BEVERLEY (R-H)
Thursday, April 27

OFFICIAL GOING: Good to firm (firm in places)
The ground had dried out and was generally described as 'genuine good to firm' but others thought it was even quicker than that.
Wind: Light, half-behind Weather: Fine and sunny.

1248 RACING AGAIN ON 13TH MAY CLAIMING STKS 5f
2:20 (2:22) (Class 5) 2-Y-0 **£3,335** (£992; £495; £247) **Stalls** High

Form RPR
06 **1** **Mr Klick (IRE)**[7] [1096] 2-8-13 .... JamieSpencer 7 73
(M J Wallace) *chsd ldrs: edgd rt and styd on to ld ins last* **9/2**[2]
4 **2** 1½ **Jord (IRE)**[10] [1040] 2-8-4 .... FrancisNorton 1 58
(C A Dwyer) *in tch: hung rt and styd on fnl f to take 2nd nr line* **8/1**
3 **3** ½ **Picture Frame**[10] [1040] 2-9-3 .... JoeFanning 3 69
(N Tinkler) *chsd ldrs: led 1f out: hdd and no ex ins last* **9/1**
52 **4** 2½ **Tokyo Jo (IRE)**[10] [1040] 2-8-8 .... RobertWinston 5 50
(K R Burke) *chsd ldrs: fdd fnl f* **9/4**[1]
6 **5** *1* **Foxxy**[20] [908] 2-8-12 .... NCallan 2 50
(K A Ryan) *swvd lft s: hdwy fnl 2f: nvr nr ldrs* **9/1**
05 **6** ¾ **All Talk**[23] [877] 2-8-4 .... ChrisCatlin 11 39
(I A Wood) *led tl hdd & wknd 1f out* **5/1**[3]
05 **7** 1¼ **Baytown Paikea**[1] [1229] 2-8-2 .... FrancisFerris 12 32
(P S McEntee) *chsd ldrs: wknd over 1f out* **20/1**
8 *shd* **Nicada (IRE)** 2-8-13 .... DaleGibson 6 43
(M W Easterby) *cmpt: s.i.s: hdwy and edgd lft 1f out: nvr on terms* **25/1**
06 **9** *hd* **Emma Told Lies**[10] [1040] 2-8-5 .... PaulMulrennan(3) 4 37
(M W Easterby) *in tch: outpcd fnl 2f* **25/1**

10 2 ½ **Pirner's Brig** 2-8-6 .... AdeleRothery(7) 9 32
(M W Easterby) *leggy: s.v.s: sme hdwy on wd outside 2f out: nvr a factor* **50/1**

0 11 2 **Milly Beat**[10] [1040] 2-8-2 .... PaulFessey 8 13
(C Grant) *uns rdr and led to s: sn outpcd and bhd* **66/1**

00 12 12 **Citoyen (IRE)**[8] [1074] 2-9-7 .... MickyFenton 10 —
(Ronald Thompson) *sn outpcd and wl bhd* **25/1**

63.58 secs (-0.42) **Going Correction** -0.275s/f (Firm) 12 Ran SP% **116.5**
Speed ratings (Par 92):92,89,88,84,83 82,80,79,79,75 72,53
CSF £35.85 TOTE £4.70: £1.80, £2.30, £2.70; EX 44.00.The winner was claimed by N. Wilson for £8,000. Jord was claimed by M. J. Polglase for £6,000.
Owner Pedro Rosas **Bred** Hyde Park Stud **Trained** Newmarket, Suffolk

FOCUS
A run-of-the-mill claimer run in a moderate time with the second, third and fourth renewing Redcar rivalry. The form looks weak.

NOTEBOOK
Mr Klick(IRE), who has plenty of size and strength, was restless in the stalls. In the end he won going away and was claimed by Noel Wilson. He will benefit from being gelded and will be suited by a sixth furlong. (op 5-1)
Jord(IRE), who had the worst of the draw, stayed on to snatch second spot on the line and was subsequently claimed by Mark Polglase. She is crying out for a sixth furlong. (op 5-1)
Picture Frame showed plenty of toe from an unfavourable draw. He can find a similar event. (op 8-1)
Tokyo Jo(IRE), having her third outing, was unable to confirm Redcar placings with the second and third. (op 2-1)
Foxxy, drawn one from the outside, again gave away ground at the start. She would not need to improve much to find a seller. (tchd 10-1)
All Talk, taken to post early, showed bags of toe and a seller on a less-stiff track looks a better option. (op 6-1)

1249 GO RACING IN YORKSHIRE FILLIES' H'CAP 1m 1f 207y
2:50 (2:50) (Class 5) (0-70,63) 4-Y-0+ **£3,400** (£1,011; £505; £252) **Stalls** High

Form RPR

-042 1 **Gramada (IRE)**[16] [965] 4-9-1 **60** .... NCallan 10 67
(P A Blockley) *led: qcknd over 3f out: edgd lft fnl f: jst hld on* **2/1**[1]

43-1 2 shd **Shekan Star**[22] [891] 4-8-4 **49** oh4 .... PaulHanagan 4 56
(K G Reveley) *lw: s.s: hld up in rr: hdwy on ins over 2f out: styd on fnl f: jst hld* **11/2**

454- 3 nk **Calamari (IRE)**[258] [4339] 4-8-12 **57** .... TonyCulhane 3 63
(Mrs A Duffield) *trckd ldrs: nt clr run and swtchd lft over 1f out: no room and swtchd ins 1f out: styd on ins last* **11/1**

304- 4 ¾ **Westcourt Dream**[173] [6262] 6-8-4 **52** .... PaulMulrennan(3) 9 57
(M W Easterby) *trckd ldrs: t.k.h: kpt on same pce fnl f* **7/2**[2]

-440 5 nk **Dispol Veleta**[10] [1045] 5-9-1 **63** .... BenSwarbrick(3) 5 67
(T D Barron) *hld up: effrt over 3f out: styd on same pce fnl f* **9/1**

310- 6 1 ½ **Awaken**[222] [5321] 5-8-5 **50** .... AdrianMcCarthy 2 51
(Miss Tracy Waggott) *hld up in tch: effrt 3f out: styd on same pce: nvr able chal* **14/1**

363- 7 12 **World At My Feet**[218] [5409] 4-8-5 **50** .... JoeFanning 8 28
(N Bycroft) *trckd ldrs on outer: lost pl over 1f out* **16/1**

023- 8 2 **Eminence Gift**[199] [5790] 4-8-7 **52** .... FrancisNorton 7 27
(K R Burke) *chsd ldrs: hrd drvn over 3f out: lost pl over 2f out* **5/1**[3]

1/00 9 27 **Snugfit Dubarry**[42] [650] 6-8-10 **55** .... DaleGibson 6 —
(M W Easterby) *stdd s: sn detached in last: t.o 5f out* **66/1**

2m 5.64s (-1.66) **Going Correction** -0.275s/f (Firm) 9 Ran SP% **120.0**
Speed ratings (Par 100):95,94,94,94,93 92,83,81,59
CSF £14.10 CT £100.34 TOTE £3.10: £1.40, £2.00, £2.50; EX 14.70.
Owner Pedro Rosas **Bred** John Osborne **Trained** Lambourn, Berks

FOCUS
A tactical affair resulting in a modest winning time. The winner was in pole position throughout and sets the standard, but the form looks unconvincing.
Snugfit Dubarry Official explanation: jockey said mare was unsuited by the good to firm (firm in places) ground

1250 GOOD LUCK PHILIP AND ANNIE STKS (H'CAP) 7f 100y
3:20 (3:20) (Class 3) (0-90,82) 3-Y-0 **£9,067** (£2,697; £1,348; £673) **Stalls** High

Form RPR

41- 1 **Sir Gerard**[197] [5832] 3-9-4 **82** .... JamieSpencer 4 93+
(J R Fanshawe) *hdw: t.k.h: effrt and hung rt over 1f out: styd on wl ins last: led post* **13/8**[1]

15-5 2 shd **Call My Number (IRE)**[12] [1016] 3-9-2 **80** .... TonyCulhane 6 86
(M R Channon) *w ldr: t.k.h: led and hung rt over 1f out: hrd rdn and jst ct* **4/1**[3]

2115 3 nk **Rebellion**[26] [831] 3-9-1 **79** .... JoeFanning 3 84
(M Johnston) *led after 1f: qcknd over 3f out: hdd and bmpd over 1f out: no ex wl ins last* **15/2**

14 4 1 ¼ **Dame Hester (IRE)**[9] [1067] 3-9-2 **80** .... ChrisCatlin 7 82+
(E J O'Neill) *led 1f: trckd ldr: t.k.h: nt clr run on inner over 1f out: kpt on same pce* **7/2**[2]

441- 5 7 **Crosby Vision**[218] [5407] 3-8-12 **76** .... DarryllHolland 5 61
(J R Weymes) *hdw: rrd s: hld up: effrt 3f out: wknd 2f out* **7/1**

-553 6 10 **Memphis Man**[26] [831] 3-9-2 **80** .... MichaelHills 2 40
(G C Bravery) *hld up in rr: hdwy on outer over 5f out: lost pl 2f out: eased* **20/1**

1m 32.41s (-1.90) **Going Correction** -0.275s/f (Firm) 6 Ran SP% **109.3**
Speed ratings (Par 102):99,98,98,97,89 77
CSF £7.87 TOTE £2.20: £1.40, £2.20; EX 9.00.
Owner Miss Rose-Anne Galligan **Bred** Whitsbury Manor Stud And Stowell Hill Ltd **Trained** Newmarket, Suffolk

FOCUS
Just a steady pace to halfway but the winner will go on to better things. The race has been rated positively through the fourth.

NOTEBOOK
Sir Gerard ◆, who has done really well from two to three, took a keen grip due to the lack of pace. He took time to get organised but really picked up inside the last and put his head in front on the line. Likely to be suited by the full mile, he will go on from here. (op 7-4 tchd 6-4)
Call My Number(IRE) was another keen to get on with it. With everything thrown at him, in the end he just missed out. (op 5-1)
Rebellion, who looked very fit, was soon dictating things. He stepped up the pace coming off the home turn and battled all the way to the line. (op 10-1 tchd 7-1)
Dame Hester(IRE), keen to get on with it, found herself on the heels of the two leaders up the home straight and lacked the pace to do anything about it. A much stronger gallop would have helped her. (op 11-4 tchd 4-1 in a place)
Crosby Vision, who looks to have thrived over the winter, reared leaving the stalls and looked unhappy on the quick ground. He should do a lot better in due course. (op 11-2)
Memphis Man, who looked very fit indeed, almost bolted going to post.

1251 WESTWOOD H'CAP 1m 1f 207y
3:50 (3:50) (Class 5) (0-75,75) 3-Y-0 **£4,210** (£1,252; £625; £312) **Stalls** High

Form RPR

04-2 1 **Dark Planet**[19] [918] 3-8-4 **61** .... JoeFanning 1 65
(C E Brittain) *sn trcking ldrs: effrt 3f out: rdn to ld over 1f out: edgd lft: hld on towards fin* **6/1**[3]

4332 2 nk **Mambo Sun**[10] [1052] 3-8-8 **65** .... PaulHanagan 3 68
(P A Blockley) *hld up in rr: hdwy 3f out: chal 1f out: carried lft ins last: styd on towards fin* **10/3**[2]

0112 3 nk **Marachi Band (USA)**[4] [1162] 3-8-12 **69** 6ex ....(b) RichardMullen 4 71
(E J O'Neill) *w ldr: chal over 2f out: no ex ins last* **3/1**[1]

30-0 4 2 **On Air (USA)**[17] [948] 3-8-13 **70** .... KDarley 6 70+
(M Johnston) *in tch in last: sn pushed along: outpcd over 3f out: rallied over 1f out: kpt on ins last* **20/1**

30-5 5 2 ½ **Carr Hall (IRE)**[10] [1044] 3-8-5 **62** .... DavidAllan 5 56
(T D Easterby) *led tl: qcknd over 3f out: hdd over 1f out: wknd jst ins last* **16/1**

321- 6 1 ¼ **Qualify**[184] [6102] 3-9-4 **75** .... TonyCulhane 8 67
(M R Channon) *sn trcking ldrs: effrt on inner over 2f out: n.m.r over 1f out: wknd jst ins last* **3/1**[1]

30-3 7 5 **Sunbolt (IRE)**[27] [817] 3-9-0 **71** .... PaulFessey 7 53
(T D Barron) *t.k.h: trckd ldrs: drvn along over 5f out: outpcd over 3f out: n.d after* **6/1**[3]

2m 4.07s (-3.23) **Going Correction** -0.275s/f (Firm) 7 Ran SP% **112.3**
Speed ratings (Par 98):101,100,100,98,96 95,91
CSF £25.25 CT £70.65 TOTE £7.30: £3.50, £2.70; EX 25.00.
Owner Sheikh Marwan Al Maktoum **Bred** Darley **Trained** Newmarket, Suffolk
■ Stewards' Enquiry : Joe Fanning one-day ban: careless riding (May 9)

FOCUS
Just a steady gallop until turning in. Ordinary form, rated through the runner-up, and a messy race in the closing stages.

1252 CONSTANT SECURITY MAIDEN STKS 1m 100y
4:20 (4:21) (Class 5) 3-Y-0+ **£3,886** (£1,156; £577; £288) **Stalls** High

Form RPR

2- 1 **Sharplaw Autumn (USA)**[202] [5711] 3-8-6 .... JamieSpencer 3 77+
(W J Haggas) *hld up in mid-field: hdwy over 3f out: led jst ins last: drvn out* **4/7**[1]

6-5 2 ½ **Madaares (USA)**[15] [978] 3-8-11 .... KDarley 6 73
(M Johnston) *lw: chsd ldr: rdn to ld over 2f out: hdd jst ins last: kpt on wl* **4/1**[2]

0-6 3 2 **Velvet Valley (USA)**[15] [981] 3-8-11 .... RobertWinston 5 69+
(Sir Michael Stoute) *trckd ldrs: chal 1f out: styd on same pce* **11/2**[3]

5-4 4 2 **Emilion**[16] [963] 3-8-6 .... MichaelHills 7 59+
(W J Haggas) *hld up in rr: hdwy over 2f out: hung rt over 1f out: styd on* **14/1**

0- 5 ½ **Bollin Dolly**[284] [3561] 3-8-6 .... DavidAllan 1 58
(T D Easterby) *swvd lft s: hdwy over 3f out: hung rt: kpt on: nvr nr ldrs* **50/1**

0-0 6 1 **Lennoxtown (IRE)**[10] [1055] 3-8-11 .... NCallan 4 61
(M A Jarvis) *chsd ldrs: rdn and one pce whn sltly hmpd 2f out* **20/1**

06-0 7 6 **Mccormack (IRE)**[51] [612] 4-9-11 **49** .... FergalLynch 2 51
(Micky Hammond) *stdd s: t.k.h in rr: sme hdwy 2f out: nvr a factor* **100/1**

/00 8 nk **Aqua**[11] [1032] 4-9-6 .... MickyFenton 10 45
(P T Midgley) *led: qcknd over 3f out: hdd over 2f out: lost pl over 1f out* **125/1**

6 9 1 ¼ **Chateau (IRE)**[15] [978] 4-9-11 .... PaulQuinn 11 47
(G A Swinbank) *t.k.h in rr: sme hdwy 2f out: nvr on terms* **33/1**

00 10 shd **Megalo Maniac**[11] [1032] 3-8-11 .... DeanMcKeown 8 43
(K G Reveley) *t.k.h in rr: outpcd fnl 3f* **100/1**

0 11 9 **Delamead (IRE)**[7] [1100] 3-8-11 .... TonyHamilton 12 23
(B Ellison) *a bhd* **100/1**

00 12 1 ¼ **Rainbow Prince**[7] [1100] 3-8-8 .... DanielTudhope(3) 9 20
(A Dickman) *t.k.h: in tch: hung rt over 2f out: sn lost pl* **100/1**

1m 45.75s (-1.65) **Going Correction** -0.275s/f (Firm)
WFA 3 from 4yo 14lb 12 Ran SP% **120.1**
Speed ratings (Par 103):97,96,94,92,92 91,85,84,83,83 74,73
CSF £3.02 TOTE £1.60: £1.10, £1.90, £1.50; EX 4.40.
Owner F C T Wilson **Bred** Morgan's Ford Farm & Grand Slam Farm **Trained** Newmarket, Suffolk

FOCUS
Just a steady pace until in line for home. The winner will go on to better things and the first six were clear of dead wood in an ordinary maiden.

1253 GEORGE RAMSHAW LOYAL RACEDAY SERVICE H'CAP 7f 100y
4:50 (4:51) (Class 6) (0-60,58) 4-Y-0+ **£3,335** (£992; £495; £247) **Stalls** High

Form RPR

500- 1 **Mount Usher**[216] [5431] 4-9-3 **57** .... DeanMcKeown 11 64
(G A Swinbank) *stdd s: hld up in rr: hdwy over 2f out: styd on to ld ins last: r.o* **20/1**

00-6 2 1 **Flaxby**[27] [818] 4-8-11 **51** ....(b) AdrianTNicholls 4 56
(J D Bethell) *mid-div: effrt on outside over 2f out: styd on wl ins last* **20/1**

020- 3 ½ **Uhuru Peak**[269] [3990] 5-8-13 **56** ....(t) PaulMulrennan(3) 16 59
(M W Easterby) *reluctant to enter stalls: hld up in mid-field: hdwy over 2f out: styd on wl ins last* **14/1**

53-5 4 shd **Just Bond (IRE)**[69] [440] 4-9-1 **55** .... DerekMcGaffin 1 58+
(B Smart) *t.k.h: w ldrs: edgd lft over 1f out: led 1f out: hdd and no ex ins last* **16/1**

10-1 5 1 ¼ **Attacca**[27] [818] 5-9-0 **54** .... JoeFanning 3 54
(J R Weymes) *in tch: effrt over 2f out: kpt on fnl f* **13/2**[2]

00-0 6 ¾ **Grandos (IRE)**[6] [1123] 4-9-4 **58** .... FergalLynch 7 56
(T D Easterby) *in rr: hdwy 2f out: styd on ins last* **20/1**

/05- 7 hd **Leighton Buzzard**[195] [5880] 4-9-1 **58** .... DanielTudhope(3) 5 56
(Mrs A Duffield) *bhd: kpt on fnl 2f: nvr nr ldrs* **12/1**

0210 8 hd **Desert Fury**[20] [906] 9-8-12 **52** .... PaulHanagan 9 49
(R Bastiman) *s.i.s: hdwy on outer over 2f out: styng on fin* **20/1**

012- 9 nk **Spanish Law**[311] [2760] 4-8-13 **53** ....(b) PhillipMakin 15 49
(M Dods) *chsd ldrs: wkng whn hmpd over 1f out* **15/2**

036- 10 ¾ **Parchment (IRE)**[248] [4628] 4-9-2 **56** .... TonyHamilton 6 50
(A J Lockwood) *in rr: kpt on fnl 2f: nvr on terms* **40/1**

-003 11 nk **Motu (IRE)**[8] [1073] 5-8-7 **52** ....(v) NataliaGemelova(5) 12 46+
(I W McInnes) *in tch: effrt on inner whn n.m.r over 1f out: no threat after* **16/1**

404- 12 1 ¼ **Paris Heights**[210] [5564] 4-8-6 **53** .... MichaelJStainton(7) 10 44
(R M Whitaker) *rr-div: sme hdwy over 2f out: sn lost pl* **11/1**

5434 **13** 1/2 **Kew The Music**[10] 1057 6-9-4 **58**........(v) ChrisCatlin 8 47
(M R Channon) *dwlt: sn bhd: hdwy on inner 2f out: hung rt: nvr on terms* **9/2**[1]

-246 **14** 1 **Burton Ash**[19] 917 4-9-4 **58**........(v) MickyFenton 14 45
(J G Given) *led tl over 1f out: wknd* **7/1**[3]

4-04 **15** 3/4 **First Rhapsody (IRE)**[27] 818 4-9-2 **56**........ KDarley 13 41
(T J Etherington) *chsd ldrs: lost pl over 1f out* **10/1**

0364 **16** 2 **Gem Bien (USA)**[5] 1148 8-8-13 **53**........(p) PaulQuinn 2 33
(D W Chapman) *chsd ldr: chal 3f out: lost pl over 1f out* **11/1**

1m 30.83s (-3.48) **Going Correction** -0.275s/f (Firm) **16** Ran SP% **129.1**
Speed ratings (Par 101):108,106,106,106,104 103,103,103,103,102 101,100,99,98,97 95
CSF £371.97 CT £5930.32 TOTE £36.80: £8.70, £6.40, £2.90, £4.20; EX 1060.60 TRIFECTA Not won. Place 6 £158.08, Place 5 £52.21.
Owner Mrs F H Crone **Bred** Juddmonte Farms **Trained** Melsonby, N Yorks

FOCUS
A strong pace resulting in a decent winning time for a race like this, 1.58 seconds faster than the earlier three-year-old handicap. The sixth and seventh sets the standard.
Kew The Music Official explanation: jockey said gelding was unsuited by the good to firm (firm in places) ground
Burton Ash Official explanation: jockey said filly had no more to give
T/Jkpt: £82,423.00 to a £1 stake. Pool: £116,088.75. 1.00 winning ticket. T/Plt: £724.80 to a £1 stake. Pool: £47,216.25. 47.55 winning tickets. T/Qpdt: £123.90 to a £1 stake. Pool: £2,511.60. 15.00 winning tickets. WG

1216 SOUTHWELL (L-H)
Thursday, April 27

OFFICIAL GOING: Standard
Wind: Virtually nil

1254 BETFRED MILLION MEDIAN AUCTION MAIDEN STKS 7f (F)
5:40 (5:42) (Class 6) 3-4-Y-O **£2,730** (£806; £403) **Stalls** Low

Form RPR

3 **1** **Snowy Day (FR)**[38] 677 3-8-13........ TonyCulhane 5 70+
(W J Haggas) *trckd ldng pair: smooth hdwy 2f out: led over 1f out: sn rdn and kpt on* **7/2**[3]

0202 **2** 2 1/2 **Mind Out (USA)**[57] 551 3-8-6 54........(v[1]) AshleyHamblett(7) 6 63
(J T Stimpson) *cl up: led wl over 2f out: sn rdn: hdd over 1f out: drvn and kpt on same pce ins last* **4/1**

5- **3** 4 **Local Spirit (USA)**[300] 3095 3-8-8........ DarryllHolland 1 48
(C E Brittain) *in tch: pushed along 1/2-way: rdn and flashed tail over 2f out: drvn and no imp fr over 1f out* **7/4**[1]

3356 **4** 5 **Pop Music (IRE)**[10] 1055 3-8-10 72........ SaleemGolam(3) 3 40
(Miss J Feilden) *chsd ldrs: rdn along wl over 2f out: sn outpcd* **2/1**[2]

06-0 **5** 6 **Mystic Queen (IRE)**[59] 536 3-8-3 35........ AndrewElliott(5) 4 19
(A P Jarvis) *led: rdn along 3f out: sn hdd & wknd* **40/1**

00 **6** 11 **Very Clear**[6] 1110 4-9-7........ GrahamGibbons 2 —
(R M H Cowell) *outpcd and bhd fr 1/2-way* **33/1**

7 19 **Salawat** 3-8-8........ TPQueally 8 —
(T T Clement) *sn outpcd and bhd* **33/1**

1m 28.98s (-1.82) **Going Correction** -0.275s/f (Stan)
WFA 3 from 4yo 13lb **7** Ran SP% **109.3**
Speed ratings (Par 101):99,96,91,85,79 66,44
CSF £32.24 TOTE £3.50: £1.60, £2.70; EX 15.60.
Owner W J Haggas **Bred** G Lehmann **Trained** Newmarket, Suffolk

FOCUS
A modest maiden in which the performance of the 54-rated runner-up anchors the form.

1255 BETFRED MILLION CLAIMING STKS 6f (F)
6:10 (6:10) (Class 6) 3-Y-0+ **£2,730** (£806; £403) **Stalls** Low

Form RPR

1000 **1** **Blakeshall Quest**[24] 858 6-9-1 52........(b) TomEaves 7 56
(R Brotherton) *mde all: rdn 2f out: drvn over 1f out: styd on gamely* **33/1**

4020 **2** hd **Orchestration (IRE)**[10] 1054 5-9-6 55........(v) RobbieFitzpatrick 12 60
(M J Attwater) *in tch: hdwy on outer 2f out: sn rdn: styd on strly ins last* **10/1**

056- **3** shd **Gracie's Gift (IRE)**[256] 4392 4-9-4 62........ FergusSweeney 4 58
(A G Newcombe) *chsd ldrs: rdn and sltly outpcd 2f out: styd on u.p ins last* **7/1**

2511 **4** shd **Soba Jones**[38] 674 9-9-5 65........ JasonEdmunds(3) 6 62
(J Balding) *trckd ldrs: hdwy to chse wnr over 2f out: swtchd lft and rdn wl over 1f out: drvn and ev ch ins last: no ex* **5/2**[1]

0201 **5** 1/2 **Penel (IRE)**[23] 873 5-9-1 49........(p) LeeEnstone 3 53
(P T Midgley) *chsd ldrs: rdn along 2f out: drvn over 1f out and ev ch tl no ex wl ins last* **10/1**

0-00 **6** 1/2 **Domirati**[10] 1047 6-9-6 63........ GrahamGibbons 9 57
(J D Bethell) *in tch: hdwy to chse ldrs 2f out: sn rdn and kpt on ins last* **10/1**

2500 **7** 1 1/2 **Shadow Jumper (IRE)**[27] 824 5-9-1 57........(v) AshleyHamblett(7) 8 54
(J T Stimpson) *towards rr: pushed along and sme hdwy 2f out: sn rdn and kpt on ins last* **14/1**

0250 **8** shd **Majik**[7] 1102 7-9-4 66........ CraigCarver 2 50
(P A Blockley) *towards rr: hdwy 2f out: swtchd lft and rdn over 1f out: kpt on ins last* **5/1**[3]

4401 **9** shd **Chickado (IRE)**[20] 907 5-8-12 50........ RobertHavlin 5 43
(D Haydn Jones) *a towards rr* **9/2**[2]

000- **10** 22 **Born For Diamonds (IRE)**[284] 3567 4-8-8 49........ MarkCoumbe(7) 1 —
(R E Barr) *midfield: rdn along and wknd 1/2-way: sn bhd* **66/1**

1m 16.42s (-0.48) **Going Correction** -0.275s/f (Stan) **10** Ran SP% **114.3**
Speed ratings (Par 101):92,91,91,91,90 90,88,88,87,58
CSF £325.00 TOTE £43.40: £7.90, £3.40, £2.20; EX 389.60.
Owner Droitwich Jokers **Bred** M P Bishop **Trained** Elmley Castle, Worcs

FOCUS
An ordinary claimer run in a very moderate winning time, even for a race like this, and resulting in a bunch finish. The form looks ordinary with the fifth the best guide.

1256 BETFRED "THE BONUS KING" H'CAP 1m 4f (F)
6:40 (6:40) (Class 6) (0-60,60) 4-Y-0+ **£2,730** (£806; £403) **Stalls** Low

Form RPR

512- **1** **Zoripp (IRE)**[159] 6381 4-8-9 **51**........(b) MickyFenton 10 59
(J G Given) *a.p: led wl over 3f out: rdn 2f out: drvn and edgd rt ins last: kpt on* **17/2**

6430 **2** 3/4 **Jackie Kiely**[10] 1058 5-9-5 **60**........ TonyCulhane 7 67
(P Howling) *in tch: hdwy over 4f out: chsd wnr over 2f out: chal and rdn wl over 1f out: drvn and ev ch tl no ex last 50 yds* **11/2**[3]

0230 **3** 5 **Eforetta (GER)**[17] 939 4-8-2 **47** oh1 ow1........ EdwardCreighton(3) 5 47
(D J Wintle) *hld up in rr: hdwy over 4f out: wd st: rdn 2f out: styd on fnl f: nrst fin* **20/1**

0014 **4** 3 **Royal Axminster**[20] 911 11-8-10 **51**........ RobertHavlin 6 46
(Mrs P N Dutfield) *trckd ldrs: effrt 3f out: sn rdn and wknd fnl 2f* **8/1**

6520 **5** 7 **Blue Opal**[17] 939 4-8-6 **48** ow1........ RobbieFitzpatrick 9 33
(Miss S E Hall) *in tch: effrt and hdwy 5f out: rdn along 3f out: btn 2f out* **5/1**[2]

0/20 **6** 1 3/4 **King's Crest**[10] 1045 8-8-7 **48**........ GrahamGibbons 3 30
(J J Quinn) *towards rr: effrt and sme hdwy 4f out: sn rdn and no further prog* **10/1**

15-1 **7** 1 **Mad Maurice**[86] 258 5-8-12 **53**........ TPQueally 1 33
(B J Curley) *keen: trckd ldrs on inner: effrt 4f out: sn rdn along and wknd 3f out* **4/1**[1]

00-0 **8** 1/2 **Hezaam (USA)**[84] 276 5-9-5 **60**........ PaulFessey 2 40
(Mrs A Duffield) *a rr* **14/1**

6320 **9** 2 1/2 **High Frequency (IRE)**[3] 1199 5-8-3 **47**........(b) BenSwarbrick(3) 4 23
(T D Barron) *led: rdn along over 4f out: hdd over 3f out and sn wknd* **4/1**[1]

06P- **10** dist **Lady Stratagem**[196] 5855 7-8-2 **46** oh11........ JohnMcAuley(3) 8 —
(E W Tuer) *chsd ldrs: rdn along and wknd 1/2-wy: sn bhd* **100/1**

2m 38.21s (-3.88) **Going Correction** -0.275s/f (Stan)
WFA 4 from 5yo+ 1lb **10** Ran SP% **115.2**
Speed ratings (Par 101):101,100,97,95,90 89,88,88,86,—
CSF £54.05 CT £909.73 TOTE £8.60: £2.00, £1.80, £6.50; EX 45.30.
Owner P A Horton **Bred** Bryan Ryan **Trained** Willoughton, Lincs

FOCUS
A moderate handicap notable for the weakness in the betting and poor performance from morning-line favourite Mad Maurice. The form looks reliable enough, rated through the runner-up.
King's Crest Official explanation: jockey said gelding never travelled

1257 BETFREDPOKER.COM H'CAP 1m (F)
7:10 (7:10) (Class 5) (0-75,75) 4-Y-0+ **£3,238** (£963; £481; £240) **Stalls** Low

Form RPR

-111 **1** **Tyzack (IRE)**[24] 860 5-9-4 **75**........ MickyFenton 8 90
(Stef Liddiard) *trckd ldrs: hdwy to chse ldr 1/2-way: led wl over 1f out: rdn ins last and styd on strly* **6/4**[1]

2061 **2** 1 1/2 **Exit Smiling**[20] 906 4-8-8 **65** ow1........ TonyCulhane 3 77
(P T Midgley) *cl up: led after 3f: rdn along 3f out: hdd wl over 1f out: sn drvn and kpt on same pce fnl f* **8/1**[3]

-221 **3** 5 **Sir Bond (IRE)**[14] 1002 5-8-6 **63**........ RobertWinston 4 65
(B Smart) *dwlt: in tch: hdwy to chse ldng pair 2f out: sn rdn and no imp appr last* **13/8**[2]

1602 **4** 3 **Quiet Reading (USA)**[20] 906 9-7-11 **61** oh4........(v) SophieDoyle(7) 7 57
(M R Bosley) *trckd ldrs: effrt 3f out: rdn along over 2f out and sn wknd* **16/1**

46U0 **5** 10 **Monte Mayor Boy**[14] 1002 4-8-6 **63** ow1........(p) RobertHavlin 6 39
(D Haydn Jones) *a rr* **16/1**

000- **6** nk **Inchloss (IRE)**[222] 5317 5-8-6 **63** oh1 ow2........ AdrianTNicholls 2 38
(C N Kellett) *led 3f: chsd ldrs tl rdn along 3f out and sn wknd* **33/1**

-000 **7** 11 **Rawaabet (IRE)**[4] 1164 4-8-10 **67**........ ChrisCatlin 1 20
(P W Hiatt) *chsd ldrs: rdn along over 3f out: sn wknd* **14/1**

8 hd **First Boy (GER)**[160] 7-8-2 **62** oh1 ow1........ EdwardCreighton(3) 5 15
(D J Wintle) *sn outpcd and bhd* **40/1**

1m 41.44s (-3.16) **Going Correction** -0.275s/f (Stan) **8** Ran SP% **113.0**
Speed ratings (Par 103):104,102,97,94,84 84,73,73
CSF £14.05 CT £21.11 TOTE £2.00: £1.10, £1.90, £1.10; EX 11.50.
Owner Simon Mapletoft Racing I **Bred** Rabea Syndicate **Trained** Great Shefford, Berks

FOCUS
Not a bad little handicap and the form looks pretty solid rated around the runner-up and fourth.

1258 BETFREDCASINO.COM H'CAP 7f (F)
7:40 (7:40) (Class 5) (0-70,70) 4-Y-0+ **£3,238** (£963; £481; £240) **Stalls** Low

Form RPR

-31 **1** **Crimson King (IRE)**[79] 331 5-9-2 **68**........ NCallan 6 89+
(T T Clement) *trckd ldrs: hdwy 3f out: rdn to ld over 1f out: sn clr* **10/11**[1]

45-5 **2** 5 **Sedge (USA)**[51] 606 6-8-4 **56** oh4........(p) RobbieFitzpatrick 1 62+
(P T Midgley) *in tch on inner: hdwy over 2f out: sn rdn: styd on ins last: no ch w wnr* **11/1**

5635 **3** shd **Pawn In Life (IRE)**[10] 1050 8-8-4 **56** oh5........(v) FrancisNorton 8 61
(M J Polglase) *sn pushed along in rr: hdwy over 2f out: sn rdn and styd on wl fnl f* **25/1**

2510 **4** 1 3/4 **Count Cougar (USA)**[17] 950 6-8-10 **62**........ AdrianTNicholls 7 62
(S P Griffiths) *cl up: led after 2f: rdn along 3f out: drvn and hdd over 1f out: wknd ins last* **16/1**

2235 **5** 1 1/4 **Roman Empire**[5] 1152 6-7-12 **57**........(v) KevinGhunowa(7) 9 54
(P A Blockley) *midfield: rdn along and wd st: styd on u.p appr last: nt rch ldrs* **8/1**[2]

0000 **6** 3 **Pamir (IRE)**[17] 949 4-9-0 **66**........(p) RobertWinston 11 55
(P R Chamings) *cl up: rdn along 3f out: drvn and wknd over 2f out* **14/1**

0-50 **7** nk **Nan Jan**[33] 721 4-9-4 **70**........(t) ChrisCatlin 5 58
(R Ingram) *rdn along towards rr: hdwy over 2f out: drvn and edgd lft ent last: nt rch ldrs* **14/1**

3200 **8** 5 **Shifty Night (IRE)**[24] 862 5-8-7 **59** ow1........(v) MickyFenton 12 34
(Mrs C A Dunnett) *chsd ldrs: rdn along 3f out: sn wknd* **12/1**

3120 **9** 8 **Zorn**[25] 845 7-8-10 **62**........ J-PGuillambert 2 17
(P Howling) *in tch: rdn along 3f out: sn wknd* **10/1**[3]

-000 **10** 1/2 **Newsround**[10] 1042 4-8-8 **60**........(p) TonyCulhane 4 13
(D W Chapman) *s.i.s: a rr* **50/1**

210- **11** nk **Filey Buoy**[133] 6587 4-8-2 **57** oh3 ow1........ StanleyChin(3) 10 9
(R M Whitaker) *in tch: rdn along over 3f out: sn wknd* **22/1**

-030 **12** 3 1/2 **Second Reef**[10] 1041 4-8-9 **61**........ PaulQuinn 3 4
(E J Alston) *led 2f: cl up tl rdn along 1/2-way and sn wknd* **25/1**

1m 28.11s (-2.69) **Going Correction** -0.275s/f (Stan) **12** Ran SP% **121.8**
Speed ratings (Par 103):104,98,98,96,94 91,90,85,76,75 75,71
CSF £11.71 CT £173.29 TOTE £1.80: £1.10, £2.90, £3.80; EX 10.10.
Owner Rothmere Racing Limited **Bred** Hazel Kelly **Trained** Newmarket, Suffolk
■ Stewards' Enquiry : J-P Guillambert one-day ban: careless riding (May 8)

FOCUS
An uncompetitive handicap as the favourite turned out to have been let in lightly. The form is not that strong but fairly reliable.
Second Reef Official explanation: jockey said gelding hung right and changed legs home straight

1259 BETFRED MILLION H'CAP 1m (F)
8:10 (8:10) (Class 6) (0-60,59) 3-Y-O £2,730 (£806; £403) Stalls Low

Form RPR
004- 1 **Stolen Glance**[163] 6358 3-8-8 52 PaulMulrennan(3) 14 58
(M W Easterby) *chsd ldrs on outer: rdn along over 2f out: hdwy to ld 11/2f out: hung lft and styd on ins last* 16/1
000- 2 3 **Lovely Hidenka (USA)**[184] 6097 3-8-12 53 DarryllHolland 12 53
(C E Brittain) *chsd ldrs: rdn along over 2f out: swtchd lft and drvn over 1f out: kpt on ins last* 11/1
3100 3 1 1/2 **Monte Mayor Junior**[10] 1052 3-9-4 59 (p) RobertHavlin 10 56
(D Haydn Jones) *chsd ldrs: rdn along 2f out: drvn and kpt on ins last* 15/2
-032 4 hd **Hillbilly Cat (USA)**[72] 415 3-9-1 56 PaulFessey 2 53
(T D Barron) *led: rdn along over 2f out: drvn and hdd 1 1/2f out: one pce ins last* 7/2[1]
5-00 5 shd **Pactolos Way**[15] 984 3-9-0 55 FrancisNorton 6 51
(P R Chamings) *s.i.s and bhd: wd st: hdwy 2f out: styd on u.p ins last* 20/1
-063 6 3 **Peephole**[15] 984 3-9-0 55 (v) FergusSweeney 9 45
(P J Makin) *cl up: effrt and ev ch over 2f out: sn rdn and grad wknd* 6/1[3]
065- 7 4 **Bond Cruz**[138] 6538 3-9-0 55 (b[1]) RobertWinston 11 37
(B Smart) *towards rr: hdwy 3f out: rdn to chse ldrs wl over 1f out: sn drvn and no imp* 11/2[2]
-050 8 2 1/2 **Captivate**[15] 979 3-8-9 50 (p) DeanMcKeown 13 27
(M J Polglase) *a midfield* 25/1
604- 9 1 1/2 **Dream Of Paradise (USA)**[133] 6585 3-8-11 52 TomEaves 1 26
(Mrs L Williamson) *in tch: rdn along 3f out: sn no imp* 33/1
2640 10 1 3/4 **Cool Isle**[24] 859 3-8-12 53 (b) TonyCulhane 7 24
(P Howling) *in tch: rdn along 1/2-way: sn outpcd* 14/1
004- 11 9 **Devon Ruby**[157] 6403 3-8-11 52 TPQueally 3 5
(Mrs A Duffield) *chsd ldrs on inner: rdn along wl over 2f out: sn drvn and wknd* 25/1
0012 12 6 **Dylan (IRE)**[23] 874 3-8-11 52 KimTinkler 8 —
(N Tinkler) *a rr* 8/1
40 13 3 1/2 **Tullochrome**[8] 1073 3-8-11 52 ChrisCatlin 5 —
(E J O'Neill) *cl up: rdn along 3f out: sn wknd* 10/1
00-0 14 16 **Chisom**[20] 910 3-8-13 54 DaleGibson 4 —
(M W Easterby) *s.i.s: a rr* 66/1

1m 43.47s (-1.13) **Going Correction** -0.275s/f (Stan) 14 Ran SP% **121.6**
Speed ratings (Par 96):94,91,89,89,89 86,82,79,78,76 67,61,57,41
CSF £173.04 CT £964.71 TOTE £29.80: £7.20, £4.10, £3.60; EX 391.30 Place 6 £1,709.89, Place 5 £294.53..
Owner R S Cockerill (Farms) Ltd **Bred** R S Cockerill (farms) Ltd **Trained** Sheriff Hutton, N Yorks
FOCUS
An ordinary handicap run in a very moderate winning time for the grade, rated around the third and fourth to previous course form.
T/Plt: £1,216.20 to a £1 stake. Pool: £36,069.70. 21.65 winning tickets. T/Qpdt: £61.70 to a £1 stake. Pool: £4,157.90. 49.80 winning tickets. JR

1053 YARMOUTH (L-H)
Thursday, April 27

OFFICIAL GOING: Good to firm
Wind: Fresh, behind Weather: Fine and sunny, but chilly

1260 HAPPY BIRTHDAY TO LUCY AND BARRY MAIDEN STKS 1m 3f 101y
5:25 (5:27) (Class 4) 3-Y-O £5,505 (£1,637; £818; £408) Stalls Low

Form RPR
465- 1 **Mont Etoile (IRE)**[182] 6120 3-8-12 83 NickyMackay 2 75+
(W J Haggas) *a.p: nt clr run fr over 2f out: swtchd rt ins fnl f: r.o wl to ld towards fin* 13/8[1]
5 2 1 1/4 **Congestion Charge**[24] 850 3-8-12 TedDurcan 1 68
(E A L Dunlop) *hld up: hdwy over 3f out: rdn and hung rt over 2f out: hung lft over 1f out: led ins fnl f: hdd towards fin* 15/8[2]
3- 3 3/4 **Materialize (USA)**[166] 6319 3-8-12 LDettori 6 67
(P J McBride) *hld up in tch: racd keenly: rdn and ev ch fr over 1f out tl no ex wl ins fnl f* 6/1[3]
0- 4 1/2 **Empire Dancer (IRE)**[180] 6142 3-8-10 KirstyMilczarek(7) 4 71
(C N Allen) *led: rdn and hdd ins fnl f: no ex* 80/1
033- 5 6 **Meantime (USA)**[236] 4955 3-9-0 73 AdamKirby(3) 7 61
(G Prodromou) *chsd ldrs: rdn over 3f out: wknd 2f out* 22/1
6 15 **Monmouthshire** 3-9-3 RyanMoore 5 37
(M L W Bell) *dwlt: sn prom: rdn to chse ldr 10f out: ev ch tl wknd over 1f out* 6/1[3]
7 dist **Grand Mempari** 3-8-12 SebSanders 8 —
(Mrs C A Dunnett) *s.s: bhd: rdn and wknd 4f out* 50/1

2m 32.97s (5.47) **Going Correction** -0.025s/f (Good) 7 Ran SP% **109.0**
Speed ratings (Par 100):79,78,77,77,72 61,—
CSF £4.38 TOTE £2.60: £1.40, £1.90; EX 3.80.
Owner Tony Hirschfeld Des Scott L K Piggott **Bred** Paget Bloodstock **Trained** Newmarket, Suffolk
FOCUS
A muddling race, as Empire Dancer, an 80/1 shot, was allowed the run of the race at just a steady pace and was still in contention a furlong out. Along with the tine he limits the form, which is rated around the placed horses.

1261 SCROBY SANDS WIND FARM MAIDEN STKS 6f 3y
5:55 (5:59) (Class 4) 3-Y-O+ £5,297 (£1,586; £793; £396; £198; £99) Stalls High

Form RPR
3- 1 **Tawaassol (USA)**[339] 1955 3-9-1 RHills 10 91+
(Sir Michael Stoute) *trckd ldrs: led on bit over 1f out: r.o wl: eased towards fin* 4/6[1]
53-0 2 4 **Chanteuse Noire (USA)**[10] 1055 3-8-10 69 (v[1]) ShaneKelly 7 61
(J Noseda) *chsd ldrs: led over 3f out: rdn and hdd over 1f out: sn outpcd* 16/1
5-02 3 4 **Oneiro Way (IRE)**[68] 449 4-9-12 68 IanMongan 11 57
(P R Chamings) *chsd ldrs: lost pl and hung lft over 4f out: hdwy u.p and hung lft over 1f out: n.d* 7/1[3]
000- 4 hd **Great Belief (IRE)**[177] 6217 4-9-12 50 MartinDwyer 1 56
(T D McCarthy) *led: hdd over 3f out: rdn and wknd over 1f out* 66/1
5 1 3/4 **Perfect Cover (IRE)** 3-8-10 AlanMunro 3 43
(J A R Toller) *dwlt: outpcd: styd on ins fnl f: nvr nrr* 33/1
0-00 6 3 1/2 **Master Malarkey**[7] 1100 3-9-1 35 (b[1]) JohnEgan 8 37
(Mrs C A Dunnett) *mid-div: outpcd 1/2-way: hdwy u.p and hung lft 2f out: sn wknd* 66/1
444- 7 shd **Finsbury**[166] 6332 3-9-1 73 GeorgeBaker 12 37
(C F Wall) *s.s: hdwy and hung lft fr over 2f out: sn rdn and nt run on* 5/1[2]
00-0 8 6 **Atticus Trophies (IRE)**[33] 722 3-9-1 65 LDettori 2 19
(K McAuliffe) *sn pushed along in rr: edgd rt wl over 3f out: n.d* 22/1
9 3 1/2 **Crimson Year (USA)** 4-9-7 RyanMoore 5 6
(C E Brittain) *chsd ldrs over 3f* 16/1
0/ 10 1 1/2 **Nellie Gwyn**[537] 6569 4-9-7 SebSanders 9 —
(J G Given) *chsd ldrs over 3f* 66/1
00-0 11 3 **Dancing Beauty (IRE)**[30] 778 4-9-2 35 JamesDoyle(5) 4 —
(T T Clement) *chsd ldrs to 1/2-way* 100/1
000- 12 3 **Runaway Ruby**[253] 4470 12-9-2 40 MarcHalford(5) 6 —
(B J McMath) *s.s: outpcd: hmpd wl over 3f out* 100/1

1m 13.17s (-0.53) **Going Correction** -0.025s/f (Good)
WFA 3 from 4yo+ 11lb 12 Ran SP% **114.7**
Speed ratings (Par 105):102,96,91,91,88 84,83,75,71,69 65,61
CSF £12.64 TOTE £1.70: £1.10, £3.70, £1.90; EX 11.10.
Owner Hamdan Al Maktoum **Bred** James T Gottwald **Trained** Newmarket, Suffolk
FOCUS
A weak maiden in which Tawaassol defied his near year-long absence to win as expected, but the form is limited by the fourth.
Master Malarkey Official explanation: jockey said gelding lost its action
Finsbury Official explanation: trainer said gelding was unsuited by the good to firm ground
Atticus Trophies(IRE) Official explanation: jockey said gelding hung right-handed

1262 M BROCK LIMITED 15TH ANNIVERSARY H'CAP 7f 3y
6:25 (6:26) (Class 3) (0-95,88) 4-Y-O+ £11,217 (£3,358; £1,679; £840; £419; £210) Stalls High

Form RPR
3-12 1 **Akona Matata (USA)**[26] 826 4-9-0 84 SebSanders 10 94
(C E Brittain) *hld up in tch: rdn to ld and hung lft over 1f out: r.o* 10/1
/P-0 2 1 1/4 **Surwaki (USA)**[26] 826 4-8-8 78 PhilipRobinson 8 85
(C G Cox) *chsd ldrs: rdn over 1f out: r.o* 25/1
0-00 3 1 **Lord Of The East**[5] 1143 7-9-1 88 PatrickMathers(3) 2 92
(I W McInnes) *led: rdn and hdd over 1f out: styd on* 66/1
110- 4 nk **Banjo Patterson**[243] 4764 4-9-3 87 LDettori 5 90+
(G A Huffer) *hld up in tch: rdn to chse wnr fnl f: no ex towards fin* 7/2[1]
30-6 5 1 3/4 **Trafalgar Square**[17] 946 4-8-10 80 AlanMunro 6 79+
(J Akehurst) *mid-div: hdwy 1/2-way: rdn over 1f out: styd on same pce* 13/2[3]
0 6 2 1/2 **Marajaa (IRE)**[26] 828 4-9-4 88 LPKeniry 1 80
(W J Musson) *hld up: hdwy over 1f out: wknd fnl f* 25/1
6022 7 shd **Tanforan**[10] 1042 4-8-0 75 (b) JamesDoyle(5) 4 67
(K McAuliffe) *hld up: hdwy 3f out: rdn: hung lft and wknd over 1f out* 9/1
140- 8 3 1/2 **Call Me Max**[216] 5440 4-8-12 82 TedDurcan 3 65
(E A L Dunlop) *hld up: a in rr* 18/1
0-22 9 4 **Namroc (IRE)**[10] 1043 5-8-12 82 JamieSpencer 9 54
(N A Callaghan) *hld up: rdn 4f out: a in rr* 7/2[1]
1100 10 6 **H Harrison (IRE)**[11] 1035 6-8-9 79 RoystonFfrench 7 36
(I W McInnes) *prom: rdn 1/2-way: wknd over 2f out* 50/1
0121 11 3 1/2 **Mr Lambros**[19] 913 5-9-1 85 MartinDwyer 11 33
(A M Balding) *chsd ldrs over 5f* 4/1[2]

1m 25.36s (-1.24) **Going Correction** -0.025s/f (Good) 11 Ran SP% **113.3**
Speed ratings (Par 107):106,104,103,103,101 98,98,94,89,82 78
CSF £230.70 CT £14776.29 TOTE £10.10: £2.50, £4.70, £8.20; EX 1095.60.
Owner Sheikh Hamdan Bin Mohammed Al Maktoum **Bred** Jayeff 'B' Stables **Trained** Newmarket, Suffolk
FOCUS
A good handicap run at a strong pace from the start and the form looks reliable.
NOTEBOOK
Akona Matata(USA) ◆, 2lb higher than when second over a mile on Kempton's Polytrack on his previous start, showed himself every bit as effective on turf with a ready success. He is clearly still improving and his trainer thinks he could be a Royal Hunt Cup horse. (op 11-1)
Surwaki(USA), well behind Akona Matata when that one was second on his return from nearly a year off a mile on Kempton's Polytrack, showed the benefit of that run and got much closer this time. With the possibility of even more to come, he should be able to win off his current sort of mark. (tchd 33-1)
Lord Of The East, given his usual positive ride, ran his best race of the year so far and would appear to be running into form. He did not exactly appear well handicapped coming into this, so it was a very creditable effort. (op 50-1)
Banjo Patterson, below form when last seen 243 days previously, ran creditably on his return to the track and should be better for the outing. (tchd 3-1 and 4-1 in places)
Trafalgar Square, as on his reappearance, ran with credit. He only needs to improve a touch to be up to winning in this sort of company. (op 7-1 tchd 6-1)
Namroc(IRE) has been in good form lately, but this is the shortest trip he has ever raced over and he could never get competitive in a race run at a very strong pace. Official explanation: trainer had no explanation for the poor form shown (op 5-2)
Mr Lambros has never won on turf, but he has proven he acts on the surface and this was disappointing considering he was able to race off a mark 10lb lower than on sand. Official explanation: jockey said gelding was unsuited by the good to firm ground

1263 BBC RADIO NORFOLK H'CAP 6f 3y
6:55 (6:55) (Class 6) (0-60,60) 3-Y-O £3,238 (£963; £481; £240) Stalls High

Form RPR
2225 1 **Smile For Us**[20] 910 3-9-4 60 (b) JamieSpencer 7 73
(C Drew) *mde all: sn clr: rdn over 1f out: unchal* 13/2
0-32 2 5 **George The Second**[23] 879 3-8-8 55 RichardKingscote(5) 16 53
(Mrs H Sweeting) *chsd wnr thrght: rdn and hung lft over 2f out: no imp* 4/1[2]
500- 3 3 **Young Bertie**[176] 6226 3-9-4 60 SteveDrowne 14 49+
(H Morrison) *hmpd s: hdwy over 1f out: nrst fin* 7/2[1]
-000 4 1 **Left Nostril (IRE)**[73] 396 3-8-7 49 BrianReilly 4 35
(P S McEntee) *chsd ldrs: rdn over 2f out: styd on same pce* 100/1
0-35 5 1/2 **Royal Tavira Girl (IRE)**[30] 776 3-8-13 60 JerryO'Dwyer(5) 2 45
(M G Quinlan) *chsd ldrs: rdn over 2f out: sn outpcd* 18/1
66-6 6 shd **Mr Cellophane**[16] 969 3-9-1 60 DeanCorby(3) 10 52+
(J R Jenkins) *hmpd s: hdwy and nt clr run fr over 1f out: nvr nr to chal* 12/1
50-5 7 3/4 **Tuscany Queen (IRE)**[36] 692 3-8-13 55 RyanMoore 5 37
(R Hannon) *chsd ldrs: rdn over 2f out: sn outpcd* 15/2
00-0 8 shd **Forces Sweetheart**[52] 595 3-9-2 58 HayleyTurner 9 40
(M L W Bell) *wnt rt and caused havoc s: styd on appr fnl f: nvr nrr* 16/1
0005 9 4 **Lucys Lady**[21] 893 3-8-8 50 (p) PatCosgrave 15 20+
(K R Burke) *hmpd s: outpcd* 33/1
60-0 10 2 1/2 **Woolfall King (IRE)**[29] 796 3-8-5 47 (v[1]) NickyMackay 1 9
(G G Margarson) *s.s: sn mid-div: wknd 1/2-way* 28/1

606- **11** *1* **That Look**[117] 6694 3-8-13 **55**........ ShaneKelly 11 14+
(D E Cantillon) *hmpd s: outpcd* **25/1**

6000 **12** *6* **Galaxy Bound (IRE)**[24] 861 3-8-10 **55**........(v) PatrickMathers(3) 8 —
(D Shaw) *s.s: sn mid-div: wknd 1/2-way* **66/1**

6-00 **13** *21* **Captain Torrance (IRE)**[23] 880 3-8-8 **50**........ AlanMunro 12 —+
(P W Chapple-Hyam) *hmpd s: outpcd* **11/2**[3]

0100 **14** *19* **Teddy Monty (IRE)**[21] 893 3-8-8 **50**........(v) MartinDwyer 13 —+
(M Quinn) *hmpd s: outpcd* **28/1**

1m 13.3s (-0.40) **Going Correction** -0.025s/f (Good) **14** Ran SP% **117.7**
Speed ratings (Par 96):101,94,90,89,88 88,87,87,81,78 77,69,41,15
CSF £30.01 CT £109.64 TOTE £7.40: £2.70, £1.70, £1.90; EX 29.90.

Owner C Drew **Bred** B Mills **Trained** Rampton, Cambs

FOCUS
A race to treat with real caution form wise as Forces Sweetheart, drawn nine, swerved badly right as the stalls opened and badly hampered all those draw above her, except George The Second, who sets the level for the form and avoided the trouble by breaking quickly. Jamie Spencer took full advantage on Smile For Us and that one is flattered by such an authoritative success.

1264 BETFRED SPRINT SERIES QUALIFIER (H'CAP) 5f 43y
7:25 (7:29) (Class 4) (0-85,84) 3-Y-O **£8,096** (£2,408; £1,203; £601) **Stalls** High

Form RPR

641- **1** **Empress Jain**[228] 5151 3-8-11 **77**........ PhilipRobinson 8 96
(M A Jarvis) *mde all: rdn clr fnl f* **7/2**[2]

200- **2** *5* **Fisola (IRE)**[206] 5668 3-8-9 **78**........ AdamKirby(3) 5 79
(C G Cox) *hld up: hdwy 2f out: rdn to chse wnr fnl f: no imp* **11/1**

-060 **3** *nk* **Smooch**[17] 954 3-8-11 **82**........ JamesDoyle(5) 6 82
(R M H Cowell) *s.i.s: outpcd: r.o ins fnl f: nrst fin* **28/1**

331- **4** *shd* **Woodnook**[219] 5378 3-8-7 **73**........ AlanMunro 1 73
(J A R Toller) *s.i.s: sn prom: rdn over 1f out: styd on same pce* **4/1**[3]

503- **5** *hd* **Brunelleschi**[182] 6124 3-8-13 **79**........ JohnEgan 3 78+
(P L Gilligan) *s.i.s: sn outpcd: r.o ins fnl f: nvr trbld ldrs* **10/1**

20-0 **6** *shd* **Azygous**[12] 1020 3-8-10 **83**........ JamesMillman(7) 4 82
(J Akehurst) *chsd wnr over 3f: styd on same pce* **8/1**

335- **7** *2 1/2* **Smart Cassie**[177] 6214 3-8-13 **79**........ JamieSpencer 7 69
(D Shaw) *hld up: rdn over 1f out: n.d* **12/1**

410- **8** *1 1/2* **Laith (IRE)**[228] 5151 3-9-4 **84**........ RHills 2 68
(B W Hills) *chsd ldrs over 3f* **10/3**[1]

4-10 **9** *1 1/4* **City For Conquest (IRE)**[5] 1146 3-8-13 **79**........(v) PatCosgrave 9 59
(K R Burke) *chsd ldrs: rdn 2f out: sn wknd* **9/1**

62.09 secs (-0.71) **Going Correction** -0.025s/f (Good) **9** Ran SP% **115.0**
Speed ratings (Par 100):104,96,95,95,95 94,90,88,86
CSF £41.29 CT £924.12 TOTE £4.30: £1.70, £2.50, £5.30; EX 37.40.

Owner Dennis Yardy **Bred** D A Yardy **Trained** Newmarket, Suffolk

FOCUS
This looked a reasonable sprint handicap beforehand, but Empress Jain was the only one to stick to the near-side rail and finished clear having had the run of the race. The form is rated at face value for the moment.

Smart Cassie Official explanation: jockey said filly lost its action in closing stages

1265 PKF (UK) LLP H'CAP 1m 3y
7:55 (7:57) (Class 5) (0-70,68) 4-Y-O+ **£3,238** (£963; £481; £240) **Stalls** High

Form RPR

60-0 **1** **Polish Index**[16] 972 4-8-8 **58**........(p) RyanMoore 10 74
(J R Jenkins) *racd stands' side: mde all that gp and overall ldr 2f out: rdn clr over 1f out: 1st of 6 that side* **22/1**

-446 **2** *6* **Fasylitator (IRE)**[15] 992 4-9-4 **68**........ JohnEgan 7 70
(D K Ivory) *racd stands' side: chsd ldrs: rdn and edgd lft over 2f out: styd on same pce appr fnl f: 2nd of 6 that side* **3/1**[2]

502- **3** *2 1/2* **Peruvian Prince (USA)**[266] 4080 4-9-4 **68**........ AlanMunro 4 64
(J A R Toller) *racd stands' side: chsd ldrs: rdn over 1f out: sn wknd: 3rd of 6 that side* **11/2**[3]

024 **4** *1 1/4* **Devil's Island**[73] 405 4-8-12 **62**........ SebSanders 1 55
(Sir Mark Prescott) *racd centre: chsd ldrs: rdn and edgd rt over 1f out: wknd fnl f: 1st of 4 that side* **11/4**[1]

-500 **5** *1* **Panshir (FR)**[10] 1058 5-7-13 **54** oh1........ JamesDoyle(5) 9 45
(Mrs C A Dunnett) *racd stands' side: hld up: rdn over 1f out: n.d: 4th of 6 that side* **11/2**[3]

0400 **6** *nk* **Blue Empire (IRE)**[15] 985 5-8-9 **59**........ HayleyTurner 3 49
(C R Dore) *led centre: hdd over 6f out: chsd ldr: rdn and wknd over 1f out: 2nd of 4 that gp* **16/1**

0000 **7** *4* **Agilete**[3] 1201 4-8-4 **54** oh4........(p) MartinDwyer 2 35
(R A Harris) *led centre and overall ldr over 6f out: hdd 2f out: wknd over 1f out: 3rd of 4 that gp* **16/1**

6400 **8** *1/2* **King Of Music (USA)**[16] 972 5-8-5 **58** ow2........(v) AdamKirby(3) 6 38
(G Prodromou) *prom stands' side over 6f: 5th of 6 that gp* **16/1**

5060 **9** *shd* **The Rebound Kid**[10] 1057 4-8-8 **63**........(b[1]) DerekNolan(5) 11 43
(G A Huffer) *prom stands' side over 6f: last of 6 that side* **16/1**

0600 **10** *10* **Duxford**[16] 972 5-8-5 **55**........(b[1]) JimmyQuinn 5 12
(D K Ivory) *racd centre: sn outpcd: last of 4 that gp* **33/1**

1m 39.69s (-0.21) **Going Correction** -0.025s/f (Good) **10** Ran SP% **113.3**
Speed ratings (Par 103):100,94,91,90,89 88,84,84,84,74
CSF £84.97 CT £433.39 TOTE £23.30: £7.20, £1.70, £1.20; EX 249.90 Place 6 £382.93, Place 5 £292.84..

Owner Mrs Stella Peirce **Bred** Michael Ng **Trained** Royston, Herts

FOCUS
A moderate handicap. Just as in the previous race, the winner raced tight against the near-side rail throughout, but four of these tried their luck down the centre of the track and unsurprisingly finished up well beaten - Devil's Island fared best of them. The runner-up is the best guide to the level in a relatively weak contest.

Agilete Official explanation: jockey said gelding hung right-handed

T/Plt: £115.90 to a £1 stake. Pool: £41,249.20. 259.80 winning tickets. T/Qpdt: £66.40 to a £1 stake. Pool: £2,809.20. 31.30 winning tickets. CR

SANDOWN (R-H)
Friday, April 28

OFFICIAL GOING: Good (good to firm in places)
Wind: Moderate, across Weather: Fine **Other races under Rules of Jump racing**

1267 BETFRED GORDON RICHARDS STKS (GROUP 3) 1m 2f 7y
1:45 (1:48) (Class 1) 4-Y-O+
£28,390 (£10,760; £5,385; £2,685; £1,345; £675) **Stalls** High

Form RPR

212- **1** **Day Flight**[174] 6255 5-9-3 115........ RichardHughes 3 119+
(J H M Gosden) *b.hind: trckd ldrs: pushed along and prog over 2f out: rdn and r.o to ld last 100yds: readily* **10/3**[2]

013- **2** *1* **Notable Guest (USA)**[224] 5270 5-9-3 110........ PhilipRobinson 7 117
(Sir Michael Stoute) *lw: trckd ldrs: rdn and prog over 2f out: led jst over 1f out: hdd and outpcd last 100yds* **3/1**[1]

6035 **3** *nk* **Crosspeace (IRE)**[16] 991 4-9-0 106........ RoystonFfrench 10 113
(M Johnston) *settled in midfield: rdn 3f out: prog u.p jst over 2f out: chsd ldng pair ent fnl f: styd on* **11/1**

21-6 **4** *1 3/4* **Enforcer**[19] 934 4-9-3 109........ MartinDwyer 5 113
(W R Muir) *hld up in last trio: rdn and prog over 2f out: kpt on fr over 1f out: nt pce to chal* **13/2**

655- **5** *2 1/2* **Weightless**[219] 5403 6-9-0 110........ KDarley 1 105
(Mrs A J Perrett) *led: kicked on 3f out: drvn and hdd jst over 1f out: fdd* **14/1**

102- **6** *2* **Admiral's Cruise (USA)**[188] 6025 4-9-0 96........ JimmyFortune 6 102
(B J Meehan) *trckd ldr: rdn 3f out: wknd jst over 1f out* **14/1**

103- **7** *3/4* **Orcadian**[45] 6255 5-9-0 102........ TedDurcan 9 103+
(J M P Eustace) *trckd ldrs: rdn 3f out: lost pl and btn over 2f out* **33/1**

00-0 **8** *1/2* **Bahar Shumaal (IRE)**[9] 1084 4-9-0 105........ RyanMoore 4 99
(C E Brittain) *stdd s: hld up in detached last: shkn up and no prog 3f out: no ch after: r.o last 100yds* **66/1**

5/1- **9** *1/2* **Tau Ceti**[182] 6131 7-9-0 107........ LDettori 8 98
(R M Beckett) *settled in last trio: rdn 3f out: no prog* **12/1**

14-2 **10** *nk* **Rohaani (USA)**[13] 1017 4-9-0 99........ RHills 2 98
(Sir Michael Stoute) *lw: t.k.h: racd wd: trckd ldrs: shkn up over 2f out: fnd nil and sn wknd* **7/2**[3]

2m 8.17s (-2.07) **Going Correction** +0.075s/f (Good) **10** Ran SP% **117.4**
Speed ratings (Par 113):111,110,109,108,106 104,104,103,103,103
CSF £13.89 TOTE £4.30: £1.80, £1.50, £3.70; EX 12.00.

Owner K Abdulla **Bred** Juddmonte Farms **Trained** Newmarket, Suffolk

FOCUS
A competitive renewal of this Group 3 prize, run at a strong gallop, and the form looks solid enough.

NOTEBOOK
Day Flight, who won on his reappearance over this trip last year, repeated that feat and ran out a ready winner to get his season off to a perfect start. He proved easy to back, mainly on account of the drying surface, but he went on it without fuss and there was a lot to like about the manner in which he knuckled down to get on top inside the last 100 yards. He should improve for this outing, plus for the return to a longer trip, and is most likely to now head towards a crack at the Ormonde Stakes at Chester, which he won last year. He will no doubt take a deal of beating. (op 3-1 tchd 7-2)
Notable Guest(USA), a most progressive colt last season, turned in a solid return to action and only gave way to the winner inside the final 100 yards. He is a very likeable performer and, on this evidence, he may need a stiffer test this year. (op 7-2 tchd 4-1)
Crosspeace(IRE), who failed to stay 14 furlongs at Nottingham in Listed company last time, showed much improved form back over this more suitable trip and lost little in defeat. He came into this with the benefit four previous outings under his belt, however, and does look a little short of Group-class. (op 10-1)
Enforcer showed the benefit of his recent seasonal bow in France, but was never quite doing enough to threaten the leaders at any stage. He remains progressive and, with a return to a less-demanding track likely to prove to his advantage in due course, he looks up to landing a race at this level during the summer. (op 7-1)
Weightless, who made all to land this event in 2005, was returning from a 219-day break and set a strong gallop down the far side, and after slowing it down on the bend he quickened it up again in the straight.He was found out on the climb for home and is likely to continue hard to place from his current mark. (op 12-1)
Admiral's Cruise(USA), returning from a 188-day break, was unable to dominate as he prefers and never looked a serious threat. He faced a very stiff task at the weights this time, however, and it is unlikely we have seen the best of him just yet. (op 18-1)
Orcadian, last seen running down the field in the Supreme Novice at Cheltenham in March, not surprisingly found this an inadequate test of stamina and was well beaten.
Rohaani(USA), having his first outing in Group company, spoilt his chances by refusing to settle through the early stages and proved most disappointing. His attitude will rightly come under close scrutiny now, but he is capable of better than this, and is not one to be writing off just yet. (op 4-1 tchd 9-2)

1268 BETFRED ESHER CUP (H'CAP) 1m 14y
2:55 (2:58) (Class 2) (0-100,100) 3-Y-O
£7,288 (£7,288; £1,679; £840; £419; £210) **Stalls** High

Form RPR

316- **1** **King's Head (IRE)**[193] 5942 3-8-7 **89**........ PhilipRobinson 1 98
(M A Jarvis) *hld up in last trio: prog on outer 2f out: str run fnl f to force dead-heat last stride* **11/2**[3]

21-6 **1** *dht* **Yarqus**[13] 1016 3-8-4 **86** oh1........ MartinDwyer 6 95
(C E Brittain) *trckd ldng pair: effrt on inner to ld wl over 1f out: drvn fnl f: jnd last stride* **13/2**

5-12 **3** *1 1/2* **Direct Debit (IRE)**[53] 592 3-8-4 **86** oh1........ HayleyTurner 9 92
(M L W Bell) *led: rdn and hdd wl over 1f out: edgd lft and kpt on same pce* **8/1**

40-3 **4** *2 1/2* **Silver Blue (IRE)**[8] 1093 3-8-13 **95**........ RyanMoore 4 95
(R Hannon) *lw: chsd ldng trio: rdn 3f out: hanging rt and one pce fr 2f out* **9/4**[1]

310- **5** *1 1/2* **Genari**[202] 5731 3-8-11 **93**........ KFallon 2 90
(P F I Cole) *hld up in last trio: shkn up over 2f out: one pce and no imp on ldrs over 1f out* **7/2**[2]

454- **6** *2* **Doctor Scott**[181] 6144 3-8-1 **86**........ StanleyChin(3) 5 78
(M Johnston) *b.bkwd: chsd ldr to over 2f out: wknd u.p* **14/1**

35-1 **7** *hd* **South Cape**[35] 717 3-9-4 **100**........ TonyCulhane 7 91
(M R Channon) *plld hrd: chsd ldrs: effrt anc cl up over 2f out: wknd over 1f out* **9/1**

100- **8** *1* **Doctor Dash**[202] 5731 3-9-0 **96** .... LPKeniry 3 85
(D R C Elsworth) *b.bkwd: stdd s: t.k.h and hld up in last trio: rdn wl over 2f out: no prog* **20/1**

1m 43.33s (-0.62) **Going Correction** +0.075s/f (Good) **8** Ran SP% **114.2**
Speed ratings (Par 104):106,106,104,102,100 98,98,97
WIN: King's Head £3.50, Yarqus £4.00. PL: KH £2.10, Y £2.10, Direct Debit £2.40. EX: KH/Y £23.60, Y/KH £22.30. CSF: KH/Y £20.33, Y/KH £20.89. TRIC: KH/Y/DD £143.29, Y/KH/DD £146.25..
Owner A D Spence **Bred** London Thoroughbred Services Ltd **Trained** Newmarket, Suffolk
Owner Saeed Manana **Bred** Mrs M Burrell **Trained** Newmarket, Suffolk

FOCUS
A good renewal of what is traditionally a strong three-year-old handicap. It was run at a sound pace, and the form should work out.

NOTEBOOK
King's Head(IRE) ◆, put in his place in Listed company on his final outing as a juvenile last term, was flying at the finish and eventually did just enough to get up for a share of the spoils. He has clearly improved during the off-season and, with a step-up in trip most likely to play to his strengths, he looks one to follow as he should not be put up too much by the Handicapper for this success. (op 13-2)
Yarqus looked all over the winner when hitting the front approaching the final furlong, but his stride shortened close home, and he was joined on the line by the fast-finishing King's Head. He had clearly benefited from his recent comeback at Kempton and the stiffer track clearly proved more to his liking. This must rate a personal best from 1lb out of the handicap, but the danger now is that he will be aimed too high. Chester's Dee Stakes is said to be next on the agenda. (op 13-2)
Direct Debit(IRE), fit from the All-Weather, held every chance from the front and posted a solid effort in defeat back at this shorter trip. He still has few miles on the clock and it would be a surprise were he not to find another race from this sort of mark. (tchd 17-2)
Silver Blue(IRE), whose stable won this event last season, did his rider few favours by hanging right under pressure when it mattered and was well held. He was probably flattered by his Feilden third, and as he is already due to race from a 4lb higher mark in the future he will probably find life hard for the time being. Official explanation: jockey said colt hung right (op 2-1 tchd 5-2)
Genari, very well backed for this three-year-old debut, failed to make an impact from off the pace and shaped as though he may have needed the outing. He is clearly thought capable of better from his current mark and may well be in need of a stiffer test on this evidence. (op 11-2)
South Cape refused to settle through the early parts and never looked like following up his comeback success at Southwell on this much faster ground. (op 7-1)

1269 BETFREDCASINO.COM CONDITIONS STKS (C&G) 1m 14y
4:05 (4:09) (Class 3) 3-Y-O
£9,348 (£2,799; £1,399; £700; £349; £175) **Stalls** High

Form RPR
1 **1** **Ivy Creek (USA)**[24] 880 3-9-0 83 .... SteveDrowne 1 98+
(G Wragg) *scope: lw: hld up in last pair: prog on outer to chse ldr wl over 1f out: rdn to ld narrowly last 100yds: jst hld on* **2/1**[1]
12- **2** *hd* **Tell**[221] 5367 3-9-0 92 .... LDettori 3 98+
(J L Dunlop) *b.bkwd: trckd ldr for 2f: rdn over 2f out: effrt u.p over 1f out: r.o ins fnl f: jst hld* **5/1**
100- **3** *nk* **West Of Amarillo (USA)**[211] 5572 3-9-0 102 .... JimmyFortune 2 97+
(J H M Gosden) *trckd ldr after 2f: led wl over 2f out: hrd rdn over 1f out: narrowly hdd last 100yds: kpt on* **5/2**[2]
3- **4** *2* **Hopeful Purchase (IRE)**[181] 6148 3-8-10 .... RHills 6 88+
(W J Haggas) *b.bkwd: b.hind: t.k.h: hld up in last pair: effrt and nt clr run wl over 1f out: shkn up and kpt on: nt pce to chal* **10/3**[3]
06-0 **5** *6* **Bramcote Lorne**[11] 1055 3-8-10 .... KFallon 4 75?
(S Parr) *chsd ldrs: outpcd and dropped to last 2f out: n.d after* **50/1**
502- **6** *6* **Pinch Of Salt (IRE)**[201] 5753 3-8-10 82 .... DarryllHolland 5 61
(A M Balding) *sn led: hdd wl over 2f out: wknd rapidly over 1f out* **12/1**

1m 42.58s (-1.37) **Going Correction** +0.075s/f (Good) **6** Ran SP% **111.3**
Speed ratings (Par 102):109,108,108,106,100 94
CSF £12.21 TOTE £2.70: £1.50, £2.20; EX 8.30.
Owner Mollers Racing **Bred** Eleanor Drake Rose Trust Et Al **Trained** Newmarket, Suffolk

FOCUS
A decent little conditions event - won by smart performers such as Kahyasi and Medicean in the past - and the first three came nicely clear.

NOTEBOOK
Ivy Creek(USA) ◆, who looked a colt with a future when winning his maiden on debut at Warwick 24 days previously, followed up with a narrow success in this much better race, despite again running distinctly green under pressure. He settled better this time, with a cross noseband fitted, and with further improvement assured he looks an exciting prospect for a stable that often does well at the upcoming Chester meeting. The Dee Stakes is likely to be his assignment there, and the longer trip looks sure to be within his compass if he settles again. (op 9-4)
Tell ◆, making his seasonal return after a 221-day break, looked to hit a flat spot when the race became serious two from home, but duly stuck to his task, and was ultimately only just denied a winning comeback. He has done very little wrong in his three outings to date, and the step up to this trip clearly suited. He looks set to reach greater heights as a three-year-old. (op 11-2 tchd 6-1)
West Of Amarillo(USA), who had by far the highest BHB rating, held every chance on this return to action and was not beaten at all far. He may just be more at home over this trip on a less-demanding track in the future, and still has few miles on the clock, but does look a little flattered by his current official rating. (op 3-1)
Hopeful Purchase(IRE), a very promising third on his sole outing as a two-year-old, was not at all disgraced on this step up in class and seasonal bow, considering he proved hard to settle early on and then met trouble nearing the final furlong. While his Derby entry may be ambitious, he has plenty of scope, and looks sure to make his mark this year. It will be little surprise to see him upped in trip again before too long. (op 11-4 tchd 7-2 in a place)
Bramcote Lorne appeared to excel himself, but will not have done his prospective handicap mark much good after this.
Pinch Of Salt(IRE), returning from a 201-day break with the tongue tie left off, dropped out tamely when headed and has a fair deal to prove now. (op 11-1 tchd 14-1)

1270 BETFRED 570 SHOPS NATIONWIDE H'CAP 1m 2f 7y
4:35 (4:39) (Class 3) (0-90,83) 3-Y-O **£9,348** (£2,799; £1,399; £700; £349) **Stalls** High

Form RPR
41-2 **1** **Linas Selection**[8] 1095 3-9-4 **83** .... KDarley 1 89+
(M Johnston) *lw: mde virtually all: rdn 3f out: sn jnd: forged ahd again over 1f out: styd on wl* **1/1**[1]
221- **2** *1 3/4* **Salute The General**[127] 6659 3-8-12 **77** .... SteveDrowne 6 80
(W R Muir) *b.bkwd: sn restrained in last: effrt on inner over 2f out: styd on to take 2nd last 75yds: unable to chal* **8/1**
33-5 **3** *1/2* **Tumbleweed Glory (IRE)**[7] 1108 3-8-12 **77** .... JimmyFortune 4 79
(B J Meehan) *trckd wnr: chal and upsides wl over 2f out to over 1f out: one pce after* **11/1**
1 **4** *1 3/4* **Faversham**[22] 897 3-9-1 **80** .... PhilipRobinson 2 79
(M A Jarvis) *t.k.h: hld up in 4th: shkn up and nt qckn over 2f out: no imp after* **5/1**[3]
564- **5** *1 3/4* **Naughty By Nature**[224] 5279 3-8-8 **73** .... KFallon 5 68
(Sir Michael Stoute) *b.bkwd: trckd ldng pair: rdn and no rspnse 2f out: wknd fnl f* **3/1**[2]

2m 11.94s (1.70) **Going Correction** +0.075s/f (Good) **5** Ran SP% **111.1**
Speed ratings (Par 102):96,94,94,92,91
CSF £9.77 TOTE £2.00: £1.30, £2.70; EX 8.10 Place 6 £31.83, Place 5 £27.72.
Owner Mrs R J Jacobs **Bred** Newsells Park Stud Limited **Trained** Middleham Moor, N Yorks

FOCUS
Just a fair three-year-old handicap, and the winner may not have needed to reproduce his Newmarket form.

NOTEBOOK
Linas Selection, due to go up 6lb for his highly pleasing second to Papal Bull in a good-looking handicap at Newmarket, made the running again and gradually wound it up to ultimately win with a little bit up his sleeve. There may be even more to come on a slightly kinder surface, and he is one to keep on-side. (op 4-5 tchd 11-10 in a place)
Salute The General ◆ posted a most encouraging seasonal reappearance, especially as many of his yard's horses have been needing their first outing. He will no doubt improve for this experience and he could well pick up a fair prize off this sort of mark during the summer. (op 20-1)
Tumbleweed Glory(IRE) had the benefit of a previous outing on the All-Weather at Kempton a week ago, and certainly settled better on this occasion. He moved up to challenge the winner and may have nosed fractionally ahead, but had nothing left for the final climb to the line. There is clearly a race in him, and it will be interesting to see if he is ridden with a little more restraint in future. (op 14-1)
Faversham refused to settle early on but momentarily threatened to make a move in the straight, before looking a little bit tentative on the quick ground and in the end proving disappointing. He may have more to offer back on slower ground. (op 9-2 tchd 11-2)
Naughty By Nature, making his seasonal and handicap debut, could only offer the one pace under pressure and appeared to get tired in the final furlong. He needed the run, but it would still have been nice to see a little more. (op 7-2)
T/Plt: £97.90 to a £1 stake. Pool: £57,896.20. 431.65 winning tickets. T/Qpdt: £44.10 to a £1 stake. Pool: £3,152.80. 52.90 winning tickets. JN

1223 WOLVERHAMPTON (A.W) (L-H)
Friday, April 28

OFFICIAL GOING: Standard
Wind: Moderate, against Weather: Cloudy with sunny spells

1271 BETFRED MILLION APPRENTICE (S) STKS 1m 4f 50y(P)
2:10 (2:11) (Class 6) 4-Y-O+ **£2,388** (£705; £352) **Stalls** Low

Form RPR
4343 **1** **Chater Knight (IRE)**[52] 607 5-9-0 56 ....(p) JamieHamblett(5) 4 58
(R A Harris) *trckd ldrs: racd keenly: rdn to ld and hung lft fr over 1f out: r.o* **3/1**[1]
5142 **2** *1 1/4* **York Cliff**[21] 911 8-9-5 56 .... TolleyDean 9 57+
(W M Brisbourne) *dwlt: sn pushed along in rr: hdwy over 3f out: rdn over 1f out: styng on whn hmpd ins fnl f: nt rcvr* **3/1**[1]
6340 **3** *1 1/4* **Molly's Secret**[25] 857 8-8-8 45 ....(p) RonanKeogh 10 43
(Miss S J Wilton) *a.p: led over 2f out: hdd and hmpd over 1f out: styd on same pce* **14/1**
660- **4** *nk* **Teutonic (IRE)**[33] 6691 5-8-8 30 .... ThomasO'Brien 3 43
(R F Fisher) *s.i.s: hld up: hdwy 5f out: styd on same pce appr fnl f* **50/1**
5400 **5** *1 3/4* **Kirkhammerton (IRE)**[33] 603 4-8-9 49 ....(v) JemmaMarshall(3) 5 45
(M J Polglase) *led over 9f: styd on same pce appr fnl f* **8/1**[3]
0/35 **6** *18* **Bhutan (IRE)**[21] 904 11-8-8 47 .... WilliamCarson(5) 7 16
(Jim Best) *chsd ldr: rdn and ev ch over 2f out: sn wknd* **10/1**
0043 **7** *2* **Paso Doble**[21] 904 8-9-5 60 .... JamesMillman 11 19
(B R Millman) *hld up: n.d* **8/1**[3]
0500 **8** *16* **Rythm N Rhyme (IRE)**[30] 791 7-8-8 40 .... LukeMorris(5) 12 —
(John A Harris) *chsd ldrs: rdn 1/2-way: wknd 4f out* **33/1**
00 **9** *shd* **King Of Scots**[18] 937 5-8-8 .... JosephWalsh(5) 1 —
(R J Price) *hld up: rdn and wknd 4f out* **100/1**
0-40 **10** *3 1/2* **Venetian Romance (IRE)**[3] 1224 5-8-3 40 ....(p) SophieDoyle(5) 8 —
(M R Bosley) *mid-div: hdwy 8f out: wknd over 5f out* **25/1**
0000 **11** *14* **Age Of Kings (USA)**[17] 965 4-8-12 60 ....(b[1]) AshleyHamblett 6 —
(A B Haynes) *plld hrd and prom: rdn and wknd 4f out* **11/2**[2]
05- **12** *1/2* **Oberon's Prize**[257] 4388 4-8-6 ow4 .... TJHowell(10) 2 —
(V Smith) *s.i.s: hld up: a bhd* **20/1**

2m 39.79s (-2.63) **Going Correction** -0.125s/f (Stan)
WFA 4 from 5yo+ 1lb **12** Ran SP% **117.9**
Speed ratings (Par 101):103,102,101,101,99 87,86,75,75,73 64,63
CSF £10.44 TOTE £3.30: £1.50, £1.50, £3.00; EX 12.30 TRIFECTA Not won..There was no bid for the winner.
Owner www.gardenshedracing.com **Bred** John McLoughlin **Trained** Earlswood, Monmouths
■ Stewards' Enquiry : Jemma Marshall one-day ban: failed to keep straight from stalls (May 9)
Jamie Hamblett four-day ban: careless riding (May 9-12)

FOCUS
A very modest seller confined to apprentices who had not ridden more than ten winners coming into this. The form look sound but is limited by the proximity of the fourth.
Venetian Romance(IRE) Official explanation: jockey said, regarding the running and riding, mare is difficult and tends to lose interest in her races, adding that she rode the mare vigorously approaching winning post on first circuit to ensure that she did not drop herself out, and she assured the panel that she was totally aware of the distance of the race

1272 BETFRED MILLION MAIDEN CLAIMING STKS 5f 20y(P)
2:45 (2:46) (Class 6) 3-Y-O+ **£2,730** (£806; £403) **Stalls** Low

Form RPR
05-6 **1** **Limited Magician**[99] 144 5-8-10 30 ....(v) RobbieFitzpatrick 8 50
(C Smith) *mid-div: hdwy 1/2-way: rdn to ld wl ins fnl f: jst hld on* **50/1**
0-56 **2** *shd* **Sarah's Art (IRE)**[31] 779 3-8-3 40 ....(b[1]) ChrisCatlin 10 49
(N A Callaghan) *in rr: rdn over 1f out: r.o ins fnl f: jst failed* **14/1**
50-0 **3** *1 1/4* **Chiselled (IRE)**[16] 978 4-9-1 62 .... PatCosgrave 5 50
(K R Burke) *chsd ldr: rdn to ld and edgd lft over 1f out: hdd wl ins fnl f* **3/1**[2]
0030 **4** *hd* **Danish Blues (IRE)**[21] 901 3-8-13 69 ....(p) NCallan 6 54
(N P Littmoden) *trckd ldrs: rdn and ev ch ins fnl f: nt run on* **11/4**[1]
6403 **5** *1 1/4* **Katie Killane**[27] 870 4-8-12 40 ow2 .... DaneO'Neill 3 42
(M Wellings) *chsd ldrs: rdn over 1f out: n.m.r: styd on same pce* **8/1**
00-4 **6** *1 3/4* **The Salwick Flyer (IRE)**[7] 1126 3-8-13 54 .... FergalLynch 1 43
(A Berry) *mid-div: sn pushed along: styd on ins fnl f: nt trble ldrs* **9/2**[3]
0/00 **7** *2 1/2* **Kussharro**[25] 853 5-8-10 35 ....(t) EdwardCreighton(3) 4 28
(Mrs L J Young) *s.s: outpcd: nvr nrr* **33/1**
P-00 **8** *3/4* **Mind That Fox**[6] 1150 4-9-5 .... MickyFenton 2 31
(T Wall) *led over 3f: wknd ins fnl f* **10/1**

0-00 **9** *1 ¼* **Cayman Mischief**[77] [360] 6-8-1 40..................(b[1]) GemmaAnderson(7) 9 16
(James Moffatt) *mid-div: hdwy 1/2-way: hung rt and wknd 2f out: hung lft over 1f out* **100/1**
0-60 **10** *10* **Champagne Moment**[30] [796] 3-7-12 58..................... MatthewHenry 7 —
(V Smith) *sn outpcd* **7/1**
62.49 secs (-0.33) **Going Correction** -0.125s/f (Stan)
WFA 3 from 4yo+ 10lb **10** Ran SP% **115.1**
Speed ratings (Par 101):97,96,94,94,92 89,85,84,82,66
CSF £620.72 TOTE £53.60: £6.90, £2.60, £1.60; EX 206.80 TRIFECTA Not won..
Owner Nicholas Baines **Bred** P And Mrs Russell **Trained** Temple Bruer, Lincs
■ Stewards' Enquiry : Gemma Anderson caution: careless riding
FOCUS
A poor maiden claimer, but a cracking finish, although the form looks shaky. Unusually for this sharp five furlongs, the principals both came from well off the pace having both started from wide draws.
Champagne Moment Official explanation: jockey said filly sustained a back injury

1273 BETFRED MILLION H'CAP 7f 32y(P)
3:20 (3:22) (Class 6) (0-60,60) 4-Y-O+ **£2,730** (£806; £403) **Stalls** High

Form RPR
0030 **1** **Iced Diamond (IRE)**[11] [1057] 7-9-0 **56**........................... JamieSpencer 7 66
(W M Brisbourne) *hld up: hdwy over 2f out: r.o to ld wl ins fnl f* **8/1**
2003 **2** *1* **Taranaki**[3] [1209] 8-9-1 **57**... SebSanders 4 64
(P D Cundell) *chsd ldrs: led over 1f out: sn rdn and edgd rt: edgd lft and hdd wl ins fnl f* **4/1**[1]
1-40 **3** *¾* **Edin Burgher (FR)**[11] [1057] 5-8-13 **55**............................ SamHitchcott 3 60
(T T Clement) *hld up: hdwy over 2f out: rdn over 1f out: r.o* **4/1**[1]
05-4 **4** *1* **Arian's Lad**[5] [1165] 5-8-11 **53**... FrancisFerris 6 56
(B Palling) *chsd ldrs: rdn and ev ch over 1f out: edgd rt and no ex ins fnl f* **8/1**
3422 **5** *1 ¾* **Beneking**[21] [903] 6-8-11 **56**...............................(p) EdwardCreighton(3) 12 54
(D Burchell) *chsd ldrs: led over 4f out: rdn and hdd over 1f out: no ex* **10/1**
0624 **6** *½* **Miskina**[21] [902] 5-9-1 **57**... ShaneKelly 5 54
(W M Brisbourne) *mid-div: hdwy 1/2-way: rdn over 1f out: styd on same pce* **13/2**[3]
2103 **7** *¾* **Golden Spectrum (IRE)**[18] [953] 7-8-8 **57**..................(b) TolleyDean(7) 2 52
(R A Harris) *s.i.s: outpcd: styd on ins fnl f: nrst fin* **6/1**[2]
5000 **8** *3* **I Wish**[27] [837] 8-8-11 **53**.. PaulFitzsimons 9 40
(Miss J R Tooth) *mid-div: rdn 1/2-way: hdwy over 2f out: wknd over 1f out* **20/1**
0500 **9** *2* **Shannon Arms (USA)**[11] [1057] 5-8-13 **60**................(p) JamesDoyle(5) 11 42
(P Howling) *w ldrs: led 6f out: hdd over 4f out: rdn and wknd over 1f out* **16/1**
-000 **10** *8* **Danielle's Lad**[52] [606] 10-9-1 **57**.............................(b) FergusSweeney 10 18
(B Palling) *mid-div: sn drvn along: wknd 2f out* **16/1**
000- **11** *½* **Mirage Prince (IRE)**[314] [2719] 4-9-1 **60**.................... PatrickMathers(3) 8 20
(D Shaw) *sn outpcd* **50/1**
00-0 **12** *1 ½* **Geordie Dancer (IRE)**[16] [977] 4-9-2 **58**.......................(p) FergalLynch 1 14
(A Berry) *led 1f: chsd ldrs tl wknd 1/2-way* **25/1**
1m 29.66s (-0.74) **Going Correction** -0.125s/f (Stan) **12** Ran SP% **121.3**
Speed ratings (Par 101):99,97,97,95,93 93,92,89,86,77 77,75
CSF £40.14 CT £151.87 TOTE £7.20: £1.80, £1.80, £1.60; EX 38.00 Trifecta £178.60 Pool: £389.91 - 1.55 winning tickets..
Owner Gary Dewhurst **Bred** Mrs Kathleen McElroy **Trained** Great Ness, Shropshire
FOCUS
Plenty of front-runners in this line-up, so the pace was always likely to be strong and so it proved with a four-horse war for the early lead involving Shannon Arms, Geordie Dancer, Beneking and Arian's Lad. The form is modest but sound enough.
Geordie Dancer(IRE) Official explanation: jockey said gelding hung right-handed

1274 BETFREDPOKER.COM MAIDEN STKS 7f 32y(P)
3:55 (3:58) (Class 5) 3-Y-O **£3,238** (£963; £481; £240) **Stalls** High

Form RPR
2- **1** **Juror (USA)**[261] [4262] 3-9-3 .... RobertWinston 10 65+
(Sir Michael Stoute) *chsd ldr 6f out: led 2f out: r.o* **8/15**[1]
0-4 **2** *¾* **Captain Xaar (FR)**[16] [981] 3-9-3 .... JamieSpencer 6 63+
(J R Fanshawe) *trckd ldrs: rdn to chse wnr fnl f: r.o* **11/4**[2]
06 **3** *3 ½* **Postage (USA)**[35] [710] 3-8-12 ....(p) JamesDoyle(5) 9 54
(K A Morgan) *sn led: rdn and hdd 2f out: styd on same pce fnl f* **66/1**
0-0 **4** *2 ½* **Maidford (IRE)**[17] [971] 3-8-12 .... FergusSweeney 5 42
(M Meade) *chsd ldrs: rdn over 2f out: wknd over 1f out* **150/1**
00 **5** *¾* **Grand Palace (IRE)**[3] [1218] 3-9-0 .... PatrickMathers(3) 3 45
(D Shaw) *hld up: rdn over 2f out: styd on ins fnl f: nrst fin* **66/1**
00- **6** *½* **Emily's Pet (IRE)**[130] [6610] 3-9-3 .... DaneO'Neill 1 44
(B W Duke) *hld up: styd on ins fnl f: nvr nrr* **100/1**
7 *shd* **Tranos (USA)** 3-9-3 .... NickyMackay 8 44+
(L M Cumani) *s.s: styd on ins fnl f: nvr nrr* **16/1**
8 *½* **Plush** 3-9-3 .... SebSanders 4 42+
(Sir Mark Prescott) *s.s: swvd lft sn after s: styd on ins fnl f: nvr nrr* **14/1**[3]
-600 **9** *½* **Nilsatisoptimum (USA)**[2] [1232] 3-9-3 55........................... JimmyQuinn 2 41
(M Mullineaux) *prom: rdn and lost pl 1/2-way: wknd over 1f out* **33/1**
10 *1 ¼* **Squirrel Tail** 3-9-3 .... GrahamGibbons 7 38
(E S McMahon) *s.s: hdwy 4f out: wknd over 2f out* **66/1**
-430 **11** *6* **Next Ness (IRE)**[53] [604] 3-9-3 56.................................... FrancisNorton 12 22
(R F Fisher) *plld hrd and prom: rdn over 2f out: sn wknd* **25/1**
1m 29.79s (-0.61) **Going Correction** -0.125s/f (Stan) **11** Ran SP% **117.4**
Speed ratings (Par 98):98,97,93,90,89 88,88,88,87,86 79
CSF £2.02 TOTE £1.60: £1.10, £1.30, £6.90; EX 2.40 Trifecta £49.20 Pool: £576.01 - 8.31 winning tickets..
Owner Highclere Thoroughbred Racing XXVII **Bred** Waterville Lake Stable **Trained** Newmarket, Suffolk
FOCUS
An interesting maiden with several big Newmarket yards represented, but very few ever got into this and the first four were always up with the pace. The winning time was fractionally slower than the preceding handicap and the form looks banded grade apart from the first three.
Maidford(IRE) Official explanation: jockey said filly hung left-handed
Next Ness(IRE) Official explanation: jockey said gelding hung right-handed

1275 BETFREDPOKER.COM H'CAP 7f 32y(P)
4:25 (4:26) (Class 5) (0-75,75) 4-Y-O+ **£3,886** (£1,156; £577; £288) **Stalls** High

Form RPR
4043 **1** **Parkview Love (USA)**[7] [1123] 5-8-9 **69**..................(v) PatrickMathers(3) 3 77
(D Shaw) *chsd ldrs: led over 5f out: hdd over 2f out: rallied to ld over 1f out: r.o* **6/1**[3]
0034 **2** *nk* **Island Rapture**[20] [915] 6-8-12 **69**.................................... JamieSpencer 2 76
(J A R Toller) *led: hdd over 5f out: chsd ldrs: rdn over 1f out: hung lft ins fnl f: r.o* **5/1**[2]
-420 **3** *½* **Hits Only Cash**[17] [970] 4-9-0 **71**....................................... JimmyQuinn 11 77
(J Pearce) *hld up: plld hrd: hdwy over 1f out: r.o wl* **14/1**
00-0 **4** *¾* **Play The Ball (USA)**[48] [632] 4-9-2 **73**............................ NickyMackay 1 77
(G A Butler) *chsd ldrs: lost pl over 5f out: hdwy over 2f out: rdn and hung rt over 1f out: r.o* **16/1**
103- **5** *shd* **What-A-Dancer (IRE)**[256] [4416] 9-9-2 **73**...................(p) RobertWinston 7 77
(D J S Ffrench Davis) *s.i.s: hld up: hdwy over 1f out: r.o* **16/1**
5240 **6** *1 ¼* **Lincolneurocruiser**[27] [826] 4-8-8 **72**............... RussellKennemore(7) 12 72
(Mrs N Macauley) *chsd ldr: led over 2f out: rdn and hdd over 1f out: no ex ins fnl f* **25/1**
0200 **7** *shd* **General Feeling (IRE)**[27] [826] 5-9-4 **75**......................... GeorgeBaker 10 75
(M Mullineaux) *hld up: r.o ins fnl f: nvr nrr* **16/1**
050- **8** *½* **Miss Meggy**[194] [5923] 4-9-4 **75**...................................(p) TomEaves 4 74
(Miss J A Camacho) *prom: lost pl 1/2-way: n.d after* **16/1**
2540 **9** *shd* **Stoic Leader (IRE)**[12] [1035] 6-8-11 **71**................................. DNolan(3) 5 70
(R F Fisher) *hld up: rdn over 1f out: n.d* **12/1**
33- **10** *2 ½* **Mozakhraf (USA)**[206] [5687] 4-8-7 **64**.. NCallan 9 56
(K A Ryan) *prom: racd keenly: rdn over 2f out: wknd fnl f: eased* **13/8**[1]
3335 **11** *1 ½* **Mission Affirmed (USA)**[15] [1002] 5-8-7 **64**.............(b) AdrianMcCarthy 8 52
(R A Harris) *prom: rdn 1/2-way: hung rt and wknd over 1f out* **12/1**
-010 **12** *16* **Mandarin Spirit (IRE)**[34] [721] 6-9-0 **71**.......................(b) OscarUrbina 6 18
(G C H Chung) *unruly in stalls: rrd s and rel to r: a wl bhd* **14/1**
1m 29.13s (-1.27) **Going Correction** -0.125s/f (Stan) **12** Ran SP% **125.1**
Speed ratings (Par 103):102,101,101,100,100 98,98,98,97,95 93,75
CSF £38.26 CT £423.69 TOTE £7.90: £2.10, £2.30, £3.90; EX 27.40 Trifecta £167.10 Part won. Pool: £235.36 - 0.75 winning tickets..
Owner Danethorpe Racing Ltd **Bred** Mark Johnston Racing Ltd **Trained** Danethorpe, Notts
FOCUS
A competitive little handicap and once again those that raced prominently held an advantage. The winning time was over half a second faster than the previous two races over the same trip, but the form may not prove that solid.

1276 BETFREDCASINO.COM H'CAP 1m 141y(P)
5:00 (5:00) (Class 6) (0-60,60) 4-Y-O+ **£2,730** (£806; £403) **Stalls** Low

Form RPR
-035 **1** **The Bonus King**[4] [1186] 6-9-3 **59**..................................... JamieSpencer 2 69
(J Jay) *hld up: hdwy over 2f out: r.o to ld wl ins fnl f* **7/2**[1]
0-00 **2** *¾* **Primeshade Promise**[5] [1204] 5-8-10 **52**........................ MichaelTebbutt 3 60
(D Burchell) *a.p: chsd ldr 2f out: rdn over 1f out: styd on* **14/1**
400- **3** *shd* **Terenzium (IRE)**[196] [5883] 4-8-1 **50**....................... AshleyHamblett(7) 8 58
(L M Cumani) *chsd ldr: led over 6f out: rdn over 1f out: hdd and unable qck ins fnl f* **9/1**
00-2 **4** *½* **Bond Diamond**[9] [1073] 9-9-4 **60**.. MickyFenton 1 67
(P T Midgley) *hld up: hdwy over 1f out: hmpd ins fnl f: nvr able to chal* **12/1**
21-6 **5** *shd* **Kings Topic (USA)**[18] [955] 6-9-4 **60**...................................... PatDobbs 11 67
(A B Haynes) *hld up: hdwy over 3f out: rdn and hung lft over 1f out: styd on* **7/1**[3]
045- **6** *1 ½* **Band**[127] [6654] 6-9-0 **56**... SebSanders 7 60
(E S McMahon) *hld up: hdwy over 2f out: rdn over 1f out: styd on same pce ins fnl f* **5/1**[2]
1000 **7** *2* **Gallego**[6] [1152] 4-8-11 **53**.. ShaneKelly 13 53
(R J Price) *hld up: rdn over 2f out: styd on ins fnl f: nt trble ldrs* **10/1**
6040 **8** *nk* **Mister Benji**[15] [1002] 7-9-3 **59**... DarrenWilliams 4 58
(B P J Baugh) *hld up: rdn over 2f out: n.d* **14/1**
5000 **9** *1 ½* **Lucius Verrus (USA)**[18] [950] 6-8-13 **58**..............(v) PatrickMathers(3) 6 54
(D Shaw) *prom: rdn over 3f out: wknd over 1f out* **14/1**
-635 **10** *2* **Choristar**[21] [906] 5-8-3 **52**................................... RussellKennemore(7) 12 44
(J Mackie) *chsd ldrs: rdn and ev ch over 2f out: wknd over 1f out* **8/1**
600- **11** *3* **Newcorp Lad**[172] [6283] 6-8-13 **55**.. NCallan 5 40
(Mrs G S Rees) *sn led: hdd over 6f out: wknd over 1f out* **16/1**
2450 **12** *2* **Preskani**[18] [950] 4-8-10 **57**...................................(p) DuranFentiman(5) 10 38
(Mrs N Macauley) *hld up: n.d* **25/1**
10-0 **13** *½* **Ferrara Flame (IRE)**[15] [1002] 4-8-13 **55**............................... TomEaves 9 35
(R Brotherton) *s.s: a in rr* **40/1**
1m 50.05s (-1.71) **Going Correction** -0.125s/f (Stan) **13** Ran SP% **121.5**
Speed ratings (Par 101):102,101,101,100,100 99,97,97,96,94 91,89,89
CSF £55.84 CT £433.38 TOTE £4.30: £2.20, £5.40, £3.80; EX 111.30 TRIFECTA Not won. Place 6 £63.39, Place 5 £43.08.
Owner Mrs Mo Done & Mrs Janet Martin **Bred** Red House Stud **Trained** Newmarket, Suffolk
■ Stewards' Enquiry : Pat Dobbs one-day ban: careless riding (May 9)
FOCUS
A low-grade, but competitive handicap run at a solid pace and it resulted in a victory for the sponsors. The form looks pretty sound with the runner-up and fifth to their marks.
Gallego Official explanation: jockey said gelding moved badly
T/Plt: £43.20 to a £1 stake. Pool: £37,837.20. 637.95 winning tickets. T/Qpdt: £7.80 to a £1 stake. Pool: £3,271.50. 309.20 winning tickets. CR

HAYDOCK (L-H)
Saturday, April 29
OFFICIAL GOING: Good (good to firm in places)
Wind: Almost nil Weather: Fine

1278 EBF FAREWELL TO RON MAIDEN FILLIES' STKS 5f
5:45 (5:47) (Class 5) 2-Y-O **£3,238** (£963; £481; £240) **Stalls** Centre

Form RPR
4 **1** **Amber Valley**[12] [1053] 2-9-0 .... NCallan 1 75
(K A Ryan) *mde all: rdn 2f out: r.o* **1/1**[1]
2 *1* **Feelin Foxy** 2-8-11 .... PatrickMathers(3) 4 71
(D Shaw) *s.s: sn in tch: hdwy and hung lft over 1f out: ev ch ins fnl f: nt qckn towards fin* **12/1**
6 **3** *4* **Esprit D'Amour (IRE)**[10] [1074] 2-9-0 .... RichardMullen 7 57
(T D Easterby) *wnt rt s: chsd wnr: rdn over 2f out: ev ch over 1f out: wknd ins fnl f* **13/2**[3]
4 *½* **Fongs Gazelle** 2-9-0 .... RobertWinston 3 55+
(M Johnston) *chsd ldrs: rn green: rdn over 2f out: wknd over 1f out* **9/4**[2]
5 *3* **Galaxy Of Stars** 2-9-0 .... TomEaves 6 44
(D Shaw) *s.s: a outpcd* **14/1**

6 12 **Just Chrissie** 2-9-0 .... JosedeSouza 2 —
(G Fierro) *s.i.s: a outpcd* **25/1**

63.17 secs (1.10) **Going Correction** -0.075s/f (Good) **6** Ran SP% **112.3**
Speed ratings (Par 89):88,86,80,79,74 55
CSF £14.48 TOTE £2.00: £1.40, £2.10; EX 18.50.
Owner T G & Mrs M E Holdcroft **Bred** Bearstone Stud **Trained** Hambleton, N Yorks
■ A race run as a tribute to course inspector and ex-champion jump jockey Ron Barry, who was retiring.

FOCUS
A modest juvenile fillies' contest run 1.82 sec slower than the following handicap and little to go on form-wise.

NOTEBOOK
Amber Valley, a well-backed favourite, made all the running but was made to work hard to score. Her previous experience proved the decisive factor, but she will have to improve to follow up under a penalty. (op 6-4 tchd 13-8 in a place)
Feelin Foxy ◆, a half-sister to a couple of juvenile winners, looked as if the race would bring her on and gave the winner a race. She looks capable of picking up a similar contest with this experience behind her. (tchd 11-1)
Esprit D'Amour(IRE) improved on her debut on soft ground and looked a big danger to the winner before fading from over a furlong out. She may well find her best opportunities lie in nurseries later on. (op 6-1)
Fongs Gazelle was supported against the favourite but showed her inexperience in the race, running green and struggling to go the pace before keeping on in the closing stages. An extra furlong at least will be in her favour. (op 7-4)
Galaxy Of Stars, a stable companion of the runner-up, ran green and was soon outpaced. However, she kept on once finding her feet under a considerate ride, and should pay back that kindness in due course. (op 12-1)

1279 NORTHERN RACING DISCOUNT CARD H'CAP 5f
6:15 (6:17) (Class 5) (0-75,80) 3-Y-O **£3,238** (£963; £481; £240) **Stalls** Centre

Form RPR
61- **1** **Terentia**[206] 5696 3-8-13 **70** .... RichardMullen 4 86+
(E S McMahon) *a.p: rdn to ld over 1f out: r.o wl* **14/1**
4-02 **2** 3 **Scooby Dude (IRE)**[7] 1146 3-9-4 **80** .... DerekNolan(5) 7 85
(Ms Deborah J Evans) *chsd ldrs: rdn 2f out: edgd lft and wnt 2nd ins fnl f: nt pce of wnr* **13/2**[2]
0-43 **3** 3 1/2 **Highland Song (IRE)**[13] 1036 3-8-10 **67** .... FrancisNorton 12 59
(R F Fisher) *racd alone towards stands' side: chsd ldrs: rdn over 2f out: outpcd and edgd lft over 1f out* **7/1**[3]
2213 **4** 1/2 **Garlogs**[17] 988 3-8-10 **67** .... RobertWinston 5 58
(A Bailey) *led: rdn and hdd over 1f out: sn edgd lft: wknd ins fnl f* **7/2**[1]
066- **5** 3 **Mouchoir**[189] 6024 3-9-1 **75** ....(b) AmirQuinn(3) 10 55
(P J Makin) *s.i.s: chsd ldrs: rdn over 2f out: wknd over 1f out* **9/1**
02-6 **6** shd **Immaculate Red**[17] 988 3-8-8 **65** .... TomEaves 3 44
(R Bastiman) *dwlt and hmpd s: towards rr: rdn over 2f out: sme hdwy and hung rt ins fnl f: nt trble ldrs* **16/1**
020- **7** nk **Bernie's Beau (IRE)**[202] 5755 3-8-4 **68** .... RussellKennemore(7) 11 46
(R Hollinshead) *in tch: rdn 3f out: sn outpcd* **25/1**
540- **8** 1 1/4 **Newkeylets**[201] 5791 3-8-4 **61** oh8 .... PaulFessey 8 35
(I Semple) *dwlt: wnt rt s and bmpd: in rr: rdn over 2f out: swtchd lft over 1f out: hung lft ins fnl f: nt pce to chal* **33/1**
12-1 **9** 1 1/2 **Egyptian Lord**[112] 66 3-8-5 **69** .... RonanKeogh(7) 1 37
(Peter Grayson) *in tch: rdn and edgd rt over 2f out: wknd over 1f out* **15/2**
4535 **10** 1/2 **Amber Glory**[17] 988 3-8-8 **65** ....(b) NCallan 2 32
(K A Ryan) *prom: rdn 2f out: sn wknd* **11/1**
000 **11** 2 **Danethorpe (IRE)**[22] 901 3-8-1 **61** oh3 .... PatrickMathers(3) 6 20
(D Shaw) *s.i.s and wnt lft s: outpcd: hung lft whn n.d ins fnl f* **66/1**

61.35 secs (-0.72) **Going Correction** -0.075s/f (Good) 11 Ran SP% **99.0**
Speed ratings (Par 98):102,97,91,90,86 85,85,83,80,80 76
CSF £72.60 CT £442.94 TOTE £16.10: £3.40, £1.90, £2.30; EX 106.40.
Owner Dr Hugh Jones **Bred** Mrs F S Williams **Trained** Hopwas, Staffs
■ Fayr Sky was withdrawn after playing up in the stalls, deduction 15p in £.
■ Stewards' Enquiry : N Callan one-day ban: careless riding (May 10)

FOCUS
A fair handicap run at a decent gallop, much faster than the opening juvenile contest, and up with the pace was the place to be. The runner-up is the best guide to the form.
Mouchoir Official explanation: jockey said gelding had no more to give
Amber Glory Official explanation: jockey said filly had no more to give

1280 LLOYD MORRIS ELECTRICAL H'CAP 1m 30y
6:45 (6:46) (Class 4) (0-80,80) 4-Y-O+ **£6,477** (£1,927; £963; £481) **Stalls** Low

Form RPR
00-3 **1** **Jubilee Street (IRE)**[12] 1043 7-9-1 **77** .... PaulFessey 1 85
(Mrs A Duffield) *s.s and wnt rt s: midfield: rdn and hdwy over 2f out: led over 1f out: r.o* **11/2**[2]
101- **2** 1/2 **Along The Nile**[258] 4397 4-9-0 **76** .... JamieSpencer 16 83
(K G Reveley) *hld up: swtchd rt over 2f out: edgd lft and hdwy over 1f out: ev ch ins fnl f: nt qckn cl home* **5/1**[1]
0303 **3** 1 **Speed Dial Harry (IRE)**[7] 1143 4-8-11 **78** ....(v) AndrewElliott(5) 5 83
(K R Burke) *chsd ldrs: rdn over 1f out: styd on ins fnl f* **17/2**
-655 **4** nk **Boundless Prospect (USA)**[31] 800 7-9-2 **78** .... MickyFenton 17 82
(Miss Gay Kelleway) *towards rr: hdwy on wd outside over 2f out: rdn over 1f out: edgd lft ins fnl f: kpt on: nt pce of ldrs cl home* **12/1**
0030 **5** 3/4 **Anduril**[45] 641 5-8-12 **74** ....(b) FrancisNorton 2 76
(Miss M E Rowland) *racd keenly: chsd ldrs: rdn and ev ch over 1f out: nt qckn ins fnl f* **16/1**
-010 **6** 1/2 **Following Flow (USA)**[28] 826 4-8-7 **76** .... RussellKennemore(7) 4 77
(R Hollinshead) *s.s: in rr: hdwy and nt clr run 2f out: styd on ins fnl f* **50/1**
06-0 **7** 1 1/4 **Society Music (IRE)**[12] 1043 4-9-0 **76** .... PhillipMakin 9 78+
(M Dods) *midfield: hdwy whn nt clr run 3f out and over 1f out: kpt on ins fnl f: nvr rchd ldrs* **20/1**
4-10 **8** 3/4 **Mezuzah**[12] 1043 6-8-13 **78** .... PaulMulrennan(3) 3 75
(M W Easterby) *wnt rt s: hld up: hdwy over 2f out: rdn over 1f out: wknd wl ins fnl f* **12/1**
4330 **9** 2 **Always Esteemed (IRE)**[35] 726 6-9-1 **77** ....(b) NCallan 8 69
(K A Ryan) *led: rdn over 2f out: hdd over 1f out: wknd fnl f* **10/1**
150- **10** hd **Nevada Desert (IRE)**[154] 6437 6-8-13 **75** .... DeanMcKeown 13 66
(R M Whitaker) *prom: rdn and ev ch 2f out: wknd over 1f out* **16/1**
000- **11** 1 1/4 **European (ARG)**[259] 4360 6-9-1 **80** .... NelsonDeSouza(3) 15 69
(R M Beckett) *plld hrd: midfield: effrt and hung lft over 2f out: wknd over 1f out* **28/1**
10-0 **12** 1/2 **Dark Charm (FR)**[12] 1043 7-8-13 **75** .... PaulHanagan 7 62
(R A Fahey) *hld up: hdwy over 2f out: nt clr run over 1f out and ins fnl f: no imp after* **16/1**
2000 **13** 1 1/2 **General Feeling (IRE)**[1] 1275 5-8-13 **75** .... PatDobbs 6 59
(M Mullineaux) *s.s: in rr: rdn over 2f out: no imp* **20/1**
60-0 **14** nk **Sea Storm (IRE)**[13] 1035 8-8-12 **77** ....(p) DNolan(3) 14 60
(D R MacLeod) *chsd ldrs: rdn over 2f out: wkng whn n.m.r wl over 1f out* **33/1**
1403 **15** 1/2 **Alfonso**[13] 1035 5-8-13 **75** ....(b) TomEaves 12 57
(I Semple) *midfield: rdn and sme hdwy over 2f out: wknd over 1f out* **8/1**[3]
06-6 **16** 3/4 **Flighty Fellow (IRE)**[29] 815 6-9-3 **79** ....(b) TonyCulhane 10 59
(Miss J A Camacho) *stdd s: hld up: hdwy 2f out: wknd fnl f* **20/1**
443- **17** 2 1/2 **Qaasi (USA)**[245] 4768 4-8-5 **72** .... GregFairley(5) 11 47
(Mrs K Walton) *prom: rdn over 2f out: sn wknd* **12/1**

1m 42.42s (-3.09) **Going Correction** -0.375s/f (Firm) **17** Ran SP% **126.1**
Speed ratings (Par 105):100,99,98,98,97 96,95,94,92,92 91,91,89,89,88 87,85
CSF £30.73 CT £249.84 TOTE £5.60: £1.70, £1.40, £2.30, £3.10; EX 15.90.
Owner D W Holdsworth & J A McMahon **Bred** My Firebird Syndicate **Trained** Constable Burton, N Yorks

FOCUS
A fair handicap run at a reasonable gallop which resulted in a battle between those at the head of the market. The form is rated around the principals.
Dark Charm(FR) Official explanation: jockey said gelding was denied a clear run

1281 BROWNS MITSUBISHI H'CAP 1m 2f 120y
7:15 (7:16) (Class 4) (0-85,87) 4-Y-O+ **£6,477** (£1,927; £963; £481) **Stalls** High

Form RPR
56-0 **1** **Active Asset (IRE)**[31] 800 4-8-6 **73** .... RobertWinston 10 84
(M R Channon) *midfield: hdwy 3f out: led 2f out: edgd lft over 1f out: r.o* **10/1**
-051 **2** 2 **Prince Samos (IRE)**[7] 1133 4-9-6 **87** .... PatDobbs 6 94
(R Hannon) *in tch: rdn over 2f out: wnt 2nd over 1f out: kpt on* **6/1**[2]
00/0 **3** 1 **Blue Sky Thinking (IRE)**[14] 1017 7-9-3 **84** .... RichardMullen 2 89
(K R Burke) *in tch: rdn over 2f out: edgd lft over 1f out: kpt on same pce ins fnl f* **14/1**
2-00 **4** 3/4 **Instructor**[12] 1043 5-8-12 **79** .... PaulHanagan 12 83
(R A Fahey) *midfield: hdwy over 2f out: hmpd over 1f out: styd on ins fnl f* **16/1**
/00- **5** nk **Sunisa (IRE)**[84] 6621 5-8-12 **79** .... DaleGibson 5 82
(J Mackie) *hld up: rdn and hdwy over 2f out: kpt on same pce ins fnl f* **50/1**
35-2 **6** 4 **Shape Up (IRE)**[25] 867 6-8-12 **79** ....(b) PaulFessey 13 75
(R Craggs) *prom: rdn and ev ch 2f out: wknd over 1f out* **8/1**
623- **7** 3/4 **Goodbye Mr Bond**[182] 6147 6-9-1 **82** .... FrancisNorton 4 76+
(E J Alston) *hld up: pushed along 4f out: hdwy over 2f out: nt clr run over 1f out: one pce ins fnl f* **13/2**[3]
012- **8** nk **Sharp Reply (USA)**[305] 2998 4-9-2 **83** .... DeanMcKeown 3 77
(R M Whitaker) *midfield: rdn 2f out: no imp* **25/1**
030- **9** 1 **Kames Park (IRE)**[258] 4397 4-9-3 **84** .... TomEaves 1 76+
(I Semple) *s.s: in rr: swtchd lft 2f out: nt clr run ins fnl f: no imp* **10/1**
1312 **10** 1 **Eloquent Knight (USA)**[17] 983 4-8-8 **75** .... JamieSpencer 11 65
(W R Muir) *led: rdn and hdd 2f out: wknd over 1f out: btn whn n.m.r ins fnl f* **9/2**[1]
1346 **11** hd **Hawkit (USA)**[10] 1075 5-8-1 **71** oh5 .... NelsonDeSouza(3) 8 60
(A Bailey) *hld up: hdwy over 3f out: rdn over 2f out: wknd over 1f out* **14/1**
460- **12** 1 **Dancer's Serenade (IRE)**[204] 5715 4-9-2 **83** .... TonyCulhane 7 70
(T P Tate) *hld up: hdwy over 4f out: rdn over 3f out: wknd over 1f out* **6/1**[2]
0-00 **13** 13 **Habanero**[35] 404 5-9-3 **84** ....(t) MickyFenton 9 47
(Miss S J Wilton) *prom: rdn over 3f out: wknd over 2f out* **50/1**

2m 13.47s (-4.26) **Going Correction** -0.375s/f (Firm) **13** Ran SP% **116.4**
Speed ratings (Par 105):100,98,97,97,97 94,93,93,92,91 91,91,81
CSF £66.22 CT £842.96 TOTE £12.20: £3.90, £2.70, £4.70; EX 102.40.
Owner aAIM Racing Syndicate **Bred** Rathasker Stud **Trained** West Ilsley, Berks
■ Stewards' Enquiry : Richard Mullen one-day ban: careless riding (May 10)

FOCUS
Another fair handicap run 2.1 sec faster than the following race over the same trip, and the principals all raced close to the pace. The form looks solid and reliable, rated around the first two.
Instructor Official explanation: jockey said gelding was denied a clear run
Goodbye Mr Bond Official explanation: jockey said gelding was denied a clear run
Eloquent Knight(USA) Official explanation: jockey said colt lost its action
Habanero Official explanation: jockey said horse lost its action

1282 WARRINGTON GUARDIAN H'CAP 1m 2f 120y
7:45 (7:46) (Class 5) (0-75,75) 3-Y-O **£3,238** (£963; £481; £240) **Stalls** High

Form RPR
041- **1** **Idarah (USA)**[177] 6234 3-9-4 **75** .... RobertWinston 9 93+
(W J Haggas) *led after 1f: mde rest: clr over 1f out: easily* **4/6**[1]
1-15 **2** 7 **Reveur**[99] 160 3-8-12 **69** .... JamieSpencer 6 69
(M Mullineaux) *s.i.s: hld up: swtchd rt and hdwy over 2f out: wnt 2nd over 1f out: no ch w wnr* **8/1**[3]
000- **3** 1 1/2 **Cartoonist (IRE)**[178] 6228 3-8-1 **61** oh2 .... RichardThomas(3) 3 58
(A King) *cl up: rdn 3f out: btn 2f out* **11/2**[2]
14-0 **4** nk **Hearthstead Dancer (USA)**[8] 1122 3-9-4 **75** .... JoeFanning 8 71
(M Johnston) *prom: rdn 3f out: edgd lft 2f out: sn btn* **11/2**[2]
0-00 **5** 1 3/4 **Sweet Boulangere**[6] 1162 3-8-10 **67** ow1 .... PatDobbs 1 61
(R Hannon) *led for 1f: sn settled bhd ldrs: rdn and hdwy over 2f out: sn n.m.r and lost pl: eased whn n.d ins fnl furlog* **10/1**

2m 15.57s (-2.16) **Going Correction** -0.375s/f (Firm) **5** Ran SP% **111.0**
Speed ratings (Par 98):92,86,85,85,84
CSF £6.78 TOTE £1.70: £1.30, £2.20; EX 6.40.
Owner Hamdan Al Maktoum **Bred** Shadwell Farm LLC **Trained** Newmarket, Suffolk
■ Stewards' Enquiry : Joe Fanning caution: careless riding

FOCUS
A fair handicap made less competitive by the withdrawal of nearly half of the field, but a very easy winner, although the time was 2.1sec slower than the previous race over the same trip. The third sets the level for the form.

1283 ST HELENS STAR MAIDEN STKS 1m 3f 200y
8:15 (8:16) (Class 5) 3-Y-O **£3,238** (£963; £481; £240) **Stalls** High

Form RPR
4- **1** **Kassiopeia (IRE)**[190] 6007 3-8-12 .... TonyCulhane 2 83+
(M R Channon) *hld up: hdwy 4f out: led over 2f out: clr over 1f out: eased towards fin* **4/1**[3]
005- **2** 1 1/4 **Shipmaster**[227] 5228 3-9-3 70 .... JamieSpencer 1 82
(A King) *trckd ldrs: chsd ldr over 4f out: rdn and ev ch over 2f out: styd on same pce fnl f* **13/8**[1]
3 shd **Rainbow's Edge** 3-8-12 .... PaulHanagan 3 77
(R Charlton) *hld up: rdn whn hdwy and hung lft over 2f out: swtchd rt over 1f out: r.o ins fnl f* **8/1**

0-0 **4** *3* **Baltic Princess (FR)**^{9} [1100] 3-8-7 .... GregFairley$^{(5)}$ 8 72
(M Johnston) *led: hdd over 2f out: rdn whn hung lft over 1f out: one pce after* **20/1**

020- **5** *4* **Moonhawk**^{192} [5977] 3-9-3 78................ RobertWinston 5 71
(J Howard Johnson) *in tch: clsd 4f out: rdn and ev ch over 2f out: wknd ins fnl f* **7/2^{2}**

0- **6** *2* **Maysoor**^{176} [6246] 3-9-3 .... JoeFanning 6 67+
(M Johnston) *s.i.s: in rr: effrt over 4f out: wknd 2f out* **14/1**

05- **7** *3/4* **Hurry Up Helen (IRE)**^{195} [5919] 3-8-12 .... TomEaves 7 61
(Mrs L Stubbs) *hld up: niggled along and rn wd on bnd over 5f out: nvr on terms* **33/1**

0-5 **8** *3 1/2* **Lord Adonis (IRE)**^{22} [909] 3-9-3 .... MickyFenton 4 61
(M J Attwater) *prom tl wknd over 4f out* **66/1**

2m 32.59s (-2.40) **Going Correction** -0.375s/f (Firm) **8** Ran SP% **107.3**
Speed ratings (Par 98):93,92,92,90,87 86,85,83
CSF £9.45 TOTE £3.50: £1.10, £1.50, £2.10; EX 6.50 Place 6 £59.12, Place 5 £38.85.
Owner Jackie & George Smith **Bred** G A E And J Smith (bloodstock) **Trained** West Ilsley, Berks

FOCUS
A fair maiden run at a steady early gallop. The winner is value for more than the official margin and can rate higher.
T/Plt: £42.10 to a £1 stake. Pool: £43,310.80. 750.10 winning tickets. T/Qpdt: £4.70 to a £1 stake. Pool: £3,588.90. 553.50 winning tickets. DO

^{892}LEICESTER (R-H)
Saturday, April 29

OFFICIAL GOING: Good (good to soft in places)
Wind: Light, against Weather: Cloudy with sunny spells

1284 FOSTERS SUPERCHILLED MEDIAN AUCTION MAIDEN STKS 5f 2y
2:20 (2:20) (Class 5) 2-Y-O **£3,886** (£1,156; £577; £288) **Stalls** Low

Form RPR

4 **1** **Fool Me (IRE)**^{23} [892] 2-9-3 .... RichardMullen 8 83
(E S McMahon) *broke wl: chsd ldrs: stmbld wl over 2f out: sn rdn: led over 1f out: r.o* **15/8^{1}**

0 **2** *1/2* **Cavort (IRE)**^{12} [1046] 2-8-12 .... SebSanders 11 76+
(Pat Eddery) *a.p: rdn to chse wnr fnl f: r.o* **16/1**

3 *2 1/2* **Blue Monkey (IRE)** 2-9-3 .... JamieSpencer 7 72
(M L W Bell) *s.i.s: sn pushed along in rr: hdwy over 1f out: styd on same pce fnl f* **3/1^{2}**

0 **4** *3 1/2* **Tom Paris**^{23} [892] 2-9-3 .... KFallon 4 60+
(W R Muir) *s.i.s: in rr whn hmpd over 3f out: nt clr run over 1f out: swtchd rt: r.o: nt rch ldrs* **10/1**

0 **5** *1/2* **Mystery World**^{10} [1074] 2-9-3 .... KDarley 1 58
(M Johnston) *chsd ldr: led 2f out: rdn and hdd over 1f out: wknd ins fnl f* **11/1**

6 *1* **Tarif (IRE)** 2-9-3 .... MickyFenton 12 54
(Mrs P Sly) *unruly in stalls: outpcd: r.o ins fnl f: nvr nrr* **40/1**

7 *1/2* **Persian Fox (IRE)** 2-8-12 .... DerekNolan$^{(5)}$ 6 52
(G A Huffer) *hld up: nvr trbld ldrs* **33/1**

8 *1* **Merlins Quest** 2-9-3 .... PaulFitzsimons 9 49+
(J M Bradley) *s.s: sn pushed along in rr: n.d* **40/1**

25 **9** *1 1/4* **Suhayl Star (IRE)**^{8} [1113] 2-9-3 .... TedDurcan 5 44+
(M R Channon) *mid-div: rdn 1/2-way: wknd over 1f out* **6/1^{3}**

5 **10** *1 1/4* **Little Tommy Fella**^{17} [987] 2-9-3 .... J-PGuillambert 10 40
(S C Williams) *prom: rdn over 3f out: wknd wl over 1f out* **20/1**

0 **11** *nk* **Tagula Music (IRE)**^{18} [961] 2-8-12 .... FrancisFerris 2 34
(B Palling) *sn led: hdd 2f out: sn edgd lft and wknd* **33/1**

63 **12** *5* **Our Toy Soldier**^{10} [1074] 2-9-3 .... PaulEddery 3 21+
(B Smart) *prom: rdn over 3f out: wkng whn hung rt and hmpd over 1f out* **16/1**

62.78 secs (1.88) **Going Correction** +0.175s/f (Good) **12** Ran SP% **118.8**
Speed ratings (Par 92):91,90,86,80,79 78,77,75,73,71 71,63
CSF £33.20 TOTE £3.00: £1.30, £2.50, £1.90; EX 24.70.
Owner J C Fretwell **Bred** David Barry **Trained** Hopwas, Staffs

FOCUS
Probably just a modest maiden, but little to gop on form-wise, although the time suggests it could be higher.

NOTEBOOK
Fool Me(IRE), green when fourth on his debut here, showed the benefit of that experience and won a shade cosily. This did not look a great maiden but he should make a nursery sort in time. (op 10-3 tchd 7-4 and 7-2 in places)
Cavort(IRE) was slowly away on her debut but knew a lot more this time and was always towards the fore. Her breeding suggests she will come into her own over further. (op 14-1)
Blue Monkey(IRE), a half-brother to Araafa, a seven-furlong winner and very smart performer at two, was coltish beforehand. Green in the race itself, he was running on towards the end of the race without being given a hard time, and he looks sure to improve a deal for this outing. (tchd 10-3)
Tom Paris did not get the best of runs and looks capable of better than the bare form suggests. Nurseries later in the season look likely to be his game eventually. (op 9-1)
Mystery World showed good speed from the rails draw and is another likely to do better later in the season when nurseries become an option. (op 8-1)
Tarif(IRE), a cheap purchase, was fractious in the stalls and struggled with the early pace before running on late in the day. (op 50-1)

1285 JOHN SMITH'S EXTRA SMOOTH H'CAP 5f 218y
2:55 (2:55) (Class 4) (0-85,83) 4-Y-0+
£6,232 (£1,866; £933; £467; £233; £117) **Stalls** Low

Form RPR

31-4 **1** **Swinbrook (USA)**^{18} [970] 5-9-1 **80**................ (v) SebSanders 3 97
(J A R Toller) *hld up: hdwy over 2f out: led over 1f out: rdn clr* **7/2^{2}**

21-0 **2** *2 1/2* **Zidane**^{19} [949] 4-8-7 **72**................ JamieSpencer 8 81+
(J R Fanshawe) *s.i.s: hld up: swtchd rt and hdwy over 1f out: sn ev ch: styd on same pce ins fnl f* **3/1^{1}**

2532 **3** *3/4* **Lake Chini (IRE)**^{19} [949] 4-8-12 **77**................ (p) PhilipRobinson 10 84
(M A Jarvis) *chsd ldrs: rdn over 2f out: led briefly over 1f out: no ex ins fnl f* **13/2^{3}**

-300 **4** *3/4* **Sir Desmond**^{18} [970] 8-8-9 **74**................ (p) KFallon 5 79
(Rae Guest) *hld up: hdwy over 1f out: nt rch ldrs* **16/1**

040- **5** *1 1/4* **Kingscross**^{190} [6014] 8-9-2 **81**................ FergusSweeney 14 82
(M Blanshard) *hld up: hdwy over 1f out: nt rch ldrs* **25/1**

12-0 **6** *nk* **Pure Imagination (IRE)**^{18} [970] 5-9-0 **79**................ RyanMoore 7 79
(J M Bradley) *s.i.s: hld up: r.o ins fnl f: nrst fin* **20/1**

00-5 **7** *3* **Capricho (IRE)**^{18} [970] 9-8-12 **77**................ PaulDoe 2 75+
(J Akehurst) *s.i.s: hld up: hdwy over 2f out: nt clr run over 1f out: styd on same pce* **16/1**

-402 **8** *1 1/2* **Willhewiz**^{18} [967] 6-8-12 **77**................ DaneO'Neill 6 64
(M S Saunders) *led: rdn: edgd rt and hdd over 1f out: wknd ins fnl f* **14/1**

00-6 **9** *1 1/4* **Bond Boy**^{13} [1031] 9-9-1 **80**................ TonyCulhane 4 63
(B Smart) *mid-div: rdn 3f out: hdwy and hung rt over 2f out: wknd fnl f* **33/1**

41-4 **10** *nk* **Raymond's Pride**^{12} [1042] 6-8-13 **83**................ (b) AndrewMullen$^{(5)}$ 17 65
(K A Ryan) *w ldr: rdn over 1f out: wknd fnl f* **14/1**

00-0 **11** *1 1/2* **Briannsta (IRE)**^{12} [1042] 4-9-4 **83**................ SamHitchcott 12 60
(M R Channon) *prom: rdn over 2f out: wknd fnl f* **40/1**

00-0 **12** *shd* **Distant Times**^{23} [898] 5-8-4 **69** oh1................ (b) JamieMackay 11 46
(T D Easterby) *chsd ldrs: rdn over 2f out: wknd fnl f* **33/1**

00-5 **13** *hd* **Melalchrist**^{10} [1076] 4-8-11 **79**................ DNolan$^{(3)}$ 1 56
(J J Quinn) *prom: rdn 1/2-way: wknd over 1f out* **18/1**

0600 **14** *nk* **Bo McGinty (IRE)**^{12} [1042] 5-9-4 **83**................ TonyHamilton 9 59
(R A Fahey) *mid-div: effrt: hdwy and hmpd over 1f out: n.d* **20/1**

00-0 **15** *4* **Royal Orissa**^{27} [846] 4-9-1 **80**................ RobertHavlin 13 44
(D Haydn Jones) *prom 4f* **33/1**

30-0 **16** *1/2* **Fun To Ride**^{5} [1183] 5-8-9 **74**................ TQuinn 15 36
(M W Easterby) *chsd ldrs: rdn over 2f out: wkng whn hmpd over 1f out* **33/1**

00-0 **17** *nk* **Sabrina Brown**^{23} [898] 5-8-12 **77**................ (t) StephenCarson 16 38
(J A Geake) *s.i.s: hld up: a in rr* **33/1**

1m 13.03s (-0.17) **Going Correction** +0.175s/f (Good) **17** Ran SP% **121.4**
Speed ratings (Par 105):108,104,103,102,101 100,96,94,92,92 90,90,90,89,84 83,83
CSF £12.10 CT £69.79 TOTE £4.40: £1.60, £1.50, £2.10, £4.20; EX 19.90.
Owner Lady Sophia Topley **Bred** B Bronstad **Trained** Newmarket, Suffolk

FOCUS
Despite the big field, only three were of interest to the punters, and the finish was dominated by that trio with the winner quite impressive.
Bond Boy Official explanation: jockey said gelding hung right
Royal Orissa Official explanation: trainer said gelding had breathing problem
Fun To Ride Official explanation: jockey said mare was interfered with at start and bumped later in race

1286 KRONENBOURG 1664 COLD PREMIERE H'CAP 1m 3f 183y
3:30 (3:31) (Class 3) (0-95,90) 3-Y-O **£11,217** (£3,358; £1,679; £840) **Stalls** High

Form RPR

1 **1** **Hero Worship (IRE)**^{25} [863] 3-9-2 **85**................ PhilipRobinson 1 93
(M A Jarvis) *chsd ldr: rdn over 2f out: hung lft over 1f out: styd on to ld nr fin* **5/1^{3}**

2121 **2** *1* **Soapy Danger**^{10} [1077] 3-9-7 **90**................ KDarley 2 96
(M Johnston) *sn led: rdn over 1f out: hdd nr fin* **8/15^{1}**

16-2 **3** *3/4* **Gee Dee Nen**^{35} [730] 3-8-10 **79**................ RHills 3 84
(M H Tompkins) *hld up: hdwy over 2f out: rdn and hung lft over 1f out: styd on same pce* **7/2^{2}**

04-5 **4** *5* **Pukka Tique**^{5} [1182] 3-8-2 **71** oh1................ NickyMackay 4 68
(R Hollinshead) *chsd ldrs: rdn over 2f out: wknd over 1f out* **25/1**

2m 37.8s (3.30) **Going Correction** +0.175s/f (Good) **4** Ran SP% **108.0**
Speed ratings (Par 102):96,95,94,91
CSF £8.36 TOTE £4.60; EX 6.30.
Owner Jumeirah Racing **Bred** Duncan A McGregor **Trained** Newmarket, Suffolk
■ Stewards' Enquiry : Philip Robinson caution: used whip with excessive frequency

FOCUS
A decent handicap despite the small field, but the early pace was not particularly strong. The form should prove reasonable and could be rated a little higher.

NOTEBOOK
Hero Worship(IRE) wore down the long-time leader close home and looks a progressive type who just does enough. He could well be capable of further improvement in a stronger-run race, and the King George V Handicap at Royal Ascot looks a suitable target. (op 11-2 tchd 9-2)
Soapy Danger, raised 7lb for his Beverley success, enjoyed the run of the race out in front and appeared to have stolen a decisive advantage when quickening things up three furlongs out, but the winner found a turn of foot to beat him. His stable does well with tough front-running types like him, though, and it will be a surprise if he does not improve as the season progresses. (op 4-6)
Gee Dee Nen, narrowly denied at Redcar last time out, ran well enough but he would have preferred a stronger pace, and that was always going to be unlikely in this small-field contest. (op 11-4 tchd 4-1)
Pukka Tique again failed to convince over the trip. (tchd 20-1)

1287 TOTESPORT.COM LEICESTERSHIRE STKS (LISTED RACE) 7f 9y
4:00 (4:01) (Class 1) 4-Y-0+
£17,034 (£6,456; £3,231; £1,611; £807; £405) **Stalls** Low

Form RPR

00-1 **1** **Etlaala**^{12} [1050] 4-8-12 110................ RHills 5 111+
(B W Hills) *racd centre: chsd ldr: led 5f out: rdn and hung lft fr over 1f out: all out: 1st of 4 that gp* **6/5^{1}**

00-1 **2** *3/4* **Philharmonic**^{36} [718] 5-8-12 100................ KDarley 2 109
(R A Fahey) *chsd ldr stands' side: rdn to ld that trio over 1f out: edgd lft: r.o: 1st of 3 that side* **9/1**

-220 **3** *1* **Quito (IRE)**^{11} [1069] 9-9-1 110................ (b) TonyCulhane 7 109
(D W Chapman) *trckd ldrs centre: rdn over 2f out: edgd lft fnl f: stayed on: 2nd of 4 that gp* **8/1**

316- **4** *1 3/4* **Polar Ben**^{182} [6146] 7-8-12 109................ JamieSpencer 6 102
(J R Fanshawe) *trckd ldrs centre: rdn over 1f out: no ex fnl f: 3rd of 4 that gp* **5/1^{3}**

130- **5** *1/2* **New Seeker**^{196} [5900] 6-9-1 111................ (b) PhilipRobinson 1 104
(C G Cox) *led stands' side: rdn and hdd over 1f out: no ex: 2nd of 3 that gp* **11/4^{2}**

003- **6** *hd* **Xtra Torrential (USA)**^{399} [717] 4-8-12 .... RyanMoore 3 100
(D M Simcock) *racd stands' side: sn outpcd: edgd rt over 1f out: styd on ins fnl f: nvr nrr: last of 3 that gp* **40/1**

05-0 **7** *3 1/2* **Coconut Squeak**^{35} [729] 4-8-10 98................ (v) MickyFenton 4 89
(Stef Liddiard) *led centre 2f: rdn and edgd lft 1/2-way: wknd over 1f out: last of 4 that gp* **50/1**

1m 26.45s (0.35) **Going Correction** +0.175s/f (Good) **7** Ran SP% **114.3**
Speed ratings (Par 111):105,104,103,101,100 100,96
CSF £13.47 TOTE £1.90: £1.50, £4.60; EX 14.80.
Owner Hamdan Al Maktoum **Bred** Matthews Breeding And Racing Ltd **Trained** Lambourn, Berks

FOCUS
Not a bad Listed race but a modest winning time for the class of contest tempers enthusiasm over the strength of the form.

NOTEBOOK

Etlaala, impressive in a conditions event at Warwick on his reappearance, made much of the running up the centre of the track, and while that was perhaps not the best place to be, given the way the runner-up finished strongly near the rail, he had enough in hand at the finish to follow up. The impression left, though, was that he will not mind dropping back to six furlongs. (op 11-10 tchd 5-4)

Philharmonic had a bit to find at this level, but he was running on well at the finish and came out best of those that raced next to the stands'-side rail. He had no trouble with the extra distance, recording a personal best, and this effort should open up a few more opportunites. (op 10-1 tchd 11-1)

Quito(IRE) could have done with a stronger pace and the field sticking together as he likes to weave a passage through from the back. He remains in good form, though, and perfectly capable of landing a contest of this nature when things fall right. (op 5-1)

Polar Ben can run well fresh, as when runner-up in this race two years ago, but he needs softer ground to be seen at his best. (tchd 11-2)

New Seeker made the running on the stands' side but dropped away in the closing stages. This was a bit disappointing, but he is entitled to come on for his seasonal reappearance, and he looks sure to be more of a force as the ground gets quicker. (op 4-1)

Xtra Torrential(USA), a lightly-raced four-year-old having his first outing since finishing third in the Easter Stakes last March, clearly retains plenty of ability, and hopefully he can build on this promising reappearance. (op 50-1)

1288 STRONGBOW SIRRUS H'CAP — 1m 1f 218y

4:30 (4:32) (Class 5) (0-70,70) 4-Y-O+ £3,886 (£1,156; £577; £288) Stalls High

Form — RPR

0-31 **1** **Tagula Blue (IRE)**[5] [1187] 6-8-8 **60** ... KFallon 10 — 72+
(Ian Williams) *s.s: hld up: nt clr run over 2f out: swtchd lft and hdwy over 1f out: r.o to ld wl ins fnl f: readily* **2/1**[1]

00-0 **2** *1 ¼* **Soufah (IRE)**[23] [897] 4-8-8 **60** ... SebSanders 11 — 69+
(J L Dunlop) *hld up: hdwy over 3f out: r.o* **50/1**

1631 **3** *shd* **Latif (USA)**[7] [1148] 5-9-4 **70** ... SamHitchcott 15 — 79
(Ms Deborah J Evans) *hld up in tch: led over 1f out: hdd wl ins fnl f* **10/1**

030- **4** *½* **Charlie Kennet**[168] [6337] 8-9-2 **68** ... GeorgeBaker 14 — 76
(Mrs H Sweeting) *led: hdd over 4f out: led over 2f out: rdn: edgd lft and hdd over 1f out: styd on same pce* **25/1**

211- **5** *3 ½* **Halla San**[238] [4944] 4-9-1 **67** ... TonyHamilton 3 — 68
(R A Fahey) *hld up: hdwy over 2f out: rdn and hung rt over 1f out: wknd ins fnl f* **9/2**[2]

3-05 **6** *shd* **Ermine Grey**[17] [992] 5-8-13 **65** ... TPQueally 5 — 66
(A W Carroll) *hld up: hdwy over 3f out: styd on same pce fnl f* **25/1**

/60- **7** *1 ½* **Mutamaasek (USA)**[192] [5990] 4-9-4 **70** ... (t) JamieSpencer 6 — 68+
(Lady Herries) *hld up: hdwy over 1f out: nt trble ldrs* **20/1**

525- **8** *3* **Damburger Xpress**[190] [6008] 4-8-7 **62** ... (t) AdamKirby(3) 4 — 55
(D M Simcock) *mid-div: hdwy 1/2-way: rdn over 2f out: sn wknd* **25/1**

-040 **9** *shd* **Bollin Michael**[17] [977] 4-8-11 **63** ... PhilipRobinson 13 — 55
(T D Easterby) *chsd ldrs: rdn over 2f out: wknd over 1f out* **12/1**

2331 **10** *3 ½* **Jakarmi**[4] [1204] 5-9-1 **67** 5ex ... TonyCulhane 9 — 53
(B Palling) *chsd ldr tl led over 4f out: hdd over 2f out: wknd over 1f out* **11/2**[3]

2244 **11** *¾* **Libre**[17] [992] 6-9-3 **69** ... PaulFitzsimons 2 — 53
(F Jordan) *chsd ldrs: rdn over 2f out: wknd over 1f out* **25/1**

4-15 **12** *1 ½* **Oakley Absolute**[21] [915] 4-9-3 **69** ... RyanMoore 16 — 51
(R Hannon) *chsd ldrs: rdn over 3f out: wknd over 1f out* **14/1**

6035 **13** *shd* **Duelling Banjos**[17] [983] 7-9-0 **66** ... TQuinn 12 — 47
(J Akehurst) *prom: wkng whn hmpd over 1f out* **20/1**

3362 **14** *10* **Perez (IRE)**[16] [1002] 4-9-2 **68** ... PatDobbs 8 — 30
(Pat Eddery) *hld up: rdn over 3f out: wknd 2f out* **18/1**

2m 8.12s (-0.18) **Going Correction** +0.175s/f (Good) 14 Ran SP% **122.5**
Speed ratings (Par 103):107,106,105,105,102 102,101,99,98,96 95,94,94,86
CSF £150.11 CT £869.03 TOTE £2.90: £1.50, £11.60, £2.90; EX 103.60.
Owner Boston R S Ian Bennett **Bred** Michael Conlon **Trained** Portway, Worcs
■ Stewards' Enquiry : T P Queally caution: careless riding

FOCUS
An ordinary handicap rated through the third and fourth, but sound enough form.

1289 C.I.U. MAIDEN STKS (DIV I) — 1m 1f 218y

5:00 (5:00) (Class 5) 3-Y-O+ £4,100 (£1,227; £613; £306; £152) Stalls High

Form — RPR

3- **1** **Futun**[221] [5392] 3-8-9 ... NickyMackay 10 — 80+
(L M Cumani) *hld up in tch: plld hrd: led 2f out: edgd rt: r.o* **8/11**[1]

0- **2** *1 ¼* **Thalberg**[204] [5711] 3-8-9 ... PhilipRobinson 6 — 78+
(M A Jarvis) *hld up: hdwy over 2f out: rdn to chse wnr fnl f: styd on* **14/1**

3 *nk* **Mobaasher (USA)** 3-8-9 ... RHills 1 — 77+
(Sir Michael Stoute) *hld up: hdwy over 2f out: styd on* **6/1**[2]

20-0 **4** *5* **Woolfall Blue (IRE)**[12] [1048] 3-8-9 82 ... TQuinn 5 — 68
(G G Margarson) *led 1f: chsd ldr: led over 2f out: sn hdd: wknd fnl f* **11/1**[3]

0 **5** *2* **Kathleen Kennet**[23] [897] 6-9-7 ... GeorgeBaker 8 — 62
(Mrs H Sweeting) *hld up: hdwy over 2f out: nt trble ldrs* **50/1**

4 **6** *¾* **The Grey Man**[22] [909] 5-9-12 ... SebSanders 12 — 66
(E S McMahon) *chsd ldrs over 8f* **40/1**

0- **7** *nk* **Colinette**[192] [5968] 3-8-4 ... JamieMackay 9 — 57+
(H Candy) *hld up: hdwy and nt clr run over 1f out: nt rch ldrs* **33/1**

8 *1* **Shadow Aspect** 3-8-2 ... JamieHamblett(7) 2 — 60+
(Sir Michael Stoute) *hld up: hdwy over 3f out: wknd over 1f out* **20/1**

9 *2* **Queen Isabella** 3-8-6 ow2 ... OscarUrbina 3 — 53
(J R Fanshawe) *hld up: rdn over 4f out: n.d* **16/1**

00- **10** *2* **Billanroy (IRE)**[198] [5850] 3-8-9 ... TPQueally 13 — 53
(M H Tompkins) *hld up: hdwy u.p over 3f out: wknd over 2f out* **33/1**

42-5 **11** *5* **My Putra (USA)**[16] [1006] 4-9-12 74 ... RyanMoore 11 — 46
(P F I Cole) *hld up in tch: rdn over 3f out: wknd over 2f out* **11/1**[3]

6 **12** *1* **For No One (IRE)**[13] [1032] 3-8-9 ... KDarley 7 — 41
(M Johnston) *chsd ldrs: rdn over 4f out: wknd over 1f out* **16/1**

0 **13** *¾* **Sheikh Shakey**[16] [1006] 5-9-12 ... DaneO'Neill 4 — 43
(R Hannon) *led 9f out: rdn and hdd over 2f out: sn wknd* **66/1**

2m 8.36s (0.06) **Going Correction** +0.175s/f (Good)
WFA 3 from 4yo+ 17lb 13 Ran SP% **123.8**
Speed ratings (Par 103):106,105,104,100,99 98,98,97,95,94 90,89,88
CSF £12.57 TOTE £2.00: £1.10, £5.20, £2.30; EX 18.90.
Owner Scuderia Rencati Srl **Bred** Azienda Agricola Francesca **Trained** Newmarket, Suffolk

FOCUS
Probably a decent maiden and marginally the quicker of the two divisions. The first three could all rate higher.

1290 C.I.U. MAIDEN STKS (DIV II) — 1m 1f 218y

5:35 (5:36) (Class 5) 3-Y-O+ £4,100 (£1,227; £613; £306; £152) Stalls High

Form — RPR

1 **Tam Lin** 3-8-9 ... RyanMoore 1 — 77+
(Sir Michael Stoute) *s.i.s: hld up: hdwy over 3f out: led 2f: pushed clr fnl f* **4/1**[2]

4-5 **2** *4* **Altenburg (FR)**[23] [897] 4-9-7 ... JamesDoyle(5) 4 — 72
(Mrs N Smith) *hld up: hdwy 1/2-way: rdn and hung rt over 1f out: styd on same pce* **12/1**

3 *1 ¾* **Aspasias Tizzy (USA)** 3-8-1 ... StanleyChin(3) 2 — 61
(M Johnston) *chsd ldrs: rdn over 3f out: no ex fnl f* **20/1**

0-5 **4** *2 ½* **Impostor (IRE)**[19] [948] 3-8-9 ... OscarUrbina 3 — 61+
(J R Fanshawe) *hld up: rdn over 3f out: styd on same pce fnl 2f* **7/1**[3]

403- **5** *shd* **Chalentina**[191] [5993] 3-8-4 70 ... HayleyTurner 11 — 56
(H R A Cecil) *led 2f: chsd ldr: led over 2f out: sn hdd: wknd over 1f out* **10/1**

6 *5* **Petito (IRE)** 3-8-9 ... RobbieFitzpatrick 7 — 51
(Ian Williams) *s.s: nvr nrr* **50/1**

7 *1 ½* **Moonshine Creek** 4-9-12 ... LPKeniry 12 — 51
(P W Hiatt) *hld up: rdn over 3f out: n.d* **66/1**

0/ **8** *1 ¼* **Lake Imperial (IRE)**[106] [6810] 5-9-12 ... FergusSweeney 10 — 49
(Heather Dalton) *led 8f out: rdn and hdd over 2f out: wknd over 1f out* **50/1**

9 *¾* **Seeking Kali (IRE)** 3-8-6 ow2 ... KFallon 6 — 42
(Sir Michael Stoute) *hld up: effrt over 3f out: sn btn* **4/5**[1]

0- **10** *1 ¼* **Delorain (IRE)**[182] [6148] 3-8-9 ... TPQueally 5 — 42
(J A R Toller) *hld up: rdn and wknd over 3f out* **33/1**

11 *3* **Whiston Lad (IRE)** 3-8-9 ... PaulEddery 9 — 37
(S R Bowring) *chsd ldrs over 7f* **50/1**

000- **12** *16* **Forever Rocky**[226] [5251] 3-8-9 45 ... PaulFitzsimons 8 — 6
(F Jordan) *hld up: rdn 1/2-way: wknd over 3f out* **100/1**

2m 8.77s (0.47) **Going Correction** +0.175s/f (Good)
WFA 3 from 4yo+ 17lb 12 Ran SP% **120.9**
Speed ratings (Par 103):105,101,100,98,98 94,93,92,91,90 88,75
CSF £49.06 TOTE £5.10: £1.80, £2.40, £3.40; EX 122.30.
Owner Gainsborough Stud **Bred** Gainsborough Stud Management Ltd **Trained** Newmarket, Suffolk

FOCUS
A fair maiden won in taking style by Tam Lin, the supposed Stoute second string, but the overall form is not that strong given the reservations about the runner-up.

1291 JOHN SMITH'S CENTRAL H'CAP — 1m 60y

6:05 (6:06) (Class 5) (0-75,73) 3-Y-O £4,416 (£1,321; £660; £330; £164) Stalls High

Form — RPR

034- **1** **Pleasing**[145] [6502] 3-8-9 **64** ... DaneO'Neill 3 — 69+
(J L Dunlop) *prom: lost pl 4f out: hdwy over 2f out: rdn and hung rt over 1f out: r.o to ld post* **20/1**

66-2 **2** *shd* **Woolly Bully**[31] [797] 3-8-13 **68** ... NickyMackay 11 — 73+
(G A Huffer) *hld up in tch: rdn over 1f out: led wl ins fnl f: hdd post* **15/8**[1]

050- **3** *nk* **Sicilian (IRE)**[225] [5271] 3-9-2 **71** ... RyanMoore 2 — 75
(B W Hills) *sn drvn to ld: rdn over 1f out: hdd wl ins fnl f* **12/1**

50-0 **4** *nk* **Floodlight Fantasy**[17] [993] 3-8-11 **66** ... TedDurcan 8 — 69
(E S McMahon) *chsd ldrs: rdn over 1f out: styd on* **20/1**

640- **5** *1 ¼* **Pagan Crest**[202] [5761] 3-8-3 **63** ... JamesDoyle(5) 10 — 64+
(Mrs A J Perrett) *hld up: hdwy over 3f out: rdn over 1f out: eased whn hld nr fin* **9/1**[3]

54-6 **6** *hd* **Vodkatini**[91] [228] 3-9-4 **73** ... (v) FergusSweeney 4 — 73
(P J Makin) *hld up: r.o ins fnl f: nrst fin* **33/1**

044- **7** *1 ¾* **Summer Lodge**[245] [4745] 3-9-2 **71** ... RHills 5 — 67+
(M H Tompkins) *hld up: hdwy over 2f out: nt clr run and swtchd lft over 1f out: nt trble ldrs* **14/1**

530- **8** *shd* **Night Cru**[211] [5582] 3-8-13 **68** ... TPQueally 12 — 64
(C F Wall) *hld up: hdwy over 3f out: sn rdn: styd on same pce fnl f* **28/1**

55-2 **9** *2 ½* **Cape Diamond (IRE)**[16] [1004] 3-9-4 **73** ... SebSanders 14 — 63
(W R Swinburn) *chsd ldrs over 6f* **10/3**[2]

000- **10** *½* **Desert Sea (IRE)**[192] [5988] 3-8-9 **67** ... NeilChalmers(3) 6 — 56
(C Tinkler) *s.i.s: hld up: n.d* **50/1**

0-33 **11** *1 ½* **Cantabilly (IRE)**[17] [993] 3-9-0 **69** ... TQuinn 9 — 54
(M R Channon) *hld up: hdwy u.p 3f out: sn edgd rt: wknd over 1f out* **9/1**[3]

002- **12** *2 ½* **Orphina (IRE)**[254] [4492] 3-9-0 **69** ... PaulEddery 1 — 49
(Pat Eddery) *hld up: a in rr* **25/1**

001- **13** *6* **Dancing Guest (IRE)**[192] [5976] 3-9-4 **73** ... PhilipRobinson 13 — 39
(G G Margarson) *chsd ldr: rdn over 2f out: wkng whn hmpd over 1f out* **25/1**

0250 **14** *12* **Marcello**[12] [1052] 3-8-11 **66** ... (t) KDarley 7 — 4
(P F I Cole) *prom: rdn over 3f out: wknd over 2f out* **10/1**

1m 47.66s (2.36) **Going Correction** +0.175s/f (Good) 14 Ran SP% **126.9**
Speed ratings (Par 98):95,94,94,94,93 92,91,88,88 86,84,78,66
CSF £56.85 CT £530.54 TOTE £23.20: £5.50, £1.40, £3.80; EX 102.10 Place 6 £43.36, Place 5 £30.12.
Owner Mrs W H Carson & Mrs J L Dunlop **Bred** Minster Enterprises Ltd **Trained** Arundel, W Sussex

FOCUS
An ordinary handicap run in a modest time for the grade, but the first two could be a bit better than the bare form and the race has been rated through the fifth.
Pagan Crest Official explanation: jockey said gelding hung
Dancing Guest(IRE) Official explanation: jockey said filly lost its action
T/Plt: £42.90 to a £1 stake. Pool: £42,734.55. 725.80 winning tickets. T/Qpdt: £25.60 to a £1 stake. Pool: £2,069.20. 59.60 winning tickets. CR

1096 RIPON (R-H)

Saturday, April 29

OFFICIAL GOING: Good (good to firm in places)
Wind: Moderate, against

1292 TOTESCOOP6 H'CAP — 6f

2:30 (2:30) (Class 3) (0-95,95) 3-Y-O
£10,906 (£3,265; £1,632; £817; £407; £204) Stalls High

Form — RPR

1-2 **1** **Obe Brave**[11] [1067] 3-9-3 **94** ... ChrisCatlin 10 — 107
(M R Channon) *trckd ldrs on outer: hdwy 1/2-way: effrt to chal 2f out: sn rdn: drvn and edgd lft ins last: led nr fin* **5/2**[1]

60-0 **2** *shd* **High Curragh**[9] 1091 3-8-4 **81** .... DO'Donohoe 7 93
(K A Ryan) *cl up: led 1/2-way: rdn wl over 1f out: edgd lft and drvn ent last: hdd nr fin* **11/2**[3]

30-3 **3** *6* **Ryedale Ovation (IRE)**[9] 1097 3-8-5 **82** .... DavidAllan 8 76
(T D Easterby) *in tch: hdwy on outer over 2f out: sn rdn and kpt on same pce appr last* **11/2**[3]

31-1 **4** *½* **Antica (IRE)**[9] 1097 3-8-9 **89** .... SaleemGolam(3) 2 82
(M H Tompkins) *in tch: hdwy over 2f out: rdn to chse ldrs wl over 1f out: sn drvn and one pce* **3/1**[2]

021- **5** *nk* **Skhilling Spirit**[190] 6004 3-9-4 **95** .... PaulFessey 5 87
(T D Barron) *hld up: effrt and nt clr run over 2f out: sn rdn and kpt on same pce* **7/1**

20-0 **6** *1 ¼* **Choysia**[7] 1146 3-8-10 **87** .... FergalLynch 6 75
(D W Barker) *hld up in rr: hdwy over 2f out: swtchd rt to outer over 1f: nrst fin* **50/1**

210- **7** *3* **Princess Cleo**[218] 5430 3-8-4 **81** .... PaulQuinn 1 60
(T D Easterby) *led: pushed along and hdd 1/2-way: rdn over 2f out: sn wknd* **33/1**

040- **8** *¾* **Green Park (IRE)**[255] 4480 3-8-10 **87** .... PaulHanagan 4 64
(R A Fahey) *chsd ldrs: rdn along over 2f out: grad wknd* **20/1**

0-00 **9** *18* **Ooh Aah Camara (IRE)**[28] 827 3-8-8 **85** ....(v[1]) ShaneKelly 3 8
(T J Pitt) *prom: rdn along over 3f out: sn wknd* **33/1**

1m 11.78s (-1.22) **Going Correction** -0.075s/f (Good) 9 Ran SP% **109.4**
Speed ratings (Par 102):105,104,96,96,95 94,90,89,65
CSF £14.77 CT £60.65 TOTE £2.90: £1.60, £1.90, £1.60; EX 14.40 Trifecta £109.70 Pool: £340.20 - 2.20 winning units..
Owner BDR Partnership **Bred** Helshaw Grange Stud, E Kent And Mrs E Connelly **Trained** West Ilsley, Berks

FOCUS
A fair three-year-old sprint for the class and the form looks sound with this first two coming clear.

NOTEBOOK
Obe Brave, who turned in a very encouraging reappearance when runner-up at Newmarket 11 days previously, duly went one better, albeit most narrowly, with a dogged display from a 4lb higher mark. The drop back to this trip proved no problem, he deserves extra credit considering he was drawn widest of all, and is clearly still improving. (op 15-8 tchd 11-4 in a place)
High Curragh showed the benefit of his seasonal bow at Newmarket and was only denied by the smallest of margins. He was well clear of the remainder, is capable of holding his form well, and is clearly well up to adding to his tally from this sort of mark. (tchd 5-1)
Ryedale Ovation(IRE), popular in the betting ring, ran close to his mark in defeat and reversed recent course and distance form with Antica on these 7lb better terms. He helps set the level for this form. (op 7-1)
Antica(IRE), up 7lb for her success over course and distance nine days previously, failed to raise her game on this quicker ground and just failed to confirm recent form with the third horse. She did leave the impression she would appreciate the return to slightly easier ground, however, and is not without hope off this new mark. (op 11-4 tchd 5-2)
Skhilling Spirit Official explanation: jockey said gelding was unsuited by the track
Choysia Official explanation: jockey said filly was unsuited by the track

1293 TOTEEXACTA (S) STKS 1m 1f 170y
3:05 (3:06) (Class 6) 3-4-Y-O **£3,238** (£963; £481; £240) **Stalls** Low

Form RPR

40-5 **1** **Zabeel Tower**[19] 945 3-8-7 70 .... ChrisCatlin 3 59
(M R Channon) *hld up in midfield: hdwy over 3f out: rdn over 1f out: edgd rt and styd on to ld ent last: sn drvn and jst hld on* **4/1**[1]

650- **2** *shd* **Alisdanza**[229] 5179 4-9-5 55 .... DeanMcKeown 5 57
(G A Swinbank) *a.p: effrt to ld wl over 1f out: rdn and hdd ent last: sn drvn and kpt on gamely: jst hld* **16/1**

1033 **3** *3 ½* **Sol Rojo**[12] 1058 4-10-0 50 ....(v) NCallan 7 59+
(J Pearce) *hld up in midfield: hdwy over 3f out: chsd ldrs and rdn whn nt clr appr last: swtchd lft and drvn: sn one pce* **9/2**[2]

-504 **4** *3* **Augustus Livius (IRE)**[17] 974 3-8-7 45 .... PaulFessey 10 47
(W Storey) *trckd ldrs: effrt 3f out and ch tl rdn wl over 1f out and kpt on same pce* **25/1**

-000 **5** *½* **Lewis Lloyd (IRE)**[19] 945 3-8-7 48 ....(t) JoeFanning 12 46
(I A Wood) *bmpd s: sn chsng ldrs on inner: rdn along 3f out: kpt on same pce fnl 2f* **25/1**

0-60 **6** *nk* **Ever Special (IRE)**[81] 329 3-8-2 40 .... LeanneKershaw(5) 8 45
(P C Haslam) *in tch: hdwy on outer to chse ldrs 3f out: rdn along over 2f out and sn no imp* **40/1**

2333 **7** *3* **Franky'N'Jonny**[25] 879 3-8-2 53 .... AdrianTNicholls 1 34
(I A Wood) *trckd ldrs on outer: hdwy to ld 3f out: sn rdn: hdd wl over 1f out and sn wknd* **6/1**[3]

056- **8** *1 ¼* **Flying Doctor**[262] 4250 3-8-7 56 .... ShaneKelly 2 37
(G M Moore) *towards rr: hdwy over 2f out: sn rdn along and kpt on appr last: nt rch ldrs* **16/1**

360- **9** *3* **Azahara**[185] 5979 4-9-5 45 .... DavidAllan 6 29
(K G Reveley) *chsd ldrs: rdn along wl over 2f out: sn wknd* **12/1**

00-0 **10** *7* **Move On (IRE)**[7] 1140 3-8-2 50 .... PaulHanagan 13 13
(B Ellison) *dwlt: wd bnd after 5f and a rr* **25/1**

000- **11** *hd* **Obstreperous Way**[196] 4045 4-9-10 52 .... PhillipMakin 16 21
(Miss Tracy Waggott) *a rr* **50/1**

-006 **12** *2 ½* **Trew Flight (USA)**[12] 1058 4-9-7 53 ....(b[1]) SaleemGolam(3) 14 16
(M H Tompkins) *wnt lft s: keen and sn cl up: led after 3f: rdn along and hdd 3f out: sn wknd* **13/2**

00-0 **13** *23* **Baron De Hoyland**[93] 193 3-8-9 35 ow2 .... DarrenWilliams 9 —
(J R Norton) *led 3f: cl up tl rdn along over 3f out and sn wknd* **100/1**

000- **14** *4* **Mister Fizzbomb (IRE)**[175] 6251 3-8-7 40 .... TomEaves 17 —
(J S Wainwright) *a bhd* **66/1**

0-01 **15** *18* **Secret Tender (IRE)**[40] 676 3-8-11 60 .... RobertWinston 15 —
(J R Weymes) *midfield: rdn along 4f out: sn wknd* **13/2**

2m 4.66s (-0.34) **Going Correction** -0.075s/f (Good)
WFA 3 from 4yo 17lb 15 Ran SP% **117.0**
Speed ratings (Par 101):98,97,95,92,92 92,89,88,86,80 80,78,60,56,42
CSF £62.60 TOTE £4.50: £2.30, £4.90, £1.90; EX 48.50 Trifecta £187.10 Part won. Pool: £263.65 - 0.10 winning units..The winner was sold to James Moffatt for 10,200gns.
Owner Mohammed Jaber **Bred** Gainsborough Stud Management Ltd **Trained** West Ilsley, Berks

FOCUS
A weak affair, run at a fair pace, and the first two came nicely clear in a thrilling finish.
Move On(IRE) Official explanation: jockey said filly hung left-handed throughout
Secret Tender(IRE) Official explanation: jockey said gelding was hampered shortly after the start and lost its action latterly

1294 TOTESPORT.COM H'CAP 2m
3:40 (3:40) (Class 2) (0-100,96) 4-Y-0+
£12,464 (£3,732; £1,866; £934; £466; £234) **Stalls** High

Form RPR

11-1 **1** **Greenwich Meantime**[7] 1144 6-8-11 **80** .... PaulHanagan 2 93+
(R A Fahey) *hld up towards rr: hdwy on outer 4f out: smooth run to ld 21/2f out: rdn and edgd rt over 1f out: kpt on* **5/2**[1]

24-3 **2** *1* **Numero Due**[17] 976 4-8-4 **77** oh4 .... ChrisCatlin 8 83
(G M Moore) *in tch on inner: rdn along over 7f out: hdwy 3f out: swtchd lft and rdn over 1f out: drvn to chse wnr ins last: kpt on wl* **11/2**[3]

1/4- **3** *½* **Stoop To Conquer**[70] 1655 6-8-11 **80** .... NCallan 9 85
(J L Dunlop) *trckd ldrs: hdwy 4f out: ev ch wl over 2f out: sn rdn: drvn and kpt on fnl f* **9/1**

12-0 **4** *1 ½* **Toldo (IRE)**[25] 867 4-8-13 **86** .... ShaneKelly 10 89
(G M Moore) *a.p: led over 3f out: sn rdn and hdd 21/2f out: drvn over 1f out: kpt on same pce* **16/1**

06-6 **5** *5* **Lets Roll**[11] 1071 5-9-6 **89** .... DeanMcKeown 1 86
(C W Thornton) *in tch: hdwy 4f out: effrt and ev ch over 2f out tl rdn and wknd wl over 1f out* **13/2**

043- **6** *1 ¾* **Most Definitely (IRE)**[222] 5357 6-9-6 **89** .... DavidAllan 12 84
(T D Easterby) *hld up in rr: stdy hdwy 3f out: rdn 2f out and sn no imp* **8/1**

000- **7** *3 ½* **Balyan (IRE)**[82] 4149 5-9-3 **89** .... PaulMulrennan(3) 3 80
(J Howard Johnson) *led 7f: prom tl rdn along over 3f out and sn wknd* **33/1**

230- **8** *2 ½* **Ten Carat**[196] 5903 6-9-7 **90** .... RoystonFfrench 11 78
(M Todhunter) *sn rdn along: a rr* **20/1**

6/0- **9** *5* **Sahem (IRE)**[336] 2072 9-8-6 **78** .... SaleemGolam(3) 4 60
(Robert Gray) *a towards rr* **66/1**

00/0 **10** *¾* **Savannah Bay**[14] 1021 7-9-13 **96** .... TomEaves 5 77
(B Ellison) *a towards rr* **50/1**

4/40 **11** *¾* **Double Obsession**[11] 1071 6-9-7 **90** ....(v) AdrianTNicholls 6 70
(D Nicholls) *prom: led after 7f: rdn along and hdd over 3f out: sn wknd* **33/1**

062- **12** *25* **Dr Sharp (IRE)**[203] 5744 6-9-3 **86** .... RobertWinston 7 36
(T P Tate) *prom: rdn along over 4f out and sn wknd* **9/2**[2]

3m 29.32s (-3.68) **Going Correction** -0.075s/f (Good)
WFA 4 from 5yo+ 4lb 12 Ran SP% **116.6**
Speed ratings (Par 109):106,105,105,104,102 101,99,98,95,95 94,82
CSF £14.88 CT £106.94 TOTE £2.70: £1.40, £2.00, £2.70; EX 15.20 Trifecta £105.80 Pool: £506.86 - 3.40 winning units..
Owner K Lee **Bred** Juddmonte Farms **Trained** Musley Bank, N Yorks

FOCUS
A decent staying handicap, run at a sound enough gallop, and the form looks solid.

NOTEBOOK
Greenwich Meantime ◆, up 6lb for winning on debut for his new yard at Thirsk a week previously, relished the return to this longer trip and followed-up in ready fashion. This must rate as a personal-best effort, his ability to quicken over this sort of trip is a notable advantage and, as his trainer tends to excel with such performers, a bold bid for the five-timer can now be expected. (tchd 3-1)
Numero Due showed the benefit of his recent seasonal return and was another who relished the return to this longer trip. He was put in his place by the winner's turn of foot, but was closing again at the finish, and is more than capable of winning again from this mark. He could be set to reach greater heights this season.
Stoop To Conquer, back with his former trainer after an unsuccessful spell over hurdles, was doing all of his best work at the finish and turned in a promising return to the Flat. He should be placed to advantage on this evidence, especially when reverting to his favoured easy ground.
Toldo(IRE) tired in the final furlong, but still improved on the form of his recent seasonal bow, and clearly appreciated the stiffer test. He will appreciate the return to softer ground in the future. (op 12-1)
Lets Roll failed to really improve on the level of his seasonal debut at Newmarket 11 days previously and was a little disappointing. He is entitled to come on again a touch for this outing, however. (op 11-2)
Dr Sharp(IRE) Official explanation: jockey said gelding was unsuited by the good, good to firm in places ground

1295 PARKER ENGINEERING AND TRANSMISSIONS MAIDEN AUCTION FILLIES' STKS 5f
4:10 (4:10) (Class 5) 2-Y-0 **£3,886** (£1,156; £577; £288) **Stalls** High

Form RPR

4 **1** **Riverside Dancer (USA)**[14] 1019 2-8-12 .... NCallan 2 82+
(K A Ryan) *cl up: led after 2f: rdn clr and hung rt ent last: styd on* **7/2**[2]

2 **2** *2 ½* **Voodoo Moon**[5] 1181 2-8-6 .... JoeFanning 5 66+
(M Johnston) *chsd ldrs: rdn and swtchd lft over 1f out: chsd wnr ins last: no imp* **7/4**[1]

4 **3** *1 ¾* **Fly So Free (IRE)**[8] 1121 2-8-8 .... AdrianTNicholls 4 61
(D Nicholls) *led 2f: cl up tl rdn over 1f out and grad wknd* **9/2**[3]

4 *5* **Hucking Hope (IRE)** 2-8-7 ow1 .... SteveDrowne 8 40
(J R Best) *chsd ldrs: rdn along over 2f out: sn edgd lft and one pce* **13/2**

5 *1 ½* **Loch Clutha (IRE)** 2-8-1 .... AndrewElliott(5) 1 33
(K R Burke) *s.i.s: hdwy and in tch 1/2-way: sn rdn: edgd rt and no further prog* **12/1**

6 *1 ¾* **Flower Of Cork (IRE)** 2-8-8 .... FergalLynch 7 28
(T D Easterby) *sn outpcd: a rr* **12/1**

7 *1 ¾* **First Valentini** 2-7-13 .... SuzzanneFrance(7) 6 19
(N Bycroft) *sn outpcd and a rr* **50/1**

8 *5* **Lovers Kiss** 2-8-6 .... GrahamGibbons 9 —
(N Wilson) *chsd ldrs on outer: rdn along 1/2-way: sn wknd* **18/1**

9 *1 ¾* **Inch Forward** 2-8-4 .... NeilPollard 3 —
(D W Barker) *chsd ldrs: rdn along 1/2-way: sn wknd* **33/1**

60.30 secs (0.10) **Going Correction** -0.075s/f (Good) 9 Ran SP% **115.7**
Speed ratings (Par 89):96,92,89,81,78 76,73,65,62
CSF £10.02 TOTE £4.80: £1.60, £1.20, £1.60; EX 8.60 Trifecta £18.00 Pool: £157.05 - 6.19 winning units..
Owner J K Shannon **Bred** Dr Walter W And Mrs Zent **Trained** Hambleton, N Yorks

FOCUS
A moderate fillies' juvenile maiden, but the winner did the job nicely and may rate higher.

NOTEBOOK
Riverside Dancer(USA), fourth on debut at Kempton against the colts last time, took the race by the scruff of the neck approaching halfway and readily broke her duck at the second attempt. She wandered about in front entering the final furlong, suggesting she ought to improve again for this experience, and another furlong should be within her compass in due course. (op 6-1)
Voodoo Moon, runner-up on debut at Pontefract five day previously, emerged to finish a clear second-best to the winner and ran to a similar level. She already looks in need of another furlong. (op 13-8 tchd 2-1)

Fly So Free(IRE) broke better than had been the case on her recent debut and showed decent early speed before tiring inside the final furlong. She is modest, but will no doubt be placed to advantage over this trip in due course. (op 11-2)

Hucking Hope(IRE), the first foal of a mile-plus performer, showed up well enough until weakening nearing the final furlong and suggested this debut experience was much-needed. (op 5-1)

1296 TOTESPORT 0800 221 221 MAIDEN STKS — 1m 1f 170y

4:40 (4:45) (Class 5) 3-Y-O — **£3,886** (£1,156; £577; £288) **Stalls** Low

Form				RPR
6	**1**		**Dream Prize (IRE)**^{19} 948 3-9-3 ... RobertWinston 2 (Sir Michael Stoute) *trckd ldrs: hdwy 3f out: rdn to ld jst ins last whn rdr dropped whip: kpt on wl* **4/6**^{1}	76+
302-	**2**	*shd*	**Macorville (USA)**^{213} 5548 3-9-3 74 ... ShaneKelly 5 (G M Moore) *led: rdn along 3f out: drvn over 1f out: hdd jst ins last: rallied gamely* **7/1**^{3}	76
345-	**3**	*2 ½*	**Grand Opera (IRE)**^{222} 5356 3-9-3 77 ... DO'Donohoe 7 (J Howard Johnson) *stmbld s and hld up in rr: hdwy 3f out: swtchd wd and str run over 1f out: rdn and one pce ins last* **5/1**^{2}	71+
6	**4**	*1 ¼*	**Luck In Running (USA)**^{29} 817 3-9-3 ... JoeFanning 3 (M Johnston) *cl up: effrt 3f out and ev ch tl rdn and wknd over 1f out* **9/1**	69
320-	**5**	*nk*	**Myrtle Bay (IRE)**^{243} 4825 3-9-3 77 ... PatCosgrave 8 (K R Burke) *keen: trckd ldrs: rdn along 3f out: wknd wl over 1f out* **8/1**	68
0	**6**	*1 ¼*	**Keisha Kayleigh (IRE)**^{29} 817 3-8-12 ... RoystonFfrench 1 (B Ellison) *keen: chsd ldrs: rdn along 3f out: sn btn* **50/1**	61
	7	*23*	**Northern Promise (IRE)** 3-9-3 ... ChrisCatlin 6 (J Parkes) *a rr: lost tch fnl 3f* **33/1**	22
	8	*2 ½*	**Tammy** 3-8-9 ... DanielTudhope$^{(3)}$ 4 (C W Thornton) *s.i.s: sn in tch: rdn along 4f out: sn wknd and bhd* **100/1**	12

2m 6.29s (1.29) **Going Correction** -0.075s/f (Good) **8** Ran SP% **116.2**

Speed ratings (Par 98):91,90,88,87,87 86,68,66

CSF £6.23 TOTE £1.70: £1.10, £2.00, £1.90; EX 5.30 Trifecta £6.60 Pool: £128.63 - 13.79 winning units..

Owner Saeed Suhail **Bred** Alexander Pereira **Trained** Newmarket, Suffolk

FOCUS

A fair maiden, lacking real strength in depth and the time was moderate, but the first two came clear. The form should work out.

1297 JAMES MARSHALL 40TH BIRTHDAY H'CAP — 5f

5:10 (5:13) (Class 5) (0-75,75) 4-Y-O+ — **£3,886** (£1,156; £577; £288) **Stalls** High

Form				RPR
00-6	**1**		**Pomfret Lad**^{8} 1125 8-9-2 **73** ... GrahamGibbons 3 (J J Quinn) *trckd ldrs stands side: hdwy to ld over 1f out: sn rdn and styd on* **6/1**^{1}	82
5030	**2**	*¾*	**Fizzlephut (IRE)**^{4} 1211 4-9-1 **75** ... RichardThomas$^{(3)}$ 16 (Miss J R Tooth) *a.p far side: effrt wl over 1f out: rdn to ld that gp ent last and ev ch tl no ex last 100 yds* **14/1**	82
40-0	**3**	*½*	**Henry Hall (IRE)**^{8} 1125 10-8-11 **68** ... KimTinkler 1 (N Tinkler) *trckd ldrs stands side: hdwy wl over 1f out: sn rdn and kpt on ins last* **9/1**^{3}	73+
1-03	**4**	*½*	**Aegean Dancer**^{53} 605 4-8-9 **66** ... ChrisCatlin 11 (B Smart) *in tch far side: hdwy over 1f out: sn rdn and kpt on ins last* **10/1**	69
234-	**5**	*hd*	**Conjecture**^{264} 4216 4-9-1 **72** ... RoystonFfrench 15 (R Bastiman) *led far side: rdn along 2f out: hdd and drvn over 1f out: kpt on same pce* **9/1**^{3}	74
000-	**6**	*½*	**Chatshow (USA)**^{245} 4746 5-8-13 **73** ... DanielTudhope$^{(3)}$ 5 (D Carroll) *overall ldr stands side: rdn and hdd ovwr 1f out: one pce ins last* **20/1**	73+
0240	**7**	*hd*	**El Potro**^{7} 1151 4-8-5 **65** ... BenSwarbrick$^{(3)}$ 8 (E S McMahon) *chsd ldrs stands side: rdn along wl over 1f out: kpt on same pce* **25/1**	65+
5-60	**8**	*nk*	**Blackheath (IRE)**^{9} 1102 10-8-11 **68** ... AdrianTNicholls 19 (D Nicholls) *in tch far side: rdn along wl over 1f out: kpt on same pce* **14/1**	67
02-6	**9**	*hd*	**Trojan Flight**^{12} 1042 5-9-4 **75** ... PaulQuinn 17 (D W Chapman) *hld up and bhd far side: hdsway over 1f out: styd on strly ins last* **9/1**^{3}	77+
05-6	**10**	*½*	**Salviati (USA)**^{6} 1161 9-9-0 **71** ... ShaneKelly 18 (J M Bradley) *s.i.s: sn in tch far side: rdn along 2f out: kpt on same pce* **12/1**	67
0-00	**11**	*1*	**Trick Cyclist**^{9} 1102 5-8-8 **65** ... DaleGibson 20 (M W Easterby) *chsd ldrs far side: rdn along 1/2-way: grad wknd* **28/1**	58
0-00	**12**	*1*	**Whistler**^{12} 1047 9-9-1 **72** ... (p) SteveDrowne 13 (Miss J R Tooth) *towards rr far side tl styd on appr last* **22/1**	61
0005	**13**	*½*	**No Time (IRE)**^{6} 1161 6-8-13 **70** ... J-PGuillambert 7 (M J Polglase) *prom stands side: rdn along 2f out: sn wknd* **20/1**	57+
3221	**14**	*hd*	**Ashes (IRE)**^{19} 954 4-8-9 **66** ... PatCosgrave 14 (K R Burke) *cl up far side: rdn and ev ch 2f out: sn wknd* **8/1**^{2}	52
000-	**15**	*hd*	**Baron Rhodes**^{175} 6248 5-9-1 **72** ... (p) DO'Donohoe 12 (J S Wainwright) *chsd ldrs stands side: rdn along 2f out: sn wknd* **20/1**	58+
00-0	**16**	*1*	**Catch The Cat (IRE)**^{8} 1125 7-8-8 **65** ... GylesParkin 6 (Robert Gray) *chsd ldrs stands side to 1/2-way: sn wknd* **14/1**	47+
64-0	**17**	*nk*	**Diamond Katie (IRE)**^{9} 1102 4-8-11 **68** ... JoeFanning 4 (N Tinkler) *chsd ldrs stands side to 1/2-way: sn wknd* **25/1**	49+

59.51 secs (-0.69) **Going Correction** -0.075s/f (Good) **17** Ran SP% **122.0**

Speed ratings (Par 103):102,100,100,99,98 98,97,97,96,96 94,92,92,91,91 89,89

CSF £78.32 CT £789.37 TOTE £7.30: £2.00, £4.00, £3.00, £3.10; EX 138.10 Trifecta £146.70 Part won. Pool: £206.70 - 0.10 winning units..

Owner Maxilead Limited **Bred** R G Percival And Miss S M Rhodes **Trained** Settrington, N Yorks

FOCUS

A modest sprint, which saw those drawn high at a slight advantage, and the form looks fair for the class.

Whistler Official explanation: jockey said gelding was unsuited by the good, good to firm in places ground

1298 TOTESPORTCASINO.COM CONDITIONS STKS — 1m 4f 10y

5:40 (5:40) (Class 3) 4-Y-O+ — **£7,790** (£2,332; £1,166; £583; £291; £146) **Stalls** Low

Form				RPR
102-	**1**		**Hearthstead Wings**^{177} 6237 4-8-8 100 ... (v) JoeFanning 4 (M Johnston) *cl up: led over 3f out: rdn wl over 1f out: styd on strly ins last* **11/4**^{1}	107
536-	**2**	*2*	**Palomar (USA)**^{210} 5637 4-8-8 105 ... SteveDrowne 1 (R Charlton) *hld up: hdwy 3f out: rdn to chse wnr over 1f out: kpt on same pce ins last* **3/1**^{2}	104
603-	**3**	*2 ½*	**Motive (FR)**^{83} 4476 5-8-9 92 ... DO'Donohoe 2 (J Howard Johnson) *hld up: hdwy 3f out: rdn to chse ldng pair wl over 1f out: kpt on same pce* **11/2**	100
520-	**4**	*6*	**Brahminy Kite (USA)**^{196} 5905 4-8-8 106 ... RoystonFfrench 6 (M Johnston) *led: rdn along and hdd over 3f out: grad wknd* **9/2**	90
402-	**5**	*22*	**Akarem**^{96} 6254 5-8-9 102 ... PatCosgrave 5 (K R Burke) *trckd ldrs: rdn along over 3f out: wknd wl over 2f out* **4/1**^{3}	55
6-	**6**	*12*	**Motafarred (IRE)**^{195} 5929 4-9-3 ... FergalLynch 3 (Micky Hammond) *cl up: rdn along 4f out: sn wknd* **40/1**	45

2m 32.06s (-4.94) **Going Correction** -0.075s/f (Good)

WFA 4 from 5yo 1lb **6** Ran SP% **107.7**

Speed ratings (Par 107):113,111,110,106,91 83

CSF £10.29 TOTE £2.90: £1.80, £2.20; EX 12.00 Place 6 £8.52, Place 5 £5.51.

Owner Hearthstead Homes Ltd **Bred** M P B Bloodstock Ltd **Trained** Middleham Moor, N Yorks

FOCUS

A decent little conditions event run in a good time and the form looks sound enough based around the first three.

NOTEBOOK

Hearthstead Wings ◆, returning from a 177-day break, posted a successful return to action - over a trip short of his best - and was full value for his winning margin. Given that he was not that well in with several of his rivals at the weights, he deserves extra credit and, with the promise of better to come when reverting to a stiffer test, this could well be his year. He may reportedly turn out quickly in the Sagaro Stakes at Lingfield and is also a possible contender for the Chester Cup. (op 5-2)

Palomar(USA), a recent 350,000gns purchase making his British debut for new connections, looked a threat to the winner when making ground at the top of the straight, yet he failed to sustain his effort and was ultimately well held. He is likely to prove better when reverting to a stiffer test, should appreciate the return to easier ground, and was entitled to have needed this outing. (op 5-2 tchd 10-3)

Motive(FR), last seen on the Flat 255 days earlier, turned in a decent effort considering he faced a stiff task at the weights and only tired nearing the final furlong. He can build on this.

Brahminy Kite(USA), making his return from a 196-day break, dropped out tamely when headed in the straight and has to rate disappointing as he had a leading chance according to official figures. He is well-regarded by connections, and despite not living up to expectations as of yet, he is surely capable of better with this outing under his belt. (op 4-1 tchd 7-2)

Akarem, last seen disappointing over hurdles in January, was well backed for this return to the Flat yet his fate was sealed with three furlongs to run. He has it to prove now. (op 13-2 tchd 7-1)

T/Plt: £10.40 to a £1 stake. Pool: £59,719.75. 4,179.40 winning tickets. T/Qpdt: £3.50 to a £1 stake. Pool: £3,170.00. 670.20 winning tickets. JR

1267 SANDOWN (R-H)

Saturday, April 29

OFFICIAL GOING: Jumps courses - good to firm; flat course - good (good to firm in places)

Wind: Moderate, across Weather: Fine **Other races under Rules of Jump racing**

1299 BETFRED.COM MILE (GROUP 2) — 1m 14y

3:55 (3:57) (Class 1) 4-Y-O+

£51,102 (£19,368; £9,693; £4,833; £2,421; £1,215) **Stalls** High

Form				RPR
310-	**1**		**Rob Roy (USA)**^{196} 5902 4-9-0 111 ... MJKinane 4 (Sir Michael Stoute) *trckd ldr: pushed into ld wl over 1f out: idled and shkn up: in command ins fnl f* **6/4**^{1}	114+
05-6	**2**	*1*	**Babodana**^{35} 728 6-9-0 106 ... DarryllHolland 6 (M H Tompkins) *trckd ldng pair: effrt 2f out: hrd rdn over 1f out: r.o to take 2nd last 100yds: nt rch wnr* **11/1**	112
16-4	**3**	*1 ¼*	**Kings Point (IRE)**^{10} 1084 5-9-0 105 ... (p) RichardHughes 5 (R A Fahey) *led at gd pce: hdd wl over 1f out: kpt on wl tl no ex ins fnl f* **14/1**	109
-003	**4**	*shd*	**Democratic Deficit (IRE)**^{6} 1171 4-9-0 ... (t) KJManning 7 (J S Bolger, Ire) *hld up in midfield: rdn and prog wl over 2f out: chsd ldng pair over 1f out: styd on same pce* **9/2**^{2}	109
/21-	**5**	*2*	**Take A Bow**^{332} 2193 5-9-0 108 ... JimmyQuinn 2 (P R Chamings) *lw: t.k.h: hld up midfield: rdn and nt qckn over 2f out: n.d after: kpt on ins fnl f* **14/1**	104
0-11	**6**	*4*	**Something (IRE)**^{42} 667 4-9-0 105 ... IanMongan 1 (T G Mills) *lw: dwlt: t.k.h: hld up in last pair: rdn over 2f out: no real prog: wknd fnl f* **7/1**	95
210-	**7**	*2 ½*	**Momtic (IRE)**^{210} 5607 5-9-0 106 ... AlanMunro 3 (W Jarvis) *t.k.h: trckd ldng pair: rdn over 2f out: sn wknd* **5/1**^{3}	89
3313	**8**	*4*	**Azarole (IRE)**^{37} 704 5-9-0 107 ... JohnEgan 8 (J S Moore) *lw: hld up in last pair: rdn and no rspnse over 2f out: hanging and wknd over 1f out* **16/1**	80

1m 41.98s (-1.97) **Going Correction** +0.10s/f (Good) **8** Ran SP% **114.9**

Speed ratings (Par 115):113,112,110,110,108 104,102,98

CSF £19.97 TOTE £2.10: £1.20, £3.00, £2.80; EX 19.40.

Owner Philip Newton **Bred** Millsec, Ltd **Trained** Newmarket, Suffolk

■ Stewards' Enquiry : K J Manning one-day ban: careless riding (May 10)

FOCUS

Not a strong renewal, and the early pace was only steady, resulting in a bit of a sprint finish. The third sets the standard, but there is a strong suspicion the winner will leave this behind when stepping back up in class.

NOTEBOOK

Rob Roy(USA) was back at a mile, having failed to see out the ten furlongs of the Champion Stakes on his final run of an injury-plagued three-year-old season. Reported to have been working well prior to this reappearance, he tracked the leader, racing a little keenly as the pace was not strong, before being angled out for a run with two furlongs to go. Soon in front, he was always going to win from then on, but he did get a little tired at the end and will definitely improve for the run. (op 7-4 tchd 15-8)

Babodana is on a long losing run and has had plenty of chances at this sort of level, including when sixth and third in the last two runnings of this event. Travelling well enough on the inside, he took time to pick up when asked for his effort and was back in fourth passing the furlong pole before staying on well for second. (tchd 12-1)

Kings Point(IRE) was able to dictate the pace but could not counter when headed by the winner with over a furlong and a half to run. This was a respectable effort, but he will continue to prove vulnerable at this level. (tchd 12-1)

Democratic Deficit(IRE), who was giving Rob Roy 3lb when beating him a head in the Craven Stakes a year ago, was not suited by the way the race panned out and could only keep on without quite getting to the leaders. (op 5-1 tchd 11-2)

Take A Bow had an eleven-month absence to overcome after running just twice last season. He looked a threat when making his move but the effort soon amounted to little.

Something(IRE) was taking a rise in both trip and grade after landing a brace of seven-furlong handicaps on the Lingfield Polytrack. Slow away and another to race keenly early on, he could never get in a blow and still has something to prove. (op 11-2)

The Form Book, Raceform Ltd, Compton, RG20 6NL

Momtic(IRE) made great strides after landing a handicap off 86 on this card a year ago. On his seasonal bow, he got no cover from his wide pitch in the early stages and raced keenly. Under pressure with a quarter of a mile to run, he was soon in trouble. (op 13-2)

1300 BETFRED CLASSIC TRIAL (GROUP 3) 1m 2f 7y

4:25 (4:26) (Class 1) 3-Y-O **£28,390** (£10,760; £5,385; £2,685; £1,345) **Stalls High**

Form				RPR
110-	**1**		**Primary (USA)**[196] [5901] 3-9-0 91 DarryllHolland 4 (W J Haggas) *mde virtually all: strly pressed and edgd lft fnl 2f: hld on gamely nr fin* **4/1**[3]	104
5-1	**2**	*nk*	**The Last Drop (IRE)**[19] [948] 3-9-0 92 MichaelHills 3 (B W Hills) *dwlt: hld up in last: prog 2f out: chal wnr jst over 1f out : nt qckn and hld nr fin* **7/2**[2]	103
21-6	**3**	*hd*	**Baan (USA)**[10] [1083] 3-9-0 101 MartinDwyer 5 (M Johnston) *lw: chsd ldng pair: rdn over 3f out: rallied on inner wl over 1f out: pressed ldrs ins fnl f: nt qckn nr fin* **5/1**	103
134-	**4**	*1 ½*	**Private Business (USA)**[189] [6023] 3-9-0 104 RichardHughes 2 (B W Hills) *trckd wnr: rdn to chal over 2f out to over 1f out: wknd ins fnl f* **15/8**[1]	102+
021-	**5**	*1*	**Jadalee (IRE)**[215] [5503] 3-9-0 86 LDettori 1 (M P Tregoning) *t.k.h: hld up in tch: effrt over 2f out: nt qckn and edgd lft fr over 1f out: fdd* **5/1**	98

2m 9.40s (-0.84) **Going Correction** +0.10s/f (Good) **5 Ran SP% 110.3**
Speed ratings (Par 108):107,106,106,105,104
CSF £17.87 TOTE £5.40: £2.40, £2.00; EX 21.70.
Owner Highclere Thoroughbred Racing XXVI **Bred** G W Humphrey & Louise I Humphrey **Trained** Newmarket, Suffolk

FOCUS
A weak renewal of a trial whose significance seems to be on the wane. It has been rated around the third and the fourth, but the first two home were both big improvers and could well rate higher still.

NOTEBOOK
Primary(USA), who looked big and well beforehand but will definitely come on for the run, won his first two starts as a juvenile for David Loder but was a well-beaten last of eight in the Dewhurst on his final outing. Setting the pace, he was strongly pressed by his four rivals in the last two furlongs but, edging left, stuck his head out to get the verdict. There is improvement to come from him. (op 7-2 tchd 9-2 in a place)
The Last Drop(IRE), successful in a maiden on his reappearance and therefore fit, was slowly away and was still last turning for home. Although a little short of room when first attempting to close, he came through to press the winner but was always just being held. (op 4-1 tchd 9-2 in a place)
Baan(USA), upped in trip after finding the seven furlongs of the Free Handicap insufficient on his return, was the first of the five to come under pressure. Finding his stride, he rallied well, racing in isolation up inside the rail, and almost forced his head in front.
Private Business(USA), the pick on official figures, looked fit enough in the paddock and was in there fighting until fading inside the last. He was short of room when held, accentuating the margin of defeat. (tchd 2-1)
Jadalee(IRE), who looked very fit beforehand, had plenty to find on official figures and, although he finished last, this was probably his best run yet. He was in with every chance with two furlongs to run but his effort petered out going to the last. (op 4-1)

1301 BETFREDPOKER.COM H'CAP 1m 14y

4:55 (5:00) (Class 2) (0-100,99) 4-Y-0+
£11,217 (£3,358; £1,679; £840; £419; £210) **Stalls High**

Form				RPR
1/1-	**1**		**Public Forum**[344] [1854] 4-8-11 92 RichardHughes 8 (Sir Michael Stoute) *bit bkwd: trckd ldng pair: effrt and rdn 2f out: styd on wl fnl f to ld last strides* **7/1**[3]	101+
1111	**2**	*nk*	**Hail The Chief**[8] [1111] 9-8-1 85 oh1 RichardSmith(3) 11 (R Hannon) *led at gd pce: hrd pressed fr 2f out: battled on wl u.p: looked like holding on tl pushed along and hdd nr fin* **8/1**	93
150-	**3**	*1 ¼*	**Tanzanite (IRE)**[155] [6025] 4-8-6 87 AlanMunro 2 (D W P Arbuthnot) *cl up: effrt to join ldr 2f out tl nt qckn and hld wl ins fnl f* **25/1**	92
2243	**4**	*¾*	**Red Spell (IRE)**[7] [1129] 5-8-12 93 MJKinane 3 (R Hannon) *lw: hld up in last pair: n.m.r 2f out and stl in last trio: swtchd rt 1f out: rdn and r.o: no ch of rching ldrs* **7/2**[2]	96+
21-1	**5**	*shd*	**Cashier**[86] [278] 4-9-4 99 JimmyFortune 12 (J H M Gosden) *dwlt: pushed up to chse ldrs: rdn over 2f out: kpt on same pce* **11/4**[1]	102+
400-	**6**	*1 ½*	**Look Again**[198] [5848] 5-8-4 85 oh1 MartinDwyer 5 (R A Fahey) *dwlt: hld up in last pair: rdn over 2f out: no prog tl styd on ins fnl f* **14/1**	85+
0133	**7**	*nk*	**Binanti**[8] [1111] 6-8-4 85 oh1 JimmyQuinn 1 (P R Chamings) *hld up towards rr: effrt on outer over 2f out: cl enough wl over 1f out: fnd nil* **20/1**	84
03-4	**8**	*1 ¾*	**Zohar (USA)**[10] [1086] 4-8-9 90 LDettori 9 (B J Meehan) *hld up towards rr: nt qckn fr over 2f out and no prog* **9/1**	85
/1-1	**9**	*1*	**Fortunate Isle (USA)**[25] [865] 4-8-10 91 MichaelHills 10 (B W Hills) *lw: swtg: trckd ldrs: effrt and cl up wl over 1f out: wknd fnl f* **7/2**[2]	84
44-0	**10**	*7*	**Fiefdom (IRE)**[35] [728] 4-8-11 92 JohnEgan 4 (I W McInnes) *pressed ldr: shkn up and lost pl over 2f out: sn eased* **50/1**	68

1m 42.14s (-1.81) **Going Correction** +0.10s/f (Good) **10 Ran SP% 122.0**
Speed ratings (Par 109):113,112,111,110,110 109,108,107,106,99
CSF £63.28 CT £1372.23 TOTE £8.40: £2.30, £2.00, £5.60; EX 78.30.
Owner K Abdulla **Bred** Juddmonte Farms **Trained** Newmarket, Suffolk

FOCUS
A decent winning time for the type of race, only fractionally slower than the Group 2, although it didn't look that strongly run. The form is not all that solid but the winner can definitely rate higher. The second improved on his turf form while the third ran to her mark.

NOTEBOOK
Public Forum ◆ retained his unbeaten status on only his third racecourse appearance and first since last May. Racing over a trip very much on the sharp side, he finally won a shade more cosily than the neck margin would indicate, and he should have considerable improvement in him when stepped back up in trip. He will also come on plenty for this as paddock inspection suggested he would definitely improve for the run. (op 7-2 tchd 15-2)
Hail The Chief, who was 9lb higher than in his last race on turf, came close to completing a nap hand of victories. Reverting to front-running tactics, he fought off the challenge of the third but his rider then put down his stick and the combination succumbed well inside the last. (tchd 9-1)
Tanzanite(IRE), who had a fine season last year, had one run over hurdles in November. She delivered her challenge with a quarter of a mile to run but could not get past a determined leader. Easy ground is ideal for her. (op 50-1)
Red Spell(IRE) ◆, held up at the back, struggled to find racing room and, when in the clear, he had been left with too much to do, although he kept on for fourth without being knocked about. Despite having been raised 2lb since his last run he is still reasonably treated on turf. (op 9-2)
Cashier was 5lb higher than when scoring in Dubai nearly three months ago. He was always in a similar position and there appeared no real excuse. (op 4-1)
Look Again was sold out of Amanda Perrett's yard for 38,000gns after his final run last season. He has dropped to a handy mark, and although he failed to settle in the early stages he was keeping on at the end over this inadequate trip. Official explanation: jockey said saddle slipped (tchd 16-1)
Fortunate Isle(USA), who was 7lb higher than when scoring in heavy ground on his reappearance, became very warm beforehand. Asked for his effort with two furlongs to run, his response was disappointing. (op 10-3 tchd 4-1 and 9-2 in a place)
Fiefdom(IRE) Official explanation: jockey said gelding had no more to give

1302 BETFREDCASINO.COM FLAT V JUMP JOCKEYS H'CAP 1m 14y

5:30 (5:31) (Class 4) (0-80,80) 4-Y-0+ **£6,477** (£1,927; £963; £481) **Stalls High**

Form				RPR
4/	**1**		**Corran Ard (IRE)**[685] [2922] 5-11-2 78 MJKinane 3 (Evan Williams) *t.k.h: pressed ldrs: chal over 2f out: drvn over 1f out : r.o wl to gain upper hand last 150yds* **25/1**	88
0401	**2**	*½*	**Undeterred**[16] [1001] 10-10-9 71 JimmyFortune 4 (K J Burke) *hld up wl in rr: gd prog over 2f out: led narrowly over 1f out: hdd and hld last 150yds* **16/1**	80
505-	**3**	*2*	**Rowan Lodge (IRE)**[210] [5603] 4-11-0 76 DarryllHolland 7 (M H Tompkins) *wl plcd: effrt over 2f out: rdn to chse ldng pair over 1f out: no imp* **16/1**	80
00-2	**4**	*nk*	**Firesong**[17] [992] 4-10-13 75 LDettori 9 (Pat Eddery) *hld up wl in rr: last and drvn 3f out: no prog tl styd on fr over 1f out: nrst fin* **5/4**[1]	79+
530-	**5**	*nk*	**Brief Goodbye**[259] [4373] 6-10-11 73 TimmyMurphy 12 (John Berry) *s.i.s: sn in tch on inner: shkn up and kpt on same pce fnl 2f* **16/1**	76
45-0	**6**	*1*	**Della Salute**[4] [1207] 4-10-13 75 LeightonAspell 8 (Miss E C Lavelle) *dwlt: hld up wl in rr: gng wl enough whn nt clr run 2f out: swtchd lft over 1f out: styd on fnl f: nvr nrr* **16/1**	76+
30-0	**7**	*½*	**Arry Dash**[56] [108] 6-11-3 79 (v) APMcCoy 2 (M J Wallace) *chsd ldrs: rdn 2f out: one pce and no imp after* **10/1**[3]	79
261-	**8**	*1 ½*	**Kingsholm**[194] [5948] 4-11-2 78 RichardJohnson 1 (A M Balding) *racd freely: led over 5f out tl hdd & wknd over 1f out* **5/1**[2]	74
20-0	**9**	*1 ¼*	**Bold Diktator**[19] [946] 4-10-8 70 RichardHughes 11 (W R Muir) *led tl over 5f out: styd prom tl wknd 2f out* **14/1**	63
1-00	**10**	*1 ½*	**Wing Commander**[12] [1043] 7-11-0 76 RobertThornton 6 (I W McInnes) *racd on outer: in tch: effrt over 2f out: wknd over 1f out* **20/1**	66
00-0	**11**	*1 ¼*	**Barathea Dreams (IRE)**[35] [726] 5-11-4 80 MickFitzgerald 5 (J S Moore) *trckd ldrs tl wknd 2f out* **10/1**[3]	67
5550	**12**	*15*	**Northern Desert (IRE)**[27] [843] 7-10-10 72 AlanMunro 10 (P W Hiatt) *a towards rr: wknd rapidly 2f out* **12/1**	24

1m 43.48s (-0.47) **Going Correction** +0.10s/f (Good) **12 Ran SP% 125.8**
Speed ratings (Par 105):106,105,103,103,102 101,101,99,98,97 95,80
CSF £398.30 CT £6480.93 TOTE £31.60: £4.90, £3.30, £4.20; EX 281.90 Place 6 £2,045.78, Place 5 £749.78.
Owner E Salmon **Bred** Eamon Salmon **Trained** Cowbridge, Vale Of Glamorgan
■ A winner with his first runner on the Flat for Evan Williams, who has been making such a big impression over jumps.
■ Stewards' Enquiry : Darryll Holland two-day ban: careless riding (May 10-11)

FOCUS
A novelty event run at a fair pace, the finish of which was dominated by Flat jockeys. The form looks solid.
T/Jkpt: Not won. T/Plt: £2,264.80 to a £1 stake. Pool: £138,680.70. 44.70 winning tickets.
T/Qpdt: £52.70 to a £1 stake. Pool: £8,402.10. 117.95 winning tickets. JN

1271 WOLVERHAMPTON (A.W) (L-H)

Saturday, April 29

OFFICIAL GOING: Standard changing to standard to fast after race 2 (7.30)
Wind: Almost nil Weather: Fine

1303 KYLIE TRIBUTE AMATEUR RIDERS' H'CAP 5f 216y(P)

7:00 (7:01) (Class 6) (0-60,60) 4-Y-0+ **£2,637** (£811; £405) **Stalls Low**

Form				RPR
3206	**1**		**Obe Bold (IRE)**[25] [876] 5-10-7 46 oh1 MrsCBartley 2 (A Berry) *a.p: led 3f out: rdn and edgd rt fr over 1f out: r.o wl* **14/1**	62
5516	**2**	*5*	**Piccleyes**[12] [1054] 5-10-11 55 MrPCollington(5) 7 (M J Polglase) *hld up towards rr: hdwy over 2f out: sn swtchd rt: rdn and wnt 2nd 1f out: no ch w wnr* **10/1**	56
4225	**3**	*2 ½*	**Beneking**[1] [1273] 6-10-10 56 (p) MrPaulDavies(7) 13 (D Burchell) *chsd ldrs: ev ch over 2f out: sn rdn: one pce* **9/2**[2]	50+
1054	**4**	*1*	**Winning Venture**[29] [821] 9-10-10 54 ow2 MrMJJSmith(5) 8 (A W Carroll) *s.i.s: hdwy over 3f out: rdn over 2f out: kpt on same pce fnl f* **8/1**	45
00-3	**5**	*1*	**Mill By The Stream**[26] [862] 4-11-5 58 (p) MrSWalker 6 (P T Midgley) *hld up in tch: rdn over 1f out: wknd ins fnl f* **4/1**[1]	46
3-06	**6**	*1*	**Tipsy Lad**[3] [1245] 4-10-10 56 ow1 (bt) MrSJEdwards(7) 5 (D J S Ffrench Davis) *s.i.s: outpcd: hdwy over 1f out: n.d* **9/1**	41
0-04	**7**	*1*	**Fraternity**[16] [1001] 9-11-0 60 MissKJames(7) 1 (J A Pickering) *prom tl rdn and wknd wl over 1f out* **5/1**[3]	42
0000	**8**	*½*	**Vandal**[16] [1001] 6-10-0 46 oh1 MrsDButler(7) 3 (M Appleby) *s.i.s: nvr nr ldrs* **80/1**	26
2303	**9**	*1 ¾*	**Byo (IRE)**[40] [674] 8-10-11 57 MissFGuillambert(7) 11 (P Howling) *racd wd: hld up in mid-div: bhd fnl 3f* **14/1**	32
0-00	**10**	*¾*	**Silver Visage (IRE)**[98] [164] 4-10-8 54 (p) MrRBirkett(7) 12 (Miss J Feilden) *led: hdd 3f out: sn rdn: wknd wl over 1f out* **16/1**	27
005-	**11**	*2 ½*	**Fly More**[242] [4852] 9-10-0 46 MissSBradley(7) 4 (J M Bradley) *s.i.s: outpcd* **16/1**	11
005-	**12**	*1*	**Beau Marche**[233] [5062] 4-10-3 49 MissSGoldsmith(7) 10 (G G Margarson) *prom over 2f* **16/1**	11
0010	**13**	*1 ½*	**Fizzy Lizzy**[31] [793] 6-10-8 47 MissEJJones 9 (H E Haynes) *mid-div whn hmpd and lost pl over 3f out: sn bhd* **16/1**	—

1m 14.8s (-1.01) **Going Correction** -0.15s/f (Stan) **13 Ran SP% 123.1**
Speed ratings (Par 101):100,93,90,88,87 86,84,84,81,80 77,76,74
CSF £151.70 CT £771.71 TOTE £13.90: £2.90, £4.00, £2.20; EX 125.10.
Owner Alan Berry **Bred** Saud Bin Saad **Trained** Cockerham, Lancs
■ Stewards' Enquiry : Miss S Goldsmith one-day ban: failed to keep straight from stalls (May 11)

FOCUS
A very moderate amateurs' race, run at a good tempo but the form is not all that strong.

1304 PUT YOUR HAND ON YOUR HEART H'CAP — 5f 20y(P)
7:30 (7:31) (Class 6) (0-65,65) 3-Y-O — £3,071 (£906; £453) Stalls Low

Form			Horse	RPR
4032	1		**Glenviews Youngone (IRE)**[8] 1109 3-9-3 **64**.......... RobbieFitzpatrick 5 (Peter Grayson) *chsd ldr: led wl over 1f out: pushed clr fnl f* **5/2**[1]	83
005-	2	3 ½	**Fantasy Explorer**[288] 3509 3-8-12 **59**.......... JimmyQuinn 1 (J J Quinn) *t.k.h: prom: hmpd on ins over 1f out: rdn 2f out: chsd wnr fnl f: no imp* **7/2**[2]	65
0042	3	5	**Mister Incredible**[22] 910 3-8-12 **62**..........(b[1]) SaleemGolam(3) 4 (C A Dwyer) *hld up: hdwy over 2f out: one pce fnl f* **11/2**	50
060-	4	1	**Gift Aid**[192] 5969 3-8-4 **54** ow3.......... EdwardCreighton(3) 6 (P J Makin) *s.i.s: bhd tl kpt on fnl f: n.d* **14/1**	38
6043	5	nk	**Thoughtsofstardom**[4] 1210 3-8-11 **61**..........(v) AdamKirby(3) 7 (P S McEntee) *s.i.s: nvr nr ldrs* **13/2**	44
30-1	6	nk	**Twinned (IRE)**[16] 1003 3-9-4 **65**..........(p) LPKeniry 2 (J S Moore) *led: hdd wl over 1f out: sn rdn and wknd* **9/2**[3]	47
250-	7	¾	**Miss Dixie**[154] 6433 3-8-13 **60**.......... TonyHamilton 8 (Miss J A Camacho) *hld up in tch: rdn 3f out: sn wknd* **16/1**	40
06-0	8	2 ½	**Jackie Francis (IRE)**[44] 653 3-8-4 **51** oh1.......... AdrianMcCarthy 3 (P Howling) *bhd fnl 3f* **33/1**	22

60.82 secs (-2.00) **Going Correction** -0.15s/f (Stan) — 8 Ran SP% **113.2**
Speed ratings (Par 96):110,104,96,94,94 93,92,88
CSF £11.04 CT £42.64 TOTE £3.20: £1.40, £1.40, £1.70; EX 15.70.
Owner Mrs M Shaughnessy and Mrs S Grayson **Bred** Leslie Young **Trained** Formby, Lancs
FOCUS
A modest handicap but the time was a new course record for the distance, so the form is likely to be fairly reliable.

1305 DUNSTALL PARK SPRING PARTY NIGHT (S) STKS — 1m 141y(P)
8:00 (8:00) (Class 6) 3-Y-O+ — £2,388 (£705; £352) Stalls Low

Form			Horse	RPR
6002	1		**Bijou Dan**[7] 1148 5-9-9 63..........(b) DuranFentiman(5) 3 (W G Harrison) *a.p: rdn to ld ins fnl f: drvn out* **11/4**[1]	66
00-0	2	¾	**Finished Article (IRE)**[6] 1164 9-9-4 70.......... StephenDonohoe(5) 9 (W J Musson) *hld up and bhd: rdn and hdwy wl over 1f out: styd on towards fin* **5/1**[2]	59
0100	3	1 ¾	**Merdiff**[16] 1001 7-10-0 52.......... ShaneKelly 2 (W M Brisbourne) *led early: prom: led over 2f out: rdn over 1f out: hdd and no ex ins fnl f* **6/1**	61
0605	4	1 ½	**Granary Girl**[40] 683 4-9-9 48.......... JimmyQuinn 4 (J Pearce) *hld up: hdwy over 2f out: sn rdn: one pce fnl f* **8/1**	53
-002	5	2	**Frank's Quest (IRE)**[35] 734 6-9-2 51.......... JosephWalsh(7) 7 (A B Haynes) *hld up and bhd: hdwy over 2f out: sn rdn: wknd ins fnl f* **12/1**	48
530-	6	½	**Mescalera (GER)**[131] 6613 5-9-4 40.......... GeorgeBaker 5 (B G Powell) *hld up in tch: rdn over 2f out: wknd 1f out* **25/1**	42
1300	7	2 ½	**Joe Jo Star**[22] 906 4-10-0 51.......... RobbieFitzpatrick 1 (B P J Baugh) *sn led: hdd over 2f out: wknd wl over 1f out* **11/2**[3]	47
5645	8	1	**Zariano**[39] 689 6-9-6 47.......... BenSwarbrick(3) 6 (T D Barron) *prom tl rdn and wknd over 2f out* **13/2**	40
-600	9	1 ¾	**Angel River**[5] 1198 4-9-1 45..........(v[1]) SaleemGolam(3) 11 (J Ryan) *a bhd* **40/1**	31
0	10	dist	**Princess Rioja**[95] 184 6-9-4 35.......... PaulFitzsimons 10 (J M Bradley) *bhd: rdn 4f out: sn lost tch: t.o* **66/1**	—

1m 50.36s (-1.40) **Going Correction** -0.15s/f (Stan) — 10 Ran SP% **112.9**
Speed ratings (Par 101):100,99,97,96,94 94,92,91,89,—
CSF £15.40 TOTE £3.40: £1.70, £2.20, £2.40; EX 15.80.There was no bid for the winner.
Owner Bert Markey **Bred** James Thom And Sons **Trained** Lesmahagow, S Lanarks
FOCUS
A modest seller and weak form, with the third and sixth the best guide to the form.

1306 I SHOULD BE SO LUCKY MAIDEN STKS — 1m 1f 103y(P)
8:30 (8:32) (Class 5) 3-Y-O+ — £3,238 (£963; £481; £240) Stalls Low

Form			Horse	RPR
4-	1		**Oscillator**[177] 6234 3-8-12.......... NickyMackay 5 (G A Butler) *hld up: hdwy 3f out: rdn to ld wl over 1f out: drvn out* **3/1**[2]	77+
44	2	½	**Scotland Yard (UAE)**[19] 952 3-8-12.......... KDarley 4 (M Johnston) *w ldr: rdn and outpcd over 2f out: rallied 1f out: styd on u.p* **7/4**[1]	76
0-0	3	3	**Oporto (UAE)**[19] 948 3-8-7.......... MatthewHenry 1 (M A Jarvis) *stmbld s: hld up in tch: swtchd rt wl over 1f out: sn rdn: one pce fnl f* **33/1**	65
	4	5	**Volaire**[35] 4-9-5.......... AdamKirby(3) 8 (A J Lidderdale) *s.i.s: bhd: rdn over 2f out: styd on fnl f: n.d* **150/1**	59?
63-0	5	¾	**Diamond Diggins (GER)**[12] 1051 4-9-8 73.......... JamesDoyle(5) 3 (V Smith) *led: rdn and hdd over 2f out: wknd fnl f* **16/1**[3]	62
5-	6	1 ½	**Strawberry Lolly**[207] 5692 3-8-7.......... RyanMoore 6 (Sir Michael Stoute) *w ldrs: led over 2f out: rdn and hdd wl over 1f out: wknd fnl f* **7/4**[1]	52
	7	12	**Top Level (IRE)** 3-8-7.......... TPQueally 7 (M G Quinlan) *hld up and bhd: rdn 3f out: sn struggling* **66/1**	29

2m 0.58s (-2.04) **Going Correction** -0.15s/f (Stan)
WFA 3 from 4yo 15lb — 7 Ran SP% **108.7**
Speed ratings (Par 103):103,102,99,95,94 93,82
CSF £7.76 TOTE £3.60: £2.40, £1.70; EX 3.60.
Owner Future In Mind Partnership **Bred** P D Player **Trained** Blewbury, Oxon
FOCUS
A fair maiden for the course, in which the winner, a Derby entrant, won with a little in hand. The runner-up sets the standard.

1307 SPINNING AROUND DUNSTALL PARK FILLIES' H'CAP — 1m 141y(P)
8:55 (8:57) (Class 5) (0-70,70) 3-Y-O — £3,238 (£963; £481; £240) Stalls Low

Form			Horse	RPR
1620	1		**Magical Music**[16] 1005 3-9-4 **70**.......... JimmyQuinn 2 (J Pearce) *hld up in tch: rdn to ld over 1f out: drvn out* **11/8**[1]	74
-234	2	1 ¼	**Crazy Bear (IRE)**[35] 735 3-9-2 **68**.......... NCallan 3 (K A Ryan) *hld up in tch: rdn over 2f out: kpt on same pce fnl f* **11/4**[2]	69
200-	3	hd	**Blushing Hilary (IRE)**[194] 5939 3-9-3 **69**..........(p) TonyHamilton 1 (Miss J A Camacho) *set slow pce: rdn and hdd over 1f out: sn edgd rt: nt qckn ins fnl f* **12/1**	70
020-	4	1 ½	**Welsh Cake**[182] 6143 3-8-11 **63**.......... RyanMoore 4 (Mrs A J Perrett) *hld up in rr: rdn over 2f out: hung lft over 1f out: styd on same pce fnl f* **4/1**[3]	60
020-	5	2 ½	**Shinko (IRE)**[217] 5463 3-8-9 **66**.......... JamesDoyle(5) 5 (Miss J Feilden) *w ldr: rdn and ev ch over 2f out: wknd fnl f* **25/1**	58
6100	6	12	**Living On A Prayer**[32] 781 3-8-10 **62**.......... ShaneKelly 7 (J Pearce) *hld up in tch: rdn over 3f out: wknd over 2f out* **10/1**	29

1m 52.66s (0.90) **Going Correction** -0.15s/f (Stan) — 6 Ran SP% **109.4**
Speed ratings (Par 95):90,88,88,87,85 74
CSF £5.01 TOTE £2.50: £1.10, £2.40; EX 5.40.
Owner Killarney Glen & Mrs E M Clarke **Bred** Peter Taplin **Trained** Newmarket, Suffolk
FOCUS
A modest fillies-only handicap, run at a very-slow early gallop. The form must be rated as suspect.

1308 ESPECIALLY FOR YOU AT DUNSTALL PARK H'CAP — 1m 4f 50y(P)
9:20 (9:21) (Class 6) (0-60,62) 4-Y-O+ — £2,730 (£806; £403) Stalls Low

Form			Horse	RPR
300-	1		**Explosive Fox (IRE)**[152] 6448 5-9-1 **56**.......... AlanDaly 5 (S Curran) *a.p: led over 1f out: rdn out* **16/1**	64
1422	2	1 ½	**York Cliff**[1] 1271 8-8-8 **56**.......... LiamJones(7) 1 (W M Brisbourne) *hld up and bhd: rdn wl over 1f out: gd hdwy fnl f: fin wl* **7/2**[2]	62+
5022	3	½	**Lady Taverner**[18] 972 5-9-0 **60**.......... NataliaGemelova(5) 2 (J E Long) *hld up in mid-div: n.m.r over 3f out: hdwy on ins over 2f out: rdn and ev ch over 1f out: nt qckn* **8/1**	65
00-6	4	1 ½	**Star Rising**[38] 696 4-8-5 **52**.......... StephenDonohoe(5) 11 (W J Musson) *plld hrd early: a.p: rdn and one pce fnl 2f* **7/1**[3]	54
0224	5	2 ½	**Valeureux**[17] 990 8-8-13 **54**.......... MichaelTebbutt 6 (J Hetherton) *set mod pce: qcknd 5f out: rdn over 2f out: hdd over 1f out: wknd ins fnl f* **8/1**	52
145-	6	5	**Ocean Rock**[173] 6283 5-8-12 **53**.......... OscarUrbina 4 (C A Horgan) *stdd s: hld up in rr: nt clr run over 2f out tl wl over 1f out: nvr nrr* **7/1**[3]	43
60-4	7	¾	**Archirondel**[19] 955 8-8-10 **54**.......... DNolan(3) 3 (N Wilson) *hld up and bhd: hdwy over 3f out: rdn and wknd 2f out* **12/1**	43
525-	8	1 ¾	**Persian Carpet**[269] 4065 4-9-1 **57**.......... LPKeniry 12 (B I Case) *nvr nr ldrs* **50/1**	43
0421	9	¾	**Scottish River (USA)**[7] 1152 7-9-7 **62**.......... HayleyTurner 8 (M D I Usher) *t.k.h: prom: ev ch over 2f out: wknd wl over 1f out* **5/2**[1]	47
5014	10	8	**Reminiscent (IRE)**[35] 733 7-9-0 **55**..........(p) PaulEddery 7 (B P J Baugh) *hld up: hdwy 7f out: rdn over 4f out: wknd 3f out* **20/1**	27
516-	11	3 ½	**Turner**[286] 3563 5-9-5 **60**.......... RobbieFitzpatrick 10 (W M Brisbourne) *hld up in mid-div: rdn over 4f out: wknd over 2f out* **20/1**	27

2m 39.63s (-2.79) **Going Correction** -0.15s/f (Stan)
WFA 4 from 5yo+ 1lb — 11 Ran SP% **123.1**
Speed ratings (Par 101):103,102,101,100,99 95,95,94,93,88 85
CSF £73.32 CT £504.82 TOTE £14.00: £3.50, £1.30, £2.20; EX 112.40 Place 6 £45.24, Place 5 £9.21.
Owner L M Power **Bred** Swettenham Stud, Caradale Trading Co And T Stack **Trained** Faringdon, Oxon
■ Sean Curran saddled his first winner with his first-ever runner.
FOCUS
Low-grade stuff, but a very easy winner. The form appears fairly sound rated around those in the frame behind the winner.
Scottish River(USA) Official explanation: jockey said she was unable to get gelding covered up and it ran too free
T/Plt: £27.80 to a £1 stake. Pool: £48,009.70. 1,258.65 winning tickets. T/Qpdt: £6.60 to a £1 stake. Pool: £3,446.00. 382.60 winning tickets. KH

BRIGHTON (L-H)
Sunday, April 30

OFFICIAL GOING: Firm (good to firm in places)
Wind: Moderate, against

1309 EUROPEAN BREEDERS FUND MAIDEN STKS — 5f 59y
2:10 (2:11) (Class 5) 2-Y-O — £4,533 (£1,348; £674; £336) Stalls Low

Form			Horse	RPR
2	1		**Mind The Style**[11] 1080 2-9-0.......... RobertMiles(3) 2 (W G M Turner) *mde all: hrd rdn fnl f: hld on gamely* **15/8**[2]	73
22	2	nk	**Rippling River**[9] 1107 2-9-3.......... AlanMunro 3 (W Jarvis) *t.k.h: trckd ldrs: hung right from hlfway: rdn to chse winner from over 1f out: ran on fnl 100 yrds* **5/6**[1]	72
64	3	3	**She Wont Wait**[13] 1046 2-8-12.......... FergusSweeney 4 (T M Jones) *w wnr to over 1f out: wknd ins fnl f* **25/1**	55
50	4	1 ¾	**Mrs Crossy (IRE)**[13] 1046 2-8-12.......... RyanMoore 1 (R Hannon) *chsd ldrs: rdn ½-wy: wkng whn hung lft fnl f* **9/1**[3]	48
4	5	4	**River Prince**[8] 1136 2-8-11 ow1.......... RichardGordon(7) 5 (W G M Turner) *s.i.s: sn prom on outside: rdn ½-wy: wknd over 1f out* **33/1**	39

62.36 secs **Going Correction** 0.0s/f (Good) — 5 Ran SP% **106.1**
Speed ratings (Par 92):99,98,93,90,84
CSF £3.46 TOTE £2.70: £1.50, £1.10; EX 3.50.
Owner Stephen Bell and Tracy Turner **Bred** N And L Warburton **Trained** Sigwells, Somerset
■ Stewards' Enquiry : Robert Miles one-day ban: used whip with excessive frequency (May 11)
FOCUS
A typical Brighton juvenile event; just ordinary form but straightforward with the first two and the fourth close to their previous best.
NOTEBOOK
Mind The Style, a promising second on his debut at Beverley nearly two weeks previously, showed the benefit of that run to win in determined fashion. He had the run of the race while the runner-up did not appear suited by the track, so things will be tougher next time. (tchd 7-4)
Rippling River, second on both his previous starts, raced keenly and did not appear ideally suited by the track. He again found one too good despite running on at the finish and can be given another chance on a more conventional course. (op 4-5 tchd 10-11)
She Wont Wait was no match for the front two late on. She has ability, but may just need to be dropped a touch in grade. (op 33-1)
Mrs Crossy(IRE) has held an entry in a claimer and will be better off in that sort of company by the look of things. (op 8-1 tchd 10-1)
River Prince failed to build on the promise he showed on his debut at Nottingham and looks very limited. (op 40-1)

1310 RACECOURSE VIDEO SERVICES (S) STKS — 5f 213y
2:45 (2:49) (Class 6) 3-Y-O+ — £2,266 (£674; £337; £168) Stalls Low

Form			Horse	RPR
4251	1		**Boanerges (IRE)**[8] 1150 9-9-12 55.......... RyanMoore 10 (J M Bradley) *hld up in mid-div: swtchd rt 2f out: rdn and r.o to ld ins fnl f* **9/2**[2]	61

4604 **2** ½ **Hadath (IRE)**[18] 982 9-9-12 54 (b) GeorgeBaker 7 59
(B G Powell) *in rr: plenty to do 2f out: hdwy over 1f out: fin fast: nvr nrr* **8/1**[3]

00-0 **3** ¾ **Renegade (IRE)**[25] 886 5-9-6 47 (p) IanMongan 3 51
(Mrs L J Mongan) *trckd ldrs: ev ch ent fnl f: rdn and r.o* **16/1**

1604 **4** *hd* **Imperium**[13] 1054 5-9-12 51 (p) FrancisNorton 2 56
(Stef Liddiard) *a.p on ins: led 2f out: hdd and no ex ins fnl f* **3/1**[1]

5440 **5** ¾ **Mulberry Lad (IRE)**[37] 708 4-9-9 46 RobertMiles(3) 12 54
(P W Hiatt) *rcd alone on stands' side: r.o fnl f: nvr nrr* **16/1**

2002 **6** ¾ **Stagnite**[30] 821 6-9-5 48 (p) SophieDoyle(7) 1 52
(K McAuliffe) *led until hdd 2f out: wknd fnl f* **9/1**

0000 **7** 3 **Revien (IRE)**[72] 446 4-9-6 50 PaulFitzsimons 8 37
(Miss J R Tooth) *in tch: rdn 2f out: wknd appr fnl f* **25/1**

0-65 **8** ¾ **Keresforth**[20] 943 4-9-6 40 (b) LPKeniry 5 35
(Mrs L C Jewell) *chsd ldr until wknd appr fnl f* **66/1**

00-0 **9** *hd* **Jasmine Pearl (IRE)**[18] 982 5-9-1 45 FergusSweeney 6 29
(T M Jones) *towards rr: effrt on ins over 1f out: sn btn* **12/1**

010- **10** ¾ **Dorn Hill**[123] 6677 4-9-4 45 DNolan(3) 11 33
(D G Bridgwater) *bhd and nvr nr to chal* **40/1**

0-00 **11** 2 **Danescourt (IRE)**[20] 951 4-9-6 40 (b) ChrisCatlin 13 26
(J M Bradley) *hld up: a bhd* **40/1**

5240 **12** 1 **Cloann (IRE)**[25] 889 4-9-1 48 (b) StephenCarson 9 18
(E A Wheeler) *chsd ldrs until wknd wl over 1f out* **8/1**[3]

000- **13** 2 **Saucepot**[138] 6570 4-9-1 35 SamHitchcott 4 12
(Miss J R Tooth) *trckd ldrs: rdn 2f out: wknd over 1f out* **66/1**

0060 **14** ½ **Silver Reign**[25] 890 5-9-3 40 (b[1]) NeilChalmers(3) 14 15
(J J Bridger) *in tch on outside until rdn and wknd 2f out* **100/1**

-000 **15** *nk* **Yorkshire Lad (IRE)**[5] 1209 4-9-3 55 (v[1]) AdamKirby(3) 15 14
(Miss Gay Kelleway) *slowly away: a bhd* **9/1**

6003 **16** 4 **Goldhill Prince**[18] 982 4-9-1 49 (p) JamesDoyle(5) 16 2
(Ernst Oertel) *in tch until wknd wl over 1f out* **12/1**

69.90 secs **Going Correction** 0.0s/f (Good) **16** Ran SP% **125.3**

Speed ratings (Par 101):101,100,99,99,98 97,93,92,91,90 88,86,84,83,83 77

CSF £40.22 TOTE £4.10: £1.80, £3.10, £6.40; EX 32.50 Trifecta £202.90 Part won. Pool: £285.90 - 0.69 winning units..There was no bid for the winner.

Owner E A Hayward **Bred** Clare Dore Ltd **Trained** Sedbury, Gloucs

FOCUS

Hand-timed. As is to be expected with a seller, moderate form with the fifth the best guide.

Renegade(IRE) Official explanation: jockey said gelding hung right in the closing stages

Yorkshire Lad(IRE) Official explanation: trainer said gelding was unsuited by the track

1311 ICEBUSTERS SERVICES H'CAP 7f 214y

3:20 (3:20) (Class 5) (0-70,70) 4-Y-0+ **£3,238** (£963; £481; £240) **Stalls** Low

Form RPR

5260 **1** **Takes Tutu (USA)**[11] 1075 7-8-10 **62** RobertWinston 7 77
(C R Dore) *hld up: swtchd rt 2f out: rdn to ld jst ins fnl f: sn clr* **5/1**[3]

25-1 **2** 4 **Molem**[27] 854 4-8-13 **70** (tp) RichardKingscote(5) 11 76
(Lady Herries) *a.p: led briefly 1f out: rdn and nt pce of wnr* **11/4**[1]

1030 **3** *nk* **Golden Spectrum (IRE)**[2] 1273 7-7-12 **57** (b) TolleyDean(7) 9 62
(R A Harris) *a.p: rdn over 1f out: one pce fnl f* **9/2**[2]

000- **4** 3 **Oh Boy (IRE)**[223] 5364 6-8-4 **56** oh3 ChrisCatlin 8 54
(J M Bradley) *led until rdn and hdd 1f out: sn wknd* **20/1**

00-5 **5** 2 ½ **Blue Line**[23] 902 4-8-6 **58** JimmyQuinn 10 50
(M Madgwick) *hld up: nvr nr to chal* **10/1**

2-00 **6** 3 ½ **Cormorant Wharf (IRE)**[92] 223 6-8-13 **65** RyanMoore 5 49
(G L Moore) *rcd wide: a towards rr* **5/1**[3]

406- **7** ¾ **Zafarshah (IRE)**[136] 6584 7-8-4 **56** oh3 (b) AdrianMcCarthy 6 39
(R A Harris) *mid-div: rdn 2f out: no hdwy after* **16/1**

-600 **8** 2 **Jools**[7] 1164 8-8-13 **68** SaleemGolam(3) 2 46
(D K Ivory) *in tch: rdn 3f out: wknd over 1f out* **8/1**

00 **9** 1 ½ **Silvo (NZ)**[7] 1163 7-8-5 **57** FrancisNorton 1 32
(M F Harris) *mid-div: bhd final 2f* **25/1**

0500 **10** ¾ **Edge Fund**[11] 1073 4-7-13 **56** oh6 (b) JamesDoyle(5) 3 29
(Miss Gay Kelleway) *bhd 2f out* **20/1**

1m 34.85s **Going Correction** 0.0s/f (Good) **10** Ran SP% **117.6**

Speed ratings (Par 103):100,96,95,92,90 86,85,83,82,81

CSF £18.74 CT £67.08 TOTE £6.30: £2.00, £1.50, £2.00; EX 20.50 Trifecta £113.40 Pool: £450.67 - 2.82 winning units..

Owner Page, Ward, Marsh **Bred** Harbor View Farm **Trained** West Pinchbeck, Lincs

FOCUS

A pretty modest handicap won in clear-cut fashion by Takes Tutu, who had dropped to a very fair mark. The third sets the standard for the form.

1312 BECK'S VIER H'CAP 6f 209y

3:55 (3:55) (Class 5) (0-75,75) 3-Y-0 **£3,886** (£1,156; £577; £288) **Stalls** Low

Form RPR

435- **1** **Pressure Putt**[152] 6467 3-9-4 **75** DarryllHolland 8 83
(W J Haggas) *trckd ldr: led over 2f out: rdn over 1f out: hld on wl fnl f* **2/1**[2]

355- **2** ½ **Neardown Beauty (IRE)**[166] 6353 3-8-9 **66** NCallan 9 73
(I A Wood) *s.i.s: hdwy 2f out: chsd wnr over 1f out: no imp ins fnl f* **14/1**

5-56 **3** 2 ½ **Spectacular Show (IRE)**[27] 851 3-9-3 **74** FrancisNorton 1 74
(M Quinn) *a in tch: kpt on u.p ins fnl f* **14/1**

1-54 **4** *nk* **Sands Of Barra (IRE)**[31] 803 3-9-1 **72** RyanMoore 6 71
(N A Callaghan) *t.k.h: hld up: rdn and hdwy 2f out: one pce ins fnl f* **6/4**[1]

6056 **5** 3 **Shannon House**[5] 1212 3-8-5 **62** FrankieMcDonald 2 53
(M J McGrath) *hld up in rr: effrt over 1f out: nvr nr to chal* **20/1**

0140 **6** ½ **African Concerto (IRE)**[31] 807 3-8-2 **64** JamesDoyle(5) 5 54
(Ernst Oertel) *hld up in rr: nvr on terms* **9/1**[3]

0-00 **7** 6 **Goodbye Girl (IRE)**[9] 1122 3-8-6 **63** oh15 ow2 (p) BrianReilly 4 38
(Mrs C A Dunnett) *led until hdd over 2f out: sn wknd* **33/1**

0020 **8** *shd* **Lady Zanzara (USA)**[18] 984 3-8-6 **63** WandersonD'Avila 7 37
(J W Hills) *t.k.h: trckd ldrs: wknd wl over 1f out* **16/1**

301- **9** 2 **Mujelle**[139] 6557 3-8-10 **67** JimmyQuinn 3 36
(D K Ivory) *in tch until wknd 2f out* **11/1**

20-0 **10** 8 **Enchanting Times (IRE)**[55] 604 3-8-8 **65** PaulEddery 10 13
(D G Bridgwater) *chsd ldrs on outside: wknd qckly wl over 2f out* **40/1**

1m 22.45s **Going Correction** 0.0s/f (Good) **10** Ran SP% **121.0**

Speed ratings (Par 98):101,100,97,97,93 93,86,86,83,74

CSF £31.17 CT £336.86 TOTE £3.00: £1.30, £3.60, £3.50; EX 34.00 Trifecta £205.80 Pool: £831.91 - 2.87 winning units..

Owner Lee Palmer **Bred** Mrs S Crompton **Trained** Newmarket, Suffolk

FOCUS

Just an ordinary handicap and the form is not that strong, rated through the third.

Mujelle Official explanation: jockey said gelding lost its action

1313 INBEV UK BECK'S VIER H'CAP 1m 3f 196y

4:30 (4:31) (Class 6) (0-60,58) 4-Y-0+ **£2,914** (£867; £433; £216) **Stalls** High

Form RPR

24-0 **1** **Figaro's Quest (IRE)**[19] 973 4-8-8 **48** (b) MartinDwyer 3 66
(P F I Cole) *s.i.s: wl in rr whn stdy hdwy 4f out: led over 2f out: sn wl clr: v. easily* **3/1**[1]

5000 **2** 10 **Chocolate Boy (IRE)**[25] 888 7-8-9 **48** (b) RyanMoore 8 54+
(G L Moore) *hld up: hdwy on outside to go 2nd over 1f out: no ch w easy wnr* **9/2**[2]

56-6 **3** 1 ½ **Ulshaw**[32] 794 9-8-5 **44** oh4 LPKeniry 5 44
(J M Bradley) *a in tch: kpt on one pce fnl 2f* **12/1**

3-00 **4** 1 **Lenwade**[32] 792 5-8-6 **45** BrianReilly 12 43
(G G Margarson) *hld up in rr: hdwy 4f out: chsd ldrs 2f out: one pce* **14/1**

000- **5** *shd* **Victor Buckwell**[314] 2760 4-8-5 **45** FrancisNorton 7 43
(G L Moore) *hld up in rr: kpt on fnl 2f: nvr nrr* **10/1**

0-00 **6** 7 **Jubilee Dream**[29] 838 4-9-3 **57** (t) IanMongan 2 44
(Mrs L J Mongan) *hld up: hdwy 4f out: rdn 3f out: sn btn* **16/1**

0-06 **7** 6 **Icannshift (IRE)**[19] 973 6-8-9 **48** FergusSweeney 10 25
(T M Jones) *trckd ldr: led 5f out: hdd over 2f out: sn wknd* **8/1**[3]

500- **8** ½ **Briannie (IRE)**[132] 6612 4-8-2 **45** (p) EdwardCreighton(3) 1 21
(P Butler) *slowly away: a bhd* **33/1**

50-0 **9** 3 **Nobbler**[18] 990 4-8-13 **53** NCallan 9 25
(N A Callaghan) *chsd ldrs: rdn 3f out: sn wknd* **8/1**[3]

010- **10** ½ **Cantrip**[182] 6184 6-9-5 **58** StephenCarson 4 29
(Miss B Sanders) *prom until rdn and wknd 3f out* **9/2**[2]

0005 **11** 7 **Ready Teddy Go**[5] 1224 4-8-3 **46** oh5 ow2 (v) SaleemGolam(3) 6 6
(J Ryan) *led until hdd 5f out: wknd 3f out* **28/1**

0-00 **12** 23 **Rhetorical**[61] 545 5-8-5 **44** oh9 (p) ChrisCatlin 11 —
(P Butler) *mid-div: wknd 5f out* **80/1**

2m 31.66s **Going Correction** 0.0s/f (Good)

WFA 4 from 5yo+ 1lb **12** Ran SP% **120.5**

Speed ratings (Par 101):101,94,93,92,92 87,83,83,81,81 76,61

CSF £16.01 CT £145.41 TOTE £3.90: £1.70, £1.90, £3.50; EX 21.70 Trifecta £161.70 Pool: £464.81 - 2.04 winning units..

Owner The Fairy Story Partnership **Bred** Deepwood Farm Stud **Trained** Whatcombe, Oxon

FOCUS

A moderate race with no strength in depth and Figaro's Quest, who had previously looked exposed, absolutely hacked up.

Nobbler Official explanation: jockey said gelding had no more to give

1314 BETFAIR H'CAP 1m 1f 209y

5:05 (5:07) (Class 6) (0-60,60) 3-Y-0 **£2,590** (£770; £385; £192) **Stalls** High

Form RPR

00-0 **1** **Precious Dancer**[19] 963 3-9-2 **58** DarryllHolland 4 67
(W R Muir) *hld up in rr: hdwy over 3f out: r.o fnl f: led nr fin* **11/1**

0000 **2** ½ **Iberian Light (USA)**[59] 558 3-8-13 **55** NCallan 8 63
(N A Callaghan) *chsd ldr: led wl over 1f out: edged rt ins fnl f: hdd nr fin* **6/1**[3]

0-10 **3** *shd* **Penang Cinta**[73] 430 3-9-2 **58** RobertWinston 10 66
(G A Butler) *mid-div: hdwy on outside over 2f out: ev ch 1f out: nt qckn cl hme* **13/2**

6363 **4** 3 **Bahhmirage (IRE)**[8] 1149 3-8-5 **47** (b) FrancisNorton 5 49
(Stef Liddiard) *t.k.h: mid-div: r.o ins fnl f: nvr nrr* **20/1**

0455 **5** 3 **Flashing Floozie**[29] 839 3-8-7 **52** RichardThomas(3) 9 48
(M F Harris) *towards rr: swtchd lft over 1f out: styd on fnl f but nvr nr to chal* **25/1**

006- **6** 1 **Sebaaq (USA)**[263] 4242 3-9-3 **59** (b[1]) MartinDwyer 6 53
(M P Tregoning) *led until hdd wl over 1f out: not run on* **8/1**

-206 **7** 1 **Emotive**[4] 1241 3-8-13 **55** (b) RyanMoore 1 48
(I A Wood) *mid-div: rdn 3f out: no danger fnl 2f* **7/2**[1]

0-00 **8** ½ **It's Basil**[22] 918 3-8-11 **53** FergusSweeney 11 45
(R M Flower) *mid-div: swtchd lft over 1f out: kpt on one pce* **25/1**

0000 **9** 5 **King's College (USA)**[33] 781 3-8-6 **55** (p) JamieJones(7) 2 37
(G L Moore) *in tch: rdn over 4 out: wknd over 2f out* **33/1**

00-0 **10** 1 ¾ **Dynamite Deano**[8] 1141 3-8-7 **52** SaleemGolam(3) 3 31
(D K Ivory) *a bhd* **25/1**

0322 **11** 1 ½ **Night Groove (IRE)**[13] 1044 3-8-13 **60** (b) JamesDoyle(5) 7 36
(N P Littmoden) *prom until wknd 3f out* **4/1**[2]

00-0 **12** 11 **Flying Penne**[8] 1140 3-8-1 **50** ThomasO'Brien(7) 14 5
(M R Channon) *rrd up leaving stalls: a bhd* **25/1**

0506 **13** 1 ¾ **Zizou (IRE)**[5] 1215 3-8-7 **52** (t) NeilChalmers(3) 13 4
(J J Bridger) *mid-div: chsd ldrs 3f out: rdn and sn wknd* **10/1**

5560 **14** ½ **Ms Rainbow Runner**[22] 918 3-8-11 **53** ChrisCatlin 12 4
(P Butler) *chsd ldrs until rdn and wknd 3f out* **20/1**

2m 3.65s **Going Correction** 0.0s/f (Good) **14** Ran SP% **126.2**

Speed ratings (Par 96):95,94,94,92,89 88,88,87,83,82 81,72,70,70

CSF £72.03 CT £481.92 TOTE £15.30: £4.40, £3.30, £2.60; EX 127.70 TRIFECTA Not won..

Owner Perspicacious Punters Racing Club **Bred** Biddestone Stud And Partner **Trained** Lambourn, Berks

■ Stewards' Enquiry : N Callan caution: careless riding

FOCUS

A moderate handicap but a few of these were unexposed and the form does not look too bad for the grade with the fourth setting the standard.

Bahhmirage(IRE) Official explanation: jockey said filly was denied a clear run

Night Groove(IRE) Official explanation: jockey said gelding did not handle the track

1315 CONSTELLATION WINES H'CAP 5f 59y

5:35 (5:36) (Class 5) (0-70,68) 4-Y-0+ **£3,886** (£1,156; £577; £288) **Stalls** Low

Form

3031 **1** **Misaro (GER)**[5] 1209 5-8-9 **59** (b) AdrianMcCarthy 7 70+
(R A Harris) *a.p: rdn to ld ins fnl f: r.o wl* **11/10**[1]

0613 **2** 1 ¼ **Red Sovereign**[20] 951 5-8-12 **65** DNolan(3) 3 71
(D G Bridgwater) *led until rdn and hdd over 1f out: edged lft ins fnl f: jst hld on for 2nd* **12/1**

212- **3** *shd* **Dance To The Blues (IRE)**[155] 6426 5-9-1 **68** (p) AdamKirby(3) 2 74
(B De Haan) *hung lft thrght but a.p: n.m.r ins fnl f but kpt on* **6/1**[2]

30-0 **4** 1 **Redwood Star**[19] 967 6-9-3 **67** (e) ChrisCatlin 1 69
(P L Gilligan) *in rr: rdn and styd on fnl f: nvr nrr* **10/1**

10-0 **5** *nk* **Cosmic Destiny (IRE)**[18] 986 4-8-9 **59** TPQueally 4 60
(E F Vaughan) *chsd ldrs: rdn to ld over 1f out: hdd and wknd ins fnl f* **10/1**

20-0 **6** *shd* **Wise Wager (IRE)**[39] 699 4-9-1 **65** RobertWinston 6 66
(Miss Z C Davison) *in tch: rdn and hung lft over 1f out: no imp fnl f* **20/1**

-000 **7** ¾ **Bold Cheverak**[18] 986 4-8-6 **56** ow1 BrianReilly 9 54
(Mrs C A Dunnett) *a in rr* **25/1**

00-4 **8** ½ **Campeon (IRE)**[4] 1243 4-9-0 **64** RyanMoore 8 60
(J M Bradley) *prom on outside: rdn 2f out: wknd over 1f out* **7/1**[3]
6065 **9** 11 **Detonate**[4] 1243 4-7-13 **54** oh4 (b[1]) JamesDoyle(5) 5 11
(Mrs C A Dunnett) *w ldr until wknd rapidly wl over 1f out* **17/2**
62.41 secs **Going Correction** 0.0s/f (Good) **9** Ran SP% **119.4**
Speed ratings (Par 103):99,97,96,95,94 94,93,92,75
CSF £17.09 CT £61.91 TOTE £2.10: £1.50, £3.80, £2.00; EX 19.80 Trifecta £38.90 Pool: £627.47 - 11.45 winning units. Place 6 £60.95, Place 5 £57.47.
Owner C Waters **Bred** Wilhelm Fasching **Trained** Earlswood, Monmouths

FOCUS
A modest sprint handicap in which Misaro followed up his recent success in an apprentice handicap at Folkestone in clear-cut fashion, having avoided a penalty. The form, rated around the third and fourth, is not that strong.
Dance To The Blues(IRE) Official explanation: jockey said mare hung left
Campeon(IRE) Official explanation: jockey said gelding lost its action
T/Plt: £73.00 to a £1 stake. Pool: £55,542.75. 555.30 winning tickets. T/Qpdt: £26.40 to a £1 stake. Pool: £3,567.15. 99.85 winning tickets. JS

1316 - 1323a (Foreign Racing) - See Raceform Interactive

NAVAN (L-H)
Sunday, April 30

OFFICIAL GOING: Good to firm (good in places)

1324a VINTAGE CROP STKS (LISTED RACE) 1m 5f
4:30 (4:30) 4-Y-0+ **£22,448** (£6,586; £3,137; £1,068) **Stalls** Far side

RPR
1 **Kastoria (IRE)**[211] 5639 5-9-1 111 (t) MJKinane 5 104+
(John M Oxx, Ire) *trckd ldrs in 5th: impr into 4th 4f out: 3rd over 2f out: led 1 1/2f out: kpt on wl u.p fnl f* **1/2**[1]
2 1 **Virginia Woolf**[21] 931 4-8-12 92 FMBerry 6 101
(John M Oxx, Ire) *cl 2nd: led early st: sn strly pressed: hdd 1 1/2f out: 3rd over 1f out: kpt on wl u.p* **8/1**[3]
3 2 **Valentina Guest (IRE)**[7] 1173 5-8-12 95 JAHeffernan 8 97
(Peter Casey, Ire) *trckd ldrs: 3rd 1/2-way: 2nd and chal early st: 3rd and no ex ins fnl f* **12/1**
4 2½ **Cairdeas (IRE)**[21] 932 5-9-1 110 DPMcDonogh 1 97
(D K Weld, Ire) *hld up in rr: prog over 4f out: 4th and rdn 2f out: no imp: kpt on same pce* **4/1**[2]
5 3½ **Imperial Rose (IRE)**[15] 1026 4-8-12 90 WSupple 4 90
(H Rogers, Ire) *hld up: last appr st: prog into 5th under 2f out: kpt on same pce* **33/1**
6 10 **Subtle Affair (IRE)**[15] 1026 4-8-12 80 KFallon 3 77
(P F Cashman, Ire) *plld hrd to 1/2-way: settled 4th: 5th appr st: no ex fr 2f out* **25/1**
7 20 **Fuerta Ventura (IRE)**[18] 991 4-8-12 95 (b[1]) RMBurke 2 51
(K J Condon, Ire) *led: hdd & wknd early st: eased 1 1/2f out* **20/1**
2m 54.7s
WFA 4 from 5yo 1lb **8** Ran SP% **117.0**
CSF £5.57 TOTE £1.60: £1.10, £3.60; DF 5.50.
Owner H H Aga Khan **Bred** H H Aga Khan's Stud's S C **Trained** Currabeg, Co Kildare

NOTEBOOK
Kastoria(IRE), successful at this level of competition and twice placed in Group Two company last year, made a successful start to her season, just doing enough after hitting the front one and a half furlongs out to hold her stablemate Virginia Woolf. The Yorkshire Cup is her next likely target. (op 4/7)
Virginia Woolf, Listed placed last year when she was twice successful and was also narrowly beaten in the Leopardstown November Handicap, had run poorly on her reappearance at The Curragh last month. This was a lot better on her part and, after racing in second place, she went to the front three furlongs out and stuck to her task well when headed by the winner, although Kastoria always had her measure. (op 8/1 tchd 10/1)
Valentina Guest(IRE), rated 3lb above the runner-up having won a handicap at Leopardstown on her previous start, was always close up and vying for the lead with Virginia Woolf over two furlongs out, but she could find no extra from over a furlong out.
Cairdeas(IRE) has a preference for easy ground. He had made the running when fourth in a ten-furlong event at The Curragh last month, but he was held up here and, after making his move on the outside early in the straight, he was unable to make much impression from over one furlong out. (op 11/4)

1325 - 1327a (Foreign Racing) - See Raceform Interactive

925 DUSSELDORF (R-H)
Sunday, April 30

OFFICIAL GOING: Soft

1328a PFERDEWETTEN.DE STUTENPREIS (GERMAN 1,000 GUINEAS) (GROUP 2) (FILLIES) 1m
3:40 (3:45) 3-Y-0 **£68,966** (£26,207; £12,414; £6,207)

RPR
1 **Lolita (GER)**[22] 925 3-9-2 AHelfenbein 5 113
(Andreas Lowe, Germany) *made all, ran on well* **58/10**
2 2 **Almerita (GER)**[189] 6051 3-9-2 EPedroza 13 109
(W Hickst, Germany) *7th straight on outside, headway well over 1f out, chased winner final f, ran on* **41/10**[2]
3 9 **Lasira (GER)**[189] 6051 3-9-2 WMongil 11 91
(P Schiergen, Germany) *mid-division, some progress final 1 1/2f to take 3rd closing stages* **17/1**
4 ¾ **Directa (GER)** 3-9-2 ADeVries 4 90
(Andreas Lowe, Germany) *towards rear to straight, some progres final 1 1/2f, never nearer* **27/1**
5 1½ **Mrs Snow**[22] 925 3-9-2 THellier 6 87
(Mario Hofer, Germany) *prominent, 2nd straight, weakened over 1f out* **114/10**
6 ¾ **Violette**[180] 6219 3-9-2 SebSanders 10 85
(Sir Mark Prescott) *mid-div early, 4th on ins str, went 3rd well over 1f out, hung left under pressure over 1f out, wknd fnl f* **38/10**[1]
7 2 **Madura (GER)** 3-9-2 AStarke 12 81
(Mario Hofer, Germany) *last at half-way, never in contention* **21/2**
8 7 **Rajeem**[10] 1093 3-9-2 TedDurcan 9 67
(C E Brittain) *prominent, 6th straight, weakened well over 1f out* **68/10**
9 ¾ **Karavel (GER)**[189] 6051 3-9-2 ASuborics 3 66
(P Schiergen, Germany) *raced in 3rd, close 5th straight, soon weakened* **5/1**[3]
10 1½ **Amateis (GER)**[189] 6051 3-9-2 TMundry 2 63
(P Rau, Germany) *rapid progress at half-way, 8th straight, weakened quickly* **19/2**
11 5 **Tech Engine (GER)**[22] 925 3-9-2 FilipMinarik 1 53
(P Schiergen, Germany) *never nearer than mid-division* **39/1**
12 shd **Manda Honor (GER)**[22] 925 3-9-2 StanleyChin 14 52
(Mario Hofer, Germany) *always in rear* **53/1**
13 20 **Shaheen (GER)**[209] 5679 3-9-2 APietsch 7 12
(P Vovcenko, Germany) *always towards rear, tailed off from over 1f out* **120/1**
14 14 **Fantastica (GER)** 3-9-2 ABoschert 8 —
(U Ostmann, Germany) *pressed winner, 3rd straight, weakened quickly, tailed off* **14/1**
1m 48.64s **14** Ran SP% **131.9**
(including 10 euro stakes): WIN 68.00; PL 21.00, 16.00, 35.00;SF 237.00.
Owner Stall Le Rastaquouere **Bred** Wilhelm Jackson **Trained** Germany

NOTEBOOK
Violette, who had her Rockfel form boosted by the success of Speciosa in the Nell Gwyn, did not get home in the testing ground. Despite the official description, her rider considered the ground to be heavy.
Rajeem won a Listed race in soft ground last autumn, but she was another who found these very testing conditions putting too much of a premium on stamina.

KYOTO (R-H)
Sunday, April 30

OFFICIAL GOING: Firm

1329a TENNO SHO SPRING (GRADE 1) (C&F) 2m
7:40 (7:40) 4-Y-0+ **£669,881** (£266,831; £165,494; £98,844; £65,143)

RPR
1 **Deep Impact (JPN)**[42] 4-9-2 YTake 7 127+
(Y Ikee, Japan) **1/10**[1]
2 3½ **Lincoln (JPN)**[126] 6-9-2 NYokoyama 11 122+
(H Otonashi, Japan) **134/10**[2]
3 5 **Stratagem (JPN)**[553] 5-9-2 GBoss 1 117
(O Hirata, Japan) **57/1**
4 ½ **Eye Popper (JPN)**[42] 6-9-2 YFukunaga 14 117
(I Shimizu, Japan) **46/1**
5 1½ **Tokai Come Come (JPN)** 5-9-2 HMiyuki 6 115
(H Tadokoro, Japan) **85/1**
6 ¾ **Fast Tateyama (JPN)**[42] 7-9-2 KTake 13 114
(I Yasuda, Japan) **107/1**
7 nk **Macky Max (JPN)**[917] 6-9-2 SFujita 2 114
(H Fujiwara, Japan) **23/1**[3]
8 nse **Rosenkreuz (JPN)**[189] 4-9-2 KAndo 4 114
(K Hashiguchi, Japan) **40/1**
9 nk **Tokai Trick (JPN)**[42] 4-9-2 JSerizawa 5 114
(S Matsumoto, Japan) **36/1**
10 2½ **Delta Blues (JPN)**[42] 5-9-2 YIwata 9 111
(Katsuhiko Sumii, Japan) **24/1**
11 1¼ **Silk Famous (JPN)**[308] 7-9-2 YShibata 15 110
(I Sameshima, Japan) **100/1**
12 ½ **Narita Century (JPN)**[518] 6761 7-9-2 HTajima 16 109
(N Fujisawa, Japan) **98/1**
13 1½ **Big Gold (JPN)**[126] 8-9-2 RWada 8 108
(T Nakao, Japan) **179/1**
14 1¾ **Admire Monarch (JPN)** 5-9-2 HShii 10 106
(H Matsuda, Japan) **105/1**
15 2 **Hi Friend Try (JPN)**[42] 6-9-2 JKobayashi 12 104
(Y Nemoto, Japan) **246/1**
16 nk **Chakra (JPN)**[42] 6-9-2 FKomaki 3 104
(A Adachi, Japan) **192/1**
17 dist **Blue Tornade (JPN)**[553] 5-9-2 KenichiIkezoe 17 —
(Kaneo Ikezoe, Japan) **197/1**
3m 13.4s
WFA 4 from 5yo+ 4lb **17** Ran SP% **122.0**
(including 100 yen stakes): WIN 110; PL 110, 170, 470; DF 380; SF 430.
Owner Kaneko Makoto Holdings Co Ltd **Bred** Northern Farm **Trained** Japan

NOTEBOOK
Deep Impact(JPN) broke the race record by a full second and, according to those who study sectional times, clocked an amazing 33.5sec for the final 600 metres. Slowly away, as usual, he made up ground on the second circuit and came wide before going to the front three furlongs out. He then powered clear, and while he clearly gets this trip well, he has plenty of speed for ten furlongs and a mile and a half too, and his trip over to Europe, where he is likely to run in either the King George or the Arc is eagerly anticipated.

1266 LONGCHAMP (R-H)
Sunday, April 30

OFFICIAL GOING: Good to soft

1330a PRIX VANTEAUX (GROUP 3) (FILLIES) 1m 1f 55y
2:20 (2:22) 3-Y-0 **£27,586** (£11,034; £8,276; £5,517; £2,759)

RPR
1 **Danzon (USA)**[34] 773 3-9-0 IMendizabal 2 106
(J-C Rouget, France) *raced in 3rd to straight, switched to rails 1 1/2f out, led approaching final f, driven out* **9/2**[3]
2 1 **Sirene Doloise (FR)**[34] 773 3-9-0 SPasquier 4 104
(A Bonin, France) *raced in 5th to straight, headway over 1f out, went 2nd 100yds out, never reached winner* **7/1**
3 shd **High Heel Sneakers**[218] 5459 3-9-0 CSoumillon 3 104
(P F I Cole) *led, hung left well over 1f out, headed approaching final f, ran on steadily under pressure* **9/4**[1]
4 2½ **Sister Trouble (FR)**[20] 959 3-9-0 DBonilla 1 100
(F Head, France) *dwelt, last to straight, some late progress, never near to challenge* **8/1**
5 2 **Chaibia (IRE)**[24] 899 3-9-0 DBoeuf 7 96+
(D Smaga, France) *went 2nd after 1f, not much room briefly over 1f out, weakened final f* **5/2**[2]

6 2 1/2 **Hurricane Mist (IRE)**[241] 3-9-0 .... C-PLemaire 5 91
(P Bary, France) *raced in 4th to straight, weakened 1 1/2f out* **7/1**

1m 59.2s **Going Correction** +0.525s/f (Yiel) **6** Ran SP% **113.6**
Speed ratings: 105,104,104,101,100 97
PARI-MUTUEL: WIN 3.00; PL 1.70, 2.60; SF 11.20.
Owner J Allen **Bred** Ecurie Woodcote Stud **Trained** Pau, France

NOTEBOOK
Danzon(USA), a provincially-trained filly, was second in a mile Listed race on her reappearance. She coped well with both the slight step up in trip and grade and ran out a clear-cut winner. She will now go directly to the Prix de Diane.
Sirene Doloise(FR), beaten three quarters of a length by Danzon in a Listed race on her reappearance, could not reverse form over this extra furlong.
High Heel Sneakers, fourth in the Fillies' Mile on her final start as a juvenile, arguably let that form down on this her reappearance. She had the run of race in front, but lacked a change of pace and only kept on when it was too late. Her rider felt that she did not appreciate the ground, which had changed to testing during the afternoon.
Sister Trouble(FR) has yet to prove up to this class.
Chaibia(IRE), a Listed winner over nine furlongs here on her reappearance, should have coped with this step up in class but was disappointing.

1331a PRIX GANAY - GRAND PRIX AIR MAURITIUS (GROUP 1) 1m 2f 110y
3:20 (3:25) 4-Y-0+ **£118,221** (£47,297; £23,648; £11,818; £5,917)

RPR

1 **Corre Caminos (FR)**[21] [934] 4-9-2 .... TJarnet 1 121
(M Delzangles, France) *tracked leader to straight, led 1 1/2f out, soon clear, ran on well* **11/2**[3]

2 5 **Royal Highness (GER)**[231] [5159] 4-8-13 .... TThulliez 4 111
(P Bary, France) *raced in 3rd to straight, chased winner from over 1f out, soon ridden & one pace* **6/1**

3 3/4 **Manduro (GER)**[21] [934] 4-9-2 .... CSoumillon 2 113
(A Fabre, France) *disputed 4th, 5th straight on outside, some headway to go 3rd over 1f out* **15/8**[1]

4 1 **Pride (FR)**[140] [6552] 6-8-13 .... C-PLemaire 6 108
(A De Royer-Dupre, France) *disputed 4th, 4th on inside straight, kept on same pace final 1 1/2f* **5/2**[2]

5 4 **Montare (IRE)**[196] [5932] 4-8-13 ....(p) TGillet 5 102
(J E Pease, France) *wore cheekpieces, held up in 6th, pushed along over 3f out, last straight, never a factor* **6/1**

6 snk **Vatori (FR)**[280] [3790] 4-9-2 .... SPasquier 7 105
(P Demercastel, France) *held up in rear, 6th straight, never a factor* **16/1**

7 3/4 **Near Honor (GER)**[16] [1014] 8-9-2 .... MSautjeau 3 104
(P Vovcenko, Germany) *led, set moderate early pace, quickened before half-way, headed 1 1/2f out* **150/1**

2m 17.1s **Going Correction** +0.525s/f (Yiel) **7** Ran SP% **113.9**
Speed ratings: 111,107,106,106,103 103,102
PARI-MUTUEL: WIN 3.80; PL 2.30, 3.80; SF 27.10.
Owner Marquise De Moratalla **Bred** Mme Renee Geffroy **Trained** France

FOCUS
This looked one of the weaker renewals of the Ganay in recent times and is unlikely to have a bearing on top-quality Group 1s.

NOTEBOOK
Corre Caminos(FR) won on his first attempt in Group 1 company. He comprehensively turned the tables on Manduro from their meeting three weeks earlier and looks open to improvement as he sprinted right away from his six rivals off a slow pace on dead ground. By Montjeu out of a Kendor mare, he is bred to improve with age and should stay a mile and a half, although whether he will have as easy a task in another Group 1 is debatable. He will now head for the Prix d'Ispahan, and connections are also looking at the Prince of Wales Stakes at Royal Ascot.
Royal Highness(GER) had chased home Shawanda in the Prix Vermeille on her last outing of 2005 and this was an encouraging reappearance. She will presumably improve a bit for this, and a longer trip will definitely be an advantage for her. She now goes on to the Grand Prix de Chantilly, followed by the Grand Prix de Saint-Cloud and the Yorkshire Oaks.
Manduro(GER) can be rated as disappointing having defeated today's winner three weeks earlier over the same trip, and he has now been beaten on both his tries at Group One level. He appeared not to appreciate the dramatic change in the ground and will be a force to be reckoned with again on good going.
Pride(FR) ended last season with excellent seconds in the Champion Stakes and Hong Kong Cup, so can also be said to have disappointed. However, she was a bit keen, and it might be worth bearing in mind that she has never won on her reappearance. Indeed, she took time to warm up last term, so it is too soon to write her off.
Montare(IRE), like Pride making her reappearance, was on a four-timer but had finished behind Royal Highness at Saint-Cloud last summer and did so again.

1332a PRIX DE BARBEVILLE - BEACHCOMBER HOTELS "ROYAL PALM" (GROUP 3) 1m 7f 110y
3:55 (3:57) 4-Y-0+ **£27,586** (£11,034; £8,276; £5,517; £2,759)

RPR

1 **Petite Speciale (USA)**[29] [842] 7-8-7 .... C-PLemaire 5 110
(E Lecoiffier, France) *held up in rear, 6th straight, headway to go 2nd well over 1f out, led 150yds out, ran on well* **33/1**

2 2 1/2 **Lord Du Sud (FR)**[29] [842] 5-9-0 .... IMendizabal 8 114
(J-C Rouget, France) *led after 1f, clear well over 1f out, headed 150 yds out, one pace* **5/2**[2]

3 5 **Reefscape**[29] [842] 5-9-6 .... OPeslier 4 115+
(A Fabre, France) *held up, disputing 6th, 5th straight, driven to take 3rd 1 1/2f out, kept on same pace* **4/1**[3]

4 5 **Shamdala (IRE)**[140] [6549] 4-8-13 .... CSoumillon 3 107
(A De Royer-Dupre, France) *held up, disputing 6th, 4th straight, disputed 3rd 2f out, soon one pace* **13/8**[1]

5 1 **Tunduru (IRE)**[38] [759] 5-9-0 .... CNora 7 103
(R Martin-Sanchez, Spain) *prominent, went 2nd 9f out, 3rd straight, weakened well over 1f out* **20/1**

6 2 **Ostankino (FR)**[189] [6055] 5-9-4 .... SPasquier 2 105
(E Lellouche, France) *raced in 4th, headway & 2nd straight, ridden 2f out, soon weakened* **8/1**

7 15 **Winged D'Argent (IRE)**[276] [3879] 5-9-0 .... KDarley 1 86
(M Johnston) *led 1f, tracked leader to 9f out, lost place 4f out, 7th & beaten straight* **12/1**

8 15 **Kindling**[178] [6237] 4-8-8 .... JoeFanning 6 69
(M Johnston) *mid-division til dropped to last 6f out, soon well behind* **16/1**

3m 24.6s **Going Correction** +0.20s/f (Good)
WFA 4 from 5yo+ 3lb **8** Ran SP% **119.1**
Speed ratings: 113,111,109,106,106 105,97,90
PARI-MUTUEL: WIN 23.60; PL 1.70, 1.10, 1.20; DF 13.80.
Owner J-P Leseigneur **Bred** Bodfari Stud **Trained** France

NOTEBOOK
Petite Speciale(USA), who has looked limited at Listed level, caused something of a shock on this second outing of the season, coming from way back to win going away. The only mare in the field, it is hard to see her confirming the form with the likes of Reefscape and Shamdala in future, but connections now have the all important winning black type. Her provincial trainer will now be looking at the Prix Vicomtesse Vigier for this seven-year-old.
Lord Du Sud(FR) really got his act together at Listed level towards the end of last season, winning three in a row, and he began this season with another victory at that level at Saint-Cloud in April. This return to Group company brought about a solid effort and he looked the likely winner when going on, but Petite Special cut him down and he had to make do with second. He is still on target for the Ascot Gold Cup.
Reefscape, giving weight all round, has the potential to develop into France's leading stayer this term in the absence of Westerner, but this was disappointing. He now has a bit to prove, but he was not given a hard race and, given that he is being specifically trained for the Ascot Gold Cup, this race can be seen as another part of his preparation.
Shamdala(IRE), taking a drop in grade for this reappearance, never really got involved but can be expected to come on for this. The ground was against her and she should still be worth keeping an eye on for the rest of the season.
Winged D'Argent(IRE) dropped away tamely and made a poor start to his season.
Kindling looked out of her grade and dropped away tamely.

1242 KEMPTON (A.W) (R-H)
Monday, May 1

OFFICIAL GOING: Standard
Wind: Breezy, against

1333 EUROPEAN BREEDERS FUND MAIDEN STKS 5f (P)
2:10 (2:11) (Class 4) 2-Y-0 **£5,181** (£1,541; £770; £384) **Stalls** High

Form RPR

1 **Mubaashir (IRE)** 2-9-3 .... LDettori 7 75+
(E A L Dunlop) *rangy: lw: trckd ldr: shkn up to chal 2f out: led jst ins fnl f: kpt on wl* **3/1**[2]

3 2 shd **Benchmark**[7] [1189] 2-9-3 .... JimmyFortune 3 75+
(R Hannon) *lw: led: rdn over 1f out: narrowly hdd jst ins fnl f: rallied gamely: no ex nr fin* **4/9**[1]

3 3 **Peggys Flower** 2-8-12 .... OscarUrbina 2 58
(N A Callaghan) *w'like: hld up: hdwy over 2f out: sn rdn: kpt on to go 3rd ins fnl f but nt pce of ldng pair* **22/1**[3]

4 2 **Loves Bidding** 2-9-3 .... RobertHavlin 6 55
(R Ingram) *neat: chsd ldrs: rdn and effrt 2f out: wknd ins fnl f* **50/1**

5 3/4 **Esteemed Prince** 2-9-3 .... ShaneKelly 4 52
(D Shaw) *leggy: scope: bit bkwd: broke wl: chsd ldrs tl outpcd 3f out: styd on fnl f* **28/1**

06 6 1 **Bentley**[19] [987] 2-9-0 .... PatrickMathers(3) 1 48
(D Shaw) *w ldr tl rn wd on bnd over 3f out: sn rdn: wknd 1f out* **66/1**

7 11 **Beat The Bully** 2-9-3 .... SebSanders 5 4
(I A Wood) *tall: str: scope: bit bkwd: s.i.s: towards rr: wknd over 1f out* **25/1**

62.32 secs (1.32) **Going Correction** +0.10s/f (Slow) **7** Ran SP% **109.3**
Speed ratings (Par 95):88,87,83,79,78 77,59
CSF £4.34 TOTE £3.60: £1.30, £1.10; EX 4.90.
Owner Atiq Ejtebi **Bred** Kildaragh Stud **Trained** Newmarket, Suffolk

FOCUS
According to the betting this only concerned two horses, and they dominated the finish. Some of those in behind, though, were not without promise.

NOTEBOOK
Mubaashir(IRE) ◆, a 60,000gns half-brother to Filimeala, a dual mile winner at three, out of a six-furlong scorer, put up a good performance to beat the Hannon horse given that one had the benefit of experience and had shown a fair level of form on his debut. He looks to have scope for improvement as the season progresses and deserves his chance in better company. (op 10-3)
Benchmark, a promising third in just an ordinary Windsor maiden on his debut, seemed to run his race but was just denied. Even though he was beaten by a potentially nice horse, it was disappointing he could not take advantage of his previous experience and it would be unwise to take such a short price again next time. (op 2-5 tchd 1-2)
Peggys Flower ◆, out of a six-furlong winner, was unfancied in the betting but made a pleasing debut. The only filly in the field, she never troubled the front two, but kept on nicely in the closing stages and should show improved form next time. (op 20-1)
Loves Bidding, out of a six-furlong winner, offered some promise on his debut and should improve with experience.
Esteemed Prince, a 16,000gns half-brother to prolific seven-furlong/mile winner Platinum Duke, and to a mile juvenile scorer Prince Shaamaal, showed ability on his racecourse debut and is the type to eventually make a fair handicapper. (op 25-1)
Bentley Official explanation: jockey said gelding hung left

1334 RUK EVENING RACING PACKAGE FOR £60 H'CAP 1m 2f (P)
2:40 (2:40) (Class 6) (0-65,63) 4-Y-0+ **£3,238** (£963; £481; £240) **Stalls** High

Form RPR

66-2 1 **Dinner Date**[14] [1058] 4-8-12 **57** .... ShaneKelly 12 67
(T Keddy) *hld up towards rr: stdy hdwy over 2f out: swtchd lft over 1f out: str run to ld ins fnl f: pushed out* **8/1**[2]

4360 2 1 1/4 **Jomus**[79] [379] 5-8-8 **53** ....(p) RobertHavlin 6 61
(L Montague Hall) *lw: keen in midfield: rdn and hdwy fr 2f out: led 1f out: sn hdd: kpt on* **16/1**

4-43 3 1 3/4 **Red Sail**[70] [461] 5-8-7 **52** ....(b) OscarUrbina 9 57
(Dr J D Scargill) *mid-div: hdwy 2f out: sn rdn: styd on fnl f* **10/1**

-130 4 nk **Bishops Finger**[83] [324] 6-9-3 **62** ....(b) PaulDoe 1 66
(Jamie Poulton) *chsd ldrs: rdn and effrt over 2f out: ev ch 1f out: no ex* **25/1**

0330 5 nk **Master'n Commander**[8] [1163] 4-9-1 **60** .... MichaelHills 4 63
(C A Cyzer) *prom: rdn to ld over 2f out: hdd 1f out: no ex* **20/1**

2-00 6 1/2 **Grande Roche (IRE)**[10] [1123] 4-8-9 **54** .... ChrisCatlin 15 56
(G A Swinbank) *lw: mid-div: rdn over 3f out: styd on fnl f* **8/1**[2]

600- 7 1 1/2 **Serramanna**[170] [6323] 5-8-4 **56** ow1 .... SladeO'Hara(7) 10 56
(Dr J R J Naylor) *chsd ldrs: rdn over 2f out: wknd ins fnl f* **25/1**

0200 8 1/2 **Blackmail (USA)**[65] [521] 8-9-4 **63** ....(b) SebSanders 2 62
(Miss B Sanders) *lw: hld up bhd: sme hdwy 5f out: rdn over 2f out: styd on fnl f* **12/1**

5002 9 1 **Flying Pass**[5] [1244] 4-8-13 **58** ....(t) LDettori 11 55
(D J S Ffrench Davis) *lw: chsd ldrs: rdn 2f out: wknd ins fnl f* **11/4**[1]

6420 10 3 1/2 **Barton Sands (IRE)**[8] [1164] 9-9-0 **59** ....(t) J-PGuillambert 5 49
(Ernst Oertel) *in tch: rdn 3f out: wknd 1f out* **14/1**

2001 11 1 1/2 **Justcallmehandsome**[26] [888] 4-8-0 **52** ....(v) DonnaCaldwell(7) 7 39
(D J S Ffrench Davis) *lw: led tl over 2f out: wkng whn n.m.r over 1f out* **16/1**

1640 **12** 1 ½ **Madhavi**[40] 696 4-8-13 **58** .... JimmyFortune 13 42
(R Hannon) *a towards rr* **25/1**

00-6 **13** 7 **Bullseye**[8] 1163 4-8-11 **56** .... AlanMunro 3 27
(A P Jarvis) *lw: a towards rr* **10/1**

0-00 **14** 1 **Asaateel (IRE)**[12] 1075 4-9-4 **63** ....(be) GeorgeBaker 14 32
(G L Moore) *a towards rr* **9/1**[3]

000- **15** ¾ **Veverka**[311] 2892 5-8-10 **55** .... LPKeniry 8 23
(J C Fox) *bit bkwd: s.i.s and a towards rr* **66/1**

2m 7.31s (-3.69) **Going Correction** +0.10s/f (Slow) **15** Ran SP% **121.0**
Speed ratings (Par 101):110,109,107,107,107 106,105,105,104,101 100,99,93,92,92
CSF £120.59 CT £1305.62 TOTE £10.00: £2.60, £8.10, £4.90; EX 226.00.
Owner Mrs H Keddy **Bred** J M Greetham **Trained** Newmarket, Suffolk

FOCUS
A moderate handicap, but the pace was good throughout and the form looks decent enough for the level, rated through the third and fourth.

1335 RUK EVENING RACING CALL 08700 50 69 47 MAIDEN STKS (DIV I) 1m (P)
3:15 (3:21) (Class 4) 3-Y-O **£5,181** (£1,541; £770; £384) **Stalls High**

Form RPR

3 **1** **Red Somerset (USA)**[12] 1087 3-9-3 .... JimmyFortune 10 78+
(R Hannon) *lw: s.i.s: sn rcvrd: prom: led over 2f out: sn hrd rdn: jst hld on* **7/4**[2]

22-5 **2** *shd* **Cousteau**[11] 1092 3-9-3 98 .... AlanMunro 6 77
(P W Chapple-Hyam) *chsd ldrs: rdn to chse wnr over 1f out: styd on strly ins fnl f: jst failed* **6/4**[1]

03- **3** 1 ½ **Bandama (IRE)**[202] 5817 3-9-3 .... LDettori 11 74+
(Mrs A J Perrett) *mid-div: sltly outpcd over 2f out: styd on to go 3rd 1f out: no further imp on ldng pair after* **7/1**[3]

0- **4** 1 ¼ **Lemon Drop Lad (USA)**[261] 4361 3-9-3 .... J-PGuillambert 7 71
(Sir Michael Stoute) *bit bkwd: chsd ldrs: rdn over 2f out: kpt on same pce fnl f* **8/1**

00- **5** 2 ½ **Satin Doll**[167] 6349 3-8-9 .... NelsonDeSouza(3) 4 60
(M P Tregoning) *chsd ldrs: rdn and effrt 2f out: sn hung rt: one pce fnl f* **50/1**

6 *hd* **Regal Sunset (IRE)** 3-9-3 .... OscarUrbina 2 65+
(W R Swinburn) *w'like: hld up towards rr: nt clr run fr 2f out: swtchd rt and styd on ins fnl f: nrst fin* **25/1**

7 1 **Mount Sinai** 3-9-3 .... RobertHavlin 1 63
(W J Knight) *lengthy: str: mid-div: hdwy 3f out: sn rdn: ev ch 2f out: wknd fnl f* **80/1**

0-0 **8** 1 ½ **Nefski Alexander (USA)**[13] 1065 3-9-3 .... SebSanders 5 59
(P F I Cole) *led: rdn and hdd over 2f out: sn hung lft: wknd fnl f* **33/1**

9 *shd* **Contra Mundum (USA)** 3-9-3 .... ChrisCatlin 12 59+
(B J Meehan) *leggy: scope: slowly away: towards rr: sme late prog: nvr trbld ldrs* **50/1**

10 *nk* **Muntada** 3-8-12 .... RHills 9 53
(M P Tregoning) *cmpt: str: lw: slowly away: bhd: sme late hdwy: nvr trbld ldrs* **16/1**

11 2 ½ **Stanley Goodspeed** 3-9-3 .... MichaelHills 14 52
(J W Hills) *w'like: hld up towards rr: hdwy over 2f out: sn rdn: wknd over 1f out* **66/1**

0 **12** 1 **Collusion (FR)**[9] 1135 3-9-3 .... ShaneKelly 8 50
(Pat Eddery) *mid-div for 4f: bhd fnl 3f* **33/1**

06 **13** 1 ¼ **Lanfredo**[93] 219 3-9-3 .... LPKeniry 13 47
(D W P Arbuthnot) *chsd ldrs tl wknd wl over 1f out* **66/1**

14 ¾ **Esteem** 3-9-3 .... PaulDoe 3 46
(W Jarvis) *w'like: lw: towards rr: hdwy on outer over 3f out: wknd 2f out* **66/1**

1m 40.76s (-1.22) **Going Correction** +0.10s/f (Slow) **14** Ran SP% **125.2**
Speed ratings (Par 101):104,103,102,101,98 98,97,95,95,95 93,92,90,90
CSF £4.66 TOTE £3.00: £1.50, £1.20, £2.00; EX 7.50.
Owner Fieldspring Racing **Bred** Haras D'Etreham **Trained** East Everleigh, Wilts

FOCUS
Quite a good maiden contested by some potentially nice types, and a boost for the form of the first division of this year's Wood Ditton, with the third from that race denying the Craven fifth. The form is rated at face value.
Satin Doll Official explanation: jockey said filly hung right in the home straight

1336 RUK EVENING RACING CALL 08700 50 69 47 MAIDEN STKS (DIV II) 1m (P)
3:45 (3:51) (Class 4) 3-Y-O **£5,181** (£1,541; £770; £384) **Stalls High**

Form RPR

5- **1** **Steppe Dancer (IRE)**[201] 5833 3-9-3 .... AlanMunro 5 82+
(D J Coakley) *gd sort: h.d.w: lw: t.k.h in mid-div: sltly outpcd over 3f out: styd on strly over 1f out: led cl home* **4/1**[1]

2 1 ¼ **Armada** 3-9-3 .... LDettori 7 79
(Sir Michael Stoute) *str: lw: chsd ldrs: rdn over 3f out: led over 1f out: no ex whn ct cl home* **6/1**[3]

02- **3** *nk* **Another Genepi (USA)**[201] 5832 3-8-12 .... MichaelHills 3 76+
(J W Hills) *swtg: mid-div: hdwy over 3f out: swtchd rt whn hmpd by loose horse over 1f out: sn drifted rt but ev ch: no ex cl home* **4/1**[1]

0-5 **4** 1 ½ **Italian Romance**[21] 952 3-9-3 .... SebSanders 10 75
(M L W Bell) *prom: hmpd by loose horse after 3f: rdn over 2f out: ev ch 1f out: sn drifted rt: kpt on* **11/2**[2]

553- **5** ¾ **Beckett Hall (IRE)**[245] 4816 3-9-3 81 .... JimmyFortune 13 73
(R Hannon) *chsd ldrs: rdn over 2f out: kpt on same pce* **8/1**

6 4 **Russian Dream (IRE)** 3-9-3 .... OscarUrbina 12 64+
(W R Swinburn) *cmpt: sn pushed along in rr: styd on fr over 2f out: nvr trbld ldrs* **20/1**

06 **7** ½ **Doctor David**[37] 720 3-9-3 .... J-PGuillambert 4 63+
(Ernst Oertel) *chsd ldrs: led over 3f out: sn rdn: hmpd by loose horse 2f out: sn hdd: wknd fnl f* **25/1**

8 4 **Mustammer** 3-9-3 .... RHills 9 53
(M P Tregoning) *neat: lw: mid-div: hdwy over 2f out: wknd fnl f* **13/2**

0-0 **9** ¾ **Misterbianco (IRE)**[11] 1094 3-9-3 .... ChrisCatlin 11 52
(B J Meehan) *led tl over 3f out: wknd over 1f out* **16/1**

10 1 ¾ **Sa Nau** 3-9-3 .... ShaneKelly 1 48
(T Keddy) *str: scope: bit bkwd: slowly away and a bhd* **40/1**

0 **11** 8 **Kapiolani (USA)**[14] 1055 3-8-12 .... RobertHavlin 6 24
(J M P Eustace) *mid div: rdn over 3f out: sn btn* **66/1**

12 2 **Mrs Solese (IRE)** 3-8-9 .... NelsonDeSouza(3) 2 20
(J R Boyle) *wl grwn: bit bkwd: v.s.a and a bhd* **66/1**

U **Ahlawy (IRE)** 3-8-10 .... AshleyHamblett(7) 8 —
(L M Cumani) *unf: bit bkwd: uns rdr sn after s (sddle slipped)* **12/1**

1m 40.92s (-1.06) **Going Correction** +0.10s/f (Slow) **13** Ran SP% **121.7**
Speed ratings (Par 101):103,101,101,99,99 95,94,90,89,88 80,78,—
CSF £27.07 TOTE £5.70: £1.90, £2.40, £1.80; EX 38.60.
Owner Chris Van Hoorn **Bred** Maggiorelli Ice Guarnieri **Trained** West Ilsley, Berks

FOCUS
Just an ordinary maiden and not as good as the first division - the winning time was slightly slower. The form is rated around the third and fifth and should work out.
Doctor David Official explanation: jockey said gelding suffered interference from the loose horse

1337 DAY TIME, NIGHT TIME, GREAT TIME H'CAP 7f (P)
4:20 (4:22) (Class 4) (0-85,83) 3-Y-O **£5,505** (£1,637; £818; £408) **Stalls High**

Form RPR

1-24 **1** **Namid Reprobate (IRE)**[16] 1016 3-9-3 **82** .... ShaneKelly 1 91
(P F I Cole) *lw: chsd ldrs: rdn over 2f out: led 1f out: kpt on: drvn out* **3/1**[1]

421- **2** *nk* **Lunar Express (USA)**[121] 6694 3-9-1 **80** .... AlanMunro 2 88+
(W J Haggas) *lw: in tch: rdn and hdwy over 2f out: chsd wnr 1f out: kpt on wl cl home* **7/2**[2]

33-3 **3** ¾ **Multakka (IRE)**[20] 964 3-9-3 **82** .... RHills 4 88
(M P Tregoning) *mid-div: rdn over 2f out: no imp and hung rt over 1f out: styd on wl ins fnl f: wnt 3rd fnl strides* **7/1**

1215 **4** ½ **Tamagin (USA)**[10] 1122 3-8-9 **77** ....(p) PatrickMathers(3) 7 82
(P D Evans) *led: rdn over 2f out: hdd 1f out: no ex* **9/1**

-311 **5** *nk* **Orchard Supreme**[60] 558 3-9-4 **83** .... JimmyFortune 11 87+
(R Hannon) *lw: hld up bhd: swtchd lft 2f out: sn rdn: styd on strly fr 1f out: nrst fin* **11/2**[3]

01-0 **6** ½ **Rubenstar (IRE)**[13] 1067 3-9-1 **80** .... MichaelHills 8 83+
(M H Tompkins) *lw: hld up towards rr: nt clr run briefly over 2f out: rdn and hdwy over 1f out: styd on: nrst fin* **10/1**

6-00 **7** *hd* **Obscene**[7] 1185 3-8-1 **69** oh9 .... NelsonDeSouza(3) 6 71?
(M J Polglase) *lw: mid-div: rdn and hdwy 2f out: kpt on fnl f* **66/1**

22-2 **8** 1 ¼ **Cloud Atlas (IRE)**[34] 776 3-8-10 **75** .... ChrisCatlin 10 74
(S Kirk) *hld up towards rr: hdwy on rails fr 2f out: kpt on same pce fnl f* **16/1**

130- **9** 8 **Vegas Boys**[223] 5395 3-8-13 **78** .... LDettori 5 56
(N A Callaghan) *lw: hld up towards rr: sme hdwy u.p over 2 out: wknd fnl f* **8/1**

-060 **10** 1 ¼ **Bucharest**[11] 1097 3-8-7 **75** .... JohnMcAuley(3) 9 50
(M Wigham) *chsd ldrs: rdn over 2f out: wknd fnl f* **66/1**

03-0 **11** *nk* **Surely Truly (IRE)**[11] 1097 3-9-0 **79** .... SebSanders 12 53
(K R Burke) *in tch: rdn over 2f out: wknd over 1f out* **20/1**

-060 **12** ¾ **Littledodayno (IRE)**[11] 1097 3-8-10 **75** .... FrancisNorton 3 47
(M Wigham) *a towards rr* **40/1**

1m 27.24s (-1.02) **Going Correction** +0.10s/f (Slow) **12** Ran SP% **121.4**
Speed ratings (Par 101):101,100,99,99,98 98,98,96,87,86 85,84
CSF £13.35 CT £68.88 TOTE £4.80: £1.60, £2.00, £2.20; EX 15.40.
Owner Richard Aston Associates **Bred** A P Jarvis **Trained** Whatcombe, Oxon

FOCUS
A fair handicap but, despite the gallop being very strong throughout, it paid to be close to the pace. The fifth and sixth give the form a solid look.

1338 FELTHAM FILLIES' H'CAP 6f (P)
4:50 (4:52) (Class 4) (0-85,83) 4-Y-O+ **£5,505** (£1,228; £1,228; £408) **Stalls High**

Form RPR

50-3 **1** **Bird Over**[20] 970 4-9-3 **82** .... SebSanders 4 87
(R M Beckett) *hld up: rdn and hdwy over 1f out: str run ins fnl f: led cl home* **10/3**[2]

3220 **2** ½ **Sahara Silk (IRE)**[8] 1161 5-8-1 **69** oh2 ....(v) PatrickMathers(3) 3 73
(D Shaw) *chsd ldrs: rdn 2f out: disp ld thrght fnl f: ct cl home* **18/1**

2210 **2** *dht* **Ashes (IRE)**[2] 1297 4-8-4 **69** oh3 .... ChrisCatlin 7 73
(K R Burke) *lw: plld hrd bhd ldrs: swtchd lft and hdwy to dispute ld 1f out: sn drifted lft: ct cl home* **11/1**

20-4 **4** 2 **Golden Asha**[12] 1076 4-9-1 **80** .... LDettori 2 78
(N A Callaghan) *lw: hld up: rdn and hdwy 2f out: kpt on same pce* **6/5**[1]

50-1 **5** 1 **Auwitesweetheart**[21] 947 4-9-4 **83** .... AlanMunro 1 78
(B R Millman) *lw: prom: led 2f: sn hung lft: hdd 1f out: wknd* **8/1**

000- **6** ¾ **Honey Ryder**[198] 5891 4-9-3 **82** .... FrancisNorton 5 74?
(Stef Liddiard) *led: rdn and hdd 2f out: wknd fnl f* **16/1**

0-02 **7** 2 ½ **Aastral Magic**[19] 985 4-8-6 **71** .... RHills 6 56
(R Hannon) *s.i.s: hld up: short lived effrt 2f out* **13/2**[3]

1m 14.28s (-1.99) **Going Correction** +0.10s/f (Slow) **7** Ran SP% **112.5**
Speed ratings (Par 102):100,99,99,96,95 94,91
TRIFECTA WIN: £4.10. PL: £2.20, Sahara Silk £2.50, Ashes £1.80. EX: Bird Over/SS £32.40. BO/A £21.50. CSF: BO/SS £27.30, BO/A £18.40..
Owner Mrs Robert Langton **Bred** Mrs Robert Langton **Trained** Whitsbury, Hants
■ Stewards' Enquiry : Seb Sanders three-day ban: used whip with excessive frequency and without giving filly time to respond (May 12, 13, 15)

FOCUS
Just the seven runners, but a pretty competitive fillies' handicap. The runner-up looks the best guide to the level.

1339 FAMILY DAY H'CAP 2m (P)
5:25 (5:25) (Class 5) (0-75,71) 4-Y-O+ **£3,238** (£963; £481; £240) **Stalls High**

Form RPR

-502 **1** **Linden Lime**[6] 1213 4-8-7 **55** .... PaulDoe 10 63
(Jamie Poulton) *lw: wnt lft s: hld up bhd: stdy hdwy fr over 5f out: led 3f out: sn rdn: drifted lft ins fnl f but styd on wl* **7/1**[3]

6553 **2** 2 **Dovedon Hero**[29] 847 6-9-8 **67** ....(b) JimmyFortune 11 73
(P J McBride) *hld up bhd: hdwy over 4f out: trckd wnr and gng wl over 2f out: rdn to chal 1f out: sn hld* **11/2**[1]

4330 **3** *shd* **Madiba**[6] 1219 7-8-12 **57** .... ShaneKelly 5 64+
(P Howling) *mid-div: hdwy over 4f out: nt clr run on rails over 2f out: sn swtchd rt: styd on wl fnl f* **14/1**

105- **4** ½ **Bobsleigh**[205] 5007 7-8-13 **58** .... AlanMunro 7 63
(H S Howe) *lw: chsd ldrs: drvn along to hold position 1/2 way: outpcd over 3f out: styd on wl fnl f* **12/1**

1500 **5** *nk* **Lady Pilot**[8] 1163 4-8-6 **61** ow1 ....(v) SladeO'Hara(7) 2 66
(Dr J R J Naylor) *lw: mid-div: rdn over 3f out: wnt 3rd over 2f out: kpt on same pce* **16/1**

104- **6** 10 **Papeete (GER)**[212] 5598 5-9-8 **67** .... SebSanders 9 60
(Miss B Sanders) *lw: bmpd s: hld up bhd: rdn and hdwy 3f out: wknd fnl f* **6/1**[2]

23-0 **7** 5 **Dark Parade (ARG)**[20] 973 5-8-10 **62** ....(b[1]) JamieJones(7) 12 49
(G L Moore) *lw: chsd ldrs: rdn whn n.m.r over 2f out: sn wknd* **10/1**

The Form Book, Raceform Ltd, Compton, RG20 6NL

1550 **8** *1 ½* **Indian Chase**[20] [966] 9-8-11 **56**.. BrianReilly 8 41
(Dr J R J Naylor) *hld up and a towards rr* **25/1**
610- **9** *2* **Our Monogram**[210] [5661] 10-9-6 **68**..................... NelsonDeSouza(3) 6 50
(R M Beckett) *bit bkwd: led tl 6f out: grad fdd* **16/1**
1255 **10** *hd* **Monte Cristo (FR)**[5] [1247] 8-9-12 **71**.................................(v) ChrisCatlin 4 53
(Mrs L C Taylor) *prom: led 6f out tl 3f out: wknd over 1f out* **6/1**[2]
4405 **11** *12* **River Gypsy**[20] [965] 5-9-3 **62**... LPKeniry 3 30
(D R C Elsworth) *mid-div tl 4f out* **12/1**
2414 **12** *dist* **Montosari**[8] [1167] 7-9-10 **69**... GeorgeBaker 1 —
(P Mitchell) *chsd ldrs tl wknd qckly 4f out: eased fnl 2f* **11/2**[1]

3m 31.41s (-11.59) **Going Correction** +0.10s/f (Slow)
WFA 4 from 5yo+ 3lb **12** Ran SP% **118.6**
Speed ratings (Par 103):103,102,101,101,101 96,94,93,92,92 86,—
CSF £45.31 CT £532.52 TOTE £7.00: £1.80, £2.10, £3.50; EX 30.20.
Owner R C Moules **Bred** R C Moules **Trained** Telscombe, E Sussex

FOCUS
A modest staying handicap run at what looked a reasonable enough pace throughout, but the form appears ordinary.
Monte Cristo(FR) Official explanation: trainer's representative said gelding was struck into during the race
Montosari Official explanation: trainer's representative had no explanation for the poor form shown

1340 LONDON MILE JUBILEE H'CAP (QUALIFIER) 1m (P)
5:55 (5:58) (Class 3) (0-90,90) 4-Y-O+
£11,217 (£3,358; £1,679; £840; £419; £210) **Stalls** High

Form RPR
4104 **1** **Waterside (IRE)**[10] [1111] 7-8-12 **84**.................................... SebSanders 8 93
(G L Moore) *lw: a.p: led over 2f out: kpt on gamely: rdn out* **6/1**[3]
011- **2** *1 ¼* **Banknote**[247] [4760] 4-9-0 **86**... LDettori 5 92+
(A M Balding) *chsd ldrs: rdn over 2f out: ev ch 1f out: no ex* **5/2**[1]
6032 **3** *1 ¼* **Outer Hebrides**[10] [1112] 5-8-12 **84**.............................. FrancisNorton 3 87
(Stef Liddiard) *lw: hld up: rdn and outpcd over 2f out: hung rt but styd on wl fnl f: wnt 3rd cl home* **7/1**
0-04 **4** *nk* **Davenport (IRE)**[6] [1207] 4-8-8 **80**..................................... AlanMunro 6 83
(B R Millman) *in tch: rdn and hdwy over 2f out: kpt on same pce fnl f* **13/2**
15-6 **5** *1 ¼* **Isidore Bonheur (IRE)**[9] [1143] 5-8-11 **83**...................... JimmyFortune 1 83
(G A Swinbank) *hld up bhd: hdwy over 2f out: sn rdn: kpt on same pce fnl f* **7/2**[2]
60-0 **6** *1 ¼* **Landucci**[10] [1111] 5-8-9 **81**.. MichaelHills 4 78
(J W Hills) *lw: hld up: hdwy over 2f out: sn rdn: one pce fnl f* **9/1**
000- **7** *¾* **Mineral Star (IRE)**[210] [5660] 4-8-13 **85**................................. RHills 7 80
(M H Tompkins) *trckd ldrs: rdn over 2f out: wknd over 1f out* **8/1**
0 **8** *6* **Major League (USA)**[30] [828] 4-9-4 **90**......................... J-PGuillambert 9 71?
(K Bishop) *lw: led: rdn and narrowly hdd over 2f out: wknd over 1f out* **66/1**

1m 41.15s (-0.83) **Going Correction** +0.10s/f (Slow) **8** Ran SP% **113.5**
Speed ratings (Par 107):102,100,99,99,97 96,95,89
CSF £21.08 CT £107.72 TOTE £7.20: £2.00, £1.10, £2.40; EX 17.30 Place 6 £38.84, Place 5 £37.86.
Owner Nigel Shields **Bred** Yeomanstown Stud **Trained** Woodingdean, E Sussex

FOCUS
Not a great turnout for the first running of the historic Jubilee Handicap on sand - now a qualifier for the London Mile series - which is disappointing considering there was added prize money of £18,000. The form looks reasonable enough, although not the most solid.

NOTEBOOK
Waterside(IRE) Is holding his form very well and this is the highest mark he has ever won off. He proved game in seeing off Banknote, but had the advantage of race fitness and will find things tougher when reassessed and faced with strong opposition. (tchd 13-2)
Banknote progressed into a useful handicapper last season and, on this evidence, looks like continuing where he left off. Switched to Polytrack for the first time on his return from a 247-day break, he handled the surface well but could not get by Waterside, who had the benefit of race fitness. (op 2-1)
Outer Hebrides, 3lb higher than when second over seven furlongs here on his previous start, had the tongue-tie and visor left off this time but seemed to run his race. (op 8-1 tchd 9-1)
Davenport(IRE)'s three wins have come on turf and he does not look attractively handicapped. (op 5-1)
Isidore Bonheur(IRE), switched to Polytrack for the first time, did not really build on the form he showed on his reappearance at Thirsk. (op 10-3 tchd 3-1)
T/Plt: £36.80 to a £1 stake. Pool: £44,046.85. 872.20 winning tickets. T/Qpdt: £7.60 to a £1 stake. Pool: £2,229.70. 215.00 winning tickets. TM

NEWCASTLE (L-H)
Monday, May 1

OFFICIAL GOING: Good to firm
Wind: Breezy, half-against

1341 LOVELY BUBBLY APPRENTICE CLAIMING STKS 7f
2:05 (2:05) (Class 6) 3-Y-O+ **£2,266** (£674; £337; £168) **Stalls** High

Form RPR
2201 **1** **Up Tempo (IRE)**[14] [1054] 8-9-11 63...........................(b) AndrewMullen 17 78
(K A Ryan) *mde all stands rail: pushed along over 1f out: kpt on wl* **3/1**[1]
0631 **2** *2* **Onlytime Will Tell**[6] [1217] 8-9-4 68.............................. VictoriaBehan(5) 1 71
(D Nicholls) *in tch: effrt and chsd wnr 2f out: kpt on fnl f* **5/1**[2]
4050 **3** *7* **Amazin**[19] [977] 4-9-6 59..(p) JemmaMarshall(5) 11 55
(N P Littmoden) *dwlt: hdwy and edgd lft over 1f out: kpt on fnl f: no ch w first two* **11/1**
05-0 **4** *½* **Fit To Fly (IRE)**[7] [1198] 5-8-10 45..............................(p) RobbieMills(5) 4 43
(R C Guest) *dwlt and sn outpcd: n.m.r wl over 2f out: hdwy over 1f out: n.d* **25/1**
00/0 **5** *hd* **Haulage Man**[31] [818] 8-9-7 48.. MarkLawson 10 49
(Karen McLintock) *midfield: effrt over 2f out: sn no imp* **33/1**
00-0 **6** *hd* **Drum Dance (IRE)**[28] [862] 4-9-7 50........................... DuranFentiman 16 48
(N Tinkler) *trckd ldrs on ins rail tl rdn and outpcd fr 2f out* **25/1**
-006 **7** *3* **Kalani Star (IRE)**[12] [1073] 6-8-10 45.......................(vt) KevinGhunowa(5) 6 34
(I W McInnes) *hld up: effrt centre over 1f out: nvr rchd ldrs* **20/1**
0530 **8** *1 ½* **Triple Zero (IRE)**[24] [902] 4-9-3 55..........................(v) AndrewElliott(3) 14 36
(A P Jarvis) *keen: cl up tl wknd fr 2f out* **8/1**[3]
-500 **9** *1* **Sapphire Storm (IRE)**[47] [642] 3-7-11 50............. LeanneKershaw(3) 7 25
(P T Midgley) *bhd: rdn 1/2-way: sme late hdwy: nvr on terms* **50/1**
250- **10** *hd* **Dispol Peto**[4] [474] 6-9-0 53..................................(p) PatrickDonaghy(5) 13 31
(R Johnson) *trckd ldrs tl wknd over 2f out* **50/1**
43-0 **11** *shd* **Inside Story (IRE)**[9] [1143] 4-9-8 78............................ RonanKeogh(5) 12 39
(M W Easterby) *missed break: sn midfield: rdn and wknd fr wl over 2f out* **10/1**
60-0 **12** *½* **Spring Time Girl**[39] [706] 4-8-9 47...........................(p) KristinStubbs(3) 9 23
(B Ellison) *s.i.s: outpcd: nvr on terms* **20/1**
-006 **13** *¾* **Atlantic Ace**[37] [734] 9-9-0 49.....................................(p) GaryWales(7) 5 30
(B Smart) *missed break: sme hdwy centre 2f out: sn btn* **50/1**
0516 **14** *¾* **True Night**[10] [1124] 9-9-10 72... HMuya(3) 2 34
(D Nicholls) *keen: chsd ldrs to 3f out: sn rdn and btn* **5/1**[2]
060/ **15** *hd* **Quicks The Word**[514] [6800] 6-9-0 .... GemmaAnderson(7) 3 27
(T A K Cuthbert) *keen: cl up tl wknd over 2f out* **100/1**
-000 **16** *11* **Mr Marucci (USA)**[18] [1001] 4-8-10 45..........................(b) NeilBrown(5) 15 —
(B Ellison) *keen: trckd ldrs tl wknd over 2f out* **66/1**

1m 28.61s (-1.39) **Going Correction** -0.025s/f (Good)
WFA 3 from 4yo+ 12lb **16** Ran SP% **115.4**
Speed ratings (Par 101):106,103,95,95,94 94,91,89,88,88 88,87,86,85,85 72
CSF £13.98 TOTE £3.70: £1.80, £2.00, £4.40; EX 19.60 Trifecta £90.30 Part won. Pool: £127.21 - 0.69 winning tickets..The winner was claimed by C. R. Dore for £10,000.
Owner Yorkshire Racing Club & Derek Blackhurst **Bred** T Burns **Trained** Hambleton, N Yorks
■ Stewards' Enquiry : H Muya one-day ban: failed to ride to draw (May 12)
Victoria Behan one-day ban: failed to ride to draw (May 12)
Gemma Anderson one-day ban: failed to ride to draw (May 12)
Robbie Mills one-day ban: used whip with excessive frequency and down the shoulder in the forehand position (May 12)

FOCUS
An ordinary event but a fair time for a claimer with the winner setting the standard. The gallop seemed sound and the field raced towards the stands side.

1342 PARAMOUNT WINDOWS & CONSERVATORIES E B F MEDIAN AUCTION MAIDEN STKS 5f
2:35 (2:37) (Class 6) 2-Y-O **£2,590** (£770; £385; £192) **Stalls** High

Form RPR
1 **Ingleby Princess** 2-8-12 .... PaulFessey 1 71
(T D Barron) *chsd far side ldrs: rdn 2f out: kpt on to ld wl ins fnl f* **9/1**[3]
2 *1 ½* **Smirfys Diamond** 2-9-0 .... SilvestreDeSousa(3) 4 70
(D Nicholls) *prom far side: led that gp 2f out: hdd wl ins fnl f: r.o: fin 2nd in gp* **14/1**
3 *nk* **Domino Dancer (IRE)** 2-9-3 .... RobertWinston 2 69
(J Howard Johnson) *set decent pce far side to 2f out: one pce fnl f: fin 3rd in gp* **4/1**[2]
4 **4** *¾* **Onenightinlisbon (IRE)**[9] [1142] 2-8-12 .... LeeEnstone 13 61
(P T Midgley) *pressed stands side ldr: led that gp over 1f out: kpt on fnl f: first in that gp* **9/1**[3]
0 **5** *nk* **Poniard (IRE)**[9] [1142] 2-8-12 .... AndrewMullen(5) 12 65
(D W Barker) *chsd stands side ldrs: drvn over 2f out: kpt on fnl f: 2nd in that gp* **50/1**
4 **6** *1 ½* **The Nifty Fox**[15] [1030] 2-9-3 .... DavidAllan 7 59
(T D Easterby) *led stands side to over 1f out: kpt on same pce fnl f: fin 3rd in that gp* **9/4**[1]
7 *1 ¼* **Blue Madeira** 2-9-3 .... TomEaves 8 54
(Mrs L Stubbs) *in tch on outside of stands side gp tl rdn and no ex over 1f out: 4th in that gp* **50/1**
8 *2* **Amelie Brown (IRE)** 2-8-12 .... TonyCulhane 6 41
(N Tinkler) *in tch far side gp: effrt and green 2f out: sn outpcd: 4th in that gp* **16/1**
9 *1 ¾* **The Mighty Ogmore** 2-8-12 .... JoeFanning 14 34
(R C Guest) *prom stands side gp: pushed along and hd high over 2f out: sn no imp: 5th in gp* **25/1**
06 **10** *1* **Jojesse**[14] [1053] 2-9-3 .... DeanMcKeown 3 35
(S Parr) *w far side ldr to over 2f out: sn wknd: last in that gp* **16/1**
0 **11** *2* **Homes By Woodford**[12] [1074] 2-9-0 .... PaulMulrennan(3) 9 27
(M W Easterby) *prom stands side tl edgd lft and wknd over 2f out: sixth in gp* **20/1**
12 *¾* **Dolly Coughdrop (IRE)** 2-8-12 .... PatCosgrave 11 19
(K R Burke) *missed break: bhd stands side: rdn and no imp fr 1/2-way: seventh in gp* **14/1**
13 *3 ½* **Mundo's Magic** 2-9-3 .... FergalLynch 5 10
(D W Barker) *dwlt: racd on outside of stands side gp: rn green and wknd over 2f out: eighth in gp* **16/1**
14 *11* **Devilfishpoker Com** 2-8-10 .... RobbieMills(7) 10 —
(R C Guest) *dwlt: a bhd stands side: ninth and last that gp* **25/1**

62.84 secs (1.34) **Going Correction** -0.025s/f (Good) **14** Ran SP% **118.1**
Speed ratings (Par 91):88,85,85,83,83 81,79,75,73,71 68,67,61,43
CSF £118.47 TOTE £11.50: £2.70, £3.80, £1.70; EX 127.60 Trifecta £140.30 Part won. Pool: £197.62 - 0.95 winning tickets..
Owner Dave Scott **Bred** Wheelersland Stud **Trained** Maunby, N Yorks

FOCUS
An ordinary event in which the pace was sound and the first three to finish were on the far side. The form looks modest.

NOTEBOOK
Ingleby Princess, a half-sister to a couple of winners up to a mile and a quarter, created a favourable impression on this racecourse debut. A step up in trip will be in her favour and she is the type to win more races. (op 10-1)
Smirfys Diamond ◆, a half-brother to three winners, including fair turf and useful All-Weather performer Hail The Chief, was easy to back on this racecourse debut but showed more than enough to suggest a similar race can be found. (op 12-1)
Domino Dancer(IRE), out of a dam who won over middle distances at three years, did well given he was up with the fair gallop throughout. A step up in trip will suit in due course and he looks capable of winning a similar event. (tchd 9-2)
Onenightinlisbon(IRE) improved on the form of her racecourse debut and may be a bit better than this bare result suggests given she headed the group to race on the stands side. She should stay six furlongs and is capable of winning a seller.
Poniard(IRE), well beaten on his racecourse debut, fared much better this time but his proximity does hold this bare form down. However, he will be suited by six furlongs and may be capable of winning a seller on this evidence.
The Nifty Fox had the run of the race near the stands rail but proved a bit of a disappointment in view of his debut promise. This may have come too quickly after his debut effort and he is not one to write off just yet. (op 2-1)

1343 HARLANDS NORTHERN ACCOUNTANCY FIRM OF THE YEAR 2006/2007 MAIDEN STKS 1m 2f 32y
3:10 (3:13) (Class 5) 3-Y-O+ **£3,238** (£963; £481; £240) **Stalls** Centre

Form RPR
36- **1** **Abbondanza (IRE)**[205] [5748] 3-8-8 .... PaulMulrennan(3) 8 79
(J Howard Johnson) *pressed ldr: led over 2f out: sn hrd pressed: hld on gamely fnl f* **11/1**
03- **2** *nk* **Spell Casting (USA)**[205] [5748] 3-8-8 .... SaleemGolam(3) 9 78
(M H Tompkins) *trckd ldrs: effrt and ev ch fr 2f out: kpt on but a hld* **6/1**[2]

4 **3** ½ **Belanak (IRE)**[21] [948] 3-8-11 .... RobertWinston 13 77+
(Sir Michael Stoute) *hld up midfield: stdy hdwy 3f out: effrt and shkn up wl over 1f out: kpt on wl towards fin* **1/2**[1]
4 4 **Follow On** 4-9-12 .... DarrenWilliams 6 70+
(A P Jarvis) *hld up: smooth hdwy 3f out: rdn wl over 1f out: nt rch first three* **10/1**[3]
0- **5** 5 **Give It Time**[192] [6007] 3-8-6 .... JoeFanning 12 55
(J G Given) *hld up: rdn over 2f out: sn outpcd* **25/1**
00- **6** 5 **Gala Casino King (IRE)**[222] [5407] 3-8-11 .... TomEaves 10 50
(M Dods) *hld up in tch: outpcd over 5f out: n.d after* **100/1**
0- **7** hd **Revolving World (IRE)**[222] [5407] 3-8-11 .... PatCosgrave 1 50
(T J Fitzgerald) *prom tl rdn and wknd over 2f out* **100/1**
0-0 **8** 2 ½ **Osolomio (IRE)**[9] [1153] 3-8-11 .... FergalLynch 7 45
(J G Given) *towards rr: rdn over 5f out: sn btn* **100/1**
0-4 **9** 7 **Torgiano (IRE)**[15] [1032] 5-9-12 .... LeeEnstone 4 33
(P Monteith) *led to over 2f out: wknd* **50/1**
0 **10** 2 **Moon Melody (GER)**[10] [1120] 3-8-11 .... PaulHanagan 5 28
(M L W Bell) *plld hrd: prom tl wknd fr 2f out* **10/1**[3]
00-0 **11** 12 **Follingworth (IRE)**[6] [1226] 3-8-6 45 .... DavidAllan 3 —
(A D Brown) *in tch to 1/2-way: wknd over 4f out* **100/1**
12 6 **Auburndale** 4-9-12 .... TonyCulhane 11 —
(K G Reveley) *missed break: hld up: wknd fr 1/2-way* **66/1**
13 dist **Kellys Double Gold (IRE)** 3-8-6 .... DaleGibson 2 —
(Mrs H O Graham) *dwlt: keen in rr: lost tch fr 1/2-way* **66/1**

2m 12.43s (0.63) **Going Correction** -0.025s/f (Good)
WFA 3 from 4yo+ 15lb **13** Ran SP% **120.2**
Speed ratings (Par 103):96,95,95,92,88 84,84,82,76,74 65,60,—
CSF £74.55 TOTE £15.40: £3.30, £2.00, £1.02; EX 62.80 Trifecta £35.70 Pool: £549.19 - 10.91 winning tickets..
Owner Transcend Bloodstock LLP **Bred** M Nolan **Trained** Billy Row, Co Durham

FOCUS
Little strength in depth and the modest pace meant those racing prominently held the edge. Consequently this bare form, rated through the runner-up, looks less than reliable.

1344 BETFRED POKER SPRINT SERIES H'CAP (QUALIFIER) 6f
3:40 (3:44) (Class 5) (0-70,71) 3-Y-O **£4,210** (£1,252; £625; £312) **Stalls** High

Form RPR
1 **Damika (IRE)**[227] 3-9-0 65 .... DeanMcKeown 5 75
(R M Whitaker) *trckd far side ldrs: led over 1f out: r.o strly* **9/1**
64-1 **2** 3 **Mulligan's Gold (IRE)**[19] [978] 3-9-4 69 .... FergalLynch 8 70+
(T D Easterby) *cl up far side: led over 2f to over 1f out: kpt on same pce ins fnl f: 2nd in gp* **5/1**[1]
06-0 **3** shd **Silk Merchant (IRE)**[19] [978] 3-8-9 60 .... RobertWinston 1 61
(J Howard Johnson) *in tch far side: effrt over 2f out: kpt on far side: nrst fin: 3rd in gp* **10/1**
0-23 **4** nk **Dasheena**[18] [1004] 3-8-11 62 .... PaulHanagan 7 62+
(M J Polglase) *dwlt: bhd far side: hdwy fr 2f out: nrst fin: 4th in gp* **12/1**
45-0 **5** 1 ¼ **Final Tune (IRE)**[38] [716] 3-9-0 65 .... PaulQuinn 13 61
(D Nicholls) *hld up stands side: hdwy to ld that gp appr fnl f: kpt on: no ch w far side: 1st in gp* **20/1**
0-36 **6** 1 **Trombone Tom**[47] [646] 3-8-11 62 .... DarrenWilliams 3 55
(J R Norton) *prom far side tl rdn and nt qckn fr 2f out: 5th in gp* **14/1**
0-41 **7** ¾ **Mormeatmic**[19] [980] 3-8-8 62 .... PaulMulrennan(3) 11 53
(M W Easterby) *swtchd to r and hld up far side: effrt over 2f out: no imp: 6th in gp* **9/1**
00-0 **8** 1 **Jellytot (USA)**[19] [980] 3-8-4 60 .... AndrewMullen(5) 6 48
(K A Ryan) *hld up in tch far side: outpcd over 2f out: n.d after: 7th in gp* **12/1**
0021 **9** 2 ½ **Sunderland Echo (IRE)**[7] [1185] 3-9-6 71 6ex .... TomEaves 15 52
(B Ellison) *cl up stands side: led that gp 2f out to appr fnl f: sn one pce: 2nd in gp* **8/1**[3]
54-3 **10** 1 **Northern Chorus (IRE)**[19] [980] 3-8-13 64 .... DavidAllan 12 42
(A Dickman) *prom stands side: effrt over 2f out: sn one pce: 3rd in gp* **9/1**
200 **11** 1 ¼ **Kings Cavalier (USA)**[15] [1036] 3-9-4 69 .... (v) RoystonFfrench 9 43
(I W McInnes) *in tch far side tl edgd lft and outpcd fr 1/2-way: 8th in gp* **40/1**
0-60 **12** ½ **Beverley Polo (IRE)**[12] [1078] 3-8-6 57 .... (b[1]) DaleGibson 17 29
(M W Easterby) *trckd stands side ldrs: rdn over 2f out: sn one pce: 4th in gp* **20/1**
0-40 **13** 1 **Coalite (IRE)**[9] [1147] 3-9-0 65 .... TonyCulhane 16 34
(A D Brown) *led stands side to 2f out: sn outpcd: 5th in gp* **20/1**
020- **14** hd **Hypnosis**[192] [6004] 3-8-12 63 .... PatCosgrave 4 32
(D W Barker) *led far side to over 2f out: sn btn: 9th in gp* **25/1**
603- **15** 7 **Emily's Place (IRE)**[196] [5945] 3-9-0 68 .... SaleemGolam(3) 10 16
(M H Tompkins) *swtchd and hld up in tch stands side: rdn 1/2-way: sn btn: 6th in gp* **13/2**[2]
00-0 **16** 7 **One Trick Pony**[19] [980] 3-8-11 62 .... (v[1]) TonyHamilton 14 —
(Karen McLintock) *bhd far side: drvn over 2f out: sn btn: 10th in gp* **33/1**

1m 15.14s (0.05) **Going Correction** -0.025s/f (Good) **16** Ran SP% **125.8**
Speed ratings (Par 99):98,94,93,93,91 90,89,88,84,83 81,81,79,79,70 60
CSF £49.93 CT £477.68 TOTE £12.10: £2.50, £2.20, £2.60, £2.90; EX 68.20 TRIFECTA Not won..
Owner G B Bedford **Bred** Patrick J Monahan **Trained** Scarcroft, W Yorks
■ Stewards' Enquiry : Fergal Lynch two-day ban: careless riding (May 12-13)

FOCUS
A run-of-the-mill handicap in which the pace was sound and the first four home finished on the far side. The fourth is the best guide to the level with the winner unexposed and could do better.
Coalite(IRE) Official explanation: jockey said gelding hung left-handed throughout

1345 TYNE TUNNEL ENGINEERING H'CAP 1m 3y(S)
4:15 (4:15) (Class 5) (0-70,70) 3-Y-O **£5,181** (£1,541; £770; £384) **Stalls** High

Form RPR
54-2 **1** **European Dream (IRE)**[19] [993] 3-9-2 68 .... FergalLynch 10 82+
(R C Guest) *hld up and bhd: smooth hdwy over 2f out: qcknd to ld appr fnl f: readily* **4/1**[1]
54-5 **2** 3 ½ **Superior Star**[31] [819] 3-8-10 62 .... PaulHanagan 14 68
(R A Fahey) *hld up: hdwy over 2f out: chsd wnr ins fnl f: r.o* **14/1**
00-6 **3** 2 ½ **William John**[19] [979] 3-8-4 56 oh3 .... RoystonFfrench 15 56
(B Ellison) *hld up: rdn 3f out: kpt on fr 2f out: nrst fin* **16/1**
6-05 **4** 1 **Bramcote Lorne**[3] [1269] 3-8-8 60 .... DeanMcKeown 7 58
(S Parr) *w ldr: led 3f out to over 1f out: one pce* **10/1**
020- **5** 1 ½ **Mister Maq**[231] [5177] 3-8-11 63 .... (b) TomEaves 5 57
(M Dods) *midfield: effrt 3f out: no imp fr 2f out* **50/1**
00-1 **6** 1 ¾ **Viva Volta**[12] [1078] 3-9-3 69 .... DavidAllan 12 59
(T D Easterby) *midfield: effrt over 2f out: rdn and no ex over 1f out* **7/1**[3]
0050 **7** ¾ **Eliminator**[19] [993] 3-8-3 60 .... NataliaGemelova(5) 8 49
(I W McInnes) *bhd: rdn 1/2-way: sme late hdwy: n.d* **50/1**
00-6 **8** 2 **Shore Thing (IRE)**[33] [795] 3-8-10 65 .... SaleemGolam(3) 6 49
(M H Tompkins) *led to 3f out: wknd over 1f out* **13/2**[2]
3-00 **9** nk **Bacharach (IRE)**[18] [1004] 3-8-13 68 .... PaulMulrennan(3) 3 51
(R F Fisher) *hld up: rdn over 3f out: n.d* **33/1**
336- **10** 1 **Lady Disdain**[196] [5939] 3-9-1 70 .... DanielTudhope(3) 16 51
(G M Moore) *hld up: rdn and edgd lft 3f out: sn btn* **14/1**
004- **11** 3 ½ **Andorran (GER)**[226] [5295] 3-8-6 58 .... RobertWinston 13 31+
(A Dickman) *hld up: effrt whn nt clr run over 2f out: n.d after* **10/1**
0500 **12** ½ **Captivate**[4] [1259] 3-8-4 56 oh6 .... (b) DavidKinsella 4 28
(M J Polglase) *chsd ldrs tl wknd over 2f out* **50/1**
-100 **13** ½ **Mystified (IRE)**[18] [1005] 3-8-9 64 .... DNolan(3) 11 35
(R F Fisher) *trckd ldrs tl wknd over 2f out* **25/1**
550- **14** 5 **Snowberry Hill (USA)**[236] [5047] 3-8-12 69 .... AndrewMullen(5) 17 28
(K A Ryan) *in tch tl rdn and wknd over 2f out* **16/1**
35-2 **15** ½ **Marmooq**[14] [1049] 3-9-2 68 .... JoeFanning 1 26
(M Johnston) *prom: outpcd over 3f out: rallied over 2f out: sn btn* **4/1**[1]
00-0 **16** 6 **Mycenean Prince (USA)**[10] [1122] 3-7-13 56 oh4 .... AndrewElliott(5) 2 —
(R C Guest) *chsd ldrs tl wknd over 3f out* **50/1**

1m 42.17s (0.27) **Going Correction** -0.025s/f (Good) **16** Ran SP% **123.7**
Speed ratings (Par 99):97,93,91,90,88 86,86,84,83,82 79,78,78,73,72 66
CSF £61.50 CT £816.27 TOTE £5.00: £1.70, £3.30, £2.70, £1.90; EX 65.70 Trifecta £170.50 Pool: £240.15 - 1.00 winning tickets..
Owner You Trotters **Bred** Limetree Stud Ltd **Trained** Brancepeth, Co Durham
■ Stewards' Enquiry : D Nolan one-day ban: failed to ride to draw (May 12)

FOCUS
An ordinary handicap in which the whole field raced centre to far side but the winner scored with plenty in hand and is the type to win more races. The form looks sound rated around the placed horses.
Bacharach(IRE) Official explanation: jockey said gelding hung right-handed throughout

1346 CAMAIR INTERNATIONAL FREIGHT FORWARDERS H'CAP 1m 4f 93y
4:45 (4:46) (Class 5) (0-70,70) 4-Y-O+ **£4,210** (£1,252; £625; £312) **Stalls** Low

Form RPR
110- **1** **Balwearie (IRE)**[179] [6236] 5-8-5 57 .... RoystonFfrench 16 66
(Miss L A Perratt) *cl up: led over 2f out: sn rdn: kpt on strly* **11/1**
0000 **2** 1 ¼ **Fort Churchill (IRE)**[19] [990] 5-9-0 66 .... (bt) RobertWinston 4 78+
(B Ellison) *keen: prom ins: no room fr 3f out to over 1f out: kpt on wl to chse wnr ins fnl f: unlucky* **7/1**[2]
64-0 **3** 1 **Caymans Gift**[63] [414] 6-8-0 57 oh3 ow1 .... AndrewMullen(5) 6 62
(A C Whillans) *hld up: hdwy to chse wnr over 1f out: hung lft: kpt on same pce ins fnl f* **33/1**
4360 **4** 1 ½ **Our Choice (IRE)**[19] [976] 4-8-10 62 .... JoeFanning 10 65
(N P Littmoden) *chsd ldrs: effrt 3f out: one pce over 1f out* **6/1**[1]
00-4 **5** ½ **Mr Majestic**[14] [1045] 4-8-6 58 .... DeanMcKeown 13 60
(R M Whitaker) *midfield: rdn over 2f out: edgd lft and sn outpcd: kpt on fnl f: no imp* **10/1**
31-0 **6** 1 ¼ **Melvino**[9] [1144] 4-9-0 66 .... PaulFessey 17 66
(T D Barron) *hld up: hdwy fr 2f out: nvr rchd ldrs* **9/1**
50-1 **7** 1 **Duroob**[9] [1138] 4-8-12 69 .... AndrewElliott(5) 11 67
(K R Burke) *in tch on ins: rdn 3f out: sn outpcd: n.d after* **7/1**[2]
4/0- **8** hd **Shares (IRE)**[16] [5983] 6-8-6 58 .... DavidAllan 15 56
(P Monteith) *hld up: rdn over 3f out: n.d* **12/1**
240- **9** 1 ¼ **Intavac Boy**[140] [6563] 5-8-4 56 oh1 .... DavidKinsella 3 52
(C W Thornton) *cl up tl wknd fr 2f out* **20/1**
U-05 **10** 2 ½ **Fiddlers Creek (IRE)**[14] [412] 7-8-6 58 .... (vt) TonyHamilton 12 50
(R Allan) *in tch: effrt over 2f out: wknd over 1f out* **20/1**
44-0 **11** 1 ½ **Royal Melbourne (IRE)**[35] [767] 6-8-6 58 ow2 .... TomEaves 8 47
(Miss J A Camacho) *hld up: effrt whn hung lft over 2f out: sn btn* **8/1**[3]
230- **12** ½ **Let It Be**[177] [6267] 5-8-10 62 .... TonyCulhane 5 51
(K G Reveley) *hld up: shkn up 3f out: sn btn* **6/1**[1]
-650 **13** 8 **Court Of Appeal**[9] [1144] 9-8-13 65 .... PatCosgrave 1 41
(B Ellison) *led to over 2f out: sn lost pl* **20/1**
00-0 **14** 8 **Bramantino (IRE)**[5] [1233] 6-8-13 65 .... FergalLynch 14 28
(T A K Cuthbert) *hld up: rdn over 3f out: sn btn* **25/1**
056- **15** 9 **Oman Gulf (USA)**[202] [5822] 5-8-8 60 .... DaleGibson 2 9
(Micky Hammond) *plld hrd: in tch tl wknd over 3f out* **20/1**

2m 41.39s (-2.16) **Going Correction** -0.025s/f (Good) **15** Ran SP% **125.6**
Speed ratings (Par 103):106,105,104,103,103 102,101,101,100,99 98,97,92,87,81
CSF £79.75 CT £2509.65 TOTE £16.30: £3.90, £3.80, £18.90; EX 199.20 TRIFECTA Not won. Place 6 £153.03, Place 5 £89.96.
Owner N J Angus **Bred** Ms Amy Mulligan **Trained** Ayr, S Ayrshire

FOCUS
Just a fair pace to this ordinary handicap and those held up seemed at a disadvantage. The runner-up looked most unlucky and the form is limited by the proximity of the third.
Bramantino(IRE) Official explanation: jockey said gelding was unsuited by the good to firm going
T/Plt: £281.50 to a £1 stake. Pool: £51,748.05. 134.15 winning tickets. T/Qpdt: £71.30 to a £1 stake. Pool: £3,070.20. 31.85 winning tickets. RY

1046 WARWICK (L-H)
Monday, May 1

OFFICIAL GOING: Good (good to firm in places)
Wind: Light, across Weather: Cloudy with sunny spells

1347 EUROPEAN BREEDERS FUND PRIMROSE MAIDEN FILLIES' STKS 5f
2:20 (2:26) (Class 5) 2-Y-O **£3,886** (£1,156; £577; £288) **Stalls** Low

Form RPR
6 **1** **Nina Blini**[7] [1189] 2-9-0 .... EddieAhern 6 77
(B J Meehan) *edgd rt s: chsd ldrs: rdn to ld wl ins fnl f* **5/1**[2]
0 **2** hd **Frisky Talk (IRE)**[12] [1082] 2-9-0 .... MartinDwyer 13 76
(B W Hills) *trckd ldr: racd keenly: led over 1f out: rdn: edgd rt and hdd wl ins fnl f* **8/1**[3]
3 **3** 2 ½ **Isobel Rose (IRE)**[12] [1082] 2-9-0 .... RichardHughes 14 66
(E A L Dunlop) *wnt rt s and s.i.s: sn chsng ldrs: rdn over 1f out: no ex ins fnl f* **11/8**[1]
4 1 ¼ **Check Tou** 2-9-0 .... GrahamGibbons 11 61
(P A Blockley) *wnt lft s: sn led: rdn and hdd over 1f out: styd on same pce* **50/1**
5 ¾ **Tiara Boom De Ay (IRE)** 2-8-11 .... RichardSmith(3) 8 58+
(R Hannon) *s.i.s: rn green and sn outpcd: hdwy over 1f out: nvr nrr* **14/1**
6 hd **Cyprus Rose** 2-9-0 .... JimmyQuinn 9 57
(V Smith) *dwlt and hmpd s: outpcd: hdwy over 1f out: nrst fin* **20/1**

0 **7** *hd* **Montemayorprincess (IRE)**[6] 1203 2-9-0 .... FrankieMcDonald 2 57
(D Haydn Jones) *prom: rdn and lost pl over 3f out: n.d after* **66/1**
0 **8** *1* **Cotswold Traveller**[14] 1046 2-9-0 .... SteveDrowne 7 53
(Tom Dascombe) *prom over 3f* **20/1**
9 *3* **Going Straight (IRE)** 2-9-0 .... TedDurcan 10 41
(I A Wood) *dwlt and hmpd s: outpcd: nvr nrr* **50/1**
02 **10** *nk* **Peppin's Gold (IRE)**[14] 1046 2-9-0 .... MickyFenton 4 39+
(B R Millman) *chsd ldrs: rdn 1/2-way: sn wknd* **9/1**
11 *7* **Vanatina (IRE)** 2-9-0 .... JamieMackay 5 11
(A Bailey) *s.i.s: sn outpcd* **33/1**

61.36 secs (1.16) **Going Correction** +0.075s/f (Good) **11** Ran SP% **104.4**
Speed ratings (Par 90):93,92,88,86,85 85,84,83,78,77 66
CSF £29.96 TOTE £4.80: £1.70, £2.60, £1.10; EX 28.50.
Owner Mrs T S M Cunningham **Bred** R And Mrs S J Turner **Trained** Manton, Wilts
■ Samahir (9/2), Shreddy Shrimpster (33/1) & Musical Affair (100/1) w/d after giving trouble at the stalls. R4, deduct 15p in the £.

FOCUS
Not an easy race to rate, with little solid form to go on, but the first three could turn out to be reasonable juveniles. The time was decent.

NOTEBOOK
Nina Blini showed the benefit of her Windsor debut. Pushed along entering the straight, where she stuck to the inside, she mastered the leader near the line. She should get another furlong. (op 7-1)
Frisky Talk(IRE) ◆, who finished behind today's third at Newmarket, showed ahead early in the straight but was just run out of it. She has plenty of pace and should soon find an opportunity. (op 11-1)
Isobel Rose(IRE) was unable to build on the form of her debut effort at Newmarket. She soon recovered from a slow start but, after having her chance, could only keep on at the same pace in the latter stages. (op 6-4 tchd 13-8)
Check Tou, out of a mare who was placed at up to ten furlongs, did well to get to the lead from her high draw but her measure was taken approaching the final furlong.
Tiara Boom De Ay(IRE), whose dam was a smart sprinting juvenile, should improve with this debut behind her and can leave this bare form behind. (op 16-1)
Cyprus Rose, a half-sister to five winners, the pick of them high-class sprinter Croft Pool, was never nearer after a tardy start and will know more about what is required next time.
Peppin's Gold(IRE) Official explanation: jockey said filly missed the break

1348 RACING UK FILLIES' H'CAP — 7f 26y
2:50 (2:56) (Class 5) (0-70,69) 3-Y-0+ **£3,238** (£963; £481; £240) **Stalls** Low

Form RPR
140- **1** **Oceancookie (IRE)**[323] 2523 4-9-12 **67** ....(t) RichardHughes 11 75
(A M Balding) *dwlt: outpcd: hdwy over 1f out: rdn to ld ins fnl f: edgd rt: jst hld on* **8/1**
650- **2** *shd* **Peace Lily**[230] 5207 4-9-0 **55** .... EddieAhern 10 65+
(R F Johnson Houghton) *hld up: hdwy over 1f out: r.o* **16/1**
14-6 **3** *¾* **Rakata (USA)**[14] 1056 4-10-0 **69** .... SteveDrowne 4 75
(P F I Cole) *hld up: hdwy over 2f out: rdn over 1f out: styd on* **5/1**[2]
2122 **4** *1* **Meditation**[14] 1057 4-9-4 **64** .... DerekNolan(5) 13 67
(I A Wood) *disp ld tl led 4f out: rdn and hdd ins fnl f: unable qckn* **4/1**[1]
000- **5** *6* **Linden's Lady**[226] 5299 6-9-0 **55** oh2 ....(v) KDarley 6 42
(J R Weymes) *chsd ldrs: rdn over 2f out: wknd fnl f* **12/1**
300- **6** *shd* **Lady Edge (IRE)**[209] 5686 4-9-3 **58** .... TedDurcan 1 45
(A W Carroll) *mid-div: hung rt: hdwy 1/2-way: rdn and wknd over 1f out* **16/1**
0035 **7** *1¾* **Tiviski (IRE)**[6] 1209 4-9-3 **58** ....(p) PhilipRobinson 2 41
(G G Margarson) *chsd ldrs: rdn over 2f out: wknd over 1f out* **8/1**
5051 **8** *shd* **Ektishaaf**[19] 985 4-9-3 **58** .... JamieMackay 9 40
(C F Wall) *sn outpcd: styd on ins fnl f: nvr nrr* **11/2**[3]
60-6 **9** *1¼* **Dancing Storm**[28] 861 3-8-7 **60** .... FergusSweeney 7 39
(W S Kittow) *prom: carried rt 1/2-way: sn lost pl* **20/1**
000- **10** *1¼* **Zafantage**[193] 5994 3-9-2 **69** .... FrankieMcDonald 8 45
(S Kirk) *sn pushed along: in rr: n.d* **12/1**
6204 **11** *¾* **Grezie**[24] 903 4-9-0 **55** oh1 .... MartinDwyer 5 29
(T D McCarthy) *disp ld 3f: rdn and wknd fnl f* **7/1**
100- **12** *1¼* **Jolie (IRE)**[216] 5532 4-9-9 **64** .... JimmyQuinn 12 35
(R Dickin) *s.s: outpcd* **40/1**
/00- **13** *21* **Fei Mah**[367] 1341 4-8-11 **55** oh25 .... DeanCorby(3) 3 —
(J R Jenkins) *plld hrd and prom: hung rt 1/2-way: sn wknd* **100/1**

1m 25.69s (0.69) **Going Correction** +0.125s/f (Good)
WFA 3 from 4yo+ 12lb **13** Ran SP% **122.1**
Speed ratings (Par 100):101,100,100,98,92 91,89,89,88,86 86,84,60
CSF £130.17 CT £736.70 TOTE £9.20: £2.70, £4.40, £2.00; EX 142.60.
Owner Miss Clare Balding **Bred** I A Balding **Trained** Kingsclere, Hants

FOCUS
This was run at a good pace. The first four finished clear and three of them were drawn high. The time was the best of the older-horse events and the race has been rated a shade more positively than it might have been.

1349 COVENTRY CUP H'CAP — 7f 26y
3:25 (3:26) (Class 4) (0-85,84) 3-Y-0 **£6,477** (£1,927; £963; £481) **Stalls** Low

Form RPR
40-5 **1** **Adeje Park (IRE)**[11] 1091 3-9-4 **84** .... EddieAhern 1 89
(P W Chapple-Hyam) *chsd ldrs: rdn to ld ins fnl f: r.o* **4/1**[2]
245- **2** *¾* **Carmenero (GER)**[215] 5540 3-8-13 **79** .... SteveDrowne 3 82
(W R Muir) *hld up: hdwy over 1f out: r.o* **20/1**
16-3 **3** *1* **Jaad**[11] 1099 3-9-1 **81** .... MartinDwyer 7 81
(M Johnston) *chsd ldr: rdn to ld over 1f out: edgd lft: hdd and unable qck ins fnl f* **7/4**[1]
000- **4** *½* **Tora Petcha (IRE)**[206] 5716 3-8-11 **77** .... GrahamGibbons 6 76
(R Hollinshead) *led over 5f: no ex fnl f* **16/1**
613- **5** *1¾* **Pure Fiction**[283] 3693 3-8-8 **77** .... RichardSmith(3) 5 71
(R Hannon) *prom: rdn over 1f out: styd on same pce* **12/1**
2-35 **6** *3½* **Broken Spur (FR)**[28] 852 3-8-8 **74** .... KDarley 8 59
(B W Hills) *chsd ldrs: rdn and hung rt over 1f out: sn wknd* **9/1**
41-0 **7** *11* **Savernake Blue**[13] 1067 3-9-3 **83** .... TedDurcan 9 40
(M R Channon) *prom: hung rt 1/2-way: wknd wl over 1f out* **9/2**[3]
00-6 **8** *5* **Musical Guest (IRE)**[32] 803 3-8-11 **77** .... JimmyQuinn 4 21
(G G Margarson) *hld up: wknd 2f out* **28/1**
106- **9** *2½* **Your Amount (IRE)**[191] 6016 3-8-11 **77** .... JDSmith 2 14
(A King) *hld up: hdwy 2f out: sn wknd* **11/1**

1m 25.49s (0.49) **Going Correction** +0.125s/f (Good) **9** Ran SP% **114.7**
Speed ratings (Par 101):102,101,100,99,97 93,80,75,72
CSF £77.88 CT £187.49 TOTE £5.10: £1.80, £4.50, £1.10; EX 88.10.
Owner Marco Bozzi **Bred** Marco Bozzi **Trained** Newmarket, Suffolk
■ Stewards' Enquiry : Martin Dwyer caution: careless riding

FOCUS
The time was moderate and this is ordinary form, rated around the fourth and fifth.
Your Amount(IRE) Official explanation: jockey said gelding lost its action

1350 EDGECOTE H'CAP — 1m 4f 134y
4:00 (4:02) (Class 5) (0-70,70) 3-Y-0 **£3,238** (£963; £481; £240) **Stalls** Low

Form RPR
45-6 **1** **Spring Dream (IRE)**[12] 1079 3-9-0 **66** .... TedDurcan 7 72
(M R Channon) *chsd ldrs: swtchd rt over 2f out: rdn to ld and hung rt ins fnl f: sn hdd: rallied to ld post* **16/1**
00-5 **2** *shd* **Squirtle (IRE)**[12] 1079 3-8-10 **62** .... RobbieFitzpatrick 5 68
(W M Brisbourne) *hld up: outpcd 5f out: hdwy over 1f out: rdn to ld wl ins fnl f: hdd post* **11/1**
0633 **3** *2* **Alexian**[14] 1052 3-9-2 **68** .... GrahamGibbons 1 71
(R Hollinshead) *s.i.s: hld up: hdwy 4f out: rdn to ld over 1f out: hdd and no ex ins fnl f* **11/4**[1]
00-0 **4** *1¾* **Girardii**[21] 948 3-8-12 **64** ....(b[1]) RichardHughes 6 64
(R Charlton) *sn rdn to chse ldr: led over 10f out: rdn and hdd over 1f out: wknd wl ins fnl f* **8/1**
0544 **5** *1¼* **Wise Choice**[19] 979 3-8-4 **56** .... MartinDwyer 11 54
(N P Littmoden) *s.i.s: hld up: hdwy over 1f out: nt rch ldrs* **7/1**[2]
000- **6** *2½* **Fonic Rock (IRE)**[290] 3516 3-8-4 **56** oh1 .... JamieMackay 4 50
(M L W Bell) *mid-div: rdn and hung lft over 1f out: nvr trbld ldrs* **28/1**
0-33 **7** *3* **Synonymy**[19] 979 3-8-13 **65** .... FergusSweeney 8 54
(M Blanshard) *prom: chsd ldr 8f out tl rdn 2f out: wknd fnl f* **15/2**[3]
400 **8** *7* **Darker Than Blue**[9] 1139 3-8-4 **56** oh6 .... JimmyQuinn 9 34
(B J Meehan) *mid-div: hdwy 8f out: rdn and wknd 2f out* **50/1**
-345 **9** *¾* **King's Fable (USA)**[19] 979 3-8-6 **58** .... KDarley 13 35
(M Johnston) *chsd ldrs over 9f* **8/1**
-500 **10** *1¾* **Earth Master (IRE)**[60] 558 3-9-0 **66** .... FrankieMcDonald 12 40
(S Kirk) *s.i.s: hld up: a in rr* **28/1**
40-5 **11** *hd* **Beauchamp United**[65] 515 3-9-4 **70** ....(b) NickyMackay 3 44
(G A Butler) *led 2f: chsd ldr to 8f out: rdn and wknd over 1f out* **16/1**
0-20 **12** *7* **Left Hand Drive**[34] 781 3-8-2 **57** ow1 ....(t) EdwardCreighton(3) 10 20
(B W Duke) *hld up: rdn 8f out: a in rr* **33/1**
00-0 **13** *14* **Vice Admiral**[9] 1140 3-8-4 **56** .... DO'Donohoe 2 —
(M W Easterby) *hld up in tch: plld hrd: lost pl 8f out: wknd over 4f out* **15/2**[3]

2m 47.71s (4.11) **Going Correction** +0.30s/f (Good) **13** Ran SP% **116.8**
Speed ratings (Par 99):99,98,97,96,95 94,92,88,87,86 86,82,73
CSF £171.78 CT £636.53 TOTE £14.60: £3.30, £3.70, £1.60; EX 116.90.
Owner W H Ponsonby **Bred** R N Auld **Trained** West Ilsley, Berks

FOCUS
Just a modest handicap, run at a good pace, with the third and fifth helping set the standard.

1351 STRATSTONE CADILLAC MAIDEN FILLIES' STKS — 1m 22y
4:30 (4:35) (Class 5) 3-Y-0+ **£3,238** (£963; £481; £240) **Stalls** Low

Form RPR
44- **1** **Balloura (USA)**[198] 5886 3-8-9 .... MartinDwyer 2 76
(W J Haggas) *led 3f: chsd ldr: led over 3f out: drvn out* **16/1**
2- **2** *nk* **Magic Peak (IRE)**[186] 6122 3-8-9 .... TedDurcan 5 75
(Sir Michael Stoute) *a.p: rdn to chse wnr fnl f: r.o* **85/40**[1]
3 *5* **Stepping Stones** 3-8-9 .... RichardHughes 8 64
(H R A Cecil) *w ldr: led 5f out to over 3f out: sn rdn and hung rt: wknd fnl f* **15/2**
0- **4** *1* **Vino**[175] 6282 3-8-9 .... KDarley 11 62+
(B W Hills) *hld up: hdwy 3f out: nvr nr to chal* **66/1**
0- **5** *½* **Royal Fantasy (IRE)**[209] 5688 3-8-9 .... JamieSpencer 17 60+
(J R Fanshawe) *s.i.s: hld up: r.o ins fnl f: nvr nr to chal* **8/1**
0-5 **6** *2* **Sea Of Calm (USA)**[14] 1055 3-8-9 .... SteveDrowne 1 56+
(E A L Dunlop) *chsd ldrs: rdn and wknd over 1f out* **9/2**[3]
7 *hd* **Maria Antonia (IRE)** 3-8-9 ow5 .... DerekNolan(5) 15 60
(M J Wallace) *s.i.s: hld up: r.o ins fnl f: nvr trbld ldrs* **100/1**
0-0 **8** *½* **Polish Welcome**[12] 1085 3-8-9 .... GrahamGibbons 13 54
(S C Williams) *prom: rdn 1/2-way: wknd over 1f out* **100/1**
000- **9** *1* **The Flying Peach**[199] 5878 3-8-2 40 .... LiamJones(7) 12 52?
(W M Brisbourne) *hld up: plld hrd: hdwy 3f out: sn rdn and wknd* **40/1**
0- **10** *½* **Dance A Daydream**[150] 6484 3-8-4 .... RoryMoore(5) 10 51
(J R Fanshawe) *prom to 1/2-way* **66/1**
11 *nk* **Atwirl** 3-8-9 .... EddieAhern 4 50+
(D J Daly) *s.s: hld up: effrt and nt clr run over 3f out: n.d* **40/1**
12 *½* **Kinvara Lass (IRE)** 3-8-9 .... NickyMackay 9 49
(L M Cumani) *hld up in tch: wknd wl over 1f out* **7/2**[2]
3 **13** *5* **Bride To Be (USA)**[44] 668 3-8-9 .... JimmyQuinn 6 37
(C E Brittain) *s.s: hld up: effrt over 3f out: sn wknd* **10/1**
0- **14** *hd* **Meohmy**[266] 4220 3-8-6 .... EdwardCreighton(3) 14 37
(M R Channon) *hld up: a in rr* **50/1**
00 **15** *1* **Kilmeena Magic**[20] 964 4-9-8 .... RobbieFitzpatrick 3 35
(J C Fox) *prom over 5f* **200/1**
00 **16** *9* **Wild Lass**[20] 963 5-9-8 .... FergusSweeney 16 14
(J C Fox) *a in rr* **200/1**
17 *3½* **Vettori Dancer** 3-8-9 .... JamieMackay 7 6
(G G Margarson) *sn outpcd* **100/1**

1m 41.93s (2.33) **Going Correction** +0.40s/f (Good)
WFA 3 from 4yo+ 13lb **17** Ran SP% **122.6**
Speed ratings (Par 100):104,103,98,97,97 95,95,94,93,93 92,92,87,87,86 77,73
CSF £50.15 TOTE £15.80: £3.70, £1.50, £3.00; EX 52.50.
Owner Hamdan Al Maktoum **Bred** Shadwell Farm LLC **Trained** Newmarket, Suffolk

FOCUS
A decent winning time for a race like this and the quickest of the three races over the trip on the day. The first two finished clear but this looks a pretty weak race, limited by the ninth home.
Stepping Stones Official explanation: jockey said filly ducked to the right in the home straight

1352 ENTERTAIN CLIENTS AT WARWICK RACECOURSE H'CAP — 1m 22y
5:00 (5:07) (Class 6) (0-60,60) 3-Y-0 **£2,730** (£806; £403) **Stalls** Low

Form RPR
0-15 **1** **Leamington Lad (IRE)**[12] 1078 3-9-1 **60** .... RichardThomas(3) 8 67
(J A Geake) *chsd ldrs: led over 1f out: sn rdn and edgd lft: jst hld on* **9/4**[1]
0-54 **2** *½* **Murrumbidgee (IRE)**[92] 234 3-9-4 **60** .... EddieAhern 13 66+
(J W Hills) *hld up: hdwy and hung rt over 1f out: r.o* **8/1**[3]
60-6 **3** *shd* **Noble Nova**[33] 797 3-8-12 **54** .... SamHitchcott 12 60
(M R Channon) *hld up: hdwy over 2f out: rdn over 1f out: r.o* **16/1**
3004 **4** *2½* **Grecianette (IRE)**[19] 984 3-8-12 **54** .... JamieSpencer 11 54
(W J Musson) *led: hdd over 6f out: chsd ldrs: rdn over 1f out: styd on same pce* **7/1**[2]
6000 **5** *1¼* **They All Laughed**[26] 890 3-9-2 **58** .... SteveDrowne 9 55
(P W Hiatt) *hld up: r.o ins fnl f: nt rch ldrs* **33/1**
000- **6** *nk* **Dark Moon**[245] 4816 3-9-2 **58** .... NickyMackay 3 55
(A M Balding) *prom: rdn over 3f out: styd on same pce appr fnl f* **16/1**

00-0 **7** *1 ¼* **Great Composer (IRE)**[9] 1140 3-8-11 **53**........................ JimCrowley 15 47
(Mrs A J Perrett) *prom: rdn over 2f out: wknd over 1f out* **12/1**

-504 **8** *hd* **Blue Army (IRE)**[20] 964 3-8-13 **55**........................ AdrianMcCarthy 4 48
(Jane Southcombe) *prom: rdn over 2f out: wknd over 1f out* **12/1**

004 **9** *1* **Tilsworth Charlie**[30] 835 3-8-10 **55**........................ DeanCorby(3) 2 46
(J R Jenkins) *hld up: hdwy over 3f out: rdn and wknd over 1f out* **20/1**

5-65 **10** *¾* **Cheveley Flyer**[19] 984 3-8-13 **55**........................ JimmyQuinn 17 44
(J Pearce) *hld up: rdn over 2f out: n.d* **8/1[3]**

005 **11** *nk* **Ronaldo**[14] 1049 3-9-2 **58**........................ MartinDwyer 10 47
(W R Muir) *mid-div: rdn over 3f out: wknd 2f out* **12/1**

30-0 **12** *2 ½* **Twentyfirst Dansar**[92] 241 3-9-1 **57**........................(v) FergusSweeney 14 40
(A D Smith) *chsd ldrs: rdn to ld over 2f out: hdd: hung lft and wknd over 1f out* **33/1**

-005 **13** *1 ¼* **Tallyhobye**[31] 817 3-8-12 **54**........................ KDarley 6 34
(J R Weymes) *led over 6f out: hdd over 2f out: rdn and wknd over 1f out* **16/1**

50-0 **14** *6* **Under Fire (IRE)**[80] 364 3-8-12 **54**........................ TedDurcan 7 20
(A W Carroll) *s.i.s: hld up a in rr* **33/1**

00-0 **15** *shd* **Leo McGarry (IRE)**[38] 709 3-8-13 **55**........................ RobbieFitzpatrick 5 21
(S C Williams) *hld up: wknd over 3f out* **25/1**

1m 43.37s (3.77) **Going Correction** +0.40s/f (Good) **15** Ran SP% **123.6**
Speed ratings (Par 97):97,96,96,93,92 92,91,90,89,89 88,86,85,79,79
CSF £18.48 CT £236.50 TOTE £2.60: £1.50, £2.90, £4.20; EX 16.10.
Owner Three Off The Tee Partnership **Bred** Daniel Galavan **Trained** Kimpton, Hants

FOCUS
Modest form, but sound enough rated through the third.
Blue Army(IRE) Official explanation: trainer said gelding could not handle the sticky ground and was never travelling
Cheveley Flyer Official explanation: jockey said colt was denied a clear run
Twentyfirst Dansar Official explanation: jockey said gelding had a breathing problem

1353 KNOWLE APPRENTICE H'CAP 1m 22y
5:30 (5:35) (Class 6) (0-60,60) 4-Y-0+ £2,388 (£705; £352) Stalls Low

Form RPR

-140 **1** **Golden Square**[67] 492 4-8-5 **50**........................ DeanWilliams(3) 8 57
(A W Carroll) *chsd ldrs: led on bit over 1f out: rdn out* **16/1**

000- **2** *1 ¼* **Tuning Fork**[153] 6461 6-8-13 **55**........................ RoryMoore 10 60
(T M Jones) *led: hung rt and hdd over 2f out: sn rdn: styd on* **16/1**

044- **3** *1 ¼* **Elopement (IRE)**[322] 2537 4-8-10 **55**........................ LiamJones(3) 12 57
(W M Brisbourne) *chsd ldrs: rdn over 2f out: styd on* **25/1**

003- **4** *¾* **Prince Of The May**[312] 2862 4-8-12 **57**........................ TravisBlock(3) 7 57
(H Morrison) *hld up in tch: rdn over 2f out: styd on* **9/1**

00-5 **5** *hd* **Joshua's Gold (IRE)**[21] 950 5-8-13 **60**........................(v) DanielleMcCreery(5) 1 60
(D Carroll) *chsd ldr: led over 2f out: rdn and hdd over 1f out: no ex ins fnl f* **7/1[3]**

-000 **6** *¾* **Huxley (IRE)**[33] 792 7-7-12 **47**........................(t) FrankiePickard(7) 13 45
(D J Wintle) *s.i.s: hld up: hdwy over 1f out: nt rch ldrs* **33/1**

1530 **7** *¾* **Physical (IRE)**[5] 1245 4-8-8 **55**........................(p) JamieHamblett(5) 2 51
(Mrs A J Perrett) *hld up: hdwy over 3f out: rdn over 1f out: styd on same pce* **6/1[2]**

000/ **8** *1 ¼* **Major Blade (GER)**[58] 3997 8-8-0 **47** oh1 ow1........ ThomasO'Brien(5) 4 40
(Heather Dalton) *chsd ldrs: rdn over 2f out: wknd fnl f* **20/1**

0366 **9** *1 ¼* **Prince Of Gold**[26] 889 6-8-3 **48**........................ RussellKennemore(3) 16 38
(R Hollinshead) *s.i.s: hld up: hdwy and hung lft over 1f out: nt trble ldrs* **11/1**

0124 **10** *1* **Lord Chamberlain**[5] 1245 13-9-2 **58**........................(b) StephenDonohoe 3 46
(J M Bradley) *s.i.s: hld up: rdn over 1f out: nvr nrr* **6/1[2]**

400 **11** *nk* **Samson Quest**[24] 906 4-8-8 **57**........................(v) JackDean(7) 11 44
(A W Carroll) *s.s: outpcd* **14/1**

0340 **12** *hd* **Taminoula (IRE)**[23] 917 5-8-10 **52**........................ MarcHalford 14 39
(J G Given) *hld up: nt clr run over 3f out and over 2f out: n.d* **12/1**

00-0 **13** *1* **Mirage Prince (IRE)**[3] 1273 4-9-1 **60**........................ DerekNolan(3) 17 45
(D Shaw) *hld up: effrt over 2f out: sn wknd* **66/1**

20-3 **14** *1 ¾* **Uhuru Peak**[4] 1253 5-8-9 **56**........................(t) AdeleRothery(5) 5 37
(M W Easterby) *hld up: a in rr* **9/2[1]**

050- **15** *1 ½* **Didoe**[219] 5447 7-8-1 **48**........................ MarkCoumbe(5) 6 25
(P W Hiatt) *chsd ldrs: lost pl 6f out: rdn and wknd over 2f out* **25/1**

/600 **16** *5* **Jewel Of India**[47] 640 7-8-8 **55**........................(p) HugoFellows(5) 15 21
(Mrs A L M King) *s.i.s: hld up: a in rr* **66/1**

0 **17** *7* **Numidas (POL)**[19] 982 4-7-13 **46** oh1........................ JosephWalsh(5) 9 —
(Mrs A L M King) *mid-div: effrt over 3f out: sn rdn and wknd* **66/1**

1m 42.48s (2.88) **Going Correction** +0.40s/f (Good) **17** Ran SP% **123.6**
Speed ratings (Par 101):101,99,98,97,97 96,96,94,93,92 92,92,91,89,87 82,75
CSF £238.54 CT £6238.98 TOTE £19.90: £3.10, £4.10, £3.40, £2.70; EX 359.70 Place 6 £40.74, Place 5 £34.02.
Owner Mr & Mrs J B **Bred** J R And Mrs P Good **Trained** Cropthorne, Worcs

FOCUS
A weak event with something of a ragged start, and nothing got into it from behind. The race has been rated through the third and fourth.
T/Jkpt: Not won. T/Plt: £15.50 to a £1 stake. Pool: £48,948.15. 2,301.85 winning tickets. T/Qpdt: £5.30 to a £1 stake. Pool: £1,973.70. 273.80 winning tickets. CR

1188 WINDSOR (R-H)
Monday, May 1

OFFICIAL GOING: Good to soft
Wind: Moderate behind

1354 FRENCH BROTHERS NOVICE AUCTION STKS 5f 10y
2:00 (2:00) (Class 5) 2-Y-0 £3,886 (£1,156; £577; £288) Stalls High

Form RPR

1 **1** **Espartano**[21] 944 2-9-3........................ JamieSpencer 1 83+
(M J Wallace) *hld up in cl 5th: swtchd lft over 2f out: shkn up and qcknd to ld jst ins fnl: kpt on wl: comf* **1/3[1]**

1 **2** *½* **No Worries Yet (IRE)**[20] 962 2-8-6........................ FrancisNorton 2 70
(J L Spearing) *t.k.h: trck ld tl slt advantage fr 2f out: rdn over 1f out: hdd jst ins last: kpt on but nt pce of wnr* **20/1**

212 **3** *2* **Spoof Master (IRE)**[10] 1121 2-8-12........................ JamesDoyle(5) 5 74
(W G M Turner) *chsd ldrs tl drvn and outpcd over 2f out: swtchd lft and styd on again ins last but nvr a danger* **9/2[2]**

4 *1 ¼* **Scented Present** 2-8-12........................ TPQueally 3 65
(B J Meehan) *chsd ldrs: drvn to chal 2 out: outpcd ins fnl f* **25/1**

10 **5** *3* **Il Palio (IRE)**[13] 1066 2-8-13........................ DaneO'Neill 4 55
(B R Millman) *led tl narrowly hdd 2f out: sn rdn: wknd fnl f* **14/1[3]**

61.64 secs (0.54) **Going Correction** -0.05s/f (Good) **5** Ran SP% **108.5**
Speed ratings (Par 93):93,92,89,87,82
CSF £8.47 TOTE £1.20: £1.10, £5.80; EX 7.70.
Owner Mrs M Findlay **Bred** Barton Stud Partnership **Trained** Newmarket, Suffolk

FOCUS
Not the most competitive of races, but the favourite won with a bit more in hand than the winning margin might suggest and the third sets the level for the form.

NOTEBOOK
Espartano ◆, saddled with the number one stall again as when winning over course and distance last month, was up against fewer rivals this time but he was still forced to circle his field and make his run down the middle of the track. He won comfortably enough in the end, despite the narrow margin, and will stay further. He remains a nice prospect. (op 4-11 tchd 4-9 in places)
No Worries Yet(IRE), whose Bath selling victory has since been boosted, stepped up considerably on that. Despite taking a good hold early, she made sure the winner had to find plenty in order to get the better of her and she is obviously a lot better than a plater.
Spoof Master(IRE), the most experienced in the field, is also the most exposed and he never looked like winning this. He is going to continue to be difficult to place. (op 4-1 tchd 7-2 in places)
Scented Present, a 26,000gns half-brother to the winning juvenile Gifted Gamble, faced a stiff task in taking on four previous winners on his debut but showed enough to suggest his turn will come.
Il Palio(IRE) made much of the running before getting swamped. He got away with it when winning on his Polytrack debut, but his two efforts on turf since suggest he barely gets the trip. (op 16-1)

1355 ATTHERACES.COM MEDIAN AUCTION MAIDEN STKS 6f
2:30 (2:30) (Class 5) 3-4-Y-0 £3,238 (£963; £481; £240) Stalls High

Form RPR

3-5 **1** **Starlight Gazer**[11] 1089 3-8-11........................ RichardThomas(3) 9 73+
(J A Geake) *chsd ldrs: led jst ins fnl 2f: rdn and hung bdly lft to far rail fnl f: r.o strly* **7/1[3]**

2 *1 ½* **Fleeting Passion** 3-8-9........................ JamesDoyle(5) 4 68
(N P Littmoden) *bhd: hdwy 2f out: r.o wl to chse wnr ins fnl f but a hld* **25/1**

2- **3** *1 ¼* **Grecian Gold (IRE)**[328] 2374 4-9-7........................ AdamKirby(3) 6 67
(C G Cox) *s.i.s: sn rcvrd to chse ldrs: ev chnace 2f out: sn chsng wnr and hung lft fnl f: sn one pce* **8/1**

0-00 **4** *1 ¼* **Atticus Trophies (IRE)**[4] 1261 3-8-7 65........................(p) SophieDoyle(7) 7 60
(K McAuliffe) *racd alone centre to far side: in tch: rdn and kpt on fnl f but nvr gng pce to chal* **33/1**

0-0 **5** *2* **North Fleet**[14] 1048 3-9-0........................ AdrianTNicholls 1 54
(J M Bradley) *c to stands aide after 1f: in tch: rdn over 2f out: kpt on ins last but nvr gng pce to chal* **100/1**

00- **6** *½* **Colton**[237] 5027 3-9-0........................ NCallan 5 53
(J M P Eustace) *keen hold: hld up in rr: hdwy ins fnl 2f: kpt on ins last but nvr gng pce to rch ldrs* **20/1**

0- **7** *½* **Jill Dawson (IRE)**[177] 6251 3-8-9........................ FrancisNorton 3 46
(John Berry) *c to stands side: in tch: rdn 1/2-way: styd on fr over 1f out but nvr gng pce of ldrs* **25/1**

25-2 **8** *¾* **Danawi (IRE)**[40] 692 3-8-11 74........................ StephaneBreux(3) 14 49
(R Hannon) *s.i.s: bhd: pushed along and kpt on fr over 1f out: n.d* **3/1[1]**

330- **9** *nk* **Balian**[234] 5092 3-9-0 72........................ IanMongan 12 48
(G L Moore) *in tch: rdn 3f out: wknd fnl f* **14/1**

524/ **10** *hd* **Optimus (USA)**[550] 6453 4-9-10 75........................ JamieSpencer 10 50
(G A Butler) *bhd: pushed along over 2f out: styd on ins last but nvr in contention* **7/2[2]**

36-0 **11** *1* **Squadron Leader (IRE)**[24] 900 3-9-0 68........................ PatDobbs 15 44
(R Hannon) *slt ld on stands side tl hd jst ins fnl 2f: wknd fnl f* **14/1**

4-6 **12** *1 ½* **Ocean Valentine**[29] 844 3-9-0........................ DaneO'Neill 8 40
(B R Millman) *pressed ldrs 4f: wknd fnl f* **25/1**

0 **13** *hd* **Lady Duxyana**[10] 1110 3-8-9........................ HayleyTurner 11 34
(M D I Usher) *in tch 4f* **33/1**

0- **14** *3* **Way To The Stars**[209] 5688 3-8-6........................ NeilChalmers(3) 16 25
(A M Balding) *s.i.s: sn recovered to press ldrs: wknd appr fnl f* **14/1**

00-0 **15** *7* **Charles Street Lad (IRE)**[40] 692 3-9-0 60........................ PaulEddery 13 9
(M R Bosley) *chsd ldrs over 3f* **66/1**

0-5 **16** *1 ¾* **Eldori**[30] 835 3-8-6........................ RobertMiles(3) 2 —
(M S Saunders) *s.i.s: c stands side after 2f: a in rr* **100/1**

1m 13.67s **Going Correction** -0.05s/f (Good)
WFA 3 from 4yo 10lb **16** Ran SP% **116.5**
Speed ratings (Par 103):98,96,94,92,90 89,88,87,87,87 85,83,83,79,70 67
CSF £175.30 TOTE £4.70: £1.80, £6.90, £2.60; EX 479.90.
Owner The Burning Stars **Bred** Dr J M Leigh **Trained** Kimpton, Hants
■ Stewards' Enquiry : Jamie Spencer one-day ban: careless riding (May 12)
Sophie Doyle two-day ban: careless riding (May 12-13)

FOCUS
A moderate contest and a rather messy one. Initially a group of four went far side, but a few soon had a change of heart and within a couple of furlongs the group had been reduced to one. Due to a couple, including the winner, taking a wayward course the action eventually unfolded next to the far rail. The winning time was 1.41 seconds slower than the later handicap over the same trip but the form appears reasonably sound.
Grecian Gold(IRE) Official explanation: jockey said gelding hung left
Charles Street Lad(IRE) Official explanation: trainer said gelding ran without declared tongue-strap, which came adrift at start and could not be refitted

1356 ARENA LEISURE PLC H'CAP 1m 3f 135y
3:05 (3:05) (Class 4) (0-85,85) 3-Y-0 £5,505 (£1,637; £818; £408) Stalls Low

Form RPR

03-1 **1** **Remember Ramon (USA)**[15] 1034 3-9-4 **85**........................ JamieSpencer 6 95+
(M J Wallace) *led 9f out: drvn and qcknd 3f out: edgd rt to stands rail 1f out and rdn: kpt on wl fnl 100yds* **2/1[2]**

611 **2** *nk* **Lightning Strike (GER)**[32] 805 3-8-13 **80**........................ IanMongan 5 90+
(T G Mills) *hld up in 5th:in tch: hdwy 5f out: chsd wnr over 2 out: styng on whn hmpd and swtchd lft 1f out: kpt on but a jst hld* **6/4[1]**

055- **3** *5* **Rajaall**[156] 6428 3-8-7 **74**........................ TQuinn 4 76
(M R Channon) *plld hrd: chsd ldrs: wnt 2nd 6f out tl rdn over 2f out: sn outpcd* **10/1**

3-13 **4** *1* **Soho Square**[32] 805 3-8-6 **78**........................ GregFairley(5) 2 78
(M Johnston) *led tl hdd 9f out: rdn and outpcd over 4f out: styd on again over 2f out: wknd fnl f* **5/1[3]**

2016 **5** *shd* **Jebel Ali (IRE)**[10] 1108 3-8-7 **79**........................ JamesDoyle(5) 1 79
(B Gubby) *chsd ldrs: rdn 3f out: wknd 2f out* **12/1**

2m 34.85s (4.75) **Going Correction** +0.375s/f (Good) **5** Ran SP% **106.8**
Speed ratings (Par 101):99,98,95,94,94
CSF £5.03 TOTE £2.80: £1.70, £1.60; EX 3.50.
Owner Mrs M Findlay **Bred** B T Hundley **Trained** Newmarket, Suffolk
■ Stewards' Enquiry : Jamie Spencer caution: careless riding

Greg Fairley one-day ban: used whip down the shoulder in the forehand position (May 12)

FOCUS

Some unexposed and progressives type in opposition in a race not run at a particularly strong gallop, which resulted in a few taking a good hold early. The quintet shaped as though they were going to come up the far rail turning for home, but eventually ended up on the stands' side. The form is rated at face value for now.

Jebel Ali(IRE) Official explanation: jockey said colt hung left

1357 ROYAL WINDSOR H'CAP — 1m 2f 7y

3:35 (3:35) (Class 3) (0-90,90) 4-Y-O+ **£8,096** (£2,408; £1,203; £601) **Stalls** Low

Form / RPR

101- **1** **Miss Provvidence (IRE)**[189] [6073] 4-9-1 **87** .... TQuinn 13 — 95+
(W R Swinburn) *bhd: hdwy whn carried lft 3f out: c rt fr 2f out: led appr fnl f: drvn out* **6/1**[2]

011- **2** ½ **Blue Bajan (IRE)**[151] [6127] 4-8-8 **80** .... AdrianTNicholls 12 — 87+
(Andrew Turnell) *s.i.s: t.k.h: hld up in rr: hdwy 3f out: hmpd fr ins fnl 2f tl 1f out:swtchd lft: fin wl: nt rcvr* **14/1**

301- **3** 1 **Mustajed**[204] [5757] 5-8-5 **84** .... JamesMillman(7) 9 — 89
(B R Millman) *chsd ldrs: wnt sharply lft to far rail 3f out: styd pressing ldrs: stl ev ch ins last: one pce cl home* **13/2**[3]

3-00 **4** ¾ **Pevensey (IRE)**[9] [1129] 4-8-6 **83** .... RichardKingscote(5) 5 — 87
(M A Buckley) *chsd ldrs: n.m.r on stands side 2f out: kpt on ins last but nvr gng pce to chal* **8/1**

401- **5** hd **Solent (IRE)**[268] [4173] 4-9-4 **90** .... DaneO'Neill 2 — 93
(R Hannon) *led 1f: styd chsng ldrs: nt mcuh room 3f out: sn one pce: kpt on again fr over 1f out but nvr gng pce to trble ldrs* **6/1**[2]

-006 **6** nk **Nero's Return (IRE)**[14] [1043] 5-8-8 **85** .... GregFairley(5) 7 — 88
(M Johnston) *mid-div: rdn 4f out: styd on u.p fnl 2f but nvr gng pce to trble ldrs* **5/1**[1]

250- **7** nk **Day To Remember**[240] [4939] 5-8-11 **83** .... (t) TPQueally 6 — 85+
(E F Vaughan) *bhd: hdwy 4f out: chal and edgd lft 2f out: sn led: hdd appr fnl f: wknd ins last* **8/1**

300- **8** 1¾ **Humble Opinion**[233] [5116] 4-8-13 **85** .... MichaelTebbutt 4 — 84
(B J Meehan) *chsd ldrs: chal 3f out tl led 2f out: sn hdd wknd fnl f* **16/1**

01-0 **9** 1 **Krugerrand (USA)**[10] [1111] 7-8-12 **89** .... StephenDonohoe(5) 10 — 86
(W J Musson) *bhd: rdn and styd on to chse ldrs over 2f out: wknd fnl f* **12/1**

30-0 **10** 3½ **Terminate (GER)**[14] [1051] 4-7-13 **76** oh1 .... JamesDoyle(5) 8 — 66
(N P Littmoden) *bhd: rdn 3f out: nvr in contention* **20/1**

0/36 **11** ¾ **Mudawin (IRE)**[11] [1098] 5-9-1 **87** .... NCallan 3 — 76
(Jane Chapple-Hyam) *chsd ldr: chal 6f out to 3f out: wkng whn hmpd 1f out* **25/1**

0-00 **12** 3 **Ringsider (IRE)**[16] [1017] 5-9-4 **90** .... (tp) HayleyTurner 1 — 73
(G A Butler) *led after 1f: hdd 2f out and sn wknd* **20/1**

2m 9.61s (1.31) **Going Correction** +0.375s/f (Good) **12** Ran SP% **114.4**

Speed ratings (Par 107):109,108,107,107,107 106,106,105,104,101 100,98

CSF £80.92 CT £561.68 TOTE £4.50: £2.10, £4.50, £2.50; EX 30.30.

Owner The Double V Partnership **Bred** Camma S A S **Trained** Aldbury, Herts

■ Stewards' Enquiry : T P Queally three-day ban: careless riding (May 12-13,15)

James Millman two-day ban: careless riding (May 12,25)

FOCUS

A competitive handicap run at a solid pace and rated through the third. Once again there seemed to be a bias towards the far side of the track in the home straight and the front three all ended up racing there.

NOTEBOOK

Miss Provvidence(IRE) ◆, weak in the market, looked a most progressive filly last autumn and made light of the six-month break. She did take a rather zig-zag course over the last three furlongs, though not all of that was of her own making, and the fact she managed to score despite the negative market vibes bodes well for the near future. (op 4-1)

Blue Bajan(IRE), not seen since a spin over hurdles in December, had anything bit a clear run over the last three furlongs especially when persistently trying for a run between the winner and Day To Remember. He finished well after being switched, but ran out of time. This was still a decent effort on ground that may have been easier than ideal. (op 16-1)

Mustajed was kept over on the far side of the track after turning for home and that probably helped him reach his final position. He won on his racecourse debut, but needed his reappearance last term so is likely to come on for this first run in six months. (op 15-2)

Pevensey(IRE), back over a more suitable trip, did best of those that stayed on the nearside in the home straight and this was an improvement on his two previous outings this term. Official explanation: jockey said gelding was denied a clear run (op 10-1)

Solent(IRE) ran with credit on this first outing in nine months, but he had won first time out in each of the previous two seasons so he may not come on a lot for this. (op 9-2)

Nero's Return(IRE), sliding down the handicap, is now 2lb lower than for his last win and ran with credit though he is yet to win over as far as this. (op 6-1)

Day To Remember looked a possible winner when just about hitting the front in the centre of the course around two furlongs from home, but was inclined to hang away from the whip soon afterwards and when it was apparent he had lost forward momentum he was allowed to coast home. (op 9-1)

1358 JOAN QUESNEL SPECIAL BIRTHDAY CONDITIONS STKS — 1m 67y

4:10 (4:12) (Class 3) 3-Y-O **£8,724** (£2,612; £1,306; £653) **Stalls** High

Form / RPR

40-4 **1** **Upper Hand**[11] [1094] 3-8-12 **100** .... TQuinn 4 — 99
(M R Channon) *plld hrd in rr: settled 5f out: hdwy 3f out: qcknd to ld 1f out: sn in command: readily* **5/4**[1]

1226 **2** 1¼ **Chief Commander (FR)**[23] [914] 3-9-1 **98** .... NCallan 5 — 99
(Jane Chapple-Hyam) *led: rdn and qcknd whn chal over 2f out: hdd 1f out: kpt on but nt pce of wnr* **11/4**[3]

01- **3** 2 **Arminius (IRE)**[310] [2930] 3-9-1 **90** .... DaneO'Neill 1 — 94
(R Hannon) *trckd ldr 5f out: rdn to chal 2f out: wknd ins fnl f* **9/4**[2]

\- **4** 5 **Sabah** 3-8-4 ow3 .... NeilChalmers(3) 3 — 75
(A M Balding) *chsd ldr to 5f out: pushed along 3f out: hung lft and wknd fr 2f out* **12/1**

1m 47.81s (2.21) **Going Correction** +0.375s/f (Good) **4** Ran SP% **109.6**

Speed ratings (Par 103):103,101,99,94

CSF £5.04 TOTE £2.50; EX 4.90.

Owner Wood Street Syndicate II **Bred** J Repard **Trained** West Ilsley, Berks

FOCUS

A reasonable little conditions event and they finished very much as adjusted official ratings suggested they should. Despite the small field, the pace was solid enough and the form looks sound.

NOTEBOOK

Upper Hand, all the better for his Newmarket reappearance and best in at the weights, was content to sit last of the quartet and, once switched for his effort furthest off the stands' rail, found plenty. He saw the longer trip out well enough. (op 11-8 tchd 13-8)

Chief Commander(FR), having only his second outing on turf in his seventh race, was allowed an uncontested lead but found the favourite, with whom he would have been 5lb better off in a handicap, too strong inside the last furlong. He is not proving the easiest to place. (op 4-1 tchd 9-2 in a place)

Arminius(IRE), returning from an 11-month break, also had plenty to do with the race-fit front pair at the weights so probably achieved as much as could reasonably have been expected under the circumstances. (op 13-8)

Sabah, a 39,000gns half-sister to several winners including Vanderlin, got herself into quite a state in the stalls but managed to keep tabs on her three rivals until lack of peak fitness took its toll. She faced a stiff task on this debut and her next outing should tell us more. (tchd 14-1)

1359 COME RACING HERE EVERY MONDAY EVENING H'CAP — 6f

4:40 (4:41) (Class 4) (0-85,85) 4-Y-O+ **£5,505** (£1,637; £818; £408) **Stalls** High

Form / RPR

122- **1** **Judd Street**[227] [5263] 4-9-2 **83** .... DaneO'Neill 16 — 94+
(R F Johnson Houghton) *chsd ldrs: chal over 1f out: hung lft u.p and led ins last: drvn out* **11/2**[2]

0220 **2** ½ **Tanforan**[4] [1262] 4-8-6 **78** .... (b) JamesDoyle(5) 2 — 87
(K McAuliffe) *t.k.h: chsd ldrs: led over 1f out: hrd drvn and hdd ins last: no ex nr fin* **10/1**

30-0 **3** 3 **Chinalea (IRE)**[21] [949] 4-8-5 **75** ow3 .... (t) AdamKirby(3) 7 — 75
(C G Cox) *chsd ldrs: led appr fnl 2f: hdd over 1f out: wknd last half f* **12/1**

0-30 **4** 1 **Thurlestone Rock**[62] [541] 6-8-10 **77** .... (t) MichaelTebbutt 5 — 74
(B J Meehan) *chsd ldrs: rdn 1/2-way: kpt in fnl f but nvr gng pce to rch ldrs* **14/1**

00-0 **5** 1¾ **Guildenstern (IRE)**[20] [970] 4-8-11 **78** .... MickyFenton 11 — 70
(H Morrison) *chsd ldrs: rdn over 2f out: sn one pce* **7/1**[3]

2006 **6** ½ **Who's Winning (IRE)**[10] [1112] 5-8-10 **77** .... TQuinn 15 — 67
(B G Powell) *chsd ldrs: rdn 1/2-way and one pce: kpt on again fnl f* **8/1**

2-40 **7** ½ **Desert Dreamer (IRE)**[10] [1112] 5-9-1 **82** .... PatDobbs 9 — 71
(P R Chamings) *bhd: hdwy fr 2f out: nvr gng pce to rch ldrs* **14/1**

2P-0 **8** 1½ **Grizedale (IRE)**[25] [898] 7-8-9 **76** .... (t) FrancisFerris 6 — 60
(J Akehurst) *s.i.s: drvn to chse ldrs after 1f: wknd over 1f out* **33/1**

606- **9** nk **Romany Nights (IRE)**[132] [6631] 6-8-5 **77** .... (b) GregFairley(5) 1 — 60
(Miss Gay Kelleway) *in tch: rdn 1/2-way: sn outpcd* **33/1**

10-2 **10** 1¾ **Fisberry**[21] [947] 4-9-1 **82** .... NCallan 3 — 60
(M S Saunders) *bhd: pushed along 1/2-way: nvr in contention* **9/2**[1]

300- **11** shd **Pitch Up (IRE)**[229] [5224] 4-8-9 **76** .... IanMongan 8 — 54
(T G Mills) *bhd fr 1/2-way* **50/1**

0-42 **12** 1½ **Hiccups**[19] [977] 6-8-9 **76** .... AdrianTNicholls 12 — 49
(D Nicholls) *spd over 3f* **7/1**[3]

00/0 **13** 7 **Silver Prelude**[8] [1161] 5-8-10 **77** .... TPQueally 10 — 29
(D K Ivory) *led tl hdd appr fnl 2f: sn wknd* **80/1**

031- **14** 1¼ **Goodenough Mover**[167] [6350] 10-9-4 **85** .... HayleyTurner 14 — 34
(Andrew Turnell) *chsd ldrs: rdn 1/2-way: sn bhd* **14/1**

1m 12.26s (-1.41) **Going Correction** -0.05s/f (Good) **14** Ran SP% **115.5**

Speed ratings (Par 105):107,106,102,101,98 98,97,95,94,92 92,90,81,79

CSF £56.42 CT £656.16 TOTE £5.70: £3.50, £5.00, £3.10; EX 93.80 Place 6 £117.61, Place 5 £91.69.

Owner R F Johnson Houghton **Bred** R F Johnson Houghton **Trained** Blewbury, Oxon

FOCUS

A competitive sprint handicap in which the field spread out across the track, though they were inclined to stay away from both rails. The principals all finished their races towards the far side of the track and the form looks straightforward, rated through the third.

Who's Winning(IRE) Official explanation: jockey said gelding hung left

Fisberry Official explanation: jockey said colt ran flat

T/Plt: £109.90 to a £1 stake. Pool: £52,430.85. 348.00 winning tickets. T/Qpdt: £10.20 to a £1 stake. Pool: £2,793.10. 201.70 winning tickets. ST

1360 - 1361a (Foreign Racing) - See Raceform Interactive

926 CURRAGH (R-H)

Monday, May 1

OFFICIAL GOING: Good to yielding

1362a ROCK OF GIBRALTAR EUROPEAN BREEDERS FUND TETRARCH STKS (GROUP 3) (ENTIRE COLTS & FILLIES) — 7f

3:00 (3:02) 3-Y-O **£40,406** (£11,855; £5,648; £1,924)

RPR

1 **Decado (IRE)**[22] [928] 3-9-1 **111** .... DPMcDonogh 6 — 116+
(Kevin Prendergast, Ire) *hld up: 8th and drvn along 1/2-way: hdwy on stand's side 2f out: led over 1f out: styd on wl* **9/4**[1]

2 3½ **Sir Xaar (IRE)**[11] [1092] 3-9-1 .... PJSmullen 2 — 107
(B Smart) *hld up in tch: 6th and hdwy 2f out: 2nd over 1f out: kpt on* **8/1**

3 1 **Hurricane Cat (USA)**[191] [6023] 3-9-1 **109** .... KFallon 3 — 104+
(A P O'Brien, Ire) *in rr: trailing bef 1/2-way: styd on wl fr 1 1/2f out* **9/2**[2]

4 4½ **Kingsdale Ocean (IRE)**[9] [1158] 3-9-1 **97** .... FMBerry 7 — 93
(W M Roper, Ire) *sn trckd ldrs: 4th 1/2-way: chal over 2f out: led 1 1/2f out: hdd over 1f out: no ex* **9/1**

5 3 **An Tadh (IRE)**[22] [928] 3-9-1 **102** .... TPO'Shea 4 — 85
(G M Lyons, Ire) *cl 3rd: chal 2 1/2f out: no ex fr 1 1/2f out* **40/1**

6 2 **Nastrelli (IRE)**[18] [1011] 3-9-1 .... JMurtagh 8 — 80
(M Halford, Ire) *hld up in tch: chal on inner 2 1/2f out: 2nd 2f out: no ex fr over 1f out* **7/1**

7 7 **Amadeus Mozart (IRE)**[36] [752] 3-9-1 **104** .... CO'Donoghue 9 — 61
(A P O'Brien, Ire) *sn disp ld: led 2 1/2f out: hdd 1 1/2f out: sn no ex and eased* **12/1**

8 ¾ **Silent Times (IRE)**[37] [757] 3-9-4 .... RichardMullen 5 — 62
(E J O'Neill) *led and disp: hdd 2 1/2f out: sn wknd: eased fnl f* **5/1**[3]

9 2 **Namaya (IRE)**[36] [751] 3-9-1 **110** .... (b[1]) KJManning 1 — 54
(J S Bolger, Ire) *upset in stalls: chsd ldrs on outer: 5th 1/2-way: wknd over 2f out: eased fnl f* **16/1**

1m 27.1s **9** Ran SP% **115.2**

CSF £21.06 TOTE £3.40: £1.10, £4.40, £1.50; DF 61.80.

Owner Mrs Catherine O'Flynn **Bred** Stonehorn Stud Farms Ltd **Trained** Friarstown, Co Kildare

NOTEBOOK

Decado(IRE) was settled towards the rear in the early stages and was being niggled along after halfway, but he picked up in good style when he was asked to raise his effort. He came with a sustained challenge on the stands' side over the final quarter of a mile and went to the front with a furlong to run. He stayed on strongly in the closing stages and the extra furlong of the Irish 2,000 Guineas will hold no fears for him. He has yet to race on anything other than an easy surface but he is clearly a very talented colt and, if taking to quicker conditions in the Irish Guineas, he could well emerge as a contender for that race. (op 5/2)

Sir Xaar(IRE) ran an honourable race in defeat and improved on his seventh behind Killybegs in the Craven Stakes. Like the winner, he launched his challenge with a quarter of a mile to run and kept pace with Decado until that rival asserted inside the distance. This was an encouraging performance from this six-furlong Listed winner and he looks capable of further Stakes race success.
Hurricane Cat(USA) was appearing for the first time since his Horris Hill victory and ran with promise. He looked to be toiling as the runners neared halfway but stayed on well over the final two furlongs. He will improve considerably for this run and a step up in trip could see him adding to his Group race haul. (op 3/1)
Kingsdale Ocean(IRE) was stepping up in trip following two good runs over the minimum distance. He improved to challenge for the lead nearing the final quarter of a mile and led shortly afterwards, but his stamina started to give out shortly afterwards. (op 8/1)
An Tadh(IRE) was well below his best on testing ground here on his reappearance but ran much better this time. (op 50/1 tchd 66/1)
Nastrelli(IRE) was taking a big step up in class having won a Tipperary maiden on his previous start. After moving into a challenging position with two furlongs to run, he had no more to offer from the furlong pole, but he was not disgraced.
Amadeus Mozart(IRE) was a spent force with well over a furlong to run. (op 10/1)
Silent Times(IRE) was a Group Two winner last year but has been well below his best on both his starts this year and it looks as though he will struggle to make an impact at this level. (op 5/1 tchd 11/2)
Namaya(IRE) got upset in the stalls beforehand and had no more to give with over two furlongs to run. He looked a smart juvenile when finishing a close third in the Railway Stakes last year but has not matched that form in three subsequent starts. (op 20/1)

1363a ORATORIO EUROPEAN BREEDERS FUND ATHASI STKS (GROUP 3) (F&M) 7f

3:30 (3:30) 3-Y-O+ **£40,344** (£11,793; £5,586; £1,862)

			RPR
1		**Jazz Princess (IRE)**[256] [4525] 4-9-9 106 .... JMurtagh 4 (M Halford, Ire) *cl 2nd: led over 2f out: sn rdn and strly pressed: styd on wl fnl f* 9/4[2]	109
2	*1 ½*	**Ardbrae Lady**[22] [928] 3-8-11 105 .... FMBerry 5 (Joseph G Murphy, Ire) *hld up in tch: 4th travelling wl 1/2-way: impr into 2nd 2f out: sn chal: no imp fnl f: kpt on* 7/1	101
3	*7*	**Sandie (IRE)**[36] [753] 3-8-11 103 .... KJManning 1 (J S Bolger, Ire) *hld up in tch: prog into 3rd u.p 2f out: sn oupced: no ex fnl f* 6/1[3]	83
4	*1*	**Polished Gem (IRE)**[182] [6204] 3-8-11 .... PJSmullen 2 (D K Weld, Ire) *cl 3rd: pushed along and lost pl 1/2-way: no imp fr 2f out* 5/4[1]	80
5	*2*	**Gemini Gold (IRE)**[16] [1026] 3-8-11 98 .... NGMcCullagh 3 (M J Grassick, Ire) *sn led: hdd 2f out: wknd 1 1/2f out* 13/2	75

1m 27.7s
WFA 3 from 4yo 12lb 5 Ran SP% **115.3**
CSF £17.90 TOTE £4.20: £2.40, £3.60; DF 35.30.
Owner T Curran **Bred** Kilnamoragh Stud **Trained** the Curragh, Co Kildare

NOTEBOOK

Jazz Princess(IRE), the only four-year-old in the field, bagged her second Group Three win and her first success since she landed the C L Weld Park Stakes over this course and distance in October 2004. Having her first run since joining trainer Michael Halford, she raced prominently and went to the front just under two furlongs out, from where she kept on well to win driven out. Plans are uncertain, although her trainer believes she will stay further and will handle quicker ground. (op 5/2)
Ardbrae Lady, a maiden winner at Gowran Park last season, had put up her best performance when third in the Group One Moyglare Stud Stakes over this course and distance in September. She showed good improvement for her first run of the season, moving through smoothly from behind to press the winner a furlong and a half out, and looking as if she would take her measure. However, she failed to find much inside the final furlong and was eventually well held. She should improve again on better ground and will take her chance in the Irish 1000 Guineas next month. (op 6/1)
Sandie(IRE), beaten a long way when last in a one mile Group Three event on heavy ground here last month, was alongside the runner-up at the back of the field three furlongs out and, although moving into third place over a furlong out, could make no impression on the first two. (op 11/2)
Polished Gem(IRE), successful over seven furlongs on heavy ground at Leopardstown on her second and final start last year, was soon close up, but she was ridden under three furlongs out and soon struggling. Official explanation: trainer said filly was found to be in season (op 6/4)
Gemini Gold(IRE), placed in a one mile Group Three event on heavy ground here in March before being well beaten when upped in trip at Leopardstown, made the running. She was ridden to quicken the tempo under three furlongs out but was done with once the winner headed her under two furlongs from home. (op 6/1)

1365a HIGH CHAPARRAL EUROPEAN BREEDERS FUND MOORESBRIDGE STKS (GROUP 3) 1m 2f

4:30 (4:30) 4-Y-O+ **£40,344** (£11,793; £5,586; £1,862)

			RPR
1		**Alayan (IRE)**[37] [741] 4-9-4 .... MJKinane 3 (John M Oxx, Ire) *sn led: rdn ent st: kpt on wl fr over 1f out* 7/2[2]	118
2	*1*	**Ace (IRE)**[184] [6168] 5-9-1 122 .... KFallon 1 (A P O'Brien, Ire) *settled 3rd: 4th into st: impr into 2nd 1 1/2f out: no imp ins fnl f: kpt on* 4/5[1]	113
3	*3 ½*	**Near Dock (GER)**[16] [1018] 5-9-1 .... JohnEgan 6 (K R Burke) *hld up in tch: last and nt clr run 2f out: impr into 3rd 1f out: kpt on same pce* 20/1	107
4	*2 ½*	**Arch Rebel (USA)**[22] [932] 5-9-1 109 .... JMurtagh 5 (Noel Meade, Ire) *hld up in rr: 5th and rdn early st: no imp fr 1 1/2f out: kpt on same pce* 10/1	102
5	*4*	**Simple Exchange (IRE)**[16] [1018] 5-9-1 108 .... PJSmullen 4 (D K Weld, Ire) *settled 2nd: rdn st: no ex under 1 1/2f out: eased ins fnl f* 7/1	95
6	*10*	**Tropical Lady (IRE)**[267] [4201] 6-9-3 109 .... KJManning 2 (J S Bolger, Ire) *trckd ldrs in 4th: 3rd into st: sn rdn: wknd under 2f out* 13/2[3]	79

2m 13.0s 6 Ran SP% **117.5**
CSF £7.13 TOTE £5.90: £2.10, £1.10; DF 15.60.
Owner H H Aga Khan **Bred** His Highness The Aga Khan's Studs S C **Trained** Currabeg, Co Kildare

NOTEBOOK

Alayan(IRE) came out on top to record his second victory at this level. He came here fit following three runs in Dubai and set out to make all the running. With three furlongs to run he was being ridden along but he kept finding under pressure and proved too strong for Ace when that rival moved off the rail to deliver his challenge with over a furlong to run. A tough, genuine and versatile performer, he is very smart sort and could well prove good enough to strike at Group Two level at some stage. He is also effective at up to a mile and a half.
Ace(IRE), who performed with distinction at the highest level throughout last year, was running in a Group Three for the first time since he won the 2004 Desmond Stakes at Leopardstown. He raced a little keenly in the early stages but still looked to be going quite well early in the straight. However, his lack of a recent run told against him in the closing stages and he was unable to get to the winner. This was still a satisfactory return from him and he can be expected to improve considerably on this effort next time. (op Evs)
Near Dock(GER) was patiently ridden and another that looked to be going well heading into the final quarter of a mile when he briefly had nowhere to go. He kept on under pressure over the final furlong and a half out to secure third and reverse Magnolia Stakes form with Simple Exchange. He was a Listed winner during his time in Germany and should be up to making his mark at that level this season.
Arch Rebel(USA) came here having won the Alleged Stakes over this course and distance last month. He was being ridden along early in the straight before keeping on over the final furlong and a half. He can continue to prove a force at Listed level with some ease in the ground.
Simple Exchange(IRE) won the Magnolia Stakes at Kempton last month. After racing in second, he came under pressure with over a quarter of a mile to run and soon had no more to offer. This former American Grade Two winner will be seen to much better effect on quick ground (op 6/1)
Tropical Lady(IRE) had no more to give over the final quarter of a mile. However, this was her first run since winning the Royal Whip Stakes here last August and she can be expected to improve significantly from this run and on quicker ground. (op 11/2)

1364 - 1367a (Foreign Racing) - See Raceform Interactive

1175 CAPANNELLE (R-H)

Monday, May 1

OFFICIAL GOING: Good to soft

1368a PREMIO CARLO CHIESA (GROUP 3) (F&M) 1m

3:45 (3:47) 4-Y-O+ **£42,201** (£19,096; £10,571; £5,285)

			RPR
1		**Kykuit (IRE)**[190] [6053] 4-8-12 .... MDemuro 6 (L Brogi, Italy) *always close up, 3rd straight, led approaching final furlong, soon clear, pushed out* 176/100[2]	96
2	*1 ½*	**La Vriga**[197] [5936] 5-8-12 .... SMulas 1 (B Grizzetti, Italy) *5th straight, headway over 1f out, chased winner final f, no impression* 9/2[3]	93
3	*1*	**Mary Pekan (IRE)** 4-8-12 .... CColombi 3 (V Valiani, Italy) *held up, 7th straight, headway on outside 2f out, kept on final furlong* 10/1	91
4	*½*	**Opatja**[190] [6053] 4-8-12 .... SLandi 7 (L Camici, Italy) *tracked leader, 2nd straight, every chance approaching final f, soon one pace* 49/10	90
5	*½*	**Alicia Higgins (IRE)** 4-8-12 .... SBasile 4 (M Massimi Jr, Italy) *raced in 4th to straight, no extra from over 1f out* 17/1	89
6	*snk*	**Liset (IRE)**[197] [5936] 4-8-12 .... EBotti 5 (A & G Botti, Italy) *held up, 5th straight, never able to challenge* 7/5[1]	89
7	*2 ½*	**Arma Di Taggia (IRE)** 5-8-12 .... GTemperini 2 (Sabrina Ducci, Italy) *last straight, always behind* 59/1	84
8	*2*	**Safanya (IRE)**[351] [1737] 4-8-12 .... OFancera 8 (A & G Botti, Italy) *led to approaching final f, weakened quickly* 7/5[1]	80

1m 40.8s 8 Ran SP% **171.0**
(including one euro stakes): WIN 2.76; PL 1.48, 1.73, 2.33; DF 7.13.
Owner Allevamento La Nuova Sbarra **Bred** Allevamento La Nuova Sbarra **Trained** Italy

COLOGNE (R-H)

Monday, May 1

OFFICIAL GOING: Soft

1369a GERLING-PREIS (GROUP 2) 1m 4f

4:15 (4:26) 4-Y-O+ **£27,586** (£10,345; £4,138; £2,759)

			RPR
1		**All Spirit (GER)**[211] [5645] 4-8-11 .... EPedroza 4 (N Sauer, Germany) *in touch, 5th straight, driven & headway 2f out, ran on to lead 1 1/2f out, driven out* 451/10	111
2	*¾*	**Expensive Dream (GER)**[247] [4774] 7-8-11 .... APietsch 9 (P Vovcenko, Germany) *held up, ran on on wide outside from over 2f out, went 2nd over 1f out, kept on* 47/1	110
3	*2 ½*	**Birkspiel (GER)**[17] [1014] 5-8-11 .... DarryllHolland 5 (S Dow) *close 3rd half-way, led 2f out, soon ridden, headed 1 1/2f out, kept on til no extra final 100yds* 13/10[1]	106
4	*½*	**El Tango (GER)**[211] [5645] 4-8-11 .... WMongil 8 (P Schiergen, Germany) *prominent, 4th straight, driven over 2f out, kept on one pace* 27/10[2]	105
5	*½*	**Wurfscheibe (GER)**[204] [5786] 4-8-7 .... TMundry 7 (P Rau, Germany) *held up tracking leaders, no impression final 2 1/2f* 53/10	101
6	*6*	**Bailamos (GER)**[17] [1014] 6-8-11 .... FilipMinarik 3 (P Schiergen, Germany) *raced in 2nd, led half-way to 2f out, one pace final 1 1/2f* 74/10	96
7	*1 ¾*	**Nicaron (GER)**[218] [5500] 4-9-4 .... ABoschert 6 (H Steinmetz, Germany) *missed break, raced in mid-division, pushed along & 3rd straight, no extra final 2f* 42/10[3]	100
8	*14*	**Harar (GER)**[183] [6191] 4-8-11 .... AHelfenbein 1 (Andreas Lowe, Germany) *led to half-way, behind final 2f* 92/10	72

2m 37.5s 8 Ran SP% **131.6**
(including ten euro stakes): WIN 461; PL 46, 63, 18; SF 3068..
Owner Stall Lowenherz **Bred** E Schulz **Trained** Germany

NOTEBOOK

Birkspiel(GER), who won a Group Three race on his debut for the stable at Bremen, goes well in soft ground and ran well in this higher grade, but he is perhaps at his best over slightly shorter.

[1072]SAINT-CLOUD (L-H)

Monday, May 1

OFFICIAL GOING: Soft

1370a PRIX CLEOPATRE (GROUP 3) (FILLIES) 1m 2f 110y
1:55 (1:54) 3-Y-O **£27,586** (£11,034; £8,276; £5,517; £2,759)

RPR

1 **Alloway**[231] [5193] 3-8-9 .... SPasquier 4 107
(A Fabre, France) *raced in 2nd, pushed along appr str, ran on to lead 2f out, rdn and qcknd 1 1/2f out, kpt on well* **83/10**

2 *1* **Sanaya (IRE)**[21] [959] 3-8-9 .... CSoumillon 5 105
(A De Royer-Dupre, France) *disp 3rd, 3rd and pushed along straight, went 2nd 2f out, rdn and ran on fnl f but not rch wnr* **9/10**[1]

3 *1 ½* **Wingspan (USA)**[25] [899] 3-8-9 .... OPeslier 3 102
(A Fabre, France) *disputed 3rd, 4th straight, pushed along 2f out, ridden over 1f out, stayed on but never a threat* **62/10**[3]

4 *hd* **Miss Salvador (FR)**[32] 3-8-9 .... TJarnet 7 102
(S Wattel, France) *held up in last, ridden and ran on final furlong, nearest at finish* **77/10**

5 *2* **Penne (FR)** 3-8-9 .... IMendizabal 6 98
(J-C Rouget, France) *held up in 6th, effort 1 1/2f out, no impression* **36/10**[2]

6 *1 ½* **Pearl Sky (FR)**[32] 3-8-9 .... TThulliez 1 96
(Y De Nicolay, France) *led to 2f out, weakened over 1 1/2f out* **27/1**

7 *½* **Ziride (FR)**[14] 3-8-9 .... C-PLemaire 2 95
(H-A Pantall, France) *raced in 5th, pushed along over 2f out, no impression* **10/1**

2m 14.5s **7 Ran SP% 123.2**

PARI-MUTUEL: WIN 9.30; PL 2.30, 1.30; SF 22.70.

Owner Haras De La Perelle **Bred** Haras De La Perelle **Trained** Chantilly, France

NOTEBOOK

Alloway put up a fine performance considering she had not been out for over seven months. She galloped on bravely up the rail to hold off the odds-on favourite, and has now been specifically marked down for the Irish Oaks in July. She may well take in the Prix de Malleret en route.

Sanaya(IRE) bided her time in second place just behind the winner and took up the challenge a furlong and a half out, but she could never quite peg back her rival and stayed on rather one-paced.

Wingspan(USA) was always well up but outpaced in the straight. She just stayed on in the final stages and never looked like threatening the winner or runner-up.

Miss Salvador(FR), last into the straight, was outpaced before running on at the finish.

1371a PRIX DU MUGUET (GROUP 2) 1m
3:00 (3:03) 4-Y-O+ **£51,103** (£19,724; £9,414; £6,276; £3,138)

RPR

1 **Krataios (FR)**[30] [841] 6-8-12 .... MBlancpain 2 115
(C Laffon-Parias, France) *tracked leader to straight, led well over 1f out, ran on well* **9/2**[2]

2 *2 ½* **Kendor Dine (FR)**[22] [934] 4-8-12 .... TThulliez 10 110
(Y De Nicolay, France) *led to well over 1f out, hung right approaching final furlong, stayed on same pace under pressure* **9/1**

3 *nk* **Svedov (FR)**[30] [841] 5-8-12 .... SPasquier 5 109
(E Lellouche, France) *6th str, hdwy on ins to go 3rd wl over 1f out, edging out whn hmpd appr fnl f, swtchd to rails, ran on one pace* **76/10**

4 *hd* **Valentino (FR)**[25] 7-8-12 .... TJarnet 6 109
(A De Royer-Dupre, France) *held up, 7th straight, stayed on final 1 1/2f, nearest at finish* **29/1**

5 *1* **Helios Quercus (FR)**[30] [841] 4-8-12 .... OPeslier 4 107
(C Diard, France) *dwelt, last straight, headway approaching final furlong, nearest at finish* **10/1**

6 *2* **Ryono (USA)**[151] [6476] 7-8-12 .... TCastanheira 3 103
(S Smrczek, Germany) *8th straight, some late progress* **75/1**

7 *½* **Special Kaldoun (IRE)**[54] [655] 7-9-1 .... DBoeuf 1 105
(D Smaga, France) *5th straight, not much room 2f out, ridden and beaten 1 1/2f out* **71/10**[3]

8 *1* **Art Master (USA)**[30] [841] 5-8-12 .... CSoumillon 7 100
(A Fabre, France) *raced in 4th to straight, ridden 1 1/2f out, beaten 1f out, eased* **1/1**[1]

9 *snk* **Rageman**[30] [841] 6-8-12 .... C-PLemaire 8 100
(M Cheno, France) *9th straight, always behind* **16/1**

10 *2* **Zero Tolerance (IRE)**[37] [728] 6-8-12 .... PhillipMakin 9 96
(T D Barron) *disputed 2nd, 3rd straight, weakened well over 1f out* **44/1**

1m 41.5s **10 Ran SP% 124.0**

PARI-MUTUEL: WIN 5.50; PL 2.30, 2.40, 2.40; DF 25.00.

Owner L Marinopoulos **Bred** Stilvi Compania Financiera **Trained** Chantilly, France

NOTEBOOK

Krataios(FR) won this race with plenty in hand. Always in the leading group, he took control halfway up the straight and was never threatened inside the final furlong. He was unlucky in his previous race and put the record straight on this occasion. He now heads for the Prix d'Ispahan.

Kendor Dine(FR), supplemented into this mile contest, put up a brave performance. He tried to make all and, after being passed by the winner, still stuck to his guns until the finishing post.

Svedov(FR) can be described as rather unlucky as he was blocked on the rail and had to be snatched up at the furlong marker. Eventually, though, he returned to the rail to make his run and progressed throughout the final furlong.

Valentino(FR), given a waiting race, was a little keen early on and did not appear on the scene until the furlong marker. He quickened well and this was a good effort from the seven-year-old.

Zero Tolerance(IRE), prominent early on, was in trouble by the straight and gradually fell back on the rail. He looked out of his depth in this race.

[1203]BATH (L-H)

Tuesday, May 2

OFFICIAL GOING: Good to firm

Wind: Slight ahead.

1372 M J CHURCH MAIDEN AUCTION STKS 5f 11y
2:00 (2:02) (Class 6) 2-Y-O **£2,590** (£770; £385; £192) **Stalls Low**

Form RPR

4 1 **Deadshot Keen (IRE)**[14] [1066] 2-8-13 .... LDettori 5 76
(B J Meehan) *wnt rt s: sn pressing ldrs: led jst ins fnl 2f: shkn up and r.o strly fnl f: readily* **4/7**[1]

2 *1* **Lipocco** 2-8-6 .... NelsonDeSouza(3) 7 68
(R M Beckett) *s.i.s: sn rcvrd to trck ldrs: effrt and wnt lft 1f out: continued to edge lft u.p ins last: kpt on* **18/1**

3 *½* **Kyle (IRE)** 2-9-2 .... RichardHughes 1 76+
(R Hannon) *s.i.s: sn trcking ldrs: effrt whn nt clr run 1f out: kpt on ins last and pushed lft: nt rcvr and one pce* **7/2**[2]

0 4 *4* **Private Peachey (IRE)**[21] [961] 2-8-9 .... AlanMunro 4 50
(B R Millman) *slt advantage tl hdd jst ins fnl 2f: wknd fnl f* **40/1**

0 5 *nk* **Splendidio**[15] [1046] 2-8-6 .... RyanMoore 6 46
(M R Channon) *s.i.s: chsd ldrs: rdn 2f out: wknd fnl f* **16/1**

6 *hd* **Red Flare (IRE)** 2-8-9 .... TQuinn 3 48
(M R Channon) *w ldr: stl upsides and rdn 2f out: wknd fnl f* **14/1**[3]

0 7 *6* **Gibsons**[11] [1107] 2-8-9 .... RobertHavlin 2 24
(Mrs P N Dutfield) *s.i.s: a outpcd* **200/1**

62.60 secs (0.10) **Going Correction** -0.025s/f (Good) **7 Ran SP% 106.6**

Speed ratings (Par 91):98,96,95,89,88 88,78

CSF £11.20 TOTE £1.50: £1.20, £4.30; EX 12.90.

Owner The Comic Strip Heroes **Bred** R N Auld **Trained** Manton, Wilts

FOCUS

A fair maiden for the track in which the first three came nicely clear and the winner sets the standard.

NOTEBOOK

Deadshot Keen(IRE), fourth in a stronger race than this at Newmarket on his debut, was only workmanlike in victory, but a stronger pace in better company should see him to better effect. (tchd 8-15 and 8-13 in places)

Lipocco, whose dam won over a mile and is a half-sister to high-class sprinter Don't Worry Me, is a brother to Scotch N'Dry, a seven-furlong winner at two. He tended to hang left into the eventual third inside the final furlong, but kept on well enough, and normal improvement should see him off the mark in a similar event. (op 22-1)

Kyle(IRE), whose dam is an unraced half-sister to high-class dual US juvenile winner She's Classy, travelled well for much of the race, but he was inconvenienced when trying for a run by the eventual runner-up hanging into him. He shaped with plenty of promise, nevertheless, and it will be a surprise if he cannot win his maiden. (tchd 4-1)

Private Peachey(IRE), whose dam is a half-sister to three winners from the family of smart US juvenile Mystery Mood, showed the benefit of his debut outing and does not look short of speed.

Splendidio, whose dam is a half-sister to very useful juvenile winner Flanders and was successful over ten furlongs at three, is likely to do better in time over a longer trip. (op 22-1)

1373 SOUTH WEST IMAGING (S) STKS 1m 2f 46y
2:30 (2:31) (Class 6) 3-Y-O+ **£2,266** (£674; £337; £168) **Stalls Low**

Form RPR

0-00 1 **Danish Monarch**[25] [904] 5-9-2 45 .... ChrisCavanagh(7) 11 56
(David Pinder) *mde all: rdn over 2f out: hung rt to stands rails fr 1f out: hld on wl* **66/1**

4660 2 *1 ½* **Eijaaz (IRE)**[15] [1058] 5-9-9 50 .... EddieAhern 10 53
(Mrs L Stubbs) *bhd: rdn over 3f out: styd on u.p fnl 2f to chse wnr cl home but nvr a danger* **3/1**[1]

10-0 3 *1* **Louve Heureuse (IRE)**[22] [940] 5-9-4 56 .... LDettori 8 46
(J R Boyle) *chsd ldrs: wnt 2nd ins fnl 3f: sn rdn: effrt over 1f out: sn one pce: wknd and lost 2nd nr fin* **13/2**[3]

060- 4 *1 ½* **Murrieta**[15] [6681] 4-9-4 47 .... (b[1]) JohnEgan 1 43
(Miss J R Gibney) *in tch: rdn to chse wnr briefly over 3f out: sn hung lft u.p: one pce fnl 2f* **33/1**

5606 5 *shd* **Piquet**[25] [904] 8-9-4 40 .... J-PGuillambert 4 43
(J J Bridger) *plld hrd in rr: hdwy 3f out: rdn over 2f out: sn no ex* **20/1**

U0-0 6 *4* **Wujood**[22] [946] 4-9-9 68 .... (p) SteveDrowne 13 41
(H Morrison) *bhd: pushed along and sme hdwy over 2f out: nvr gng pce to rch ldrs* **7/2**[2]

-435 7 *4* **Count The Trees**[56] [609] 3-7-12 50 .... MarcHalford(5) 7 28
(W G M Turner) *bhd: rdn over 3f out: nvr gng pce to rch ldrs* **11/1**

5000 8 *¾* **Supreme Salutation**[7] [1227] 10-9-6 52 .... SaleemGolam(3) 3 32
(D K Ivory) *s.i.s: plld hrd in rr: effrt 4f out: nvr in contention* **14/1**

0060 9 *shd* **Trew Flight (USA)**[3] [1293] 4-9-9 53 .... MichaelHills 2 31
(M H Tompkins) *chsd ldrs: rdn over 3f out: wknd over 2f out* **7/1**

0000 10 *7* **King's Melody**[22] [945] 3-8-8 45 .... (b[1]) AlanMunro 5 18
(B R Millman) *chsd ldrs to 3f out* **18/1**

3600 11 *5* **Alzarma**[35] [783] 4-9-4 40 .... JerryO'Dwyer(5) 9 9
(J Gallagher) *chsd ldrs: wnt 2nd 6f out tl over 3f out: sn wknd* **80/1**

00 12 *dist* **Lol Draper**[15] [1049] 3-8-3 .... MartinDwyer 12 —
(P D Evans) *in tch 5f: sn wknd: t.o* **14/1**

2m 11.05s (0.05) **Going Correction** -0.025s/f (Good)

WFA 3 from 4yo+ 15lb **12 Ran SP% 110.4**

Speed ratings (Par 101):98,96,96,94,94 91,88,87,87,82 78,—

CSF £238.26 TOTE £90.00: £16.90, £1.30, £2.50; EX 287.40 TRIFECTA Not won..There was no bid for the winner. Wujood was claimed by A.E Jones for £6,000. Louve Heureuse was claimed by B.G Powell for £6,000.

Owner Little Farm Partnership II **Bred** The National Stud **Trained** Kingston Lisle, Oxon

■ Stewards' Enquiry : Chris Cavanagh two-day ban: used whip with excessive frequency (May 13-15)

FOCUS

A moderate seller which provided a shock winner. The form looks dubious and fairly weak.

Trew Flight(USA) Official explanation: jockey said gelding slipped on bend

1374 RACECOURSE VIDEO SERVICES MAIDEN STKS 1m 2f 46y
3:00 (3:09) (Class 5) 3-Y-O **£3,238** (£963; £481; £240) **Stalls Low**

Form RPR

4 1 **Adventuress**[13] [1085] 3-8-12 .... LDettori 5 86+
(B J Meehan) *trckd ldrs: qcknd to ld ins fnl 2f: c clr last: eased cl home* **1/1**[1]

2 *3 ½* **Sweet Spot**[9] [1169] 3-8-12 .... MCHussey 7 74
(Eamon Tyrrell, Ire) *led: rdn and hdd ins fnl 2f: no ch w wnr fnl f but hld on wl for 2nd* **28/1**

5- **3** *hd* **Salesin**[195] 5987 3-9-3 NickyMackay 6 79+
(L M Cumani) *sn trcking ldrs: outpcd 3f out: kpt on wl fr over 1f out: clsng on 2nd cl home but no ch w wnr* **13/2**[3]

43- **4** *2 ½* **Tennis Star (IRE)**[220] 5455 3-9-3 SteveDrowne 1 74
(R Charlton) *t.k.h: in tch: pushed along over 2f out: nvr gng pce to trble wnr: wknd fnl f* **8/1**

0 **5** *1 ¼* **Alqaab (USA)**[11] 1120 3-9-3 RHills 2 72
(M P Tregoning) *slowly away: bhd: pushed along 3f out: mod prog fnl 2f but nvr in contention* **3/1**[2]

6 *hd* **Electric Storm** 3-9-3 RichardHughes 9 72
(R Charlton) *sn chsng ldr: rdn over 2f out: wknd sn after* **16/1**

003- **7** *nk* **Adage**[225] 5356 3-8-12 75 HayleyTurner 4 66
(David Pinder) *chsd ldrs: rdn3f out: wknd fr 2f out* **50/1**

8 *7* **Light Dreams** 3-8-12 EddieAhern 8 53
(W J Knight) *s.i.s: bhd: pushed along 3f out: nvr in contention* **33/1**

0 **9** *dist* **Mukaaber**[10] 1134 3-9-3 MartinDwyer 3 —
(M P Tregoning) *chsd ldrs to 1/2-way: sn bhd: t.o* **33/1**

2m 10.01s (-0.99) **Going Correction** -0.025s/f (Good) **9** Ran SP% **116.6**
Speed ratings (Par 99):102,99,99,97,96 95,95,90,—
CSF £41.29 TOTE £2.30: £1.10, £3.50, £2.40; EX 23.70 Trifecta £85.70 Pool: £874.90 - 7.24 winning units.
Owner Wyck Hall Stud **Bred** Wyck Hall Stud Ltd **Trained** Manton, Wilts

FOCUS
Not a bad maiden on paper but the pace was not that strong and, although the final time was fairly ordinary, the form appears sound enough.

1375 WEATHERBYS BANK H'CAP 1m 2f 46y
3:30 (3:35) (Class 5) (0-70,70) 3-Y-O **£3,886** (£1,156; £577; £288) **Stalls** Low

Form RPR

006- **1** **High Seasons**[197] 5949 3-8-11 **66** SaleemGolam(3) 8 70+
(B R Millman) *bhd: stl plenty to do whn swtchd rt to outside 2f out: str run u.p fnl f to ld last stride* **14/1**

040- **2** *shd* **Tangarita**[222] 5419 3-8-5 **57** MartinDwyer 7 61
(A M Balding) *chsd ldrs: drvn to chal 1f out: led ins last: ct last stride* **16/1**

4-34 **3** *1* **Conservation (FR)**[15] 1055 3-9-3 **69** AlanMunro 9 74+
(P W Chapple-Hyam) *bhd: drvn and hdwy over 2f out: styng on whn edgd lft and bdly hmpd 1f out and ins last: swtchd rt: r.o wl nt rcvr* **4/1**[1]

00-0 **4** *shd* **Constant Cheers (IRE)**[10] 1141 3-8-9 **61** TedDurcan 3 63
(W R Swinburn) *chsd ldrs: chal ins fnl 2f: edgd rt 1f out: ev ch ins last: one pce* **14/1**

3653 **5** *1* **Coda Agency**[24] 918 3-8-8 **60** RyanMoore 2 61+
(D W P Arbuthnot) *chsd ldrs: rdn and outpcd over 2f out: rallied to chse ldrs whn bdly hmpd 1f out: kpt on but nt rcvr* **8/1**

00-3 **6** *hd* **Lester Leaps In (USA)**[10] 1141 3-8-13 **65** RichardHughes 14 64
(R Hannon) *chsd ldrs: rdn to press ldrs 2f out: kpt on same pce fnl f* **7/1**[3]

2323 **7** *shd* **Sky High Guy (IRE)**[38] 735 3-9-4 **70** JimmyFortune 12 69
(S Kirk) *in tch: rdn and lost position 3f out: stl plenty to do 2f out: fin wl: nt rch ldrs* **5/1**[2]

00-0 **8** *shd* **Generous Lad (IRE)**[15] 1052 3-8-8 **65** JamesDoyle(5) 13 64
(Miss J S Davis) *chsd ldrs: chal fr 2f out: stl ev ch 1f out: one pce whn n.m.r last half f* **22/1**

-345 **9** *½* **Stellenbosch (USA)**[69] 483 3-9-3 **69** (v[1]) MichaelHills 5 67
(J W Hills) *sn led: hdd ins last: sn one pce* **16/1**

00-6 **10** *¾* **Wannabe Posh (IRE)**[20] 993 3-8-9 **61** EddieAhern 6 64+
(J L Dunlop) *bhd: hdwy on rails over 2f out: styng on whan hmpd 1f out: nt rcvr and n.d after* **8/1**

4-55 **11** *4* **Endless Night**[20] 993 3-9-0 **66** SteveDrowne 1 55
(H Morrison) *sn chsng ldrs: rdn over 2f out: wknd over 1f out* **9/1**

000- **12** *nk* **South Hill**[236] 5058 3-8-4 **56** oh9 FrancisNorton 11 45
(M Blanshard) *a in rr: nvr in contention* **150/1**

000- **13** *24* **Kolhapur (IRE)**[211] 5667 3-8-11 **63** TQuinn 4 6
(J L Dunlop) *wl bhd fr 1/2-way* **16/1**

2m 12.64s (1.64) **Going Correction** -0.025s/f (Good) **13** Ran SP% **117.4**
Speed ratings (Par 99):92,91,91,91,90 90,90,89,89,88 85,85,66
CSF £216.78 CT £1069.15 TOTE £20.70: £6.60, £5.30, £1.80; EX 396.20 TRIFECTA Not won..
Owner Seasons Holidays **Bred** Darley **Trained** Kentisbeare, Devon

FOCUS
An unsatisfactory race featuring plenty of trouble in running. It was run in a moderate time for the type of race, 2.63 seconds slower than the preceding maiden over the same trip, and is form to treat with caution.
Conservation(FR) Official explanation: jockey said colt was denied a clear run
Kolhapur(IRE) Official explanation: jockey said colt never travelled

1376 WEATHERBYS INSURANCE FILLIES' H'CAP 1m 3f 144y
4:00 (4:03) (Class 4) (0-85,85) 4-Y-O+ **£6,309** (£1,888; £944; £472; £235) **Stalls** Low

Form RPR

030- **1** **Desert Island Disc**[173] 6308 9-8-1 **71** oh3 RichardThomas(3) 6 75
(Dr J R J Naylor) *bhd: drvn and hdwy over 2f out: led 1f out: pushed along and kpt on wl cl home* **20/1**

035- **2** *1 ¼* **Simonda**[189] 6100 5-9-4 **85** RyanMoore 8 87
(Mrs A J Perrett) *stmbld s rr: hdwy u.p 2f out: hung lft u.p ins last: tk 2nd lst strides but no imp on wnr* **5/2**[1]

0421 **3** *hd* **Gramada (IRE)**[5] 1249 4-8-5 **67** 6ex ow1 JohnEgan 2 74
(P A Blockley) *led: sn 5l clr: rdn 3f out: hdd 1f out: styd on same pce* **15/2**

1-0 **4** *¾* **Quizzical Question (IRE)**[9] 1162 4-8-9 **76** NickyMackay 5 76
(L M Cumani) *bhd: hrd drvn ins fnl 3f: styd on fnl f but nvr in contention* **5/1**[3]

1121 **5** *3 ½* **Shaunas Vision (IRE)**[20] 983 7-8-13 **80** MartinDwyer 3 75
(D K Ivory) *chsd ldrs: rdn over 3f out: wknd fnl f* **13/2**

3-00 **6** *2 ½* **Spinning Coin**[10] 1132 4-8-5 **77** JamesDoyle(5) 7 68
(J G Portman) *chsd ldrs tl dropped rr 6f out: styd on fr over 2f out: nvr a danger* **11/2**

403- **7** *8* **Sand And Stars (IRE)**[207] 5720 5-8-8 **75** MichaelHills 4 53
(M H Tompkins) *n.m.r s: sn chsng ldr: rdn over 3f out: wknd over 2f out* **9/2**[2]

2m 30.57s (0.27) **Going Correction** -0.025s/f (Good) **7** Ran SP% **108.7**
Speed ratings (Par 102):98,97,97,96,94 92,87
CSF £63.14 CT £377.76 TOTE £23.70: £6.40, £1.70; EX 89.40 Trifecta £340.20 Part won. Pool: £479.16 - 0.20 winning units..
Owner W Wood **Bred** Southill Stud **Trained** Shrewton, Wilts

FOCUS
A fair fillies' handicap run at a good pace, resulting in the first two coming from well off the pace. Despite that the form appears dubious.

1377 EUROPEAN BREEDERS FUND LANSDOWN FILLIES' STKS (LISTED RACE) 5f 11y
4:30 (4:33) (Class 1) 3-Y-O+
£15,898 (£6,025; £3,015; £1,503; £753; £378) **Stalls** Low

Form RPR

-320 **1** **Indian Maiden (IRE)**[14] 1069 6-9-4 104 TedDurcan 11 107
(M S Saunders) *bhd: stdy hdwy 2f out: qcknd to ld last half f: readily* **3/1**[1]

130- **2** *nk* **Dhekraa (IRE)**[213] 5613 3-8-5 90 RHills 8 98
(M A Jarvis) *chsd ldrs: led 1f out: kpt on u.p: hdd and outpcd last half f* **7/1**[3]

/10- **3** *1* **Clear Impression (IRE)**[381] 1045 4-9-0 AlanMunro 7 98
(S C Williams) *hmpd s: sn rcvrd to chsd ldrs: drvn to chal 1f out: one pce ins last* **18/1**

041- **4** *½* **Sierra Vista**[201] 5853 6-9-0 101 JohnEgan 9 97
(D W Barker) *sn slt advantage: rdn 2f out: hdd 1f out: no ex last half f* **9/1**

3-12 **5** *1 ½* **Angus Newz**[12] 1091 3-8-5 94 (v) FrancisNorton 10 87
(M Quinn) *chsd ldrs: rdn 2f out: wknd ins fnl f* **7/1**[3]

20-2 **6** *½* **Yomalo (IRE)**[121] 6 6-9-0 94 TQuinn 2 89
(Rae Guest) *hmpd s: bhd: stl plenty to do 2f out: kpt on fr over 1f out: fin wl* **8/1**

200- **7** *1 ½* **Sweet Afton (IRE)**[215] 5571 3-8-5 MCHussey 14 80
(Eamon Tyrrell, Ire) *bhd: stl plenty to o 2f out: kpt on fr over 1f out: gng on cl home* **16/1**

642- **8** *1 ½* **Nigella**[199] 5888 3-8-6 88 ow1 DarryllHolland 13 76
(E S McMahon) *chsd ldrs: rdn 2f out: wknd fnl f* **14/1**

000- **9** *2 ½* **Enchantment**[255] 4587 5-9-0 (p) RyanMoore 12 70
(J M Bradley) *chsd ldr: rdn over 2f out: wknd appr fnl f* **25/1**

00-0 **10** *1* **Waterline Twenty (IRE)**[17] 1020 3-8-5 80 MartinDwyer 6 62
(P D Evans) *outpcd tl sme hdwy form over 1f out* **125/1**

0/3- **11** *1 ½* **Jewel In The Sand (IRE)**[325] 2503 4-9-0 103 RichardHughes 15 50
(R Hannon) *hmpd s: towards rr: sme hdwy over 2f out: nvr nr ldrs: wknd over 1f out* **5/1**[2]

14-0 **12** *½* **Neverletme Go (IRE)**[20] 989 4-9-0 84 SteveDrowne 4 59
(G Wragg) *hmpd s: sn prom: wknd 2f out* **20/1**

526- **13** *8* **Siena Gold**[354] 1668 4-9-0 90 JimmyFortune 1 30
(J G Given) *wnt bdly rt s: a bhd* **50/1**

00-0 **14** *shd* **Right Answer**[13] 1076 4-9-0 87 EddieAhern 3 30
(T D Easterby) *hmpd s: a in rr* **25/1**

61.06 secs (-1.44) **Going Correction** -0.025s/f (Good)
WFA 3 from 4yo+ 9lb **14** Ran SP% **120.8**
Speed ratings (Par 108):110,109,107,107,104 103,101,99,95,93 91,90,77,77
CSF £22.34 TOTE £4.30: £2.10, £3.10, £4.90; EX 34.50 TRIFECTA Not won..
Owner Chris Scott & Peter Hall **Bred** Shadwell Estate Co Ltd **Trained** Green Ore, Somerset

FOCUS
A pretty competitive Listed sprint for fillies, and it was run at a good pace throughout, resulting in a winning time which was well up to scratch for a race of its stature. The winner is the best guide to last year's winning mark.

NOTEBOOK
Indian Maiden(IRE), who won this race last year, defied a penalty to repeat. Suited by the strong pace, she saw it out really well despite the ground riding quicker than ideal. She has now won five times in Listed grade and deserves a success at Group Three level, but opportunities against her own sex at that level are limited. (op 7-2)
Dhekraa(IRE), whose stable is going well, showed improved form on her seasonal reappearance. She appears to have progressed well from two to three and there could be better to come on a sharper track, especially back against fellow three-year-olds. (op 8-1)
Clear Impression(IRE), who was highly regarded by her previous trainer, had not run for over a year but this was a very promising return to action. Hopefully she can finally begin to fulfill her potential this season. (op 20-1 tchd 16-1)
Sierra Vista, who progressed throughout last season, winning a handicap off 97 on her final start, showed plenty of speed on her reappearance, but just got a bit tired in the closing stages. She is entitled to come on for this and looks up to winning at this level. (op 8-1)
Angus Newz, beaten in a handicap off 93 last time out, had the benefit of race fitness over a number of her rivals, but she is arguably a bit better over another furlong. (op 11-2)
Yomalo(IRE) is a difficult mare to place off her current mark and she is better suited to six furlongs. Official explanation: jockey said mare suffered interference at start (op 10-1)
Sweet Afton(IRE) is another who looks likely to be difficult to place this season off what looks a stiff mark.
Jewel In The Sand(IRE), who was restricted to just one outing last year, in June, proved disappointing on her first run since, and it remains to be seen whether she retains her smart juvenile ability which saw her win the Group Two Cherry Hinton Stakes. (op 9-2 tchd 11-2)
Siena Gold Official explanation: jockey said mare jumped right on leaving stalls

1378 EXPRESS CAFES H'CAP 5f 11y
5:00 (5:00) (Class 5) (0-70,70) 3-Y-O **£3,886** (£1,156; £577; £288) **Stalls** Low

Form RPR

64-2 **1** **Mannikko (IRE)**[20] 988 3-9-4 **70** SteveDrowne 8 79+
(G Wragg) *trckd ldrs: led 1f out: hrd drvn ins last: hld on wl* **1/1**[1]

4216 **2** *hd* **Lucayos**[11] 1109 3-8-8 **65** (b) RichardKingscote(5) 4 73
(Mrs H Sweeting) *trckd ldrs: led 2f out: sn rdn: edgd lft and hdd 1f out: rallied and edgd lft ins last: no ex cl home* **5/1**[3]

405- **3** *5* **Ceredig**[214] 5581 3-9-1 **67** EddieAhern 9 64+
(W R Muir) *hld up in tch: hdwy whn whn nt clr run and swtchd rt over 1f out: kpt on but nvr gng pce to trble ldrs after* **4/1**[2]

60-4 **4** *3* **Danny The Dip**[7] 1210 3-8-5 **57** FrankieMcDonald 5 36
(J J Bridger) *s.i.s: sn chsng ldrs: rdn 1/2-way: wknd over 1f out* **20/1**

40-0 **5** *shd* **Sunset Ridge (IRE)**[21] 969 3-8-5 **57** AlanMunro 6 36
(Rae Guest) *bhd: rdn sme hdwy and hung lft over 1f out: styd on cl home but nvr in contention* **16/1**

-550 **6** *½* **Dora's Green**[20] 980 3-8-6 **58** FrancisNorton 2 35
(M Blanshard) *led tl hdd 2f out: sn btn* **33/1**

0-34 **7** *4* **Pride Of Joy**[11] 1110 3-9-4 **70** MartinDwyer 1 33
(D K Ivory) *bhd: 1/2-way: sn wknd* **16/1**

0260 **8** *2 ½* **Par Excellence**[57] 595 3-7-13 **56** oh2 MarcHalford(5) 7 10
(W G M Turner) *chsd ldrs to 1/2-way* **28/1**

53-0 **9** *3 ½* **Arkadia Honey**[21] 969 3-8-6 **61** ow1 RobertMiles(3) 3 2
(J L Spearing) *in tch to 1/2-way* **20/1**

61.72 secs (-0.78) **Going Correction** -0.025s/f (Good) **9** Ran SP% **114.3**
Speed ratings (Par 99):105,104,96,91,91 90,84,80,74
CSF £5.65 CT £14.17 TOTE £1.80: £1.10, £2.20, £1.70; EX 7.90 Trifecta £19.00 Pool: £469.05 - 17.47 winning units. Place 6 £34.24, Place 5 £24.02.
Owner Trevor C Stewart **Bred** T Stewart **Trained** Newmarket, Suffolk

FOCUS
The winning time was decent for a race of its type, being only 0.66sec slower than that taken by Indian Maiden to win the preceding Listed contest and the runner-up is the best guide to the form.
Lucayos Official explanation: jockey said colt hung left-handed

T/Jkpt: Not won. T/Plt: £33.30 to a £1 stake. Pool: £49,512.65. 1,084.90 winning tickets. T/Qpdt: £11.80 to a £1 stake. Pool: £3,070.70. 191.00 winning tickets. ST

1333 KEMPTON (A.W) (R-H)

Tuesday, May 2

OFFICIAL GOING: Standard
Wind: Moderate, half behind

1379 JUBILEE CLAIMING STKS — 5f (P)

7:00 (7:01) (Class 5) 2-Y-O — £3,238 (£963; £481; £240) Stalls High

Form — RPR

504 **1** **Mrs Crossy (IRE)**[2] 1309 2-8-1 .... StephaneBreux(3) 8 — 58
(R Hannon) *mde virtually all: rdn and responded wl whn chal appr fnl f* — 5/1[3]

06 **2** 1 **Circle Of Truth**[21] 962 2-8-4 .... SaleemGolam(3) 1 — 57
(W G M Turner) *racd in cl 3rd: kpt on to go 2nd ins fnl f* — 12/1

2 **3** ¾ **Go On Jessica (IRE)**[10] 1142 2-8-6 .... AdrianTNicholls 7 — 53+
(D Nicholls) *leggy: b.hind: s.i.s: sn trckd ldrs: swtchd lft over 1f out: hung lft but kpt on fnl f* — 1/1[1]

056 **4** 1¼ **All Talk**[5] 1248 2-8-2 .... NickyMackay 2 — 44
(I A Wood) *trckd ldrs: swtchd lft over 1f out: one pce after* — 16/1

3325 **5** hd **Diminuto**[11] 1107 2-8-6 .... HayleyTurner 3 — 47
(M D I Usher) *w wnr tl wknd fnl f* — 7/2[2]

00 **6** 3 **Three Mates**[15] 1040 2-7-9 .... DuranFentiman(5) 6 — 29
(W G M Turner) *in tch: outpcd fr 1/2-way* — 20/1

7 2 **Moody Goose** 2-8-8 .... FergusSweeney 9 — 29
(M Meade) *unf: bit bkwd: s.i.s: a in rr* — 25/1

0 **8** 3 **Beatani**[8] 1189 2-7-10 .... NataliaGemelova(5) 5 — 10
(P D Evans) *w'like: v.s.a: a bhd* — 33/1

62.52 secs **Going Correction** -0.075s/f (Stan) — **8** Ran SP% **114.0**
Speed ratings (Par 93):80,78,77,75,74 70,66,62
CSF £58.43 TOTE £4.70: £1.40, £3.10, £1.10; EX 58.30.The winner and Circle Of Truth were subject to friendly claims.
Owner A C Pickford, David Mort & N A Woodcock **Bred** Mrs C L Weld **Trained** East Everleigh, Wilts
■ Stewards' Enquiry : Saleem Golam one-day ban: used whip with excessive frequency (May 13)

FOCUS
A weak event, run at a solid pace, and the form, rated through the fourth, looks worth treating with a degree of caution.

NOTEBOOK
Mrs Crossy(IRE), fourth at Brighton just two days previously, found this drop in class right up her street and duly lost her maiden tag at the fourth attempt. She found an extra gear when pressed by the runner-up in the final furlong, had something up her sleeve at the finish, and has clearly found her level. (op 9-2)
Circle Of Truth, beaten in a seller last time, looked a big danger to the winner nearing the final furlong yet ultimately failed to see out the race as well as that rival. This was his best effort to date, but his proximity at the finish rather sums up this form.
Go On Jessica(IRE), runner-up on debut in this class ten days previously and making her debut for new connections, once again did herself few favours with a sluggish start and ultimately paid late on for refusing to settle through the first half of the race. This must rate as disappointing and she does look tricky. Official explanation: jockey said filly hung left throughout (op 6-5 tchd 5-4)
Diminuto again looked a short-runner and failed to improve for this drop in class. Official explanation: jockey said filly ran too free early (tchd 10-3)

1380 RUK EVENING RACING PACKAGE FOR £60 H'CAP — 1m 2f (P)

7:28 (7:29) (Class 4) (0-85,85) 4-Y-O+ — £7,790 (£2,332; £1,166; £583; £291; £146) Stalls High

Form — RPR

425- **1** **Tabadul (IRE)**[185] 6147 5-9-3 84 .... RHills 3 — 103+
(E A L Dunlop) *hld up: hdwy 4f out: gng wl whn qcknd to ld appr fnl f: sn clr* — 11/4[1]

60-5 **2** 5 **Desert Cristal (IRE)**[7] 1207 5-9-1 82 .... LDettori 10 — 89
(J R Boyle) *a in front rnk: ev ch over 1f out: nt pce of wnr* — 5/1[3]

00-2 **3** ¾ **Snowed Under**[15] 1051 5-8-6 73 .... TQuinn 4 — 79
(J D Bethell) *led for 2f: rdn and outpcd 2f out: kpt on fnl f* — 11/2

0500 **4** nk **Dower House**[61] 556 11-9-1 82 ....(t) ChrisCatlin 5 — 87
(Andrew Turnell) *hld up: hdwy and styd on fnl f: nvr nrr* — 20/1

2226 **5** nk **Red Birr (IRE)**[15] 1051 5-8-7 74 .... DaneO'Neill 11 — 78
(P R Webber) *prom: rdn 2f out: wknd fnl f* — 4/1[2]

22-0 **6** 1 **Fabrian**[7] 1207 8-8-1 73 .... JamesDoyle(5) 2 — 76
(R J Price) *led after 2f: rdn and hdd appr fnl f: wknd ins fnl f* — 14/1

500- **7** shd **Chancellor (IRE)**[186] 6131 8-9-4 85 ....(t) J-PGuillambert 7 — 87
(Ernst Oertel) *hld up in mid-div: hdwy on ins whn checked appr fnl f: kpt on but nvr a danger* — 25/1

0100 **8** ½ **Berkhamsted (IRE)**[11] 1112 4-8-10 80 ....(v) RichardThomas(3) 1 — 81
(M F Harris) *lw: a towards rr* — 16/1

5240 **9** hd **Gingko**[21] 965 9-8-7 74 .... RyanMoore 9 — 75
(P R Webber) *lw: a bhd* — 8/1

60-0 **10** 2½ **Hypnotic**[15] 1043 4-8-8 75 .... AdrianTNicholls 8 — 71
(D Nicholls) *in tch early: bhd fnl 4f* — 20/1

540- **11** 2½ **Scutch Mill (IRE)**[184] 6183 4-8-1 71 oh5 .... NelsonDeSouza(3) 6 — 63
(Karen George) *t.k.h: mid-div: wknd over 2f out* — 33/1

2m 6.06s **Going Correction** -0.075s/f (Stan) — **11** Ran SP% **118.7**
Speed ratings (Par 105):108,104,103,103,102 102,102,101,101,99 97
CSF £15.61 CT £71.98 TOTE £3.70: £1.40, £1.90, £1.90; EX 20.30.
Owner Hamdan Al Maktoum **Bred** Shadwell Estate Company Limited **Trained** Newmarket, Suffolk

FOCUS
A fair handicap, run at a solid pace, and the clear-cut winner is value for further, although there was not much strength in depth behind.
Chancellor(IRE) Official explanation: jockey said horse was denied a clear run

1381 HAPPY 25TH ANNIVERSARY TONY & BEVERLEY H'CAP — 1m 2f (P)

7:56 (7:56) (Class 4) (0-80,80) 3-Y-O — £7,790 (£2,332; £1,166; £583; £291; £146) Stalls High

Form — RPR

-111 **1** **Royal Amnesty**[19] 1005 3-8-6 68 .... OscarUrbina 6 — 74
(G C H Chung) *hld up in tch: rdn 2f out: led ins fnl f: r.o wl* — 10/3[1]

630- **2** 1¾ **Arabian Sea (IRE)**[224] 5393 3-9-2 78 .... RyanMoore 3 — 81
(C E Brittain) *trckd ldrs: led 2f out: rdn and hdd ins fnl f: kpt on* — 14/1

216- **3** 1½ **Ahmedy (IRE)**[217] 5524 3-9-4 80 .... TonyCulhane 8 — 80
(M R Channon) *a in tch: rdn 2f out: kpt on one pce* — 9/2[3]

000- **4** shd **Phone In**[181] 6224 3-8-4 66 oh1 .... JamieMackay 2 — 66
(Sir Mark Prescott) *swtg: trckd ldrs on outside: rdn 2f out: styd on one pce* — 6/1

1246 **5** 2 **Orvietan (IRE)**[15] 1052 3-8-4 66 ....(b[1]) JoeFanning 7 — 62
(M Johnston) *slowly away: in rr: effrt wl over 1f out: nvr nr to chal* — 8/1

15-0 **6** ½ **Sivivatu (USA)**[14] 1067 3-9-4 80 .... DarryllHolland 5 — 75
(J Noseda) *led tl rdn andd hdd 2f out: wknd fnl f* — 7/2[2]

1050 **7** shd **Casablanca Minx (IRE)**[8] 1190 3-8-9 76 .... JamesDoyle(5) 4 — 71
(N P Littmoden) *chsd ldrs: rdn 2f out: wknd appr fnl f* — 20/1

01- **8** 6 **Entranced**[171] 6334 3-8-9 71 .... TomEaves 1 — 54
(Miss J A Camacho) *lw: slowly away: hld up: bhd fnl 3f* — 7/1

2m 7.95s **Going Correction** -0.075s/f (Stan) — **8** Ran SP% **112.8**
Speed ratings (Par 101):101,99,98,98,96 96,96,91
CSF £47.57 CT £209.24 TOTE £4.00: £1.60, £2.80, £1.50; EX 59.70.
Owner H C Chung **Bred** Brick Kiln Stud, Mrs L Hicks And Partners **Trained** Newmarket, Suffolk

FOCUS
A decent enough handicap for the grade, featuring some unexposed three-year-olds, and the form, rated through the third, looks just fair.
Orvietan(IRE) Official explanation: jockey said colt suffered interference shortly after start

1382 SPONSOR AT KEMPTON H'CAP — 7f (P)

8:24 (8:24) (Class 5) (0-75,75) 4-Y-O+ — £5,505 (£1,637; £818; £408) Stalls High

Form — RPR

0144 **1** **Quantum Leap**[20] 985 9-8-13 70 ....(v) JimmyQuinn 13 — 78
(S Dow) *a in tch: drvn to ld 1f out: all out* — 12/1

4301 **2** nk **Adantino**[8] 1188 7-8-10 74 ....(b) JamesMillman(7) 9 — 81
(B R Millman) *t.k.h: a in tch: pressed wnr through out fnl f* — 14/1

22-2 **3** nk **Cross The Line (IRE)**[9] 1164 4-8-13 70 .... JamieSpencer 12 — 80+
(A P Jarvis) *lw: a.p on ins: nt clr run fr 2f out tl r.o ins fnl f* — 2/1[1]

4510 **4** 1 **Goose Chase**[20] 985 4-8-12 69 .... DaneO'Neill 14 — 73+
(A M Hales) *bhd: rdn and hdwy on ins whn n.m.r over 1f out: r.o: nvr nrr* — 14/1

0463 **5** hd **Serieux**[20] 977 7-9-1 72 ....(v) AdrianTNicholls 2 — 75
(D Nicholls) *trckd ldrs: led over 2f out tl rdn and hdd 1f out: no ex ins fnl f* — 14/1

0424 **6** 1¼ **Aperitif**[8] 1186 5-8-9 66 .... FrancisNorton 11 — 72+
(D Nicholls) *rrd up leaving stalls: in rr tl mde late hdwy* — 11/2[2]

00-0 **7** hd **Elkhorn**[20] 992 4-8-12 69 ....(v) TomEaves 1 — 69
(Miss J A Camacho) *hld up in rr: mde sme late hdwy* — 33/1

0631 **8** 1 **Norcroft**[10] 1151 4-8-10 72 ....(p) JamesDoyle(5) 7 — 69
(Mrs C A Dunnett) *mid-div: rdn 3f out: nt qckn over 1f out* — 16/1

0-00 **9** nk **Acomb**[30] 846 6-8-13 73 .... RichardThomas(3) 10 — 69
(Mrs L Richards) *hmpd s: in rr: styd on fnl f* — 40/1

363- **10** shd **Logsdail**[173] 6305 6-9-4 75 .... RyanMoore 3 — 71
(G L Moore) *bhd: rdn 1/2-way: mde sme late hdwy* — 7/1[3]

00-5 **11** 1 **Regal Dream (IRE)**[20] 985 4-8-12 69 .... EddieAhern 4 — 62
(J W Hills) *mid-div: rdn 2f out: wknd over 1f out* — 7/1[3]

040- **12** 1½ **Missed A Beat**[164] 6376 4-8-13 70 .... TedDurcan 5 — 60
(M Blanshard) *a bhd* — 25/1

010- **13** 2 **Nephetriti Way (IRE)**[143] 6544 5-9-2 73 .... IanMongan 6 — 57
(P R Chamings) *trckd ldr: led over 3f out: hdd over 2f out: sn rdn and btn* — 25/1

26-0 **14** 12 **Life's A Whirl**[15] 1056 4-8-13 70 .... ChrisCatlin 8 — 23
(Mrs C A Dunnett) *led tl hdd over 3f out: wknd rapidly and eased* — 50/1

1m 25.94s **Going Correction** -0.075s/f (Stan) — **14** Ran SP% **122.3**
Speed ratings (Par 103):101,100,100,99,98 97,97,96,95,95 94,92,90,76
CSF £163.55 CT £482.99 TOTE £14.40: £3.10, £5.10, £1.40; EX 129.70.
Owner Mrs M E O'Shea **Bred** L C And Mrs A E Sigsworth **Trained** Epsom, Surrey

FOCUS
A modest handicap, which saw the first three fight out a thrilling finish, and the form is a bit messy and should be treated with a degree of caution.
Cross The Line(IRE) Official explanation: jockey said gelding was denied a clear run
Aperitif Official explanation: jockey said gelding reared leaving stalls
Acomb Official explanation: jockey said gelding missed the break
Missed A Beat Official explanation: jockey said filly hung left

1383 RUK EVENING RACING CALL 08700 50 69 47 H'CAP — 6f (P)

8:52 (8:53) (Class 6) (0-65,65) 4-Y-O+ — £3,238 (£963; £481; £240) Stalls High

Form — RPR

00-0 **1** **Pippa's Dancer (IRE)**[25] 902 4-9-4 65 .... MartinDwyer 10 — 75
(W R Muir) *t.k.h: a.p: rdn to ld ins fnl f: all out* — 14/1

-665 **2** hd **Seneschal**[10] 1151 5-9-1 62 .... JamieSpencer 9 — 71
(A B Haynes) *hld up: rdn and hdwy over 1f out: r.o u.p to go 2nd cl home* — 4/1[1]

0141 **3** ¾ **Desert Light (IRE)**[25] 903 5-9-1 62 ....(v) DaneO'Neill 7 — 69
(D Shaw) *mid-div: hdwy on ins over 1f out: ev ch ins fnl f: nt qckn cl home* — 11/2[2]

015- **4** ¾ **Bens Georgie (IRE)**[216] 5539 4-9-1 62 .... DarryllHolland 4 — 67
(D K Ivory) *trckd ldr: led wl over 1f out: hdd ins fnl f: no ex* — 11/1

2620 **5** ½ **Times Review (USA)**[6] 1243 5-9-4 65 .... FrancisNorton 11 — 68
(C A Dwyer) *led tl hdd 2f out: one pce ins fnl f* — 10/1

3100 **6** ¾ **Patternmaker (USA)**[33] 806 4-9-1 62 .... ChrisCatlin 2 — 63
(A M Hales) *trckd ldr: led briefly 2f out: fdd ins fnl f* — 20/1

-420 **7** nk **Loupho le**[67] 501 4-9-4 65 .... SebSanders 3 — 65
(P J Makin) *lw: s.i.s: hdwy whn n.m.r over 1f out: wknd ins fnl f* — 7/1[3]

-300 **8** shd **Hard To Catch (IRE)**[87] 292 8-8-13 63 ....(b) SaleemGolam(3) 12 — 63
(D K Ivory) *prom tl rdn and no danger in fnl 2f* — 16/1

010- **9** ½ **Perfect Solution (IRE)**[210] 5686 4-9-1 62 .... LDettori 8 — 60
(J A R Toller) *chsd ldrs: rdn over 2f out: n.d afterwards* — 11/1

600- **10** ¾ **Sergeant Lewis**[187] 6126 4-9-1 62 .... EddieAhern 1 — 58
(R M Flower) *a bhd* — 33/1

-215 **11** hd **Scuba (IRE)**[68] 492 4-9-1 62 ....(v) SteveDrowne 5 — 57
(H Morrison) *in tch: rdn 1/2-way: no hdwy on outside fnl 2f* — 11/2[2]

45/0 **12** 2 **Grand Place**[22] 949 4-9-4 65 .... RyanMoore 6 — 54
(R Hannon) *hld up: bhd fnl 2f* — 20/1

1m 13.24s **Going Correction** -0.075s/f (Stan) — **12** Ran SP% **114.0**
Speed ratings (Par 101):100,99,98,97,97 96,95,95,94,93 93,90
CSF £64.86 CT £351.23 TOTE £20.60: £4.30, £1.60, £2.40; EX 99.20.
Owner Perspicacious Punters Racing Club **Bred** Clody Norton And Mrs Con Collins **Trained** Lambourn, Berks

FOCUS
A modest handicap which produced a blanket finish. The form looks straightforward with the first five close to their marks.

1384 LONDON MILE QUALIFIER H'CAP 1m (P)

9:20 (9:20) (Class 4) (0-85,82) 3-Y-O

£7,790 (£2,332; £1,166; £583; £291; £146) **Stalls** High

Form RPR

2-12 **1** **Kalankari (IRE)**[29] 855 3-9-1 **79** MartinDwyer 9 92+
(A M Balding) *lw: chsd ldr and clr 2nd tl led 2f out: sn clr: pushed out fnl f* **5/2**[1]

45-1 **2** *5* **Tempsford Flyer (IRE)**[22] 952 3-9-4 **82** EddieAhern 7 84+
(J W Hills) *prom in chsng gp: styd on to go 2nd ins fnl f: no ch w wnr* **5/1**[3]

-010 **3** *2* **Li Shih Chen**[40] 702 3-8-10 **74** JamieSpencer 5 71
(A P Jarvis) *chsd ldng pair: rdn 2f out: styd on one pce* **11/1**

3-1 **4** *shd* **Herring (IRE)**[25] 900 3-9-1 **79** LDettori 6 76
(D J Coakley) *bhd tl hdwy on ins 1f out: r.o: nvr nrr* **8/1**

-230 **5** *½* **Lake Poet (IRE)**[14] 1067 3-8-10 **74** RyanMoore 2 70
(C E Brittain) *in rr: mde sme late hdwy* **12/1**

2154 **6** *½* **Tamagin (USA)**[1] 1337 3-8-8 **77** (p) StephenDonohoe(5) 4 72
(P D Evans) *set str pce tl hdd 2f out: rdn and wknd ins fnl f* **13/2**

600- **7** *3* **Skyelady**[192] 6016 3-9-4 **82** TomEaves 1 70
(Miss J A Camacho) *a struggling in rr* **33/1**

034- **8** *2½* **Secret Liaison**[225] 5362 3-8-13 **77** SebSanders 8 59
(Sir Mark Prescott) *rdn 1/2-way: wknd 2f out* **16/1**

1-10 **9** *nk* **Royal Reservation**[12] 1095 3-9-4 **82** AlanMunro 3 63
(P W Chapple-Hyam) *lw: hld up in rr: nvr gng pce* **7/2**[2]

1m 38.16s **Going Correction** -0.075s/f (Stan) **9** Ran SP% **116.8**
Speed ratings (Par 101):110,105,103,102,102 101,98,96,96
CSF £15.40 CT £117.11 TOTE £4.60: £1.60, £2.10, £2.80; EX 17.90 Place 6 £15.53, Place 5 £11.41.
Owner Dubai Thoroughbred Racing **Bred** B Kennedy **Trained** Kingsclere, Hants

FOCUS
A fair three-year-old handicap, which saw few get into the race from off the pace, and the form looks reasonable, rated around the third and fourth. However, the winner is still capable of rating higher.
Royal Reservation Official explanation: jockey said colt hung right
T/Plt: £6.50 to a £1 stake. Pool: £47,607.15. 5,268.05 winning tickets. T/Qpdt: £3.50 to a £1 stake. Pool: £2,856.60. 593.00 winning tickets. JS

1254 SOUTHWELL (L-H)

Tuesday, May 2

OFFICIAL GOING: Standard
Wind: Moderate across

1385 SOUTHWELL-RACECOURSE.CO.UK CLAIMING STKS 1m 4f (F)

2:40 (2:40) (Class 6) 4-Y-0+ **£2,730** (£806; £403) **Stalls** Low

Form RPR

6554 **1** **Starcross Maid**[22] 939 4-8-3 40 ow1 ChrisCatlin 3 56
(J F Coupland) *hld up in rr: hdwy over 4f out: rdn to chal wl over 1f out: drvn to ld ins last: all out* **11/1**

2510 **2** *hd* **Romil Star (GER)**[20] 975 9-8-4 57 (v) AndrewElliott(5) 7 62
(K R Burke) *a.p: hdwy 4f out: led over 2f out: sn rdn: hdd ins last: kpt on gamely* **5/2**[1]

0000 **3** *11* **Afadan (IRE)**[15] 847 8-8-7 60 ow1 (vt) DeanCorby(3) 9 45
(J R Jenkins) *s.i.s: sn in tch: hdwy 4f out: rdn along 3f out: n.d* **14/1**

00 **4** *hd* **Gawrosz (POL)**[7] 1219 7-8-4 50 RoryMoore(5) 8 44
(G J Smith) *chsd ldrs: rdn along 4f out: plugged on same pce fnl 3f* **40/1**

20-0 **5** *¾* **Distant Cousin**[9] 1163 9-8-7 58 (v) RichardMullen 6 41
(M A Buckley) *prom: led 1/2-way: rdn along and hdd over 2f out: sn wknd* **4/1**[2]

3403 **6** *17* **Molly's Secret**[4] 1271 8-7-11 45 (p) JohnMcAuley(3) 5 7
(Miss S J Wilton) *in tch: pushed along 5f out: rdn 4f out and sn wknd* **11/1**

050/ **7** *15* **Saltrio**[21] 5639 8-8-11 JamieSpencer 1 —
(W M Brisbourne) *trckd ldrs: effrt over 4f out: sn rdn and btn 3f out* **9/2**[3]

2-46 **8** *25* **Shingle Street (IRE)**[21] 966 4-9-7 64 (b) SebSanders 2 —
(Miss Venetia Williams) *led: hdd 1/2-way: wknd over 4f out* **9/2**[3]

9 *dist* **Big Bad Bill (IRE)**[11] 6-8-11 LeeEnstone 4 —
(P T Midgley) *s.i.s: sn in tch: rdn along 1/2-way: sn wknd* **100/1**

2m 41.12s (-0.97) **Going Correction** 0.0s/f (Stan) **9** Ran SP% **111.7**
Speed ratings (Par 101):103,102,95,95,94 83,73,56,—
CSF £37.02 TOTE £12.10: £2.90, £1.10, £3.60; EX 49.40.
Owner J F Coupland **Bred** D M Beresford **Trained** Grimsby, Lincs

FOCUS
A modest claimer, but the pace was decent and it took its toll as the field were spread out over half of Nottinghamshire.

1386 BUY TICKETS ON LINE MAIDEN STKS 1m (F)

3:10 (3:13) (Class 5) 3-Y-O **£3,238** (£963; £481; £240) **Stalls** Low

Form RPR

4- **1** **Tears Of A Clown (IRE)**[187] 6123 3-9-3 JamieSpencer 3 85+
(J A Osborne) *trckd ldrs: smooth hdwy to ld wl over 2f out: pushed clr over 1f out: easily* **1/1**[1]

0 **2** *10* **Plush**[4] 1274 3-9-3 SebSanders 6 54
(Sir Mark Prescott) *in tch: hdwy 3f out: sn rdn: styd on ins last: no ch w wnr* **18/1**

0-3 **3** *¾* **Blacktoft (USA)**[10] 1153 3-9-3 RichardMullen 9 52
(E A L Dunlop) *dwlt: hld up: hdwy over 3f out: rdn to chse ldrs 2f out: kpt on u.p ins last* **15/2**[3]

4-2 **4** *hd* **Red Diadem**[30] 844 3-8-12 ChrisCatlin 7 47
(W J Haggas) *trckd ldrs: hdwy and n.m.r 3f out: sn chsng wnr: rdn wl over 1f out: drvn and wknd ent last* **9/4**[2]

0-5 **5** *3* **Tabulate**[10] 1153 3-8-5 NicolPolli(7) 2 40
(P L Gilligan) *cl up: led after 3f: rdn along 3f out: sn hdd & wknd fnl 2f* **25/1**

0-00 **6** *1¼* **Millbrook Star (IRE)**[7] 1216 3-8-10 30 JamieHamblett(7) 10 42?
(M C Chapman) *chsd ldrs on outer: rdn along 1/2-way: sn wknd* **100/1**

0-00 **7** *2½* **Night Reveller (IRE)**[65] 528 3-8-7 30 EmmettStack(5) 4 31?
(M C Chapman) *led 3f: cl up tl rdn along over 3f out and sn wknd* **100/1**

8 *19* **Alan The Aussie** 3-9-3 StephenCarson 8 —
(G Prodromou) *s.i.s: a bhd* **80/1**

00- **9** *nk* **Navajo Warrior (IRE)**[220] 5455 3-9-3 DavidAllan 1 —
(T D Easterby) *sn outpcd and bhd* **66/1**

1m 44.38s (-0.22) **Going Correction** 0.0s/f (Stan) **9** Ran SP% **106.4**
Speed ratings (Par 99):101,91,90,90,87 85,83,64,64
CSF £17.32 TOTE £2.40: £1.10, £3.90, £1.10; EX 20.00.
Owner Mountgrange Stud **Bred** A Stroud And J Hanly **Trained** Upper Lambourn, Berks
■ Ten To The Dozen (9/1, broke out of stalls) was withdrawn. R4 applies, deduct 10p in the £.

FOCUS
A two-horse race according to the market, but a one-horse race on the track and the favourite could hardly have done it any easier. The beaten horses look moderate to say the least.

1387 DINE IN THE QUEEN MOTHER RESTAURANT (S) STKS 1m (F)

3:40 (3:41) (Class 6) 3-Y-O+ **£2,388** (£705; £352) **Stalls** Low

Form RPR

2040 **1** **Shrine Mountain (USA)**[13] 1073 4-9-10 48 (v[1]) RichardMullen 11 65
(J R Holt) *trckd ldrs: hdwy 3f out: led wl over 2f out: rdn clr over 1f out: styd on wl* **6/1**[2]

04U1 **2** *9* **Musical Gift**[8] 1194 6-9-9 48 (v) KevinGhunowa(7) 10 53
(P A Blockley) *towards rr: hdwy on outer 1/2-way: rdn wl over 2f out: styd on ins last: no ch w wnr* **7/1**[3]

0646 **3** *hd* **Veneer (IRE)**[7] 1217 4-9-5 45 DerekNolan(5) 8 47
(Miss Gay Kelleway) *cl up: rdn along 2f out: sn drvn and one pce* **7/1**[3]

0000 **4** *3* **Castanza**[7] 1217 4-9-5 40 (b[1]) TPQueally 12 36
(M Wellings) *chsd ldrs on outer: rdn along 3f out: drvn over 2f out and sn no imp* **50/1**

00-3 **5** *3½* **Aventura (IRE)**[7] 1217 6-9-5 61 StephenDonohoe(5) 2 34
(S R Bowring) *cl up: led after 3f: rdn along and hdd wl over 2f out: sn drvn and wknd* **9/2**[1]

0260 **6** *6* **Kokila**[7] 1221 3-8-6 59 (b[1]) GrahamGibbons 1 17
(W J Haggas) *a rr* **9/2**[1]

0 **7** *hd* **Lets Be Lucky (IRE)**[26] 897 4-9-7 JohnMcAuley(3) 4 21
(F Jordan) *s.i.s: a rr* **66/1**

0240 **8** *1* **Colonel Bilko (IRE)**[42] 689 4-9-10 46 ChrisCatlin 3 19
(Miss S J Wilton) *a rr* **8/1**

-400 **9** *10* **Hows That**[91] 261 4-9-5 40 SebSanders 9 —
(K R Burke) *a rr* **11/1**

006 **10** *3* **Shaika**[21] 971 3-8-6 45 StephenCarson 5 —
(G Prodromou) *sn rdn along and a bhd* **33/1**

500- **11** *nk* **Arms Acrossthesea**[213] 5621 7-9-7 40 (p) JasonEdmunds(3) 6 —
(J Balding) *chsd ldrs: rdn along 3f out: sn wknd* **12/1**

00-0 **P** **Look Here's May**[11] 1126 4-9-5 40 JamieSpencer 7 —
(R Hollinshead) *sn led: hdd and lost pl after 3f: p.u 3f out* **33/1**

1m 44.48s (-0.12) **Going Correction** 0.0s/f (Stan)
WFA 3 from 4yo+ 13lb **12** Ran SP% **112.1**
Speed ratings (Par 101):100,91,90,87,84 78,78,77,67,64 63,—
CSF £43.76 TOTE £7.00: £1.80, £2.00, £3.20; EX 92.20.The winner was bought in for 6,800gns
Owner G J Oliver **Bred** WinStar Farm Llc **Trained** Peckleton, Leics
■ Stewards' Enquiry : Derek Nolan one-day ban: failed to keep straight from stalls (May 13)

FOCUS
A moderate seller in which the field finished well spread out behind the easy winner, who along with the runner-up sets the standard.
Lets Be Lucky(IRE) Official explanation: jockey said gelding ran green
Look Here's May Official explanation: jockey said filly hung badly right

1388 EXPERIENCE NOTTINGHAMSHIRE H'CAP 6f (F)

4:10 (4:12) (Class 5) (0-70,70) 4-Y-O+ **£3,238** (£963; £481; £240) **Stalls** Low

Form RPR

5104 **1** **Count Cougar (USA)**[5] 1258 6-8-10 **62** ChrisCatlin 10 72
(S P Griffiths) *cl up: led wl over 2f out: rdn clr wl over 1f out: drvn out* **5/1**[2]

-030 **2** *1¼* **Vienna's Boy (IRE)**[59] 575 5-8-9 **66** StephenDonohoe(5) 7 72
(W J Musson) *towards rr: hdwy over 2f out: sn rdn and styd on strly ins last* **15/2**

5114 **3** *2½* **Soba Jones**[5] 1255 9-8-10 **65** JasonEdmunds(3) 1 64
(J Balding) *dwlt: hdwy and n.m.r on inner over 3f out: rdn and nt clr run wl over 1f out: kpt on ins last: nrst fin* **8/1**

2500 **4** *1¾* **Majik**[5] 1255 7-8-7 **66** (p) KevinGhunowa(7) 11 59
(P A Blockley) *outpcd and towards rr: wd st: rdn and hdwy on outer wl over 1f out: kpt on ins lasty: nrst fin* **14/1**

46-0 **5** *hd* **Unlimited**[12] 1102 4-8-11 **63** JamieSpencer 6 56
(Mrs A Duffield) *midfield: hdwy to chse ldrs over 2f out: sn rdn and no imp* **11/2**[3]

2000 **6** *1¾* **Shifty Night (IRE)**[5] 1258 5-7-13 **58** (v) KirstyMilczarek(7) 3 45
(Mrs C A Dunnett) *led: rdn along 3f out: sn hdd and grad wknd fnl 2f* **12/1**

5016 **7** *nk* **Desert Opal**[29] 862 6-8-10 **62** PhillipMakin 8 49
(D W Chapman) *cl up: rdn along wl over 2f out: grad wknd* **25/1**

1200 **8** *1½* **Zorn**[5] 1258 7-8-10 **62** SebSanders 2 44
(P Howling) *prom on inner: rdn along 3f out: sn wknd* **7/1**

-006 **9** *7* **Domirati**[5] 1255 6-8-8 **60** GrahamGibbons 5 21
(J D Bethell) *chsd ldrs: rdn over 2f out: drvn and wknd over 1f out* **16/1**

5000 **10** *nk* **Shadow Jumper (IRE)**[5] 1255 5-8-0 **57** (v) RoryMoore(5) 9 17
(J T Stimpson) *sn outpcd and bhd* **20/1**

0-05 **11** *3½* **Johnston's Diamond (IRE)**[8] 1183 8-9-4 **70** DavidAllan 4 20
(E J Alston) *dwlt: chsng ldrs whn squeezed out after 1f: sn rdn along and rr after* **7/2**[1]

1m 17.01s (0.11) **Going Correction** 0.0s/f (Stan) **11** Ran SP% **118.5**
Speed ratings (Par 103):99,97,94,91,91 89,88,86,77,76 72
CSF £42.78 CT £304.63 TOTE £6.00: £1.80, £4.00, £2.40; EX 96.60.
Owner M Grant **Bred** Angus Glen Farm (1996) Ltd **Trained** Easingwold, N Yorks

FOCUS
A strong early pace for this ordinary sprint handicap that contained several Fibresand regulars. The first two were to their marks and the form appears sound.
Domirati Official explanation: jockey said gelding hung left in straight
Shadow Jumper(IRE) Official explanation: jockey said gelding hit its head on stalls and missed break
Johnston's Diamond(IRE) Official explanation: jockey said gelding resented kick-back

1389 JUMPING ON THE 5TH H'CAP 1m 3f (F)

4:40 (4:40) (Class 5) (0-70,70) 4-Y-O+ **£3,238** (£963; £481; £240) **Stalls** Low

Form RPR

-402 **1** **Mceldowney**[6] 1233 4-8-11 **68** GregFairley(5) 1 76
(M Johnston) *chsd ldr: pushed along 5f out: rdn to ld over 2f out: drvn and edgd lft ent last: styd on gamely* **9/4**[1]

0015 **2** *1¼* **Sand Repeal (IRE)**[7] 1222 4-9-4 **70** JamieSpencer 7 76
(Miss J Feilden) *trckd ldng pair: hdwy 3f out: chal 2f out: rdn and edgd lft over 1f out: drvn and no ex wl ins last* **5/2**[2]

3460 **3** *nk* **Hawkit (USA)**[3] [1281] 5-9-0 **66** DavidAllan 5 72
(A Bailey) *hld up in rr: hdwy 3f out: effrt 2f out: rdn and n.m.r ent last: sn drvn and one pce* **4/1**[3]

2055 **4** *1¾* **Amwell Brave**[9] [1163] 5-8-8 **63** DeanCorby(3) 3 66
(J R Jenkins) *trckd ldrs: effrt 3f out: sn rdn along and kpt on same pce appr last* **8/1**

0114 **5** *5* **Mossmann Gorge**[47] [647] 4-8-10 **62** (v) SebSanders 6 57
(M Wellings) *hld up: hdwy 4f out: rdn along to chse ldrs 2f out: sn one pce* **8/1**

120- **6** *8* **Plenty Cried Wolf**[227] [5296] 4-8-11 **63** TonyHamilton 4 45
(R A Fahey) *led: rdn along 3f out: hdd over 2f out: sn wknd and eased* **20/1**

0020 **7** *9* **Mi Odds**[62] [549] 10-8-11 **63** PhillipMakin 2 31
(Mrs N Macauley) *in tch: rdn along over 4f out: wknd wl over 2f out* **12/1**

2m 27.96s (-0.94) **Going Correction** 0.0s/f (Stan) 7 Ran SP% **114.0**
Speed ratings (Par 103):103,102,101,100,96 91,84
CSF £8.10 TOTE £2.40: £1.10, £1.90; EX 5.80.
Owner C G Maybury **Bred** St Clare Hall Stud **Trained** Middleham Moor, N Yorks

FOCUS
There early pace was only ordinary for much of the contest and it developed into a bit of a sprint. There was still only a length covering six horses passing the two-furlong pole but the form appears sound enough.

1390 BOOK HOSPITALITY APPRENTICE H'CAP 7f (F)
5:10 (5:10) (Class 6) (0-60,60) 4-Y-0+ **£2,730** (£806; £403) **Stalls** Low

Form RPR

6353 **1** **Pawn In Life (IRE)**[5] [1258] 8-8-8 **53** ow2 (v) DerekNolan(3) 3 63
(M J Polglase) *sn pushed along in rr: hdwy on outer 3f out: rdn 2f out: styd on wl to ld ins last* **4/1**[2]

2420 **2** *1½* **Contented (IRE)**[21] [972] 4-8-10 **57** (p) RonanKeogh(5) 6 63
(Mrs L C Jewell) *dwlt: rr tl hdwy wl over 2f out: sn rdn and kpt on ins last* **11/1**

2031 **3** *¾* **La Musique**[22] [941] 4-8-3 **48** LiamJones(3) 4 52
(P J McBride) *cl up: led after 3f: rdn along and hdd 2f out: sn drvn and ev ch tl one pce ins last* **7/1**[3]

1000 **4** *¾* **Christian Bendix**[7] [1209] 4-8-13 **55** StephenDonohoe 2 57
(P Howling) *midfield: hdwy over 2f out: rdn to chse ldrs over 1f out: one pce ins last* **14/1**

0512 **5** *shd* **Favouring (IRE)**[22] [940] 4-8-3 **50** (v) LukeMorris(5) 7 52
(M C Chapman) *hld up and bhd: hdwy over 2f out: sn rdn and kpt on fnl f: nrst fin* **11/4**[1]

00-5 **6** *½* **Extemporise (IRE)**[22] [940] 6-7-13 **46** JosephWalsh(5) 9 47
(T T Clement) *chsd ldrs: hdwy to ld 2f out: sn rdn: hdd & wknd ins last* **15/2**

21-0 **7** *5* **Sea Frolic (IRE)**[111] [95] 5-8-5 **47** (p) GregFairley 5 35
(Jennie Candlish) *led 3f: rdn along 3f out: sn wknd* **12/1**

3100 **8** *½* **Faithisflying**[7] [1225] 4-8-1 **46** oh1 (p) AndrewElliott(3) 1 32
(D W Chapman) *chsd ldrs on inner: rdn along 3f out: wknd fnl 2f* **16/1**

00 **9** *2½* **Khetaab (IRE)**[11] [1124] 4-9-4 **60** RoryMoore 8 40
(E J Alston) *cl up: rdn along 1/2-way: wknd over 2f out* **15/2**

1m 31.59s (0.79) **Going Correction** 0.0s/f (Stan) 9 Ran SP% **111.3**
Speed ratings (Par 101):95,93,92,91,91 90,85,84,81
CSF £44.48 CT £287.48 TOTE £2.70: £1.90, £5.20, £3.10; EX 28.70 Place 6 £76.45, Place 5 £31.00.
Owner Geraldine Degville & Lawrence Degville **Bred** Lt-Col W L Newell **Trained** Babworth, Notts
■ Stewards' Enquiry : Liam Jones three-day ban: used whip with excessive frequency (May 13, 15-16)

FOCUS
A poor race and the leaders might have gone off too quick as the front pair came from well back. The winning time was moderate for the grade but the form looks fairly solid, rated around those in the frame behind the winner.

T/Plt: £72.50 to a £1 stake. Pool: £35,675.90. 358.80 winning tickets. T/Qpdt: £26.00 to a £1 stake. Pool: £2,426.00. 68.80 winning tickets. JR

1303 WOLVERHAMPTON (A.W) (L-H)
Tuesday, May 2

OFFICIAL GOING: Standard
Wind: Fresh; half behind Weather: Some drizzle

1391 HOLIDAY INN GARDEN COURT WOLVERHAMPTON BANDED STKS 5f 216y(P)
2:20 (2:20) (Class 7) 4-Y-0+ **£1,365** (£403; £201) **Stalls** Low

Form RPR

30-0 **1** **Jahia (NZ)**[42] [686] 7-8-8 45 StanleyChin(3) 4 52
(P T Midgley) *mde virtually all: rdn over 1f out: drvn out* **10/1**

4330 **2** *1¼* **St Ivian**[36] [772] 6-8-11 45 (v) MickyFenton 5 48
(Mrs N Macauley) *sn chsng ldrs: rdn over 3f out: wnt 2nd wl over 1f out: kpt on same pce ins fnl f* **3/1**[1]

0640 **3** *1* **Spanish Music**[9] [1165] 4-8-11 45 DaneO'Neill 2 45
(R Ingram) *bhd: rdn and hdwy whn swtchd rt over 1f out: r.o ins fnl f* **4/1**[2]

006- **4** *½* **Attila The Hun**[200] [5883] 7-8-11 40 PaulHanagan 6 44+
(F Watson) *bhd: rdn and swtchd lft whn hdwy on ins over 2f out: one pce fnl f* **25/1**

-035 **5** *¾* **Grand View**[28] [873] 10-8-8 45 (p) PaulMulrennan(3) 12 42
(J R Weymes) *hdwy over 4f out: rdn wl over 1f out: one pce fnl f* **9/1**

000 **6** *3* **Princess Arwen**[28] [876] 4-8-11 40 (p) SamHitchcott 9 33
(Mrs Barbara Waring) *bhd: rdn whn nt clr run and swtchd rt over 3f out: hdwy over 1f out: no imp fnl f* **16/1**

-600 **7** *½* **Petana**[7] [1228] 6-8-11 45 (p) RobbieFitzpatrick 1 31
(Peter Grayson) *mid-div: lost pl 4f out: hdwy over 1f out: n.d* **8/1**

0060 **8** *2½* **Indian Gem**[15] [1054] 5-8-11 40 DeanMcKeown 8 24
(A J Chamberlain) *s.i.s: sn mid-div: hmpd and lost pl over 3f out: n.d after* **8/1**

000- **9** *2* **Lucky Emerald (IRE)**[146] [6526] 4-8-11 45 FrancisFerris 11 18
(B Palling) *prom: rdn and ev ch over 2f out: wknd wl over 1f out* **25/1**

00-0 **10** *¾* **Graceful Flight**[11] [1127] 4-8-8 40 DanielTudhope(3) 3 15
(P T Midgley) *hld up in tch: lost pl over 4f out: bhd fnl 2f* **14/1**

-050 **11** *1½* **Danethorpe Lady (IRE)**[59] [588] 4-8-8 40 PatrickMathers(3) 13 11
(D Shaw) *outpcd: swtchd lft 4f out: a bhd* **50/1**

0000 **12** *5* **On The Trail**[22] [943] 9-8-11 45 (p) TonyCulhane 7 —
(D W Chapman) *prom tl rdn and wknd over 2f out* **10/1**

-000 **13** *½* **Fox Covert (IRE)**[20] [974] 5-8-11 45 RobertWinston 10 —
(D W Barker) *w wnr: rdn 3f out: wknd 2f out: eased fnl f* **6/1**[3]

1m 16.14s (0.33) **Going Correction** -0.10s/f (Stan) 13 Ran SP% **131.9**
Speed ratings (Par 97):93,91,90,89,88 84,83,80,77,76 74,68,67
CSF £43.66 TOTE £8.30: £2.00, £1.70, £1.90; EX 40.40.
Owner Enjoy A Day Out Partnership **Bred** A K Illston **Trained** Westow, N Yorks
■ The first winner in Britain since 2004 for Stanley Chin, who drew a blank last year.

FOCUS
This took little winning.
Fox Covert(IRE) Official explanation: jockey said gelding ran flat

1392 WOLVERHAMPTON RACECOURSE - A CONFERENCE CENTRE TOO BANDED STKS 1m 5f 194y(P)
2:50 (2:50) (Class 7) 4-Y-0+ **£1,876** (£554; £277) **Stalls** Low

Form RPR

0052 **1** **Rose Bien**[8] [1199] 4-8-13 48 (p) TonyCulhane 3 61
(P J McBride) *a.p: rdn 3f out: led wl over 1f out: sn edgd rt: drvn out* **9/4**[1]

6661 **2** *1* **Lake Wakatipu**[8] [1199] 4-9-4 47 JimmyQuinn 6 65
(M Mullineaux) *hld up and bhd: hdwy whn nt clr run and swtchd rt over 2f out: styd on ins fnl f* **12/1**

4402 **3** *2½* **Lysander's Quest (IRE)**[27] [891] 8-8-11 45 DaneO'Neill 2 53
(R Ingram) *mid-div: rdn over 3f out: hdwy over 2f out: one pce ins fnl f* **3/1**[2]

500- **4** *3* **Red River Rebel**[232] [5185] 8-8-13 47 DarrenWilliams 13 51
(J R Norton) *led: rdn over 3f out: hdd wl over 1f out: wknd ins fnl f* **12/1**

1044 **5** *1¾* **Ice And Fire**[8] [1199] 7-8-12 46 MickyFenton 12 47
(J T Stimpson) *hld up and bhd: rdn and c wd st: hdwy over 1f out: nvr trbld ldrs* **15/2**[3]

-304 **6** *1½* **Iamback**[21] [973] 6-8-11 45 (t) JamieMackay 8 44
(Miss D A McHale) *mid-div: rdn over 3f out: sn lost pl: rallied over 1f out: n.d* **20/1**

2043 **7** *1* **Makarim (IRE)**[22] [938] 10-8-13 47 (p) FergusSweeney 4 45
(M R Bosley) *hld up towards rr: stdy hdwy over 5f out: wknd over 2f out* **16/1**

5360 **8** *1½* **Jadeeron**[57] [599] 7-8-13 47 (p) AlanDaly 9 43
(Miss D A McHale) *mid-div: stdy hdwy over 5f out: rdn over 3f out: wknd over 2f out* **12/1**

4400 **9** *1¼* **Noble Mind**[8] [1199] 5-8-13 47 (p) RobertWinston 10 41
(P G Murphy) *prom: rdn over 3f out: wknd wl over 1f out* **20/1**

630- **10** *3½* **Barnbrook Empire (IRE)**[105] [5301] 4-8-10 45 AdrianMcCarthy 1 34
(R A Harris) *prom tl rdn and wknd over 2f out* **14/1**

6-01 **11** *7* **Hillfield Flyer (IRE)**[34] [791] 6-8-9 46 DanielTudhope(3) 5 25
(Samuel Murphy, Ire) *s.s: bhd: short-lived effrt over 2f out* **16/1**

-065 **12** *½* **Keltic Rainbow (IRE)**[25] [911] 5-8-4 40 (v) DonnaCaldwell(7) 7 24
(D Haydn Jones) *a bhd* **25/1**

-000 **13** *17* **Futoo (IRE)**[10] [1152] 5-9-2 50 (p) PaulQuinn 11 5
(D W Chapman) *hld up in tch: rdn over 5f out: wknd over 3f out* **25/1**

3m 6.30s (-1.07) **Going Correction** -0.10s/f (Stan)
WFA 4 from 5yo+ 1lb 13 Ran SP% **126.3**
Speed ratings (Par 97):99,98,97,95,94 93,92,92,91,89 85,85,75
CSF £31.22 TOTE £2.90: £1.10, £4.50, £1.80; EX 14.30.
Owner P J Pateman **Bred** Mrs J F Budgett **Trained** Newmarket, Suffolk
■ Stewards' Enquiry : Jimmy Quinn caution: used whip with excessive frequency

FOCUS
Only a short head had separated the first two in a similar event over two miles here last week.
Ice And Fire Official explanation: jockey said gelding hung right

1393 TO SPONSOR A RACE CALL 0870 220 2242 BANDED STKS 7f 32y(P)
3:20 (3:20) (Class 7) 4-Y-0+ **£1,365** (£403; £201) **Stalls** High

Form RPR

0000 **1** **Inescapable (USA)**[29] [853] 5-8-11 40 MickyFenton 3 49
(A W Carroll) *hld up in mid-div: rdn over 3f out: hdwy over 2f out: led wl ins fnl f: drvn out* **20/1**

30-6 **2** *nk* **Mescalera (GER)**[3] [1305] 5-8-11 40 PaulHanagan 11 49
(B G Powell) *hld up in mid-div: rdn and hdwy over 2f out: r.o ins fnl f* **14/1**

0002 **3** *1* **Margaret's Dream (IRE)**[36] [768] 5-8-8 45 DanielTudhope(3) 9 49+
(D Carroll) *hld up and bhd: hmpd and swtchd rt over 2f out: hdwy over 1f out: sn rdn: kpt on ins fnl f* **3/1**[2]

53 **4** *½* **Midmaar (IRE)**[34] [793] 5-8-11 45 JamieMackay 8 45
(M Wigham) *a.p: rdn to ld wl over 1f out: hdd and no ex wl ins fnl f* **2/1**[1]

536/ **5** *¾* **Limit Down (IRE)**[818] [678] 5-8-8 45 StanleyChin(3) 6 43
(John Berry) *a.p: led 3f out: rdn and hdd wl over 1f out: no ex ins fnl f* **25/1**

0000 **6** *shd* **Dutch Key Card (IRE)**[7] [1228] 5-8-11 45 (b) RobbieFitzpatrick 2 42
(C Smith) *t.k.h in tch: rdn over 2f out: one pce fnl f* **7/1**[3]

3330 **7** *hd* **Sergeant Slipper**[15] [1054] 9-8-11 45 (v) DeanMcKeown 1 42+
(C Smith) *s.i.s: hld up and bhd: nt clr run on ins over 3f out and over 2f out: hdwy wl over 1f out: sn swtchd rt: one pce* **12/1**

-000 **8** *1¾* **Dematraf (IRE)**[85] [315] 4-8-11 45 SamHitchcott 4 37
(Ms Deborah J Evans) *led: rdn and hdd 3f out: wknd towards fin* **9/1**

0050 **9** *4* **Mytton's Dream**[8] [1197] 4-8-11 45 (b) TomEaves 5 27
(R Brotherton) *s.i.s: a bhd* **14/1**

00-0 **10** *¾* **Mazindar (USA)**[8] [1197] 4-8-11 45 TonyCulhane 7 25
(P T Midgley) *hld up in tch: rdn and wknd over 2f out* **28/1**

0006 **11** *1¼* **Annals**[8] [1197] 4-8-4 45 (be) RobbieMills(7) 12 22
(R C Guest) *s.i.s: t.k.h: hdwy on outside 3f out: wknd wl over 1f out* **14/1**

30-0 **12** *16* **Warren Place**[8] [1185] 6-8-11 45 (b) RobertWinston 10 —
(A D Brown) *t.k.h in tch: wknd over 2f out* **66/1**

1m 31.6s (1.20) **Going Correction** -0.10s/f (Stan) 12 Ran SP% **122.1**
Speed ratings (Par 97):89,88,87,86,86 85,85,83,79,78 76,58
CSF £272.87 TOTE £45.30: £6.20, £3.90, £1.90; EX 199.20.
Owner David M Thornton **Bred** J R Perrotta **Trained** Cropthorne, Worcs

FOCUS
A very moderate winning time for what was a desperate affair.

1394 HOTEL & CONFERENCING AT WOLVERHAMPTON RACECOURSE BANDED STKS 1m 141y(P)
3:50 (3:51) (Class 7) 4-Y-0+ **£1,876** (£554; £277) **Stalls** Low

Form RPR

-602 **1** **Magic Warrior**[8] [1194] 6-9-2 50 PatDobbs 11 65
(J C Fox) *hld up: hdwy over 3f out: rdn to ld over 2f out: sn clr: r.o wl* **15/2**

0010 **2** *6* **Wanna Shout**[8] [1194] 8-9-1 49 TonyCulhane 2 51
(R Dickin) *hld up towards rr: rdn and hdwy on ins 2f out: r.o ins fnl f: no ch w wnr* **14/1**

3635 **3** *1* **Musiotal**^{10} [1148] 5-8-12 46..........(p) RobbieFitzpatrick 7 46
(P A Blockley) *s.i.s: bhd: rdn over 2f out: hdwy on ins wl over 1f out: one pce fnl f* **6/1**^{2}

6-41 **4** *hd* **Merlins Profit**^{7} [1227] 6-9-7 49.......... DeanMcKeown 1 55
(G A Swinbank) *broke wl: led early: a.p: rdn over 2f out: one pce* **7/4**^{1}

0133 **5** *1* **Ballare (IRE)**^{8} [1194] 7-9-0 48..........(v) FergusSweeney 12 46
(P J Makin) *hld up in tch: rdn over 2f out: one pce* **12/1**

0030 **6** *2* **Luciferous (USA)**^{8} [1194] 4-8-13 47..........(v) FergalLynch 10 41
(P G Murphy) *stdd s: sn swtchd lft: hld up and bhd: rdn over 3f out: hdwy and hung lft over 1f out: n.d* **66/1**

6450 **7** *½* **Zariano**^{3} [1305] 6-8-13 47..........(p) PaulFessey 8 40
(T D Barron) *prom: rdn and ev ch over 2f out: wknd wl over 1f out* **9/1**

3500 **8** *4* **Pending (IRE)**^{22} [953] 5-8-13 47.......... PaulHanagan 4 31
(R A Harris) *sn led: hdd over 6f out: led over 4f out: rdn and hdd over 2f out: wknd over 1f out* **7/1**^{3}

0006 **9** *4* **Qobtaan (USA)**^{7} [1225] 7-8-11 45..........(v) LPKeniry 9 21
(M R Bosley) *hld up in mid-div: rdn 3f out: wknd over 1f out* **33/1**

4000 **10** *2 ½* **House Martin**^{23} [586] 4-8-13 47..........(v^{1}) RobertWinston 6 17
(C R Dore) *hld up and bhd: short-lived effrt over 2f out* **16/1**

4-00 **11** *nk* **Icecap**^{8} [1194] 6-8-13 50.......... AmirQuinn(3) 3 20
(W G M Turner) *prom: led over 6f out: rdn and hdd over 4f out: wknd over 3f out* **16/1**

130- **12** *12* **Noorain**^{196} [5957] 4-8-13 47.......... MickyFenton 5 —
(Stef Liddiard) *prom: lost pl 6f out: bhd fnl 3f* **12/1**

1m 50.22s (-1.54) **Going Correction** -0.10s/f (Stan) **12** Ran SP% **123.2**
Speed ratings (Par 97):102,96,95,95,94 92,92,88,85,83 82,72
CSF £112.19 TOTE £10.30: £2.30, £2.70, £2.60; EX 85.40.
Owner Miss H J Flower **Bred** Patrick Eddery Ltd **Trained** Collingbourne Ducis, Wilts

FOCUS
This turned into something of a one horse race.
Zariano Official explanation: jockey said gelding hung right
Qobtaan(USA) Official explanation: jockey said gelding had no more to give
House Martin Official explanation: jockey said filly had no more to give
Noorain Official explanation: trainer said filly hit its head leaving stalls

1395 RINGSIDE SUITE 700 THEATRE STYLE CONFERENCE BANDED STKS 1m 1f 103y(P)

4:20 (4:20) (Class 7) 4-Y-0+ **£1,365** (£403; £201) **Stalls** Low

Form RPR

-660 **1** **Boogie Magic**^{59} [579] 6-8-8 45.......... AdamKirby(3) 11 52
(T Keddy) *hld up and bhd: rdn and hdwy over 2f out: led wl ins fnl f: drvn out* **16/1**

0-41 **2** *nk* **Wood Fern (UAE)**^{7} [1224] 6-9-3 45.......... ShaneKelly 3 57
(W M Brisbourne) *hld up in tch: rdn over 2f out: ev ch wl ins fnl f: r.o* **9/4**^{1}

0522 **3** *1 ¾* **Danum**^{8} [1198] 6-8-4 45..........(p) RussellKennemore(7) 4 48
(R Hollinshead) *led: rdn clr 2f out: hrd rdn and edgd rt whn hdd wl ins fnl f* **7/1**

50-5 **4** *1 ¾* **Adalar (IRE)**^{22} [941] 6-8-11 40..........(t) JimmyQuinn 2 44
(P W D'Arcy) *a.p: rdn to chse ldr 3f out to 1f out: one pce* **12/1**

0030 **5** *hd* **Dishdasha (IRE)**^{27} [891] 4-8-11 45.......... RobertWinston 12 44
(C R Dore) *s.i.s: sn swtchd lft: hdwy over 3f out: rdn over 2f out: one pce fnl f* **13/2**^{3}

0060 **6** *2 ½* **Paper Doll**^{8} [1197] 4-8-4 45..........(p) SoniaEaton(7) 9 39
(B P J Baugh) *hld up and bhd: hdwy on ins 2f out: no further prog fnl f* **20/1**

-000 **7** *¾* **Fortunes Favourite**^{8} [1198] 6-8-6 45.......... NataliaGemelova(5) 1 38
(J E Long) *hld up in tch: rdn over 3f out: wknd ins fnl f* **33/1**

5402 **8** *7* **Tuscan Treaty**^{8} [1197] 6-8-11 45..........(tp) TonyCulhane 10 24
(P J McBride) *hld up and bhd: rdn over 3f out: short-lived effrt over 2f out* **7/2**^{2}

00-0 **9** *5* **Printsmith (IRE)**^{86} [304] 9-8-11 35..........(v) DarrenWilliams 6 15
(J R Norton) *sn chsng ldr: rdn over 3f out: wknd over 2f out* **33/1**

4-06 **10** *2* **Parisian Playboy**^{34} [792] 6-8-11 40.......... PaulHanagan 7 11
(A D Brown) *hld up in mid-div: hdwy over 4f out: rdn 3f out: wknd 2f out* **16/1**

050- **11** *2* **Fairy Monarch (IRE)**^{225} [5359] 7-8-11 45..........(b) MickyFenton 8 7
(P T Midgley) *a bhd* **11/1**

-435 **12** *3* **Emperor Cat (IRE)**^{7} [1225] 5-8-11 45..........(p) VinceSlattery 5 2
(Mrs N S Evans) *hld up in tch: rdn over 4f out: wknd over 3f out* **22/1**

2m 1.65s (-0.97) **Going Correction** -0.10s/f (Stan) **12** Ran SP% **121.6**
Speed ratings (Par 97):100,99,98,96,96 94,93,87,82,81 79,76
CSF £51.31 TOTE £20.40: £3.60, £1.20, £2.20; EX 66.30.
Owner Mrs L M Thomas **Bred** B A McMahon **Trained** Newmarket, Suffolk

FOCUS
They went a fair pace in what can only be described as a modest affair.

1396 WOLVERHAMPTON-RACECOURSE.CO.UK BANDED STKS 5f 20y(P)

4:50 (4:50) (Class 7) 4-Y-0+ **£1,876** (£554; £277) **Stalls** Low

Form RPR

5054 **1** **Edged In Gold**^{8} [1195] 4-8-13 50..........(e) AmirQuinn(3) 5 58
(P J Makin) *s.i.s: hld up and bhd: hdwy on ins over 2f out: led jst ins fnl f: sn rdn: jst hld on* **6/1**^{2}

0-01 **2** *shd* **Compton Classic**^{7} [1228] 4-9-3 45..........(p) FergalLynch 8 59
(J S Goldie) *bhd tl rdn and hdwy over 1f out: r.o wl ins fnl f: jst failed* **8/1**

-002 **3** *1 ½* **New Options**^{8} [1195] 9-8-13 47..........(b) RobbieFitzpatrick 7 49
(Peter Grayson) *s.i.s: hld up and bhd: rdn and hdwy on ins over 1f out: r.o ins fnl f* **6/1**^{2}

6000 **4** *nk* **Blue Moon Hitman (IRE)**^{8} [1195] 5-9-2 50..........(b) PaulHanagan 2 51
(R Brotherton) *led: rdn wl over 1f out: hdd jst ins fnl f: one pce* **13/2**^{3}

4201 **5** *nk* **Muktasb (USA)**^{8} [1195] 5-9-4 49..........(v) PatrickMathers(3) 11 55
(D Shaw) *hld up and bhd: rdn and edgd lft over 1f out: late hdwy: nrst fin* **11/2**^{1}

005- **6** *½* **Tartan Special**^{274} [3995] 4-9-2 50..........(v) PatCosgrave 4 48
(K R Burke) *chsd ldrs: rdn and hung lft over 1f out: one pce* **13/2**^{3}

000- **7** *1* **Rosie's Result**^{239} [4999] 6-8-11 45.......... RoystonFfrench 1 40
(M Todhunter) *chsd ldrs: rdn over 2f out: bmpd jst ins fnl f: fdd towards fin* **7/1**

5210 **8** *7* **Prime Recreation**^{8} [1195] 9-9-2 50.......... RobertWinston 3 19
(P S Felgate) *w ldr: ev ch over 2f out: hung rt ent st: sn wknd* **8/1**

-000 **9** *1 ½* **Torrent**^{7} [1228] 11-8-11 45..........(b) TonyCulhane 6 9
(D W Chapman) *chsd ldrs tl wknd wl over 1f out* **14/1**

504/ **10** *shd* **Aegean Mist**^{584} [5801] 6-8-11 45.......... ShaneKelly 10 9
(M Mullineaux) *bhd fnl 3f* **33/1**

62.80 secs (-0.02) **Going Correction** -0.10s/f (Stan) **10** Ran SP% **115.0**
Speed ratings (Par 97):96,95,93,92,92 91,90,78,76,76
CSF £52.48 TOTE £8.80: £3.90, £2.20, £2.00; EX 38.60.
Owner Weldspec Glasgow Limited **Bred** Mrs P J Makin **Trained** Ogbourne Maisey, Wilts

FOCUS
A strong pace in this wide-open sprint led to the fastest time of the day compared with standard.
Prime Recreation Official explanation: jockey said gelding hung right

1397 ZONGALERO RESTAURANT OVERLOOKS THE RACETRACK BANDED STKS 5f 216y(P)

5:20 (5:20) (Class 7) 4-Y-0+ **£1,876** (£554; £277) **Stalls** Low

Form RPR

-022 **1** **Geojimali**^{7} [1227] 4-9-2 50.......... FergalLynch 8 66+
(J S Goldie) *dwlt: hld up in rr: swtchd lft wl over 1f out: rdn and hdwy ent fnl f: str run to ld last strides* **6/4**^{1}

0000 **2** *½* **Marshallspark (IRE)**^{12} [1102] 7-8-13 47..........(p) PaulHanagan 3 54
(R A Fahey) *chsd ldrs: rdn and edgd lft over 1f out: led wl ins fnl f: hdd last strides* **9/2**^{2}

6-30 **3** *¾* **Weakest Link**^{77} [411] 5-8-13 47..........(p) MickyFenton 12 52
(E J Alston) *led: rdn 2f out: hdd wl ins fnl f: kpt on* **12/1**

0-10 **4** *½* **Sharp Hat**^{8} [1195] 12-8-13 47.......... TonyCulhane 13 50
(D W Chapman) *hld up: sn bhd: hdwy over 3f out: rdn wl over 1f out: ev ch ins fnl f: nt qckn* **20/1**

006- **5** *¾* **Kahlua Bear**^{196} [5964] 4-9-2 50..........(b) PaulDoe 4 51
(Miss K B Boutflower) *prom: rdn whn n.m.r over 3f out: sn lost pl: rallied fnl f: r.o* **33/1**

5004 **6** *hd* **Lady Hopeful (IRE)**^{10} [1150] 4-9-2 50..........(b) RobbieFitzpatrick 9 50
(Peter Grayson) *hld up and bhd: hdwy over 2f out: rdn wl over 1f out: one pce ins fnl f* **5/1**^{3}

0-16 **7** *1 ¼* **Magical Mimi**^{8} [1196] 5-8-13 47..........(t) LPKeniry 7 44
(K G Wingrove) *s.i.s: sn mid-div: hdwy on ins whn nt clr run 2f out: sn rdn: wknd wl ins fnl f* **12/1**

0505 **8** *½* **Carcinetto (IRE)**^{36} [766] 4-8-11 45..........(p) FrancisFerris 5 40
(B Palling) *s.i.s: bhd: rdn over 2f out: hdwy on ins over 1f out: no imp fnl f* **14/1**

00-0 **9** *3 ½* **Princess Kai (IRE)**^{27} [886] 5-8-11 45..........(b) SamHitchcott 11 30
(R Ingram) *rdn over 2f out: a bhd* **33/1**

0-00 **10** *2 ½* **Bold Maggie**^{81} [360] 4-8-4 40.......... RussellKennemore(7) 1 22
(J A Pickering) *w ldr: rdn over 2f out: wknd wl over 1f out* **33/1**

0-66 **11** *½* **Wolfman**^{28} [873] 4-9-0 48..........(p) RobertWinston 6 24
(D W Barker) *hld up in tch: rdn and wknd over 2f out* **9/1**

-506 **12** *¾* **Roko**^{22} [943] 4-8-11 35..........(b) DeanMcKeown 10 18
(S R Bowring) *prom tl wknd 2f out* **100/1**

1m 15.53s (-0.28) **Going Correction** -0.10s/f (Stan) **12** Ran SP% **121.5**
Speed ratings (Par 97):97,96,95,94,93 93,91,91,86,83 82,81
CSF £7.73 TOTE £2.10: £1.30, £2.60, £2.90; EX 14.00 Place 6 £143.84, Place 5 £76.57.
Owner Mrs D I Goldie **Bred** Jim Goldie **Trained** Uplawmoor, E Renfrews
■ Stewards' Enquiry : Paul Hanagan one-day ban: used whip with excessive frequency (May 13)

FOCUS
The winner came from last to first in the home straight.
Magical Mimi Official explanation: bled from the nose
T/Plt: £54.70 to a £1 stake. Pool: £37,113.55. 494.85 winning tickets. T/Qpdt: £29.00 to a £1 stake. Pool: £1,995.80. 50.90 winning tickets. KH

1277 CHANTILLY (R-H)

Tuesday, May 2

OFFICIAL GOING: Good to soft

1398a PRIX ALLEZ FRANCE (GROUP 3) (F&M) 1m 2f

1:50 (1:49) 4-Y-0+ **£27,586** (£11,034; £8,276; £5,517; £2,759)

RPR

1 **Paita**^{198} [5932] 4-8-9 .... OPeslier 7 109
(E Lellouche, France) *with leader early, settled in 3rd to straight, led 1 1/2f out, pushed out* **6/4**^{1}

2 *2* **Bastet (IRE)**^{22} [960] 4-8-7 .... SPasquier 4 103
(E Lellouche, France) *raced in 4th to straight, chased winner final f, kept on but could never reach her* **5/1**

3 *½* **Ysoldina (FR)**^{31} [841] 4-8-9 .... C-PLemaire 3 105
(A De Royer-Dupre, France) *hooded, pulled early, restrained in 5th to straight, held up for late run, ridden to take 3rd inside last 100y* **49/10**^{3}

4 *nk* **In Clover**^{189} [6104] 4-9-0 .... DBonilla 2 109
(F Head, France) *held up, 7th straight, some progress on outside from 2f out, never able to challenge* **34/10**^{2}

5 *¾* **Saishu (IRE)**^{22} [960] 4-8-7 .... CSoumillon 1 101
(E Libaud, France) *held up, 6th straight, closed up on inside over 2f out, never able to challenge* **81/10**

6 *5* **Aunt Julia**^{258} [4479] 4-8-7 .... DBoeuf 8 92
(R Hannon) *led 1f, 2nd straight, driven to lead 2f out, headed 1 1/2f out, soon weakened* **19/1**

7 *1 ½* **Afaf (FR)**^{22} [960] 4-8-7 .... TThulliez 6 89
(M Delzangles, France) *led after 1f, headed & weakened 2f out* **14/1**

8 *2* **Chavela (IRE)**^{22} [960] 4-8-7 .... CNora 5 85
(R Martin-Sanchez, Spain) *slowly into stride, last throughout* **32/1**

2m 4.80s **8** Ran SP% **122.0**
PARI-MUTUEL: WIN 2.50; PL 1.30, 1.60, 1.60; DF 7.90.
Owner T Yoshida **Bred** Gestut Fahrhof **Trained** Lamorlaye, France

NOTEBOOK
Paita, who did not win in 2005, looks sure to have a good season this year as she produced her best form to win this Group Three race in style. She relaxed in third place early on before taking control of the race halfway up the straight, and quickened well. Never tested in the final stages, she will now be kept to a similar distance and will run next in the Prix Corrida.
Bastet(IRE) put up another decent performance. She was given every chance but could not quicken in the same manner as her stablemate.
Ysoldina(FR) once again pulled a lot early on before battling well to hold third place.
In Clover, giving weight to the rest of the field, was brought up the centre of the track in the straight and flattered a little at the furlong marker before just failing to hold third place. She had had a setback, so in the circumstances this was a very promising run which augers well for the future.
Aunt Julia, smartly into her stride, raced in second place and took the lead at the two-furlong marker. She did not hold it for long, though, and faded on the rail as the race came to an end. Her rider felt she was in need of the outing.

1379 **KEMPTON (A.W)** (R-H)
Wednesday, May 3

OFFICIAL GOING: Standard
Wind: Nil

1399 RUK EVENING RACING PACKAGE FOR £60 H'CAP 5f (P)
7:00 (7:00) (Class 4) (0-85,85) 4-Y-O+

£6,232 (£1,866; £933; £467; £233; £117) **Stalls** High

Form RPR
4410 **1** **Wicked Uncle**16 1047 7-8-8 **75** (v) TQuinn 8 87
(S Gollings) *in tch: rdn and hung rt wl over 1f out: r.o wl ins fnl f: led cl home* **10/1**
5001 **2** *nk* **Trinculo (IRE)**14 1076 9-9-1 **82** AdrianTNicholls 2 93
(D Nicholls) *lw: sn swtchd rt after s: led: rdn 2f out: drifted lft ins fnl f: no ex whn hdd cl home* **12/1**
1-26 **3** *1 1/4* **After The Show**22 967 5-8-6 **73** ChrisCatlin 9 79+
(Rae Guest) *bhd: hmpd 3f out: sn drvn along: kpt on wl ins fnl f: wnt 3rd cl home: nrst fin* **5/1**2
0050 **4** *1 1/4* **No Time (IRE)**4 1297 6-8-10 **77** (p) FrancisNorton 10 79
(M J Polglase) *b.hind: chsd ldr: rdn and effrt over 2f out: kpt on same pce fnl f* **20/1**
2/1 **5** *hd* **Financial Times (USA)**62 553 4-8-9 **76** NCallan 7 77
(Stef Liddiard) *lw: wnt lft s: sn chsng ldrs: rdn and effrt over 2f out: one pce fnl f* **11/2**3
-202 **6** *1/2* **Golden Dixie (USA)**10 1161 7-9-4 **85** (p) AdrianMcCarthy 4 84
(R A Harris) *hmpd sn after s: towards rr: rdn over 2f out: kpt on ins fnl f* **3/1**1
-243 **7** *1 1/2* **Lindbergh**10 1161 4-9-3 **84** RichardHughes 1 78
(R Hannon) *lw: in tch on outer tl lost pl over 3f out: no imp after* **11/2**3
101 **8** *3/4* **Silver Dane (IRE)**10 1161 4-8-9 **76** 6ex (v) DaneO'Neill 6 67
(Mrs C A Dunnett) *hmpd sn after s: sn chsng ldrs: rdn over 2f out: wknd fnl f* **7/1**
2000 **9** *3* **Law Maker**22 967 6-8-4 **78** (v) JamieHamblett(7) 5 58+
(A Bailey) *hmpd sn after s and sddle slipped: nvr rcvrd* **16/1**

59.91 secs (-1.09) **Going Correction** -0.10s/f (Stan) **9** Ran SP% **112.4**
Speed ratings (Par 105):99,98,96,94,94 93,91,89,85
CSF £117.88 CT £672.77 TOTE £15.20: £3.20, £3.00, £1.80; EX 182.30.
Owner Roy G Gibney, P & Mrs A Allen **Bred** Lady Jennifer Green **Trained** Scamblesby, Lincs
■ Stewards' Enquiry : Adrian T Nicholls two-day ban: careless riding (May 15-16)

FOCUS
A fair handicap and there were plenty of front-runners in this race and that ensured that it was run at a good gallop. The form looks straightforward, rated through the first two.
Law Maker Official explanation: jockey said saddle slipped

1400 RUK EVENING RACING CALL 08700 50 69 47 H'CAP 1m 2f (P)
7:28 (7:28) (Class 6) (0-60,60) 4-Y-O+ **£3,238** (£963; £481; £240) **Stalls** High

Form RPR
000- **1** **Wild Pitch**133 6644 5-9-4 **60** (b) RichardHughes 6 68
(P Mitchell) *hld up towards rr: rdn over 2f out: hdwy over 1f out: styd on strly ins fnl f: led fnl stride* **20/1**
0633 **2** *shd* **Seattle Robber**11 1152 4-8-13 **55** (p) NCallan 14 63
(P A Blockley) *lw: hld up towards rr: hdwy 3f out: rdn 2f out: styd on strly to ld briefly cl home: hdd fnl stride* **7/1**2
3602 **3** *nk* **Jomus**2 1334 5-8-11 **53** (p) RobertHavlin 12 60
(L Montague Hall) *hld up mid-div: smooth hdwy to trck ldrs over 2f out: rdn to ld 1f out: ct cl home* **6/1**1
6166 **4** *2* **Treetops Hotel (IRE)**7 1244 7-8-12 **54** RyanMoore 15 58
(B R Johnson) *hld up towards rr: rdn 3f out: styd on wl fnl f to go 4th cl home: nt rch ldrs* **9/1**
0-60 **5** *1/2* **Bullseye**2 1334 4-9-0 **56** (v1) FrankieMcDonald 1 59
(A P Jarvis) *lw: chsd ldrs: rdn over 2f out: kpt on same pce* **25/1**
5100 **6** *hd* **Christmas Truce (IRE)**7 1245 7-8-9 **56** (v) JamesDoyle(5) 7 58
(Ms J S Doyle) *chsd ldrs: led 2f out: sn rdn and drifted lft: hdd 1f out: wknd fnl 75yds* **33/1**
40-6 **7** *3/4* **Tayman (IRE)**27 894 4-9-4 **60** SteveDrowne 4 61
(G Wragg) *rn in snatches in mid-div: rdn over 2f out: styd on fnl f: nvr trbld ldrs* **8/1**3
3232 **8** *nk* **Glendale**11 1152 5-8-12 **57** SaleemGolam(3) 10 57
(D K Ivory) *chsd ldrs: rdn 2f out: one pce sn after* **6/1**1
0020 **9** *1/2* **Flying Pass**2 1334 4-9-2 **58** (p) LDettori 13 57
(D J S Ffrench Davis) *hld up towards rr: rdn and hdwy fr 2f out: wknd ins fnl f* **6/1**1
0-05 **10** *shd* **Play Up Pompey**7 1244 4-8-7 **52** NeilChalmers(3) 9 51
(J J Bridger) *chsd ldrs: rdn 2f out: wknd fnl f* **20/1**
0000 **11** *3/4* **Meelup (IRE)**8 1204 6-8-13 **58** (p) AmirQuinn(3) 2 56
(P G Murphy) *squeezed out s: nvr rcvrd and a towards rr* **33/1**
2250 **12** *shd* **Cherished Number**20 1001 7-9-1 **57** (b) DaneO'Neill 16 55
(A M Hales) *a towards rr* **16/1**
00-0 **13** *2 1/2* **Just A Fluke (IRE)**41 706 5-8-10 **52** (t) FergusSweeney 11 45
(M R Bosley) *in tch tl wknd 2f out* **50/1**
0/00 **14** *2 1/2* **Hallings Overture (USA)**23 950 7-9-0 **56** ChrisCatlin 8 44
(C A Horgan) *led: rdn and hdd 2f out: sn wknd* **25/1**
1313 **15** *11* **Competitor**10 1163 5-9-4 **60** (v) TQuinn 3 27
(J Akehurst) *hmpd sn after s and a towards rr* **8/1**3
155- **16** *5* **Saucy**338 2121 5-8-13 **55** JimmyFortune 5 13
(A W Carroll) *b: chsd ldrs tl wknd over 2f out* **16/1**

2m 7.39s (-3.61) **Going Correction** -0.10s/f (Stan) **16** Ran SP% **124.4**
Speed ratings (Par 101):102,101,101,100,99 99,98,98,98,98 97,97,95,93,84 80
CSF £147.53 CT £969.67 TOTE £29.00: £4.20, £2.40, £2.00, £3.00; EX 349.60.
Owner Mrs Julie Auletta **Bred** Wyck Hall Stud Ltd **Trained** Epsom, Surrey

FOCUS
A moderate handicap in which the principals came from off the pace. The placed horses set the standard.
Meelup(IRE) Official explanation: jockey said gelding was hampered leaving stalls
Competitor Official explanation: jockey said horse was hampered after start and lost interest

1401 HANWORTH MEDIAN AUCTION MAIDEN STKS 1m (P)
7:56 (7:57) (Class 5) 3-4-Y-O **£3,238** (£963; £481; £240) **Stalls** High

Form RPR
5-22 **1** **Scot Love (IRE)**18 1016 3-9-0 81 LDettori 4 83
(J Noseda) *sn prom: drvn into narrow advantage over 2f out: hrd pressed fr 1f out: all out* **4/7**1
360- **2** *shd* **Plum Pudding (IRE)**202 5850 3-9-0 74 RyanMoore 9 83
(R Hannon) *bit bkwd: h.d.w: chsd ldrs: rdn 2f out: r.o strly fr jst over 1f out: ev ch ins fnl f: no ex cl home* **20/1**
5- **3** *1* **Danski**186 6142 3-9-0 SebSanders 6 81+
(P J Makin) *lw: keen in mid-div: rdn and drifted lft fr 2f out: r.o wl ins fnl f: nt rch ldrs* **6/1**2
4 *2 1/2* **Equator** 3-9-0 RichardHughes 5 75+
(Mrs A J Perrett) *w'like: hld up towards rr: smooth hdwy on rails fr 4f out: rdn to chse ldrs 2f out: wknd ins fnl f* **12/1**
23- **5** *2 1/2* **Bold Act (IRE)**198 5952 4-9-13 DaneO'Neill 12 72
(H Candy) *chsd ldrs: rdn over 2f out: one pce fr over 1f out* **7/1**3
320- **6** *1/2* **Semi Detached (IRE)**201 5870 3-8-11 79 AmirQuinn(3) 10 68
(J R Boyle) *swtg: led tl over 2f out: sn rdn: wknd fnl f* **14/1**
0- **7** *5* **October Ben**258 4492 3-8-9 ChrisCatlin 8 52
(M D I Usher) *b: keen in mid-div: sme hdwy over 2f out: sn rdn: wknd over 1f out* **66/1**
56- **8** *1* **Moon On A Spoon**202 5850 3-8-9 JamieSpencer 3 49
(J R Fanshawe) *chsd ldrs: rdn over 2f out: wknd over 1f out* **14/1**
62-0 **9** *2* **Sky At Night (IRE)**119 31 3-9-0 54 JimmyFortune 11 50
(P Mitchell) *a towards rr* **66/1**
10 *1* **Helen Wood** 3-8-9 DavidKinsella 1 42
(M D I Usher) *unf: b: bhd: sme hdwy on outer 4f out: wknd over 1f out* **66/1**
11 *1 1/4* **Flying Visitor** 3-8-9 NCallan 2 39
(J M P Eustace) *leggy: mid-div: rdn 3f out: sn wknd* **66/1**
0- **12** *17* **Eathie**232 5210 4-9-13 RobbieFitzpatrick 7 —
(M J Attwater) *sn outpcd in rr* **100/1**

1m 39.39s (-2.59) **Going Correction** -0.10s/f (Stan)
WFA 3 from 4yo 13lb **12** Ran SP% **123.2**
Speed ratings (Par 103):103,102,101,99,96 96,91,90,88,87 86,69
CSF £21.81 TOTE £1.60: £1.10, £4.10, £2.20; EX 19.90.
Owner Vimal Khosla **Bred** Eclipse Thoroughbreds Ireland Ltd **Trained** Newmarket, Suffolk

FOCUS
Just an ordinary maiden and Scot Love did not have to run up to his official mark of 81 to get off the mark. However, the form looks sound enough, rated through the runner-up.

1402 SUBSCRIBE TO RACING UK H'CAP 6f (P)
8:24 (8:33) (Class 6) (0-65,65) 4-Y-O+ **£3,238** (£963; £481; £240) **Stalls** High

Form RPR
0-01 **1** **Circuit Dancer (IRE)**7 1235 6-9-4 **65** AdrianTNicholls 3 73
(D Nicholls) *b.hind: chsd ldrs: rdn over 2f out: kpt on to go 2nd ins fnl f fin 2nd, 1½l: awrdd r* **4/1**1
5104 **2** *2¼* **Desert Lover (IRE)**21 977 4-9-1 **62** ShaneKelly 8 68
(R J Price) *in tch: drvn over 1f out: kpt on one pce: fin 3rd, 1½l & 3/4l: pl 2nd* **8/1**2
240- **3** *1 1/2* **Vindication**200 5893 6-9-4 **65** (t) LDettori 6 68+
(R M H Cowell) *hld up: swtchd lft and stdy prog 2f out: sn hung rt: styd on same pce fnl f: fin 4th, plcd 3rd* **8/1**2
0143 **4** *3 1/2* **Hello Roberto**23 954 5-9-1 **62** (p) AdrianMcCarthy 11 53
(R A Harris) *chsd ldrs: rdn over 2f out: wknd fnl f: fin 5th, plcd 4th* **10/1**3
3000 **5** *1 1/4* **Hard To Catch (IRE)**1 1383 8-8-13 **63** (b) SaleemGolam(3) 1 50
(D K Ivory) *sn led: rdn 2f out: hdd over 1f out: wknd: fin 6th, plcd 5th* **25/1**
-206 **6** *8* **Cherokee Nation**85 323 5-9-3 **64** JPGadsby 5 27
(P W D'Arcy) *rrd stalls: a bhd: fin 7th, plcd 6th* **16/1**
6-00 **7** *4* **Dr Synn**9 1188 5-8-13 **65** RoryMoore(5) 2 16
(J Akehurst) *lw: sn drvn along in tch: wknd 2f out: fin 8th, plcd 7th* **12/1**
000- **8** *8* **New Proposal (IRE)**351 1785 4-8-11 **58** TPQueally 12 —
(A P Jarvis) *s.i.s: a in rr: fin 9th, plcd 8th* **20/1**
6652 **D** **Seneschal**1 1383 5-9-1 **62** JamieSpencer 4 75
(A B Haynes) *in tch: rdn and hdwy to ld over 1f out: r.o but drifted rt ins fnl f: rdn out : fin 1st, 1½l: disq (prohibit substance)* **4/1**1

1m 13.1s (-3.17) **Going Correction** -0.10s/f (Stan) **9** Ran SP% **93.5**
Speed ratings (Par 101):98,97,95,90,88 78,72,62,100
CSF £12.28 CT £60.06 TOTE £4.30: £1.20, £1.70, £1.70; EX 14.70.
Owner David Fish **Bred** Michael Staunton **Trained** Sessay, N Yorks
■ Auentraum (5/1), Val De Maal (12/1) & Savile's Delight (16/1) withdrawn (passed post after false start). R4, deduct 20p in £. Stewards Enq: Seneschal disq: prohibited substance in urine.

FOCUS
There was a false start. A modest handicap, run at a solid pace, and the form looks sound for the class.
Cherokee Nation Official explanation: jockey said gelding reared as stalls opened
Dr Synn Official explanation: vet said gelding bled from the nose
New Proposal(IRE) Official explanation: trainer said gelding finished lame

1403 KEENELAND H'CAP 1m 4f (P)
8:52 (8:56) (Class 4) (0-85,76) 3-Y-O **£6,477** (£1,927; £963; £481) **Stalls** Low

Form RPR
0-61 **1** **Cool Customer (USA)**27 894 3-8-12 **70** JamieSpencer 2 81+
(E A L Dunlop) *lw: trckd ldr: led over 2f out: shkn up over 1f out: r.o wl and a in command fnl f: comf* **8/11**1
3424 **2** *1 1/2* **Katchit (IRE)**9 1192 3-9-4 **76** TQuinn 1 85
(M R Channon) *hld up bhd ldng trio: rdn to chse wnr 2f out: kpt on but a hld fnl f* **5/2**2
40-0 **3** *8* **Hoh Bla Daa**23 948 3-8-12 **70** JimmyFortune 6 66
(S Kirk) *trckd ldng pair: rdn over 3f out: nt clr run on rails over 2f out: sn swtchd lft: one pce after* **16/1**
04-6 **4** *3 1/2* **Truly Fruitful (IRE)**20 1005 3-9-0 **72** PatCosgrave 5 63
(K R Burke) *led tl over 2f out: grad fdd* **10/1**3
6035 **5** *3* **Archimboldo (USA)**14 1077 3-9-0 **72** SebSanders 4 58
(T Wall) *t.k.h bhd ldng quartet: brief effrt over 3f out* **12/1**

2m 35.23s (-7.77) **Going Correction** -0.10s/f (Stan) **5** Ran SP% **109.1**
Speed ratings (Par 101):101,100,94,92,90
CSF £2.67 TOTE £1.60: £1.60, £1.30; EX 3.20.
Owner Gainsborough Stud **Bred** Dell Ridge Farm **Trained** Newmarket, Suffolk

FOCUS
A modest handicap, run at a sound pace, and the first two came clear. The winner should rate higher.

1404 KEMPTON PARK STKS (HERITAGE H'CAP) 7f (P)
9:20 (9:23) (Class 2) (0-105,104) 3-Y-O

£28,044 (£8,397; £4,198; £2,101; £1,048; £526) **Stalls** High

Form RPR
-110 **1** **Dingaan (IRE)**46 665 3-8-5 **88** ChrisCatlin 9 94
(A M Balding) *in tch and keen early: restrained to rr after 3f: outpcd 4f out: styd on strly fr jst over 1f out: sn veered rt: led fnl st* **16/1**
10-3 **2** *nk* **Advanced**14 1083 3-9-3 **100** DaneO'Neill 8 105+
(R Charlton) *plld hrd bhd ldrs: drvn to ld 1f out: r.o: ct fnl strides* **10/3**1

-244 **3** *2* **Secret Night**[25] [914] 3-8-5 **88** ..... JimmyQuinn 4 88
(J A R Toller) *mid-div: rdn over 2f out: hdwy over 1f out: styd on to go 3rd ins fnl f* **16/1**

34-1 **4** *½* **Critic (IRE)**[114] [70] 3-8-3 **86** ..... NickyMackay 3 85
(M L W Bell) *mid-div: rdn over 2f out: sn hung rt: styd on ins fnl f* **8/1**

-211 **5** *¾* **Total Impact**[18] [1020] 3-8-4 **87** ..... AlanMunro 5 84
(C A Cyzer) *chsd ldrs: rdn and effrt 2f out: one pce fnl f* **12/1**

16-5 **6** *1 ¾* **Manston (IRE)**[14] [1083] 3-9-7 **104** ..... LDettori 2 96
(B J Meehan) *led after 1f: rdn over 2f out: hdd 1f out: wknd* **5/1**[2]

2-12 **7** *½* **Porters (USA)**[32] [831] 3-8-7 **90** ..... RichardHughes 1 81
(R Hannon) *hld up bhd: rdn and hdwy fr over 2f out: no further imp ins fnl f* **13/2**[3]

04-0 **8** *1 ¾* **Ans Bach**[18] [1016] 3-8-7 **90** ..... (p) PhilipRobinson 7 76
(M A Jarvis) *prom early: chsd ldrs after 2f: rdn 2f out: wknd fnl f* **8/1**

30-2 **9** *hd* **Angel Voices (IRE)**[13] [1100] 3-7-12 **81** oh2 ..... HayleyTurner 6 67
(K R Burke) *hld up towards rr: hdwy and nt clr run over 2f out: wknd over 1f out* **16/1**

12-4 **10** *1 ½* **Johannes (IRE)**[14] [1083] 3-9-6 **103** ..... AdrianTNicholls 10 85
(D Nicholls) *led for 1f: prom: rdn over 2f out: wknd ovr 1f out* **10/1**

13-0 **11** *15* **Mutamarres**[18] [1016] 3-8-1 **84** ..... RoystonFfrench 11 27
(Sir Michael Stoute) *mid-div: hdwy on rails to chse ldrs over 3f out: rdn over 2f out: wknd qckly: t.o* **9/1**

1m 25.41s (-2.85) **Going Correction** -0.10s/f (Stan) **11** Ran SP% **119.7**
Speed ratings (Par 105):103,102,100,99,98 96,96,94,94,92 75
CSF £70.13 CT £912.89 TOTE £30.80: £6.00, £1.30, £4.10; EX 109.70 Place 6 £37.68, Place 5 £6.97.
Owner Lady C S Cadbury **Bred** Mrs Gill Wilson **Trained** Kingsclere, Hants

FOCUS
The inaugural running of this Heritage Handicap, which was run at a decent pace, and the form looks solid for the class with the first two coming clear.

NOTEBOOK
Dingaan(IRE), despite refusing to settle under restraint through the early parts, flew home on the outside of the pack in the home straight to mow down the eventual runner-up. He looked to hit a flat spot just after halfway, but he responded to his rider's urgings, and indeed looked to have a little up his sleeve at the finish. While he is developing into a versatile performer on this surface, he is clearly tricky, and it is hard to accurately assess just how much further improvement he has in him.
Advanced ◆, third in the Free Handicap on his seasonal bow last time, proved keen through the early parts, yet still came to have every chance in the final furlong and simply met one too good at the weights on this All-Weather bow. This must rate a slightly-improved effort and he will most likely be placed to go one better before too long. (op 3-1)
Secret Night was doing her best work at the finish and lost nothing in defeat. She looked to run right up to her mark and is a decent benchmark for this form. (op 12-1)
Critic(IRE), last seen comfortably breaking his duck at Wolverhampton in January, was not disgraced on this step-up in class and shaped as though he would come on again for this experience. He has started handicap life on a fair mark. (op 7-1)
Total Impact, searching for a third straight success on this surface, acquitted himself with credit off a 5lb higher mark but still may have been better suited by a slightly more patient ride on this first attempt at the longer trip. (op 11-1 tchd 14-1)
Manston(IRE), fifth in the Free Handicap on his comeback last time, ran close to that form on this All-Weather debut despite being on 2lb better terms with the runner-up. He looks in need of further respite from the Handicapper on this evidence. (op 6-1 tchd 13-2)
Johannes(IRE), fourth in the Free Handicap on his seasonal debut last time, was again ridden handily yet once more left the impression he needs to revert to six furlongs to be seen at his best.
T/Plt: £61.10 to a £1 stake. Pool: £48,835.60. 583.45 winning tickets. T/Qpdt: £3.20 to a £1 stake. Pool: £3,806.10. 879.30 winning tickets. TM

981 LINGFIELD (L-H)
Wednesday, May 3

OFFICIAL GOING: Turf course - good (good to firm in places); all-weather - standard
Wind: Moderate, behind Weather: Warm sunny spells

1405 CLEMATIS CONDITIONS STKS 5f (P)
2:00 (2:00) (Class 3) 2-Y-O **£7,478** (£2,239; £1,119; £560; £279) **Stalls** High

Form RPR

21 **1** **Gradetime (IRE)**[26] [908] 2-8-6 ..... NCallan 1 81
(M J Wallace) *mde all: rdn and qcknd over 2f out: hld on wl fnl f* **4/1**[3]

2 **2** *¾* **Crystal Gazer (FR)**[7] [1242] 2-8-6 ..... RichardHughes 4 79
(R Hannon) *dwlt: sn trcking ldng pair: effrt on rail ent st: drvn to chal fnl f: nt qckn fnl 50 yds* **13/8**[1]

41 **3** *1 ¼* **Fairfield Princess**[7] [1242] 2-8-10 ..... DaneO'Neill 5 78
(N A Callaghan) *in tch: outpcd and wd st: kpt on again fnl f* **15/8**[2]

4221 **4** *nk* **Hucking Hill (IRE)**[12] [1107] 2-8-11 ..... TQuinn 2 78
(J R Best) *lw: trckd wnr: hrd rdn over 1f out: one pce* **6/1**

5 *7* **Daruma (IRE)** 2-8-11 ..... RobbieFitzpatrick 3 53
(Peter Grayson) *w'like: bit bkwd: s.s: outpcd in rr thrght* **66/1**

59.56 secs (-0.22) **Going Correction** +0.075s/f (Slow) **5** Ran SP% **108.7**
Speed ratings (Par 97):104,102,100,100,89
CSF £10.68 TOTE £4.30: £1.70, £1.20; EX 8.40.
Owner Mrs E O'Leary **Bred** Noel O'Callaghan **Trained** Newmarket, Suffolk

FOCUS
A small field, but containing some speedy types with early-season form already in the book. Fillies filled the first three places.

NOTEBOOK
Gradetime(IRE), small but speedy, made full use of her rail draw under a fine ride, though she came towards the centre off the final bend. Now a winner on Fibresand and Polytrack, as well as a runner-up on turf, this tough filly looks a reliable and versatile sort and should continue to go well until scopier rivals begin to have the edge. (op 7-2)
Crystal Gazer(FR) got a dream run on the rail when the winner came off the fence turning for home, but could not quite finish the job off. However, she should have little trouble finding a maiden. (op 15-8)
Fairfield Princess became a bit unbalanced and was thrown wide on on the home turn, but for which she would have finished closer. She looked happier around right-handed Kempton, but still ran well. (tchd 2-1 and 85-40 in a place)
Hucking Hill(IRE), the most experienced in the field, ran well enough but was just outclassed in the home straight. (op 15-2 tchd 8-1)
Daruma(IRE) has plenty of speed in his pedigree at distances up to a mile, but he was a relatively cheap yearling at 6,000 guineas, and has already been gelded. This was a tough debut, but he showed enough to give connections hope at a slightly lower level. (op 50-1)

1406 AUNTIE LYNE IS 80 TODAY CONDITIONS STKS (FILLIES) 7f 140y
2:30 (2:30) (Class 3) 3-Y-O **£8,724** (£2,612; £1,306) **Stalls** Centre

Form RPR

51- **1** **Spinning Ruby**[222] [5428] 3-8-12 77 ..... NelsonDeSouza(3) 2 94
(R M Beckett) *lw: trckd ldr: led on bit 2f out: qcknd 2 l ahd 1f out: rdn fnl f: a holding runner-up* **10/3**[2]

610- **2** *½* **Arm Candy (IRE)**[200] [5904] 3-9-1 91 ..... AlanMunro 3 93
(J A R Toller) *lw: cl up in 3rd: rdn 3f out: edgd rt and wnt 2nd 2f out: clsd on wnr fnl f: a hld* **8/13**[1]

520- **3** *15* **Sensuous**[228] [5307] 3-8-12 79 ..... RyanMoore 1 53+
(R Hannon) *led and sn c to stands' rail: rdn and hdd 2f out: sn btn: eased whn no ch fnl f* **7/2**[3]

1m 30.1s (-1.36) **Going Correction** -0.125s/f (Firm) **3** Ran SP% **107.2**
Speed ratings (Par 100):101,100,85
CSF £5.94 TOTE £3.30; EX 9.00.
Owner Axis Partnership **Bred** Stowell Hill Ltd And S P Tindall **Trained** Whitsbury, Hants

FOCUS
A disappointing turnout for the money but the first two could still be improving.

NOTEBOOK
Spinning Ruby would have have been receiving a stone from the runner-up in a handicap, and appears to be improving. Though the lack of opposition makes it hard to be too effusive, this was an encouraging start to the season. (op 3-1)
Arm Candy(IRE) had the conditions of the race of her favour, and would have been conceding weight in a handicap, so this defeat has to be a shade disappointing. That said, she went down gamely and deserves another chance to show what she can do this season. (tchd 8-11)
Sensuous went out rather tamely when headed, and now needs to show she has trained on. She had only three runs as a juvenile, so there is every hope that she can do much better than this if not aimed too high. (op 4-1 tchd 9-2)

1407 V DRINKS TRANSYLVANIAN WINES PARADISE STKS (LISTED RACE) 7f 140y
3:00 (3:00) (Class 1) 4-Y-O+
£17,034 (£6,456; £3,231; £1,611; £807; £405) **Stalls** Centre

Form RPR

110- **1** **Stronghold**[235] [5107] 4-9-0 102 ..... RichardHughes 3 114+
(J H M Gosden) *h.d.w: bhd: rdn and hdwy over 2f out: led jst over 1f out: styd on wl* **7/2**[2]

220- **2** *1 ½* **Vortex**[145] [6530] 7-9-5 109 ..... (e[1]) LDettori 2 113
(Miss Gay Kelleway) *hld up in 5th: hdwy 3f out: led briefly over 1f out: nt pce of wnr fnl f* **14/1**

531- **3** *nk* **St Andrews (IRE)**[186] [6146] 6-9-3 106 ..... PhilipRobinson 5 110
(M A Jarvis) *chsd ldrs: led ins fnl 2f tl over 1f out: one pce* **5/1**[3]

121- **4** *nk* **Mostashaar (FR)**[321] [2634] 4-9-0 109 ..... RHills 7 107+
(Sir Michael Stoute) *lw: hld up in 4th: n.m.r and lost pl over 2f out: swtchd lft over 1f out: styd on* **11/10**[1]

24-4 **5** *1 ¾* **Three Wrens (IRE)**[18] [1015] 4-8-9 85 ..... DaneO'Neill 4 97
(D J Daly) *towards rr: hdwy to chse ldrs ins fnl 2f: no ex fnl f* **14/1**

100- **6** *4* **Pintle**[208] [5713] 6-8-9 79 ..... KerrinMcEvoy 1 87
(J L Spearing) *bit bkwd: led and set gd pce: hdd ins fnl 2f: sn hrd rdn and btn* **66/1**

2245 **7** *9* **Royal Storm (IRE)**[15] [1069] 7-9-0 100 ..... RyanMoore 6 70
(Mrs A J Perrett) *chsd ldr: hrd rdn 3f out: wknd 2f out: eased whn no ch 1f out* **11/1**

1m 28.8s (-2.66) **Going Correction** -0.125s/f (Firm) **7** Ran SP% **109.7**
Speed ratings (Par 111):108,106,106,105,104 100,91
CSF £44.43 TOTE £4.30: £2.70, £2.30; EX 55.30.
Owner K Abdulla **Bred** Juddmonte Farms **Trained** Newmarket, Suffolk

FOCUS
Hand timed. A solid-quality Listed race with some proven performers on show, and run at a good gallop, allowing the winner to come from last to first.

NOTEBOOK
Stronghold, a progressive handicapper last season, appreciated the strong gallop and went away to score well after being one of the first off the bridle. He looks well up to tackling higher grade this season, and a return to a mile will suit him even more. (tchd 10-3)
Vortex made an encouraging start to the season, and there was no disgrace in being beaten by the progressive winner, especially as he was conceding weight. He looks as good as ever.
St Andrews(IRE), a winner in Listed company at Newmarket last year, saw his race out well, and will be suited by a return to a mile. A good seasonal debut. (op 6-1)
Mostashaar(FR) had no luck in running and may well have finished second with a clear passage. He will be ready to win next time and should have a good season. (op Evens tchd 5-4)
Three Wrens(IRE) followed up a promising return to action in Listed company at Kempton. Though not quite up to it in the end, she ran with great credit as usual. (op 10-1)
Pintle did not do badly considering the quality of the opposition, but her attempt to burn off these rivals was never likely to succeed.

1408 V DRINKS TRANSYLVANIAN RED VODKA PAVILION STKS (LISTED RACE) 6f
3:30 (3:30) (Class 1) 3-Y-O **£17,034** (£6,456; £3,231; £1,611; £807) **Stalls** High

Form RPR

63-3 **1** **Assertive**[11] [1131] 3-9-1 106 ..... RichardHughes 1 108
(R Hannon) *lw: chsd ldr: led wl over 1f out: rdn out* **13/8**[2]

1142 **2** *1 ¼* **Kingsgate Prince (IRE)**[25] [914] 3-9-1 105 ..... GeorgeBaker 4 104
(J R Best) *hld up in 4th: rdn to chal over 1f out: nt qckn fnl f* **11/2**[3]

21-0 **3** *shd* **Strike Up The Band**[14] [1083] 3-9-4 108 ..... AdrianTNicholls 3 107
(D Nicholls) *hmpd s: in rr tl swtchd lft and hdwy over 1f out: disp 2nd fnl f: one pce* **7/1**

212- **4** *6* **Northern Empire (IRE)**[301] [3243] 3-8-11 107 ..... JimmyFortune 6 82
(B J Meehan) *lw: hmpd on rail after 100 yds: chsd ldrs tl hrd rdn and wknd over 1f out* **6/4**[1]

56-0 **5** *1* **Clare Hills (IRE)**[18] [1020] 3-8-10 97 ..... (p) PatCosgrave 2 78
(K R Burke) *wnt rt s: led and sn c to stands' rail: hdd wl over 1f out: sn wknd* **25/1**

69.03 secs (-2.64) **Going Correction** -0.125s/f (Firm) **5** Ran SP% **109.8**
Speed ratings (Par 107):112,110,110,102,100
CSF £10.56 TOTE £2.50: £1.10, £2.40; EX 12.50.
Owner A J Ilsley, K T Ivory & Lady Whent **Bred** Raffin Bloodstock **Trained** East Everleigh, Wilts
■ Stewards' Enquiry : Pat Cosgrave caution: careless riding

FOCUS
Hand timed A modest turnout for the class, but run at a decent gallop and the form appears reasonable, rated through the third.

NOTEBOOK
Assertive looked at least as effective returned to this trip, and was safely on top in the last 100 yards despite the relatively narrow margin. The Golden Jubilee at Royal Ascot is a possible target, which looks optimistic at this stage, but he has trained on well and should make his mark back in Group 3 company. (tchd 6-4 and 15-8 and 2-1 in a place)

Kingsgate Prince(IRE) has had a marvellous winter on Polytrack, and this excellent run behind a proven quality performer amply demonstrated just how much he has improved. He looks just as effective on grass these days, and it is just a question of long he can be kept going before he needs a rest. (op 9-2 tchd 6-1)
Strike Up The Band looked fitter than he did at Newmarket on his reappearance, but had still not come in his coat. Given he did not have the run of the race but still threatened to take second place, this was a creditable effort. He may have the stamina for six furlongs, but five could prove to be his tour de force for the time being. (tchd 13-2)
Northern Empire(IRE) made a fair seasonal debut, with the early interference not being significant. He is entitled to improve for the run, but needs to in order to become competitive again at this level. (op 15-8 tchd 2-1 in a place)
Clare Hills(IRE) has not recaptured last season's form in two efforts so far this year. (op 18-1 tchd 16-1 and 28-1)

1409 HESMONDS STUD SAGARO STKS (GROUP 3) 2m
4:00 (4:00) (Class 1) 4-Y-0+
£28,390 (£10,760; £5,385; £2,685; £1,345; £675) **Stalls** Low

Form RPR
401- **1** **Cover Up (IRE)**^{200} [5905] 9-9-2 108 KFallon 1 112
(Sir Michael Stoute) *trckd ldng pair: drvn along fnl 2f: styd on strly to ld fnl strides* **4/1**^{3}
102- **2** *hd* **Tungsten Strike (USA)**^{200} [5905] 5-8-13 106 RyanMoore 3 109
(Mrs A J Perrett) *led: kpt on gamely u.p fnl 2f: hdd fnl strides* **7/4**^{1}
02-1 **3** *2* **Hearthstead Wings**^{4} [1298] 4-8-10 100 (v) JoeFanning 4 106
(M Johnston) *trckd ldr: drvn level over 2f out: sustained chal tl no ex fnl 50 yds* **10/3**^{2}
32-4 **4** *1/2* **Larkwing (IRE)**^{21} [991] 5-8-13 102 SteveDrowne 6 106
(G Wragg) *lw: hld up in tch: hrd rdn over 2f out: styd on same pce* **10/3**^{2}
14-0 **5** *1 3/4* **Casual Glance**^{21} [991] 4-8-7 83 RichardHughes 2 101?
(A M Balding) *hld up towards rr: effrt in centre 2f out: hrd rdn and no imp appr fnl f* **20/1**
5-0 **6** *2 1/2* **Sworn In (USA)**^{21} [991] 5-8-13 NCallan 8 101?
(N I M Rossiter) *b: in rr: outpcd and rdn 4f out: n.d after: fin lame* **100/1**
7 *14* **Openide**^{13} 5-8-13 DaneO'Neill 7 84?
(B W Duke) *hld up in 5th: rdn 6f out: bhd fnl 4f* **100/1**

3m 34.68s (1.42) **Going Correction** -0.075s/f (Good)
WFA 4 from 5yo+ 3lb 7 Ran SP% **109.3**
Speed ratings (Par 113):93,92,91,91,90 89,82
CSF £10.38 TOTE £3.60: £4.30, £1.10; EX 8.80 Trifecta £16.40 Pool: £381.59 - 16.52 winning tickets..
Owner Ballymacoll Stud **Bred** Ballymacoll Stud Farm Ltd **Trained** Newmarket, Suffolk

FOCUS
A modest Group Three, but a heroic win for the ever-popular Cover Up, who is now reaching the veteran stage. The pace was modest for the first mile and a half and the race is rated around the principals.

NOTEBOOK
Cover Up(IRE) did not have the race run in his favour, since the pace was modest and this track would be sharper than ideal. In the circumstances, it was a heroic performance under a never-say-die ride from Fallon, confirming him as one of the most popular horses in training and a strong contender again in the Queen Alexandra at Royal Ascot. (op 3-1)
Tungsten Strike(USA) did everything but win and deserves to get home in front in similar races this season. Just how many battles like this he can take remains to be seen, but this game performance merits full marks. (op 5-2)
Hearthstead Wings, happy to take a lead from the runner-up, was engaged in an epic battle with him all the way up the home straight, only to crack in the last 50 yards. A game effort. (op 5-2)
Larkwing(IRE) kept staying on without ever looking likely to quicken enough to take a serious hand. The stiffer the test, the better for him this season. (op 4-1)
Casual Glance looked very fit but faced a tough task and, though doing her best, was never quite up to it. (tchd 16-1)
Sworn In(USA) was thrown in at the deep end but, after looking likely to be beaten some way early in the straight, kept on reasonably well in the final quarter-mile. It was a pity he should finish lame but, if recovering soon, he can make his mark back in lesser company. Official explanation: vet said horse finished lame in front

1410 DEREK TAYLOR BIRTHDAY CELEBRATION ROSE STKS (H'CAP) 1m (P)
4:30 (4:30) (Class 4) (0-85,83) 4-Y-0+ **£6,477** (£1,927; £963; £481) **Stalls** High

Form RPR
1121 **1** **Fajr (IRE)**^{25} [915] 4-8-11 76 LDettori 7 85+
(Miss Gay Kelleway) *b: b.hind: lw: chsd ldrs on outside: effrt 2f out: rdn to ld fnl 50 yds* **7/4**^{1}
2510 **2** *nk* **Star Magnitude (USA)**^{11} [1133] 5-9-1 80 TQuinn 3 88
(S Dow) *led 1f: styd w ldr: drvn to ld ins fnl f: hdd and nt qckn fnl 50 yds* **7/1**
1103 **3** *nk* **Merrymadcap (IRE)**^{8} [1207] 4-8-12 77 FrancisNorton 6 84
(M Blanshard) *hld up in midfield: rdn and r.o fnl 2f: nvr nrr* **10/1**
1350 **4** *1/2* **Farewell Gift**^{8} [1207] 5-8-7 75 (b) StephaneBreux$^{(3)}$ 4 81
(R Hannon) *led after 1f and dictated stdy tempo: qcknd over 2f out: hdd and one pce ins fnl f* **11/1**
2310 **5** *nk* **Glad Big (GER)**^{23} [946] 4-9-3 82 SteveDrowne 5 87
(J A Osborne) *hld up in midfield: effrt on ins ent st: kpt on fnl f* **4/1**^{2}
0200 **6** *1* **Trifti**^{12} [1111] 5-9-4 83 NCallan 1 86
(C A Cyzer) *dwlt: sn rdn up to trck ldrs on rail: hrd rdn wl over 1f out: sn outpcd* **9/1**
25-4 **7** *shd* **Dry Ice (IRE)**^{12} [1112] 4-9-1 80 DaneO'Neill 2 83
(H Candy) *hld up in tch: effrt ent st: no ex fnl f* **11/2**^{3}
8 *1/2* **Return In Style (IRE)**^{336} 5-8-10 75 RHills 8 77
(J W Hills) *t.k.h towards rr: rdn 2f out: styd on fnl f* **50/1**
4-00 **9** *2 1/2* **Asharon**^{12} [1112] 4-8-13 78 RichardHughes 9 74
(C E Brittain) *stdd in rr: shkn up and nt trble ldrs fnl 2f* **40/1**

1m 40.28s (0.85) **Going Correction** +0.075s/f (Slow) 9 Ran SP% **116.1**
Speed ratings (Par 105):98,97,97,96,96 95,95,95,92
CSF £14.81 CT £96.74 TOTE £2.30: £1.10, £3.10, £4.20; EX 17.80 Trifecta £87.30 Pool: £461.13 - 3.75 winning tickets..
Owner The New Dawn Partnership **Bred** Shadwell Estate Company Limited **Trained** Exning, Suffolk

FOCUS
A routine handicap on Polytrack run at a muddling tempo, with Farewell Gift steadying it up in front. The form looks reasonable with the first three as the guide.
Star Magnitude(USA) Official explanation: jockey said gelding hung left final furlong
Asharon Official explanation: jockey said gelding had no more to give

1411 LINGFIELD-RACECOURSE.CO.UK H'CAP 6f (P)
5:00 (5:00) (Class 5) (0-75,75) 3-Y-0 **£3,238** (£963; £481; £240) **Stalls** Low

Form RPR
1530 **1** **Garstang**^{21} [980] 3-8-12 69 (b) RobbieFitzpatrick 2 79
(Peter Grayson) *mde all: qcknd clr 2f out: drvn to hold on fnl 100 yds* **7/1**
50-3 **2** *1* **Tous Les Deux**^{8} [1208] 3-9-4 75 StephenCarson 4 82
(R F Johnson Houghton) *chsd ldng pair: wnt 2nd over 1f out: clsd on wnr fnl f: jst hld* **4/1**^{2}
61-3 **3** *3* **Guilded Warrior**^{22} [969] 3-8-12 69 FergusSweeney 7 67
(W S Kittow) *wd: hdwy to chse ldrs over 3f out: one pce fnl 2f* **11/2**^{3}
520- **4** *hd* **Imperial Gain (USA)**^{203} [5836] 3-9-1 72 TQuinn 1 69
(W R Swinburn) *in rr: outpcd and rdn 1/2-way: styd on wl fnl f* **17/2**
2322 **5** *1/2* **Gavarnie Beau (IRE)**^{8} [1208] 3-8-13 70 FrancisNorton 5 66
(M Blanshard) *chsd wnr over 3f: rdn and btn whn n.m.r jst over 1f out* **11/4**^{1}
3210 **6** *1 1/4* **Cool Sting (IRE)**^{8} [1208] 3-9-4 75 LDettori 3 67
(A M Balding) *hld up towards rr: mod effrt 2f out: nt pce to chal* **11/2**^{3}
00-0 **7** *4* **Catspraddle (USA)**^{7} [1241] 3-9-1 72 RichardHughes 8 52
(R Hannon) *stdd s: sn in tch: lost pl over 2f out: n.d after* **11/1**
2610 **8** *1 3/4* **Sigismundus (IRE)**^{34} [803] 3-8-12 72 AmirQuinn$^{(3)}$ 6 47
(J R Boyle) *spd over 3f: sn lost pl* **20/1**

1m 12.43s (-0.38) **Going Correction** +0.075s/f (Slow) 8 Ran SP% **113.6**
Speed ratings (Par 99):105,103,99,99,98 97,91,89
CSF £34.57 CT £166.95 TOTE £10.50: £2.60, £1.90, £2.40; EX 44.00 Trifecta £157.60 Pool: £355.33 - 1.60 winning tickets. Place 6 £197.25, Place 5 £107.48.
Owner The Foulrice Twenty **Bred** Mrs S E Barclay **Trained** Formby, Lancs
■ Stewards' Enquiry : Stephen Carson caution: careless riding

FOCUS
An ordinary three-year-old handicap on Polytrack rated through the third and fourth to form.
T/Plt: £120.50 to a £1 stake. Pool: £39,187.05. 237.35 winning tickets. T/Qpdt: £19.70 to a £1 stake. Pool: £3,205.10. 119.90 winning tickets. LM

1136 NOTTINGHAM (L-H)
Wednesday, May 3

OFFICIAL GOING: Good (good to firm in places) changing to good to firm after race 3 (3.10)
Wind: Light, against Weather: Sunny

1412 BESTWOOD PARK MAIDEN STKS 6f 15y
2:10 (2:14) (Class 5) 3-Y-0 **£3,238** (£963; £481; £240) **Stalls** High

Form RPR
24-2 **1** **Mr Sandicliffe**^{13} [1089] 3-9-3 90 (p) JamieSpencer 5 74
(B W Hills) *chsd ldr: led wl over 1f out: sn rdn: jst hld on* **2/1**^{2}
22- **2** *shd* **Storm On The Run (IRE)**^{205} [5801] 3-9-3 PatDobbs 11 74+
(R Hannon) *dwlt: hld up: hdwy over 2f out: rdn and swtchd lft ins fnl f: r.o* **11/8**^{1}
3 *1* **Cape** 3-8-12 OscarUrbina 6 66
(J R Fanshawe) *dwlt: hld up: hdwy over 2f out: styd on* **20/1**
4 *3 1/2* **Falmassim** 3-9-3 NickyMackay 9 61+
(L M Cumani) *hld up: r.o ins fnl f: nvr nrr* **14/1**
3 **5** *1 3/4* **Spinning**^{85} [331] 3-9-3 PaulFessey 4 55
(T D Barron) *hld up in tch: effrt and nt clr run over 1f out: nvr trbld ldrs* **20/1**
6 *1/2* **Tender Process (IRE)** 3-9-3 DarryllHolland 2 54
(E S McMahon) *s.s: hld up: hdwy and hung lft over 1f out: wknd ins fnl f* **33/1**
0-6 **7** *2* **Free Silver (IRE)**^{12} [1110] 3-8-12 PaulDoe 8 43
(Miss K B Boutflower) *hld up: nvr trbld ldrs* **50/1**
000 **8** *nk* **Bournonville**^{64} [538] 3-9-0 40 (t) SaleemGolam$^{(3)}$ 10 47?
(J Ryan) *chsd ldrs: rdn over 2f out: wknd over 1f out* **200/1**
000- **9** *5* **At The Bar**^{206} [5768] 3-9-3 50 VinceSlattery 3 32
(A J Chamberlain) *sn led: hdd wl over 1f out: edgd rt: sn wknd* **200/1**
3-2 **10** *3 1/2* **Macademy Royal (USA)**^{25} [916] 3-9-3 JohnEgan 12 22
(H Morrison) *prom: rdn and wknd over 1f out* **6/1**^{3}

1m 15.6s (0.60) **Going Correction** -0.025s/f (Good) 10 Ran SP% **111.8**
Speed ratings (Par 99):95,94,93,88,86 85,83,82,76,71
CSF £4.51 TOTE £3.00: £1.10, £1.20, £4.30; EX 5.30.
Owner Henry Barton **Bred** Rosyground Stud **Trained** Lambourn, Berks

FOCUS
A fair three-year-old maiden, run at a solid pace, and the first three came clear. However, the bare form is only ordinary.

1413 NOTTINGHAMSHIRE CHAMBER OF COMMERCE AND INDUSTRY FILLIES' H'CAP 6f 15y
2:40 (2:42) (Class 5) (0-70,67) 3-Y-0+ **£3,886** (£1,156; £577; £288) **Stalls** High

Form RPR
156- **1** **Daniella**^{229} [5277] 4-9-12 65 (p) FrancisFerris 6 78
(Rae Guest) *mde all far side: rdn over 1f out: r.o: 1st of 6 that side* **12/1**
3134 **2** *1 1/2* **Riquewihr**^{12} [1124] 6-9-13 66 (p) TomEaves 1 74
(J S Wainwright) *chsd wnr far side: rdn over 1f out: styd on: 2nd of 6 that side* **8/1**
00-0 **3** *1 1/2* **Tagula Bay (IRE)**^{29} [864] 4-9-9 62 FergalLynch 4 66
(T D Easterby) *racd far side: chsd ldrs: rdn over 1f out: styd on: 3rd of 6 that side* **16/1**
0-12 **4** *1 1/4* **Dorn Dancer (IRE)**^{13} [1102] 4-9-11 64 JamieSpencer 8 64+
(D W Barker) *swtchd to r stands' side: hld up: hdwy over 2f out: led that side 1f out: no ch w far side: 1st of 9 that side* **9/2**^{2}
63-0 **5** *1 3/4* **Cerulean Rose**^{16} [1047] 7-10-0 67 TedDurcan 5 62
(A W Carroll) *racd far side: hld up: styd on ins fnl f: nvr nrr: 4th of 6 that side* **14/1**
00-4 **6** *1 1/4* **Desertina (IRE)**^{13} [1102] 4-9-0 53 oh3 HayleyTurner 7 44
(R M Whitaker) *racd far side: chsd ldrs: rdn over 2f out: wknd over 1f out: 4th of 6 that side* **16/1**
0-00 **7** *3/4* **African Gift**^{11} [1151] 4-9-8 61 EddieAhern 9 50+
(J G Given) *racd stands' side: hld up: hdwy 2f out: rdn over 1f out: wknd ins fnl f: 2nd of 9 that side* **15/2**^{3}
3-66 **8** *1 1/4* **Angelofthenorth**^{13} [1102] 4-9-10 63 (b) IanMongan 3 48
(J D Bethell) *racd far side: hld up: rdn over 2f out: sn wknd: last of 6 that side* **14/1**
0-00 **9** *1 3/4* **Rancho Cucamonga (IRE)**^{13} [1102] 4-9-10 63 (b) PaulFessey 16 43+
(T D Barron) *racd stands' side: chsd ldrs: rdn over 1f out: sn wknd: 3rd of 9 that side* **15/2**^{3}
000- **10** *1 3/4* **Mis Chicaf (IRE)**^{231} [5222] 5-9-9 65 (t) SaleemGolam$^{(3)}$ 15 39+
(Robert Gray) *led stands' side over 4f: sn wknd: 4th of 9 that side* **20/1**
0500 **11** *1 1/2* **Danethorpe Lady (IRE)**^{1} [1391] 4-8-11 53 oh13 PatrickMathers$^{(3)}$ 11 23+
(D Shaw) *racd stands' side: mid-div: rdn 1/2-way: edgd lft and wknd over 1f out: 5th of 9 that side* **100/1**

412- **12** ¾ **Portmeirion**[229] 5277 5-9-11 **64** .... MartinDwyer 13 32+
(S C Williams) *racd stands' side: chsd ldrs: led that gp over 1f out: sn rdn and hdd: wknd qckly: 6th of 9 that side* **7/2**[1]

0-00 **13** 2 **Ruby's Dream**[7] 1243 4-9-1 **54** .... (p) JohnEgan 17 16+
(J M Bradley) *racd stands' side: chsd ldrs: wkng whn nt clr run over 1f out: 7th of 9 that side* **22/1**

00-0 **14** 9 **Maayafushi**[7] 1234 3-8-4 **53** oh1 .... NickyMackay 14 —+
(Micky Hammond) *racd stands' side: a in rr: 8th of 9 that side* **50/1**

/00- **15** 14 **Ms Polly Garter**[352] 1764 4-9-0 **53** oh18 .... ChrisCatlin 10 —+
(J M Bradley) *racd stands' side: sn outpcd: last of 9 that side* **66/1**

1m 14.14s (-0.86) **Going Correction** -0.025s/f (Good)
WFA 3 from 4yo+ 10lb **15** Ran SP% **121.4**
Speed ratings (Par 100):104,102,100,98,96 94,93,91,89,87 85,84,81,69,50
CSF £100.86 CT £1010.71 TOTE £15.50: £4.40, £2.50, £5.30; EX 175.30.
Owner Ms E Reffo & B Cooper **Bred** Amethyst Stud **Trained** Newmarket, Suffolk

FOCUS
A moderate sprint, which saw those drawn low at a clear advantage, and the overall form should be treated with caution.
Maayafushi Official explanation: jockey said filly was outpaced

1414 COLWICK PARK H'CAP 5f 13y
3:10 (3:13) (Class 6) (0-60,60) 4-Y-0+ **£2,730** (£806; £403) **Stalls** High

Form RPR

40-6 **1** **Lady Algarhoud (FR)**[12] 4 4-8-12 **53** .... MartinDwyer 3 63
(D K Ivory) *racd far side: chsd ldr: led and hung rt over 1f out: rdn and bmpd ins fnl f: hdd post: 2nd of 10 that side: fin 2nd, shd: awrdd r* **10/1**

05-0 **2** shd **Drumming Party (USA)**[26] 903 4-8-11 **55** .... (t) NeilChalmers(3) 10 65+
(A M Balding) *racd far side: a.p: chal edgd lft and bmpd ins ins fnl f: r.o to ld post: 1st of 10 that side: fin 1st,shd: plcd 2nd* **22/1**

340- **3** 1¼ **Never Without Me**[156] 6447 6-9-4 **59** .... LPKeniry 2 65
(J F Coupland) *racd far side: chsd ldrs: rdn over 1f out: styd on: 3rd of 10 that side* **10/1**

056- **4** ½ **Tadlil**[258] 4495 4-9-4 **59** .... TomEaves 1 63+
(J M Bradley) *racd far side: hld up: r.o and nt clr run ins fnl f: nrst fin: 4th of 10 that side* **20/1**

4541 **5** 1¼ **Cashel Mead**[7] 1243 6-9-5 **60** 6ex .... JamieSpencer 14 65+
(J L Spearing) *racd stands' side: dwlt: hld up: hdwy to ld that gp over 1f out: no ch w far side: 1st of 7 that gp* **7/1**[1]

0005 **6** shd **Namir (IRE)**[21] 986 4-9-3 **58** .... (v) EddieAhern 4 57
(Stef Liddiard) *racd far side: prom: rdn over 1f out: styd on: 5th of 10 that side* **8/1**[3]

2000 **7** nk **Borzoi Maestro**[23] 951 5-9-3 **58** .... (v[1]) HayleyTurner 6 56
(M Wellings) *led far side over 3f: no ex ins fnl f: 6th of 10 that side* **50/1**

0030 **8** shd **Monte Major (IRE)**[33] 824 5-8-10 **54** .... (v) PatrickMathers(3) 8 51
(D Shaw) *racd far side: dwlt and hmpd s: hld up: running on whn hmpd ins fnl f: nvr able to chal: 7th of 10 that side* **33/1**

03-0 **9** ¾ **Pyramid**[10] 1165 4-8-13 **54** .... (b[1]) JohnEgan 16 55+
(P L Gilligan) *racd stands' side: mid-div: hung lft over 2f out: sn rdn: nt clr run over 1f out: r.o ins fnl f: 2nd of 7 that side* **25/1**

0-05 **10** nk **Cosmic Destiny (IRE)**[3] 1315 4-9-4 **59** .... TPQueally 5 53
(E F Vaughan) *racd far side: chsd ldrs: rdn over 1f out: wknd ins fnl f: 8th of 10 that gp* **7/1**[1]

-023 **11** hd **Mynd**[13] 1102 6-8-9 **57** .... MichaelJStainton(7) 17 56+
(R M Whitaker) *racd stands' side: mid-div: hdwy 2f out: rdn over 1f out: wknd ins fnl f: 3rd of 7 that side* **15/2**[2]

010- **12** ½ **My Rascal (IRE)**[205] 5793 4-8-12 **56** .... (p) JasonEdmunds(3) 7 47
(J Balding) *racd far side: chsd ldrs: rdn over 1f out: no ex: 9th of 10 that side* **20/1**

0000 **13** 1½ **I Wish**[5] 1273 8-8-12 **53** .... PaulFitzsimons 13 45+
(Miss J R Tooth) *racd stands' side: prom: rdn over 2f out: wknd fnl f: 4th of 7 that side* **20/1**

6-00 **14** hd **Pro Tempore**[23] 954 4-8-11 **52** .... ChrisCatlin 12 43+
(David Pinder) *led stands' side over 3f: wknd fnl f: 5th of 7 that side* **14/1**

0-03 **15** 1½ **Vague Star (ITY)**[30] 858 4-9-3 **58** .... (b) RobertHavlin 9 38
(R Ingram) *wnt lft s: hld up: a in rr: last of 10 that side* **11/1**

3140 **16** 1¾ **Mambazo**[8] 1209 4-8-13 **57** .... (e) SaleemGolam(3) 15 36+
(S C Williams) *racd stands' side: hld up: swtchd lft and sme hdwy over 1f out: sn wknd: 6th of 7 that side* **12/1**

050- **17** nk **Heavens Walk**[258] 4507 5-8-12 **53** .... (t) DarryllHolland 11 31+
(P J Makin) *racd stands' side: trckd ldrs: rdn and ev ch that gp over 1f out: sn wknd: last of 7 that side* **16/1**

60.59 secs (-1.21) **Going Correction** -0.025s/f (Good) **17** Ran SP% **122.0**
Speed ratings (Par 101):107,108,105,105,103 102,102,102,101,100 100,99,97,96,94 91,91
CSF £217.82 CT £2334.81 TOTE £9.30: £2.30, £6.60, £3.60, £5.40; EX 372.50.
Owner P A Urban **Bred** S Hope **Trained** Radlett, Herts

FOCUS
A weak sprint, which again saw those drawn low at a real advantage, but the form looks reasonable.
My Rascal(IRE) Official explanation: jockey said gelding lost its action

1415 BUY YOUR TICKETS ONLINE @NOTTINGHAMRACECOURSE.CO.UK H'CAP 1m 6f 15y
3:40 (3:41) (Class 6) (0-60,60) 4-Y-0+ **£2,388** (£705; £352) **Stalls** Low

Form RPR

1135 **1** **Mister Completely (IRE)**[17] 482 5-8-6 46 .... EdwardCreighton(3) 17 56+
(Miss Sheena West) *led after 1f: clr over 1f out: rdn out* **12/1**

P026 **2** 3½ **Cemgraft**[9] 1199 5-8-8 48 .... (tp) RichardThomas(3) 7 53
(A J Lidderdale) *hld up: hdwy and hung lft fr over 2f out: nt rch wnr* **22/1**

4066 **3** hd **Smoothie (IRE)**[8] 1204 8-8-13 50 .... ChrisCatlin 9 55
(Ian Williams) *dwlt: hld up: hdwy over 1f out: nrst fin* **14/1**

00-3 **4** 1 **Senor Set (GER)**[8] 1219 5-8-8 45 .... MartinDwyer 10 50+
(J Pearce) *hld up: rdn 1/2-way: hdwy 5f out: outpcd 3f out: rallied and nt clr run over 1f out: styd on* **7/1**[3]

0/0 **5** nk **Lets Try Again (IRE)**[9] 966 9-9-1 52 .... RobertHavlin 1 55
(R A Farrant) *hld up: hdwy over 7f out: chsd wnr 2f out: sn rdn: no ex ins fnl f* **33/1**

006- **6** 3 **Calfraz**[36] 3630 4-8-12 50 .... NickyMackay 8 49
(Micky Hammond) *hld up: rdn over 4f out: nvr nrr* **20/1**

00-4 **7** nk **Ruling Reef**[8] 1204 4-8-13 51 .... HayleyTurner 3 50
(M D I Usher) *prom: rdn over 3f out: wknd over 1f out* **28/1**

60-5 **8** nk **Hugs Destiny (IRE)**[7] 1233 5-9-2 53 .... DarryllHolland 6 51
(M A Barnes) *mid-div: hdwy 9f out: rdn over 3f out: wknd over 1f out* **14/1**

0040 **9** shd **Aristi (IRE)**[9] 1184 5-8-11 53 .... (p) RoryMoore(5) 13 51
(M Quinn) *sn chsng wnr: rdn over 3f out: wknd wl over 1f out* **20/1**

000- **10** ¾ **Gidam Gidam (IRE)**[12] 5892 4-8-12 50 .... (p) DaleGibson 12 47
(J Mackie) *chsd ldrs: rdn over 3f out: wknd 2f out* **13/2**[2]

0-34 **11** ¾ **My Legal Eagle (IRE)**[11] 1138 12-8-7 51 .... LiamJones(7) 11 47
(E G Bevan) *chsd ldrs: rdn over 4f out: wknd 2f out* **11/1**

0022 **12** shd **Robbie Can Can**[11] 1138 7-8-13 57 .... JackDean(7) 4 53
(A W Carroll) *hld up: rdn over 3f out: styng on whn hmpd ins fnl f: n.d* **8/1**

003- **13** 1 **Primondo (IRE)**[254] 4635 4-9-7 59 .... JamieSpencer 2 53
(J R Fanshawe) *hld up: rdn over 3f out: n.d* **5/1**[1]

4302 **14** 1 **Jackie Kiely**[6] 1256 5-9-9 60 .... J-PGuillambert 15 53
(P Howling) *hld up in tch: rdn over 3f out: wknd over 2f out* **10/1**

6406 **15** 13 **Real Chief (IRE)**[16] 675 8-8-13 50 .... FrancisFerris 16 25
(Miss M E Rowland) *sn led: hdd after 1f: remained handy tl wknd over 4f out* **100/1**

05-0 **16** 6 **Harlestone Linn**[22] 966 4-9-0 52 .... IanMongan 14 18
(J L Dunlop) *dwlt: hld up: rdn over 4f out: sn wknd* **10/1**

3m 6.65s (-0.45) **Going Correction** -0.025s/f (Good)
WFA 4 from 5yo+ 1lb **16** Ran SP% **122.4**
Speed ratings (Par 101):100,98,97,97,97 95,95,95,95,94 94,94,93,92,85 82
CSF £264.17 CT £3716.68 TOTE £21.20: £3.20, £8.60, £5.60, £1.10; EX 355.60.
Owner Michael Moriarty **Bred** Eamonn Griffin **Trained** Falmer, E Sussex
■ Stewards' Enquiry : Francis Ferris four-day ban: careles riding (May 15-18)

FOCUS
A moderate staying handicap, run at an even pace and the form is sound, with the winner value for slightly further.

1416 CARLTON H'CAP 1m 54y
4:10 (4:10) (Class 5) (0-70,70) 3-Y-0 **£3,238** (£963; £481; £240) **Stalls** Centre

Form RPR

24-5 **1** **Luckylover**[29] 880 3-9-2 **68** .... TPQueally 10 74
(M G Quinlan) *chsd ldrs: led over 1f out: sn rdn: hung rt ins fnl f: all out* **11/2**[2]

033- **2** shd **Catbang (IRE)**[138] 6591 3-8-11 **63** .... JamieSpencer 9 68
(N A Callaghan) *a.p: rdn and ev ch ins fnl f: hung rt: styd on* **5/2**[1]

4502 **3** 1½ **Rebellious Spirit**[11] 1141 3-9-3 **69** .... DarrenWilliams 17 74+
(P W Hiatt) *hld up: hdwy over 2f out: nt clr run over 1f out: styd on* **7/1**[3]

00-5 **4** nk **Temperance (IRE)**[12] 1114 3-9-3 **69** .... MartinDwyer 1 70
(S Kirk) *chsd ldrs: led 7f out: rdn and hdd over 2f out: stl ev ch tl no ex ins fnl f* **10/1**

24-0 **5** 1¾ **Bold Cross (IRE)**[16] 1049 3-9-4 **70** .... MichaelTebbutt 4 67
(E G Bevan) *dwlt: hld up: hdwy over 2f out: rdn and hung lft over 1f out: sn ev ch: wknd wl ins fnl f* **10/1**

0-00 **6** 1¼ **Croft (IRE)**[16] 1048 3-9-1 **67** .... EddieAhern 5 61
(J W Hills) *chsd ldrs: rdn over 2f out: styd on same pce appr fnl f* **12/1**

300- **7** 1½ **Tiptoeing**[186] 6150 3-8-11 **66** .... SaleemGolam(3) 6 57
(M H Tompkins) *mid-div: rdn over 2f out: nvr trbld ldrs* **14/1**

025- **8** ¾ **Lady Lochinver (IRE)**[169] 6360 3-8-4 **56** .... NickyMackay 2 45
(Micky Hammond) *hld up: hdwy over 3f out: wknd over 1f out* **15/2**

3065 **9** 1½ **Salisbury World (IRE)**[81] 378 3-8-8 **60** .... LPKeniry 3 46
(J F Coupland) *dwlt: hld up: rdn over 2f out: n.d* **25/1**

50-0 **10** 1¼ **Paddy Moon**[11] 1141 3-8-6 **58** .... NeilPollard 16 41
(J G Given) *led 1f: chsd ldrs: led over 2f out: rdn and hdd over 1f out: wknd fnl f* **66/1**

056- **11** 3½ **Blandford Flyer**[173] 6316 3-8-11 **63** .... TedDurcan 14 38
(W R Swinburn) *hld up: rdn over 3f out: n.d* **16/1**

000- **12** hd **Thomas A Beckett (IRE)**[149] 6501 3-8-12 **64** .... IanMongan 11 38
(P R Chamings) *hld up: plld hrd: hdwy over 3f out: rdn over 2f out: sn wknd* **40/1**

3-00 **13** ½ **Puteri Sas (IRE)**[12] 1118 3-8-12 **64** .... JosedeSouza 12 37
(P F I Cole) *mid-div: rdn over 3f out: sn wknd* **18/1**

1m 45.61s (-0.79) **Going Correction** -0.025s/f (Good) **13** Ran SP% **119.7**
Speed ratings (Par 99):102,101,100,100,98 97,95,94,93,92 88,88,87
CSF £19.28 CT £104.18 TOTE £7.20: £2.00, £1.60, £2.10; EX 27.50.
Owner Giuliano Manfredini **Bred** Shutford Stud **Trained** Newmarket, Suffolk

FOCUS
The bare form of this handicap is just modest, but a few of these were unexposed and it looked a reasonable enough race for the grade and should prove sound.

1417 NOTTINGHAM RACECOURSE CONFERENCE CENTRE MAIDEN FILLIES' STKS (DIV I) 1m 54y
4:40 (4:41) (Class 5) 3-Y-0 **£4,210** (£1,252; £625; £312) **Stalls** Centre

Form RPR

4- **1** **Harvest Queen (IRE)**[239] 5032 3-9-0 .... EddieAhern 2 79+
(P J Makin) *plld hrd: led: hdd over 6f out: chsd ldr: led over 2f out: clr over 1f out: eased ins fnl f* **14/1**

2 5 **Rose Lady (IRE)** 3-9-0 .... TedDurcan 7 65
(M R Channon) *chsd ldrs: led over 3f out: rdn and hdd over 2f out: styd on same pce appr fnl f* **12/1**

3 ½ **Dear Gracie (IRE)** 3-9-0 .... JamieSpencer 6 63
(J R Fanshawe) *hld up: hdwy over 1f out: edgd lft: nrst fin* **10/1**[3]

4 shd **Adraaj (USA)** 3-9-0 .... MartinDwyer 10 63
(E A L Dunlop) *hld up: hdwy 5f out: rdn over 2f out: carried hd awkwardly over 1f out: kep on* **12/1**

0 **5** nk **Panic Stations**[21] 981 3-9-0 .... HayleyTurner 1 62
(M L W Bell) *chsd ldrs: rdn over 2f out: sn outpcd* **25/1**

3- **6** shd **Miss Thailand**[231] 5230 3-9-0 .... DarryllHolland 4 62+
(G Wragg) *hld up: hdwy over 3f out: nt clr run over 2f out: swtchd rt and sn rdn: no ch whn nt clr run ins fnl f* **4/7**[1]

00- **7** 4 **Valerie**[172] 6318 3-9-0 .... NickyMackay 13 53
(L M Cumani) *hld up: nvr nrr* **9/1**[2]

0-00 **8** ½ **Silvabella (IRE)**[65] 534 3-9-0 30 .... (p) FrankieMcDonald 8 52?
(D Haydn Jones) *chsd ldrs: led over 6f out: rdn and hdd over 3f out: wknd wl over 1f out* **100/1**

9 nk **Gaze** 3-9-0 .... PaulDoe 3 51+
(W Jarvis) *s.s: outpcd* **28/1**

0- **10** hd **Platinum Hound (IRE)**[228] 5315 3-9-0 .... RobertHavlin 9 51
(H Morrison) *hld up: hdwy 1/2-way: wknd 2f out* **66/1**

0 **11** 1 **Prophet Preacher (IRE)**[13] 1101 3-8-7 .... StacyRenwick(7) 5 48
(M J Attwater) *hld up: hdwy over 3f out: sn wknd* **100/1**

0- **12** 1¼ **Prima Markova**[159] 6417 3-9-0 .... RoystonFfrench 12 46
(D J Daly) *hld up: a in rr* **66/1**

13 1¼ **Sophie James** 3-9-0 .... TPQueally 11 43
(M G Quinlan) *hld up: hdwy over 3f out: wknd over 2f out* **50/1**

1m 47.84s (1.44) **Going Correction** -0.025s/f (Good) **13** Ran SP% **119.0**
Speed ratings (Par 96):91,86,85,85,85 85,81,80,80,80 79,77,76
CSF £163.60 TOTE £14.30: £3.00, £2.60, £2.20; EX 141.90.

Owner Bakewell Bloodstock Ltd **Bred** Bakewell Bloodstock **Trained** Ogbourne Maisey, Wilts

FOCUS

A modest maiden and, even allowing for a steady early pace, the winning time was poor - over three seconds slower than the second division, and over two seconds slower than the mile handicap for three-year-olds earlier on the card. As a result the form is not solid.

Miss Thailand Official explanation: jockey said filly was denied a clear run

Gaze Official explanation: jockey said filly was slowly away

1418 NOTTINGHAM RACECOURSE CONFERENCE CENTRE MAIDEN FILLIES' STKS (DIV II) 1m 54y

5:10 (5:13) (Class 5) 3-Y-O **£4,210** (£1,252; £625; £312) **Stalls** Centre

Form	Pos	Dist	Horse / Trainer / Comment	Jockey	SP	RPR
022-	1		**Princess Nada**[205] [5788] 3-9-0 77 (L M Cumani) *hld up: hdwy over 3f out: led over 1f out: r.o: eased nr fin*	NickyMackay 6	7/1[3]	82+
-	2	1 ¾	**Caressed** 3-9-0 (J R Fanshawe) *hld up: hdwy over 2f out: hung lft fnl f: styd on*	JamieSpencer 1	14/1	78
2-	3	¾	**Heather Moor (USA)**[188] [6120] 3-9-0 (Sir Michael Stoute) *trckd ldr: racd keenly: led over 3f out: hdd over 1f out: styd on same pce*	TedDurcan 11	3/1[2]	76
	4	2 ½	**Dallma (IRE)** 3-9-0 (C E Brittain) *prom: chsdv ldr over 2f out: sn rdn: styd on same pce appr fnl f*	DarryllHolland 10	40/1	71
	5	6	**True West (USA)** 3-9-0 (J Noseda) *hld up: rdn over 2f out: sn edgd lft: nvr trbld ldrs*	TPQueally 2	33/1	57+
	6	¾	**Inchmahome** 3-9-0 (G Wragg) *s.s: hld up: nvr nrr*	JohnEgan 13	25/1	55
4	7	1	**Star Jasmine**[22] [971] 3-9-0 (M L W Bell) *hld up: effrt over 2f out: n.d*	HayleyTurner 3	33/1	53
30	8	¾	**Capriolla**[12] [1114] 3-9-0 (P F I Cole) *dwlt: hld up: hdwy over 3f out: wknd over 2f out*	JosedeSouza 12	66/1	51
23-	9	1	**Tawaafud**[225] [5391] 3-9-0 (B W Hills) *prom: pushed along over 5f out: sn edgd lft: wknd and eased wl over 1f out*	MartinDwyer 8	10/11[1]	49+
0	10	5	**Rada (IRE)**[12] [1119] 3-9-0 (R Hannon) *led after 1f: rdn and hdd over 3f out: wknd over 2f out*	PatDobbs 5	80/1	37
0	11	7	**Sujana (USA)**[14] [1085] 3-9-0 (B J Meehan) *led 1f: chsd ldrs: pushed along and hmpd 5f out: wknd over 2f out*	EddieAhern 4	16/1	21
0	12	6	**Hippolyte (USA)**[11] [1153] 3-9-0 (J G Given) *hld up: a in rr*	NeilPollard 9	100/1	7

1m 44.61s (-1.79) **Going Correction** -0.025s/f (Good) **12 Ran SP% 118.3**

Speed ratings (Par 96):107,105,104,102,96 95,94,93,92,87 80,74

CSF £93.04 TOTE £7.10: £2.30, £2.80, £1.40; EX 61.80.

Owner Sheikh Mohammed Obaid Al Maktoum **Bred** Darley **Trained** Newmarket, Suffolk

FOCUS

This looked a better maiden that the first division and the winning time was over three seconds faster and the form looks more solid.

Tawaafud Official explanation: jockey said filly ducked left and lost its action in straight

Sujana(USA) Official explanation: trainer's representative said filly had been unsuited by the fast ground

1419 NETHERFIELD FILLIES' H'CAP 1m 1f 213y

5:40 (5:40) (Class 4) (0-85,80) 3-Y-O+ **£6,477** (£1,927; £963; £481) **Stalls** Low

Form	Pos	Dist	Horse / Trainer / Comment	Jockey	SP	RPR
026-	1		**Solva**[205] [5795] 3-8-8 75 (B J Meehan) *chsd ldrs: rdn over 1f out: led ins fnl f: r.o*	EddieAhern 5	16/1	81
2133	2	1	**Captain Margaret**[21] [983] 4-9-7 73 (J Pearce) *chsd ldr 2f: remained handy: rdn over 2f out: nt clr run ins fnl f: swtchd rt: r.o*	JimmyQuinn 3	9/2[2]	80
1	3	nk	**Wagtail**[40] [710] 3-8-6 73 (E A L Dunlop) *dwlt: hdwy to chse ldr 8f out: led over 2f out: rdn and hdd ins fnl f: no ex*	JamieSpencer 4	10/11[1]	76
04-2	4	3 ½	**My Lovely Lady (IRE)**[16] [1055] 3-8-3 70 (M L W Bell) *hld up: rdn over 3f out: hdwy and hung lft 2f out: styd on same pce appr fnl f*	HayleyTurner 2	6/1[3]	67
043-	5	2 ½	**Michaels Pride (IRE)**[186] [6137] 4-9-4 70 (M Johnston) *led over 7f: wknd over 1f out*	RoystonFfrench 6	10/1	65
300-	6	4	**Lysandra (IRE)**[221] [5456] 4-10-0 80 (N Tinkler) *hld up: stmbld 8f out: wknd over 2f out*	MartinDwyer 1	17/2	67

2m 11.75s (2.05) **Going Correction** -0.025s/f (Good)

WFA 3 from 4yo 15lb **6 Ran SP% 110.4**

Speed ratings (Par 102):90,89,88,86,84 80

CSF £81.10 TOTE £16.50: £3.90, £2.10; EX 65.80 Place 6 £893.99, Place 5 £704.04.

Owner Usk Valley Stud **Bred** Usk Valley Stud **Trained** Manton, Wilts

FOCUS

Just an ordinary fillies' handicap for the grade and the form does not look up to much.

T/Plt: £10,970.60 to a £1 stake. Pool: £39,824.80. 2.65 winning tickets. T/Qpdt: £434.10 to a £1 stake. Pool: £2,640.10. 4.50 winning tickets. CR

1181 PONTEFRACT (L-H)

Wednesday, May 3

OFFICIAL GOING: Good to firm (firm in places)

The ground had dried out and was described as 'quick, rough in places where repairs had been made'.

Wind: Light, half-behind Weather: Sunny and warm

1420 EUROPEAN BREEDERS FUND BETFRED.COM MAIDEN STKS 5f

2:20 (2:20) (Class 4) 2-Y-O **£5,181** (£1,541; £770; £384) **Stalls** Low

Form	Pos	Dist	Horse / Trainer / Comment	Jockey	SP	RPR
	1		**Steady As A Rock (FR)** 2-9-3 (M Johnston) *tall: leggy: scope: mde all: kpt on wl: jst hld on*	KDarley 5	5/1[3]	81+
3	2	½	**Jack Rackham**[17] [1030] 2-9-3 (B Smart) *chsd ldrs: swtchd rt 1f out: styd on wl ins last: jst hld*	RobertWinston 7	11/4[1]	79+
3	3	1 ½	**Josr's Magic (IRE)**[13] [1096] 2-9-3 (Mrs A Duffield) *chsd wnr: kpt on same pce fnl f*	SebSanders 10	3/1[2]	73
3	4	3 ½	**Calloff The Search**[11] [1136] 2-9-0 (W G M Turner) *chsd ldrs: hung rt over 1f out: wknd jst ins last*	RobertMiles[(3)] 6	10/1	59
0	5	2	**Tom Tower (IRE)**[22] [961] 2-9-3 (M R Channon) *chsd ldrs: one pce fnl 2f*	TonyCulhane 9	17/2	51
	6	3	**Skye But N Ben** 2-9-3 (T D Barron) *leggy: scope: s.i.s: in rr tl styd on wl fnl f*	PhillipMakin 1	9/1	39
	7	1	**Vodkat** 2-8-12 (N Tinkler) *leggy: unf: s.i.s: hdwy on inner over 1f out: nvr nr ldrs*	KimTinkler 13	40/1	30
	8	1 ½	**Seriously Lucky (IRE)** 2-9-0 (D Nicholls) *lengthy: unf: scope: sn outpcd on outer: nvr a factor*	SilvestreDeSousa[(3)] 12	20/1	29
	9	1	**Johannesburg Jack (IRE)** 2-8-12 (H Morrison) *cmpt: mid-div: hung lft and wknd over 1f out*	TravisBlock[(5)] 8	16/1	25
5	10	¾	**Avoncreek**[11] [1136] 2-9-3 (B P J Baugh) *prom on outside: lost pl over 3f out: sn bhd*	DeanMcKeown 11	100/1	22
0	11	shd	**Marryl**[14] [1080] 2-9-0 (M W Easterby) *sn drvn along and outpcd: a bhd*	PaulMulrennan[(3)] 4	100/1	22
	12	shd	**Joella's Lad** 2-8-12 (Ms Deborah J Evans) *unf: bkwd: mid-div: wandered and lost pl over 2f out*	DerekNolan[(5)] 3	33/1	21

63.24 secs (-0.56) **Going Correction** -0.075s/f (Good) **12 Ran SP% 116.0**

Speed ratings (Par 95):101,100,97,92,89 84,82,80,78,77 77,77

CSF £17.98 TOTE £4.70: £1.90, £1.70, £1.90; EX 14.90.

Owner A D Spence **Bred** Janus Bloodstock Inc **Trained** Middleham Moor, N Yorks

■ A first winner for first-season sire Rock Of Gibraltar.

FOCUS

An above average two-year-old maiden. The winner is sure to progress and the two placed horses will surely make their mark.

NOTEBOOK

Steady As A Rock(FR), an April foal, is rather a gangly type. He knew his job and with the rail to help did just enough. He has plenty of toe and will go on from here. (op 9-2)

Jack Rackham, quite keen to post, was pulled out entering the final furlong. He was closing the gap all the way to the line and is crying out for a sixth furlong. (op 3-1)

Josr's Magic(IRE), noisy in the paddock, again showed ability but is not quite the finished article yet. (tchd 10-3 in a place)

Calloff The Search, a moderate walker, looked to be feeling the much quicker ground and tired in the closing stages.

Tom Tower(IRE), racing on totally different ground, stepped up a good deal on his debut effort. (op 8-1 tchd 9-1)

Skye But N Ben ◆, a March foal, missed the break but made considerable late debut. The market support suggested he had shown a fair bit at home and he will improve a good deal on this. (op 28-1)

1421 TOTESPORT.COM MAIDEN STKS 1m 2f 6y

2:50 (2:53) (Class 5) 3-Y-O **£4,533** (£1,348; £674; £336) **Stalls** Low

Form	Pos	Dist	Horse / Trainer / Comment	Jockey	SP	RPR
6	1		**Balanced Budget**[11] [1134] 3-9-3 (J Noseda) *lw: dwlt: t.k.h: sn trcking ldrs: wnt 2nd 3f out: led 1f out: styd on strly: readily*	ShaneKelly 2	4/1[1]	90
42-	2	2 ½	**Barodine**[204] [5821] 3-9-3 (H R A Cecil) *lw: t.k.h: trckd ldr: led 6f out tl 1f out: no ex*	JimmyQuinn 10	4/1[1]	85
0	3	5	**Hasayaz (IRE)**[15] [1070] 3-9-3 (Sir Michael Stoute) *dwlt: hdwy over 3f out: wnt mod 3rd over 1f out: kpt on*	RobertWinston 4	5/1[2]	76+
00-	4	¾	**Great Tidings**[206] [5769] 3-9-3 (M Johnston) *set mod pce: hdd 6f out: outpcd over 3f out: kpt on one pce*	KDarley 9	66/1	74
	5	nk	**Riff Raff** 3-8-12 (W Jarvis) *lengthy: unf: sn in rr: hdwy over 1f out: styd on wl ins last*	SebSanders 7	25/1	69+
	6	shd	**Mustamad** 3-9-3 (Sir Michael Stoute) *rangy: wl grwn: bhd and drvn along 6f out: hdwy over 3f out: edgd rt and styd on fnl f*	JamieMackay 12	17/2[3]	73+
0	7	½	**Ghallab**[27] [897] 3-9-3 (E A L Dunlop) *hld up in rr: hdwy and pushed along over 4f out: nvr rchd ldrs*	RichardMullen 5	17/2[3]	72
36-6	8	5	**Nelsons Column (IRE)**[11] [1139] 3-9-3 72 (G M Moore) *w ldrs: lost pl over 2f out*	DO'Donohoe 11	10/1	63
00-	9	7	**Arcangela**[205] [5788] 3-8-12 (J G Given) *chsd ldrs: hung bdly rt and lost pl over 5f out*	DeanMcKeown 1	50/1	45
50-3	10	½	**Hunting Party (IRE)**[23] [952] 3-9-3 73 (B W Hills) *trckd ldrs: t.k.h: lost pl 2f out*	MichaelHills 3	4/1[1]	49
	11	¾	**Agent Eleven (IRE)** 3-9-3 (B J McMath) *rangy: unf: a in rr*	JDSmith 6	125/1	47
6	12	10	**Every Inch (IRE)**[39] [731] 3-9-3 (T D Easterby) *mid-div: drvn and lost pl over 3f out: sn bhd*	DavidAllan 8	125/1	28

2m 12.77s (-1.31) **Going Correction** -0.075s/f (Good) **12 Ran SP% 115.7**

Speed ratings (Par 99):102,100,96,95,95 95,94,90,85,84 84,76

CSF £18.84 TOTE £5.70: £2.00, £1.60, £2.00; EX 22.60.

Owner Hesmonds Stud **Bred** Hesmonds Stud Ltd **Trained** Newmarket, Suffolk

FOCUS

Just a steady gallop but the first two pulled clear in the end. The race is rated around the placed horses and the form could prove reasonable.

Ghallab Official explanation: jockey said colt was unsuited by the good to firm (firm in places) ground

Hunting Party(IRE) Official explanation: jockey said colt was unsuited by the good to firm (firm in places) ground

1422 SKYBET.COM H'CAP 1m 4y

3:20 (3:20) (Class 5) (0-70,70) 4-Y-O+ **£3,886** (£1,156; £577; £288) **Stalls** Low

Form	Pos	Dist	Horse / Trainer / Comment	Jockey	SP	RPR
0-03	1		**Hula Ballew**[12] [1124] 6-8-8 60 (M Dods) *hld up in tch: effrt 2f out: edgd lft and led jst ins last: r.o*	PhillipMakin 16	15/2[3]	73
45-0	2	2	**Champain Sands (IRE)**[12] [1123] 7-8-4 56 oh5 (E J Alston) *hld up and bhd: hdwy on outer 2f out: styd on to take 2nd ins last: no real imp*	DavidAllan 1	12/1	64
2601	3	hd	**Takes Tutu (USA)**[3] [1311] 7-9-2 68 6ex (C R Dore) *hld up towards rr: hdwy on inner 2f out: styd on strly ins last*	RobertWinston 12	11/2[1]	76+
006-	4	1 ¼	**Dvinsky (USA)**[211] [5687] 5-8-11 66 (D Carroll) *chsd ldrs: kpt on same pce fnl f*	DNolan[(3)] 3	25/1	71
00-1	5	nk	**Mount Usher**[6] [1253] 4-8-11 63 6ex (G A Swinbank) *hld up in tch: effrt 2f out: kpt on same pce*	DeanMcKeown 15	10/1	67
41-2	6	1 ¼	**Time To Regret**[12] [1123] 6-8-4 56 oh1 (J S Wainwright) *chsd ldrs: led over 2f out: hdd jst ins last: no ex*	DO'Donohoe 11	10/1	57
0002	7	1	**Selective**[8] [1220] 7-9-4 70 (A W Carroll) *trckd ldrs: effrt over 1f out: keeping on same pce whn n.m.r ins last*	SebSanders 8	13/2[2]	74+
10-5	8	shd	**Shifty**[12] [1123] 7-8-8 63 (D Carroll) *rr-div: effrt on outer 2f out: kpt on: nvr nr ldrs*	DanielTudhope[(3)] 18	14/1	62
0-05	9	nk	**Apache Point (IRE)**[16] [1045] 9-8-5 57 (N Tinkler) *bhd: hdwy on inner over 2f out: kpt on fnl f: nvr nrr*	KimTinkler 5	50/1	55

3-00 **10** *2* **Crail**[105] [140] 6-9-1 **67** .... KDarley 9 60
(C F Wall) *chsd ldrs: effrt over 2f out: wknd appr fnl f* **9/1**

00-5 **11** *nk* **Foolish Groom**[14] [1075] 5-8-3 **62** ow1 .... RussellKennemore(7) 7 55
(R Hollinshead) *rrd s: kpt on fnl 2f: nvr on terms* **10/1**

1325 **12** *2 ½* **Blue Hedges**[22] [972] 4-8-6 **58** .... JimmyQuinn 17 45
(H J Collingridge) *s.i.s: swtchd lft after s: sme hdwy 2f out: nvr on terms* **25/1**

00-0 **13** *1 ½* **Tidy (IRE)**[57] [611] 6-8-13 **65** .... ShaneKelly 14 48
(Micky Hammond) *a in rr* **100/1**

00 **14** *2* **Spirit Guide (FR)**[11] [1148] 4-8-5 **57** .... PaulEddery 6 36
(R C Guest) *stdd s: t.k.h in rr* **200/1**

00/0 **15** *¾* **Travelling Band (IRE)**[18] [955] 8-8-8 **60** .... JamieMackay 2 37
(J Mackie) *a in rr* **22/1**

-050 **16** *1* **Sforzando**[12] [1123] 5-8-5 **64** .... KristinStubbs(7) 10 39
(Mrs L Stubbs) *s.i.s: a in rr and sn pushed along* **33/1**

10-0 **17** *11* **Kabis Amigos**[12] [1124] 4-8-12 **67** .... SilvestreDeSousa(3) 13 16
(D Nicholls) *chsd ldrs: wknd qckly over 1f out: sn bhd: eased* **80/1**

0-06 **18** *13* **Wayward Shot (IRE)**[16] [1041] 4-8-7 **62** .... PaulMulrennan(3) 4 —
(M W Easterby) *set str pce: hdd over 2f out: wknd qckly: sn bhd: eased* **25/1**

1m 43.92s (-1.78) **Going Correction** -0.075s/f (Good) **18** Ran SP% **115.6**
Speed ratings (Par 103):105,103,102,101,101 100,99,98,98,96 96,93,92,90,89 88,77,64
CSF £79.96 CT £552.41 TOTE £8.60: £1.90, £3.30, £2.20, £9.00; EX 144.80.
Owner Mrs J W Hutchinson & Mrs P A Knox **Bred** T K & Mrs P A Knox **Trained** Denton, Co Durham
■ Stewards' Enquiry : D Nolan caution: careless riding

FOCUS
A modest handicap run at a strong gallop but a messy affair with horses getting in each others' way in the home straight and limited by the runner-up, racing from out of the handicap.
Wayward Shot(IRE) Official explanation: jockey said gelding ran too free early

1423 LADBROKES FILLIES' H'CAP 1m 2f 6y
3:50 (3:51) (Class 3) (0-90,89) 3-Y-O
£11,217 (£3,358; £1,679; £840; £419; £210) **Stalls** Low

Form RPR

231- **1** **Shortest Day**[198] [5949] 3-9-4 **89** .... RobertWinston 7 96+
(Sir Michael Stoute) *trckd ldr: chal 4f out: led 2f out: edgd rt and pushed out fnl f* **11/10**[1]

215- **2** *1 ½* **Maroussies Wings (IRE)**[186] [6145] 3-9-2 **87** .... KDarley 2 90
(P C Haslam) *trckd ldrs: wnt 2nd over 1f out: carried hd high and hung lft: no imp* **14/1**

013- **3** *2* **Missoula (IRE)**[230] [5252] 3-8-6 **77** .... MichaelHills 6 76
(M H Tompkins) *hld up in rr: effrt 3f out: kpt on to take 3rd jst ins last: one pce* **7/1**[3]

0-24 **4** *¾* **Ellesappelle**[12] [1122] 3-7-13 **75** oh7 .... AndrewElliott(5) 3 73?
(K R Burke) *s.s: hld up in rr: drvn over 4f out: kpt on one pce fnl 2f* **16/1**

00-4 **5** *5* **Damelza (IRE)**[13] [1099] 3-8-11 **82** .... DavidAllan 4 70
(T D Easterby) *trckd ldrs: effrt over 3f out: wknd over 1f out* **9/1**

40-2 **6** *2 ½* **Distinctive Look (IRE)**[12] [1118] 3-8-10 **81** .... SebSanders 1 64
(B J Meehan) *set modest pce: qcknd over 5f out: hdd 2f out: sn lost pl* **11/4**[2]

2m 12.03s (-2.05) **Going Correction** -0.075s/f (Good) **6** Ran SP% **109.3**
Speed ratings (Par 100):105,103,102,101,97 95
CSF £16.81 TOTE £1.90: £1.10, £4.60; EX 21.00.
Owner K Abdulla **Bred** Juddmonte Farms Ltd **Trained** Newmarket, Suffolk

FOCUS
No gallop to halfway but a ready winner who can make her mark in Listed company. The form is rated at face value through the third.

NOTEBOOK
Shortest Day, 5lb higher than when taking a nursery at Windsor in October on her fourth and final start at two, is a tall filly and a good mover. She made this look relatively simple and can add to her stud value by taking a Listed race. (op 5-4 tchd 13-8 and 7-4 in a place)
Maroussies Wings(IRE), a big filly, has an ungainly action. She put her head in the air and looked uncomfortable on the quick ground but kept battling away all the way to the line. (op 12-1)
Missoula(IRE), dropped in at the start, did just enough to secure third spot without ever threatening the first two. (tchd 6-1)
Ellesappelle, fitted with a rope haltar, was racing from 7lb out of the handicap. After giving away ground at the start she never looked a threat, but to her credit kept going all the way to the line albeit in her own time. (tchd 18-1)
Damelza(IRE), still backward in her coat, is looking fully exposed and has yet to show she truly stays this far. (op 7-1)
Distinctive Look(IRE), a big filly, set her own pace on her handicap debut but dropped out in most disappointing fashion when headed by the winner. (tchd 2-1)

1424 WILLIAM HILL H'CAP 1m 4f 8y
4:20 (4:20) (Class 5) (0-70,68) 3-Y-O **£4,533** (£1,348; £674; £336) **Stalls** Low

Form RPR

0-21 **1** **Bollin Derek**[8] [1221] 3-8-5 **55** 5ex .... DavidAllan 3 61+
(T D Easterby) *in rr: drvn along over 5f out: hdwy over 2f out: squeezed through on innner 1f out: led last 75yds: styd on strly* **11/10**[1]

2526 **2** *1* **Noble Edge**[8] [1221] 3-8-6 **59** .... DanielTudhope(3) 6 64
(Robert Gray) *hld up: hdwy on outsider over 3f out: wnt 2nd over 2f out: led over 1f out: hdd and no ex wl ins last* **12/1**

-662 **3** *3 ½* **Northerner (IRE)**[9] [1182] 3-8-4 **54** oh1 .... DeanMcKeown 11 53+
(J R Norton) *set str pce: hdd over 1f out: edgd lft 1f out: one pce* **7/1**[3]

0-06 **4** *4* **Cora Pearl (IRE)**[9] [1182] 3-8-5 **55** oh9 ow1 .... GrahamGibbons 2 48
(M J Polglase) *hld up in tch: effrt on inner over 2f out: wknd appr fnl f* **80/1**

4-63 **5** *4* **Special Moment (IRE)**[14] [1079] 3-9-3 **67** .... TonyCulhane 5 53
(B W Hills) *s.i.s: drvn over 5f out: nvr on terms* **10/1**

00-3 **6** *19* **Ritsi**[9] [1193] 3-9-4 **68** .... KDarley 4 24+
(Mrs A J Perrett) *trckd ldrs: wknd 2f out* **9/2**[2]

055- **7** *3 ½* **Don'Tcallmeginger (IRE)**[238] [5051] 3-9-3 **67** .... MichaelHills 10 17
(M H Tompkins) *s.i.s: effrt over 3f out: sn btn* **12/1**

-450 **8** *8* **Aboyne (IRE)**[23] [945] 3-8-10 **65** .... DerekNolan(5) 12 2
(M G Quinlan) *trckd ldrs: lost pl over 2f out: sn bhd* **33/1**

-500 **9** *6* **Cragganmore Creek**[35] [797] 3-8-8 **58** .... RobertWinston 9 —
(D Morris) *s.i.s: hld up in rr: effrt over 3f out: sn lost pl and bhd* **33/1**

0066 **10** *26* **Sahara Style**[8] [1216] 3-8-4 **54** oh6 .... (v) PaulQuinn 7 —
(R Hollinshead) *trckd ldrs: wknd over 3f out: sn bhd: virtually p.u* **66/1**

2m 38.19s (-2.11) **Going Correction** -0.075s/f (Good) **10** Ran SP% **111.4**
Speed ratings (Par 99):104,103,101,98,95 83,80,75,71,54
CSF £14.70 CT £61.91 TOTE £2.00: £1.10, £3.00, £2.10; EX 19.10.
Owner Sir Neil Westbrook **Bred** Sir Neil And Lady Westbrook **Trained** Great Habton, N Yorks

FOCUS
A strong gallop and they came home well strung out. The winner is a progressive young stayer who will be seen to much greater effect on less-firm ground and the form is rated positively through the second.
Cragganmore Creek Official explanation: jockey said gelding was unsuited by the good to firm (firm in places) ground

1425 FRIENDS OF THE NORTHERN RACING COLLEGE H'CAP 1m 2f 6y
4:50 (4:52) (Class 5) (0-70,70) 4-Y-O+ **£4,533** (£1,348; £674; £336) **Stalls** Low

Form RPR

36-0 **1** **Thorny Mandate**[22] [965] 4-8-8 **60** .... KDarley 2 69
(R F Johnson Houghton) *sn trcking ldrs: qcknd to ld 1f out: drvn out* **8/1**[3]

4006 **2** *1 ¼* **Eastborough (IRE)**[11] [1132] 7-9-1 **67** .... TonyCulhane 15 74+
(B G Powell) *swtchd lft after s: bhd: gd hdwy over 1f out: nt clr run: styd on strly ins last: nt rch wnr* **12/1**

450- **3** *1* **To Arms**[242] [4944] 4-8-8 **60** .... DavidAllan 7 65
(T D Easterby) *bhd: hdwy and n.m.r over 1f out: styd on wl ins last* **33/1**

0000 **4** *nk* **Monash Lad (IRE)**[9] [1187] 4-9-1 **67** .... (b[1]) MichaelHills 14 71
(M H Tompkins) *bhd: hdwy on outer 2f out: styd on ins last* **25/1**

1046 **5** *shd* **Stage Manager (IRE)**[67] [521] 4-8-13 **70** .... DerekNolan(5) 4 74
(M J Wallace) *trckd ldrs: led over 1f out: sn hdd and no ex* **8/1**[3]

-060 **6** *½* **Fame**[14] [1075] 6-9-1 **67** .... (t) RobertWinston 9 70
(W Jarvis) *chsd ldrs: kpt on same pce appr fnl f* **11/1**

602- **7** *½* **Purple Dancer (FR)**[178] [5244] 4-8-5 **57** .... DeanMcKeown 13 59
(G A Swinbank) *in rr: hdwy on inner over 1f out: nvr rchd ldrs* **10/1**

40-4 **8** *shd* **Silverhay**[14] [1075] 5-8-13 **68** .... PaulMulrennan(3) 1 70
(T D Barron) *chsd ldrs: styd on same pce over 1f out* **7/2**[1]

03-0 **9** *½* **Bright Sun (IRE)**[14] [1075] 5-9-1 **67** .... (t) KimTinkler 3 68
(N Tinkler) *trckd ldrs: t.k.h: one pce fnl 2f* **16/1**

030- **10** *1* **Wizard Looking**[271] [4122] 5-8-11 **63** .... TonyHamilton 11 62
(J S Wainwright) *uns rdr gng to s: in rr: sme hdwy over 1f out: nvr on terms* **28/1**

300- **11** *nk* **El Rey Royale**[200] [5892] 4-8-4 **56** oh2 .... RichardMullen 8 54
(Micky Hammond) *in rr: effrt on outer 2f out: nvr a factor* **66/1**

26-6 **12** *1 ½* **Abstract Folly (IRE)**[11] [1152] 4-8-7 **59** .... (b) GrahamGibbons 12 55
(J D Bethell) *trckd ldrs: led over 2f out: hdd over 1f out: sn lost pl* **25/1**

00-6 **13** *1* **Inchloss (IRE)**[6] [1257] 5-8-8 **60** .... PaulEddery 16 54
(C N Kellett) *led tl over 2f out: lost pl over 1f out* **33/1**

13-0 **14** *½* **Qualitair Wings**[14] [1075] 7-8-10 **62** .... PhillipMakin 6 55
(J Hetherton) *trckd ldrs: one pce whn hmpd jst ins last* **9/1**

46-3 **15** *21* **Zarova (IRE)**[7] [1233] 4-8-4 **56** oh1 .... JamieMackay 10 9
(M W Easterby) *chsd ldrs: lost pl over 2f out: sn bhd and eased* **5/1**[2]

2m 12.51s (-1.57) **Going Correction** -0.075s/f (Good) **15** Ran SP% **120.6**
Speed ratings (Par 103):103,102,101,100,100 100,100,100,99,98 98,97,96,96,79
CSF £92.63 CT £3003.33 TOTE £9.20: £3.10, £3.90, £7.30; EX 119.60 Place 6 £46.66, Place 5 £37.49.
Owner R C Naylor **Bred** Major W R Hern And W H Carson **Trained** Blewbury, Oxon

FOCUS
A messy race in the home straight with the winner getting first run and the bare form looks ordinary.
Bright Sun(IRE) Official explanation: jockey said horse was struck into
Zarova(IRE) Official explanation: trainer had no explanation for the poor form shown
T/Jkpt: £27,184.00 to a £1 stake. Pool: £57,431.00. 1.50 winning tickets. T/Plt: £73.50 to a £1 stake. Pool: £45,960.50. 456.40 winning tickets. T/Qpdt: £62.70 to a £1 stake. Pool: £2,070.60. 24.40 winning tickets. WG

1426 - 1428a (Foreign Racing) - See Raceform Interactive

[1209]FOLKESTONE (R-H)
Thursday, May 4

OFFICIAL GOING: Good to firm (firm in places)
The ground was riding particularly fast and four horses were withdrawn because the conditions were deemed unsuitable.

1429 FOLKESTONE-RACECOURSE.CO.UK MAIDEN AUCTION STKS 5f
2:30 (2:32) (Class 5) 2-Y-O **£3,238** (£963; £481; £240) **Stalls** Low

Form RPR

2 **1** **Karayel (IRE)**[12] [1136] 2-8-13 .... RichardHughes 2 84
(R Hannon) *cl up on inner: effrt to ld over 1f out: edgd rt and rdn out fnl f* **5/2**[2]

2 **2** *¾* **See In The Dark (IRE)**[13] [1113] 2-8-13 .... LDettori 1 81
(B J Meehan) *led: edgd rt and hdd over 1f out: hrd rdn and nt qckn fnl f* **8/11**[1]

2 **3** *1 ¼* **Racing Stripes (IRE)**[37] [775] 2-8-10 .... PatDobbs 11 73
(A B Haynes) *racd on outer: outpcd and hanging rt: swtchd rt and gd prog over 1f out: r.o fnl f: nrst fin* **9/1**[3]

4 *nk* **Hythe Bay** 2-8-5 ow1 .... SteveDrowne 8 70
(R T Phillips) *s.i.s: in tch towards rr: pushed along 2f out: kpt on steadily: nrst fin* **50/1**

5 *¾* **Ten Dollars More (IRE)** 2-8-11 .... ShaneKelly 5 70
(J A Osborne) *dwlt: racd against nr side rail and sn in tch in rr: outpcd 2f out: kpt on fnl f* **66/1**

2 **6** *¾* **Hucking Hot**[9] [1223] 2-8-5 .... LPKeniry 4 61
(J R Best) *pressed ldrs: hanging and lost pl 2f out: one pce after* **9/1**[3]

0 **7** *1* **Cesc**[9] [1203] 2-8-11 .... SebSanders 10 63
(P J Makin) *racd on outer: chsd ldrs: effrt and cl up over 1f out: wknd fnl f* **16/1**

8 *1 ½* **Down The Well (IRE)** 2-8-5 .... RichardKingscote(5) 6 56
(J A Osborne) *hanging and green: outpcd and bhd: kpt on fnl f* **66/1**

0 **9** *9* **Sunstroke (IRE)**[9] [1223] 2-7-13 .... RoryMoore(5) 7 14
(M G Quinlan) *pressed ldrs tl wknd rapidly jst over 2f out* **66/1**

0 **10** *1 ¼* **Catweasel**[42] [701] 2-8-9 .... RobertMiles(3) 9 17
(W G M Turner) *s.s: outpcd and a wl bhd* **100/1**

60.50 secs (-0.30) **Going Correction** -0.325s/f (Firm) **10** Ran SP% **119.8**
Speed ratings (Par 93):89,87,85,85,84 82,81,78,64,62
CSF £4.77 TOTE £3.50: £1.30, £1.02, £2.40; EX 5.80 Trifecta £22.70 Pool: £515.76 - 16.08 winning units.
Owner Kemal Kurt **Bred** Stall A And R **Trained** East Everleigh, Wilts

FOCUS
Hand timed. Just an ordinary maiden and the winner can rate higher, but assessed around the placed horses for now.

The Form Book, Raceform Ltd, Compton, RG20 6NL

NOTEBOOK

Karayel(IRE), a beaten favourite when second in an ordinary soft-ground maiden at Nottingham on his debut, handled this faster surface well enough and proved good enough to get off the mark at the second attempt. He deserves his chance in better company and connections think a return to slightly easier ground will not go amiss. (op 11-4 tchd 3-1)

See In The Dark(IRE), in finding Karayel too good, did not do a great deal for the form of that one's stablemate, Cav Okay, whom he was a five-length second to on his debut at Newbury. A maiden should come his way, but he does not look above average. (op 10-11)

Racing Stripes(IRE), who would surely have won a modest four-runner course and distance maiden on soft ground on his debut had he not veered across the track, found a couple too good this time but still appeared to put up an improved effort. He was noted to be hanging right, and certainly looks to have his quirks, but he has races in him and could make a fair nursery type later in the season. (op 10-1)

Hythe Bay, a 13,000gns first foal of a winning miler, hails from a National Hunt-orientated yard but showed plenty of promise. She is open to improvement and it will be disappointing if she does not find a race or two this season. (tchd 66-1)

Ten Dollars More(IRE), a 15,000euros first foal of a half-sister to multiple six to seven-furlong winner Puma, was totally unfancied in the betting, but made a pleasing debut and should be better for the experience. (op 50-1)

Hucking Hot did not really build on the promise he showed on his debut in what would appear to be a modest maiden at Wolverhampton. (op 8-1 tchd 10-1)

Cesc, well supported on his debut at Bath but only seventh, filled the same position once again but was not totally without promise. He has presumably shown something at home and is not one to give up on just yet.

1430 TEMPLE LIFTS LTD MAIDEN STKS — 5f
3:00 (3:01) (Class 5) 3-Y-0+ — **£3,886** (£1,156; £577; £288) **Stalls** Low

Form			Horse / Details	RPR
323	**1**		**Pititana (IRE)**[14] 1089 3-8-9 76 .... RichardHughes 10 (R Hannon) *mde virtually all: rdn and def advantage over 1f out: styd on wl* **5/4**[1]	66
0-	**2**	1 ½	**Cheney Hill**[251] 4724 3-9-0 .... DaneO'Neill 5 (H Candy) *w wnr tl over 1f out: hanging rt and nt qckn fnl f* **8/1**[3]	65
60-	**3**	1 ¼	**Lii Najma**[211] 5694 3-8-9 .... RyanMoore 3 (C E Brittain) *chsd ldrs: effrt on outer over 1f out: drvn and kpt on same pce* **12/1**	55
5-50	**4**	1	**Elusive Warrior (USA)**[8] 1241 3-9-0 72 .... JimCrowley 2 (Mrs A J Perrett) *chsd ldrs: rdn 2f out: one pce and no imp* **8/1**[3]	56
00-4	**5**	hd	**Great Belief (IRE)**[7] 1261 4-9-6 50 .... RobertMiles(3) 1 (T D McCarthy) *swvd s: sn in tch: effrt 2f out: hanging bdly rt: kpt on* **20/1**	59
3-4	**6**	2	**Hang Loose**[27] 901 3-9-0 .... SteveDrowne 7 (R Charlton) *prom tl wknd wl over 1f out* **7/2**[2]	47
0-04	**7**	3 ½	**Sorrel Point**[82] 380 3-9-0 62 .... JimmyQuinn 6 (H J Collingridge) *scratchy to post: hld up: nvr on terms: pushed along and no prog 2f out* **20/1**	33
-	**8**	hd	**Opus Magnus (IRE)** 3-9-0 .... SebSanders 8 (P J Makin) *scratchy to post: s.v.s: a wl bhd* **11/1**	32
	9	1 ½	**Maylea Gold (IRE)** 3-8-9 .... JamesDoyle(5) 9 (Miss J Feilden) *taken down early: dwlt: sn outpcd: drvn and no prog 2f out* **33/1**	26

59.00 secs (-1.80) **Going Correction** -0.325s/f (Firm)
WFA 3 from 4yo 9lb — 9 Ran SP% **117.4**
Speed ratings (Par 103):101,98,96,95,94 91,85,85,83
CSF £12.05 TOTE £2.00: £1.10, £2.50, £2.70; EX 14.80 Trifecta £197.70 Pool: £479.11 - 1.72 winning units.
Owner William Durkan **Bred** 6 C Stallions Ltd And L D'Alessandri **Trained** East Everleigh, Wilts

FOCUS
Hand timed. Fifth-placed Great Belief may be a little better than his official rating of 50 suggests, but his proximity still suggests this was a pretty ordinary maiden and the fifth is the best guide to the level.

1431 INVICTA MOTORS FILLIES' H'CAP — 6f
3:30 (3:37) (Class 5) (0-70,70) 3-Y-0 — **£3,238** (£963; £481; £240) **Stalls** Low

Form			Horse / Details	RPR
65-2	**1**		**Spirit Of Arosa (IRE)**[13] 1110 3-9-4 70 .... SebSanders 10 (J Akehurst) *t.k.h: hld up in rr: prog on outer over 2f out: hrd rdn and r.o to ld last 100yds* **9/2**[1]	78+
64-5	**2**	¾	**Light Mozart**[13] 1109 3-8-8 60 .... MartinDwyer 8 (C E Brittain) *trckd ldrs: rdn 2f out: effrt to ld jst over 1f out: styd on but hdd and outpcd last 100yds* **7/1**[3]	66
040-	**3**	2	**Dona Vitoria**[189] 6120 3-9-1 67 .... RichardHughes 2 (S Kirk) *stmbld s: trckd ldrs against nr side rail: rdn 2f out: outpcd over 1f out: kpt on* **9/1**	67
5200	**4**	nk	**Kellys Dream (IRE)**[13] 1110 3-8-10 62 .... ShaneKelly 1 (M Quinn) *pressed ldr: led over 3f out to jst over 1f out: fdd* **25/1**	61
00-5	**5**	shd	**Arculinge**[50] 646 3-8-4 56 .... AlanMunro 13 (M Blanshard) *dwlt: racd on wd outside: sn chsd ldrs: rdn 2f out: kpt on same pce* **9/1**	55+
0-36	**6**	1 ¼	**Piccostar**[24] 954 3-8-10 65 .... RichardSmith(3) 4 (A B Haynes) *racd against nr side rail: in tch: hanging rt fr 1/2-way: outpcd 2f out: kpt on ins fnl f* **8/1**	60+
64-0	**7**	1 ¼	**Divine White**[13] 1110 3-8-7 59 .... RyanMoore 12 (Mrs A J Perrett) *racd on outer: pressed ldrs: drvn and nt qckn 2f out: wknd fnl f* **12/1**	50
103-	**8**	shd	**Miss Brush**[283] 3805 3-8-13 65 .... OscarUrbina 11 (J R Fanshawe) *t.k.h: hld up bhd ldrs: cl up wl over 1f out: wknd* **13/2**[2]	56
2-65	**9**	3	**Halfwaytoparadise**[30] 868 3-9-2 68 .... LDettori 7 (M L W Bell) *in tch: rdn 2f out: no prog over 1f out: n.m.r and heavily eased fnl f* **7/1**[3]	50
04-6	**10**	5	**Miss Redactive**[17] 1049 3-8-8 60 .... HayleyTurner 6 (M D I Usher) *dwlt: a in last trio: bhd fnl 2f* **12/1**	27
040-	**11**	6	**Whisper Inthe Wind (IRE)**[227] 5370 3-8-11 63 .... ChrisCatlin 5 (Miss J Feilden) *led to over 3f out: wknd rapidly* **16/1**	12

1m 12.3s (-1.30) **Going Correction** -0.325s/f (Firm) — 11 Ran SP% **112.7**
Speed ratings (Par 96):95,94,91,90,90 89,87,87,83,76 68
CSF £33.50 CT £273.32 TOTE £3.60: £1.60, £2.10, £3.60; EX 29.50 Trifecta £192.70 Pool: £391.03 - 1.44 winning units.
Owner R P Tullett and Partners **Bred** Twelve Oaks Stud Establishment **Trained** Epsom, Surrey

FOCUS
Hand timed. A modest sprint handicap for fillies and the form looks limited.
Divine White Official explanation: jockey said filly lost its action
Miss Redactive Official explanation: jockey said filly suffered early interference

1432 PROVINCE OF EAST KENT H'CAP — 6f
4:00 (4:01) (Class 5) (0-75,75) 4-Y-0+ — **£3,238** (£963; £481; £240) **Stalls** Low

Form			Horse / Details	RPR
040-	**1**		**High Ridge**[156] 6465 7-8-12 69 .... (p) LDettori 1 (J M Bradley) *towards rr: rdn and prog 2f out: effrt to chal between two rivals fnl f: drvn to ld last strides* **15/2**[3]	80
6400	**2**	hd	**Franksalot (IRE)**[62] 569 6-8-3 63 .... RichardThomas(3) 6 (Miss B Sanders) *s.s: in tch in rr: prog over 2f out: rdn to ld last 150yds: hdd fnl strides* **16/1**	73
000-	**3**	shd	**Blue Tomato**[241] 4995 5-8-12 69 .... RyanMoore 4 (J M Bradley) *cl up: led over 1f out: hanging and idled in front: hdd last 150yds: nt qckn nr fin* **16/1**	79
600-	**4**	1 ¾	**Keyaki (IRE)**[219] 5526 5-9-4 75 .... GeorgeBaker 11 (C F Wall) *dwlt: hld up in last pair: stdy prog over 2f out: shuffled along to chse ldng trio fnl f: nvr nr them* **16/1**	79+
035-	**5**	nk	**Danehill Stroller (IRE)**[241] 4995 6-8-12 69 .... SebSanders 9 (R M Beckett) *stmbld s: wl in rr: effrt 2f out: hanging rt but styd on fnl f* **15/2**[3]	73
0022	**6**	½	**Ivory Lace**[27] 902 5-8-5 67 .... JamesDoyle(5) 10 (S Woodman) *towards rr: rdn over 2f out: plugged on fnl f: n.d* **12/1**	69
0311	**7**	nk	**Misaro (GER)**[4] 1315 5-8-9 66 7ex .... (b) AdrianMcCarthy 5 (R A Harris) *pressed ldr: led 2f out: hdd and nt qckn over 1f out: sn btn* **7/4**[1]	67
2202	**8**	3	**Canadian Danehill (IRE)**[9] 1211 4-8-13 70 .... AlanMunro 2 (R M H Cowell) *racd against nr side rail: cl up: rdn and hanging fr 2f out: wkng whn n.m.r 1f out* **4/1**[2]	62
340-	**9**	½	**Coranglais**[219] 5532 6-8-4 61 .... (p) MartinDwyer 3 (J M Bradley) *led to 2f out: sn wknd* **33/1**	52
4340	**10**	1 ¾	**Kew The Music**[7] 1253 6-8-4 61 oh2 .... (v) ChrisCatlin 7 (M R Channon) *early reminders to chse ldrs: wknd u.p 2f out* **10/1**	46
5-00	**11**	9	**Burhaan (IRE)**[11] 1164 4-8-8 68 .... (t) AmirQuinn(3) 8 (J R Boyle) *racd on outer: chsd ldrs to 1/2-way: wknd rapidly* **40/1**	26

1m 10.7s (-2.90) **Going Correction** -0.325s/f (Firm) — 11 Ran SP% **119.7**
Speed ratings (Par 103):106,105,105,103,102 102,101,97,97,94 82
CSF £122.74 CT £1911.30 TOTE £9.50: £3.10, £5.00, £5.00; EX 228.20 TRIFECTA Not won..
Owner James Leisure Ltd **Bred** Buckram Thoroughbred Enterprises Inc **Trained** Sedbury, Gloucs

FOCUS
Hand timed. Just a modest sprint handicap, but the form looks solid for the grade and reliable.
Burhaan(IRE) Official explanation: jockey said colt lost its action

1433 EASTWELL MANOR H'CAP — 7f (S)
4:30 (4:30) (Class 6) (0-60,60) 3-Y-0 — **£2,730** (£806; £403) **Stalls** Low

Form			Horse / Details	RPR
000-	**1**		**Strife (IRE)**[197] 5970 3-8-5 50 .... RichardSmith(3) 7 (R Hannon) *pressed nr side ldr: led gp over 2f out: drvn and r.o fnl f to ld nr fin* **10/1**	56
2000	**2**	nk	**Simpsons Ross (IRE)**[78] 422 3-9-4 60 .... FergusSweeney 13 (R M Flower) *hld up last of far side gp: prog against rail 2f out: overall ldr ins fnl f: hung lft and hdd nr fin* **16/1**	65
60-0	**3**	½	**The Grey One (IRE)**[30] 879 3-8-10 52 .... (p) ShaneKelly 14 (J M Bradley) *led far side gp: overall ldr and hung bdly lft fr 2f out: hdd and no ex ins fnl f* **8/1**	56
55-0	**4**	2	**Captain Bolsh**[12] 1141 3-9-3 59 .... JimmyQuinn 10 (J Pearce) *trckd far side ldr: rdn and edgd lft fr 2f out: edgd rt and one pce fnl f* **4/1**[1]	58
5-56	**5**	1 ¾	**Alwariah**[12] 1140 3-8-13 55 .... RyanMoore 1 (C E Brittain) *trckd nr side ldrs: effrt 2f out: outpcd fr over 1f out* **9/2**[2]	49
00-0	**6**	¾	**Double Valentine**[27] 901 3-8-13 55 .... RobertHavlin 2 (R Ingram) *hld up last of nr side gp: outpcd fr 2f out: n.d after: kpt on* **22/1**	47
0-50	**7**	1 ½	**Tuscany Queen (IRE)**[7] 1263 3-8-13 55 .... RichardHughes 6 (R Hannon) *scratchy to post: led nr side gp to over 2f out: wknd fnl f* **9/1**	43
0-04	**8**	1 ½	**Moonlight Fantasy (IRE)**[8] 1232 3-8-10 52 .... LDettori 12 (N Tinkler) *taken down early: chsd ldrs far side: hung lft fr 2f out: wknd* **4/1**[1]	37
006-	**9**	½	**Royal Agreement**[241] 4990 3-8-8 55 .... JamesDoyle(5) 4 (B G Powell) *chsd nr side ldrs: rdn over 2f out: wknd over 1f out* **7/1**[3]	38
00-0	**10**	2	**Compton Flyer**[11] 1166 3-8-12 54 .... DaneO'Neill 9 (J M Bradley) *chsd far side ldrs: drvn fr 3f out: hung lft wl over 1f out: wknd* **20/1**	32
00-0	**11**	8	**Paddy's Place (IRE)**[65] 544 3-8-8 50 .... ChrisCatlin 5 (M Blanshard) *chsd ldrs nr side to 1/2-way: struggling in rr 2f out: wknd* **33/1**	7
-000	**12**	½	**Smart Golden Boy (IRE)**[59] 595 3-8-6 48 .... LPKeniry 8 (Mrs L C Jewell) *racd on outer of nr side gp: in tch to 3f out: wknd rapidly* **25/1**	4
0-00	**13**	hd	**Flying Penne**[4] 1314 3-8-1 50 .... ThomasO'Brien(7) 3 (M R Channon) *dwlt: a in rr nr side: bhd fnl 2f* **20/1**	5

1m 26.7s (-1.20) **Going Correction** -0.325s/f (Firm) — 13 Ran SP% **127.4**
Speed ratings (Par 97):93,92,92,89,87 86,85,83,82,80 71,70,70
CSF £155.90 CT £1408.15 TOTE £12.90: £2.80, £5.10, £3.20; EX 433.10 TRIFECTA Not won..
Owner Lucayan Stud **Bred** Mrs Mary Gallagher **Trained** East Everleigh, Wilts

FOCUS
Hand timed. A pretty moderate handicap in which the field split into two groups. Although the winner came from the larger near-side group, the next three home came from the five who elected to race far side, despite all of them wandering to their left close home, suggesting they raced on the better ground. Those immediately behind the first two suggest the form is sound enough.
Simpsons Ross(IRE) Official explanation: jockey said bit slipped through gelding's mouth
The Grey One(IRE) Official explanation: jockey said colt hung left
Moonlight Fantasy(IRE) Official explanation: jockey said gelding hung left

1434 RICHARD FLOWER MEDIAN AUCTION MAIDEN STKS — 1m 1f 149y
5:00 (5:00) (Class 6) 3-4-Y-0 — **£2,730** (£806; £403) **Stalls** Low

Form			Horse / Details	RPR
23-2	**1**		**Just Observing**[24] 952 3-8-9 77 .... LDettori 2 (E A L Dunlop) *sn led: mde rest: in command fr 3f out: clr over 1f out: eased nr fin* **2/11**[1]	61+
-000	**2**	4	**Silver Court**[9] 1225 4-9-10 40 .... ShaneKelly 5 (A W Carroll) *t.k.h: chsd wnr after 2f: rdn and no imp 3f out: jst hld on for 2nd* **16/1**[3]	46
	3	shd	**Loriinae** 3-8-4 .... AlanMunro 1 (T G Mills) *hld up: chsd ldng pair 1/2-way: shkn up and no imp 3f out: kpt on ins fnl f* **6/1**[2]	41+

\- **4** *25* **Greenacre Legend**[46] 4-9-10 .... MichaelTebbutt 6 —
(D B Feek) *s.s: last and off the pce: lost tch over 3f out: sn t.o: snatched remote 4th nr fin* **66/1**

06/ **5** *1* **Glads Image**[572] 6060 4-9-5 .... BrianReilly 3 —
(J Ryan) *chsd wnr for 2f: wknd rapidly 3f out: t.o* **33/1**

2m 2.78s (-2.45) **Going Correction** -0.325s/f (Firm)
WFA 3 from 4yo 15lb **5** Ran SP% **109.2**
Speed ratings (Par 101):96,92,92,72,71
CSF £4.51 TOTE £1.20: £1.10, £3.30; EX 3.90 TRIFECTA Part won. Pool: £297.45 - 0.10 winning units..
Owner The Wily Partnership **Bred** Stratford Place Stud **Trained** Newmarket, Suffolk

FOCUS
As uncompetitive a maiden as you are likely to see, with 37lb separating the front two on official ratings. The winning time was modest, 2.74 seconds slower than the following handicap.

1435 COME EVENING RACING AT FOLKESTONE H'CAP — 1m 1f 149y
5:30 (5:32) (Class 4) (0-80,80) 4-Y-0+ **£5,505** (£1,637; £818; £408) **Stalls** Low

Form RPR

50-5 **1** **Secretary General (IRE)**[32] 843 5-8-8 **70** .... SteveDrowne 12 80
(P F I Cole) *chsd ldng pair: pushed along 4f out: effrt u.p 2f out: styd on to ld last 150yds: drvn out* **9/4**[1]

0500 **2** *1 1/4* **Alekhine (IRE)**[22] 983 5-8-7 **69** ....(p) AlanMunro 7 76
(J R Boyle) *hld up in midfield and off the pce: prog over 3f out: drvn to chal and upsides 1f out: nt qckn u.p* **20/1**

0-30 **3** *hd* **South O'The Border**[12] 1133 4-8-11 **73** .... IanMongan 3 80
(T G Mills) *led after 1f and set decent pce: drvn over 2f out: kpt on u.p: hdd and one pce last 150yds* **3/1**[3]

0-45 **4** *1 1/2* **Top Spec (IRE)**[82] 385 5-8-10 **72** .... JimmyQuinn 11 76
(J Pearce) *s.s: hld up in last pair and wl off the pce: rdn 3f out: hanging but prog 2f out: kpt on: nt rch ldrs* **11/4**[2]

0-06 **5** *3/4* **The Gaikwar (IRE)**[12] 1148 7-8-10 **72** ....(b) AdrianMcCarthy 5 75
(R A Harris) *chsd ldrs: rdn 4f out: lost pl sn after and struggling: kpt on again fr over 1f out* **33/1**

400- **6** *shd* **Yo Pedro (IRE)**[216] 5588 4-9-4 **80** .... OscarUrbina 9 83
(J R Fanshawe) *s.i.s: hld up towards rr and off the pce: sme prog over 2f out: shkn up briefly over 1f out: nvr nr ldrs* **16/1**

5S-6 **7** *hd* **Hatch A Plan (IRE)**[50] 641 5-8-4 **66** .... ChrisCatlin 4 68
(Mrs A J Hamilton-Fairley) *hld up in last trio and off the pce: effrt over 3f out: plugged on: n.d* **22/1**

1000 **8** *3/4* **Berkhamsted (IRE)**[2] 1380 4-9-4 **80** ....(v) SebSanders 6 81
(M F Harris) *led for 1f: chsd ldr: rdn to chal 2f out: fnd nil: wknd rapidly fnl f* **16/1**

0400 **9** *1 1/2* **Admiral Compton**[38] 764 5-8-4 **66** oh2......................(v) MartinDwyer 10 64
(J R Boyle) *trckd ldrs: rdn over 2f out: fdd over 1f out* **25/1**

50-6 **10** *3/4* **Lizarazu (GER)**[9] 1207 7-8-6 **75** ....(b[1]) TolleyDean[(7)] 8 71
(R A Harris) *s.v.s: hld up in last pair and wl off the pce: rdn over 3f out: plugged on fnl 2f: nrst fin* **16/1**

105- **11** *9* **Native American**[344] 2007 4-8-7 **69** .... RobertHavlin 2 48
(T D McCarthy) *hld up in midfield: wknd wl over 2f out* **40/1**

2m 0.04s (-5.19) **Going Correction** -0.325s/f (Firm) **11** Ran SP% **118.4**
Speed ratings (Par 105):107,106,105,104,104 103,103,103,102,101 94
CSF £55.37 CT £141.38 TOTE £3.40: £1.30, £5.30, £1.30; EX 81.20 Trifecta £211.10 Place 6 £153.97, Place 5 £135.72.
Owner The Blenheim Partnership **Bred** Mrs C L Weld **Trained** Whatcombe, Oxon

FOCUS
A fair handicap run at a reasonable pace and ordinary form rated through the third.
Top Spec(IRE) Official explanation: jockey said gelding missed the break
Admiral Compton Official explanation: jockey said gelding was unsuited by the good to firm (firm in places) ground
Lizarazu(GER) Official explanation: jockey said gelding missed the break and would not face the blinkers
T/Jkpt: Not won. T/Plt: £474.40 to a £1 stake. Pool: £45,076.45. 69.35 winning tickets. T/Qpdt: £294.50 to a £1 stake. Pool: £2,427.90. 6.10 winning tickets. JN

1030 MUSSELBURGH (R-H)
Thursday, May 4

OFFICIAL GOING: Good to firm
Wind: Virtually nil

1436 EDINBURGH EVENING NEWS H'CAP — 1m 6f
6:00 (6:00) (Class 6) (0-65,62) 4-Y-0+ **£3,412** (£1,007; £504) **Stalls** High

Form RPR

06-0 **1** **Whoopsie**[12] 1138 4-8-12 **51** .... DeanMcKeown 9 59
(S Parr) *mde virtually all: pushed along over 3f out: rdn and hung lft wl over 1f out: drvn ins last: hld on gamely* **7/1**[3]

00-0 **2** *nk* **Toss The Caber (IRE)**[17] 1045 4-9-2 **55** ....(t) TomEaves 11 63
(K G Reveley) *prom: trckd wnr fr over 4f out: chal wl over 2f out: rdn over 1f out and ev ch tl drvn and no ex last 50 yds* **16/1**

-500 **3** *1 1/2* **Mary Gray**[12] 1138 4-8-11 **50** .... KDarley 1 55
(M Johnston) *trckd ldrs: hdwy 3f out: rdn and ev ch over 1f out: edgd lft and drvn ins last: one pce* **7/2**[1]

4 *3/4* **Thoutmosis (USA)**[25] 7-9-3 **55** .... PaulHanagan 7 59
(L Lungo) *in tch: hdwy 4f out: rdn to chse ldrs over 2f out: sn drvn and kpt on same pce* **16/1**

3200 **5** *2 1/2* **High Frequency (IRE)**[7] 1256 5-8-9 **47** ....(p) PhillipMakin 2 48
(T D Barron) *hld up in midfield: hdwy on outer 3f out: sn rdn along and no imp appr last* **7/1**[3]

00-0 **6** *1 1/2* **Minivet**[22] 975 11-8-3 **46** ow1 .... AndrewMullen[(5)] 4 45
(R Allan) *bhd tl styd on u.p fnl 3f: nrst fin* **28/1**

/000 **7** *1* **Delta Force**[62] 570 7-8-7 **45** .... AdrianTNicholls 8 42
(P A Blockley) *prom: rdn along 4f out: wknd 3f out* **33/1**

4520 **8** *1* **Brockhole (IRE)**[30] 882 4-9-3 **56** .... JohnEgan 6 52
(J G Given) *hld up: effrt and sme hdwy over 3f out: sn rdn along and no imp fr wl over 1f out* **8/1**

/5-0 **9** *shd* **Royal Glen (IRE)**[10] 1034 8-8-7 **45** .... RoystonFfrench 3 41
(W S Coltherd) *in tch: hdwy to chse ldrs over 3f out: rdn over 2f out: grad wknd* **33/1**

2005 **10** *1 1/4* **Three Boars**[43] 696 4-8-12 **51** ....(b) DarryllHolland 5 45
(S Gollings) *in tch: rdn along over 3f out and sn wknd* **4/1**[2]

50/4 **11** *24* **Sconced (USA)**[6] 816 11-8-8 **46** ow1 ....(b) FergalLynch 10 7
(R C Guest) *a rr* **14/1**

20-0 **12** *2 1/2* **Royal Auditon**[69] 503 5-9-10 **62** .... NCallan 12 19
(T T Clement) *a rr* **25/1**

3m 5.69s (-0.01) **Going Correction** +0.025s/f (Good)
WFA 4 from 5yo+ 1lb **12** Ran SP% **109.9**
Speed ratings (Par 101):101,100,99,99,98 97,96,96,96,95 81,80
CSF £99.30 CT £426.63 TOTE £8.00: £2.20, £6.40, £2.40; EX 102.40.
Owner Mrs M Slater **Bred** Mrs G Slater **Trained** Carburton, Notts

FOCUS
A poor handicap in which very few ever got into it and the first four virtually occupied those places throughout.
Three Boars Official explanation: jockey said gelding was unsuited by the good to firm ground
Sconced(USA) Official explanation: jockey said gelding was unsuited by the good to firm ground
Royal Auditon Official explanation: jockey said mare lost its action

1437 MURRAY BEITH MURRAY MAIDEN STKS — 5f
6:30 (6:30) (Class 5) 3-Y-0+ **£4,095** (£1,209; £604) **Stalls** Low

Form RPR

54-2 **1** **Sea Salt**[12] 1147 3-9-0 82 .... PhillipMakin 2 70
(T D Barron) *mde all: rdn wl over 1f out: drvn ins last and jst hld on* **4/6**[1]

2 *shd* **Urbe Condita (IRE)** 3-9-0 .... KDarley 4 69
(T J Etherington) *dwlt: towards rr: hdwy over 2f out: swtchd rt and rdn over 1f out: styd on strly ins last: jst failed* **20/1**

0-00 **3** *4* **Jun Fan (USA)**[90] 290 4-9-9 50 .... PatCosgrave 1 57
(B Ellison) *chsd ldrs: rdn over 1f out: styd on same pce ins last* **25/1**

33-0 **4** *1 1/4* **Mozakhraf (USA)**[6] 1275 4-9-9 64 .... NCallan 7 52
(K A Ryan) *cl up: pushed along 2f out: sn rdn and wknd appr last* **9/4**[2]

000- **5** *2 1/2* **Sokoke**[241] 4997 5-9-9 45 .... DerekMcGaffin 5 42
(D A Nolan) *cl up: rdn along 1/2-way: sn wknd* **100/1**

60-0 **6** *4* **Pensata**[8] 1234 3-8-9 45 .... RoystonFfrench 3 17
(Miss L A Perratt) *in tch: rdn along 1/2-way: sn wknd* **50/1**

020- **7** *2* **Midnight Pearl (USA)**[234] 5182 3-8-9 68 .... DarryllHolland 9 9
(J Howard Johnson) *chsd ldrs: swtchd rt and rdn 2f out: sn btn* **12/1**[3]

000- **8** *3* **Crystal Bay (IRE)**[202] 5881 3-8-9 30 .... JohnEgan 8 —
(A Berry) *sn outpcd and bhd* **100/1**

460- **9** *8* **Once In A Bluemoon (IRE)**[231] 5237 3-8-9 30 .... FergalLynch 6 —
(A Berry) *s.i.s: a bhd* **100/1**

58.30 secs (-2.20) **Going Correction** -0.325s/f (Firm)
WFA 3 from 4yo+ 9lb **9** Ran SP% **112.0**
Speed ratings (Par 103):104,103,97,95,91 85,81,77,64
CSF £19.98 TOTE £1.80: £1.02, £3.00, £4.20; EX 15.50.
Owner J H Tattersall **Bred** D R Tucker **Trained** Maunby, N Yorks

FOCUS
A modest maiden on paper and a two-horse race according to the market, but the front pair pulled well clear off the rest and the winning time was decent when compared with the handicap that followed.

1438 WEATHERBYS INSURANCE H'CAP — 5f
7:00 (7:00) (Class 3) (0-90,90) 3-Y-0+
£11,217 (£3,358; £1,679; £840; £419; £210) **Stalls** Low

Form RPR

05-2 **1** **Highland Warrior**[18] 1031 7-9-3 **79** .... TonyCulhane 8 88
(J S Goldie) *dwlt: hld up in rr: smooth hdwy 1/2-way: str run ent last: led last 100 yds* **7/1**

1-00 **2** *1* **Harry Up**[83] 362 5-9-1 **77** .... NCallan 9 82+
(K A Ryan) *cl up: led wl over 1f out: sn rdn: drvn ins last: hdd and nt qckn last 100 yds* **17/2**

0-00 **3** *1* **Catch The Cat (IRE)**[5] 1297 7-8-4 **71** oh6............(v) AndrewMullen[(5)] 10 72
(Robert Gray) *chsd ldrs on outer: rdn along wl over 1f out: kpt on wl u.p ins last* **25/1**

00-4 **4** *nk* **Merlin's Dancer**[42] 705 6-10-0 **90** .... AdrianTNicholls 6 90
(D Nicholls) *chsd ldrs: rdn along wl over 1f out: one pce appr last* **9/1**

000- **5** *1* **Ptarmigan Ridge**[200] 5922 10-9-0 **76** .... RoystonFfrench 5 72
(Miss L A Perratt) *in tch: hdwy to chse ldrs 2f out: sn rdn and no imp appr last* **20/1**

34-0 **6** *3/4* **Grigorovitch (IRE)**[18] 1031 4-9-8 **84** .... TomEaves 4 77+
(I Semple) *towards rr: hdwy 2f out: sn swtchd rt and rdn: no imp* **13/2**[3]

3-00 **7** *1* **Mr Wolf**[10] 1183 5-9-8 **84** ....(p) JamieSpencer 7 73
(D W Barker) *led: rdn along over 2f out: hdd wl over 1f out and sn wknd* **7/1**

02-0 **8** *nk* **The Leather Wedge (IRE)**[18] 1031 7-8-6 **71** oh3.... PatrickMathers[(3)] 2 59
(R Johnson) *cl up: rdn along 2f out: drvn and wknd over 1f out* **33/1**

21-3 **9** *1 1/2* **Fullandby (IRE)**[32] 846 4-9-12 **88** .... KDarley 1 70+
(T J Etherington) *s.i.s: a rr* **3/1**[1]

16-4 **10** *nk* **Come Out Fighting**[19] 1020 3-9-5 **90** .... GrahamGibbons 11 70
(P A Blockley) *in tch: hdwy on outer to chse ldrs over 2f out: sn rdn and btn* **11/2**[2]

604- **11** *2* **Sentiero Rosso (USA)**[182] 6238 4-9-1 **77** .... PatCosgrave 12 49
(B Ellison) *sn outpcd: a rr* **40/1**

58.02 secs (-2.48) **Going Correction** -0.325s/f (Firm)
WFA 3 from 4yo+ 9lb **11** Ran SP% **113.2**
Speed ratings (Par 107):106,104,102,102,100 99,97,97,95,94 91
CSF £59.53 CT £1391.98 TOTE £6.80: £1.80, £3.80, £4.20; EX 86.10.
Owner Frank & Annette Brady **Bred** Rowcliffe Stud **Trained** Uplawmoor, E Renfrews

FOCUS
A competitive handicap run at a solid pace. The front three were all drawn high, but they took varied routes and the result was not due to a draw bias.

NOTEBOOK
Highland Warrior had everything go right for him this time, a strong pace to run at and the gaps appearing at the right time. His rider looked confident even before he got to the leader, so he can be rated a bit better than the winning margin. (tchd 8-1)
Harry Up, returning from a three-month break, eventually came out best after a three-way battle for the lead but the winner swamped him well inside the last furlong. He has not won on turf for nearly three years, but is still well handicapped on the very best of his form and there should be other days. (tchd 10-1)
Catch The Cat(IRE) ◆, with the visor back on, ran a solid race out in the centre of the track from 6lb out of the handicap. His current proper mark is 4lb lower than for this last three victories and, now that the ground has come right for him, is one to watch.
Merlin's Dancer has gained all five of his victories over six and it was noticeable that he was struggling to go the pace from some way out. He stuck to his guns well enough though, and should eventually find another opportunity back over an extra furlong. (tchd 10-1)
Ptarmigan Ridge has always needed his seasonal reappearance since making a successful racecourse debut as a two-year-old, so this return performance on ground that would have been faster than ideal suggests he is no back number yet.
Grigorovitch(IRE) could never land an effective blow and could do with some help from the Handicapper. (op 8-1)

Fullandby(IRE) could ill-afford to miss the break over this trip so he should not be judged too harshly on this. Official explanation: jockey said gelding was slow away (op 11-4 tchd 100-30 in a place)

Come Out Fighting, the only three-year-old in the line-up, faced a stiff task against his elders. He is still relatively unexposed and should do better back against his own age group. (tchd 9-2)

1439 FORTH ONE H'CAP — 1m 4f

7:30 (7:30) (Class 4) (0-80,77) 4-Y-0+ **£7,772** (£2,312; £1,155; £577) **Stalls** High

Form				RPR
4-21	**1**		**Saif Sareea**[8] [1233] 6-8-11 **67** 6ex ... PaulHanagan 1 (R A Fahey) *keen: mde all: shkn up 2f out and styd on strly* **4/7**[1]	80+
1114	**2**	*6*	**Polish Power (GER)**[22] [983] 6-9-4 **74** ... JohnEgan 6 (J S Moore) *trckd ldng pair: hdwy to chse wnr over 3f out: rdn 2f out: drvn and one pce appr last* **7/1**[3]	77
360-	**3**	*1 1/4*	**Incursion**[196] [5451] 5-9-7 **77** ... AdrianTNicholls 3 (D Nicholls) *hld up in rr: hdwy over 3f out: rdn 2f out: edgd lft and kpt on same pce* **33/1**	78
-622	**4**	*5*	**Platinum Charmer (IRE)**[9] [1222] 6-8-2 **63** ... (p) AndrewElliott(5) 4 (K R Burke) *trckd ldrs: effrt on outer 3f out: sn rdn and wknd fnl 2f* **5/1**[2]	56
446-	**5**	*5*	**Thistle**[271] [4141] 5-9-2 **72** ... DarryllHolland 2 (J Howard Johnson) *chsd wnr: rdn along 4f out: drvn and wknd wl over 2f out* **20/1**	57
-050	**6**	*3/4*	**Fiddlers Creek (IRE)**[3] [1346] 7-8-2 **58** ... (t) RoystonFfrench 7 (R Allan) *hld up in tch: hdwy over 4f out: rdn along 3f out and sn btn* **20/1**	42

2m 37.02s (0.12) **Going Correction** +0.025s/f (Good) **6** Ran SP% **105.3**
Speed ratings (Par 105):100,96,95,91,88 88
CSF £4.00 TOTE £1.50: £1.10, £2.40; EX 4.00.
Owner The Ipso Facto Syndicate **Bred** Mrs M Beddis **Trained** Musley Bank, N Yorks

FOCUS
A very uncompetitive handicap with half of the six runner starting at 20/1 or longer. The outcome was as predictable as the betting had suggested from a very long way out.

1440 RUK EVENING RACING FOR £60 H'CAP — 1m

8:00 (8:00) (Class 4) (0-85,85) 3-Y-0 **£7,772** (£2,312; £1,155; £577) **Stalls** Low

Form				RPR
1-	**1**		**Crime Scene (IRE)**[313] [2927] 3-9-4 **85** ... KDarley 5 (M Johnston) *trckd ldng pair: effrt over 2f out: rdn wl over 1f out: styd on strly ins last to ld nr fin* **13/2**[3]	92+
-123	**2**	*hd*	**Direct Debit (IRE)**[6] [1268] 3-9-4 **85** ... JamieSpencer 1 (M L W Bell) *trckd ldr: hdwy over 3f out: rdn to ld ent last: sn drvn: hdd and no ex nr line* **2/1**[2]	92
55-1	**3**	*1 1/4*	**King Of The Moors (USA)**[18] [1032] 3-9-3 **84** ... PhillipMakin 6 (T D Barron) *led: rdn along wl over 2f out: drvn and hdd ent last: kpt on same pce* **20/1**	88
4-21	**4**	*1*	**European Dream (IRE)**[3] [1345] 3-8-7 **74** 6ex ... FergalLynch 4 (R C Guest) *hld up in tch: hdwy and swtchd rt over 2f out: effrt wl over 1f out: swtchd lft and rdn ent last: kpt on same pce* **13/8**[1]	76
2-46	**5**	*1 1/2*	**Creative Mind (IRE)**[26] [925] 3-8-11 **78** ... DarryllHolland 2 (E J O'Neill) *hld up: hdwy over 2f out: sn rdn and no imp appr last* **16/1**	76
35-5	**6**	*1 1/4*	**Zabeel House**[14] [1095] 3-9-4 **85** ... RobertWinston 7 (E A L Dunlop) *s.i.s: a towards rr* **8/1**	81
400-	**7**	*15*	**Cape Gold (IRE)**[237] [5086] 3-8-4 **71** ... PaulHanagan 3 (R A Fahey) *chsd ldrs: rdn along 3f out: wknd over 2f out* **33/1**	32

1m 42.54s (0.04) **Going Correction** +0.025s/f (Good) **7** Ran SP% **109.5**
Speed ratings (Par 101):100,99,98,97,96 94,79
CSF £18.22 TOTE £9.10: £2.20, £2.20; EX 18.00.
Owner Gainsborough Stud **Bred** Gainsborough Stud Management Ltd **Trained** Middleham Moor, N Yorks

FOCUS
A decent little three-year-old handicap though the pace looked ordinary. A couple of these are likely to carry on improving.

1441 FORTH TWO H'CAP — 7f 30y

8:30 (8:30) (Class 6) (0-65,65) 3-Y-0 **£3,238** (£963; £481; £240) **Stalls** Low

Form				RPR
00-2	**1**		**Angaric (IRE)**[22] [978] 3-9-4 **65** ... TonyCulhane 5 (B Smart) *a.p: effrt 2f out: sn rdn: drvn to ld ins last: hld on wl* **13/2**[3]	70
3004	**2**	*nk*	**Beowulf**[22] [978] 3-9-3 **64** ... KDarley 7 (M Johnston) *in tch: hdwy over 2f out: rdn over 1f out: styd on to dispute ld ins last and ev ch tl drvn and no ex nr fin* **11/2**[2]	68
0-66	**3**	*nk*	**Sgt Schultz (IRE)**[21] [1004] 3-9-3 **64** ... RobertWinston 4 (J S Moore) *hld up: pushed along 3f out: gd hdwy on outer 2f out: sn rdn and ev ch over 1f out tl drvn and no ex wl ins last* **5/2**[1]	68
5-00	**4**	*1 3/4*	**Quaker Boy**[8] [1232] 3-8-13 **60** ... TomEaves 10 (M Dods) *cl up: rdn to ld wl over 1f out: drvn and hdd ins last: wknd towards fin* **16/1**	59
00-0	**5**	*1*	**Boy Dancer (IRE)**[22] [980] 3-8-7 **54** ow2 ... JamieSpencer 6 (D W Barker) *keen: hld up in rr: hdwy and n.m.r over 2f out: swtchd lft wl over 1f out: styd on ins last: nrst fin* **7/1**	50+
060-	**6**	*shd*	**Gifted Glori**[187] [6136] 3-8-4 **51** oh1 ... GrahamGibbons 12 (J J Quinn) *chsd ldrs on inner: rdn along over 2f out: kpt on same pce appr last* **15/2**	47
200-	**7**	*1 1/2*	**Sea Grain (IRE)**[274] [4052] 3-9-3 **64** ... RoystonFfrench 8 (Robert Gray) *midfield tl styd on fnl 2f: nrst fin* **100/1**	56
0-40	**8**	*nk*	**Penny Glitters**[15] [1085] 3-9-4 **65** ... DeanMcKeown 13 (S Parr) *led: rdn along wl over 2f out: drvn and hdd wl over 1f out: wknd ent last* **14/1**	56
-000	**9**	*1 3/4*	**Obscene**[3] [1337] 3-8-13 **60** ... NCallan 1 (M J Polglase) *in tch on outer: rdn along wl over 2f out: no imp* **12/1**	47
562-	**10**	*3 1/2*	**Laphonic (USA)**[184] [6212] 3-8-8 **55** ow1 ... DarryllHolland 11 (T J Etherington) *chsd ldrs: rdn along over 2f out: grad wknd* **16/1**	33
0-00	**11**	*3*	**Mycenean Prince (USA)**[3] [1345] 3-8-5 **52** ... JohnEgan 2 (R C Guest) *a rr* **66/1**	22
1600	**12**	*dist*	**Tilen (IRE)**[36] [796] 3-8-4 **51** oh2 ... PaulHanagan 3 (S Parr) *stdd s: hld up and a bhd* **20/1**	—

1m 30.25s (0.31) **Going Correction** +0.025s/f (Good) **12** Ran SP% **114.9**
Speed ratings (Par 97):99,98,98,96,95 95,93,93,91,87 83,—
CSF £40.28 CT £113.10 TOTE £8.20: £2.50, £1.80, £1.80; EX 25.80.
Owner Anthony D Gee **Bred** Humphrey Okeke **Trained** Hambleton, N Yorks

FOCUS
A moderate handicap, but very competitive and there were six in a line across the track a furlong from home.

Mycenean Prince(USA) Official explanation: jockey said gelding had a breathing problem

T/Plt: £36.10 to a £1 stake. Pool: £40,070.15. 808.50 winning tickets. T/Qpdt: £12.90 to a £1 stake. Pool: £3,169.10. 181.70 winning tickets. JR

1040 REDCAR (L-H)

Thursday, May 4

OFFICIAL GOING: Firm (good to firm in places)
The ground was described as 'just on the quick side of good with a very good cover of grass'.
Wind: Moderate; half behind Weather: Fine and sunny but breezy

1442 REDCARRACING.CO.UK MAIDEN AUCTION STKS — 5f

2:20 (2:21) (Class 5) 2-Y-0 **£3,238** (£963; £481; £240) **Stalls** Centre

Form				RPR
6	**1**		**Major Third (IRE)**[15] [1080] 2-8-12 ... DavidAllan 6 (T D Easterby) *mde virtually all: hld on wl* **5/1**[3]	66
24	**2**	*3/4*	**Fractured Foxy**[14] [1096] 2-8-4 ... GrahamGibbons 11 (J J Quinn) *mid-div: hdwy over 2f out: styd on ins last* **9/4**[1]	55
0	**3**	*1*	**Flamestone**[15] [1080] 2-8-9 ... TedDurcan 9 (J D Bethell) *sn outpcd and in rr: hdwy 2f out: styd on ins last* **20/1**	56
	4	*shd*	**Riotous (IRE)** 2-8-9 ... DanielTudhope(3) 5 (A Dickman) *str: cmpt: dwlt: hdwy over 2f out: kpt on fnl f* **20/1**	59
	5	*3/4*	**Ishibee (IRE)** 2-8-7 ... PaulFessey 10 (Mrs A Duffield) *lengthy: scope: swtchd rt after s and racd stands' side: sn chsng ldrs: edgd lft and kpt on fnl f* **14/1**	51
	6	*shd*	**Luscivious** 2-8-12 ... DeanMcKeown 12 (M J Polglase) *rangy: unf: dwlt: hdwy over 2f out: kpt on fnl f: nt rch ldrs* **4/1**[2]	55
	7	*nk*	**La Vecchia Scuola (IRE)** 2-8-7 ... AdrianTNicholls 8 (D Nicholls) *rangy: scope: chsd ldrs: kpt on same pce fnl 2f* **14/1**	49
	8	*3/4*	**Laguna Reef** 2-8-9 ... RobertWinston 3 (T D Easterby) *rangy: unf: scope: chsd ldrs: hung lft over 1f out: one pce* **14/1**	48
00	**9**	*1/2*	**Homes By Woodford**[3] [1342] 2-8-6 ... PaulMulrennan(3) 1 (M W Easterby) *sn outpcd: hdwy on outside 2f out: nvr trbld ldrs* **80/1**	46
	10	*2 1/2*	**Practicallyperfect (IRE)** 2-8-7 ... JoeFanning 4 (M Johnston) *lengthy: unf: w ldrs: hung lft 2f out: sn lost pl* **8/1**	34+
	11	*2 1/2*	**Silly Gilly (IRE)** 2-8-4 ... FrancisNorton 2 (A Berry) *rangy: unf: s.s: a in rr* **25/1**	21
5	**12**	*1 1/4*	**Bowl Em Over**[15] [1080] 2-8-4 ... NeilPollard 7 (M E Sowersby) *w wnr: hung bdly lft and lost pl over 1f out* **14/1**	16

59.99 secs (1.29) **Going Correction** +0.025s/f (Good) **12** Ran SP% **119.8**
Speed ratings (Par 93):90,88,87,87,85 85,85,84,83,79 75,73
CSF £16.01 TOTE £7.50: £2.10, £1.40, £9.20; EX 21.20.
Owner John & Marilyn Williams **Bred** Kilian Farm **Trained** Great Habton, N Yorks

FOCUS
Probably a very ordinary maiden auction race but the winner will improve again.

NOTEBOOK

Major Third(IRE) had clearly learnt plenty first time. He really knuckled down and will improve again. (op 7-1)

Fractured Foxy, who looked very fit indeed, stayed on from off the pace but her late challenge was always being held. (op 11-4 tchd 3-1)

Flamestone, a fair sort, showed the benefit of his initial outing and will improve again. (tchd 25-1)

Riotous(IRE), a February foal, was first into the paddock and, with his trainer at his side, was noisy and coltish. After missing a beat at the start, he stuck on and this will have taught him plenty. (op 16-1)

Ishibee(IRE), a February foal, looked to be carrying plenty of condition. Switched to race virtually alone down the stands' side, she went looking for company but this will have taught her plenty.

Luscivious, a February foal, was heavily supported to give her trainer a welcome first-time-out juvenile scorer. After a tardy start he was never doing anything like enough but is clearly thought capable of a fair bit better. (op 5-1 tchd 7-2)

Silly Gilly(IRE) (op 16-1)

Bowl Em Over Official explanation: jockey said filly was unsuited by the firm (good to firm in places) ground

1443 RACING UK (S) STKS — 7f

2:50 (2:50) (Class 6) 3-Y-0+ **£2,388** (£705; £352) **Stalls** Centre

Form				RPR
000-	**1**		**Cd Europe (IRE)**[215] [5625] 8-9-4 80 ... RobertWinston 8 (G A Swinbank) *hld up: hdwy over 2f out: led 1f out: shkn up and styd on* **6/4**[1]	64+
-004	**2**	*2*	**Green Pirate**[8] [1235] 4-9-4 53 ... PaulFessey 3 (R Craggs) *trckd ldrs: chal over 1f out: kpt on same pce ins last* **7/1**	59
000-	**3**	*nk*	**Petite Mac**[164] [6407] 6-8-6 52 ... SuzzanneFrance(7) 4 (N Bycroft) *w ldrs: led over 2f out: hdd 1f out: no ex* **16/1**	53
1020	**4**	*nk*	**Banjo Bay (IRE)**[12] [1150] 8-9-3 60 ... KellyHarrison(7) 10 (D Nicholls) *trckd ldrs: kpt on same pce fnl f* **5/1**[2]	63
0206	**5**	*4*	**Aswan (IRE)**[87] [315] 8-8-13 55 ... (t) MarcHalford(5) 1 (S R Bowring) *led tl over 2f out: wknd over 1f out* **16/1**	47
0-00	**6**	*1 1/2*	**Dispol Valentine**[84] [347] 3-7-8 45 ... LiamJones(7) 7 (P T Midgley) *trckd ldrs: wknd over 1f out* **66/1**	38
0-00	**7**	*2 1/2*	**Downland (IRE)**[13] [1124] 10-9-4 56 ... KimTinkler 11 (N Tinkler) *in tch: reminders over 3f out: nvr rchd ldrs* **13/2**[3]	37
0-00	**8**	*1*	**Lord Conyers (IRE)**[69] [501] 7-8-13 45 ... JamieSpencer 6 (G Woodward) *in rr: rdn and kpt on fnl 3f: nvr on terms* **12/1**	29
520-	**9**	*1 3/4*	**Splodger Mac (IRE)**[197] [5979] 7-9-4 47 ... (b) FrancisNorton 2 (N Bycroft) *s.s: hdwy to chse ldrs after 2f: lost pl over 1f out* **20/1**	29
-000	**10**	*2*	**Nebraska City**[22] [974] 5-9-1 40 ... (b[1]) PaulMulrennan(3) 9 (D W Thompson) *a outpcd and in rr* **125/1**	24
34-0	**11**	*12*	**Luke After Me (IRE)**[22] [974] 6-9-1 48 ... BenSwarbrick(3) 5 (Miss Tracy Waggott) *s.v.s: hdwy and in tch over 3f out: sn lost pl and bhd* **25/1**	—

1m 24.62s (-0.28) **Going Correction** +0.025s/f (Good)
WFA 3 from 4yo+ 12lb **11** Ran SP% **112.9**
Speed ratings (Par 101):102,99,99,99,94 92,89,88,86,84 70
CSF £11.09 TOTE £2.00: £1.20, £1.90, £4.70; EX 14.50.There was no bid for the winner.
Owner Gary Flitcroft **Bred** Airlie Stud **Trained** Melsonby, N Yorks

FOCUS
A one-sided contest on official ratings but how good the winner is now remains to be seen. The race is rated through the runner-up.

Luke After Me(IRE) Official explanation: jockey said gelding was slowly away

1444 JOHN SMITH'S REDCAR STRAIGHT-MILE CHAMPIONSHIP STKS (H'CAP) (QUALIFIER) 1m
3:20 (3:21) (Class 5) (0-75,75) 3-Y-O £3,238 (£963; £481; £240) Stalls Centre

Form RPR
5-03 **1** **Methusaleh (IRE)**[13] 1122 3-9-4 **75** DavidAllan 8 79
(T D Easterby) *hld up: hdwy 2f out: styd on wl to ld last 75yds* **7/1**[3]
50-0 **2** ½ **Il Castagno (IRE)**[21] 1004 3-9-4 **75** PhilipRobinson 3 78
(B Smart) *led after 1f: hung lft over 1f out: hdd and no ex wl ins last* **20/1**
1-60 **3** 1 ½ **Suits Me**[14] 1097 3-9-2 **73** GrahamGibbons 6 73
(J J Quinn) *hld up: hdwy over 2f out: kpt on wl fnl f* **14/1**
411 **4** 3 **Piano Player (IRE)**[33] 839 3-9-2 **73** EddieAhern 9 66
(J A Osborne) *trckd ldrs: hung bdly lft over 1f out: sn btn* **4/1**[2]
004- **5** 1 ¼ **Ayam Jantan**[230] 5264 3-8-5 **62** JoeFanning 4 52
(M Johnston) *led 1f: chsd ldrs: wknd over 1f out* **15/2**
0500 **6** 1 ¾ **Eliminator**[3] 1345 3-7-13 **61** oh1 NataliaGemelova[(5)] 2 47
(I W McInnes) *prom: sn drvn along: one pce whn sltly hmpd over 1f out* **50/1**
00-1 **7** ¾ **Malech (IRE)**[36] 797 3-9-1 **72** JamieSpencer 7 56
(M L W Bell) *s.s: bhd: drvn along over 3f out: nvr on terms* **11/10**[1]
34-0 **8** 1 ½ **Dream Rose (IRE)**[15] 1085 3-9-2 **73** TonyCulhane 1 54
(M R Channon) *stmbld s: sn trcking ldrs: wkng whn carried lft over 1f out* **16/1**
510- **9** nk **Grandad Bill (IRE)**[279] 3898 3-8-12 **74** DuranFentiman[(5)] 5 54
(T D Easterby) *trckd ldrs over 3f: grad wknd* **28/1**

1m 37.54s (-0.26) **Going Correction** +0.025s/f (Good) **9** Ran SP% **114.6**
Speed ratings (Par 99):102,101,100,97,95 94,93,91,91
CSF £130.92 CT £1902.76 TOTE £8.00: £2.50, £5.30, £4.00; EX 113.70.
Owner bellhouseracing.com **Bred** Stall A And R **Trained** Great Habton, N Yorks

FOCUS
The complexion of the race changed when the traps opened and the favourite missed the break, but full marks to the winner who was breaking his duck. The form is ordinary but straightforward with the placed horses to form.
Malech(IRE) Official explanation: jockey said gelding missed the break

1445 TRANSMORE VAN HIRE MEDIAN AUCTION MAIDEN STKS 7f
3:50 (3:53) (Class 5) 3-Y-O £3,238 (£963; £481; £240) Stalls Centre

Form RPR
1 **La Matanza** 3-8-9 BenSwarbrick[(3)] 6 73
(T D Barron) *leggy: trckd ldrs: effrt over 2f out: styd on to ld jst ins last* **50/1**
35 **2** 1 ¾ **Five Two**[12] 1135 3-9-3 TedDurcan 2 73
(M R Channon) *sn trcking ldrs: hung lft over 1f out: kpt on same pce* **11/2**[2]
005- **3** 1 ¾ **Our Sheila**[203] 5857 3-8-12 65 RobertWinston 10 63
(B Smart) *swvd rt s: sn trcking ldrs: led over 2f out tl jst ins last: no ex* **8/1**
6- **4** nk **Ruse**[170] 6360 3-8-12 JamieSpencer 4 62
(J R Fanshawe) *trckd ldrs: rdn and outpcd over 2f out: kpt on fnl f* **6/1**[3]
3-2 **5** 1 **Compromiznotension (IRE)**[9] 1212 3-9-3 PhilipRobinson 8 65
(M A Jarvis) *led tl over 2f out: wknd over 1f out* **4/7**[1]
6 5 **Xpres Maite** 3-9-3 PaulEddery 5 52
(S R Bowring) *rangy: s.i.s: bhd: kpt on fnl 2f: nvr on terms* **100/1**
00-0 **7** 2 ½ **Nimble Star**[24] 936 3-8-12 45 LeeEnstone 7 40
(C W Fairhurst) *s.i.s: hdwy over 3f out: rdn and lost pl 2f out* **200/1**
0 **8** 2 ½ **Centreofattention**[9] 1218 3-8-9 SaleemGolam[(3)] 1 34
(Mrs A Duffield) *sn trcking ldrs on outside: lost pl 2f out* **50/1**
5- **9** 7 **Jenise (IRE)**[159] 6435 3-8-7 DuranFentiman[(5)] 9 15
(Mark Campion) *unruly in stalls: chsd ldrs: lost pl over 2f out* **33/1**
00- **10** hd **Deserted Island (IRE)**[325] 2541 3-8-9 DNolan[(3)] 3 15
(N Wilson) *w ldrs: hung lft and lost pl over 2f out* **200/1**

1m 24.79s (-0.11) **Going Correction** +0.025s/f (Good) **10** Ran SP% **113.3**
Speed ratings (Par 99):101,99,97,96,95 89,86,84,76,75
CSF £295.02 TOTE £50.90: £10.00, £1.60, £2.30; EX 290.30.
Owner J G Brown **Bred** A C M Spalding **Trained** Maunby, N Yorks

FOCUS
A weak maiden rated around the placed horses, but anchored by the proximity of the 45-rated seventh.
Jenise(IRE) Official explanation: jockey said filly was unsuited by the firm (good to firm in places) ground

1446 JACKSONS-CPL SOLICITORS AMIGOS H'CAP 1m 2f
4:20 (4:20) (Class 3) (0-95,87) 3-Y-O £8,096 (£2,408; £1,203; £601) Stalls Low

Form RPR
0-1 **1** **Pearly King (USA)**[17] 1055 3-9-4 **87** RobertWinston 1 92+
(Sir Michael Stoute) *trckd ldrs: effrt over 3f out: led over 1f out: r.o wl* **8/13**[1]
110- **2** nk **Nihal (IRE)**[238] 5064 3-9-1 **84** JoeFanning 3 89
(M Johnston) *trckd ldrs: effrt over 3f out: led over 2f out: hdd over 1f out: no ex ins last* **13/2**[3]
01-0 **3** 4 **Participation**[19] 1016 3-9-3 **86** (t) JamieSpencer 4 83?
(M J Wallace) *hld up: hdwy to ld 7f out: shkn up and qcknd 3f out: one pce* **7/2**[2]
210- **4** 4 **Heureux (USA)**[195] 6005 3-8-13 **82** EddieAhern 2 71
(J Howard Johnson) *set mod pce: hdd 7f out: drvn and outpcd 3f out: no threat after* **10/1**

2m 8.65s (1.85) **Going Correction** +0.025s/f (Good) **4** Ran SP% **106.6**
Speed ratings (Par 103):93,92,89,86
CSF £4.81 TOTE £1.50; EX 3.10.
Owner Gainsborough Stud **Bred** Swettenham Stud **Trained** Newmarket, Suffolk

FOCUS
A pathetic turnout for a race carrying £12,500 prize money including a fourth-place prize, and the winning time was very moderate for a race of its type, but the first two are all right and the winner could be very useful.

NOTEBOOK
Pearly King(USA) ◆, happy to get a lead, was always doing enough. An Irish Derby entry, he will be seen to much greater effect coming off a stronger pace over a mile and a half. (op 4-7 tchd 4-6 in a place)
Nihal(IRE), 8lb higher than when winning a nursery at York in August, looked in good order. She went down fighting to an unknown quantity and deserves to win a race or two this year. (op 6-1)
Participation, with the visor left off, was dropped in but with the pace sedate the champion took things into his own hands. He looks weighted to the limit but will be better off in a bigger field with a stronger pace. (tchd 3-1)
Heureux(USA), who needs quick ground, did not impress as a stayer and his win at two was over six. (op 12-1 tchd 14-1)

1447 REDCAR CONFERENCE CENTRE APPRENTICE CLAIMING STKS 6f
4:50 (4:51) (Class 6) 3-4-Y-O £2,388 (£705; £352) Stalls Centre

Form RPR
0005 **1** **Chairman Rick (IRE)**[100] 180 4-8-13 40 SilvestreDeSousa 2 53
(D Nicholls) *s.i.s: sn chsng ldrs: led over 1f out: kpt on wl* **14/1**
0045 **2** 1 **Suhezy (IRE)**[8] 1234 3-8-4 53 SaleemGolam 4 48
(P T Midgley) *chsd ldrs: outpcd over 2f out: hdwy over 1f out: styd on ins last* **11/4**[1]
0240 **3** nk **Beverley Beau**[10] 1196 4-8-10 46 KristinStubbs[(5)] 1 51
(Mrs L Stubbs) *led tl over 1f out: styd on same pce* **11/2**[3]
0251 **4** nk **Midge's Girl (IRE)**[44] 690 3-7-5 49 (v) LukeMorris[(7)] 9 40
(Mrs A Duffield) *s.i.s: hdwy and wnt lft over 1f out: kpt on wl* **13/2**
0022 **5** 1 ¾ **Desert Lightning (IRE)**[9] 1217 4-8-10 57 PatrickDonaghy[(7)] 10 47
(K R Burke) *swtchd lft s: hld up: hdwy over 2f out: bmpd and carried lft ent fnl f: kpt on same pce* **10/3**[2]
0000 **6** 1 ½ **Straffan (IRE)**[17] 1054 4-8-10 45 (b) MarcHalford[(3)] 5 38
(J Hetherton) *s.i.s: hdwy on wd outside over 2f out: upsides over 1f out: wknd fnl 150yds* **12/1**
00-0 **7** 3 **Sweetly Sharp (IRE)**[22] 980 3-7-12 47 KevinGhunowa[(5)] 3 26
(A Berry) *chsd ldrs: rdn over 2f out: wknd over 1f out* **22/1**
30-0 **8** ½ **Haroldini (IRE)**[10] 1196 4-9-2 45 (p) GregFairley[(3)] 7 34
(J Balding) *trckd ldrs: rdn 2f out: sn wknd* **10/1**
0-60 **9** ¾ **Coquet Island**[22] 980 3-8-0 57 DuranFentiman[(3)] 8 23
(G M Moore) *chsd ldrs: wknd over 1f out* **28/1**
0/0- **10** 3 ½ **Apetite**[233] 5207 4-8-10 52 SuzzanneFrance[(5)] 11 17
(N Bycroft) *bhd: sme hdwy 3f out: sn lost pl* **33/1**
06- **11** 19 **Desert Bounty**[339] 2130 3-8-4 PaulMulrennan 6 —
(G M Moore) *chsd ldrs: lost pl over 3f out: sn bhd: virtually p.u* **16/1**

1m 11.8s (0.10) **Going Correction** +0.025s/f (Good)
WFA 3 from 4yo 10lb **11** Ran SP% **118.5**
Speed ratings (Par 101):100,98,98,97,95 93,89,88,87,83 57
CSF £51.91 TOTE £11.50: £3.50, £1.60, £2.30; EX 82.20.
Owner J Higginson & Mrs A Nicholls **Bred** Philip Brady **Trained** Sessay, N Yorks
■ Stewards' Enquiry : Luke Morris caution: careless riding

FOCUS
They don't come much worse than this yet it was the best time performance of the day. The form appears sound with the placed horses close to their marks.
Sweetly Sharp(IRE) Official explanation: jockey said filly hung left

1448 WE'RE BACKING THE BORO FILLIES' H'CAP 5f
5:20 (5:22) (Class 4) (0-85,85) 3-Y-O+ £5,505 (£1,637; £818; £408) Stalls Centre

Form RPR
5054 **1** **Bonne De Fleur**[13] 1125 5-9-9 **72** (b) RobertWinston 2 83
(B Smart) *mde all: rdn and hung lft over 1f out: kpt on* **2/1**[1]
120- **2** 1 **Millinsky (USA)**[182] 6238 5-9-1 **71** RobbieMills[(7)] 7 78
(Rae Guest) *sn outpcd: hdwy 2f out: styd on ins last: no ex* **5/2**[2]
-000 **3** nk **Ooh Aah Camara (IRE)**[5] 1292 3-9-13 **85** FrancisNorton 4 87
(T J Pitt) *chsd ldrs: reminders after 1f: kpt on same pce appr fnl f* **16/1**
600- **4** hd **Lyndalee (IRE)**[237] 5086 3-8-11 **69** DavidAllan 6 70
(T D Easterby) *chsd ldrs: kpt on same pce appr fnl f* **8/1**
0-14 **5** 1 ¼ **True Magic**[24] 954 5-9-8 **71** TedDurcan 5 71
(J D Bethell) *in rr: hdwy 2f out: n.m.r over 1f out: nvr rchd ldrs* **9/2**[3]
0603 **6** shd **Smooch**[7] 1264 3-9-3 **82** DeanWilliams[(7)] 1 78
(R M H Cowell) *sn outpcd and bhd: wnt rt over 1f out: styd on ins last* **10/1**
21-0 **7** ½ **Rothesay Dancer**[18] 1036 3-8-11 **72** DanielTudhope[(3)] 3 66
(J S Goldie) *in tch: effrt 2f out: nvr trbld ldrs* **11/1**
600- **8** 3 ½ **Safranine (IRE)**[166] 6380 9-8-6 **62** oh12 (p) AnnStokell[(7)] 9 46
(Miss A Stokell) *chsd ldrs: lost pl over 1f out: eased towards fin* **40/1**

58.49 secs (-0.21) **Going Correction** +0.025s/f (Good)
WFA 3 from 4yo+ 9lb **8** Ran SP% **116.9**
Speed ratings (Par 102):102,100,99,99,97 97,96,91
CSF £7.36 CT £60.41 TOTE £2.80: £1.10, £1.60, £2.90; EX 9.20 Place 6 £200.00, Place 5 £102.01.
Owner Miss N Jefford **Bred** Miss N A Jefford **Trained** Hambleton, N Yorks

FOCUS
A fair handicap but ordinary form, rated through the runner-up.
T/Plt: £408.10 to a £1 stake. Pool: £33,689.10. 60.25 winning tickets. T/Qpdt: £524.50 to a £1 stake. Pool: £2,055.50. 2.90 winning tickets. WG

1449 - 1452a (Foreign Racing) - See Raceform Interactive

1436 MUSSELBURGH (R-H)
Friday, May 5

OFFICIAL GOING: Straight course - good to firm (firm in places); round course - firm (good to firm in places)
Wind: Virtually nil

1453 WATCH LIVE RACING ON RACING UK H'CAP 5f
2:20 (2:20) (Class 5) (0-70,69) 3-Y-O £3,886 (£1,156; £577; £288) Stalls Low

Form RPR
00-4 **1** **Welcome Approach**[19] 1036 3-9-1 **66** DarryllHolland 2 73
(J R Weymes) *rr and pushed along 1/2-way: hdwy wl over 1f out: swtchd rt and rdn ent last: styd on wl to ld nr fin* **5/2**[2]
-433 **2** nk **Highland Song (IRE)**[6] 1279 3-9-2 **67** FrancisNorton 3 73
(R F Fisher) *cl up: rdn over 1f out: drvn to ld ent last: hdd and no ex nr fin* **3/1**[3]
-221 **3** 1 ¼ **Toy Top (USA)**[9] 1234 3-9-4 **69** 6ex (b) PhillipMakin 1 70
(M Dods) *chsd ldrs: hdwy 2f out: swtchd rt and rdn to chal over 1f out: drvn and one pce ins last* **2/1**[1]
20-0 **4** 1 **Hypnosis**[4] 1344 3-8-12 **63** RobertWinston 6 60
(D W Barker) *led: rdn along 2f out: drvn and hdd ent last: wknd* **11/1**
00-6 **5** 11 **Howards Prince**[19] 1036 3-9-4 **69** (p) TomEaves 4 22
(I Semple) *chsd ldrs: rdn along 2f out: sn wknd* **9/1**

59.80 secs (-0.70) **Going Correction** -0.15s/f (Firm) **5** Ran SP% **105.2**
Speed ratings (Par 99):99,98,96,94,77
CSF £9.30 TOTE £3.90: £1.90, £2.40; EX 8.90.
Owner T A Scothern **Bred** P Wyatt And Ranby Hall **Trained** Middleham Moor, N Yorks

FOCUS
A modest sprint handicap, but it was run at a fast early pace, the form looks sound, and the winner came from last to first.
Hypnosis Official explanation: jockey said filly hung right-handed in final 2f

1454 RECTANGLE GROUP MEDIAN AUCTION MAIDEN STKS 5f
2:50 (2:50) (Class 5) 2-Y-O **£3,238** (£963; £481; £240) **Stalls** Low

Form RPR

6 **1** **Avertuoso**[14] 1121 2-9-3 ... PhilipRobinson 7 80
(B Smart) *chsd ldng pair: hdwy 2f out: rdn to chal and edgd lft ins last: led last 100 yds* **7/2**[2]

4 **2** 1 **Tencendur (IRE)**[10] 1203 2-9-3 ... KDarley 3 76
(M Johnston) *led: pushed along and edgd rt 2f out: rdn ins last: hdd and nt qckn last 100 yds* **2/1**[1]

42 **3** 1 ½ **Joseph Locke (IRE)**[15] 1096 2-9-3 ... FergalLynch 4 70
(M Dods) *cl up: effrt 2f out and sn rdn: ev ch tl hld whn n.m.r wl ins last* **2/1**[1]

4 3 **Kunte Kinteh** 2-9-3 ... AdrianTNicholls 1 58
(D Nicholls) *s.i.s and bhd: hdwy on outer: 1/2-way: styd on appr last: nrst fin* **25/1**

5 shd **Kaladar (IRE)** 2-9-3 ... NCallan 5 58
(K A Ryan) *chsd ldrs: rdn along 2f out: sn one pce* **9/1**[3]

6 6 **Flushed** 2-9-3 ... DeanMcKeown 6 34
(M J Polglase) *slowly away: a rr* **33/1**

7 5 **Perfect Reflection** 2-8-12 ... FrancisNorton 2 —
(A Berry) *in tch: rdn along 1/2-way: sn outpcd* **25/1**

61.15 secs (0.65) **Going Correction** -0.15s/f (Firm) 7 Ran SP% **109.5**
Speed ratings (Par 93):88,86,84,79,79 69,61
CSF £9.92 TOTE £4.10: £2.30, £1.80; EX 10.70.
Owner Pinnacle Averti Partnership **Bred** P A Mason **Trained** Hambleton, N Yorks

FOCUS
A pretty ordinary maiden run in a modest winning time for a race of its type and dominated by those who had the benefit of previous racecourse experience. The form is difficult to rate and could be slightly higher.

NOTEBOOK
Avertuoso had been too green to do himself justice on his debut, but he had been sent off as joint second-favourite that day, so was clearly thought to have some ability. Pretty solid in the market on this second start, he put up a more professional display, having clearly learnt plenty from that initial outing. (tchd 4-1)
Tencendur(IRE), fourth in a Bath maiden on his debut, grabbed the rail and attempted to make every yard. He hung right in the closing stages, though, and could not hold off the eventual winner. He should get six furlongs and make a nursery type in time. (op 7-4)
Joseph Locke(IRE), whose stable is in good form and who, having raced twice previously, had the most experience of these, looked to hold every chance a furlong and a half out, but he found less than had looked likely under pressure and was getting the worst of the argument when squeezed for room. His previous runs had been on much softer ground than this. (op 9-4)
Kunte Kinteh, a brother to Native American, a winner over ten furlongs at three, is bred to need much further than this in time, so this was a promising debut. (op 33-1)
Kaladar(IRE), for whom there was some market support, is out of a mare who is a half-sister to the top-class juvenile Beckett, from the family of 2000 Guineas winner Entrepreneur and top-class fillies Exclusive and Chic. However, his sire imparts stamina and his progeny tend to do better with time. (op 14-1)

1455 EDMONDS.CO.UK H'CAP 1m
3:20 (3:20) (Class 5) (0-75,75) 4-Y-0+ **£4,533** (£1,348; £674; £336) **Stalls** Low

Form RPR

0-00 **1** **Royal Dignitary (USA)**[13] 1143 6-9-4 **75** ... RobertWinston 2 87
(D Nicholls) *mde all: qcknd clr over 3f out: rdn 2f out and styd on strly* **25/1**

6020 **2** 2 ½ **Sawwaah (IRE)**[10] 1220 9-9-2 **73** ...(v) AdrianTNicholls 8 79
(D Nicholls) *in tch: hdwy on inner 3f out: sn rdn: chse wnr ins last: kpt on* **8/1**[3]

-304 **3** 1 **Defi (IRE)**[63] 571 4-8-12 **69** ...(b) TomEaves 1 73
(I Semple) *chsd wnr: wd st: rdn along over 2f out: drvn over 1f out: kpt on same pce* **8/1**[3]

5-44 **4** 1 **Ballyhurry (USA)**[19] 1035 9-8-11 **68** ... FergalLynch 3 70+
(J S Goldie) *hld up and bhd: hdwy 3f out: rdn and kpt on fnl 2f: nrst fin* **13/2**[2]

600- **5** 3 ½ **Brace Of Doves**[208] 5774 4-8-12 **69** ... PhillipMakin 9 63
(T D Barron) *chsd ldng pair: rdn along 3f out: drvn and wknd fnl 2f* **25/1**

5-61 **6** shd **Major Magpie (IRE)**[11] 1186 4-8-13 **70** 6ex ... PaulFessey 5 63
(M Dods) *hld up in rr: effrt over 3f out: sn rdn and no hdwy* **6/5**[1]

64-0 **7** 2 **Cordage (IRE)**[63] 571 4-8-6 **63** ... JoeFanning 7 52
(Karen McLintock) *chsd ldrs: rdn along 3f out: wknd fnl 2f* **100/1**

0310 **8** shd **Mystic Man (FR)**[34] 826 8-9-4 **75** ...(b) PaulHanagan 6 64
(I W McInnes) *wnt lft s: in tch: rdn along 3f out: sn btn* **14/1**

0-04 **9** 1 ¼ **Play The Ball (USA)**[7] 1275 4-9-2 **73** ... NickyMackay 4 59
(G A Butler) *a rr* **13/2**[2]

1m 39.72s (-2.78) **Going Correction** -0.15s/f (Firm) 9 Ran SP% **109.7**
Speed ratings (Par 103):107,104,103,102,99 98,96,96,95
CSF £195.19 CT £1654.07 TOTE £22.60: £6.00, £2.20, £2.60; EX 63.50.
Owner Middleham Park Racing XXXVI **Bred** Bentley Smith, J Michael O'Farrell Jr , Joan Thor **Trained** Sessay, N Yorks

FOCUS
An ordinary handicap in which the winner was gifted an uncontested lead. The form may not be reliable, although the time was decent and the winner sets the level.
Royal Dignitary(USA) Official explanation: trainer's representative said, regarding the improved form shown, gelding was better suited by the quicker ground and got the run of the race
Brace Of Doves Official explanation: jockey said gelding had no more to give
Major Magpie(IRE) Official explanation: trainer had no explanation for the poor form shown

1456 "DAILY RECORD FIRST FOR SCOTTISH RACING" H'CAP 7f 30y
3:50 (3:51) (Class 3) (0-90,88) 4-Y-0+
£8,101 (£2,425; £1,212; £607; £302; £152) **Stalls** Low

Form RPR

41-3 **1** **Will He Wish**[14] 1112 10-9-6 **87** ... DarryllHolland 1 96
(S Gollings) *bhd and pushed along 1/2-way: rdn 3f out: swtchd outside and gd hdwy over 1f out: styd on wl to ld nr fin ish* **11/1**

5400 **2** nk **Stoic Leader (IRE)**[7] 1275 6-8-13 **80** ... FrancisNorton 6 88
(R F Fisher) *towards rr: hdwy 3f out: rdn wl over 1f out: drvn and styd on to ld wl ins last: hdd nr fin* **10/1**

0422 **3** ½ **Commando Scott (IRE)**[11] 1183 5-8-11 **81** ... PatrickMathers(3) 9 88+
(I W McInnes) *chsd ldrs: hdwy to ld 2f out: sn rdn: drvn ins last: hdd and no ex wl ins last* **11/2**[2]

-400 **4** 1 ¾ **Prince Tum Tum (USA)**[13] 1143 6-9-3 **84** ... FergalLynch 2 86
(D W Barker) *hld up and bhd: hdwy 3f out: rdn to chse ldrs over 1f out: kpt on same pce ins last* **16/1**

05-0 **5** shd **Regent's Secret (USA)**[19] 1035 6-8-9 **76** ... NickyMackay 8 78
(J S Goldie) *s.i.s and sn wl bhd: hdwy over 2f out: styd on strly ins last: nrst fin* **16/1**

5112 **6** 5 **Byron Bay**[31] 865 4-9-3 **84** ... TomEaves 10 73
(I Semple) *led to 1/2-way: cl up tl rdn over 2f out and grad wknd* **6/1**[3]

05-0 **7** 2 **Sky Crusader**[13] 1129 4-9-7 **88** ... JohnEgan 3 72
(R Ingram) *hld up: effrt and hdwy 3f out: rdn 2f out: sn btn* **3/1**[1]

-003 **8** ¾ **Lord Of The East**[8] 1262 7-9-6 **87** ... SebSanders 7 69
(I W McInnes) *chsd ldng pair: rdn along wl over 2f out: grad wknd* **8/1**

0-10 **9** ¾ **Vicious Knight**[13] 1156 8-9-3 **84** ...(v) AdrianTNicholls 4 64
(D Nicholls) *chsd ldrs: rdn along wl over 2f out: sn wknd* **10/1**

45-5 **10** 5 **Dispol Katie**[19] 1035 5-9-1 **82** ... PhillipMakin 5 49
(T D Barron) *cl up: led 1/2-way: rdn along 3f out: hdd 2f out and sn wknd* **12/1**

1m 27.52s (-2.42) **Going Correction** -0.15s/f (Firm) 10 Ran SP% **111.8**
Speed ratings (Par 107):107,106,106,104,103 98,95,95,94,88
CSF £110.85 CT £678.63 TOTE £8.00: £2.40, £3.10, £2.00; EX 100.20.
Owner Mrs D Dukes **Bred** Mrs C Buckland **Trained** Scamblesby, Lincs
■ Stewards' Enquiry : Francis Norton two-day ban: used whip with excessive frequency and without giving gelding time to respond (May 16-17)

FOCUS
A strong early pace led to this fairly decent handicap being fought out by a couple of hold-up performers. The form is rated around the winner but not with total confidence.

NOTEBOOK
Will He Wish, at his best when able to challenge from off the pace over a strongly-run seven furlongs, had the race run to suit him ideally. He came widest of all in the straight and mowed his rivals down to get his head in front close home, and despite his advancing years he clearly retains plenty of ability. (op 12-1)
Stoic Leader(IRE) was suited by the frantic early pace as he too was held up towards the back of the field in the first half of the race. He won his first three starts of the season on turf last spring and was running off a 5lb lower mark than for the third of them here.
Commando Scott(IRE) did best of those who tried to track the pace and for that he deserves credit. His best form is all with some cut in the ground, too, so conditions would not have been ideal. (op 4-1 tchd 13-2)
Prince Tum Tum(USA) popped up in a claimer over nine furlongs here last summer but has been mainly disappointing otherwise. The race fell his way this time as he was held up towards the back in a race run at a scorching early pace, but he would not be one to bank on repeating this performance. (op 20-1)
Regent's Secret(USA) needs further than this and so it was no surprise to see him putting in his best work when the race was all but over. Official explanation: jockey said gelding missed the break and was never travelling (op 18-1 tchd 20-1)
Byron Bay helped set an unsustainably fast gallop which set the race up for the hold-up horses. (tchd 7-1)
Sky Crusader was the disappointment of the race as he appeared to have the race run to suit. Official explanation: jockey said, regarding the apparent tender ride in the final 2f, colt had no more to give (op 7-2 tchd 11-4)

1457 RUK EVENING RACING FOR £60 H'CAP 1m 6f
4:20 (4:20) (Class 5) (0-75,73) 4-Y-0+ **£5,181** (£1,541; £770; £384) **Stalls** High

Form RPR

/11- **1** **Silvertown**[293] 3526 11-9-10 **73** ... RobertWinston 4 84
(L Lungo) *set stdy pce: qcknd over 3f out: qcknd and qcknd wl over 1f out: styd on strly* **11/4**[2]

06-1 **2** 2 **Reluctant Suitor**[19] 1033 4-9-4 **68** ... NickyMackay 1 76
(J S Goldie) *hld up in rr: hdwy 3f out: rdn to chse wnr whn hung rt over 1f out: sn drvn and kpt on same pce* **11/8**[1]

31-2 **3** 10 **Hernando's Boy**[28] 816 5-9-5 **68** ... PaulHanagan 2 62+
(K G Reveley) *trckd wnr: effrt 3f out and sn pushed along: rdn 2f out: drvn and wknd over 1f out* **11/4**[2]

2306 **4** 7 **Beauchamp Trump**[10] 1213 4-9-2 **66** ...(bt) FrancisNorton 3 50+
(G A Butler) *chsd ldng pair: pushed along 3f out: rdn over 2f out and sn wknd* **9/1**[3]

3m 5.91s (0.21) **Going Correction** -0.15s/f (Firm)
WFA 4 from 5yo+ 1lb 4 Ran SP% **105.4**
Speed ratings (Par 103):93,91,86,82
CSF £6.63 TOTE £3.20; EX 6.90.
Owner R J Gilbert & SW Group Logistics Limited **Bred** Juddmonte Farms **Trained** Carrutherstown, D'fries & G'way

FOCUS
A small field and the winner was gifted an easy lead. He set a modest pace and recorded a very moderate winning time for a race of its class, but sets the standard form-wise.

1458 NEWHAILES MAIDEN STKS 1m 1f
4:50 (4:50) (Class 5) 3-Y-0+ **£3,238** (£963; £481; £240) **Stalls** High

Form RPR

0- **1** **Jidaar (IRE)**[282] 3842 3-8-13 ... JoeFanning 5 82
(M Johnston) *trckd ldr: led over 2f out: sn rdn and wandered over 1f out: drvn and kpt on gamely ins last* **7/1**[2]

0-2 **2** shd **Otelcaliforni (USA)**[11] 1191 3-8-8 ... ShaneKelly 6 77
(J Noseda) *trckd ldrs: hdwy whn nt clr run and squeezed through 2f out: sn rdn: drvn and ev ch ins last: jst hld* **30/100**[1]

42-5 **3** 7 **Grey Outlook**[19] 1032 3-8-8 69 ... RobertWinston 2 66+
(Miss L A Perratt) *keen: trckd ldrs: effrt on outer and ev ch whn edgd rt 2f out: sn rdn and wknd appr last* **8/1**[3]

-020 **4** 12 **Cuesta Canyon (IRE)**[31] 874 3-8-13 40 ... DeanMcKeown 4 44
(M J Polglase) *led: rdn along and hdd over 2f out: sn hmpd and wknd* **66/1**

0/40 **5** 12 **Chiracahua (IRE)**[10] 1225 4-9-13 45 ... PaulEddery 7 22
(B Smart) *plld hrd: in tch: rdn along over 3f out: sn wknd* **66/1**

00- **6** 16 **Pappas Ruby (USA)**[302] 3286 3-8-8 ... NickyMackay 1 —
(J S Goldie) *sn outpcd and bhd fr 1/2-way* **50/1**

00 **7** 18 **Delamead (IRE)**[8] 1252 3-8-13 ... TomEaves 3 —
(B Ellison) *s.i.s: a bhd* **200/1**

1m 53.56s (-2.44) **Going Correction** -0.15s/f (Firm)
WFA 3 from 4yo 14lb 7 Ran SP% **106.0**
Speed ratings (Par 103):104,103,97,87,76 62,46
CSF £8.38 TOTE £7.70: £2.50, £1.10; EX 15.00.
Owner Hamdan Al Maktoum **Bred** Shadwell Estate Company Limited **Trained** Middleham Moor, N Yorks

FOCUS
An ordinary maiden but they came home well strung out behind the front two and the form looks modest but solid enough.

1459 RUK EVENING RACING CALL 08700 50 69 47 H'CAP 7f 30y
5:20 (5:20) (Class 6) (0-65,65) 4-Y-0+ **£2,730** (£806; £403) **Stalls** Low

Form RPR

0-15 **1** **Attacca**[8] 1253 5-8-7 **54** ... DarryllHolland 4 60
(J R Weymes) *chsd ldng pair: hdwy over 2f out: rdn wl over 1f out: swtchd lft and drvn ins last: styd on to ld nr line* **5/2**[1]

0-55 **2** *hd* **Joshua's Gold (IRE)**[4] [1353] 5-8-13 **60** ... (v) TomEaves 7 65
(D Carroll) *chsd ldr: led over 3f out: rdn clr 2f out: drvn ins last: hdd and no ex nr fin* **3/1**[2]

0-25 **3** *shd* **Insubordinate**[18] [1041] 5-8-10 **57** ... FergalLynch 5 62
(J S Goldie) *hld up: hdwy to chse ldrs over 2f out: rdn wl over 1f out: drvn and styd on strly ins last* **7/2**[3]

600- **4** *3* **Ulysees (IRE)**[140] [6593] 7-9-4 **65** ... PaulHanagan 2 62
(I Semple) *hld up: effrt 3f out: rdn to chse ldrs wl over 1f out: sn no imp* **11/1**

500- **5** *5* **Proud Western (USA)**[242] [4999] 8-7-11 **51** oh6 ... (t) KristinStubbs[(7)] 6 35
(B Ellison) *a rr* **28/1**

00-4 **6** *1 1/4* **Obe One**[31] [864] 6-8-8 **55** ... RobertWinston 1 36
(D Nicholls) *led: rn wd home bnd and sn hdd: rdn along over 2f out and sn wknd* **4/1**

1m 28.37s (-1.57) **Going Correction** -0.15s/f (Firm) **6** Ran SP% **107.6**
Speed ratings (Par 101):102,101,101,98,92 91
CSF £9.33 TOTE £2.90: £1.90, £2.20; EX 12.60 Place 6 £241.66, Place 5 £143.30.
Owner High Moor Racing 2 **Bred** Pigeon House Stud **Trained** Middleham Moor, N Yorks
FOCUS
A moderate handicap made up of exposed performers and the form is ordinary but sound.
Obe One Official explanation: jockey said gelding hung badly left-handed on the final bend
T/Plt: £277.80 to a £1 stake. Pool: £42,317.05. 111.20 winning tickets. T/Qpdt: £65.40 to a £1 stake. Pool: £2,352.90. 26.60 winning tickets. JR

1391 WOLVERHAMPTON (A.W) (L-H)
Friday, May 5

OFFICIAL GOING: Standard
Wind: Light, behind Weather: Fine and sunny

1460 DUNSTALL PARK MAIDEN CLAIMING STKS 1m 1f 103y(P)
2:00 (2:00) (Class 7) 4-Y-O+ **£1,365** (£403; £201) **Stalls** Low

Form RPR

-540 **1** **Scamperdale**[25] [953] 4-8-13 **52** ... JimmyFortune 5 55
(B P J Baugh) *mid-div: hdwy over 3f out: rdn and hung lft fr over 1f out: r.o to ld nr fin* **5/2**[1]

-000 **2** *nk* **Royal Lustre**[32] [857] 5-8-6 **40** ... DanielTudhope[(3)] 9 50
(Robert Gray) *disp ld tl led over 3f out: rdn clr over 1f out: hdd nr fin* **9/1**

-434 **3** *1* **Heathyards Joy**[11] [1197] 5-8-6 **40** ... (p) GrahamGibbons 11 45
(R Hollinshead) *hld up: rdn over 3f out: hdwy over 2f out: styd on* **9/2**[3]

6444 **4** *6* **Queue Up**[10] [1224] 4-8-13 **40** ... (p) FergusSweeney 6 41
(A G Newcombe) *prom: rdn over 2f out: hung lft and wknd over 1f out* **9/1**

-000 **5** *hd* **Grandma Ryta**[25] [953] 4-8-8 **40** ... MickyFenton 10 35
(John Berry) *chsd ldrs: rdn: hung lft and nt clr run over 1f out: sn wknd* **11/1**

00-6 **6** *shd* **Pitsi Kahtoh**[10] [1224] 4-8-4 **40** ... ChrisCatlin 13 31
(P W Hiatt) *s.i.s: rdn 1/2-way: styd on fnl f: nvr nrr* **20/1**

0-00 **7** *2 1/2* **Guadiana (GER)**[102] [175] 4-8-9 **40** ow1 ... DaneO'Neill 8 31
(A W Carroll) *hld up: hdwy over 3f out: rdn and wknd over 1f out* **10/1**

000/ **8** *6* **Superfling**[12] [6696] 5-8-8 ... RoryMoore[(5)] 2 24
(H J Manners) *prom to 1/2-way* **33/1**

0-20 **9** *2 1/2* **King Zafeen (IRE)**[30] [889] 4-8-13 **52** ... (b[1]) DaleGibson 7 19
(M W Easterby) *trckd ldrs: plld hrd: rdn and wknd over 1f out* **7/2**[2]

060- **10** *4* **Rocket (IRE)**[269] [4237] 5-8-8 **50** ... RichardKingscote[(5)] 4 12
(H J Manners) *disp ld 6f: wknd over 2f out* **25/1**

11 *1 3/4* **Gessecapade**[62] 4-8-8 ... FrancisFerris 12 3
(P S McEntee) *dwlt: outpcd* **33/1**

00 **12** *1 1/4* **Red Ruth Lady**[30] [890] 4-8-5 ... NelsonDeSouza[(3)] 1 —
(D L Williams) *a in rr: bhd fr 1/2-way* **33/1**

000- **13** *9* **Ardasnails (IRE)**[197] [1983] 4-8-10 **35** ... (bt) NeilChalmers[(3)] 3 —
(K G Wingrove) *sn outpcd* **50/1**

2m 2.67s (0.05) **Going Correction** -0.175s/f (Stan) **13** Ran SP% **125.8**
Speed ratings (Par 97):92,91,90,85,85 85,83,77,75,71 70,69,61
CSF £25.67 TOTE £3.40: £1.20, £2.70, £1.60; EX 45.10 Trifecta £234.70 Part won. Pool: £330.59 - 0.69 winning tickets..
Owner Miss S M Potts **Bred** Mrs J A Prescott **Trained** Audley, Staffs
FOCUS
The early pace was decent, but that appeared to tell in the latter stages of the contest and in the end the winning time was modest, even for a race like this. The front three pulled a very long way clear of the rest but the form is weak.

1461 WOLVERHAMPTON RACECOURSE - A CONFERENCE CENTRE TOO BANDED STKS 1m 1f 103y(P)
2:30 (2:30) (Class 7) 4-Y-O+ **£1,706** (£503; £252) **Stalls** Low

Form RPR

05-6 **1** **Cottingham (IRE)**[31] [875] 5-8-8 **45** ... BenSwarbrick[(3)] 1 51
(T D Barron) *chsd ldrs: led 2f out: rdn and hung lft ins fnl f: r.o* **9/1**

6021 **2** *1 1/2* **Magic Warrior**[3] [1394] 6-9-8 **50** ... PatDobbs 2 59+
(J C Fox) *hld up in tch: rdn and hung lft over 1f out: styd on: nt pce to chal* **13/8**[1]

2 **3** *3/4* **Hillhall (IRE)**[11] [1201] 4-8-7 **48** ... LiamJones[(7)] 4 50
(W M Brisbourne) *led: rdn and hdd 2f out: no ex ins fnl f* **15/2**[3]

310- **4** *5* **Phoenix Eye**[172] [6343] 5-8-13 **47** ... TPQueally 5 40
(M Mullineaux) *hld up: hdwy u.p and edgd rt wl over 1f out: nvr trbld ldrs* **20/1**

2320 **5** *nk* **Majehar**[30] [888] 4-8-8 **47** ... StephenDonohoe[(5)] 10 39
(A G Newcombe) *hld up in tch: rdn and wknd over 1f out* **8/1**

0015 **6** *1 1/4* **Diamond Dan (IRE)**[11] [1201] 4-8-12 **49** ... DanielTudhope[(3)] 6 39
(P D Evans) *s.i.s: hld up: hdwy over 3f out: rdn and wknd over 1f out* **11/4**[2]

3 **7** *nk* **Ivorbella (IRE)**[39] [771] 4-8-12 **46** ... (t) OscarUrbina 8 35
(M Botti) *chsd ldrs: rdn over 2f out: wknd over 1f out* **12/1**

060- **8** *shd* **Magic Charm**[151] [6510] 8-8-11 **30** ... ChrisCatlin 9 34
(K G Wingrove) *a in rr* **100/1**

-010 **9** *1 3/4* **Hillfield Flyer (IRE)**[3] [1392] 6-8-5 **46** ... KellyHarrison[(7)] 3 31
(Samuel Murphy, Ire) *mid-div: rdn and wknd 3f out* **20/1**

504- **10** *1 3/4* **Brendan's Surprise**[108] [6258] 4-8-6 **45** ... EmmettStack[(5)] 7 27
(K J Burke) *chsd ldrs: rdn over 3f out: sn wknd* **33/1**

2m 1.92s (-0.70) **Going Correction** -0.175s/f (Stan) **10** Ran SP% **118.8**
Speed ratings (Par 97):96,94,94,89,89 88,87,87,86,84
CSF £23.71 TOTE £9.60: £3.20, £1.10, £2.90; EX 39.60 Trifecta £365.90 Part won. Pool: £515.39 - 0.69 winning tickets..
Owner Twinacre Nurseries Ltd **Bred** B Kennedy **Trained** Maunby, N Yorks
FOCUS
Just a fair pace but the winning time was 0.75 seconds faster than the preceding maiden claimer and rated through the winner. As with that contest, the front three pulled well clear.

1462 HOLD YOUR CONFERENCE AT DUNSTALL PARK BANDED STKS 1m 141y(P)
3:00 (3:00) (Class 7) 4-Y-O+ **£1,535** (£453; £226) **Stalls** Low

Form RPR

050- **1** **Gala Sunday (USA)**[80] [6651] 6-8-8 **45** ... (b) PaulMulrennan[(3)] 2 46
(M W Easterby) *mde all: rdn over 1f out: edgd rt ins fnl f: r.o* **15/2**

6531 **2** *1 1/4* **Bob Baileys**[11] [1197] 4-9-3 **40** ... (b) JimmyQuinn 3 49
(P R Chamings) *hld up in tch: rdn to chse wnr fnl f: styd on* **6/1**[3]

0060 **3** *2 1/2* **Kalani Star (IRE)**[4] [1341] 6-8-11 **45** ... (vt) RoystonFfrench 1 38
(I W McInnes) *a.p: chsd wnr 2f out: sn rdn: styd on same pce fnl f* **13/2**

144/ **4** *nk* **Royal Indulgence**[596] [5585] 6-8-11 **45** ... RobbieFitzpatrick 5 37
(W M Brisbourne) *s.i.s: hld up: hdwy and nt clr run over 2f out: swtchd rt over 1f out: r.o* **8/1**

6242 **5** *1/2* **Dexileos (IRE)**[10] [1225] 7-8-11 **45** ... (t) FergusSweeney 7 36
(David Pinder) *chsd wnr: rdn over 3f out: hung lft and no ex fr over 1f out* **9/4**[1]

-054 **6** *5* **Viscount Rossini**[10] [1225] 4-8-11 **40** ... JimmyFortune 9 26
(A W Carroll) *hld up: rdn 1/2-way: hung lft ins fnl f: nvr nrr* **9/1**

5022 **7** *7* **Tommytyler (IRE)**[25] [937] 7-8-8 **45** ... (t) DanielTudhope[(3)] 4 11
(D Carroll) *trckd ldrs: racd keenly: rdn and wknd over 1f out* **4/1**[2]

0-03 **8** *6* **Iceni Warrior**[10] [1225] 4-8-11 **45** ... J-PGuillambert 8 —
(P Howling) *prom: rdn 1/2-way: wknd wl over 2f out* **16/1**

050- **9** *1* **Dolly**[263] [4418] 4-8-4 **40** ... RichardRowe[(7)] 6 —
(W J Knight) *s.i.s: hld up: plld hrd: bhd fr 1/2-way* **50/1**

1m 50.63s (-1.13) **Going Correction** -0.175s/f (Stan) **9** Ran SP% **119.1**
Speed ratings (Par 97):98,96,94,94,93 89,83,77,77
CSF £53.58 TOTE £10.40: £2.20, £2.50, £2.10; EX 50.60 Trifecta £248.00 Pool: £398.21 - 1.14 winning tickets..
Owner M W Easterby **Bred** Juddmonte Farms Inc **Trained** Sheriff Hutton, N Yorks
FOCUS
A fair pace for this banded contest and the form is sound enough.

1463 PARADE RESTAURANT BANDED STKS 7f 32y(P)
3:30 (3:31) (Class 7) 4-Y-O+ **£1,706** (£503; £252) **Stalls** High

Form RPR

4405 **1** **Mulberry Lad (IRE)**[5] [1310] 4-8-12 **46** ... ChrisCatlin 1 51
(P W Hiatt) *chsd ldrs: lost pl 6f out: hdwy 1/2-way: rdn to ld and edgd lft wl ins fnl f: r.o* **11/8**[1]

0-50 **2** *hd* **Glenviews Babalou (USA)**[10] [1227] 4-9-0 **48** ... RobbieFitzpatrick 2 53
(Peter Grayson) *hld up: hdwy over 2f out: rdn to ld and edgd rt ins fnl f: sn hdd: styd on* **8/1**

0100 **3** *3/4* **Fizzy Lizzy**[6] [1303] 6-8-13 **47** ... DavidAllan 3 50
(H E Haynes) *chsd ldrs: rdn to ld over 1f out: hdd and unable qck ins fnl f* **7/1**[3]

400- **4** *4* **Kirstys Lad**[151] [6512] 4-8-11 **40** ... (b[1]) TPQueally 4 38
(M Mullineaux) *led: hrd rdn and hdd over 1f out: wknd fnl f* **25/1**

-104 **5** *hd* **Wings Of Morning (IRE)**[38] [784] 5-8-9 **46** ... (v) DanielTudhope[(3)] 5 38
(D Carroll) *chsd ldr: rdn and ev ch over 2f out: hung rt and wknd fnl f* **7/1**[3]

4010 **6** *1* **Chickado (IRE)**[8] [1255] 5-9-2 **50** ... (p) RobertHavlin 8 39
(D Haydn Jones) *chsd ldrs: rdn over 2f out: wknd over 1f out* **4/1**[2]

00-0 **7** *1* **Super Canyon**[52] [638] 8-8-11 **35** ... (t) JimmyQuinn 9 32
(J Pearce) *sn outpcd* **20/1**

6-00 **8** *dist* **Come On**[25] [940] 7-8-11 **40** ... MichaelTebbutt 6 —
(J Hetherton) *chsd ldrs: rdn 1/2-way: wknd over 2f out* **14/1**

0-00 **9** *12* **Kris Spring**[14] [1110] 4-8-11 **40** ... (p) MickyFenton 10 —
(R M H Cowell) *s.s: hdwy 5f out: wknd 3f out* **33/1**

1m 30.22s (-0.18) **Going Correction** -0.175s/f (Stan) **9** Ran SP% **116.4**
Speed ratings (Par 97):94,93,92,88,88 86,85,—,—
CSF £13.05 TOTE £2.20: £1.10, £2.00, £2.30; EX 15.20 Trifecta £36.90 Pool: £489.48 - 9.40 winning tickets..
Owner P W Hiatt **Bred** Mountarmstrong Stud **Trained** Hook Norton, Oxon
FOCUS
A routine banded contest in which the pace was ordinary. Once again the front three pulled well clear and the first five finished in draw order with the placed horses setting the standard.
Kris Spring Official explanation: jockey said filly lost its action

1464 WOLVERHAMPTON-RACECOURSE.CO.UK TRI-BANDED STKS 5f 20y(P)
4:00 (4:01) (Class 7) 3-Y-O **£1,382** (£408; £204) **Stalls** Low

Form RPR

562 **1** **Sarah's Art (IRE)**[7] [1272] 3-8-7 **40** ... (b) ChrisCatlin 6 52
(N A Callaghan) *bmpd s: hld up: hdwy over 1f out: hmpd ins fnl f: rdn to ld wl ins fnl f* **7/4**[1]

0601 **2** *shd* **Red Vixen (IRE)**[11] [1200] 3-8-11 **45** 6ex ... KirstyMilczarek[(7)] 3 63
(C N Allen) *hld up: swtchd rt and hdwy 1/2-way: rdn and hung lft ins fnl f: sn ev ch: r.o* **10/3**[2]

4000 **3** *1 1/4* **Sanders Boy**[29] [893] 3-8-4 **40** ... PaulMulrennan[(3)] 1 48
(J R Norton) *led 1f: chsd ldr: rdn to ld ins fnl f: sn hdd and unable qck* **14/1**

5045 **4** *5* **Stoneacre Girl (IRE)**[25] [936] 3-8-7 **40** ... (b) RobbieFitzpatrick 4 30
(Peter Grayson) *led 4f out: clr 2f out: sn rdn: hdd: edgd rt and hmpd ins fnl f: sn wknd* **13/2**[3]

0445 **5** *3/4* **Jazz At The Sands (USA)**[11] [1200] 3-8-12 **45** ... (v) DaneO'Neill 5 32
(D Shaw) *s.i.s and wnt rt s: outpcd: nvr nrr* **8/1**

0500 **6** *3/4* **My Reflection**[11] [1200] 3-8-12 **45** ... JimmyFortune 8 29
(D Shaw) *chsd ldrs: rdn 2f out: sn edgd rt and wknd* **9/1**

-003 **7** *hd* **Stanley Wolfe (IRE)**[9] [1234] 3-8-12 **45** ... RoystonFfrench 9 28
(James Moffatt) *in tch: rdn 1/2-way: sn wknd* **12/1**

0-00 **8** *2 1/2* **Lough Arrow (IRE)**[52] [637] 3-8-2 **30** ... DaleGibson 2 9
(P S Felgate) *chsd ldrs: rdn 1/2-way: wknd over 1f out* **66/1**

-006 **9** *5* **Baytown Valentina**[46] [676] 3-8-0 **40** ... LiamJones[(7)] 7 —
(R Brotherton) *sn outpcd* **28/1**

62.64 secs (-0.18) **Going Correction** -0.175s/f (Stan) **9** Ran SP% **113.2**
Speed ratings (Par 93):94,93,91,83,82 81,81,77,69
CSF £7.21 TOTE £2.50: £1.40, £1.30, £3.90; EX 6.60 Trifecta £83.30 Pool: £376.93 - 3.21 winning tickets..
Owner Matthew Green **Bred** Newtownbarry House Stud **Trained** Newmarket, Suffolk
FOCUS
There was no hanging about in this, but that did rather set the race up for the closers. The first two set the level for the form.

1465 TO SPONSOR A RACE CALL 0870 220 2442 BANDED STKS 5f 216y(P)
4:30 (4:30) (Class 7) 4-Y-O+ £1,535 (£453; £226) Stalls Low

Form RPR
0355 1 Grand View[3] 1391 10-8-8 45 (p) PaulMulrennan(3) 2 53
(J R Weymes) chsd ldrs: rdn to ld 1f out: all out 9/2[2]
34 2 shd Midmaar (IRE)[3] 1393 5-8-11 45 (v[1]) JamieMackay 6 53
(M Wigham) trckd ldrs: hrd rdn and hung lft ins fnl f: sn ev ch: nt run on 2/1[1]
00-0 3 2 1/2 Justenjoy Yourself[46] 680 4-8-11 40 SamHitchcott 12 45
(R W Price) chsd ldrs: led over 2f out: rdn and hdd 1f out: no ex 50/1
5423 4 2 A Teen[10] 1228 8-8-11 45 J-PGuillambert 11 39
(P Howling) chsd ldrs: rdn over 2f out: styng on same pce whn hung lft ins fnl f 6/1[3]
5000 5 1 Danethorpe Lady (IRE)[2] 1413 4-8-11 40 (v) DaneO'Neill 3 36
(D Shaw) s.s: hdwy u.p over 1f out: nvr nrr 25/1
0500 6 3/4 Mytton's Dream[3] 1393 4-8-11 45 ChrisCatlin 8 34
(R Brotherton) sn outpcd: sme late hdwy: nvr nrr 18/1
500- 7 2 Pride Of Kinloch[167] 6383 6-8-9 35 ow1 (p) DNolan(3) 9 29
(N Wilson) chsd ldr: rdn over 2f out: wknd over 1f out 7/1
5600 8 3/4 Sapphire Dream[45] 691 4-8-11 45 DavidAllan 4 26
(A Bailey) led over 3f: rdn and wknd over 1f out 11/1
00-0 9 3/4 Sound That Alarm[45] 691 4-8-11 45 (bt[1]) JimmyFortune 10 23
(P D Evans) sn pushed along in rr: hdwy 4f out: rdn and wknd 2f out 11/1
0430 10 6 Headland (USA)[31] 876 8-8-11 40 (be) PaulQuinn 7 5
(D W Chapman) in rr whn hmpd 5f out: bhd fr 1/2-way 10/1
60-0 11 4 Mickledo[37] 789 4-8-11 35 (b) MickyFenton 5 —
(A Bailey) sn outpcd 66/1

1m 15.64s (-0.17) **Going Correction** -0.175s/f (Stan) 11 Ran SP% 116.6
Speed ratings (Par 97):94,93,90,87,86 85,82,81,80,72 67
CSF £13.56 TOTE £7.00: £2.10, £1.20, £10.40; EX 18.50 Trifecta £176.90 Pool: £431.13 - 1.73 winning tickets..
Owner Sporting Occasions **Bred** The Wickfield Stud Ltd **Trained** Middleham Moor, N Yorks
FOCUS
An ordinary banded sprint in which the pace was fairly average and the second sets the standard.

1466 NAME A RACE TO ENHANCE YOUR BRAND BANDED STKS 5f 20y(P)
5:00 (5:00) (Class 7) 3-Y-O+ £1,365 (£403; £201) Stalls Low

Form RPR
0000 1 Rock Fever (IRE)[37] 789 4-8-7 45 (b) RonanKeogh(7) 6 51
(Peter Grayson) w ldrs: rdn over 1f out: edgd lft and r.o to ld wl ins fnl f 14/1
4035 2 1/2 Katie Killane[7] 1272 4-9-0 40 (v) MickyFenton 8 49
(M Wellings) chsd ldrs: rdn over 1f out: edgd lft: r.o 20/1
-034 3 1/2 Maromito (IRE)[10] 1228 9-9-0 45 RoystonFfrench 2 47
(R Bastiman) led: rdn over 1f out: hdd and unable qckn wl ins fnl f 11/2[3]
0022 4 shd Comic Tales[10] 1228 5-9-0 40 (b) TPQueally 4 47+
(M Mullineaux) s.i.s and hmpd s: hld up: swtchd rt and hdwy over 1f out: sn rdn: edgd lft: r.o: nt rch ldrs 3/1[1]
050- 5 1 Piper Lily[193] 6082 4-9-0 45 RyanMoore 1 43
(M Blanshard) chsd ldrs: rdn over 1f out: styd on same pce 4/1[2]
6000 6 3/4 Petana[3] 1391 6-9-0 45 (p) RobbieFitzpatrick 9 41
(Peter Grayson) s.i.s: in rr: r.o ins fnl f: nrst fin 15/2
00-5 7 1 3/4 King Egbert (FR)[10] 1228 5-9-0 45 JimmyFortune 10 34
(A W Carroll) s.i.s: rdn over 1f out: nvr nrr 6/1
5-40 8 1 1/2 So Sober (IRE)[31] 872 8-9-0 45 DaneO'Neill 3 29
(D Shaw) prom: rdn 1/2-way: wknd over 1f out 10/1
0000 9 1 On The Trail[3] 1391 9-9-0 45 (p) PaulQuinn 7 25
(D W Chapman) w ldrs to 1/2-way: wknd over 1f out 18/1
5006 10 2 Town House[10] 1228 4-8-7 45 SoniaEaton(7) 5 18
(B P J Baugh) hmpd s: hld up: a in rr 14/1

62.45 secs (-0.37) **Going Correction** -0.175s/f (Stan) 10 Ran SP% 118.9
Speed ratings (Par 97):95,94,93,93,91 90,87,85,83,80
CSF £263.97 TOTE £23.30: £5.20, £3.70, £2.30; EX 218.60 Trifecta £193.60 Pool: £283.59 - 1.04 winning tickets..
Owner Mrs Sarah Grayson **Bred** Liam Phelan **Trained** Formby, Lancs
FOCUS
With so many front-runners in opposition, the early pace was always going to be solid but that took its toll towards the end of the contest. The form is ordinary.

1467 HOLIDAY INN GARDEN COURT WOLVERHAMPTON BANDED STKS 1m 4f 50y(P)
5:30 (5:30) (Class 7) 4-Y-O+ £1,706 (£503; £252) Stalls Low

Form RPR
4-01 1 Figaro's Quest (IRE)[5] 1313 4-9-3 45 (b) RyanMoore 12 60
(P F I Cole) chsd ldr tl led over 9f out: clr 2f out: rdn out 5/6[1]
2332 2 2 1/2 Zaffeu[74] 470 5-9-2 50 J-PGuillambert 6 55
(A G Juckes) hld up: hdwy over 2f out: styd on ins fnl f: nt rch wnr 13/2[3]
0260 3 3/4 Pharaoh Prince[11] 1201 5-8-7 48 (v) KirstyMilczarek(7) 3 52
(G Prodromou) a.p: chsd wnr over 3f out: rdn over 1f out: styd on same pce 14/1
-412 4 1/2 Wood Fern (UAE)[3] 1395 6-8-10 45 LiamJones(7) 1 54
(W M Brisbourne) hld up in tch: rdn and bmpd over 2f out: styd on same pce fnl f 15/2
054- 5 2 Silver Prophet (IRE)[20] 6029 7-9-2 50 GeorgeBaker 2 50
(M R Bosley) sn pushed along and prom: rdn and bmpd over 2f out: no ex fnl f 7/2[2]
0310 6 3 High (IRE)[11] 1199 4-8-11 50 StephenDonohoe(5) 7 45
(W J Musson) hld up: styd on appr fnl f: nvr nrr 16/1
5-00 7 7 Candy Anchor (FR)[39] 771 7-8-11 40 JimmyQuinn 4 29
(R E Peacock) hld up: a in rr 80/1
0510 8 1/2 Mustakhlas (USA)[37] 794 5-8-7 48 SoniaEaton(7) 8 31
(B P J Baugh) prom: rdn over 8f 40/1
000- 9 3 Pearson Glen (IRE)[125] 6534 7-9-2 50 RoystonFfrench 10 28
(James Moffatt) hld up: hdwy over 3f out: wknd over 2f out 100/1
040- 10 6 Norman Norman[165] 6399 4-9-0 48 ChrisCatlin 5 17
(W S Kittow) hld up: a in rr 28/1
310- 11 8 Cyber Santa[326] 2549 8-8-11 45 DerekMcGaffin 9 1
(J Hetherton) led: hdd over 9f out: wknd over 2f out 66/1

2m 40.12s (-2.30) **Going Correction** -0.175s/f (Stan) 11 Ran SP% 124.0
Speed ratings (Par 97):100,98,97,97,96 94,89,89,87,83 77
CSF £7.49 TOTE £2.00: £1.40, £1.70, £3.10; EX 11.00 Trifecta £51.50 Pool: £389.22 - 5.36 winning tickets. Place 6 £18.40, Place 5 £11.27.
Owner The Fairy Story Partnership **Bred** Deepwood Farm Stud **Trained** Whatcombe, Oxon
FOCUS
Not a particularly competitive banded contest, but a solid pace thanks to the favourite. The form is sounder than most banded contests.

T/Plt: £33.30 to a £1 stake. Pool: £35,005.15. 766.45 winning tickets. T/Qpdt: £26.70 to a £1 stake. Pool: £1,989.40. 55.00 winning tickets. CR

1468 - (Foreign Racing) - See Raceform Interactive

1059 CORK (R-H)
Friday, May 5

OFFICIAL GOING: Sprint course - soft; remainder - yielding to soft

1469a CORK STKS (LISTED RACE) 6f
5:50 (5:53) 3-Y-O+ £22,448 (£6,586; £3,137; £1,068)

RPR
1 Miss Sally (IRE)[208] 5776 4-9-9 111 JMurtagh 6 114+
(M Halford, Ire) in tch: prog 1 1/2f out: rdn to ld under 1f out: kpt on wl 9/2[1]
2 1/2 Senor Benny (USA)[4] 1361 7-9-7 103 WMLordan 4 111+
(M McDonagh, Ire) hld up in tch: prog on stand's side 1 1/2f out: 2nd and kpt on wl ins fnl f 10/1
3 3 Majestic Times (IRE)[13] 1158 6-9-10 103 VRDeSouza 14 105
(Liam McAteer, Ire) trckd ldrs on outer: 3rd 1 1/2f out: sn rdn to chal: no ex ins fnl f 10/1
4 1/2 Moon Unit (IRE)[13] 1158 5-9-9 106 WSupple 12 102
(H Rogers, Ire) mid-div: 5th travelling wl after 1/2-way: led under 1 1/2f out: hdd under 1f out: no ex 6/1[2]
5 4 Common World (USA)[26] 930 7-9-12 111 FMBerry 8 93
(T Hogan, Ire) outpcd early: prog 2f out: mod 5th and kpt on fnl f 8/1[3]
6 nk Kay Two (IRE)[13] 1158 4-9-7 96 PJSmullen 3 87
(Ms F M Crowley, Ire) chsd ldrs: 5th and rdn under 1 1/2f out: no imp fnl f 33/1
7 1 Pout (IRE)[40] 753 4-9-4 92 DMGrant 1 81
(John Joseph Murphy, Ire) towards rr: kpt on fr 1 1/2f out 33/1
8 hd Waterways (IRE)[208] 5777 3-8-11 106 NGMcCullagh 5 84
(P J Prendergast, Ire) led: hdd bef 1/2-way: rdn 2f out: sn no ex 14/1
9 2 1/2 Chained Emotion (IRE)[194] 6043 5-9-7 100 DPMcDonogh 2 76
(Kevin Prendergast, Ire) hld up on stand's rail: swtchd under 2f out: kpt on same pce 20/1
10 shd Turnkey[26] 930 4-9-7 (b) TonyCulhane 11 76
(M R Channon) prom: cl 4th 1/2-way: chal 2f out: hmpd and lost pl 1 1/2f out: no ex 8/1[3]
11 3 1/2 Moone Cross (IRE)[18] 1060 3-8-8 85 TPO'Shea 7 62
(Mrs John Harrington, Ire) cl up: led bef 1/2-way: hdd over 1 1/2f out: sn wknd 20/1
12 6 Moyenne (IRE)[180] 6270 4-9-7 98 KJManning 9 47
(Timothy Doyle, Ire) nvr a factor 33/1
13 2 1/2 Noelani (IRE)[208] 5776 4-9-9 105 MJKinane 13 42
(John M Oxx, Ire) chsd ldrs on outer: rdn and wknd fr 1/2-way 6/1[2]
14 3 Fontanally Springs (IRE)[194] 6043 4-9-4 86 JAHeffernan 10 28
(H Rogers, Ire) prom: 3rd bef 1/2-way: rdn to ld over 1 1/2f out: sn hdd: wknd over 1f out 40/1

1m 16.2s
WFA 3 from 4yo+ 10lb 14 Ran SP% 114.6
CSF £42.38 TOTE £3.50: £1.70, £2.30, £6.10; DF 63.60.
Owner Mrs M Mullen **Bred** Miss Hilary Mullen **Trained** the Curragh, Co Kildare

NOTEBOOK
Miss Sally(IRE) produced a cracking performance to score on her seasonal debut and may well have announced herself as an emerging force in the sprinting division. A dual Group Three winner over seven furlongs last season, she also landed a Listed race at this trip on her final start of 2005. She stayed on well close home to hold off the late charge of Senor Benny and her trainer felt that, given that she had suffered a minor setback two weeks ago, she should improve significantly for this run, and the Greenlands Stakes at the Curragh later this month is the next target. (op 9/2 tchd 5/1)
Senor Benny(USA) ran a fine race in second just four days after winning a five-furlong Curragh handicap off a mark of 95. A former Listed winner over this course and distance, he has looked at least as good as ever this term and is a very decent sort with ease in the ground. (op 7/1)
Majestic Times(IRE) showed good speed to lie up with the pace on the outer and challenged for the lead with over a furlong to run, but he was soon unable to raise his effort. He should be able to make his mark at Listed level this term. (op 8/1)
Moon Unit(IRE), who won a Listed race at Naas on her reappearance, was travelling well at halfway and led with over a furlong to run, but she was unable to sustain that effort. Nonetheless, she remains a force to be reckoned with. (op 4/1)
Common World(USA) was outpaced early on but stuck to his task over the final quarter of a mile. The Gladness Stakes winner will be seen to better effect over further.
Waterways(IRE) was one of only two three-year-olds in the line up and will improve for this reappearance run. She showed good early speed but had no more to offer heading towards the final furlong. (op 10/1 tchd 16/1)
Turnkey had no more to offer after being hampered and losing his place well over a furlong from home. (op 7/1)

GOODWOOD (R-H)
Saturday, May 6

OFFICIAL GOING: Good
Wind: Nil Weather: Overcast

1472 32RED.COM LUPE STKS (LISTED RACE) (FILLIES) 1m 1f 192y
2:20 (2:21) (Class 1) 3-Y-O
£13,702 (£13,702; £3,769; £1,879; £941; £472) Stalls High

Form RPR
-365 1 Rising Cross[28] 914 3-9-0 98 GeorgeBaker 3 103
(J R Best) trckd ldng pair: effrt 3f out: rdn to ld over 1f out: kpt on wl fnl f: jnd on line 8/1
010- 1 dht Soft Centre[196] 6027 3-9-0 84 DaneO'Neill 6 103+
(Mrs A J Perrett) lw: hld up in last pair: effrt on outer over 2f out: drvn and r.o wl fnl f to force dead-heat last stride 25/1
61-3 3 3 Nyarhini[35] 827 3-9-0 95 TedDurcan 1 97
(G Wragg) t.k.h: cl up: trckd ldr over 5f out: rdn to chal over 2f out: upsides over 1f out: nt qckn 3/1[2]
45-4 4 3/4 Suzy Bliss[35] 827 3-9-0 97 TQuinn 2 96
(W R Swinburn) led: rdn and pressed over 2f out: hdd over 1f out: fdd fnl f 7/2[3]
103- 5 3 1/2 Jaish (USA)[189] 6145 3-9-0 92 JimmyFortune 4 89
(J L Dunlop) bit bkwd: hld up in last pair: rdn 3f out: hanging and no prog: sn btn 8/1

63-5 **6** *3* **Deveron (USA)**[79] [436] 3-9-0 110....(t) KerrinMcEvoy 7 84
(Saeed Bin Suroor) *swtg: trckd ldr to over 5f out: lost pl 4f out: rdn and no rspnse over 2f out: sn wknd* **7/4**[1]

2m 9.67s (1.92) **Going Correction** +0.20s/f (Good) **6** Ran SP% **109.7**
Speed ratings (Par 104):100,100,97,97,94 91
WIN: Rising Cross £5.60, Soft Centre £11.90. PL: RC £3.80, SC £3.70. EX: RC/SC £127.10, SC/RC £151.60. CSF: RC/SC £69.41, SC/RC £93.62..
Owner Heading For The Rocks Partnership **Bred** J R Wills **Trained** Hucking, Kent
Owner Nicholas Cooper **Bred** Normandie Stud Ltd **Trained** Pulborough, W Sussex

FOCUS
A pretty weak race for the class and a modest winning time for a race of this stature. The third and fourth were roughly to their marks and the form is sound enough but limited.

NOTEBOOK
Rising Cross has been exposed at Pattern level on many occasions but this was a weak Listed race and, with the favourite disappointing, it took little winning. She looked likely to win outright going into the final furlong, but Soft Centre's strong finish resulted in her having to share the spoils. Connections will be pleased to have got a win at this level out of her, though, and she clearly goes well here, having recorded her best performance at two when runner-up to Nannina here in the Prestige Stakes. (op 9-1 tchd 10-1)
Soft Centre had a lot to find at this level in theory, but this was not the strongest Listed race ever run and she found the necessary improvement to finish strongly and share the spoils on the line. Indeed, given that her dam won this race five years ago and that she is bred to appreciate this sort of trip, it could be argued that she had no right to be sent off at such a long price. A mile and a half should suit her in time. (op 9-1 tchd 10-1)
Nyarhini, third and in front of Rising Cross in the Masaka Stakes last time out, could not confirm the form on this different surface and over this longer trip despite having previously shaped as though it would suit her. (op 10-3 tchd 7-2)
Suzy Bliss finished a length and a half behind Nyarhini in the Masaka, and ran roughly to that form over this longer trip. She had the run of the race in front, not having to set a strong gallop, and her limitations have been seemingly exposed, but faster ground might see her in a better light. (op 10-3 tchd 4-1 in a place)
Jaish(USA) looked in need of the run beforehand and never really threatened. Official explanation: jockey said filly was never travelling
Deveron(USA) had by far the best form coming into this having finished third in the Marcel Boussac on her final start at two. Having her first start for Godolphin, she was denied the lead her rider had been keen to get but she still travelled well enough into the straight. She found little under pressure, though, and proved bitterly disappointing. Official explanation: jockey said filly ran flat (op 13-8 tchd 15-8 in places)

1473 LETHEBY & CHRISTOPHER PREDOMINATE STKS (LISTED RACE) (C&G) 1m 3f
2:50 (2:52) (Class 1) 3-Y-O **£19,873** (£7,532; £3,769; £1,879; £941) **Stalls** Low

Form RPR
112- **1** **Championship Point (IRE)**[259] [4598] 3-9-3 105....TedDurcan 6 112+
(M R Channon) *trckd ldr for 2f: styd cl up: effrt to ld 3f out: rdn clr fr 2f out: eased last 75yds* **4/5**[1]
10-3 **2** *4* **Sienna Storm (IRE)**[10] [1237] 3-9-0 80....DarryllHolland 4 98
(M H Tompkins) *lw: hld up in last pair: rdn and effrt 3f out: outpcd 2f out: hung rt after: kpt on to take 2nd last 100yds* **14/1**
54-4 **3** *½* **Senor Dali (IRE)**[18] [1070] 3-9-0 95....TQuinn 1 97
(J L Dunlop) *lw: hld up in last pair: prog to chal and w wnr 3f out: btn 2f out: wknd: lost 2nd last 100yds* **5/1**[3]
2-12 **4** *4* **London Express (IRE)**[10] [1231] 3-9-0 97....StanleyChin 2 91
(M Johnston) *lw: led: urged along over 5f out: rdn and hdd 3f out: sn btn* **3/1**[2]
3154 **5** *10* **Fiddlers Wood**[16] [1095] 3-9-0 86....(v) DaneO'Neill 5 75
(V Smith) *dwlt: drvn frntically and jnd ldr after 2f: wknd over 3f out* **20/1**

2m 26.78s (-0.43) **Going Correction** +0.20s/f (Good) **5** Ran SP% **108.7**
Speed ratings (Par 107):109,106,105,102,95
CSF £12.50 TOTE £1.60: £1.30, £2.30; EX 9.60.
Owner John Livock Bloodstock Limited **Bred** Mount Coote Stud **Trained** West Ilsley, Berks
■ This race, and the Lupe, have been switched to this fixture from the mid-May meeting.

FOCUS
A perfectly acceptable winning time for a race like this, 0.82 seconds faster than the 80-rated five-year-old Top Seed took to win the last. The winner was impressive but the placed form does not look that solid.

NOTEBOOK
Championship Point(IRE) was 5lb and upwards clear of his nearest rivals based on official ratings and was well backed to make a successful reappearance. He won in the manner of a smart colt, drawing clear easily from two furlongs out, and it is no surprise that connections fancy their Epsom chances. He will get a mile and a half without much trouble, and while this race is not the strongest Listed form around, it was the way he won which impressed. There are worse 25-1 shots for the Derby. (op 10-11 tchd Evens)
Sienna Storm(IRE), last of three in the Blue Riband Trial on his reappearance, had a mountain to climb in this company according to the official ratings, but he stayed on from off the pace to grab a flattering second place. (op 11-1)
Senor Dali(IRE), whose Newmarket form is working out well enough, had his chance but was outclassed by the winner in the end. He is still without a win next to his name after four starts but a maiden should be a formality before stepping into decent handicap company. (tchd 11-2, 6-1 in a place)
London Express(IRE) was raised 12lb for his heavy-ground handicap win against older horses last month, and his efforts since on quicker ground suggest that that may have been harsh. (op 11-4)
Fiddlers Wood is a fairly exposed handicapper, albeit a useful one, and he was found out in this company. (op 25-1)

1474 ROYAL SUSSEX REGIMENT STKS (H'CAP) 6f
3:25 (3:26) (Class 4) (0-85,89) 3-Y-O+ **£7,124** (£2,119; £1,059; £529) **Stalls** Low

Form RPR
06-0 **1** **Romany Nights (IRE)**[5] [1359] 6-9-6 77....(b) KerrinMcEvoy 7 92
(Miss Gay Kelleway) *trckd ldng trio: led gng easily over 1f out: shkn up and wl in command fnl f* **33/1**
014- **2** *2 ½* **Pic Up Sticks**[227] [5402] 7-10-0 85....TQuinn 8 92
(B G Powell) *hld up in midfield: smooth prog 2f out: chsd wnr jst ins fnl f: nt qckn and no imp* **7/1**[2]
0-03 **3** *shd* **Chinalea (IRE)**[5] [1359] 4-9-1 72....(t) DaneO'Neill 2 79
(C G Cox) *w ldrs: led 3f out to 2f out: kpt on same pce u.p* **7/1**[2]
0066 **4** *1* **Kempsey**[11] [1211] 4-8-11 71 oh1....(v) NeilChalmers(3) 6 75
(J J Bridger) *lw: w ldr: led 2f out to over 1f out: one pce* **66/1**
0-03 **5** *hd* **Royal Challenge**[12] [1183] 5-9-5 76....DarryllHolland 12 79+
(M H Tompkins) *t.k.h: hld up fr wd draw and wl off the pce: drvn 2f out: styd on fr over 1f out: no ch* **6/1**[1]
P-00 **6** *½* **Grizedale (IRE)**[5] [1359] 7-9-5 76....(t) PaulDoe 4 78
(J Akehurst) *dwlt: wl in rr: rdn and effrt 2f out: kpt on: nt pce to rch ldrs* **66/1**
-350 **7** *nk* **Digital**[19] [1041] 9-8-7 71 oh2....JamieJones(7) 14 72+
(M R Channon) *dwlt: wl off the pce in last pair fr wd draw: rdn over 2f out: kpt on: nrst fin* **20/1**
000- **8** *5* **Oranmore Castle (IRE)**[252] [4755] 4-9-0 78....(t) SladeO'Hara(7) 1 64
(B W Hills) *swtg: racd against nr side rail: led to 3f out: reluctant and wknd over 1f out* **14/1**
0-50 **9** *1 ¾* **Capricho (IRE)**[7] [1285] 9-9-0 76....RoryMoore(5) 13 56+
(J Akehurst) *swtg: wl off the pce on outer fr wd draw: effrt over 2f out: wknd over 1f out* **7/1**[2]
2026 **10** *hd* **Golden Dixie (USA)**[3] [1399] 7-9-13 89....LiamTreadwell(5) 15 69+
(R A Harris) *wl off the pce on outer fr wd draw: effrt to chse ldrs 2f out: sn wknd* **10/1**
0-00 **11** *1 ¼* **Briannsta (IRE)**[7] [1285] 4-9-9 80....SamHitchcott 9 56
(M R Channon) *lw: racd towards outer and nvr beyond midfield: rdn over 2f out: wknd over 1f out* **16/1**
40-5 **12** *hd* **Kingscross**[7] [1285] 8-9-10 81....TedDurcan 3 57
(M Blanshard) *dwlt: hld up against nr side rail: rdn and no prog over 2f out: wknd over 1f out* **12/1**
0-55 **13** *1* **Marker**[12] [1188] 6-8-11 71 oh1....RichardThomas(3) 11 44
(J A Geake) *lw: racd towards outer fr wd draw and sn wl off the pce: rdn and struggling over 2f out* **8/1**[3]
1066 **14** *½* **Silent Storm**[42] [721] 6-9-0 71 oh2....JimmyFortune 5 42
(C A Cyzer) *hld up in midfield: rdn and wkng whn squeezed out 2f out* **12/1**
060- **15** *4* **Buy On The Red**[252] [4755] 5-9-8 82....RobertMiles(3) 10 41
(W R Muir) *lw: hld up in last: detached after 2f: wandering and wkng 2f out* **11/1**

1m 11.01s (-1.84) **Going Correction** -0.075s/f (Good) **15** Ran SP% **118.9**
Speed ratings (Par 105):109,105,105,104,103 103,102,96,93,93 91,91,90,89,84
CSF £242.41 CT £1863.19 TOTE £19.00: £5.80, £2.30, £2.40; EX 141.90.
Owner John W Farley **Bred** The Lloyd Farm Stud **Trained** Exning, Suffolk

FOCUS
A competitive sprint handicap in which they went a decent pace. The form looks solid for the grade rated through the third and fourth.
Oranmore Castle(IRE) Official explanation: jockey said gelding hung right last 2f
Buy On The Red Official explanation: jockey said gelding was unsuited by the good going

1475 RACINGUK.TV STKS (H'CAP) 5f
4:00 (4:03) (Class 3) (0-90,89) 4-Y-O+ **£10,201** (£3,035; £1,516; £757) **Stalls** Low

Form RPR
30-0 **1** **Peopleton Brook**[15] [1125] 4-8-6 77....TedDurcan 8 89
(J M Bradley) *lw: w ldr: led 1/2-way: drvn and styd on wl fnl f* **9/2**[1]
0302 **2** *1 ¼* **Fizzlephut (IRE)**[7] [1297] 4-8-6 77....PaulFitzsimons 10 84
(Miss J R Tooth) *awkward s: sn pressed ldrs: rdn to chse wnr wl over 1f out: kpt on but hld ins fnl f* **7/1**[3]
1100 **3** *½* **Graze On**[10] [1246] 4-9-3 88....(b) AdrianMcCarthy 5 93
(R A Harris) *bmpd twice sn after s: chsd ldrs: effrt and cl up 2f out: kpt on same pce u.p fr over 1f out* **9/1**
0-60 **4** *1 ½* **Fast Heart**[10] [1246] 5-9-0 85....(bt[1]) JimmyFortune 11 85+
(B J Meehan) *swtg: racd on outer fr wd draw: hld up and nvr on terms: drvn and kpt on fnl 2f: no ch* **5/1**[2]
0/00 **5** *shd* **Purus (IRE)**[15] [1112] 4-9-3 88....DarryllHolland 2 87+
(P Mitchell) *chsd ldrs: bdly outpcd after 2f and sn last: r.o wl fnl f* **10/1**
2430 **6** *1* **Lindbergh**[3] [1399] 4-9-1 86....(b[1]) PatDobbs 9 82
(R Hannon) *chsd ldrs: rdn 1/2-way: outpcd and btn wl over 1f out* **11/1**
2/00 **7** *1* **First Order**[10] [1246] 5-9-1 86....TPQueally 1 78
(Ernst Oertel) *b: b.hind: a towards rr: hrd rdn and no prog over 2f out* **12/1**
-000 **8** *2 ½* **Whistler**[7] [1297] 9-8-4 75 oh5....(p) FrankieMcDonald 7 58
(Miss J R Tooth) *sn struggling in last pair: nvr a factor* **25/1**
0-00 **9** *2* **Night Prospector**[13] [1161] 6-9-2 87....(p) GeorgeBaker 3 63
(G L Moore) *lw: wnt rt sn after s: chsd ldrs tl wknd 2f out* **7/1**[3]
00-0 **10** *hd* **Hornpipe**[35] [836] 4-9-4 89....(p) DaneO'Neill 6 64
(M S Saunders) *lw: led to 1/2-way: sn wknd* **16/1**

58.34 secs (-0.71) **Going Correction** -0.075s/f (Good) **10** Ran SP% **104.7**
Speed ratings (Par 107):102,100,99,96,96 95,93,89,86,85
CSF £29.01 CT £200.14 TOTE £5.50: £2.10, £2.00, £2.70; EX 25.00.
Owner G S Thompson & P Banfield **Bred** Lower Hill Farm Stud **Trained** Sedbury, Gloucs
■ Quality Street was withdrawn (8/1, refused to enter stalls). R4 applies, deduct 10p in the £.

FOCUS
Sound form and pretty straightforward to rate, with the third running close to his recent All-Weather best.

NOTEBOOK
Peopleton Brook, who crossed over from his stall in eight to race one off the rail, responded well when asked to go and take his race and, in victory, recorded a personal best according to RPRs. A winner of his first two starts last season, he has once again hit form early, and it would not be a surprise to see him follow up. (op 11-2)
Fizzlephut(IRE) had every chance but once again found one too good. He has been fairly consistent off this sort of mark over the minimum trip. (op 13-2)
Graze On, who has enjoyed a successful campaign on the All-Weather earlier this year, was reappearing on turf off a 17lb higher mark than when last seen on it winning a claimer at Bath in October. He showed that he can be competitive, recording an RPR close to his recent best. (tchd 10-1)
Fast Heart, who last won in a nursery off a mark of 90 in August 2003, is now only 5lb lower, but it did not stop people backing him into 5-1 in the belief that the first-time blinkers would spring a revival. He is an useful sort but not one to rely on.
Purus(IRE) finished best of all having got himself outpaced when the principals stepped on the gas. He had winning form in France last autumn over a mile, so it was hardly surprising to see him get outpaced, but the way he finished suggests there is a race to be won with him when he steps back up in trip.
Lindbergh struggles to win but is consistent enough that the Handicapper gives him little slack.
First Order Official explanation: jockey said gelding hung right

1476 MARRIOTT GOODWOOD PARK HOTEL MAIDEN STKS 7f
4:30 (4:32) (Class 5) 3-Y-O **£3,562** (£1,059; £529; £264) **Stalls** High

Form RPR
224- **1** **Illustrious Blue**[224] [5463] 3-9-3 78....TPQueally 6 82
(J A Osborne) *b: in tch: shkn up over 2f out: prog to press ldr over 1f out: led last 150yds: styd on wl* **14/1**
3 **2** *¾* **Mumaathel (IRE)**[19] [1048] 3-9-3....TedDurcan 7 86+
(M P Tregoning) *s.s: hld up in tch: nt clr run over 2f out tl twice swtchd lft over 1f out: r.o to take 2nd nr fin: nt rcvr* **10/3**[2]
3-4 **3** *hd* **Music By Mozart**[16] [1089] 3-9-3....AdrianMcCarthy 4 80
(P W Chapple-Hyam) *b.hind: cl up: effrt to ld wl over 1f out: hdd and one pce last 150yds* **25/1**

4 3 1/2 **Gulf Of Gold (USA)** 3-9-3 ....(t) KerrinMcEvoy 3 71+
(Saeed Bin Suroor) *cmpt: bit bkwd: led: shkn up over 2f out: hdd wl over 1f out: sn btn* **11/10**[1]

03-2 5 1 1/2 **Chronomatic**[42] 731 3-9-3 76.... DarryllHolland 8 67
(M H Tompkins) *prom: n.m.r briefly on inner over 2f out: wknd over 1f out* **14/1**

0-0 6 3/4 **Jamaahir (USA)**[14] 1134 3-9-3 .... TQuinn 5 65
(J L Dunlop) *plld hrd: hld up in last pair: stl keen 3f out: nt keen and hanging fnl 2f* **33/1**

7 1 1/4 **Accompanist** 3-9-3 .... JimmyFortune 2 62
(J H M Gosden) *str: bit bkwd: hld up in last pair: shkn up and no prog over 2f out* **15/2**[3]

40-6 8 1/2 **Urban Tiger (GER)**[12] 1190 3-9-3 76.... DaneO'Neill 1 61
(A King) *swtg: awkward s: sn chsd ldr: wknd jst over 2f out* **11/1**

1m 28.15s (0.11) **Going Correction** +0.20s/f (Good) **8** Ran SP% **110.9**
Speed ratings (Par 99):107,106,105,101,100 99,97,97
CSF £56.79 TOTE £12.50: £2.20, £1.50, £2.60; EX 36.40.
Owner Mr & Mrs I H Bendelow **Bred** B J And Mrs Crangle **Trained** Upper Lambourn, Berks

FOCUS
An ordinary maiden won by an exposed performer with a rating of 78. The time was decent and the runner-up was somewhat unlucky.
Mumaathel(IRE) ◆ Official explanation: jockey said colt was denied a clear run
Jamaahir(USA) Official explanation: jockey said colt ran in snatches

1477 EUROPEAN BREEDERS FUND FILLIES' AND MARES' CONQUEROR STKS (LISTED RACE) 1m
5:05 (5:05) (Class 1) 3-Y-0+
£17,034 (£6,456; £3,231; £1,611; £807; £405) **Stalls** High

Form RPR
330- 1 **Nantyglo**[217] 5605 3-8-5 103.... TQuinn 4 103
(M L W Bell) *lw: trckd ldr: led over 2f out and gng easily: shkn up and pressed over 1f out: rdn out and styd on wl* **7/2**[1]

645- 2 1 1/4 **Sweet Treat (IRE)**[181] 6270 4-9-4 .... OscarUrbina 3 103
(J R Fanshawe) *bit bkwd: hld up in 4th: prog over 2f out: pressed wnr over 1f out: nt qckn and readily hld ins fnl f* **7/2**[1]

00-5 3 2 **Salamanca**[21] 1015 4-9-7 98.... JimmyFortune 2 101
(S Kirk) *lw: hld up in 6th: rdn wl over 2f out: outpcd wl over 1f out: kpt on* **4/1**[2]

220- 4 shd **Little Miss Gracie**[188] 6181 4-9-4 98.... DaneO'Neill 7 98
(A B Haynes) *bit bkwd: led: set stdy pce to 5f out: rdn and hdd over 2f out: outpcd over 1f out* **6/1**[3]

040- 5 1 3/4 **Favourita**[224] 5462 4-9-4 90....(t) KerrinMcEvoy 6 94
(J W Hills) *trckd ldng pair to over 2f out: nt qckn and btn wl over 1f out* **8/1**

54-6 6 hd **Heat Of The Night**[21] 1015 4-9-4 86.... AdrianMcCarthy 1 94?
(P W Chapple-Hyam) *t.k.h and hld up in last: effrt 3f out: nt qckn and btn wl over 1f out* **6/1**[3]

040- 7 nk **Love Thirty**[223] 5492 4-9-4 88.... TedDurcan 5 93
(M R Channon) *hld up in 5th: rdn over 2f out: sn struggling* **14/1**

1m 40.46s (0.19) **Going Correction** +0.20s/f (Good)
WFA 3 from 4yo 13lb **7** Ran SP% **110.8**
Speed ratings (Par 108):107,105,103,103,101 101,101
CSF £14.83 TOTE £3.30: £2.50, £2.20; EX 9.60.
Owner Usk Valley Stud **Bred** Usk Valley Stud **Trained** Newmarket, Suffolk

FOCUS
Not a particularly strong Listed contest, and the early pace was far from frenetic. The winner is the best guide to the level.

NOTEBOOK
Nantyglo, the only three-year-old in the field, had the highest official rating of these and won a shade cosily having been well positioned throughout in a race not run at a great early pace. She finished third in the Mill Reef last year so was entitled to win in this sort of company, and connections will no doubt be after Group-race success now.
Sweet Treat(IRE), who raced in Ireland for John Oxx last year, ran a pleasing race on her debut for her new stable, especially as paddock inspection suggested she would come on for the run. She was not up to conceding 13lb to the three-year-old but this was a solid effort. (tchd 4-1)
Salamanca, who, in contrast to all but one of her rivals, had the benefit of a recent outing, had to give weight all round owing to her success in a Listed race last year. Held up off the pace in a race run at a modest early gallop, she was out of her ground when the leaders kicked for home.
Little Miss Gracie, who looked in need of the outing beforehand, enjoyed the run of the race in front as she was able to dictate a steady gallop for much of the way.
Favourita, tongue tied for the first time, could have settled better. She has been placed a number of times in Pattern races but finds winning difficult. (op 11-1)
Heat Of The Night, who had the lowest official rating in the field, was sent off at quite a short price in the circumstances. She did, however, have the benefit of a recent outing on her side. She failed to settle off the modest early gallop, though, and never really threatened. (op 11-2 tchd 5-1)

1478 GOODWOOD.CO.UK STKS (H'CAP) 1m 3f
5:40 (5:44) (Class 4) (0-80,80) 4-Y-0+ **£6,800** (£2,023; £1,011; £505) **Stalls** Low

Form RPR
0-51 1 **Top Seed (IRE)**[11] 1206 5-9-4 80.... SamHitchcott 13 90+
(M R Channon) *hld up in last trio: plenty to do and rdn 3f out: sustained prog after: swtchd lft wl over 1f out: r.o to ld last 100yds* **2/1**[1]

050- 2 1 1/4 **Ocean Avenue (IRE)**[194] 6073 7-8-11 73.... TQuinn 15 81
(C A Horgan) *allowed unchal ld: gng wl 3f out: rdn and pressed over 1f out: hdd and outpcd last 100yds* **33/1**

2-60 3 hd **Mister Right (IRE)**[20] 1033 5-8-6 71.... NelsonDeSouza(3) 7 79
(D J S Ffrench Davis) *swtg: trckd ldr: rdn to chal over 1f out: kpt on but outpcd ins fnl f* **14/1**

1-30 4 3 1/2 **Prime Contender**[14] 1132 4-8-9 71.... TedDurcan 11 73
(B W Hills) *swtg: trckd ldrs: nt qckn 2f out: one pce and btn over 1f out: fdd* **6/1**[2]

10-0 5 hd **Prime Powered (IRE)**[122] 37 5-7-13 66.... RobynBrisland(5) 8 68
(G L Moore) *t.k.h: trckd ldrs: nt qckn over 2f out: one pce after* **25/1**

5150 6 1 1/4 **Zamboozle (IRE)**[18] 1071 4-9-3 79.... JohnEgan 9 79
(D R C Elsworth) *lw: dwlt: hld up in last pair: rdn and sme prog over 2f out: no imp over 1f out: kpt on again ins fnl f* **8/1**[3]

00-6 7 1/2 **Mixing**[12] 1187 4-7-11 66 oh1.... BRoper(7) 12 65
(W Jarvis) *s.s: t.k.h: hld up in last: sme prog on inner 3f out: bmpd along fnl 2f: r.o ins fnl f* **50/1**

000- 8 3/4 **Azizam**[194] 6073 4-9-1 77.... AdrianMcCarthy 1 75
(P W Chapple-Hyam) *bit bkwd: pressed ldrs: rdn over 2f out: steadily wknd* **33/1**

05/0 9 3/4 **North Lodge (GER)**[13] 1167 6-8-13 75.... DaneO'Neill 6 72
(A King) *bit bkwd: trckd ldrs: rdn wl over 2f out: sn btn* **16/1**

-056 10 shd **Burgundy**[24] 983 9-8-9 71....(b) TPQueally 4 67
(P Mitchell) *lw: dwlt: wl in rr: hrd rdn wl over 2f out: one pce and no real prog* **16/1**

315- 11 1/2 **Alessano**[197] 6003 4-9-1 77.... JimmyFortune 16 77+
(G L Moore) *lw: hld up in rr: pushed along & nt clr run over 2f out: sme prog 2f out: gng wl enough but no ch whn nt clr run over 1f ou* **8/1**[3]

120- 12 1 **Hawk Arrow (IRE)**[280] 3956 4-8-5 67.... KerrinMcEvoy 14 61
(Miss Sheena West) *hld up in midfield: shuffled along and no prog over 2f out: steadily lost pl* **12/1**

5240 13 1 1/4 **The Violin Player (USA)**[40] 765 5-9-1 77.... DarryllHolland 2 69
(H J Collingridge) *swtg: racd on outer in midfield: drvn wl over 2f out: sn btn* **10/1**

5-00 14 1 1/2 **Love Angel (USA)**[19] 1051 4-8-7 69.... J-PGuillambert 10 59
(J J Bridger) *rousted along early to rch midfield: rdn and struggling 3f out* **33/1**

00-0 15 1 1/2 **Harcourt (USA)**[31] 33 6-8-3 68.... NeilChalmers(3) 3 55
(M Madgwick) *a towards rr: detached in last over 2f out* **50/1**

2m 27.6s (0.39) **Going Correction** +0.20s/f (Good) **15** Ran SP% **121.6**
Speed ratings (Par 105):106,105,104,102,102 101,100,100,99,99 99,98,97,96,95
CSF £92.33 CT £767.06 TOTE £2.20: £1.30, £10.40, £4.80; EX 86.50 Place 6 £898.74, Place 5 £46.97.
Owner John Livock Bloodstock Limited **Bred** Hugo Merry And Jack Dorrian **Trained** West Ilsley, Berks
■ Augustine was withdrawn (10/1, rdr uns & inj). R4 applies, deduct 5p in the £. New market formed.

FOCUS
An ordinary handicap run at a modest gallop and the winner did well to win from off the pace. The runner-up sets the standard but the form could rate higher.
The Violin Player(USA) Official explanation: jockey said gelding hung right
T/Plt: £1,307.80 to a £1 stake. Pool: £54,375.35. 30.35 winning tickets. T/Qpdt: £14.80 to a £1 stake. Pool: £3,093.70. 154.35 winning tickets. JN

1278 HAYDOCK (L-H)
Saturday, May 6

OFFICIAL GOING: Flat course - good to firm; hurdle course - good
Wind: Fresh, half-behind Weather: Fine **Other races under Rules of Jump racing**

1479 BETFRED MILLION SPRING TROPHY STKS (LISTED RACE) 7f 30y
2:25 (2:28) (Class 1) 3-Y-0+ **£17,034** (£6,456; £3,231) **Stalls** Low

Form RPR
235- 1 **Majors Cast (IRE)**[189] 6166 5-9-7 117.... ShaneKelly 2 113+
(J Noseda) *hld up in last pl: impr in bit to go upsides 1f out: sn led: easily* **2/7**[1]

0-12 2 1 1/2 **Philharmonic**[7] 1287 5-9-7 100.... PaulHanagan 4 109
(R A Fahey) *racd in 2nd pl: led wl over 1f out: hdd ent fnl f: no ch w wnr after* **5/1**[2]

3-00 3 4 **My Paris**[42] 728 5-9-7 105.... MickyFenton 1 99
(K A Ryan) *led: rdn and hdd wl over 1f out: outpcd fnl f* **8/1**[3]

1m 30.33s (-1.73) **Going Correction** -0.175s/f (Firm) **3** Ran SP% **105.5**
Speed ratings (Par 111):102,100,95
CSF £1.97 TOTE £1.40; EX 1.40.
Owner Mrs Susan Roy **Bred** Joe Fogarty **Trained** Newmarket, Suffolk

FOCUS
A very disappointing turnout for a Listed contest with half of those declared to run overnight missing for various reasons. A predictable result and not surprisingly the winning time was very moderate for a race of its class with the runner-up setting the standard.

NOTEBOOK
Majors Cast(IRE), having his first race since finishing fifth in last year's Breeders' Cup Mile, had upwards of 12lb in hand of his two rivals on official ratings and, given the most confident of rides, he had little difficulty in picking them off without his jockey having to work very hard. Things will get a lot tougher now, but this was a nice way to start the campaign. (op 3-10 tchd 1-3)
Philharmonic sat in second place until quickening to the front over a furlong from home, but the favourite was always toying with him. Technically he performed above himself at the weights, but contests like this are notoriously misleading. (op 4-1)
My Paris set just a modest pace yet was still easily picked off by his two rivals. He had 5lb in hand of Philharmonic on official ratings, which shows that he has not started off this campaign at the top of his game and finds himself on an awkward mark.

1480 BETFREDCASINO.COM FLAT V JUMP JOCKEYS H'CAP 1m 30y
3:00 (3:00) (Class 5) (0-70,73) 4-Y-0+ **£5,505** (£1,637; £818; £408) **Stalls** Low

Form RPR
6013 1 **Takes Tutu (USA)**[3] 1422 7-11-2 65 3ex.... PhilipRobinson 1 75+
(C R Dore) *hld up in rr: hdwy over 2f out: led ins fnl f: r.o wl* **2/1**[1]

6313 2 1 3/4 **Latif (USA)**[7] 1288 5-11-10 73.... PhillipMakin 8 79
(Ms Deborah J Evans) *hld up: rdn and hdwy over 2f out: styd on to take 2nd ins fnl f: nt pce of wnr cl home* **11/2**[2]

1-26 3 1 1/2 **Time To Regret**[3] 1422 6-10-7 56 oh1.... PJBrennan 7 59+
(J S Wainwright) *trckd ldrs: led wl over 3f out: rdn and hung lft over 2f out: hdd ins fnl f: no ex cl home* **16/1**

0-40 4 1 1/4 **Silverhay**[3] 1425 5-11-5 68.... ShaneKelly 6 68
(T D Barron) *in tch: rdn over 2f out: styd on same pce fnl f* **6/1**[3]

6006 5 nk **Burnley Al (IRE)**[12] 1186 4-10-10 59.... PadgeWhelan 2 58
(R A Fahey) *prom: ev ch over 3f out: kpt on same fnl f* **16/1**

-056 6 1 1/4 **Ermine Grey**[7] 1288 5-11-1 64.... DavidO'Meara 4 60
(A W Carroll) *hld up: rdn and hdwy over 2f out: hung lft over 1f out: one pce ins fnl f* **12/1**

0612 7 nk **Exit Smiling**[9] 1257 4-11-5 68.... CarlLlewellyn 12 63
(P T Midgley) *in tch: rdn over 2f out: bmpd whn wkng over 1f out* **12/1**

0-06 8 4 **Grandos (IRE)**[9] 1253 4-10-9 58.... PaulHanagan 11 44
(T D Easterby) *midfield: rdn over 3f out: no imp* **14/1**

00-3 9 2 1/2 **Sake (IRE)**[19] 1041 4-10-11 60.... KimTinkler 5 40
(N Tinkler) *in rr: rdn over 4f out: nvr on terms* **14/1**

403- 10 nk **Credential**[190] 6134 4-10-12 61.... AndrewTinkler 3 41
(John A Harris) *midfield: rdn over 3f out: sn wknd* **16/1**

003- 11 3/4 **Threezedzz**[250] 4814 8-11-5 68....(t) WayneHutchinson 9 46
(P D Evans) *led: hdd wl over 3f out: wknd over 1f out* **20/1**

6-0 12 49 **Quasimodo (IRE)**[26] 946 4-11-5 68....(v) FergusSweeney 10 —
(A W Carroll) *midfield: wknd over 4f out: t.o: btn 49l by 11th horse* **33/1**

1m 43.44s (-2.07) **Going Correction** -0.175s/f (Firm) **12** Ran SP% **117.1**
Speed ratings (Par 103):103,101,99,98,98 96,96,92,90,89 89,40
CSF £11.82 CT £138.38 TOTE £2.90: £1.50, £2.00, £4.70; EX 14.90.

Owner Page, Ward, Marsh **Bred** Harbor View Farm **Trained** West Pinchbeck, Lincs
FOCUS
A novelty contest in which the form can be dubious and, as was the case in a similar event at Sandown the previous week, it was the Flat jockeys who had the edge. At least with several front-runners in opposition, the pace was always going to be solid and the form appears ordinary but sound enough for a race of its type.
Quasimodo(IRE) Official explanation: jockey said gelding lost its action

1481 BETFRED MILLION CONDITIONS STKS 6f
3:35 (3:36) (Class 3) 3-Y-O+
£10,906 (£3,265; £1,632; £817; £407; £204) Stalls Centre

Form RPR
23-6 1 **One Putra (IRE)**[18] 1069 4-9-0 100 (t) PhilipRobinson 3 108+
(M A Jarvis) *led: hdd wl over 2f out: qckly to regain ld over 1f out: r.o wl: shyed rt cl home whn in command* 4/5[1]
-434 2 1 1/4 **Peace Offering (IRE)**[14] 1158 6-9-0 95 PhillipMakin 4 101
(D Nicholls) *racd keenly: w wnr: led wl over 2f out: rdn and hdd over 1f out: sn outpcd by wnr: flattered* 7/2[2]
006- 3 5 **Jonny Ebeneezer**[343] 2079 7-9-0 (b) MickyFenton 1 86
(M Wellings) *in tch: effrt 2f out: outpcd by ldrs fnl f* 14/1
000- 4 shd **Chookie Heiton (IRE)**[217] 5614 8-9-12 105 TomEaves 6 98
(I Semple) *trckd ldrs: rdn over 1f out: sn outpcd by ldrs* 10/1
0-20 5 9 **Bahamian Pirate (USA)**[14] 1158 11-9-0 102 PaulHanagan 2 59
(D Nicholls) *in rr: rdn 2f out: nvr on terms* 11/2[3]
0650 6 2 **Smirfys Party**[38] 793 8-9-0 40 (v) ShaneKelly 5 53?
(W M Brisbourne) *chsd ldrs tl outpcd over 3f out* 150/1

1m 11.26s (-3.64) **Going Correction** -0.475s/f (Firm) 6 Ran SP% 109.6
Speed ratings (Par 107):105,103,96,96,84 81
CSF £3.61 TOTE £1.70: £1.40, £2.10; EX 3.70.
Owner H R H Sultan Ahmad Shah **Bred** Mount Coote Stud, Richard Pegum & M Bell Racing **Trained** Newmarket, Suffolk
FOCUS
A fair little conditions event run at just an ordinary pace with the favourite making all. Although the stalls were in the centre, the runners were inclined to edge towards the far side of the track. The form does not appear that strong and is best assessed through the runner-up.
NOTEBOOK
One Putra(IRE), with the tongue tie back on following his encouraging return in the Abernant without it, was crucially able to get straight to the front this time and, sticking to the far rail throughout, always seemed to have everything in control. (op evens tchd 11-10)
Peace Offering(IRE) was always closest to the winner and though he always looked held, never stopped trying. He would have been 5lb better off with the winner in a handicap and it must be infuriating to connections that he keeps on doing his best yet cannot get his head in front. (op 11-2)
Jonny Ebeneezer was not disgraced on this first outing for a year, but he does given the impression he is going to be a nightmare to place unless the Handicapper shows even more sympathy. (op 11-1 tchd 10-1)
Chookie Heiton(IRE) faced a stiff task under his big penalty, but was entitled to need this reappearance effort. In recent years he has tended to come into his own later in the season. (op 8-1 tchd 15-2)
Bahamian Pirate(USA) would have preferred softer ground, but even so is going to struggle to find an opportunity at his age. (op 10-3)
Smirfys Party was predictably outclassed. (op 100-1)

1482 BETFRED "THE BONUS KING" H'CAP 6f
4:10 (4:12) (Class 4) (0-85,85) 3-Y-O £6,477 (£1,927; £963; £481) Stalls Centre

Form RPR
40-1 1 **Borehan**[14] 1147 3-9-4 85 PhilipRobinson 5 93+
(M A Jarvis) *mde all: rdn 1f out: r.o* 11/4[1]
01-0 2 1 1/4 **John Keats**[18] 1067 3-9-0 81 TomEaves 8 85
(I Semple) *cl up: rdn over 1f out: wnt 2nd wl ins fnl f: styd on: nt pce of wnr* 9/1
100- 3 nk **Signor Peltro**[197] 6010 3-8-10 77 FergusSweeney 4 80
(H Candy) *towards rr: rdn over 2f out: hdwy over 1f out: styd on ins fnl f* 7/1
40-0 4 3/4 **Glasshoughton**[20] 1032 3-8-3 73 BenSwarbrick(3) 3 74
(M Dods) *in tch: effrt to chse wnr over 2f out: lost 2nd and no ex wl ins fnl f* 33/1
1-15 5 2 **Jimmy The Guesser**[14] 1146 3-8-12 79 PaulHanagan 9 74
(N P Littmoden) *hld up: rdn and hdwy 2f out: hung lft fr over 1f out: one pce ins fnl f* 9/2[2]
0-31 6 2 **Shes Minnie**[15] 1110 3-8-5 72 DavidKinsella 6 61
(J G M O'Shea) *in tch: rdn 2f out: wknd fnl f* 14/1
030- 7 1 1/2 **Charlie Delta**[137] 6627 3-8-7 77 DanielTudhope(3) 10 61
(D Carroll) *dwlt: in rr: rdn over 1f out: no imp* 25/1
00-6 8 3 **Cheap N Chic**[14] 1146 3-8-12 79 MickyFenton 2 54
(T D Easterby) *chsd ldrs: rdn over 2f out: wknd over 1f out* 12/1
0-00 9 1 1/4 **Sleeping Storm (IRE)**[16] 1091 3-9-0 81 MichaelTebbutt 1 53
(B J Meehan) *chsd ldrs: rdn over 2f out: wknd over 1f out* 10/1
0-00 10 7 **Danjet (IRE)**[14] 1146 3-8-10 77 ShaneKelly 7 28
(P D Evans) *cl up: rdn over 2f out: sn wknd* 25/1
4-1 11 8 **Rondo**[15] 1127 3-8-10 77 PhillipMakin 11 4
(T D Barron) *midfield early: outpcd fr 1/2-way* 5/1[3]

1m 11.59s (-3.31) **Going Correction** -0.475s/f (Firm) 11 Ran SP% 118.1
Speed ratings (Par 101):103,101,100,99,97 94,92,88,86,77 66
CSF £27.92 CT £160.06 TOTE £3.80: £1.60, £3.10, £2.90; EX 44.30.
Owner Sheikh Ahmed Al Maktoum **Bred** Stratford Place Stud **Trained** Newmarket, Suffolk
■ Borehan completed a just over 19-1 treble for jockey Philip Robinson.
FOCUS
A fairly competitive handicap in which the field once again tended to edge towards the far side of the track. The form is solid rated around those in the frame behind the winner, whereas the winner can rate higher.
Danjet(IRE) Official explanation: jockey said filly was unsuited by the good to firm ground
Rondo Official explanation: jockey said gelding hung right throughout

1483 BETFREDPOKER.COM MAIDEN STKS 1m 2f 120y
4:40 (4:41) (Class 5) 3-Y-O £3,238 (£963; £481; £240) Stalls High

Form RPR
0 1 **Great Hawk (USA)**[17] 1087 3-9-3 TomEaves 8 85
(Sir Michael Stoute) *trckd ldrs: swtchd rt to take 2nd over 2f out: rdn to ld 1f out: r.o* 6/4[1]
0-5 2 1 **New Guinea**[12] 1192 3-9-3 PhilipRobinson 1 84
(M A Jarvis) *midfield: hdwy 3f out: rdn and ev ch fr over 1f out: nt qckn cl home* 4/1[3]
32- 3 2 1/2 **My Petra**[199] 5988 3-8-12 JDSmith 7 74
(A King) *led: rdn 2f out: hdd 1f out: no ex wl ins fnl f* 3/1[2]
6 4 2 1/2 **Soulard (USA)**[12] 1192 3-9-3 ShaneKelly 3 75
(J Noseda) *trckd ldrs: rdn over 2f out: one pce fr over 1f out* 7/1
0 5 7 **Garrulous (UAE)**[14] 1139 3-8-12 GregFairley(5) 10 62
(M Johnston) *prom: rdn over 3f out: edgd lft and wknd 2f out* 20/1
6 2 1/2 **Forever Autumn** 3-9-3 MichaelTebbutt 5 57+
(B J Meehan) *dwlt: hld up: rdn over 4f out: hung lft over 3f out: nvr on terms* 12/1
7 1 3/4 **Naval Hero (IRE)** 3-9-3 RobbieFitzpatrick 6 54?
(Mrs L Williamson) *dwlt: a bhd* 100/1
54 8 2 1/2 **King Of Rhythm (IRE)**[11] 1216 3-9-0 DanielTudhope(3) 4 50
(D Carroll) *midfield: effrt over 2f out: wknd over 1f out* 50/1
060- 9 47 **Inchmarlow (IRE)**[197] 6001 3-9-3 58 PaulHanagan 2 —
(T H Caldwell) *s.i.s: towards rr: rdn 4f out: lft bhd 3f out: t.o: btn 47l by 8th horse* 66/1

2m 13.26s (-4.47) **Going Correction** -0.175s/f (Firm) 9 Ran SP% 114.4
Speed ratings (Par 99):109,108,106,104,99 97,96,94,60
CSF £7.50 TOTE £2.50: £1.10, £1.90, £1.80; EX 9.00 Place 6 £14.08, Place 5 £5.88.
Owner Saeed Suhail **Bred** Clover Iv Llc **Trained** Newmarket, Suffolk
■ Stewards' Enquiry : Tom Eaves one-day ban: careless riding (May 17)
FOCUS
Only half the field could be given a serious chance, but this may have been a good maiden and the winning time was very decent for a race of its type. The third sets the standard and the form appears sound.
T/Plt: £27.40 to a £1 stake. Pool: £59,299.39. 1,574.15 winning tickets. T/Qpdt: £5.00 to a £1 stake. Pool: £2,257.50. 328.35 winning tickets. DO

1089 NEWMARKET (ROWLEY) (R-H)
Saturday, May 6

OFFICIAL GOING: Good to firm (firm in places)
Wind: Light, against Weather: Overcast

1484 STANJAMESUK.COM H'CAP 1m 2f
2:05 (2:06) (Class 2) (0-100,99) 4-Y-O+
£18,696 (£5,598; £2,799; £1,401; £699; £351) Stalls Low

Form RPR
623- 1 **Wild Savannah**[158] 6459 4-9-4 99 RyanMoore 9 108
(J H M Gosden) *a.p: led over 2f out: edgd lft over 1f out: drvn out* 11/2[3]
31-3 2 nk **Chantaco (USA)**[14] 1133 4-8-7 88 MartinDwyer 5 96+
(A M Balding) *b.hind: lw: hld up: nt clr run fr over 2f out: swtchd lft over 1f out: sn rdn: r.o wl: edgd rt towards fin* 5/1[2]
313- 3 3/4 **Thunder Rock (IRE)**[252] 4765 4-8-6 87 RobertWinston 3 94
(Sir Michael Stoute) *lw: hld up: hdwy 4f out: rdn over 1f out: styd on* 9/4[1]
1123 4 1 1/2 **Young Mick**[21] 1017 4-8-9 90 (v) JimmyQuinn 2 95+
(G G Margarson) *trckd ldrs: rdn and nt clr run over 1f out: styng on same pce whn hmpd towards fin* 10/1
165- 5 3 **I'm So Lucky**[287] 3730 4-9-3 98 JoeFanning 1 96
(M Johnston) *led 3f: chsd ldr: led 3f out: sn rdn and hdd: wknd over 1f out* 9/1
10-0 6 5 **Prime Number (IRE)**[14] 1129 4-8-7 88 (t) JamieSpencer 10 77
(G A Butler) *s.s: hld up: hdwy over 2f out: wknd over 1f out* 12/1
0-00 7 5 **Coup D'Etat**[14] 1129 4-8-4 85 KDarley 4 64
(J L Dunlop) *lw: hld up: rdn over 3f out: wknd over 1f out* 16/1
00-6 8 1/2 **Crow Wood**[53] 518 7-9-3 98 GrahamGibbons 11 76
(J J Quinn) *chsd ldrs: rdn 4f out: wknd over 1f out* 18/1
40-5 9 1 **Go Tech**[32] 867 6-8-9 90 MJKinane 8 66
(T D Easterby) *lw: chsd ldr: led 7f out: rdn and hdd 3f out: wknd over 1f out* 20/1
3502 10 1 **Impeller (IRE)**[10] 1239 7-8-13 94 SteveDrowne 6 69
(W R Muir) *lw: hld up: hdwy over 4f out: rdn and wknd over 1f out* 11/1
0060 11 1/2 **Shahzan House (IRE)**[10] 1239 7-8-5 86 (p) JohnEgan 7 60
(P G Murphy) *hld up in tch: lost pl 5f out: rdn over 2f out: sn wknd* 66/1

2m 3.92s (-1.79) **Going Correction** -0.025s/f (Good) 11 Ran SP% 115.3
Speed ratings (Par 109):106,105,105,103,101 97,93,93,92,91 91
CSF £32.46 CT £79.30 TOTE £6.80: £2.40, £2.40, £1.30; EX 39.70 Trifecta £48.50 Pool £1,080.88, 15.80 w/u.
Owner A E Oppenheimer **Bred** Hascombe And Valiant Studs **Trained** Newmarket, Suffolk
■ Stewards' Enquiry : Martin Dwyer two-day ban: careless riding (May 17-18)
Ryan Moore caution: careless riding
FOCUS
A decent handicap but most looked pretty exposed beforehand. It has been rated through the fourth.
NOTEBOOK
Wild Savannah had the visor that he wore when successful over this trip on the July course last summer left off on this reappearance, but it made little difference and he won well, albeit fairly narrowly in the end. Handicaps may well be a thing of the past for him now, but there should be no reason why he cannot continue to progress into Listed company. (op 13-2)
Chantaco(USA) would have won with a clear run. Continually denied a clear passage from three furlongs out, he had to be switched again and again, but finished strongly and was only denied by a neck. He can win off this sort of mark, and his proven ability to win on soft ground and fast should make finding a winning opportunity easier, but this is the second time in a row he has been beaten by finding trouble, and he is clearly not the easiest of rides. (op 9-2 tchd 11-2)
Thunder Rock(IRE) ◆ travelled well in behind the leaders for much of the way and looked a big danger a furlong and a half out, but he could not quite claw back the winner, and he lost second place in the closing stages. The lightest-raced runner in the field, he stays further than this, is fully entitled to come on for this seasonal reappearance, and it will be a big surprise if he does not win a similar contest in the coming weeks. (op 2-1 tchd 5-2)
Young Mick had to delay his challenge just inside the final two furlongs as his run was blocked, but he had enough time to get there if good enough. He ran a solid race, right up there with his best according to RPRs, and is a pretty good benchmark for the form. Official explanation: jockey said gelding suffered interference (op 12-1)
I'm So Lucky enjoyed the run of the race next to the stands'-side rail and showed up well up to a point. It appeared that lack of a recent outing found him out, although he also looks quite high in the handicap these days too. (op 12-1)
Prime Number(IRE) was well held in the end and still has his stamina to prove over this trip. (tchd 14-1)
Coup D'Etat had looked worth a try over this trip but he did not appear to get it.

1485 STAN JAMES PALACE HOUSE STKS (GROUP 3) 5f
2:35 (2:41) (Class 1) 3-Y-O+

£28,390 (£10,760; £5,385; £2,685; £1,345; £675) Stalls Low

Form				RPR
-2	1		**Dandy Man (IRE)**[14] 1158 3-8-4 .... NGMcCullagh 16 (C Collins, Ire) *gd sort: lw: racd centre: chsd ldrs: rdn to ld wl ins fnl f: r.o: 1st of 13 that gp* **25/1**	114
0-44	2	1 ¼	**Pivotal Flame**[18] 1069 4-8-13 105..........................(p) GrahamGibbons 23 (E S McMahon) *racd centre: chsd ldrs: led that gp and edgd lft over 1f out: hdd wl ins fnl f: 2nd of 13 that gp* **33/1**	113
111-	3	½	**Tax Free (IRE)**[252] 4764 4-8-13 99.............................. AdrianTNicholls 5 (D Nicholls) *led stands' side: rdn and edgd lft over 1f out: r.o: 1st of 9 in gp* **10/1**	114+
1-31	4	shd	**Reverence**[24] 989 5-8-13 108.. KDarley 18 (E J Alston) *racd centre: mid-div: outpcd 1/2-way: nt clr run over 1f out: rdn and r.o ins fnl f: nrst fin: 3rd of 13 in gp* **8/1**[2]	111+
65-0	5	shd	**The Tatling (IRE)**[18] 1069 9-9-2 114.......................... RyanMoore 14 (J M Bradley) *lw: racd centre: hld up: hdwy 1/2-way: r.o: 4th of 13 in gp* **16/1**	113
154-	6	hd	**Patavellian (IRE)**[204] 5873 8-8-13 110........................(b) SteveDrowne 22 (R Charlton) *b: racd centre: hld up: hdwy over 1f out: r.o: 5th of 13 in gp* **16/1**	109
42-0	7	nk	**Baltic King**[18] 1069 6-8-13 107..(t) EddieAhern 19 (H Morrison) *lw: racd centre: hld up: swtchd rt and hdwy over 1f out: r.o: 6th of 13 in gp* **14/1**	108
/00-	8	1 ¼	**Pivotal Point**[303] 3271 6-8-13 .... SebSanders 21 (P J Makin) *racd centre: chsd ldrs: rdn over 1f out: styd on same pce ins fnl f: 7th of 13 in gp* **33/1**	103
013-	9	hd	**Tabaret**[232] 5261 3-8-4 103... JimmyQuinn 3 (R M Whitaker) *lw: chsd ldr stands' side: rdn and edgd rt over 1f out: styd on same pce: 2nd of 9 in gp* **50/1**	101
23-2	10	½	**Corridor Creeper (FR)**[15] 1116 9-8-13 108..............(p) TonyCulhane 10 (J M Bradley) *racd centre: prom: rdn 2f out: styd on 8th of 13 in gp* **16/1**	100
631-	11	1	**Boogie Street**[219] 5573 5-8-13 110............................ RichardHughes 17 (R Hannon) *lw: led centre over 3f: wkng whn hmpd 1f out: 9th of 13 in gp* **17/2**[3]	96
10-0	12	nk	**Nota Bene**[15] 1116 4-8-13 107...(t) LPKeniry 20 (D R C Elsworth) *chsd ldr centre: rdn and ev ch over 1f out: wknd fnl f: 10th of 13 in gp* **33/1**	95
053-	13	¾	**Moss Vale (IRE)**[204] 5873 5-8-13 109.................................... JMurtagh 1 (D Nicholls) *lw: racd stands' side: hld up: hdwy over 1f out: r.o: 3rd of 9 in gp* **14/1**	95
120-	14	3	**Majestic Missile (IRE)**[216] 5647 5-8-13 112........................(t) LDettori 6 (W J Haggas) *racd stands' side: prom: rdn 2f out: wknd over 1f out: 4th of 9 in gp* **4/1**[1]	83
360-	15	shd	**The Trader (IRE)**[216] 5647 8-9-5 111.........................(b) JamieSpencer 13 (M Blanshard) *s.s: racd centre: n.d: 11th of 13 in gp* **33/1**	86
-256	16	hd	**Slip Dance (IRE)**[71] 506 4-8-10 .... MCHussey 12 (Eamon Tyrrell, Ire) *s.i.s and hmpd s: swtchd to racd stands' side: n.d: 5th of 9 in gp* **66/1**	79
0-36	17	½	**Beckermet (IRE)**[14] 1145 4-8-13 110............................ MartinDwyer 2 (R F Fisher) *raecd stands' side: chsd ldrs over 3f: 6th of 9 in gp* **12/1**	80
000-	18	1 ¾	**Texas Gold**[216] 5647 8-8-13 104.. NCallan 4 (W R Muir) *lw: racd stands' side: chsd ldrs over 3f: 7th of 9 in gp* **33/1**	73
031-	19	1 ¾	**Celtic Mill**[171] 6370 8-8-13 110.................................... RobertWinston 11 (D W Barker) *racd centre: chsd ldrs 3f: 12th of 13 in gp* **20/1**	63
14-1	20	5	**Paradise Isle**[18] 1069 5-8-10 103... AlanMunro 8 (C F Wall) *racd stands' side: chsd ldrs over 3f: 8th of 9 in gp* **14/1**	43
130-	21	4	**Classic Encounter (IRE)**[210] 5732 3-8-4 101................. JoeFanning 15 (D M Simcock) *lw: racd centre: chsd ldrs 3f: last of 13 in gp* **66/1**	23
00-0	22	12	**Captain Hurricane**[42] 729 4-8-13 98.............................(b¹) MJKinane 9 (P W Chapple-Hyam) *lw: racd stands' side: prom to 1/2-way: last of 9 in gp* **66/1**	—

58.41 secs (-2.06) **Going Correction** -0.025s/f (Good)
WFA 3 from 4yo+ 9lb **22 Ran SP% 125.8**
Speed ratings (Par 113):115,113,112,112,111 111,111,109,108,107 106,105,104,99,99 99,98,95,93,85 78,59
CSF £677.95 TOTE £32.50: £6.70, £15.70, £2.80; EX 879.80 TRIFECTA Not won..
Owner A McLean **Bred** Mountarmstrong Stud **Trained** The Curragh, Co Kildare
■ Treasure Cay (66/1) was withdrawn after refusing to enter the stalls.

FOCUS
A competitive Group Three sprint, well up to scratch, and a perfectly acceptable winning time for a contest of this class. The form is not totally rock solid, but with the fourth to seventh close to their marks it should prove reasonable form.

NOTEBOOK
Dandy Man(IRE) had run well behind the older Moon Unit on his reappearance and, racing in the bigger group up the centre, won with a bit up his sleeve. He was only the fourth three-year-old to win this race in the last 24 renewals and, providing he can build on this, he should have a decent part to play in the King's Stand Stakes. There is certainly room for an improving three-year-old to emerge and boss a relatively ordinary bunch of older sprinters. (tchd 20-1 in places)
Pivotal Flame, fourth in a couple of Listed events already this season, had the benefit of being race-fit and had a good draw to boot. Easier ground has appeared to suit him better in the past, though, and the drop back to five furlongs was not sure to be in his favour, but he handled both well and posted a personal best in defeat.
Tax Free(IRE) ♦, a progressive sprint handicapper last season, was pitched in at the deep end on his reappearance over a trip which looked on the short side for him, but he ran a race full of promise. Drawn on the wrong side, he showed good pace throughout, finished clear of his group, and was the only horse drawn in single figures to make the first eight, and all this on his seasonal reappearance. On this evidence he will have no trouble winning in Group company this season and, given that this was only his sixth-ever start and that six furlongs is possibly his best trip, his connections can look forward to him improving again as the year progresses. (op 9-1)
Reverence had never before run on ground officially described as faster than good but he seemed to run very close to his best despite that. Finishing strongly having not enjoyed the clearest of runs, he remains capable of winning in Pattern company when things fall right.
The Tatling(IRE), conceding weight to most of the field, has never won before June in his life so it was not a surprise that he found a few too good. He did, however, shape with plenty of promise and, while he is no longer in the first flush of youth, he appears to still have what it takes to mix it with the best at this trip. (op 14-1)
Patavellian(IRE), representing a stable which has only sent out two winners so far this turf season, looked likely to need this seasonal reappearance outing. In the circumstances he ran a promising race, but since his Prix de l'Abbaye win in 2003 he has only won a small-field conditions race at Yarmouth, which shows how difficult he has been to place.
Baltic King finished a little closer to Pivotal Flame than he did in the Abernant over an extra furlong here last month, but he is another who has proven difficult to place over the past 18 months. (op 12-1)
Pivotal Point won the Group 2 Diadem Stakes by three lengths in 2004 but he has had his problems since, and two outings in 2005 suggested he had lost his ability. This was a far more promising performance, though, and hopefully he can build on it.
Tabaret, a Listed race winner at two, was second home on the stands' side. If he can build on this seasonal reappearance there could be another success for him at Pattern level.
Corridor Creeper(FR) was a bit disappointing, although he does seem to prefer some cut in the ground these days. (op 20-1)
Boogie Street is at his best when able to dominate in a small field. His record over the minimum trip in fields of ten runners or fewer reads 1111741, while his record in all other races reads 5343264205294630. It is fairly clear when he should be backed. Official explanation: jockey said horse had stumbled (op 10-1 tchd 11-1)
Nota Bene finished up well held on his side and has yet to recapture his three-year-old best.
Moss Vale(IRE), third on the stands' side, was running on at the finish and will be suited by a return to six furlongs. (op 12-1)
Majestic Missile(IRE) was representing an in-form yard but, not for the first time in his career, proved disappointing. He has been sent off at 5-1 or shorter eight times in the last two years and has only won once, at 13-8. Sometimes it is best just to let go. Official explanation: jockey said horse had run too freely (op 11-2 tchd 6-1 in places)
The Trader(IRE) Official explanation: jockey said gelding had been unsuited by the good to firm, firm in places ground
Paradise Isle Official explanation: jockey said mare slipped leaving the stalls and lost her action

1486 STAN JAMES 2000 GUINEAS STKS (GROUP 1) (ENTIRE COLTS & FILLIES) 1m
3:15 (3:20) (Class 1) 3-Y-O

£187,374 (£71,016; £35,541; £17,721; £8,877; £4,455) Stalls Centre

Form				RPR
111-	1		**George Washington (IRE)**[230] 5346 3-9-0 .... KFallon 6 (A P O'Brien, Ire) *nice colt: lw: hld up: rcd knly: hdwy over 2f out: led over 1f out: hung rt ins fnl f: rdn out* **6/4**[1]	127+
111-	2	2 ½	**Sir Percy**[203] 5901 3-9-0 121... MartinDwyer 4 (M P Tregoning) *lw: chsd ldrs: rdn and hung lft over 1f out: styd on same pce* **4/1**[2]	120
21-2	3	1 ½	**Olympian Odyssey**[16] 1093 3-9-0 100.......................... JamieSpencer 2 (B W Hills) *led: rdn and hdd over 1f out: no ex ins fnl f* **33/1**	117
263-	4	¾	**Araafa (IRE)**[196] 6023 3-9-0 106... AlanMunro 1 (J Noseda) *lw: hld up in tch: racd keenly: outpcd 2f out: sn rdn and edgd rt: r.o ins fnl f: nt trble ldrs* **66/1**	115
01-1	5	½	**Misu Bond (IRE)**[17] 1083 3-9-0 106............................... TonyCulhane 14 (B Smart) *hld up: outpcd 1/2-way: hdwy u.p over 1f out: no ex towards fin* **66/1**	114
422-	6	½	**Final Verse**[196] 6023 3-9-0 107...................................... RobertWinston 5 (Sir Michael Stoute) *h.d.w: hld up: plld hrd: rdn over 2f out: styd on: nvr able to chal* **50/1**	113
211-	7	¾	**Amadeus Wolf**[218] 5591 3-9-0 120... NCallan 12 (K A Ryan) *h.d.w: chsd ldrs: rdn over 2f out: wknd fnl f* **9/1**	111
112-	8	nk	**Horatio Nelson (IRE)**[203] 5901 3-9-0 .... MJKinane 11 (A P O'Brien, Ire) *chsd ldrs: rdn over 2f out: wknd fnl f* **6/1**[3]	110
13-1	9	shd	**Asset (IRE)**[35] 829 3-9-0 107...................................... RichardHughes 9 (R Hannon) *lw: hld up: plld hrd: hdwy over 2f out: rdn and wknd over 1f out* **10/1**	110+
10-1	10	hd	**Close To You (IRE)**[28] 914 3-9-0 113............................... IanMongan 7 (T G Mills) *lw: trckd ldrs: racd keenly: rdn over 2f out: wknd over 1f out* **80/1**	110
32-1	11	1	**Killybegs (IRE)**[16] 1092 3-9-0 110..................................... MichaelHills 8 (B W Hills) *lw: chsd ldrs: rdn over 2f out: wknd over 1f out* **16/1**	108+
24-1	12	¾	**Red Clubs (IRE)**[14] 1131 3-9-0 117... RHills 3 (B W Hills) *lw: chsd ldrs: rdn and hung lft over 1f out: sn wknd* **25/1**	106
31-	13	9	**Frost Giant (USA)**[187] 6205 3-9-0 .... JMurtagh 10 (A P O'Brien, Ire) *gd sort: lw: s.i.s: sn prom: wknd over 3f out* **50/1**	85
123-	14	1 ½	**Opera Cape**[203] 5901 3-9-0 ....(t) LDettori 13 (Saeed Bin Suroor) *hld up in tch: rdn over 2f out: sn wknd* **16/1**	81

1m 36.86s (-2.51) **Going Correction** -0.025s/f (Good) **14 Ran SP% 120.1**
Speed ratings (Par 113):111,108,107,106,105 105,104,104,104,103 102,102,93,91
CSF £6.58 TOTE £2.70: £1.50, £2.00, £7.00; EX 11.00 Trifecta £346.70 Pool £25,148.50, 51.50 w/u.
Owner Mrs John Magnier, M Tabor & D Smith **Bred** Lael Stables **Trained** Ballydoyle, Co Tipperary

FOCUS
A good renewal and an impressive winner, who has been allotted an RPR which was bettered only by King's Best in the last ten years. The early pace was not that strong and that resulted in a winning time which was acceptable, but not spectacular, for a race of this stature. With Sir Percy looking the best guide to the form, the next four were all showing improved form, but there were grounds for expecting them to.

NOTEBOOK
George Washington(IRE), last year's Champion two-year-old, had been a solid favourite for this race all winter and was heavily supported from 2-1 on the day. However, backers were happily accommodated by many who believed that the Ballydoyle colt's stamina was questionable and that his price was based more on hype than substance. They were wrong, as Fallon's mount proved to be in a different league to the rest and was one of the most impressive winners of the 2000 Guineas in the last ten years. Despite not settling in the early stages, he produced a devastating turn of foot a furlong and a half out which saw him pull clear of his field and come home with a healthy gap back to Sir Percy, and while he has his share of quirks - he would not enter the winner's enclosure afterwards - he is undoubtedly an extremely talented individual. Some bookmakers quoted him at single figures for the Derby afterwards, but it would be a great surprise if connections decide to go down that route, as he would surely fail for stamina, and a campaign based around the top mile races looks the likely option. (op 2-1 tchd 11-8 in places)
Sir Percy, last year's Dewhurst winner, had wintered well and was the subject of good reports. Always close to the pace, he took a little time to get into top gear but stayed on really strongly from the bottom of the Dip. He would probably have won an ordinary Guineas and was a little unlucky to run into a potential star. On the evidence of this run and his breeding, he is going to appreciate stepping up in trip, and it was no surprise that this performance catapulted him to Derby favouritism in most lists. He should not have any trouble getting ten furlongs, but 12 might stretch him a bit, so while his Classic form justifies his prominent position in the Derby market, he might just find one or two too strong again at Epsom. (op 10-3)
Olympian Odyssey, the moral winner of the Feilden Stakes, led the field for most of the way, setting an ordinary pace, and kept on well once headed, as befits a son of Sadler's Wells. His trainer is keen to take him to the Derby now, but one would have thought that the Irish 2000 Guineas might provide him with a better chance of Classic glory. (tchd 40-1 in places)
Araafa(IRE), third in the Horris Hill on his final start at two, was another who was a bit keen in the early stages but he saw the mile out really well in the end. He is in the Irish Guineas and it would not come as a surprise to see him run well there. Easier ground should not inconvenience him.
Misu Bond(IRE), winner of the Free Handicap on his reappearance, struggled to stay in touch when the pace quickened, but he got going in the closing stages and was running on well at the finish. His previous form and pedigree suggest that he will not want to be stepped up in trip, though.

Final Verse, whose trainer's representatives in this race rarely go off at 50-1, looked to have plenty to find to compete at this level but, like Araafa, who finished just behind him in last year's Horris Hill, he was far from disgraced. He made things difficult for himself by pulling hard in the early stages, but he stayed on and is the type who could build on this and make his mark at Group level, perhaps over ten furlongs, later this year. (op 33-1)
Amadeus Wolf had his chance two furlongs out but simply failed to stay. It was always likely that he would turn out to be a sprinter this season, and this performance appears to confirm that. His two-year-old form over six furlongs was very smart and he could yet develop into a top-class colt over sprint distances, as it is a division which for many years now has lacked a star performer. The Golden Jubilee is apparently his next target. (tchd 10-1 and 11-1 in a place)
Horatio Nelson(IRE), who looked unlucky not to win the Dewhurst last season, could be given about the same chance as Sir Percy on that form, but he has apparently been slow to come to hand this spring and that was evident in this performance. There is only a week between the Irish Guineas and the Derby this year so it would be a surprise to see him run in both of those races, a la Oratorio last year, and perhaps the Dante or Derrinstown Derby Trial will prove more suitable targets en route to Epsom. Nevertheless, he is going to have to find a fair amount of improvement for this run to get back on the Derby trail. (op 7-1 tchd 15-2)
Asset(IRE) was visually impressive in quickening off a steady pace in the Easter Stakes on the sand last time, but he beat very little, and he disappointed in this stronger contest having pulled hard early. He might be better off using his finishing kick in sprint races or over seven furlongs. (op 11-1 tchd 12-1 in a place)
Close To You(IRE) looked outclassed, but he might have done better on easier ground and connections plan to have another crack at a Group 1 in the St James's Palace Stakes. (op 100-1)
Killybegs(IRE) won the Craven over this course and distance last month, but was well and truly put in his place. He probably ran his Guineas in the Craven.
Red Clubs(IRE), the Greenham winner, was pretty exposed at two and had his stamina to prove over a mile. He did not get it and is another who was probably trained to the minute to win his trial in the knowledge that he would struggle in the real thing.
Frost Giant(USA), who won the Group Three Killavullan Stakes last season, the same race Footstepsinthesand won prior to his Guineas glory, is a nice type but he was reported as likely to need this run, and his performance backed that up. He acted well in soft ground last year so better should be expected of him as the season progresses and conditions come in his favour. Official explanation: jockey said colt missed the break (op 40-1)
Opera Cape finished third in the Dewhurst last season but his new connections were hardly bullish about his chance here. The horses his stable has run so far have not set the world alight and perhaps they need more time to acclimatise following a winter in Dubai. Official explanation: jockey said colt had run flat

1487 STANJAMESUK.COM STKS (HERITAGE H'CAP) 6f

3:50 (3:54) (Class 2) 3-Y-0+

£31,160 (£9,330; £4,665; £2,335; £1,165; £585) **Stalls** Low

Form				RPR
10-1	**1**		**Mutamared (USA)**^{35} [836] 6-8-11 **92** NCallan 14 (K A Ryan) *racd centre: hld up in tch: swtchd lft over 1f out: r.o to ld wl ins fnl f: 1st of 17 in gp* **12/1**	106+
10-4	**2**	½	**Ice Planet**^{12} [1183] 5-8-8 **89** RobertWinston 7 (D Nicholls) *b: dwlt: racd centre: hld up: hdwy over 1f out: r.o: 2nd of 17 in gp* **10/1**^{3}	98
1320	**3**	*hd*	**Bahiano (IRE)**^{14} [1129] 5-9-5 **100** RyanMoore 8 (C E Brittain) *lw: racd centre: sn pushed along in rr: r.o ins fnl f: nt rch ldrs* **40/1**	108
0-44	**4**	*shd*	**Golden Asha**^{5} [1338] 4-7-13 **80** FrancisFerris 20 (N A Callaghan) *racd centre: hld up: rdn 1/2-way: hdwy and swtchd rt over 1f out: r.o: 4th of 17 in gp* **33/1**	88
0-46	**5**	*hd*	**Pieter Brueghel (USA)**^{35} [836] 7-8-10 **91** AdrianTNicholls 5 (D Nicholls) *led centre: rdn over 1f out: hdd and unable qck wl ins fnl f: 5th of 17 in gp* **25/1**	98
00-0	**6**	*hd*	**Continent**^{42} [729] 9-8-11 **92** TonyCulhane 17 (D Nicholls) *racd centre: chsd ldrs: rdn and ev ch 1f out: no ex towards fin: 6th of 17 in gp* **50/1**	99
6000	**7**	*hd*	**Bo McGinty (IRE)**^{7} [1285] 5-8-0 **81** (b) HayleyTurner 3 (R A Fahey) *lw: racd centre: chsd ldrs: rdn and ev ch 1f out: no ex towards fin* **50/1**	87
3300	**8**	¾	**One More Round (USA)**^{15} [1116] 8-8-9 **95** (b) JamesDoyle$^{(5)}$ 19 (N P Littmoden) *swtg: racd centre: hld up: r.o ins fnl f: nrst fin: 8th of 17 in gp* **33/1**	99
-512	**9**	*nk*	**Idle Power (IRE)**^{10} [1246] 8-8-9 **90** LDettori 4 (J R Boyle) *racd centre: chsd ldrs: rdn and ev ch 1f out: no ex ins fnl f: 9th of 17 in gp* **25/1**	94+
240-	**10**	*nk*	**Greenslades**^{191} [6125] 7-8-13 **94** SebSanders 9 (P J Makin) *lw: racd centre: chsd ldrs: rdn over 1f out: styd on same pce: 10th of 17 in gp* **25/1**	96
0-11	**11**	*shd*	**Spanish Ace**^{11} [1211] 5-8-4 **85** JimmyQuinn 21 (J M Bradley) *b: racd far side: chsd ldrs: led that gp and edgd lft over 2f out: styd on same pce fnl f: 1st of 7 in gp* **12/1**	87
-311	**12**	*hd*	**Bayeux (USA)**^{56} [627] 5-9-0 **95** JamieSpencer 12 (G A Butler) *racd centre: hld up: rdn over 1f out: nt trble ldrs: 11th of 17 in gp* **9/2**^{1}	96
10-4	**13**	*1*	**Banjo Patterson**^{9} [1262] 4-8-6 **87** RichardHughes 22 (G A Huffer) *racd far side: prom: rdn and nt clr run over 1f out: styd on same pce: 2nd of 7 in gp* **12/1**	85
000-	**14**	½	**Woodcote (IRE)**^{241} [5044] 4-8-8 **92** AdamKirby$^{(3)}$ 16 (C G Cox) *racd centre: chsd ldrs: rdn over 2f out: no ex fnl f: 12th of 17 in gp* **25/1**	88
50-0	**15**	*shd*	**Rising Shadow (IRE)**^{12} [1183] 5-8-9 **90** JoeFanning 18 (T D Barron) *lw: racd centre: s.i.s: hld up: rdn over 2f out: n.d: 13th of 17 in gp* **25/1**	86
-116	**16**	¾	**Something (IRE)**^{7} [1299] 4-9-10 **105** IanMongan 29 (T G Mills) *lw: racd far side: chsd ldrs over 4f: 3rd of 7 in gp* **8/1**^{2}	99
2202	**17**	*1*	**Tanforan**^{5} [1359] 4-7-12 **79** oh1 (b) MatthewHenry 11 (K McAuliffe) *racd centre: hld up: n.d: 14th of 17 in gp* **25/1**	70
0646	**18**	½	**Moayed**^{35} [828] 7-8-5 **89** (b) SaleemGolam$^{(3)}$ 24 (N P Littmoden) *racd far side: dwlt: outpcd: 4th of 7 in gp* **22/1**	78
2450	**19**	*shd*	**Royal Storm (IRE)**^{3} [1407] 7-9-5 **100** MJKinane 1 (Mrs A J Perrett) *racd alone stands' side: prom over 3f* **25/1**	89
2-32	**20**	*nk*	**King's Gait**^{17} [1076] 4-9-0 **95** (b) KDarley 2 (T D Easterby) *racd centre: chsd ldrs over 4f: 15th of 17 in gp* **20/1**	83
601-	**21**	*shd*	**Kenmore**^{204} [5874] 4-8-12 **93** EddieAhern 6 (D Nicholls) *racd centre: hld up: wknd 2f out: 16th of 17 in gp* **25/1**	81
10-0	**22**	*nk*	**Intoxicating**^{97} [238] 4-9-5 **100** StephenCarson 27 (R F Johnson Houghton) *racd far side: sn pushed along in rr: n.d: 5th of 7 in gp* **28/1**	87
0-	**23**	*2*	**Enfield Chase (IRE)**^{231} [5329] 5-8-4 **85** WMLordan 26 (T Stack, Ire) *racd far side: chsd ldrs over 4f: 6th of 7 in gp* **33/1**	66
00-3	**24**	*1 ¼*	**High Reach**^{10} [1236] 6-8-12 **93** MartinDwyer 28 (W R Muir) *led far side over 3f: wknd over 1f out: last of 7 in gp* **12/1**	70
U00-	**25**	*6*	**Fantasy Believer**^{196} [6021] 8-8-9 **90** GrahamGibbons 15 (J J Quinn) *racd centre: chsd ldr over 3f: wknd wl over 1f out: last of 17 in gp* **40/1**	49
300-	**U**		**Coeur Courageux (FR)**^{280} [3932] 4-9-5 **100** JMurtagh 13 (D Nicholls) *rrd and uns rdr in stalls* **40/1**	—

1m 11.43s (-1.67) **Going Correction** -0.025s/f (Good) **26** Ran SP% **132.5**
Speed ratings (Par 109):110,109,109,108,108 108,108,107,106,106 106,105,104,103,103 102,101,100,100,100 100,99,97,95,8
CSF £99.85 CT £4683.08 TOTE £11.40: £2.70, £2.60, £10.60, £9.30; EX 134.40 TRIFECTA Not won..
Owner Errigal Racing **Bred** E J Hudson Jr, Irrevocable Trust & Kilroy T'Bred **Trained** Hambleton, N Yorks

FOCUS
A competitive sprint handicap, run at a strong pace, in which the place to be was up the centre of the track. It has been rated through the runner-up and fourth and the form looks solid.

NOTEBOOK
Mutamared(USA), only 2lb higher for his latest All-Weather win, continues to progress and won his fourth race from six starts for Kevin Ryan. He does not like to be in front a long time and that has helped him with the Handicapper's attentions in mind, as he has only been raised 10lb since the first of those four wins. He has a smart turn of foot on fast ground and the Wokingham, in which he will surely hold strong claims, is the next big target. (tchd 14-1 in a place)
Ice Planet improved from a modest performer to a useful handicapper last term and it looks as though he has improved again over the winter. He saw his race out strongly and further success this season looks a given, with all the big sprint handicaps likely to be on his agenda. (op 11-1)
Bahiano(IRE) has only won two races in his career and is high in the handicap, but he has not raced over sprint distances much. He gets further than this so the fact that the race was strongly run suited him, and he finished well from off the pace. (op 33-1)
Golden Asha, who ran well from a poor draw at Beverley on her reappearance before disappointing on the All-Weather next time, was another who kept on well from off the pace.
Pieter Brueghel(USA) did well to stick around given the strong pace he went. A tough old gelding who finished runner-up in both the Great St Wilfrid and Portland Handicaps during the course of a busy season last year, he will pick up a race again sometime this term, granted the opportunity of a less-contested lead.
Continent, a head behind his stable companion Pieter Brueghel in the Portland last September, was 1lb better off at the weights this time, but the result was exactly the same. He has only won one of his last 23 starts but clearly retains the ability to win a race of this nature when things fall right.
Bo McGinty(IRE) is back on the mark he last won off and likes fast ground, so it was not a great surprise to see him run a lot better than his place in the market suggested he would. A stiff six furlongs suits him best.
One More Round(USA) never wins but ran his usual staying-on all too late kind of race.
Idle Power(IRE) ran a solid race but the Handicapper may just have him for the time being off a mark of 90, although he runs so well at Goodwood that perhaps he can find the necessary improvement to defy that sort of mark at his favourite track.
Greenslades, who ran a series of good races in competitive handicaps last season, posted a perfectly reasonable effort on his reappearance. He is entitled to come on for the run and may well be capable of defying a mark that is currently 4lb higher than for his last win.
Spanish Ace ◆, raised a total of 10lb for a couple of wins in Class 5 handicaps earlier this spring, did not appear to be found out by the rise in class but rather by the extra furlong. He still did best of the seven who raced more towards the far side, though, and is just the sort his trainer does well with. Further success looks a certainty, especially if he is dropped back to the minimum trip. (tchd 11-1 in places)
Bayeux(USA), another who has gone up 10lb in the weights for two wins earlier this year, in his case on the All-Weather, was a well-supported favourite, but he failed to translate his improvement on sand back to the turf. (op 11-2 tchd 6-1 in places)
Something(IRE) was giving weight to all his rivals but was still very well supported in the market. He found himself racing in a smaller group of seven towards the far side, though, when the place to be turned out to be the middle. (op 7-1 tchd 9-1 in places)

1488 STANSPOKER.CO.UK NEWMARKET STKS (LISTED RACE) (COLTS) 1m 2f

4:20 (4:23) (Class 1) 3-Y-0

£17,034 (£6,456; £3,231; £1,611; £807; £405) **Stalls** Low

Form				RPR
11-6	**1**		**Mulaqat**^{16} [1092] 3-8-12 97 MartinDwyer 4 (M P Tregoning) *h.d.w: hld up in tch: rdn to ld over 1f out: hung rt ins fnl f: r.o* **4/1**^{2}	108
1	**2**	*2 ½*	**Purple Moon (IRE)**^{14} [1135] 3-8-12 88 MJKinane 6 (Sir Michael Stoute) *lw: hld up: plld hrd: rdn over 2f out: hdwy over 1f out: styd on same pce ins fnl f* **11/10**^{1}	103+
1-6	**3**	*2*	**Morghim (IRE)**^{16} [1093] 3-8-12 96 RHills 2 (J L Dunlop) *chsd ldr: rdn over 2f out: no ex fnl f* **11/2**^{3}	99
4-	**4**	*1 ¼*	**Blue Ksar (FR)**^{210} [5750] 3-8-12 (t) LDettori 1 (Saeed Bin Suroor) *chsd ldrs: rdn over 2f out: wknd over 1f out* **13/2**	97
10-3	**5**	*1 ¾*	**Criminal Act (USA)**^{15} [1117] 3-8-12 92 MichaelHills 5 (B W Hills) *lw: led: rdn and hung rt and hdd over 1f out: wknd fnl f* **16/1**	93
0-34	**6**	*15*	**Silver Blue (IRE)**^{8} [1268] 3-8-12 99 RyanMoore 3 (R Hannon) *chsd ldrs: rdn over 2f out: wkng whn stmbld wl over 1f out* **10/1**	65

2m 4.79s (-0.92) **Going Correction** -0.025s/f (Good) **6** Ran SP% **111.3**
Speed ratings (Par 107):102,100,98,97,96 84
CSF £8.70 TOTE £5.40: £2.20, £1.40; EX 11.80.
Owner Sheikh Ahmed Al Maktoum **Bred** Darley **Trained** Lambourn, Berks

FOCUS
Fair form for a Listed contest rated around the third and fourth, but the winning time was only modest for a race like this.

NOTEBOOK
Mulaqat, whose galloping companion had earlier finished runner-up in the Guineas, put behind him a disappointing effort in the Craven, where the steady early pace proved all against him, and improved for the step up in trip. He stretched out well in the closing stages, has regained his progressive profile and should get a mile and a half on this evidence. (op 9-2)
Purple Moon(IRE), a well-supported favourite, tried to go faster than his rider wanted him to in the early stages and the result was that he used up valuable energy pulling. This was still a step up on his debut form, though, and he can improve further if he settles better. (op 11-8 tchd 6-4 in places)
Morghim(IRE), sixth in a steadily-run Feilden Stakes on his reappearance, had every chance but was left behind by the first two in the closing stages. It remains to be seen what his best trip will turn out to be, and he might prove difficult to place off a mark in the mid-90s. (op 5-1 tchd 6-1)
Blue Ksar(FR), fourth in a Group 3 at two when trained in France by Andre Fabre, was having his first start for Godolphin, but he holds no big-race entries and is clearly not thought to be one of their stars. He failed to shine and may well need more time to acclimatise properly. (op 9-2)
Criminal Act(USA) enjoyed the run of the race next to the rail but was easily brushed aside in the closing stages. He may prove difficult to place. (op 14-1)
Silver Blue(IRE) is another who is high in the handicap but not up to competing successfully at this level. Official explanation: jockey said colt stumbled at the 2f marker (tchd 11-1 and 12-1 in a place)

1489 STANSCASINO.CO.UK CONDITIONS STKS — 1m 2f
4:55 (4:56) (Class 2) 4-Y-0+

£12,464 (£3,732; £1,866; £934; £466; £234) Stalls Low

Form				RPR
140-	1		**Mountain High (IRE)**[203] [5906] 4-8-7 105 ...... RobertWinston 6 (Sir Michael Stoute) *lw: a.p: chsd ldr 6f out: led over 2f out: rdn and edgd lft over 1f out: r.o wl* **11/10**[1]	116+
0344	2	5	**Boule D'Or (IRE)**[58] [622] 5-8-7 ...... MichaelHills 1 (J Akehurst) *hld up: swtchd rt 3f out: hdwy over 1f out: sn rdn: styd on same pce fnl f* **5/1**[3]	105+
0-10	3	nk	**Blythe Knight (IRE)**[14] [1129] 6-8-7 101 ...... GrahamGibbons 4 (J J Quinn) *lw: led over 7f: rdn and nt clr run over 1f out: no ex* **12/1**	104
26-0	4	7	**Hattan (IRE)**[58] [622] 4-8-7 ...... RyanMoore 2 (C E Brittain) *dwlt: hld up: hdwy over 6f out: rdn and wknd over 1f out* **7/1**	91
4402	5	2 ½	**Colisay**[14] [1129] 7-8-7 105 ...... MJKinane 3 (Mrs A J Perrett) *hld up: rdn over 2f out: wknd over 1f out* **10/3**[2]	86
006-	6	35	**Colinca's Lad (IRE)**[162] [6418] 4-8-7 75 ...... AlanMunro 5 (J Ryan) *chsd ldr 4f: rdn and wknd 3f out* **100/1**	19

2m 2.94s (-2.77) **Going Correction** -0.025s/f (Good) 6 Ran SP% **108.5**
Speed ratings (Par 109):110,106,105,100,98 70
CSF £6.50 TOTE £2.00: £1.40, £2.20; EX 6.60.
Owner Mrs John Magnier & M Tabor **Bred** Ballymacoll Stud Farm Ltd **Trained** Newmarket, Suffolk

FOCUS
A decent conditions race won in impressive style by Mountain High, who recorded the quickest time of the three races run over the distance on the card.

NOTEBOOK
Mountain High(IRE) proved disappointing last season following an easy win in a Chester maiden - he was sent off 11-10 for the King Edward VII Stakes - but his trainer excels with his older horses and it was no surprise that he has improved over the winter and marked himself down as a horse to follow on this reappearance. A return to Group company beckons, and the Brigadier Gerard Stakes at the end of the month looks a suitable target for this well-bred four-year-old. (op 5-4 tchd Evens and 11-8 in a place)
Boule D'Or(IRE), fit from a campaign in Dubai, is a smart performer but a very difficult horse to place these days. He is at his best challenging from off the pace in a strongly-run race, so conditions were not ideal here, but he has still been rated as having run close to his best in defeat. (op 9-2 tchd 11-2)
Blythe Knight(IRE), the Lincoln winner, needs easier ground than this to be seen at his best, but he did enjoy the run of the race next to the stands' rail. He has never been the easiest to win with, and his three-figure mark is only going to make things more difficult in that respect. (op 8-1 tchd 14-1 in places)
Hattan(IRE) could be given a big chance in this company on his best form, but he might well have needed this run, and another two furlongs in on easier ground might be ideal. He is bred to improve with age and could still progress. Official explanation: jockey said colt missed the break and hung left (op 8-1)
Colisay, runner-up in the Spring Cup off a mark of 102, deserved to return to conditions company, but he proved very disappointing. A strongly-run big-field handicap probably suits him better than a more tactical small-field race. (op 7-2 tchd 4-1)

1490 STAN JAMES H'CAP — 1m
5:25 (5:26) (Class 2) (0-100,100) 3-Y-0 £16,192 (£4,817; £2,407; £1,202) Stalls Low

Form				RPR
31-3	1		**Dunelight (IRE)**[16] [1095] 3-8-6 **88** ...... KDarley 8 (C G Cox) *mde virtually all: rdn out* **10/3**[2]	98
10-0	2	1 ½	**Regal Royale**[18] [1067] 3-8-8 **90** ...... MJKinane 10 (Sir Michael Stoute) *lw: hld up: hdwy over 1f out: r.o: nt rch wnr* **15/2**	96+
4005	3	1	**Wovoka (IRE)**[41] [758] 3-8-10 **95** ...... EdwardCreighton(3) 1 (M R Channon) *swtg: s.i.s: hld up: swtchd rt and hdwy over 1f out: r.o* **20/1**	99
21-2	4	1	**Acheekyone (IRE)**[15] [1115] 3-8-4 **86** oh1 ...... AlanMunro 4 (B J Meehan) *s.i.s: hld up: hdwy 1/2-way: swtchd rt over 2f out: rdn to chse wnr over 1f out: no ex ins fnl f* **3/1**[1]	88
310-	5	1	**Beau Nash (USA)**[196] [6023] 3-8-9 **91** ...... JamieSpencer 7 (P W Chapple-Hyam) *chsd ldrs: rdn over 2f out: edgd rt and wknd ins fnl f* **16/1**	90
00-4	6	nk	**Louie Louie (IRE)**[16] [1091] 3-7-13 **86** oh1 ...... JamesDoyle(5) 6 (N A Callaghan) *lw: chsd ldrs: nt clr run over 2f out: rdn and wknd fnl f* **6/1**[3]	85
22-0	7	4	**Aamaaq**[16] [1095] 3-8-6 **88** ...... RHills 12 (J L Dunlop) *chsd ldrs: rdn over 2f out: wknd fnl f* **16/1**	78
3-22	8	3	**Kaveri (USA)**[19] [1056] 3-8-4 **86** oh3 ...... MartinDwyer 3 (C E Brittain) *prom: hmpd over 7f out: sn lost pl: effrt and nt clr run fr over 2f out: eased over 1f out* **9/1**	69
050-	9	1 ¼	**Guest Connections**[196] [6023] 3-9-4 **100** ...... TonyCulhane 5 (M R Channon) *hld up: rdn over 2f out: sn wknd* **20/1**	80
3-50	10	2	**Ocean Pride (IRE)**[21] [1016] 3-8-1 **86** oh3 ...... StephaneBreux(3) 9 (R Hannon) *w wnr 5f: rdn and wknd over 1f out* **33/1**	61
163-	11	9	**Jamieson Gold (IRE)**[238] [5103] 3-8-8 **90** ...... MichaelHills 11 (B W Hills) *lw: s.i.s: hld up: rdn and wknd wl over 2f out* **12/1**	44

1m 38.2s (-1.17) **Going Correction** -0.025s/f (Good) 11 Ran SP% **116.1**
Speed ratings (Par 105):104,102,101,100,99 99,95,92,90,88 79
CSF £27.38 CT £441.67 TOTE £3.40: £1.60, £3.00, £6.30; EX 37.20 Place 6 £157.36, Place 5 £122.55.
Owner Mr and Mrs P Hargreaves **Bred** D And Ms B Egan **Trained** Lambourn, Berks

FOCUS
A decent handicap, rated through the exposed third and the form should work out.

NOTEBOOK
Dunelight(IRE), third in a ten-furlong handicap which is working out well here last month, did not have to struggle to get the lead and was able to set a sensible gallop in front. Appreciating the drop back to a mile, he saw the trip out strongly and looks a likely type for the Britannia Handicap at Royal Ascot. (tchd 7-2 and 3-1 in places)
Regal Royale, who ran poorly when drawn on the wrong side in a seven-furlong handicap here at the last meeting, ran a much better race this time, coming from well off the pace to chase the winner home. A lightly-raced type, he is capable of further improvement. (op 7-1)
Wovoka(IRE), a lot more exposed than the first two, also stayed on well from off the pace. His trouble is that he is likely to continue running into more progressive, unexposed rivals who have been let in lightly by the Handicapper.
Acheekyone(IRE), raised 6lb for finishing runner-up at Newbury on his reappearance, was held in this arguably stronger contest. He is going to have to find further improvement to defy his current mark, but that is entirely possible as he is still relatively lightly raced. (op 11-4 tchd 7-2 in places and 100-30 in places)
Beau Nash(USA), out the back in the Horris Hill on his final start last season, ran a solid race on his reappearance. He is considered to be a middle-distance prospect by his trainer and can improve on this when stepped up in trip.
Louie Louie(IRE) did not get a clear run and shaped better than his finishing position suggests. He has been tried over a variety of distances but seemed to get the mile well enough. (tchd 13-2 in places)
Aamaaq is still winless and connections would be well advised to go back and try and pick up a maiden at a minor track with him, for with a rating in the mid-80s he would probably set a decent standard.
Kaveri(USA) raced next to the stands' rail and was denied a clear run. Her rider soon gave up and her finishing position underestimates her ability. She is not one to give up on yet. Official explanation: jockey said filly was unsuited by the good to firm, firm in places ground (op 14-1)
Guest Connections pulled too hard in the early stages and did not get home as a result. (op 25-1)
T/Jkpt: Not won. T/Plt: £169.80 to a £1 stake. Pool: £125,694.45. 540.20 winning tickets. T/Qpdt: £15.70 to a £1 stake. Pool: £6,754.20. 317.40 winning tickets. CR

1142 THIRSK (L-H)
Saturday, May 6

OFFICIAL GOING: Firm
The going was officially described as 'firm' and some jockeys felt that 'very' should be added to that description. There were 19 non-runners.
Wind: Virtually nil

1491 TOTEPLACEPOT EUROPEAN BREEDERS FUND NOVICE STKS — 5f
2:30 (2:31) (Class 3) 2-Y-0 £7,772 (£2,312; £1,155; £577) Stalls High

Form				RPR
1	1		**Eloquent Rose (IRE)**[12] [1181] 2-8-11 ...... PaulFessey 1 (Mrs A Duffield) *cl up: rdn to ld ent last: sn edgd lft and hld on towards fin* **5/2**[2]	79
	2	shd	**We'll Confer** 2-8-12 ...... DO'Donohoe 7 (K A Ryan) *trckd ldrs: pushed along 1/2-way: hdwy over 1f out: rdn to chal and hung lft ent last: ev ch tl no ex nr line* **9/4**[1]	80+
2	3	¾	**Feelin Foxy**[7] [1278] 2-8-4 ...... PatrickMathers(3) 6 (D Shaw) *in tch: hdwy 2f out: swtchd lft and rdn over 1f out: kpt on ins last* **15/2**	72
1	4	¾	**Stolt (IRE)**[20] [1030] 2-9-2 ...... DNolan(3) 5 (N Wilson) *led: rdn along wl over 1f out: drvn and hdd ent last: sn drvn and wknd* **3/1**[3]	81
	5	¾	**Bollin Franny** 2-8-12 ...... DavidAllan 3 (T D Easterby) *cl up: ev ch 2f out: sn rdn and wknd over 1f out* **14/1**	71
	6	1 ¼	**Danum Dancer** 2-8-12 ...... ChrisCatlin 4 (N Bycroft) *chsd ldrs: rdn over 2f out: sn wknd* **50/1**	66
	7	3	**Hawaii Prince** 2-8-12 ...... FrancisNorton 2 (D Nicholls) *sn outpcd: a rr* **12/1**	54

58.93 secs (-0.97) **Going Correction** -0.25s/f (Firm) 7 Ran SP% **112.4**
Speed ratings (Par 97):97,96,95,94,93 91,86
CSF £8.25 TOTE £3.80: £3.10, £1.20; EX 12.90.
Owner Mrs D Addison and Mr & Mrs P Addison **Bred** Colin Kennedy **Trained** Constable Burton, N Yorks
■ Stewards' Enquiry : Paul Fessey one-day ban: failed to keep straight from stalls (May 17)

FOCUS
A fair juvenile contest where they finished quite close together, and the runner-up could be the one to take from the race.

NOTEBOOK
Eloquent Rose(IRE), having won over the stiff five at Pontefract, was sharp enough for this much quicker track and she showed plenty of courage to just prevail in what was probably a fairly decent affair. Connections had intended to give her a longer break after that first race but she came out of it better than expected. She will be effective over six furlongs and she is likely to have a crack at a better race at some stage. (op 11-4 tchd 3-1)
We'll Confer, for whom there was good support, looked to be running a bit green at halfway but then picked up to mount a serious challenge only to edge left under pressure. He will be better for the experience and can soon go one better. (tchd 2-1, 5-2 in a place)
Feelin Foxy had run well first time at Haydock and she showed that was no fluke with another good effort. She may appreciate another furlong.
Stolt(IRE), a winner first time out, ran another fine race conceding weight all round. This track and the very fast ground may not have been completely ideal for him. (op 11-4 tchd 10-3)
Bollin Franny, out of a sprinter who was a half-sister to Bollin Eric, showed good speed and it was an encouraging debut. Official explanation: jockey said colt lost its action (tchd 12-1)
Danum Dancer never looked like getting in a serious blow, but it was not a bad first effort. (op 40-1)

1492 TOTECOURSE TO COURSE MAIDEN STKS — 1m 4f
3:05 (3:07) (Class 5) 3-Y-0+ £5,181 (£1,541; £770; £384) Stalls Low

Form				RPR
3	1		**Aspasias Tizzy (USA)**[7] [1290] 3-8-2 ...... RoystonFfrench 5 (M Johnston) *in tch: hdwy to chse clr ldr 4f out: rdn to ld wl over 1f out: sn clr* **15/8**[2]	79+
34	2	7	**Som Tala**[15] [1120] 3-8-7 ...... ChrisCatlin 1 (M R Channon) *in tch: pushed along over 4f out: rdn along and outpcd 3f out: kpt on u.p appr last: no ch w wnr* **5/6**[1]	73
24/0	3	9	**Tamatave (IRE)**[20] [1032] 4-9-12 70 ...... DO'Donohoe 7 (K A Ryan) *plld hrd: sn led and clr: rdn along over 2f out: hdd wl over 1f out: sn wknd* **10/1**	66+
46	4	3 ½	**The Grey Man**[7] [1289] 5-9-12 ...... WSupple 2 (E S McMahon) *in tch: pushed along 4f out: rdn over 3f out and sn outpcd* **7/1**[3]	53
0	5	dist	**Celtic Jig (IRE)**[42] [731] 3-8-7 ...... DavidAllan 8 (T D Easterby) *sn rdn along in rr: wl bhd fr 1/2-way* **40/1**	—
	6	dist	**Master Pip**[160] 4-9-9 ...... PaulMulrennan(3) 3 (T H Caldwell) *chsd ldr to 1/2-way: sn wknd and wl bhd fnl 3f* **100/1**	—

2m 32.5s (-2.70) **Going Correction** -0.25s/f (Firm)
WFA 3 from 4yo+ 19lb 6 Ran SP% **114.4**
Speed ratings (Par 103):99,94,88,86,— —
CSF £3.88 TOTE £2.80: £1.60, £1.10; EX 3.70.
Owner Mrs R J Jacobs **Bred** Newsells Park Stud **Trained** Middleham Moor, N Yorks

FOCUS
A modest maiden in which they finished well strung out. The runner-up is the best guide to the level, but the form does not look solid.
Master Pip Official explanation: jockey said gelding lost its action

1493 TOTESPORT 0800 221 221 MAIDEN STKS — 7f
3:40 (3:43) (Class 5) 3-Y-0 £5,181 (£1,541; £770; £384) Stalls Low

Form				RPR
05-2	1		**Royal Envoy (IRE)**[14] [1135] 3-9-3 80 ...... WSupple 7 (B W Hills) *a.p: led 2f out: sn rdn: drvn ins last and styd on wl towards fin* **2/7**[1]	75

43-3 **2** *1* **Bel Cantor**[11] 1218 3-8-12 74 .... RichardKingscote(5) 14 72
(W J H Ratcliffe) *chsd ldrs: gd hdwy over 2f out: rdn to chal over 1f out and ev ch tl drvn and nt qckn wl ins last* **6/1**[2]

043- **3** *½* **Great Chieftain (IRE)**[247] 4886 3-9-3 75 .... TonyHamilton 1 71
(R A Fahey) *keen: led: rdn along and hdd 2f out: cl up tl drvn and no ex wl ins last* **8/1**[3]

0 **4** *nk* **Regal Raider (IRE)**[18] 1065 3-9-3 .... FergalLynch 8 70
(I Semple) *in tch: hdwy over 2f out: rdn to chse ldrs whn n.m.r over 1f out: swtchd rt and kpt on ins* **16/1**

5 *3* **Just Lille (IRE)** 3-8-12 .... PaulFessey 13 57
(Mrs A Duffield) *towards rr tl styd on fnl 2f* **20/1**

0 **6** *nk* **Light Sentence**[10] 1230 3-9-3 .... DeanMcKeown 11 61
(G A Swinbank) *towards rr tl styd on fnl 2f* **50/1**

0- **7** *7* **Miss Lemon (IRE)**[225] 5427 3-8-12 .... RoystonFfrench 6 38
(J Hetherton) *chsd ldrs: rdn along 3f out: sn wknd* **100/1**

8 *7* **Heavy Seas** 3-9-0 .... PaulMulrennan(3) 4 25
(P D Niven) *s.i.s: a bhd* **50/1**

9 *5* **Thornton Welcome** 3-8-12 .... AndrewMullen(5) 12 12
(B S Rothwell) *s.i.s: a bhd* **80/1**

1m 26.85s (-0.25) **Going Correction** -0.25s/f (Firm) **9** Ran SP% **119.9**
Speed ratings (Par 99):91,89,89,88,85 85,77,69,63
CSF £2.67 TOTE £1.30: £1.02, £1.70, £1.90; EX 2.70.
Owner Gainsborough Stud **Bred** Northern Lights Bloodstock **Trained** Lambourn, Berks

FOCUS
A fair maiden but a very moderate winning time for a race like this, 2.39 seconds slower than the following handicap. The runner-up set the standard for the form.

1494 TOTEPOOL "A BETTER WAY TO BET" H'CAP 7f
4:15 (4:17) (Class 4) (0-85,85) 3-Y-O+ **£8,096** (£2,408; £1,203; £601) **Stalls** Low

Form RPR

30-2 **1** **Malcheek (IRE)**[14] 1143 4-9-9 80 .... DavidAllan 3 88+
(T D Easterby) *trckd ldng pair: hdwy to chse ldr 3f out: led wl over 1f out: rdn ins last and kpt on* **5/4**[1]

104- **2** *nk* **Gallantry**[290] 3646 4-10-0 85 .... FergalLynch 8 92
(D W Barker) *s.i.s and bhd: stdy hdwy 3f out: rdn to chse ldrs over 1f out: kpt on wl fnl f* **20/1**

0-63 **3** *nk* **Bobski (IRE)**[38] 798 4-9-6 82 .... DerekNolan(5) 1 88
(G A Huffer) *s.i.s: sn in midfield: hdwy 3f out: rdn to chse wnr ent last: kpt on u.p* **9/2**[2]

-004 **4** *2½* **Danzig River (IRE)**[14] 1143 5-9-4 78 .... SilvestreDeSousa(3) 2 77
(D Nicholls) *led: rdn along over 2f out: hdd wl over 1f out: drvn and kpt on same pce ent last* **11/1**

60-0 **5** *1¼* **Zarabad (IRE)**[119] 64 4-9-6 77 .... PatCosgrave 4 73
(K R Burke) *chsd ldrs on inner: rdn along wl over 2f out: grad wknd* **20/1**

0-00 **6** *1½* **Dark Charm (FR)**[7] 1280 7-9-2 73 .... TonyHamilton 5 65
(R A Fahey) *prom: rdn along 3f out: grad wknd fnl 2f* **20/1**

2-60 **7** *nk* **Trojan Flight**[7] 1297 5-9-3 74 .... PaulQuinn 14 65
(D W Chapman) *stdd s: hld up and bhd: hdwy on inner 2f out: styd on ins last: nrst fin* **11/1**

46-0 **8** *shd* **Go Solo**[19] 1043 5-9-6 77 .... DeanMcKeown 11 68
(G A Swinbank) *hld up: effrt and sme hdwy over 2f out: sn edgd lft and btn* **20/1**

00-0 **9** *nk* **Apex**[19] 1042 5-9-1 75 .... PaulMulrennan(3) 9 65
(N Tinkler) *chsd ldrs: rdn along 3f out: sn wknd* **40/1**

00-5 **10** *1¾* **Tough Love**[11] 1220 7-9-1 72 .... WSupple 13 57
(T D Easterby) *midfield: pushed along over 3f out: sn btn* **9/1**

-330 **11** *2½* **Hits Only Heaven (IRE)**[10] 1246 4-9-10 81 .... (e) FrancisNorton 7 59
(D Nicholls) *a towards rr* **8/1**[3]

1m 24.46s (-2.64) **Going Correction** -0.25s/f (Firm) **11** Ran SP% **121.9**
Speed ratings (Par 105):105,104,104,101,100 98,97,97,97,95 92
CSF £37.33 CT £99.92 TOTE £1.90: £1.50, £4.60, £1.60; EX 35.60.
Owner Mrs Susie Dicker **Bred** Carrigbeg Stud **Trained** Great Habton, N Yorks

FOCUS
Just a fair handicap and not all that strong, rated around the winner and fourth.
Go Solo Official explanation: jockey said gelding hung left in straight
Hits Only Heaven(IRE) Official explanation: jockey said gelding was unsuited by the firm ground

1495 TOTESPORT.COM THIRSK HUNT CUP (H'CAP) 1m
4:50 (4:51) (Class 2) (0-100,97) 3-Y-O+ **£16,192** (£4,817; £2,407; £1,202) **Stalls** Low

Form RPR

221- **1** **Minority Report**[211] 5713 6-9-3 86 .... NickyMackay 6 100+
(L M Cumani) *hld up in tch: hdwy on outer over 2f out: rdn to ld jst ins last: drvn and kpt on* **2/1**[1]

23-0 **2** *1* **Flipando (IRE)**[19] 1043 5-9-4 87 .... PaulFessey 14 98
(T D Barron) *trckd ldrs: hdwy over 2f out: rdn to ld wl over 1f out: hdd jst ins last: kpt on gamely* **14/1**

5-00 **3** *nk* **Kings Quay**[14] 1129 4-9-7 93 .... DNolan(3) 5 104
(J J Quinn) *hld up in rr: stdy hdwy 3f out: rdn to chse ldrs over 1f out: swtchd lft and styd on ins last: nrst fin* **20/1**

16-3 **4** *1¾* **Game Lad**[17] 1086 4-9-9 92 .... DavidAllan 3 99
(T D Easterby) *trckd ldrs: hdwy on inner over 2f out: rdn over 1f out: kpt on same pce ins last* **11/2**[2]

0-22 **5** *¾* **Granston (IRE)**[15] 1111 5-9-5 88 .... RichardMullen 17 93
(J D Bethell) *prom: effrt and ev ch over 2f out tl rdn and one pce appr last* **12/1**

451- **6** *3* **Hartshead**[211] 5717 7-9-9 92 .... DeanMcKeown 8 90
(G A Swinbank) *in tch: hdwy to chse ldrs over 2f out: sn rdn: edgd lft and no imp* **8/1**

-130 **7** *nk* **Capable Guest (IRE)**[14] 1129 4-9-11 94 .... ChrisCatlin 12 91+
(M R Channon) *hld up towards rr: hdwy over 2f out: swtchd lft and rdn over 1f out: kpt on ins last: nt rch ldrs* **7/1**[3]

5-20 **8** *nk* **Emerald Bay (IRE)**[19] 1043 4-9-1 84 .... FergalLynch 4 81
(I Semple) *led: rdn along over 2f out: drvn and hdd wl over 1f out: sn wknd* **12/1**

-005 **9** *nk* **Uhoomagoo**[15] 1111 8-9-12 95 .... (b) DO'Donohoe 10 91
(K A Ryan) *a towards rr* **14/1**

5-65 **10** *1* **Isidore Bonheur (IRE)**[5] 1340 5-9-0 83 .... PaulQuinn 11 77
(G A Swinbank) *a rr* **25/1**

6-00 **11** *1¼* **Shot To Fame (USA)**[14] 1129 7-9-8 91 .... FrancisNorton 1 82
(D Nicholls) *prom: effrt over 2f out: sn rdn and wknd wl over 1f out* **14/1**

-050 **12** *2* **Lord Mayor**[10] 1239 5-9-7 97 .... DeanWilliams(7) 7 83
(R M H Cowell) *dwlt:. a rr* **100/1**

0-00 **13** *7* **Traytonic**[16] 1098 5-9-12 95 .... PatCosgrave 2 65
(D Nicholls) *dwlt: hdwy on inner and in tch whn hmpd bnd after 3f: bhd after* **40/1**

1m 35.97s (-3.73) **Going Correction** -0.25s/f (Firm) **13** Ran SP% **119.8**
Speed ratings (Par 109):108,107,106,104,104 101,100,100,100,99 98,96,89
CSF £32.04 CT £470.14 TOTE £2.50: £1.70, £4.00, £7.20; EX 35.00.
Owner G Shiel **Bred** Fittocks Stud **Trained** Newmarket, Suffolk
■ Stewards' Enquiry : D Nolan caution: careless riding

FOCUS
A good, competitive handicap run at a sound pace and the form looks solid and reliable, with the second, fourth and fifth to form.

NOTEBOOK
Minority Report ◆ continued where he left off last season with a decisive win. It would be no surprise to see him continue to progress and land another decent handicap this season. (op 15-8 tchd 7-4)
Flipando(IRE) ran a splendid race from a bad draw, coping with all but the winner. He has not won since September 2004 but surely he will soon end that sequence.
Kings Quay is another not to have won since 2004 and he had not fared too well on his two previous appearances this term. However, this was a much-improved performance even though he would probably appreciate an easier surface. (op 33-1)
Game Lad came with what looked like a winning run on the rails but could not find any more inside the final furlong. Seven furlongs appears to be the ideal trip for him and the Victoria Cup could be a suitable target.
Granston(IRE) was another to run a good race despite a bad draw. He is in good heart this term and this consistent sort deserves to pick up a decent handicap.
Hartshead made progress on the outside without looking as if he could get into serious contention, but it was a promising enough first run of the campaign. (op 10-1)
Capable Guest(IRE), whose only win since 2004 was on Polytrack, is running reasonably but looks to need a drop in the handicap. (op 13-2 tchd 6-1)
Emerald Bay(IRE) had cried enough a furlong or so out, but he is not one to write off by any means. (op 16-1)

1496 TOTEEXACTA H'CAP 5f
5:20 (5:20) (Class 4) (0-80,80) 3-Y-O+ **£6,477** (£1,927; £963; £481) **Stalls** High

Form RPR

03-4 **1** **Matsunosuke**[11] 1211 4-8-11 71 .... LukeMorris(7) 13 82
(A B Coogan) *hld up: hdwy over 2f out: rdn over 1f out: styd on wl fnl f to ld nr fin* **6/1**

-000 **2** *nk* **Handsome Cross (IRE)**[15] 1125 5-9-10 77 .... FrancisNorton 1 87
(D Nicholls) *cl: led 2f out: sn rdn: drvn ins last: hdd and nt qckn nr fin* **11/1**

225- **3** *½* **Raccoon (IRE)**[234] 5222 6-9-0 67 .... WSupple 10 75
(T D Barron) *trckd ldrs: hdwy 2f out: rdn and ev ch appr last: drvn and nt qckn towards fin* **10/3**[1]

3056 **4** *nk* **Plateau**[10] 1236 7-9-9 79 .... SilvestreDeSousa(3) 2 86
(D Nicholls) *cl up on outer: effrt 2f out and sn ev ch tl rdn ins last and no ex towards fin* **8/1**

-034 **5** *1¼* **Aegean Dancer**[7] 1297 4-8-13 66 .... ChrisCatlin 3 68
(B Smart) *sltly hmpd s: chsd ldrs: rdn along wl over 1f out: kpt on same pce* **11/2**[3]

4-00 **6** *1* **Diamond Katie (IRE)**[7] 1297 4-8-13 66 oh1 .... KimTinkler 6 64
(N Tinkler) *in tch: pushed along 1/2-way: rdn and kpt on same pce appr last* **33/1**

0-63 **7** *shd* **Bold Marc (IRE)**[15] 1125 4-9-5 77 .... AndrewElliott(5) 14 74
(K R Burke) *chsd ldrs: rdn along wl over 1f out: sn one pce* **7/2**[2]

60-0 **8** *¾* **Throw The Dice**[20] 1035 4-9-13 80 .... FergalLynch 7 74+
(D W Barker) *hmpd s and bhd tl sme late hdwy* **40/1**

00-6 **9** *hd* **Chatshow (USA)**[7] 1297 5-9-2 72 .... DNolan(3) 5 66
(D Carroll) *led: rdn along 1/2-way: hdd 2f out and grad wknd* **16/1**

0050 **10** *hd* **Whinhill House**[15] 1125 6-9-3 75 .... (p) MarkLawson(5) 9 68
(D W Barker) *midfield: rdn along 1/2-way: sn drvn and btn* **12/1**

-000 **11** *1½* **Ryedane (IRE)**[15] 1125 4-9-8 75 .... DavidAllan 11 62
(T D Easterby) *a rr* **20/1**

200- **12** *hd* **Special Gold**[280] 3930 4-8-10 68 .... DuranFentiman(5) 8 54
(T D Easterby) *midfield: rdn along 2f out: sn wknd* **50/1**

26/0 **13** *¾* **Shank On Fourteen (IRE)**[15] 1125 5-9-10 77 .... PatCosgrave 4 60
(K R Burke) *a rr* **66/1**

58.05 secs (-1.85) **Going Correction** -0.25s/f (Firm) **13** Ran SP% **121.6**
Speed ratings (Par 105):104,103,102,102,100 98,98,97,96,96 94,93,92
CSF £68.38 CT £267.79 TOTE £6.90: £2.60, £3.60, £2.20; EX 109.40.
Owner A B Coogan **Bred** R Coogan **Trained** Soham, Cambs

FOCUS
A fair handicap and competitive enough, although the form is unexceptional.

1497 ANGELA HOLT'S SPECIAL BIRTHDAY H'CAP 6f
5:50 (5:50) (Class 5) (0-75,75) 3-Y-O **£3,886** (£1,156; £577; £288) **Stalls** High

Form RPR

100- **1** **Greek Secret**[186] 6214 3-8-11 68 .... FergalLynch 13 78
(T D Easterby) *trckd ldrs: swtchd lft and hdwy over 1f out: rdn and n.m.r ent last: styd on to ld last 100 yds* **6/1**[3]

5401 **2** *1* **Peter Island (FR)**[15] 1109 3-9-3 74 .... ChrisCatlin 9 81
(J Gallagher) *led: rdn along 2f out: drvn ent last: hdd and nt no ex last 100 yds* **6/1**[3]

116- **3** *3* **The Terrier**[197] 6004 3-9-3 74 .... DeanMcKeown 10 72+
(G A Swinbank) *hld up: hdwy 2f out: rdn over 1f out: kpt on ins last* **4/1**[1]

30-2 **4** *1* **Imperial Sword**[20] 1036 3-9-4 75 .... PaulFessey 7 70+
(T D Barron) *in tch towards outer: hdwyt 2f out: sn rdn and kpt on same pce fnl f* **6/1**[3]

1216 **5** *¾* **Danetime Lord (IRE)**[17] 1078 3-8-12 69 .... (p) DO'Donohoe 3 62
(K A Ryan) *cl up: rdn along 2f out: drvn and wknd over 1f out* **9/2**[2]

026- **6** *hd* **Rosita Mia (IRE)**[185] 6225 3-8-8 65 .... NeilPollard 11 57
(D W Barker) *towards rr: hdwy 2f out: swtchd rt and rdn ent last: nrst fin* **33/1**

-100 **7** *nk* **Grafton (IRE)**[17] 1078 3-8-8 65 .... WSupple 1 56
(J D Bethell) *prom: rdn along 2f out: grad wknd* **16/1**

50-0 **8** *nk* **Soto**[16] 1097 3-9-1 75 .... PaulMulrennan(3) 6 65
(M W Easterby) *cl up: pushed along 1/2-way: sn rdn and wknd fnl 2f* **12/1**

10-0 **9** *4* **Making Music**[16] 1097 3-8-11 68 .... DavidAllan 14 46
(T D Easterby) *a rr* **16/1**

356- **10** *1½* **Crusader's Gold (FR)**[231] 5295 3-8-9 66 .... RichardMullen 2 40
(T D Easterby) *in tch: pushed along over 2f out: sn wknd* **20/1**

06-0 **11** *21* **Bold Tiger (IRE)**[38] 796 3-8-4 61 oh6 .... FrancisNorton 12 —
(D Nicholls) *a rr: bhd fr 1/2-way* **33/1**

The Form Book, Raceform Ltd, Compton, RG20 6NL

10-0 **12** *1* **The Thrifty Bear**[16] 1097 3-9-1 72 LeeEnstone 4 —
(C W Fairhurst) *cl up: rdn along over 2f out: sn wknd and eased* **14/1**

1m 10.81s (-1.69) **Going Correction** -0.25s/f (Firm) **12** Ran SP% **117.8**

Speed ratings (Par 99):101,99,95,94,93 93,92,92,86,84 56,55

CSF £40.70 CT £161.08 TOTE £9.40: £1.70, £2.70, £2.30; EX 51.70 Place 6 £5.92, Place 5 £4.13.

Owner Maurice P Lindsay & G Liles **Bred** James Clark **Trained** Great Habton, N Yorks

FOCUS

Only a moderate handicap, but it looked a competitive enough at its level and the form appears solid.

Rosita Mia(IRE) Official explanation: jockey said filly was denied a clear run

T/Plt: £6.40 to a £1 stake. Pool: £33,435.80. 3,803.95 winning tickets. T/Qpdt: £4.10 to a £1 stake. Pool: £1,761.10. 312.00 winning tickets. JR

CHURCHILL DOWNS (L-H)

Saturday, May 6

OFFICIAL GOING: Turf course - firm; dirt course - fast

1498a KENTUCKY DERBY (GRADE 1) 1m 2f (D)

11:04 (11:15) 3-Y-O **£844,884** (£232,558; £116,279; £46,512; £46,512)

RPR

1 **Barbaro (USA)**[35] 3-9-0 EPrado 8 129+
(M Matz, U.S.A) *disputed 3rd, led 2f out, soon clear, pushed out, impressive* **61/10**[2]

2 *6 1/2* **Bluegrass Cat (USA)**[21] 3-9-0 RADominguez 13 118
(T Pletcher, U.S.A) *always close up, 5th straight towards outside, went 2nd over 1f out, no chance with winner* **30/1**

3 *2* **Steppenwolfer (USA)**[21] 3-9-0 RAlbarado 2 114
(D Peitz, U.S.A) *bumped start, 19th early, headway over 4f out, 8th straight on outside, kept on to take 3rd 100y out* **163/10**

4 *1* **Brother Derek (USA)**[28] 3-9-0 ASolis 18 115+
(Dan L Hendricks, U.S.A) *drawn wide, mid-division on outside, came wide into straight, stayed on one pace, never nearer* **77/10**[3]

4 *dht* **Jazil (USA)**[28] 3-9-0 FJara 1 112
(K McLaughlin, U.S.A) *last early, in rear til slipped through on inside to go 7th entering straight, kept on under pressure, nearest at finish* **24/1**

6 *1/2* **Showing Up (USA)**[14] 3-9-0 CVelasquez 6 111
(B Tagg, U.S.A) *disputed 3rd, 4th & ridden straight, disputed 2nd 1f out, gradually weakened* **26/1**

7 *3* **Sweetnorthernsaint (USA)**[28] 3-9-0 (b) KDesormeaux 11 106
(M Trombetta, U.S.A) *squeezed back early, rapid headway on inside to go 5th 1/2-way, disputed 3rd 3f out, ridden & 3rd straight, weakened final f* **11/2**[1]

8 *1* **Deputy Glitters (USA)**[28] 3-9-0 JLezcano 14 104
(T Albertrani, U.S.A) *behind to straight, some headway under pressure when hung left approaching final f & bumped rival, no further progress* **61/1**

9 *1 1/4* **Point Determined (USA)**[28] 3-9-0 (b) RBejarano 5 102
(B Baffert, U.S.A) *mid-division on inside, closed up over 3f out, 7th straight, soon weakened* **94/10**

10 *hd* **Seaside Retreat (USA)**[21] 3-9-0 PHusbands 15 101
(M Casse, Canada) *mid-division to half-way, behind final 3f* **53/1**

11 *4 1/2* **Storm Treasure (USA)**[21] 3-9-0 DFlores 19 93
(S Asmussen, U.S.A) *always behind* **52/1**

12 *1 3/4* **Lawyer Ron (USA)**[21] 3-9-0 JohnMcKee 17 90
(R Holthus, U.S.A) *mid-division, 9th straight, soon beaten* **102/10**

13 *nse* **Cause To Believe (USA)**[28] 3-9-0 RBaze 16 90
(J Hollendorfer, U.S.A) *last after 3f, always behind* **26/1**

14 *3* **Flashy Bull (USA)**[35] 3-9-0 MESmith 20 85
(K McLaughlin, U.S.A) *drawn widest, towards rear on outside, came widest into straight, no headway* **43/1**

15 *2 1/2* **Private Vow (USA)**[21] 3-9-0 SBridgmohan 12 80
(S Asmussen, U.S.A) *always towards rear* **41/1**

16 *2 3/4* **Sinister Minister (USA)**[21] 3-9-0 (b) VEspinoza 4 75
(B Baffert, U.S.A) *pressed leader, led over 2 1/2f out to 2f out, 5th & weakening straight* **97/10**

17 *1 1/2* **Bob And John (USA)**[28] 3-9-0 (b) GKGomez 7 73
(B Baffert, U.S.A) *never nearer than mid-division* **129/10**

18 *nk* **A. P. Warrior (USA)**[28] 3-9-0 CNakatani 10 72
(J Shirreffs, U.S.A) *raced wide, mid-division & under pressure when bumped & carried left at distance* **141/10**

19 *1 1/2* **Sharp Humor (USA)**[35] 3-9-0 MGuidry 9 69
(Dale Romans, U.S.A) *in touch on outside til weakening over 3f out, last straight, tailed off* **30/1**

20 *7 1/2* **Keyed Entry (USA)**[28] 3-9-0 PValenzuela 3 56
(T Pletcher, U.S.A) *led to over 2 1/2f out, 6th & weakening straight, eased* **29/1**

2m 1.36s **20** Ran SP% **119.6**

PARI-MUTUEL: WIN 14.20; PL (1-2) 8.00, 28.40; SHOW (1-2-3) 6.00,15.40, 7.80; SF 587.00.

Owner Lael Stable **Bred** Mr & Mrs M Roy Jackson **Trained** USA

■ Barbaro recorded the biggest winning margin in 60 years. A first Derby winner at the first attempt for Michael Matz.

FOCUS

A good renewal on paper and it is quite possible Barbaro could emerge as a potential Triple Crown winner. Unbeaten coming into it, he produced a jaw-dropping performance, sprinting clear without his rider reaching for the whip to record the biggest winning margin in 60 years. He travels with supreme ease, has a turn of foot, and stays extremely well, all the attributes of a Triple Crown winner. Brother Derek was scuppered by stall 18 and probably emerges as the second best horse in the line-up. He had been highly progressive coming into this and looks the winner's biggest danger in the Preakness. Bluegrass Cat stayed on well into second, but was chasing shadows, while Steppenwolfer continues to run well in defeat. Favourite Sweetnorthernsaint made his ground too quickly having lost his place and was done no favours by the winning owner's second-string, who helped keep him on the inside.

NOTEBOOK

Barbaro(USA) ◆, a huge, imposing colt, came into this unbeaten following a cosy win from Sharp Humour in the Florida Derby, and he appeared to hold obvious claims from a reasonable berth. Nobody, however, could have been aware of what we were about to witness as, having held a good early pitch just off of the gallop, he made smooth headway to challenge turning in and burst clear in the manner of a top quality performer, making him a rare winner of this prestigious race both not to have run at two, and to be returning from a five-week break. The way in which he stretched out under hands and heels riding took the breath away, and the further he went the better it got. Therefore the 12-furlong Belmont Stakes should suit him, but equally he has the necessary speed to cope with the Preakness and he appears to hold strong claims of completing the Triple Crown, a feat that has not been achieved since Affirmed in 1978.

Bluegrass Cat(USA), below his best in the Blue Grass Stakes at Keeneland last month, was never far away and he moved into what would ordinarily have been a challenging position well over a furlong out, but Barbaro had flown and he had to make do with second. He beat the remainder well enough and, given he saw his first try at ten furlongs out well, it is reasonable to expect him to stay the 12 furlongs of the Belmont Stakes.

Steppenwolfer(USA), a closer who has been running well in defeat of late, was able to reverse Arkansas Derby form with Lawyer Ron and may have challenged for second had he not got so far behind early - bumped at the start and last but one through the early stages. He may well take a hand in one of the remaining Triple Crown legs if going the right way from this.

Brother Derek(USA), a tough and highly progressive colt whose only previous defeat over a mile plus came when fourth behind Stevie Wonderboy in the Breeders' Cup Juvenile, landed his second Grade 1 contest when taking the Santa Anita Derby in impressive fashion last month and would probably have been sent off favourite for this had it not been for a horror draw in box 18. This ultimately ended any winning chance he held as he was forced to race wide and was unable to get into the mix - just 16th rounding for home. He may well have been second had the draw been kinder and as a result he is worthy of strong consideration for the Preakness, with the Breeders' Cup Classic later in the year looking within his capabilities.

Jazil(USA) posted a fair effort latest when second in the Wood Memorial, but he was given plenty to do here and did well to finish as close as he did considering he was the early back-marker. He showed tremendous mid-pace but any future success is likely to come at a slightly lower level.

Showing Up(USA), the winning owner's second string, played an invaluable part as he did his best to hinder the chances of Sweetnorthernsaint by keeping him in, and once Barbaro had kicked he edged out to keep any potential challengers wide. He was not beaten far in sixth and is clearly a smart sort in him own right.

Sweetnorthernsaint(USA), well-fancied on the back of crushing his field in the Illinois Derby, was heavily supported in the moments before the off and was forced into favourite. However, things did not quite go to plan as he got squeezed back through the field early before quickly making stealthy headway. This effort clearly took its toll though as he had nothing in reserve once asked to go in pursuit of the rampant winner and he faded into seventh. He is better than this and probably deserves another chance.

Point Determined(USA), runner-up to Brother Derek at Santa Anita, was a popular place selection, but he proved most disappointing and never really threatened.

Lawyer Ron(USA), smooth winner of the Arkansas Derby, was done no favours by a wide draw and was unable to confirm placings with Steppenwolfer. He too deserves another chance.

Sinister Minister(USA), a 12 3/4 length winner of the Blue Grass Stakes, was soon pressing early leader Keyed Entry and he went into the lead after three-out, but his time in front was short-lived and he folded tamely in the straight.

Bob And John(USA), winner of the Wood Memorial, should really have fared better for top connections and he was clearly below his best.

A. P. Warrior(USA) is a strong stayer at this sort of distance and he was another popular place selection, but he was forced wide and he was already beaten when suffering interference.

Sharp Humor(USA), runner-up to Barbaro in the Florida Derby, was beaten out of sight and it would not surprise to learn something was amiss.

Keyed Entry(USA) could be given a chance of sorts on the best of his form, but he was always likely to be vulnerable to something coming from off the pace. He was running on empty from the turn-in and in the end he was eased right down.

HAMILTON (R-H)

Sunday, May 7

OFFICIAL GOING: Good (good to soft in places)

The times and jockey comments suggested that the ground was a bit softer than the official version.

Wind: Almost nil

1499 DAVIE COOPER MAIDEN AUCTION STKS (A QUALIFIER FOR THE HAMILTON PARK 2-Y-O NURSERY SERIES FINAL) 5f 4y

2:05 (2:05) (Class 5) 2-Y-O **£3,886** (£1,156; £577; £288) **Stalls** Centre

Form RPR

2 **1** **Hill Of Lujain**[18] 1074 2-8-10 DaleGibson 1 70
(M W Easterby) *chsd ldrs: drvn and outpcd 1/2-way: rallied over 1f out: kpt on wl to ld cl home* **6/1**[2]

33 **2** *nk* **Picture Frame**[10] 1248 2-8-10 JoeFanning 5 69
(N Tinkler) *pressed ldrs: rdn to ld 1f out: kpt on: hdd cl home* **13/2**[3]

22 **3** *3* **My Mirasol**[21] 1030 2-8-7 NCallan 10 55+
(K A Ryan) *disp ld to 1f out: kpt on same pce* **4/6**[1]

6 **4** *1* **Top Tier**[21] 1030 2-8-6 ow2 TomEaves 8 50+
(I Semple) *prom: drvn and outpcd over 2f out: kpt on fnl f: no imp* **20/1**

5 *hd* **Animated** 2-9-0 AdrianTNicholls 9 58+
(D Nicholls) *keen: slt ld to 1f out: fdd* **10/1**

6 *5* **Danni Di Guerra (IRE)** 2-8-13 LeeEnstone 3 39
(P C Haslam) *checked s: sn rdn in rr: nvr rchd ldrs* **20/1**

7 *2* **Perilore (IRE)** 2-8-4 FrancisNorton 7 22
(A Berry) *s.i.s: nvr on terms* **28/1**

0 **8** *9* **Makeusabuck**[21] 1030 2-8-4 PaulFessey 2 —
(A Berry) *wnt rt s: sn outpcd* **100/1**

62.53 secs (1.33) **Going Correction** +0.15s/f (Good) **8** Ran SP% **110.7**

Speed ratings (Par 93):95,94,89,88,87 79,76,62

CSF £39.66 TOTE £6.10: £1.60, £2.00, £1.02; EX 26.50.

Owner Pertemps Group Limited **Bred** S J Curtis **Trained** Sheriff Hutton, N Yorks

FOCUS

A modest bunch on looks and rated conservatively so just ordinary form. The field raced on the far side.

NOTEBOOK

Hill Of Lujain confirmed debut promise when showing the right attitude to score from another unfavourable berth. She will stay six furlongs but this bare form is nothing special and she is likely to look vulnerable under a penalty. (op 7-2)

Picture Frame, having his first run on easy ground, ran his race and looks a good guide to the worth of this form. Although capable of winning a similar race, he is likely to remain vulnerable to the better types in this grade. (op 9-1)

My Mirasol looked to have plenty in her favour but she proved a disappointment in this ordinary event. She lacks anything in the way of physical scope and, although capable of winning a race of this nature, may not be one to lump on at short odds. (op 10-11 tchd evens in places and 11-10 in a place)

Top Tier got much closer to My Mirasol than on her debut at Musselburgh and she left the impression that a stiffer test of stamina would be more to her liking. She will be of more interest when her stable is in better form.

Animated ◆, a half-brother to seven furlong winner Shava, was just about the pick of the paddock and showed more than enough, despite racing keenly, to suggest a similar race can be found with this experience behind him. (op 11-1 tchd 9-1)

Danni Di Guerra(IRE), the first foal of a dam placed in France, did not show much on this debut but left the impression that he would do better in ordinary nursery company over further in due course. (op 16-1)

1500 SUNDAY MAIL ANNUAL JUMP JOCKEYS H'CAP (TO BE RIDDEN BY NATIONAL HUNT JOCKEYS) 1m 65y

2:40 (2:42) (Class 5) (0-70,68) 4-Y-0+ **£3,886** (£1,156; £577; £288) **Stalls** High

Form RPR

4405 **1** **Dispol Veleta**[10] 1249 5-10-12 **62** .... TonyDobbin 12 78+
(T D Barron) *hld up: stdy hdwy over 3f out: led gng wl 1f out: shkn up and r.o strly* **10/3**[1]

-006 **2** *5* **Grande Roche (IRE)**[6] 1334 4-10-4 **54** .... DominicElsworth 6 58
(G A Swinbank) *hld up: hdwy over 2f out: rdn and hung rt: chsd wnr ins fnl f: r.o* **9/2**[3]

20-6 **3** *3* **Jordans Elect**[21] 1035 6-11-4 **68** .... WilsonRenwick 11 65
(P Monteith) *chsd clr ldr: led over 2f out to 1f out: sn no ex* **7/2**[2]

5415 **4** *1 ¾* **Scotty's Future (IRE)**[12] 1217 8-10-8 **58** .... NeilMulholland 9 51
(A Berry) *s.i.s: reluctant and sn t.o: gd hdwy fnl 2f: nrst fin* **12/1**

30-0 **5** *nk* **Royal Pardon**[16] 1123 4-10-4 **54** oh1 .... BarryKeniry 1 46
(R C Guest) *hld up: effrt 3f out: nvr rchd ldrs* **20/1**

000- **6** *3 ½* **Inch High**[42] 4824 8-10-4 **54** oh19 .... RichardMcGrath 10 38
(J S Goldie) *prom: outpcd 4f out: rallied over 2f out: no imp* **100/1**

060- **7** *1 ¼* **Compton Dragon (USA)**[109] 5772 7-10-10 **60** ....(b) KennyJohnson 7 41
(R Johnson) *hld up: hdwy and prom over 2f out: sn rdn and wknd* **16/1**

54-3 **8** *12* **Calamari (IRE)**[10] 1249 4-10-7 **57** .... TonyCulhane 2 11
(Mrs A Duffield) *in tch: rdn over 3f out: sn btn* **5/1**

000- **9** *nk* **Anthemion (IRE)**[223] 5509 9-10-4 **54** oh3 .... PeterBuchanan 4 7
(Mrs J C McGregor) *chsd ldrs tl rdn and wknd over 2f out* **40/1**

325/ **10** *½* **Tipu Sultan**[11] 6-10-4 **54** oh4 .... DNolan 3 6
(Micky Hammond) *bhd: rdn 1/2-way: nvr on terms* **40/1**

30-0 **11** *6* **Barataria**[25] 992 4-11-2 **66** .... PadgeWhelan 8 4
(R Bastiman) *sn led and clr: hdd & wknd qckly over 2f out* **12/1**

1m 54.16s (4.86) **Going Correction** +0.50s/f (Yiel) **11** Ran SP% **112.0**
Speed ratings (Par 103):95,90,87,85,84 81,80,68,67,67 61
CSF £16.93 CT £54.79 TOTE £4.00: £1.80, £2.20, £1.70; EX 31.70.
Owner W B Imison **Bred** B N And Mrs Toye **Trained** Maunby, N Yorks
■ Stewards' Enquiry : Tony Dobbin caution: careless riding

FOCUS
A low-grade handicap but one in which the pace was sound throughout. The placed horses help set a solid standard although the sixth limits the form.
Calamari(IRE) Official explanation: trainer said filly was unsuited by the good (good to soft places) ground

1501 PETER SCAHILL MEMORIAL (S) STKS 1m 65y

3:15 (3:15) (Class 5) 3-Y-0 **£3,238** (£963; £481; £240) **Stalls** High

Form RPR

60-4 **1** **Scuzme (IRE)**[39] 796 3-8-12 50 .... TomEaves 5 52+
(B Ellison) *midfield: hdwy over 2f out: led ins fnl f: r.o wl* **3/1**[1]

0050 **2** *1 ¼* **Lucys Lady**[10] 1263 3-8-7 48 .... PatCosgrave 6 44
(K R Burke) *hld up: hdwy 3f out: rdn 2f out: kpt on wl to take 2nd cl home* **14/1**

5044 **3** *hd* **Augustus Livius (IRE)**[8] 1293 3-8-12 45 .... PaulFessey 8 49
(W Storey) *chsd ldr: rdn over 3f out: rallied and ch ins fnl f: kpt on same pce* **8/1**

2362 **4** *1 ½* **The Jailer**[12] 1226 3-8-7 45 ....(p) DavidKinsella 11 41
(J G M O'Shea) *keen: led: rdn over 2f out: hdd and no ex ins fnl f* **4/1**[3]

-606 **5** *3* **Ever Special (IRE)**[8] 1293 3-8-7 45 .... LeanneKershaw(5) 10 39
(P C Haslam) *prom: rdn over 2f out: one pce over 1f out* **16/1**

6405 **6** *7* **Royal Moon (USA)**[15] 1149 3-8-12 55 .... PhillipMakin 1 23
(T D Barron) *s.i.s: effrt over 2f out: no imp over 1f out* **15/2**

00-0 **7** *1 ¾* **Red Iris (IRE)**[11] 1230 3-8-7 49 .... DaleGibson 4 14
(G A Swinbank) *hld up: rdn over 3f out: edgd rt and sn no imp* **20/1**

65-0 **8** *2* **Bond Cruz**[10] 1259 3-8-12 53 ....(b) RobertWinston 7 14
(B Smart) *prom: effrt over 2f out: wknd wl over 1f out* **7/2**[2]

00- **9** *6* **Mandarin Dancer (IRE)**[231] 5338 3-8-2 .... AndrewMullen(5) 12 —
(Miss L A Perratt) *prom tl rdn and wknd over 3f out* **66/1**

060- **10** *2* **Mandarin Grand (IRE)**[190] 6135 3-8-7 40 .... PaulHanagan 9 —
(Miss L A Perratt) *midfield: rdn 4f out: sn btn* **66/1**

0 **11** *5* **Frank Cartwright (IRE)**[21] 1032 3-8-12 .... FrancisNorton 2 —
(A Berry) *hld up: rdn over 4f out: nvr on terms* **100/1**

12 *23* **Wilmas Gal** 3-8-7 ....(t) RoystonFfrench 3 —
(R Bastiman) *missed break: nvr on terms* **33/1**

1m 54.55s (5.25) **Going Correction** +0.50s/f (Yiel) **12** Ran SP% **114.3**
Speed ratings (Par 99):93,91,91,90,87 80,78,76,70,68 63,40
CSF £42.95 TOTE £3.50: £2.10, £2.40, £2.80; EX 31.00.The winner was bought in for 7,000gns.
Owner Black and White Diamond Partnership **Bred** John Osborne **Trained** Norton, N Yorks

FOCUS
A modest event in which the gallop was soon sound but a modest winning time for the grade. The form os poor, with the third and fourth setting the standard.
Bond Cruz Official explanation: jockey said gelding lost its action final furlong

1502 IAN STEVENSON H'CAP 1m 5f 9y

3:50 (3:50) (Class 4) (0-80,78) 4-Y-0+ **£8,096** (£2,408; £1,203; £601) **Stalls** High

Form RPR

34-5 **1** **Tilt**[25] 976 4-9-0 **74** .... FrancisNorton 10 88+
(B Ellison) *midfield: gd hdwy to ld 2f out: edgd rt: sn clr* **3/1**[1]

6- **2** *3* **First Look (FR)**[49] 5511 6-8-8 **68** .... RobertWinston 2 75
(P Monteith) *hld up: hdwy on outside 1/2-way: effrt and cl up 2f out: chsd wnr ins fnl f: kpt on: no imp* **9/2**[2]

3156 **3** *1 ¼* **Cotton Eyed Joe (IRE)**[15] 1144 5-8-10 **70** .... DeanMcKeown 6 75
(G A Swinbank) *prom: effrt and ev ch 2f out: one pce ins fnl f* **14/1**

-400 **4** *¾* **Haatmey**[15] 1144 4-8-10 **70** .... TonyCulhane 8 74
(M R Channon) *bhd tl hdwy over 2f out: kpt on wl fnl f to take 4th cl home* **20/1**

4-22 **5** *nk* **Charlotte Vale**[15] 1144 5-9-1 **75** .... PaulHanagan 15 80+
(Micky Hammond) *in tch on ins: effrt and cl up 2f out: one pce ins fnl f: eased and lost 4th cl home* **5/1**[3]

0016 **6** *7* **John Forbes**[21] 1033 4-9-1 **75** .... PatCosgrave 3 69
(B Ellison) *led tl hdd 2f out: sn btn* **16/1**

610- **7** *¾* **Cripsey Brook**[210] 5772 8-8-11 **78** .... JamesReveley(7) 13 71
(K G Reveley) *hld up: rdn over 4f out: sme late hdwy: nvr rchd ldrs* **25/1**

566- **8** *2* **Absolutelythebest (IRE)**[32] 5502 5-8-9 **69** .... DavidKinsella 9 59
(J G M O'Shea) *hld up: pushed along 3f out: nvr on terms* **16/1**

/0-0 **9** *1 ¾* **Protective**[21] 1033 5-9-3 **77** ....(b) FergalLynch 7 64
(J G Given) *bhd: rdn over 4f out: nvr on terms* **66/1**

35-0 **10** *2* **Estrelle (GER)**[15] 1132 4-8-12 **72** .... JimmyQuinn 11 57
(H R A Cecil) *midfield: nt clr run over 3f out: sn rdn and wknd over 2f out* **6/1**

60-3 **11** *1* **Incursion**[3] 1439 5-9-3 **77** .... AdrianTNicholls 12 60
(D Nicholls) *cl up tl rdn and wknd wl over 1f out* **16/1**

40-0 **12** *6* **Rule For Ever**[21] 1033 4-8-9 **69** .... JoeFanning 14 44
(M Johnston) *chsd ldrs to over 3f out: sn struggling* **12/1**

/0-0 **13** *10* **Sahem (IRE)**[8] 1294 9-9-1 **75** .... RoystonFfrench 4 36
(Robert Gray) *hld up: rdn over 4f out: sn btn* **50/1**

000- **14** *¾* **Nerone (GER)**[11] 5983 5-8-4 **64** oh8 .... PaulFessey 1 24
(P Monteith) *cl up tl rdn and wknd over 3f out* **66/1**

2m 57.98s (4.58) **Going Correction** +0.50s/f (Yiel) **14** Ran SP% **119.7**
Speed ratings (Par 105):105,103,102,101,101 97,96,95,94,93 92,89,82,82
CSF £14.80 CT £165.05 TOTE £4.60: £3.10, £1.50, £3.40; EX 24.90.
Owner The Seasiders **Bred** Cheveley Park Stud Ltd **Trained** Norton, N Yorks
■ Stewards' Enquiry : Paul Hanagan four-day ban: dropped hands and lost 4th place (May 18-21)

FOCUS
A decent gallop throughout and an improved performance from the winner, who is one to keep on the right side. The form looks solid rated around the third and fifth.
Absolutelythebest(IRE) Official explanation: jockey said gelding hung right-handed throughout

1503 LORD ADVOCATE MEDIAN AUCTION MAIDEN STKS 1m 4f 17y

4:25 (4:25) (Class 5) 3-5-Y-0 **£3,412** (£1,007; £504) **Stalls** High

Form RPR

5- **1** **Power Of Future (GER)**[190] 6143 3-8-2 .... JimmyQuinn 3 79+
(H R A Cecil) *prom: smooth hdwy to ld over 2f out: sn clr: eased nr fin* **10/3**[2]

-222 **2** *3* **Dream Champion**[12] 1216 3-8-7 75 .... TonyCulhane 4 76
(M R Channon) *chsd ldrs: drvn and effrt over 3f out: wnt 2nd over 2f out: kpt on: no imp* **10/11**[1]

4 **3** *8* **Accordello (IRE)**[21] 1034 5-9-0 .... JamesReveley(7) 2 63+
(K G Reveley) *hld up: outpcd over 4f out: rallied over 2f out: no imp* **7/1**

0 **4** *14* **Now Tell Me This**[21] 1034 3-8-7 ....(v[1]) TomEaves 6 41
(I Semple) *led to over 2f out: sn btn* **50/1**

6-00 **5** *2* **Mccormack (IRE)**[10] 1252 4-9-12 49 .... FergalLynch 5 40
(Micky Hammond) *in tch: drvn over 3f out: sn outpcd* **100/1**

64 **6** *2* **Luck In Running (USA)**[8] 1296 3-8-7 .... JoeFanning 1 34
(M Johnston) *cl up tl rdn and wknd fr 3f out* **6/1**[3]

7 *1* **Special Ballot (IRE)**[107] 5-9-7 .... DeanMcKeown 7 30
(G A Swinbank) *keen: cl up tl wknd fr 3f out* **33/1**

2m 47.42s (8.24) **Going Correction** +0.50s/f (Yiel)
WFA 3 from 4yo+ 19lb **7** Ran SP% **108.1**
Speed ratings (Par 103):92,90,84,75,74 72,72
CSF £5.97 TOTE £4.80: £1.80, £1.40; EX 8.10.
Owner G Schoeningh **Bred** Gestut Elite **Trained** Newmarket, Suffolk

FOCUS
An uncompetitive event in which the gallop was fair and not surprisingly a moderate winning time for the type of race. The race is rated through the runner-up to previous form.

1504 HOWARD MCDOWALL MEMORIAL H'CAP 6f 5y

5:00 (5:01) (Class 5) (0-70,69) 3-Y-0+ **£4,533** (£1,348; £674; £336) **Stalls** Centre

Form RPR

-005 **1** **George The Best (IRE)**[17] 1102 5-9-0 **55** oh7 .... JimmyQuinn 3 67
(Micky Hammond) *mde all stands side: rdn and r.o strly fr 2f out* **14/1**

-600 **2** *3 ½* **Blackheath (IRE)**[8] 1297 10-9-12 **67** .... FrancisNorton 5 69
(D Nicholls) *cl up stands side: effrt over 2f out: kpt on fnl f: no ch w wnr: 2nd in gp* **16/1**

60-3 **3** *1* **Primarily**[16] 1127 4-9-10 **65** ....(p) JoeFanning 4 64
(A Berry) *prom stands side: effrt over 2f out: kpt on fnl f: no imp: 3rd in gp* **33/1**

000- **4** *1* **Dizzy In The Head**[131] 6668 7-9-5 **60** ....(b) PaulHanagan 1 56
(I Semple) *chsd stands side ldrs tl rdn and no ex over 1f out: 4th in gp* **16/1**

50-0 **5** *2 ½* **Dispol Peto**[6] 1341 6-8-7 **55** oh2 ....(v[1]) PatrickDonaghy(7) 2 43
(R Johnson) *in tch stands side: effrt over 2f out: sn no imp: 5th and last in gp* **100/1**

-124 **6** *1 ½* **Dorn Dancer (IRE)**[4] 1413 4-9-9 **64** .... RobertWinston 15 48+
(D W Barker) *bhd far side: hdwy 2f out: kpt on fnl f: no ch w far side: 1st in gp* **5/2**[1]

230- **7** *shd* **Glencairn Star**[297] 3463 5-9-8 **66** .... DanielTudhope(3) 11 49+
(J S Goldie) *prom far side: effrt and led that gp over 1f out: kpt on same pce fnl f: 2nd in gp* **16/1**

0-00 **8** *hd* **Yorkshire Blue**[16] 1124 7-9-2 **57** .... FergalLynch 9 40+
(J S Goldie) *s.i.s: bhd far side tl kpt on fr 2f out: nrst fin: 3rd in gp* **25/1**

6-05 **9** *2* **Unlimited**[5] 1388 4-9-8 **63** .... TonyCulhane 14 40+
(Mrs A Duffield) *cl up far side: ev ch over 2f out: no ex fnl f: 4th in gp* **9/1**

400- **10** *nk* **Viewforth**[190] 6140 8-9-7 **62** ....(b) TomEaves 8 38+
(I Semple) *led far side to over 2f out: sn no ex: 5th in gp* **16/1**

6312 **11** *hd* **Onlytime Will Tell**[6] 1341 8-9-9 **64** .... AdrianTNicholls 10 39+
(D Nicholls) *in tch far side: effrt over 2f out: no imp: 6th in gp* **6/1**[2]

030- **12** *1 ¾* **Cd Flyer (IRE)**[200] 5986 9-9-11 **69** .... PaulMulrennan(3) 6 39+
(R C Guest) *racd on outside of far side gp: effrt 1/2-way: no imp: 7th in gp* **20/1**

00-0 **13** *½* **Dunn Deal (IRE)**[20] 1047 6-9-10 **65** .... PaulQuinn 12 33+
(W M Brisbourne) *cl up far side tl rdn fr 2f out: 8th in gp* **7/1**[3]

0000 **14** *¾* **Blue Knight (IRE)**[15] 1151 7-9-10 **65** ....(v) PhillipMakin 7 31+
(D Nicholls) *in tch far side tl rdn and no ex over 2f out: 9th in gp* **33/1**

5162 **15** *6* **Piccleyes**[8] 1303 5-9-0 **55** oh1 ....(b) DeanMcKeown 16 3+
(M J Polglase) *cl up far side tl wknd fr 2f out: 10th in gp* **16/1**

00-0 **16** *14* **Mister Marmaduke**[21] 1031 5-8-13 **57** ....(t) DNolan(3) 13 —
(D A Nolan) *s.i.s: a bhd far side: 11th in gp* **150/1**

1m 13.83s (0.73) **Going Correction** +0.15s/f (Good) **16** Ran SP% **117.6**
Speed ratings (Par 103):101,96,95,93,90 88,88,87,85,84 84,82,81,80,72 53
CSF £201.05 CT £3845.43 TOTE £17.30: £3.40, £3.90, £5.50, £3.50; EX 241.20 Place 6 £27.99, Place 5 £25.02.
Owner M D Hammond **Bred** E R Breeding **Trained** Middleham Moor, N Yorks

FOCUS
A dubious result as the stands' side, usually unfavoured on easy ground in large fields, proved the place to be with every one to race on that side finishing ahead of the far-side bunch.

T/Plt: £129.10 to a £1 stake. Pool: £44,788.85. 253.15 winning tickets. T/Qpdt: £72.90 to a £1 stake. Pool: £2,436.20. 24.70 winning tickets. RY

1484 **NEWMARKET (ROWLEY) (R-H)**
Sunday, May 7

OFFICIAL GOING: Soft
Wind: Light, behind Weather: Raining

1505 STAN JAMES TELEBETTING H'CAP — 7f
1:45 (1:48) (Class 2) (0-100,94) 3-Y-O **£19,431** (£5,781; £2,889; £1,443) **Stalls** Low

Form | | | | RPR
21-1 **1** **Levera**[19] 1067 3-9-2 **92** JamieSpencer 6 — 102+
(A King) *lw: mde all centre: rdn over 1f out: edgd lft towards fin: r.o: 1st of 6 in gp* **9/4**[1]
34-5 **2** *nk* **Layazaal (IRE)**[19] 1067 3-9-0 **90** RHills 7 — 98
(J L Dunlop) *racd centre: a.p: chsd wnr over 2f out: rdn over 1f out: styng on whn hmpd towards fin: 2nd of 6 in gp* **11/1**
52-6 **3** *3/4* **The Snatcher (IRE)**[19] 1067 3-9-0 **90** RyanMoore 4 — 96
(R Hannon) *lw: led stands' side: rdn and ev ch over 1f out: r.o: 1st of 3 that side* **5/1**[3]
3-02 **4** *1 1/4* **Star Crowned (USA)**[19] 1065 3-8-11 **87** (bt) AlanMunro 1 — 90
(B J Meehan) *chsd ldr stands' side: rdn and hung rt over 2f out: styd on: 2nd of 3 that side* **22/1**
031- **5** *shd* **Cactus King**[176] 6319 3-8-8 **84** JimmyFortune 9 — 87
(J H M Gosden) *racd centre: prom: outpcd 3f out: hdwy over 1f out: styd on same pce ins fnl f: 3rd of 6 in gp* **13/2**
03-1 **6** *5* **Dream Theme**[35] 844 3-8-11 **87** RichardHughes 5 — 78
(B W Hills) *lw: racd stands' side: hld up in tch: rdn over 1f out: wknd fnl f: last of 3 in gp* **4/1**[2]
110- **7** *1 3/4* **Military Cross**[197] 6023 3-9-2 **92** LDettori 8 — 78
(W J Haggas) *racd centre: hld up: hdwy 1/2-way: hung lft and wknd over 1f out: 4th of 6 in gp* **9/1**
0-06 **8** *1/2* **Salute Him (IRE)**[16] 1115 3-8-9 **85** ChrisCatlin 3 — 70
(M R Channon) *lw: swtchd to racd centre over 6f out: sn chsng wnr: rdn over 2f out: hung lft and wknd over 1f out: 5th of 6 in gp* **14/1**
14-0 **9** *8* **Cape Presto (IRE)**[16] 1115 3-8-13 **89** SebSanders 10 — 54
(R Hannon) *racd centre: hld up: plld hrd: wknd 3f out: last of 6 in gp* **33/1**

1m 27.87s (1.37) **Going Correction** +0.325s/f (Good) **9** Ran SP% **113.1**
Speed ratings (Par 105):105,104,103,102,102 96,94,93,84
CSF £28.03 CT £111.37 TOTE £2.90: £1.50, £3.20, £1.60; EX 31.90 Trifecta £126.60 Pool £945.42 - 5.30 winning units..

Owner Four Mile Racing **Bred** Cheveley Park Stud Ltd **Trained** Barbury Castle, Wilts

FOCUS
Quite a good three-year-old handicap, although soft ground was an unknown for many of these and they split into two groups. The first two home emerged from the larger group down the middle of the track, although the three who raced stands' side did not seem too disadvantaged; later results certainly suggest that was case. The form looks strong enough, with the first three coming from a similar contest at the Craven meeting.

NOTEBOOK
Levera, having travelled as well as anything for most of the way, quickly got tired when coming under serious pressure - his jockey later suggested this ground was far from ideal - but he never really looked like being caught and defied a 10lb rise in the weights for his two-length success in a course and distance handicap at the Craven meeting. The winner of his last three starts, he is progressing very nicely indeed, although talk of the Jersey Stakes is a touch ambitious at this stage and he is probably best off in handicaps for the time being. (op 15-8 tchd 5-2, 11-4 in places)

Layazaal(IRE), around four lengths behind Levera in a similar event over course and distance on his reappearance, only just failed to reverse placings on 10lb better terms. He handled the soft ground quite well and, although slightly hampered when trying to stay on, did not look unlucky. (op 12-1)

The Snatcher(IRE), a neck behind Layazaal and just over four lengths behind Levera in a similar event over course and distance on his reappearance, failed to reverse placings but still emerged with plenty of credit in faring best of the three who raced on the stands' side. However, it could be worth keeping in mind later results suggested it was no disadvantage to race against the near-side rail. (op 11-1)

Star Crowned(USA), second in a course and distance maiden at 33/1 on his turf debut at the Craven meeting, had no easy task against this opposition off a mark of 87 on his first start in handicap company. This was by no means a bad effort and he is open to improvement. (op 20-1)

Cactus King, a comfortable four-length winner of a mile maiden on Lingfield's Polytrack when last seen 176 days previously, made a satisfactory return to action on his debut in handicap company. He can be expected to improve for the run and better ground may also suit. (op 9-2)

Dream Theme looked a nice prospect when winning a seven-furlong Polytrack maiden at Kempton on his reappearance, but failed to build on that form on his handicap debut and was presumably unsuited by the testing conditions. (tchd 9-2 in places)

1506 STAN JAMES DAHLIA STKS (GROUP 3) (F&M) — 1m 1f
2:15 (2:19) (Class 1) 4-Y-O+
£28,390 (£10,760; £5,385; £2,685; £1,345; £675) **Stalls** Low

Form | | | | RPR
02-2 **1** **Violet Park**[22] 1015 5-8-12 92 RichardHughes 1 — 104+
(B J Meehan) *hld up: hdwy over 1f out: r.o to ld wl ins fnl f: hung lft nr fin* **15/2**
23-1 **2** *1/2* **Royal Alchemist**[22] 1015 4-8-12 103 JimmyFortune 9 — 103
(M D I Usher) *chsd ldr tl led over 2f out: rdn and hung lft fr over 1f out: hdd wl ins fnl f: hmpd nr fin* **6/1**[3]
504- **3** *shd* **Mango Mischief (IRE)**[183] 6253 5-9-1 103 LDettori 8 — 106
(J L Dunlop) *led over 6f: sn rdn: hmpd over 1f out and ins fnl f: r.o* **9/1**
20-0 **4** *1 1/4* **Bon Nuit (IRE)**[22] 1015 4-8-12 102 AlanMunro 6 — 100
(G Wragg) *b.off hind: chsd ldrs: rdn over 1f out: styd on same pce ins fnl f* **25/1**
44-0 **5** *1 3/4* **Bahia Breeze**[42] 753 4-8-12 108 JMurtagh 5 — 97
(Rae Guest) *lw: hld up: hdwy over 2f out: rdn over 1f out: no ex ins fnl f* **12/1**
11/ **6** *2 1/2* **Mamela (GER)**[367] 5-8-12 NickyMackay 7 — 92
(L M Cumani) *prom: racd keenly: rdn over 2f out: wknd fnl f* **11/2**[2]
113- **7** *hd* **Musicanna**[218] 5606 5-8-12 106 (t) JamieSpencer 4 — 91
(J R Fanshawe) *lw: hld up: rdn over 2f out: sn rdn: wknd fnl f* **15/8**[1]
514- **8** *22* **Zayn Zen**[169] 6378 4-8-12 99 PhilipRobinson 2 — 47
(M A Jarvis) *hld up: rdn over 3f out: wknd over 2f out* **13/2**

1m 54.24s (2.29) **Going Correction** +0.525s/f (Yiel) **8** Ran SP% **111.1**
Speed ratings (Par 113):110,109,109,108,106 104,104,84
CSF £48.60 TOTE £8.80: £2.00, £1.80, £2.90; EX 31.60 Trifecta £290.10 Pool £1,021.62 - 2.50 winning units..

Owner Mrs J Cash **Bred** D E And Mrs J Cash **Trained** Manton, Wilts

FOCUS
The soft ground would not have bothered the majority of these and this was not that bad a Group 3 by fillies/mares standards, although at the same time it could have been better had the likes of Musicanna run to form. They all raced down the centre of the track and the winning time was as you would expect for a race like this in the conditions, indicating that the form is pretty sound.

NOTEBOOK
Violet Park has her quirks and underachieved in handicaps last year, but she has improved since switched to Pattern company and reversed recent Kempton placings with Royal Alchemist under a terrifically confident ride from Hughes. Having been held up well off the pace, she was produced with a well-timed run and had little choice but to put her head in front, although she did not like the idea and slightly hampered the runner-up when hanging left. Clearing progressing, she should have a good season in fillies/mares company if her riders can continue to get the best out of her, and her main aim could be the Nassau Stakes at Goodwood, a ten-furlong Group One. (op 9-1)

Royal Alchemist, the winner of a mile Listed race on Kempton's Polytrack on her reappearance, ran well upped in grade but was unable to confirm form with Violet Park, who was half a length away in second last time. She was hampered by the eventual winner near the line, but it made no difference. She is another who should have a good season in fillies/mares company. (tchd 7-1)

Mango Mischief(IRE), returning from a 183-day break, would not have minded the ground and has the run of the race. She can be expected to come on for the run. (op 11-1)

Bon Nuit(IRE) ran better than when a beaten favourite in a mile Listed race on Kempton's Polytrack on her reappearance and was clearly suited by the return to turf.

Bahia Breeze, racing beyond a mile for the first time, did not run badly but never looked like winning and may not have stayed. (op 14-1)

Mamela(GER), ex-German trained who won has twice won in Listed company, would not have minded this ground but finished up well beaten on her debut for Luca Cumani. This was her first run in just over a year, and she may have needed the outing. (op 5-1)

Musicanna, highly progressive last year but perhaps flattered by her third in the Group 1 Sun Chariot Stakes on her final start, had conditions to suit for her first run in 218 days but was very disappointing. (op 13-8 tchd 2-1)

Zayn Zen Official explanation: jockey said filly was unsuited by the soft ground

1507 STANJAMESUK.COM JOCKEY CLUB STKS (GROUP 2) — 1m 4f
2:50 (2:52) (Class 1) 4-Y-O+
£51,102 (£19,368; £9,693; £4,833; £2,421; £1,215) **Stalls** High

Form | | | | RPR
341- **1** **Shirocco (GER)**[190] 6168 5-9-3 CSoumillon 6 — 129+
(A Fabre, France) *nice colt: lw: chsd ldr tl led over 2f out: shkn up over 1f out: styd on wl* **10/11**[1]
13-2 **2** *3 1/2* **Munsef**[15] 1128 4-8-12 107 RHills 2 — 117
(J L Dunlop) *lw: hld up: hdwy and hung rt over 1f out: sn rdn to chse wnr: styd on same pce ins fnl f* **7/2**[2]
124- **3** *1 1/2* **Bandari (IRE)**[246] 4948 7-9-1 118 KDarley 5 — 118
(M Johnston) *led: rdn and hdd over 2f out: no ex fnl f* **11/1**
202- **4** *1/2* **Self Defense**[92] 6026 9-8-12 110 AlanMunro 7 — 114
(Miss E C Lavelle) *chsd ldrs: rdn over 2f out: styng ons ame pce whn n.m.r fnl f* **16/1**
1-64 **5** *shd* **Enforcer**[9] 1267 4-8-12 109 LDettori 4 — 114
(W R Muir) *hld up in tch: rdn over 2f out: no ex fnl f* **12/1**
23-0 **6** *17* **Gulf (IRE)**[15] 1128 7-8-12 105 (t) LPKeniry 1 — 90
(D R C Elsworth) *lw: hld up: wknd over 2f out* **100/1**
115- **7** *4* **Hard Top (IRE)**[239] 5109 4-9-1 115 MJKinane 3 — 88
(Sir Michael Stoute) *prom: racd keenly: rdn edgd lft and hmpd over 1f out: sn wknd and eased* **11/2**[3]

2m 36.25s (2.75) **Going Correction** +0.525s/f (Yiel) **7** Ran SP% **112.9**
Speed ratings (Par 115):111,108,107,107,107 95,93
CSF £4.15 TOTE £1.80: £1.30, £2.00; EX 4.10.

Owner Baron G Von Ullmann **Bred** Baron G Von Ullmann **Trained** Chantilly, France

FOCUS
The ground came in Shirocco's favour and, the only previous Group 1 winner in the line up, he totally outclassed his six rivals without having to be seriously asked. The pace was just ordinary, which resulted in a modest winning time for a Group 2, even allowing for the conditions. However, the form looks sound with the second, fourth and fifth to form.

NOTEBOOK
Shirocco(GER) ◆, fourth in last year's Arc before winning the Breeders' Cup Turf at Belmont Park, had a Group 1 penalty for his first run in England and had to give weight away all round. However, heavy rain turned conditions well and truly in his favour and none of these could match his form. He was duly hammered into odds-on in the betting and, always going well just off Bandari, he eased his way to the front without having to be asked a serious question, or being hit by the whip. He won as he liked to confirm Andre Fabre's theory that he has strengthened up over the winter and is an improved horse this year. His connections will no doubt have left something to work on and this should put him right for a return to Group 1 company. He should be a leading player in many of the top middle-distance races this season, the only imponderable being he still has to prove his effectiveness on ground with 'firm' in the description His next target is the Coronation Cup at Epsom and connections have already mapped out plans for later in the campaign. In the longer term he is a "possibility" for the King George, but the Arc followed by a repeat bid in the Breeders' Cup Turf are his two main aims. (op 11-8 tchd 6-4 in places)

Munsef, a highly-progressive sort last year who was second to Mubtaker in the John Porter at Newbury on his reappearance, ran a creditable race behind the top-class Shirocco, especially considering his rider gave that one a bit of a head start in a race run at no more than an ordinary pace. (tchd 4-1)

Bandari(IRE), returning from a 246-day break, had the run of the race and ran about as well as could have been expected. He should come on for the race. (op 12-1 tchd 10-1)

Self Defense, given another chance on the Flat after running some creditable races in defeat over hurdles during the winter, acquitted himself with credit and may be able to do even better in a stronger-run race. He deserves to find a race at Listed/Group 3 level, and could well do so. (op 20-1)

Enforcer is a likeable sort and perhaps still improving, but he had never raced over a trip this far and had it all to do in this company. (op 10-1)

Hard Top(IRE), last year's Great Voltigeur winner, was reported to have been unsuited by heavy ground when down the field in the St Leger on his last start, so it was a surprise to see him take his chance. He floundered badly when coming off the bridle and can be given another chance back on a decent surface. Official explanation: jockey said colt was unsuited by the soft ground (op 4-1 tchd 6-1)

1508 STAN JAMES 1000 GUINEAS STKS (GROUP 1) (FILLIES) — 1m
3:30 (3:32) (Class 1) 3-Y-O
£187,374 (£71,016; £35,541; £17,721; £8,877; £4,455) **Stalls** Centre

Form | | | | RPR
31-1 **1** **Speciosa (IRE)**[19] 1068 3-9-0 109 MickyFenton 3 — 114
(Mrs P Sly) *lw: mde all towards stands' side: hung lft over 2f out: rdn out* **10/1**
210- **2** *2 1/2* **Confidential Lady**[217] 5649 3-9-0 109 SebSanders 5 — 108
(Sir Mark Prescott) *lw: chsd wnr towards stands' side: rdn and hung lft over 1f out: styd on* **12/1**

13-1 **3** *1* **Nasheej (USA)**[15] 1130 3-9-0 107 .... RyanMoore 11 106
(R Hannon) *lw: racd centre: chsd ldr: led that gp over 3f out: rdn and hung lft to join stands' side gp over 1f out: no ex ins fnl f* **16/1**

511- **4** *1 ½* **Silca's Sister**[259] 4618 3-9-0 .... LDettori 4 103+
(Saeed Bin Suroor) *lw: racd towards stands' side: hld up in tch: rdn over 2f out: styd on same pce appr fnl f* **13/2**[2]

212- **5** *1 ½* **Wake Up Maggie (IRE)**[220] 5571 3-9-0 113 .... AlanMunro 1 99
(C F Wall) *h.d.w: racd towards stands' side: chsd ldrs: rdn over 1f out: wknd ins fnl f* **25/1**

06-2 **6** *2* **Spinning Queen**[19] 1068 3-9-0 104 .... MichaelHills 13 94
(B W Hills) *lw: b.hind: hld up: racd centre: hdwy and hung lft over 1f out: wknd ins fnl f* **50/1**

111- **7** *2 ½* **Rumplestiltskin (IRE)**[217] 5649 3-9-0 .... KFallon 7 89
(A P O'Brien, Ire) *neat: bmpd s: racd towards stands' side: hld up: rdn over 2f out: nvr nrr* **3/1**[1]

01- **8** *1 ½* **Race For The Stars (USA)**[218] 5605 3-9-0 .... JMurtagh 12 85
(A P O'Brien, Ire) *w'like: leggy: racd centre: hld up: sme hdwy u.p over 1f out: wknd fnl f* **12/1**

142- **9** *3 ½* **La Chunga (USA)**[262] 4511 3-9-0 113 .... DarryllHolland 9 77
(J Noseda) *racd towards stands' side: hld up: racd keenly: hdwy over 2f out: rdn and wknd over 1f out* **33/1**

1- **10** *5* **Alexander Alliance (IRE)**[210] 5777 3-9-0 .... WMLordan 8 66
(T Stack, Ire) *gd sort: h.d.w: wnt lft s: racd towards stands' side: hld up: plld hrd: rdn and wknd over 2f out* **9/1**

123- **11** *shd* **Flashy Wings**[220] 5571 3-9-0 115 .... JamieSpencer 2 65
(M R Channon) *lw: racd towards stands' side: s.i.s: hld up: rdn over 2f out: sn wknd* **7/1**[3]

311- **12** *3* **Nannina**[225] 5459 3-9-0 113 .... JimmyFortune 6 59
(J H M Gosden) *racd towards stands' side: trckd ldrs: racd keenly: rdn over 2f out: wknd over 1f out* **7/1**[3]

211- **13** *10* **Donna Blini**[220] 5571 3-9-0 114 .... MJKinane 10 36
(B J Meehan) *led centre: racd keenly: hdd that gp over 3f out: wknd over 2f out* **16/1**

1m 40.53s (1.16) **Going Correction** +0.525s/f (Yiel) **13** Ran SP% **118.3**
Speed ratings (Par 110):115,112,111,110,108 106,104,102,99,94 93,90,80
CSF £121.30 TOTE £11.80: £2.90, £3.80, £5.30; EX 139.30 Trifecta £4164.40 Pool £7,038.59 - 1.20 winning units..

Owner Michael H Sly Dr T Davies Mrs Pam Sly **Bred** K And Mrs Cullen **Trained** Thorney, Cambs
■ Pam Sly became the first British-based woman to train a classic winner, & a first domestic classic success for Michael Fenton.

FOCUS
Despite the soft ground compromising the chances of a few of these, most notably Race For The Stars, Flashy Wings and Nannina, this still looked like a reasonable renewal of the 1000 Guineas - the three horses who chased home Speciosa home had won five Group races between them - and the winning time was very creditable given the conditions. The field split into two distinct groups in the early stages, with Nasheej, Spinning Queen, Race For The Stars and Donna Blini racing down the middle of the track, and the other nine racing a little way off the stands'-side rail. Speciosa led the larger group and drifted towards the rail in the latter stages, gradually bring most of the others with her. Speciosa's RPR has been bettered only by Russian Rhythm in recent years and the placed horses were roughly to form.

NOTEBOOK
Speciosa(IRE) ◆ third to Nasheej in the May Hill off the back of her maiden success before winning the Rockfel over seven furlongs here towards the end of last season, showed she had trained on with a clear-cut success in the Nell Gwyn on her reappearance, despite her tendency to hang left under pressure being as pronounced as ever. Off the back of that sort of preparation she would surely have been sent off at single-figure odds were she trained by one of the big 'names', but her little-known trainer, who turned down big-money bids over the winter, managed to get the very best out of her. Well drawn in stall three, given her tendency to drift left, she was allowed her own way in front and gradually made her way to the stands'-side rail without any fuss; a good bit of horsemanship from Fenton. Once she had the rail to help, she never looked in any danger and bounded clear without having to be asked a major question - the race was won by the time her rider resorted to the whip. Her connections all but ruled out the Irish 1000 Guineas, as the track is unlikely to suit, and she is not entered in the Oaks, although there is a chance she will be supplemented. It is clear, then, that she will not be that easy to place given her tendency to hang, but she will deserve the utmost respect wherever she turns up. (tchd 11-1 in places)
Confidential Lady was below form in the Marcel Boussac behind Rumplestiltskin when last seen 217 days previously, but she had by then progressed into a very smart filly and showed her best form when winning a seven-furlong Group 3 at Deauville. Remarkably her trainer's first-ever domestic Classic runner, she justified the decision to stay at home with a fine second. She looked likely to pose a threat when asked for her challenge, but Speciosa had plenty left and she could make little impact in the last quarter mile. She is in the Oaks at Epsom, but her stamina is not totally guaranteed and her trainer suggested the French version over an extended ten furlongs could be the preferred option. (op 14-1)
Nasheej(USA) had Speciosa just over a length away in third when winning the May Hill last season but that one has clearly progressed quite significantly since then and she could not confirm form. The form of her Fred Darling success did not amount to much, but that run clearly brought her on and this was a fine effort in defeat. Her effort is all the more creditable given she was one of only four who raced down the middle of the track in the early stages and she was still about five horse widths away from the eventual winner when under maximum pressure. She should give a good account in the Irish 1000 Guineas if taking her chance at the Curragh. (tchd 20-1 in places)
Silca's Sister ◆ had not been seen since winning Group 1 Prix Morny against the colts on bad ground for Mick Channon and had since been privately purchased by Godolphin. Making her debut for new connections off the back of a 259-day break, she did not appear to handle the dip all that well, but kept on for pressure right the way to the line. Her effort is all the more creditable considering the majority of her stable's horses ran disappointingly over the Guineas weekend. This run can also be expected to have sharpened her up and she will go for Coronation Stakes at Royal Ascot with a leading chance. (op 7-1 tchd 15-2 in a place)
Wake Up Maggie(IRE), the winner of a valuable Sales race in Ireland before finding only Donna Blini too good in the Cheveley Park on her last start as a juvenile, made a pleasing reappearance, upped to a mile for the first time and faced with the softest ground she has encountered. Alan Munro reported to the trainer that she was struggling a little on the testing ground and may turn out to be better suited by seven furlongs.
Spinning Queen, sixth to Speciosa in the Rockfel on her last start as a juvenile and a length second to that one on her reappearance in the Nell Gwyn, had no right to reverse form with that rival and was duly well held. However, this was still a very respectable effort, not least because she was one of the four who raced away from the main pack down the centre of the track early on, and was still pitched very wide at the line. (op 66-1)
Rumplestiltskin(IRE), successful at the highest level in both the Moyglare Stud Stakes and the Marcel Boussac in a juvenile campaign that saw her win five of her six starts, had been ante-post favourite all winter and was well supported on the day as well. However, she was never really seen with a chance and only passed beaten horses in the closing stages. This is the softest ground she has ever encountered, but her dam is a full-sister to Kingmambo, who handled this sort of surface well and, given her only defeat last year came on fast ground, is it hard to blame the ground. Perhaps a more valid point worth noting is that her trainer said the previous day she was showing signs of coming into season. Whatever the case, she still has to prove she has trained on. (op 4-1 tchd 9-2 in places)
Race For The Stars(USA) ◆ looked an ideal type for the 1000 Guineas when winning the same Curragh race her stablemate Virginia Waters landed during her juvenile campaign en-route to success at Newmarket, and followed that up with a smart victory in the Listed Oh So Sharp Stakes over seven furlongs here on her final outing. However, although that win came on easy ground, she needs a fast surface to be seen at her best and these conditions were totally against her - she duly drifted alarmingly in the betting. This run is best forgotten and she must be given another chance to build on the promise she showed at two. With the ground unlikely to be in her favour in the Irish 1000 Guineas, she looks made for the Coronation Stakes at Ascot and could be worth taking a chance on. (op 8-1)
La Chunga(USA) showed some smart form as a juvenile, most notably when winning the Albany Stakes and finishing second to Flashy Wings in the Lowther. However, upped in trip and faced with the softest ground she has encountered off the back of a 262-day break, she failed to show her best.
Alexander Alliance(IRE) showed smart form at two when finishing second to Art Museum before comfortably winning a Listed race over six furlongs at the Curragh, but her pedigree gave her no hope of staying and she finished well beaten after racing keenly. She really took the eye in the paddock, however, and can be given another chance back over sprint trips. (op 11-1)
Flashy Wings looked like a high-class juvenile when taking both the Queen Mary and Lowther Stakes, but she was then beaten in a sales race at Newbury and again met with defeat in the Cheveley Park on her final outing, albeit somewhat unluckily. Her pedigree gave plenty of hope for her training on and staying this trip, but as it turned out the ground was totally against her and she finished up well beaten. (op 13-2 tchd 15-2)
Nannina, successful in the Prestige Stakes before landing the Group 1 Fillies' Mile, when she had today' third Nasheej just over three lengths away, was reported by her trainer to have "hated the ground". She will now be aimed at the Coronation Stakes and can be given another chance back on a decent surface. Official explanation: jockey said filly was unsuited by the soft ground (op 6-1)
Donna Blini, the winner of the Group 2 Cherry Hinton and Group 1 Cheveley Park during a juvenile campaign in which she was beaten only once, had it all to prove over this trip on such testing ground and seemed to hate the conditions.

1509 STANSPOKER.CO.UK PRETTY POLLY STKS (LISTED RACE) (FILLIES) 1m 2f

4:05 (4:07) (Class 1) 3-Y-O

£17,034 (£6,456; £3,231; £1,611; £807; £405) **Stalls** Low

Form RPR

2- **1** **Riyalma (IRE)**[243] 5022 3-8-12 .... MJKinane 6 106+
(Sir Michael Stoute) *chsd ldr: led over 7f out: rdn and edgd lft over 1f out: r.o* **7/2**[3]

12- **2** *2 ½* **Bunood (IRE)**[190] 6145 3-8-12 95 .... RHills 7 101
(J L Dunlop) *hld up in tch: chsd wnr 1/2-way: rdn over 1f out: styd on same pce* **5/2**[1]

3 *3 ½* **Park Esteem (IRE)** 3-8-12 .... DarryllHolland 2 95
(J Noseda) *b. nr hind: sn pshd along in rr: rdn 4f out: outpcd fnl 2f* **10/1**

0-26 **4** *1* **Saabiq (USA)**[19] 1068 3-8-12 97 .... RyanMoore 3 93
(C E Brittain) *lw: hld up: hdwy over 3f out: sn rdn: hung rt and wknd fnl f* **13/2**

214- **5** *13* **Stage Flight**[204] 5904 3-8-12 102 .... RichardHughes 9 70+
(B J Meehan) *chsd ldrs: rdn over 2f out: wknd over 1f out* **10/3**[2]

011- **6** *dist* **Under The Rainbow**[190] 6144 3-9-3 88 .... JamieSpencer 4 —+
(P W Chapple-Hyam) *lw: stmbld st: sn led: hdd over 7f out: chsd ldrs: rdn over 3f out: wknd over 2f out: virtually p.u* **6/1**

2m 10.34s (4.63) **Going Correction** +0.525s/f (Yiel) **6** Ran SP% **110.6**
Speed ratings (Par 104):102,100,97,96,86 —
CSF £12.26 TOTE £4.10: £2.40, £2.30; EX 15.00.

Owner H H Aga Khan **Bred** His Highness The Aga Khan's Studs S C **Trained** Newmarket, Suffolk

FOCUS
A fair renewal of this Listed event - and well-established Oaks Trial - which saw the field come home fairly strung out and it produced an ordinary winning time for a race of its type. The first three rate as smart prospects with the fourth setting the level for the form.

NOTEBOOK
Riyalma(IRE), runner-up on her sole outing as a juvenile, showed how she has improved during the off-season and duly got off the mark on this marked step-up in class. The longer trip proved much to her liking and, as her pedigree strongly suggested it would, and she appeared to relish the softened ground. Her connections cited that she was a possible contender for the Epsom Oaks - although the yard may well have stronger candidates - and the longer trip there ought to be well within her compass. (op 3-1 tchd 4-1 in places and 5-2 in places)
Bunood(IRE), who won on debut before finishing a game second in Listed company on both her starts over a mile at this venue last term, was well backed for this three-year-old debut and duly posted a career-best in defeat. She could not live with the winner, but got this longer trip well enough and has done little wrong in her career to date. (op 11-4 tchd 10-3)
Park Esteem(IRE), half-sister to several winners notably high-class stayer Central Park and Lupe winner Mellow Park, was pitched in at a very high level for this debut and was not at all disgraced in defeat. She came off the bridle at an early stage, but kept to her task under pressure, and looks sure to improve a deal for the experience and the switch to better ground. (op 8-1)
Saabiq(USA) looked a non-stayer on this marked step-up in trip and was well held at the finish. She is proving hard to catch right, but will prove happier again when reverting to a shorter distance. (op 9-1 tchd 10-1 in places)
Stage Flight, fourth behind Speciosa in the Rockfel at this venue on her final outing last term, dropped out tamely at the business end of the race and has to rate disappointing. While she might not have got home over the longer trip, she lacks any big-race entries, and it may be that she is flattered by her official rating. Official explanation: vet said filly returned stiff behind (op 4-1 tchd 3-1)
Under The Rainbow, who landed a Listed event at this track on her third and final start last season, shaped as though something may well have been amiss and was eased right down after passing the two furlong marker. She has it all to prove now. Official explanation: jockey said filly bled from the nose (op 5-1 tchd 9-2)

1510 STAN JAMES MAIDEN STKS 5f

4:40 (4:40) (Class 3) 2-Y-O **£7,772** (£2,312; £1,155; £577) **Stalls** Low

Form RPR

1 **Sonny Red (IRE)** 2-9-3 .... RichardHughes 6 88+
(R Hannon) *w'like: scope: chsd ldr: rdn to ld 1f out: r.o* **9/2**[3]

2 *nk* **Conquest (IRE)** 2-9-3 .... NickyMackay 8 87+
(W J Haggas) *wl grwn: bit bkwd: prom: rdn over 1f out: chsd wnr ins fnl f: r.o* **3/1**[2]

3 *2 ½* **Winning Spirit (IRE)** 2-9-3 .... LDettori 3 78+
(J Noseda) *w'like: lw: chsd ldrs: led over 1f out: sn rdn and hdd: no ex ins fnl f* **11/4**[1]

4 *1* **Christmas Tart (IRE)** 2-8-12 .... ChrisCatlin 7 69+
(V Smith) *lt-f: scope: hld up: hdwy over 1f out: nt rch ldrs* **20/1**

6 **5** *3 ½* **The Illies (IRE)**[16] 1113 2-9-3 .... MichaelHills 1 62
(B W Hills) *lw: s.i.s: hdwy 1/2-way: wknd fnl f* **6/1**

6 *2 ½* **Bookiesindex Boy** 2-9-0 .... DeanCorby(3) 2 53+
(J R Jenkins) *gd sort: lw: led over 3f: wknd fnl f* **50/1**

7 shd **Tres Hombres** 2-9-3 .... RyanMoore 4 52
(Tom Dascombe) *cmpt: scope: bkwd: sn pushed along and prom: wkng whn n.m.r over 1f out* **25/1**

8 ¾ **Napoleon Dynamite (IRE)** 2-9-3 .... EddieAhern 5 50
(J W Hills) *leggy: scope: hld up: sme hdwy over 1f out: sn hung lft and wknd* **12/1**

9 ¾ **Silver Hotspur** 2-9-3 .... AlanMunro 9 47
(P W Chapple-Hyam) *neat: wnt rt s: sn prom: hung rt and wknd over 1f out* **12/1**

62.71 secs (2.24) **Going Correction** +0.525s/f (Yiel) 9 Ran SP% **110.1**
Speed ratings (Par 97):103,102,98,96,91 87,87,85,84
CSF £16.86 TOTE £5.50: £1.90, £1.30, £1.60; EX 24.40.

Owner Michael Pescod & J A Leek **Bred** Denis Bergin **Trained** East Everleigh, Wilts

FOCUS
This bunch have a lot to live up to given George Washing filled third on his debut in last year's renewal, but it looked a pretty good maiden. The ground was not ideal for such inexperienced horses, but the winning time was decent for a race of its type and a few winners should emerge.

NOTEBOOK
Sonny Red(IRE), a 26,000gns half-brother to six-furlong three-year-old winner Molly Ellen, and Raise A Tune, a mile scorer at two, was quite well supported on course and proved good enough to make a winning debut from some nice types. He is held in high regard and will apparently have one more race before being aimed at the Coventry Stakes. (op 8-1 tchd 9-1 in a place)

Conquest(IRE) ◆, a 135,000gns yearling, out of a 12-furlong three-year-old winner, was the subject of very good reports prior to this debut and duly ran a big race. He is open to improvement and really should find a race before stepping up in class. (op 2-1)

Winning Spirit(IRE) ◆, a 50,000gns half-brother to speedy and precocious juvenile Waterline Twenty, out of a triple six/seven-furlong winner, moved quite well in the early stages, but seemed to lose his action somewhat when coming off the bridle and appeared totally unsuited by the soft ground. He is clearly well thought of and should win next time providing the ground is decent. (op 5-2 tchd 3-1 in places)

Christmas Tart(IRE), a half-sister to six winners, most notably high-class sprinter Andreyev, was the only filly in the line up and made a most encouraging debut. She really should be placed to effect before much longer and could be useful. (op 25-1)

The Illies(IRE), not given a hard time when down the field in a Newbury maiden that has yet to work out on his debut, failed to build on that. He was beaten by some nice types, but it was disappointing he could put his experience to better use. (op 13-2)

Bookiesindex Boy, a 13,000gns purchase, out of a triple five-furlong winner, took the eye in the paddock. He showed decent pace early and could be one to watch for.

Tres Hombres, an 11,000gns half-brother to five-furlong juvenile winner Music Teacher, looked as though this run would bring him on significantly.

1511 STAN JAMES H'CAP 1m 4f
5:15 (5:18) (Class 2) (0-100,100) 4-Y-0+**£16,192** (£4,817; £2,407; £1,202) **Stalls** High

Form RPR
314- 1 **Tartouche**[238] [5164] 5-9-2 **98** .... SebSanders 10 109+
(Lady Herries) *lw: hld up in tch: rdn to ld 1f out: hung lft and rt ins fnl f: r.o* **7/4**[1]

023- 2 3½ **Camrose**[206] [5848] 5-9-3 **99** ....(b) JimmyFortune 7 105
(J L Dunlop) *a.p: chsd ldr 5f out: led 3f out: rdn and hdd 1f out: styd on same pce* **4/1**[2]

6-21 3 3 **Country Pursuit (USA)**[36] [834] 4-8-4 **86** .... AlanMunro 12 88
(C E Brittain) *lw: chsd ldrs: rdn over 2f out: wknd over 1f out* **9/2**[3]

020/ 4 1¾ **Pretty Star (GER)**[52] [4831] 6-8-8 **90** ow1 .... RichardHughes 2 89
(A King) *hld up: reminders over 7f out: hdwy u.p over 3f out: wknd over 1f out* **12/1**

150- 5 5 **Idealistic (IRE)**[194] [6100] 5-8-11 **93** .... NickyMackay 5 84
(L M Cumani) *s.i.s: hld up: hdwy over 2f out: rdn and wknd over 1f out* **13/2**

00-0 6 29 **Given A Choice (IRE)**[15] [1133] 4-8-4 **86** oh2 .... EddieAhern 9 34
(J G Given) *led: rdn and hdd 3f out: wknd qckly* **25/1**

000- 7 4 **Massif Centrale**[108] [5496] 5-9-0 **96** ....(t) DarryllHolland 1 38
(D R C Elsworth) *s.i.s: rdn over 3f out: swtchd lft and wknd over 2f out* **16/1**

00-6 8 6 **Wunderwood (USA)**[22] [1018] 7-9-4 **100** .... RyanMoore 6 33
(Lady Herries) *lw: chsd ldr 7f: rdn and wknd over 2f out* **14/1**

2m 37.66s (4.16) **Going Correction** +0.525s/f (Yiel) 8 Ran SP% **116.7**
Speed ratings (Par 109):107,104,102,101,98 78,76,72
CSF £8.28 CT £25.33 TOTE £2.50: £1.20, £1.60, £1.70; EX 9.80 Place 6 £94.71, Place 5 £54.50.

Owner Lady Herries and Friends **Bred** Angmering Park Stud **Trained** Patching, W Sussex

FOCUS
Just the eight runners and by no means a strong handicap for the grade, but Tartouche still posted a smart effort. The placed horses were close to relevant form which suggests it is sound enough.

NOTEBOOK
Tartouche ◆ had won in Group company since she was last seen in handicap company, yet somehow she was still able to race off an official mark of just 98 and, with conditions well and truly in her favour, she duly took advantage. The runner-up kicked for home soon enough and she always looked like picking that one up, although Sanders had to very much make her mind up. The Handicapper will surely take note and she will probably return to Pattern company next time. (op 2-1 tchd 9-4 and 5-2 in places)

Camrose, 10lb higher than when last winning, committed for home plenty soon enough, especially for one fitted with blinkers and returning from a 206-day break, and he never really looked like holding off Tartouche. A pleasing enough return, but he is not exactly well handicapped. (op 5-1)

Country Pursuit(USA), 6lb higher than when winning over a mile and a half on Lingfield's Polytrack on his previous start, proved no match for the front two and this ground may not have been ideal. (op 4-1)

Pretty Star(GER), three times a winner over hurdles since he was last seen on the Flat 628 days previously, was under pressure some way out and never looked like winning. The ground should not have been too much of a problem. (tchd 11-1)

Idealistic(IRE) beat only two home on her only previous start on testing ground and was again well beaten. This was her first start in 194 days and she can do better when returned to decent ground. (op 7-1)

Massif Centrale Official explanation: jockey said gelding lost its action

T/Jkpt: Not won. T/Plt: £162.20 to a £1 stake. Pool: £113,645.95. 511.35 winning tickets. T/Qpdt: £27.10 to a £1 stake. Pool: £6,568.50. 179.15 winning tickets. CR

SALISBURY (R-H)
Sunday, May 7

OFFICIAL GOING: Firm (good to firm in places)
Wind: Light across

1512 TOTESPORT.COM H'CAP 6f
2:30 (2:31) (Class 2) (0-100,100) 3-Y-0
£13,398 (£4,011; £2,005; £1,004; £500; £251) **Stalls** High

Form RPR
1-2 1 **Bentong (IRE)**[17] [1097] 3-8-1 **86** oh2 .... NelsonDeSouza(3) 6 104
(P F I Cole) *w ldr: rdn to ld wl over 1f out: pushed clr fnl f* **5/2**[1]

1 2 3 **Pearly Wey**[17] [1089] 3-8-3 **88** ow1 .... AdamKirby(3) 11 97
(C G Cox) *s.i.s: sn trckd ldrs: rdn and styd on to chse wnr over 1f out* **6/1**[3]

641- 3 1½ **Trafalgar Bay (IRE)**[197] [6024] 3-8-7 **89** .... MartinDwyer 3 97+
(S Kirk) *mid-div: rdn over 3f out: styd on to go 3rd ins fnl f: nvr nrr* **8/1**

66-2 4 1½ **Gamble In Gold (IRE)**[31] [896] 3-8-9 **91** ow1 .... DaneO'Neill 9 91
(R Hannon) *in tch: rdn and swtchd rt wl over 1f out: one pce ins fnl f* **5/1**[2]

6-30 5 ¾ **Puskas (IRE)**[17] [1091] 3-8-13 **95** .... TQuinn 7 93
(M R Channon) *sn rdn in mid-div: nt pce to chal fr over 1f out* **14/1**

400- 6 1½ **Jeanmaire (IRE)**[191] [6129] 3-8-12 **94** .... SteveDrowne 5 87
(H Morrison) *trckd ldrs tl rdn and wknd over 1f out* **20/1**

01- 7 ½ **Dark Missile**[227] [5418] 3-8-2 **87** oh3 ow1 .... NeilChalmers(3) 10 79
(A M Balding) *led tl hdd 2f out: wknd appr fnl f* **12/1**

1- 8 ¾ **Makabul**[407] [720] 3-8-4 **86** oh1 .... RobertHavlin 2 76
(B R Millman) *a towards rr* **11/1**

45-4 9 ½ **Charles Darwin (IRE)**[31] [896] 3-8-8 **90** .... FergusSweeney 8 78
(M Blanshard) *chsd ldrs: wkng whn n.m.r wl over 1f out* **28/1**

5-26 10 16 **Scarlet Knight**[17] [1091] 3-8-4 **86** .... JohnEgan 1 26
(P Mitchell) *a towards rr* **16/1**

00-0 11 ½ **Ba Foxtrot**[18] [1083] 3-9-4 **100** .... TedDurcan 4 39
(M R Channon) *a struggling in rr* **12/1**

1m 11.3s (-3.68) **Going Correction** -0.475s/f (Firm) course record 11 Ran SP% **115.1**
Speed ratings (Par 105):105,101,99,97,96 94,93,92,91,70 69
CSF £16.49 CT £106.07 TOTE £3.20: £1.50, £2.40, £2.50; EX 21.20.
Owner H R H Sultan Ahmad Shah **Bred** J Egan, J Corcoran And J Judd **Trained** Whatcombe, Oxon

FOCUS
A course record, but still just an average time for the grade given the conditions. This is usually a good race - Goodricke and Resplendent Glory dead-heated last year - and this looks strong, solid form with the first three ahead of the Handicapper.

NOTEBOOK
Bentong(IRE) ◆, raised 5lb after finishing runner-up at Ripon, had no problem with this very different surface and, in front entering the final two furlongs, came clear for a comprehensive victory. Unexposed and progressive, he will stay further and may not be running in handicaps for much longer. (op 4-1)
Pearly Wey soon recovered from a tardy start and came through to chase the favourite over a furlong out, but was no match for that unexposed opponent. His maiden win at Newmarket has worked out really well with the next three home all winning, and there is more to come from him. (op 4-1)
Trafalgar Bay(IRE), withdrawn after bolting to post on his intended reappearance at the Craven meeting, was taken to the start early. Doing his best work at the end, he might be most effective back over further. Official explanation: jockey said colt slipped shortly after leaving stalls (op 7-1)
Gamble In Gold(IRE), from a decent draw, ran her race again but could not find a change of gear in the final furlong. She seems best on an easy surface. (op 13-2)
Puskas(IRE), soon pushed along and keeping on without being able to challenge, still looks high enough in the weights despite a 2lb drop since his last run.
Jeanmaire(IRE), who tackled Group or Listed company on her last four starts at two, was not disgraced but might not be easy to place this term from her present sort of mark.
Scarlet Knight Official explanation: jockey said gelding was unsuited by the firm (good to firm in places) ground

1513 TOTECOURSE TO COURSE MAIDEN STKS 6f
3:05 (3:07) (Class 4) 3-Y-0+ **£5,505** (£1,637; £818; £408) **Stalls** High

Form RPR
02-5 1 **Loyal Royal (IRE)**[19] [1065] 3-9-0 84 .... JohnEgan 15 90+
(D R C Elsworth) *led after 1f: clr whn veered bdly lft ins fnl f* **3/1**[2]

42- 2 6 **Always Emirates (USA)**[235] [5231] 3-9-0 ....(t) KerrinMcEvoy 3 72
(Saeed Bin Suroor) *in tch: rdn to chse wnr fnl f* **5/2**[1]

00- 3 2½ **Diamond World**[192] [6120] 3-8-9 .... ShaneKelly 8 60
(C A Horgan) *led for 1f: styd prom: one pce ins fnl 2f* **25/1**

24-5 4 nk **You Call That Art (USA)**[18] [1085] 3-8-9 86 .... DaneO'Neill 12 59+
(R Hannon) *a in tch: rdn 2f out: styd on one pce fnl f* **7/2**[3]

0 5 1¼ **Serene Dancer**[16] [1119] 3-8-9 .... RobertHavlin 11 55
(Mrs P N Dutfield) *slowly away: racd wd: hdwy over 2f out: kpt on but nt pce to chal* **100/1**

0 6 1 **Good Turn**[16] [1119] 3-8-9 .... PatDobbs 13 52
(R Hannon) *in tch: rdn 2f out: one pce after* **20/1**

3- 7 nk **Rogue**[159] [6462] 4-9-5 .... AdrianMcCarthy 10 54
(Jane Southcombe) *chsng ldrs whn hmpd after 2f: nvr on terms after* **40/1**

- 8 ½ **Highland Belle** 3-8-6 ....(v[1]) NeilChalmers(3) 14 49
(A M Balding) *chsd ldrs: rdn over 2f out: sn btn* **25/1**

06- 9 shd **Catabound (USA)**[188] [6200] 3-9-0 .... IanMongan 7 54
(B R Millman) *s.i.s: in rr: mde sme late hdwy* **22/1**

10 1 **Cabriole** 3-8-9 .... TQuinn 4 46+
(H R A Cecil) *nvr bttr than mid-div* **7/1**

0-3 11 5 **Dream Forest (IRE)**[29] [916] 3-9-0 .... TPQueally 6 36+
(Mrs P N Dutfield) *prom tl wknd 2f out* **20/1**

12 1¼ **Bare Rambler** 3-9-0 .... SteveDrowne 17 32
(Stef Liddiard) *slowly away: a bhd* **25/1**

0/00 13 1½ **Melmott**[11] [1240] 6-9-3 30 .... JosephLoveridge(7) 16 31
(R Ingram) *hmpd after 2f and bhd after* **100/1**

14 1 **Art Man** 3-9-0 .... TedDurcan 5 25
(Mrs A J Perrett) *s.i.s: a bhd* **16/1**

15 14 **Stingray (IRE)**[94] 4-9-3 .... MarkCoumbe(7) 2 —
(N I M Rossiter) *t.k.h: prom tl wknd rapidly 2f out* **100/1**

1m 13.1s (-1.88) **Going Correction** -0.475s/f (Firm)
WFA 3 from 4yo+ 10lb 15 Ran SP% **125.0**
Speed ratings (Par 105):93,85,81,81,79 78,77,77,77,75 69,67,65,64,45
CSF £9.98 TOTE £4.10: £1.50, £1.50, £16.10; EX 11.60.
Owner W V & Mrs E S Robins **Bred** J F Tuthill **Trained** Newmarket, Suffolk
■ Stewards' Enquiry : Joseph Loveridge one-day ban: used whip when out of contention (May 18)

FOCUS
A very moderate winning time for the type of contest, 1.8 seconds slower than the opener. The winner impressed and this was an improved effort if the second and the fourth ran their races, but there is some doubt that they did. Not many got into the race.

Cabriole Official explanation: jockey said filly lost its action a furlong out

1514 TOTEQUADPOT FILLIES' CONDITIONS STKS — 5f

3:40 (3:42) (Class 3) 2-Y-O — **£7,124** (£2,119; £1,059; £529) **Stalls** High

Form					RPR
411	1		**Gilded (IRE)**[19] 1066 2-9-3 .... DaneO'Neill 2		95+
			(R Hannon) *trckd ldr: led after 2f: pushed out fnl f: comf*	**4/7**[1]	
	2	2	**Pretty Majestic (IRE)** 2-8-6 .... TedDurcan 6		76
			(M R Channon) *hld up: rdn and hdwy to chse wnr over 1f out: kpt on*	**8/1**[3]	
	3	1 ½	**Elizabeth Street (USA)** 2-8-3 .... NelsonDeSouza(3) 1		70
			(P F I Cole) *trckd ldrs: rdn over 1f out: kpt on one pce*	**7/2**[2]	
35	4	1 ½	**Queen Of Narnia**[26] 968 2-8-9 .... SamHitchcott 5		67
			(M R Channon) *led for 2f: sn rdn and one pce after*	**18/1**	
	5	hd	**Harvest Joy (IRE)** 2-8-6 .... RobertHavlin 3		63
			(B R Millman) *slowly away: a bhd*	**28/1**	
	6	5	**Colchium (IRE)** 2-8-6 .... SteveDrowne 4		43
			(H Morrison) *t.k.h: in tch: rdn and wknd 2f out*	**20/1**	

60.35 secs (-1.24) **Going Correction** -0.475s/f (Firm) **6** Ran SP% **110.5**
Speed ratings (Par 94):90,86,84,82,81 73
CSF £5.77 TOTE £1.50: £1.10, £2.50; EX 3.30.
Owner Mrs J Wood **Bred** Tally-Ho Stud **Trained** East Everleigh, Wilts

FOCUS
Solid form for the type of race, with another good effort from the winner and nice enough debuts from the next two.

NOTEBOOK
Gilded(IRE), tackling firm ground for the first time, enjoyed the edge on experience and had little problem landing the hat-trick. Her trainer believes she will get six furlongs but she could go to Ascot first. (tchd 8-11)
Pretty Majestic(IRE) is a half-sister to three winners, best of them five-furlong juvenile scorer Tent. She made sure the favourite did not have things all her own way and should not be long in getting off the mark. (op 4-1 tchd 7-2)
Elizabeth Street(USA), the most expensive of these at 80,000gns, is a half-sister to six winners in the United States out of a decent dual winner there. Well supported, she ran as if in need of the experience and could never quite get in a challenge. (op 8-1)
Queen Of Narnia, a stablemate of the runner-up, probably ran to a similar level of form as when third to Gilded on her debut at Warwick. (op 14-1 tchd 20-1)
Harvest Joy(IRE), a cheap yearling, was slowly away and outpaced at the back of the field until finding her feet in the latter stages. There is improvement to come from her. (op 20-1)
Colchium(IRE), whose dam was a high-class miler in South Africa, showed no great promise on this debut but may improve if settling better. (op 18-1)

1515 TOTESPORT 0800 221 221 H'CAP — 1m 1f 198y

4:15 (4:19) (Class 4) (0-85,82) 3-Y-O — **£7,124** (£2,119; £1,059; £529) **Stalls** High

Form					RPR
44-3	1		**Snoqualmie Boy**[16] 1120 3-9-4 82 .... JohnEgan 1		90+
			(D R C Elsworth) *a in tch: wnt 2nd over 6f out: led over 2f out: rdn and styd on wl*	**2/1**[2]	
2-13	2	1 ¼	**Awatuki (IRE)**[16] 1108 3-9-3 81 .... TPQueally 5		87+
			(A P Jarvis) *led after 2f: rdn and qcknd over 4f out: hdd over 2f out: kpt on one pce*	**1/1**[1]	
035-	3	2	**Smart Gal (IRE)**[222] 5524 3-8-7 71 .... ShaneKelly 4		73+
			(J L Dunlop) *led for 2f: outpcd over 4f out: rallied and styd on on fnl f*	**5/1**[3]	
50-0	4	1 ¼	**Mujood**[22] 1016 3-9-2 80 ....(b) StephenCarson 2		80
			(R F Johnson Houghton) *hld up: effrt over 3f out: no hdwy fnl 2f*	**20/1**	
50-0	5	3 ½	**Mister Benedictine**[16] 1115 3-9-3 81 .... MartinDwyer 7		77+
			(W R Muir) *hld up: hdwy over 4f out: outpcd 2f out and no imp after*	**16/1**	

2m 11.1s (2.64) **Going Correction** +0.05s/f (Good) **5** Ran SP% **119.7**
Speed ratings (Par 101):91,90,88,87,84
CSF £4.41 TOTE £2.70: £1.40, £1.30; EX 4.60.
Owner J C Smith **Bred** Littleton Stud **Trained** Newmarket, Suffolk

FOCUS
They went no pace, resulting in a muddling affair and a very moderate winning time for the class of contest. The bare form is not up to much, rated through the fourth, but the first three are all unexposed and likely to rate higher.

1516 TOTEEXACTA MAIDEN STKS — 1m 4f

4:50 (4:51) (Class 4) 3-Y-O — **£5,505** (£1,637; £818; £408) **Stalls** High

Form					RPR
02-2	1		**Degas Art (IRE)**[19] 1070 3-9-3 95 .... JohnEgan 2		94+
			(D R C Elsworth) *led tl slipped on bnd and hdd briefly 6f out: styd on strly ins fnl 3f*	**2/5**[1]	
	2	8	**Nimra (USA)** 3-8-9 .... AdamKirby(3) 6		76
			(G A Butler) *sn trckd ldr: plugged on one pce but no ch w wnr ins fnl 3f*	**10/1**[3]	
	3	5	**Sybella** 3-8-12 .... IanMongan 7		68
			(J L Dunlop) *went lft s: hdwy 5f out: styd on one pce fr over 2f out*	**14/1**	
	4	8	**Artist's Muse (USA)** 3-8-12 .... TedDurcan 1		55
			(Mrs A J Perrett) *trckd ldrs: led briefly over 6f out: wknd wl over 1f out*	**15/2**[2]	
0	5	1	**Dipped Wings (IRE)**[19] 1070 3-8-12 .... TQuinn 5		54+
			(J L Dunlop) *mid-div: lost tch 4f out*	**40/1**	
	6	1 ½	**Galibard (IRE)** 3-9-3 .... FergusSweeney 3		56
			(A M Balding) *a bhd: lost tch 4f out*	**16/1**	
0-0	7	59	**El Faro (FR)**[16] 1120 3-9-3 .... SamHitchcott 4		—
			(M R Channon) *a bhd: lost tch 5f out: t.o*	**18/1**	

2m 34.2s (-2.16) **Going Correction** +0.05s/f (Good) **7** Ran SP% **112.5**
Speed ratings (Par 101):109,103,100,95,94 93,54
CSF £5.21 TOTE £1.40: £1.10, £3.90; EX 5.40.
Owner Matthew Green **Bred** Millsec Limited **Trained** Newmarket, Suffolk
■ A treble for David Elsworth, his first winners since leaving Whitsbury for Newmarket.

FOCUS
A decent pace and a very smart winning time for the type of contest. Pretty weak form as it stands, the winner rated having improved slightly on his reappearance effort, but more will be known when the second and third run again.

1517 TOTEPOOL "A BETTER WAY TO BET" H'CAP — 1m 6f 15y

5:25 (5:25) (Class 2) (0-105,93) 4-Y-O+
£11,217 (£3,358; £1,679; £840; £419; £210) **Stalls** Far side

Form					RPR
10-4	1		**Ebtikaar (IRE)**[19] 1071 4-9-10 93 .... MartinDwyer 4		95+
			(J L Dunlop) *hld up: swtchd lft 2f out: hdwy and hung rt ins fnl f: styd on to ld nr fin*	**8/13**[1]	
21-0	2	nk	**Michabo (IRE)**[22] 1021 5-9-2 84 .... SteveDrowne 2		86
			(H Morrison) *led: rdn over 1f out: kpt on: hdd nr fin*	**6/1**[2]	
1/5-	3	1 ¼	**Croon**[176] 6325 4-8-4 73 .... JohnEgan 5		74+
			(H Morrison) *hld up: hdwy 5f out: chsd ldr over 3f out: nt qckn and squeezed up wl ins fnl f*	**11/1**	
000-	4	3 ½	**Ocean Of Storms (IRE)**[82] 4730 11-7-13 74 oh8 ow1 MarkCoumbe(7) 3		69?
			(N I M Rossiter) *hld up: one pce fnl 2f*	**50/1**	
10-0	5	½	**Baddam**[19] 1071 4-9-9 92 .... IanMongan 8		86
			(M R Channon) *trckd ldr tl rdn over 3f out: sn outpcd and btn*	**7/1**[3]	
10-4	6	17	**Tender Falcon**[11] 1238 6-9-3 85 .... TQuinn 9		56
			(R J Hodges) *sn on tch: lost pl 4f out and wl bhd after*	**8/1**	

3m 3.73s (-2.50) **Going Correction** +0.05s/f (Good)
WFA 4 from 5yo+ 1lb **6** Ran SP% **110.1**
Speed ratings (Par 109):109,108,108,106,105 96
CSF £4.56 CT £17.37 TOTE £1.50: £1.30, £2.60; EX 4.30 Place 6 £2.55, Place 5 £1.75.
Owner Hamdan Al Maktoum **Bred** Shadwell Estate Company Limited **Trained** Arundel, W Sussex
■ Stewards' Enquiry : Martin Dwyer one-day ban: careless riding (May 19)

FOCUS
There was a flip start. The pace was modest and the form is suspect, with the principals not at their best given the way the race was run and the fourth too close for comfort.

NOTEBOOK
Ebtikaar(IRE) ◆, tackling this trip for the first time, looked like he might not get there entering the final furlong but he stuck his neck out gamely as he answered his rider's calls and edged ahead near the line. A truer test at this trip will suit him well and he should be kept on the right side. (op 8-11)
Michabo(IRE), having his second run for this yard, was down in trip for this return to turf. Responsible for setting the modest gallop before gradually winding things up, he fought off the challenge of the eventual third before succumbing to the winner's late thrust. (op 15-2)
Croon, lightly raced when with Luca Cumani, refused to go into the stalls on his intended reappearance at Warwick. Making his debut on turf and tackling his longest trip to date, he threw down a challenge with two to run but could not get past the leader, and was held in third when squeezed up close home. (op 17-2)
Ocean Of Storms(IRE), beaten in selling hurdles since last in action on the Flat and racing from out of the weights, stayed on in the latter stages without posing at threat. He gives trouble at the stalls so was suited by the flip start here. (op 66-1)
Baddam, having his second run since leaving John Dunlop, looks held from this mark but the lack of a true gallop here was no help to him. (tchd 13-2)
Tender Falcon Official explanation: jockey said gelding was unsuited by the firm (good to firm places) ground
T/Plt: £3.50 to a £1 stake. Pool: £42,387.50. 8,718.90 winning tickets. T/Qpdt: £2.00 to a £1 stake. Pool: £2,149.10. 793.35 winning tickets. JS

1518 - 1525a (Foreign Racing) - See Raceform Interactive

FRANKFURT (L-H)

Sunday, May 7

OFFICIAL GOING: Good

1526a FRUHJAHRSPREIS DES BANKHAUS METZLER - STADTRAT ALBERT VON METZLER-RENNEN (GROUP 3) — 1m 2f

4:00 (4:08) 3-Y-O — **£22,069** (£6,897; £3,448; £2,069)

				RPR
1		**Prince Flori (GER)**[28] 3-9-0 .... HGrewe 9		99
		(S Smrczek, Germany) *reluctant to ld, hld up, 6th str, hdwy on outside to chal 200yds out, led wl ins fnl f, driven out*	**177/10**	
2	hd	**Sommertag (GER)** 3-9-0 .... THellier 7		98
		(P Schiergen, Germany) *hmpd s, towards rr, 7th str, hdwy on outside over 1f out, ev ch fnl f til unable to qckn cl home*	**71/10**	
3	nk	**Saddex** 3-9-0 .... TMundry 2		98
		(P Rau, Germany) *always close up, 5th straight, led approaching final f til well inside final f, no extra close home*	**17/10**[1]	
4	2	**Lucidor (GER)**[203] 5931 3-9-0 .... StanleyChin 1		94
		(Frau E Mader, Germany) *tracked leader, 3rd straight, ran on same pace*	**78/10**	
5	6	**El Paso (GER)**[250] 3-9-0 .... WMongil 8		83
		(P Schiergen, Germany) *hdwy to go 2nd 4f out, led ent str (wl over 1f out), headed appr fnl f, wknd quickly*	**32/10**[2]	
6	1 ¼	**Protettore (GER)**[28] 3-9-0 .... JParize 6		81
		(Frau D Breuer, Germany) *swerved right start, headway 3f out, 4th straight, soon one pace*	**29/1**	
7	2	**Tschaikowskij (GER)**[231] 5351 3-9-0 .... EPedroza 3		77
		(W Kujath, Germany) *led to well over 1f out*	**15/1**	
8	½	**Ponticello (GER)**[21] 3-9-0 .... J-PCarvalho 10		76
		(Mario Hofer, Germany) *always behind, last & beaten straight*	**21/1**	
9	7	**Sagunt (GER)**[203] 5931 3-9-0 .... ASuborics 4		64
		(W Hickst, Germany) *always in rear, 8th straight, soon beaten*	**113/10**	
U		**Mannico (GER)**[14] 1176 3-9-0 .... AStarke 5		—
		(Mario Hofer, Germany) *behind when ran out on first bend, slipped up and unseated rider*	**43/10**[3]	

2m 7.81s **10** Ran SP% **131.0**
(including 10 euro stakes): WIN 187.00; PL 35.00, 22.00, 15.00;SF 1750.00.
Owner Stall Reni **Bred** H A Wacek **Trained** Germany

1180 SHA TIN (R-H)

Sunday, May 7

OFFICIAL GOING: Good to firm

1527a CHAMPIONS MILE (HONG KONG GROUP 1) — 1m

8:50 (8:50) 3-Y-O+
£338,092 (£135,237; £60,105; £33,809; £22,539; £11,270)

				RPR
1		**Bullish Luck (USA)**[14] 1180 7-9-0 ....(b) BPrebble 2		121
		(A S Cruz, Hong Kong)	**45/4**	
2	1 ½	**Danacourt (NZ)** 4-9-0 .... DWhyte 12		118
		(J Size, Hong Kong)	**37/10**[2]	
3	1	**Joyful Winner (AUS)**[22] 6-9-0 .... SDye 5		116
		(J Moore, Hong Kong)	**48/10**[3]	
4	nse	**Russian Pearl (NZ)**[14] 1180 6-9-0 .... RFradd 11		116
		(A S Cruz, Hong Kong)	**34/1**	

5 nse **Vanderlin**[45] [704] 7-9-0 .... GSchofield 9 116
(A M Balding) *raced in 4th to straight, ran on to dispute 3rd 100y out, kept on same pace* **138/1**
6 3/4 **Seihali (IRE)**[43] [742] 7-9-0 .... WCMarwing 4 114
(D Selvaratnam, UAE) **67/1**
7 shd **Sunny Sing (IRE)**[42] 4-9-0 .... GMosse 3 114
(J Moore, Hong Kong) **86/10**
8 1 1/2 **High Intelligent (AUS)**[22] 6-9-0 .... (b) CMunce 6 111
(J Size, Hong Kong) **45/1**
9 1 **Silent Witness (AUS)**[22] 7-9-0 .... FCoetzee 7 109
(A S Cruz, Hong Kong) **6/4**[1]
10 1 **Art Trader (USA)**[49] 5-9-0 .... ESaint-Martin 13 107
(J Moore, Hong Kong) **16/1**
11 1/2 **Dave's Best**[22] 6-9-0 .... DDunn 1 106
(C H Yip, Hong Kong) **38/1**
12 1 **Niconero (AUS)**[15] 4-9-0 .... (b) CraigWilliams 10 104
(D Hayes, Australia) **11/1**
13 4 **Perfect Partner (AUS)**[105] 6-9-0 .... ODoleuze 8 96
(A S Cruz, Hong Kong) **78/1**

1m 33.7s **13** Ran SP% **122.4**
(including $HK10 stakes): WIN 122.50; PL 35.00, 21.50, 22.00; DF353.50.
Owner Wong Wing Keung **Bred** Max Morris & Isabel Morris **Trained** Hong Kong

NOTEBOOK
Vanderlin seems to love travelling. He may have been the complete outsider but he had no trouble finding a good position and keeping it. Only inches separated him from third prize.

AYR (L-H)
Monday, May 8

OFFICIAL GOING: Good
Wind: Fresh, half-behind

1528 AYR RACECOURSE CHAMPAGNE & SEAFOOD BAR H'CAP 6f
6:10 (6:11) (Class 6) (0-65,65) 4-Y-O+ **£3,238** (£963; £481; £240) **Stalls** High

Form RPR
363- **1** **Indian Spark**[222] [5552] 12-8-13 **60** .... TonyCulhane 6 77
(J S Goldie) *trckd ldrs: led over 1f out: shkn up to go clr: readily* **16/1**
620- **2** 4 **Quantica (IRE)**[185] [6243] 7-8-5 **52** .... KimTinkler 1 57
(N Tinkler) *led to over 2f out: sn rdn: rallied over 1f out: kpt on: no ch w wnr* **25/1**
0230 **3** nk **Mynd**[5] [1414] 6-8-3 **57** .... MichaelJStainton(7) 12 61
(R M Whitaker) *cl up: led over 2f to over 1f out: kpt on same pce* **7/1**[3]
04-0 **4** 1 **Divine Spirit**[17] [1125] 5-9-4 **65** .... PhillipMakin 14 66
(M Dods) *in tch: effrt over 2f out: edgd lft and no ex over 1f out* **4/1**[1]
6000 **5** 3 **Enjoy The Buzz**[13] [1209] 7-8-4 **51** oh1 .... NickyMackay 7 43
(J M Bradley) *bhd on outside: effrt over 2f out: no imp over 1f out* **50/1**
-000 **6** 2 1/2 **Rancho Cucamonga (IRE)**[5] [1413] 4-9-2 **63** .... (b) PaulFessey 11 48
(T D Barron) *dwlt: sn rdn in rr: kpt on fr over 1f out: nvr on terms* **10/1**
-000 **7** 1 1/4 **Trick Cyclist**[9] [1297] 5-9-2 **63** .... DaleGibson 8 44
(M W Easterby) *midfield: n.m.r whn rdn over 2f out: sn no imp* **40/1**
40-0 **8** 2 1/2 **Coranglais**[4] [1432] 6-9-0 **61** .... (p) RobertWinston 2 34
(J M Bradley) *prom tl edgd rt and wknd fr 2f out* **12/1**
5215 **9** 1/2 **Piccolo Prince**[12] [1235] 5-8-12 **59** .... DavidAllan 13 31
(E J Alston) *midfield: sn drvn along: outpcd over 2f out: n.d after* **7/1**[3]
046 **10** nk **Nova Tor (IRE)**[16] [1150] 4-8-8 **55** .... (b) RobbieFitzpatrick 10 26
(Peter Grayson) *chsd ldrs tl rdn and wknd over 2f out* **25/1**
532- **11** hd **Yorkie**[153] [6514] 7-8-12 **59** .... DeanMcKeown 3 29
(J Pearce) *bhd: rdn 1/2-way: nvr on terms* **14/1**
0221 **12** 3/4 **Geojimali**[6] [1397] 4-8-11 **58** 6ex .... FergalLynch 5 26+
(J S Goldie) *stdd and swtchd rt sn after s: hld up ins: repeatedly denied room fr 1/2-way: nvr on terms* **6/1**[2]
0600 **13** 1/2 **Queens Rhapsody**[65] [585] 6-8-12 **59** .... PaulHanagan 9 26
(A Bailey) *midfield: outpcd 1/2-way: sn btn* **12/1**
0000 **14** 1 1/2 **Oeuf A La Neige**[72] [514] 6-8-4 **51** oh1 .... RoystonFfrench 4 13
(G C H Chung) *bhd: struggling fr 1/2-way* **10/1**

1m 12.46s (-1.21) **Going Correction** -0.075s/f (Good) **14** Ran SP% **117.5**
Speed ratings (Par 101):105,99,99,97,93 90,88,85,84,84 84,83,82,80
CSF £371.01 CT £3104.24 TOTE £20.80: £5.60, £6.70, £2.90; EX 675.20.
Owner Frank Brady **Bred** H Young **Trained** Uplawmoor, E Renfrews

FOCUS
An ordinary event in which the field raced centre to stands' side. There was a fair breeze behind the runners and it paid to race close to the pace. The form looks sound enough.
Geojimali Official explanation: jockey said gelding continually denied a clear run

1529 WEDDINGS AT WESTERN HOUSE H'CAP 5f
6:40 (6:40) (Class 4) (0-85,79) 3-Y-O **£8,096** (£2,408; £1,203; £601) **Stalls** High

Form RPR
24-4 **1** **Rainbow Bay**[13] [1218] 3-8-9 **70** .... PaulHanagan 5 79
(R A Fahey) *trckd ldrs: rdn to ld over 1f out: kpt on wl fnl f* **11/2**
62-5 **2** 1 **Blazing Heights**[22] [1036] 3-8-11 **72** .... FergalLynch 7 77
(J S Goldie) *hld up: hdwy to press ldrs whn nt clr run and swtchd lft ent fnl f: kpt on: hld towards fin* **6/1**
00-0 **3** 2 **Mytton's Pride**[22] [1036] 3-8-7 **68** .... PaulFessey 8 66
(A Bailey) *set decent gallop to appr fnl f: kpt on same pce* **50/1**
0321 **4** 4 **Glenviews Youngone (IRE)**[9] [1304] 3-8-13 **74** .... RobbieFitzpatrick 4 57
(Peter Grayson) *prom: effrt over 2f out: outpcd fnl f* **4/1**[2]
04-0 **5** 1 1/2 **Inca Soldier (FR)**[54] [645] 3-8-5 **66** .... PaulEddery 2 44
(R C Guest) *s.i.s: hld up: shkn up over 2f out: nvr nrr* **33/1**
00-1 **6** 1 **Sandwith**[22] [1036] 3-8-12 **73** .... RobertWinston 9 47
(I Semple) *hld up in tch: effrt over 2f out: hung lft: wknd over 1f out* **3/1**[1]
-155 **7** 7 **Jimmy The Guesser**[2] [1482] 3-9-4 **79** .... (b) TomEaves 3 28
(N P Littmoden) *hld up in tch on outside: rdn over 2f out: sn btn* **5/1**[3]
2-10 **8** 1 1/2 **Egyptian Lord**[9] [1279] 3-8-8 **69** .... (v[1]) TonyCulhane 6 13
(Peter Grayson) *w ldr to 2f out: sn rdn and btn* **10/1**
10 **9** 14 **Swiper Hill (IRE)**[25] [1004] 3-8-12 **73** .... PatCosgrave 1 —
(B Ellison) *wnt bdly lft leaving stalls: hung lft in rr thrght: lost tch fr 1/2-way* **9/1**

60.37 secs (-0.07) **Going Correction** -0.075s/f (Good) **9** Ran SP% **115.3**
Speed ratings (Par 101):97,95,92,85,83 81,70,68,45
CSF £38.34 CT £1484.33 TOTE £8.00: £3.00, £2.80, £6.90; EX 58.20.
Owner K Lee **Bred** Ms R A Myatt **Trained** Musley Bank, N Yorks

FOCUS
A field of exposed three-year-olds and the strong pace set by the two leaders set this up for something coming from just behind the pace.
Sandwith Official explanation: jockey said gelding hung left-handed throughout
Swiper Hill(IRE) Official explanation: trainer said gelding was found to have mucus on its lungs

1530 XMAS PARTY NIGHTS AT AYR RACECOURSE MEDIAN AUCTION MAIDEN STKS 1m
7:10 (7:10) (Class 4) 3-5-Y-O **£5,505** (£1,637; £818; £408) **Stalls** Low

Form RPR
34-0 **1** **Secret Liaison**[6] [1384] 3-8-12 77 .... JamieMackay 4 73+
(Sir Mark Prescott) *chsd ldr: led over 1f out: drvn out* **2/1**[1]
5 **2** 3/4 **Prince Egor (IRE)**[18] [1101] 3-8-12 .... PhillipMakin 8 71
(M Dods) *s.i.s: hld up: shkn up and hdwy over 2f out: kpt on wl fnl f: improve* **4/1**[2]
00 **3** 1/2 **Azurine (IRE)**[42] [762] 3-8-7 .... RoystonFfrench 5 65
(M Johnston) *led to over 1f out: rallied: no ex ins fnl f* **10/1**
2-53 **4** 1 3/4 **Grey Outlook**[3] [1458] 3-8-7 69 .... RobertWinston 6 61
(Miss L A Perratt) *prom: rdn over 2f out: hung lft: one pce fnl f* **2/1**[1]
00 **5** hd **Electron Pulse**[22] [1032] 3-8-7 .... NickyMackay 1 61
(J S Goldie) *prom: effrt over 2f out: one pce fnl f* **7/1**[3]
00-0 **6** 16 **Cashema (IRE)**[38] [818] 5-9-3 40 .... DNolan(3) 2 27
(D R MacLeod) *hld up: rdn over 3f out: wknd over 2f out* **100/1**
000- **7** 19 **Borsch (IRE)**[352] [1878] 4-9-11 .... TomEaves 3 —
(Miss L A Perratt) *bhd: lost tch fr 1/2-way* **100/1**

1m 45.33s (1.84) **Going Correction** +0.125s/f (Good)
WFA 3 from 4yo+ 13lb **7** Ran SP% **110.2**
Speed ratings (Par 105):95,94,93,92,91 75,56
CSF £9.66 TOTE £3.10: £1.60, £2.60; EX 18.80.
Owner W E Sturt - Osborne House **Bred** Cheveley Park Stud Ltd **Trained** Newmarket, Suffolk

FOCUS
An uncompetitive race run at a modest gallop resulted in a moderate winning time for the grade, just over two seconds slower than the following handicap.

1531 SCOTTISH WOMAN STKS (H'CAP) 1m
7:40 (7:40) (Class 5) (0-75,75) 4-Y-O+ **£5,505** (£1,637; £818; £408) **Stalls** Low

Form RPR
036- **1** **Vicious Warrior**[163] [6431] 7-9-4 **75** .... DeanMcKeown 1 87
(R M Whitaker) *mde all: rdn 2f out: r.o strly* **7/1**[2]
4603 **2** nk **Hawkit (USA)**[6] [1389] 5-8-9 **66** .... RobertWinston 5 78
(A Bailey) *hld up: effrt over 2f out: kpt on wl fnl f: jst hld* **8/1**[3]
12-1 **3** 1 1/4 **Stellite**[17] [1124] 6-8-10 **67** .... TonyCulhane 11 76
(J S Goldie) *pressed ldr: rdn over 2f out: one pce fnl f* **4/1**[1]
00-0 **4** 1 **Queen's Echo**[21] [1041] 5-8-4 **61** oh1 .... PaulFessey 13 68
(M Dods) *hld up: hdwy 3f out: rdn and kpt on fnl f* **12/1**
0400 **5** 2 **Bollin Michael**[9] [1288] 4-8-4 **61** oh1 .... (b[1]) DavidAllan 2 63
(T D Easterby) *in tch: drvn over 3f out: effrt over 2f out: no imp fnl f* **16/1**
0200 **6** 3 **Corky (IRE)**[14] [1186] 5-8-12 **72** .... PatrickMathers(3) 6 67
(I W McInnes) *missed break: bhd tl hdwy over 2f out: kpt on: nvr rchd ldrs* **33/1**
50-0 **7** 1 3/4 **Nevada Desert (IRE)**[9] [1280] 6-9-2 **73** .... StanleyChin 4 64
(R M Whitaker) *trckd ldrs: effrt over 2f out: fdd over 1f out* **8/1**[3]
0-00 **8** 3 **Sea Storm (IRE)**[9] [1280] 8-9-1 **75** .... (p) DNolan(3) 12 59
(D R MacLeod) *prom: outpcd over 2f out: n.d after* **25/1**
3451 **9** 5 **Dispol Isle (IRE)**[21] [1041] 4-8-6 **66** .... BenSwarbrick(3) 10 39
(T D Barron) *hld up: rdn outside over 2f out: nvr rchd ldrs* **14/1**
3100 **10** 2 1/2 **Mystic Man (FR)**[3] [1455] 8-9-4 **75** .... PaulHanagan 14 42
(I W McInnes) *hld up: rdn 3f out: n.d* **25/1**
062- **11** 3 **Sovereignty (JPN)**[206] [5880] 4-8-5 **69** .... StephenCairns(7) 9 29
(I Semple) *keen: trckd ldrs tl wknd over 2f out* **16/1**
112- **12** 1 1/4 **Mystical Ayr (IRE)**[191] [6139] 4-7-13 **61** oh3 .... AndrewMullen(5) 3 18
(Miss L A Perratt) *prom: rdn over 3f out: wknd over 2f out* **7/1**[2]
0305 **13** 9 **Anduril**[9] [1280] 5-9-2 **73** .... (b) FergalLynch 7 9
(Miss M E Rowland) *s.v.s and flyj. leaving stalls: nvr on terms* **16/1**
6-00 **14** 2 1/2 **Society Music (IRE)**[9] [1280] 4-9-4 **75** .... PhillipMakin 8 6
(M Dods) *midfield: drvn over 3f out: btn 2f out* **7/1**[2]

1m 43.28s (-29.21) **Going Correction** +0.125s/f (Good) **14** Ran SP% **122.4**
Speed ratings (Par 103):106,105,104,103,101 98,96,93,88,86 83,81,72,70
CSF £61.85 CT £266.67 TOTE £10.70: £3.80, £3.70, £2.30; EX 133.60.
Owner sportaracing.com **Bred** Hellwood Stud Farm **Trained** Scarcroft, W Yorks

FOCUS
No progressive performers on show but the pace was sound and this form should prove reliable.
Society Music(IRE) Official explanation: jockey said filly never travelled

1532 HORSERACING BREAKS H'CAP 7f 50y
8:10 (8:10) (Class 3) (0-90,87) 4-Y-O+ **£11,658** (£3,468; £1,733; £865) **Stalls** Low

Form RPR
4223 **1** **Commando Scott (IRE)**[3] [1456] 5-8-10 **82** .... PatrickMathers(3) 7 93
(I W McInnes) *keen: prom: rdn to ld ent fnl f: kpt on wl* **11/2**[2]
00-3 **2** 3/4 **Breaking Shadow (IRE)**[13] [1220] 4-8-9 **78** .... PhillipMakin 9 87
(T D Barron) *keen: prom: effrt and ev ch 1f out: kpt on: hld towards fin* **9/2**[1]
00-0 **3** 1 1/4 **Tagula Sunrise (IRE)**[16] [1143] 4-8-13 **82** .... PaulHanagan 1 88
(R A Fahey) *midfield: effrt over 2f out: rdn and edgd lft over 1f out: n.m.r and swtchd rt ins fnl f: r.o fin* **8/1**
0-31 **4** shd **Jubilee Street (IRE)**[9] [1280] 7-8-12 **81** .... PaulFessey 11 87
(Mrs A Duffield) *rrd s: bhd tl gd hdwy 2f out: kpt on wl fnl f: nrst fin* **8/1**
00-0 **5** nk **Steel Blue**[21] [1042] 6-8-11 **80** .... TonyCulhane 6 85
(R M Whitaker) *chsd ldrs: smooth hdwy to ld over 2f out: hdd ent fnl f: one pce* **16/1**
2-06 **6** 3 **Pure Imagination (IRE)**[9] [1285] 5-8-9 **78** .... RobertWinston 5 75
(J M Bradley) *hld up: hdwy 3f out: rdn and no ex fnl f* **10/1**
-000 **7** 3 **Lake Andre (IRE)**[21] [1043] 5-8-12 **86** .... AndrewMullen(5) 4 75
(K A Ryan) *set str pce to over 2f out: sn outpcd* **11/1**
004- **8** shd **Chief Scout**[191] [6149] 4-8-10 **79** .... TomEaves 2 68
(I Semple) *midfield: rdn over 2f out: nvr able to chal* **16/1**
-344 **9** 3 **Harvest Warrior**[21] [1043] 4-8-13 **82** .... (b) DavidAllan 3 63
(T D Easterby) *hld up outside: rdn and edgd lft over 2f out: sn no imp* **7/1**[3]
06-0 **10** 3 **Loaderfun (IRE)**[19] [1076] 4-9-0 **86** .... DNolan(3) 14 59
(N Wilson) *hld up: rdn over 3f out: sn btn* **100/1**
16-3 **11** 13 **Dakota Rain (IRE)**[38] [815] 4-8-9 **78** .... PaulEddery 10 18
(R C Guest) *midfield tl rdn over 2f out: sn btn* **12/1**
0030 **12** 2 **Lord Of The East**[3] [1456] 7-9-4 **87** .... RoystonFfrench 8 21
(I W McInnes) *pressed ldr tl wknd over 2f out* **16/1**
234- **13** 4 **Looks Could Kill (USA)**[150] [6530] 4-9-1 **84** .... NickyMackay 12 8
(E J Alston) *in tch on outside: rdn over 2f out: wkng whn short of room wl over 1f out: eased* **20/1**

020- **14** *19* **Doric (USA)**[233] [5285] 5-9-4 **87**.. PatCosgrave 13 —
(B Ellison) *bhd: lost tch fr over 3f out* **16/1**

1m 32.33s (-0.39) **Going Correction** +0.125s/f (Good) **14** Ran SP% **122.7**
Speed ratings (Par 107):107,106,104,104,104 100,97,97,93,90 75,73,68,47
CSF £31.00 CT £209.83 TOTE £6.80: £1.90, £2.40, £3.40; EX 35.80.
Owner Mrs Ann Morris **Bred** Noel Finegan **Trained** Catwick, E Yorks

FOCUS
A race full of exposed performers but, although the pace was sound throughout, those attempting to come from off the pace were at a disadvantage.

NOTEBOOK
Commando Scott(IRE), better than the bare form in a strongly-run race at Musselburgh last time, had the race run to suit and showed the right attitude to break a losing run. He should not be going up too much for this and should continue to run well. (op 9-2 tchd 6-1)
Breaking Shadow(IRE) had conditions in his favour and the race run to suit and fully confirmed reappearance promise. Although he has not always proved reliable, he is capable of winning again around this trip from this sort of mark. (op 11-2)
Tagula Sunrise(IRE) bettered her reappearance form in a race that was run to suit but did not really look to be helping her rider in the closing stages as she just wanted to edge to the far rail. She has little margin for error from this mark. (op 15-2)
Jubilee Street(IRE) ◆, a consistent sort on a sound surface with a good strike-rate, did well to get as close as he did given he was already in the air as the stalls opened. He made up a good deal of ground late on and is the type to win more races this year. Official explanation: jockey said gelding reared as stalls opened
Steel Blue ◆ remains on a fair mark and, judged by the way he tanked along through this race, he will be very much of interest in the near future when returned to ordinary handicap company over six furlongs. (tchd 20-1)
Pure Imagination(IRE), a winner over six furlongs and a mile last year, was not disgraced in a race where it paid to race prominently, but he may have to drop a few pounds in the weights before returning to winning ways.
Lake Andre(IRE), who looked in tremendous condition, paid the price for going off too quickly but remains plenty high enough in the weights at present. (op 10-1)

1533 LADIES NIGHT ON SATURDAY 12TH AUGUST H'CAP 1m 2f
8:40 (8:40) (Class 6) (0-65,65) 3-Y-O **£3,412** (£1,007; £504) **Stalls** Low

Form RPR
00-0 **1** **Bauer (IRE)**[28] [952] 3-8-13 **60**.......................... NickyMackay 7 65+
(L M Cumani) *trckd ldrs: rdn to ld over 1f out: styd on wl* **15/2**
0102 **2** *1 ¾* **Hits Only Life (USA)**[16] [1140] 3-8-8 **55**........................ DeanMcKeown 1 56
(J Pearce) *keen: hld up in tch on ins: effrt over 2f out: edgd lft: kpt on ins fnl f* **5/2**[1]
0-63 **3** *¾* **William John**[7] [1345] 3-8-6 **53**.. TomEaves 9 53+
(B Ellison) *hld up: hdwy over 2f out: rdn and r.o ins fnl f* **7/2**[2]
5440 **4** *½* **Tirol Livit (IRE)**[13] [1221] 3-8-4 **51** oh4.............................. DaleGibson 5 50
(N Wilson) *hld up towards rr: effrt and rdn over 2f out: one pce ins fnl f* **25/1**
000- **5** *3 ½* **Rivetting**[193] [6121] 3-8-4 **51** oh2.. JamieMackay 3 43
(Sir Mark Prescott) *led to over 2f out: rallied: fdd ins fianl f* **7/1**
033- **6** *3* **Linton Dancer (IRE)**[240] [5125] 3-8-7 **54**........................ RobertWinston 8 41
(J R Weymes) *sn pressing ldr: led over 2f to over 1f out: wknd ins fnl f* **5/1**[3]
000- **7** *1 ¾* **Katsumoto (IRE)**[164] [6417] 3-9-4 **65**.................................. StanleyChin 4 48
(N P Littmoden) *s.i.s: keen and sn cl up: rdn over 2f out: btn over 1f out* **25/1**
2140 **8** *½* **Subsidise (IRE)**[21] [1044] 3-8-12 **59**................................ PaulHanagan 2 41
(F P Murtagh) *bhd: drvn 1/2-way: btn over 2f out* **20/1**
-600 **9** *25* **Gigs Magic (USA)**[13] [1215] 3-8-8 **55**............................ RoystonFfrench 10 —
(M Johnston) *in tch on outside tl wknd fr 4f out: t.o* **10/1**

2m 15.88s (4.16) **Going Correction** +0.125s/f (Good) **9** Ran SP% **113.3**
Speed ratings (Par 97):88,86,86,85,82 80,79,78,58
CSF £25.39 CT £76.65 TOTE £6.70: £2.00, £1.20, £1.30; EX 35.60 Place 6 £211.63, Place 5 £30.31 .
Owner Aston House Stud **Bred** Aston House Stud **Trained** Newmarket, Suffolk

FOCUS
A modest handicap and a modest pace resulted in a very moderate winning time for the type of race.
T/Plt: £175.30 to a £1 stake. Pool: £45,896.15. 191.05 winning tickets. T/Qpdt: £3.90 to a £1 stake. Pool: £4,340.20. 803.40 winning tickets. RY

1399 KEMPTON (A.W) (R-H)
Monday, May 8

OFFICIAL GOING: Standard
Wind: Light, behind

1534 LAKE VIEW BANDED STKS 5f (P)
1:50 (1:50) (Class 7) 3-Y-O+ **£1,706** (£503; £252) **Stalls** High

Form RPR
5046 **1** **Secret Vision (USA)**[13] [1209] 5-9-0 45.......................... JamieSpencer 10 53
(R M H Cowell) *chsd ldr: rdn and r.o wl to ld ins fnl f* **9/2**[2]
4234 **2** *½* **A Teen**[3] [1465] 8-9-0 45.. IanMongan 9 51
(P Howling) *chsd ldrs: hrd rdn and swtchd lft appr fnl f: kpt on to go 2nd wl ins fnl f* **9/1**
0352 **3** *¾* **Katie Killane**[3] [1466] 4-9-0 40..(v) MickyFenton 2 49
(M Wellings) *chsd ldrs: rdn over 1f out: kpt on u.p* **10/1**
-006 **4** *1* **Master Malarkey**[11] [1261] 3-8-5 40.................................(b) JohnEgan 8 41
(Mrs C A Dunnett) *s.i.s: rdn 2f out: hdwy and r.o fnl f: nvr nrr* **33/1**
0000 **5** *hd* **Legal Set (IRE)**[18] [1102] 10-8-8 45 ow1........................(bt) AnnStokell(7) 1 45
(Miss A Stokell) *led: clr 1/2-way: rdn over 1f out: no ex and hdd ins fnl f* **20/1**
0-00 **6** *nk* **Stephanie's Mind**[77] [465] 4-9-0 45..................................... RyanMoore 11 43
(M Quinn) *a in tch: rdn whn hmpd ent fnl f: no ex* **5/1**[3]
0-03 **7** *1 ¼* **Justenjoy Yourself**[3] [1465] 4-9-0 40................................ SamHitchcott 5 39
(R W Price) *chsd ldrs: hmpd ent fnl f: one pce after* **14/1**
0-00 **8** *1 ¼* **Jasmine Pearl (IRE)**[8] [1310] 5-9-0 45............................ FergusSweeney 3 34
(T M Jones) *in tch: rdn whn carried lft ent fnl f: no ex* **20/1**
342 **9** *nk* **Midmaar (IRE)**[3] [1465] 5-9-0 45.................................(b[1]) JamieMackay 12 33
(M Wigham) *trckd ldrs: rdn wl over 1f out: sn btn* **9/4**[1]
0001 **10** *1* **Rock Fever (IRE)**[3] [1466] 4-9-6 45...................................(b) GylesParkin 4 35
(Peter Grayson) *slowly away: a bhd* **12/1**
5-40 **11** *2 ½* **Victoriana**[13] [1228] 5-8-11 40.....................................(p) NeilChalmers(3) 6 20
(H J Collingridge) *a bhd* **66/1**
-650 **12** *hd* **Keresforth**[8] [1310] 4-9-0 40..(b) DaneO'Neill 7 20
(Mrs L C Jewell) *a bhd* **33/1**

60.47 secs **Going Correction** -0.075s/f (Stan)
WFA 3 from 4yo+ 9lb **12** Ran SP% **116.0**
Speed ratings (Par 97):96,95,94,92,92 91,89,87,87,85 81,81
CSF £40.49 TOTE £6.20: £2.10, £2.10, £2.70; EX 53.10.
Owner Mrs J M Penney **Bred** Juddmonte Farms Inc **Trained** Six Mile Bottom, Cambs
■ Stewards' Enquiry : Ian MonganE two-day ban: careless riding (May 19,21)

FOCUS
Just a typical banded sprint run at a strong pace.
Legal Set(IRE) Official explanation: jockey said gelding hung right
Jasmine Pearl(IRE) Official explanation: jockey said mare hung right and was found to be lame post-race

1535 KEMPTON.CO.UK MEDIAN AUCTION MAIDEN STKS 5f (P)
2:20 (2:22) (Class 7) 2-Y-O **£1,706** (£503; £252) **Stalls** High

Form RPR
5 **1** **Juan Bol (IRE)**[21] [1053] 2-9-3 .... ChrisCatlin 7 80
(V Smith) *chsd ldr: rdn and edgd rt bef led ins fnl f: r.o* **4/1**[2]
0 **2** *1 ½* **Going Straight (IRE)**[7] [1347] 2-8-12 .... RyanMoore 1 69
(I A Wood) *sn led: rdn over 1f out: hdd ins fnl f: no ex* **4/1**[2]
3 *1* **Whiskey Junction** 2-9-0 .... NeilChalmers(3) 3 70
(A M Balding) *mid-div: hdwy over 1f out: r.o fnl f: nvr nrr* **10/1**
4 *5* **Early Promise (IRE)** 2-8-12 .... BrianReilly 10 45
(P L Gilligan) *s.i.s: rdn 1/2-way: mde sme late hdwy* **20/1**
5 *nk* **Aggresive** 2-9-3 .... JohnEgan 6 49
(Ernst Oertel) *prom: rdn 2f out: edgd rt appr fnl f: wknd ins* **14/1**
533 **6** *1 ¼* **Our Susie (IRE)**[13] [1223] 2-8-12 .... HayleyTurner 5 39
(M D I Usher) *chsd ldrs: rdn 1/2-way: rdn d wknd appr fnl f* **4/1**[2]
4 **7** *3* **Dotty's Daughter**[13] [1223] 2-8-12 .... JamieSpencer 9 27
(Mrs A Duffield) *chsd ldrs: rdn and hmpd appr fnl f: no ex* **3/1**[1]
40 **8** *1* **Princely Royal**[14] [1189] 2-9-3 .... TPQueally 8 28
(J J Bridger) *rdn 1/2-way: a towards rr* **8/1**[3]
9 *¾* **Brynris** 2-9-0 .... RobertMiles(3) 2 25
(W G M Turner) *sojnn struggling in rr* **20/1**
10 *1* **Champagne Perry** 2-9-3 .... MichaelTebbutt 4 21
(V Smith) *slowly away: a bhd* **33/1**

61.11 secs **Going Correction** -0.075s/f (Stan) **10** Ran SP% **124.3**
Speed ratings (Par 87):91,88,87,79,78 76,71,70,68,67
CSF £21.42 TOTE £4.80: £1.70, £1.80, £3.20; EX 30.40.
Owner David Jenkins **Bred** Denis And Mrs Teresa Bergin **Trained** Exning, Suffolk

FOCUS
Just a modest maiden, but the quality of horse was much better than you would often see at a banded meeting and the front three were clear. The winning time was slightly quicker than the previous race for older horses.

NOTEBOOK
Juan Bol(IRE), fifth in a Yarmouth maiden that has already produced a couple of winners on her debut three weeks previously, stepped up on that effort to get off the mark on this switch to Polytrack, and was backed to do so. Although this was a banded meeting, this was not a bad race and he should not be underestimated next time. (op 7-1)
Going Straight(IRE), down the field in a half-decent maiden at Warwick on her debut just a week previously, was backed to improve on that and duly did so. She showed tremendous early pace, but had to use up plenty of energy to get to the front from the lowest stall of all and that ultimately looked to cost her. (op 11-2)
Whiskey Junction, a half-brother to five/seven-furlong winner Victory Spin, and Lara Falana, a dual mile to ten-furlong scorer, never threatened the front two but kept on nicely to finish well clear of the remainder. He is open to plenty of improvement.
Early Promise(IRE), a full-sister to six-furlong scorer Pompey Blue, made a satisfactory debut.
Aggresive, a half-brother to a six-furlong juvenile winner in Italy, who was later successful over hurdles, out of triple seven-furlong/mile winner, was well held but offered some promise. (op 25-1)
Our Susie(IRE) ran well below the form she had shown on her previous three starts. (op 7-2 tchd 9-2)
Dotty's Daughter failed to build on the promise she showed when fourth on her debut at Wolverhampton, and that looks like a pretty moderate race now. (tchd 11-4 and 10-3)

1536 SUNBURY BANDED STKS 1m 2f (P)
2:50 (2:50) (Class 7) 4-Y-O+ **£2,047** (£604; £302) **Stalls** High

Form RPR
10-1 **1** **Revolve**[84] [395] 6-8-12 45...(p) IanMongan 2 54
(Mrs L J Mongan) *trckd ldr after 2f: led over 2f out: rdn out fnl f* **7/2**[1]
0/0- **2** *1 ½* **Expected Bonus (USA)**[481] [87] 7-8-12 40.............................. JohnEgan 7 51
(Jamie Poulton) *hld up towards rr: hdwy over 2f out: chsd wnr fnl f* **7/1**[2]
-304 **3** *nk* **Amnesty**[22] [972] 7-8-12 45...(be) RyanMoore 5 50+
(G L Moore) *bmpd leaving stalls: hld up in rr: hdwy over 1f out: r.o wl fnl f: nvr nrr* **7/2**[1]
05-0 **4** *½* **Zeena**[13] [1224] 4-8-12 45..(p) AlanDaly 8 49
(C A Horgan) *led tl hdd over 6f out: styd prom: nt qckn fnl f* **20/1**
0-43 **5** *1* **Nobelmann (GER)**[13] [1224] 7-8-12 45.................................. JimmyQuinn 9 48
(A W Carroll) *mid-div: rdn over 1f out: styd on fnl f* **7/1**[2]
0305 **6** *shd* **Dishdasha (IRE)**[6] [1395] 4-8-12 45.............................. MickyFenton 14 47+
(C R Dore) *hld up: swtchd lft and hdwy over 1f out: r.o fnl f* **9/1**[3]
41-0 **7** *1* **Wodhill Gold**[77] [468] 5-8-12 45...(v) ChrisCatlin 4 45
(D Morris) *hld up in rr: sme hdwy over 2f out: kpt on one pce after* **20/1**
0-06 **8** *shd* **Longing For Cindy (USA)**[14] [1198] 4-8-12 45............(b[1]) EddieAhern 12 45
(W M Brisbourne) *in tch: rdn over 2f out: wknd ent fnl f* **12/1**
6065 **9** *1 ¼* **Piquet**[6] [1373] 8-8-12 45.. TPQueally 1 43
(J J Bridger) *prom tl wknd appr fnl f* **12/1**
560 **10** *1* **Vizulize**[13] [1227] 7-8-12 45.. JimmyFortune 13 41
(A W Carroll) *nvr bttr than mid-div* **12/1**
0403 **11** *½* **Homebred Star**[14] [1198] 5-8-7 45...........................(p) RobynBrisland(5) 6 40
(G P Enright) *a bhd* **12/1**
/0-0 **12** *5* **Last Chapter (IRE)**[34] [875] 4-8-12 45............................ VinceSlattery 3 31
(C A Dwyer) *a bhd* **100/1**
-000 **13** *½* **Queen Tara**[13] [1222] 4-8-12 40.. HayleyTurner 10 30
(Mrs C A Dunnett) *trckd ldrs: led over 6f out: hdd over 2f out: wknd over 1f out* **66/1**

2m 11.97s **Going Correction** -0.075s/f (Stan) **13** Ran SP% **122.2**
Speed ratings (Par 97):85,83,83,83,82 82,81,81,80,79 79,75,74
CSF £27.55 TOTE £3.60: £1.70, £2.60, £2.40; EX 37.70.
Owner Mrs P J Sheen **Bred** Wickfield Farm Partnership **Trained** Epsom, Surrey

FOCUS
An ordinary banded event and, with the pace just ordinary, the winning time was significantly slower than the only other ten-furlong race on the card, won by Brave Dane.
Dishdasha(IRE) Official explanation: jockey said gelding was denied a clear run

1537 GREENHAM BANDED STKS — 1m 2f (P)

3:20 (3:21) (Class 7) 4-Y-0+ — £1,706 (£503; £252) Stalls High

Form — RPR

500- **1** **Brave Dane (IRE)**[220] 5587 8-9-2 50 — JimmyFortune 7 — 64+
(A W Carroll) *hld up wl in rr: stdy hdwy fr 4f out: shkn up to ld 1f out: rdn clr* **10/1**

P-60 **2** 3 **Ferrando**[15] 1166 4-9-2 50 — JamieSpencer 1 — 58
(D J Daly) *mid-div: hdwy to go 2nd 4f out: led over 2f out: rdn and hdd 1f out: nt pce of wnr* **8/1**[3]

6054 **3** 2½ **Granary Girl**[9] 1305 4-9-0 48 — JimmyQuinn 12 — 51
(J Pearce) *led for 1f: styd prom: rdn and outpcd fnl f* **14/1**

2-06 **4** ¾ **Prince Valentine**[84] 395 5-8-11 45 — (be) RyanMoore 9 — 47
(G L Moore) *hld up: hdwy 5f out: kpt on one pce fr over 1f out* **25/1**

0-64 **5** ¾ **Star Rising**[9] 1308 4-8-11 50 — StephenDonohoe(5) 10 — 50
(W J Musson) *prom: rdn 4f out: one pce ins fnl 2f* **6/1**[2]

-635 **6** ¾ **Mad**[12] 1245 5-9-2 50 — JohnEgan 8 — 49
(Ernst Oertel) *mid-div: hung rt and wknd appr fnl f* **6/1**[2]

4651 **7** 3 **Abbeygate**[14] 1201 5-8-13 50 — (p) AdamKirby(3) 5 — 43
(T Keddy) *a towards rr* **3/1**[1]

0155 **8** hd **Elms Schoolboy**[13] 1227 4-8-13 47 — (b) IanMongan 4 — 40
(P Howling) *a bhd* **33/1**

6-00 **9** 1½ **Aberdeen Park**[14] 1194 4-9-0 48 — (b) GeorgeBaker 3 — 38
(Mrs H Sweeting) *slowly away: led after 1f: headed over 2f out: wknd over 1f out* **20/1**

0-04 **10** ½ **Kinsman (IRE)**[84] 394 9-8-10 47 — RobertMiles(3) 11 — 36
(T D McCarthy) *a bhd* **16/1**

555- **11** ½ **Loup Sifflet (IRE)**[221] 5564 4-9-0 48 — TonyHamilton 2 — 36
(R A Fahey) *mid-div: rdn and wknd over 2f out* **10/1**

1045 **12** 1¾ **Ringarooma**[30] 917 4-9-1 49 — MartinDwyer 6 — 34
(C N Allen) *slowly away: a bhd* **6/1**[2]

2m 8.98s **Going Correction** -0.075s/f (Stan) — 12 Ran SP% **121.2**
Speed ratings (Par 97):97,94,92,92,91 90,88,88,87,86 86,84
CSF £87.68 TOTE £14.40: £4.20, £2.30, £2.50; EX 104.80.

Owner Exhall Dodgers **Bred** Gainsborough Stud Management Ltd **Trained** Cropthorne, Worcs

FOCUS
Not a bad banded event and a reasonable enough pace resulted in a winning time just short of three seconds faster than the only other ten-furlong race on the card.

Abbeygate Official explanation: jockey said gelding got kicked in stalls and hung right throughout
Ringarooma Official explanation: vet said filly returned with cut leg sustained in stalls

1538 ALL WEATHER RACING BANDED STKS — 7f (P)

3:50 (3:50) (Class 7) 4-Y-0+ — £2,047 (£604; £302) Stalls High

Form — RPR

6-03 **1** **Tamora**[14] 1197 4-8-11 45 — (v) JamieSpencer 7 — 57
(A P Jarvis) *led for 2f: led again over 2f out: pushed out fnl f: comf* **7/1**[3]

6463 **2** 1¾ **Veneer (IRE)**[6] 1387 4-8-11 45 — JimmyQuinn 5 — 52
(Miss Gay Kelleway) *hld up: gd hdwy over 1f out: to chse wnr fnl f* **5/1**[1]

0664 **3** 1½ **Gaudalpin (IRE)**[33] 889 4-8-11 45 — (t) JohnEgan 9 — 48
(Ernst Oertel) *mid-div: rdn and hdwy appr fnl f: kpt on* **15/2**

000- **4** 1 **Zantero**[131] 6677 4-8-11 45 — ChrisCatlin 8 — 46
(W M Brisbourne) *hld up in rr: hdwy on outside over 1f out: r.o: nvr nrr* **33/1**

6403 **5** nk **Spanish Music**[6] 1391 4-8-11 45 — DaneO'Neill 12 — 45
(R Ingram) *hld up: hdwy whn sltly hmpd ins fnl f* **8/1**

0001 **6** 1¼ **Inescapable (USA)**[6] 1393 5-9-3 40 — MickyFenton 10 — 47
(A W Carroll) *chsd ldrs tl fdd appr fnl f* **16/1**

00-0 **7** ¾ **African Star**[13] 1212 5-8-11 45 — RyanMoore 2 — 40
(J M Bradley) *bhd: mde sme late hdwy but nvr on terms* **50/1**

4-66 **8** ½ **Orpen Quest (IRE)**[117] 92 4-8-11 45 — EddieAhern 6 — 38
(M J Attwater) *bhd: effrt 2f out: one pce after* **11/2**[2]

00-0 **9** hd **Bakke**[13] 1227 4-8-11 45 — (bt) LPKeniry 11 — 38
(B I Case) *prom: rdn over 2f out: wknd over 1f out* **25/1**

6000 **10** 1½ **Angel River**[9] 1305 4-8-4 40 — (b[1]) DonnaCaldwell(7) 4 — 34
(J Ryan) *bhd: making hdwy whn n.m.r over 1f out: nvr a danger* **66/1**

6004 **11** 1½ **Barachois Gaudy**[41] 778 4-8-11 45 — OscarUrbina 13 — 30
(Mrs N Smith) *mid-div: rdn over 2f out: wknd over 1f out* **5/1**[1]

00-0 **12** 2 **Savernake Brave (IRE)**[49] 682 5-8-6 45 — (b) RichardKingscote(5) 1 — 25
(Mrs H Sweeting) *led after 2f: hdd 2f out: sn wknd* **25/1**

0-62 **13** 1 **Mescalera (GER)**[6] 1393 5-8-11 40 — JimmyFortune 14 — 22
(B G Powell) *in tch: wknd over 2f out* **8/1**

0300 **14** 9 **Wodhill Be**[13] 1227 6-8-11 45 — MichaelTebbutt 3 — —
(D Morris) *trckd ldrs tl wknd over 2f out* **16/1**

1m 26.67s **Going Correction** -0.075s/f (Stan) — 14 Ran SP% **121.1**
Speed ratings (Par 97):97,95,93,92,91 90,89,88,88,87 85,83,81,71
CSF £40.28 TOTE £9.40: £2.80, £2.50, £5.20; EX 34.40.

Owner Eurostrait Ltd **Bred** Miss S N Ralphs **Trained** Twyford, Bucks

FOCUS
A standard banded contest run at a reasonable pace, and the form looks sound enough.

1539 RACING UK BANDED STKS — 6f (P)

4:20 (4:21) (Class 7) 4-Y-0+ — £1,706 (£503; £252) Stalls High

Form — RPR

01-2 **1** **Forest Dane**[33] 886 6-9-2 50 — OscarUrbina 3 — 59
(Mrs N Smith) *hld up in tch: hdwy to ld wl over 1f out: rdn out* **5/1**[2]

30-3 **2** ½ **Rowanberry**[14] 1195 4-8-13 47 — JamieSpencer 8 — 54
(R M H Cowell) *t.k.h in mid-div: hdwy over 1f out: rdn to go 2nd nr fin* **4/1**[1]

0002 **3** hd **Marshallspark (IRE)**[6] 1397 7-8-13 47 — (p) TonyHamilton 1 — 53
(R A Fahey) *a front rnk: led briefly 2f out: r.o but lost 2nd nr fin* **13/2**[3]

6000 **4** 3 **Jennverse**[33] 889 4-8-12 46 — JohnEgan 7 — 43
(D K Ivory) *hld up in rr: rdn and hdwy over 1f out: nvr nrr* **12/1**

-451 **5** nk **Lauren Louise**[84] 396 4-8-12 49 — AdamKirby(3) 5 — 46
(T T Clement) *towards rr: mde sme late hdwy: nvr nrr* **20/1**

0026 **6** 1¼ **Stagnite**[8] 1310 6-9-0 48 — (p) MatthewHenry 4 — 41
(K McAuliffe) *led tl over 2f out: wknd appr fnl f* **10/1**

0043 **7** 1 **Double M**[33] 886 9-8-13 50 — (v) RichardThomas(3) 2 — 40
(Mrs L Richards) *hld up in tch: rdn 2f out: sn wknd* **10/1**

2141 **8** shd **Misty Princess**[14] 1196 4-9-1 49 — EddieAhern 10 — 38
(M J Attwater) *in tch tl wknd over 1f out* **8/1**

0030 **9** ½ **Goldhill Prince**[8] 1310 4-9-1 49 — (p) JimmyFortune 6 — 37
(Ernst Oertel) *in tch tl rdn and wknd appr fnl f* **25/1**

0023 **10** ½ **New Options**[6] 1396 9-8-13 47 — (b) GylesParkin 9 — 33
(Peter Grayson) *a bhd* **16/1**

5023 **11** 1¼ **Border Artist**[14] 1196 7-9-1 49 — (b) GeorgeBaker 12 — 32
(B G Powell) *in tch: rdn 2f out: noyt much room appr fnl f: sn btn* **7/1**

05-0 **12** 3½ **Beau Marche**[9] 1303 4-8-12 46 — JimmyQuinn 11 — 18
(G G Margarson) *prom: wkng whn hmpd over 1f out* **25/1**

1m 13.88s **Going Correction** -0.075s/f (Stan) — 12 Ran SP% **117.8**
Speed ratings (Par 97):95,94,94,90,89 88,86,86,85,85 83,78
CSF £24.39 TOTE £5.00: £2.10, £2.30, £2.50; EX 34.20.

Owner The Ember Partnership **Bred** Loan And Development Corporation **Trained** Bury, W Sussex

■ Stewards' Enquiry : George Baker two-day ban: careless riding (May 19,21)

FOCUS
An ordinary banded sprint and pretty sound form rated around the runner-up and third.

Goldhill Prince Official explanation: jockey said gelding was short of room first bend

1540 KEMPTON FOR TEAM BUILDING EVENTS BANDED STKS — 2m (P)

4:50 (4:53) (Class 7) 4-Y-0+ — £1,706 (£503; £252) Stalls High

Form — RPR

010 **1** **Galantos (GER)**[13] 1219 5-9-4 49 — GeorgeBaker 7 — 60+
(G L Moore) *mid-div: rdn and hdwy to ld 2f out: rdn out fnl f* **15/2**

-300 **2** 2½ **Olivino (GER)**[75] 482 5-9-5 50 — JamieSpencer 11 — 58
(S Dow) *hld up in tch: hdwy 2f out to chse wnr over fr over 1f out* **10/3**[1]

0233 **3** 1½ **Twentytwosilver (IRE)**[14] 891 6-9-0 45 — MichaelTebbutt 12 — 54+
(D B Feek) *slowly away and hld up in rr: hmpd 2f out: styd on fr over 1f out: nvr nrr* **8/1**

4023 **4** 3½ **Lysander's Quest (IRE)**[6] 1392 8-9-0 45 — DaneO'Neill 3 — 47
(R Ingram) *hld up: hdwy to chse ldrs over 3f out: ever ch 2f out: wknd fnl f* **9/2**[2]

0-00 **5** 2 **War Feather**[33] 891 4-8-11 45 — RobertHavlin 9 — 44
(T D McCarthy) *in rr: hdwy and styd on fnl 2f: nvr nrr* **20/1**

3046 **6** 2½ **Iamback**[6] 1392 6-9-0 45 — (t) TPQueally 4 — 41
(Miss D A McHale) *in tch: rdn over 2f out: one pce after* **16/1**

00-5 **7** 5 **Victor Buckwell**[8] 1313 4-8-11 45 — RyanMoore 5 — 35
(G L Moore) *slowly away: bhd: effrt 2f out: one pce after* **6/1**[3]

6-63 **8** 6 **Ulshaw**[8] 1313 9-9-0 40 — LPKeniry 14 — 28
(J M Bradley) *mid-div: wknd 2f out* **14/1**

3-00 **9** 2 **Garple Burn**[31] 904 4-8-8 45 — (p) AmirQuinn(3) 2 — 26
(Jim Best) *trckd ldrs: wkng whn hmpd over 1f out* **50/1**

23-0 **10** ½ **Trials 'n Tribs**[21] 1058 4-9-2 50 — MartinDwyer 1 — 30
(C A Cyzer) *prom tl wknd over 1f out* **8/1**

0050 **11** 8 **Ready Teddy Go**[8] 1313 4-8-11 40 — (p) MickyFenton 10 — 16
(J Ryan) *led tl hdd 2f out: wknd rapidly* **100/1**

000- **12** 13 **Looking Great (USA)**[10] 3595 4-8-11 45 — StephenCarson 6 — —
(R F Johnson Houghton) *trckd ldrs: rdn over 5f out: sn dropped rr* **25/1**

0/0- **13** 3½ **Valet**[387] 1054 4-8-11 40 — FergusSweeney 8 — —
(J G M O'Shea) *in tch: hung rt on bnds turning away fr stands: bhd fnl 5f* **50/1**

3m 31.3s **Going Correction** -0.075s/f (Stan)
WFA 4 from 5yo+ 3lb — 13 Ran SP% **115.6**
Speed ratings (Par 97):97,95,95,93,92 91,88,85,84,84 80,73,72
CSF £30.17 TOTE £9.30: £3.80, £1.50, £2.60; EX 49.20.

Owner David Allen **Bred** R Zimmer **Trained** Woodingdean, E Sussex

FOCUS
Not that bad a race by banded standards, and the winner could have more to offer.

Twentytwosilver(IRE) Official explanation: jockey said, regarding the running and riding, his orders were to hold gelding up and come between horses in the home straight, but he met with interference several times and by the time he got a clear run the race was effectively over
Valet Official explanation: jockey said gelding hung badly left

1541 R.H.T. BANDED STKS — 1m 4f (P)

5:20 (5:22) (Class 7) 4-Y-0+ — £1,706 (£503; £252) Stalls Low

Form — RPR

1-00 **1** **Ndola**[77] 469 7-8-11 45 — (v[1]) JamieSpencer 11 — 50+
(B J Curley) *led for 1f: styd prom: rdn to ld over 1f out: kpt up to work* **5/4**[1]

4505 **2** 2½ **Opera Knight**[14] 1198 6-8-11 45 — JimmyFortune 7 — 46
(A W Carroll) *hld up in tch: racd 2nd fr 1/2-way tl over 1f out: rallied to regain 2nd wl ins fnl f* **13/2**

-060 **3** 1¼ **Icannshift (IRE)**[8] 1313 6-8-11 40 — FergusSweeney 5 — 44
(T M Jones) *led after 1f: rdn and hdd over 1f out: lost 2nd wl ins fnl f* **14/1**

0/3- **4** shd **Misbehaviour**[60] 1107 7-8-11 35 — TPQueally 1 — 44+
(G L Moore) *hld up: hdwy over 1f out: styd on: fnl f: nvr nrr* **9/2**[2]

3/00 **5** ¾ **One Alone**[40] 794 5-8-11 35 — (b) StephenCarson 10 — 43
(Jean-Rene Auvray) *hld up: hdwy over 3f out: rdn and wknd ent fnl f* **50/1**

00-0 **6** shd **Plain Champagne (IRE)**[13] 1214 4-8-8 45 — RichardThomas(3) 2 — 42
(Dr J R J Naylor) *t.k.h: prom tl hung rt and wknd over 1f out* **33/1**

6-45 **7** ¾ **Ambersong**[8] 284 8-8-11 45 — MickyFenton 3 — 41
(A W Carroll) *hld up in rr: effort 2f out but nt pce to chal* **16/1**

600- **8** ½ **Our Glenard**[159] 5656 7-8-11 40 — SamHitchcott 8 — 40
(J E Long) *slowly away: nvr on terms* **33/1**

504- **9** 3½ **Top Trees**[131] 6678 8-8-11 45 — LPKeniry 9 — 35
(W S Kittow) *chsd ldrs tl rdn and wknd 2f out* **11/2**[3]

0000 **10** 5 **Fortunes Favourite**[6] 1395 6-8-6 40 — NataliaGemelova(5) 12 — 27
(J E Long) *a in rr* **66/1**

000- **11** shd **Gran Clicquot**[168] 6394 11-8-6 40 — RobynBrisland(5) 4 — 27
(G P Enright) *mid-div: rdn 2f out: sn wknd* **66/1**

/356 **12** 1¾ **Bhutan (IRE)**[10] 1271 11-8-8 45 — AmirQuinn(3) 6 — 24
(Jim Best) *chsd ldrs tl wknd over 2f out* **16/1**

2m 36.85s **Going Correction** -0.075s/f (Stan) — 12 Ran SP% **120.6**
Speed ratings (Par 97):97,95,94,94,93 93,93,93,90,87 87,86
CSF £9.71 TOTE £2.80: £1.40, £1.10, £3.80; EX 12.90 Place 6 £219.47, Place 5 £71.51.

Owner Curley Leisure **Bred** Loan And Development Corporation **Trained** Newmarket, Suffolk

FOCUS
An ordinary banded event, but Ndola is a cut-above this level.

Our Glenard Official explanation: jockey said gelding had a breathing problem
Fortunes Favourite Official explanation: jockey said mare was hampered shortly after start

T/Plt: £335.70 to a £1 stake. Pool: £28,995.65. 63.05 winning tickets. T/Qpdt: £33.20 to a £1 stake. Pool: £2,429.70. 54.10 winning tickets. JS

[1354]WINDSOR (R-H)

Monday, May 8

OFFICIAL GOING: Soft

Wind: Nil Weather: Fine but cloudy

1542 WELCOME TO MONDAY NIGHTS WITH VCCASINO.COM MAIDEN AUCTION FILLIES' STKS 5f 10y

5:50 (5:51) (Class 5) 2-Y-O **£3,238** (£963; £481; £240) **Stalls** High

Form RPR

25 **1** **Camissa**[14] 1189 2-8-6 MartinDwyer 16 71
(D K Ivory) *racd nr side: led gp thrght: overall ldr fr 3f out: drvn and flashed tail over 1f out: styd on* **11/2**[2]

2 *2 ½* **Princess Ileana (IRE)** 2-8-8 FrancisNorton 8 64+
(K R Burke) *dwlt: sn chsd ldrs on far side: effrt to ld gp 1f out: styd on but nt on terms w wnr* **28/1**

3 *nk* **Baltic Belle (IRE)** 2-8-13 RichardHughes 3 68+
(R Hannon) *dwlt: w far side ldrs: led gp over 1f out to 1f out: kpt on same pce* **8/1**

3 **4** *shd* **Cassiara**[32] 892 2-8-6 JimmyQuinn 1 61+
(J Pearce) *racd far side: w ldrs: one pce u.p fnl f* **9/4**[1]

5 *hd* **Whipchord (IRE)** 2-8-6 RyanMoore 14 60
(R Hannon) *racd nr side: nvr on terms w wnr: kpt on u.p fnl f* **9/1**

6 *shd* **Our Ruby** 2-8-8 AdrianMcCarthy 13 61
(P W Chapple-Hyam) *mostly chsd wnr nr side but no imp fr 1/2-way: kpt on u.p* **16/1**

7 *1 ¼* **Lady Firecracker (IRE)** 2-8-6 TQuinn 9 55+
(J R Best) *chsd far side ldrs: swtchd rt and rdn over 1f out: styd on but nvr able to chal* **25/1**

8 *1* **River Rosie (IRE)** 2-8-6 EddieAhern 10 51
(J G Portman) *dwlt: racd nr side: a last of quartet: kpt on* **33/1**

9 *5* **Inflight (IRE)** 2-8-3 NelsonDeSouza(3) 15 33
(R M Beckett) *dwlt: swtchd to r far side over 3f out and w ldrs: wknd over 1f out* **10/1**

04 **10** *nk* **Banana Belle**[35] 856 2-8-4 AlanMunro 6 30
(A J Lidderdale) *racd far side: overall ldr for 2f: led gp to over 1f out: wknd* **66/1**

3 **11** *¾* **Three Decades (IRE)**[12] 1242 2-8-13 LDettori 11 37+
(C A Cyzer) *swtchd to r far side after 1f and w ldrs: wknd over 1f out* **13/2**[3]

12 *1 ¼* **Party Palace** 2-8-10 ShaneKelly 7 29
(J A Osborne) *racd far side: off the pce and pushed along 3f out: no prog* **40/1**

13 *1 ½* **Suzieblue (IRE)** 2-8-6 JohnEgan 4 20
(J S Moore) *s.s: racd far side: a struggling* **25/1**

14 *¾* **Auction Oasis** 2-8-4 FrancisFerris 5 15
(B Palling) *racd far side: sn outpcd and wl off the pce: sme prog 2f out: wknd and eased fnl f* **50/1**

15 *25* **Fair 'n Square (IRE)** 2-8-4 ChrisCatlin 2 —
(J L Spearing) *sn outpcd far side: t.o and green fr 1/2-way* **25/1**

62.04 secs (0.94) **Going Correction** +0.05s/f (Good) **15** Ran SP% **119.4**
Speed ratings (Par 90):94,90,89,89,89 88,86,85,77,76 75,73,71,70,30
CSF £157.98 TOTE £6.00: £2.30, £7.70, £3.90; EX 307.20.
Owner K T Ivory **Bred** D K Ivory **Trained** Radlett, Herts

FOCUS
A modest fillies' maiden, which saw no real advantage with the draw, and the winner did the job nicely.

NOTEBOOK
Camissa stuck to the favoured stands'-side rail and readily broke her duck at the third attempt. She appreciated racing against her own sex once again, handled the easy ground without fuss, and should be high on confidence for the step up to a higher level now. (op 9-2 tchd 6-1 in places)
Princess Ileana(IRE), bred to make her mark as a juvenile, took time to find her stride after a sluggish start yet was keeping on with promise towards the finish. Being by Danetime, it was little surprise she proved suited by the easy surface, and she is entitled to improve a deal for this debut experience.
Baltic Belle(IRE), a half-sister to winning spinter Gone'N'Dunnet among others, showed promise and looks assured to improve for the experience. She ought to be placed to break her duck in the coming weeks. (op 5-1 tchd 9-1)
Cassiara, a promising third at Leicester on her debut 32 days previously, did nothing wrong in defeat and turned in another sound effort. She has shown in her last two outings that she handles cut in the ground, but her dam's best efforts came on a quick surface, so she may be capable of better when encountering faster underfoot conditions. (op 5-2 tchd 11-4)
Whipchord(IRE), bred to appreciate further than this, chased the winner throughout on the stands' side and ought to come into her own when faced with a sixth furlong. (op 11-1)

1543 PLAY BLACKJACK AT VCCASINO.COM H'CAP 1m 3f 135y

6:20 (6:20) (Class 5) (0-75,75) 3-Y-O **£3,238** (£963; £481; £240) **Stalls** Low

Form RPR

50-1 **1** **Free To Air**[13] 1216 3-9-4 **75** LDettori 2 84+
(A M Balding) *hld up: prog over 3f out: rdn to ld narrowly 1f out: jst hld upper hand last 150yds* **10/3**[1]

6-34 **2** *hd* **Strategic Mount**[14] 1193 3-9-1 **72** TQuinn 6 81
(P F I Cole) *pressed ldr: rdn to ld jst over 2f out: narrowly hdd 1f out: battled on wl but jst hld ins fnl f* **9/2**[3]

004- **3** *5* **Cape Secret (IRE)**[189] 6199 3-8-2 **62** NelsonDeSouza(3) 11 63+
(R M Beckett) *hld up: last pair 5f out: swtchd lft and rdn over 3f out: kpt on u.p fnl 2f: no imp ldng pair* **7/1**

000- **4** *1 ¾* **Rehearsed (IRE)**[200] 5995 3-8-8 **65** MickyFenton 4 63
(H Morrison) *in tch: rdn to chse ldng pair over 3f out to over 2f out: one pce* **14/1**

1035 **5** *6* **Ballybeg (IRE)**[14] 1193 3-8-10 **67** RichardHughes 9 56
(R Hannon) *led to jst over 2f out: hanging lft and wknd over 1f out* **11/1**

4-21 **6** *5* **Dark Planet**[11] 1251 3-8-7 **64** RyanMoore 10 45
(C E Brittain) *trckd ldrs: rdn 4f out: wknd over 2f out* **6/1**

-061 **7** *3 ½* **Raise The Heights (IRE)**[16] 1140 3-8-6 **63** EddieAhern 8 38
(C Tinkler) *trckd ldrs: rdn over 3f out: wknd over 2f out* **4/1**[2]

-404 **8** *9* **Eclipse Park**[51] 668 3-8-12 **69** ShaneKelly 5 30
(M J McGrath) *v s.i.s: in tch in last pair after 3f: pushed lft over 3f out: no prog over 2f out: wknd* **25/1**

0-50 **9** *shd* **Life Peer**[21] 1052 3-8-6 **63** JohnEgan 1 23
(J G Portman) *hld up: shkn up and no prog over 3f out: wknd and eased fnl 2f* **25/1**

2m 30.48s (0.38) **Going Correction** +0.05s/f (Good) **9** Ran SP% **110.7**
Speed ratings (Par 99):100,99,96,95,91 88,85,79,79
CSF £17.09 CT £91.51 TOTE £3.10: £1.60, £1.70, £2.70; EX 13.10.
Owner Miss Clare Balding **Bred** Robert Charles Key **Trained** Kingsclere, Hants

FOCUS
A fair handicap for the class, run at an average pace, and the first two came clear. Solid enough form.
Eclipse Park Official explanation: jockey said gelding had thrown its head back leaving the stalls
Life Peer Official explanation: jockey said gelding had had no more to give

1544 VCCASINO.COM H'CAP 1m 2f 7y

6:50 (6:50) (Class 4) (0-85,85) 4-Y-O+ **£6,477** (£1,927; £963; £481) **Stalls** Low

Form RPR

40-0 **1** **Cool Hunter**[16] 1133 5-8-11 **78** JamieSpencer 15 90
(W R Swinburn) *trckd ldng pair: led on inner 2f out: drvn and in command fnl f* **15/2**[3]

220- **2** *1 ¼* **Folio (IRE)**[203] 5948 6-8-9 **76** TPQueally 7 86
(W J Musson) *hld up in rr: stdy prog fr over 2f out: rdn to chse wnr fnl f: styd on but no imp* **50/1**

332- **3** *1* **Feed The Meter (IRE)**[318] 2888 6-8-5 **75** SaleemGolam(3) 11 83
(J Ryan) *hld up wl in rr: prog on wd outside fr over 2f out: drvn and styd on: nvr nrr* **12/1**

50-0 **4** *hd* **Day To Remember**[7] 1357 5-9-2 **83** (t) SebSanders 13 91
(E F Vaughan) *trckd ldng gp: prog 3f out: rdn to chal 2f out: hung lft and nt qckn over 1f out: one pce after* **5/1**[1]

00-4 **5** *1 ¾* **Transvestite (IRE)**[16] 1133 4-8-9 **76** EddieAhern 9 81+
(J W Hills) *chsd ldng gp: effrt over 2f out: nt clr run briefly wl over 1f out: styd on: nt pce to rch ldrs* **15/2**[3]

61-0 **6** *2 ½* **Kingsholm**[9] 1302 4-8-11 **78** MartinDwyer 5 78
(A M Balding) *racd freely: led for 2f: chsd ldr to over 2f out: wknd fnl f* **7/1**[2]

2011 **7** *½* **Kylkenny**[62] 610 11-8-6 **78** TravisBlock(5) 14 77
(P D Cundell) *led after 2f to 2f out: wknd jst over 1f out* **12/1**

1-00 **8** *¾* **Parnassian**[21] 1051 6-8-2 **72** RichardThomas(3) 6 70
(J A Geake) *rrd s: hld up wl in rr: prog on outer over 3f out: cl up 2f out: wknd sn after* **9/1**

450/ **9** *½* **First Centurion**[57] 6396 5-8-2 **72** oh1 ow1 EdwardCreighton(3) 17 69
(Ian Williams) *dwlt: hld up in last pair: stl in last pair over 2f out: taken to outer and kpt on: no ch* **66/1**

60-0 **10** *½* **Liakoura (GER)**[16] 1133 4-9-2 **83** RyanMoore 3 79
(Mrs A J Perrett) *chsd ldrs: rdn over 3f out: grad fdd fnl 2f* **10/1**

/0-0 **11** *¾* **Eldorado**[13] 1206 5-8-5 **72** FrankieMcDonald 19 67
(S Kirk) *chsd ldrs: rdn on inner 3f out: wknd and hanging 2f out* **33/1**

3-05 **12** *¾* **Diamond Diggins (GER)**[9] 1306 4-8-4 **71** oh1 ChrisCatlin 2 64
(V Smith) *prom: drvn 3f out: lost pl and struggling over 2f out* **40/1**

306- **13** *hd* **Evolution Ex (USA)**[232] 5342 4-8-11 **78** FrancisNorton 12 71+
(K R Burke) *hld up towards rr: shuffled along briefly over 2f out: eased fnl f* **16/1**

30-0 **14** *5* **Takafu (USA)**[13] 1206 4-8-10 **77** FergusSweeney 16 61
(W S Kittow) *chsd ldng gp: rdn 3f out: wknd rapidly jst over 2f out* **50/1**

41-1 **15** *2* **Let Slip**[15] 1162 4-8-8 **75** AlanMunro 1 55
(W Jarvis) *prom: chsng ldrs over 3f out: wknd rapidly over 2f out* **15/2**[3]

241- **16** *6* **Stolen Hours (USA)**[312] 3035 6-8-10 **77** TQuinn 18 47
(J Akehurst) *dwlt: a in last pair: no prog fnl 3f* **16/1**

2m 8.19s (-0.11) **Going Correction** +0.05s/f (Good) **16** Ran SP% **121.5**
Speed ratings (Par 105):102,101,100,100,98 96,96,95,95,94 94,93,93,89,87 83
CSF £362.04 CT £4415.06 TOTE £10.20: £2.70, £15.10, £2.90, £1.40; EX 582.00.
Owner Mrs P W Harris **Bred** Cheveley Park Stud Ltd **Trained** Aldbury, Herts

FOCUS
A fair handicap, run at a sound pace, and the form looks straightforward enough.
Evolution Ex(USA) Official explanation: jockey said gelding was unsuited by the soft going
Stolen Hours(USA) Official explanation: jockey said horse was unsuited by the soft going

1545 PLAY AT VCCASINO.COM H'CAP 6f

7:20 (7:20) (Class 4) (0-80,79) 4-Y-O+ **£6,477** (£1,927; £963; £481) **Stalls** High

Form RPR

3004 **1** **Sir Desmond**[9] 1285 8-8-12 **73** (p) ChrisCatlin 9 83
(Rae Guest) *towards rr: rdn 1/2-way: prog on outer over 1f out: styd on strly fnl f to ld nr fin* **6/1**[1]

4013 **2** *hd* **Nautical**[14] 1188 8-8-8 **74** JamesDoyle(5) 7 83
(A W Carroll) *hld up wl in rr: prog over 1f out: styd on strly fnl f w wnr: jst hld* **15/2**[3]

-406 **3** *¾* **Roman Quintet (IRE)**[28] 949 6-8-10 **71** EddieAhern 15 78
(D W P Arbuthnot) *trckd ldr on inner: led 2f out: clr 1f out: wknd and hdd nr fin* **15/2**[3]

0-00 **4** *2 ½* **Extremely Rare (IRE)**[14] 1188 5-8-10 **71** MickyFenton 16 71
(M S Saunders) *led: hung lft and hdd 2f out: continued to hang lft and fdd fnl f* **7/1**[2]

005- **5** *1 ¼* **Ingleton**[186] 6238 4-8-11 **72** TPQueally 1 68
(G L Moore) *hld up wl in rr: effrt on outer 2f out: hanging bdly lft but kpt on: n.d* **10/1**

000- **6** *nk* **Loyal Tycoon (IRE)**[190] 6182 8-9-1 **76** MartinDwyer 5 71
(D K Ivory) *prom: drvn and outpcd fr 2f out: n.d after* **16/1**

0-00 **7** *1* **Royal Orissa**[9] 1285 4-9-2 **77** (t) RobertHavlin 12 69+
(D Haydn Jones) *dwlt: chsd ldng gp: nt on terms and struggling fr 2f out* **25/1**

00-0 **8** *1 ¼* **Prince Cyrano**[28] 949 7-8-10 **71** LPKeniry 14 59
(W J Musson) *dwlt: chsd ldng gp on inner: outpcd fr 2f out: n.d after* **33/1**

30-3 **9** *1* **Devon Flame**[28] 947 7-9-3 **78** RichardHughes 6 63
(R J Hodges) *prom tl lost pl u.p over 2f out: no ch after* **6/1**[1]

4160 **10** *1* **Marko Jadeo (IRE)**[51] 667 8-8-13 **74** DaneO'Neill 10 56
(S Dow) *s.v.s: nvr any ch to rcvr: r.o ins fnl f* **14/1**

404- **11** *1* **Born To Be Bold**[203] 5951 4-8-8 **72** RichardSmith(3) 13 51
(R Hannon) *chsd ldrs to 1/2-way: sn wknd* **14/1**

046- **12** *½* **Go Mo (IRE)**[190] 6182 4-9-3 **78** JimmyFortune 8 56
(S Kirk) *dwlt: nvr beyond midfield: struggling over 2f out* **12/1**

020- **13** *2* **Bowness**[217] 5660 4-9-4 **79** SebSanders 3 51
(J G Given) *chsd ldrs to 1/2-way: wknd* **14/1**

450- **14** *1 ½* **Meikle Barfil**[184] 6263 4-8-13 **74** RyanMoore 11 41
(J M Bradley) *racd freely: w ldrs to 1/2-way: wknd rapidly* **20/1**

1m 13.2s (-0.47) **Going Correction** +0.05s/f (Good) **14** Ran SP% **118.8**
Speed ratings (Par 105):105,104,103,100,98 98,97,95,94,92 91,90,88,86
CSF £47.50 CT £355.75 TOTE £6.80: £2.50, £2.60, £3.40; EX 26.00.
Owner Davies, Guest and Mccabe **Bred** M G T Stokes **Trained** Newmarket, Suffolk

FOCUS
A fair sprint for the grade, which again saw no distinct advantage with the draw, and the first three came clear. Pretty straightforward form to rate through the third.
Devon Flame Official explanation: jockey said gelding was unsuited by the soft going
Marko Jadeo(IRE) Official explanation: jockey said gelding missed the break

1546 VCCASINO.COM MAIDEN STKS 1m 2f 7y
7:50 (7:53) (Class 5) 3-Y-0 £3,886 (£1,156; £577; £288) Stalls Low

Form RPR
6 1 **Sixties Icon**[20] 1070 3-9-3 ShaneKelly 4 89
(J Noseda) *pressed ldr: rn green and hanging lft 2f out: shkn up to ld ent fnl f: r.o wl* 6/4[1]
6- 2 ¾ **Fleeting Memory**[230] 5391 3-8-12 (t) RyanMoore 13 83
(Sir Michael Stoute) *led: set stdy pce tl kicked on over 3f out: drvn over 1f out: hdd ent fnl f: r.o but readily hld* 3/1[2]
22- 3 7 **Pigeon Island**[143] 6588 3-9-3 DaneO'Neill 10 75
(H Candy) *trckd ldrs: effrt over 2f out: easily outpcd by ldng pair fr over 1f out* 7/2[3]
54-3 4 3 ½ **Forroger (CAN)**[18] 1100 3-9-3 80 ChrisCatlin 14 69
(V Smith) *chsd ldrs: pushed along over 3f out: rdn and outpcd fnl 2f* 4/1
6 5 1 ¾ **Petito (IRE)**[9] 1290 3-9-3 FergusSweeney 2 66
(Ian Williams) *dwlt: hld up in last trio: shuffled along fr over 2f out: kpt on steadily but easily outpcd by ldrs* 100/1
6 6 ¾ **Monmouthshire**[11] 1260 3-9-3 HayleyTurner 3 64
(M L W Bell) *prom: chsd ldng pair 4f out to over 2f out: wknd wl over 1f out* 66/1
00 7 1 ¾ **Jack Absolute (IRE)**[17] 1120 3-9-3 MichaelTebbutt 7 61
(B J Meehan) *hld up in midfield: shkn up over 2f out: sn wknd* 50/1
8 ¾ **Dab Hand (IRE)** 3-9-3 LPKeniry 5 60
(D M Simcock) *dwlt: hld up in midfield: shkn up over 2f out: wknd wl over 1f out* 100/1
9 5 **Woolsey** 3-9-3 FrancisNorton 11 51
(M Blanshard) *dwlt: hld up in last trio: shkn up and lft bhd fr over 2f out* 100/1
05- 10 11 **Sahf London**[219] 5597 3-8-12 RobynBrisland(5) 12 31
(G L Moore) *plld hrd: in tch to 3f out: sn bhd: sddle slipped* 100/1
11 24 **With Admiration** 3-9-3 TPQueally 1 —
(C Drew) *hld up in rr: wd bnds 6f out and 5f out: wknd rapidly 3f out: t.o* 100/1

2m 11.0s (2.70) **Going Correction** +0.05s/f (Good) 11 Ran SP% 115.6
Speed ratings (Par 99):91,90,84,82,80 80,78,78,74,65 46
CSF £6.12 TOTE £2.40: £1.10, £2.20, £1.50; EX 8.80.
Owner Mrs Susan Roy **Bred** Lordship Stud **Trained** Newmarket, Suffolk
FOCUS
A fair maiden that produced a very moderate winning time for the class, almost three seconds slower than the earlier handicap, due to the sedate early pace. The first two came clear.
Sahf London Official explanation: jockey said saddle slipped

1547 MONDAY NIGHT RACING WITH VCCASINO.COM H'CAP 1m 67y
8:20 (8:20) (Class 5) (0-75,75) 3-Y-0 £3,238 (£963; £481; £240) Stalls High

Form RPR
34-0 1 **Ingratitude (IRE)**[21] 1048 3-9-4 75 SebSanders 11 94
(R M Beckett) *hld up in midfield: prog over 2f out: drvn to chse ldr over 1f out: narrow ld ins fnl f: jst hld on* 11/1
60-2 2 shd **Plum Pudding (IRE)**[5] 1401 3-9-3 74 RyanMoore 13 93
(R Hannon) *chsd ldng pair: pushed along over 3f out: clsd to ld 2f out: hrd rdn over 1f out: hdd ins fnl f: jst pipped* 10/11[1]
0-04 3 12 **Miss Wedge**[12] 1241 3-8-9 66 IanMongan 4 61
(T G Mills) *pressed ldr at str pce: led briefly over 2f out: wknd over 1f out* 12/1
06-5 4 2 ½ **Fratt'n Park (IRE)**[12] 1241 3-8-9 66 TPQueally 10 56
(J J Bridger) *led at str pce: hdd over 2f out: sn wknd* 25/1
040- 5 nk **Gillipops (IRE)**[228] 5419 3-8-7 67 StephaneBreux(3) 5 56
(R Hannon) *chsd clr ldrs: hanging and no prog over 2f out: wknd* 25/1
550- 6 1 ½ **High Class Problem (IRE)**[223] 5524 3-8-10 67 ShaneKelly 2 53
(P F I Cole) *hld up towards rr and wl off the pce: hrd rdn over 2f out: no prog* 11/2[2]
400- 7 1 ¼ **The Struie**[193] 6120 3-8-10 67 OscarUrbina 1 51
(Miss J R Gibney) *hld up towards rr and off the pce: shkn up and no prog over 2f out: bhd after* 50/1
031- 8 nk **Altilhar (USA)**[193] 6121 3-9-4 75 GeorgeBaker 8 58
(G L Moore) *dwlt: hld up in last and wl off the pce: pushed along and no prog 3f out* 8/1[3]
640- 9 shd **Mad Professor (IRE)**[146] 6569 3-8-8 65 TQuinn 14 48
(D J S Ffrench Davis) *hld up in last pair and wl off the pce: nudged along fnl 2f: kpt on: nvr nr ldrs* 50/1
0-45 10 1 ¾ **Hill Of Almhuim (IRE)**[18] 1099 3-9-2 73 (v) FrancisNorton 3 53
(K R Burke) *settled in midfield and off the pce: hrd rdn over 3f out: no rspnse* 9/1

1m 44.25s (-1.35) **Going Correction** +0.05s/f (Good) 10 Ran SP% 116.5
Speed ratings (Par 99):108,107,95,93,93 91,90,90,89,88
CSF £20.93 CT £132.42 TOTE £12.80: £3.70, £1.10, £2.10; EX 30.60 Place 6 £43.43, Place 5 £9.51.
Owner Young Guns Syndicate **Bred** Mount Coote Stud **Trained** Whitsbury, Hants
FOCUS
A very decent winning time for a race of its type and the first two came well clear. The form should be treated with a degree of caution.
T/Plt: £45.10 to a £1 stake. Pool: £58,597.15. 946.85 winning tickets. T/Qpdt: £10.70 to a £1 stake. Pool: £4,936.60. 341.05 winning tickets. JN

1460 WOLVERHAMPTON (A.W) (L-H)
Monday, May 8

OFFICIAL GOING: Standard
Wind: Almost nil Weather: Raining first 4 races

1548 NAME A RACE TO ENHANCE YOUR BRAND CLAIMING STKS 1m 4f 50y(P)
2:30 (2:30) (Class 6) 4-Y-0+ £2,730 (£806; £403) Stalls Low

Form RPR
4210 1 **Zalkani (IRE)**[26] 983 6-9-3 72 KerrinMcEvoy 8 66
(J R Boyle) *s.i.s: hld up and bhd: smooth hdwy over 2f out: swtchd rt wl over 1f out: r.o wl to ld cl home* 7/2[2]
-120 2 nk **Principal Witness (IRE)**[96] 264 5-9-11 64 SteveDrowne 5 74
(Tom Dascombe) *a.p: rdn wl over 1f out: led ins fnl f: hdd cl home* 7/1
60-4 3 1 ¾ **Murrieta**[6] 1373 4-8-3 47 ow2 (v[1]) EdwardCreighton(3) 3 52
(Miss J R Gibney) *hld up in mid-div: hdwy on ins 3f out: rdn wl over 1f out: kpt on same pce fnl f* 40/1
3431 4 ½ **Chater Knight (IRE)**[10] 1271 5-8-11 57 (p) NCallan 2 56
(R A Harris) *t.k.h in tch: led 2f out: sn rdn: hdd ins fnl f: no ex* 2/1[1]
4222 5 3 ½ **York Cliff**[9] 1308 8-8-6 56 LiamJones(7) 4 53
(W M Brisbourne) *hld up in mid-div: rdn and hdwy on outside over 2f out: no real prog fnl f* 4/1[3]
2045 6 4 **Soviet Sceptre (IRE)**[14] 1199 5-9-0 50 (t) DarryllHolland 1 47
(R T Phillips) *set mod pce: qcknd over 6f out: hdd 2f out: sn rdn: wknd over 1f out* 13/2
0003 7 7 **Afadan (IRE)**[6] 1385 8-8-12 60 (vt) DeanCorby(3) 7 37
(J R Jenkins) *stdd s: t.k.h in rr: hdwy over 4f out: rdn over 2f out: sn wknd* 25/1
30-0 8 7 **Xacobeo (IRE)**[13] 1204 4-9-3 53 PatDobbs 11 28
(R Hannon) *hld up towards rr: hdwy over 4f out: rdn and wknd over 3f out* 50/1
430- 9 3 **Lazzaz**[318] 2877 8-8-6 48 SaleemGolam(3) 10 15
(P W Hiatt) *t.k.h: prom: rdn over 6f out: wknd 3f out* 25/1
0/0- 10 8 **Bevier**[287] 3797 12-8-5 40 ow3 StephanieHollinshead(5) 6 3
(T Wall) *a bhd* 40/1
000- 11 3 ½ **Millkom Elegance**[138] 6643 7-7-13 40 ow2 (v) JamesDoyle(5) 9 —
(G A Ham) *hld up in tch: rdn over 5f out: sn lost pl* 66/1

2m 40.81s (-1.61) **Going Correction** -0.125s/f (Stan) 11 Ran SP% 117.4
Speed ratings (Par 101):100,99,98,98,95 93,88,83,81,76 74
CSF £26.11 TOTE £4.90: £1.10, £3.00, £7.00; EX 36.90 Trifecta £254.70 Part won. Pool: £358.77 - 0.54 winning tickets..Zalkani was claimed by Jeff Pearce for £10,000. Principal Witness was claimed by R. E. R. Williams for £14,000.
Owner M Khan X2 **Bred** His Highness The Aga Khan's Studs S C **Trained** Epsom, Surrey
FOCUS
A mixed bag of abilities, but victory still went to the horse best in at the weights.
Millkom Elegance Official explanation: jockey said mare had no more to give

1549 STAY AT THE WOLVERHAMPTON HOLIDAY INN H'CAP 5f 216y(P)
3:00 (3:01) (Class 6) (0-60,60) 3-Y-0 £2,730 (£806; £403) Stalls Low

Form RPR
0-00 1 **Seesawmilu (IRE)**[13] 1226 3-8-4 46 oh1 AdrianTNicholls 12 57
(E J Alston) *hld up in tch: rdn 2f out: led ins fnl f: rdn out* 66/1
064- 2 1 ½ **Wednesdays Boy (IRE)**[182] 6282 3-8-13 58 PaulMulrennan(3) 9 64
(P D Niven) *hld up in mid-div: rdn over 2f out: hdwy over 1f out: r.o ins fnl f: nt rch wnr* 33/1
6631 3 1 **Spirit Of Coniston**[13] 1210 3-8-8 57 ow2 (v) RonanKeogh(7) 6 60
(Peter Grayson) *w ldr: hung lft and led over 1f out: hdd ins fnl f: nt qckn* 7/1[3]
1501 4 1 ¼ **Inaminute (IRE)**[16] 1149 3-8-13 60 AndrewElliott(5) 1 59+
(K R Burke) *chsd ldrs: rdn 2f out: nt clr run on ins and swtchd rt jst over 1f out: kpt on ins fnl f* 9/2[2]
040- 5 1 **Jakeini (IRE)**[163] 6435 3-9-4 60 GrahamGibbons 2 56
(E S McMahon) *led: hdd and bmpd over 1f out: wknd ins fnl f* 9/1
1000 6 1 **Drink To Me Only**[73] 500 3-8-10 52 DarryllHolland 4 45
(J R Weymes) *hld up in mid-div: rdn and no real prog fnl 2f* 9/2[2]
4302 7 nk **Otis B Driftwood**[13] 1210 3-8-13 55 (b) ShaneKelly 7 47
(M Quinn) *prom: rdn over 2f out: wkng whn edgd lft over 1f out* 16/1
6000 8 3 ½ **Nilsatisoptimum (USA)**[10] 1274 3-8-10 52 (b[1]) TedDurcan 5 34
(M Mullineaux) *nvr nr ldrs* 20/1
003- 9 nk **Creambiscuit**[236] 5219 3-8-13 60 JamesDoyle(5) 3 41
(N P Littmoden) *n.d: a bhd* 3/1[1]
0045 10 shd **Mon Petite Amour**[54] 642 3-8-6 48 FrankieMcDonald 8 29
(D W P Arbuthnot) *a bhd* 33/1
00-6 11 2 **Black Jade**[13] 1218 3-8-11 53 (p) PhilipRobinson 13 28
(M A Jarvis) *bhd fnl 3f* 9/1
-600 12 nk **Champagne Moment**[10] 1272 3-8-12 57 ow2 RossStudholme(3) 11 31
(V Smith) *a bhd* 100/1
000- 13 5 **Pink Pyjamas**[150] 6528 3-8-5 47 oh1 ow1 KerrinMcEvoy 10 6
(J A R Toller) *a bhd* 33/1

1m 15.42s (-0.39) **Going Correction** -0.125s/f (Stan) 13 Ran SP% 115.8
Speed ratings (Par 97):97,95,93,92,90 89,88,84,83,83 81,80,74
CSF £1455.04 CT £16432.50 TOTE £87.00: £12.80, £10.40, £1.60; EX 1944.90 TRIFECTA Not won..
Owner John And Maria Thompson, John Jackson **Bred** Gerard Keane **Trained** Longton, Lancs
■ Stewards' Enquiry : Ronan Keogh caution: careless riding
FOCUS
A moderate sprint handicap, but a solid pace thanks to a three-way battle for the early lead involving Jakeini, Spirit Of Coniston and Otis B Driftwood. It has been rated through the third.

1550 YOU CAN GET MARRIED AT WOLVERHAMPTON RACECOURSE (S) STKS 7f 32y(P)
3:30 (3:30) (Class 6) 3-Y-0+ £2,388 (£705; £352) Stalls High

Form RPR
1003 1 **Million Percent**[12] 1235 7-9-7 59 AndrewElliott(5) 3 78
(K R Burke) *hld up in tch: rdn to ld over 1f out: drvn clr ins fnl f* 12/1
3350 2 4 **Mission Affirmed (USA)**[10] 1275 5-9-6 60 (b) NCallan 4 62
(R A Harris) *sn chsng ldrs: rdn over 2f out: kpt on ins fnl f: no ch w wnr* 6/1[2]
20- 3 1 ½ **Pantomime Prince**[234] 5268 3-8-9 ow1 PatDobbs 6 55
(R Hannon) *hld up towards rr: rdn 4f out: hdwy on ins wl over 1f out: kpt on same pce fnl f* 16/1
5000 4 ¾ **Resplendent Prince**[13] 1217 4-9-12 60 (v) AdrianTNicholls 5 62
(P Howling) *led: hdd 4f out: rdn over 2f out: one pce* 33/1
0430 5 nk **Paso Doble**[10] 1271 8-8-13 57 (b) JamesMillman(7) 7 55
(B R Millman) *bhd tl hdwy over 1f out: n.d* 25/1
220- 6 shd **Prince Dayjur (USA)**[215] 5701 7-9-6 77 TedDurcan 11 55+
(J Pearce) *sn chsng ldrs: n.m.r 4f out: sn rdn and lost pl: rallied over 1f out: nvr trbld ldrs: fin lame* 10/11[1]
4432 7 nk **Wiltshire (IRE)**[33] 889 4-9-6 54 (v) GrahamGibbons 1 54
(P A Blockley) *prom: led 4f out: rdn and hdd over 1f out: wknd ins fnl f* 6/1[2]
0544 8 11 **Winning Venture**[9] 1303 9-9-7 52 JamesDoyle(5) 10 31
(A W Carroll) *sn w ldr: rdn over 3f out: wknd over 2f out* 33/1
1003 9 6 **Merdiff**[9] 1305 7-9-12 54 ShaneKelly 12 16
(W M Brisbourne) *hld up in tch: hung rt over 2f out: sn wknd* 20/1
00-0 10 1 ¾ **Desert Fantasy (IRE)**[16] 1129 7-9-6 97 DarryllHolland 9 5
(M Meade) *hld up and bhd: short-lived effrt on outside over 3f out* 10/1[3]
4130 11 50 **Jalouhar**[33] 889 6-9-5 50 KylieManser(7) 8 —
(J R Best) *s.i.s and n.m.r s: a bhd: t.o* 33/1

1m 29.16s (-1.24) **Going Correction** -0.125s/f (Stan)
WFA 3 from 4yo+ 12lb 11 Ran SP% 121.1
Speed ratings (Par 101):102,97,95,94,94 94,94,81,74,72 15
CSF £79.40 TOTE £19.20: £5.80, £2.50, £4.70; EX 94.50 TRIFECTA Not won..There was no bid for the winner. Pantomime Prince was claimed by C. A. Dwyer for £6,000.

Owner Spigot Lodge Partnership **Bred** D J And Mrs Deer **Trained** Middleham Moor, N Yorks
FOCUS
An above-average seller in which the pace was decent and the outcome dominated by those drawn in the lowest half of the field.
Prince Dayjur(USA) Official explanation: jockey said gelding finished lame behind
Winning Venture Official explanation: jockey said gelding ran too free
Desert Fantasy(IRE) Official explanation: jockey said gelding was reluctant to race

1551 WOLVERHAMPTON-RACECOURSE.CO.UK FILLIES' H'CAP 7f 32y(P)
4:00 (4:01) (Class 5) (0-70,70) 3-Y-O **£3,886** (£1,156; £577; £288) **Stalls** High

Form RPR
04-2 **1** **Deira (USA)**[19] 1078 3-9-4 **70** KerrinMcEvoy 3 81+
(C E Brittain) *led early: a.p: led over 1f out: pushed out* **9/4**[1]
531- **2** *3/4* **Imperial Lucky (IRE)**[216] 5681 3-8-9 **66** ow1 DerekNolan(5) 4 75
(M J Wallace) *hld up and bhd: hdwy on ins wl over 1f out: rdn to chse wnr fnl f: nt qckn* **9/1**
1-13 **3** *5* **Tour D'Amour (IRE)**[19] 1078 3-8-11 **66** PaulMulrennan(3) 10 62
(R Craggs) *a.p: rdn over 2f out: one pce* **9/1**
341- **4** *3/4* **Foreplay (IRE)**[133] 6661 3-9-2 **68** TedDurcan 6 62
(E A L Dunlop) *hld up in mid-div: rdn and hdwy over 1f out: one pce fnl f* **8/1**[3]
20-5 **5** *nk* **Shinko (IRE)**[9] 1307 3-8-6 **63** JamesDoyle(5) 11 56
(Miss J Feilden) *s.i.s: rdn over 3f out: hdwy on outside over 2f out: one pce fnl f* **33/1**
454- **6** *hd* **Fortress**[219] 5626 3-8-12 **64** GrahamGibbons 9 57
(E J Alston) *hld up in mid-div: rdn wl over 1f out: no hdwy* **16/1**
002- **7** *1/2* **Diamond De Triano (USA)**[185] 6242 3-8-12 **67** DanielTudhope(3) 7 58+
(P W Chapple-Hyam) *hld up towards rr: sme hdwy whn nt clr run 1f out: stmbld ins fnl f: nvr nrr* **7/2**[2]
20-5 **8** *nk* **Musical Romance (IRE)**[25] 1004 3-8-13 **65** DarryllHolland 12 56
(B J Meehan) *led after 1f: rdn and hdd over 1f out: wknd fnl f* **20/1**
2050 **9** *3/4* **Fangorn Forest (IRE)**[14] 1190 3-8-13 **65** (p) NCallan 5 54+
(R A Harris) *a bhd* **14/1**
36-4 **10** *1 1/4* **La Fanciulla**[41] 776 3-9-2 **68** PatDobbs 8 53
(R Hannon) *prom tl rdn and wknd over 1f out* **14/1**
244 **11** *nk* **Kasumi**[52] 658 3-8-10 **62** AdrianTNicholls 1 47
(H Morrison) *hld up in tch: lost pl over 3f out: sn bhd* **12/1**
1m 29.38s (-1.02) **Going Correction** -0.125s/f (Stan) **11** Ran SP% **118.7**
Speed ratings (Par 96):100,99,93,92,92 92,91,91,90,88 88
CSF £23.68 CT £160.97 TOTE £2.80: £1.50, £1.80, £2.30; EX 29.30 Trifecta £484.40 Part won. Pool: £682.30 - 0.40 winning tickets..
Owner Ali Saeed **Bred** Darley **Trained** Newmarket, Suffolk
FOCUS
An ordinary fillies' handicap, but the pace was solid and the time was very creditable for the type of contest. The front two pulled a mile clear and are probably capable of more.
Diamond De Triano(USA) Official explanation: jockey said filly was denied a clear run
Fangorn Forest(IRE) Official explanation: jockey said filly suffered interference at start

1552 HOLD YOUR CONFERENCE AT WOLVERHAMPTON RACECOURSE MEDIAN AUCTION MAIDEN STKS 1m 141y(P)
4:30 (4:32) (Class 5) 3-Y-O **£3,238** (£963; £481; £240) **Stalls** Low

Form RPR
30-6 **1** **King's Revenge**[21] 1048 3-9-3 75 TedDurcan 7 57+
(T D Easterby) *hld up in mid-div: pushed along over 5f out: rdn over 3f out: hdwy on outside over 1f out: styd on to ld nr fin* **6/5**[1]
0-4 **2** *1/2* **Empire Dancer (IRE)**[11] 1260 3-8-10 KirstyMilczarek(7) 4 56
(C N Allen) *t.k.h: led early: led over 6f out: rdn over 1f out: hdd nr fin* **8/1**[3]
0 **3** *nk* **Even Bolder**[16] 1134 3-9-3 PatDobbs 8 56+
(S Kirk) *sn led: hdd over 6f out: ev ch over 2f out: sn rdn: edgd lft 1f out: kpt on* **66/1**
3634 **4** *3/4* **Bahhmirage (IRE)**[8] 1314 3-8-12 47 (b) GrahamGibbons 6 49
(Stef Liddiard) *a.p: rdn over 2f out: hung lft ins fnl f: nt qckn* **14/1**
5 *1 1/4* **Polite Reply (USA)** 3-8-12 NCallan 3 46
(D M Simcock) *s.i.s: stdy hdwy over 5f out: rdn over 2f out: one pce whn hmpd ins fnl f* **25/1**
6 *hd* **Mexican Bob** 3-8-12 GregFairley(5) 9 51
(Heather Dalton) *hld up and bhd: rdn and hdwy 2f out: one pce fnl f* **40/1**
350- **7** *1 1/4* **Giverny Spring**[233] 5307 3-8-12 71 DarryllHolland 10 43
(J W Hills) *prom: rdn over 2f out: sn wknd* **13/8**[2]
00-0 **8** *nk* **Moonlight (GER)**[15] 1165 3-8-5 47 SladeO'Hara(7) 2 43
(Dr J R J Naylor) *hld up in mid-div: lost pl and rdn over 3f out: n.d after* **66/1**
0 **9** *6* **Terrys Alfie**[25] 1006 3-8-12 JamesDoyle(5) 5 35
(N P Littmoden) *rdn over 3f out: a bhd* **66/1**
1m 51.36s (-0.40) **Going Correction** -0.125s/f (Stan) **9** Ran SP% **112.1**
Speed ratings (Par 99):96,95,95,94,93 93,92,91,86
CSF £10.87 TOTE £2.60: £1.40, £1.10, £7.60; EX 10.00 Trifecta £216.90 Pool: £583.64 - 1.91 winning tickets..
Owner W H Ponsonby **Bred** Helshaw Grange Farm And C J Whiston **Trained** Great Habton, N Yorks
FOCUS
A modest maiden in which the pace was ordinary and only a little over four lengths covered the first eight.

1553 TELETEXT RACING "HANDS AND HEELS" APPRENTICE H'CAP 1m 1f 103y(P)
5:00 (5:01) (Class 6) (0-60,60) 4-Y-0+ **£2,730** (£806; £403) **Stalls** Low

Form RPR
00/0 **1** **Major Blade (GER)**[7] 1353 8-7-13 **46** oh1 ChrisHough(5) 8 53
(Heather Dalton) *chsd ldrs: rdn over 2f out: styd on to ld last strides* **16/1**
0303 **2** *hd* **Golden Spectrum (IRE)**[8] 1311 7-8-12 **57** (b) TolleyDean(3) 1 63
(R A Harris) *hld up: hdwy on ins to chse ldr over 2f out: sn rdn: sustained chal to ld cl home: hdd last strides* **9/1**
5000 **3** *shd* **Shannon Arms (USA)**[10] 1273 5-9-1 **57** RobbieMills 10 63
(P Howling) *led: rdn over 1f out: hdd cl home* **25/1**
10-4 **4** *1/2* **Phoenix Eye**[3] 1461 5-8-7 **49** ow2 RonanKeogh 12 54
(M Mullineaux) *s.i.s: hld up towards rr: rdn and hdwy over 2f out: r.o ins fnl f* **14/1**
42 **5** *shd* **At The Helm (IRE)**[30] 917 4-8-2 **52** RichardRowe(8) 7 57
(W J Knight) *hld up towards rr: rdn and hdwy over 2f out: r.o ins fnl f* **12/1**
500- **6** *1/2* **Lauro**[235] 5250 6-9-1 **60** DawnRankin(3) 11 64
(Miss J A Camacho) *stdd s: sn swtchd lft: hdwy over 1f out: r.o* **16/1**
0304 **7** *1* **Ardea Brave (IRE)**[16] 1152 4-9-1 **57** (p) JamieHamblett 3 59
(M Botti) *mid-div: no real prog fnl 2f* **9/2**[2]
5440 **8** *1/2* **Nimello (USA)**[25] 1001 10-9-4 **60** JamesMillman 4 61
(A G Newcombe) *bhd tl late hdwy: nrst fin* **16/1**
5000 **9** *1/2* **Sorbiesharry (IRE)**[12] 1244 7-8-8 **50** (p) WilliamCarson 2 50
(Mrs N Macauley) *hld up towards rr: sme hdwy on ins whn swtchd rt over 1f out: n.d* **8/1**
0450 **10** *1 1/4* **King Of Knight (IRE)**[21] 1058 5-8-13 **55** KirstyMilczarek 5 53
(G Prodromou) *mid-div: hdwy over 4f out: rdn over 2f out: wkng whn edgd lft jst over 1f out* **11/2**[3]
0004 **11** *2* **Midshipman**[15] 1164 8-9-4 **60** (vt) ChrisCavanagh 6 54
(A W Carroll) *dwlt: a bhd* **7/2**[1]
500- **12** *3/4* **Zando**[164] 4885 4-9-1 **57** ThomasO'Brien 13 49
(E G Bevan) *hld up in tch: lost pl 4f out: n.d after* **100/1**
-040 **13** *3/4* **Fraternity**[9] 1303 9-9-2 **58** KevinGhunowa 9 49
(J A Pickering) *chsd ldr tl rdn and wknd over 2f out* **14/1**
2m 1.64s (-0.98) **Going Correction** -0.125s/f (Stan) **13** Ran SP% **120.4**
Speed ratings (Par 101):99,98,98,98,98 97,96,96,95,94 93,92,91
CSF £154.37 CT £3583.70 TOTE £24.40: £8.90, £2.50, £7.40; EX 409.90 TRIFECTA Not won. Place 6 £3,479.82, Place 5 £1,131.05.
Owner G Lloyd, G Allmond, R Barrs **Bred** Wilhelm Fasching **Trained** Norton, Shropshire
■ Stewards' Enquiry : William Carson seven-day ban: improper riding - used whip in a prohibited manner in a hands and heels race (May 19-25)
FOCUS
A modest event in which the pace was ordinary and they finished in a bit of a heap. Sound enough form rated through the runner-up, fourth and fifth.
Midshipman Official explanation: jockey said horse was slowly away
T/Jkpt: Not won. T/Plt: £527.20 to a £1 stake. Pool: £44,780.20. 62.00 winning tickets. T/Qpdt: £61.60 to a £1 stake. Pool: £3,755.20. 45.10 winning tickets. KH

1554 - 1556a (Foreign Racing) - See Raceform Interactive

1330 LONGCHAMP (R-H)
Monday, May 8

OFFICIAL GOING: Very soft

1557a PRIX HOCQUART (GROUP 2) (C&F) 1m 3f
2:20 (2:22) 3-Y-O **£51,103** (£19,724; £9,414; £6,276; £3,138)

RPR
1 **Numide (FR)**[51] 672 3-9-2 IMendizabal 4 113
(J-C Rouget, France) *held up in last, finished well from 2f out, challenged final 100 yards, driven to lead on line* **71/10**
2 *snk* **Gentlewave (IRE)**[21] 1064 3-9-2 CSoumillon 1 113
(A Fabre, France) *in touch, 3rd half-way, pushed along 2f out, ran on to lead over 1f out, headed on line* **9/10**[1]
3 *6* **Sudan (IRE)**[28] 3-9-2 SPasquier 6 103
(E Lellouche, France) *led, pushed along and ran on 2f out, headed over 1f out, kept on to just hold 3rd* **11/1**
4 *nse* **Nordic Thunder (GER)**[29] 935 3-9-2 OPeslier 5 103
(A Fabre, France) *prominent, 2nd half-way, pushed along to chase leader 2f out, kept on final stages, just missed 3rd* **46/10**[3]
5 *hd* **Kentucky Dynamite (USA)**[20] 3-9-2 C-PLemaire 7 103
(A De Royer-Dupre, France) *held up in 6th, ridden and ran on from over 1f out, nearest at finish* **39/10**[2]
6 *3* **Royal Pennekamp (FR)** 3-9-2 TThulliez 2 98
(H-A Pantall, France) *midfield, 5th half-way, never in contention* **13/1**
7 *4* **Double Eagle (FR)**[24] 3-9-2 TJarnet 3 92
(R Gibson, France) *in touch, 4th half-way, weakened over 1 1/2f out* **22/1**
2m 23.0s **7** Ran SP% **123.1**
PARI-MUTUEL: WIN 8.10; PL 2.70, 1.40; SF 19.60.
Owner Ecurie I M Fares **Bred** Scea Haras De Manneville **Trained** Pau, France

NOTEBOOK
Numide(FR) was slowly into his stride as usual and lost several lengths at the start, but his rider was happy to bowl along in last place for much of the race. He was still last two furlongs out but came with a sweeping late run to get up in the last few strides. Clearly suited by very soft ground, he will now go for the Jockey Club.
Gentlewave(IRE) was beautifully placed early on just behind the leaders entering the straight. He quickened rapidly from a furlong and a half out and led at the furlong marker, but it was then that his jockey dropped his whip. He was caught in the final 10 metres and was probably an unlucky loser. He will have his chance for revenge in the Jockey Club.
Sudan(IRE) reluctantly was asked to make the running. He stayed at the head of affairs until a furlong and a half out and then ran on one-paced to the line. Probably not aided by the testing ground, this was only his second race, and he will improve.
Nordic Thunder(GER) was settled in second place and made his effort soon after entering the straight. He was then outpaced, but stayed on late, only missing out on third place by inches.

1558a PRIX D'HEDOUVILLE (GROUP 3) 1m 4f
2:50 (2:51) 4-Y-O+ **£27,586** (£11,034; £8,276; £5,517; £2,759)

RPR
1 **Bellamy Cay**[20] 1072 4-8-9 CSoumillon 4 113
(A Fabre, France) *made all, pushed along and ran on 1 1/2f out, kept on well* **14/10**[1]
2 *3/4* **Salutino (GER)**[29] 4-8-11 OPeslier 2 114
(A Fabre, France) *disp 2nd, 4th on ins in str, pushed along to chase leader and soon went 2nd, ran on to line but not pace of wnr* **37/10**[3]
3 *1* **Walk In The Park (IRE)**[29] 934 4-8-11 TGillet 8 112
(J E Hammond, France) *held up in last, effort on outside 1 1/2f out, went 3rd final 100 yards, nearest at finish* **46/10**
4 *nk* **Marend (FR)**[253] 4806 5-9-4 DBoeuf 6 119
(D Sepulchre, France) *held up in 7th, ran on in straight to go 3rd approaching final furlong, lost place narrowly 100 yards out* **81/10**
5 *2* **Policy Maker (IRE)**[20] 1072 6-8-11 SPasquier 3 109
(E Lellouche, France) *disputed 4th, disputing 5th straight, slightly short of room over 1f out but never in challenging position* **34/10**[2]
6 *1/2* **Coventgarden (FR)**[20] 1072 6-8-9 IMendizabal 1 106
(D Sepulchre, France) *disputed 4th on inside, disputing 5th straight, never a threat* **81/10**
7 *15* **Alost (FR)**[29] 934 6-8-11 FSpanu 7 86
(A Spanu, France) *disputed 4th on outside, 3rd and pushed along straight, one pace final 1 1/2f* **17/1**
8 *2* **Farouge (FR)**[239] 5164 5-9-2 FJohansson 5 88
(Mme Pia Brandt, France) *disputed 2nd, 2nd and ridden straight, weakened over 1f out* **30/1**
2m 39.1s **8** Ran SP% **134.3**
PARI-MUTUEL: WIN 2.40; PL 1.20, 1.40, 1.70; DF 4.10.
Owner K Abdulla **Bred** Juddmonte Farms **Trained** Chantilly, France

NOTEBOOK
Bellamy Cay is getting better with age and was given a confident ride by his jockey, who decided to make all. Things were quickened up early in the straight and the four-year-old was never really threatened thereafter, eventually winning with a little in hand. He now goes for the Grand Prix de Chantilly and still looks a progressive sort.
Salutino(GER) was caught for speed early in the straight and then began to run on again at the furlong marker. He finished best of all and has plenty of scope for further improvement.
Walk In The Park(IRE) put up a fine effort in defeat. Dropped out last, he still held the same position in the straight, but he then started a progressive run and made up a considerable amount of late ground up the centre of the track. He was not given a hard race and his program will be determined by the ground, which must be on the soft side.
Marend(FR), considering he was giving weight all round and four kilos to the winner, posted a fine effort. This performance augurs well for the future, and he does like to get his toe in.

[1229] CATTERICK (L-H)
Tuesday, May 9

OFFICIAL GOING: Good to firm (good in places)
Wind: Nil

1559 CATTERICKBRIDGE.CO.UK MAIDEN AUCTION STKS — 5f
6:10 (6:12) (Class 6) 2-Y-0 — **£2,730** (£806; £403) **Stalls Low**

Form — RPR
3 **1** **Diamond Hurricane (IRE)**[18] [1121] 2-8-6 .... DanielTudhope(3) 8 — 67
(P D Evans) *chsd ldrs on outer: pushed along and sltly outpcd 2f out: rdn over 1f out: styd on ins last to ld nr fin* **3/1**[2]
0 **2** *hd* **The Italian Job**[15] [1181] 2-8-6 .... DavidAllan 5 — 63
(T D Easterby) *cl up: led wl over 1f out: drvn ins last: hdd and no ex nr line* **4/1**[3]
3 *1 ¼* **Sunken Rags** 2-8-4 .... FrancisNorton 7 — 56
(K R Burke) *towards rr: hdwy 2f out: sn rdn and styd on ins last: nrst fin* **25/1**
33 **4** *shd* **Josr's Magic (IRE)**[6] [1420] 2-8-11 .... TonyCulhane 6 — 63
(Mrs A Duffield) *cl up: rdn along and sltly outpcd 1/2-way: chsd ldrs over 1f out: drvn: edge lft and one pce ins last* **3/1**[2]
5 *3* **Ten For Tosca (IRE)** 2-8-13 .... ShaneKelly 3 — 53
(J A Osborne) *trckd ldrs: hdwy 2f out and sn ev ch: rdn over 1f out and sn wknd* **12/1**
6 *nk* **Denton Hawk** 2-8-9 .... PhillipMakin 10 — 48
(M Dods) *s.i.s: towards rr tl styd on appr last* **33/1**
34 **7** *2* **Hart Of Gold**[27] [987] 2-8-11 .... JamieSpencer 4 — 50+
(M J Wallace) *led: rdn along 1/2-way: hdd wl over 1f out and sn wknd* **5/2**[1]
8 *5* **Lost Inheritance** 2-8-6 .... MickyFenton 2 — 17
(P T Midgley) *s.i.s: a bhd* **50/1**

61.12 secs (0.52) **Going Correction** -0.15s/f (Firm) **8 Ran SP% 115.0**
Speed ratings (Par 91):89,88,86,86,81 81,78,70
CSF £15.28 TOTE £4.30: £1.70, £1.60, £5.40; EX 19.60.
Owner Diamond Racing Ltd **Bred** Rathasker Stud **Trained** Pandy, Abergavenny

FOCUS
Ordinary maiden form.

NOTEBOOK
Diamond Hurricane(IRE) had made a pleasing debut at Thirsk last time and, although this sharp track probably was not ideal, he stayed on well in the closing stages to just edge it. He will improve for a stiffer course and/or six furlongs. (op 10-3 tchd 7-2 and 4-1 in a place)
The Italian Job was another who had the benefit of a previous outing but, in contrast to the winner, this sharp track suited her down to the ground. Only narrowly denied, she can win an ordinary race under similar circumstances. (op 11-2 tchd 6-1)
Sunken Rags, a half-sister to Ace Baby, a winner over five furlongs at two, was running on at the finish and shaped with promise. She should come on for the outing. (op 28-1 tchd 33-1)
Josr's Magic(IRE) was beaten for the third time and, while he has shown fair form, he is beginning to look a little exposed. (op 5-2 tchd 7-2)
Ten For Tosca(IRE), a half-brother to two winners including triple sprinting juvenile-winner Evangelist, had the rail to help in the straight and had every chance. His stable's juveniles usually improve for their debuts. (tchd 14-1)
Denton Hawk, who only cost 1,500gns as a foal, is likely to need more time. (op 40-1)
Hart Of Gold got warm beforehand and was disappointing, failing to run to the form of his previous two outings. Official explanation: jockey said colt hung left-handed throughout (op 3-1 tchd 9-4)

1560 BOOK RACEDAY HOSPITALITY ON 01748 810165 CLAIMING STKS — 1m 3f 214y
6:40 (6:40) (Class 6) 4-Y-0+ — **£3,412** (£1,007; £504) **Stalls Low**

Form — RPR
3036 **1** **Oldenway**[14] [1222] 7-9-3 67 .... PaulHanagan 10 — 75+
(R A Fahey) *a cl up: led 4f out: rdn clr over 1f out* **4/1**[2]
500- **2** *4* **Bronze Dancer (IRE)**[174] [6218] 4-8-13 60 .... DeanMcKeown 11 — 64
(G A Swinbank) *keen: trckd ldrs: effrt to chse wnr over 2f out: sn rdn and no imp appr last* **6/1**
666- **3** *hd* **Shamrock Bay**[18] [4780] 4-8-6 69 .... RobertWinston 2 — 56+
(L Lungo) *hld up in midfield: effrt and pushed along over 3f out: rdn 2f out swtchd rt over 1f out: styd on u.p: nrst fin* **11/4**[1]
5102 **4** *2* **Romil Star (GER)**[7] [1385] 9-8-0 45 ....(v) AndrewElliott(5) 13 — 52
(K R Burke) *led: rdn along and hdd 4f out: drvn over 2f out and kpt on same pce* **9/1**
6500 **5** *nk* **Court Of Appeal**[8] [1346] 9-8-9 65 ....(tp) TomEaves 15 — 56
(B Ellison) *chsd ldrs on outer: pushed along over 3f out: rdn along 2f out: kpt on same pce* **11/2**[3]
5541 **6** *shd* **Starcross Maid**[7] [1385] 4-8-4 40 .... AdrianTNicholls 8 — 50
(J F Coupland) *hld up in rr: hdwy over 5f pout: rdn to chse ldrs over 2f out: sn drvn and one pce appr last* **14/1**
/0-0 **7** *¾* **Siena Star (IRE)**[63] [610] 8-8-4 70 .... PaulMulrennan(3) 5 — 52
(Miss Tracy Waggott) *hld up in rr: hdwy 4f out: rdn along over 2f out: nt rch ldrs* **22/1**
1145 **8** *½* **Mossmann Gorge**[7] [1389] 4-9-1 62 ....(v) NCallan 14 — 59
(M Wellings) *towards rr: hdwy 4f out: rdn along over 2f out: nt rch ldrs* **14/1**
00-0 **9** *nk* **Sovereign State (IRE)**[3] [1184] 9-8-4 48 ....(p) GregFairley(5) 3 — 53
(D W Thompson) *trckd ldrs: rdn along over 4f out: wknd over 2f out* **25/1**
-040 **10** *2* **Comeintothespace (IRE)**[17] [1152] 4-8-7 58 ow2 .... ShaneKelly 4 — 48
(J A Osborne) *chsd ldrs: rdn along over 3f out: wknd over 2f out* **22/1**
536- **11** *nk* **Rouge Et Noir**[225] [5518] 8-8-7 47 ....(t) DavidAllan 6 — 47
(K G Reveley) *dwlt: a towards rr* **16/1**
50-6 **12** *nk* **Airedale Lad (IRE)**[27] [974] 5-8-7 40 .... StanleyChin 12 — 47
(R M Whitaker) *in tch: rdn al0ong over 4f out: sn wknd* **66/1**
400- **13** *1 ¾* **Loaded Gun**[128] [5409] 6-8-3 48 .... RoystonFfrench 9 — 40
(W Storey) *chsd ldrs: pushed alpong 5f out: sn wknd* **100/1**
340- **14** *8* **The Wizard Mul**[128] [5980] 6-8-9 48 ....(t) PaulFessey 7 — 33
(W Storey) *in tch: hdwy to chse ldrs 1/2-way: rdn along over 3f out and sn wknd* **40/1**
/00- **15** *8* **Richie Boy**[367] [1532] 5-8-5 60 .... RobbieFitzpatrick 1 — 16
(Jennie Candlish) *dwlt: a rr* **100/1**

2m 37.2s (-1.80) **Going Correction** -0.10s/f (Good) **15 Ran SP% 124.0**
Speed ratings (Par 101):102,99,99,97,97 97,97,96,96,95 95,94,93,88,83
CSF £27.42 TOTE £5.10: £1.50, £2.50, £1.70; EX 49.70.Shamrock Bay Mr C. R. Dore for £9,000
Owner J J Staunton **Bred** Snailwell Stud Co Ltd **Trained** Musley Bank, N Yorks
■ Stewards' Enquiry : Stanley Chin three-day ban: careless riding (May 21-23)

FOCUS
A standard claimer and ordinary form.
The Wizard Mul Official explanation: jockey said gelding was unsuited by the good to firm (good in places) ground

1561 "BE THE BEST DRESSED LADY" H'CAP — 7f
7:10 (7:10) (Class 4) (0-80,79) 4-Y-0+ — **£7,772** (£2,312; £1,155; £577) **Stalls Low**

Form — RPR
4246 **1** **Aperitif**[7] [1382] 5-8-5 66 .... AdrianTNicholls 3 — 77+
(D Nicholls) *trckd ldrs: hdwy on inner 2f out: swtchd rt and nt clr run ent last: squeezed through and styd on to ld last 50 yds* **8/1**
300- **2** *½* **Grey Boy (GER)**[189] [6216] 5-8-9 70 .... TonyHamilton 7 — 80
(R A Fahey) *trckd ldrs: hdwy to chse ldr 2f out: rdn: edgd lft and led ent last: sn drvn: hdd and no ex last 50 yds* **13/2**[3]
4002 **3** *½* **Stoic Leader (IRE)**[4] [1456] 6-9-4 79 .... NCallan 5 — 88+
(R F Fisher) *hld up towards rr: hdwy over 2f out: rdn and n.m.r over 1f out: swtchd rt and styd on ins last* **4/1**[2]
0-35 **4** *2 ½* **Titinius (IRE)**[18] [1124] 6-8-11 72 .... RobertWinston 6 — 74
(Micky Hammond) *hld up towards rr: hdwy 2f out: rdn over 1f out: kpt on ins last: nrst fin* **14/1**
4104 **5** *½* **Bessemer (JPN)**[14] [1220] 5-9-1 79 .... DanielTudhope(3) 12 — 80
(D Carroll) *hld up in rr: stdy hdwy on outer wl over 1f out: styd on ins last: nrst fin* **25/1**
00-0 **6** *shd* **King Harson**[17] [1143] 7-9-0 75 ....(v) AlanMunro 2 — 76
(J D Bethell) *chsd ldr: rdn along 2f out: drvn edgd rt and one pce appr last* **10/1**
-116 **7** *½* **Border Music**[14] [1220] 5-9-4 79 ....(b) JamieSpencer 11 — 78
(A M Balding) *sn led and sn clr: rdn along wl over 1f out: edgd rt: hdd and hmpd ent last: sn wknd* **9/4**[1]
00-5 **8** *shd* **Kirkby's Treasure**[39] [815] 8-8-11 72 .... FergalLynch 9 — 71
(A Berry) *hld uo in rr tl styd on fnl 2f* **33/1**
120- **9** *1 ¾* **Alchemist Master**[155] [6504] 7-9-2 77 .... DeanMcKeown 8 — 72
(R M Whitaker) *chsd ldrs on outer: rdn along over 2f out: sn wknd* **50/1**
-600 **10** *nk* **Trojan Flight**[3] [1494] 5-8-13 74 .... TonyCulhane 10 — 68
(D W Chapman) *in tch: pushed along 2f out: sn btn* **9/1**
330/ **11** *3* **Watching**[577] [6070] 9-9-2 77 .... PaulHanagan 4 — 63
(R A Fahey) *a rr* **20/1**
40-5 **12** *2 ½* **Zhitomir**[27] [977] 8-8-7 68 .... PhillipMakin 1 — 47
(M Dods) *chsd ldrs on inner: rdn along 3f out: sn wknd* **16/1**

1m 25.33s (-2.03) **Going Correction** -0.10s/f (Good) **12 Ran SP% 120.4**
Speed ratings (Par 105):107,106,105,103,102 102,101,101,99,99 95,93
CSF £57.84 CT £243.90 TOTE £9.40: £3.90, £2.90, £2.30; EX 138.60.
Owner Constellation Racing **Bred** A B Barraclough **Trained** Sessay, N Yorks

FOCUS
A fair handicap, and pretty competitive.
Border Music Official explanation: trainer's rep said gelding appeared unsuited by turf as opposed to all-weather
Zhitomir Official explanation: jockey said gelding was unsuited by the good to firm (good in places) ground

1562 GORACING.CO.UK H'CAP — 1m 7f 177y
7:40 (7:40) (Class 6) (0-65,65) 4-Y-0+ — **£3,412** (£1,007; £504) **Stalls Low**

Form — RPR
0-00 **1** **Prairie Sun (GER)**[15] [1184] 5-9-7 63 .... SaleemGolam(3) 10 — 75
(Mrs A Duffield) *trckd ldrs: hdwy 3f out: rdn over ld over 1f out: drvn ins last and styd on wl* **4/1**[1]
0-34 **2** *1 ¼* **Senor Set (GER)**[6] [1415] 5-8-7 46 .... DeanMcKeown 11 — 56
(P A Blockley) *hld up in tch: hdwy 3f out: swtchd rt and rdn wl over 1f out: chse wnr and hung lft ent last: kpt on* **4/1**[1]
5350 **3** *4* **College Rebel**[29] [938] 5-8-7 46 oh1 .... DavidAllan 7 — 51
(J F Coupland) *a.p: rdn to ld over 2f out: drvn and hdd over 1f out: kpt on same pce* **18/1**
402- **4** *3 ½* **Singhalongtasveer**[30] [4144] 4-8-5 47 ....(tp) PaulFessey 4 — 48
(W Storey) *hld up: hdwy over 3f out: rdn and kpt on fnl 2f: nt rch ldrs* **10/1**[3]
0-50 **5** *2 ½* **Hugs Destiny (IRE)**[6] [1415] 5-9-0 53 ....(t) PaulHanagan 6 — 51
(M A Barnes) *led: rdn along over 3f out: hdd over 2f out and grad wknd* **12/1**
3146 **6** *½* **Champion Lion (IRE)**[27] [975] 7-9-0 53 .... MickyFenton 9 — 50
(James Moffatt) *hld up in rr: gd hdwy on outer 5f out: rdn to chse ldrs over 2f out: sn no imp* **16/1**
/00- **7** *¾* **Sun King**[13] [5983] 9-8-10 56 ....(t) JamesReveley(7) 3 — 53+
(K G Reveley) *hld up and bhd tl sme late hdwy* **4/1**[1]
5-00 **8** *1 ½* **William Tell (IRE)**[22] [1045] 4-9-4 60 .... TonyCulhane 1 — 55
(Micky Hammond) *in tch on inner: rdn along 4f out: sn wknd* **20/1**
0 **9** *hd* **Spy Game (IRE)**[64] [589] 6-9-7 60 ....(b) RobbieFitzpatrick 8 — 54
(Jennie Candlish) *nvr nr ldrs* **100/1**
0015 **10** *1* **Bill Bennett (FR)**[17] [1138] 5-9-12 65 .... JamieSpencer 12 — 58
(J Jay) *a towards rr* **7/1**[2]
050- **11** *6* **Wise Tale**[183] [6280] 7-8-5 47 ....(v) PaulMulrennan(3) 14 — 33
(P D Niven) *prom: rdn along 4f out: drvn 3f out and sn wknd* **12/1**
-000 **12** *2* **My Boo**[50] [684] 4-7-13 46 oh1 ....(bt[1]) DuranFentiman(5) 2 — 30
(T Keddy) *dwlt: a rr* **20/1**

3m 32.09s (0.69) **Going Correction** -0.10s/f (Good)
WFA 4 from 5yo+ 3lb **12 Ran SP% 118.6**
Speed ratings (Par 101):94,93,91,89,88 88,87,87,86,86 83,82
CSF £18.17 CT £261.52 TOTE £4.60: £2.10, £1.70, £4.80; EX 24.70.
Owner Miss Helen Wynne **Bred** Gestut Isarland **Trained** Constable Burton, N Yorks

FOCUS
A moderate staying handicap run in a moderate time.
Bill Bennett(FR) Official explanation: jockey said gelding was unsuited by the good to firm (good in places) ground

1563 "JOSEPH M LADIES NIGHT" H'CAP 5f

8:10 (8:11) (Class 5) (0-70,69) 4-Y-0+ £5,460 (£1,612; £806) Stalls Low

Form RPR

54-1 **1** **Our Little Secret (IRE)**[19] 1102 4-8-4 **62**.................. KevinGhunowa(7) 9 75
(A Berry) *mde all: rdn wl over 1f out: kpt on strly* **17/2**

0160 **2** 1 ½ **Desert Opal**[7] 1388 6-8-11 **62**.......................... TonyCulhane 3 69
(D W Chapman) *chsd ldrs: hdwy 2f out: sn rdn: kpt on ins last* **9/1**

222- **3** ½ **Brut**[211] 5793 4-9-0 **65**.................................... FergalLynch 13 70+
(D W Barker) *hld up in rr and swtchd lft to far rail after 1f: smooth hdwy 1/2-way: rdn over 1f out: kpt on ins last: nrst fin* **16/1**

25-3 **4** 1 ½ **Raccoon (IRE)**[3] 1496 6-9-2 **67**.................................(v) NCallan 16 66+
(T D Barron) *chsd wnr centre: rdn along 2f out: drvn and one pce appr last* **9/2**[1]

6-53 **5** nk **Seven No Trumps**[14] 1211 9-8-10 **61**.......................... JamieSpencer 2 59
(J M Bradley) *in tch: pushed along 1/2-way: rdn wl over 1f out: kpt on ins last: nrst fin* **5/1**[2]

40-3 **6** 1 ½ **Never Without Me**[6] 1414 6-8-8 **59**........................ DavidAllan 7 51
(J F Coupland) *chsd ldrs centre: rdn along 2f out: drvn and no imp appr last* **9/1**

2102 **7** ½ **Ashes (IRE)**[8] 1338 4-9-1 **66**.................................. PatCosgrave 6 56
(K R Burke) *chsd ldrs: rdn along 2f out: kpt on same pce* **9/1**

1335 **8** ¾ **Almaty Express**[22] 1047 4-8-11 **65**.........................(b) PaulMulrennan(3) 1 52
(J R Weymes) *prom on ins rail: rdn along 2f out: drvn and wknd over 1f out* **8/1**[3]

600- **9** ¾ **Kings College Boy**[187] 6238 6-9-4 **69**.......................... PaulHanagan 5 53
(R A Fahey) *towards rr tl sme late hdwy* **12/1**

00-0 **10** 1 **Compton Plume**[18] 1124 6-9-1 **66**.............................. DaleGibson 15 46
(M W Easterby) *a towards rr* **33/1**

350- **11** 1 **Snow Wolf**[162] 6447 5-9-1 **66**.................................. RobertWinston 4 42
(J M Bradley) *in tch: rdn along 2f out: sn btn* **14/1**

310- **12** 1 **Bahamian Ballet**[158] 6483 4-9-4 **69**.......................... RichardMullen 17 41
(E S McMahon) *dwlt: a rr* **14/1**

000- **13** nk **Chairman Bobby**[260] 4625 8-7-13 **55**..................... DuranFentiman(5) 14 26
(D W Barker) *chsd ldrs to 1/2-way: sn wknd* **50/1**

306- **14** 3 ½ **Strensall**[206] 5891 9-9-3 **68**..................................... TomEaves 12 25
(R E Barr) *dwlt: a rr* **33/1**

59.35 secs (-1.25) **Going Correction** -0.15s/f (Firm) 14 Ran SP% **121.2**
Speed ratings (Par 103):104,101,100,98,97 95,94,93,92,90 89,87,87,81
CSF £82.54 CT £1248.46 TOTE £10.80: £3.50, £2.90, £5.80; EX 145.30.
Owner J Berry **Bred** Camogue Stud Ltd **Trained** Cockerham, Lancs

FOCUS
A modest sprint handicap but competitive enough on paper. The winner scored in similar fashion to on her reappearance, though.

1564 WHY NOT SPONSOR AT CATTERICK MAIDEN STKS 7f

8:40 (8:41) (Class 5) 3-Y-0 £3,886 (£1,156; £577; £288) Stalls Low

Form RPR

200- **1** **Sir Orpen (IRE)**[214] 5716 3-9-3 78.......................... PhillipMakin 8 74+
(T D Barron) *cl up: rdn to ld wl over 1f out: clr ins last* **11/8**[1]

5- **2** 2 ½ **Wind Shuffle (GER)**[271] 4283 3-9-3 .... RobertWinston 1 68+
(T P Tate) *dwlt and bhd: gd hdwy over 2f out: rdn to chse wnr over 1f out: edgd lft and kpt on* **6/1**[3]

400- **3** 2 **Ya Late Maite**[237] 5217 3-8-12 50.......................... RichardMullen 12 57
(E S McMahon) *led 3f: rdn along over 2f out: kpt on same pce* **33/1**

4 1 **Penzo (IRE)** 3-9-3 .... PatCosgrave 13 60
(J Howard Johnson) *prom on outer: rdn along over 2f out: drvn and kpt on same pce fr wl over 1f out* **50/1**

-400 **5** nk **Coalite (IRE)**[8] 1344 3-9-0 65.......................... SilvestreDeSousa(3) 7 59
(A D Brown) *chsd ldrs: rdn along over 2f out: sn drvn and one pce* **40/1**

22 **6** 1 ¼ **Hams (USA)**[13] 1230 3-8-12 .... RoystonFfrench 5 51
(M Johnston) *cl up on inner: led after 3f: rdn along over 2f out: drvn and hdd wl over 1f out: sn wknd* **2/1**[2]

00- **7** 1 **Little Britain (USA)**[246] 4996 3-9-0 .... PaulMulrennan(3) 6 53
(J Howard Johnson) *a towards rr* **40/1**

5 **8** 7 **Artie's Son (IRE)**[17] 1147 3-8-12 .... DuranFentiman(5) 4 35+
(T D Easterby) *in tch: rdn along 1/2-way: sn wknd* **20/1**

6-4 **9** 2 ½ **Bolckow**[13] 1230 3-9-3 .... NCallan 9 28+
(K A Ryan) *midfield: hdwy on outer 1/2-way: rdn along wl over 2f out and sn wknd* **6/1**[3]

10 dist **Millwood Lad (IRE)** 3-9-3 .... MickyFenton 2 —
(B S Rothwell) *s.i.s: a outpcd and bhd* **50/1**

1m 27.54s (0.18) **Going Correction** -0.10s/f (Good) 10 Ran SP% **120.5**
Speed ratings (Par 99):94,91,88,87,87 85,84,76,73,—
CSF £10.16 TOTE £2.60: £1.20, £2.20, £5.80; EX 14.80 Place 6 £149.79, Place 5 £54.78.
Owner Owen Boyle **Bred** Mrs Ann Stack **Trained** Maunby, N Yorks

FOCUS
A low-grade maiden.
T/Plt: £219.80 to a £1 stake. Pool: £45,489.20. 151.05 winning tickets. T/Qpdt: £50.30 to a £1 stake. Pool: £3,639.30. 53.50 winning tickets. JR

CHEPSTOW (L-H)

Tuesday, May 9

OFFICIAL GOING: Soft
Wind: Virtually nil

1565 ARMY BENEVOLENT FUND MAIDEN STKS 6f 16y

2:10 (2:11) (Class 5) 3-Y-0 £3,238 (£963; £481; £240) Stalls High

Form RPR

00-3 **1** **Proud Killer**[42] 776 3-9-3 70.......................... EddieAhern 6 73
(J R Jenkins) *in tch: swtchd lft 3f out: chsd ldr over 2f out: led jst ins fnl f: drvn out* **8/1**

20-3 **2** nk **Sensuous**[6] 1406 3-8-12 79.......................... RyanMoore 2 67
(R Hannon) *wnt lft s: sn hld slt ld: rdn and hdd jst ins last: kpt on under presure but no imp on wnr cl home* **7/2**[3]

240- **3** 2 **Bellanora**[194] 6122 3-8-12 67.......................... StephenCarson 1 61
(R F Johnson Houghton) *bmpd s: sn trcking ldrs: rdn to dispute cl 2nd over 1f out: wknd ins last* **11/4**[2]

4 **4** 1 ½ **Dragon Flame (IRE)**[17] 1147 3-9-3 .... SebSanders 5 62
(M Quinn) *bhd: rdn and hdwy 2f out: chsd ldrs 1f out but nvr gng pce to chal: styd on same pce* **9/2**

5-20 **5** 2 **Danawi (IRE)**[8] 1355 3-9-3 74.......................... RichardHughes 4 56
(R Hannon) *hld up in rr: shkn up 2f out and no rspnse* **5/2**[1]

0 **6** 19 **Silvanella (IRE)**[71] 533 3-8-12 .... DaneO'Neill 3 —
(M S Saunders) *w ldr over 3f: wknd qckly 2f out* **40/1**

1m 15.57s (3.17) **Going Correction** +0.575s/f (Yiel) 6 Ran SP% **109.2**
Speed ratings (Par 99):101,100,97,95,93 67
CSF £33.68 TOTE £8.90: £2.90, £2.00; EX 35.40.
Owner Nolan's Bar Racing Syndicate **Bred** Grove Stud Farm **Trained** Royston, Herts

FOCUS
The winner has been rated as improving 10lb, but the second and third might not have been at their best in the conditions.

1566 BRISTOL ARMY BENEVOLENT FUND CLAIMING STKS 1m 2f 36y

2:40 (2:40) (Class 6) 4-Y-0+ £2,266 (£674; £337; £168) Stalls Low

Form RPR

20-5 **1** **Ionian Spring (IRE)**[17] 1133 11-9-7 80.......................... AdamKirby(3) 1 88
(C G Cox) *mid-div: hdwy 5f out: trckd ldr ins fnl 3f: shkn up to chal 1f out: edgd lft and sn led: pushed out: readily* **8/15**[1]

0-36 **2** 2 ½ **Nuit Sombre (IRE)**[53] 659 6-9-10 77.......................... DarryllHolland 6 84
(J G M O'Shea) *led: 5l clr 4f out: drvn over 1f out: hdd and no ex ins last but kpt on for clr 2nd* **12/1**[3]

0600 **3** 11 **Weet A Head (IRE)**[27] 990 5-8-10 58.......................... FergusSweeney 3 51
(R Hollinshead) *bhd: hdwy and rdn 3f out: styd on to take 3rd appr fnl f but nvr nr ldrs* **16/1**

000- **4** 1 ¾ **Arabian Moon (IRE)**[165] 6419 10-8-10 48.......................... DaneO'Neill 5 48
(R Brotherton) *bhd: pushed along 3f out: styd on fr over 1f out but nvr a danger* **40/1**

542- **5** 1 ½ **Financial Future**[11] 2009 6-8-11 57.......................... KevinGhunowa(7) 8 54
(C Roberts) *in tch: rdn fr 4f out: no imp on ldrs: wknd fr 2f out* **20/1**

00-0 **6** 2 ½ **Lights Out (DEN)**[43] 765 6-9-10 90.......................... (t) EddieAhern 2 56
(C A Horgan) *wnt 2nd 6f out: rdn and dropped to 3rd ins fnl 3f: wknd fr 2f out* **20/1**

0500 **7** 7 **Zinging**[34] 889 7-7-13 40.......................... MarcHalford(5) 11 24
(J J Bridger) *prom early: sn bhd and n.d* **150/1**

540/ **8** 2 **Uncle Max (IRE)**[11] 4822 6-8-6 57.......................... HayleyTurner 7 22
(N A Twiston-Davies) *in tch: rdn fr 7f out: wknd over 3f out* **40/1**

0-00 **9** 4 **Cool Bathwick (IRE)**[17] 283 7-8-6 40.......................... (b) ChrisCatlin 9 15
(G H Yardley) *bhd fr 1/2-way* **200/1**

242- **10** 12 **Sovereign Dreamer (USA)**[310] 3164 6-9-0 58.......................... RyanMoore 4 3
(P F I Cole) *chsd ldr 4f: wknd 5f out* **5/1**[2]

2m 19.12s (9.22) **Going Correction** +0.95s/f (Soft) 10 Ran SP% **111.0**
Speed ratings (Par 101):101,99,90,88,87 85,80,78,75,65
CSF £6.50 TOTE £1.60: £1.10, £2.10, £3.20; EX 7.70.The winner was claimed by Declan Carroll for £15,000.
Owner Elite Racing Club **Bred** Ballymacoll Stud Farm Ltd **Trained** Lambourn, Berks

FOCUS
Only the first two ran to form in this claimer, finishing well clear of the rest. The winner ran close to last year's best.
Zinging Official explanation: trainer said gelding was unsuited by the track

1567 FINANCE WALES BUSINESS H'CAP 6f 16y

3:10 (3:12) (Class 6) (0-65,65) 3-Y-0 £2,590 (£770; £385; £192) Stalls High

Form RPR

-322 **1** **George The Second**[12] 1263 3-8-3 **55**.......................... RichardKingscote(5) 4 64
(Mrs H Sweeting) *mde virtually all: strly pressed tl asserted fnl f and r.o wl* **5/1**[2]

0-03 **2** ½ **The Grey One (IRE)**[5] 1433 3-8-5 **52**.......................... (p) RyanMoore 7 59
(J M Bradley) *pressed ldrs: pressed wnr appr fnl f: no ex u.p ins last* **5/1**[2]

00-0 **3** 1 ¾ **Wizby**[35] 879 3-8-6 **53** ow1.......................... (t) GrahamGibbons 10 55
(P D Evans) *bhd: hdwy over 2f out: str run on rails over 1f out: tk 3rd fnl f but nvr gng pce to rch ldrs* **7/1**[3]

600- **4** 1 ¾ **Mull Of Dubai**[199] 6024 3-8-7 **61**.......................... JosephWalsh(7) 2 58
(J S Moore) *s.i.s: rr: hdwy over 2f out: chsd ldrs 1f out: sn one pce* **22/1**

0565 **5** 1 ¾ **Shannon House**[9] 1312 3-8-12 **59**.......................... FrankieMcDonald 3 50
(M J McGrath) *s.i.s: bhd: rdn and hdwy over 1f out: styd on ins last but nvr a danger* **20/1**

000- **6** 1 ¾ **Mannello**[221] 5583 3-8-7 **54**.......................... FrancisFerris 6 40
(B Palling) *pressed ldrs: rdn over 2f out: wknd appr fnl f* **16/1**

-000 **7** 3 ½ **Just Down The Road (IRE)**[18] 1109 3-9-1 **62**.......... AdrianMcCarthy 9 38
(R A Harris) *in tch: rdn over 3f out: nvr gng pce to rch ldrs: no ch fnl 2f* **22/1**

2600 **8** 3 **Par Excellence**[7] 1378 3-8-2 **54**.......................... MarcHalford(5) 12 21
(W G M Turner) *pressed ldrs 3f: wknd ins fnl 2f* **40/1**

65-0 **9** shd **Waiting For Mary (IRE)**[17] 1141 3-8-9 **61**.......................... JamesDoyle(5) 13 27
(J G M O'Shea) *prssed ldrs 3f: wknd over 2f out* **10/1**

004- **10** 6 **Premier Cru**[139] 6642 3-8-12 **59**.......................... ChrisCatlin 8 7
(Andrew Turnell) *unruly bef s: a outpcd* **10/1**

0-00 **11** ¾ **Compton Flyer**[5] 1433 3-8-5 **52** ow1.......................... (p) LPKeniry 5 —
(J M Bradley) *pressed ldrs over 3f* **28/1**

0-00 **12** ¾ **Enchanting Times (IRE)**[9] 1312 3-8-11 **65**.......... (v) MarkCoumbe(7) 15 9
(D G Bridgwater) *wnt lft s: sn hanging lft and repeatedly bmpd for over 1f: a in rr* **66/1**

6000 **13** 6 **Bollywood (IRE)**[28] 969 3-9-3 **64**.......................... DarryllHolland 14 —
(J J Bridger) *bmpd s and continually bmpd for over 1f: a in rr* **12/1**

5-10 **14** 2 ½ **Miltons Choice**[14] 1208 3-9-2 **63**.......................... KDarley 11 —
(J M Bradley) *a outpcd* **9/2**[1]

1m 15.35s (2.95) **Going Correction** +0.575s/f (Yiel) 14 Ran SP% **116.6**
Speed ratings (Par 97):103,102,100,97,95 93,88,84,84,76 75,74,66,62
CSF £26.39 CT £181.11 TOTE £4.30: £1.80, £2.20, £2.40; EX 22.30.
Owner The Kennet Connection **Bred** R Withers **Trained** Lockeridge, Wilts

FOCUS
Pretty ordinary form, but solid enough, with the winner and third running similar races relative to Warwick last month. The form should be reliable.
Miltons Choice Official explanation: jockey said colt missed the break

1568 T & G WOODWARE 30TH ANNIVERSARY H'CAP 1m 14y

3:40 (3:43) (Class 6) (0-65,65) 4-Y-0+ £2,590 (£770; £385; £192) Stalls High

Form RPR

0121 **1** **Indian Edge**[13] 1245 5-8-8 **55**.......................... FrancisFerris 5 74
(B Palling) *mde all but hrd pressed to 1/2-way: sn rdn: r.o strly fr over 1f out* **13/2**[2]

5100 **2** 1 ¾ **Azreme**[72] 526 6-8-12 **59**.......................... KDarley 6 74
(P Howling) *trckd ldrs: rdn to chse wnr 2f out: r.o wl u.p fnl f but a hld* **16/1**

4202 **3** 6 **Contented (IRE)**[7] 1390 4-8-10 **57**.......................... (p) DaneO'Neill 16 60
(Mrs L C Jewell) *bhd: hdwy 3f out: sn rdn: kpt on to take 3rd fnl f but nvr in contention* **12/1**

3000 **4** 1 1/4 **Measured Response**[28] 965 4-9-1 62 SebSanders 13 63
(J G M O'Shea) *pressed wnr to 3f out: lost 2nd 2f out and sn btn* **14/1**
06-0 **5** 2 1/2 **Zafarshah (IRE)**[9] 1311 7-8-6 53 (b) AdrianMcCarthy 11 49
(R A Harris) *bhd: hrd drvn and styd on 2f out: nvr in contention* **12/1**
-000 **6** 3/4 **Stamford Blue**[14] 1217 5-8-2 56 (b) TolleyDean(7) 1 50
(R A Harris) *chsd ldrs: rdn 3f out: wknd 2f out* **20/1**
1-13 **7** 2 **Redeye Special**[13] 1245 4-9-1 62 HayleyTurner 9 52
(M L W Bell) *chsd ldrs: drvn along 3f out: no rspnse: sn btn* **3/1**[1]
000- **8** nk **Pittsburgh**[144] 6594 4-9-1 65 NeilChalmers(3) 15 54
(A M Balding) *bhd tl kpt on fr over 1f out: nvr in contention* **25/1**
630- **9** shd **My Michelle**[174] 6372 5-8-13 60 EddieAhern 3 49
(B Palling) *chsd ldrs over 3f* **12/1**
3- **10** 1 **Glory Be (ITY)**[332] 2511 4-8-3 53 ow1 EdwardCreighton(3) 12 40
(J L Spearing) *bhd: rdn and effrt into mid-div 3f out: sn btn* **7/1**[3]
0-00 **11** 3 **Bogaz (IRE)**[35] 882 4-8-3 55 RichardKingscote(5) 10 36
(Mrs H Sweeting) *sn in tch: rdn 3f out: sn btn* **40/1**
130- **12** 2 1/2 **Will The Till**[250] 4900 4-8-11 58 RyanMoore 4 34
(J M Bradley) *chsd ldrs over 3f: wknd over 2f out* **9/1**
6042 **13** 3 1/2 **Hadath (IRE)**[9] 1310 9-8-7 54 TQuinn 8 23
(B G Powell) *bhd most of way* **10/1**

1m 39.92s (3.92) **Going Correction** +0.575s/f (Yiel) 13 Ran SP% **116.6**
Speed ratings (Par 101):103,101,95,94,91 90,88,88,88,87 84,81,78
CSF £100.75 CT £1262.30 TOTE £5.80: £1.90, £4.90, £3.40; EX 128.90.
Owner Nigel Thomas and Christopher Mason **Bred** Christopher J Mason **Trained** Tredodridge, Vale Of Glamorgan
FOCUS
Good efforts from the first two to pull clear, with the winner clearly on a high at present and the runner-up rated to last year's turf best.
Redeye Special Official explanation: jockey said filly may have been unsuited by the soft ground

1569 AVONMOUTH & PORTBURY OCCUPATIONAL HEALTH LTD H'CAP 1m 14y
4:10 (4:11) (Class 4) (0-85,85) 3-Y-O **£6,309** (£1,888; £944; £472; £235) **Stalls** High

Form RPR
3-62 **1** **Bin Rahy (IRE)**[18] 1122 3-8-10 77 ChrisCatlin 5 85
(M R Channon) *chsd ldrs tl hrd drvn and lost position over 3f out: styd on u.p fr 2f out: to ld jst ins last: drvn out* **7/2**[2]
40-0 **2** 3 **Glenmuir (IRE)**[21] 1067 3-8-13 80 DaneO'Neill 3 82+
(B R Millman) *pressed ldrs tl led over 3f out: rdn 2f out: hdd and outpcd jst ins last* **4/1**[3]
-242 **3** 1/2 **Time For Life (USA)**[80] 448 3-9-4 85 DarryllHolland 8 86
(H J Collingridge) *s.i.s: wl bhd 1/2-way: hdwy fr 3f out: kpt on ins last tl no ex cl home* **13/2**
-500 **4** 2 1/2 **Ocean Pride (IRE)**[3] 1490 3-9-2 83 RichardHughes 11 79
(R Hannon) *towards rr tl hdwy over 3f out: kpt on fr 2f out: outpcd fnl f* **12/1**
135- **5** 2 **Nawaqees**[200] 6005 3-8-9 76 RHills 10 68
(J L Dunlop) *pressed ldrs: chal 4f out tl over 3f out: wknd ins fnl 2f* **3/1**[1]
1-45 **6** 2 1/2 **Bathwick Emma (IRE)**[33] 896 3-8-8 75 GrahamGibbons 1 62
(P D Evans) *behud: sme hdwy fr 3f out: nvr gng pce to rch ldrs: wknd ins fnl 2f* **40/1**
001- **7** 3 **Grey Paint (USA)**[192] 6158 3-8-9 76 (t) RyanMoore 4 57
(R Hannon) *chsd ldrs: rdn over 3f out: wknd 2f out* **20/1**
61-0 **8** 2 **Kings Heir (IRE)**[15] 1190 3-8-10 77 SebSanders 12 54
(R M Beckett) *slt ld tl hdd over 3f out: sn wknd* **10/1**
5-1 **9** 15 **Drawback (IRE)**[119] 76 3-8-8 75 AdrianMcCarthy 2 22
(R A Harris) *bhd: effrt and rdn 1/2-way: nvr in contention and sn bhd* **40/1**
020- **10** 6 **Pairumani's Girl (IRE)**[204] 5949 3-8-10 77 PaulDoe 6 12
(J L Dunlop) *pressed ldrs to 1/2-way: sn bhd* **28/1**
050- **11** 1/2 **Corrib (IRE)**[223] 5556 3-8-9 76 FrancisFerris 9 10
(B Palling) *bhd: sme hdwy and rdn 1/2-way: nvr in contention and sn bhd* **22/1**

1m 41.67s (5.67) **Going Correction** +0.575s/f (Yiel) 11 Ran SP% **114.8**
Speed ratings (Par 101):94,91,90,88,86 83,80,78,63,57 57
CSF £16.14 CT £84.47 TOTE £4.20: £1.90, £2.20, £2.70; EX 21.30.
Owner Sheikh Ahmed Al Maktoum **Bred** Darley **Trained** West Ilsley, Berks
FOCUS
The time was modest and the race has been rated at face value with the winner improving for this stiffer test.

1570 SUPPORT THE ARMY BENEVOLENT FUND H'CAP 7f 16y
4:40 (4:40) (Class 5) (0-75,69) 4-Y-O+ **£3,886** (£1,156; £577; £288) **Stalls** High

Form RPR
2011 **1** **Up Tempo (IRE)**[8] 1341 8-8-7 63 (b) AndrewMullen(5) 14 77
(C R Dore) *led stands side and wl clr of that gp fr 2f out: styd on strly fnl f to take overall ld cl home* **4/1**[1]
000- **2** hd **Blue Java**[175] 6362 5-8-11 67 TravisBlock(5) 10 80
(H Morrison) *racd centre crse:chsd ldr that gp over 2f out: led and marginal overall ldr appr fnl f: hdd cl home* **7/1**[3]
010- **3** 3 **Inka Dancer (IRE)**[190] 6202 4-8-7 58 DarryllHolland 11 64
(B Palling) *racd in centre crse: led that gp and marginal overall ldr tl hdd over 1f out: wknd ins last* **14/1**
5-44 **4** 6 **Arian's Lad**[11] 1273 5-8-4 55 FrancisFerris 2 46
(B Palling) *rced centre crse and chsd ldrs: rdn 3f out: wknd fr 2f out* **8/1**
5501 **5** 2 1/2 **Charlie Bear**[22] 1057 5-8-8 59 AdrianMcCarthy 13 43
(Miss Z C Davison) *racd stands side: chsd ldrs tl wknd fr 2f out* **7/1**[3]
3400 **6** nk **Kew The Music**[5] 1432 6-8-7 58 ChrisCatlin 3 42
(M R Channon) *racd centre crse: rr: rdn and sme hdwy 1/2-way: nvr in contention: wknd 2f out* **10/1**
502- **7** 2 **Morgan Lewis (IRE)**[196] 6103 5-9-1 66 (p) SteveDrowne 16 45
(J A Geake) *chsd ldrs stands side over 3f* **9/2**[2]
00-3 **8** 1 **Blue Tomato**[5] 1432 5-9-4 69 RyanMoore 1 45
(J M Bradley) *racd centre crse: towards rr tl sme hday 1/2-way: nvr in contention and sn bhd* **7/1**[3]
0-04 **9** 2 **Peruvian Style (IRE)**[14] 1209 5-8-5 56 ow1 LPKeniry 15 27
(J M Bradley) *chsd ldr stands side over 3f out tl wknd qckly 2f out* **12/1**
00-0 **10** 11 **Moon Forest (IRE)**[18] 1124 4-9-0 65 KDarley 8 9
(J M Bradley) *racd centre crse: hdwy to chse ldrs 1/2-way: sn wknd* **25/1**
000- **11** 11 **Cleveland**[278] 4099 4-8-12 63 FergusSweeney 12 —
(R Hollinshead) *racd stands side: bhd fr 1/2-way* **40/1**
5/00 **12** 5 **Grand Place**[7] 1383 4-9-0 65 RichardHughes 5 —
(R Hannon) *racd centre crse: a outpcd* **40/1**

1m 27.47s (4.17) **Going Correction** +0.575s/f (Yiel) 12 Ran SP% **119.0**
Speed ratings (Par 103):99,98,95,88,85 85,83,81,79,67 54,48
CSF £31.55 CT £357.90 TOTE £3.80: £2.00, £3.10, £5.10; EX 47.40 Place 6 £161.99, Place 5 £42.55.
Owner Andrew Page **Bred** T Burns **Trained** West Pinchbeck, Lincs
FOCUS
The field split into two distinct groups, with five, including the winner, going down the stands' side and seven racing centre-to-far side. The winner ran to form with the second improving. The third only showed her form once last year so the placed form is not rock solid.
Grand Place Official explanation: jockey said gelding lost its action
T/Jkpt: £17,761.20 to a £1 stake. Pool: £50,031.74. 2.00 winning tickets. T/Plt: £74.90 to a £1 stake. Pool: £47,565.30. 463.35 winning tickets. T/Qpdt: £16.80 to a £1 stake. Pool: £3,351.60. 147.20 winning tickets. ST

1385 SOUTHWELL (L-H)
Tuesday, May 9

OFFICIAL GOING: Standard
Wind: Light, across Weather: Hazy sunshine

1571 SOUTHWELL-RACECOURSE.CO.UK BANDED STKS 5f (F)
2:00 (2:00) (Class 7) 3-Y-O+ **£1,706** (£503; £252) **Stalls** High

Form RPR
5-00 **1** **Estoille**[15] 1195 5-9-0 45 (t) RobertWinston 1 56
(Mrs S Lamyman) *chsd ldr: led 1/2-way: rdn out* **3/1**[1]
5014 **2** 1 1/2 **Laurel Dawn**[15] 1196 8-9-2 47 (b) JimmyQuinn 3 53
(C N Kellett) *led to 1/2-way: rdn over 1f out: edgd rt ins fnl f: styd on same pce* **3/1**[1]
-006 **3** 2 **Shopfitter**[18] 1127 3-8-5 40 (b) RobbieFitzpatrick 2 40
(Mrs C A Dunnett) *chsd ldrs: rdn 1/2-way: styd on same pce appr fnl f* **25/1**
-000 **4** 2 **Goodbye Girl (IRE)**[9] 1312 3-8-9 45 ow4 (b[1]) BrianReilly 8 37
(Mrs C A Dunnett) *mid-div: sn drvn along: hdwy u.p over 1f out: nvr nrr* **25/1**
-104 **5** 1 **Sharp Hat**[7] 1397 12-9-2 47 TonyCulhane 10 36
(D W Chapman) *free to post: sn outpcd: r.o ins fnl f: nrst fin* **5/1**[2]
0-00 **6** 1 **Zap Attack**[14] 1217 6-8-11 45 (tp) DNolan(3) 4 31
(J Parkes) *s.i.s: outpcd: nvr nrr* **20/1**
3540 **7** 3/4 **Eternally**[14] 1228 4-9-0 45 (p) ShaneKelly 13 28
(R M H Cowell) *prom over 3f* **11/2**[3]
-000 **8** 1/2 **Mind That Fox**[11] 1272 4-9-3 48 MickyFenton 7 29
(T Wall) *chsd ldrs over 3f* **14/1**
005- **9** 3 **Miss Mujahid Times**[142] 6605 3-8-7 47 PaulEddery 5 14
(A D Brown) *s.i.s: outpcd* **18/1**
0-00 **10** 1/2 **Grasslandik**[96] 271 10-8-7 35 (p) AnnStokell(7) 11 14
(Miss A Stokell) *mid-div: sn rdn along: wknd wl over 1f out* **100/1**
06-0 **11** nk **Arisea (IRE)**[17] 1150 3-8-5 45 (v[1]) JohnEgan 6 13
(R C Guest) *s.i.s: outpcd* **33/1**
0-00 **12** 2 1/2 **Valiant Romeo**[15] 1195 6-9-0 45 (p) RoystonFfrench 12 5
(R Bastiman) *prom: rdn 1/2-way: wknd wl over 1f out* **12/1**
00-0 **13** 1 3/4 **Fei Mah**[8] 1348 4-8-11 30 DeanCorby(3) 9 —
(J R Jenkins) *sn outpcd* **40/1**

60.39 secs (0.09) **Going Correction** -0.025s/f (Stan)
WFA 3 from 4yo+ 9lb 13 Ran SP% **120.5**
Speed ratings (Par 97):98,95,92,89,87 86,84,84,79,78 77,73,71
CSF £10.41 TOTE £4.00: £1.70, £1.40, £6.90; EX 18.10 Trifecta £236.10 Part won. Pool: £332.54 - 0.54 winning tickets..
Owner B C S Kemp **Bred** B And Mrs H Kemp **Trained** Ruckland, Lincs
FOCUS
A very weak sprint that saw the lowest three stalls dominate.

1572 DINE IN THE QUEEN MOTHER RESTAURANT MAIDEN CLAIMING STKS 1m 4f (F)
2:30 (2:30) (Class 7) 4-Y-O+ **£1,365** (£403; £201) **Stalls** Low

Form RPR
4655 **1** **Bold Trump**[16] 939 5-9-0 45 J-PGuillambert 7 51
(Mrs N S Evans) *a.p: chsd ldr 1/2-way: led over 3f out: hrd rdn fr over 1f out: styd on* **2/1**[1]
030- **2** 3/4 **Ben Bacchus (IRE)**[164] 6434 4-9-0 47 (b) NCallan 6 50
(P A Blockley) *s.s: hld up: hdwy 1/2-way: hrd rdn fr over 1f out: styd on* **11/4**[2]
0000 **3** 3/4 **Agilete**[12] 1265 4-8-11 47 AmirQuinn(3) 5 49
(J R Boyle) *hld up in tch: nt clr run and lost pl over 6f out: hdwy over 4f out: rdn over 1f out: styd on same pce* **5/1**
06-0 **4** 13 **Gravardlax**[15] 1198 5-9-0 40 (t) JamieMackay 3 28
(Miss D A McHale) *chsd ldrs: rdn over 4f out: wknd over 2f out* **9/2**[3]
5000 **5** 6 **Rythm N Rhyme (IRE)**[11] 1271 7-8-10 40 (p) PaulEddery 1 14
(John A Harris) *led: hdd over 3f out: rdn and wknd 2f out* **18/1**
600- **6** 24 **Stylish Sunrise (IRE)**[291] 3681 5-8-12 40 DeanMcKeown 2 —
(A J Chamberlain) *hld up: rdn and wknd 4f out* **10/1**
05-0 **P** **Oberon's Prize**[11] 1271 4-8-9 40 ow1 (p) MichaelTebbutt 4 —
(V Smith) *trckd ldr: racd keenly: lost pl over 6f out: sn bhd: t.o whn p.u and dismntd 3f out* **16/1**

2m 44.53s (2.44) **Going Correction** -0.025s/f (Stan) 7 Ran SP% **115.1**
Speed ratings (Par 97):90,89,89,80,76 60,—
CSF £7.81 TOTE £2.40: £1.40, £2.00; EX 8.10.The winner was the subject of a friendly claim.
Owner Gerald Statham **Bred** Worksop Manor Stud **Trained** Pandy, Gwent
■ A first Flat winner for Nicki Evans.
FOCUS
A dire contest which saw the first three come well clear. The winning time was moderate, even for a race like this.

1573 BOOK TICKETS ON LINE BANDED STKS 1m (F)
3:00 (3:00) (Class 7) 4-Y-O+ **£1,365** (£403; £201) **Stalls** Low

Form RPR
4005 **1** **Kirkhammerton (IRE)**[11] 1271 4-8-12 45 (v) DeanMcKeown 2 53
(M J Polglase) *sn led: hdd over 2f out: rdn to ld ins fnl f: r.o* **4/1**[2]
0220 **2** nk **Tommytyler (IRE)**[4] 1462 7-8-10 46 ow1 (t) DNolan(3) 4 53
(D Carroll) *hld up: hdwy over 4f out: led on bit over 2f out: rdn and hdd ins fnl f: styd on* **15/2**
5-04 **3** 1 1/2 **Fit To Fly (IRE)**[8] 1341 5-8-12 45 (p) JohnEgan 6 49
(R C Guest) *sn pushed along in rr: hdwy u.p over 2f out: styd on same pce ins fnl f* **11/4**[1]
4524 **4** 2 1/2 **Spy Gun (USA)**[13] 1198 6-8-12 45 J-PGuillambert 8 44
(T Wall) *a.p: chsd wnr 5f out: rdn over 2f out: edgd lft and no ex fnl f* **11/4**[1]
0206 **5** 1 1/2 **Ming Vase**[15] 1194 4-8-12 45 StanleyChin 11 41
(P T Midgley) *chsd ldrs: rdn 1/2-way: sn outpcd: styd on u.p fnl f* **9/2**[3]

000- **6** *4* **Tantien**[238] [5211] 4-8-12 40 RobertWinston 7 33
(John A Harris) *chsd ldr 3f: rdn over 2f out: wknd over 1f out* **20/1**

000- **7** *5* **On Every Street**[284] [3907] 5-8-12 45 RoystonFfrench 3 23
(R Bastiman) *hld up: hdwy over 3f out: rdn and wknd over 2f out* **22/1**

0/0- **8** *1 3/4* **Green Ginger**[481] [113] 10-8-9 30 JasonEdmunds(3) 10 20
(J T Stimpson) *prom: lost pl over 6f out: rdn and wknd over 3f out* **150/1**

5/00 **9** *11* **Hello Tiger**[22] [941] 5-8-12 30 MickyFenton 9 —
(J A Supple) *hld up: hdwy u.p over 3f out: sn wknd* **100/1**

-060 **10** *1 3/4* **Parisian Playboy**[7] [1395] 6-8-12 40 PaulEddery 1 —
(A D Brown) *hld up: bhd fr 1/2-way* **33/1**

1m 45.25s (0.65) **Going Correction** -0.025s/f (Stan) **10** Ran SP% **117.0**
Speed ratings (Par 97):95,94,93,90,89 85,80,78,67,65
CSF £32.01 TOTE £6.40: £2.10, £2.60, £1.40; EX 32.30 Trifecta £123.40 Part won. Pool: £173.90 - 0.54 winning tickets..
Owner Paul J Dixon **Bred** Barronstown Stud And Orpendale **Trained** Babworth, Notts

FOCUS
Typical form for the class and the first two came clear.

1574 GOLF AND RACING AT SOUTHWELL BANDED STKS 1m (F)
3:30 (3:30) (Class 7) 4-Y-0+ **£1,706** (£503; £252) **Stalls** Low

Form RPR

0401 **1** **Shrine Mountain (USA)**[7] [1387] 4-9-6 48 (v) RichardMullen 1 67
(J R Holt) *dwlt: sn chsng ldrs: rdn over 2f out: led and hung lft over 1f out: styd on: eased nr fin* **10/11**[1]

4415 **2** *5* **Legal Lover (IRE)**[20] [1073] 4-8-9 50 RussellKennemore(7) 7 53
(R Hollinshead) *sn rdn to ld: hdd over 1f out: edgd lft and wknd ins fnl f* **5/2**[2]

0000 **3** *2* **Sorbiesharry (IRE)**[1] [1553] 7-9-2 50 (p) MickyFenton 5 49
(Mrs N Macauley) *hld up: hdwy over 4f out: rdn over 2f out: sn outpcd* **9/1**

1660 **4** *1 3/4* **Priorina (IRE)**[34] [889] 4-9-1 49 (v) RobertHavlin 3 45
(D Haydn Jones) *chsd ldrs: rdn over 2f out: wknd over 1f out* **14/1**

3556 **5** *2 1/2* **Galley Law**[29] [939] 6-8-12 46 PaulFessey 6 37
(R Craggs) *prom to 1/2-way* **11/2**[3]

1-00 **6** *5* **Sea Frolic (IRE)**[7] [1390] 5-8-13 47 (v) RobbieFitzpatrick 4 28
(Jennie Candlish) *hld up: effrt over 3f sn wknd* **20/1**

0/0- **7** *48* **Shardda**[348] [2026] 6-8-11 35 RobertWinston 2 —
(F Watson) *chsd ldrs to 1/2-way* **100/1**

1m 44.09s (-0.51) **Going Correction** -0.025s/f (Stan) **7** Ran SP% **118.8**
Speed ratings (Par 97):101,96,94,92,89 84,36
CSF £3.63 TOTE £1.80: £1.40, £1.80; EX 3.30.
Owner G J Oliver **Bred** WinStar Farm Llc **Trained** Peckleton, Leics

FOCUS
A poor affair, run at a sound pace, and the in-form winner was value for further.

1575 HOSPITALITY PACKAGES AVAILABLE BANDED STKS 7f (F)
4:00 (4:00) (Class 7) 4-Y-0+ **£1,706** (£503; £252) **Stalls** Low

Form RPR

2005 **1** **Feast Of Romance**[22] [1054] 9-8-11 45 (b) NCallan 2 59
(G A Huffer) *chsd ldrs: rdn to ld 2f out: r.o: eased nr fin* **5/1**[2]

30-0 **2** *2 1/2* **Noorain**[7] [1394] 4-8-13 47 (t) MickyFenton 5 54
(Stef Liddiard) *s.s: hdwy 3f out: rdn to chse wnr and edgd lft fnl f: styd on same pce* **12/1**

1045 **3** *3 1/2* **Wings Of Morning (IRE)**[4] [1463] 5-8-10 46 ow1 (v) DNolan(3) 1 45
(D Carroll) *s.i.s: sn prom: rdn 1/2-way: styd on same pce fnl 2f* **8/1**[3]

0005 **4** *hd* **Barzak (IRE)**[62] [618] 6-8-13 47 (bt) MichaelTebbutt 6 44
(S R Bowring) *chsd ldrs: rdn over 1f out: wknd ins fnl f* **8/1**[3]

0313 **5** *2 1/2* **La Musique**[7] [1390] 4-9-0 48 DaleGibson 8 39
(P J McBride) *trckd ldrs: racd keenly: led over 4f out: rdn and hdd 2f out: edgd lft and wknd fnl f* **6/4**[1]

3320 **6** *3* **Rocky Reppin**[14] [1225] 6-8-8 45 (b) JasonEdmunds(3) 7 28
(J Balding) *in rr: effrt 3f out: n.d* **10/1**

5000 **7** *11* **Pending (IRE)**[7] [1394] 5-8-10 47 (p) AmirQuinn(3) 4 —
(J R Boyle) *s.i.s: rdn 3f out: sn lost tch* **5/1**[2]

0060 **8** *4* **Annals**[7] [1393] 4-8-11 45 (v[1]) JohnEgan 3 —
(R C Guest) *led: hdd over 4f out: rdn and wknd 2f out* **25/1**

1m 29.91s (-0.89) **Going Correction** -0.025s/f (Stan) **8** Ran SP% **116.2**
Speed ratings (Par 97):104,101,97,96,94 90,78,73
CSF £62.72 TOTE £5.70: £1.90, £3.80, £2.30; EX 54.80 Trifecta £284.80 Part won. Pool: £401.15 - 0.54 winning tickets..
Owner Robert Stevens **Bred** Aramstone Stud **Trained** Newmarket, Suffolk

FOCUS
A poor event, but run at a fair pace and in a decent time for a banded race. The field trailed home behind the easy winner.
La Musique Official explanation: jockey said gelding ran flat
Annals Official explanation: jockey said filly had no more to give

1576 EXPERIENCE NOTTINGHAMSHIRE TRI-BANDED STKS 7f (F)
4:30 (4:30) (Class 7) 3-Y-0 **£1,365** (£403; £201) **Stalls** Low

Form RPR

005- **1** **Markestino**[189] [6212] 3-8-9 40 GylesParkin 5 42
(T D Easterby) *s.i.s: hld up: hdwy u.p over 1f out: hung lft: styd on to ld wl ins fnl f* **10/1**

6-00 **2** *1/2* **Fallal Parc**[17] [1149] 3-8-6 40 RichardThomas(3) 4 41
(M F Harris) *chsd ldrs: led over 5f out: hdd 4f out: rdn to ld 2f out: edgd lft: hdd wl ins fnl f* **14/1**

-006 **3** *1 1/4* **Boucheen**[14] [1226] 3-9-0 45 SamHitchcott 11 43
(Ms Deborah J Evans) *dwlt: sn prom: rdn and rdr dropped reins over 1f out: sn ev ch: edgd lft and n.m.r ins fnl f: no ex* **5/1**[2]

6600 **4** *shd* **Moraadi**[29] [936] 3-8-4 30 (b) PaulQuinn 9 32
(D W Chapman) *s.i.s: hld up: r.o ins fnl f: nrst fin* **80/1**

0-64 **5** *1/2* **October Sun**[35] [874] 3-8-4 35 AlanDaly 12 31
(Miss D Mountain) *dwlt: outpcd and bhd: r.o ins fnl f: nrst fin* **7/1**

63-0 **6** *2 1/2* **Ten Commandments (IRE)**[14] [1226] 3-8-6 40 JasonEdmunds(3) 6 30
(J Balding) *led: hdd over 5f out: rdr over 2f out: styd on same pce appr fnl f* **18/1**

660- **7** *3/4* **Macs All Heart (IRE)**[133] [6670] 3-9-0 45 JDSmith 7 33
(A B Coogan) *mid-div: rdn over 2f out: nvr trbld ldrs* **12/1**

2310 **8** *nk* **Beginners Luck (IRE)**[14] [1226] 3-9-0 45 LeeEnstone 10 32
(D Carroll) *prom: lost pl over 4f out: n.d after* **13/2**

-060 **9** *3/4* **Master Ben (IRE)**[14] [1216] 3-9-0 45 (bt) PaulEddery 3 30
(S R Bowring) *s.i.s: hdwy 4f out: rdn over 1f out: wknd fnl f* **14/1**

0-00 **10** *1 1/4* **Baron De Hoyland**[10] [1293] 3-8-5 35 ow1 JosedeSouza 14 18
(J R Norton) *chsd ldrs: rdn over 2f out: wknd fnl f* **80/1**

1533 **11** *1 1/2* **Berties Brother**[15] [1200] 3-9-0 45 DaleGibson 8 23
(D G Bridgwater) *prom to 1/2-way* **9/2**[1]

0-00 **12** *1 1/2* **Distant Mind (IRE)**[19] [1101] 3-9-0 45 (p) RichardMullen 2 19
(Mrs C A Dunnett) *prom: led 4f out: hdd and hung lft 2f out: sn wknd* **25/1**

04-0 **13** *1 1/2* **Devon Ruby**[12] [1259] 3-9-0 45 MichaelTebbutt 1 15
(Mrs A Duffield) *prom: rdn 1/2-way: wknd 2f out* **6/1**[3]

1m 32.21s (1.41) **Going Correction** -0.025s/f (Stan) **13** Ran SP% **116.7**
Speed ratings (Par 93):90,89,88,87,87 84,83,83,82,80 79,77,75
CSF £137.68 TOTE £17.80: £4.00, £4.90, £2.30; EX 237.10 TRIFECTA Not won..
Owner Mrs Jennifer E Pallister **Bred** Deerfield Farm **Trained** Great Habton, N Yorks

FOCUS
A weak event, but the winner has scope and could prove better than this class.
Berties Brother Official explanation: jockey said gelding was unsuited by the fibresand

1577 SEE YOU ON 16TH BANDED STKS 6f (F)
5:00 (5:00) (Class 7) 4-Y-0+ **£1,706** (£503; £252) **Stalls** Low

Form RPR

2215 **1** **Union Jack Jackson (IRE)**[15] [1196] 4-9-1 49 (b) DaleGibson 4 58+
(J G Given) *hld up: hdwy to ld 1f out: sn clr: eased nr fin* **1/1**[1]

3300 **2** *1 3/4* **Sergeant Slipper**[7] [1393] 9-8-11 45 (v) GylesParkin 3 46
(C Smith) *s.i.s: outpcd: r.o ins fnl f: nt rch wnr* **11/1**

6100 **3** *nk* **Sundried Tomato**[15] [1196] 7-8-12 46 (p) PaulQuinn 1 46
(D W Chapman) *chsd ldr: led over 3f out: rdn edgd lft and hdd 1f out: styd on same pce* **11/2**[3]

5060 **4** *1 3/4* **Roko**[7] [1397] 4-8-11 35 (bt) MichaelTebbutt 6 40
(S R Bowring) *s.i.s: sn trcking ldrs: rdn over 1f out: no rspnse* **66/1**

6065 **5** *1/2* **Off Hire**[29] [942] 10-8-8 40 (v) JasonEdmunds(3) 5 39
(C Smith) *led: hdd over 3f out: rdn over 1f out: no ex* **16/1**

20-5 **6** *4* **Cayman King**[106] [178] 4-9-0 48 (b[1]) PatCosgrave 10 30
(R Craggs) *s.i.s: hdwy over 4f out: rdn: hung lft and wknd over 1f out* **11/4**[2]

0000 **7** *3* **Dematraf (IRE)**[7] [1393] 4-8-11 45 SamHitchcott 9 18
(Ms Deborah J Evans) *prom over 4f* **10/1**

06-0 **8** *4* **Tuscan Flyer**[15] [1196] 8-8-12 46 LeeEnstone 8 7
(R Bastiman) *chsd ldrs: rdn over 3f out: wknd 2f out* **20/1**

0-00 **9** *3 1/2* **Warren Place**[7] [1393] 6-8-11 45 (b) PaulEddery 7 —
(A D Brown) *chsd ldrs over 3f* **80/1**

050- **10** *12* **Frogs' Gift (IRE)**[285] [3869] 4-8-11 45 JamieMackay 2 —
(G M Moore) *s.i.s: a in rr* **28/1**

1m 17.15s (0.25) **Going Correction** -0.025s/f (Stan) **10** Ran SP% **126.3**
Speed ratings (Par 97):97,94,94,91,91 85,81,76,71,55
CSF £15.75 TOTE £2.10: £1.20, £2.60, £1.90; EX 13.80 Trifecta £59.40 Pool: £456.84 - 5.46 winning units. Place 6 £52.39, Place 5 £30.38.
Owner Andy Clarke **Bred** Tom Foley **Trained** Willoughton, Lincs

FOCUS
A fair event for the class, run at a sound pace, and the winner was value for further.
T/Plt: £124.60 to a £1 stake. Pool: £26,380.65. 154.45 winning tickets. T/Qpdt: £41.00 to a £1 stake. Pool: £1,699.40. 30.60 winning tickets. CR

1578 - 1581a (Foreign Racing) - See Raceform Interactive

CHESTER (L-H)
Wednesday, May 10

OFFICIAL GOING: Good to firm
Wind: Almost nil Weather: Warm & sunny

1582 JOSEPH HELER CHEESE LILY AGNES CONDITIONS STKS 5f 16y
1:50 (1:50) (Class 2) 2-Y-0
£13,087 (£3,918; £1,959; £980; £489; £245) **Stalls** Low

Form RPR

1 **1** **Mubaashir (IRE)**[9] [1333] 2-9-1 LDettori 5 92
(E A L Dunlop) *w'like: chsd ldrs: rdn over 1f out: led ins fnl f: r.o* **5/1**[2]

1 **2** *1 1/2* **Cav Okay (IRE)**[19] [1113] 2-9-1 RichardHughes 2 87
(R Hannon) *w ldr: rdn to ld 1f out: hdd ins fnl f: nt qckn towards fin* **4/11**[1]

21 **3** *nk* **Mind The Style**[10] [1309] 2-9-1 RobertMiles 7 86
(W G M Turner) *w ldrs on outside tl over 3f out: racd bhd ldrs after: rdn over 1f out: ev ch ins fnl f: nt qckn* **28/1**

12 **4** *1* **Lord Charles**[22] [1066] 2-8-12 AmirQuinn 1 79
(W G M Turner) *led: rdn and hdd 1f out: no ex towards fin* **8/1**[3]

4 **5** *3* **Smirfy's Silver**[21] [1074] 2-8-12 JamieSpencer 6 69
(W M Brisbourne) *sn pushed along towards rr: kpt on ins fnl f: nt pce to trble ldrs* **66/1**

2214 **6** *3 1/2* **Hucking Hill (IRE)**[7] [1405] 2-8-12 SteveDrowne 3 59+
(J R Best) *s.s: sn wl bhd and outpcd: nvr on terms* **33/1**

1 **7** *2 1/2* **Ask Don't Tell (IRE)**[15] [1223] 2-8-7 JohnEgan 4 49+
(Tom Dascombe) *leggy: s.i.s: a outpcd* **40/1**

61.34 secs (-0.71) **Going Correction** 0.0s/f (Good) **7** Ran SP% **111.4**
Speed ratings (Par 99):105,102,102,100,95 90,86
CSF £6.96 TOTE £5.20: £1.80, £1.10; EX 7.60.
Owner Atiq Ejtebi **Bred** Kildaragh Stud **Trained** Newmarket, Suffolk

FOCUS
This has been rated very much as an average renewal. Impressive Newbury winner Cav Okay was taken on for the lead by Lord Charles, and those two basically ended up setting the race up for Mubasshir, who impressed with his attitude just as he had at Kempton on his debut.

NOTEBOOK
Mubaashir(IRE) ◆, who showed a likeable attitude when winning on his debut over this trip on Kempton's Polytrack, raced in the ideal position given how fast the leaders went off and took advantage to ultimately run out a convincing winner. While he looks a touch flattered by the manner of this victory, this was still a fine effort considering he looks almost sure to improve when stepped up to six furlongs in due course. Both the Woodcote Stakes and the Coventry at Royal Ascot were mentioned as possible targets. (op 9-2)
Cav Okay(IRE) looked so impressive when bolting up on his debut at Newbury, but that form had not quite worked out as one might have hoped and he failed to justify his very short odds. On his debut nothing could lay up with him and he basically had the race won by half way, but he was taken on this time by Lord Charles, who was drawn on his inside and would not allow him to grab the favoured rail. Although he eventually saw that one off, he was softened up and was unable to resist the very useful winner. He is better than he was able to show and can bounce back when things fall right for him, as they did first time up. (op 2-5 tchd 4-9 in a place)
Mind The Style improved significantly on the form he showed when winning a weak maiden at Brighton on his previous start with a tremendous effort from the widest stall of all. There could be even better to come. (op 25-1)
Lord Charles, who came from well off the pace to win a five-furlong maiden on his debut at Lingfield before again starting slowly when second in a decent conditions race at Newmarket, broke very fast this time to make full use of his rails draw, but he was hassled by Cav Okay throughout and got tired late on. Still, he finished clear of the remainder and could have a reasonable race or two in him this season.

Smirfy's Silver shaped well on his debut when fourth at Beverley, but that was a modest race and this was asking a bit much. Still, he should have benefited from the further experience and should be respected when returned to maiden company. (op 50-1)
Hucking Hill(IRE) had some fair form in the book on turf and Polytrack, but this company was too hot for him and he was never sighted after starting slowly. Official explanation: jockey said colt missed the break
Ask Don't Tell(IRE), whose Wolverhampton maiden success has not worked out at all, lost any chance she may have had in this company when she fell out of the stalls. (tchd 33-1)

1583 WEATHERBYS BANK CHESHIRE OAKS (FOR THE ROBERT SANGSTER MEMORIAL CUP) (LISTED RACE) (FILLIES) 1m 3f 79y
2:20 (2:21) (Class 1) 3-Y-O
£22,712 (£8,608; £4,308; £2,148; £1,076; £540) **Stalls** Low

Form RPR
03-1 **1** **Time On**[29] 971 3-8-12 82 .... LDettori 1 94
(J L Dunlop) *mde all: rdn to qckn clr over 1f out: r.o wl* **2/1**[1]
65-1 **2** *3* **Mont Etoile (IRE)**[13] 1260 3-8-12 83 .... NickyMackay 10 89+
(W J Haggas) *midfield: hdwy 2f out: r.o to take 2nd ins fnl f: nt trble wnr* **10/1**
40- **3** *nk* **Prowess (IRE)**[232] 5391 3-8-12 .... MichaelHills 2 88+
(B W Hills) *unf: in tch: pushed along and n.m.r 2f out: r.o u.p ins fnl f* **12/1**
06- **4** *nk* **Kaylianni**[200] 6027 3-8-12 .... TonyCulhane 6 88
(M R Channon) *in tch: pushed along 3f out: hdwy 2f out: kpt on u.p ins fnl f: nt qckn cl home* **16/1**
1123 **5** *1 1/4* **Marachi Band (USA)**[13] 1251 3-8-12 72 .... (b) JamieSpencer 3 86
(E J O'Neill) *lw: prom: rdn over 1f out: no ex ins fnl f* **25/1**
5- **6** *hd* **Allegretto (IRE)**[201] 6007 3-8-12 .... RyanMoore 9 86+
(Sir Michael Stoute) *lw: hld up in rr: pushed along over 2f out: swtchd rt and hdwy over 1f out: r.o ins fnl f: nrst fin* **7/1**[3]
4122 **7** *1/2* **Fusili (IRE)**[21] 1077 3-8-12 82 .... JamesDoyle 4 85
(N P Littmoden) *midfield: rdn and nt clr run 2f out: hdwy over 1f out: one pce ins fnl f* **12/1**
144- **8** *hd* **Auction Room (USA)**[201] 6010 3-8-12 79 .... RichardHughes 8 85
(B W Hills) *hld up: rdn and sme hdwy over 1f out: no imp* **14/1**
0-1 **9** *hd* **Cortesia (IRE)**[19] 1114 3-8-12 80 .... AlanMunro 11 84
(P W Chapple-Hyam) *lw: in tch: pushed along over 4f out: outpcd over 1f out* **14/1**
1 **10** *3 1/2* **Off Message (IRE)**[82] 445 3-8-12 80 .... EddieAhern 7 79
(E A L Dunlop) *w'like: scope: b.bkwd: hld up: rdn over 1f out: no imp* **5/1**[2]
4 **11** *1 1/4* **Shout (IRE)**[19] 1114 3-8-12 .... SteveDrowne 5 77
(R Charlton) *hld up: rdn over 3f out: btn 2f out* **10/1**
34- **12** *1 1/2* **Wassfa**[251] 4896 3-8-12 .... SebSanders 12 74
(C E Brittain) *racd keenly: prom: rdn 2f out: wknd over 1f out* **33/1**

2m 26.06s (0.27) **Going Correction** 0.0s/f (Good) 12 Ran SP% **122.1**
Speed ratings (Par 104):99,96,96,96,95 95,94,94,94,92 91,90
CSF £23.89 TOTE £2.90: £1.50, £2.80, £3.90; EX 25.30 Trifecta £437.00 Pool: £984.80 - 1.60 winning tickets.
Owner R Barnett **Bred** W And R Barnett Ltd **Trained** Arundel, W Sussex

FOCUS
A very weak renewal of the Cheshire Oaks - fifth-placed Marachi Band came into this officially rated 72 - and Time On ran out an easy winner after being allowed her own way up front and leading at an ordinary pace. Quite predictably they were well bunched in behind and the form does not look very reliable. The winning time was modest for a race of its type.

NOTEBOOK
Time On, off the mark in an extended nine-furlong maiden at Folkestone on her reappearance, showed significantly improved form on this step up in class, but had things very much her own way. Left alone up front, she set just an ordinary pace and never looked like being caught when suddenly quickening up inside the final two furlongs. While she was impressive on the eye, the manner of this success flatters her, and the opposition was weak by Listed standards. She may be supplemented for the Oaks at a cost of £20,000 but, while she deserves her chance given it does not always take a great performance to place at Epsom, and the track will suit, the single-figure price offered by Ladbrokes does not appeal at all. (op 5-2 tchd 11-4)
Mont Etoile(IRE), who overcame trouble in running to make a successful reappearance in maiden company at Yarmouth, fared best of those in behind the comfortable winner to pick up some valuable black type. The form of this race does not look very reliable but she deserves another chance to further boost her value.
Prowess(IRE), who showed promise in a couple of runs at up to a mile in maiden company as a juvenile, made a pleasing return from a 232-day break and will no doubt have delighted her connections in picking up some valuable black type. This form is not to be relied upon but she is open to improvement. (op 14-1)
Kaylianni, who showed improved form on her second run at two when sixth of nine in a seven-furlong Newbury Listed race, was taking quite a jump up in trip on her return from a 200-day break, so the steady pace may not have been that much of an inconvenience, and she ran well.
Marachi Band(USA) has progressed nicely at a modest level of late, but none of her form entitled her to finish so close in a race like the Cheshire Oaks and her proximity does little for the form. (op 28-1)
Allegretto(IRE), a really well-bred filly who offered promise when fifth in a backend maiden at Doncaster on her only start at two, did not have the race run to suit and is better than she was able to show. She apparently finished lame, but should be given another chance if there are no serious problems. Official explanation: vet said filly spread front plate and returned lame (op 11-2 tchd 8-1)
Fusili(IRE) raced in mid-division throughout and could not pick up when asked. While this company was a bit hot, she was entitled to finish in front of the fifth-placed Marachi Band.
Auction Room(USA) was said to look fit enough for its first run of the season, but was on its toes before the race. (op 16-1)
Off Message(IRE) created a good impression when winning an extended nine-furlong maiden at Wolverhampton on her debut nearly three months previously, but had no chance upped in class given that she was held up near last throughout in a race run at a steady pace. Official explanation: vet said filly sustained cut on near foreleg (op 11-2)

1584 TOTESPORT CHESTER CUP (HERITAGE H'CAP) 2m 2f 147y
2:50 (2:56) (Class 2) 4-Y-O+
£74,784 (£22,392; £11,196; £5,604; £2,796; £1,404) **Stalls** High

Form RPR
/50- **1** **Admiral (IRE)**[32] 5421 5-8-1 85 ow1 .... JohnEgan 1 92
(T J Pitt) *mde all: rdn over 1f out: styd on gamely* **28/1**
432- **2** *1 1/4* **Vinando**[74] 6339 5-9-3 101 .... (bt) LDettori 2 107
(C R Egerton) *lw: trckd ldrs: rdn 3f out: wnt 2nd 2f out: styd on u.p ins fnl f* **7/1**
1-11 **3** *hd* **Greenwich Meantime**[11] 1294 6-7-13 83 3ex .... PaulHanagan 11 88+
(R A Fahey) *lw: hld up: hdwy over 3f out: rdn on wd outside over 2f out: r.o ins fnl f* **11/2**[3]
44-2 **4** *hd* **Dancing Bay**[28] 991 9-9-5 103 .... JamieSpencer 13 108
(N J Henderson) *s.i.s: midfield: hdwy 4f out: rdn 2f out: r.o ins fnl f* **20/1**
00-0 **5** *1/2* **Winged D'Argent (IRE)**[10] 1332 5-9-5 108 .... GregFairley(5) 5 113
(M Johnston) *a.p: pushed along 4f out: styd on u.p ins fnl f: no ex cl home* **25/1**
21-5 **6** *1 1/4* **Bulwark (IRE)**[22] 1071 4-8-4 92 .... (be) KerrinMcEvoy 15 95+
(Mrs A J Perrett) *lw: hld up in rr: hdwy whn nt clr run and swtchd rt over 2f out: carried hd awkwardly: fin wl* **9/1**
4511 **7** *hd* **Cold Turkey**[25] 1021 6-8-11 95 .... RyanMoore 17 98
(G L Moore) *swtchd lft s: hld up: wnt into midfield after 2f: nt clr run over 2f out: rdn and hdwy over 1f out: styd on: nt trble ldrs* **16/1**
1P-2 **8** *1 1/2* **The Nawab (IRE)**[17] 1167 4-8-1 89 .... JimmyQuinn 7 90
(J L Dunlop) *in tch: lost pl wl over 7f out: rdn over 3f out: styd on one pce fr over 1f out* **9/2**[1]
453- **9** *1* **Elusive Dream**[186] 6250 5-8-6 90 .... SebSanders 6 90
(Sir Mark Prescott) *lw: midfield: rdn and hdwy 3f out: n.m.r over 2f out: hung lft fr over 1f out: one pce ins fnl f* **5/1**[2]
2021 **10** *3/4* **Trance (IRE)**[18] 1132 6-7-12 82 oh2 .... (p) PaulFessey 3 81+
(T D Barron) *s.i.s: hld up: rdn over 2f out: kpt on fnl f: nvr able to chal* **25/1**
62-0 **11** *nk* **Dr Sharp (IRE)**[11] 1294 6-8-2 86 .... RoystonFfrench 16 85
(T P Tate) *midfield: hdwy 10f out: rdn whn chsd ldrs 3f out: wknd over 1f out* **50/1**
000- **12** *1* **Big Moment**[34] 5594 8-8-5 89 .... (p) PhilipRobinson 9 87
(Mrs A J Perrett) *hld up: nt clr run and hmpd over 2f out: rdn over 1f out: no imp* **20/1**
41-1 **13** *5* **Mikao (IRE)**[22] 1071 5-8-0 87 .... SaleemGolam(3) 18 80
(M H Tompkins) *in tch: effrt 3f out: wknd 2f out* **16/1**
5053 **14** *1 3/4* **High Point (IRE)**[14] 1247 8-7-7 82 oh9 .... RobynBrisland(5) 10 73
(G P Enright) *racd keenly: hld up: pushed along over 3f out: nvr on terms* **50/1**
2-66 **15** *7* **Hiddensee (USA)**[17] 1167 4-8-4 92 .... JoeFanning 14 75
(M Johnston) *midfield: rdn 4f out: wknd over 3f out* **33/1**
0635 **16** *shd* **Kristensen**[16] 1184 7-7-13 83 oh10 ow1 .... (v) FrankieMcDonald 8 66
(Karen McLintock) *racd keenly: prom tl rdn and wknd over 3f out* **50/1**
300- **17** *2 1/2* **Contact Dancer (IRE)**[23] 2925 7-8-8 92 .... (p) KFallon 4 72
(C F Swan, Ire) *a bhd* **10/1**

4m 3.34s (-2.23) **Going Correction** 0.0s/f (Good)
WFA 4 from 5yo+ 4lb 18 Ran SP% **123.1**
Speed ratings (Par 109):109,108,108,108,108 107,107,106,106,106 105,105,103,102,99 99,98
CSF £196.62 CT £1261.34 TOTE £44.80: £5.70, £2.10, £2.00, £3.20; EX 320.80 Trifecta £2075.20 Part won. Pool: £2,922.90 - 0.10 winning tickets..
Owner Chris Roper & Willie McKay **Bred** R Lee **Trained** Bawtry, S Yorks
■ Stewards' Enquiry : Kerrin McEvoy two-day ban: careless riding (May 21-22)

FOCUS
This looked a reasonable renewal beforehand, but the draw played a huge part with stall one beating stall two, and the form may not be that reliable. Greenwich Meantime and Dancing Bay fared best of those in double-figure stalls, and best of those who raced off the pace.

NOTEBOOK
Admiral(IRE) looked like making a smart hurdler at the beginning of the last jumps season, but was faced with some stiff tasks and soon lost his way. However, returned to the level and having just his second start for his current trainer, he was soon booted into the lead to take full advantage of stall one and, very much allowed his own way, found plenty in the straight to dispel any stamina doubts. He had to be re-shod at the start, but it did not bother him in the slightest and he showed no ill effects in the race itself. Although flattered by the bare form given that he had the best draw and was allowed an uncontested lead, he is clearly up to making a very useful stayer now that he has proven his stamina, and he should not look too harshly treated when reassessed, given that he only raced off a mark of 85 here. (op 33-1)
Vinando, back on the Flat following three unsuccessful spins over hurdles, returned from a 74-day break in good form and ran well from his favourable draw. This was a very good effort, but plenty of those in behind did not enjoy clear runs from less favourable positions and it remains to be seen whether he will confirm this. (op 8-1 tchd 9-1)
Greenwich Meantime, chasing a five-timer following a couple of victories for the Ramsdens last season and two wins for his new connections this term, was 2lb well in under his penalty but still racing off a career-high mark, a rating 16lb higher than when starting his winning run. He broke well enough, but his rider was keen not to be caught wide and dropped him in. Given the winner hardly saw another horse, he did well to pick up sufficiently to grab a place and he is clearly still improving. (op 5-1)
Dancing Bay, second in a Nottingham Listed race on his return to the Flat, ran a fine race under his big weight from his double-figure stall.
Winged D'Argent(IRE) was never far away and kept on to run a good race under his big weight. (op 28-1)
Bulwark(IRE) ◆ is not an easy ride, but he has bags of talent and Kerrin McEvoy was four from four aboard him coming into this. That sequence was broken, but he still ran a big race and may well have won had he enjoyed a clear run. His jockey cannot be blamed for the way things developed as he needs kidding along and had an awful draw, but the way he finished despite meeting trouble suggests he is still very much improving. There is a decent race or two to be won with him the season, and races like the Ascot Stakes and Northumberland Plate look ideal targets. He looks one to follow, despite his quirkiness.
Cold Turkey, in great form on Polytrack recently, had a terrible draw and his style of running would not have been suited to this track. Considering he raced off a mark just 1lb lower than that of his highest ever, this was a very respectable effort.
The Nawab(IRE) has run well here in the past and looked an obvious type for this contest, but he was below form and proved a little disappointing. (tchd 5-1 in a place)
Elusive Dream may have been closer with a clearer run, but it remains to be seen just how well handicapped he is.
Contact Dancer(IRE), an Irish raider who had cheekpieces fitted on his return to the level, would have preferred softer ground and could not repeat last year's third in this race.

1585 BREITLING WATCHES & WALTONS OF CHESTER H'CAP 1m 2f 75y
3:20 (3:24) (Class 2) (0-100,99) 4-Y-~~0~~**£13,248** (£3,964; £1,982; £991; £493) **Stalls** High

Form RPR
-203 **1** **Divine Gift**[14] 1239 5-8-11 92 .... JamieSpencer 8 101
(K A Ryan) *lw: mde all: rdn to qckn clr over 1f out: r.o* **11/2**[1]
4123 **2** *1 1/4* **Nice Tune**[25] 1015 4-8-4 85 .... AlanMunro 10 92
(C E Brittain) *b: lw: midfield: hdwy over 4f out: rdn over 1f out: nt qckn fnl f* **7/1**[3]
/1-0 **3** *nk* **Focus Group (USA)**[36] 865 5-8-8 89 .... JimmyQuinn 5 95
(J J Quinn) *in tch: rdn and nt qckn 2f out: r.o towards fin* **7/1**[3]
10-0 **4** *nk* **Ofaraby**[14] 1239 6-9-4 99 .... PhilipRobinson 4 104
(M A Jarvis) *b.hind: cl up: rdn and nt qckn 2f out: r.o towards fin* **7/1**[3]
000- **5** *3/4* **Alfie Noakes**[218] 5690 4-8-5 86 .... KerrinMcEvoy 12 90
(Mrs A J Perrett) *midfield: wnt prom wl over 7f out: rdn over 1f out: hung rt and no ex ins fnl f* **14/1**
-206 **6** *1 1/2* **Sew'N'So Character (IRE)**[19] 1111 5-8-5 86 .... PaulHanagan 3 87
(M Blanshard) *racd keenly: sn dropped to midfield: rdn over 1f out: styd on ins fnl f: nt rch ldrs* **6/1**[2]

-016 **7** *hd* **Yakimov (USA)**[15] 1206 7-8-1 **85** oh1 .... EdwardCreighton(3) 11 86
(D J Wintle) *hld up: rdn and styd on ins fnl f: nvr nrr* **16/1**

300- **8** *3/4* **Temple Place (IRE)**[33] 5137 5-8-10 **91** ....(t) RichardHughes 13 90
(D McCain) *lw: hld up: rdn and swtchd rt over 1f out: kpt on ins fnl f: nvr trbld ldrs* **33/1**

30-0 **9** *3/4* **Kames Park (IRE)**[11] 1281 4-8-6 **87** oh1 ow2 ....(p) TomEaves 1 85
(I Semple) *t.k.h: prom: rdn and carried hd high over 1f out: sn wknd* **20/1**

10-0 **10** *2 1/2* **Fairmile**[22] 1071 4-8-7 **88** .... SebSanders 7 81
(W R Swinburn) *midfield: lost pl 2f out: n.d after* **9/1**

-105 **11** *1/2* **Tiger Tiger (FR)**[95] 296 5-9-1 **96** .... SteveDrowne 14 88
(Jamie Poulton) *swtg: hld up: pushed along over 2f out: nvr on terms* **14/1**

12 *2 1/2* **Magnum Opus (IRE)**[211] 4-8-4 **85** .... JohnEgan 9 73
(T J Pitt) *midfield: rdn over 2f out: sn nt clr run: wknd over 1f out* **16/1**

60-0 **13** *2* **Diamonds And Dust**[18] 1129 4-8-2 **86** .... SaleemGolam(3) 2 70
(M H Tompkins) *midfield: rdn over 2f out: sn wknd* **14/1**

00-0 **14** *12* **Artistic Style**[25] 1017 6-8-11 **92** .... RoystonFfrench 6 53
(B Ellison) *rel to r and lost 27l s: bhd: hdwy wl over 7f out and hung bdly rt: midfield over 5f out: wknd over 2f out* **25/1**

2m 12.82s (-0.32) **Going Correction** 0.0s/f (Good) **14** Ran SP% **120.5**
Speed ratings (Par 109):101,100,99,99,98 97,97,96,96,94 93,91,90,80
CSF £41.93 CT £278.59 TOTE £5.00: £2.10, £2.50, £3.00; EX 18.40 Trifecta £437.80 Pool: £986.74 - 1.60 winning units.

Owner Sporting Gunners Syndicate Two **Bred** Bloomsbury Stud **Trained** Hambleton, N Yorks

FOCUS
A competitive handicap, but the pace was not at all strong and the winning time was moderate, so it is difficult to be confident about the form. Yet again the winner made all of the running, the third consecutive race in which that had happened.

NOTEBOOK
Divine Gift confirmed the promise of his Epsom effort, but this victory is totally down to him being left alone in front and able to set his own pace on a track that was very much favouring front-runners. That is not to say he cannot win again, though, as his new yard seems to have found the key to him. (op 6-1)

Nice Tune is running consistently well just now and stayed on to snatch second place, but the enterprisingly-ridden winner had gone beyond recall. It does appear that this is her best trip now. (op 6-1)

Focus Group(USA) ◆, who seemed to get bogged down in the heavy ground on his reappearance and first start for the yard, performed a lot better back on a quick surface over this extra quarter-mile. He finished in great style once switched and remains relatively unexposed. (op 8-1)

Ofaraby ◆ ran a fine race in defeat especially as he would have preferred some cut. This should have put him spot on. (op 13-2)

Alfie Noakes showed up for a very long way, but he had nothing more to offer inside the last furlong. He was returning from a seven-month break, but won after an even longer layoff last season so may not come on a great deal for this. (op 16-1)

Sew'N'So Character(IRE), who has done most of his racing over a mile in recent seasons, could never land an effective blow but was up against it in trying to come from off the pace given the way the track was riding. (op 7-1)

Kames Park(IRE) was said not to have come in his coat yet.

Artistic Style stood still as the stalls opened and, when eventually underway, he proved virtually unrideable.

1586 WALKER SMITH WAY H'CAP — 1m 4f 66y
4:00 (4:00) (Class 3) (0-95,91) 3-Y-O **£10,039** (£2,986; £1,492; £745) **Stalls** High

Form RPR

0-1 **1** **Galient (IRE)**[21] 1081 3-9-7 **89** .... PhilipRobinson 6 101+
(M A Jarvis) *lw: led after 1f: mde rest: rdn over 1f out: pressed ins fnl f: r.o gamely* **15/8**[1]

421- **2** *1* **Daylami Star**[219] 5658 3-8-12 **80** .... JimmyFortune 1 90
(J H M Gosden) *trckd ldrs: rdn to chse wnr 2f out: ev ch ins fnl f: nt qckn towards fin* **3/1**[2]

6-23 **3** *1 1/2* **Gee Dee Nen**[11] 1286 3-8-8 **79** .... SaleemGolam(3) 3 87
(M H Tompkins) *in tch: pushed along over 5f out: carried sltly wd on bnd 2f out: rdn whn chsd ldrs over 1f out: sn hung lft: styd on* **9/1**

501- **4** *3* **Dynacam (USA)**[187] 6246 3-8-13 **81** .... RyanMoore 2 84
(Sir Michael Stoute) *hld up: hdwy 2f out: sn rdn: wknd ins fnl f* **5/1**

-152 **5** *17* **Reveur**[11] 1282 3-7-12 **71** oh1 ow1 .... JamesDoyle(5) 4 47
(M Mullineaux) *stdd s: pushed along over 5f out: a bhd* **33/1**

3-11 **6** *9* **Remember Ramon (USA)**[9] 1356 3-9-9 **91** 6ex........... JamieSpencer 5 52+
(M J Wallace) *racd keenly: led for 1f: remained prom: hung rt most of way: w ldr 6f out: wknd qckly ent fnl 2f: sn eased* **7/2**[3]

2m 36.58s (-4.07) **Going Correction** 0.0s/f (Good) **6** Ran SP% **111.6**
Speed ratings (Par 103):113,112,111,109,98 92
CSF £7.64 TOTE £2.30: £1.70, £1.90; EX 8.20.

Owner Mr & Mrs Kevan Watts **Bred** Cliveden Stud Ltd **Trained** Newmarket, Suffolk

FOCUS
Although not given an easy lead, the winner just about made all to demonstrate once again how much the track was favouring front-runners. The winning time was very smart for the type of contest and the form looks strong despite the small field.

NOTEBOOK
Galient(IRE) ◆, making his handicap debut, adopted the same tactics that served him so well at Newmarket and found the track helping him in that respect. He did not have an easy time of it over the last half-mile, though, and had to battle very hard to prevail, so this victory should not be seen as merely the result of a track bias. The winning time suggests the form is strong and he can continue to progress. The Queen's Vase remains his target and the longer trip looks certain to suit him. (op 7-4 after 13-8 in a place, tchd 2-1)

Daylami Star ◆, up in trip and returning from a seven-month break, gave it everything and tried very hard to close the winner down in the home straight, but found him very determined. He should go one better before too long, but was reported to look very fit prior to the race. (tchd 11-4 and 10-3)

Gee Dee Nen, racing on fast ground for the first time, had every chance but did seem to find conditions rather quicker than he would have liked. He is worth another chance back on an easier surface. (op 10-1)

Dynacam(USA), easy winner of a heavy-ground Yarmouth maiden on her third outing as a juvenile, found these conditions very different, and a brief effort rounding the home turn came to nothing. (op 7-1)

Reveur, the most experienced in the field, was always out the back and seemed to find this company too hot. (op 50-1)

Remember Ramon(USA), bidding for a hat-trick under his penalty, looked very unhappy on the track but was still in with a chance when suddenly coming to a halt rounding the home turn. It transpired that the bit had slipped through his mouth so he can be forgiven this. Official explanation: jockey said bit pulled through colt's mouth (tchd 10-3)

1587 GRANT THORNTON UK E B F MAIDEN STKS — 5f 16y
4:35 (4:36) (Class 2) 2-Y-O **£8,582** (£2,553; £1,275; £637) **Stalls** Low

Form RPR

3 **1** **Captain Marvelous (IRE)**[20] 1090 2-9-3 .... MichaelHills 4 81+
(B W Hills) *in tch: rdn and hdwy over 1f out: sn hung lft: r.o to ld wl ins fnl f* **11/8**[1]

0 **2** *1 1/4* **Benllech**[15] 1203 2-9-3 .... JimmyFortune 9 76
(S Kirk) *lw: s.i.s and carried rt s: sn in midfield: hdwy and edgd lft over 1f out: swtchd rt ins fnl f: fin wl* **33/1**

3 **3** *shd* **Kyle (IRE)**[8] 1372 2-9-3 .... RichardHughes 7 76
(R Hannon) *lw: bmpd s: a.p: rdn whn carried sltly wd on bnd over 1f out: sn led: hdd wl ins fnl f: nt qckn* **2/1**[2]

4 *1* **Tang** 2-8-12 .... RobertMiles 5 67
(W G M Turner) *leggy: led: rdn whn edgd rt on bnd over 1f out: sn hdd: no ex towards fin* **40/1**

05 **5** *1 1/2* **Baileys Hilight (IRE)**[20] 1096 2-9-3 .... JoeFanning 3 66
(M Johnston) *prom: rdn over 1f out: fdd towards fin* **16/1**

0 **6** *3/4* **Crystal Ice (IRE)**[15] 1223 2-8-12 .... TomEaves 6 58
(Mrs L Williamson) *wnt rt s: chsd ldrs: rdn over 1f out: one pce ins fnl f* **66/1**

7 *1 3/4* **Northern Fling** 2-9-3 .... FrancisNorton 10 56+
(D Nicholls) *w'like: midfield: pushed along whn rn green and lost pl over 3f out: kpt on ins fnl f: no imp* **66/1**

6 **8** *3/4* **Luscivious**[6] 1442 2-9-3 .... EddieAhern 8 53
(M J Polglase) *wnt rt s: midfield: pushed along over 2f out: nt pce to chal* **33/1**

44 **9** *1/2* **Miss Kool Kat (USA)**[21] 1080 2-8-12 .... PhilipRobinson 1 46
(K A Ryan) *chsd ldrs: rdn over 1f out: sn wknd* **5/1**[3]

10 *shd* **Harriets Dream** 2-8-12 .... RobbieFitzpatrick 11 45+
(Peter Grayson) *leggy: bit bkwd: s.i.s: sn in midfield: n.m.r over 3f out: no hdwy* **100/1**

11 *nk* **Pat Will (IRE)** 2-8-12 .... JamieSpencer 15 44+
(P D Evans) *leggy: s.i.s: hld up: kpt on whn racd on wd outside ins fnl f: nt trble ldrs* **28/1**

12 *2* **Not For Me (IRE)** 2-9-3 .... JohnEgan 2 41
(T J Pitt) *b: dwlt: a bhd* **14/1**

13 *1/2* **Mandurah (IRE)** 2-9-3 .... SilvestreDeSousa 14 39
(D Nicholls) *w'like: str: bit bkwd: s.i.s: a bhd* **80/1**

14 *hd* **Cheshire Prince** 2-9-3 .... SebSanders 13 38
(W M Brisbourne) *leggy: s.i.s: a bhd* **66/1**

15 *3/4* **Delta Queen** 2-8-12 .... JimmyQuinn 12 30
(C N Kellett) *wnt rt s: a bhd* **80/1**

61.84 secs (-0.21) **Going Correction** 0.0s/f (Good) **15** Ran SP% **124.4**
Speed ratings (Par 99):101,99,98,97,94 93,89,88,87,87 86,83,82,82,81
CSF £64.36 TOTE £2.30: £1.20, £6.80, £1.30; EX 66.60 Place 6 £16.87, Place 5 £15.84.

Owner R J Arculli **Bred** Duncan A McGregor **Trained** Lambourn, Berks

■ Stewards' Enquiry : Joe Fanning three-day ban: careless riding (May 21-23)

FOCUS
A big field of two-year-olds and not surprisingly the draw played its part. Also, those with previous experience did best on this tricky track. Although the winner is value for more than the official margin, the form does not look that solid.

NOTEBOOK
Captain Marvelous(IRE) ◆ confirmed the promise of his Newmarket debut despite not everything going right for him. He was well drawn but missed the break and was forced to make his effort wide, especially rounding the home bend. He also looked less than happy on the track, but still found enough to win with a degree of comfort in the end. This performance can be considered even better than it looked. (tchd 6-4, 13-8 in places)

Benllech ◆ finished in great style and deserves plenty of credit considering his modest draw and the fact that he met trouble at the start. A maiden should come his way before too long.

Kyle(IRE) was always in a good position but, after hitting the front a furlong out, he could do nothing do repel the favourite and unfortunately lost second place right on the line. (op 9-4)

Tang, a half-sister to Arabian Dancer, tried to make every yard and made a good fist of it. She did much the best of the newcomers and should soon make her mark. (op 50-1)

Baileys Hilight(IRE), more experienced than most, was well drawn to run a big race given his proven early pace. He duly raced prominently for a long way before running out of puff and may still need more time, so nurseries later in the season may be his thing.

Crystal Ice(IRE) caught the eye on her Wolverhampton Polytrack debut, despite only finishing seventh of 11, and again demonstrated that she does possess some ability.

Miss Kool Kat(USA) appeared to have no excuses from the plum draw and does not seem to be progressing. (op 6-1 after 7-1 in a place)

T/Jkpt: Not won. T/Plt: £17.20 to a £1 stake. Pool: £100,693.80. 4,256.50 winning tickets. T/Qpdt: £6.70 to a £1 stake. Pool: £4,606.70. 503.20 winning tickets. DO

1341 NEWCASTLE (L-H)
Wednesday, May 10

OFFICIAL GOING: Good (good to firm in places) changing to good to firm after race 4 (3.35)
Wind: Light; half behind Weather: Fine and sunny

1588 EVERSHEDS LLP MEDIAN AUCTION MAIDEN STKS — 6f
2:00 (2:01) (Class 6) 2-Y-O **£2,914** (£867; £433; £216) **Stalls** High

Form RPR

1 **Vital Equine (IRE)** 2-9-3 .... ChrisCatlin 5 80+
(E J O'Neill) *w'like: leggy: scope: chsd ldrs far side: led over 1f out: r.o strly* **4/1**[2]

3 **2** *2* **Domino Dancer (IRE)**[9] 1342 2-9-3 .... RobertWinston 4 74
(J Howard Johnson) *mde most far side: hdd over 1f out: no ex* **7/2**[1]

5 **3** *1 1/2* **Ten Dollars More (IRE)**[6] 1429 2-9-3 .... ShaneKelly 8 70
(J A Osborne) *racd far side: in tch: hdwy over 2f out: styd on fnl f* **6/1**[3]

4 *3/4* **Top Bid** 2-9-3 .... DavidAllan 6 67
(T D Easterby) *rangy: scope: racd far side: w ldr: kpt on same pce fnl 2f* **12/1**

5 *2* **Middleham (IRE)** 2-9-3 .... KDarley 11 67+
(M Johnston) *w'like: leggy: racd stands's side: w ldrs: led that gp over 2f out: edgd lft: kpt on same pce* **12/1**

6 *nk* **Soviet Palace (IRE)** 2-9-3 .... DO'Donohoe 13 65+
(K A Ryan) *led stands' side: kpt on same pce appr fnl f* **33/1**

7 *1* **Ebn Reem** 2-9-3 .... MatthewHenry 10 57
(M A Jarvis) *w'like: chsd ldrs far side: effrt over 2f out: one pce* **4/1**[2]

0 **8** *3/4* **Soundasapound**[21] 1074 2-8-9 .... PatrickMathers(3) 16 56+
(I W McInnes) *racd stands' side: mid-div: kpt on fnl 2f* **100/1**

9 shd **Eddie Jock (IRE)** 2-9-3 ... HayleyTurner 1 55
(M L W Bell) *lengthy: unf: racd far side: sn outpcd and bhd: kpt on fnl 2f: nvr nr ldrs* **16/1**

10 hd **Seaton Snooks** 2-9-3 ... GrahamGibbons 3 54
(T D Easterby) *leggy: scope: mid-div: kpt on fnl 2f: nvr a threat* **66/1**

11 nk **Just Oscar (GER)** 2-9-3 ... DarrenWilliams 14 59+
(W M Brisbourne) *leggy: scope: dwlt: racd stands' side: nvr nr ldrs* **40/1**

12 nk **Straight Face (IRE)** 2-9-3 ... MartinDwyer 12 58+
(W J Knight) *w'like: cmpt: racd stands' side: sn outpcd: kpt on fnl 2f: nvr on terms* **25/1**

000 13 ½ **Homes By Woodford**[6] 1442 2-9-0 ... PaulMulrennan(3) 9 51
(M W Easterby) *racd far side: chsd ldrs: outpcd fnl 2f* **100/1**

6 14 1¼ **Pietersen (IRE)**[20] 1090 2-9-3 ... PhillipMakin 7 47
(T D Barron) *racd far side: sn outpcd: nvr on terms* **18/1**

0 15 1 **Mundo's Magic**[9] 1342 2-9-3 ... FergalLynch 17 50+
(D W Barker) *racd stands' side: chsd ldrs 4f: sn wknd* **66/1**

16 2½ **Bowman's Boy (IRE)** 2-9-3 ... DaleGibson 2 37
(M W Easterby) *leggy: unf: racd far side: sn outpcd and bhd* **50/1**

17 27 **Ashover Rock (IRE)** 2-9-3 ... TonyHamilton 15 —+
(I W McInnes) *leggy: unf: s.v.s: racd stands' side: sn outpcd* **100/1**

1m 13.21s (-1.88) **Going Correction** -0.55s/f (Hard) **17** Ran SP% **120.2**
Speed ratings (Par 91):90,87,85,84,81 81,79,78,78,78 78,77,77,75,74 70,34
CSF £17.01 TOTE £6.20: £1.50, £1.80, £2.60; EX 30.60 Trifecta £69.80 Part won. Pool: £98.35 - 0.53 winning units..
Owner Fasthandle Ltd **Bred** John Costello **Trained** Averham Park, Notts

FOCUS
The first six-furlong race of the season for juveniles. Those drawn low seemed to have a massive advantage and the placed horses are the best guide with the stands'-side group likely to do better on a level playing field.

NOTEBOOK
Vital Equine(IRE) showed a tidy change of gear to come through and take it up a furlong out, stretching away for a comfy success. Considering his trainer was expressing doubts over his readiness beforehand, it is reasonable to expect improvement, and he should be capable of seeing out at least seven furlongs if the dam's side of his pedigree is anything to go by. (op 9-2 tchd 5-1)
Domino Dancer(IRE) showed plenty of speed when third over five furlongs on his debut here last week, and he was equally effective at this sixth furlong, simply finding the winner too classy. He should have little trouble finding a race if continuing to head the right way. (op 10-3 tchd 4-1)
Ten Dollars More(IRE) showed the benefit of last week's promising Folkestone outing, appreciating the step up to six furlongs and keeping on well inside the final quarter mile. He can probably find a small maiden, but his future will ultimately lie in nurseries. (op 7-1)
Top Bid, who looked exceptionally well in the paddock beforehand, shaped most promisingly back in fourth, showing good early speed before keeping on at the one pace. He may improve for a softer surface and is one to watch next time. (op 9-1)
Middleham(IRE), who has been given an entry in the Grade One Phoenix Stakes, was weak in the market throughout the day and he showed typical traits of a Johnston newcomer, running green and looking unsure of what was required of him. He wandered into the middle of the course and ended up nearer those on the far side, but the experience should not be lost on him. (op 9-1)
Soviet Palace(IRE), who is bred to appreciate a mile, fared best of those who raced on the stands' side, leading his group and staying on right the way to the line. His trainer's juveniles usually benefit from a run and seven furlongs will help in time. (op 40-1)
Ebn Reem was providing Michael Jarvis with his first juvenile runner of the season, but he looked in need of the outing beforehand and confirmed that impression in the race itself. There was promise to be taken from this and better can be expected next time. (op 7-2 tchd 10-3)
Eddie Jock(IRE) never got into things early, but stayed on well enough in the latter stages to suggest he is capable of improving for the experience. (op 12-1)
Seaton Snooks Official explanation: jockey said colt ran green
Mundo's Magic Official explanation: jockey said colt hung left-handed from 3f out
Ashover Rock(IRE) Official explanation: jockey said gelding hung left-handed throughout

1589 CROFT TECHNOLOGY PLC MEDIAN AUCTION MAIDEN STKS 5f
2:30 (2:31) (Class 6) 3-4-Y-O **£2,590** (£770; £385; £192) **Stalls** High

Form RPR

00-0 1 **Moorhouse Lad**[18] 1147 3-9-0 78 ... RobertWinston 6 86+
(G Woodward) *mde all: hung lft over 2f out: forged clr fnl f: readily* **13/2**

25-2 2 2½ **Lucksin (IRE)**[19] 1127 3-9-0 75 ... KDarley 3 73
(N Tinkler) *w ldr: rdn over 2f out: rallied to take 2nd nr fin* **10/3**[2]

3-3 3 nk **Monashee Brave (IRE)**[18] 1147 3-9-0 ... GrahamGibbons 1 72
(J J Quinn) *chsd ldrs: carried hd high over 1f out: no ex* **9/4**[1]

3536 4 1½ **Arzaag**[20] 1089 3-9-0 72 ... MartinDwyer 5 67
(D M Simcock) *sn outpcd: hdwy over 2f out: nvr nr ldrs* **7/2**[3]

434- 5 nk **Opera Writer (IRE)**[269] 4393 3-9-0 75 ... DavidAllan 4 65
(T D Easterby) *sn outpcd: sme hdwy over 2f out: nvr a threat* **4/1**

650- 6 6 **Chunky Bell**[254] 4829 3-9-0 ... LeeEnstone 2 44
(P T Midgley) *sn outpcd: sme hdwy over 2f out: sn wknd* **100/1**

5 7 5 **Ailsa**[19] 1126 4-9-4 ... DeanMcKeown 7 25
(C W Thornton) *stdd s: a last* **33/1**

59.35 secs (-2.15) **Going Correction** -0.55s/f (Hard)
WFA 3 from 4yo 9lb **7** Ran SP% **113.3**
Speed ratings (Par 101):95,91,90,88,87 78,70
CSF £27.83 TOTE £8.10: £3.50, £1.80; EX 26.60.
Owner Ron Hull **Bred** P Onslow **Trained** Conisbrough, S Yorks

FOCUS
An ordinary maiden and the form, rated through the second, is unlikely to be that strong.

1590 NEWCASTLE INTERNATIONAL AIRPORT H'CAP 1m 4f 93y
3:00 (3:00) (Class 6) (0-60,56) 4-Y-0+ **£2,914** (£867; £433; £216) **Stalls** Low

Form RPR

6-50 1 **Darghan (IRE)**[18] 1138 6-9-3 55 ... TPQueally 13 63
(W J Musson) *t.k.h in mid div: stdy hdwy 3f out: styd on wl to ld last 75yds* **14/1**

4-03 2 nk **Caymans Gift**[9] 1346 6-8-10 53 ... AndrewMullen(5) 5 61
(A C Whillans) *t.k.h in rr: hdwy over 3f out: led 1f out: hdd and no ex wl ins last* **15/2**[2]

40-0 3 1¾ **Intavac Boy**[9] 1346 5-9-3 55 ... RobertWinston 8 60
(C W Thornton) *chsd ldrs: hung lft and led over 1f out: sn hdd: kpt on same pce* **8/1**[3]

-011 4 1 **Figaro's Quest (IRE)**[5] 1467 4-9-2 54 6ex ...(b) MartinDwyer 10 57
(P F I Cole) *mid-div: hdwy over 2f out: kpt on same pce fnl f* **11/10**[1]

00-2 5 ½ **Archie Babe (IRE)**[16] 1187 10-9-1 53 ... GrahamGibbons 4 56
(J J Quinn) *trckd ldrs: led over 2f out: hdd over 1f out: one pce* **9/1**

0-00 6 shd **Hezaam (USA)**[13] 1256 5-9-4 56 ... DO'Donohoe 12 58
(Mrs A Duffield) *chsd ldrs: drvn along over 3f out: kpt on one pce fnl 2f* **16/1**

100- 7 ½ **Dimashq**[143] 6606 4-8-7 45 ... ChrisCatlin 1 47
(Ronald Thompson) *hld up in rr: hdwy over 2f out: styd on wl fnl f* **66/1**

3-12 8 2 **Shekan Star**[13] 1249 4-8-12 50 ... PaulEddery 6 48
(K G Reveley) *hld up in rr: hdwy on ins over 2f out: swtchd rt over 1f out: nvr rchd ldrs* **12/1**

0-00 9 1 **Mirage Prince (IRE)**[9] 1353 4-9-0 55 ... PatrickMathers(3) 7 52
(D Shaw) *hld up in rr: nvr on terms* **100/1**

-040 10 5 **Saameq (IRE)**[16] 1199 5-8-6 47 ... DanielTudhope(3) 15 36
(D W Thompson) *swtchd lft s: bhd: sme hdwy on outer 5f out: nvr on terms* **50/1**

00-4 11 1½ **Red River Rebel**[8] 1392 8-9-0 52 ... DarrenWilliams 9 38
(J R Norton) *led tl over 2f out: sn lost pl* **20/1**

P-60 12 3½ **Nakwa (IRE)**[72] 537 8-9-3 55 ... DavidAllan 3 36
(E J Alston) *chsd ldrs: rdn over 3f out: sn btn* **33/1**

234- 13 1½ **Onyergo (IRE)**[190] 6215 4-9-3 55 ... KDarley 14 33
(J R Weymes) *mid-div: effrt 3f out: sn btn* **25/1**

12-1 14 2 **Zoripp (IRE)**[13] 1256 4-9-4 56 ...(b) NeilPollard 11 31
(J G Given) *chsd ldrs: lost pl over 2f out* **12/1**

2m 42.42s (-1.13) **Going Correction** -0.10s/f (Good) **14** Ran SP% **124.4**
Speed ratings (Par 101):99,98,97,96,96 96,96,94,94,90 89,87,86,85
CSF £113.34 CT £921.09 TOTE £19.60: £5.80, £2.90, £3.30; EX 402.20 TRIFECTA Not won..
Owner S Rudolf **Bred** His Highness The Aga Khan's Studs S C **Trained** Newmarket, Suffolk

FOCUS
A competitive handicap, despite the favourite being fairly short in the market. The form looks sound rated through the third and fifth, and should prove reliable.
Red River Rebel Official explanation: trainer said gelding returned sore

1591 FIRST CHOICE HOLIDAYS H'CAP 1m 2f 32y
3:35 (3:37) (Class 6) (0-65,65) 4-Y-0+ **£2,914** (£867; £433; £216) **Stalls** Centre

Form RPR

10-4 1 **Dium Mac**[19] 1123 5-8-7 61 ... SuzzanneFrance(7) 14 73
(N Bycroft) *in rr: hdwy on outside over 3f out: hung lft and led 1f out: kpt on wl* **8/1**

3-00 2 3 **Rotuma (IRE)**[21] 1075 7-8-8 55 ...(b) PhillipMakin 7 62
(M Dods) *prom: effrt over 2f out: nt qckn ins last* **7/1**[2]

05-0 3 nk **Trouble Mountain (USA)**[23] 1045 9-8-12 59 ...(t) DaleGibson 1 65
(M W Easterby) *hld up towards rr: hdwy on inner over 2f out: styd on ins last* **14/1**

0-15 4 ½ **Donna's Double**[16] 1187 11-8-6 53 ...(p) TonyHamilton 4 58
(Karen McLintock) *chsd ldrs: one pce appr fnl f* **11/1**

00-0 5 hd **Ariodante**[16] 1186 4-9-4 65 ... ShaneKelly 6 70
(J M P Eustace) *chsd clr ldrs: led over 1f out: sn hdd and no ex* **33/1**

-050 6 shd **Apache Point (IRE)**[7] 1422 9-8-10 57 ... KimTinkler 13 61+
(N Tinkler) *mid-div: hdwy over 2f out: nt clr run over 1f out: styd on ins last* **14/1**

65-0 7 1¼ **Nabir (FR)**[75] 505 6-8-12 62 ...(t) PaulMulrennan(3) 11 64
(P D Niven) *chsd ldrs: one pce fnl 2f* **20/1**

66-6 8 ½ **San Deng**[23] 1045 4-9-1 62 ... RobertWinston 3 67+
(Micky Hammond) *mid-div: drvn along 5f out: kpt on: nvr rchd ldrs* **9/2**[1]

0500 9 ¾ **Street Life (IRE)**[18] 1144 8-9-4 65 ... TPQueally 5 65
(W J Musson) *hld up in rr: stdy hdwy on ins over 2f out: nt clr run 1f out: styd on ins last* **15/2**[3]

25-0 10 hd **Damburger Xpress**[11] 1288 4-8-13 60 ...(t) LPKeniry 15 59
(D M Simcock) *bhd: hdwy over 2f out: nvr nr ldrs* **12/1**

00/6 11 3½ **Bukit Fraser (IRE)**[38] 847 5-9-4 65 ...(t) MartinDwyer 8 58
(P F I Cole) *chsd ldrs: pushed along 5f out: nvr a threat* **7/1**[2]

500 12 1¾ **Bookman (IRE)**[16] 1185 4-8-8 60 ...(t) LeanneKershaw(5) 10 49
(P C Haslam) *s.i.s: a bhd* **25/1**

500- 13 8 **Woolly Back (IRE)**[295] 3609 5-8-9 56 ... AdrianTNicholls 12 30
(A C Whillans) *led: sn clr: put hd in air: hdd over 1f out: wknd: heavily eased ins last* **14/1**

2100 14 11 **Desert Fury**[13] 1253 9-8-5 52 ...(b) DO'Donohoe 2 5
(R Bastiman) *s.i.s: sn detached in rr* **16/1**

004- 15 5 **Red River Rock (IRE)**[296] 3586 4-8-8 55 ... GrahamGibbons 17 —
(T J Fitzgerald) *chsd ldrs: lost pl over 3f out: sn bhd* **40/1**

00-0 16 3½ **Celtic Shadow (IRE)**[14] 1233 4-8-7 54 ...(t) KDarley 9 —
(K G Reveley) *sn bhd* **16/1**

2m 9.83s (-1.97) **Going Correction** -0.10s/f (Good) **16** Ran SP% **127.8**
Speed ratings (Par 101):103,100,100,99,99 99,98,98,97,97 94,93,86,78,74 71
CSF £63.55 CT £800.85 TOTE £11.50: £2.20, £2.20, £3.80, £2.80; EX 82.30 TRIFECTA Not won..
Owner J A Swinburne **Bred** T Umpleby **Trained** Brandsby, N Yorks

FOCUS
An ordinary handicap run in a modest winning time for the grade and, although the form appears sound enough, it is not totally convincing..
Donna's Double Official explanation: jockey said gelding was unsuited by the good (good to firm places) ground
San Deng Official explanation: jockey said gelding was denied a clear run
Bukit Fraser(IRE) Official explanation: jockey said gelding was unsuited by the good (good to firm in places) ground
Woolly Back(IRE) Official explanation: jockey said gelding ran too free

1592 THOMAS COOK H'CAP 7f
4:10 (4:17) (Class 5) (0-75,75) 3-Y-0 **£3,886** (£1,156; £577; £288) **Stalls** High

Form RPR

43-6 1 **Abbey Cat (IRE)**[19] 1122 3-8-12 69 ... RobertWinston 9 83
(G A Swinbank) *swtchd lft after 1f and racd far side: sn trcking ldrs: led 2f out* **10/3**[1]

30-6 2 2½ **Royal Composer (IRE)**[16] 1185 3-8-8 65 ... DavidAllan 5 72
(T D Easterby) *racd far side: chsd ldr: led 2f out: sn hdd: no ch w wnr* **11/2**[3]

3-30 3 3 **Esoterica (IRE)**[16] 1185 3-8-2 62 ... BenSwarbrick(3) 4 61
(T D Barron) *racd far side: chsd ldrs: one pce fnl 2f* **10/1**

41-5 4 shd **Crosby Vision**[13] 1250 3-9-4 75 ... MartinDwyer 14 74+
(J R Weymes) *led stands' side: kpt on fnl 2f* **15/2**

053- 5 2½ **Moonstreaker**[213] 5769 3-8-11 68 ... DeanMcKeown 15 60+
(R M Whitaker) *racd stands' side: chsd ldr: hung lft over 1f out: one pce* **10/1**

55-2 6 nk **Neardown Beauty (IRE)**[10] 1312 3-8-9 66 ...(p) TPQueally 11 58+
(I A Wood) *swtchd rt and racd stands' side: one pce fnl 2f* **11/2**[3]

220- 7 1¼ **Strong Approach (IRE)**[251] 4880 3-9-3 74 ... PhillipMakin 8 62
(T D Barron) *racd far side: trckd ldrs: one pce fnl 2f* **16/1**

040- 8 7 **King Faz (IRE)**[236] 5275 3-8-3 65 ...(t) LeanneKershaw(5) 13 35+
(P C Haslam) *racd stands' side: chsd ldrs: hung lft over 2f out: sn wknd* **50/1**

030- 9 1¼ **Apache Nation (IRE)**[224] 5546 3-8-6 63 ... DO'Donohoe 2 30
(M Dods) *hld up far side: nvr a threat* **25/1**

0042 **10** *1 ½* **Beowulf**[6] [1441] 3-8-7 **64**........(b[1]) KDarley 6 27
(M Johnston) *hmpd s: racd far side: hdwy over 3f out: sn wknd* **9/2**[2]
040- **11** *4* **Madam Moschata**[294] [3624] 3-8-8 **65**........ NeilPollard 7 18
(D W Barker) *swtchd lft s: led far side: hdd over 2f out: sn lost pl* **50/1**
000 **12** *1 ¾* **Bacharach (IRE)**[9] [1345] 3-8-11 **68**........ ChrisCatlin 3 16
(R F Fisher) *racd far side: a in rr* **50/1**
100- **13** *32* **River Crossing**[267] [4456] 3-9-1 **72**........ FergalLynch 12 —
(T D Easterby) *racd stands' side: sn bhd: virtually p.u: t.o* **25/1**

1m 25.18s (-4.82) **Going Correction** -0.55s/f (Hard) 13 Ran SP% **121.4**
Speed ratings (Par 99):105,102,98,98,95 95,93,85,84,82 78,76,39
CSF £20.84 CT £167.39 TOTE £3.80: £1.90, £2.10, £3.50; EX 28.10 Trifecta £176.20 Pool: £354.96 - 1.43 winning units.
Owner Abbadis Racing Club **Bred** Mrs Marion Daly **Trained** Melsonby, N Yorks

FOCUS
A decent winning time for a race of its type, in which those who raced on the far side again had the advantage. The form looks above average and those on the stands' side can be rated better than the bare form.
Moonstreaker Official explanation: jockey said gelding hung left-handed throughout
Bacharach(IRE) Official explanation: jockey said gelding hung right-handed throughout
River Crossing Official explanation: jockey said filly lost its action

1593 NEWCASTLE TO LONDON CITY WITH EASTERN AIRWAYS H'CAP 1m 3y(S)
4:45 (4:47) (Class 6) (0-60,60) 3-Y-O **£1,680** (£1,680; £385; £192) **Stalls** High

Form RPR
64-0 **1** **Moody Tunes**[36] [879] 3-9-2 **58**........ PatCosgrave 12 63
(K R Burke) *hld up in mid-div: hdwy to ld and j. shadow 1f out: jnd on line* **11/2**[3]
03-0 **1** *dht* **Punjabi**[18] [1141] 3-9-2 **58**........ J-PGuillambert 14 63
(Mrs G S Rees) *swtchd lft after 1f: hld up: hdwy over 2f out: styd on fnl f: jnd ldr on line* **25/1**
0-05 **3** *1 ½* **Boy Dancer (IRE)**[6] [1441] 3-8-10 **52**........ FergalLynch 3 54+
(D W Barker) *dwlt: hld up in rr: hdwy over 2f out: swtchd rt over 1f out: styd on ins last* **5/1**[2]
04-1 **4** *shd* **Stolen Glance**[13] [1259] 3-9-0 **59**........ PaulMulrennan[(3)] 7 62+
(M W Easterby) *mid-div: drvn along over 3f out: sn chsng ldrs: one pce whn n.m.r ins last* **10/1**
565- **5** *½* **Inchdhuaig (IRE)**[176] [6357] 3-8-11 **58**........ LeanneKershaw[(5)] 13 58
(P C Haslam) *swtchd lft after 1f: sn trcking ldrs: nt qckn fnl f* **11/1**
535- **6** *1 ½* **Touch Of Ivory (IRE)**[206] [5921] 3-8-12 **54**........ TonyHamilton 15 51
(R A Fahey) *rea -div: kpt on fnl 2f: nt rch ldrs* **14/1**
000- **7** *1 ¾* **Lambency (IRE)**[172] [6374] 3-8-13 **55**........ GrahamGibbons 17 48
(J G Given) *swtchd lft after 1f: sn led: hdd 1f out: fdd* **16/1**
0-04 **8** *4* **Sparkbridge (IRE)**[40] [817] 3-9-4 **60**........ MartinDwyer 2 43
(R F Fisher) *trckd ldrs: wknd over 1f out* **10/1**
200 **9** *1* **Trumpita**[19] [1126] 3-8-13 **55**........ DavidAllan 6 36
(T D Easterby) *rr-div: sme hdwy over 2f out: sn btn* **20/1**
200- **10** *shd* **Distinctly Jim (IRE)**[257] [4735] 3-9-4 **60**........ DerekMcGaffin 4 41
(B Smart) *mid-div: drvn along over 3f out: nvr on terms* **33/1**
0-63 **11** *1* **Noble Nova**[9] [1352] 3-8-12 **54**........ SamHitchcott 16 33
(M R Channon) *swtchd lft after s: bhd and drvn along: nvr on terms* **11/2**[3]
-103 **12** *1 ½* **Penang Cinta**[10] [1314] 3-9-2 **58**........(b[1]) RobertWinston 10 33
(G A Butler) *trckd ldrs: chal over 2f out: wkng whn n.m.r over 1f out* **7/2**[1]
500- **13** *8* **Lazzoom (IRE)**[208] [5879] 3-8-10 **55**........ BenSwarbrick[(3)] 1 12
(Miss Tracy Waggott) *led over 1f: lost pl 2f out* **33/1**
000- **14** *5* **Our Serendipity**[218] [5680] 3-8-11 **53**........ TPQueally 8 —
(K G Reveley) *swtchd lft after 1f: a bhd* **25/1**

1m 41.3s (-0.60) **Going Correction** -0.55s/f (Hard) 14 Ran SP% **127.1**
Speed ratings (Par 97):81,81,79,79,78 77,75,71,70,70 69,68,60,55
Trifecta not won. Place 6 £253.16, Place 5 £159.69 TRIFECTA W: MT 4.5, P 23. Pl: MT 2.7, P 8.5, 2.3; Ex: MT/P 74.73, P/MT 176.4; CSF: MT/P 74.73, P/MT 78.99; Tri: MT/P/BD 384.39, P/MT/BD 425..
Owner Capt James Wilson **Bred** Capt J H Wilson **Trained** Sollom, Lancs
Owner Geoffrey Hamilton **Bred** Llety Stud **Trained** Middleham Moor, N Yorks
■ Stewards' Enquiry : Ben Swarbrick one-day ban: failed to keep straight from stalls (May 21)
Pat Cosgrave one-day ban: careless riding (May 21)

FOCUS
A moderate handicap run in a pedestrian winning time for a race of its class. The form, rated around fifth and sixth, does not look solid.
Noble Nova Official explanation: jockey said filly was unsuited by the good to firm ground
Penang Cinta Official explanation: jockey said gelding hung left in latter stages
Our Serendipity Official explanation: jockey said filly was unsuited by the good to firm ground
T/Plt: £1,524.60 to a £1 stake. Pool: £35,506.45. 17.00 winning tickets. T/Qpdt: £158.60 to a £1 stake. Pool: £2,187.00. 10.20 winning tickets. WG

1292 RIPON (R-H)
Wednesday, May 10

OFFICIAL GOING: Good
Wind: virtually nil

1594 NIDDERDALE APPRENTICE (S) STKS 6f
6:05 (6:06) (Class 6) 3-4-Y-O **£2,590** (£770; £385; £192) **Stalls** Low

Form RPR
00-0 **1** **Maison Dieu**[19] [1127] 3-8-10 53........ NeilBrown[(3)] 17 61
(J Howard Johnson) *trckd ldrs far side: hdwy to ld that gp wl over 1f out: sn overall ldr and pushed clr ent last: easily* **50/1**
0-60 **2** *3 ½* **Tequila Sheila (IRE)**[102] [227] 4-9-4 49........ AndrewElliott 2 49
(K R Burke) *overall ldr stands side: rdn along over 2f out: hdd wl over 1f out: sn drvn and kpt on same pce* **13/2**[3]
430- **3** *½* **Sister Gee (IRE)**[204] [5957] 4-9-4 45........ RussellKennemore 6 47
(R Hollinshead) *in tch stands side: hdwy to chse ldrs 2f out: sn rdn and kpt on ins last* **33/1**
0-06 **4** *2* **Drum Dance (IRE)**[9] [1341] 4-10-0 50........ TravisBlock 11 51
(N Tinkler) *swtchd to r far side: cl up tl rdn along and one pce fr wl over 1f out* **12/1**
3 **5** *1 ½* **Diamond Winnie**[19] [1126] 3-8-3........ WilliamCarson[(5)] 16 34
(Mrs A Duffield) *dwlt and bhd far side: hdwy wl over 1f out: styd on strly ins last: nrst fin* **11/2**[2]
0-46 **6** *1* **Desertina (IRE)**[7] [1413] 4-9-9 50........ DonnaCaldwell 15 39
(R M Whitaker) *led far side gp: rdn along over 2f out: sn hdd and grad wknd* **5/1**[1]
-000 **7** *hd* **Danescourt (IRE)**[10] [1310] 4-9-9 40........(b) RonanKeogh 1 38
(J M Bradley) *chsd ldrs stands side: rdn along over 2f out: sn wknd* **40/1**
00-0 **8** *shd* **Born For Diamonds (IRE)**[13] [1255] 4-8-13 45........ RobbieMills[(5)] 7 33
(R E Barr) *cl up stands side: rdn along over 2f out: sn wknd* **100/1**
00-0 **9** *nk* **Make Us Flush**[28] [974] 4-9-1 45........ KevinGhunowa[(3)] 13 32
(A Berry) *bhd far side tl sme late hdwy* **33/1**
0452 **10** *¾* **Suhezy (IRE)**[6] [1447] 3-8-13 52........(p) LiamJones 9 31
(P T Midgley) *chsd ldrs stands side: rdn along over 2f out and sn wknd* **15/2**
0051 **11** *hd* **Chairman Rick (IRE)**[6] [1447] 4-9-9 40........ HMuya 10 34
(D Nicholls) *racd towards centre: nvr nr ldrs* **10/1**
10-0 **12** *nk* **Dorn Hill**[10] [1310] 4-9-4 45........(p) JemmaMarshall[(5)] 14 33
(D G Bridgwater) *cl up far side: rdn along over 2f out: sn wknd* **40/1**
4051 **13** *5* **Mulberry Lad (IRE)**[5] [1463] 4-10-0 46........ DerekNolan 8 23
(P W Hiatt) *chsd ldrs stands side: rdn 2f out: sn wknd* **5/1**[1]
000- **14** *4* **King Henrik (USA)**[11] [3567] 4-9-9 45........ SladeO'Hara 12 6
(A Crook) *racd towards centre: bhd fr 1/2-way* **100/1**
66P- **15** *2* **Lord Mayfair (USA)**[179] [6331] 4-9-9 40........(b[1]) KellyHarrison 5 —
(Miss A Stokell) *in tch stands side to 1/2-way: sn bhd* **100/1**
2334 **16** *12* **Silver Nun**[16] [1200] 3-8-3 45........ PatrickDonaghy[(5)] 3 —
(T D Easterby) *dwlt and a rr stands side* **14/1**

1m 14.31s (1.31) **Going Correction** +0.05s/f (Good)
WFA 3 from 4yo 10lb 16 Ran SP% **113.0**
Speed ratings (Par 101):93,88,87,85,83 81,81,81,80,79 79,79,72,67,64 48
CSF £322.06 TOTE £42.70: £11.90, £2.10, £8.20; EX 634.40.The winner was bought by Eric Alston for 9,000gns.
Owner Transcend Bloodstock LLP **Bred** Andy Miller **Trained** Billy Row, Co Durham

FOCUS
Plenty of runners, but a moderate seller. The field split into two groups, but the winner raced far side and the next two stayed on the near side, suggesting there was no real difference in the ground and the form makes sense.
King Henrik(USA) Official explanation: jockey said gelding hung left throughout

1595 UREDALE MAIDEN STKS 6f
6:35 (6:36) (Class 5) 2-Y-O **£3,886** (£1,156; £577; £288) **Stalls** Low

Form RPR
1 **Always Fruitful** 2-9-3........ KDarley 7 87+
(M Johnston) *bmpd s and towards rr: hdwy and in tch whn swtchd wd and wandered wl over 1f out: rdn and styd on ins last: led nrfin* **8/1**
24 **2** *nk* **Rouen (IRE)**[30] [944] 2-9-3........ TonyCulhane 5 86
(M R Channon) *cl up stands side: led that gp 2f out: sn rdn and ev ch tl drvn and nt qckn towards fin* **5/1**[2]
22 **3** *shd* **Dimboola**[20] [1090] 2-9-3........ RHills 13 86
(B W Hills) *unruly stalls: racd alone far side and overall ldr: rdn and hung bdly lft ent last: hdd and eased nr fin* **5/4**[1]
4 *1 ¾* **Prince Golan (IRE)** 2-9-3........ TedDurcan 4 81+
(K A Ryan) *chsd ldrs stands side: hdwy 2f out and ev ch tl rdn and one pce ins last* **9/1**
5 *2* **Rainbow Mirage (IRE)** 2-9-3........ RoystonFfrench 3 75+
(E S McMahon) *in touch stands side: hdwy 2f out: sn rdn and kpt on same pce appr last* **25/1**
6 *1* **Rosbay (IRE)** 2-9-3........ DavidAllan 1 72+
(T D Easterby) *midfield stands side: hdwy 2f out: styd on ins last: nrst fin* **25/1**
7 *3 ½* **Umpa Loompa (IRE)** 2-9-3........ AdrianTNicholls 6 61
(D Nicholls) *hld up stands side: hdwy 2f out: sn rdn and no imp appr last* **33/1**
8 *nk* **Nota Liberata** 2-9-3........ ShaneKelly 2 60
(G M Moore) *led stands side gp: rdn along and hdd 2f out: sn wknd* **66/1**
9 *2 ½* **Cadeaux Du Monde** 2-9-3........ ChrisCatlin 9 53
(E J O'Neill) *a towards rr* **6/1**[3]
10 *6* **Bellapais Boy** 2-9-3........ PaulQuinn 10 35
(T D Easterby) *s.i.s: a rr* **50/1**
11 *2* **Fire In Cairo (IRE)** 2-8-12........ LeeEnstone 8 24
(P C Haslam) *wnt lft s: a rr* **100/1**
00 **12** *½* **Marryl**[7] [1420] 2-9-3........ DaleGibson 11 27
(M W Easterby) *a rr* **150/1**
13 *3* **Hunting Call** 2-9-3........ PaulHanagan 12 18
(K A Ryan) *a rr* **33/1**

1m 14.74s (1.74) **Going Correction** +0.05s/f (Good) 13 Ran SP% **115.2**
Speed ratings (Par 93):90,89,89,87,84 83,78,78,74,66 64,63,59
CSF £43.34 TOTE £8.70: £3.30, £1.90, £1.10; EX 44.90.
Owner Always Trying Partnership III **Bred** Mark Johnston Racing Ltd **Trained** Middleham Moor, N Yorks

FOCUS
A reasonable maiden by Ripon's standards but not that solid form-wise. The favourite raced alone on the far side early but threw his chance away by hanging across the track under pressure; he could be one to avoid.

NOTEBOOK
Always Fruitful ◆, a 10,000gns full-brother to Fruit Salad, who over seven furlongs for Mark Johnston as a juvenile, received a bump soon after the start and had a bit to do from there on, but he showed the right attitude when switched for a run to get up close home. His stable has a tremendous record in this maiden - they had won the race for the previous two years with debutants - and, with plenty of improvement likely, he deserves his chance in better company. (op 7-1)
Rouen(IRE), a beaten favourite on his first two starts in maiden company, seemed to benefit from the step up to six furlongs and was just held. He has been expensive to follow so far, but should win a maiden before too much longer. (op 9-2 tchd 11-2)
Dimboola, beaten at odds-on at Newmarket on his previous start, again disappointed and is not going the right way mentally. After dumping his jockey in the stalls, he raced alone on the far side before hanging his chance away and ending up on the stands' side of the track with all the others. He would surely have won but for hanging and looks one to avoid. (op 6-5 tchd 11-10 and 11-8)
Prince Golan(IRE), a 55,000gns half-brother to Satchem, very smart over six and seven furlongs, made a very pleasing debut in fourth. He is open to plenty of improvement as the season progresses and looks one to keep on the right side of. (op 13-2)
Rainbow Mirage(IRE), out of a half-sister to a multiple seven/eight-furlong winner, made a respectable debut and should progress. (tchd 22-1)
Rosbay(IRE), a 12,000gns first foal of an unraced half-sister to a useful multiple winner over a mile in the US, gave the impression this run will bring him on.
Cadeaux Du Monde, a 42,000gns of an 11-furlong winner, was quite well backed but never showed and may have needed this more than some people thought. (op 10-1)

1596 BETRESCUE.COM H'CAP 1m
7:05 (7:07) (Class 4) (0-80,80) 3-Y-O **£6,309** (£1,888; £944; £472; £235) **Stalls** High

Form RPR
352- **1** **Flying Clarets (IRE)**[213] [5769] 3-8-5 **67**........ PaulHanagan 9 74
(R A Fahey) *hld up: hdwy 3f out: rdn along 2f out: styd on wl u.p ins last to ld last 50 yds* **20/1**

603- **2** *nk* **Formal Decree (GER)**[205] 5939 3-8-8 **70** .... TedDurcan 10 76+
(G A Swinbank) *hld up in rr: effrt and n clr run over 2f out: swtchd lft and hdwy over 1f out: rdn and kpt on wl fnl f* **8/1**

6-52 **3** *nk* **Madaares (USA)**[13] 1252 3-9-0 **76** .... RHills 8 81
(M Johnston) *hld up: hdwy and in tch 1/2-way: effrt to chal 2f out: rdn to ld ent last: drvn: edgd rt and hdd last 50 yds* **7/2**[1]

20-4 **4** *1* **Fire Two**[20] 1101 3-9-4 **80** .... TonyCulhane 3 83
(M R Channon) *chsd ldrs: pushed along 1/2-way: rdn along 3f out: drvn and kpt on same pce fnl 2f* **6/1**

0-02 **5** *½* **Il Castagno (IRE)**[6] 1444 3-8-13 **75** .... KDarley 6 77+
(B Smart) *cl up: led over 4f out: pushed along 3f out: sn rdn: drvn and hdd ent last: wknd* **8/1**

0-44 **6** *5* **Stainley (IRE)**[23] 1044 3-8-6 **68** ow1 .... GrahamGibbons 7 58
(J D Bethell) *chsd ldng pair: rdn along on inner 3f out: drvn 2f out and sn wknd* **11/1**

10-2 **7** *3 ½* **Top Jaro (FR)**[20] 1099 3-9-1 **77** .... RobertWinston 1 59
(T P Tate) *led: hdd over 4f out: rdn along over 3f out: sn wknd* **4/1**[2]

50-3 **8** *2* **Sicilian (IRE)**[11] 1291 3-8-10 **72** .... RoystonFfrench 4 50
(B W Hills) *chsd ldrs: rdn along 1/2-way: sn wknd* **11/2**[3]

13-0 **9** *½* **North Walk (IRE)**[20] 1097 3-9-4 **80** .... DO'Donohoe 2 57
(K A Ryan) *in tch: hdwy to chse ldrs 4f out: rdn along 3f out and sn wknd* **20/1**

550- **10** *1* **Orange Stravinsky**[187] 6244 3-8-8 **70** .... LeeEnstone 5 44
(P C Haslam) *a rr* **50/1**

1m 39.71s (-1.39) **Going Correction** -0.10s/f (Good) **10** Ran SP% **113.9**
Speed ratings (Par 101):102,101,101,100,99 94,91,89,88,87
CSF £164.28 CT £561.64 TOTE £19.40: £4.80, £3.00, £1.40; EX 138.40.
Owner The Matthewman Partnership **Bred** Gabriel Bell **Trained** Musley Bank, N Yorks

FOCUS
A reasonable-looking handicap run at a strong pace and the form should prove reliable, with the fourth the best guide.
Formal Decree(GER) Official explanation: jockey said gelding became unbalanced
Stainley(IRE) Official explanation: jockey said gelding lost its action

1597 NICK WILMOT-SMITH MEMORIAL H'CAP 6f
7:35 (7:43) (Class 3) (0-90,89) 4-Y-0+
£9,348 (£2,799; £1,399; £700; £349; £175) **Stalls** Low

Form RPR

000- **1** **Dazzling Bay**[291] 3756 6-9-1 **86** .... DavidAllan 12 97
(T D Easterby) *hld up far side: hdwy 2f out: swtchd lft and rdn ins last: styd on to ld last 50 yds* **20/1**

4004 **2** *1* **Prince Tum Tum (USA)**[5] 1456 6-8-13 **84** .... FergalLynch 15 92
(D W Barker) *trckd ldrs far side: hdwy to ld and overall ldr wl over 1f out: rdn ent last: hdd and no ex last 50 yds* **12/1**

0-01 **3** *nk* **Paris Bell**[23] 1042 4-8-6 **77** .... PaulQuinn 13 84
(T D Easterby) *trckd ldrs far side: hdwy 2f out: sn rdn and kpt on ins last* **7/1**[3]

000- **4** *4* **Smokin Beau**[175] 6370 9-8-11 **87** .... JamesDoyle(5) 14 82
(N P Littmoden) *overall ldr far side: rdn along 2f out: sn hdd & wknd appr last* **12/1**

00-0 **5** *shd* **Ellens Academy (IRE)**[23] 1042 11-8-7 **78** .... KDarley 10 73
(E J Alston) *hld up far side: hdwy 2f out: sn rdn and no imp fnl f* **25/1**

0-61 **6** *½* **Pomfret Lad**[11] 1297 8-8-7 **78** .... GrahamGibbons 9 71
(J J Quinn) *cl up far side: rdn along 2f out: grad wknd* **11/2**[2]

0-00 **7** *shd* **Inter Vision (USA)**[18] 1143 6-8-12 **86** .... DanielTudhope(3) 5 79+
(A Dickman) *chsd ldrs stands side: hdwy to ld that gp over 1f out: sn rdn and kpt on: no ch w far side* **12/1**

50-0 **8** *4* **Artie**[21] 1076 7-8-10 **81** .... RobertWinston 11 62
(T D Easterby) *cl up far side: rdn along 2f out: sn wknd* **16/1**

60-0 **9** *¾* **Gifted Gamble**[16] 1183 4-9-3 **88** .... (b) DO'Donohoe 1 67+
(K A Ryan) *led stands side gp: hdd over 3f out and sn rdn: grad wknd fnl 2f* **14/1**

00-0 **10** *nk* **Folga**[21] 1076 4-9-0 **85** .... TedDurcan 4 63+
(J G Given) *chsd ldrs stands side: rdn along over 2f out and sn wknd* **25/1**

505- **11** *2* **Imperial Echo (USA)**[186] 6248 5-8-4 **75** .... PaulFessey 2 47+
(T D Barron) *racd stands side: bhd fr 1/2-way* **7/1**[3]

0-0 **12** *nk* **Betsen (IRE)**[47] 719 4-8-7 **78** .... AdrianTNicholls 7 49+
(D Nicholls) *in tch stands side: hdwy and cl up 2f out: sn rdn and wknd* **50/1**

-420 **13** *1 ¼* **Hiccups**[9] 1359 6-8-5 **76** .... PaulHanagan 8 43+
(D Nicholls) *chsd ldrs stands side: cl up 2f out: sn rdn and wknd* **12/1**

0-05 **14** *1 ¼* **Steel Blue**[2] 1532 6-8-9 **80** .... TonyCulhane 6 43+
(R M Whitaker) *cl up stands side: led that gp over 3f out: ridfden 2f out: hdd over 1f out and sn wknd* **5/1**[1]

1m 12.1s (-0.90) **Going Correction** +0.05s/f (Good) **14** Ran SP% **114.8**
Speed ratings (Par 107):108,106,106,100,100 100,100,94,93,93 90,90,88,86
CSF £224.47 CT £1215.11 TOTE £24.80: £6.10, £3.30, £2.50; EX 198.90.
Owner Ghmw Racing **Bred** T And M A Bibby **Trained** Great Habton, N Yorks

FOCUS
A decent sprint handicap but seven of the first eight came from the group that raced on the far side. The form looks reasonable rated through the third.

NOTEBOOK
Dazzling Bay, having his first outing since last July, finally bounced back to winning ways following a barren spell lasting almost three years. Impressive in coming from behind to win comfortably, he is well handicapped on his best form and could have a major prize in him this summer. The Wokingham looks a suitable short-term assignment. (new market)
Prince Tum Tum(USA) appreciated the drop back to sprinting and was unfortunate to run into a well-handicapped rival returning to his best. He is on a fair mark and should continue to run well in this sort of company. (old market op 10-1 new market op 8-1)
Paris Bell, 4lb higher for his win at Redcar last time, coped with the drying ground well enough, but was not in his element like his successful stablemate. His performance suggests he might be able to win off this higher mark when he gets his toe in. (old market op 7-1 tchd 15-2 new market op 6-1)
Smokin Beau, returning from his winter break, showed good speed for much of the way and should be sharper next time for this seasonal reappearance. (new market tchd 14-1)
Ellens Academy(IRE), who last won in October 2003, ran a better race on his second race back, but he is not getting any younger and was obviously helped by racing on the favoured far side. (new market)
Pomfret Lad, a winner here over five last time, was drawn in the middle, raced on the far side and did not get home. (old market op 5-1 new market op 6-1 tchd 5-1)
Inter Vision(USA) ◆ came home well in front of the rest of his group on the stands' side and put up a better performance than his finishing position suggests. A winner over this course and distance last summer off a 2lb lower mark, he looks one to keep in mind for a similar event. (new market)
Gifted Gamble had the blinkers back on and was not disgraced in finishing second on the stands' side. (new market op 16-1)

1598 WHARFEDALE MAIDEN FILLIES' STKS 1m 1f 170y
8:05 (8:08) (Class 5) 3-Y-0+
£3,886 (£1,156; £577; £288) **Stalls** High

Form RPR

6- **1** **Grain Of Truth**[218] 5688 3-8-11 .... RobertWinston 4 79+
(Sir Michael Stoute) *hld up in tch: hdwy on outer 4f out: led wl over 1f out: rdn appr last: styd on* **4/9**[1]

05- **2** *¾* **Tasjeel (USA)**[225] 5535 3-8-11 .... RHills 9 77+
(W J Haggas) *chsd ldr: hdwy 3f out: rdn and ev ch 2f out tl drvn and one pce ins last* **8/1**[3]

0- **3** *5* **Takanewa (IRE)**[208] 5881 3-8-8 .... PaulMulrennan(3) 10 67
(J Howard Johnson) *led: rdn along 3f out: drvn and hdd wl over 1f out: kpt on same pce* **100/1**

32- **4** *2* **Cheviot Heights**[202] 5993 3-8-11 .... RyanMoore 14 63
(Mrs A J Perrett) *dwlt: sn in tch: hdwy 3f out to chse ldrs 3f out: rdn over 2f out and sn one pce* **4/1**[2]

0 **5** *1* **Blessings Count (USA)**[19] 1114 3-8-11 .... ShaneKelly 11 61
(E A L Dunlop) *prom: rdn along 3f out: grad wknd* **20/1**

0-5 **6** *hd* **Bollin Dolly**[13] 1252 3-8-11 .... DavidAllan 8 61
(T D Easterby) *chsd ldrs: rdn along 3f out: grad wknd fnl 2f* **20/1**

7 *3 ½* **Princess Toto** 3-8-11 .... LeeEnstone 3 54
(P C Haslam) *bhd tl sme late hdwy* **125/1**

3- **8** *2 ½* **Graze On Too (IRE)**[190] 6212 3-8-11 .... GrahamGibbons 15 49
(J J Quinn) *a rr* **33/1**

00 **9** *shd* **Prophet Preacher (IRE)**[7] 1417 3-8-11 .... RobbieFitzpatrick 6 49
(M J Attwater) *a rr* **100/1**

05- **10** *hd* **Tender The Great (IRE)**[145] 6588 3-8-11 .... ChrisCatlin 12 48
(V Smith) *in tch on inner: rdn alo ng 4f out: sn wknd* **50/1**

0 **11** *1 ¾* **Tammy**[11] 1296 3-8-8 .... DanielTudhope(3) 1 45
(C W Thornton) *s.i.s: a bhd* **200/1**

0 **12** *3 ½* **Little Lily Morgan**[20] 1101 3-8-11 .... RoystonFfrench 5 38
(R Bastiman) *a rr: bhd fr 1/2-way* **100/1**

0- **13** *1 ¾* **Coronation Flight**[203] 5976 3-8-11 .... DeanMcKeown 7 34
(F P Murtagh) *s.i.s: a towards rr* **200/1**

050- **14** *69* **Intavac Girl**[229] 5427 3-8-11 40 .... PaulHanagan 2 —
(C W Thornton) *s.i.s: a bhd* **200/1**

2m 5.38s (0.38) **Going Correction** -0.10s/f (Good) **14** Ran SP% **120.0**
Speed ratings (Par 100):94,93,89,87,87 86,84,82,81,81 80,77,76,21
CSF £4.53 TOTE £1.60: £1.10, £2.00, £15.90; EX 9.10.
Owner Gainsborough Stud **Bred** W And R Barnett Ltd **Trained** Newmarket, Suffolk

FOCUS
A modest maiden with some likely platers not beaten that far. The race has been rated around the fourth and sixth.
Graze On Too(IRE) Official explanation: jockey said filly hung left
Intavac Girl Official explanation: jockey said filly was unsuited by the undulating track

1599 WENSLEYDALE H'CAP 1m 1f 170y
8:35 (8:36) (Class 5) (0-70,70) 3-Y-0
£3,886 (£1,156; £577; £288) **Stalls** High

Form RPR

03-6 **1** **Capistrano**[36] 880 3-8-13 **65** .... RHills 7 77
(B W Hills) *a cl up: rdn along over 2f out: drvn over 1f out: styd on to ld ins last* **15/8**[1]

5-44 **2** *¾* **Fann (USA)**[19] 1108 3-9-4 **70** .... RyanMoore 3 81
(C E Brittain) *trckd ldrs: hdwy 3f out: rdn to ld wl over 1f out: sn edgd rt: drvn and hdd ins last: no ex* **9/1**

5023 **3** *3 ½* **Rebellious Spirit**[7] 1416 3-9-3 **69** .... DarrenWilliams 8 73
(P W Hiatt) *chsd ldrs: rdn along 2f out: drvn and wandered over 1f out: sn one pce* **7/1**[3]

00-6 **4** *1 ¾* **Princess Cocoa (IRE)**[14] 1230 3-8-6 **58** .... PaulHanagan 9 59+
(R A Fahey) *hld up: hdwy on inner over 2f out: effrt and hmpd over 1f out: styd on ins last: nrst fin* **20/1**

-244 **5** *shd* **Ellesappelle**[7] 1423 3-9-2 **68** .... RobertWinston 2 68
(K R Burke) *dwlt and towards rr: hdwy on outer 3f out: rdn and edgd rt 2f out: sn drvn and no imp appr last* **5/1**[2]

-225 **6** *1 ½* **Rose Muwasim**[37] 855 3-9-3 **69** .... TedDurcan 5 67
(E A L Dunlop) *hld up in rr: hdwy 3f out: rdn 2f out: styd on ins last: nrst fin* **10/1**

0-30 **7** *hd* **Sunbolt (IRE)**[13] 1251 3-9-4 **70** .... PaulFessey 12 67
(T D Barron) *led: rdn along 3f out: drvn and hdd wl over 1f out: hung rt and wknd* **16/1**

450 **8** *½* **Russian Mist (IRE)**[23] 1049 3-8-7 **64** .... DerekNolan(5) 6 60
(M J Wallace) *chsd ldrs: rdn along over 3f out: grad wknd* **8/1**

053- **9** *1 ¼* **Farne Island**[170] 6395 3-8-13 **65** .... NickyMackay 10 59
(J J Quinn) *hld up: hdwy 3f out: rdn to chse ldrs whn n.m.r wl over 1f out: sn wknd* **20/1**

425- **10** *shd* **Makai**[134] 6673 3-9-4 **70** .... KDarley 4 64
(M Johnston) *chsd ldng pair: rdn along wl over 2f out: sn drvn and wknd* **16/1**

5-00 **11** *5* **Boss Mak (IRE)**[42] 795 3-8-6 **58** .... (p) ChrisCatlin 1 42
(V Smith) *a bhd* **50/1**

060- **12** *7* **Loch Awe**[189] 6227 3-8-10 **62** ow1 .... FergalLynch 11 33
(J G Given) *s.i.s: a bhd* **50/1**

2m 5.45s (0.45) **Going Correction** -0.10s/f (Good) **12** Ran SP% **119.4**
Speed ratings (Par 99):94,93,90,89,89 87,87,87,86,86 82,76
CSF £18.78 CT £100.09 TOTE £3.10: £1.30, £3.50, £2.20; EX 26.60 Place 6 £205.36, Place 5 £19.58..
Owner Guy Reed **Bred** G Reed **Trained** Lambourn, Berks

■ Stewards' Enquiry : Paul Fessey caution: careless riding

FOCUS
A modest winning time, fractionally slower than the preceding fillies' maiden, but the first two came clear and could be open to improvement.
Loch Awe Official explanation: jockey said filly was never travelling

T/Plt: £343.10 to a £1 stake. Pool: £50,485.15. 107.40 winning tickets. T/Qpdt: £25.90 to a £1 stake. Pool: £4,777.90. 136.10 winning tickets. JR

1398 CHANTILLY (R-H)

Wednesday, May 10

OFFICIAL GOING: Very soft

1600a PRIX DE GUICHE (GROUP 3) (COLTS) — 1m 1f
3:05 (3:04) 3-Y-O **£27,586** (£11,034; £8,276; £5,517; £2,759)

RPR

1 **Boris De Deauville (IRE)**[25] 3-9-2 .... YBarberot 4 — 105
(S Wattel, France) *held up in 5th, 6th straight on inside, headway bewtween rivals to lead 1f out, driven out* **268/10**

2 *1* **Poquelin (FR)**[39] [840] 3-9-2 .... SPasquier 6 — 103
(F-X de Chevigny, France) *raced in 4th, headway to lead narrowly over 1f out, headed 1f out, stayed on final f* **24/1**

3 *1* **Lateral**[206] [5935] 3-9-2 .... WMongil 5 — 101
(P Schiergen, Germany) *racd in 6th, 5th str, hdwy towards outside 2f out, edgd left 1 1/2f out, ev ch over 1f out, sn rdn and one pace* **17/10**[1]

4 *shd* **Racinger (FR)**[23] 3-9-2 .... DBonilla 9 — 101
(F Head, France) *hld up in rr, last str, swtchd to outside and hdwy 2f out, slightly hmpd 1 1/2f out, kept on steadily fnl f* **53/10**[3]

5 *3* **Beringoer (FR)**[210] 3-9-2 .... OPeslier 2 — 95
(A Fabre, France) *racd in 3rd, n.m.r and outpcd towards inside 1 1/2f out, shuffled back to 6th, modest late hdwy* **31/10**[2]

6 *½* **Gin Jockey (FR)**[20] [1092] 3-9-2 .... CSoumillon 8 — 94
(R Hannon) *raced in 2nd, led just over 2f out til headed over 1f out, weakened* **53/10**[3]

7 *5* **Pegase Jem (FR)**[17] [1179] 3-9-2 .... C-PLemaire 1 — 85
(P Bary, France) *held up in 7th, never a factor* **6/1**

8 *15* **Turcci (FR)**[47] 3-9-2 .... J-BEyquem 3 — 56
(R Avial Lopez, Spain) *led to just over 2f out, weakened* **14/1**

1m 55.2s — **8** Ran SP% **121.7**
PARI-MUTUEL: WIN 27.80; PL PL 4.00, 4.50, 1.90; DF 75.90.
Owner Mme M Bryant **Bred** Petra Bloodstock Agency Ltd **Trained** France

NOTEBOOK
Boris De Deauville(IRE), bought as a potential jumper shortly before this race, made it at Group level with authority. He was given a patient ride and began his move forward at the two-furlong marker before taking the advantage running into the last furlong. Connections have no idea where this colt will go now as he was a maiden before the race.
Poquelin(FR), provincially trained, was settled behind the leaders before quickening halfway up the straight, but he did not have the finishing speed of the winner.
Lateral, who looked to be going easily in sixth place rounding the final turn, was brought with a run up the centre of the track and battled well to hold third place.
Racinger(FR), waited with at the back of the field, was a bit free early on. He had every chance and only missed third place by inches.
Gin Jockey(FR) took the advantage two out and stayed at the head of affairs for about a furlong. He then faded quickly and his jockey felt he was not suited by the very soft ground.

1582 CHESTER (L-H)

Thursday, May 11

OFFICIAL GOING: Good to firm
Wind: Almost nil Weather: Sunny and warm

1601 JARDINE LLOYD THOMPSON HUXLEY STKS (FOR THE TRADESMAN'S CUP) (GROUP 3) — 1m 2f 75y
1:50 (1:50) (Class 1) 4-Y-O+ **£36,907** (£13,988; £7,000; £3,490) **Stalls** High

Form — RPR

3-03 **1** **Maraahel (IRE)**[19] [1128] 5-9-0 120 .... (v) RHills 2 — 117+
(Sir Michael Stoute) *lw: s.i.s: rcvrd to ld after 1f: hdd wl over 7f out: racd in 2nd pl tl led over 3f out: rdn over 1f out: r.o wl* **4/11**[1]

-305 **2** *3* **Counsel's Opinion (IRE)**[15] [1239] 9-9-0 100 .... GeorgeBaker 3 — 111
(C F Wall) *hld up in rr: hdwy whn nt clr run over 2f out: sn wnt 2nd: rdn over 1f out: no imp on wnr fnl f* **16/1**

5022 **3** *2½* **Kew Green (USA)**[22] [1084] 8-9-0 109 .... DaneO'Neill 1 — 106
(P R Webber) *lw: sn trckd ldrs: ev ch 3f out: rdn 2f out: edgd lft over 1f out: wknd ins fnl f* **9/2**[2]

5333 **4** *14* **Near Dock (GER)**[10] [1365] 5-9-0 106 .... JohnEgan 4 — 80+
(K R Burke) *racd keenly: led for 1f: regained ld wl over 7f out: hdd over 3f out: losing pl whn n.m.r over 2f out: sn btn: eased fnl f* **9/1**[3]

2m 7.92s (-5.22) **Going Correction** -0.225s/f (Firm) — **4** Ran SP% **107.4**
Speed ratings (Par 113):111,108,106,95
CSF £6.86 TOTE £1.30; EX 5.90.
Owner Hamdan Al Maktoum **Bred** Shadwell Estate Company Limited **Trained** Newmarket, Suffolk
■ Stewards' Enquiry : George Baker caution careless riding

FOCUS
Just the four runners, which was normal for this race until a couple of years ago, but despite the small field the pace was very solid with the lead changing on a regular basis and the final time was perfectly acceptable for a race of its stature. Maraahel was better class and did no more that he was entitled to.

NOTEBOOK
Maraahel(IRE), with upwards of 11lb in hand of his rivals on official ratings and with six fewer rivals to contend with than when winning this last year, never had the luxury of an easy lead after missing the break with both he and Near Dock taking turns out in front. He held the advantage where it mattered though, and had the race in safe-keeping all the way up the home straight. He kept on finding one or two to beat him in many of the world's top ten-furlong races after winning this last year and will no doubt be given a similar campaign from now on. (op 2-5 after 4-9 in a place)
Counsel's Opinion(IRE) had a mountain to climb on official ratings, but the trip and ground were ideal and crucially he got the strong pace he needs despite the small field. That enabled him to come from the back and pass two higher-rated rivals over the last couple of furlongs but the winner, who is rated 20lb higher than him, proved far superior.
Kew Green(USA), runner-up in a sub-standard Earl Of Sefton last time, has a good record on turning tracks but he appeared to have every chance with no real excuses and does not look quite good enough to win at this level.
Near Dock(GER) took a good hold early and, after swapping the lead with the favourite a couple of times, merely succeeded in running himself into the ground.

1602 BETFRED H'CAP — 5f 16y
2:20 (2:21) (Class 2) (0-100,100) £16,141 (£4,531; £2,265; £1,132; £564) **Stalls** Low

Form — RPR

0-44 **1** **Merlin's Dancer**[7] [1438] 6-8-8 **90** .... AdrianTNicholls 2 — 103
(D Nicholls) *mde all: rdn over 1f out: kpt on wl* **11/2**[2]

22-1 **2** *¾* **Judd Street**[10] [1359] 4-8-7 **89** 6ex .... StephenCarson 4 — 99
(R F Johnson Houghton) *chsd ldrs: rdn to take 2nd over 1f out: r.o u.p* **4/1**[1]

-661 **3** *1¾* **Green Manalishi**[20] [1116] 5-9-4 **100** .... PhilipRobinson 8 — 104
(D W P Arbuthnot) *lw: wnt rt s: sn bmpd: midfield: hdwy 2f out: rdn over 1f out: styd on ins fnl f: nt pce of ldng pair* **7/1**[3]

160- **4** *½* **Mine Behind**[255] [4831] 6-8-6 **88** .... AlanMunro 11 — 90+
(J R Best) *sn outpcd and bhd: swtchd rt and hdwy over 1f out: fin wl* **50/1**

-310 **5** *hd* **Desert Lord**[15] [1236] 6-8-10 **92** .... (b) NCallan 16 — 93+
(K A Ryan) *hung lft sn after s: in tch: rdn and lost pl over 2f out: styd on ins fnl f* **25/1**

0130 **6** *nk* **Qadar (IRE)**[20] [1116] 4-8-13 **100** .... JamesDoyle[(5)] 10 — 100+
(N P Littmoden) *hld up: rdn and hdwy over 1f out: r.o ins fnl f* **20/1**

336- **7** *hd* **Pivotal's Princess (IRE)**[224] [5573] 4-8-13 **95** .... RichardMullen 7 — 94
(E S McMahon) *in tch: rdn over 1f out: no ex ins fnl f* **8/1**

1040 **8** *½* **The Lord**[20] [1116] 6-8-11 **93** .... TonyCulhane 12 — 91
(W G M Turner) *n.m.r sn after s: midfield: rdn over 1f out: kpt on ins fnl f: nt pce to chal* **33/1**

000- **9** *hd* **Caribbean Coral**[234] [5369] 7-8-4 **86** oh3 .... GrahamGibbons 9 — 83+
(J J Quinn) *bit bkwd: hmpd s: hld up: hdwy whn nt clr run over 1f out: no ch and nt knocked abt after* **25/1**

0-30 **10** *½* **Wanchai Lad**[15] [1236] 5-8-4 **86** oh4 .... PaulQuinn 6 — 81+
(D Nicholls) *sn pushed along: hdwy 3f out: rdn and nt clr run over 1f out: kpt on u.p: nvr able to chal* **16/1**

4342 **11** *½* **Peace Offering (IRE)**[5] [1481] 6-8-13 **95** .... FrancisNorton 13 — 88
(D Nicholls) *hmpd sn after s: midfield: rdn and lost pl 2f out: keeping on whn nt clr run ins fnl f: sn eased* **14/1**

00-0 **12** *½* **Enchantment**[9] [1377] 5-8-10 **92** .... (p) LDettori 5 — 83
(J M Bradley) *w wnr tl over 2f out: rdn over 1f out: wknd fnl f* **12/1**

0012 **13** *1* **Trinculo (IRE)**[8] [1399] 9-8-6 **88** .... PaulFessey 15 — 76
(D Nicholls) *lw: in rr: rdn and swtchd lft over 1f out: sn nt clr run: n.d* **25/1**

0502 **14** *shd* **Cape Royal**[15] [1236] 6-9-1 **97** .... (t) RyanMoore 3 — 85
(J M Bradley) *midfield: rdn over 1f out: wknd fnl f* **11/2**[2]

0-00 **15** *1* **Right Answer**[9] [1377] 4-8-5 **87** .... JohnEgan 1 — 71+
(T D Easterby) *chsd ldrs: rdn over 1f out: hld whn eased ins fnl f* **16/1**

59.75 secs (-2.30) **Going Correction** -0.225s/f (Firm) — **15** Ran SP% **121.7**
Speed ratings (Par 109):109,107,105,104,103 103,103,102,101,101 100,99,97,97,96
CSF £25.31 CT £164.26 TOTE £5.00: £1.80, £1.90, £3.10; EX 20.20 Trifecta £142.90 Pool: £1,731.10 - 8.60 winning tickets..
Owner Chalfont Foodhalls Ltd **Bred** Cheveley Park Stud Ltd **Trained** Sessay, N Yorks

FOCUS
A typically competitive sprint handicap in which the draw and luck in running typically played their part. The form looks reasonably sound.

NOTEBOOK
Merlin's Dancer, well drawn, especially for a front-runner, pinged the gates and quickly managed to grab pole position against the inside rail. From then on it was just a question as to whether he was good enough to defend the position he had established and, showing the right attitude, the answer was yes. (op 6-1 tchd 13-2 in a place)
Judd Street, carrying a 6lb penalty for his Windsor victory, was always in a good position just behind the winner from his decent draw, but he could never quite overhaul him. This was a decent effort considering he may prefer an extra furlong and he does not know how to run a bad race. (op 9-2 tchd 7-2 in a place)
Green Manalishi, raised 5lb for his Newbury victory, had an ordinary draw and was trying to come from off the pace in race in which the front pair were always at the sharp end. Under the circumstances this was a fine effort, but he will need to be better than ever to win off this sort of mark. (op 13-2)
Mine Behind ◆, reappearing from a nine-month break though he was won after a similar layoff in the past and looked fit enough, ran a remarkable race from a poor draw. Stone last turning for home, after being switched wide he passed 11 horses in the last furlong to reach his final position. Eye-catching performances like this on this track are not always confirmed elsewhere, this was still a most encouraging return.
Desert Lord ◆ had the worst draw once again, but even though he was eventually able to get across to the inside rail, he would have had to cover a lot of ground in order to do it, so still emerges from this contest with a lot of credit.
Qadar(IRE), another with an ordinary draw, did not have a lot of room to play with a furlong out but was noted finishing well. His previous form shows that he is well suited by a sharp, turning track like this.
Pivotal's Princess(IRE), who looked fit, made a very encouraging return to action following an eight-month break, but she is now 10lb higher than for her last win following her purple patch last summer, so will need to have improved if she is to win off this sort of mark.
Caribbean Coral ◆, another returning from an eight-month break on ground that would have been faster than ideal, endured a nightmare passage and gave the impression he would have finished a lot closer with a clear run. He is now 10lb lower than for his last win and is one to keep an eye on. (op 20-1)
Cape Royal had a couple of those that finished behind him at Epsom last time finish ahead of him on this occasion and he should really have performed a lot better from his decent draw. (tchd 6-1)
Right Answer Official explanation: jockey said filly lost its action

1603 MBNA EUROPE BANK CHESTER VASE (GROUP 3) (C&G) — 1m 4f 66y
2:50 (2:50) (Class 1) 3-Y-O **£36,907** (£13,988; £7,000; £3,490; £1,748) **Stalls** Low

Form — RPR

21-1 **1** **Papal Bull**[21] [1095] 3-8-12 99 .... KFallon 1 — 107+
(Sir Michael Stoute) *lw: s.i.s: in tch: niggled along fr 4f out: rdn over 2f out: led wl ins fnl f: sn hung lft: r.o* **6/4**[1]

0-32 **2** *¾* **Dragon Dancer**[20] [1120] 3-8-12 95 .... AlanMunro 2 — 104
(G Wragg) *lw: chsd ldr: upsides 3f out: rdn over 2f out: led 1f out: hdd wl ins fnl f: nt qckn cl home* **7/2**[3]

62-3 **3** *1* **Mashaahed**[23] [1070] 3-8-12 95 .... RHills 5 — 102
(B W Hills) *hld up: rdn over 2f out: hdwy over 1f out: sn chalng: nt qckn ins fnl f* **7/1**

1-61 **4** *1¼* **Yarqus**[13] [1268] 3-8-12 90 .... RyanMoore 4 — 100
(C E Brittain) *chsd ldrs: rdn over 2f out: kpt on same pce ins fnl f* **16/1**

10-1 **5** *nk* **Primary (USA)**[12] [1300] 3-8-12 105 .... LDettori 3 — 100
(W J Haggas) *lw: led: rdn over 2f out: hdd 1f out: wknd cl home* **9/4**[2]

2m 35.24s (-5.41) **Going Correction** -0.225s/f (Firm) — **5** Ran SP% **111.4**
Speed ratings (Par 109):109,108,107,107,106
CSF £7.21 TOTE £2.00: £1.20, £1.80; EX 6.70.

Owner Mrs J Magnier, D Smith & M Tabor **Bred** B H And C F D Simpson **Trained** Newmarket, Suffolk

FOCUS
As in the first race, a decent pace despite the small field, and the final time was very much par for the grade. Even though the pace was solid, all five runners were within a length of each other passing the furlong pole and the form does not appear anything more than ordinary for the grade.

NOTEBOOK
Papal Bull, stepping up from handicap company though the form of his Newmarket victory has worked out wonderfully well, was also stepping up a couple of furlongs. Not best away, he never looked that comfortable but even so he managed to stay in touch and when the gap appeared between the two leaders a furlong out, he took full advantage. He is obviously a decent colt, perfectly capable of winning again at Group level, but he will still need to significantly improve again if he is to be considered a serious Derby candidate. (op 7-4)
Dragon Dancer, on the shoulder of the favourite throughout, had every chance but was inclined to hang to his right in the home straight which let the winner through. He is still a maiden, but this good mover looks more of a stayer whilst easier ground would probably help him also. This performance still paid a compliment to his Newbury conqueror Hala Bek. (op 3-1)
Mashaahed, held up out the back, tried to come around his four rivals in the home straight but lacked the pace to make it count. He also remains a maiden, but should find a race or two given a suitable test of stamina. (op 13-2 tchd 8-1 in a place)
Yarqus, representing last year's successful owner and trainer, was the lowest-rated and most exposed of the quintet, so probably did as much as could be expected. (op 18-1)
Primary(USA), bidding to match Shergar by winning this after landing the Sandown Classic Trial, was able to set his own pace out in front but he could never shake off his rivals and was eventually swamped. First impressions were that he did not stay. (op 5-2 tchd 11-4 in places)

1604 HALIFAX H'CAP — 5f 16y
3:20 (3:22) (Class 2) (0-100,95) 3-Y-O **£14,897** (£4,432; £2,214; £1,106) **Stalls** Low

Form	Pos	Dist	Horse	Jockey	RPR
41-1	1		**Empress Jain**[14] 1264 3-9-4 **92** (M A Jarvis) *mde all: edgd rt most of way: rdn over 1f out: all out* **13/8**[1]	PhilipRobinson 1	100
40-0	2	nk	**Green Park (IRE)**[12] 1292 3-8-11 **85** (R A Fahey) *midfield: swtchd rt and hdwy over 1f out: r.o strly ins fnl f* **10/1**	PaulHanagan 5	92
-022	3	1 ¼	**Scooby Dude (IRE)**[12] 1279 3-8-6 **80** (Ms Deborah J Evans) *lw: chsd ldrs: rdn over 1f out: nt qckn towards fin* **8/1**[3]	JohnEgan 9	83
42-0	4	1 ¼	**Nigella**[9] 1377 3-8-13 **87** (E S McMahon) *bit bkwd: prom: ev ch 2f out: sn rdn: no ex towards fin* **7/1**[2]	RichardMullen 2	85
-100	5	¾	**City For Conquest (IRE)**[14] 1264 3-7-11 **76** (v) (K R Burke) *wnt lft and bmpd s: bhd: rdn and r.o ins fnl f: nrst fin* **33/1**	AndrewElliott(5) 8	71+
500-	6	nk	**Grazeon Gold Blend**[202] 6004 3-8-13 **87** (J J Quinn) *wnt rt s: midfield: nt clr run 2f out: rdn over 1f out: styd on ins fnl f: nt rch ldrs* **50/1**	GrahamGibbons 11	81+
12-1	7	1 ¾	**Guto**[19] 1146 3-9-7 **95** (K A Ryan) *chsd ldrs: hung rt over 2f out: rdn over 1f out: fdd* **8/1**[3]	NCallan 10	83+
445-	8	½	**Christa Bee**[236] 5286 3-8-11 **85** (A Berry) *s.i.s: midfield: n.m.r and lost pl 3f out: kpt on ins fnl f: nt trble ldrs* **16/1**	FrancisNorton 3	71
451-	9	nk	**Triskaidekaphobia**[207] 5920 3-9-2 **90** (Miss J R Tooth) *prom: rdn 2f out: wknd fnl f* **17/2**	PaulFitzsimons 4	75
22-0	10	½	**Brandywell Boy (IRE)**[26] 1020 3-8-12 **86** (D J S Ffrench Davis) *bmpd s: midfield: rdn over 1f out: wknd fnl f* **16/1**	JimmyFortune 6	69
-133	11	6	**Stoneacre Lad (IRE)**[26] 1020 3-8-10 **84** (b) (Peter Grayson) *swtg: bmpd s: a bhd: eased whn n.d ins fnl f* **17/2**	RobbieFitzpatrick 7	46+
3110	12	6	**Sands Crooner (IRE)**[19] 1146 3-8-1 **78** (v) (D Shaw) *lw: s.i.s: a wl bhd* **33/1**	PatrickMathers(3) 12	18

60.49 secs (-1.56) **Going Correction** -0.225s/f (Firm) 12 Ran SP% **122.6**
Speed ratings (Par 105):103,102,100,98,97 96,94,93,92,91 82,72
CSF £19.60 CT £111.34 TOTE £2.30: £1.40, £3.40, £1.70; EX 24.80 Trifecta £179.60 Pool: £1,315.60 - 5.20 winning tickets..
Owner Dennis Yardy **Bred** D A Yardy **Trained** Newmarket, Suffolk

FOCUS
Another competitive sprint handicap run at a furious pace and the draw again had a major impact on the outcome. The form is not totally convincing but should prove as good as rated.

NOTEBOOK
Empress Jain started a very short price for a race like this, but she was a front-runner bidding for a hat-trick starting from stall one, so it was perhaps understandable. The only question was whether a whopping 15lb rise for her Yarmouth victory would stop her, but she pinged the lids and then showed plenty of grit to hold off her rivals. She had plenty going for her here and will find things very tough in her bid for a four-timer back on a more conventional track. (tchdc 15-8 in places)
Green Park(IRE) ◆, all the better for his Ripon reappearance, stayed on very strongly once in line for home but found the favourite had just built up too much of a lead. He is down to a more feasible mark now and will appreciate a return to six. (tchd 11-1)
Scooby Dude(IRE) ran a fine race in defeat considering his moderate draw, but despite his consistency he is not proving easy to win with and is unlikely to get much help from the Handicapper as a result of this. (op 10-1)
Nigella, who has not yet come in her coat, was making her handicap debut and was always up with the pace from her decent draw. Her only win so far came on Polytrack and she would be of obvious interest back on that surface given her prominent style of racing, but she does have the ability to win on turf.
City For Conquest(IRE) burst the stalls by anticipating the start and then cannoned into Stoneacre Lad after she exited them. Despite all of that, she stayed on very well in the closing stages and finished much closer to the winner that she did at Yarmouth, although she was entitled to on the revised terms.
Grazeon Gold Blend ◆, fifth in last season's Group Two Champagne Stakes at Doncaster, had a bad draw to start with and then made things even worse by diving out to his right leaving the stalls. To his great credit he finished in good style and is entitled to benefit from this first run in seven months. (op 40-1)
Guto likes to be up with the pace, but his high draw meant he was forced to race wide and that eventually took its toll. (op 9-1)
Christa Bee, who looked fit despite the eight-month absence, was making her handicap debut and was not disgraced. She may prefer an easier surface to this.
Triskaidekaphobia tried to serve it up to the favourite right from the start, but lack of a recent race eventually took its toll. (op 8-1)
Stoneacre Lad(IRE) was badly hampered by City For Conquest leaving the stalls and had no real chance after that. (op 10-1)
Sands Crooner(IRE) had it all to do from the outside stall, but he took a broadside from Grazeon Gold Blend leaving the gate, knocking him back to last, making this performance look even worse than it was.

1605 BOODLES DIAMOND MAIDEN STKS — 1m 2f 75y
4:00 (4:00) (Class 4) 3-Y-O **£7,124** (£2,119; £1,059; £529) **Stalls** High

Form	Pos	Dist	Horse	Jockey	RPR
62-4	1		**Numeric (GER)**[19] 1134 3-9-3 80 (J H M Gosden) *lw: mde all: rdn over 1f out: r.o* **6/4**[1]	JimmyFortune 7	79+
3	2	2 ½	**Mobaasher (USA)**[12] 1289 3-9-3 (Sir Michael Stoute) *w'like: rangy: scope: lw: prom: rdn and outpcd by ldrs 2f out: hung lft ent fnl f: styd on wl towards fin* **2/1**[2]	RHills 3	74+
5-	3	nk	**Zero (IRE)**[193] 6178 3-9-3 (M A Jarvis) *tall: racd keenly: a.p: ev ch 2f out: sn rdn: hung lft ins fnl f: no ex towards fin* **11/4**[3]	PhilipRobinson 8	73+
04-0	4	1 ¼	**Dream Of Paradise (USA)**[14] 1259 3-8-12 49 (Mrs L Williamson) *swtg: in tch: chsd ldrs 2f out: sn rdn: kpt on same pce fnl f* **100/1**	PaulHanagan 4	66?
-244	5	3	**Markington**[28] 1005 3-9-3 73 (J D Bethell) *in tch: pushed along over 3f out: wknd 2f out* **25/1**	GrahamGibbons 9	65
404-	6	1 ½	**Cresta Gold**[167] 6420 3-8-12 72 (A Bailey) *stdd s: hld up: hdwy 3f out: rdn and wknd 2f out* **25/1**	NCallan 5	57
0-	7	16	**Skit**[220] 5667 3-9-3 (W M Brisbourne) *bit bkwd: pushed along 3f out: a bhd: eased whn n.d ins fnl f* **66/1**	DavidAllan 6	32
00	8	hd	**Debord (FR)**[15] 1240 3-9-3 (Jamie Poulton) *lw: hld up: pushed along 4f out: wknd 2f out: eased whn n.d ins fnl f* **33/1**	JohnEgan 1	32
60-	9	1 ¼	**Yes Dear**[255] 4809 3-8-12 (W M Brisbourne) *bit bkwd: midfield: pushed along over 4f out: wknd over 2f out: eased whn n.d ins fnl f* **40/1**	RobbieFitzpatrick 2	24

2m 11.91s (-1.23) **Going Correction** -0.225s/f (Firm) 9 Ran SP% **115.6**
Speed ratings (Par 101):95,93,92,91,89 88,75,75,74
CSF £4.50 TOTE £2.80: £1.10, £1.20, £1.30; EX 5.00.
Owner Highclere Thoroughbred Racing XXX **Bred** Dr Chr Berglar **Trained** Newmarket, Suffolk

FOCUS
Not a very competitive maiden with only the front three starting at less than 25-1. The proxity of the 49-rated Dream Of Paradise does not do a great deal for the form and a moderate pace resulted in a modest winning time for the type of contest.
Cresta Gold Official explanation: jockey said filly was unbalanced throughout

1606 SENIOR WRIGHT H'CAP — 6f 18y
4:35 (4:35) (Class 3) (0-90,90) 3-Y-O **£10,039** (£2,986; £1,492; £745) **Stalls** Low

Form	Pos	Dist	Horse	Jockey	RPR
0003	1		**Ooh Aah Camara (IRE)**[7] 1448 3-8-8 **80** (T J Pitt) *lw: chsd ldrs: rdn over 2f out: r.o to ld towards fin* **7/1**	JohnEgan 9	84
013-	2	hd	**Orpsie Boy (IRE)**[180] 6320 3-8-7 **84** (N P Littmoden) *midfield: rdn and hdwy over 1f out: ev ch wl ins fnl f: r.o* **5/1**[3]	JamesDoyle(5) 4	88
1-20	3	hd	**Figaro Flyer (IRE)**[19] 1146 3-9-3 **89** (P Howling) *towards rr: n.m.r after 1f: rdn and hdwy over 1f out: str run wl ins fnl f* **7/1**	TonyCulhane 6	92
4012	4	nk	**Peter Island (FR)**[5] 1497 3-8-4 **76** oh2 (J Gallagher) *lw: led: rdn over 1f out: hrd pressed ins fnl f: hdd towards fin* **7/2**[2]	FrancisNorton 7	78
0-00	5	nk	**Waterline Twenty (IRE)**[9] 1377 3-8-8 **80** (P D Evans) *in tch: rdn and lost pl 3f out: rallied and swtchd lft jst ins fnl fulong: r.o* **33/1**	SteveDrowne 5	81
050-	6	hd	**Zennerman (IRE)**[236] 5289 3-8-10 **82** (W M Brisbourne) *chsd ldrs: rdn 3f out: nt qckn ins fnl f* **25/1**	DavidAllan 3	83
60-0	7	½	**Calypso King**[21] 1091 3-9-2 **88** (J W Hills) *edgy: s.i.s: in rr: rdn over 1f out: styd on and hung lft ins fnl f: eased whn nt clr run towards fin* **25/1**	RyanMoore 11	89+
31-0	8	1 ¼	**Night In (IRE)**[19] 1146 3-8-4 **76** oh1 (t) (N Tinkler) *w ldr: rdn and ev ch over 1f out: wknd wl ins fnl f* **8/1**	AlanMunro 2	71
41-	9	3	**Makfly**[187] 6251 3-8-7 **79** (R Hollinshead) *lw: chsd ldrs: rdn over 3f out: wknd ins fnl f: sn eased* **3/1**[1]	NCallan 1	65+
300-	10	2	**Colorus (IRE)**[222] 5613 3-9-4 **90** (R A Fahey) *bit bkwd: s.i.s: swtcd lft sn after s: n.m.r after 1f: in rr: rdn over 1f out: no imp whn nt clr run ins fnl* **11/1**	PaulHanagan 10	70+

1m 13.5s (-2.15) **Going Correction** -0.225s/f (Firm) 10 Ran SP% **119.0**
Speed ratings (Par 103):105,104,104,104,103 103,102,101,97,94
CSF £41.93 CT £259.14 TOTE £7.20: £1.70, £2.20, £2.70; EX 39.20 Place 6 £12.17, Place 5 £8.71.
Owner Willie McKay **Bred** Michael Murphy **Trained** Bawtry, S Yorks

FOCUS
Another competitive sprint handicap, but the draw had less of an effect over this six furlongs than the five and a large horse blanket would have covered the first seven at the line. That said the form looks pretty solid.

NOTEBOOK
Ooh Aah Camara(IRE), winner of the Lily Agnes Stakes at this meeting last year for a different trainer, was gaining her first victory since for her new and in-form handler. The Handicapper had given her a chance and, having raced up with the pace throughout, she forced her head in front where it mattered. (op 11-2)
Orpsie Boy(IRE), another with winning form on this quirky track as a juvenile, was minus the tongue tie on this return to action and was one of several brought with a late effort, but he just failed to get there. He should derive some benefit from this first outing in six months. (op 6-1)
Figaro Flyer(IRE) probably found himself further back than ideal in the early stages and was attempting to buck the trend by coming from quite so far off the pace. However, he did his best and, with his rider giving it everything, he put in a strong late effort on the inside that only just failed to succeed. (op 8-1 tchd 9-1 in a place)
Peter Island(FR), 2lb wrong, was given a very positive ride, but he was given no peace by Night In which might well have eventually cost him. Still in front 50 yards from the line, he was swallowed up on both sides and amazingly did not even make the first three. (tchd 4-1)
Waterline Twenty(IRE) ◆, who has faced some stiff tasks in her short career, was making her handicap debut on turf and was staying on in pleasing style at the line. She is dropping to the sort of mark she can be competitive off.
Zennerman(IRE) ◆ made a most encouraging return after eight months off. He won over seven furlongs on soft ground as a juvenile, so is likely to benefit from a longer trip now. (op 22-1)
Calypso King Official explanation: jockey said gelding missed the break
Makfly found this very different to the sort of ground he was successful on in his second and final outing at two, but not being able to make full use of the inside stall in the early stages was also no help. He should still come on for this first outing in five months. (tchd 11-4 and 100-30 in a place)
T/Jkpt: £1,849.80 to a £1 stake. Pool: £23,449.00. 9.00 winning tickets. T/Plt: £15.50 to a £1 stake. Pool: £89,639.55. 4,198.85 winning tickets. T/Qpdt: £6.50 to a £1 stake. Pool: £3,770.10. 428.10 winning tickets. DO

1499 HAMILTON (R-H)

Thursday, May 11

OFFICIAL GOING: Good to firm (good on loop)

Wind: Light, across

1607 HAMILTON PARK AMATEUR RIDERS' H'CAP 6f 5y

6:15 (6:15) (Class 6) (0-65,65) 4-Y-0+ £2,637 (£811; £405) Stalls Centre

Form RPR

2061 1 **Obe Bold (IRE)**12 1303 5-10-11 50 MrsCBartley 4 63
(A Berry) *mde all far side: effrt over 2f out: kpt on wl fnl f* 4/1[2]

0031 2 2 1/2 **Million Percent**3 1550 7-11-7 65 6ex MissKellyBurke(5) 3 71+
(K R Burke) *racd centre: cl up: hung rt 1/2-way: pressed wnr over 1f out: kpt on ins fnl f* 9/4[1]

60-0 3 1 **Quicks The Word**10 1341 6-10-7 51 MissHCuthbert(5) 1 54
(T A K Cuthbert) *trckd ldrs far side: effrt over 2f out: kpt on ins fnl f* 33/1

4060 4 1/2 **Louisiade (IRE)**24 1041 5-10-11 55 MissARyan(5) 5 56+
(K A Ryan) *in tch far side: drvn 1/2-way: r.o fnl f: no imp* 4/1[2]

0462 5 1 1/4 **Briery Lane (IRE)**17 1185 5-11-0 60 MissHWragg(7) 8 57
(Mrs K Walton) *trckd far side ldrs tl rdn and no ex over 1f out* 12/1

2330 6 1 **Wainwright (IRE)**110 164 6-11-4 60 MissFayeBramley(3) 10 54
(P A Blockley) *hld up bhd far side ldrs: rdn over 2f out: nt pce to chal* 6/1[3]

0003 7 1 1/2 **Jun Fan (USA)**7 1437 4-10-8 50 MissLEllison(3) 7 40
(B Ellison) *towards rr far side: rdn over 2f out: no imp over 1f out* 8/1

0224 8 3/4 **Comic Tales**6 1466 5-10-0 46 oh1 (b) MissMMullineaux(7) 2 34
(M Mullineaux) *s.i.s: bhd centre: drvn 1/2-way: n.d* 25/1

0006 9 1 1/4 **Tappit (IRE)**157 6511 7-10-0 46 oh6 (vt) MrKJames(7) 6 30
(L R James) *trckd ldrs tl wknd over 1f out* 100/1

0000 10 5 **Pays D'Amour (IRE)**29 974 9-10-3 49 oh6 ow3 (tp) MrCMcGaffin(7) 9 18
(D A Nolan) *s.i.s: a bhd far side* 100/1

1m 11.76s (-1.34) **Going Correction** -0.325s/f (Firm) 10 Ran SP% 112.6
Speed ratings (Par 101):95,91,90,89,88 86,84,83,82,75
CSF £12.64 CT £233.90 TOTE £3.00: £1.70, £1.10, £8.20; EX 10.10.
Owner Alan Berry **Bred** Saud Bin Saad **Trained** Cockerham, Lancs

FOCUS
An ordinary event in which the majority raced towards the far rail. The pace was fair but it paid to race prominently and the form looks reasoanble, rated around the winner and fifth.

1608 JOEL NATTY CLAIMING STKS 1m 1f 36y

6:45 (6:45) (Class 6) 3-Y-0+ £2,730 (£806; £403) Stalls High

Form RPR

0050 1 **Double Ransom**36 888 7-9-3 47 (b) MickyFenton 6 56
(Mrs L Stubbs) *hld up in tch: effrt over 2f out: edgd rt: kpt on fnl f to ld towards fin* 7/1[3]

0506 2 nk **Fiddlers Creek (IRE)**7 1439 7-9-8 58 (tp) DanielTudhope(3) 5 63
(R Allan) *cl up: led 1/2-way: hrd pressed fr over 2f out: kpt on: hdd towards fin* 11/2[2]

6502 3 nk **Alisdanza**12 1293 4-8-12 53 DeanMcKeown 4 50
(G A Swinbank) *trckd ldrs: chal over 2f out: rdn over 1f out: kpt on: hld towards fin* 4/7[1]

04U0 4 3 **Templet (USA)**15 6621 6-8-13 52 (v) DuranFentiman(5) 2 50
(W G Harrison) *hld up in tch: effrt over 2f out: nt qckn fnl f* 20/1

0300 5 5 **Mercari**85 5564 4-8-8 46 AndrewMullen(5) 1 35
(Mrs J C McGregor) *hld up: rdn 3f out: no imp over 1f out* 20/1

0455 6 3 **Rossin Gold (IRE)**119 5568 4-9-8 48 PaulMulrennan(3) 8 41
(P Monteith) *led to 1/2-way: sn rdn: rallied: wknd over 1f out* 12/1

5000 7 5 **Lucky Largo (IRE)**47 734 6-9-3 30 (b) DerekMcGaffin 7 23
(D A Nolan) *sn trcking ldrs: rdn over 3f out: wknd over 2f out* 150/1

2m 0.30s (0.64) **Going Correction** -0.175s/f (Firm) 7 Ran SP% 109.4
Speed ratings (Par 101):90,89,89,86,82 79,75
CSF £39.77 TOTE £8.30: £2.20, £2.80; EX 67.40.
Owner Tyme Partnership **Bred** Limestone Stud **Trained** Norton, N. Yorks

FOCUS
A low-grade event and a muddling gallop resulted in a moderate time, even for a claimer and the form is not that solid.

1609 MEARNS CASTLE GOLF ACADEMY OPEN MAIDEN STKS 6f 5y

7:20 (7:20) (Class 5) 3-4-Y-O £3,886 (£1,156; £577; £288) Stalls Centre

Form RPR

3643 1 **Sunrise Safari (IRE)**25 1032 3-8-12 82 (v1) TomEaves 8 70+
(I Semple) *mde virtually all: rdn over 1f out: kpt on fnl f* 10/11[1]

40 2 5 **Mandarin Rocket (IRE)**241 5175 3-8-12 TonyHamilton 4 55
(Miss L A Perratt) *disp ld to over 2f out: sn drvn along: rallied to chse wnr ins fnl f: r.o* 50/1

5 3 1 1/4 **Josarty**17 1185 3-8-9 DNolan(3) 7 51
(J J Quinn) *prom: effrt over 2f out: chsd wnr over 1f out to ins fnl f: no ex* 9/1[3]

246 4 1/2 **Royal Bandit**33 916 3-8-12 70 ChrisCatlin 5 50
(N A Callaghan) *hld up: effrt over 2f out: nvr rchd ldrs* 11/4[2]

4 5 3/4 **Eternal Legacy (IRE)**17 1185 4-9-3 MickyFenton 3 46
(J Parkes) *prom: rdn over 2f out: wknd over 1f out* 10/1

60 6 shd **Chateau (IRE)**14 1252 4-9-8 DeanMcKeown 6 50+
(G A Swinbank) *hld up: shkn up over 2f out: nvr nr ldrs* 20/1

000 7 2 **Active Audience (IRE)**25 1036 3-8-7 58 JoeFanning 2 39+
(A Berry) *dwlt: sn in tch: wknd over 2f out* 33/1

50 8 3 1/2 **Nautico**224 5562 3-8-7 PatCosgrave 1 26
(Miss L A Perratt) *chsd ldrs: n.m.r on ins 1/2-way: sn rdn and wknd* 50/1

0050 9 7 **Tallyhobye**10 1352 3-8-9 54 (b1) PaulMulrennan(3) 9 10
(J R Weymes) *dwlt: sn in tch on outside: rdn and wknd fr 1/2-way* 33/1

1m 11.91s (-1.19) **Going Correction** -0.325s/f (Firm)
WFA 3 from 4yo 10lb 9 Ran SP% 112.7
Speed ratings (Par 103):94,87,85,85,84 83,81,76,67
CSF £72.68 TOTE £1.60: £1.10, £15.10, £2.10; EX 62.20.
Owner Mrs J Penman **Bred** Mervyn Stewkesbury **Trained** Carluke, S Lanarks

FOCUS
Another uncompetitive race in which the clear form choice finally got off the mark. The time was moderate and the race has been rated negatively.
Tallyhobye Official explanation: jockey said gelding hung right-handed throughout; trainer said gelding did not face the blinkers

1610 DAILY RECORD H'CAP 1m 3f 16y

7:55 (7:55) (Class 5) (0-75,75) 4-Y-0+ £5,505 (£1,637; £818; £408) Stalls High

Form RPR

-360 1 **Aleron (IRE)**77 318 8-8-11 71 (p) DNolan(3) 2 78
(J J Quinn) *hld up: hdwy 3f out: led ins fnl f: hld on wl* 7/1

0200 2 hd **Lucayan Dancer**16 1220 6-9-4 75 AdrianTNicholls 6 82
(D Nicholls) *hld up in tch: smooth hdwy to ld over 2f out: hdd ins fnl f: flashed tail: kpt on towards fin* 5/2[1]

5400 3 1 3/4 **Easibet Dot Net**111 5875 6-8-13 70 (p) TomEaves 4 74
(I Semple) *cl up: disp ld over 2f out: no ex ins fnl f* 9/1

2000 4 1 3/4 **Kiama**16 1213 4-8-4 61 oh1 JoeFanning 7 62
(M Johnston) *prom: effrt and rdn over 3f out: one pce fr over 1f out* 8/1

1044 5 2 **Phoenix Eye**3 1553 5-8-4 61 oh16 ChrisCatlin 5 59?
(M Mullineaux) *hld up: effrt whn hung rt over 2f out: kpt on: no imp* 25/1

5450 6 5 **Bollin Thomas**10 1033 8-8-5 65 DanielTudhope(3) 8 55
(R Allan) *mde most to over 2f out: sn btn* 4/1[3]

6-3 7 5 **Andre Chenier (IRE)**32 5983 5-8-8 65 PaulFessey 1 47
(P Monteith) *trckd ldrs tl rdn and wknd over 2f out* 10/3[2]

2m 24.44s (-1.82) **Going Correction** -0.175s/f (Firm) 7 Ran SP% 109.1
Speed ratings (Par 103):99,98,97,96,94 91,87
CSF £22.57 CT £142.86 TOTE £9.70: £6.00, £2.30; EX 33.30.
Owner Grahame Liles **Bred** Sheikh Mohammed Bin Rashid Al Maktoum **Trained** Settrington, N Yorks

FOCUS
A moderate gallop to this ordinary event and a modest winning time. The placed horses set the level for the form, but it does not look all that solid.
Andre Chenier(IRE) Official explanation: jockey said gelding was unsuited by the good to firm (good in places) ground

1611 RECTANGLE GROUP H'CAP 5f 4y

8:25 (8:26) (Class 6) (0-65,65) 4-Y-0+ £3,238 (£963; £481; £240) Stalls Centre

Form RPR

0004 1 **Dizzy In The Head**4 1504 7-8-13 60 (b) TomEaves 11 71+
(I Semple) *racd w one other far side: overall ldr: rdn 2f out: hld on wl fnl f* 7/2[2]

0003 2 nk **Catch The Cat (IRE)**7 1438 7-8-10 62 (v) AndrewMullen(5) 6 72
(Robert Gray) *trckd stands side ldrs: led that gp over 1f out: edgd rt ins fnl f: kpt on: jst hld by far side wnr* 3/1[1]

3000 3 1 **Tribute (IRE)**231 5420 5-8-9 63 KevinGhunowa(7) 9 69
(P A Blockley) *dwlt: sn prom stands side: effrt over 2f out: one pce ins fnl f* 16/1

0300 4 nk **Monte Major (IRE)**8 1414 5-8-4 54 (v) PatrickMathers(3) 7 59
(D Shaw) *bhd and rdn stands side 1/2-way: hdwy over 1f out: kpt on wl fnl f* 14/1

0000 5 shd **Telepathic (IRE)**268 4447 6-8-4 51 oh6 JoeFanning 1 56
(A Berry) *trckd stands side ldrs: effrt over 1f out: nt qckn fnl f* 25/1

0012 6 nk **Compton Classic**9 1396 4-8-4 51 oh5 (p) ChrisCatlin 12 55
(J S Goldie) *swtchd to stands side: bhd tl hdwy over 1f out: kpt on fnl f* 7/1[3]

2015 7 1 **Muktasb (USA)**9 1396 5-8-5 52 (v) DeanMcKeown 2 52
(D Shaw) *hld up stands side: effrt over 2f out: no imp fnl f* 10/1

0030 8 hd **Champagne Cracker**25 1031 5-9-4 65 TonyHamilton 4 65
(I Semple) *chsd stands side ldrs tl wknd over 1f out* 16/1

1664 9 3 **Navigation (IRE)**189 6235 4-9-0 64 SaleemGolam(3) 5 53
(T J Etherington) *in tch on outside of stands side gp: rdn over 2f out: sn btn* 7/1[3]

0060 10 2 **Mutayam**268 4448 6-8-5 52 oh4 ow1 (t) NeilPollard 8 34
(D A Nolan) *led stands side to over 1f out: sn btn* 100/1

0400 11 5 **Vijay (IRE)**331 2568 7-8-4 51 oh6 PaulFessey 10 15
(Mrs J C McGregor) *racd far side: chsd wnr to 1/2-way: sn wknd* 50/1

59.17 secs (-2.03) **Going Correction** -0.325s/f (Firm) 11 Ran SP% 106.5
Speed ratings (Par 101):103,102,100,100,100 99,98,97,93,89 81
CSF £12.19 CT £119.19 TOTE £4.70: £2.00, £1.10, £5.70; EX 11.20.
Owner Gordon McDowall **Bred** Bearstone Stud And T Herbert Jackson **Trained** Carluke, S Lanarks
■ Oeuf A La Neige was withdrawn (14/1, vet's advice). R4 applies, deduct 5p in the £.

FOCUS
An ordinary event in which there was nothing between the two sides. The pace was sound but the form appears unsatisfactory.

1612 HASTE YE BACK TOMORROW H'CAP 5f 4y

8:55 (8:58) (Class 6) (0-60,60) 3-Y-O £3,238 (£963; £481; £240) Stalls Centre

Form RPR

621 1 **Sarah's Art (IRE)**6 1464 3-8-13 55 6ex (b) ChrisCatlin 6 62
(N A Callaghan) *prom far side: qcknd to ld 1f out: kpt on strly* 7/2[2]

5400 2 1 1/2 **Newkeylets**12 1279 3-8-11 53 TomEaves 8 55
(I Semple) *led far side to 1f out: kpt on same pce: 2nd of 6 in gp* 10/1[3]

2105 3 2 **Quadrophenia**19 1137 3-9-4 60 DaleGibson 4 55+
(J G Given) *mde virtually all stands side: rdn and kpt on fnl f: nt rch far side: 1st of 6 in gp* 7/2[2]

5620 4 hd **Laphonic (USA)**7 1441 3-8-12 54 PatCosgrave 3 48+
(T J Etherington) *cl up stands side: ev ch that gp over 1f out: kpt on ins fnl f: 2nd of 6 in gp* 14/1

0030 5 nk **Stanley Wolfe (IRE)**6 1464 3-7-13 46 oh1 AndrewMullen(5) 2 39+
(James Moffatt) *in tch stands side: effrt 2f out: kpt on ins fnl f: 3rd of 6 in gp* 20/1

0300 6 nk **Signor Whippee**77 487 3-7-13 48 KevinGhunowa(7) 1 40+
(A Berry) *trckd stands side ldrs: effrt 1/2-way: kpt on u.p fnl f: 4th of 6 in gp* 40/1

0502 7 1 **Soviet Legend (IRE)**15 1234 3-8-5 50 (v) SaleemGolam(3) 9 38
(T J Etherington) *trckd far side ldrs tl rdn and no ex wl over 1f out: 3rd of 6 that gp* 3/1[1]

000 8 5 **Eldon Outlaw**285 3957 3-8-10 52 DeanMcKeown 7 22+
(B Storey) *in tch on outside of stands side gp: effrt over 2f out: no imp fnl f: 5th of 6 in gp* 33/1

5006 9 2 1/2 **My Reflection**6 1464 3-8-2 47 oh1 ow1 PatrickMathers(3) 5 8+
(D Shaw) *hld up in tch stands side: effrt over 2f out: hung rt and sn no imp: last of 6 in that gp* 14/1

0600 10 hd **Liberation Square**213 5791 3-8-4 46 oh1 JoeFanning 10 7
(J S Goldie) *racd bhd far side ldrs tl rdn and wknd fr 2f out: 4th of 6 in gp* 14/1

006 11 nk **Networker**20 1126 3-8-4 46 oh6 PaulFessey 12 6
(K G Reveley) *unruly bef s: w far side ldrs to 1/2-way: sn rdn and btn: 5th of 6 in gp* 20/1

0660 **12** *12* **Compton Lad**[228] [5486] 3-8-10 **52** .... DerekMcGaffin 11 —
(D A Nolan) *cl up to 1/2-way far side tl wknd fr 1/2-way: last of 6 in gp* **50/1**

59.74 secs (-1.46) **Going Correction** -0.325s/f (Firm) **12** Ran SP% **115.4**
Speed ratings (Par 97):98,95,92,92,91 91,89,81,77,77 76,57
CSF £34.49 CT £131.00 TOTE £4.70: £1.10, £3.30, £1.60; EX 53.00 Place 6 £65.61, Place 5 £36.30.
Owner Matthew Green **Bred** Newtownbarry House Stud **Trained** Newmarket, Suffolk

FOCUS
A run-of-the-mill handicap in which the first two finished far side but there was again little between the two wings and the form is modest.
Networker Official explanation: jockey said gelding hung left
T/Plt: £109.30 to a £1 stake. Pool: £44,177.40. 294.85 winning tickets. T/Qpdt: £5.90 to a £1 stake. Pool: £4,006.20. 495.20 winning tickets. RY

[1260] YARMOUTH (L-H)
Thursday, May 11

OFFICIAL GOING: Good to firm
Wind: Moderate, across Weather: Sunny

1613 WEATHERBYS INSURANCE MAIDEN STKS 1m 3f 101y
2:00 (2:02) (Class 4) 3-Y-O+ **£6,477** (£1,927; £963; £481) **Stalls** Low

Form RPR
02 **1** **Duty (IRE)**[17] [1192] 3-8-9 .... KerrinMcEvoy 11 82+
(Sir Michael Stoute) *hld up midfield: rdn over 3f out: styd on steadily fnl 2f: led wl ins fnl f* **8/11**[1]
0 **2** *½* **Ermine Sea**[209] [5870] 3-8-9 .... RobertHavlin 7 82
(J H M Gosden) *cl up: rdn 3f out: led 2f out: hdd and nt qckn wl ins fnl f* **8/1**[3]
3 *¾* **Moonshadow** 3-8-4 .... EddieAhern 10 75
(H R A Cecil) *prom: rdn to ld over 4f out: hdd 2f out: ev ch tl no ex wl ins fnl f* **12/1**
65 **4** *2 ½* **Alasoun (IRE)**[19] [1139] 3-8-9 .... NickyMackay 4 76
(Sir Michael Stoute) *sn pushed along: prom: rdn 3f out: ev ch 1f out: wknd fnl 100 yds* **11/2**[2]
5 **5** *1 ½* **Riff Raff**[8] [1421] 3-8-4 .... JimmyQuinn 12 69
(W Jarvis) *hld up and bhd: effrt to chse ldrs fnl 3f: sn rdn: no imp fnl 2f* **9/1**
00 **6** *18* **Call Me George**[35] [897] 3-8-9 .... KDarley 8 45
(M Johnston) *bhd: disp t.o last ent st: plodded on* **33/1**
0 **7** *1 ¾* **Vettori Dancer**[10] [1351] 3-8-4 .... JamieMackay 3 37
(G G Margarson) *midfield: rdn and wknd 4f out: t.o over 2f out* **125/1**
8 *¾* **Mamonta** 3-8-5 ow1 .... LPKeniry 5 37
(D M Simcock) *s.s: nvr nr ldrs: hrd rdn and fnd nil over 3f out: t.o* **28/1**
0335 **9** *21* **Meantime (USA)**[14] [1260] 3-8-6 72 ....(v[1]) AdamKirby[(3)] 1 8
(G Prodromou) *led tl crossed to stands rails and r alone st: promptly hdd and sn t.o* **40/1**
0 **10** *4* **Alan The Aussie**[9] [1386] 3-8-2 .... KirstyMilczarek[(7)] 6 1
(G Prodromou) *awkward in preliminaries: pressed ldr tl brought wd to r centre st: sn t.o* **150/1**
0 **11** *39* **Grand Mempari**[14] [1260] 3-8-4 .... HayleyTurner 9 —
(Mrs C A Dunnett) *s.i.s: sn drvn and nvr gng pce: disp t.o last st: btn 88l* **150/1**

2m 27.67s (0.17) **Going Correction** +0.05s/f (Good) **11** Ran SP% **113.0**
Speed ratings (Par 105):101,100,100,98,97 84,82,82,67,64 35
CSF £6.44 TOTE £1.60: £1.10, £2.40, £2.10; EX 9.20 Trifecta £41.40 Pool: £339.60 - 5.82 winning tickets..
Owner Highclere Thoroughbred Racing XXX **Bred** 6c Stallions Ltd **Trained** Newmarket, Suffolk

FOCUS
A reasonable maiden in which Duty confirmed the improved form he showed at Windsor on his previous start, but had to work hard enough to see off Ermine Sea, who improved for the step up to middle-distances on his reappearance.

1614 WEATHERBYS BANK H'CAP 1m 3f 101y
2:30 (2:30) (Class 5) (0-75,72) 4-Y-O+ **£5,505** (£1,637; £818; £408) **Stalls** Low

Form RPR
065 **1** **Captain General**[244] [5096] 4-8-8 **62** .... KerrinMcEvoy 2 73+
(J A R Toller) *bhd: swtchd rt over 1f out: rapid burst on outside fnl f: drvn past five rivals last 100 yds to ld nr post* **16/1**
0601 **2** *hd* **Summer Charm**[24] [1045] 4-9-0 **68** .... JamieSpencer 7 76
(W Jarvis) *hld up and bhd: effrt and swtchd rt 2f out: edging lft fnl f: led 50 yds out: jst ct* **5/1**[3]
4016 **3** *1 ¼* **Magic Amigo**[43] [799] 5-9-4 **72** .... EddieAhern 4 78
(J R Jenkins) *prom: drvn to ld over 1f out: hdd fnl 50 yds: nt qckn* **33/1**
2250 **4** *½* **Velvet Waters**[196] [6127] 5-8-13 **67** .... TQuinn 5 72
(R F Johnson Houghton) *led: rdn and hdd wl over 1f out: stl ev ch tl no ex wl ins fnl f* **9/2**[2]
0000 **5** *1* **Tata Naka**[18] [1162] 6-8-4 **58** oh8 .... HayleyTurner 1 62?
(Mrs C A Dunnett) *midfield: rdn 2f out: ev ch on heels of ldrs 100 yds out: no ex* **33/1**
0002 **6** *½* **Fort Churchill (IRE)**[10] [1346] 5-8-12 **66** ....(bt) RobertWinston 3 69
(B Ellison) *t.k.h chsng ldrs: effrt 2f out: kpt hanging lft after: fnd nil fnl f* **2/1**[1]
0001 **7** *1 ¾* **Migration**[16] [1222] 10-8-5 **62** .... RichardThomas[(3)] 6 62
(Mrs S Lamyman) *bhd: detached last st: prog on outside fnl f: styd on* **25/1**
2004 **8** *3* **Santando**[39] [847] 6-8-8 **62** .... MartinDwyer 9 57
(C E Brittain) *towrds rr: rdn over 3f out: btn 2f out* **11/2**
0166 **9** *1 ½* **Boxhall (IRE)**[225] [5559] 4-9-3 **71** .... SebSanders 8 64
(W R Swinburn) *pressed ldr: hrd rdn over 3f out: lost pl 2f out* **8/1**
0100 **10** *9* **Domenico (IRE)**[172] [5903] 8-8-7 **64** ow4 .... DeanCorby[(3)] 10 42
(J R Jenkins) *cl up: drvn 3f out: carried hd high after: nt run on and sn btn* **40/1**

2m 29.87s (2.37) **Going Correction** +0.05s/f (Good) **10** Ran SP% **112.7**
Speed ratings (Par 103):93,92,91,91,90 90,89,87,85,79
CSF £87.86 CT £2599.71 TOTE £23.70: £4.10, £1.90, £4.20; EX 140.20 TRIFECTA Not won..
Owner M E Wates **Bred** M E Wates **Trained** Newmarket, Suffolk

FOCUS
Just a modest handicap and a steady pace resulted in a very moderate winning time for the type of contest, 2.2 seconds slower than the preceding maiden. Thye form is ordinary, rated around the placed horses to form.
Migration Official explanation: jockey said gelding was unsuited by the good to firm ground

1615 BET365 CALL 08000 322 365 H'CAP 1m 2f 21y
3:00 (3:00) (Class 3) (0-90,86) 3-Y-O **£11,217** (£3,358; £1,679; £840; £419; £210) **Stalls** Low

Form RPR
0321 **1** **Stage Gift (IRE)**[20] [1108] 3-9-0 **82** .... RobertWinston 4 98+
(Sir Michael Stoute) *trckd ldrs: 2nd st: led 2f out: pushed clr over 1f out: readily* **6/4**[1]
2305 **2** *1 ¾* **Lake Poet (IRE)**[9] [1384] 3-8-11 **79** .... SebSanders 8 86
(C E Brittain) *hld up: last st: styd on up far rails fr 2f out: wnt 2nd over 1f out: nt extend wnr* **25/1**
14 **3** *2* **Merveilles**[237] [5271] 3-9-4 **86** .... RobertHavlin 7 89
(J H M Gosden) *stdd s: 5th st: tending to edge lft whn pushed along fr over 2f out: wnt 3rd ins fnl f: kpt on steadily* **7/1**
4546 **4** *1 ¼* **Doctor Scott**[13] [1268] 3-9-2 **84** .... StanleyChin 5 85
(M Johnston) *led: drvn and hdd 2f out: fdd ins fnl f* **14/1**
5004 **5** *½* **Mujood**[4] [1515] 3-8-12 **80** .... TQuinn 1 80
(R F Johnson Houghton) *prom: 3rd st: drvn 2f out: wl hld after* **18/1**
5021 **6** *1* **Airbuss (IRE)**[15] [1241] 3-8-9 **77** .... TedDurcan 6 75
(M R Channon) *hld up: 4th st: rdn 2f out: one pced after* **4/1**[2]
1102 **7** *¾* **Nihal (IRE)**[7] [1446] 3-9-2 **84** .... KDarley 2 80
(M Johnston) *6th st: rdn 3f out: btn over 2f out* **9/2**[3]

2m 12.52s (4.42) **Going Correction** +0.05s/f (Good) **7** Ran SP% **106.5**
Speed ratings (Par 103):84,82,81,80,79 78,78
CSF £36.12 CT £163.89 TOTE £2.10: £1.40, £4.10; EX 36.20 Trifecta £179.10 Pool: £517.25 - 2.05 winning tickets..
Owner Ballymacoll Stud **Bred** Ballymacoll Stud Farm Ltd **Trained** Newmarket, Suffolk

FOCUS
Although both Airbuss and Nihal disappointed, that should not detract from what was a taking performance from the progressive Stage Gift, who never looked in any danger despite pricking his ears throughout the final furlongs. They went a steady pace for most of the way, so it was no surprise the time was slow and as such the form behind is not the most solid.

NOTEBOOK
Stage Gift(IRE) ◆, who showed improved form when upped to this trip on his reappearance/handicap debut on Kempton's Polytrack, confirmed that progression returned to turf with a decisive success off a 6lb higher mark. He had his ears pricked almost throughout the last furlong and won very much in the style of a horse who has plenty more to offer. His trainer has plenty of similarly nice middle-distance three-year-olds in his care this season, so he should know where he stands with this one and he must be kept on the right side. Something like the King George V handicap at Royal Ascot could be a good target; his breeding suggests the extra couple of furlongs will not be problem. (op 13-8 tchd 11-8)
Lake Poet(IRE), a maiden after nine starts coming into this, proved suited by the step up to ten furlongs and just ran into a very nice horse. (op 22-1 tchd 20-1)
Merveilles ◆, upped in trip and making his debut in handicap company off the back of a 237-day break, made a pleasing return to action. Racing on ground that could be considered fast enough, he was not subjected to a hard ride and can do better. (op 6-1 tchd 15-2)
Doctor Scott, back up in trip, had the run of the race at just a steady gallop and can have few excuses. (tchd 16-1)
Mujood again failed to prove his stamina. (op 20-1)
Airbuss(IRE), 5lb higher, failed to build on the form he showed when winning on his handicap debut at Epsom and was disappointing. (op 7-2)
Nihal(IRE) shaped well on her reappearance when second at Redcar, but failed to build on that and was disappointing. (op 7-2 tchd 5-1)

1616 CUSTOM KITCHENS H'CAP 1m 3y
3:35 (3:36) (Class 6) (0-65,65) 3-Y-O **£3,238** (£963; £481; £240) **Stalls** High

Form RPR
000 **1** **Prince Picasso**[219] [5680] 3-8-9 **56** .... SebSanders 5 71
(Sir Mark Prescott) *prom: led wl over 3f out: clr fnl f: styd on stoutly* **15/2**[3]
0332 **2** *5* **Catbang (IRE)**[8] [1416] 3-9-2 **63** .... JamieSpencer 6 66
(N A Callaghan) *chsd ldrs: hrd drvn over 1f out: wnt 2nd ins fnl f: no ch w wnr* **11/4**[1]
000 **3** *nk* **Carpeting**[92] [337] 3-8-10 **57** ....(v[1]) TedDurcan 10 59
(D Morris) *stdd s: last early: swtchd rt and gd prog over 1f out: kpt on wl ins fnl f* **100/1**
0640 **4** *hd* **Black Sea Pearl**[37] [879] 3-8-10 **57** .... KerrinMcEvoy 3 59
(P W D'Arcy) *chsd ldrs: rdn over 1f out: kpt on ins fnl f* **20/1**
0155 **5** *¾* **Al Rayanah**[24] [1056] 3-8-10 **64** .... KirstyMilczarek[(7)] 1 64
(G Prodromou) *prom: drvn over 1f out: kpt on same pce* **33/1**
4044 **6** *3 ½* **Lisfannon**[22] [1078] 3-9-2 **63** .... MichaelHills 2 55
(B W Hills) *mde most for over 4f: prom tl fdd ins fnl f* **12/1**
504 **7** *3 ½* **Air Biscuit (IRE)**[19] [1141] 3-9-4 **65** .... EddieAhern 13 49
(C F Wall) *plld hrd: chsd ldrs tl wknd wl over 1f out* **10/1**
0204 **8** *9* **Welsh Cake**[12] [1307] 3-9-0 **61** .... TQuinn 7 24
(Mrs A J Perrett) *midfield: effrt over 2f out: sn rdn: btn wl over 1f out* **20/1**
5412 **9** *2 ½* **Musicmaestroplease (IRE)**[15] [1232] 3-8-10 **62** .... DerekNolan[(5)] 9 20
(S Parr) *bhd fr 1/2-way* **9/1**
5650 **10** *3 ½* **Cheveley Flyer**[10] [1352] 3-8-8 **55** .... JimmyQuinn 11 5
(J Pearce) *slowly away: nvr on terms* **10/1**
0045 **11** *3* **Ayam Jantan**[7] [1444] 3-9-1 **62** .... KDarley 4 5
(M Johnston) *plld hrd: jnd ldr after 2f: rdn over 3f out: rapidly lost pl: t.o* **40/1**
1006 **12** *1* **Living On A Prayer**[12] [1307] 3-8-12 **59** .... RoystonFfrench 12 —
(J Pearce) *sn drvn along: nvr gng wl: t.o* **100/1**
0050 **13** *1 ¾* **Ronaldo**[10] [1352] 3-8-11 **58** .... MartinDwyer 8 —
(W R Muir) *prom: drvn after 3f: sn lost pl: t.o* **33/1**
0650 **14** *3 ½* **Almowj**[29] [984] 3-8-10 **57** .... TPQueally 15 —
(C E Brittain) *drvn and struggling 1/2-way: t.o* **25/1**
0663 **15** *15* **Sgt Schultz (IRE)**[7] [1441] 3-9-3 **64** .... RobertWinston 16 —
(J S Moore) *bhd: eased 2f out: virtually p.u fnl f* **5/1**[2]
5140 **16** *47* **Super Frank (IRE)**[16] [1215] 3-9-3 **64** ....(b) NickyMackay 14 —
(G A Butler) *plld hrd early: struggling 1/2-way: t.o and virtually p.u over 1f out: btn 97l* **11/1**

1m 38.1s (-1.80) **Going Correction** -0.25s/f (Firm) **16** Ran SP% **123.0**
Speed ratings (Par 97):99,94,93,93,92 89,85,76,74,70 67,66,65,61,46 —
CSF £26.18 CT £1976.20 TOTE £9.70: £2.20, £1.30, £14.50, £5.30; EX 36.10 TRIFECTA Not won..
Owner Syndicate 2004 **Bred** Cheveley Park Stud Ltd **Trained** Newmarket, Suffolk

FOCUS
Prince Picasso, last seen over five furlongs, showed improved form stepped up in trip on his handicap debut and looks capable of rating much higher. The placed horses set a solid enough standard.
Prince Picasso ◆ Official explanation: trainers rep said, regarding the improved form shown, the gelding may have benefited from the step up in trip
Musicmaestroplease(IRE) Official explanation: jockey said colt lost a front shoe
Ronaldo Official explanation: jockey said colt had no more to give
Sgt Schultz(IRE) Official explanation: jockey said gelding ran flat

Super Frank(IRE) Official explanation: jockey said colt lost its action; vet said colt finished lame

1617 LETHEBY & CHRISTOPHER H'CAP 7f 3y

4:10 (4:13) (Class 4) (0-85,84) 3-Y-O

£7,790 (£2,332; £1,166; £583; £291; £146) **Stalls** High

Form				RPR
1544	**1**		**Sands Of Barra (IRE)**[11] 1312 3-8-6 **72** .... KerrinMcEvoy 2 (N A Callaghan) *mde all and waited in front: pushed along ins fnl f: kpt on gamely* **20/1**	78
31	**2**	1 1/2	**Tawaassol (USA)**[14] 1261 3-9-2 **82** .... MartinDwyer 6 (Sir Michael Stoute) *cl up: rdn to chse wnr wl over 1f out: drvn and a hld fnl f* **4/6**[1]	84
1013	**3**	1/2	**Celebration Song (IRE)**[47] 724 3-9-4 **84** .... TedDurcan 3 (W R Swinburn) *pressed ldr tl rdn wl over 1f out: kpt on same pce after* **16/1**[3]	85
5210	**4**	2 1/2	**Aspen Falls (IRE)**[215] 5733 3-9-2 **82** .... SebSanders 5 (Sir Mark Prescott) *chsd ldrs: rdn and effrt over 1f out: wknd ins fnl f* **33/1**	77
3213	**5**	2 1/2	**Bomber Command (USA)**[26] 1016 3-9-2 **82** .... EddieAhern 7 (J W Hills) *towards rr: rdn wl over 2f out: sn btn* **5/2**[2]	70
4230	**6**	1	**Categorical**[21] 1091 3-9-0 **80** .... JamieSpencer 8 (J A R Toller) *hld up last: struggling fr 1/2-way* **25/1**	65
2004	**7**	3	**Woolfall Blue (IRE)**[12] 1289 3-9-2 **82** .... TQuinn 9 (G G Margarson) *cl up: rdn 3f out: sn btn* **25/1**	60
4100	**8**	1	**Local Fancy**[234] 5370 3-9-1 **81** .... RobertWinston 1 (J M P Eustace) *shkn up after 3f: sn racing awkwardly: no ch fr 1/2-way* **80/1**	56
5536	**9**	3	**Memphis Man**[14] 1250 3-8-9 **75** .... MichaelHills 4 (G C Bravery) *taken down early: a bhd: no ch fnl 3f* **50/1**	42

1m 24.67s (-1.93) **Going Correction** -0.25s/f (Firm) **9** Ran SP% **113.0**
Speed ratings (Par 101):101,99,98,95,93 91,88,87,83
CSF £32.49 CT £245.67 TOTE £23.50: £2.90, £1.10, £3.00; EX 45.20 Trifecta £420.00 Part won. Pool: £591.61 - 0.68 winning tickets..
Owner Alan Brazil Racing Club Ltd **Bred** Sunderland Holdings Inc **Trained** Newmarket, Suffolk
■ A treble on the card for Kerrin McEvoy.

FOCUS
This looked a straightforward opportunity for Tawaassol to follow up his recent course maiden success, but Kerrin McEvoy stole this on Sands Of Barra with a very good ride from the front. As a result, the bare form does not look very reliable, although the third and fourth were close to form.
Woolfall Blue(IRE) Official explanation: jockey said colt had no more to give
Local Fancy Official explanation: jockey said filly hung left

1618 DOCWRAS ROCK H'CAP 5f 43y

4:45 (4:46) (Class 6) (0-65,63) 4-Y-O+ **£3,238** (£963; £481; £240) **Stalls** High

Form				RPR
4126	**1**		**Mystery Pips**[44] 782 6-8-7 **52** ....(v) KimTinkler 2 (N Tinkler) *pushed along and pressing ldr: kpt on to ld ins fnl f: r.o* **16/1**	65
0600	**2**	3/4	**Smiddy Hill**[189] 6235 4-9-3 **62** .... RoystonFfrench 1 (R Bastiman) *mde most: drvn and hdd ins fnl f: r.o one pce* **20/1**	73
5415	**3**	1 1/4	**Cashel Mead**[8] 1414 6-8-13 **58** .... KerrinMcEvoy 15 (J L Spearing) *midfield: rdn and prog over 1f out: styd on to go 3rd fnl stride* **15/8**[1]	64+
0650	**4**	shd	**Detonate**[11] 1315 4-7-12 **50** .... KirstyMilczarek(7) 13 (Mrs C A Dunnett) *chsd ldrs: rdn over 1f out: nt qckn after* **16/1**	56
0050	**5**	3/4	**Cosmic Destiny (IRE)**[8] 1414 4-9-0 **59** .... EddieAhern 12 (E F Vaughan) *chsd ldrs: rdn over 1f out: no imp* **12/1**	62
0050	**6**	1 3/4	**Russian Rocket (IRE)**[16] 1211 4-9-4 **63** .... HayleyTurner 9 (Mrs C A Dunnett) *chsd ldrs over 3f: sn btn* **11/1**	60
0000	**7**	2	**Bold Cheverak**[11] 1315 4-8-7 **55** .... AdamKirby(3) 16 (Mrs C A Dunnett) *taken to post early: effrt 2f out: nvr able to chal* **16/1**	44
0564	**8**	1 1/2	**Tadlil**[8] 1414 4-9-0 **59** .... TedDurcan 10 (J M Bradley) *sn pushed along: nvr on terms* **15/2**[3]	43
0000	**9**	nk	**Belrose (IRE)**[17] 1194 4-8-4 **49** oh4 ....(b[1]) JimmyQuinn 7 (Mrs C A Dunnett) *missed break: a bhd* **66/1**	32
0004	**10**	7	**Bahamian Breeze**[31] 951 5-8-8 **53** .... LPKeniry 11 (D M Simcock) *missed break: nt rcvr* **14/1**	11
2100	**11**	1	**Prime Recreation**[9] 1396 9-8-6 **51** ow1 .... RobertWinston 8 (P S Felgate) *spd to 1/2-way: edgd rt and sn fdd: eased fnl f* **33/1**	—
3030	**12**	2 1/2	**Byo (IRE)**[12] 1303 8-8-10 **55** .... JamieSpencer 14 (P Howling) *struggling 1/2-way: eased fnl f* **8/1**	—
5400	**13**	1	**Victoriana**[3] 1534 5-8-4 **49** oh9 ....(p) JamieMackay 4 (H J Collingridge) *sn labouring bdly in rr* **100/1**	—
0040	**14**	1 1/4	**Flaran**[163] 6455 6-8-12 **57** .... SebSanders 3 (J A R Toller) *a struggling* **7/1**[2]	—

61.46 secs (-1.34) **Going Correction** -0.25s/f (Firm) **14** Ran SP% **120.7**
Speed ratings (Par 101):100,98,96,96,95 92,89,87,86,75 73,69,68,66
CSF £308.96 CT £908.81 TOTE £19.90: £3.10, £5.90, £1.60; EX 251.50 TRIFECTA Not won. Place 6 £56.68, Place 5 £43.39.
Owner Paglia & Fieno Racing **Bred** Michael Worton **Trained** Langton, N Yorks

FOCUS
A moderate sprint dominated by the fillies/mares and the form looks sound, rated through the fourth and fifth.
Prime Recreation Official explanation: jockey said gelding hung right
Byo(IRE) Official explanation: jockey said gelding lost its action
Flaran Official explanation: jockey said gelding lost its action
T/Plt: £13.60 to a £1 stake. Pool: £37,827.40. 2,018.00 winning tickets. T/Qpdt: £5.90 to a £1 stake. Pool: £2,701.00. 336.75 winning tickets. IM

1619 - 1625a (Foreign Racing) - See Raceform Interactive

1601 CHESTER (L-H)

Friday, May 12

OFFICIAL GOING: Good to soft

Wind: Light, across Weather: Heavy rain race 1 (1.50), stormy but dry thereafter

1626 EDWARDS HOMES STKS (H'CAP) 7f 122y

1:50 (1:50) (Class 2) (0-100,94) 3-Y-O **£14,510** (£4,342; £2,171; £1,085; £540) **Stalls** Low

Form				RPR
41	**1**		**Song Of Passion (IRE)**[248] 5032 3-8-5 **81** .... RyanMoore 6 (R Hannon) *sn led: edgd rt ins fnl f: drvn out* **12/1**	92
3150	**2**	3/4	**Collateral Damage (IRE)**[24] 1067 3-8-4 **80** .... GrahamGibbons 4 (T D Easterby) *led early: trckd ldrs after: wnt 2nd wl over 1f out: sn rdn r.o ins fnl f: a hld* **9/1**[3]	89
4214	**3**	3/4	**European Dream (IRE)**[8] 1440 3-7-13 **80** 6ex .... AndrewMullen(5) 5 (R C Guest) *in tch: niggled along briefly over 4f out: nt clr run 2f out: rdn over 1f out: r.o towards fin* **9/1**[3]	90+
11	**4**	nk	**Easy Air**[39] 852 3-8-10 **86** .... LDettori 3 (E A L Dunlop) *lw: hld up: hdwy 2f out: rdn over 1f out: one pce wl ins fnl f* **11/8**[1]	92
016	**5**	3 1/2	**Champions Gallery**[216] 5731 3-9-2 **92** .... TQuinn 2 (D R C Elsworth) *lw: hld up: rdn over 1f out: nvr able to chal* **4/1**[2]	90
4012	**6**	11	**Silidan**[213] 5818 3-8-12 **88** .... JohnEgan 1 (T P Tate) *prom: rdn and ev ch over 2f out: wknd over 1f out* **4/1**[2]	60

1m 37.65s (2.90) **Going Correction** +0.525s/f (Yiel) **6** Ran SP% **109.8**
Speed ratings (Par 105):106,105,104,104,100 89
CSF £100.99 TOTE £12.30: £3.60, £3.10; EX 99.30.
Owner Thurloe Thoroughbreds XVI **Bred** Mrs Stephanie Hanly **Trained** East Everleigh, Wilts

FOCUS
Just the six runners and Champions Gallery and Silidan did not seem happy on the easy ground, but still a decent effort from Song Of Passion and the form should prove reasonable.

NOTEBOOK
Song Of Passion(IRE), who showed promise on her debut at Windsor before getting off the mark in a seven-furlong Polytrack maiden on her final start at two, defied a 248-day break to make a winning return. The only filly in the field, this was a very good effort and she should be able to defy a rise in the weights. (op 10-1)
Collateral Damage(IRE), ninth of 17 on his reappearance in a decent handicap at Newmarket, stepped up on that from and was just held having travelled well for much of the way. The ground had come on his favour, though, and it remains to be seen if he can confirm this sort of form back on a faster surface. (op 12-1)
European Dream(IRE), carrying a penalty but still 6lb out of the handicap, would not have minded the soft ground and ran well; he would have been even closer had he enjoyed a clear run when beginning to pick up about two furlongs out. (tchd 11-1)
Easy Air's half-brother Court Masterpiece has won on soft ground, so he is bred to handle this sort of surface, but this was his first run on turf following two wins on Polytrack, and perhaps the experience was just needed. He did not exactly look well handicapped either following a 9lb rise in the weights for just a workmanlike success on his most recent start, and maybe he just needs more time. (op 5-4 tchd 6-4 in places)
Champions Gallery, who won his maiden before finishing sixth of 12 in the Autumn Stakes on his final start as a juvenile, did not look too harshly treated on a mark of 92 for his return, but was well held. He can be given another chance back on a sound surface. (op 6-1)
Silidan, returning from a 213-day break, had never raced on ground worse than good and his two wins came on a fast surface, so this can be forgiven. He also got a little warm. (op 5-2)

1627 CHESHIRE REGIMENT DEE STKS (SPONSORED BY ELIFAR FOUNDATION) (GROUP 3) (C&G) 1m 2f 75y

2:20 (2:21) (Class 1) 3-Y-O

£36,907 (£13,988; £7,000; £3,490; £1,748; £877) **Stalls** High

Form				RPR
12	**1**		**Art Deco (IRE)**[247] 5046 3-8-12 **95** .... LDettori 6 (C R Egerton) *a.p: led over 2f out: rdn clr over 1f out: hld on gamely cl home* **8/1**	113
11	**2**	nk	**Ivy Creek (USA)**[14] 1269 3-8-12 **103** .... SteveDrowne 1 (G Wragg) *lw: in tch: nt clr run & lost pl 3f out: nt clr run 2f out: rdn & hdwy whn swtchd rt over 1f out: ran on strongly ins fnl f* **15/8**[1]	115+
03	**3**	7	**Alhaajes (USA)**[23] 1081 3-8-12 .... RHills 4 (B W Hills) *hld up: hdwy over 3f out: rdn whn bmpd over 1f out: one pce one pce ins fnl f* **11/1**	99
1140	**4**	hd	**City Of Troy**[22] 1092 3-8-12 **102** .... KFallon 8 (Sir Michael Stoute) *s.i.s: hld up: pushed along whn n.m.r 2f out: hdwy whn swtchd lft over 1f out: one pce ins fnl f* **11/4**[2]	99+
2252	**5**	2 1/2	**Cousteau**[11] 1335 3-8-12 **98** .... AlanMunro 3 (P W Chapple-Hyam) *lw: racd keenly: in tch: rdn to cl over 2f out: wknd ins fnl f* **10/1**	94
01	**6**	6	**Gandor (IRE)**[16] 1240 3-8-12 **89** .... JimmyFortune 7 (J H M Gosden) *in tch: effrt to chal over 2f out: wkng whn bmpd over 1f out* **5/1**[3]	83
5103	**7**	1 1/2	**Dubai Typhoon (USA)**[41] 829 3-8-12 **95** .... RyanMoore 9 (C E Brittain) *wnt rt s: hld up in rr: rdn over 2f out: nvr on terms* **40/1**	81
6	**8**	hd	**Sandton City (IRE)**[27] 1027 3-8-12 .... NCallan 2 (Francis Ennis, Ire) *trckd ldrs: rdn over 3f out: nt clr run and lost pl over 2f out: sn wknd* **20/1**	80+
0000	**9**	23	**Grand Jour (IRE)**[27] 1016 3-8-12 **85** .... JohnEgan 5 (K McAuliffe) *led: rdn and hdd over 2f out: sn wknd* **66/1**	39

2m 16.15s (3.01) **Going Correction** +0.525s/f (Yiel) **9** Ran SP% **115.3**
Speed ratings (Par 109):108,107,102,102,100 95,94,93,75
CSF £23.10 TOTE £6.50: £1.80, £1.30, £2.90; EX 23.30 Trifecta £424.00 Pool: £836.20 - 1.40 winning tickets..
Owner Mrs Evelyn Hankinson **Bred** C H Wacker Iii **Trained** Chaddleworth, Berks

FOCUS
By no means a bad renewal and a good effort from Art Deco on his seasonal reappearance, although he was a fortunate winner as Ivy Creek was most unlucky in running. That one can be rated as a clear-cut winner and looks a high-class prospect.

NOTEBOOK
Art Deco(IRE), a winner on his debut on soft ground at Sandown before finding only City Of Troy too good in a conditions event at Doncaster on his final start as a juvenile, looked fit enough for his return rom a 247-day break and, with conditions to suit, he ran out a narrow winner. He had a dream passage all the way and can count himself most fortunate to have beaten Ivy Creek, as that one had quite the opposite, but the pair were clear and this still must rate as a very smart effort. (op 9-1 tchd 9-2)
Ivy Creek(USA) ◆, a winner on his debut at Warwick before following up in a decent conditions race at Sandown, would not have minded this soft ground at all and was a most unlucky loser. He got absolutely no run through when beginning to respond to pressure and, when finally in the clear, still looked a touch green and just failed to reel in the Art Deco. He did extremely well to get as close as did, as well as finish so far clear of the remainder, and he looks a high-class prospect. (op 2-1 tchd 9-4, 5-2 in places)
Alhaajes(USA), who would have been second at least but for clipping heels close home in a decent mile and a half maiden at Newmarket on his reappearance, would not have minded the drop in trip, but this was a tough ask. Still, he ran with credit and, although no match for the front two, showed himself to be very useful in grabbing a place. (op 14-1)
City Of Troy, disappointing when a beaten favourite in both the Royal Lodge on his final start at two and in the Craven on his reappearance, looked interesting upped in trip and switched to Chester, but the ground that came would not have been in his favour and he never looked happy. He has not progressed as one might have hoped, having looked so promising on his first two starts - not least when he beat today's winner in a Doncaster conditions race - but things did not go his way this time and it would be unwise to give up on him just yet. (op 9-4 tchd 3-1 in places)
Cousteau, the Craven fifth, shaped as though this sort of trip would suit when beaten in a Kempton maiden on his latest start, and he would not have minded the ground, but he finished up well held after racing keenly. While this was still a useful effort strictly on the figures, he does not seem to be progressing. (op 12-1)
Gandor(IRE) would have found this much tougher than the extended-mile maiden he won on his reappearance and was well held. (tchd 9-2)

1628 BLUE SQUARE ORMONDE STKS (GROUP 3) 1m 5f 89y
2:50 (2:51) (Class 1) 4-Y-0+ £42,585 (£16,140; £8,077; £4,027; £2,017) Stalls Low

Form RPR

3205 **1** **The Whistling Teal**[20] [1128] 10-9-0 114 ..... SteveDrowne 5 108+
(G Wragg) *hld up in tch: hmpd 5f out: sn pushed along: wnt 2nd over 1f out: led ins fnl f: styd on* 7/2[2]

1030 **2** ½ **Orcadian**[14] [1267] 5-9-0 102 ..... NCallan 2 107+
(J M P Eustace) *sn led: clr whn hung rt fr over 7f out: rel to r & hdd 5f out: rallied over 3f out: led 2f out: edgd lft: hdd ins fnl f: no* 10/1[3]

-521 **3** 7 **Arbella**[29] [1006] 4-8-11 87 ..... JimmyFortune 4 94
(W R Swinburn) *chsd ldr: swtchd rt and lft in ld 5f out: rdn and hdd 2f out: hmpd over 1f out: wknd fnl f* 16/1

2000 **4** 10 **Compton Bolter (IRE)**[20] [1128] 9-9-3 109 .....(b) LDettori 1 86
(G A Butler) *broke wl: sn hld up in tch: rdn 3f out: sn btn* 12/1

1041 **5** 13 **Mubtaker (USA)**[20] [1128] 9-9-3 115 ..... RHills 3 68
(M P Tregoning) *lw: hld up: hdwy whn bmpd and lft in 2nd pl 5f out: rdn and wknd qckly 3f out* 1/2[1]

3m 0.71s (5.29) **Going Correction** +0.525s/f (Yiel) 5 Ran SP% 111.6
Speed ratings (Par 113):104,103,99,93,85
CSF £32.97 TOTE £4.80: £1.90, £3.50; EX 45.00.
Owner Mrs F A Veasey **Bred** Mrs F A Veasey **Trained** Newmarket, Suffolk

FOCUS
A bizarre renewal of the Ormonde Stakes. Mubtaker looked a good thing to add to his recent John Porter success before the rain arrived, but the change in going from the previous two days made him vulnerable. One of those who would have been suited by the easy ground was Orcadian, but he did everything he could to get beat, and just succeeded. Having led the field at a good gallop, he dropped himself out with just over half a mile to race before picking up the bit once more and very nearly managing to get back up and win. The Whistling Teal was left to gain a deserved success, but the fact he could only scrape home by half a length says little for the level of form he achieved.

NOTEBOOK
The Whistling Teal is not very consistent these days, but he showed he retains plenty of ability when second in last season's Irish St Leger and fifth to Mubtaker in the John Porter at Newbury on his reappearance. He could, though, have been expected to win this more easily given Orcadian dropped himself out to last place at one stage, and the favourite ran no sort of race. While he should continue to go well, but things are unlikely to fall so kindly for him at this sort of level again. (op 4-1)
Orcadian, with conditions well and truly in his favour, quickly became the one to beat when seemingly enjoying himself out in front, and had the others on the stretching when quickening the pace going out on the final circuit, but he appeared to get bored with just over half a mile to run and dropped himself right out to last. Remarkably, he responded to Callan's urgings and was soon back in front, but the whole episode eventually just took its toll. The ability is there, but his attitude is most suspect. (tchd 11-1)
Arbella, finally off the mark in a mile and a half maiden at Wolverhampton maiden on her reappearance, had never raced on ground this soft, but she seemed to handle it and ran about as well as could have been expected. She picked up some valuable black type and could find further opportunities to do so in fillies-only company. (op 20-1)
Compton Bolter(IRE) was well below form and may not have taken to the re-fitting of blinkers. (tchd 10-1, 14-1 in a place)
Mubtaker(USA) showed he retains a high level of ability when winning the John Porter on his reappearance, but the soft ground made him vulnerable, and he had a hard enough race at Newbury. Still, he should have run a lot better than this and something may have been amiss - his rider eased him up in the straight and was looking down. He is a popular horse, and hopefully he can bounce back. (tchd 4-7, 8-13 in places)

1629 WARWICK INTERNATIONAL H'CAP 7f 122y
3:20 (3:20) (Class 2) (0-100,91) 4-Y-0+ £14,826 (£4,436; £2,218; £1,109; £552) Stalls Low

Form RPR

4231 **1** **Dabbers Ridge (IRE)**[20] [1143] 4-9-0 87 ..... MichaelHills 10 108+
(B W Hills) *trckd ldrs gng wl: led over 2f out: qcknd clr over 1f out: eased cl home* 6/4[1]

6000 **2** 5 **Shot To Fame (USA)**[6] [1495] 7-9-1 91 ..... SilvestreDeSousa(3) 4 97+
(D Nicholls) *trckd ldrs: swtchd rt whn nt clr run over 1f out: wnt 2nd wl ins fnl f: no ch w wnr* 10/1

2010 **3** ¾ **Mina A Salem**[20] [1133] 4-8-4 77 oh3 ..... AlanMunro 8 81
(C E Brittain) *lw: hld up: rdn over 2f out: forced wd off bnd over 1f out: r.o ins fnl f: nrst fin* 12/1

0054 **4** shd **Roman Maze**[25] [1050] 6-9-2 89 ..... RyanMoore 2 93
(W M Brisbourne) *midfield: hdwy 2f out: rdn to chse wnr but no imp over 1f out: lost 2nd wl ins fnl f: no ex* 7/2[2]

4635 **5** 2 **Serieux**[10] [1382] 7-8-4 77 oh5 ..... AdrianTNicholls 9 76
(D Nicholls) *racd keenly: hld up: hdwy over 3f out: sn rdn: one pce fnl f* 16/1

4400 **6** 1¾ **Fiefdom (IRE)**[13] [1301] 4-9-1 88 ..... JohnEgan 1 83
(I W McInnes) *midfield: rdn whn nt clr run over 1f out: edgd lft ins fnl f: n.d* 16/1

0400 **7** 2½ **Nashaab (USA)**[217] [5717] 9-8-10 83 ..... JimmyFortune 6 72
(P D Evans) *rdn over 2f out: a bhd* 16/1

0001 **8** hd **Royal Dignitary (USA)**[7] [1455] 6-8-8 81 6ex ..... SteveDrowne 3 69
(D Nicholls) *lw: led: hdd over 2f out: rdn over 1f out: wknd and eased fnl f* 9/1

3021 **9** 1¼ **Malcheek (IRE)**[6] [1494] 4-8-13 86 6ex ..... GrahamGibbons 7 71
(T D Easterby) *racd keenly: prom: ev ch over 2f out: rdn whn n.m.r over 1f out: sn wknd* 7/1[3]

1m 36.83s (2.08) **Going Correction** +0.525s/f (Yiel) 9 Ran SP% 119.2
Speed ratings (Par 109):110,105,104,104,102 100,97,97,96
CSF £18.88 CT £140.12 TOTE £2.80: £1.30, £3.10, £3.90; EX 31.90 Trifecta £251.90 Pool: £1,348.54 - 3.80 winning tickets..
Owner Maurice Mogg **Bred** Franco Castelfranci **Trained** Lambourn, Berks

FOCUS
This looked a decent enough handicap beforehand, but nothing could live with the well-backed Dabbers Ridge, who had been nominated by connections as their best chance of the meeting and looks near Listed class on this evidence. THe form behind however, is not the most solid.

NOTEBOOK
Dabbers Ridge(IRE) ◆ would not have minded the soft ground in the slightest and defied a 6lb higher mark than when winning at Thirsk on his previous start in some style. The Handicapper will hit him hard for this, but he still appeals as the type to go well in something like the Victoria Cup. (op 7-4 tchd 2-1, 9-4 in places)
Shot To Fame(USA) had not been in much form so far this season, but he had conditions to suit and ran well in second. He met with some trouble in running, but would not have beaten the winner under any circumstances.
Mina A Salem's best form has come over a little further on Polytrack and he just got going too late after being forced wide into the straight. (op 11-1 tchd 14-1)
Roman Maze did not exactly look favourably handicapped coming into this and it may be that he really wants better ground. Still, this was a reasonable performance. (op 4-1)
Serieux, with the visor left off, had it to do from 5lb out of the handicap and was well held after taking a bit of a pull early.

Malcheek(IRE) Official explanation: vet said colt bled from the nose

1630 RIPPLEFFECT MAIDEN FILLIES' STKS 7f 2y
4:00 (4:01) (Class 4) 3-Y-O £7,124 (£2,119; £1,059; £529) Stalls Low

Form RPR

6 **1** **Tawaajud (USA)**[21] [1119] 3-9-0 ..... RHills 3 79+
(B W Hills) *a.p: led 2f out: edgd lft ins fnl f: drvn out* 5/4[1]

2 1 **Las Beatas** 3-9-0 ..... AlanMunro 5 76+
(W R Swinburn) *w'like: s.i.s: bhd: rdn and hdwy 1f out: r.o strly to take 2nd ins fnl f: nt rch wnr* 10/1

00 **3** 1½ **Princess Lavinia**[23] [1085] 3-9-0 ..... SteveDrowne 6 72
(G Wragg) *lw: chsd ldrs: rdn to take 2nd and hung lft over 1f out: lost 2nd and no ex ins fnl f* 4/1[3]

4 **4** ½ **Dallma (IRE)**[9] [1418] 3-9-0 ..... RyanMoore 1 71
(C E Brittain) *lw: led: rdn and hdd 2f out: no ex ins fnl f* 11/4[2]

6 **5** ¾ **Cordelia**[38] [868] 3-9-0 ..... MichaelHills 2 69
(B W Hills) *bit bkwd: chsd ldrs: rdn over 1f out: one pce* 5/1

1m 31.88s (3.41) **Going Correction** +0.525s/f (Yiel) 5 Ran SP% 116.9
Speed ratings (Par 98):101,99,98,97,96
CSF £15.18 TOTE £2.30: £1.40, £3.60; EX 18.80.
Owner Hamdan Al Maktoum **Bred** Shadwell Farm LLC **Trained** Lambourn, Berks

FOCUS
Just an ordinary maiden in which Tawaajud was made to work hard enough to justify her short odds. The form looks fairly sound, based around the third and fourth.

1631 OWEN PROMOTIONS H'CAP 1m 4f 66y
4:35 (4:36) (Class 4) (0-85,85) 4-Y-0+ £8,420 (£2,505; £1,251; £625) Stalls Low

Form RPR

0210 **1** **Stretton (IRE)**[177] [6371] 8-8-10 77 ..... TQuinn 11 86
(J D Bethell) *hld up in rr: hdwy over 3f out: led ins fnl f: r.o* 16/1

0065 **2** 1 **Jack Of Trumps (IRE)**[17] [1206] 6-9-2 83 ..... SteveDrowne 2 91
(G Wragg) *lw: in tch: rdn to ld 1f out: hdd ins fnl f: nt qckn* 7/2[1]

0150 **3** 1½ **Merrymaker**[200] [6073] 6-8-7 74 ow1 ..... NCallan 4 79
(W M Brisbourne) *reminders after 2f: hld up: hdwy whn swtchd lft over 2f out: nt clr run over 1f out: swtchd lft ins fnl f: styd on* 14/1

1-22 **4** shd **River Alhaarth (IRE)**[20] [1133] 4-9-4 85 ..... AlanMunro 6 93+
(P W Chapple-Hyam) *b.hind: midfield: rdn over 4f out: lost pl over 3f out: hdwy over 1f out: struck by rival's whip ins fnl f: r.o* 7/2[1]

0404 **5** nk **Silverhay**[6] [1480] 5-8-4 71 oh3 .....(p) GrahamGibbons 1 76
(T D Barron) *sn led: rdn and hdd 1f out: kpt on same pce after* 14/1

0005 **6** 1¾ **Quizzene (USA)**[16] [1238] 4-9-2 83 ..... RoystonFfrench 7 85
(M Johnston) *midfield: rdn over 4f out: hdwy over 3f out: ev ch over 2f out: fdd wl ins fnl f* 8/1[3]

2064 **7** 5 **Gringo**[25] [1051] 4-8-8 75 ..... MichaelHills 14 69
(B W Hills) *hld up: hdwy over 3f out: ev ch on outside wl over 2f out: wknd over 1f out: eased whn btn ins fnl f* 6/1[2]

0-56 **8** 1¼ **Petrula**[220] [5685] 7-8-0 72 .....(p) AndrewMullen(5) 10 64
(K A Ryan) *in tch: rdn 7f out: lost pl over 3f out: n.d after* 33/1

0606 **9** ½ **Nessen Dorma (IRE)**[30] [976] 5-8-13 80 .....(v) MickyFenton 12 71
(J G Given) *broke wl: prom: pushed along over 7f out: ev ch over 2f out: rdn and wknd 1f out* 9/1

403 **10** 1¾ **Sporting Gesture**[16] [1238] 9-8-11 81 ..... PaulMulrennan(3) 3 69
(M W Easterby) *hld up: rdn over 3f out: n.m.r over 2f out: nvr on terms* 12/1

6001 **11** 2 **Mr Aitch (IRE)**[228] [5505] 4-8-5 72 ow1 ..... JohnEgan 5 57
(R T Phillips) *plld hrd: hld up: rdn over 1f out: nvr on terms* 20/1

500 **12** 5 **Le Corvee (IRE)**[24] [1071] 4-9-4 85 ..... AdrianTNicholls 8 62+
(A King) *lw: prom: rdn and lost pl over 2f out: nt clr run over 1f out: sn wknd* 20/1

1544 **13** 5 **Graham Island**[83] [454] 5-9-1 82 ..... JDSmith 13 51
(G Wragg) *racd keenly: midfield: hdwy 6f out: wkng whn n.m.r over 2f out* 16/1

2m 45.78s (5.13) **Going Correction** +0.525s/f (Yiel) 13 Ran SP% 125.1
Speed ratings (Par 105):103,102,101,101,101 99,96,95,95,94 92,89,86
CSF £72.97 CT £844.63 TOTE £22.30: £5.10, £1.70, £5.70; EX 101.00 Place 6 £1,335.25, Place 5 £44.89.
Owner M J Dawson **Bred** Burton Agnes Stud Co Ltd **Trained** Middleham Moor, N Yorks

FOCUS
The finish was dominated by horses that were not obviously well-handicapped, but at least they went a good pace and the form looks sound enough, rated around the third and fifth.
T/Jkpt: Not won. T/Plt: £913.60 to a £1 stake. Pool: £94,999.30. 75.90 winning tickets. T/Qpdt: £47.20 to a £1 stake. Pool: £6,664.00. 104.35 winning tickets. DO

1607 HAMILTON (R-H)
Friday, May 12

OFFICIAL GOING: Good to firm (firm in places)
Wind: Fresh; half against

1632 MITIE TWO-YEAR-OLD MAIDEN STKS (QUALIFIER FOR THE HAMILTON PARK 2-Y-O NURSERY SERIES FINAL) 5f 4y
6:15 (6:15) (Class 5) 2-Y-O £3,886 (£1,156; £577; £288) Stalls Centre

Form RPR

2 **1** **Mood Music**[17] [1203] 2-9-3 ..... RichardMullen 6 86
(E J O'Neill) *mde all: rdn over 1f out: kpt on wl fnl f* 6/4[1]

32 **2** ½ **Jack Rackham**[9] [1420] 2-9-3 ..... RobertWinston 2 84
(B Smart) *keen: trckd ldrs: edgd rt and chal appr fnl f: no ex wl ins fnl f* 5/2[2]

3 3 **Steelcut** 2-9-3 ..... PaulHanagan 3 73+
(R A Fahey) *keen: sn prom: effrt over 1f out: no ex ins fnl f* 25/1

4 1½ **Nufoudh (IRE)** 2-9-3 ..... JoeFanning 1 67
(M Johnston) *keen: cl up: effrt and ev ch over 1f out: sn hmpd and no ex* 9/2[3]

46 **5** nk **The Nifty Fox**[11] [1342] 2-9-3 ..... DavidAllan 7 66
(T D Easterby) *chsd ldrs tl rdn and wknd over 1f out* 25/1

6 8 **Howards Tipple** 2-9-3 ..... TonyHamilton 4 35
(I Semple) *s.i.s: outpcd and struggling after 2f: nvr on terms* 66/1

P **New Destiny (IRE)** 2-9-3 ..... DarryllHolland 5 —
(J Howard Johnson) *in tch whn broke leg over 2f out: dead* 6/1

59.75 secs (-1.45) **Going Correction** -0.375s/f (Firm) 7 Ran SP% 110.2
Speed ratings (Par 93):96,95,90,88,87 74,—
CSF £4.94 TOTE £2.40: £1.40, £1.50; EX 5.00.
Owner J C Fretwell **Bred** R T And Mrs Watson **Trained** Averham Park, Notts
■ Stewards' Enquiry : Robert Winston one-day ban: careless riding (May 23)

FOCUS
A fair event for the track and the pace was sound. The runner-up looks a good marker and this form should prove reliable.

NOTEBOOK
Mood Music attracted plenty of support and fully confirmed debut promise. He showed a pleasing attitude for pressure, should have no problems with six furlongs and appeals as the type to win more races. (op 5-2 tchd 11-4 in places)
Jack Rackham ran creditably, despite failing to settle and edging off a true line under pressure. He is vulnerable to the better types in this grade but looks a good guide to the form and is capable of winning a small race. (tchd 11-4)
Steelcut ◆, a 16,000gns half brother to a couple of sprint winners, looked as though the race would do him good beforehand but shaped with a fair bit of promise and is sure to win a similar event in the coming weeks. (tchd 20-1)
Nufoudh(IRE), a 130,000 euros half-brother to classy sprinter Pipalong, showed ability, despite failing to settle, on this racecourse debut and is a bit better than the bare form given he met trouble late on. He is sure to win a race. (op 3-1 after 5-2 in a place early)
The Nifty Fox was not disgraced after enjoying the run of the race but again underlined his vulnerability in this sort of event. However, he is not a bad sort on looks and may do better in modest nursery company in due course. (op 33-1)
Howards Tipple, very coltish in the paddock, is from a stable that is back among the winners but showed nothing on this racecourse debut. (op 40-1)
New Destiny(IRE), related to a winner abroad, took the eye in the paddock but sadly broke a leg and had to be destroyed. (op 5-1)

1633 MITIE CONDITIONS STKS — 6f 5y
6:45 (6:49) (Class 3) 3-Y-O
£9,971 (£2,985; £1,492; £747; £372; £187) Stalls Centre

Form — RPR
3041 **1** **Ingleby Arch (USA)**[22] 1091 3-8-9 97 .... PaulFessey 7 — 102
(T D Barron) *cl up: rdn over 2f out: outpcd over 1f out: kpt on wl fnl f to ld post* **5/2**[2]
121 **2** *shd* **Obe Brave**[13] 1292 3-8-12 99 .... TonyCulhane 6 — 105+
(M R Channon) *led: rdn over 2f out: hung to far rail ins last: tied up and hdd post* **10/11**[1]
1000 **3** *3/4* **Pacific Pride**[202] 6020 3-8-12 93 .... DarryllHolland 4 — 102
(J Howard Johnson) *trckd ldrs: outpcd over 2f out: kpt on wl fnl f* **11/1**
2302 **4** *3/4* **Gallery Girl (IRE)**[196] 6129 3-8-4 99 .... DavidAllan 10 — 92
(T D Easterby) *chsd ldrs: effrt and ev ch over 1f out: no ex ins fnl f* **9/1**[3]
1000 **5** *3 1/2* **Titus Alone (IRE)**[244] 5108 3-9-2 100 .... JoeFanning 1 — 94
(B Smart) *unruly bef s: keen: chsd ldrs tl rdn and no ex fr 2f out* **25/1**
4401 **6** *9* **The Bear**[298] 3579 3-8-12 96 .... RobertWinston 9 — 63+
(I Semple) *prom tl rdn and wknd over 2f out* **20/1**
7 *4* **Onlybayinvillage (IRE)** 3-8-6 .... TonyHamilton 8 — 45
(A Berry) *missed break: nvr on terms* **200/1**
4000 **8** *nk* **Isharram (IRE)**[256] 4829 3-8-4 40 .... PaulQuinn 5 — 42
(A Berry) *s.i.s: a outpcd* **200/1**
00 **9** *1/2* **Frank Cartwright (IRE)**[5] 1501 3-8-9 .... RobbieFitzpatrick 3 — 45
(A Berry) *s.i.s: a struggling* **200/1**

1m 10.92s (-2.18) **Going Correction** -0.375s/f (Firm) — **9** Ran SP% **109.4**
Speed ratings (Par 103):99,98,97,96,92 80,74,74,73
CSF £4.57 TOTE £3.50: £1.40, £1.10, £3.00; EX 6.00.
Owner Dave Scott **Bred** Alexander-Groves Thoroughbreds **Trained** Maunby, N Yorks
■ Stewards' Enquiry : Tony Culhane caution: careless riding

FOCUS
A couple of useful sorts and a sound pace, although the form is not totally rock-solid. The field raced centre to far side but things changed dramatically late on.

NOTEBOOK
Ingleby Arch(USA) ◆ fully confirmed his reappearance improvement with a career-best effort to nail a progressive sort in the last stride. A more conventional track and the step up to seven furlongs could bring about further progress. (op 9-4)
Obe Brave, a progressive sort, looked sure to win when asserting on the rising ground but looked to throw things away by hanging to the far rail and either idling or weakening in the closing stages. Conditions may have been plenty quick enough but, given his progressive nature, he is well worth another chance back on better ground. (tchd 4-5 and Evens in places)
Pacific Pride, who disappointed on his final three starts of last year, took the eye in the preliminaries and ran creditably on this first run since October. He may be suited by a flatter track and the step up to seven furlongs. (op 8-1 tchd 12-1)
Gallery Girl(IRE), a model of consistency last year, showed she retains plenty of ability on her reappearance and is a good guide to this form but, given her current rating of 99, may not be easy to place in handicap company this season. (op 10-1 tchd 11-1)
Titus Alone(IRE) looked to have a stiff task conceding weight all round on this reappearance and did not really impress with his attitude before the start or the fact he failed to settle in the race. He may not be easy to place this year. (tchd 33-1)
The Bear, a fair sort last year, was soundly beaten on this reappearance outing and first run since last July and, given his current rating of 96, may not find things very easy this term. Official explanation: jockey said gelding was unsuited by the good to firm (firm in places) ground (op 25-1)

1634 MITIE SCOTTISH H'CAP — 1m 4f 17y
7:15 (7:17) (Class 5) (0-70,65) 3-Y-O
£3,886 (£1,156; £577; £288) Stalls High

Form — RPR
3630 **1** **Winds Of Change**[34] 918 3-9-0 61 .... JoeFanning 4 — 71
(M Johnston) *set stdy pce: mde all: rdn over 3f out: sn hrd pressed: edgd lft and hld on gamely fnl f* **11/1**
0052 **2** *1/2* **Squirtle (IRE)**[11] 1350 3-9-1 62 .... RobbieFitzpatrick 3 — 71
(W M Brisbourne) *prom: effrt 2f out: ev ch ins fnl f: hld towards fin* **4/1**[3]
0002 **3** *4* **Iberian Light (USA)**[12] 1314 3-8-8 55 .... DarryllHolland 5 — 58
(N A Callaghan) *hld up: effrt and rdn over 2f out: kpt on fnl f: nt rch first two* **3/1**[2]
000 **4** *4* **Liberate**[193] 6200 3-8-9 56 .... DavidAllan 6 — 53+
(Sir Mark Prescott) *chsd ldrs: niggled fr 1/2-way: rdn and outpcd 3f out: n.d after* **15/8**[1]
0135 **5** *1 1/2* **Beauchamp Unique**[97] 294 3-9-3 64 ....(p) PaulHanagan 1 — 58
(G A Butler) *hld up: rdn over 2f out: sn n.d* **8/1**
4051 **6** *5* **Zabeel Tower**[13] 1293 3-9-4 65 .... RobertWinston 2 — 51+
(James Moffatt) *chsd ldrs: ev ch whn hung rt and blkd over 2f out: sn eased* **9/1**

2m 47.1s (7.92) **Going Correction** +0.10s/f (Good) — **6** Ran SP% **109.2**
Speed ratings (Par 99):77,76,74,71,70 67
CSF £50.63 TOTE £11.00: £3.50, £2.60; EX 40.10.
Owner Gainsborough Stud **Bred** Gainsborough Stud Management Ltd **Trained** Middleham Moor, N Yorks

FOCUS
An uncompetitive event in which the pace was on the steady side, resulting in a pedestrian time,and the bare form, rated around the placed horses, may not prove reliable.
Zabeel Tower Official explanation: jockey said gelding lost its action

1635 MITIE MAIDEN STKS — 1m 1f 36y
7:45 (7:45) (Class 5) 3-5-Y-O
£3,238 (£963; £481; £240) Stalls High

Form — RPR
0 **1** **Baizically (IRE)**[217] 5708 3-8-10 .... ShaneKelly 2 — 85+
(J A Osborne) *hld up: stdy hdwy over 3f out: rdn and rn green over 2f out: led ins fnl f: sn clr: readily* **10/11**[1]
4220 **2** *5* **Zaharath Al Bustan**[22] 1099 3-8-6 76 ow1 .... TonyCulhane 3 — 71
(M R Channon) *cl up: ev ch fr over 3f out to 1f out: kpt on: no ch w wnr* **7/1**[3]
5 **3** *1/2* **Sir Arthur (IRE)**[300] 3524 3-8-10 .... JoeFanning 7 — 74
(M Johnston) *led to ins fnl f: kpt on same pce* **12/1**
4 *3* **Greyside (USA)** 3-8-10 .... DarryllHolland 5 — 68
(J Howard Johnson) *hld up: outpcd 4f out: rallied over 1f out: kpt on: nt rch ldrs* **33/1**
222 **5** *5* **Shamila**[81] 459 3-8-5 80 ....(b[1]) PaulHanagan 8 — 53
(G A Butler) *plld hrd: prom: rdn and hung rt 3f out: sn btn* **2/1**[2]
6 *5* **Brief Statement (IRE)**[231] 5442 4-9-10 .... RobbieFitzpatrick 6 — 50
(W M Brisbourne) *chsd ldrs tl wknd over 2f out* **50/1**
060 **7** *2 1/2* **The Dunion**[225] 5562 3-8-10 30 .... PatCosgrave 4 — 43?
(Miss L A Perratt) *keen early: prom tl wknd over 3f out* **200/1**
040 **8** *30* **Torgiano (IRE)**[11] 1343 5-9-10 .... RobertWinston 1 — —
(P Monteith) *bhd: lost tch fr 1/2-way* **50/1**

1m 58.82s (-0.84) **Going Correction** +0.10s/f (Good)
WFA 3 from 4yo+ 14lb — **8** Ran SP% **113.3**
Speed ratings (Par 103):107,102,102,99,95 90,88,61
CSF £8.05 TOTE £2.00: £1.10, £1.40, £2.70; EX 13.00.
Owner Mountgrange Stud **Bred** G And Mrs Middlebrook **Trained** Upper Lambourn, Berks

FOCUS
Not the most competitive of races and the second favourite disappointed but hard not to be impressed with the well-backed winner, who is the sort to hold his own in stronger company.

1636 MITIE MILE FILLIES' STKS (H'CAP) — 1m 65y
8:15 (8:15) (Class 4) (0-80,78) 4-Y-O+ — £8,096 (£2,408; £1,203; £601) Stalls High

Form — RPR
0360 **1** **Mistress Twister**[205] 5983 5-8-11 68 .... PaulFessey 2 — 72
(T D Barron) *in tch: hdwy to ld 2f out: kpt on wl fnl f* **8/1**
3005 **2** *2* **Royal Pardon**[5] 1500 4-8-2 59 oh6 ....(p) JoeFanning 4 — 58
(R C Guest) *hld up: hdwy over 2f out: chsd wnr ins fnl f: no imp* **20/1**
0031 **3** *1 1/4* **Hula Ballew**[9] 1422 6-8-9 66 6ex .... PhillipMakin 1 — 62
(M Dods) *trckd ldrs: effrt over 2f out: one pce over 1f out* **3/1**[2]
0006 **4** *1/2* **Hansomelle (IRE)**[236] 5339 4-8-6 63 .... DaleGibson 8 — 58
(B Mactaggart) *led: styd alone far rail in st: hdd over 3f out: rallied: no ex over 1f out* **12/1**
0020 **5** *1* **Grande Terre (IRE)**[21] 1123 5-8-2 59 .... PaulHanagan 6 — 52
(R A Fahey) *hld up in tch: effrt over 2f out: sn no imp* **4/1**[3]
3104 **6** *7* **My Princess (IRE)**[25] 1056 4-9-7 78 .... DarryllHolland 7 — 55
(N A Callaghan) *trckd ldrs tl rdn and wknd over 2f out* **5/2**[1]
5101 **7** *1 3/4* **Ignition**[239] 5242 4-8-9 66 .... RobertWinston 3 — 39
(W M Brisbourne) *pressed ldr: led over 3f to 2f out: sn wknd* **7/1**

1m 49.21s (-0.09) **Going Correction** +0.10s/f (Good) — **7** Ran SP% **109.6**
Speed ratings (Par 102):104,102,100,100,99 92,90
CSF £127.37 CT £544.00 TOTE £10.70: £4.50, £9.00; EX 116.20.
Owner Dave Scott **Bred** Mrs F A Veasey **Trained** Maunby, N Yorks

FOCUS
An ordinary event in which the pace was just fair and the form looks shaky, based around the runner-up.

1637 MITIE H'CAP (QUALIFIER FOR THE HAMILTON PARK HANDICAP SERIES FINAL) — 1m 1f 36y
8:45 (8:45) (Class 5) (0-70,69) 4-Y-O+ — £3,886 (£1,156; £577; £288) Stalls High

Form — RPR
6004 **1** **Ulysees (IRE)**[7] 1459 7-9-0 65 .... PaulHanagan 1 — 73
(I Semple) *hld up: pushed along over 2f out: hdwy to ld ins fnl f: kpt on strly* **9/1**
2063 **2** *1 1/4* **Jordans Elect**[5] 1500 6-9-3 68 .... RobertWinston 2 — 73
(P Monteith) *keen early: led to ins fnl f: kpt on same pce* **11/4**[2]
0056 **3** *1* **Barbirolli**[194] 6183 4-8-13 64 .... ShaneKelly 4 — 67
(W M Brisbourne) *prom: rdn over 2f out: edgd rt and outpcd over 1f out: r.o fnl f* **8/1**
5002 **4** *hd* **Alekhine (IRE)**[8] 1435 5-9-4 69 ....(p) JoeFanning 6 — 72
(J R Boyle) *chsd ldrs: effrt and ev ch over 1f out: no ex ins fnl f* **2/1**[1]
4000 **5** *1/2* **Admiral Compton**[8] 1435 5-8-13 64 ....(b) PatCosgrave 7 — 66
(J R Boyle) *trckd ldrs: rdn over 3f out: wknd over 1f out* **11/1**
1300 **6** *1/2* **Qualitair Wings**[9] 1425 7-8-11 62 .... DerekMcGaffin 3 — 63
(J Hetherton) *hld up in tch: hdwy over 3f out: outpcd over 2f out: rallied and edgd rt appr fnl f: btn ins last* **9/2**[3]
0000 **7** *16* **Wood Dalling (USA)**[229] 5491 8-8-4 55 oh10 .... PaulFessey 5 — 24
(Mrs J C McGregor) *hld up: rdn over 3f out: sn wknd* **100/1**

1m 59.79s (0.13) **Going Correction** +0.10s/f (Good) — **7** Ran SP% **108.6**
Speed ratings (Par 103):103,101,101,100,100 99,85
CSF £30.59 TOTE £7.70: £3.00, £2.00; EX 11.70 Place 6 £771.83, Place 5 £589.15.
Owner The Farmer Boys (Jock, Danny & Ally) **Bred** Sweetmans Bloodstock **Trained** Carluke, S Lanarks

FOCUS
Several unreliable sorts in this low-grade event and the gallop was a muddling one, so it is unlikely the form is strong.
T/Plt: £491.30 to a £1 stake. Pool: £48,796.25. 72.50 winning tickets. T/Qpdt: £355.80 to a £1 stake. Pool: £2,692.90. 5.60 winning tickets. RY

1405 LINGFIELD (L-H)
Friday, May 12

OFFICIAL GOING: Turf course - good (good to firm in places); all-weather - standard
Wind: Nil Weather: Fine and warm

1638 THE DERBY TRIAL HERE TOMORROW FILLIES' H'CAP — 1m 2f (E)
1:40 (1:40) (Class 5) (0-70,68) 3-Y-O+ — £3,238 (£963; £481; £240) Stalls Low

Form — RPR
4433 **1** **Red Sail**[11] 1334 5-8-13 54 oh2 ....(b) OscarUrbina 2 — 62
(Dr J D Scargill) *lw: hld up in midfield: prog over 2f out: rdn to ld narrowly over 1f out: drvn out* **9/2**[1]

5300 **2** *nk* **Aimee Vibert**[16] 1244 4-9-9 **64** TedDurcan 11 71
(W R Swinburn) *lw: trckd ldrs: rdn and effrt over 2f out: w wnr over 1f out: nt qckn and jst hld ins fnl f* **10/1**

050 **3** *3/4* **Kalatime (IRE)**[18] 1192 3-8-12 **68** MartinDwyer 5 73
(A M Balding) *lw: mde most: rdn 2f out: hdd on inner over 1f out: kpt on wl but hld ins fnl f* **8/1**

420 **4** *1/2* **Nikki Bea (IRE)**[18] 1191 3-8-2 **58** ow1 ChrisCatlin 7 62
(Jamie Poulton) *rn in snatches towards rr: last and drvn over 2f out: r.o u.p over 1f out: gaining at fin* **9/1**

0004 **5** *2* **Overjoy Way**[34] 917 4-8-13 **54** oh2 (b) IanMongan 3 55
(P R Chamings) *hld up in last trio: rdn over 3f out: prog on outer wl over 1f out: no imp u.str.p fnl f* **16/1**

0135 **6** *1/2* **Bowled Out (GER)**[197] 6127 4-9-13 **68** (p) J-PGuillambert 4 68
(P J McBride) *trckd ldrs: rdn over 3f out: wnt 2nd briefly 2f out: sn lost pl and btn* **11/2**[2]

4005 **7** *1/2* **Uig**[19] 1162 5-9-11 **66** DaneO'Neill 9 65
(H S Howe) *unable to ld: chsd ldr over 7f out to 2f out: wknd fnl f* **11/2**[2]

2250 **8** *shd* **Siwa**[35] 902 3-8-11 **67** NickyMackay 8 65+
(E A L Dunlop) *trckd ldr to over 7f out: lost pl 3f out: rdn and cl up in 5th but hld whn hmpd 1f out* **7/1**[3]

000 **9** *3 1/2* **Arsad (IRE)**[21] 1114 3-8-3 **59** HayleyTurner 1 51
(C E Brittain) *chsd ldrs: drvn 1/2-way: wknd 2f out* **50/1**

0005 **10** *1* **Sweet Boulangere**[13] 1282 3-8-4 **63** StephaneBreux(3) 10 53
(R Hannon) *hld up in last trio: brief effrt over 2f out: no prog and btn over 1f out* **50/1**

5505 **11** *nk* **Future Deal**[188] 6265 5-9-7 **62** GeorgeBaker 6 52
(C A Horgan) *hld up in last: prog on wd outside over 2f out: rdn and no imp over 1f out: wknd fnl f* **10/1**

2m 8.15s (0.36) **Going Correction** +0.05s/f (Slow)
WFA 3 from 4yo+ 15lb **11** Ran SP% **110.5**
Speed ratings (Par 100):100,99,99,98,97 96,96,96,93,92 92
CSF £46.49 CT £329.16 TOTE £4.50: £2.40, £2.60, £2.20; EX 19.80 TRIFECTA Not won..
Owner Silent Partners **Bred** London Thoroughbred Services Ltd **Trained** Newmarket, Suffolk

FOCUS
A moderate handicap featuring a number of unexposed fillies, but the race went to a mare breaking her duck at the 17th attempt, suggesting the form is not that strong.
Siwa Official explanation: jockey said filly was denied a clear run
Future Deal Official explanation: jockey said mare hung right

1639 EUROPEAN BREEDERS FUND MAIDEN STKS 5f
2:10 (2:11) (Class 5) 2-Y-O **£3,886** (£1,156; £577; £288) **Stalls** High

Form RPR

4 **1** **King's Bastion (IRE)**[22] 1090 2-9-3 HayleyTurner 5 84+
(M L W Bell) *lw: chsd ldng pair over 3f out: pushed along to cl fr 1/2-way: led over 1f out: in command after: rdn out last 100yds* **6/4**[2]

22 **2** *1 1/2* **See In The Dark (IRE)**[8] 1429 2-9-3 ChrisCatlin 4 78
(B J Meehan) *racd against nr side rail: pressed ldr: rdn 2f out: kpt on same pce u.p fr over 1f out* **5/4**[1]

66 **3** *1 1/2* **Wrecking Crew (IRE)**[36] 892 2-9-3 DaneO'Neill 8 72
(B R Millman) *sn off the pce in midfield: effrt 2f out: rdn and styd on fr over 1f out to take 3rd nr fin* **8/1**[3]

643 **4** *1 3/4* **She Wont Wait**[12] 1309 2-8-12 FergusSweeney 1 60
(T M Jones) *led: rdn and hdd over 1f out: wknd rapidly last 100yds* **20/1**

5 *2* **Aggbag** 2-9-3 J-PGuillambert 9 57
(M J Wallace) *leggy: scope: dwlt: sn wl off the pce in last: pushed along and rn green fr 1/2-way: styd on steadily fr over 1f out: bttr* **25/1**

6 *3/4* **Fort Worth (IRE)** 2-9-3 MartinDwyer 6 54
(B Gubby) *str: bit bkwd: s.s: rn green in rr: kpt on one pce fr over 1f out: n.d* **40/1**

065 **7** *3 1/2* **Chip Leader**[17] 1203 2-9-3 PatDobbs 2 40
(R Hannon) *fractious bef ent stalls: outpcd and struggling over 3f out: wknd fnl f* **25/1**

8 *1* **Queensgate** 2-8-12 TedDurcan 7 31
(M Blanshard) *wl-grwn: lw: chsd ldng pair to over 3f out: sn lost pl and struggling* **50/1**

9 *1 1/4* **Joint Expectations (IRE)** 2-8-10 KirstyMilczarek(7) 3 31
(Mrs C A Dunnett) *str: bkwd: s.s: mostly racd wd and nvr on terms: wknd fnl f* **66/1**

58.46 secs (-0.48) **Going Correction** -0.225s/f (Firm) **9** Ran SP% **113.9**
Speed ratings (Par 93):94,91,89,86,83 82,76,74,72
CSF £3.32 TOTE £2.40: £1.10, £1.10, £1.70; EX 4.50 Trifecta £47.80 Part won. Pool: £67.40 - 0.70 winning tickets..
Owner Edward J Ware **Bred** Floors Farming And Dominic Burke **Trained** Newmarket, Suffolk

FOCUS
Solid enough maiden form rated around the runner-up and fourth.

NOTEBOOK
King's Bastion(IRE), who has an entry in the Group One Phoenix Stakes in Ireland, was nicely on top at the finish but he made hard work of it. He shapes as though he will improve for a step up to six furlongs. (op 13-8 tchd 2-1)
See In The Dark(IRE), whose five-length second to Cav Okay on his debut does not look such strong form any more, was beaten again by a Hannon-trained juvenile on his second start, and this effort extended that string of twos next to his name. He did not look over-keen and is becoming expensive to follow. (tchd 6-5)
Wrecking Crew(IRE) had shown only modest form on his first two starts and this looked an improvement. Out of a mare who placed over 12 furlongs at 3 in France, he unsurprisingly shapes as though he will appreciate a step up in trip, and nurseries are likely to be his game in time. (op 10-1 tchd 7-1)
She Wont Wait, whose dam was a triple seven-furlong winner at three, is beginning to look fairly exposed.
Aggbag, whose dam was a dual winner over a mile at three, is a half-brother to four winners in Germany, including Eucalyptos, a multiple winner over a mile to ten furlongs and Equinox and Emblade, both dual winners at three to four. Friendless in the market, he was too green to do himself justice on this debut, but he still shaped with promise, and with this experience under his belt, better should be seen from him next time, especially if stepped up to six furlongs.

1640 WEATHERBYS INSURANCE MAIDEN STKS (DIV I) 7f
2:40 (2:42) (Class 5) 3-Y-O **£2,914** (£867; £433; £216) **Stalls** High

Form RPR

2 **1** **Mobsir**[343] 2258 3-9-3 MartinDwyer 12 70+
(E A L Dunlop) *lw: trckd ldrs: prog to ld wl over 1f out: pushed along and sn clr* **6/5**[1]

020 **2** *2 1/2* **Midnight Traveller**[174] 6392 3-9-3 NickyMackay 5 67+
(L M Cumani) *hld up in rr: stdy prog gng wl fr 2f out: nt clr run jst over 1f out: nudged along and kpt on to take 2nd nr fin* **9/1**[3]

0 **3** *hd* **Grateful**[195] 6143 3-8-12 FergusSweeney 1 58
(R M Beckett) *bit bkwd: hld up in midfield: pushed along and prog 2f out: chsd wnr ins fnl f: no imp: lost 2nd nr fin* **100/1**

4 *3/4* **Quintrell** 3-8-12 DaneO'Neill 3 56
(H Candy) *neat: hld up wl in rr: stdy prog on outer fr 2f out: shkn up and kpt on same pce fnl f* **33/1**

40 **5** *nk* **Eagle Eye**[25] 1055 3-9-3 OscarUrbina 7 61+
(G Wragg) *lw: trckd ldrs: shkn up and effrt 2f out: chsd wnr briefly 1f out: one pce after* **28/1**

6 *hd* **Mcnairobi** 3-8-12 LPKeniry 4 55+
(P D Cundell) *lengthy: s.s: hld up wl in rr: prog over 2f out: nt clr run over 1f out: pushed along and kpt on steadily* **100/1**

6223 **7** *1 1/4* **Alhaitham (USA)**[24] 1065 3-9-3 86 IanMongan 8 57+
(J L Dunlop) *lw: hld up in rr: nt clr run over 3f out: pushed along and no real prog 2f out: n.d after* **13/8**[2]

0440 **8** *2* **Diktatorship (IRE)**[22] 1089 3-9-3 67 GeorgeBaker 9 52
(Miss Gay Kelleway) *w ldr to 2f out: wknd over 1f out* **50/1**

3 **9** *shd* **Titian Dancer**[19] 1166 3-9-3 TedDurcan 10 51+
(W R Swinburn) *dwlt: t.k.h: hld up in midfield: stl keen over 2f out: fdd and eased over 1f out* **12/1**

0060 **10** *1/2* **Batchworth Fleur**[38] 880 3-8-12 45 StephenCarson 2 45
(E A Wheeler) *mde most to wl over 1f out: wknd rapidly fnl f* **100/1**

11 *2* **Shoshoni** 3-8-12 MatthewHenry 13 40+
(M A Jarvis) *lengthy: str: scope: bit bkwd: t.k.h early and rn green: pressed ldrs: lost pl 3f out: no ch whn nt clr run 1f out* **33/1**

0000 **12** *29* **New Blood (IRE)**[254] 4861 3-9-3 35 ChrisCatlin 6 —
(J M Bradley) *in tch to 3f out: wknd rapidly: t.o* **100/1**

1m 23.57s (-0.64) **Going Correction** -0.225s/f (Firm) **12** Ran SP% **116.5**
Speed ratings (Par 99):94,91,90,90,89 89,88,85,85,85 82,49
CSF £12.54 TOTE £2.50: £1.30, £2.20, £10.70; EX 13.70 Trifecta £36.70 Pool: £103.52 - 2.00 winning tickets..
Owner Hamdan Al Maktoum **Bred** David John Brown **Trained** Newmarket, Suffolk

FOCUS
The winner was impressive, albeit he had the run of the race, and the winning was 0.64 seconds slower than the second division, and modest for the grade and the form looks somewhat shaky.
Mcnairobi Official explanation: jockey said filly was denied a clear run
Titian Dancer Official explanation: jockey said colt suffered interference in running

1641 WEATHERBYS INSURANCE MAIDEN STKS (DIV II) 7f
3:10 (3:15) (Class 5) 3-Y-O **£2,914** (£867; £433; £216) **Stalls** High

Form RPR

0430 **1** **Lavenham (IRE)**[247] 5042 3-8-12 75 DaneO'Neill 2 75+
(R Hannon) *lw: t.k.h: w ldr: led over 2f out: rdn clr over 1f out: in n.d after* **7/1**[3]

2 *2 1/2* **Don Pietro** 3-9-3 StephenCarson 7 73
(D J Coakley) *leggy: unf: dwlt: hld up in last and wl off the pce: swtchd to outer and stdy prog fr 1/2-way: chsd wnr over 1f out: kpt on* **50/1**

3 *1* **Moves Goodenough** 3-9-3 DeanMcKeown 10 70
(Andrew Turnell) *str: scope: bit bkwd: off the pce in midfield: rdn over 2f out: prog wl over 1f out: kpt on* **50/1**

0 **4** *2* **Tranos (USA)**[14] 1274 3-9-3 NickyMackay 9 65+
(L M Cumani) *dwlt: hld up in last trio: reminder wl over 2f out: prog whn nt clr run over 1f out: kpt on: do bttr* **20/1**

3240 **5** *3/4* **Cabourg (IRE)**[18] 1192 3-9-3 80 J-PGuillambert 4 63
(C R Egerton) *chsd ldrs and racd towards outer: effrt over 2f out: disp 2nd over 1f out: fdd* **11/2**[2]

00 **6** *4* **Levin (IRE)**[17] 1212 3-9-3 IanMongan 6 53
(J L Dunlop) *a towards rr: outpcd fr 3f out: plugged on fr over 1f out* **50/1**

05 **7** *nk* **Panic Stations**[9] 1417 3-8-12 HayleyTurner 5 47
(M L W Bell) *prom: shkn up over 2f out: wknd over 1f out* **25/1**

5 **8** *nk* **Some Diva**[178] 6351 3-8-12 TedDurcan 1 46+
(W R Swinburn) *prom: rdn over 2f out: wknd over 1f out: eased fnl f* **16/1**

06 **9** *nk* **Nahaar (IRE)**[272] 4356 3-9-3 PatDobbs 11 51
(M P Tregoning) *chsd ldrs: outpcd 1/2-way: rdn over 2f out: no prog* **16/1**

0 **10** *3* **Ebraam (USA)**[234] 5392 3-9-3 MartinDwyer 12 43+
(E A L Dunlop) *lw: led against nr side rail: hdd over 2f out: shkn up and no response: wknd and eased over 1f out* **8/11**[1]

02 **11** *11* **Digger Boy**[43] 802 3-9-3 MatthewHenry 3 14
(M A Jarvis) *a in last trio and nvr gng wl: wknd over 2f out: t.o* **12/1**

1m 22.93s (-1.28) **Going Correction** -0.225s/f (Firm) **44** Ran SP% **119.7**
Speed ratings (Par 99):98,95,94,91,90 86,85,85,85,81 69
CSF £322.99 TOTE £8.80: £2.00, £7.10, £7.80; EX 359.00 TRIFECTA Not won..
Owner Mrs J Wood **Bred** M Ervine **Trained** East Everleigh, Wilts

FOCUS
On paper this looked the weaker of the two divisions, but a truer pace led to a winning time that was 0.64 seconds quicker than the first division. The form looks ordinary at this stage.
Panic Stations Official explanation: jockey said filly lost a front shoe
Ebraam(USA) Official explanation: trainer said colt finished distressed
Digger Boy Official explanation: jockey said colt never travelled

1642 LINGFIELD-RACECOURSE.CO.UK H'CAP 7f
3:45 (3:55) (Class 5) (0-70,71) 3-Y-O **£3,886** (£1,156; £577; £288) **Stalls** High

Form RPR

1 **1** **Damika (IRE)**[11] 1344 3-9-5 **71** 6ex DeanMcKeown 7 81+
(R M Whitaker) *lw: hld up bhd ldrs: prog over 2f out: led over 1f out: shkn up and in command fnl f* **2/1**[1]

01 **2** *1 1/4* **Apply Dapply**[38] 868 3-9-1 **67** TedDurcan 2 74
(H Morrison) *lw: w ldr: led 2f out to over 1f out: chsd wnr after: styd on but readily hld* **10/1**

6666 **3** *1 1/2* **Mr Cellophane**[15] 1263 3-8-8 **60** J-PGuillambert 12 63
(J R Jenkins) *lw: hld up towards rr: effrt and threaded through fr 2f out: r.o to take 3rd wl ins fnl f* **9/1**[3]

0000 **4** *1* **The London Gang**[21] 1109 3-9-1 **67** (v) GeorgeBaker 11 67
(P D Evans) *hld up in rr: prog on outer over 2f out: rdn and kpt on same pce fr over 1f out* **10/1**

0002 **5** *1/2* **Simpsons Ross (IRE)**[8] 1433 3-8-8 **60** FergusSweeney 13 59+
(R M Flower) *hld up towards rr: shkn up and effrt 2f out: styd on wl fr over 1f out: unable to chal* **14/1**

004 **6** *2* **Good Companion (IRE)**[205] 5985 3-8-12 **64** IanMongan 1 58
(J L Dunlop) *chsd ldrs: rdn over 2f out: outpcd and btn over 1f out* **25/1**

000 **7** *nk* **Bon Viveur**[224] 5592 3-9-2 **68** DaneO'Neill 10 67+
(R Hannon) *settled in midfield: lost pl and wl in rr 3f out: nt clr run 2f out: 12th 1f out: shuffled along and r.o: nvr nr ldrs* **16/1**

0444 **8** *nk* **Patavium Prince (IRE)**[73] 540 3-8-11 **63** ChrisCatlin 15 55
(J R Best) *chsd ldrs: hrd rdn over 2f out: fdd over 1f out* **20/1**

063 **9** *nk* **Dawaleeb (IRE)**^{217} [5710] 3-9-2 **68** MartinDwyer 18 60
(M P Tregoning) *pressed ldrs: rdn over 2f out: steadily wknd* **6/1**^{2}

450 **10** *1 ½* **Just Tallulah**^{43} [801] 3-8-8 **60** NickyMackay 9 48
(N P Littmoden) *mde most to 2f out: sn wknd u.p* **25/1**

5040 **11** *shd* **Simplified**^{49} [709] 3-8-6 **58** PaulDoe 17 45
(J Pearce) *s.i.s: hld up in rr: effrt on outer over 2f out: no imp on ldrs over 1f out: fdd* **40/1**

5100 **12** *3 ½* **Miltons Choice**^{3} [1567] 3-8-11 **63** LPKeniry 6 41
(J M Bradley) *lw: wl in rr: effrt on outer fr 3f out: no imp on ldrs over 1f out: eased whn btn fnl f* **20/1**

200 **13** *1 ¼* **Little Miss Daisy**^{30} [993] 3-9-0 **66** PatDobbs 3 41
(A B Haynes) *racd on wd outside: nvr on terms w ldrs: bhd fnl 2f* **33/1**

013 **14** *2 ½* **Solicitude**^{143} [6634] 3-8-12 **67** RichardThomas$^{(3)}$ 14 36
(D Haydn Jones) *bit bkwd: a wl in rr: bhd fnl 2f* **20/1**

5020 **15** *2* **High Octave (IRE)**^{25} [1048] 3-9-4 **70** (b^{1}) StephenCarson 4 33
(B G Powell) *lw: prom: rdn and wknd rapidly fr wl over 2f out* **33/1**

1m 22.96s (-1.25) **Going Correction** -0.225s/f (Firm) **15** Ran SP% **118.6**
Speed ratings (Par 99):98,96,94,93,93 90,90,90,89,88 88,84,82,79,77
CSF £18.15 CT £156.17 TOTE £2.90: £2.00, £4.30, £2.00; EX 19.60 Trifecta £172.80 Part won. Pool: £243.44 - 0.10 winning tickets..
Owner G B Bedford **Bred** Patrick J Monahan **Trained** Scarcroft, W Yorks

FOCUS
An ordinary handicap but the result reads well with the first two among the least exposed in the line-up. The race has been rated through the fourth to his late 2005 form.
Bon Viveur Official explanation: jockey said gelding was denied a clear run
Solicitude Official explanation: jockey said filly was unsuited by the track

1643 RICHARDSON H'CAP 5f
4:20 (4:23) (Class 4) (0-85,84) 4-Y-O+ **£5,505** (£1,637; £818; £408) **Stalls** High

Form RPR

3001 **1** **Peopleton Brook**^{6} [1475] 4-9-4 **84** 7ex TedDurcan 7 93
(J M Bradley) *lw: pressed ldr: led 2f out: sn jnd: drvn and gained upper hand wl ins fnl f* **5/4**^{1}

0004 **2** *¾* **Bluebok**^{25} [1047] 5-8-7 **73** (t) LPKeniry 2 79
(J M Bradley) *hld up: prog 1/2-way: jnd wnr wl over 1f out: no ex wl ins fnl f* **5/1**^{2}

010 **3** *1 ½* **Silver Dane (IRE)**^{9} [1399] 4-8-10 **76** (v) J-PGuillambert 1 77
(Mrs C A Dunnett) *t.k.h: hld up on outer: hrd rdn 2f out: kpt on to take 3rd ins fnl f* **11/1**

3000 **4** *¾* **Pitch Up (IRE)**^{11} [1359] 4-8-10 **76** IanMongan 9 74
(T G Mills) *chsd ldrs: drvn 2f out: kpt on same pce after* **10/1**

2-15 **5** *¾* **Financial Times (USA)**^{9} [1399] 4-8-10 **76** NickyMackay 5 72
(Stef Liddiard) *lw: chsd ldrs: rdn 2f out: one pce and n.d fr over 1f out* **7/1**

5466 **6** *nk* **Intriguing Glimpse**^{76} [517] 5-9-4 **84** HayleyTurner 3 79+
(Miss B Sanders) *hld up in last: gng wl 2f out: effrt but hanging lft over 1f out: nt clr run after: fin full of running* **11/2**^{3}

0-00 **7** *1 ¾* **Silver Prelude**^{11} [1359] 5-8-8 **74** MartinDwyer 8 62
(D K Ivory) *led to 2f out: wknd over 1f out* **25/1**

2006 **8** *6* **Wise Wager (IRE)**^{12} [1315] 4-8-1 **70** oh5 RichardThomas$^{(3)}$ 4 37
(Miss Z C Davison) *sn pushed along: struggling fr 1/2-way: sn wknd* **20/1**

57.39 secs (-1.55) **Going Correction** -0.225s/f (Firm) **8** Ran SP% **115.0**
Speed ratings (Par 105):103,101,99,98,97 96,93,84
CSF £7.75 CT £46.81 TOTE £2.40: £1.10, £2.10, £3.20; EX 5.90 Trifecta £19.00 Pool: £152.57 - 5.69 winning tickets..
Owner G S Thompson & P Banfield **Bred** Lower Hill Farm Stud **Trained** Sedbury, Gloucs

FOCUS
A fair sprint handicap and sound form rated around the runner-up.
Silver Dane(IRE) Official explanation: jockey said gelding suffered interference in running
Intriguing Glimpse Official explanation: jockey said mare was denied a clear run

1644 SATURDAY NIGHT RACING AT LINGFIELD H'CAP 1m (P)
4:55 (4:55) (Class 5) (0-70,70) 4-Y-O+ **£3,238** (£963; £481; £240) **Stalls** High

Form RPR

5030 **1** **Bee Stinger**^{267} [4494] 4-8-11 **63** IanMongan 3 83
(I A Wood) *bit bkwd: trckd ldrs: wnt 2nd over 2f out and gng easily: led wl over 1f out: rdn clr* **20/1**

2000 **2** *5* **Samuel Charles**^{17} [1220] 8-9-2 **68** FergusSweeney 1 76
(C R Dore) *swtg: s.s: sn in tch in rr: prog on inner over 2f out: drvn and styd on to take 2nd wl ins fnl f* **10/1**

5340 **3** *½* **Hollow Jo**^{30} [985] 6-8-13 **65** MartinDwyer 12 72
(J R Jenkins) *lw: t.k.h: prom: led over 4f out to wl over 1f out: sn outpcd and btn* **4/1**^{2}

0244 **4** *¾* **Devil's Island**^{15} [1265] 4-8-10 **62** (b^{1}) J-PGuillambert 8 67
(Sir Mark Prescott) *s.s: sn in tch in rr: prog on inner over 2f out: drvn and nt qckn over 1f out: plugged on* **9/2**^{3}

0230 **5** *1* **Aggravation**^{34} [915] 4-8-13 **70** StephanieHollinshead$^{(5)}$ 7 73+
(D R C Elsworth) *lw: hld up in rr: nt clr run over 2f out tl swtchd to inner over 1f out: styd on: no ch* **8/1**

5104 **6** *1* **Goose Chase**^{10} [1382] 4-9-3 **69** DaneO'Neill 6 70
(A M Hales) *chsd ldrs: drvn 1/2-way: no prog 2f out: sn outpcd and btn* **8/1**

1403 **7** *1 ¼* **Edin Burgher (FR)**^{14} [1273] 5-8-1 **56** oh1 EdwardCreighton$^{(3)}$ 4 54
(T T Clement) *lw: in tch: rdn over 2f out: effrt u.p and sme prog 1f out: no ch whn squeezed out nr fin* **7/2**^{1}

1304 **8** *2* **Bishops Finger**^{11} [1334] 6-8-10 **62** (b) PaulDoe 9 55
(Jamie Poulton) *s.i.s: sn wl in tch: drvn and effrt on outer over 2f out: no prog over 1f out: wknd* **11/1**

4006 **9** *2 ½* **Blue Empire (IRE)**^{15} [1265] 5-8-7 **59** HayleyTurner 10 46
(C R Dore) *led to over 4f out: wknd over 2f out* **25/1**

3531 **10** *nk* **Pawn In Life (IRE)**^{10} [1390] 8-8-4 **56** oh1 (v) ChrisCatlin 5 43
(M J Polglase) *walked to post and mounted at s: hld up last of main gp: drvn on outer 3f out: no prog* **14/1**

3066 **11** *5* **Tipsy Lad**^{13} [1303] 4-8-4 **56** oh2 (bt) AlanDaly 2 31
(D J S Ffrench Davis) *s.v.s and lost all ch: a detached in last pair* **25/1**

006 **12** *1 ½* **Must Be Keen**^{19} [1166] 7-8-8 **60** TedDurcan 11 32
(Ernst Oertel) *b: t.k.h: trckd ldr for 2f: wknd v rapidly over 2f out* **50/1**

1m 38.56s (-0.87) **Going Correction** +0.05s/f (Slow) **12** Ran SP% **121.1**
Speed ratings (Par 103):106,101,100,99,98 97,96,94,92,91 86,85
CSF £204.22 CT £992.62 TOTE £30.00: £9.00, £3.50, £2.60; EX 319.00 Trifecta £165.80 Part won. Pool: £233.58 - 0.50 winning tickets. Place 6 £47.45, Place 5 £18.49.
Owner Neardown Stables **Bred** Templeton Stud **Trained** Upper Lambourn, Berks

FOCUS
A modest handicap but run at a decent gallop and won in good style by Bee Stinger. Sound form rated around the placed horses.
T/Plt: £51.90 to a £1 stake. Pool: £36,558.60. 513.35 winning tickets. T/Qpdt: £22.00 to a £1 stake. Pool: £2,238.40. 75.10 winning tickets. JN

1412 NOTTINGHAM (L-H)
Friday, May 12

OFFICIAL GOING: Good to firm (good in places)
Wind: Light, against Weather: Apart from a shower between the first two races it was mainly dry and sunny

1645 COME RACING AGAIN NEXT WEEKEND APPRENTICE H'CAP 6f 15y
2:00 (2:03) (Class 6) (0-60,60) 4-Y-O+ **£2,388** (£705; £352) **Stalls** High

Form RPR

4250 **1** **Joy And Pain**^{32} [950] 5-8-5 **52** (v^{1}) KevinGhunowa$^{(5)}$ 15 68
(M J Attwater) *racd stands' side: chsd ldrs: led that gp and overall ldr over 1f out: rdn out* **12/1**

0005 **2** *1 ¼* **Enjoy The Buzz**^{4} [1528] 7-8-5 **50** RonanKeogh$^{(3)}$ 13 62
(J M Bradley) *racd stands' side: hld up: hdwy 2f out: rdn and ev ch 1f out : styd on same pce: 2nd in gp* **14/1**

0501 **3** *3* **Drumming Party (USA)**^{9} [1414] 4-8-13 **55** (t) StephenDonohoe 8 58+
(A M Balding) *racd far side: chsd ldr tl rdn and hung rt fr over 1f out: ended up stands' side fnl f: styd on same pce: 3rd in gp* **4/1**^{2}

1242 **4** *1 ¼* **Hammer Of The Gods (IRE)**^{56} [657] 6-9-1 **60** (bt) LiamJones$^{(3)}$ 6 59
(P S McEntee) *led far side: rdn over 2f out: edgd rt over 1f out: no ex fnl f: 1st home that side* **7/2**^{1}

5222 **5** *1 ¼* **Mina**^{17} [1209] 4-9-1 **60** DerekNolan$^{(3)}$ 9 56
(Rae Guest) *racd far side: chsd ldrs: rdn and nt clr run over 1f out: styd on same pce: 2nd in gp* **7/1**^{3}

0340 **6** *hd* **Crystal Mystic (IRE)**^{16} [1235] 4-8-9 **56** JosephWalsh$^{(5)}$ 11 51
(B Palling) *racd stands' side: chsd ldr: led 5f out: overall ldr 1/2-way: rdn and hdd over 1f out: sn wknd: 4th in gp* **20/1**

4650 **7** *1 ¾* **Kingsmaite**^{66} [611] 5-8-13 **55** MarcHalford 10 45
(S R Bowring) *racd far side: prom: rdn over 2f out: wknd over 1f out: 3rd in gp* **18/1**

0510 **8** *½* **Ektishaaf**^{11} [1348] 4-9-2 **58** RichardKingscote 7 46
(C F Wall) *racd far side: in rr tl styd on ins fnl f: nvr nrr 4th in gp* **9/1**

0004 **9** *½* **Christian Bendix**^{10} [1390] 4-8-8 **53** (p) DonnaCaldwell$^{(3)}$ 1 40
(P Howling) *racd far side: sn pushed along in rr: n.d: 5th in gp* **80/1**

0462 **10** *shd* **Doctor's Cave**^{16} [1243] 4-8-12 **57** (b) DeanWilliams$^{(3)}$ 5 43
(K O Cunningham-Brown) *racd far side: sn outpcd: 6th in gp* **14/1**

0000 **11** *2* **Portacarron (IRE)**^{20} [1155] 4-8-11 **60** (p) SJWilliams$^{(7)}$ 17 40
(Eamon Tyrrell, Ire) *racd stands' side: dwlt: outpcd: 5th in gp* **33/1**

0501 **12** *shd* **Ardkeel Lass (IRE)**^{11} [1623] 5-8-7 **52** 7ex MichaelJStainton$^{(3)}$ 16 32
(P D Evans) *led stands' side 1f: wknd wl over 1f out: 6th in gp* **25/1**

245 **13** *1 ½* **Val De Maal (IRE)**^{39} [862] 6-8-13 **60** (v) DawnRankin$^{(5)}$ 2 36
(Miss J A Camacho) *racd far side: chsd ldrs 4f: 7th in gp* **11/1**

0300 **14** *1 ½* **Mansiya**^{51} [693] 4-8-13 **60** WilliamCarson$^{(5)}$ 3 31
(C E Brittain) *racd far side: s.s: outpcd: 8th in gp* **80/1**

0501 **15** *nk* **Chantelle's Dream**^{30} [982] 4-8-8 **50** JamesDoyle 4 20
(Ms J S Doyle) *racd far side: chsd ldrs 4f: last in gp* **33/1**

P02- **16** *12* **Beresford Boy**^{571} [6280] 5-8-10 **55** RussellKennemore$^{(3)}$ 12 —
(J A Pickering) *racd stands' side: bhd fr 1/2-way: last in gp* **40/1**

1m 14.01s (-0.99) **Going Correction** -0.225s/f (Firm) **16** Ran SP% **118.7**
Speed ratings (Par 101):97,95,91,89,88 87,85,84,84,83 81,81,79,77,76 60
CSF £155.54 CT £797.18 TOTE £19.70: £3.40, £3.60, £1.60, £1.30; EX 127.00.
Owner Phones Direct Partnership **Bred** Jonathan Shack **Trained** Wysall, Notts

FOCUS
This was by no means a strong race, even allowing for many of the best apprentices around taking rides. Most of the field are better known for their exploits on the All-Weather, and predictably the field did split. THe runner-up sets the standard.

1646 BUY YOUR TICKETS ON-LINE @NOTTINGHAMRACECOURSE.CO.UK MEDIAN AUCTION MAIDEN STKS 6f 15y
2:30 (2:31) (Class 5) 3-Y-O **£3,238** (£963; £481; £240) **Stalls** High

Form RPR

0 **1** **Stanley Goodspeed**^{11} [1335] 3-9-0 DeanCorby$^{(3)}$ 11 77
(J W Hills) *hld up in tch: rdn to ld wl ins fnl f* **25/1**

42 **2** *nk* **Royal Citadel (IRE)**^{219} [5694] 3-8-12 PhilipRobinson 10 71
(C G Cox) *led: rdn and edgd lft fr over 3f out: hdd wl ins fnl f* **10/11**^{1}

3 **3** *nk* **Namoos (USA)**^{336} [2453] 3-8-12 EddieAhern 4 70
(J L Dunlop) *chsd ldrs: rdn over 2f out: hung lft ins fnl f: r.o* **5/1**^{2}

005 **4** *1* **Bold Argument (IRE)**^{34} [916] 3-9-3 70 RobertHavlin 3 72
(Mrs P N Dutfield) *prom: rdn over 1f out: no ex ins fnl f* **22/1**

6 **5** *2* **Tender Process (IRE)**^{9} [1412] 3-9-3 RichardMullen 1 66
(E S McMahon) *swvd lft s: hdwy to joine ldrs over 4f out: rdn and ev ch over 1f out: sn edgd lft: and wknd* **10/1**

05 **6** *½* **Athena's Dream**^{227} [5531] 3-8-12 RichardHughes 5 60
(C F Wall) *hld up in tch: rdn over 1f out: wknd ins fnl f* **17/2**

00 **7** *4* **Two Acres (IRE)**^{17} [1218] 3-9-3 SamHitchcott 8 53
(A G Newcombe) *hld up: swtchd lft over 2f out: n.d* **150/1**

5 **8** *1 ¼* **Wendals**^{223} [5611] 3-8-12 KDarley 9 44
(Rae Guest) *s.i.s: hld up: n.d* **8/1**^{3}

6000 **9** *2 ½* **Captain Torrance (IRE)**^{15} [1263] 3-9-3 50 AdrianMcCarthy 6 41
(P W Chapple-Hyam) *mid-div: nt clr run 4f out: sn pushed along: bhd fr 1/2-way* **22/1**

0 **10** *1 ¾* **Bare Rambler**^{5} [1513] 3-9-3 FrancisNorton 7 36
(Stef Liddiard) *s.i.s: bhd fr 1/2-way: hung lft over 2f out* **66/1**

0 **11** *1 ½* **Bee Magic**^{17} [1218] 3-9-3 PaulEddery 2 32
(C N Kellett) *disp ld 4f: sn wknd* **100/1**

1m 14.29s (-0.71) **Going Correction** -0.225s/f (Firm) **11** Ran SP% **115.5**
Speed ratings (Par 99):95,94,94,92,90 89,84,82,79,76 74
CSF £46.37 TOTE £31.50: £5.00, £1.10, £1.30; EX 65.40.
Owner R J Tufft **Bred** Burton Agnes Stud Co Ltd **Trained** Upper Lambourn, Berks

FOCUS
An ordinary but interesting maiden, which could produce a few winners in time, rated through the fourth for the moment.
Athena's Dream ◆ Official explanation: jockey said, regarding the running and riding, his orders were to hold filly up and deliver his challenge between horses, adding that filly had given her all with about a furlong to run; trainer said he was content with the ride, adding, in his opinion, the filly is fairly moderate

The Form Book, Raceform Ltd, Compton, RG20 6NL

1647 EUROPEAN BREEDERS FUND MEDIAN AUCTION MAIDEN FILLIES' STKS — 5f 13y

3:00 (3:02) (Class 5) 2-Y-O **£3,886** (£1,156; £577; £288) **Stalls** High

Form — RPR

0 **1** **Down The Well (IRE)**^{8} [1429] 2-8-9 .... RichardKingscote(5) 10 — 77
(J A Osborne) *chsd ldr: rdn to ld over 1f out: styd on* **28/1**

02 **2** ¾ **Frisky Talk (IRE)**^{11} [1347] 2-9-0 .... RichardHughes 4 — 74
(B W Hills) *led: clr 1/2-way: hdd over 1f out: rdn ins fnl f: styd on* **4/6**^{1}

3 1 ½ **Bijouterie** 2-9-0 .... KerrinMcEvoy 12 — 69
(G A Swinbank) *chsd ldrs: rdn over 1f out: styd on* **8/1**^{3}

4 ¾ **Cuppacocoa** 2-8-11 .... AdamKirby(3) 8 — 66+
(C G Cox) *rrd s: outpcd: hdwy over 1f out: r.o* **12/1**

5 2 ½ **Spirit Of Venus (FR)** 2-9-0 .... RichardMullen 9 — 57+
(E A L Dunlop) *mid-div: hdwy 2f out: sn rdn: wknd fnl f* **7/1**^{2}

6 5 **Dee Cee Elle** 2-9-0 .... KDarley 6 — 39+
(M Johnston) *s.i.s: sn hung lft and outpcd: nvr nrr* **20/1**

7 2 **Smash N'Grab (IRE)** 2-9-0 .... DO'Donohoe 2 — 32
(K A Ryan) *mid-div: rdn 1/2-way: wknd over 1f out* **28/1**

8 1 ¾ **La Marmotte (IRE)** 2-9-0 .... EddieAhern 11 — 26
(J W Hills) *prom: rdn: hung lft and wknd 1/2-way* **25/1**

9 1 ¼ **Red** 2-8-11 .... NelsonDeSouza(3) 3 — 21
(R M Beckett) *s.i.s: outpcd* **16/1**

03 **10** shd **Piccolo Prezzo**^{35} [908] 2-9-0 .... FrancisNorton 7 — 21
(Stef Liddiard) *s.i.s: outpcd* **33/1**

0 **11** 2 ½ **Suntan Lady (IRE)**^{18} [1181] 2-9-0 .... NeilPollard 1 — 12
(Miss V Haigh) *chsd ldrs to 1/2-way* **66/1**

00 **12** 2 **Sainara (IRE)**^{25} [1046] 2-9-0 .... (p) TomEaves 5 — 5
(J M Bradley) *s.i.s: outpcd* **200/1**

62.11 secs (0.31) **Going Correction** -0.225s/f (Firm) **12** Ran SP% **117.6**
Speed ratings (Par 90):88,86,84,83,79 71,68,65,63,63 59,55
CSF £45.30 TOTE £29.60: £5.70, £1.10, £1.90; EX 91.50.
Owner Danny Durkan **Bred** Rathasker Stud **Trained** Upper Lambourn, Berks

FOCUS
This looked to be an ordinary juvenile maiden and difficult to assess form-wise, with the favourite possibly not running to her previous mark.

NOTEBOOK
Down The Well(IRE) , who clearly benefited from her first run at Folkestone where she was very green, chased the pacemaker throughout and stuck to the task really well when asked to quicken. She should hold her own in slightly better company.
Frisky Talk(IRE) was on her toes leaving the paddock and looks to be an excitable sort. Hughes was motionless over a furlong out but soon had to get to work when challenged on his outside. It might well be that she used up too much energy from her low draw to get to the stands' side, but is one to treat with caution all the same. (tchd 4-5)
Bijouterie ran a really nice race on her debut, but she had the best of the draw to help her. Her stable rarely has a juvenile wound-up first-time-out, making the effort all the more encouraging.
Cuppacocoa is the first offspring of the useful but quirky Coffee Time and showed some of her mother's traits leaving the stalls. However, she got back into the race slowly and was on the heels of the leaders at the finish.
Spirit Of Venus(FR), whose dam is an unraced half-sister to the very useful sprinter Three Points, came into the race on the back of some decent gallops reports, and was not given a hard time when her chance had gone. She looks capable of better.
Dee Cee Elle, who has plenty of size and scope for improvement, did not get away from the stalls very quickly and became outpaced but, once back on an even keel, she stayed on nicely to suggest there is better to come.
La Marmotte(IRE) Official explanation: jockey said filly hung to the left

1648 RHINO RISK H'CAP — 1m 6f 15y

3:35 (3:36) (Class 5) (0-75,72) 3-Y-O **£5,181** (£1,541; £770; £384) **Stalls** Low

Form — RPR

5332 **1** **At The Money**^{17} [1221] 3-8-7 **58** .... FrancisNorton 1 — 68
(J M P Eustace) *mde virtually all: rdn over 1f out: styd on* **7/2**^{2}

5221 **2** shd **Meadow Mischief (FR)**^{35} [909] 3-9-7 **72** .... EddieAhern 9 — 82
(E A L Dunlop) *chsd wnr over 4f: rdn over 2f out: chsd wnr again over 1f out: styd on wl* **9/2**^{3}

5445 **3** 6 **Wise Choice**^{11} [1350] 3-8-0 **56** .... JamesDoyle(5) 7 — 58
(N P Littmoden) *sn pushed along and prom: chsd wnr over 9f out: rdn over 2f out: wknd fnl f* **10/1**

4003 **4** 5 **Hoh Bla Daa**^{9} [1403] 3-9-5 **70** .... RichardHughes 10 — 65
(S Kirk) *hld up: hdwy 10f out: rdn over 3f out: wknd over 1f out* **28/1**

5603 **5** 3 ½ **Shardia (IRE)**^{20} [1140] 3-8-3 **54** oh1 ow1 .... PaulEddery 3 — 44
(J Jay) *hld up: hdwy over 2f out: wknd over 1f out* **25/1**

0064 **6** 2 ½ **Cora Pearl (IRE)**^{9} [1424] 3-8-2 **56** oh8 ow3 .... SaleemGolam(3) 11 — 42
(M J Polglase) *chsd ldrs: rdn 4f out: wknd 2f out* **28/1**

0000 **7** ½ **Sunny Disposition (IRE)**^{37} [887] 3-7-13 **53** oh8 .... NelsonDeSouza(3) 2 — 39
(E F Vaughan) *s.s: hld up: n.d* **100/1**

0055 **8** ½ **Cool Ebony**^{26} [1034] 3-9-7 **72** .... TomEaves 5 — 57
(M Dods) *s.i.s: hld up: hdwy 3f out: wknd wl over 1f out* **33/1**

000 **9** 2 **Chess Board**^{190} [6233] 3-8-7 **58** .... JamieMackay 12 — 40
(Sir Mark Prescott) *hld up in tch: racd keenly: pushed along 8f out: wknd over 3f out* **7/4**^{1}

0305 **10** 1 ¾ **Patavium (IRE)**^{17} [1216] 3-9-5 **70** .... RichardMullen 8 — 50
(E J O'Neill) *hld up: hdwy over 4f out: rdn and wknd over 2f out* **16/1**

0600 **11** 1 ½ **Queen Of Diamonds (IRE)**^{23} [1079] 3-8-2 **53** oh4 .... DavidKinsella 4 — 30
(Mrs P N Dutfield) *hld up: a in rr* **66/1**

3004 **12** 14 **On Air (USA)**^{15} [1251] 3-9-4 **69** .... KDarley 6 — 27
(M Johnston) *chsd ldrs: lost pl 6f out: wknd 3f out* **12/1**

3m 6.80s (-0.30) **Going Correction** +0.025s/f (Good) **12** Ran SP% **115.6**
Speed ratings (Par 99):101,100,97,94,92 91,90,90,89,88 87,79
CSF £17.85 CT £142.98 TOTE £4.50: £1.70, £1.70, £3.50; EX 16.50.
Owner Harold Nass **Bred** Rockville Pike Partnership **Trained** Newmarket, Suffolk

FOCUS
A wide range of ability on show here with almost 30lb separating the top and bottom horses on unadjusted official figures. The race time was not particulary quick either, but the first two were clear of a consistent sort, suggesting the form may prove sound.
On Air(USA) Official explanation: jockey said filly lost its action

1649 HARRY RICHMOND & PARTNER LTD MAIDEN FILLIES' STKS (DIV I) — 1m 54y

4:10 (4:12) (Class 5) 3-Y-O **£4,210** (£1,252; £625; £312) **Stalls** Centre

Form — RPR

66 **1** **Abhisheka (IRE)**^{203} [6007] 3-9-0 .... KerrinMcEvoy 6 — 84+
(Saeed Bin Suroor) *a.p: chsd ldr over 2f out: rdn to ld over 1f out: r.o wl: eased nr fin* **15/8**^{1}

4035 **2** 3 ½ **Chalentina**^{13} [1290] 3-9-0 70 .... RichardHughes 2 — 69
(H R A Cecil) *led: rdn and hdd over 1f out: outpcd ins fnl f* **4/1**^{2}

0 **3** nk **Lilac Star**^{21} [1119] 3-9-0 .... PaulEddery 8 — 68
(Pat Eddery) *hld up in tch: rdn over 1f out: hung lft ins fnl f: styd on* **4/1**^{2}

3 **4** 1 ½ **Reflecting (IRE)**^{197} [6122] 3-9-0 .... EddieAhern 10 — 65
(J W Hills) *hld up: plld hrd: hdwy over 3f out: rdn over 1f out: styd on same pce* **13/2**^{3}

0 **5** 3 **Rose Briar (IRE)**^{23} [1085] 3-9-0 .... JimmyQuinn 5 — 58+
(R Charlton) *hld up: nt clr run fr over 3f out tl over 1f out: nvr trbld ldrs* **17/2**

00 **6** nk **Ciccone**^{256} [4816] 3-9-0 .... KDarley 7 — 57
(W Jarvis) *hld up: hdwy over 1f out: hung lft ins fnl f: n.d* **22/1**

0 **7** 1 ¾ **Dunlin**^{18} [1191] 3-9-0 .... RobertHavlin 9 — 53+
(H Morrison) *hld up: nt clr run over 3f out: nvr trbld ldrs* **40/1**

5 **8** nk **Sharpe Image (IRE)**^{192} [6213] 3-9-0 .... TomEaves 3 — 53
(G Woodward) *w ldr 5f: rdn and wknd over 1f out* **33/1**

40 **9** ½ **Star Jasmine**^{9} [1418] 3-9-0 .... JamieMackay 11 — 51
(M L W Bell) *hld up: n.d* **16/1**

00 **10** hd **Dance A Daydream**^{11} [1351] 3-8-9 .... RoryMoore(5) 4 — 51
(J R Fanshawe) *prom: rdn over 2f out: wknd over 1f out* **40/1**

0020 **11** 3 ½ **Kissi Kissi**^{67} [604] 3-9-0 57 .... FrancisFerris 1 — 43
(M J Attwater) *chsd ldrs: rdn: hung lft and wknd over 2f out* **50/1**

1m 46.65s (0.25) **Going Correction** +0.025s/f (Good) **11** Ran SP% **118.7**
Speed ratings (Par 96):99,95,95,93,90 90,88,88,87,87 84
CSF £8.87 TOTE £2.60: £1.30, £1.80, £1.60; EX 15.10.
Owner Godolphin **Bred** Gainsborough Stud Management Ltd **Trained** Newmarket, Suffolk

FOCUS
The early tempo was not great and the time was particularly slow, so with the possible exception of the winner the form appears ordinary, rated through the second.

1650 HARRY RICHMOND & PARTNER LTD MAIDEN FILLIES' STKS (DIV II) — 1m 54y

4:45 (4:47) (Class 5) 3-Y-O **£4,210** (£1,252; £625; £312) **Stalls** Centre

Form — RPR

1 **Missisipi Star (IRE)**^{12} [1317] 3-9-0 .... MCHussey 6 — 81
(Eamon Tyrrell, Ire) *a.p: rdn 2f out: r.o to ld wl ins fnl f* **14/1**

32 **2** 1 **Safqa**^{21} [1114] 3-9-0 .... EddieAhern 1 — 79
(B W Hills) *sn led: hdd over 2f out: rdn to ld over 1f out: hdd whn hit over hd by rivals whip wl ins fnl f* **5/4**^{1}

3 **3** 1 ½ **Stepping Stones**^{11} [1351] 3-9-0 .... RichardHughes 9 — 75
(H R A Cecil) *hld up: racd keenly: hdwy 1/2-way: rdn over 1f out: styd on same pce* **8/1**

5 **4** ½ **Regent's Park**^{21} [1119] 3-9-0 .... KDarley 5 — 74
(R Charlton) *hld up: hdwy over 3f out: rdn over 1f out: styd on same pce* **16/1**

02 **5** shd **Zaafran**^{16} [1240] 3-9-0 .... PhilipRobinson 10 — 74
(M A Jarvis) *chsd ldrs: led over 2f out: rdn and hdd over 1f out: wknd wl ins fnl f* **5/2**^{2}

6 1 ¼ **Peppertree** 3-9-0 .... KerrinMcEvoy 4 — 71
(J R Fanshawe) *sn pushed along in rr: outpcd over 2f out: edgd lft over 1f out: styd on ins fnl f: nvr trbld ldrs* **6/1**^{3}

00 **7** 2 **Generosia**^{211} [5850] 3-9-0 .... (t) JimmyQuinn 8 — 67
(A M Balding) *hld up: hdwy over 3f out: wknd fnl f* **40/1**

6344 **8** ½ **Bahhmirage (IRE)**^{4} [1552] 3-9-0 47 .... (b) FrancisNorton 3 — 65?
(Stef Liddiard) *trckd ldr: rdn over 2f out: wknd wl over 1f out* **150/1**

9 6 **Louise Dupin (IRE)** 3-8-11 .... NelsonDeSouza(3) 7 — 52
(R M Beckett) *s.s: outpcd: hdwy 3f out: wkng whn hung lft over 1f out* **66/1**

10 ¾ **Tejareb (IRE)** 3-9-0 .... StanleyChin 2 — 50
(C E Brittain) *hld up in tch: plld hrd: wknd 3f out* **80/1**

1m 44.95s (-1.45) **Going Correction** +0.025s/f (Good) **49** Ran SP% **116.8**
Speed ratings (Par 96):108,107,105,105,104 103,101,101,95,94
CSF £32.20 TOTE £17.30: £3.40, £1.30, £1.80; EX 48.50.
Owner M McLoughlin **Bred** P F Kelly And Sean Madigan **Trained** The Curragh, Co Kildare

FOCUS
This looked the slightly weaker of the two divisions, but still had plenty of interesting types lining up. The pace was much better, resulting in a decent time for the type of race and 1.7 seconds quicker than the first division. The runner-up and fifth set a fair standard.

1651 COLWICK PARK H'CAP — 1m 1f 213y

5:15 (5:19) (Class 5) (0-75,75) 4-Y-O+ **£4,210** (£1,252; £625; £312) **Stalls** Low

Form — RPR

340 **1** **Count Kristo**^{241} [5200] 4-8-11 **71** .... AdamKirby(3) 11 — 77+
(C G Cox) *hld up: hdwy 1/2-way: rdn over 2f out: r.o to ld wl ins fnl f* **25/1**

1201 **2** ½ **Press Express (IRE)**^{215} [5772] 4-9-4 **75** .... KDarley 8 — 80
(M L W Bell) *plld hrd and prom: lost pl over 6f out: hdwy over 4f out: rdn and edgd lft ins fnl f: sn ev ch: r.o* **11/2**^{2}

4540 **3** hd **Smooth Jazz**^{305} [3391] 4-8-7 **67** .... NelsonDeSouza(3) 5 — 72
(R M Beckett) *chsd ldrs: led 8f out: rdn over 1f out: hdd wl ins fnl f* **20/1**

4 ½ **Olimpo (FR)**^{197} 5-8-11 **68** .... KerrinMcEvoy 9 — 72+
(B R Millman) *hld up: hdwy over 1f out: r.o* **40/1**

0530 **5** nk **Tribe**^{17} [1206] 4-8-13 **70** .... TomEaves 7 — 73
(Sir Michael Stoute) *chsd ldrs: outpcd 3f out: rallied over 1f out: r.o* **11/2**^{2}

2206 **6** ½ **Fabrian**^{10} [1380] 8-8-10 **72** .... JamesDoyle(5) 6 — 75
(R J Price) *led 2f: chsd ldrs: rdn over 2f out: styd on same pce ins fnl f* **10/1**^{3}

4430 **7** 1 ½ **Qaasi (USA)**^{13} [1280] 4-8-13 **70** .... NeilPollard 15 — 70
(Mrs K Walton) *hld up: nt clr run 3f out: swtchd rt and hdwy over 1f out: no imp ins fnl f* **100/1**

3050 **8** 4¾ **Anduril**^{4} [1531] 5-9-2 **73** .... FrancisNorton 3 — 64
(Miss M E Rowland) *hld up:: plld hrd: effrt over 2f out: nvr trbld ldrs* **28/1**

-320 **9** 3½ **Phoebe Woodstock (IRE)**^{18} [1186] 4-9-4 **75** .... JimmyQuinn 16 — 59
(W R Swinburn) *hld up: nt clr run over 3f out: n.d: fin 10th, plcd 9th* **22/1**

40-0 **10** 1 ¾ **Personify**^{17} [1207] 4-9-1 **72** .... PhilipRobinson 2 — 53
(C G Cox) *chsd ldrs 7f: fin 11th, plcd 10th* **25/1**

1000 **11** 8 **Wing Commander**^{13} [1302] 7-8-13 **73** .... (v) PatrickMathers(3) 4 — 38
(I W McInnes) *hld up: rdn and hung rt 1/2-way: a in rr : fin 12th plcd 11th* **40/1**

0613 **12** 15 **Cordier**^{66} [610] 4-8-13 **75** .... DerekNolan(5) 13 — 12
(J Mackie) *hld up in tch: rdn and wknd over 2f out: fin 13th, plcd 12th* **16/1**

1/ **D** ¾ **Jake The Snake (IRE)**^{884} [6158] 5-9-4 **75** .... EddieAhern 12 — 73
(G A Huffer) *chsd ldrs: ev ch over 2f out: sn rdn: no ex whn hmpd ins fnl f: fin 8th: disq (prohibited substance)* **85/40**^{1}

0000 **R** **Arabie**^{77} [505] 8-9-1 **72** .... DO'Donohoe 10 — —
(Ian Williams) *ref to r* **25/1**

2m 9.64s (-0.06) **Going Correction** +0.025s/f (Good) **14** Ran SP% **107.7**
Speed ratings (Par 103):101,100,100,100,99 99,98,94,91,90 83,71,—,97
CSF £114.30 CT £2081.98 TOTE £24.10: £4.40, £1.90, £5.60; EX 112.10.
Owner Mr and Mrs P Hargreaves **Bred** Millsec Limited **Trained** Lambourn, Berks
■ Custodian was withdrawn (6/1, refused to enter stalls). R4 applies, deduct 5p in the £.

FOCUS
A fair handicap that may produce a couple of winners, but the form is ordinary. Non-runner Custodian is one to be very wary of in the future, as he flatly refused to go into the stalls and reared up, while Arabie flatly refused to leave the stalls and is on a sharp decline.
Fabrian Official explanation: jockey said gelding was denied a clear run
Anduril Official explanation: jockey said gelding was unsuited by the good to firm ground
Personify Official explanation: jockey said gelding hung left up home straight
Wing Commander Official explanation: jockey said gelding was denied a clear run
Jake The Snake(IRE) ◆ Official explanation: vet said horse finished stiff behind

1652 NOTTINGHAM RACECOURSE CONFERENCE CENTRE H'CAP 1m 1f 213y
5:45 (5:48) (Class 6) (0-60,60) 3-Y-O **£2,730** (£806; £403) **Stalls** Low

Form RPR
0500 **1** **Unasuming (IRE)**[127] [49] 3-8-8 **50** .... KDarley 8 58
(J Pearce) *a.p: rdn over 1f out: edgd lft and led wl ins fnl f* **100/1**
0402 **2** *nk* **Tangarita**[10] [1375] 3-9-1 **57** .... RichardHughes 6 64
(A M Balding) *led 1f: chsd ldr: led over 3f out: rdn over 1f out: hdd wl ins fnl f* **7/2**[1]
0000 **3** *1 ½* **Sarwin (USA)**[20] [1140] 3-8-13 **55** .... PhilipRobinson 15 59
(W J Musson) *hld up: plld hrd: hdwy over 2f out: sn rdn: edgd lft ins fnl f: styd on* **9/1**
5050 **4** *1 ¼* **Citelle (IRE)**[18] [1193] 3-9-0 **56** ....(t) RobertHavlin 3 58
(Mrs P N Dutfield) *led 9f out: hdd over 3f out: sn rdn: styd on same pce ins fnl f* **33/1**
0005 **5** *1 ¼* **They All Laughed**[11] [1352] 3-8-13 **58** .... RobertMiles[(3)] 4 58
(P W Hiatt) *chsd ldrs: rdn over 1f out: wknd ins fnl f* **16/1**
0542 **6** *½* **Murrumbidgee (IRE)**[11] [1352] 3-9-4 **60** .... EddieAhern 1 59
(J W Hills) *hld up in tch: stmbld 8f out: rdn over 2f out: styd on same pce appr fnl f* **9/2**[2]
0060 **7** *2* **Haiti Dancer**[20] [1141] 3-8-12 **57** .... AdamKirby[(3)] 5 52
(C G Cox) *s.i.s: hld up: hdwy over 3f out: sn hrd rdn: styd on same pce fnl 2f* **8/1**
0500 **8** *nk* **Royal Premier (IRE)**[25] [1052] 3-9-0 **56** ....(v[1]) JimmyQuinn 9 50
(H J Collingridge) *prom: rdn 3f out: wknd over 1f out* **28/1**
0000 **9** *1* **Master Mark**[20] [1141] 3-8-8 **55** .... StephenDonohoe[(5)] 12 47
(P D Evans) *hld up: rdn and hung lft over 2f out: n.d* **16/1**
5000 **10** *shd* **Cragganmore Creek**[9] [1424] 3-8-13 **58** .... SaleemGolam[(3)] 13 50
(D Morris) *hld up: n.d* **66/1**
0002 **11** *3* **Lovely Hidenka (USA)**[15] [1259] 3-8-12 **54** .... KerrinMcEvoy 10 41
(C E Brittain) *hld up: effrt over 3f out: sn wknd* **8/1**
0004 **12** *¾* **Changiz**[20] [1140] 3-8-13 **55** .... DavidKinsella 11 40
(J A Geake) *chsd ldrs over 7f* **20/1**
0000 **13** *¾* **Wings Of Dawn**[233] [5408] 3-8-11 **56** .... NelsonDeSouza[(3)] 2 40
(M P Tregoning) *hld up: rdn over 4f out: a in rr* **10/1**
000 **14** *2 ½* **Maraval**[193] [6198] 3-8-9 **54** .... NeilChalmers[(3)] 14 33
(M Wellings) *hld up: a in rr* **66/1**
0003 **15** *7* **King's Charter (USA)**[129] [20] 3-8-10 **52** .... PaulFitzsimons 16 18
(S Dow) *hld up: a in rr* **66/1**
000 **16** *7* **Spaceman**[25] [1055] 3-9-3 **59** .... JamieMackay 7 11
(L M Cumani) *s.s: outpcd* **7/1**[3]
2m 11.25s (1.55) **Going Correction** +0.025s/f (Good) **16** Ran SP% **122.6**
Speed ratings (Par 97):94,93,92,91,90 90,88,88,87,87 85,84,83,81,76 70
CSF £424.43 CT £3595.99 TOTE £76.00: £9.60, £1.40, £2.90, £5.30; EX 351.90 Place 6 £8.35, Place 5 £4.36.
Owner J P Hayes **Bred** Gerry Aherne **Trained** Newmarket, Suffolk
■ Stewards' Enquiry : Richard Hughes caution: careless riding
FOCUS
It was worrying that quite a few horses had last-placed finishes in their previous form, some on more than one occasion, so the race is worth treating with caution in the short-term, especially with the time ordinary.
Master Mark Official explanation: trainer's rep said gelding was unsuited by the good to firm ground
T/Plt: £10.50 to a £1 stake. Pool: £34,314.55. 2,383.95 winning tickets. T/Qpdt: £4.90 to a £1 stake. Pool: £1,782.50. 268.35 winning tickets. CR

1653 - 1658a (Foreign Racing) - See Raceform Interactive

JAGERSRO (R-H)
Friday, May 12
OFFICIAL GOING: Standard

1659a PRAMMS MEMORIAL (LISTED RACE) (DIRT) 1m 143y(D)
8:10 (8:10) 4-Y-O+ **£43,924** (£14,641; £7,321; £4,392; £2,928)

RPR
1 **Binary File (USA)**[587] [5968] 8-9-4 .... KAndersen 11 110
(L Kelp, Sweden) **219/10**
2 *5* **Red Spell (IRE)**[13] [1301] 5-9-4 .... FJohansson 1 100
(R Hannon) *raced in 4th in inside, went 3rd 3f out, led briefly entering straight 2f out, soon headed, kept on but not pace of winner* **2/1**[1]
3 *1 ½* **Salt Track (ARG)**[211] 6-9-4 .... LHammer-Hansen 8 97
(Niels Petersen, Norway) **143/10**
4 *2* **Maybach**[25] 5-9-4 .... GSolis 5 93
(O Stenstrom, Sweden) **175/10**
5 *hd* **Avie Pimiento (IRE)** 5-9-4 ....(b) JMSanchez 10 93
(Eva Olofsson, Sweden) **27/1**
6 *3* **Hovman (DEN)**[208] 7-9-4 .... ESki 2 87
(Ms C Erichsen, Norway) **6/1**
7 *2* **Limit Up (GR)**[68] 8-9-4 .... JPalik 6 83
(Dr A Bolte, Germany) **20/1**
8 *hd* **Damachida (IRE)**[55] [667] 7-9-4 .... MSantos 4 83
(Eva Sundbye, Sweden) **24/1**
9 *10* **Apeiron (GER)**[11] 5-9-6 .... AStarke 7 65
(Mario Hofer, Germany) **36/10**[3]
10 *4* **Billy Allen (IRE)**[15] [1266] 5-9-4 .... SPasquier 12 55
(F Chappet, France) **7/2**[2]
11 *18* **Tiberius Caesar (FR)**[132] 6-9-4 .... YvonneDurant 3 19
(F Reuterskiold, Sweden) **148/10**
1m 47.6s **11** Ran SP% **126.6**
(including 1Kr stake): WIN 22.88; PL 4.17, 1.59, 4.06; DF 147.18.
Owner Stald Milo & Light Valley Stud **Bred** Juddmonte Farms **Trained** Sweden

NOTEBOOK
Red Spell(IRE), who had some narrow misses on Polytrack earlier in the year, has been holding his form on turf. He had no chance with the winner, but picked up some good place money.

[1248] BEVERLEY (R-H)
Saturday, May 13
OFFICIAL GOING: Good (good to soft in places) changing to good to soft (soft in places) after race 2 (2.45)
After 8mm water had been put on the track over the previous three days, another 8mm overnight rain turned the ground to 'almost soft'.
Wind: Moderate, half behind Weather: Overcast, occasional light rain

1660 C.G.I. STAYERS H'CAP 2m 35y
2:15 (2:15) (Class 5) (0-75,75) 4-Y-O+ **£4,533** (£1,348; £674; £336) **Stalls** High

Form RPR
0001 **1** **Prairie Sun (GER)**[4] [1562] 5-9-1 **69** 6ex .... GregFairley[(5)] 3 77+
(Mrs A Duffield) *chsd ldrs: styd on to ld over 1f out: drew clr: eased towards fin* **5/4**[1]
1100 **2** *6* **Isa'Af (IRE)**[17] [1247] 7-9-7 **75** .... LiamTreadwell[(5)] 7 76
(P W Hiatt) *hld up: hdwy to join ldrs 7f out: led over 2f out: hdd and no ex over 1f out* **8/1**
0601 **3** *3* **Whoopsie**[9] [1436] 4-8-5 **57** oh2 ow1 .... DeanMcKeown 6 54
(S Parr) *trckd ldr: jnd ldr 7f out: led over 3f out: hdd over 2f out: one pce* **3/1**[2]
0000 **4** *3* **Delta Force**[9] [1436] 7-8-0 **56** oh16 .... KevinGhunowa[(7)] 2 50
(P A Blockley) *t.k.h: hdwy to trck ldrs 5f out: one pce fnl 2f* **40/1**
3045 **5** *5* **Arch Folly**[18] [1219] 4-8-4 **56** oh3 .... GrahamGibbons 4 44
(J G Portman) *chsd ldrs: effrt 4f out: wknd over 1f out* **7/1**[3]
0166 **6** *27* **John Forbes**[6] [1502] 4-9-9 **75** .... PatCosgrave 1 30
(B Ellison) *set mod pce: keen: rdn over 5f out: hdd over 3f out: lost pl over 2f out: sn bhd* **7/1**[3]
0300 **7** *4* **Scarrabus (IRE)**[15] [1233] 5-8-2 **58** oh4 ow2 .... SladeO'Hara[(7)] 5 8
(A Crook) *hld up: racd wd: lost pl over 4f out: sn wl bhd* **40/1**
3m 44.3s (4.80) **Going Correction** +0.45s/f (Yiel)
WFA 4 from 5yo+ 3lb **7** Ran SP% **110.4**
Speed ratings (Par 103):106,103,101,100,97 84,82
CSF £11.35 TOTE £2.00: £1.40, £3.70; EX 12.20.
Owner Miss Helen Wynne **Bred** Gestut Isarland **Trained** Constable Burton, N Yorks
FOCUS
A very steady pace and ordinary form, but in the end a most decisive, bang in-form winner.

1661 COACHMAN LASER TOURER OF THE YEAR (S) STKS 1m 1f 207y
2:45 (2:45) (Class 5) 3-Y-O **£3,400** (£1,011; £505; £252) **Stalls** High

Form RPR
06 **1** **Keisha Kayleigh (IRE)**[14] [1296] 3-8-7 .... TomEaves 7 48
(B Ellison) *hld up: hdwy over 2f out: led over 1f out: edgd lft: kpt on* **9/4**[1]
0000 **2** *2* **Mister Fizzbomb (IRE)**[14] [1293] 3-8-12 35 ....(b[1]) TonyHamilton 11 49
(J S Wainwright) *trckd ldrs: styd on to go 2nd 1f out: no real imp* **33/1**
0204 **3** *2 ½* **Cuesta Canyon (IRE)**[8] [1458] 3-8-12 40 .... DeanMcKeown 8 44
(M J Polglase) *chsd ldrs: effrt on wd outside over 2f out: styd on same pce appr fnl f* **20/1**
0660 **4** *3 ½* **Sahara Style**[10] [1424] 3-8-12 48 ....(v) GrahamGibbons 1 37
(R Hollinshead) *w ldr: led over 3f out: hung rt and hdd over 1f out: wknd ins last* **15/2**
0304 **5** *5* **Archidona (FR)**[33] [945] 3-9-0 48 .... ShaneKelly 6 30
(M Quinn) *chsd ldrs: effrt over 3f out: wknd over 1f out* **7/2**[2]
0000 **6** *¾* **Silver Bank**[18] [1221] 3-8-4 45 .... PaulMulrennan[(3)] 12 21
(M W Easterby) *led tl over 3f out: lost pl over 1f out* **20/1**
0056 **7** *9* **Tesoro**[88] [415] 3-8-5 45 .... KevinGhunowa[(7)] 4 9
(P A Blockley) *sn chsng ldrs: wknd over 2f out* **9/1**
5000 **8** *1* **Captivate**[12] [1345] 3-8-7 45 ....(p) AdamCarter[(7)] 2 9
(M J Polglase) *s.i.s: bhd and sn drvn along* **14/1**
4350 **9** *8* **Count The Trees**[11] [1373] 3-8-4 46 .... RobertMiles[(3)] 9 —
(W G M Turner) *trckd ldrs: lost pl 4f out: sn bhd* **8/1**
5000 **10** *24* **Valentino Taffi**[21] [1140] 3-8-12 47 ....(v[1]) J-PGuillambert 5 —
(S C Williams) *s.i.s: a bhd: t.o 4f out* **7/1**[3]
00 **11** *9* **Fox Flight (IRE)**[283] [4062] 3-8-12 .... NeilPollard 3 —
(D W Barker) *racd wd: sn chsng ldrs: lost pl over 4f out: t.o 2f out* **66/1**
2m 11.38s (4.08) **Going Correction** +0.45s/f (Yiel) **11** Ran SP% **119.0**
Speed ratings (Par 99):101,99,97,94,90 90,82,82,75,56 49
CSF £95.15 TOTE £2.80: £1.50, £5.80, £2.90; EX 107.20.There was no bid for the winner.
Owner Black and White Diamond Partnership **Bred** Ronnie Boland **Trained** Norton, N Yorks
FOCUS
Rock bottom stuff but a sound gallop and the form is not entirely straightforward, with the third the best guide.
Count The Trees Official explanation: jockey said filly was unsuited by the good (good to soft places) ground

1662 LEISURE FURNISHINGS SPRINT (H'CAP) 5f
3:15 (3:15) (Class 4) (0-85,85) 4-Y-O+ **£7,772** (£2,312; £1,155; £577) **Stalls** High

Form RPR
3060 **1** **Prince Namid**[22] [1125] 4-8-8 **75** .... PaulFessey 13 90
(Mrs A Duffield) *chsd ldrs: led jst ins last: r.o wl* **12/1**
0110 **2** *2* **Spanish Ace**[7] [1487] 5-9-4 **85** .... KDarley 16 93
(J M Bradley) *w ldr: led over 2f out: edgd lft: hdd and no ex last 150yds* **9/4**[1]
3406 **3** *2* **Grigorovitch (IRE)**[9] [1438] 4-9-1 **82** ....(p) TomEaves 11 83
(I Semple) *chsd ldrs: kpt on wl fnl f* **8/1**
0002 **4** *1* **Handsome Cross (IRE)**[7] [1496] 5-8-12 **79** .... AdrianTNicholls 14 76
(D Nicholls) *led: hdd over 2f out: edgd lft and kpt on same pce fnl f* **15/2**[3]
0564 **5** *hd* **Plateau**[7] [1496] 7-8-9 **79** .... SilvestreDeSousa[(3)] 7 75+
(D Nicholls) *chsd ldrs on outer: kpt on fnl 2f* **20/1**
0000 **6** *¾* **Ryedane (IRE)**[7] [1496] 4-8-5 **72** ....(e) DavidAllan 6 66+
(T D Easterby) *sn in rr: hdwy 2f out: styd on towards fin* **66/1**
0060 **7** *½* **Chatshow (USA)**[7] [1496] 5-7-13 **71** oh1 .... DuranFentiman[(5)] 5 63
(D Carroll) *mid-div: kpt on fnl 2f* **100/1**
1600 **8** *1 ¼* **Brigadore**[26] [1042] 7-8-5 **72** .... DaleGibson 3 59+
(J G Given) *swtchd rt s: bhd tl styd on fnl 2f* **66/1**
6040 **9** *shd* **Sentiero Rosso (USA)**[9] [1438] 4-8-8 **75** .... PatCosgrave 18 62
(B Ellison) *mid-div: kpt on fnl f* **25/1**
0003 **10** *1* **Armagnac**[232] [5439] 8-8-7 **74** .... ShaneKelly 15 58
(M A Buckley) *rr-div: kpt on fnl 2f* **25/1**
1115 **11** *¾* **Holbeck Ghyll (IRE)**[52] [699] 4-8-6 **73** .... FergusSweeney 17 54
(A M Balding) *chsd ldrs: wknd over 1f out* **5/1**[2]
2502 **12** *nk* **Countdown**[22] [1125] 4-8-11 **78** ....(b) TonyHamilton 9 58
(Miss J A Camacho) *rr-div: sme hdwy over 1f out: nvr on terms* **11/1**

The Form Book, Raceform Ltd, Compton, RG20 6NL

0000 **13** *nk* **Whistler**[7] [1475] 9-8-5 **72** oh1 ow1....(p) PaulFitzsimons 1 51
(Miss J R Tooth) *swtchd rt s: bhd: sme hdwy 2f out: nvr a factor* **50/1**

0050 **14** *3/4* **Melalchrist**[14] [1285] 4-8-11 **78**.... GrahamGibbons 4 54
(J J Quinn) *sn outpcd and bhd: sme hdwy on inner 2f out: nvr on terms* **33/1**

0341 **15** *1 1/4* **Matsunosuke**[7] [1496] 4-8-1 **75**.... LukeMorris(7) 10 46
(A B Coogan) *in tch: wknd over 1f out* **14/1**

0541 **16** *1* **Bonne De Fleur**[9] [1448] 5-8-10 **77**....(b) RobertWinston 2 45
(B Smart) *in tch on outer: lost pl over 1f out* **16/1**

4101 **17** *1/2* **Wicked Uncle**[10] [1399] 7-8-13 **80**....(v) DeanMcKeown 12 46
(S Gollings) *a in rr* **16/1**

0560 **18** *3* **Salviati (USA)**[14] [1297] 9-8-4 **71** oh1.... FrancisFerris 8 26
(J M Bradley) *s.s: a bhd* **40/1**

63.65 secs (-0.35) **Going Correction** +0.075s/f (Good) 18 Ran SP% **128.5**
Speed ratings (Par 105):105,101,98,97,96 95,94,92,92,90 89,89,88,87,85 83,83,78
CSF £37.65 CT £250.28 TOTE £16.50: £3.40, £1.50, £3.10, £1.70; EX 73.00.
Owner S Adamson **Bred** Mrs R D Peacock **Trained** Constable Burton, N Yorks

FOCUS
Very few got into this and the high-drawn horses, as usual, came out on top. The form should prove sound, rated around the first two.
Holbeck Ghyll(IRE) Official explanation: jockey said gelding lost its action

1663 COACHMAN CARAVANS CONDITIONS STKS 5f
3:45 (3:46) (Class 2) 3-Y-0+
£12,464 (£3,732; £1,866; £934; £466; £234) **Stalls** High

Form RPR

2320 **1** **Corridor Creeper (FR)**[7] [1485] 9-8-12 108....(p) ShaneKelly 7 112
(J M Bradley) *w ldrs: styd on to ld last 75yds* **11/4**[1]

0414 **2** *1/2* **Sierra Vista**[11] [1377] 6-8-7 101.... RobertWinston 6 105
(D W Barker) *chsd ldrs: led 2f out: hdd and no ex wl ins last* **5/1**[2]

2100 **3** *1 1/4* **Out After Dark**[25] [1069] 5-8-12 104....(b[1]) KDarley 2 106
(C G Cox) *s.i.s: sn chsng ldrs: styd on same pce fnl f* **5/1**[2]

2024 **4** *1/2* **Lafi (IRE)**[21] [1145] 7-8-12 105.... PaulFessey 4 104+
(D Nicholls) *sn in rr: hdwy and swtchd outside over 1f out: hung rt and kpt on wl* **10/1**[3]

5202 **5** *3/4* **Fonthill Road (IRE)**[238] [5288] 6-8-12 103.... TonyHamilton 9 101
(R A Fahey) *mid-div: sn drvn along: kpt on same pce fnl 2f* **11/4**[1]

0205 **6** *1 3/4* **Bahamian Pirate (USA)**[7] [1481] 11-8-12 102.... AdrianTNicholls 3 95
(D Nicholls) *dwlt: swtchd rt s: sme hdwy and nt clr run 2f out: n.m.r on inner 1f out: nvr nr ldrs* **14/1**

0050 **7** *3/4* **Pawan (IRE)**[18] [1220] 6-8-12 74.... AnnStokell 1 92?
(Miss A Stokell) *s.s: outpcd and bhd: sme hdwy on wd outside 2f out: nvr nr ldrs* **100/1**

0636 **8** *1 3/4* **If Paradise**[22] [1116] 5-8-12 98.... PatDobbs 8 86
(R Hannon) *w ldrs: lost pl over 1f out* **14/1**

1-20 **9** *shd* **Hoh Hoh Hoh**[232] [5438] 4-8-12 88.... FergusSweeney 10 85
(A M Balding) *led: hung lft thrght: hdd 2f out: sn btn* **18/1**

0004 **10** *10* **Chookie Heiton (IRE)**[7] [1481] 8-9-9 105.... TomEaves 5 60
(I Semple) *mid-div: lost pl over 1f out: heavily eased ins last* **20/1**

63.18 secs (-0.82) **Going Correction** +0.075s/f (Good) 10 Ran SP% **120.1**
Speed ratings (Par 109):109,108,106,105,104 101,100,97,97,81
CSF £17.23 TOTE £4.10: £1.90, £1.90, £2.30; EX 21.30.
Owner G & L Johnson **Bred** J Byng **Trained** Sedbury, Gloucs

FOCUS
The first two were in the firing line throughout, and although the time was reasonable, the form although decent is not totally rock-solid.

NOTEBOOK
Corridor Creeper(FR), suited by the give underfoot, put his head down and battled to nail the runner-up in the closing stages. He is a credit to his trainer. (op 7-2)
Sierra Vista, who started last year rated just 75, is all speed and with the ground conditions to suit, it took all the winner's strength to get the better of her. (op 9-2)
Out After Dark, who has won here in the past, was tried in blinkers but from his outside draw was always seeing too much daylight. (op 6-1)
Lafi(IRE), still carrying tons of condition, did not look entirely happy on the rain-soaked ground. He stuck on steadily and is clearly on the way back. There may well be another big handicap to be won with him this time. (op 9-1 tchd 11-1)
Fonthill Road(IRE), narrowly denied in both the Stewards Cup and the Ayr Gold Cup, was ring-rusty but this will have put him spot on when he steps back to six at York. (tchd 5-2)
Bahamian Pirate(USA), who took this two years ago, showed that even in his 12th year he is no back number. (op 16-1)
Pawan(IRE) did amazingly well considering he had a mountain to climb. Official explanation: jockey said gelding was slowly away from stalls
Hoh Hoh Hoh Official explanation: jockey said gelding hung left

1664 COACHMAN AMARA MEDIAN AUCTION MAIDEN STKS 5f
4:20 (4:20) (Class 4) 2-Y-0 **£5,181** (£1,541; £770; £384) **Stalls** High

Form RPR

1 **Supreme Speedster** 2-9-0.... PaulMulrennan(3) 12 77
(K A Ryan) *cmpt: unf: mde all: qcknd clr over 1f out: pushed out* **8/1**[3]

2 *3/4* **Cherri Fosfate** 2-9-0.... RobertMiles(3) 4 74
(W G M Turner) *rangy: unf: mid-div: hdwy to chse wnr 1f out: styd on towards fin* **25/1**

5 **3** *5* **Ishibee (IRE)**[9] [1442] 2-8-12.... PaulFessey 8 51
(Mrs A Duffield) *chsd wnr: kpt on same pce fnl f* **7/1**[2]

3 **4** *1/2* **Argentine (IRE)**[24] [1080] 2-9-3.... KDarley 9 54
(M Johnston) *chsd ldrs: sn drvn along: one pce fnl 2f* **4/6**[1]

5 *3 1/2* **Dickie Le Davoir** 2-9-3.... RobertWinston 5 41
(K R Burke) *cmpt: in tch on inner: drvn 2f out: wknd over 1f out* **12/1**

6 **6** *2* **Reflective Glory (IRE)**[19] [1181] 2-8-12.... GrahamGibbons 1 29
(J J Quinn) *chsd ldrs: lost pl over 1f out* **14/1**

7 *hd* **Fire Alarm** 2-9-3.... TonyHamilton 3 33
(J J Quinn) *rangy: scope: s.i.s: kpt on fnl 2f: nvr nr ldrs* **33/1**

0 **8** *1* **Lovers Kiss**[14] [1295] 2-8-9.... DNolan(3) 10 24
(N Wilson) *chsd ldrs: wknd over 1f out* **33/1**

9 *1 1/2* **Mystic** 2-8-12.... TomEaves 6 19
(D W Barker) *s.i.s: bhd tl sme hdwy fnl 2f* **50/1**

10 *1 3/4* **Billy Ruffian** 2-9-3.... DavidAllan 2 17
(T D Easterby) *w'like: bit bkwd: chsd ldrs: lost pl over 1f out* **16/1**

11 *2* **Alavana (IRE)** 2-8-8 ow1.... MarkLawson(5) 7 6
(D W Barker) *leggy: unf: s.i.s: a in rr* **50/1**

12 *6* **Ruthles Philly** 2-8-12.... NeilPollard 11 —
(D W Barker) *leggy: a bhd* **33/1**

65.25 secs (1.25) **Going Correction** +0.075s/f (Good) 12 Ran SP% **120.4**
Speed ratings (Par 95):93,91,83,83,77 74,73,72,69,67 63,54
CSF £197.09 TOTE £10.30: £2.70, £7.80, £2.00; EX 266.60.
Owner Ryder Racing Ltd **Bred** Rainsbrook Bloodstock **Trained** Hambleton, N Yorks

FOCUS
Probably just an ordinary median auction maiden event but the first two finished clear in a fair time.

NOTEBOOK
Supreme Speedster, a sharp April foal, had the plum draw. After going three lengths clear, in the end he was pleased to cross the finishing line. (op 9-1)
Cherri Fosfate, an April foal, stands over plenty of ground. He showed a choppy action going down and had a poor draw. He went in pursuit of the winner and was closing him down all the way to the line.
Ishibee(IRE) again showed ability and should improve again. (op 6-1)
Argentine(IRE), who made his debut just 24 days previously, looked to be carrying plenty of condition. He never really went in the ground but must be given another chance. (op 8-11 tchd 4-5)
Dickie Le Davoir, a close-coupled April foal, showed ability on his debut from an unfavourable draw. (op 16-1)
Reflective Glory(IRE), worst drawn, will appreciate a return to better ground. (op 10-1)

1665 POWERPART H'CAP 1m 100y
4:55 (4:56) (Class 5) (0-70,70) 4-Y-0+ **£4,533** (£1,348; £674; £336) **Stalls** High

Form RPR

1003 **1** **Bridgewater Boys**[30] [1002] 5-8-10 **65**....(b) PaulMulrennan(3) 8 70
(K A Ryan) *led 1f: trckd ldrs: led over 1f out: sn clr: readily* **4/1**[1]

5200 **2** *3* **Splodger Mac (IRE)**[9] [1443] 7-7-11 **56** oh11....(b) SuzzanneFrance(7) 10 55
(N Bycroft) *hld up in mid-field: hdwy on outer to ld over 2f out: hdd over 1f out: no ex* **33/1**

4236 **3** *1* **Torquemada (IRE)**[20] [1164] 5-8-11 **63**.... MichaelTebbutt 11 60
(W Jarvis) *hld up in tch: nt clr run over 2f out: effrt appr fnl f: r.o same pce* **4/1**[1]

4150 **4** *1* **Oakley Absolute**[14] [1288] 4-9-2 **68**.... PatDobbs 7 63
(R Hannon) *sn trcking ldrs: kpt on same pce appr fnl f* **8/1**[3]

3040 **5** *1/2* **Gifted Flame**[206] [5991] 7-9-4 **70**.... GrahamGibbons 1 64
(J J Quinn) *swtchd rt s: hld up in rr: effrt 3f out: kpt on: nvr trbld ldrs* **20/1**

0351 **6** *3/4* **The Bonus King**[15] [1276] 6-8-12 **64**.... ShaneKelly 3 56
(J Jay) *in tch: effrt over 2f out: nvr a real threat* **6/1**[2]

4040 **7** *3/4* **Paris Heights**[16] [1253] 4-8-4 **56** oh4.... StanleyChin 9 47
(R M Whitaker) *chsd ldrs: lost pl over 1f out* **14/1**

3130 **8** *nk* **Distant Country (USA)**[21] [1148] 7-8-9 **61**....(b) KDarley 6 51
(B D Leavy) *hld up in rr: effrt 3f out: nvr a factor* **16/1**

2030 **9** *6* **Uhuru Peak**[12] [1353] 5-8-4 **56**....(t) DaleGibson 2 33
(M W Easterby) *swvd lft s: in rr: drvn 3f out: no rspnse* **10/1**

0064 **10** *4* **Dvinsky (USA)**[10] [1422] 5-8-11 **66**.... DanielTudhope(3) 12 35
(D Carroll) *t.k.h: trckd ldrs: led after 1f: hdd over 2f out: wknd 1f out: eased* **4/1**[1]

1m 51.28s (3.88) **Going Correction** +0.45s/f (Yiel) 10 Ran SP% **114.7**
Speed ratings (Par 103):98,95,94,93,92 91,91,90,84,80
CSF £141.17 CT £560.38 TOTE £4.40: £2.10, £6.50, £1.70; EX 169.50.
Owner Bishopthorpe Racing **Bred** Southill Stud **Trained** Hambleton, N Yorks

FOCUS
A modest handicap and the form looks a little shaky.
Dvinsky(USA) Official explanation: trainer had no explanation for the poor form shown other than gelding ran a little too freely in the early stages

1666 COACHMAN VIP LADY AMATEUR RIDERS' H'CAP 1m 1f 207y
5:30 (5:30) (Class 5) (0-70,70) 4-Y-0+ **£3,435** (£1,065; £532; £266) **Stalls** High

Form RPR

4154 **1** **Scotty's Future (IRE)**[6] [1500] 8-9-12 **58**.... MrsCBartley 3 69
(A Berry) *sn in rr: gd hdwy on outer 3f out: wnt rt and led over 1f out: sn clr* **5/1**[2]

/206 **2** *1 3/4* **King's Crest**[16] [1256] 8-9-11 **57**.... MissADeniel 5 65
(J J Quinn) *hld up in tch: hdwy 3f out: wnt 2nd 1f out: styd on wl: nt rch wnr* **9/1**

3103 **3** *3* **Great View (IRE)**[222] [5663] 7-9-10 **59**....(p) MissLEllison(3) 9 62
(Mrs A L M King) *hld up in rr: hdwy 3f out: kpt on same pce fnl 2f* **8/1**

6332 **4** *1 1/2* **Seattle Robber**[10] [1400] 4-9-13 **62**....(p) MissFayeBramley(3) 8 62
(P A Blockley) *in tch: hdwy 4f out: wnt 2nd over 1f out: one pce* **13/2**

6040 **5** *2 1/2* **Archirondel**[14] [1308] 8-9-3 **56** oh4.... MissWGibson(7) 7 52
(N Wilson) *s.s: kpt on fnl 2f: nvr nr ldrs* **10/1**

6224 **6** *8* **Platinum Charmer (IRE)**[9] [1439] 6-9-11 **62**....(p) MissKellyBurke(5) 11 43
(K R Burke) *chsd ldrs: led over 3f out: hdd over 1f out: sn wknd* **4/1**[1]

1340 **7** *6* **Richtee (IRE)**[294] [3760] 5-10-3 **70**.... MissFrancesHarper(7) 2 40
(R A Fahey) *chsd ldrs: wknd fnl 2f* **10/1**

5066 **8** *nk* **Spitfire Bob (USA)**[40] [857] 7-9-10 **63** oh16 ow7.... MissKSearby(7) 4 33
(M E Sowersby) *mid-div: sn drvn along: lost pl over 2f out* **33/1**

0000 **9** *5* **Jidiya (IRE)**[187] [6280] 7-9-6 **57**.... MissARyan(5) 1 18
(S Gollings) *trckd ldrs on outer: lost pl over 2f out* **16/1**

0000 **10** *4* **Loves Travelling (IRE)**[17] [1233] 6-10-1 **68**.... MissSLWatson(7) 10 22
(N Wilson) *hld up in rr: bhd fnl 3f* **20/1**

5200 **11** *5* **Emperor's Well**[216] [5773] 7-9-7 **60**....(b) MissJCoward(7) 6 5
(M W Easterby) *set str pce: hdd over 3f out: lost pl 2f out* **11/2**[3]

2m 11.45s (4.15) **Going Correction** +0.45s/f (Yiel) 11 Ran SP% **118.3**
Speed ratings (Par 103):101,99,97,96,94 87,82,82,78,75 71
CSF £49.91 CT £358.78 TOTE £4.30: £1.50, £4.00, £2.60; EX 67.20 Place 6 £61.92, Place 5 £36.54.
Owner E Nisbet **Bred** William J Hamilton **Trained** Cockerham, Lancs

FOCUS
A strong early pace for this moderate contest. Those that raced up there paid the price in the end, but the form looks reasonably sound with the third and fourth running to their marks.
T/Plt: £144.60 to a £1 stake. Pool: £48,116.60. 242.85 winning tickets. T/Qpdt: £39.30 to a £1 stake. Pool: £2,421.10. 45.50 winning tickets. WG

1638 LINGFIELD (L-H)
Saturday, May 13

OFFICIAL GOING: Good (good to firm in places)
Wind: Moderate, across

1667 TOTESPORT 0800 221 221 STKS (HERITAGE H'CAP) 7f
2:10 (2:11) (Class 2) 4-Y-0+
£37,392 (£11,196; £5,598; £2,802; £1,398; £702) **Stalls** High

Form RPR

022 **1** **Kostar**[127] [54] 5-8-11 **89**.... AdamKirby(3) 1 99
(C G Cox) *lw: a.p on outside: shkn up over 1f out: r.o to ld ins fnl f* **14/1**

21-0 **2** *3/4* **Munaddam (USA)**[211] [5874] 4-9-6 **95**.... MartinDwyer 6 103
(E A L Dunlop) *a.p: rdn to ld over 1f out: hdd ins fnl f* **10/1**

0601 **3** *nk* **Romany Nights (IRE)**[7] [1474] 6-8-9 **84**............................(b) JohnEgan 10 91
(Miss Gay Kelleway) *hld up in mid-div: hrd rdn over 1f out: styd on fnl f* **16/1**

5002 **4** *nk* **Coleorton Dancer**[50] [718] 4-9-2 **96**.......................... AndrewMullen(5) 4 102
(K A Ryan) *a front rnk: led briefly 2f out: edgd lft u.p and no ex nr fin* **20/1**

4111 **5** *hd* **Bonus (IRE)**[104] [238] 6-9-2 **91**.. KFallon 8 97
(G A Butler) *lw: hld up in mid-div: rdn over 2f out: r.o fnl f: nvr nrr* **4/1**[1]

3065 **6** *hd* **Trafalgar Square**[16] [1262] 4-8-3 **78**.................................. DavidKinsella 9 83+
(J Akehurst) *lw: in rr: n.m.r fr 2f out tl swtchd rt ins fnl f: r.o wl* **33/1**

2400 **7** *½* **Desert Dreamer (IRE)**[12] [1359] 5-8-5 **80**................... StephenCarson 14 84
(P R Chamings) *hld up in rr: hdwy over 1f out: r.o: nvr nrr* **25/1**

06 **8** *½* **Marajaa (IRE)**[16] [1262] 4-8-10 **85**...................................... TonyCulhane 3 88
(W J Musson) *hld up on outside: shkn up over 2f out: kpt on one pce* **40/1**

1206 **9** *1* **Kamanda Laugh**[21] [1129] 5-9-6 **95**... NCallan 11 95
(K A Ryan) *chsd ldrs tl wknd over 1f out* **9/1**

1400 **10** *nk* **Jalamid (IRE)**[78] [511] 4-9-9 **98**.......................................(t) RobertHavlin 7 97
(J H M Gosden) *hld up: a bhd* **18/1**

6460 **10** *dht* **Moayed**[7] [1487] 7-8-11 **86**...(b) ChrisCatlin 13 85
(N P Littmoden) *a bhd* **16/1**

2000 **12** *shd* **Cool Panic (IRE)**[42] [828] 4-9-5 **94**.................................. DaneO'Neill 16 93
(M L W Bell) *mid-div: rdn over 1f out: nt qckn* **50/1**

0011 **13** *3 ½* **Into The Breeze (IRE)**[22] [1112] 6-8-10 **85**................ FrankieMcDonald 5 75
(J W Hills) *chsd ldrs: rdn over 3f out: wknd over 1f out* **20/1**

2215 **14** *½* **All Ivory**[24] [1086] 4-9-6 **95**.. RichardHughes 12 84
(R Charlton) *lw: prom tl wknd over 1f out* **9/2**[2]

0003 **15** *shd* **Tagula Sunrise (IRE)**[5] [1532] 4-8-7 **82**............................. TedDurcan 15 71
(R A Fahey) *a bhd* **12/1**

0501 **16** *nk* **Visionist (IRE)**[42] [828] 4-9-10 **99**.................................... CSoumillon 17 87
(Pat Eddery) *prom: t.k.h: rdn over 2f out: wknd over 1f out* **6/1**[3]

0500 **17** *hd* **Lord Mayor**[7] [1495] 5-9-5 **94**.. MickyFenton 2 81
(R M H Cowell) *led after 2f: hdd & wknd qckly 2f out* **66/1**

1m 21.88s (-2.33) **Going Correction** -0.10s/f (Good) **17** Ran SP% **125.1**
Speed ratings (Par 109):109,108,107,107,107 107,106,105,104,104 104,104,100,99,99 99,99
CSF £140.17 CT £2370.25 TOTE £19.80: £3.10, £2.60, £2.90, £4.30; EX 269.50 TRIFECTA Not won..

Owner Mrs P Scott-Dunn And Mrs F J Ryan **Bred** Mrs P Scott-Dunn **Trained** Lambourn, Berks

■ Stewards' Enquiry : Andrew Mullen one-day ban: failed to keep straight from the stalls (May 24)

FOCUS
They went a pretty ordinary pace for most of the way and the bare form does not look as strong, or as reliable as one might expect for such a valuable handicap. They all raced towards the stands'-side rail, although somewhat surprisingly the first six home were all drawn ten or lower.

NOTEBOOK
Kostar, returning from a 127-day break, had never previously raced beyond six furlongs, so the steady pace would not have bothered him and Kirby did well to get him across towards the stands' side rail from the lowest stall of all. Once there, he was a little keen but found plenty under pressure and ultimately won decisively. He should stay this trip in a stronger-run race and something like the Victoria Cup could be a worthwhile target, although that will be tougher. (op 16-1)

Munaddam(USA), 19th of 23 in a Newmarket handicap on his only start last year, was just run out of it on his reappearance. He has clearly had his problems, but retains plenty of ability and could go on from this. (tchd 11-1)

Romany Nights(IRE) ran well off a 7lb higher mark than when causing a surprise in a seven-furlong handicap at Goodwood on his previous start and continues in good form. (op 14-1)

Coleorton Dancer, an unlucky second on his reappearance at Southwell, ran well but looks better suited to sprint trips on easy ground. (op 16-1)

Bonus(IRE), the winner of both his starts on Polytrack over the winter having been claimed after winning at Windsor last season, could not take advantage of a mark 7lb lower than that of his sand rating on his return to turf. A stronger pace would have suited better. (op 9-2)

Trafalgar Square ◆ stepped up on the form of his two reappearance efforts off bottom weight and would probably have been second at the very least with a clear run. Although this was a muddling contest, this effort can probably be taken at face value. Official explanation: jockey said colt was denied a clear run

Desert Dreamer(IRE) is back on a reasonable mark and was not beaten far. Official explanation: jockey said gelding was denied a clear run (op 33-1)

All Ivory failed to build on the form he showed on his reappearance at Newmarket and was disappointing, even allowing for the way the race was run. Official explanation: jockey said colt saw too much daylight early (op 5-1)

Tagula Sunrise(IRE) Official explanation: jockey said filly was denied a clear run

Visionist(IRE), 7lb higher than winning on Kempton's Polytrack on his reappearance, had a good draw but was unable to take advantage and proved very disappointing. (op 11-2)

1668 TOTESPORT.COM DERBY TRIAL STKS (GROUP 3) (C&G) 1m 3f 106y
2:40 (2:41) (Class 1) 3-Y-O **£34,471** (£13,315; £6,865; £3,625) **Stalls** High

Form RPR

2114 **1** **Linda's Lad**[26] [1064] 3-9-3 .... CSoumillon 2 116+
(A Fabre, France) *unf: hld up in last pl: hdwy over 3f out: rdn appr fnl f: drvn to ld post* **15/8**[1]

511 **2** *hd* **Hazeymm (IRE)**[22] [1117] 3-8-10 107.................................... TedDurcan 5 109
(M R Channon) *lw: racd keenly: trckd ldr: led over 2f out: rdn and rallied whn chal fnl f: hdd post* **7/1**

2163 **3** *5* **Baan (USA)**[14] [1300] 3-8-10 104... MartinDwyer 1 101
(M Johnston) *led: pushed along 4f out: hdd over 2f out: wknd fnl f* **9/1**

1211 **4** *nk* **Before You Go (IRE)**[17] [1237] 3-8-10 100......................... IanMongan 3 101
(T G Mills) *racd in 4th pl: rdn over 3f out: wknd appr fnl f* **9/2**[3]

31 **F** **Botteen**[227] [5554] 3-8-10 89.. KFallon 4 —
(M P Tregoning) *lw: racd in 3rd pl: rdn 5f out: wkng & last whn broke nr-fore & fell wl over 1f out: dead* **2/1**[2]

2m 29.25s (-0.67) **Going Correction** +0.025s/f (Good) **5** Ran SP% **108.8**
Speed ratings (Par 109):103,102,99,99,—
CSF £14.20 TOTE £2.40: £1.20, £3.10; EX 13.00.

Owner S Mulryan **Bred** The Niarchos Family **Trained** Chantilly, France

■ Stewards' Enquiry : C Soumillon one-day ban: used whip with excessive frequency and without giving colt time to respond (May 24)

FOCUS
Four of the five runners came into this entered in the Derby, and this year's renewal offered some clues, not least because Linda's Lad is a stablemate of the current ante-post favourite Visindar, but the bare form is a little way short of what will be required at Epsom. Having said that, it would be unwise to dismiss Linda's Lad totally, as he was conceding 7lb all round, and he would be a real player if the ground happened to be riding on the soft side. They went just an ordinary pace and the winning time was modest for a race of this stature - almost a second slower than the fillies half an hour later, but the form appears reasonable, if not rock-solid.

NOTEBOOK
Linda's Lad, carrying a 7lb penalty for his success in last season's Group 1 Criterium de St-Cloud, stepped up significantly on the form he showed on his reappearance when a beaten favourite in a Group 3 at Longchamp, but was made to work hard. Having travelled as well as anything towards the rear for most of the way, he looked likely to win easily at the top of the straight, but he would have preferred more give in the ground and only just did enough. His aim now is the Derby itself, but this form is a little way short of what is likely to be required at Epsom and, while it would be unwise to dismiss him totally, he could only really be backed with confidence if the ground is riding on the soft side. His stable also have the current ante-post favourite Visindar. (op 2-1 tchd 5-2 and 11-4 in a place)

Hazeymm(IRE) is not a particularly flashy type, as he showed when only scraping home in his maiden last season and again in a conditions race on his reappearance, but he battles well and was just held. He is clearly still progressing and deserves his chance in something like the King Edward VII Stakes at Royal Ascot. (op 11-2 tchd 15-2)

Baan(USA) was not beaten far into third in the Group 3 Sandown Classic Trial on his previous start, but that looked a weak race for the grade and he was no match for the front two here. He lacks size and things will not get any easier. (op 8-1)

Before You Go(IRE), winner of a Polytrack handicap off a mark of 82 before following up in the Blue Riband Trial at Epsom, would have found this much tougher and was well held. Still, he is probably a little better than he showed and can be given another chance on easier ground. (op 6-1)

Botteen, a Salisbury maiden winner on his final start at two, was really well regarded coming into this but sadly broke a leg and had to be put down. (tchd 7-4)

1669 TOTESCOOP6 OAKS TRIAL (LISTED RACE) (FILLIES) 1m 3f 106y
3:10 (3:12) (Class 1) 3-Y-O
£28,390 (£10,760; £5,385; £2,685; £1,345; £675) **Stalls** High

Form RPR

14 **1** **Sindirana (IRE)**[196] [6145] 3-8-10 88.................................. CSoumillon 5 95+
(Sir Michael Stoute) *lw: hld up in mid-div: hdwy to trck ldrs 1/2-way: wnt 2nd over 2f out: rdn to ld jst ins fnl f: carried rt: hld on* **7/4**[1]

1220 **2** *nk* **Fusili (IRE)**[3] [1583] 3-8-10 82.. NCallan 9 94
(N P Littmoden) *trckd ldrs: led 3f out: rallied wl whn hdd jst ins fnl f but edgd rt and jst hld* **20/1**

021 **3** *2 ½* **Summer's Eve**[18] [1214] 3-8-10 80.. DaneO'Neill 7 90+
(H Candy) *hld up: hdwy 2f out: rdn and styd on to go 3rd fnl f* **14/1**

3155 **4** *3 ½* **Cross Channel (USA)**[42] [827] 3-8-10 97................(b[1]) SteveDrowne 10 84
(E A L Dunlop) *s.i.s but ld after 1f: hdd 3f out: rdn and wknd 1f out* **10/1**[3]

41 **5** *¾* **Kassiopeia (IRE)**[14] [1283] 3-8-10 78................................ TonyCulhane 6 83
(M R Channon) *w'like: led for 1f: trckd ldr to over 2f out: rdn and wknd over 1f out* **15/2**[2]

2 **6** *1* **Nimra (USA)**[6] [1516] 3-8-10 .... KFallon 4 82
(G A Butler) *in rr and nvr nr to chal* **20/1**

0 **7** *½* **Wabra (USA)**[24] [1087] 3-8-10 .... TedDurcan 1 81
(C E Brittain) *mid-div: rdn 3f out: no hdwy after* **100/1**

2311 **8** *1 ¼* **Shortest Day**[10] [1423] 3-8-10 89.................................... RichardHughes 8 79
(Sir Michael Stoute) *lw: hld up: hung lft fr 2f out and nvr on terms* **7/4**[1]

0 **9** *4* **In On The Act (IRE)**[40] [850] 3-8-10 .... JohnEgan 2 72
(Jamie Poulton) *chsd ldrs tl rdn and wknd 2f out* **66/1**

33 **10** *shd* **Materialize (USA)**[16] [1260] 3-8-10 ....(p) ChrisCatlin 3 72
(P J McBride) *a bhd* **100/1**

2m 28.27s (-1.65) **Going Correction** +0.025s/f (Good) **10** Ran SP% **113.2**
Speed ratings (Par 104):107,106,104,102,101 101,100,99,96,96
CSF £44.09 TOTE £2.60: £1.10, £5.20, £3.50; EX 59.60 Trifecta £318.01 Pool: £752.85 - 1.68 winning units..

Owner H H Aga Khan **Bred** His Highness The Aga Khan's Studs S C **Trained** Newmarket, Suffolk

■ A big-race double for Christophe Soumillon following his success on Linda's Lad, on what was his first visit to Lingfield.

■ Stewards' Enquiry : N Callan two-day ban: used whip with excessive frequency and down the shoulder in the forehand position (May 24-25)

FOCUS
As likeable as Fusili is, she is some way short of an Oaks filly (as her rating of 82 suggests) and her proximity indicates this was a very weak trial for Epsom. Sindirana looked an Oaks type when winning on her debut, but has not yet progressed in the manner one might have hoped. She still looked quite green, however, and the winning time was nearly a second quicker than the colts half an hour earlier, despite the pace not appearing to be all that strong.

NOTEBOOK
Sindirana(IRE) looked a potential Oaks filly when winning on her debut at Leicester, but disappointed on soft ground in a Newmarket Listed race on her final start at two. Stepped up to middle distances and returned to better ground on her reappearance, she was made to work very hard to see off a filly rated just 82, and it was disappointing she could not stamp herself as a serious Oaks contender. There are positives, though, in that she still looked green under pressure and the winning time was good, but it will still be surprising were she to find enough improvement to play a hand in the finish at Epsom. (tchd 6-4 and 15-8 in a place)

Fusili(IRE), who did not get the run of things when upped to this class in the Cheshire Oaks just three days earlier, enjoyed a much better trip this time and ran a huge race. This was, though, the 20th start of her career and it is unlikely she has suddenly improved significantly, so her proximity strongly suggests this was a very soft race for the class. However, she is a very likeable little filly and her connections will be delighted to have picked up some black type.

Summer's Eve ◆ has not had the run of things so far this season - she hit the front too soon at Windsor on her reappearance and was then disqualified at Folkestone - but she is held in high regard and ran creditably to take third. She was probably given a bit too much to do, although in her rider's defence very few managed to get into this. Being a full-sister to Ascot Gold Cup winner Papineau, this black type was very valuable, but a win would furthest increase her paddock worth and she does appear to have more to offer. She ought to land a maiden before stepping back up in class. (tchd 16-1)

Cross Channel(USA), a beaten favourite in the Masaka Stakes on her reappearance, had blinkers fitted and was stepped up significantly in trip. She found little under pressure and either failed to stay or was not putting it in. She looks one to watch. (op 17-2 tchd 11-1)

Kassiopeia(IRE) failed to build on the form she showed when winning at Haydock on her reappearance. (op 7-1 tchd 8-1)

Shortest Day ran nowhere near the form she showed to win a Pontefract handicap off a mark of 89 on her reappearance and was a major disappointment. Official explanation: trainer said filly failed to come down hill and lost a shoe (op 9-4)

1670 TOTECOURSE TO COURSE MAIDEN STKS 1m 2f
3:40 (3:42) (Class 5) 3-Y-O+ **£3,886** (£1,156; £577; £288) **Stalls** Low

Form RPR

05 **1** **Alqaab (USA)**[11] [1374] 3-8-11 .... MartinDwyer 6 85
(M P Tregoning) *trckd ldrs: rdn and styd on to ld jst ins fnl f: pushed out* **8/1**[3]

2634 **2** *1 ½* **Areyoutalkingtome**[23] [1092] 3-8-11 100................................. NCallan 4 82
(C A Cyzer) *lw: t.k.h: led tl rdn and hdd jst ins fnl f: kpt on one pce* **10/11**[1]

3 **3** *4* **Montpellier (IRE)**[19] [1192] 3-8-11 .... TedDurcan 10 74
(E A L Dunlop) *w'like: gd-bodied: s.i.s: sn prom on outside: chsd ldr over 2f out tl wknd fnl f* **13/8**[2]

4 2 **Soubriquet (IRE)** 3-8-11 .... IanMongan 9 71+
(T G Mills) *w'like: bit bkwd: mid-div: hdwy 1/2-way: plugged on one pce fnl 2f* **20/1**

00 5 11 **Montage (IRE)**[285] [4006] 4-9-12 .... RobertHavlin 7 51
(J Akehurst) *bhd and nvr on terms* **100/1**

6 1 ½ **Secret Moment**[122] 4-9-9 .... AdamKirby(3) 3 48
(C G Cox) *leggy: mid-div but wknd 4f out and sn btn* **40/1**

4 7 5 **Volaire**[14] [1306] 4-9-4 .... RichardThomas(3) 2 33
(A J Lidderdale) *a bhd* **100/1**

00 8 7 **Kapiolani (USA)**[12] [1336] 3-8-6 .... JohnEgan 11 19
(J M P Eustace) *a in rr* **66/1**

0 9 4 **Crimson Year (USA)**[16] [1261] 4-9-7 .... MickyFenton 1 12
(C E Brittain) *w'like: lw: a bhd: lost tch 4f out* **100/1**

10 1 ¾ **Marlion (FR)**[26] 4-9-12 .... PaulDoe 8 14
(B R Johnson) *w'like: slowly away: a wl bhd* **100/1**

20 11 ¾ **Steady Rain**[78] [503] 4-9-7 .... RichardHughes 5 8
(P S McEntee) *trckd ldr tl rdn 3f out: wknd qckly* **50/1**

2m 8.29s (-1.43) **Going Correction** +0.025s/f (Good)
WFA 3 from 4yo 15lb **11 Ran SP% 116.2**
Speed ratings (Par 103):106,104,101,100,91 90,86,80,77,75 75
CSF £15.43 TOTE £8.60: £1.70, £1.10, £1.10; EX 17.60 Trifecta £18.10 Pool: £414.68 - 16.22 winning units..
Owner Hamdan Al Maktoum **Bred** London Thoroughbred Services Ltd **Trained** Lambourn, Berks

FOCUS
This maiden lacked strength in depth and they finished well strung out. Areyoutalkingtome has twice shown smart for in Group company, but this was also the second time he has failed to land the odds in maiden company. For the purposes of assessing this form, his lofty official rating should be ignored and the third is the best guide.
Crimson Year(USA) Official explanation: jockey said filly had a breathing problem
Steady Rain Official explanation: jockey said filly lost its action

1671 TOTEPOOL CHARTWELL FILLIES' STKS (GROUP 3) 7f
4:15 (4:16) (Class 1) 3-Y-0+
£28,390 (£10,760; £5,385; £2,685; £1,345; £675) **Stalls High**

Form RPR

2141 1 **Echelon**[230] [5492] 4-9-3 103 .... KFallon 7 104+
(Sir Michael Stoute) *lw: in tch: sn pushed along: swtchd lft over 1f out: led ins fnl f: in command cl home* **8/15**[1]

2400 2 1 **Chantilly Beauty (FR)**[202] [6053] 4-9-3 ....(b) TJarnet 4 100
(R Pritchard-Gordon, France) *w'like: trckd ldrs: rdn and wl hld over 1f out but rallied and burst through to go 2nd wl ins fnl f* **12/1**

1434 3 nk **Strut**[21] [1130] 3-8-5 101 .... SteveDrowne 3 96
(R Charlton) *lw: racd wd: chsd ldrs: effrt appr fnl f: kpt on* **7/1**[3]

0500 4 hd **Coconut Squeak**[14] [1287] 4-9-3 97 ....(v) MickyFenton 6 99
(Stef Liddiard) *led tl rdn and hdd over 1f out: no ex fnl stages* **33/1**

3046 5 shd **Shersha (IRE)**[13] [1325] 7-9-3 .... JohnEgan 2 99
(Kevin F O'Donnell, Ire) *trckd ldr: led briefly appr fnl f: no ex ins* **20/1**

3201 6 nk **Indian Maiden (IRE)**[11] [1377] 6-9-3 104 .... TedDurcan 5 98
(M S Saunders) *hld up: effrt over 1f out but nt pce to chal* **11/2**[2]

6010 7 1 ¼ **My Amalie (IRE)**[21] [1130] 3-8-5 95 .... MartinDwyer 1 91
(C E Brittain) *a in rr* **33/1**

6624 8 hd **Gamble In Gold (IRE)**[6] [1512] 3-8-6 90 ow1 .... NCallan 8 91
(R Hannon) *hld up: rdn over 1f out: nvr on terms* **25/1**

1m 21.75s (-2.46) **Going Correction** -0.10s/f (Good)
WFA 3 from 4yo+ 12lb **8 Ran SP% 115.3**
Speed ratings (Par 110):110,108,108,108,108 107,106,106
CSF £7.76 TOTE £1.60: £1.10, £2.40, £1.60; EX 9.10 Trifecta £42.20 Pool: £705.37 - 11.86 winning units..
Owner Cheveley Park Stud **Bred** Cheveley Park Stud Ltd **Trained** Newmarket, Suffolk

FOCUS
A weak Group 3 and there was only around three lengths separating the entire field at the line, despite them having gone what looked an even pace, and the form does look somewhat limited.

NOTEBOOK
Echelon, twice a winner in Listed company last season, was found a soft option for her return to Group company and duly outclassed her seven rivals. She was having to be niggled along by the former champion jockey from some way out, but never looked in any real danger and found plenty when asked to pick up. This was a nice starting point and she should have a good season in fillies/mares company. (op 8-11 tchd 4-5 in a place)
Chantilly Beauty(FR), a Listed winner in her native France last season, appeared to run right up to her best on her return from a 202-day break. (op 10-1)
Strut, fourth behind the subsequent 1000 Guineas third Nasheej in the Fred Darling on her reappearance, seemed to step up a little on that effort. She is running creditably, but in the longer term may turn out to be a sprinter. (op 5-1 tchd 15-2)
Coconut Squeak kept on well once headed and just missed out on a place. She should continue to go well in fillies/mares only company when allowed her own way. (op 40-1 tchd 25-1)
Shersha(IRE), a winner in Listed company in her native Ireland last year, ran a creditable race and was not beaten far. (op 22-1)
Indian Maiden(IRE), upped to seven furlongs for the first time, did not appear to stay. (op 5-1)

1672 LINGFIELD PARK TRIALS DAY H'CAP 6f
4:50 (4:50) (Class 4) (0-80,78) 3-Y-0 **£6,477** (£1,927; £963; £481) **Stalls High**

Form RPR

2220 1 **Didn't We (IRE)**[23] [1091] 3-9-3 77 ....(v) IanMongan 7 87
(T G Mills) *mde all: rdn out fnl f: a in control* **7/2**[2]

0562 2 1 ¾ **Burning Incense (IRE)**[18] [1218] 3-9-0 74 .... KFallon 1 79+
(R Charlton) *lw: hld up on outside: rdn over 1f out and r.o to go 2nd ins fnl f* **5/1**[3]

6421 3 ½ **Mannikko (IRE)**[11] [1378] 3-9-3 77 .... SteveDrowne 8 80
(G Wragg) *lw: a in tch: chsd wnr over 1f out tl ins fnl f* **11/4**[1]

5035 4 1 ¾ **Brunelleschi**[16] [1264] 3-9-4 78 .... JohnEgan 11 76
(P L Gilligan) *lw: prom: chaased ldr 1/2-way to over 1f out: no ex ins fnl f* **20/1**

3231 5 ½ **Pititana (IRE)**[9] [1430] 3-9-1 75 .... RichardHughes 5 72
(R Hannon) *hld up: swtchd lft over 1f out: kpt on but nvr a danger* **8/1**

310 6 1 ¾ **Nudrah**[218] [5716] 3-9-1 75 .... MartinDwyer 2 66+
(J L Dunlop) *outpcd: nvr nr to chal* **14/1**

0600 7 1 ½ **Bucharest**[12] [1337] 3-8-7 70 .... JohnMcAuley(3) 10 57
(M Wigham) *trckd wnr to 1/2-way: sn struggling and outpcd* **33/1**

14 8 nk **What Do You Know**[134] [6688] 3-9-2 76 .... NCallan 3 62
(G A Butler) *hld up: a bhd* **16/1**

4444 9 nk **Waddon (IRE)**[18] [1208] 3-8-8 71 ....(p) AdamKirby(3) 4 56
(C G Cox) *in tch to 1/2-way* **10/1**

0122 10 2 **Matterofact (IRE)**[216] [5755] 3-9-2 76 .... RobertHavlin 9 55
(Mrs P N Dutfield) *a bhd* **20/1**

0234 11 6 **Dasheena**[12] [1344] 3-7-13 64 oh2 .... NataliaGemelova(5) 6 25
(M J Polglase) *rcd wd: chsd ldrs to over 2f out* **25/1**

69.91 secs (-1.76) **Going Correction** -0.10s/f (Good) **11 Ran SP% 114.6**
Speed ratings (Par 101):107,104,104,101,101 98,96,96,95,93 85
CSF £19.50 CT £54.95 TOTE £4.90: £2.10, £1.70, £1.60; EX 19.90 Trifecta £17.80 Pool: £555.74 - 22.09 winning units..
Owner T G Mills **Bred** Mrs John McEnery **Trained** Headley, Surrey

FOCUS
A fair sprint handicap won in good style by Didn't We, who made all at a decent pace from the start. Improved form from the less-exposed second and third, but it can be expected to work out.
What Do You Know Official explanation: jockey said gelding suffered interference in running

1673 OCS GROUP LADIES H'CAP (LADY AMATEUR RIDERS) 7f
5:25 (5:25) (Class 5) (0-75,75) 4-Y-0+ **£3,123** (£968; £484; £242) **Stalls High**

Form RPR

2040 1 **Greenwood**[19] [1188] 8-10-1 69 .... MrsSMoore 14 79
(P G Murphy) *hld up: hdwy 2f out: r.o to ld post* **22/1**

5024 2 nk **Cusoon**[195] [6183] 4-9-11 70 .... MissHayleyMoore(5) 11 79
(G L Moore) *hld up: hdwy 2f out: r.o to go 2nd post* **25/1**

1 3 shd **Massaro Pape (IRE)**[20] [1165] 4-10-3 74 .... MrsSCumani(3) 7 83+
(L M Cumani) *lw: a.p: led 2f out: hdd and lost 2nd v nr fin* **11/10**[1]

0500 4 hd **Tiber Tiger (IRE)**[26] [1041] 6-9-8 62 ....(b) MrsEmmaLittmoden 12 71
(N P Littmoden) *hld up: hdwy over 2f out: r.o fnl f* **9/1**[3]

1534 5 1 **Arctic Desert**[37] [898] 6-10-0 73 .... MissMSowerby(5) 10 79
(A M Balding) *chsd ldrs: rdn 2f out: one pce fnl f* **8/1**[2]

1224 6 ½ **Meditation**[12] [1348] 4-9-10 64 .... MrsSBosley 4 69+
(I A Wood) *led far side gp thrght: kpt on one pce fnl f* **12/1**

0204 7 1 ½ **Banjo Bay (IRE)**[9] [1443] 8-9-0 61 oh1 .... MissNathalieNorgren(7) 16 62
(Miss Gay Kelleway) *a prom: hung bdly rt over 1f out and wknd fnl f* **33/1**

0032 8 1 ¼ **Taranaki**[15] [1273] 8-9-7 61 oh2 .... MissSBrotherton 2 59+
(P D Cundell) *chsd far side ldr: no ch fnl 2f* **14/1**

3250 9 1 **Billy One Punch**[22] [1124] 4-9-4 65 .... MissKMargarson(7) 15 60
(G G Margarson) *w ldrs: rdn 2f out: sn wknd* **33/1**

2150 10 ½ **Scuba (IRE)**[11] [1383] 4-9-1 62 oh1 ow1 ....(v) MissVCartmel(7) 9 56
(H Morrison) *led tl hdd & wknd 2f out* **20/1**

5064 11 ½ **Full Of Zest**[20] [1163] 4-9-0 61 oh1 ....(b) MissLauraGray(7) 13 53
(Mrs L J Mongan) *in rr: wnt into centre of crse 1/2-way: nvr on terms* **66/1**

331 12 1 **Toffee Vodka (IRE)**[279] [4189] 4-10-7 75 .... MissEJJones 8 65
(J W Hills) *t.k.h: prom: rdn 2f out: sn wknd* **14/1**

0006 13 1 ½ **Jubilee Dream**[13] [1313] 4-9-3 64 oh6 ow3 ....(t) MissSSawyer(7) 18 50
(Mrs L J Mongan) *a bhd* **100/1**

1035 14 ¾ **What-A-Dancer (IRE)**[15] [1275] 9-9-9 68 ....(p) MrsMarieKing(5) 5 52
(D J S Ffrench Davis) *rrd up s: a bhd* **20/1**

0616 15 shd **Danger Zone**[75] [530] 4-10-0 71 .... MrsLucindaCrowley(3) 17 55
(Mrs A J Perrett) *prom on stands side tl wknd over 2f out* **16/1**

4012 16 3 ½ **Undeterred**[14] [1302] 10-10-3 74 .... MissEALalor(3) 6 49
(K J Burke) *racd far side: a bhd* **12/1**

0000 17 2 ½ **Hey Presto**[17] [1245] 6-9-6 65 .... MissJFerguson(5) 1 33
(R Rowe) *racd far side: bhd fnl 2f* **66/1**

0000 18 6 **Silver Visage (IRE)**[14] [1303] 4-9-7 61 oh9 ....(p) MrsACooke 3 13
(Miss J Feilden) *racd far side: wl bhd fr 1/2-way* **100/1**

1m 23.3s (-3.11) **Going Correction** -0.10s/f (Good) **18 Ran SP% 131.9**
Speed ratings (Par 103):101,100,100,100,99 98,96,95,94,93 93,92,90,89,89 85,82,75
CSF £489.78 CT £1170.71 TOTE £40.40: £7.20, £4.70, £1.10, £2.30; EX 430.40 TRIFECTA Not won. Place 6 £19.39, Place 5 £3.35.
Owner The Golden Anorak Partnership **Bred** Britton House Stud And C Gregson **Trained** East Garston, Berks

FOCUS
A modest but highly competitive amateur riders' handicap. The field split into two distinct groups early on, with five horses staying far side and the remainder racing stands' side, but they were spread all over the place at the finish. Those that raced stands' side from the start appeared to be at an advantage and the winner and fifth set the standard for the form.
T/Plt: £64.50 to a £1 stake. Pool: £77,100.20. 871.80 winning tickets. T/Qpdt: £3.80 to a £1 stake. Pool: £4,429.10. 859.30 winning tickets. JS

1505 NEWMARKET (ROWLEY) (R-H)
Saturday, May 13

OFFICIAL GOING: Good
Wind: Fresh, behind Weather: Overcast

1674 PLAY ONLINE AT 32RED MAIDEN STKS (DIV I) 1m
1:25 (1:29) (Class 5) 3-Y-0 **£4,857** (£1,445; £722; £360) **Stalls High**

Form RPR

1 **Bold Alaska (IRE)** 3-9-3 .... RichardMullen 3 85
(E A L Dunlop) *racd centre: s.i.s: hld up: hdwy over 3f out: overall ldr over 1f out: r.o* **33/1**

0 2 1 ¾ **Smart Enough**[211] [5870] 3-9-3 .... EddieAhern 14 81
(M A Magnusson) *racd far side: led that trio over 4f out: rdn and ev ch over 1f out: one pce ins fnl f: 1st of 3 that side* **7/2**[2]

2 3 1 ¾ **Minister Of State**[24] [1088] 3-9-3 .... PhilipRobinson 6 77
(M A Jarvis) *led and overall ldr in centre: hung lft and hdd over 1f out: styd on same pce: 2nd of 8 in gp* **4/6**[1]

4 ½ **Marbaa (IRE)** 3-9-3 .... RHills 2 76
(E A L Dunlop) *racd centre: dwlt: hld up: hdwy over 2f out: styd on: 3rd of 8 in gp* **16/1**

5 nk **Avelian (IRE)** 3-9-3 .... NickyMackay 10 75
(W J Haggas) *racd centre: hld up in tch: effrt over 2f out: styd on: 4th of 8 in gp* **25/1**

0 6 3 ½ **Nassar (IRE)**[26] [1055] 3-8-10 .... KirstyMilczarek(7) 4 67
(G Prodromou) *chsd ldr centre over 5f: wknd fnl f: 5th of 8 in gp* **66/1**

7 3 ½ **Salonga (IRE)** 3-8-12 .... RyanMoore 1 54
(C F Wall) *racd centre: chsd ldrs: rdn 1/2-way: sn outpcd: 6th of 8 in gp* **50/1**

0 8 1 **Convallaria (FR)**[24] [1085] 3-8-12 .... AlanMunro 13 52
(G Wragg) *racd far side: hld up: hdwy to chse ldr over 2f out: wknd over 1f out: 2nd of 3 in gp* **50/1**

9 1 **Bedizen** 3-9-3 .... KerrinMcEvoy 5 54
(Sir Michael Stoute) *racd centre: chsd ldrs: rdn over 2f out: wknd over 1f out: 7th of 8 in gp* **8/1**[3]

0 10 8 **Florida Legend (IRE)**[260] [4717] 3-8-7 .... JamesDoyle(5) 12 31
(Miss J Feilden) *led far side over 3f: wknd over 2f out: last of 3 in gp* **66/1**

11 *27* **Pelican Hill (IRE)** 3-9-3 .... DO'Donohoe 9 —
(T H Caldwell) *s.s: racd centre: outpcd: last of 8 in gp* **100/1**

1m 38.0s (-1.37) **Going Correction** +0.05s/f (Good) **11** Ran SP% **113.9**
Speed ratings (Par 99):108,106,104,104,103 100,96,95,94,86 59
CSF £139.27 TOTE £26.70: £5.20, £1.40, £1.10; EX 210.30.
Owner Gainsborough Stud **Bred** Michael Boland **Trained** Newmarket, Suffolk

FOCUS
The field split into two, with eight including the winner racing down the centre and the other three, headed by the runner-up, going down the far side. This was run a second faster than division two and looks good maiden form.

1675 BET ON 32RED EBF MAIDEN FILLIES' STKS 5f
1:55 (1:55) (Class 4) 2-Y-O **£4,533** (£1,348; £674; £336) **Stalls** High

Form RPR

1 **Bahama Mama (IRE)** 2-9-0 .... DarryllHolland 3 80+
(J Noseda) *dwlt: hdwy over 3f out: hung rt over 1f out: r.o wl to ld nr fin* **15/2**

2 *hd* **Bicoastal (USA)** 2-9-0 .... JimmyFortune 4 79
(B J Meehan) *chsd ldrs: rdn 1/2-way: outpcd over 1f out: r.o wl ins fnl f* **10/3**[2]

0 3 *½* **Bridge It Jo**[24] 1082 2-8-9 .... JamesDoyle[(5)] 9 77
(Miss J Feilden) *plld hrd and prom: led over 1f out: hung lft ins fnl f: hdd nr fin* **25/1**

2 4 *3* **Tarkamara (IRE)**[24] 1082 2-9-0 .... JoeFanning 7 67
(P F I Cole) *led: rdn, hung lft and hdd over 1f out: wknd ins fnl f* **7/4**[1]

5 *1 ½* **Duskiness (FR)** 2-9-0 .... JamieSpencer 5 61
(M J Wallace) *chsd ldr: rdn and nt clr run over 1f out: wknd ins fnl f* **8/1**

0 6 *3 ½* **Absent Love**[19] 1181 2-9-0 .... BrianReilly 6 49
(G G Margarson) *mid-div: rdn 1/2-way: sn wknd* **66/1**

7 *¾* **Grand Lucre** 2-9-0 .... RichardMullen 2 46
(E J O'Neill) *dwlt: outpcd* **12/1**

8 *5* **Dubai's Fairy** 2-9-0 .... RyanMoore 8 28
(R Hannon) *s.i.s: wknd 3f out* **11/2**[3]

9 *13* **Hessian (IRE)** 2-9-0 .... HayleyTurner 1 —
(M L W Bell) *s.s: outpcd* **25/1**

60.15 secs (-0.32) **Going Correction** +0.05s/f (Good) **9** Ran SP% **114.6**
Speed ratings (Par 92):95,94,93,89,86 81,79,71,51
CSF £31.94 TOTE £8.00: £2.40, £1.70, £5.40; EX 38.90.
Owner Lucayan Stud **Bred** C J Foy **Trained** Newmarket, Suffolk

FOCUS
A tricky race to assess, with the favourite below form and several of these showing quirks and/or inexperience.

NOTEBOOK
Bahama Mama(IRE) is a half-sister to several winners at between six and ten furlongs. Running distinctly green on her debut, she was hanging to her right inside the last but the two fillies in front of her were hanging left and she ran on to snatch the race near the line. There should be improvement in her. (op 7-1)
Bicoastal(USA), a $425,000 yearling out of a Grade 3 winner, represents the stable of last year's winner Donna Blini and holds an entry in the Group 1 Phoenix Stakes. She became a little outpaced by the leaders and was only fifth passing the furlong pole, but came through with the winner as those in front faltered. She will have learned a good deal from this. (op 7-2 tchd 4-1 in places)
Bridge It Jo obviously has ability but is a hard ride. After failing to settle early on, she seemed set to score when showing ahead only to hang badly to her left inside the last and throw it away. (op 20-1)
Tarkamara(IRE), who made a promising debut at the Craven meeting, tried to make all but began to hang when challenged and put up little resistance. She is one to be wary of on this evidence. (op 6-4 tchd 15-8 in places)
Duskiness(FR), first foal of a dual winner in France, showed pace behind the leaders before weakening inside the last. (op 9-1)
Dubai's Fairy, a half-sister to the high-class but quirky Just James, who was best at seven furlongs, started slowly and was soon trailing on this debut. (op 7-1 tchd 15-2 in places)

1676 32RED.COM H'CAP 1m
2:25 (2:25) (Class 3) (0-95,92) 4-Y-0+ **£9,067** (£2,697; £1,348; £673) **Stalls** High

Form RPR

1211 1 **Fajr (IRE)**[10] 1410 4-8-6 **80** .... JimmyQuinn 2 86+
(Miss Gay Kelleway) *hld up: hdwy to ld over 1f out: hung left ins fnl f: rdn out* **4/1**[2]

24 2 *hd* **Putra Kuantan**[248] 5052 6-9-1 **89** .... PhilipRobinson 3 95
(M A Jarvis) *hld up: hdwy over 1f out: r.o* **7/1**[3]

5020 3 *shd* **Skidrow**[21] 1129 4-9-1 **89** .... HayleyTurner 4 95
(M L W Bell) *chsd ldrs: rdn and hung rt over 1f out: r.o* **9/1**

6504 4 *¾* **Indian Steppes (FR)**[56] 667 7-8-11 **85** .... EddieAhern 6 90+
(P S McEntee) *hld up: nt clr run fr over 1f out tl swtchd lft ins fnl f: r.o: nvr able to chal* **25/1**

1050 5 *½* **Wigwam Willie (IRE)**[21] 1143 4-8-8 **82** ....(b[1]) DO'Donohoe 9 85
(K A Ryan) *chsd ldrs: rdn over 1f out: styd on same pce ins fnl f* **11/1**

5060 6 *½* **Ettrick Water**[211] 5876 7-9-3 **91** ....(v) NickyMackay 7 93
(L M Cumani) *racd keenly: led over 6f out: rdn and hdd over 1f out: styd on same pce* **8/1**

0625 7 *hd* **Norton (IRE)**[245] 5116 9-9-4 **92** .... JimmyFortune 1 93
(T G Mills) *w ldr: rdn over 2f out: btn whn hmpd ins fnl f* **12/1**

1112 8 *shd* **Hail The Chief**[14] 1301 9-9-0 **88** .... RyanMoore 5 89
(R Hannon) *led: hdd over 6f out: chsd ldrs: rdn and nt clr run over 1f out: swtchd rt and styd on same pce* **13/8**[1]

1m 37.95s (-1.42) **Going Correction** +0.05s/f (Good) **8** Ran SP% **111.6**
Speed ratings (Par 107):109,108,108,107,107 106,106,106
CSF £30.25 CT £229.87 TOTE £4.80: £1.70, £2.30, £2.40; EX 33.30 Trifecta £345.50 Part won. Pool: £486.66 - 0.80 winning units..
Owner The New Dawn Partnership **Bred** Shadwell Estate Company Limited **Trained** Exning, Suffolk

FOCUS
The field raced a little away from the rail. There was not much pace on and it resulted in a bunch finish, with the whole field separated by not much more than two lengths. The second and third have been rated to last year's best but the form is unconvincing.

NOTEBOOK
Fajr(IRE) ◆, last seen on turf back in October, has since proved a real success story on Polytrack. From a mark 4lb higher than when winning at Lingfield earlier in the month, he was held up on the outer of the bunch. Making good headway to show in front, he idled under pressure but was always holding on. He should be even more effective on fast ground and should be kept on the right side. (op 7-2 tchd 9-2)
Putra Kuantan, who has been gelded and has undergone a wind operation since last year, was without the cheekpieces. Running on strongly from the back of the field but just held, he will be suited by the return to ten furlongs. (tchd 15-2)
Skidrow, in midfield in the Newbury Spring Cup on his reappearance, ran a solid race on ground that suited but could not quite force his head in front.
Indian Steppes(FR) ◆, tackling a mile for the first time since 2002, was having her first start for this trainer having run just once for Lucinda Featherstone. Ridden to get the trip and as a result meeting with traffic problems, she came home well once in the clear and is capable of landing a similar race. (op 16-1)
Wigwam Willie(IRE), in blinkers for the first time and returning to a mile, ran his race with no obvious excuses. (op 10-1)
Ettrick Water, now 3lb lower than when last successful, showed plenty of zest on this reappearance and should come on for the outing. (op 9-1 tchd 15-2)
Norton(IRE) was taken on for the lead and eventually faded inside the last. He remains high enough in the weights. (op 11-1)
Hail The Chief, 3lb higher, soon lost his early lead but continued to race prominently. Shuffled back with two furlongs to run, he was forced to switch around the pack and could not counter. Although finishing last, he was not beaten far and this was just one of those days. (op 7-4 tchd 2-1)

1677 32RED POKER CONDITIONS STKS 1m 4f
2:55 (2:59) (Class 2) 4-Y-0+
£12,464 (£3,732; £1,866; £934; £466; £234) **Stalls** High

Form RPR

1026 1 **Admiral's Cruise (USA)**[15] 1267 4-8-13 97 .... JimmyFortune 6 113+
(B J Meehan) *chsd ldr: led 2f out: r.o wl* **4/1**

5362 2 *3* **Palomar (USA)**[14] 1298 4-8-13 102 .... RyanMoore 2 107
(R Charlton) *trckd ldrs: racd keenly: led 3f out: rdn and hdd 2f out: styd on same pce fnl f* **10/3**[2]

0-00 3 *5* **Asian Heights**[225] 5589 8-8-10 105 .... DarryllHolland 1 96
(G Wragg) *sn pushed along in rr: hdwy over 2f out: hung rt over 1f out: wknd fnl f* **12/1**

6241 4 *2 ½* **Balkan Knight**[252] 4939 6-8-10 103 .... LPKeniry 4 92
(D R C Elsworth) *chsd ldrs: rdn over 2f out: wknd over 1f out* **2/1**[1]

2212 5 *6* **Foreign Affairs**[216] 5781 8-9-3 105 .... JamieMackay 5 89
(Sir Mark Prescott) *led: rdn and hdd 3f out: wknd 2f out* **7/2**[3]

323 6 *½* **Feed The Meter (IRE)**[5] 1544 6-8-5 75 .... JimmyQuinn 3 77
(J Ryan) *s.s: hld up: wknd over 2f out* **25/1**

2m 31.86s (-1.64) **Going Correction** +0.05s/f (Good) **6** Ran SP% **110.2**
Speed ratings (Par 109):107,105,101,100,96 95
CSF £16.89 TOTE £5.40: £2.50, £2.40; EX 20.20.
Owner Joe L Allbritton **Bred** Lazy Lane Stables Inc **Trained** Manton, Wilts

FOCUS
Decent form for the grade, the winner impressive, although the form is not rock solid with the runner-up the only other to run his race.

NOTEBOOK
Admiral's Cruise(USA), found wanting in a Group 3 last time, was down to a more suitable level but tackling 12 furlongs for the first time. After challenging going well, he was ridden clear in the final furlong to score with something in hand. He should be a force in Listed races at this trip. (tchd 9-2)
Palomar(USA), reported by his trainer to have been unsuited by the course at Ripon, travelled strongly before taking it up, but he did not last long in front and edged over to the rail when headed by the winner. A return to further might help. (op 7-2 tchd 3-1)
Asian Heights has been lightly raced and well beaten since landing the Ormonde Stakes at Chester three years ago and this was little more encouraging, although he is not going to be easy to place. (tchd 10-1)
Balkan Knight, who had a fine campaign in handicaps last year, might have found this trip too sharp on his seasonal bow. (op 9-4 tchd 11-4)
Foreign Affairs was fit for this seasonal debut - he is the yard's lead horse - but he sweated up beforehand. Attempting to concede weight to all his rivals, he tried to make all but was unable to put up much resistance when headed. (op 3-1 tchd 4-1)
Feed The Meter(IRE) was out of her depth. (tchd 16-1 and 28-1)

1678 32RED ONLINE CASINO SUFFOLK STKS (HERITAGE H'CAP) 1m 1f
3:30 (3:32) (Class 2) 3-Y-0+
£31,160 (£9,330; £4,665; £2,335; £1,165; £585) **Stalls** High

Form RPR

1210 1 **Star Of Light**[224] 5607 5-8-11 **93** .... AlanMunro 17 104
(B J Meehan) *hld up in tch: rdn to ld ins fnl f: r.o* **9/1**

4006 2 *½* **Look Again**[14] 1301 5-8-2 **84** .... RoystonFfrench 9 94+
(R A Fahey) *s.i.s: hld up: nt clr run over 2f out: hdwy over 1f out : n.m.r ins fnl f: r.o wl* **10/1**

2620 3 *1* **Langford**[224] 5607 6-9-0 **96** .... MichaelHills 11 104
(M H Tompkins) *hld up: hdwy over 1f out: hung lft ins fnl f: r.o* **33/1**

3121 4 *shd* **Akona Matata (USA)**[16] 1262 4-8-8 **90** .... KerrinMcEvoy 14 98
(C E Brittain) *a.p: chsd ldr over 3f out: led over 2f out: rdn and hdd ins fnl f: unable qckn* **10/1**

3003 5 *½* **My Paris**[7] 1479 5-9-6 **102** .... DO'Donohoe 13 109
(K A Ryan) *led over 6f: rdn over 1f out: styd on* **16/1**

1302 6 *½* **Great Plains**[206] 5989 4-8-8 **90** .... DarryllHolland 6 96
(Mrs A J Perrett) *hld up: hdwy and hung rt over 1f out: styd on* **16/1**

1050 7 *¾* **Ace Of Hearts**[21] 1129 7-9-6 **102** .... EddieAhern 2 106
(C F Wall) *hld up: hdwy over 3f out: rdn whn carried rt and nt clr run over 1f out: styd on ins fnl f* **25/1**

5000 8 *shd* **Johnny Jumpup (IRE)**[34] 930 4-8-12 **97** .... NelsonDeSouza[(3)] 8 101
(R M Beckett) *hld up: hdwy over 1f out: styd on* **40/1**

0450 9 *hd* **Audience**[21] 1129 6-8-5 **87** ....(p) JimmyQuinn 1 91
(J Akehurst) *hld up: hdwy 2f out: sn rdn and edgd rt: styd on same pce* **18/1**

2115 10 *shd* **Cashier**[14] 1301 4-9-3 **99** .... JimmyFortune 10 103
(J H M Gosden) *chsd ldrs: rdn over 1f out: no ex fnl f* **6/1**[2]

1503 11 *shd* **Tanzanite (IRE)**[14] 1301 4-8-5 **87** .... TQuinn 4 92+
(D W P Arbuthnot) *trckd ldrs: racd keenly: rdn over 1f out: eased whn btn nr fin* **14/1**

4251 12 *¾* **Tabadul (IRE)**[11] 1380 5-8-8 **90** .... RHills 12 92+
(E A L Dunlop) *hld up: nt clr run over 2f out: rdn over 1f out: nvr trbld ldrs* **9/2**[1]

4020 13 *1* **Royal Island (IRE)**[28] 1017 4-9-7 **103** .... JoeFanning 16 105+
(M Johnston) *chsd ldrs: rdn over 2f out: btn whn hmpd ins fnl f* **20/1**

1654 14 *¾* **Bravo Maestro (USA)**[28] 1017 5-8-8 **95** .... JamesDoyle[(5)] 15 93
(N P Littmoden) *mid-div: rdn over 2f out: sn wknd* **20/1**

0400 15 *nk* **Spanish Don**[24] 1084 8-9-1 **97** .... LPKeniry 3 95
(D R C Elsworth) *chsd ldrs 7f* **22/1**

0512 16 *1 ¾* **Prince Samos (IRE)**[14] 1281 4-8-5 **87** .... RyanMoore 5 81
(R Hannon) *hld up: rdn over 2f out: sn wknd* **12/1**

5313 **17** 3/4 **St Andrews (IRE)**[10] 1407 6-9-10 **106**.......................... PhilipRobinson 7 99
(M A Jarvis) *hld up: effrt over 2f out: wknd over 1f out* **13/2**[3]

1m 50.26s (-1.69) **Going Correction** +0.05s/f (Good) **17** Ran SP% **128.5**
Speed ratings (Par 109):109,108,107,107,107 106,106,105,105,105 105,104,104,103,103 101,100
CSF £91.46 CT £2984.49 TOTE £12.20: £2.70, £2.50, £9.90, £2.50; EX 125.10 Trifecta £3828.00 Pool: £43,133.34 - 8.00 winning units..
Owner J H Widdows **Bred** J H Widdows **Trained** Manton, Wilts

FOCUS
A fiercely competitive handicap and the form should work out, although it is not as strong as it might have been.

NOTEBOOK
Star Of Light went into this fairly weighted, being only 4lb higher than when landing another Heritage Handicap at Newbury in the autumn. Racing on the outer of the pack, he came under pressure with two to run and got on top inside the last. Connections have ambitious plans for him which include a possible tilt at the Arlington Million in August. (op 12-1)
Look Again ◆, at the back of the field when hampered with over two furlongs to run, weaved his way through inside the last and flew home, but just too late. Things have not gone his way this season and he can find compensation even after he is reassessed. (op 9-1)
Langford made a very pleasing return and was running on at the death. He is higher in the weights than he has ever been but there could be a decent handicap in him.
Akona Matata(USA), 6lb higher than at Yarmouth, travelled strongly on the heels of the leader before going on plenty soon enough over this longer trip. Only collared inside the last, he was relegated two more places near the line. (op 11-1 tchd 12-1)
My Paris, 3lb lower than when third over course and distance in the autumn, was soon in front and kept on willingly when headed.
Great Plains did not look wholly straightforward but was doing some decent late work. He is lightly raced and there is further improvement in him.
Ace Of Hearts has been held from this mark four times now, and can do with dropping a pound or two. He will also appreciate genuine fast ground. (op 20-1)
Johnny Jumpup(IRE) had finished last on his latest three starts, and this ease in grade produced a more encouraging run. He appeared to get this longer trip. (op 33-1)
Tabadul(IRE), 6lb higher than at Kempton, was looking for room when trying to improve from out of the pack with over two furlongs to run. When free, he failed to pick up anything like well enough. (op 11-2)
St Andrews(IRE) Official explanation: jockey said horse was unsuited by the good ground

1679 32RED CASINO AND POKER ROOM H'CAP 5f
4:05 (4:06) (Class 4) (0-80,77) 3-Y-O **£5,505** (£1,637; £818; £408) **Stalls** High

Form				RPR
0144	**1**		**Rochdale**[23] 1097 3-9-4 **77**.......... PhilipRobinson 7 (M A Jarvis) *chsd ldrs: led 1f out: rdn out* **7/4**[1]	89+
3314	**2**	1	**Woodnook**[16] 1264 3-9-0 **73**.......... AlanMunro 3 (J A R Toller) *s.i.s: hdwy 1/2-way: rdn over 1f out: r.o* **6/1**[3]	80
015	**3**	nk	**Blue Aura (IRE)**[18] 1208 3-9-2 **75**.......... RyanMoore 5 (R Charlton) *prom: rdn and edgd lft over 2f out: r.o* **9/2**[2]	81
0015	**4**	1	**Overwing (IRE)**[115] 136 3-8-12 **71**.......... EddieAhern 9 (R M H Cowell) *trckd ldrs: rdn over 1f out: r.o* **20/1**	73
644	**5**	nk	**Yellow Card**[175] 6374 3-8-11 **70**.......... JimmyFortune 6 (N A Callaghan) *hld up: swtchd lft over 1f out: r.o ins fnl f: nvr nr to chal* **12/1**	71+
3230	**6**	1/2	**Don't Tell Sue**[18] 1208 3-8-13 **72**.......... MichaelHills 10 (B W Hills) *disp ld tl led over 1f out: sn rdn and hdd: no ex ins fnl f* **9/1**	71
6040	**7**	3/4	**Ochre Bay**[23] 1097 3-8-10 **76**.......... RussellKennemore(7) 1 (R Hollinshead) *s.i.s: outpcd: styd on ins fnl f: nvr trbld ldrs* **25/1**	72
2250	**8**	hd	**Hits Only Jude (IRE)**[19] 1183 3-9-2 **75**.......... JimmyQuinn 8 (J Pearce) *hld up: nvr nr to chal* **28/1**	71
0240	**9**	1	**Gwilym (GER)**[18] 1208 3-9-0 **73**.......... JamieSpencer 2 (D Haydn Jones) *hld up: hdwy and hung rt 1/2-way: wknd fnl f* **11/1**	65
6100	**10**	1/2	**Xaluna Bay (IRE)**[18] 1208 3-8-13 **72**.......... DarryllHolland 11 (W R Muir) *disp ld over 3f: wknd ins fnl f* **12/1**	62
4050	**11**	nk	**Tiber Tilly**[148] 6591 3-8-11 **75**.......... JamesDoyle(5) 4 (N P Littmoden) *hld up: hdwy and hmpd 1/2-way: sn lost pl: n.d after* **20/1**	64

59.39 secs (-1.08) **Going Correction** +0.05s/f (Good) **11** Ran SP% **119.4**
Speed ratings (Par 101):101,99,98,97,96 96,94,94,92,92 91
CSF £11.55 CT £42.38 TOTE £2.60: £1.60, £1.90, £2.00; EX 14.80.
Owner Jumeirah Racing **Bred** R F And S D Knipe **Trained** Newmarket, Suffolk

FOCUS
A fair handicap in which the winner was a bit more convincing than the bare margin. The fourth and sixth are fair guides to the form.
Yellow Card Official explanation: jockey said gelding moved poorly throughout
Gwilym(GER) Official explanation: jockey said colt never travelled

1680 PLAY ONLINE AT 32RED MAIDEN STKS (DIV II) 1m
4:40 (4:43) (Class 5) 3-Y-O **£4,857** (£1,445; £722; £360) **Stalls** High

Form				RPR
02	**1**		**Supaseus**[204] 6013 3-9-3.......... JimmyFortune 5 (H Morrison) *s.i.s and hmpd s: plld hrd and sn w ldr: led 3f out: rdn and hdd over 1f out: rallied to ld post* **9/4**[1]	78
43	**2**	hd	**Incidentally (IRE)**[21] 1134 3-9-3.......... RyanMoore 11 (R Hannon) *led 5f: rdn to ld ins fnl f: hdd post* **11/4**[2]	78
305	**3**	3/4	**Hill Spirit**[22] 1115 3-9-3 75.......... LPKeniry 8 (D R C Elsworth) *chsd ldrs: led over 1f out: hdd and unable qckn ins fnl f* **9/2**[3]	76
4	**4**	2	**Archiestown (USA)**[24] 1087 3-9-3.......... TQuinn 13 (J L Dunlop) *hld up: hdwy over 3f out: rdn and edgd lft 2f out: styd on same pce fnl f* **6/1**	71
	5	1/2	**Stumped** 3-9-3..........(t) MichaelHills 7 (W J Haggas) *hld up: outpcd over 2f out: r.o ins fnl f: nrst fin* **33/1**	70+
	6	1	**Benandonner (USA)** 3-9-3.......... JamieSpencer 2 (E A L Dunlop) *hld up: hdwy over 3f out: rdn and hung rt over 1f out: styd on same pce* **10/1**	68
	7	1	**Disco Ball** 3-8-12.......... AlanMunro 10 (G Wragg) *mid-div: rdn over 2f out: styd on same pce appr fnl f* **33/1**	61
00	**8**	1/2	**Prince Zafonic**[25] 1065 3-9-3.......... DarryllHolland 6 (W Jarvis) *prom over 6f* **66/1**	65
	9	4	**Mathoor** 3-9-3.......... RHills 12 (Sir Michael Stoute) *hld up: hdwy 5f out: wkng whn hmpd 2f out* **12/1**	55+
0	**10**	6	**Mozie Cat (IRE)**[24] 1085 3-8-12.......... JamieMackay 3 (D J Daly) *hld up: plld hrd: wknd over 2f out* **66/1**	37
	11	1	**Saratoga** 3-8-10.......... JamieHamblett(7) 1 (Sir Michael Stoute) *prom over 5f* **25/1**	39

1m 39.05s (-0.32) **Going Correction** +0.05s/f (Good) **44** Ran SP% **119.4**
Speed ratings (Par 99):103,102,102,100,99 98,97,97,93,87 86
CSF £8.29 TOTE £3.20: £1.50, £1.40, £2.20; EX 11.70.
Owner Ben & Sir Martyn Arbib **Bred** Arbib Bloodstock Partnership **Trained** East Ilsley, Berks
■ Stewards' Enquiry : L P Keniry one-day ban: careless riding (May 24)

FOCUS
This was not as strongly run as the first division and the proximity of the third suggests the form is nothing out of the ordinary, the first two not having run to their previous form.

1681 32RED ONLINE POKER ROOM H'CAP 1m
5:15 (5:17) (Class 5) (0-75,80) 3-Y-O **£3,886** (£1,156; £577; £288) **Stalls** High

Form				RPR
6022	**1**		**Plum Pudding (IRE)**[5] 1547 3-9-9 **80**.......... RyanMoore 11 (R Hannon) *chsd ldr: led over 2f out: clr over 1f out: rdn out* **5/2**[1]	95
0010	**2**	5	**Malech (IRE)**[9] 1444 3-9-1 **72**.......... DarryllHolland 16 (M L W Bell) *a.p: rdn to chse wnr 2f out: edgd rt over 1f out: styd on same pce* **14/1**	75
5300	**3**	hd	**Night Cru**[14] 1291 3-8-9 **66**.......... KerrinMcEvoy 17 (C F Wall) *hld up: hdwy over 2f out: swtchd lft ins fnl f: styd on* **14/1**	69
032	**4**	shd	**Ebert**[201] 6072 3-9-2 **73**.......... JimmyFortune 9 (P J Makin) *chsd ldrs: rdn and hung rt over 1f out: styd on same pce* **25/1**	76
0440	**5**	2 1/2	**Summer Lodge**[14] 1291 3-8-13 **70**.......... MichaelHills 15 (M H Tompkins) *mid-div: outpcd 3f out: styd on ins fnl f* **25/1**	67
042	**6**	3/4	**Captain Xaar (FR)**[15] 1274 3-9-0 **71**.......... JamieSpencer 10 (J R Fanshawe) *hld up: hdwy over 3f out: rdn over 1f out: wknd ins fnl f* **11/4**[2]	69+
006	**7**	1 3/4	**Madame Medusa (IRE)**[23] 1094 3-8-11 **75**.......... RonanKeogh(7) 13 (J A R Toller) *chsd ldrs: rdn over 2f out: hung rt and wknd over 1f out* **25/1**	66
0400	**8**	1 3/4	**Possessed**[40] 855 3-8-9 **66**.......... NickyMackay 12 (T D McCarthy) *hld up: hdwy over 3f out: rdn and wknd over 1f out* **50/1**	53
2451	**9**	9	**Luckylover**[10] 1416 3-8-9 **71**.......... JerryO'Dwyer(5) 2 (M G Quinlan) *hld up: hdwy and hung rt over 2f out: sn wknd* **12/1**	38
6201	**10**	3 1/2	**Magical Music**[14] 1307 3-9-2 **73**.......... JimmyQuinn 3 (J Pearce) *hld up: nvr trbld ldrs* **16/1**	31
606	**11**	nk	**Height Of Fury (IRE)**[214] 5817 3-9-2 **73**.......... TQuinn 7 (J L Dunlop) *s.i.s: hld up: bhd fnl 3f* **8/1**[3]	31
2050	**12**	1/2	**Golden Alchemist**[22] 1122 3-9-3 **74**.......... HayleyTurner 1 (M D I Usher) *hld up: rdn over 3f out: sn wknd* **28/1**	31
006	**13**	nk	**Lennoxtown (IRE)**[16] 1252 3-8-8 **65**..........(b[1]) PhilipRobinson 14 (M A Jarvis) *led over 5f: hung rt and wknd over 1f out* **25/1**	21
0300	**14**	nk	**Mystic Roll**[19] 1190 3-9-2 **73**.......... LPKeniry 8 (B J Meehan) *prom: rdn over 2f out: sn wknd* **20/1**	28
0006	**15**	1 3/4	**Chris Corsa**[23] 1099 3-9-0 **71**.......... JamieMackay 4 (M L W Bell) *bhd fnl 3f* **25/1**	22
2220	**16**	hd	**Cloud Atlas (IRE)**[12] 1337 3-9-3 **74**.......... OscarUrbina 5 (S Kirk) *mid-div: rdn and hung rt over 2f out: sn wknd* **25/1**	25

1m 38.09s (-1.28) **Going Correction** +0.05s/f (Good) **16** Ran SP% **126.5**
Speed ratings (Par 99):108,103,102,102,100 99,97,95,86,83 83,82,82,82,80 80
CSF £34.14 CT £439.01 TOTE £3.30: £1.10, £2.80, £3.70, £5.00; EX 42.30 Place 6 £90.79, Place 5 £76.36.
Owner Hyde Sporting Promotions Limited **Bred** Tom Deane **Trained** East Everleigh, Wilts

FOCUS
The time compared favourably with the maidens over the same trip and this is solid form with the second, third and fifth all running to their marks. The winner is much improved this year.
Height Of Fury(IRE) Official explanation: jockey said colt was unsuited by the good ground
T/Jkpt: Not won. T/Plt: £170.30 to a £1 stake. Pool: £76,405.55. 327.35 winning tickets. T/Qpdt: £57.30 to a £1 stake. Pool: £4,702.60. 60.70 winning tickets. CR

1491 THIRSK (L-H)
Saturday, May 13

OFFICIAL GOING: Good
Wind: Virtually nil

1682 QUADNETICS CLAIMING STKS 5f
6:15 (6:16) (Class 5) 2-Y-O **£4,533** (£1,348; £674; £336) **Stalls** High

Form				RPR
	1		**Best Woman** 2-8-2.......... PaulQuinn 10 (M W Easterby) *s.i.s and bhd: hdwy and rdn along 2f out: styd on strly ent last: led nr fin* **50/1**	52
40	**2**	1/2	**Dotty's Daughter**[5] 1535 2-8-5..........(v[1]) PaulFessey 8 (Mrs A Duffield) *led: rdn clr over 1f out: edgd lft ins last: eased and ct nr fin* **8/1**	54+
	3	1 1/4	**Bridget's Team** 2-7-13.......... LeanneKershaw(5) 13 (P C Haslam) *rr and hmpd after 1f: swtchd outside and hdwy 2f out: rdn and kpt on ins last: nrst fin* **40/1**	47
03	**4**	1/2	**Minnie Magician**[17] 1229 2-7-7.......... DuranFentiman(5) 2 (C Grant) *midfield: hdwy 2fout: sn rdn and kpt on ins last* **40/1**	39
4	**5**	1 3/4	**Argent Danseur**[17] 1229 2-8-6..........(p) DavidAllan 9 (B S Rothwell) *prom and swtchd rt after 1f: cl up: rdn wl over 1f out: drvn and wknd ent last* **22/1**	40
31	**6**	1 1/4	**Auction Time**[21] 1142 2-8-3.......... AdrianTNicholls 6 (J L Spearing) *in tch whn hmpd after 1f: hdwy 2f out: sn rdn: hung bdly lft and btn* **2/1**[1]	32
0	**7**	1	**Fath And Furiouth (IRE)**[24] 1074 2-8-11.......... LeeEnstone 11 (P C Haslam) *chsd ldrs: rdn along over 2f out: grad wknd* **40/1**	36
	8	2	**Coy Joy (IRE)** 2-8-7.......... TomEaves 4 (M Dods) *in tch: rdn along 2f out: sn no imp* **20/1**	24
	9	5	**Spinning Game** 2-8-3.......... FrancisFerris 14 (K A Ryan) *midfield: rdn along over 2f out: sn wknd* **16/1**	—
05	**10**	5	**Poniard (IRE)**[12] 1342 2-8-13.......... RobertWinston 5 (D W Barker) *chsd ldrs whn hmpd after 1f: rdn along 2f out: hmpd over 1f out and sn wknd* **9/2**[3]	—
	11	5	**Don't Try It On** 2-8-7.......... PatCosgrave 7 (M W Easterby) *s.i.s: a rr* **50/1**	—
23	**U**		**Go On Jessica (IRE)**[11] 1379 2-7-12.......... SilvestreDeSousa(3) 12 (D Nicholls) *chsd ldrs whn stmbld: swvd bdly lft and uns rdr after 1f* **5/2**[2]	—

63.86 secs (3.96) **Going Correction** +0.65s/f (Yiel) **12** Ran SP% **117.4**
Speed ratings (Par 93):94,93,91,90,87 85,84,80,72,64 56,—
CSF £389.83 TOTE £42.10: £6.00, £2.60, £6.40; EX 790.50.The winner was claimed by Paul Howling for £9,000. Go On Jessica was claimed by Alan Juckes for £8,000.
Owner Stephen J Curtis **Bred** S J Curtis **Trained** Sheriff Hutton, N Yorks
■ Stewards' Enquiry : Paul Fessey 28-day ban: failed to ride out for first place (May 24-Jun 20)
David Allan seven-day ban: careless riding (May 24-30)

FOCUS
A moderate claimer, but incident packed. The second favourite Go On Jessica unseated her rider after a furlong, while Dotty's Daughter would surely have made all, having set a good pace, had her rider not stopped riding near the line.

NOTEBOOK

Best Woman, a half-sister to Business Mind, who was unplaced over five and six furlongs as a juvenile, started slowly and looked set to finish no better than mid-division when seemingly going nowhere well inside the final two furlongs, but the penny well and truly dropped late on and he just caught Dotty's Daughter, who was eased near the line. This was a moderate race, but she can be expected to come on quite a bit for this experience and can do even better over six furlongs.
Dotty's Daughter, who failed to build on the promise she showed on her debut at Wolverhampton when a beaten favourite in maiden company at Kempton on her previous start, showed good pace in the first-time visor and, although getting tired late on, would surely have held on had her rider not stopped riding near the line. This was her first run on turf and she handled the surface well enough to suggest she can win in similar company. (op 11-1 tchd 12-1)
Bridget's Team, an 8,000gns half-sister to triple mile winner Brace Of Doves, out of a ten-furlong scorer, made an encouraging debut and was probably unlucky not to have finished even closer as she was hampered early on by the unseated rider. (op 33-1)
Minnie Magician ran well and seems to be going the right way at this lowly level. (op 33-1)
Argent Danseur, with cheekpieces on for the first time, could not reverse Catterick placings with Minnie Magician and does not appear to have progressed. (op 16-1)
Auction Time, already on her third trainer, hung left under pressure and was well below the form she showed when winning a similar event over course and distance on her previous start. She looks best watched now. (op 13-8)
Fath And Furiouth(IRE) Official explanation: jockey said gelding hung left-handed throughout
Poniard(IRE), returned to claiming company, did not recover after being hampered soon after the start. Official explanation: jockey said colt lost its action (op 5-1 tchd 11-2)
Go On Jessica(IRE), a beaten favourite in this grade at Kempton on her previous start, stumbled after about a furlong and unseated her rider. She may have clipped heels. (op 7-2)

1683 HYDRA FOOD GROUP H'CAP 7f
6:45 (6:55) (Class 6) (0-60,60) 3-Y-O+ **£3,238** (£963; £481; £240) **Stalls** Low

Form RPR
4655 **1** **Bollin Edward**[215] [5794] 7-9-12 **58** PatCosgrave 13 71
(K A Ryan) *hld up in rr: gd hdwy over 2f out: swtchd outside and str run to ld ins last: styd on* **14/1**
6502 **2** *2* **Peace Lily**[12] [1348] 4-9-11 **57** ShaneKelly 8 65
(R F Johnson Houghton) *in tch: hdwy to chse ldrs over 2f out: sn rdn: kpt on to chse wnr ins last: no imp* **11/2**[1]
5502 **3** *1 ½* **Confide (IRE)**[290] [3853] 4-9-12 **58** RobertWinston 14 62
(G A Swinbank) *hld up: hdwy on outer over 2f out: sn rdn and ev ch fr wl over 1f out tl drvn and one pce ent last* **6/1**[2]
1401 **4** *1* **Golden Square**[12] [1353] 4-9-1 **54** DeanWilliams(7) 4 56
(A W Carroll) *prom: effrt over 2f out: rdn to ld 1 1/2f out: sn hung lft: hdd ent last and wknd* **13/2**[3]
0042 **5** *¾* **Green Pirate**[9] [1443] 4-9-5 **54** PaulMulrennan(3) 3 54
(R Craggs) *cl up: rdn and ev ch 2f out: wkng whn n.m.r appr last* **15/2**
0024 **6** *nk* **Bond Diamond**[15] [1276] 9-9-13 **59** RobbieFitzpatrick 10 58+
(P T Midgley) *hld up in tch: smooth hdwy on inner whn nt clr run wl over 1f out: swtchd rt and styd on ins last* **14/1**
-050 **7** *1 ¼* **Leighton Buzzard**[16] [1253] 4-9-12 **58** PaulFessey 6 54
(Mrs A Duffield) *chsd ldrs: rdn along over 2f out: sn one pce* **7/1**
0552 **8** *nk* **Joshua's Gold (IRE)**[8] [1459] 5-9-11 **60** (v) DanielTudhope(3) 7 55
(D Carroll) *in tch: hdwy on outer 3f out: sn rdn along and no imp fr wl over 1f out* **11/2**[1]
3620 **9** *1 ¼* **Borodinsky**[26] [1041] 5-9-8 **54** DavidAllan 11 45
(R E Barr) *prom: rdn along 2f out: wknd appr last* **25/1**
1005 **10** *3* **Fuel Cell (IRE)**[138] [5997] 5-9-5 **58** (b) JamesO'Reilly(7) 5 42
(J O'Reilly) *a rr* **22/1**
4500 **11** *nk* **Preskani**[15] [1276] 4-9-4 **55** (p) DuranFentiman(5) 9 38
(Mrs N Macauley) *a rr* **80/1**
0040 **12** *½* **Peruvian Style (IRE)**[4] [1570] 5-9-9 **55** KDarley 1 37
(J M Bradley) *led: rdn along over 2f out: drvn and hdd 1 ½f out: sn wknd* **8/1**
3601 **13** *11* **Ellens Princess (IRE)**[284] [4025] 4-9-10 **56** TomEaves 12 9
(J S Wainwright) *a rr* **33/1**

1m 30.21s (3.11) **Going Correction** +0.65s/f (Yiel) 13 Ran SP% **119.5**
Speed ratings (Par 101):108,105,104,102,102 101,100,99,98,95 94,94,81
CSF £86.40 CT £541.66 TOTE £16.40: £4.90, £2.10, £2.70; EX 71.80.
Owner N O'Brien,T Fawcett and J Ryan **Bred** Sir Neil And Lady Westbrook **Trained** Hambleton, N Yorks

FOCUS
Just a moderate race, but the form looks straightforward and good for the grade, rated around the third and fourth, and Bollin Edward won in the style of a well-handicapped horse on just his third start for Kevin Ryan.
Bond Diamond ◆ Official explanation: jockey said gelding was denied a clear run

1684 GLISTEN MAIDEN STKS 1m
7:15 (7:23) (Class 5) 3-Y-O+ **£4,533** (£1,348; £674; £336) **Stalls** Low

Form RPR
5 **1** **Motaraqeb**[24] [1088] 3-8-13 RobertWinston 4 84+
(Sir Michael Stoute) *dwlt and in rr till stdy hdwy 3f out: swtchd outside and effrt 2f out: rdn to ld over 1f out: styd on* **7/4**[2]
5026 **2** *1 ¾* **Pinch Of Salt (IRE)**[15] [1269] 3-8-13 80 (t) FergusSweeney 8 80
(A M Balding) *midfield: hdwy 3f out: rdn to chse ldrs 2f out: cl up over 1f out: kpt on u.p ins last* **9/1**[3]
02 **3** *1 ¼* **Montjeu Man**[279] [4181] 3-8-13 JamieSpencer 9 77
(E A L Dunlop) *trckd ldrs: hdwy over 2f out: led briefly wl over 1f out: sn rdn and hdd: edgd lft and one pce ent last* **6/5**[1]
U **4** *2* **Ahlawy (IRE)**[12] [1336] 3-8-13 NickyMackay 10 73
(L M Cumani) *in tch: pushed along and outpcd wl over 2f out: styd on strly appr last: nrst fin* **20/1**
6000 **5** *1 ½* **Three Strings (USA)**[234] [5408] 3-8-10 45 PaulMulrennan(3) 11 69?
(P D Niven) *keen: cl up: led after 3f: rdn along 3f out: hdd 2f out and grad wknd* **150/1**
6 **6** *4* **Virginia Rose (IRE)**[206] [5976] 3-8-8 KDarley 12 55
(J G Given) *prom: rdn along 3f out: wknd fnl 2f* **33/1**
0035 **7** *¾* **World In Action (IRE)**[259] [4745] 3-8-13 72 DarrenWilliams 2 58
(A P Jarvis) *in tch: rdn along wl over 2f out: sn no imp* **20/1**
50 **8** *½* **Kavachi (IRE)**[248] [5051] 3-8-13 TomEaves 15 57+
(E A L Dunlop) *stdd and swtchd lft s: hld up in rr tl sme late hdwy* **28/1**
00 **9** *3* **Eathie**[10] [1401] 4-9-12 RobbieFitzpatrick 13 53?
(M J Attwater) *bhd tl sme late hdwy* **200/1**
10 *nk* **Bold Medicean** 3-8-13 DeanMcKeown 1 49+
(T P Tate) *s.i.s: a rr* **50/1**
0 **11** *½* **Zingbat (IRE)**[206] [5987] 3-8-13 NeilPollard 5 48
(J G Given) *bhd fr 1/2-way* **100/1**
0 **12** *9* **Azerley (IRE)**[22] [1126] 3-8-8 GrahamGibbons 14 23
(J D Bethell) *a towards rr* **100/1**
0 **13** *8* **Mount Sinai**[12] [1335] 3-8-13 ShaneKelly 7 9
(W J Knight) *led 3f: cl up tl rdn over 2f out and sn wknd* **28/1**
0-00 **14** *1 ¼* **Mister Minty (IRE)**[355] [1958] 4-9-5 35 JamesO'Reilly(7) 6 6
(J O'Reilly) *a rr* **200/1**
15 *11* **Genevieve** 4-9-7 BrianReilly 3 —
(Mrs C A Dunnett) *chsd ldrs: rdn along 3f out: sn wknd* **150/1**

1m 44.32s (4.62) **Going Correction** +0.65s/f (Yiel)
WFA 3 from 4yo 13lb 15 Ran SP% **117.4**
Speed ratings (Par 103):102,100,99,97,95 91,90,90,87,86 86,77,69,68,57
CSF £15.32 TOTE £2.80: £1.40, £1.90, £1.60; EX 13.20.
Owner Hamdan Al Maktoum **Bred** Lady Bamford **Trained** Newmarket, Suffolk

FOCUS
This looked an ordinary maiden beforehand and 45-rated Three Strings does little for the form in fifth, although there is obviously a chance he has improved over the winter, and otherwise it makes sense.
Three Strings(USA) Official explanation: jockey said gelding hung right-handed throughout
Mount Sinai Official explanation: jockey said saddle slipped

1685 CALVERTS CARPETS H'CAP 2m
7:45 (7:52) (Class 4) (0-85,85) 4-Y-O+ **£6,477** (£1,927; £963; £481) **Stalls** Low

Form RPR
2432 **1** **Numero Due**[14] [1294] 4-9-4 **78** JamieSpencer 5 91+
(G M Moore) *trckd ldrs: niggled along 1/2-way: rdn along 4f out: hdwy to ld wl over 2f out: rdn clr over 1f out: eased ins last* **1/1**[1]
0550 **2** *1 ½* **Hue**[31] [976] 5-8-9 **66** (b[1]) PatCosgrave 7 70
(B Ellison) *hld up: hdwy 4f out: rdn and hung rt 2f out: drvn to chse wnr ins last: kpt on* **33/1**
-400 **3** *1 ¼* **Double Obsession**[14] [1294] 6-9-12 **83** (v) AdrianTNicholls 6 86?
(D Nicholls) *led after 3f: rdn along 4f out: hdd wl over 2f out: sn drvn and kpt on same pce* **40/1**
6001 **4** *1 ¼* **Finalmente**[258] [4795] 4-9-9 **83** NickyMackay 3 84+
(N A Callaghan) *hld up: rdn along and wl outpcd 4f out: styd on fnl 2f: nrst fin* **8/1**
1204 **5** *9* **Toldo (IRE)**[14] [1294] 4-9-11 **85** ShaneKelly 2 75
(G M Moore) *led 3f: prom tl rdn along 3f out and sn wknd* **4/1**[2]
0210 **6** *5* **Wasalat (USA)**[315] [3144] 4-8-10 **75** MarkLawson(5) 1 59
(D W Barker) *bhd fr 1/2-way* **100/1**
4000 **7** *9* **Rule For Ever**[6] [1502] 4-8-9 **69** KDarley 8 42
(M Johnston) *prom: rdn along over 4f out: sn wknd* **9/1**
0220 **8** *19* **Spanish Ridge (IRE)**[21] [1132] 4-9-0 **74** RobertWinston 4 25
(J L Dunlop) *trckd ldrs: hdwy and cl up 1/2-way: rdn along 4f out: wkng whn lost action and virtually p.u 2f out* **6/1**[3]

3m 41.17s (9.97) **Going Correction** +0.65s/f (Yiel)
WFA 4 from 5yo+ 3lb 8 Ran SP% **111.8**
Speed ratings (Par 105):101,100,99,99,94 92,87,78
CSF £40.77 CT £804.07 TOTE £1.80: £1.20, £2.60, £3.80; EX 29.90.
Owner Trattoria Due/Valueplace Ltd **Bred** London Thoroughbred Services Ltd **Trained** Middleham Moor, N Yorks
■ Stewards' Enquiry : Adrian T Nicholls caution: careless riding

FOCUS
A fair staying handicap, although the pace was just steady for most of the way and the form looks weak for the grade.
Spanish Ridge(IRE) Official explanation: jockey said gelding cocked its jaw and hung violently right

1686 DICK PEACOCK SPRINT H'CAP 6f
8:15 (8:23) (Class 5) (0-75,74) 3-Y-O+ **£5,505** (£1,637; £818; £408) **Stalls** High

Form RPR
2102 **1** **Zidane**[14] [1285] 4-10-0 **74** JamieSpencer 6 86+
(J R Fanshawe) *stdd and swtchd rt to stands rail s: bhd tl swtchd lft and hdwy wl over 1f out: str run ins last: led nr line* **3/1**[1]
1342 **2** *hd* **Riquewihr**[10] [1413] 6-9-3 **68** (p) GregFairley(5) 4 79
(J S Wainwright) *swtchd rt s: chsd ldrs stands side: hdwy 2f out and sn overall ldr: rdn and hung lft over 1f out: drvn:ct nr line* **12/1**
6002 **3** *1 ½* **Blackheath (IRE)**[6] [1504] 10-9-7 **67** PaulQuinn 16 74
(D Nicholls) *chsd ldrs stands side: hdwy and ev ch wl over 1f out tl rdn and nt qckn ins last* **20/1**
1246 **4** *¾* **Dorn Dancer (IRE)**[6] [1504] 4-9-4 **64** PhillipMakin 9 69+
(D W Barker) *in tch far side: hdwy to ld that gp 2f out: sn rdn and kpt on ins last* **10/1**
0000 **5** *1 ½* **Apex**[7] [1494] 5-9-10 **70** KimTinkler 14 70
(N Tinkler) *chsd ldrs stands side: rdn 2f out: kpt on same pce appr last* **28/1**
0000 **6** *½* **Baron Rhodes**[14] [1297] 5-9-9 **69** (p) TomEaves 15 68
(J S Wainwright) *in tch stands side: rdn along 2f out: kpt on same pce* **33/1**
2406 **7** *4* **Lincolneurocruiser**[15] [1275] 4-9-11 **71** RobbieFitzpatrick 20 58
(Mrs N Macauley) *chsd ldrs stands side: rdn along over 2f out: sn wknd* **25/1**
300 **8** *½* **Glencairn Star**[6] [1504] 5-9-3 **66** DanielTudhope(3) 5 51+
(J S Goldie) *hld up far side: hdwy 2f out: sn rdn and no imp* **14/1**
0245 **9** *1 ½* **Summer Recluse (USA)**[162] [6483] 7-9-8 **68** (t) ShaneKelly 17 49
(J M Bradley) *in tch stands side: swtchd lft and hdwy over 2f out: sn rdn and no imp* **33/1**
4005 **10** *1 ½* **Kennington**[104] [244] 6-9-7 **67** (b) BrianReilly 7 43
(Mrs C A Dunnett) *led stands side: gp: rdn along and hdd 2f out: grad wknd* **66/1**
5342 **11** *¾* **Winthorpe (IRE)**[21] [1151] 6-9-9 **69** GrahamGibbons 8 43
(J J Quinn) *cl up stands side: rdn over 2f out and sn wknd* **18/1**
0012 **12** *½* **Circuit Dancer (IRE)**[10] [1402] 6-9-10 **70** AdrianTNicholls 18 42
(D Nicholls) *in tch stands side: rdn along 1/2-way: sn btn* **7/1**[2]
6310 **13** *3 ½* **Norcroft**[11] [1382] 4-9-12 **72** (p) J-PGuillambert 3 34+
(Mrs C A Dunnett) *chsd ldrs far side: rdn along ½-wy: sn wknd* **33/1**
1600 **14** *nk* **Joyeaux**[31] [977] 4-9-8 **68** DerekMcGaffin 13 29
(J Hetherton) *in tch stands side: hdwy on outer ½-way: sn rdn and wknd 2f out* **125/1**
2223 **15** *1 ¼* **Brut**[4] [1563] 4-9-0 **65** MarkLawson(5) 1 22+
(D W Barker) *overall ldr far side: edgd rt to centre ½-way: sn rdn: hdd 2f out: sddle slipped and wknd over 1f out* **12/1**
0145 **16** *5* **True Magic**[9] [1448] 5-9-4 **71** WilliamCarson(7) 2 13+
(J D Bethell) *chsd ldr far side: rdn along ½-wy: sn wknd* **50/1**
0401 **17** *¾* **High Ridge**[9] [1432] 7-9-13 **73** (p) KDarley 19 13
(J M Bradley) *a rr stands side* **8/1**[3]

1561 **18** *2 ½* **Daniella**[10] 1413 4-9-11 **71**..........(p) FrancisFerris 10 4+
(Rae Guest) *swtchd to far side: in tch tl rdn along and wknd over 2f out* **16/1**

0500 **19** *½* **Whinhill House**[7] 1496 6-9-12 **72**..........(p) RobertWinston 12 3
(D W Barker) *chsd ldrs stands side: rdn along ½-way: sn wknd* **20/1**

0541 **20** *25* **Kool Ovation**[324] 2855 4-9-10 **70**.......... DavidAllan 11 —
(A Dickman) *a rr stands side* **50/1**

1m 15.46s (2.96) **Going Correction** +0.65s/f (Yiel) **20** Ran SP% **122.7**
Speed ratings (Par 103):106,105,103,102,100 100,94,94,92,90 89,88,83,83,81 75,74,70,70,36
CSF £32.96 CT £647.37 TOTE £3.40: £2.00, £2.80, £3.70, £2.40; EX 70.10.
Owner Mrs Jan Hopper **Bred** Mrs J P Hopper And Mrs E M Grundy **Trained** Newmarket, Suffolk

FOCUS
No more than a fair sprint handicap, but the time was decent and the form looks solid, rated around those in the frame behind the winner. A small group of horses opted to race far side, but were at a disadvantage with the larger pack towards the stands' side.
Summer Recluse(USA) Official explanation: jockey said gelding suffered interference in running
Circuit Dancer(IRE) Official explanation: jockey said gelding was denied a clear run
Brut Official explanation: jockey said saddle slipped
High Ridge Official explanation: jockey said gelding suffered interference in running
Whinhill House Official explanation: jockey said gelding hung right-handed

1687 MICHAEL BURROWS 65TH BIRTHDAY MAIDEN STKS — 6f
8:45 (8:49) (Class 5) 3-Y-0+ **£4,533** (£1,348; £674; £336) **Stalls** High

Form RPR

1 **Nusoor (IRE)** 3-8-13.......... ShaneKelly 7 71+
(W J Haggas) *dwlt: hdwy on outer over 2f out: rdn to ld ent last: edgd rt and drvn out* **12/1**

35 **2** *½* **Spinning**[10] 1412 3-8-13.......... PaulFessey 11 70+
(T D Barron) *hld up in rr: hdwy on inner 2f out: swtchd lft and rdn ins last: styd on wl nr fin* **4/1**[3]

02 **3** *1 ¼* **Loch Verdi**[206] 5969 3-8-8.......... FergusSweeney 5 61+
(A M Balding) *led: rdn along 2f out: hdd ent last: kpt on same pce u.p* **5/4**[1]

4 **4** *½* **Falmassim**[10] 1412 3-8-13.......... NickyMackay 1 65+
(L M Cumani) *trckd ldrs: hdwy 2f out and sn ev ch tl rdn and nt qckn ent last* **9/4**[2]

3300 **5** *3 ½* **Montana**[17] 1235 6-9-9 **50**.......... LeeEnstone 4 57
(C W Fairhurst) *cl up: rdn along over 2f out: grad wknd* **22/1**

4 **6** *2* **Forestelle (IRE)**[22] 1127 3-8-5.......... BenSwarbrick(3) 6 43
(M Dods) *towards rr: hdwy over 2f out: sn rdn and no imp* **33/1**

0660 **7** *nk* **Desert Hunter (IRE)**[215] 5791 3-8-13 **51**.......... RobertWinston 9 47
(Micky Hammond) *hld up towards rr: hdwy over 2f out: sn rdn and no imp* **25/1**

00 **8** *nk* **Missouri (USA)**[21] 1147 3-8-10.......... DanielTudhope(3) 8 46
(G M Moore) *nvr nr ldrs* **125/1**

0000 **9** *¾* **Cape Sydney (IRE)**[40] 861 3-8-8 **45**.......... NeilPollard 3 39
(D W Barker) *chsd ldrs to 1/2-way: sn wknd* **100/1**

0000 **10** *2* **Night Reveller (IRE)**[11] 1386 3-8-3 **30**.......... EmmettStack(5) 10 33
(M C Chapman) *in tch to 1/2-way: sn wknd* **200/1**

11 *15* **Soba Fella** 3-8-13.......... RobbieFitzpatrick 2 —
(P T Midgley) *wnt lft s: a bhd* **80/1**

1m 16.51s (4.01) **Going Correction** +0.65s/f (Yiel)
WFA 3 from 6yo 10lb **11** Ran SP% **117.6**
Speed ratings (Par 103):99,98,96,96,91 88,88,87,86,84 64
CSF £57.72 TOTE £12.10: £2.40, £2.00, £1.30; EX 51.50 Place 6 £102.14, Place 5 £6.93.
Owner Hamdan Al Maktoum **Bred** Shadwell Estate Company Limited **Trained** Newmarket, Suffolk

FOCUS
As tends to be the case with older-horse sprint maidens, an ordinary affair. The fifth home came into this rated just 50, and looks the best guide to the strength of the form. They all raced stands' side.
Desert Hunter(IRE) Official explanation: jockey said gelding ran too free early stages
T/Plt: £823.20 to a £1 stake. Pool: £42,009.80. 37.25 winning tickets. T/Qpdt: £3.80 to a £1 stake. Pool: £4,576.70. 872.55 winning tickets. JR

1347 WARWICK (L-H)
Saturday, May 13

OFFICIAL GOING: Good (good to firm in places) changing to good (good to soft in places) after race 2 (6.30)
Wind: Nil

1688 SPONSOR AT WARWICK MAIDEN AUCTION STKS — 5f 110y
6:00 (6:02) (Class 5) 2-Y-0 **£3,412** (£1,007; £504) **Stalls** Low

Form RPR

1 **Arnie's Joint (IRE)** 2-8-4.......... JamesDoyle(5) 6 73
(N P Littmoden) *trckd ldr: chal halfay: led 1f out: edgd rt ins last: readily* **18/1**

2 *1* **Gremlin** 2-8-11.......... JDSmith 14 72
(A King) *wnt lft s:prom:pushed wd bnd over 2f out: str run over 1f out to chse wnr ins last: edgd lft: kpt on but a hld* **7/2**[1]

3 *1 ¾* **Apollo Five** 2-8-11.......... StephenCarson 9 66
(D J Coakley) *s.i.s: bhd: rdn and hdwy fr 2f out: kpt on ins last but nt pce to rch ldrs* **14/1**

05 **4** *shd* **Mystery World**[14] 1284 2-8-11.......... JoeFanning 1 66
(M Johnston) *slt ld: rdn over 2f out: headed 1f out: wknd ins last* **7/2**[1]

5 *1 ½* **Sans Reward (IRE)** 2-8-8.......... ChrisCatlin 7 58
(B J Meehan) *chsd ldrs: rdn and outpcd 2f out: styd on again ins last and kpt on cl home* **13/2**[3]

0 **6** *hd* **Shes Millie**[21] 1136 2-8-4.......... FrankieMcDonald 11 53
(J G M O'Shea) *bhd: sn drvn along: kpt on wl fnl f but nvr gng pce to rch ldrs* **33/1**

7 *¾* **Copper King** 2-8-13.......... NeilChalmers(3) 8 63+
(A M Balding) *sn chsng ldrs: rdn 2f out: j. path appr fnl f and sn btn* **25/1**

0 **8** *¾* **Persian Fox (IRE)**[14] 1284 2-8-10.......... NelsonDeSouza(3) 10 57
(G A Huffer) *chsd ldrs: rdn 1/2-way: wknd fnl f* **25/1**

0 **9** *hd* **Party Palace**[5] 1542 2-8-1.......... FrankiePickard(7) 5 52
(J A Osborne) *chsd ldrs: pushed along 1/2-way: wknd fnl f* **33/1**

0 **10** *¾* **Emergency Services**[50] 707 2-8-11.......... JimCrowley 4 52
(Tom Dascombe) *bhd: sn rdn: kpt on fnl 2f but nvr gng pce to rch ldrs* **11/1**

11 *1 ¼* **Jost Van Dyke** 2-8-9.......... TonyCulhane 13 46+
(B R Millman) *s.i.s: outpcd most of way* **25/1**

12 *5* **Brierley Lil** 2-8-11.......... SamHitchcott 2 32
(J L Spearing) *s.i.s: bhd and sn drvn: outpcd most of way* **16/1**

13 *2 ½* **Wendy's Boy** 2-8-11.......... DaneO'Neill 12 23
(R Hannon) *chsd ldrs: rn wd bnd over 2f out: wknd over 1f out* **5/1**[2]

14 *7* **Spirit Rising** 2-8-6.......... RichardThomas(3) 3 —
(J M Bradley) *v.s.a: a wl bhd* **33/1**

68.70 secs (4.39) **Going Correction** +0.625s/f (Yiel) **14** Ran SP% **121.0**
Speed ratings (Par 93):95,93,91,91,89 88,87,86,86,85 84,77,74,64
CSF £74.80 TOTE £27.40: £6.70, £1.60, £5.90; EX 104.40.
Owner Mrs Linda Francis **Bred** Martin Francis Ltd **Trained** Newmarket, Suffolk

FOCUS
A modest event and the form does not loos strong, but it should still produce winners.

NOTEBOOK
Arnie's Joint(IRE), a first two-year-old runner of the season for the yard, knew his job and was soon chasing the tails of the leaders. He went on over a furlong out and, despite going out to his right under pressure, was always holding the well-supported runner-up. This was a highly pleasing first effort and, with a rise in distance unlikely to hinder him, he looks one to keep on side. (op 14-1)
Gremlin, a positive in the market beforehand despite having a very wide draw to overcome, was trapped out wide the whole way and did mightily well to finish as close as he did. His stable is a shrewd operation and it is highly likely to he will pick up a maiden before going handicapping. (op 5-2 tchd 9-4)
Apollo Five, a relatively cheap purchase, is bred for speed, but he lacked the knowhow of the winner early on and was doing his best work late. Natural progression may see him pick up a small contest, probably over six furlongs. (op 12-1 tchd 11-1)
Mystery World has looked all about speed so far and the sixth furlong proved beyond him on this occasion. He still looks a little weak and it is likely he will be capable of better in nurseries later in the year. (op 6-1)
Sans Reward(IRE), who is related to some classy middle-distance performers, will no doubt have delighted connections with this debut effort, keeping on close home having been outpaced, and it is highly likely she will benefit from a greater distance. She is one to have onside in future. (op 7-1 tchd 15-2 and 6-1)
Shes Millie made a little late headway and will be better off once contesting nurseries. (tchd 40-1)
Copper King, already a gelding, showed up well to a point and is likely to benefit from the outing. (op 22-1)
Wendy's Boy comes from a stable who demand obvious respect in these races, but he was unable to justify market support, running wide on the bend, and may deserve another chance. Official explanation: jockey said colt lost its action home straight (op 8-1)
Spirit Rising Official explanation: jockey said gelding missed the break

1689 LARRY KIELY IS 60 H'CAP — 5f 110y
6:30 (6:33) (Class 6) (0-65,65) 3-Y-0+ **£3,238** (£963; £481; £240) **Stalls** Low

Form RPR

0000 **1** **Dunn Deal (IRE)**[6] 1504 6-9-13 **65**.......... EddieAhern 5 76
(W M Brisbourne) *rr but in tch: hdwy 2f out: styd on under prssure fnl f to ld cl home* **9/2**[2]

4153 **2** *¾* **Cashel Mead**[2] 1618 6-9-6 **58**.......... SamHitchcott 2 66+
(J L Spearing) *burst out of stalls bef s: chsd ldrs: rdn over 2f out: led 1f out: hdd and no ex cl home* **9/4**[1]

4200 **3** *1 ¼* **Louphole**[11] 1383 4-9-9 **64**.......... AmirQuinn(3) 17 68
(P J Makin) *chsd ldrs: hrd rdn fr 2f out: edgd lft u.p 1f out and sn one pce* **12/1**

0000 **4** *hd* **Trace Clip**[173] 6407 8-8-8 **53**.......... MarkCoumbe(7) 12 56
(N I M Rossiter) *s.i.s: bhd: hdway and nt clr run over 1f out:swtchd rt to stands rail and r.o wl fnl f: nt rch ldrs* **33/1**

4400 **5** *¾* **Starduster**[26] 1047 4-9-12 **64**.......... GeorgeBaker 1 65
(B R Millman) *led: rdn 2f out: hdd 1f out: wknd last half f* **14/1**

0030 **6** *nk* **Jun Fan (USA)**[2] 1607 4-9-6 **58**.......... RoystonFfrench 13 58
(B Ellison) *chsd ldrs: rdn and one pce whn n.m.r 1f out: sn one pce* **20/1**

2400 **7** *1 ½* **El Potro**[14] 1297 4-9-5 **64**.......... GaryEdwards(7) 14 59
(E S McMahon) *in tch: hdwy on outside over 2f out: wknd ins last* **10/1**

6000 **8** *1 ¼* **Pro Tempore**[10] 1414 4-8-13 **51** oh1.......... ChrisCatlin 6 42
(David Pinder) *s.i.s: bhd: sn drvn along: sme hdwy fnl f but n.d* **28/1**

0040 **9** *¾* **Campeon (IRE)**[13] 1315 4-9-6 **63**.......... JamesDoyle(5) 11 51
(J M Bradley) *pressed ldrs 3f: wknd fnl f* **11/1**

1050 **10** *½* **Ballybunion (IRE)**[147] 6597 7-9-5 **62**.......... LiamTreadwell(5) 8 49
(R A Harris) *prssed ldrs 3f: wknd fnl f* **14/1**

3000 **11** *¾* **Gavioli (IRE)**[18] 1209 4-9-3 **55**.......... PaulFitzsimons 9 39
(J M Bradley) *s.i.s: sn prom: rdn 1/2-way: wknd fnl f* **50/1**

1006 **12** *hd* **Patternmaker (USA)**[11] 1383 4-9-8 **60**.......... DaneO'Neill 10 44
(A M Hales) *s.i.s: bhd: rdn 1/2-way: mod prog fnl f* **9/1**[3]

0-00 **13** *1 ½* **Willofcourse**[311] 3235 5-9-5 **62**.......... AurelioMedeiros(5) 15 41
(H Candy) *hood late off: s.i.s and wnt rt s: hday 1/2-way: wknd over 1f out* **40/1**

0000 **14** *7* **Borzoi Maestro**[10] 1414 5-9-4 **56**..........(v) JoeFanning 4 12
(M Wellings) *s.i.s: sn chsd ldrs ldrs: wknd over 1f out: eased whn no ch* **25/1**

3330 **15** *2 ½* **Parkside Pursuit**[211] 5869 8-9-13 **65**.......... TonyCulhane 3 12
(J M Bradley) *a outpcd* **14/1**

100 **16** *hd* **Firework**[272] 4392 8-9-3 **55**.......... StephenCarson 7 2
(E A Wheeler) *early spd: hung lft 1/2-way: lost action and eased fr 2f out* **28/1**

68.19 secs (3.88) **Going Correction** +0.625s/f (Yiel) **16** Ran SP% **126.9**
Speed ratings (Par 101):99,98,96,96,95 94,92,91,90,89 88,88,86,76,73 73
CSF £14.35 CT £126.57 TOTE £6.10: £2.20, £1.10, £3.20, £9.30; EX 24.60.
Owner Raymond McNeill **Bred** John Cullinan **Trained** Great Ness, Shropshire

FOCUS
A typically competitive sprint handicap. Ordinary form, but sound enough.
Borzoi Maestro Official explanation: jockey said gelding stumbled coming out of stalls and saddle slipped
Firework Official explanation: jockey said gelding hung badly right-handed

1690 WORLD BET EXCHANGE LAUNCHING SOON AT WBX.COM H'CAP — 1m 6f 213y
7:00 (7:00) (Class 4) (0-80,80) 4-Y-0+ **£6,477** (£1,927; £963; £481) **Stalls** Low

Form RPR

0100 **1** **Maystock**[17] 1247 6-8-10 **65**.......... TedDurcan 12 73
(B G Powell) *chsd ldrs: slt ld 4f out: hdd 2f out: rallied to ld 1f out: styd on u.p: all out* **22/1**

0062 **2** *nk* **Eastborough (IRE)**[10] 1425 7-8-10 **70**.......... JamesDoyle(5) 9 78
(B G Powell) *stdd s:t.k.h and plld way to ld over 1m out:narrowly hdd 4f out: led 2f out: narrowly hdd 1f out: styd on: no ex nr fin* **3/1**[1]

0030 **3** *2* **Salute (IRE)**[17] 1247 7-9-8 **77**.......... TonyCulhane 11 82
(P G Murphy) *prom: outpcd and rdn 4f out: styd on under pressuse fr 2f out: nt rch ldrs* **16/1**

0-02 **4** *nk* **Archduke Ferdinand (FR)**[17] 1247 8-9-11 **80**.......... DaneO'Neill 6 84
(A King) *in tch: rdn and outpcd 4f out: styd on u.p fnl 3f: nt rch ldrs* **7/2**[2]

5021 **5** ¾ **Linden Lime**[12] 1339 4-8-4 **61** oh3 .... PaulDoe 1 64
(Jamie Poulton) *t.k.h in rr: hdwy 5f out: pressed ldrs over 3f out tl over 1f out: wknd ins last* **11/2**[3]

1054 **6** 1 ¼ **Bobsleigh**[12] 1339 7-8-6 **61** oh3 .... ChrisCatlin 13 63
(H S Howe) *ken hold: chsd ldrs: chal after 3f tl 9f out: styd prom tl over 2f out* **9/1**

0301 **7** nk **Desert Island Disc**[11] 1376 9-9-1 **73** .... RichardThomas(3) 7 74
(Dr J R J Naylor) *in tch: rdn to chse ldrs 5f out: wknd 2f out* **8/1**

1103 **8** ¾ **Frontlinefinancier**[278] 4229 6-7-13 **61** oh7 .... MarkCoumbe(7) 2 61
(N I M Rossiter) *t.k.h: chsd ldrs: rdn 3f out: wknd fr 2f out* **16/1**

2460 **9** ½ **Shingle Street (IRE)**[11] 1385 4-8-5 **62** .... (b) EddieAhern 5 61
(Miss Venetia Williams) *bhd: rdn and sme hday over 3f out: n.d* **16/1**

/400 **10** ½ **Blue Away (IRE)**[18] 1213 8-9-1 **70** .... FrankieMcDonald 8 69
(S Kirk) *bhd: pushed along over 4f out: nver in contention* **22/1**

1520 **11** 3 ½ **Mt Desert**[13] 5533 4-9-5 **76** .... VinceSlattery 10 70
(C J Mann) *chsd ldrs tl outpcd 5f out: sn rdn and rallieed to chal 4f out: wknd fr 3f out* **14/1**

2300 **12** hd **Ganymede**[20] 1163 5-8-7 **62** .... JoeFanning 4 56
(J G M O'Shea) *sn led: hdd over 1m out: wknd 3f out* **33/1**

0003 **13** 44 **Love Beauty (USA)**[9] 4458 4-8-13 **70** .... (b[1]) SamHitchcott 3 2
(M F Harris) *bhd fr 1/2-way: t.o* **50/1**

3m 24.22s (8.32) **Going Correction** +0.60s/f (Yiel)
WFA 4 from 5yo+ 2lb **13** Ran SP% **121.6**
Speed ratings (Par 105):101,100,99,99,99 98,98,97,97,97 95,95,72
CSF £86.18 CT £1138.58 TOTE £23.10: £5.40, £1.90, £7.80; EX 132.90.
Owner Stock Hill Racing **Bred** Stock Hill Stud **Trained** Morestead, Hants

FOCUS
A modest handicap run at a steady gallop. The form may not work out, with the fifth and eighth not beaten far from out of the handicap.

1691 HBG CONSTRUCTION LTD MAIDEN STKS — 1m 2f 188y
7:30 (7:30) (Class 4) 3-Y-O — **£5,505** (£1,637; £818; £408) **Stalls** Low

Form RPR

422 **1** **Barodine**[10] 1421 3-9-3 85 .... EddieAhern 4 81
(H R A Cecil) *trckd ldr: pushed along over 2f out:and c stands side: led over 1f out: readily* **8/11**[1]

6 **2** 3 **Mustamad**[10] 1421 3-9-3 .... RHills 6 76
(Sir Michael Stoute) *chsd ldrs: outpcd 3f out: styd far side: styd on again to take 2nd ins last but no chnace w wnr* **9/4**[2]

50 **3** nk **Calcutta Cup (UAE)**[37] 894 3-9-3 .... JoeFanning 5 75
(M Johnston) *led: c stands side and rdn over 2f out: hdd over 1f out: sn outpcd: lost 2nd cl home* **14/1**

00 **4** 9 **Ghallab**[10] 1421 3-9-3 .... MartinDwyer 2 59
(E A L Dunlop) *in tch: pushed along and outpcd over 5f out: styd in centre crse and drvn over 2f out: nvr in contention* **10/1**[3]

00 **5** 5 **Moon Melody (GER)**[12] 1343 3-9-3 .... TedDurcan 7 50
(M L W Bell) *in tch: rdn and effrt 4f out: wknd 3f out* **40/1**

0 **6** ½ **Project Sunshine (GER)**[19] 1192 3-9-3 .... DaneO'Neill 1 49
(J A Osborne) *a in rr: no ch whn styd far side fr over 2f out* **20/1**

0 **7** ½ **Mika's Fable (FR)**[19] 1192 3-8-7 .... JamesDoyle(5) 3 43
(M Meade) *t.k.h in rr: rdn and lost tch 3f out:no ch whn c centre crse: hung lft and continually flashed tail fr over 2f out* **66/1**

2m 24.82s (5.42) **Going Correction** +0.60s/f (Yiel) **7** Ran SP% **113.1**
Speed ratings (Par 101):104,101,101,95,91 91,90
CSF £2.43 TOTE £1.70: £1.10, £1.80; EX 2.60.
Owner P Van Belle **Bred** Mrs A M Jenkins And E D Kessly **Trained** Newmarket, Suffolk

FOCUS
An uncompetitive maiden won in good style by Barodine, who probably did not need to reproduce his Pontefract run.

1692 WENDY AND NEIL GREEN H'CAP — 7f 26y
8:00 (8:01) (Class 4) (0-85,87) 4-Y-O+ — **£6,477** (£1,927; £963; £481) **Stalls** Low

Form RPR

5060 **1** **Lizarazu (GER)**[9] 1435 7-8-0 **74** .... (p) TolleyDean(7) 6 82
(R A Harris) *slowly ino stride: t.k.h and sn chsng ldr: led ins fnl 2f: drvn out* **20/1**

1330 **2** ½ **Binanti**[14] 1301 6-9-2 **83** .... GeorgeBaker 10 90
(P R Chamings) *in tch: hdwy whn bmpd ins fnl 2f: swtchd lft 1f out: styd on to chse wnr ins last: one pce cl home* **8/1**

0000 **3** 1 ¼ **Irony (IRE)**[218] 5713 7-8-13 **83** .... NeilChalmers(3) 1 87
(A M Balding) *chsd ldrs: drvn to chal 2f out: edge rt fr over 1f out: one pce ins last* **12/1**

0020 **4** 2 ½ **Aastral Magic**[12] 1338 4-8-9 **76** .... RyanMoore 8 73
(R Hannon) *led 1f. prssed ldrs: stl ev chnace 2f out: wknd fnl f* **20/1**

0001 **5** 1 **Phluke**[18] 1220 5-8-8 **75** .... StephenCarson 11 70
(R F Johnson Houghton) *chsd ldrs: styng on whn n.m.r over 1f out and stdd: n.d after* **8/1**

1000 **6** shd **Atlantic Quest (USA)**[22] 1111 7-9-0 **86** ow1 .... (p) LiamTreadwell(5) 13 80
(R A Harris) *bhd: hdwy on ins and rdn 2f out: one pce u.p fnl f* **20/1**

-105 **7** ½ **Puya**[37] 898 4-9-0 **81** .... DaneO'Neill 5 74+
(H Candy) *led after 1f: hdd ins fnl 2f: hung lft over 1f out and sn wknd* **11/4**[1]

0633 **8** shd **Bobski (IRE)**[7] 1494 4-9-2 **83** .... (b[1]) MartinDwyer 7 76+
(G A Huffer) *s.i.s: rr but in tch: hdwy whn bdly hmpd appr fnl f: nt rcvr* **11/2**[3]

4000 **9** 1 ½ **Bow Wave**[22] 1112 4-8-6 **73** .... ChrisCatlin 14 62
(H Candy) *chsd ldrs: rdn outpcd over 3f out: n.d after* **28/1**

3040 **10** ½ **Jalissa**[228] 5525 4-8-8 **78** .... NelsonDeSouza(3) 9 66
(R M Beckett) *t.k.h in rr: bhd: pushed along 2f out: sme hdwy fnl f* **16/1**

1042 **11** 7 **Gallantry**[7] 1494 4-9-6 **87** .... NCallan 12 56
(D W Barker) *in tch: hdwy to chse ldrs 3f out: wknd over 1f out* **4/1**[2]

04 **12** nk **Zarakash (IRE)**[15] 913 6-8-12 **79** .... VinceSlattery 3 48
(Jonjo O'Neill) *slowly away: nt keen and a bhd* **33/1**

1m 26.26s (1.26) **Going Correction** +0.35s/f (Good) **12** Ran SP% **118.5**
Speed ratings (Par 105):106,105,104,101,100 99,99,99,97,96 88,88
CSF £161.30 CT £2049.53 TOTE £33.90: £9.50, £3.10, £4.70; EX 681.30.
Owner Mrs Jan Adams **Bred** W Schunzel **Trained** Earlswood, Monmouths

FOCUS
Just a fair handicap, but pretty sound form with the winner running his best race yet.
Bobski(IRE) Official explanation: jockey said gelding suffered interference in running

1693 RACING UK H'CAP — 7f 26y
8:30 (8:31) (Class 5) (0-75,75) 3-Y-O — **£3,238** (£963; £481; £240) **Stalls** Low

Form RPR

0500 **1** **Fangorn Forest (IRE)**[5] 1551 3-8-6 **70** .... (p) TolleyDean(7) 7 75
(R A Harris) *bhd: rdn and outpcd 4f out: stl plenty to do over 2f out: rdn and str run fnl f to ld cl home* **14/1**

0021 **2** nk **Angaric (IRE)**[9] 1441 3-8-10 **67** .... TonyCulhane 1 71
(B Smart) *in tch: rdn over 2f out: str run fnl f to chal cl home: nt pce of wnr fnl strides* **7/4**[1]

6440 **3** 1 ¼ **Bathwick Alice**[18] 1208 3-9-1 **72** .... DaneO'Neill 8 73
(B R Millman) *led: rdn 2f out: hdd over 1f out: styd on same pce* **11/1**

0210 **4** hd **Mimiteh (USA)**[183] 6312 3-9-0 **74** .... NelsonDeSouza(3) 2 74+
(R M Beckett) *trckd ldrs: qcknd to ld over 1f out: rdn ins last: wknd qckly and hdd nr fin* **8/1**

0304 **5** ½ **Mocha Java**[31] 993 3-8-8 **65** .... JosedeSouza 6 64
(P F I Cole) *chsd ldrs and sn t.k.h: wnt 2nd 3f out: rdn 2f out and kpt on same pce* **9/2**[3]

3410 **6** 3 ½ **Billy Bling (IRE)**[18] 1208 3-8-9 **66** .... RyanMoore 4 56
(R Hannon) *bhd: rdn over 2f out: switcjed lft appr fnl f: styd on u.p but nvr gng pce to rch ldrs* **10/3**[2]

510 **7** 11 **Drawback (IRE)**[4] 1569 3-9-4 **75** .... AdrianMcCarthy 5 36
(R A Harris) *s.i.s: bhd: sme hdwy 3f out: nvr rchd ldrs and sn wknd* **25/1**

6100 **8** 5 **Penny Whisper (IRE)**[31] 993 3-8-6 **63** .... RoystonFfrench 9 11
(I W McInnes) *chsd ldrs: rdn 3f out: sn wknd* **16/1**

1m 27.93s (2.93) **Going Correction** +0.35s/f (Good) **8** Ran SP% **113.5**
Speed ratings (Par 99):97,96,95,95,94 90,77,72
CSF £38.41 CT £291.39 TOTE £19.20: £4.50, £1.50, £2.50; EX 46.10 Place 6 £166.26, Place 5 £53.70.
Owner Peter A Price **Bred** Mrs C M Tinkler **Trained** Earlswood, Monmouths

FOCUS
A steady gallop and it turned into a dash for the line. A strange race, with the winner and second looking forlorn hopes a furlong out, and just fair form.
T/Plt: £256.00 to a £1 stake. Pool: £36,945.05. 105.35 winning tickets. T/Qpdt: £72.20 to a £1 stake. Pool: £2,880.10. 29.50 winning tickets. ST

1705 - 1707a (Foreign Racing) - See Raceform Interactive

1168 LEOPARDSTOWN (L-H)
Sunday, May 14

OFFICIAL GOING: Yielding

1708a DERRINSTOWN STUD DERBY TRIAL STKS (GROUP 2) — 1m 2f
3:55 (3:55) 3-Y-O — **£56,034** (£16,379; £7,758; £2,586)

RPR

1 **Dylan Thomas (IRE)**[204] 6019 3-9-1 101 .... JAHeffernan 1 114
(A P O'Brien, Ire) *cl 2nd: disp ld 1/2-way: led ent st: rdn clr over 1f out: styd on wl* **11/2**

2 1 ½ **Mountain (IRE)**[21] 1172 3-9-1 101 .... CO'Donoghue 7 111
(A P O'Brien, Ire) *chsd ldrs in 4th: 5th and rdn 3f out: hdwy under 2f out: 2nd and kpt on fnl f* **8/1**

3 shd **Youmzain (IRE)**[18] 1231 3-9-1 .... TonyCulhane 2 111
(M R Channon) *trckd ldrs in 6th: styd on wl on inner fr 1 /2f out* **9/1**

4 3 **Caribbean**[29] 1025 3-9-1 95 .... MJKinane 4 106
(John M Oxx, Ire) *hld up in rr: rdn and kpt on st* **16/1**

5 2 **Golden Arrow (IRE)**[21] 1172 3-9-1 111 .... PJSmullen 6 102
(D K Weld, Ire) *settled 5th: 4th and prog 3f out: rdn and no imp st: no ex over 1f out* **9/2**[3]

6 nk **Rekaab (IRE)**[29] 1025 3-9-1 107 .... DPMcDonogh 5 101
(Kevin Prendergast, Ire) *hld up in tch: 7th and rdn over 3f out: no imp st* **7/2**[2]

7 nk **Altius (IRE)**[21] 1172 3-9-1 103 .... WMLordan 8 101
(A P O'Brien, Ire) *led: jnd 1/2-way: hdd ent st: sn wknd* **16/1**

8 25 **Heliostatic (IRE)**[29] 1025 3-9-1 107 .... KJManning 3 56
(J S Bolger, Ire) *cl 3rd: wknd u.p early st: virtually p.u fr over 1f out* **11/4**[1]

2m 7.80s **Going Correction** 0.0s/f (Good) **8** Ran SP% **115.3**
Speed ratings: 110,108,108,106,104 104,104,84
CSF £48.74 TOTE £7.30: £2.10, £3.40, £1.70; DF 84.20.
Owner Mrs John Magnier **Bred** Tower Bloodstock **Trained** Ballydoyle, Co Tipperary

FOCUS
A race won in recent years by the likes of Sinndar, Galileo, High Chaparral and Alamshar, but this looked an ordinary renewal. Still, this was a smart effort from Dylan Thomas on his reappearance, and he deserves to take his chance in the Epsom Derby.

NOTEBOOK
Dylan Thomas(IRE) flopped on his final start at two when just a 6-1 shot for the Group One Racing Post Trophy, but he had previously won his first two starts and finished runner-up in the Group Three Autumn Stakes. Upped in trip for his reappearance, he was always close to the pace and kept on in likeable fashion when asked to win quite decisively. His stamina for a mile and a half is far from guaranteed strictly on breeding, but he runs as though he could get it and deserves his chance in the Epsom Derby given the recent record of winners of this race. (op 9/2)
Mountain(IRE) ◆, a beaten favourite and a little disappointing in the Ballysax Stakes over the course and distance on his previous start, showed improved form to reverse placings with his stablemate Altius, who was one place in front of him that day, but found another O'Brien horse too good. A big, likeable type, he should continue to progress throughout the season and is almost sure to stay further. (op 8/1 tchd 9/1)
Youmzain(IRE) showed a smart level of form when winning a three-runner race at Catterick on his reappearance and looked to improve a little on that effort to take a creditable third. (op 10/1)
Caribbean, last in a 2000 Guineas Trial over a mile here on his reappearance, showed improved form on this step up in trip.
Golden Arrow(IRE) was well below the form he showed to finish a neck-second in the Ballysax on his reappearance.
Rekaab(IRE) could not confirm 2000 Guineas Trial form with Caribbean and was a little disappointing. (op 4/1)
Altius(IRE) was below the form he showed when third in the Ballysax on his reappearance and just set the race up for stablemate Dylan Thomas.
Heliostatic(IRE), a neck-second in the 2000 Guineas Trial at Leopardstown on his reappearance, looked sure to be suited by this step up in trip but ran no sort of race. He is much better than this and something must have been amiss. (op 9/4)

1709a DERRINSTOWN STUD 1,000 GUINEAS TRIAL (GROUP 3) (FILLIES) 1m

4:25 (4:26) 3-Y-O £38,162 (£11,196; £5,334; £1,817)

RPR

1 Queen Cleopatra (IRE)[21] 1177 3-9-0 106 JAHeffernan 5 105
(A P O'Brien, Ire) *cl 2nd: led early st: styd on wl whn strly pressed ins fnl f* **6/4**[1]

2 ¾ Modeeroch (IRE)[227] 5571 3-9-0 108 KJManning 8 103
(J S Bolger, Ire) *hld up in 5th: 3rd and prog ent st: 2nd and chal fnl f: kpt on wl u.p* **3/1**[2]

3 ½ Tamazug[35] 929 3-9-0 DPMcDonogh 6 102+
(Kevin Prendergast, Ire) *trckd ldrs in 3rd: 4th and rdn early st: 3rd 1f out: kpt on wl* **10/1**

4 ½ Be My Queen (IRE)[205] 6007 3-9-0 CO'Donoghue 4 101+
(A P O'Brien, Ire) *hld up in 6th: rdn early st: 4th 1f out: kpt on wl* **14/1**

5 3 Sandie (IRE)[13] 1363 3-9-0 100 DJMoran 3 95
(J S Bolger, Ire) *hld up in rr: rdn ent st: kpt on same pce* **12/1**

6 ½ Lifetime Romance (IRE)[202] 6083 3-9-0 MJKinane 1 94
(John M Oxx, Ire) *trckd ldrs: 4th 3f out: no ex st* **6/1**[3]

7 2 Queen Of Rap (IRE)[24] 1104 3-9-0 PJSmullen 2 90
(D K Weld, Ire) *led: hdd early st: sn wknd: eased ins fnl f* **6/1**[3]

1m 44.5s **Going Correction** -0.10s/f (Good) **8** Ran SP% **117.0**
Speed ratings: 95,94,93,93,90 89,87
CSF £6.41 TOTE £3.60: £2.10, £2.60; DF 6.60.
Owner Mrs John Magnier **Bred** Western Bloodstock **Trained** Ballydoyle, Co Tipperary

FOCUS
A solid renewal of this Irish 1000 Guineas trial.

NOTEBOOK
Queen Cleopatra(IRE) produced a gritty display to land this Group 3 prize. Although she came into this race looking for her first victory, she had already proven herself in good company this season. She quickened into the lead early in the straight to open up a useful advantage and ran on well under pressure to repel the challenge of the runner-up. She is improving with racing and will be well worth her place in the Irish 1000, where a big run looks entirely possible. (op 7/4)
Modeeroch(IRE) was having her first run since finishing fourth in last year's Cheveley Park Stakes. The Tyros Stakes winner and Debutante Stakes runner-up improved into a challenging position early in the straight and soon went in pursuit of the leader. She found plenty under pressure but just could not reel in the winner. She can be expected to improve on this and appeals as another who can run a big race at The Curragh in two weeks' time. (op 9/4)
Tamazug came here off a narrow victory in a useful-looking Curragh maiden last month. She held every chance early in the straight and was putting in her best work at the finish. A step up to ten furlongs looks as though it could suit.
Be My Queen(IRE) was another maiden but she had shown plenty of promise when finishing close up in last year's C L Weld Park Stakes. She will improve from this reappearance and a first success will not be long in coming her way.
Lifetime Romance(IRE) raced close to the pace but had no more to give inside the final quarter-mile. She can be expected to come on for this but more will be needed if she is to make her mark in Pattern company.

1710 - 1711a (Foreign Racing) - See Raceform Interactive

1368 CAPANNELLE (R-H)
Sunday, May 14

OFFICIAL GOING: Good

1712a PREMIO PRESIDENTE DELLA REPUBBLICA AT THE RACES (GROUP 1) 1m 2f

3:15 (3:35) 4-Y-0+ £157,379 (£75,276; £42,828; £21,414)

RPR

1 Distant Way (USA)[13] 5-9-2 MDemuro 1 118
(L Brogi, Italy) *held up in last, pushed along and ran on 2f out, went 2nd 150 yards out, ran on to lead 50 yards out* **242/100**[2]

2 1 Soldier Hollow[30] 1014 6-9-2 WMongil 7 116
(P Schiergen, Germany) *racd in 6th, easy prog to press ldrs 2f out, led 1 1/2f out, rdn and ran on fnl f, hdd 50y out* **43/10**

3 ¾ Groom Tesse[13] 5-9-2 (b) SLandi 2 115
(L Camici, Italy) *disp 3rd, 4th str, hdwy on ins over 2f out, wnt 2nd over 1f out, crossed by Soldier Hollow ins fnl f, kpt on* **4/1**[3]

4 2 Rocamadour[25] 1084 4-9-2 RobertWinston 6 111
(M R Channon) *led, pushed along 3f out, headed 1 1/2f out, stayed on at one pace to line* **6/4**[1]

5 hd Bening (FR)[22] 6-9-2 CColombi 5 111
(O Pessi, Italy) *disputed 3rd, 3rd straight, kept on til no extra final furlong* **46/10**

6 5 Los Bonitos (GER)[157] 4-9-2 (b) GMarcelli 3 102
(L A Berretta, Italy) *raced in 5th, pushed along 3f out, weakened 2f out* **45/1**

7 15 Nonno Carlo (IRE)[189] 6278 6-9-2 MPasquale 4 75
(M Grassi, Italy) *raced in 2nd til lost place 3f out, eased final 1 1/2f* **47/1**

2m 0.90s **7** Ran SP% **130.2**
(Including 1 Euro stake): WIN 3.42; PL 1.86, 2.42; SF 9.88.
Owner Allevamento La Nuova Sbarra **Bred** Grundy Bloodstock Ltd **Trained** Italy

NOTEBOOK
Distant Way(USA) was favourite and ridden with plenty of confidence from the rear of the field. His jockey timed his challenge particlarly well, and there is no doubt he was a worthy winner.
Rocamadour turned in a creditable effort trying to make all, but he could not cope with the pace of the first two in the final furlong and a half.

1713a PREMIO REGINA ELENA EMIRATES AIRLINE (GROUP 2) (FILLIES) 1m

4:20 (4:47) 3-Y-O £95,552 (£48,948; £28,724; £14,362)

RPR

1 Windhuk (GER)[49] 758 3-8-11 SLandi 1 106
(P Giannotti, Italy) *mid-division, headway 3f out, finished well final 1 1/2f, led just inside final furlong, pushed out* **66/1**

2 1 Musa Golosa[308] 3383 3-8-11 SMulas 14 104
(B Grizzetti, Italy) *held up, ran on well through field from 2f out, went 2nd inside final furlong, kept on to line* **64/1**

3 1 ½ Sabana Perdida (IRE)[42] 3-8-11 MTellini 7 101
(R Feligioni, Italy) *soon led, ridden 2f out, headed just inside final furlong, kept on* **13/10**[1]

4 nk Hands Clean (IRE)[217] 5787 3-8-11 OFancera 15 100
(A Candi, Italy) *held up, headway 2f out, ran on to take 4th final furlong* **119/1**

5 4 Golden System (IRE)[175] 3-8-11 WMongil 13 92
(M Fratini, Italy) *raced in close 2nd, driven 2 1/2f out, kept on til no extra 1 1/2f out* **39/1**

6 ¾ Dionisia (USA)[21] 3-8-11 CFiocchi 12 91
(R Menichetti, Italy) *in touch, 4th straight, effort 3f out, one pace final 2f* **16/10**[2]

7 1 Adeje Park (IRE)[13] 1349 3-8-11 EddieAhern 10 89
(P W Chapple-Hyam) *mid-division, never in contention* **20/1**

8 nse Bahalita (IRE) 3-8-11 GMarcelli 2 89
(L Riccardi, Italy) *held up, effort 2 1/2f out, never in contention* **10/1**

9 1 ½ Capannacce (IRE)[217] 5787 3-8-11 FBranca 11 86
(Francesca Falco, Italy) *always mid-division* **49/1**

10 ¾ Miss Lorella (IRE)[47] 3-8-11 MPasquale 3 84
(M Grassi, Italy) *never dangerous* **41/1**

11 1 Percristina (IRE)[42] 3-8-11 DVargiu 16 82
(B Grizzetti, Italy) *towards rear, ridden 2f out, never threatened* **24/1**

12 3 Winga (IRE)[194] 6222 3-8-11 MEsposito 4 76
(B Grizzetti, Italy) *held up, driven along straight, one pace* **31/1**

13 ½ Reina De Mexico 3-8-11 GTemperini 18 75
(E Russo, Italy) *never better than mid-division* **116/1**

14 2 Stella Celtica (ITY) 3-8-11 EBotti 17 71
(A Botti, Italy) *mid-division, never dangerous* **10/1**

15 2 Fusijama (USA) 3-8-11 MDemuro 6 67
(L Brogi, Italy) *prominent in 4th, 4th straight, effort 3f out, weakened 2f out* **20/1**

16 nk Cinzia Vegas (IRE) 3-8-11 MSimonaggio 5 67
(S Santella, Italy) *always towards rear* **155/1**

17 12 Salar Violet (IRE) 3-8-11 SGandini 19 43
(R Feligioni, Italy) *prominent in 3rd til weakened over 2f out* **13/10**[1]

F Mrs Snow[14] 1328 3-8-11 RobertWinston 9 —
(Mario Hofer, Germany) *mid-division when tripped and fell 3f out* **11/2**[3]

1m 37.0s **18** Ran SP% **187.9**
WIN 67.65; PL 11.61, 10.54, 1.66; DF 1,328.00.
Owner P L Giannotti **Bred** Gestut Romerhof **Trained** Italy

NOTEBOOK
Windhuk(GER) was a shock winner but she turned in an excellent effort. Connections have no future targets in mind.
Adeje Park(IRE) never managed to get into the race.

1369 COLOGNE (R-H)
Sunday, May 14

OFFICIAL GOING: Good

1714a SCHWARZGOLD-RENNEN (EX DIANA-TRIAL - DEUTSCHER STUTEN-PREIS) (GROUP 2) (FILLIES) 1m 3f

3:05 (3:11) 3-Y-O £27,568 (£10,345; £4,138; £2,759)

RPR

1 Quelle Amore (GER)[27] 3-9-0 EPedroza 1 104
(A Wohler, Germany) *first to show, tracked leader 4f, 3rd on inside straight, led 2f out, driven out* **54/10**

2 nk Nordtanzerin (GER)[203] 6051 3-9-0 FilipMinarik 7 104
(P Schiergen, Germany) *raced in 4th to straight, stayed on under pressure but too late to worry winner* **24/10**[1]

3 1 ¼ Souvenance[208] 5967 3-9-0 SebSanders 9 102
(Sir Mark Prescott) *soon led, headed 2f out, kept on steadily under pressure, lost 2nd in last 100 yards* **43/10**[3]

4 1 ¾ Samerous (FR)[217] 5787 3-9-0 ADeVries 8 99
(H Blume, Germany) *in rear when hampered after 2f, 7th straight, stayed on final 2f, nearest at finish* **134/10**

5 1 Auenprincess (GER) 3-9-0 ABoschert 4 98
(U Ostmann, Germany) *always close up, went 2nd after 4f, 2nd straight, one pace from well over 1f out* **67/10**

6 2 Turning Light (GER)[27] 3-9-0 AStarke 5 94
(Mario Hofer, Germany) *held up in rear, 8th straight, never a factor* **26/10**[2]

7 3 Jade Rheinberg (GER)[203] 6051 3-9-0 AHelfenbein 2 90
(M Trybuhl, Germany) *disputed 4th, 5th straight, never a factor* **34/1**

8 5 Zakopane (GER)[27] 3-9-0 THellier 6 82
(P Schiergen, Germany) *towards rear when hampered after 2f, soon racing in mid-division, 6th straight, never a factor* **7/1**

9 6 Elounesse (GER) 3-9-0 ASuborics 3 72
(Mario Hofer, Germany) *pulling hard towards rear and caused interference after 2f, always behind thereafter* **22/1**

2m 21.46s **9** Ran SP% **131.3**
(Including 10 Euro stake): WIN 64; PL 19, 15, 22; SF 210.
Owner Stiftung Gestut Fahrhof **Bred** Gestut Park Wiedingen **Trained** Germany

NOTEBOOK
Souvenance, racing for the first time since October, set off in front and would not give in when headed by the winner two furlongs out. She was rallying at the end and should find a good staying prize before long.

1715a MEHL-MUHLENS-RENNEN (GERMAN 2,000 GUINEAS) (GROUP 2) (ENTIRE COLTS & FILLIES) 1m

4:10 (4:18) 3-Y-O £68,966 (£26,207; £12,414; £3,103; £3,103)

RPR

1 Royal Power (IRE)[21] 1175 3-9-2 ChrisCatlin 6 106
(M R Channon) *tracked leader, 2nd straight, led 2f out, driven out* **38/10**[2]

2 hd Aspectus (IRE)[21] 1176 3-9-2 ADeVries 5 106
(H Blume, Germany) *held up in 5th to straight, not clear run over 1f out, driven to take 2nd inside final furlong, ran on* **4/5**[1]

3 1 Lord Of England (GER)[21] 1176 3-9-2 AStarke 1 104
(Mario Hofer, Germany) *hld up, 6th str, tried to get through on rails 2f out, swtchd left 1 1/2f out, ran on to take 3rd cl home* **46/10**

4 ¾ Sovereign Dancer (GER)[238] 5351 3-9-2 THellier 4 103
(Mario Hofer, Germany) *led to 2f out, kept on one pace, no extra last 100 yards* **34/1**

4 dht Chief Commander (FR)[13] 1358 3-9-2 JimmyQuinn 2 103
(Jane Chapple-Hyam) *a cl up, 3rd straight, hard ridden and every chance 2f out to appr fnl f, one pace* **23/1**

6 ¾ Saldenblatt[13] 3-9-2 ASuborics 3 101
(Mario Hofer, Germany) *held up, 9th straight, some late progress, never nearer* **43/10**[3]

7 1 **Silex (GER)**[21] 1176 3-9-2 .... FilipMinarik 9 99
(P Schiergen, Germany) *prominent, 4th straight, beaten well over 1f out* **39/1**

8 1 1/2 **Mharadono (GER)**[21] 1176 3-9-2 .... TMundry 11 96
(P Hirschberger, Germany) *towards rear to straight, effort 2f out, weakened approaching final furlong* **54/1**

9 shd **Annunzio**[13] 3-9-2 .... EPedroza 8 96
(W Baltromei, Germany) *always towards rear* **33/1**

10 2 **World's Mission (GER)**[21] 1176 3-9-2 .... AHelfenbein 10 92
(Mario Hofer, Germany) *last straight, always behind* **29/1**

1m 38.04s 10 Ran SP% **130.7**
WIN 48; PL 14, 11, 13; SF 98.
Owner Jaber Abdullah **Bred** Denis McDonnell **Trained** West Ilsley, Berks

NOTEBOOK
Royal Power(IRE) tracked the leader most of the way. He took a narrow lead with two furlongs to run but had to work hard to shake off Chief Commander and Sovereign Dancer before the furlong marker. He went at least a length up but then had to battle to hold the favourite's late run. He deserved this narrow success after a sequence of four seconds.
Chief Commander(FR) was level with the winner two furlongs out. He had edged off the rails at that point, tempting Lord of England to go for a gap, which he soon closed. He battled on under strong pressure and only lost second halfway through the final furlong.

KRANJI (L-H)
Sunday, May 14
OFFICIAL GOING: Yielding

1716a SINGAPORE AIRLINES INTERNATIONAL CUP (GROUP 1) 1m 2f
1:35 (1:36) 3-Y-0+
£557,895 (£210,526; £105,263; £52,632; £15,789; £10,526)

RPR

1 **Cosmo Bulk (JPN)**[140] 5-9-0 .... FIgarashi 1 121
(K Tabe, Japan) *raced in 2nd, driven straight, ran on to lead 1f out, ran on well to line, driven out* **58/10**[3]

2 1 3/4 **King And King (AUS)** 5-9-0 .... (p) RLim 13 117
(S Burridge, Singapore) *mid-division, 7th on outside straight, ran on 1 1/2f out, went 2nd on line* **144/10**

3 hd **Bowman's Crossing (IRE)**[21] 1180 7-9-0 .... GMosse 3 117
(C Fownes, Hong Kong) *mid-div, hdwy 2 1/2f out, 6th str, rdn and ran on 1 1/2f out, pressing ldrs fnl f, kpt on, lost 2nd on line* **102/10**

4 5 **Vroom Vroom (ARG)**[36] 5-9-0 .... CraigWilliams 6 108
(D Hayes, Australia) *led, driven and ran on 1 1/2f out, headed 1f out, ridden and no extra final 100 yards* **32/10**[1]

5 3/4 **Diamond Dust (JPN)** 5-9-0 .... CSegeon 11 107
(H Takaoka, Japan) *towards rear, ran on straight but never dangerous* **37/1**

6 3/4 **Terfel**[79] 509 7-9-0 .... KBSoo 10 105
(Daniel J Murphy, Singapore) *last til progress 3f out, driven 2 1/2f out, 4th on inside straight, stayed on same pace* **34/1**

7 3/4 **Falstaff (IRE)**[21] 1180 4-9-0 .... (b) BVorster 5 104
(M F De Kock, South Africa) *in touch, headway 3f out, 3rd straight, no extra from over 1f out* **96/10**

8 8 **War Horn (ARG)** 4-9-0 .... MDuPlessis 4 90
(P Shaw, Singapore) *prominent, 4th half-way, ridden 2 1/2f out, 5th straight, no extra* **22/1**

9 nk **Chiquitin (ARG)**[50] 743 6-9-0 .... WCMarwing 2 89
(I Jory, Saudi Arabia) *raced in 3rd til lost place 3f out, 10th and beaten straight* **7/1**

10 3 1/4 **Zankel (NZ)**[92] 4-9-0 .... (b) NCallow 9 83
(D Koh, Singapore) *towards rear, 9th and driven straight, never a factor* **28/1**

11 nk **Big Easy (NZ)**[79] 513 5-9-0 .... (b) JSaimee 12 83
(L Laxon, Singapore) *mid-division, driven to chase leaders 3f out, 8th towards outside straight, no extra final 1 1/2f* **176/10**

12 10 **Mount Street (NZ)**[182] 5-9-0 .... JohnPowell 8 65
(L Laxon, Singapore) *mid-division, driven 3f out, unable to quicken* **96/10**

13 3 **Valixir (IRE)**[50] 742 5-9-0 .... (b) LDettori 7 59
(Saeed Bin Suroor) *in tch early, 8th half-way, lost place and under pressure appr str, last str, sn rdn and btn* **38/10**[2]

2m 6.50s 13 Ran SP% **124.8**
(Including S$5 stake): WIN 34; PL 12, 19, 16, DF 180.
Owner M Okada **Bred** Kano Bokujo **Trained** Japan

FOCUS
Rain before the race softened the ground markedly
NOTEBOOK
Cosmo Bulk(JPN) always had a good position and ran on well once hitting the front. This horse shows the strength in depth of Japanese racing, as he is a NAR horse, the racing body considered second fiddle to JRA racing.
King And King(AUS) previously raced in Australia under the name Beau Jack.
Valixir(IRE) was a major disappointment, with the writing on the wall turning for home. There seemed some pessimism about his chances beforehand, and this tame display must be of concern to connections.

1557 LONGCHAMP (R-H)
Sunday, May 14
OFFICIAL GOING: Good to soft
Racing began two and a half hours late after a strike by on-course PMU staff.

1717a PRIX DE SAINT-GEORGES (GROUP 3) 5f (S)
2:20 (4:34) 3-Y-0+ **£27,586** (£11,034; £8,276; £5,517; £2,759)

RPR

1 **Latona (FR)**[20] 1202 4-8-11 .... TGillet 7 110
(J E Pease, France) *always close up on outside, led well over 2f out, pushed out & ran on well* **9/4**[2]

2 1 1/2 **Matrix (GER)**[20] 1202 5-9-0 .... DBoeuf 1 108
(W Baltromei, Germany) *led after 1f, headed well over 2f out, kept on under pressure* **9/1**

3 hd **Biniou (IRE)**[16] 1277 3-8-5 .... CSoumillon 5 103
(Robert Collet, France) *always in touch, headway over 2f out, one pace final f* **12/1**

4 1 **The Tatling (IRE)**[8] 1485 9-9-7 .... RyanMoore 8 111
(J M Bradley) *always in touch, went 3rd ahlf-way, one pace from over 1f out* **7/4**[1]

5 shd **Alyzea (IRE)**[16] 1277 3-8-4 .... DBonilla 2 99
(C Laffon-Parias, France) *always about same place, not much room on rails inside final f* **8/1**[3]

6 hd **Tycoon's Hill (IRE)**[219] 5729 7-9-0 .... OPeslier 9 103
(Robert Collet, France) *last early, closed up half-way, never able to cahllenge* **8/1**[3]

7 1/2 **Headache (FR)**[16] 1277 3-8-12 .... SMaillot 3 104
(Robert Collet, France) *led 1f, weakened well over 1f out* **16/1**

8 3/4 **Meliksah (IRE)**[7] 12-9-0 .... TRicher 4 99
(Mrs D Smith, Germany) *always outpaced* **33/1**

56.70 secs **Going Correction** -0.075s/f (Good)
WFA 3 from 4yo+ 9lb 8 Ran SP% **115.9**
Speed ratings: 113,110,110,108,108 108,107,106
PARI-MUTUEL: WIN 4.30; PL 1.40, 1.60, 1.40; DF 14.60.
Owner J Goelet **Bred** John Goelet **Trained** Chantilly, France

NOTEBOOK
Latona(FR) was smartly into her stride and never far from the lead which she took a furlong and a half out. She was never really troubled thereafter and won in style. She now heads for the Prix de Gros Chene and has also been entered in the King's Stand Stakes at Ascot. She is certainly one to watch this season.
Matrix(GER) was the quickest into his stride and took the field along until passed by the winner. He battled really well in the final stages to hold second place, although he is probably better suited to faster ground.
Biniou(IRE) was not too quick out of the stalls and then in mid-division before making an effort with 300 yards left to run. He had to change course close to the post and only missed second place by a head.
The Tatling(IRE), fifth at the halfway stage, he ran on from one and a half furlongs out but never threatened to get any closer. His stride shortened in the last 50 yards and his jockey felt he was a bit flat on this occasion.

1718a GAINSBOROUGH POULE D'ESSAI DES POULAINS (GROUP 1) (COLTS) 1m
2:50 (5:04) 3-Y-0 **£157,628** (£63,062; £31,531; £15,752; £7,890)

RPR

1 **Aussie Rules (USA)**[21] 1178 3-9-2 .... KFallon 5 117+
(A P O'Brien, Ire) *held up, 6th on inside straight, headway 2f out, led on rails 100 yds out, ran on well* **4/1**[2]

2 1/2 **Marcus Andronicus (USA)**[22] 1131 3-9-2 .... CSoumillon 2 116
(A P O'Brien, Ire) *always close up, 3rd straight, 2nd 2f out, kept on under pressure to regain 2nd last strides* **14/1**

3 hd **Stormy River (FR)**[21] 1178 3-9-2 .... TThulliez 7 116
(N Clement, France) *tracked leader, led over 2f out, headed 100 yds out, lost 2nd last strides* **4/6**[1]

4 1 **West Of Amarillo (USA)**[16] 1269 3-9-2 .... JimmyFortune 6 113
(J H M Gosden) *held up, 9th straight, progress under pressure approaching final f, no extra last 100y* **33/1**

5 1 **Garnica (FR)**[19] 3-9-2 .... IMendizabal 9 111
(J-C Rouget, France) *soon racing in 4th, 4th straight, one pace final f* **25/1**

6 nk **Porto Santo (FR)**[21] 1178 3-9-2 .... SPasquier 10 110
(P Demercastel, France) *held up in rear, last straight, stayed on final 2f, nearest at finish* **12/1**

7 1 1/2 **Ivan Denisovich (IRE)**[21] 1178 3-9-2 .... OPeslier 8 107
(A P O'Brien, Ire) *held up in rear, 10th straight, some late progress, never a factor* **9/1**[3]

8 hd **Dream In Blue (FR)**[21] 1178 3-9-2 .... JAuge 3 106+
(Robert Collet, France) *close up, 5th straight, beaten over 1f out* **16/1**

9 hd **Yasoodd**[29] 1025 3-9-2 .... TedDurcan 4 106
(M R Channon) *mid-division, 8th straight, soon ridden & one pace* **10/1**

10 3/4 **Fenice (IRE)**[40] 884 3-9-2 .... C-PLemaire 11 104
(Robert Collet, France) *9th straight, always in rear* **66/1**

11 15 **James Joyce (IRE)**[29] 1025 3-9-2 .... DavidMcCabe 1 70
(A P O'Brien, Ire) *led to over 2f out* **50/1**

1m 37.0s **Going Correction** -0.35s/f (Firm) 11 Ran SP% **129.6**
Speed ratings: 113,112,112,111,110 110,108,108,108,107 92
PARI-MUTUEL: WIN 3.70 (coupled with Marcus Andronicus, James Joyce, Ivan Denisovich); PL 1.60, 2.10, 1.20; DF 31.50.
Owner Mrs J Magnier,M Tabor,F Salman **Bred** Belgrave Bloodstock Ltd **Trained** Ballydoyle, Co Tipperary

NOTEBOOK
Aussie Rules(USA) looked in great shape in the paddock and had come on enormously since his previous trip to France. He was given a fine waiting ride, for he still had plenty to do on entering the straight but made his run up the far rail and took it up with 100 yards left. He will now run over a longer trip in the Prix du Jockey-Club.
Marcus Andronicus(USA), another who looked in great condition in the preliminaries, was well away and soon behind the leaders. He pulled out to challenge halfway up the straight and ran on really well inside the final furlong to take second place close home. He will now go to the Irish 2000 Guineas at the end of the month.
Stormy River(FR) had every chance but ran rather free in the early part of this mile. In second position before taking command halfway up the straight, he fought well but did not have the same zip as in his previous race. His trainer will see how he comes out this before making any plans.
West Of Amarillo(USA) put up a decent performance and was doing his best work up the far rail at the finish, having been held up early on. He has now been marked down for the Jersey Stakes at Royal Ascot.
Yasoodd was never seen with a real chance and failed to run his race. He was always towards the rear of the field and made little progress in the straight.

1719a GAINSBOROUGH POULE D'ESSAI DES POULICHES (GROUP 1) (3YO FILLIES) 1m
3:30 (5:43) 3-Y-0 **£157,628** (£63,062; £31,531; £15,752; £7,890)

RPR

1 **Tie Black (IRE)**[19] 3-9-0 .... J-BEyquem 1 111
(F Rohaut, France) *mid-div, 9th st, gd hdwy wl over 1f out, led briefly 150y out, brushed with 3rd 100y out, kept on, fin 2nd, 1 1/2l, awrdd r* **20/1**

2 **Impressionnante**[32] 3-9-0 .... OPeslier 11 111
(C Laffon-Parias, France) *hld up, gd hdwy wl over 1f out, ev ch ins fnl f, squeezed up and brushed with 2nd ins final 100y, fin 3rd, 1 1/2l & snk, plcd 2nd* **8/1**

3 **Price Tag**[21] 1177 3-9-0 .... TThulliez 10 114
(P Bary, France) *hld up, 12th st, gd hdwy wl over 1f out, hung right, ran on to lead 100y out, driven out, fin 1st, 1½l & snk, plcd 3rd* **33/1**

4 ½ **Daltaya (FR)**[21] 1177 3-9-0 .... CSoumillon 2 110
(A De Royer-Dupre, France) *always close up, 5th straight, 4th & ridden over 1f out, one pace* **4/1**[2]

5 ½ **Mauralakana (FR)**[40] 883 3-9-0 .... IMendizabal 12 108
(J-C Rouget, France) *mid-division, 8th straight, headway on inside 2f out, disputed 4th over 1f out, one pace* **8/1**

6 4 **New Girlfriend (IRE)**[266] 4618 3-9-0 .... C-PLemaire 3 101
(Robert Collet, France) *led to 150y out, one pace* **5/1**[3]

7 ¾ **Damoiselle (USA)**[226] 5595 3-9-0 ....(b) DBonilla 5 100
(F Head, France) *prominent, 2nd straight, weakened well over 1f out* **16/1**

8 2 **Beauty Bright (IRE)**[29] 1023 3-9-0 .... TJarnet 13 96
(A P O'Brien, Ire) *towards rear to straight, never a factor* **16/1**

9 3 **Daaly Babet (FR)**[38] 3-9-0 .... DBoeuf 8 90
(C Scandella, France) *never nearer than mid-division* **11/1**

10 6 **Dama'A (IRE)**[20] 1191 3-9-0 .... JimmyFortune 6 78
(J H M Gosden) *6th straight, weakened well over 1f out* **50/1**

11 1 ½ **Kamarinskaya (USA)**[29] 1023 3-9-0 .... KFallon 4 75
(A P O'Brien, Ire) *4th straight, weakened well over 1f out* **3/1**[1]

12 2 ½ **Silva (FR)**[16] 1277 3-9-0 .... MBlancpain 7 70
(C Laffon-Parias, France) *prominent, 3rd straight, soon weakened* **16/1**

13 dist **Silver Touch (IRE)**[23] 1119 3-9-0 .... TedDurcan 9 —
(M R Channon) *11th over 4f out, dropped to last over 3f out, tailed off* **9/1**

1m 36.6s **Going Correction** -0.25s/f (Firm) 13 Ran SP% **129.5**
Speed ratings: 117,117,119,116,116 112,111,109,106,100 99,96,—
PARI-MUTUEL: WIN 9.70; PL 3.20, 4.30, 6.40; DF 72.10.
Owner J Gispert **Bred** Stone Ridge Farm **Trained** Sauvagnon, France

NOTEBOOK
Tie Black(IRE) still had plenty to do at the entrance to the straight. Asked to make a forward move a furlong and a half out, she ran on well up the far rail. Beaten fairly and squarely, she was awarded this Classic when the Stewards harshly disqualified the winner. She may now be rested, and one of her main targets later on could be the Group One Prix d'Astarte.
Impressionnante was not easy to extract to challenge halfway up the straight. She then ran on and veered right when the winner hung inside the final furlong. She was moved up to second place by the Stewards. Still quite green, she is open to improvement, but connections have no fixed plans at the moment.
Price Tag still had plenty to do coming into the straight in a race that had early pace, but made rapid late progress from one and a half out and joined the leaders at the furlong marker. She won this race fair and square but was demoted for hanging to the right and hampering the third, a decision her connections unsuccesfully appealed against. She will definitely stay further and is one to watch for the future.
Daltaya(FR) raced just behind the leaders on the rail and didn't have the clearest of runs, but she did stay on bravely throughout the final stages. She is now likely to be tried over a longer distance, which should be an advantage.
Mauralakana(FR) was trying a mile for the first time and was back up to Group 1 company, having met her only two defeat when she had been tried at that level at two. She appeared to get the trip but wasn't quite good enough.
New Girlfriend(IRE) had easily the best two-year-old form, and although she had not been out since pulling too hard and finishing only fifth on soft ground in the Morny at Deauville in August, she had reportedly enjoyed a good preparation. Jumped straight off in front, she raced clear of the field until well into the straight, seemingly not pulling too hard, but the writing was on the wall going to the 200 metre mark and she was ultimately swamped. The Prix du Jockey-Club had been the target, but on this evidence she is more likely to drop back in trip. Quicker ground would help too.
Dama'A(IRE) was never seen with a real chance and certainly ran below expectations.
Kamarinskaya(USA) raced prominently in the chasing group but started to struggle straightening for home and gradually dropped back through the field. She has run as many bad races as good ones.
Silver Touch(IRE) was in trouble well before the straight and made no show

1720 - (Foreign Racing) - See Raceform Interactive

HOLLYWOOD PARK (L-H)

Saturday, May 13

OFFICIAL GOING: Turf course - firm; dirt course - fast

1721a JIM MURRAY MEMORIAL H'CAP (GRADE 2) (TURF) 1m 4f (T)

11:50 (11:53) 3-Y-0+ **£87,209** (£29,070; £17,442; £8,721; £2,907)

RPR

1 **Grey Swallow (IRE)**[202] 6059 5-8-9 .... ASolis 3 124
(D K Weld, Ire) *tracked leader in 2nd, ridden to lead straight, ran clear inside final furlong, ridden out* **3/5**[1]

2 5 **Brecon Beacon**[119] 4-7-13 ....(b) AGryder 2 106
(Doug O'Neill, U.S.A) **72/10**

3 1 **Runaway Dancer (USA)**[35] 7-8-3 .... JValdivia 6 109
(Dan L Hendricks, U.S.A) **69/10**[3]

4 nk **Golden Rahy (USA)**[20] 7-8-3 .... OFigueroa 4 108
(Doug O'Neill, U.S.A) **26/1**

5 1 ½ **One Off**[20] 6-8-2 ....(b) JKCourt 5 105
(N Drysdale, U.S.A) **26/10**[2]

2m 27.33s 5 Ran SP% **118.8**
PARI-MUTUEL (Including $2 stake): WIN 3.20; PL (1-2) 2.60, 4.60;SHOW (1-2-3) 2.10, 2.80, 2.40; SF 14.20.
Owner Vega FZE **Bred** Mrs C L Weld **Trained** The Curragh, Co Kildare

NOTEBOOK
Grey Swallow(IRE) made a fine start to his US career and, getting a good lead from the runner-up, won in fine style. He will head for the Grade One Manhattan Handicap at Belmont, after which he will remain in America in the care of Richard Dutrow jnr.

1534 KEMPTON (A.W) (R-H)

Monday, May 15

OFFICIAL GOING: Standard
Wind: Light, half-behind

1722 KEMPTON FOR EXHIBITIONS BANDED STKS 5f (P)

2:00 (2:01) (Class 7) 3-Y-0+ **£1,706** (£503; £252) **Stalls** High

Form RPR

3523 1 **Katie Killane**[7] 1534 4-9-6 45 ....(v) DaneO'Neill 4 51
(M Wellings) *led after 1f: clr over 1f out: hrd rdn fnl f: jst hld on* **10/1**

0050 2 shd **King Egbert (FR)**[10] 1466 5-9-6 40 .... ShaneKelly 8 51
(A W Carroll) *s.i.s: stong hdwy u.p over 1f out: fin fast: jst failed* **12/1**

0343 3 nk **Maromito (IRE)**[10] 1466 9-9-6 45 .... RoystonFfrench 1 50
(R Bastiman) *trckd wnr: rdn over 1f out: kpt on but lost 2nd post* **12/1**

4060 4 1 ¾ **Davids Mark**[20] 1209 6-9-3 45 ....(vt) DeanCorby(3) 10 43
(J R Jenkins) *s.i.s: hdwy over 1f out: kpt on one pce fnl f* **9/2**[1]

2342 5 shd **A Teen**[7] 1534 8-9-6 45 .... IanMongan 6 43
(P Howling) *led for 1f: rdn and one pce fr over 1f out* **5/1**[2]

2403 6 nk **Beverley Beau**[11] 1447 4-8-13 45 .... KristinStubbs(7) 5 42
(Mrs L Stubbs) *chsd ldrs tl rdn and nt qckn fr over 1f out* **7/1**

0006 7 2 ½ **Petana**[10] 1466 6-9-6 40 ....(p) RobbieFitzpatrick 3 33
(Peter Grayson) *bhd: rdn 2f out: nvr on terms* **33/1**

0005 8 shd **Legal Set (IRE)**[7] 1534 10-8-13 45 ....(bt) AnnStokell(7) 11 32
(Miss A Stokell) *trckd ldrs on ins: rdn over 1f out: wknd ins fnl f* **14/1**

0006 9 2 ½ **Stephanie's Mind**[7] 1534 4-9-6 45 .... JohnEgan 9 23
(M Quinn) *mid-div: sn rdn: struggling fnl 2f* **13/2**[3]

6100 10 hd **Maluti**[209] 5966 5-8-13 45 .... RobbieMills(7) 2 23
(Rae Guest) *slowly away: a bhd* **12/1**

0050 11 13 **Fly More**[16] 1303 9-9-6 45 .... JamieSpencer 7 —
(J M Bradley) *a wl bhd and eased wl over 1f out* **9/1**

60.80 secs **Going Correction** -0.05s/f (Stan) **11** Ran SP% **112.5**
Speed ratings (Par 97):94,93,93,90,90 89,85,85,81,81 60
CSF £118.43 TOTE £7.40: £2.20, £6.10, £3.30; EX 123.10.
Owner Mark Wellings Racing **Bred** Peter Balding **Trained** Six Ashes, Shropshire

FOCUS
A weak event, run at a solid pace, and the first three came clear, giving the form a sound appearance.
Fly More Official explanation: jockey said gelding never travelled

1723 KEMPTON FOR WEDDINGS BANDED STKS 1m 2f (P)

2:30 (2:31) (Class 7) 4-Y-0+ **£1,706** (£503; £252) **Stalls** High

Form RPR

5001 1 **Brave Dane (IRE)**[7] 1537 8-9-8 50 .... JamieSpencer 11 66
(A W Carroll) *hld up: hdwy on outside 2f out: rdn and r.o to ld ins fnl f* **6/4**[1]

0561 2 ¾ **Cottingham (IRE)**[10] 1461 5-8-12 49 .... BenSwarbrick(3) 13 58
(T D Barron) *hld up: rdn and hdwy 3f out: outled over 1f out: rdn and hdd ins fnl f* **4/1**[2]

2301 3 ½ **Miss Glory Be**[21] 1198 8-9-0 48 ....(p) DarryllHolland 2 56
(Ernst Oertel) *t.k.h: prom: shkn up over 1f out: kpt on but nt pce to chal* **12/1**

6601 4 3 **Boogie Magic**[13] 1395 6-8-13 47 .... J-PGuillambert 14 49
(T Keddy) *in rr tl hdwy on outside over 1f out: styd on: nt rch first 3* **12/1**

1550 5 1 ¾ **Elms Schoolboy**[7] 1537 4-8-13 47 ....(b) IanMongan 1 46
(P Howling) *towards rr tl hdwy 1/2-way: led briefly 2f out: fdd fnl f* **25/1**

2064 6 3 **Prince Valentine**[7] 1537 5-8-11 45 ....(be) ShaneKelly 6 38
(G L Moore) *mid-div: effrt 2f out: no further hdwy* **14/1**

2600 7 shd **Fantasy Defender (IRE)**[101] 290 4-9-0 48 ....(v) LPKeniry 3 41
(Ernst Oertel) *towards rr: some hdwy over 2f out: nvr nr to chal* **25/1**

5312 8 6 **Bob Baileys**[10] 1462 4-9-2 50 ....(b) StephenCarson 5 31
(P R Chamings) *s.i.s: hdwy to ld 1/2-way: hdd 2f out: sn btn* **25/1**

-014 9 nk **Heathers Girl**[10] 1201 7-8-13 47 .... HayleyTurner 12 28
(R Dickin) *mid-div: rdn and wknd over 2f out* **12/1**

-000 10 3 ½ **Attishoe**[257] 4864 4-8-13 50 .... RichardThomas(3) 8 24
(Miss B Sanders) *in rr: rdn over 4f out: no ch fnl 3f* **66/1**

-055 11 ¾ **Cotton Easter**[363] 1789 5-9-0 48 ....(t) SteveDrowne 4 21
(Mrs A J Bowlby) *slowly away: sn trckd ldrs: rdn over 3f out: sn wknd* **50/1**

1000 12 ½ **Ferrara Flame (IRE)**[17] 1276 4-9-2 50 ....(v) DaneO'Neill 10 22
(R Brotherton) *slowly away: a bhd* **66/1**

000 13 ½ **Silvo (NZ)**[5] 1311 7-9-2 50 .... JohnEgan 7 21
(M F Harris) *trckd ldr to over 2f out: rdn and wknd qckly* **16/1**

0501 14 ¾ **Gala Sunday (USA)**[10] 1462 6-8-10 47 ....(b) PaulMulrennan(3) 9 16
(M W Easterby) *led to 1/2-way: wknd over 2f out* **10/1**[3]

2m 8.22s **Going Correction** -0.05s/f (Stan) **14** Ran SP% **121.2**
Speed ratings (Par 97):101,100,100,97,96 93,93,88,88,85 85,84,84,83
CSF £6.26 TOTE £2.30: £1.40, £1.60, £3.60; EX 10.10.
Owner Exhall Dodgers **Bred** Gainsborough Stud Management Ltd **Trained** Cropthorne, Worcs
■ Stewards' Enquiry : Shane Kelly one-day ban: careless riding (May 26)

FOCUS
This looks to be good form for the class, rated around the placed horses, and the finish was dominated by four previous winners.
Silvo(NZ) Official explanation: jockey said gelding had no more to give

1724 ST PAUL'S CATHOLIC COLLEGE BANDED STKS 1m 2f (P)

3:00 (3:01) (Class 7) 4-Y-0+ **£1,706** (£503; £252) **Stalls** High

Form RPR

0240 1 **Dagola (IRE)**[11] 891 5-8-11 45 .... JohnEgan 5 56
(C A Dwyer) *a in tch on outside: rdn to ld 1f out: r.o strly* **8/1**

0-01 2 2 **Major Blade (GER)**[7] 1553 8-8-11 45 .... LPKeniry 9 52
(Heather Dalton) *trckd ldr: led 3f out: rdn and hdd 1f out: nt pce of wnr* **6/1**[2]

-000 3 2 **Last Chapter (IRE)**[7] 1536 4-8-8 45 ....(b[1]) EdwardCreighton(3) 12 48
(C A Dwyer) *chsd ldrs thrght: rdn and one pce fnl f* **100/1**

6000 4 ½ **Karrnak**[82] 309 4-8-11 45 .... ChrisCatlin 11 47
(Miss J Feilden) *hld up: hdwy 2f out: styd on: nvr nrr* **20/1**

30 5 ½ **Ivorbella (IRE)**[10] 1461 4-8-11 45 ....(t) OscarUrbina 1 47
(M Botti) *hld up towards rr: hdwy over 1f out: kpt on but nvr nr to chal* **25/1**

44-4 6 2 **Royal Indulgence**[10] 1462 6-8-11 45 .... RobbieFitzpatrick 7 43
(W M Brisbourne) *t.k.h in mid-div: kpt on one pce ins fnl 2f* **12/1**

0504 7 nk **Zeena**[7] 1536 4-8-11 45 ....(p) DarryllHolland 8 42
(C A Horgan) *nvr bttr than mid-div* **16/1**

3043 8 1 ½ **Amnesty**[7] 1536 7-8-11 45 ....(be) IanMongan 2 39
(G L Moore) *s.i.s: in rr: mde sme late hdwy* **9/2**[1]

0060 9 6 **Longing For Cindy (USA)**[7] 1536 4-8-11 45 ....(v) DaneO'Neill 14 28
(W M Brisbourne) *led tl hdd 3f out: rdn and wkng whn bdly hmpd over 1f out: nt rcvr* **33/1**

060 10 1 **Earl Of Spectrum (GER)**[152] 5998 5-8-11 45 .... SteveDrowne 6 26
(J L Spearing) *a towards rr* **13/2**[3]

6000 11 6 **Didnt Tell My Wife**[54] 697 7-8-11 45 .... JamieSpencer 4 15
(G C H Chung) *mid-div: wknd over 3f out* **8/1**

0000 12 6 **Supreme Salutation**[13] 1373 10-8-7 45 ow3........ JamesMillman(7) 10 6
(D K Ivory) *bolted to s: a bhd* **20/1**

3535 **13** ½ **Semper Paratus (USA)**[104] 258 7-8-11 45 ow3(v) RossStudholme(3) 13 — 5
(V Smith) *trckd ldrs: wknd 4f out* **16/1**

0435 **P** **Nobelmann (GER)**[7] 1536 7-8-11 45 ShaneKelly 3 —
(A W Carroll) *bhd: t.o whn p.u and dismntd 2f out* **10/1**

2m 8.46s **Going Correction** -0.05s/f (Stan) **14** Ran SP% **113.9**
Speed ratings (Par 97):100,98,96,96,96 94,94,92,88,87 82,77,77,—
CSF £48.71 TOTE £11.50: £3.40, £2.20, £20.90; EX 57.70.
Owner S B Components (international) Ltd **Bred** Patrick Hughes **Trained** Burrough Green, Cambs

FOCUS
A poor affair, run at a decent early pace, and the field came home fairly strung out as a result. The runner-up sets the standard.
Last Chapter(IRE) Official explanation: jockey said gelding hung right-handed
Supreme Salutation Official explanation: jockey said gelding was very free to post
Nobelmann(GER) Official explanation: jockey said gelding lost its action

1725 BISHOP WAND SCHOOL BANDED STKS 1m (P)
3:30 (3:32) (Class 7) 4-Y-0+ **£2,047** (£604; £302) **Stalls** High

Form — RPR

0102 **1** **Wanna Shout**[13] 1394 8-9-1 49 JamieSpencer 3 58
(R Dickin) *mid-div: hdwy 3f out: rdn to ld 1f out: rdn out* **5/1**[2]

2003 **2** 1 **King Of Meze (IRE)**[20] 1227 5-8-13 47 (p) TonyHamilton 10 54
(J S Wainwright) *led tl rdn and hdd 1f out: nt pce of wnr* **8/1**

0025 **3** ¾ **Frank's Quest (IRE)**[16] 1305 6-9-2 50 SamHitchcott 2 55
(A B Haynes) *mid-div: rdn and hdwy 2f out: kpt on one pce fnl f* **12/1**

6510 **4** nk **Abbeygate**[7] 1537 5-9-2 50 J-PGuillambert 11 54
(T Keddy) *hld up: rdn and hdwy over 2f out: styd on: nvr nrr* **7/2**[1]

5000 **5** nk **Postmaster**[20] 1204 4-9-2 50 DaneO'Neill 7 54
(R Ingram) *trckd ldr: rdn over 1f out: fdd fnl f* **16/1**

0040 **6** nk **Kinsman (IRE)**[7] 1537 9-8-10 47 SaleemGolam(3) 1 50
(T D McCarthy) *hld up on outside: rdn and kpt on ins fnl 2f* **14/1**

3002 **7** 1 **Noorain**[6] 1575 4-8-13 47 (t) ChrisCatlin 5 48
(Stef Liddiard) *hld up: hdwy over 2f out: kpt on one pce* **10/1**

0100 **8** 1½ **Riviera Red (IRE)**[91] 398 6-8-12 46 (v) SteveDrowne 6 43
(L Montague Hall) *a towards rr* **11/1**

2660 **9** nk **The Job**[68] 618 5-9-0 48 (v) AdrianMcCarthy 4 44
(A D Smith) *hld up: effrt 2f out: nvr nr to chal* **11/1**

0003 **10** hd **Renegade (IRE)**[15] 1310 5-8-13 47 IanMongan 14 43
(Mrs L J Mongan) *chsd ldrs: rdn over 2f out: sn btn* **7/1**[3]

0000 **11** nk **Fortiszamo**[19] 1244 4-9-1 49 ShaneKelly 9 44
(A W Carroll) *prom tl wknd 2f out* **33/1**

0502 **12** 10 **Glenviews Babalou (USA)**[10] 1463 4-9-2 50 RobbieFitzpatrick 8 22
(Peter Grayson) *a bhd* **25/1**

54-0 **13** 12 **Love's Design (IRE)**[336] 2554 9-8-13 47 (v) OscarUrbina 12 —
(Miss J Feilden) *a towards rr: lost tch 3f out: t.o* **33/1**

1m 41.17s **Going Correction** -0.05s/f (Stan) **13** Ran SP% **118.2**
Speed ratings (Par 97):96,95,94,93,93 93,92,90,90,90 90,80,68
CSF £43.44 TOTE £4.20: £2.20, £2.00, £3.10; EX 26.30.
Owner E R C Beech & B Wilkinson **Bred** C C Bromley And Son **Trained** Atherstone on Stour, Warwicks
■ Stewards' Enquiry : J-P Guillambert three-day ban: careless riding (May 26-28)

FOCUS
Typical form for the class, which looks pretty sound rated through the second and fourth, and the winner is value for slightly further.
Riviera Red(IRE) Official explanation: jockey said gelding hung left-handed
The Job Official explanation: jockey said gelding suffered interference in running
Fortiszamo Official explanation: jockey said gelding lost its action
Love's Design(IRE) Official explanation: jockey said gelding lost its action

1726 KEMPTON FOR OUTDOOR EVENTS TRI-BANDED STKS 1m (P)
4:00 (4:02) (Class 7) 3-Y-0 **£1,706** (£503; £252) **Stalls** High

Form — RPR

004 **1** **Maidford (IRE)**[17] 1274 3-9-0 45 FergusSweeney 8 56
(M Meade) *hld up: hdwy on ins to ld over 1f out: sn clr* **8/1**[2]

0056 **2** 4 **Cecchetti (IRE)**[23] 1149 3-8-9 45 RichardKingscote(5) 9 47
(Mrs H Sweeting) *hld up: hdwy 3f out: rdn and r.o to chse wnr ins fnl f* **8/1**[2]

3624 **3** 3 **The Jailer**[8] 1501 3-9-0 45 (p) DarryllHolland 3 40
(J G M O'Shea) *led tl rdn and hdd over 1f out: fdd and lost 2nd ins fnl f* **11/4**[1]

3040 **4** 3½ **Three Feathers**[40] 890 3-8-11 45 SaleemGolam(3) 6 32
(M Salaman) *in tch: rdn over 2f out: wknd appr fnl f* **12/1**[3]

0004 **5** 1¼ **Joy In The Guild (IRE)**[20] 1226 3-9-0 45 LPKeniry 4 29
(W S Kittow) *trckd ldrs: rdn and wknd wl over 1f out* **8/1**[2]

0000 **6** 1¼ **King's Melody**[13] 1373 3-8-7 45 JamesMillman(7) 10 26
(B R Millman) *mid-div: rdn over 2f out: no hdwy after* **14/1**

0000 **7** 2 **Flying Penne**[11] 1433 3-9-0 45 SamHitchcott 13 22
(M R Channon) *in tch tl wknd over 2f out* **20/1**

0205 **8** ¾ **Skin Sure Thing**[20] 1226 3-9-0 45 (v) AdrianMcCarthy 2 20
(A D Smith) *trckd ldr: rdn over 3f out: wknd wl over 1f out* **25/1**

6040 **9** 5 **Coffin Dodger**[20] 1226 3-8-7 45 (b[1]) KirstyMilczarek(7) 1 8
(C N Allen) *racd wd: lost tch w ldrs fr 1/2-way* **12/1**[3]

0000 **10** 5 **Forever Rocky**[16] 1290 3-9-0 45 PaulFitzsimons 7 —
(F Jordan) *in tch tl wknd over 3f out* **33/1**

050 **11** shd **By Storm**[221] 5703 3-9-0 45 HayleyTurner 12 —
(John Berry) *mid-div: wknd 4f out* **20/1**

0000 **12** 21 **The Flying Peach**[14] 1351 3-9-0 45 RobbieFitzpatrick 11 —
(W M Brisbourne) *a bhd: lost tch 1/2-way: t.o* **25/1**

6003 **13** 17 **Skye Boat Song**[20] 1226 3-9-0 45 (t) ShaneKelly 5 —
(J Jay) *mid-div: lost tch sn after 1/2-way: t.o* **8/1**[2]

005 **14** 5 **Topflight Wildbird**[203] 6077 3-9-0 45 (b[1]) J-PGuillambert 14 —
(Mrs G S Rees) *outpcd and a wl bhd: t.o* **12/1**[3]

1m 41.67s **Going Correction** -0.05s/f (Stan) **14** Ran SP% **121.0**
Speed ratings (Par 93):93,89,86,82,81 80,78,77,72,67 67,46,29,24
CSF £65.50 TOTE £13.50: £3.20, £2.90, £1.30; EX 117.70.
Owner Ladyswood Stud **Bred** T Wada **Trained** Sherston,Wilts
■ Martyn Meade's first winner since resuming training.
■ Stewards' Enquiry : Shane Kelly one-day ban (reduced from three on appeal): careless riding (May 27)

FOCUS
This was run at a strong gallop and few, bar the impressive winner, managed to get competitive from off the pace.
King's Melody Official explanation: jockey said gelding hung right-handed
The Flying Peach Official explanation: jockey said filly suffered interference in running
Skye Boat Song Official explanation: jockey said colt had a breathing problem
Topflight Wildbird Official explanation: jockey said filly lost its action

1727 ISLEWORTH AND SYON SCHOOL FOR BOYS BANDED STKS 7f (P)
4:30 (4:34) (Class 7) 4-Y-0+ **£2,047** (£604; £302) **Stalls** High

Form — RPR

2425 **1** **Dexileos (IRE)**[10] 1462 7-8-11 45 (t) FergusSweeney 7 54
(David Pinder) *a.p: led over 2f out: drvn out fnl f: all out* **6/1**[2]

6643 **2** shd **Gaudalpin (IRE)**[7] 1538 4-8-11 45 (t) JohnEgan 6 54
(Ernst Oertel) *hld up: hdwy 2f out: pressed wnr thrght fnl f* **9/1**[3]

4440 **3** 2 **Start Of Authority**[219] 5740 5-8-11 45 J-PGuillambert 2 49
(J Gallagher) *mid-div: rdn and kpt on one pce fnl 2f* **16/1**

0000 **4** ¾ **Angel River**[7] 1538 4-8-4 40 (b) DonnaCaldwell(7) 12 47
(J Ryan) *a in tch: rdn wl over 1f out: kpt on one pce* **66/1**

36-5 **5** nk **Limit Down (IRE)**[13] 1393 5-8-11 45 StanleyChin 3 46
(John Berry) *a.p: ev ch over 1f out: no ex fnl fnl f* **25/1**

0650 **6** shd **Piquet**[7] 1536 8-8-11 45 SteveDrowne 8 46
(J J Bridger) *mid-div: rdn and kpt on one pce fr over 1f out* **18/1**

4035 **7** 1 **Spanish Music**[7] 1538 4-8-11 45 (b) DaneO'Neill 5 43
(R Ingram) *hld up in rr: hdwy 2f out: nvr nr to chal* **20/1**

0023 **8** 1 **Margaret's Dream (IRE)**[13] 1393 5-8-8 45 DanielTudhope(3) 1 40
(D Carroll) *hld up: rdn over 2f out: nvr nr to chal* **10/1**

6031 **9** 2½ **Tamora**[7] 1538 4-9-3 45 (v) JamieSpencer 4 40
(A P Jarvis) *hld up: rdn 1/2-way: effrt whn n.m.r over 2f out: swtchd rt over 1f out: no hdwy* **10/11**[1]

0000 **10** 1½ **African Star**[7] 1538 5-8-11 45 ShaneKelly 13 30
(J M Bradley) *in tch: rdn over 2f out: wknd over 1f out* **33/1**

5304 **11** 1 **Multahab**[138] 6677 7-8-8 45 (t) SaleemGolam(3) 11 27
(Miss D A McHale) *racd wd in tch: wknd wl over 1f out* **11/1**

0400 **12** nk **Sunset Dreamer (USA)**[131] 35 5-8-11 45 DarryllHolland 10 27
(P Mitchell) *a bhd* **25/1**

0006 **13** 13 **Princess Arwen**[13] 1391 4-8-11 40 (p) RobbieFitzpatrick 14 —
(Mrs Barbara Waring) *led tl hdd over 2f out: wknd qckly: eased ins fnl f* **33/1**

4066 **14** 3 **Unprecedented (IRE)**[86] 449 5-8-11 45 SamHitchcott 9 —
(T T Clement) *w ldr: wknd qckly wl over 1f out: eased* **50/1**

1m 27.39s **Going Correction** -0.05s/f (Stan) **14** Ran SP% **127.0**
Speed ratings (Par 97):94,93,91,90,90 90,89,88,85,83 82,81,67,63
CSF £58.28 TOTE £8.00: £2.20, £2.10, £3.60; EX 75.40.
Owner Mrs Angela Pinder **Bred** A Christodoulou **Trained** Kingston Lisle, Oxon
■ Stewards' Enquiry : Stanley Chin four-day ban: used whip with excessive force (May 26-29)

FOCUS
A typically weak event for the grade, run at a sound pace, and the first two came clear. The form is ordinary but sound enough, rated through those immediately behind the first two.
Gaudalpin(IRE) Official explanation: jockey said filly had no more to give
Tamora Official explanation: jockey said he couild offer no explanation for the poor form shown
African Star Official explanation: jockey said gelding hung left under pressure

1728 DAY TIME, NIGHT TIME, GREAT TIME, BANDED STKS 6f (P)
5:00 (5:01) (Class 7) 4-Y-0+ **£1,706** (£503; £252) **Stalls** High

Form — RPR

0004 **1** **Jennverse**[7] 1539 4-8-12 46 JohnEgan 5 54
(D K Ivory) *hld up: hdwy to go 2nd 2f out but stl plenty to do: hrd rdn and r.o to ld post* **8/1**[3]

0065 **2** hd **Kahlua Bear**[13] 1397 4-9-0 48 (b) DarryllHolland 3 56
(Miss K B Boutflower) *sn led: clr over 1f out: rdn and kpt on: hdd post* **16/1**

0121 **3** 1½ **Forest Dane**[7] 1539 6-9-8 50 OscarUrbina 9 59
(Mrs N Smith) *hld up: rdn and hdwy over 2f out: kpt on fnl f* **5/4**[1]

0430 **4** 2 **Double M**[7] 1539 9-8-13 50 (v) RichardThomas(3) 2 47
(Mrs L Richards) *hld up: hdwy on outside 2f out: r.o one pce fnl f* **11/1**

6200 **5** nk **Peggys First**[21] 1194 4-9-0 48 ChrisCatlin 7 44
(D E Cantillon) *chsd ldrs: rdn over 1f out: wknd fnl f* **20/1**

5060 **6** 2 **Cut Ridge (IRE)**[228] 5566 7-8-12 46 TonyHamilton 8 36
(J S Wainwright) *bhd: effrt over 1f out: nvr on terms* **16/1**

4515 **7** 2½ **Lauren Louise**[7] 1539 4-9-1 49 SamHitchcott 12 32
(T T Clement) *in tch tl wknd wl over 1f out* **16/1**

0046 **8** nk **Lady Hopeful (IRE)**[13] 1397 4-9-0 48 (b) RobbieFitzpatrick 11 30
(Peter Grayson) *mid-div: rdn over 2f out: sn btn* **9/1**

3551 **9** ½ **Grand View**[10] 1465 10-8-11 48 (p) PaulMulrennan(3) 6 28
(J R Weymes) *chsd ldrs: rdn over 2f out: sn bhd* **15/2**[2]

0102 **10** 3½ **Arfinnit (IRE)**[219] 5738 5-9-1 49 (p) RoystonFfrench 10 19
(Mrs A L M King) *chsd ldr: rdn 1/2-way: wknd over 1f out* **12/1**

0000 **11** 8 **Westlake Bond (IRE)**[107] 232 4-9-1 49 StephenCarson 4 —
(G R Oldroyd) *prom: wkng whn hmpd over 2f out* **40/1**

1m 13.8s **Going Correction** -0.05s/f (Stan) **11** Ran SP% **118.2**
Speed ratings (Par 97):97,96,94,92,91 89,85,85,84,79 69
CSF £128.85 TOTE £9.90: £2.40, £2.60, £1.70; EX 116.50.
Owner Mrs J A Cornwell **Bred** Mrs J A Cornwell **Trained** Radlett, Herts

FOCUS
This weak event was run at a stop-start gallop but the form makes sense and looks sound.

1729 ST MARK'S CATHOLIC SCHOOL BANDED STKS 1m 4f (P)
5:30 (5:33) (Class 7) 4-Y-0+ **£1,706** (£503; £252) **Stalls** Centre

Form — RPR

2333 **1** **Twentytwosilver (IRE)**[7] 1540 6-8-11 45 MichaelTebbutt 7 54
(D B Feek) *mid-div: hdwy 2f out: rdn to ld ins fnl f: styd on* **8/1**

2223 **2** 2½ **Larad (IRE)**[21] 1199 5-8-13 47 (b) JohnEgan 10 52+
(J S Moore) *a in tch: led over 2f out: rdn and hdd ins fnl f* **4/1**[2]

3106 **3** nk **High (IRE)**[10] 1467 4-9-0 48 (b[1]) LPKeniry 4 53
(W J Musson) *in tch: hdwy 1/2-way: ev ch over 1f out: one pce ins fnl f* **25/1**

5052 **4** ½ **Opera Knight**[7] 1541 6-8-11 45 ChrisCatlin 2 49
(A W Carroll) *t.k.h: in touch: rdn 2f out: styd on one pce fnl f* **11/1**

0002 **5** 2 **Chocolate Boy (IRE)**[15] 1313 7-8-12 46 (be) IanMongan 8 47
(G L Moore) *towards rr: hdwy over 3f out: rdn and nt qckn fr over 1f out* **10/1**

3002 **6** hd **Olivino (GER)**[7] 1540 5-9-2 50 DarryllHolland 9 50+
(S Dow) *mid-div: styd on ins fnl 2f: nvr nr to chal* **3/1**[1]

3120 **7** 1¾ **Shekan Star**[5] 1590 4-8-13 50 DanielTudhope(3) 13 47+
(K G Reveley) *v.s.a: bhd: mde sme late hdwy* **5/1**[3]

23 **8** 5 **Hillhall (IRE)**[10] 1461 4-9-0 48 RobbieFitzpatrick 3 37
(W M Brisbourne) *sn led: hdd over 2f out: rdn and wknd over 1f out* **25/1**

5140 **9** 1¾ **Summer Bounty**[20] 1204 10-9-0 48 PaulFitzsimons 11 35
(F Jordan) *hld up in rr: nvr on terms* **14/1**

0013 **10** ½ **Fiore Di Bosco (IRE)**[21] 1201 5-8-11 48 BenSwarbrick(3) 6 34
(T D Barron) *a towards rr* **14/1**

0005 **11** 1 1/4 **Flyingwithoutwings**[20] 1204 7-9-2 50 .... DaneO'Neill 5 34
(A King) *trckd ldrs: wnt 2nd 4f out: ev ch 3f out: hung rt and sn dropped out* **20/1**
-200 **12** 13 **Middlethorpe**[23] 1144 9-8-11 48 .... (b) PaulMulrennan(3) 14 11
(M W Easterby) *trckd ldrs tl rdn and wknd qckly over 3f out* **20/1**
5000 **13** 17 **Jamaican (UAE)**[290] 3910 4-9-2 50 .... FrankieMcDonald 12 —
(M J McGrath) *trckd ldr tl rdn and wknd over 3f out: eased over 1f out* **50/1**

2m 37.71s **Going Correction** -0.05s/f (Stan) **13** Ran SP% **122.7**
Speed ratings (Par 97):95,93,93,92,91 91,90,86,85,85 84,75,64
CSF £38.30 TOTE £8.30: £2.60, £2.10, £6.30; EX 45.10 Place 6 £691.18, Place 5 £75.32.
Owner Chegwidden Systems Ltd **Bred** Dr Paschal Carmody **Trained** Brightling, E Sussex
FOCUS
A fair event for class, run at a sound pace, and the first four came clear. The winner is value for further and the form is solid with the placed horses to their marks.
Shekan Star Official explanation: jockey said filly reared on leaving stalls
Hillhall(IRE) Official explanation: jockey said gelding hung left-handed
Jamaican(UAE) Official explanation: jockey said gelding finished lame
T/Plt: £401.70 to a £1 stake. Pool: £32,166.45. 58.45 winning tickets. T/Qpdt: £51.40 to a £1 stake. Pool: £2,143.00. 30.80 winning tickets. JS

1442 REDCAR (L-H)
Monday, May 15

OFFICIAL GOING: Good (good to soft in places)
The ground was changed after the first race. At that stage it was described as 'on the easy side'. By the last it was described as 'definitely soft'.
Wind: Light, half-behind Weather: Persistent rain.

1730 MIDDLESBROUGH SUPER CASINO BID MEDIAN AUCTION MAIDEN STKS 5f
2:20 (2:20) (Class 6) 2-Y-O **£2,388** (£705; £352) **Stalls** Centre

Form RPR
1 **Opal Noir** 2-9-3 .... RobertWinston 3 84+
(J Howard Johnson) *leggy: unf: s.s: hdwy over 2f out: led over 1f out: r.o strly: readily* **20/1**
42 **2** 4 **Tencendur (IRE)**[10] 1454 2-9-3 .... KDarley 4 70
(M Johnston) *led tl over 1f out: kpt on: no ch w wnr* **7/4**[1]
3 **3** 1 **Startolini**[21] 1181 2-8-12 .... PaulEddery 10 61
(B Smart) *w ldr: nt qckn appr fnl f* **4/1**[3]
63 **4** hd **Esprit D'Amour (IRE)**[16] 1278 2-8-12 .... DavidAllan 8 60
(T D Easterby) *t.k.h: sn trcking ldrs: kpt on same pce appr fnl f* **22/1**
5 1 1/2 **Sophie's Dream** 2-9-3 .... MickyFenton 9 60
(J G Given) *lengthy: unf: scope: chsd ldrs: one pce fnl 2f* **33/1**
6 nk **Gold Spirit (IRE)** 2-9-3 .... RichardMullen 2 59
(E J O'Neill) *w'like: tall: unf: chsd ldrs: hung lft over 1f out: kpt on same pce* **7/2**[2]
7 1 1/4 **Woodland Symphony** 2-9-3 .... FrancisNorton 5 54
(N Tinkler) *cmpt: outpcd and lost pl after 1f: kpt on wl fnl f* **10/1**
8 1 **High Style** 2-9-3 .... RyanMoore 1 51
(R Hannon) *rangy: scope: v green to post: sn chsng ldrs: wknd over 1f out* **13/2**
9 9 **Dockside Dancer (IRE)** 2-8-12 .... LeeEnstone 6 13
(P T Midgley) *leggy: unf: s.i.s: hung lft and a bhd* **100/1**
10 7 **Inmarysfootsteps** 2-8-12 .... JoeFanning 7 —
(N Tinkler) *neat: sn outpcd and bhd: detached fnl 2f* **100/1**

61.25 secs (2.55) **Going Correction** +0.45s/f (Yiel) **10** Ran SP% **115.0**
Speed ratings (Par 91):97,90,89,88,86 85,83,82,67,56
CSF £53.29 TOTE £12.80: £4.40, £1.10, £1.40; EX 40.70.
Owner Transcend Bloodstock LLP **Bred** J K And Mrs Keegan **Trained** Billy Row, Co Durham
FOCUS
The rain had barely arrived and the time was good compared with later on. It was an ordinary median auction maiden race but the form appears fairly sound and the winner looks a decent prospect.
NOTEBOOK
Opal Noir, a March foal, is short-backed, on the leg and narrow. After missing the break he sprinted clear and looks potentially useful. (op 16-1)
Tencendur(IRE), not the best of walkers, ran an honest race but had no answer when the winner swept by. (op 9-4)
Startolini, who looked very well, again gave a good account of herself but this may be as good as she is. (op 10-3)
Esprit D'Amour(IRE), having her third run, was very keen and could only stick on in her own time. When she learns to settle better, a sixth furlong will be in her favour. (op 20-1 tchd 25-1)
Sophie's Dream, a February foal, is long in the back. He made a satisfactory debut and should improve for the outing. (op 25-1)
Gold Spirit(IRE), a tall, narrow type, was noisy in the paddock. He looked very inexperienced and the outing should have taught him plenty. (op 4-1 tchd 9-2 in a place)
Woodland Symphony, a sharp sort, looked all at sea on the easy ground. He picked up in encouraging fashion late on. (op 7-1)
High Style, a well-made March foal, was as green as grass both in the paddock and on the way to the start. He became very tired late on but ought to be be capable of much better in due course. (op 10-1)

1731 RACING UK CHANNEL 432 (S) STKS 1m 2f
2:50 (2:51) (Class 6) 3-Y-O **£2,388** (£705; £352) **Stalls** Low

Form RPR
000 **1** **English City (IRE)**[26] 1078 3-8-12 55 .... PaulEddery 3 59
(B Smart) *s.i.s: hdwy and swtchd rt over 2f out: led 1f out: kpt on* **7/1**
0000 **2** 1 1/4 **Elite Land**[213] 5878 3-8-5 45 .... SuzzanneFrance(7) 6 57
(N Bycroft) *in rr: hdwy 4f out: led over 1f out: sn hdd and no ex* **9/1**
4000 **3** 8 **Darker Than Blue**[14] 1350 3-8-7 50 .... (b[1]) KDarley 2 36
(B J Meehan) *chsd ldrs: led over 3f out: hdd over 1f out: sn wknd* **7/1**
0400 **4** 2 **Devon Ruby**[6] 1576 3-8-7 45 .... (p) DavidAllan 5 33
(Mrs A Duffield) *hld up in mid-div: hdwy to chse ldrs over 3f out: wknd over 1f out* **12/1**
0560 **5** 5 **Wensleydale Star**[19] 1232 3-8-12 50 .... PaulFessey 9 28
(T D Barron) *led tl over 5f out: wknd over 2f out* **5/1**[2]
0005 **6** 2 **Lewis Lloyd (IRE)**[16] 1293 3-8-12 45 .... (t) RyanMoore 8 24
(I A Wood) *trckd ldrs: wnt 2nd over 3f out: wknd 2f out* **7/2**[1]
0000 **7** 5 **Ebony Lady**[20] 1221 3-8-7 45 .... RichardMullen 1 10
(R M Whitaker) *w ldr: led over 5f out: hdd over 3f out: sn lost pl* **11/2**[3]
0010 **8** 13 **Secret Tender (IRE)**[16] 1293 3-9-4 60 .... RobertWinston 10 —
(J R Weymes) *hld up in midfield: effrt on outer over 3f out: wknd and heavily eased over 1f out* **7/1**
00 **9** 11 **Tina's Magic**[150] 6588 3-8-7 .... MickyFenton 7 —
(Mrs G S Rees) *t.k.h: trckd ldrs: lost pl over 3f out: sn bhd* **66/1**
00 **10** 29 **Il Divo**[365] 1722 3-8-12 .... PaulHanagan 4 —
(C Grant) *s.i.s: reminders after 3f: t.o 4f out: virtually p.u* **50/1**

2m 11.1s (4.30) **Going Correction** +0.45s/f (Yiel) **10** Ran SP% **112.9**
Speed ratings (Par 97):100,99,92,91,87 85,81,71,62,39
CSF £66.08 TOTE £8.00: £2.60, £3.30, £2.50; EX 119.90.There was no bid for the winner.
Owner Mick White Partnership **Bred** Troy Cullen **Trained** Hambleton, N Yorks
FOCUS
A very poor race even by selling race standards, although the form appears sound enough for the level.
Secret Tender(IRE) Official explanation: jockey said gelding lost its action

1732 HERALD & POST H'CAP 1m 2f
3:20 (3:20) (Class 5) (0-70,70) 3-Y-O **£3,238** (£963; £481; £240) **Stalls** Low

Form RPR
0660 **1** **Swayze (IRE)**[33] 993 3-8-11 63 .... KDarley 2 67
(N P Littmoden) *trckd ldrs: effrt and swtchd outside over 2f out: styd on to ld jst ins last: hung lft: kpt on* **9/2**[3]
6050 **2** 1 **Apt To Run (USA)**[24] 1108 3-9-4 70 .... (b[1]) RichardMullen 3 72
(E A L Dunlop) *trckd ldrs: led over 2f out: edgd rt over 1f out: hdd and no ex jst ins last* **9/1**
2003 **3** 1 1/4 **Blushing Hilary (IRE)**[16] 1307 3-9-3 69 .... (p) TomEaves 6 69
(Miss J A Camacho) *set modest pce: qcknd over 3f out: hdd over 2f out: kpt on same pce appr fnl f* **11/2**
0205 **4** shd **Mister Maq**[14] 1345 3-8-9 61 .... (b) PhillipMakin 1 61
(M Dods) *hld up in rr: effrt on inner over 3f out: one pce fnl 2f* **9/1**
000 **5** 11 **Machhapuchhare**[171] 6417 3-8-4 56 oh1 .... DavidAllan 8 35
(W M Brisbourne) *hld up in rr: drvn along over 5f out: lost pl over 3f out* **14/1**
0355 **6** 2 1/2 **Ballybeg (IRE)**[7] 1543 3-9-1 67 .... (b[1]) RyanMoore 7 41
(R Hannon) *hld up in rr: effrt on inner 4f out: lost pl 3f out* **4/1**[2]
2465 **7** 7 **Orvietan (IRE)**[13] 1381 3-8-13 65 .... JoeFanning 5 26
(M Johnston) *trckd ldrs: jnd ldr 7f out: outpcd over 3f out: lost pl over 2f out: sn bhd and eased* **3/1**[1]
256 **8** 8 **Baileys Polka**[25] 1100 3-9-4 70 .... MickyFenton 4 15
(J G Given) *hld up in midfield: hdwy to trck ldrs 5f out: lost pl 3f out: sn bhd and eased* **14/1**

2m 11.46s (4.66) **Going Correction** +0.45s/f (Yiel) **8** Ran SP% **111.9**
Speed ratings (Par 99):99,98,97,97,88 86,80,74
CSF £41.97 CT £223.23 TOTE £4.90: £1.60, £2.30, £2.00; EX 39.90.
Owner Kent Design & Build Ltd **Bred** Gerard Callinan **Trained** Newmarket, Suffolk
FOCUS
A moderate pace in the deteriorating conditions and the form looks very modest, rated through the third.
Swayze(IRE) Official explanation: trainers rep said, regarding the improved form shown, the gelding had benefited from the step up in trip and better ground
Baileys Polka Official explanation: trainer said, following race, filly was found to be in season

1733 REDCAR CONFERENCE CENTRE MAIDEN FILLIES' STKS 6f
3:50 (3:50) (Class 5) 3-Y-O+ **£3,238** (£963; £481; £240) **Stalls** Centre

Form RPR
1 **Pick A Nice Name** 4-9-0 .... MichaelJStainton(7) 7 74
(R M Whitaker) *rangy: scope: s.s: hdwy on wd outside over 2f out: led jst ins last: hld on towards fin* **40/1**
0053 **2** 3/4 **Our Sheila**[11] 1445 3-8-11 65 .... RobertWinston 1 69
(B Smart) *dwlt and swvd lft s: hdwy 3f out: chal 1f out: no ex wl ins last* **7/4**[1]
5302 **3** 2 **Chanteuse Noire (USA)**[18] 1261 3-8-11 65 .... (v) KDarley 9 63
(J Noseda) *led tl jst ins last: fnd little* **5/2**[2]
2300 **4** 6 **Yorke's Folly (USA)**[203] 6076 5-9-2 45 .... LeanneKershaw(5) 6 48
(C W Fairhurst) *hld up in midfield: hdwy over 2f out: sn chsng ldrs: wknd fnl f* **16/1**
36 **5** 1 3/4 **Mullady Penelope**[233] 5465 3-8-11 .... PaulFessey 8 40
(Mrs A Duffield) *chsd ldrs: lost pl over 1f out* **16/1**
06 **6** 2 1/2 **Good Turn**[8] 1513 3-8-11 .... RyanMoore 5 32
(R Hannon) *chsd ldrs: outpcd over 2f out: sn btn* **6/1**[3]
6600 **7** 1 **Underthemistletoe (IRE)**[198] 6154 4-9-7 45 .... TomEaves 3 32
(R E Barr) *trckd ldrs: effrt over 2f out: lost pl over 1f out* **20/1**
0 **8** 3 1/2 **Maria Antonia (IRE)**[14] 1351 3-8-7 ow1 .... DerekNolan(5) 4 20
(M J Wallace) *sn outpcd and drvn along: swtchd rt after 1f: nvr on terms* **8/1**
0500 **9** 1/2 **Value Plus (IRE)**[69] 612 4-9-0 48 .... (vt[1]) MarkCoumbe(7) 2 20
(C J Teague) *swvd lft s: hld up: hdwy over 2f out: sn wknd* **50/1**
0-0 **10** 1 1/2 **Nellie Gwyn**[18] 1261 4-9-7 .... MickyFenton 10 16
(J G Given) *trckd ldrs: lost pl 2f out* **66/1**

1m 14.32s (2.62) **Going Correction** +0.45s/f (Yiel)
WFA 3 from 4yo+ 10lb **10** Ran SP% **112.8**
Speed ratings (Par 100):100,99,96,88,86 82,81,76,76,74
CSF £105.22 TOTE £29.60: £7.40, £1.10, £1.20; EX 130.50.
Owner John W Ford **Bred** J W Ford **Trained** Scarcroft, W Yorks
FOCUS
A modest sprint maiden with 65-rated Our Sheila the best guide to the form.

1734 EVENING GAZETTE FILLIES' H'CAP 7f
4:20 (4:20) (Class 4) (0-85,82) 3-Y-O+ **£6,477** (£1,927; £963; £481) **Stalls** Centre

Form RPR
0500 **1** **Miss Meggy**[17] 1275 4-9-10 74 .... (b) TomEaves 8 86
(Miss J A Camacho) *hld up in tch: stdy hdwy to ld over 1f out: rdn out* **20/1**
1133 **2** 1 **Tour D'Amour (IRE)**[7] 1551 3-8-4 66 .... PaulFessey 2 71
(R Craggs) *trckd ldrs: outpcd over 2f out: kpt on fnl f: no ex ins last* **10/1**
4361 **3** 1 3/4 **Abbey Cat (IRE)**[5] 1592 3-8-13 75 6ex .... RobertWinston 7 75
(G A Swinbank) *w ldrs: led and hung lft over 2f out: hdd over 1f out: nt qckn* **1/1**[1]
1001 **4** 3/4 **Polliwilline (IRE)**[21] 1190 3-9-6 82 .... RyanMoore 4 83+
(R Hannon) *trckd ldrs: kpt on same pce appr fnl f* **10/3**[2]
2545 **5** 3 **Passion Fruit**[198] 6139 5-9-4 68 .... PaulHanagan 3 63
(C W Fairhurst) *s.i.s: effrt over 2f out: nvr nr ldrs* **8/1**[3]
4550 **6** 11 **Dispol Katie**[10] 1456 5-10-0 78 .... PhillipMakin 1 44
(T D Barron) *swvd rt s: led after 1f: hdd over 2f out: wknd over 1f out* **12/1**
5200 **7** 1 **Kudbeme**[242] 5250 4-8-10 67 .... (b[1]) SuzzanneFrance(7) 6 31
(N Bycroft) *s.s: sn t.k.h: jnd ldrs after 3f: lost pl over 2f out* **25/1**

4303 **8** *nk* **Elegant Times (IRE)**[19] 1230 3-8-9 71 .... FergalLynch 5 30
(T D Easterby) *led 1f: w ldrs: lost pl and eased over 1f out* **25/1**

1m 27.55s (2.65) **Going Correction** +0.45s/f (Yiel)
WFA 3 from 4yo+ 12lb **8** Ran SP% **113.4**
Speed ratings (Par 102):102,100,98,98,94 82,80,80
CSF £194.77 CT £390.07 TOTE £18.60: £5.70, £2.10, £1.10; EX 212.60.
Owner David W Armstrong **Bred** Trickledown Stud **Trained** Norton, N Yorks

FOCUS
A very steady early pace and not totally convincing, although the runner-up and fourth were close to their marks.
Elegant Times(IRE) Official explanation: jockey said filly had no more to give

1735 REDCAR LIVE CLAIMING STKS — 6f
4:50 (4:50) (Class 6) 3-Y-O+ — **£2,388** (£705; £352) **Stalls** Centre

Form — RPR

3120 **1** **Onlytime Will Tell**[8] 1504 8-9-9 64 .... JoeFanning 4 79
(D Nicholls) *trckd ldrs: led jst ins last: r.o wl* **4/1**[2]

0312 **2** *2* **Million Percent**[4] 1607 7-9-0 59 .... AndrewElliott(5) 6 69
(K R Burke) *racd stands' side: chsd ldrs: styd on to ld over 1f out: hdd jst ins last: no ex* **9/2**[3]

0001 **3** *1* **Cd Europe (IRE)**[11] 1443 8-9-1 75 .... RobertWinston 7 62
(G A Swinbank) *hld up: stdy hdwy over 2f out: shkn up over 1f out: nt qckn* **5/4**[1]

2610 **4** *2 ½* **Further Outlook (USA)**[24] 1125 12-9-2 74 .... DNolan(3) 1 59
(D Carroll) *charged gate: led: hdd over 2f out: wknd fnl f* **8/1**

0006 **5** *¾* **Zap Attack**[6] 1571 6-8-13 45 ....(tp) MickyFenton 5 50
(J Parkes) *chsd ldrs: led over 2f out: hdd over 1f out: sn fdd* **100/1**

0003 **6** *2* **Tagula Bay (IRE)**[12] 1413 4-9-8 61 .... DavidAllan 3 53
(T D Easterby) *hld up: hdwy over 2f out: hit on hd by rdr's whip over 1f out: sn wknd* **9/1**

0000 **7** *1 ¾* **Chairman Bobby**[6] 1563 8-8-13 55 .... FergalLynch 8 39
(D W Barker) *racd stands' side: chsd ldrs: wknd over 1f out* **33/1**

0604 **8** *5* **Louisiade (IRE)**[4] 1607 5-9-9 55 ....(p) DO'Donohoe 2 34
(K A Ryan) *chsd ldrs: rdn over 2f out: wknd and eased over 1f out* **12/1**

1m 13.86s (2.16) **Going Correction** +0.45s/f (Yiel) **8** Ran SP% **115.4**
Speed ratings (Par 101):103,100,99,95,94 92,89,83
CSF £22.58 TOTE £4.50: £1.90, £1.40, £1.10; EX 20.00.Million Percent was the subject of a friendly claim.
Owner Mrs E G Faulkner **Bred** L C And Mrs A E Sigsworth **Trained** Sessay, N Yorks

FOCUS
A strongly-run claimer rated around the second, but the form is held down by the fifth.
Tagula Bay(IRE) Official explanation: jockey said filly suffered interference in running

1736 GO RACING IN YORKSHIRE 30TH ANNIVERSARY H'CAP — 1m
5:20 (5:21) (Class 6) (0-60,62) 3-Y-O — **£2,388** (£705; £352) **Stalls** Centre

Form — RPR

0560 **1** **Queen Jean**[223] 5681 3-8-12 **54** .... MickyFenton 11 64
(J G Given) *mde all: edgd rt over 1f out: styd on wl towards fin* **40/1**

000 **2** *¾* **Mystic Storm**[22] 1165 3-9-4 **60** .... KDarley 14 68+
(Lady Herries) *mid-div: hrd drvn over 3f out: hrd rdn and hdwy over 2f out: styd on wl to go 2nd ins last: no ex* **6/1**[2]

3 *3 ½* **Ai Hawa (IRE)**[254] 4965 3-8-7 **49** .... MCHussey 18 49
(Eamon Tyrrell, Ire) *hld up in mid-div: hdwy over 2f out: kpt on same pce fnl f* **33/1**

006 **4** *4* **Dado Mush**[22] 1165 3-8-12 **54** .... JoeFanning 16 45
(T T Clement) *chsd ldrs: wknd fnl f* **50/1**

0001 **5** *3 ½* **Prince Picasso**[4] 1616 3-9-6 **62** 6ex .... JamieMackay 5 45
(Sir Mark Prescott) *sn chsng ldrs: rdn over 2f out: wknd fnl f* **10/11**[1]

0000 **6** *½* **Jenny Soba**[41] 868 3-8-7 **56** .... MichaelJStainton(7) 13 38
(R M Whitaker) *sn wl bhd: hdwy over 2f out: styd on fnl f* **40/1**

2060 **7** *¾* **Emotive**[15] 1314 3-8-10 **52** ....(p) TomEaves 2 32
(I A Wood) *hld up towards rr: hdwy over 2f out: nvr nr ldrs* **11/1**

0001 **8** *4* **Strife (IRE)**[11] 1433 3-8-11 **53** .... RyanMoore 8 24
(R Hannon) *chsd ldrs: lost pl over 1f out* **10/1**[3]

0400 **9** *nk* **Casonova (IRE)**[19] 1232 3-8-11 **53** .... FergalLynch 17 23
(T D Easterby) *hld up towards rr: sme hdwy over 2f out: nvr on terms* **50/1**

500 **10** *5* **Gala Jackpot (USA)**[245] 5170 3-8-5 **50** .... PatrickMathers(3) 4 9
(W M Brisbourne) *mid-div: drvn over 2f out: nvr on terms* **50/1**

406 **11** *2* **Money Mate (IRE)**[33] 980 3-8-8 **57** .... MarkCoumbe(7) 10 11
(C J Teague) *in tch: effrt over 2f out: sn btn* **66/1**

000 **12** *½* **Madam Mac (IRE)**[33] 981 3-8-8 **50** .... FrancisNorton 1 3
(B J Meehan) *sn bhd: sme hdwy 3f out: wknd and eased 2f out* **40/1**

2000 **13** *¾* **Sea Grain (IRE)**[11] 1441 3-8-13 **60** ....(t) GregFairley(5) 15 11
(Robert Gray) *w ldrs: drvn along 4f out: lost pl over 2f out* **33/1**

0000 **14** *1 ¾* **Pontefract Glory**[19] 1232 3-8-8 **50** .... PhillipMakin 3 —
(M Dods) *w ldrs: lost pl over 2f out* **50/1**

3055 **15** *6* **Carr Hall (IRE)**[18] 1251 3-9-3 **59** .... DavidAllan 7 —
(T D Easterby) *chsd ldrs: lost pl over 2f out* **11/1**

0043 **16** *2 ½* **Desert Dust**[93] 373 3-9-2 **58** .... RobertWinston 12 —
(R M H Cowell) *s.s: a in rr* **20/1**

000 **17** *25* **Prince Richard**[208] 5988 3-8-9 **51** .... PaulHanagan 6 —
(B Smart) *mid-div: lost pl after 3f: sn bhd: t.o: virtually p.u* **50/1**

1m 42.22s (4.42) **Going Correction** +0.45s/f (Yiel) **17** Ran SP% **121.7**
Speed ratings (Par 97):95,94,90,86,83 82,82,78,77,72 70,70,69,67,61 59,34
CSF £247.47 CT £8157.14 TOTE £53.60: £10.20, £1.80, £4.20, £7.80; EX 414.90 Place 6 £46.15, Place 5 £28.29.
Owner M J Dawson **Bred** Slatch Farm Stud **Trained** Willoughton, Lincs

FOCUS
The rain had really got into the ground by now and the riders were adamant it was soft, the Clek Of The Course had other ideas however, and refused to change the ground despite over two hours persistent rain. A moderate contest and an orsdinary pace, but the form appears sound enough, rated through the third and fourth.
Queen Jean Official explanation: trainer said, regarding the improved form shown, filly was having her first run for the yard
Desert Dust Official explanation: jockey said colt was unsuited by the good (good to soft in places) ground

T/Plt: £11.10 to a £1 stake. Pool: £34,633.80. 2,267.05 winning tickets. T/Qpdt: £4.40 to a £1 stake. Pool: £2,501.40. 414.10 winning tickets. WG

1542 WINDSOR (R-H)
Monday, May 15

OFFICIAL GOING: Good to firm
The last race was abandoned due to slippery ground.
Wind: Almost nil. Weather: Overcast becoming fine.

1737 VCCASINO.COM NOVICE STKS — 5f 10y
6:00 (6:01) (Class 4) 2-Y-O — **£4,533** (£1,348; £674; £336) **Stalls** High

Form — RPR

2 **1** **Hoh Mike (IRE)**[21] 1189 2-8-12 .... JamieSpencer 8 96+
(M L W Bell) *trckd ldr after 2f: shkn up to chal over 1f out: led jst ins fnl f: pushed clr* **4/5**[1]

4 **2** *2 ½* **Scented Present**[14] 1354 2-8-12 .... LDettori 1 87+
(B J Meehan) *fast away: led and sn crossed to nr side rail: clr w wnr over 1f out: hdd jst ins fnl f: r.o but no ch* **5/2**[2]

21 **3** *6* **Karayel (IRE)**[11] 1429 2-9-2 .... RichardHughes 9 69+
(R Hannon) *chsd ldrs: rdn and outpcd fr 2f out: plugged on* **7/1**[3]

4 *nk* **Capannina** 2-8-7 .... ShaneKelly 6 59
(J Noseda) *in tch in rr: outpcd and rdn 1/2-way: r.o ins fnl f* **20/1**

5 *nk* **Road To Recovery** 2-8-9 .... NeilChalmers(3) 7 63
(A M Balding) *hld up in tch: outpcd 2f out: shuffled along and kpt on one pce* **40/1**

00 **6** *nk* **Cesc**[11] 1429 2-8-12 .... FergusSweeney 4 62
(P J Makin) *restrained s: t.k.h and hld up: rdn and outpcd 2f out: fnd ni* **66/1**

12 **7** *2 ½* **No Worries Yet (IRE)**[14] 1354 2-8-9 .... SteveDrowne 2 50
(J L Spearing) *chsd ldr for 2f: outpcd 2f out: wknd fnl f* **12/1**

8 *5* **Sagassa** 2-8-7 .... AdrianMcCarthy 3 30
(W De Best-Turner) *s.s: racd wd: rdn and struggling 1/2-way: wknd fnl f* **100/1**

9 *7* **Ella Y Rossa** 2-8-4 .... SaleemGolam(3) 5 —
(P D Evans) *s.s: sn t.o* **66/1**

58.75 secs (-2.35) **Going Correction** -0.575s/f (Hard) 2y crse rec **9** Ran SP% **115.5**
Speed ratings (Par 95):95,91,81,80,80 79,75,67,56
CSF £2.79 TOTE £1.90: £1.10, £1.30, £2.00; EX 4.20.
Owner David Allport & Michael Lynch **Bred** John Malone **Trained** Newmarket, Suffolk

FOCUS
A decent enough novice event and a useful effort from the front pair to finish so far clear and they can rate higher.

NOTEBOOK
Hoh Mike(IRE) ◆ stepped up on the form he showed when second in a course and distance maiden on his debut to win well. He had to work to get by the eventual runner-up, but ultimately won well and there was eight and a half lengths back to the third. He looks decent and deserves to step up in class. (tchd 5-8-11 and 5-6 in places)
Scented Present, fourth in a reasonable course and distance novice event on his debut, showed improved form with the benefit of that run and finished well clear of all bar the winner. He really should be a good thing for a maiden. (op 4-1)
Karayel(IRE) would have found this tougher than the Folkestone maiden he won on his previous start and was left behind by the front two. (op 13-2 tchd 10-1)
Capannina, the first foal of a smart multiple six to eight-furlong winner, was soon struggling but kept to her task in likeable fashion when it was all over. She should come on significantly for the run and can go close in maiden company next time. (op 10-1)
Road To Recovery, a 23,000gns half-brother to six-furlong juvenile winner Mafaheem, made a pleasing debut and can be found easier opportunities to get off the mark. (op 33-1)
Cesc did not find as much as had looked like and is proving frustrating. The ability would appear to be there, but he has plenty to prove. (op 50-1)
No Worries Yet(IRE) Official explanation: jockey said filly slipped after 2f

1738 VCCASINO.COM H'CAP — 1m 2f 7y
6:30 (6:32) (Class 5) (0-75,75) 3-Y-O — **£3,886** (£1,156; £577; £288) **Stalls** Low

Form — RPR

4144 **1** **Abstract Art (USA)**[26] 1077 3-9-1 **72** .... JamieSpencer 14 78
(N A Callaghan) *a in ldng trio: led on inner wl over 2f out: drvn over 1f out: kpt on wl fnl f* **5/1**[2]

4343 **2** *½* **Conservation (FR)**[13] 1375 3-9-0 **71** .... AlanMunro 8 76
(P W Chapple-Hyam) *t.k.h: prom: effrt to chal 3f out: nt qckn w wnr sn after: rallied fnl f: a jst hld* **85/40**[1]

010 **3** *1* **Snark (IRE)**[21] 1190 3-9-4 **75** .... FergusSweeney 12 78
(P J Makin) *sn trckd ldrs: rdn: hanging lft and nt qckn over 2f out: r.o ins fnl f: nrst fin* **16/1**

2304 **4** *½* **Feu D'Artifice (USA)**[19] 1240 3-9-1 **72** .... RichardHughes 4 74
(R Hannon) *hld up towards rr: rdn and effrt over 2f out: prog over 1f out: styd on same pce fnl f: nt rch ldrs* **12/1**

3450 **5** *1 ¼* **Stellenbosch (USA)**[13] 1375 3-8-11 **68** ....(v) EddieAhern 5 68
(J W Hills) *led and sn clr: hdd wl over 2f out: fdd over 1f out* **25/1**

6403 **6** *hd* **Salvestro**[20] 1215 3-8-7 **64** .... KerrinMcEvoy 10 63
(Mrs A J Perrett) *hld up towards rr: prog on outer 3f out: shkn up and one pce fnl 2f* **6/1**[3]

5004 **7** *2 ½* **Floodlight Fantasy**[16] 1291 3-8-9 **66** .... ChrisCatlin 9 61
(E S McMahon) *awkward s: hld up in last pair: rdn over 2f out: sme prog over 1f out: n.d* **8/1**

033 **8** *1 ¼* **Blacktoft (USA)**[13] 1386 3-8-11 **68** .... ShaneKelly 2 60
(E A L Dunlop) *t.k.h: hld up in midfield: wd bnd 6f out: prog 4f out: nt qckn over 2f out: fdd* **16/1**

4000 **9** *5* **Mighty Moon**[217] 5795 3-8-8 **65** .... TedDurcan 11 48
(Lady Herries) *settled midfield: shkn up 4f out: struggling fr 3f out: wknd* **16/1**

050 **10** *shd* **Gateland**[22] 1165 3-8-10 **67** .... TQuinn 13 50
(W R Swinburn) *hld up in rr: pushed along 4f out: no prog: wknd 2f out* **16/1**

4006 **11** *½* **Dancing Melody**[23] 1141 3-8-1 **61** oh1 .... RichardThomas(3) 1 43
(J A Geake) *chsd ldrs tl wknd u.p over 2f out* **50/1**

060 **12** *1 ¾* **Lanfredo**[14] 1335 3-8-4 **61** oh1 ....(p) StephenCarson 6 39
(D W P Arbuthnot) *t.k.h: hld up in last: rdn over 2f out: no ch* **50/1**

000 **13** *2* **Billanroy (IRE)**[16] 1289 3-8-5 **65** .... SaleemGolam(3) 15 40
(M H Tompkins) *a towards rr: rdn and struggling 3f out* **33/1**

0000 **14** *6* **Generous Lad (IRE)**[13] 1375 3-8-7 **64** ....(p) MartinDwyer 7 27
(Miss J S Davis) *mostly chsd ldr to over 3f out: sn wknd rapidly* **25/1**

2m 6.15s (-2.15) **Going Correction** -0.35s/f (Firm) **14** Ran SP% **119.8**
Speed ratings (Par 99):94,93,92,92,91 91,89,88,84,84 83,82,80,75
CSF £15.03 CT £160.61 TOTE £6.90: £2.50, £1.50, £5.00; EX 20.10.
Owner Matthew Green **Bred** Ms J L Mills **Trained** Newmarket, Suffolk
■ Stewards' Enquiry : Alan Munro one-day ban: used whip without giving colt time to respond (May 26)

FOCUS
A fair handicap and the form looks reasonable enough for the grade, using the fourth and fifth as the guide.
Feu D'Artifice(USA) Official explanation: jockey said colt slipped on bend
Stellenbosch(USA) Official explanation: jockey said colt hung left
Gateland Official explanation: jockey said colt was hampered on bend
Billanroy(IRE) Official explanation: jockey said colt lost a front shoe

1739 VCCASINO.COM ROYAL WINDSOR STKS (LISTED RACE) 1m 67y
7:00 (7:00) (Class 1) 3-Y-O+ **£16,595** (£6,274; £3,136; £1,568) **Stalls** High

Form RPR
3406 **1** **Home Affairs**[227] 5590 4-9-2 109 RichardHughes 1 96+
(Sir Michael Stoute) *led after 1f: mde rest: clr whn shkn up over 1f out: unchal* **4/6**[1]
2100 **2** 2 ½ **Momtic (IRE)**[16] 1299 5-9-2 105 AlanMunro 5 90+
(W Jarvis) *dwlt: chsd wnr 6f out: rdn and no imp 2f out: kpt on* **9/2**[3]
-215 **3** 2 ½ **Take A Bow**[16] 1299 5-9-2 107 JimmyQuinn 3 84+
(P R Chamings) *stmbld s: led for 1f: stmbld bnd 6f out: rdn and one pce over 2f out* **10/3**[2]
0120 **4** ½ **Undeterred**[2] 1673 10-9-2 74 JimCrowley 4 83?
(K J Burke) *hld up in last: effrt on outer 3f out: one pce and no imp fnl 2f* **50/1**
6-2 **5** 19 **Dalpe**[229] 5543 5-9-2 RichardThomas 6 65?
(A J Lidderdale) *t.k.h: hld up: slipped bnd over 5f out: wknd 2f out: heavily eased 1f out* **100/1**
1m 40.81s (-4.79) **Going Correction** -0.35s/f (Firm) **5** Ran SP% **104.2**
Speed ratings (Par 111):109,106,104,103,84
CSF £3.50 TOTE £1.40: £1.10, £2.60; EX 3.50.
Owner K Abdulla **Bred** Juddmonte Farms **Trained** Newmarket, Suffolk

FOCUS
With the ten-year-old Undeterred, who is rated just 74, only five and a half lengths away in fourth, this was quite clearly a weak Listed race, but Home Affairs never looked in danger.

NOTEBOOK
Home Affairs, who progressed from a handicapper to run some creditable races in defeat in Pattern company last season, found this an easy opportunity on his return from a 227-day break and won well. Given a horse rated 74 was only five and a half lengths behind in fourth, he did not have to be at his best, but this should have boosted his confidence and he will no doubt be returned to Group company at some stage. (tchd 4-7, 8-11 in places)
Momtic(IRE), a progressive handicapper last season but down the field behind Home Affairs' stablemate Rob Roy in a Group 2 at Sandown on his reappearance, was never a threat and did not appear to run up to his mark. (tchd 11-2)
Take A Bow, fifth in a Group 2 at Sandown on his reappearance, could not confirm form with Momtic and has to be considered a little disappointing. Official explanation: jockey said horse stumbled leaving stalls and slipped on bend (op 3-1)
Undeterred beat only two home in a seven-furlong amateur riders' handicap at Lingfield just two days earlier, so to be beaten just five and a half lengths in this company suggests the form is not what one would expect for the grade. (tchd 66-1)

1740 PLAY AT VCCASINO.COM H'CAP 1m 3f 135y
7:30 (7:33) (Class 5) (0-75,72) 3-Y-O **£3,238** (£963; £481; £240) **Stalls** Low

Form RPR
0053 **1** **Ogee**[20] 1205 3-9-4 **72** KFallon 9 84+
(Sir Michael Stoute) *trckd ldng pair 7f out: clsd over 2f out: pushed into ld jst ins fnl f: wl in command after* **11/10**[1]
002 **2** 1 ½ **Brabazon (IRE)**[21] 1193 3-9-0 **68** SteveDrowne 3 77
(R Charlton) *chsd ldr: rdn to cl over 2f out: relegated to 3rd over 1f out: kpt on to take 2nd again nr fin* **10/1**
5432 **3** ½ **Deutschland (USA)**[38] 909 3-9-0 **68** (p) PhilipRobinson 4 76
(M A Jarvis) *led at str pce: 4l clr 4f out: kpt on u.p over 2f out: hdd and no ex jst ins fnl f* **8/1**[3]
0001 **4** 3 **Precious Dancer**[15] 1314 3-8-9 **63** MartinDwyer 11 67
(W R Muir) *hld up towards rr: rdn over 3f out: effrt to chse ldrs over 2f out: kpt on same pce* **12/1**
0061 **5** ¾ **High Seasons**[13] 1375 3-8-11 **68** SaleemGolam(3) 6 70
(B R Millman) *chsd ldrs: rdn over 3f out: effrt to chse ldrs 2f out: one pce after* **6/1**[2]
033 **6** hd **Italic**[20] 1214 3-9-2 **70** KerrinMcEvoy 10 72
(Mrs A J Perrett) *hld up in last pair: plld to outer and rdn 2f out: hanging lft after: kpt on same pce* **10/1**
3230 **7** 2 ½ **Sky High Guy (IRE)**[13] 1375 3-9-1 **69** JimmyFortune 2 71+
(S Kirk) *chsd ldng pair to 7f out: rdn over 3f out: chsd ldrs over 2f out: wl hld whn lost action over 1f out* **16/1**
6004 **8** 5 **Asbury Park**[28] 1052 3-8-11 **65** ChrisCatlin 5 55
(E S McMahon) *nvr beyond midfield: wknd u.p over 2f out* **14/1**
300 **9** 10 **Capriolla**[12] 1418 3-8-11 **65** RichardHughes 8 39
(P F I Cole) *hld up in last pair: rdn and no prog wl over 3f out: t.o* **20/1**
5000 **10** 18 **Earth Master (IRE)**[14] 1350 3-8-9 **63** EddieAhern 7 8
(S Kirk) *nvr beyond midfield: rdn and wknd 4f out: t.o* **66/1**
2m 26.59s (-3.51) **Going Correction** -0.35s/f (Firm) **10** Ran SP% **117.7**
Speed ratings (Par 99):97,96,95,93,93 93,91,88,81,69
CSF £13.45 CT £64.13 TOTE £2.00: £1.10, £3.20, £2.70; EX 15.10.
Owner Sir Evelyn De Rothschild **Bred** Hesmonds Stud Ltd **Trained** Newmarket, Suffolk

FOCUS
Quite a competitive handicap, run at a decent pace, and the form looks pretty sound with the first three clear, and should work out.
Earth Master(IRE) Official explanation: jockey said gelding had no more to give

1741 PLAY BLACKJACK AT VCCASINO.COM MEDIAN AUCTION MAIDEN STKS 1m 2f 7y
8:00 (8:03) (Class 5) 3-Y-O **£3,238** (£963; £481; £240) **Stalls** Low

Form RPR
0 **1** **Masterofthecourt (USA)**[23] 1135 3-9-3 SteveDrowne 1 79+
(H Morrison) *chsd ldrs: shkn up over 3f out: effrt to chse ldr over 1f out: drvn to ld ins fnl f: kpt on* **4/1**[2]
5535 **2** nk **Beckett Hall (IRE)**[14] 1336 3-9-3 77 RichardHughes 7 79
(R Hannon) *mde most: rdn 3f out: kpt on wl: hdd ins fnl f: jst hld* **5/1**[3]
2 **3** 1 ½ **Alcyon (IRE)**[42] 850 3-9-3 LDettori 3 76
(E A L Dunlop) *pressed ldr: upsides over 3f out to over 2f out: nt qckn over 1f out : kpt on same pce fnl f* **11/4**[1]
024 **4** shd **Island Myth (IRE)**[150] 6595 3-9-3 79 MartinDwyer 13 76
(M P Tregoning) *chsd ldrs: rdn 3f out: cl up over 1f out: nt pce to chal fnl f* **9/1**
06 **5** ½ **Enjoy The Moment**[236] 5401 3-9-3 ShaneKelly 16 75
(J A Osborne) *trckd ldrs: effrt over 2f out: hanging bdly lft fnl 2f: styd on* **20/1**
000 **6** 1 ½ **Nefski Alexander (USA)**[14] 1335 3-9-3 73 JimmyFortune 6 73+
(P F I Cole) *prom: rdn and nt qckn over 3f out: clsd u.p 2f out: nt run on fnl f* **14/1**
5 **7** 4 **Fondness**[24] 1118 3-8-12 EddieAhern 10 59
(R Charlton) *settled in midfield: pushed along and outpcd 3f out: one pce and n.d after* **7/1**
8 hd **Himba** 3-9-3 JimCrowley 14 64+
(Mrs A J Perrett) *hld up towards rr: outpcd 3f out: shuffled along and kpt on fnl 2f* **50/1**
04 **9** 1 **Bamboo Banks (IRE)**[23] 1139 3-9-3 DaneO'Neill 15 62
(J L Dunlop) *settled in midfield: outpcd 3f out: shuffled along and one pce after* **25/1**
10 5 **Camp Attack** 3-9-3 StephenCarson 11 53
(S Dow) *dwlt: hld up in last pair: wl off the pce 4f out: taken to wd outside over 2f out: pushed along and one pce* **100/1**
11 3 **Gavanello** 3-9-3 TedDurcan 5 47
(W R Swinburn) *hld up towards rr: outpcd over 3f out: shuffled along and nvr on terms after* **25/1**
0000 **12** 1 ¾ **Peak Seasons (IRE)**[22] 1166 3-9-3 52 AdrianMcCarthy 12 44
(W De Best-Turner) *rapid prog on outer to press ldrs 5f out: wknd 3f out: eased 2f out* **200/1**
00 **13** 1 **Delorain (IRE)**[16] 1290 3-9-3 AlanMunro 4 42
(J A R Toller) *a wl in rr: outpcd over 3f out: bhd after* **100/1**
14 ½ **Fiction Factory (IRE)**[204] 6047 3-8-12 45 JimmyQuinn 9 36
(J Pearce) *hld up towards rr: outpcd over 3f out: shuffled along and no prog after: wknd over 1f out* **66/1**
15 2 **Top Award** 3-9-3 JamieSpencer 2 37
(J R Fanshawe) *a wl in rr: rn green and bhd over 3f out* **18/1**
65 **16** 3 ½ **Petito (IRE)**[7] 1546 3-9-3 FergusSweeney 17 30
(Ian Williams) *wnt rt s: prog to chse ldrs 6f out: wknd 4f out* **50/1**
17 27 **Gatecrasher** 3-8-12 EmmettStack(5) 8 —
(Pat Eddery) *s.s: rn v green in last: t.o* **66/1**
2m 6.98s (-1.32) **Going Correction** -0.35s/f (Firm) **17** Ran SP% **119.6**
Speed ratings (Par 99):91,90,89,89,89 87,84,84,83,79 77,75,75,74,73 70,48
CSF £22.00 TOTE £5.80: £1.70, £2.60, £1.20; EX 41.70 Place 6 £2.66, Place 5 £2.48 .
Owner Mrs B Oppenheimer **Bred** B D Oppenheimer **Trained** East Ilsley, Berks

FOCUS
Probably a decent maiden but a very slow time, partially due to the bottom bend being slippery, and the sixth is the best guide to the level.
Nefski Alexander(USA) Official explanation: jockey said colt hung left
Petito(IRE) Official explanation: jockey said gelding was unsuited by the good to firm going

1742 MONDAY NIGHT RACING WITH VCCASINO.COM H'CAP 1m 67y
() (Class 5) (0-70,) 3-Y-O £

T/Plt: £2.80 to a £1 stake. Pool: £62,016.85. 15,987.25 winning tickets. T/Qpdt: £1.70 to a £1 stake. Pool: £3,425.60. 1,423.40 winning tickets. JN

[1548] WOLVERHAMPTON (A.W) (L-H)
Monday, May 15

OFFICIAL GOING: Standard
Wind: Almost nil

1743 ROOFTOP HOUSING GROUP MAIDEN AUCTION FILLIES' STKS 5f 20y(P)
2:10 (2:13) (Class 5) 2-Y-O **£3,238** (£963; £481; £240) **Stalls** Low

Form RPR
3 **1** **Sunken Rags**[6] 1559 2-8-6 PatCosgrave 1 63
(K R Burke) *t.k.h: a.p: rdn to ld jst over 1f out: drvn out* **5/2**[2]
2 shd **Drifting Gold** 2-8-3 ow1 AdamKirby(3) 7 63
(C G Cox) *bhd: rdn 3f out: hdwy on ins wl over 1f out: ev ch wl ins fnl f: r.o* **12/1**
40 **3** 2 **Elizabeth Garrett**[26] 1082 2-8-4 AlanMunro 2 53
(R M H Cowell) *sn led: rdn and hdd jst over 1f out: no ex wl ins fnl f* **13/2**[3]
6 **4** nk **Flower Of Cork (IRE)**[16] 1295 2-8-9 EddieAhern 6 57
(T D Easterby) *bhd: rdn and hdwy over 2f out: r.o one pce fnl f* **14/1**
4 **5** 1 ¾ **Tang**[5] 1587 2-8-4 ow2 RobertMiles(3) 5 49
(W G M Turner) *led early: w ldr: rdn 2f out: wknd ins fnl f* **2/1**[1]
4 **6** nk **Autumn Storm**[19] 1242 2-8-7 RobertHavlin 8 48
(R Ingram) *hmpd s: hld up and bhd: rdn over 2f out: c wd st: hung lft over 1f out: nvr trbld ldrs* **16/1**
4 **7** 1 ¼ **Check Tou**[14] 1347 2-8-6 GrahamGibbons 9 42
(P A Blockley) *wnt lft s: prom: rdn over 2f out: wknd over 1f out* **7/1**
50 **8** 6 **Caj (IRE)**[21] 1181 2-8-9 NCallan 4 24
(M Quinn) *prom: rdn over 2f out: wknd over 1f out: eased whn no ch ins fnl f* **17/2**
63.53 secs (0.71) **Going Correction** -0.025s/f (Stan) **8** Ran SP% **118.5**
Speed ratings (Par 90):93,92,89,89,86 85,83,74
CSF £33.59 TOTE £4.10: £1.50, £2.70, £1.90; EX 43.00 Trifecta £136.80 Pool: £329.55 - 1.71 winning tickets..
Owner Market Avenue Racing Club Ltd **Bred** Peter Balding **Trained** Middleham Moor, N Yorks

FOCUS
An ordinary maiden designed for fillies bought cheaply. The form appears weak and has been rated conservatively.

NOTEBOOK
Sunken Rags built on the promise of her debut and held on in a close-run thing after racing keenly. (op 11-4 tchd 3-1)
Drifting Gold ◆, a half-sister to a winner three times in Turkey, took a while to get the hang of things on her debut. She may well have prevailed had Kirby been able to make full use of his allowance and a similar contest would appear to be there for the taking. (op 10-1)
Elizabeth Garrett ran much better but could not take full advantage of a drop in class on this switch to sand. (op 9-2 tchd 7-1)
Flower Of Cork(IRE) stepped up considerably on her Ripon debut. Out of a mare who won over six furlongs first time out at two, a longer trip may help. (op 16-1)
Tang may have found this coming too soon after her promising debut at Chester last week. (op 5-2 tchd 3-1)

1744 HOMEZONE HOT SHOTS CLAIMING STKS 5f 20y(P)
2:40 (2:40) (Class 6) 2-Y-O **£2,730** (£806; £403) **Stalls** Low

Form RPR
4132 **1** **Granny Peel (IRE)**[19] 1229 2-8-7 NCallan 4 65
(K A Ryan) *mde all: rdn clr over 1f out: r.o wl* **7/4**[1]
0 **2** 4 **Bathwick Style**[41] 878 2-8-7 GrahamGibbons 3 51
(B R Millman) *mid-div: rdn over 3f out: hdwy on ins over 2f out: kpt on to take 2nd last strides* **14/1**

062 **3** *nk* **Circle Of Truth**[13] [1379] 2-8-8 .... RobertMiles(3) 1 54
(W G M Turner) *a.p: chsng wnr whn n.m.r on ins over 3f out: rdn over 1f out: one pce* **3/1**[2]

0 **4** *3/4* **Nicada (IRE)**[18] [1248] 2-8-12 .... JimmyQuinn 9 52
(M W Easterby) *s.i.s: hdwy and hung lft over 1f out: r.o ins fnl f* **20/1**

5041 **5** *1 1/4* **Mrs Crossy (IRE)**[13] [1379] 2-8-4 .... StephaneBreux(3) 8 43
(R Hannon) *prom tl rdn and wknd over 1f out* **9/2**[3]

0564 **6** *1* **All Talk**[13] [1379] 2-7-13 ow1 .... JamesDoyle(5) 2 36
(I A Wood) *prom: rdn over 2f out: wknd over 1f out* **10/1**

0 **7** *5* **Brynris**[7] [1535] 2-8-4 .... MarcHalford(5) 7 23
(W G M Turner) *a bhd* **33/1**

8 *1 1/4* **Put It On The Card** 2-9-2 .... JimmyFortune 5 26
(P D Evans) *outpcd* **20/1**

0 **9** *1/2* **Pirner's Brig**[18] [1248] 2-8-12 .... DaleGibson 6 20
(M W Easterby) *sn bhd: hung lft over 1f out* **22/1**

10 *17* **Answer Back** 2-8-5 .... PaulDoe 10 —
(Miss J R Tooth) *s.i.s: sn chsng ldrs: rdn and wknd over 2f out* **33/1**

63.28 secs (0.46) **Going Correction** -0.025s/f (Stan) **10** Ran SP% **115.1**
Speed ratings (Par 91):95,88,88,86,84 83,75,73,72,45
CSF £25.14 TOTE £2.60: £1.10, £3.00, £1.30; EX 24.20 Trifecta £163.10 Pool: £328.58 - 1.43 winning tickets..The winner was the subject of a friendly claim. Nicada was claimed by Miss Gay Kelleway for £10,000.
Owner J Hopkinson and R Peel **Bred** Tally-Ho Stud **Trained** Hambleton, N Yorks
■ Stewards' Enquiry : N Callan two-day ban: careless riding (May 26-27)

FOCUS
A modest claimer in which the third sets the standard.

NOTEBOOK
Granny Peel(IRE), without the cheekpieces this time, ran these rivals ragged on this switch to sand. (op 6-4)
Bathwick Style is quite stoutly bred on her dam's side and gave the impression she would appreciate a longer trip.
Circle Of Truth managed to turn around a length defeat by Mrs Crossy at Kempton on a pound worse terms but proved no match for the winner. (op 5-1)
Nicada(IRE) was claimed for £10,000 by Gaye Kelleway and looks the type who could improve for a step up in distance. (op 14-1)
Mrs Crossy(IRE) could not confirm her length defeat of Circle Of Truth at Kempton despite meeting her old rival on a pound better terms. (op 3-1)
All Talk could not reverse the Kempton form with either Circle Of Truth or Mrs Crossy despite being better off at the weights. (tchd 8-1)
Answer Back Official explanation: jockey said filly had no more to give

1745 NICOL THOMAS LTD H'CAP 1m 5f 194y(P)
3:10 (3:10) (Class 6) (0-65,65) 4-Y-0+ **£3,071** (£906; £453) **Stalls** Low

Form RPR

0342 **1** **Senor Set (GER)**[6] [1562] 5-8-12 **55** .... DeanMcKeown 8 66
(J Pearce) *hld up in mid-div: hdwy 9f out: rdn over 2f out: led and hung lft over 1f out: rdn out* **9/1**

1023 **2** *2* **Taxman (IRE)**[44] [838] 4-9-5 **63** .... (p) JimmyFortune 5 71
(C E Brittain) *a.p: led 9f out: rdn and hdd over 1f out: nt qckn ins fnl f* **5/1**[2]

6612 **3** *nk* **Lake Wakatipu**[13] [1392] 4-8-12 **56** .... AlanMunro 2 64
(M Mullineaux) *hld up in rr: rdn and hdwy over 2f out: styd on ins fnl f* **12/1**

0521 **4** *nk* **Rose Bien**[13] [1392] 4-8-8 **52** .... (p) TonyCulhane 10 59
(P J McBride) *hld up in mid-div: sltly hmpd after 3f: rdn and outpcd 5f out: rallied 1f out: styd on* **7/1**[3]

2226 **5** *3 1/2* **Pee Jay's Dream**[23] [1138] 4-8-12 **56** .... DaleGibson 13 58
(M W Easterby) *led: hdd 9f out: rdn over 2f out: wknd ins fnl f* **8/1**

0554 **6** *1 1/2* **Amwell Brave**[13] [1389] 5-9-3 **60** .... EddieAhern 9 60
(J R Jenkins) *hld up and bhd: rdn and hdwy over 2f out: wknd fnl f* **14/1**

1202 **7** *hd* **Principal Witness (IRE)**[7] [1548] 5-9-4 **64** .... AdamKirby(3) 4 64
(Evan Williams) *hld up in tch: clipped heels and stmbld after 2f: rdn over 2f out: wknd fnl f* **5/2**[1]

0632 **8** *1/2* **Screen Test**[18] [881] 4-9-0 **58** .... GeorgeBaker 11 57
(B G Powell) *prom: jnd ldr 8f out: rdn 3f out: wknd 2f out* **8/1**

5005 **9** *hd* **Lady Pilot**[14] [1339] 4-8-9 **60** .... (v) SladeO'Hara(7) 1 59
(Dr J R J Naylor) *hld up in tch: rdn over 3f out: wknd over 2f out* **16/1**

6000 **10** *6* **Duxford**[18] [1265] 5-8-12 **55** .... JimmyQuinn 6 46
(D K Ivory) *a bhd* **66/1**

5500 **11** *11* **Indian Chase**[14] [1339] 9-8-10 **53** .... BrianReilly 12 28
(Dr J R J Naylor) *hld up and bhd: sltly hmpd after 3f: hdwy 6f out: rdn over 3f out: sn wknd* **33/1**

40/0 **12** *12* **Uncle Max (IRE)**[6] [1566] 6-9-8 **65** .... VinceSlattery 7 24
(N A Twiston-Davies) *hld up towards rr: rdn 5f out: sn struggling* **66/1**

10-0 **13** *26* **Only For Sue**[23] [1138] 7-8-9 **52** .... NCallan 3 —
(W S Kittow) *prom: rdn over 4f out: wknd 3f out: t.o* **10/1**

3m 4.90s (-2.47) **Going Correction** -0.025s/f (Stan)
WFA 4 from 5yo+ 1lb **13** Ran SP% **125.2**
Speed ratings (Par 101):106,104,104,104,102 101,101,101,101,97 91,84,69
CSF £55.92 CT £561.02 TOTE £11.80: £2.60, £1.70, £4.90; EX 58.10 Trifecta £220.70 Part won. Pool: £310.96 - 0.10 winning tickets..
Owner sportaracing.com **Bred** Gestut Graditz **Trained** Newmarket, Suffolk

FOCUS
They went no great pace in this poor handicap and the form is not rock-solid.
Only For Sue Official explanation: jockey said gelding had no more to give

1746 MIDLAND HEART GROUP (S) STKS 7f 32y(P)
3:40 (3:40) (Class 6) 3-Y-0+ **£2,388** (£705; £352) **Stalls** High

Form RPR

0000 **1** **Downland (IRE)**[11] [1443] 10-9-8 59 .... KimTinkler 7 59
(N Tinkler) *hld up in mid-div: hdwy over 3f out: rdn 2f out: r.o to ld post* **16/1**

0030 **2** *shd* **Merdiff**[7] [1550] 7-9-13 54 .... EddieAhern 4 64
(W M Brisbourne) *hld up in tch: wnt 2nd 2f out: rdn over 1f out: struck on hd by rival jockey's whip ins fnl f: led cl home: hdd post* **8/1**

2065 **3** *1* **Aswan (IRE)**[11] [1443] 8-9-5 60 .... (t) AmirQuinn(3) 6 56
(S R Bowring) *a.p: led wl over 2f out: sn rdn: hdd cl home* **7/1**[3]

6353 **4** *2* **Musiotal**[13] [1394] 5-9-1 45 .... (p) KevinGhunowa(7) 1 51
(P A Blockley) *mid-div: lost pl on ins over 3f out: rdn and hdwy 2f out: one pce fnl f* **9/2**[2]

0600 **5** *2* **Indian Gem**[13] [1391] 5-9-3 40 .... AlanDaly 5 41
(A J Chamberlain) *s.i.s: sn chsng ldrs: n.m.r and lost pl 4f out: rdn and hdwy on ins over 2f out: no imp fnl f* **40/1**

0220 **6** *7* **Midnight Lace**[42] [853] 4-9-3 61 .... NCallan 8 23
(J R Boyle) *bhd: rdn 3f out: nvr nr ldrs* **9/2**[2]

0004 **7** *1 1/2* **Resplendent Prince**[7] [1550] 4-9-13 60 .... (v) TonyCulhane 9 29
(P Howling) *chsd ldrs tl rdn and wknd wl over 1f out* **11/1**

0000 **8** *1 1/4* **Lucky Emerald (IRE)**[13] [1391] 4-9-3 40 .... JimmyQuinn 3 15
(B Palling) *led: hdd wl over 2f out: wknd wl over 1f out* **40/1**

0030 **9** *1 1/4* **Hit's Only Money (IRE)**[33] [977] 6-9-8 65 .... (t) DeanMcKeown 11 17
(J Pearce) *s.i.s: rdn and short-lived effrt 4f out* **7/4**[1]

0000 **10** *1* **Bennanabaa**[25] [1102] 7-9-8 40 .... (t) RobertHavlin 10 15
(S C Burrough) *a bhd* **100/1**

0000 **11** *11* **At The Bar**[12] [1412] 3-8-10 50 .... VinceSlattery 12 —
(A J Chamberlain) *rdn 4f out: a bhd* **66/1**

000 **12** *13* **Lol Draper**[13] [1373] 3-8-5 45 .... (v1) GrahamGibbons 2 —
(P D Evans) *w ldr 3f: sn rdn and wknd* **33/1**

1m 29.93s (-0.47) **Going Correction** -0.025s/f (Stan)
WFA 3 from 4yo+ 12lb **12** Ran SP% **120.9**
Speed ratings (Par 101):101,100,99,97,95 87,85,84,82,81 68,54
CSF £137.35 TOTE £18.20: £4.30, £3.00, £2.70; EX 125.80 TRIFECTA Not won..There was no bid for the winner. Hit's Only Money was claimed by R. A. Harris for £6,000.
Owner A Graham **Bred** Yeomanstown Stud **Trained** Langton, N Yorks

FOCUS
Only a seller but a cracking finish, however the fourth and fifth tend to limit the form.
Midnight Lace Official explanation: jockey said filly suffered interference in running

1747 GLEESON BUILDING LTD FILLIES' H'CAP 1m 141y(P)
4:10 (4:10) (Class 5) (0-70,70) 3-Y-0 **£3,886** (£1,156; £577; £288) **Stalls** Low

Form RPR

003 **1** **Oporto (UAE)**[16] [1306] 3-8-13 **65** .... NCallan 1 69
(M A Jarvis) *mde all: rdn wl over 1f out: r.o* **11/2**[3]

0621 **2** *2* **Ruffie (IRE)**[156] [6543] 3-9-1 **67** .... JimmyQuinn 3 67
(Miss Gay Kelleway) *a.p: rdn over 2f out: chsd wnr wl over 1f out: no imp fnl f* **9/1**

005 **3** *1/2* **Starboard Light**[327] [2819] 3-8-1 **56** .... NelsonDeSouza(3) 2 55
(R M Beckett) *chsd wnr tl rdn wl over 1f out: one pce fnl f* **50/1**

544 **4** *1* **Emilion**[18] [1252] 3-8-13 **65** .... TonyCulhane 5 63+
(W J Haggas) *hld up: rdn over 3f out: hdwy on ins wl over 1f out: no imp fnl f* **4/1**[2]

055 **5** *1 1/4* **Tabulate**[13] [1386] 3-7-11 **56** oh1 .... NicolPolli(7) 7 50
(P L Gilligan) *hld up: n.m.r ent st: sn rdn: no hdwy* **33/1**

0561 **6** *1* **Christmas Player (USA)**[51] [735] 3-9-4 **70** .... JimmyFortune 4 62
(J H M Gosden) *hld up in tch: rdn over 2f out: wknd over 1f out: fin lame* **4/6**[1]

4036 **7** *7* **Lucidity Light (IRE)**[193] [6233] 3-9-1 **67** .... GrahamGibbons 8 44
(J D Bethell) *hld up: rdn 3f out: bhd fnl 2f* **40/1**

1m 51.6s (-0.16) **Going Correction** -0.025s/f (Stan) **7** Ran SP% **112.7**
Speed ratings (Par 96):99,97,96,95,94 93,87
CSF £48.59 CT £2197.15 TOTE £7.10: £3.00, £1.10; EX 35.40 Trifecta £180.10 Pool: £794.27 - 3.13 winning tickets..
Owner Jumeirah Racing **Bred** Darley **Trained** Newmarket, Suffolk

FOCUS
A steadily-run modest affair with the winner benefiting from a soft lead and the form is not strong.
Christmas Player(USA) Official explanation: vet said filly was found to be lame

1748 EXTRACARE CHARITABLE TRUST AMATEUR RIDERS' H'CAP 1m 4f 50y(P)
4:40 (4:40) (Class 6) (0-60,60) 4-Y-0+ **£2,637** (£811; £405) **Stalls** Low

Form RPR

5632 **1** **Ramsgill (USA)**[44] [833] 4-11-2 **60** .... MrSPearce(5) 8 74+
(J Pearce) *hld up in tch: led wl over 1f out: clr whn rdn and edgd lft ent fnl f: r.o wl* **11/2**[3]

3322 **2** *5* **Zaffeu**[10] [1467] 5-10-11 **50** .... MrSWalker 11 56
(A G Juckes) *hld up and bhd: hdwy over 3f out: rdn over 2f out: chsd wnr fnl f: no imp* **5/1**[2]

0-00 **3** *3/4* **Celtic Star (IRE)**[225] [2747] 8-10-6 **48** .... (p) MissFayeBramley(3) 7 53
(Mrs L Williamson) *hld up in mid-div: hdwy on outside 4f out: one pce fnl 2f* **50/1**

/00- **4** *1 1/4* **Kristoffersen**[15] [984] 6-11-0 **60** .... MrJRavenall(7) 2 63
(Ian Williams) *hld up in mid-div: lost pl over 5f out: hdwy over 1f out: styd on fnl f* **14/1**

2225 **5** *1/2* **York Cliff**[7] [1548] 8-10-10 **56** .... MrBenBrisbourne(7) 6 58
(W M Brisbourne) *hld up in tch: lost pl 4f out: hdwy over 1f out: nvr trbld ldrs* **10/1**

-412 **6** *2* **Hilltime (IRE)**[303] [3213] 6-10-8 **52** .... MrRTierney(5) 5 51
(J J Quinn) *led: rdn whn swtchd rt over 2f out: sn wknd* **7/1**

5003 **7** *3/4* **Mary Gray**[11] [1436] 4-10-11 **50** .... MrWHogg 12 48
(M Johnston) *w ldr: led 9f out: qcknd over 5f out: rdn and hdd wl over 1f out: wknd ins fnl f* **5/1**[2]

3001 **8** *4* **Explosive Fox (IRE)**[16] [1308] 5-11-2 **60** .... MrSPJones(5) 10 51
(S Curran) *prom: rdn over 3f out: wknd over 2f out* **7/2**[1]

0050 **9** *1 1/4* **Ardglass (IRE)**[28] [6127] 4-10-11 **55** .... (p) MrsCThompson(5) 9 44
(Mrs P Townsley) *dwlt: rdn over 4f out: a bhd* **25/1**

1456 **10** *3 1/2* **Ocean Rock**[16] [1308] 5-11-0 **53** .... GerardTumelty 4 37
(C A Horgan) *dwlt: a bhd* **5/1**[2]

2m 41.59s (-0.83) **Going Correction** -0.025s/f (Stan) **10** Ran SP% **121.7**
Speed ratings (Par 101):101,97,97,96,96 94,94,91,90,88
CSF £34.77 CT £1272.66 TOTE £5.90: £3.00, £1.50, £7.80; EX 41.50 Trifecta £220.20 Part won. Pool: £310.23 - 0.34 winning tickets. Place 6 £1,392.99, Place 5 £652.28.
Owner Mrs M Miller **Bred** C L Kidder, J K Griggs And N M Cole **Trained** Newmarket, Suffolk

FOCUS
A modest pace until past halfway in what was not much better than a banded-class handicap, with the runner-up the best guide to the level.
T/Jkpt: Not won. T/Plt: £494.60 to a £1 stake. Pool: £43,877.80. 64.75 winning tickets. T/Qpdt: £211.70 to a £1 stake. Pool: £3,175.70. 11.10 winning tickets. KH

1370 SAINT-CLOUD (L-H)
Monday, May 15

OFFICIAL GOING: Good

1749a PRIX GREFFULHE MITSUBISHI MOTORS (GROUP 2) (C&F) 1m 2f
2:50 (2:53) 3-Y-0 **£51,103** (£19,724; £9,414; £9,276; £3,138)

RPR

1 **Visindar**[28] 3-9-2 .... CSoumillon 2 117+
(A Fabre, France) *racd in 4th early, 3rd halfway, ran on easily fr 2f out to chal 1 1/2f out, led appr fnl f, qcknd clr, easily* **1/5**[1]

2 *4* **Onerous**[51] 3-9-2 .... IMendizabal 1 106
(J-C Rouget, France) *disp last early, last half-way, ridden and ran on 1 1/2f out, took 2nd 50 yards out* **83/10**[3]

The Form Book, Raceform Ltd, Compton, RG20 6NL

3 *hd* **Hello Sunday (FR)**28 1064 3-9-2 RonanThomas 6 106
(Mme C Head-Maarek, France) *disp last early, 5th halfway, ran on fr 1 1/2f out, rdn fnl f, ev ch of 2nd place fnl 50y, stayed on* **39/1**
4 *nk* **Zatonic (FR)**22 1179 3-9-2 SPasquier 4 105
(P Demercastel, France) *racd in 2nd, led and pushed along str, hdd appr fnl f, rdn and stayed on under pressure til no ex fnl 50y* **14/1**
5 *2 1/2* **Bremen**28 1064 3-9-2 OPeslier 3 101
(A Fabre, France) *raced in 3rd early, 4th straight, ridden 2f out, unable to quicken* **4/1**2
6 *1 1/2* **Moon Mix (FR)**31 3-9-2 MSautjeau 5 98
(A Fabre, France) *set good pace until headed entering straight, eased final 1 1/2f* **1/5**1

2m 3.10s **6** Ran SP% **206.6**
PARI-MUTUEL: WIN 1.20 (coupled with Moon Mix); PL 1.10, 1.20; SF 4.50.
Owner H H Aga Khan **Bred** M Lagardere **Trained** Chantilly, France

FOCUS
Visindar was already ante-post favourite for the Epsom Derby coming into this, and a comfortable four-length success ensured his price only got shorter. He is developing into a high-class colt, and fully deserves his place at the head of the market, although strictly on breeding he is not guaranteed to be as effective over a mile and a half, despite his sire Sinndar having been an impressive winner of the Derby.

NOTEBOOK
Visindar ◆, a stylish winner of a newcomers' race here on his only start as a juvenile and impressive again when upped to nine furlongs at Longchamp on his reappearance, took his first Group race in style. Settled quite close to what was an unusally good pace by French standards, he took control about a furlong and a half out and only had to be pushed out to win by a good margin. He did not exactly display an electric change of pace, but was never in any danger and saw his race out very well indeed over the furthest trip he has tried to date. Already ante-post favourite for the Epsom Derby, his price shortened further off the back of this display. He is rapidly developing into a high-class colt and looks very much the one to beat at Epsom, the only niggling concern being his stamina for a truly-run mile and a half, as there is plenty of speed on the dam's side of his pedigree.
Onerous, unbeaten previously in two races in the Provinces and racing at a Paris track for the first time, finished well but was no match for the comfortable winner.
Hello Sunday(FR), given a waiting ride, was outpaced early in the straight but ran on again at the finish and looks to be finding his true form.
Zatonic(FR), still a maiden, but a high-class one, ran another good race in defeat. Settled behind the pacemaker, he quickened early in the straight but could not go with the winner when it mattered. He only lost second place in the last few strides.

1309 BRIGHTON (L-H)
Tuesday, May 16

OFFICIAL GOING: Firm (good to firm in places) changing to good to soft after race 5 (4.10)
Wind: Virtually nil Weather: Rainy

1750 STS FLOORING MAIDEN STKS 5f 213y
2:10 (2:11) (Class 5) 3-Y-O+ **£3,238** (£963; £481; £240) **Stalls** Low

Form RPR
025 **1** **Perfect Treasure (IRE)**129 60 3-8-9 70 AlanMunro 2 54
(J A R Toller) *keen: w ldr: hrd rdn to ld ins fnl f: all out* **5/1**2
3306 **2** *nk* **Glenargo (USA)**61 651 3-9-0 49 AdrianMcCarthy 4 59+
(R A Harris) *trckd ldrs: rdn 2f out: nt clr run ins fnl f: swtchd rt and r.o strly cl home* **66/1**
5504 **3** *nk* **Elusive Warrior (USA)**12 1430 3-9-0 65 JimCrowley 5 58
(Mrs A J Perrett) *trckd ldrs: ev ch and bmpd 2f out: nt qckn u.p last 100 yds* **13/2**3
600 **4** *hd* **Riolo (IRE)**23 1166 4-9-4 50 JamesDoyle(5) 3 62+
(K F Clutterbuck) *outpcd: drvn 3f out: sn hung lft: str run fnl f: n.m.r nr fin* **100/1**
2032 **5** *nk* **Sensuous**7 1565 3-8-9 79 RyanMoore 1 51
(R Hannon) *slt ld: hrd rdn 2f out: hdd ins fnl f: wknd cl home* **8/13**1
2536 **6** *1 1/4* **Phinerine**21 1208 3-8-7 63 (b) TolleyDean(7) 6 52
(R A Harris) *hld up in tch: effrt and wnt lft 2f out: wknd last 100 yds* **9/1**
00 **7** *27* **Mustang Lil**168 6462 5-9-1 AdamKirby(3) 7 —
(Ms J S Doyle) *a bhd: drvn 4f out: t.o 2f out* **20/1**

69.90 secs (-0.20) **Going Correction** -0.075s/f (Good)
WFA 3 from 4yo+ 9lb **7** Ran SP% **109.2**
Speed ratings (Par 103):98,97,97,96,96 94,58
CSF £217.93 TOTE £5.40: £2.00, £7.90; EX 112.10.
Owner John Drew **Bred** Patrick F Kelly **Trained** Newmarket, Suffolk
■ Stewards' Enquiry : Alan Munro two-day ban: used whip with excessive frequency, without giving filly time to recover and with whip arm above shoulder height (May 27-28)

FOCUS
A weak maiden producing a blanket finish and rated around the runner-up and fourth.
Riolo(IRE) Official explanation: jockey said gelding hung left
Mustang Lil Official explanation: jockey said mare was unsuited by the track and the firm (good to firm in places) ground

1751 WEATHERBYS INSURANCE H'CAP 5f 59y
2:40 (2:40) (Class 5) (0-70,70) 3-Y-O **£3,886** (£1,156; £577; £288) **Stalls** Low

Form RPR
0010 **1** **Devine Dancer**24 1137 3-9-4 70 DaneO'Neill 8 81
(H Candy) *mde all: rdn over 1f out: in command after: eased nr fin* **11/1**
6445 **2** *1* **Yellow Card**3 1679 3-9-4 70 ChrisCatlin 9 77
(N A Callaghan) *chsd ldrs: wnt 2nd 2f out: sn rdn: hld hd high: no imp* **11/4**2
6313 **3** *2 1/2* **Spirit Of Coniston**8 1549 3-8-11 63 (v) RobbieFitzpatrick 7 61
(Peter Grayson) *midfield: rdn 3f out: hung lft and kpt on fnl f* **10/1**
0003 **4** *1* **Mytton's Pride**8 1529 3-9-2 68 SebSanders 5 62+
(A Bailey) *chsd ldrs: drvn 2f out: hmpd 1f out: wknd* **8/1**3
6044 **5** *1/2* **Danny The Dip**14 1378 3-8-4 59 ow2 NeilChalmers(3) 1 52+
(J J Bridger) *hld up: rdn 2f out: nt clr run fnl f: n.d* **20/1**
5560 **6** *1/2* **Watch Out Jess**239 5363 3-8-2 57 EdwardCreighton(3) 3 48
(M Madgwick) *hld up and bhd: nvr trbld ldrs* **66/1**
0435 **7** *nk* **Thoughtsofstardom**17 1304 3-8-8 60 (v) BrianReilly 4 50
(P S McEntee) *hld up: plld out and rdn 2f out: hung lft: nvr trbld ldrs* **33/1**
2162 **8** *1* **Lucayos**14 1378 3-8-13 70 (b) RichardKingscote(5) 6 56
(Mrs H Sweeting) *scratchy to post: slowly away: sn drvn and nvr gng wl in rr* **9/4**1
3600 **9** *3/4* **Squadron Leader (IRE)**15 1355 3-8-13 65 RyanMoore 2 48
(R Hannon) *a bhd* **14/1**
005 **10** *1* **North Fleet**15 1355 3-8-9 61 TQuinn 10 41
(J M Bradley) *chsd ldr tl rdn 2f out: sn wknd* **9/1**

61.43 secs (-0.87) **Going Correction** -0.075s/f (Good) **10** Ran SP% **111.8**
Speed ratings (Par 99):103,101,97,95,95 94,93,92,90,89
CSF £39.05 CT £268.19 TOTE £13.40: £2.80, £1.30, £2.60; EX 35.00 Trifecta £118.70 wu.
Owner John Simms **Bred** J Simms **Trained** Kingston Warren, Oxon

FOCUS
A modest sprint handicap but sound enough, with the third and fourth close to recent efforts.
Thoughtsofstardom Official explanation: jockey said gelding ran too free
Lucayos Official explanation: jockey said colt missed the break and ran flat; vet said colt lost a shoe and finished lame in front
North Fleet Official explanation: jockey said gelding lost its action

1752 EXPRESS CAFE (S) STKS 6f 209y
3:10 (3:12) (Class 6) 3-Y-O+ **£2,266** (£674; £337; £168) **Stalls** Low

Form RPR
0450 **1** **Mon Petite Amour**8 1549 3-8-0 50 ow2 (p) FrankieMcDonald 5 49
(D W P Arbuthnot) *trckd ldrs: rdn 2f out: led ins fnl f: jst hld on* **33/1**
0420 **2** *hd* **Hadath (IRE)**7 1568 9-9-0 54 (b) SebSanders 4 55
(B G Powell) *wl bhd: rdn 1/2-way: hrd drvn and stl plenty to do over 1f out: str burst fnl f: jst hld* **11/2**3
0000 **3** *1* **Moon Forest (IRE)**7 1570 4-9-0 65 (p) RyanMoore 2 53
(J M Bradley) *led: rdn over 2f out: hdd & wknd last 100 yds* **12/1**
0230 **4** *2* **Border Artist**8 1539 7-9-0 49 (b) TQuinn 8 47
(B G Powell) *hld up: c wd st: effrt and flattered 2f out: sn nt qckn: kpt on again ins fnl f* **17/2**
0000 **5** *hd* **Princess Kai (IRE)**14 1397 5-8-9 40 RobertHavlin 10 42
(R Ingram) *midfield: effrt whn bmpd 2f out: kpt on one pce* **66/1**
0500 **6** *nk* **Beau Marche**8 1539 4-9-0 45 (b1) BrianReilly 3 46
(G G Margarson) *chsd ldr: rdn over 2f out: hung lft and lost 2nd ins fnl f* **33/1**
0605 **7** *1/2* **Zafarshah (IRE)**7 1568 7-8-7 53 (b) TolleyDean(7) 12 45
(R A Harris) *hld up midfield: rdn and bmpd 2f out: no imp after* **8/1**
6044 **8** *3/4* **Imperium**16 1310 5-9-6 51 (p) SteveDrowne 7 49
(Stef Liddiard) *hld up midfield: rdn 1/2-way: wl hld whn sltly hmpd ins fnl f* **5/1**2
3502 **9** *2* **Mission Affirmed (USA)**8 1550 5-9-0 50 (b) AdrianMcCarthy 6 37
(R A Harris) *midfield: drvn 1/2-way: wknd 2f out* **4/1**1
5000 **10** *1 1/2* **Edge Fund**16 1311 4-8-11 49 (b) AdamKirby(3) 11 33
(Miss Gay Kelleway) *a wl bhd* **12/1**
000 **11** *3/4* **Kings Cavalier (USA)**15 1344 3-8-3 64 (v) RoystonFfrench 1 27
(I W McInnes) *trckd ldrs: rdn 2f out: wkng whn hmpd over 1f out* **16/1**
000 **12** *8* **Bournonville**13 1412 3-8-3 50 (tp) MatthewHenry 9 6
(J Ryan) *sn wl bhd* **66/1**
0510 **13** *1 1/2* **Mulberry Lad (IRE)**6 1594 4-9-6 49 ChrisCatlin 13 12
(P W Hiatt) *chsd ldrs: rdn over 2f out: sn wknd* **8/1**

1m 22.5s **Going Correction** -0.025s/f (Good)
WFA 3 from 4yo+ 11lb **13** Ran SP% **114.9**
Speed ratings (Par 101):100,99,98,96,96 95,95,94,92,90 89,80,78
CSF £197.13 TOTE £36.00: £7.50, £1.90, £4.40; EX 193.80.There was no bid for the winner.
Owner Noel Cronin **Bred** Branston Stud Ltd **Trained** Upper Lambourn, Berks

FOCUS
A moderate seller, with all but two of the runners wearing headgear of some type. The form is rated negatively through the winner.
Border Artist Official explanation: jockey said gelding hung right

1753 BLUE CHIP H'CAP 7f 214y
3:40 (3:43) (Class 6) (0-60,57) 4-Y-O+ **£3,238** (£963; £481; £240) **Stalls** Low

Form RPR
1006 **1** **Christmas Truce (IRE)**13 1400 7-8-10 54 (v) JamesDoyle(5) 6 68
(Ms J S Doyle) *drvn along briefly: in tch: hrd rdn 3f out: styd on to chal 1f out: led last 100 yds: sn clr* **16/1**
2015 **2** *4* **Whatatodo**246 5179 4-9-2 55 HayleyTurner 7 60
(M L W Bell) *chsd ldng pair: led wl over 1f out: hdd and no ex fnl 100 yds* **11/1**
0030 **3** *1 1/4* **Motu (IRE)**19 1253 5-8-12 51 (v) SebSanders 3 53
(I W McInnes) *keen: hld up in tch: rdn 2f out: fnd little and hung lft: kpt on fnl 100 yds* **7/1**2
0212 **4** *1 1/2* **Magic Warrior**11 1461 6-9-2 55 PatDobbs 14 54
(J C Fox) *midfield: rdn 3f out: kpt on fnl f: nvr on terms* **5/1**1
0004 **5** *nk* **Oh Boy (IRE)**16 1311 6-9-0 53 ChrisCatlin 12 51
(J M Bradley) *chsd ldr: led over 2f out: hdd over 1f out: wknd fnl f* **9/1**3
0000 **6** *nk* **Miss Madame (IRE)**55 696 5-9-4 57 IanMongan 5 54
(T G Mills) *led: rdn and hdd over 2f out: wknd over 1f out* **10/1**
50 **7** *1 1/2* **Hill Of Clare (IRE)**295 3803 4-8-8 47 RyanMoore 4 41
(P R Webber) *midfield: rdn over 2f out: no imp after* **10/1**
3032 **8** *1/2* **Golden Spectrum (IRE)**8 1553 7-8-11 57 (b) TolleyDean(7) 11 50
(R A Harris) *midfield: hrd rdn 2f out: no rspnse* **5/1**1
0400 **9** *2 1/2* **Megalala (IRE)**75 557 5-8-10 52 NeilChalmers(3) 8 39
(J J Bridger) *midfield: shkn up 2f out: no rspnse* **66/1**
4060 **10** *nk* **Elvina Hills (IRE)**38 917 4-9-1 54 DaneO'Neill 10 40
(P Mitchell) *rr: rdn over 4f out: nvr on terms* **12/1**
0000 **11** *5* **Bogaz (IRE)**7 1568 4-9-2 55 (p) GeorgeBaker 9 30
(Mrs H Sweeting) *a wl bhd* **20/1**
3050 **12** *10* **Pheckless**57 681 7-8-7 46 StephenCarson 13 —
(J M Bradley) *midfield: rdn over 2f out: wandered and wknd: t.o* **20/1**
0040 **13** *2 1/2* **Barachois Gaudy**8 1538 4-8-8 50 EdwardCreighton(3) 15 —
(Mrs N Smith) *a wl bhd: t.o* **25/1**
000 **14** *15* **Maya's Prince**23 1166 4-9-0 53 RobertHavlin 2 —
(M D I Usher) *a wl bhd: t.o* **80/1**

1m 34.46s (-0.58) **Going Correction** -0.025s/f (Good) **14** Ran SP% **112.0**
Speed ratings (Par 101):101,97,95,94,93 93,92,91,89,88 83,73,71,56
CSF £143.90 CT £1008.06 TOTE £17.60: £6.40, £3.20, £2.20; EX 278.60.
Owner Gaylor William Chambers **Bred** John McDonnell **Trained** Upper Lambourn, Berks
■ Pepper Road was withdrawn (8/1, broke through stalls). R4 applies, deduct 10p in the £.
■ Stewards' Enquiry : Hayley Turner one-day ban: used whip in an incorrect place (May 27)

FOCUS
A moderate handicap but run at a strong pace and probably sound, rated around the third and fourth.

1754 WEATHERBYS PRINTING H'CAP 1m 3f 196y
4:10 (4:13) (Class 5) (0-70,69) 4-Y-O+ **£3,886** (£1,156; £577; £288) **Stalls** High

Form RPR
1003 **1** **Gambling Spirit**20 1244 4-8-9 60 DaneO'Neill 4 67
(H Candy) *led 1f: chsd ldr: led in centre over 2f out: hung lft fnl f: styd on wl* **11/4**1

4413 **2** 3/4 **Ten-Cents**[84] [471] 4-8-7 **58** .... SteveDrowne 9 64
(C F Wall) *hld up last: prog over 2f out: ev ch 1f out: no ex ins fnl f* **6/1**

6663 **3** 3 1/2 **Shamrock Bay**[7] [1560] 4-9-0 **65** .... RyanMoore 8 65
(C R Dore) *hld up and bhd: effrt over 2f out: 3rd and one pce fnl f* **8/1**

2000 **4** 1 1/2 **Blackmail (USA)**[15] [1334] 8-8-10 **61** .... (b) SebSanders 6 59
(Miss B Sanders) *hld up in rr: rdn and fnd little 3f out: kpt on fnl f* **7/2**[2]

6043 **5** 3/4 **Murrieta**[8] [1548] 4-8-3 **57** oh10 ow2 .... (v) NeilChalmers[(3)] 5 54
(Miss J R Gibney) *t.k.h: trckd ldrs: rdn to ld in centre 3f out: hdd 2f out: hung lft and wknd* **33/1**

5S60 **6** 9 **Hatch A Plan (IRE)**[12] [1435] 5-8-13 **64** .... ChrisCatlin 2 46
(Mrs A J Hamilton-Fairley) *hld up in tch: rdn 3f out: wl btn whn hung lft fnl f* **11/1**

66-0 **7** nk **Garston Star**[21] [1204] 5-7-11 **55** .... JosephWalsh[(7)] 1 37
(J S Moore) *taken down early: t.k.h: trckd ldng pair: rdn 3f out: wknd 2f out* **50/1**

1351 **8** 2 **Mister Completely (IRE)**[10] [1415] 5-8-1 **55** oh1... EdwardCreighton[(3)] 3 34
(Miss Sheena West) *missed break: rcvrd to ld after 1f: hdd 3f out: wknd 2f out: eased fnl f* **5/1**[3]

000 **9** 16 **Factual Lad**[24] [1152] 8-9-4 **69** .... AlanMunro 7 22
(B R Millman) *trckd ldrs on outer: wknd rapidly 3f out: eased* **14/1**

2m 33.16s (0.96) **Going Correction** +0.175s/f (Good) **9** Ran SP% **110.9**
Speed ratings (Par 103):103,102,100,99,98 92,92,91,80
CSF £18.30 CT £109.67 TOTE £3.90: £1.40, £1.80, £2.30; EX 20.10 Trifecta £108.50 wu.
Owner Simon Broke And Partners **Bred** Beech Park Bloodstock Ltd **Trained** Kingston Warren, Oxon

FOCUS
A typical Brighton handicap, run on softening ground following two hours of rain. The bare form is ordinary with the fifth to form.
Factual Lad Official explanation: jockey said gelding was unsuited by the firm (good to firm in places) ground

1755 TELETEXT RACING "HANDS AND HEELS" APPRENTICE H'CAP 1m 1f 209y
4:40 (4:40) (Class 6) (0-60,60) 4-Y-0+ **£2,266** (£674; £337; £168) **Stalls** High

Form RPR

5000 **1** **Zinging**[7] [1566] 7-8-5 **46** oh6 .... RobbieMills 1 51
(J J Bridger) *t.k.h: plld to ld after 1f: mde rest: styd on gamely fnl f* **33/1**

0054 **2** nk **Miss Monica (IRE)**[85] [468] 5-8-5 **46** oh1 .... TolleyDean 9 50
(P W Hiatt) *dwlt: hld up: c wd and hdwy 3f out: chal 1f out: hld last 100yds* **9/1**

1664 **3** 3 1/2 **Treetops Hotel (IRE)**[13] [1400] 7-8-12 **53** .... JamesMillman 7 51
(B R Johnson) *hld up: effrt on bit 2f out: hung lft and no imp fnl f* **5/2**[1]

0350 **4** 1 1/2 **Fantasy Crusader**[148] [6614] 7-8-6 **47** .... LukeMorris 5 42
(R M H Cowell) *led on suffernce 1f: chsd ldr tl 6f out: c wd and ev ch 2f out: hung lft and wknd fnl f* **10/1**

0600 **5** 1 **Carpet Ride**[23] [421] 4-9-3 **58** .... (p) JosephWalsh 2 52
(B G Powell) *chsd ldrs: chal in centre 3f out: sn rdn: hung lft and wknd wl over 1f out* **12/1**

3004 **6** 1 3/4 **Lenwade**[16] [1313] 5-8-5 **46** oh1 .... JamieHamblett 10 37
(G G Margarson) *dwlt: hld up in last: shkn up 3f out: kpt on: nvr rchd ldrs* **6/1**[2]

0000 **7** 6 **Asaateel (IRE)**[15] [1334] 4-9-5 **60** .... (b) JemmaMarshall 8 40
(G L Moore) *chsd ldrs: c wd and rdn 3f out: wknd 2f out* **13/2**[3]

0003 **8** 1/2 **Agilete**[7] [1572] 4-8-6 **47** .... KevinGhunowa 4 26
(J R Boyle) *chsd ldrs: c wd and rdn 3f out: wknd over 1f out* **8/1**

4000 **9** 1 1/4 **Icecap**[14] [1394] 6-8-7 **48** .... ThomasO'Brien 3 25
(W G M Turner) *plld hrd: chsd ldrs after 2f: wnt 2nd 6f out tl 3f out: sn wknd* **10/1**

3620 **10** 1 1/4 **Bauhinia**[85] [462] 4-8-6 **50** .... RonanKeogh[(3)] 6 24
(J A R Toller) *dwlt: hld up and bhd: drvn 3f out: sn no ch* **10/1**

2m 6.33s (3.73) **Going Correction** +0.40s/f (Good) **10** Ran SP% **115.2**
Speed ratings (Par 101):101,100,97,96,95 94,89,89,88,87
CSF £300.92 CT £1025.47 TOTE £18.80: £4.40, £3.30, £1.30; EX 465.40 Place 6 £826.72, Place 5 £153.92.
Owner J J Bridger **Bred** M P Bishop **Trained** Liphook, Hants

FOCUS
A modest race run under hands-and-heels rules and probably not that solid.
Agilete Official explanation: jockey said gelding hung right
T/Plt: £929.20 to a £1 stake. Pool: £43,916.05. 34.50 winning tickets. T/Qpdt: £49.80 to a £1 stake. Pool: £3,853.80. 57.20 winning tickets. SP

[1588] NEWCASTLE (L-H)
Tuesday, May 16

OFFICIAL GOING: Good to soft (good in places)
Softer ground than the official and, given the steady pace of the majority of races, it was a meeting where the prominent racers held the edge.
Wind: Light; half behind

1756 MOTORSHOW AT HERRINGTON COUNTRY PARK H'CAP 1m 4f 93y
2:20 (2:20) (Class 5) (0-75,80) 4-Y-0+ **£4,210** (£1,252; £625; £312) **Stalls** Centre

Form RPR

1142 **1** **Polish Power (GER)**[12] [1439] 6-9-4 **74** .... JohnEgan 6 83
(J S Moore) *hld up: effrt over 2f out: edgd lft and led ins fnl f: hld on wl* **11/1**

0404 **2** nk **Rocket Force (USA)**[24] [1144] 6-8-11 **70** .... DNolan[(3)] 12 79
(N Wilson) *prom: rdn and led over 1f out: hdd ins fnl f: r.o* **14/1**

451 **3** hd **Tilt**[9] [1502] 4-9-10 **80** 6ex .... TomEaves 5 89+
(B Ellison) *midfield: effrt 3f out: hdwy over 1f out: kpt on wl fnl f* **85/40**[1]

2336 **4** 4 **Tannenberg (IRE)**[260] [4826] 5-9-0 **70** .... DeanMcKeown 14 72+
(G A Swinbank) *dwlt: bhd tl kpt on fnl 2f: nvr rchd ldrs* **20/1**

5546 **5** 1/2 **Royal Flynn**[20] [1233] 4-8-6 **62** .... TonyHamilton 3 63
(M Dods) *keen: hld up: rdn 3f out: kpt on fnl 2f: nrst fin* **33/1**

5303 **6** 1 **Ego Trip**[24] [1144] 5-8-4 **60** oh1 .... (b) DaleGibson 8 60
(M W Easterby) *keen: cl up: led over 2f to over 1f out: wknd ins fnl f* **8/1**[3]

4003 **7** 2 **Intavac Boy**[6] [1590] 5-8-4 **60** oh6 .... JoeFanning 7 57
(C W Thornton) *keen: chsd ldrs: ev ch 3f out tl wknd over 1f out* **20/1**

6-30 **8** 1 **Andre Chenier (IRE)**[5] [1610] 5-8-9 **65** .... DavidAllan 10 60
(P Monteith) *hld up: shkn up 3f out: hdwy over 1f out: nvr rchd ldrs* **33/1**

3106 **9** 3 **Melvino**[15] [1346] 4-8-9 **65** .... PhillipMakin 1 55
(T D Barron) *missed break: bhd: shortlived effrt over 2f out: no imp* **12/1**

2300 **10** 2 **Let It Be**[15] [1346] 5-8-5 **61** .... PaulHanagan 9 48
(K G Reveley) *hld up: rdn 3f out: n.d* **25/1**

4021 **11** 5 **Mceldowney**[14] [1389] 4-8-10 **71** .... GregFairley[(5)] 2 50
(M Johnston) *midfield: niggled along fr 1/2-way: outpcd fr 3f out* **9/1**

5150 **12** 6 **Leslingtaylor (IRE)**[207] [6006] 4-8-13 **69** .... GrahamGibbons 4 38
(J J Quinn) *keen: in tch tl rdn and wknd fr 3f out* **25/1**

3006 **13** 5 **Mister Arjay (USA)**[122] [4873] 6-8-6 **62** .... PatCosgrave 15 23
(B Ellison) *cl up: rdn and led over 3f out: hdd over 2f out: wknd over 1f out* **66/1**

00-6 **14** 9 **Rajam**[234] [4030] 8-8-11 **70** .... PaulMulrennan[(3)] 11 17
(G A Harker) *led to over 3f out: wknd over 2f out* **100/1**

1112 **15** 3 **Whispering Death**[209] [5983] 4-8-12 **68** .... TonyCulhane 13 10
(W J Haggas) *hld up midfield: rdn 4f out: edgd lft and wknd over 2f out* **7/1**[2]

2m 44.77s (1.22) **Going Correction** +0.25s/f (Good) **15** Ran SP% **113.9**
Speed ratings (Par 103):105,104,104,102,101 101,99,99,97,95 92,88,85,79,77
CSF £131.06 CT £451.99 TOTE £12.70: £2.50, £4.40, £1.70; EX 192.40.
Owner Mrs Fitri Hay **Bred** Gestut Hofgut Mappen **Trained** Upper Lambourn, Berks

FOCUS
An ordinary handicap in which the pace was fair and the form looks sound, with the first three clear.
Mceldowney Official explanation: jockey said gelding never travelled
Mister Arjay(USA) Official explanation: jockey said gelding had no more to give
Whispering Death Official explanation: jockey said gelding had no more to give

1757 REG VARDY SUNDERLAND RENAULT CLAIMING STKS 1m 2f 32y
2:50 (2:52) (Class 6) 4-Y-0+ **£2,266** (£674; £337; £168) **Stalls** Centre

Form RPR

0300 **1** **Mobane Flyer**[232] [5509] 6-8-9 62 .... PaulHanagan 8 63
(R A Fahey) *set stdy pce: mde all: rdn 2f out: hld on wl* **9/2**[3]

5060 **2** 3/4 **Airedale Lad (IRE)**[7] [1560] 5-8-5 40 .... DeanMcKeown 13 58
(R M Whitaker) *cl up: rdn over 2f out: kpt on same pce ins fnl f* **33/1**

0154 **3** hd **Donna's Double**[6] [1591] 11-8-5 53 .... (p) KDarley 1 58?
(Karen McLintock) *hld up bhd ldng gp: effrt over 2f out: kpt on fnl f: nrst finh* **4/1**[2]

-000 **4** 3 1/2 **Siena Star (IRE)**[7] [1560] 8-8-7 70 .... MickyFenton 9 53
(Miss Tracy Waggott) *bhd: rdn over 3f out: hdwy on outside over 1f out: nvr rchd ldrs* **14/1**

0000 **5** 3 **Berkhamsted (IRE)**[12] [1435] 4-8-13 78 .... (v) JohnEgan 6 54
(M F Harris) *prom tl rdn and no ex fr wl over 1f out* **9/4**[1]

5043 **6** 1 **Fit To Fly (IRE)**[7] [1573] 5-8-3 45 .... (p) JoeFanning 2 42
(R C Guest) *trckd ldrs: lost pl over 3f out: n.d after* **10/1**

4300 **7** nk **Inside Story (IRE)**[15] [1341] 4-8-6 70 .... PaulMulrennan[(3)] 10 48
(M W Easterby) *trckd ldrs tl wknd over 2f out* **9/1**

6000 **8** hd **Spring Time Girl**[15] [1341] 4-7-7 45 .... (p) DuranFentiman[(5)] 7 36
(B Ellison) *bhd: rdn 4f out: nvr rchd ldrs* **20/1**

0500 **9** 32 **Ruby Legend**[209] [5980] 8-8-7 48 .... TomEaves 4 —
(K G Reveley) *bhd: struggling 1/2-way: nvr on terms* **11/1**

0 **10** hd **Galloping Gertie**[57] [677] 4-8-6 .... TonyHamilton 5 —
(J Hetherton) *bhd: struggling 1/2-way: t.o* **100/1**

0060 **11** 36 **Atlantic Ace**[15] [1341] 9-8-9 47 ow2 .... (p) TonyCulhane 12 —
(B Smart) *trckd ldrs tl wknd over 2f out: virtually p.u ins fnl f* **33/1**

2m 14.66s (2.86) **Going Correction** +0.25s/f (Good) **11** Ran SP% **114.7**
Speed ratings (Par 101):98,97,97,94,92 91,91,90,65,65 36
CSF £147.79 TOTE £4.80: £1.60, £8.00, £1.80; EX 242.00.Berkhamsted (IRE) was claimed by Mr T. Dascombe for £10,000. Siena Star (IRE) was claimed by Mrs Stef Liddiard for £7,000.
Owner R A Fahey **Bred** Cheveley Park Stud Ltd **Trained** Musley Bank, N Yorks

FOCUS
An ordinary event in which the early pace was steady but overall the time was reasonable and this bare form should not prove reliable, rated around the third.

1758 REG VARDY STONEYGATE RENAULT H'CAP 2m 19y
3:20 (3:20) (Class 5) (0-75,69) 4-Y-0+ **£3,886** (£1,156; £577; £288) **Stalls** Centre

Form RPR

3303 **1** **Madiba**[15] [1339] 7-8-8 **48** .... JoeFanning 11 60
(P Howling) *hld up in tch: hdwy 1/2-way: led over 3f out: hld on wl fnl f* **11/1**[3]

5502 **2** 1/2 **Dhehdaah**[23] [990] 5-9-4 **58** .... MickyFenton 1 69
(Mrs P Sly) *hld up in tch: smooth hdwy to press wnr over 2f out: rdn ent last: fnd little* **7/2**[2]

2035 **3** 4 **Zeloso**[11] [5707] 8-8-5 **45** .... (v) JohnEgan 2 51
(M F Harris) *dwlt: bhd: hdwy to chse clr ldrs 2f out: no imp fnl f* **33/1**

0011 **4** 8 **Prairie Sun (GER)**[3] [1660] 5-9-10 **69** 6ex .... GregFairley[(5)] 4 66
(Mrs A Duffield) *prom: drvn over 4f out: one pce fr over 2f out* **2/1**[1]

4 **5** 3 **Thoutmosis (USA)**[12] [1436] 7-8-12 **55** .... PaulMulrennan[(3)] 10 48
(L Lungo) *trckd ldrs: lost pl over 5f out: n.d after* **14/1**

1633 **6** 3/4 **Gone Too Far**[7] [816] 8-9-6 **60** .... (v) KDarley 6 52
(P Monteith) *hld up: rdn 5f out: nvr rchd ldrs* **16/1**

0006 **7** 1 3/4 **Hezaam (USA)**[6] [1590] 5-9-2 **56** .... DO'Donohoe 8 46
(Mrs A Duffield) *led to over 3f out: wknd over 2f out* **16/1**

1401 **8** 6 **Celtic Carisma**[21] [1219] 4-9-1 **57** .... PaulHanagan 3 40
(K G Reveley) *prom on ins: no room and shuffled bk over 4f out: n.d after* **7/2**[2]

10-0 **9** 13 **Zoltano (GER)**[46] [816] 8-9-9 **63** .... TomEaves 7 30
(M Todhunter) *pressed ldr tl wknd over 3f out* **16/1**

3m 40.41s (5.21) **Going Correction** +0.40s/f (Good)
WFA 4 from 5yo+ 2lb **9** Ran SP% **113.4**
Speed ratings (Par 103):102,101,99,95,94 93,93,90,83
CSF £48.50 CT £1236.42 TOTE £10.40: £3.00, £1.10, £6.70; EX 66.10.
Owner Eastwell Manor Racing Ltd **Bred** M L Roberts **Trained** Newmarket, Suffolk

FOCUS
An ordinary event in which the pace was fair but, with two of the three market leaders below par, this did not take much winning. However, the form should prove sound, rated around the winner and third.
Zoltano(GER) Official explanation: trainer said gelding finished lame

1759 BENFIELD MOTORS RENAULT MEDIAN AUCTION MAIDEN STKS 1m 2f 32y
3:50 (3:54) (Class 6) 3-Y-0 **£2,590** (£770; £385; £192) **Stalls** Centre

Form RPR

4 **1** **Adraaj (USA)**[13] [1417] 3-8-12 .... RHills 4 78
(E A L Dunlop) *unruly bef s: mde all: pushed along over 2f out: hld on wl fnl f* **9/2**[3]

20 **2** 3 1/2 **Moonlight Music (IRE)**[241] [5307] 3-8-12 .... RichardMullen 10 71
(E J O'Neill) *cl up: rdn over 2f out: edgd lft: one pce fnl f* **9/4**[1]

3453 **3** 3 1/2 **Grand Opera (IRE)**[17] [1296] 3-9-3 77 .... DarryllHolland 2 69+
(J Howard Johnson) *dwlt: rdn over 4f out: hdwy outside over 3f out: hung lft and chsd clr ldrs over 2f out: no imp fnl f* **3/1**[2]

06 **4** 1 1/2 **Chief Argent (IRE)**[209] [5977] 3-9-0 .... PaulMulrennan[(3)] 3 67+
(J Howard Johnson) *keen in rr: rdn over 4f out: hdwy over 2f out: edgd lft and no imp* **10/1**

52 **5** *10* **Prince Egor (IRE)**[8] 1530 3-9-3 .... PhillipMakin 9 48+
(M Dods) *keen in tch: effrt whn nt clr run over 2f out: no ch after* **9/2**[3]
6 *1* **Midnight Diamond (IRE)** 3-9-3 .... TomEaves 12 46
(Mrs L Williamson) *prom tl wknd over 2f out* **100/1**
7 *3 ½* **Moving Story** 3-9-3 .... MickyFenton 8 39
(T J Fitzgerald) *hld up: effrt whn hung rt 4f out: wknd 3f out* **100/1**
0 **8** *13* **Travelling Fox**[22] 1192 3-9-3 .... EddieAhern 1 14
(H Morrison) *plld hrd bhd ldrs tl wknd over 4f out* **16/1**
0 **9** *5* **Flying Visitor**[13] 1401 3-8-12 .... NCallan 11 —
(J M P Eustace) *prom tl wknd over 2f out* **33/1**
65 **10** *7* **Little Eyecatcher (IRE)**[321] 3010 3-9-3 .... DavidAllan 6 —
(T D Easterby) *bhd: rdn over 4f out: sn btn* **25/1**
0 **11** *68* **Millwood Lad (IRE)**[7] 1564 3-9-3 .... PatCosgrave 7 —
(B S Rothwell) *s.i.s: struggling after 3f: t.o* **66/1**

2m 16.43s (4.63) **Going Correction** +0.40s/f (Good) **11** Ran SP% **117.4**
Speed ratings (Par 97):97,94,91,90,82 81,78,68,64,58 4
CSF £14.68 TOTE £5.50: £1.70, £1.80, £1.10; EX 16.10.
Owner Hamdan Al Maktoum **Bred** Shadwell Farm LLC **Trained** Newmarket, Suffolk

FOCUS
A mixed bag and the modest pace suited those racing close to the pace. The placed horses appeared to run to form, suggesting it was a fair maiden.

1760 BETFRED POKER SPRINT SERIES H'CAP (QUALIFIER) 7f
4:20 (4:23) (Class 5) (0-75,75) 4-Y-O+ **£4,210** (£1,252; £625; £312) **Stalls** Centre

Form RPR
0030 **1** **Sake (IRE)**[10] 1480 4-8-4 **61** oh1 .... KimTinkler 5 76
(N Tinkler) *set stdy pce: mde all: qcknd 2f out: edgd rt ins last: hld on wl* **25/1**
3002 **2** *½* **Grey Boy (GER)**[7] 1561 5-8-13 **70** .... PaulHanagan 6 84
(R A Fahey) *in tch: effrt over 2f out: chsd wnr 1f out: rdn and kpt on towards fin* **6/1**[2]
0005 **3** *2 ½* **Guildenstern (IRE)**[15] 1359 4-9-4 **75** .... EddieAhern 12 83
(H Morrison) *trckd ldrs tl rdn and one pce fr over 1f out* **15/2**
4060 **4** *2* **Lincolneurocruiser**[3] 1686 4-9-0 **71** .... RHills 4 73
(Mrs N Macauley) *in tch: effrt whn n.m.r over 2f out: no imp whn clr over 1f out* **16/1**
6521 **5** *1* **Seneschal**[13] 1402 5-8-11 **68** .... DarryllHolland 2 68
(A B Haynes) *cl up tl rdn and no ex fr 2f out* **4/1**[1]
4003 **6** *shd* **Ask The Clerk (IRE)**[22] 1186 5-8-13 **70** .... MickyFenton 9 69+
(Mrs P Sly) *hld up: nt clr run over 2f out: effrt over 1f out: kpt on ins fnl f: no imp* **7/1**[3]
0620 **7** *¾* **Sovereignty (JPN)**[8] 1531 4-8-12 **69** .... TomEaves 3 66
(I Semple) *keen: hld up: effrt over 2f out: n.d* **33/1**
1200 **8** *2 ½* **Out Of India**[94] 381 4-8-8 **65** .... KDarley 14 56
(B Smart) *hld up: effrt on outside over 2f out: sn no imp* **16/1**
0000 **9** *2 ½* **Young Mr Grace (IRE)**[25] 1123 6-8-4 **61** oh1 .... DavidAllan 1 45
(T D Easterby) *bhd: drvn over 3f out: sn n.d* **8/1**
1140 **10** *1 ½* **Dig Deep (IRE)**[200] 6134 4-9-4 **75** .... TonyCulhane 8 56
(W J Haggas) *keen in midfield: rdn and edgd lft over 2f out: wknd* **8/1**
0000 **11** *2 ½* **Elkhorn**[14] 1382 4-8-10 **67** ....(v) TonyHamilton 15 41
(Miss J A Camacho) *bhd: effrt over 2f out: sn rdn and btn* **14/1**
0253 **12** *3 ½* **Insubordinate**[11] 1459 5-8-4 **61** oh4 .... JoeFanning 11 26
(J S Goldie) *hld up: rdn outside over 2f out: sn btn* **7/1**[3]
300 **13** *8* **Cd Flyer (IRE)**[9] 1504 9-8-9 **69** ....(p) PaulMulrennan(3) 13 13
(R C Guest) *prom tl rdn and wknd over 2f out* **33/1**

1m 31.18s (1.18) **Going Correction** +0.40s/f (Good) **13** Ran SP% **121.4**
Speed ratings (Par 103):97,96,93,91,90 90,89,86,83,81 78,74,65
CSF £169.33 CT £1260.66 TOTE £31.90: £5.60, £2.40, £3.60; EX 301.80.
Owner Mrs Lara Dales **Bred** Illuminatus Investments **Trained** Langton, N Yorks

FOCUS
An ordinary and moderately-run handicap in which those held up were at a big disadvantage. The form has been rated negatively around the runner-up.
Young Mr Grace(IRE) Official explanation: jockey said horse anticipated start and hit its head on the gates
Dig Deep(IRE) Official explanation: jockey said gelding was denied a clear run

1761 RENAULT VANS FILLIES' H'CAP 1m (R)
4:50 (4:53) (Class 6) (0-65,68) 3-Y-O+ **£2,914** (£867; £433; £216) **Stalls** Centre

Form RPR
0414 **1** **Stolen Glance**[6] 1593 3-8-10 **59** .... PaulMulrennan(3) 12 68
(M W Easterby) *prom: effrt whn swtchd lft 2f out: rdr dropped whip: led ins fnl f: r.o wl* **6/1**[3]
406/ **2** *2* **Whittinghamvillage**[865] 408 5-9-2 **55** .... GregFairley(5) 15 63
(D W Whillans) *midfield: hdwy to ld over 2f out: hdd ins fnl f: no ex* **66/1**
0052 **3** *1 ¼* **Royal Pardon**[4] 1636 4-9-5 **53** ....(p) JoeFanning 14 58
(R C Guest) *hld up: hdwy 2f out: one pce fnl f* **8/1**
0500 **4** *¾* **Sforzando**[13] 1422 5-9-7 **62** .... KristinStubbs(7) 6 65
(Mrs L Stubbs) *dwlt: bhd tl kpt on fnl 2f: nrst fin* **16/1**
0004 **5** *4* **Queen's Echo**[8] 1531 5-9-12 **60** .... TomEaves 7 55
(M Dods) *in tch: effrt on ins over 2f out: sn outpcd: no imp after* **11/4**[1]
4051 **6** *2* **Dispol Veleta**[9] 1500 5-10-6 **68** 6ex .... PhillipMakin 5 59+
(T D Barron) *hld up ins: effrt whn no room over 2f out: sn rdn and no ch after* **4/1**[2]
0000 **7** *1* **She's Our Lass (IRE)**[151] 6594 5-9-7 **62** .... KellyHarrison(7) 3 51
(D Carroll) *hld up: stdy hdwy over 2f out: nvr nr ldrs* **10/1**
004 **8** *¾* **Lady Georgette (IRE)**[26] 1100 3-9-5 **65** .... EddieAhern 1 49
(E J O'Neill) *chsd ldrs tl wknd over 2f out* **9/1**
0460 **9** *12* **Karashino (IRE)**[42] 873 4-9-4 **52** ....(b) TonyHamilton 2 14
(Mrs L Williamson) *led to over 2f out: wknd* **66/1**
-000 **10** *10* **Aqua**[19] 1252 4-9-5 **53** .... MickyFenton 4 —
(P T Midgley) *cl up: ev ch over 3f out: outpcd whn hmpd over 2f out* **33/1**
6260 **11** *nk* **Teide Lady**[27] 1079 3-9-3 **63** .... KDarley 11 —
(Rae Guest) *bhd: effrt outside 3f out: sn rdn and btn* **12/1**
4000 **12** *1* **Princess Galadriel**[217] 5824 5-9-12 **60** .... NCallan 10 —
(J M P Eustace) *chsd ldrs: ev ch over 2f out: sn rdn and btn* **20/1**
0000 **13** *1 ¼* **Our Serendipity**[6] 1593 3-8-7 **53** .... PaulHanagan 9 —
(K G Reveley) *bhd: rdn 4f out: sn btn* **66/1**

1m 45.4s (1.92) **Going Correction** +0.40s/f (Good)
WFA 3 from 4yo+ 12lb **13** Ran SP% **116.9**
Speed ratings (Par 98):106,104,102,102,98 96,95,94,82,72 71,70,69
CSF £370.09 CT £2139.86 TOTE £7.50: £2.20, £14.00, £2.90; EX 421.90 Place 6 £213.72, Place 5 £121.70.
Owner R S Cockerill (Farms) Ltd **Bred** R S Cockerill (farms) Ltd **Trained** Sheriff Hutton, N Yorks
■ Stewards' Enquiry : Kelly Harrison ten-day ban: in breach of Rule 158 (May 27-Jun 5)
Paul Mulrennan four-day ban: careless riding (May 27-30)

FOCUS
An ordinary event in which the two market leaders failed to run to form.
She's Our Lass(IRE) ◆ Official explanation: jockey said, regarding the apparent tender ride, her orders were to drop mare in and get her travelling early on, but she took a pull coming out of stalls and thereafter struggled to go the early gallop; she added that mare was unsuited by the ground early on but stayed on well home straight; trainer added his orders were to drop the mare in, but felt that she should have been handier than she was and, as a result, he was not happy with the ride
Lady Georgette(IRE) Official explanation: jockey said filly was denied a clear run
T/Jkpt: Not won. T/Plt: £403.20 to a £1 stake. Pool: £60,521 - 109.55 winning units. T/Qpdt: £81.40 to a £1 stake. Pool: £3,091 - 28.10 winning units. RY

1571 SOUTHWELL (L-H)
Tuesday, May 16

OFFICIAL GOING: Standard
Wind: Light, across Weather: Overcast

1762 EXPERIENCE NOTTINGHAMSHIRE BANDED STKS 5f (F)
2:30 (2:31) (Class 7) 3-Y-O+ **£1,876** (£554; £277) **Stalls** High

Form RPR
4041 **1** **Axis Shield (IRE)**[42] 870 3-8-6 50 .... EmmettStack(5) 2 53
(M C Chapman) *disp ld tl led over 1f out: rdn out* **10/1**
6636 **2** *1* **Global Achiever**[34] 982 5-9-1 46 ....(b) MichaelTebbutt 6 45
(G C H Chung) *a.p: rdn to chse wnr fnl f: styd on* **9/2**[2]
2240 **3** *hd* **Comic Tales**[5] 1607 5-9-0 45 .... LeeEnstone 4 44
(M Mullineaux) *chsd ldrs: outpcd 3f out: swtchd rt and hdwy over 1f out: r.o* **9/1**
0000 **4** *nk* **Newsround**[19] 1258 4-9-5 50 ....(b) PaulQuinn 3 48
(D W Chapman) *s.s: outpcd: hdwy over 1f out: r.o* **13/2**[3]
5001 **5** *½* **Estoille**[7] 1571 5-9-3 45 ....(t) RichardThomas(3) 11 47
(Mrs S Lamyman) *chsd ldrs: rdn over 1f out: styd on same pce* **7/2**[1]
6000 **6** *1 ¼* **Safranine (IRE)**[12] 1448 9-8-8 40 ow1 ....(p) AnnStokell(7) 1 37
(Miss A Stokell) *mde most over 3f out: no ex ins fnl f* **20/1**
0142 **7** *¾* **Laurel Dawn**[7] 1571 8-9-2 47 ....(b) SamHitchcott 5 36
(C N Kellett) *chsd ldrs: rdn 1/2-way: no ex fr over 1f out* **13/2**[3]
0060 **8** *6* **Lady Palma Nova**[81] 499 3-8-11 50 .... JosedeSouza 7 17
(G P Kelly) *s.s: outpcd* **66/1**
0004 **9** *½* **Blue Moon Hitman (IRE)**[14] 1396 5-9-1 46 ....(b) PaulFessey 8 11
(R Brotherton) *chsd ldrs over 3f* **9/2**[2]
0000 **10** *5* **Ronnie From Donny (IRE)**[259] 4851 6-8-11 35 .... JasonEdmunds(3) 10 —
(C J Teague) *dwlt: sn outpcd* **18/1**

59.81 secs (-0.49) **Going Correction** -0.05s/f (Stan)
WFA 3 from 4yo+ 8lb **10** Ran SP% **115.9**
Speed ratings (Par 97):101,99,99,98,97 95,94,85,84,76
CSF £54.28 TOTE £13.20: £2.50, £1.50, £2.70; EX 47.30.
Owner Dr A Shubsachs **Bred** Mrs P Grubb **Trained** Market Rasen, Lincs

FOCUS
A pretty competitive banded sprint in which, as usual, it paid to be drawn low. The form seems sound rated through the third.
Estoille Official explanation: jockey said mare hung left-handed throughout
Blue Moon Hitman(IRE) Official explanation: trainer said gelding was unsuited by fibresand

1763 LADBROKESCASINO.COM MAIDEN CLAIMING STKS 6f (F)
3:00 (3:00) (Class 7) 4-Y-O+ **£1,365** (£403; £201) **Stalls** Low

Form RPR
3000 **1** **Haroldini (IRE)**[12] 1447 4-8-10 48 ....(p) JasonEdmunds(3) 8 64+
(J Balding) *sn pushed along in rr: nt clr run over 3f out: hdwy over 1f out: led ins fnl f: r.o wl* **7/2**[2]
5264 **2** *5* **Fir Tree**[56] 687 6-8-11 47 ....(p) MichaelTebbutt 9 47
(S R Bowring) *trckd ldrs: led over 2f out: rdn over 1f out: hdd and no ex ins fnl f* **9/4**[1]
66P0 **3** *6* **Lord Mayfair (USA)**[6] 1594 4-8-8 40 ow2 ....(b) AnnStokell(7) 2 33
(Miss A Stokell) *sn led: hdd over 2f out: wknd over 1f out* **18/1**
6650 **4** *1* **Fayrz Please (IRE)**[6] 974 5-8-2 40 ....(t) EmmettStack(5) 1 22
(M C Chapman) *sn pushed along and prom: outpcd over 3f out: n.d after* **17/2**
0000 **5** *¾* **Kris Spring**[11] 1463 4-8-4 40 ....(v[1]) PaulFessey 7 17
(R M H Cowell) *s.i.s and hmpd s: hdwy u.p over 2f out: wknd over 1f out* **33/1**
-405 **6** *3* **Chiracahua (IRE)**[11] 1458 4-8-13 40 ....(b[1]) PaulEddery 4 17
(B Smart) *trckd ldrs: plld hrd: rdn over 2f out: wknd over 1f out* **5/1**[3]
255- **7** *7* **Russian Servana (IRE)**[643] 4651 4-8-8 .... JimmyQuinn 5 —
(J Pearce) *dwlt: outpcd* **15/2**
2000 **8** *2* **She Who Dares Wins**[82] 487 6-7-12 45 .... DonnaCaldwell(7) 6 —
(L R James) *chsd ldrs: hmpd over 3f out: sn rdn and wknd* **10/1**
000- **9** *11* **Mermaid's Cry**[540] 6715 4-8-8 35 .... SamHitchcott 3 —
(R Brotherton) *chsd ldr: hmpd over 3f out: sn wknd* **20/1**

1m 16.51s (-0.39) **Going Correction** -0.10s/f (Stan) **9** Ran SP% **114.0**
Speed ratings (Par 97):98,91,83,82,81 77,67,65,50
CSF £11.60 TOTE £5.00: £2.40, £1.10, £6.30; EX 10.60.Kris Spring was claimed by K. R. Burke for £3,000.
Owner Tykes And Terriers Racing Club **Bred** Michael O'Mahony **Trained** Scrooby, Notts

FOCUS
A very poor race and little to enthuse about for the future, with the second the best guide.
Lord Mayfair(USA) Official explanation: jockey said gelding hung right around the bend
Russian Servana(IRE) Official explanation: jockey said filly ran too freely to post

1764 LADBROKESPOKER.COM BANDED STKS 7f (F)
3:30 (3:33) (Class 7) 4-Y-O+ **£1,876** (£554; £277) **Stalls** Low

Form RPR
0453 **1** **Wings Of Morning (IRE)**[7] 1575 5-8-8 45 ....(v) DanielTudhope(3) 8 53
(D Carroll) *chsd ldrs: hmpd over 4f out: rdn over 1f out: styd on to ld wl ins fnl f* **10/1**
5125 **2** *½* **Favouring (IRE)**[14] 1390 4-8-11 50 ....(v) RoryMoore(5) 9 57
(M C Chapman) *led: hdwy 1/2-way: sn edgd lft: led over 2f out: rdn over 1f out: hdd wl ins fnl f* **7/2**[1]
4516 **3** *1* **Thornaby Green**[157] 6542 5-8-12 46 .... PaulFessey 5 50
(T D Barron) *hld up: hdwy 1/2-way: rdn and edgd rt 1f out: sn ev ch: no ex wl ins fnl f* **5/1**[3]
0051 **4** *2* **Feast Of Romance**[7] 1575 9-8-12 45 ....(b) DerekNolan(5) 4 50
(G A Huffer) *chsd ldrs: hmpd over 4f out: bmpd 3f out: rdn and edgd lft over 1f out: styd on same pce* **4/1**[2]
3002 **5** *shd* **Sergeant Slipper**[7] 1577 9-8-11 45 ....(v) GylesParkin 2 44
(C Smith) *s.s: hdwy u.p over 1f out: nt rch ldrs* **12/1**
6 *½* **Tackcoat (IRE)**[24] 1155 6-8-11 40 ....(t) ShaneKelly 3 42
(Eoin Doyle, Ire) *s.i.s: hld up: hdwy u.p over 1f out: nt trble ldrs* **16/1**

2151 **7** *1 ¼* **Union Jack Jackson (IRE)**[7] 1577 4-9-7 49................(b) FergalLynch 1 49
(J G Given) *hld up: hdwy over 2f out: rdn over 1f out: styd on same pce* **7/2**[1]

2015 **8** *½* **Penel (IRE)**[19] 1255 5-9-1 49...(p) LeeEnstone 10 42
(P T Midgley) *led 2f: led 3f out: sn hdd: rdn whn nt clr run 1f out: sn wknd and eased* **12/1**

1003 **9** *10* **Fizzy Lizzy**[11] 1463 6-8-13 47... SamHitchcott 6 14
(H E Haynes) *mid-div: sn drvn along: n.d* **28/1**

4004 **10** *1 ½* **Kirstys Lad**[11] 1463 4-8-11 40..................................(b) DarrenWilliams 13 8
(M Mullineaux) *chsd ldrs: led 5f out: hdd 3f out: sn rdn: wknd wl over 1f out* **50/1**

0600 **11** *1 ¼* **Dysonic (USA)**[120] 121 4-8-8 40.........................(p) JasonEdmunds(3) 11 5
(J Balding) *trckd ldrs: plld hrd: wknd wl over 2f out* **28/1**

-060 **12** *10* **Diamond Heritage**[25] 1127 4-8-11 45.......................... J-PGuillambert 7 —
(S Parr) *s.i.s: sn pushed along in rr: bhd fr 1/2-way* **50/1**

60-0 **13** *33* **Hiats**[383] 1326 4-8-4 35.. MarkCoumbe(7) 12 —
(C J Teague) *chsd ldrs to 1/2-way* **100/1**

1m 29.9s (-0.90) **Going Correction** -0.10s/f (Stan) **13** Ran SP% **123.3**
Speed ratings (Par 97):101,100,99,97,96 96,94,94,82,81 79,68,30
CSF £45.19 TOTE £12.80: £2.70, £1.60, £2.80.
Owner L Ibbotson **Bred** Limestone Stud **Trained** Warthill, N Yorks
■ Stewards' Enquiry : Lee Enstone three-day ban: careless riding (May 27-29)

FOCUS
A competitive banded event featuring a number of the usual suspects but pretty sound.
Penel(IRE) Official explanation: vet said gelding had been struck into

1765 LADBROKES FREEPHONE 0800 524 524 BANDED STKS 1m (F)
4:00 (4:02) (Class 7) 4-Y-0+ **£1,706** (£503; £252) **Stalls** Low

Form RPR

4100 **1** **Wodhill Gold**[8] 1536 5-8-11 45....................................(v) DerekMcGaffin 6 54
(D Morris) *a.p: chsd ldr 2f out: sn rdn: led ins fnl f: r.o* **25/1**

0051 **2** *1 ½* **Kirkhammerton (IRE)**[7] 1573 4-9-3 45............................(v) ShaneKelly 7 57
(M J Polglase) *sn pushed along and prom: led 6f out: rdn over 1f out: hdd and unable qckn ins fnl f* **5/1**[3]

0506 **3** *6* **Shami**[63] 636 7-8-11 45...(b) VinceSlattery 8 37
(D W Chapman) *s.i.s: bhd and rel to r: r.o u.p ins fnl f: nrst fin* **12/1**

2202 **4** *2 ½* **Tommytyler (IRE)**[7] 1573 7-8-8 45.......................(t) DanielTudhope(3) 12 31
(D Carroll) *hld up: hdwy 1/2-way: chsd ldr over 2f out: rdn over 1f out: sn wknd* **9/2**[2]

5223 **5** *2 ½* **Danum**[14] 1395 6-8-4 45....................................(p) RussellKennemore(7) 13 25
(R Hollinshead) *s.i.s: outpcd: hdwy over 2f out: n.d* **12/1**

2065 **6** *nk* **Ming Vase**[7] 1573 4-8-11 45... LeeEnstone 10 25
(P T Midgley) *s.i.s: hld up: nt clr run over 3f out: hdwy over 2f out: sn hung lft: n.d* **12/1**

1000 **7** *½* **Faithisflying**[14] 1390 4-8-11 45..(p) PaulQuinn 4 23
(D W Chapman) *mid-div: hdwy 3f out: wknd over 1f out* **16/1**

4632 **8** *1 ½* **Veneer (IRE)**[8] 1538 4-8-11 45....................................... JimmyQuinn 11 20
(Miss Gay Kelleway) *mid-div: hdwy 5f out: rdn over 2f out: wknd over 1f out* **2/1**[1]

3206 **9** *½* **Rocky Reppin**[7] 1575 6-8-8 45................................(b) JasonEdmunds(3) 9 19
(J Balding) *hld up: effrt over 2f out: nt run on* **12/1**

0000 **10** *6* **Bakke**[8] 1538 4-8-11 45...(e1) LPKeniry 14 5
(B I Case) *mid-div: hdwy 5f out: wknd 3f out* **25/1**

0004 **11** *3 ½* **Castanza**[14] 1387 4-8-11 35..(b) TPQueally 5 —
(M Wellings) *chsd ldr 6f out: rdn and wknd over 2f out* **33/1**

4000 **12** *28* **Campbells Lad**[217] 5827 5-8-11 40............................ J-PGuillambert 2 —
(Mrs G S Rees) *chsd ldrs: lost pl over 5f out: bhd fnl 3f* **18/1**

06-5 **13** *3* **Glads Image**[12] 1434 4-8-8 40....................................... StephaneBreux(3) 3 —
(J Ryan) *led 2f: wknd 1/2-way* **80/1**

0000 **14** *50* **Super Canyon**[11] 1463 8-8-11 35.................................(t) MichaelTebbutt 1 —
(J Pearce) *chsd ldrs: sn pushed along: lost pl 6f out: hung rt and wknd wl over 4f out* **66/1**

1m 42.69s (-1.91) **Going Correction** -0.10s/f (Stan) **14** Ran SP% **123.5**
Speed ratings (Par 97):105,103,97,95,92 92,91,90,89,83 80,52,49,—
CSF £145.70 TOTE £16.70: £3.70, £2.20, £4.90; EX 176.10.
Owner Miss S Graham **Bred** Wodhill Stud **Trained** Newmarket, Suffolk

FOCUS
Recent winning form was very thin on the ground in this ordinary banded event, but the time was good and the form looks sound.

1766 COME EVENING RACING ON 31ST BANDED STKS 1m 6f (F)
4:30 (4:31) (Class 7) 4-Y-0+ **£1,876** (£554; £277) **Stalls** Low

Form RPR

2303 **1** **Eforetta (GER)**[19] 1256 4-8-11 45.................................... VinceSlattery 2 63
(D J Wintle) *a.p: rdn over 4f out: led 2f out: drvn clr fnl f* **10/1**

0430 **2** *9* **Makarim (IRE)**[14] 1392 10-8-11 45...........................(p) FergusSweeney 4 50
(M R Bosley) *hld up: hdwy to chse ldr over 4f out: led over 2f out: sn rdn and hdd: wknd ins fnl f* **10/1**

0466 **3** *2 ½* **Iamback**[8] 1540 6-8-11 40...(t) JamieMackay 10 47
(Miss D A McHale) *chsd ldrs: rdn over 3f out: wknd over 1f out* **18/1**

0445 **4** *¾* **Ice And Fire**[14] 1392 7-8-11 45.......................................(b) ShaneKelly 1 46
(J T Stimpson) *chsd ldrs: rdn over 3f out: wknd over 1f out* **9/1**

0400 **5** *2* **Aristi (IRE)**[13] 1415 5-8-11 50..(p) RoryMoore(5) 7 48
(M Quinn) *chsd ldr tl led 6f out: rdn and hdd over 2f out: sn wknd* **4/1**[2]

004 **6** *½* **Gawrosz (POL)**[14] 1385 7-8-11 45................................. MichaelTebbutt 6 42
(G J Smith) *hld up: outpcd over 4f out: n.d* **50/1**

2005 **7** *2* **High Frequency (IRE)**[12] 1436 5-8-11 45......................(b) PaulFessey 3 40
(T D Barron) *hld up: effrt over 3f out: wknd over 2f out* **5/1**[3]

0012 **8** *7* **Smart Boy Prince (IRE)**[17] 938 5-8-5 46......... RussellKennemore(7) 5 31
(C Smith) *led 8f: sn rdn: wknd wl over 3f out* **11/8**[1]

4455 **9** *4* **Verstone (IRE)**[91] 5294 4-8-11 35.................................... PaulEddery 8 24
(R F Fisher) *s.i.s: hld up: rdn 6f out: wknd over 4f out* **28/1**

0-00 **10** *27* **Valet**[8] 1540 4-8-8 40... BenSwarbrick(3) 9 —
(J G M O'Shea) *s.s: hld up: plld hrd: hdwy 8f out: rdn 6f out: sn wknd* **66/1**

3m 6.33s (-3.27) **Going Correction** -0.10s/f (Stan) **10** Ran SP% **119.1**
Speed ratings (Par 97):105,99,98,98,96 96,95,91,89,73
CSF £106.02 TOTE £15.50: £3.10, £2.80, £3.10; EX 103.20.
Owner John W Egan **Bred** Gestut Rietberg **Trained** Naunton, Gloucs

FOCUS
A modest staying race made even weaker by the failure of the favourite to run his race and the form is very limited.
Smart Boy Prince(IRE) Official explanation: trainer said, regarding the poor form shown, gelding had been unable to dominate and as a result dropped the bit

1767 LADBROKES.COM BANDED STKS 1m 3f (F)
5:00 (5:00) (Class 7) 4-Y-0+ **£1,706** (£503; £252) **Stalls** Low

Form RPR

4320 **1** **Yashin (IRE)**[50] 770 5-8-11 45... PaulFessey 9 44
(P A Blockley) *chsd ldrs: led over 6f out: rdn and edgd lft over 1f out: all out* **3/1**[1]

6604 **2** *nk* **Teutonic (IRE)**[18] 1271 5-8-11 45...................................... GylesParkin 10 44
(R F Fisher) *s.i.s: sn prom: chsd wnr 5f out: rdn 3f out: styd on u.p ins fnl f* **6/1**[3]

0000 **3** *1 ¼* **On Every Street**[7] 1573 5-8-6 45................................ AndrewMullen(5) 6 42
(R Bastiman) *sn led: hdd over 9f out: remined handy: rdn over 3f out: styd on* **16/1**

0020 **4** *1* **Kentucky Bullet (USA)**[36] 939 10-8-11 45........................ LPKeniry 2 40+
(A G Newcombe) *hld up: hdwy over 2f out: rdn over 1f out: styd on* **7/2**[2]

0000 **5** *1 ¾* **Guadiana (GER)**[11] 1460 4-8-11 40.................................... ShaneKelly 5 37
(A W Carroll) *a.p: rdn over 1f out: no ex fnl f* **9/1**

0042 **6** *5* **Sudden Impulse**[21] 1224 5-8-11 45.................................... PaulEddery 1 29
(A D Brown) *hld up: hdwy u.p over 3f out: wknd fnl f* **7/2**[2]

0604 **7** *2 ½* **Gravardlax**[7] 1572 5-8-11 40..(vt1) JamieMackay 4 25
(Miss D A McHale) *sn drvn to chse ldrs: led over 9f out: rdn and hdd over 6f out: nt run on* **16/1**

0000 **8** *8* **Dejeeje (IRE)**[126] 78 5-8-11 30... PaulQuinn 8 12
(D W Chapman) *hld up: hdwy over 4f out: wknd over 3f out* **25/1**

0066 **9** *½* **Pitsi Kahtoh**[11] 1460 4-8-11 35...................................... DarrenWilliams 7 12
(P W Hiatt) *hld up: hdwy over 4f out: wknd over 3f out* **11/1**

0-00 **10** *45* **Mikes Mate**[269] 4582 5-8-4 30..................................... MarkCoumbe(7) 3 —
(C J Teague) *chsd ldrs to 1/2-way* **66/1**

2m 27.91s (-0.99) **Going Correction** -0.10s/f (Stan) **10** Ran SP% **119.2**
Speed ratings (Par 97):99,98,97,97,95 92,90,84,84,51
CSF £22.02 TOTE £3.40: £1.20, £2.10, £8.00; EX 33.30.
Owner Nigel Shields **Bred** Wickfield Farm Partnership **Trained** Lambourn, Berks
■ Stewards' Enquiry : Gyles Parkin two-day ban: used whip with excessive frequency (May 27-28)

FOCUS
A very ordinary banded contest, featuring very few who could be described as being in-form, and another limited contest.

1768 LADIES NIGHT ON 22ND JUNE TRI-BANDED STKS 6f (F)
5:30 (5:34) (Class 7) 3-Y-0 **£1,672** (£493; £246) **Stalls** Low

Form RPR

6300 **1** **Mister Becks (IRE)**[21] 1218 3-8-11 45....................... JohnMcAuley(3) 3 51
(M C Chapman) *chsd ldr: rdn over 1f out: styd on to ld wl ins fnl f* **14/1**

5610 **2** *1* **Bekoning (IRE)**[48] 790 3-9-0 45...................................... NeilPollard 2 48
(M Quinn) *chsd ldrs: led over 4f out: rdn and hung lft over 1f out: hdd wl ins fnl f* **4/1**[1]

0063 **3** *1 ½* **Shopfitter**[7] 1571 3-8-9 40..(b) GylesParkin 10 39
(Mrs C A Dunnett) *s.i.s: sn trcking ldrs: rdn and hung rt over 1f out: r.o* **8/1**

000 **4** *shd* **Sunny Haze**[219] 5752 3-8-4 30.. AlanDaly 8 33
(Mrs P N Dutfield) *led: hdd over 4f out: rdn over 2f out: styd on* **25/1**

0010 **5** *nk* **Joking John**[22] 1200 3-8-9 40.. LeeEnstone 5 37
(C W Fairhurst) *chsd ldrs: rdn over 3f out: styd on* **15/2**[3]

0003 **6** *½* **Sanders Boy**[11] 1464 3-9-0 45...................................... MichaelTebbutt 4 41
(J R Norton) *sn outpcd: running on whn nt clr run ins fnl f: nrst fin* **14/1**

0004 **7** *nk* **Goodbye Girl (IRE)**[7] 1571 3-9-0 45............................(v) PaulFessey 14 40
(Mrs C A Dunnett) *chsd ldrs: rdn and hung lft over 1f out: styd on same pce* **11/2**[2]

0000 **8** *¾* **Baron De Hoyland**[7] 1576 3-8-4 35............................... JosedeSouza 9 28
(J R Norton) *chsd ldrs: rdn 1/2-way: nt clr run over 1f out: styd on* **40/1**

3340 **9** *1 ¼* **Silver Nun**[6] 1594 3-9-0 45... PaulQuinn 1 34
(T D Easterby) *s.i.s: outpcd: styd on fnl f: nvr nrr* **8/1**

0600 **10** *1 ½* **Dangermouse**[57] 677 3-9-0 45..................................... SamHitchcott 11 29
(A G Newcombe) *sn outpcd: styd on ins fnl f: nvr nrr* **11/1**

0064 **11** *1 ¼* **Master Malarkey**[8] 1534 3-9-0 45...............................(b) JamieMackay 7 26
(Mrs C A Dunnett) *s.i.s: pulled hrd and hdwy over 3f out: rdn and wknd 2f out* **9/1**

6306 **12** *1* **Ten Commandments (IRE)**[7] 1576 3-8-6 40.......... JasonEdmunds(3) 6 18
(J Balding) *s.s: outpcd* **10/1**

0000 **13** *2 ½* **Vincent Vegas**[209] 5988 3-8-1 30........................... RichardThomas(3) 12 5
(Mrs S Lamyman) *sn outpcd* **22/1**

1m 18.09s (1.19) **Going Correction** -0.10s/f (Stan) **13** Ran SP% **120.8**
Speed ratings (Par 93):88,86,84,84,84 83,83,82,80,78 76,75,72
CSF £68.64 TOTE £16.80: £3.90, £2.70, £2.80; EX 106.20 Place 6 £1,019.46, Place 5 £268.18.
Owner Eric Knowles **Bred** Tally-Ho Stud **Trained** Market Rasen, Lincs

FOCUS
A competitive sprint in which the principals raced prominently throughout. The placed horses were close to form suggesting the race can be taken at face value.
Goodbye Girl(IRE) Official explanation: jockey said filly hung left-handed throughout
T/Plt: £539.40 to a £1 stake. Pool: £36,283.55. 49.10 winning tickets. T/Qpdt: £144.00 to a £1 stake. Pool: £2,230.10. 11.50 winning tickets. CR

1372 BATH (L-H)
Wednesday, May 17

OFFICIAL GOING: Good to soft changing to soft after race 4 (7.40pm)
Wind: Strong, ahead

1769 BATHWICK TYRES LADY RIDERS' H'CAP 1m 2f 46y
6:10 (6:12) (Class 6) (0-65,65) 4-Y-0+ **£2,637** (£811; £405) **Stalls** Low

Form RPR

2006 **1** **Cormorant Wharf (IRE)**[17] 1311 6-9-13 **62**................ MissJPowell(5) 6 72
(G L Moore) *in tch: hdwy over 3f out: edgd rt to stands' side then carried rt 3f out: led 2f out: drvn out* **12/1**

3324 **2** *2 ½* **Seattle Robber**[4] 1666 4-10-1 **62**...................(b) MissFayeBramley(3) 12 67
(P A Blockley) *chsd ldrs: rdn and kpt on fnl 2f: tk 2nd cl home but a hld by wnr* **8/1**

0000 **3** *1 ¼* **Gallego**[19] 1276 4-9-8 **52**..................................... MissSBrotherton 8 55
(R J Price) *chsd ldrs: wnt 2nd 2f out: no imp on wnr ins fnl f: ct for 2nd cl home* **15/2**[3]

5400 **4** *2 ½* **Wind Chime (IRE)**[49] 792 9-10-3 **61**........................ MissCHannaford 15 59
(A G Newcombe) *mid-div: rdn and hdwy over 2f out: styd on fnl f but nt rch ldrs* **50/1**

0011 **5** *1* **Brave Dane (IRE)**[2] 1723 8-9-12 **56** 6ex........................... MrsSBosley 5 52
(A W Carroll) *bhd: hdwy on rails over 2f out: kpt on fnl f but nvr gng pce to rch ldrs* **7/2**[1]

2400 **6** 4 **Gingko**[15] 1380 9-9-5 **56** MissVGraham(7) 13 45
(P R Webber) *bhd: c rt towards stands' side: rdn over 2f out: n.d* **8/1**
0000 **7** 2 **Vandal**[18] 1303 6-9-2 **53** oh6 ow2 MrsDButler(7) 14 39
(M Appleby) *bhd: styd on fnl 2f: n.d* **100/1**
0500 **8** 1 1/4 **Didoe**[16] 1353 7-9-2 **51** oh4 MrsMarieKing(5) 4 34
(P W Hiatt) *bhd: hdwy 3f out: sn rdn: one pce fnl 2f* **14/1**
0010 **9** 2 1/2 **Justcallmehandsome**[16] 1334 4-9-0 **51** oh1 (v) MissJGeeson(7) 7 30
(D J S Ffrench Davis) *sn led: hdd 2f out: sn wknd* **16/1**
3331 **10** 3/4 **Mr Belvedere**[93] 399 5-9-7 **51** oh11 (p) MrsSMoore 1 29
(A J Lidderdale) *pressed ldrs: ev ch 3f out: wknd over 2f out* **9/1**
0500 **11** 4 **Ardglass (IRE)**[2] 1748 4-9-9 **58** (b) MrsCThompson(5) 9 28
(Mrs P Townsley) *a in rr* **40/1**
2246 **12** 1/2 **Platinum Charmer (IRE)**[4] 1666 6-9-13 **62** (v) MissKellyBurke(5) 10 31
(K R Burke) *in tch: rdn 3f out: sn wknd* **5/1**[2]
5160 **13** 14 **Turner**[18] 1308 5-10-2 **60** MissEJJones 2 4
(W M Brisbourne) *chsd ldrs: chal 4f out to 3f out: sn wknd* **25/1**
0015 **14** 43 **Liberty Run (IRE)**[12] 6236 4-10-0 **58** MrsEmmaLittmoden 11 —
(Mrs A J Hamilton-Fairley) *a in rr: t.o* **20/1**
530 **U** **Luis Melendez (USA)**[39] 915 4-10-2 **65** (t) MissMSowerby(5) 16 —
(Tom Dascombe) *stmbld and uns rdr s* **14/1**

2m 13.35s (2.35) **Going Correction** +0.275s/f (Good) 15 Ran SP% **123.8**
Speed ratings (Par 101):101,99,98,96,95 92,90,89,87,86 83,83,72,37,—
CSF £102.76 CT £788.11 TOTE £17.20: £6.00, £4.20, £5.10; EX 193.80.
Owner Miss J Powell **Bred** Marlinstown Syndicate **Trained** Woodingdean, E Sussex

FOCUS
This lady riders' handicap was run in thick mist and as they emerged from the gloom Cormorant Wharf was running on particularly strongly to run out a decisive winner. The form is only modest rated around the runner-up.

1770 EUROPEAN BREEDERS FUND MAIDEN STKS 5f 11y
6:40 (6:42) (Class 5) 2-Y-O **£3,886** (£1,156; £577; £288) **Stalls** Low

Form RPR
1 **Baby Strange** 2-9-3 RobbieFitzpatrick 8 85+
(P A Blockley) *trckd ldr tl lft in front ins fnl 2f: c clr ins fnl f: easily* **8/1**
3 **2** 4 **Grand Prix**[22] 1203 2-9-3 RichardHughes 2 71
(R Hannon) *prom: rdn and lft chsng wnr ins fnl 2f: kpt on to hold 2nd but wl hld ins fnl f* **2/1**[1]
2 **3** hd **Lipocco**[15] 1372 2-9-3 SebSanders 1 70
(R M Beckett) *chsd ldrs: rdn and sltly hmpd ins fnl 2f: styd on to press for 2nd wl ins fnl f but no ch w wnr* **7/2**[3]
4 3 **Vadinka** 2-9-3 JimCrowley 9 59
(P Winkworth) *sn drvn along and outpcd: swtchd lft and styd on fnl f: nvr gng pce to rch ldrs* **40/1**
5 3/4 **Auction Boy** 2-9-3 FergusSweeney 13 56
(B Palling) *pressed ldrs: rdn 3f out: wknd appr fnl f* **22/1**
0 **6** 3 **Merlins Quest**[18] 1284 2-9-3 LPKeniry 12 46
(J M Bradley) *chsd ldrs: rdn 3f out: wknd over 1f out: edgd lft u.p ins fnl f* **40/1**
7 shd **Regal Ovation** 2-9-3 RyanMoore 10 45
(W R Muir) *s.i.s: sn rdn: kpt on fnl f but nvr in contention* **33/1**
4 **8** 1 1/4 **Loves Bidding**[16] 1333 2-9-3 RobertHavlin 11 48+
(R Ingram) *chsd ldrs: n.m.r 2f out: hld whn hmpd on rails ins fnl f* **25/1**
9 nk **Cashcade (IRE)** 2-9-0 NeilChalmers(3) 5 40
(A M Balding) *s.i.s: outpcd and rdn: sme late hdwy* **40/1**
10 3 **Avery** 2-8-12 TravisBlock(5) 4 29
(R J Hodges) *in rr and v green thrght* **50/1**
11 nk **Alloro** 2-9-3 MickyFenton 7 28
(D J S Ffrench Davis) *a outpcd* **40/1**
242 **P** **Rouen (IRE)**[7] 1595 2-9-3 ChrisCatlin 3 —
(M R Channon) *led tl p.u ins fnl 2f: destroyed* **3/1**[2]

62.82 secs (0.32) **Going Correction** +0.125s/f (Good) 12 Ran SP% **114.5**
Speed ratings (Par 93):102,95,95,90,89 84,84,82,81,77 76,—
CSF £21.78 TOTE £9.50: £2.20, £1.80, £1.20; EX 31.90.
Owner Market Avenue Racing Club Ltd **Bred** Michael John Williamson **Trained** Lambourn, Berks

FOCUS
A typical Bath juvenile maiden in which Baby Strange justified market support with a clear-cut success. There should be a race or two in some of those in behind.

NOTEBOOK
Baby Strange, a 20,000gns half-brother to seven-furlong juvenile winner Mambo Sun, out of dual seven-furlong/mile winner, was entered in a seller at Beverley the following week, but not too much should be read into that as he landed a bit of a gamble in what was not a bad maiden. Always handy enough, he readily drew clear when asked and clearly knew his job. He deserves to step up in class off the back of this, although it remains to be see how much improvement there is to come. (op 7-1)
Grand Prix, third in a course and distance maiden on his debut, did not really improve a great deal on that effort and may not have appreciated the easy ground. (op 5-2)
Lipocco, a length second in a course and distance maiden on his debut, did not build on that effort but can be forgiven this as he was badly hampered by the stricken Rouen. (op 11-4 tchd 9-4)
Vadinka, a 12,000gns first foal of a multiple sprint winner, hails from a stable that did well with its juveniles last season and shaped with some promise.
Auction Boy does not offer much on breeding, but his trainer can get the odd decent two-year-old and he ran quite well. (op 25-1 tchd 20-1)
Loves Bidding Official explanation: jockey said colt was denied a clear run
Rouen(IRE) showed good pace until sadly appearing to break a leg. (op 7-2 tchd 4-1)

1771 STEVE VICK INTERNATIONAL 25TH ANNIVERSARY CLAIMING STKS 5f 161y
7:10 (7:18) (Class 6) 3-Y-O **£2,266** (£674; £337; £168) **Stalls** Low

Form RPR
5366 **1** **Phinerine**[1] 1750 3-8-12 63 (b) TolleyDean(7) 12 66
(R A Harris) *chsd ldrs: led over 2f out: hung bdly lft fr over 1f out: drvn out* **4/1**[2]
05 **2** 2 1/2 **Silvertown Sky (IRE)**[57] 687 3-7-7 NicolPolli(7) 10 39
(P L Gilligan) *s.i.s: bhd and reminders after 1f: c to stands' side and styd on fr over 2f out: tk 2nd cl home but no ch w wnr* **50/1**
3020 **3** 3/4 **Otis B Driftwood**[9] 1549 3-8-5 55 (b) KerrinMcEvoy 4 42
(M Quinn) *prom: rdn 1/2-way: styd on u.p fnl f but nvr gng pce to rch ldrs* **5/2**[1]
6600 **4** 1 **Macs All Heart (IRE)**[8] 1576 3-7-7 50 (t) LukeMorris(7) 7 34
(A B Coogan) *bhd: rdn over 3f out: kpt on u.p fr over 1f out: nvr gng pce to rch ldrs* **11/1**
0620 **5** nk **Safari**[22] 1226 3-8-0 45 FrankieMcDonald 3 33
(R J Hodges) *chsd ldrs: rdn 1/2-way: one pce fnl 2f* **16/1**
0006 **6** 1 **First Among Equals**[21] 1234 3-8-0 55 AdrianMcCarthy 5 30
(Miss J R Tooth) *sn slt ld: hdd over 2f out: wknd ins fnl f* **12/1**
3220 **7** 1/2 **Song Huntress**[103] 287 3-7-11 52 RoryMoore(5) 6 30
(D G Bridgwater) *chsd ldrs: sn rdn: wknd 2f out* **10/1**
0206 **8** nk **Bertie Bear**[23] 1200 3-8-0 40 (bt) JamesDoyle(5) 8 32
(G G Margarson) *sn rdn and outpcd in rr* **33/1**
4 **9** 3 1/2 **Neardown Queen**[24] 1166 3-8-4 ChrisCatlin 2 20
(I A Wood) *in tch: rdn 1/2-way: wknd fr 2f out* **6/1**[3]
0242 **10** 4 **In Fashion**[16] 1623 3-8-10 48 JimCrowley 1 13
(R J Hodges) *sn w ldr: rdn 3f out: wknd 2f out* **10/1**
1000 **11** 1 **Teddy Monty (IRE)**[20] 1263 3-8-5 50 (b) RobbieFitzpatrick 9 5
(M Quinn) *chsd ldrs to 1/2-way* **25/1**

1m 13.1s (1.90) **Going Correction** +0.25s/f (Good) 11 Ran SP% **111.7**
Speed ratings (Par 97):97,93,92,91,90 89,88,88,83,78 77
CSF £187.38 TOTE £5.10: £1.60, £12.90, £1.60; EX 239.40.
Owner Mr & Mrs I D Evans **Bred** Mrs Celia Miller **Trained** Earlswood, Monmouths
■ Stewards' Enquiry : Nicol Polli one-day ban: careless riding (May 28)

FOCUS
A very moderate claimer in which Phinerine was gaining his second success at the 21st attempt, despite having finished down the field in a maiden the previous day. The third represents the best guide to the level.
Teddy Monty(IRE) Official explanation: jockey said saddle slipped

1772 WEATHERBYS PRINTING H'CAP 1m 3f 144y
7:40 (7:41) (Class 6) (0-65,65) 4-Y-O+ **£2,590** (£770; £385; £192) **Stalls** Low

Form RPR
0040 **1** **Lewis Island (IRE)**[36] 589 7-9-1 **62** RyanMoore 6 68
(G L Moore) *in tch 4f out: sn rdn: styd on to ld wl ins fnl f* **5/1**[2]
0026 **2** 1/2 **Sabbiosa (IRE)**[35] 990 4-9-4 **65** KerrinMcEvoy 2 70
(J L Dunlop) *chsng ldrs 4f out: sn wnt 2nd: kpt on u.p to chse wnr wl ins fnl f: no ex cl home* **4/1**[1]
6403 **3** nk **Kathryn Janeway (IRE)**[22] 1204 4-9-2 **63** SebSanders 12 68
(W R Muir) *mid-div: hdwy over 2f out: drvn to ld ins fnl f: hdd and no ex wl ins fnl f* **8/1**
6400 **4** 1 1/2 **Madhavi**[16] 1334 4-8-9 **56** RichardHughes 3 58
(R Hannon) *led: hrd rdn over 2f out: hdd ins fnl f and sn btn* **16/1**
1450 **5** hd **Mossmann Gorge**[8] 1560 4-8-13 **60** (v) DaneO'Neill 14 62
(M Wellings) *mid-div 4f out: rdn 3f out: kpt on fr over 1f out: nt rch ldrs* **25/1**
2032 **6** 1/2 **Nina Fontenail (FR)**[22] 1204 5-8-13 **60** RobertHavlin 8 61
(B R Millman) *chsng ldrs 4f out: sn rdn: wknd fnl f* **4/1**[1]
0000 **7** shd **Harcourt (USA)**[11] 1478 6-9-1 **65** NeilChalmers(3) 7 66
(M Madgwick) *chsng ldrs 4f out: rdn 3f out: wknd over 1f out* **40/1**
0300 **8** 5 **Arthurs Dream (IRE)**[22] 1204 4-8-4 **56** JamesDoyle(5) 10 49
(A W Carroll) *bhd 4f out: sme hdwy fnl 2f: n.d* **10/1**
6000 **9** 11 **Serramanna**[16] 1334 5-8-5 **55** RichardThomas(3) 5 30
(Dr J R J Naylor) *in tch 4f out: sn rdn: wknd 2f out* **12/1**
0043 **10** 1/2 **Sovietta (IRE)**[22] 1222 5-8-7 **54** (t) LPKeniry 13 29
(A G Newcombe) *mid-div 4f out: sn rdn: n.d* **15/2**[3]
0-00 **11** 2 **Salisbury Plain**[45] 847 5-8-8 **62** MarkCoumbe(7) 4 33
(N I M Rossiter) *chsng ldrs 4f out: sn outpcd: hdwy 2f out: sn wknd* **66/1**
0006 **12** 16 **Romanova (IRE)**[22] 1214 4-8-6 **60** SladeO'Hara(7) 16 6
(Dr J R J Naylor) *in tch and styd far side fr 4f out: sn no ch* **66/1**
00-0 **13** 1 1/4 **Lawood (IRE)**[35] 990 6-9-4 **65** (v[1]) VinceSlattery 15 9
(L P Grassick) *bhd fr 4f out* **50/1**
00 **14** 2 1/2 **Spy Game (IRE)**[8] 1562 6-8-13 **60** (b) RobbieFitzpatrick 11 —
(Jennie Candlish) *bhd fr 4f out* **40/1**
0000 **15** 3 1/2 **Mirage Prince (IRE)**[7] 1590 4-8-5 **55** PatrickMathers(3) 9 —
(D Shaw) *bhd fr 4f out* **50/1**

2m 34.85s (4.55) **Going Correction** +0.275s/f (Good) 15 Ran SP% **117.8**
Speed ratings (Par 101):95,94,94,93,93 93,92,89,82,81 80,69,69,67,65
CSF £23.41 CT £158.33 TOTE £6.80: £2.40, £1.90, £2.40; EX 35.30.
Owner Ashley Carr **Bred** Emmet Beston **Trained** Woodingdean, E Sussex

FOCUS
Visibility was particularly poor for this race and close-ups comments are limited. The runner-up and the third ran to form but the winner did not need to be at his best.

1773 CHARLES SAUNDERS FOOD SERVICE BE HOPEFUL H'CAP 1m 5y
8:10 (8:25) (Class 5) (0-70,70) 4-Y-O+ **£4,210** (£1,252; £625; £312)

Form RPR
1211 **1** **Indian Edge**[8] 1568 5-8-9 **61** 6ex FergusSweeney 9 73
(B Palling) *led fr 6f out: hrd rdn fr over 1f out: hld on all out* **10/3**[1]
1033 **2** 1/2 **Merrymadcap (IRE)**[14] 1410 4-9-4 **70** RyanMoore 4 81
(M Blanshard) *trckd ldrs 6f out: rdn and gd hdwy 2f out: str chal ins fnl f: no ex cl home* **11/2**[2]
1300 **3** 2 **Will The Till**[8] 1568 4-8-3 **58** RichardThomas(3) 12 64
(J M Bradley) *in tch 6f out: hrd drvn and hdwy fr 2f out: kpt on ins fnl f: nt pce to rch ldrs* **16/1**
4 nk **Full Victory (IRE)**[205] 6090 4-9-0 **66** DaneO'Neill 14 72
(R A Farrant) *chsd ldrs 6f out: rdn over 2f out: one pce ins fnl f* **20/1**
0 **5** 1 1/4 **Kickahead (USA)**[25] 1148 4-8-10 **62** RobbieFitzpatrick 8 65
(Ian Williams) *chsd ldrs 6f out: rdn 3f out: one pce fnl f* **16/1**
1043 **6** 1 **Desert Lover (IRE)**[14] 1402 4-8-5 **62** JamesDoyle(5) 3 62
(R J Price) *chsd ldrs 6f out: rdn over 3f out: wknd fnl f* **8/1**
6U05 **7** 2 **Monte Mayor Boy**[20] 1257 4-8-8 **60** (p) RobertHavlin 13 56
(D Haydn Jones) *bhd 5f out: rdn over 3f out: styd on u.p fr over 1f out: n.d* **20/1**
0065 **8** shd **The Gaikwar (IRE)**[13] 1435 7-8-11 **70** (b) TolleyDean(7) 11 66
(R A Harris) *in tch 5f out: rdn over 3f out: n.d* **7/1**[3]
-000 **9** 2 1/2 **Hallings Overture (USA)**[14] 1400 7-8-7 **59** HayleyTurner 16 49
(C A Horgan) *chsd ldrs 6f out to 3f out: sn rdn: wknd 2f out* **25/1**
-000 **10** 1/2 **Bridegroom**[220] 5762 4-8-10 **62** SebSanders 5 51
(Lady Herries) *bhd 5f out: nvr in contention* **9/1**
5000 **11** nk **Connotation**[22] 1220 4-8-12 **67** NeilChalmers(3) 10 55
(A G Newcombe) *bhd fr 6f out* **50/1**
0000 **12** 1 1/4 **Lockstock (IRE)**[22] 1204 8-8-7 **59** MickyFenton 7 44
(M S Saunders) *chsd ldrs 6f out: rdn 3f out: sn wknd* **12/1**
0110 **13** 49 **Lord Of Dreams (IRE)**[22] 1204 4-8-13 **65** KerrinMcEvoy 2 —
(D W P Arbuthnot) *styd alone far side: chsd ldrs 6f out tl wknd 3f out: t.o* **8/1**

1m 41.91s **Going Correction** +0.275s/f (Good) 13 Ran SP% **118.0**
Speed ratings (Par 103):106,105,103,103,101 100,98,98,96,95 95,94,45
CSF £19.03 CT £267.95 TOTE £3.70: £1.60, £1.90, £4.80; EX 16.30.
Owner Nigel Thomas and Christopher Mason **Bred** Christopher J Mason **Trained** Tredodridge, Vale Of Glamorgan

FOCUS
There was a flip start after problems with the stalls and the runners did not line up in anything like their stalls order. The field again came over to the stands' side. This was a modest handicap but the form appears solid.

Connotation Official explanation: trainer said filly was unsuited by the soft ground

1774 WEATHERBYS INSURANCE FILLIES' H'CAP 5f 161y

8:40 (8:51) (Class 5) (0-70,70) 3-Y-0+ **£3,886** (£1,156; £577; £288) **Stalls** Low

Form				RPR
1532	**1**		**Cashel Mead**[4] 1689 6-9-1 **58** ... KerrinMcEvoy 15 (J L Spearing) *in tch: hdwy over 2f out: led appr fnl f: hld on all out* **9/4**[1]	72
5360	**2**	*nk*	**Linda Green**[50] 777 5-9-2 **62** ... EdwardCreighton(3) 12 (M R Channon) *bhd: hdwy over 2f out: chsd wnr fnl f: str chal wl ins fnl f: no ex cl home* **9/2**[3]	75
1435	**3**	*2 ½*	**Hello Roberto**[14] 1402 5-8-12 **62** ... (p) TolleyDean(7) 1 (R A Harris) *chsd ldrs: racd alone far side: str chal ins fnl f: sn one pce* **16/1**	67
1020	**4**	*5*	**Ashes (IRE)**[8] 1563 4-9-10 **67** ... PatCosgrave 5 (K R Burke) *slt ld tl hdd over 1f out: wknd ins fnl f* **16/1**	56
0260	**5**	*2 ½*	**Nazaaha (USA)**[116] 164 4-8-13 **56** oh2 ... LPKeniry 13 (A G Newcombe) *bhd: hdwy 2f out: kpt on fnl f: nvr gng pce to rch ldrs* **33/1**	37
3422	**6**	*½*	**Riquewihr**[4] 1686 6-9-11 **68** ... (p) RyanMoore 2 (J S Wainwright) *chsd ldrs over 3f* **3/1**[2]	47
0000	**7**	*2 ½*	**Ruby's Dream**[14] 1413 4-8-13 **56** oh6 ... (p) ChrisCatlin 14 (J M Bradley) *pressed ldrs: chal 3f out: wknd fnl 2f* **33/1**	27
0154	**8**	*nk*	**Bens Georgie (IRE)**[15] 1383 4-9-5 **62** ... DaneO'Neill 16 (D K Ivory) *pressed ldrs: rdn 3f out: wknd ins fnl 2f* **12/1**	32
6132	**9**	*shd*	**Red Sovereign**[17] 1315 5-9-2 **66** ... MarkCoumbe(7) 4 (D G Bridgwater) *chsd ldrs over 3f* **28/1**	36
6305	**10**	*3 ½*	**Cerulean Rose**[14] 1413 7-9-7 **64** ... MickyFenton 11 (A W Carroll) *a outpcd* **12/1**	23
0000	**11**	*1 ½*	**Jinksonthehouse**[261] 4815 5-8-13 **56** oh6 ... HayleyTurner 8 (M D I Usher) *chsd ldrs 3f* **66/1**	10
2202	**12**	*14*	**Sahara Silk (IRE)**[16] 1338 5-9-7 **67** ... (v) PatrickMathers(3) 6 (D Shaw) *v.s.a: a bhd* **16/1**	—

1m 12.89s **Going Correction** +0.375s/f (Good) 12 Ran SP% **117.8**
Speed ratings (Par 100):103,102,99,92,89 88,85,84,84,80 78,59
CSF £11.86 CT £132.83 TOTE £3.60: £1.50, £2.20, £5.00; EX 15.30 Place 6 £31.83, Place 5 £6.59.
Owner Masonaires **Bred** D R Tucker **Trained** Kinnersley, Worcs
■ Stewards' Enquiry : Tolley Dean one-day ban: used whip with excessive frequency (May 28)

FOCUS
The going was officially to soft amended before this race. The field fanned out across the course in the straight in this ordinary handicap. The first two finished clear and the winner ran to last year's best.
Sahara Silk(IRE) Official explanation: jockey said mare sat down in the stalls and missed the break
T/Plt: £41.60 to a £1 stake. Pool: £53,523.45. 938.45 winning tickets. T/Qpdt: £5.80 to a £1 stake. Pool: £3,801.80. 484.40 winning tickets. ST

YORK (L-H)

Wednesday, May 17

OFFICIAL GOING: Good to soft
The going was described as 'soft side of good, very dead'.
Wind: Fresh; half behind Weather: Overcast and blustery, rain last 2.

1775 NEWTON INVESTMENT MANAGEMENT STKS (H'CAP) 1m 2f 88y

1:45 (1:46) (Class 2) (0-100,96) 4-Y-0+ **£16,516** (£4,913; £2,455; £1,226) **Stalls** Low

Form				RPR
0003	**1**		**Blue Spinnaker (IRE)**[43] 865 7-8-9 **90** ... PaulMulrennan(3) 5 (M W Easterby) *hld up in midfield: smooth hdwy 4f out: rdn along to chse wnr wl over 1f out: styd on wl fnl f to ld last 50 yds* **7/1**[3]	108
0062	**2**	*½*	**Look Again**[4] 1678 5-8-6 **84** ... PaulHanagan 14 (R A Fahey) *lw: keen: hld up in midfield gng wl: hdwy on bit over 3f out: led over 2f out and sn clr: rdn ins last: hdd and no ex last* **5/1**[1]	101
-103	**3**	*13*	**Focus Group (USA)**[7] 1585 5-8-11 **89** ... GrahamGibbons 2 (J J Quinn) *lw: hld up in tch: hdwy 4f out: rdn along wl over 2f out: kpt on same pce u.p* **7/1**[3]	81
2403	**4**	*2*	**Wingman (IRE)**[29] 1071 4-8-9 **87** ... EddieAhern 4 (J W Hills) *chsd ldng pair: hdwy 3f out: led briefly wl over 2f out: sn rdn and hdd: grad wknd appr last* **9/1**	76
1011	**5**	*2 ½*	**Miss Provvidence (IRE)**[16] 1357 4-8-12 **90** ... TQuinn 6 (W R Swinburn) *lw: in tch: hdwy 4f out: sn rdn and no imp* **11/2**[2]	74
4050	**6**	*hd*	**Go Tech**[11] 1484 6-8-10 **88** ... DavidAllan 7 (T D Easterby) *hld up in rr: hdwy 4f out: sn rdn and no imp* **33/1**	71
1050	**7**	*1 ¾*	**Tiger Tiger (FR)**[7] 1585 5-9-4 **96** ... JohnEgan 10 (Jamie Poulton) *hld up: a towards rr* **25/1**	76
1662	**8**	*nk*	**Red Racketeer (USA)**[21] 1238 4-9-3 **95** ... LDettori 13 (E A L Dunlop) *chsd ldrs: rdn along over 3f out: sn wknd* **8/1**	75
4600	**9**	*1*	**Dancer's Serenade (IRE)**[18] 1281 4-8-5 **83** ow1 ... RobertWinston 8 (T P Tate) *dwlt: a rr* **20/1**	61
4130	**10**	*5*	**Blaise Hollow (USA)**[315] 3244 4-8-12 **90** ... SteveDrowne 11 (R Charlton) *in tch: rdn along over 4f out and sn wknd* **33/1**	58
1306	**11**	*¾*	**Consular**[259] 4870 4-8-12 **90** ... PhilipRobinson 9 (M A Jarvis) *chsd ldrs: rdn along 4f out: sn wknd* **10/1**	57
0066	**12**	*5*	**Nero's Return (IRE)**[16] 1357 5-8-6 **84** ... KDarley 12 (M Johnston) *nt rt in coat: a rr* **16/1**	41
1050	**13**	*6*	**Torrens (IRE)**[228] 5608 4-8-4 **82** oh1 ... RoystonFfrench 3 (R A Fahey) *bit bkwd: cl up: rdn along 4f out: drvn 3f out and sn wknd* **33/1**	28
6020	**14**	*2 ½*	**Cardinal Venture (IRE)**[53] 728 8-8-10 **88** ... NCallan 1 (K A Ryan) *led: rdn along over 3f out: hdd wl over 2f out ou6t and sn wknd* **40/1**	29

2m 11.7s (1.22) **Going Correction** +0.35s/f (Good) 14 Ran SP% **113.0**
Speed ratings (Par 109):109,108,98,96,94 94,93,92,92,88 87,83,78,76
CSF £35.71 CT £253.15 TOTE £7.90: £2.40, £2.20, £2.40; EX 32.20 Trifecta £188.20 Pool: £1,352.54 - 5.10 winning units..
Owner G Sparkes G Hart S Curtis & T Dewhirst **Bred** M3 Elevage And Haras D'Etreham **Trained** Sheriff Hutton, N Yorks
■ Jockey Paul Mulrennan lost his claim with victory on Blue Spinnaker.

FOCUS
A decent handicap but, of those who counted, only the front two produced their best on the easy ground and they pulled well clear. The pace looked reasonable given the conditions and the winning time was nearly four seconds faster than the Musidora, and over five seconds quicker than the concluding three-year-old handicap.

NOTEBOOK
Blue Spinnaker(IRE) was comfortably held in the Lincoln on his reappearance, but he offered plenty of promise when third over a mile at Pontefract on his previous start and, back up to what is probably a more suitable trip these days, he was able to take advantage of a handicap mark 8lb lower than when last winning. The eventual runner-up looked to have his measure when looming up travelling very strongly, but he ran on most gamely for pressure and wore than one down close home. There was a massive 13 lengths back of third, so he will take quite a rise in the weights for this, but he was rated 104 in his prime. His trainer suggested he could drop back to a mile once more for the Royal Hunt Cup. (tchd 13-2)
Look Again ◆, 3lb lower than in future following a good second in a nine-furlong handicap at Newmarket just four days earlier, looked like hacking up when moving to the front still hard on the bridle, but he proved unable to shake off Blue Spinnaker despite finding enough to pull upwards of 13 lengths clear of the remainder. Although run out of it this time, he travelled like a very useful horse for much of the way and he should still be competitive when the Handicapper grabs hold of him for this effort. (op 9-2 tchd 11-2 in a place)
Focus Group(USA) failed to build on the promise he showed when third at Chester on his previous start and probably found this ground softer than he would have liked. He has won on an easy surface, but was disappointing on heavy ground on his reappearance this season. (op 11-2)
Wingman(IRE) had the ground to suit and did not look on a bad mark, but he was made to look one paced in the closing stages. His chance may not have been helped by his rider appearing slightly hesitant about coming to the stands' side of the track in the straight, but he could still have been expected to finish a little closer and remains with just a maiden success to his name. (tchd 10-1)
Miss Provvidence(IRE), 3lb higher than when winning over this trip on similarly easy ground on her reappearance, ran below that form and was a little disappointing. She was, though, the only filly in the field and can be given another chance, perhaps against her own sex. Official explanation: jockey said filly was never travelling (tchd 5-1)
Go Tech ◆, just 2lb higher than when last winning, caught the eye keeping on without managing to pose a threat. He could be one to look out for when returned to better ground.
Red Racketeer(USA), 2lb higher than when second over a mile and a half at Epsom on his previous start, failed to build on that dropped back in trip and was a little disappointing. He may prefer genuinely good ground.

1776 BLUE SQUARE STKS (H'CAP) (REGISTERED AS THE MERRION STAKES) (LISTED RACE) 7f

2:15 (2:18) (Class 1) (0-110,100) 3-Y-0 **£17,781** (£6,723; £3,360; £1,680) **Stalls** Low

Form				RPR
2111	**1**		**Levera**[10] 1505 3-8-13 **95** 3ex ... JamieSpencer 2 (A King) *lw: mde all: qcknd clr 2f out: easily* **10/11**[1]	109+
3114	**2**	*5*	**Antica (IRE)**[18] 1292 3-8-7 **89** ... DarryllHolland 6 (M H Tompkins) *hld up in rr: effrt and nt clr run wl over 2f out: swtchd lft and hdwy 2f out: sn rdn and kpt on ins last* **13/2**[3]	93+
4041	**3**	*1*	**Upper Hand**[16] 1358 3-9-4 **100** ... TQuinn 5 (M R Channon) *lw: hld up in rr: hdwy wl over 2f out: rdn to chse wnr wl over 1f out: sn drvn and no imp* **7/2**[2]	95
500	**4**	*½*	**Guest Connections**[11] 1490 3-9-1 **97** ... TonyCulhane 3 (M R Channon) *chsd wnr: rdn along over 2f out: sn drvn and one pce* **25/1**	91
3510	**5**	*4*	**South Cape**[19] 1268 3-9-1 **97** ... TedDurcan 4 (M R Channon) *chsd ldrs: rdn along 3f out: sn btn* **14/1**	80
3414	**6**	*nk*	**Critic (IRE)**[14] 1404 3-8-4 **86** ... NickyMackay 1 (M L W Bell) *chsd ldrs: rdn along wl over 2f out: sn drvn and wknd* **13/2**[3]	69

1m 26.0s (0.60) **Going Correction** +0.275s/f (Good) 6 Ran SP% **111.8**
Speed ratings (Par 107):107,101,100,99,95 94
CSF £7.43 TOTE £1.60: £1.10, £2.40; EX 5.20.
Owner Four Mile Racing **Bred** Cheveley Park Stud Ltd **Trained** Barbury Castle, Wilts

FOCUS
A relatively weak Listed handicap, but Levera won easily under the 3lb penalty in a reasonable time for the grade and is progressing into a very smart colt.

NOTEBOOK
Levera ◆ was 2lb well-in under the penalty he picked up for winning a decent handicap at Newmarket on 1000 Guineas day and hacked up on this step up to Listed company. While this may not have been as strong a race as one might have expected for the grade, he could hardly have won any easier. Now successful on his last four starts, he is progressing into a very smart colt and fully deserves his chance in the Group 3 Jersey Stakes, although he does still have to prove himself fully effective on fast ground. (tchd 11-10)
Antica(IRE), stepped up to seven furlongs for the first time, is a little better than the bare form as she had to wait an age for a clear run and the eventual winner was long gone by the time she hit full stride, although she is unlikely to have beaten that one under any circumstances. Still, at least she proved her stamina, and should have more options. (op 7-1 tchd 6-1)
Upper Hand, successful in a conditions race over a mile at Windsor on his previous start, would have found this tougher under top weight, but he did not appear suited by this drop back in trip in any case. (op 4-1)
Guest Connections, dropped a furlong in trip, ran better than when too keen on his reappearance but was still well held.
South Cape would have been suited by the easy ground, but he proved disappointing and did little to justify his official mark of 97. (op 10-1)
Critic(IRE), returned to turf having been in good form on Polytrack, should not have minded the ground but he proved disappointing. Perhaps this competition was hot enough for him at this stage of his career. (op 8-1)

1777 TATTERSALLS MUSIDORA STKS (GROUP 3) (FILLIES) 1m 2f 88y

2:45 (2:48) (Class 1) 3-Y-0

£34,068 (£12,912; £6,462; £3,222; £1,614; £810) **Stalls** Low

Form				RPR
10	**1**		**Short Skirt**[214] 5904 3-8-12 99 ... MJKinane 4 (Sir Michael Stoute) *lw: prom: effrt and nt clr run 2f out: swtchd lft and hdwy over 1f out: rdn and styd on to ld ins last* **7/2**[2]	112+
632	**2**	*1 ¼*	**Alexandrova (IRE)**[235] 5459 3-8-12 ... KFallon 5 (A P O'Brien, Ire) *clipped heels and stmbld after 100 yds: rr tl gd hdwy over 3f out rdn to ld and edgd rt over 1f out: hdd and no ex ins last* **8/15**[1]	105+
2152	**3**	*2 ½*	**Maroussies Wings (IRE)**[14] 1423 3-8-12 88 ... KDarley 2 (P C Haslam) *trckd ldr: rdn to ld wl over 2f out: drvn and hdd over 1f out: kpt on same pce ins last* **33/1**	100
1	**4**	*9*	**Lake Shabla (USA)**[95] 374 3-8-12 76 ... LDettori 3 (E A L Dunlop) *lw: hld up in tch: hdwy 3f out: rdn along over 2f out: sn wknd* **8/1**[3]	86+
2243	**5**	*16*	**High Heel Sneakers**[17] 1330 3-8-12 104 ... JamieSpencer 6 (P F I Cole) *edgy: led: rdn along 3f out: sn hdd: wknd 2f out and sn eased* **16/1**	53+
	6	*dist*	**Jabbara (IRE)** 3-8-12 ... TedDurcan 1 (C E Brittain) *w'like: leggy: unf: towards rr: outpcd and bhd fnl 3f* **100/1**	—

2m 15.63s (5.15) **Going Correction** +0.725s/f (Yiel) 6 Ran SP% **108.4**
Speed ratings (Par 106):108,107,105,97,85 —
CSF £5.30 TOTE £4.10: £1.80, £1.10; EX 6.50.
Owner J M Greetham **Bred** J M Greetham **Trained** Newmarket, Suffolk
■ Stewards' Enq: Spencer two-day ban: careless riding (May 29-30) interf. to Alexandrova

The Form Book, Raceform Ltd, Compton, RG20 6NL

FOCUS
An interesting renewal of the Musidora, but it posed more questions than it answered with regards the Oaks. Maroussies Wings does little for the form in third at first glance given she came into this rated just 88. As is to be expected in a small field, the pace was just ordinary and the winning time was nearly four seconds slower than the earlier handicap won by Blue Spinnaker.

NOTEBOOK
Short Skirt ◆, an easy six-length winner of a seven-furlong July course maiden on her racecourse debut, but disappointing on her final start of last season when a beaten favourite behind subsequent 1000 Guineas Speciosa in the Rockfel Stakes, proved well suited by the step up to middle-distances and won nicely. She had to wait for a gap in the straight, but her rider is one of the last to panic in that sort of situation and she picked up well when switched wide. Alexandrova was quite clearly below the form she showed when second in last year's Fillies' Mile, and the third was rated just 88, but this was still a smart effort and, with physical scope and the race likely to bring her on, she looks capable of progressing throughout the season. She is in the Oaks, although her trainer was reluctant to commit her to Epsom as he considers she needs plenty of give in the ground, and he also has the likes of Scottish Stage and Riyalma towards the head of the Epsom betting. Wherever she goes, though, she looks one to keep very much on the right side of and this is unlikely to be her last Pattern-race victory. (tchd 10-3)
Alexandrova(IRE), a ten-length winner of a Tralee maiden on her third start as a juvenile before failing by just a short-head to Nannina in the Group 1 Fillies' Mile at Newmarket, was the clear form pick and looked capable of improving further over middle-distances this year, but she disappointed. Her chance was not helped when she clipped heels with High Heel Sneakers and stumbled quite badly soon after the start, but it is impossible to know just how much that took out of her. When asked to go and win her race, she responded well enough to take it up, but did not clear away as one might have expected and always looked like being picked off by Short Skirt once that one had got in the clear. It may be that she does little in front - she was caught after leading about a furlong out in the Fillies' Mile - and she could also have been expected to need this first run of the season, but one would like to have seen more from a filly who came into the race a well-backed ante-post favourite for the Oaks. Many firms left her at the head of the market for the second fillies' Classic of the season, but she will need to improve significantly on the bare form of this effort to justify that position. (op 1-2 tchd 4-7 and 8-13 in places)
Maroussies Wings(IRE)who looked fit, appeared to have plenty to find given Shortest Day, who beat her a length and a half in a Pontefract handicap on her reappearance, had subsequently finished well beaten in the Lingfield Oaks Trial. However, the return to softer ground brought around significant improvement and she ran a cracker to pick up some black type. A Ribblesdale entry, her stable did well with another filly in the same colours, Kinnaird, just a couple of years back, and it would be unwise to underestimate this one. (tchd 40-1)
Lake Shabla(USA), a big, strong filly who is not the best of walkers, came from a mile off the pace to win on her debut over a mile on Polytrack just over three months previously, looked worth a try in this sort of company, but she came up short. It may be that she needs decent ground, and she can be given another chance. (tchd 9-1)
High Heel Sneakers, four and a quarter lengths behind Alexandrova in the Fillies' Mile on her final start as a juvenile, was a little disappointing when a beaten favourite on her reappearance in a nine-furlong Group 3 in France, but should still have run better than this. She may just have ended up setting the race up for the bigger names. (tchd 14-1)
Jabbara(IRE), a 65,000euros sister to Baie Des Flamandes, a nine-furlong winner who later scored over hurdles, out of a high-class 12-furlong winner, had little chance in this company first time up.

1778 DUKE OF YORK HEARTHSTEAD HOMES STKS (GROUP 2) 6f
3:15 (3:18) (Class 1) 3-Y-O+

£56,780 (£21,520; £10,770; £5,370; £2,690; £1,350) **Stalls** Centre

Form RPR
5055 **1** **Steenberg (IRE)**^{38} [930] 7-9-2 105 .... MichaelHills 2 116
(M H Tompkins) *hld up towards rr: gd hdwy on outer over 2f out: rdn to ld ent last: kpt on wl* **25/1**
2203 **2** *½* **Quito (IRE)**^{18} [1287] 9-9-2 110 .... (b) TonyCulhane 13 115
(D W Chapman) *lw: bhd: pushed along and hdwy over 2f out: sn rdn: styd on strly ins last* **10/1**
0465 **3** *2* **Somnus**^{214} [5900] 6-9-2 111 .... MJKinane 9 109
(T D Easterby) *hld up in rr: swtchd outside and gd hdwy 2f out: sn rdn nd styd on wl fnl f: nrst fin* **7/1**^{3}
5220 **4** *1 ¾* **Fayr Jag (IRE)**^{228} [5614] 7-9-2 111 .... TQuinn 3 103
(T D Easterby) *chsd ldrs: hdwy 2f out: rdn to ld jst over 1f out: hdd ent last: wknd* **40/1**
3110 **5** *¾* **Gift Horse**^{256} [4940] 6-9-2 106 .... EddieAhern 7 101+
(D Nicholls) *trckd ldrs: hdwy 2f out: sn rdn and kpt on same pce ins last* **12/1**
2103 **6** *½* **Eisteddfod**^{25} [1145] 5-9-2 110 .... LDettori 6 100
(P F I Cole) *towards rr: pushed along 1/2-way: rdn and hdwy 2f out: kpt on ins last* **11/2**^{1}
0122 **7** *1* **Philharmonic**^{11} [1479] 5-9-2 100 .... KDarley 4 97
(R A Fahey) *lw: cl up: ev ch 2f out: sn rdn and wknd appr last* **16/1**
5000 **8** *hd* **The Kiddykid (IRE)**^{53} [729] 6-9-2 104 .... JamieSpencer 1 96
(P D Evans) *lw: prom tl rdn along and wkng whn n.m.r wl over 1f out* **20/1**
3602 **9** *¾* **Mecca's Mate**^{216} [5853] 5-8-13 101 .... FergalLynch 14 91
(D W Barker) *bhd tl styd on fnl 2f* **66/1**
2025 **10** *shd* **Fonthill Road (IRE)**^{4} [1663] 6-9-2 103 .... PaulHanagan 15 93
(R A Fahey) *a towards rr* **16/1**
0530 **11** *1 ¼* **Moss Vale (IRE)**^{11} [1485] 5-9-2 109 .... AdrianTNicholls 11 90
(D Nicholls) *chsd ldrs: rdn 2f out: wknd appr last* **12/1**
0360 **12** *1 ¼* **Beckermet (IRE)**^{11} [1485] 4-9-2 110 .... JohnEgan 10 86
(R F Fisher) *led to 1/2-way: sn rdn along and wknd 2f out* **33/1**
0011 **13** *1 ¾* **Etlaala**^{18} [1287] 4-9-2 110 .... RHills 5 81
(B W Hills) *lw: chsd ldrs: led 1/2-way: rdn 2f out: hdd & wknd over 1f out* **11/2**^{1}
121 **14** *nk* **Welsh Emperor (IRE)**^{25} [1145] 7-9-2 110 .... RobertWinston 16 80
(T P Tate) *lw: in tch: rdn along 2f out: grad wknd* **6/1**^{2}
6011 **15** *5* **Balthazaar's Gift (IRE)**^{197} [6220] 3-8-11 111 .... NCallan 12 69
(K A Ryan) *hdw: in tch: rdn along 1/2-way: sn wknd* **10/1**
4060 **16** *2* **Royal Millennium (IRE)**^{29} [1069] 8-9-2 103 .... TedDurcan 8 59
(M R Channon) *a rr* **33/1**

1m 12.54s (-0.02) **Going Correction** +0.375s/f (Good)
WFA 3 from 4yo+ 9lb **16** Ran SP% **121.3**
Speed ratings (Par 115):115,114,111,109,108 107,106,106,105,104 103,101,99,98,92 89
CSF £244.49 TOTE £37.50: £7.80, £3.30, £3.00; EX 330.00 Trifecta £1678.90 Part won. Pool: £2,364.70 - 0.20 winning units..
Owner Kenneth Macpherson **Bred** B Ryan **Trained** Newmarket, Suffolk

FOCUS
A good competitive renewal of Duke Of York in which Steenberg was getting it right at the fourth attempt having run sixth in 2003, and the finished runner-up in both 2004 and 2005. The time was decent and the form looks sound.

NOTEBOOK
Steenberg(IRE), sixth in this race in 2003, and then runner-up in both the last two seasons, got it right at the fourth attempt and fully deserved this first Group-race success. He looked set to win very nicely when hitting the front, but was closed down fast by the slightly unlucky in-running Quito. While this could have boosted his confidence, his overall record suggests he cannot really be backed to follow up.
Quito(IRE), at the age of nine, is still capable of running up to his very best form and this was a fine effort. His running style requires a certain amount of luck and he was closing fast at the line, after having to be switched with his effort. (tchd 9-1)
Somnus ◆ failed to win last year and never quite reached his best form but this was a very pleasing return to action. He can be expected to come on for this first outing in 214 days and could well return to his best this season. (op 15-2)
Fayr Jag(IRE) ◆ has not won for almost two years now but this performance suggests he retains plenty of ability, especially as this ground would not have been to his liking. He needs a quick surface to be seen at his best and, providing he can build on this, further Pattern-race success should be on the cards. (op 33-1)
Gift Horse, who enjoyed such a successful season in handicap company last year, travelled strongly for much of the race but was found out by a lack of a recent run. The impression left, though, was that he should very much be able to hold his own at Group level this season. (tchd 14-1)
Eisteddfod stepped up on the form he showed on his reappearance and gave the impression he can do better again. (op 7-1)
Philharmonic has been in good form lately and had conditions to suit, but he had a bit to find at this level. He had every chance if good enough and the conclusion must be that he is a touch short of the class required to win in Group company.
The Kiddykid(IRE), whose latest success came in this event last year, failed to sustain his effort at the business end of the race, but still stepped-up on this level of his comeback in Listed company at Redcar in March. Official explanation: jockey said gelding hung right
Beckermet(IRE) Official explanation: jockey said gelding had no more to give
Etlaala, dropping back in trip in this quest for the hat-trick, showed decent early speed yet ultimately appeared to pay for running too freely. He may have also found this ground a touch too soft for his liking. (tchd 6-1)
Welsh Emperor(IRE), a winner on his recent seasonal reappearance at Thirsk and who had finished fourth and third respectively in the past two runnings of this event, proved disappointing on the ground that should have been right up his street. He is better than this. (tchd 13-2)
Balthazaar's Gift(IRE), the only three-year-old in the field and saddled with a 4lb penalty for his win in a French Group 2 race last season, was disappointing, but his trainer had suggested beforehand that the run would be needed, so it is too early to write him off. (op 11-1)

1779 BLUE SQUARE STKS (H'CAP) 1m 4f
3:50 (3:50) (Class 3) (0-95,93) 4-Y-O+ **£9,067** (£2,697; £1,348; £673) **Stalls** Centre

Form RPR
0033 **1** **Millville**^{179} [6377] 6-9-4 **93** .... PhilipRobinson 3 101
(M A Jarvis) *lw: trckd ldrs: styd on wl fnl 2f: led last strides* **8/1**^{3}
0665 **2** *hd* **Lets Roll**^{18} [1294] 5-8-13 **88** .... DeanMcKeown 16 96
(C W Thornton) *racd wd and led 2f: chsd ldr: styd on to ld ins last: hdd post* **12/1**
134 **3** *1 ¾* **Tcherina (IRE)**^{35} [976] 4-8-5 **80** .... GrahamGibbons 5 85
(T D Easterby) *swtchd lft after 1f: led after 2f: hdd and no ex ins last* **7/1**^{2}
3-00 **4** *1 ½* **Akritas**^{21} [1247] 5-8-4 **79** .... JoeFanning 4 82
(P F I Cole) *b: hmpd after 1f: trckd ldrs: edgd lft fnl 2f: no ex fnl f* **28/1**
0000 **5** *1 ¼* **Mirjan (IRE)**^{25} [5903] 10-9-1 **90** .... PaulHanagan 10 91+
(L Lungo) *in rr: hdwy over 2f out: styd on strly: nt rch ldrs* **20/1**
0210 **6** *½* **Cruise Director**^{42} [5451] 6-8-13 **88** .... KFallon 9 88
(Ian Williams) *mid-div: hdwy over 3f out: kpt on same pce fnl 2f* **7/1**^{2}
0015 **7** *¾* **Group Captain**^{193} [6254] 4-9-0 **89** .... DarryllHolland 14 88+
(R Charlton) *in tch: effrt over 2f out: one pce* **10/1**
0444 **8** *8* **Wiggy Smith**^{15} [5436] 7-8-9 **84** .... EddieAhern 15 70
(O Sherwood) *mid-div:hdwy to chse ldrs 6f out: wknd over 1f out* **20/1**
030 **9** *4* **Sporting Gesture**^{5} [1631] 9-8-6 **81** .... DaleGibson 8 60
(M W Easterby) *mid-div: hdwy 5f out: wknd over 1f out* **25/1**
0511 **10** *4* **Top Seed (IRE)**^{11} [1478] 5-8-11 **86** .... SamHitchcott 12 59
(M R Channon) *hld up towards rr: hdwy 6f out: sn drvn along: lost pl over 1f out* **7/1**^{2}
0436 **11** *1 ¾* **Most Definitely (IRE)**^{18} [1294] 6-8-12 **87** .... DavidAllan 6 57
(T D Easterby) *rr-div: sme hdwy 3f out: sn lost pl* **14/1**
6000 **12** *8* **Nordwind (IRE)**^{21} [1238] 5-8-11 **86** .... TedDurcan 11 43
(W R Swinburn) *nt rt in coat: hld up in rr: drvn 4f out: nvr on terms* **33/1**
3006 **13** *½* **Lysandra (IRE)**^{14} [1419] 4-8-4 **79** oh1 .... KimTinkler 13 36
(N Tinkler) *warm: edgy: rr-div: sme hdwy 4f out: sn lost pl* **50/1**
5022 **14** *5* **Self Respect (USA)**^{291} [3931] 4-8-9 **84** .... JamieSpencer 1 33
(A King) *s.i.s: bdly hmpd after 1f: effrt and mid-field 5f out: sn wknd: eased* **9/2**^{1}
5-41 **15** *21* **Seyaadi**^{392} [1143] 4-8-12 **87** .... NCallan 2 2
(Robert Gray) *trckd ldrs: hmpd after 1f: wknd over 2f out: heavily eased* **33/1**
0010 **P** **El Tiger (GER)**^{95} [377] 5-9-0 **89** .... TPQueally 7 —
(B J Curley) *trckd ldrs: lost pl over 3f out: heavily eased and p.u ins last* **20/1**

2m 37.63s (5.23) **Going Correction** +0.725s/f (Yiel) **16** Ran SP% **119.7**
Speed ratings (Par 107):111,110,109,108,107 107,107,101,99,96 95,89,89,86,72 —
CSF £86.49 CT £713.42 TOTE £11.70: £2.70, £3.10, £1.60, £8.90; EX 203.10.
Owner T G Warner **Bred** Red House Stud **Trained** Newmarket, Suffolk
■ Stewards' Enquiry : Dean McKeown two-day ban: used whip with excessive frequency (May 29-30)
Philip Robinson two-day ban: used whip with excessive frequency (May 29-30)
Graham Gibbons three-day ban: careless riding (May 28-30)

FOCUS
A decent handicap in which Tcherina crossed over at the start and caused a domino effect. She set just a steady pace until the turn for home but even so they came home well strung out with the first seven clear. Few got into it from off the pace and as such the races is not rated as positively as it could have been.

NOTEBOOK
Millville, knocked back early on, really put his head down and battled to lead on the line. He is even better over further. (op 11-1)
Lets Roll, 5lb higher than when third a year ago, had the worst of the draw. Racing wide in the back straight and up the centre once in line for home, in the end he just missed out. He thoroughly deserves to go one better.
Tcherina(IRE), well backed on the morning line, went left after a furlong on to the running rail, hampering the four drawn on her inside. She set just a steady pace until winding it up turning in and in the end could not quite see it out. She loves to get her toe in.
Akritas, back on turf, edged left in the final quarter mile and ended up on the far rail. He has clearly had his problems and this was much more encouraging. (op 25-1)
Mirjan(IRE), 4lb higher than when winning the 2004 Northumberland Plate, showed that even at his advanced age he is no back number. He was the only one to make serious inroads from off the pace. (op 22-1)

Cruise Director, 6lb higher than when taking this a year ago, was fit from hurdling and had no apparent excuse.
Group Captain, 3lb higher than the last of his four wins last year, has changed stables. A rangy type likely to make an even better four-year-old, he made a highly satisfactory return. (tchd 11-1)
Self Respect(USA), runner-up to Group Captain at Goodwood in July when fitted with a first-time visor, has changed stables. Knocked right out of his stride early on, he never fully recovered. (tchd 5-1 in places)
Seyaadi Official explanation: jockey said gelding had no more to give
El Tiger(GER) Official explanation: jockey said gelding felt wrong behind

1780 BLUE SQUARE EBF NOVICE STKS 5f
4:25 (4:26) (Class 3) 2-Y-O **£8,420** (£2,505; £1,251; £625) **Stalls** Centre

Form				RPR
13	**1**		**Chief Editor**[29] [1066] 2-9-0 .... JamieSpencer 3 (M J Wallace) *lw: mde all: qcknd over 1f out: hld on wl towards fin* **13/8**[1]	87+
61	**2**	*1 ½*	**Avertuoso**[12] [1454] 2-9-2 .... PhilipRobinson 1 (B Smart) *b. hind: racd wd: t.k.h: w ldrs: kpt on wl ins last* **15/2**	84
061	**3**	*hd*	**Mr Klick (IRE)**[20] [1248] 2-9-2 .... GrahamGibbons 2 (N Wilson) *dwlt: sn trcking ldrs: rdn and hung lft over 2f out: kpt on fnl f* **50/1**	83
6	**4**	*3*	**Danum Dancer**[11] [1491] 2-8-12 .... NCallan 5 (N Bycroft) *chsd ldrs: outpcd over 2f out: kpt on fnl f* **33/1**	68
21	**5**	*3*	**Hill Of Lujain**[10] [1499] 2-9-2 .... KFallon 6 (M W Easterby) *chsd ldrs: effrt 2f out: sn hmpd and lost pl* **5/1**[3]	61
	6	*½*	**Dubai's Touch** 2-8-12 .... JoeFanning 4 (M Johnston) *rangy: scope: s.i.s: hdwy to chse ldrs over 3f out: lost pl over 1f out* **9/1**	55
21	**7**	*1 ¼*	**Alternative**[22] [1203] 2-9-2 .... NelsonDeSouza(3) 7 (R M Beckett) *neat: trckd ldrs: effrt on inner 2f out: sn wknd* **9/4**[2]	58

61.60 secs (2.28) **Going Correction** +0.375s/f (Good) **7 Ran SP% 112.2**
Speed ratings (Par 97):96,93,93,88,83 82,80
CSF £14.10 TOTE £2.70: £1.50, £4.50; EX 16.00.
Owner Mrs P Good **Bred** J R And Mrs P Good **Trained** Newmarket, Suffolk

FOCUS
The winner had his own way and is value for more than the official margin. The third, a claiming race winner, should have given him more to do.

NOTEBOOK
Chief Editor, who towered over his rivals in the paddock, was allowed to set his own pace and was always doing more than enough. His action suggests he will always need some give underfoot. (op 7-4 tchd 15-8 in places)
Avertuoso, drawn one, was always tending to race wide. He really knuckled down inside the last and is clearly going the right way. (op 11-2)
Mr Klick(IRE), awkward to load, hung violently left and ended up racing up the centre. A bargain claim, he has the ability but needs to be gelded soon. (op 40-1)
Danum Dancer again showed ability but this will not have done his potential nursery mark any good.
Hill Of Lujain was struggling to make an impact when knocked right out of his stride. He is crying out for six furlongs. (op 7-1)
Dubai's Touch ◆, a good-bodied March foal, stands over plenty of ground and was noisy in the paddock. After a tardy start he showed plenty of toe until tiring. He will be a different proposition next time. (op 10-1)
Alternativea sprinting type, was quite keen tucked away on the inner. Giving weight away all round, he fell in a heap soon after the two furlong from home marker. Official explanation: trainer said colt was found to be lame the following morning (op 5-2)

1781 CHRIS WRIGHT "STILL NOT TOO OLD TO ROCK'N'ROLL" H'CAP 1m 2f 88y
4:55 (4:56) (Class 3) (0-90,85) 3-Y-O **£8,096** (£2,408; £1,203; £601) **Stalls** Low

Form				RPR
021	**1**		**Reem Three**[25] [1153] 3-8-11 **78** .... NickyMackay 5 (L M Cumani) *leggy: trckd ldrs: led over 2f out: styd on wl fnl f* **9/1**	92+
0606	**2**	*2*	**Quince (IRE)**[27] [1095] 3-8-13 **80** ....(p) JimmyQuinn 7 (J Pearce) *hld up in rr: hdwy over 2f out: chsd wnr fnl f: no real imp* **33/1**	89
41	**3**	*3*	**Tears Of A Clown (IRE)**[15] [1386] 3-9-4 **85** .... JamieSpencer 10 (J A Osborne) *w'like: trckd ldrs: chal on inner and n.m.r over 2f out: hung rt and kpt on same pce fnl f* **4/1**[2]	89+
3022	**4**	*½*	**Macorville (USA)**[18] [1296] 3-8-11 **78** .... ShaneKelly 6 (G M Moore) *bit bkwd: chsd ldrs: hmpd over 2f out: styd on ins last* **25/1**	81
5221	**5**	*1 ¼*	**Scot Love (IRE)**[14] [1401] 3-9-0 **81** .... LDettori 3 (J Noseda) *lw: hld up: stdy hdwy over 3f out: edgd lft over 2f out: one pce appr fnl f* **4/1**[2]	82
3602	**6**	*shd*	**Charlie Tokyo (IRE)**[212] [5949] 3-8-11 **78** .... PaulHanagan 13 (R A Fahey) *hld up in rr: stdy hdwy over 2f out: nt clr run over 1f out: r.o* **16/1**	86+
0011	**7**	*4*	**Gracechurch (IRE)**[22] [1205] 3-9-1 **82** .... TonyCulhane 11 (M R Channon) *fit: in rr: effrt over 3f out: kpt on fnl 2f: nvr nr ldrs* **8/1**[3]	75
2132	**8**	*hd*	**Awatuki (IRE)**[10] [1515] 3-9-0 **81** .... KFallon 2 (A P Jarvis) *lw: t.k.h: trckd ldrs: led after 2f: rdn and wnt lft over 2f out: sn hdd & wknd* **10/3**[1]	74
5022	**9**	*3*	**Maggies Farm (USA)**[234] [5489] 3-9-2 **83** .... JoeFanning 1 (M Johnston) *lw: nt grwn: led 2f: chsd ldrs: wknd over 1f out* **25/1**	71
015	**10**	*16*	**Zilcash**[22] [1205] 3-8-10 **77** .... EddieAhern 12 (A King) *on toes: fit: mid-div: hdwy to chse ldrs over 5f out: lost pl over 2f out: sn bhd and eased* **20/1**	36
0014	**11**	*7*	**Twill (IRE)**[41] [895] 3-9-1 **82** .... SteveDrowne 9 (H Morrison) *b.hind: sn chsng ldrs: lost pl over 3f out: sn bhd and eased* **16/1**	28
0131	**12**	*dist*	**Fregate Island (IRE)**[169] [6457] 3-9-0 **81** .... DarryllHolland 8 (W J Haggas) *sn chsng ldrs: lost pl over 3f out: sn bhd: virtually p.u: t.o: btn 50l* **20/1**	—

2m 16.95s (6.47) **Going Correction** +0.725s/f (Yiel) **12 Ran SP% 116.1**
Speed ratings (Par 103):103,101,99,98,97 97,94,94,91,78 73,—
CSF £279.94 CT £1372.55 TOTE £9.10: £2.90, £8.60, £1.70; EX 276.00 Place 6 £75.48, Place 5 £45.69.
Owner Sheikh Mohammed Obaid Al Maktoum **Bred** Darley **Trained** Newmarket, Suffolk

FOCUS
A fair handicap run at just a steady pace and the form is not that strong. The winner should continue to progress, Charlie Tokyo was the eye-catcher.

NOTEBOOK
Reem Three, on her handicap bow, is clearly on the up and took this in most decisive fashion.
Quince(IRE), with the headgear back on, stepped up markedly on his return effort staying on from way off the pace but at the line he was very much second best.
Tears Of A Clown(IRE), done no favours on his handicap bow from a mark of 85, was tightened up on the inner and then tended to hang. He is still learning. Official explanation: jockey said colt hung left
Macorville(USA), squeezed out at a vital stage, is well worth a try over a mile and a half.
Scot Love(IRE), in no hurry to join issue, seemed to struggle to see out this extended trip especially in this ground.
Charlie Tokyo(IRE) ◆, who has changed stables, was asked to race from a career-high mark. He was staying on in eye-catching style when running out of racing room and was definitely not knocked about. He is well worth keeping an eye on. Official explanation: jockey said gelding was denied a clear run 2f out
Awatuki(IRE) would not settle and pulled his way to the front. He came off a straight line when put under pressure and looks to have wayward tendencies. (op 3-1 tchd 7-2)
Fregate Island(IRE) Official explanation: jockey said gelding hung right
T/Jkpt: Not won. T/Plt: £102.90 to a £1 stake. Pool: £120,047.00. 850.95 winning tickets. T/Qpdt: £32.30 to a £1 stake. Pool: £4,806.00. 109.85 winning tickets. JR

1154 NAAS (L-H)
Wednesday, May 17
OFFICIAL GOING: Round course - yielding to soft; sprint course - yielding changing to yielding to soft after race 3 (6.50)

1785a IRISH STALLION FARMS EUROPEAN BREEDERS FUND BLUE WIND STKS (GROUP 3) (F&M) 1m 2f
7:20 (7:20) 3-Y-0+ **£40,344** (£11,793; £5,586; £1,862)

			RPR
1		**Galatee (FR)**[10] [1521] 3-8-9 .... KJManning 6 (J S Bolger, Ire) *trckd ldr in 2nd: rdn to chal and ld over 2f out: sn clr: styd on wl u.p: comf* **11/4**[2]	113+
2	*3 ½*	**Allexina**[25] [1128] 4-9-9 106 .... MJKinane 5 (John M Oxx, Ire) *led: strly pressed and hdd over 2f out: sn no imp: kpt on same pce u.p* **5/2**[1]	107
3	*3 ½*	**Gift Range (IRE)**[38] [932] 4-9-9 101 .... FMBerry 3 (John M Oxx, Ire) *chsd ldrs in 5th: clsr in 4th wl bef st: no imp u.p fr 2f out: kpt on wout threatening into 3rd fr over 1f out* **16/1**	101
4	*1 ½*	**Chelsea Rose (IRE)**[206] [6053] 4-9-9 112 .... WSupple 1 (C Collins, Ire) *trckd ldrs in 3rd: no imp u.p fr 2f out: kpt on same pce and dropped to 4th fr over 1f out* **4/1**[3]	98
5	*20*	**Sacrosanct (IRE)**[32] [1022] 3-8-9 .... JAHeffernan 2 (A P O'Brien, Ire) *racd in 4th: dropped to 5th and swished tail bef st: sn no imp u.p: eased fr over 1f out* **9/2**	62
6	*¾*	**Million Waves (IRE)**[32] [1026] 3-8-9 94 .... DPMcDonogh 4 (Kevin Prendergast, Ire) *chsd ldrs in 6th: rdn and no imp fr bef st: sn n.d* **20/1**	61
7	*dist*	**Saintly Rachel (IRE)**[32] [1026] 8-9-9 97 .... JMurtagh 7 (C F Swan, Ire) *dwlt: a trailing: rdn 4f out: sn bhd: virtually p.u fnl f: t.o* **14/1**	—

2m 18.2s
WFA 3 from 4yo+ 14lb **7 Ran SP% 110.7**
CSF £9.38 TOTE £3.60: £2.20, £1.50; DF 14.10.
Owner Mrs Claudia Jungo-Corpataux **Bred** M Jean-Pierre Dubois **Trained** Coolcullen, Co Carlow

NOTEBOOK
Galatee(FR) extended her unbeaten record with a very taking effort that makes her a leading contender for the Irish Oaks, which is to be her next start. She stayed on well over the final furlong and looks as though she will be even better going a mile and a half. She has yet to encounter good ground but is clearly a very high class filly and has every chance of giving her trainer a third Irish Oaks. (op 9/4)
Allexina came into this off a run in a Group Three at Newbury last month. The three-time Listed winner had no answer when Galatee moved past but she stayed on under pressure to make sure of second and finished nicely clear of the remainder. She can win again back in Listed company. (op 9/4)
Gift Range(IRE) improved markedly on her sixth behind Arch Rebel in the Alleged Stakes last month. She has yet to win at Listed level but this effort bodes well for her future prospects in that sphere. (op 12/1)
Chelsea Rose(IRE), the former Moyglare winner, was running for the first time since finishing third in an Italian Group One last October. She held third place for much of the race but eventually had to surrender that position to Gift Range. All her victories have come on better ground and she can be expected to leave this form behind under her favoured conditions. (op 3/1)
Sacrosanct(IRE) was being ridden along with half a mile to run and could make no further impression in the straight. (op 9/2 tchd 5/1)
Saintly Rachel(IRE) Official explanation: jockey said mare hung badly right

1786 - 1788a (Foreign Racing) - See Raceform Interactive

883 MAISONS-LAFFITTE (R-H)
Wednesday, May 17
OFFICIAL GOING: Good to soft

1789a PRIX D'ANGERVILLE (LISTED RACE) (FILLIES) (LEFT-HANDED) 1m (S)
2:35 (2:37) 3-Y-0 **£17,241** (£6,897; £5,172; £3,448; £1,724)

			RPR
1		**Phantom Rose (USA)**[27] 3-8-12 .... CSoumillon 8 (A Fabre, France) **7/5**[1]	100
2	*1 ½*	**Heaven's Cause (USA)**[23] 3-8-12 .... TThulliez 1 (N Clement, France)	97
3	*1*	**Blue Blue Sky (IRE)**[51] [773] 3-9-2 .... DBonilla 10 (Y De Nicolay, France)	99
4	*hd*	**Galma (FR)**[24] [1177] 3-8-12 .... SPasquier 5 (E Lellouche, France)	95
5	*shd*	**Folle Biche (FR)**[9] 3-8-12 .... RonanThomas 9 (Mme N Rossio, France)	94
6	*snk*	**Flor Y Nata (USA)**[265] [4688] 3-8-12 .... J-BEyquem 3 (Sir Mark Prescott) *hld up in last bhd fast pace, 9th str, rdn on outside 1 1/2f out, kpt on under pressure fnl f (31/1)* **31/1**[2]	94
7	*¾*	**Drosia (IRE)**[24] 3-8-12 .... MBlancpain 4 (C Laffon-Parias, France)	93
8	*4*	**Nantes (GER)**[16] 3-8-12 .... JVictoire 2 (A Fabre, France)	85
9	*3*	**Indian Fun**[51] [773] 3-9-2 ....(b) OPeslier 6 (F Head, France)	83
10	*hd*	**Beau Monde**[24] [1177] 3-8-12 ....(b) C-PLemaire 7 (H-A Pantall, France)	78

1m 41.8s **10 Ran SP% 44.8**
PARI-MUTUEL: WIN 2.40; PL 1.50, 2.60, 3.80; DF 14.20.
Owner K Abdulla **Bred** Juddmonte Farms Inc **Trained** Chantilly, France

The Form Book, Raceform Ltd, Compton, RG20 6NL

NOTEBOOK
Flor Y Nata(USA) appeared to be outpaced in the early stages before making good progress rounding the final turn. She looked dangerous a furlong and a half out but just stayed on one-paced during the final 100 yards. She was not beaten far by the third-placed filly, and this was a good performance on ground that was not soft enough for her to show her best. Her rider felt she would come on a lot for the run and will stay further.

CARLISLE (R-H)

Thursday, May 18

OFFICIAL GOING: Good to soft (good in places)

The round course needed time to recover from winter wear and all the races were run over 5f & 6f. Running rail moved in by 5 yards.

Wind: fresh, half against Weather: Overcast, frequent heavy showers.

1790 EUROPEAN BREEDERS FUND MAIDEN STKS 5f

6:30 (6:31) (Class 5) 2-Y-O £3,886 (£1,156; £577; £288) Stalls High

Form RPR

5 1 **Middleham (IRE)**8 1588 2-9-3 .... JoeFanning 4 76+
(M Johnston) mde all: edgd sltly lft fr over 1f out: shkn up and r.o wl ins fnl f **4/7**1

2 1 3/4 **My Valerina (IRE)** 2-8-12 .... GrahamGibbons 1 65
(Mrs A Duffield) cmpt: trckd ldng pair: chsd wnr and wandered over 1f out: styd on ins fnl f: no imp **6/1**2

3 2 1/2 **Davaye** 2-8-12 .... PatCosgrave 2 56
(K R Burke) lengthy: unf: t.k.h: w wnr tl rdn over 1f out: one pce ins fnl f **12/1**

0 4 3/4 **The Mighty Ogmore**17 1342 2-8-12 .... FergalLynch 5 53
(R C Guest) s.i.s: hld up on outside: styd on ins fnl 2f: nvr gng pce to trble ldrs **14/1**

5 12 **Muncaster Castle (IRE)** 2-9-3 .... FrancisNorton 6 15
(R F Fisher) leggy: trckd ldrs: pushed along 3f out: wknd over 2f out **8/1**3

0 6 3 **Joella's Lad**15 1420 2-9-3 .... StanleyChin 7 —
(Ms Deborah J Evans) trckd ldrs on ins: sltly hmpd over 3f out: rdn and wknd over 2f out **25/1**

0 7 10 **Devilfishpoker Com**17 1342 2-9-3 .... PaulEddery 3 —
(R C Guest) hld up in tch: pushed along over 2f out: sn wknd **50/1**

63.78 secs (2.28) **Going Correction** +0.30s/f (Good) 7 Ran SP% **109.2**
Speed ratings (Par 93):93,90,86,85,65 61,45
CSF £3.88 TOTE £1.50: £1.10, £1.80; EX 3.50.
Owner Jumeirah Racing **Bred** Johnston King **Trained** Middleham Moor, N Yorks
■ Stewards' Enquiry : Joe Fanning caution: careless riding

FOCUS
A modest maiden but not easy to assess with confidence. The winner, who had clearly learnt plenty first time, holds a Group 1 entry but he will need to improve a good deal to reach anywhere near that level.

NOTEBOOK
Middleham(IRE), who had clearly learnt plenty first time, dominated throughout and will improve again. A sixth furlong will not come amiss. (tchd 8-15 and 8-13 in a place)
My Valerina(IRE), withdrawn on her intended debut at Catterick after giving a rodeo display and getting rid of her rider, was again tricky beforehand. Drawn on the outside, she tended to wander but stuck on to bustle up the winner. Hopefully racing will help settle down this good-bodied March foal. (op 7-1)
Davaye, long in the back and narrow, would not settle and took on the winner but it was clear that she was not good enough. The outing will have taught her a fair bit. (op 9-1)
The Mighty Ogmore, a weak-looking filly, stayed on steadily up the wide outside and is still learning the ropes. (op 16-1)
Muncaster Castle(IRE), an April foal, is on the leg and was noisy and on his toes beforehand. (op 15-2)
Joella's Lad, backward in his coat, was tightened up on the bend and was soon on the retreat.

1791 PINK LADIES (S) STKS 5f 193y

7:00 (7:01) (Class 6) 3-4-Y-O £2,590 (£770; £385; £192) Stalls High

Form RPR

540 1 **Dancing Deano (IRE)**226 5687 4-9-0 59 ....(v) MichaelJStainton(7) 11 59
(R M Whitaker) prom: led 1/2-way: rdn over 2f out: styd on wl for press ins fnl f **9/4**1

0064 2 1 **Drum Dance (IRE)**8 1594 4-9-7 46 .... KimTinkler 6 56
(N Tinkler) n.m.r briefly leaving stalls: in rr: hdwy 3f out: rdn over 2f out: hung rt and chsd wnr ins fnl f: styd on **9/2**3

0000 3 1 1/4 **Sweetly Sharp (IRE)**14 1447 3-8-7 45 .... GrahamGibbons 8 47
(A Berry) sn trcking ldrs: rdn to chse wnr 2f out: one pce ins fnl f **20/1**

5000 4 2 **Sapphire Storm (IRE)**17 1341 3-8-7 45 ow3 .... PaulMulrennan(3) 2 44
(P T Midgley) trckd ldrs: rdn 2f out: styd on same pce ins fnl f **25/1**

6400 5 2 1/2 **Boumsong (IRE)**259 4880 3-8-12 45 .... FergalLynch 3 39
(R C Guest) hld up: drvn wl over 2f out: effrt over 1f out: nvr nr ldrs **25/1**

0050 6 1 1/2 **Miss Mujahid Times**9 1571 3-8-7 47 ....(b1) PaulEddery 4 29
(A D Brown) mid-div: rdn and hdwy over 2f out: edgd rt 1f out: no ex fnl f **50/1**

3250 7 2 **Alpaga Le Jomage (IRE)**54 732 4-9-12 65 .... FrancisNorton 10 33
(M J Polglase) led 1f: prom: rdn over 2f out: wknd 1f out **4/1**2

0-00 8 1/2 **Apetite**14 1447 4-9-0 48 ....(b1) SuzzanneFrance(7) 12 27
(N Bycroft) in tch: lost pl bef 1/2-way: no imp after **20/1**

3400 9 3 1/2 **Silver Nun**2 1768 3-8-2 45 ....(p) DuranFentiman(5) 13 11
(T D Easterby) s.i.s: hld up towards rr: rdn over 3f out: sn struggling **14/1**

3250 10 3/4 **Glendening**50 797 3-8-12 57 .... AdrianTNicholls 1 14
(D Nicholls) hld up: rdn over 3f out: sn btn **7/1**

4200 11 3 1/2 **True Valentine**44 870 3-8-7 45 .... GylesParkin 9 —
(A Berry) prom 3f **20/1**

6P03 12 1 3/4 **Lord Mayfair (USA)**2 1763 4-9-0 40 ....(b) AnnStokell(7) 5 —
(Miss A Stokell) wnt rt s: led after 1f: hdd 1/2-way: wknd over 2f out **20/1**

0000 13 41 **Crystal Bay (IRE)**14 1437 3-8-7 30 .... JoeFanning 7 —
(A Berry) hmpd s: a wl bhd **50/1**

1m 17.0s (3.39) **Going Correction** +0.30s/f (Good)
WFA 3 from 4yo 9lb 13 Ran SP% **118.8**
Speed ratings (Par 101):89,87,86,83,80 78,75,74,70,69 64,62,7
CSF £10.15 TOTE £3.00: £2.00, £1.80, £5.20; EX 15.20.There was no bid for the winner.
Owner Craig and Amanda Harrison **Bred** Mrs Olivia Farrell **Trained** Scarcroft, W Yorks

FOCUS
A poor race even by selling race standards with just three having a realistic chance beforehand on official ratings. Lord Mayfair dived right at the start causing problems for those on his inside and behind the principals the form is not that solid.
Alpaga Le Jomage(IRE) Official explanation: jockey said gelding moved poorly throughout
Crystal Bay(IRE) Official explanation: jockey said filly suffered interference leaving the stalls

1792 CUMBRIA COMMUNITY FOUNDATION H'CAP 5f 193y

7:30 (7:31) (Class 6) (0-60,60) 3-Y-O £3,238 (£963; £481; £240) Stalls Low

Form RPR

0305 1 **Stanley Wolfe (IRE)**7 1612 3-7-13 46 oh1 .... AndrewMullen(5) 2 51
(James Moffatt) sn trcking ldrs: led over 2f out: rdn and strly pressed fr wl over 1f out: drvn out **25/1**

5004 2 1 **Quaker Boy**14 1441 3-9-2 58 .... TomEaves 3 60
(M Dods) mid-div: hdwy over 2f out: rdn and edgd rt over 1f out: kpt on towards fin **6/1**3

0006 3 hd **Drink To Me Only**10 1549 3-8-10 52 .... PhillipMakin 11 53
(J R Weymes) a.p: rdn over 2f out: styd on towards fin **11/1**

1053 4 nk **Quadrophenia**7 1612 3-9-4 60 .... MickyFenton 8 60
(J G Given) a.p: chal fr 3f out: rdn over 1f out: stl ev ch ins fnl f: nt qckn towards fin **4/1**1

0000 5 1 1/4 **Cape Sydney (IRE)**5 1687 3-8-4 46 oh1 .... NeilPollard 13 42
(D W Barker) mid-div: rdn over 2f out: hdwy and edgd sltly lft wl over 1f out: styd on: nt rch ldrs **25/1**

0016 6 nk **Taras Tornado**22 1232 3-8-11 53 .... GrahamGibbons 1 48
(J J Quinn) hld up: swtchd rt over 3f out: hdwy whn nt clr run wl over 1f out: nvr able to chal **5/1**2

3006 7 1 1/4 **Signor Whippee**7 1612 3-8-6 48 .... JoeFanning 6 40
(A Berry) prom: led 3f out: rdn and hdd over 2f out: fdd ins fnl f **20/1**

0600 8 2 **Beverley Polo (IRE)**17 1344 3-8-7 52 ....(b) PaulMulrennan(3) 7 38
(M W Easterby) mid-div: rdn over 2f out: rdn and hdwy whn nt clr run wl over 1f out: wknd ins fnl f **16/1**

0600 9 5 **Arisea (IRE)**9 1571 3-8-5 47 oh1 ow1 ....(p) PaulEddery 9 18
(R C Guest) hld up: struggling fr 1/2-way **40/1**

0001 10 nk **Seesawmilu (IRE)**10 1549 3-8-9 51 6ex .... AdrianTNicholls 12 21
(E J Alston) w ldr over 1f: prom tl wknd over 2f out **5/1**2

0324 11 2 **Hillbilly Cat (USA)**21 1259 3-9-2 58 .... PaulFessey 10 22
(T D Barron) led: hdd over 3f out: rdn over 2f out: wknd over 1f out **5/1**2

000 12 shd **Cuccinello (IRE)**249 5148 3-8-2 47 oh16 ow1 .... PatrickMathers(3) 4 10
(K W Hogg) rrd up and wnt rt leaving stalls: a bhd **100/1**

005 13 9 **Flaming Cat (IRE)**342 2440 3-9-1 57 .... PatCosgrave 5 —
(J Wade) hmpd s: rdn wl over 2f out: a bhd **25/1**

1m 17.35s (3.74) **Going Correction** +0.30s/f (Good) 13 Ran SP% **118.2**
Speed ratings (Par 97):87,85,85,85,83 82,81,78,71,71 68,68,56
CSF £158.21 CT £1832.96 TOTE £29.10: £5.20, £2.10, £3.00; EX 211.80.
Owner J W Barrett **Bred** Ballyhane Stud **Trained** Cartmel, Cumbria
■ Stewards' Enquiry : Paul Eddery one-day ban: using whip when out of contention (May 29)

FOCUS
A low-grade sprint handicap, no better than a seller and the form is weak. The middle of the track seemed to be the place to be.

1793 PENRITH BUILDING SUPPLIES H'CAP 5f

8:00 (8:00) (Class 5) (0-70,70) 3-Y-O £3,886 (£1,156; £577; £288) Stalls High

Form RPR

0410 1 **Mormeatmic**17 1344 3-8-7 62 .... PaulMulrennan(3) 7 69
(M W Easterby) mde most: rdn over 1f out: edgd lft ins fnl f: hld on **5/2**1

1000 2 nk **Making Music**12 1497 3-8-12 64 .... DavidAllan 5 70
(T D Easterby) hld up: hdwy over 2f out: rdn and ev ch fr over 1f out: edgd rt ins fnl f: r.o **13/2**

2004 3 1 1/4 **Hypnosis**13 1453 3-8-8 60 .... TomEaves 6 62
(D W Barker) trckd ldrs: rdn over 1f out: styd on **6/1**3

6006 4 3 1/2 **Alugat (IRE)**190 6296 3-9-4 70 .... TonyCulhane 2 59
(Mrs A Duffield) hld up: hdwy 2f out: rdn over 1f out: edgd rt and no imp on ldrs ins fnl f **5/1**2

4332 5 2 1/2 **Highland Song (IRE)**13 1453 3-9-4 70 .... FrancisNorton 3 51
(R F Fisher) chsd ldrs: rdn whn nt clr run briefly wl over 1f out: sn btn **5/2**1

0036 6 8 **Obergurgl (IRE)**188 6311 3-9-0 66 .... PaulFessey 1 19
(Mrs A Duffield) slt jump bef stalls opened: w wnr after 1f: rdn over 2f out: edgd lft wl over 1f out: sn wknd **10/1**

64.04 secs (2.54) **Going Correction** +0.30s/f (Good) 6 Ran SP% **110.5**
Speed ratings (Par 99):91,90,88,82,78 66
CSF £18.51 TOTE £3.40: £1.90, £3.30; EX 15.50.
Owner M Broad & Mrs M E Attwood **Bred** A C Birkle **Trained** Sheriff Hutton, N Yorks
■ Stewards' Enquiry : Paul Mulrennan one-day ban: used whip with excessive frequency and without giving gelding time to respond (May 31)

FOCUS
A modest sprint handicap with three in line a furlong out. The time was moderate and the form is ordinary.

1794 DOBIES FOR VAUXHALL H'CAP 5f

8:30 (8:31) (Class 6) (0-60,60) 4-Y-O+ £2,730 (£806; £403) Stalls Low

Form RPR

0003 1 **Petite Mac**14 1443 6-8-2 51 .... SuzzanneFrance(7) 13 69
(N Bycroft) trckd ldrs: drvn to ld 1f out: sn clr: r.o wl **16/1**

0126 2 4 **Compton Classic**7 1611 4-8-9 51 ow1 ....(p) FergalLynch 7 55
(J S Goldie) hld up: swtchd rt and nt clr run briefly jst ins 2f out: hdwy over 1f out: rdn 2nd wl ins fnl f: nt trble wnr **9/1**

3004 3 1 **Monte Major (IRE)**7 1611 5-8-8 53 ....(v) PatrickMathers(3) 9 54
(D Shaw) sn drvn towards rr: rdn and hdwy 1f out: kpt on **14/1**

6000 4 3/4 **Grey Cossack**295 3847 9-9-4 60 .... TomEaves 6 58
(Mrs L Stubbs) s.i.s: hld up: hdwy and edgd rt wl over 1f out: styd on ins fnl f **25/1**

2030 5 1 **Blue Maeve**22 1235 6-8-7 52 .... SilvestreDeSousa(3) 15 46
(A D Brown) s.i.s: hdwy over 3f out: rdn 2f out: one pce ins fnl f **14/1**

4000 6 nk **Harrington Bates**28 1102 5-8-6 48 .... DavidAllan 10 41
(R M Whitaker) in rr: rdn over 2f out: n.m.r over 1f out: kpt on wl ins fnl f **22/1**

6050 7 3/4 **Unlimited**11 1504 4-9-4 60 .... TonyCulhane 17 51
(Mrs A Duffield) chsd ldrs: rdn wl over 1f out: no ex ins fnl f **9/1**

5200 8 1/2 **Percy Douglas**22 1243 6-8-6 55 ow1 ....(bt) AnnStokell(7) 4 44
(Miss A Stokell) w ldrs: rdn 2f out: wknd ins fnl f **25/1**

0150 9 1/2 **Muktasb (USA)**7 1611 5-8-10 52 ....(v) JoeFanning 1 39
(D Shaw) hld up: rdn 2f out: nvr on terms **12/1**

6202 10 shd **Quantica (IRE)**10 1528 7-8-10 52 .... KimTinkler 16 39
(N Tinkler) in tch: drvn along and lost pl wl over 2f out: no imp whn edgd rt over 1f out **11/2**2

1620 11 shd **Piccleyes**11 1504 5-8-12 54 .... DeanMcKeown 2 41
(M J Polglase) mid-div: rdn 2f out: n.d **20/1**

0013 12 1 3/4 **Coconut Moon**138 6696 4-9-0 56 .... PaulQuinn 14 36
(E J Alston) sn led: rdn over 1f out: sn hdd: wknd ins fnl f **5/1**1

0000 13 1 3/4 **Chairman Bobby**3 1735 8-8-8 55 .... AndrewMullen(5) 8 29
(D W Barker) prom: rdn 3f out: wknd wl over 1f out **20/1**

0422 **14** ½ **He's A Rocket (IRE)**[26] 1150 5-8-12 **54**....................(b) FrancisNorton 11 27
(K R Burke) *led early: hmpd over 3f out: rdn and wknd over 1f out: eased whn no ch ins fnl f* **7/1**[3]

0035 **15** *11* **Mill By The Stream**[19] 1303 4-8-7 **49**............................ MickyFenton 12 —
(P T Midgley) *chsd ldrs over 2f* **14/1**

300 **16** *29* **Pyramid**[15] 1414 4-8-8 **53**.........................(b) PaulMulrennan(3) 3 —
(P L Gilligan) *s.i.s: a bhd: lost tch wl over 3f out* **14/1**

62.26 secs (0.76) **Going Correction** +0.30s/f (Good) **16** Ran SP% **126.4**
Speed ratings (Par 101):105,98,97,95,94 93,92,91,90,90 90,87,85,84,66 20
CSF £146.56 CT £2090.77 TOTE £23.20: £3.70, £2.10, £3.50, £7.60; EX 261.40.
Owner N Bycroft **Bred** T Umpleby **Trained** Brandsby, N Yorks

FOCUS
A low-grade sprint handicap, no better than a seller, but the form looks sound rated around the placed horses. The winner found a real kick to record career win number three but she will have a lot more on her plate when she is reassessed.
Coconut Moon Official explanation: jockey said filly was unsuited by the good to soft, good in places ground

1795 BOOK NOW FOR MUSIC NIGHT 8TH JULY H'CAP 5f 193y
9:00 (9:01) (Class 5) (0-70,70) 4-Y-0+ **£3,238** (£963; £481; £240) **Stalls** High

Form RPR

2210 **1** **Geojimali**[10] 1528 4-8-4 **56** oh2.. JoeFanning 15 69+
(J S Goldie) *hld up: nt clr run 2f out: hdwy over 1f out: r.o wl to ld wl ins fnl f: won gng away* **6/1**[2]

0000 **2** *2* **Distant Times**[19] 1285 5-8-13 **65**..................................(b) FergalLynch 12 72
(T D Easterby) *hld up: drvn 3f out: hdwy over 1f out: r.o wl ins fnl f to take 2nd last stride* **18/1**

0330 **3** *nk* **Word Perfect**[36] 977 4-8-12 **64**.. DaleGibson 1 70
(M W Easterby) *trckd ldrs: rdn 2f out: wnt 2nd wl ins fnl f tl last stride* **11/1**

0005 **4** ¾ **Apex**[5] 1686 5-9-4 **70**.. KimTinkler 3 74
(N Tinkler) *dwlt: bhd: rdn and hdwy over 1f out: kpt on ins fnl f* **10/1**

1602 **5** *nk* **Desert Opal**[9] 1563 6-8-9 **61**... TonyCulhane 6 64
(D W Chapman) *led early: w ldr: drvn to ld over 1f out: hdd wl ins fnl f: no ex* **7/1**[3]

0006 **6** ½ **Baron Rhodes**[5] 1686 5-9-3 **69**.......................................(p) TomEaves 16 70
(J S Wainwright) *in tch: rdn wl over 2f out: hung lft jst over 1f out: styd on same pce* **16/1**

5005 **7** 1 ¼ **Dispol Peto**[11] 1504 6-7-13 **58** oh7 ow2.................(v) PatrickDonaghy(7) 5 56
(R Johnson) *mid-div: drvn over 3f out: hdwy and hung rt ins fnl f: nt trble ldrs* **66/1**

2464 **8** *nk* **Dorn Dancer (IRE)**[5] 1686 4-8-12 **64**.............................. PhillipMakin 17 61
(D W Barker) *prom on ins: rdn and edgd lft 2f out: fdd wl ins fnl f* **7/4**[1]

600 **9** ½ **Dazzler Mac**[248] 5189 5-8-5 **57** oh1 ow1............................ NeilPollard 14 52
(N Bycroft) *hld up: rdn and edgd rt over 1f out: nvr on terms* **33/1**

4040 **10** ½ **First Rhapsody (IRE)**[21] 1253 4-8-1 **56** oh4......... SilvestreDeSousa(3) 4 50
(T J Etherington) *dwlt: hld up: hmpd ins fnl f: nvr able to chal* **25/1**

6240 **11** *1* **Millsy**[244] 5277 4-8-6 **58**.. AdrianTNicholls 8 49
(J L Spearing) *sn led: rdn and hdd over 1f out: wknd wl ins fnl f* **20/1**

3201 **12** ½ **Flying Edge (IRE)**[236] 5469 6-9-0 **66**.............................. FrancisNorton 7 55
(E J Alston) *hld up in tch: rdn 2f out: wknd ins fnl f* **12/1**

0030 **13** 1 ½ **Bundy**[44] 864 10-8-4 **56** oh1.. PaulFessey 10 41
(M Dods) *mid-div: rdn and wknd over 2f out* **16/1**

1606 **14** *nk* **Mind Alert**[41] 903 5-8-2 **57** oh9 ow1....................(v) PatrickMathers(3) 13 41
(D Shaw) *chsd ldrs over 2f* **50/1**

1413 **15** *hd* **Desert Light (IRE)**[16] 1383 5-8-12 **64**.........................(v) MickyFenton 2 47
(D Shaw) *hld up and bhd: drvn wl over 2f out: no rspnse* **16/1**

0000 **16** *1* **Jadan (IRE)**[32] 1031 5-9-2 **68**.. DavidAllan 11 48
(E J Alston) *plld v hrd in mid-div: rdn over 1f out: wknd fnl f* **25/1**

0504 **17** ½ **No Time (IRE)**[15] 1399 6-9-1 **67**.................................(p) DeanMcKeown 9 46
(M J Polglase) *prom tl rdn and lost pl over 1f out: wknd fnl f* **28/1**

1m 15.49s (1.88) **Going Correction** +0.30s/f (Good) **17** Ran SP% **133.5**
Speed ratings (Par 103):99,96,95,94,94 93,92,91,91,90 89,88,86,86,85 84,83
CSF £111.36 CT £1242.24 TOTE £7.60: £1.70, £5.90, £3.70, £3.30; EX 308.70 Place 6 £481.34, Place 5 £429.54..
Owner Mrs D I Goldie **Bred** Jim Goldie **Trained** Uplawmoor, E Renfrews

FOCUS
The fastest race of the night and the winner was quite impressive. The form looks solid and should work out.
T/Plt: £590.40 to a £1 stake. Pool: £48,611.05. 60.10 winning tickets. T/Qpdt: £260.70 to a £1 stake. Pool: £3,136.00. 8.90 winning tickets. DO

1512 SALISBURY (R-H)
Thursday, May 18
OFFICIAL GOING: Good to soft (good in places)
Wind: fairly strong, slightly across (a drying wind)

1796 KNIGHTS & CO MAIDEN STKS 5f
1:55 (1:56) (Class 4) 2-Y-0 **£4,857** (£1,445; £722; £360) **Stalls** Centre

Form RPR

1 **Strategic Prince** 2-9-3 .... EddieAhern 13 84+
(P F I Cole) *a.p: led 2f out: drifted lft ins fnl f: r.o: rdn out* **12/1**

4 **2** 1 ¼ **Longquan (IRE)**[24] 1189 2-9-0 .... AmirQuinn(3) 7 80
(P J Makin) *prom: rdn and hung rt over 1f out: r.o wl ins fnl f: tk 2nd fnl stride* **4/1**[1]

3 *shd* **Dazed And Amazed** 2-9-3 .... RyanMoore 12 79
(R Hannon) *led tl over 3f out: prom: rdn and ev ch over 1f out: drifted lft and no ex ins fnl f* **5/1**[2]

4 ½ **Vital Statistics** 2-8-12 .... TQuinn 6 72
(D R C Elsworth) *chsd ldrs: rdn over 2f out: kpt on same pce fnl f* **8/1**

02 **5** *nk* **Benllech**[8] 1587 2-9-3 .... JimmyFortune 1 76
(S Kirk) *mid div: stdy prog fr over 2f out: r.o fnl 75yds: nrst fin* **4/1**[1]

6 **6** 1 ¼ **Bahamian Love**[23] 1203 2-8-12 .... RHills 9 67
(B W Hills) *prom: led over 3f out tl 2f out: sn rdn: wknd ins fnl f* **13/2**[3]

7 *5* **Buzbury Rings** 2-9-3 .... TPQueally 5 54
(A M Balding) *a mid div* **25/1**

8 *1* **Compton Fields** 2-9-3 .... SteveDrowne 11 50
(R Charlton) *wnt rt s: nvr bttr than mid div* **16/1**

9 1 ¼ **Dee Jay Wells** 2-9-3 .... PatDobbs 2 46
(R Hannon) *s.i.s: a towards rr* **33/1**

10 *shd* **Pas De Trois** 2-9-3 .... StephenCarson 10 45
(R F Johnson Houghton) *s.i.s: sn chsng ldrs: wknd over 1f out* **10/1**

11 *1* **Two Sips Sue** 2-8-7 .... StephenDonohoe(5) 3 37
(P D Evans) *slowy into stride: a bhd* **50/1**

12 *8* **Briarwood Bear** 2-9-3 .... FergusSweeney 4 13
(M Blanshard) *a towards rr* **66/1**

62.27 secs (0.68) **Going Correction** +0.075s/f (Good) **12** Ran SP% **114.0**
Speed ratings (Par 95):97,95,94,94,93 91,83,81,79,79 78,65
CSF £55.88 TOTE £12.30: £3.90, £1.60, £2.20; EX 108.40.
Owner H R H Sultan Ahmad Shah **Bred** The Ausherra Partnership **Trained** Whatcombe, Oxon

FOCUS
A mixed bunch, but the form looks sound rated around the second and fifth. The first three home are probably quite useful and there will be other winners in the field too.

NOTEBOOK
Strategic Prince, a strongly-made, scopey son of Dansili, carried condition but showed excellent pace throughout and saw it out really well. He should be even better over an extra furlong, and the Coventry Stakes at Royal Ascot must be an option following this encouraging debut. (op 11-1)
Longquan(IRE) looks as if a step up to six furlongs would be in his favour. This well-grown youngster is stronger than many of his rivals at present and should soon be off the mark.
Dazed And Amazed is a nippier-looking sort than the first two home, but he should still be better for the run. He has a speedy pedigree, and lived up to it, and must have a good chance of finding a similar race. (op 10-3)
Vital Statistics was recovering at the finish after struggling to hold her handy position entering the last quarter-mile. This was creditable debut against the colts, and an extra furlong should suit. (op 7-1 tchd 13-2 and 9-1)
Benllech was doing his best work at the end, and should find a race over an extra furlong. (op 5-1)
Bahamian Love again ran well enough to suggest she can break her duck if not aimed too high. She has plenty of early pace, so the minimum trip suits her well at present. (op 17-2 tchd 9-1)
Compton Fields muffed the start and never fully recovered, but this son of Compton Place has many winners in the family and he can significantly improve on this debut effort. (op 14-1)

1797 WINDSOR PLC MAIDEN FILLIES' STKS (DIV I) 1m 1f 198y
2:25 (2:26) (Class 4) 3-Y-0+ **£5,181** (£1,541; £770; £384) **Stalls** High

Form RPR

1 **Novellara** 3-8-9 .... EddieAhern 4 88+
(H R A Cecil) *travelled wl bhd ldrs: wnt 2nd over 3f out: shkn up to ld jst ins fnl f: styd on wl: pushed out* **9/2**[3]

0 **2** 1 ½ **Dayrose**[201] 6143 3-8-9 .... RyanMoore 1 85
(Sir Michael Stoute) *trckd ldr: led over 4f out: rdn 2f out: hdd jst ins fnl f: no ex* **7/2**[2]

3 1 ½ **Jewaar (USA)** 3-8-9 .... RHills 8 82+
(M A Jarvis) *t.k.h: sn in tch: trckd ldng pair over 2f out: swtchd lft and effrt over 1f out: 3rd and hld whn pitched ins fnl f* **6/4**[1]

03 **4** *7* **Dimelight**[173] 6428 3-8-9 .... TQuinn 10 69
(D R C Elsworth) *trckd ldrs: rdn over 2f out: wknd fnl f* **5/1**

5 *5* **Dream Witness (FR)** 3-8-9 .... SteveDrowne 11 60
(W R Muir) *stdd s: towards rr: sme hdwy over 3f out: rdn and no further imp fr 2f out* **50/1**

00 **6** 1 ½ **Colinette**[19] 1289 3-8-9 .... DaneO'Neill 7 57
(H Candy) *hld up towards rr: sme hdwy over 3f out: no further imp fr 2f out* **20/1**

3 **7** *7* **Loriinae**[14] 1434 3-8-9 .... IanMongan 3 43
(T G Mills) *in tch: rdn and effrt 3f out: wknd 2f out* **20/1**

05 **8** 1 ¼ **Kathleen Kennet**[19] 1289 6-9-9 .... FergusSweeney 2 41
(Mrs H Sweeting) *hld up towards rr: brief effrt over 3f out: wknd 2f out* **25/1**

40 **9** *shd* **Volaire**[5] 1670 4-9-6 .... RichardThomas(3) 5 41
(A J Lidderdale) *sn drvn along in rr: hdwy over 3f out: wknd 2f out* **100/1**

00 **10** *27* **Phills Pearl**[73] 590 3-8-6 .... AdamKirby(3) 9 —
(D Burchell) *led: rn wd on bnd 6f out: rdn and hdd over 4f out: sn wknd* **200/1**

2m 9.11s (0.65) **Going Correction** +0.075s/f (Good)
WFA 3 from 4yo+ 14lb **10** Ran SP% **113.9**
Speed ratings (Par 102):100,98,97,92,88 86,81,80,80,58
CSF £18.73 TOTE £5.30: £1.90, £1.90, £1.10; EX 24.40.
Owner K Abdulla **Bred** Juddmonte Farms Ltd **Trained** Newmarket, Suffolk

FOCUS
An above average maiden bdespite the ordinary gallop, so it helped to be handy, and the form should work out. Novellara made a stylish debut and has some fancy entries - she was as low as 33-1 for the Oaks after this.
Phills Pearl Official explanation: jockey said filly hung left-handed

1798 WINDSOR PLC MAIDEN FILLIES' STKS (DIV II) 1m 1f 198y
2:55 (2:58) (Class 4) 3-Y-0+ **£5,181** (£1,541; £770; £384) **Stalls** High

Form RPR

00 **1** **Oh Glory Be (USA)**[187] 6319 3-8-6 .... StephaneBreux(3) 8 74+
(R Hannon) *s.i.s: towards rr: gd hdwy fr 3f out: hung lft and led over 1f out: r.o wl* **14/1**

3 **2** 2 ½ **Garafena**[27] 1118 3-8-9 .... ShaneKelly 10 67
(Pat Eddery) *trckd ldrs: led over 3f out: sn rdn: hdd over 1f out: kpt on but no ch w wnr* **11/4**[2]

3 **3** *nk* **Gouranga**[232] 5555 3-8-9 .... DaneO'Neill 3 66
(H Candy) *chsd ldrs: carried wd on bnd 6f out: riden to chal wl over 2f out: kpt on same pce fnl f* **11/8**[1]

4 1 ¾ **Mawazeen (IRE)**[596] 5-9-2 .... MarkCoumbe(7) 6 64
(N I M Rossiter) *towards rr: tk clsr order 5f out: outpcd over 3f out: styd on fr 2f out: nrst fin* **66/1**

0 **5** *nk* **Consuelita**[24] 1191 3-8-9 .... JimmyFortune 1 62
(B J Meehan) *led tl over 3f out: sn rdn: wknd ins fnl f* **13/2**[3]

6 3 ½ **Knotted** 3-8-9 .... SteveDrowne 9 55
(R Charlton) *mid div: trckd ldrs 5f out: rdn 3f out: wknd 1f out* **8/1**

7 *1* **Tiz Timely (USA)** 3-8-6 .... NeilChalmers(3) 2 54
(A M Balding) *restrained s: bhd: hdwy 5f out: rdn over 2f out: wknd over 1f out* **16/1**

00 **8** ½ **Platinum Hound (IRE)**[15] 1417 3-8-9 .... RobertHavlin 7 53
(H Morrison) *mid div tl 4f out* **25/1**

500 **9** *23* **Khyber Knight (IRE)**[223] 5708 3-8-9 48 .... PaulFitzsimons 4 9
(Jane Southcombe) *plld v hrd: prom: rn wd on bnd 6f out: wknd over 3f out: t.o* **100/1**

2m 11.04s (2.58) **Going Correction** +0.075s/f (Good)
WFA 3 from 5yo 14lb **9** Ran SP% **112.1**
Speed ratings (Par 102):92,90,89,88,88 85,84,84,65
CSF £50.61 TOTE £20.10: £3.30, £1.50, £1.40; EX 62.40.
Owner I A N Wight **Bred** W S Farish **Trained** East Everleigh, Wilts

FOCUS
A fair fillies' maiden run at a routine gallop in the rain-softened ground. The form is rated around the placed horses.

1799 JOHN SCOTT MEMORIAL CLAIMING STKS 6f 212y
3:30 (3:30) (Class 5) 3-Y-O £3,562 (£1,059; £529; £264) Stalls Centre

Form RPR
3640 **1** **La Fanciulla**[10] 1551 3-9-0 68 .... RyanMoore 2 66
(R Hannon) *hld up bhd: smooth hdwy over 3f out: led over 2f out: sn rdn and hung rt: r.o: rdn out* **9/2**[3]
0030 **2** 1 ¼ **Mucho Loco (IRE)**[93] 415 3-9-0 57 .... (p) RichardMullen 1 63
(J G Portman) *hld up towards rr: hdwy over 3f out: rdn and ev ch 2f out: 2nd and hld whn n.m.r ins 1f out: hung rt cl home* **25/1**
2000 **3** 5 **Radius**[23] 1208 3-9-5 70 .... (t) SteveDrowne 12 55
(H Morrison) *led tl 4f out: sn rdn: ev ch 2f out: kpt on same pce* **9/1**
3045 **4** 4 **Mocha Java**[5] 1693 3-9-5 65 .... TQuinn 4 45
(P F I Cole) *in tch: rdn 3f out: ev ch over 2f out: one pce after* **11/4**[1]
0500 **5** hd **Tuscany Queen (IRE)**[14] 1433 3-8-3 50 .... RichardSmith(3) 7 31
(R Hannon) *chsd ldrs: outpcd over 3f out and stmbld: sme late prog but nvr a danger after* **20/1**
6002 **6** 1 ½ **Fallal Parc**[9] 1576 3-8-4 40 .... RichardThomas(3) 11 28
(M F Harris) *chsd ldrs: rdn over 3f out: one pce fnl 2f* **10/1**
0006 **7** 1 ¼ **Croft (IRE)**[15] 1416 3-8-11 64 .... EddieAhern 5 29
(J W Hills) *mid div: rdn over 3f out: wknd over 1f out* **9/2**[3]
1163 **8** ½ **The City Kid (IRE)**[128] 76 3-8-9 75 .... (b[1]) StephenDonohoe(3) 10 31
(P D Evans) *prom: led 4f out tl over 2f out: sn wknd* **4/1**[2]
3000 **9** dist **Twentyfirst Dansar**[17] 1352 3-8-9 54 .... (vt) FergusSweeney 8 —
(A D Smith) *prom for 4f: t.o and p.u to a walk ins fnl f* **50/1**

1m 29.85s (0.79) **Going Correction** +0.075s/f (Good) **9** Ran SP% **112.7**
Speed ratings (Par 99):98,96,90,86,86 84,82,82,—
CSF £107.09 TOTE £6.40: £1.80, £5.60, £3.50; EX 116.60.La Fanciulla was the subject of a friendly claim.
Owner Roger Barby **Bred** Lostford Manor Stud **Trained** East Everleigh, Wilts

FOCUS
A modest claimer run at a good gallop, setting the race up for two finishers from the rear. The form does not look that strong.
Twentyfirst Dansar Official explanation: jockey said gelding had a breathing problem

1800 BRIDGEND HOTEL, ISLAY FILLIES' H'CAP 1m 4f
4:05 (4:05) (Class 4) (0-85,78) 4-Y-O+ £7,124 (£2,119; £1,059; £529) Stalls High

Form RPR
005 **1** **Sunisa (IRE)**[19] 1281 5-9-2 76 .... NickyMackay 8 82
(J Mackie) *in tch: rdn 3f out: swtchd lft over 1f out: styd on wl to ld cl home: rdn out* **9/1**
1001 **2** 1 **Maystock**[5] 1690 6-8-11 71 6ex .... TedDurcan 9 75
(B G Powell) *chsd ldr: led over 2f out: sn rdn: hdd 1f out: rallied to ld again sn after: no ex whn ct cl home* **13/2**[3]
5104 **3** 1 **Queen Of Iceni**[26] 1132 4-8-12 72 .... TQuinn 4 75
(J L Dunlop) *trckd ldrs: rdn to chal 3f out: led briefly 1f out: no ex nr fin* **4/1**[2]
4 shd **Trompette (USA)**[22] 4-9-0 74 .... EddieAhern 5 79+
(N J Henderson) *hld up: smooth hdwy on rails to join ldrs 4f out: outpcd over 2f out: swtchd lft over 1f out: fin strly* **7/2**[1]
600- **5** 1 ¼ **Almah (SAF)**[28] 5784 8-9-1 75 .... (b) RyanMoore 2 76
(Miss Venetia Williams) *sn drvn into clr ld: rdn and hdd over 2f out: kpt on same pce* **12/1**
1166 **6** ½ **Ti Adora (IRE)**[183] 6371 4-8-13 73 .... SteveDrowne 7 73
(P W D'Arcy) *hld up in tch: rdn and effrt 3f out: kpt on same pce fnl 2f* **9/1**
4100 **7** 1 ¼ **Aoninch**[181] 5559 6-8-6 66 .... RobertHavlin 6 64
(Mrs P N Dutfield) *hld up bhd: stdy prog on bit fr 3f out: rdn and effrt over 1f out: wknd ins fnl f* **11/1**
1234 **8** 3 **Pine Cone (IRE)**[220] 5799 4-9-4 78 .... DaneO'Neill 1 73+
(A King) *in tch: rdn over 3f out: wknd over 1f out: eased whn btn ins fnl f* **4/1**[2]

2m 35.93s (-0.43) **Going Correction** +0.075s/f (Good) **8** Ran SP% **111.6**
Speed ratings (Par 102):104,103,102,102,101 101,100,98
CSF £62.48 CT £266.74 TOTE £12.50: £3.30, £2.00, £1.70; EX 72.50.
Owner G A Greaves **Bred** H De Bromhead **Trained** Church Broughton , Derbys

FOCUS
A fair race in which Sunisa's stamina won the day. The form is not that strong and rated around the first two back to their old form.

1801 JORDAN BROOKES CHARTERED ACCOUNTANTS H'CAP 6f
4:35 (4:38) (Class 5) (0-70,69) 3-Y-O £3,562 (£1,059; £529; £264) Stalls Centre

Form RPR
4440 **1** **Patavium Prince (IRE)**[6] 1642 3-8-12 63 .... TQuinn 3 73
(J R Best) *outpcd towards rr early: hdwy and swtchd lft to centre 2f out: r.o strly to ld fnl 100yds* **14/1**
0055 **2** 1 ½ **Arculinge**[14] 1431 3-8-4 55 .... NickyMackay 8 61
(M Blanshard) *mid div: hdwy over 2f out: sn rdn: ev ch ins fnl f: nt pce of wnr fnl 100yds* **20/1**
0000 **3** 1 ¼ **Catherines Cafe (IRE)**[45] 851 3-9-2 67 .... RobertHavlin 14 69
(Mrs P N Dutfield) *in tch: rdn to ld over 1f out: no ex whn hdd fnl 100yds* **20/1**
6133 **4** 2 **Guilded Warrior**[15] 1411 3-9-4 69 .... FergusSweeney 20 65+
(W S Kittow) *chsd ldrs: rdn 3f out: ev ch over 1f out: kpt on same pce* **6/1**[2]
1331 **5** ½ **Buzzin'Boyzee (IRE)**[22] 1232 3-8-8 59 .... RichardMullen 17 53
(P D Evans) *mid div: hdwy over 2f out: sn rdn: styd on ins fnl f* **14/1**
6004 **6** ½ **Mull Of Dubai**[9] 1567 3-8-10 61 .... LPKeniry 13 54
(J S Moore) *mid div: outpcd 3f out: styd on again ins fnl f:nrst fin* **12/1**
3221 **7** ¾ **George The Second**[9] 1567 3-8-7 61 6ex .... AdamKirby(3) 10 52
(Mrs H Sweeting) *w ldrs: rdn 3f out: ev ch 2f out: kpt on same pce* **7/2**[1]
000 **8** ¾ **Tamino (IRE)**[213] 5946 3-8-11 62 .... SteveDrowne 15 50+
(H Morrison) *bmpd s: sn prom: led 3f out: sn rdn: hdd over 1f out: wknd ins fnl f* **7/1**[3]
0000 **9** ½ **Montzando**[23] 1208 3-8-8 66 .... JamesMillman(7) 19 53+
(B R Millman) *bhd: hdwy and nt clr run over 1f out: nt a danger after* **20/1**
21 **10** shd **Bingo One (IRE)**[335] 2645 3-8-9 69 .... SaleemGolam(3) 4 55
(W J H Ratcliffe) *outpcd in rr: sme late prog: n.d* **14/1**
4106 **11** nk **Billy Bling (IRE)**[5] 1693 3-9-1 66 .... RyanMoore 12 52
(R Hannon) *in tch: rdn and effrt 3f out: wknd fnl f* **8/1**
0654 **12** 1 ¾ **Fratt'n Park (IRE)**[10] 1547 3-9-1 66 .... TPQueally 7 46
(J J Bridger) *chsd ldrs tl wknd 2f out* **14/1**
0460 **13** 2 **Miss Redactive**[14] 1431 3-8-4 55 .... HayleyTurner 16 29
(M D I Usher) *wnt lft s: sn chsng ldrs: wknd over 1f out* **33/1**
346 **14** 2 ½ **Hang Loose**[14] 1430 3-9-4 69 .... (b[1]) DaneO'Neill 18 36
(R Charlton) *led tl 3f out: sn wknd* **12/1**
5000 **15** 2 ½ **Sprouston (FR)**[27] 1109 3-8-2 60 .... JosephWalsh(7) 1 19
(J S Moore) *rrd s: a in rr* **40/1**
0200 **16** 3 ½ **Bella Bertolini**[313] 3346 3-9-4 69 .... IanMongan 11 18
(T G Mills) *mid div: hdwy over 2f out: wknd over 1f out* **25/1**

1m 15.24s (0.26) **Going Correction** +0.075s/f (Good) **16** Ran SP% **125.7**
Speed ratings (Par 99):101,99,97,94,94 93,92,91,90,90 90,87,85,81,78 73
CSF £281.04 CT £5727.05 TOTE £16.10: £3.30, £4.60, £4.90, £2.10; EX 275.70.
Owner Mr B Cains Mr C Purnell Mr Clements **Bred** J P Hardiman **Trained** Hucking, Kent

FOCUS
A modest handicap and the form looks sound, despite the leaders set off too fast, allowing Patavium Prince to sweep down the centre, and win going away.
Hang Loose Official explanation: jockey said saddle slipped

1802 AXMINSTER CARPETS APPRENTICE H'CAP 6f 212y
5:05 (5:06) (Class 5) (0-70,70) 4-Y-O+ £3,724 (£1,108; £553; £276) Stalls Centre

Form RPR
0002 **1** **Blue Java**[9] 1570 5-9-2 67 .... TravisBlock 16 78
(H Morrison) *chsd ldrs: rdn to ld over 1f out: kpt on wl* **7/4**[1]
-000 **2** 1 **Treasure House (IRE)**[26] 1151 5-9-1 66 .... LiamJones 10 74
(M Blanshard) *chsd ldrs: rdn 3f out: kpt on to go 2nd ins fnl f* **33/1**
2246 **3** ¾ **Meditation**[5] 1673 4-8-8 64 .... JamieHamblett(5) 8 70
(I A Wood) *chsd ldrs: led 3f out: sn rdn: hdd over 1f out: kpt on same pce* **5/1**[3]
1463 **4** hd **Rakata (USA)**[17] 1348 4-9-5 70 .... AndrewElliott 11 75
(P F I Cole) *in tch: rdn: hdwy and ev ch over 1f out: no ex* **9/2**[2]
0000 **5** 1 **Linda's Colin (IRE)**[101] 316 4-8-11 65 .... TolleyDean(3) 5 68
(R A Harris) *towards rr: rdn and no imp 3f out: styd on wl fnl f : nrst fin* **11/1**
0000 **6** 1 ½ **Simplify**[37] 972 4-8-5 56 .... (p) RonanKeogh 1 55
(T M Jones) *hld up towards rr: hdwy over 3f out: styd on fnl f* **20/1**
0055 **7** 1 ¾ **Blue Line**[18] 1311 4-8-2 56 oh1 .... ThomasO'Brien(3) 4 50
(M Madgwick) *bhd: rdn 3f out: styd on fr over 1f out: nvr trbld ldrs* **22/1**
4610 **8** ½ **Greenmeadow**[220] 5808 4-8-12 63 .... NicolPolli 18 56
(S Kirk) *in tch: rdn over 2f out: wknd fnl f* **25/1**
5000 **9** 1 ½ **Celtic Spa (IRE)**[23] 1207 4-9-2 67 .... StephanieHollinshead 7 56
(Mrs P N Dutfield) *hld up towards rr: sme prog over 2f out: no further imp fr over 1f out* **14/1**
0030 **10** 3 **Threezedzz**[12] 1480 8-9-3 68 .... (t) KevinGhunowa 12 49
(P D Evans) *led tl 3f out: grad fdd* **20/1**
0004 **11** shd **Trace Clip**[5] 1689 8-8-0 56 oh3 .... MarkCoumbe(5) 14 37
(N I M Rossiter) *dwlt: bhd: gd hdwy to trck ldrs over 4f out: wknd over 1f out* **16/1**
3300 **12** 1 **Pink Bay**[41] 902 4-8-9 65 .... LukeMorris(5) 17 44
(W S Kittow) *chsd ldrs for 4f* **20/1**
6000 **13** 4 **Yorkies Boy**[227] 5653 11-8-0 56 oh16 .... SophieDoyle(5) 2 24
(N E Berry) *mid div tl 3f out* **66/1**

1m 28.67s (-0.39) **Going Correction** +0.075s/f (Good) **13** Ran SP% **119.0**
Speed ratings (Par 103):105,103,103,102,101 99,97,97,95,92 92,90,86
CSF £83.08 CT £260.70 TOTE £2.40: £1.50, £6.80, £2.30; EX 85.50 Place 6 £99.99, Place 5 £48.33..
Owner Pangfield Partners **Bred** T J Billington **Trained** East Ilsley, Berks

FOCUS
An ordinary handicap and solid enough form rated through the winner and fourth.
Celtic Spa(IRE) Official explanation: jockey said filly was unsuited by the going - good to soft, good in places
T/Plt: £122.10 to a £1 stake. Pool: £34,179.35. 204.30 winning tickets. T/Qpdt: £51.40 to a £1 stake. Pool: £2,029.90. 29.20 winning tickets. TM

1775 YORK (L-H)
Thursday, May 18

OFFICIAL GOING: Soft
Wind: strong, half across

1803 TOTESPORT.COM H'CAP 5f
1:45 (1:46) (Class 2) (0-100,100) 3-Y-O+ £16,516 (£4,913; £2,455; £1,226) Stalls Centre

Form RPR
0120 **1** **Trinculo (IRE)**[7] 1602 9-8-12 88 .... AdrianTNicholls 5 99
(D Nicholls) *a.p: rdn to ld over 1f out: kpt on wl* **16/1**
6064 **2** ¾ **Orientor**[27] 1116 8-9-10 100 .... KFallon 11 108+
(J S Goldie) *lw: towards rr: gd hdwy wl over 1f out: rdn and styd on strly ins lastr* **5/1**[3]
0000 **3** ½ **Enchantment**[7] 1602 5-8-12 88 .... (p) LDettori 4 95
(J M Bradley) *led 2f: cl up: rdn and ev ch over 1f out: drvn and nt qckn ins last* **20/1**
4255 **4** ½ **Fromsong (IRE)**[27] 1116 8-9-8 98 .... JohnEgan 2 103
(D K Ivory) *in tch: hdwy and pushed along 2f out: sn rdn and kpt on ins last* **25/1**
2320 **5** 1 ½ **King's Gait**[12] 1487 4-9-5 95 .... (b) DavidAllan 10 95
(T D Easterby) *chsd ldrs: rdn along 2f out: grad wknd appr last* **8/1**
0101 **6** ¾ **Zowington**[22] 1236 4-9-4 94 .... GeorgeBaker 9 91
(C F Wall) *in tch: pushed along and outpcd over 2f out: sn riddn: styd on ins last: nrst fin* **15/2**
3141 **7** 2 ½ **Swinbrook (USA)**[19] 1285 5-8-12 88 .... (v) SebSanders 7 77
(J A R Toller) *towards rr and sn pushed along: rdn along 2f out: nvr nr ldrs* **7/2**[1]
5020 **8** 1 ¾ **Cape Royal**[7] 1602 6-9-7 97 .... (t) KDarley 1 80
(J M Bradley) *cl up: led after 2f: rdn along and hdd over 1f out: sn wknd* **11/1**
61-1 **9** 3 ½ **Desert Commander (IRE)**[27] 1125 4-8-13 89 .... NCallan 8 60
(K A Ryan) *lw: chsd ldrs: rdn along 2f out: sn wknd* **4/1**[2]
0000 **10** 15 **Just James**[243] 5288 7-9-10 100 .... RichardHughes 6 20
(D Nicholls) *lw: dwlt: a rr: hung bdly lft and eased fnl 2f* **33/1**
3160 **11** 16 **Desperate Dan**[89] 450 5-9-0 90 .... (b) JamieSpencer 3 —
(J A Osborne) *chsd ldrs: rdn along 1/2-way: sn wknd and eased wl over 1f out* **14/1**

60.20 secs (0.88) **Going Correction** +0.475s/f (Yiel) **11** Ran SP% **114.2**
Speed ratings (Par 109):111,109,109,108,105 104,100,97,92,68 42
CSF £89.37 CT £1647.88 TOTE £19.30: £3.60, £1.70, £4.30; EX 99.90 Trifecta £1076.40 Part won. Pool £1,516.10 - 0.40 winning units..
Owner Nigel Shields **Bred** Humphrey Okeke **Trained** Sessay, N Yorks

FOCUS
A competitive sprint handicap in which, as is usual for this track, it paid to race prominently. The form is not rock-solid.

NOTEBOOK
Trinculo(IRE) has been in good form this spring and could easily be excused his latest effort at Chester when he was drawn out wide and unsurprisingly did not get a clear run. The ground was also more in his favour this time as he likes to get his toe in.
Orientor is a smart performer but he rarely wins and, despite having conditions to suit, he once again found one too good. He still did much the best of those who were held up for a late run, though, on a track which regularly favours pacesetters.
Enchantment, who is back down to a mark in the 80s for the first time in almost two years, was perhaps helped by the easier ground and ran her best race for some time. She is a prominent racer, suited by the way races are ofen won over sprint distances here. (tchd 18-1)
Fromsong(IRE), who probably ran a bit better than the bare form suggested at Newbury last time, ran another solid race, but the impression left was that he remains in the grip of the Handicapper.
King's Gait had conditions to suit but his performances this season very much suggest that the Handicapper has got his measure now.
Zowington, despite being by Zafonic, is perfectly happy on this sort of ground, but he struggled to pick up when the pace quickened inside the final three furlongs and failed to make up much ground from the rear. On this track it pays to race more prominently. (op 8-1)
Swinbrook(USA), whose Leicester form had been boosted by the subsequent successes of the second and fourth, looked to hold a strong chance in this company off an 8lb higher mark, but he was dropping back in trip from six furlongs and simply could not go the early pace. That cost him in a race where early speed was crucial and those at the head of affairs dominated. (op 4-1)
Cape Royal, another infrequent winner who looks handicapped up to the hilt, had ground conditions to suit and was up there for a lot of the way, but he weakened disappointingly from a furlong out. (op 12-1)
Desert Commander(IRE), put up 11lb for his Thirsk win on his first outing since August 2004, proved disappointing. He may have 'bounced' or perhaps the ground proved too soft for this son of Green Desert. (op 7-2 tchd 9-2 after 3-1 and early 10-3 in a place)
Just James Official explanation: jockey said gelding was never travelling
Desperate Dan was eased down by Spencer as though something had gone amiss. Official explanation: jockey said gelding was unsuited by the soft ground (op 20-1)

1804 TOTEPOOL MIDDLETON STKS (GROUP 3) (F&M) 1m 2f 88y
2:15 (2:15) (Class 1) 4-Y-O+

£28,390 (£10,760; £5,385; £2,685; £1,345; £675) **Stalls** Low

Form RPR
1001 **1** **Strawberry Dale (IRE)**[194] 6253 4-8-12 104 JamieSpencer 4 109
(J D Bethell) *mde all: rdn clr wl over 1f out: comf* **8/1**
5043 **2** *3* **Mango Mischief (IRE)**[11] 1506 5-9-0 103 SebSanders 1 106
(J L Dunlop) *trckd winenr: hdwy to chal 3f out and ev ch tl rdn and one pce fr over 1f out* **6/1**[3]
25-1 **3** *2 ½* **Portrayal (USA)**[217] 5849 4-8-12 112 LDettori 3 103+
(Saeed Bin Suroor) *hld up in tch: hdwy to trck ldrs 3f out: rdn and ch wl over 1f out: drvn and wknd ins last* **5/4**[1]
3216 **4** *3 ½* **Red Bloom**[228] 5648 5-9-2 111 KFallon 7 98
(Sir Michael Stoute) *trckd ldrs: rapid hdwy to join ldrs 1/2-way: cl up 4f out: rdn along 3f out and sn wknd* **9/4**[2]
5451 **5** *½* **Ma'Am (USA)**[25] 1164 4-8-12 72 MickyFenton 2 93?
(I A Wood) *a rr* **100/1**
0010 **6** *5* **Tarandot (IRE)**[194] 6254 5-8-12 93 NCallan 6 84
(G G Margarson) *chsd ldrs: rdn along over 3f out: sn outpcd* **33/1**
1 **7** *22* **Umthoulah (IRE)**[273] 4502 4-8-12 80 RobertWinston 5 47
(K R Burke) *dwlt: a rr* **66/1**

2m 19.41s (8.93) **Going Correction** +1.00s/f (Soft) **7** Ran SP% **106.0**
Speed ratings (Par 113):104,101,99,96,96 92,74
CSF £45.49 TOTE £8.70: £3.00, £2.40; EX 41.20.
Owner M J Dawson **Bred** Bryan Ryan **Trained** Middleham Moor, N Yorks

FOCUS
With the first two in the betting failing to run to their best this probably did not take that much winning. The form, rated through the runner-up for now, is not that solid.

NOTEBOOK
Strawberry Dale(IRE), a progressive performer last season whose campaign was capped with a win in Listed company at Doncaster, had Mango Mischief over ten lengths behind her that day, and had no trouble confirming that form on her reappearance. She loves this sort of ground, and, while the form may not be the soundest, she will always be of interest when conditions are in her favour. She apparently heads to Cork next for a similar contest.
Mango Mischief(IRE), over ten lengths behind Strawberry Dale at Doncaster on her final start last season, had the benefit of a recent outing over that rival this time, but she could not make it pay. She is, however, reasonably comfortable running in soft ground, and that was enough to ensure a prominent display in a race where the market leaders failed to run to their best. (op 8-1)
Portrayal(USA), a winner on her only start at three in a Listed contest at Newmarket, should not have had a problem with the ground, but her stable's runners have not been firing this spring and she is not the first to disappoint despite fairly strong market support. She could well leave this form behind later in the season. (tchd 11-10, 11-8 in a place)
Red Bloom, who had to give weight all round following her success in a Group 2 race last season, is by Selkirk, but she has a clear preference for quick ground so conditions were hardly ideal. (op 2-1 tchd 5-2 in a place)
Ma'Am(USA), a winner of an All-Weather handicap off a mark of 68 last time, was chasing some black type and had a mountain to climb at the weights. On the face of it she ran well, but the form is almost certainly misleading.
Tarandot(IRE) likes this sort of ground but she had a job on at the weights and was running over a trip a long way short of her best. She should come on for the run. (tchd 28-1)
Umthoulah(IRE) beat a modest bunch when winning her maiden on fast ground at Chester last summer so this was a big jump in class, and the ground may well have been softer than she wants. Official explanation: jockey said filly was unsuited by the soft ground (op 50-1)

1805 TOTESPORT DANTE STKS (GROUP 2) 1m 2f 88y
2:45 (2:46) (Class 1) 3-Y-O

£82,331 (£31,204; £15,616; £7,786; £3,900; £1,957) **Stalls** Low

Form RPR
130 **1** **Septimus (IRE)**[25] 1179 3-9-0 KFallon 4 119
(A P O'Brien, Ire) *lw: scope: trckd ldrs: hdwy 4f out: rdn to ld 2f out: drvn clr ent last and styd on wl* **13/8**[1]
0314 **2** *8* **Best Alibi (IRE)**[208] 6019 3-9-0 103 MJKinane 5 106+
(Sir Michael Stoute) *h.d.w: prom: hdwy to ld over 6f out: rdn along 3f out: hdd 2f out: rallied over 1f out: sn one pce* **6/1**
4431 **3** *11* **Snoqualmie Boy**[11] 1515 3-9-0 82 JohnEgan 1 88
(D R C Elsworth) *lw: hld up: hdwy 4f out: sn rdn and plugged on one pce fnl 2f* **16/1**
1 **4** *1 ½* **Leningrad (IRE)**[45] 850 3-9-0 JamieSpencer 2 86
(M L W Bell) *hld up: hdwy 4f out: rdn along 3f out and no imp* **9/2**[3]
512 **5** *8* **The Last Drop (IRE)**[19] 1300 3-9-0 92 MichaelHills 3 73
(B W Hills) *prom: rdn along over 4f out: sn wknd* **10/1**
1351 **6** *29* **Palace Episode (USA)**[208] 6019 3-9-0 LDettori 6 27
(Saeed Bin Suroor) *led 4f: rdn along to chse wnr over 3f out: sn drvn and wknd qckly: eased and virtually p.u fnl 2f* **10/3**[2]

2m 17.55s (7.07) **Going Correction** +1.00s/f (Soft) **6** Ran SP% **108.6**
Speed ratings (Par 111):111,104,95,94,88 65
CSF £10.96 TOTE £2.70: £1.70, £3.10; EX 14.70.
Owner D Smith, Mrs J Magnier & M Tabor **Bred** Barronstown Stud & Orpendale **Trained** Ballydoyle, Co Tipperary

FOCUS
Perhaps not the classiest of renewals on paper but Septimus has been rated up to scratch for a Dante winner. Four of the last 12 Derby winners won the Dante on their previous start.

NOTEBOOK
Septimus(IRE), whose trainer's runners have been improving for their reappearance outings, stepped up considerably on his effort in France and ran out the most convincing winner of any of the Derby trials run in this country. Off a good pace in testing ground, he saw the trip out strongly, giving every indication that, as his breeding suggests, he will only improve further for a step up to a mile and a half. Fallon suggested that faster ground would hold no fears for him. While he does not do anything quickly, a likely strong pace at Epsom will suit him very well, and few will be staying on stronger at the finish. He may turn out to be a Leger horse, but at this stage no horse in the Derby betting looks more certain to make the frame, at least, in the Blue Riband. (op 15-8 tchd 2-1 in places)
Best Alibi(IRE), one place behind Septimus in the Racing Post Trophy on his final start at two, helped make it a proper test in the ground by stepping on the gas once he hit the front. He did not see it out as well as the winner in the end, but he could well improve for this seasonal reappearance and for faster ground. With Epsom in mind, though, it is worth noting that no horse beaten in the Dante has ever gone on to win the Derby. (op 11-2 tchd 13-2)
Snoqualmie Boy, a handicap winner off a mark of 82 last time, tried to go with the first two in the straight but was soon left behind. He still ran well enough, though, given that he had plenty on his plate strictly on the book, and on faster ground he may well prove himself up to competing in Listed company later this season.
Leningrad(IRE), whose place in the market was certainly not based on his form as he only had a minor Polytrack maiden success to his name, was found out on this step up in grade. However, it would be wrong to judge a horse too harshly on his performance in these testing conditions, and he may yet prove himself Group class on quicker ground later in the year. (tchd 4-1 and 5-1 in a place)
The Last Drop(IRE), whose Sandown Classic Trial form has been let down a number of times and who looked very fit for this, may not have liked the ground much but he may well be overrated anyhow.
Palace Episode(USA) was the one to beat on his Racing Post Trophy victory in heavy ground, when he had Septimus and Best Alibi behind, but he has not grown much over the winter and his stable is woefully out of form. Needless to say this was a very disappointing effort and Godolphin will be hoping that something will come to light, as otherwise it looks like they have bought a dud. Official explanation: trainer had no explanation for the poor form shown (op 3-1 tchd 7-2 in places)

1806 BANK OF SCOTLAND CORPORATE HAMBLETON STKS (H'CAP) (LISTED RACE) 1m
3:15 (3:15) (Class 1) (0-110,108) 4-Y-O+**£20,744** (£7,843; £3,920; £1,960) **Stalls** Low

Form RPR
3140 **1** **Zero Tolerance (IRE)**[17] 1371 6-9-1 102 JamieSpencer 8 111
(T D Barron) *lw: mde all: qcknd over 2f out: rdn over 1f out: styd on strly ins last* **9/2**[2]
0562 **2** *hd* **Babodana**[19] 1299 6-9-7 108 DarryllHolland 4 117
(M H Tompkins) *trckd ldrs: hdwy 3f out: rdn wl over 1f out:d riven and styd on wl fnl furlong: edgd rt and hld nr fin* **6/1**[3]
2311 **3** *2 ½* **Dabbers Ridge (IRE)**[6] 1629 4-8-7 93 3ex MichaelHills 6 98
(B W Hills) *lw: trckd wnr: effrt to chal over 2f out: sn rdna nd ev ch tl drvn and wknd ent last* **15/8**[1]
0103 **4** *½* **Blythe Knight (IRE)**[12] 1489 6-9-0 101 GrahamGibbons 10 104
(J J Quinn) *lw: trckd ldrs: effrt over 2f out: sn rdn: kpt on same pce u.p fnl f* **10/1**
0000 **5** *5* **Cool Panic (IRE)**[5] 1667 4-8-7 94 RobertWinston 7 87
(M L W Bell) *t.k.h: chsd ldrs: hdwy 3f out: sn rdn along and no imp fnl 2f* **20/1**
1643 **6** *hd* **Kings Point (IRE)**[19] 1299 5-9-4 105 TonyHamilton 2 97
(R A Fahey) *in tch: hdwy over 3f out: sn rdn along and no imp fnl 2f* **16/1**
3103 **7** *2 ½* **Chrysander**[28] 1098 4-9-4 105 ChrisCatlin 9 92
(M R Channon) *nvr bttr than midfield* **33/1**
0005 **8** *¾* **Tucker**[29] 1084 4-9-2 103 JohnEgan 13 89
(D R C Elsworth) *chsd ldrs: rdn along 4f out: sn wknd* **16/1**
0310 **9** *3* **Pentecost**[97] 370 7-9-4 105 LDettori 1 85
(A M Balding) *lw: a towards rr* **18/1**
4300 **10** *11* **Imperialistic (IRE)**[93] 412 5-8-7 94 oh17 KerrinMcEvoy 12 52
(K R Burke) *a rr* **100/1**
0000 **11** *5* **Traytonic**[12] 1495 5-8-7 94 oh4 AdrianTNicholls 5 42
(D Nicholls) *a rr* **66/1**
1101 **12** *½* **Stronghold**[15] 1407 4-9-7 108 RichardHughes 11 55
(J H M Gosden) *lw: in tch: hdwy to chse ldrs over 3f out: rdn wl over 2f out and sn wknd* **10/1**
0036 **13** *18* **Xtra Torrential (USA)**[19] 1287 4-8-13 100 NCallan 3 11
(D M Simcock) *swtg: a rr* **28/1**

1m 42.32s (2.82) **Going Correction** +0.65s/f (Yiel) **13** Ran SP% **116.1**
Speed ratings (Par 111):111,110,108,107,102 102,100,99,96,85 80,79,61
CSF £29.21 CT £67.23 TOTE £4.70: £1.70, £2.10, £1.50; EX 25.80 Trifecta £41.50 Pool £2,145.34 - 36.70 winning units..
Owner The Hornsey Warriors Racing Syndicate **Bred** Cliveden Stud Ltd **Trained** Maunby, N Yorks

FOCUS
A decent handicap, run at a fair pace, and the first four came clear. The runner-up sets the standard.

NOTEBOOK
Zero Tolerance(IRE), who made all to score over ten furlongs at this meeting last year, resumed winning ways under a fine ride from Spencer - again doing it from the front - and landed a gamble in the process. This ground is key to him, he clearly has a liking for this venue, and is a smart handicapper on his day. Whether he can do the business in Pattern company remains to be seen, but he reportedly failed to travel well when disappointing in France last time, and he is well worth another shot at Group 3 level when the ground is soft. (op 6-1)
Babodana, runner-up in Group 2 company last time, ran another brave race and, while he was always being held by the winner late on, it must be noted he was conceding 7lb to that rival. He is a tough performer and, while he is clearly not the easiest to place from his current mark, he is in grand form at present and his turn may not be far off again. (tchd 13-2)
Dabbers Ridge(IRE), officially 6lb "well-in" for this under his penalty for winning easily at Chester six days previously, held every chance under a positive ride yet failed to see out the extra furlong as well as the first two. He may have found this coming a touch too soon, and it could be that he is a real seven furlong specialist, but his life is obviously going to be a deal harder off his higher future mark. (op 7-4 tchd 2-1)

Blythe Knight(IRE) posted another solid effort in defeat, but failed to really improve for this return to his favoured soft ground and the drop back to a mile. He is 6lb higher than when winning the Lincoln in March, but he clearly remains in great heart, and has developed into a likeable performer for current connections.
Cool Panic(IRE), who ran better than the bare form suggested when unplaced at Lingfield five days previously, spoilt his chances of getting home on this first attempt at the longer trip by refusing to settle through the early parts. This must still rate another improved effort, however, and he is clearly coming back to form now. (op 25-1)
Kings Point(IRE), just behind the runner-up in a Group 2 at Sandown previously, was not disgraced on ground he would have found plenty soft enough. He is capable of getting closer again when reverting to a faster surface. (op 20-1)
Traytonic Official explanation: jockey said gelding had no more to give
Stronghold, up 6lb for comfortably taking a Listed event at Lingfield last time, failed to raise his game and could not quicken on this much easier ground under the burden of top weight. He is capable of better than he showed this time. Official explanation: jockey said colt was unsuited by the soft ground (op 17-2)
Xtra Torrential(USA) Official explanation: jockey said gelding was unsuited by the soft ground

1807 GNER 10TH BIRTHDAY EBF MAIDEN STKS 6f
3:50 (3:52) (Class 3) 2-Y-O **£7,837** (£2,331; £1,165; £582) **Stalls** Centre

Form RPR
1 **Sadeek** 2-9-3 NCallan 4 90+
(K A Ryan) *unf: cl up: led over 2f out: rdn and hdd ent last: drvn and rallied wl to ld nr line* **9/2**[3]
2 *hd* **Abraham Lincoln (IRE)**[17] 1360 2-9-3 KFallon 1 89+
(A P O'Brien, Ire) *lw: w'like: scope: trckd ldrs: hdwy over 2f out: rdnto chal over 1f out: led ins last: edgd lft and hdd nr line* **10/11**[1]
3 *9* **Silkie Smooth (IRE)** 2-8-12 JamieSpencer 7 57+
(B W Hills) *unf: scope: trckd ldrs: smooth hdwy over 2f out and sn ev ch tl rdn and one pce over 1f out* **10/3**[2]
4 *5* **Alberts Story (USA)** 2-9-3 RobertWinston 3 47
(R A Fahey) *w'like; b.bkwd: hld up: hdwy over 2f out: sn rdn and no imp* **20/1**
5 *8* **Gallows Hill (USA)** 2-9-3 TonyHamilton 2 23
(R A Fahey) *w'like: b.bkwd: chsd ldrs: rdn along wl over 2f out: sn wknd* **33/1**
6 6 *1* **Flushed**[13] 1454 2-9-3 DeanMcKeown 6 20
(M J Polglase) *sn led: rdn along: edgd lft and hdd over 2f out: sn wknd* **66/1**
7 *13* **Autograph Hunter** 2-9-3 JoeFanning 5 —
(M Johnston) *w'like: dwlt: a rr* **10/1**

1m 16.26s (3.70) **Going Correction** +0.475s/f (Yiel) 7 Ran SP% **111.9**
Speed ratings (Par 97):94,93,81,75,64 63,45
CSF £8.63 TOTE £5.70: £2.20, £1.30; EX 10.00.
Owner John Browne **Bred** T K And Mrs P A Knox **Trained** Hambleton, N Yorks

FOCUS
A decent juvenile maiden, run at a solid pace on the easy ground, and the first two came well clear. Both look colts capable of rating much higher in due course.

NOTEBOOK
Sadeek ◆, a 40,000gns purchase whose dam won over this trip at two and has produced numerous sprint winners, was well backed on course and duly rewarded his followers with a game success at the first time of asking. He was notably sweating, and ran freely at the head of affairs, but stuck to his task most professionally when pressed by the eventual runner-up and was always going to prevail inside the final 50 yards. The soft ground proved to his liking, and he looks a colt of real promise on this evidence, with a shot at the Coventry Stakes at Royal Ascot rightly on the agenda. However, his ability to act as well on the likely faster surface in that event must be taken on trust at this stage. (op 13-2)
Abraham Lincoln(IRE), fifth in Listed company at the Curragh on his recent debut, looked the most likely winner when looming up to challenge Sadeek approaching the final furlong, yet despite getting his head in front, he could not cope with the renewed challenge of that rival and was just held. He was noted as still being green in the preliminaries, and does look assured to come on again for this experience, but he had the benefit of a previous outing for this, and whether he can reverse form with the winner in the future has to be a doubt. (op Evens tchd 11-10 in a place)
Silkie Smooth(IRE), a 48,000gns purchase and whose dam is related to smart middle-distance performers, travelled sweetly until coming under pressure nearing the final furlong and was ultimately firmly put in her place by the front pair. She will appreciate further in due course, but should have learnt plenty for the experience, and ought to be placed to score before too long. (op 7-2)
Alberts Story(USA), a $125,000 purchase and the first foal of a smart multiple seven furlong winner in the US, shaped as though he would benefit greatly for the outing and probably needs faster ground. He has a future. (op 11-1)
Autograph Hunter, a 32,000gns half-brother to very smart juvenile winner Abigail Pett, proved easy to back and it was not hard to see why as he ran distinctly green thoughout and never looked like playing a part. Juveniles from his yard tend to improve from their debut efforts, but this colt may need a fair bit of time before the penny actually drops. (tchd 9-1)

1808 THE SPORTSMAN RACING STKS (H'CAP) 2m 4f
4:25 (4:25) (Class 4) (0-80,80) 4-Y-0+ **£7,772** (£2,312; £1,155; £577) **Stalls** Centre

Form RPR
0612 1 **Kayf Aramis**[24] 1184 4-8-0 **61** oh1 PaulQuinn 16 73
(J L Spearing) *hld up towards rr: hdwy 1/2-way: effrt on wd outside 3f out: rdn to ld 1f out: styd on* **9/1**
0060 2 *1 1/2* **Overstrand (IRE)**[12] 4001 7-7-13 **61** oh3 AndrewMullen(5) 3 71
(Robert Gray) *hld up: hdwy over 6f out: chsd ldrs over 4f out: rdn and ev ch over 1f out: drvn and kpt on ins last* **33/1**
30-5 3 *1* **Monolith**[26] 1882 8-9-3 **79** GregFairley(5) 7 88
(L Lungo) *lw: a.p: led over 5f out: rdn along 3f out: drvn and hdd 1f out: kpt on u.p* **11/1**
0013 4 *5* **Great As Gold (IRE)**[24] 1184 7-8-8 **65** (p) TomEaves 8 69
(B Ellison) *in tch: hdwy to chse ldrs over 3f out: sn rdn along and kpt on appr last* **9/1**
2225 5 *7* **All Star (GER)**[23] 4159 6-9-5 **76** KFallon 2 73
(N J Henderson) *trckd ldrs: hdwy 5f out: rdn to chse ldrs 3f out: drvn 2f out and sn one pce* **9/2**[1]
5-00 6 *nk* **Fiddlers Ford (IRE)**[22] 1247 5-8-7 **64** J-PGuillambert 1 61
(T Keddy) *midfield: hdwy over 7f out: rdn along 4f out: kpt on same pce fnl 2f* **25/1**
1400 7 *1/2* **Heathcote**[32] 4424 4-8-9 **70** RichardHughes 6 69+
(G L Moore) *hld up in midfield: hdwy on inner to chse ldrs over 4f out: rdn along wl over 2f out: sn btn* **15/2**[3]
6005 8 *27* **Siegfrieds Night (IRE)**[18] 975 5-7-13 **61** oh9 (t) EmmettStack(5) 5 30
(M C Chapman) *a rr* **66/1**
4001 9 *1 3/4* **Villago (GER)**[24] 1184 6-8-5 **62** RobertWinston 4 29
(E W Tuer) *hld up in midfield: effrt and sme hdwy 5f out: rdn along over 3f out and sn wknd* **15/2**[3]
1002 10 *1* **Isa'Af (IRE)**[5] 1660 7-9-4 **75** PhillipMakin 11 41
(P W Hiatt) *in tch: hdwy to join ldrs over 6f out: rdn along over 3f out and sn wknd* **25/1**
200- 11 *1* **Pipssalio (SPA)**[28] 6084 9-8-4 **61** oh16 JohnEgan 15 26
(Jamie Poulton) *nvr a factor* **33/1**
1-43 12 *1 3/4* **Stoop To Conquer**[19] 1294 6-9-9 **80** NCallan 17 44
(J L Dunlop) *trckd ldrs: effrt 5f out: rdn along 4f out and sn wknd* **5/1**[2]
0-06 13 *3 1/2* **Halland**[22] 1247 8-9-2 **73** (e) MickyFenton 14 33
(T J Fitzgerald) *trckd ldr: led 12f out: rdn along and hdd over 5f out: sn drvn and wknd over 3f out* **33/1**
-032 14 *46* **Jolizero**[23] 1219 5-8-4 **61** oh3 KerrinMcEvoy 10 —
(John Berry) *led 8f: rdn along over 6f out and sn wknd* **9/1**
3120 15 *61* **He's A Star**[63] 652 4-8-9 **70** DarrylHolland 13 —
(Miss Gay Kelleway) *chsd ldrs: rdn along over 7f out: sn wknd* **33/1**
4320 16 *1/2* **Peak Park (USA)**[117] 168 6-8-4 **61** oh1 ChrisCatlin 12 —
(P L Gilligan) *midfield lost pl 1/2-way and sn bhd* **50/1**

4m 43.97s (30.97)
WFA 4 from 5yo+ 4lb 16 Ran SP% **119.6**
CSF £285.46 CT £3280.64 TOTE £12.00: £2.20, £7.60, £3.20, £2.00; EX 540.80.
Owner Mrs Isobel Phipps Coltman **Bred** Mrs Isobel Phipps Coltman **Trained** Kinnersley, Worcs

FOCUS
A modest marathon handicap, run at a solid gallop, and it favoured those to be held up off the pace. The form is best rated through the fourth.
Heathcote Official explanation: jockey said gelding suffered from cramp during the race
Villago(GER) Official explanation: trainer had no explanation for the poor form shown
Halland Official explanation: jockey said gelding had no more to give
Jolizero Official explanation: jockey said gelding ran too free early on

1809 TOTEEXACTA H'CAP 1m 5f 197y
4:55 (4:56) (Class 4) (0-85,85) 4-Y-0+ **£8,096** (£2,408; £1,203; £601) **Stalls** Low

Form RPR
0015 1 **Sphinx (FR)**[26] 1132 8-8-3 **67** (b) JohnEgan 13 83+
(Jamie Poulton) *lw: hld up: stdy hdwy over 5f out: trckd ldrs on bit 3f out: rdn to ld over 1f out and sn clr* **17/2**
2161 2 *4* **Wing Collar**[260] 4868 5-9-6 **84** DavidAllan 5 91
(T D Easterby) *hld up: hdwy over 4f out: effrt and n.m.r wl over 1f out: switrchd lft and rdn to chse wnr ins last: kpt on* **20/1**
3453 3 *1* **Modaffaa**[23] 1206 6-9-0 **78** LDettori 3 84
(P R Webber) *trckd ldrs on inner: hdwy over 3f out: rdn to ld over 2f out: drvn and hdd over 1f out: kpt on same pce* **8/1**[3]
1563 4 *3/4* **Cotton Eyed Joe (IRE)**[11] 1502 5-8-6 **70** DeanMcKeown 7 75
(G A Swinbank) *in tch:. hdwy to chse ldrs over 4f out: rdn along and outpcd 3f out: styd on u.p appr last* **12/1**
0612 5 *12* **Reluctant Suitor**[13] 1457 4-8-6 **70** KerrinMcEvoy 15 59
(J S Goldie) *hld up: stdy hdwy 6f out: effrt to chal over 2f out: sn rdn and ev ch tl drvn and wknd appr last: eased* **10/1**
5010 6 *3* **Duroob**[17] 1346 4-8-4 **68** ChrisCatlin 8 54
(K R Burke) *towards rr tl styd on fnl 4f: nvr a factor* **12/1**
5000 7 *5* **Ski Jump (USA)**[36] 976 6-9-2 **80** (v) TonyHamilton 6 59
(R A Fahey) *prominent: rdn along over 3f out: sn wknd* **14/1**
2436 8 *3* **Sualda (IRE)**[262] 4819 7-8-12 **76** RoystonFfrench 17 51
(R A Fahey) *trckd ldrs: smooth hdwy 5f out: cl up 3f out: rdn along 2f out and sn wknd* **33/1**
6200 9 *2 1/2* **Dr Sharp (IRE)**[8] 1584 6-9-7 **85** RobertWinston 2 57
(T P Tate) *led: rdn along 4f out: drvn over 2f out: sn hdd & wknd* **13/2**[2]
4244 10 *8* **Zaville**[309] 3444 4-8-4 **68** ow1 PhilipRobinson 1 29
(M A Jarvis) *prom: rdn along 4f out: sn wknd* **12/1**
1S15 11 *5* **Maneki Neko (IRE)**[26] 1144 4-8-10 **74** JamieSpencer 9 29
(E W Tuer) *hld up in rr: hdwy over 5f out: rdn and in tch on wd outside over 3f out: sn rdn and btn* **8/1**[3]
3210 12 *21* **Top Man Tee**[70] 6458 4-9-0 **78** VinceSlattery 10 6
(D J Daly) *a bhd* **66/1**
66 13 *10* **Motafarred (IRE)**[19] 1298 4-9-7 **85** MJKinane 4 —
(Micky Hammond) *nvr bttr than midfield* **33/1**
5-63 14 *50* **Indonesia**[407] 902 4-8-8 **72** ow2 DarrylHolland 16 —
(T D Walford) *promient: rdn along over 5f out: sn wknd* **66/1**
3321 15 *42* **Velvet Heights (IRE)**[22] 1247 4-9-4 **82** KDarley 14 —
(J L Dunlop) *hld up: hdwy and in tch 5f out: rdn along over 3f out: sn wknd: lost action and virtually p.u fnl 2f* **7/2**[1]

3m 8.14s (9.70) **Going Correction** +1.00s/f (Soft) 15 Ran SP% **120.8**
Speed ratings (Par 105):112,109,109,108,101 100,97,95,94,89 86,74,69,40,16
CSF £176.21 CT £1417.82 TOTE £10.60: £2.90, £5.90, £3.90; EX 261.40 Place 6 £560.56, Place 5 £133.21..
Owner R W Huggins **Bred** M Arbib **Trained** Telscombe, E Sussex

FOCUS
A fair handicap, run at a decent pace, and the first four came clear. The winner is value for further and the third and fourth are the best guides to the form.
Dr Sharp(IRE) Official explanation: jockey said gelding ran flat
Velvet Heights(IRE) Official explanation: jockey said colt lost its action
T/Jkpt: Part won. £168,644.80 to a £1 stake. Pool: £237,528.00. 0.50 winning tickets. T/Plt: £365.70 to a £1 stake. Pool: £126,298.25. 252.05 winning tickets. T/Qpdt: £12.80 to a £1 stake. Pool: £7,876.90. 455.15 winning tickets. JR

1632 HAMILTON (R-H)
Friday, May 19

OFFICIAL GOING: Good (good to soft in places)
Wind: Light; half behind

1811 CHARD CONSTRUCTION EBF MAIDEN STKS (A QUALIFIER FOR THE HAMILTON PARK 2-Y-O SERIES FINAL) 6f 5y
6:25 (6:25) (Class 5) 2-Y-O **£3,886** (£1,156; £577; £288) **Stalls** Centre

Form RPR
5 1 **As One Does**[29] 1090 2-9-3 DO'Donohoe 1 82+
(K A Ryan) *mde virtually all: pushed along over 1f out: styd on strly fnl f* **3/1**[2]
2 *3* **Dowlleh** 2-9-3 TonyCulhane 4 73
(M R Channon) *keen: cl up tl rn green and outpcd after 2f: rallied to chse wnr 1f out: kpt on: no imp* **15/2**
53 3 *1* **Ten Dollars More (IRE)**[9] 1588 2-9-3 JoeFanning 2 70
(J A Osborne) *cl up: effrt over 2f out: one pce appr fnl f* **4/1**[3]
322 4 *3* **Jack Rackham**[7] 1632 2-9-3 RobertWinston 5 61
(B Smart) *plld hrd: w ldrs tl edgd rt and wknd over 1f out* **5/4**[1]

5 3 **Atheneum (IRE)** 2-9-3 .... KDarley 3 52
(M Johnston) *dwlt: sn prom: effrt and ev ch over 2f out: edgd rt and wknd over 1f out* **11/1**

1m 16.26s (3.16) **Going Correction** +0.275s/f (Good) 5 Ran SP% **109.5**
Speed ratings (Par 93):89,85,83,79,75
CSF £22.95 TOTE £3.80: £2.30, £4.40; EX 33.80.
Owner Colm Gavin and Henry Bourke **Bred** Daniel James **Trained** Hambleton, N Yorks

FOCUS
A fair race in which the winner appeals as the type to improve again, but the time was modest.

NOTEBOOK
As One Does ◆, upped in distance, bettered the form of his promising debut win to acore with something in hand. He will stay further than six furlongs, is open to improvement and appeals as the type to win more races. (op 5-2)
Dowlleh, a half-brother to a couple of winners, looked as though the race would do him good but shaped well, despite his inexperience and left the impression that he could win a similar race, especially when upped to seven furlongs. (op 7-1 tchd 8-1)
Ten Dollars More(IRE) again showed ability and looks a good guide to the worth of this form. Although likely to remain vulnerable to the better types in this grade, he looks capable of winning a small race and should stay seven furlongs. (op 5-1)
Jack Rackham looked sure to be suited by the step up to six furlongs but pulled far too hard to give himself any chance of lasting home over it. He is capable of winning a small race but looks one to have reservations about. (op 13-8 tchd 7-4 in places)
Atheneum(IRE), related to a couple of winners in France and out of a mile and a half winner, was easy to back but showed up well for a long way on this debut. He is not a bad sort and will come into his own over further in due course. (op 8-1)

1812 MCGRATTAN PILING H'CAP 6f 5y
6:55 (6:55) (Class 4) (0-85,82) 3-Y-O **£7,772** (£2,312; £1,155; £577) **Stalls** Centre

Form RPR
3024 1 **Imperial Sword**[13] [1497] 3-8-11 **75** .... RobertWinston 5 85
(T D Barron) *bhd and outpcd after 2f: gd hdwy to ld ins fnl f: comf* **13/2**
414 2 2 ½ **Westport**[46] [852] 3-8-6 **70** .... DO'Donohoe 8 73
(K A Ryan) *cl up: led 2f out: rdn and edgd rt: hdd ins fnl f: no ch w wnr* **8/1**
5000 3 shd **Soto**[13] [1497] 3-8-5 **72** .... PaulMulrennan(3) 1 75
(M W Easterby) *chsd ldrs: effrt 2f out: kpt on same pce fnl f* **12/1**
010 4 ½ **The History Man (IRE)**[29] [1097] 3-8-11 **75** ....(b) DaleGibson 2 76
(M W Easterby) *keen: cl up: outpcd whn checked 2f out: kpt on fnl f: no imp* **10/1**
0102 5 nk **John Keats**[13] [1482] 3-9-4 **82** .... TomEaves 6 82
(I Semple) *led to 2f out: one pce* **5/2**[1]
2441 6 2 ½ **Rainbow Bay**[11] [1529] 3-8-12 **76** 6ex........ PatCosgrave 3 69
(R A Fahey) *keen: chsd ldrs tl rdn and no ex fr over 1f out* **6/1**[3]
4100 7 4 **Savernake Blue**[18] [1349] 3-9-2 **80** .... TonyCulhane 9 61
(M R Channon) *s.i.s: outpcd: nvr rchd ldrs* **12/1**
1163 8 ½ **The Terrier**[13] [1497] 3-8-10 **74** .... DeanMcKeown 7 53
(G A Swinbank) *keen: cl up tl edgd rt and wknd over 1f out* **5/1**[2]
5410 9 5 **Violent Velocity (IRE)**[29] [1091] 3-9-0 **78** .... GrahamGibbons 4 42
(J J Quinn) *hld up bhd ldrs: effrt over 2f out: wknd over 1f out* **12/1**

1m 14.15s (1.05) **Going Correction** +0.275s/f (Good) **9** Ran SP% **116.1**
Speed ratings (Par 101):104,100,100,99,99 96,90,90,83
CSF £57.61 CT £616.12 TOTE £7.90: £2.00, £2.40, £3.50; EX 71.90.
Owner J Stephenson **Bred** David John Brown **Trained** Maunby, N Yorks

FOCUS
An ordinary handicap but the overly strong pace teed things up for the winner. Those in the frame behind the winner were to form and encourage it to be rated at face value.

1813 ICON HOLDINGS GLASGOW STKS (LISTED RACE) (C&G) 1m 3f 16y
7:30 (7:30) (Class 1) 3-Y-O **£19,873** (£7,532; £3,769; £1,879) **Stalls** High

Form RPR
1 1 **Tam Lin**[20] [1290] 3-8-11 90 .... RobertWinston 1 96+
(Sir Michael Stoute) *stdd in tch: hdwy over 2f out: hung rt and led over 1f out: carried hd high and flashed tail repeatedly: kpt on* **8/11**[1]
31 2 2 **Futun**[20] [1289] 3-8-11 89 .... NickyMackay 2 93+
(L M Cumani) *plld hrd to 1/2-way: chsd ldrs: effrt over 2f out: n.m.r briefly over 1f out: chsd wnr ins fnl f: r.o* **15/8**[2]
3105 3 2 **Genari**[21] [1268] 3-8-11 93 .... JoeFanning 3 90
(P F I Cole) *set stdy pce: rdn over 2f out: hdd over 1f out: no ex* **8/1**[3]
032 4 1 ¾ **Spell Casting (USA)**[18] [1343] 3-8-11 85 .... KDarley 4 87
(M H Tompkins) *chsd ldr: rdn and hung lft over 2f out: n.m.r and no ex over 1f out* **25/1**

2m 28.04s (1.78) **Going Correction** +0.35s/f (Good) **4** Ran SP% **107.6**
Speed ratings (Par 107):107,105,104,102
CSF £2.31 TOTE £1.80; EX 2.20.
Owner Gainsborough Stud **Bred** Gainsborough Stud Management Ltd **Trained** Newmarket, Suffolk

FOCUS
A weak event by Listed standards and a muddling gallop means this bare form is unreliable with the third the best guide. Although the winner won with a bit in hand and is open to improvement, he looked less than straightforward.

NOTEBOOK
Tam Lin looked anything but straightforward on only this second run but he has already achieved a fair level of form in two starts and is open to plenty of improvement, especially over a mile and a half in a contest run at a better gallop. He is the type to win more races but, on this evidence may not be one to lump on at short odds in stronger company next time. (op 4-6)
Futun bettered the form of his maiden win and may be a bit better than the bare form as he failed to settle in a race that was not really run to suit. He will be of more interest granted a stronger gallop in similar company next time. (tchd 2-1 and 9-4 in places)
Genari was the pick on ratings but is vulnerable to more progressive sorts in this type of event and he was readily left behind after enjoying the run of the race over this longer trip. He may not be the easiest to place this term. (op 11-1 tchd 12-1)
Spell Casting(USA) was not disgraced in the face of a stiff task on this first run out of maiden company. He may be flattered by his proximity in this muddling event and is sure to do better in ordinary handicaps around this trip. (op 20-1)

1814 LUDDON CONSTRUCTION MAIDEN STKS 1m 1f 36y
8:00 (8:00) (Class 5) 3-Y-O+ **£3,886** (£1,156; £577; £288) **Stalls** High

Form RPR
04 1 **Lemon Drop Lad (USA)**[18] [1335] 3-8-12 .... RobertWinston 5 80+
(Sir Michael Stoute) *prom: effrt over 1f out: kpt on wl fnl f to ld cl home* **6/4**[2]
23 2 ½ **O'Tara (IRE)**[29] [1101] 3-8-12 .... JoeFanning 8 79+
(M H Tompkins) *cl up: led over 2f out: kpt on wl fnl f: hdd cl home* **5/4**[1]
3 ¾ **My Arch**[57] 4-9-11 .... DO'Donohoe 3 79+
(K A Ryan) *hld up: rdn over 4f out: rn green: hdwy over 2f out: kpt on wl fnl f* **20/1**
4 19 **Claudia May**[136] 5-9-3 .... PaulMulrennan(3) 2 36
(Miss Lucinda V Russell) *s.i.s: bhd: rdn over 4f out: n.d* **100/1**
00 5 1 ½ **Coronation Flight**[9] [1598] 3-8-7 .... DeanMcKeown 4 31
(F P Murtagh) *hld up: effrt over 3f out: wknd 2f out* **200/1**
04 6 2 ½ **Now Tell Me This**[12] [1503] 3-8-12 ....(b[1]) TomEaves 6 31
(I Semple) *cl up tl rdn and wknd over 2f out* **25/1**
0000 7 5 **Lucky Largo (IRE)**[8] [1608] 6-9-11 30........(b) DerekMcGaffin 1 23
(D A Nolan) *in tch tl wknd over 2f out* **200/1**
34 8 3 **Stormy Love (IRE)**[240] [5412] 4-9-11 .... KDarley 7 17
(M Johnston) *plld hrd early: led to over 2f out: wknd* **6/1**[3]

2m 1.87s (2.21) **Going Correction** +0.35s/f (Good)
WFA 3 from 4yo+ 13lb **8** Ran SP% **109.3**
Speed ratings (Par 103):104,103,102,86,84 82,78,75
CSF £3.28 TOTE £2.60: £1.10, £1.10, £4.30; EX 3.40.
Owner Saeed Suhail **Bred** G W Humphrey And Louise I Humphrey **Trained** Newmarket, Suffolk

FOCUS
An uncompetitive maiden in which the gallop was only fair. The firs three finished clear so it may prove sound enough.

1815 BRAVEHEART STKS (H'CAP) (LISTED RACE) 1m 4f 17y
8:35 (8:35) (Class 1) (0-110,105) 4-Y-O+
£17,034 (£6,456; £3,231; £1,611; £807; £405) **Stalls** High

Form RPR
4025 1 **Akarem**[20] [1298] 5-9-4 **102** .... PatCosgrave 5 108
(K R Burke) *chsd ldrs: effrt over 2f out: led ins fnl f: hld on wl* **20/1**
1111 2 nk **Ouninpohja (IRE)**[236] [5496] 5-9-7 **105** .... DeanMcKeown 6 114+
(G A Swinbank) *stdd in rr: keen: smooth hdwy to ld over 2f out: rdn: edgd rt and hdd ins fnl f: rallied: jst hld* **6/4**[1]
0014 3 ½ **Profit's Reality (IRE)**[23] [1239] 4-9-2 **100** .... RobbieFitzpatrick 2 105
(P A Blockley) *keen: in tch: effrt and rdn whn hmpd over 2f out: edgd to stands side and kpt on wl fnl f* **7/1**
0324 4 1 ¾ **Rehearsal**[23] [296] 5-8-9 **93** .... RobertWinston 3 95
(L Lungo) *hld up in tch: smooth hdwy 1/2-way: ev ch over 2f out: one pce fnl f* **6/1**[3]
1655 5 5 **I'm So Lucky**[13] [1484] 4-8-13 **97** .... JoeFanning 1 91
(M Johnston) *keen: cl up tl rdn and outpcd over 2f out: n.d after* **11/4**[2]
5204 6 nk **Brahminy Kite (USA)**[20] [1298] 4-9-4 **102** .... KDarley 4 96
(M Johnston) *set stdy pce to over 2f out: sn btn* **7/1**

2m 40.23s (1.05) **Going Correction** +0.35s/f (Good) **6** Ran SP% **110.7**
Speed ratings (Par 111):110,109,109,108,104 104
CSF £49.50 TOTE £19.40: £4.80, £1.20; EX 76.80.
Owner Mrs M Gittins **Bred** Kilcarn Stud **Trained** Middleham Moor, N Yorks

FOCUS
Not the most competitive races for the money on offer and a muddling gallop means this bare form is best not taken at face value.

NOTEBOOK
Akarem disappointed at Ripon on his previous start but showed that to be all wrong with a workmanlike success. He showed a good attitude but he did have the run of this fairly uncompetitive event and may be one to take on from a higher mark in stronger company next time. Official explanation: trainer's representative said, regarding the improved form shown, horse had been unsuited by the good ground at Ripon last time
Ouninpohja(IRE) ◆, who looked as though the run would do him good, showed he retains all his ability on this reappearance run. A more strongly-run race will see him in a better light and he is the type to win a decent handicap this term. (op 11-8tchd 2-1 in a place)
Profit's Reality(IRE) looks a bit better than the bare form given he was hampered at a crucial stage but, although running creditably, he is likely to find life much tougher back in competitive handicap company. (op 9-1)
Rehearsal had the run of the race and ran creditably but, on this evidence, is likely to prove vulnerable to progressive or well-handicapped types from his current mark. (op 4-1)
I'm So Lucky proved a disappointment but, given this race may have come too quickly after his reappearance run, is worth another chance back on a more conventional track granted a better gallop. (op 4-1 tchd 9-2 in a place)
Brahminy Kite(USA), who looked in tremendous shape, had the run of the race on this second fairly quick run after a break but dropped away tamely. He will have to show more before he is a betting proposition again. (op 6-1)

1816 BRANDON HOMES H'CAP 5f 4y
9:10 (9:11) (Class 5) (0-70,68) 4-Y-O+ **£3,886** (£1,156; £577; £288) **Stalls** Centre

Form RPR
3302 1 **Taboor (IRE)**[23] [1235] 8-8-8 **58** .... RobertWinston 3 65
(R M H Cowell) *chsd ldrs: effrt over 1f out: led ins fnl f: kpt on wl* **5/1**[2]
2101 2 nk **Geojimali**[1] [1795] 4-8-10 **60** .... FergalLynch 4 66+
(J S Goldie) *sn outpcd and hung rt: hdwy on outside over 1f out: edgd lft: kpt on wl fnl f* **5/2**[1]
0200 3 nk **The Leather Wedge (IRE)**[15] [1438] 7-9-1 **68**........ PaulMulrennan(3) 5 73
(R Johnson) *set decent gallop to ins fnl f: no ex towards fin* **9/1**
3660 4 5 **Angelofthenorth**[16] [1413] 4-8-3 **60** .... MarkCoumbe(7) 1 47
(C J Teague) *bhd tl hdwy over 1f out: no imp fnl f* **16/1**
6033 5 shd **Primarily**[12] [1504] 4-9-1 **65** ....(p) JoeFanning 6 51
(A Berry) *prom tl rdn and outpcd over 1f out* **12/1**
0005 6 5 **Sokoke**[15] [1437] 5-8-4 **54** oh9........ RobbieFitzpatrick 8 22
(D A Nolan) *in tch on outside tl wknd 2f out* **100/1**
0051 7 1 ¼ **George The Best (IRE)**[12] [1504] 5-8-4 **54** 6ex........ DeanMcKeown 2 18
(Micky Hammond) *cl up tl wknd fr 2f out* **5/2**[1]
4000 8 1 ½ **Viewforth**[12] [1504] 8-8-12 **62** ....(b) TomEaves 7 21
(I Semple) *prom tl rdn and wknd fr 2f out* **6/1**[3]

60.37 secs (-0.83) **Going Correction** +0.275s/f (Good) **8** Ran SP% **112.7**
Speed ratings (Par 103):103,102,102,94,93 85,83,81
CSF £17.36 CT £107.05 TOTE £5.60: £1.70, £1.80, £3.10; EX 30.20 Place 6 £81.00, Place 5 £20.83.
Owner T W Morley **Bred** Rathasker Stud **Trained** Six Mile Bottom, Cambs

FOCUS
An ordinary handicap but one in which the pace was sound throughout and the form appears solid enough.

George The Best(IRE) Official explanation: trainer said, regarding poor form shown, gelding was not quick enough over this trip and needs softer going

T/Plt: £314.10 to a £1 stake. Pool: £49,042.50 - 113.95 winning units T/Qpdt: £7.80 to a £1 stake. Pool: £5,126.40 - 218.60 winning units RY

[1128]NEWBURY (L-H)

Friday, May 19

OFFICIAL GOING: Good (good to soft in places)

Wind: Strong ahead

1817 SPREADFAIR.COM FILLIES' CONDITIONS STKS 5f 34y

1:55 (1:56) (Class 3) 2-Y-O

£6,855 (£2,052; £1,026; £513; £256; £128) **Stalls** High

Form RPR

1 **Sunley Gift** 2-8-5 .... SamHitchcott 4 72
(M R Channon) *w'like: w ldr: drvn to take slt advantage over 1f out: kpt on strly ins last* **8/1**[3]

2 ½ **Silca Soprano** 2-8-2 .... EdwardCreighton(3) 3 70
(M R Channon) *w'like: s.i.s: rr: outpcd after 2f: swtchd lft and hdwy over 1f out: str run ins last: gng on cl home* **12/1**

22 3 shd **Crystal Gazer (FR)**[16] [1405] 2-8-8 .... RyanMoore 5 73
(R Hannon) *lw: slt ld and t.k.h: hdd appr fnl f: kpt on same pce ins last* **9/4**[1]

4 4 nk **Christmas Tart (IRE)**[12] [1510] 2-8-8 .... ChrisCatlin 6 72
(V Smith) *t.k.h trckd ldrs: nt much room 2f out: rdn over 1f out: styd on u.p ins last but nvr gng pce to chal* **9/4**[1]

5 ¾ **Yerevan** 2-8-0 ow2... ThomasO'Brien(7) 2 68
(M R Channon) *leggy: b.bkwd: chsd ldrs: drvn along fr 1/2-way: styd on same pce fnl f* **25/1**

6 nk **Candyland (IRE)** 2-8-5 .... TQuinn 1 65
(M R Channon) *unf: chsd ldrs: rdn and edgd lft over 1f out: sn one pce* **3/1**[2]

66.96 secs (4.40) **Going Correction** +0.40s/f (Good) **6** Ran SP% **109.2**

Speed ratings (Par 94):80,79,79,78,77 76

CSF £83.67 TOTE £9.20: £3.20, £3.40; EX 53.80.

Owner John B Sunley **Bred** Whitsbury Manor Stud **Trained** West Ilsley, Berks

FOCUS

Mick Channon saddled four of the six runners in what was in all probability just an average conditions event for fillies. It was run at only a modest gallop, and the field were closely covered at the finish.

NOTEBOOK

Sunley Gift, whose stable had landed the past three runnings of this event, got her career off to a perfect start with a ready success under a positive ride. She showed a decent attitude when asked to win her race, looks sure to improve for the experience, and should have no trouble in staying further in due course. (op 12-1)

Silca Soprano ◆, a half-sister to smart hurdler/chaser Keltic Bard, who was effective over a mile to ten furlongs on the Flat, was doing all of her best work at the finish having been restrained at the rear until being asked to improve nearing the final furlong. This must rate a promising start to her career and a sixth furlong should be well within her compass. She ought to go very close next time. (op 20-1)

Crystal Gazer(FR), runner-up on both her previous outings on Polytrack, held every chance up against the stands' rail and had no apparent excuse. She appeared to be doing little for her rider in the final two furlongs, and may not be all that straightforward, but does help set the level of this form.

Christmas Tart(IRE), well backed to improve on her recent debut effort at Newmarket, proved free through the early parts and then met trouble when attempting to challenge the leaders two from home. She still had every chance if good enough when in the clear, however, and most likely needs a stronger overall gallop over this trip to be seen at best. (tchd 5-2)

Yerevan, related to winning sprinters, ran green from halfway and lacked the necessary chance of gear. She looks to need a little more time. (tchd 33-1)

Candyland(IRE), seemingly the most fancied of his trainer's four runners, was unable to get any cover throughout the race from the outside draw and her fate was sealed with two furlongs to run. She boasts an entry in the Group 1 Phoenix Stakes and is presumably thought capable of a great deal better. (op 2-1)

1818 PADDYPOWERPOKER.COM CARNARVON STKS (LISTED RACE) 6f 8y

2:25 (2:26) (Class 1) 3-Y-O

£15,898 (£6,025; £3,015; £1,503; £753; £378) **Stalls** High

Form RPR

1422 1 **Kingsgate Prince (IRE)**[16] [1408] 3-9-1 105.............................. TQuinn 2 108
(J R Best) *bhd: hdwy on outside over 1f out: str run u.p to ld wl ins last: readily* **10/1**

6331 2 ½ **Assertive**[16] [1408] 3-9-1 109.. RyanMoore 7 107
(R Hannon) *lw: w ldr tl def advantage over 2f out: sn rdn: kpt on gamely tl hdd wl ins last* **9/4**[1]

2103 3 hd **Strike Up The Band**[16] [1408] 3-9-4 108....................... AdrianTNicholls 5 109
(D Nicholls) *chsd ldrs: str chal fr over 1f out tl ins last: no ex nr fin* **10/1**

0251 4 2 **Loyal Royal (IRE)**[12] [1513] 3-8-11 84.............................. JohnEgan 8 96
(D R C Elsworth) *lw: chsd ldrs: rdn 2f out: outpcd ins last* **10/1**

1640 5 1 **Mutawajid (IRE)**[258] [4946] 3-8-11 103................................. PatDobbs 3 93
(R Hannon) *s.i.s: hld up in rr: hdwy 2f out: chsd ldrs 1f out: one pce u.p ins last* **20/1**

2155 6 3½ **Racer Forever (USA)**[223] [5732] 3-8-11 101..................... RobertHavlin 9 83+
(J H M Gosden) *hld up in rr: nt clr run fr over 2f out and stl no room tl ins last: kpt on nr fin but nvr in contention* **20/1**

1300 7 ¾ **River Thames**[31] [1069] 3-8-11 98..................................... SebSanders 10 80+
(J A R Toller) *chsd ldrs: rdn over 2f out: wknd over 1f out* **11/1**

1656 8 2 **Manston (IRE)**[16] [1404] 3-9-1 102.................................... SteveDrowne 6 78
(B J Meehan) *slt ld tl hdd over 2f out: wkng over 1f out whn n.m.r on rails* **5/1**[3]

00 9 5 **Grand Parrot**[195] [6251] 3-8-11 .... AdrianMcCarthy 1 59?
(W De Best-Turner) *b.bkwd: chsd ldrs: rdn 4f out: wknd ins fnl 3f* **100/1**

0121 10 5 **Murfreesboro**[232] [5570] 3-8-11 98................................... JimmyFortune 4 44
(J H M Gosden) *s.i.s: sn pressing ldrs: rdn 3f out: wknd qckly over 2f out* **7/2**[2]

1m 15.62s (1.30) **Going Correction** +0.40s/f (Good) **10** Ran SP% **115.8**

Speed ratings (Par 107):107,106,106,103,102 97,96,93,87,80

CSF £31.95 TOTE £14.10: £2.90, £1.50, £2.30; EX 39.00.

Owner John Mayne **Bred** P G Lyons **Trained** Hucking, Kent

■ Stewards' Enquiry : John Egan caution: careless riding

FOCUS

A decent three-year-old Listed event, run at a solid pace, and the form looks straightforward.

NOTEBOOK

Kingsgate Prince(IRE), second to Assertive on his return to turf at Lingfield last time, produced a telling late turn of foot to get on top and reverse form despite racing on identical terms. He enjoyed this slightly easier ground and this confirmed his effectiveness on turf. He deserves his place in the Jersey Stakes at Royal Ascot next month, where he could again lock horns with the runner-up, and the return to seven furlongs should suit. (tchd 11-1)

Assertive, who had the winner behind when resuming winning ways at Lingfield last time, held every chance under a positive ride yet failed to confirm that form despite racing on identical terms. He probably wants faster ground, but whether he can reverse form with the winner over another furlong in the Jersey Stakes next month is doubtful. (op 15-8 tchd 5-2)

Strike Up The Band, third behind the winner and runner-up at Lingfield last time, ran a solid race in defeat again but was once more found out by the penalty for his Group win at two. He was nicely clear of the rest at the finish, and this was another step in the right direction. (op 7-1)

Loyal Royal(IRE), finally off the mark in maiden company at Salisbury, once again looked a tricky ride and was keeping on all too late in the day. He has talent, and this must rate improved form, but he also has temperament to boot. (op 14-1)

Mutawajid(IRE), returning from a 258-day break, did not shape without promise and ought to come on a bundle for the experience. (op 25-1)

Racer Forever(USA) ◆, making his seasonal return after a 223-day absence, was restrained in rear and got no sort of run when attempting to make a challenge around two out. He must be rated a deal better than the bare form and should come on a deal for this run, so he is one to keep an eye on. Official explanation: jockey said colt ran too free (op 22-1)

Manston(IRE), popular in the betting ring, failed to raise his game for the drop back in trip and has yet to conclusively prove that he has fully trained on. (tchd 11-2)

Murfreesboro, well backed, recovered quickly from a sluggish start yet weakened dramatically with more than two to run. He may need faster ground, but this was a most disappointing seasonal bow and he has it to prove now. Official explanation: jockey said colt ran too free (op 9-2)

1819 SWETTENHAM STUD FILLIES' TRIAL STKS (LISTED RACE) 1m 2f 6y

3:00 (3:02) (Class 1) 3-Y-O

£15,898 (£6,025; £3,015; £1,503; £753; £378) **Stalls** High

Form RPR

12 1 **Scottish Stage (IRE)**[230] [5605] 3-8-9 100......................... RyanMoore 10 107
(Sir Michael Stoute) *lw: hld up off pce in rr: pushed along and str hdwy to chse ldrs 3f out: led 2f out: kpt on wl fnl f: jst hld on* **4/6**[1]

1 2 hd **Guilia**[248] [5203] 3-8-9 .... SteveDrowne 1 106
(Rae Guest) *leggy: hld up in rr: hdwy 3f out: n.m.r and edgd lft 2f out: swtchd rt and str run fnl f: fin wl: jst failed* **33/1**

31 3 2½ **Makderah (IRE)**[27] [1134] 3-8-9 81... RHills 9 102
(M P Tregoning) *lw: bhd: hdwy 6f out: trckd ldrs 3f out: chal fr 2f out tl ins last: sn one pce* **9/2**[2]

1035 4 3½ **Jaish (USA)**[13] [1472] 3-8-9 92.. TQuinn 8 95
(J L Dunlop) *chsd ldrs: hrd drvn fr 5f out: styd on to chse ldrs over 2f out: wknd fnl f* **50/1**

421 5 nk **Innocent Air**[280] [4331] 3-8-12 104.................................. JimmyFortune 4 97
(J H M Gosden) *led tl hdd 2f out: wknd appr fnl f* **13/2**[3]

41 6 11 **Adventuress**[17] [1374] 3-8-9 89.. ChrisCatlin 2 74
(B J Meehan) *chsd ldrs: rdn 4f out: wknd fr 3f out* **20/1**

5502 7 ½ **Hanoona (IRE)**[23] [1237] 3-8-9 99.................................... TedDurcan 7 73
(M R Channon) *bhd: rdn 4f out: nvr in contention* **25/1**

8 2 **Karlovy** 3-8-9 .... PhilipRobinson 3 69
(M A Jarvis) *unf: chsd ldrs tl wknd 4f out* **25/1**

6102 9 7 **Arm Candy (IRE)**[16] [1406] 3-8-9 91.................................. SebSanders 6 55
(J A R Toller) *chsd ldr to tl over 3f out: sn wknd* **14/1**

2231 10 12 **Annabelle Ja (FR)**[149] [6641] 3-8-9 85............................. JohnEgan 5 33
(D R C Elsworth) *chsd ldrs: rdn 4f out: sn wknd* **40/1**

2m 9.03s (0.32) **Going Correction** +0.25s/f (Good) **10** Ran SP% **118.0**

Speed ratings (Par 104):108,107,105,103,102 94,93,92,86,76

CSF £40.50 TOTE £1.70: £1.10, £4.60, £1.50; EX 48.50.

Owner Ballymacoll Stud **Bred** Ballymacoll Stud Farm Ltd **Trained** Newmarket, Suffolk

■ Scottish Stage maintained Sir Michael Stoute's superb run in the Oaks trials after wins with Riyalma, Sindirana and Short Skirt.

FOCUS

The last of the recognised Oaks Trials. It was run at a fair pace, and the first two came clear, but the level of form they showed is a long way short of what is usually required at Epsom.

NOTEBOOK

Scottish Stage(IRE) ◆, a market mover in the Epsom Oaks prior to this much anticipated three-year-old debut, ultimately just did enough to hold off the late challenge of the runner-up. While more might have been expected from a serious Oaks candidate, she was given a lot to do from off the pace and she responded well for pressure to make up ground quickly from four out to two out. What's more, she didn't appear to be doing do a great deal in front and might want producing later, but she dug deep when pressed inside the closing stages. The longer distance and possibly better ground may also prove to her liking at Epsom. (op 5-6)

Guilia, unfancied when winning her sole outing last year at Thirsk over seven furlongs, responded kindly to pressure when switched inside the final furlong and was eventually only just denied. She has clearly done very well during the off-season, relished the step up to this longer trip, and was nicely clear of the remainder at the finish. There is no reason to believe this was a fluke effort, as her trainer tends to excel with his three-year-old fillies, and she looks fully entitled to take her place in the Oaks next month. (op 25-1)

Makderah(IRE) ◆, off the mark on her seasonal return in maiden company at this venue 27 days previously, travelled sweetly and looked a big danger when making her challenge, then did not get home nearly as well as the first two. Further improvement looks likely, and the return to a mile in the Coronation Stakes at Royal Ascot should be right up her street. (op 5-1 tchd 6-1)

Jaish(USA), well held in the Lupe on her recent return to action, stuck to her task under pressure and returned to last year's best level. She is likely to continue to prove vulnerable in this type of event, however. (op 40-1)

Innocent Air, last seen breaking her duck in Listed company over seven furlongs at this venue last year, showed up well from the front until finding nothing when pressed nearing two out. She may well have needed the race, but her pedigree suggests the longer trip should have been well within her compass, and she does not appeal as a likely type for an Oaks now. (op 7-1 tchd 6-1)

Adventuress, off the mark in a Bath maiden 17 days previously, was firmly put in her place on this step up in class. (op 16-1)

Karlovy, a half-sister to Arc winner Marienbard and from a stable that took this last year with subsequent Oaks heroine Eswarah, shaped as though the experience was badly needed and can be expected to be plenty sharper next time out. (tchd 28-1)

Annabelle Ja(FR) Official explanation: jockey said filly had no more to give

1820 STAN JAMES H'CAP 6f 8y

3:30 (3:35) (Class 4) (0-85,85) 4-Y-O+ **£6,477** (£1,927; £963; £481) **Stalls** High

Form RPR

0020 1 **Exmoor**[25] [1183] 4-8-8 75.. SteveDrowne 12 86
(R Charlton) *hld up in rr: gd hdwy over 1f out: str run u.p fnl f to ld last strides* **8/1**[3]

4050 2 nk **Kingscross**[13] [1474] 8-8-12 79...................................... FergusSweeney 5 89
(M Blanshard) *hld up in rr: stdy hdwy fr 2f out: drvn to ld last half f: ct last strides* **20/1**

0132 3 hd **Nautical**[11] [1545] 8-8-7 74.. PatDobbs 17 84
(A W Carroll) *hld up in rr: gd hdwy fr 2f out: chal ins last: kpt on but no ex cl home* **7/1**[2]

5323 4 1½ **Lake Chini (IRE)**[20] [1285] 4-8-10 77.........................(b) PhilipRobinson 14 82
(M A Jarvis) *chsd ldrs: rdn 2f out: chal appr fnl f: wknd cl home* **6/1**[1]

0055 **5** *hd* **Ingleton**[11] [1545] 4-8-5 **72** .... RyanMoore 9 76
(G L Moore) *lw: slt ld: rdn 2f out: kpt on tl hdd last half f: wknd nr fin* **6/1**[1]

0000 **6** *1 ¼* **Oranmore Castle (IRE)**[13] [1474] 4-8-8 **75** .... (t) SamHitchcott 15 76
(B W Hills) *chsd ldrs: rdn to chse ldrs 1f out: styd on one pce ins last* **33/1**

4040 **7** *nk* **Born To Be Bold**[11] [1545] 4-8-2 **72** .... StephaneBreux(3) 10 72
(R Hannon) *lw: chsd ldrs: rdn 2f out: one pce ins fnl f* **66/1**

5060 **8** *¾* **Malapropism**[30] [1076] 6-8-8 **78** .... EdwardCreighton(3) 8 76
(M R Channon) *chsd ldrs: drvn to chal over 1f out: wknd ins last* **25/1**

0000 **9** *nk* **Mutawaqed (IRE)**[279] [4377] 8-9-1 **82** .... (t) JimmyFortune 2 79+
(M A Magnusson) *bhd: drvn and hdwy over 1f out: styd on ins last but nvr gng pce to rch ldrs* **28/1**

3630 **10** *½* **Logsdail**[17] [1382] 6-8-10 **77** .... TPQueally 4 72
(G L Moore) *in tch: drvn and hdwy to chse ldrs 2f out: wknd fnl f* **28/1**

5031 **11** *½* **Bird Over**[18] [1338] 4-9-4 **85** .... SebSanders 1 79
(R M Beckett) *bhd: hdwy on outside over 2f out: sn one pce: wknd ins fnl f* **14/1**

0000 **12** *½* **Royal Orissa**[11] [1545] 4-8-10 **77** .... (p) RobertHavlin 11 69
(D Haydn Jones) *chsd ldrs: rdn 1/2-way: wknd fnl f* **25/1**

2066 **13** *3 ½* **Pure Imagination (IRE)**[11] [1532] 5-8-11 **78** .... TedDurcan 13 60
(J M Bradley) *chsd ldrs: rdn over 2f out: wknd over 1f out* **14/1**

0000 **14** *1* **Briannsta (IRE)**[13] [1474] 4-8-8 **75** .... (v[1]) ChrisCatlin 16 54
(M R Channon) *w ldr: rdn over 2f out: stl ev ch over 1f out: wknd sn after* **20/1**

1450 **15** *2* **Wrighty Almighty (IRE)**[264] [4787] 4-8-12 **82** .... AmirQuinn(3) 7 55
(P R Chamings) *chsd ldrs: rdn 1/2-way: wknd ins fnl 2f* **14/1**

0142 **16** *¾* **Pic Up Sticks**[13] [1474] 7-9-4 **85** .... TQuinn 3 55
(B G Powell) *fly-jmpd s: bhd: hdwy to press ldrs 3f out: wknd ins fnl 2f* **11/1**

0600 **17** *18* **Buy On The Red**[13] [1474] 5-8-12 **79** .... JohnEgan 6 —
(W R Muir) *chsd ldrs over 4f* **40/1**

0044 **18** *5* **Danzig River (IRE)**[13] [1494] 5-8-10 **77** .... AdrianTNicholls 18 —
(D Nicholls) *chsd ldrs: hrd drvn fr 1/2-way: sn btn* **7/1**[2]

1m 14.93s (0.61) **Going Correction** +0.40s/f (Good) **18** Ran SP% **124.0**
Speed ratings (Par 105):111,110,110,108,108 106,106,105,104,103 103,102,97,96,93 92,68,62
CSF £165.93 CT £1225.76 TOTE £9.40: £2.50, £5.20, £1.80, £2.10; EX 208.30.
Owner D J Deer **Bred** D J And Mrs Deer **Trained** Beckhampton, Wilts

FOCUS
A competitive sprint for the grade. There was no apparent draw bias or interference, and the form looks sound.
Exmoor Official explanation: trainer said, regarding improved form shown, gelding was better suited change of tactics, having been ridden too prominently at Pontefract.
Buy On The Red Official explanation: jockey said gelding had no more to give
Danzig River(IRE) Official explanation: jockey said gelding hung badly right-handed

1821 STANJAMESUK.COM H'CAP 1m 2f 6y
4:05 (4:06) (Class 5) (0-70,70) 4-Y-0+ **£4,533** (£1,348; £674; £336) **Stalls** High

Form RPR

1005 **1** **Prime Powered (IRE)**[13] [1478] 5-9-0 **66** .... RyanMoore 13 78
(G L Moore) *bhd: drvn along over 4f out: swtchd to outside over 2f out and str run to ld ins last: drvn out* **15/2**

6323 **2** *1* **Compton Court**[42] [905] 4-9-2 **68** .... SebSanders 4 78+
(A M Balding) *chsd ldrs: led over 2f out: sn hrd drvn: hdd ins last: one pce nr fin* **7/1**[3]

5320 **3** *2 ½* **Double Spectre (IRE)**[168] [4789] 4-9-1 **67** .... SteveDrowne 1 72
(Jean-Rene Auvray) *lw: bhd: rdn and hdwy over 2f out: r.o wl fnl f: nt pce to rch ldrs* **33/1**

2440 **4** *¾* **Libre**[20] [1288] 6-9-1 **67** .... PaulFitzsimons 3 71
(F Jordan) *hld up in tch: trckd ldrs gng wl appr fnl 2f: sn rdn: no ex fnl f* **16/1**

5305 **5** *¾* **Tribe**[7] [1651] 4-9-4 **70** .... JimmyFortune 14 72+
(Sir Michael Stoute) *lw: chsd ldrs: led over 3f out: hdd over 2f out: wknd fnl f* **4/1**[2]

4046 **6** *2 ½* **Desert Reign**[42] [905] 5-9-3 **69** .... TPQueally 12 66
(A P Jarvis) *bhd: hdwy 4f out: chsd ldrs 2f out: sn rdn: wknd fnl f* **10/1**

0606 **7** *2* **Fame**[16] [1425] 6-9-0 **66** .... (t) ChrisCatlin 6 60
(W Jarvis) *bhd: pushed along over 3f out: kpt on fr over 1f out but nvr gng pce to rch ldrs* **16/1**

0311 **8** *2 ½* **Tagula Blue (IRE)**[20] [1288] 6-9-1 **67** .... FergusSweeney 7 56
(Ian Williams) *slowly away and lost 4l: hdwy 3f out: nvr gng pce to rch ldrs: wknd over 1f out* **7/2**[1]

0000 **9** *7* **Final Promise**[37] [992] 4-9-0 **66** .... RobertHavlin 10 42
(J A Geake) *in tch: rdn 3f out: wknd over 2f out* **33/1**

2246 **10** *10* **Ticki Tori (IRE)**[342] [2488] 4-9-3 **69** .... TQuinn 11 26
(G C H Chung) *b.bkwd: in tch: rdn over 3f out: sn btn* **33/1**

0304 **11** *½* **Charlie Kennet**[20] [1288] 8-9-4 **70** .... VinceSlattery 9 26
(Mrs H Sweeting) *disp unsustainable pce tl definte advantage over 4f out: hdd over 3f out and sn btn* **11/1**

1050 **12** *3 ½* **Native American**[15] [1435] 4-8-12 **67** .... RobertMiles(3) 5 16
(T D McCarthy) *chsd clr ldrs: rdn over 3f out: sn btn* **100/1**

0560 **13** *¾* **Burgundy**[13] [1478] 9-9-3 **69** .... (b) JohnEgan 2 17
(P Mitchell) *hld up in rr: effrt over 3f out: sn wknd* **14/1**

050- **14** *2* **Shosolosa (IRE)**[559] [6574] 4-8-7 **66** .... KMay(7) 8 10
(B J Meehan) *b.bkwd: set unsustainable gallop and slt advantage tl hdd over 4f out: sn wknd* **66/1**

1504 **15** *½* **Oakley Absolute**[6] [1665] 4-9-2 **68** .... PatDobbs 16 11
(R Hannon) *chsd ldrs: rdn and btn 3f out* **20/1**

2m 9.40s (0.69) **Going Correction** +0.25s/f (Good) **15** Ran SP% **118.4**
Speed ratings (Par 103):107,106,104,103,103 101,99,97,91,83 83,80,80,78,78
CSF £54.44 CT £1643.18 TOTE £10.20: £3.00, £2.10, £6.60; EX 85.20.
Owner Prime Power GB Ltd **Bred** Caribbean Quest Partnership **Trained** Woodingdean, E Sussex

FOCUS
This was run at a strong pace, which suited those held up, but the form looks ordinary by Newbury standards.
Tagula Blue(IRE) Official explanation: jockey said gelding missed break
Ticki Tori(IRE) Official explanation: jockey said filly hung right-handed
Burgundy Official explanation: jockey said gelding had no more to give

1822 SPREADFAIR.COM MAIDEN STKS (DIV I) 1m 2f 6y
4:40 (4:42) (Class 5) 3-Y-0 **£4,210** (£1,252; £625; £312) **Stalls** High

Form RPR

1 **Simondiun** 3-9-3 .... PhilipRobinson 9 91+
(Mrs A J Perrett) *w'like: bhd: swtchd rt to outside and rapid hdwy fr 2f out to ld 1f out: sn pushed clr: easily* **16/1**[3]

4 **2** *6* **Valverde (IRE)**[30] [1088] 3-9-3 .... SebSanders 10 76
(J L Dunlop) *in tch: drvn to chal over 1f out: sn no ch w wnr but kpt on wl for 2nd* **5/2**[1]

5352 **3** *hd* **Beckett Hall (IRE)**[4] [1741] 3-9-3 77 .... RyanMoore 6 76
(R Hannon) *chsd ldrs: slt advantage ins fnl 2f tl hdd 1f out: sn no ch w wnr and styd on same pce* **5/2**[1]

5 **4** *shd* **His Honour (IRE)**[27] [1134] 3-9-3 .... SteveDrowne 3 76
(R Charlton) *lw: sn slt advantage: narrowly hdd ins fnl 2f: styd chalng and ev ch 1f out: sn no ch w wnr and one pce* **3/1**[2]

0 **5** *1 ¼* **Queen Isabella**[20] [1289] 3-8-12 .... OscarUrbina 4 71+
(J R Fanshawe) *lw: trckd ldrs tl lost position ins fnl 3f: nvr in contention after but n.m.r on rail ins fnl f and kpt on* **25/1**

6 *hd* **Cape Maya** 3-8-5 .... KMay(7) 8 68
(B J Meehan) *unf: b.bkwd: s.i.s: sn t.k.h and chsd ldrs after 3f: disp ld 3f out: stl ev ch over 1f out: wknd fnl f* **25/1**

7 *nk* **Stotsfold** 3-9-3 .... TedDurcan 2 72
(W R Swinburn) *w'like: b.bkwd: in tch: outpcd 3f out: edgd rt and green ins fnl 2f: kpt on fnl f but nvr a danger* **18/1**

8 *1 ¾* **Dance Spirit (IRE)** 3-9-3 .... JimmyFortune 5 69
(B J Meehan) *w'like: tall: chsd ldrs: drvn along 3f out: chal fr 2f out tl over 1f out: wknd ins last* **20/1**

9 *16* **Rockatorri** 3-8-12 .... ChrisCatlin 11 34
(M R Channon) *leggy: bhd most of way* **22/1**

10 *¾* **Dark Emotion** 3-9-3 .... AdrianMcCarthy 7 37
(W De Best-Turner) *leggy: a in rr* **100/1**

2m 13.93s (5.22) **Going Correction** +0.25s/f (Good) **10** Ran SP% **111.1**
Speed ratings (Par 99):89,84,84,83,82 82,82,81,68,67
CSF £48.01 TOTE £22.60: £3.60, £1.30, £1.60; EX 63.60.
Owner S P Tindall **Bred** Simon Tindall **Trained** Pulborough, W Sussex

FOCUS
This first division of the maiden was run at just a moderate early gallop and saw plenty still in with chances nearing the final furlong. The form should be treated with caution, but the winner still impressed nevertheless.
Queen Isabella Official explanation: jockey said filly was denied clear run
Stotsfold Official explanation: jockey said gelding hung right-handed

1823 SPREADFAIR.COM MAIDEN STKS (DIV II) 1m 2f 6y
5:10 (5:11) (Class 5) 3-Y-0 **£4,210** (£1,252; £625; £312) **Stalls** High

Form RPR

033 **1** **Bandama (IRE)**[18] [1335] 3-9-3 85 .... RyanMoore 8 85
(Mrs A J Perrett) *lw: in tch: hdwy on outside to ld 2f out: rdn 1f out: styd on strly ins last* **2/1**[1]

40 **2** *1 ½* **King Of Argos**[28] [1120] 3-9-3 .... SteveDrowne 6 82
(E A L Dunlop) *lw: t.k.h: in tch: hdwy over 2f out: chsd wnr and edgd lft ins last: no imp* **13/2**

0 **3** *2* **Contra Mundum (USA)**[18] [1335] 3-9-3 .... JimmyFortune 9 78
(B J Meehan) *chsd ldr 6f out: chal and rdn over 2f out: outpcd fnl f* **16/1**

4 *hd* **Millistar** 3-8-12 .... PhilipRobinson 3 73+
(M A Jarvis) *leggy: in tch: hdwy to chse ldrs 2f out: kpt on same pce fnl f* **7/2**[2]

5 *4* **Topjeu (IRE)** 3-9-3 .... TedDurcan 1 70+
(L M Cumani) *unf: scope: b.bkwd: s.i.s: sn mid-div: outpcd 3f out: styng on whn n.m.r on rail appr fnl f: kpt on again cl home* **11/2**[3]

6230 **6** *3 ½* **Dyanita**[24] [1214] 3-8-12 74 .... SamHitchcott 10 59
(B W Hills) *led after 2f: rdn over 3f out: hdd over 2f out: sn btn* **20/1**

36 **7** *shd* **Just Devine (IRE)**[28] [1118] 3-8-12 .... JohnEgan 4 59
(B Palling) *t.k.h in rr: hdwy to trck ldrs 3f out: sn rdn: wknd 2f out* **12/1**

00 **8** *1 ¾* **Meohmy**[18] [1351] 3-8-9 .... EdwardCreighton(3) 5 55+
(M R Channon) *a towards rr: rdn and no ch fnl 2f* **100/1**

9 *2* **Rifaat** 3-9-3 .... TQuinn 7 56
(C A Horgan) *w'like: b.bkwd: led 2f: chsd ldrs to 3f out: wkng whn bmpd 2f out* **28/1**

0 **10** *14* **Kirkstall Lane**[206] [6102] 3-9-3 .... PatDobbs 11 30
(R Hannon) *unf: s.i.s: a bhd* **66/1**

0 **11** *1 ½* **Mustammer**[18] [1336] 3-9-3 .... RHills 2 27
(M P Tregoning) *in tch: rdn 3f out: sn wknd* **12/1**

2m 11.9s (3.19) **Going Correction** +0.25s/f (Good) **11** Ran SP% **116.2**
Speed ratings (Par 99):97,95,94,94,90 88,87,86,84,73 72
CSF £14.73 TOTE £2.70: £1.20, £1.90, £5.10; EX 20.10 Place 6 £419.91, Place 5 £22.18.
Owner Lady Clague **Bred** Newberry Stud Farm Ltd **Trained** Pulborough, W Sussex

FOCUS
This second division of the maiden was run at a more generous gallop, and the form looks sound enough.
Just Devine(IRE) Official explanation: trainer's representative said filly had bled from nose
Rifaat Official explanation: jockey said gelding suffered interference in running
T/Plt: £484.60 to a £1 stake. Pool: £50,219.95. 75.65 winning tickets. T/Qpdt: £9.30 to a £1 stake. Pool: £4,780.70. 379.00 winning tickets. ST

[1645] NOTTINGHAM (L-H)
Friday, May 19

OFFICIAL GOING: Soft (good to soft in places)
Showers in the morning had eased the ground and a headwind in the straight made conditions more testing.
Wind: Fresh, against Weather: Overcast

1824 EUROPEAN BREEDERS FUND NOVICE STKS 6f 15y
2:05 (2:06) (Class 5) 2-Y-0 **£4,533** (£1,348; £674; £336) **Stalls** High

Form RPR

0 **1** **Fontana Amorosa**[30] [1082] 2-8-7 .... EddieAhern 7 79+
(K A Ryan) *a.p: rdn to chse ldr and hung lft fr over 2f out: led over 1f out: styd on u.p* **13/8**[1]

1 **2** *nk* **Everymanforhimself (IRE)**[30] [1080] 2-9-2 .... MickyFenton 1 87
(J G Given) *s.i.s: rn green in rr: hdwy over 2f out: rdn and ev ch fr over 1f out: edgd rt ins fnl f: styd on* **4/1**[2]

61 **3** *5* **Beckenham's Secret**[34] [1019] 2-9-5 .... DaneO'Neill 6 75
(B R Millman) *sn led: hung lft thrght: rdn and hdd over 1f out: wknd ins fnl f* **12/1**

10 **4** *1 ½* **Ask Don't Tell (IRE)**[9] [1582] 2-8-7 .... StephenCarson 3 59
(Tom Dascombe) *s.i.s: sn pushed along in rr: hdwy over 2f out: rdn and wknd over 1f out* **9/1**

31 **5** *1 ¼* **Diamond Hurricane (IRE)**[10] [1559] 2-8-11 .... DanielTudhope(3) 2 62
(P D Evans) *chsd ldrs over 4f* **4/1**[2]

51 **6** *12* **Juan Bol (IRE)**[11] 1535 2-8-12 .... MichaelTebbutt 5 24
(V Smith) *fly-leapt leaving stalls: plld hrd and prom: rdn 1/2-way: hung lft and wknd 2f out* **8/1**[3]

5 **7** *28* **Esteemed Prince**[18] 1333 2-8-12 .... ShaneKelly 4 —
(D Shaw) *chsd ldr to 1/2-way: sn rdn and wknd* **20/1**

1m 19.77s (4.77) **Going Correction** +0.45s/f (Yiel) **7** Ran SP% **111.7**
Speed ratings (Par 93):86,85,78,76,75 59,21
CSF £7.79 TOTE £2.40: £1.60, £1.50; EX 7.60.
Owner Joy And Valentine Feerick **Bred** Meon Valley Stud **Trained** Hambleton, N Yorks

FOCUS
A fair juvenile contest in which five of the seven runners were previous winners. The easy ground and headwind made this a real test, but the first two came clear and could prove useful. The third and fourth set the level for the form.

NOTEBOOK
Fontana Amorosa ◆had clearly been showing plenty of ability since her debut as she started favourite in a contest with five previous winners in opposition. She had to work hard to get the better of the runner-up, but showed the right attitude and, well-bred, being from the family of Stagecraft and Bella Colora, has secured her paddock value and may be given a break until later in the season. (op 7-4 tchd 15-8)
Everymanforhimself(IRE) ◆ ran with plenty of credit, having to come around his field to mount a challenge and only just losing out. Although a previous winner, he still looked green and has more improvement in him. There is a possibility he will go to Royal Ascot, and better ground will suit.
Beckenham's Secret set the pace and ran creditably on this turf debut, but may not have got home on easy ground made more testing by a headwind. Official explanation: jockey said gelding hung left throughout (op 14-1 tchd 16-1)
Ask Don't Tell(IRE) ran on to collar Diamond Hurricane, who faded in the closing stages, for fourth place, (op 10-1 tchd 11-1)
Diamond Hurricane(IRE), a fast-ground winner at Catterick, faded in the closing stages, and may have found the easy surface against him. Official explanation: jockey said gelding hung right (op 7-2 tchd 3-1)
Esteemed Prince Official explanation: jockey said gelding lost action

1825 RACING UK ON CHANNEL 432 H'CAP 6f 15y
2:35 (2:37) (Class 5) (0-70,69) 3-Y-O **£3,238** (£963; £481; £240) **Stalls** High

Form RPR

0210 **1** **Sunderland Echo (IRE)**[18] 1344 3-8-9 **65**............ StephenDonohoe(5) 7 76
(B Ellison) *mde all far side: rdn clr fnl f: 1st of 9 in gp* **7/1**[2]

4434 **2** *2 1/2* **Bobby Rose**[38] 969 3-8-12 **63**.. DaneO'Neill 6 67
(D K Ivory) *racd far side: hld up: hdwy 2f out: rdn to chse wnr and edgd lft fnl f: r.o: 2nd of 9 in gp* **8/1**[3]

6452 **3** *1 1/2* **Light Mozart**[15] 1431 3-8-11 **62**.. EddieAhern 3 61
(C E Brittain) *racd far side: a.p: chsd wnr over 2f out: rdn over 1f out: no ex fnl f: 3rd of 9 in gp* **8/1**[3]

6000 **4** *1/2* **Squadron Leader (IRE)**[3] 1751 3-9-0 **65**.......................... ShaneKelly 2 63
(R Hannon) *racd far side: s.i.s: hld up: hdwy over 2f out: rdn over 1f out: styd on same pce: 4th of 9 in gp* **10/1**

3315 **5** *3* **Buzzin'Boyzee (IRE)**[1] 1801 3-8-8 **59**......................... J-PGuillambert 14 48
(P D Evans) *racd stands' side: chsd ldrs: rdn to ld that side over 1f out: styd on: no ch w far side: 1st of 4 in gp* **7/1**[2]

0633 **6** *5* **Shopfitter**[3] 1768 3-8-4 **55** oh15....................................(b) HayleyTurner 5 29
(Mrs C A Dunnett) *racd far side: chsd ldrs: rdn over 2f out: sn wknd: 5th of 9 in gp* **50/1**

0105 **7** *nk* **Joking John**[3] 1768 3-7-13 **55** oh15.......................... LeanneKershaw(5) 1 28
(C W Fairhurst) *racd far side: in rr: rdn 1/2-way: n.d: 6th of 9 in gp* **50/1**

0266 **8** *2 1/2* **Immaculate Red**[20] 1279 3-8-8 **62**............................... SaleemGolam(3) 8 27
(R Bastiman) *racd far side: s.i.s: sn prom: hung rt and wknd over 2f out: 7th of 9 in gp* **20/1**

1050 **9** *3 1/2* **Xpres Boy (IRE)**[27] 1140 3-8-5 **56**................................... PaulEddery 10 11
(S R Bowring) *racd far side: s.i.s: sn chsng ldrs: rdn and wknd 2f out: 8th of 9 in gp* **28/1**

0250 **10** *1/2* **Ours (IRE)**[216] 5889 3-8-8 **62**... AdamKirby(3) 12 15
(J D Bethell) *racd stands' side: led 1f: remined handy tl wknd wl over 1f out: 2nd of 4 in gp* **8/1**[3]

0514 **11** *nk* **Roman Quest**[28] 1109 3-9-3 **68**.. MickyFenton 13 20
(H Morrison) *racd stands' side: led 5f out: rdn and hdd over 1f out: sn wknd: 3rd of 4 in gp* **9/2**[1]

2251 **12** *1 1/4* **Smile For Us**[22] 1263 3-9-4 **69**...................................(b) BrianReilly 11 17
(C Drew) *racd stands' side: s.i.s: sn chsng ldrs: hung lft 1/2-way: rdn and wknd wl over 1f out: last of 4 in gp* **17/2**

350 **13** *3* **Jucebabe**[212] 5984 3-8-12 **63**... FrancisFerris 9 —
(J L Spearing) *racd far side: chsd ldrs over 3f: last of 9 in gp* **20/1**

1m 16.88s (1.88) **Going Correction** +0.45s/f (Yiel) **13** Ran SP% **113.0**
Speed ratings (Par 99):105,101,99,99,95 88,87,84,79,79 78,77,73
CSF £54.48 CT £453.52 TOTE £5.60: £2.40, £1.90, £2.60; EX 69.00.
Owner Black and White Diamond Partnership **Bred** Ms Audrey Barlow **Trained** Norton, N Yorks

FOCUS
A modest sprint handicap in which the field split into two groups. The majority went far side and they held a significant advantage. The form seems sound rated around the placed horses.
Ours(IRE) Official explanation: jockey said gelding was unsuited by soft, good to soft in places ground
Smile For Us Official explanation: jockey said gelding missed break and hung

1826 JOHN SMITHS EXTRA SMOOTH MAIDEN STKS (DIV I) 1m 6f 15y
3:05 (3:06) (Class 5) 3-Y-O+ **£2,914** (£867; £433; £216) **Stalls** Low

Form RPR

0052 **1** **Shipmaster**[20] 1283 3-8-6 76.. EddieAhern 8 72+
(A King) *chsd ldrs: rdn over 2f out: led over 1f out: styd on wl: eased fnl half-f* **4/6**[1]

2 *3 1/2* **Contemplation** 3-8-6 .... StanleyChin 7 64+
(M Johnston) *dwlt: hld up: hdwy over 5f out: led over 2f out: rdr sn dropped whip: hdd over 1f out: edgd lft fnl f: eased whn btn* **6/1**[3]

0 **3** *6* **Openide**[16] 1409 5-9-12 .... DaneO'Neill 2 54
(B W Duke) *chsd ldrs: rdn over 2f out: sn wknd* **9/2**[2]

0446 **4** *1/2* **Esquillon**[72] 614 4-9-7 40... MickyFenton 1 48
(S Parr) *w ldr tl led 12f out: rdn and hdd over 2f out: sn wknd* **28/1**

05 **5** *8* **Dipped Wings (IRE)**[12] 1516 3-8-1 .... JamieMackay 6 36
(J L Dunlop) *sn drvn along in rr: lost tch 6f out: mod late prog* **16/1**

4 **6** *1/2* **Greenacre Legend**[15] 1434 4-9-7 .... MarcHalford(5) 9 41
(D B Feek) *slowly in to stride: hld up: effrt over 3f out: sn wknd* **100/1**

0 **7** *4* **Moonshine Creek**[20] 1290 4-9-12 .... ShaneKelly 10 36
(P W Hiatt) *hld up: plld hrd: hdwy over 5f out: rdn and wknd over 2f out* **20/1**

050 **8** *13* **Lord Adonis (IRE)**[20] 1283 3-8-6 55................................ FrancisFerris 3 16
(M J Attwater) *plld hrd and prom: lost pl over 6f out: wknd 4f out* **20/1**

00 **9** *dist* **Star Of Erhaab**[25] 1192 3-8-6 .... StephenCarson 4 —
(E A Wheeler) *led 2f: remained w ldr tl rdn 4f out: wknd qckly* **150/1**

3m 12.57s (5.47) **Going Correction** +0.275s/f (Good)
WFA 3 from 4yo+ 20lb **9** Ran SP% **113.0**
Speed ratings (Par 103):95,93,89,89,84 84,82,74,—
CSF £4.49 TOTE £1.40: £1.02, £1.80, £1.20; EX 5.60.
Owner Nigel Bunter **Bred** Newsells Park Stud Limited **Trained** Barbury Castle, Wilts

FOCUS
An uncompetitive staying maiden limited by the proximity of the fourth, but the first two could develop in to decent sorts.

1827 JOHN SMITHS EXTRA SMOOTH MAIDEN STKS (DIV II) 1m 6f 15y
3:40 (3:42) (Class 5) 3-Y-O+ **£2,914** (£867; £433; £216) **Stalls** Low

Form RPR

24 **1** **Souffleur**[30] 1081 3-8-6 .... HayleyTurner 2 66
(M L W Bell) *trckd ldrs: racd keenly: led over 4f out: edgd lft ins fnl f: rdn out* **3/1**[2]

43 **2** *1* **Accordello (IRE)**[12] 1503 5-9-0 .... JamesReveley(7) 9 60+
(K G Reveley) *hld up: hdwy 8f out: lost pl over 6f out: hdwy over 3f out: rdn and nt clr run ins fnl f: styd on* **12/1**

0044 **3** *1 3/4* **Encrypt (IRE)**[206] 6099 4-9-4 40.................................. AdamKirby(3) 10 58
(O Brennan) *sn led: hdd over 4f out: rdn over 2f out: no ex ins fnl f* **150/1**

52 **4** *7* **Congestion Charge**[22] 1260 3-8-1 .... FrancisNorton 5 47
(E A L Dunlop) *hld up: hdwy 10f out: rdn over 2f out: sn wknd* **4/1**[3]

0 **5** *1 1/4* **Magnum Opus (IRE)**[9] 1585 4-9-12 85.............................. EddieAhern 1 51
(T J Pitt) *chsd ldrs: rdn and nt clr run over 3f out: wknd fnl f* **11/4**[1]

64 **6** *16* **Soulard (USA)**[13] 1483 3-8-6 .... ShaneKelly 8 28
(J Noseda) *hld up: hdwy over 5f out: rdn and wknd over 2f out* **11/4**[1]

3 **7** *2 1/2* **Dawn Spirit**[23] 1231 3-7-13 ow3................................ AndrewMullen(5) 4 23
(J R Weymes) *chsd ldrs: rdn over 6f out: hmpd over 4f out: sn wknd* **20/1**

0 **8** *nk* **Kentuckian**[43] 897 4-9-12 .... StephenCarson 3 25
(P W Hiatt) *hld up: plld hrd: hdwy and hmpd over 4f out: wknd 3f out* **200/1**

9 *dist* **Devonia Plains (IRE)**[21] 4-9-9 .... RichardThomas(3) 6 —
(Mrs P N Dutfield) *s.i.s: a bhd: t.o fnl 5f* **40/1**

3m 12.77s (5.67) **Going Correction** +0.275s/f (Good)
WFA 3 from 4yo+ 20lb **9** Ran SP% **114.4**
Speed ratings (Par 103):94,93,92,88,87 78,77,76,—
CSF £36.17 TOTE £3.70: £1.20, £2.30, £12.60; EX 20.30.
Owner Baron F C Oppenheim **Bred** Baron Von Oppenheim **Trained** Newmarket, Suffolk

FOCUS
The second division of this maiden was run at a steady gallop, as was the first leg, and the time was just a fifth of a second slower. The form is weak with the third limiting the form.
Magnum Opus(IRE) Official explanation: jockey said gelding was unsuited by soft, good to soft in places ground
Soulard(USA) Official explanation: trainer's representative had no explanation for poor form shown

1828 BROWNE JACOBSON H'CAP 1m 54y
4:15 (4:16) (Class 4) (0-85,84) 3-Y-O **£6,477** (£1,927; £963; £481) **Stalls** Centre

Form RPR

421 **1** **Baskerville**[32] 1049 3-9-0 **80**.. EddieAhern 1 86
(P W Chapple-Hyam) *mde virtually all: rdn and edgd rt over 1f out: r.o* **5/1**[3]

3401 **2** *nk* **Ingratitude (IRE)**[11] 1547 3-9-1 **81** 6ex............................ MickyFenton 3 86+
(R M Beckett) *trckd ldrs: nt clr run over 1f out: rdn and ev ch ins fnl f: r.o* **7/4**[1]

2143 **3** *1* **European Dream (IRE)**[7] 1626 3-8-10 **76**........................... ShaneKelly 8 79+
(R C Guest) *hld up: nt clr run fr over 2f out tl r.o ins fnl f: nvr able to chal* **7/2**[2]

5004 **4** *1* **Ocean Pride (IRE)**[10] 1569 3-8-12 **81**..................... RichardSmith(3) 11 82
(R Hannon) *chsd wnr: rdn and ev ch over 1f out: no ex ins fnl f* **20/1**

5466 **5** *1* **Vodkatini**[20] 1291 3-8-6 **72**...................................(v) JimmyQuinn 4 71
(P J Makin) *plld hrd and prom: rdn and hung lft fr over 1f out: styd on same pce* **10/1**

1060 **6** *2* **Your Amount (IRE)**[18] 1349 3-8-10 **76**................................. JDSmith 2 71
(A King) *s.i.s: hld up: hdwy 5f out: rdn over 2f out: wknd ins fnl f* **20/1**

0415 **7** *shd* **Daaweitza**[114] 188 3-7-13 **70**..................................... AndrewMullen(5) 7 65
(B Ellison) *chsd ldrs: lost pl over 6f out: effrt over 1f out: wknd ins fnl f* **12/1**

0310 **8** *1/2* **Cinematic (IRE)**[224] 5716 3-8-12 **81**......................... SaleemGolam(3) 9 75
(M H Tompkins) *hld up: hdwy over 4f out: wknd over 1f out* **18/1**

6312 **9** *6* **Shogun Prince (IRE)**[292] 3973 3-9-4 **84**.......................... DaneO'Neill 6 66
(A King) *hld up: hdwy over 3f out: wknd 2f out* **14/1**

1m 46.66s (0.26) **Going Correction** +0.275s/f (Good) **9** Ran SP% **113.5**
Speed ratings (Par 101):109,108,107,106,105 103,103,103,97
CSF £13.85 CT £33.41 TOTE £5.30: £2.10, £1.10, £1.90; EX 9.60.
Owner Hintlesham Racing **Bred** Mrs J A Prescott **Trained** Newmarket, Suffolk

FOCUS
A decent handicap run fastest of the three races over the trip on the day and the form looks sound with the fourth and fifth close to recent form.

1829 COME RACING TOMORROW (S) H'CAP 1m 54y
4:50 (4:52) (Class 6) (0-60,60) 3-Y-O **£2,730** (£806; £403) **Stalls** Centre

Form RPR

0636 **1** **Peephole**[22] 1259 3-8-11 **53**...(v) JamieMackay 8 59
(P J Makin) *a.p: chsd ldr and hung lft fr over 2f out: rdn to ld ins fnl f: r.o* **9/1**[3]

0000 **2** *2 1/2* **Jellytot (USA)**[18] 1344 3-8-10 **57**............................ AndrewMullen(5) 2 58
(K A Ryan) *sn led: rdn over 1f out: hdd and unable qckn ins fnl f* **10/1**

6041 **3** *3* **Sczume (IRE)**[12] 1501 3-8-9 **56** 6ex.................. StephenDonohoe(5) 3 58+
(B Ellison) *hld up: hdwy and hung lft fr over 1f out: nrst fin* **7/2**[1]

0460 **4** *2 1/2* **Rock Of Cloonavery (IRE)**[27] 1141 3-8-13 **55**.......... J-PGuillambert 14 45
(S C Williams) *chsd ldrs: rdn over 2f out: sn outpcd* **9/1**[3]

6200 **5** *1 1/2* **Sky At Night (IRE)**[16] 1401 3-8-12 **54**............................ DaneO'Neill 1 43+
(P Mitchell) *hld up: rdn over 4f out: nt clr run over 2f out: nvr nrr* **9/1**[3]

500 **6** *3/4* **Just Tilly**[42] 900 3-8-8 **50**.. JimmyQuinn 9 36
(P R Chamings) *hdwy over 6f out: rdn over 2f out: sn wknd* **25/1**

0400 **7** *1* **Coffin Dodger**[4] 1726 3-7-11 **46** oh1.................... KirstyMilczarek(7) 15 30
(C N Allen) *s.i.s: rdn and hung lft 2f out: nvr nrr* **66/1**

3330 **8** *1 1/2* **Franky'N'Jonny**[20] 1293 3-8-11 **53**...........................(p) MickyFenton 4 34
(I A Wood) *s.s: outpcd: nvr nrr* **11/2**[2]

0600 **9** *1* **Bold Love**[46] 861 3-8-5 **47**.. FrancisNorton 5 26
(J D Bethell) *plld hrd and prom: rdn and wknd over 2f out* **22/1**

1004 **10** *1/2* **Crush On You**[45] 879 3-8-10 **52**... LPKeniry 12 30
(R Hollinshead) *mid-div: hdwy over 3f out: rdn and wknd 2f out* **12/1**

4500 **11** *3* **Aboyne (IRE)**[16] 1424 3-8-13 **60**............................(b1) JerryO'Dwyer(5) 11 32
(M G Quinlan) *chsd ldr tl rdn over 2f out: sn wknd* **33/1**
0400 **12** *3/4* **Simplified**[7] 1642 3-9-2 **58**.. EddieAhern 10 28
(J Pearce) *mid-div: rdn and wknd over 2f out* **25/1**
0120 **13** *3* **Dylan (IRE)**[22] 1259 3-8-10 **52**... KimTinkler 6 16
(N Tinkler) *sn outpcd* **10/1**
6000 **14** *3/4* **Champagne Moment**[11] 1549 3-8-9 **51** ow1..........(p) MichaelTebbutt 13 14
(V Smith) *mid-div: effrt over 3f out: sn wknd* **50/1**
2600 **15** *9* **Mr Cheers**[48] 839 3-8-6 **55**..(b) TolleyDean(7) 17 —
(R A Harris) *hld up: rdn over 3f out: sn wknd* **20/1**
000 **16** *30* **Ferroli**[27] 1149 3-8-4 **46**...(p) PaulQuinn 9 —
(J Balding) *hld up: rdn and wknd over 3f out* **66/1**

1m 47.53s (1.13) **Going Correction** +0.275s/f (Good) **16** Ran SP% **118.2**
Speed ratings (Par 97):105,102,99,97,95 94,93,92,91,90 87,87,84,83,74 44
CSF £84.25 CT £377.99 TOTE £12.10: £3.70, £2.50, £2.10, £2.60; EX 153.00.The winner was sold to J Pearce for 4,500gns. Scuzme was claimed by G. Doel for £6,000.
Owner Ten Horsepower **Bred** Mrs P Harford **Trained** Ogbourne Maisey, Wilts

FOCUS
A moderate seller for three-year-olds run nearly a second slower than the previous contest, but a race that very few got into. The first two set the level for the form.
Franky'N'Jonny Official explanation: jockey said filly suffered interference on leaving stalls

1830 HAPPY BRITHDAY BRITT HAUSELT H'CAP 1m 54y
5:20 (5:21) (Class 5) (0-75,80) 4-Y-O+ **£3,886** (£1,156; £577; £288) **Stalls** Centre

Form RPR
0201 **1** **Commitment Lecture**[28] 1123 6-8-10 **67**........................(t) PhillipMakin 5 77
(M Dods) *chsd ldrs: rdn to ld over 1f out: hung lft ins fnl f: all out* **5/1**[2]
0566 **2** *shd* **Ermine Grey**[13] 1480 5-8-4 **61**.. FrancisNorton 4 71
(A W Carroll) *mid-div: hdwy over 4f out: rdn over 2f out: r.o* **8/1**
235 **3** *shd* **Bold Act (IRE)**[16] 1401 4-8-13 **70**....................................... DaneO'Neill 14 80
(H Candy) *hld up in tch: lost pl over 3f out: hdwy over 2f out: sn rdn: hung lft ins fnl f: r.o* **12/1**
3052 **4** *3/4* **Topatoo**[25] 1186 4-9-1 **75**....................................... SaleemGolam(3) 15 83+
(M H Tompkins) *hld up: hdwy 2f out: rdn over 1f out: r.o* **11/2**[3]
1050 **5** *2 1/2* **Shifty**[16] 1422 7-7-12 **62**.. DanielleMcCreery(7) 8 65
(D Carroll) *sn led: rdn and hdd over 1f out: no ex ins fnl f* **22/1**
0106 **6** *1/2* **Following Flow (USA)**[20] 1280 4-8-11 **75**......... RussellKennemore(7) 9 77
(R Hollinshead) *s.i.s: hld up: hdwy over 2f out: sn hrd rdn: no ex fnl f* **50/1**
3260 **7** *shd* **Cantarna (IRE)**[137] 15 5-8-5 **62**................................. JamieMackay 16 64
(J Mackie) *hld up: hdwy over 3f out: rdn over 1f out: styd on same pce fnl f* **12/1**
2006 **8** *1 1/2* **Corky (IRE)**[11] 1531 5-9-1 **72**.. JimmyQuinn 11 71
(I W McInnes) *dwlt: hld up: hdwy over 2f out: wknd ins fnl f* **25/1**
0601 **9** *nk* **Lizarazu (GER)**[6] 1692 7-9-2 **80** 6ex..............................(p) TolleyDean(7) 2 79
(R A Harris) *s.i.s: hdwy 6f out: rdn over 1f out: wknd fnl f* **12/1**
0000 **10** *1/2* **Riley Boys (IRE)**[24] 1220 5-9-3 **74**.................................. MickyFenton 7 72
(J G Given) *s.i.s: hld up: hdwy over 3f out: rdn over 1f out: wknd and eased ins fnl f* **16/1**
2066 **11** *2 1/2* **Fabrian**[7] 1651 8-8-9 **71**.. JamesDoyle(5) 12 64
(R J Price) *plld hrd: sn w ldr: hung rt over 4f out: wknd 2f out* **10/1**
0006 **12** *nk* **Dark Charm (FR)**[13] 1494 7-8-13 **70**.............................. GylesParkin 13 62
(R A Fahey) *mid-div: rdn over 2f out: sn wknd* **28/1**
6030 **13** *hd* **Tom Forest**[203] 6134 4-8-8 **70**................................... AndrewMullen(5) 17 62
(K A Ryan) *mid-div: rdn over 4f out: wknd over 2f out* **16/1**
0066 **14** *1 1/4* **Soviet Threat (IRE)**[97] 381 5-8-6 **63**........................... J-PGuillambert 1 52
(A G Juckes) *plld hrd and prom: wknd 2f out* **40/1**
0024 **15** *1/2* **Firesong**[20] 1302 4-8-13 **75**.. EmmettStack(5) 10 63
(Pat Eddery) *trckd ldrs: racd keenly: wknd 2f out* **9/2**[1]

1m 48.0s (1.60) **Going Correction** +0.275s/f (Good) **15** Ran SP% **121.3**
Speed ratings (Par 103):103,102,102,102,99 99,98,97,97,96 94,93,93,92,91
CSF £42.21 CT £475.38 TOTE £7.90: £2.90, £2.30, £4.00; EX 70.10 Place 6 £30.45, Place 5 £20.85.
Owner Mrs B Riddell **Bred** Mrs Ian Pilkington **Trained** Denton, Co Durham

FOCUS
An ordinary handicap run slowest of the three races over the trip on the day, but the form looks sound with the runner-up and fifth the best guides. The field raced up the centre of the track in the straight.
Riley Boys(IRE) Official explanation: jockey said gelding missed break
Fabrian Official explanation: jockey said gelding hung right
T/Plt: £27.20 to a £1 stake. Pool: £33,283.10. 893.15 winning tickets. T/Qpdt: £7.10 to a £1 stake. Pool: £1,773.70. 182.30 winning tickets. CR

1803 YORK (L-H)
Friday, May 19
OFFICIAL GOING: Soft (heavy in places in back straight)
Wind: Strong; half against

1831 LANGLEYS SOLICITORS E B F MARYGATE STKS (LISTED RACE) (FILLIES) 5f
1:45 (1:45) (Class 1) 2-Y-O **£14,817** (£5,602; £2,800; £1,400) **Stalls** Centre

Form RPR
4111 **1** **Gilded (IRE)**[12] 1514 2-9-1 .... RichardHughes 5 94
(R Hannon) *cl up: rdn 2f out: swtchd sharply rt over 1f out: styd on u.p to ld ins last* **11/8**[1]
41 **2** *1/2* **Amber Valley**[20] 1278 2-8-12 .... NCallan 6 89
(K A Ryan) *lw: chsd ldrs: rdn along 2f out: styd on u.p ins last* **12/1**
34 **3** *3/4* **Cassiara**[11] 1542 2-8-12 .... JimmyQuinn 3 87?
(J Pearce) *in tch: rdn along 1/2-way: styd on wl appr last: nrst fin* **11/1**
1 **4** *1 3/4* **Kerry's Dream**[29] 1096 2-8-12 .... DavidAllan 7 80
(T D Easterby) *lw: led: rdn whn hung bdly lft wl over 1f out: hdd ins last and sn wknd* **7/2**[2]
01 **5** *5* **Down The Well (IRE)**[7] 1647 2-8-12 .... JamieSpencer 8 62
(J A Osborne) *a towards rr* **15/2**
23 **6** *3* **Feelin Foxy**[13] 1491 2-8-12 .... PatrickMathers 4 51
(D Shaw) *dwlt: a rr* **25/1**
251 **7** *6* **Camissa**[11] 1542 2-8-12 .... KDarley 1 30
(D K Ivory) *chsd ldrs: rdn along 2f out: sn wknd* **6/1**[3]

62.67 secs (3.35) **Going Correction** +0.70s/f (Yiel) **7** Ran SP% **110.2**
Speed ratings (Par 98):101,100,99,96,88 83,73
CSF £18.01 TOTE £2.10: £1.50, £4.70; EX 13.90 Trifecta £72.90 Pool: £521.70 - 5.08 winning units.
Owner Mrs J Wood **Bred** Tally-Ho Stud **Trained** East Everleigh, Wilts

FOCUS
Just an average Listed event with Amber Valley, Cassiara and Kerry's Dream all appearing to improve significantly on their maiden form, but Gilded did well to overcome trouble in running and defy her 3lb penalty and she is bordering on a three-figure RPR.

NOTEBOOK
Gilded(IRE), upped to Listed company following success in a maiden and a couple of reasonable conditions races, gamely completed the four-timer. Always handy, she came under pressure some way before the early leader Kerry's Dream, and had to be switched quite sharply when that one began to drift, but she kept finding under pressure to defy her 3lb penalty. She will now be aimed at the Queen Mary Stakes at Royal Ascot and the Super Sprint at Newbury. (op Evens tchd 6-4 in places)
Amber Valley, off the mark in just a modest fillies' maiden at Haydock on her second start, improved significantly and was just held. Connections will be delighted to pick up some black type and there should be even more to come. (op 10-1)
Cassiara, a promising third on her debut at Leicester but a beaten favourite next time at Windsor, confirmed that initial promise with a fine effort in third. She should win her maiden before stepping back up in class. (op 14-1)
Kerry's Dream, off the mark on her debut under similar conditions in a modest Ripon maiden, looked the one to beat when still travelling strongly in front around two furlongs out, but she seemed to get tired quite quickly and blew her chance by veering badly left. It may be that did just a bit too much in front, given the conditions, and she can be given another chance to pick up some black type. (op 5-1)
Down The Well(IRE), a surprise winner on fast ground at Nottingham on her previous start, was found out by the step up in class and switch to a soft surface. (op 8-1)
Camissa could not repeat the form she showed to win at Windsor on her previous start and was disappointing. (op 8-1)

1832 VC CASINO.COM STKS (H'CAP) 1m
2:15 (2:15) (Class 2) (0-100,91) 3-Y-O **£16,516** (£4,913; £2,455; £1,226) **Stalls** Low

Form RPR
331 **1** **Peppertree Lane (IRE)**[29] 1101 3-8-11 **84**............................ KDarley 3 99
(M Johnston) *mde virtually all: rdn over 2f out: drvn ent last and styd on wl* **11/8**[1]
1411 **2** *3 1/2* **Anna Pavlova**[253] 5064 3-9-4 **91**.................................... TonyHamilton 2 99
(R A Fahey) *trckd ldrs: hdwy 2f out: rdn to chal over 1f out and ev ch tl drvn and one pce ins last* **12/1**
4151 **3** *5* **Kinsya**[29] 1099 3-8-9 **82**... DarryllHolland 5 80
(M H Tompkins) *lw: hld up in tch: hdwy over 2f out: sn rdn and one pce* **9/4**[2]
0045 **4** *3* **Damelza (IRE)**[16] 1423 3-8-7 **80**.. DavidAllan 1 72
(T D Easterby) *hld up: hdwy to chse ldrs over 3f out: sn rdn and wknd fnl 2f* **16/1**
1144 **5** *11* **Bonnie Prince Blue**[28] 1115 3-9-2 **89**............................... MichaelHills 6 59
(B W Hills) *cl up: rdn along 3f out: drvn and wknd 2f out* **7/1**[3]
4512 **6** *12* **Tempsford Flyer (IRE)**[17] 1384 3-8-11 **84**.............................. KFallon 4 30
(J W Hills) *chsd ldng pair: rdn along over 3f out: sn wknd* **7/1**[3]

1m 44.81s (5.31) **Going Correction** +0.825s/f (Soft) **6** Ran SP% **111.4**
Speed ratings (Par 105):106,102,97,94,83 71
CSF £18.33 TOTE £2.10: £1.50, £2.90; EX 13.90.
Owner P D Savill **Bred** Gestut Wittekindshof **Trained** Middleham Moor, N Yorks

FOCUS
Just the six runners, but this looked like a strong handicap for the grade. Peppertree Lane followed up his recent Ripon maiden success in most decisive fashion from Irish Oaks entry Anna Pavlova. Both look ahead of the Handicapper.

NOTEBOOK
Peppertree Lane(IRE) ◆, off the mark on his reappearance under similar conditions in a maiden at Ripon, showed himself on a very fair mark on his handicap debut. He was seriously challenged early in the straight and looked set for a continued battle to the line, but found plenty to draw right away. He should stay further and looks capable of defying a rise in the weights. (tchd 6-4)
Anna Pavlova ◆, who progressed well as a juvenile to win three of her five starts, interestingly has an Irish Oaks entry. Racing on soft ground for the first time, she could not live with the winner late on, but was entitled to get tired given this was her first run in 253 days. This must rate as a very promising return and presumably connections think she could have even more to offer over further. (op 14-1)
Kinsya, 7lb higher than when winning at Ripon on his reappearance, had the ground in his favour but proved disappointing. Admittedly the front two both look very useful, but he could still have been expected to finish closer. (op 11-4)
Damelza(IRE), dropped a couple of furlongs in trip, could not reverse Ripon placings with Kinsya. (op 20-1)
Bonnie Prince Blue could not build on the promise he showed on his reappearance at Newbury, and a mile on this ground probably stretched his stamina. (op 11-2)

1833 EMIRATES AIRLINE YORKSHIRE CUP (GROUP 2) 1m 5f 197y
2:45 (2:45) (Class 1) 4-Y-O+
£79,492 (£30,128; £15,078; £7,518; £3,766; £1,890) **Stalls** Low

Form RPR
5-20 **1** **Percussionist (IRE)**[118] 2633 5-8-12 109..................... DarryllHolland 4 117
(J Howard Johnson) *hld up in tch: hdwy over 5f out: chal over 3f out: rdn to ld over 2f out: drvn and styd on wl ent last* **9/1**
1214 **2** *3* **Sergeant Cecil**[27] 1128 7-8-12 112.................................... AlanMunro 6 113
(B R Millman) *lw: hld up in rr: hdwy 5f out: rdn to chse ldrs 3f out: drvn to chal and ev ch over 1f out: one pce ins last* **9/2**[3]
0302 **3** *6* **Orcadian**[7] 1628 5-8-12 102.. NCallan 5 105
(J M P Eustace) *chsd ldr: hdwy 4f out: rdn to ld over 3f out: hdd over 2f out: sn drvn and wknd over 1f out* **7/1**
1221 **4** *1 1/4* **Kastoria (IRE)**[19] 1324 5-8-9 ....(t) MJKinane 10 101
(John M Oxx, Ire) *lw: hld up in rr: hdwy 5f out: rdn to chse ldrs over 2f out: sn drvn and no imp* **11/4**[1]
1224 **5** *6* **The Geezer**[230] 5637 4-8-12 .... LDettori 9 96
(Saeed Bin Suroor) *lw: trckd ldng pair: pushed along 5f out: rdn over 3f out and sn btn* **7/2**[2]
0100 **6** *5* **Cherry Mix (FR)**[78] 562 5-9-3 ....(t) KerrinMcEvoy 8 94
(Saeed Bin Suroor) *led: rdn along over 4f out: hdd over 3f out and sn wknd* **13/2**
0005 **7** *134* **Winged D'Argent (IRE)**[9] 1584 5-8-12 108.............................. KDarley 7 —
(M Johnston) *chsd ldrs: rdn along after 5f: outpcd and bhd fr 5f out* **12/1**

3m 12.41s (13.97) **Going Correction** +1.35s/f (Soft) **7** Ran SP% **110.6**
Speed ratings (Par 115):114,112,108,108,104 101,—
CSF £45.49 TOTE £11.40: £3.50, £2.70; EX 56.40 Trifecta £193.90 Pool: £1,630.74 - 6 winning units.
Owner Transcend Bloodstock LLP **Bred** Swettenham Stud **Trained** Billy Row, Co Durham

FOCUS
This looked a decent renewal, but they finished well strung out after Cherry Mix had set a strong pace in the testing ground. The form has been rated conservatively owing to the conditions.

NOTEBOOK

Percussionist(IRE), beaten a neck into second in this race last year, had since shown just modest form in four runs over hurdles. Returned to the Flat, he had conditions in his favour and showed he retains all of his ability with a good staying display. He should remain very competitive in these types of races when there is 'soft' in the going description, and the Irish St Leger looks a good long-term target. (op 10-1)

Sergeant Cecil ◆, fourth in the John Porter on his reappearance at Newbury, ran a terrific race on ground much softer than he cares for. He has made the step up from handicapper to Group performer with no problems at all and can do even better on faster ground. He looks an ideal type for the Ascot Gold Cup. (op 4-1)

Orcadian, who would surely have won the Ormonde Stakes at Chester on his previous start but for nearly pulling himself up inside the final mile, was better behaved this time and seemed to run his race. He was unable to dominate, but looked happy enough getting a lead and can have few excuses. (op 9-1)

Kastoria(IRE), successful in an ordinary Listed race over a mile and five at Navan on her reappearance, would have found this much tougher and failed to return to the sort of form she showed in Group company last year. (tchd 5-2 and 3-1 in places)

The Geezer, a length second to Scorpion in the St Leger for David Elsworth last season, ran a shocker on his debut for Godolphin. He looked very fit beforehand, but many of his stable's horses have not been running well so far this season and he was beaten a fair way out. A really likeable type last year, he deserves another chance and connections will have plenty of options as he is by no means just a one-dimensional stayer. (op 10-3 tchd 4-1)

Cherry Mix(FR) set a good pace but dropped out tamely. His stamina was unproven, but his yard is basically badly out of form. (op 8-1)

Winged D'Argent(IRE) Official explanation: jockey said gelding ran flat

1834 MICHAEL SEELY MEMORIAL FILLIES' STKS (LISTED RACE) 1m

3:15 (3:16) (Class 1) 3-Y-O **£17,781** (£6,723; £3,360; £1,680) **Stalls** Low

Form RPR

1413 **1** **Short Dance (USA)**[27] 1130 3-9-1 100 .... RichardHughes 5 107
(B W Hills) *lw: mde all: pushed clr over 2f out: rdn over 1f out: styd on strly* **9/2**[2]

2263 **2** *12* **Salut D'Amour (IRE)**[31] 1068 3-8-12 104 .... KFallon 4 90
(J Noseda) *lw: j. awkwardly and in rr: gd hdwy 3f out: rdn to chse wnr over 1f out: sn drvn: hung rt and no imp: eased ins last* **6/4**[1]

1400 **3** *5* **Queen Of Fire**[244] 5286 3-8-12 97 .... JamieSpencer 1 70
(M R Channon) *chsd wnr: effrt 3f out: rdn over 2f out and sn one pce* **16/1**

511 **4** *6* **Spinning Ruby**[16] 1406 3-8-12 93 .... NelsonDeSouza 3 58
(R M Beckett) *chsd wnr: rdn along 3f out: sn outpcd* **11/2**

031 **5** *17* **Heaven Sent**[25] 1191 3-8-12 82 .... MJKinane 6 24
(Sir Michael Stoute) *chsd ldrs: rdn along over 3f out: sn wknd* **5/1**[3]

16 **6** *13* **Dictatrix**[27] 1130 3-8-12 94 .... NCallan 2 —
(J M P Eustace) *dwlt: hdwy 1/2-way: chsd ldrs over 3f out: sn rdn and wknd qckly* **6/1**

1m 44.73s (5.23) **Going Correction** +0.825s/f (Soft) **6** Ran SP% **110.4**

Speed ratings (Par 104):106,94,89,83,66 53

CSF £11.33 TOTE £6.10: £2.90, £1.50; EX 13.50.

Owner K Abdulla **Bred** Juddmonte Farms Inc **Trained** Lambourn, Berks

FOCUS

With both Heaven Sent and Dictatrix running well below the form they showed on their respective reappearances, and Salut D'Amour never looking happy, this fillies' Listed race did not take much winning. However, Short Dance could do no more than win by 12 lengths and Richard Hughes was impressed enough to think she will be worth her place in the Irish 1000 Guineas.

NOTEBOOK

Short Dance(USA), just over a length behind subsequent 1000 Guineas third Nasheej in the Fred Darling on her reappearance, improved on the bare form of that effort upped to a mile for the first time with a facile success. She had the run of the race in front, but still looked set for a race when Salut D'Armour began to stay on and did well to find so much under pressure, although the beaten distances are obviously exaggerated given the testing ground (she has been rated value for 7 lengths over the easeed runner-up). Richard Hughes was very complimentary afterwards and suggested she will be well worth her place in the Irish 1000 Guineas. (op 4-1)

Salut D'Amour(IRE), third behind subsequent 1000 Guineas winner Speciosa in the Nell Gwyn on her reappearance, nearly got rid of her rider when awkward away from the stalls and never looked happy thereafter. When finally beginning to stay on, she hung to her left and the eventual winner soon cleared away. She is better than this, but may not be straightforward. (op 13-8 tchd 7-4)

Queen Of Fire, racing beyond six furlongs for the first time on her return from a 244-day break, was well beaten but picked up some valuable black type. (op 14-1)

Spinning Ruby would have found this tougher than the three-runner conditions event she won on her reappearance, but ran well below form in any case. A mile on ground this soft probably stretched her. (op 5-1)

Heaven Sent, off the mark in a Windsor maiden on her reappearance, ran no sort of race upped to Listed company. She is by Pivotal, so it is disappointing she did not appear to handle the ground, and she has something to prove now. (op 7-1)

Dictatrix, the winner of a heavy ground maiden at Yarmouth on her only start at two, and sixth in the Fred Darling on her reappearance, ran a shocker. She may have failed to stay. Official explanation: trainer said filly finished distressed (op 13-2)

1835 COUNTRYWIDE FREIGHT STKS (H'CAP) 6f

3:50 (3:50) (Class 2) (0-100,100) 4-Y-0+ **£12,954** (£3,854; £1,926; £962) **Stalls** Centre

Form RPR

1231 **1** **Borderlescott**[223] 5745 4-9-1 97 .... RoystonFfrench 7 109
(R Bastiman) *mde all: rdn 2f out: drvn ins last and kpt on gamely* **12/1**

5000 **2** *½* **Rising Shadow (IRE)**[13] 1487 5-8-6 88 .... PaulFessey 8 98
(T D Barron) *dwlt and towards rr: hdwy 2f out: rdn over 1f out: styd on strly u.p ins last* **8/1**

6000 **3** *nk* **Gifted Gamble**[9] 1597 4-8-6 88 ....(b) NCallan 9 97
(K A Ryan) *chsd wnr: rdn and ev ch over 1f out: drvn and nt qckn wl ins last* **16/1**

0000 **4** *¾* **Mutawaffer**[224] 5717 5-8-5 87 .... TonyHamilton 10 94
(R A Fahey) *in tch: hdwy 2f out: sn rdn and kpt on u.p ins last: nrst fin* **10/1**

1042 **5** *shd* **Ice Planet**[13] 1487 5-8-9 91 .... KFallon 12 98
(D Nicholls) *midfield: hdwy 2f out: styd on ins last: nrst fin* **5/1**[1]

1420 **6** *½* **Intrepid Jack**[238] 5438 4-9-1 97 .... JamieSpencer 11 102
(H Morrison) *chsd ldrs: rdn along 2f out: drvn and one pce ent last* **14/1**

2130 **7** *1¼* **Fullandby (IRE)**[15] 1438 4-8-6 88 ow1 .... RichardHughes 3 89
(T J Etherington) *chsd ldrs: rdn along wl over 1f out: wknd ent last* **12/1**

2231 **8** *3* **Commando Scott (IRE)**[11] 1532 5-8-1 85 3ex oh1 PatrickMathers(3) 14 78
(I W McInnes) *in tch: rdn along 2f out: sn drvn and no imp* **9/1**

300U **9** *3* **Coeur Courageux (FR)**[13] 1487 4-8-13 100 .... LiamTreadwell(5) 5 83
(D Nicholls) *rrd s and bhd: hdwy 2f out: kpt on ins last: nrst fin* **50/1**

0000 **10** *hd* **Funfair Wane**[47] 846 7-8-4 89 .... SilvestreDeSousa(3) 17 72
(D Nicholls) *cl up: rdn along over 2f out: grad wknd* **40/1**

0465 **11** *5* **Pieter Brueghel (USA)**[13] 1487 7-8-9 91 .... MJKinane 4 59
(D Nicholls) *lw: chsd ldrs: rdn along over 2f out: sn wknd* **15/2**[3]

0006 **12** *¾* **Continent**[13] 1487 9-8-10 92 .... DarryllHolland 2 57
(D Nicholls) *a towards rr* **20/1**

U000 **13** *2½* **Fantasy Believer**[13] 1487 8-8-5 87 .... AlanMunro 6 45
(J J Quinn) *in tch: pushed along 1/2-way: sn wknd* **40/1**

1633 **14** *2* **Beaver Patrol (IRE)**[23] 1246 4-8-8 90 .... LDettori 1 42
(R F Johnson Houghton) *chsd ldrs: pushed along 1/2-way: sn wknd* **7/1**[2]

0600 **15** *6* **Josh**[30] 1086 4-8-8 90 .... KerrinMcEvoy 15 24
(K A Ryan) *bhd fr 1/2-way* **16/1**

0063 **16** *2* **Jonny Ebeneezer**[13] 1481 7-8-12 94 ....(b) MichaelHills 13 22
(M Wellings) *a rr* **33/1**

0200 **17** *39* **Doric (USA)**[11] 1532 5-8-5 87 .... RichardMullen 16 —
(B Ellison) *a rr* **66/1**

1m 15.39s (2.83) **Going Correction** +0.70s/f (Yiel) **17** Ran SP% **121.0**

Speed ratings (Par 109):109,108,107,106,106 106,104,100,96,96 89,88,85,82,74 71,19

CSF £97.74 CT £1561.23 TOTE £13.90: £2.80, £3.00, £5.20, £3.20; EX 202.00.

Owner Border Rail & Plant Limited **Bred** James Clark **Trained** Cowthorpe, N Yorks

FOCUS

A really competitive sprint handicap in which Borderlescott sustained a strong pace from the start to finish. He progressed into a very useful sprinter last season and he is still improving. The second and the fifth set the standard, and the form is solid.

NOTEBOOK

Borderlescott ◆ won his first handicap off a mark of 64, but progressed throughout last season to land four of his eight starts, including on his final outing off a mark of 92 over this course and distance. Racing off a 5lb higher mark on his first run in 223 days, he set a very strong pace and had just enough left to hold on, though getting tired close home. He is entitled to come on for this and he has the potential to make the step up to pattern company at some stage. (op 14-1)

Rising Shadow(IRE), down the field on both his starts so far this year, stepped up on those efforts and finished faster than anything. On this evidence he certainly looks one to be with in future, but he has managed to win just twice in 26 starts and is not one to get carried away with. (op 9-1)

Gifted Gamble, due to be dropped 3lb, had every chance and ran right up to his best. However, he only has a juvenile maiden success to his name. (op 12-1)

Mutawaffer ◆ made a very pleasing return from a 224-day break. He was rated 100 as a juvenile and his connections will surely be able to exploit his current mark. (op 11-1)

Ice Planet just hit full stride too late, but he was not beaten far and this was another highly creditable effort. (op 4-1)

Intrepid Jack made a pleasing reappearance off the back of a 238-day break.

Coeur Courageux(FR) ◆ lost his chance when rearing up leaving the stalls, but caught the eye running on nicely. There could be a decent race or two in him this year.

Pieter Brueghel(USA) was not at his best and seems better suited by a faster surface. (tchd 8-1)

Beaver Patrol(IRE) failed to build on the from he showed on his reappearance and was disappointing. (op 10-1)

Doric(USA) Official explanation: jockey said gelding was unsuited by soft (heavy in places in the straight) ground

1836 PLAY VC CASINO.COM STKS (H'CAP) 7f

4:25 (4:26) (Class 3) (0-95,95) 3-Y-O **£9,715** (£2,890; £1,444; £721) **Stalls** Low

Form RPR

1502 **1** **Collateral Damage (IRE)**[7] 1626 3-8-4 81 oh1 .... DavidAllan 4 93
(T D Easterby) *lw: trckd ldrs: gd hdwy 3f out: led 2f out: sn rdn clr and kpt on* **5/1**[3]

0215 **2** *2½* **Skhilling Spirit**[20] 1292 3-9-4 95 .... PaulFessey 6 101
(T D Barron) *hld up towards rr: hdwy wl over 2f out: rdn and bmpd over 1f out: chsd wnr ins last: kpt on* **16/1**

5263 **3** *8* **The Snatcher (IRE)**[12] 1505 3-8-13 90 .... RichardHughes 2 77
(R Hannon) *led: rdn along and hdd 3f out: drvn and one pce fnl 2f* **10/3**[2]

3020 **4** *2½* **Angel Voices (IRE)**[16] 1404 3-8-4 81 oh3 .... RichardMullen 3 62
(K R Burke) *chsd ldrs: rdn along 3f out: drvn 2f out and sn wknd* **20/1**

2006 **5** *1¼* **Choysia**[20] 1292 3-8-9 86 ow1 .... FergalLynch 8 64
(D W Barker) *in tch: hdwy on outer to ld 3f out: rdn and hdd 2f out: sn wandered and wknd* **40/1**

2421 **6** *2* **Mr Sandicliffe**[16] 1412 3-8-9 86 .... AlanMunro 5 59
(B W Hills) *a rr* **12/1**

121 **7** *7* **Bentong (IRE)**[12] 1512 3-8-12 89 5ex .... JamieSpencer 1 45
(P F I Cole) *lw: chsd ldrs on inner: rdn along wl over 2f out: sn wknd* **11/8**[1]

3110 **8** *15* **Ludovico**[34] 1016 3-8-11 88 .... NCallan 7 8
(K A Ryan) *cl up: rdn along 1/2-way: sn wknd* **12/1**

1m 28.78s (3.38) **Going Correction** +0.70s/f (Yiel) **8** Ran SP% **110.3**

Speed ratings (Par 103):108,105,96,93,91 89,81,64

CSF £72.75 CT £287.70 TOTE £5.40: £1.40, £3.20, £1.50; EX 49.30.

Owner Middleham Park Racing Xxv **Bred** Minch Bloodstock And Castletown Stud **Trained** Great Habton, N Yorks

FOCUS

This looked a reasonable handicap beforehand but, with both The Snatcher and Betong running below their best, the form does not look very strong. Still, the front two both appeared to show improved form and came a long way clear.

NOTEBOOK

Collateral Damage(IRE) showed improved form when second under similar conditions in a similar event at Chester on his previous start and progressed again to run out a clear-cut winner. He will find things tougher off higher marks back on fast ground. (op 13-2)

Skhilling Spirit, upped to seven furlongs for the first time, stepped up on the form he showed on his reappearance and saw the trip out well.

The Snatcher(IRE) had conditions to suit but could not build on the form he showed when third at Newmarket on his previous start. (op 4-1)

Angel Voices(IRE) should not have minded the ground, but would have found this a tough enough ask from 3lb out of the handicap. (op 25-1)

Choysia's two career wins came over five furlongs on fast ground, so these conditions are unlikely to have suited.

Bentong(IRE), 7lb well-in under the penalty he picked up for winning a good six-furlong handicap on fast ground on his previous start, should not have minded the step back up in trip or return to easier ground, but ran a stinker. Official explanation: jockey said colt was unsuited by soft (heavy in places in the straight) ground (op 11-10 tchd 6-4 and evens in a place early)

1837 RIPLEYCOLLECTION.COM STKS (H'CAP) 1m 4f

5:00 (5:00) (Class 4) (0-80,80) 3-Y-O **£7,772** (£2,312; £1,155; £577) **Stalls** Centre

Form RPR

042 **1** **Swan Queen**[24] 1214 3-8-13 75 .... LDettori 6 83+
(J L Dunlop) *hld up: hdwy over 4f out: chsd ldrs 3f out: rdn to ld 2f out: sn drvn and edgd rt over 1f out: kpt on ins last* **5/1**[3]

0611 **2** *hd* **Cool Customer (USA)**[16] 1403 3-9-1 77 .... JamieSpencer 3 84+
(E A L Dunlop) *lw: hld up: gd hdwy 5f out: led over 3f out: rdn and hdd 2f out: drvn: bmpd and hit by rival's whip over 1f out: kpt on gamely* **3/1**[1]

0660 **3** *6* **Rebelling (IRE)**[32] 1052 3-8-6 68 .... AlanMunro 1 67
(R F Johnson Houghton) *keen: hld up in rr: hdwy over 3f out: sn rdn and kpt on appr last: nrst fin* **22/1**

0205 **4** *13* **Moonhawk**[20] 1283 3-9-2 78 DarryllHolland 9 59
(J Howard Johnson) *chsd ldrs: hdwy and cl up 4f out: rdn along 3f out: drvn and wknd fnl 2f* **20/1**
3215 **5** *6* **Regal Connection (USA)**[214] 5939 3-8-13 75 RoystonFfrench 8 47
(M Johnston) *led: rdn along over 4f out: hdd over 3f out and sn wknd* **16/1**
14 **6** *15* **Samurai Jack (IRE)**[49] 822 3-8-10 72 (t) DavidAllan 7 23
(John A Quinn, Ire) *hld up in rr: hdwy 4f out: rdn along wl over 2f out and nvr a factor* **12/1**
1235 **7** *shd* **Marachi Band (USA)**[9] 1583 3-8-10 72 (b) RichardMullen 4 23
(E J O'Neill) *chsd ldrs on inner: rdn along 4f out: drvn and wknd 3f out* **11/2**
0514 **8** *14* **Unique Moment**[30] 1079 3-8-9 76 GregFairley(5) 12 8
(M Johnston) *chsd ldrs: rdn along over 5f out: sn wknd* **7/1**
0033 **9** *26* **Karlani (IRE)**[25] 1182 3-8-5 67 (v1) MJKinane 11 —
(Sir Michael Stoute) *prom: rdn along 4f out: drvn and wknd 3f out* **4/1**[2]
3205 **10** *10* **Myrtle Bay (IRE)**[20] 1296 3-9-0 76 NCallan 5 —
(K R Burke) *lw: chsd ldrs: rdn along 5f out: sn wknd* **25/1**

2m 48.04s (15.64) **Going Correction** +1.35s/f (Soft) **10** Ran SP% **116.1**
Speed ratings (Par 101):101,100,96,88,84 74,74,64,47,40
CSF £19.68 CT £302.74 TOTE £5.30: £1.90, £1.60, £7.40; EX 23.30 Place 6 £156.06, Place 5 £80.77.
Owner Sir Thomas Pilkington **Bred** Sir Thomas Pilkington **Trained** Arundel, W Sussex

FOCUS
This looked like a fair middle-distance handicap but, the front two apart, they finished well strung out. The third sets the standard.
Myrtle Bay(IRE) Official explanation: jockey said gelding had no more to give
T/Jkpt: £87,698.80 to a £1 stake. Pool: £247,039.00. 2.00 winning tickets. T/Plt: £283.40 to a £1 stake. Pool: £117,475.05. 302.50 winning tickets. T/Qpdt: £73.60 to a £1 stake. Pool: £5,178.50. 52.00 winning tickets. JR

1817 NEWBURY (L-H)
Saturday, May 20

OFFICIAL GOING: Soft
Wind: Strong against

1838 PADDYPOWERCASINO.COM MAIDEN STKS 6f 8y
1:35 (1:36) (Class 4) 2-Y-O **£6,477** (£1,927; £963; £481) **Stalls** Centre

Form RPR
1 **Major Cadeaux** 2-9-3 RichardHughes 12 90+
(R Hannon) *w'like: scope: trckd ldrs: squeezed between horses to chal 1f out: sn led: rdn and styd on strly ins last* **7/1**[2]
2 *1 ¼* **Jo'Burg (USA)** 2-9-3 MJKinane 15 86
(Mrs A J Perrett) *cmpt: str: scope: lw: sn trcking ldrs: led 2f out: rdn over 1f out: hdd jst ins last: kpt on but nt pce of wnr* **14/1**
3 *¾* **Champlain** 2-9-3 PhilipRobinson 6 84
(M A Jarvis) *tall: str: swtg: chsd ldrs: chal fr 2f out: stl ev ch ins last: one pce last half f* **14/1**
4 *1* **Endiamo (IRE)** 2-9-3 MartinDwyer 17 81
(M P Tregoning) *neat: b.bkwd: chsd ldrs: rdn over 2f out: kpt on same pce fnl f* **7/1**[2]
2 **5** *1* **Conquest (IRE)**[13] 1510 2-9-3 KFallon 19 78
(W J Haggas) *lw: t.k.h in rr: hld up: gd hdwy to press ldrs 2f out: sn rdn and edgd lft: carried hd high and wknd ins fnl f* **1/1**[1]
6 *1 ¼* **Marine Parade** 2-9-3 RyanMoore 14 74+
(R Hannon) *str: lw: s.i.s: bhd: hdwy 2f out: kpt on fnl f but nvr gng pce to trble ldrs* **40/1**
7 *1 ½* **Al Khaleej (IRE)** 2-9-3 LDettori 2 70+
(E A L Dunlop) *well grwn: str: b.bkwd: hld up in rr: c towards stands side and kpt on wl fr over 1f out: nt pce to rch ldrs* **10/1**[3]
8 *shd* **Tudor Prince (IRE)** 2-9-3 JimmyFortune 11 69
(B J Meehan) *w'like: scope: t.k.h early: hld up towards rr: pushed along over 2f out and one pce: hdwy fnl f: kpt on wl cl home* **33/1**
9 *2* **Montalembert (USA)** 2-9-3 LPKeniry 8 63
(J S Moore) *tall: b.bkwd: s.i.s: sn mid-div: pushed along 1/2-way: nvr gng pce to be competitive* **100/1**
10 *1 ½* **Proper (IRE)** 2-9-0 EdwardCreighton(3) 13 59
(M R Channon) *unf: scope: led tl hdd 2f out: sn wknd* **50/1**
5 **11** *1 ¼* **Right Option (IRE)**[57] 707 2-9-3 TPQueally 1 55+
(A P Jarvis) *s.i.s: rdn 1/2-way: nvr gng pce to get beyond mid-div* **66/1**
12 *shd* **Venir Rouge** 2-9-0 NeilChalmers(3) 18 55+
(M Salaman) *rangy: lw: hmpd s: bhd: sn rdn: styd on fr over 1f out but nvr gng pce to rch ldrs* **100/1**
3 **13** *3* **Make Me An Offer (IRE)**[29] 1113 2-9-3 MichaelHills 16 46
(B W Hills) *lw: chsd ldrs: rdn 1/2-way: wknd ins fnl 2f* **16/1**
14 *3 ½* **Colditz (IRE)** 2-9-3 TedDurcan 7 35
(M R Channon) *w'like: early spd: sn outpcd* **28/1**
15 *shd* **Six Shots** 2-9-3 DaneO'Neill 4 35
(J A Osborne) *tall: scope: b.bkwd: s.i.s: outpcd most of way* **66/1**
16 *2 ½* **Joburg Gold (USA)** 2-9-3 RHills 10 28
(B W Hills) *rangy: scope: b.bkwd: plld hrd early: bhd most of way* **33/1**
00 **17** *nk* **Emergency Services**[7] 1688 2-9-3 JimCrowley 9 27
(Tom Dascombe) *in tch early: bhd fr 1/2-way* **100/1**
18 *3 ½* **Law Of The Land (IRE)** 2-9-3 SteveDrowne 5 16
(W R Muir) *leggy: scope: chsd ldrs over 3f* **100/1**

1m 18.05s (3.73) **Going Correction** +0.725s/f (Yiel) **18** Ran SP% **124.0**
Speed ratings (Par 95):104,102,101,100,98 97,95,94,92,90 88,88,84,79,79 76,75,71
CSF £96.28 TOTE £9.80: £2.90, £4.00, £4.20; EX 144.70.
Owner N A Woodcock, A C Pickford & David Mort **Bred** R Evain **Trained** East Everleigh, Wilts

FOCUS
This is usually a good race, and paddock inspection suggested it will prove well up to standard. It looks sure to throw up plenty of winners.

NOTEBOOK
Major Cadeaux ◆, whose dam is a half-sister to Cape Beino, a smart winner over six furlongs to a mile at three in the US, knew his job first time out and won what was is likely to turn out to be a decent maiden in good style. As a son of Cadeaux Genereux he might have been expected to handle conditions better than a few of the others, but he is clearly a useful prospect, and the Coventry Stakes looks the logical target. (op 9-1)
Jo'Burg(USA) ◆, whose dam was a high-class multiple winner in Italy and the US over six furlongs to a mile, was the highest priced of these at the sales. The stable's juveniles invariably improve for their debut outings so this was a highly encouraging performance, and a maiden win should be a formality. (op 12-1 tchd 16-1 in places)
Champlain ◆, a half-brother to Sovereignty, who won over seven furlongs at three, is out of a mare who won the May Hill at two and was later a smart performer at up to ten furlongs. Not given a hard time in third, he was the only one of the first six home to be drawn in single figures, and his breeding suggests that faster ground will see him in an even better light. He should not have any trouble winning his maiden en route to Royal Ascot. (op 9-1)
Endiamo(IRE), whose dam won over six furlongs at two and three and is a sister to Makfool, a dual winner over a mile, should have been suited by the cut in the ground, but he was a little tapped for toe when the pace quickened and ran green. He should come on for the run. (op 6-1)
Conquest(IRE), runner-up at Newmarket on his debut, looked set to take the beating with the benefit of that experience, but while he travelled strongly and came to have every chance, he did not seem to go through with his effort. He may still be green, but he carried his head high and perhaps is not the most straightforward. (op 5-4 tchd 11-8 in places)
Marine Parade, whose dam was a triple winner on the All-Weather over a mile at three to four, was the lesser fancied of the Hannon pair, but he was keeping on well at the finish and shaped with definite promise. (op 33-1)
Al Khaleej(IRE), a half-brother to four winners, is by Sakhee and bred to need further than this. He ended up racing next to the stands'-side rail despite having been drawn in two and was keeping on well at the finish, not unduly knocked about. He should do better in time, especially when stepping up to seven furlongs.
Tudor Prince(IRE), a half-brother to London Follies, a dual winner at two over six furlongs; kept on well enough at the finish despite having raced keenly early. He looks another who will be happier over seven furlongs in time. (op 25-1)
Montalembert(USA), a half-brother to Blarney Stream, a dual winner over ten furlongs in the US, and to Portorosa, a winner in France over an extended nine furlongs, is himself by Kalanisi. It is to his credit that he ran so well over this trip on his debut given that his pedigree screams middle-distance three-year-old. (op 66-1)

1839 PADDY POWER STKS (REGISTERED AS THE ASTON PARK STAKES) (LISTED RACE) 1m 5f 61y
2:10 (2:10) (Class 1) 4-Y-0+
£18,169 (£6,886; £3,446; £1,718; £860; £432) **Stalls** High

Form RPR
1260 **1** **Distinction (IRE)**[200] 6223 7-9-7 MJKinane 5 121
(Sir Michael Stoute) *b.bkwd: racd 3rd: wnt 2nd over 2 out: rdn and styd on to ld wl ins fnl f* **3/1**[3]
2414 **2** *hd* **Balkan Knight**[7] 1677 6-8-12 103 LPKeniry 6 112
(D R C Elsworth) *lw: hld up: hdwy to ld on bit wl over 2f out: rdn and hdd wl ins fnl f: kpt on gamely* **11/4**[2]
34 **3** *7* **Avalon**[96] 5569 4-8-12 113 FMBerry 1 102
(Jonjo O'Neill) *b.bkwd: hld up in rr: rdn and styd on to go 3rd 1f out: nvr nrr* **10/1**
0353 **4** *2* **Crosspeace (IRE)**[22] 1267 4-9-1 108 RoystonFfrench 7 102
(M Johnston) *lw: trckd ldrs: led wl over 3f out to wl over 2f out: rdn and wknd over 1f out* **15/8**[1]
0440 **5** *6* **High Action (USA)**[238] 5458 6-8-12 101 RichardHughes 3 91
(Ian Williams) *hw: led: rdn clr over 5f out: hdd wl over 3 out: rdn and sn wknd* **16/1**
0000 **6** *4* **Bahar Shumaal (IRE)**[22] 1267 4-8-12 99 RyanMoore 2 85
(C E Brittain) *lw: hld up in last pl: wknd over 2f out* **20/1**

3m 3.45s (12.46) **Going Correction** +0.85s/f (Soft) **6** Ran SP% **106.2**
Speed ratings (Par 111):95,94,90,89,85 83
CSF £10.31 TOTE £3.30: £2.00, £1.90; EX 11.30.
Owner Highclere Thoroughbred Racing Ltd **Bred** Orpendale And Minch Bloodstock **Trained** Newmarket, Suffolk
■ Stewards' Enquiry : L P Keniry two-day ban: used whip with excessive force and frequency (May 31-Jun 1)

FOCUS
While this distance would be the minimum for most stayers, it took plenty of getting in these testing conditions. The time was slow for a race of this class but the form looks sound enough.

NOTEBOOK
Distinction(IRE) had never won on his seasonal reappearance before but his stable can do little wrong at present and, despite drifting badly in the market, he showed plenty of tenacity to wear down Balkan Knight close home. This was a good effort under his 9lb penalty, and he should definitely improve for the run. He was a close second to Westerner in last year's Gold Cup and, with that top-class rival now retired, he looks the one to beat this time around. (op 15-8)
Balkan Knight has always liked to get his toe in and, in receipt of plenty of weight from his principal market rivals, he looked to hold every chance. He went to the front travelling well, but got there too soon and was ultimately worn down by Distinction. However, with the pair finishing well clear this was probably still another personal best from a horse who keeps improving steadily. He should be able to win at this level when conditions allow. (op 4-1)
Avalon, whose close third in the Great Voltigeur when trained by Aidan O'Brien last season is responsible for his mark of 113, was a disappointment over hurdles earlier this year. Never a threat here, he is flattered by his finishing position as he merely stayed on past tired rivals who had shot their bolt. (op 11-1 tchd 9-1)
Crosspeace(IRE), who won a race of this class at the end of last season in desperate ground, appeared to have conditions to suit, but his stamina for this sort of distance remains in question and his rating makes him a difficult horse to place. (tchd 7-4)
High Action(USA) won first time up last season, so he can go well fresh, but his best form is all on quicker ground and he soon dropped away when the principals came alongside in the straight. (op 14-1)
Bahar Shumaal(IRE), who has been aggressively campaigned since his maiden success at Sandown last year, is another who has a rating which makes him tricky to place now. He also prefers faster ground. (op 28-1)

1840 JUDDMONTE LOCKINGE STKS (GROUP 1) 1m (S)
2:45 (2:45) (Class 1) 4-Y-0+
£113,560 (£43,040; £21,540; £10,740; £5,380; £2,700) **Stalls** Centre

Form RPR
1314 **1** **Peeress**[217] 5900 5-8-11 114 KFallon 10 122
(Sir Michael Stoute) *lw: hld up rr but in tch: stdy hdwy to ld over 1f out: drvn and styd on gamely* **4/1**[2]
2351 **2** *1 ¾* **Majors Cast (IRE)**[14] 1479 5-9-0 117 LDettori 2 121
(J Noseda) *lw: hld up in rr: stdy hdwyfr 2f out to chse wnr fnl f: kpt on u.p but a hld last half f* **9/2**[3]
3156 **3** *3 ½* **Court Masterpiece**[56] 738 6-9-0 114 GMosse 3 114
(E A L Dunlop) *lw: hld up in rr: smooth hdwy to press ldrs ins fnl 2f: stl ev ch over 1f out: wknd ins last* **7/1**
-312 **4** *1 ½* **Soviet Song (IRE)**[297] 3837 6-8-11 119 JamieSpencer 4 108
(J R Fanshawe) *swtg: trckd ldrs: qcknd to chal 2f out: sn rdn: wknd ins fnl f* **7/2**[1]
0011 **5** *1 ¼* **Kandidate**[35] 1017 4-9-0 110 (t) SebSanders 9 109
(C E Brittain) *lw: trckd ldrs: led over 2f out: hdd over 1f out: sn wknd* **33/1**
3101 **6** *5* **Rob Roy (USA)**[21] 1299 4-9-0 111 MJKinane 6 99
(Sir Michael Stoute) *wnt rt s: t.k.h: trckd ldrs: rdn to chal over 2f out: wknd ins fnl quarter m* **9/2**[3]

0015 **7** *3* **Common World (USA)**[15] [1469] 7-9-0 .... FMBerry 8 93
(T Hogan, Ire) *bmpd s: hmpd after half a f: sn in tch: rdn over 3f out: sn btn* **12/1**

1305 **8** *9* **New Seeker**[21] [1287] 6-9-0 110....................................(v) PhilipRobinson 5 75
(C G Cox) *lw: led tl hdd over 2f out: sn btn* **25/1**

4364 **9** *11* **Rocamadour**[6] [1712] 4-9-0 112.. TedDurcan 7 53
(M R Channon) *lw: bmpd s: in tch: rdn 3f out: sn btn* **14/1**

1m 44.57s (3.95) **Going Correction** +0.725s/f (Yiel) **9** Ran SP% **112.2**
Speed ratings (Par 117):109,107,103,102,101 96,93,84,73
CSF £21.52 TOTE £5.10: £2.00, £1.90, £2.40; EX 28.30 Trifecta £283.30 Pool £17,438.83, 43.70 winning units.
Owner Cheveley Park Stud **Bred** Cheveley Park Stud Ltd **Trained** Newmarket, Suffolk

FOCUS
A far from vintage renewal. Three of the nine runners had a previous Group 1 success to their names, and they filled three of the first four places. Majors Cast and Court Masterpiece set the standard.

NOTEBOOK
Peeress, from a stable in flying form, handles soft ground and has clearly improved again over the winter, as this took more winning than her Sun Chariot success did, given that she only had other members of her own sex to beat there and had the benefit of a huge draw bias. Once she hit the front she was never going to be caught, and she saw the mile out strongly. The Queen Anne is the next obvious target, and faster ground will not bother her, but a bit more will be needed against the top milers. (op 7-2)
Majors Cast(IRE) may have won on fast ground, but in these conditions he did not see out the mile as well as the winner. He is basically at his best over seven furlongs on fast ground, but Group 1 contests under those conditions are very few and far between and the Prix Maurice de Gheest (six and a half furlongs) at Deauville and the Prix de la Foret at Longchamp are usually run on softish ground. He does not look short of speed and the sprinting division is relatively weak, so with races like the Golden Jubilee, July Cup and Haydock Sprint Cup usually run at a strong gallop it could well pay to drop him back to six furlongs.
Court Masterpiece had the ground to suit but he is another at his best over a furlong shorter. Ridden to get the trip, he came there to have every chance but flattened out inside the last. His best chance of another Group 1 win this year is likely to be when he attempts to repeat in the Prix de la Foret on Arc weekend. (op 8-1)
Soviet Song(IRE), the best horse in the race according to official ratings and the only prolific Group 1 winner in the field, had needed the run on her seasonal debut in 2004 and 2005, and the market suggested that the same scenario was likely again this year, for although she started favourite, her form entitled her to start much shorter than 7-2. It will be a surprise if she does not improve plenty for the run, and the Queen Anne could well see her reverse placings with the winner, although she also has the Windsor Forest as an option. (tchd 4-1 in places)
Kandidate, in the form of his life on the All-Weather recently, ran well under far from optimum conditions, confirming his current wellbeing.
Rob Roy(USA), whose Group 2 success at Sandown on his reappearance suggested that he was ready for another crack at the big time, once again disappointed at the highest level. He may well need faster ground than this to be seen at his best, but he now has a few questions to answer. (op 4-1 tchd 5-1 in a place)
Common World(USA), a wide-margin winner of the Group 3 Gladness Stakes last month, saw that form given a timely boost when Steenberg won the Group 2 Duke of York Stakes earlier in the week. With the ground to suit, it was no surprise to see him backed at long prices, but he got messed about a bit in the early stages and in the end simply looked outclassed. (op 11-1)
New Seeker needs quicker ground than this to be seen at his best but he was probably outclassed in this company anyway. Official explanation: jockey said gelding was unsuited by soft ground
Rocamadour had not run on ground as soft as this before but he gets further than this, so presumably those who supported him into 14-1 believed that the greater stamina test would be in his favour. He proved disappointing, and looks likely to be a difficult horse to place this season. Official explanation: jockey said colt had no more to give (op 25-1)

1841 LONDON PADDY POWER GOLD CUP (HERITAGE H'CAP) 1m 2f 6y
3:20 (3:21) (Class 2) (0-105,95) 3-Y-0
£31,160 (£9,330; £4,665; £2,335; £1,165; £585) **Stalls** High

Form RPR

011 **1** **Pearly King (USA)**[16] [1446] 3-9-2 **90**.. KFallon 1 99+
(Sir Michael Stoute) *lw: t.k.h: hld up: hdwy over 2f out: r.o wl to ld ins fnl f* **9/2**[2]

2212 **2** *½* **Salute The General**[22] [1270] 3-8-4 **78**............................ MartinDwyer 15 86
(W R Muir) *lw: t.k.h: hdwy to go 2nd 1/2-way: led over 2f out: rdn and hdd ins fnl f* **10/1**

0211 **3** *1 ½* **High Command**[44] [895] 3-9-1 **89**.................................. JamieSpencer 8 95+
(E A L Dunlop) *lw: prom tl outpcd over 3f out: rallying whn short of room and swtchd lft appr fnl f: r.o to go 3rd ins* **4/1**[1]

6241 **4** *2* **Numeric (GER)**[9] [1605] 3-8-9 **83**.................................. JimmyFortune 6 85
(J H M Gosden) *trckd ldrs: rdn 2 out: styd on one pce fnl f* **4/1**[1]

3105 **5** *hd* **Beau Nash (USA)**[14] [1490] 3-9-2 **90**.................................. AlanMunro 11 91
(P W Chapple-Hyam) *hld up: hdwy on outside 3f out: nt pce to chal fnl f* **16/1**

0262 **6** *1* **Pinch Of Salt (IRE)**[7] [1684] 3-8-6 **80**.......................(t) RichardHughes 10 80
(A M Balding) *mid-div: rdn over 1f out: one pce after* **20/1**

2124 **7** *shd* **Acheekyone (IRE)**[14] [1490] 3-8-11 **85**.................................. LDettori 12 84
(B J Meehan) *lw: hld up: hdwy on outside over 2f out: no ex fnl f* **7/1**[3]

5434 **8** *½* **Forroger (CAN)**[12] [1546] 3-8-4 **78**...................................... ChrisCatlin 14 76
(V Smith) *lw: prom: rdn over 1f out: fdd fnl f* **25/1**

1114 **9** *3 ½* **Prince Charlemagne (IRE)**[25] [1205] 3-8-2 **81**............. JamesDoyle(5) 4 73
(N P Littmoden) *slowly away: sn mid-div: rdn over 2f out: wknd over 1f out* **25/1**

1035 **10** *shd* **Criminal Act (USA)**[14] [1488] 3-9-4 **92**.............................. MichaelHills 9 84
(B W Hills) *mid-div: t.k.h: hdwy over 2f out: wknd appr fnl f* **25/1**

0053 **11** *2* **Wovoka (IRE)**[14] [1490] 3-9-4 **95**.............................. EdwardCreighton(3) 7 83
(M R Channon) *hld up: effrt on outside over 2f out: wknd over 1f out* **14/1**

0103 **12** *7* **Participation**[16] [1446] 3-8-11 **85**..................................(bt[1]) RyanMoore 13 61
(M J Wallace) *rrd up leaving stalls: a bhd* **33/1**

6302 **13** *8* **Arabian Sea (IRE)**[18] [1381] 3-8-6 **80**................................. SebSanders 5 41
(C E Brittain) *sn led: rdn and hdd over 2f out: sn btn* **16/1**

300 **14** *1 ½* **Time Out (IRE)**[28] [1134] 3-8-5 **79**...................................... LPKeniry 3 38
(A M Balding) *b.bkwd: trckd ldr to 1/2-way: styd prom tl wknd wl over 1f out* **66/1**

1111 **15** *1 ½* **Royal Amnesty**[18] [1381] 3-8-2 **76**................................. RoystonFfrench 2 32
(G C H Chung) *a bhd: lost tch 2f out* **22/1**

2m 15.88s (7.17) **Going Correction** +0.85s/f (Soft) **15** Ran SP% **123.3**
Speed ratings (Par 105):105,104,103,101,101 100,100,100,97,97 95,90,83,82,81
CSF £45.39 CT £200.69 TOTE £4.80: £2.20, £3.40, £2.30; EX 72.90 Trifecta £243.60 Pool £1,887.32 - 5.50 winning units.
Owner Gainsborough Stud **Bred** Swettenham Stud **Trained** Newmarket, Suffolk

FOCUS
A decent-looking handicap but the pace was fairly steady in the early stages before they quickened things up in the straight, and many riders struggled to settle their mounts. The first five all improved to some extent, with the winner and third the most interesting of them.

NOTEBOOK
Pearly King(USA), raised 3lb for his narrow Redcar win, was quite weak in the market on account of the different ground conditions, but he coped admirably and could be called the likeliest winner from some way out. He is going to be suited by a step up to a mile and a half, and the King George V Handicap at Royal Ascot is a tempting target. (op 4-1)
Salute The General, a very consistent performer, took a fairly keen grip towards the head of affairs, but he found himself in the right position when the steady early pace developed into a sprint to the line. While he could not hold off the potentially smart winner, this was a very creditable performance, and he should continue to be a threat in races like this off a mark around 80. (op 9-1)
High Command ◆ would have gone close with a clear run and remains a progressive colt capable of defying his current mark. He will be better served by coming off a stronger pace and may well be another who could take his chance in the King George V Handicap at Royal Ascot. (op 9-2)
Numeric(GER), who enjoyed the run of the race when getting off the mark at Chester last time, was the best backed horse in the race, but the ground was much softer this time and he failed to live up to market expectations. He might be worth another chance back on a faster surface. (op 13-2)
Beau Nash(USA) reversed Newmarket form with Wovoka and Acheekyone but one wonders whether he is that well handicapped on a mark of 90. (op 14-1)
Pinch Of Salt(IRE) stayed on well in the closing stages and a stronger all-round pace would have suited him better. On this evidence his trainer should be able to find a handicap for him off this sort of mark. (op 16-1)
Acheekyone(IRE) could not confirm Newmarket form with Beau Nash over this extra two furlongs and he shaped like a non-stayer. A return to a mile will suit. (op 15-2 tchd 8-1)
Forroger(CAN), running in a handicap for the first time, weakened out of things in the closing stages and perhaps this was a little too competitive for him. (tchd 28-1)
Prince Charlemagne(IRE) may not have been at home on the soft ground and it is too early to write him off on turf. Official explanation: jockey said colt was unsuited by soft ground (op 20-1)
Criminal Act(USA), who has been highly tried since his maiden win, is on a tricky mark and is likely to prove difficult to place. This trip appears to stretch his stamina, though.
Wovoka(IRE) raced keenly and did not get home over this longer trip. (op 16-1)

1842 PADDYPOWER.COM STKS (H'CAP) 1m 4f 5y
3:55 (3:55) (Class 2) (0-100,95) 4-Y-0+
£12,464 (£3,732; £1,866; £934; £466; £234) **Stalls** High

Form RPR

4015 **1** **Solent (IRE)**[19] [1357] 4-8-13 **90**.. DaneO'Neill 9 99
(R Hannon) *trckd ldr: led ins fnl 4f: drvn and styd on strly fnl 2f* **5/1**

2 *3* **Castle Howard (IRE)**[236] 4-8-12 **89**.................................. TPQueally 1 94
(W J Musson) *b.bkwd: rr but in tch: rdn and hdwy 3f out: chsd wnr 2f out: styd on but a readily hld* **11/1**

0260 **3** *2 ½* **Danehill Willy (IRE)**[32] [1071] 4-8-11 **88**..........................(p) ChrisCatlin 7 90
(N A Callaghan) *swtg: led tl hdd ins fnl 4f: lost 2nd 2f out and sn no ch w ldrs* **7/2**[3]

2106 **4** *½* **Cruise Director**[3] [1779] 6-8-11 **88**.. KFallon 2 89
(Ian Williams) *lw: rr but in tch: rdn over 3f out: swtchd rt and hdwy 2f out: nvr gng pce to rch ldrs and sn one pce* **3/1**[2]

2526 **5** *8* **Chocolate Caramel (USA)**[211] [6012] 4-8-7 **84**..................... MJKinane 5 74
(Mrs A J Perrett) *lw: s.i.s: hld up in rr: drvn along 3f out: no rspnse and btn 2f out* **9/4**[1]

5103 **6** *10* **Llamadas**[27] [1167] 4-7-11 **81** oh1.. LukeMorris(7) 8 57
(C Roberts) *chsd ldrs tl c wd and racd alone in centre crse over 4f out: no ch fnl 3f* **16/1**

2m 42.61s (6.62) **Going Correction** +0.85s/f (Soft) **6** Ran SP% **108.9**
Speed ratings (Par 109):111,109,107,107,101 95
CSF £49.99 CT £194.06 TOTE £4.80: £2.20, £2.80; EX 27.70 Trifecta £118.10 Pool £565.58 - 3.40 winning units.
Owner Mrs J Wood **Bred** Quay Bloodstock And Samac Ltd **Trained** East Everleigh, Wilts

FOCUS
A depleted field for this middle-distance handicap, in which the first two were sired by Montjeu. The form does not look terribly strong.

NOTEBOOK
Solent(IRE) found the necessary improvement from his reappearance effort to run out a clear winner. This may not have taken too much winning, but he has now shown versatility regarding ground conditions, having now won on soft, good and good to firm surfaces, and another two furlongs will probably not frighten him. (op 7-1)
Castle Howard(IRE) was having his first start for his new stable, having previously been trained in France by Andre Fabre, who sent him out to win over a mile seven on his final start at three. This was a promising seasonal reappearance and there is likely to be better to come when he is stepped up in trip again. (tchd 10-1 and 12-1)
Danehill Willy(IRE) has run his best races since being raised in the handicap for a couple of wins last summer when gifted an uncontested lead, and that was the case here. He was unable to capitalise, though, and the impression left is that he remains high in the handicap. (op 4-1)
Cruise Director, who is at his best challenging from off the pace in a race run at a decent clip, was making a quick reappearance and remains on a rating only 1lb lower than his career-high mark. He gives the impression that he needs some assistance from the Handicapper. (op 9-4)
Chocolate Caramel(USA) had trip and ground conditions to suit, and the fact that he was sent off favourite suggests he was thought ready to do himself justice first time up. This must be considered a very disappointing effort. Official explanation: trainer's representative was unable to offer any explanation for poor form shown (tchd 15-8)
Llamadas showed why he has been very lightly raced on turf over the last couple of seasons. (tchd 20-1)

1843 CATRIDGE FARM STUD & MANOR FARM PACKERS FILLIES' H'CAP 7f (S)
4:25 (4:27) (Class 4) (0-85,84) 3-Y-0 **£6,477** (£1,927; £963; £481) **Stalls** Centre

Form RPR

011 **1** **Red Evie (IRE)**[33] [1056] 3-9-3 **83**.................................. JamieSpencer 11 104+
(M L W Bell) *lw: b.hind: hld up: smooth hdwy to ld 2f out: sn clr: idled in front fnl f: easily* **11/2**[1]

6521 **2** *1 ½* **Spirit Of Arosa (IRE)**[16] [1431] 3-8-9 **75**.................................. KFallon 9 86
(J Akehurst) *wnt lft s: hld up: rdn and hdwy to chse wnr fnl f* **7/1**

4301 **3** *2 ½* **Lavenham (IRE)**[8] [1641] 3-8-11 **77**.............................. RichardHughes 19 81+
(R Hannon) *lw: set stdy pce tl hdd 2 out: kpt on one pce fnl f* **13/2**[3]

6400 **4** *1 ¼* **Tara Too (IRE)**[203] [6145] 3-9-4 **84**.. LDettori 20 85
(D W P Arbuthnot) *hld up in rr: rdn over 3f out: hdwy under press over 1f out: r.o fnl f: nvr nrr* **14/1**

1000 **5** *½* **Local Fancy**[9] [1617] 3-8-11 **77**.. AlanMunro 18 77
(J M P Eustace) *hld up in rr: hdwy over 1f out: nvr nr to chal* **33/1**

16 **6** *hd* **Mango Music**[30] [1097] 3-8-9 **75**.. TedDurcan 5 74+
(M R Channon) *t.k.h: in tch tl fdd over 1f out* **6/1**[2]

5316 **7** *¾* **Right Ted (IRE)**[275] [4516] 3-8-12 **78**.................................. PatDobbs 13 75
(R Hannon) *lw: hld up in rr: effrt over 1f out: nvr on terms* **40/1**

010 **8** *shd* **Silver Dip**[245] [5307] 3-9-0 **80**.. MichaelHills 12 77
(B W Hills) *t.k.h: prom tl wknd over 1f out* **10/1**

4306 **9** ½ **Dune Melody (IRE)**[44] [896] 3-8-9 **75** .... LPKeniry 2 71
(J S Moore) *hld up in rr: mde mod late hdwy* **100/1**

0421 **10** 3 **Deira (USA)**[12] [1551] 3-8-7 **73** .... RyanMoore 7 61
(C E Brittain) *lw: in tch tl wknd over 1f out* **8/1**

5001 **11** 2½ **Fangorn Forest (IRE)**[7] [1693] 3-8-1 **74** ....(p) TolleyDean(7) 15 55
(R A Harris) *lw: hld up in rr: nvr on terms* **14/1**

4150 **12** ¾ **Violet Ballerina (IRE)**[231] [5604] 3-8-11 **77** .... JimmyFortune 17 56
(B J Meehan) *s.i.s: t.k.h: sn chsd ldrs: rdn over 2f out: sn wknd* **33/1**

1030 **13** ¾ **Marriage Value (IRE)**[32] [1067] 3-9-2 **82** .... SteveDrowne 14 59
(J A Osborne) *t.k.h in mid-div: wknd over 2f out* **20/1**

024 **14** ¾ **Laqataat (IRE)**[213] [5978] 3-8-9 **75** .... RHills 6 51
(J L Dunlop) *lw: trckd ldr: rdn 2f out: wknd qckly* **14/1**

025 **15** 2 **Felin Gruvy (IRE)**[259] [4941] 3-8-9 **75** .... StephenCarson 4 45
(R F Johnson Houghton) *hld up: a bhd* **20/1**

210 **16** 13 **Pearly Poll**[166] [6501] 3-8-12 **78** .... SebSanders 3 15
(R M Beckett) *chsd ldrs: rdn 3f out: sn wknd: eased ins fnl f* **20/1**

1m 31.07s (4.07) **Going Correction** +0.725s/f (Yiel) **16** Ran SP% **119.3**
Speed ratings (Par 98):105,103,100,99,98 98,97,97,96,93 90,89,88,87,85 70
CSF £38.22 CT £270.93 TOTE £4.00: £1.40, £2.10, £1.90, £3.20; EX 43.40.
Owner Terry Neill **Bred** Dermot Cantillon And Forenaghts Stud **Trained** Newmarket, Suffolk

FOCUS
This looked a competitive fillies' handicap on paper, but it was won easily by the progressive Red Evie. The form looks sound, rated through the third to eighth.

1844 PADDY POWER DIAL-A-BET MAIDEN STKS (DIV I) 7f (S)
4:55 (4:58) (Class 5) 3-Y-O **£4,857** (£1,445; £722; £360) **Stalls** Centre

Form RPR

1 **Bosset (USA)** 3-8-12 .... TPQueally 12 80+
(J Noseda) *neat: lw: in tch: hdwy 2f out: qcknd ins last to ld fnl 50yds: readily* **20/1**

2 ¾ **Third Set (IRE)** 3-9-3 .... SteveDrowne 14 83+
(R Charlton) *gd sort: str: rangy: scope: chsd ldrs: drvn to ld 1f out: hung lft ins last: hdd and outpcd fnl 50yds* **33/1**

4 **3** hd **Lindenburgh Way (IRE)**[211] [6011] 3-9-3 .... LDettori 5 82
(B J Meehan) *in tch: hdwy over 1f out: qcknd to press ldrs ins last: one pce cl home* **4/1**[3]

043 **4** 2 **Pirouetting**[31] [1085] 3-8-12 86 .... MichaelHills 8 72+
(B W Hills) *led tl hdd 1f out: wknd ins last* **3/1**[1]

33 **5** 1¼ **Vacation (IRE)**[113] [215] 3-9-0 .... RossStudholme(3) 6 74
(V Smith) *s.i.s: t.k.h in rr: pushed along 2f out: hdwy over 1f out: kpt on ins last: nt pce to rch ldrs* **40/1**

0 **6** shd **Greek Renaissance (IRE)**[246] [5271] 3-9-3 .... MartinDwyer 4 73+
(M P Tregoning) *trckd ldrs: rdn 2f out: chal jst ins fnl f: sn wknd* **10/3**[2]

7 1 **Gold Flame** 3-9-3 .... DaneO'Neill 9 71
(H Candy) *str: rangy: bkwd: hld up in rr: hdwy over 1f out: kpt on wl fnl f but nvr in contention* **20/1**

00 **8** nk **Way To The Stars**[19] [1355] 3-8-12 .... RyanMoore 3 65
(A M Balding) *s.i.s: towards rr: hdwy fr 2f out: kpt on fnl f but nvr in contention* **100/1**

9 ¾ **Royal Oath (USA)** 3-9-3 .... JimmyFortune 1 68
(J H M Gosden) *leggy: scope: wnt lft s: rcvrd to chse ldrs 1/2-way: chal over 1f out: outpcd ins last: fdd* **5/1**

0 **10** hd **Reeling N' Rocking (IRE)**[31] [1085] 3-8-12 .... AlanMunro 13 62
(B W Hills) *bhd: pushed along 3f out: styd on fnl f: nvr a danger* **66/1**

11 nk **Hassaad** 3-9-3 .... RHills 10 67
(W J Haggas) *str: lengthy: b.bkwd: b.hind: bhd tl sme hdwy fr over 1f out* **16/1**

12 1 **Mambonow (USA)** 3-9-3 .... JamieSpencer 15 64
(J Noseda) *cmpt: b.bkwd: chsd ldrs: ev chance 2f out: wknd over 1f out* **16/1**

06 **13** 1 **Blues In The Night (IRE)**[225] [5708] 3-9-3 .... SebSanders 11 62
(P J Makin) *chsd ldrs over 4f* **50/1**

00 **14** ¾ **Lady Duxyana**[19] [1355] 3-8-12 .... ChrisCatlin 2 55?
(M D I Usher) *s.i.s: a in rr* **100/1**

2 **15** 1 **Rose Lady (IRE)**[17] [1417] 3-8-12 .... TedDurcan 7 52
(M R Channon) *lw: chsd ldrs over 4f* **12/1**

1m 32.77s (5.77) **Going Correction** +0.725s/f (Yiel) **15** Ran SP% **124.5**
Speed ratings (Par 99):96,95,94,92,91 91,89,89,88,88 88,87,85,85,83
CSF £548.44 TOTE £34.70: £7.10, £8.80, £2.00; EX 802.10.
Owner Budget Stable **Bred** L Jones **Trained** Newmarket, Suffolk

FOCUS
Perhaps not a great maiden for the track, but arguably the stronger of the two divisions, despite being run in a time 0.39sec slower.

1845 PADDY POWER DIAL-A-BET MAIDEN STKS (DIV II) 7f (S)
5:25 (5:31) (Class 5) 3-Y-O **£4,857** (£1,445; £722; £360) **Stalls** Centre

Form RPR

02 **1** **Master Pegasus**[201] [6200] 3-9-3 .... GeorgeBaker 6 88
(C F Wall) *lw: hld up in tch: shkn up to ld over 1f out: sn clr* **7/1**[2]

0 **2** 3½ **Usk Poppy**[186] [6351] 3-8-12 .... LPKeniry 5 74
(D R C Elsworth) *lw: hld up in rr: hdwy over 2f out: styd on to chse wnr fnl f* **12/1**

4 **3** nk **Mashaair (IRE)**[221] [5817] 3-9-3 .... RHills 9 78+
(B W Hills) *lw: a.p: wnt 2nd 3f out: tl one pce fnl f* **5/4**[1]

620 **4** 2 **And I**[245] [5307] 3-8-12 71 .... MartinDwyer 10 68
(M P Tregoning) *t.k.h: led tl hdd over 1f out: wknd ins fnl f* **15/2**[3]

5 shd **Bombardier Bush (IRE)** 3-9-3 .... SebSanders 3 73+
(J L Dunlop) *lengthy: str: lw: slowly away: hld up in rr: hdwy fr over 1f out: nvr nrr* **9/1**

24 **6** 2 **Woodcote Place**[220] [5832] 3-9-3 .... AlanMunro 2 68
(P R Chamings) *trckd ldr to 3f out: rdn 2f out: wknd over 1f out* **8/1**

4 **7** ¾ **Bijli (IRE)**[403] [983] 3-9-3 .... TPQueally 4 66
(J Noseda) *bkwd: steadied s: settled in mid-div: wknd 2f out* **16/1**

8 ½ **Hanella (IRE)** 3-8-12 .... NickyMackay 1 59
(R M Beckett) *neat: b.bkwd: mid-div: rdn 3f out: wknd 2f out* **25/1**

00 **9** 1 **October Ben**[17] [1401] 3-8-5 .... FrankiePickard(7) 14 57
(M D I Usher) *prom: rdn over 2f out: sn wknd* **33/1**

10 hd **Burnt Orange (IRE)** 3-9-0 .... RobertMiles(3) 8 61
(T D McCarthy) *cmpt: bkwd: slowly away: a bhd* **50/1**

0 **11** 1½ **Towerofcharlemagne (IRE)**[196] [6251] 3-9-3 .... JimmyQuinn 11 57
(Miss Gay Kelleway) *b.bkwd: s.i.s: plld hrd and sn prom: wknd over 2f out* **14/1**

0 **12** shd **Reinstated (IRE)**[203] [6143] 3-8-12 .... MichaelHills 15 52
(B W Hills) *b.bkwd: slowly away: a bhd* **22/1**

1m 32.38s (5.38) **Going Correction** +0.725s/f (Yiel) **12** Ran SP% **123.2**
Speed ratings (Par 99):98,94,93,91,91 88,88,87,86,86 84,84
CSF £87.77 TOTE £9.00: £2.40, £2.70, £1.30; EX 87.80 Place 6 £485.89, Place 5 £114.41.

Owner Mrs J Roberts **Bred** Mrs Sally Roberts **Trained** Newmarket, Suffolk

FOCUS
The quicker of the two divisions, but the form only looks fair at best.
T/Jkpt: Not won. T/Plt: £663.40 to a £1 stake. Pool: £121,560.30. 133.75 winning tickets. T/Qpdt: £37.00 to a £1 stake. Pool: £9,282.45. 185.25 winning tickets. ST

1824 NOTTINGHAM (L-H)
Saturday, May 20

OFFICIAL GOING: Soft (heavy in places)
After 10mm overnight rain the ground was described as 'heavy in the back straight, soft in the home straight'.
Wind: Fresh, half-against Weather: Overcast, occasional light showers

1846 TOTEPLACEPOT H'CAP 5f 13y
1:55 (1:57) (Class 5) (0-70,70) 3-Y-O+ **£4,533** (£1,348; £674; £336) **Stalls** High

Form RPR

5321 **1** **Cashel Mead**[3] [1774] 6-9-6 **67** 6ex .... AdamKirby(3) 5 75+
(J L Spearing) *mid-div: nt clr run: swtchd rt and stmbld 2f out: r.o to ld last 100yds* **7/2**[1]

3516 **2** 1 **Gilded Cove**[28] [1151] 6-9-3 **68** .... RussellKennemore(7) 3 77+
(R Hollinshead) *mid-div: nt clr run over 2f out and over 1f out: swtchd rt ins last: styd on wl: nt rch wnr* **14/1**

0050 **3** shd **Kennington**[7] [1686] 6-9-7 **65** ....(b) JohnEgan 1 69
(Mrs C A Dunnett) *w ldrs: kpt on wl ins last* **12/1**

0506 **4** nk **Russian Rocket (IRE)**[9] [1618] 4-9-3 **61** .... HayleyTurner 12 64
(Mrs C A Dunnett) *chsd ldrs: led over 1f out: edgd lft and hdd ins last: no ex* **16/1**

0600 **5** 2 **Chatshow (USA)**[7] [1662] 5-9-7 **68** .... DanielTudhope(3) 10 64
(D Carroll) *in tch: effrt 2f out: kpt on fnl f* **8/1**[3]

0400 **6** 1 **Campeon (IRE)**[7] [1689] 4-9-3 **61** .... ShaneKelly 6 54
(J M Bradley) *led tl over 1f out: wknd last 150yds* **5/1**[2]

6000 **7** hd **Kings College Boy**[11] [1563] 6-9-8 **66** ....(v) TonyHamilton 2 58+
(R A Fahey) *in tch: effrt over 2f out: wkng whn n.m.r ins last* **10/1**

2000 **8** ½ **Special Gold**[14] [1496] 4-9-2 **65** ....(b) DuranFentiman(5) 4 55
(T D Easterby) *chsd ldrs: wknd fnl f* **20/1**

4000 **9** shd **El Potro**[7] [1689] 4-9-4 **62** .... WSupple 11 52
(E S McMahon) *hld up towards rr: sme hdwy 2f out: nvr nr ldrs* **16/1**

0000 **10** 2 **Mis Chicaf (IRE)**[17] [1413] 5-9-1 **62** ....(t) SaleemGolam(3) 8 45
(Robert Gray) *dwlt: nvr a factor* **40/1**

6535 **11** ¾ **Seven No Trumps**[11] [1563] 9-8-8 **59** .... BarrySavage(7) 15 40
(J M Bradley) *racd stands side: hung lft and jnd main gp over 3f out: wknd over 1f out* **16/1**

4203 **12** 1¼ **Hits Only Cash**[22] [1275] 4-9-12 **70** .... J-PGuillambert 17 46
(J Pearce) *swtchd lft s: a bhd* **14/1**

0000 **13** ¾ **Whistler**[7] [1662] 9-9-11 **69** ....(p) PaulFitzsimons 9 43
(Miss J R Tooth) *a in rr* **20/1**

0000 **14** ½ **Oceanico Dot Com (IRE)**[50] [813] 4-9-4 **62** ....(t) FrancisNorton 7 34
(A Berry) *chsd ldrs: lost pl over 1f out* **50/1**

3500 **15** 1 **Snow Wolf**[11] [1563] 5-9-5 **63** ....(p) TQuinn 13 32
(J M Bradley) *swtchd lft after s: a bhd* **16/1**

63.65 secs (1.85) **Going Correction** +0.45s/f (Yiel) **15** Ran SP% **117.6**
Speed ratings (Par 103):103,101,101,100,97 95,95,94,94,91 90,88,87,86,84
CSF £49.47 CT £410.18 TOTE £4.00: £1.40, £5.50, £2.80; EX 67.90.
Owner Masonaires **Bred** D R Tucker **Trained** Kinnersley, Worcs

FOCUS
A modest handicap in which they all eventually raced towards the far side, and so a low draw proved an advantage. Sound form for the grade.
Kings College Boy Official explanation: jockey said gelding was denied clear run

1847 TOTECOURSE TO COURSE H'CAP 1m 6f 15y
2:25 (2:25) (Class 4) (0-80,76) 4-Y-O+ **£6,477** (£1,927; £963; £481) **Stalls** Low

Form RPR

0151 **1** **Sphinx (FR)**[2] [1809] 8-9-4 **73** 6ex ....(b) JohnEgan 1 88+
(Jamie Poulton) *hld up in mid-field: hdwy over 4f out: led on bit over 2f out: shkn up and wnt clr over 1f out: heavily eased towards fin* **4/6**[1]

6633 **2** 3 **Shamrock Bay**[4] [1754] 4-8-7 **62** .... RobbieFitzpatrick 11 67
(C R Dore) *bhd: hdwy 4f out: styd on to go 2nd 1f out: kpt on wl: no ch w wnr* **20/1**

3236 **3** 5 **Feed The Meter (IRE)**[7] [1677] 6-9-3 **75** .... SaleemGolam(3) 2 73
(J Ryan) *chsd ldrs: led briefly 3f out: one pce* **8/1**[2]

0240 **4** ½ **Master Cobbler (IRE)**[204] [6133] 4-9-4 **73** ....(p) TQuinn 5 70
(J Akehurst) *w ldrs: chal 3f out: wknd over 1f out* **16/1**

6100 **5** 3 **Cripsey Brook**[13] [1502] 8-9-0 **76** .... JamesReveley(7) 8 69
(K G Reveley) *hld up in rr: hdwy over 2f out: kpt on: nt rch ldrs* **25/1**

6123 **6** 5 **Lake Wakatipu**[5] [1745] 4-8-2 **57** oh2 .... FrancisNorton 10 43
(M Mullineaux) *mid-div: drvn 5f out: nvr on terms* **20/1**

0-60 **7** 1¼ **Bukit Fraser (IRE)**[10] [1591] 5-8-8 **63** .... EddieAhern 7 47
(P F I Cole) *rrd and swtchd lft s: hld up in rr: hdwy 4f out: rdn and edgd rt over 2f out: sn btn* **9/1**[3]

0010 **8** 6 **Migration**[9] [1614] 10-8-2 **60** .... RichardThomas(3) 4 36
(Mrs S Lamyman) *in rr: drvn along 7f out: edgd rt 3f out: nvr a factor* **20/1**

3-00 **9** 1 **Burning Moon**[187] [5433] 5-9-3 **72** .... BrianReilly 3 47
(J Ryan) *led tl 3f out: sn wknd* **100/1**

464 **10** 1½ **The Grey Man**[14] [1492] 5-8-13 **68** .... WSupple 6 40
(E S McMahon) *chsd ldrs: lost pl over 2f out* **25/1**

0152 **11** 17 **Sand Repeal (IRE)**[18] [1389] 4-9-1 **70** .... MickyFenton 9 19
(Miss J Feilden) *chsd ldrs: lost pl over 3f out: sn bhd and eased* **11/1**

3m 15.07s (7.97) **Going Correction** +0.625s/f (Yiel) **11** Ran SP% **118.3**
Speed ratings (Par 105):102,100,97,97,95 92,91,88,87,87 77
CSF £22.89 CT £70.24 TOTE £1.80: £1.10, £5.00, £2.60; EX 18.90.
Owner R W Huggins **Bred** M Arbib **Trained** Telscombe, E Sussex

FOCUS
The overall form of this staying contest looks pretty weak, but the winner did it easily again and is clearly very progressive.

1848 TOTESCOOP6 H'CAP 6f 15y
3:00 (3:01) (Class 3) (0-95,92) 3-Y-O **£11,658** (£3,468; £1,733; £865) **Stalls** High

Form RPR

140 **1** **Hogmaneigh (IRE)**[30] [1091] 3-8-11 **85** .... J-PGuillambert 6 96+
(S C Williams) *hld up: hdwy and nt clr run over 2f out: rdn to ld 1f out: styd on wl* **4/1**[2]

0436 **2** 1 **Phantom Whisper**[35] [1020] 3-8-4 **81** .... SaleemGolam(3) 8 87
(B R Millman) *led over 2f: chsd ldrs: kpt on wl ins last* **14/1**

0031 **3** 1 ¼ **Ooh Aah Camara (IRE)**[9] 1606 3-8-11 **85**........................ JohnEgan 1 87
(T J Pitt) *chsd ldrs: rdn over 2f out: edgd lft and kpt on same pce fnl f* **9/2**[3]

3033 **4** ¾ **Ryedale Ovation (IRE)**[21] 1292 3-8-8 **82**........................ WSupple 5 82
(T D Easterby) *dwlt: swvd lft after s: hdwy 3f out: kpt on same pce appr fnl f* **7/2**[1]

3201 **5** *nk* **Spiritual Peace (IRE)**[25] 1218 3-8-6 **80**........................ DO'Donohoe 3 79
(K A Ryan) *led over 2f: chsd ldrs: one pce fnl f* **9/2**[3]

6305 **6** *14* **Puskas (IRE)**[13] 1512 3-9-4 **92**........................ TQuinn 4 49
(M R Channon) *chsd ldrs: rdn: hung lft and wknd 2f out* **17/2**

6000 **7** *hd* **Calypso King**[9] 1606 3-9-0 **88**........................ EddieAhern 2 45
(J W Hills) *hld up: effrt and wnt lft over 2f out: lost pl over 1f out* **17/2**

2200 **8** ½ **Brandywell Boy (IRE)**[9] 1604 3-8-10 **84**........................ MickyFenton 7 39
(D J S Ffrench Davis) *chsd ldrs: lost pl over 2f out* **22/1**

1m 18.54s (3.54) **Going Correction** +0.625s/f (Yiel) **8** Ran SP% **110.7**
Speed ratings (Par 103):101,99,98,97,96 77,77,77
CSF £53.02 CT £249.39 TOTE £3.80: £1.30, £4.20, £1.50; EX 58.90.
Owner Mrs Lucille Bone **Bred** John Malone **Trained** Newmarket, Suffolk

FOCUS
Pretty ordinary form all told for the class of contest, but the winner is unexposed and could be capable of better.

NOTEBOOK
Hogmaneigh(IRE), racing on softish ground for the first time since winning on his racecourse debut last year, was a market mover from a yard that is to be respected when the money is down. He overcame a troubled passage to score and could be capable of better still as he is relatively unexposed. (op 6-1 after 13-2 in places)
Phantom Whisper has struggled since his win in the Brocklesby last spring, but he is finally dropping back to a realistic mark, and there might be a race for him back over five. (op 12-1 tchd 16-1)
Ooh Aah Camara(IRE), who won twice with cut in the ground at two, was 5lb higher for her Chester win and ran a fair race. She is probably a fair guide to the level of the form. (op 5-1)
Ryedale Ovation(IRE) is a fairly consistent type but whether he was ideally served by the soft conditions underfoot is open to question. Official explanation: jockey said gelding was unsuited by soft, heavy in places ground (op 11-4)
Spiritual Peace(IRE), off the mark in an ordinary Southwell maiden last time, has arguarby been given quite a stiff mark off which to begin his career in handicap company. (op 4-1 tchd 7-2)
Puskas(IRE) Official explanation: jockey said gelding hung left and had no more to give
Calypso King Official explanation: jockey said gelding was unsuited by soft, heavy in places ground
Brandywell Boy(IRE) Official explanation: jockey said colt was unsuited by soft, heavy in places ground

1849 TOTESPORT.COM FILLIES' STKS (REGISTERED AS THE KILVINGTON STAKES) (LISTED RACE) 6f 15y
3:35 (3:36) (Class 1) 3-Y-O+
£17,034 (£6,456; £3,231; £1,611; £807; £405) **Stalls** High

Form RPR
3125 **1** **Angus Newz**[18] 1377 3-8-7 94........................(v) ShaneKelly 5 101
(M Quinn) *led: swtchd lft after 1f and racd far side: sn clr: kpt on fnl f: hld on towards fin* **10/1**

2016 **2** ¾ **Indian Maiden (IRE)**[7] 1671 6-9-6 104........................ FrancisNorton 7 103
(M S Saunders) *hld up: swtchd far side after 2f: wnt 2nd appr fnl f: styd on: nt quite able chal* **13/8**[1]

5460 **3** *6* **Cape Columbine**[32] 1069 4-9-2 105........................ TQuinn 6 81
(D R C Elsworth) *chsd ldrs: outpcd over 3f out: styd on fnl f: tk modest 3rd on line* **85/40**[2]

-103 **4** *shd* **Clear Impression (IRE)**[18] 1377 4-9-2 94........................ WSupple 2 80
(S C Williams) *trckd ldrs: t.k.h: wnt 2nd over 2f out: wknd fnl f* **5/1**[3]

5004 **5** 1 ½ **Coconut Squeak**[7] 1671 4-9-6 97........................(v) MickyFenton 1 80
(Stef Liddiard) *chsd wnrs: rdn and outpcd over 2f out: kpt on fnl f* **13/2**

4450 **6** *17* **Christa Bee**[9] 1604 3-8-7 85........................ FergusSweeney 3 25
(A Berry) *s.i.s: sn chsng ldrs: lost pl over 3f out: sn bhd* **50/1**

0006 **7** *3* **Shifty Night (IRE)**[18] 1388 5-9-2 48........................(v) HayleyTurner 4 16
(Mrs C A Dunnett) *trckd ldrs: rdn and lost pl 3f out: sn bhd* **100/1**

1m 17.18s (2.18) **Going Correction** +0.625s/f (Yiel)
WFA 3 from 4yo+ 9lb **7** Ran SP% **112.1**
Speed ratings (Par 108):110,109,101,100,98 76,72
CSF £25.75 TOTE £10.70: £4.10, £1.10; EX 39.50.
Owner J G Dooley **Bred** Henry And Mrs Rosemary Moszkowicz **Trained** Newmarket, Suffolk

FOCUS
A race won by jockey tactics as much as anything and the form may not be totally reliable.

NOTEBOOK
Angus Newz, who looked in peak condition beforehand, was the beneficiary of a fine tactical ride by Kelly, who bounced her out quickly, took her to race on the favoured far side and soon had his rivals in trouble. In receipt of plenty of weight from the favourite, she was always going to hold on, and reversed Bath form with both her and Clear Impression on this softer ground. (op 8-1)
Indian Maiden(IRE), who had the winner back in fifth when successful at Bath earlier in the month, acts well in soft ground and put up a fine effort in second, but she was simply beaten by Shane Kelly's enterprising ride on Angus Newz. (op 15-8 tchd 2-1)
Cape Columbine was best in at the weights according to official adjusted ratings, but she was disappointing at Newmarket on her reappearance and it was a similar story here. Her three-year-old best would have seen her win this and there has to be some doubt as to whether she has trained on, as the ground should have been to her liking. (op 2-1 tchd 9-4 in places)
Clear Impression(IRE) was up against it strictly on the ratings but that had been the case at Bath when she was an admirable third to Indian Maiden, only beaten just over a length. She raced too keenly on this occasion, though and the ground took its toll over this longer distance. In time she will probably prove to be at her best over the minimum trip. (op 13-2)
Coconut Squeak, who ran well in a Group Three at Lingfield on her previous start, had to work hard to get to the front of the main group that raced up the centre of the track, and that effort seemed to take its toll. When she won at Newmarket last autumn she was able to make the running more easily.

1850 TOTEEXACTA H'CAP 1m 1f 213y
4:10 (4:11) (Class 6) (0-60,60) 4-Y-O+ **£3,238** (£963; £481; £240) **Stalls** Low

Form RPR
0503 **1** **Trouble Mountain (USA)**[10] 1591 9-9-3 **59**........................(t) DaleGibson 7 73
(M W Easterby) *mid-div: hdwy to ld over 1f out: drvn out* **11/2**[2]

4505 **2** 3 ½ **Mossmann Gorge**[3] 1772 4-9-2 **58**........................(b) EddieAhern 11 66
(M Wellings) *hld up in tch: smooth hdwy over 2f out: wnt over 1f out: fnd little and unable to trble wnr* **7/1**[3]

3002 **3** 1 ½ **Rotuma (IRE)**[10] 1591 7-8-13 **55**........................(b) FergalLynch 4 62+
(M Dods) *hld up: stdy hdwy on ins over 3f out: rdn over 1f out: one pce* **9/2**[1]

0506 **4** *3* **Apache Point (IRE)**[10] 1591 9-8-13 **55**........................ KimTinkler 3 55
(N Tinkler) *keen in tch: hdwy on inner to ld 3f out: hdd and edgd rt over 1f out: one pce* **7/1**[3]

0050 **5** *8* **Foolish Groom**[17] 1422 5-9-4 **60**........................(p) FrancisNorton 2 45
(R Hollinshead) *s.i.s: hdwy over 2f out: kpt on same pce: eased nr fin* **9/1**

2000 **6** 1 ½ **Middlethorpe**[5] 1729 9-9-2 **58**........................(b) DO'Donohoe 14 41
(M W Easterby) *s.s: bhd tl sme hdwy fnl 2f: nvr on terms* **16/1**

4030 **7** *5* **Credential**[14] 1480 4-8-12 **59**........................ GregFairley[(5)] 5 33
(John A Harris) *chsd ldrs: chal over 3f out: wknd over 2f out* **10/1**

0340 **8** *nk* **Padre Nostro (IRE)**[80] 549 7-8-7 **56**........................ ChrisGlenister[(7)] 15 29
(J R Holt) *mid-div: hdwy on outer to chse ldrs over 5f out: lost pl over 3f out* **20/1**

0000 **9** ¾ **Pianoforte (USA)**[28] 1144 4-8-13 **60**........................ TravisBlock[(5)] 13 32
(E J Alston) *led: hdd 3f out: lost pl 2f out* **33/1**

0034 **10** 1 ½ **Prince Of The May**[19] 1353 4-8-13 **55**........................ MickyFenton 12 24
(H Morrison) *chsd ldrs: lost pl over 3f out* **8/1**

0005 **11** 2 ½ **Tata Naka**[9] 1614 6-8-13 **55**........................ HayleyTurner 16 19
(Mrs C A Dunnett) *chsd ldrs: chal over 3f out: lost pl over 2f out* **20/1**

5-00 **12** *6* **Danzatrice**[347] 2359 4-9-2 **58**........................ NeilPollard 10 12
(C W Thornton) *s.i.s: sn mid-div: rdn 4f out: sn lost pl* **100/1**

0005 **13** *6* **Unsuited**[265] 4789 7-8-13 **60**........................ NataliaGemelova[(5)] 6 3
(J E Long) *a in rr* **33/1**

-000 **14** *17* **Richie Boy**[11] 1560 5-9-1 **57**........................ RobbieFitzpatrick 8 —
(Jennie Candlish) *s.i.s: a in rr: bhd and eased fnl 2f* **40/1**

2m 15.76s (6.06) **Going Correction** +0.625s/f (Yiel) **14** Ran SP% **113.5**
Speed ratings (Par 101):100,97,96,93,87 86,82,81,81,79 77,73,68,54
CSF £37.60 CT £186.37 TOTE £6.80: £2.40, £2.60, £2.10; EX 55.00.
Owner Mrs Jean Turpin **Bred** Robert B Berger **Trained** Sheriff Hutton, N Yorks

FOCUS
A modest handicap rated around the third.
Prince Of The May Official explanation: jockey said gelding was unsuited by soft, heavy in places ground
Tata Naka Official explanation: jockey said mare was unsuited by soft, heavy in places ground
Unsuited Official explanation: trainer said mare had breathing problem

1851 TOTEPOOL "A BETTER WAY TO BET" H'CAP 1m 54y
4:40 (4:42) (Class 5) (0-70,70) 3-Y-O **£4,533** (£1,348; £674; £336) **Stalls** Centre

Form RPR
0020 **1** **Diamond De Triano (USA)**[12] 1551 3-8-12 **67**........ DanielTudhope[(3)] 7 74
(P W Chapple-Hyam) *hld up in tch: effrt over 3f out: styd on to ld last 75yds: hld on nr fin* **5/1**[2]

0330 **2** *nk* **Cantabilly (IRE)**[21] 1291 3-9-2 **68**........................ TQuinn 2 75
(M R Channon) *rr-div: hdwy over 2f out: edgd rt over 1f out: styd on wl towards fin* **8/1**

0446 **3** 1 ¼ **Stainley (IRE)**[10] 1596 3-8-13 **65**........................ WSupple 10 69
(J D Bethell) *led tl over 2f out: rallied ins last: tk 3rd on line* **12/1**

0341 **4** *hd* **Pleasing**[21] 1291 3-9-0 **66**........................ ShaneKelly 15 70+
(J L Dunlop) *trckd ldr: led over 2f out: hdd and no ex wl ins last* **9/2**[1]

3521 **5** *5* **Flying Clarets (IRE)**[10] 1596 3-9-4 **70**........................ TonyHamilton 9 64+
(R A Fahey) *towards rr: pushed along and hdwy over 5f out: hung lft and kpt on fnl 2f: nvr nr ldrs* **7/1**[3]

0400 **6** 1 ¼ **Henchman**[25] 1215 3-8-9 **66**........................ RichardKingscote[(5)] 16 57
(Lady Herries) *awkward to load: chsd ldrs: rdn and wknd over 2f out* **20/1**

5400 **7** 2 ½ **Dancing Flame**[29] 1122 3-8-6 **58**........................ FrancisNorton 3 44
(E J Alston) *chsd ldrs: wknd 2f out* **33/1**

1525 **8** *1* **Reveur**[10] 1586 3-9-2 **68**........................ JohnEgan 5 52
(M Mullineaux) *s.i.s: bhd tl sme hdwy fnl 2f: nvr on terms* **25/1**

460 **9** 1 ¼ **Ocean Valentine**[19] 1355 3-8-8 **60**........................ RobertHavlin 14 42
(B R Millman) *t.k.h in mid-div: effrt 3f out: sn wknd* **50/1**

1022 **10** *hd* **Hits Only Life (USA)**[12] 1533 3-8-5 **57** oh1 ow1........ RobbieFitzpatrick 8 38
(J Pearce) *sn bhd: detached 5f out: sme hdwy fnl 2f: nvr on terms* **8/1**

000 **11** *1* **Freeze The Flame (GER)**[33] 1049 3-8-8 **60**........................ MickyFenton 17 39
(C R Egerton) *in rr: pushed along and sme hdwy over 5f out: lost pl 3f out* **33/1**

2405 **12** 1 ½ **Bold Cross (IRE)**[17] 1416 3-9-2 **68**........................ MichaelTebbutt 11 44
(E G Bevan) *t.k.h in rr: rn wd bnd over 6f out: nvr on terms* **16/1**

400 **13** *7* **Star Jasmine**[8] 1649 3-8-6 **58**........................ HayleyTurner 13 20
(M L W Bell) *sn chsng ldrs: sn pushed along: lost pl over 3f out* **10/1**

0505 **14** 1 ¼ **Deep Sleep**[39] 969 3-8-11 **66**........................ SaleemGolam[(3)] 6 26
(M H Tompkins) *t.k.h: in tch: lost pl over 2f out* **10/1**

0000 **15** *35* **Kolhapur (IRE)**[18] 1375 3-8-11 **63**........................(b[1]) IanMongan 4 —
(J L Dunlop) *s.i.s: a bhd: t.o and virtually p.u: btn 35 l* **33/1**

1m 51.23s (4.83) **Going Correction** +0.625s/f (Yiel) **15** Ran SP% **120.7**
Speed ratings (Par 99):100,99,98,98,93 92,89,88,87,87 86,84,77,76,41
CSF £40.97 CT £475.69 TOTE £5.00: £2.10, £2.60, £3.80; EX 60.40.
Owner Diamond Racing Ltd **Bred** Swettenham Stud **Trained** Newmarket, Suffolk
■ Rebellious Spirit was withdrawn (7/1, spread plate at s). R4 applies, deduct 10p in the £.

FOCUS
An ordinary handicap in which few figured. The form looks reliable enough, though.
Reveur Official explanation: jockey said filly had no more to give
Freeze The Flame(GER) Official explanation: jockey said gelding hung left

1852 TOTESPORT 0800 221 221 APPRENTICE MAIDEN H'CAP 1m 54y
5:10 (5:16) (Class 6) (0-60,59) 4-Y-O+ **£3,412** (£1,007; £504) **Stalls** Centre

Form RPR
4005 **1** **Bollin Michael**[12] 1531 4-9-2 **59**........................(b) DuranFentiman[(3)] 1 72+
(T D Easterby) *led after 1f: wnt clr over 2f out: shkn up wl ins last: unchal* **4/1**[2]

4660 **2** 2 ½ **Orpen Quest (IRE)**[12] 1538 4-8-0 **45**........................(v) KevinGhunowa[(5)] 6 53
(M J Attwater) *s.i.s: hld up in mid-div: swtchd outside 3f out: hung lft and wnt 2nd 1f out: styd on: no ch w wnr* **15/2**

0602 **3** 3 ½ **Airedale Lad (IRE)**[4] 1757 5-8-2 **47** ow2............ MichaelJStainton[(5)] 15 48
(R M Whitaker) *n.m.r and lost pl after 1f: hdwy 3f out: kpt on same pce* **7/2**[1]

2460 **4** *2* **Burton Ash**[23] 1253 4-8-12 **55**........................(v) GregFairley[(3)] 3 52
(J G Given) *s.i.s: sn trcking ldrs: wnt 2nd 4f out: wknd 1f out* **6/1**[3]

0400 **5** *5* **Rapid Flow**[24] 1235 4-8-10 **53**........................ StephenDonohoe[(3)] 4 40
(P D Evans) *mid-div: hdwy 4f out: wknd over 1f out* **40/1**

5033 **6** 1 ¼ **Drumroll (IRE)**[86] 493 4-9-1 **58**........................(p) JerryO'Dwyer[(3)] 7 43
(Miss J Feilden) *led 1f: chsd ldrs: wknd over 1f out* **12/1**

30 **7** *2* **Glory Be (ITY)**[11] 1568 4-8-9 **49**........................ DanielTudhope 16 30
(J L Spearing) *chsd ldrs: wknd over 2f out* **12/1**

2024 **8** *2* **Tommytyler (IRE)**[4] 1765 7-8-0 **45**........................(t) KellyHarrison[(5)] 17 22
(D Carroll) *trckd ldrs on outer: outpcd 4f out: kpt on fnl 2f: nvr a threat* **10/1**

0006 **9** *6* **Tantien**[11] [1573] 4-8-0 **47** oh5 ow2 JamieHamblett(7) 12 — 12
(John A Harris) *s.i.s: a in rr* **50/1**
000 **10** *1 3/4* **Arpetcheeo (USA)**[152] [6623] 4-9-1 **55** SaleemGolam 9 — 16
(D Carroll) *a towards rr* **33/1**
5550 **11** *1/2* **Loup Sifflet (IRE)**[12] [1537] 4-8-7 **47** DeanCorby 10 — 7
(R A Fahey) *s.i.s: a in rr* **8/1**
0000 **12** *1 3/4* **Zambezi River**[27] [1165] 7-7-12 **45** oh10 PietroRomeo(7) 14 — 2
(J M Bradley) *t.k.h in rr: hdwy 4f out: lost pl over 2f out* **66/1**
4060 **13** *4* **Tod Sloan (IRE)**[61] [682] 4-7-12 **45** oh5 BarrySavage(7) 13 — —
(J M Bradley) *trckd ldrs: t.k.h: lost pl over 3f out* **20/1**
0400 **14** *13* **Red Lantern**[150] [6649] 5-8-0 **45** oh5 StacyRenwick(5) 5 — —
(M J Attwater) *w ldrs: wknd over 3f out: sn bhd* **33/1**

1m 50.27s (3.87) **Going Correction** +0.625s/f (Yiel) **14** Ran SP% **120.4**
Speed ratings (Par 101):105,102,99,97,92 90,88,86,80,79 78,76,72,59
CSF £31.98 CT £120.06 TOTE £5.80: £2.40, £2.80, £1.60 Place 6 £67.61, Place 5 £29.89.
Owner Sir Neil Westbrook **Bred** Sir Neil And Lady Westbrook **Trained** Great Habton, N Yorks
■ For Life was withdrawn (14/1, bolted two circuits bef s). R4 applies, deduct 5p in the £.
FOCUS
A moderate heat, but the winner is relatively lightly raced and open to some improvement.
T/Plt: £175.50 to a £1 stake. Pool: £68,903.30. 286.55 winning tickets. T/Qpdt: £40.50 to a £1 stake. Pool: £2,932.00. 53.50 winning tickets. WG

1682 THIRSK (L-H)
Saturday, May 20

OFFICIAL GOING: Heavy
A couple of hours of rain in the morning resulted in the going becoming heavy.
Wind: Virtually nil.

1853 EUROPEAN BREEDERS FUND CARLTON MINIOTT MAIDEN FILLIES' STKS — 5f
2:35 (2:35) (Class 4) 2-Y-O **£6,477** (£1,927; £963; £481) **Stalls** High

Form — RPR
1 **Eliza May** 2-9-0 NCallan 6 — 66+
(K A Ryan) *cl up: led after 2f: rdn clr wl over 1f out: kpt on* **11/4**[1]
2 *1 1/4* **Fly Time** 2-9-0 TonyCulhane 3 — 62+
(M R Channon) *chsd ldrs: hdwy to chse wnr wl over 1f out: sn rdn and kpt on ins last* **10/3**[2]
00 **3** *4* **Lovers Kiss**[7] [1664] 2-9-0 GrahamGibbons 5 — 47
(N Wilson) *pushed along in midfield 1/2-way: styd on fnl 2f* **14/1**
4 *2* **Moonlight Applause** 2-9-0 DavidAllan 4 — 40
(T D Easterby) *s.i.s and outpcd in rr: hdwy 2f out: rdn: edgd lft and kpt on same pce appr last* **11/2**[3]
0 **5** *3* **First Valentini**[21] [1295] 2-8-7 SuzzanneFrance(7) 2 — 29
(N Bycroft) *chsd ldrs on outer: rdn along over 2f out: sn wknd* **11/1**
50 **6** *2* **Bowl Em Over**[16] [1442] 2-9-0 TomEaves 8 — 22
(M E Sowersby) *led 2f: cl up tl rdn over 2f out and grad wknd* **8/1**
7 *2 1/2* **Autour Du Monde** 2-9-0 LeeEnstone 7 — 13
(P C Haslam) *s.i.s: sn in tch: rdn along over 2f out and sn wknd* **8/1**
8 *12* **Theoretical** 2-9-0 DeanMcKeown 1 — —
(M J Polglase) *wnt lft s: a rr* **10/1**

65.44 secs (5.54) **Going Correction** +0.70s/f (Yiel) **8** Ran SP% **111.4**
Speed ratings (Par 92):83,81,74,71,66 63,59,40
CSF £11.28 TOTE £3.30: £1.70, £1.10, £5.20; EX 8.00.
Owner Mrs T Marnane **Bred** Lostford Manor Stud **Trained** Hambleton, N Yorks
FOCUS
An ordinary juvenile fillies' contest but the first two both look to have a future, although the level is somewhat guessy.
NOTEBOOK
Eliza May ◆, speedily-bred, by a champion sprinter out of a triple juvenile winner, was an uneasy favourite. However, she showed all the pace that her pedigree suggested and, clear over a furlong out, won nicely despite getting a little tired in the ground late on. She can be expected to improve from this, and it would be no surprise to see her take her chance in races like the Hilary Needler and possibly the Queen Mary. (op 7-4 tchd 3-1)
Fly Time, not as speedily-bred as the winner, had to be ridden along at halfway, but picked up from that point and was gradually closing down that rival as the line came. She should come on for the run and can find a maiden with this under her belt. (op 4-1)
Lovers Kiss, the most experienced in the field, put up her best effort so far, and although never a danger to the first two, does tend to limit the form. (op 20-1)
Moonlight Applause, like the winner bred to be a sprinter, never really threatened on this debut. However, her stable's juveniles normally come on for the outing and she is likely to follow that pattern. (op 5-1 tchd 6-1)
Bowl Em Overon much easier ground than when finishing well beaten last time. Showed speed until past halfway. (op 10-1 tchd 15-2)

1854 ATKINSON MAIDEN STKS — 1m 4f
3:10 (3:11) (Class 5) 3-Y-0+ **£5,181** (£1,541; £770; £384) **Stalls** Low

Form — RPR
1 **Alfie Flits**[42] 4-9-12 RobertWinston 1 — 98+
(G A Swinbank) *trckd ldrs: smooth hdwy over 3f out: led over 2f out: easily* **11/10**[1]
2 *2 1/2* **Riodan (IRE)**[19] 4-9-7 GrahamGibbons 3 — 76
(J J Quinn) *hld up in tch: hdwy to trck ldrs over 4f out: chsd wnr over 2f out: sn rdn and no imp* **28/1**
22 **3** *8* **Virgin Islands (IRE)**[39] [971] 3-8-4 KerrinMcEvoy 5 — 64
(M A Jarvis) *trckd ldrs: effrt 3f out: sn rdn along and outpcd: plugged on u.p fnl 2f* **5/4**[2]
06 **4** *1 1/4* **Maysoor**[21] [1283] 3-8-9 JoeFanning 9 — 67
(M Johnston) *dwlt: sn chsng ldr: led 3f out: rdn and hdd over 2f out: drvn and grad wknd* **14/1**[3]
05 **5** *7* **Industrial Star (IRE)**[56] [2260] 5-9-12 PaulHanagan 6 — 58
(Micky Hammond) *trckd ldrs: rn wd bnd after 11/2f: hdwy over 3f out: sn rdn and nvr a factor* **25/1**
60 **6** *24* **Every Inch (IRE)**[17] [1421] 3-8-9 DavidAllan 2 — 24
(T D Easterby) *keen: chsd ldrs: rn wd bnd after 11/2f: rdn along over 4f out and sn wknd* **66/1**
00 **7** *15* **Tammy**[10] [1598] 3-8-5 ow1 DeanMcKeown 4 — —
(C W Thornton) *a rr: bhd fr 1/2-way* **200/1**
05 **8** *8* **Celtic Jig (IRE)**[14] [1492] 3-8-9 (b[1]) KDarley 7 — —
(T D Easterby) *led: rdn along 4f out: hdd over 3f out and wknd qckly* **50/1**
0500 **9** *1* **Intavac Girl**[10] [1598] 3-8-4 40 AdrianTNicholls 8 — —
(C W Thornton) *a bhd* **200/1**

2m 48.7s (13.50) **Going Correction** +1.00s/f (Soft)
WFA 3 from 4yo+ 17lb **9** Ran SP% **110.5**
Speed ratings (Par 103):95,93,88,87,82 66,56,51,50
CSF £34.81 TOTE £2.20: £1.10, £4.40, £1.10; EX 30.60.
Owner Dom Flit **Bred** Shadwell Estate Company Limited **Trained** Melsonby, N Yorks
FOCUS
A moderate and uncompetitive maiden with a very easy winner. The fourth is the best guide to the level.
Virgin Islands(IRE) Official explanation: jockey said filly was unsuited by the heavy ground

1855 DOUG MOSCROP RETIREMENT H'CAP — 1m
3:45 (3:47) (Class 4) (0-80,78) 3-Y-O **£6,477** (£1,927; £963; £481) **Stalls** Low

Form — RPR
531 **1** **Heaven Knows**[175] [6435] 3-9-4 **78** DarryllHolland 5 — 91+
(W J Haggas) *sn pushed along in rr: hdwy on outer 3f out: rdn and edgd lft over 1f out: sn drvn and styd on ent last to ld last 150 yds* **7/4**[1]
1300 **2** *1 3/4* **North Walk (IRE)**[10] [1596] 3-8-13 **78** AndrewMullen(5) 9 — 82
(K A Ryan) *in tch: hdwy 3f out: rdn to chse ldr 2f out: drvn and ev ch over 1f out tl no ex wl ins last* **20/1**
4655 **3** *3/4* **The Osteopath (IRE)**[252] [5122] 3-8-11 **71** TomEaves 4 — 74+
(M Dods) *dwlt and bhd: hdwy over 2f out: styd on u.p ins last: nrst fin* **33/1**
2220 **4** *shd* **Queen's Composer (IRE)**[40] [952] 3-8-12 **72** RobertWinston 12 — 74
(B Smart) *in tch: hdwy 3f out: rdn wl over 1f out: drvn and ev ch ins last tl wknd towards fin* **12/1**
2001 **5** *3/4* **Sir Orpen (IRE)**[11] [1564] 3-9-4 **78** PhillipMakin 8 — 79
(T D Barron) *cl up: led after 1f: rdn clr wl over 2f out: drvn over 1f out: hdd & wknd last 150 yds* **8/1**
3444 **6** *3 1/2* **Crimson Flame (IRE)**[26] [1190] 3-9-1 **75** TonyCulhane 11 — 69
(M R Channon) *in tch: hdwy 3f out: rdn 2f out and kpt on same pce* **16/1**
006 **7** *3/4* **Electric Warrior (IRE)**[40] [952] 3-8-7 **67** PatCosgrave 6 — 59
(K R Burke) *in tch: rdn along 3f out: sn no imp* **15/2**[3]
0433 **8** *2* **Great Chieftain (IRE)**[14] [1493] 3-8-13 **73** PaulHanagan 3 — 61
(R A Fahey) *nvr bttr than midfield* **20/1**
5441 **9** *5* **Sands Of Barra (IRE)**[9] [1617] 3-9-3 **77** KerrinMcEvoy 13 — 55
(N A Callaghan) *chsd ldrs: rdn along wl over 2f out: sn edgd lft and wknd* **13/2**[2]
3215 **10** *20* **Manouche**[37] [1005] 3-8-12 **72** NCallan 7 — 10
(K A Ryan) *chsd ldrs: rdn along wl over 2f out: sn wknd* **13/2**[2]
4000 **11** *12* **Cape Gold (IRE)**[16] [1440] 3-8-4 **67** PaulMulrennan(3) 14 — —
(R A Fahey) *led 1f: cl up tl rdn along 3f out and sn wknd* **50/1**
3360 **12** *2 1/2* **Lady Disdain**[19] [1345] 3-8-8 **68** DavidAllan 1 — —
(G M Moore) *towards rr: hmpd in inner after 2f and bhd after* **25/1**
0230 **13** *dist* **Sinner Or Saint (IRE)**[31] [1077] 3-8-13 **73** KDarley 2 — —
(T D Easterby) *chsd ldrs: rdn along over 3f out: sn wknd* **25/1**

1m 47.47s (7.77) **Going Correction** +1.00s/f (Soft) **13** Ran SP% **121.6**
Speed ratings (Par 101):101,99,98,98,97 94,93,91,86,66 54,51,—
CSF £47.99 CT £907.64 TOTE £2.60: £1.30, £7.30, £8.30; EX 69.70.
Owner B Haggas **Bred** Southcourt Stud **Trained** Newmarket, Suffolk
■ Stewards' Enquiry : Pat Cosgrave two-day ban: careless riding (May 31, Jun 1)
FOCUS
A fair handicap that appeared to be run at a decent gallop, but was a somewhat rough race, especially on the bend. However, the form appears sound enough with the second, fourth and fifth close to their marks.
Sands Of Barra(IRE) Official explanation: jockey said gelding was unsuited by the heavy ground
Sinner Or Saint(IRE) Official explanation: jockey said colt lost its action

1856 POLAR FORD H'CAP — 5f
4:15 (4:16) (Class 4) (0-85,85) 3-Y-O+ **£6,477** (£1,927; £963; £481) **Stalls** High

Form — RPR
0060 **1** **Bond Boy**[21] [1285] 9-9-4 **77** (b[1]) RobertWinston 7 — 92
(B Smart) *hld up stands side: swtchd rt and hdwy 2f out: str run ent last: led last 100 yds* **7/1**[3]
0006 **2** *2* **Our Fugitive (IRE)**[204] [6132] 4-9-4 **77** KerrinMcEvoy 8 — 85
(A W Carroll) *cl up stands side: led that gp and overall ldr 1/2-way: rdn over 1f out: hdd and nt qucken last 100 yds* **12/1**
0405 **3** *1/2* **Mimi Mouse**[217] [5891] 4-9-12 **85** DavidAllan 10 — 92
(T D Easterby) *in tch stands side: hdwy 2f out: sn rdn and kpt on ins last* **25/1**
0630 **4** *1 3/4* **Bold Marc (IRE)**[14] [1496] 4-9-3 **76** PaulHanagan 2 — 77
(K R Burke) *led far side gp 2f: cl up tl rdn and ch over 1f out: kpt on same pce ins last* **15/2**
0601 **5** *hd* **Prince Namid**[7] [1662] 4-9-11 **84** PaulFessey 1 — 84
(Mrs A Duffield) *cl up far side: led that gp after 2f: rdn and ch over 1f out: sn one pce* **5/1**[1]
3145 **6** *nk* **Efistorm**[29] [1125] 5-9-6 **79** DarryllHolland 11 — 78
(J Balding) *chsd ldrs stands side: rdn wl over 1f out: wknd entetring last* **11/2**[2]
0300 **7** *3/4* **Wanchai Lad**[9] [1602] 5-9-9 **82** AdrianTNicholls 3 — 78
(D Nicholls) *trckd ldng pair far side: effrt 2f out: sn rdn and one pce appr last* **15/2**
0005 **8** *shd* **Ptarmigan Ridge**[16] [1438] 10-9-1 **74** TomEaves 6 — 70
(Miss L A Perratt) *chsd ldrs stands side: rdn wl over 1f out: wknd ent last* **8/1**
0616 **9** *5* **Pomfret Lad**[10] [1597] 8-9-5 **78** GrahamGibbons 12 — 57
(J J Quinn) *dwlt: a rr stands side* **10/1**
3000 **10** *1/2* **Fun To Ride**[21] [1285] 5-8-9 **71** oh1 PaulMulrennan(3) 9 — 48
(M W Easterby) *chsd ldrs stands side: rdn along 1/2-way: sn wknd* **33/1**
0042 **11** *4* **Bluebok**[8] [1643] 5-9-1 **74** (t) NCallan 14 — 38
(J M Bradley) *overall ldr stansds side: hdd 1/2-way: sn wknd and eased fnl f* **11/2**[2]
0-00 **12** *13* **Capped For Victory (USA)**[287] [4166] 5-9-0 **73** LeeEnstone 5 — —
(W S Cunningham) *racd stands side: a bhd* **66/1**

62.10 secs (2.20) **Going Correction** +0.70s/f (Yiel) **12** Ran SP% **119.6**
Speed ratings (Par 105):110,106,106,103,102 102,101,101,93,92 85,65
CSF £87.56 CT £1993.61 TOTE £7.50: £2.20, £3.90, £4.40; EX 99.30.
Owner R C Bond **Bred** D E And Mrs J Cash **Trained** Hambleton, N Yorks
FOCUS
A fair sprint handicap in which the field split into two groups - three went far side, but the stands'-side group held a clear advantage. The form looks pretty solid backed up by a decent time.
Bluebok Official explanation: jockey said gelding was unsuited by the heavy ground

1857 THIRSK H'CAP — 5f
4:50 (4:51) (Class 2) (0-100,93) 3-Y-O **£12,954** (£3,854; £1,926; £962) **Stalls** High

Form — RPR
4002 **1** **Green Park (IRE)**[9] [1604] 3-9-4 **90** PaulHanagan 2 — 96+
(R A Fahey) *trckd ldrs: effrt and nt clr run 2f out: swtchd lft and rdn over 1f out: qcknd ent last to ld last 100 yds* **10/1**

5006 **2** *2* **Grazeon Gold Blend**[9] [1604] 3-9-0 **86**........................ GrahamGibbons 4 84
(J J Quinn) *cl up:rdn 2f out: drvn and ev ch ent last tl one pce last 100 yds* **8/1**

0223 **3** *nk* **Scooby Dude (IRE)**[9] [1604] 3-8-9 **81**............................ DarryllHolland 1 78
(Ms Deborah J Evans) *trckd ldrs: hdwy on outer 2f out: rdn to ld ent last: hdd and one pce last 100 yds* **7/1**[3]

010 **4** *3* **Dark Missile**[13] [1512] 3-8-11 **83**.. JoeFanning 5 70
(A M Balding) *cl up: led 1/2-way: rdn wl over 1f out: hdd & wknd ent last* **12/1**

13 **5** *3/4* **King Orchisios (IRE)**[30] [1094] 3-9-7 **93**.................................. NCallan 7 77
(K A Ryan) *dwlt: sn trcking ldrs: effrt and nt clr run 2f out: swtchd lft and rdn ent last: no hdwy* **1/1**[1]

5421 **6** *nk* **Sea Salt**[16] [1437] 3-8-8 **80**.. PhillipMakin 6 63
(T D Barron) *led to 1/2-way: sn rdn along and wknd wl over 1f out* **15/2**

6412 **7** *1 1/4* **Mulligan's Gold (IRE)**[19] [1344] 3-8-2 **74** oh4..................... PaulFessey 3 53
(T D Easterby) *cl up: rdn along 2f out: sn wknd* **5/1**[2]

62.31 secs (2.41) **Going Correction** +0.70s/f (Yiel) 7 Ran SP% **118.8**
Speed ratings (Par 105):108,104,104,99,98 97,95
CSF £88.41 TOTE £10.50: £4.80, £3.80; EX 70.80.
Owner G A Fixings Ltd **Bred** James Burns And A Moynan **Trained** Musley Bank, N Yorks

FOCUS
A decent handicap but a slightly disappointing turnout numbers-wise. The form looks sound enough rated around the placed horses.

NOTEBOOK
Green Park(IRE), who was narrowly touched off at Chester the previous week, gained compensation on the most testing ground he has faced. He picked up really well in the closing stages and once hitting the front quickly went clear. He will go up again for this effort but it would be no surprise to see him score again, with the big handicap on York's charity day an obvious target. (op 8-1 tchd 12-1)
Grazeon Gold Blend, who was 6lb better off with today's winner for just under four lengths, ran close to that form having been prominent all the way. He helps give the form a sound appearance. (op 7-1)
Scooby Dude(IRE)was 2lb worse off with the runner-up but 4lb better off with Green Park compared with Chester, and looked the winner when striking the front. However, he tired in the final furlong as if finding this ground too testing. (op 13-2 tchd 6-1 and 8-1)
Dark Missileshowed plenty of speed until fading in the closing stages. (op 10-1 tchd 9-1)
King Orchisios(IRE) was slowly into his stride, but after tracking the leaders got a gap near the rail and looked sure to figure in the finish. However, he could not pick up from that point. The ground may have been too soft for him, but he has something to prove now. (op 11-8)
Sea Salt, who was well-backed, set the pace until dropping out in the last quarter mile. (op 10-1)
Mulligan's Gold(IRE), racing from 4lb out of the handicap, was another who was supported in the ring but dropped away after racing up all the pace. (op 7-1)

1858 ARMY BENEVOLENT FUND H'CAP 6f
5:20 (5:20) (Class 3) (0-90,89) 3-Y-0+ **£9,067** (£2,697; £1,348; £673) **Stalls** High

Form RPR

0050 **1** **Johnston's Diamond (IRE)**[18] [1388] 8-9-2 **78**.............. DarryllHolland 2 92
(E J Alston) *racd alone far side: a cl up: overall ldr wl over 1f out and sn clr* **16/1**

4140 **2** *5* **Raymond's Pride**[21] [1285] 6-9-2 **83**.........................(b) AndrewMullen(5) 5 89
(K A Ryan) *cl up stands siude: overall ldr 1/2-way: rdn and hdd wl over 1f out: sn drvn and kpt on ins last: no chanvce w far side* **5/1**[2]

0013 **3** *shd* **Paris Bell**[10] [1597] 4-9-1 **77**.. PaulQuinn 12 83
(T D Easterby) *dwlt: hdwy 1/2-way: rdn to chse ldr stands side 2f out: drvn and kpt on fnl f* **7/2**[1]

0000 **4** *6* **Inter Vision (USA)**[10] [1597] 6-9-10 **86**.......................... RobertWinston 3 74
(A Dickman) *in tch stands side: swtchd rt and hdwy over 2f out: sn rdn and one pce* **14/1**

0000 **5** *3* **Bo McGinty (IRE)**[14] [1487] 5-9-5 **81**...........................(v) PaulHanagan 13 60
(R A Fahey) *hld up stands rail: hdwy 2f out: styd on appr last: nvr a factor* **9/1**

0444 **6** *1 1/4* **Golden Asha**[14] [1487] 4-9-5 **81**...................................... KerrinMcEvoy 11 56
(N A Callaghan) *hld up stands side: hdwy over 2f out: sn rdn and nvr nr ldrs* **7/2**[1]

0400 **7** *hd* **Sentiero Rosso (USA)**[7] [1662] 4-8-13 **75** oh3................. PatCosgrave 6 49
(B Ellison) *bhd stands side tl styd on fnl 2f* **28/1**

6000 **8** *3* **Throw The Dice**[14] [1496] 4-9-2 **78**....................................... JoeFanning 9 43
(D W Barker) *chsd ldrs stands side: rdn along over 2f out: sn wknd* **25/1**

1003 **9** *7* **Graze On**[14] [1475] 4-9-12 **88**......................................(b) AdrianMcCarthy 4 32
(R A Harris) *prom stands side: rdn along 1/2-way: sn wknd* **16/1**

0000 **10** *1 1/4* **Lake Andre (IRE)**[12] [1532] 5-9-7 **83**.. NCallan 7 24
(K A Ryan) *overall ldr stands side: hdd 1/2-way: sn rdn and wknd 2f out* **8/1**[3]

0000 **11** *5* **Currency**[212] [5999] 9-9-2 **78**... TonyCulhane 1 —
(J M Bradley) *chsd ldrs stands side: rdn along 1/2-way: sn wknd* **40/1**

0005 **12** *1 3/4* **Ellens Academy (IRE)**[10] [1597] 11-8-13 **75**........................ DavidAllan 8 —
(E J Alston) *dwlt: a rr stands side* **20/1**

0600 **13** *5* **Loaderfun (IRE)**[12] [1532] 4-9-6 **82**............................ GrahamGibbons 14 —
(N Wilson) *a bhd stands side* **22/1**

0 **14** *11* **Pachello (IRE)**[24] [1246] 4-9-11 **87**.. TomEaves 10 —
(J M Bradley) *a b ehind stands side* **50/1**

1m 16.06s (3.56) **Going Correction** +0.70s/f (Yiel) 14 Ran SP% **121.5**
Speed ratings (Par 107):104,97,97,89,85 83,83,79,69,68 61,59,52,37
CSF £87.85 CT £363.24 TOTE £18.30: £3.90, £1.60, £2.00; EX 50.30.
Owner Mollington Golf Club Boys **Bred** Sos Investments **Trained** Longton, Lancs

FOCUS
A fair handicap in which apart from one the field stayed on the stands' side. However, that one was the winner and he is rated to best with those stands' side half a stone off.

NOTEBOOK
Johnston's Diamond(IRE), whose rider, despite the evidence of earlier in the day, went to the 'unfavoured' far side, and somewhat surprisingly ran our a clear-cut winner. He likes to race up with the pace and being on his own may have been in his favour. (op 14-1)
Raymond's Pride ran a fine race on ground that suits him well, and battled well to hold his narrow advantage over the third but would not have seen the winner on the opposite side of the track. He remains 4lb above his highest winning mark. (op 8-1)
Paris Bell, most of whose wins have been on similar ground, ran his race and sets the standard for the form. (op 4-1 tchd 9-2 in a place)
Inter Vision(USA), who moved into contention after halfway, was then unable to pick up on ground that was much softer than he prefers. (op 12-1)
Bo McGinty(IRE) merely stayed on past beaten rivals but was never in contention. (op 8-1)
Golden Ashahas form on easy ground but her best efforts have been on a sound surface and she never really figured. Official explanation: jockey said filly was unsuited by the heavy ground (op 10-3)
Graze On , who is holding his form well, set the early pace towards the centre before fading. (op 14-1)

1859 DARRON AND PAULA'S WEDDING DAY H'CAP 1m
5:50 (5:51) (Class 6) (0-65,66) 3-Y-0 **£2,590** (£770; £385; £192) **Stalls** Low

Form RPR

401 **1** **Moody Tunes**[10] [1593] 3-9-2 **62**....................................... PatCosgrave 15 76
(K R Burke) *in tch on outer: gd hdwy 3f out: led 2f out: rdn clr over 1f out: kpt on* **6/1**[2]

4141 **2** *1 1/4* **Stolen Glance**[4] [1761] 3-9-3 **66** 6ex............................ PaulMulrennan(3) 6 77
(M W Easterby) *midfield: hdwy over 3f out: rdn to chse wnr wl over 1f out: drvn and kpt on fnl f* **2/1**[1]

0300 **3** *6* **Apache Nation (IRE)**[10] [1592] 3-8-13 **59**.......................... PhillipMakin 8 58
(M Dods) *midfield: hdwy 3f out: rdn to chse ldng pair and hung lft over 1f out: kpt on same pce* **20/1**

3046 **4** *2 1/2* **Impeccable Guest (IRE)**[75] [604] 3-8-6 **57**........... LeanneKershaw(5) 4 51
(P C Haslam) *towards rr: hdwy over 2f out: sn rdn and kpt on wl appr last: nrst fin* **25/1**

5024 **5** *3/4* **Jaassey**[252] [5125] 3-9-0 **60**.. TomEaves 11 53
(T D Walford) *dwlt: towards rr: hdwy over 2f out: sn rdn and kpt on appr last: nrst fin* **33/1**

0614 **6** *3 1/2* **Hi Dancer**[93] [430] 3-8-8 **54**.. LeeEnstone 5 40
(P C Haslam) *towards rr tl styd on fnl 2f* **20/1**

0032 **7** *2 1/2* **The Grey One (IRE)**[11] [1567] 3-8-9 **55**......................(p) TonyCulhane 16 36
(J M Bradley) *stdd s and bhd tl styd on fnl 2f* **13/2**[3]

063 **8** *2 1/2* **Carloman**[208] [6077] 3-8-12 **61**.................................. NelsonDeSouza(3) 18 37
(R M Beckett) *prom tl rdn along and wknd 3f out* **11/1**

0000 **9** *1 1/2* **Obscene**[16] [1441] 3-8-11 **57**.. DarryllHolland 17 30
(M J Polglase) *chsd ldrs: rdn along 3f out: sn wknd* **12/1**

0530 **10** *1* **Farne Island**[10] [1599] 3-9-4 **64**...................................... GrahamGibbons 7 35
(J J Quinn) *nvr nr ldrs* **20/1**

0566 **11** *7* **Stormingmichaelori**[214] [5961] 3-8-8 **54**......................... RobertWinston 14 11
(N Wilson) *chsd ldrs: rdn along 3f out: sn wknd* **66/1**

640 **12** *4* **Walnut Grove**[228] [5680] 3-8-5 **54**.................................. BenSwarbrick(3) 1 3
(T D Barron) *a rr* **16/1**

0000 **13** *3 1/2* **Danethorpe (IRE)**[21] [1279] 3-8-6 **55**.......................... PatrickMathers(3) 9 —
(D Shaw) *dwlt: a rr* **100/1**

4600 **14** *11* **Fancy You (IRE)**[231] [5613] 3-8-8 **54**................................ PaulHanagan 13 —
(T J Pitt) *prom: rdn along 1/2-way: snw eakened* **11/1**

3030 **15** *5* **Eskimo Nell**[31] [1079] 3-8-10 **56**.. DavidAllan 2 —
(T D Easterby) *chsd ldrs: rdn along over 3f out: sn wknd* **25/1**

3560 **16** *3* **Crusader's Gold (FR)**[14] [1497] 3-9-2 **62**................................ NCallan 12 —
(T D Easterby) *loed: rdn along 1/2-way: hdd 2f out and sn wknd* **16/1**

1m 46.94s (7.24) **Going Correction** +1.00s/f (Soft) 16 Ran SP% **124.5**
Speed ratings (Par 97):103,101,95,93,92 89,86,84,82,81 74,70,67,56,51 48
CSF £16.68 CT £249.03 TOTE £8.70: £2.30, £1.70, £4.80, £4.40; EX 28.10 Place 6 £725.16, Place 5 £432.64.
Owner Geoffrey Hamilton **Bred** Llety Stud **Trained** Middleham Moor, N Yorks
■ Stewards' Enquiry : Nelson De Souza one-day ban: careless riding (May 31)

FOCUS
A moderate handicap in which the leaders went off too quick in the conditions and the principals came from off the pace. The first two came clear and look progressive and the fourth helps set the standard.
T/Plt: £295.80 to a £1 stake. Pool: £50,715.05. 125.15 winning tickets. T/Qpdt: £264.80 to a £1 stake. Pool: £2,684.30. 7.50 winning tickets. JR

BADEN-BADEN (L-H)
Saturday, May 20

OFFICIAL GOING: Soft

1860a BETTY BARCLAY-RENNEN (GROUP 3) 2m
4:00 (4:22) 4-Y-0+ **£24,138** (£10,345; £4,138; £2,759)

RPR

1 **Bussoni (GER)**[19] 5-8-12 .... ADeVries 8 111
(H Blume, Germany) *tracked leader, led well over 1f out, driven out & ran on well* **46/10**[3]

2 *5* **Frank Sonata**[28] [1128] 5-8-12 .... AStarke 6 106
(M G Quinlan) *raced in 7th, 5th straight, stayed on to take 2nd well inside final f* **33/10**[2]

3 *nk* **Tirwanako (FR)**[20] 4-8-12 .... GBocksai 4 108
(Frau C Bocskai, Switzerland) *always in touch, 4th straight on outside, chased winner from 1 1/2f out, one pace & lost 2nd well inside final f* **31/2**

4 *2 1/2* **Tartouche**[13] [1511] 5-8-10 .... ASuborics 11 102
(Lady Herries) *held up in rear, some headway on outside from over 1f out, took 4th on line* **8/5**[1]

5 *nse* **Soterio (GER)**[189] [6339] 6-8-12 .... ABoschert 1 103
(W Baltromei, Germany) *held up, good headway well over 1f out, lost 4th on line* **15/1**

6 *hd* **Kasus (GER)**[19] 8-8-12 ....(b) FilipMinarik 2 103
(P Vovcenko, Germany) *7th straight on inside, effort well over 1f out, soon one pace* **58/10**

7 *1 1/2* **Bailamos (GER)**[19] [1369] 6-8-12 .... TMundry 9 102
(P Schiergen, Germany) *6th straight, never able to challenge* **103/10**

8 *1 1/2* **Liquido (GER)**[19] 7-8-12 .... WMongil 3 100
(H Steinmetz, Germany) *prominent, 3rd straight on inside, beaten over 1f out* **13/1**

9 *10* **Harar (GER)**[19] [1369] 4-8-12 .... AHelfenbein 10 92
(Andreas Lowe, Germany) *always towards rear* **21/1**

10 *4 1/2* **Palais Tiff (GER)**[36] [1014] 7-8-10 .... NRichter 12 84
(Frau M Fechner, Germany) *led to well over 1f out* **61/1**

11 *84* **Notte Italiana (IRE)**[207] [6099] 4-8-5 .... TBitala 7 —
(H J Koll, Germany) *mid-division, weakened quickly 4f out, soon tailed off* **65/1**

3m 28.57s
WFA 4 from 5yo+ 2lb 11 Ran SP% **130.3**
(including ten euro stakes): WIN 56; PL 18, 18, 25; SF 148.
Owner Stall Kaiserberg **Bred** Gestut Karlshof **Trained** Germany

FOCUS
They used a flag to get this Group 3 underway.

NOTEBOOK
Frank Sonata made progress approaching the straight and stayed on to grab second close home. He was never going to threaten the winner but might have finished closer a few hours earlier when conditions were more in his favour. The official going was changed to soft after a wet morning but the wind blew so hard that it had dried up quite a bit by the time of the race.

Tartouche spent about 20 minutes down at the start not doing very much after her stall was slow to open. The others ran at least half a mile before pulling up but Suborics pulled Tartouche up after a few strides. She firmed in the market as a result but was never happy in the race, which had to be started by flag. She was last until starting the final turn but made a little progress on the outside to take fourth on the line. Her jockey said she hated the wind and she will soon do better than this.

PIMLICO (L-H)

Saturday, May 20

OFFICIAL GOING: Turf course - firm; dirt course - fast

1861a PREAKNESS STKS (GRADE 1) 1m 1f 110y(D)

11:10 (11:19) 3-Y-O £377,907 (£116,279; £58,140; £29,070)

RPR

1 **Bernardini (USA)**[21] 3-9-0 .... JCastellano 8 124+
(T Albertrani, U.S.A) *always close up, good headway to go 2nd approaching straight, led well over 1f out, soon clear, ridden out* **129/10**

2 5 ¼ **Sweetnorthernsaint (USA)**[14] [1498] 3-9-0 ....(b) KDesormeaux 7 115
(M Trombetta, U.S.A) *tracked leader, disputed lead over 5f out, led 2 1/2f out to well over 1f out, one pace* **84/10**[3]

3 6 **Hemingway's Key (USA)**[28] 3-9-0 .... JRose 3 104
(N Zito, U.S.A) *outpaced to half-way, 6th straight, stayed on under pressure to take 3rd inside final f* **294/10**

4 4 **Brother Derek (USA)**[14] [1498] 3-9-0 .... ASolis 5 97
(Dan L Hendricks, U.S.A) *s.i.s & slightly hmpd, sn cl up, pressed ldrs on outside 5f out, outpcd 3f out, 5th str, went 3rd 1 1/2f out, one pace* **32/10**[2]

5 7 **Greeley's Legacy (USA)**[28] 3-9-0 ....(b) RMigliore 4 84
(G Weaver, U.S.A) *7th straight, no real progress* **35/1**

6 nk **Platinum Couple (USA)**[42] 3-9-0 .... JLEspinoza 2 84
(J Lostritto, U.S.A) *last straight, always behind* **33/1**

7 3 ½ **Like Now (USA)**[28] 3-9-0 .... GKGomez 1 78
(K McLaughlin, U.S.A) *led to 2 1/2f out, 3rd straight, soon weakened* **17/1**

8 2 ¼ **Diabolical (USA)**[25] 3-9-0 .... RADominguez 9 74
(Steven B Klesaris, U.S.A) *raced in 5th, 4th & ridden on inside straight, soon weakened* **26/1**

P **Barbaro (USA)**[14] [1498] 3-9-0 .... EPrado 6 —
(M Matz, U.S.A) *broke through gate, soon pulled up, 4th when broke down on off hind after 1f, pulled up* **1/2**[1]

1m 54.65s (-0.94) **9** Ran SP% **126.6**

PARI-MUTUEL (including $2 stakes): WIN 27.80; PL (1-2) 9.40, 7.80;SHOW (1-2-3) 5.80, 5.00, 8.00; SF 171.60.

Owner Darley Stable **Bred** Darley **Trained** USA

FOCUS

A race marred by the serious injury to the Kentucky Derby winner Barabaro, but nothing should be taken away from Bernardini, who won in fine style.

NOTEBOOK

Bernardini(USA), a progressive performer but untested at the top level coming into this, ran out a decisive winner and marked himself down as a very smart horse indeed. His rider showed good patience to delay his challenge until the optimum moment and the colt soon put the race to bed once asked to go on. He will get further and the Belmont Stakes looks the ideal target.

Sweetnorthernsaint(USA), who ran well in the Derby, was unable to hold off the challenge of the winner in the straight having gone fast towards the head of affairs for much of the race. He was later reported to have possibly suffered an overreach during the race.

Hemingway's Key(USA) stayed on from off the strong pace to take a third place which faltters him.

Brother Derek(USA), rushed up to chase the pace, used up too much energy in the early parts of the race and had nothing left for the finish.

Barbaro(USA), who won the Kentucky Derby so impressively, was made a hot favourite for this second leg of the Triple Crown, but he was edgy beforehand, burst the gates before the start, and sadly sustained multiple fractures of his off-hind early in the race itself.

1594 RIPON (R-H)

Sunday, May 21

OFFICIAL GOING: Heavy

Very testing ground and the bare form of all the races is best treated with caution.
Wind: Light, half-behind Weather: Overcast, raining

1862 SKYBET.COM WOODEN SPOON CHARITY (S) STKS 6f

2:10 (2:11) (Class 5) 2-Y-O £3,238 (£963; £481; £240) Stalls Low

Form RPR

0 **1** **Spinning Game**[8] [1682] 2-8-9 .... NCallan 9 61
(K A Ryan) *cl up far side: led that gp over 2f out: edgd lft and overall ldr over 1f out: hld on wl fnl f* **8/1**

524 **2** ½ **Tokyo Jo (IRE)**[24] [1248] 2-8-9 .... RobertWinston 6 59
(K R Burke) *chsd far side ldrs: edgd lft and ev ch over 1f out: kpt on fnl f: hld cl home: 2nd of 5 in gp* **9/4**[1]

060 **3** 4 **Emma Told Lies**[24] [1248] 2-8-9 .... PaulMulrennan 3 47+
(M W Easterby) *led stands side and overall ldr to over 1f out: no ex fnl f: 1st of 5 in gp* **6/1**[2]

00 **4** ½ **Catweasel**[17] [1429] 2-8-11 ....(t) RobertMiles[(3)] 8 51
(W G M Turner) *dwlt: sn prom far side: effrt over 2f out: sn no ex: 3rd of 5 in gp* **6/1**[2]

6240 **5** 5 **Sad Times (IRE)**[25] [1229] 2-8-2 .... LiamJones[(7)] 4 31
(W G M Turner) *chsd stands side ldrs tl edgd rt and outpcd fr over 2f out: 2nd of 5 in gp* **6/1**[2]

046 **6** 15 **Minimum Fuss (IRE)**[29] [1142] 2-8-9 .... DaleGibson 7 —
(M W Easterby) *keen: led far side gp to over 2f out: sn btn: 4th of 5 in gp* **17/2**

00 **7** 5 **Makeusabuck**[14] [1499] 2-8-9 .... FrancisNorton 10 —
(A Berry) *outpcd far side: nvr on terms: last of 5 in gp* **50/1**

034 **8** ½ **Minnie Magician**[8] [1682] 2-8-9 .... TonyHamilton 5 —
(C Grant) *chsd stands side ldr tl wknd over 2f out: 3rd of 5 in gp* **13/2**[3]

0 **9** 18 **Mister Cricket (IRE)**[29] [1142] 2-9-0 .... NeilPollard 1 —
(M E Sowersby) *in tch stands side tl wknd fr 1/2-way: 4th of 5 in gp* **100/1**

10 12 **Herons Kiss (IRE)** 2-8-9 .... TomEaves 2 —
(B S Rothwell) *dwlt: a bhd stands side: last of 5 in gp* **33/1**

1m 19.1s (6.10) **Going Correction** +0.85s/f (Soft) **10** Ran SP% **114.5**

Speed ratings (Par 93):93,92,87,86,79 59,53,52,28,12

CSF £25.70 TOTE £11.20: £2.80, £1.40, £2.60; EX 26.50 Trifecta £128.00 Part won. Pool of £180.32 - 0.78 winning units..There was no bid for the winner. Tokyo Jo was the subject of a friendly claim of £6,000.

Owner T G & Mrs M E Holdcroft **Bred** Bearstone Stud **Trained** Hambleton, N Yorks

FOCUS

A weak event in which the field split evenly but the far side held sway in the last furlong and a half.

NOTEBOOK

Spinning Game, up in trip and in much more testing conditions than on her debut, turned in an improved effort and showed the right attitude to prevail. However this was a weak event and it remains to be seen whether she will be able to build on this back on a sound surface. (op 15-2)

Tokyo Jo(IRE), up to this trip for the first time and back in heavy ground, has had a few chances but again showed enough to suggest she is capable of winning a similar event. She is a good guide to the worth of this form. (op 15-8 tchd 5-2)

Emma Told Lies, up in trip and in testing ground for the first time, shaped better than the bare form as she did the best of those racing in the stands side group and probably did too much too soon. She is capable of winning a small race. (op 8-1 tchd 17-2)

Catweasel, up in trip and racing in heavy ground for the first time, failed to justify the market support dropped to this grade for the first time with the tongue-tie fitted. He may do better back on a sound surface. (op 16-1)

Sad Times(IRE) may be a bit better than the bare form upped in trip and in the unfavoured stands side group but she has had a few chances now and is not really one to be placing much faith in at shortish odds. (op 5-1)

Minimum Fuss(IRE) was again soundly beaten in these testing conditions but, although a sound surface may suit better, she will have to improve to win even a similar event. (op 8-1 tchd 9-1)

1863 GO SUNDAY RACING IN YORKSHIRE MAIDEN STKS 6f

2:40 (2:41) (Class 4) 2-Y-O £4,533 (£1,348; £674; £336) Stalls Low

Form RPR

4 **1** **Prince Golan (IRE)**[11] [1595] 2-9-3 .... NCallan 7 85+
(K A Ryan) *chsd far side ldrs: led that gp 2f out: edgd lft ins fnl f: styd on wl* **8/11**[1]

2 2 **Prince Rossi (IRE)** 2-9-3 .... GrahamGibbons 4 76
(J D Bethell) *cl up far side: effrt 2f out: kpt on ins fnl f: 2nd of 6 in gp* **11/1**

4 **3** shd **Fongs Gazelle**[22] [1278] 2-8-12 .... KDarley 6 71
(M Johnston) *w far side ldr: ev ch 2f out: kpt on same pce ins fnl f: 3rd of 6 in gp* **7/1**[3]

5 **4** 12 **Perlachy**[30] [1121] 2-9-3 .... DavidAllan 2 58+
(T D Easterby) *led stands side: hung rt thrght: outpcd fr 2f out: eased whn hld fnl f: 1st of 3 in gp* **4/1**[2]

0 **5** 5 **Amelie Brown (IRE)**[20] [1342] 2-8-12 .... TonyCulhane 9 20
(N Tinkler) *led far side to 2f out: sn btn: 4th of 6 in gp* **20/1**

0 **6** 17 **Only A Grand**[26] [1223] 2-8-12 .... RoystonFfrench 8 —
(R Bastiman) *in tch far side: outpcd after 2f: sn btn: 5th of 6 in gp* **50/1**

7 13 **Cicada (IRE)** 2-9-3 .... PhillipMakin 5 —
(J R Weymes) *s.i.s: outpcd far side: no ch fr 1/2-way: last of 6 in gp* **28/1**

8 1 ¼ **Focus Star** 2-9-3 .... TomEaves 3 —
(J M Jefferson) *s.i.s: nvr on terms stands side: 2nd of 3 in gp* **33/1**

9 13 **Bidders Itch** 2-8-12 .... FrancisNorton 1 —
(A Berry) *chsd stands side ldr: wknd 1/2-way: last of 3 in gp* **40/1**

1m 18.98s (5.98) **Going Correction** +0.85s/f (Soft) **9** Ran SP% **114.3**

Speed ratings (Par 95):94,91,91,75,68 45,28,26,9

CSF £9.04 TOTE £1.70: £1.10, £2.90, £1.40; EX 11.90 Trifecta £21.10 Pool £162.98 - 5.48 winning units..

Owner Mr and Mrs J D Cotton **Bred** K Molloy **Trained** Hambleton, N Yorks

FOCUS

An uncompetitive event in which the action again unfolded in the centre to the far side.

NOTEBOOK

Prince Golan(IRE) ◆ fully confirmed debut promise to win an uncompetitive event and, given the way he saw out this event, should prove equally effective when upped to seven furlongs plus. He is in good hands and is capable of winning again. (tchd 5-6 and 10-11 in places)

Prince Rossi(IRE), who is related to a couple of winners over sprint distances, travelled strongly in these testing conditions on this racecourse debut and showed enough to suggest a similar event can be found. (op 16-1)

Fongs Gazelle duly proved suited by the step up to this trip and bettered the form of her debut on good ground at Haydock last month. She should stay seven furlongs and, given she is in good hands, appeals as the type to win a small race. (op 9-2)

Perlachy looks a bit better than the bare form given he fared the best of those that raced against the stands side and that he was bang there till the last furlong and a half. Not knocked about when his chance had gone, he looks the type to do better in nurseries on better ground. (op 11-2)

Amelie Brown(IRE) showed up well for a fair way but failed to build on her debut run and, although a run in this ground can always be excused, she is likely to remain vulnerable in this type of event.

1864 MIDDLEHAM TRAINERS ASSOCIATION H'CAP 1m 1f 170y

3:10 (3:13) (Class 4) (0-85,83) 4-Y-0 £7,570 (£2,265; £1,132; £566; £282) Stalls High

Form RPR

6230 **1** **Goodbye Mr Bond**[22] [1281] 6-9-1 **80** .... FrancisNorton 12 95
(E J Alston) *midfield: smooth hdwy and swtchd lft over 3f out: led over 2f out: pushed out fnl f* **6/1**[3]

2113 **2** 4 **Augustine**[27] [1187] 5-8-11 **76** .... RobertWinston 6 84
(P W Hiatt) *midfield: hdwy over 2f out: chsd wnr ins fnl f: no imp* **6/1**[3]

3033 **3** 2 ½ **Speed Dial Harry (IRE)**[22] [1280] 4-8-13 **78** ....(v) NCallan 10 82
(K R Burke) *chsd ldrs: smooth hdwy and disp ld over 2f out: wknd ins fnl f* **12/1**

4 7 **Auenmoon (GER)**[24] 5-8-9 **74** .... KDarley 15 66
(P Monteith) *keen: mde most to over 2f out: wknd over 1f out* **7/2**[1]

2130 **5** nk **Webbow (IRE)**[27] [1186] 4-8-7 **72** .... DavidAllan 2 63
(T D Easterby) *chsd ldrs: effrt and ev ch over 3f out: wknd over 2f out* **20/1**

2002 **6** ¾ **Lucayan Dancer**[10] [1610] 6-8-12 **77** .... AdrianTNicholls 5 67
(D Nicholls) *towards rr on ins: drvn over 4f out: sme hdwy 3f out: nvr rchd ldrs* **12/1**

0516 **7** shd **Dispol Veleta**[5] [1761] 5-8-7 **72** .... PaulFessey 3 62
(T D Barron) *hld up: pushed along over 4f out: nvr rchd ldrs* **20/1**

0-00 **8** hd **Buddy Brown**[96] [412] 4-8-11 **76** .... PaulMulrennan 14 66
(J Howard Johnson) *prom tl rdn and wknd over 3f out* **50/1**

5030 **9** 5 **Little Jimbob**[99] [375] 5-8-13 **78** .... TonyHamilton 4 59
(R A Fahey) *bhd: drvn over 4f out: nvr on terms* **33/1**

4650 **10** 14 **Typhoon Ginger (IRE)**[212] [6008] 11-7-13 **69** oh10.. AndrewMullen[(5)] 13 26
(G Woodward) *s.i.s: nvr on terms* **100/1**

4-03 **11** 21 **Tamatave (IRE)**[15] [1492] 4-8-5 **70** .... DO'Donohoe 11 —
(K A Ryan) *w ldr tl wknd over 3f out: eased whn btn over 1f out* **25/1**

140 **12** *25* **Little Bob**[39] [992] 5-8-4 **69** oh2....................................(b) NickyMackay 9 —
(J D Bethell) *prom early: sn lost pl: no ch fr 1/2-way* **6/1**[3]
4001 **13** *14* **Cool Hunter**[13] [1544] 5-9-4 **83**.. TedDurcan 8 —
(W R Swinburn) *dwlt: hld up: rdn over 4f out: nvr on terms* **9/2**[2]
2m 12.76s (7.76) **Going Correction** +0.925s/f (Soft) **13** Ran SP% **117.9**
Speed ratings (Par 105):105,101,99,94,93 93,93,93,89,77 61,41,29
CSF £37.99 CT £423.43 TOTE £7.00: £2.10, £2.30, £3.50; EX 52.50 Trifecta £253.00 Pool £483.42 - 1.30 winning units..
Owner Peter J Davies **Bred** Michael Ng **Trained** Longton, Lancs

FOCUS
Mainly exposed types a fair pace but those attempting to come from behind were at a disadvantage.
Little Bob Official explanation: jockey said gelding was never travelling
Cool Hunter Official explanation: jockey said gelding was unsuited by the heavy ground

1865 C. B. HUTCHINSON MEMORIAL CHALLENGE CUP (FILLIES' H'CAP) 6f
3:40 (3:57) (Class 3) (0-95,88) 3-Y-O£11,217 (£3,358; £1,679; £840; £419) **Stalls** Low

Form RPR
0030 **1** **Tagula Sunrise (IRE)**[8] [1667] 4-9-7 **82**.......................... TonyHamilton 7 92
(R A Fahey) *swtchd to r alone far side s: overall ldr over 2f out: r.o strly fnl f* **6/5**[1]
5506 **2** *3 1/2* **Dispol Katie**[6] [1734] 5-9-3 **78**.. PhillipMakin 4 78
(T D Barron) *chsd ldrs stands side: led that gp over 1f out: kpt on: nt rch far side* **11/2**[3]
4- **3** *6* **Tajaathub (USA)**[296] 4-9-12 **87**.. KDarley 5 69
(M Johnston) *w stands side ldr: led that gp over 2f to over 1f out: no ex* **4/1**[2]
2100 **4** *hd* **Princess Cleo**[22] [1292] 3-8-9 **79**.. DavidAllan 2 60
(T D Easterby) *led stands side to over 2f out: sn wknd* **11/2**[3]
1302 **5** *14* **Howards Princess**[199] [6235] 4-8-13 **74** oh2.......................... TomEaves 3 13
(I Semple) *prom stands side tl wknd over 2f out* **8/1**
1m 18.16s (5.16) **Going Correction** +1.05s/f (Soft)
WFA 3 from 4yo+ 9lb **5** Ran SP% **107.3**
Speed ratings (Par 104):107,102,94,94,75
CSF £7.63 TOTE £2.10: £1.20, £2.50; EX 6.70.
Owner David M Knaggs & Mel Roberts **Bred** Thomas Doherty **Trained** Musley Bank, N Yorks

FOCUS
Not the most competitive of handicaps and a muddling result as the wide-margin winner was the only one to tack across to the far rail.

NOTEBOOK
Tagula Sunrise(IRE) had conditions to suit and, under an enterprising ride, proved far too good for a field of mainly exposed sorts. She had plenty in her favour, though, and may be vulnerable in stronger company on better ground after reassessment. (op 13-8 tchd 7-4 and 11-10 in places)
Dispol Katie, from a stable in tremendous form, may be a bit better than the bare facts as she finished ahead of those to race on the stands side. She may be better sutied by seven furlongs and will be of interest in similar company away from progressive sorts. (op 13-2 tchd 7-1)
Tajaathub(USA), having her first start for her new stable, was not totally disgraced in these very testing conditions but may be happier on better ground and over a bit further. She is not one to write off yet. (op 11-4)
Princess Cleo was again below her best, this time on her first start in very testing ground and she is likely to continue to look vulnerable in handicaps from her current mark. (op 5-1 tchd 4-1)
Howards Princess, from a stable back among the winners, was well beaten on her first start since November and on her first run in ground as testing as this. She is not one to write off just yet. (op 6-1 tchd 10-1)

1866 RIPON-RACES.CO.UK MAIDEN STKS (DIV I) 1m 1f
4:15 (4:22) (Class 5) 3-Y-O **£4,210** (£1,252; £625; £312) **Stalls** High

Form RPR
53 **1** **Sir Arthur (IRE)**[9] [1635] 3-9-3 .... KDarley 2 78
(M Johnston) *sn led: hrd pressed fr over 2f out: hld on gamely fnl f* **11/4**[2]
22 **2** *3/4* **Speedy Sam**[225] [5748] 3-9-3 .... FrancisNorton 10 76
(K R Burke) *hld up in tch: hdwy over 2f out: ev ch ins fnl f: no ex towards fin* **15/8**[1]
3 *2 1/2* **Ha'Penny Beacon** 3-8-9 .... DanielTudhope[(3)] 12 66+
(D Carroll) *dwlt: bhd tl styd on wl fnl 2f: nrst fin* **20/1**
3600 **4** *1 1/2* **Rainbow's Classic**[30] [1122] 3-9-3 **70**.................................... NCallan 5 68
(K A Ryan) *chsd ldrs: ev ch over 2f out: no ex ins fnl f* **10/3**[3]
54 **5** *10* **Find It Out (USA)**[245] [5338] 3-9-3 .... PhillipMakin 8 48
(T D Barron) *midfield: outpcd and edgd rt over 3f out: nvr rchd ldrs* **12/1**
00 **6** *3/4* **Little Lily Morgan**[11] [1598] 3-8-12 .... RoystonFfrench 13 42
(R Bastiman) *towards rr: drvn 1/2-way: nvr on terms* **100/1**
00 **7** *nk* **Revolving World (IRE)**[20] [1343] 3-9-3 .... PaulMulrennan 11 46
(T J Fitzgerald) *prom tl rdn and wknd over 3f out* **33/1**
06 **8** *2* **Tiltili (IRE)**[218] [5889] 3-8-12 .... LeeEnstone 3 37
(P C Haslam) *towards rr: drvn over 4f out: sn btn* **50/1**
0 **9** *7* **Quintin**[263] [4871] 3-8-12 .... DavidAllan 7 23
(T D Easterby) *hld up: rdn over 4f out: sn btn* **25/1**
0 **10** *7* **Heavy Seas**[15] [1493] 3-9-3 .... RobertWinston 6 14
(P D Niven) *dwlt: bhd: effrt outside over 3f out: sn btn* **50/1**
0 **11** *18* **Flick N Flack**[265] [4823] 3-9-3 .... JosedeSouza 14 —
(D W Thompson) *cl up tl wknd over 3f out* **100/1**
12 *18* **Smoke It (IRE)** 3-9-3 .... FergalLynch 1 —
(A Berry) *s.i.s: nvr on terms* **50/1**
2m 5.36s (11.51) **Going Correction** +1.075s/f (Soft) **12** Ran SP% **111.6**
Speed ratings (Par 99):91,90,88,86,77 77,76,75,68,62 46,30
CSF £7.13 TOTE £3.50: £1.40, £1.10, £4.60; EX 5.90 Trifecta £32.30 Pool £154.14 - 3.38 winning units..
Owner Mrs Mary Keaney **Bred** Lodge Park Stud **Trained** Middleham Moor, N Yorks

FOCUS
An uncompetitive event in which the market leaders dominated but the winner appeals as the sort to progress again.

1867 GARDEN RACECOURSE H'CAP 1m 4f 10y
4:45 (4:47) (Class 5) (0-75,75) 3-Y-O **£5,362** (£1,604; £802; £401; £199) **Stalls** High

Form RPR
0211 **1** **Bollin Derek**[18] [1424] 3-8-5 **62** oh2 ow1.......................... DavidAllan 1 79
(T D Easterby) *mde virtually all: drew clr fr over 2f out: eased ins fnl f* **11/10**[1]
2321 **2** *13* **Juniper Girl (IRE)**[27] [1182] 3-8-7 **71**.............................. LukeMorris[(7)] 3 76
(M L W Bell) *keen early: chsd ldrs: effrt over 3f out: one pce fr 2f out* **5/2**[2]
004 **3** *19* **Great Tidings**[18] [1421] 3-9-4 **75**.. KDarley 6 53
(M Johnston) *trckd ldrs: drvn 4f out: sn one pce* **20/1**
1555 **4** *3/4* **Al Rayanah**[10] [1616] 3-8-0 **64**.............................. KirstyMilczarek[(7)] 7 34
(G Prodromou) *keen: hld up: drvn over 4f out: n.d* **22/1**
0300 **5** *42* **Sunbolt (IRE)**[11] [1599] 3-8-10 **67**.............................. PaulFessey 2 —
(T D Barron) *keen: cl up: lost pl after 3f: n.d after* **16/1**
3216 **6** *27* **Qualify**[24] [1251] 3-9-3 **74**.. TonyCulhane 8 —
(M R Channon) *sn drvn in rr: hdwy and prom after 3f: wknd fr 4f out* **5/1**[3]
5500 **7** *24* **Snowberry Hill (USA)**[20] [1345] 3-8-10 **67**..........................(b[1]) NCallan 4 —
(K A Ryan) *plld hrd: sn cl up: rdn and wknd over 3f out* **33/1**
2m 50.03s (13.03) **Going Correction** +1.075s/f (Soft) **7** Ran SP% **110.8**
Speed ratings (Par 99):99,90,77,77,49 31,15
CSF £3.62 CT £26.60 TOTE £2.10: £2.20, £1.60; EX 6.50 Trifecta £27.70 Pool £257.52 - 6.58 winning units..
Owner Sir Neil Westbrook **Bred** Sir Neil And Lady Westbrook **Trained** Great Habton, N Yorks

FOCUS
A one sided event with a very easy winner in the progressive Bollin Derek, who is open to further improvement.

1868 RIPON-RACES.CO.UK MAIDEN STKS (DIV II) 1m 1f
5:15 (5:16) (Class 5) 3-Y-O **£4,210** (£1,252; £625; £312) **Stalls** High

Form RPR
0224 **1** **Macorville (USA)**[4] [1781] 3-9-3 78.............................. ShaneKelly 12 81+
(G M Moore) *cl up: led 1/2-wayy: drew clr fr over 2f out: eased ins fnl f* **1/2**[1]
0 **2** *8* **Riverhill (IRE)**[275] [4528] 3-9-3 .... PaulMulrennan 11 62
(J Howard Johnson) *keen: led to 1/2-way: cl up tl rdn and one pce fr 2f out* **14/1**
0006 **3** *17* **Silver Bank**[8] [1661] 3-8-12 45.. DaleGibson 6 23
(M W Easterby) *cl up on outside tl edgd rt and outpcd fr 3f out* **33/1**
0 **4** *8* **Naval Hero (IRE)**[15] [1483] 3-9-3 .... TomEaves 10 12
(Mrs L Williamson) *chsd ldrs tl rdn and wknd fr 3f out* **25/1**
65 **5** *nk* **Decree Nisi**[235] [5548] 3-9-3 .... PaulFessey 4 11
(Mrs A Duffield) *bhd: drvn over 4f out: nvr on terms* **7/1**[2]
000 **6** *3/4* **Frank Cartwright (IRE)**[9] [1633] 3-9-3 40.......................... DavidAllan 13 10
(A Berry) *midfield: drvn over 4f out: sn btn* **100/1**
60 **7** *18* **Wild Fell Hall (IRE)**[214] [5987] 3-9-3 .... TedDurcan 9 —
(W R Swinburn) *hld up: pushed along over 3f out: wknd* **10/1**[3]
8 *nk* **Weet For Ever (USA)** 3-9-3 .... GrahamGibbons 2 —
(P A Blockley) *prom tl rdn and wknd fr 3f out* **10/1**[3]
00 **9** *9* **Millwood Lad (IRE)**[5] [1759] 3-8-12 ....(v[1]) JerryO'Dwyer[(5)] 8 —
(B S Rothwell) *missed break: bhd and sn rdn along: nvr on terms* **80/1**
0 **10** *43* **Wilmas Gal**[14] [1501] 3-8-12 ....(t) RoystonFfrench 1 —
(R Bastiman) *hld up: rdn 1/2-way: sn btn* **50/1**
2m 3.58s (9.73) **Going Correction** +1.075s/f (Soft) **10** Ran SP% **115.0**
Speed ratings (Par 99):99,91,76,69,69 68,52,52,44,6
CSF £8.49 TOTE £1.60: £1.10, £3.70, £3.30; EX 8.00 TRIFECTA Not won. Place 6 £10.07, Place 5 £5.66.
Owner Geoff & Sandra Turnbull **Bred** Brookdale Thoroughbreds Inc **Trained** Middleham Moor, N Yorks

FOCUS
Another uncompetitive event and another wide margin winner.
T/Jkpt: £4,207.00 to a £1 stake. Pool: £20,739.00. 3.50 winning tickets. T/Plt: £20.00 to a £1 stake. Pool: £67,296.20. 2,455.10 winning tickets. T/Qpdt: £10.70 to a £1 stake. Pool: £3,489.30. 239.60 winning tickets. RY

1860 BADEN-BADEN (L-H)
Sunday, May 21

OFFICIAL GOING: Good

1869a BADENER MEILE (GROUP 3) 1m
4:00 (4:10) 3-Y-O+ **£24,138** (£10,345; £4,138; £2,759)

RPR
1 **Idealist (GER)**[370] [1773] 4-9-1 .... ASuborics 4 109
(P Schiergen, Germany) *hld up, 5th str, pushed along and ran on fr over 1 1/2f out, stayed on on outside to lead 100 yards out* **7/10**[1]
2 *1/2* **Willingly (GER)**[239] [5483] 7-9-1 .... FilipMinarik 2 108
(M Trybuhl, Germany) *soon led, pushed along straight, ran on 1 1/2f out, stayed on til headed 100 yards out* **71/10**
3 *1/2* **Lazio (GER)**[203] [6193] 5-9-3 .... ADeVries 5 109
(A Trybuhl, Germany) *held up in last, in touch straight, soon pushed along, stayed on steadily* **43/10**[3]
4 *1/2* **Apeiron (GER)**[9] [1659] 5-9-3 ....(b) AStarke 1 108
(Mario Hofer, Germany) *disputing 3rd half-way, driven straight, ran on at one pace* **28/10**[2]
5 *5* **Austrian (GER)**[287] [4212] 5-9-1 .... AHelfenbein 3 96
(M Sowa, Germany) *prominent, 2nd half-way, pushed along straight, challenged 1 1/2f out, no extra inside final furlong* **142/10**
6 *7* **Sambaprinz (GER)**[71] 7-9-1 ....(b) JBojko 6 82
(H Horwart, Germany) *first to show, disputing 3rd half-way, 3rd and pushed along straight, weakened over 1f out* **88/10**
1m 42.33s **6** Ran SP% **133.1**
(Including 10 Euro Stake): WIN 17; PL 14, 22; SF 92.
Owner Gestut Schlenderhan **Bred** Gestut Schlenderhan **Trained** Germany

1712 CAPANNELLE (R-H)
Sunday, May 21

OFFICIAL GOING: Good

1870a PREMIO CARLO D'ALESSIO (GROUP 3) 1m 4f
2:50 (2:57) 4-Y-O+ **£47,197** (£21,768; £12,167; £6,084)

RPR
1 **Groom Tesse**[7] [1712] 5-8-9 ....(b) SLandi 4 110
(L Camici, Italy) *mid-division, 6th straight, headway 3f out, led just inside fianl 2f, soon in command, ran on well* **76/100**[1]
2 *2* **Cocodrail (IRE)**[98] [393] 5-8-9 .... FBranca 2 107
(F Brogi, Italy) *4th straight, headway with winner over 2f out, every chance just inside final 2f, soon one pace* **144/10**
3 *1* **Urgente**[259] 4-8-9 .... MDemuro 7 106
(L Brogi, Italy) *5th straight, stayed on one pace from well over 1f out* **84/10**

4 ¾ **Clasem Di San Jore (IRE)**[26] 5-8-9 .... DVargiu 6 104
(A & G Botti, Italy) *held up, 7th straight, headway on outside from well over 1f out, never nearer* **128/10**

5 3 **Senex (GER)**[217] 5937 6-9-2 .... EPedroza 5 107
(H Blume, Germany) *8th straight, never near to challenge* **39/10**[2]

6 1 ½ **Nonno Carlo (IRE)**[7] 1712 6-8-9 ....(p) GMarcelli 1 98
(M Grassi, Italy) *wore cheek pieces, led, clear 5f out, hung left & headed over 3f out, one pace* **36/1**

7 1 ½ **Lord Nash** 4-8-9 .... MTellini 3 95
(M Grassi, Italy) *raced in 2nd to straight, left in lead over 3f out, headed just inside final 2f, eased final f* **37/1**

8 4 **Rhodesian Winner (GER)**[218] 5905 7-8-9 .... EBotti 9 89
(Frau Marion Rotering, Germany) *raced in 3rd to straight, weakened over 2f out* **48/10**[3]

9 8 **Dovizioso (IRE)**[201] 4-9-2 .... ACarboni 10 84
(P Caravati, Italy) *always in rear* **94/10**

2m 28.9s 9 Ran SP% **133.8**
(including 1 euro stake): WIN 1.76; PL 1.25, 2.62, 2.89; DF 12.93.
Owner Scuderia L3c **Bred** Azienda Agricola Rosati Colarieti **Trained** Italy

1871a PREMIO TUDINI (GROUP 3) 6f
3:25 (3:34) 3-Y-0+ **£32,990** (£15,122; £8,426; £4,213)

RPR

1 **Kuaicoss (IRE)**[181] 6408 4-9-0 .... MTellini 8 101
(A Renzoni, Italy) *made most, driven out* **459/10**

2 1 **Krisman (IRE)**[196] 6277 7-9-3 .... SMulas 3 101
(M Ciciarelli, Italy) *always in touch, headway over 1f out, stayed on to take 2nd close home* **69/10**

3 nk **Great Uncle Ted (USA)**[28] 1175 3-8-8 .... DVargiu 12 100
(B Grizzetti, Italy) *always prominent, every chance 1f out, lost 2nd close home* **54/10**[3]

4 nk **Golden West (IRE)** 3-8-8 ....(b) PAragoni 10 99
(G Fratini, Italy) *slowly into stride, soon prominent on outside, every chance over 1f out, one pace final f* **29/2**

5 ¾ **Lift Cape (IRE)** 3-8-8 .... MEsposito 11 97
(V Caruso, Italy) *always close up, stayed on same pace final f* **30/1**

6 1 ½ **T E Lawrence (USA)**[364] 1935 6-9-3 .... MMonteriso 6 92
(A Renzoni, Italy) *close up til one pace approaching final f* **66/10**

7 shd **Polish Magic**[196] 6277 6-9-3 .... EPedroza 7 92
(A Wohler, Germany) *mid-division, never able to challenge* **15/1**

8 2 ½ **Crucial**[196] 6277 6-9-3 .... EBotti 13 85
(Frank Sheridan, Italy) *prominent on outside til weakened quickly well over 1f out* **53/10**[2]

9 ½ **Patapan (USA)**[308] 3577 4-9-3 ....(b) MPasquale 1 83
(R Brogi, Italy) *speed on rails 4f* **59/10**

10 1 **Dream Impact (USA)**[44] 5-9-3 .... GMarcelli 9 80
(L Riccardi, Italy) *never a factor* **11/2**

11 4 **San Dany (IRE)**[196] 6277 6-9-3 .... FBranca 4 68
(M Massimi Jr, Italy) *speed over 3f* **44/1**

12 1 **Slapper (ITY)**[392] 1233 4-9-3 .... SLandi 5 65
(R Brogi, Italy) *behind final 2f* **118/10**

13 1 ½ **Rychter (ITY)**[917] 6009 5-9-3 ....(b) MDemuro 2 61
(F & L Brogi, Italy) *prominent til weakened 2f out* **7/2**[1]

69.00 secs
WFA 3 from 4yo+ 9lb 13 Ran SP% **137.5**
WIN 46.87; PL 10.71, 3.03, 2.72; DF 247.67.
Owner Scuderia Parco Srl **Bred** Agricola Del Parco **Trained** Italy

1872a DERBY ITALIANO (GROUP 1) (C&F) 1m 4f
4:35 (4:48) 3-Y-0 **£330,505** (£170,913; £100,701; £50,350)

RPR

1 **Gentlewave (IRE)**[13] 1557 3-9-2 .... MMonteriso 9 116+
(A Fabre, France) *held up towards rear to straight, good headway on outside over 2f out, led well over 1f out, soon clear, comfortably* **71/100**[1]

2 4 **Storm Mountain (IRE)**[253] 5144 3-9-2 .... DVargiu 11 110
(B Grizzetti, Italy) *5th straight, every chance well over 1f out, one pace* **21/4**[3]

3 3 ½ **Rockmaster (IRE)** 3-9-2 .... MDemuro 7 104
(F Brogi, Italy) *in rear to straight, stayed on final 2f, never near first two* **26/1**

4 1 ½ **Monachesi (IRE)** 3-9-2 .... FBranca 5 102
(F & L Camici, Italy) *hooded in preliminaries, always prom, 4th straight, chal 3f out, slight lead 2 1/2f out to well over 1f out, one pace* **76/10**

5 nse **Miles Gloriosus (USA)**[210] 6052 3-9-2 .... CFiocchi 3 102
(R Menichetti, Italy) *headway 3f out, no extra from well over 1f out* **31/1**

6 1 ½ **Yarqus**[10] 1603 3-9-2 .... RyanMoore 12 100
(C E Brittain) *raced in 3rd to straight, disputing lead when hampered by 4th 2 1/2f out, weakened well over 1f out* **106/10**

7 nk **Carobene (IRE)**[210] 6052 3-9-2 .... MMimmocchi 4 99
(R Mimmocchi, Italy) *always mid-division, one pace final 2f* **139/1**

8 2 ½ **Adorabile Fong**[28] 1175 3-9-2 .... FSpanu 13 96
(M Guarnieri, Italy) *never a factor* **25/1**

9 ¾ **Pressing (IRE)**[56] 758 3-9-2 .... MTellini 6 94
(R Feligioni, Italy) *prominent 7f* **35/1**

10 1 ½ **Rattle And Hum (ITY)**[28] 1175 3-9-2 .... SLandi 10 92
(F & L Camici, Italy) *6th straight, weakened over 2f out* **9/2**[2]

11 2 **Rumsfeld (ITY)**[30] 1117 3-9-2 .... EBotti 8 89
(M Botti) *mid-division, effort 3f out, weakened 2f out* **11/1**

12 2 **Golden Stud (IRE)**[337] 2733 3-9-2 ....(b) PAragoni 14 86
(M Fratini, Italy) *always in rear* **131/1**

13 10 **Carlomagno (IRE)**[28] 1175 3-9-2 .... SMulas 2 71
(B Grizzetti, Italy) *led to over 2f out* **21/4**[3]

14 8 **Diarius (GER)**[218] 3-9-2 .... EPedroza 1 59
(H Blume, Germany) *tracked leader til weakening quickly over 3f out* **88/1**

2m 27.4s 14 Ran SP% **153.3**
(including one euro stakes): WIN 1.71; PL 1.25, 1.84, 3.52; DF 5.34 (Storm Mountain (2nd) and Carlomagno (13th) were coupled for betting purposes).
Owner Gary A Tanaka **Bred** Haras De La Perelle **Trained** Chantilly, France
■ Gentlewave became the first French winner of this race since Houmayoun in 1990.

FOCUS
Gentlewave, supplemented just three days earlier, ran out a most convincing winner of this year's Italian Derby.

NOTEBOOK
Gentlewave(IRE) took advantage of a new race condition allowing horses to be supplemented three days before the race. He won most convincingly, this result underlining what a strong hand Andre Fabre holds in the three-year-old colt middle-distance division this year.
Storm Mountain(IRE), whose stable-companion Carlomagno set a good pace, challenged at the same time as the winner but was soon left behind.
Yarqus suffered only minor interference in the home straight, and ran an honest race, but simply did not stay.
Rumsfeld(ITY) may be flattered by his close second to Hazeymm at Newbury and does not seem up to this class.

1810 LONGCHAMP (R-H)
Sunday, May 21

OFFICIAL GOING: Soft

1873a PRIX D'ISPAHAN (GROUP 1) 1m 1f 55y
2:20 (2:22) 4-Y-0+ **£98,517** (£39,414; £19,707; £9,845; £4,931)

RPR

1 **Laverock (IRE)**[28] 1180 4-9-2 .... DBonilla 5 121
(C Laffon-Parias, France) *held up, 9th straight, headway from 1 1/2f out, ridden over 1f out and went 2nd final f, led 50 yards out, ridden out* **16/1**

2 snk **Manduro (GER)**[21] 1331 4-9-2 .... OPeslier 9 121
(A Fabre, France) *hld up, 10th str, pushed along and hdwy on outside fr over 1 1/2f out, wnt 3rd 150 yds out, rdn and ran on to line, nrst at* **9/2**[3]

3 ½ **Krataios (FR)**[20] 1371 6-9-2 .... MBlancpain 2 120
(C Laffon-Parias, France) *prom, 3rd half-way, pushed along and 2nd staight, led 2f out, rdn and ran on 1 1/2f out, hdd 50 yards out, kept on* **7/1**

4 3 **Archange D'Or (IRE)**[42] 934 4-9-2 .... CSoumillon 3 114
(A Fabre, France) *in touch, disputing 4th straight, pushed along to chase leader 2f out, one pace final furlong* **7/2**[2]

5 2 **Corre Caminos (FR)**[21] 1331 4-9-2 .... TJarnet 8 111
(M Delzangles, France) *prom and raced freely early, disp 4th straight, went 2nd 2f out, soon pushed along and lost place 1f out, no extra* **13/8**[1]

6 ¾ **Vatori (FR)**[21] 1331 4-9-2 .... SPasquier 4 109
(P Demercastel, France) *held up, disputing 6th straight, pushed along on inside to chase leaders 2f out, one pace from over 1f out* **33/1**

7 ½ **Turtle Bowl (IRE)**[322] 3171 4-9-2 .... C-PLemaire 1 109
(F Rohaut, France) *held up in last, pushed along 1 1/2f out, never dangerous* **11/1**

8 snk **Helios Quercus (FR)**[20] 1371 4-9-2 .... IMendizabal 11 108
(C Diard, France) *mid-division, towards outside, disputing 6th straight, some headway 2f out to over 1f out, no extra* **22/1**

9 2 **Special Kaldoun (IRE)**[20] 1371 7-9-2 .... DBoeuf 7 105
(D Smaga, France) *mid-division, 8th straight, never a factor* **20/1**

10 3 **Kendor Dine (FR)**[20] 1371 4-9-2 .... TThulliez 10 99
(Y De Nicolay, France) *2nd after 3f, pushed along and 3rd straight, driven 1 1/2f out, weakened over 1f out* **16/1**

11 **Thistle Suite**[17] 8-9-2 .... TGillet 6 99?
(M Cheno, France) *led to 2f out, eased once headed* **100/1**

1m 52.2s 11 Ran SP% **124.1**
PARI-MUTUEL: WIN 27.60; PL 7.80, 3.10, 3.40; DF 103.90.
Owner Gainsborough Stud Management Ltd **Bred** Gainsborough Stud Management Ltd **Trained** Chantilly, France

FOCUS
This did not look to be a great renewal of the Prix d'Ispahan.

NOTEBOOK
Laverock(IRE), towards the tail of the field early on, came with a progressive run to lead a 100 yards out before pulling out all the stops to hold off the runner up. He is likely to be supplemented for the Prince of Wales's Stakes at Royal Ascot.
Manduro(GER), given a waiting ride, raced on the outside because of his high draw but picked up well from halfway up the straight and was cutting down the winner in the final stages. There are no plans for the moment and he may well have a little rest.
Krataios(FR) quickened to lead about a furlong and a half out and battled on really well against the rail when headed. He might have just run out of stamina at the end and will now revert to a mile.
Archange D'Or(IRE), always just behind the leaders, was caught for speed early in the straight and then stayed on at the one. He looks just short of this level.
Corre Caminos(FR) was below the form he showed to win the Prix Ganay over slightly further here on his previous start.

1874a MONTJEU COOLMORE PRIX SAINT-ALARY (GROUP 1) (FILLIES) 1m 2f
2:55 (2:55) 3-Y-0 **£98,517** (£39,414; £19,707; £9,845; £4,931)

RPR

1 **Germance (USA)**[41] 959 3-9-0 .... IMendizabal 8 110
(J-C Rouget, France) *hld up mid-div, disp 5th str, pushed along & hdwy 1 1/2f out, 2nd ovr 1f out, rdn to chal 100yds out, led near fin, drvn out* **11/8**[1]

2 ½ **Sanaya (IRE)**[20] 1370 3-9-0 ....(p) CSoumillon 6 109
(A De Royer-Dupre, France) *raced in close 2nd, pushed along to lead 2f out, ridden and 2 lengths clear 1 1/2f out, kept on til headed near finish* **3/1**[2]

3 snk **Alix Road (FR)**[41] 959 3-9-0 .... TThulliez 1 109
(Mme M Bollack-Badel, France) *held up, disputing 5th straight, ridden and finished well from over 1f out, nearest at finish* **12/1**

4 2 ½ **Chaibia (IRE)**[21] 1330 3-9-0 .... DBoeuf 7 105
(D Smaga, France) *held up, 7th straight, stayed on from 1 1/2f out to take 4th 50 yards out* **8/1**

5 ¾ **Fauvelia (FR)**[41] 959 3-9-0 .... SPasquier 5 103
(Y De Nicolay, France) *prominent, 3rd straight, pushed along to chase leader over 1 1/2f out, lost 2nd over 1f out, one pace* **12/1**

6 6 **Mayoress**[18] 3-9-0 .... OPeslier 3 92
(A Fabre, France) *prominent, 4th and pushed along straight, one pace 1 1/2f out* **4/1**[3]

7 8 **Top Wave (FR)**[169] 6491 3-9-0 .... TCastanheira 2 78
(Mme M Bollack-Badel, France) *held up in rear, last straight, never a factor* **33/1**

8 4 **Hollywood Starlet (FR)**[20] 3-9-0 .... MCherel 4 71
(Y De Nicolay, France) *led to 2f out, soon weakened, eased over 1f out* **66/1**

2m 5.10s 8 Ran SP% **118.0**
PARI-MUTUEL: WIN 1.80; PL 1.10, 1.10, 1.60; DF 2.70.
Owner Nelson Radwan **Bred** Edmund J Loder **Trained** Pau, France

FOCUS
This Group 1 should provide some clues for the French Oaks, the Prix de Diane.

NOTEBOOK
Germance(USA), drawn on the wide outside, ran very freely early on and interfered with the fourth when her jockey tried to cover her up 350 yards after the start. Still, she quickened well in the straight and her superior speed enabled her to take the lead 50 yards from the post. She looks high class and the Prix de Diane is her next target.
Sanaya(IRE), tucked in behind the pacemaker, was sent for the post early in the straight and was only caught well inside the final furlong. There are no immediate plans for her but she will probably be raced over a longer trip next time.
Alix Road(FR) lengthened her stride from one and a half out and stayed on at the one pace until the line. She is another who could be suited by a longer distance.
Chaibia(IRE) was badly hampered and nearly brought down by the winner 350 yards after the start, so she looks better than the bare form.

1875a PRIX VICOMTESSE VIGIER (GROUP 2) 1m 7f 110y
3:25 (3:24) 4-Y-0+ **£51,103** (£19,724; £9,414; £6,276; £3,138)

RPR
1 **Shamdala (IRE)**[21] [1332] 4-8-10 CSoumillon 3 116
(A De Royer-Dupre, France) *held up in 5th, headway 3f out, disputing lead straight, led 2f out, driven and kept on final furlong, just held on* **7/2**[2]
2 *nse* **Montare (IRE)**[21] [1331] 4-8-10 TGillet 5 116
(J E Pease, France) *reluctant ldr early, in tch in 4th half-way, last straight, driven and ran on 1 1/2f out, chal close home, just failed* **5/1**
3 *1 ½* **Reefscape**[21] [1332] 5-9-2 OPeslier 6 118
(A Fabre, France) *prominent, 2nd half-way, 3rd straight, driven 1 1/2f out, ran on steadily to line* **3/1**[1]
4 *½* **Ostankino (FR)**[21] [1332] 5-9-0 SPasquier 2 116
(E Lellouche, France) *3rd half-way, 4th straight, ridden and ran on on rail from 1 1/2f out, 2nd 1f out, stayed on* **11/1**
5 *nse* **Petite Speciale (USA)**[21] [1332] 7-8-8 C-PLemaire 4 109
(E Lecoiffier, France) *held up in last, ridden 1 1/2f out, stayed on steadily but never a danger* **4/1**[3]
6 *1 ½* **Alcazar (IRE)**[210] [6055] 11-9-2 MickyFenton 1 116
(H Morrison) *prominent, led after 3f, joined straight, headed 2f out and ridden, ran on til no extra final furlong* **7/2**[2]

3m 22.5s
WFA 4 from 5yo+ 1lb **6** Ran SP% **114.4**
PARI-MUTUEL: WIN 4.90; PL 2.60, 3.50; SF 27.70.
Owner H H Aga Khan **Bred** His Highness The Aga Khan's Studs S C **Trained** Chantilly, France

NOTEBOOK
Shamdala(IRE) was always going well within herself and, after buiding up a lead of several lengths in the straight, she only just held on. She may now be aimed at the Grand Prix de Saint-Cloud and the Yorkshire Oaks.
Montare(IRE), after racing keenly, became outpaced when things quickened up early in the straight but finished well and only just failed. The Yorkshire Oaks and Prix Vermeille have been mentioned as possible targets.
Reefscape got outpaced at the start of the straight before running on well in the final stages. He should be just about spot on for the Ascot Gold Cup next time out.
Ostankino(FR) was running on at the finish and the Ascot Gold Cup is also on the cards for him
Alcazar(IRE) tried to make all the running but never really tested the stamina of his opponents. He was passed by the winner before the straight and then gradually dropped away at the end of the race. This was his first run for nearly seven months and it will have done him the power of good. The Henry II Stakes is now a possibility and later in the year the Prix Kergolay.

[1769]BATH (L-H)
Monday, May 22

OFFICIAL GOING: Soft
Wind: Strong, ahead

1876 EUROPEAN BREEDERS FUND NOVICE STKS 5f 11y
2:00 (2:00) (Class 5) 2-Y-0 **£3,562** (£1,059; £529; £264) **Stalls Low**

Form RPR
105 1 **Il Palio (IRE)**[21] [1354] 2-9-2 AlanMunro 5 78+
(B R Millman) *mde all: pushed along ins fnl f and sn clr: unchal* **11/10**[1]
000 2 *5* **Emergency Services**[2] [1838] 2-8-7 JamesDoyle(5) 1 56
(Tom Dascombe) *disp 2nd but nvr gng pce to rch wnr: jst asserted for mod 2nd last strides* **12/1**
3 *shd* **Bush Breakfast** 2-8-12 JimCrowley 4 56
(P Winkworth) *nvr gng pce to rch wnr but jst hld narrow 2nd tl no ex and lost that position last strides* **4/1**[2]
4 *8* **Cleobury** 2-8-7 RobertHavlin 3 22
(M Meade) *chsd ldrs but nvr in contetion: no ch fnl 2f* **13/2**
5 *34* **Lucknam (IRE)** 2-8-7 FergusSweeney 2 —
(M Meade) *v.s.a and a t.o* **5/1**[3]

67.80 secs (5.30) **Going Correction** +0.80s/f (Soft) **5** Ran SP% **105.3**
Speed ratings (Par 93):89,81,80,68,13
CSF £13.07 TOTE £1.90: £1.10, £4.20; EX 10.30.
Owner Mrs L S Millman **Bred** Blue Bloodstock Limited **Trained** Kentisbeare, Devon
■ Stewards' Enquiry : James Doyle one-day ban: used whip with excessive force (Jun 4)

FOCUS
A very weak novice event in which the clear form pick, Il Palio, proved in a different league and won as expected. He is rated to his previous best. They all came stands' side in the straight.

NOTEBOOK
Il Palio(IRE) had been well held in two runs in better company since winning on his debut, but found this a pretty simple task. He had hung left at Newmarket two starts previously, but stayed straight this time and was not inconvenienced by coming stands' side. (op 5-6 tchd 5-4)
Emergency Services had been well beaten on all three of his previous starts, but was well supported on his debut and is clearly thought to have some ability. He was no match for the easy winner, but kept on for second and may stay six furlongs. (op 14-1 tchd 16-1)
Bush Breakfast, an 18,500gns first foal of a quite useful five-furlong juvenile winner, hails from a stable that does well with its two-year-olds, including at Bath. This was a respectable debut and he can be expected to improve. (op 7-2 tchd 11-4)
Cleobury, an 8,5000gns half-sister to a six-furlong juvenile winner, out of a five-furlong two-year-old winner, showed little. (op 9-1)
Lucknam(IRE), a 7,000gns half-sister to a dual sprinter, offered little. (op 6-1)

1877 PARTNERS EMPLOYMENT 10TH ANNIVERSARY CHALLENGE MEDIAN AUCTION MAIDEN STKS 5f 11y
2:30 (2:31) (Class 6) 3-4-Y-0 **£2,590** (£770; £385; £192) **Stalls Low**

Form RPR
02 1 **Cheney Hill**[18] [1430] 3-9-0 DaneO'Neill 1 73+
(H Candy) *cl 3rd tl qcknd to ld ins fnl 2f: sn in command: easily* **15/8**[1]
65 2 *2 ½* **Tender Process (IRE)**[10] [1646] 3-9-0 RichardMullen 3 63
(E S McMahon) *chsd ldrs tl rdn and one pce over 2f out: styd on again fr over 1f out to chse wnr ins last but nvr any ch* **2/1**[2]
0000 3 *2 ½* **Mostanad**[28] [1196] 4-9-8 47 AlanMunro 5 56
(J M Bradley) *rr but in tch: rdn 1/2-way: hdwy fnl f and styd on to take n.d 3rd last strides* **11/1**
44 4 *nk* **Dragon Flame (IRE)**[13] [1565] 3-9-0 SebSanders 4 52
(M Quinn) *led tl hdd ins fnl 2f: wknd fnl f* **4/1**[3]
04 5 *5* **The Cayterers**[217] [5950] 4-9-8 SteveDrowne 2 38
(J M Bradley) *s.i.s: sn rcvrd to chse ldrs: wknd ins fnl 2f* **10/1**
06 6 *hd* **Silvanella (IRE)**[13] [1565] 3-8-9 FergusSweeney 6 29
(M S Saunders) *chsd ldr to 2f out: sn wknd* **66/1**
0060 7 *nk* **Just Bonnie**[299] [3844] 4-9-8 32 RyanMoore 7 36
(J M Bradley) *s.i.s: chsd ldrs to 1/2-way* **40/1**

66.26 secs (3.76) **Going Correction** +0.80s/f (Soft)
WFA 3 from 4yo 8lb **7** Ran SP% **109.5**
Speed ratings (Par 101):101,97,93,92,84 84,83
CSF £5.35 TOTE £3.20: £1.70, £1.70; EX 7.60.
Owner C J Burley **Bred** Barton Stud Partnership **Trained** Kingston Warren, Oxon

FOCUS
The proximity of the 47-rated Mostanad in third suggests this was a weak maiden, but Cheney Hill won nicely and showed improved form. They all came stands' side in the straight.

1878 JOHN SMITH'S EXTRA SMOOTH H'CAP 5f 161y
3:00 (3:02) (Class 5) (0-70,70) 3-Y-0+ **£3,562** (£1,059; £529; £264) **Stalls Low**

Form RPR
3500 1 **Digital**[16] [1474] 9-9-12 **69** SamHitchcott 7 81
(M R Channon) *bhd: gd hdwy on outside fr 2f out to ld jst ins last: edgd lft u.p but sn clr: raedily* **12/1**
6000 2 *2 ½* **Brigadore**[9] [1662] 7-9-13 **70** SebSanders 9 74
(J G Given) *s.i.s: bhd: swtchd lft to outside and hdwy over 1f out: styd on to chse wnr ins last but no ch* **16/1**
0563 3 *2 ½* **Gracie's Gift (IRE)**[25] [1255] 4-9-3 **60** FergusSweeney 2 56
(A G Newcombe) *prom: rdn over 2f out: styd on fnl f but nvr gng pce to rch ldrs* **50/1**
5602 4 *nk* **Cesar Manrique (IRE)**[35] [1047] 4-9-10 **67** MichaelHills 5 62
(B W Hills) *chsd ldrs: rdn and ev ch over 1f out: no ex ins last* **11/2**[2]
3602 5 *1* **Linda Green**[5] [1774] 5-9-2 **62** EdwardCreighton(3) 12 54+
(M R Channon) *hld up in rr: gd hdwy on stands rail fr 2f out to ld 1f out: sn hdd and no ex* **11/4**[1]
5215 6 *1 ¼* **Seneschal**[6] [1760] 5-9-11 **68** RichardHughes 13 56+
(A B Haynes) *in tch: hdwy to trck ldrs 1/2-way: drvn and ev chnace over 1f out: wknd ins last* **8/1**
4000 7 *1 ¼* **Coranglais**[14] [1528] 6-9-1 **58** (p) RyanMoore 14 42
(J M Bradley) *chsd ldrs: rdn fr 1/2-way: chal over 1f out: wknd ins last* **25/1**
6005 8 *½* **Chatshow (USA)**[2] [1846] 5-9-8 **68** DNolan(3) 3 50
(D Carroll) *chsd ldrs: rdn over 2f out: wknd fnl f* **14/1**
0000 9 *nk* **Cree**[28] [1188] 4-9-7 **64** SteveDrowne 10 45
(W R Muir) *bhd: rdn and sme hdwy over 2f out: nvr gng pce to rch ldrs* **20/1**
4620 10 *½* **Doctor's Cave**[10] [1645] 4-8-13 **56** (b) LPKeniry 4 36
(K O Cunningham-Brown) *chsd ldrs: sn rdn: wknd ins fnl 2f* **66/1**
0001 11 *1 ¼* **Dunn Deal (IRE)**[9] [1689] 6-9-13 **70** ShaneKelly 15 46
(W M Brisbourne) *bhd: sme hdwy on stands rail whn hmpd ins fnl f: n.d after* **12/1**
5640 12 *¾* **Tadlil**[11] [1618] 4-9-1 **58** AlanMunro 8 31
(J M Bradley) *bhd: rdn and sme hdwy over 2f out: nvr rchd ldrs: wknd over 1f out* **12/1**
0003 13 *5* **Tribute (IRE)**[11] [1611] 5-9-6 **63** RobbieFitzpatrick 1 20
(P A Blockley) *w ldr tl slt advantage over 3f out: hdd 2f out: wknd qckly over 1f out* **66/1**
0304 14 *1 ½* **Savile's Delight (IRE)**[79] [588] 7-9-10 **67** (b) ChrisCatlin 6 19
(R Brotherton) *s.i.s: sn chsng ldrs: ev ch 2f out: wknd over 1f out* **20/1**
0004 15 *3* **Extremely Rare (IRE)**[14] [1545] 5-9-13 **70** FrancisNorton 16 13
(M S Saunders) *slt ld tl hdd over 3f out: styd pressing ldr tl slt ld again 2f out: hdd 1f out and wknd rapidly* **7/1**[3]

1m 15.12s (3.92) **Going Correction** +0.80s/f (Soft) **15** Ran SP% **119.6**
Speed ratings (Par 103):105,101,98,97,96 94,93,92,92,91 89,88,82,80,76
CSF £174.50 CT £9072.33 TOTE £14.40: £3.60, £5.10, £8.60; EX 206.80 TRIFECTA Not won..
Owner W G R Wightman **Bred** W G R Wightman **Trained** West Ilsley, Berks
■ Stewards' Enquiry : L P Keniry caution: careless riding

FOCUS
An ordinary handicap in which those to race more towards the centre and drawn low were at an advantage. The level of the form is not rock solid but the winner is rated back to the level of last year's early form.

1879 VIC & JAN JOHNSON 14TH ANNIVERSARY FILLIES' H'CAP 1m 5f 22y
3:30 (3:31) (Class 5) (0-70,60) 4-Y-0+ **£4,210** (£939; £939; £312) **Stalls High**

Form RPR
0550 1 **Cotton Easter**[7] [1723] 5-8-9 **51** (t) ChrisCatlin 3 57
(Mrs A J Bowlby) *bhd: drvn and hdwy fr 3f out: racd in centre crse and chal ins fnl f: led last stride: all out* **11/2**
0430 2 *shd* **Sovietta (IRE)**[5] [1772] 5-8-12 **54** (t) LPKeniry 6 60
(A G Newcombe) *prom: wnt 2nd 7f out: chal stands side gng wl 3f out:led over 2f out:narrowly hdd 1f out: styd upsides: no ex cl home* **7/2**[2]
6000 2 *dht* **Rafelite**[29] [1163] 4-9-2 **58** SebSanders 4 64
(Lady Herries) *led tl hdd over 2f out: racd in centre crse: drvn to take narrow ld again 1f out: kpt on: hdd last stride* **7/2**[2]
0223 4 *nk* **Lady Taverner**[23] [1308] 5-8-13 **60** NataliaGemelova(5) 5 66
(J E Long) *chsd ldrs: dropped rr 7f out: hdwy over 3f out: c to stands side and chal fr 2f out tl no ex last strides* **3/1**[1]
0000 5 *2 ½* **Just Beware**[111] [6681] 4-8-4 **46** oh6 (p) AdrianMcCarthy 2 48?
(Miss Z C Davison) *bhd: hdwy 6f out: hung lef to far side and ev ch fr 2f out tl wknd ins last* **33/1**
2000 6 *1 ¾* **Royal Audition**[18] [1436] 5-9-4 **60** SamHitchcott 1 60
(T T Clement) *behund: hdwy 5f out: pressed ldrs and styd towards far side over 2f out: wknd fnl f* **14/1**
0435 7 *¾* **Murrieta**[6] [1754] 4-8-3 **48** ow1 (v) NeilChalmers(3) 7 47
(Miss J R Gibney) *sn chsng ldr tl 7f out: lost pl 5f out: rallied u.p in centre crse and effrt over 2f out: wknd over 1f out* **9/2**[3]

3m 6.64s (15.14) **Going Correction** +0.60s/f (Yiel) **7** Ran SP% **112.6**
Speed ratings (Par 100):77,76,76,76,75 74,73
PL: Rafelite £1.70, Sovietta £1.20; EX: Rafelite £15.50, Sovietta £13.50; CSF: Rafelite £12.10; Sovietta £12.10 TOTE £6.60: £2.60.
Owner Mrs Amanda Bowlby **Bred** S R Hope And D Erwin **Trained** Kingston Lisle, Oxon
■ Stewards' Enquiry : L P Keniry two-day ban: used whip with excessive frequency (Jun 4-5)

FOCUS
A modest fillies' handicap run at a steady pace almost throughout and, with just over a neck separating the first four home, the form looks suspect. Very ordinary form, rated through Rafelite for now.

1880 FOREVER FRIENDS APPEAL CT SCANNER MEDIAN AUCTION MAIDEN STKS 1m 2f 46y
4:00 (4:01) (Class 6) 3-Y-0 **£2,590** (£770; £385; £192) **Stalls** Low

Form RPR
53 **1** **Salesin**[20] [1374] 3-9-3 ... NickyMackay 3 96+
(L M Cumani) *mde all: pushed clr over 1f out: unchal* **11/4**[1]
4242 **2** *7* **Katchit (IRE)**[19] [1403] 3-9-3 78 ... TQuinn 6 79
(M R Channon) *chsd wnr fr 6f out: rdn fr 3f out: no imp 2f out: sn no ch* **3/1**[2]
5 **3** *4* **Wulimaster (USA)**[258] [5027] 3-9-3 ... RyanMoore 8 72
(Sir Michael Stoute) *rr but in tch: rdn and hdwy 3f out: nvr gng pce to rch ldrs* **7/2**[3]
4 **4** *nk* **Equator**[19] [1401] 3-9-3 ... RichardHughes 7 72
(Mrs A J Perrett) *in tch: hdwy to dispute 2nd 3f out but nvr gng pce to rch wnr: wknd ins fnl 2f* **11/2**
050 **5** *2* **Roya**[276] [4542] 3-9-3 72 ... DaneO'Neill 4 68
(R Hannon) *bhd: rdn and hdwy to chse ldrs over 3f out: sn outpcd and no ch* **25/1**
44 **6** *9* **Star Of The Desert (IRE)**[30] [1135] 3-9-0 ... AdamKirby(3) 2 61+
(C G Cox) *chsd wnr to 6f out: outpcd 4f out: rallied 3f out: wknd 2f out: eased whn no ch fnl f* **7/1**
7 *57* **Spiritwind (IRE)** 3-9-3 ... AlanMunro 1 —
(W R Swinburn) *slowly away: a bhd: t.o fnl 5f* **25/1**

2m 15.73s (4.73) **Going Correction** +0.60s/f (Yiel) 7 Ran SP% **109.5**
Speed ratings (Par 97):105,99,96,95,94 87,41
CSF £10.24 TOTE £3.60: £2.20, £1.90; EX 11.30 Trifecta £36.80 Pool: £700.51 - 13.49 winning units..
Owner Scuderia Rencati Srl **Bred** Ban Partnership **Trained** Newmarket, Suffolk

FOCUS
This looked just an ordinary maiden beforehand, but nothing could go with Salesin, who was allowed an easy lead and recorded a time slightly faster than the following handicap won by Mae Cigan. There is more to come from him and the form is solid.
Star Of The Desert(IRE) Official explanation: trainer said gelding was unsuited by the soft ground

1881 YFM GROUP H'CAP 1m 2f 46y
4:30 (4:30) (Class 5) (0-75,74) 3-Y-0 **£3,562** (£1,059; £529; £264) **Stalls** Low

Form RPR
2430 **1** **Mae Cigan (FR)**[39] [1005] 3-8-4 60 oh1 ... FrancisNorton 4 69
(M Blanshard) *hld up in rr:hdwy 3f out:rdn 2f out:led jst ins fnl f: r.o strly* **25/1**
0001 **2** *1 ½* **Bauer (IRE)**[14] [1533] 3-8-9 65 ... NickyMackay 5 71+
(L M Cumani) *in tch: hdwy 3f out: styd on u.p to chse wnr ins last but a hld* **7/4**[1]
14 **3** *3* **Looker**[221] [5852] 3-9-2 72 ... SebSanders 1 73
(R M Beckett) *led: rdn 2f out: hdd jst ins last: wknd nr fin* **9/2**[3]
5010 **4** *nk* **Risk Runner (IRE)**[28] [1193] 3-9-4 74 ... (v) JDSmith 7 74
(A King) *in tch: hdwy 3f out: chsd ldr over 2f out: wknd fnl f* **6/1**
0361 **5** *17* **Capistrano**[12] [1599] 3-9-2 72 ... MichaelHills 6 41
(B W Hills) *chsd ldr 7f out tl over 2f out: sn wknd* **11/4**[2]
0326 **6** *10* **Historic Appeal (USA)**[33] [1077] 3-9-1 71 ... (v[1]) TQuinn 2 22
(M R Channon) *chsd ldr to 7f out: wknd ins fnl 3f* **12/1**

2m 16.16s (5.16) **Going Correction** +0.60s/f (Yiel) 6 Ran SP% **107.0**
Speed ratings (Par 99):103,101,99,99,85 77
CSF £63.16 TOTE £26.70: £5.00, £1.30; EX 115.10.
Owner A D Jones **Bred** J Jay **Trained** Upper Lambourn, Berks

FOCUS
The bottom weight Mae Cigan, who was a maiden after nine starts coming into this, won comfortably, showing improvement to the tune of 8lb. The form looks solid. They came up the middle of the track in the straight.
Capistrano Official explanation: jockey said colt lost its action

1882 BATH MARQUEES H'CAP 1m 5y
5:00 (5:02) (Class 5) (0-70,70) 4-Y-0+ **£3,562** (£1,059; £529; £264) **Stalls** Low

Form RPR
2111 **1** **Indian Edge**[5] [1773] 5-9-1 67 6ex ... FrancisFerris 2 79
(B Palling) *mde all: hrd drvn fnl 2f: hld on gamely thrght fnl f* **4/1**[2]
0332 **2** *½* **Merrymadcap (IRE)**[5] [1773] 4-9-4 70 ... FrancisNorton 9 81
(M Blanshard) *hld up in tch: hday on bit 2f out: trckd ldrs and n.m.r over 1f out: pressed wnr ins last: fnd no ex fnl 100yds* **7/2**[1]
0000 **3** *3* **Lockstock (IRE)**[5] [1773] 8-8-4 59 ... (p) AdamKirby(3) 10 64
(M S Saunders) *chsd ldr: rdn over 2f out: kpt on u.p fr over 1f out: outpcd fnl f* **9/1**
2-00 **4** *1* **Three Welshmen**[27] [1204] 5-8-1 56 oh7 ... EdwardCreighton(3) 4 59
(D Burchell) *bhd: hdwy 3f out: chsd ldrs over 1f out: styd on same pce* **25/1**
3240 **5** *nk* **Smoothly Does It**[24] [3021] 5-8-6 63 ... TravisBlock(5) 14 65
(Mrs A J Bowlby) *bhd: rdn and hdwy over 2f out: kpt on same pce fnl f* **7/1**
0000 **6** *nk* **Hallings Overture (USA)**[5] [1773] 7-8-7 59 ... FergusSweeney 6 61
(C A Horgan) *bhd: hdwy over 2f out: sn rdn: kpt on again ins last but nvr gng pce to rch ldrs* **50/1**
0002 **7** *shd* **Primeshade Promise**[24] [1276] 5-8-4 56 oh2 ... NickyMackay 3 58
(D Burchell) *chsd ldrs: rdn 3f out: wknd fnl f* **14/1**
0640 **8** *1* **Dvinsky (USA)**[9] [1665] 5-8-9 64 ... DNolan(3) 12 64
(D Carroll) *chsd ldrs: rdn and effrt 2f out: nvr gng pce to chal: wknd fnl f* **16/1**
5020 **9** *1 ¼* **Morgan Lewis (IRE)**[13] [1570] 5-8-13 65 ... (p) SteveDrowne 7 62
(J A Geake) *bhd: pushed along 1/2-way: sme prog fnl f* **12/1**
3003 **10** *½* **Will The Till**[5] [1773] 4-8-1 56 oh1 ... RichardThomas(3) 1 52
(J M Bradley) *bhd: sme hdwy 3f out: sn rdn: nvr in contention* **6/1**[3]
0000 **11** *hd* **Sound That Alarm**[17] [1465] 4-7-11 56 oh14 ... LiamJones(7) 8 52
(P D Evans) *bhd: sme hdwy over 2f out: nvr in contention* **66/1**
2060 **12** *2* **Trevian**[196] [6286] 5-7-11 56 oh3 ... PietroRomeo(7) 11 48
(J M Bradley) *racd wd into st: nvr in contention* **66/1**
0004 **13** *36* **Red Contact (USA)**[56] [763] 5-8-10 62 ... AlanMunro 13 —
(J R Best) *chsd ldrs: wknd 1/2-way: t.o* **10/1**

1m 46.26s (5.16) **Going Correction** +0.60s/f (Yiel) 13 Ran SP% **117.1**
Speed ratings (Par 103):98,97,94,93,93 92,92,91,90,90 89,87,51
CSF £17.58 CT £122.06 TOTE £4.30: £1.50, £2.00, £3.10; EX 9.70 Trifecta £92.10 Pool: £941.85 - 7.26 winning units. Place 6 £113.92, Place 5 £67.56.
Owner Nigel Thomas and Christopher Mason **Bred** Christopher J Mason **Trained** Tredodridge, Vale Of Glamorgan

FOCUS
A modest but competitive handicap in which Indian Edge improved again and gamely landed his fifth race of the year. The form of this is probably not as solid as that of his previous win here. They raced middle to stands' side in the straight.
Will The Till Official explanation: trainer said gelding was unsuited by tacky (soft) ground
Red Contact(USA) Official explanation: trainer said gelding was unsuited by the soft ground
T/Plt: £311.60 to a £1 stake. Pool: £69,537.15. 162.90 winning tickets. T/Qpdt: £122.70 to a £1 stake. Pool: £5,737.40. 34.60 winning tickets. ST

[1453] MUSSELBURGH (R-H)
Monday, May 22

OFFICIAL GOING: Straight course - good to soft; round course - good (good to soft in places)
Wind: Virtually nil

1883 GULLANE APPRENTICE H'CAP 2m
6:30 (6:30) (Class 6) (0-65,65) 4-Y-0+ **£3,238** (£963; £481; £240) **Stalls** Low

Form RPR
0050 **1** **High Frequency (IRE)**[6] [1766] 5-7-11 44 oh1 ... (p) DeanHeslop(7) 8 45
(T D Barron) *trckd ldrs: hdwy and cl up 1/2-way: rdn to ld 1/2f out: clr ins last* **9/2**[3]
1200 **2** *2 ½* **Compton Eclaire (IRE)**[40] [975] 6-8-9 52 ... (v) MarkLawson(3) 5 50
(B Ellison) *hld up towards rr: hdwy to trck ldrs over 6f out: rdn over 2f out: styd on ins last* **13/2**
060- **3** *nk* **Copplestone (IRE)**[449] [3099] 10-8-0 47 oh12 ow3(p) PatrickDonaghy(7) 6 45
(A C Whillans) *led: pushed clr over 3f out: rdn over 2f out: hdd 11/2f out and kpt on same pce* **20/1**
6042 **4** *¾* **Teutonic (IRE)**[6] [1767] 5-8-1 44 oh2 ... AndrewMullen(3) 3 41
(R F Fisher) *s.i.s: sn in tch: pushed along and hdwy over 3f out: sn rdn: swtchd lft over 1f out: kpt on same pce ins last* **11/2**
0000 **5** *½* **Rule For Ever**[9] [1685] 4-9-6 65 ... GregFairley(3) 9 62
(M Johnston) *trckd ldrs: pushed along over 4f out: rdn 3f out: plugged on same pce* **4/1**[2]
4U04 **6** *1 ¾* **Templet (USA)**[11] [1608] 6-8-7 50 ... (b) DuranFentiman(3) 11 44
(W G Harrison) *trckd ldrs: effrt 3f out: sn rdn along and no imp* **16/1**
0353 **7** *hd* **Zeloso**[6] [1758] 8-8-4 44 oh2 ... (v) BenSwarbrick 7 38
(M F Harris) *hld up in tch: effrt over 3f out: swtchd lft and rdn 2f out: sn btn* **7/2**[1]
0000 **8** *2* **Baileys Honour**[42] [940] 4-8-5 48 oh1 ow2 ... DanielTudhope 4 39
(A G Newcombe) *hld up in rr: hdwy on outer 4f out: rdn along 2f out: sn no imp* **10/1**
0000 **9** *24* **Dejeeje (IRE)**[6] [1767] 5-8-4 44 oh22 ... SilvestreDeSousa 10 7
(D W Chapman) *in tch: rdn along 4f out: sn wknd* **66/1**
0400 **10** *27* **Howards Dream (IRE)**[136] [6236] 8-7-13 44 oh24(t) LeanneKershaw(5) 12 —
(D A Nolan) *a rr* **100/1**

3m 40.22s (6.32) **Going Correction** +0.275s/f (Good)
WFA 4 from 5yo+ 2lb 10 Ran SP% **111.3**
Speed ratings (Par 101):95,93,93,93,92 92,92,91,79,65
CSF £31.70 CT £509.52 TOTE £5.90: £1.90, £2.80, £6.10; EX 89.20.
Owner S Knighton & A Kundi **Bred** Laurent Cottrell **Trained** Maunby, N Yorks
■ Dean Heslop's first winner.

FOCUS
No pace on at all in this low-grade event and it rather turned into a sprint down the home straight. As a result the winning time was moderate and the form looks highly dubious.

1884 BROOKE CHARITY MAIDEN AUCTION STKS 5f
7:00 (7:00) (Class 5) 2-Y-0 **£3,238** (£963; £481; £240) **Stalls** Low

Form RPR
1 **Fathom Five (IRE)** 2-8-10 ... PaulEddery 9 63+
(B Smart) *sn rdn along and outpcd towards rr: swtchd rt and hdwy 2f out: sn rdn and styd on wl to ld last 100 yds* **8/1**
0 **2** *nk* **Nota Liberata**[12] [1595] 2-8-9 ... DanielTudhope(3) 2 64
(G M Moore) *led 1f: cl up: rdn 2f out: led again appr last: sn drvn and hdd last 100 yds* **20/1**
332 **3** *¾* **Picture Frame**[15] [1499] 2-8-12 ... TonyCulhane 3 61
(N Tinkler) *chsd ldrs: rdn along 1/2-way: styd on u.p ent last* **4/1**[2]
4 *nk* **Sweet Candy** 2-8-11 ... RobertWinston 4 59
(K A Ryan) *dwlt: hdwy and led after 1f: rdn wl over 1f out: sn hdd and no ex ins last* **2/1**[1]
0 **5** *3* **Hawaii Prince**[16] [1491] 2-8-11 ... SilvestreDeSousa(3) 1 51
(D Nicholls) *dwlt: sn rdn along in rr: hdwy 2f out: no imp appr last* **16/1**
054 **6** *hd* **Mystery World**[9] [1688] 2-9-0 ... RoystonFfrench 6 51
(M Johnston) *chsd ldrs: rdn along 2f out: drvn and wknd appr last* **7/1**
5 **7** *nk* **Loch Clutha (IRE)**[23] [1295] 2-8-7 ... PatCosgrave 7 43
(K R Burke) *chsd ldrs: rdn along 1/2-way: sn wknd* **14/1**
5 **8** *5* **Aggbag**[10] [1639] 2-8-11 ow4 ... DerekNolan(5) 5 34
(M J Wallace) *chsd ldrs: rdn along 1/2-way: sn wknd* **6/1**[3]
0 **9** *10* **Perilore (IRE)**[15] [1499] 2-8-6 ow1 ... JohnEgan 8 —
(A Berry) *s.i.s: a bhd* **66/1**

62.18 secs (1.68) **Going Correction** +0.15s/f (Good) 9 Ran SP% **110.0**
Speed ratings (Par 93):92,91,90,89,85 84,84,76,60
CSF £139.96 TOTE £9.90: £3.40, £4.80, £1.10; EX 131.80.
Owner Hintlesham Racing **Bred** Eamonn Connolly **Trained** Hambleton, N Yorks

FOCUS
A modest maiden and with a little over a length covering the first four the form looks ordinary. The winner is capable of better , however.

NOTEBOOK
Fathom Five(IRE) ♦, a half-brother to a multiple sprint winner in Italy, ran a remarkable race. After giving away a significant amount of ground at the start, he eventually managed to get himself back into the race and put in a strong finish down the centre of the track to snatch the spoils. The form looks ordinary, but he was one of only two newcomers in the field and given his problems at the start he can be rated a bit better than the winning margin. (op 9-1)
Nota Liberata was always up with the pace and kept on all the way to the line. He seemed to appreciate dropping back a furlong from his debut. (op 25-1)
Picture Frame stayed on to fill the frame for the fourth time in as many starts. He shapes as though an extra furlong would suit, but is obviously of limited ability. (op 10-3)
Sweet Candy, the other newcomer in the field and an 18,000gns half-sister to Desert Royal and Imperial Sword, was backed to make a winning debut and ran well enough in defeat. She should come on for the experience. (op 5-2 tchd 15-8)

Hawaii Prince, well beaten on very fast ground on his debut, ran a bit better on this easier surface. His dam comes from a very successful family and he looks more of a long-term prospect. (op 20-1)
Mystery World is still not getting home and is beginning to look exposed. (op 13-2 tchd 6-1)

1885 BRIDGEWELL SECURITIES H'CAP — 7f 30y
7:30 (7:31) (Class 5) (0-70,70) 4-Y-0+ — **£3,886** (£1,156; £577; £288) **Stalls** Low

Form — RPR

4510 **1** **Dispol Isle (IRE)**[14] 1531 4-8-10 **65** BenSwarbrick(3) 6 — 73
(T D Barron) *cl up: rdn over 2f out: drvn and edgd lft ent last: styd on to ld nr fin* **14/1**

1201 **2** *nk* **Onlytime Will Tell**[7] 1735 8-9-2 **68** 6ex RobertWinston 5 — 75
(D Nicholls) *hld up: hdwy on outer over 2f out: rdn over 1f out and ev ch ins last tl no ex nr fin* **9/2**[1]

5520 **3** *hd* **Joshua's Gold (IRE)**[9] 1683 5-8-5 **60** (v) DanielTudhope(3) 7 — 67
(D Carroll) *led: rdn 2f out: drvn ins last: hdd and no ex nr fin* **8/1**[3]

0041 **4** *½* **Ulysees (IRE)**[10] 1637 7-9-3 **69** TomEaves 10 — 74
(I Semple) *trckd ldrs: hdwy 3f out: rdn 2f out: swtchd rt and drvn ins last: kpt wl towards fin* **10/1**

2530 **5** *shd* **Insubordinate**[6] 1760 5-8-0 **57** DuranFentiman(5) 9 — 62
(J S Goldie) *hld up towards rr: hdwy on inner over 2f out: rdn wl over 1f out: swtchd lft and drvn ins last: styd on wl towards fin* **11/2**[2]

0151 **6** *7* **Attacca**[17] 1459 5-8-5 **57** oh1 ow1 JohnEgan 1 — 44
(J R Weymes) *chsd ldrs: hdwy 3f out: rdn 2f out: drvn and wknd appr last* **11/2**[2]

1504 **7** *2* **Arnie De Burgh**[28] 1188 4-9-1 **67** RoystonFfrench 3 — 49
(D J Daly) *plld hrad: chsd ldng pair: rdn along over 2f out: grad wknd* **10/1**

4000 **8** *nk* **Peters Delite**[276] 4557 4-8-13 **65** TonyHamilton 8 — 46
(R A Fahey) *chsd ldrs: rdn along 3f out: drvn and wknd 2f out* **16/1**

5000 **9** *6* **Diktatit**[268] 3850 4-7-13 **56** oh11 AndrewElliott(5) 2 — 21
(R C Guest) *v.s.a and bhd: hdwy on outer 1/2-way: rdn and in tch over 2f out: sn wknd* **100/1**

0050 **10** *54* **Kirkby's Treasure**[13] 1561 8-9-4 **70** FergalLynch 4 — —
(A Berry) *hld up: rdn along in rr wl over 2f out: nvr a factor* **9/2**[1]

1m 30.7s (0.76) **Going Correction** +0.275s/f (Good) **10** Ran SP% **110.0**
Speed ratings (Par 103):106,105,105,104,104 96,94,94,87,25
CSF £70.61 CT £510.00 TOTE £14.80: £3.40, £2.30, £3.70; EX 59.00.
Owner W B Imison **Bred** Mrs I A Balding **Trained** Maunby, N Yorks

FOCUS
A fair little handicap and though there was little covering the front five at the line, they did pull a long way clear of the rest. Ordinary but sound form.
Diktatit Official explanation: jockey said filly missed break when stalls blindfold got stuck on bridle
Kirkby's Treasure Official explanation: trainer had no explanation for the poor form shown

1886 LONGNIDDRY (S) STKS — 5f
8:00 (8:00) (Class 6) 3-Y-0+ — **£2,730** (£806; £403) **Stalls** Low

Form — RPR

6104 **1** **Further Outlook (USA)**[7] 1735 12-9-1 74 DanielTudhope(3) 1 — 73
(D Carroll) *mde all: rdn clr and hung bdly rt ent last: styd on strly* **5/2**[1]

0306 **2** *2½* **Jun Fan (USA)**[9] 1689 4-9-4 56 PatCosgrave 10 — 64
(B Ellison) *prom: effrt and ev ch 2f out: sn rdn and kpt on same pce appr last* **6/1**

0000 **3** *shd* **Atlantic Viking (IRE)**[43] 11-9-4 RobertWinston 7 — 64
(D Nicholls) *in tch tl pushed along and outpcd after 1f: rdn 1/2-way: styd on appr last: nrst fin* **3/1**[2]

1000 **4** *3* **Rudi's Pet (IRE)**[258] 5026 12-8-11 76 VictoriaBehan(7) 6 — 53
(D Nicholls) *chsd ldrs: rdn 2f out: sn one pce* **8/1**

5003 **5** *3* **Chiselled (IRE)**[24] 1272 4-8-13 58 AndrewElliott(5) 3 — 42
(K R Burke) *cl up: rdn along 2f out: sn wknd* **5/1**[3]

0000 **6** *hd* **Rosie's Result**[20] 1396 6-8-13 43 GregFairley(5) 5 — 41
(M Todhunter) *chsd ldrs: rdn along and outpcd fr 1/2-way* **16/1**

U000 **7** *2½* **Northern Svengali (IRE)**[238] 5508 10-9-4 41 (t) DerekMcGaffin 4 — 32
(D A Nolan) *s.i.s: a rr* **100/1**

0000 **8** *6* **Mister Marmaduke**[15] 1504 5-9-4 50 (p) JohnEgan 2 — 11
(D A Nolan) *chsd ldrs: rdn along 2f out: sn wknd* **33/1**

1000 **9** *nk* **Shatin Leader**[238] 5507 4-8-13 46 RoystonFfrench 9 — 5
(Miss L A Perratt) *a towards rr* **25/1**

61.02 secs (0.52) **Going Correction** +0.15s/f (Good) **9** Ran SP% **109.3**
Speed ratings (Par 101):101,97,96,92,87 86,82,73,72
CSF £16.11 TOTE £2.80: £1.20, £2.20, £1.10; EX 17.50.The winner was bought in for 7,200gns.
Owner Diamond Racing Ltd **Bred** Gainsborough Farm Inc **Trained** Warthill, N Yorks

FOCUS
A moderate seller and a whole range of abilities with 46lb covering the field. The level hinges on whether or not the runner-up improved.

1887 TALK 107 H'CAP — 1m 4f
8:30 (8:30) (Class 5) (0-75,75) 4-Y-0+ — **£5,181** (£1,541; £770; £384) **Stalls** High

Form — RPR

4135 **1** **Crathorne (IRE)**[26] 4030 6-8-7 **61** RobertWinston 4 — 71
(M Todhunter) *hld up in rr: hdwy over 3f out: rdn to chse ldr over 1f out: drvn and styd on ins last to ld last 100 yds* **4/1**[2]

2062 **2** *1* **King's Crest**[9] 1666 8-8-3 **57** PaulFessey 6 — 65
(J J Quinn) *in tch: hdwy over 3f out: rdn to ld over 2f out: drvn ent last: hdd and no ex last 100 yds* **4/1**[2]

0361 **3** *1¾* **Oldenway**[13] 1560 7-9-4 **72** TonyHamilton 1 — 77
(R A Fahey) *led: rdn along and hdd over 3f out: drvn over 2f out and kpt on same pce appr last* **5/1**[3]

4003 **4** *5* **Easibet Dot Net**[11] 1610 6-9-2 **70** (p) TomEaves 2 — 67
(I Semple) *chsd ldrs: effrt on outer 3f out: sn rdn and outpcd fnl 2f* **8/1**

6030 **5** *3½* **Incursion**[15] 1502 5-9-0 **75** VictoriaBehan(7) 5 — 67
(D Nicholls) *hld up: hdwy over 3f out: rdn to chse ldrs over 2f out: sn wknd* **8/1**

1101 **6** *1½* **Balwearie (IRE)**[21] 1346 5-8-6 **60** (p) RoystonFfrench 7 — 49
(Miss L A Perratt) *cl up: effrt to ld over 3f out: rdn and hdd over 2f out: sn drvna nd grad wknd* **10/3**[1]

0004 **7** *13* **Fardi (IRE)**[26] 1233 4-8-0 **59** DuranFentiman(5) 3 — 27
(K W Hogg) *a towards rr* **33/1**

0300 **8** *¾* **Red Chairman**[320] 3230 4-9-0 **68** (t) PaulEddery 8 — 35
(R Johnson) *plld hrd: chsd ldrs tl wknd over 3f out* **50/1**

2m 39.95s (3.05) **Going Correction** +0.275s/f (Good) **8** Ran SP% **106.9**
Speed ratings (Par 103):100,99,98,94,92 91,82,82
CSF £17.59 CT £66.27 TOTE £6.00: £1.90, £1.60, £2.00; EX 31.00.
Owner The Centaur Group Partnership IX **Bred** Shirley Blue Syndicate **Trained** Orton, Cumbria

FOCUS
A fair handicap run at a fair pace and the first three came well clear of the rest. Pretty sound form.

1888 ESK MILLS H'CAP — 1m
9:00 (9:00) (Class 6) (0-60,60) 3-Y-0 — **£3,071** (£906; £453) **Stalls** Low

Form — RPR

0600 **1** **Jordan's Light (USA)**[263] 4887 3-9-3 **59** JohnEgan 1 — 67
(T J Pitt) *keen: cl up: rdn and edgd rt 2f out: sn drvn: led 1f out and kpt on gamely* **7/2**[1]

1000 **2** *hd* **Feelin Irie (IRE)**[30] 1141 3-9-4 **60** KimTinkler 9 — 67
(N Tinkler) *keen: led: rdn along over 2f out: edgd lft and drvn over 1f out: hdd 1f out: hung lft and kpt on gamely towards fin* **16/1**

0336 **3** *1¾* **Linton Dancer (IRE)**[14] 1533 3-8-11 **53** RobertWinston 10 — 56
(J R Weymes) *hld up towards rr: hdwy 3f out: rdn to chse ldrs wl over 1f out: sn drvn: edgd rta nd kpt on same pce ins last* **4/1**[2]

0450 **4** *nk* **Ayam Jantan**[11] 1616 3-9-2 **58** RoystonFfrench 7 — 60
(M Johnston) *trckd ldng pair: rdn along over 2f out: swtchd lft and drvn over 1f out: kpt on same pce ins last* **16/1**

5356 **5** *hd* **Touch Of Ivory (IRE)**[12] 1593 3-8-11 **53** TonyHamilton 8 — 55+
(R A Fahey) *hld up towards rr: hdwy 3f out: rdn to chse ldrs 2f out: drvn and kpt on fnl f* **7/1**[3]

000 **6** *5* **Eurana**[40] 978 3-8-5 **50** DanielTudhope(3) 12 — 40
(Jedd O'Keeffe) *bhd: hdwy on outer over 2f out: sn rdn and no imp appr last* **33/1**

0040 **7** *1¾* **Sparkbridge (IRE)**[12] 1593 3-8-11 **58** AndrewMullen(5) 6 — 44
(R F Fisher) *in tch: hdwy to chse ldrs over 3f out: sn rdn and wknd* **12/1**

0135 **8** *1¼* **Mid Valley**[27] 1215 3-8-12 **54** TonyCulhane 2 — 37
(J R Jenkins) *trckd ldrs: hdwy over 3f out: sn rdn and wknd fnl 2f* **7/1**[3]

600 **9** *1* **Collette's Choice**[254] 5125 3-8-10 **52** PatCosgrave 4 — 33
(R A Fahey) *a rr* **33/1**

0000 **10** *5* **Lambency (IRE)**[12] 1593 3-8-11 **53** PaulFessey 13 — 23
(J G Given) *dwlt and towards rr: sme hdwy 1/2-way: sn rdn along and wknd wl over 2f out* **10/1**

0432 **11** *1½* **Chicherova (IRE)**[63] 676 3-8-4 **49** BenSwarbrick(3) 5 — 15
(T D Barron) *hld up: a rr* **7/1**[3]

1m 43.49s (0.99) **Going Correction** +0.275s/f (Good) **11** Ran SP% **114.2**
Speed ratings (Par 97):106,105,104,103,103 98,96,95,94,89 88
CSF £58.94 CT £233.33 TOTE £2.70: £1.20, £3.60, £2.00; EX 48.20 Place 6 £120.77, Place 5 £40.75.
Owner B A Jordan **Bred** Lantern Hill Farm Llc **Trained** Bawtry, S Yorks
■ Stewards' Enquiry : Kim Tinkler one-day ban: careless riding (Jun 4)
John Egan caution: careless riding

FOCUS
A modest handicap, but a gamble landed if only just. The front five pulled a long way clear of the rest and the race has been rated a bit more positively than it might have been, with the winner showing improved form.
Jordan's Light(USA) Official explanation: trainer said, regarding the improved form shown, gelding was having its first run for the yard
Sparkbridge(IRE) Official explanation: jockey said gelding hung right-handed throughout
T/Plt: £125.10 to a £1 stake. Pool: £63,734.15. 371.80 winning tickets. T/Qpdt: £12.60 to a £1 stake. Pool: £4,651.80. 272.30 winning tickets. JR

1730 REDCAR (L-H)
Monday, May 22

1889 Meeting Abandoned - Waterlogged

1737 WINDSOR (R-H)
Monday, May 22

OFFICIAL GOING: Good to soft (soft in places)
Wind: Blustery, behind Weather: Frequent heavy showers

1896 BEDLAM ASSET MANAGEMENT EBF MAIDEN FILLIES' STKS — 5f 10y
6:10 (6:11) (Class 5) 2-Y-0 — **£4,533** (£1,348; £674; £336) **Stalls** High

Form — RPR

1 **Miss Otis** 2-9-0 JimCrowley 1 — 76
(P Winkworth) *sn trckd ldrs on outer: effrt gng wl 2f out: rdn to ld last 75yds: jst hld on* **20/1**

5 **2** *shd* **Top Royelle**[33] 1082 2-9-0 RichardHughes 7 — 76
(R Hannon) *prom: rdn to chse ldr wl over 1f out: led jst ins fnl f: hdd last 75yds: kpt on wl: jst failed* **3/1**[2]

3 *½* **Relkida** 2-9-0 ChrisCatlin 4 — 74+
(M R Channon) *s.i.s: sn pushed along in rr: prog 1/2-way: styd on fr over 1f out: gaining at fin* **14/1**

4 *¾* **Lorena Wood (USA)** 2-9-0 LDettori 11 — 71
(B J Meehan) *led against nr side rail: hanging lft fr 2f out: hdd jst ins fnl f: no ex* **11/4**[1]

5 *¾* **Samahir (USA)** 2-9-0 PhilipRobinson 5 — 68+
(M A Jarvis) *sn chsd ldrs: rdn and cl up 1f out: fdd ins fnl f* **9/2**[3]

6 *3½* **Babylon Sister (IRE)** 2-9-0 RyanMoore 12 — 56
(R Hannon) *dwlt: off the pce in last pair: kpt on fr over 1f out: n.d* **15/2**

7 *2½* **Bluebelle Dancer (IRE)** 2-9-0 MartinDwyer 10 — 47
(W R Muir) *chsd ldr to wl over 1f out: sn wknd* **16/1**

0 **8** *hd* **Pat Will (IRE)**[12] 1587 2-8-9 StephenDonohoe(5) 3 — 46
(P D Evans) *in tch: effrt on outer 1/2-way: wknd over 1f out* **20/1**

9 *1* **Maid Of Ale (IRE)** 2-9-0 JimmyFortune 8 — 43
(B J Meehan) *chsd ldrs: shkn up and no imp wl over 1f out: wknd fnl f* **11/1**

10 *2* **Doubly Guest** 2-9-0 JamieMackay 9 — 35
(G G Margarson) *dwlt: outpcd and a in last pair: no prog fnl 2f* **33/1**

61.93 secs (0.83) **Going Correction** +0.025s/f (Good) **10** Ran SP% **115.0**
Speed ratings (Par 90):94,93,93,91,90 85,81,80,79,75
CSF £76.77 TOTE £23.20: £4.00, £1.50, £2.80; EX 100.00.
Owner Kennet Valley Thoroughbreds VII **Bred** D R Botterill **Trained** Chiddingfold, Surrey

FOCUS
An interesting juvenile fillies' maiden, run at a decent pace, and the first three came nicely clear late on. The form looks fair rated through the runner-up.

NOTEBOOK
Miss Otis, a 20,000gns half-sister to juvenile debutant winner Hoh Hoh Hoh, emulated that individual and got her career off to a perfect start. She was always travelling sweetly before knuckling down when asked to win her race and the soft ground clearly proved to her liking. She has scope and really should have a fair bit more to offer this term over this trip.

Top Royelle was given a positive ride, and had every chance against the stands' rail, but was always just being held by the winner inside the closing stages. This must rate an improvement on her debut effort at Newmarket, she seemed to act without fuss on the totally different surface, and clearly has a maiden within her compass. (op 9-4)

Relkida ◆, whose dam is a half-sister to several winners, most notably the smart miler Brunel, ran green throughout the first half of the race, yet was noted finishing her race in taking style and this must rate a promising debut effort. The soft ground was to her liking and, granted the normal improvement, she looks nailed on to shed her maiden tag in a similar event in the coming weeks. (tchd 16-1)

Lorena Wood(USA), a $90,000 purchase bred to make her mark at two and whose pedigree suggests a mix of speed and stamina, showed decent early dash before finding just the same pace when put under pressure nearing two out. She may well need better ground and can leave this form behind with further experience under her belt. (op 7-2)

Samahir(USA), closely related to numerous winners from seven furlongs to a mile, proved easy to back ahead of this debut and shaped as though the race would be of real benefit. A sixth furlong will no doubt be much to her liking in due course. (op 4-1)

Babylon Sister(IRE), from a decent sprinting family, was well backed on course ahead of this debut but her fate was sealed after she fell out of the stalls and lost vital ground. She was never a serious factor thereafter, but should learn from this experience, and can be expected to be a lot sharper next time. (op 10-1)

1897 WEATHERBYS BANK CONDITIONS STKS — 5f 10y

6:40 (6:42) (Class 2) 2-Y-O — **£12,464** (£3,732; £1,866; £934; £466) **Stalls High**

Form				RPR
21	**1**		**Hoh Mike (IRE)**^{7} [1737] 2-9-0 .... JamieSpencer 1 (M L W Bell) *s.i.s: cl up: trckd ldr 2f out: nudged into ld ins fnl f: nt really extended* **1/4**^{1}	96+
124	**2**	1 ¼	**Lord Charles**^{12} [1582] 2-8-11 .... AmirQuinn 2 (W G M Turner) *led after 1f: rdn over 1f out: hdd ins fnl f: styd on but no ch w wnr* **11/1**^{3}	84
1	**3**	5	**Bazroy (IRE)**^{59} [707] 2-8-11 .... ShaneKelly 5 (P D Evans) *led for 1f: pressed ldr to 2f out: fdd u.p over 1f out* **7/1**^{2}	66
325	**4**	5	**Pernomente (IRE)**^{41} [961] 2-8-11 .... MartinDwyer 4 (J S Moore) *t.k.h early: chsd ldrs: shkn up over 2f out: wknd over 1f out* **25/1**	48
1	**5**	7	**Best Woman**^{9} [1682] 2-8-6 .... EddieAhern 6 (P Howling) *uns rdr and bolted bef s: mostly last: rdn and wknd 2f out* **25/1**	17

61.39 secs (0.29) **Going Correction** +0.025s/f (Good) — 5 Ran SP% **108.5**

Speed ratings (Par 99):98,96,88,80,68

CSF £3.74 TOTE £1.20: £1.10, £2.40; EX 2.90.

Owner David Allport & Michael Lynch **Bred** John Malone **Trained** Newmarket, Suffolk

FOCUS

This was weakened by the withdrawal of Sonny Red, but it was hard not to be very impressed with the easy winner, who ought to rate higher. The runner-up ran to his sound Newmarket form.

NOTEBOOK

Hoh Mike(IRE), off the mark at the second attempt with a facile success on much faster ground over course and distance a week previously, confirmed that promise with a classy display and proved his versatility as regards underfoot conditions. He looked to be toying with the runner-up inside the final furlong, being value for at least double his winning margin, and looks assured to improve again for this experience. Royal Ascot will be his next port of call, where the Norfolk Stakes looks an ideal target, and it will no doubt take a very smart juvenile to deny him the hat-trick in that event. It should be noted that 2004 Norfolk hero Blue Dakota won the same two races at this venue en-route to success at Ascot. (op 2-7)

Lord Charles posted another sound effort in defeat, but he held no chance with the winner, and must rate as flattered by his proximity to that rival at the finish. He is an imposing two-year-old, and handled this softer ground without fuss, but is most likely going to prove hard to successfully place in the short-term. (op 10-1 tchd 12-1)

Bazroy(IRE), last seen winning comfortably on his debut at Lingfield in March, showed early speed but was readily brushed aside passing the two-furlong marker. He most likely needs a sound surface to be seen at his best and can be given another chance to prove his worth. (op 11-2)

Pernomente(IRE) gave himself little chance of getting home on the deep surface by pulling hard through the early parts. (op 33-1)

Best Woman not surprisingly failed to figure after her antics before the start and she is clearly one to tread carefully with.

1898 SMITH & WILLIAMSON H'CAP — 1m 3f 135y

7:10 (7:10) (Class 4) (0-85,85) 3-Y-O — **£6,477** (£1,927; £963; £481) **Stalls Low**

Form				RPR
0531	**1**		**Ogee**^{7} [1740] 3-8-11 78 6ex .... RyanMoore 3 (Sir Michael Stoute) *pressed ldr after 3f: led 3f out: sn in command: clr and pushed out fr over 1f out* **7/4**^{1}	96+
323	**2**	5	**My Petra**^{16} [1483] 3-8-7 74 .... JamieSpencer 5 (A King) *trckd ldr for 3f: rdn 4f out: outpcd 3f out: kpt on to take 2nd again 1f out: no ch w wnr* **6/1**	83
4241	**3**	1 ¼	**Island Odyssey**^{28} [1193] 3-8-10 77 .... LDettori 2 (E A L Dunlop) *led: rdn and hdd 3f out: swtchd lft over 2f out: lost 2nd 1f out: kpt on u.p* **11/2**^{3}	84
6112	**4**	5	**Lightning Strike (GER)**^{21} [1356] 3-9-4 85 .... IanMongan 4 (T G Mills) *chsd ldrs: rdn 5f out: outpcd 3f out: one pce and no imp after* **9/4**^{2}	85
2300	**5**	5	**Sky High Guy (IRE)**^{7} [1740] 3-8-4 71 oh2 .... MartinDwyer 7 (S Kirk) *in tch in rr: rdn 5f out and sn struggling: no hdwy fnl 3f* **20/1**	64
1322	**6**	3	**Go Figure (IRE)**^{27} [1205] 3-8-10 77 .... (t) JimmyFortune 6 (B J Meehan) *in tch in rr: rdn over 4f out: no prog 3f out: wknd 2f out* **10/1**	66
0620	**7**	18	**China Pearl**^{243} [5401] 3-8-8 75 .... SteveDrowne 1 (John Berry) *a last and nvr gng wl: t.o over 3f out* **50/1**	39

2m 33.5s (3.40) **Going Correction** +0.325s/f (Good) — 7 Ran SP% **112.6**

Speed ratings (Par 101):101,97,96,93,90 88,76

CSF £12.48 TOTE £2.80: £1.80, £3.40; EX 9.80.

Owner Sir Evelyn De Rothschild **Bred** Hesmonds Stud Ltd **Trained** Newmarket, Suffolk

FOCUS

Hand timed. Not the strongest form for the grade, but the winner was impressive and can rate higher still. The pace was sound.

1899 SUNLEY CLAIMING STKS — 6f

7:40 (7:40) (Class 5) 3-Y-O+ — **£3,238** (£963; £481; £240) **Stalls High**

Form				RPR
4002	**1**		**Franksalot (IRE)**^{18} [1432] 6-9-12 66 .... SebSanders 9 (Miss B Sanders) *racd nr side: trckd ldr: led gp and overall ldr 2f out: rdn and styd on wl fnl f: 1st of 5 stands' side* **5/1**^{2}	76
0004	**2**	1 ½	**The London Gang**^{10} [1642] 3-8-8 66 .... (v) StephenDonohoe$^{(5)}$ 8 (P D Evans) *s.i.s: racd centre and wl off the pce in rr: prog over 2f out: c to nr side and chsd wnr fnl f: kpt on: 2nd of 5 stands' si* **5/1**^{2}	66
0000	**3**	1 ½	**Endless Summer**^{153} [6631] 9-9-8 74 .... JimmyFortune 12 (A W Carroll) *racd nr side: chsd other pair: effrt 2f out: styd on same pce over 1f out: 3rd of 5 stands' side* **4/1**^{1}	63
0266	**4**	½	**Stagnite**^{14} [1539] 6-9-0 46 .... (b) MatthewHenry 10 (K McAuliffe) *racd in centre: overall ldr to over 3f out: edgd across to nr side over 1f out: one pce: 4th of 5 stands' side* **25/1**	54
2040	**5**	3	**Banjo Bay (IRE)**^{9} [1673] 8-8-13 59 .... JamesDoyle$^{(5)}$ 11 (Miss Gay Kelleway) *led nr side trio: overall ldr over 3f out to 2f out: wknd and fin last of 5 stands' side* **4/1**^{1}	49
0100	**6**	2 ½	**Piddies Pride (IRE)**^{35} [1057] 4-9-3 62 .... (p) JimmyQuinn 3 (Miss Gay Kelleway) *dwlt: wl in rr on far side: styd on fr over 1f out to ld gp of 7 nr fin: no ch with near side* **11/1**^{3}	40
3330	**7**	½	**Kitchen Sink (IRE)**^{89} [485] 4-9-8 50 .... (e) FergusSweeney 4 (P J Makin) *trckd far side ldrs: drvn to ld gp jst ins fnl f tl nr fin: 2nd of 7 his side, but nvr on terms w nr side* **14/1**	44
030	**8**	1	**Vague Star (ITY)**^{19} [1414] 4-9-4 57 .... (b) RobertHavlin 6 (R Ingram) *cl up far side: led gp 2f out and kicked on: no ch w nr side: hdd & wknd jst ins fnl f: 3rd of 7 his group* **12/1**	37
5005	**9**	hd	**Tuscany Queen (IRE)**^{4} [1799] 3-8-1 50 .... StephaneBreux$^{(3)}$ 5 (R Hannon) *off the pce on far side: rdn over 2f out: plugged on fnl f: 4th of 7 her group* **16/1**	29
0030	**10**	¾	**Renegade (IRE)**^{7} [1725] 5-9-4 47 .... (p) IanMongan 7 (Mrs L J Mongan) *sn rdn in rr of far side gp: nvr on terms and no ch: 5th of 7 his group* **16/1**	34
0300	**11**	½	**Byo (IRE)**^{11} [1618] 8-9-4 52 .... J-PGuillambert 1 (P Howling) *led far side gp to over 2f out: no ch and steadily wknd u.p: 6th of 7 his group* **16/1**	32
6000	**12**	19	**Sergeant Lewis**^{20} [1383] 4-9-8 55 .... (b) ShaneKelly 2 (R M Flower) *dwlt: sn prom far side: led gp over 2f out to 2f out: wknd rapidly: eased fnl f* **40/1**	—

1m 14.95s (1.28) **Going Correction** +0.225s/f (Good)

WFA 3 from 4yo+ 9lb — 12 Ran SP% **120.0**

Speed ratings (Par 103):100,98,96,95,91 88,87,86,85,84 84,58

CSF £30.63 TOTE £4.00: £2.80, £2.30, £1.60; EX 17.20.The winner was claimed by I. W. McInnes for £12,000.

Owner Peter Crate And Jane Byers **Bred** J P Hardiman **Trained** Headley, Surrey

FOCUS

A moderate event, which saw those who kept to the stands' side at a distinct advantage. The form is fair and not rock solid.

Byo(IRE) Official explanation: jockey said gelding was unsuited by the good to soft (soft in places) ground

Sergeant Lewis Official explanation: jockey said gelding had a breathing problem

1900 TOTESPORT H'CAP — 5f 10y

8:10 (8:10) (Class 4) (0-85,82) 3-Y-O — **£6,477** (£1,927; £963; £481) **Stalls High**

Form				RPR
611	**1**		**Terentia**^{23} [1279] 3-9-2 80 .... RichardMullen 5 (E S McMahon) *mde all: clr and in command over 1f out: pushed out: unchal* **15/8**^{1}	91+
0316	**2**	1 ½	**Shes Minnie**^{16} [1482] 3-8-7 71 .... JamieSpencer 9 (J G M O'Shea) *squeezed out s: wl in rr: prog against nr side rail over 1f out: styd on to take 2nd nr fin: no ch w wnr* **6/1**^{3}	75+
011	**3**	1	**Queen Cobra (IRE)**^{209} [6098] 3-8-12 76 .... SteveDrowne 7 (H Morrison) *bmpd s: t.k.h: cl up: chsd wnr 2f out: hld whn hung bdly lft fnl f: lost 2nd nr fin* **5/1**^{2}	77
0000	**4**	¾	**Supercast (IRE)**^{30} [1146] 3-9-2 80 .... (p) MartinDwyer 4 (J S Moore) *t.k.h: trckd ldrs: rdn and nt qckn over 1f out: one pce after* **20/1**	78
2500	**5**	1	**Hits Only Jude (IRE)**^{9} [1679] 3-8-9 73 .... JimmyQuinn 3 (J Pearce) *settled in last: outpcd 1/2-way: shuffled along over 1f out: reminder and styd on ins fnl f: nvr nr ldrs* **11/1**	68
10	**6**	½	**Makabul**^{15} [1512] 3-9-4 82 .... AlanMunro 2 (B R Millman) *racd on outer: chsd ldrs: rdn 2f out: no prog and btn over 1f out* **7/1**	75
3015	**7**	2	**Spearit (IRE)**^{174} [6456] 3-8-13 77 .... JamieMackay 10 (D R C Elsworth) *wnt sharply lft s and bmpd rival: chsd ldrs: pushed along 3f out: wknd over 1f out* **12/1**	64
3150	**8**	nk	**Sofinella (IRE)**^{206} [6132] 3-8-6 70 .... ChrisCatlin 1 (A W Carroll) *racd freely: chsd wnr to 2f out: wknd over 1f out* **20/1**	56
0000	**9**	1 ¼	**Sleeping Storm (IRE)**^{16} [1482] 3-8-13 77 .... (b^{1}) JimmyFortune 6 (B J Meehan) *bmpd twice sn after s: wl in rr: hrd rdn and struggling 2f out* **8/1**	58

61.75 secs (0.65) **Going Correction** +0.225s/f (Good) — 9 Ran SP% **114.9**

Speed ratings (Par 101):103,100,99,97,96 95,92,91,89

CSF £13.10 CT £46.77 TOTE £3.20: £1.50, £1.50, £1.60; EX 13.60.

Owner Dr Hugh Jones **Bred** Mrs F S Williams **Trained** Hopwas, Staffs

FOCUS

A fair handicap, which saw one or two hampered at the start, and the form should be treated with a desgree of caution. That said, the winner is progressing and can rate higher still.

Queen Cobra(IRE) Official explanation: jockey said filly hung left

Hits Only Jude(IRE) Official explanation: jockey said gelding lost a shoe

1901 RUINART CHAMPAGNE MAIDEN FILLIES' STKS — 1m 67y

8:40 (8:40) (Class 5) 3-Y-O+ — **£3,886** (£1,156; £577; £288) **Stalls High**

Form				RPR
22	**1**		**Magic Peak (IRE)**^{21} [1351] 3-8-9 .... RyanMoore 8 (Sir Michael Stoute) *mde all: pushed along and in command 2f out: rdn out nr fin* **8/11**^{1}	70
3	**2**	1	**Dear Gracie (IRE)**^{19} [1417] 3-8-9 .... JamieSpencer 7 (J R Fanshawe) *chsd wnr after 3f: rdn over 2f out: styd on and clsd ins fnl f but a readily hld* **9/2**^{2}	68
4	**3**	2	**And Again (USA)**^{274} [4601] 3-8-9 .... MartinDwyer 13 (J R Fanshawe) *hld up in midfield: effrt over 2f out: shkn up and styd on fr over 1f out: nrst fin* **10/1**^{3}	63
	4	½	**Valdemosa** 3-8-9 .... ShaneKelly 10 (B I Case) *chsd wnr for 3f: styd in tch: pushed along over 2f out: btn whn swtchd lft ins fnl f* **50/1**	62
	5	½	**Selkirk Lady** 3-8-9 .... OscarUrbina 2 (W R Swinburn) *hld up wl in rr: taken to wd outside and pushed along over 2f out: kpt on steadily: nvr nrr* **25/1**	61
	6	2	**Princess Danah (IRE)** 3-8-9 .... SebSanders 14 (W R Swinburn) *dwlt: wl in rr: pushed along over 4f out: styd on fnl 2f: nvr nrr* **20/1**	57
	7	1 ¼	**Jiminor Mack** 3-8-4 .... RichardKingscote$^{(5)}$ 6 (W J H Ratcliffe) *prom tl hung bdly lft bnd 5f out and lost pl: ended on far side and nvr on terms after* **66/1**	54

8 hd **Lady Galadriel (USA)** 3-8-9 .... AlanMunro 12 53
(J M P Eustace) *dwlt: sn chsd ldrs: shkn up 3f out: wknd over 1f out* **20/1**
54 9 nk **Musical Echo**[253] [5148] 3-8-9 .... SteveDrowne 9 52+
(G C H Chung) *t.k.h: cl up tl over 2f out: wknd and eased* **14/1**
10 nk **Juicy Fruits** 3-8-9 .... RichardMullen 11 52
(E A L Dunlop) *trckd ldrs: effrt wl over 2f out: wknd over 1f out* **20/1**
11 4 **Indian Pride** 4-9-7 .... JimmyQuinn 3 43
(D J Coakley) *s.s: detached in last 5f out: nvr a factor* **33/1**
0 12 15 **Spinning Dancer (IRE)**[299] [3846] 3-8-9 .... J-PGuillambert 1 8
(Ian Williams) *s.s and rrd: a towards rr: wknd over 2f out: t.o* **66/1**
13 1/2 **Silk Purse** 3-8-9 .... FrancisFerris 4 7
(Rae Guest) *a in rr: wknd 3f out: t.o* **33/1**

1m 50.23s (4.63) **Going Correction** +0.675s/f (Yiel)
WFA 3 from 4yo 12lb **13** Ran SP% **120.8**
Speed ratings (Par 100):103,102,100,99,99 97,95,95,95,94 90,75,75
CSF £3.21 TOTE £1.70: £1.10, £1.70, £2.80; EX 4.00 Place 6 £11.03, Place 5 £2.74.
Owner Cheveley Park Stud **Bred** Airlie Stud **Trained** Newmarket, Suffolk

FOCUS
This was run at a sound pace, but the form is far from solid and probably modest for the track.
Jiminor Mack Official explanation: jockey said filly hung left
Musical Echo Official explanation: jockey said filly hung left
Spinning Dancer(IRE) Official explanation: jockey said filly missed the break
T/Plt: £4.70 to a £1 stake. Pool: £75,443.20. 11,709.35 winning tickets. T/Qpdt: £2.30 to a £1 stake. Pool: £5,023.90. 1,609.70 winning tickets. JN

1660 BEVERLEY (R-H)
Tuesday, May 23
1902 Meeting Abandoned - Waterlogged

1722 KEMPTON (A.W) (R-H)
Tuesday, May 23

OFFICIAL GOING: Standard
This was the last banded meeting until the autumn.

Wind: Moderate; half against

1909 KEMPTON FOR TEAM BUILDING EVENTS BANDED STKS 5f (P)
2:00 (2:00) (Class 7) 4-Y-0+ **£1,706** (£503; £252) **Stalls** High

Form RPR
0502 1 **King Egbert (FR)**[8] [1722] 5-8-11 40 .... ShaneKelly 3 60
(A W Carroll) *stdd s and w.w: hdwy over 1f out: rdn and str burst to ld ins fnl f: won gng away* **4/1**[1]
2 2 1/2 **Stone Arch (IRE)**[19] [1450] 6-8-11 45 .... JohnEgan 10 51
(Jarlath P Fahey, Ire) *chsd ldrs: rdn 2f out: styd on to go 2nd ins fnl f: no ch w wnr* **6/1**[3]
0006 3 1 1/4 **Safranine (IRE)**[7] [1762] 9-8-7 38 ow3 .... (p) AnnStokell[(7)] 8 50
(Miss A Stokell) *w ldr: rdn 2f out: one pce fnl f* **50/1**
1045 4 shd **Sharp Hat**[14] [1571] 12-8-11 45 .... TonyCulhane 5 46
(D W Chapman) *in rr tl rdn and hdwy over 1f out: r.o: nvr nrr* **12/1**
5231 5 nk **Katie Killane**[8] [1722] 4-9-3 43 .... (v) DaneO'Neill 9 51
(M Wellings) *led tl rdn and hdd ins fnl f: fdd* **7/1**
4036 6 3/4 **Beverley Beau**[8] [1722] 4-8-4 45 .... KristinStubbs[(7)] 6 42
(Mrs L Stubbs) *chsd ldrs: rdn and one pce fr over 1f out* **10/1**
0000 7 hd **On The Trail**[18] [1466] 9-8-11 41 .... (p) PaulQuinn 11 42
(D W Chapman) *fly-jmpd s: nvr on terms* **33/1**
0050 8 1/2 **Saintly Place**[222] [5854] 5-8-11 40 .... GylesParkin 12 40
(C Smith) *a towards rr* **50/1**
0010 9 1 1/4 **Rock Fever (IRE)**[15] [1534] 4-8-4 45 .... (b) RonanKeogh[(7)] 1 35
(Peter Grayson) *mid-div: rdn 1/2-way: sn outpcd* **16/1**
0230 10 shd **New Options**[15] [1539] 9-8-11 45 .... (b) RobbieFitzpatrick 7 35
(Peter Grayson) *slowly away: a bhd* **8/1**
3433 11 1 **Maromito (IRE)**[8] [1722] 9-8-11 42 .... RoystonFfrench 4 31
(R Bastiman) *mid-div: rdn 1/2-way: sn outpcd* **5/1**[2]
3425 12 1 1/4 **A Teen**[8] [1722] 8-8-11 44 .... J-PGuillambert 2 27
(P Howling) *prom on outside tl wknd fr 1/2-way* **14/1**

60.38 secs **Going Correction** -0.05s/f (Stan) **12** Ran SP% **115.2**
Speed ratings (Par 97):98,94,92,91,91 90,89,89,87,86 85,83
CSF £26.34 TOTE £6.10: £2.00, £2.20, £8.70; EX 39.10.
Owner Bob Dean **Bred** Eric Puerari **Trained** Cropthorne, Worcs

FOCUS
Some old favourites on show here but few of these can be relied upon nowadays. An above-average effort for the grade from the winner, and the race has been rated through the fifth.

1910 SPONSOR AT KEMPTON BANDED STKS 1m 2f (P)
2:30 (2:31) (Class 7) 4-Y-0+ **£2,047** (£604; £302) **Stalls** High

Form RPR
3504 1 **Fantasy Crusader**[7] [1755] 7-8-13 47 .... DaneO'Neill 10 55
(R M H Cowell) *hld up: hdwy over 3f out: rdn to ld ins fnl f: r.o* **14/1**
1011 2 1 1/4 **Revolve**[15] [1536] 6-8-11 48 .... (p) AmirQuinn[(3)] 8 54
(Mrs L J Mongan) *trckd ldrs: led over 1f out: rdn and hdd ins fnl f* **13/2**[3]
500 3 1 **Hill Of Clare (IRE)**[7] [1753] 4-8-13 47 .... FergusSweeney 4 51
(P R Webber) *in rr tl hdwy on outside 2f out: styd on fnl f: nvr nrr* **10/1**
0000 4 1/2 **Southern Tide (USA)**[283] [4353] 4-8-13 47 .... JimmyQuinn 9 50
(J Pearce) *mid-div: rdn and hdwy appr fnl f: r.o: nvr nr to chal* **18/1**
6014 5 1 **Boogie Magic**[8] [1723] 6-8-10 47 .... RichardThomas[(3)] 11 48
(T Keddy) *in tch: rdn over 1f out: one pce fnl f* **12/1**
1001 6 2 **Ndola**[15] [1541] 7-8-13 47 .... (v) TPQueally 3 44
(B J Curley) *mid-div: but in tch tl wknd appr fnl f* **6/1**[2]
2232 7 1 1/2 **Larad (IRE)**[8] [1729] 5-8-13 47 .... (b) JohnEgan 7 41
(J S Moore) *chsd ldrs: rdn whn short of room over 1f out: nowhere to go and nt persevered w* **4/1**[1]
0156 8 1 **Diamond Dan (IRE)**[18] [1461] 4-8-11 48 .... JohnMcAuley[(3)] 13 41
(P D Evans) *mid-div: lost pl over 3f out: rdn over 1f out and nvr nr to chal* **12/1**
0002 9 1 1/4 **Silver Court**[19] [1434] 4-9-0 48 .... ShaneKelly 5 38
(A W Carroll) *slowly away: in rr tl rapid hdwy to disp ld after 4f: led 3f out: rdn and hdd over 1f out: wknd qckly* **25/1**
0003 10 2 1/2 **Sorbiesharry (IRE)**[14] [1574] 7-9-0 48 .... MickyFenton 2 33
(Mrs N Macauley) *a in rr* **20/1**
0000 11 3 **Futoo (IRE)**[21] [1392] 5-9-0 48 .... (p) TonyCulhane 1 28
(D W Chapman) *led tl rdn and hdd 3f out: sn wknd* **33/1**
3013 12 1 **Miss Glory Be**[8] [1723] 8-9-0 48 .... (p) DarryllHolland 6 26
(Ernst Oertel) *a bhd* **7/1**
0040 13 4 **Ruling Reef**[20] [1415] 4-9-2 50 .... HayleyTurner 12 20
(M D I Usher) *trckd ldrs: riden 1/2-way: wknd 3f out* **16/1**
2006 14 7 **Farnborough (USA)**[29] [1201] 5-8-10 47 .... RobertMiles[(3)] 14 4
(R J Price) *a bhd* **20/1**

2m 9.22s **Going Correction** -0.05s/f (Stan) **14** Ran SP% **118.7**
Speed ratings (Par 97):97,96,95,94,94 92,91,90,89,87 85,84,81,75
CSF £95.86 TOTE £17.90: £6.10, £3.30, £4.10; EX 229.40.
Owner The Fantasy Fellowship **Bred** J R C And Mrs Wren **Trained** Six Mile Bottom, Cambs

FOCUS
They appeared to go a good clip here but the time was around three seconds slower than the average for this trip on limited evidence thus far. Pretty sound form, average for the grade.
Larad(IRE) Official explanation: jockey said, regarding the running and riding, his orders were to sit 4th or 5th and cover gelding up, but on the turn for home he chose to switch inside and was denied a clear run

1911 KEMPTON FOR BANQUETING BANDED STKS 1m 2f (P)
3:00 (3:03) (Class 7) 4-Y-0+ **£2,388** (£705; £352) **Stalls** High

Form RPR
0524 1 **Opera Knight**[8] [1729] 6-8-11 43 .... ShaneKelly 2 52
(A W Carroll) *hld up: hdwy on outside 2f out: rdn to ld ins fnl f: kpt up to work* **5/1**[1]
0-02 2 nk **Expected Bonus (USA)**[15] [1536] 7-8-11 44 .... JohnEgan 9 51+
(Jamie Poulton) *hld up: hdwy on ins over 1f out: r.o to go 2nd ins fnl f* **6/1**[3]
0426 3 1 **Sudden Impulse**[7] [1767] 5-8-11 42 .... PaulEddery 4 49
(A D Brown) *trckd ldr: led 4f out: hdd ins fnl f and sn lost 2nd* **20/1**
0006 4 1 1/4 **Plain Champagne (IRE)**[15] [1541] 4-8-8 43 .... RichardThomas[(3)] 1 47
(Dr J R J Naylor) *plld hrd: hdwy on outside to trck ldrs after 4f: rdn and nt qckn appr fnl f* **33/1**
3201 5 1 1/2 **Yashin (IRE)**[7] [1767] 5-9-3 45 .... PaulFessey 11 50
(P A Blockley) *trckd ldr: rdn over 2f out: kpt on one pce* **13/2**
5063 6 nk **Shami**[7] [1765] 7-8-11 45 .... (v) TonyCulhane 14 44
(D W Chapman) *trckd ldrs: rdn over 1f out: one pce after* **10/1**
0004 7 shd **Karrnak**[8] [1724] 4-8-11 45 .... (p) DaneO'Neill 7 43
(Miss J Feilden) *bhd: mde som late hdwy but nvr on terms* **14/1**
0000 8 shd **Vandal**[6] [1769] 6-8-4 43 .... LiamJones[(7)] 5 43
(M Appleby) *a in rr* **50/1**
9 nk **All Square (IRE)**[27] [6019] 6-8-11 44 .... (t) DarryllHolland 13 43
(R A Farrant) *mid-div: wknd over 2f out* **10/1**
2401 10 1/2 **Dagola (IRE)**[8] [1724] 5-9-0 43 .... SaleemGolam[(3)] 6 48
(C A Dwyer) *racd wd: effrt 2f out but nvr on terms* **11/2**[2]
0016 11 3/4 **Artzola (IRE)**[169] [6509] 6-8-11 45 .... MickyFenton 8 40
(C A Horgan) *stdd s: a bhd* **20/1**
4030 12 1 1/4 **Homebred Star**[15] [1536] 5-8-6 45 .... (p) RobynBrisland[(5)] 10 38
(G P Enright) *mid-div: wknd over 2f out* **25/1**
0600 13 1 1/2 **Opera Belle**[103] [350] 4-8-11 45 .... JimmyQuinn 12 35
(Miss Gay Kelleway) *t.k.h: in tch tl fnl 3f* **6/1**[3]
0304 14 3/4 **Legacy (JPN)**[7] [1625] 6-8-6 45 .... (b) StephenDonohoe[(5)] 3 34
(P D Evans) *slowly away: plld hrd: a bhd* **16/1**

2m 10.22s **Going Correction** -0.05s/f (Stan) **14** Ran SP% **123.0**
Speed ratings (Par 97):93,92,91,90,89 89,89,89,89,88 88,87,85,85
CSF £32.78 TOTE £6.30: £2.50, £2.00, £8.50; EX 38.40.
Owner Frontrunner Syndicate **Bred** M Bin Hendi **Trained** Cropthorne, Worcs
■ Stewards' Enquiry : Stephen Donohoe one-day ban: used whip when out of contention (Jun 4)

FOCUS
The early pace was not strong here resulting in a few pulling for their heads, and the overall time was a second slower than the previous contest, which was itself particularly slow. Ordinary form, the winner back to his winter best.
Plain Champagne(IRE) Official explanation: jockey said filly had run too freely
Artzola(IRE) Official explanation: jockey said mare was denied a clear run

1912 JUBILEE PANORAMIC BAR & RESTAURANT MAIDEN AUCTION STKS 6f (P)
3:30 (3:44) (Class 7) 2-Y-0 **£1,706** (£503; £252) **Stalls** High

Form RPR
2 1 **Cherri Fosfate**[10] [1664] 2-8-8 .... RobertMiles[(3)] 11 67+
(W G M Turner) *chsd ldrs: rdn over 2f out: rallied and r.o to ld post* **8/15**[1]
4 2 shd **Callisto Moon**[32] [1113] 2-8-11 .... DaneO'Neill 5 67+
(R Curtis) *hld up: rdn and hdwy over 2f out: led over 1f out: kpt on: hdd post* **9/1**[3]
5 3 5 **Aggresive**[15] [1535] 2-8-10 .... DarryllHolland 8 48
(Ernst Oertel) *trckd ldrs: ev ch 2f out: rdn and outpcd fnl f* **14/1**
0 4 1 **Ella Y Rossa**[8] [1737] 2-8-7 .... ShaneKelly 12 41
(P D Evans) *led tl rdn and hdd over 1f out: wknd ins fnl f* **50/1**
03 5 3 **Flamestone**[19] [1442] 2-8-10 .... AdrianTNicholls 7 33
(J D Bethell) *chsd ldrs: rdn 1/2-way: wknd 2f out* **7/1**[2]
6 hd **Foxy Games** 2-8-1 .... EdwardCreighton[(3)] 1 27
(D J S Ffrench Davis) *wnt lft s: a bhd* **50/1**
7 3 1/2 **Gifted Heir (IRE)** 2-8-8 .... SaleemGolam[(3)] 4 21
(I A Wood) *slowly away: a bhd* **40/1**
8 3 1/2 **Kerswell** 2-8-6 .... RobertHavlin 3 3
(B R Millman) *in tch on outside to 1/2-way* **20/1**
9 5 **Zameliana** 2-8-1 .... RichardThomas[(3)] 9 —
(Dr J R J Naylor) *slowly away: and outpcd thrght* **66/1**

1m 16.07s **Going Correction** -0.05s/f (Stan) **9** Ran SP% **107.0**
Speed ratings (Par 87):82,81,75,73,69 69,64,60,53
CSF £4.41 TOTE £1.40: £1.02, £2.40, £2.00; EX 5.60.
Owner C McKenna **Bred** The Newchange Syndicate **Trained** Sigwells, Somerset
■ Outsiders Auction Oasis & Cookies Quiff (unruly in stalls) and Early Promise (refused to enter stalls) were withdrawn. No R4.

FOCUS
There were all sorts of problems loading this field of maidens up and quite a few were left standing in the stalls for some time before they were unloaded, after Kerswell got herself trapped under the stalls. Decent efforts from the front two and the race could be rated 10lb higher, but the third and fourth hold down the form.

NOTEBOOK
Cherri Fosfate made a promising start to his career at Beverley and that form stood head and shoulders above what any of his rivals had achieved, but he was made to work extremely hard and he only got up in the final ten yards. He was shaken up passing the two-furlong pole and, although the response was not immediate, he gradually wound up and was clawing the leader back with every stride inside the final half-furlong. Connections insist that he is not an All-Weather horse, and the only reason they came here was because it appeared to be a weak race. He needs a stiff six furlongs on turf to be seen at his best. (op 4-6)

Callisto Moon, who had looked worth a try over this extra furlong, ran a cracker in defeat, pulling some five lengths clear to give the form a solid look. He was shaken up to lead entering the final furlong and, having battled bravely all the way to the line, was only headed in the final strides. (tchd 10-1)
Aggresive had his chance with two to run but was soon swamped by the front two and was never a factor thereafter. (op 16-1)
Ella Y Rossa showed more than on her debut and made the running until collared with a furlong and a half to run. A drop back to five might suit.
Flamestone wandered left under pressure in the home straight and does not seem to be progressing. (op 13-2)
Foxy Games, who looked green and in need of the experience, was not knocked about. Official explanation: jockey said filly hung right-handed
Kerswell, a cheap buy as a yearling, became trapped in the stalls beforehand. (op 16-1)
Zameliana Official explanation: jockey said filly missed the break

1913 KEMPTON FOR CONFERENCES BANDED STKS 6f (P)
4:00 (4:12) (Class 7) 4-Y-0+ **£2,388** (£705; £352) **Stalls** High

Form				RPR
4304	**1**		**Double M**[8] 1728 9-8-12 49....(v) RichardThomas(3) 8 (Mrs L Richards) *hld up in tch: rdn and hdwy 2f out: led 1f out: r.o wl* **11/1**	58
3032	**2**	2	**Rowanberry**[15] 1539 4-9-0 48.... DarryllHolland 3 (R M H Cowell) *in tch on outside: rdn whn nt much toom over 1f out: swtchd rt and r.o wl to o 2nd ins fnl f* **10/3**[1]	57+
2005	**3**	shd	**Peggys First**[8] 1728 4-9-0 48.... DaneO'Neill 11 (D E Cantillon) *stdd s and in rr tl gd hdwy on outside over 1f out: r.o wl: nvr nrr* **8/1**[3]	51
0001	**4**	½	**Haroldini (IRE)**[7] 1763 4-9-3 48....(p) JasonEdmunds(3) 5 (J Balding) *hld up: hdwy on outside over 1f out: kpt on fnl f* **10/1**	56
0004	**5**	1	**Newsround**[7] 1762 4-9-2 50....(p) TonyCulhane 10 (D W Chapman) *trckd ldrs: led 2f out: rdn and hdd 1f out: no ex fnl f* **17/2**	49
0460	**6**	1	**Lady Hopeful (IRE)**[8] 1728 4-8-7 48....(b) RonanKeogh(7) 6 (Peter Grayson) *hld up: mde sme late hdwy* **16/1**	44
1530	**7**	1	**Trouble Maker**[50] 854 5-9-2 50....(v[1]) ShaneKelly 1 (A M Balding) *in rr: effrt over 2f out: nvr nr to chal* **5/1**[2]	43
0000	**8**	nk	**Boisdale (IRE)**[63] 691 8-8-13 47.... MickyFenton 12 (K A Morgan) *led tl hdd 2f out: wknd ent fnl f* **33/1**	39
3420	**9**	1 ¼	**Midmaar (IRE)**[15] 1534 5-8-13 47.... JamieMackay 2 (M Wigham) *chsd ldrs tl wknd over 1f out* **12/1**	35
6504	**10**	1	**Detonate**[12] 1618 4-9-0 48.... JimmyQuinn 4 (Mrs C A Dunnett) *chsd ldrs tl wknd 2f out* **8/1**[3]	33
6000	**11**	½	**Madrasee**[9] 8-8-13 50.... AmirQuinn(3) 7 (P G Murphy) *stdd s: a bhd* **20/1**	33
0000	**12**	1 ½	**Pro Tempore**[10] 1689 4-9-1 49.... FergusSweeney 9 (David Pinder) *trckd ldr: rdn 2f out: wknd 1/2-way* **16/1**	28

1m 13.61s **Going Correction** -0.05s/f (Stan) 12 Ran SP% **117.1**
Speed ratings (Par 97):98,95,95,94,93 91,90,90,88,87 86,84
CSF £46.88 TOTE £12.20: £3.50, £1.80, £2.80; EX 49.80.
Owner Bryan Mathieson **Bred** M G Tebbitt **Trained** Funtington, W Sussex
FOCUS
Pretty sound form, the winner back to his best winter form, with the runner-up unlucky.
Boisdale(IRE) Official explanation: jockey said gelding hung left

1914 SUPPORT RETRAINING OF RACEHORSES BANDED STKS 7f (P)
4:30 (4:39) (Class 7) 4-Y-0+ **£1,706** (£503; £252) **Stalls** High

Form				RPR
0056	**1**		**Extemporise (IRE)**[21] 1390 6-8-11 43.... TPQueally 1 (T T Clement) *chsd ldr: rdn to ld 2f out: in command after* **7/1**[3]	56
6320	**2**	1 ¾	**Veneer (IRE)**[7] 1765 4-8-11 45....(p) DarryllHolland 2 (Miss Gay Kelleway) *in rr tl hdwy 3f out: r.o to chse wnr over 1f out: kpt on* **9/2**[1]	51
4403	**3**	1	**Start Of Authority**[8] 1727 5-8-11 42.... ShaneKelly 11 (J Gallagher) *mid-div: rdn and hdwy 2f out to chse first 2 fnl f* **6/1**[2]	49
005	**4**	5	**Proud Western (USA)**[18] 1459 8-8-11 43....(t) DaneO'Neill 7 (B Ellison) *hld up: mde sme late hdwy past btn horses* **14/1**	36
0000	**5**	nk	**Icecap**[7] 1755 6-8-11 44....(p) AlanDaly 10 (W G M Turner) *slowly away: in rr tl sme late hdwy* **16/1**	35
0604	**6**	1 ¼	**Davids Mark**[8] 1722 6-8-8 44....(vt) DeanCorby(3) 14 (J R Jenkins) *bhd and nvr on terms* **8/1**	32
6432	**7**	2 ½	**Gaudalpin (IRE)**[8] 1727 4-8-11 45....(t) JohnEgan 4 (Ernst Oertel) *chsd ldrs: rdn over 2f out: sn btn* **9/2**[1]	25
4000	**8**	shd	**Sunset Dreamer (USA)**[8] 1727 5-8-11 42....(p) JimmyQuinn 8 (P Mitchell) *a bhd* **50/1**	25
0600	**9**	hd	**Tuscan Flyer**[14] 1577 8-8-11 45.... RoystonFfrench 5 (R Bastiman) *in tch tl rdn over 2f out: sn btn* **40/1**	25
0050	**10**	1	**Legal Set (IRE)**[8] 1722 10-8-7 44 ow3....(bt) AnnStokell(7) 12 (Miss A Stokell) *led tl hung rt and hdd 2f out: wknd qckly appr fnl f* **33/1**	25
0016	**11**	2	**Inescapable (USA)**[15] 1538 5-8-11 45.... MickyFenton 13 (A W Carroll) *mid-div: lost tch over 2f out* **11/1**	17
0025	**12**	5	**Sergeant Slipper**[7] 1764 9-8-11 44....(v) GylesParkin 6 (C Smith) *mid-div: bhd fr over 2f out* **25/1**	4
0230	**13**	7	**Margaret's Dream (IRE)**[8] 1727 5-8-8 44.... DanielTudhope(3) 9 (D Carroll) *chsd ldrs tl wknd over 2f out* **10/1**	—
0620	**14**	3	**Mescalera (GER)**[15] 1538 5-8-11 44.... TonyCulhane 3 (B G Powell) *trckd ldrs to 1/2-way* **25/1**	—

1m 26.53s **Going Correction** -0.05s/f (Stan) 14 Ran SP% **119.3**
Speed ratings (Par 97):99,97,95,90,89 88,85,85,85,84 81,76,68,64
CSF £36.16 TOTE £6.80: £2.60, £3.20, £2.60; EX 52.30.
Owner S Anrude **Bred** Paradime Ltd **Trained** Newmarket, Suffolk
FOCUS
The pace was strong, they were soon well strung out and few got into this from behind. The form seems pretty sound.
Legal Set(IRE) Official explanation: jockey said gelding hung right-handed in the last 2f

1915 COMBINE BUSINESS WITH PLEASURE APPRENTICE BANDED STKS 1m (P)
5:00 (5:08) (Class 7) 4-Y-0+ **£2,388** (£705; £352) **Stalls** High

Form				RPR
4003	**1**		**Terenzium (IRE)**[25] 1276 4-8-9 50.... HeatherMcGee(7) 3 (L M Cumani) *t.k.h: wnt 2nd 1/2-way: led appr fnl f: won w smething in hand* **8/1**	60
0253	**2**	½	**Frank's Quest (IRE)**[8] 1725 6-9-2 50.... JamieJones 11 (A B Haynes) *hld up in rr: gd hdwy over 1f out: r.o to go 2nd ins fnl f* **7/1**[3]	59
6000	**3**	¾	**Fantasy Defender (IRE)**[8] 1723 4-8-9 48....(v) JamieHamblett(5) 2 (Ernst Oertel) *mid-div: rdn and hdwy over 1f out: kpt on ins fnl f* **14/1**	55
6600	**4**	nk	**The Job**[8] 1725 5-8-11 48....(v) ThomasO'Brien(3) 12 (A D Smith) *t.k.h: trckd ldr: led 1/2-way: hdd appr fnl f: nt qckn ins* **33/1**	54
2066	**5**	shd	**Sriology (IRE)**[63] 689 5-8-11 48....(t) KirstyMilczarek(3) 13 (G Prodromou) *sn rdn in mid-div: r.o fnl f* **16/1**	54
3310	**6**	nk	**Mr Belvedere**[6] 1769 5-8-9 48....(p) SophieDoyle(5) 14 (A J Lidderdale) *led to 1/2-way: ev ch 2f out: one pce fnl f* **5/1**[2]	53
0033	**7**	¾	**Harare**[139] 43 5-9-0 48.... LiamJones 1 (R J Price) *bhd: rdn over 3f out: mde sme late hdwy* **8/1**	52
4U12	**8**	½	**Musical Gift**[21] 1387 6-9-1 49....(p) KevinGhunowa 4 (P A Blockley) *in tch: rdn 3f out: wknd wl over 1f out* **9/2**[1]	52
1021	**9**	1 ¼	**Wanna Shout**[8] 1725 8-9-2 49.... JosephWalsh(5) 5 (R Dickin) *chsd ldrs tl wknd over 1f out* **9/1**	55
5060	**10**	nk	**Savoy Chapel**[101] 382 4-8-9 48.... PatrickDonaghy(5) 8 (D Carroll) *hld up: a in rr* **12/1**	47
5000	**11**	1 ¼	**Preskani**[10] 1683 4-8-11 50.... LukeMorris(5) 7 (Mrs N Macauley) *s.i.s: a bhd* **12/1**	46
4050	**12**	1 ½	**Limonia (GER)**[133] 81 4-8-9 48.... JemmaMarshall(5) 10 (N P Littmoden) *sn outpcd and a bhd* **14/1**	41

1m 41.37s **Going Correction** -0.05s/f (Stan) 12 Ran SP% **117.1**
Speed ratings (Par 97):95,94,93,93,93 93,92,91,90,90 89,87
CSF £62.27 TOTE £6.20: £3.00, £2.30, £5.70; EX 53.50 Place 6 £58.89, Place 5 £27.63.
Owner Mrs Luca Cumani **Bred** Azienda Agricola Patrizia **Trained** Newmarket, Suffolk
■ A winner on her first ride in public for Heather McGee.
■ Stewards' Enquiry : Kevin Ghunowa one-day ban: failed to keep straight from stalls (Jun 4)
FOCUS
The field finished in something of a bunch at the line so the form should be treated with caution, although it has been rated at face value for now.
T/Plt: £127.60 to a £1 stake. Pool: £45,978.00. 262.90 winning tickets. T/Qpdt: £10.60 to a £1 stake. Pool: £4,174.00. 288.70 winning tickets. JS

1284 LEICESTER (R-H)
Tuesday, May 23
1916 Meeting Abandoned - Waterlogged

1667 LINGFIELD (L-H)
Tuesday, May 23
OFFICIAL GOING: Standard
Wind: Moderate behind Weather: Mostly fine

1922 TRACKSIDE RESTAURANT MAIDEN AUCTION FILLIES' STKS 5f (P)
2:10 (2:16) (Class 5) 2-Y-0 **£3,238** (£963; £481; £240) **Stalls** Low

Form				RPR
02	**1**		**Going Straight (IRE)**[15] 1535 2-8-5 ow1.... RyanMoore 5 (I A Wood) *trckd ldr: led over 1f out: drvn and edgd rt fnl f: hld on* **5/1**[3]	73
5	**2**	¾	**Sans Reward (IRE)**[10] 1688 2-8-7.... RichardHughes 1 (B J Meehan) *sn rdn to chse ldrs: effrt over 1f out: r.o to take 2nd nr fin and gaining on wnr* **4/1**[2]	72
30	**3**	1	**Three Decades (IRE)**[15] 1542 2-8-10.... LDettori 6 (C A Cyzer) *chsd ldng pair 3f out: drvn and nt qckn over 1f out: chsd wnr ins fnl f: no imp: lost 2nd nr fin* **7/1**	72
03	**4**	4	**Bridge It Jo**[10] 1675 2-8-4.... ChrisCatlin 7 (Miss J Feilden) *led at furious pce: hdd & wknd over 1f out* **10/3**[1]	51
	5	nk	**Ioweyou** 2-8-7.... MartinDwyer 4 (J S Moore) *outpcd and off the pce towards rr: kpt on fr over 1f out: n.d* **16/1**	53
46	**6**	1	**Autumn Storm**[8] 1743 2-8-4.... RobertHavlin 9 (R Ingram) *chsd ldrs on outer: rdn 3f out: effrt 2f out: sn wknd* **50/1**	47
4	**7**	nk	**Cuppacocoa**[11] 1647 2-8-4.... AdamKirby(3) 10 (C G Cox) *unruly stalls and jockey nt ready whn stalls opened: s.s: a off the pce: kpt on fnl f* **7/1**	49
5	**8**	½	**Spirit Of Venus (FR)**[11] 1647 2-8-7.... EddieAhern 2 (E A L Dunlop) *chsd ldrs: rdn 1/2-way: wknd wl over 1f out* **7/1**	47
0	**9**	5	**River Rosie (IRE)**[15] 1542 2-8-1.... StephaneBreux(3) 8 (J G Portman) *s.s: a outpcd in last pair* **20/1**	26
6	**10**	shd	**Baytown Rosie (IRE)**[50] 856 2-7-11.... DonnaCaldwell(7) 3 (P S McEntee) *v s.i.s: a outpcd in last pair* **80/1**	25

59.47 secs (-0.31) **Going Correction** -0.15s/f (Stan) 10 Ran SP% **111.1**
Speed ratings (Par 90):96,94,93,86,86 84,84,83,75,75
CSF £23.63 TOTE £5.50: £1.70, £2.20, £2.30; EX 18.40 Trifecta £226.10 Pool: £532.01 - 1.67 winning units.
Owner Christopher Shankland **Bred** Kilnamoragh Stud **Trained** Upper Lambourn, Berks
FOCUS
A modest maiden for juvenile fillies, which was run at a strong early pace, and the first three came clear.
NOTEBOOK
Going Straight(IRE), well backed when second at Kempton last time, was given a slightly more patient ride which clearly paid dividends, as she got the run of the race and duly broke her duck at the third attempt. She is going the right way, looks the type to get six furlongs in due course, and could turn out quickly in a conditions event at Ascot later this week. (op 6-1)
Sans Reward(IRE) hit a flat spot at a crucial stage and was staying on again all too late in the day. She looks the one to take from the race with the future in mind and, on this evidence, will relish the step-up to a sixth furlong. (op 9-2 tchd 5-1 in places)
Three Decades(IRE) showed improved form for this return to a sound surface and was not disgraced considering she was giving away weight to her rivals. She has not really progressed as could have been expected from her debut back in April, however. (op 8-1 tchd 17-2)
Bridge It Jo, who hung her chance away at Newmarket last time, proved very easy to back despite the fact this course should have proved much more to her liking. She ultimately went off too fast for her own good, and does look a headstrong filly, but she now qualifies for a nursery mark and has a race within her compass on a sharp track in due course. (op 5-2 tchd 7-2 in a place)
Ioweyou, the first foal of a dual winner at two who is herself a half-sister to top-class miler Le Vie Dei Colori, showed temperament in the preliminaries and was not that surprisingly very green through the early parts of the race. She still finished her race well enough, however, and appeals as the type to progress with further experience under her belt.
Cuppacocoa, as had been the case on her recent debut, lost all chance at the start and is clearly tricky.
Spirit Of Venus(FR) failed to build on the level of her recent debut and looks in need of more time. (op 11-2)

1923 ARENA LEISURE PLC CLAIMING STKS 7f (P)
2:40 (2:46) (Class 5) 3-Y-0+ £3,238 (£963; £481; £240) Stalls Low

Form RPR
3055 1 **Labelled With Love**[41] 982 6-9-0 52....(t) LDettori 3 59
(J R Boyle) *hld up in midfield: effrt on outer and n.m.r briefly 2f out: rdn to ld jst over 1f out: drvn out* 10/1
4501 2 1 1/2 **Mon Petite Amour**[7] 1752 3-8-0 45....(p) FrankieMcDonald 11 48
(D W P Arbuthnot) *trckd ldrs: rdn on outer 2f out: styd on fnl f to take 2nd nr fin* 20/1
2060 3 1/2 **Cherokee Nation**[20] 1402 5-9-3 62.... AdamKirby(3) 9 60
(P W D'Arcy) *hld up in tch: nt clr run wl over 1f out: nt look keen sn after: rdn to dispute 2nd fnl f: one pce* 20/1
4202 4 hd **Hadath (IRE)**[7] 1752 9-9-2 53....(b) TQuinn 12 55
(B G Powell) *hld up wl in rr: drvn 3f out: prog on outer fnl f: nvr nrr* 8/1[3]
3300 5 3/4 **Always Esteemed (IRE)**[24] 1280 6-10-0 92....(b) NCallan 1 65
(K A Ryan) *w ldr: led 4f out: nvr able to dominate: edgd rt wl over 1f out: hdd jst over 1f out: nt qckn* 8/11[1]
0350 6 3/4 **What-A-Dancer (IRE)**[10] 1673 9-9-10 72....(p) GeorgeBaker 4 66+
(D J S Ffrench Davis) *hld up wl in rr: stdy prog on inner 2f out: clsng on ldrs whn hmpd jst ins fnl f: nt rcvr* 7/1[2]
1060 7 3/4 **Ockums Razor (IRE)**[66] 665 3-8-13 77.... EddieAhern 2 53
(M J Polglase) *t.k.h: trckd ldng pair: drvn to chal and upsides over 1f out: hld whn edgd lft and bmpd jst ins fnl f* 8/1[3]
4-00 8 6 **Love's Design (IRE)**[8] 1725 9-9-0 47....(v) OscarUrbina 8 32
(Miss J Feilden) *hld up in midfield: sltly hmpd 5f out: wknd over 1f out* 66/1
0000 9 1 1/4 **Charles Street Lad (IRE)**[22] 1355 3-9-1 50.... IanMongan 7 37
(M R Bosley) *prom: drvn to chal 2f out: wknd rapidly jst over 1f out* 100/1
2400 10 6 **Cloann (IRE)**[23] 1310 4-8-9 47....(b) StephenCarson 6 8
(E A Wheeler) *led to 4f out: pressed ldr tl wknd rapidly over 1f out* 50/1
1050 11 4 **Frenchmans Lodge**[192] 6330 6-9-0 36....(b) PaulDoe 10 3
(L A Dace) *s.s: a towards rr: lost tch over 2f out* 100/1
-000 12 13 **Kussharro**[25] 1272 5-9-0 35....(t) ChrisCatlin 5 —
(Mrs L J Young) *sn struggling in last: t.o 3f out* 100/1

1m 25.72s (-0.17) **Going Correction** -0.15s/f (Stan)
WFA 3 from 4yo+ 11lb 12 Ran SP% **117.7**
Speed ratings (Par 103):94,92,91,91,90 89,88,82,80,73 69,54
CSF £185.54 TOTE £10.30: £2.30, £4.70, £4.40; EX 144.90 TRIFECTA Not won..
Owner Inside Track Racing Club **Bred** Mascalls Stud **Trained** Epsom, Surrey

FOCUS
A weak event, run at a decent early pace, and the form looks suspect with the favourite way below his best.

1924 OXTED VETERINARY CLINIC H'CAP 7f (P)
3:10 (3:15) (Class 3) (0-95,94) 3-Y-0
£11,217 (£3,358; £1,679; £840; £419; £210) Stalls Low

Form RPR
3115 1 **Orchard Supreme**[22] 1337 3-8-7 83.... RichardHughes 3 92
(R Hannon) *t.k.h: hld up in 5th: effrt 2f out: shkn up to ld last 150yds: sn jnd: fnd ex and hld on wl* 11/2[2]
114 2 hd **Easy Air**[11] 1626 3-8-10 86.... LDettori 5 94
(E A L Dunlop) *wl in tch: pushed along to chse ldng pair over 3f out: effrt 2f out: drvn to join wnr last 100yds: jst hld* 1/1[1]
32 3 1 1/4 **Dark Islander (IRE)**[33] 1094 3-9-4 94.... EddieAhern 6 99
(J W Hills) *t.k.h: hld up in last pair: rdn and effrt over 2f out: nt qckn over 1f out: r.o to take 3rd last 75yds* 6/1[3]
2115 4 1 1/2 **Total Impact**[20] 1404 3-8-11 87.... MartinDwyer 4 88
(C A Cyzer) *pressed ldr: chal fr 3f out: led over 1f out: hdd & wknd last 150yds* 14/1
2443 5 1/2 **Secret Night**[20] 1404 3-8-12 88.... OscarUrbina 7 88
(J A R Toller) *hld up in last pair: pushed along 3f out: outpcd 2f out: kpt on ins fnl f* 12/1
1101 6 3/4 **Dingaan (IRE)**[20] 1404 3-9-4 94.... ChrisCatlin 2 92
(A M Balding) *led: hrd pressed fr 3f out: hdd & wknd over 1f out* 6/1[3]
5520 7 7 **Charlton**[38] 1016 3-8-11 87.... IanMongan 1 67
(T G Mills) *chsd ldng pair to over 3f out: sn struggling* 20/1

1m 24.57s (-1.32) **Going Correction** -0.15s/f (Stan) 7 Ran SP% **113.1**
Speed ratings (Par 103):101,100,99,97,97 96,88
CSF £11.18 TOTE £5.70: £2.10, £1.30; EX 10.40.
Owner Brian C Oakley **Bred** Mrs M H Goodrich **Trained** East Everleigh, Wilts

FOCUS
A decent little handicap for three-year-olds, which was run at a frantic early pace, and the first two came clear. The form makes sense.

NOTEBOOK
Orchard Supreme, slightly unfortunate at Kempton in his quest for the hat-trick last time, found the race run to suit and just did enough to prevail under a well-judged ride. This was his fourth success from his last six outings - indeed he has now won on his last three starts at this venue - and he is evidently still progressive on this surface. (op 6-1 tchd 5-1)
Easy Air, who lost his unbeaten record on softening ground on his turf debut at Chester, failed to really improve for this return to this course and distance yet was only just thwarted. He may have fared better with a slightly more patient ride and is not one to give up on just yet. (op 11-10 tchd 6-5 in a place)
Dark Islander(IRE), despite refusing to settle early on, turned in his best effort to date on the All-Weather and was not disgraced under joint top weight. He is a consistent colt, who is thought by his connections to be much more effective on turf, and he really does deserve to find another race. (op 11-2 tchd 7-1 in a places)
Total Impact posted an improved effort and reversed his recent Kempton form with Secret Night and Dingaan. He is most likely going to prove hard to successfuly place from his current mark, however.
Secret Night did not run up to her best on this return to this venue and shaped as though she may benefit from the step-up to another furlong again now. (op 14-1)
Dingaan(IRE), raised 6lb for winning a valuable handicap at Kempton last time, was not helped by being hassled for the early lead on this switch back to more positive tactics and not surprisingly faded when pressed in the home straight. (tchd 13-2)

1925 MARSH GREEN H'CAP 1m 2f (P)
3:40 (3:46) (Class 6) (0-65,65) 3-Y-0 £3,238 (£963; £481; £240) Stalls Low

Form RPR
0002 1 **Mystic Storm**[8] 1736 3-8-13 60.... SebSanders 6 79+
(Lady Herries) *trckd ldrs: swept into ld wl over 2f out: sn clr: won w plenty in hand* 9/4[1]
4204 2 4 **Nikki Bea (IRE)**[11] 1638 3-8-10 57.... PaulDoe 4 64
(Jamie Poulton) *trckd ldrs: stmbld 4f out: rdn to chse wnr over 1f out: no ch but kpt on* 7/1[2]
0036 3 nk **Lester Leaps In (USA)**[21] 1375 3-9-4 65.... RyanMoore 9 71+
(R Hannon) *hld up in last trio: stl wl in rr 2f out: prog on wd outside over 1f out: r.o fnl f: hopeless task* 10/1
4216 4 1 3/4 **Dark Planet**[15] 1543 3-9-3 64.... MartinDwyer 12 67
(C E Brittain) *hld up in last trio: prog over 2f out: drvn and kpt on same pce over 1f out* 7/1[2]
000 5 1 **Muckle**[62] 692 3-8-11 58.... SteveDrowne 5 59
(S C Williams) *hld up in midfield: outpcd and drvn over 2f out: kpt on again over 1f out* 14/1
0500 6 1 3/4 **Life Peer**[15] 1543 3-8-8 60.... JamesDoyle(5) 1 58
(J G Portman) *trckd ldrs: pushed along 4f out: outpcd u.p 2f out: one pce after* 20/1
2202 7 nk **Mighty Dancer (IRE)**[28] 1215 3-9-1 62.... JimmyFortune 14 59
(S Kirk) *forced to r wd early in midfield: drvn 3f out: sn outpcd and btn* 8/1[3]
0004 8 1 3/4 **Constant Cheers (IRE)**[21] 1375 3-9-0 61.... TedDurcan 7 55
(W R Swinburn) *pressed ldr: upsides fr 5f out to wl over 2f out: wknd over 1f out* 10/1
4022 9 1 3/4 **Tangarita**[11] 1652 3-8-13 60.... RichardHughes 3 51
(A M Balding) *mde most to wl over 2f out: wknd over 1f out* 7/1[2]
500 10 2 1/2 **Hazium (IRE)**[23] 1327 3-9-1 62.... LDettori 11 48
(Patrick Morris, Ire) *settled in last: nvr looked happy: rdn and effrt on inner over 2f out : sn btn: hung rt fnl f* 11/1
0000 11 8 **Kinetic Power (IRE)**[29] 1192 3-8-11 58.... TQuinn 8 29
(D R C Elsworth) *pressed ldrs: wkng whn n.m.r 2f out* 33/1
4000 12 nk **The Struie**[15] 1547 3-9-3 64.... OscarUrbina 13 34
(Miss J R Gibney) *racd v wd: in tch tl wknd 3f out* 33/1

2m 7.08s (-0.71) **Going Correction** -0.15s/f (Stan) 12 Ran SP% **123.2**
Speed ratings (Par 97):96,92,92,91,90 88,88,87,85,83 77,77
CSF £18.15 CT £136.19 TOTE £2.90: £1.10, £2.70, £5.20; EX 16.80 Trifecta £301.70 Part won. Pool: £425.01 - 0.79 winning tickets..
Owner P D Savill **Bred** Mountgrange Stud Ltd **Trained** Patching, W Sussex

FOCUS
A moderate handicap, a shade above average for the grade, run at a fair gallop. The progressive winner is value for further.
Hazium(IRE) Official explanation: jockey said filly hung right throughout

1926 EDENBRIDGE H'CAP 1m 2f (P)
4:10 (4:16) (Class 6) (0-65,65) 4-Y-0+ £3,238 (£963; £481; £240) Stalls Low

Form RPR
443 1 **Lisathedaddy**[30] 1165 4-9-2 63.... GeorgeBaker 6 76
(B G Powell) *hld up wl in rr: stdy prog on outer wl over 2f out: led jst over 1f out: shkn up and r.o wl* 11/2[2]
5400 2 2 **Scutch Mill (IRE)**[21] 1380 4-9-3 64....(t) LDettori 14 73
(Karen George) *dwlt: hld up wl in rr: stdy prog on outer fr 3f out: led briefly over 1f out: outpcd by wnr fnl f* 20/1
0040 3 4 **Santando**[12] 1614 6-9-4 65....(b) RyanMoore 11 66
(C E Brittain) *drvn to chse ldr: led 1/2-way: kicked 3 l clr over 3f out: hdd and outpcd over 1f out* 7/1[3]
4050 4 1/2 **River Gypsy**[22] 1339 5-8-8 60.... StephanieHollinshead(5) 13 60
(D R C Elsworth) *t.k.h: trckd ldrs: rdn and fnd nil over 2f out: hanging over 1f out: kpt on fnl f* 33/1
0000 5 shd **Pittsburgh**[14] 1568 4-8-13 60.... RichardHughes 1 60
(A M Balding) *settled in midfield: drvn over 2f out: kpt on one pce over 1f out* 20/1
0060 6 1/2 **Piano Man**[158] 6594 4-8-13 60....(b[1]) PatDobbs 9 59
(J C Fox) *settled midfield: rdn over 2f out: one pce and nvr on terms w ldrs* 12/1
4562 7 shd **Night Storm**[105] 327 5-9-3 64.... ChrisCatlin 2 63+
(S Dow) *hld up wl in rr: trapped bhd wkng rival over 3f out: effrt on inner 2f out: styd on: nvr nr ldrs* 10/1
0350 8 1 **Duelling Banjos**[24] 1288 7-9-3 64.... TQuinn 12 61
(J Akehurst) *chsd ldng pair: rdn wl over 2f out: steadily wknd wl over 1f out* 9/1
3040 9 1 **Bishops Finger**[11] 1644 6-9-0 61....(b) SteveDrowne 10 56
(Jamie Poulton) *dwlt: hld up wl in rr: outpcd over 2f out: no ch after* 10/1
0060 10 hd **Whitgift Rock**[27] 1244 5-9-2 63.... IanMongan 4 58
(S Dow) *led to 1/2-way: drvn and outpcd by ldr over 3f out: wknd 2f out* 7/1[3]
3212 11 1 1/2 **Montjeu Baby (IRE)**[215] 5997 4-9-0 61.... JimmyFortune 7 53
(S Kirk) *settled in tch: rdn over 2f out: wknd* 15/2
600- 12 2 1/2 **Danakil**[606] 5764 11-8-11 65.... ThomasBubb(7) 3 52
(S Dow) *hld up in last: bmpd along and no prog over 2f out* 66/1
3601 13 7 **Thorny Mandate**[20] 1425 4-9-3 64.... StephenCarson 5 38
(R F Johnson Houghton) *trckd ldrs: rdn 4f out: wknd fr 3f out* 5/1[1]

2m 6.12s (-1.67) **Going Correction** -0.15s/f (Stan) 13 Ran SP% **118.6**
Speed ratings (Par 101):100,98,95,94,94 94,94,93,92,92 91,89,83
CSF £115.86 CT £786.36 TOTE £4.50: £2.20, £5.50, £2.70; EX 103.30 TRIFECTA Not won..
Owner Mrs Patricia Wilson **Bred** M Barrett **Trained** Morestead, Hants

FOCUS
A modest handicap which saw the first two come clear inside the final furlong. The winner was a notable improver and the overall form looks sound. The early pace was solid.
Thorny Mandate Official explanation: trainer's rep had no explanation for the poor form shown

1927 ARENA LEISURE PLC H'CAP 1m 4f (P)
4:40 (4:45) (Class 4) (0-85,83) 4-Y-0+ £6,477 (£1,927; £963; £481) Stalls Low

Form RPR
1-53 1 **Croon**[16] 1517 4-8-8 73.... SteveDrowne 6 85
(H Morrison) *trckd ldrs: effrt over 2f out and forced wd bnd sn after: drvn to ld 1f out: styd on wl* 5/1
2030 2 3/4 **Mandatum**[248] 5320 5-9-1 80.... NickyMackay 2 90
(L M Cumani) *trckd ldr for 3f: styd prom: effrt on inner and led briefly over 1f out: kpt on u.p but hld last 150yds* 7/2[2]
1422 3 hd **Prince Vector**[28] 1206 4-9-4 83.... EddieAhern 1 93
(A King) *hld up in 5th: rdn and effrt 2f out: styd on on fnl f: nt rch ldng pair* 2/1[1]
2603 4 4 **Mister Right (IRE)**[17] 1478 5-8-6 74.... NelsonDeSouza(3) 8 78
(D J S Ffrench Davis) *t.k.h: sn led: rdn 3f out: edgd rt and hdd over 1f out : sn btn* 14/1
1215 5 1 3/4 **Shaunas Vision (IRE)**[21] 1376 7-9-1 80.... SebSanders 5 81
(D K Ivory) *trckd ldr after 3f: drvn to chal over 2f out: wknd fnl f* 7/1
4100 6 4 **Cash On (IRE)**[25] 5764 4-8-7 72.... RichardHughes 4 66
(Karen George) *hld up in 6th: cajoled along and no rspnse 3f out: carried hd to one side and wl btn over 1f out* 25/1

0622 7 4 **Eastborough (IRE)**[10] 1690 7-8-8 **73** .... RyanMoore 3 61
(B G Powell) *dwlt: hld up in last and detached to 1/2-way: rdn 3f out: sn btn* **4/1**[3]

2m 31.38s (-3.01) **Going Correction** -0.15s/f (Stan) **7** Ran SP% **115.2**
Speed ratings (Par 105):104,103,103,100,99 96,94
CSF £23.15 CT £45.90 TOTE £6.70: £3.00, £3.90; EX 18.10 Trifecta £19.10 Pool: £619.63 - 22.95 winning tickets.
Owner de La Warr Racing **Bred** D J And Mrs Deer **Trained** East Ilsley, Berks

FOCUS
A fair handicap run at a decent pace and the form looks solid enough with the first three largely progressive and pulling clear.
Eastborough(IRE) Official explanation: jockey said gelding ran flat

1928 LINGFIELD-RACECOURSE.CO.UK H'CAP 5f (P)
5:10 (5:15) (Class 4) (0-85,84) 3-Y-0+ **£6,477** (£1,927; £963; £481) **Stalls** Low

Form RPR
4400 1 **The Jobber (IRE)**[108] 295 5-9-4 **82** .... TedDurcan 6 93
(M Blanshard) *trckd ldng pair: effrt to chal over 1f out: led last 150yds: styd on wl* **15/2**
-155 2 ¾ **Financial Times (USA)**[11] 1643 4-8-10 **74** .... SteveDrowne 4 82
(Stef Liddiard) *chsd ldr: clsd 2f out: rdn to ld over 1f out: hdd and one pce last 150yds* **8/1**
5026 3 1 **Zarzu**[57] 761 7-9-6 **84** .... RyanMoore 10 88
(C R Dore) *hld up and sn wl off the pce: prog on inner 2f out: styd on to take 3rd last 100yds: unable to chal* **7/1**
1150 4 nk **Stoneacre Boy (IRE)**[31] 1146 3-8-9 **81** ....(b) RobbieFitzpatrick 3 81
(Peter Grayson) *chsd ldrs: rdn 1/2-way: kpt on same pce fr over 1f out* **5/1**[2]
1010 5 ½ **Wicked Uncle**[10] 1662 7-9-2 **80** ....(v) JimmyFortune 2 82
(S Gollings) *mistimed s sltly: rdn in midfield 3f out: kpt on fr over 1f out: n.d* **5/1**[2]
0103 6 1 **Silver Dane (IRE)**[11] 1643 4-8-11 **75** ....(v) ChrisCatlin 5 73
(Mrs C A Dunnett) *off the pce in midfield: rdn 1/2-way: c wd bnd 2f out: no real imp* **12/1**
5040 7 ½ **No Time (IRE)**[5] 1795 6-8-11 **75** ....(p) LDettori 1 71
(M J Polglase) *led at fast pce: hdd & wknd over 1f out* **11/2**[3]
2006 8 1 **Azygous**[26] 1264 3-8-10 **82** .... TQuinn 7 72
(J Akehurst) *sn scrubbed along in last pair and hanging lft: nvr a factor* **10/1**
4666 9 3 **Intriguing Glimpse**[11] 1643 5-9-6 **84** .... SebSanders 9 66+
(Miss B Sanders) *lft s and lost 10 l: nvr rcvrd* **9/2**[1]

58.12 secs (-1.66) **Going Correction** -0.15s/f (Stan)
WFA 3 from 4yo+ 8lb **9** Ran SP% **119.1**
Speed ratings (Par 105):107,105,104,103,102 101,100,98,94
CSF £67.86 CT £446.62 TOTE £10.50: £3.40, £2.50, £2.10; EX 141.10 TRIFECTA Not won. Place 6 £405.17, Place 5 £210.19.
Owner Mrs R Wilkerson, Mrs J Breton & Partners **Bred** Dr T J Molony **Trained** Upper Lambourn, Berks

FOCUS
Not a bad sprint handicap and it was run at a strong pace. The form is solid.
Azygous Official explanation: jockey said gelding missed the break
Intriguing Glimpse Official explanation: jockey said mare anticipated start, jumped at gate, was rocked back and missed the break
T/Jkpt: Not won. T/Plt: £2,135.10 to a £1 stake. Pool: £65,810.00. 22.50 winning tickets. T/Qpdt: £23.50 to a £1 stake. Pool: £6,136.00. 192.50 winning tickets. JN

COMPIEGNE (L-H)
Tuesday, May 23

OFFICIAL GOING: Heavy

1929a PRIX DU FRANCPORT 1m 6f
2:20 (2:26) 4-Y-0+ **£8,276** (£3,310; £2,483; £1,655; £828)

RPR
1 **Trezene (USA)**[35] 1072 4-9-1 .... DBoeuf 9 103
(D Smaga, France)
2 6 **Biwa (FR)**[16] 5-8-11 .... YGourraud 7 91
(J-P Gallorini, France)
3 4 **The Devil (GER)**[216] 5992 4-9-1 .... DBonilla 6 90
(U Suter, France)
4 5 **Staramix (FR)**[18] 5-9-4 .... SPasquier 1 87
(E Lellouche, France)
5 2½ **Stradivari (USA)**[13] 4-8-11 .... ABonnefoy 8 77
(D Bressou, France)
6 5 **Bill Bennett (FR)**[14] 1562 5-8-11 .... MBlancpain 3 70
(J Jay) *raced in 4th, 5th halfway, ridden and beaten 3f out (8/1)* **8/1**[1]

3m 13.8s **6** Ran SP% **11.1**
PARI-MUTUEL (including 1 Euro stake): WIN 2.90; PL 1.90, 4.20;DF 16.70.
Owner Woodside Farms Llc **Bred** Edward Stephenson **Trained** Lamorlaye, France

NOTEBOOK
Bill Bennett(FR) has shown his best form on a testing surface in Britain, but found these conditions all too much.

1472 GOODWOOD (R-H)
Wednesday, May 24

OFFICIAL GOING: Good to soft (soft in places)
Wind: Strong, against Weather: Showers

1930 CASCO E B F MAIDEN FILLIES' STKS 6f
2:10 (2:10) (Class 4) 2-Y-0 **£5,343** (£1,589; £794; £396) **Stalls** Low

Form RPR
02 1 **Cavort (IRE)**[25] 1284 2-8-9 .... EmmettStack(5) 4 76
(Pat Eddery) *leggy: racd keenly: trckd ldrs: led jst over 1f out: edgd sltly lft ins fnl f: rdn out* **13/2**
3 2 nk **Baltic Belle (IRE)**[16] 1542 2-9-0 .... RichardHughes 6 75
(R Hannon) *str: lw: a.p: led over 2f out: hdd jst over 1f out: edgd sltly rt ins fnl f: r.o u.p* **3/1**[2]
6 3 1¾ **La Roca (IRE)**[37] 1046 2-8-11 .... NelsonDeSouza(3) 2 70
(R M Beckett) *leggy: led: hdd over 3f out: swtchd rt over 2f out: rallied over 1f out: no ex towards fin* **16/1**
5 4 1 **Harvest Joy (IRE)**[17] 1514 2-9-0 .... AlanMunro 1 67
(B R Millman) *leggy: s.i.s: sn trckd ldrs: rdn over 3f out: kpt on ins fnl f: nt pce to chal* **10/1**
5 1¼ **Bathwick Fancy (IRE)** 2-9-0 .... RyanMoore 7 63
(J G Portman) *leggy: swtchd lft jst after s: racd keenly: hld up: sme hdwy 2f out: eased whn no ex ins fnl f* **50/1**
6 6 **Fine Day** 2-9-0 .... MartinDwyer 3 45
(M P Tregoning) *w'like: str: bit bkwd: hld up: pushed along over 3f out: nvr trbld ldrs* **11/2**[3]
7 ½ **Majestic Roi (USA)** 2-9-0 .... TedDurcan 5 44
(M R Channon) *unf: scope: racd keenly: w ldr: led over 3f out: hdd over 2f out: wknd over 1f out* **13/8**[1]
8 1¼ **Spanish Air** 2-9-0 .... MichaelHills 8 40
(J W Hills) *w'like: hld up: outpcd over 2f out* **25/1**

1m 18.28s (5.43) **Going Correction** +0.725s/f (Yiel) **8** Ran SP% **112.6**
Speed ratings (Par 92):92,91,89,87,86 78,77,75
CSF £25.50 TOTE £6.50: £1.90, £1.20, £4.00; EX 15.80.
Owner Pat Eddery Racing (Lady Carla) **Bred** Tally-Ho Stud **Trained** Nether Winchendon, Bucks

FOCUS
An ordinary maiden for the course where the early pace was modest. Sound enough form on the face of it.

NOTEBOOK
Cavort(IRE) made her experience count, staying on well in the easy ground in the latter stages. She is likely to be a nursery sort by the end of the season and should get a bit further as well. (op 8-1)
Baltic Belle(IRE) travelled nicely for much of the race but found less off the bridle than looked likely. She can be given another chance over either the minimum distance or on a much sounder surface. (tchd 10-3)
La Roca(IRE) was not disgraced after making much of the running. This was the second time in a row that she has shown enough talent to pick up a race, and handicaps are likely to be her objective in time. (op 14-1)
Harvest Joy(IRE) ran much better than she had done on her debut, but looks to need more time. (op 9-1)
Bathwick Fancy(IRE) came with an effort two furlongs from home before not getting home. She is entitled to come on for her first racecourse effort and should be wiser next time.
Fine Day never got into the race at any stage and looks to have only minimal ability at the moment. However, she has the pedigree of a horse that should progress with racing, and might be worth another chance if given time. (op 5-1)
Majestic Roi(USA), quite an athletic type, did not shape too badly even though she was beaten a fair way. She travelled like a good horse until weakening quickly inside the final two furlongs, possibly finding the going testing enough for her - she has an American pedigree - and time may show she was one of the better fillies in this race. Official explanation: jockey said filly had no more to give (op 7-4 tchd 15-8 and 2-1 in places)

1931 INTERNATIONAL BUREAU OF AVIATION STKS (H'CAP) 2m
2:40 (2:41) (Class 3) (0-90,88) 4-Y-0+ **£8,420** (£2,505; £1,251; £625) **Stalls** Low

Form RPR
5502 1 **Hue**[11] 1685 5-8-4 **69** oh3........(b) KerrinMcEvoy 4 76
(B Ellison) *hld up: hdwy whn nt clr run over 2f out: sn swtchd rt: nt clr run again over 1f out: sn swtchd lft: led ins fnl f:* **8/1**
3-00 2 1¼ **San Hernando**[20] 182 6-7-13 **69** oh5........(v) JamesDoyle(5) 1 75
(Miss E C Lavelle) *trckd ldrs: rdn over 4f out: led over 1f out: hdd and edgd rt ins fnl f: nt qckn cl home* **10/1**
4144 3 1½ **Establishment**[28] 1247 9-8-12 **77** .... MartinDwyer 10 81
(C A Cyzer) *midfield: n.m.r and hmpd after 3f: nt clr run over 2f out: hdwy wl over 1f out: styd on ins fnl f* **9/1**
3010 4 ½ **Desert Island Disc**[11] 1690 9-8-4 **72** .... RichardThomas(3) 7 75
(Dr J R J Naylor) *midfield: hdwy whn nt clr run 3f out: swtchd lft over 1f out: styd on ins fnl f* **16/1**
0303 5 ½ **Salute (IRE)**[11] 1690 7-8-12 **77** .... TonyCulhane 9 83+
(P G Murphy) *trckd ldrs: n.m.r and hmpd after 3f: led over 2f out: hdd over 1f out: stl cl 3rd but u.p whn n.m.r* **12/1**
0632 6 3 **Theatre (USA)**[256] 5118 7-8-6 **71** .... JohnEgan 11 70
(Jamie Poulton) *lw: hld up: pushed along 5f out: hdwy over 3f out: one pce fr over 1f out* **5/1**[1]
20-4 7 1½ **Pretty Star (GER)**[17] 1511 6-9-9 **88** .... RichardHughes 2 85
(A King) *prom: rdn over 4f out: led 3f out: hdd over 2f out: wknd ins fnl f* **8/1**
/060 8 1½ **Global Challenge (IRE)**[29] 1213 7-8-4 **69** .... DavidKinsella 3 65
(P G Murphy) *hld up: pushed along bhd 7f out: kpt on fnl f: nvr trbld ldrs* **66/1**
0401 9 8 **Lewis Island (IRE)**[7] 1772 7-8-4 **68** 6ex........ FrancisNorton 8 55
(G L Moore) *hld up: n.m.r and hmpd after 3f: rdn and hdwy 4f out: wknd over 1f out* **7/1**[3]
1132 10 8 **Reggae Rhythm (IRE)**[79] 589 12-8-7 **75** .... AdamKirby(3) 13 51
(A J Lidderdale) *in tch: n.m.r and hmpd after 3f: rdn 3f out: wknd over 1f out* **11/1**
0352 11 7 **Simonda**[22] 1376 5-9-6 **85** .... RyanMoore 5 53
(Mrs A J Perrett) *trckd ldrs: rdn over 3f out: wknd 2f out:* **13/2**[2]
4003 12 10 **Double Obsession**[11] 1685 6-9-3 **82** ....(v) AdrianTNicholls 12 38
(D Nicholls) *led: rdn and hdd 3f out: wknd 2f out: sn eased* **9/1**
0004 13 84 **Ocean Of Storms (IRE)**[17] 1517 11-7-13 **71** oh2 ow2 MarkCoumbe(7) 6 —
(N I M Rossiter) *rel to r and s.v.s: a t.o* **66/1**

3m 39.44s (8.65) **Going Correction** +0.75s/f (Yiel) **13** Ran SP% **118.7**
Speed ratings (Par 107):108,107,106,106,106 104,103,103,99,95 91,86,44
CSF £85.13 CT £739.31 TOTE £10.50: £3.60, £3.60, £2.80; EX 165.20 Trifecta £514.50 Part won. Pool: £724.78 - 0.50 winning tickets..
Owner Mike Ashton **Bred** Juddmonte Farms **Trained** Norton, N Yorks

FOCUS
A messy staying handicap run at a slow early tempo. The form is not straight forward despite those immediately behind the front two running close to form.

NOTEBOOK
Hue was given an excellent waiting ride by his jockey and hardly knew he was in a race. This was his first success of any description and he may well need things to go his way to be at his best. Given that he was a maiden before the race, the form is probably not reliable in the short-term. (op 15-2)
San Hernando, who was given an ordinary ride over hurdles when last seen, does not look the most straightforward of characters, but kept on strongly enough after being vigorously ridden along turning for home. He is not an obvious candidate to reproduce this effort next time unless they can employ a jockey like Spencer or Hughes to switch him off until the last second. (op 12-1)
Establishment, the winner of the race 12 months ago off an 11lb lower mark, has been running consistently well still at the age of nine, so it was slightly disappointing that he could not pick up the front two given their profiles. However, he was giving them plenty of weight and looks sure to head to Royal Ascot again for one of the long-distance handicaps again. (op 10-1)

Desert Island Disc did not have the best of runs down the home straight and can be rated slightly better than her final position suggests. Official explanation: jockey said mare was denied a clear run 2f out

Salute(IRE) has yet to fully convince that he stays two miles on the Flat, but he shaped with promise all the same and would have finished a bit closer had he not been hampered by San Hernando inside the final furlong. (op 14-1)

Theatre(USA) has a good record at Goodwood, without winning, and held every chance before not getting home. He often runs his race but only has three career successes to his name and clearly finds getting his head in front difficult.

Simonda Official explanation: jockey said mare had no more to give

Double Obsession faded badly after pulling fairly hard in front and has not shown anywhere near the form he was once capable of. In fairness, though, he is better suited by a sounder surface and is one to keep an eye on for a handicap when the ground starts to get quicker, now his handicap mark has spiralled downwards. The Ascot Stakes at the Royal meeting would be the obvious next race for him, given that he won the race in 2004 off a similar mark. Official explanation: jockey said gelding had no more to give (op 7-1)

1932 BERNARD BENHAM BIRTHDAY STKS (H'CAP) 7f
3:15 (3:17) (Class 4) (0-80,79) 4-Y-0+ **£7,124** (£2,119; £1,059; £529) **Stalls** High

Form RPR

3012 **1** **Wavertree Warrior (IRE)**[29] [1207] 4-8-13 **79** .... JamesDoyle(5) 7 93
(N P Littmoden) *in tch: led over 1f out: drvn out* **9/2**[2]

2223 **2** 1 1/4 **Cross The Line (IRE)**[22] [1382] 4-8-11 **72** .... TPQueally 1 83
(A P Jarvis) *lw: hld up: hdwy over 2f out: chsd wnr 1f out: nt qckn towards fin* **15/2**

0020 **3** 3 **Selective**[21] [1422] 7-8-11 **72** .... (t) RyanMoore 11 75
(A W Carroll) *trckd ldrs: rdn over 2f out: kpt on same pce fnl f* **13/2**[3]

0021 **4** 1 **Blue Java**[6] [1802] 5-8-4 **70** .... TravisBlock(5) 4 70+
(H Morrison) *lw: hld up: hdwy whn nt clr run over 2f out: rdn whn n.m.r over 1f out: one pce ins fnl f* **2/1**[1]

0000 **5** 2 **Chateau Nicol**[85] [541] 7-9-0 **75** .... TedDurcan 6 70
(B G Powell) *in rr of main gp: rdn over 1f out: kpt on fnl f: nvr able to chal* **14/1**

P006 **6** 5 **Grizedale (IRE)**[18] [1474] 7-8-13 **74** .... (t) PaulDoe 5 56
(J Akehurst) *prom: rdn and ev ch over 1f out: wknd fnl f* **12/1**

6010 **7** shd **Lizarazu (GER)**[5] [1830] 7-8-10 **78** .... (p) TolleyDean(7) 9 60
(R A Harris) *prom: led over 2f out: rdn and hdd over 1f out: wknd fnl f* **14/1**

1000 **8** shd **Border Edge**[105] [343] 8-7-13 **65** oh1 .... (v) MarcHalford(5) 10 47
(J J Bridger) *led: rdn and hdd over 2f out: sn n.m.r whn wkng* **25/1**

0460 **9** 1/2 **Go Mo (IRE)**[16] [1545] 4-9-1 **76** .... MartinDwyer 2 56
(S Kirk) *hld up: pushed along 3f out: no imp* **20/1**

0060 **10** 38 **Corky (IRE)**[5] [1830] 5-8-9 **70** .... (b1) TonyCulhane 3 —
(I W McInnes) *rel to r and s.v.s: a wl bhd: t.o* **17/2**

1m 32.15s (4.11) **Going Correction** +0.75s/f (Yiel) **10** Ran SP% **116.8**
Speed ratings (Par 105):106,104,101,100,97 92,91,91,91,47
CSF £38.32 CT £224.21 TOTE £5.50: £2.20, £1.80, £2.40; EX 30.90.
Owner Wavertree Racing Partnership C **Bred** Liam Queally **Trained** Newmarket, Suffolk
■ Stewards' Enquiry : Tolley Dean caution: careless riding

FOCUS
An ordinary handicap, in which the time was slower than a seven-runner race later on the card. The first two came clear and the form has been rated through the runner-up, with the winner improving a few pounds.

Blue Java Official explanation: jockey said gelding was denied a clear run 2f out
Corky(IRE) Official explanation: jockey said gelding did not face the blinkers

1933 THOMAS EGGAR STKS (H'CAP) 1m 4f
3:45 (3:47) (Class 2) (0-100,96) 4-Y-0+
£11,217 (£3,358; £1,679; £840; £419; £210) **Stalls** Low

Form RPR

4630 **1** **Gavroche (IRE)**[68] [661] 5-9-2 **94** .... MartinDwyer 1 100
(J R Boyle) *stdd s: hld up in rr: hdwy 2f out: led ins fnl f: sn edgd lft: r.o* **10/1**

2342 **2** 3/4 **Nawamees (IRE)**[18] [1071] 8-8-11 **89** .... (p) RyanMoore 5 94
(G L Moore) *hld up in tch: rdn and nt qckn over 2f out: styd on strly towards fin* **11/4**[2]

0005 **3** 1 **Alfie Noakes**[14] [1585] 4-8-7 **85** .... KerrinMcEvoy 4 88
(Mrs A J Perrett) *lw led: rdn 1f out: hdd ins fnl f: no ex towards fin* **9/4**[1]

0000 **4** 1 1/4 **Massif Centrale**[17] [1511] 5-9-4 **96** .... (t) JohnEgan 3 97
(D R C Elsworth) *lw: a.p: rdn and ev ch 1f out: nt qckn ins fnl f* **8/1**

-3P6 **5** 5 **Diego Cao (IRE)**[28] [1239] 5-8-3 **86** .... JamesDoyle(5) 2 79
(Mrs N Smith) *hld up in tch: rdn over 2f out: wknd fnl f* **7/2**[3]

0405 **6** 14 **Favourita**[18] [1477] 4-8-12 **90** .... (t) MichaelHills 6 61
(J W Hills) *prom: rdn over 2f out: wknd over 1f out* **15/2**

2m 47.88s (8.96) **Going Correction** +0.75s/f (Yiel) **6** Ran SP% **111.6**
Speed ratings (Par 109):100,99,98,98,94 85
CSF £37.05 TOTE £11.80: £3.20, £1.80; EX 36.50.
Owner M Khan X2 **Bred** John O'Connor **Trained** Epsom, Surrey

FOCUS
This was spoilt by the lack of pace and the form is not that strong. The second sets the standard.

NOTEBOOK
Gavroche(IRE) looked to prove his effectiveness at the trip and did the job nicely after travelling well during the race. However, it must be worth noting that the time for the race was very slow and it appeared to turn into a sprint, so in the short term his stamina must still be open to question. He likes Epsom and there is a mile and a half handicap on Derby day that may well be his next port of call if the Handicapper does not overreact. (op 9-1)

Nawamees(IRE) got outpaced early in the straight, but fought back strongly late on to make the winner battle all the way to the line. The slow early tempo would not have suited him. (op 9-4)

Alfie Noakes had the run of the race but has yet to prove he stays a mile and a half and is still flying a bit high in the weights on his only piece of winning form. (op 5-2 tchd 11-4 in places)

Massif Centrale ran much better than he had done on his seasonal debut and shaped a bit more encouragingly. A more galloping track suits him better. (op 9-1)

Diego Cao(IRE) had his chance but was nowhere near good enough on the day. (op 9-2)

Favourita must be considered disappointing even though the pace was muddling. (op 13-2)

1934 LOVELLS STKS (H'CAP) 1m
4:20 (4:23) (Class 4) (0-85,80) 3-Y-0 **£7,124** (£2,119; £1,059; £529) **Stalls** High

Form RPR

3360 **1** **Zamala**[50] [880] 3-8-12 **74** .... MartinDwyer 1 82
(J L Dunlop) *trckd ldrs: rdn to ld over 1f out: sn edgd rt: r.o* **12/1**

432 **2** 1 1/2 **Incidentally (IRE)**[11] [1680] 3-9-4 **80** .... RyanMoore 7 84+
(R Hannon) *led: rdn and hdd over 1f out: nt qckn ins fnl f* **7/4**[1]

6523 **3** 1 **Follow The Colours (IRE)**[28] [1241] 3-8-7 **69** ow1 .... MichaelHills 4 71
(J W Hills) *lw: hld up in rr: rdn and hdwy over 1f out: lugged rt ins fnl f: styd on* **4/1**[3]

421 **4** hd **Lucky Token (IRE)**[54] [823] 3-8-12 **74** .... TedDurcan 3 76
(E A L Dunlop) *t.k.h: trckd ldrs: rdn over 2f out: styd on same pce fnl f* **10/1**

3206 **5** 2 1/2 **Semi Detached (IRE)**[21] [1401] 3-8-12 **77** .... AmirQuinn(3) 5 73
(J R Boyle) *hld up: rdn over 2f out: one pce fnl f* **12/1**

4002 **6** 1 **Glenmuir (IRE)**[15] [1569] 3-9-4 **80** .... AlanMunro 2 73
(B R Millman) *lw: prom: rdn over 2f out: wknd fnl f* **11/4**[2]

0010 **7** 3/4 **Fangorn Forest (IRE)**[4] [1843] 3-8-5 **74** .... (p) TolleyDean(7) 6 66
(R A Harris) *s.s: hld up: effrt 3f out: hung rt and wknd over 1f out* **16/1**

1m 46.28s (6.01) **Going Correction** +0.75s/f (Yiel) **7** Ran SP% **113.4**
Speed ratings (Par 101):99,97,96,96,93 92,92
CSF £32.98 TOTE £14.60: £4.70, £1.60; EX 46.20.
Owner Hamdan Al Maktoum **Bred** Shadwell Estate Company Limited **Trained** Arundel, W Sussex

FOCUS
A handicap that can produce winners. The third looks the best guide to the form.
Zamala Official explanation: trainer had no explanation for the improved form shown

1935 GOODWOOD AERO CLUB STKS (H'CAP) 7f
4:55 (4:55) (Class 3) (0-95,95) 3-Y-0+ **£9,715** (£2,890; £1,444; £721) **Stalls** High

Form RPR

2053 **1** **Polar Magic**[241] [5497] 5-9-6 **92** .... RyanMoore 6 106
(J R Fanshawe) *plld hrd: hld up: swtchd lft and hdwy 2f out: led 1f out: sn hung rt: r.o wl* **6/4**[1]

0200 **2** 3 1/2 **Material Witness (IRE)**[190] [6354] 9-9-2 **88** .... MartinDwyer 3 93
(W R Muir) *led: rdn and hdd 1f out: nt pce of wnr ins fnl f* **14/1**

3302 **3** nk **Binanti**[11] [1692] 6-8-13 **85** .... FrancisNorton 4 89
(P R Chamings) *a.p: rdn and ev ch whn n.m.r and hmpd 1f out: kpt on* **11/1**

4342 **4** nk **Red Spell (IRE)**[12] [1659] 5-9-7 **93** .... RichardHughes 2 96
(R Hannon) *lw: in tch: effrt and cl 4th whn n.m.r and hmpd 1f out: kpt on* **3/1**[2]

0002 **5** 2 **Shot To Fame (USA)**[12] [1629] 7-9-5 **91** .... AdrianTNicholls 7 89
(D Nicholls) *prom: rdn and ev ch over 1f out: wknd ins fnl f* **5/1**[3]

0360 **6** 3/4 **Marshman (IRE)**[179] [6431] 7-8-10 **85** .... SaleemGolam(3) 5 81
(M H Tompkins) *rrd s and slowly away: a bhd* **13/2**

-640 **7** shd **Stagbury Hill (USA)**[368] [1892] 4-9-9 **95** .... MichaelHills 1 91
(J W Hills) *hld up: rdn 2f out: no imp* **33/1**

1m 31.39s (3.35) **Going Correction** +0.75s/f (Yiel) **7** Ran SP% **112.9**
Speed ratings (Par 107):110,106,105,105,103 102,102
CSF £23.82 TOTE £2.30: £1.60, £3.40; EX 28.60.
Owner R C Thompson **Bred** Cheveley Park Stud Ltd **Trained** Newmarket, Suffolk

FOCUS
A good handicap won in emphatic style by favourite Polar Magic and best rated around the second and fourth.

NOTEBOOK
Polar Magic did not really progress as once anticipated last season, but he was well supported for this reappearance on his favoured ground and, despite pulling hard in the early stages, he came through with a strong run to win going away. He may be capable of fulfilling his potential this season and could develop into a Pattern peformer with a little further progression. (op 13-8 tchd 7-4 in places)

Material Witness(IRE) did not have the best of seasons last year, but this was a bright start and it was only the very useful winner that he found too strong. He is likely to remain difficult to place, but capable when there is some cut in the ground.

Binanti has been in decent form since the turn of the year and this was another sound effort. He was bumped when a bit short of room over a furlong out, but it did not affect his winning chance. (op 10-1)

Red Spell(IRE) is a consistent performer in good handicaps and, although only fourth here, he was not beaten far. His rating will continue to make winning difficult, but he should at least continue to pay his way. (op 7-2)

Shot To Fame(USA), although running well in defeat on his latest start, again looked vulnerable off this sort of mark and he probably needs some further assistance from the Handicapper before being able to win again. (op 4-1)

Marshman(IRE) held claims on this reappearance, but he reared at the gate and lost several lengths, effectively ending his chance. Official explanation: jockey said gelding reared as gates opened (op 6-1 tchd 7-1)

Stagbury Hill(USA) faced a stiff task under top weight on this reappearance, especially with the ground being soft, but he was not beaten all that far, despite finishing last, and a little assistance from the Handicapper would make him interesting.

1936 GOODWOOD FLYING SCHOOL STKS (H'CAP) 5f
5:30 (5:30) (Class 2) (0-100,96) 3-Y-0+
£11,217 (£3,358; £1,679; £840; £419; £210) **Stalls** Low

Form RPR

0400 **1** **The Lord**[13] [1602] 6-9-8 **92** .... TonyCulhane 3 108
(W G M Turner) *s.s due to late removal of blindfold: in rr: hdwy 2f out: led over 1f out: r.o wl* **9/2**[2]

0000 **2** 2 1/2 **Night Prospector**[18] [1475] 6-9-0 **84** .... GylesParkin 1 91+
(G L Moore) *hld up in rr: hdwy whn nt clr run and swtchd rt 2f out: wnt 2nd 1f out: nt pce of wnr* **14/1**

6360 **3** hd **If Paradise**[11] [1663] 5-9-12 **96** .... (b1) RichardHughes 2 102
(R Hannon) *hld up in tch bhd ldrs: rdn and hdwy over 1f out: styd on ins fnl f* **8/1**

1315 **4** 2 **Angel Sprints**[237] [5575] 4-9-5 **89** .... AlanMunro 9 88
(B R Millman) *cl up: rdn and ev ch over 1f out: no ex ins fnl f* **11/1**

0004 **5** hd **Smokin Beau**[14] [1597] 9-8-10 **85** .... JamesDoyle(5) 8 83
(N P Littmoden) *in tch: rdn over 1f out: nt pce to chal* **8/1**

0003 **6** 1/2 **Enchantment**[6] [1803] 5-9-4 **88** .... (p) RyanMoore 4 85
(J M Bradley) *in tch: rdn 2f out: wknd over 1f out* **4/1**[1]

0260 **7** hd **Golden Dixie (USA)**[18] [1474] 7-8-9 **86** .... TolleyDean(7) 7 82
(R A Harris) *lw: racd freely: cl up: rdn over 1f out: wknd fnl f* **17/2**

0011 **8** 3/4 **Peopleton Brook**[12] [1643] 4-9-5 **89** .... TedDurcan 5 82
(J M Bradley) *lw: prom: led over 2f out: rdn and hdd over 1f out: sn wknd* **6/1**

1201 **9** 6 **Trinculo (IRE)**[6] [1803] 9-9-9 **93** 7ex .... AdrianTNicholls 6 65
(D Nicholls) *lw: led: hdd over 2f out: sn hung rt: wknd over 1f out* **11/2**[3]

61.26 secs (2.21) **Going Correction** +0.725s/f (Yiel) **9** Ran SP% **115.6**
Speed ratings (Par 109):111,107,106,103,103 102,102,100,91
CSF £64.78 CT £386.54 TOTE £5.80: £2.00, £4.10, £2.40; EX 84.50 Place 6 £265.58, Place 5 £111.29.
Owner Mrs M S Teversham **Bred** Mrs M S Teversham **Trained** Sigwells, Somerset
■ Stewards' Enquiry : Richard Hughes one-day ban: used whip with excessive frequency (Jun 4)

FOCUS
A competitive sprint handicap likely to produce winners. The first two, who came from off the pace, had finished second and third in this race last year and the form should prove reliable.

NOTEBOOK
The Lord, who has always gone well with some cut in the ground, did not get the start he wanted because his rider was slow to remove his blind, but it may have done him a favour in the end as he came through strongly from off the pace to win going away. (op 11-2)
Night Prospector has been out of sorts for some time and, until now, had failed to improve for a switch to current connections, but the change in tactics brought about an improved effort and he was a little unlucky not to get closer to the winner. He is a winner waiting to happen, but is far from certain to reproduce the effort. (tchd 12-1)
If Paradise showed a bit more in the first-time blinkers and a return to more aggressive tactics is likely to help in future. (op 17-2)
Angel Sprints will no doubt have delighted connections with this seasonal return and natural progression should see her going close in a decent sprint handicap. (tchd 10-1 and 12-1)
Smokin Beau ran as well as could have been expected and is beginning to look a little long in the tooth to be winning races such as this. (tchd 17-2)
Enchantment was the major disappointment of the race as, following a highly pleasing effort when second at York last week, she failed to race as sweetly on this occasion and could only plug on at the one pace having been unable to lead. (op 9-2 tchd 7-2)
Golden Dixie(USA), still 13lb higher than when last successful, raced too enthusiastically for his own good and failed to see his race out as a result. (tchd 8-1 and 9-1)
Peopleton Brook has been on a roll but this further 5lb rise proved beyond him. (op 13-2)
Trinculo(IRE), who beat Enchantment into second last week, failed to see his race out on this occasion, and the way he stopped suggested something may have been amiss. Official explanation: vet said gelding returned lame right-fore (op 9-2 tchd 4-1)
T/Plt: £197.70 to a £1 stake. Pool: £64,604.70. 238.50 winning tickets. T/Qpdt: £28.30 to a £1 stake. Pool: £3,622.10. 94.55 winning tickets. DO

1909 KEMPTON (A.W) (R-H)
Wednesday, May 24

OFFICIAL GOING: Standard
Wind: Fresh, half-against

1937 BOOK NOW FOR WEDNESDAY EVENING 7TH JUNE H'CAP — 5f (P)
2:20 (2:22) (Class 6) (0-65,65) 3-Y-O — **£3,238** (£963; £481; £240) **Stalls** High

Form — RPR
0052 **1** **Fantasy Explorer**[25] 1304 3-8-12 **59** ... GrahamGibbons 6 — 71
(J J Quinn) *hung lft early: wnt 2nd 1/2-way: rdn to ld over 1f out: jst hld on* **4/1**[1]
4523 **2** *nk* **Light Mozart**[5] 1825 3-9-1 **62** ... EddieAhern 7 — 73
(C E Brittain) *a in tch: rdn to go 2nd 1f out: r.o and clsng on wnr post* **9/2**[2]
6211 **3** *2 1/2* **Sarah's Art (IRE)**[13] 1612 3-9-2 **63** ... (b) ChrisCatlin 11 — 65
(N A Callaghan) *mid-div: rdn over 1f out: r.o to go 3rd wl ins fnl f: no ch w first 2* **9/2**[2]
3016 **4** *1* **Twinned (IRE)**[25] 1304 3-9-4 **65** ... (p) JamieSpencer 4 — 63
(J S Moore) *led tl rdn and hdd over 1f out: fdd ins fnl f* **11/1**
2200 **5** *nk* **Shunkawakhan (IRE)**[203] 6226 3-9-4 **65** ... OscarUrbina 8 — 62
(G C H Chung) *hld up: rdn and hdwy over 1f out: one pce after* **16/1**
0304 **6** *3/4* **Danish Blues (IRE)**[26] 1272 3-9-4 **65** ... (p) IanMongan 12 — 60
(N P Littmoden) *t.k.h: hld up: sme hdwy over 1f out: nvr nr to chal* **16/1**
4350 **7** *hd* **Thoughtsofstardom**[8] 1751 3-8-13 **60** ... HayleyTurner 5 — 54
(P S McEntee) *in rr: mde sme late hdwy* **20/1**
8 *shd* **Sarah's Prince (IRE)**[224] 5840 3-8-9 **56** ow1 ... DaneO'Neill 1 — 50
(D K Ivory) *bhd: rdn 1/2-way: nvr on terms* **40/1**
2050 **9** *1* **Musical Romance (IRE)**[16] 1551 3-9-2 **63** ... LDettori 10 — 53
(B J Meehan) *trckd ldr to 1/2-way: wknd over 1f out* **11/2**[3]
6000 **10** *hd* **Supreme Kiss**[227] 5755 3-9-4 **65** ... SebSanders 3 — 54
(Miss B Sanders) *slowly away: a bhd* **14/1**
4400 **11** *1 3/4* **Diktatorship (IRE)**[12] 1640 3-8-13 **60** ... DarryllHolland 9 — 43
(Miss Gay Kelleway) *s.i.s: a bhd* **12/1**
003 **12** *1/2* **Diamond World**[17] 1513 3-9-1 **62** ... ShaneKelly 2 — 43
(C A Horgan) *in tch: rdn 2f out: sn btn* **20/1**
60.28 secs **Going Correction** -0.075s/f (Stan) — 12 Ran SP% **118.2**
Speed ratings (Par 97):97,96,92,90,90 89,88,88,87,86 84,83
CSF £20.93 CT £86.32 TOTE £5.20: £1.50, £1.90, £1.90; EX 36.50.
Owner The Fantasy Fellowship E **Bred** Sexton Enterprises **Trained** Settrington, N Yorks
FOCUS
A competitive if modest sprint handicap which was dominated by those that raced handily.
Musical Romance(IRE) Official explanation: jockey said filly ran too free to post

1938 WEDNESDAY EVENING SERIES H'CAP — 7f (P)
2:55 (2:56) (Class 4) (0-85,84) 4-Y-O+
£7,790 (£2,332; £1,166; £583; £291; £146) **Stalls** High

Form — RPR
1114 **1** **Spectait**[293] 4101 4-9-4 **84** ... SebSanders 1 — 109+
(Sir Mark Prescott) *hld up: shkn up and str hdwy to ld over 1f out: sn clr: v easily* **4/1**[2]
4000 **2** *6* **Desert Dreamer (IRE)**[11] 1667 5-9-0 **80** ... GeorgeBaker 5 — 89
(P R Chamings) *slowly away: wl bhd tl weaved way through on ins fr 2f out to go 2nd to v easy wnr ins fnl f* **11/1**
0003 **3** *3/4* **Irony (IRE)**[11] 1692 7-9-3 **83** ... JamieSpencer 7 — 90
(A M Balding) *chsd ldrs: outpcd 2f out: kpt on fnl f* **8/1**
3105 **4** *1 3/4* **Glad Big (GER)**[21] 1410 4-9-2 **82** ... SteveDrowne 11 — 85
(J A Osborne) *squeezed out s: in rr tl hdwy over 1f out: nvr nrr* **9/1**
0303 **5** *nk* **Ali Bruce**[68] 659 6-8-11 **77** ... (p) IanMongan 3 — 79
(G L Moore) *t.k.h: settled in mid-div: sme late hdwy: nvr on terms* **33/1**
3315 **6** *1 1/2* **Glencalvie (IRE)**[137] 64 5-8-12 **78** ... (v) TQuinn 6 — 76
(J Akehurst) *trckd ldrs tl rdn 2f out: sn outpcd* **20/1**
2111 **7** *nk* **Fajr (IRE)**[11] 1676 4-9-2 **82** ... LDettori 10 — 79
(Miss Gay Kelleway) *wnt rt s: hld up: rdn over 2f out: sme late hdwy* **3/1**[1]
1400 **8** *nk* **Call Me Max**[27] 1262 4-9-0 **80** ... JimmyFortune 2 — 76
(E A L Dunlop) *mid-div: nvr on terms* **33/1**
6002 **9** *shd* **Kabeer**[83] 559 8-8-10 **76** ... (t) RichardMullen 13 — 72
(P S McEntee) *led after 2f: hung lft and hdd over 1f out: wknd qckly* **33/1**
2011 **10** *3 1/2* **Raza Cab (IRE)**[58] 764 4-8-10 **76** ... DarryllHolland 8 — 63
(Karen George) *a towards rr* **6/1**[3]
0323 **11** *1 1/2* **Outer Hebrides**[23] 1340 5-9-3 **83** ... (tp) EddieAhern 14 — 66
(Stef Liddiard) *s.i.s: a bhd* **11/1**
1441 **12** *1 3/4* **Quantum Leap**[22] 1382 9-8-7 **73** ... (v) JimmyQuinn 12 — 51
(S Dow) *prom tl rdn and wknd 2f out* **20/1**
0220 **13** *13* **Te Quiero**[33] 1112 8-9-2 **82** ... (t) ShaneKelly 4 — 27
(Miss Gay Kelleway) *led for 2f: wknd wl over 2f out: sn wl bhd* **50/1**
1m 24.69s **Going Correction** -0.075s/f (Stan) — 13 Ran SP% **117.4**
Speed ratings (Par 105):109,102,101,99,98 97,96,96,96,92 90,88,73
CSF £42.03 CT £350.64 TOTE £3.70: £1.70, £3.50, £3.10; EX 87.70.
Owner Edward S A Belcher **Bred** B Tait **Trained** Newmarket, Suffolk
FOCUS
This looked a decent-quality handicap on paper and the form should work out, and with several front runners in opposition a strong pace was assured. Unlike in the opener, the way this race was run suited those held up.
Fajr(IRE) Official explanation: jockey said gelding ran flat
Te Quiero Official explanation: jockey said gelding had no more to give

1939 RACING UK H'CAP — 6f (P)
3:25 (3:26) (Class 4) (0-85,85) 4-Y-O+
£7,790 (£2,332; £1,166; £583; £291; £146) **Stalls** High

Form — RPR
1346 **1** **Algharb**[243] 5438 4-9-2 **83** ... RHills 1 — 99+
(W J Haggas) *hld up in rr: hdwy on outside over 1f out: r.o to ld nr fin* **9/1**
-000 **2** *hd* **First Order**[18] 1475 5-9-3 **84** ... RobertWinston 5 — 93
(Ernst Oertel) *hld up in rr: hdwy over 1f out: rdn and led ins fnl f: hdd nr fin* **33/1**
0000 **3** *3/4* **Folga**[14] 1597 4-9-2 **83** ... MickyFenton 10 — 90
(J G Given) *plld hrd in mid-div: effrt over 1f out: r.o ins fnl f* **33/1**
5120 **4** *1/2* **Idle Power (IRE)**[18] 1487 8-9-3 **84** ... LDettori 7 — 90
(J R Boyle) *sn led: rdn and hdd ins fnl f: no ex* **4/1**[1]
-005 **5** *1/2* **Purus (IRE)**[18] 1475 4-9-0 **81** ... DarryllHolland 4 — 85
(P Mitchell) *prom: chsd ldr 1/2-way tl wknd ins fnl f* **9/1**
0405 **6** *1 1/4* **Jayanjay**[28] 1236 7-8-13 **80** ... TQuinn 9 — 80
(Miss B Sanders) *nvr bttr than mid-div: kpt on one pce ins fnl 2f* **12/1**
3012 **7** *shd* **Adantino**[22] 1382 7-8-9 **76** ... (b) DaneO'Neill 3 — 76
(B R Millman) *in tch: rdn over 2f out: wknd appr fnl f* **11/1**
0042 **8** *1/2* **Prince Tum Tum (USA)**[14] 1597 6-9-4 **85** ... FergalLynch 12 — 83
(D W Barker) *in rr: effrt 2f out: sn btn* **13/2**
0660 **9** *1* **Silent Storm**[18] 1474 6-8-8 **75** ... ChrisCatlin 2 — 70
(C A Cyzer) *a in rr: nvr on terms* **25/1**
0030 **10** *1/2* **Blue Tomato**[15] 1570 5-8-12 **79** ... JamieSpencer 8 — 73
(J M Bradley) *t.k.h: ev ch 2f out: edgd rt: wknd ins fnl f* **16/1**
1335 **11** *2 1/2* **Rezzago (USA)**[85] 541 6-8-10 **77** ... SebSanders 11 — 83+
(W R Swinburn) *prom tl bdly hmpd on ins over 1f out: nt rcvr* **11/2**[3]
0003 **12** *9* **Gifted Gamble**[5] 1835 4-9-4 **85** ... (b) DO'Donohoe 6 — 44
(K A Ryan) *squeezed out s: nvr got into r* **9/2**[2]
1m 13.33s **Going Correction** -0.075s/f (Stan) — 12 Ran SP% **118.5**
Speed ratings (Par 105):99,98,97,96 94,94,93,92,91 88,76
CSF £278.23 CT £9127.46 TOTE £11.70: £3.00, £5.10, £5.70; EX 213.20.
Owner Hamdan Al Maktoum **Bred** D R Botterill **Trained** Newmarket, Suffolk
FOCUS
A competitive sprint handicap, but something of a rough race. Despite that the form looks sound with the third and fourth to form.
Jayanjay Official explanation: jockey said gelding was denied a clear run
Adantino Official explanation: jockey said gelding hung right
Prince Tum Tum(USA) Official explanation: jockey said gelding was denied a clear run

1940 DAY TIME, NIGHT TIME, GREAT TIME MAIDEN STKS — 1m 4f (P)
4:00 (4:00) (Class 4) 3-Y-O — **£5,505** (£1,637; £818; £408) **Stalls** Centre

Form — RPR
03 **1** **Hasayaz (IRE)**[21] 1421 3-9-3 ... RobertWinston 2 — 82+
(Sir Michael Stoute) *mid-div: hdwy 4f out: hung lft on bnd over 3f out: rallied and wnt 2nd over 1f out: rdn to ld wl ins fnl f* **6/4**[2]
02 **2** *1/2* **Ermine Sea**[13] 1613 3-9-3 ... JimmyFortune 6 — 81
(J H M Gosden) *led after 1f: rdn and kpt on whn hdd wl ins fnl f* **11/8**[1]
54 **3** *1 1/4* **Monets Masterpiece (USA)**[225] 5821 3-9-3 ... (b[1]) SebSanders 8 — 79
(Mrs A J Perrett) *t.k.h: prom: wnt 2nd briefly 2f out: one pce fnl f* **5/1**[3]
4 *11* **Ship Mate (IRE)**[13] 1619 3-8-12 ... MCHussey 4 — 61+
(Eamon Tyrrell, Ire) *wnt 2nd after 3f: rdn and wknd 2f out* **20/1**
50 **5** *nk* **Fondness**[9] 1741 3-8-12 ... SteveDrowne 10 — 56
(R Charlton) *led for 1f: prom tl wknd over 2f out* **25/1**
6 *1 1/2* **Raffiene (IRE)** 3-8-12 ... RichardMullen 5 — 54
(E J O'Neill) *mid-div: reminders after 2f: rdn and wknd wl over 2f out* **50/1**
6 **7** *2* **Galibard (IRE)**[17] 1516 3-9-3 ... LDettori 1 — 55
(A M Balding) *s.i.s: a bhd* **20/1**
06 **8** *3* **Project Sunshine (GER)**[11] 1691 3-9-3 ... ShaneKelly 9 — 59+
(J A Osborne) *hld up: rdn 4f out: sn lost pl* **50/1**
00 **9** *1* **Vettori Dancer**[13] 1613 3-8-12 ... JamieMackay 7 — 44
(G G Margarson) *a bhd* **100/1**
10 *58* **Sansel** 3-8-5 ... DonnaCaldwell[(7)] 3 — —
(J Ryan) *a in rr: lost tch 4f out: t.o:* **100/1**
2m 36.92s **Going Correction** -0.075s/f (Stan) — 10 Ran SP% **118.0**
Speed ratings (Par 101):96,95,94,87,87 86,84,82,82,43
CSF £3.69 TOTE £2.70: £1.30, £1.30, £1.60; EX 4.30.
Owner H H Aga Khan **Bred** His Highness The Aga Khan's Studs S C **Trained** Newmarket, Suffolk
FOCUS
Some big stables were represented in this maiden and the first three pulled miles clear of the others. They probably all have a future and the placed horses set the standard.

1941 TRAVEL BY TRAIN FROM WATERLOO H'CAP — 1m (P)
4:35 (4:35) (Class 6) (0-65,65) 3-Y-O — **£3,238** (£963; £481; £240) **Stalls** High

Form — RPR
603 **1** **Lii Najma**[20] 1430 3-9-1 **62** ... SebSanders 6 — 71
(C E Brittain) *hld up: hdwy on outside over 2f out: hrd rdn to ld post* **7/1**
6030 **2** *shd* **Emily's Place (IRE)**[23] 1344 3-9-4 **65** ... RHills 2 — 74
(M H Tompkins) *towards rr tl hdwy on ins over 2f out: short of room and swtchd lft over 1f out: rdn to ld ins fnl f: hdd post* **16/1**
520 **3** *3* **Ten Shun**[51] 855 3-9-3 **64** ... RobertWinston 11 — 66
(P D Evans) *hld up: hdwy on ins over 2f out: ev ch 1f out: one pce ins fnl f* **10/1**
0305 **4** *hd* **Davidia (IRE)**[32] 1141 3-9-1 **62** ... JimmyFortune 4 — 64
(S Kirk) *trckd ldrs: wnt 2nd 3f out: ev ch 1f out: no ex ins fnl f* **9/2**[1]
0043 **5** *1* **Miss Wedge**[16] 1547 3-9-3 **64** ... IanMongan 3 — 63
(T G Mills) *trckd ldrs: led over 4f out: rdn and hdd ins fnl f: no ex* **8/1**
5426 **6** *hd* **Murrumbidgee (IRE)**[12] 1652 3-9-1 **62** ... (v[1]) EddieAhern 14 — 61
(J W Hills) *mid-div: rdn over 2f out: kpt on one pce* **13/2**[3]
0530 **7** *3* **Golden Sprite**[228] 5733 3-9-3 **64** ... DaneO'Neill 9 — 56
(B R Millman) *bhd: sme hdwy 2f out: nvr on terms* **20/1**
405 **8** *nk* **Eagle Eye**[12] 1640 3-9-1 **62** ... SteveDrowne 8 — 53
(G Wragg) *mid-div: no hdwy fnl 2f* **6/1**[2]
000 **9** *1* **Storm Of Arabia (IRE)**[238] 5541 3-9-2 **63** ... OscarUrbina 13 — 52
(W R Swinburn) *s.i.s: nvr on terms* **20/1**
6025 **10** *3* **Welcome Releaf**[60] 735 3-9-2 **63** ... TQuinn 1 — 45
(G C H Chung) *a in rr* **20/1**

0060 **11** *3* **Kick And Prance**[42] 993 3-9-0 **61**.....(t) StephenCarson 10 36
(J A Geake) *prom tl lost pl over 3f out: sn in rr* **25/1**

0521 **12** *2 1/2* **Titus Lumpus (IRE)**[42] 984 3-9-0 **61**..... FergusSweeney 7 30
(R M Flower) *led tl hdd over 4f out: wknd over 2f out* **8/1**

0050 **13** *4* **Smokey Blue**[42] 993 3-8-12 **64**..... DerekNolan(5) 5 24
(M J Wallace) *slowly away: a bhd* **25/1**

203 **14** *3/4* **Pantomime Prince**[16] 1550 3-9-0 **61**..... GeorgeBaker 12 19
(C A Dwyer) *hld up: a bhd* **11/1**

1m 40.26s **Going Correction** -0.075s/f (Stan) **14** Ran SP% **125.8**
Speed ratings (Par 97):99,98,95,95,94 94,91,91,90,87 84,81,77,76
CSF £108.56 CT £1163.71 TOTE £6.90: £2.50, £3.70, £3.00; EX 126.90.
Owner Saeed Manana **Bred** Zubieta Ltd **Trained** Newmarket, Suffolk

FOCUS
A very moderate handicap containing several maidens including those at the top of the weights. There were five in a line across the track a furlong out, but the front two eventually pulled clear and the form looks sound rated through the fourth and fifth.

Eagle Eye Official explanation: jockey said colt had no more to give
Titus Lumpus(IRE) Official explanation: jockey said gelding hung left

1942 KEMPTON PARK FILLIES' CONDITIONS STKS 1m 4f (P)
5:10 (5:10) (Class 2) 3-Y-O **£11,217** (£3,358; £1,679; £840; £419) **Stalls** Centre

Form RPR
1 **1** **Alessandria**[239] 5534 3-8-12 85..... LDettori 2 104+
(E A L Dunlop) *hld up: hdwy over 3f out: led 2f out: qcknd clr: kpt up to work tl eased wl ins fnl f: easily* **13/8**[2]

3 **2** *1 3/4* **Park Esteem (IRE)**[17] 1509 3-8-12..... DarryllHolland 4 97
(J Noseda) *t.k.h: sn trckd ldr: led briefly over 2f out: kpt on but sn outpcd by wnr* **10/11**[1]

10 **3** *12* **Off Message (IRE)**[14] 1583 3-8-12 80.....(b[1]) EddieAhern 1 78
(E A L Dunlop) *led after 2f: rdn and hdd over 2f out: sn wknd* **9/1**[3]

50 **4** *30* **Overlook**[207] 6145 3-8-12..... JamieSpencer 6 30
(A M Balding) *led for 1f: rdn over 4f out: sn lost tch* **20/1**

10 **5** *10* **Hosiva (GER)**[227] 5787 3-8-12..... TPQueally 5 14
(M G Quinlan) *t.k.h: hld up: lost tch over 3f out* **33/1**

2m 34.32s **Going Correction** -0.075s/f (Stan) **5** Ran SP% **108.2**
Speed ratings (Par 102):105,103,95,75,69
CSF £3.29 TOTE £2.30: £1.20, £1.10; EX 3.10.
Owner Gainsborough Stud **Bred** Gainsborough Stud Management Ltd **Trained** Newmarket, Suffolk

FOCUS
A very interesting conditions event, but margins between the five runners at the line normally associated with three-mile chasers. The winning time was 2.6 seconds quicker than the earlier maiden and the winner looks capable of going on to better things.

NOTEBOOK
Alessandria ◆, off for eight months since her debut victory, quickened up really well to leave the favourite standing. The form of her win last season has already produced winners and the fact that she won this so well, despite being expected to come on for the race, bodes very well for the future. She is in the Ribblesdale, but it remains to be seen if she takes up that option. (op 2-1 tchd 6-4)
Park Esteem(IRE) was popular in the market following her encouraging debut in the Pretty Polly, but after having seemed to travel well she was made to look woefully one-paced by the winner. It must be a case of back to the drawing board now. (op 4-6 tchd 8-13)
Off Message(IRE) was allowed a soft lead, but was eventually swamped by the front two. She has now been well and truly found out twice in better company since making a winning debut on the Wolverhampton Polytrack and needs her sights lowering. (op 10-1)
Overlook found this company far too hot following her seven-month absence. (op 16-1)
Hosiva(GER), racing in this country for the first time after two outings in Italy at two, was well and truly put in her place. (op 25-1)

1943 SPONSOR AT KEMPTON H'CAP 1m 4f (P)
5:40 (5:41) (Class 4) (0-85,84) 4-Y-O+
£7,790 (£2,332; £1,166; £583; £291; £146) **Stalls** Centre

Form RPR
-360 **1** **Mudawin (IRE)**[23] 1357 5-9-2 **82**..... JohnEgan 5 92
(Jane Chapple-Hyam) *mid-div: hdwy over 1f out: r.o u.p to ld nr fin* **20/1**

0006 **2** *3/4* **Given A Choice (IRE)**[17] 1511 4-9-4 **84**..... RobertWinston 3 93
(J G Given) *sn trckd ldr: led over 2f out: strly rdn: hdd nr fin* **20/1**

3133 **3** *shd* **Nobelix (IRE)**[252] 5220 4-8-8 **74** ow2..... JamieSpencer 2 83
(J R Fanshawe) *a.p: ev ch 1f out tl no ex nr fin* **6/1**[3]

4533 **4** *1 3/4* **Modaffaa**[6] 1809 6-8-12 **78**..... DaneO'Neill 1 84
(P R Webber) *stdd s fr outside draw: sn in tch: effrt 2f out: styd on fnl f* **9/2**[2]

5532 **5** *5* **Dovedon Hero**[23] 1339 6-8-4 **70** oh3.....(b) RichardMullen 11 68
(P J McBride) *slowly away: in rr tl kpt on past btn horses ins fnl 2f* **14/1**

3115 **6** *1 1/4* **Annibale Caro**[287] 4253 4-8-12 **78**..... SebSanders 4 74
(Sir Mark Prescott) *mid-div: rdn over 2f out: no hdwy after* **15/8**[1]

0502 **7** *1* **Ocean Avenue (IRE)**[18] 1478 7-8-10 **76**..... LDettori 10 70
(C A Horgan) *led tl hdd over 2f out: wknd over 1f out* **10/1**

2101 **8** *1* **Stretton (IRE)**[12] 1631 8-8-6 **72**..... TQuinn 6 65
(J D Bethell) *in rr: rdn 3f out: nvr on terms* **6/1**[3]

5004 **9** *shd* **Dower House**[22] 1380 11-9-2 **82**.....(t) ChrisCatlin 9 75
(Andrew Turnell) *a bhd: brief effrt 2f out* **14/1**

4446 **10** *8* **Yankeedoodledandy (IRE)**[214] 5437 5-8-0 **73**..... LukeMorris(7) 7 53
(C Roberts) *in rr: rdn 3f out: lost tch 2f out* **25/1**

3000 **11** *1 1/2* **Crail**[21] 1422 6-8-11 **77**..... EddieAhern 8 54
(C F Wall) *in tch tl wknd over 2f out* **25/1**

0205 **12** *6* **Hawridge Star (IRE)**[37] 1051 4-8-8 **74** ow1..... DarryllHolland 12 42
(W S Kittow) *trckd ldr tl rdn and wknd over 3f out* **16/1**

2m 34.02s **Going Correction** -0.075s/f (Stan) **12** Ran SP% **127.1**
Speed ratings (Par 105):106,105,105,104,100 100,99,98,98,93 92,88
CSF £375.62 CT £2701.54 TOTE £38.90: £7.70, £4.70, £2.80; EX 296.30 Place 6 £233.63, Place 5 £152.81.
Owner Franconson Partners **Bred** Shadwell Estate Company Limited **Trained** Newmarket, Suffolk

FOCUS
A decent pace for this handicap and the fastest of the three races over the trip on the day. The form should prove sound with the fourth a reliable guide.

Dovedon Hero Official explanation: trainer said gelding finished distressed
Stretton(IRE) Official explanation: jockey said gelding was unsuited by the slow pace and needed a stronger gallop

T/Jkpt: Not won. T/Plt: £211.60 to a £1 stake. Pool: £48,207.65. 166.25 winning tickets. T/Qpdt: £35.40 to a £1 stake. Pool: £2,700.80. 56.40 winning tickets. JS

1749 SAINT-CLOUD (L-H)
Wednesday, May 24

OFFICIAL GOING: Very soft

1944a PRIX DE PONTARME (LISTED) (C&G) 1m
2:05 (2:13) 3-Y-O **£17,241** (£6,897; £5,172; £3,448; £1,724)

RPR
1 **Indianski (IRE)**[16] 3-8-11..... OPeslier 1 106
(C Laffon-Parias, France)

2 *1/2* **Major Grace (FR)**[31] 1178 3-8-11..... TThulliez 6 105
(Mme J Laurent-Joye Rossi, France)

3 *1* **Chief Commander (FR)**[10] 1715 3-8-11..... IMendizabal 5 103
(Jane Chapple-Hyam) *racd in 2nd, pushed along to chal str, rdn and not pass ldr 1 1/2f out, stayed on at one pace (34-10)* **34/10**[1]

4 *hd* **Reve Lunaire (USA)**[32] 1131 3-8-11..... TJarnet 4 103
(A Fabre, France)

5 *shd* **Auzi (FR)**[66] 3-8-11..... SPasquier 2 102
(X Thomas-Demeaulte, France)

6 *shd* **Fenice (IRE)**[10] 1718 3-8-11..... C-PLemaire 3 102
(Robert Collet, France)

1m 47.2s **6** Ran SP% **22.7**
PARI-MUTUEL: WIN 4.20; PL 2.10, 3.60; SF 37.50.
Owner Wertheimer Et Frere **Bred** Wertheimer Et Frere **Trained** Chantilly, France

NOTEBOOK
Chief Commander(FR), totally unsuited by the early lack of pace, was settled in second place soon after the start before making an effort early in the straight and staying on gamely. He should win a race like this in the future, but is now to be rested after a busy start to the season.

1528 AYR (L-H)
Thursday, May 25

OFFICIAL GOING: Soft (heavy in places)
Wind: Fresh; half against

1945 TENNENTS LAGER MAIDEN AUCTION STKS 6f
2:20 (2:21) (Class 4) 2-Y-O **£5,801** (£1,712; £856) **Stalls** High

Form RPR
0 **1** **Blue Madeira**[24] 1342 2-8-9..... TomEaves 1 70
(Mrs L Stubbs) *hld up last: rdn 1/2-way: effrt outside over 1f out: led wl ins fnl f: hld on wl* **50/1**

2 *hd* **Orpen Prince (IRE)** 2-8-12..... DO'Donohoe 7 72+
(K A Ryan) *missed break: bhd tl hdwy and swtchd lft over 1f out: styd on wl fnl f: jst hld* **12/1**[3]

3 *nk* **Kay Gee Be (IRE)** 2-8-12..... KFallon 6 72
(D J Daly) *dwlt: sn niggled in tch: hdwy to ld over 1f out: hdd and no ex wl ins fnl f* **1/1**[1]

6 **4** *shd* **Rosbay (IRE)**[15] 1595 2-8-11..... GrahamGibbons 8 70+
(T D Easterby) *trckd ldrs on ins: effrt whn hmpd over 1f out: sn swtchd lft: kpt on strly fnl f* **14/1**

0 **5** *2 1/2* **Eddie Jock (IRE)**[15] 1588 2-9-0..... DarryllHolland 3 66
(M L W Bell) *cl up: effrt and ev ch over 1f out: sn rdn and btn* **14/1**

22 **6** *2* **Voodoo Moon**[26] 1295 2-8-5..... KDarley 5 51
(M Johnston) *unruly in paddock: led tl hdd and no ex over 1f out* **5/2**[2]

7 *10* **Todwick Owl** 2-8-10..... MickyFenton 4 26
(J G Given) *dwlt: rn green in rr: effrt outside over 2f out: sn wknd* **12/1**[3]

6 **8** *4* **Red Flare (IRE)**[23] 1372 2-8-11..... TonyCulhane 2 15
(M R Channon) *pressed ldr: rdn over 2f out: sn btn* **25/1**

1m 19.48s (5.81) **Going Correction** +0.775s/f (Yiel) **8** Ran SP% **113.1**
Speed ratings (Par 95):92,91,91,91,87 85,71,66
CSF £531.59 TOTE £45.10: £6.30, £3.10, £1.10; EX 287.70.
Owner D M Smith **Bred** Barry Minty **Trained** Norton, N. Yorks

FOCUS
A mixed bag on looks and, with about half a length covering the first four home, this bare form looks nothing special.

NOTEBOOK
Blue Madeira, who lacks in physical scope, turned in a much-improved effort on this second start on his first run on soft ground. He won with little to spare and, although he should stay seven, is likely to prove vulnerable under a penalty.
Orpen Prince(IRE) ◆, related to winners over a variety of distances, took the eye in the paddock as a strong sort with scope and, although looking as though the run would do him good, showed more than enough after fluffing the start to suggest he can win a similar event at the very least. (op 16-1 tchd 20-1 in places)
Kay Gee Be(IRE), who is related to several winners, looked on the leg but fit for this racecourse debut. He attracted plenty of support under Fallon and showed enough to suggest he can win a similar event. (op 5-4 tchd 11-8 in places)
Rosbay(IRE) ◆, who showed ability on his racecourse debut, bettered that and looked unlucky as he was hampered when asked for his effort. He stuck on in a manner that suggested seven furlongs would suit and he looks sure to win a similar event. (op 10-1)
Eddie Jock(IRE), who has little in the way of physical scope, bettered the form of his debut effort but left the impression that he is likely to remain vulnerable in this type of event. (op 12-1)
Voodoo Moon had looked sure to be suited by the step up to this trip but, after getting very fractious in the paddock, proved the disappointment of the race and folded tamely once headed. She has had a few chances now. (op 2-1 tchd 11-4 in places)
Todwick Owl was well beaten in the end but took the eye in the preliminaries, despite looking as though in need of the run, and showed ability. He has plenty of scope and is likely to leave this form a fair way behind in due course. (op 11-1 tchd 14-1 in places)

1946 COCA COLA RATING RELATED MAIDEN STKS 1m 2f
2:50 (2:50) (Class 5) 3-Y-O+ **£5,505** (£1,637; £818; £408) **Stalls** Low

Form RPR
4323 **1** **Deutschland (USA)**[10] 1740 3-8-12 68.....(p) PhilipRobinson 3 83
(M A Jarvis) *mde all: qcknd 3f out: kpt on wl: unchal* **11/8**[1]

0502 **2** *12* **Apt To Run (USA)**[10] 1732 3-8-12 70.....(b) SebSanders 7 63
(E A L Dunlop) *hld up: smooth hdwy over 4f out: chsd wnr over 3f out: sn rdn and hung lft: no imp fr 2f out* **9/2**[3]

4405 **3** *8* **Summer Lodge**[12] 1681 3-8-12 68..... DarryllHolland 5 49
(M H Tompkins) *prom: effrt and edgd lft over 3f out: sn no ex* **4/1**[2]

0424 **4** *11* **My Lovely Lady (IRE)**[22] 1419 3-8-2 70..... ChrisHough(7) 1 27
(M L W Bell) *trckd ldrs: outpcd 4f out: no ch after* **7/1**

2534 **5** *12* **Grey Outlook**[17] [1530] 3-8-9 65 .... RoystonFfrench 9 — 7
(Miss L A Perratt) *bhd: drvn and outpcd 1/2-way: sme hdwy over 2f out: nvr on terms* **20/1**

003 **6** *25* **Azurine (IRE)**[17] [1530] 3-8-9 67 .... JoeFanning 4 — —
(M Johnston) *chsd ldr tl wknd fr 4f out* **12/1**

0040 **7** *2 ½* **Nimrana Fort**[38] [1044] 3-8-12 66 .... PaulHanagan 6 — —
(I Semple) *chsd ldrs: drvn over 4f out: sn btn* **14/1**

0400 **8** *7* **Sparkbridge (IRE)**[3] [1888] 3-8-12 58 .... PaulMulrennan 8 — —
(R F Fisher) *in tch tl rdn and wknd fr 4f out* **66/1**

0000 **9** *54* **Borsch (IRE)**[17] [1530] 4-9-12 30 .... PatCosgrave 2 — —
(Miss L A Perratt) *bhd and sn struggling: t.o fr 1/2-way* **200/1**

2m 20.26s (8.54) **Going Correction** +0.975s/f (Soft)
WFA 3 from 4yo 14lb — 9 Ran SP% **113.9**
Speed ratings (Par 103):104,94,88,79,69 49,47,42,—
CSF £7.47 TOTE £2.30: £1.10, £1.80, £1.60; EX 6.80.
Owner Jumeirah Racing **Bred** Darley **Trained** Newmarket, Suffolk

FOCUS
An uncompetitive event in which the winner had the run of the race but nevertheless turned in an improved display.

1947 RED SQUARE VODKA H'CAP — 1m

3:25 (3:26) (Class 6) (0-60,60) 4-Y-0+ — **£3,238** (£963; £481; £240) **Stalls** Low

Form — RPR

0006 **1** **Inch High**[18] [1500] 8-8-4 **46** oh5 .... PaulHanagan 4 — 57
(J S Goldie) *keen: prom: effrt and led appr fnl f: pushed out ins last* **16/1**

1120 **2** *3* **Mystical Ayr (IRE)**[17] [1531] 4-8-11 **58** .... AndrewMullen(5) 11 — 63
(Miss L A Perratt) *chsd ldrs: led 2f out to appr fnl f: one pce ins last* **11/2**[3]

0021 **3** *2* **Bijou Dan**[26] [1305] 5-8-5 **52** .... (b) DuranFentiman(5) 3 — 53
(W G Harrison) *hld up: hdwy over 2f out: kpt on fnl f: nt rch first two* **9/1**

5163 **4** *shd* **Thornaby Green**[9] [1764] 5-7-11 **46** .... DeanHeslop(7) 5 — 47
(T D Barron) *prom: effrt over 2f out: kpt on fnl f: no imp* **5/1**[2]

5000 **5** *4* **Pride Of Kinloch**[20] [1465] 6-8-10 **55** ow2 .... (p) DNolan(3) 9 — 48
(N Wilson) *cl up tl rdn and outpcd fr wl over 1f out* **40/1**

3640 **6** *¾* **Gem Bien (USA)**[28] [1253] 8-8-8 **50** .... (p) TonyCulhane 2 — 41
(D W Chapman) *midfield: effrt outside over 2f out: no imp over 1f out* **9/1**

1263 **7** *2 ½* **Time To Regret**[19] [1480] 6-8-13 **55** .... TonyHamilton 8 — 41
(J S Wainwright) *led tl hdd 2f out: sn btn* **7/2**[1]

0050 **8** *2* **Star Sign**[227] [5790] 4-8-4 **46** oh6 .... DaleGibson 12 — 28
(D W Barker) *chsd ldrs tl rdn and wknd over 2f out* **100/1**

0501 **9** *3* **Jordans Spark**[201] [5979] 5-8-5 **47** .... DO'Donohoe 7 — 23
(P Monteith) *bhd: pushed along 1/2-way: nvr rchd ldrs* **10/1**

3005 **10** *1 ½* **Mercari**[14] [1608] 4-8-4 **46** oh2 .... GrahamGibbons 1 — 19
(Mrs J C McGregor) *hld up ins: drvn 3f out: sn btn* **33/1**

2430 **11** *11* **Charlie Tango (IRE)**[31] [1187] 5-9-2 **58** .... JoeFanning 13 — 9
(D W Thompson) *hld up on outside: drvn over 2f out: sn btn* **12/1**

3000 **12** *hd* **Barataria**[18] [1500] 4-9-4 **60** .... RoystonFfrench 10 — 11
(R Bastiman) *bhd: drvn over 3f out: sn btn* **14/1**

0440 **13** *33* **In Rhubarb**[302] [3850] 4-8-4 **46** oh5 .... PaulQuinn 6 — —
(D Nicholls) *bhd: drvn over 3f out: wknd* **20/1**

1m 50.86s (7.37) **Going Correction** +0.975s/f (Soft) — 13 Ran SP% **114.7**
Speed ratings (Par 101):102,99,97,96,92 92,89,87,84,83 72,71,38
CSF £95.00 CT £881.35 TOTE £22.90: £5.70, £1.90, £2.70; EX 102.10.
Owner J S Goldie **Bred** Jim Goldie **Trained** Uplawmoor, E Renfrews

FOCUS
An ordinary event and, although the gallop was just fair, those racing prominently held the edge. The form is modest with the runner-up the best guide.

1948 SMIRNOFF VODKA H'CAP — 1m 2f

3:55 (3:55) (Class 4) (0-80,78) 3-Y-0 — **£8,096** (£2,408; £1,203; £601) **Stalls** Low

Form — RPR

4046 **1** **Norman Beckett**[58] [781] 3-8-6 **66** .... TomEaves 1 — 71
(I Semple) *keen early: trckd ldrs: drvn over 4f out: rallied 3f out: led ent fnl f: styd on wl* **16/1**

0325 **2** *7* **Chronomatic**[19] [1476] 3-8-13 **73** .... DarryllHolland 5 — 66
(M H Tompkins) *sn drvn towards rr: hdwy outside over 3f out: kpt on fnl f: nt rch wnr* **5/1**[1]

3401 **3** *1 ¾* **Secret Liaison**[17] [1530] 3-9-1 **75** .... SebSanders 2 — 65+
(Sir Mark Prescott) *led: clr over 3f out: hdd ent fnl f: sn btn* **5/1**[1]

3061 **4** *hd* **King's Revenge**[17] [1552] 3-9-1 **75** .... GrahamGibbons 3 — 65
(T D Easterby) *hld up ins: effrt 4f out: no imp fr 2f out* **6/1**[2]

0450 **5** *12* **Hill Of Almhuim (IRE)**[17] [1547] 3-8-10 **70** .... (p) PatCosgrave 4 — 39
(K R Burke) *chsd ldrs: lost pl over 4f out: sn rdn and n.d after* **10/1**

4413 **6** *40* **Shaydreambeliever**[242] [5489] 3-8-11 **71** .... PaulHanagan 8 — —
(R A Fahey) *bhd: drvn over 5f out: nvr on terms* **5/1**[1]

10 **7** *14* **Lucky Lark**[61] [730] 3-9-4 **78** .... KDarley 6 — —
(M Johnston) *sn bhd and rdn along: no ch fr 1/2-way* **10/1**

5500 **8** *½* **Orange Stravinsky**[15] [1596] 3-8-7 **67** .... DaleGibson 10 — —
(P C Haslam) *prom tl rdn and wknd fr over 3f out* **33/1**

2202 **9** *3* **Zaharath Al Bustan**[13] [1635] 3-8-12 **72** .... TonyCulhane 7 — —
(M R Channon) *chsd ldrs tl wknd over 3f out* **11/1**

6103 **10** *51* **Ransom Strip (USA)**[38] [1044] 3-8-9 **69** .... JoeFanning 9 — —
(M Johnston) *cl up tl lost pl over 4f out: t.o* **7/1**[3]

2m 22.77s (11.05) **Going Correction** +0.975s/f (Soft) — 10 Ran SP% **112.1**
Speed ratings (Par 101):94,88,87,86,77 45,34,33,31,—
CSF £90.57 CT £462.49 TOTE £21.50: £4.40, £1.80, £1.60; EX 79.80.
Owner Robert Reid **Bred** Mike Channon Bloodstock Ltd **Trained** Carluke, S Lanarks

FOCUS
An ordinary event and a fair gallop but a surprise winner, who was showing much-improved form in the conditions. The runner-up looks the best guide to the form.
Zaharath Al Bustan Official explanation: jockey said filly was unsuited by the soft (good to soft places) ground

1949 MAGNER'S IRISH CIDER H'CAP — 6f

4:30 (4:30) (Class 3) (0-90,88) 4-Y-0+ — **£11,658** (£3,468; £1,733; £865) **Stalls** High

Form — RPR

2310 **1** **Commando Scott (IRE)**[6] [1835] 5-9-2 **86** .... FergalLynch 7 — 99
(I W McInnes) *cl up: led over 1f out: pushed out ins fnl f* **7/1**

0002 **2** *1 ¾* **Rising Shadow (IRE)**[6] [1835] 5-9-4 **88** .... PaulHanagan 3 — 96
(T D Barron) *bhd: hdwy over 1f out: wnt 2nd ins fnl f: nt rch wnr* **3/1**[1]

1402 **3** *3 ½* **Raymond's Pride**[5] [1858] 6-8-8 **83** .... (b) AndrewMullen(5) 8 — 80
(K A Ryan) *keen: led to over 1f out: one pce fnl f* **4/1**[2]

3631 **4** *2* **Indian Spark**[17] [1528] 12-8-4 **74** oh4 .... JoeFanning 2 — 65
(J S Goldie) *midfield: effrt over 2f out: no imp over 1f out* **12/1**

0035 **5** *½* **Royal Challenge**[19] [1474] 5-8-6 **76** .... DarryllHolland 10 — 66
(M H Tompkins) *in tch: effrt and rdn over 2f out: no imp over 1f out* **7/1**

0133 **6** *9* **Paris Bell**[5] [1858] 4-8-7 **77** .... PaulQuinn 4 — 40
(T D Easterby) *keen: chsd ldrs tl rdn and wknd wl over 1f out* **6/1**[3]

1510 **7** *2* **Local Poet**[62] [719] 5-8-4 **74** oh1 .... (bt) RoystonFfrench 9 — 31
(I Semple) *bhd: drvn 1/2-way: nvr rchd ldrs* **25/1**

0626 **8** *9* **Glaramara**[62] [718] 5-8-11 **81** .... MickyFenton 5 — 11
(A Bailey) *cl up tl rdn and wknd 2f out* **16/1**

1126 **9** *3* **Byron Bay**[20] [1456] 4-9-0 **84** .... TomEaves 1 — 5
(I Semple) *in tch on outside tl wknd over 2f out* **7/1**

0000 **10** *9* **Queen's Lodge (IRE)**[201] [6248] 6-8-11 **81** .... TonyHamilton 6 — —
(J S Wainwright) *bhd and sn outpcd: no ch fr 1/2-way* **33/1**

1m 16.94s (3.27) **Going Correction** +0.775s/f (Yiel) — 10 Ran SP% **117.1**
Speed ratings (Par 107):109,106,102,99,98 86,84,72,68,56
CSF £28.42 CT £98.84 TOTE £10.60: £3.10, £1.50, £2.00; EX 42.20.
Owner Mrs Ann Morris **Bred** Noel Finegan **Trained** Catwick, E Yorks

FOCUS
Exposed performers in this fair handicap. The field raced stands' side and those racing prominently held the edge. The runner-up, backed up by the third, sets the standard.

NOTEBOOK
Commando Scott(IRE) proved disappointing at York last week but comprehensively reversed placings with the runner-up, who was just touched off on the Knavesmire. Essentially consistent, he goes on most ground and should continue to give a good account. (op 13-2)
Rising Shadow(IRE) invariably gives himself plenty to do but was far from disgraced in a race where it paid to race close to the pace. He is the type that needs things to fall just right and, as such, is not really one to place maximum faith in.
Raymond's Pride had plenty in his favour regarding ground, trip, draw and current form and ran creditably, despite proving a shade keen early on. He should continue to go well away from progressive sorts when getting his favoured soft ground . (op 3-1)
Indian Spark, who broke a long losing run over course and distance last time, was found out from this 14lb higher mark in this better race. Although not disgraced, he is the type that needs things to fall just right.
Royal Challenge has little margin for error from this mark and a modest recent wins-to-runs ratio but again left the impression that the return to seven furlongs would be in his favour. (tchd 15-2)
Paris Bell was closely matched with Raymond's Pride on last weekend's Thirsk form and had conditions to suit but ran poorly after jumping off on terms this time. He has never been the most predictable. (op 7-1)
Byron Bay attracted support dropped to this trip for the first time since his debut but, although well beaten, will be of more interest from a better draw returned to seven furlongs next time. (op 14-1 tchd 16-1)

1950 BLACK BOTTLE SCOTCH WHISKY H'CAP — 7f 50y

5:05 (5:06) (Class 6) (0-65,67) 3-Y-0 — **£3,238** (£963; £481; £240) **Stalls** Low

Form — RPR

011 **1** **Moody Tunes**[5] [1859] 3-9-7 **67** 5ex .... PatCosgrave 3 — 85+
(K R Burke) *trckd ldrs on ins: nt clr run over 2f out: led over 1f out: pushed clr fnl f: eased towards fin* **5/4**[1]

0642 **2** *5* **Wednesdays Boy (IRE)**[17] [1549] 3-8-6 **52** .... PaulMulrennan 14 — 51
(P D Niven) *hld up: hdwy on outside to ld over 2f out: hdd over 1f out: kpt on: no ch w wnr* **16/1**

006 **3** *3 ½* **Pappas Ruby (USA)**[20] [1458] 3-8-4 **50** oh12 .... JoeFanning 6 — 41
(J S Goldie) *trckd ldrs: effrt and ev ch over 2f out: no ex over 1f out* **100/1**

0630 **4** *hd* **Noble Nova**[15] [1593] 3-8-9 **55** .... TonyCulhane 13 — 45
(M R Channon) *bhd: rdn 1/2-way: hdwy over 2f out: kpt on fnl f: no imp* **20/1**

0053 **5** *nk* **Boy Dancer (IRE)**[15] [1593] 3-8-7 **53** .... TomEaves 8 — 42
(D W Barker) *hld up in tch: effrt over 2f out: kpt on fnl f: nvr rchd ldrs* **13/2**[3]

6001 **6** *5* **Jordan's Light (USA)**[3] [1888] 3-9-4 **64** 5ex .... KFallon 9 — 41
(T J Pitt) *sn drvn towards rr: hdwy on outside over 2f out: edgd lft: nvr able to chal* **10/3**[2]

0600 **7** *1* **The Dunion**[13] [1635] 3-8-0 **51** oh10 ow1 .... AndrewMullen(5) 1 — 26
(Miss L A Perratt) *led to over 2f out: sn rdn and btn* **66/1**

4300 **8** *1 ¾* **Next Ness (IRE)**[27] [1274] 3-8-8 **54** .... RoystonFfrench 5 — 25
(R F Fisher) *in tch tl wknd over 2f out* **66/1**

5000 **9** *8* **Paddy Moon**[22] [1416] 3-8-9 **55** .... MickyFenton 10 — 7
(J G Given) *chsd ldrs tl wknd over 2f out* **66/1**

3000 **10** *5* **Tiptoeing**[22] [1416] 3-9-4 **64** .... DarryllHolland 2 — 4
(M H Tompkins) *s.i.s: sn midfield: effrt over 2f out: sn btn* **16/1**

000 **11** *¾* **Bacharach (IRE)**[15] [1592] 3-9-0 **60** .... PaulHanagan 11 — —
(R F Fisher) *hld up ins: short-lived effrt on ins over 2f out: wknd* **33/1**

0000 **12** *3* **King Of Chav's (IRE)**[29] [1232] 3-8-6 **52** .... DaleGibson 7 — —
(A Bailey) *towards rr: drvn over 3f out: sn btn* **16/1**

0606 **13** *14* **Gifted Glori**[21] [1441] 3-8-4 **50** oh1 .... GrahamGibbons 12 — —
(J J Quinn) *towards rr: drvn 1/2-way: nvr on terms* **25/1**

063 **14** *nk* **Postage (USA)**[27] [1274] 3-8-9 **55** .... (p) DO'Donohoe 4 — —
(K A Morgan) *keen: cl up tl wknd qckly over 3f out* **25/1**

1m 40.42s (7.70) **Going Correction** +0.975s/f (Soft) — 14 Ran SP% **119.4**
Speed ratings (Par 97):95,89,85,85,84 79,77,75,66,61 60,56,40,40
CSF £23.11 CT £1434.32 TOTE £2.50: £1.10, £4.60, £9.20; EX 33.40 Place 6 £44.57, Place 5 £27.24.
Owner Geoffrey Hamilton **Bred** Llety Stud **Trained** Middleham Moor, N Yorks

FOCUS
A modest bunch but another improved effort from Moody Tunes, who is in tremendous form. The pace was just fair and the form does not look rock-solid.
T/Plt: £60.30 to a £1 stake. Pool: £46,913.60. 567.30 winning tickets. T/Qpdt: £18.80 to a £1 stake. Pool: £3,148.40. 123.30 winning tickets. RY

1930 GOODWOOD (R-H)

Thursday, May 25

OFFICIAL GOING: Soft
Wind: Light across Weather: Fine

1951 SEALINE STKS (HERITAGE H'CAP) — 1m 1f

2:10 (2:13) (Class 2) (0-105,93) 3-Y-0
£28,044 (£8,397; £4,198; £2,101; £1,048; £526) **Stalls** High

Form — RPR

3452 **1** **Layazaal (IRE)**[18] [1505] 3-9-7 **93** .... RHills 8 — 99
(J L Dunlop) *hld up in rr: hdwy 2f out: r.o to ld last stride* **5/1**[2]

3333 **2** *hd* **Multakka (IRE)**[24] [1337] 3-8-11 **83** .... MartinDwyer 5 — 89
(M P Tregoning) *racd keenly: midfield: hdwy 4f out: rdn 2f out: led narrowly over 1f out: hdd last stride* **10/1**

6311 **3** *nk* **Night Crescendo (USA)**[34] [1115] 3-9-5 **91** .... RyanMoore 6 — 96
(Mrs A J Perrett) *lw: hld up: hdwy 4f out: rdn and nt qckn whn nt clr run over 2f out: swtchd lft over 1f out: r.o towards fin* **5/1**[2]

0216 **4** *hd* **Airbuss (IRE)**[14] 1615 3-8-5 77 ChrisCatlin 10 82
(M R Channon) *hld up: rdn and hdwy over 2f out: ev ch ins fnl f: nt qckn last strides* **17/2**[3]

0165 **5** *3* **Champions Gallery**[13] 1626 3-9-6 92 TQuinn 7 91
(D R C Elsworth) *lw: racd keenly: trcked ldrs: rdn and ev ch ent fnl f: sn no ex* **9/1**

615 **6** *½* **Punta Galera (IRE)**[251] 5271 3-9-3 89 RichardHughes 9 87
(R Hannon) *led: hdd 3f out: rdn and stl ev ch over 1f out: fdd ins fnl f* **20/1**

2113 **7** *½* **High Command**[5] 1841 3-9-3 89 JamieSpencer 4 86
(E A L Dunlop) *prom: led 3f out: sn rdn: hdd over 1f out: fdd ins fnl f* **15/8**[1]

1545 **8** *9* **Fiddlers Wood**[19] 1473 3-8-11 86 (v) AdamKirby(3) 1 65
(V Smith) *hld up: rdn 3f out: sn btn* **33/1**

0554 **9** *½* **Blu Manruna**[171] 6501 3-7-12 70 oh6 (b) DavidKinsella 3 48
(J Akehurst) *racd keenly: prom: lost pl 3f out: n.m.r over 2f out: struggling after* **66/1**

3353 **10** *45* **Tumbleweed Glory (IRE)**[27] 1270 3-8-5 77 (b[1]) AlanMunro 2 —
(B J Meehan) *plld hrd: cl up: lost pl 3f out: bhd after: t.o* **12/1**

2m 3.60s (6.74) **Going Correction** +0.775s/f (Yiel) 10 Ran SP% **114.6**
Speed ratings (Par 105):101,100,100,100,97 97,96,88,88,48
CSF £51.82 CT £262.12 TOTE £6.70: £1.80, £2.20, £2.10; EX 35.10 Trifecta £145.10 Pool: £1,042.64 - 5.10 winning units.
Owner Hamdan Al Maktoum **Bred** Mrs Anne Marie Burns **Trained** Arundel, W Sussex

FOCUS
The field tacked over to the stands' rail in the home straight as they often do in soft conditions. The race cannot be rated too highly with the field finishing in something of a heap off the modest pace, but this is usually a good race and the form should prove sound.

NOTEBOOK
Layazaal(IRE), second to subsequent winner Levera last time, went one better with a last-gasp victory over this longer trip. Improving from the rear in the straight, he was stuck behind a wall of five opponents heading to the furlong pole but he ran on well when free to get up on the line. (tchd 11-2)
Multakka(IRE), carrying the second colours of Hamdan Al Maktoum, took a narrow lead over a furlong out and, after edging to his right and carrying his head slightly high, he was just touched off. He is not straightforward but his turn will come. (op 11-1)
Night Crescendo(USA) was 6lb higher than when making a winning reappearance on very different ground at Newbury. He came home in good style once switched to the stands' rail for a run and saw out this slightly longer trip well. (tchd 11-2)
Airbuss(IRE), back down in trip, was in there fighting inside the last but had to settle for fourth place in the end. He loses little in defeat. (op 8-1 tchd 9-1)
Champions Gallery, whose maiden win last term came on firm ground, was battling for the lead approaching the furlong pole but did not quite see out this longer trip. (op 17-2)
Punta Galera(IRE), who had ground conditions against him on this return to action, tried to make all but was collared early in the home straight and gradually faded out of contention. (op 22-1 tchd 25-1)
High Command took over as the field tacked over in the straight and was able to grab the stands' rail, but he could not hold off a host of challenges going to the last. This might have come too soon for him. Official explanation: trainer said colt was unsuited by the soft (heavy in places) ground (tchd 85-40 in places and 9-4 in places)
Blu Manruna, returning from a 171-day break, looked fit enough but had not quite come in his coat. He travelled quite well but did not find much in the straight. (tchd 100-1)
Tumbleweed Glory(IRE) Official explanation: jockey said gelding was unsuited by the soft (heavy in places) ground

1952 PETERS PLC STKS (REGISTERED AS THE ACHILLES STAKES) (LISTED RACE) 5f
2:40 (2:40) (Class 1) 3-Y-O+ **£17,034** (£6,456; £3,231; £1,611) **Stalls** Low

Form RPR
4001 **1** **The Lord**[1] 1936 6-9-3 92 JohnEgan 4 108
(W G M Turner) *trckd ldrs: led over 1f out: edgd lft ins fnl f: r.o* **9/2**[3]

6613 **2** *1 ¼* **Green Manalishi**[14] 1602 5-9-3 100 LDettori 2 106+
(D W P Arbuthnot) *lw: hld up: swtchd rt and hdwy over 1f out: sn chsd wnr: ev ch ins fnl f: nt qckn towards fin* **9/2**[3]

3201 **3** *2* **Corridor Creeper (FR)**[12] 1663 9-9-3 108 (p) ShaneKelly 1 97
(J M Bradley) *w ldr: ev ch wl over 1f out: kpt on same pce fnl f* **11/10**[1]

3500 **4** *12* **Fire Up The Band**[37] 1069 7-9-10 107 AdrianTNicholls 3 63
(D Nicholls) *led: pushed along 2f out: hdd over 1f out: sn wknd: eased whn btn ins fnl f* **10/3**[2]

60.84 secs (1.79) **Going Correction** +0.65s/f (Yiel) 4 Ran SP% **107.1**
Speed ratings (Par 111):111,109,105,86
CSF £21.38 TOTE £5.70; EX 15.10.
Owner Mrs M S Teversham **Bred** Mrs M S Teversham **Trained** Sigwells, Somerset

FOCUS
This was run at a good clip and the winner confirmed his improvement of the previous day. The runner-up has been assessed as being beaten three-quarters of a length and sets the standard.

NOTEBOOK
The Lord achieved a notable double at the meeting in the space of 21 hours. Taking first run on the second, he was always going to hold him at bay. Well suited by soft ground, he is set for a rise in the handicap after this improved performance. (op 5-1)
Green Manalishi ran a good race on this step up in grade but he had to be pulled around horses for a run and, although he was cutting back the winner's lead, he was always being held. (op 5-1)
Corridor Creeper(FR) had no problem with the ground and ran his race with no apparent excuses other than that he might have gone too fast up front in a duel with the fourth. (op 5-4 tchd 11-8 in places)
Fire Up The Band, to whom Nicholls switched after stablemate Tax Free was taken out, still did not look quite right in his coat. Soon leading after an awkward break from the stalls, he had no answers when headed and was eased right down in the final furlong. Penalised for his win in last year's King George Stakes here, he has yet to recapture his form. Official explanation: vet said gelding returned sore (op 5-2)

1953 RAYMARINE STKS (REGISTERED AS THE HERON STAKES) (LISTED RACE) 1m
3:15 (3:15) (Class 1) 3-Y-O **£17,034** (£6,456; £3,231; £1,611; £807) **Stalls** High

Form RPR
4226 **1** **Final Verse**[19] 1486 3-8-12 109 RobertWinston 1 106
(Sir Michael Stoute) *mde all at stdy pce: rdn over 1f out: r.o* **1/2**[1]

421 **2** *2 ½* **Deepwater Bay (USA)**[32] 1166 3-8-12 86 MartinDwyer 3 101
(A M Balding) *racd keenly: sn trckd ldrs: chsd wnr over 2f out: rdn and edgd rt over 1f out: no imp towards fin* **15/2**

1142 **3** *7* **Antica (IRE)**[8] 1776 3-8-7 89 MichaelHills 6 82
(M H Tompkins) *racd keenly: hld up: effrt to chse ldrs over 2f out: wknd ins fnl f* **11/2**[2]

31 **4** *5* **Red Somerset (USA)**[24] 1335 3-8-12 89 RichardHughes 4 77
(R Hannon) *lw: prom: rdn over 2f out: wknd wl over 1f out* **6/1**[3]

6300 **5** *13* **Renderoc (USA)**[104] 368 3-8-12 90 JohnEgan 2 51
(J S Moore) *hld up: n.m.r after 2f: rdn over 2f out: sn lft bhd* **40/1**

1m 45.28s (5.01) **Going Correction** +0.775s/f (Yiel) 5 Ran SP% **110.5**
Speed ratings (Par 107):105,102,95,90,77
CSF £5.01 TOTE £1.50: £1.10, £2.80; EX 4.80.
Owner Saeed Suhail **Bred** A Christodoulou **Trained** Newmarket, Suffolk

FOCUS
The pace was only steady and the field again came stands' side. The form is not easy to pin down but it is doubtful whether the winner had to run to near his best.

NOTEBOOK
Final Verse, sixth in the 2000 Guineas last time, was on his toes beforehand. Making his own running, he ran on willingly when asked and too strongly for his only serious challenger. He may go for the St James's Palace Stakes now and should get further in time. (op 2-5 tchd 4-7)
Deepwater Bay(USA), keen as the pace was pretty moderate in the early stages, went after the favourite with over two to run but was always being held. This was a big improvement on his previous form and his handicap mark will take a hit. (op 10-1)
Antica(IRE), another who wanted to go faster in the early parts, ran respectably but was found out by this step up in grade. This did not really tell us whether she stayed or not. (op 13-2 tchd 7-1)
Red Somerset(USA), winner of a decent maiden on Kempton's Polytrack, was found out in this better grade and appeared unhappy on the ground in the latter stages. (op 13-2)
Renderoc(USA), facing a stiff task on this first run since February and encountering soft ground for the first time, was well beaten. (op 50-1 tchd 66-1)

1954 DE NOVO STKS (H'CAP) 7f
3:45 (3:46) (Class 4) (0-85,85) 3-Y-O **£7,124** (£2,119; £1,059; £529) **Stalls** High

Form RPR
331 **1** **Days Of My Life (IRE)**[30] 1212 3-8-7 74 SteveDrowne 2 90+
(R Charlton) *a.p: led jst over 2f out: r.o: in command towards fin* **11/4**[2]

3060 **2** *¾* **Dune Melody (IRE)**[5] 1843 3-8-8 75 JohnEgan 3 82
(J S Moore) *in tch: rdn and ev ch fr over 2f out tl nt qckn towards fin* **10/1**

2241 **3** *5* **Illustrious Blue**[19] 1476 3-8-13 80 LDettori 1 75
(J A Osborne) *swtg: hld up: rdn over 3f out: hdwy over 2f out: chsd ldng pair fr over 1f out: no imp ins fnl f* **7/4**[1]

3556 **4** *2* **Zabeel House**[21] 1440 3-9-2 83 JamieSpencer 5 73+
(E A L Dunlop) *prom: n.m.r 2f out: sn rdn and lost pl: n.d after* **9/2**[3]

5260 **5** *1 ½* **Scarlet Knight**[18] 1512 3-9-4 85 RyanMoore 4 72
(P Mitchell) *hld up: effrt 2f out: no imp fr over 1f out* **10/1**

6100 **6** *4* **Sigismundus (IRE)**[22] 1411 3-8-4 71 (p) MartinDwyer 7 48
(J R Boyle) *led: hdd jst over 2f out: sn rdn: wknd over 1f out* **12/1**

2000 **7** *½* **Reviving (IRE)**[93] 473 3-8-7 74 StephenCarson 6 50
(R F Johnson Houghton) *plld hrd: in tch: rdn over 2f out: wknd wl over 1f out* **40/1**

1m 31.8s (3.76) **Going Correction** +0.775s/f (Yiel) 7 Ran SP% **109.5**
Speed ratings (Par 101):109,108,102,100,98 93,93
CSF £26.86 TOTE £3.80: £2.10, £3.60; EX 43.50.
Owner Mountgrange Stud **Bred** Sir E J Loder **Trained** Beckhampton, Wilts

FOCUS
The runners stayed on the far side in the straight. Not easy to assess, this has been rated through the runner-up. The winner is going to rate higher.

1955 AVON INFLATABLES MAIDEN FILLIES' STKS 1m 1f
4:20 (4:21) (Class 5) 3-Y-O **£3,562** (£1,059; £529; £264) **Stalls** High

Form RPR
0213 **1** **Summer's Eve**[12] 1669 3-9-0 86 DaneO'Neill 5 85+
(H Candy) *midfield: hdwy gng wl 6f out: led over 1f out: r.o wl to draw clr towards fin* **1/1**[1]

2 *3 ½* **Quenched** 3-9-0 RichardHughes 8 78+
(J H M Gosden) *unf: scope: hld up: shkn up and hdwy 3f out: kpt on to take 2nd towards fin: no ch w wnr* **7/2**[2]

0 **3** *1* **Muntada**[24] 1335 3-9-0 RHills 6 76
(M P Tregoning) *soon led: rdn and hdd over 1f out: no ex ins fnl f* **8/1**[3]

4 *2 ½* **Kentucky Warbler (IRE)** 3-9-0 SteveDrowne 11 71
(H Morrison) *leggy: trckd ldrs: rdn and outpcd 2f out: kpt on same pce fnl f* **12/1**

00 **5** *¾* **Dunlin**[13] 1649 3-9-0 RobertHavlin 1 69
(H Morrison) *w ldr: rdn 3f out: btn over 1f out* **50/1**

03 **6** *4* **Gower Song**[194] 6319 3-9-0 TQuinn 10 61
(D R C Elsworth) *hld up in midfield: rdn over 2f out: no imp on ldrs* **8/1**[3]

7 *6* **Dream Shared** 3-9-0 RichardMullen 4 49
(E A L Dunlop) *leggy: in tch: rdn 3f out: wknd wl over 1f out* **16/1**

0 **8** *¾* **Virginia Plain**[33] 1139 3-9-0 ShaneKelly 13 48
(Miss Diana Weeden) *in tch: lost pl 4f out: n.d after* **100/1**

0 **9** *½* **Coronation Queen**[216] 6009 3-9-0 FrankieMcDonald 3 47
(S Kirk) *t.k.h: hld up: rdn over 3f out: nvr on terms* **40/1**

00 **10** *1 ¼* **Forest Lodge (IRE)**[216] 6013 3-9-0 LPKeniry 2 44
(D R C Elsworth) *bit bkwd: hld up: hdwy over 3f out: rdn 2f out: wknd over 1f out* **50/1**

0000 **11** *11* **Whistleupthewind**[31] 1200 3-9-0 39 AlanMunro 12 22
(J M P Eustace) *trckd ldrs: rdn 3f out: sn wknd* **100/1**

0 **12** *4* **Rockatorri**[6] 1822 3-9-0 ChrisCatlin 7 14
(M R Channon) *a bhd* **50/1**

2m 3.68s (6.82) **Going Correction** +0.775s/f (Yiel) 12 Ran SP% **118.3**
Speed ratings (Par 96):100,96,96,93,93 89,84,83,83,82 72,68
CSF £4.24 TOTE £2.30: £1.10, £1.30, £2.60; EX 6.70.
Owner Mrs S E Lakin **Bred** Lakin Bloodstock **Trained** Kingston Warren, Oxon

FOCUS
A straightforward opportunity for the winner and the form is not all that strong, rated around the sixth. The pace was only moderate.
Virginia Plain Official explanation: jockey said filly was unsuited by the soft (heavy in places) ground
Whistleupthewind Official explanation: jockey said filly hung left

1956 EXHIBAR MAIDEN FILLIES' STKS 7f
4:55 (4:56) (Class 5) 3-Y-O **£4,533** (£1,348; £674; £336) **Stalls** High

Form RPR
3 **1** **Rydal Mount (IRE)**[34] 1119 3-9-0 FergusSweeney 4 82
(W S Kittow) *lw: w ldr: led over 2f out: r.o fnl f* **4/1**[2]

4 **2** *2 ½* **Quintrell**[13] 1640 3-9-0 DaneO'Neill 10 76
(H Candy) *hld up: hdwy 3f out: swtchd lft whn nt clr run over 2f out: r.o to take 2nd towards fin: nt rch wnr* **7/1**

0203 **3** *¾* **First Approval**[29] 1240 3-9-0 74 MichaelHills 2 74
(B W Hills) *trckd ldrs: rdn to chse wnr 2f out: kpt on same pce ins fnl f: lost 2nd towards fin* **6/1**[3]

0 **4** *4* **Shangazi (USA)**[36] 1087 3-9-0 MartinDwyer 8 64
(B W Hills) *hld up: hdwy 2f out: kpt on fnl f: nt trble ldrs* **12/1**

	5	1 ½	**Sajaaya (AUS)** 3-9-0 .... RobertWinston 1	66+
			(Sir Michael Stoute) *w'like: bit bkwd: hld up: hdwy over 3f out: chsd ldrs 2f out: wknd ins fnl f* **7/1**	
33	6	shd	**Namoos (USA)**[13] [1646] 3-9-0 .... RHills 11	61
			(J L Dunlop) *trckd ldrs: rdn over 2f out: wknd over 1f out* **11/4**[1]	
05	7	shd	**Rose Briar (IRE)**[13] [1649] 3-8-9 .... RichardKingscote(5) 9	60+
			(R Charlton) *lw: in tch: rdn 3f out: sn wknd* **12/1**	
3	8	1 ½	**Summertime Parkes**[167] [6531] 3-9-0 .... ChrisCatlin 5	57
			(H Candy) *swtg: t.k.h: hld up: rdn over 2f out: nvr on terms* **8/1**	
0	9	8	**Ameliore (IRE)**[306] [3723] 3-8-11 .... AdamKirby(3) 7	38
			(S Woodman) *led: hdd over 2f out: wknd wl over 1f out* **100/1**	

1m 34.01s (5.97) **Going Correction** +0.775s/f (Yiel) 9 Ran SP% **113.4**
Speed ratings (Par 96):96,93,92,87,86 85,85,84,74
CSF £31.46 TOTE £5.20: £1.60, £2.30, £2.10; EX 46.10.
Owner Reg Gifford **Bred** D R Tucker **Trained** Blackborough, Devon

FOCUS
There was not much pace and the runners stayed far side in the straight. The form is only ordinary, rated through the third, but the first two should do better.

1957 FINNING POWER STKS (H'CAP) 1m

5:30 (5:30) (Class 4) (0-85,85) 4-Y-0+ **£7,124** (£2,119; £1,059; £529) **Stalls** High

Form				RPR
0656	1		**Trafalgar Square**[12] [1667] 4-8-11 **78** .... DavidKinsella 2	92
			(J Akehurst) *lw: a cl up gng wl: led wl over 1f out: r.o wl* **9/2**[3]	
0044	2	4	**Davenport (IRE)**[24] [1340] 4-8-12 **79** .... AlanMunro 8	85
			(B R Millman) *hld up: rdn and hdwy over 1f out: styd on to take 2nd ins fnl f: nt trble wnr* **11/4**[2]	
2302	3	½	**First Show**[45] [946] 4-8-8 **75** .... ShaneKelly 6	80
			(J Noseda) *trckd ldr: rdn over 2f out: ev ch wl over 1f out: lost 2nd whn no ex ins fnl f* **13/8**[1]	
0400	4	5	**Jalissa**[12] [1692] 4-8-5 **75** .... NelsonDeSouza(3) 7	70
			(R M Beckett) *racd keenly: hld up: rdn over 2f out: wl outpcd over 1f out* **12/1**	
6106	5	2	**Kingsholm**[17] [1544] 4-8-9 **76** .... MartinDwyer 1	67
			(A M Balding) *b.hind: racd keenly: led: hdd wl over 1f out: sn rdn: wknd fnl f* **5/1**	

1m 45.24s (4.97) **Going Correction** +0.775s/f (Yiel) 5 Ran SP% **107.3**
Speed ratings (Par 105):106,102,101,96,94
CSF £16.11 TOTE £4.50: £1.60, £1.70; EX 13.40 Place 6 £106.15, Place 5 £44.57.
Owner Canisbay Bloodstock **Bred** Matthews Breeding And Racing Ltd **Trained** Epsom, Surrey

FOCUS
Only ordinary form, the winner confirming himself an improved performer. The second and third were not quite at their best.
T/Jkpt: £1,518.00 to a £1 stake. Pool: £28,865.00. 13.50 winning tickets. T/Plt: £199.30 to a £1 stake. Pool: £81,576.50. 298.80 winning tickets. T/Qpdt: £6.10 to a £1 stake. Pool: £4,830.70. 581.40 winning tickets. DO

1922 LINGFIELD (L-H)

Thursday, May 25

OFFICIAL GOING: Standard

1958 LINGFIELD-RACECOURSE.CO.UK H'CAP 1m 4f (P)

6:05 (6:05) (Class 5) (0-70,70) 4-Y-0+ **£3,886** (£1,156; £577; £288) **Stalls** Low

Form				RPR
2300	1		**Dark Parade (ARG)**[24] [1339] 5-8-3 **62** ow1 .... JamieJones(7) 2	73
			(G L Moore) *hld up.hdwy on ins wl over 1f out: r.o to ld post* **14/1**	
0403	2	hd	**Santando**[2] [1926] 6-8-13 **65** .... (b) TedDurcan 3	75
			(C E Brittain) *trckd ldrs: wnt 2nd 4f out: led over 2f out: hrd rdn: hdd post* **11/2**	
5546	3	2 ½	**Amwell Brave**[10] [1745] 5-8-8 **60** .... EddieAhern 7	66
			(J R Jenkins) *racd mid-div: rdn over 1f out: r.o wl to go 3rd ins fnl f* **5/1**[3]	
1161	4	¾	**Turner's Touch**[32] [1163] 4-9-0 **66** .... (be) RyanMoore 9	71
			(G L Moore) *mid-div: rdn and hdwy over 2f out: nt rch ldrs* **3/1**[2]	
5600	5	shd	**Burgundy**[6] [1821] 9-9-4 **70** .... (b) GeorgeBaker 6	75
			(P Mitchell) *hld up: hdwy to go 2nd over 2f out:: rdn and wknd fnl f* **9/1**	
6005	6	1	**Carpet Ride**[9] [1755] 4-8-6 **58** .... HayleyTurner 1	61
			(B G Powell) *trckd ldrs: rdn over 2f out: wknd over 1f out* **16/1**	
5130	7	10	**Fen Game (IRE)**[99] [420] 4-9-3 **69** .... JimmyFortune 5	56
			(J H M Gosden) *hld up: rdn 3f out: sn wl bhd* **5/2**[1]	
1053	8	1	**Mostarsil (USA)**[120] [186] 8-8-5 **57** .... (p) StephenCarson 8	43
			(G L Moore) *trckd ldrs: led over 4f out: hdd over 2f out: wknd qckly* **10/1**	
0450	9	17	**Ringarooma**[17] [1537] 4-7-11 **56** oh7 .... (t) KirstyMilczarek(7) 10	14
			(C N Allen) *v.s.a: lost at least 25l: a toiling in rr* **20/1**	
46-0	10	6	**Dancing Bear**[100] [147] 5-8-4 **56** oh11 .... FrancisFerris 4	5
			(P S McEntee) *led tl hdd over 4f out: wknd sn after* **100/1**	

2m 32.87s (-1.52) **Going Correction** -0.05s/f (Stan) 10 Ran SP% **123.0**
Speed ratings (Par 103):103,102,101,100,100 99,93,92,81,77
CSF £94.05 CT £453.25 TOTE £18.50: £10.00, £2.10, £1.70; EX 169.30.
Owner N J Jones **Bred** Firmamento **Trained** Woodingdean, E Sussex

FOCUS
A modest middle-distance handicap run at just a steady pace, but sound enough rated through the third and fourth to previous course form.

1959 NEXT MEETING JUNE 6TH MAIDEN AUCTION STKS 6f (P)

6:35 (6:36) (Class 5) 2-Y-0 **£3,886** (£1,156; £577; £288) **Stalls** Low

Form				RPR
2	1		**We'll Confer**[19] [1491] 2-8-13 .... JamieSpencer 4	90+
			(K A Ryan) *trckd ldr: led over 1f out: sn clr: comf* **1/2**[1]	
3	2	3 ½	**Whiskey Junction**[17] [1535] 2-8-6 .... NeilChalmers(3) 5	73
			(A M Balding) *led tl rdn and hdd over 1f out: outpcd by wnr* **7/1**[2]	
4	3	nk	**Hythe Bay**[21] [1429] 2-8-6 .... SteveDrowne 9	69
			(R T Phillips) *trckd ldrs: rdn over 1f out: one pce after* **16/1**	
	4	½	**Rosie Cross (IRE)** 2-8-4 .... StephenCarson 1	65
			(R F Johnson Houghton) *s.i.s: sn on tch: rdn and wknd appr fnl f* **50/1**	
	5	nk	**Prince Of Elegance** 2-9-2 .... JimCrowley 7	76
			(Mrs A J Perrett) *in tch: tl rdn over 1f out: no further hdwy* **7/1**[2]	
	6	¾	**Zeeuw (IRE)** 2-8-13 .... JimmyQuinn 12	71
			(D J Coakley) *bhd: rdn 2f out: kpt on one pce* **28/1**	
	7	nk	**Vintage (IRE)** 2-8-11 .... NickyMackay 6	68
			(P Mitchell) *s.i.s: sn mid-div: no prog ins fnl 2f* **40/1**	
	8	shd	**Recruit** 2-8-13 .... RyanMoore 8	70
			(R Hannon) *slowly away: in rr* **8/1**[3]	
	9	1 ½	**Lascelles** 2-9-2 .... EddieAhern 2	68
			(J A Osborne) *slowly away: a in rr* **22/1**	
	10	3 ½	**Cavallo Di Ferro (IRE)** 2-8-9 .... HayleyTurner 3	51
			(J R Boyle) *slowly away: a bhd* **50/1**	

1m 12.47s (-0.34) **Going Correction** -0.05s/f (Stan) 10 Ran SP% **122.8**
Speed ratings (Par 93):100,95,94,94,93 92,92,92,90,85
CSF £4.77 TOTE £1.60: £1.30, £1.80, £2.50; EX 6.70.
Owner P Byrne **Bred** Slatch Farm Stud **Trained** Hambleton, N Yorks

FOCUS
This looked a reasonable maiden auction beforehand, so We'll Confer looked impressive in getting off the mark in such comfortable fashion and should be capable of going on to better things. The form is not totally solid but the time was good.

NOTEBOOK
We'll Confer ◆, who was beaten just a short head when favourite for a five-furlong novice event at Thirsk on his debut, showed the benefit of that run with a very comfortable success. Always up with the pace, he found plenty in the straight without having to be asked a serious question and looks ready for a step up in class. He could be decent. (op 8-11)
Whiskey Junction's debut third in a five-furlong maiden at Kempton received a boost when the runner-up that day landed a maiden round here, and this was a good effort. He probably ran into a useful sort and ought to find a race before long. (op 10-1)
Hythe Bay, who shaped with plenty of promise in an ordinary five-furlong maiden at Folkestone on her debut, again ran with credit. She may be up to finding a maiden, and should make a fair nursery type later in the season. (op 14-1)
Rosie Cross(IRE), out of an unraced mare from a good family, shaped with plenty of promise and is open to improvement. (op 40-1)
Prince Of Elegance, a 45,000gns purchase, out of a six-furlong three-year-old winner, made a satisfactory introduction. (op 11-2)
Recruit, a 32,000gns half-brother to Radius, who was placed over six furlongs at two, out of an unraced half-sister to the fairly useful sprinter Sheer Precocity, was well held on his debut. Official explanation: jockey said colt was denied a clear run in straight (op 15-2 tchd 7-1)
Lascelles, a 42,000gns purchase, out of a dual five-furlong winner at two and three, gave the impression he will be better for the run. Official explanation: jockey said colt was slowly away (op 16-1)

1960 LINGFIELD PARK GOLF CLUB MEDIAN AUCTION MAIDEN STKS 6f (P)

7:05 (7:08) (Class 5) 3-4-Y-0 **£3,238** (£963; £481; £240) **Stalls** Low

Form				RPR
222	1		**Storm On The Run (IRE)**[22] [1412] 3-8-10 82 .... RyanMoore 10	81
			(R Hannon) *in tch: rdn over 2f out: kpt on u.str p to ld nr fin* **2/5**[1]	
402	2	1	**Leopoldine**[220] [5946] 3-8-6 73 ow1 .... SteveDrowne 1	74
			(H Morrison) *led: rdn clr over 1f out: hdd nr fin* **9/2**[2]	
30	3	shd	**Titian Dancer**[13] [1640] 3-8-10 .... TedDurcan 11	78
			(W R Swinburn) *hld up: rdn 2f out: picked up bit and r.o strly fnl f: jst failed to go 2nd* **12/1**[3]	
5	4	10	**John Bratby (USA)**[166] [6545] 4-9-2 .... (t) AmirQuinn(3) 6	50
			(P J Makin) *trckd ldr tl rdn and wknd qckly 1f out* **20/1**	
	5	1	**Divo Nero (IRE)** 3-8-10 .... NickyMackay 7	45+
			(L M Cumani) *hld up: rdn 1/2-way: nvr on terms* **12/1**[3]	
	6	hd	**Tajjree** 3-8-5 .... (p) StephenCarson 4	39
			(Miss K B Boutflower) *v.s.a: sme hdwy over 2f out: nvr on terms* **66/1**	
00	7	2	**Terrys Alfie**[17] [1552] 3-8-5 .... (b[1]) JamesDoyle(5) 8	38
			(N P Littmoden) *chsd ldrs: rdn over 2f out: sn btn* **80/1**	
	8	¾	**Kansas Gold** 3-8-10 .... EddieAhern 9	36
			(W R Muir) *mid-div: bhd fnl 2f* **33/1**	
500	9	3	**Elli Lewtia**[224] [5850] 3-8-7 40 ow2 .... ShaneKelly 2	24
			(J Jay) *a bhd* **66/1**	
	10	2	**Royal Senga** 3-8-5 .... JimmyQuinn 5	16
			(C A Horgan) *outpcd thrght* **33/1**	

1m 12.02s (-0.79) **Going Correction** -0.05s/f (Stan)
WFA 3 from 4yo 9lb 10 Ran SP% **119.9**
Speed ratings (Par 103):103,101,101,88,86 86,83,82,78,76
CSF £2.41 TOTE £1.30: £1.02, £1.40, £2.00; EX 2.90.
Owner Jaber Abdullah **Bred** Knocktoran Stud **Trained** East Everleigh, Wilts

FOCUS
Older horse sprint maidens tend to be modest events, but this did not look too bad a race and the front three pulled well clear.
John Bratby(USA) Official explanation: trainer later said colt had choked during race
Royal Senga Official explanation: jockey said filly was slowly away

1961 LINGFIELD PARK LEISURE CLUB H'CAP 6f (P)

7:35 (7:35) (Class 4) (0-80,78) 3-Y-0+ **£5,505** (£1,637; £818; £408) **Stalls** Low

Form				RPR
4010	1		**High Ridge**[12] [1686] 7-9-8 **73** .... (p) JamieSpencer 2	80
			(J M Bradley) *hld up: strly rdn to ld over 1f out: rdn out* **11/4**[2]	
0001	2	1 ¼	**Pippa's Dancer (IRE)**[23] [1383] 4-9-5 **70** .... MartinDwyer 6	73
			(W R Muir) *plld hrd: trckd ldrs: rdn to go 2nd ins fnl f* **2/1**[1]	
500	3	nk	**Depressed**[84] [555] 4-9-2 **67** .... (tp) JohnEgan 7	69
			(Ernst Oertel) *chsd ldrs: rdn over 1f out: kpt on fnl f* **7/1**	
0610	4	½	**Humility**[29] [1245] 5-8-13 **64** oh13 .... RyanMoore 4	65?
			(C A Cyzer) *hld up in rr: hdwy on ins over 1f out: nt qckn ins fnl f* **6/1**[3]	
0000	5	nk	**Elrafa Mujahid**[32] [1164] 4-8-11 **65** .... (b) SaleemGolam(3) 3	65
			(Ernst Oertel) *racd wd: r.o wl fnl f: nvr nrr* **10/1**	
0000	6	1 ¼	**Currency**[5] [1858] 9-9-11 **76** .... TedDurcan 1	72
			(J M Bradley) *led tl rdn and hdd over 1f out: wknd ins fnl f* **13/2**	
0006	7	1 ¼	**Honey Ryder**[24] [1338] 4-9-13 **78** .... SteveDrowne 5	70
			(Stef Liddiard) *trckd ldr tl wknd ent fnl f* **12/1**	

1m 12.54s (-0.27) **Going Correction** -0.05s/f (Stan) 7 Ran SP% **116.9**
Speed ratings (Par 105):99,97,96,96,95 94,92
CSF £9.06 TOTE £2.90: £2.10, £1.50; EX 7.50.
Owner James Bookmakers Ltd **Bred** Buckram Thoroughbred Enterprises Inc **Trained** Sedbury, Gloucs

FOCUS
Not a very strong sprint handicap - Humility was beaten less than two lengths from 13lb out of the weights - and the pace was just steady for much of the way, making the form look shaky.
Depressed Official explanation: jockey said filly hung left home straight

1962 ARENA LEISURE PLC FILLIES' H'CAP 7f (P)

8:05 (8:05) (Class 4) (0-85,83) 3-Y-0+ **£6,477** (£1,927; £963; £481) **Stalls** Low

Form				RPR
3220	1		**Kaveri (USA)**[19] [1490] 3-10-0 **83** .... JimmyFortune 4	86
			(C E Brittain) *trckd ldr: led over 1f out: drvn out* **3/1**[2]	
0204	2	¾	**Aastral Magic**[12] [1692] 4-9-13 **71** .... RyanMoore 6	76
			(R Hannon) *in rr tl rdn and hdwy over 1f out: r.o to go 2nd ins fnl f* **8/1**	
211	3	1 ¼	**Famcred**[254] [5209] 3-9-13 **82** .... NickyMackay 5	80+
			(L M Cumani) *hld up: racd wd: rdn wl over 1f out: kpt on fnl f but nvr nr to chal* **5/4**[1]	

0-00 4 shd **A Woman In Love**[82] 576 7-9-0 58 .... SebSanders 7 59
(Miss B Sanders) *hld up and t.k.h: rdn and hdwy over 1f out: kpt on* **16/1**
0342 5 ½ **Island Rapture**[27] 1275 6-9-13 71 .... EddieAhern 1 71
(J A R Toller) *led tl hdd over 1f out: fdd ins fnl f* **7/2**[3]
0410 6 2½ **Stormy Monday**[260] 5042 3-9-2 71 .... JamieSpencer 2 61
(J W Hills) *chsd ldrs tl rdn and wknd ins fnl f* **16/1**
0600 7 3 **Saxon Lil (IRE)**[43] 977 4-10-0 72 .... SteveDrowne 3 58
(J L Spearing) *a in rr* **16/1**

1m 25.76s (-0.13) **Going Correction** -0.05s/f (Stan)
WFA 3 from 4yo+ 11lb **7** Ran SP% **120.4**
Speed ratings (Par 102):98,97,95,95,95 92,88
CSF £28.69 TOTE £4.30: £3.40, £4.10; EX 29.20.
Owner Shamsudeen **Bred** Glory Days Breeding Inc **Trained** Newmarket, Suffolk

FOCUS
Just the seven runners, but this looked a reasonable enough fillies' handicap, although the form is not that strong with the runner-up the best guide.

1963 FURLONGS AND FAIRWAYS H'CAP 7f (P)
8:35 (8:35) (Class 4) (0-80,81) 3-Y-O **£5,505** (£1,637; £818; £408) **Stalls** Low

Form RPR
1546 1 **Tamagin (USA)**[23] 1384 3-8-10 77 .... (p) StephenDonohoe(5) 7 86
(P D Evans) *led: rdn clr 2f out: unchal* **11/4**[1]
1550 2 1¼ **Jimmy The Guesser**[17] 1529 3-9-5 81 .... HayleyTurner 4 87
(N P Littmoden) *chsd ldrs: wnt 2nd wl over 1f out: kpt on but no ch w wnr* **10/1**
550 3 ½ **Southport Star (IRE)**[32] 1166 3-8-11 73 .... JamieSpencer 10 78+
(J R Fanshawe) *hld up: hdwy appr fnl f: rdn and r.o: nvr nrr* **7/1**
2104 4 3 **Aspen Falls (IRE)**[14] 1617 3-9-4 80 .... SebSanders 9 77
(Sir Mark Prescott) *hld up on outside: hdwy 2f out: styd on: nvr nr to chal* **4/1**[2]
16 5 nk **Sir Douglas**[61] 725 3-9-1 77 .... ShaneKelly 5 73+
(J A Osborne) *hld up: nt clr run over 2f out: hung rt over 1f out: nvr nr to chal* **7/1**
010 6 ¾ **Kahlua Kiss**[229] 5733 3-9-2 78 .... MartinDwyer 8 72+
(W R Muir) *hld up: nvr on terms* **14/1**
030 7 1¼ **Dream Forest (IRE)**[18] 1513 3-8-8 70 .... JohnEgan 1 61
(Mrs P N Dutfield) *slowly away: a bhd* **20/1**
0000 8 1 **Bollywood (IRE)**[16] 1567 3-7-13 66 oh4 .... JamesDoyle(5) 2 54
(J J Bridger) *prom tl rdn and wknd wl over 1f out* **25/1**
6135 9 2½ **Pure Fiction**[24] 1349 3-9-0 76 .... RyanMoore 6 58
(R Hannon) *mid-div: rdn 1/2-way: btn whn hmpd wl over 1f out* **5/1**[3]
2405 10 7 **Cabourg (IRE)**[13] 1641 3-8-13 75 .... (b) SteveDrowne 3 39
(C R Egerton) *trckd wnr to wl over 1f out: rdn and wknd qckly* **12/1**

1m 24.75s (-1.14) **Going Correction** -0.05s/f (Stan) **10** Ran SP% **120.4**
Speed ratings (Par 101):104,102,102,98,98 97,95,94,91,83
CSF £32.88 CT £184.67 TOTE £4.50: £1.40, £3.50, £2.80; EX 44.40 Place 6 £37.47, Place 5 £7.71.
Owner Jordan E Lund **Bred** Stonehaven Farm Llc **Trained** Pandy, Abergavenny

FOCUS
This looked a reasonable handicap for the grade beforehand and although there was some trouble in behind the form looks sound enough and the time was reasonable.
T/Plt: £53.70 to a £1 stake. Pool: £64,066.30. 870.55 winning tickets. T/Qpdt: £15.60 to a £1 stake. Pool: £5,833.20. 275.60 winning tickets. JS

[1796]SALISBURY (R-H)
Thursday, May 25
1964 Meeting Abandoned - Waterlogged

1970 - 1972a (Foreign Racing) - See Raceform Interactive

[1869]BADEN-BADEN (L-H)
Thursday, May 25

OFFICIAL GOING: Good

1973a BENAZET-RENNEN (GROUP 3) 6f
4:00 (4:06) 3-Y-O+ **£24,138** (£10,345; £4,138; £2,759)

RPR
1 **Soave (GER)**[185] 6408 7-9-6 .... OPeslier 4 114
(A Trybuhl, Germany) *close up, disputed lead 2f out til led over 1f out, soon quickened clear* **51/10**[2]
2 4½ **Donatello (GER)**[51] 885 5-9-6 .... JVictoire 8 101
(W Baltromei, Germany) *raced in midfield, ran on strongly from over 1f out to go 2nd inside final furlong* **33/1**
3 2½ **Lucky Strike**[270] 4804 8-9-6 .... ADeVries 10 93
(A Trybuhl, Germany) *close up on wide outside, hung right and disputed lead 2f out, headed over 1f out, one pace* **7/10**[1]
4 1½ **Shinko's Best (IRE)**[214] 6049 5-9-6 .... JHillis 9 89
(A Kleinkorres, Germany) *always close up, 5th 2f out, kept on at one pace* **16/1**
5 hd **Matrix (GER)**[11] 1717 5-9-6 .... DBoeuf 7 88
(W Baltromei, Germany) *close 3rd 2f out, one pace* **51/10**[2]
6 ½ **Key To Pleasure (GER)**[200] 6277 6-9-6 .... J-PCarvalho 6 86
(Mario Hofer, Germany) *always midfield* **18/1**
7 1¼ **Omasheriff (IRE)**[31] 1202 4-9-6 .... THellier 2 83
(Bruce Hellier, Germany) *speed to 2f out* **86/10**[3]
8 nk **Diable**[242] 7-9-6 .... JBojko 11 82
(H Hesse, Germany) *in rear, some late headway* **27/1**
9 2 **Moyenne (IRE)**[20] 1469 4-9-2 .... CatherineGannon 1 72
(Timothy Doyle, Ire) *always in rear* **41/1**
10 5 **Lamargue (GER)**[270] 4804 4-9-6 .... AHelfenbein 5 61
(Andreas Lowe, Germany) *led 4f out, soon weakened* **16/1**
11 1½ **Miss Lips (GER)**[327] 3161 5-9-2 .... CCzachary 3 52
(P Hirschberger, Germany) *pressed leader to over 2f out* **47/1**

69.26 secs (-1.03) **11** Ran SP% **130.0**
(including ten euro stakes): WIN 61; PL 16, 35, 12; SF 1205.
Owner Stall Magic **Bred** Gestut Etzean **Trained** Germany

[1526]FRANKFURT (L-H)
Thursday, May 25

OFFICIAL GOING: Soft

1974a FRANKFURTER STUTEN-MEILE (LISTED) (F&M) 1m
3:30 (3:33) 4-Y-O+ **£18,621** (£7,586; £4,138; £2,759; £1,379)

RPR
1 **Molly Art (GER)**[356] 4-8-9 .... (b) ABoschert 8 104
(U Ostmann, Germany) **54/10**[3]
2 ¾ **Toamasina (FR)**[31] 5-9-0 .... MSautjeau 10 108
(M Rulec, Germany) **36/1**
3 hd **Delora (GER)** 5-8-9 .... JPalik 6 102
(M Weber, Germany) **20/1**
4 5 **New Inspiration (GER)**[641] 5-8-9 .... KKerekes 12 92
(W Kujath, Germany) **16/1**
5 hd **The Spring Flower (GER)**[200] 6279 4-8-9 .... HGrewe 9 92
(Andreas Lowe, Germany) **77/10**
6 3 **Norwegian Pride (FR)**[51] 4-9-4 .... AGoritz 13 95
(P Schiergen, Germany) **18/1**
7 ½ **Wonderful Day (GER)**[217] 6000 4-8-9 .... JParize 3 85
(C Brandstatter, Germany) **24/1**
8 2 **Ticina (GER)**[228] 5785 6-9-0 .... DVSmith 7 86
(G Sybrecht, Germany) **35/1**
9 1 **Quadrupa (GER)**[40] 1015 4-9-4 .... MTimpelan 4 88
(C Von Der Recke, Germany) **29/10**[2]
10 8 **Golden Rose (GER)**[228] 6-8-9 .... GBatistic 2 63
(H Hesse, Germany) **117/10**
11 27 **Ruby Hill (GER)**[237] 5596 4-9-4 .... ACrastus 5 18
(W Baltromei, Germany) **25/1**
12 9 **Three Wrens (IRE)**[22] 1407 4-9-0 .... TPQueally 1 —
(D J Daly) *racing in 4th on inside when squeezed up and almost fell after 3f, dropped right out and no chance after* **54/10**[3]
P **Sorrent (GER)**[212] 6104 4-8-9 .... NRichter 11 —
(P Schiergen, Germany) **28/10**[1]

1m 38.35s **13** Ran SP% **131.8**
(including ten euro stakes): WIN 64; PL 29, 92, 58; SF 2636.
Owner Gestut Auenquelle **Bred** Gestut Auenquelle **Trained** Germany

NOTEBOOK
Three Wrens(IRE), on her travels in a continued search for black type, was badly hampered over half a mile out and her race was soon over.

[1951]GOODWOOD (R-H)
Friday, May 26

OFFICIAL GOING: Soft
Wind: Strong, against Weather: Overcast becoming fine late on

1975 GET BETTER SHOW PRICES WITH BLUE SQUARE STKS (H'CAP) 1m 3f
2:10 (2:12) (Class 4) (0-85,82) 3-Y-O **£7,772** (£2,312; £1,155; £577) **Stalls** High

Form RPR
003 1 **Madroos**[219] 5988 3-8-10 74 .... MartinDwyer 6 82
(J L Dunlop) *lw: hld up: rdn and hdwy over 2f out: led over 1f out: edgd lft ins fnl f: hld on wl* **9/2**[2]
6112 2 ½ **Cool Customer (USA)**[7] 1837 3-8-13 77 .... JamieSpencer 5 84
(E A L Dunlop) *lw: led for 1f: remained prom: rdn over 2f out: ev ch ins fnl f: a hld* **5/4**[1]
5011 3 2½ **Free To Air**[18] 1543 3-9-2 80 .... DarryllHolland 2 83
(A M Balding) *trckd ldr: led after 1f: rdn 2f out: hdd over 1f out: sn lugged lft: 3rd but hld whn n.m.r ins fnl f: no ex* **11/2**[3]
0244 4 ¾ **Island Myth (IRE)**[11] 1741 3-9-1 79 .... DaneO'Neill 1 81
(M P Tregoning) *trckd ldrs: rdn and outpcd over 2f out: kpt on ins fnl f* **10/1**
054 5 2½ **Impostor (IRE)**[27] 1290 3-9-1 79 .... RyanMoore 3 77
(J R Fanshawe) *hld up in rr: rdn and hdwy over 2f out: fdd ins fnl f* **14/1**

2m 36.72s (9.51) **Going Correction** +0.85s/f (Soft) **5** Ran SP% **93.8**
Speed ratings (Par 101):99,98,96,96,94
CSF £7.60 TOTE £4.90: £1.90, £1.20; EX 6.50.
Owner Hamdan Al Maktoum **Bred** Five Horses Ltd **Trained** Arundel, W Sussex

FOCUS
A race weakened by the late withdrawal of Elise (9/2, unruly at s). They went a sensible pace in the conditions and the field made for the centre of the track on reaching the home straight. Possibly not the strongest of handicap form, although the winner is unexposed.

1976 BLUE SQUARE EXCLUSIVE PRICES FESTIVAL STKS (LISTED RACE) 1m 1f 192y
2:40 (2:44) (Class 1) 4-Y-O+
£17,034 (£6,456; £3,231; £1,611; £807; £405) **Stalls** High

Form RPR
4212 1 **Blue Monday**[36] 1098 5-8-12 108 .... SteveDrowne 2 116+
(R Charlton) *hld up: hdwy whn nt clr run 2f out: sn swtchd lft: led ins fnl f: r.o wl: won gng away* **10/3**[2]
1401 2 3 **Mountain High (IRE)**[20] 1489 4-8-12 111 .... DarryllHolland 4 107
(Sir Michael Stoute) *lw: a.p: led over 2f out: edgd lft fr over 1f out: hdd ins fnl f: nt qckn towards fin* **10/11**[1]
2440 3 2 **Vol De Nuit**[201] 6278 5-8-12 .... JamieSpencer 3 104
(L M Cumani) *w'like: racd keenly: hld up: trckd ldrs 5f out: rdn and ev ch fr 2f out tl no ex wl ins fnl f* **4/1**[3]
0500 4 2½ **Tiger Tiger (FR)**[9] 1775 5-8-12 94 .... JohnEgan 5 99
(Jamie Poulton) *prom: niggled along 5f out: rdn and lost pl over 4f out: bhd 2f out: kpt on but no imp on ldrs ins fnl f* **33/1**
5/10 5 ½ **Tau Ceti**[28] 1267 7-9-1 107 .... MartinDwyer 6 101
(R M Beckett) *s.i.s: hld up in rr: rdn over 3f out: hdwy and effrt to chse ldrs 2f out: wknd ins fnl f* **20/1**
6555 6 18 **Weightless**[28] 1267 6-8-12 108 .... RyanMoore 1 66
(Mrs A J Perrett) *led: rdn and hdd over 2f out: wknd over 1f out* **14/1**

2m 14.71s (6.96) **Going Correction** +0.85s/f (Soft) **6** Ran SP% **109.8**
Speed ratings (Par 111):106,103,102,100,99 85
CSF £6.45 TOTE £4.10: £1.80, £1.40; EX 7.20.
Owner Mountgrange Stud **Bred** Darley **Trained** Beckhampton, Wilts
■ Stewards' Enquiry : Darryll Holland caution: used whip down shoulder in forehand position

FOCUS
A modest winning time for a Listed race, but given the size of the field and the conditions it is perfectly understandable. Unlike in the first race, the field stayed on the far side of the track on reaching the straight. A good effort from Blue Monday, who was value for a bit more, but the form overall is anchored by Tiger Tiger, and neither the second or the third ran to their best.

NOTEBOOK
Blue Monday, on his toes beforehand, came off the bridle at halfway and then found himself stuck in a pocket approaching the final quarter-mile, but once switched left he quickened up in impressive style. His stable is going much better now and he looks well worth a try in Group company. (op 4-1)

Mountain High(IRE), best in at the weights and all the rage following his Newmarket victory, was never far away and held every chance but was completely swamped by the winner's turn of foot. He may not have wanted the ground as soft as this and should be given another chance to confirm the impression he created at headquarters. (op 4-5)

Vol De Nuit, an ex-Italian entire making his debut for the yard off the back of a six-month break, had been beaten less than a length by Electrocutionist at San Siro last summer. He held every chance on this first start in Britain, but was found wanting for pace over the last furlong or so. The ground should not have bothered him too much - although his fine second to Electrocutionist was on fast ground, he won several times on soft going in his native land - but lack of a recent run might have, so he is well worth another chance. (tchd 5-1, 11-2 in a place)

Tiger Tiger(FR), worst in at the weights, looked likely to finished tailed off passing the two-furlong pole, but eventually ran on past a couple of flagging rivals and was not beaten far at the end. It remains to be seen whether this performance flatters him.

Tau Ceti should have handled these conditions without a problem, but he could never get involved down the outside of the track and is yet to catch fire this season. (op 16-1)

Weightless had his ground and was able to establish his usual position out in front, but he still faded very tamely once losing the advantage. (op 16-1 tchd 12-1)

1977 BAKER TILLY TROPHY STKS (REGISTERED AS THE AUBIGNY STAKES) (LISTED RACE) 5f
3:15 (3:15) (Class 1) 2-Y-O

£14,195 (£5,380; £2,692; £1,342; £672; £337) **Stalls** Low

Form | | | | RPR
1 **1** **Sonny Red (IRE)**[19] [1510] 2-9-0 .... RyanMoore 5 98+
(R Hannon) *lw: w ldrs: led over 2f out: pressed 1f out: edgd rt ins fnl f: r.o wl and won gng away towards fin* **11/10**[1]

131 **2** *3* **Chief Editor**[9] [1780] 2-9-0 .... JamieSpencer 4 89+
(M J Wallace) *swtg: trckd ldrs: chsd wnr wl over 1f out: upsides 1f out: edgd rt ins fnl f: outpcd by wnr towards fin* **11/4**[2]

236 **3** *2 ½* **Feelin Foxy**[7] [1831] 2-8-9 .... DaneO'Neill 1 71
(D Shaw) *hld up in rr: hdwy wl over 1f out: sn chsd ldng pair: nt pce to chal* **33/1**

400 **4** *5* **Princely Royal**[18] [1535] 2-9-0 .... SteveDrowne 6 58
(J J Bridger) *hld up: rdn over 2f out: outpcd over 1f out* **100/1**

213 **5** *2 ½* **Mind The Style**[16] [1582] 2-9-0 .... RobertMiles 3 49
(W G M Turner) *edgy in stalls: sn led: hdd over 2f out: rdn and wknd over 1f out* **9/1**

1 **6** *1 ¼* **Elhamri**[32] [1189] 2-9-0 .... DPMcDonogh 2 45+
(S Kirk) *led early: remained prom: rdn over 2f out: wknd over 1f out* **3/1**[3]

62.07 secs (3.02) **Going Correction** +0.65s/f (Yiel) 6 Ran SP% **113.2**
Speed ratings (Par 101):101,96,92,84,80 78
CSF £4.51 TOTE £1.90: £1.30, £1.60; EX 5.20.

Owner Michael Pescod & J A Leek **Bred** Denis Bergin **Trained** East Everleigh, Wilts

FOCUS
This looked well up to standard for a Listed race and the winner was very impressive, but there did seem to be a bias against those that raced closest to the stands' rail. The third and fourth set the level for the form.

NOTEBOOK
Sonny Red(IRE) ◆, whose debut victory in soft ground at Newmarket has not worked out as well as expected, looked outstanding in the paddock and put matters right with a convincing success. The most impressive aspect was the way he quickened for a second time when the runner-up ranged alongside and he now looks to be a leading player for next month's Coventry Stakes provided he can handle quicker ground, though his rider believes he has the speed to win the Norfolk. (op 5-4 tchd 11-8)

Chief Editor stalked the favourite the whole way and when eventually pulled out for his effort it looked as though he was going to cause his rival a real problem. However, the winner merely engaged the afterburner and left him choking on his dust. He will not always bump into one so smart. (op 5-2 tchd 3-1)

Feelin Foxy, on her toes and edgy beforehand, stayed on to snatch third prize and on the face of it her proximity holds the form down, but she probably just handled these conditions better then those behind her and at least one of them did not run their race.

Princely Royal never looked like getting involved and achieved very little. (op 66-1)

Mind The Style, who managed to get right down in the stalls beforehand, set the early pace but eventually fell in a heap and almost certainly failed to handle this much softer ground. Official explanation: trainer said gelding was unsuited by the soft ground (op 8-1)

Elhamri showed up for a while but never looked happy - tending to carry his head to one side - and eventually fell in a complete hole. This was very disappointing, but he was probably racing on the slowest ground against the stands' rail. His Windsor win has worked out well and he deserves a chance to make amends. (op 7-2)

1978 M-REAL MAIDEN STKS 1m
3:50 (3:50) (Class 4) 3-Y-O **£7,124** (£2,119; £1,059; £529) **Stalls** High

Form | | | | RPR
02 **1** **Smart Enough**[13] [1674] 3-9-3 .... SteveDrowne 4 91+
(M A Magnusson) *lw: mde all: shkn up over 1f out: r.o wl* **11/10**[1]

53 **2** *4* **Danski**[23] [1401] 3-9-3 .... RyanMoore 6 81
(P J Makin) *lw: trckd ldrs: rdn to take 2nd over 2f out: edgd lft over 1f out: no ch w wnr ins fnl f* **6/4**[2]

3 *1 ¾* **Paraguay (USA)**[36] 3-9-0 .... EdwardCreighton(3) 1 78
(M R Channon) *hld up: hdwy over 2f out: rdn whn chsng ldrs over 1f out: one pce ins fnl f* **15/2**[3]

000 **4** *6* **Debord (FR)**[15] [1605] 3-9-3 54 .... JohnEgan 5 66
(Jamie Poulton) *in tch: pushed along 5f out: edgd lft u.p and wknd over 2f out* **50/1**

0 **5** *9* **Press The Button (GER)**[33] [1165] 3-9-0 .... AmirQuinn(3) 3 48
(J R Boyle) *prom: rdn over 3f out: wknd over 1f out* **33/1**

0 **6** *nk* **Xenophile**[277] [4629] 3-9-3 .... DaneO'Neill 2 47
(J L Dunlop) *hld up: rdn over 2f out: sn btn* **25/1**

1m 45.66s (5.39) **Going Correction** +0.85s/f (Soft) 6 Ran SP% **108.1**
Speed ratings (Par 101):107,103,101,95,86 85
CSF £2.69 TOTE £2.00: £1.40, £1.30; EX 3.20.

Owner East Wind Racing Ltd **Bred** Whitsbury Manor Stud And Mrs M E Slade **Trained** Upper Lambourn, Berks

FOCUS
As in the first race the field made for the centre of the track on turning in. The winning time was decent race for a race like this and they finished well spread out.

1979 BLUE SQUARE PRICES V THE REST CONDITIONS STKS 7f
4:20 (4:22) (Class 3) 3-Y-O+ **£8,420** (£2,505; £1,251; £625) **Stalls** High

Form | | | | RPR
3164 **1** **Polar Ben**[27] [1287] 7-9-8 108 .... JamieSpencer 2 116
(J R Fanshawe) *hld up in rr: rdn and hdwy over 1f out: led ins fnl f: sn edgd rt: r.o* **2/1**[1]

0330 **2** *2* **Turnkey**[21] [1469] 4-9-1 100 .... SamHitchcott 3 104
(M R Channon) *a.p: pushed along 3f out: led over 1f out: hdd ins fnl f: nt qckn towards fin* **9/2**

520 **3** *1 ¾* **Andronikos**[223] [5900] 4-9-1 108 .... (t) RyanMoore 4 100
(P F I Cole) *swtg: bit bkwd: trckd ldrs: rdn and ev ch 1f out: no ex ins fnl f* **9/4**[2]

0325 **4** *1* **Squaw Dance**[254] [5234] 4-8-10 102 .... KFallon 1 93
(W J Haggas) *racd keenly: led: rdn and hdd over 1f out: sn btn* **3/1**[3]

1m 32.34s (4.30) **Going Correction** +0.85s/f (Soft) 4 Ran SP% **107.3**
Speed ratings (Par 107):109,106,104,103
CSF £10.33 TOTE £2.30; EX 8.30.

Owner Simon Gibson **Bred** Worksop Manor Stud **Trained** Newmarket, Suffolk

FOCUS
Only four runners, but a fair pace in the circumstances and the winning time was very acceptable for the grade. The quartet stayed far side in the home straight. Arguably improved form from the winner, but there were doubts over his rivals.

NOTEBOOK
Polar Ben was not that well in at the weights with a couple of these rivals under his penalty, but he relishes this sort of ground and that counted for plenty. Held up last, he quickened up in grand style once switched wide for his effort and looks sure to continue to pay his way. (op 13-8 tchd 9-4 in a place)

Turnkey, worst in at the weights, also loves this ground and though he was the first to come off the bridle, he kept on pretty well to finish second. He will remain a difficult horse to place and will probably have to go back on his travels. (op 4-1)

Andronikos was best in on adjusted official ratings and handles this ground, but he was returning from a seven-month break and was forced to give best to two race-fit rivals. (tchd 5-2)

Squaw Dance set off in front, but she eventually found trying to make all in these conditions following a nine-month break all to much. She can be expected to last longer back on better ground with this run under her belt. (op 9-2)

1980 BET@BLUESQ.COM FOR EXCLUSIVE LIVE SHOW PRICES E B F MAIDEN STKS 6f
4:55 (4:55) (Class 4) 2-Y-O **£4,857** (£1,445; £722; £360) **Stalls** Low

Form | | | | RPR
1 **Samorra (IRE)** 2-8-12 .... MartinDwyer 4 70+
(M P Tregoning) *w'like: dwlt: sn prom: led 3f out: hdd over 2f out: rallied gamely to regain ld wl ins fnl f* **7/4**[2]

2 *nk* **Caldra (IRE)** 2-9-3 .... DPMcDonogh 5 74+
(S Kirk) *w'like: cl up on outside: led over 2f out: edgd lft over 1f out: hdd wl ins fnl f: r.o u.p* **6/5**[1]

3 *2* **Paymaster General (IRE)** 2-9-3 .... DaneO'Neill 2 68
(M D I Usher) *w'like: str: s.s: in rr: rdn and hdwy over 2f out: ev ch ins fnl f: no ex towards fin* **11/1**

0 **4** *1 ¾* **Alloro**[9] [1770] 2-9-3 .... JohnEgan 1 63+
(D J S Ffrench Davis) *w'like: bit bkwd: w ldr: pushed along and lost pl 3f out: sn outpcd: kpt on again ins fnl f* **16/1**

04 **5** *3 ½* **Nicada (IRE)**[11] [1744] 2-9-3 .... SteveDrowne 3 52+
(Miss Gay Kelleway) *b.hind: led: hdd 3f out: sn rdn: wknd over 1f out* **17/2**[3]

1m 19.74s (6.89) **Going Correction** +0.65s/f (Yiel) 5 Ran SP% **106.6**
Speed ratings (Par 95):80,79,76,74,69
CSF £3.90 TOTE £2.40: £1.40, £1.40; EX 3.80.

Owner Sheikh Ahmed Al Maktoum **Bred** Darley **Trained** Lambourn, Berks

FOCUS
The pair with previous experience looked moderate and the race was eventually dominated by the three newcomers. The winning time was very slow, even allowing for the ground and the form is well below average for the track.

NOTEBOOK
Samorra(IRE), a half-sister to several winners, including Zahrat Dubai, took over at halfway but looked well and truly cooked when the favourite went past her. To her credit, she never gave up and eventually got back on top near the line. The winning time does not suggest the form is anything special, but her breeding and the style of her victory suggests she is going to improve for further in the longer term. (tchd 2-1)

Caldra(IRE), a half-brother to Kestrel Cross out of a winner over middle distances, raced keenly but still looked the likely winner when taking it up two furlongs from home, but for some reason he then tended to pull up in front and was worried out of it. Perhaps the ground was too testing or he was just green, but whatever the reason he should be given another chance. (op 6-4 tchd 11-10, 13-8 in a place)

Paymaster General(IRE), out of a winning half-sister to Tolpuddle, completely fluffed the start but still managed to give himself every chance if unable to quicken in the final furlong. There should be a race in him in due course. (op 8-1 tchd 12-1)

Alloro, well beaten on his debut, probably did not achieve a great deal more this time in view of the moderate time. (op 11-1)

Nicada(IRE), claimed out of Mick Easterby's stable after finishing fourth at Wolverhampton the previous week, set the early pace but was easily picked off and looks moderate. (op 8-1)

1981 CHECK BLUESQ.COM BEFORE EVERY RACE APPRENTICE STKS (H'CAP) 5f
5:30 (5:31) (Class 5) (0-70,70) 3-Y-O+ **£3,886** (£1,156; £577; £288) **Stalls** Low

Form | | | | RPR
3211 **1** **Cashel Mead**[6] [1846] 6-9-11 68 7ex .... TravisBlock 11 84+
(J L Spearing) *hld up in midfield: hdwy and gng wl over 2f out: led ins fnl f: r.o wl* **6/4**[1]

1220 **2** *1 ¾* **Zazous**[31] [1209] 5-8-13 56 oh3 .... MarcHalford 10 60
(J J Bridger) *swtg: hld up: rdn and hdwy over 1f out: nt clr run briefly ins fnl f: r.o to take 2nd towards fin: nt trble wnr* **33/1**

0052 **3** *nk* **Enjoy The Buzz**[14] [1645] 7-8-10 56 oh4 .... RonanKeogh(3) 8 59+
(J M Bradley) *lw: hld up in midfield: hdwy whn nt clr run and hmpd over 1f out: r.o ins fnl f* **12/1**

0664 **4** *nk* **Kempsey**[20] [1474] 4-9-13 70 .... (v) StephenDonohoe 6 72
(J J Bridger) *led: rdn over 1f out: hdd ins fnl f: kpt on same pce* **9/1**

0000 **5** *½* **Coranglais**[4] [1878] 6-8-12 58 .... (p) LiamJones(3) 12 58
(J M Bradley) *swtg: s.s: towards rr: rdn and hdwy over 1f out: swtchd rt ins fnl f: styd on* **16/1**

0600 **6** ¾ **Free Wheelin (IRE)**[158] 6611 6-8-13 **56** oh11 .... RoryMoore 5 54
(T M Jones) *s.i.s: sn trckd ldrs: rdn and edgd rt over 1f out: one pce after* **33/1**

110 **7** *shd* **Auentraum (GER)**[49] 903 6-8-12 **60** ....(p) JosephWalsh(5) 9 57
(K McAuliffe) *in tch: clsd over 2f out: rdn and ev ch 1f out: hung rt ins fnl f: wknd towards fin* **14/1**

0040 **8** *nk* **Trace Clip**[8] 1802 8-8-8 **56** oh3 .... MarkCoumbe(5) 1 52
(N I M Rossiter) *lw: s.s: hld up: hdwy whn nt clr run over 1f out: kpt on ins fnl f* **25/1**

5350 **9** 1¾ **Seven No Trumps**[6] 1846 9-8-9 **59** .... BarrySavage(7) 4 49
(J M Bradley) *prom tl rdn and wknd over 1f out* **8/1**[3]

4353 **10** ½ **Hello Roberto**[9] 1774 5-9-0 **62** ....(p) TolleyDean(5) 3 51
(R A Harris) *hld up: rdn over 2f out: nvr on terms* **6/1**[2]

4130 **11** 2 **Desert Light (IRE)**[8] 1795 5-9-4 **64** ....(v) DerekNolan(3) 7 46
(D Shaw) *swtg: trckd ldrs: rdn over 2f out: wknd over 1f out* **28/1**

4005 **12** ¾ **Starduster**[13] 1689 4-9-0 **62** .... JamesMillman(5) 2 41
(B R Millman) *hld up: rdn over 1f out: nvr on terms* **12/1**

61.76 secs (2.71) **Going Correction** +0.65s/f (Yiel) 12 Ran SP% **116.5**
Speed ratings (Par 103):104,101,100,100,99 98,98,97,94,94 90,89
CSF £70.64 CT £444.52 TOTE £2.20: £1.40, £4.40, £2.50; EX 60.20 Place 6 £2.64, Place 5 £2.26.
Owner Masonaires **Bred** D R Tucker **Trained** Kinnersley, Worcs

FOCUS
An ordinary sprint handicap and those that were drawn closest to the stands' rail seemed at a major disadvantage. The winner impressed again, but several of her closest rivals were racing from out of the proper handicap.
T/Plt: £4.80 to a £1 stake. Pool: £70,274.00. 10,580.45 winning tickets. T/Qpdt: £3.30 to a £1 stake. Pool: £2,103.60. 466.10 winning tickets. DO

1479 HAYDOCK (L-H)
Friday, May 26

OFFICIAL GOING: Heavy (soft in places)
The ground was described as heavy at the start but on a drying day it ended up 'tacky and like glue'.
Wind: Fresh, half-against Weather: Fine and becoming sunny but breezy

1982 SLATERS OF ABERGELE RENAULT MAIDEN AUCTION STKS 5f
2:30 (2:31) (Class 5) 2-Y-O **£3,238** (£963; £481; £240) Stalls High

Form RPR

5 **1** **Dickie Le Davoir**[13] 1664 2-8-11 .... RobertWinston 5 76
(K R Burke) *trckd ldrs: led over 1f out: edgd lft ins last: hld on towards fin* **10/3**[1]

2 *hd* **Invincible Force (IRE)** 2-8-9 .... FrancisNorton 7 73
(Ms Deborah J Evans) *leggy: trckd ldrs: effrt over 2f out: hung lft over 1f out: no ex towards fin* **14/1**

0 **3** 2½ **Seaton Snooks**[16] 1588 2-8-9 .... FergalLynch 4 64
(T D Easterby) *led tl over 1f out: kpt on same pce* **6/1**[3]

4 12 **Fiddlers Spirit (IRE)** 2-8-9 .... PaulHanagan 10 21+
(J G M O'Shea) *cmpt: swvd lft s: in tch: outpcd over 2f out: sn n.d* **14/1**

00 **5** 1¼ **Emefdream**[35] 1107 2-8-11 .... DO'Donohoe 1 19
(K A Ryan) *w ldrs: lost pl over 1f out* **9/2**[2]

6 3 **Windjammer** 2-8-11 .... GrahamGibbons 9 8
(T D Easterby) *rangy: dwlt: sn prom: lost pl over 1f out* **17/2**

0 **7** 1½ **Vodkat**[23] 1420 2-8-4 .... KimTinkler 3 —
(N Tinkler) *squeezed out s: sn in tch: wknd 2f out* **7/1**

8 30 **Tullythered (IRE)** 2-8-9 .... JoeFanning 8 —
(A Berry) *rangy: swvd bdly lft s: a bhd: eased fnl 2f: t.o* **20/1**

5 **9** 1½ **Stepaside (IRE)**[40] 1030 2-8-13 .... KDarley 2 —
(M Johnston) *chsd ldrs on outer: sn pushed along: lost pl over 2f out: bhd and eased ins last: t.o* **6/1**[3]

67.18 secs (5.11) **Going Correction** +0.95s/f (Soft) 9 Ran SP% **111.0**
Speed ratings (Par 93):97,96,92,73,71 66,64,16,13
CSF £48.20 TOTE £3.40: £1.70, £3.10, £2.30; EX 40.70.
Owner Bigwigs Bloodstock II **Bred** P And Mrs A G Venner **Trained** Middleham Moor, N Yorks

FOCUS
An ordinary maiden auction with the first three a long way clear in the testing conditions. The form is difficult to assess but the winner will improve again.

NOTEBOOK
Dickie Le Davoir, much fitter, always looked like doing just enough though it was a close call in the end. A laid-back individual, he will improve again. (op 7-2)
Invincible Force(IRE), a March foal, is on the leg. He showed his inexperience and in the end just missed out. (op 12-1)
Seaton Snooks, dropping back in trip, took them along and had no excuse. (op 11-2)
Fiddlers Spirit(IRE), a March foal, is a close-coupled type. He went sideways at the start and was left well behind from soon after halfway. (op 12-1)
Emefdream, now a gelding, showed bags of toe before falling in a heap in the bad ground. (op 13-2)
Windjammer, a January foal, has a pedigree a mixture of speed and stamina. He moved poorly to post and finished very tired in the testing conditions. (op 8-1 tchd 9-1)
Vodkat Official explanation: jockey said filly suffered interference shortly after gates opened
Stepaside(IRE), a lazy walker, was soon pushed along to keep up on the outer and stopping to nothing, in the end struggled to cross the winning line. He is not the first from this yard to disappoint badly recently and this was simply too bad to be true. (op 11-2)

1983 RENAULT MANCHESTER H'CAP 6f
3:05 (3:08) (Class 4) (0-80,78) 3-Y-O **£6,477** (£1,927; £963; £481) Stalls High

Form RPR

3225 **1** **Gavarnie Beau (IRE)**[23] 1411 3-9-3 **77** .... FrancisNorton 6 82
(M Blanshard) *hld up: hdwy: nt clr run and swtchd lft over 2f out: led ins last: jst hld on* **13/2**[3]

5301 **2** *hd* **Garstang**[23] 1411 3-8-6 **66** ow2 ....(b) RobbieFitzpatrick 7 70
(Peter Grayson) *in rr: hdwy on ins to ld over 1f out: hdd ins last: hung rt and rallied: jst hld* **9/1**

410 **3** ¾ **Makfly**[15] 1606 3-9-4 **78** .... RobertWinston 8 80
(R Hollinshead) *swtchd lft after 2f: hdwy on outside over 2f out: upsides jst ins last: no ex* **11/2**[2]

4004 **4** 6 **Glasshoughton**[20] 1482 3-8-9 **72** .... BenSwarbrick(3) 1 56
(M Dods) *w ldrs on outer: led 2f out: sn hdde and wknd* **7/1**

11 **5** 5 **Damika (IRE)**[14] 1642 3-9-4 **78** .... DeanMcKeown 2 47
(R M Whitaker) *sltly hmpd s: w ldrs: led over 2f out: sn hdd & wknd* **3/1**[1]

0000 **6** 6 **Canina**[44] 988 3-8-7 **67** .... AdrianTNicholls 5 18
(Ms Deborah J Evans) *chsd ldrs: rdn and wknd 2f out* **33/1**

1050 **7** 1½ **Observatory Star (IRE)**[283] 4456 3-9-0 **74** .... GrahamGibbons 3 21
(T D Easterby) *bmpd s: w ldrs: wekaneing whn n.m.r wl over 1f out* **16/1**

104 **8** 1¾ **The History Man (IRE)**[7] 1812 3-9-1 **75** ....(b) DaleGibson 4 16
(M W Easterby) *swvd lft s: led tl hdd & wknd over 2f out* **3/1**[1]

1m 20.96s (6.06) **Going Correction** +0.95s/f (Soft) 8 Ran SP% **110.0**
Speed ratings (Par 101):97,96,95,87,81 73,71,68
CSF £57.77 CT £261.28 TOTE £7.90: £1.90, £2.40, £1.60; EX 73.30.
Owner Lloyd Hill **Bred** Seamus Murphy **Trained** Upper Lambourn, Berks

FOCUS
Ordinary fare, the first three clear and rated at face value for now.

1984 LOOKERS STOCKPORT MAIDEN STKS 1m 30y
3:40 (3:44) (Class 4) 3-Y-O+ **£6,477** (£1,927; £963; £481) Stalls Low

Form RPR

1 **Future's Dream**[281] 3-8-12 66 .... PatCosgrave 8 84
(K R Burke) *mid-div: effrt over 3f out: styd on to ld ins last: kpt on wl* **33/1**

32 **2** 2 **Northern Boy (USA)**[255] 5203 3-8-12 .... PaulHanagan 3 80
(T D Barron) *led: hdd and no ex ins last* **4/1**[2]

32 **3** ¾ **Escape Clause (USA)**[33] 1166 3-8-12 .... RobertWinston 7 79
(Sir Michael Stoute) *trckd ldng pair: t.k.h: rdn and hung lft over 1f out: no ex* **2/5**[1]

4 8 **Gobi King** 4-9-10 .... NickyMackay 4 66
(L M Cumani) *rangy: tall: hld up in mid-div: effrt over 3f out: nvr on terms* **20/1**

02 **5** 5 **Zurbaran (IRE)**[205] 6227 3-8-12 .... MickyFenton 2 53
(K A Morgan) *chsd ldr: wknd over 1f out* **14/1**[3]

66 **6** 8 **Virginia Rose (IRE)**[13] 1684 3-8-7 .... KDarley 10 32
(J G Given) *in rr: sme hdwy over 3f out: nvr on terms* **50/1**

00 **7** 4 **Zingbat (IRE)**[13] 1684 3-8-12 .... NeilPollard 9 29
(J G Given) *hld up in rr: effrt over 3f out: nvr on terms* **150/1**

0 **8** 4 **Smoke It (IRE)**[5] 1866 3-8-12 .... FrancisNorton 6 21
(A Berry) *s.i.s: a bhd* **200/1**

0 **9** 30 **Pelican Hill (IRE)**[13] 1674 3-8-12 .... DO'Donohoe 1 —
(T H Caldwell) *s.s: a bhd: t.o 4f out* **100/1**

1m 49.1s (3.59) **Going Correction** +0.625s/f (Yiel)
WFA 3 from 4yo 12lb 9 Ran SP% **109.9**
Speed ratings (Par 105):107,105,104,96,91 83,79,75,45
CSF £147.29 TOTE £34.50: £5.50, £1.10, £1.02; EX 158.80.
Owner Mrs M Gittins **Bred** Mrs D Du Feu **Trained** Middleham Moor, N Yorks

FOCUS
A sound gallop, the first three clear, the form looks sound rated through the runner-up and the ex-French winner will be well treated under a penalty.

1985 LEWIS REED STKS (H'CAP) 1m 30y
4:10 (4:11) (Class 3) (0-90,90) 4-Y-O+ **£9,715** (£2,890; £1,444; £721) Stalls Low

Form RPR

2211 **1** **Pride Of Nation (IRE)**[31] 1207 4-9-1 **87** .... NickyMackay 2 110+
(L M Cumani) *trckd ldrs: led on bit 2f out: pushed out: v comf* **11/8**[1]

2301 **2** 2 **Goodbye Mr Bond**[5] 1864 6-8-11 **83** 3ex .... FrancisNorton 9 99
(E J Alston) *hld up in rr: shkn up 3f out: wnt 2nd over 1f out: no imp* **7/2**[2]

0203 **3** 4 **Skidrow**[13] 1676 4-9-3 **89** .... HayleyTurner 6 97
(M L W Bell) *trckd ldrs: effrt over 2f out: one pce* **10/1**

2066 **4** 3 **Sew'N'So Character (IRE)**[16] 1585 5-8-13 **85** .... PaulHanagan 8 87
(M Blanshard) *trckd ldrs: effrt 2f out: wknd last 150yds* **11/1**

0040 **5** 1¼ **Chief Scout**[18] 1532 4-8-6 **78** ow1 .... TomEaves 4 78
(I Semple) *t.k.h: led early: trckd ldrs: lost pl over 1f out* **20/1**

4100 **6** 5 **Mezuzah**[27] 1280 6-8-5 **77** .... PaulMulrennan 3 67
(M W Easterby) *sn led: hdd 2f out: sn wknd* **7/1**[3]

1111 **7** 3½ **Tyzack (IRE)**[29] 1257 5-8-10 **82** .... MickyFenton 10 65
(Stef Liddiard) *racd wd: trckd ldrs: lost pl over 2f out* **16/1**

3440 **8** 1½ **Harvest Warrior**[18] 1532 4-8-10 **82** ow2 ....(b) FergalLynch 5 62
(T D Easterby) *hld up: hdwy on ins over 3f out: sn chsng ldrs: lost pl 2f out* **14/1**

1m 48.05s (2.54) **Going Correction** +0.625s/f (Yiel) 8 Ran SP% **111.6**
Speed ratings (Par 107):112,110,106,103,101 96,93,91
CSF £5.70 CT £30.79 TOTE £2.30: £1.10, £1.30, £2.50; EX 5.20.
Owner Equibreed S.R.L. **Bred** Deni S R L **Trained** Newmarket, Suffolk

FOCUS
A sound gallop and solid form with a very comfortable winner who will progress again.

NOTEBOOK
Pride Of Nation(IRE) ◆, who accounted for a subsequent winner at Bath, was racing from an 11lb higher mark. He travelled supremely well and made this looks very simple. He will win in stronger company than this. (op 5-4 tchd 6-4)
Goodbye Mr Bond, back in trip, ran well under his penalty but the winner was much too good. (op 4-1)
Skidrow ran right up to his best but he looks weighted to the very limit now.
Sew'N'So Character(IRE), who lasted tasted success a year ago, handles these conditions and put three poor efforts behind him. (op 12-1)
Chief Scout, having his second outing in two weeks after a six-month break, has slipped down the rtaings. He was too keen for his own good and seven might suit him better. (op 18-1)
Mezuzah, 7lb higher than Redcar, took them along at a good clip but he is no great battler. (op 8-1 tchd 9-1 in a place)
Tyzack(IRE) Official explanation: jockey said gelding was unsuited by the heavy (soft in places) ground

1986 SUNWIN RENAULT H'CAP 7f 30y
4:45 (4:45) (Class 3) (0-95,87) 3-Y-O **£9,715** (£2,890; £1,444) Stalls Low

Form RPR

51 **1** **River Bravo (IRE)**[221] 5946 3-9-3 **86** .... AdrianMcCarthy 2 100+
(P W Chapple-Hyam) *trckd ldr: chal on bit over 2f out: shkn up to ld over 1f out: r.o strly* **7/4**[2]

0241 **2** 1½ **Imperial Sword**[7] 1812 3-8-12 **81** 6ex .... RobertWinston 1 88
(T D Barron) *hld up in last: trckd ldrs: effrt over 2f out: rdn and hung lft 1f out: no real imp* **2/1**[3]

1241 **3** 9 **Namid Reprobate (IRE)**[25] 1337 3-9-4 **87** .... JoeFanning 3 72
(P F I Cole) *led: drvn and qcknd over 2f out: hdd over 1f out: wknd and eased 1f out* **13/8**[1]

1m 39.85s (7.79) **Going Correction** +0.625s/f (Yiel) 3 Ran SP% **107.8**
Speed ratings (Par 103):80,78,68
CSF £5.22 TOTE £2.70; EX 3.90.
Owner R J Arculli **Bred** Max Morris **Trained** Newmarket, Suffolk

FOCUS
A decent handicap but a very steady gallop with the second the best guide to the form. The winner, who clearly handles the mud, has the potential to go on to better things.

NOTEBOOK

River Bravo(IRE), winner at Windsor in October on just his second start, travelled strongly and made this look very straightforward. He clearly appreciates getting his toe in and has a fair amount of potential. (op 11-8 tchd 15-8)

Imperial Sword, under his penalty, was stepping up a furlong in trip and in the un-exposed winner, simply met one much too good.

Namid Reprobate(IRE), 5lb higher, set just a steady pace but was readily brushed aside and with all chance gone, was allowed to complete in his own time. This was still a very disappointing effort. (op 15-8)

1987 RENAULT LIVERPOOL H'CAP — 1m 2f 120y

5:20 (5:20) (Class 5) (0-75,74) 4-Y-0+ — **£3,238** (£963; £481; £240) — **Stalls** High

Form — RPR

5000 **1** — **The Composer**[34] [1132] 4-8-9 **65** .... FrancisNorton 6 — 78
(M Blanshard) *chsd ldrs: drvn along and lost pl over 6f out: hdwy to go 2nd over 2f out: led 1f out: styd on* — **11/2**[2]

2430 **2** 1 3/4 **Greenbelt**[44] [976] 5-8-11 **67** .... JoeFanning 4 — 77
(G M Moore) *hld up: hdwy to ld 3f out: hdd 1f out: no ex* — **7/1**

045- **3** 7 **Tudor Bell (IRE)**[463] [6534] 5-9-1 **74** .... BenSwarbrick(3) 5 — 72
(J G M O'Shea) *s.i.s: detached in rr: hdwy over 2f out: styd on fnl f: tk modest 3rd cl home* — **20/1**

0060 **4** 2 **Mixing**[20] [1478] 4-8-7 **63** .... PaulHanagan 7 — 58
(W Jarvis) *trckd ldrs: wknd appr fnl f* — **9/2**[1]

5000 **5** hd **Nevada Desert (IRE)**[18] [1531] 6-9-1 **71** .... DeanMcKeown 3 — 65
(R M Whitaker) *trckd ldrs: chal over 3f out: wknd over 1f out* — **6/1**[3]

3132 **6** 4 **Latif (USA)**[20] [1480] 5-9-0 **73** .... AdamKirby(3) 2 — 61
(Ms Deborah J Evans) *stdd s: sn trcking ldrs: effrt over 3f out: wknd 2f out* — **9/2**[1]

400 **7** 9 **Little Bob**[5] [1864] 5-8-11 **67** .... (b) GrahamGibbons 8 — 39
(J D Bethell) *mde most: hdd 3f out: wknd and eased* — **8/1**

0000 **8** 12 **Intricate Web (IRE)**[171] [6520] 10-8-12 **68** .... AdrianMcCarthy 9 — 20
(E J Alston) *trckd ldrs: hung lft over 2f out: sn lost pl and eased* — **10/1**

3154 **9** 30 **Buscador (USA)**[31] [1222] 7-7-11 **60** oh8 .... LukeMorris(7) 1 — —
(W M Brisbourne) *w ldr: drvn over 5f out: lost pl over 3f out: hung rt and sn bhd: virtually p.u: t.o:* — **14/1**

2m 22.33s (4.60) **Going Correction** +0.625s/f (Yiel) — 9 Ran SP% **110.2**

Speed ratings (Par 103):108,106,101,100,100 97,90,81,60

CSF £40.38 CT £666.01 TOTE £6.50: £1.80, £2.30, £4.40; EX 71.10.

Owner A D Jones **Bred** D A And Mrs Hicks **Trained** Upper Lambourn, Berks

FOCUS

An ordinary handicap run at a sound pace, in the end the first two clear. The runner-up sets the standard.

Tudor Bell(IRE) Official explanation: jockey said gelding hung right

Latif(USA) Official explanation: jockey said gelding was unsuited by the heavy (soft in places) ground

1988 WAINHOMES MAIDEN STKS — 1m 3f 200y

5:50 (5:50) (Class 5) 3-Y-0+ — **£3,238** (£963; £481; £240) — **Stalls** High

Form — RPR

3 **1** — **Rainbow's Edge**[27] [1283] 3-8-4 .... PaulHanagan 5 — 77+
(R Charlton) *trckd ldrs: wnt 2nd over 4f of out: led on bit over 2f out: clr 1f out: easily* — **8/13**[1]

0050 **2** 8 **Minthare (IRE)**[219] [5987] 3-8-9 50 .... TonyHamilton 4 — 64
(C Grant) *s.i.s: t.k.h: effrt over 4f out: wnt 2nd over 2f out: no ch w wnr* — **25/1**

4360 **3** 2 **Discord**[15] [652] 5-9-12 61 .... FrancisNorton 6 — 63
(T H Caldwell) *hld up: hdwy to chse ldrs 5f out: one pce fnl 2f* — **25/1**

2 **4** 20 **Contemplation**[7] [1826] 3-8-9 .... JoeFanning 7 — 33
(M Johnston) *trckd ldrs: hdwy to ld over 5f out: hdd over 2f out: sn lost pl and bhd* — **7/4**[2]

6 **5** 8 **Brief Statement (IRE)**[14] [1635] 4-9-12 .... RobbieFitzpatrick 1 — 24
(W M Brisbourne) *led: hdd over 5f out: lost pl over 3f out* — **20/1**[3]

0000 **6** 62 **Vincent Vegas**[10] [1768] 3-8-7 25 ow5 .... JohnCavanagh(7) 3 — —
(Mrs S Lamyman) *w ldr: lost pl over 4f out: t.o 2f out: btn 100l* — **100/1**

2m 44.22s (9.23) **Going Correction** +0.625s/f (Yiel)
WFA 3 from 4yo+ 17lb — 6 Ran SP% **111.7**

Speed ratings (Par 103):94,88,87,74,68 27

CSF £19.45 TOTE £1.60: £1.20, £4.80; EX 26.00 Place 6 £76.96, Place 5 £39.55.

Owner The Queen **Bred** The Queen **Trained** Beckhampton, Wilts

■ Stewards' Enquiry : John Cavanagh one-day ban: used whip when out of contention (Jun 6)

FOCUS

A sound gallop and a facile winner. The runner-up is rated just 50 and limits the form, with the third the best guide.

T/Plt: £114.90 to a £1 stake. Pool: £48,356.30. 307.15 winning tickets. T/Qpdt: £18.30 to a £1 stake. Pool: £2,577.80. 103.80 winning tickets. WG

1674 NEWMARKET (ROWLEY) (R-H)

Friday, May 26

OFFICIAL GOING: Soft

Wind: Fresh, half-behind Weather: Cloudy with sunny spells

1989 UNICORN E B F MAIDEN FILLIES' STKS — 6f

2:20 (2:22) (Class 5) 2-Y-0 — **£4,533** (£1,348; £674; £336) — **Stalls** Low

Form — RPR

2 **1** — **Bicoastal (USA)**[13] [1675] 2-9-0 .... JimmyFortune 2 — 79+
(B J Meehan) *leggy: scope: mde all: rdn over 1f out: r.o* — **2/1**[1]

2 1 **Buddies Girl (IRE)** 2-9-0 .... MichaelHills 14 — 76+
(R Hannon) *cmpt: bit bkwd: hdwy 4f out: ev ch over 1f out: styd on same pce towards fin* — **40/1**

3 1 1/2 **Alzerra (UAE)** 2-9-0 .... TedDurcan 7 — 72+
(M R Channon) *leggy: scope: lw: chsd wnr: rdn and ev ch over 1f out: no ex ins fnl f* — **10/1**[2]

4 2 1/2 **Sander Camillo (USA)** 2-9-0 .... LDettori 4 — 64+
(J Noseda) *w'like: scope: hld up: outpcd over 2f out: styd on ins fnl f* — **2/1**[1]

4 **5** shd **Miss Ippolita**[52] [878] 2-9-0 .... RichardMullen 8 — 64
(J R Jenkins) *hld up in tch: plld hrd: rdn over 1f out: wknd fnl f* — **33/1**

6 nk **Lady Lily (IRE)** 2-9-0 .... EddieAhern 6 — 63+
(H R A Cecil) *leggy: scope: chsd ldrs: outpcd over 2f out: styd on ins fnl f* — **12/1**

6 **7** 1 1/2 **Our Ruby**[18] [1542] 2-9-0 .... SebSanders 1 — 58
(P W Chapple-Hyam) *chsd ldrs over 4f* — **12/1**

8 3/4 **Scarlet Runner** 2-9-0 .... KerrinMcEvoy 12 — 56
(J L Dunlop) *w'like: cmpt: mid-div: rdn 1/2-way: wknd wl over 1f out* — **20/1**

9 1 **Don't Tell (IRE)** 2-9-0 .... TQuinn 3 — 53
(M L W Bell) *neat: prom: lost pl over 3f out: n.d after* — **20/1**

10 1/2 **Miss Saafend Plaza (IRE)** 2-9-0 .... RHills 5 — 52
(R Hannon) *w'like: s.i.s: nvr trbld ldrs* — **11/1**[3]

11 hd **Moist** 2-9-0 .... ChrisCatlin 10 — 51
(N A Callaghan) *small: s.s: outpcd* — **66/1**

12 5 **Silver Flame** 2-9-0 .... MichaelTebbutt 9 — 36
(B J Meehan) *w'like: s.i.s: a in rr* — **50/1**

1m 16.0s (2.90) **Going Correction** +0.175s/f (Good) — **12** Ran SP% **117.8**

Speed ratings (Par 90):87,85,83,80,80 79,77,76,75,74 74,67

CSF £116.75 TOTE £3.20: £1.30, £7.90, £3.40; EX 108.20.

Owner Andrew Rosen **Bred** Summer Wind Farm **Trained** Manton, Wilts

FOCUS

This looked a fair maiden for the course, possibly spoilt by the ground. The winner looks decent and sets the standard, and winners should come from the race.

NOTEBOOK

Bicoastal(USA), stepping up in trip, went one better than she had done on her debut with a gritty display. She looked in trouble with a furlong to go after leading throughout the early stages, but stuck to the task well under strong pressure to win all out. A seventh furlong should be within her compass and she could well be an above-average sort. (op 11-4 tchd 3-1)

Buddies Girl(IRE), the second string of the stable on jockey bookings, looked all set to collect inside the final furlong before not quite getting home. This was a fine first effort and she should have learnt plenty.

Alzerra(UAE) kept on really strongly in the latter stages after tracking the pace. She has a really attractive pedigree and should have little trouble finding a maiden. (op 11-1 tchd 8-1)

Sander Camillo(USA) was well supported in the market for her debut, but appeared to flounder in the ground. Given that she was clearly expected to run well prior to the race, she can be given another chance on better going. (op 15-8)

Miss Ippolita, who was pretty keen in the early stages, kept on fairly well for pressure after racing prominently. It would be a surprise if some of those that finished behind do not improve past her, and she may well need a bit further in time given the way she was outpaced by the leaders. That said, she clearly has more than enough ability to win any ordinary maiden.

Lady Lily(IRE) stayed on nicely late in the day after being left behind when the pace increased. It was a satisfactory first effort without suggesting she will have a clear chance of winning next time. (op 9-1)

Scarlet Runner Official explanation: jockey said filly ran green and hung right

Moist may have been beaten quite decisively in the end, but she was very green throughout and never gave herself a sensible chance of getting involved. She should have enough ability to pick up a race of some description.

1990 UNICORNAM.COM CONDITIONS STKS — 1m

2:55 (2:57) (Class 4) 3-Y-0 — **£6,477** (£1,927; £963; £481) — **Stalls** Low

Form — RPR

15 **1** — **After You**[34] [1130] 3-8-7 95 .... MichaelHills 7 — 96
(B W Hills) *lw: mde all: qcknd 2f out: rdn over 1f out: r.o* — **4/1**[2]

152 **2** 1 3/4 **Metropolitan Man**[36] [1092] 3-8-12 108 .... KerrinMcEvoy 4 — 97
(D M Simcock) *hld up in tch: rdn over 1f out: edgd rt ins fnl f: r.o: nt rch wnr* — **7/2**[1]

024 **3** shd **Star Crowned (USA)**[19] [1505] 3-8-12 86 .... (bt) JimmyFortune 3 — 97?
(B J Meehan) *chsd wnr: rdn and edgd lft over 1f out: styd on same pce* — **15/2**

0100 **4** 3 **My Amalie (IRE)**[13] [1671] 3-8-7 95 .... SebSanders 2 — 86
(C E Brittain) *hld up: rdn over 2f out: nvr trbld ldrs* — **8/1**

51 **5** 2 **Illuminise (IRE)**[37] [1085] 3-8-7 89 .... LDettori 6 — 82
(E A L Dunlop) *lw: s.i.s: sn chsng ldrs: rdn and wknd over 1f out* — **9/2**[3]

1 **6** 1 1/2 **Bold Alaska (IRE)**[13] [1674] 3-8-12 .... RichardMullen 5 — 84
(E A L Dunlop) *b: lw: s.i.s: sn chsng ldrs: rdn over 2f out: wknd over 1f out* — **4/1**[2]

013 **7** 3 1/2 **Arminius (IRE)**[25] [1358] 3-8-12 90 .... (v[1]) RHills 1 — 77
(R Hannon) *lw: s.i.s: hld up: rdn over 3f out: wknd 2f out* — **12/1**

1m 41.0s (1.63) **Going Correction** +0.175s/f (Good) — 7 Ran SP% **111.0**

Speed ratings (Par 101):98,96,96,93,91 89,86

CSF £17.22 TOTE £5.00: £2.30, £1.90; EX 20.20.

Owner Guy Reed **Bred** G Reed **Trained** Lambourn, Berks

FOCUS

A decent little contest fought out by the two 'form' horses. The first two home look to be above average on their respective favoured going. The form is not rated too positively with the time slow.

1991 UNICORN ASSET MANAGEMENT H'CAP — 1m 4f

3:30 (3:37) (Class 3) (0-90,90) 4-Y-0+ — **£8,096** (£2,408; £1,203; £601) — **Stalls** High

Form — RPR

212 **1** — **Signatory (USA)**[229] [5764] 4-9-2 **88** .... JimmyFortune 8 — 105+
(J H M Gosden) *mde all: rdn clr over 1f out: styd on wl* — **7/2**[3]

-224 **2** 3 **River Alhaarth (IRE)**[14] [1631] 4-8-13 **85** .... EddieAhern 2 — 95
(P W Chapple-Hyam) *chsd wnr 4f: rdn over 3f out: outpcd over 1f out: styd on ins fnl f* — **5/2**[1]

6652 **3** 1 **Lets Roll**[9] [1779] 5-8-13 **88** .... SaleemGolam(3) 6 — 97
(C W Thornton) *a.p: chsd wnr 8f out: rdn and ev ch over 2f out : no ex fnl f* — **11/4**[2]

3150 **4** 3 **Alessano**[20] [1478] 4-8-4 **76** .... (b) RichardMullen 7 — 81
(G L Moore) *chsd ldrs: rdn over 2f out: edgd lft and wknd over 1f out* **25/1**

0000 **5** 1 **Balyan (IRE)**[27] [1294] 5-8-12 **84** .... TQuinn 11 — 87
(J Howard Johnson) *hld up: rdn over 3f out: nvr trbld ldrs* — **20/1**

1030 **6** 1/2 **Sweet Indulgence (IRE)**[223] [5903] 5-8-7 **79** .... TPQueally 9 — 82
(W J Musson) *lw: hld up: rdn over 2f out: n.d* — **14/1**

051 **7** nk **Sunisa (IRE)**[8] [1800] 5-8-5 82 6ex .... JamesDoyle(5) 3 — 84
(J Mackie) *hld up in tch: rdn over 2f out: edgd rt and wknd over 1f out* — **12/1**

-004 **8** 14 **Akritas**[9] [1779] 5-8-7 **79** .... SebSanders 4 — 62
(P F I Cole) *b: mid-div: rdn 3f out: wknd over 2f out: eased fnl f* **11/1**

304/ **9** 21 **Wavertree Boy (IRE)**[479] [5254] 6-9-4 **90** .... LPKeniry 10 — 43
(D R C Elsworth) *lw: s.i.s: hld up: wknd over 3f out* — **40/1**

2m 32.02s (-1.48) **Going Correction** +0.175s/f (Good) — 9 Ran SP% **111.2**

Speed ratings (Par 107):111,109,108,106,105 105,105,95,81

CSF £11.80 CT £25.12 TOTE £3.60: £1.50, £1.40, £1.20; EX 15.30 Trifecta £17.10 Pool: £826.31 - 34.17 winning tickets..

Owner Sheikh Mohammed **Bred** Waterville Lake Stables Limited **Trained** Newmarket, Suffolk

FOCUS

A fair handicap run at a slow early tempo but the overall time was decent. The winner may have been slightly flattered, but was impressive all the same and the form is rated at face value through those in the frame behind him. Feed The Meter was withdrawn after she bolted on the way to the start.

NOTEBOOK

Signatory(USA) ◆, who was quite weak in the market before the race, had it all his own way in front and won by a wide margin. He clearly has potential to progress further, given that he was unraced at two, and one would think that he will be aimed at a major handicap next, probably the Duke Of Edinburgh at Royal Ascot. (op 11-4 tchd 4-1)

The Form Book, Raceform Ltd, Compton, RG20 6NL

River Alhaarth(IRE), who was a positive in the market, never looked like getting to the head of affairs after being niggled at various stages of the race. The slow early tempo may not have suited him. (op 10-3)
Lets Roll looked to be niggled along quite early in the race and never really threatened to win at any stage. He is high enough in the weights at the moment. (op 3-1)
Alessano was always close to the pace but could not confirm places with Signatory on last season's form, even though he had the benefit of a run. However, he is yet to prove he handles ground with ease and can be excused the effort for that reason.
Balyan(IRE) showed a bit of promise in behind but never threatened to get involved. As a whole, the stable's horses are running quite well now after a lull, and he might be capable of better in the near future.
Sweet Indulgence(IRE), who has an odd head-carriage, did not shape too badly on his first run of the season, but probably needs to come down the weights a touch to be of really serious interest. (op 16-1)

1992 UNICORN FREE SPIRIT PARTNERSHIP H'CAP — 1m 2f
4:00 (4:06) (Class 4) (0-85,85) 4-Y-O+ **£5,505** (£1,637; £818; £408) **Stalls** Low

Form — RPR
5004 **1** **Day To Remember**[18] 1544 5-9-2 **83**....(t) EddieAhern 4 — 98
(E F Vaughan) *chsd ldrs: led 3f out: rdn clr over 1f out* **7/1**[1]
2202 **2** *4* **Folio (IRE)**[18] 1544 6-8-10 **77**.... TPQueally 5 — 85
(W J Musson) *lw: hld up: hdwy over 2f out: styd on ins fnl f: no ch w wnr* **8/1**[2]
0045 **3** *½* **Transvestite (IRE)**[18] 1544 4-8-9 **76**.... MichaelHills 1 — 83
(J W Hills) *lw: hld up: hdwy over 2f out: rdn to chse wnr and edgd rt over 1f out: styd on same pce ins fnl f* **7/1**[1]
6200 **4** *3* **Reaching Out (IRE)**[43] 5698 4-8-6 **73**.... KerrinMcEvoy 11 — 75
(N J Henderson) *chsd ldrs: rdn over 3f out: wknd over 1f out* **9/1**[3]
6052 **5** *hd* **Desert Cristal (IRE)**[24] 1380 5-9-2 **83**.... LDettori 9 — 85
(J R Boyle) *chsd ldr over 6f: sn rdn: wknd over 1f out* **7/1**[1]
6500 **6** *5* **Winners Delight**[69] 670 5-8-8 **75**.... RichardHughes 14 — 68
(C F Wall) *s.i.s: hld up: rdn over 2f out: nvr trbld ldrs* **25/1**
5601 **7** *1 ¼* **Active Asset (IRE)**[27] 1281 4-8-11 **78**.... ChrisCatlin 13 — 69
(M R Channon) *hld up: rdn over 2f out: n.d* **8/1**[2]
0220 **8** *1* **Namroc (IRE)**[29] 1262 5-9-4 **85**.... OscarUrbina 10 — 74
(N A Callaghan) *lw: hld up: hdwy 1/2-way: wknd over 2f out* **12/1**
3000 **9** *3* **Terminate (GER)**[25] 1357 4-8-1 **73**.... JamesDoyle(5) 12 — 57
(N P Littmoden) *s.s: hld up: rdn over 2f out: a in rr* **33/1**
5100 **10** *1 ¾* **Rawdon (IRE)**[38] 1071 5-9-4 **85**....(v) TQuinn 2 — 66
(M L W Bell) *hld up: rdn over 2f out: sn wknd* **9/1**[3]
0404 **11** *1 ¾* **Solo Flight**[31] 1206 9-9-4 **85**.... JimmyFortune 3 — 63
(H Morrison) *s.s: hld up: wknd over 2f out* **8/1**[2]
1020 **12** *3 ½* **Almanshood (USA)**[119] 214 4-8-5 **72**.... AllanMackay 6 — 44
(P L Gilligan) *led: clr 6f out: edgd lft 5f out: hdd 3f out: sn hung rt and wknd* **25/1**
0603 **13** *shd* **Foodbroker Founder**[151] 5948 6-8-13 **80**.... LPKeniry 8 — 52
(D R C Elsworth) *chsd ldrs over 6f* **16/1**

2m 5.66s (-0.05) **Going Correction** +0.175s/f (Good) **13** Ran SP% **115.0**
Speed ratings (Par 105):107,103,103,101,100 96,95,95,92,91 89,87,86
CSF £57.60 CT £407.38 TOTE £5.50: £1.90, £3.30, £2.40; EX 45.10.
Owner Racing For Gold **Bred** Stratford Place Stud **Trained** Newmarket, Suffolk

FOCUS
A solid-looking handicap run at a fair pace. This is a race that, although rated at face value, is one to treat with caution in the short-term when the ground changes, as the winner was always perfectly placed, while his final challengers came from too far off the pace.

1993 UNICORN "RACING FOR FUN" H'CAP — 1m
4:35 (4:39) (Class 5) (0-75,75) 4-Y-O+ **£3,886** (£1,156; £577; £288) **Stalls** Low

Form — RPR
6000 **1** **Rain Stops Play (IRE)**[32] 1186 4-9-1 **72**.... SebSanders 19 — 89
(M Quinn) *lw: racd alone far side: mde all: rdn clr fr over 1f out* **12/1**
4462 **2** *6* **Fasylitator (IRE)**[29] 1265 4-8-7 **67**.... SaleemGolam(3) 9 — 72
(D K Ivory) *lw: racd centre: chsd ldrs: hung rt over 1f out: led that gp ins fnl f: styd on same pce* **8/1**[3]
0111 **3** *¾* **Up Tempo (IRE)**[17] 1570 8-8-6 **68**....(b) AndrewMullen(5) 14 — 72
(C R Dore) *racd centre: w ldr tl led that gp 5f out: rdn and hung rt over 1f out: styd on same pce* **8/1**[3]
5004 **4** *2* **Tiber Tiger (IRE)**[13] 1673 6-8-1 **63**....(b) JamesDoyle(5) 13 — 63+
(N P Littmoden) *racd centre: hld up: hdwy u.p over 1f out: r.o: nrst fin* **13/2**[2]
0300 **5** *1 ½* **Littleton Telchar (USA)**[226] 5834 6-8-13 **70**.... KerrinMcEvoy 10 — 67
(Hugh O'Driscoll, Ire) *racd centre: s.i.s: hld up: hdwy over 2f out: wknd fnl f* **14/1**
1046 **6** *¾* **My Princess (IRE)**[14] 1636 4-9-4 **75**....(b[1]) JimmyFortune 3 — 70
(N A Callaghan) *lw: racd centre: chsd ldrs: hung rt and wknd over 1f out* **25/1**
1000 **7** *2* **Parnassian**[18] 1544 6-8-10 **70**.... RichardThomas(3) 8 — 61
(J A Geake) *b: racd centre: hld up: rdn over 2f out: wknd over 1f out* **5/1**[1]
2215 **8** *5* **Golden Applause (FR)**[259] 5095 4-9-1 **72**.... JimmyQuinn 2 — 53
(Mrs A L M King) *racd centre: hld up: effrt over 2f out: sn edgd rt and wknd* **14/1**
6001 **9** *1 ½* **Polish Index**[29] 1265 4-8-10 **67**....(p) RichardHughes 4 — 45
(J R Jenkins) *led centre 3f: hung rt and wknd over 1f out* **11/1**
3400 **10** *hd* **Kareeb (FR)**[209] 6161 9-8-11 **68**.... TPQueally 15 — 46
(W J Musson) *bkwd: racd centre: hld up: rdn and wknd over 2f out* **33/1**
0604 **11** *shd* **Lincolneurocruiser**[10] 1760 4-8-12 **69**.... RHills 17 — 46
(Mrs N Macauley) *racd centre: prom over 5f* **14/1**
1- **12** *1 ½* **Inch Lodge**[559] 6646 4-8-13 **70**.... LDettori 6 — 44
(Miss D Mountain) *b: racd centre: s.i.s: sn chsng ldrs: wknd over 2f out* **12/1**
0000 **13** *1 ½* **Bow Wave**[13] 1692 4-8-13 **70**.... FergusSweeney 7 — 41
(H Candy) *racd centre: hld up: rdn over 3f out: sn wknd* **16/1**
0 **14** *1 ¾* **Return In Style (IRE)**[23] 1410 5-9-3 **74**.... MichaelHills 11 — 42
(J W Hills) *racd centre: s.i.s: hld up: wknd 3f out* **33/1**
0500 **15** *6* **Nan Jan**[29] 1258 4-8-10 **67**....(t) RobertHavlin 16 — 23
(R Ingram) *racd centre: mid-div: wknd 3f out* **50/1**
6005 **16** *25* **Out For A Stroll**[33] 1164 7-8-6 **63**.... JamieMackay 1 — —
(S C Williams) *racd centre: sooon pushed along in rr: wknd over 3f out* **20/1**

1m 38.45s (-0.92) **Going Correction** +0.175s/f (Good) **16** Ran SP% **118.3**
Speed ratings (Par 103):111,105,104,102,100 100,98,93,91,91 91,89,88,86,80 55
CSF £95.71 CT £859.31 TOTE £14.90: £3.20, £2.30, £1.80, £2.10; EX 143.80.
Owner Paul Montgomery & Brian Morton **Bred** Lucayan Stud Ltd **Trained** Newmarket, Suffolk

FOCUS
A modest handicap but a smart piece of riding by Seb Sanders. As with the previous race, the form should be treated with caution on any other ground.
Up Tempo(IRE) Official explanation: jockey said gelding hung right
My Princess(IRE) Official explanation: jockey said filly ran too free
Parnassian Official explanation: jockey said gelding never travelled
Polish Index Official explanation: jockey said gelding hung right

1994 PETER WEBB MAIDEN STKS — 1m 2f
5:10 (5:16) (Class 5) 3-Y-O **£5,181** (£1,541; £770; £384) **Stalls** Low

Form — RPR
6 **1** **Invention (USA)**[37] 1087 3-9-3.... RichardHughes 8 — 89
(J H M Gosden) *led 8f: rdn over 1f out: sn hung lft: styd on u.p to ld nr fin* **4/1**[3]
033 **2** *nk* **Alhaajes (USA)**[14] 1627 3-9-3 97.... RHills 6 — 88
(B W Hills) *a.p: chsd wnr over 3f out: led 2f out: rdn and edgd lft ins fnl f: hdd nr fin* **6/5**[1]
24 **3** *1 ¼* **Dan Dare (USA)**[231] 5709 3-9-3.... KerrinMcEvoy 12 — 86
(Sir Michael Stoute) *chsd ldrs: outpcd 2f out: r.o ins fnl f* **7/2**[2]
4 **4** *2 ½* **Thumpers Dream**[209] 6143 3-8-12.... EddieAhern 7 — 76
(H R A Cecil) *chsd ldrs: rdn over 2f out: styd on same pce appr fnl f* **7/1**
5 *hd* **Ivory Gala (FR)** 3-8-12.... MichaelTebbutt 4 — 76
(B J Meehan) *gd sort: neat: s.i.s: hld up: hdwy over 2f out: nt rch ldrs* **66/1**
6 *8* **Miss Trinidad (USA)** 3-8-12.... JimmyFortune 2 — 61
(B J Meehan) *w'like: s.i.s: hld up: nvr nrr* **50/1**
7 *1* **Triple Bluff** 3-9-3.... JimCrowley 13 — 64
(Mrs A J Perrett) *gd sort: bkwd: s.i.s: hld up: hdwy 1/2-way: hung lft and wknd over 2f out: hung rt over 1f out* **50/1**
0 **8** *¾* **Gaze**[23] 1417 3-8-12.... MichaelHills 1 — 57
(W Jarvis) *s.i.s: hld up: rdn and wknd 3f out* **50/1**
0 **9** *28* **Top Award**[11] 1741 3-9-3.... OscarUrbina 3 — 9
(J R Fanshawe) *lw: chsd ldrs over 7f* **100/1**
0 **10** *4* **Mohtarres (USA)**[238] 5592 3-9-3.... MatthewHenry 9 — 2
(M A Jarvis) *b: bit bkwd: s.i.s: sn pushed along in rr: wknd over 3f out* **28/1**
66 **11** *18* **Monmouthshire**[18] 1546 3-9-3.... TQuinn 10 — —
(M L W Bell) *lw: prom 7f* **50/1**
12 *5* **Gallant Sir** 3-9-3.... SebSanders 11 — —
(J R Fanshawe) *w'like: scope: hld up: rdn 1/2-way: wknd over 3f out* **25/1**

2m 6.78s (1.07) **Going Correction** +0.175s/f (Good) **12** Ran SP% **117.8**
Speed ratings (Par 99):102,101,100,98,98 92,91,90,68,65 50,46
CSF £8.70 TOTE £5.30: £1.60, £1.20, £1.40; EX 10.50.
Owner K Abdulla **Bred** Juddmonte Farms Inc **Trained** Newmarket, Suffolk

FOCUS
Almost certainly a decent maiden that should produce winners in a similar grade or later on in handicap company.
Monmouthshire Official explanation: jockey said colt was unsuited by the soft ground
Gallant Sir Official explanation: jockey said colt had no more to give

1995 BOLLINGER CHAMPAGNE CHALLENGE SERIES H'CAP (FOR GENTLEMAN AMATEUR RIDERS) — 1m 2f
5:40 (5:41) (Class 5) (0-75,75) 4-Y-O+ **£3,747** (£1,162; £580; £290) **Stalls** Low

Form — RPR
0051 **1** **Prime Powered (IRE)**[7] 1821 5-11-1 **71** 5ex.... MrDHutchison(5) 6 — 80
(G L Moore) *hld up: hdwy over 2f out: styd on to ld post* **9/2**[2]
0000 **2** *shd* **Asaateel (IRE)**[10] 1755 4-10-10 **61** oh1.... MrWHogg 2 — 70
(G L Moore) *chsd ldrs: led over 3f out: rdn and hung rt over 2f out: swished tail: hdd post* **14/1**
1-12 **3** *1 ½* **Authority (IRE)**[371] 1870 6-11-7 **72**.... MrSWalker 13 — 78
(Lady Herries) *lw: chsd ldrs: rdn and ev ch whn hmpd over 2f out: swtchd lft over 1f out: styd on same pce ins fnl f* **11/4**[1]
0001 **4** *1 ¾* **Wild Pitch**[23] 1400 5-10-8 **64**....(b) JackMitchell(5) 7 — 70+
(P Mitchell) *lw: s.s: hdwy over 3f out: outpcd over 2f out: nt clr run wl over 1f out: r.o ins fnl f: nt trble ldrs* **12/1**
0454 **5** *nk* **Top Spec (IRE)**[22] 1435 5-11-1 **71**.... MrSPearce(5) 8 — 73
(J Pearce) *s.i.s: outpcd: rdn and hung lft over 2f out: hdwy and hung rt over 1f out: styd on* **9/2**[2]
0660 **6** *5* **Fabrian**[7] 1830 8-10-13 **71**.... MrMPrice(7) 1 — 64
(R J Price) *chsd ldrs over 7f* **16/1**
5051 **7** *½* **Secretary General (IRE)**[22] 1435 5-11-4 **74**.... MrOCole(5) 14 — 66
(P F I Cole) *led 3f: chsd ldrs tl wknd over 2f out* **5/1**[3]
0050 **8** *½* **Forthright**[128] 135 5-11-1 **71**.... MrMJJSmith(5) 3 — 63
(A W Carroll) *hld up: effrt over 2f out: sn wknd* **33/1**
4055 **9** *3* **Russalka**[203] 6245 5-10-3 **61** oh15.... MrAChahal(7) 4 — 47
(M Wigham) *b.hind: hld up: hdwy over 3f out: hung rt and wknd 2f out* **66/1**
0000 **10** *hd* **Entailment**[156] 6644 4-10-7 **63**.... MrPCollington(5) 10 — 49
(Miss Gay Kelleway) *hld up in tch: rdn and wkng whn n.m.r 2f out* **33/1**
040 **11** *2 ½* **Zarakash (IRE)**[13] 1692 6-11-10 **75**.... MrAJBerry 9 — 56
(Jonjo O'Neill) *s.s: a bhd* **33/1**
0050 **12** *7* **Halcyon Magic**[58] 794 8-10-5 **61** oh9....(b) MrSRees(5) 11 — 30
(M Wigham) *b: b.hind: chsd ldr: led 7f out: hdd over 3f out: wkng whn hmpd 2f out* **50/1**
000 **13** *hd* **Akash (IRE)**[5] 4920 6-10-10 **68**.... MrRBirkett(7) 5 — 36
(Miss J Feilden) *b.hind: mid-div: rdn 1/2-way: wknd over 3f out* **25/1**

2m 8.55s (2.84) **Going Correction** +0.175s/f (Good) **13** Ran SP% **116.1**
Speed ratings (Par 103):95,94,93,92,92 88,87,87,84,84 82,77,76
CSF £58.99 CT £204.91 TOTE £6.90: £2.30, £3.20, £1.70; EX 71.60 Place 6 £16.65, Place 5 £7.90.
Owner Prime Power GB Ltd **Bred** Caribbean Quest Partnership **Trained** Woodingdean, E Sussex
■ Stewards' Enquiry : Mr W Hogg one-day ban: used whip above shoulder height (Jun 14)

FOCUS
Only a modest race run in a time almost three seconds slower than the earlier handicap over the distance. Unlike earlier races, several of the principals came from off the pace.

T/Jkpt: Not won. T/Plt: £12.50 to a £1 stake. Pool: £66,013.60. 3,840.35 winning tickets. T/Qpdt: £5.30 to a £1 stake. Pool: £3,850.00. 536.30 winning tickets. CR

1420 PONTEFRACT (L-H)

Friday, May 26

OFFICIAL GOING: Good to soft

Wind: Virtually nil

1996 CONSTANT SECURITY SERVICES H'CAP — 1m 4y

6:35 (6:35) (Class 6) (0-65,65) 4-Y-0+ — **£3,238** (£963; £481; £240) **Stalls** Low

Form — RPR

6120 **1** — **Exit Smiling**[20] [1480] 4-9-4 **65** — MickyFenton 2 — 77
(P T Midgley) *trckd ldrs: hdwy 3f out: swtchd rt and rdn to chse ldr over 1f out: drvn ins last: styd on wl to ld nr line* **12/1**

0301 **2** *shd* **Sake (IRE)**[10] [1760] 4-9-3 **64** 5ex — KimTinkler 8 — 76
(N Tinkler) *mde most: rdn clr wl over 1f out: drvn ins last: hdd and no ex nr fin* **10/1**

1002 **3** *1 ¾* **Azreme**[17] [1568] 6-9-0 **61** — TonyCulhane 4 — 69+
(P Howling) *towards rr: rdn along 1/2-way: hdwy into midfield over 2f out: swtchd outside and rdn over 1f out: fin strly* **8/1**[3]

0000 **4** *1 ½* **Kaymich Perfecto**[39] [1041] 6-8-10 **64** — MichaelJStainton(7) 5 — 69
(R M Whitaker) *midfield: hdwy on inner 3f out: rdn to chse ldrs wl over 1f out: kpt on same pce ent last* **25/1**

2660 **5** *¾* **Abstract Folly (IRE)**[23] [1425] 4-8-9 **56** — AdrianTNicholls 18 — 59+
(J D Bethell) *stdd and swtchd lft s: bhd tl hdwy on inner over 2f out: sn rdn and styd on ins last: nrst fin* **25/1**

0456 **6** *3* **Band**[28] [1276] 6-8-8 **55** — NickyMackay 9 — 51
(E S McMahon) *trckd ldrs: hdwy 1/2-way: cl up 3f out: rdn along over 2f out: drvn and grad wknd appr last* **12/1**

3006 **7** *shd* **Qualitair Wings**[14] [1637] 7-8-13 **60** — DerekMcGaffin 3 — 56
(J Hetherton) *midfield: hdwy 2f out: sn rdn and kpt on ins last: nrst fin* **14/1**

4502 **8** *1 ¼* **Champain Sands (IRE)**[23] [1422] 7-8-10 **57** — DarryllHolland 1 — 50
(E J Alston) *in tch: hdwy to chse ldrs over 2f out: sn rdn and wknd ent last* **13/2**[2]

0000 **9** *nk* **Tidy (IRE)**[23] [1422] 6-8-8 **60** — GregFairley(5) 12 — 52
(Micky Hammond) *stdd s and towards rr: hdwy 3f out: rdn along to chse ldrs 2f out: wkng whn n.m.r over 1f out* **20/1**

0000 **10** *4* **Young Mr Grace (IRE)**[10] [1760] 6-8-13 **60** — (v[1]) FergalLynch 17 — 43
(T D Easterby) *in tch: hdwy on outer to chse ldrs 2f out: sn rdn and no imp appr last* **14/1**

5023 **11** *3 ½* **Confide (IRE)**[13] [1683] 4-8-11 **58** — DaleGibson 7 — 47+
(G A Swinbank) *dwlt: sn trcking ldrs: effrt over 2f out: sn rdn and wknd wl over 1f out* **5/1**[1]

0530 **12** *1 ½* **Height Of Spirits**[30] [1245] 4-8-10 **57** — PhillipMakin 11 — 28
(T D McCarthy) *a midfield* **40/1**

0360 **13** *10* **Parchment (IRE)**[29] [1253] 4-8-8 **55** — PaulMulrennan 6 — 3
(A J Lockwood) *a towards rr* **80/1**

3310 **14** *1* **My Obsession (IRE)**[39] [1041] 4-9-4 **65** — TedDurcan 15 — 11
(John Berry) *racd wd: a rr* **18/1**

3516 **15** *½* **The Bonus King**[13] [1665] 6-9-1 **62** — KDarley 16 — 7
(J Jay) *midfield: rdn along over 3f out: sn wknd* **12/1**

0050 **16** *2 ½* **Fuel Cell (IRE)**[13] [1683] 5-8-7 **54** — (b) GylesParkin 13 — —
(J O'Reilly) *a rr* **50/1**

0053 **17** *5* **Etoile Russe (IRE)**[15] [5382] 4-8-9 **61** — (t) LeanneKershaw(5) 14 — —
(P C Haslam) *a rr* **10/1**

1000 **18** *19* **Kabis Amigos**[23] [1422] 4-8-8 **62** — VictoriaBehan(7) 10 — —
(D Nicholls) *cl up: rdn along over 3f out: sn wknd* **40/1**

1m 47.22s (1.52) **Going Correction** +0.325s/f (Good) — **18** Ran SP% **121.5**
Speed ratings (Par 101):105,104,103,101,100 97,97,96,96,92 88,87,77,76,75 73,68,49
CSF £116.93 CT £1033.96 TOTE £17.10: £3.20, £2.50, £2.20, £8.90; EX 213.10.
Owner Peter Mee **Bred** Mrs D O Joly **Trained** Westow, N Yorks

FOCUS
A moderate but competitive handicap and the form looks solid. The pace looked reasonable, but the first two home were always close up.
Confide(IRE) Official explanation: jockey said gelding lost its action
My Obsession(IRE) Official explanation: jockey said gelding had no more to give

1997 MSK FILLIES' H'CAP — 1m 2f 6y

7:05 (7:05) (Class 5) (0-70,68) 3-Y-0+ — **£4,533** (£1,348; £674; £336) **Stalls** Low

Form — RPR

3000 **1** — **Epicurean**[234] [5685] 4-10-0 **64** — MickyFenton 4 — 71
(Mrs K Walton) *hld up in rr: hdwy on outer over 2f out: rdn to ld jstr ins last: sn drvn and kpt on wl* **20/1**

061 **2** *1* **Keisha Kayleigh (IRE)**[13] [1661] 3-8-10 **60** — TomEaves 8 — 63
(B Ellison) *trckd ldrs: hdwy 3f out: rdn along over 1f out: ev ch ins last: sn drvn and kpt on* **6/1**[3]

1200 **3** *1 ½* **Shekan Star**[11] [1729] 4-9-0 **50** oh1 — TonyCulhane 6 — 52
(K G Reveley) *prom: hdwy 1/2-way: cl up 3f out: rdn to ld 2f out: drvn and hdd ins last: kpt on* **7/2**[1]

3000 **4** *1* **Wolds Dancer**[279] [4565] 4-8-11 **52** — (b) DuranFentiman(5) 2 — 52
(T D Easterby) *chsd ldrs: rdn along and outpcd on inner over 3f out: kpt on ins last: nrst fin* **12/1**

0600 **5** *5* **Loch Awe**[16] [1599] 3-8-9 **59** — DaleGibson 9 — 48
(J G Given) *hld up towards rr: effrt 3f out: sn rdn along: kpt on fnl 2f: nvr nr ldrs* **25/1**

0503 **6** *nk* **Kalatime (IRE)**[14] [1638] 3-9-4 **68** — DarryllHolland 1 — 56
(A M Balding) *trckd ldrs: hdwy to ld over 3f out: rdn and hdd 2f out: drvn and wknd ent last* **7/2**[1]

000 **7** *13* **Saluscraggie**[323] [3287] 4-9-1 **51** — RobertWinston 7 — 16
(K G Reveley) *hld up: hdwy 1/2-way: cl up 3f out: sn rdn and wknd fnl 2f* **12/1**

5500 **8** *17* **Laheen (IRE)**[30] [1241] 3-8-5 **55** — KDarley 5 — —
(M H Tompkins) *a rr* **8/1**

2256 **9** *9* **Rose Muwasim**[16] [1599] 3-9-2 **66** — (b[1]) TedDurcan 3 — —
(E A L Dunlop) *led: rdn along and hdd over 3f out: sn wknd* **9/2**[2]

2m 20.14s (6.06) **Going Correction** +0.325s/f (Good)
WFA 3 from 4yo 14lb — **9** Ran SP% **112.0**
Speed ratings (Par 100):88,87,86,85,81 80,70,56,49
CSF £129.94 CT £524.70 TOTE £20.60: £4.10, £2.10, £1.70; EX 125.30.
Owner Keep The Faith Partnership **Bred** Worksop Manor Stud **Trained** Middleham Moor, N Yorks

FOCUS
A weak fillies' handicap rated around the third and fourth, but not really a race to dwell on.

1998 YOUNGSTERS CONDITIONS STKS — 6f

7:35 (7:35) (Class 2) 2-Y-0 — **£9,348** (£2,799; £1,399; £700) **Stalls** Low

Form — RPR

1 **1** — **Hellvelyn**[50] [892] 2-8-11 — TedDurcan 3 — 98+
(B Smart) *trckd ldr: smooth hdwy to ld over 1f out: sn clr* **4/6**[1]

1 **2** *4* **Always Fruitful**[16] [1595] 2-9-1 — KDarley 1 — 87
(M Johnston) *led: rdn along 2f out: hdd over 1f out: kpt on same pce* **4/1**[2]

3 *2 ½* **Tombi (USA)** 2-8-8 — DarryllHolland 4 — 73
(J Howard Johnson) *trckd ldng pair: effrt 2f out: sn rdn and kpt on same pce* **9/2**[3]

2215 **4** *10* **Urban Warrior**[38] [1066] 2-8-11 — RobertWinston 2 — 52+
(J R Best) *dwlt: in tch: rdn along 2f out: wknd and eased over 1f out* **9/1**

1m 19.27s (1.87) **Going Correction** +0.325s/f (Good) — **4** Ran SP% **108.2**
Speed ratings (Par 99):100,94,91,78
CSF £3.63 TOTE £1.70; EX 2.50.
Owner H E Sheikh Rashid Bin Mohammed **Bred** N E and Mrs Poole and Trickledown Stud **Trained** Hambleton, N Yorks

FOCUS
Just the four runners, but the front three are nice types and Hellvelyn confirmed the good impression he made when winning on his debut at Leicester with a comfortable success. The third is possibly the best guide to the level of the form.

NOTEBOOK
Hellvelyn, off the mark on his debut in a reasonable five-furlong Leicester maiden 50 days previously, took this step up in class in his stride with a comfortable success. His trainer won this race last year with Sir Xaar, who went on to finish fourth in the Coventry Stakes, and this one deserves his chance at Royal Ascot. (op 5-6)
Always Fruitful would have found this tougher than the six-furlong Ripon maiden he won on his debut and was ultimately no match for comfortable winner. He can be found easier opportunities. (op 10-3)
Tombi(USA) ◆, a 475,000euros half-brother to a few winners, including Tour Of The Cat, a high-class sprint winner in the US, and Cat On Tour, a smart sprinter/miler in the US, out of a triple winner in the States, is by the brilliant juvenile Johannesburg. Pitched in at the deep end on his debut, this was a pleasing introduction and, with the benefit of this experience, he should win his maiden before stepping up back up in class. (tchd 5-1)
Urban Warrior, already having his sixth start, was out of his depth but below form in any case. (tchd 17-2)

1999 PONTEFRACT IRISH NIGHT MONDAY 12TH JUNE H'CAP — 1m 4y

8:05 (8:05) (Class 4) (0-85,80) 3-Y-0 — **£6,477** (£1,927; £963; £481) **Stalls** Low

Form — RPR

6032 **1** — **Formal Decree (GER)**[16] [1596] 3-8-10 **72** — RobertWinston 2 — 82+
(G A Swinbank) *lost 10l s: stdy hdwy and w field at 1/2-way: prog on inner over 2f out: rdn to ld over 1f out: drvn and kpt on wl* **11/4**[2]

5215 **2** *1 ¼* **Flying Clarets (IRE)**[6] [1851] 3-8-8 **70** — PaulHanagan 5 — 77
(R A Fahey) *dwlt and plld hrd in rr: hdwy 3f out: rdn over 1f out: swtchd lft and drvn ins last: ch tl no ex towards fin* **10/1**

0202 **3** *2 ½* **Midnight Traveller**[14] [1640] 3-8-12 **74** — NickyMackay 4 — 75+
(L M Cumani) *hld up: pushed along and sltly outpcd 3f out: styd on u.p ins last: nrst fin* **2/1**[1]

2104 **4** *nk* **Heureux (USA)**[22] [1446] 3-9-4 **80** — DarryllHolland 3 — 81
(J Howard Johnson) *trckd ldrs: hdwy 3f out: rdn to ld briefly wl over 1f out: sn hdd: drvn and wknd ins last* **20/1**

0035 **5** *1 ½* **Baileys Encore**[213] [6102] 3-8-9 **71** — JoeFanning 6 — 68
(M Johnston) *prom: cl up 3f out: rdn and ev ch 2f out tl drvn and wknd ent last* **12/1**

0233 **6** *2 ½* **Rebellious Spirit**[16] [1599] 3-8-7 **69** — DarrenWilliams 1 — 65+
(P W Hiatt) *led: rdn along 3f out: drvn and hdd wl over 1f out: sn wknd* **9/1**

2204 **7** *12* **Queen's Composer (IRE)**[6] [1855] 3-8-10 **72** — PhilipRobinson 7 — 36
(B Smart) *keen: chsd ldrs: hdwy 3f out: rdn 2f out and sn wknd* **6/1**[3]

4154 **8** *14* **Crosby Vision**[16] [1592] 3-8-13 **75** — KDarley 8 — 7
(J R Weymes) *chsd ldrs on ouiter: rdn along wl over 2f out and sn wknd* **16/1**

1m 47.95s (2.25) **Going Correction** +0.325s/f (Good) — **8** Ran SP% **111.7**
Speed ratings (Par 101):101,99,97,96,95 92,80,66
CSF £28.60 CT £63.56 TOTE £3.50: £1.30, £2.30, £1.30; EX 33.90.
Owner Mrs Karen S Pratt **Bred** Gestut Olympia **Trained** Melsonby, N Yorks

FOCUS
A fair handicap in which Formal Decree overcame losing around eight lengths at the start to get up and win. The form is ordinary but sound.
Queen's Composer(IRE) Official explanation: jockey said colt was unsuited by the track

2000 CONSTANT SECURITY SERVING YORKSHIRE RACECOURSES H'CAP — 1m 4f 8y

8:35 (8:35) (Class 4) (0-80,80) 4-Y-0+ — **£6,477** (£1,927; £963; £481) **Stalls** Low

Form — RPR

3364 **1** — **Tannenberg (IRE)**[10] [1756] 5-8-8 **70** — DeanMcKeown 8 — 88+
(G A Swinbank) *dwlt: hld up in rr: gd hdwy on outer over 4f out: led wl over 2f out and sn rdn clr: styd on wl* **5/1**[3]

4042 **2** *6* **Rocket Force (USA)**[10] [1756] 6-8-5 **70** — DanielTudhope(3) 6 — 78
(N Wilson) *trckd ldrs: hdwy 4f out and sn cl up: rdn along over 2f out: drvn to chse wnr fr wl over 1f out: no imp* **5/1**[3]

1132 **3** *4* **Augustine**[5] [1864] 5-9-0 **76** — RobertWinston 3 — 78
(P W Hiatt) *hld up in tch: hdwy 3f out: rdn along over 2f out: sn drvn and one pce* **2/1**[1]

1343 **4** *¾* **Tcherina (IRE)**[9] [1779] 4-9-4 **80** — FergalLynch 5 — 80
(T D Easterby) *trckd ldrs: hdwy 4f out: sn rdn along and outpcd fr wl over 2f out* **5/2**[2]

6060 **5** *3* **Nessen Dorma (IRE)**[14] [1631] 5-9-1 **77** — (v) MickyFenton 1 — 73
(J G Given) *led: rdn along over 3f out: hdd wl over 2f out and sn wknd* **17/2**

6130 **6** *13* **Cordier**[14] [1651] 4-8-11 **73** — DaleGibson 2 — 48
(J Mackie) *chsd ldrs on inner: rdn along 4f out and sn btn* **33/1**

1356 **7** *63* **Bowled Out (GER)**[14] [1638] 4-8-5 **67** — (p) KDarley 4 — —
(P J McBride) *cl up: rdn along over 4f out: sn wknd: bhd and eased fnl 3f* **16/1**

2m 43.62s (3.32) **Going Correction** +0.325s/f (Good) — **7** Ran SP% **114.6**
Speed ratings (Par 105):101,97,94,93,91 83,41
CSF £29.97 CT £65.43 TOTE £6.60: £3.70, £2.20; EX 46.40.
Owner Nick Shutts **Bred** Darley **Trained** Melsonby, N Yorks

FOCUS
This looked a reasonable handicap beforehand but Tannenberg, who was a maiden coming into this, ran out a ready winner and they were well strung out behind. The form is taken at face value with the third and fourth coming here in decent form.

The Form Book, Raceform Ltd, Compton, RG20 6NL

2001 BARBICAN MAIDEN STKS 6f
9:05 (9:05) (Class 5) 3-Y-O £5,181 (£1,541; £770; £384) Stalls Low

Form RPR
4332 1 **Bel Cantor**[20] [1493] 3-8-12 74 RichardKingscote(5) 6 72
(W J H Ratcliffe) *mde all: rdn clr 2f out: drvn ins last and kpt on wl* 9/2[3]
4 2 1 **Penzo (IRE)**[17] [1564] 3-9-3 DarryllHolland 1 69
(J Howard Johnson) *trckd ldrs on inner: hdwy to chse wnr 2f out: drvn and kpt on wl fnl f* 8/1
3 1 1/4 **Our Putra** 3-9-3 PhilipRobinson 11 65
(M A Jarvis) *chsd ldrs: rdn 2f out: kpt on u.p fnl f* 11/4[2]
352 4 3 1/2 **Spinning**[13] [1687] 3-9-3 73 PhillipMakin 4 55
(T D Barron) *chsd ldrs: rdn along and outpcd 1/2-way: styd on appr last* 9/4[1]
5 3 **Liskaveen Beauty** 3-8-12 MickyFenton 9 41
(T J Fitzgerald) *s.i.s and bhd: stdy hdwy on inner over 2f out: kpt on appr last: nrst fin* 50/1
4345 6 3/4 **Opera Writer (IRE)**[16] [1589] 3-9-3 73 FergalLynch 2 44
(T D Easterby) *in tch: hdwy to chse ldrs 2f out: sn rdn and wknd over 1f out* 7/1
00 7 6 **Centreofattention**[22] [1445] 3-8-12 RoystonFfrench 10 21
(Mrs A Duffield) *a towards rr* 40/1
53 8 1/2 **Josarty**[15] [1609] 3-9-3 GrahamGibbons 8 24
(J J Quinn) *a towards rr* 11/1
0 9 1 3/4 **Honor Me (IRE)**[206] [6212] 3-8-9 DNolan(3) 3 14
(J J Quinn) *a towards rr* 50/1
0650 10 5 **Salisbury World (IRE)**[23] [1416] 3-9-3 57 DarrenWilliams 5 4
(J F Coupland) *prom: rdn along 3f out: wknd 2f out* 50/1
0 11 16 **Soba Fella**[13] [1687] 3-9-3 LeeEnstone 7 —
(P T Midgley) *s.i.s: a rr* 100/1

1m 18.91s (1.51) **Going Correction** +0.325s/f (Good) 11 Ran SP% 116.9
Speed ratings (Par 99):102,100,99,94,90 89,81,80,78,71 50
CSF £38.91 TOTE £6.70: £1.80, £2.50, £1.90; EX 37.20 Place 6 £ 124.60, Place 5 £ 34.48.
Owner W J H Ratcliffe **Bred** Henry And Mrs Rosemary Moszkowicz **Trained** Leyburn, N Yorks

FOCUS
A standard older horse sprint maiden rated around the winner.
T/Plt: £130.10 to a £1 stake. Pool: £54,333.00. 304.70 winning tickets. T/Qpdt: £20.60 to a £1 stake. Pool: £3,468.90. 124.40 winning tickets. JR

2002 - 2008a (Foreign Racing) - See Raceform Interactive

ASCOT (R-H)
Saturday, May 27

OFFICIAL GOING: Straight course - good to firm; round course - good to soft
The first meeting since Ascot's £200 million redevelopment. Bizarre ground; the straight described as good to firm, and the round course on the easy side.
Wind: Light across Weather: Rain

2009 MCGEE GROUP CONDITIONS STKS 6f
12:50 (12:52) (Class 3) 2-Y-O £7,772 (£2,312; £1,155; £577) Stalls Low

Form RPR
1 1 **Baby Strange**[10] [1770] 2-9-2 GrahamGibbons 5 95+
(P A Blockley) *w'like: trckd ldrs: led against nr side rail over 1f out: r.o wl* 9/4[1]
1 2 1 3/4 **La Neige**[35] [1136] 2-9-2 TedDurcan 4 90+
(M R Channon) *w'like: s.s: wl in rr: gd prog on outside 2f out: styd on fnl f* 9/2[2]
1 3 1 1/2 **Chjimes (IRE)**[26] [1360] 2-9-2 PatCosgrave 10 85
(K R Burke) *strong: lw: w ldr: led 2f out to over 1f out: outpcd* 9/4[1]
4 shd **The Old Fella** 2-8-8 RyanMoore 3 77+
(R Hannon) *w'like: leggy: hld up: prog over 2f out: styd on same pce fnl f* 12/1
41 5 3/4 **King's Bastion (IRE)**[15] [1639] 2-9-2 MartinDwyer 11 83
(M L W Bell) *lw: pressed ldrs on outer: styd on same pce fnl 2f* 15/2[3]
6 shd **Dumas (IRE)** 2-8-8 FrankieMcDonald 6 74
(A P Jarvis) *w'like: b.bkwd: chsd ldrs: rdn and one pce fr over 2f out* 50/1
0613 7 5 **Mr Klick (IRE)**[10] [1780] 2-8-11 DNolan(3) 1 65
(N Wilson) *swtg: led to 2f out: wknd* 33/1
0 8 nk **Venir Rouge**[7] [1838] 2-8-8 AdamKirby(3) 8 62
(M Salaman) *w ldrs over 3f: wknd* 100/1
9 5 **Revisionist (IRE)** 2-8-5 RichardSmith(3) 7 44
(R Hannon) *b.bkwd: chsd ldrs: wknd 2f out* 33/1
10 1 1/2 **Ceris Star (IRE)** 2-8-8 TQuinn 2 39
(B R Millman) *b.bkwd: a wl bhd* 25/1

1m 16.66s **Going Correction** +0.075s/f (Good) 10 Ran SP% 111.9
Speed ratings (Par 97):98,95,93,93,92 92,85,85,78,76
CSF £11.54 TOTE £3.10: £1.40, £1.60, £1.60; EX 17.20 Trifecta £42.80 Pool: £647.58 - 10.74 winning units.
Owner Market Avenue Racing Club Ltd **Bred** Michael John Williamson **Trained** Lambourn, Berks
■ Baby Strange, for Paul Blockley and Graham Gibbons, became the first winner at Ascot since its £200 million redevelopment.

FOCUS
With the odd exception, they did not look a great bunch in the paddock and this was probably just an ordinary conditions race, certainly by Ascot's previous standards. Chjimes was the form pick judged on his Listed second at the Curragh, but he failed to produce his best. Still, Baby Strange continued his progression and looks ready for a further step up in class.

NOTEBOOK
Baby Strange, who landed a gamble on his debut in a five-furlong maiden at Bath, showed he has gone the right way since with a ready success on this step up in class. Settled just behind the leaders, he got a dream with through tight against the near-side rail and picked up well to take full advantage. The winning rider, Graham Gibbons, said he compared favourably with Always Hopeful, who won last year's Group 2 Richmond Stakes, and he deserves to take his chance in something like the Coventry Stakes back over this course and distance at the Royal meeting. (op 2-1 tchd 11-4)
La Neige, an athletic sort off the mark on his debut in a five-furlong maiden at Nottingham, was probably unlucky not to have finished closer as he was the slowest away from the stalls and had to come wide of the entire field with his run. He is clearly useful and deserves another chance in similar company. (op 11-2)
Chjimes(IRE) ran below the form he showed when second in a Listed race at the Curragh on his previous start. His trainer was of the opinion he may have been better suited by easier ground or a stronger pace. (tchd 5-2 in places)
The Old Fella, a 75,000gns half-brother to five-furlong juvenile winner Service, out of a two-year-old sprint scorer, fared best of the newcomers and offered plenty of promise. He may have been even closer had he enjoyed a clear run when initially beginning to pick up and he will be hard to beat if switched to maiden company next time.
King's Bastion(IRE), off the mark at the second attempt in a five-furlong maiden on Lingfield's turf course, seemed to find this tougher but may prove better back over the minimum trip. (op 7-1)
Dumas(IRE) ◆, a 20,000gns half-brother to Distinctly Jim, who was placed over six furlongs at two, out of a multiple seven to ten-furlong winner in Italy, caught the eye travelling well for much of the way, but was just found out by his inexperience late on. There should be much better to come.
Revisionist(IRE) ◆, a 33,000gns half-brother to three seven-furlong juvenile winners, as well as the prolific middle-distance/stayer Trance, out of a ten-furlong scorer, was one of the few who took the eye in the paddock and can do better over further in time.

2010 BOVIS HOMES BUCKHOUNDS STKS (LISTED RACE) 1m 4f
1:20 (1:24) (Class 1) 4-Y-O+
£28,390 (£10,760; £5,385; £2,685; £1,345; £675) Stalls High

Form RPR
0251 1 **Akarem**[8] [1815] 5-9-1 102 PatCosgrave 9 115
(K R Burke) *hld up in tch: effrt on inner over 2f out: led over 1f out: rdn clr* 16/1
3162 2 4 **Frank Sonata**[7] [1860] 5-9-1 106 RyanMoore 2 108
(M G Quinlan) *lw: hld up last: rdn and prog 3f out: styd on to take 2nd fnl f* 11/2[2]
0143 3 hd **Profit's Reality (IRE)**[8] [1815] 4-8-12 100 GrahamGibbons 6 105
(P A Blockley) *hld up in tch: rdn 2f out: styd on: no ch w wnr* 18/1
0261 4 2 **Admiral's Cruise (USA)**[14] [1677] 4-8-12 107 LDettori 4 102
(B J Meehan) *lw: prom: led over 2f out to over 1f out: wknd* 5/4[1]
2024 5 2 1/2 **Self Defense**[20] [1507] 9-8-12 110 MartinDwyer 3 98
(Miss E C Lavelle) *lw: racd wd: in tch: drvn 3f out: wknd over 1f out* 6/1[3]
3023 6 2 1/2 **Orcadian**[8] [1833] 5-9-1 105 TedDurcan 1 97
(J M P Eustace) *led: clr after 3f: hdd over 2f out: wknd over 1f out* 15/2
3345 7 3/4 **Acropolis (IRE)**[134] [5493] 5-8-12 RoystonFfrench 5 93
(J Howard Johnson) *chsd ldrs: wknd over 2f out* 20/1
6213 8 14 **Birkspiel (GER)**[26] [1369] 5-9-4 108 TQuinn 8 76+
(S Dow) *chsd ldr to over 3f out: eased whn btn 2f out* 12/1
20-0 P **Maktub (ITY)**[385] [1543] 7-8-12 105 DaneO'Neill 7 —
(Ernst Oertel) *a bhd: t.o 4f out: p.u and dismounted: lame* 50/1

2m 35.65s (2.22) **Going Correction** +0.45s/f (Yiel) 9 Ran SP% 111.4
Speed ratings (Par 111):110,107,107,105,104 102,102,92,—
CSF £96.48 TOTE £17.80: £4.10, £1.60, £4.20; EX 81.60 Trifecta £819.10 Part won. Pool: £1,153.69 - 0.54 winning units..
Owner Mrs M Gittins **Bred** Kilcarn Stud **Trained** Middleham Moor, N Yorks

FOCUS
This Listed contest could have been stronger, with the likes of Admiral's Cruise and Self Defense running below their best, while Frank Sonata was given plenty to do. However, Profit's Reality gives the form some substance and Akarem looked to produce a career-best effort. Orcadian set a reasonable enough pace before weakening out of contention on the turn into the straight.

NOTEBOOK
Akarem did not really progress in three runs over hurdles during the winter, and was beaten a long way on his return to the Flat at Ripon, but he has really turned the corner since then and followed up his recent Hamilton Listed success, where he was just too good for the highly progressive Ouninpohja, with what has to rate as a career-best effort. He deserves his chance in Group company now. (op 14-1)
Frank Sonata appeared to be given far too much to do by Ryan Moore, especially considering he was placed over two miles in a German Group 3 on his previous start. He is better than he was able to show. (op 4-1)
Profit's Reality(IRE), who has run well in defeat in a couple of high-class handicaps since taking the scalp of last year's Cambridgeshire and subsequent Listed scorer Blue Monday, including when behind Akarem at Hamilton last time, was unlucky not to have finished a little closer as he appeared to go for the same gap against the far rail as the eventual winner. However, he is unlikely to have beaten that one under any circumstances and basically helps set the standard. (op 20-1)
Admiral's Cruise(USA), the convincing winner of a conditions race over this trip at Newmarket on his previous start, travelled well into the straight but found disappointingly little. Perhaps he was not ideally suited to the ground riding on the fast side in the straight. (op 13-8 tchd 7-4 in places)
Self Defense was well below the form he showed when fourth in the Jockey Club Stakes at Newmarket on his previous start and was disappointing. (op 11-2)
Orcadian set a decent enough pace, but offered no more in the straight and was maybe not on a going day. In his defence, though, he has had a couple of tough races this month, including when third in the Yorkshire Cup last time. (op 7-1 tchd 8-1)
Birkspiel(GER) Official explanation: jockey said horse hung left and lost near-fore shoe
Maktub(ITY) Official explanation: jockey said horse finished lame

2011 JOHN DOYLE FILLIES' STKS (HERITAGE H'CAP) 1m (S)
1:50 (1:59) (Class 2) 3-Y-O+ £29,146 (£8,671; £4,333; £2,164) Stalls Low

Form RPR
5044 1 **Indian Steppes (FR)**[14] [1676] 7-8-7 85 TQuinn 6 97
(P S McEntee) *trckd ldrs: prog to ld over 1f out: rdn out* 8/1
10 2 1 **Kelucia (IRE)**[36] [1111] 5-8-2 83 NelsonDeSouza(3) 7 93
(R M Beckett) *hld up: prog to chal over 2f out: flashed tail and nt qckn fnl f* 9/1
5030 3 hd **Tanzanite (IRE)**[14] [1678] 4-8-8 86 JoeFanning 4 96
(D W P Arbuthnot) *led to over 5f out: led 3f otu to over 1f out: outpcd* 7/2[1]
310 4 4 **Toffee Vodka (IRE)**[14] [1673] 4-7-12 76 oh3 FrankieMcDonald 5 76
(J W Hills) *plld hrd: hld up: effrt 2f out: sn btn* 20/1
5 hd **Astronomia (NZ)**[205] 4-9-9 103 LDettori 3 101
(Saeed Bin Suroor) *lw: trckd ldrs: effrt 2f out: sn btn* 4/1[2]
0053 6 hd **Salamanca**[21] [1477] 4-9-6 98 RyanMoore 10 97
(S Kirk) *lw: wl in rr: prog u.p over 2f out: one pce* 9/2[3]
7 3/4 **Maria Luisa (IRE)**[13] [1710] 4-8-0 78 NickyMackay 8 76
(David P Myerscough, Ire) *prom: rdn 2f out: wknd* 6/1
0400 8 11 **Love Thirty**[21] [1477] 4-8-10 88 TedDurcan 1 60
(M R Channon) *in tch tl wknd over 2f out* 25/1
5236 9 5 **River Of Babylon**[232] [5713] 5-8-2 80 JimmyQuinn 9 41
(M L W Bell) *pulled hrd: led over 5f out to over 3f out: wknd* 14/1

1m 43.05s (1.19) **Going Correction** +0.075s/f (Good) 9 Ran SP% 111.1
Speed ratings (Par 96):97,96,95,91,91 91,90,79,74
CSF £72.96 CT £287.68 TOTE £9.40: £2.70, £3.40, £1.60; EX 67.80 Trifecta £806.40 Pool: £1,362.93 - 1.20 winning units.
Owner Meddler Bloodstock **Bred** Sentinel Bloodstock **Trained** Newmarket, Suffolk

FOCUS
They went just a steady pace early on - the winning time was moderate for a race of its class - and the form looks ordinary for the grade, even for a fillies/mares only contest.

NOTEBOOK
Indian Steppes(FR) had never previously won beyond seven furlongs, but she saw this mile out well to confirm the promise she showed when fourth at Newmarket on her return from a break. She is clearly useful when things fall right, but this did not look a great race for the grade and things will be a lot tougher if she turns up in the Royal Hunt Cup. (op 6-1)
Kelucia(IRE) stepped up on the form she showed on her debut for Ralph Beckett, but worryingly flashed her tail under pressure. She could do better again when getting a stronger pace, but one could question her resolution. (op 11-1 tchd 12-1)

Tanzanite(IRE) ◆ did very well to finish as close as she did given her best previous form was on easy ground and she stays ten furlongs. She can do even better next time granted more suitable conditions. (tchd 4-1)
Toffee Vodka(IRE), 3lb out of the handicap, was too keen and would have preferred a stronger pace.
Astronomia(NZ) showed some smart form when trained in Australia, including when second in a Group 2, but this was a disappointing British debut. Her yard are badly out of form and she has some way to go to justify entries in the Windsor Forest Stakes and July Cup. (op 7-2 tchd 9-2)
Salamanca was another to run disappointingly. Maybe a stronger pace would have suited better. (op 4-1)
Maria Luisa(IRE) travelled quite nicely, but found little under pressure and may have preferred easier ground. (op 11-2)

2012 TOTESPORT VICTORIA CUP (HERITAGE H'CAP) 7f
2:20 (2:32) (Class 2) 4-Y-0+

£52,972 (£15,861; £7,930; £3,969; £1,980; £994) **Stalls** Low

Form				RPR
0000	**1**		**Partners In Jazz (USA)**[38] [1086] 5-9-1 **94** RyanMoore 12 (T D Barron) *hld up: prog over 2f out: led over 1f out: drvn out* **8/1**[3]	105
5005	**2**	1 ¼	**Marching Song**[70] [667] 4-8-13 **92** DaneO'Neill 5 (R Hannon) *lw: hld up wl in rr: prog on outer 2f out: styd on wl to take 2nd nr fin* **25/1**	100
4002	**3**	nk	**Prince Of Thebes (IRE)**[38] [1086] 5-9-0 **93** PaulDoe 7 (J Akehurst) *lw: a.p: chsd wnr fnl f: lost 2nd nr fin* **33/1**	100
1251	**4**	nk	**Pinpoint (IRE)**[231] [5730] 4-9-1 **94** TedDurcan 15 (W R Swinburn) *hld up: prog and swtchd lft over 2f out: hmpd 1f out: r.o: nt rcvr* **12/1**	103+
1340	**5**	hd	**Paper Talk (USA)**[38] [1086] 4-9-0 **93** NickyMackay 1 (B W Hills) *hld up: prog and nt clr run 2f out: styd on: nrst fin* **16/1**	98
2120	**6**	¾	**Notability (IRE)**[345] [2634] 4-9-7 **100** LDettori 2 (M A Jarvis) *lw: hld up: hmpd 2f out: running on whn nt clr run ins fnl f: nt rcvr* **5/1**[1]	109+
0000	**7**	hd	**Mine (IRE)**[35] [1129] 8-9-10 **103** (v) TQuinn 20 (J D Bethell) *hld up wl in rr: prog on outer 2f out: hung lft and nt qckn fnl f* **14/1**	106
3101	**8**	2	**Commando Scott (IRE)**[2] [1949] 5-8-13 **92** 6ex RoystonFfrench 6 (I W McInnes) *towards rr: kpt on fnl 2f: nrst fin* **16/1**	90
4601	**9**	½	**Zomerlust**[33] [1183] 4-9-2 **95** GrahamGibbons 4 (J J Quinn) *towards rr: styd on fnl 2f: n.d* **10/1**	91+
0024	**10**	½	**Coleorton Dancer**[14] [1667] 4-8-12 **96** AndrewMullen(5) 10 (K A Ryan) *prom: led 3f out and sn clr: hdd & wknd over 1f out* **12/1**	91
2440	**11**	hd	**Compton's Eleven**[38] [1086] 5-9-2 **98** EdwardCreighton(3) 9 (M R Channon) *dwlt: hld up: nt clr run 2f out: kpt on* **50/1**	92+
3000	**12**	shd	**One More Round (USA)**[21] [1487] 8-9-1 **94** (b) IanMongan 18 (N P Littmoden) *dwlt: swtchd lft s: wl in rr tl kpt on fnl 2f* **40/1**	88
1634	**13**	nk	**Game Lad**[21] [1495] 4-8-13 **92** PhillipMakin 14 (T D Easterby) *chsd ldrs fdd fnl 2f* **7/1**[2]	85
4000	**14**	¾	**Jalamid (IRE)**[14] [1667] 4-9-4 **97** (t) RobertHavlin 3 (J H M Gosden) *keen early: hld up wl in rr: nvr on terms* **20/1**	88
0005	**15**	5	**Cool Panic (IRE)**[9] [1806] 4-8-13 **92** JoeFanning 8 (M L W Bell) *nvr beyond midfield: wknd 2f out* **20/1**	70
340	**16**	1 ½	**Zohar (USA)**[28] [1301] 4-8-11 **90** MichaelTebbutt 17 (B J Meehan) *hld up: a wl in rr* **50/1**	64
5000	**17**	5	**Lord Mayor**[14] [1667] 5-8-8 **90** AdamKirby(3) 11 (R M H Cowell) *rdn in rr 1/2-way: sn btn* **66/1**	50
2001	**18**	¾	**King's Caprice**[38] [1086] 5-8-11 **90** (t) StephenCarson 13 (J A Geake) *led to 3f out: wknd* **20/1**	48
1-02	**19**	8	**Munaddam (USA)**[14] [1667] 4-9-4 **97** MartinDwyer 16 (E A L Dunlop) *in tch tl wknd 2f out* **9/1**	33
2060	**20**	2	**Kamanda Laugh**[14] [1667] 5-9-1 **94** PatCosgrave 19 (K A Ryan) *racd wd in tch to 1/2-way* **20/1**	25

1m 28.11s **Going Correction** +0.075s/f (Good) **20** Ran SP% **126.9**
Speed ratings (Par 109):108,106,106,105,105 104,104,102,101,101 100,100,100,99,93 92,86,85,76,74
CSF £202.21 CT £6303.12 TOTE £11.30: £2.80, £5.90, £6.10, £3.70; EX 268.00 Trifecta £6090.10 Part won. Pool: £8,086.67 - 0.10 winning unit..
Owner Sporting Occasions Racing No 2 **Bred** Charles Nuckols Jr And Sons **Trained** Maunby, N Yorks

FOCUS
This looked like a decent enough renewal, and they went a good pace from the outset, with the action toowards the stands' side. A few of these look better than the bare form. Partners In Jazz clearly produced a smart effort, but Marching Song can be rated higher given he came widest of all, and both Pinpoint and Paper Talk were denied clear runs. Nothing, though, was as unlucky as Notability. It was a pretty wet afternoon, and the ground was perhaps no longer as fast as the official description, but it was by no means on the soft side.

NOTEBOOK
Partners In Jazz(USA) did not offer a great deal on his reappearance over this trip at Newmarket, but that run clearly brought him on quite significantly and he returned to best to win decisively. However, he is likely to be raised to around a career-high mark and, given he has never followed up, things will be tougher next time. (op 7-1)
Marching Song, fifth in a decent seven-furlong Polytrack handicap on his only other start this season 70 days previously, stepped up on that effort and is probably even better than the bare form, as he was switched widest of all with his run. He has never won over this trip, but saw it out well and connections will have plenty of options.
Prince Of Thebes(IRE), having just his third start for his current trainer, ran well off a mark 2lb higher than when second at Newmarket on his previous start, although he could not confirm form with Partners In Jazz, who was down the field that day.
Pinpoint(IRE)'s six previous runs had all come over a mile but, dropped in trip for his belated reappearance, he ran well and would have been even closer with a trouble-free passage. Considering he was returning from a 231-day break, and racing off a 9lb higher mark than when winning on his final start last season, this was a good effort. He is still lightly raced and there could be better to come. (op 11-1)
Paper Talk(USA), disappointing when a beaten favourite on his reappearance at Newmarket, yet still only one place behind Partners In Jazz that day, stepped up on that effort and probably would have finished even closer with a clearer run. There could be better to come.
Notability(IRE) ◆, not seen since apparently returning wrong behind when a disappointing ninth in the Britannia at last year's Royal Ascot at York, looked very unlucky, a view backed up by his jockey Frankie Dettori. He was picking up very nicely when running into the back of the tiring Coleorton Dancer and being kept in by Paper Talk, and would have finished second at the very least with a clear run. This must rate as a most encouraging comeback and he looks one to be with from now on. He looked potentially Group class last season, but connections clearly want to take advantage of his handicap mark before stepping him up in class and he will take some beating in the Royal Hunt Cup, provided the ground is not too firm. (tchd 11-2)
Mine(IRE), winner of this off a mark of 99 in 2004, ran well off top weight and clearly retains plenty of ability. Official explanation: jockey said horse hung (op 16-1)
Commando Scott(IRE), who crept into this race after picking up a penalty for winning over six furlongs at Ayr on his previous start, did not run badly but seems better suited by more cut in the ground.
Zomerlust never really threatened off a mark 5lb higher than when winning over six furlongs at Pontefract on his previous start and is another who seems better on easier ground.
Coleorton Dancer ◆ showed up well for longer than one might have expected and is one to look out for when returned to sprinting on easier ground.
Compton's Eleven did not enjoy a clear run and is better than the bare form.
Game Lad looked the ideal type for this race, but he failed to produce his best and was disappointing. (op 13-2)
Zohar(USA) Official explanation: jockey said gelding hung right
Munaddam(USA) failed to build on the form he showed on his reappearance at Lingfield and was a major disappointment. He has been very lightly raced in recent times and may have his problems.

2013 TONI AND DAVID EYLES H'CAP 2m
2:50 (3:06) (Class 2) (0-105,102) 4-Y-0+

£12,464 (£3,732; £1,866; £934; £466; £234) **Stalls** High

Form				RPR
2045	**1**		**Toldo (IRE)**[14] [1685] 4-8-4 **83** NickyMackay 4 (G M Moore) *prom: lost pl over 2f out: rallied to ld over 1f out: drvn out* **12/1**	93
4530	**2**	¾	**Elusive Dream**[17] [1584] 5-8-13 **90** JamieMackay 8 (Sir Mark Prescott) *lw: rrd s: chsd ldrs: chal 2f out: styd on: a hld* **9/1**	99
4050	**3**	nk	**Odiham**[136] [5903] 5-8-10 **92** TravisBlock(5) 5 (H Morrison) *hld up midfield: prog 4f out: led over 2f out to over 1f out: one pce* **10/1**	101
1031	**4**	1 ¼	**Sirce (IRE)**[34] [1167] 4-8-12 **91** (v) JimmyQuinn 9 (D J Coakley) *hld up in rr: gd prog 2f out: pressed ldrs 1f out: nt qckn* **9/1**	98
1041	**5**	½	**Ebtikaar (IRE)**[20] [1517] 4-9-2 **95** MartinDwyer 15 (J L Dunlop) *lw: towards rr: rdn and styd on fnl 2f: nt rch ldrs* **9/2**[1]	102
-501	**6**	½	**Admiral (IRE)**[17] [1584] 5-8-11 **88** LDettori 10 (T J Pitt) *keen: prom: lost pl 3f out: rallied 2f out: one pce* **13/2**[3]	94
5011	**7**	½	**Colloquial**[218] [6012] 5-8-11 **88** DaneO'Neill 6 (H Candy) *hld up midfield: rdn and kpt on same pce fnl 3f* **5/1**[2]	93
3622	**8**	2 ½	**Palomar (USA)**[14] [1677] 4-9-9 **102** RyanMoore 1 (R Charlton) *lw: dwlt: hld up last: effrt 3f out: one pce* **13/2**[3]	104
1005	**9**	nk	**Baddam**[20] [1517] 4-8-11 **90** IanMongan 2 (M R Channon) *prom: w ldr 4f out to over 2f out: fdd* **33/1**	92
0/	**10**	1 ¼	**Caracciola (GER)**[21] 9-8-13 **90** TQuinn 7 (N J Henderson) *a midfield: one pce fnl 3f* **20/1**	91
2300	**11**	13	**Ten Carat**[28] [1294] 6-8-12 **89** RoystonFfrench 11 (M Todhunter) *lw: a towards rr: wknd over 2f out* **66/1**	74
4230	**12**	1 ¾	**Spear Thistle**[42] [1021] 4-8-6 **85** GrahamGibbons 3 (Mrs N Smith) *pressed ldr: led 4f out to over 2f out: wknd rapidly* **33/1**	68
0500	**13**	16	**Jeepstar**[39] [1071] 6-8-8 **85** TedDurcan 12 (S C Williams) *led to 4f out: wknd* **33/1**	49
0040	**14**	59	**Ocean Of Storms (IRE)**[3] [1931] 11-8-0 **84** oh14 ow3 MarkCoumbe(7) 14 (N I M Rossiter) *virtually ref to r: a t.o* **100/1**	—
4020	**15**	16	**Fortune Island (IRE)**[42] [1021] 7-9-1 **92** (vt) JoeFanning 13 (D E Pipe) *chsd ldrs: wknd 5f out: sn t.o* **25/1**	—

3m 34.92s (2.92) **Going Correction** +0.45s/f (Yiel)
WFA 4 from 5yo+ 2lb **15** Ran SP% **118.2**
Speed ratings (Par 109):110,109,109,108,108 108,108,106,106,106 99,98,90,61,53
CSF £106.08 CT £1130.98 TOTE £16.00: £4.20, £3.10, £4.10; EX 92.40 Trifecta £698.20 Part won..
Owner J W Armstrong **Bred** Mrs C A Moore **Trained** Middleham Moor, N Yorks

FOCUS
A good staying handicap, but they could probably have gone a stronger pace and there was just over three and a half lengths covering the first seven home. A few of these will no doubt re-oppose in the Northumberland Plate later in the season.

NOTEBOOK
Toldo(IRE) was disappointing with no obvious excuse in a weaker race than this at Thirsk just two week previously, but the slightly muddling conditions would not have bothered him at all given he has won on both good to form and heavy ground, and he showed a good attitude to win narrowly. He is progressive and the Northumberland Plate is his long-term target.
Elusive Dream, who did not enjoy a clear run in the Chester Cup on his previous start, got a much better run through this time and ran well. He will also probably take his chance in the Northumberland Plate. (op 8-1)
Odiham, back on the Flat after three respectable runs in defeat over hurdles, ran a cracker off the back of a 136-day break. There could be better to come and he is another who will probably run in the Northumberland Plate - he was fifth last year. (op 12-1)
Sirce(IRE) seems at her best in a strongly run race, so this was a decent enough effort off a mark 7lb higher mark than when winning at Kempton on her previous start. (op 8-1)
Ebtikaar(IRE) ◆, upped to two miles for the first time, was held up and just got going too late off a mark only 2lb higher than when winning at Salisbury on his previous start. He can do better again, ridden handier or in a stronger-run race. The Northumberland Plate could be a good race for him as well. (tchd 5-1 in places)
Admiral(IRE) was only 3lb higher than when winning the Chester Cup on his previous start, but things did not fall as kindly this time and he probably would have benefited from a stronger pace. (op 6-1 tchd 7-1)
Colloquial, who progressed nicely to win his final two starts last season, looked fit enough in the paddock but could not produce his best off the back of a 218-day break off a 7lb higher mark. He can be expected to come on for the run. (tchd 11-2 in a place)
Palomar(USA) ran better than the bare form suggests, as he was dropped in at the back on the rail from his outside draw and made his effort widest of all. (op 5-1)

2014 ALFRED FRANKS & BARTLETT SUNGLASSES H'CAP 6f
3:25 (3:43) (Class 3) (0-95,91) 3-Y-0 **£9,715** (£2,890; £1,444; £721) **Stalls** Low

Form				RPR
6413	**1**		**Trafalgar Bay (IRE)**[20] [1512] 3-9-2 **89** LDettori 7 (S Kirk) *hld up: plenty to do over 1f out: chsd ldr ins fnl f: led nr fin: cleverly* **4/1**[1]	100
12	**2**	½	**Pearly Wey**[20] [1512] 3-9-0 **90** AdamKirby(3) 11 (C G Cox) *lw: w ldr: led 2f out: sn clr: hdd nr fin* **7/1**[3]	99
5622	**3**	1 ½	**Burning Incense (IRE)**[14] [1672] 3-8-4 **77** oh1 NickyMackay 2 (R Charlton) *hld up: effrt over 1f out: styd on same pce* **4/1**[1]	82
1	**4**	2	**Bajan Parkes**[243] [5501] 3-8-12 **85** DaneO'Neill 5 (H Candy) *w ldrs: one pce over 1f out* **10/1**	84
351	**5**	shd	**Starlight Gazer**[26] [1355] 3-8-5 **78** RichardThomas 4 (J A Geake) *hld up: hmpd over 1f out: styd on: nvr nrr* **16/1**	76+
2633	**6**	1	**The Snatcher (IRE)**[8] [1836] 3-9-4 **91** RyanMoore 8 (R Hannon) *hld up in rr: prog 2f out: one pce fnl f* **11/2**[2]	86
11	**7**	nk	**Matuza (IRE)**[156] [6653] 3-8-8 **81** MartinDwyer 9 (W R Muir) *keen: hld up: prog to chse ldr over 1f out: wknd fnl furlog* **8/1**	75

2201 **8** 3 **Didn't We (IRE)**[14] [1672] 3-8-10 **83**....................(v) IanMongan 1 68
(T G Mills) *led to 2f out: sn btn* **9/1**
1203 **9** 3/4 **Figaro Flyer (IRE)**[16] [1606] 3-9-3 **90**.................... TedDurcan 10 73
(P Howling) *racd on outer: in tch: wknd fnl f* **40/1**
5032 **10** 6 **Tous Les Deux**[24] [1411] 3-8-5 **78**.................... StephenCarson 6 43
(R F Johnson Houghton) *keen: w ldrs: wknd 2f out* **18/1**
2605 **11** 11 **Scarlet Knight**[2] [1954] 3-8-12 **85**....................(b) JoeFanning 3 17
(P Mitchell) *a rr: wknd 2f out* **33/1**
3056 **12** 3 **Puskas (IRE)**[7] [1848] 3-9-2 **89**.................... TQuinn 12 12
(M R Channon) *pressed ldrs over 3f: wknd* **33/1**

1m 15.23s **Going Correction** +0.075s/f (Good) **12** Ran SP% **117.6**
Speed ratings (Par 103):108,107,105,102,102 101,100,96,95,87 73,69
CSF £31.06 CT £121.90 TOTE £3.90: £1.90, £3.00, £2.00; EX 35.50 Trifecta £90.00 Pool: £987.12 - 7.78 winning units. Place 6 £627.44, Place 5 £544.65.
Owner M Nicolson, G Doran, A Wilson **Bred** Patrick Hennessy **Trained** Upper Lambourn, Berks

FOCUS
A very strong three-year-old sprint handicap featuring any number of progressive types. Although the rain had appeared to get into the ground a little bit, the winning time was still significantly faster than the opening juvenile contest. The form should work out.

NOTEBOOK
Trafalgar Bay(IRE) ◆, a length and a half behind Pearly Way in a good six-furlong handicap at Salisbury on his reappearance, was 2lb better off with that one, with the benefit of that reappearance fitness wide, and just reversed form. Having bolted to post on his intended reappearance at the Craven meeting, he went to the start very early this time, and the plan worked a treat. Now connections have got the key to him, there could be plenty more to come. (tchd 7-2 and 9-2)
Pearly Wey ◆ was a 40/1 winner on his debut at Newmarket in maiden that worked out well, before running second in a decent handicap at Salisbury. He was just caught here off a 2lb higher mark, having looked all over the winner at the furlong pole when kicking clear. He possibly hit the front a touch too soon, but he was going so well, his rider may have had little choice. He remains highly progressive and has a very good race or two in him. He must be followed, although he may just want riding with a little more patience. (tchd 8-1)
Burning Incense(IRE) reversed recent Lingfield placings with Didn't We on 3lb better terms, but basically ran into two very useful sorts. He can find easier opportunities and does not look badly handicapped. (tchd 9-2 and 5-1 in a place)
Bajan Parkes, the winner of his only start as a juvenile in an extended five-furlong maiden at Bath, ran well in this hot contest on his first run in 243 days and is open to plenty of improvement, especially considering he looked in need of the outing. (op 6-1)
Starlight Gazer would have found this tougher than the Windsor maiden he won on his previous start, but ran very well and was unlucky not to finish closer.
The Snatcher(IRE) ran creditably dropped back from seven furlongs but was unable to concede weight to success progressive types. (op 13-2)
Matuza(IRE) looked a nice prospect when winning both his starts in minor company on sand towards the end of last year, but this was his first experience of turf and he faced pretty stiff competition off the back of a 156-day break. He can do better. (op 9-1)
Didn't We(IRE) ran below the form he showed when beating Burning Incense at Lingfield on his previous start, and his recent busy spell may have found him out against this kind of opposition.
T/Jkpt: Not won. T/Plt: £458.30 to a £1 stake. Pool: £93,701.80. 149.25 winning tickets. T/Qpdt: £102.30 to a £1 stake. Pool: £6,685.10. 48.35 winning tickets. JN

1559 CATTERICK (L-H)
Saturday, May 27

OFFICIAL GOING: Good to soft
Wind: Fresh, against

2015 TOTEPLACEPOT (S) STKS 5f 212y
2:15 (2:15) (Class 6) 2-Y-O £2,730 (£806; £403) **Stalls** Low

Form RPR
5242 **1** **Tokyo Jo (IRE)**[6] [1862] 2-8-1 ....(v1) AndrewElliott(5) 5 60+
(K R Burke) *cl up: led 2f out: sn rdn clr: kpt on* **10/11**[1]
5 **2** 2 1/2 **Burlington Fayr (IRE)**[38] [1074] 2-8-6 .... KimTinkler 8 53+
(N Tinkler) *cl up on outer whn bumped after 1f and lost pl: hdwy 2f out: sn rdn and styd on wl fnl f* **11/2**[3]
0603 **3** 1 **Emma Told Lies**[6] [1862] 2-8-6 .... DaleGibson 4 50
(M W Easterby) *led: rdn along and hdd 2f out: sn drvn and one pce* **4/1**[2]
4 5 **Mollyanko** 2-8-1 .... MarcHalford(5) 3 35
(W G M Turner) *dwlt and bhd tl styd on fnl 2f* **16/1**
45 **5** 2 **Argent Danseur**[14] [1682] 2-8-6 ....(p) GregFairley(5) 7 34
(B S Rothwell) *chsd ldrs: rdn along 2f out: grad wknd* **14/1**
6 2 1/2 **Dispol Truly (IRE)** 2-8-3 .... BenSwarbrick(3) 2 21
(P T Midgley) *s.i.s: a rr* **20/1**
0 **7** 1 **Inch Forward**[28] [1295] 2-8-6 .... TomEaves 6 18
(D W Barker) *prom: rdn along 1/2-way: sn wknd* **16/1**
00 **8** 3 1/2 **Brynris**[12] [1744] 2-8-11 .... TonyHamilton 1 13
(W G M Turner) *chsd ldrs on inner: rdn along over 2f out: sn wknd* **16/1**

1m 16.14s (2.14) **Going Correction** 0.0s/f (Good) 8 Ran SP% **116.8**
Speed ratings (Par 91):85,81,80,73,71 67,66,61
CSF £6.56 TOTE £1.70: £1.10, £1.10, £1.50; EX 8.20.There was no bid for the winner.
Owner Bigwigs Bloodstock II **Bred** E Campion **Trained** Middleham Moor, N Yorks

FOCUS
A very low-grade affair won by the form pick. The race is unlikely to prove very informative in the future, although the runner-up seems to possess enough ability to win a race.

NOTEBOOK
Tokyo Jo(IRE), who had proved to be slightly frustrating until now, made a move two furlongs from home and soon had the race in safe keeping. The first-time visor surely helped but it remains to be seen whether it will have the same effect next time. (op 6-5 tchd 5-4)
Burlington Fayr(IRE) still had plenty to do rounding the home turn, but stayed on to good effect, catching the leader all the way to the line. A similar affair would see her go close next time. (op 5-1 tchd 6-1)
Emma Told Lies has never managed to get her head in front of Tokyo Jo at the end of a race in the past, and did not look like doing so again despite leading early. She is fully exposed now and will need a very weak race to have an obvious chance of winning. (tchd 7-2)
Mollyanko was staying on nicely when badly chopped for room just over a furlong from home. Clearly no star, she did show just enough promise to suggest she can progress for the race and have a chance in a similar race. (op 12-1)
Dispol Truly(IRE) did really well to beat any horses given how slowly she started. That said, she will need to make amazing progress for the run to have any chance next time. (op 18-1)

2016 TOTECOURSE TO COURSE MEDIAN AUCTION MAIDEN STKS 5f
2:45 (2:46) (Class 6) 3-Y-O £2,730 (£806; £403) **Stalls** Low

Form RPR
0405 **1** **Jakeini (IRE)**[19] [1549] 3-9-3 **58**.................... FergalLynch 7 73
(E S McMahon) *trckd ldrs: hdwy on outer 2f out: rdn and edgd lft over 1f out: styd on ins last to ld on line* **7/1**
0043 **2** shd **Hypnosis**[9] [1793] 3-8-12 **59**.................... TomEaves 8 68
(D W Barker) *cl up: rdn to ld ent last: drvn: hdd and no ex on line* **8/1**
2522 **3** 1 1/2 **Lucksin (IRE)**[17] [1589] 3-9-3 **75**.................... KimTinkler 6 68
(N Tinkler) *led: rdn along 2f out: drvn and hdd ent last: one pce* **5/2**[2]
50 **4** 3 **Artie's Son (IRE)**[18] [1564] 3-8-12 .... DuranFentiman(5) 4 57
(T D Easterby) *sn pushed along and outpcd towards rr: hdwy wl over 1f out: styd on ins last: nrst fin* **25/1**
00 **5** nk **Steel City Boy (IRE)**[35] [1147] 3-9-0 .... DanielTudhope(3) 3 56
(D Carroll) *chsd ldrs: rdn along over 2f out: sn btn* **25/1**
325 **6** 5 **Compromiznotension (IRE)**[23] [1445] 3-9-3 **70**........(p) MatthewHenry 2 38
(M A Jarvis) *trckd ldrs: rdn along and lost pl after f: sn bhd* **9/4**[1]
7 shd **Orpenlina (IRE)** 3-8-12 .... TonyHamilton 5 32
(R A Fahey) *chsd ldrs: rdn along 1/2-way: sn wknd* **12/1**
4546 **8** 2 **Fortress**[19] [1551] 3-8-12 **62**.................... DeanMcKeown 1 25
(E J Alston) *cl up: rdn along 1/2-way: sn wknd* **11/2**[3]

60.24 secs (-0.36) **Going Correction** -0.125s/f (Firm) 8 Ran SP% **113.7**
Speed ratings (Par 97):97,96,94,89,89 81,81,77
CSF £60.22 TOTE £7.10: £2.40, £1.90, £1.10; EX 65.60.
Owner Martin W Crane **Bred** Gestut Roemerhof **Trained** Hopwas, Staffs

FOCUS
A moderate contest run in a fair time. Apart from Artie's Son, the form is likely to prove very moderate, with the principals the best guides.
Compromiznotension(IRE) Official explanation: jockey said gelding hit its head on stalls

2017 TOTEQUADPOT H'CAP 7f
3:15 (3:16) (Class 2) (0-100,92) 4-Y-O+ **£12,954** (£3,854; £1,926; £962) **Stalls** Low

Form RPR
3000 **1** **Imperialistic (IRE)**[9] [1806] 5-7-13 **78** oh1.................... AndrewElliott(5) 6 96
(K R Burke) *hld up towards rr: gd hdwy on inner over 2f out: n.m.r and swtchd rt over 1f out: rdn to ld ins last: sn clr* **12/1**
4516 **2** 3 1/2 **Hartshead**[21] [1495] 7-9-4 **92**.................... DeanMcKeown 4 101
(G A Swinbank) *hld up in tch: hdwy over 2f out: sn rdn and styd on ins last: no ch w wnr* **10/1**
0032 **3** 1 1/2 **Breaking Shadow (IRE)**[19] [1532] 4-8-3 **80**.................... BenSwarbrick(3) 1 85
(T D Barron) *chsd ldrs: hdwy to ld 11/2f out: sn rdn and edgd lft: drvn and hdd ins last: wknd* **15/8**[1]
0600 **4** 1/2 **Primo Way**[35] [1143] 5-8-8 **82**....................(b) TomEaves 9 86
(I Semple) *dwlt and rr tl styd on fnl 2f: nrst fin* **14/1**
0600 **5** 1/2 **Rainbow Rising (IRE)**[217] [6021] 4-8-9 **83**.................... NeilPollard 5 86
(J Howard Johnson) *chsd ldrs: rdn along over 2f out: sn one pce* **20/1**
0050 **6** 1/2 **Steel Blue**[17] [1597] 6-8-5 **79**.................... DaleGibson 10 80
(R M Whitaker) *towards rr: rdn along and styd on fnl 2f: nvr a factor* **25/1**
0301 **7** 1 1/4 **Tagula Sunrise (IRE)**[6] [1865] 4-9-0 **88** 6ex.................... TonyHamilton 8 86
(R A Fahey) *in tch: rdn along over 2f out: sn rdn and btn* **8/1**[2]
4650 **8** hd **Pieter Brueghel (USA)**[8] [1835] 7-9-2 **90**.................... AdrianTNicholls 3 87
(D Nicholls) *led: rdn along 2f out: hdd 11/2f out: sn wknd* **9/1**[3]
0420 **9** 1 **Prince Tum Tum (USA)**[3] [1939] 6-8-6 **85**.................... GregFairley(5) 2 80
(D W Barker) *trckd ldrs: rdn over 2f out: sn wknd* **9/1**[3]
3001 **10** 2 **Baylaw Star**[41] [1035] 5-8-12 **89**.................... DanielTudhope(3) 7 79
(K A Ryan) *cl up: rdn over 2f out: sn wknd* **8/1**[2]
0544 **11** 7 **Roman Maze**[15] [1629] 6-9-0 **88**.................... FergalLynch 11 59
(W M Brisbourne) *a towards rr* **10/1**

1m 25.74s (-1.62) **Going Correction** 0.0s/f (Good) 11 Ran SP% **118.2**
Speed ratings (Par 109):109,105,103,102,102 101,100,99,98,96 88
CSF £126.93 CT £334.40 TOTE £15.70: £3.10, £3.50, £1.50; EX 186.00.
Owner Bigwigs Bloodstock II **Bred** B H Bloodstock **Trained** Middleham Moor, N Yorks

FOCUS
A fair winning time, even for a valuable handicap like this and the form appears sound, rated around the placed horses.

NOTEBOOK
Imperialistic(IRE), who is reportedly in-foal, absolutely flew away from her field when asked to quicken and won in great style. If she turns out quickly after this run, it would take a good one to lower her colours, despite her being a very in-and-out character in recent seasons. (tchd 11-1)
Hartshead ran a really decent race on ground that is arguably against him and off a very high handicap mark. Unfortunately, he will get no respite for the good effort and is likely to struggle next time unless he is genuinely improving. (tchd 11-1)
Breaking Shadow(IRE) looked to have an excellent chance on his last run, when splitting two fair handicappers at Ayr. He had every chance from his good stall position but, despite his good effort last time, he looks too high in the weights at the moment, and he failed to get home. (op 9-4)
Primo Way, who still had the blindfold on when the stalls opened last time, is now much closer to a realistic handicap mark and can be placed to advantage soon. He is most likely to be suited by a stiff course given his running style.
Rainbow Rising(IRE) did not shaped without promise on his first try at seven furlongs, and is entitled to come on for the run.
Steel Blue seems to be slightly out of sorts at the moment, despite finishing well from off the pace, as he was on a winning mark and never actually threatened to trouble the leaders. He obviously has the ability to win and will probably pop up when least expected.
Tagula Sunrise(IRE) has not won off a mark higher than the low eighties before, so seems likely to struggle to get his head back in front until he comes back down the weights. (op 13-2 tchd 6-1)
Pieter Brueghel(USA) is probably being lined up for a sprint later in the season, as he showed plenty of dash on ground he has no winning form in before fading badly. This run should see him dropped a pound or two, which would then make him of interest if raced on his ideal conditions. (op 8-1)

2018 TOTESPORT.COM H'CAP 1m 5f 175y
3:50 (3:50) (Class 4) (0-80,74) 4-Y-O+ **£6,477** (£1,927; £963; £481) **Stalls** Low

Form RPR
0210 **1** **Mceldowney**[11] [1756] 4-8-12 **70**.................... GregFairley(5) 8 82
(M Johnston) *cl up: led over 3f out: qcknd clr 2f out: styd on strly* **7/1**
4225 **2** 3 1/2 **Charlotte Vale**[20] [1502] 5-9-7 **74**.................... DeanMcKeown 6 81
(Micky Hammond) *hld up in rr: hdwy 3f out: rdn 2f out: kpt on u.p ins last* **11/4**[1]
002 **3** nk **Bronze Dancer (IRE)**[18] [1560] 4-8-2 **60**.................... AndrewElliott(5) 1 67
(G A Swinbank) *trckd ldrs: pushed along wl over 2f out: sn rdn and kpt on ins last* **5/1**[2]
3601 **4** 2 **Aleron (IRE)**[16] [1610] 8-9-4 **74**....................(p) DanielTudhope(3) 7 78
(J J Quinn) *trckd ldrs: effrt 3f out: rdn over 2f out and sn one pce* **11/2**[3]
1503 **5** 1 1/4 **Merrymaker**[15] [1631] 6-9-7 **74**.................... FergalLynch 5 76
(W M Brisbourne) *hld up in rr: hdwy 4f out: effrt on outer over 2f out: sn rdn and no imp* **5/1**[2]
5050 **6** shd **Just Waz (USA)**[38] [1075] 4-8-2 **55** oh2.................... DaleGibson 10 57
(R M Whitaker) *plld hrd: chsd ldrs: hdwy and cl up 4f out: rdn along over 2f out and sn wknd* **11/1**
/00- **7** 3 **Compton Commander**[31] [971] 8-9-2 **69**.................... TonyHamilton 9 67
(E W Tuer) *in tch: rdn along 4f out: sn btn* **33/1**

-606 **8** *hd* **Thewhirlingdervish (IRE)**[355] 2338 8-9-0 **72**......... DuranFentiman(5) 2 69
(T D Easterby) *a rr* **16/1**
2106 **9** *nk* **Wasalat (USA)**[14] 1685 4-9-1 **73**......................... MarkLawson(5) 3 70
(D W Barker) *v.s.a: keen: hdwy 4f out: rdn along 3f out: nvr a factor* **40/1**
1500 **10** *25* **Leslingtaylor (IRE)**[11] 1756 4-9-0 **67**................................ TomEaves 4 29
(J J Quinn) *led: rdn along 4f out: hdd over 3f out: wknd over 2f out* **12/1**
3m 6.44s (1.94) **Going Correction** 0.0s/f (Good) **10** Ran SP% **115.2**
Speed ratings (Par 105):94,92,91,90,89 89,88,88,87,73
CSF £26.20 CT £105.86 TOTE £7.80: £2.00, £2.80, £2.00; EX 29.40.
Owner C G Maybury **Bred** St Clare Hall Stud **Trained** Middleham Moor, N Yorks
FOCUS
A moderate winning time for a race like this. The winner is progressive, but he was in the right place when the sprint for the line unfolded, and might be a touch flattered by the bare result. The form makes sense but is not strong.

2019 TOTEEXACTA MEDIAN AUCTION MAIDEN FILLIES' STKS 5f 212y
4:25 (4:27) (Class 6) 3-4-Y-O **£2,730** (£806; £403) **Stalls** Low

Form RPR
0532 **1** **Our Sheila**[12] 1733 3-8-10 65.. TomEaves 11 66
(B Smart) *led 2f: cl up tl rdn to ld ins last: drvn out* **2/1**[1]
3030 **2** *1 ½* **Elegant Times (IRE)**[12] 1734 3-8-10 67............................ FergalLynch 1 62
(T D Easterby) *trckd ldrs: hdwy on inner to ld after 2f: rdn 2f out: sn drvn: hdd ins last: kpt on* **5/2**[2]
0266 **3** *1 ½* **Rosita Mia (IRE)**[21] 1497 3-8-10 65...................................... NeilPollard 7 57
(D W Barker) *in tch: hdwy to chse ldng pair over 2f out: sn rdn and kpt on fnl f* **9/2**[3]
0500 **4** *1 ½* **Thornton Princess**[229] 5791 3-8-5 52........................ GregFairley(5) 4 53
(B S Rothwell) *towards rr: hdwy over 2f out: sn rdn and kpt on appr last* **12/1**
60 **5** *1* **Charming Princess**[135] 99 3-8-7 .... DanielTudhope(3) 9 50
(J S Wainwright) *towards rr: hdwy over 2f out: sn rdn and kpt on same pce appr last* **66/1**
50 **6** *nk* **Ailsa**[17] 1589 4-9-5 .... DeanMcKeown 12 51
(C W Thornton) *outpcd and towards rr tl styd on fnl 2f: nrst fin* **25/1**
0000 **7** *6* **Born For Diamonds (IRE)**[17] 1594 4-9-0 42............. AndrewElliott(5) 6 33
(R E Barr) *cl up: rdn along 1/2-way: grad wknd fnl 2f* **40/1**
2 **8** *3* **Catherine Medici**[56] 835 3-8-10 .... TonyHamilton 10 22
(R M H Cowell) *a towards rr* **7/1**
0400 **9** *1 ¼* **Madam Moschata**[17] 1592 3-8-6 60 ow1..................... MarkLawson(5) 3 19
(D W Barker) *s.i.s and bhd: sme hdwy over 2f out: sn rdn and wknd* **16/1**
00 **10** *7* **Miss Lemon (IRE)**[21] 1493 3-8-10 .... DaleGibson 5 —
(J Hetherton) *chsd ldrs to 1/2-way: sn wknd* **40/1**
6000 **11** *3 ½* **Underthemistletoe (IRE)**[12] 1733 4-8-12 42........ MichaelJStainton(7) 2 —
(R E Barr) *chsd ldrs: rdn along 1/2-way: sn wknd* **40/1**
1m 15.12s (1.12) **Going Correction** 0.0s/f (Good)
WFA 3 from 4yo 9lb **11** Ran SP% **118.8**
Speed ratings (Par 98):92,90,88,86,84 84,76,72,70,61 56
CSF £6.84 TOTE £2.60: £1.20, £1.60, £1.90; EX 9.60.
Owner Anthony D Gee **Bred** Mrs C R Philipson **Trained** Hambleton, N Yorks
FOCUS
A very ordinary affair, unlikely to be that informative in the future, rated around the winner and third.

2020 TOTESPORT 0800 221 221 H'CAP 7f
5:00 (5:01) (Class 6) (0-65,65) 4-Y-0+ **£3,412** (£1,007; £504) **Stalls** Low

Form RPR
0400 **1** **First Rhapsody (IRE)**[9] 1795 4-8-0 **52**...................... AndrewElliott(5) 11 63
(T J Etherington) *hld up: hdwy on outer wl over 1f out: rdn and styd on strly ins last to ld nr line* **25/1**
401 **2** *shd* **Dancing Deano (IRE)**[9] 1791 4-8-5 **59**............(v) MichaelJStainton(7) 12 70
(R M Whitaker) *chsd ldrs: hdwy over 2f out: led wl over 1f out: sn rdn: drvn ins last: ct nr line* **12/1**
4640 **3** *1* **Dorn Dancer (IRE)**[9] 1795 4-8-11 **63**...................... MarkLawson(5) 1 71
(D W Barker) *chsd ldrs: effrt 2f out: sn rdn and ev ch over 1f out tl drvn and nt qckn ins last* **12/1**
6400 **4** *1* **Dvinsky (USA)**[5] 1882 5-9-0 **64**............................... DanielTudhope(3) 4 70
(D Carroll) *chsd ldrs: hdwy over 2f out: sn rdn and ev ch over 1f out: drvn and one pce ins last* **15/2**[3]
0500 **5** *¾* **No Grouse**[158] 6638 6-9-0 **64**................................... JasonEdmunds(3) 16 68
(E J Alston) *bhd tl hdwy wl over 1f out: rdn and styd on ins last: nrst fin* **33/1**
0015 **6** *1* **Mount Usher**[24] 1422 4-9-0 **61**.................................... DeanMcKeown 15 62
(G A Swinbank) *s.i.s and bhd tl styd on ins last: nrst fin* **13/2**[2]
4625 **7** *hd* **Briery Lane (IRE)**[16] 1607 5-8-7 **59**.......................... GregFairley(5) 17 59
(Mrs K Walton) *in tch: hdwy over 2f out: sn rdn to chse ldrs: one pce appr last* **22/1**
-000 **8** *nk* **Bond Playboy**[32] 1220 6-9-1 **62**...(p) TomEaves 9 62
(G R Oldroyd) *cl up: led over 2f out: sn rdn: edgd lft and hdd wl over 1f out: drvn and grad wknd* **25/1**
0000 **9** *½* **Compton Plume**[18] 1563 6-9-2 **63**.................................. DaleGibson 10 61
(M W Easterby) *chsd ldrs: rdn along 2f out: grad wknd appr last* **50/1**
6025 **10** *3* **Desert Opal**[9] 1795 6-9-2 **63**.. PaulQuinn 6 54
(D W Chapman) *chsd ldrs: rdn along 2f out: grad wknd appr last* **10/1**
2012 **11** *hd* **Onlytime Will Tell**[5] 1885 8-9-1 **62**............................. AdrianTNicholls 8 52
(D Nicholls) *a midfield* **13/8**[1]
5160 **12** *hd* **Cool Sands (IRE)**[36] 1124 4-8-9 **59**.......................(v) BenSwarbrick(3) 13 49
(D Shaw) *nvr nr ldrs* **100/1**
0000 **13** *1 ½* **Oddsmaker (IRE)**[184] 5549 5-8-8 **62**............................(t) JamieJones(7) 2 48
(M A Barnes) *a towards rr* **14/1**
2230 **14** *2 ½* **Brut**[14] 1686 4-9-4 **65**... FergalLynch 7 44
(D W Barker) *s.i.s: a rr* **14/1**
10 **15** *5* **Heartcrusher (IRE)**[134] 106 4-8-13 **60**............................. NeilPollard 5 26
(G A Swinbank) *led: rdn and hdd over 2f out: sn wknd* **50/1**
6000 **16** *½* **Joyeaux**[14] 1686 4-9-4 **65**.. DerekMcGaffin 3 30
(J Hetherton) *chsd ldrs: rdn along 3f out: sn wknd* **50/1**
5300 **17** *16* **Slavonic (USA)**[193] 6356 5-9-1 **62**...........................(p) TonyHamilton 14 —
(B Storey) *a bhd* **100/1**
1m 27.42s (0.06) **Going Correction** 0.0s/f (Good) **17** Ran SP% **123.8**
Speed ratings (Par 101):99,98,97,96,95 94,94,94,93,90 89,89,87,85,79 78,60
CSF £287.98 CT £3916.63 TOTE £40.90: £5.50, £2.50, £3.00, £2.10; EX 554.50 Place 6 £33.89, Place 5 £29.22.
Owner Ownaracehorse Ltd (ownaracehorse.co.uk) **Bred** Ballyhane Stud **Trained** Norton, N Yorks
FOCUS
A low-grade handicap run at a fair tempo and the form appears sound.
Mount Usher Official explanation: jockey said gelding was denied a clear run
Onlytime Will Tell Official explanation: trainer's rep had no explanation for the poor form shown
T/Plt: £45.70 to a £1 stake. Pool: £42,318.75. 675.55 winning tickets. T/Qpdt: £13.90 to a £1 stake. Pool: £1,979.50. 105.30 winning tickets. JR

1982 HAYDOCK (L-H)
Saturday, May 27
OFFICIAL GOING: Heavy (soft in places)
Wind: Light, across Weather: Overcast and light showers becoming fine later

2021 RECTANGLE GROUP H'CAP 5f
2:10 (2:13) (Class 2) (0-105,96) 3-Y-0+ **£19,431** (£5,781; £2,889; £1,443) **Stalls** High

Form RPR
6015 **1** **Prince Namid**[7] 1856 4-9-0 **84**.. TPQueally 5 94
(Mrs A Duffield) *a.p: led jst over 1f out: rdn out* **6/1**[3]
1330 **2** *½* **Stoneacre Lad (IRE)**[16] 1604 3-8-4 **82**..................(b) RobbieFitzpatrick 3 88
(Peter Grayson) *in rr: rdn and hdwy whn hung bdly lft over 1f out: chsd wnr ins fnl f: r.o* **33/1**
0601 **3** *½* **Bond Boy**[7] 1856 9-8-13 **83**..(b) JamieSpencer 9 93+
(B Smart) *in rr: pushed along 3f out: rdn and hdwy over 1f out: nt clr run ins fnl f: fin wl: nrst fin* **2/1**[1]
2233 **4** *2 ½* **Scooby Dude (IRE)**[7] 1857 3-8-4 **82** oh2...................... PaulHanagan 10 78
(Ms Deborah J Evans) *led: rdn and hdd jst over 1f out: no ex ins fnl f* **9/1**
0200 **5** *1 ½* **Cape Royal**[9] 1803 6-9-11 **95**...(t) KDarley 2 88
(J M Bradley) *cl up: rdn over 1f out: wknd ins fnl f* **12/1**
0501 **6** *1 ½* **Johnston's Diamond (IRE)**[7] 1858 8-9-1 **85**................ FrancisNorton 7 73
(E J Alston) *in tch: rdn and wknd over 1f out* **13/2**
40-0 **7** *1 ½* **Next Time Around (IRE)**[45] 989 4-9-6 **90**...................... MickyFenton 4 73
(Mrs L Stubbs) *a bhd: nvr on terms* **50/1**
3360 **8** *4* **Pivotal's Princess (IRE)**[16] 1602 4-9-9 **93**................... RichardMullen 8 63
(E S McMahon) *cl up tl rdn and wknd over 1f out* **5/1**[2]
3603 **9** *5* **If Paradise**[3] 1936 5-9-12 **96**...(b) SebSanders 1 49
(R Hannon) *hld up: rdn and lft bhd over 1f out* **7/1**
63.95 secs (1.88) **Going Correction** +0.65s/f (Yiel)
WFA 3 from 4yo+ 8lb **9** Ran SP% **112.7**
Speed ratings (Par 109):110,109,108,104,102 99,97,90,82
CSF £168.06 CT £529.98 TOTE £7.40: £2.30, £6.80, £1.20; EX 290.70.
Owner S Adamson **Bred** Mrs R D Peacock **Trained** Constable Burton, N Yorks
FOCUS
Testing conditions, but a good pace for this decent handicap and not that many got into it. The form appears solid, but with various problems affecting the second and third, the form may not be totally reliable.
NOTEBOOK
Prince Namid, proven in the ground, was undone by the draw at Thirsk last time but everything went right for him on this occasion. Always up with the pace, he stayed on well but would surely have faced a sterner test had the runner-up kept straight and the third not been stopped in his run. (op 13-2)
Stoneacre Lad(IRE), who, like the winner, had valid excuses for his most recent defeat, came from off the pace but hung badly left as he did so and he would probably have won otherwise. This is not the first time he has done this, and it does appear as though he will either need to be drawn close to a left-hand rail or race around a left-hand bend to show his best. (op 25-1)
Bond Boy, with the blinkers unsurprisingly retained following his Thirsk victory, was not in the most cooperative of moods and the champion jockey was after him some way home. He was hampered against the stands' rail by the weakening Scooby Dude a furlong from home, but it is hard to say that he would have won otherwise. (op 5-2 tchd 11-4)
Scooby Dude(IRE) ran well for a long way from the stands'-side draw, but he seems to have difficulty staying the trip on soft ground. (op 10-1)
Cape Royal was not totally disgraced out in the middle of the track, but the Handicapper is not giving him an inch. (op 10-1)
Johnston's Diamond(IRE) likes this ground, but he was raised 7lb for his Thirsk victory and that found him out. (op 6-1 tchd 9-2 in a place)
Pivotal's Princess(IRE) as form on easy ground, but found this something different, especially off her inflated mark. (op 11-2 tchd 9-2)

2022 WEST PROPERTIES SANDY LANE STKS (LISTED RACE) 6f
2:40 (2:41) (Class 1) 3-Y-0
£15,898 (£6,025; £3,015; £1,503; £753; £378) **Stalls** High

Form RPR
2152 **1** **Skhilling Spirit**[8] 1836 3-8-11 95.. JamieSpencer 6 100
(T D Barron) *in rr: rdn 3f out: hdwy over 1f out: wnt rt ins fnl f: r.o to ld cl home* **3/1**[1]
1210 **2** *nk* **Guto**[16] 1604 3-8-11 95.. DO'Donohoe 4 99
(K A Ryan) *led: rdn over 2f out: hung lft 1f out: hdd cl home* **16/1**
0021 **3** *1 ¾* **Green Park (IRE)**[7] 1857 3-8-11 90................................ PaulHanagan 1 94
(R A Fahey) *s.i.s: in rr: rdn 2f out: hdwy over 1f out: styd on ins fnl f: nt qckn towards fin* **7/2**[2]
2101 **4** *1* **Sunderland Echo (IRE)**[8] 1825 3-8-6 65........................ SamHitchcott 8 91+
(B Ellison) *handy for 1f: sn lost pl: rdn over 2f out: hdwy over 1f out: running on whn n.m.r and hmpd ins fnl f: nt rcvr* **25/1**
1251 **5** *1* **Angus Newz**[7] 1849 3-8-9 94.......................................(v) MickyFenton 7 86
(M Quinn) *trckd ldrs: wnt 2nd 2f out: rdn and hung lft over 1f out: ev ch ins fnl f: wknd towards fin* **4/1**[3]
6240 **6** *12* **Gamble In Gold (IRE)**[14] 1671 3-8-6 89................................ KDarley 3 47
(R Hannon) *in tch: rdn and wknd over 1f out* **9/1**
2256 **7** *½* **Campbeltown (IRE)**[56] 829 3-8-11 98......................... RichardMullen 2 51
(E J O'Neill) *prom: rdn over 2f out: wknd over 1f out* **14/1**
3024 **8** *¾* **Gallery Girl (IRE)**[15] 1633 3-8-6 97................................ FrancisNorton 5 43
(T D Easterby) *trckd ldrs: rdn and edgd lft 2f out: wknd over 1f out* **5/1**
1m 17.68s (2.78) **Going Correction** +0.65s/f (Yiel) **8** Ran SP% **110.3**
Speed ratings (Par 107):107,106,104,102,101 85,84,83
CSF £47.14 TOTE £3.80: £1.20, £4.20, £1.60; EX 43.00.
Owner I Hill **Bred** Pillar To Post Racing **Trained** Maunby, N Yorks
■ Stewards' Enquiry : Jamie Spencer caution: careless riding
FOCUS
A decent Listed race and the winning time was as you would expect in the conditions. The form is just fair for the grade, rated around the winner.
NOTEBOOK
Skhilling Spirit ◆, who ran so well over seven at York, was not certain to be suited by the drop back in trip but the ground brought his stamina into play and he gained a narrow, if ultimately fairly comfortable victory after having been off the bridle from some way out. A return to further should see him in an even better light. (op 7-2)
Guto made a bold bid to make every yard against the stands' rail and kept on well despite rather looking at the crowd, but was thwarted in the shadow of the post. He is yet to win beyond the minimum trip, but was not beaten here through lack of stamina. (tchd 14-1)
Green Park(IRE), who likes this ground, did have a bit to find with a few of these at the weight but he stayed on well from off the pace after switching out to the centre of the track. He is another yet to win beyond the minimum trip, but stamina does not appear to be a problem. (op 9-2)

Sunderland Echo(IRE), proven in the ground, nonetheless had a mountain to climb at these weights and can be considered unlucky not to have finished even closer, as she was totally squeezed out between the front pair when staying on a furlong out. This was a fine effort, but form shown on this sort of ground can be misleading and much will depend on how the Handicapper views this. (op 16-1)
Angus Newz, whose Nottingham victory the previous week was mainly down to receiving a shrewd ride, had every chance on this occasion, but failed to quicken sufficiently and this is probably a truer measure of her ability. (op 10-3)
Campbeltown(IRE) Official explanation: jockey said colt had no more to give
Gallery Girl(IRE) should have handled the ground and was rather disappointing. Official explanation: jockey said filly lost its action (op 9-2)

2023 EBF JOAN WESTBROOK PINNACLE STKS (LISTED RACE) (F&M) 1m 3f 200y
3:10 (3:12) (Class 1) 4-Y-0+ **£21,576** (£8,177; £4,092; £2,040; £1,022) **Stalls** High

Form — RPR
5213 **1** **Arbella**[15] [1628] 4-8-11 92 .... JamieSpencer 4 — 100
(W R Swinburn) *led: hdd narrowly 3f out: sustained chal: r.o to regain ld wl ins fnl f* **9/2**[3]
1306 **2** *nk* **Aunt Julia**[25] [1398] 4-8-11 100 .... KDarley 3 — 100
(R Hannon) *trckd ldrs: wnt 2nd over 3f out: led narrowly 3f out: continually pressed: hdd wl ins fnl f: hld cl home* **4/1**[2]
314- **3** *5* **Intrigued**[601] [5979] 4-8-11 .... SebSanders 2 — 93
(Sir Mark Prescott) *s.i.s: hld up: hdwy 3f out: rdn whn chsd ldrs over 2f out: sn lugged lft: one pce after* **4/5**[1]
0106 **4** *5* **Tarandot (IRE)**[9] [1804] 5-9-0 93 .... MickyFenton 5 — 89
(G G Margarson) *hld up: hdwy over 4f out: wknd and sn edgd lft over 3f out* **9/1**
4213 **5** *4* **Gramada (IRE)**[25] [1376] 4-8-11 70 .... RobbieFitzpatrick 1 — 80?
(P A Blockley) *trckd ldr tl over 4f out: sn wknd: lft bhd 2f out: eased ins fnl f* **33/1**

2m 37.86s (2.87) **Going Correction** +0.425s/f (Yiel) **5** Ran SP% **106.7**
Speed ratings (Par 111):107,106,103,100,97
CSF £20.49 TOTE £5.10: £1.90, £2.40; EX 11.30.
Owner Mrs P W Harris **Bred** Pendley Farm **Trained** Aldbury, Herts

FOCUS
A small field, but a solid pace given the conditions and the winning time was perfectly respectable. The form is rated around the first two, but is not rock solid. The quintet seemed keen to avoid the inside rail once into the home straight and came down the middle.

NOTEBOOK
Arbella, who was far from disgraced when finishing third of five in the Ormonde, gained a dramatic victory and beat two much higher-rated rivals in the process. After setting a reasonable pace for about a mile, she lost the advantage to Aunt Julia after turning for home and it looked as though she would have to be content with second best. However, she refused to go away and with the champion giving it everything, she managed to rally and snatch the race back near the line. On this evidence she will get further and, if she maintains her progress, she could develop into a Park Hill contender. (op 5-1)
Aunt Julia probably hit the front sooner than ideal and though she never stopped trying, she could not shake the winner off and was worried out of it. She handles cut, but her only win came on fast ground and perhaps this trip in the conditions is right on the limit of her stamina. (op 7-2)
Intrigued, who had upwards of 12lb in hand of her rivals on adjusted official ratings, had not been seen since finishing fourth behind Divine Proportions in the 2004 Prix Marcel Boussac. The way she held her position in the market suggested she was considered fit enough, but this much longer trip in the conditions was always going to be a severe test and she could never land an effective blow. She can be given another chance to show that she retains her ability back on better ground. (tchd 5-6 in places)
Tarandot(IRE) may be a Listed winner in heavy ground, but she still had plenty to do judged on official ratings and she was duly put in her place. (tchd 10-1)
Gramada(IRE) had no chance in this company and so it proved. (op 28-1 tchd 25-1)

2024 TOTEPOOL SILVER BOWL (HERITAGE H'CAP) 1m 30y
3:45 (3:49) (Class 2) 3-Y-0
£62,320 (£18,660; £9,330; £4,670; £2,330; £1,170) **Stalls** Low

Form — RPR
4112 **1** **Anna Pavlova**[8] [1832] 3-9-5 91 .... PaulHanagan 6 — 103
(R A Fahey) *in tch: rdn and hdwy over 2f out: led over 1f out: sn hung lft: kpt on wl* **4/1**[3]
411 **2** *nk* **Sir Gerard**[30] [1250] 3-9-0 86 .... JamieSpencer 1 — 100+
(J R Fanshawe) *hld up: n.m.r over 5f out: hdwy 2f out: nt clr run and swtchd rt over 1f out: r.o wl towards fin* **7/2**[2]
2121 **3** *1 ¼* **Kalankari (IRE)**[25] [1384] 3-9-4 90 .... FrancisNorton 7 — 99
(A M Balding) *racd keenly: trckd ldrs: wnt 2nd over 2f out: rdn and ev ch ent fnl f: nt qckn towards fin* **11/1**
3621 **4** *4* **Bin Rahy (IRE)**[18] [1569] 3-8-11 83 .... SamHitchcott 3 — 84
(M R Channon) *trckd ldrs: rdn 4f out: outpcd over 2f out: no imp on ldrs after* **11/1**
3311 **5** *1* **Peppertree Lane (IRE)**[8] [1832] 3-9-7 93 .... KDarley 4 — 92
(M Johnston) *led: rdn and hdd over 1f out: wknd fnl f* **13/8**[1]
4211 **6** *nk* **Baskerville**[8] [1828] 3-8-13 85 .... AdrianMcCarthy 5 — 83
(P W Chapple-Hyam) *trckd ldr tl rdn over 2f out: wknd over 1f out* **8/1**
1040 **7** *6* **Envision**[36] [1115] 3-9-2 88 .... SebSanders 2 — 74
(R Hannon) *hld up: rdn over 2f out: nvr on terms* **33/1**

1m 46.97s (1.46) **Going Correction** +0.425s/f (Yiel) **7** Ran SP% **111.0**
Speed ratings (Par 105):109,108,107,103,102 102,96
CSF £17.24 CT £133.63 TOTE £4.60: £2.20, £1.90; EX 16.90 Trifecta £220.70 Pool: £839.34 - 2.70 winning units.
Owner Galaxy Racing **Bred** Raymond Cowie **Trained** Musley Bank, N Yorks

FOCUS
A solid pace for this extremely valuable handicap; the winning time was very creditable and the form looks sound with the first three all progressive. On this occasion the runners were content to stay on the inside once into the home straight.

NOTEBOOK
Anna Pavlova, who ran so well at testing ground at York eight days earlier, was a candidate for the bounce factor considering that was her first outing in eight months, but there was no sign of it. Brought with her effort wide, she did tend to hang left under pressure and did the runner-up few favours, but she did run right to the line and was the winner on merit. She is probably capable of more, especially as she has now proved that she acts on any ground, but this was a very nice prize to win in the meantime. (op 11-2)
Sir Gerard ◆, racing on soft ground for the first time, was given a patient ride but met trouble in running on a couple of occasions, firstly on the home bend and then, probably more significantly, when the winner crossed him a furlong from home just as he was getting into the race. He stayed on strongly once gathering himself together, but the margin was still a neck at the line and the Stewards could not have been sure that he would have won with a clear run, so allowed the result to stand. He is still unexposed and remains progressive, so it should not be long before he gains compensation. The Britannia looks tailor-made for him. (op 3-1 tchd 4-1)
Kalankari(IRE), raised a whopping 11lb for his recent Kempton Polytrack success, and 13lb on sand, ran a cracker considering he saw plenty of daylight on the outside of the field and was keen enough. He never stopped battling and deserves to find another race off his revised mark if given the opportunity. (op 10-1 tchd 12-1)
Bin Rahy(IRE), raised 6lb for his victory in similar ground at Chepstow, had every chance but looked short of pace even in these conditions and probably needs a return to further now. (op 9-1)
Peppertree Lane(IRE), with the ground remaining in his favour, was well backed to complete the hat-trick and confirm recent York form with Anna Pavlova despite meeting her on 9lb worse terms. However, despite getting his own way out in front he did not put up much of a fight once the challengers arrived and perhaps this was one step too far. (op 2-1 tchd 6-4 and 9-4 in a place)
Baskerville, raised 5lb for his Nottingham win and also bidding for a hat-trick, was keen enough early and that would not have helped him in these conditions. (op 7-1)

2025 OPTION HYGIENE H'CAP 1m 30y
4:15 (4:16) (Class 5) (0-70,70) 4-Y-0+ **£3,238** (£963; £481; £240) **Stalls** Low

Form — RPR
0060 **1** **Dark Charm (FR)**[8] [1830] 7-9-1 67 .... (p) PaulHanagan 10 — 78
(R A Fahey) *in tch: rdn over 2f out: hdwy to ld over 1f out: r.o* **14/1**
5-00 **2** *2* **Wizard Of Us**[371] [1889] 6-8-4 56 oh4 .... AdrianMcCarthy 9 — 63
(M Mullineaux) *hld up: rdn 3f out: hdwy whn hung lft over 2f out: nt clr run and swtchd rt over 1f out: styd on to take 2nd last strides* **66/1**
0600 **3** *hd* **Corky (IRE)**[3] [1932] 5-9-4 70 .... SebSanders 8 — 77
(I W McInnes) *in rr: hdwy 3f out: rdn 2f out: hung lft over 1f out: chsd wnr ins fnl f tl one pce last strides* **16/1**
5662 **4** *hd* **Ermine Grey**[8] [1830] 5-8-10 62 .... FrancisNorton 7 — 68
(A W Carroll) *towards rr: hdwy 2f out: rdn and edgd rt over 1f out: kpt on ins fnl f* **6/1**[3]
6032 **5** *3 ½* **Hawkit (USA)**[19] [1531] 5-9-3 69 .... MickyFenton 4 — 68
(A Bailey) *in rr: rdn and hdwy over 1f out: kpt on: nt trble ldrs* **9/1**
0100 **6** *1 ½* **Pauline's Prince**[35] [1148] 4-8-13 65 .... KDarley 3 — 61
(R Hollinshead) *midfield: rdn over 3f out: outpcd over 1f out* **25/1**
2600 **7** *¾* **Cantarna (IRE)**[8] [1830] 5-8-8 60 .... RichardMullen 6 — 55
(J Mackie) *sn chsd ldrs: rdn and wknd over 2f out* **11/2**[2]
3310 **8** *2 ½* **Komreyev Star**[33] [1198] 4-7-11 56 oh3 .... LiamJones(7) 5 — 46
(M Mullineaux) *chsd ldrs: rdn over 3f out: wknd over 2f out* **20/1**
0051 **9** *nk* **Bollin Michael**[7] [1852] 4-8-13 65 .... (b) JamieSpencer 2 — 54
(T D Easterby) *chsd ldr: led briefly over 1f out: wknd qckly and eased ins fnl f* **6/5**[1]
0300 **10** *nk* **Second Reef**[30] [1258] 4-8-0 59 .... DonnaCaldwell(7) 11 — 48
(E J Alston) *racd keenly: led: clr 5f out: rdn over 2f out: hdd over 1f out: wknd qckly ins fnl f* **66/1**
0505 **11** *3 ½* **Shifty**[8] [1830] 7-8-8 60 .... TPQueally 1 — 42
(D Carroll) *midfield: rdn over 3f out: edgd lft over 2f out: wknd over 1f out* **16/1**

1m 48.22s (2.71) **Going Correction** +0.425s/f (Yiel) **11** Ran SP% **115.1**
Speed ratings (Par 103):103,101,100,100,97 95,94,92,92,91 88
CSF £715.97 CT £8020.03 TOTE £20.00: £4.10, £11.90, £3.70; EX 978.60.
Owner R A Fahey **Bred** Cyril Humphris **Trained** Musley Bank, N Yorks

FOCUS
A rapid early pace thanks to the antics of Second Reef, but in the end the winning time was about par for the grade in the conditions. The runner-up is the best guide to the form, which appears sound amongst the principals. The field were spread well across the track in the home straight, though as in the third race they were happy to shun the inside rail.
Dark Charm(FR) Official explanation: trainer said, regarding improved form shown, the gelding may have benefited from the re-application of cheek pieces
Bollin Michael Official explanation: trainer had no explanation for the poor form shown

2026 EBF CASINO 36 CLASSIC MAIDEN FILLIES' STKS 6f
4:50 (4:51) (Class 5) 2-Y-0 **£3,886** (£1,156; £577; £288) **Stalls** High

Form — RPR
1 **Tender Moments** 2-9-0 .... PaulHanagan 2 — 73+
(K A Ryan) *s.i.s: in rr: sn pushed along: hdwy whn nt clr run and swtchd lft ins fnl f: str run to ld towards fin* **9/1**
2 *½* **Spritza (IRE)** 2-9-0 .... JamieSpencer 3 — 72+
(M L W Bell) *swtchd rt after 1f: hld up: hdwy 2f out: led ins fnl f: hdd towards fin* **5/1**[2]
04 **3** *¾* **Angeletta**[33] [1181] 2-9-0 .... RichardMullen 9 — 70
(E S McMahon) *wnt lft s: led for 1f: remained prom: led again over 2f out: rdn and hdd 1f out: styd on* **12/1**
4 *nk* **Milliegait** 2-9-0 .... MickyFenton 5 — 69
(T D Easterby) *in tch: rdn over 2f out: swtchd lft over 1f out: ev ch ins fnl f: nt qckn towards fin* **20/1**
2 **5** *1 ¼* **My Valerina (IRE)**[9] [1790] 2-9-0 .... TPQueally 1 — 65+
(Mrs A Duffield) *chsd ldrs: rdn to ld 1f out: sn edgd lft: hdd ins fnl f: fdd towards fin* **5/1**[2]
2 **6** *½* **Silca Soprano**[8] [1817] 2-9-0 .... SamHitchcott 8 — 64
(M R Channon) *prom: rdn and ev ch over 1f out: no ex ins fnl f* **2/1**[1]
0 **7** *2 ½* **Almora Guru**[40] [1046] 2-9-0 .... RobbieFitzpatrick 4 — 56
(W M Brisbourne) *racd keenly: lost pl after 1f: hdwy and hung lft over 2f out: ev ch ins fnl f: wknd and eased towards fin* **33/1**
6 **8** *7* **Dee Cee Elle**[15] [1647] 2-9-0 .... KDarley 7 — 35
(M Johnston) *chsd ldrs: rdn over 2f out: sn wknd* **6/1**[3]
0 **9** *7* **Springtime Parkes**[40] [1046] 2-9-0 .... DO'Donohoe 6 — 14
(K A Ryan) *racd keenly: prom: led after 1f: hdd over 2f out: sn rdn and wknd* **11/1**

1m 21.6s (6.70) **Going Correction** +0.65s/f (Yiel) **9** Ran SP% **114.7**
Speed ratings (Par 90):81,80,79,78,77 76,73,63,54
CSF £53.11 TOTE £10.70: £2.50, £1.80, £3.40; EX 45.00.
Owner Leinster Partnership **Bred** J R And Mrs P Good **Trained** Hambleton, N Yorks

FOCUS
This looked a fair maiden on paper, but it did appear as though these fillies had a real problem seeing out the trip in the conditions and the moderate winning time was almost four seconds slower than the earlier Listed contest. The form has been rated conservatively.

NOTEBOOK
Tender Moments, a 30,000gns full-sister to Golden Square, was out the back and apparently going nowhere for much of the way, but those that forced the early pace rather fell in a hole and, though she had to take evasive action to avoid the backwash, she saw her race out better than her rivals. She is entitled to improve, but the slow winning time has to put a big question mark over the true value of the form. (op 14-1)
Spritza(IRE), a 135,000euros half-sister to Portrait Of A Lady, seemed to have been produced at just the right time but she could not withstand the winner's late effort. The form may not be great, but she is entitled to come on for this and her breeding suggests she is going to need further. (op 10-3)
Angeletta, stepping up a furlong, raced up with the leaders the whole way against the stands' rail and plugged on at one pace, but the two newcomers saw their races out that much better and she will need to find a very modest contest if she is to get off the mark.

Milliegait ◆, a half-sister to several winners including Bold Gait and Captain Miller, stayed on in eye-catching style down the middle of the track and is likely to come on a good deal for this initial experience.
My Valerina(IRE), runner-up on her debut, showed up for a long way but this extra furlong in testing conditions seemed to find her out. (op 6-1)
Silca Soprano, so promising on her debut, showed up well for much of the way but did not get home over this extra furlong and the ground was most likely the reason. She is worth another chance. (op 7-4 tchd 9-4)
Dee Cee Elle, an eye-catcher on her debut, was a springer in the market but was one of the first beaten. (op 16-1)

2027 GEORGE DUFFIELD APPRENTICE H'CAP — 5f
5:25 (5:25) (Class 5) (0-75,75) 3-Y-0+ — **£3,238** (£963; £481; £240) **Stalls** High

Form — RPR
3040 **1** **Balakiref**[147] [6698] 7-9-11 **73** .... LiamJones 7 — 86
(M Dods) *in tch: rdn over 1f out: edgd rt ent fnl f: r.o to ld towards fin* **9/1**
3050 **2** ¾ **Cerulean Rose**[10] [1774] 7-8-6 **61** oh1 .... JackDean(7) 4 — 71
(A W Carroll) *hld up: hdwy over 2f out: led over 1f out: sn edgd rt: hdd towards fin* **20/1**
5162 **3** 2½ **Gilded Cove**[7] [1846] 6-9-7 **69** .... RussellKennemore 13 — 71
(R Hollinshead) *hld up: rdn and hdwy 2f out: styd on ins fnl f: nt rch ldrs* **7/2**[1]
1020 **4** 3 **Knot In Wood (IRE)**[251] [5337] 4-9-8 **75** .... JamesReveley(5) 6 — 66
(R A Fahey) *led: rdn and hdd over 1f out: no ex ins fnl f* **7/1**
0000 **5** ¾ **Whistler**[7] [1846] 9-9-0 **65** .... (p) JamesMillman(3) 3 — 54
(Miss J R Tooth) *in rr: hdwy over 1f out: one pce ins fnl f* **16/1**
0000 **6** nk **Kings College Boy**[7] [1846] 6-9-2 **64** .... (b) DerekNolan 11 — 52
(R A Fahey) *in tch: rdn over 2f out: hung lft over 1f out: no imp ins fnl f* **9/2**[3]
0406 **7** ½ **Jilly Why (IRE)**[47] [950] 5-9-4 **71** .... JamieHamblett(5) 15 — 57
(Ms Deborah J Evans) *hld up: hdwy whn rdn and hung lft over 1f out: wknd ins fnl f* **16/1**
0500 **8** 1 **Unlimited**[9] [1794] 4-8-10 **61** oh4 .... TolleyDean(3) 2 — 44
(Mrs A Duffield) *w ldr: rdn whn n.m.r and hmpd over 1f out: sn wknd* **12/1**
0000 **9** 1 **Jadan (IRE)**[9] [1795] 5-9-3 **65** .... DonnaCaldwell 10 — 44
(E J Alston) *chsd ldrs: rdn 2f out: wknd ins fnl f* **20/1**
0034 **10** ½ **Mytton's Pride**[11] [1751] 3-8-10 **66** .... RonanKeogh 1 — 44
(A Bailey) *w ldrs: rdn over 1f out: wknd fnl f* **25/1**
0050 **11** ¾ **Ellens Academy (IRE)**[7] [1858] 11-9-3 **72** .... JamesRogers(7) 14 — 47
(E J Alston) *hld up: hdwy 2f out: wknd fnl f* **16/1**
2303 **12** nk **Mynd**[19] [1528] 6-8-8 **61** oh5 .... DeanHeslop(5) 8 — 35
(R M Whitaker) *s.i.s: hld up: n.m.r over 2f out: sn rdn: no imp* **4/1**[2]

64.84 secs (2.77) **Going Correction** +0.65s/f (Yiel)
WFA 3 from 4yo+ 8lb — **12** Ran SP% **121.6**
Speed ratings (Par 103):103,101,97,93,91 91,90,88,87,86 85,84
CSF £181.72 CT £770.49 TOTE £11.70: £3.70, £3.80, £2.10; EX 137.00 Place 6 £1,051.99, Place 5 £582.11.
Owner Septimus Racing Group **Bred** S R Hope And D Erwin **Trained** Denton, Co Durham
■ Winthorpe was withdrawn (12/1, no suitable jockey). R4, deduct 5p in the £. New market formed.

FOCUS
An ordinary sprint handicap and the action all unfolded down the centre of the track, with those that raced against the stands' rail looking to be at a disadvantage.
T/Plt: £2,179.00 to a £1 stake. Pool: £83,578.60. 28.00 winning tickets. T/Qpdt: £543.30 to a £1 stake. Pool: £3,671.20. 5.00 winning tickets. DO

1989 NEWMARKET (ROWLEY) (R-H)
Saturday, May 27

OFFICIAL GOING: Soft
There was a distinct advantage in racing prominently throughout the afternoon.
Wind: Fresh, half-behind Weather: Raining

2028 PERSIMMON HOMES MAIDEN STKS (DIV I) — 1m
1:25 (1:29) (Class 5) 3-Y-0 — **£4,857** (£1,445; £722; £360) **Stalls** High

Form — RPR
2525 **1** **Cousteau**[15] [1627] 3-9-3 97 .... EddieAhern 2 — 88+
(P W Chapple-Hyam) *lw: racd centre: mde all: rdn and hung rt over 1f out: sn clr* **7/4**[2]
2 3½ **Majestic Halo** 3-8-12 .... SteveDrowne 10 — 76
(E A L Dunlop) *lt-f: racd centre: a.p: rdn to chse wnr over 1f out: styd on: 2nd of 12 in gp* **66/1**
3 5 **Mighty** 3-9-3 .... RobertWinston 4 — 71+
(Sir Michael Stoute) *w'like: scope: racd centre: s.i.s: hdwy over 3f out: outpcd over 2f out : styd on ins fnl f: 3rd of 12 in gp* **10/1**[3]
432 **4** shd **Le Colombier (IRE)**[35] [1153] 3-9-3 83 .... RichardHughes 11 — 71
(J W Hills) *lw: racd alone far side: w ldrs tl rdn over 1f out: wknd fnl f* **12/1**
0 **5** 1 **Art Man**[20] [1513] 3-9-3 .... JimCrowley 3 — 69+
(Mrs A J Perrett) *racd centre: s.i.s: sn prom: outpcd over 2f out: edgd rt over 1f out: styd on ins fnl f: 4th of 12 in gp* **66/1**
3 **6** 3 **Alsadaa (USA)**[252] [5311] 3-9-3 .... (t) RHills 7 — 63
(J H M Gosden) *racd centre: prom: chsd wnr 1/2-way: rdn and wknd over 1f out: 5th of 12 in gp* **11/10**[1]
7 1½ **Mr Wiseguy** 3-9-3 .... JohnEgan 13 — 60
(G C Bravery) *cmpt: racd centre: hld up in tch: rdn 1/2-way: wknd over 2f out: 6th of 12 in gp* **100/1**
8 1 **Wizards Dream** 3-9-3 .... LPKeniry 12 — 58
(D R C Elsworth) *w'like: scope: racd centre: s.i.s: nvr nrr: 7th of 12 in gp* **66/1**
9 ½ **Fluffy** 3-8-12 .... MichaelHills 1 — 52
(B W Hills) *str: scope: s.i.s: racd centre: a in rr: 8th of 12 in gp* **33/1**
0 **10** 2 **Sand Sprite (IRE)**[210] [6143] 3-8-12 .... KerrinMcEvoy 5 — 48
(Sir Michael Stoute) *racd centre: chsd ldrs over 5f: 9th of 12 in gp* **20/1**
5 **11** ¾ **True West (USA)**[24] [1418] 3-8-12 .... DarryllHolland 6 — 47
(J Noseda) *leggy: scope: racd centre: prom over 5f: 10th of 12 in gp* **33/1**
12 10 **Dik Dik** 3-9-3 .... OscarUrbina 9 — 32
(J R Fanshawe) *cmpt: scope: bkwd: s.i.s: racd centre: sn mid-div: wknd 3f out: 11th of 12 in gp* **100/1**
0 **13** 11 **Sa Nau**[26] [1336] 3-9-3 .... TonyCulhane 8 — 10
(T Keddy) *lw: racd centre: hld up: a in rr: bhd fnl 3f: last of 12 in gp* **100/1**

1m 41.32s (1.95) **Going Correction** +0.20s/f (Good) — **13** Ran SP% **118.9**
Speed ratings (Par 99):98,94,89,89,88 85,83,82,82,80 79,69,58
CSF £131.40 TOTE £2.70: £1.30, £12.00, £2.00; EX 174.80.
Owner Charnwood Boy Partnership, B Reilly **Bred** Star Pointe Ltd,Brosnan And Williamson **Trained** Newmarket, Suffolk

FOCUS
A decent maiden run at just a steady gallop and rated through the fourth.
Le Colombier(IRE) Official explanation: jockey said bit slipped through colt's mouth
Alsadaa(USA) Official explanation: jockey said colt was unsuited by the soft ground

2029 EUROPEAN BREEDERS FUND MAIDEN STKS — 6f
1:55 (1:57) (Class 5) 2-Y-0 — **£4,533** (£1,348; £674; £336) **Stalls** High

Form — RPR
1 **Tariq** 2-9-3 .... EddieAhern 10 — 92
(P W Chapple-Hyam) *cmpt: s.i.s: sn prom: led 1f out: r.o wl* **14/1**
0 **2** 3½ **Ebn Reem**[17] [1588] 2-9-3 .... PhilipRobinson 9 — 82
(M A Jarvis) *led: rdn and hdd 1f out: styd on same pce* **7/1**[3]
0 **3** hd **Tudor Prince (IRE)**[7] [1838] 2-9-3 .... MichaelHills 3 — 81
(B J Meehan) *lw: chsd ldr: rdn and hung lft over 1f out: sn ev ch: styd on same pce* **7/2**[1]
6 **4** 5 **Fort Worth (IRE)**[15] [1639] 2-8-12 .... JamesDoyle(5) 12 — 66
(B Gubby) *bkwd: chsd ldrs: rdn over 2f out: wknd over 1f out* **40/1**
5 ¾ **Kalgoorlie (USA)** 2-9-3 .... DarryllHolland 1 — 64
(J Noseda) *gd sort: lw: hld up: rdn over 2f out: nvr trbld ldrs* **15/2**
6 **6** 2½ **Marine Parade**[7] [1838] 2-9-3 .... PatDobbs 5 — 56
(R Hannon) *w'like: leggy: s.i.s: in rr: rdn over 2f out: n.d* **7/2**[1]
7 2 **Rescue (USA)** 2-9-3 .... TonyCulhane 4 — 50+
(M R Channon) *neat: s.s: hld up: n.d* **9/1**
8 ½ **Cryptic Clue (USA)** 2-9-3 .... RichardHughes 2 — 49+
(Mrs A J Perrett) *w'like: lw: hld up in tch: rdn over 2f out: hung rt and wknd over 1f out* **12/1**
9 ½ **Strike Force** 2-9-3 .... JimmyFortune 11 — 47+
(J H M Gosden) *cmpt: mid-div: rdn 1/2-way: wknd 2f out* **6/1**[2]
10 31 **Stravinsky's Art (USA)** 2-9-3 .... JohnEgan 8 — —
(D R C Elsworth) *w'like: prom over 3f* **16/1**

1m 14.57s (1.47) **Going Correction** +0.20s/f (Good) — **10** Ran SP% **115.7**
Speed ratings (Par 93):98,93,93,86,85 82,79,78,78,36
CSF £107.64 TOTE £17.00: £3.80, £2.20, £1.70; EX 127.10.
Owner Saleh Al Homaizi & Imad Al Sagar **Bred** D R Botterill **Trained** Newmarket, Suffolk

FOCUS
A creditable winning time, slightly faster than the sprint handicap won by Borehan later on the card, although the ground softened during the day. Those who raced on the pace were seen at an advantage and the front trio drew clear of the fourth. The form looks strong for the grade.

NOTEBOOK
Tariq, a well-bred colt hailing from a stable more than capable of producing a decent juvenile, was a shade tardy at the gate, but was soon sat just off the pace-setting Ebn Reem. Ridden to challenge over a furlong out, he quickly asserted once settling into top gear and ran on strongly to make a taking debut. Bred to stay further, it was slightly surprising to hear connections are planning a tilt at the five-furlong Norfolk Stakes at Royal Ascot, but he may get away with it assuming he is able to handle the likely faster ground. Either way he a nice prospect.
Ebn Reem, too green to do himself justice in a fair event on debut at Newcastle, had clearly learned from that experience and was soon heading up the field. However, he looked in trouble when challenged on both sides running into the final quarter mile and simply lacked the winner's acceleration. A return to faster ground may bring him on again and he looks the sort connections can pick up a decent nursery with. (op 13-2)
Tudor Prince(IRE) ran on late to not be beaten all that far on his debut at Newbury the previous weekend and he stepped up on that with a one-paced third. He came to challenge over a furlong out, but lacked the pace of the winner and was unable to get by Ebn Reem for second. He can find an ordinary maiden, but nurseries will ultimately be where he ends up. (tchd 4-1 in places)
Fort Worth(IRE) appeared to step up on his initial outing at Lingfield, but whether or not he was flattered in having raced up with the leading trio early on is open to debate. Either way he should be able to find a small race once qualified for handicaps. (tchd 50-1)
Kalgoorlie(USA), whose stable introduced a debutant to win here at the last meeting, never got into it having been behind early, but he was going forward at the end and it is highly likely better ground will bring about some improvement. (op 8-1)
Marine Parade, over a length ahead of Tudor Prince at Newbury last weekend, did himself no favours with a sluggish start and was always struggling to get into it thereafter. This was disappointing, but it would come as no surprise to see him leave the form behind in future. (tchd 4-1)
Rescue(USA), who cost 130,000gns, was representing a leading two-year-old trainer and it came as no surprise to see him nibbled at in the market beforehand. However, he was slowly away and found himself unable to make any headway in the ground, but the fact there was money for him suggests he is better than this and it is hoped he learns from the experience. (op 12-1)
Cryptic Clue(USA), whose stable introduced a well-bred juvenile to finish second at Newbury the previous weekend, was a negative in the market and he raced as though the soft ground first time out was too much to handle. He should leave the form behind. (op 9-1)
Strike Force, a first juvenile runner of the season for connections, is ultimately bred to stay further, but should have the speed for six furlongs and it was disappointing to see him trail in last but one. He obviously needs to raise him game in future, but it is possible the ground was no good for him. (op 11-2)
Stravinsky's Art(USA), whose stable can ready one, was weak in the market and he ran accordingly, dropping right out in ground that clearly did not suit. He can improve for better ground, but obviously needs to. Official explanation: jockey said colt suffered a breathing problem (op 18-1 tchd 20-1)

2030 SHADWELL ESTATES FAIRWAY STKS (LISTED RACE) — 1m 2f
2:25 (2:29) (Class 1) 3-Y-0
£15,898 (£6,025; £3,015; £1,503; £753; £378) **Stalls** High

Form — RPR
0321 **1** **Red Rocks (IRE)**[33] [1192] 3-8-12 103 .... JimmyFortune 1 — 116+
(B J Meehan) *lw: chsd ldr: led over 2f out: rdn out* **15/8**[1]
0221 **2** 4 **Degas Art (IRE)**[20] [1516] 3-8-12 95 .... JohnEgan 5 — 107
(D R C Elsworth) *lw: s.i.s: sn prom: nt clr run over 2f out: rdn to chse wnr fnl f: edgd rt and no imp* **10/1**
641 **3** 3 **Markovitch**[39] [1070] 3-8-12 97 .... EddieAhern 4 — 102
(P W Chapple-Hyam) *led over 7f: wknd fnl f* **8/1**
1 **4** ½ **Book Of Music (IRE)**[210] [6142] 3-8-12 .... RobertWinston 3 — 101
(Sir Michael Stoute) *lw: s.i.s: hld up: hdwy over 3f out: rdn and wknd fnl f* **5/2**[2]
1136 **5** 11 **Gin Jockey (FR)**[17] [1600] 3-9-1 101 .... (v[1]) RichardHughes 2 — 84
(R Hannon) *trckd ldrs: racd keenly: rdn and wknd over 1f out* **12/1**
122 **6** dist **Tell**[29] [1269] 3-8-12 102 .... PhilipRobinson 6 — —
(J L Dunlop) *hld up: eased over 8f out: virtually p.u fnl 5f: t.o* **9/2**[3]

2m 5.90s (0.19) **Going Correction** +0.20s/f (Good) — **6** Ran SP% **109.4**
Speed ratings (Par 107):107,103,101,101,92 —
CSF £19.59 TOTE £2.70: £1.70, £3.90; EX 23.50.

Owner J Paul Reddam **Bred** Ballylinch Stud **Trained** Manton, Wilts

FOCUS

A decent event that threw up David Junior last year and, although he will do well to follow his stable companion in going on to Group 1 success, Red Rocks was most impressive and the third sets a reasonable standard.

NOTEBOOK

Red Rocks(IRE) ◆, whose stable took this with subsequent Champion Stakes winner David Junior a year ago, confirmed the promise show in three outings at two when running out a smooth winner of a ten-furlong maiden at Windsor in April, and he was unfazed by the rise in class, pulling clear from well over a furlong out in the style of a very smart performer. It is asking a lot for him to emulate David Junior, but he looks well worth his place at Group level and he should prove just as effective over the 12 furlongs of the King Edward VII Stakes, his next intended target and a race he is likely to take some beating in. (op 2-1 tchd 9-4)

Degas Art(IRE) ◆ has got some useful form to his name and relished every yard of the 12-furlong trip when routing his field in a Salisbury maiden last time. He too seemed at home in this grade, but he had no answer to the winner's kick at this distance and could only keep on at the one pace. A return to greater distances is going to help the scopey son of Danehill Dancer and it will be interesting to see what weight he is allocated for the King George V Handicap at the Royal meeting, as the stiff finish there is sure to suit and he would appeal as one of the more likely winners.

Markovitch, a winner over course and distance on his seasonal return, again attempted to make most of the running on this rise in class, having the rail to help, but he proved no match for the front pair and quite simply did not look good enough. He may not be the easiest to place from now on. (op 11-1)

Book Of Music(IRE) was perhaps the one of most interest in the field, the son of Sadler's Wells having his first start since making a winning debut in a seven-furlong maiden here at the backend of last season. In rear early, he made smooth headway to loom menacingly over two furlongs out, but it was evident once he came off the bridle there was little in reserve and he dropped away in the final furlong. It is possible he needed the run, but the more likely reason for his defeat is that he did not stay, his breeding very much pointing to him being a miler. He may last out the trip on better ground, but for now connections will no doubt look to drop him back in trip. (op 11-4)

Gin Jockey(FR) disappointed in similar ground in France last time and the first-time visor made little difference. He simply needs better ground. (tchd 10-1)

Tell, narrowly denied by the potentially smart Ivy Creek on his reappearance at Sandown, looked one of the more likely winners, but Robinson was never happy on the colt and was looking down to see if something was amiss at an early stage. It is possible he failed to stride out on the ground and, as a result, he deserves another chance. Official explanation: jockey said, regarding the running and riding, colt was fractious being loaded into stalls, made slight contact with a rival leaving stalls, and lost its action immediately after start; vet said colt finished sound (op 10-3 tchd 5-1 in places)

2031 CHEVELEY PARK STUD KING CHARLES II STKS (LISTED RACE) 7f

2:55 (2:58) (Class 1) 3-Y-O

£15,898 (£6,025; £3,015; £1,503; £753; £378) **Stalls** High

Form			Horse	Jockey	RPR
2122	**1**		**Jeremy (USA)**[38] 1083 3-8-12 105	RobertWinston 3	112
			(Sir Michael Stoute) *lw: trckd ldrs: led over 1f out: hdd ins fnl f: rallied to ld nr fin*	**15/8**[1]	
2125	**2**	*nk*	**Wake Up Maggie (IRE)**[20] 1508 3-8-7 113	RichardHughes 4	106
			(C F Wall) *led: hdd over 1f out: rallied to ld ins fnl f: rdn and hdd nr fin*	**10/3**[2]	
0626	**3**	*4*	**Spinning Queen**[20] 1508 3-8-7 104	MichaelHills 5	96
			(B W Hills) *b.hind: trckd ldrs: plld hrd: rdn over 1f out: styd on same pce*	**9/2**	
21	**4**	*hd*	**Aeroplane**[39] 1065 3-8-12 97	EddieAhern 1	101+
			(P W Chapple-Hyam) *lw: hld up: hdwy over 1f out: styd on same pce fnl f*	**7/2**[3]	
0003	**5**	*1*	**Pacific Pride**[15] 1633 3-8-12 98	DarryllHolland 2	99
			(J Howard Johnson) *chsd ldr: rdn over 2f out: no ex fnl f*	**25/1**	
21	**6**	*7*	**Mobsir**[15] 1640 3-8-12 86	RHills 6	82
			(E A L Dunlop) *hld up: wknd 2f out*	**16/1**	

1m 28.81s (2.31) **Going Correction** +0.425s/f (Yiel) **6** Ran SP% **108.0**

Speed ratings (Par 107):103,102,98,97,96 88

CSF £7.63 TOTE £2.30: £1.40, £2.00; EX 7.60.

Owner Mrs Elizabeth Moran **Bred** Brookdale **Trained** Newmarket, Suffolk

FOCUS

A good Listed contest with Group 1 form on offer, but the pace was modest for the class and the form may not be totally reliable.

NOTEBOOK

Jeremy(USA), slightly unlucky not to make a winning reappearance over course and distance in the Free handicap, found the necessary improvement to topple Wake Up Maggie, the attractive-looking colt looking much happier on this softer surface. He travelled through smoothly, but took his time to get on top, nosing back ahead in the dying strides having looked set to finish second 50 yards from the line. He should stay a mile, but the Jersey Stakes is his next intended target and he should have obvious claims there, as long as the going is not rock hard. (op 5-2)

Wake Up Maggie(IRE) ◆, taking a drop in grade having performed with great credit in defeat in both the Cheveley Park and 1000 Guineas on her last two starts, was made plenty of use of on this drop in distance and looked to have battled her way back to victory nearing the line, but Jeremy had kept a little bit in reserve and she was denied close home. Clear of the third, she may be able to reverse form with the winner at Ascot on better ground, and has the Coronation Stakes as another option. (op 5-2)

Spinning Queen, one place behind Wake Up Maggie in the 1000 Guineas, pulled hard early on and that dented her chance. She was keeping on close home, without threatening the front two, but winning is not going to come easily form her this year. (op 4-1)

Aeroplane confirmed connections high opinion of him when winning a fair course maiden in taking style on his reappearance and was bidding to provide connections with a treble on the card. Solid in the market beforehand, he was at a disadvantage in being held up and, although briefly threatening to make a move, he was unable to pick up in the ground. He is thought capable of better and is not one to give up on just yet. (op 4-1)

Pacific Pride has twice run well since returning as a three-year-old and a return to six furlongs on faster ground will may see some further progress, with a little help from the Handicapper likely to be appreciated. (op 16-1)

Mobsir, good winner of a modest event at Lingfield last time, may have found the ground against him, but he had a big gap to bridge on form anyhow and he should prove to be more of a handicapper. Official explanation: jockey said colt was unsuited by the soft ground (op 14-1 tchd 18-1)

2032 CORAL SPRINT (HERITAGE H'CAP) 6f

3:30 (3:30) (Class 2) (0-105,100) 3-Y-O

£28,044 (£8,397; £4,198; £2,101; £1,048; £526) **Stalls** High

Form			Horse	Jockey	RPR
4011	**1**		**Borehan**[21] 1482 3-8-12 **91**	PhilipRobinson 8	105
			(M A Jarvis) *lw: sn led: rdn over 1f out: r.o*	**5/1**[2]	
1003	**2**	*1 3/4*	**Signor Peltro**[21] 1482 3-7-12 **77**	FrancisFerris 10	85
			(H Candy) *lw: a.p: rdn to chse wnr and edgd lft 1f out: styd on same pce*	**6/1**[3]	
1401	**3**	*1 3/4*	**Hogmaneigh (IRE)**[7] 1848 3-8-9 **91**	SaleemGolam(3) 1	94+
			(S C Williams) *hld up: racd keenly: hdwy over 1f out: no ex ins fnl f*	**5/1**[2]	
1212	**4**	*hd*	**Obe Brave**[15] 1633 3-9-7 **100**	TonyCulhane 11	102+
			(M R Channon) *sn outpcd: hdwy u.p over 1f out: styd on*	**4/1**[1]	
0015	**5**	*3/4*	**Sir Orpen (IRE)**[7] 1855 3-7-12 **77**	DavidKinsella 9	77+
			(T D Barron) *mid-div: rdn: nt clr run and lost pl over 1f out: styd on ins fnl f*	**7/1**	
4343	**6**	*nk*	**Strut**[14] 1671 3-9-7 **100**	SteveDrowne 6	99
			(R Charlton) *outpcd: styd on ins fnl f: nrst fin*	**9/1**	
0132	**7**	*3/4*	**Orpsie Boy (IRE)**[16] 1606 3-8-1 **85**	JamesDoyle(5) 4	82
			(N P Littmoden) *hld up: rdn 1/2-way: nvr trbld ldrs*	**14/1**	
135	**8**	*2*	**King Orchisios (IRE)**[7] 1857 3-9-0 **93**	RobertWinston 2	84
			(K A Ryan) *w ldr tl rdn 2f out: wknd fnl f*	**8/1**	
2514	**9**	*2 1/2*	**Loyal Royal (IRE)**[8] 1818 3-9-2 **95**	JohnEgan 5	79
			(D R C Elsworth) *lw: chsd ldrs: rdn over 2f out: wknd fnl f*	**14/1**	
0100	**10**	*hd*	**Lady Livius (IRE)**[287] 4362 3-8-10 **89**	PatDobbs 3	72
			(R Hannon) *chsd ldrs: rdn over 2f out: wknd over 1f out*	**50/1**	

1m 14.66s (1.56) **Going Correction** +0.425s/f (Yiel) **10** Ran SP% **116.5**

Speed ratings (Par 105):106,103,101,101,100 99,98,96,92,92

CSF £35.09 CT £161.72 TOTE £6.10: £2.10, £2.30, £2.00; EX 35.50 Trifecta £146.00 Pool: £966.94 - 4.70 winning units.

Owner Sheikh Ahmed Al Maktoum **Bred** Stratford Place Stud **Trained** Newmarket, Suffolk

■ Stewards' Enquiry : Francis Ferris caution: careless riding

FOCUS

A good, competitive sprint handicap that usually throws up a smart sprinter, although not quite as many runners as usual. The form looks decent with the winner progressive.

NOTEBOOK

Borehan, a maiden having his second start when beaten only two lengths in a £250,000 sales race over course and distance last September, has quickly progressed into a very useful three-year-old sprinter. He won his maiden at Thirsk before collecting on fast ground at Haydock and then taking this valuable prize in impressive fashion under a fine tactical ride from Robinson, who was aware how hard it was to make headway from the rear in the soft ground. Evidently versatile ground-wise, he will suffer a further rise, but seems to be progressive enough to defy a higher mark and he is entitled to respect wherever he goes next. (op 11-2)

Signor Peltro, 6lb better off with Borehan for a length defeat at Haydock, is clearly not as progressive and was unable to reverse the form, but it was another sound effort and he has a race in him off this sort of mark. (tchd 13-2)

Hogmaneigh(IRE), a good winner in soft ground at Nottingham the previous weekend, emerged with much credit considering he was held up. He too is progressive, but he will need to be to win off this sort of mark. (op 9-2 tchd 11-2)

Obe Brave, runner-up in a competitive seven-furlong handicap at the course on his seasonal reappearance, has since done well back at this distance, but he was always struggling to lay-up on this occasion and may be open to a little further improvement back at seven. (op 5-1)

Sir Orpen(IRE), dropping back from a mile, was unsurprisingly found wanting for pace, but he was not beaten all that far and has a decent race in him off this sort of mark. (op 8-1 tchd 9-1 in places)

Strut, dropping back to this distance for the first time this season, faced no easy task giving weight to all bar Obe Brave and she simply lacked the pace to hold a prominent early position. She made a little late headway, but gives the impression she may continue to struggle, unless found a suitable Listed contest. (op 11-1)

Orpsie Boy(IRE) has been in decent form, but he was not quite as effective under these conditions.

King Orchisios(IRE) showed up well early before dropping away and connections have yet to decide on a trip for the colt, who is beginning to look vulnerable off this mark. (op 7-1)

Loyal Royal(IRE), who ran quite well in Listed company at Newbury last time, was another who did not appear to produce his form on account of the ground. Official explanation: jockey said colt had no more to give (op 11-1)

Lady Livius(IRE), shock winner of last season's Super Sprint, looked to starting out on a stiff enoguh mark for this seasonal reappearance and she trailed in well held. She is clearly in need of some assistance from the Handicapper.

2033 SUNLEY H'CAP 1m

4:05 (4:06) (Class 3) (0-90,88) 3-Y-O **£8,096** (£2,408; £902; £902) **Stalls** High

Form			Horse	Jockey	RPR
0221	**1**		**Music Note (IRE)**[253] 5279 3-8-10 **80**	TonyCulhane 6	86
			(M R Channon) *b: w ldr: led over 2f out: drvn out*	**10/1**	
51	**2**	*2 1/2*	**Motaraqeb**[14] 1684 3-9-3 **87**	RHills 5	88+
			(Sir Michael Stoute) *s.i.s: hld up in tch: rdn over 1f out: styd on*	**2/1**[1]	
2306	**3**	*shd*	**Categorical**[16] 1617 3-8-4 **77**	SaleemGolam(3) 2	78+
			(J A R Toller) *hld up: outpcd over 2f out: hrd rdn over 1f out: r.o ins fnl f*	**16/1**	
6012	**3**	*dht*	**Jumbajukiba**[217] 6016 3-9-4 **88**	EddieAhern 3	89
			(Mrs A J Perrett) *chsd ldrs: outpcd over 1f out: r.o ins fnl f*	**7/2**[2]	
0400	**5**	*3/4*	**Ans Bach**[24] 1404 3-9-3 **87**	PhilipRobinson 8	86
			(M A Jarvis) *lw: trckd ldrs: rdn over 1f out: wknd ins fnl f*	**8/1**	
2423	**6**	*5*	**Time For Life (USA)**[18] 1569 3-9-1 **85** (v[1])	DarryllHolland 4	74
			(H J Collingridge) *plld hrd: sn led: rdn and hdd over 2f out: wkng whn n.m.r over 1f out*	**7/1**	
0046	**7**	*nk*	**Louie Louie (IRE)**[21] 1490 3-9-0 **84**	KerrinMcEvoy 7	72
			(N A Callaghan) *rrd s: hld up: rdn over 1f out: n.d*	**9/2**[3]	

1m 43.0s (3.63) **Going Correction** +0.425s/f (Yiel) **7** Ran SP% **112.3**

Speed ratings (Par 103):98,95,95,95,94 89,89

Tricast: Music Note/Motaraqeb/Jumbajukiba £42.46, Music Note/Motaraqeb/Categorical £160.26 CSF £29.37 TOTE £8.20: £2.80, £1.50; EX 20.30.

Owner Jaber Abdullah **Bred** Gainsborough Stud Management Ltd **Trained** West Ilsley, Berks

FOCUS

A tricky contest in which Music Note was able to get a head start on his rivals and maintain it right the way to the line. The form is rated at face value but is not necessarily that strong.

NOTEBOOK

Music Note(IRE), winner of a mile Nottingham maiden on his fourth and final start at two, was bred to handle the ground, and he was yet another winner on the card to race prominently. Having gone on over two furlongs out, he was always doing enough to hold any challenges, but things will be tougher in future when asked to race off a higher mark. (tchd 11-1)

Motaraqeb ◆ won in the style of a good horse when making great strides from an unpromising position at Thisk last time, and he looked more than capable of defying a mark of 87 on this handicap debut. However, he was forced to settle in behind following a slow start and found himself unable to quicken out of the ground when asked to go on with the winner. Although disappointing on the face of it, the return to a faster surface is likely to bring about a much better performance and he has the makings of a typically progressive Stoute handicapper with aspirations of making up into a Group horse. The good-looking son of Grand Lodge may improve for a step up to ten furlongs, but the Britannia Stakes at Royal Ascot could be a suitable short-term target. (op 6-4)

Jumbajukiba showed himself capable of handling this ground when second at Doncaster towards the backend of last season, and he got kept on in the final furlong having been outpaced. This was a pleasing reappearance and improvement can be expected. (op 20-1)

Categorical has been waiting for this sort of ground and he left behind a couple of modest efforts, running on well in the final furlong to tie for third. He showed he stays the trip and may soon be ready to strike. (op 20-1)

Ans Bach left behind a couple of moderate efforts, coming through to throw down a challenge to the winner over a furlong out before failing to last out. He is likely to continue to find winning hard off this sort of mark, but a drop back to seven furlongs will help. (op 10-1 tchd 15-2)

Time For Life(USA) ran disappointingly in the first-time visor, pulling hard early on and failing to get home as a result (tchd 8-1)

Louie Louie(IRE) ran disappointingly and not for the first time showed he is incapable of handling the ground. (op 11-2)

2034 PERSIMMON HOMES MAIDEN STKS (DIV II) — 1m

4:40 (4:43) (Class 5) 3-Y-O — **£4,857** (£1,445; £722; £360) **Stalls** High

Form				RPR
024	**1**		**Muzher (IRE)**[39] [1065] 3-9-3 85 .... RHills 4 (B W Hills) *hld up in tch: plld hrd: rdn to ld and edgd rt over 1f out: styd on* **10/3**[1]	83
6	**2**	¾	**Uno**[38] [1085] 3-8-12 .... MichaelHills 11 (B W Hills) *b.hind: led: rdn and hdd over 1f out: styd on* **10/3**[1]	77
	3	1	**Dukedom** 3-9-3 .... RobertWinston 7 (Sir Michael Stoute) *gd sort: lw: s.i.s: hdwy over 1f out: r.o wl* **9/2**[2]	86+
020	**4**	2	**Zaif (IRE)**[35] [1134] 3-9-0 84 .... AntonyProcter(3) 3 (D R C Elsworth) *h.d.w: s.s: hld up: hdwy over 3f out: swtchd rt over 1f out: styd on* **14/1**	76
	5	4	**Imperial Star (IRE)** 3-9-3 .... JimmyFortune 8 (J H M Gosden) *gd sort: mid-div: hdwy 1/2-way: wknd fnl f* **11/2**[3]	68
6	**6**	hd	**Inchmahome**[24] [1418] 3-8-12 .... SteveDrowne 1 (G Wragg) *s.s: hld up: effrt over 3f out: n.d* **8/1**	62
0	**7**	¾	**Esteem**[26] [1335] 3-9-3 .... LPKeniry 10 (W Jarvis) *prom: chsd ldr over 2f out: rdn and wknd over 1f out* **66/1**	66
0000	**8**	11	**Peak Seasons (IRE)**[12] [1741] 3-9-3 52 .... FrancisFerris 5 (W De Best-Turner) *chsd ldr tl rdn and wknd over 2f out* **100/1**	44
	9	1 ¾	**Brief History** 3-9-3 .... FergusSweeney 9 (H Candy) *wl grwn: bkwd: s.s: hld up: effrt over 3f out: sn wknd* **14/1**	40
00	**10**	¾	**Jill Dawson (IRE)**[26] [1355] 3-8-12 .... JohnEgan 13 (John Berry) *mid-div: hdwy 1/2-way: wknd wl over 1f out* **33/1**	34
00	**11**	2	**Collusion (FR)**[26] [1335] 3-8-12 .... EmmettStack(5) 12 (Pat Eddery) *hld up: wknd over 3f out* **50/1**	35
	12	5	**Samarinda (USA)** 3-9-3 .... OscarUrbina 6 (E A L Dunlop) *gd sort: scope: s.i.s: hld up: hmpd over 5f out: wknd over 3f out* **20/1**	25

1m 42.48s (3.11) **Going Correction** +0.425s/f (Yiel) — **54** Ran SP% **116.3**
Speed ratings (Par 99):101,100,99,97,93 93,92,81,79,78 76,71
CSF £13.17 TOTE £3.80: £1.70, £1.60, £2.20; EX 13.40.

Owner Hamdan Al Maktoum **Bred** Shadwell Estate Company Limited **Trained** Lambourn, Berks

FOCUS
A fair maiden and although slower than the first division is likely to produce future winners, the form is rated around the winner.

Dukedom ◆ Official explanation: jockey said colt ran very green

Imperial Star(IRE) Official explanation: jockey said colt had no more to give

Jill Dawson(IRE) Official explanation: jockey said filly was unsuited by the soft ground

2035 NGK SPARK PLUGS H'CAP — 1m 6f

5:15 (5:19) (Class 4) (0-85,85) 4-Y-O+ — **£5,505** (£1,637; £818; £408) **Stalls** High

Form				RPR
0014	**1**		**Finalmente**[14] [1685] 4-9-5 **83** .... OscarUrbina 5 (N A Callaghan) *a.p: chsd ldr 6f out: led over 2f out: sn rdn and edgd lft: hung rt ins fnl f: styd on* **10/1**	93
0056	**2**	1	**Quizzene (USA)**[15] [1631] 4-9-3 **81** .... RoystonFfrench 9 (M Johnston) *led: rdn and hdd over 2f out: styd on* **11/1**	90
0210	**3**	1 ¼	**Trance (IRE)**[17] [1584] 6-9-1 **79** .... GeorgeBaker 6 (T D Barron) *s.s: hld up: hdwy u.p over 1f out: r.o: nt rch ldrs* **5/1**[2]	86
1511	**4**	9	**Sphinx (FR)**[7] [1847] 8-9-5 **83** .... (b) JohnEgan 3 (Jamie Poulton) *b: plld hrd and prom: stdd and lost pl 10f out: hdwy over 4f out: rdn and wknd over 1f out* **11/10**[1]	78
0026	**5**	3	**Fort Churchill (IRE)**[16] [1614] 5-7-13 **68** ow2 .... (bt) JamesDoyle(5) 4 (B Ellison) *lw: s.i.s: hld up: hdwy over 3f out: rdn and wknd over 2f out* **9/1**[3]	58
1304	**6**	3 ½	**Prime Contender**[21] [1478] 4-8-6 **70** .... MichaelHills 7 (B W Hills) *hld up: plld hrd: hdwy 7f out: rdn and wknd wl over 1f out* **25/1**	56
0232	**7**	½	**Taxman (IRE)**[12] [1745] 4-8-3 **67** oh3 ow1 .... (p) KerrinMcEvoy 10 (C E Brittain) *chsd ldr 4f: remained handy tl rdn and wknd 2f out* **12/1**	52
653/	**8**	7	**Schooner (GER)**[177] [6089] 6-8-3 **67** .... JimmyQuinn 2 (Lady Herries) *lw: prom: chsd ldr 10f out to 6f out: rdn: hung rt and wknd over 2f out* **20/1**	42
1120	**9**	1	**Whispering Death**[11] [1756] 4-8-4 **68** ow1 .... EddieAhern 8 (W J Haggas) *lw: prom: rdn over 3f out: sn wknd* **12/1**	42

3m 3.40s (3.27) **Going Correction** +0.425s/f (Yiel) — **9** Ran SP% **115.7**
Speed ratings (Par 105):107,106,105,100,98 96,96,92,92
CSF £113.41 CT £618.31 TOTE £13.10: £2.60, £2.80, £2.00; EX 120.70 Place 6 £59.24, Place 5 £19.89.

Owner Edward M Kirtland **Bred** Helshaw Grange Stud Ltd **Trained** Newmarket, Suffolk

■ Stewards' Enquiry : George Baker caution: careless riding

FOCUS
A decent staying handicap in which the front three drew clear of the hot favourite. The placed horses set a decent standard.

T/Plt: £88.70 to a £1 stake. Pool: £70,195.00. 577.70 winning tickets. T/Qpdt: £7.30 to a £1 stake. Pool: £5,217.20. 523.60 winning tickets. CR

2036 - (Foreign Racing) - See Raceform Interactive

1360 CURRAGH (R-H)

Saturday, May 27

OFFICIAL GOING: Heavy

2037a ISABEL MORRIS STKS (LISTED RACE) — 5f

2:45 (2:45) 2-Y-O — **£26,040** (£7,640; £3,640; £1,240)

			RPR
1		**Drayton (IRE)**[26] [1360] 2-9-4 .... WMLordan 5 (T Stack, Ire) *racd keenly: led over 3f out: qcknd clr over 1f out: styd on wl: impressive* **11/8**[1]	104+
2	3	**King Of Swords (IRE)**[44] [1007] 2-9-1 .... WSupple 1 (C Collins, Ire) *hld up in rr: hdwy 2f out: 3rd 1f out: mod 2nd and kpt on ins fnl f* **33/1**	90
3	1	**Little White Lie (IRE)**[10] [1784] 2-9-1 .... KFallon 2 (G M Lyons, Ire) *hld up towards rr: kpt on fr 1 1/2f out* **7/1**	87
4	1	**New Spirit (IRE)**[26] [1360] 2-8-12 .... DMGrant 3 (John Joseph Murphy, Ire) *trckd ldrs: 5th 1/2-way: prog 1 1/2f out: 2nd 1f out: sn no ex* **16/1**	80
5	½	**Snaefell (IRE)**[37] [1103] 2-9-1 .... (t) JMurtagh 6 (M Halford, Ire) *trckd ldrs in 4th: 3rd and rdn under 2f out: sn outpcd: kpt on ins fnl f* **10/3**[2]	81
6	1	**Latin Walk (IRE)**[62] [750] 2-8-12 .... KJManning 7 (J S Bolger, Ire) *prom: 2nd bef 1/2-way: sn rdn: wknd over 1f out: hmpd nr fin* **6/1**[3]	75
7	3	**Varsity Blues (IRE)**[10] [1784] 2-9-1 .... WJLee 4 (T Stack, Ire) *led: hdd over 3f out: hmpd and stmbld 2f out: no ex* **14/1**	73+

66.00 secs **Going Correction** +1.025s/f (Soft) — **7** Ran SP% **107.5**
Speed ratings: 103,98,96,95,94 92,87
CSF £43.19 TOTE £1.80: £1.50, £4.20; DF 32.60.

Owner Andrew Boyle **Bred** Rossenarra Stud **Trained** Golden, Co Tipperary

FOCUS
A race that often produces a high-class juvenile and this year's renewal looks no exception with the time good.

NOTEBOOK
Drayton(IRE) made it three wins from three starts, having been successful in the first two-year-old maiden of the season - later disqualified after testing positive - and in a Listed race over this course and distance. He again broke smartly and raced quite keenly before going to the front with over three furlongs to run and had his six rivals in trouble well before the final furlong. Connections feel that he will be better on quicker ground, he will have no trouble stepping up to six furlongs and he now has the option of the Coventry or Railway Stakes. (op 1/1)

King Of Swords(IRE) reversed the form of his debut run at Tipperary with today's third and seventh. Given a patient ride, he kept on under pressure in the closing stages and if maintaining this improvement it will not be long before he opens his account. (op 25/1)

Little White Lie(IRE) looked to be struggling inside the final two furlongs but was putting in his best work towards the finish. He has made up into a tough and reliable juvenile and can be expected to progress further when he steps back up in trip.

New Spirit(IRE) provides a good guide to the form, finishing slightly further behind the winner than on their last meeting despite being 3lb better off. She may appreciate better ground and should have no trouble winning her maiden.

Snaefell(IRE) finished further behind today's third than at Tipperary last month. He seemed to be caught a little flat footed with over a furlong to run before staying on again. He may do better over further. (op 7/2)

2038a WEATHERBYS IRELAND GREENLANDS STKS (GROUP 3) — 6f

3:20 (3:22) 3-Y-O+ — **£35,862** (£10,482; £4,965; £1,655)

			RPR
1		**Moss Vale (IRE)**[10] [1778] 5-9-9 .... KFallon 3 (D Nicholls) *mde all: qcknd clr after 1/2-way: rdn and kpt on wl fnl f: comf* **7/2**[2]	116
2	1	**Moon Unit (IRE)**[22] [1469] 5-9-9 106 .... WSupple 4 (H Rogers, Ire) *hld up in rr: hdwy 2f out: mod 2nd 1f out: kpt on wl wout threatening wnr* **5/1**[3]	113
3	2	**Miss Sally (IRE)**[22] [1469] 4-9-9 111 .... JMurtagh 6 (M Halford, Ire) *hld up: 5th and rdn appr 1/2-way: prog under 2f out: 3rd and no imp fnl f* **1/1**[1]	107
4	3 ½	**Bahamian Pirate (USA)**[14] [1663] 11-9-9 .... KJManning 5 (D Nicholls) *chsd ldr in 2nd: outpcd after 1/2-way: 4th and no ex fr over 1f out* **12/1**	97
5	6	**Cheddar Island (IRE)**[35] [1156] 4-9-9 97 .... DPMcDonogh 1 (Kevin Prendergast, Ire) *chsd ldrs: 3rd early: rdn 1/2-way: no ex fr 2f out* **14/1**	79
6	10	**Leitra (IRE)**[251] [5348] 3-8-11 104 .... RPCleary 2 (M Halford, Ire) *chsd ldrs: 4th briefly 1/2-way: no ex fr 2f out* **11/1**	44

1m 18.3s **Going Correction** +1.025s/f (Soft)
WFA 3 from 4yo+ 9lb — **6** Ran SP% **111.6**
Speed ratings: 115,113,111,106,98 85
CSF £20.59 TOTE £5.90: £2.60, £2.60; DF 38.80.

Owner Lady O'Reilly **Bred** Derek Veitch **Trained** Sessay, N Yorks

FOCUS
This race was started by flag.

NOTEBOOK
Moss Vale(IRE), runner-up in the race last year when trained by Barry Hills, reversed form with the runner-up to gain his first win at this level under an enterprising ride by Fallon. In front from the start, he was able to take up a position on the rail and quickening up just after halfway, never looked in danger of being caught. His three Listed wins were all gained on fast ground, but he has looked well suited to this ground in the past. (op 4/1)

Moon Unit(IRE), who won this race last year, was almost back to her best having been behind today's third at Cork. She is in-foal and may be able to score again at this level before she retires to the paddocks.

Miss Sally(IRE) was sent off favourite to extend her winning sequence to four after an impressive win on her seasonal debut when today's runner-up was four lengths behind. She has handled heavy ground effectively in the past, but this time she was no match for the first two and she was clearly below her best. Official explanation: trainer said filly was found to be in season post race (op 1/1 tchd 5/4)

Bahamian Pirate(USA), well into the veteran stage, would have appreciated the conditions but began to feel the pinch and got detached from the first three in the final furlong. (op 10/1)

2039a **BOYLESPORTS IRISH 2,000 GUINEAS (GROUP 1) (ENTIRE COLTS & FILLIES)** **1m**
3:55 (4:01) 3-Y-0
£154,827 (£52,758; £25,172; £8,620; £5,862; £3,103)

RPR

1 **Araafa (IRE)**[21] [1486] 3-9-0 AlanMunro 8 119
(J Noseda) *trckd ldrs: cl 4th after 1/2-way: led under 3f out: rdn clr over 1f out: styd on wl* **12/1**

2 *2* **George Washington (IRE)**[21] [1486] 3-9-0 124 KFallon 2 115
(A P O'Brien, Ire) *hld up in tch: 7th and hdwy 2f out: 3rd over 1f out: 2nd whn drifted lft ins fnl f: kpt on wout threatening wnr* **4/7**[1]

3 *1* **Decado (IRE)**[26] [1362] 3-9-0 111 DPMcDonogh 6 113
(Kevin Prendergast, Ire) *a.p: 2nd and rdn over 2f out: 3rd and no imp whn sltly hmpd ins fnl f: kpt on* **4/1**[2]

4 *1* **Yasoodd**[13] [1718] 3-9-0 ChrisCatlin 3 111
(M R Channon) *hld up towards rr: prog over 2f out: 5th whn nt clr run under 1f out: kpt on* **25/1**

5 *nk* **Golden Arrow (IRE)**[13] [1708] 3-9-0 107 (b[1]) PJSmullen 1 110
(D K Weld, Ire) *trckd ldrs on stand's side: 4th 2f out: sn rdn and no imp: sltly hmpd ins fnl f: one pce* **33/1**

6 *3* **Heliostatic (IRE)**[13] [1708] 3-9-0 105 KJManning 9 104
(J S Bolger, Ire) *chsd ldrs: 5th and drvn along 3f out: no imp fr over 2f out: kpt on same pce* **40/1**

7 *nk* **Hurricane Cat (USA)**[26] [1362] 3-9-0 109 JAHeffernan 5 104
(A P O'Brien, Ire) *hld up in tch: prog on stands' side 2f out: 6th and no ex fr over 1f out* **13/2**[3]

8 *shd* **Crookhaven**[14] [1700] 3-9-0 85 DMGrant 4 104?
(John Joseph Murphy, Ire) *sn disp ld: hdd under 3f out: no ex fr over 1 1/2f out* **200/1**

9 *1 1/2* **Caribbean**[13] [1708] 3-9-0 101 FMBerry 10 101
(John M Oxx, Ire) *trckd ldrs on far side: 7th and rdn 1 1/2f out: sn no ex* **50/1**

10 *9* **River Tiber**[20] [1523] 3-9-0 DavidMcCabe 7 83
(A P O'Brien, Ire) *s.i.s: sn disp ld: hdd under 3f out: rdn and wknd* **50/1**

11 *25* **Arabian Prince (USA)**[217] [6019] 3-9-0 101 CO'Donoghue 11 33
(A P O'Brien, Ire) *hld up towards rr: wknd fr 2f out: t.o* **66/1**

1m 49.8s **Going Correction** +1.375s/f (Soft) 11 Ran SP% **119.8**
Speed ratings: 116,114,113,112,111 108,108,108,106,97 72
CSF £19.41 TOTE £15.40: £2.50, £1.10, £1.40; DF 43.50.
Owner Saleh Al Homaizi & Imad Al Sagar **Bred** Sweetmans Bloodstock **Trained** Newmarket, Suffolk

FOCUS
This renewal lacked strength in depth and the ground was a key factor. The fourth, sixth and ninth represent the best guides to the level.

NOTEBOOK
Araafa(IRE), much improved when fourth in the Newmarket version, handled the ground and was able to turn around form with the favourite. While this may have been a Classic that lacked significant strength in depth, he has firmly established himself as a Group 1 performer when there is cut in the ground. Munro got things right tactically when going to the front under three furlongs out, getting first run on the main home-trained fancies. His mount stayed on in determined style, and an extra quarter mile should be within his range. He will now go for the St James's Palace Stakes at Royal Ascot where he will be a major contender, although it remains to be seen if he will prove as effective if faced with fast ground. (op 12/1 tchd 14/1)
George Washington(IRE), who was so impressive at Newmarket, was odds on despite the very different conditions. It was no surprise that he could not produce the acceleration that he showed at Newmarket and he was never travelling with the same fluency, and when Fallon got serious he began to drift under pressure and never looked like getting to grips with Araafa. His head carriage looked a shade ominous, but he was subsequently reported to have pulled muscles in a hip, so had excuses. Hopefully he can recover and on better ground confirm the impression he created at Newmarket, but whether he will be ready for a re-match with the winner at Royal Ascot remains to be seen. Official explanation: trainer said colt finished lame (op 4/7 tchd 8/13)
Decado(IRE), who has looked highly progressive this season and had conditions to suit, ran a bit free and would probably have been seen to better advantage off a stronger gallop. He was held when George Washington leaned in on him. He is obviously a smart colt, but his prospects for the rest of the season will hinge on how effectively he adapts to better ground, and with engagements in the Eclipse and Irish Champion Stakes, it will be no surprise to see him step up in trip. (op 7/2)
Yasoodd, who won a Leopardstown Group 3 before finishing ninth in the French Guineas, finished slightly closer than at Longchamp and is the best guide to the relative merits of the races. He appeals as the type who could pick up another Group 3 on soft ground, but this level is probably beyond him. (op 33/1)
Golden Arrow(IRE), fitted with blinkers on this drop in trip, was flattered by last season's National Stakes second to George Washington, but ran well enough and is another who looks capable of scoring at Group Three level.
Heliostatic(IRE), who ran badly in the Derrinstown, did better this time but was three lengths further behind Yasoodd, on the same terms, than he had been in the Leopardstown Guineas Trial.
Hurricane Cat(USA), who beat the winner in last year's Horris Hill, ran close to Tetrarch Stakes form with Decado and it appears others have progressed past him. (op 8/1)
Crookhaven, who is still a maiden, was again highly tried but showed up for a long way and should be able to pick up a race when his sights are lowered.

2041a **RIDGEWOOD PEARL STKS (GROUP 2) (F&M)** **1m**
5:00 (5:00) 4-Y-0+
£51,724 (£16,379; £7,758; £2,586; £1,724; £862)

RPR

1 **Pout (IRE)**[22] [1469] 4-8-12 90 DMGrant 1 105
(John Joseph Murphy, Ire) *hld up in rr: prog on stand's side 3f out: 4th 2f out: chal ins fnl f: led 100 yds out: kpt on wl* **40/1**

2 *1 1/2* **Jazz Princess (IRE)**[26] [1363] 4-8-12 106 JMurtagh 2 102
(M Halford, Ire) *chsd ldrs: 4th and drvn along over 3f out: led 2f out: kpt on u.p: hdd 100 yds out: no ex* **13/8**[1]

3 *1 1/2* **Royal Alchemist**[20] [1506] 4-8-12 PJSmullen 4 99
(M D I Usher) *led: rdn and hdd 2f out: rallied to chal 1f out: no ex cl home* **11/4**[2]

4 *1* **Little Miss Gracie**[21] [1477] 4-8-12 KFallon 6 98
(A B Haynes) *chsd ldrs on far side: 3rd 1/2-way: 5th and rdn 2f out: 4th and kpt on same pce fnl f* **8/1**

5 *4* **Sweet Treat (IRE)**[21] [1477] 4-8-12 WSupple 3 91
(J R Fanshawe) *hld up in 5th: impr into 3rd 2f out: no ex fnl f* **9/2**[3]

6 *7* **Fairy Of The Night (IRE)**[13] [1711] 4-8-12 103 FMBerry 5 79
(John M Oxx, Ire) *cl 2nd to 3f out: sn rdn and wknd* **11/2**

1m 52.1s **Going Correction** +1.375s/f (Soft) 6 Ran SP% **111.9**
Speed ratings: 105,103,102,101,97 90
CSF £105.01 TOTE £44.30: £6.30, £1.50; DF 126.10.
Owner John Joseph Murphy **Bred** Corstone Partnership **Trained** Upton, Co. Cork

FOCUS
With only one previous Group winner in the field, this was by no means a strong race for its status and the winner limits the form.

NOTEBOOK
Pout(IRE), who won a handicap off 81 last season, had a stiff task on official ratings. She handled the testing ground and step up in trip well and caused a major surprise. She may struggle to repeat this but her paddock value is assured. (op 25/1)
Jazz Princess(IRE), who set the standard in terms of form, may have found the testing ground in this grade just beyond her and was caught late on. She has not had that much racing and can win again on better ground. Official explanation: trainer said filly finished lame (op 2/1)
Royal Alchemist, who seems to run her best races fresh, kept on to prove best of the British-trained trio, none of whom had obvious credentials for success at this level. (op 5/2)
Little Miss Gracie reversed recent Goodwood form with Sweet Treat, but both of them are Listed class. (op 7/1)
Sweet Treat(IRE), who has form on soft ground, could not repeat Goodwood form with today's fourth and is another who may prefer better ground. (op 7/2)

2042 - (Foreign Racing) - See Raceform Interactive

SAN SIRO (R-H)
Saturday, May 27

OFFICIAL GOING: Good

2043a **PREMIO MARIO INCISA DELLA ROCCHETTA (GROUP 3)** **1m 2f**
3:15 (3:22) 3-Y-0 **£33,486** (£15,494; £8,674; £4,337)

RPR

1 **Dionisia (USA)**[13] [1713] 3-8-7 MDemuro 4 103
(R Menichetti, Italy) *raced in 4th or 5th, headway to lead 1f out, ridden clear, easily* **9/10**[1]

2 *3 1/2* **Wickwing** 3-8-8 ow1 EBotti 2 98
(A & G Botti, Italy) *led till headed 1f out, one pace* **67/10**

3 *3/4* **Rovana Jowe (GER)** 3-8-7 EPedroza 10 95
(A Wohler, Germany) *held up in rear, stayed on down outside from over 2f out to take 3rd inside final f, no extra closing stages* **49/10**[3]

4 *1 1/4* **Penfection (IRE)**[20] 3-8-7 IRossi 7 93
(A & G Botti, Italy) *raced in 5th or 6th, stayed on at same pace final 2f* **84/10**

5 *hd* **Black Profusion (IRE)**[60] 3-8-7 FBranca 6 93
(P Martometti, Italy) *midfield on inside, effort and not much room 2f out, switched outside, stayed on final f* **96/10**

6 *nk* **Ekagra** 3-8-7 SLandi 1 92
(F & L Camici, Italy) *raced in 3rd early, effort and one pace from over 2f out* **168/10**

7 *1 3/4* **La Bandera** 3-8-7 DVargiu 5 89
(B Grizzetti, Italy) *raced in 2nd, ridden to press leader 3f out, beaten over 1 1/2f out* **46/10**[2]

8 *shd* **So Stream (ITY)** 3-8-7 SMulas 9 89
(B Grizzetti, Italy) *never a factor* **70/1**

9 *2 1/2* **Winga (IRE)**[13] [1713] 3-8-7 GArena 3 84
(B Grizzetti, Italy) *prominent til weakened 3f out* **35/1**

10 *1 3/4* **Riabouchinska** 3-8-7 MMonteriso 11 81
(E Borromeo, Italy) *always in rear* **48/1**

11 *3 1/2* **Smorfia** 3-8-7 CColombi 8 75
(V Valiani, Italy) *always in rear* **20/1**

2m 5.80s 11 Ran SP% **137.1**
(including 1 euro stake): WIN 1.90; PL 1.29, 1.72, 1.66; DF 8.54.
Owner Scuderia Razza Dell'Olmo **Bred** E H B Lane III **Trained** Italy

2028
NEWMARKET (ROWLEY) (R-H)
Sunday, May 28

OFFICIAL GOING: Good to soft (soft in places)
Wind: Fresh, half-behind Weather: Cloudy with sunny spells

2044 **CAMBRIDGE TO LONDON WITH "ONE" RAILWAY LADIES H'CAP (IN MEMORY OF LUCINDA STOPFORD-SACKVILLE)** **1m 4f**
2:10 (2:11) (Class 5) (0-70,70) 4-Y-0+ **£3,747** (£1,162; £580; £290) **Stalls High**

Form RPR

1033 **1** **Great View (IRE)**[15] [1666] 7-9-7 59 (p) MissLEllison(3) 4 71
(Mrs A L M King) *hld up: hdwy over 4f out: led 3f out: rdn out* **15/2**

0061 **2** *2 1/2* **Cormorant Wharf (IRE)**[11] [1769] 6-9-12 66 MissJPowell(5) 2 74+
(G L Moore) *dwlt and hmpd s: hld up: plld hrd: hdwy 4f out: ev ch over 2f out: outpcd over 1f out: styd on ins fnl f* **11/2**[2]

3604 **3** *nk* **Our Choice (IRE)**[27] [1346] 4-9-12 61 MrsEmmaLittmoden 5 69
(N P Littmoden) *chsd ldrs: led 4f out: hdd 3f out: outpcd over 1f out: styd on ins fnl f* **5/1**[1]

0100 **4** *1* **Migration**[8] [1847] 10-9-9 58 MrsMMorris 6 64
(Mrs S Lamyman) *hld up: hdwy over 4f out: ev ch over 2f out: no ex fnl f* **16/1**

3242 **5** *3* **Seattle Robber**[11] [1769] 4-9-12 61 (p) MissEJJones 14 62
(P A Blockley) *hld up: hdwy over 2f out: rdn over 1f out: no imp* **7/1**

6230 **6** *1 3/4* **Last Pioneer (IRE)**[359] [2266] 4-9-8 64 MissPHermansson(7) 3 62
(R Ford) *wnt lft s: sn prom: chsd clr ldr 10f out: styd on same pce fnl 2f* **25/1**

3005 **7** *4* **Almizan (IRE)**[35] [4788] 6-9-13 67 (b[1]) MissHayleyMoore(5) 13 59
(G L Moore) *hld up: effrt and hmpd over 3f out: n.d* **10/1**

-560 **8** *shd* **Petrula**[16] [1631] 7-10-0 70 (b) MrsPCallan(7) 12 62
(K A Ryan) *chsd ldrs over 9f* **16/1**

2460 **9** *5* **Ticki Tori (IRE)**[9] [1821] 4-9-13 67 MissJCDuncan(5) 10 51
(G C H Chung) *lw: chsd ldrs over 8f* **20/1**

0640 **10** *3/4* **Full Of Zest**[15] [1673] 4-9-3 59 (b) MissLauraGray(7) 8 42
(Mrs L J Mongan) *hld up: a in rr* **25/1**

4133 **11** *nk* **Paradise Flight (IRE)**[323] [3335] 5-9-13 67 (b) MissARyan(5) 7 49
(K A Ryan) *lw: hld up: rdn over 3f out: wknd 2f out* **13/2**[3]

3000 **12** *1/2* **Love You Always (USA)**[51] [906] 6-9-9 58 MrsACooke 11 39
(Miss J Feilden) *hld up: plld hrd: hdwy 5f out: wknd over 2f out* **33/1**

0050 **13** *15* **Neptune**[55] [857] 10-9-2 56 oh28 MissSarah-JaneDurman(5) 1 13
(J C Fox) *lw: chsd ldrs: rn wd bnd 10f out: wknd 4f out* **100/1**

4250 **14** *15* **My Putra (USA)**[29] [1289] 4-10-2 65 (b[1]) MissSBrotherton 16 —
(P F I Cole) *b.hind: led: racd freely and sn clr: wknd and hdd 4f out* **10/1**

2m 36.15s (2.65) **Going Correction** +0.05s/f (Good) **14** Ran SP% **116.0**
Speed ratings (Par 103):93,91,91,90,88 87,84,84,81,80 80,80,70,60
CSF £43.71 CT £227.96 TOTE £9.20: £2.80, £2.10, £2.20; EX 36.20.

Owner All The Kings Horses **Bred** Terry McGrath **Trained** Wilmcote, Warwicks

■ Stewards' Enquiry : Miss S Brotherton three-day ban: used whip with excessive frequency on a horse showing no response and when out of contention (Jun 9-10,13)

FOCUS

An open handicap in which My Putra, who raced pretty keenly, took them along at a decent pace. Sound enough form.

2045 STANSTED EXPRESS EVERY 15 MINUTES MAIDEN STKS 5f

2:40 (2:40) (Class 4) 2-Y-O £4,533 (£1,348; £674; £336) Stalls High

Form RPR

3 **1** **Dazed And Amazed**[10] 1796 2-9-3 DaneO'Neill 3 84+
(R Hannon) *b.hind: lw: led 2f: led again 2f out: sn rdn clr* **5/4**[1]

4 **2** 3 **Vital Statistics**[10] 1796 2-8-12 TQuinn 2 67
(D R C Elsworth) *lw: s.i.s: sn prom: rdn to chse wnr and hung lft over 1f out: styd on same pce* **11/8**[2]

3 3 **Game Lady** 2-8-7 JamesDoyle(5) 11 55
(I A Wood) *neat: hld up: hdwy 1/2-way: edgd lft over 1f out: wknd fnl f* **10/1**[3]

4 ½ **Breckland Boy** 2-9-3 ChrisCatlin 1 58
(Mrs C A Dunnett) *cmpt: bkwd: dwlt: jinked lft 4f out: hdwy to ld 3f out: rdn and hdd 2f out: wknd fnl f* **33/1**

5 1 ¼ **Mint State** 2-9-0 AntonyProcter(3) 5 53
(D R C Elsworth) *w'like: leggy: s.s: a in rr* **14/1**

0 **6** 6 **Joint Expectations (IRE)**[16] 1639 2-8-10 KirstyMilczarek(7) 9 29
(Mrs C A Dunnett) *cmpt: chsd wnr 2f: wknd 2f out* **40/1**

61.64 secs (1.17) **Going Correction** +0.05s/f (Good) **6** Ran SP% **107.7**

Speed ratings (Par 95):92,87,82,81,79 70

CSF £2.90 TOTE £2.20: £1.20, £1.30; EX 2.70.

Owner Mrs R Ablett **Bred** Whitsbury Manor Stud And Pigeon House Stud **Trained** East Everleigh, Wilts

FOCUS

Plenty of non-runners left this a virtual match between the two who ran close at Salisbury ten days earlier.

NOTEBOOK

Dazed And Amazed ran with plenty of promise on his debut and put that experience to good use. Showing good speed throughout, he came home a clear winner, having produced a useful turn of foot two furlongs out, and it is no surprise that connections are now keen to take him to Royal Ascot in a bid to win the Norfolk Stakes. (tchd 11-8)

Vital Statistics, a half-sister to Emerald Lodge, a triple six-furlong winner at two to three, and to Spiritual Peace, a six-furlong winner at three, finished half a length behind Dazed And Amazed when they met at Salisbury on their debuts, and was again done for speed. Once more she shaped as though she will be seen to better effect when stepped up to six furlongs. (tchd 5-4)

Game Lady, whose dam was a winner over seven furlongs at four and is a half-sister to several winners, including prolific winning stayer Captain Miller, shaped with distinct promise, despite running green, against a couple of rivals who had the benefit of previous experience. (tchd 9-1)

Breckland Boy, a cheap purchase and already gelded, is a half-brother to Blue Minx, a dual winner over this trip at two. He showed a bit of speed and should pay his way at a more modest level in time.

Mint State, whose dam is an unraced sister to top-class multiple middle-distance winner User Friendly, is a half-brother to Angel Annie, a seven-furlong winner at three, Clueless, a dual winner over middle distances at three, and Champions Gallery, a seven-furlong winner at two. Missing the break badly, he was always playing catch-up thereafter, and he is likely to derive plenty from this experience. (op 20-1)

2046 LET'S GO WITH "ONE" RAILWAY TO NEWMARKET H'CAP 1m 2f

3:15 (3:15) (Class 2) (0-100,98) 3-Y-O £11,658 (£3,468; £1,733; £865) Stalls High

Form RPR

3052 **1** **Lake Poet (IRE)**[17] 1615 3-8-4 **84** oh2 KerrinMcEvoy 4 92
(C E Brittain) *chsd ldr: led over 1f out: rdn and hdd ins fnl f: hmpd nr fin: r.o to ld post* **14/1**

0411 **2** hd **Idarah (USA)**[29] 1282 3-8-7 **87** RHills 6 94+
(W J Haggas) *lw: led: rdn and hdd over 1f out: rallied to ld ins fnl f: hung lft: hdd post* **11/4**[1]

4221 **3** 3 **Barodine**[15] 1691 3-8-5 **85** EddieAhern 7 87
(H R A Cecil) *chsd ldrs: rdn over 1f out: styd on same pce* **6/1**[3]

01 **4** hd **Great Hawk (USA)**[22] 1483 3-8-7 **87** RobertWinston 1 88+
(Sir Michael Stoute) *lw: hld up: hdwy over 2f out: rdn and hung rt over 1f out: no ex fnl f* **3/1**[2]

6062 **5** hd **Quince (IRE)**[11] 1781 3-8-4 **84** (p) JimmyQuinn 5 85+
(J Pearce) *hld up: nt clr run over 2f out: outpcd over 1f out: r.o ins fnl f: nvr able to chal* **10/1**

61 **6** shd **Balanced Budget**[25] 1421 3-8-12 **92** ShaneKelly 9 93+
(J Noseda) *lw: hld up: nt clr run fr over 2f out tl r.o ins fnl f: nvr able to chal* **15/2**

3212 **7** 4 **Hard To Explain (IRE)**[121] 213 3-9-4 **98** NickyMackay 2 91
(L M Cumani) *prom: rdn over 2f out: wknd over 1f out* **12/1**

0530 **8** 5 **Wovoka (IRE)**[8] 1841 3-9-0 **94** TonyCulhane 3 78
(M R Channon) *prom: rdn over 2f out: wknd over 1f out* **9/1**

2m 5.80s (0.09) **Going Correction** +0.05s/f (Good) **8** Ran SP% **111.2**

Speed ratings (Par 105):101,100,98,98,98 98,94,90

CSF £49.69 CT £253.21 TOTE £17.80: £3.90, £1.20, £1.90; EX 72.80.

Owner Mohammed Rashid **Bred** Philip And Mrs Jane Myerscough And Charles O'Brien **Trained** Newmarket, Suffolk

■ Stewards' Enquiry : R Hills two-day ban: careless riding (Jun 8-9)

FOCUS

There was a steady early pace to this decent handicap, and the first three were in those positions throughout. As a result the form does not look reliable.

NOTEBOOK

Lake Poet(IRE), who was running from 2lb out of the handicap, benefited from racing in second for most of the way in a race which lacked early pace. Well positioned for the sprint for home, he just managed to nail Idarah on the line, but it would be a mistake to take this form literally. (op 16-1)

Idarah(USA), raised 12lb for his win at Haydock last month, was given a good front-running ride by Hills, who excels when he deploys these tactics. He set a steady pace before quickening things up approaching the two-furlong marker, and he was a touch unlucky not to hang on. He remains a progressive performer, though. (tchd 3-1)

Barodine, in third place on the rail for most of the way, could not pick up and go with the first two when the pace quickened. He is flattered by his finishing position given where he raced in a race which lacked a strong early gallop and it remains to be seen whether he can win off this sort of mark. (op 13-2)

Great Hawk(USA) was unsuited by the way the race was run as he had to make up ground on the outside from the tail of the field off the back of a steady early gallop. The effort cost him in the closing stages as he lost third place close home, but the impression left was that he is better than the bare form suggests. Faster ground might be more in his favour, too. Official explanation: jockey said colt slipped on leaving stalls (op 9-4 after 2- early, tchd 7-2)

Quince(IRE) ran well at York last time but he is at his best challenging from off the pace in a race run at a good gallop, and he did not get that here. He is clearly in form and has the ability to strike off this sort of mark, but he is reliant on others setting it up for him. (op 11-1)

Balanced Budget was another fast-ground maiden held up for a late run in a race run at a steady early gallop in more testing conditions. This race did not see him at his best and it would be daft to judge him on this performance. (op 8-1 tchd 7-1)

Hard To Explain(IRE), was hammered by the Handicapper for running a close second in a conditions race at Wolverhampton on his last start, and he now looks on a very stiff mark for his new stable. (op 11-1)

2047 TAKING PEOPLE PLACES WITH "ONE" RAILWAY H'CAP 6f

3:50 (3:50) (Class 2) (0-100,99) 4-Y-O+ £11,658 (£3,468; £1,733; £865) Stalls High

Form RPR

2400 **1** **Greenslades**[22] 1487 7-8-13 **94** DarryllHolland 9 103
(P J Makin) *chsd ldr: led 2f out: rdn out* **5/1**[1]

1204 **2** 1 **Idle Power (IRE)**[4] 1939 8-8-9 **90** LDettori 8 96
(J R Boyle) *sn led: rdn and hdd 2f out: unable qck ins fnl f* **5/1**[1]

1630 **3** shd **Firenze**[227] 5851 5-8-8 **89** ow1 DaneO'Neill 2 95+
(J R Fanshawe) *hld up: hdwy over 2f out: rdn over 2f out: styd on* **8/1**[3]

0400 **4** 1 ½ **Gloved Hand**[210] 6181 4-8-7 **88** OscarUrbina 5 89+
(J R Fanshawe) *hld up: rdn over 1f out: r.o ins fnl f: nt rch ldrs* **14/1**

14- **5** 1 ¾ **Seamus Shindig**[583] 6333 4-8-4 **85** oh2 ChrisCatlin 3 81+
(H Candy) *lw: hld up: r.o ins fnl f: nrst fin* **16/1**

0024 **6** shd **Excusez Moi (USA)**[274] 4764 4-9-4 **99** (p) KerrinMcEvoy 10 95
(C E Brittain) *lw: chsd ldrs: rdn over 1f out: no ex fnl f* **5/1**[1]

4600 **7** 1 ¾ **Moayed**[15] 1667 7-7-13 **85** oh1 (b) JamesDoyle(5) 7 75
(N P Littmoden) *dwlt: outpcd: nvr nrr* **11/1**

0630 **8** hd **Jonny Ebeneezer**[9] 1835 7-8-9 **90** MickyFenton 4 80
(M Wellings) *chsd ldrs: rdn over 2f out: wknd fnl f* **33/1**

1040 **9** 2 ½ **Banjo Patterson**[22] 1487 4-8-5 **86** EddieAhern 6 68
(G A Huffer) *chsd ldrs over 4f* **8/1**[3]

6013 **10** ¾ **Romany Nights (IRE)**[15] 1667 6-8-4 **85** (b) MartinDwyer 1 65
(Miss Gay Kelleway) *b.hind: hld up in tch: rdn over 2f out: wknd over 1f out* **7/1**[2]

2020 **11** 9 **Tanforan**[22] 1487 4-8-4 **85** oh4 (b) JamieMackay 11 38
(K McAuliffe) *s.i.s: sn pushed along in rr: wknd over 2f out* **18/1**

1m 11.82s (-1.28) **Going Correction** +0.05s/f (Good) **11** Ran SP% **113.8**

Speed ratings (Par 109):110,108,108,106,104 104,101,101,98,97 85

CSF £27.70 CT £198.70 TOTE £6.40: £1.90, £1.70, £2.60; EX 33.20 Trifecta £190.70 Pool £913.56 - 3.40 winning units..

Owner Four Seasons Racing Ltd **Bred** C M Oakshott **Trained** Ogbourne Maisey, Wilts

FOCUS

A decent sprint handicap, but it proved difficult to make up ground from off the pace in the softish ground, and the first two were prominent throughout.

NOTEBOOK

Greenslades, well positioned throughout, just behind the leader, does not mind a bit of cut in the ground and, off a 4lb higher mark than when last successful, proved good enough in a race in which few got competitive. No doubt he will now be aimed at the Wokingham, but it will be a surprise if there are not one or two in the race better handicapped than him. (op 6-1)

Idle Power(IRE) tried to make all next to the far-side rail. He made the most of the difficulty horses were having in making up ground from off the pace, but was unable to hold off Greenslades, who tracked him for most of the way. This was still a solid effort, though, and he looks one to keep in mind for when he returns to Goodwood. (op 11-2)

Firenze ◆, who did best of those who tried to make up ground from off the pace, could well reoppse the winner in the Wokingham, and would have strong claims of reversing the form. Quicker ground will suit, and all in all this was a very pleasing seasonal reappearance.

Gloved Hand was another making her seasonal reappearance and given the task of making up ground from off the pace in a race in which those who raced prominently dominated throughout. She raced over a mile towards the end of last season and, while her winning form is over sprint distances, she should have no trouble getting seven furlongs.

Seamus Shindig ◆, absent since finishing fourth in a Sales race at Doncaster in October 2004, gave plenty of encouragement on this return to action, staying on well from off the pace in a race in which those who were held up struggled to get into it. He would be a very interesting proposition if he can build on this promising reappearance, although one would be cautious were he to reappear quickly after this. (op 14-1 tchd 18-1)

Excusez Moi(USA) ran one or two decent races in face of stiff tasks last season and put up a fair effort on his return to action this time. He is not the easiest to place, though, and will need to find a bit of improvement to win a handicap off this sort of mark. (op 11-2 tchd 6-1)

2048 MAINTENANCE AND RESTORATION SERVICES MAIDEN STKS 7f

4:25 (4:25) (Class 5) 3-Y-O £5,181 (£1,541; £770; £384) Stalls High

Form RPR

1 **Against The Grain** 3-9-3 JoeFanning 8 90
(M Johnston) *leggy: scope: lw: led 1f: chsd ldr tl led over 2f out: r.o wl* **11/2**[2]

3 **2** 3 ½ **Villa Sonata**[242] 5542 3-8-12 OscarUrbina 4 74
(J R Fanshawe) *hld up: hdwy over 2f out: rdn to chse wnr over 1f out: no imp* **9/2**[1]

3 3 ½ **Abwaab** 3-9-3 (t) RHills 5 69+
(W J Haggas) *leggy: unf: hld up: swtchd lft 2f out: sn rdn: r.o ins fnl f: nvr nrr* **7/1**[3]

0 **4** 1 **Double Bay (USA)**[39] 1085 3-8-12 EddieAhern 9 61
(Jane Chapple-Hyam) *prom: rdn over 2f out: hung rt and wknd over 1f out* **11/2**[2]

0 **5** hd **Disco Ball**[15] 1680 3-8-12 TedDurcan 14 60
(G Wragg) *lw: chsd ldrs: rdn over 2f out: hng rt ovr 1f out: sn wknd* **9/2**[1]

36 **6** 1 **Theatre Royal**[242] 5556 3-8-9 NeilChalmers(3) 10 57
(A M Balding) *lw: s.i.s: hld up: hdwy over 2f out: rdn and wknd over 1f out* **7/1**[3]

00 **7** 1 ¼ **Pay On (IRE)**[211] 6148 3-9-3 SteveDrowne 2 58+
(W Jarvis) *dwlt: hld up: n.d* **20/1**

00 **8** ½ **Milton's Keen**[167] 6557 3-9-3 BrianReilly 7 57
(P S McEntee) *plld hrd and prom: rdn over 2f out: wknd over 1f out* **80/1**

9 3 **Don't Mind Me** 3-8-12 KerrinMcEvoy 1 43
(T Keddy) *w'like: bkwd: wnt lft s: a in rr* **16/1**

0 **10** 6 **Atwirl**[27] 1351 3-8-12 ShaneKelly 11 25
(D J Daly) *s.i.s: hdwy 6f out: wknd over 2f out* **14/1**

50 **11** ½ **Lady Ambitious**[35] 1166 3-8-12 ChrisCatlin 12 23
(D K Ivory) *a in rr* **25/1**

0 **12** 1 **With Admiration**[20] 1546 3-9-3 TPQueally 13 25
(C Drew) *b.hind: led 7f out: racd keenly: hdd over 2f out: sn rdn and wknd* **80/1**

1m 26.53s (0.03) **Going Correction** +0.05s/f (Good) **12** Ran SP% **115.8**

Speed ratings (Par 99):101,97,93,91,91 90,89,88,85,78 77,76

CSF £28.76 TOTE £5.70: £2.10, £1.60, £2.20; EX 22.90.

Owner The Right Angle Club **Bred** Mrs C F Van Straubeenzee And Miss A G **Trained** Middleham Moor, N Yorks

FOCUS

A fair maiden rated around the fourth and fifth and, although the winner enjoyed the run of the race, he did it impressively.

2049 "ONE" RAILWAY ACROSS THE EAST OF ENGLAND EBF FILLIES' H'CAP 6f

4:55 (4:59) (Class 4) (0-85,82) 3-Y-0 **£6,477** (£1,927; £963; £481) **Stalls** High

Form RPR

011 **1** **Ripples Maid**[33] [1208] 3-9-2 **80** .... RichardThomas 13 94+
(J A Geake) *trckd ldrs: led 2f out: r.o wl* **4/1**[1]

166 **2** *2 ½* **Mango Music**[8] [1843] 3-8-10 **74** .... TedDurcan 2 81
(M R Channon) *lw: hld up: hdwy 1/2-way: rdn to chse wnr fnl f: r.o* **9/2**[2]

5563 **3** *1 ½* **Spectacular Show (IRE)**[28] [1312] 3-8-8 **72** .... ShaneKelly 3 74
(M Quinn) *lw: hung rt thrght: led 1f: w ldrs: rdn over 1f out: styd on same pce fnl f* **18/1**

114 **4** *½* **Hypocrisy**[64] [725] 3-9-0 **78** .... LDettori 5 79
(S C Williams) *lw: hld up: hdwy over 2f out: rdn over 1f out: no ex ins fnl f* **5/1**[3]

5516 **5** *2* **Tilly's Dream**[216] [6071] 3-8-3 **70** ow1 .... SaleemGolam(3) 14 65
(G C H Chung) *chsd ldrs: rdn over 2f out: wknd fnl f* **25/1**

0300 **6** *shd* **Surely Truly (IRE)**[27] [1337] 3-8-9 **73** ....(p) PatCosgrave 4 67
(K R Burke) *chsd ldrs: rdn over 2f out: wknd fnl f* **11/1**

1000 **7** *¾* **Xaluna Bay (IRE)**[15] [1679] 3-8-6 **70** .... MartinDwyer 1 62
(W R Muir) *hld up: effrt over 2f out: wknd over 1f out* **28/1**

5341 **8** *shd* **Rapsgate (IRE)**[36] [1137] 3-8-10 **74** ....(b) PatDobbs 11 66
(R Hannon) *s.i.s: hld up: rdn over 2f out: n.d* **11/1**

3142 **9** *hd* **Woodnook**[15] [1679] 3-8-12 **76** .... KerrinMcEvoy 7 77+
(J A R Toller) *prom: n.m.r and wknd over 1f out* **9/2**[2]

6036 **10** *1 ¼* **Smooch**[24] [1448] 3-9-3 **81** .... RobertWinston 9 68
(R M H Cowell) *lw: a in rr* **20/1**

0500 **11** *1 ¼* **Tiber Tilly**[15] [1679] 3-8-3 **72** .... JamesDoyle(5) 12 56
(N P Littmoden) *w ldrs 4f: wknd fnl f* **22/1**

010 **12** *2* **Titian Saga (IRE)**[309] [3731] 3-9-4 **82** .... OscarUrbina 10 60
(C N Allen) *led 5f out: rdn and hdd 2f out: sn wknd* **16/1**

1m 12.55s (-0.55) **Going Correction** +0.05s/f (Good) **12** Ran SP% **117.2**

Speed ratings (Par 98): 105,101,99,99,96 96,95,95,94,93 91,88

CSF £20.15 CT £296.25 TOTE £4.70: £1.80, £2.10, £4.40; EX 27.40.

Owner Rex L Mead **Bred** Compton Down Stud **Trained** Kimpton, Hants

FOCUS

Decent form for the grade and the progressive winner was impressive in landing the hat-trick. The form looks solid, rated around the exposed third.

Tiber Tilly Official explanation: jockey said filly lost its action

2050 NEWMARKETRACECOURSES.CO.UK H'CAP 7f

5:25 (5:31) (Class 5) (0-70,70) 3-Y-0 **£3,886** (£1,156; £577; £288) **Stalls** High

Form RPR

5014 **1** **Inaminute (IRE)**[20] [1549] 3-8-8 **60** .... PatCosgrave 15 68
(K R Burke) *racd far side: a.p: rdn to ld and edgd lft ins fnl f: r.o* **16/1**

6663 **2** *½* **Mr Cellophane**[16] [1642] 3-8-8 **60** .... EddieAhern 19 67
(J R Jenkins) *lw: racd far side: hld up: hdwy over 2f out: rdn and ev ch ins fnl f: r.o* **11/2**[3]

5526 **3** *hd* **Neardown Beauty (IRE)**[18] [1592] 3-9-1 **67** .... LDettori 12 74+
(I A Wood) *lw: racd far side: hld up: hdwy over 2f out: r.o* **10/1**

422 **4** *1* **Royal Citadel (IRE)**[16] [1646] 3-9-3 **69** ....(v[1]) PhilipRobinson 16 73
(C G Cox) *racd far side: led: rdn over 1f out: hdd and unable qck ins fnl f* **5/1**[2]

0522 **5** *hd* **Wee Charlie Castle (IRE)**[143] [49] 3-9-1 **67** .... OscarUrbina 6 70
(G C H Chung) *swtchd to race far side sn after s: prom: rdn over 1f out styd on* **25/1**

3303 **6** *1 ¼* **Esoterica (IRE)**[18] [1592] 3-8-7 **62** .... BenSwarbrick(3) 11 64+
(T D Barron) *racd far side: sn chsng ldrs: riddden over 1f out: looked hld whn hmpd ins fnl f* **9/1**

5040 **7** *shd* **Air Biscuit (IRE)**[17] [1616] 3-8-12 **64** ....(t) JimmyQuinn 20 64+
(C F Wall) *racd far side: hld up: effrt and nt clr run over 2f out: hdwy over 1f out: nt rch ldrs* **10/1**

0151 **8** *1 ¼* **Leamington Lad (IRE)**[27] [1352] 3-8-13 **65** .... RichardThomas 9 68+
(J A Geake) *racd far side: hld up: nt clr run and lost pl over 2f out: r.o ins fnl f: nvr able to chal* **11/4**[1]

0010 **9** *¾* **Dancing Guest (IRE)**[29] [1291] 3-9-4 **70** .... RobertWinston 4 65
(G G Margarson) *lw: dwlt: in rr whn swtchd far side over 5f out: sme hdwy over 1f out : n.d* **33/1**

2400 **10** *½* **Glenbuck (IRE)**[39] [1078] 3-9-0 **66** .... SamHitchcott 10 59
(A Bailey) *racd far side: chsd ldrs over 5f* **28/1**

1133 **11** *nk* **Welsh Dragon**[57] [839] 3-8-8 **63** .... NeilChalmers(3) 14 56
(A M Balding) *b.hind: racd far side: prom over 5f* **14/1**

523 **12** *1 ¼* **Musical Script (USA)**[47] [963] 3-8-11 **63** .... ChrisCatlin 13 52
(Mrs A J Hamilton-Fairley) *racd far side: mid-div: nt clr run over 2f out: styd on u.p ins fnl f: n.d* **20/1**

0400 **13** *1* **Macs Ransom (USA)**[169] [6539] 3-8-11 **63** .... SteveDrowne 2 50
(N A Callaghan) *racd centre: chsd ldrs: hung rt fr over 2f out: sn wknd: 1st of 4 in gp* **25/1**

6000 **14** *5* **Bucharest**[15] [1672] 3-8-13 **65** .... JamieMackay 18 39
(M Wigham) *racd far side: plld hrd and prom: lost pl whn hmpd 1/2-way: sn bhd* **40/1**

0004 **15** *2* **Atticus Trophies (IRE)**[27] [1355] 3-8-13 **65** ....(p) DarryllHolland 5 34
(K McAuliffe) *racd centre: led that gp to 1/2-way: hung rt and wknd over 2f out: 2nd of 4 in gp* **33/1**

3010 **16** *1 ¾* **Mujelle**[28] [1312] 3-8-8 **67** .... JamesMillman(7) 1 31
(D K Ivory) *racd centre: hung rt over 2f out: n.d: 3rd of 4 in gp* **50/1**

5130 **17** *shd* **Fateful Attraction**[65] [712] 3-8-3 **60** .... JamesDoyle(5) 3 24
(I A Wood) *racd centre: chsd ldr tl led that gp 1/2-way: hung rt and wknd over 2f out: last of 4 in gp* **20/1**

0036 **18** *5* **Grand Sefton**[57] [839] 3-8-12 **64** .... TonyCulhane 7 15
(J G Portman) *racd far side: chsd ldrs over 4f* **28/1**

00P0 **19** *11* **Colourpoint (USA)**[36] [1137] 3-9-0 **66** .... KerrinMcEvoy 17 —
(C E Brittain) *racd far side: hld up: a in rr* **33/1**

1m 26.64s (0.14) **Going Correction** +0.05s/f (Good) **19** Ran SP% **136.8**

Speed ratings (Par 99): 101,100,100,99,98 97,97,95,95,94 94,92,91,85,83 81,81,75,63

CSF £98.70 CT £1000.25 TOTE £18.10: £4.40, £1.90, £2.70, £1.80; EX 88.60 Place 6 £15.23, Place 5 £8.09.

Owner Ray Bailey **Bred** R Bailey **Trained** Middleham Moor, N Yorks

■ Stewards' Enquiry : Pat Cosgrave one-day ban: careless riding (Jun 8)

FOCUS

An open, albeit modest, handicap in which those drawn high dominated. The winner showed improved form, and the next six all ran very close to their marks.

Colourpoint(USA) Official explanation: jockey said filly had no more to give

T/Jkpt: Not won. T/Plt: £46.00 to a £1 stake. Pool: £71,917.15. 1,140.55 winning tickets. T/Qpdt: £30.10 to a £1 stake. Pool: £3,117.60. 76.50 winning tickets. CR

2036 CURRAGH (R-H)

Sunday, May 28

OFFICIAL GOING: Round course - soft; straight course - heavy

2053a TATTERSALLS GOLD CUP (GROUP 1) 1m 2f 110y

3:00 (3:03) 4-Y-0+ **£118,965** (£32,758; £15,517)

RPR

1 **Hurricane Run (IRE)**[238] [5651] 4-9-0 .... KFallon 3 128+
(A Fabre, France) *mde all: rdn 2f out: drew clr fnl f: easily* **1/4**[1]

2 *7* **Alexander Goldrun (IRE)**[64] [741] 5-8-11 119 .... KJManning 1 114
(J S Bolger, Ire) *hld up in 3rd: impr into 2nd 2f out: sn rdn: no imp fr over 1f out: kpt on same pce* **7/2**[2]

3 *12* **Lord Admiral (USA)**[14] [1711] 5-9-0 111 .... FMBerry 2 101
(Charles O'Brien, Ire) *cl 2nd: rdn ent st: 3rd and wknd under 2f out* **25/1**[3]

2m 26.4s **Going Correction** +1.10s/f (Soft) **3** Ran SP% **106.1**

Speed ratings: 105,99,91

CSF £1.40 TOTE £1.30; DF 1.30.

Owner Michael Tabor **Bred** Gestut Ammerland **Trained** Chantilly, France

FOCUS

This proved a formality for Hurricane Run on his reappearance.

NOTEBOOK

Hurricane Run(IRE) took the initiative once it became clear that the outsider of three was not going to make the running, and he was in no way unsettled by a tactic that was also employed when he won at Longchamp on his first run last season before his rise to eminence. Once asked to go about his business, he picked up well to stretch clear, displaying a lovely action on the ground. He is an exceptional racehorse and this was never going to add much to what is already known about him, but the race should serve as an ideal launch-pad to the more significant tests that he will face later on in the season. (op 2/9)

Alexander Goldrun(IRE), admirable though she is as a four-time Group One winner, she is not in the same league as Hurricane Run.

Lord Admiral(USA), who needs good ground, was merely making up the numbers such as they were. (op 25/1 tchd 28/1)

2054a BOYLESPORTS IRISH 1,000 GUINEAS (GROUP 1) (FILLIES) 1m

3:35 (3:36) 3-Y-0

£154,827 (£52,758; £25,172; £8,620; £5,862; £3,103)

RPR

1 **Nightime (IRE)**[42] [1037] 3-9-0 .... PJSmullen 15 116
(D K Weld, Ire) *a.p: 5th appr 1/2-way: 3rd 3f out: 2nd 2f out: led over 1 1/2f out: rdn clr fnl f: styd on strly* **12/1**

2 *6* **Ardbrae Lady**[27] [1363] 3-9-0 105 .... FMBerry 8 104
(Joseph G Murphy, Ire) *hld up in tch: 3rd and hdwy 2f out: 2nd over 1f out: sn rdn and one pce* **50/1**

3 *1 ½* **Queen Cleopatra (IRE)**[14] [1709] 3-9-0 106 .... JAHeffernan 10 101
(A P O'Brien, Ire) *hld up: 6th and hdwy over 2f out: 4th over 1f out: kpt on* **11/1**

4 *3* **Race For The Stars (USA)**[21] [1508] 3-9-0 102 .... KFallon 9 95
(A P O'Brien, Ire) *hld up: rdn over 3f out: 7th 2f out: kpt on fnl f* **7/1**[3]

5 *3 ½* **Abigail Pett**[209] [6205] 3-9-0 108 ....(b) KJManning 11 88
(J S Bolger, Ire) *trckd ldrs: prog into 5th 3f out: 4th and rdn 2 1/2f out: no ex fr 1 1/2f out* **14/1**

6 *¾* **Confidential Lady**[21] [1508] 3-9-0 .... SebSanders 13 87
(Sir Mark Prescott) *led: strly pressed over 2f out: hdd over 1 1/2f out: sn wknd* **5/2**[1]

7 *2* **Be My Queen (IRE)**[14] [1709] 3-9-0 101 .... CO'Donoghue 5 83
(A P O'Brien, Ire) *towards rr: kpt on without threatening fr 1 1/2f out* **40/1**

8 *1* **Talwin (IRE)**[21] [1521] 3-9-0 93 .... WSupple 6 81
(Kevin Prendergast, Ire) *towards rr: pushed along 1/2-way: kpt on without threatening fr 2f out* **33/1**

9 *1* **Gist (IRE)**[43] [1023] 3-9-0 85 .... TPO'Shea 3 79
(W J Martin, Ire) *towards rr: rdn 1/2-way: kpt on same pce fr over 2f out* **200/1**

10 *3* **Kamarinskaya (USA)**[14] [1719] 3-9-0 103 .... DavidMcCabe 12 73
(A P O'Brien, Ire) *cl up in 2nd: rdn 3f out: wknd over 2f out* **25/1**

11 *3* **Ugo Fire (IRE)**[43] [1023] 3-9-0 110 .... DPMcDonogh 7 67
(Kevin Prendergast, Ire) *a towards rr* **10/1**

12 *4 ½* **Dont Dili Dali**[38] [1093] 3-9-0 .... JohnEgan 14 58
(J S Moore) *chsd ldrs: 6th 1/2-way: wknd over 2f out* **20/1**

13 *¾* **Short Dance (USA)**[9] [1834] 3-9-0 .... RichardHughes 4 56
(B W Hills) *prom: 4th 1/2-way: wknd fr 3f out* **5/1**[2]

14 *½* **Nasheej (USA)**[21] [1508] 3-9-0 .... RyanMoore 1 55
(R Hannon) *hld up: pushed along 1/2-way: no ex fr over 2f out* **7/1**[3]

15 *½* **Beauty Bright (IRE)**[14] [1719] 3-9-0 102 .... SMLevey 2 54
(A P O'Brien, Ire) *prom: 3rd 1/2-way: rdn and wknd 3f out* **66/1**

1m 48.3s **Going Correction** +1.10s/f (Soft) **15** Ran SP% **120.0**

Speed ratings: 113,107,105,102,99 98,96,95,94,91 88,83,83,82,82

CSF £523.41 TOTE £14.30: £3.30, £10.30, £4.00; DF 1049.80.

Owner Mrs C L Weld **Bred** Mrs C L Weld **Trained** The Curragh, Co Kildare

FOCUS

A reasonable renewal on paper, and the winner has been rated the equal of Gossamer.

NOTEBOOK

Nightime(IRE), had won just a Cork maiden but ran right away from her opponents to score in a style that is hard to fault, whatever the substance of the form. She is clearly a rapidly improving filly, and perhaps she will turn out to be one of the stars of the season. (op 14/1)

Ardbrae Lady exceeded general expectations to earn an honourable Group 1 placing, for which Joe Murphy deserves great credit. She has won only one of her 11 races, but is a tough and talented filly who has proved conclusively that her third in last season's Moyglare was not a fluke. (op 66/1)

Queen Cleopatra(IRE) took seven starts to open her account, but despite not getting the easiest of passages she confirmed the solid impression that she made in winning a Group 3 at Leopardstown with a sound effort to take third place by a comfortable margin. (op 10/1)

Race For The Stars(USA) did best of the three fillies who had contested the Newmarket equivalent but again ran below her two-year-old form. (op 7/1 tchd 8/1)

Abigail Pett, whose winning form at two was on good ground, ran an honest race on her first appearance of the season and should be capable of adding to her tally when the going improves.

Confidential Lady looked as if she set too strong a pace in the ground and used up too much energy in leading the pack over to the stands' side. She was soon beaten after being headed over a furlong and a half down. (op 3/1)

Ugo Fire(IRE) was very disappointing. The fact that she finished six lengths adrift of the 85-rated maiden Gist is just one of many aspects of the race that represent a bit of a puzzle from a handicapping perspective.

Dont Dili Dali was out of her depth.
Short Dance(USA), perhaps flattered by the bare form of her York win, was reappearing quite quickly after that success.
Nasheej(USA) looked in trouble by halfway, and finished with only one of the Ballydoyle outsiders behind her.

2055a AIRLE STUD GALLINULE STKS (GROUP 3) 1m 2f
4:10 (4:10) 3-Y-O **£35,917** (£10,537; £5,020; £1,710)

RPR
1 **Puerto Rico (IRE)**[21] 1522 3-9-1 .... KFallon 1 111+
(A P O'Brien, Ire) *trckd ldrs in 3rd: pushed along appr st: impr to ld 2f out: sn rdn clr: styd on wl fnl f* **9/4**[1]
2 *4* **Mon Michel (IRE)**[43] 1028 3-9-1 .... DPMcDonogh 4 102
(Kevin Prendergast, Ire) *hld up in rr: impr into 4th 1/2-way: rdn early st: mod 2nd over 1f out: kpt on u.p* **11/2**
3 *1* **King In Waiting (IRE)**[63] 756 3-9-1 .... FMBerry 5 101+
(John M Oxx, Ire) *settled 4th: last 1/2-way: prog early st: 3rd 2f out: kpt on same pce u.p* **7/2**[3]
4 *shd* **Rhythm'n Roots (IRE)**[35] 1172 3-9-4 107........(t) KJManning 2 103
(J S Bolger, Ire) *led: hdd 2f out: sn outpcd: mod 3rd fnl f: kpt on* **3/1**[2]
5 *25* **Talenti (IRE)**[11] 1786 3-9-1 .... JAHeffernan 3 55
(A P O'Brien, Ire) *cl up in 2nd: rdn appr st: sn wknd: t.o* **13/2**
2m 20.2s **Going Correction** +1.10s/f (Soft) **5** Ran SP% **106.7**
Speed ratings: 100,96,96,95,75
CSF £13.50 TOTE £3.60: £1.80, £2.20; DF 15.40.
Owner Mrs John Magnier **Bred** Southern Bloodstock **Trained** Ballydoyle, Co Tipperary

FOCUS
Not an especially strong Group Three, but it produced an emphatic winner and has been rated around the fourth.

NOTEBOOK
Puerto Rico(IRE) provided an illustration of the theory that many of the Ballydoyle colts are showing major improvement from a first run of the season. On the face of it, there was nothing very remarkable about his third behind longer-priced stablemate Poseidon Adventure over two furlongs farther at Gowran, but there was no shortage of confidence behind his chance here, and the issue was promptly settled when he took over two furlongs out. He stayed on in a manner that augurs well for a return to a mile and a half. (op 5/2)
Mon Michel(IRE), whose Leopardstown maiden win was boosted by a handicap success for Strath Gallant on Saturday, won the battle for second but had no chance with the easy winner. (op 6/1)
King In Waiting(IRE), a well-regarded type who suffered a setback after winning in good style on his debut in March, should now go on to build on this. (op 4/1)
Rhythm'n Roots(IRE) appeared to set the standard as an experienced Group Three winner, but he was found wanting after making the running until headed by the winner. He ought to have been capable of much better than this. (op 5/2)
Talenti(IRE), whose maiden win stood up to scrutiny later in the day, was beaten a long way from home and dropped right out. Official explanation: jockey said colt suffered accidental interference in the early stages and did not stride out well thereafter (op 6/1)

2056 - 2058a (Foreign Racing) - See Raceform Interactive

1973 BADEN-BADEN (L-H)
Saturday, May 27

OFFICIAL GOING: Good

2059a FESTA-RENNEN (LISTED) (FILLIES) 1m 1f
2:10 (2:12) 3-Y-O **£12,414** (£5,172; £2,069; £1,034)

RPR
1 **Sexy Lady (GER)**[20] 3-9-0 .... ABest 9 101
(P Rau, Germany) **73/10**[2]
2 *2* **Amy Storm (GER)**[216] 6051 3-8-10 .... APietsch 6 93
(P Vovcenko, Germany)
3 *1/2* **Flor Y Nata (USA)**[10] 1789 3-9-0 .... THellier 1 96
(Sir Mark Prescott) *raced in 5th, stayed on under pressure down centre from over 1f out* **3/1**[1]
4 *nk* **Imperia (GER)** 3-9-0 .... ASuborics 5 95
(W Hickst, Germany)
5 *1* **Amateis (GER)**[27] 1328 3-8-10 .... TMundry 2 90
(P Rau, Germany)
6 *5* **Madura (GER)**[27] 1328 3-9-0 .... AStarke 7 84
(Mario Hofer, Germany)
7 *1* **Navette (GER)**[216] 6051 3-9-0 .... WMongil 3 82
(P Schiergen, Germany)
8 *1/2* **Giardini** 3-8-10 .... ABoschert 8 77
(Mario Hofer, Germany)
9 *10* **Mellanie Surprise (HOL)** 3-9-0 .... NRichter 4 62
(J Pubben, Holland)
1m 55.5s **9** Ran SP% **37.0**
(including 10 euro stakes): WIN 83; PL 23, 72, 22; SF 3054.
Owner Gestut Ittlingen **Bred** Gestut Hof Ittlingen **Trained** Germany

NOTEBOOK
Flor Y Nata(USA) achieved some black type for finishing third but looks to need a step up in distance if she is to be successful at this level.

2060 - (Foreign Racing) - See Raceform Interactive

2059 BADEN-BADEN (L-H)
Sunday, May 28

OFFICIAL GOING: Soft

2061a GROSSER MERCEDES-BENZ-PREIS (GROUP 2) 1m 3f
4:00 (4:09) 4-Y-O+ **£48,276** (£19,310; £9,655; £5,517)

RPR
1 **Arcadio (GER)**[41] 4-8-12 .... ASuborics 2 118
(P Schiergen, Germany) *held up in 6th, brought widest of all to stands rail and headway entering straight, led over 1f out, ran on well* **23/10**[2]
2 *2* **Day Flight**[30] 1267 5-8-12 .... JimmyFortune 5 115
(J H M Gosden) *led, headed over 1f out, hard driven and hung right inside final f, kept on* **11/10**[1]
3 *2 1/2* **Fight Club (GER)**[252] 5352 5-9-1 .... ADeVries 1 114
(A Schutz, Germany) *always close up, 3rd straight, every chance over 1 1/2f out, one pace* **47/10**[3]
4 *1 1/2* **Expensive Dream (GER)**[27] 1369 7-8-12 .... FilipMinarik 10 109
(P Vovcenko, Germany) *held up in last, 6th staight, stayed on steadily final 1 1/2f* **97/10**
5 *1 1/2* **Chiron (GER)**[274] 4774 5-8-12 .... ABoschert 3 106
(Dr A Bolte, Germany) *close up in 4th, one pace final 2f* **17/1**
6 *nk* **Laredo Sound (IRE)**[44] 1014 4-8-12 .... AStarke 7 106
(Mario Hofer, Germany) *held ip in 6th, last straight, never a factor* **78/10**
7 *1 1/2* **El Tango (GER)**[27] 1369 4-8-12 .... WMongil 8 103
(P Schiergen, Germany) *pressed leader in 2nd, weakened 2f out* **92/10**
2m 24.01s **7** Ran SP% **131.5**
(including 10 Euro stake): WIN 33; PL 12, 13, 14; SF 53.
Owner Gestut Schlenderhan **Bred** *unknown **Trained** Germany

NOTEBOOK
Arcadio(GER), like recent big race winners Shirocco and Gentlewave, is a son of Monsun. Patiently ridden, he was brought right across to the stands rail in the straight and had matters in hand from before the furlong pole. He appeared not to stay when hot favourite for last year's German Derby and connections still feel that a mile and a quarter is his best distance. The Arlington Million is one of many options open to him at that trip.
Day Flight did his best to make this a test of stamina but was still found wanting for a turn of foot by the winner. A return to a longer trip will suit and he remains progressive.

1870 CAPANNELLE (R-H)
Sunday, May 28

OFFICIAL GOING: Good

2062a PREMIO ALESSANDRO PERRONE (LISTED) (FILLIES) 5f 110y
3:15 (3:18) 2-Y-O **£21,724** (£9,559; £5,214; £2,607)

RPR
1 **Docksil** 2-8-11 .... DVargiu 6 100
(B Grizzetti, Italy) **51/50**[1]
2 *3* **Silenia (USA)** 2-8-11 .... MEsposito 4 90
(R Menichetti, Italy) **14/1**
3 *1 1/2* **Trans Gold (IRE)** 2-8-11 .... MDemuro 3 85
(A Renzoni, Italy) **33/10**[3]
4 *1/2* **Gradetime (IRE)**[25] 1405 2-8-11 .... NCallan 1 83
(M J Wallace) *led, hung right 1 1/2f out, headed approaching final f, weakened last 100y* **29/10**[2]
5 *shd* **Iuturna (USA)** 2-8-11 .... CFiocchi 2 83
(R Menichetti, Italy) **14/1**
6 *3* **Love Profusion (USA)** 2-8-11 .... GMarcelli 7 73
(L Riccardi, Italy) **25/4**
7 *3* **Pinky Tinky (ITY)** 2-8-11 .... SLandi 8 63
(A Peraino, Italy) **41/1**
8 *5* **Golden Iron (IRE)** 2-8-11 .... MPasquale 5 46
(M Fratini, Italy) **10/1**
64.90 secs **8** Ran SP% **137.0**
(including one euro stakes): WIN 2.02; PL 1.28, 4.11, 1.64; DF 33.07.
Owner Scuderia Bogi Sas **Bred** Curtasse S N C **Trained** Italy

NOTEBOOK
Docksil had won her only previous contest by 14 lengths. She quickly put the race beyond doubt after hitting the front and is now expected to aim for the Premio Primi Passi-G3 and Prix Robert Papin-G2, races which her trainer won with Rolly Polly in 2000.
Gradetime(IRE) broke well from her railside draw and made it, albeit pressed by Golden Iron from the off. She hung right nearing the final furlong, thus allowing Docksil to quicken through the gap. The eventual second and third both went past her in the final 120yds.

1565 CHEPSTOW (L-H)
Monday, May 29

OFFICIAL GOING: Heavy changing to soft (heavy in places) after race 2 (2.55)
Wind: Moderate, half-behind Weather: Heavy shower after race 4

2063 ROTARY DISTRICT 1100 MAIDEN STKS 1m 14y
2:20 (2:22) (Class 5) 3-Y-O+ **£3,368** (£1,002; £500; £250) **Stalls** High

Form RPR
6 1 **Celtic Spirit (IRE)**[48] 964 3-8-13 .... EddieAhern 4 76
(R M Beckett) *a.p: rdn over 3f out: styd on to ld ins fnl f: rdn out* **5/2**[1]
2 *1* **Vampyrus** 3-8-13 .... DaneO'Neill 7 74+
(H Candy) *a.p: rdn over 2f out: led wl over 1f out tl ins fnl f: nt qckn* **5/1**
6 3 *3 1/2* **Scylla Cadeaux (IRE)**[35] 1191 3-8-8 .... J-PGuillambert 11 62+
(Sir Michael Stoute) *hld up in tch: led over 3f out: rdn and hdd wl over 1f out: wknd towards fin* **9/2**[3]
0045 4 *3 1/2* **Overjoy Way**[17] 1638 4-9-6 51........(b) LPKeniry 2 58
(P R Chamings) *s.i.s: sn in tch: rdn over 2f out: wknd over 1f out* **14/1**
5 *3/4* **Quel Ange (FR)**[438] 4-9-11 .... JimCrowley 3 62
(R J Hodges) *hld up in tch: rdn and wknd 2f out* **50/1**
04 6 *1* **Tranos (USA)**[17] 1641 3-8-13 .... NickyMackay 5 57
(L M Cumani) *s.s: sn mid-div: rdn over 3f out: no hdwy* **3/1**[2]
0 7 *1* **Woolsey**[21] 1546 3-8-13 .... FergusSweeney 6 55
(M Blanshard) *t.k.h in mid-div: rdn and wknd 2f out* **50/1**
60 8 *3 1/2* **Red Raptor**[34] 1212 5-9-11 ....(t) RichardThomas 12 51
(J A Geake) *hld up and bhd: rdn and hdwy over 3f out: wknd 2f out* **22/1**
06 9 *6* **Storm Prospect**[198] 6318 3-8-13 .... TedDurcan 10 36
(C Tinkler) *a bhd* **18/1**
10 *2* **Just Matty** 3-8-8 .... StephenDonohoe[(5)] 1 32
(J G M O'Shea) *s.s: outpcd: rdn and hung lft fr over 3f out: fin alone far side* **28/1**
11 *1* **Ballymena**[116] 5-9-1 .... RichardKingscote[(5)] 9 28
(R A Harris) *led over 6f out: rdn and hdd over 3f out: sn wknd* **28/1**
000 12 *166* **In Some Style (IRE)**[273] 4838 3-8-8 47........ FrancisFerris 8 —
(R A Harris) *led over 1f: wknd 4f out: virtually p.u fnl f: t.o* **100/1**
1m 41.68s (5.68) **Going Correction** +0.725s/f (Yiel)
WFA 3 from 4yo+ 12lb **12** Ran SP% **116.5**
Speed ratings (Par 103):100,99,95,92,91 90,89,85,79,77 76,—
CSF £14.00 TOTE £3.90: £1.40, £1.90, £3.10; EX 15.60 Trifecta £99.90 Pool: £311.25 - 2.21 winning tickets..
Owner Mrs H M Chamberlain **Bred** Genesis Green Stud Ltd **Trained** Whitsbury, Hants

FOCUS
A modest maiden, run in a poor time compared with the later handicap. The form limited by the fourth.
In Some Style(IRE) Official explanation: jockey said filly lost its action

2064 JOIN THE ROTARY CLUB CHEPSTOW 01291 423704 (S) STKS 6f 16y
2:55 (2:55) (Class 6) 2-Y-O **£2,266** (£674; £337; £168) **Stalls High**

Form RPR

4 **1** **Mollyanko**[2] 2015 2-8-1 .... MarcHalford(5) 5 54
(W G M Turner) *hung lft thrght: hdwy whn nt clr run over 2f out: rdn to ld 1f out: r.o* **13/2**

550 **2** *1* **Readyforone**[34] 1223 2-8-6 .... (b) StephenDonohoe(5) 7 56
(P D Evans) *led: rdn 2f out: hdd 1f out: kpt on* **10/3**[2]

0 **3** *4* **Lansdown**[48] 968 2-8-6 .... FergusSweeney 3 39
(M Meade) *prom: lost pl 4f out: rallied 3f out: one pce fnl 2f* **12/1**

0356 **4** *4* **Afric Star**[33] 1229 2-8-6 .... NickyMackay 1 27
(P D Evans) *hld up: hdwy 4f out: rdn and ev ch whn edgd rt over 2f out: wknd over 1f out* **5/1**

010 **5** *¾* **Alittleriskie (IRE)**[37] 1142 2-8-11 .... LPKeniry 2 30
(J S Moore) *prom: rdn and ev ch over 2f out: wknd over 1f out* **9/2**[3]

00 **6** *17* **Lenard Frank (IRE)**[34] 1223 2-8-11 .... (v[1]) DaneO'Neill 4 —
(M D I Usher) *prom: rdn 3f out: sn wknd* **22/1**

004 **7** *4* **Catweasel**[5] 1862 2-8-8 .... (vt[1]) RobertMiles(3) 8 —
(W G M Turner) *swvd bdly lft s: rdn 4f out: a bhd* **11/4**[1]

1m 17.69s (5.29) **Going Correction** +0.725s/f (Yiel) 7 Ran SP% **110.0**
Speed ratings (Par 91):93,91,86,81,80 57,52
CSF £26.14 TOTE £7.10: £2.50, £1.90; EX 33.90 Trifecta £149.00 Pool: £495.48 - 2.36 winning tickets..The winner was bought-in for 5,500gns.
Owner G S Tuck **Bred** G S Tuck **Trained** Sigwells, Somerset

FOCUS
Pretty average form for the grade, rated through the runner-up.

NOTEBOOK
Mollyanko was all the better for her debut just two days earlier. Hanging left throughout, she was slightly hampered at the two pole by a rival on her outer and, once switched, drifted right over towards the far rail. Running on at the same time, she collared the leader on the opposite flank with a furlong to run. (op 15-2)
Readyforone was smartly away and tried to make all against the stands' rail, but could not hold off the winner who was racing on the opposite flank. He saw out the extra furlong and his turn should come in this grade. (op 3-1)
Lansdown saw out this longer trip and if anything might need further still. (op 10-1)
Afric Star, a stablemate of the runner-up, did not see out the six furlongs in this heavy ground. (op 8-1)
Alittleriskie(IRE), penalised for her fortunate victory at Warwick, is probably happiest over the minimum trip. (tchd 4-1)
Catweasel, in a first-time visor, lost his chance at the start, but he still should have finished closer than he did. He is one to be wary of. (op 5-2 tchd 3-1)

2065 PRINCIPALITY BUILDING SERVICES H'CAP 1m 14y
3:30 (3:30) (Class 5) (0-70,70) 3-Y-O **£3,562** (£1,059; £529; £264) **Stalls High**

Form RPR

0000 **1** **The Great Delaney**[54] 887 3-8-4 **56** oh18.......... FrancisFerris 1 62
(K McAuliffe) *a.p: rdn 4f out: hung lft and led 2f out: sn edgd rt: r.o* **150/1**

0302 **2** *1* **Mucho Loco (IRE)**[11] 1799 3-8-8 **60**.......... (b[1]) NickyMackay 4 64
(J G Portman) *hld up towards rr: hdwy 3f out: rdn and ev ch over 1f out: nt qckn ins fnl f* **11/1**

0046 **3** *3* **Mull Of Dubai**[11] 1801 3-8-6 **58**.......... LPKeniry 7 56
(J S Moore) *hld up in tch: rdn 3f out: kpt on ins fnl f* **7/1**[3]

4453 **4** *¾* **Merchant Bankes**[43] 1034 3-8-11 **70**.......... RichardGordon(7) 15 67
(W G M Turner) *led: rdn and hdd 2f out: sn btn* **10/1**

0020 **5** *½* **Orphina (IRE)**[30] 1291 3-8-10 **67**.......... EmmettStack(5) 2 63
(Pat Eddery) *hld up and bhd: rdn and hdwy 3f out: one pce fnl 2f* **16/1**

0340 **6** *1 ½* **Zed Candy (FR)**[37] 1139 3-8-10 **67**.......... RoryMoore(5) 9 60
(J T Stimpson) *s.i.s: sn chsng ldrs: rdn over 3f out: no hdwy fnl 2f* **25/1**

0060 **7** *3* **Dancing Melody**[14] 1738 3-8-5 **57**.......... RichardThomas 8 44
(J A Geake) *t.k.h: prom tl wknd over 2f out* **16/1**

0000 **8** *½* **Bon Viveur**[17] 1642 3-9-2 **68**.......... DaneO'Neill 10 54
(R Hannon) *hld up in tch: rdn and wknd over 2f out* **13/2**[2]

6304 **9** *shd* **Noble Nova**[4] 1950 3-8-1 **56** oh1.......... EdwardCreighton(3) 14 41
(M R Channon) *nvr trbld ldrs* **14/1**

0000 **10** *3* **Desert Sea (IRE)**[30] 1291 3-8-12 **64**.......... TedDurcan 12 43
(C Tinkler) *nvr nr ldrs* **33/1**

3302 **11** *1* **Cantabilly (IRE)**[9] 1851 3-9-4 **70**.......... TQuinn 6 47
(M R Channon) *hld up and bhd: hdwy over 3f out: wknd over 2f out* **9/4**[1]

0000 **12** *11* **Thomas A Beckett (IRE)**[26] 1416 3-8-8 **60**.......... J-PGuillambert 3 15
(P R Chamings) *prom: rdn over 3f out: sn wknd* **50/1**

0000 **13** *1 ¾* **Montzando**[11] 1801 3-8-11 **63**.......... FergusSweeney 5 15
(B R Millman) *dwlt: hld up: hdwy over 3f out: wknd over 2f out* **14/1**

006 **14** *10* **Levin (IRE)**[17] 1641 3-8-9 **61**.......... EddieAhern 13 —
(J L Dunlop) *bhd fnl 4f* **12/1**

4040 **15** *4* **Eclipse Park**[21] 1543 3-9-2 **68**.......... FrankieMcDonald 11 —
(M J McGrath) *prom 4f* **50/1**

1m 40.34s (4.34) **Going Correction** +0.725s/f (Yiel) 15 Ran SP% **118.2**
Speed ratings (Par 99):107,106,103,102,101 100,97,96,96,93 92,81,79,69,65
CSF £1353.43 CT £12834.39 TOTE £115.80: £24.10, £2.10, £3.00; EX 855.20 TRIFECTA Not won..
Owner Alan Smith **Bred** Mrs L A Sadler **Trained** Fernham, Oxon

FOCUS
The breeze was drying the ground, which was officially changed before this race. A decent winning time for the type of race, 1.34 seconds faster than the earlier all-aged maiden, and it is doubtful if the winner is flattered by this shock victory. The form seems sound enough.
The Great Delaney Official explanation: trainer had no explanation for the improved form shown
Dancing Melody Official explanation: jockey said filly ran too free
Noble Nova Official explanation: jockey said filly was unsuited by the soft (heavy in places) ground
Cantabilly(IRE) Official explanation: jockey said colt ran flat and race may have come too soon
Levin(IRE) Official explanation: jockey said gelding lost its action

2066 REDBRIDGE MANAGEMENT SERVICES MAIDEN STKS 1m 4f 23y
4:05 (4:06) (Class 5) 3-Y-O **£3,368** (£1,002; £500; £250) **Stalls Low**

Form RPR

6 **1** **Mount Kilimanjaro (IRE)**[38] 1120 3-9-3 .... TQuinn 1 89+
(J L Dunlop) *hld up: rdn and hdwy 8f out: led over 2f out: sn edgd lft: styd on wl* **7/4**[2]

002 **2** *7* **Vehari**[53] 894 3-9-3 64.......... FergusSweeney 3 66
(M Scudamore) *hld up: sn in rr: sme hdwy over 5f out: rdn over 4f out: styd on fnl f: tk 2nd cl home: no ch w wnr* **25/1**

00 **3** *½* **Picacho (IRE)**[220] 6007 3-8-12 .... TedDurcan 5 60
(J L Dunlop) *hld up: hdwy over 5f out: rdn and outpcd 3f out: styd on fnl f* **16/1**

6342 **4** *½* **Strategic Mount**[21] 1543 3-9-3 76.......... EddieAhern 2 65
(P F I Cole) *a.p: ev ch over 2f out: sn rdn and swtchd rt: wknd fnl f* **6/4**[1]

2422 **5** *½* **Katchit (IRE)**[7] 1880 3-9-0 78.......... EdwardCreighton(3) 6 64
(M R Channon) *t.k.h: led after 1f: rdn and hdd over 2f out: wknd fnl f* **7/2**[3]

00 **6** *70* **Benjum**[198] 6334 3-9-3 .... LPKeniry 4 —
(B I Case) *led 1f: lost pl 8f out: t.o fnl 5f* **50/1**

00 **7** *73* **Kirkstall Lane**[10] 1823 3-9-3 .... DaneO'Neill 7 —
(R Hannon) *sn prom: rdn and wknd over 5f out: sn t.o* **50/1**

2m 50.62s (11.90) **Going Correction** +1.00s/f (Soft) 7 Ran SP% **112.2**
Speed ratings (Par 99):100,95,95,94,94 47,—
CSF £39.49 TOTE £2.60: £1.60, £4.40; EX 43.60.
Owner L Neil Jones **Bred** Abergwaun Farms **Trained** Arundel, W Sussex

FOCUS
An ordinary maiden. The winner can prove a fair bit better than the bare figures although he beat little in the end with the fourth and fifth over a stone off form.
Strategic Mount Official explanation: vet said colt lost an off-fore shoe and was sore

2067 EUROPEAN BREEDERS FUND FILLIES' H'CAP 1m 4f 23y
4:40 (4:40) (Class 4) (0-80,73) 4-Y-O+ **£6,477** (£1,927; £963; £481) **Stalls Low**

Form RPR

0262 **1** **Sabbiosa (IRE)**[12] 1772 4-8-12 **67**.......... TQuinn 1 80+
(J L Dunlop) *hld up: hdwy 3f out: shkn up to ld over 1f out: easily* **7/2**[2]

0104 **2** *3 ½* **Desert Island Disc**[5] 1931 9-8-10 **72**.......... SladeO'Hara(7) 4 76
(Dr J R J Naylor) *hld up: hdwy on ins over 4f out: led wl over 2f out tl over 1f out: one pce* **7/1**

5020 **3** *16* **Spectral Star**[36] 1162 4-9-3 **72**.......... OscarUrbina 5 54
(J R Fanshawe) *prom: led over 3f out tl wl over 2f out: wknd over 1f out* **11/1**

0012 **4** *14* **Maystock**[11] 1800 6-9-2 **71**.......... TedDurcan 3 33
(B G Powell) *sn chsng ldr: rdn over 3f out: wknd over 2f out* **9/2**[3]

4 **5** *12* **Trompette (USA)**[11] 1800 4-9-4 **73**.......... EddieAhern 6 18
(N J Henderson) *hld up and bhd: hdwy over 5f out: wknd over 2f out* **6/4**[1]

0050 **6** *12* **Uig**[17] 1638 5-9-1 **70**.......... DaneO'Neill 2 —
(H S Howe) *led tl over 3f out: sn wknd* **9/1**

2m 49.74s (11.02) **Going Correction** +1.00s/f (Soft) 6 Ran SP% **111.2**
Speed ratings (Par 102):103,100,90,80,72 64
CSF £26.43 TOTE £4.50: £2.30, £3.00; EX 32.70.
Owner N C Clark (Susan Abbott Racing) **Bred** Mrs Phyllis Macferran **Trained** Arundel, W Sussex

FOCUS
This was run at a sound pace and only two of the field got home in the ground. The winner is rated value for 6l and the runner-up ran to form, but this was pretty weak overall.
Maystock Official explanation: trainer said mare ran flat

2068 ROTARY INTERNATIONAL FILLIES' STKS (H'CAP) 6f 16y
5:10 (5:11) (Class 5) (0-70,70) 3-Y-O **£3,886** (£1,156; £577; £288) **Stalls High**

Form RPR

6354 **1** **Orange Dancer (IRE)**[46] 1004 3-8-11 **68**.......... TravisBlock(5) 6 73
(H Morrison) *a.p: rdn 3f out: r.o to ld cl home* **10/3**[2]

0006 **2** *shd* **Mannello**[20] 1567 3-8-4 **56** oh6.......... FrancisFerris 3 61
(B Palling) *a.p: led 3f out: hrd rdn and hdd cl home* **10/1**

0003 **3** *1 ½* **Wizby**[20] 1567 3-8-4 **56** oh4.......... (t) NickyMackay 2 56
(P D Evans) *s.i.s: hdwy over 2f out: r.o ins fnl f* **7/2**[3]

0000 **4** *5* **Just Down The Road (IRE)**[20] 1567 3-8-5 **57**.......... LPKeniry 8 42
(R A Harris) *prom: n.m.r over 2f out: swtchd lft wl over 1f out: one pce* **16/1**

6401 **5** *1 ¾* **La Fanciulla**[11] 1799 3-8-13 **65**.......... DaneO'Neill 1 45
(R Hannon) *bhd: sme late prog: n.d* **11/4**[1]

1630 **6** *shd* **The City Kid (IRE)**[11] 1799 3-8-13 **70**.......... (v) StephenDonohoe(5) 4 49
(P D Evans) *led 3f: wknd over 1f out* **15/2**

0006 **7** *2* **The Lady Caster**[97] 477 3-8-5 **57** oh1 ow1.......... EddieAhern 7 30
(R M Beckett) *plld hrd: wnt lft and hdwy over 4f out: rdn 3f out: wknd fnl f* **16/1**

3660 **8** *1 ½* **Baytown Lulu**[297] 4125 3-7-13 **56** oh1.......... EmmettStack(5) 10 25
(H S Howe) *prom: rdn over 2f out: sn wknd* **33/1**

0060 **9** *5* **Vixen Virago**[231] 5796 3-7-13 **56** oh7.......... MarcHalford(5) 5 10
(Jane Southcombe) *prom: rdn over 3f out: sn hung lft and wknd* **33/1**

1m 17.34s (4.94) **Going Correction** +0.725s/f (Yiel) 9 Ran SP% **110.5**
Speed ratings (Par 96):96,95,93,87,84 84,82,80,73
CSF £33.89 CT £116.11 TOTE £4.20: £1.60, £2.10, £1.70; EX 35.80 Trifecta £228.30 Pool: £321.55. 0.54 winning tickets. Place 6 £212.88, Place 5 £138.52.
Owner Mrs B Oppenheimer **Bred** Mrs B D Oppenheimer **Trained** East Ilsley, Berks

FOCUS
A modest handicap, run in a poor time and rated through the third. Questionable form with the second and third out of the handicap.
T/Plt: £489.80 to a £1 stake. Pool: £50,800.50. 75.70 winning tickets. T/Qpdt: £56.70 to a £1 stake. Pool: £3,211.80. 41.90 winning tickets. KH

1284 LEICESTER (R-H)
Monday, May 29

OFFICIAL GOING: Good to soft (soft in places)
Wind: Fresh, behind Weather: Sunshine and showers

2069 TOTEPLACEPOT MEDIAN AUCTION MAIDEN STKS 1m 60y
2:00 (2:07) (Class 5) 3-Y-O **£4,533** (£1,348; £674; £336) **Stalls High**

Form RPR

2 **1** **Don Pietro**[17] 1641 3-9-3 .... JimmyFortune 8 76+
(D J Coakley) *mde all: shkn up over 1f out: r.o: eased nr fin* **11/2**[3]

3440 **2** *2* **Bahhmirage (IRE)**[17] 1650 3-8-12 50.......... (b) SteveDrowne 4 65
(Stef Liddiard) *hmpd s: hld up in tch: rdn to chse wnr over 1f out: styd on same pce ins fnl f* **25/1**

40 **3** *3* **Ravish**[298] 4093 3-8-12 .... (t) MichaelHills 3 59+
(W J Haggas) *hld up: hdwy over 2f out: sn rdn: styd on same pce appr fnl f* **6/1**

4340 **4** *5* **Forroger (CAN)**[9] 1841 3-9-3 76.......... DO'Donohoe 1 54
(V Smith) *hld up: hdwy over 4f out: rdn 2f out: nt run on* **7/4**[1]

0320 **5** *5* **Ollie George (IRE)**[55] 880 3-9-3 75.......... JimmyQuinn 2 43
(A M Balding) *chsd ldrs over 5f* **7/1**

4430 **6** *6* **Power Broker**[55] 720 3-9-0 78.......... (t) NelsonDeSouza(3) 6 30
(P F I Cole) *wnt lft s: trckd wnr: plld hrd: rdn over 2f out: wknd over 1f out* **7/2**[2]

5000 **7** *12* **Under Fire (IRE)**[28] 1352 3-9-3 48.......... RobbieFitzpatrick 7 5
(A W Carroll) *plld hrd: trckd ldrs: rdn and wknd over 3f out* **125/1**

1m 50.42s (5.12) **Going Correction** +0.65s/f (Yiel) 7 Ran SP% **105.4**
Speed ratings (Par 99):100,98,95,90,85 79,67
CSF £98.35 TOTE £5.30: £2.30, £10.90; EX 51.60.

Owner Pedro Rosas **Bred** B N And Mrs Toye **Trained** West Ilsley, Berks
FOCUS
A weak maiden, run at an average pace, and the field came home strung out. The form is worth treating with caution.

2070 TOTECOURSE TO COURSE (S) STKS 1m 1f 218y
2:35 (2:35) (Class 5) 3-5-Y-O **£3,238** (£963; £481; £240) **Stalls** High

Form RPR
0060 **1** **Shaika**[27] 1387 3-7-9 45 LiamJones(7) 13 53
(G Prodromou) *hld up: swtchd lft and hdwy over 3f out: rdn to ld over 1f out: hung rt: r.o* **28/1**
0060 **2** *nk* **Broughton Buzzer**[223] 5960 5-8-13 45 NeilChalmers(3) 9 54
(A G Newcombe) *hld up: hdwy over 3f out: led wl over 1f out: sn hdd: r.o* **8/1**[3]
4000 **3** *4* **Coffin Dodger**[10] 1829 3-7-9 41 KirstyMilczarek(7) 2 44
(C N Allen) *s.i.s: hdwy 8f out: chsd ldr over 6f out: led over 2f out: rdn and hdd wl over 1f out: no ex fnl f* **12/1**
0542 **4** *nk* **Miss Monica (IRE)**[13] 1755 5-9-2 46 DarrenWilliams 14 46
(P W Hiatt) *s.i.s: hld up: hmpd over 3f out: hdwy u.p over 2f out: hung rt fr over 1f out: nt run on* **3/1**[1]
0005 **5** *1 ¾* **Guadiana (GER)**[13] 1767 4-9-2 37 JimmyFortune 4 43
(A W Carroll) *hld up: hdwy u.p over 2f out: styd on same pce appr fnl f* **9/1**
0000 **6** *2* **Moonlight (GER)**[21] 1552 3-8-4 47 ow2 AlanDaly 1 39
(Dr J R J Naylor) *plld hrd: trckd ldr 3f: rdn 2f out: wknd fnl f* **16/1**
0600 **7** *11* **Lanfredo**[14] 1738 3-8-8 57 ow1 (b[1]) SteveDrowne 8 22
(D W P Arbuthnot) *s.i.s: hld up: rdn over 4f out: n.d* **8/1**[3]
0000 **8** *1 ½* **Tonight (IRE)**[34] 1225 4-9-7 36 RobbieFitzpatrick 15 20
(W M Brisbourne) *mid-div: rdn over 3f out: wknd over 2f out* **66/1**
0000 **9** *½* **Mytass**[34] 1221 3-8-2 45 (b) AndrewElliott(5) 6 17
(J A Pickering) *led: rdn and hdd over 2f out: wknd over 1f out* **20/1**
006 **10** *7* **Marvin Gardens**[62] 776 3-8-7 45 BrianReilly 12 4
(P S McEntee) *mid-div: swtchd lft and hdwy over 2f out: sn rdn and wknd* **50/1**
0000 **11** *1* **Duxford**[14] 1745 5-9-7 48 (p) JimmyQuinn 11 4
(D K Ivory) *mid-div: lost pl and dropped rr after 2f: n.d after* **10/1**
0000 **12** *1* **Age Of Kings (USA)**[31] 1271 4-9-7 55 SamHitchcott 10 2
(A B Haynes) *prom over 7f: eased over 1f out* **6/1**[2]
0004 **13** *9* **Angel River**[14] 1727 4-8-9 39 DonnaCaldwell(7) 7 —
(J Ryan) *mid-div: hdwy 1/2-way: wknd over 2f out* **20/1**
U **Lucy Babe** 3-7-9 LukeMorris(7) 5 —
(G Prodromou) *wnt lft and uns rdr leaving stalls* **18/1**

2m 13.08s (4.78) **Going Correction** +0.65s/f (Yiel)
WFA 3 from 4yo+ 14lb **14** Ran SP% **115.9**
Speed ratings (Par 103):106,105,102,102,100 99,90,89,88,83 82,81,74,—
CSF £221.04 TOTE £40.30: £8.20, £4.30, £3.80; EX 324.60.There was no bid for the winner.
Owner Faisal Al-Nassar **Bred** Ellis Stud Partnership **Trained** East Harling, Norfolk
■ Stewards' Enquiry : Liam Jones one-day ban: careless riding (Jun 9)
FOCUS
A dire event, run at a solid gallop, and it suited those coming from off the pace. The first two came clear of the third, who anchors the form.
Duxford Official explanation: jockey said gelding moved badly
Age Of Kings(USA) Official explanation: jockey said gelding moved badly

2071 TOTEQUADPOT FILLIES' H'CAP 1m 60y
3:10 (3:10) (Class 4) (0-85,82) 4-Y-O+ **£7,478** (£2,239; £1,119; £560; £279) **Stalls** High

Form RPR
0001 **1** **Imperialistic (IRE)**[2] 2017 5-9-2 82 5ex AndrewElliott(5) 5 97+
(K R Burke) *hld up in tch: racd keenly: led over 2f out: shkn up over 1f out: r.o strly* **5/6**[1]
1506 **2** *6* **Danehill Dazzler (IRE)**[36] 1162 4-8-12 78 GregFairley(5) 2 80
(Ian Williams) *chsd ldrs: rdn over 1f out: sn outpcd* **10/1**
6000 **3** *nk* **Society Music (IRE)**[21] 1531 4-8-12 73 FergalLynch 3 75
(M Dods) *led: hdd over 6f out: chsd ldr: rdn over 1f out: sn outpcd* **8/1**[3]
4634 **4** *1 ¼* **Rakata (USA)**[11] 1802 4-8-9 70 SteveDrowne 1 69
(P F I Cole) *trckd ldr: plld hrd: led over 6f out: qcknd 3f out: hdd over 2f out: wknd fnl f* **5/2**[2]
5560 **5** *nk* **Gaelic Princess**[119] 252 6-9-4 79 SamHitchcott 4 78
(A G Newcombe) *hld up: rdn over 2f out: nvr trbld ldrs* **20/1**

1m 54.62s (9.32) **Going Correction** +0.65s/f (Yiel) **5** Ran SP% **108.1**
Speed ratings (Par 102):79,73,72,71,71
CSF £9.53 TOTE £1.80: £1.20, £4.10; EX 6.90.
Owner Bigwigs Bloodstock II **Bred** B H Bloodstock **Trained** Middleham Moor, N Yorks
FOCUS
A pedestrian winning time, 4.2 seconds slower than the opening three-year-old maiden, and the in-form winner proved in a different league. The second and third were withing a length of their recent form.

2072 TOTESPORT.COM MEDIAN AUCTION MAIDEN STKS 5f 2y
3:45 (3:47) (Class 5) 2-Y-O **£4,533** (£1,348; £674; £336) **Stalls** Low

Form RPR
4 **1** **Top Bid**[19] 1588 2-9-3 FergalLynch 4 87+
(T D Easterby) *trckd ldrs: led on bit 1/2-way: shkn up and hung lft over 1f out: r.o wl* **4/7**[1]
5 **2** *8* **Kaladar (IRE)**[24] 1454 2-9-3 DO'Donohoe 6 58
(K A Ryan) *chsd ldrs: chal 1/2-way: outpcd fr over 1f out* **10/3**[2]
0 **3** *3* **Abdu**[39] 1096 2-9-3 JimmyQuinn 3 47
(M W Easterby) *prom: racd keenly: lost pl wl over 1f out* **20/1**
0 **4** *shd* **Spirit Rising**[16] 1688 2-9-3 SteveDrowne 5 47
(J M Bradley) *chsd ldrs: rdn 1/2-way: wknd over 1f out* **33/1**
0 **5** *3 ½* **Delta Queen**[19] 1587 2-8-12 RobbieFitzpatrick 7 29
(C N Kellett) *led to 1/2-way: wknd over 1f out* **33/1**
0 **6** *3* **Yve Sam La Champ**[35] 1189 2-9-3 JimmyFortune 2 23
(A W Carroll) *s.i.s: outpcd* **22/1**
U **Kaptain Kate** 2-8-12 SamHitchcott 1 —
(R Brotherton) *dwlt: wnt rt sn after s and uns rdr* **16/1**[3]

64.70 secs (3.80) **Going Correction** +0.65s/f (Yiel) **7** Ran SP% **107.6**
Speed ratings (Par 93):95,82,77,77,71 66,—
CSF £2.06 TOTE £1.50: £1.40, £1.30; EX 2.20.
Owner John & Marilyn Williams **Bred** Southill Stud **Trained** Great Habton, N Yorks
FOCUS
No strength in depth to this maiden, but the winner was impressive and should rate higher.
NOTEBOOK
Top Bid ◆, fourth at Newcastle on his debut, came home as he pleased to break his duck and proved in a different class to his rivals. He had no trouble with this drop in trip and, while this form may prove just ordinary in time, it was hard not to be very impressed with this display. (op 4-6)
Kaladar(IRE), very easy to back, seemed to appreciate the easy ground, but could not live with the winner over this trip and clearly wants a stiffer test. (op 5-2)
Abdu spoilt his chances by racing too freely through the first half of the race and looks in need of more time. Official explanation: jockey said bit came through gelding's mouth (op 22-1 tchd 25-1)
Spirit Rising, who failed to beat a rival on his debut at Warwick last time, broke better yet still had his limitations firmly exposed. (op 25-1)

2073 TOTESPORT 0800 221 221 CLAIMING STKS 5f 2y
4:20 (4:21) (Class 5) 2-Y-O **£4,416** (£1,321; £660; £330; £164) **Stalls** Low

Form RPR
1321 **1** **Granny Peel (IRE)**[14] 1744 2-8-8 DO'Donohoe 6 63
(K A Ryan) *chsd ldrs: led over 3f out: r.o* **4/5**[1]
2 *2 ½* **Meru Camp (IRE)** 2-8-8 ow1 SteveDrowne 2 54
(P Winkworth) *a.p: chsd wnr fnl f: styd on same pce* **5/1**[3]
23U **3** *1 ½* **Go On Jessica (IRE)**[16] 1682 2-8-5 AdamKirby(3) 5 49
(A G Juckes) *a.p: chsd wnr 1/2-way: rdn over 1f out: no ex* **11/4**[2]
60 **4** *2 ½* **Baytown Rosie (IRE)**[6] 1922 2-7-5 LukeMorris(7) 3 30
(P S McEntee) *chsd ldrs: rdn 1/2-way: hung rt and wknd over 1f out* **33/1**
0 **5** *2 ½* **Job Done**[37] 1142 2-8-6 JimmyQuinn 1 29
(M W Easterby) *s.i.s: hld up in tch: hung rt thrght: wknd over 1f out* **28/1**
000 **6** *5* **Sainara (IRE)**[17] 1647 2-7-7 ow2 LiamJones(7) 7 5
(J M Bradley) *led: hdd over 3f out: wknd 2f out* **50/1**
7 *1* **Providence Farm** 2-8-3 ow3 SaleemGolam(3) 4 7
(M W Easterby) *s.s: outpcd* **14/1**

65.62 secs (4.72) **Going Correction** +0.65s/f (Yiel) **7** Ran SP% **113.9**
Speed ratings (Par 93):88,84,81,77,73 65,64
CSF £5.31 TOTE £1.60: £1.10, £3.40; EX 6.10.Meru Camp was the subject of a friendly claim.
Owner J Hopkinson and R Peel **Bred** Tally-Ho Stud **Trained** Hambleton, N Yorks
FOCUS
A moderate contest which saw the field come home in indian file behind the consistent Granny Peel, who ran to her improved turf form.
NOTEBOOK
Granny Peel(IRE) followed up her recent Wolverhampton success in this class with another decisive success under a positive ride. She is a very consistent performer at this level, has been very well placed to date by her shrewd trainer, and evidently all ground seems to come alike. (op 8-11)
Meru Camp(IRE), making his debut at a lowly level, was put in his place by the winner, but kept on nicely enough inside the final furlong to finish a clear second-best. He really ought to build on this and go one better in a similar event. (op 6-1)
Go On Jessica(IRE), well backed on this debut for new connections, was not disgraced on her Thirsk form with the winner at the weights. She did not appear overly suited by the easy ground, however. (op 10-3 tchd 7-2)
Baytown Rosie(IRE), making her turf debut, was another who did not look all that suited by the easy surface and was well beaten off. (op 22-1)

2074 TOTEEXACTA H'CAP 5f 218y
4:50 (4:51) (Class 5) (0-75,76) 4-Y-O+ **£5,362** (£1,604; £802; £401; £199) **Stalls** Low

Form RPR
0401 **1** **Balakiref**[2] 2027 7-8-11 73 LiamJones(7) 13 85
(M Dods) *hld up: hdwy over 2f out: led over 1f out: r.o* **3/1**[1]
2030 **2** *½* **Hits Only Cash**[9] 1846 4-8-11 66 JimmyQuinn 12 76
(J Pearce) *outpcd: hdwy over 1f out: r.o* **20/1**
0010 **3** *1 ½* **Dunn Deal (IRE)**[7] 1878 6-9-1 70 RobbieFitzpatrick 5 76
(W M Brisbourne) *dwlt: hld up: hdwy over 2f out: nt clr run and swtchd lft over 1f out: r.o* **22/1**
1600 **4** *1 ¼* **Cool Sands (IRE)**[2] 2020 4-7-13 59 (v) AndrewElliott(5) 9 61
(D Shaw) *chsd ldrs: led 2f out: sn rdn: hung lft and hdd: no ex ins fnl f* **33/1**
0000 **5** *1* **Sabrina Brown**[30] 1285 5-9-3 72 (t) SteveDrowne 7 71
(J A Geake) *chsd ldrs: rdn over 1f out: no ex ins fnl f* **10/1**
2000 **6** *1* **My Only Sunshine**[42] 1047 7-8-7 67 ow1 DerekNolan(5) 10 63
(M J Wallace) *chsd ldrs: rdn over 1f out: styd on same pce* **16/1**
5320 **7** *1 ¼* **Yorkie**[21] 1528 7-8-4 59 oh1 DO'Donohoe 8 51
(J Pearce) *outpcd hdwy over 1f out: nvr trbld ldrs* **28/1**
0002 **8** *nk* **Distant Times**[11] 1795 5-8-11 66 (b) FergalLynch 3 57
(T D Easterby) *mid-div: rdn over 3f out: hung lft over 1f out: hung rt ins fnl f: n.d* **8/1**
0510 **9** *5* **Calabaza**[244] 5532 4-8-11 69 (b) SaleemGolam(3) 2 45
(W Jarvis) *plld hrd: trckd ldr: led 1/2-way: hdd 2f out: sn rdn and wknd* **50/1**
0033 **10** *7* **Chinalea (IRE)**[23] 1474 4-9-0 72 (t) AdamKirby(3) 11 27
(C G Cox) *hdwy over 4f out: rdn and wknd over 1f out* **5/1**[3]
4063 **11** *1 ½* **Roman Quintet (IRE)**[21] 1545 6-9-3 72 JimmyFortune 1 23
(D W P Arbuthnot) *led to 1/2-way: wknd wl over 1f out* **9/2**[2]
5001 **12** *7* **Digital**[7] 1878 9-9-7 76 7ex SamHitchcott 4 6
(M R Channon) *hmpd sn after s: outpcd* **13/2**

1m 16.73s (3.53) **Going Correction** +0.65s/f (Yiel) **12** Ran SP% **116.7**
Speed ratings (Par 103):102,101,99,97,96 95,93,92,86,76 74,65
CSF £70.54 CT £1137.77 TOTE £3.70: £1.50, £5.10, £5.50; EX 81.50.
Owner Septimus Racing Group **Bred** S R Hope And D Erwin **Trained** Denton, Co Durham
FOCUS
A modest sprint, run at a sound pace, and the field came home fairly strung out. The form is ordinary but looks quite sound.
Chinalea(IRE) Official explanation: jockey said gelding ran flat

2075 TOTESPORTCASINO.COM APPRENTICE H'CAP 1m 3f 183y
5:20 (5:20) (Class 6) (0-60,60) 4-Y-O+ **£3,154** (£944; £472; £236; £117) **Stalls** High

Form RPR
4302 **1** **Sovietta (IRE)**[7] 1879 5-8-8 52 (t) JamesMillman(3) 13 61
(A G Newcombe) *s.s: hld up: hdwy over 3f out: led 1f out: r.o* **6/1**[3]
0645 **2** *nk* **Star Rising**[21] 1537 4-8-7 48 JamieJones 12 57
(W J Musson) *hld up: hdwy 1/2-way: led over 2f out: hung lft and hdd 1f out: r.o* **16/1**
0603 **3** *5* **General Flumpa**[48] 973 5-8-9 57 JonjoMilczarek(7) 3 58
(C F Wall) *hld up: hdwy over 3f out: rdn and ev ch over 1f out: no ex ins fnl f* **13/2**
5465 **4** *¾* **Royal Flynn**[13] 1756 4-9-2 60 TolleyDean(3) 4 60
(M Dods) *hld up: hdwy over 3f out: rdn over 1f out: styd on same pce* **8/1**
4124 **5** *1* **Wood Fern (UAE)**[24] 1467 6-8-5 46 oh1 LiamJones 2 44
(W M Brisbourne) *hld up: hdwy over 3f out: rdn over 1f out: styd on same pce* **8/1**
0660 **6** *½* **Pitsi Kahtoh**[13] 1767 4-8-0 46 oh16 LukeMorris(5) 15 43?
(P W Hiatt) *chsd ldrs: led 3f out: sn edgd rt and hdd: rdn and wknd fnl f* **100/1**
0025 **7** *nk* **Archie Babe (IRE)**[9] 1590 10-8-11 52 DerekNolan 14 49
(J J Quinn) *chsd ldrs: rdn over 2f out: weakened over 1f out* **5/1**[1]

6630 **8** 2 ½ **Ulshaw**[21] 1540 9-7-13 **47** oh10 ow1 .... BarrySavage(7) 8 40
(J M Bradley) *chsd ldrs: rdn over 2f out: sn wknd* **33/1**

0220 **9** ½ **Robbie Can Can**[26] 1415 7-8-8 **56** .... JackDean(7) 1 48
(A W Carroll) *dwlt: bhd and raced wd for 5f: nvr nrr* **11/2**[2]

0600 **10** 5 **Sharp N Frosty**[275] 3081 4-8-7 **53** .... MarkCoumbe(5) 9 37
(W M Brisbourne) *hld up: hung lft over 4f out: n.d* **40/1**

0046 **11** 6 **Gawrosz (POL)**[13] 1766 7-8-0 **46** oh6 .... JamieHamblett(5) 7 21
(G J Smith) *chsd ldrs 9f* **66/1**

3036 **12** 3 **Ego Trip**[13] 1756 5-8-12 **58** .... (b) AdeleRothery(5) 11 28
(M W Easterby) *led: rdn and hdd 3f out: sn hmpd and wknd* **15/2**

3400 **13** 6 **Padre Nostro (IRE)**[9] 1850 7-8-8 **54** .... ChrisGlenister(5) 6 14
(J R Holt) *prom: hmpd and lost pl over 9f out: hdwy 1/2-way: wknd 3f out* **33/1**

1210 **14** 24 **Zoripp (IRE)**[19] 1590 4-8-13 **54** .... (b) AndrewElliott 5 —
(J G Given) *hld up in tch: lost pl 1/2-way: sn bhd* **16/1**

000 **15** 12 **Eathie**[16] 1684 4-8-12 **53** .... KevinGhunowa 10 —
(M J Attwater) *hld up in tch: rdn and wknd over 3f out* **40/1**

2m 41.41s (6.91) **Going Correction** +0.65s/f (Yiel) **15** Ran SP% **118.7**
Speed ratings (Par 101):102,101,98,97,97 96,96,95,94,91 87,85,81,65,57
CSF £91.61 CT £649.83 TOTE £6.80: £2.10, £5.30, £2.70; EX 102.30 Place 6 £207.38, Place 5 £22.47 .
Owner S F Turton **Bred** Lawn Stud **Trained** Yarnscombe, Devon

FOCUS
A modest apprentice handicap, run at a sound pace, and the first two came clear. With the sixth home over a stone out of the handicap, the form looks far from solid.
Sharp N Frosty Official explanation: jockey said gelding hung left
Gawrosz(POL) Official explanation: jockey said gelding failed to handle the bend
Zoripp(IRE) Official explanation: jockey said gelding found very little extra when coming off the bridle

T/Plt: £378.80 to a £1 stake. Pool: £46,757.25. 90.10 winning tickets. T/Qpdt: £5.60 to a £1 stake. Pool: £3,167.30. 415.50 winning tickets. CR

1730 REDCAR (L-H)
Monday, May 29

OFFICIAL GOING: Good
Wind: Strong, against

2076 HARRY RUDLAND MEMORIAL NOVICE AUCTION STKS 5f
2:05 (2:06) (Class 5) 2-Y-O **£3,238** (£963; £481; £240) **Stalls** High

Form RPR

3 **1** **Steelcut**[17] 1632 2-8-9 .... PaulHanagan 10 86+
(R A Fahey) *trckd ldrs:hdwy over 2f out: rdn to ld and edgd lft over 1f out: styd on wl* **9/2**[2]

1 **2** 3 **Fathom Five (IRE)**[7] 1884 2-8-13 .... TonyCulhane 7 79+
(B Smart) *trckd ldrs: hdwy to ld briefly wl over 1f out: sn hdd and kpt on same pce u.p ins last* **11/4**[1]

120 **3** 2 ½ **No Worries Yet (IRE)**[14] 1737 2-8-6 .... FrancisNorton 1 63
(J L Spearing) *c lose up: rdn along 2f out: drvn and one pcefr over 1f out* **7/1**

215 **4** nk **Hill Of Lujain**[12] 1780 2-8-13 .... DaleGibson 4 69
(M W Easterby) *dwlt and bhd: hdwy 1/2-way: rdn and kpt on fnl f* **14/1**

02 **5** nk **Nota Liberata**[7] 1884 2-8-9 .... ShaneKelly 3 64
(G M Moore) *in tch: pushed along over 2f out: sn rdn and kpt on fnl f* **16/1**

05 **6** 1 **First Valentini**[9] 1853 2-8-2 .... RoystonFfrench 9 53
(N Bycroft) *a midfield* **100/1**

61 **7** 1 ½ **Major Third (IRE)**[25] 1442 2-9-1 .... KDarley 8 61
(T D Easterby) *led: rdn along 2f out: sn hdd & wknd* **12/1**

4 **8** 1 ¼ **Sweet Candy**[7] 1884 2-8-7 .... NCallan 2 49
(K A Ryan) *cl up: rdn along over 2f out: sn wknd* **5/1**[3]

3 **9** ¾ **Bijouterie**[17] 1647 2-8-5 ow1 .... RobertWinston 5 44
(G A Swinbank) *s.i.s and wnt lft s: a rr* **11/2**

10 ½ **Dispol Moonlight (IRE)** 2-8-7 .... PhillipMakin 6 44
(T D Barron) *a towards rr: rdn along and outpcd fr 1/2-way* **25/1**

60.68 secs (1.98) **Going Correction** +0.375s/f (Good) **10** Ran SP% **114.5**
Speed ratings (Par 93):99,94,90,89,89 87,85,83,82,81
CSF £16.90 TOTE £6.00: £2.20, £1.20, £2.80; EX 19.40.
Owner A Rhodes Haulage And P Timmins **Bred** Mrs B Skinner **Trained** Musley Bank, N Yorks

FOCUS
A good pace for this novice event which was dominated by the front two in the market. A decent winning time for a race like this and the winner especially looks a decent prospect.

NOTEBOOK
Steelcut ◆, who looked as though he would benefit from his debut effort, duly did so and despite edging to his left throughout the last furlong, he showed a decent turn of speed to pull away from his rivals. He has a speedy pedigree and looks potentially a nice sprinter in the making. (op 4-1)
Fathom Five(IRE) did not lose ground at the start this time and kept going all the way to the line. He was totally blitzed by the winner for finishing speed, but still beat the others hollow and there will be other days. (op 10-3 tchd 7-2)
No Worries Yet(IRE), well beaten on very fast ground at Windsor last time, ran much better back on this easier surface but found the two more-progressive colts far too good. Given her liking for cut in the ground, her best chance of winning again may be in autumn nurseries. (op 8-1)
Hill Of Lujain was the only one to make up any significant ground from off the pace and looks badly in need of further. (op 12-1)
Nota Liberata did best of the maidens, but he finished a neck behind Fathom Five at Musselburgh last time and finished much further behind him on this occasion despite meeting him on 6lb better terms. (op 14-1)
Sweet Candy, who started favourite to beat both Fathom Five and Nota Liberata on her Musselburgh debut, finished behind them then and did so again which suggests she is not as good as might have been expected. (op 9-2)
Bijouterie was disappointing in view of her promising debut, but basically lost all chance at the start.

2077 RACING UK CHANNEL 432 (S) STKS 7f
2:40 (2:41) (Class 6) 3-5-Y-O **£2,730** (£806; £403) **Stalls** High

Form RPR

606 **1** **Chateau (IRE)**[18] 1609 4-9-7 58 .... NCallan 17 63
(G A Swinbank) *hld up: hdwy 1/2-way: swtchd rt and rdn to ld over 1f out: drvn out* **9/1**

0425 **2** ¾ **Green Pirate**[16] 1683 4-9-7 53 .... RobertWinston 15 61
(R Craggs) *hld up in tch: hdwy over 2f out: swtchd rt and rdn to chal ent last: ev ch tl drvn and no ex last 100 yds* **9/2**[1]

0642 **3** 4 **Drum Dance (IRE)**[11] 1791 4-9-7 49 .... KimTinkler 8 51
(N Tinkler) *keen: trckd ldrs: hdwy over 2f out: rdn and ev ch over 1f out: drvn and wknd ins last* **8/1**

0000 **4** ¾ **Spring Time Girl**[13] 1757 4-9-2 43 .... (v[1]) TomEaves 10 44
(B Ellison) *bhd: hdwy over 2f out: swityched rt and rdn over 1f out: styd on strly ins last: nrst fin* **14/1**

6000 **5** 1 **Hamaasy**[55] 864 5-9-7 49 .... AdrianTNicholls 11 46
(D Nicholls) *led: rdn along over 2f out: drvn and hdd over 1f out: sn wknd* **9/1**

0656 **6** 1 ¼ **Ming Vase**[13] 1765 4-9-4 42 .... DanielTudhope(3) 5 43
(P T Midgley) *chsd ldrs: rdn along 2f out: drvn and wknd appr last* **14/1**

35 **7** 1 **Diamond Winnie**[19] 1594 3-8-6 ow1 .... DarryllHolland 9 36
(Mrs A Duffield) *keen: hld up: hdwy over 2f out: rdn to chse ldrs over 1f out: sn drvn and no imp* **5/1**[2]

0225 **8** 2 ½ **Desert Lightning (IRE)**[25] 1447 4-9-0 55 .... PatrickDonaghy(7) 6 34
(K R Burke) *cl up: rdn along 2f out: grad wknd* **5/1**[2]

6000 **9** 1 ¾ **Hilversum**[63] 771 4-8-9 40 .... (p) DawnRankin(7) 4 24
(Miss J A Camacho) *in tch: effrt and sme hdwy over 2f out: sn rdn and btn* **33/1**

000 **10** nk **Signor Albertini (IRE)**[276] 4713 3-8-5 35 .... LeanneKershaw(5) 3 28
(P C Haslam) *racd wd: nvr bttr than midfield* **100/1**

0400 **11** shd **Paris Heights**[16] 1665 4-9-0 52 .... MichaelJStainton(7) 12 28
(R M Whitaker) *chsd ldrs: rdn along wl over 2f out: sn wknd* **7/1**[3]

-000 **12** 5 **Apetite**[11] 1791 4-9-0 45 .... (b) SuzzanneFrance(7) 2 15
(N Bycroft) *a rr* **66/1**

00 **13** 2 **Sun Of The Glen (IRE)**[76] 634 4-8-13 .... BenSwarbrick(3) 14 5
(B D Leavy) *a rr* **100/1**

060- **14** 10 **Svenson**[591] 6200 5-9-4 28 .... JasonEdmunds(3) 7 —
(J S Wainwright) *in tch: rdn along 1/2-way: sn wknd* **100/1**

0000 **15** 20 **Cuccinello (IRE)**[11] 1792 3-8-0 30 .... DuranFentiman(5) 16 —
(K W Hogg) *dwlt: sn prom: rdn along 1/2-way and sn wknd* **100/1**

1m 27.22s (2.32) **Going Correction** +0.375s/f (Good)
WFA 3 from 4yo+ 11lb **15** Ran SP% **116.9**
Speed ratings (Par 101):101,100,95,94,93 92,91,88,86,85 85,79,77,66,43
CSF £47.02 TOTE £11.60: £3.10, £1.80, £3.00; EX 58.40.There was no bid for the winner. Green Pirate was claimed by J. Babb for £6,000.
Owner Arnie Flower Anna Noble E Todhunter **Bred** Sean Collins **Trained** Melsonby, N Yorks

FOCUS
An ordinary seller, but the big field at least ensured the pace was solid and the front pair pulled a long way clear of the others.

2078 TOTEPOOL "A BETTER WAY TO BET" H'CAP 1m 6f 19y
3:15 (3:15) (Class 5) (0-75,75) 4-Y-0+ **£3,238** (£963; £481; £240) **Stalls** Low

Form RPR

4004 **1** **Haatmey**[22] 1502 4-9-1 **69** .... TonyCulhane 4 75
(M R Channon) *trckd ldrs: hdwy over 3f out: rdn along 2f out: led over 1f out: drvn ins last and styd on gamely* **10/1**

1005 **2** hd **Cripsey Brook**[9] 1847 8-9-0 **75** .... JamesReveley(7) 2 81
(K G Reveley) *hld up in midfield: hdwy over 3f out: effrt and ev ch over 1f out: sn rdn and no ex wl ins last* **16/1**

4032 **3** 1 ½ **Caymans Gift**[19] 1590 6-7-13 **58** oh1 ow2 .... AndrewMullen(5) 6 62
(A C Whillans) *hld up in rr: hdwy 4f out: rdn and ev ch over 1f out: drvn and one pce ins last* **8/1**

3000 **4** ½ **Let It Be**[13] 1756 5-8-5 **59** .... KDarley 10 62
(K G Reveley) *hld up: hdwy on outer over 3f out: rdn 2f out and ev ch tl drvn and one pce ent last* **7/1**[3]

0045 **5** ½ **Mr Majestic**[28] 1346 4-8-2 **56** .... HayleyTurner 12 58
(R M Whitaker) *prom: rdn to ld wl over 2f out: drvn and hdd over 1f out: kpt on same pce* **20/1**

145- **6** 1 **Pay Attention**[38] 5145 5-8-4 **63** .... DuranFentiman(5) 7 64
(T D Easterby) *in tch: effrt over 3f out and sn pouched along: rdn 2f out and sn one pce* **5/1**[2]

1666 **7** ¾ **John Forbes**[16] 1660 4-9-4 **72** .... TomEaves 3 72
(B Ellison) *hld up and bhd tl styd on fnl 2f* **16/1**

6013 **8** 3 ½ **Whoopsie**[16] 1660 4-8-2 **56** oh2 .... PaulHanagan 5 51
(S Parr) *prom: chsd ldr fr 1/2-way: rdn along over 3f out: wknd fnl 2f* **8/1**

2200 **9** 8 **Spanish Ridge (IRE)**[16] 1685 4-9-6 **74** .... NCallan 11 58
(J L Dunlop) *hld up in rr: hdwy on outer over 3f out: rdiden along 2f out: sn drvn and wknd* **14/1**

031 **10** 10 **You Too**[381] 1676 4-9-4 **72** .... RoystonFfrench 9 42
(M Johnston) *led: rdn along 4f out: drvn 3f out: sn hdd and grad wknd* **12/1**

0040 **11** 20 **Fardi (IRE)**[7] 1887 4-8-3 **60** ow1 .... BenSwarbrick(3) 8 2
(K W Hogg) *chsd ldrs: rdn along over 3f out: sn wknd* **100/1**

6332 **12** 1 ¾ **Shamrock Bay**[9] 1847 4-8-9 **63** .... RobertWinston 1 2
(C R Dore) *hld up: a rr: eased fnl 2f* **4/1**[1]

3m 5.76s (0.74) **Going Correction** +0.10s/f (Good) **12** Ran SP% **112.4**
Speed ratings (Par 103):101,100,100,99,99 98,98,96,91,86 74,73
CSF £151.25 CT £1332.98 TOTE £12.00: £3.00, £4.80, £3.00; EX 147.70.
Owner M Channon **Bred** Darley **Trained** West Ilsley, Berks
■ Stewards' Enquiry : Tony Culhane one-day ban: used whip with excessive frequency (Jun 9)

FOCUS
A fairly competitive handicap, but the pace was only ordinary and there were virtually six in a line across the track passing the furlong pole. Modest form but sound enough.
Shamrock Bay Official explanation: trainer said filly was found to be coughing post-race

2079 TOTESPORT ZETLAND GOLD CUP (HERITAGE H'CAP) 1m 2f
3:50 (3:50) (Class 2) (0-105,101) 3-Y-0+**£32,385** (£9,635; £4,815; £2,405) **Stalls** Low

Form RPR

3132 **1** **Chantaco (USA)**[23] 1484 4-9-0 **91** .... MartinDwyer 16 100
(A M Balding) *hld up in midfield: hdwy 3f out: rdn over 1f out: styd on to ld last 100 yds* **4/1**[1]

0500 **2** ½ **Ace Of Hearts**[16] 1678 7-9-10 **101** .... GeorgeBaker 6 109
(C F Wall) *trckd ldrs: hdwy 2f out: rdn over 1f out: drvn to ld and edgd lft ins last: hdd and nt qckn last 100 yds* **16/1**

6010 **3** hd **Active Asset (IRE)**[3] 1992 4-8-1 **78** .... ChrisCatlin 12 86+
(M R Channon) *hld up towards rr: hdwy 3f out: rdn over 1f out: fin wl* **25/1**

4100 **4** ½ **El Coto**[37] 1129 6-9-1 **92** .... NCallan 4 99
(K A Ryan) *hld up: hdwy 3f out: rdn and squeezed through over 1f out: drvn and kpt on ins last* **20/1**

0311 **5** ½ **Dancing Lyra**[59] 815 5-8-5 **82** .... PaulHanagan 9 90+
(R A Fahey) *in tch: hdwy 4f out: led over 2f out: sn rdn and edgd lft: drvn and hdd ins last: wkng whn hmpd towards fin* **6/1**[2]

6540 **6** shd **Bravo Maestro (USA)**[16] 1678 5-8-8 **90** .... JamesDoyle(5) 5 96
(N P Littmoden) *hld up and bhd: hdwy 3f out: rdn wl over 1f out: styd on fnl f* **33/1**

1004 **7** hd **Ofaraby**[19] 1585 6-9-8 **99** .... KDarley 11 105
(M A Jarvis) *hld up towards rr: hdwy 3f out: rdn wl over 1f out: kpt on ins last: nrst fin* **8/1**[3]

3012 **8** ½ **Goodbye Mr Bond**[3] [1985] 6-8-9 **86** 6ex........................ FrancisNorton 2 95+
(E J Alston) *hld up: hdwy on inner whn nt clr run over 1f out: swtchd rt and sn rdn: styd on strly ins last: nrst fin* **6/1**[2]

0000 **9** 1 ¼ **Artistic Style**[19] [1585] 6-9-1 **92**.. TomEaves 14 94
(B Ellison) *hld up in rr tl styd on fnl 2f* **25/1**

0150 **10** ½ **Group Captain**[12] [1779] 4-8-12 **89**.............................. DarryllHolland 17 90
(R Charlton) *in tch: hdsway 3f out: rdn and ev ch 2f out: sn drvn and no ex ent last* **8/1**[3]

3435 **11** 1 ¼ **Best Prospect (IRE)**[238] [5660] 4-8-5 **82**........................... DaleGibson 1 81+
(M Dods) *prom: effrt 3f out: rdn along 2f out: wkng whn hmpd over 1f out* **12/1**

0506 **12** ¾ **Go Tech**[12] [1775] 6-8-9 **86**.. RichardMullen 15 83
(T D Easterby) *hld up and towards rr tl styd on fnl 2f* **28/1**

0120 **13** ¾ **Sharp Reply (USA)**[30] [1281] 4-8-3 **80**........................... JamieMackay 13 76
(R M Whitaker) *chsd ldrs: rdn along on outer over 3f out: grad wknd* **25/1**

0060 **14** ½ **Crow Wood**[23] [1484] 7-9-2 **96**.. DNolan(3) 10 91
(J J Quinn) *a towards rr* **20/1**

6200 **15** ¾ **Magic Sting**[42] [1051] 5-8-1 **78**.. HayleyTurner 7 72
(M L W Bell) *chsd ldr: hdwy to ld over 3f out: sn rdn: hdd over 2f out and wkng whn bmpd wl over 1f out* **25/1**

46-0 **16** 3 ½ **Bustan (IRE)**[121] [222] 7-9-4 **95**.................................... RobertWinston 3 89+
(G C Bravery) *trckd ldrs: hdwy to chse ldr 3f out: sn rdn to chal: drvn and wkng whn hmpd over 1f out and sn eased* **33/1**

-410 **17** 20 **Seyaadi**[12] [1779] 4-8-0 **82**...(v) AndrewMullen(5) 8 31
(Robert Gray) *led: rdn along 4f out: hdd 3f out and sn wknd* **66/1**

2m 5.19s (-1.61) **Going Correction** +0.10s/f (Good) **17** Ran SP% **120.1**
Speed ratings (Par 109):110,109,109,109,108 108,108,108,107,106 105,105,104,104,103 100,84
CSF £58.81 CT £1435.64 TOTE £4.20: £1.80, £3.60, £5.30, £3.30; EX 77.40 Trifecta £1109.80 Part won. Pool: £1,563.20 - 0.10 winning tickets..
Owner The Pink Hat Racing Partnership **Bred** London Thoroughbred Services **Trained** Kingsclere, Hants
■ Stewards' Enquiry : George Baker two-day ban: careless riding (Jun 9-10)

FOCUS
An ultra-competitive handicap run at a strong pace, but the leaders may have gone off too quick as those that were up with the pace early all finished in the rear. Inevitably this was also a rough race and one or two met serious interference. With most of the first eight running to form this looks solid.

NOTEBOOK
Chantaco(USA), so unlucky in both his outings so far this season, had nonetheless still crept up the handicap but this was his day as the gaps appeared just when he needed them. He had to battle hard to take full advantage, but showed the right resolution to gain what was undoubtedly a richly deserved success. He is incredibly consistent, acts on any ground, and looks well capable of adding to this. (tchd 9-2)
Ace Of Hearts, still 5lb higher than for his last win, seemed to have been produced at just the right time only to have the favourite snatch the race from him near the line. This was a cracking effort over the trip under top weight and on ground that may not have been quite fast enough for him. (op 14-1)
Active Asset(IRE) got the strong pace he needs, but his strong late finish was a few strides too late. His style of running does rely on luck, but he is capable of winning a contest like this provided the race is run to suit.
El Coto ◆, trying this trip for only the third time in his life and the first time in two and a half years, was another doing his best work late. He is well worth another try over the distance and has become well handicapped.
Dancing Lyra, bidding for a hat-trick after his two heavy-ground victories this year, hit the front passing the two-furlong pole but he could never get away from his rivals and had been passed when completely running out of room near the line. He could probably have done without the ground starting to dry out.
Bravo Maestro(USA), yet to win on turf, had to be switched wide in order to get a run after running into a bit of a pocket, but stayed on well once in the clear without quite managing to get on terms with the principals. Official explanation: jockey said gelding was denied a clear run
Ofaraby had every chance, but lacked a vital turn of foot and would have preferred it had the ground stayed genuinely soft. (op 9-1)
Goodbye Mr Bond ◆, held up for a late run, endured an absolute nightmare of a passage down the home straight and did extremely well to reach his final position. He remains in good form. Official explanation: jockey said gelding was denied a clear run
Group Captain Official explanation: jockey said gelding was unsuited by the good ground

2080 LESTER PIGGOTT MEDIAN AUCTION MAIDEN STKS 6f
4:25 (4:25) (Class 5) 3-Y-O **£3,238** (£963; £481; £240) **Stalls** High

Form RPR

25 **1** **River Kirov (IRE)**[42] [1048] 3-9-3................................. AdrianMcCarthy 1 68+
(P W Chapple-Hyam) *trckd ldrs: hdwy 1/2-way: rdn 2f out: led wl over 1f out: styd on ins last* **4/7**[1]

2 ¾ **Advancement** 3-9-3.. PaulHanagan 9 63+
(R A Fahey) *sn pushed along in rr: hdwy 2f out: sn rdn and styd on wl fnl f* **15/2**[2]

3 1 ¼ **Libor (IRE)** 3-8-10.. HeatherMcGee(7) 3 60
(L M Cumani) *trckd ldrs on outer: rdn along over 2f out: kpt on same pce appr last* **8/1**[3]

0 **4** hd **Mandarin Lady**[75] [645] 3-8-12.. TomEaves 4 54
(Miss J A Camacho) *towards rr: hdwy over 2f out: styd on ins last: nrst fin* **25/1**

00 **5** ½ **Azerley (IRE)**[16] [1684] 3-8-12.. FrancisNorton 5 53
(J D Bethell) *chsd ldrs: rdn along over 2f out: kpt on same pce* **66/1**

4500 **6** 1 ½ **Just Tallulah**[17] [1642] 3-8-7 55.................................. JamesDoyle(5) 6 48
(N P Littmoden) *chsd ldrs: rdn along 2f out: drvn and one pce appr last* **14/1**

000 **7** 2 **Grand Parrot**[10] [1818] 3-9-3 60.. NCallan 7 47
(W De Best-Turner) *led: rdn along over 2f out: hdd & wknd wl over 1f out* **20/1**

8 ¾ **Lillie Lou** 3-8-7.. DuranFentiman(5) 8 40
(T D Easterby) *in tch: rdn along wl over 2f out: sn wknd* **12/1**

0 **9** shd **Mister Jingles**[39] [1101] 3-9-3....................................... TonyCulhane 2 44
(R M Whitaker) *rr fr 1/2-way* **40/1**

1m 14.53s (2.83) **Going Correction** +0.375s/f (Good) **9** Ran SP% **113.4**
Speed ratings (Par 99):96,95,93,93,92 90,87,86,86
CSF £4.81 TOTE £1.60: £1.10, £1.90, £2.30; EX 5.00.
Owner R J Arculli and B Vuchot **Bred** Kildaragh Stud **Trained** Newmarket, Suffolk

FOCUS
A weak maiden run at just a fair pace, and rated through the sixth. A few of these may have a future once handicapped.
Mister Jingles Official explanation: jockey said gelding hung left-handed

2081 TOTESPORT 0800 221 221 H'CAP 1m 3f
4:55 (4:55) (Class 4) (0-85,84) 3-Y-O **£6,477** (£1,927; £963; £481) **Stalls** Low

Form RPR

1140 **1** **Prince Charlemagne (IRE)**[9] [1841] 3-8-13 **80**............ JamesDoyle(5) 4 87
(N P Littmoden) *hld up in rr: smooth hdwy over 3f out: led wl over 1f out: kpt on ins last* **9/2**

4300 **2** 1 ½ **Nesno (USA)**[38] [1108] 3-8-11 **73**... KDarley 6 78
(J D Bethell) *trckd ldrs: hdwy on outer to ld over 2f out: sn rdn and hdd wl over 1f out: kpt on u.p fnl f* **8/1**

2222 **3** 1 ¼ **Dream Champion**[22] [1503] 3-8-13 **75**.......................... TonyCulhane 1 78
(M R Channon) *trckd ldng pair: effrt 3f out: sn rdn and kpt on same pce fnl 2f* **4/1**[3]

2241 **4** 3 **Macorville (USA)**[8] [1868] 3-9-8 **84** 6ex......................... ShaneKelly 2 82
(G M Moore) *led: rdn along over 3f out: hdd over 2f out and grad wknd* **9/4**[1]

431 **5** 6 **Spanish Lace**[122] [215] 3-8-11 **73**...................................... TomEaves 3 62
(Miss J A Camacho) *cl up: rdn along over 3f out: drvn and wknd fnl 2f* **7/2**[2]

0036 **6** hd **Boquilobo**[43] [1034] 3-8-13 **75**.................................. RoystonFfrench 5 63
(M Johnston) *chsd ldrs: rdn along over 3f out: sn btn* **12/1**

2m 21.46s (0.46) **Going Correction** +0.10s/f (Good) **6** Ran SP% **110.0**
Speed ratings (Par 101):102,100,100,97,93 93
CSF £36.28 TOTE £6.10: £2.60, £4.50; EX 59.10.
Owner Neil Ryan **Bred** Michael O'Mahony **Trained** Newmarket, Suffolk

FOCUS
A fair pace for this handicap despite the small field and the form looks solid enough, if only ordinary.

2082 "COME RACING AT REDCAR TOMORROW!" MAIDEN H'CAP 1m 6f 19y
5:25 (5:25) (Class 6) (0-65,65) 3-Y-O **£2,730** (£806; £403) **Stalls** Low

Form RPR

006 **1** **Call Me George**[18] [1613] 3-9-0 **58**............................... RoystonFfrench 16 67
(M Johnston) *chsd ldrs: shkn up and hdwy over 3f out: rdn to ld and hung lft 2f out: sn drvn: wandered and styd on ins last* **33/1**

4453 **2** 3 **Wise Choice**[17] [1648] 3-8-5 **54**...................................... JamesDoyle(5) 2 59
(N P Littmoden) *led: rdn along 3f out: hdd and bmpd 2f out: sn drvn and one pce fnl f* **7/1**

0464 **3** 1 ¼ **Impeccable Guest (IRE)**[9] [1859] 3-8-7 **56**........... LeanneKershaw(5) 15 59
(P C Haslam) *hld up: hdwy on outer over 3f out: rdn to chse ldng pair wl over 1f out: sn drvn and no imp* **14/1**

006 **4** 1 ½ **Gala Casino King (IRE)**[28] [1343] 3-9-1 **59**...................... PhillipMakin 3 60
(M Dods) *trckd ldrs: hdwy 3f out: sn rdn and kpt on same pce fnl 2f* **50/1**

0004 **5** 1 **Rehearsed (IRE)**[21] [1543] 3-9-6 **64**............................... RobertHavlin 14 64
(H Morrison) *towards rr: hdwy over 3f out: sn rdn along and styd on fnl 2f: nrst fin* **7/1**

0005 **6** ½ **Rivetting**[21] [1533] 3-8-4 **48**... JamieMackay 13 47
(Sir Mark Prescott) *hld up in tch: hdwy over 3f out: sn rdn along and no imp fnl 2f* **9/2**[2]

050 **7** 1 ½ **Hurry Up Helen (IRE)**[30] [1283] 3-9-1 **59**........................... TomEaves 11 56
(Mrs L Stubbs) *towards rr tl sme late hdwy* **12/1**

6603 **8** ½ **Rebelling (IRE)**[10] [1837] 3-9-7 **65**................................. StephenCarson 1 61
(R F Johnson Houghton) *in tch: hdwy to chse ldrs over 4f out: rdn along 3f out and grad wknd* **6/1**[3]

000 **9** ½ **El Faro (FR)**[22] [1516] 3-9-7 **65**.. TonyCulhane 9 61
(M R Channon) *chsd ldr: rdn along over 4f out and sn wknd* **25/1**

000 **10** 2 **Jack Absolute (IRE)**[21] [1546] 3-9-6 **64**...................... MichaelTebbutt 12 57
(B J Meehan) *hld up: a towards rr* **25/1**

060 **11** nk **Peas 'n Beans (IRE)**[229] [5832] 3-9-1 **59**........................ HayleyTurner 7 51
(M L W Bell) *trckd ldrs: hdwy to chse ldr 4f out: rdn along over 3f out and sn wknd* **20/1**

600 **12** 5 **Gettysburg (IRE)**[259] [5184] 3-8-6 **50**.............................. DarryllHolland 10 35
(J Howard Johnson) *hld up: hdwy on outer and in tch over 5f out: rdn along and wknd over 3f out* **25/1**

0605 **13** 7 **Persian Conqueror (IRE)**[37] [1140] 3-8-6 **50**.......................... NCallan 5 26+
(J L Dunlop) *hld up: a towards rr* **11/4**[1]

650 **14** 2 **Little Eyecatcher (IRE)**[13] [1759] 3-8-9 **58**................ DuranFentiman(5) 6 31
(T D Easterby) *a rr* **50/1**

0045 **15** 7 **El Dee (IRE)**[34] [1221] 3-8-3 **47**...................................... PaulHanagan 8 10
(D Carroll) *a rr* **12/1**

3m 8.39s (3.37) **Going Correction** +0.10s/f (Good) **15** Ran SP% **129.3**
Speed ratings (Par 97):94,92,91,90,90 89,89,88,88,87 87,84,80,79,75
CSF £252.59 CT £3439.25 TOTE £31.00: £7.50, £2.60, £4.20; EX 235.40 Place 6 £396.98, Place 5 £245.37.
Owner Jumeirah Racing **Bred** Exors Of The Late Gerald W Leigh **Trained** Middleham Moor, N Yorks
■ Stewards' Enquiry : Royston Ffrench two-day ban: used whip with excessive frequency (Jun 9-10)

FOCUS
A moderate race run at a modest pace and the winning time was 2.63 seconds slower than the earlier handicap over the same trip. The form is modest but sound enough.
Call Me George Official explanation: trainer's rep said, regarding the improved form shown, the colt may have benefited from the step up in trip
Jack Absolute(IRE) Official explanation: jockey said, regarding the running and riding, his orders were to ride gelding in a handy position but he encountered traffic problems mid-race and so was further back than he wanted, adding that gelding subsequently stayed on one pace; trainer's rep added the ground was probably too fast
Gettysburg(IRE) Official explanation: jockey said gelding hung left throughout
Persian Conqueror(IRE) Official explanation: trainer's rep said gelding was unsuited by the good ground
T/Jkpt: Not won. T/Plt: £316.90 to a £1 stake. Pool: £63,229.35. 145.65 winning tickets. T/Qpdt: £73.20 to a £1 stake. Pool: £2,751.30. 27.80 winning tickets. JR

1299 SANDOWN (R-H)
Monday, May 29
OFFICIAL GOING: Sprint course - heavy; round course - soft (heavy in places)
Wind: Strong, against Weather: Overcast

2083 WBX.COM WORLD BET EXCHANGE EBF MAIDEN FILLIES' STKS 5f 6y
2:15 (2:17) (Class 5) 2-Y-O **£3,886** (£1,156; £577; £288) **Stalls** High

Form RPR

44 **1** **Christmas Tart (IRE)**[10] [1817] 2-9-0.................................... LDettori 1 72+
(V Smith) *lw: trckd ldr after 2f: shkn up to ld over 1f out: drew clr ins fnl f* **4/9**[1]

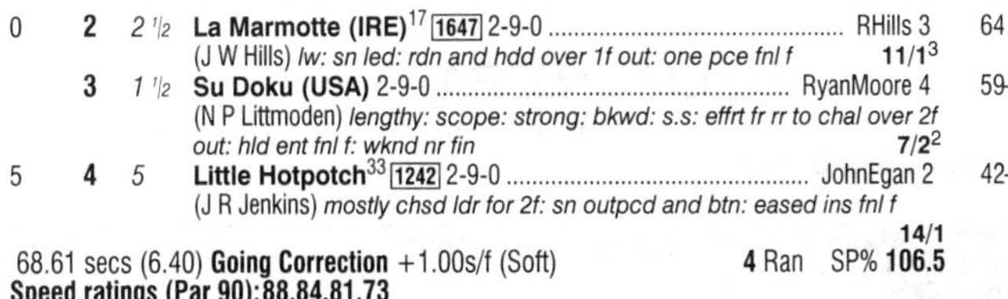

0 **2** 2 ½ **La Marmotte (IRE)**[17] 1647 2-9-0 ..... RHills 3 64
(J W Hills) *lw: sn led: rdn and hdd over 1f out: one pce fnl f* **11/1**[3]

3 1 ½ **Su Doku (USA)** 2-9-0 ..... RyanMoore 4 59+
(N P Littmoden) *lengthy: scope: strong: bkwd: s.s: effrt fr rr to chal over 2f out: hld ent fnl f: wknd nr fin* **7/2**[2]

5 **4** 5 **Little Hotpotch**[33] 1242 2-9-0 ..... JohnEgan 2 42+
(J R Jenkins) *mostly chsd ldr for 2f: sn outpcd and btn: eased ins fnl f* **14/1**

68.61 secs (6.40) **Going Correction** +1.00s/f (Soft) 4 Ran SP% **106.5**
Speed ratings (Par 90):88,84,81,73
CSF £5.70 TOTE £1.40; EX 3.90.
Owner Stephen Dartnell **Bred** T F Moorhead **Trained** Exning, Suffolk

FOCUS
A weak fillies' maiden with just the four runners. Christmas Tart was the form pick and won pretty much as expected.

NOTEBOOK
Christmas Tart(IRE) only had three rivals and confirmed the promise she showed on her two previous starts to gain a straightforward success. She is likely to find things tougher from now on, especially as the Queen Mary Stakes is said to be her next target.. (op 4-7 tchd 8-13 in places)
La Marmotte(IRE), down the field in just an ordinary maiden at Nottingham on her debut, seemed to step up on that form despite having got loose twice in the preliminaries. However, she had the run of the race out in front and connections will do well to find such an uncompetitive event next time. (op 10-1 tchd 12-1)
Su Doku(USA), a 50,000gns purchase, out of a triple sprint winner at three in the US, started slowly and was only able to produce a short-lived effort. She very much gave the impression she will show improved form on better ground, and she ought to get a little further in time. (op 5-2)
Little Hotpotch, last of five on her debut at Kempton, again failed to beat a rival and may either need more time, or dropping in grade. (op 16-1)

2084 WBX.COM WORLD BET EXCHANGE NATIONAL STKS (LISTED RACE) 5f 6y
2:50 (2:54) (Class 1) 2-Y-O **£13,343** (£5,057; £2,530; £1,261) **Stalls** High

Form RPR
1 **1** **Excellent Art**[39] 1090 2-9-0 ..... LDettori 1 100+
(N A Callaghan) *lw: trckd ldr: led over 1f out: sn wl clr: eased fnl 100yds* **8/13**[1]

12 **2** 9 **Cav Okay (IRE)**[19] 1582 2-9-0 ..... RichardHughes 4 67
(R Hannon) *lw: fast away: led: rdn and hdd over 1f out: no ch w wnr after: jst hld on for 2nd* **13/8**[2]

3 shd **Dress To Impress (IRE)** 2-9-0 ..... KerrinMcEvoy 3 67
(J R Boyle) *strong: lw: in tch in last pair: rdn and wl outpcd over 1f out: plugged on* **40/1**

2154 **4** 1 **Urban Warrior**[3] 1998 2-9-0 ..... JohnEgan 2 64
(J R Best) *lw: dwlt: in tch in last pair: rdn and wl outpcd over 1f out: no ch after* **16/1**[3]

66.49 secs (4.28) **Going Correction** +1.00s/f (Soft) 4 Ran SP% **108.3**
Speed ratings (Par 101):105,90,90,88
CSF £1.86 TOTE £1.70; EX 2.20.
Owner Matthew Green **Bred** Cheveley Park Stud Ltd **Trained** Newmarket, Suffolk

FOCUS
A very poor turnout for this year's Listed National Stakes, but the winning time was fair, 2.12 seconds quicker than the opener. Cav Okay again failed to build on the promise he showed when bolting up on his debut, perhaps this time failing to act on the ground, so Excellent Art only had the newcomer Dress To Impress and the exposed Urban Warrior to beat, and he came home alone.

NOTEBOOK
Excellent Art ◆ had next to nothing to beat with Cav Okay faltering on the testing ground and confirmed the good impression he made when winning on his debut at Newmarket with an effortless success. This was as 'soft' a Listed race as you are likely to see, but he could not have won any easier and will be worth maximum respect when faced with tougher opposition. Connections suggested afterwards he could be turned out quickly in the Woodcote Stakes on Derby day, but were not so keen on the Coventry Stakes if the ground is riding very fast. (tchd 1-2 and 4-6 in places)
Cav Okay(IRE), an impressive winner on his debut at Newbury before failing to produce his best when taken on for the lead in the Lily Agnes at Chester, got his own way this time but is basically all speed and was unable to go with a horse of Excellent Art's class on ground this testing. (tchd 2-1)
Dress To Impress(IRE) ◆, a 30,000euros first foal of a five-furlong juvenile winner, was making his debut in this company because the race had cut up so badly. Still, he showed plenty of ability, despite racing keenly, and is open to plenty of improvement. He is probably worth keeping in mind. (op 33-1)
Urban Warrior, just as in a conditions race at Pontefract three days previously, was totally outclassed. This was his seventh start of the season already. (op 20-1 tchd 22-1)

2085 WBX.COM WORLD BET EXCHANGE HENRY II STKS (GROUP 2) 2m 78y
3:25 (3:25) (Class 1) 4-Y-O+
£51,102 (£19,368; £9,693; £4,833; £2,421; £1,215)

Form RPR
1022 **1** **Tungsten Strike (USA)**[26] 1409 5-9-2 106 ..... RyanMoore 4 114
(Mrs A J Perrett) *lw: trckd ldr: led main gp over to nr side in st: drvn clr fr over 1f out* **4/1**[3]

0050 **2** 5 **Winged D'Argent (IRE)**[10] 1833 5-9-2 106 ..... JoeFanning 6 108
(M Johnston) *settled in 4th: rdn over 4f out: kpt on u.p to take 2nd nr fin* **12/1**

1-30 **3** ½ **Barolo**[347] 2633 7-9-2 109 ..... SebSanders 2 107
(W R Swinburn) *trckd ldng pair: chsd wnr on nr side in st: rdn and no imp 2f out: one pce and lost 2nd nr fin* **12/1**

5416 **4** 1 ¼ **Art Eyes (USA)**[226] 5905 4-8-11 105 ..... JohnEgan 7 103
(D R C Elsworth) *led: styd alone far side in st: nt on terms w wnr fr over 1f out* **8/1**

4322 **5** 3 **Vinando**[19] 1584 5-9-2 101 ..... (bt) LDettori 1 102
(C R Egerton) *lw: hld up in 6th: rdn over 4f out: struggling and btn over 2f out* **10/3**[2]

0415 **6** ¾ **Mubtaker (USA)**[17] 1628 9-9-2 115 ..... RHills 3 101
(M P Tregoning) *settled in 5th: rdn and effrt 3f out: no prog 2f out: wknd over 1f out* **6/1**

4011 **7** 11 **Cover Up (IRE)**[26] 1409 9-9-2 108 ..... KFallon 5 88
(Sir Michael Stoute) *lw: a last and nvr gng wl: struggling fr 3f out* **11/4**[1]

3m 45.55s (7.32) **Going Correction** +0.725s/f (Yiel)
WFA 4 from 5yo+ 2lb 7 Ran SP% **110.5**
Speed ratings (Par 115):110,107,107,106,105 104,99
CSF £45.21 TOTE £5.30: £1.90, £4.60; EX 62.60.
Owner John Connolly **Bred** Minster Stud **Trained** Pulborough, W Sussex

FOCUS
Hardly any of these were capable of producing their best on the testing ground, and this did not look a very good renewal of the Henry II Stakes, although the form does make sense. All bar Art Eyes came stands' side in the straight.

NOTEBOOK
Tungsten Strike(USA), a head second to Cover Up in the Sagaro Stakes at Lingfield on his previous start, handled the soft ground best of all and won decisively under a good ride from Ryan Moore, who made a bold bid for the stands'-side rail in the straight and never looked back. This was his first success in Group company, and he is clearly developing into a very smart stayer but, while this division seems to lack the strength of previous years, he will still find things tougher in his next intended target, the Ascot Gold Cup. (tchd 9-2)
Winged D'Argent(IRE) bounced back from an abysmal effort in the Yorkshire Cup on his previous start, but got going too late and may benefit from a return to more positive tactics. (tchd 14-1)
Barolo, tenth in the Gold Cup at York when last seen nearly a year ago, returned to action with a pleasing effort, looking second best until tiring near the finish. He would probably not have minded the ground as much as some of these, but this was still encouraging and he can do better.
Art Eyes(USA), faced with a stiff task on her return from a 226-day break, ran a cracker considering she raced alone on the far side of the track in the straight, the only one to do so all afternoon. There is no better trainer of stayers than David Elsworth, and this filly could well progress. (op 10-1)
Vinando, second in the Chester Cup on his reappearance, should not have minded the ground but was a major disappointment. (op 7-2 tchd 4-1 in places)
Mubtaker(USA), who won the John Porter on his reappearance before running no sort of race in the Ormonde Stakes, was again below form. Despite having run well on easy ground in the Arc in 2003, he appreciates a fast surface and the ground was totally against him for his first run over two miles. He can be given another chance. Official explanation: jockey said horse was unsuited by the soft (heavy in places) ground (op 11-2 tchd 5-1 and 13-2 in a place)
Cover Up(IRE) had today's winner a head away in second when winning the Sagaro Stakes at Lingfield on his reappearance, but he never looked happy this time and presumably failed to handle the ground. Official explanation: trainer's rep said gelding was unsuited by the soft (heavy in places) ground (op 2-1 tchd 3-1 in places)

2086 BUTLINS BINGO JACKPOT H'CAP 1m 14y
4:00 (4:00) (Class 3) (0-95,91) 4-Y-O+
£9,348 (£2,799; £1,399; £700; £349; £175) **Stalls** High

Form RPR
0303 **1** **Tanzanite (IRE)**[2] 2011 4-8-13 86 ..... KerrinMcEvoy 8 100
(D W P Arbuthnot) *lw: hld up in 5th: smooth prog 3f out: led 2f out: rdn clr fnl f: r.o wl* **5/1**[2]

1141 **2** 3 ½ **Spectait**[5] 1938 4-9-2 89 5ex ..... SebSanders 3 96
(Sir Mark Prescott) *lw: trckd ldng trio: effrt over 2f out: rdn to chse wnr over 1f out: nt qckn and wl btn fnl f* **8/13**[1]

4500 **3** 1 **Audience**[16] 1678 6-8-13 86 ..... (p) PaulDoe 4 91
(J Akehurst) *lw: s.i.s: hld up in last: prog on outer over 2f out: chsd ldrs over 1f out: kpt on same pce* **9/1**[3]

0660 **4** 1 **Nero's Return (IRE)**[12] 1775 5-8-9 82 ..... JoeFanning 1 85
(M Johnston) *hld up in 6th: rdn over 2f out: kpt on one pce fnl 2f* **20/1**

6250 **5** 3 **Norton (IRE)**[16] 1676 9-9-4 91 ..... IanMongan 5 88
(T G Mills) *led to 3f out: sn rdn: wknd over 1f out* **16/1**

2446 **6** ½ **San Antonio**[35] 1183 6-8-11 84 ..... (b) MickyFenton 7 80
(Mrs P Sly) *trckd ldng pair: chal 3f out: upsides 2f out: wknd* **14/1**

0112 **7** nk **Banknote**[28] 1340 4-9-0 87 ..... LDettori 2 82
(A M Balding) *lw: trckd ldr: led 3f out to 2f out: wknd over 1f out* **12/1**

1m 45.69s (1.74) **Going Correction** +0.425s/f (Yiel) 7 Ran SP% **113.6**
Speed ratings (Par 107):108,104,103,102,99 99,98
CSF £8.34 CT £25.49 TOTE £6.10: £2.50, £1.30; EX 9.60.
Owner D C Broomfield & N Cronin **Bred** Yeomanstown Stud **Trained** Upper Lambourn, Berks

FOCUS
Not that strong a handicap on the ground, but a smart winning time for a race of its grade. The form has been rated through the third, with the winner improving back on soft ground, but the runner-up around 14lb below the form he showed on the AW at Kempton.

NOTEBOOK
Tanzanite(IRE), a proven soft-ground performer, appeared only two days previously at Ascot and it remained to be seen whether she could handle this quick reappearance, but she did well in a busy spell last season and she seems to thrive on racing. Having been restrained in rear early, she made smooth headway before going on, and hot favourite Spectait was unable to match her. Tried unsuccessfully over hurdles in the winter, Flat racing is definitely her game and it would not surprise to see her gain some black type this summer. (op 6-1 tchd 13-2)
Spectait, due to be raised 14lb for a mightily impressive win on his reappearance at Kempton, missed the cut by one in the Victoria Cup at the weekend and was widely expected to gain smooth compensation in what was a lesser race. However, having travelled well into contention and got the gap, he was unable to pick up as well as the winner and flattened out under pressure. This was obviously disappointing. (tchd 4-6 and 8-11 in a place)
Audience, two places ahead of Tanzanite at Newmarket last time, was unable to confirm the form, but hardly did himself any favours with a sluggish start and may have been closer had he been able to get going earlier. He remains on a winnable mark. (tchd 10-1)
Nero's Return(IRE) left behind a poor effort at York and ran well considering he would not have been that happy in the ground. He kept on right the way to the line, and is currently 5lb lower than when last successful.
Norton(IRE) ran well on his reappearance at Newmarket, but he is probably not up to winning decent races off this sort of mark these days. (op 14-1 tchd 12-1)
San Antonio has gone over a year without a win and remains a little high in the weights. (op 16-1)
Banknote, who made a pleasing reappearance at Kempton, would have found this ground too testing and he can safely have the run ignored. Official explanation: jockey said horse was unsuited by the soft (heavy in places) ground (tchd 10-1)

2087 RANGE ROVER H'CAP 7f 16y
4:35 (4:36) (Class 4) (0-80,80) 3-Y-O **£5,505** (£1,637; £818; £408) **Stalls** High

Form RPR
210 **1** **Best Guess (USA)**[226] 5887 3-8-11 73 ..... RyanMoore 2 77+
(P W Chapple-Hyam) *hld up in last: plenty to do whn effrt 2f out: drvn and r.o fr over 1f out: led last strides* **10/1**

111 **2** nk **Moody Tunes**[4] 1950 3-9-0 76 6ex ..... PatCosgrave 1 79
(K R Burke) *lw: trckd ldng pair: rdn to chse ldr over 1f out: kpt on fnl f: upsides nr fin: jst outpcd* **5/6**[1]

0005 **3** shd **Local Fancy**[9] 1843 3-8-13 75 ..... MickyFenton 6 78
(J M P Eustace) *trckd ldng trio: prog to ld 2f out: drvn fnl f: collared last strides* **9/1**[3]

01 **4** 1 **Stanley Goodspeed**[17] 1646 3-8-10 75 ..... DeanCorby(3) 3 76+
(J W Hills) *lw: trckd ldr to 3f out: lost pl: n.m.r 2f out: hung rt over 1f out: rallied and cl up ins fnl f: one pce nr fin* **12/1**

4403 **5** 6 **Bathwick Alice**[16] 1693 3-8-10 72 ..... KerrinMcEvoy 7 58
(B R Millman) *led to 2f out: wknd over 1f out* **10/1**

5645 **6** 8 **Naughty By Nature**[31] 1270 3-8-10 72 ..... (v[1]) KFallon 4 39
(Sir Michael Stoute) *lw: s.i.s: t.k.h: hld up in 6th: shkn up and no rspnse over 2f out: sn bhd* **4/1**[2]

1m 34.24s (3.15) **Going Correction** +0.425s/f (Yiel) 6 Ran SP% **110.4**
Speed ratings (Par 101):99,98,98,97,90 81
CSF £18.45 TOTE £9.80: £3.10, £1.40; EX 21.50.

Owner Fawzi Abdulla Nass **Bred** E P Evans **Trained** Newmarket, Suffolk
FOCUS
A tricky handicap fought out by the 'right' horses. The form seems to be limited by the third and is not that straightforward.

2088 WBX.COM WORLD BET EXCHANGE H'CAP 1m 2f 7y
5:05 (5:06) (Class 5) (0-75,75) 4-Y-0+ **£3,886** (£1,156; £577; £288) **Stalls** High

Form				RPR
6012	**1**		**Summer Charm**[18] 1614 4-8-7 **71** BRoper(7) 10 (W Jarvis) *lw: hld up: last 1/2-way: stdy prog fr 3f out: shuffled along and r.o to ld last 100yds: comf* **14/1**	81
0303	**2**	¾	**South O'The Border**[25] 1435 4-9-3 **74** IanMongan 5 (T G Mills) *lw: prom: trckd ldr 1/2-way: led over 2f out: hrd rdn over 1f out: hdd last 100yds: styd on* **6/1**	83
0U46	**3**	1 ¼	**Dumaran (IRE)**[41] 578 8-9-4 **75** TPQueally 6 (W J Musson) *hld up wl in rr: prog against nr side rail fr over 2f out: drvn and styd on fnl f: nrst fin* **16/1**	82+
/000	**4**	3 ½	**Eldorado**[21] 1544 5-8-12 **69** RHills 8 (S Kirk) *hld up towards rr: prog over 2f out: chsd ldrs over 1f out: outpcd and no imp fnl f* **12/1**	69
3203	**5**	*shd*	**Double Spectre (IRE)**[10] 1821 4-8-10 **67** SebSanders 11 (Jean-Rene Auvray) *lw: hld up in midfield: prog over 3f out: chsd ldr 2f out tl ent fnl f: wknd* **6/1**	67
5600	**6**	3 ½	**African Sahara (USA)**[103] 421 7-8-10 **74** (t) ChrisCavanagh(7) 7 (Miss D Mountain) *lw: hld up wl in rr: stdy prog on outer fr 3f out: pressed ldrs over 1f out: wknd fnl f* **25/1**	68
3000	**7**	3	**Takafu (USA)**[21] 1544 4-9-3 **74** DavidKinsella 12 (W S Kittow) *hld up in midfield: effrt over 2f out: no prog and wl btn over 1f out* **33/1**	63
0023	**8**	*nk*	**Snowed Under**[27] 1380 5-9-2 **73** KerrinMcEvoy 2 (J D Bethell) *prom: rdn 3f out: struggling and btn 2f out* **9/2**[2]	61
0066	**9**	8	**Colinca's Lad (IRE)**[23] 1489 4-9-4 **75** LDettori 4 (J Ryan) *lw: led to over 2f out: sn wknd* **25/1**	49
0163	**10**	1	**Magic Amigo**[18] 1614 5-9-2 **73** RichardHughes 1 (J R Jenkins) *hld up in midfield: prog to chse ldrs over 3f out: wknd over 2f out* **5/1**[3]	45
-010	**11**	*hd*	**Cleaver**[48] 965 5-8-7 **64** RyanMoore 3 (Lady Herries) *lw: hld up last: styd alone on inner bk st: prog 3f out: clsng u.p whn jockey lost iron 1f out: lost all momentum and ch* **3/1**[1]	76+
0300	**12**	7	**Golo Gal**[37] 1152 4-8-5 **62** oh4 ow1 JohnEgan 9 (Mrs L J Mongan) *lw: chsd ldrs: rdn 3f out: wknd rapidly wl over 1f out: eased* **25/1**	21
0000	**13**	*dist*	**Shakeratteandroll (IRE)**[34] 1213 5-8-8 **65** PaulDoe 13 (Mrs L Richards) *lw: chsd ldr to 1/2-way: wknd over 3f out: t.o* **50/1**	—

2m 15.62s (5.38) **Going Correction** +0.725s/f (Yiel) **13 Ran SP% 125.1**
Speed ratings (Par 103):107,106,105,102,102 99,97,97,90,89 89,84,—
CSF £95.27 CT £1397.19 TOTE £14.80: £4.10, £2.50, £3.70; EX 77.50 Place 6 £85.92, Place 5 £58.36.
Owner William Jarvis **Bred** Blackdown Stud **Trained** Newmarket, Suffolk
■ Bradley Roper's first career winner.
FOCUS
An ordinary handicap, but sound enough form. The winner was typical of many on the round course at this two-day fixture in that she came from well off the pace.
Takafu(USA) Official explanation: jockey said horse was unsuited by the soft (heavy in places) ground
Cleaver Official explanation: jockey said gelding spooked and he lost his irons
T/Plt: £129.00 to a £1 stake. Pool: £61,883.55. 350.10 winning tickets. T/Qpdt: £46.00 to a £1 stake. Pool: £3,211.70. 51.60 winning tickets. JN

1944 SAINT-CLOUD (L-H)
Monday, May 29

OFFICIAL GOING: Good to soft

2092a PRIX CORRIDA (GROUP 2) (F&M) 1m 2f 110y
2:20 (2:19) 4-Y-0+ **£51,103** (£19,724; £9,414; £6,276; £3,138)

			RPR
1		**Pride (FR)**[29] 1331 6-9-0 C-PLemaire 3 (A De Royer-Dupre, France) *held up in 4th behind slow pace, 3rd 1f out, quickened to lead 100y out, easily* **6/10**[1]	117+
2	1 ½	**Paita**[27] 1398 4-8-11 OPeslier 5 (E Lellouche, France) *set slow pace, quickened 2 1/2f out, ridden 1 1/2f out, headed 100y out, no extra* **26/10**[2]	111
3	1 ½	**Ysoldina (FR)**[27] 1398 4-8-9 TJarnet 1 (A De Royer-Dupre, France) *held up in last, headway over 1f out, stayed on final f to take 3rd last strides* **10/1**	106
4	*snk*	**Bastet (IRE)**[27] 1398 4-8-9 SPasquier 4 (E Lellouche, France) *raced in 2nd, ridden 1 1/2f out, one pace* **69/10**[3]	106
5	¾	**In Clover**[27] 1398 4-8-11 DBonilla 2 (F Head, France) *raced keenly in 3rd on inside tracking leader, ridden 1 1/2f out, not quicken* **79/10**	107

2m 17.2s **5 Ran SP% 123.3**
PARI-MUTUEL: WIN 1.60; PL 1.10, 1.20; SF 2.70.
Owner N P Bloodstock **Bred** N P Bloodstock Ltd **Trained** Chantilly, France

NOTEBOOK
Pride(FR), who was always travelling well within herself, was brought with a smooth run a furlong and a half out and took control soon after. She totally outclassed the others, looks back to her very best and now has the option of the Prince of Wales's Stakes at Royal Ascot or the Grand Prix de Saint-Cloud.
Paita, who tried to make all the running and set a reasonable sort of pace, did absolutely nothing wrong. She quickened from two out but did not have the same speed as the winner. She could be another for the Grand Prix at Saint-Cloud.
Ysoldina(FR), who was dropped out last, still held the same position entering the straight. She made a forward move halfway up the straight and stole third place close home.
Bastet(IRE), second from the very start and never far from the leader, tried in vain to quicken when things warmed up but finally stayed on one-paced.

BELMONT PARK (L-H)
Monday, May 29

OFFICIAL GOING: Fast

2093a METROPOLITAN H'CAP (GRADE 1) (DIRT) 1m
9:48 (9:48) 3-Y-0+
£209,302 (£69,767; £34,884; £17,442; £10,465; £3,488)

			RPR
1		**Silver Train (USA)**[86] 4-8-7 EPrado 4 (R Dutrow Jr, U.S.A) **23/10**[1]	120
2	*hd*	**Sun King (USA)**[44] 4-8-6 (b) RBejarano 2 (N Zito, U.S.A) **69/10**	119
3	2 ¾	**Mass Media (USA)**[51] 5-8-4 (b) JCastellano 1 (R J Frankel, U.S.A) **61/10**	111
4	4 ½	**Bandini (USA)**[58] 4-8-7 GKGomez 3 (T Pletcher, U.S.A) **49/20**[2]	105
5	1 ¼	**Wilko (USA)**[65] 743 4-8-5 KDesormeaux 5 (J Noseda) *pushed along to go early pace, raced three wide, 6th straight, never able to challenge* **119/10**	101
6	¾	**Sir Greeley (USA)**[26] 4-8-4 ECoa 7 (J Jerkens, U.S.A) **34/10**[3]	98
7	33	**New York Hero (USA)**[912] 6-8-4 ow2 (b) CVelasquez 6 (R Dutrow Jr, U.S.A) **56/1**	32

1m 34.27s **7 Ran SP% 118.3**
PARI-MUTUEL (including $2 stakes): WIN 6.60; PL (1-2) 3.50, 6.30; SHOW (1-2-3) 2.90, 4.80, 5.00; SF 48.40.
Owner Buckram Oak Farm **Bred** Joe Sr & Joe Jr & John Mulholland **Trained** USA

NOTEBOOK
Wilko(USA), promoted to second in the Dubai World Cup on his last start, struggled to go the early pace on the drop back to a mile on this first outing back in the US. He will be suited by a return to a bit further.

2063 CHEPSTOW (L-H)
Tuesday, May 30

OFFICIAL GOING: Soft changing to good to soft (soft in places) after race 2 (3.00)
The ground was drying out all the time.
Wind: Moderate, behind Weather: Fine

2094 JOHN SMITH'S "NO NONSENSE WINNER" MAIDEN STKS 5f 16y
2:30 (2:31) (Class 5) 2-Y-0 **£3,368** (£1,002; £500; £250) **Stalls** High

Form				RPR
05	**1**		**Tom Tower (IRE)**[27] 1420 2-9-3 ChrisCatlin 1 (M R Channon) *a.p: led on bit over 2f out: rdn out ins fnl f* **8/1**[2]	72+
00	**2**	2	**Montemayorprincess (IRE)**[29] 1347 2-8-12 FrankieMcDonald 2 (D Haydn Jones) *chsd ldr: rdn to ld briefly over 2f out: r.o one pce fnl f* **9/1**[3]	60
0	**3**	½	**Copper King**[17] 1688 2-9-0 NeilChalmers(3) 7 (A M Balding) *chsd ldrs: hung lft 2f out: sn rdn: kpt on ins fnl f* **12/1**	63
4	**4**	5	**Nufoudh (IRE)**[18] 1632 2-9-3 MartinDwyer 4 (M Johnston) *led: rdn and hdd over 2f out: wknd over 1f out* **8/11**[1]	45+
00	**5**	2	**Tagula Music (IRE)**[31] 1284 2-8-12 FergusSweeney 6 (B Palling) *hld up and bhd: rdn and hung lft over 2f out: short-lived effrt over 1f out* **33/1**	33
4004	**6**	5	**Princely Royal**[4] 1977 2-9-3 SteveDrowne 8 (J J Bridger) *hld up: rdn 3f out: sn struggling* **10/1**	20
02	**7**	1 ¾	**Bathwick Style**[15] 1744 2-8-12 DaneO'Neill 3 (B R Millman) *fly-jmpd s: sn mid-div: rdn over 3f out: sn bhd* **12/1**	9
04	**8**	7	**Ella Y Rossa**[7] 1912 2-8-7 StephenDonohoe(5) 5 (P D Evans) *s.i.s: sn outpcd* **25/1**	—

63.21 secs (3.61) **Going Correction** +0.375s/f (Good) **8 Ran SP% 110.3**
Speed ratings (Par 93):86,82,82,74,70 62,60,48
CSF £70.93 TOTE £8.10: £2.70, £2.30, £2.20; EX 82.40 Trifecta £234.70 Pool: £763.73 - 2.31 winning tickets..
Owner Jumeirah Racing **Bred** C J Foy **Trained** West Ilsley, Berks
FOCUS
Not a great event with the odds-on favourite disappointing. Not easy to assess, this has been rated through the second and third.
NOTEBOOK
Tom Tower(IRE), back on soft ground, was by no means hard pressed to score. The form may not amount to much and he will have to improve if he is to live up to his Phoenix Stakes entry.
Montemayorprincess(IRE) seemed to appreciate the give in the ground and this was a significant improvement although she was clearly second best. (op 8-1 tchd 10-1)
Copper King shaped as though he requires further despite the conditions putting the emphasis on stamina. (tchd 10-1)
Nufoudh(IRE) disappointed on this totally different surface despite having winners on soft ground in his family. (op 4-5)

2095 JOHN SMITH'S EXTRA SMOOTH BITTER H'CAP 6f 16y
3:00 (3:01) (Class 6) (0-65,65) 3-Y-0+ **£2,590** (£770; £385; £192) **Stalls** High

Form				RPR
0006	**1**		**Stamford Blue**[21] 1568 5-8-8 **53** (b) TolleyDean(7) 4 (R A Harris) *s.i.s: hdwy 3f out: rdn to ld jst over 1f out: r.o wl* **16/1**	66
0502	**2**	1	**Cerulean Rose**[3] 2027 7-9-3 **60** JamesDoyle(5) 10 (A W Carroll) *mid-div: rdn over 2f out: hdwy over 1f out: r.o ins fnl f* **11/2**[1]	70
0006	**3**	½	**Pamir (IRE)**[33] 1258 4-9-11 **63** (b[1]) IanMongan 15 (P R Chamings) *prom: led over 4f out: rdn over 2f out: hdd jst over 1f out: edgd lft ins fnl f: no ex* **33/1**	72
0033	**4**	1 ¾	**Wizby**[1] 2068 3-7-12 **52** (t) DonnaCaldwell(7) 3 (P D Evans) *bhd: rdn 4f out: hdwy 2f out: one pce fnl f* **14/1**	53
2253	**5**	½	**Beneking**[31] 1303 6-9-3 **55** (p) ChrisCatlin 7 (D Burchell) *a.p: rdn and one pce fnl 2f* **28/1**	57
3303	**6**	*shd*	**Word Perfect**[12] 1795 4-9-12 **64** DaleGibson 14 (M W Easterby) *chsd ldrs: rdn and no hdwy fnl 2f* **8/1**	65
5444	**7**	1 ¼	**Arian's Lad**[21] 1570 5-9-1 **53** FrancisFerris 9 (B Palling) *prom: rdn over 2f out: wknd over 1f out* **10/1**	51
054	**8**	*nk*	**Palais Polaire**[35] 1212 4-9-8 **60** SteveDrowne 12 (J A Geake) *nvr nrr* **7/1**[2]	57

4342 **9** *1 ¼* **Bobby Rose**[11] [1825] 3-9-2 **63** .... DaneO'Neill 5 54
(D K Ivory) *s.i.s: sme hdwy over 2f out: n.d* **15/2**[3]
6025 **10** *shd* **Linda Green**[8] [1878] 5-9-10 **65** .... EdwardCreighton(3) 1 58
(M R Channon) *swtchd rt s: nvr nr ldrs* **7/1**[2]
0000 **11** *1* **Caustic Wit (IRE)**[36] [1188] 8-9-8 **63** .... (p) RobertMiles(3) 6 53
(M S Saunders) *w ldrs: rdn and ev ch 2f out: eased whn btn wl ins fnl f* **40/1**
000 **12** *2 ½* **Cate Washington**[223] [5976] 3-8-9 **56** .... J-PGuillambert 2 36
(Mrs L Williamson) *mid-div: rdn over 3f out: bhd fnl 2f* **100/1**
5023 **13** *nk* **Oneiro Way (IRE)**[33] [1261] 4-9-13 **65** .... StephenCarson 8 46
(P R Chamings) *led over 1f: rdn and wknd 2f out* **50/1**
0000 **14** *6* **Cree**[8] [1878] 4-9-12 **64** .... MartinDwyer 16 27
(W R Muir) *prom tl rdn and wknd over 2f out* **20/1**
2202 **15** *4* **Zazous**[4] [1981] 5-8-10 **53** .... MarcHalford(5) 11 4
(J J Bridger) *wnt lft s: a bhd* **9/1**
3406 **16** *1 ½* **Crystal Mystic (IRE)**[18] [1645] 4-9-2 **54** .... FergusSweeney 13 1
(B Palling) *prom tl rdn and wknd over 2f out* **14/1**

1m 13.59s (1.19) **Going Correction** +0.225s/f (Good)
WFA 3 from 4yo+ 9lb **16** Ran SP% **118.1**
Speed ratings (Par 101):101,99,99,96,96 95,94,93,92,92 90,87,86,78,73 71
CSF £92.97 CT £3002.01 TOTE £25.00: £4.40, £1.90, £6.20, £3.10; EX 209.70 TRIFECTA Not won..
Owner Brian Hicks **Bred** Mrs Wendy Miller **Trained** Earlswood, Monmouths
FOCUS
A wide-open low-grade handicap. Modest but sound form, the winner back to his best and the second running to her recent Haydock form. The winner and fourth raced more towards the far side than the second and third, but there seemed little in it.
Crystal Mystic(IRE) Official explanation: jockey said gelding had no more to give

2096 JOHN SMITH'S BACKING WINNERS CLAIMING STKS 5f 16y
3:30 (3:31) (Class 6) 3-Y-O+ **£2,266** (£674; £337; £168) **Stalls** High

Form RPR
3030 **1** **Mynd**[3] [2027] 6-8-10 56 .... MichaelJStainton(7) 9 67
(R M Whitaker) *wnt lft s: hld up: hdwy 3f out: rdn 2f out: r.o to ld nr fin* **5/2**[1]
0003 **2** *nk* **Endless Summer**[8] [1899] 9-9-2 74 .... JamesDoyle(5) 1 70
(A W Carroll) *hld up: hdwy 3f out: rdn to ld jst over 1f out: hdd nr fin* **11/4**[2]
2664 **3** *3* **Stagnite**[8] [1899] 6-8-11 46 .... (b) FrancisFerris 10 49+
(K McAuliffe) *racd alone stands' rail: prom: outpcd after 1f: r.o wl ins fnl f* **11/2**[3]
0001 **4** *1* **Blakeshall Quest**[33] [1255] 6-9-2 52 .... (b) DaneO'Neill 5 51
(R Brotherton) *led: rdn and hdd jst over 1f out: wknd ins fnl f* **8/1**
3661 **5** *3* **Phinerine**[13] [1771] 3-8-10 65 .... (b) TolleyDean(7) 8 46
(R A Harris) *carried lft s: sn prom: rdn and ev ch over 1f out: wknd ins fnl f* **11/2**[3]
0000 **6** *1* **Jinksonthehouse**[13] [1774] 5-7-13 48 .... FrankiePickard(7) 2 27
(M D I Usher) *nvr nr ldrs* **20/1**
0300 **7** *hd* **Von Wessex**[353] [2476] 4-8-12 58 .... RobertMiles(3) 7 35
(W G M Turner) *s.i.s and hmpd s: outpcd* **20/1**
0600 **8** *5* **Tiffin Deano (IRE)**[218] [6078] 4-9-3 40 .... ChrisCatlin 6 20
(H J Manners) *bhd fnl 2f* **33/1**
0000 **9** *4* **Saucepot**[30] [1310] 4-8-12 35 .... PaulFitzsimons 3 —
(Miss J R Tooth) *chsd ldrs on far rail: wknd 3f out* **66/1**
0 **10** *14* **Stingray (IRE)**[23] [1513] 4-9-6 .... MarkCoumbe(7) 4 —
(N I M Rossiter) *chsd ldr 2f: sn wknd* **66/1**

62.13 secs (2.53) **Going Correction** +0.225s/f (Good)
WFA 3 from 4yo+ 8lb **10** Ran SP% **112.6**
Speed ratings (Par 101):88,87,82,81,76 74,74,66,60,37
CSF £8.55 TOTE £3.30: £1.30, £1.20, £1.60; EX 12.50 Trifecta £34.20 Pool: £335.36 - 6.96 winning tickets..The winner was the subject of a friendly claim. Stagnite claimed by P. A. Blockley for £5,000.
Owner Derek And Jean Clee **Bred** John Rose **Trained** Scarcroft, W Yorks
FOCUS
A modest claimer with the two at the head of the market fighting out the finish. The winner is rated to last year's best. All bar the third and seventh went far side.
Stingray(IRE) Official explanation: trainer said colt had beld from the nose

2097 JOHN SMITH'S CHEPSTOW CLUB MEMBERS H'CAP 1m 2f 36y
4:00 (4:00) (Class 5) (0-75,75) 4-Y-O+ **£3,562** (£1,059; £529; £264) **Stalls** Low

Form RPR
4 **1** **Olimpo (FR)**[18] [1651] 5-8-11 **68** .... AlanMunro 6 79
(B R Millman) *hld up: hdwy over 3f out: rdn to ld 2f out: hdd over 1f out: led wl ins fnl f: r.o* **3/1**[2]
5031 **2** *¾* **Trouble Mountain (USA)**[10] [1850] 9-8-9 **66** .... (t) DaleGibson 1 76
(M W Easterby) *a.p: rdn over 3f out: led over 1f out tl wl ins fnl f: nt qckn* **11/4**[1]
50-0 **3** *3 ½* **First Centurion**[22] [1544] 5-8-12 **69** .... DaneO'Neill 4 73
(Ian Williams) *a.p: led 3f out: rdn and hdd 2f out: no ex fnl f* **7/1**
2050 **4** *1* **Hawridge Star (IRE)**[6] [1943] 4-9-2 **73** .... (v[1]) ChrisCatlin 7 75
(W S Kittow) *hld up: hdwy 3f out: sn rdn and outpcd: rallied over 1f out: styd on ins fnl f* **8/1**
0110 **5** *5* **Kylkenny**[22] [1544] 11-8-11 **75** .... (t) NBazeley(7) 8 68
(P D Cundell) *hld up: hdwy 6f out: rdn and wknd over 2f out* **13/2**[3]
5000 **6** *shd* **Love Angel (USA)**[24] [1478] 4-8-9 **66** .... J-PGuillambert 2 59
(J J Bridger) *prom: led over 3f out: sn hdd: wknd over 2f out* **12/1**
4210 **7** *17* **Scottish River (USA)**[31] [1308] 7-8-6 **70** .... FrankiePickard(7) 3 32
(M D I Usher) *s.v.s: hld up: hdwy over 5f out: wknd over 2f out* **12/1**
0000 **8** *36* **Elidore**[223] [5974] 6-8-9 **66** .... FrancisFerris 5 —
(B Palling) *led: hdd over 3f out: sn wknd: t.o* **9/1**

2m 16.72s (6.82) **Going Correction** +0.775s/f (Yiel) **8** Ran SP% **114.0**
Speed ratings (Par 103):103,102,99,98,94 94,81,52
CSF £11.63 CT £51.22 TOTE £4.10: £1.50, £1.50, £1.90; EX 12.10 Trifecta £38.70 Pool: £745.60 - 13.65 winning tickets..
Owner Christine And Aubrey Loze **Bred** Ewar Stud Farm **Trained** Kentisbeare, Devon
FOCUS
An ordinary handicap but the form looks sound, the runner-up setting the standard.

2098 JOHN SMITH'S EXTRA COLD H'CAP 1m 14y
4:30 (4:34) (Class 5) (0-70,71) 4-Y-O+ **£3,562** (£1,059; £529; £264) **Stalls** High

Form RPR
4 **1** **Full Victory (IRE)**[13] [1773] 4-8-12 **64** .... DaneO'Neill 14 83
(R A Farrant) *a.p: led on bit over 2f out: rdn and hung lft over 1f out: r.o wl* **7/1**[2]
0505 **2** *5* **Foolish Groom**[10] [1850] 5-8-6 **58** .... (v) LPKeniry 12 66
(R Hollinshead) *dwlt: sn mid-div: hdwy over 3f out: rdn and ev ch 2f out: one pce* **10/1**
1500 **3** *1 ½* **Hurricane Coast**[16] [1188] 7-8-13 **70** .... (b) JamesDoyle(5) 13 75
(K McAuliffe) *hld up and bhd: swtchd lft and hdwy 2f out: one pce fnl f* **20/1**
0020 **4** *¾* **Primeshade Promise**[8] [1882] 5-8-4 **56** oh2 .... RichardThomas 11 59
(D Burchell) *hld up in tch: rdn over 2f out: one pce* **12/1**
0003 **5** *1 ½* **Lockstock (IRE)**[8] [1882] 8-8-1 **56** oh1 .... (p) EdwardCreighton(3) 8 56
(M S Saunders) *w ldrs: rdn and ev ch over 2f out: wknd fnl f* **9/1**
1111 **6** *2 ½* **Indian Edge**[8] [1882] 5-9-5 **71** 6ex .... FrancisFerris 5 66
(B Palling) *prom: rdn and ev ch over 2f out: wknd fnl f* **11/4**[1]
0650 **7** *1 ¼* **The Gaikwar (IRE)**[13] [1773] 7-9-0 **69** .... (b) AmirQuinn(3) 16 61
(R A Harris) *s.s: rdn and hdwy 2f out: n.d* **14/1**
4014 **8** *¾* **Golden Square**[17] [1683] 4-7-13 **58** oh2 ow2 .... DeanWilliams(7) 4 49
(A W Carroll) *mid-div: rdn over 4f out: no rspnse whn hung lft over 2f out* **12/1**
6050 **9** *½* **Zafarshah (IRE)**[14] [1752] 7-7-12 **57** oh11 ow1 .... (b) TolleyDean(7) 10 47
(R A Harris) *t.k.h: prom: rdn over 2f out: sn wknd* **20/1**
4551 **10** *¾* **Welsh Whisper**[35] [1225] 7-8-4 **59** oh10 ow3 .... NeilChalmers(3) 3 47
(S A Brookshaw) *a bhd* **33/1**
2405 **11** *hd* **Smoothly Does It**[8] [1882] 5-8-11 **63** .... ChrisCatlin 2 51
(Mrs A J Bowlby) *a bhd* **15/2**[3]
0300 **12** *hd* **Threezedzz**[12] [1802] 8-8-7 **64** .... (t) StephenDonohoe(5) 15 51
(P D Evans) *led: hdd over 2f out: sn wknd* **14/1**
1000 **13** *¾* **Sand Iron (IRE)**[149] [4] 4-7-13 **56** .... NataliaGemelova(5) 7 42
(John Allen) *rdn over 3f out: a towards rr* **50/1**
3000 **14** *22* **Shortbread**[241] [5617] 4-8-12 **64** .... (t) AlanDaly 1 3
(M Salaman) *a bhd: t.o* **66/1**
U050 **15** *6* **Monte Mayor Boy**[13] [1773] 4-8-6 **58** .... FrankieMcDonald 9 —
(D Haydn Jones) *s.i.s: a bhd: t.o* **16/1**

1m 36.12s (0.12) **Going Correction** +0.10s/f (Good) **15** Ran SP% **120.5**
Speed ratings (Par 103):103,98,96,95,94 91,90,89,89,88 88,88,87,65,59
CSF £70.63 CT £896.45 TOTE £7.10: £2.30, £3.70, £6.00; EX 106.20 TRIFECTA Not won..
Owner Barnstaple Racing Club **Bred** Larry Ryan **Trained** Bampton, Devon
■ A first winner on the Flat for Rodney Farrant.
FOCUS
A third of the field were out of the handicap proper. An ordinary handicap, but solid form and an improved performance from the winner.

2099 COURAGE WEST AND WALES APPRENTICE H'CAP 1m 4f 23y
5:00 (5:00) (Class 6) (0-60,60) 4-Y-O+ **£2,590** (£770; £385; £192) **Stalls** Low

Form RPR
0 **1** **Boulevin (IRE)**[11] [688] 6-7-12 **46** oh9 .... JamesRogers(7) 2 54
(R J Price) *s.i.s: hld up and bhd: hdwy over 3f out: led over 2f out: sn rdn: r.o wl* **20/1**
5052 **2** *1 ½* **Mossmann Gorge**[10] [1850] 4-9-5 **60** .... (v) KevinGhunowa 8 66
(M Wellings) *hld up in mid-div: hdwy over 5f out: rdn and chsd wnr 2f out: edgd lft jst over 1f out: nt qckn* **5/1**[1]
0340 **3** *shd* **My Legal Eagle (IRE)**[27] [1415] 12-8-9 **50** .... LiamJones 1 56
(E G Bevan) *hld up towards rr: hdwy over 3f out: rdn 2f out: styd on towards fin* **7/1**[3]
0004 **4** *2* **Delta Force**[17] [1660] 7-8-0 **46** oh1 .... SophieDoyle(5) 10 49
(P A Blockley) *hld up in mid-div: hdwy 6f out: rdn over 1f out: one pce* **8/1**
5425 **5** *3 ½* **Financial Future**[21] [1566] 6-8-12 **56** .... ThomasO'Brien(3) 5 53
(C Roberts) *led: rdn and hdd over 2f out: wknd ins fnl f* **10/1**
0-00 **6** *1 ¼* **Only For Sue**[15] [1745] 7-8-6 **50** .... (b) TolleyDean(3) 11 45
(W S Kittow) *s.i.s: plld hrd: sn prom: swtchd lft over 4f out: rdn and ev ch over 2f out: wknd over 1f out* **6/1**[2]
5501 **7** *1* **Cotton Easter**[8] [1879] 5-8-8 **54** 6ex .... (t) MarkCoumbe(5) 12 47
(Mrs A J Bowlby) *s.i.s: sn hld up in mid-div: hdwy over 3f out: rdn over 2f out: wknd over 1f out* **7/1**[3]
010- **8** *7* **Tom Bell (IRE)**[15] [6626] 6-8-9 **55** .... JamieHamblett(5) 3 37
(J G M O'Shea) *hld up in mid-div: rdn over 3f out: sn struggling* **10/1**
0302 **9** *7* **Ben Bacchus (IRE)**[21] [1572] 4-8-0 **48** .... (b) FrankiePickard(7) 6 19
(P A Blockley) *s.s: bhd: short-lived effrt on ins 4f out* **11/1**
0000 **10** *4* **Cool Bathwick (IRE)**[21] [1566] 7-8-5 **46** oh10 .... (b) MichaelJStainton 7 11
(G H Yardley) *prom: rdn 4f out: sn wknd* **50/1**
00-0 **11** *16* **Superfling**[25] [1460] 5-8-0 **46** oh6 .... NBazeley(5) 9 —
(H J Manners) *plld hrd: prom 4f* **50/1**
0056 **12** *3 ½* **Carpet Ride**[5] [1958] 4-8-9 **55** .... (t) JosephWalsh(5) 4 —
(B G Powell) *prom: rdn over 3f out: sn wknd* **7/1**[3]

2m 49.62s (10.90) **Going Correction** +0.775s/f (Yiel) **12** Ran SP% **114.8**
Speed ratings (Par 101):94,93,92,91,89 88,87,83,78,75 65,62
CSF £112.33 CT £779.64 TOTE £23.70: £4.20, £2.10, £2.40; EX 248.90 Trifecta £237.00 Part won. Pool: £333.90 - 0.69 winning tickets. Place 6 £219.66, Place 5 £47.88.
Owner R J Price **Bred** Hugh B McGahon **Trained** Ullingswick, H'fords
■ The first career winner for James Rogers.
FOCUS
A slowly-run and very modest handicap. It is unlikely the winner was flattered as he was entitled to rate this high on some jumps and Irish form.
Carpet Ride Official explanation: jockey said gelding had bled from the nose
T/Plt: £197.40 to a £1 stake. Pool: £48,657.35. 179.85 winning tickets. T/Qpdt: £15.70 to a £1 stake. Pool: £4,737.70. 221.90 winning tickets. KH

2069 LEICESTER (R-H)
Tuesday, May 30
OFFICIAL GOING: Good to soft (good in places)
Wind: Fresh, half-behind Weather: Cloudy with sunny spells

2100 EBF LADBROKES.COM MAIDEN FILLIES' STKS 5f 2y
2:20 (2:20) (Class 4) 2-Y-O **£6,309** (£1,888; £944) **Stalls** Low

Form RPR
52 **1** **Top Royelle**[8] [1896] 2-9-0 .... RichardHughes 2 76
(R Hannon) *mde all: rdn 1f out: edgd rt ins fnl f: r.o* **4/11**[1]
2 *¾* **Vale Of Belvoir (IRE)** 2-9-0 .... PatCosgrave 4 73
(K R Burke) *chsd wnr: chal 1/2-way: rdn ins fnl f: edgd rt: r.o* **3/1**[2]
3 *29* **Feisty** 2-9-0 .... SebSanders 1 —
(Rae Guest) *s.i.s: chsd ldrs: rdn 3f out: sn outpcd* **14/1**[3]

64.24 secs (3.34) **Going Correction** +0.55s/f (Yiel) **3** Ran SP% **105.0**
Speed ratings (Par 92):95,93,47
CSF £1.65 TOTE £1.20; EX 1.30.
Owner The Hill Top Partnership **Bred** John And Susan Davis **Trained** East Everleigh, Wilts
FOCUS
An uncompetitive affair and the winner probably did not need to improve on her previous efforts to score.

NOTEBOOK
Top Royelle had shown plenty on her first two starts to suggest that she could win her maiden, and she was found a weak event here to get off the mark. She was made to work hard for it in the end, though, and did not improve to win this. Six furlongs is likely to suit her. (op 4-9)
Vale Of Belvoir(IRE), a half-sister to Mystified, a dual winner over seven to nine furlongs at two to three, gave the odds-on favourite a fright before having to accept second place on her debut. Her stable is flying at present and a little improvement should see her off the mark. (op 9-4)
Feisty, whose dam won twice over 12 furlongs as an older horse, is bred to need further in time and looked to need this debut experience. (op 10-1)

2101 LADBROKES.COM CLAIMING STKS — 1m 60y
2:50 (2:50) (Class 5) 3-Y-O — **£3,886** (£1,156; £577; £288) **Stalls** High

Form — RPR
0600 **1** **Emotive**[15] [1736] 3-8-8 50 ... SebSanders 5 — 63
(I A Wood) *a.p: chsd ldr over 2f out: led ins fnl f: r.o* **15/2**
0502 **2** *3* **Lucys Lady**[23] [1501] 3-7-12 42 ... AndrewElliott(5) 1 — 52
(K R Burke) *chsd ldrs: led 3f out: hdd and no ex ins fnl f* **15/2**
0250 **3** *4* **Cape Win (IRE)**[154] [6673] 3-9-4 72 ... RHills 3 — 58
(W J Haggas) *hld up: hmpd over 6f out: hdwy over 3f out: rdn and wknd over 1f out* **11/4**[1]
0003 **4** *11* **Darker Than Blue**[15] [1731] 3-7-13 47 ... (b) JamieMackay 8 — 16
(B J Meehan) *sn pushed along to ld: hdd over 5f out: rdn and wknd 2f out* **22/1**
U000 **5** *1* **Tay Bridge (IRE)**[35] [1221] 3-7-11 47 ... LukeMorris(7) 10 — 19
(M L W Bell) *sn pushed along in mid-div: hmpd and lost pl over 6f out: hdwy over 3f out: wknd over 2f out* **33/1**
0454 **6** *5* **Mocha Java**[12] [1799] 3-9-4 63 ... JosedeSouza 11 — 23
(P F I Cole) *mid-div: hmpd over 6f out: hdwy over 3f out: wknd over 2f out* **9/1**
2020 **7** *4* **Mighty Dancer (IRE)**[7] [1925] 3-8-12 62 ... RichardHughes 7 — 8
(S Kirk) *hld up in tch: hmpd and lost pl over 3f out: n.d after* **7/2**[2]
0562 **8** *3* **Cecchetti (IRE)**[15] [1726] 3-8-4 45 ... RichardKingscote(5) 6 — —
(Mrs H Sweeting) *chsd ldrs: led over 5f out: rdn and hdd 3f out: sn wknd* **25/1**
000 **9** *3* **Bournonville**[14] [1752] 3-8-3 43 ow2 ... (t) SaleemGolam(3) 4 — —
(J Ryan) *hld up: a in rr* **100/1**
0000 **10** *25* **The Flying Peach**[15] [1726] 3-7-10 42 ... JohnMcAuley(3) 2 — —
(W M Brisbourne) *s.i.s: a bhd* **100/1**
4604 **11** *2 ½* **Rock Of Cloonavery (IRE)**[11] [1829] 3-8-6 52 ... JamieSpencer 9 — —
(S C Williams) *chsd ldrs: rdn over 3f out: wknd over 2f out: eased* **5/1**[3]

1m 48.66s (3.36) **Going Correction** +0.40s/f (Good) — **11** Ran SP% **112.2**
Speed ratings (Par 99):99,96,92,81,80 75,71,68,65,40 37
CSF £56.59 TOTE £9.00: £2.80, £1.80, £2.00; EX 40.90.
Owner Christopher Shankland **Bred** Mrs J Mitchell **Trained** Upper Lambourn, Berks
■ Stewards' Enquiry : Jamie Mackay two-day ban: careless riding (Jun 10-11)

FOCUS
Moderate stuff and they finished well strung out. Hard to pin down, this has been rated through the runner-up.
Mighty Dancer(IRE) Official explanation: jockey said gelding suffered interference turning out of back straight
Rock Of Cloonavery(IRE) Official explanation: jockey said gelding had no more to give

2102 LADBROKESCASINO.COM H'CAP — 1m 3f 183y
3:20 (3:20) (Class 5) (0-75,72) 3-Y-O — **£4,416** (£1,321; £660; £330; £164) **Stalls** High

Form — RPR
550 **1** **Warsaw Pact (IRE)**[255] [5325] 3-8-6 60 ... SebSanders 3 — 74+
(Sir Mark Prescott) *chsd ldrs: rdn to ld over 1f out: styd on wl* **12/1**[3]
2111 **2** *1 ½* **Bollin Derek**[9] [1867] 3-8-10 64 5ex ... JamieSpencer 4 — 76
(T D Easterby) *chsd ldrs: led over 7f out: rdn and hdd over 1f out: unable qck wl ins fnl f* **4/9**[1]
043 **3** *2 ½* **Cape Secret (IRE)**[22] [1543] 3-8-7 61 ... FrancisNorton 1 — 69+
(R M Beckett) *trckd ldrs: racd keenly: outpcd over 3f out: hdwy over 2f out: rdn and edgd rt over 1f out: styd on* **7/1**[2]
024 **4** *4* **Trinity Rose**[35] [1214] 3-9-1 69 ... JoeFanning 2 — 71
(M Johnston) *chsd ldrs: rdn over 4f out: wknd over 1f out* **16/1**
3000 **5** *7* **Capriolla**[15] [1740] 3-8-5 62 ... (b[1]) NelsonDeSouza(3) 7 — 52
(P F I Cole) *hld up: hdwy over 2f out: rdn: hung rt and wknd over 1f out* **66/1**
5000 **6** *25* **Royal Premier (IRE)**[18] [1652] 3-8-4 58 oh5 ... (v) JamieMackay 6 — 8
(H J Collingridge) *chsd ldrs: rdn 1/2-way: wknd over 4f out* **100/1**
040 **7** *3* **Bamboo Banks (IRE)**[15] [1741] 3-9-4 72 ... RichardHughes 5 — 18
(J L Dunlop) *led over 4f: remained handy tl rdn and wknd over 2f out* **20/1**
0610 **8** *24* **Raise The Heights (IRE)**[22] [1543] 3-8-8 62 ... EddieAhern 8 — —
(C Tinkler) *s.s: effrt over 4f out: sn wknd* **20/1**

2m 37.8s (3.30) **Going Correction** +0.40s/f (Good) — **8** Ran SP% **107.3**
Speed ratings (Par 99):105,104,102,99,95 78,76,60
CSF £15.89 CT £34.74 TOTE £7.60: £3.00, £1.02, £1.50; EX 16.70.
Owner J Fishpool - Osborne House **Bred** Saad Bin Mishrif **Trained** Newmarket, Suffolk

FOCUS
A fair handicap. The unexposed winner showed big improvement and the runner-up was not far off his Ripon form.
Warsaw Pact(IRE) Official explanation: trainer's rep said, regarding the improved form shown, the gelding was a big backward two-year-old who had matured over the winter and had had a breathing operation since its last run
Bamboo Banks(IRE) Official explanation: jockey said gelding lost his action

2103 LADBROKES.COM FILLIES' CONDITIONS STKS — 7f 9y
3:50 (3:51) (Class 2) 3-Y-O — **£12,464** (£3,732; £1,866; £934) **Stalls** Low

Form — RPR
0111 **1** **Red Evie (IRE)**[10] [1843] 3-8-6 94 ow1 ... JamieSpencer 3 — 102+
(M L W Bell) *chsd ldrs: shkn up to ld 2f out: edgd rt ins fnl f: comf* **1/2**[1]
1 **2** *1 ½* **Star Cluster**[319] [3503] 3-8-9 ... RichardHughes 4 — 99
(H R A Cecil) *wnt rt s: hld up: hdwy over 2f out: rdn to chse wnr over 1f out: no imp* **9/4**[2]
16 **3** *11* **Melaaya (USA)**[241] [5605] 3-8-9 94 ... RHills 1 — 71
(M Johnston) *led 5f: sn rdn and wknd* **9/1**[3]
045 **4** *8* **Macho Dancer (IRE)**[75] [651] 3-8-5 52 ... EmmettStack 2 — 46
(K J Burke) *chsd ldr over 4f: wknd qckly* **100/1**

1m 29.55s (3.45) **Going Correction** +0.55s/f (Yiel) — **4** Ran SP% **108.4**
Speed ratings (Par 102):102,100,87,78
CSF £1.89 TOTE £1.40; EX 2.10.
Owner Terry Neill **Bred** Dermot Cantillon And Forenaghts Stud **Trained** Newmarket, Suffolk

FOCUS
A small field but the first two are both smart fillies and look likely to notch further success. The form cannot be considered rock solid.

NOTEBOOK
Red Evie(IRE), a progressive filly this spring, had the advantage of race-fitness over her two main rivals and that made all the difference. She won cosily in the end and the Listed Sandringham Handicap at Royal Ascot is next on the agenda, where another furlong should not pose any problems. (op 8-13 tchd 4-6)
Star Cluster, winner of her only start at two, has seen that form boosted a number of times since, but she has clearly had one or two problems in the meantime. This was a promising return to action, though, as her main rival was race-fit and received weight from her, and she had to race on ground that would have been softer than ideal. She could well improve past the winner with this run under her belt. (op 2-1)
Melaaya(USA), weak in the market beforehand on this reappearance, could not live with the first two over the final quarter mile. The stable's runners are not all firing at present and she might be better on faster ground, but she is going to have to improve quite a bit for the run to justify her current rating of 94. (op 15-2)
Macho Dancer(IRE) picked up some nice prize-money for finishing last in a race in which she was completely outclassed. (op 80-1)

2104 LADBROKES.COM FOREST H'CAP — 1m 1f 218y
4:20 (4:20) (Class 5) (0-70,70) 4-Y-O+ **£5,047** (£1,510; £566; £566; £188) **Stalls** High

Form — RPR
3040 **1** **Charlie Kennet**[11] [1821] 8-9-3 69 ... GeorgeBaker 5 — 77
(Mrs H Sweeting) *hld up: hdwy 1/2-way: outpcd over 3f out: hdwy over 2f out: r.o u.p to ld post* **9/2**[3]
0002 **2** *shd* **Soufah (IRE)**[31] [1288] 4-8-11 63 ... SebSanders 7 — 71
(J L Dunlop) *hld up: hdwy over 2f out: rdn to ld wl ins fnl f: hdd post* **4/1**[2]
0000 **3** *½* **Viable**[53] [905] 4-8-12 64 ... MickyFenton 3 — 71
(Mrs P Sly) *led: hdd over 8f out: chsd ldr: rdn and ev ch fr 3f out : styd on* **28/1**
6024 **3** *dht* **Bouquet**[297] [4165] 4-9-1 67 ... JamieSpencer 1 — 74
(J R Fanshawe) *led over 8f out: rdn over 1f out: hdd wl ins fnl f* **8/1**
3110 **5** *½* **Tagula Blue (IRE)**[11] [1821] 6-8-8 67 ... NeilBrown(7) 4 — 73
(Ian Williams) *s.s: bhd: r.o ins fnl f: nt rch ldrs* **7/2**[1]
4503 **6** *¾* **To Arms**[27] [1425] 4-8-8 60 ... JamieMackay 6 — 65
(T D Easterby) *a.p: rdn over 2f out: styd on* **10/1**
0622 **7** *¾* **King's Crest**[8] [1887] 8-8-5 57 ... JoeFanning 9 — 64+
(J J Quinn) *hld up: hdwy over 2f out: rdn over 1f out: no ex wl ins fnl f* **7/2**[1]
1506 **8** *hd* **Bill Bennett (FR)**[7] [1929] 5-8-13 65 ... DerekMcGaffin 8 — 68
(J Jay) *sn outpcd: rdn over 4f out: styd on ins fnl f: nt pce to chal* **25/1**
-000 **9** *40* **Burning Moon**[10] [1847] 5-9-4 70 ... RichardHughes 2 — —
(J Ryan) *chsd ldrs tl rdn and wknd over 2f out* **40/1**

2m 11.57s (3.27) **Going Correction** +0.40s/f (Good) — **9** Ran SP% **112.6**
Speed ratings (Par 103):102,101,101,101,101 100,99,99,67
WIN: £5.40. PL: £1.70, £1.60, Bouquet £1.50, Viable £3.50. TRIC: Charlie Kennet/Soufah/Bouquet £68.53. CK/S/V £220.58. CSF £21.74; EX 40.60.
Owner The Northleach Kennet Connection **Bred** Richard William Floyd **Trained** Lockeridge, Wilts
■ Stewards' Enquiry : Seb Sanders two-day ban: used whip with excessive frequency (Jun 10-11)

FOCUS
A competitive handicap on paper, and that proved to be the case with barely three lengths covering the first eight home. Ordinary form, rated through the third.
Burning Moon Official explanation: jockey said gelding had no more to give

2105 LADBROKES.COM H'CAP — 5f 218y
4:50 (4:50) (Class 4) (0-85,83) 3-Y-O — **£6,309** (£1,888; £944; £472; £235) **Stalls** Low

Form — RPR
2251 **1** **Gavarnie Beau (IRE)**[4] [1983] 3-9-10 83 6ex ... FrancisNorton 2 — 86
(M Blanshard) *hld up: hdwy over 1f out: rdn to ld wl ins fnl f* **7/2**[2]
040 **2** *shd* **The History Man (IRE)**[4] [1983] 3-8-8 74 ... (b) AdeleRothery(7) 7 — 77
(M W Easterby) *wnt lft s: hld up: hdwy to ld 1/2-way: rdn over 1f out: edgd lft: r.o* **12/1**
0016 **3** *2* **Viva Volta**[29] [1345] 3-8-10 69 ... MickyFenton 5 — 66
(T D Easterby) *bmpd s: led to 1/2-way: rdn over 1f out: styd on same pce* **12/1**
3410 **4** *2 ½* **Rapsgate (IRE)**[2] [2049] 3-9-1 74 ... (b) PatDobbs 4 — 64
(R Hannon) *hld up: outpcd over 2f out: styd on u.p fnl f* **10/1**
1014 **5** *¾* **Sunderland Echo (IRE)**[3] [2022] 3-8-13 72 ... PatCosgrave 3 — 59
(B Ellison) *chsd ldrs: rdn over 2f out: wknd fnl f* **7/4**[1]
0150 **6** *3* **Spearit (IRE)**[8] [1900] 3-9-4 77 ... JamieMackay 8 — 55
(D R C Elsworth) *chsd ldrs: rdn over 2f out: wknd fnl f* **14/1**
0124 **7** *3* **Peter Island (FR)**[19] [1606] 3-9-4 77 ... JamieSpencer 9 — 46
(J Gallagher) *chsd ldrs over 4f* **4/1**[3]
3300 **8** *3* **Balian**[29] [1355] 3-8-9 68 ow1 ... (p) RichardHughes 6 — 28
(G L Moore) *hmpd s: hld up in tch: rdn and wknd over 2f out* **16/1**

1m 15.8s (2.60) **Going Correction** +0.55s/f (Yiel) — **8** Ran SP% **115.6**
Speed ratings (Par 101):104,103,101,97,96 92,88,84
CSF £44.58 CT £457.06 TOTE £7.20: £1.70, £3.60, £3.80; EX 54.60 Place 6 £29.16, Place 5 £20.93.
Owner Lloyd Hill **Bred** Seamus Murphy **Trained** Upper Lambourn, Berks
■ Stewards' Enquiry : Adele Rothery four-day ban: used whip in incorrect place with whip in forehand, and without giving gelding time to respond (Jun 10-13)

FOCUS
A fair handicap run at a good gallop. With the runner-up hardly an obvious improver this has not been rated too positively.
T/Plt: £106.50 to a £1 stake. Pool: £35,355.00. 242.20 winning tickets. T/Qpdt: £41.80 to a £1 stake. Pool: £2,234.30. 39.50 winning tickets. CR

2076 REDCAR (L-H)
Tuesday, May 30

OFFICIAL GOING: Good to firm
Wind: Fresh, against

2106 EUROPEAN BREEDERS FUND MEDIAN AUCTION MAIDEN FILLIES' STKS — 6f
2:10 (2:12) (Class 5) 2-Y-O — **£3,886** (£1,156; £577; £288) **Stalls** Centre

Form — RPR
1 **Emma's Surprise** 2-9-0 ... NCallan 12 — 74+
(K A Ryan) *dwlt: gd hdwy over 2f out: rdn to chal ent last: styd on strly to ld nr line* **12/1**
2 *nk* **Ponty Rossa (IRE)** 2-9-0 ... FergalLynch 5 — 73
(T D Easterby) *dwlt: swtchd lft and gd hdwy on outer 2f out: rdn over 1f out: led ins last: hdd and no ex nr line* **33/1**
3 *1 ¼* **Princess Palatine (IRE)** 2-9-0 ... RichardMullen 14 — 69
(K R Burke) *towards rr: hdwy 2f out: sn rdn and styd on ins last: nrst fin* **16/1**

2 **4** ½ **Pretty Majestic (IRE)**[23] 1514 2-9-0 TonyCulhane 8 68
(M R Channon) *sn led: pushed clr 2f out: sn rdn and hung rt over 1f out: drvn and hdd ins last: wknd towards fin* **10/11**[1]

5 2½ **Ocean Of Champagne** 2-8-11 DanielTudhope(3) 2 60
(A Dickman) *dwlt and bhd: swtchd rta nd hdwy over 2f out: rdn and styd on wl fnl f: nrst fin* **66/1**

6 ½ **Streamer** 2-9-0 StanleyChin 3 59
(M Johnston) *prom: rdn and ev ch 2f out: grad wknd* **25/1**

7 1 **Jane Of Arc (FR)** 2-8-9 DuranFentiman(5) 1 56
(T D Easterby) *chsd ldrs: rdn alongand sltly outpcd over 2f out: kpt on ins last* **40/1**

8 1 **Up The Pole** 2-9-0 JimmyQuinn 4 53
(M W Easterby) *outpcd and bhd tl styd on fnl 2f* **66/1**

9 2 **Valley Of The Moon (IRE)** 2-9-0 PaulHanagan 15 47+
(R A Fahey) *in tch: rdn along over 2f out: sn btn* **7/1**[2]

10 1¾ **Little Miss Tara (IRE)** 2-8-9 GregFairley(5) 6 42
(A B Haynes) *chsd ldrs: rdn along 1/2-way: snw eakened* **14/1**

0 **11** 1¼ **Sagassa**[15] 1737 2-9-0 AdrianMcCarthy 13 38
(W De Best-Turner) *chsd ldrs: rdn over 2f out: sn drvn and wknd* **66/1**

00 **12** 2 **Soundasapound**[20] 1588 2-9-0 TonyHamilton 9 32
(I W McInnes) *cl up: rdn along over 2f out and sn wknd* **50/1**

13 ¾ **Ellies Faith** 2-8-7 SuzzanneFrance(7) 11 30
(N Bycroft) *chsd ldrs: rdn along 1/2-way: sn wknd* **100/1**

33 **14** 6 **Startolini**[15] 1730 2-9-0 RobertWinston 18 12
(B Smart) *chsd ldrs: oushed along 1/2-way: sn wknd and eased over 1f out* **15/2**[3]

0 **15** 9 **Dockside Dancer (IRE)**[15] 1730 2-9-0 LeeEnstone 16 —
(P T Midgley) *a rr* **100/1**

1m 14.5s (2.80) **Going Correction** +0.30s/f (Good) **15** Ran SP% **114.5**
Speed ratings (Par 90):93,92,90,90,86 86,84,83,80,78 76,74,73,65,53
CSF £354.91 TOTE £10.50: £2.60, £6.50, £4.70; EX 242.80.
Owner M G White **Bred** Red House Stud **Trained** Hambleton, N Yorks

FOCUS
From the first ten home only Pretty Majestic had run previously, and she seemed below her best this time, so it is hard to gauge the level of the form, but it looked like a race that will produce a few winners.

NOTEBOOK
Emma's Surpriseis a 28,000gns half-sister to six winners, most notably high-class juvenile/sprinter Indian Rocket, and useful juvenile sprinter The Bonus King. She started slowly but soon recovered and found plenty under pressure to make a winning debut. Her starting price would suggest she was not particularly fancied, so there should be more to come, and her trainer expects her to stay further. (op 8-1)
Ponty Rossa(IRE), a 15,000euros first foal of a mile winner France, belied her big price with a very promising debut effort. She was clear of the rest and looks well up to winning a similar race.
Princess Palatine(IRE), an 11,500gns half-sister to Woodboro Kat, a nine-furlong three-year-old winner, Countykat, a six- and seven-furlong winner, and Hill Of Almhuim, successful on debut as a juvenile, made a pleasing start in third and is open to plenty of improvement. (op 12-1)
Pretty Majestic(IRE), runner-up to the subsequent Listed winner Gilded in a five-furlong Salisbury conditions race on her debut, seemed to run below that level of form on this step up in trip. She can be given another chance, and may be better back over the minimum trip. (tchd evens in places)
Ocean Of Champagne, a half-sister to five-furlong juvenile winners Ninety Degrees and Intersky Champagne, out of a multiple winner over five to seven furlongs, made a very creditable introduction and looks capable of progressing.
Streamer, the second foal of a six-furlong four-year-old winner, made a satisfactory introduction and better can be expected with the benefit of this experience.
Valley Of The Moon(IRE), a 20,000gns half-sister to six winners, including Limanda, a smart multiple sprint winner, finished up well held on her racecourse debut, but she was solid enough in the betting and it would be no surprise to see her improve on this next time. (tchd 15-2)
Startolini ran below the form she had shown on her two previous starts and was disappointing. Official explanation: jockey said filly was struck into behind (tchd 7-1 and 8-1)

2107 REDCARRACING.CO.UK CLAIMING STKS 1m 3f
2:40 (2:41) (Class 6) 3-Y-O **£2,388** (£705; £352) **Stalls** Low

Form RPR

0500 **1** **Tallyhobye**[19] 1609 3-8-3 50 PaulHanagan 1 56
(J R Weymes) *hld up towards rr: stdy hdwy over 3f out: rdn to ld 11/2f out: sn clr* **14/1**[3]

0002 **2** 5 **Mister Fizzbomb (IRE)**[17] 1661 3-8-13 47 (b) TonyHamilton 9 58
(J S Wainwright) *trckd ldrs: hdwy to ld over 2f out: rdn and hdd 11/2f out: sn one pce* **16/1**

0000 **3** 3 **Ebony Lady**[15] 1731 3-7-12 40 (v[1]) DavidKinsella 13 38
(R M Whitaker) *in tch: hdwy to chse ldrs 4f out: rdn along 3f out: kpt on same pce fnl 2f* **18/1**

5605 **4** 3½ **Wensleydale Star**[15] 1731 3-7-12 45 ow2 DeanHeslop(7) 7 40
(T D Barron) *sn led: pushed along and hdd 5f out: sn rdn and wknd over 2f out* **9/1**[2]

2445 **5** 2 **Ellesappelle**[20] 1599 3-8-12 68 (v) RobertWinston 2 43
(K R Burke) *cl up: led 5f out: rdn along 3f out: hdd and drvn over 2f out: sn wknd* **8/13**[1]

0063 **6** 5 **Silver Bank**[9] 1868 3-7-12 41 JimmyQuinn 11 21
(M W Easterby) *trckd ldrs: hdwy over 4f out: rdn along over 2f out and sn btn* **16/1**

000 **7** 2 **Tammy**[10] 1854 3-7-7 47 DuranFentiman(5) 6 18
(C W Thornton) *a rr* **33/1**

8 1¼ **Back Too Bedlam** 3-9-0 PJMcDonald(5) 8 37
(Mrs S A Watt) *a rr* **66/1**

000 **9** ¾ **Fox Flight (IRE)**[17] 1661 3-8-0 16 ow2 (p) AndrewMullen(5) 5 22
(D W Barker) *chsd ldrs: rdn along 1/2-way: sn wknd* **100/1**

000 **10** 11 **Lucky Bamblue (IRE)**[233] 5769 3-7-12 40 LeanneKershaw(5) 3 2
(P C Haslam) *in tch: rdn along 1/2-way: sn wknd* **66/1**

0 **11** 19 **Northern Promise (IRE)**[31] 1296 3-8-4 ow1 AdrianTNicholls 12 —
(J Parkes) *a rr* **66/1**

000 **12** 16 **Katejackiera (IRE)**[357] 2364 3-7-12 45 PaulQuinn 4 —
(W M Brisbourne) *a rr* **33/1**

1400 **U** **Subsidise (IRE)**[22] 1533 3-8-6 54 (v[1]) GregFairley(5) 10 —
(F P Murtagh) *in tch: hdwy to chse ldrs whn stmbld and uns rdr 5f out* **9/1**[2]

2m 21.74s (0.74) **Going Correction** +0.125s/f (Good) **13** Ran SP% **117.0**
Speed ratings (Par 97):102,98,96,93,92 88,87,86,85,77 63,52,—
CSF £204.66 TOTE £15.60: £3.00, £3.20, £5.80; EX 198.00.The winner was claimed by M E Sowersby for £5,000.
Owner Mrs A Birkett **Bred** Mrs Deborah O'Brien **Trained** Middleham Moor, N Yorks

FOCUS
A very moderate claimer and they finished well-strung out. Low-grade stuff, with the favourite below form.
Ellesappelle Official explanation: trainer's rep said filly needs to be covered up more
Silver Bank Official explanation: jockey said filly was unsuited by the good to firm ground

2108 PERTEMPS EMPLOYMENT ALLIANCE H'CAP 1m 1f
3:10 (3:11) (Class 5) (0-70,70) 4-Y-0+ **£3,238** (£963; £481; £240) **Stalls** Low

Form RPR

1041 **1** **Dium Mac**[20] 1591 5-8-8 67 SuzzanneFrance(7) 1 73
(N Bycroft) *hld up in rr: stdy hdwy 4f out: rdn over 1f out: styd on to ld ins last: r.o* **9/2**[1]

5004 **2** *hd* **Sforzando**[14] 1761 5-8-3 62 KristinStubbs(7) 12 68
(Mrs L Stubbs) *dwlt and bhd: hdwy on outer 3f out: rdn over 1f out: styd on wl towards fin: jst hld* **14/1**

006 **3** ¾ **Lauro**[22] 1553 6-8-7 59 TomEaves 10 64
(Miss J A Camacho) *hld up towards rr: hdwy 3f out: rdn over 1f out:ev ch ins last: drvn and no ex towards fin* **9/1**

0300 **4** ½ **Bright Sun (IRE)**[27] 1425 5-9-0 66 (t) KimTinkler 5 70
(N Tinkler) *led: rdn along over 2f out: drvn over 1f out: hdd and no ex ins last* **11/2**[3]

0000 **5** ½ **Wing Commander**[18] 1651 7-9-4 70 (b) GylesParkin 8 73
(I W McInnes) *hld up towards rr: hdwy over 2f out: rdn to chse ldrs over 1f out: kpt on u.p ins last* **25/1**

0410 **6** 2½ **Fossgate**[199] 6324 5-8-8 60 AdrianTNicholls 6 58
(J D Bethell) *chsd ldrs on inner: rdn along 3f out: drvn 2f out and kpt on same pce* **20/1**

6005 **7** *nk* **Mccormack (IRE)**[23] 1503 4-8-4 56 oh7 RichardMullen 3 53
(Micky Hammond) *in tch: hdwy to chse ldrs 4f out: rdn along 3f out: sn drvn and one pce* **66/1**

3004 **8** *hd* **Wrenlane**[109] 363 5-8-4 56 oh3 JimmyQuinn 11 53
(J J Quinn) *chsd ldr: rdn along 3f out: drvn and wknd fnl 2f* **10/1**

262P **9** 3½ **Royal Master**[41] 1075 4-8-1 58 LeanneKershaw(5) 14 48
(P C Haslam) *hld up towards rr: hdwy on outer over 3f out: sn rdn and no imp fnl 2f* **40/1**

-000 **10** *shd* **Capped For Victory (USA)**[10] 1856 5-8-13 65 LeeEnstone 7 54
(W S Cunningham) *bhd tl sme late hdwy* **66/1**

0156 **11** 1 **Danceinthevalley (IRE)**[251] 5410 4-9-2 68 NCallan 4 55
(G A Swinbank) *in tch: hdwy to chse ldrs 4f out: rdn along wl over 2f out: sn wknd* **5/1**[2]

2630 **12** 1¼ **Time To Regret**[5] 1947 6-8-5 57 oh1 ow1 TonyHamilton 9 42
(J S Wainwright) *chsd ldrs: hdwy over 3f out: rdn over 2f out: sn drvn and wknd wl over 1f out* **8/1**

0000 **13** ½ **Beltane**[259] 5206 8-8-4 56 oh19 AdrianMcCarthy 16 40
(W De Best-Turner) *midfiueld: hdwy and in tch 4f out: sn rdn along and wknd wl over 2f out* **100/1**

0040 **14** *nk* **King Nicholas (USA)**[50] 940 7-7-13 56 oh15 (tp) RoryMoore(5) 13 39
(J Parkes) *a towards rr* **100/1**

3001 **15** *nk* **Mobane Flyer**[14] 1757 6-8-10 62 PaulHanagan 15 45
(R A Fahey) *chsd ldrs: rdn along over 3f out: wknd over 2f out* **7/1**

1m 53.78s (0.38) **Going Correction** +0.125s/f (Good) **15** Ran SP% **115.6**
Speed ratings (Par 103):103,102,102,101,101 99,98,98,95,95 94,93,92,92,92
CSF £61.69 CT £553.80 TOTE £7.20: £2.10, £2.90, £2.70; EX 83.70.
Owner J A Swinburne **Bred** T Umpleby **Trained** Brandsby, N Yorks

FOCUS
A modest but competitive handicap. The form seems sound enough but the seventh leads to doubts.
King Nicholas(USA) Official explanation: jockey said gelding was unsuited by the good to firm ground

2109 HOT CHOCOLATE HERE IN AUGUST H'CAP 6f
3:40 (3:41) (Class 5) (0-70,70) 3-Y-O **£3,238** (£963; £481; £240) **Stalls** Centre

Form RPR

4142 **1** **Westport**[11] 1812 3-9-4 70 NCallan 6 82
(K A Ryan) *trckd ldrs: smooth hdwy to ld 2f out: rdn clr and hung bdly lft ent last: kpt on* **13/8**[1]

0001 **2** 2½ **Maison Dieu**[20] 1594 3-8-5 60 DanielTudhope(3) 8 65
(E J Alston) *trckd ldrs: hdwy 2f out: rdn to chse wnr over 1f out: kpt on* **11/2**[2]

0002 **3** 2½ **Making Music**[12] 1793 3-8-10 67 DuranFentiman(5) 9 64
(T D Easterby) *hld up: hdwy 1/2-way: rdn to chse ldrs over 1f out: kpt on same pce* **12/1**

234 **4** ½ **Bond Angel Eyes**[344] 2759 3-8-13 65 TonyCulhane 10 61
(G R Oldroyd) *towards rr: swtchd rt and hdwy 2f out: sn rdna nd kpt on ins last: nrst fin* **20/1**

005 **5** 2 **Electron Pulse**[22] 1530 3-8-11 63 FergalLynch 11 53
(J S Goldie) *hld up towards rr: hdwy over 2f out: rdn wl over 1f out: kpt on ins last: nrst fin* **16/1**

0420 **6** 3½ **Beowulf**[20] 1592 3-8-7 64 GregFairley(5) 7 43
(M Johnston) *in tch: rdn along over 2f out: sn drvn and btn* **7/1**[3]

0000 **7** 1¾ **Countess Carmine**[41] 1073 3-7-13 56 oh1 LeanneKershaw(5) 3 30
(P C Haslam) *cl up: rdn along over 2f out: sn wknd* **33/1**

1000 **8** *hd* **The Thrifty Bear**[24] 1497 3-8-12 67 DNolan(3) 4 40
(C W Fairhurst) *led: rdn along over 2f out: sn hdd & wknd* **25/1**

0405 **9** 2½ **Inca Soldier (FR)**[22] 1529 3-8-11 63 StanleyChin 5 29
(R C Guest) *chsd ldrs: pushed along 1/2-way: sn wknd* **12/1**

465 **10** *nk* **English Archer**[40] 1100 3-8-11 63 PhillipMakin 13 28
(J R Weymes) *chsd ldrs: rdn along 1/2-way: snw eakened* **20/1**

1000 **11** 1½ **Penny Whisper (IRE)**[17] 1693 3-8-8 60 GylesParkin 12 20
(I W McInnes) *a rr* **33/1**

0400 **12** *hd* **King Faz (IRE)**[20] 1592 3-8-10 62 LeeEnstone 14 22
(P C Haslam) *chsd ldrs to 1/2-way: sn wknd* **40/1**

1000 **13** 7 **Grafton (IRE)**[24] 1497 3-8-11 63 (b[1]) AdrianTNicholls 2 —
(J D Bethell) *a rr* **12/1**

1m 13.65s (1.95) **Going Correction** +0.30s/f (Good) **13** Ran SP% **116.6**
Speed ratings (Par 99):99,95,92,91,89 84,82,81,78,78 76,75,66
CSF £8.34 CT £80.85 TOTE £2.30: £1.50, £1.70, £3.70; EX 15.00.
Owner The C H F Partnership **Bred** Agricola Ficomontanino S R L **Trained** Hambleton, N Yorks

FOCUS
Just a modest handicap, but Westport had them well-strung out and is yet another one going in the right direction from the Kevin Ryan yard. Ordinary but sound form.
Grafton(IRE) Official explanation: jockey said gelding lost its action

2110 PERTEMPS PEOPLE DEVELOPMENT GROUP H'CAP 5f
4:10 (4:10) (Class 4) (0-85,82) 3-Y-O **£6,477** (£1,927; £963; £481) **Stalls** Centre

Form RPR

31 **1** **Rare Breed**[347] 2643 3-9-2 80 TomEaves 6 89
(Mrs L Stubbs) *ledm hdd 1/2-way: rdn to ld again over 1f out: drvn and edgd lft ins last: r.o wl* **8/1**

0041 **2** 1 ½ **Welcome Approach**[25] 1453 3-8-6 **70**.............................. PhillipMakin 3 73
(J R Weymes) *trckd ldrs: hdwy 2f out: sn rdn and ev ch ent last: sn drvn and one pce* **7/2**[2]

4120 **3** shd **Mulligan's Gold (IRE)**[10] 1857 3-8-6 **70**.............................. PaulQuinn 4 73
(T D Easterby) *chsd ldrs: effrt 2f out: swtchd lft and rdn ent last: one pce* **5/1**

6252 **4** shd **Blazing Heights**[22] 1529 3-8-11 **75**.............................. FergalLynch 5 77
(J S Goldie) *trckd ldrs: swtchd rt and smooth hdwy wl over 1f out: shkn up[and ev chgance entreing last: sn rdn and nt qucken* **11/4**[1]

1005 **5** shd **City For Conquest (IRE)**[19] 1604 3-8-11 **75**..............(v) PaulHanagan 8 77
(K R Burke) *cl up: led 1/2-way: rdn and hdd over 1f out: one pce* **4/1**[3]

3100 **6** 6 **Night In (IRE)**[19] 1606 3-8-10 **74**..............................(t) KimTinkler 1 52
(N Tinkler) *wnt lft s: in tch: rdn along 2f out and sn wknd* **8/1**

60.17 secs (1.47) **Going Correction** +0.30s/f (Good) **6** Ran SP% **107.8**
Speed ratings (Par 101):100,97,97,97,97 87
CSF £32.81 CT £134.10 TOTE £9.10: £3.10, £2.10; EX 33.80.
Owner Rare Breeders **Bred** M Pennell And Mrs M Holdcroft **Trained** Norton, N. Yorks
FOCUS
Just an ordinary sprint handicap - Rare Breed won well but short-heads separated the next four home. Sound enough form.

2111 RACING UK CHANNEL 432 MAIDEN STKS 1m 2f

4:40 (4:40) (Class 5) 3-Y-O+ **£3,238** (£963; £481; £240) **Stalls** Low

Form RPR

34 **1** **Hopeful Purchase (IRE)**[32] 1269 3-8-10 .... TonyCulhane 11 93+
(W J Haggas) *trckd ldng pair: hdwy on bit over 2f out: swtchd rt and shkn up to ld ent last: sn clr* **1/4**[1]

2054 **2** 2 ½ **Moonhawk**[11] 1837 3-8-10 76.............................. TomEaves 4 73
(J Howard Johnson) *led: rdn along 3f out: hdd over 2f out: sn drvn and one pce* **9/1**[2]

0550 **3** shd **Cool Ebony**[18] 1648 3-8-10 70.............................. PhillipMakin 3 73
(M Dods) *chsd ldr: hdwy to ld over 2f out: sn rdn along: drvn and hdd ent last: one pce* **20/1**[3]

0 **4** 7 **Shy Glance (USA)**[223] 5990 4-9-10 .... AdrianTNicholls 7 61
(G A Swinbank) *hld up in tch: hdwy 3f out: rdn along over 2f out: sn no imp* **20/1**[3]

5 ¾ **Anasena** 3-8-5 .... PaulHanagan 2 53
(G G Margarson) *in tch: rdn along over 3f out and sn btn* **25/1**

6 hd **Unbridled Storm (IRE)** 3-8-10 .... PaulQuinn 6 58
(G A Swinbank) *hld up towards rr: hdwy over 2f out: nvr nr ldrs* **50/1**

60 **7** 2 **For No One (IRE)**[31] 1289 3-8-5 .... GregFairley(5) 1 54
(M Johnston) *chsd ldrs: rdn along over 3f out: sn wknd* **25/1**

0 **8** 3 **Whiston Lad (IRE)**[31] 1290 3-8-7 .... BenSwarbrick(3) 9 48?
(S R Bowring) *a rr* **100/1**

0006 **9** 43 **Paint The Lily (IRE)**[246] 5513 5-9-0 35.................... AndrewMullen(5) 8 —
(F Watson) *a rr* **100/1**

2m 8.34s (1.54) **Going Correction** +0.125s/f (Good)
WFA 3 from 4yo+ 14lb **9** Ran SP% **111.2**
Speed ratings (Par 103):98,96,95,90,89 89,87,85,51
CSF £2.01 TOTE £1.30: £1.02, £1.50, £2.60; EX 2.60.
Owner J Hanson **Bred** Barronstown Stud And Orpendale **Trained** Newmarket, Suffolk
FOCUS
A modest maiden behind Hopeful Purchase who won as expected, confirming the promise he showed in better company on his two previous starts. He was value for further and the first three finished clear.

2112 GO RACING AT BEVERLEY TOMORROW EVENING AMATEUR RIDERS' MAIDEN H'CAP 6f

5:10 (5:11) (Class 6) (0-60,60) 4-Y-O+ **£2,307** (£709; £354) **Stalls** Centre

Form RPR

6250 **1** **Briery Lane (IRE)**[3] 2020 5-10-13 **59**....................(p) MissHWragg(7) 16 69
(Mrs K Walton) *in tch: hdwy 2f out: rdn over 1f out: styd on ins last to ld nr fin* **11/1**[3]

6303 **2** nk **Weakest Link**[28] 1397 5-10-3 **47**..............................(p) MrSPearce(5) 3 56
(E J Alston) *led: rdn wl over 1f out: hdd and no ex nr fin* **12/1**

6000 **3** 1 ¾ **Dazzler Mac**[12] 1795 5-10-11 **53**.............................. MissLEllison(3) 10 57
(N Bycroft) *in tch: hdwy 2f out: rdn over 1f out: kpt on ins last* **20/1**

0036 **4** 1 **Tagula Bay (IRE)**[15] 1735 4-11-5 **58**.............................. GerardTumelty 2 59
(T D Easterby) *trckd ldrs: rdn to chse ldr over 1f out: sn drvn and one pce ins last* **12/1**

4603 **5** nk **California Laws**[182] 6460 4-10-13 **57**.................... MrPCollington(5) 7 57
(T D Barron) *midfield: hdwy wl over 1f out: sn rdn and styd on ins last: nrst fin* **11/4**[1]

2605 **6** 1 **Nazaaha (USA)**[13] 1774 4-10-13 **52**.............................. MissCHannaford 9 49
(A G Newcombe) *hld up towards rr: hdwy 2f out: rdn and kpt on ins last: nrst fin* **16/1**

0062 **7** hd **Flaxby**[33] 1253 4-10-13 **52**..............................(b) MrSWalker 5 48
(J D Bethell) *hld up: hdwy 2f out: rdn over 1f out: kpt on ins last: nrst fin* **13/2**[2]

3220 **8** ¾ **Dark Champion**[210] 6217 6-10-12 **58**.............................. MissVBarr(7) 8 52
(R E Barr) *cl up: rdn 2f out: grad wknd appr last* **14/1**

0006 **9** 1 ¾ **Harrington Bates**[12] 1794 5-10-7 **46** oh1................ MissSBrotherton 17 35
(R M Whitaker) *bhd tl styd on fnl 2f* **12/1**

0060 **10** shd **Grandos (IRE)**[24] 1480 4-10-9 **55**.............................. MissJCoward(7) 14 43
(T D Easterby) *bhd tl styd on fnl 2f* **12/1**

0056 **11** ¾ **Tartan Special**[28] 1396 4-10-4 **48**....................(p) MissKellyBurke(5) 11 34
(K R Burke) *chsd ldrs: rdn 2f out: drvn and wknd appr last* **16/1**

0000 **12** ½ **Beau Jazz**[68] 706 5-10-2 **46** oh1.............................. MrsIDeBest(5) 18 31
(W De Best-Turner) *prom stands side: rdn and ch 2f out: drvn and wknd appr last* **100/1**

2642 **13** 1 ¾ **Fir Tree**[14] 1763 6-10-7 **46** oh1..............................(p) MrsMMorris 4 25
(S R Bowring) *chsd ldrs: rdn over 2f out: snw eakened* **25/1**

2500 **14** 2 ½ **Billy One Punch**[17] 1673 4-11-0 **60**.................... MissKMargarson(7) 13 32
(G G Margarson) *a towards rr* **16/1**

3005 **15** 2 ½ **Montana**[17] 1687 6-10-11 **50**.............................. MrsSBosley 15 14
(C W Fairhurst) *a towards rr* **12/1**

400- **16** 5 **Algorithm**[575] 6515 4-10-13 **52**.............................. MrSDobson 6 1
(T D Easterby) *in tch: rdn along over 2f out: sn wknd* **33/1**

5000 **17** ¾ **Value Plus (IRE)**[15] 1733 4-10-0 **46** oh1..............(vt) JPFeatherstone(7) 1 —
(C J Teague) *a towards rr* **100/1**

0004 **18** 5 **Zantero**[22] 1538 4-10-6 **52**.............................. MrBenBrisbourne(7) 12 —
(W M Brisbourne) *s.i.s: a bhd* **40/1**

1m 14.5s (2.80) **Going Correction** +0.30s/f (Good) **18** Ran SP% **127.1**
Speed ratings (Par 101):93,92,90,88,88 87,86,85,83,83 82,81,79,76,72 66,65,58
CSF £133.64 CT £2708.47 TOTE £12.40: £3.50, £3.40, £6.50, £2.70; EX 144.10 Place 6 £1506.31, Place 5 £123.14.

Owner Mrs K Walton **Bred** Simon And Helen Plumbly **Trained** Middleham Moor, N Yorks
FOCUS
As is to be expected in a 'maiden' handicap, a weak affair. Solid form for the grade, the runner-up the best guide.
T/Jkpt: Not won. T/Plt: £582.00 to a £1 stake. Pool: £39,948.95. 50.10 winning tickets. T/Qpdt: £10.10 to a £1 stake. Pool: £3,913.60. 285.30 winning tickets. JR

2083 SANDOWN (R-H)

Tuesday, May 30

OFFICIAL GOING: Sprint course - soft; round course - good to soft (soft in places)
With the exception of Art Eyes in the Henry II Stakes, all runners in races on the round course came towards the stands' side.
Wind: Moderate, half-against Weather: Fine

2113 BETFAIRPOKER.COM FILLIES' H'CAP 1m 1f

6:10 (6:12) (Class 5) (0-75,75) 3-Y-O+ **£3,886** (£1,156; £577; £288) **Stalls** High

Form RPR

5442 **1** **Fann (USA)**[20] 1599 3-9-1 **75**.............................. RyanMoore 8 83
(C E Brittain) *hld up in last trio: prog 3f out: led 3f out and sn rdn 3 l clr: drvn out fnl f* **3/1**[1]

034 **2** 2 **Dimelight**[12] 1797 3-8-10 **70**.............................. TQuinn 7 74
(D R C Elsworth) *lw: trckd ldng pair: effrt 3f out: led briefly over 2f out: chsd wnr after: no real imp* **7/2**[2]

4110 **3** 2 **Let Slip**[22] 1544 4-10-0 **75**.............................. AlanMunro 6 77
(W Jarvis) *lw: hld up in last trio: effrt 3f out: styd on to chse ldng pair over 1f out: one pce after* **7/2**[2]

1010 **4** 1 ¾ **Ignition**[18] 1636 4-9-5 **66**.............................. ShaneKelly 3 64
(W M Brisbourne) *pressed ldr: led over 3f out to over 2f out: sn outpcd and btn* **11/1**

0000 **5** 1 **Celtic Spa (IRE)**[12] 1802 4-9-3 **64**.............................. RobertHavlin 1 60
(Mrs P N Dutfield) *chsd ldrs: rdn 3f out: no imp 2f out: outpcd after* **7/1**[3]

0030 **6** ¾ **Adage**[28] 1374 3-8-12 **72**.............................. FergusSweeney 5 65
(David Pinder) *led to over 3f out: steadily wknd fnl 2f* **20/1**

6100 **7** 16 **Greenmeadow**[12] 1802 4-9-0 **61**.............................. JimmyFortune 2 24
(S Kirk) *chsd ldrrs: pushed along 1/2-way: wknd u.p 3f out: eased fnl f* **7/1**[3]

4440 **8** 23 **Seldemosa**[38] 1152 5-9-0 **61** oh7.............................. JohnEgan 4 —
(M S Saunders) *bit bkwd: hld up: a last: shkn up and no rspnse over 3f out: eased whn no ch 2f out: t.o* **20/1**

1m 58.68s (2.57) **Going Correction** +0.25s/f (Good)
WFA 3 from 4yo+ 13lb **8** Ran SP% **112.3**
Speed ratings (Par 100):98,96,94,92,92 91,77,56
CSF £13.10 CT £36.39 TOTE £3.00: £1.30, £1.30, £1.60; EX 8.40.
Owner Saeed Manana **Bred** Skymarc Farm Inc And Castlemartin Stud **Trained** Newmarket, Suffolk
FOCUS
A modest fillies' handicap, which saw the field race stands' side in the home straight, and the form looks fairly ordinary.

2114 BETFAIRGAMES.COM H'CAP 1m 14y

6:40 (6:43) (Class 4) (0-80,80) 4-Y-O+ **£6,477** (£1,927; £963; £481) **Stalls** High

Form RPR

0442 **1** **Davenport (IRE)**[5] 1957 4-8-10 **79**.............................. JamesMillman(7) 4 87+
(B R Millman) *dwlt: hld up in last: wl off the pce 1/2-way: gd prog on outer over 2f out: led last 150yds: jst hld on* **7/2**[1]

-222 **2** hd **Master Of The Race**[321] 3433 4-9-4 **80**.............................. ShaneKelly 11 87
(Sir Michael Stoute) *lw: trckd ldrs gng wl: chsd ldr wl over 1f out to ins fnl f: chsd wnr last 100yds: gaining at fin* **7/1**

0000 **3** 1 **Barathea Dreams (IRE)**[31] 1302 5-9-2 **78**.............................. KDarley 10 83
(J S Moore) *trckd ldrs: led 2f out: drvn over 1f out: hdd last 150yds: no ex* **11/2**[2]

130 **4** 3 **Percy's Pearl (USA)**[265] 5048 4-9-3 **79**.............................. JohnEgan 9 77
(D R C Elsworth) *lw: hld up in midfield: effrt and prog over 2f out: chsd ldrs over 1f out: no imp after* **8/1**

0506 **5** nk **Freeloader (IRE)**[56] 865 6-9-4 **80**.............................. RoystonFfrench 1 77
(R A Fahey) *hld up in rr: pushed along 3f out: kpt on steadily fnl 2f: no real imp on ldrs* **11/2**[2]

0000 **6** nk **Border Edge**[6] 1932 8-7-13 **66** oh2..............................(v) MarcHalford(5) 2 63
(J J Bridger) *plld hrd early: chsd ldrs: rdn 3f out: lost pl and struggling 2f out: styd on again ins fnl f* **33/1**

5102 **7** ¾ **Star Magnitude (USA)**[27] 1410 5-9-4 **80**.............................. IanMongan 5 75
(S Dow) *lw: dwlt: hld up and wl off the pce: rdn over 3f out: no prog tl kpt on fr over 1f out: n.d* **16/1**

0103 **8** 2 ½ **Mina A Salem**[18] 1629 4-9-0 **76**.............................. RyanMoore 7 65
(C E Brittain) *lw: led at gd pce to 2f out: sn wknd* **6/1**[3]

2110 **9** ½ **Deeper In Debt**[130] 161 8-8-7 **69**.............................. TQuinn 3 57
(J Akehurst) *pressed ldr to over 2f out: sn btn* **20/1**

4035 **10** 5 **Blue Trojan (IRE)**[43] 1043 6-9-1 **77**.............................. JimmyFortune 6 54
(S Kirk) *hld up wl in rr: rdn over 3f out: sn struggling and no ch* **10/1**

0- **11** 14 **Domart (POL)**[391] 3181 6-8-4 **66** oh1.............................. AlanMunro 8 10
(J R Best) *bit bkwd: chsd ldrs for 3f: sn wl in rr and struggling: t.o* **40/1**

1m 44.85s (0.90) **Going Correction** +0.25s/f (Good) **11** Ran SP% **116.0**
Speed ratings (Par 105):105,104,103,100,100 100,99,96,96,91 77
CSF £26.95 CT £134.74 TOTE £4.30: £1.40, £1.90, £2.60; EX 22.40.
Owner M A Swift and A J Chapman **Bred** M P B Bloodstock Ltd **Trained** Kentisbeare, Devon
FOCUS
A fair handicap, run at a decent pace, and the field once more came to the stands' side in the straight, with the winner again coming from well of the pace. The form looks sound enough.

2115 BETFAIR.COM TEMPLE STKS (GROUP 2) 5f 6y

7:15 (7:18) (Class 1) 3-Y-O+
£51,102 (£19,368; £9,693; £4,833; £2,421; £1,215) **Stalls** High

Form RPR

1314 **1** **Reverence**[24] 1485 5-9-4 108.............................. KDarley 13 117
(E J Alston) *lw: racd against far side rail: a ldng trio: led 1/2-way: clr fnl f: rdn out* **9/4**[1]

3600 **2** 1 ¼ **The Trader (IRE)**[24] 1485 8-9-8 110..............................(b) TedDurcan 7 117
(M Blanshard) *lw: hld up in last: swtchd sharply lft over 1f out: gd prog to take 2nd last 75yds: no ch w wnr* **33/1**

6020 **3** ¾ **Mecca's Mate**[13] 1778 5-9-1 101.............................. MJKinane 10 107
(D W Barker) *lw: chsd ldrs: pushed along 1/2-way: prog to chse wnr over 1f out: no imp: lost 2nd last 75yds* **20/1**

0642 **4** ½ **Orientor**[12] [1803] 8-9-4 100 .... JamieSpencer 12 109
(J S Goldie) *racd against far side rail: chsd ldrs: rdn 2f out: kpt on fnl f: nvr able to chal* **7/1**[3]

1036 **5** nk **Eisteddfod**[13] [1778] 5-9-4 110 .... JimmyFortune 9 108
(P F I Cole) *sn pushed along in midfield: no prog u.p fr 2f out tl styd on ins fnl f* **8/1**

0162 **6** 1 ½ **Indian Maiden (IRE)**[10] [1849] 6-9-1 104 .... FrancisNorton 11 100+
(M S Saunders) *hld up towards rr: effrt whn nowhere to go over 1f out: kpt on ins fnl f: no ch* **12/1**

1003 **7** 2 **Out After Dark**[17] [1663] 5-9-4 104 .... (b) AdamKirby 1 96
(C G Cox) *racd on outer: wl in rr: rdn and struggling 2f out: n.d* **20/1**

1112 **8** 1 ¼ **Les Arcs (USA)**[42] [1069] 6-9-4 111 .... JohnEgan 4 92
(T J Pitt) *led for 2f: wknd u.p over 1f out: eased whn no ch* **6/1**[2]

5054 **9** nk **The Tatling (IRE)**[16] [1717] 9-9-4 113 .... RyanMoore 3 91
(J M Bradley) *dwlt: a towards rr: effrt but no ch whn hmpd 1f out: eased* **10/1**

3520 **10** 3 **Balmont (USA)**[285] [4512] 5-9-4 110 .... ShaneKelly 8 80
(J Noseda) *a wl in rr: rdn and no prog 1/2-way: wknd fnl f* **12/1**

1111 **11** 6 **Resplendent Glory (IRE)**[332] [3146] 4-9-4 110 .... IanMongan 6 60
(T G Mills) *dwlt: sn w ldrs: led 3f out to 1/2-way: wknd v rapidly fr over 1f out: dismntd after fin* **12/1**

2510 **12** 11 **Godfrey Street**[234] [5732] 3-9-0 107 .... RichardHughes 2 27
(R Hannon) *bit bkwd: chsd ldrs for 3f: wknd rapidly: t.o* **33/1**

62.10 secs (-0.11) **Going Correction** +0.375s/f (Good)
WFA 3 from 4yo+ 8lb **12** Ran SP% **116.2**
Speed ratings (Par 115):115,113,111,111,110 108,104,102,102,97 88,70
CSF £99.97 TOTE £3.30: £1.50, £8.60, £4.90; EX 118.50.
Owner Mr & Mrs G Middlebrook **Bred** G And Mrs Middlebrook **Trained** Longton, Lancs

FOCUS
A competitive renewal of this Group 2 sprint, which seemed to favour those drawn high, and the form looks straightforward enough and decent for the grade.

NOTEBOOK
Reverence ◆ readily resumed winning ways under a positive ride from Darley, who was quick to make use of his decent draw against the far-side rail. He hit the front full of running at halfway, clearly relishing this return to his favoured soft ground, and was never going to be reeled in thereafter. On this sort of ground, he is right up there with the best in this division, and he still looks to be improving. His next immediate target is most likely the King's Stand at Royal Ascot and, while the prospect of fast ground there is not ideal, he still possesses the class to go very close. (tchd 11-4 and 3-1 in a place)
The Trader(IRE) looked a brief threat when making a strong challenge from off the pace, but the stiff finish saw him put in his place by the winner. He loves this sort of ground - and this was a much-improved effort - but consistency has never been his strong suit, and he is far from certain to reverse form with Reverence if taking up his entry in the King's Stand next month, despite the fact he will be better off at the weights there.
Mecca's Mate was up there throughout and posted a solid effort from her high draw. She is versatile as regards underfoot conditions, but probably wants it soft over this trip, and this was arguably a career-best effort. It is possible she may turn out in the Vodafone Sprint Handicap at Epsom on Derby Day over another furlong, but she will have to carry top-weight in that. (op 25-1)
Orientor, second in this event last year, held every chance under a more prominent ride than is often the case and looked to run close to his best in defeat. He really deserves to get his head back in front, but is not at all easy to place from his current rating. (op 15-2 tchd 8-1)
Eisteddfod was not disgraced, but just struggled to go the pace on this drop back to the minimum trip, before keeping on again up the rising finish. (op 15-2 tchd 7-1)
Indian Maiden(IRE) would have finished closer but for enduring a troubled passage nearing the final furlong, and is better than the bare form. (tchd 11-1)
Les Arcs(USA) showed decent early dash to lead from his low draw, but he faded tamely after passing two out, and ultimately disappointed. He was later reported to have lost his action and, while he has won in Listed company on soft ground, at this level he probably needs top of the ground to be seen at best. Official explanation: jockey said gelding lost its action (op 11-2)
Balmont(USA), third in this event last year, was always struggling from off the pace on ground he would have found plenty soft enough. He has a little to prove at present, but ideally needs a quicker surface, and is entitled to come on for the run. (tchd 14-1)
Resplendent Glory(IRE), beaten just once from seven previous outings and returning from a 332-day layoff, weakened dramatically after showing good early dash and, as he was dismounted quickly after passing the finish, something was clearly amiss. Official explanation: jockey said colt lost its action (op 10-1)

2116 BETFAIR.COM BRIGADIER GERARD STKS (GROUP 3) 1m 2f 7y
7:50 (7:51) (Class 1) 4-Y-O+
£28,390 (£10,760; £5,385; £2,685; £1,345; £675) **Stalls** High

Form RPR

0211 **1** **Notnowcato**[41] [1084] 4-9-3 112 .... MJKinane 1 119+
(Sir Michael Stoute) *trckd ldr: led 2f out: rdn and in command fr over 1f out: readily* **5/4**[1]

3442 **2** 1 ¼ **Boule D'Or (IRE)**[24] [1489] 5-9-0 107 .... MichaelHills 4 112
(J Akehurst) *hld up in last: prog 2f out but sn outpcd: styd on to take 2nd last 100yds: n.d to wnr* **12/1**

2604 **3** ½ **Hattan (IRE)**[24] [1489] 4-9-0 108 .... SebSanders 2 111
(C E Brittain) *lw: dwlt: hld up in 5th: effrt 2f out: drvn and nt qckn wl over 1f out: styd on same pce fnl f* **9/1**

0150 **4** shd **Common World (USA)**[10] [1840] 7-9-3 .... FMBerry 5 114
(T Hogan, Ire) *dwlt: sn trckd ldng pair: effrt to chal and w wnr 2f out: nt qckn over 1f out: lost 2nd and fdd last 100yds* **8/1**[3]

6124 **5** 6 **Grand Passion (IRE)**[40] [1098] 6-9-0 104 .... SteveDrowne 6 100
(G Wragg) *settled in 4th: rdn 2f out: sn wknd* **20/1**

1243 **6** hd **Bandari (IRE)**[23] [1507] 7-9-5 118 .... RHills 3 105
(M Johnston) *lw: led: rdn and hdd 2f out and squeezed out sltly: sn dropped out* **9/4**[2]

2m 13.92s (3.68) **Going Correction** +0.70s/f (Yiel) **6** Ran SP% **108.8**
Speed ratings (Par 113):113,112,111,111,106 106
CSF £15.96 TOTE £1.90: £1.30, £4.40; EX 19.70.
Owner Anthony & David de Rothschild **Bred** Southcourt Stud **Trained** Newmarket, Suffolk

FOCUS
A substandard renewal of this Group 3 event - whose previous winners include such top-class performers as Mtoto, Pilsudski and Bosra Sham - and the progressive winner is full value for his winning margin.

NOTEBOOK
Notnowcato had very much the run of the race and duly made it two wins from as many starts this term. He is clearly at home on most types of ground, saw out this slightly longer trip without fuss, and he left the impression that he still has a fair deal more to offer. His trainer's record of improving older horses is second to none and, while he was entitled to win this as he did, he looks well worthy of another rise in class now. (tchd 11-10 and 11-8 in places)
Boule D'Or(IRE) was doing all of his best work towards the finish, having being very patiently ridden, and appeared to run right up to his best in defeat. He is proving very hard to win with, but on this evidence he can be found another opening when reverting to his favoured fast ground in the future. (tchd 14-1)
Hattan(IRE) turned in an improved effort and would have most likely been better served by a more positive ride over this trip. He really needs 12 furlongs. (op 11-1)
Common World(USA) had his chance, but the rising finish over this trip ultimately stretched his stamina to the limit. He is very genuine, but is best at a mile, and not at all easy to place at present. (op 7-1)
Grand Passion(IRE), fourth in this event last season, was never a serious factor on ground he would have found against him.
Bandari(IRE), who won this event in 2004, was quick to bag his favoured position at the head of affairs, but his fate was sealed nearing the two-furlong marker as he proved a sitting duck for those coming from behind. He is better than this, but has it prove now. (tchd 2-1 and 5-2)

2117 BETFAIR.COM H'CAP 1m 6f
8:20 (8:22) (Class 4) (0-85,82) 3-Y-O **£6,477** (£1,927; £963; £481) **Stalls** Low

Form RPR

241 **1** **Souffleur**[11] [1827] 3-8-11 72 .... JamieSpencer 4 81
(M L W Bell) *sn settled in midfield: stdy prog over 2f out: effrt to ld 1f out: shkn up and styd on wl: shade comf* **5/1**[2]

3321 **2** ½ **At The Money**[18] [1648] 3-8-3 64 .... FrancisNorton 2 72
(J M P Eustace) *racd freely: led after 2f: hdd over 2f out: pressed ldr after: upsides 1f out: chsd wnr after: r.o but readily hld* **11/2**[3]

6233 **3** 1 **Gee Dee Nen**[20] [1586] 3-9-4 79 .... MichaelHills 3 86
(M H Tompkins) *lw: led for 2f: styd cl up: led again over 2f out: drvn and hdd 1f out: one pce* **4/1**[1]

342 **4** 2 ½ **Som Tala**[24] [1492] 3-9-2 77 .... TedDurcan 5 81
(M R Channon) *hld up in rr but wl in tch: effrt 3f out: cl up 2f out: sn nt qckn and btn: plugged on* **20/1**

51 **5** nk **Power Of Future (GER)**[23] [1503] 3-9-3 78 .... EddieAhern 6 81
(H R A Cecil) *tall: leggy: s.i.s: sn trckd ldrs: effrt 3f out: nt qckn 2f out and btn after: one pce* **4/1**[1]

4212 **6** 4 **Daylami Star**[20] [1586] 3-9-7 82 .... JimmyFortune 8 79
(J H M Gosden) *hmpd after 1f: hld up in last: effrt 3f out: cl up but rdn whn hmpd 2f out: wknd over 1f out* **5/1**[2]

0353 **7** 14 **Smart Gal (IRE)**[23] [1515] 3-8-10 71 .... ShaneKelly 7 49
(J L Dunlop) *hld up: prog to chse ldr 8f out to 3f out: wknd rapidly over 2f out* **13/2**

3134 **8** 3 **Soho Square**[29] [1356] 3-9-2 77 .... RoystonFfrench 1 51
(M Johnston) *chsd ldr after 3f to 8f out: sn rdn: last and struggling over 4f out: sn bhd* **20/1**

3m 13.64s (9.13) **Going Correction** +0.70s/f (Yiel) **8** Ran SP% **111.6**
Speed ratings (Par 101):101,100,100,98,98 96,88,86
CSF £30.83 CT £116.84 TOTE £4.50: £1.70, £1.80, £2.00; EX 32.20.
Owner Baron F C Oppenheim **Bred** Baron Von Oppenheim **Trained** Newmarket, Suffolk

FOCUS
Quite an interesting three-year-old handicap, but it was run at an uneven pace, and the form is worth treating with a degree of caution.
Smart Gal(IRE) Official explanation: jockey said filly had a breathing problem

2118 BETFAIR BACKS BROOKE MAIDEN STKS 1m 2f 7y
8:50 (8:56) (Class 5) 3-Y-O+ **£4,533** (£1,348; £674; £336) **Stalls** High

Form RPR

5443 **1** **Senor Dali (IRE)**[24] [1473] 3-8-11 95 .... TQuinn 9 80+
(J L Dunlop) *lw: prom: led 3f out: hung lft sn after: clr and in command fr 2f out: unchal* **10/11**[1]

0 **2** 3 **Accompanist**[24] [1476] 3-8-11 .... JimmyFortune 5 74
(J H M Gosden) *hld up in midfield: prog over 2f out: rdn to chse wnr 1f out: no imp* **16/1**

452 **3** nk **Altenburg (FR)**[31] [1290] 4-9-11 80 .... RyanMoore 15 75
(Mrs N Smith) *hld up in last quartet: prog on wd outside over 2f out: rdn and styd on fr over 1f out: nrst fin* **12/1**

0006 **4** 1 **Nefski Alexander (USA)**[15] [1741] 3-8-11 73 .... SteveDrowne 14 72
(P F I Cole) *trckd ldrs: chsd wnr over 2f out to 1f out: one pce* **25/1**

5 ½ **Darenjan (IRE)** 3-8-11 .... MJKinane 8 71
(Sir Michael Stoute) *w'like: scope: sn in midfield: effrt 3f out: chsd ldrs 2f out: kpt on same pce* **4/1**[2]

6 ½ **Acts Of Grace (USA)** 3-8-6 .... SebSanders 1 69+
(J L Dunlop) *leggy: hld up in last quartet: stdy prog on inner over 2f out: nt clr run over 1f out: kpt on fnl f: bttr for experience* **14/1**

0 **7** ¾ **Mrs Solese (IRE)**[29] [1336] 3-8-6 .... EddieAhern 4 64
(J R Boyle) *prom: lost pl sltly over 2f out: kpt on steadily fnl f* **100/1**

4 **8** 3 ½ **Soubriquet (IRE)**[17] [1670] 3-8-11 .... IanMongan 7 63
(T G Mills) *prom: rdn 3f out: wknd 2f out* **10/1**[3]

03 **9** ½ **Openide**[11] [1826] 5-9-8 .... AdamKirby(3) 11 62
(B W Duke) *mde most to 3f out: sn lost pl u.p and btn* **50/1**

0 **10** shd **Salonga (IRE)**[17] [1674] 3-8-6 .... AlanMunro 13 56
(C F Wall) *dwlt: a wl in rr: rdn over 2f out: no real prog* **33/1**

0 **11** nk **Himba**[15] [1741] 3-8-11 .... JimCrowley 2 61+
(Mrs A J Perrett) *rangy: str: bit bkwd: hld up in midfield: nudged along and no prog over 2f out: nvr nr ldrs* **33/1**

0 **12** hd **Devonia Plains (IRE)**[11] [1827] 4-9-11 .... (v[1]) RobertHavlin 3 62
(Mrs P N Dutfield) *w'like: bit bkwd: dwlt: prog to trck ldr 6f out to 3f out: wknd* **100/1**

13 2 **Monsignor Fred** 4-9-11 .... DaneO'Neill 12 58
(H Candy) *w'like: bit bkwd: chsd ldrs tl wknd wl over 2f out* **25/1**

00 **14** 1 ¼ **In On The Act (IRE)**[17] [1669] 3-8-6 .... JohnEgan 6 50
(Jamie Poulton) *hld up in last quartet: nvr a factor* **22/1**

2m 15.44s (5.20) **Going Correction** +0.70s/f (Yiel)
WFA 3 from 4yo+ 14lb **14** Ran SP% **123.6**
Speed ratings (Par 103):107,104,104,103,103 102,102,99,98,98 98,98,96,95
CSF £17.74 TOTE £2.00: £1.20, £3.90, £2.70; EX 24.00 Place 6 £13.59, Place 5 £10.53 .
Owner Mrs M E Slade **Bred** Frank Dunne **Trained** Arundel, W Sussex

FOCUS
This was probably just a fair maiden for the track, and the 95-rated winner won as he was entitled to. It ought to produce its share of future winners, but the overall form is tricky to assess.
Acts Of Grace(USA) ◆ Official explanation: jockey said filly was denied a clear run

T/Plt: £14.50 to a £1 stake. Pool: £66,011.75. 3,309.25 winning tickets. T/Qpdt: £10.20 to a £1 stake. Pool: £3,301.30. 237.80 winning tickets. JN

2119 - 2122a (Foreign Racing) - See Raceform Interactive

TABY (R-H)

Tuesday, May 30

OFFICIAL GOING: Good

2123a AON STOCKHOLMS STORA PRIS (GROUP 3) 1m 1f 165y

8:10 (8:17) 4-Y-0+ £21,962 (£10,981; £5,271; £3,514; £2,196)

RPR

1 **Jubilation**[282] [4622] 7-9-2 ... FDiaz 7 110
(F Reuterskiold, Sweden) *hld up in tch, rapid prog to ld wl over 2f out, sn clr in str, pushed out, eased closing stages* **67/10**[3]

2 1 1/2 **Fly Society (DEN)**[234] [5751] 5-9-2 ... KAndersen 9 107
(S Jensen, Denmark) *in rear early, headway 4f out, took 2nd 1f out, stayed on but no chance with winner* **71/10**

3 3 **Funny Legend (NOR)**[226] 5-8-12 ... FJohansson 5 98
(Wido Neuroth, Norway) *held up in touch, outpaced 3f out, headway final 2f, never nearer* **2/1**[1]

4 2 1/2 **Alnitak (USA)**[273] 5-9-2 ...(b) LHammer-Hansen 2 97
(B Olsen, Norway) *mid-division, 5th straight, stayed on to take 4th in final furlong* **39/1**

5 2 1/2 **Eltizaam (USA)**[591] [6206] 4-9-2 ... MMartinez 6 93
(B Olsen, Norway) *mid-division, headway to go 3rd briefly over 3f out, 4th straight, one pace* **20/1**

6 hd **Maybach**[18] [1659] 5-9-2 ... GSolis 11 92
(O Stenstrom, Sweden) *never a factor* **17/1**

7 shd **Mambo King (DEN)** 4-9-2 ... MSantos 1 92
(L Kelp, Sweden) *always mid-division* **21/2**

8 1 **Passport (SWE)**[316] 5-9-2 ... JJohansen 8 90
(L Reuterskiold, Sweden) *2nd to 4f out, 6th and beaten straight* **106/10**

9 1 **Binary File (USA)**[18] [1659] 8-9-2 ... YvonneDurant 12 88
(L Kelp, Sweden) *started slowly, last to half-way, always in rear* **38/10**[2]

10 18 **Tiberius Caesar (FR)**[18] [1659] 6-9-2 ... NCordrey 10 56
(F Reuterskiold, Sweden) *close up, went 2nd briefly 4f out, 3rd straight, soon weakened* **17/1**

11 6 **Pecoiquen (CHI)**[261] [5162] 5-9-2 ...(b) JLSanchez 3 —
(F Castro, Sweden) *led to well over 2f out, weakened quickly* **86/10**

2m 2.80s **11 Ran SP% 125.6**
(including 1 SKr stakes); WIN 7.77; PL 2.22, 2.18, 1.57; DF 79.33.
Owner Stall Falk & Stall Lambada Ab **Bred** Juddmonte Farms **Trained** Sweden

[1660] BEVERLEY (R-H)

Wednesday, May 31

OFFICIAL GOING: Good (good to firm in places)

Wind: Moderate, across

2124 SUPABED QUALITY PAPER BEDDING H'CAP 1m 4f 16y

6:40 (6:40) (Class 5) (0-70,70) 3-Y-O £3,562 (£1,059; £529; £264) Stalls High

Form RPR

0004 1 **Liberate**[19] [1634] 3-8-4 **56** oh1 ... JamieMackay 2 67
(Sir Mark Prescott) *cl up: effrt 3f out: rdn to ld over 2f out: drvn and edgd rt over 1f out: sn clr* **7/1**[3]

6301 2 3 **Winds Of Change**[19] [1634] 3-8-13 **65** ... JoeFanning 4 71
(M Johnston) *led: rdn along over 3f out: hdd over 2f out: drvn and sltly hmpd over 1f out: kpt on same pce* **6/1**[1]

0064 3 1/2 **Princess Cocoa (IRE)**[21] [1599] 3-8-6 **58** ... TonyHamilton 13 63
(R A Fahey) *trckd ldrs on inner: hdwy over 2f out: sn rdn: n.m.r and swtchd rt over 1f out: drvn and kpt on same pce* **13/2**[2]

0033 4 nk **Blushing Hilary (IRE)**[16] [1732] 3-9-3 **69** ...(v) JimmyQuinn 10 74
(Miss J A Camacho) *trckd ldrs: hdwy 3f out: rdn wl over 1f out and kpt on same pce ins last* **9/1**

6054 5 hd **Bramcote Lorne**[30] [1345] 3-8-6 **58** ... DarrylIHolland 9 62
(S Parr) *hld up towards rr: hdwy 3f out: rdn wl over 1f out: kpt on ins last: nrst fin* **8/1**

5262 6 2 1/2 **Noble Edge**[28] [1424] 3-8-4 **59** ... DanielTudhope(3) 5 59
(Robert Gray) *hld up towards rr: hdwy on outer 3f out: rdn and edgd rt wl over 1f out: sn drvn and no imp fnl f* **13/2**[2]

0063 7 2 **Penmara**[246] [5536] 3-8-7 **59** ... KDarley 8 56
(M H Tompkins) *midfield: hdwy on outer over 3f out: rdn along 2f out: sn btn* **16/1**

010 8 2 **Entranced**[29] [1381] 3-9-4 **70** ... TomEaves 1 64
(Miss J A Camacho) *hld up and bhd: hdwy over 4f out: sn rdn along and nvr rch ldrs* **22/1**

0000 9 1/2 **Katsumoto (IRE)**[23] [1533] 3-8-8 **60** ... NCallan 14 53
(N P Littmoden) *chsd ldrs: rdn along 4f out: wknd wl over 2f out* **33/1**

3322 10 shd **Mambo Sun**[34] [1251] 3-8-8 **67** ... KevinGhunowa(7) 11 60
(P A Blockley) *trckd ldrs: rdn along 4f out: wknd over 2f out* **6/1**[1]

0646 11 8 **Cora Pearl (IRE)**[19] [1648] 3-8-4 **56** oh12 ... FrancisNorton 7 36
(M J Polglase) *in tch on outer: rdn along over 3f out: sn wknd* **33/1**

0003 12 2 **Cartoonist (IRE)**[32] [1282] 3-8-7 **59** ... RoystonFfrench 12 36
(A King) *trckd ldng pair on inner: rdn along over 4f out: drvn 3f out and sn wknd* **12/1**

0522 13 3/4 **Squirtle (IRE)**[19] [1634] 3-8-13 **65** ... RobbieFitzpatrick 3 41
(W M Brisbourne) *in tch on outer: rdn along 4f out: wkng whn bmpd wl over 2f out* **12/1**

2m 37.72s (-2.49) **Going Correction** -0.30s/f (Firm) **13 Ran SP% 120.3**
Speed ratings (Par 99):96,94,93,93,93 91,90,89,88,88 83,81,81
CSF £48.07 CT £289.34 TOTE £8.60: £2.70, £1.90, £2.40; EX 33.50.
Owner Eclipse Thoroughbreds-Osborne House III **Bred** Miss K Rausing **Trained** Newmarket, Suffolk
■ Stewards' Enquiry : Jamie Mackay two-day ban: used whip with excessive frequency (Jun 12-13)

FOCUS
A modest handicap run at a steady early pace that was dominated by those who raced prominently. The fourth sets the level for the form.

2125 HILARY NEEDLER TROPHY (LISTED RACE) (FILLIES) 5f

7:10 (7:11) (Class 1) 2-Y-O

£14,195 (£5,380; £2,692; £1,342; £672; £337) Stalls High

Form RPR

1 **Roxan (IRE)** 2-8-9 ... NCallan 8 90+
(K A Ryan) *dwlt: sn in tch: n.m.r and swtchd lft 2f out: hdwy to ld ent last: sn rdn and r.o wl* **3/1**[1]

1 2 1 3/4 **Just Joey**[44] [1046] 2-8-12 ... DarrylIHolland 12 84
(J R Weymes) *led: rdn along 2f out: drvn and hdd ent last: kpt on gamely* **9/1**

26 3 1/2 **Hucking Hot**[27] [1429] 2-8-12 ... JoeFanning 10 82
(J R Best) *trckd ldrs: hdwy 2f out: sn rdn: styd on wl fnl f* **40/1**

11 4 shd **Eloquent Rose (IRE)**[25] [1491] 2-8-12 ... RoystonFfrench 3 82
(Mrs A Duffield) *cl up: rdn along 2f out and ev ch tl drvn and nt qckn ins last* **12/1**

14 5 hd **Kerry's Dream**[12] [1831] 2-8-12 ... DavidAllan 1 81
(T D Easterby) *cl up on outer: rdn along wl over 1f out and ev ch tl drvn and edgd lft ins last: no ex* **6/1**[3]

343 6 1 **Cassiara**[12] [1831] 2-8-12 ... JimmyQuinn 7 78
(J Pearce) *hld up in tch: hdwy 2f out: sn rdn: kpt on ins last* **9/2**[2]

1 7 1 1/4 **Miss Otis**[9] [1896] 2-8-12 ... JimCrowley 6 73
(P Winkworth) *cl up: ev ch 2f out: sn rdn and wknd appr last* **13/2**

8 3/4 **My Lovely Lesley (USA)** 2-8-9 ... KDarley 9 67
(B J Meehan) *hld up towards rr: swtchd lft and hdwy on outer over 1f out: sn rdn and no imp ins last: eased* **14/1**

44 9 2 **Onenightinlisbon (IRE)**[30] [1342] 2-8-12 ... LeeEnstone 4 63
(P T Midgley) *stdd s: a towards rr* **100/1**

2 10 nk **Fly Time**[11] [1853] 2-8-12 ... TonyCulhane 11 62
(M R Channon) *chsd ldr on inner: rdn along wl over 1f out: grad wknd* **9/1**

31 11 5 **Sunken Rags**[16] [1743] 2-8-12 ... FrancisNorton 2 44
(K R Burke) *dwlt and swtchd rt s: a towards rr* **22/1**

62.57 secs (-1.43) **Going Correction** -0.30s/f (Firm) **11 Ran SP% 112.9**
Speed ratings (Par 98):99,96,95,95,94 93,91,90,86,86 78
CSF £28.89 TOTE £3.80: £2.00, £1.80, £6.90; EX 37.10.
Owner Highbank Equine Limited **Bred** Gamra Partnership **Trained** Hambleton, N Yorks

FOCUS
A competitive renewal on paper featuring five last-time-out winners. The previously unraced winner was impressive and is likely to be one of the main contenders for the Queen Mary. The form looks straightforward and has been rated positively.

NOTEBOOK
Roxan(IRE) hails from a stable that has enjoyed a very successful season so far with its juveniles, and it was a tip in itself that she was the chosen representative in this Listed contest, despite the fact that she had not been seen on a racecourse before. A daughter of Rock Of Gibraltar out of a mare who won over a mile, she justified favouritism in impressive fashion despite having to challenge on the outside of the field from some way out. Granted normal improvement from this debut run she should be capable of scoring in Group company, and the Queen Mary at Royal Ascot is the obvious target. (op 11-4 tchd 10-3 and 7-2 in a place)
Just Joey made full use of her favourable high draw and tried to make all the running. She ran well but was unable to give 3lb to the impressive and previously unraced winner. A step up to six furlongs should not inconvenience her. (op 10-1)
Hucking Hot stayed on well in the closing stages and posted a much-improved performance. A reproduction of this effort should see her off the mark in an average maiden, but she probably needs six furlongs now.
Eloquent Rose(IRE), a winner of her previous two starts, was poorly drawn and not disgraced. She may, however, have done her winning for the time being and find others progressing past her. (op 14-1)
Kerry's Dream had the worst of the draw and raced keenly in the early stages. That did not help her get home over this stiff five furlongs and she will be more effective on an easier track. (op 15-2)
Cassiara finished one place in front of Kerry's Dream at York when that rival set an unsustainably fast gallop, and the form was reversed this time, although there was still little in it. She is another who will not mind stepping up to six furlongs. (op 4-1)
Miss Otis was a bit dissapointing on this step up in class, but she showed speed and perhaps a sharper track, like the one where she made a winning debut, will suit her better. (op 5-1)
My Lovely Lesley(USA), a half-sister to four winners including Wonderful Days, a high-class multiple winner in Japan, and to Shin Feign, a dual winner on turf in the US, was the only other debutante in the race apart from the winner. It all proved a bit too much for her first time out, but her stable's juveniles usually improve a fair amount for their debuts.

2126 ROLLITS SOLICITORS H'CAP 7f 100y

7:40 (7:40) (Class 4) (0-85,82) 3-Y-O £6,477 (£1,927; £963; £481) Stalls High

Form RPR

0212 1 **Angaric (IRE)**[18] [1693] 3-8-6 **70** ... RobertWinston 7 77
(B Smart) *hld up in tch: hdwy 3f out: rdn over 1f out: styd on wl to ld ins last* **9/2**[2]

2465 2 1 **Creative Mind (IRE)**[27] [1440] 3-8-12 **76** ... RichardMullen 8 81
(E J O'Neill) *chsd ldr: rdn to ld 2f out: drvn over 1f out: hdd ins last: kpt on gamely* **20/1**

0106 3 nk **Rubenstar (IRE)**[30] [1337] 3-9-1 **79** ... NCallan 2 83
(M H Tompkins) *hld up in tch: swtchd lft and hdwy over 2f out: rdn over 1f out ev ch ins last tl drvn and no ex last 100 yds* **7/1**

3062 4 hd **Royal Composer (IRE)**[21] [1592] 3-8-4 **68** ... DavidAllan 6 72
(T D Easterby) *chsd ldrs: rdn along and outpcd over 2f out: swtchd lft and drvn ent last: styd on wl towards fin* **7/1**

335 5 1 1/2 **Vacation (IRE)**[11] [1844] 3-9-2 **80** ... DarrylIHolland 4 80
(V Smith) *in rr and pushed along 1/2-way: rdn 2f out: hdwy over 1f out: drvn and kpt on ins last: nrst fin* **9/1**

1552 6 1 **Call My Number (IRE)**[34] [1250] 3-9-4 **82** ... TonyCulhane 5 79
(M R Channon) *in tch: hdwy over 2f out: rdn and ev ch wl over 1f out: drvn and wknd ent last* **15/8**[1]

51 7 2 1/2 **Vanilla Delight (IRE)**[254] [5355] 3-8-13 **77** ... RoystonFfrench 3 68
(J Howard Johnson) *chsd ldrs on outer: rdn along 2f out: drvn and wknd over 1f out* **20/1**

1633 8 2 **Jaad**[30] [1349] 3-9-3 **81** ... JoeFanning 9 67
(M Johnston) *t.k.h: sn led: rdn along 3f out: hdd 2f out and wknd over 1f out* **6/1**[3]

1m 31.35s (-2.96) **Going Correction** -0.30s/f (Firm) **8 Ran SP% 111.8**
Speed ratings (Par 101):104,102,102,102,100 99,96,94
CSF £81.22 CT £617.02 TOTE £6.10: £1.40, £4.60, £2.40; EX 128.60.
Owner Anthony D Gee **Bred** Humphrey Okeke **Trained** Hambleton, N Yorks

FOCUS
A fair handicap featuring one or two progressive types and solid form with those in the frame behind the winner all to form.

2127 BRIAN YEARDLEY CONTINENTAL TWO YEAR OLD TROPHY CONDITIONS STKS (C&G) 5f

8:10 (8:10) (Class 2) 2-Y-O

£12,464 (£3,732; £1,866; £934; £466; £234) **Stalls** High

Form RPR

12 **1** **Everymanforhimself (IRE)**[12] [1824] 2-9-0 .... EddieAhern 10 94+
(J G Given) *sn outpcd in rr: swtchd wd and hdwy wl over 1f out: sn rdn and str run ent last: edgd rt and led last 50 yds* **7/1**

21 **2** *¾* **Mood Music**[19] [1632] 2-9-2 .... RichardMullen 3 93+
(E J O'Neill) *prom: hdwy 2f out: rdn to ld over 1f out: drvn and edgd rt ins last: hdd and nt qckn last 50 yds* **13/2**[3]

31 **3** *nk* **Steelcut**[2] [2076] 2-9-0 .... PaulHanagan 7 90
(R A Fahey) *chsd ldrs: hdwy on inner 2f out: rdn to chal ent last: sn drvn and ev ch tl edgd rt and no ex last 50 yds* **11/4**[1]

51 **4** *1 ¼* **Dickie Le Davoir**[5] [1982] 2-9-0 .... RobertWinston 12 87+
(K R Burke) *outpcd and pushed along towards rr after 1f: hdwy on inner 2f out: rdn to chse ldrs ent last: hld whn n.m.r nr fin* **9/1**

1 **5** *hd* **Opal Noir**[16] [1730] 2-8-12 .... DarryllHolland 1 83+
(J Howard Johnson) *in tch: pushed along 2f out: rdn over 1f out: styng on whn n.m.r wl ins last: kpt on towards fin* **14/1**

612 **6** *shd* **Avertuoso**[14] [1780] 2-9-0 .... KDarley 2 85+
(B Smart) *cl up: led after 1f: rdn along 2f out: edgd lft over 1f out and wknd ins last* **18/1**

51 **7** *1* **Middleham (IRE)**[13] [1790] 2-9-2 .... JoeFanning 4 85+
(M Johnston) *hld up: hdwy over 1f out: sn rdn and styng on whn n.m.r ins last* **20/1**

1 **8** *2 ½* **Prospect Place**[42] [1074] 2-9-0 .... PhillipMakin 11 72
(M Dods) *chsd ldrs: rdn along 2f out: sn wknd* **18/1**

14 **9** *nk* **Stolt (IRE)**[25] [1491] 2-9-2 .... DNolan 5 73+
(N Wilson) *cl up: rdn along 2f out: hld whn hmpd over 1f out* **50/1**

2146 **10** *4* **Hucking Hill (IRE)**[21] [1582] 2-9-0 .... JamieSpencer 6 57
(J R Best) *towards rr: pushed along and sme hdwy 1/2-way: sn rdn and wknd wl over 1f out* **33/1**

1 **11** *10* **Supreme Speedster**[18] [1664] 2-9-2 .... NCallan 9 23+
(K A Ryan) *led 1f: prom tl rdn along 2f out: sn drvn and wknd: eased* **3/1**[2]

62.71 secs (-1.29) **Going Correction** -0.30s/f (Firm) **11** Ran SP% **114.4**

Speed ratings (Par 99):98,96,96,94,94 93,92,88,87,81 65

CSF £49.49 TOTE £7.50: £2.30, £3.00, £1.70; EX 70.10.

Owner Pickering Properties Ltd **Bred** Denis McDonnell **Trained** Willoughton, Lincs

■ Stewards' Enquiry : Richard Mullen one-day ban: careless riding (Jun 11)

FOCUS

A fair renewal of what has recently been a disappointing race but it has been rated positively. The race time, however, was slightly slower than the Hilary Needler, which was won by a first-time out filly.

NOTEBOOK

Everymanforhimself(IRE) stayed on really strongly, passing the early leaders in the final stages, who appeared to go off very quickly in front. The way he finished suggests that the Coventry Stakes at Royal Ascot would be his most likely target if connections are seeking Group race success, although the trainer did suggest he feels his charge has plenty of speed, which would bring the Windsor Castle Stakes into play. (op 9-1)

Mood Music, giving 2lb to the winner, just failed to last out the trip and would have probably been better suited by a less demanding five furlongs against decent colts. That said, there is nothing to suggest he will not get a sixth furlong given the way he stayed on. (op 6-1 tchd 7-1)

Steelcut, making a very quick reappearance after winning nicely at Redcar earlier in the week, came to have every chance a furlong from home, but could not quite get to the head of affairs. It would have been interesting to know how he would have faired had he not had the race at Redcar, and he remains of interest in similar company. (op 7-2)

Dickie Le Davoir seemed to be a bit unlucky, threading his way through a packing field before getting squeezed again close to home by Steelcut. He can be rated slightly better than his final position suggests and has the talent to win a nice race. (tchd 10-1 in a place and 8-1 in a place)

Opal Noir had the worst of the draw but ran a race full of promise. He seems likely to stay further and should improve for it.

Avertuoso showed really good speed from his very moderate draw and had plenty of quick horses under pressure early. He failed to see out the trip, and is probably just short of the class required for top races, but, if connections fancied testing the water again in good company, a race such as The Molcomb Stakes at Glorious Goodwood could be the ideal shot at a good race for him. (op 20-1)

Stolt(IRE) did not run too badly despite finishing down the field, and is very much one to keep and eye on in lesser company, as he may go off at a price he is not entitled to due to the stable he comes from.

Supreme Speedster, who showed blistering speed on his debut, could never get to the front, even from his advantageous stalls position, and did not travel with much zest. He is worth another chance given his first run. Official explanation: trainer had no explanation for the poor form shown (op 9-4)

2128 WEATHERBYS INSURANCE H'CAP 1m 100y

8:40 (8:40) (Class 5) (0-70,70) 3-Y-O **£4,210** (£1,252; £625; £312) **Stalls** High

Form RPR

6341 **1** **Black Beauty**[36] [1215] 3-9-4 **70** .... EddieAhern 6 77
(M G Quinlan) *trckd ldng pair: smooth hdwy 3f out: led wl over 1f out: sn rdn and styd on wl fnl f* **9/4**[1]

050 **2** *1* **Tender The Great (IRE)**[21] [1598] 3-8-6 **58** .... RobertWinston 4 63+
(V Smith) *bhd and pushed along 1/2-way: hdwy 3f out: rdn over 1f out: swtchd rt ins last: styd on wl towards fin* **40/1**

0330 **3** *1 ¼* **Blacktoft (USA)**[16] [1738] 3-9-0 **66** .... JamieSpencer 10 68
(E A L Dunlop) *keen: in tch: hdwy 3f out: rdn to chal over 1f out and ev ch tl drvn and one pce ins last* **9/2**[3]

0550 **4** *1 ¼* **Carr Hall (IRE)**[16] [1736] 3-8-4 **56** .... DavidAllan 11 56
(T D Easterby) *trckd ldrs on inner: effrt 3f out: rdn 2f out and kpt on same pce appr last* **14/1**

640 **5** *nk* **Bolckow**[22] [1564] 3-8-10 **67** .... AndrewMullen[(5)] 7 66+
(K A Ryan) *towards rr: hdwy 3f out: rdn and kpt on fnl 2f: nrst fin* **28/1**

0404 **6** *¾* **Dream Of Paradise (USA)**[20] [1605] 3-8-13 **65** .... PaulHanagan 9 63
(Mrs L Williamson) *chsd ldr: rdn along 2f out: drvn and wknd over 1f out* **20/1**

2054 **7** *½* **Mister Maq**[16] [1732] 3-8-9 **61** .... (b) PhillipMakin 5 57
(M Dods) *dwlt: hld up towards rr: hdwy over 2f out: rdn and hung lft over 1f out: sn no imp* **16/1**

5655 **8** *1 ¼* **Inchdhuaig (IRE)**[21] [1593] 3-8-6 **58** .... KDarley 2 52
(P C Haslam) *chsd ldrs on outer: rdn along wl over 2f out: sn wknd* **8/1**

601 **9** *1 ¾* **Lady Romanov (IRE)**[225] [5953] 3-9-1 **67** .... DarryllHolland 8 57
(M H Tompkins) *keen: hld up: a towards rr* **18/1**

1412 **10** *hd* **Stolen Glance**[11] [1859] 3-9-4 **70** .... DaleGibson 3 60
(M W Easterby) *towards rr: rdn along 1/2-way: nvr a factor* **4/1**[2]

1153 **11** *19* **Petrichan (IRE)**[61] [822] 3-9-0 **66** .... (p) NCallan 1 16
(K A Ryan) *led: rdn along 3f out: hdd wl over 1f out and sn wknd* **11/1**

1m 45.83s (-1.57) **Going Correction** -0.30s/f (Firm) **11** Ran SP% **116.9**

Speed ratings (Par 99):95,94,92,91,91 90,89,88,86,86 67

CSF £115.91 CT £393.44 TOTE £3.50: £1.70, £7.70, £2.40; EX 362.10.

Owner Anglo Irish Racing **Bred** N E Poole And Paul Trickey **Trained** Newmarket, Suffolk

■ Stewards' Enquiry : Andrew Mullen one-day ban: careless riding (Jun 11)

FOCUS

A modest handicap with the third setting the standard for the form.

Blacktoft(USA) Official explanation: jockey said colt ran too free

2129 DIRECT-RACING.CO.UK MAIDEN FILLIES' STKS 7f 100y

9:10 (9:10) (Class 5) 3-Y-O+ **£3,886** (£1,156; £577; £288) **Stalls** High

Form RPR

2 **1** **Caressed**[28] [1418] 3-8-9 .... JamieSpencer 9 81+
(J R Fanshawe) *trckd ldrs: swtchd lft: qcknd to ld and hung rt over 1f out: sn clr* **8/11**[1]

2 *1 ¾* **Robema** 3-8-9 .... GrahamGibbons 10 73
(J J Quinn) *midfield: hdwy on inenr over 2f out: rdn and styd on to chse wnr ins last: kpt on* **40/1**

03 **3** *1* **Takanewa (IRE)**[21] [1598] 3-8-9 .... DarryllHolland 6 70
(J Howard Johnson) *led: rdn along wl over 2f out: hdd over 1f out and kpt on same pce* **16/1**[3]

23 **4** *5* **Heather Moor (USA)**[28] [1418] 3-8-9 .... RobertWinston 5 58
(Sir Michael Stoute) *trckd ldr: hdwy to chal over 2f out and ev ch tl rdn and sltly hmpd appr last:sn btn* **7/4**[2]

45 **5** *1 ¼* **Eternal Legacy (IRE)**[20] [1609] 4-9-6 .... DavidAllan 2 58
(J Parkes) *dwlt and bhd: hdwy wl over 2f out: sn rdn and kpt on appr last: nrst fin* **66/1**

46 **6** *½* **Forestelle (IRE)**[18] [1687] 3-8-6 .... BenSwarbrick[(3)] 7 53
(M Dods) *midfield: hdwy over 2f out: sn rdn and kpt on appr last: nrst fin* **50/1**

30 **7** *3* **Graze On Too (IRE)**[21] [1598] 3-8-9 .... RoystonFfrench 3 46
(J J Quinn) *chsd ldrs: rdn along wl over 2f out: sn wknd* **50/1**

000 **8** *5* **Beautiful South**[225] [5961] 3-8-9 47 ow3 .... (b[1]) DNolan[(3)] 8 36
(N Wilson) *a rr* **100/1**

40 **9** *3* **Missdevina (IRE)**[320] [3503] 3-8-9 .... EddieAhern 1 26
(M G Quinlan) *a rr* **20/1**

0 **10** *26* **Automation**[346] [2735] 3-8-9 .... NCallan 4 —
(C W Thornton) *a rr* **100/1**

1m 32.2s (-2.11) **Going Correction** -0.30s/f (Firm)

WFA 3 from 4yo 11lb **10** Ran SP% **114.7**

Speed ratings (Par 100):100,98,96,91,89 89,85,80,76,46

CSF £45.59 TOTE £1.80: £1.10, £4.20, £2.10; EX 27.80 Place 6 £54.96, Place 5 £24.00.

Owner Cheveley Park Stud **Bred** Cheveley Park Stud Ltd **Trained** Newmarket, Suffolk

FOCUS

A modest maiden run at a good pace. The winner and second are probably the two to take from the race with the third and seventh the best lines to the form.

Missdevina(IRE) Official explanation: jockey said filly hung wide round bottom bend

Automation Official explanation: jockey said filly ran too free

T/Plt: £150.20 to a £1 stake. Pool: £60,143.70. 292.30 winning tickets. T/Qpdt: £23.70 to a £1 stake. Pool: £3,972.70. 123.60 winning tickets. JR

1750 BRIGHTON (L-H)

Wednesday, May 31

OFFICIAL GOING: Good to firm (good in places)

Wind: Fresh behind

2130 EBF TATTERSALLS MAIDEN STKS 5f 213y

2:00 (2:01) (Class 5) 2-Y-O **£3,238** (£963; £481; £240) **Stalls** Low

Form RPR

0 **1** **Johannesburg Jack (IRE)**[28] [1420] 2-9-3 .... SteveDrowne 4 79+
(H Morrison) *bhd: swtchd lft 2f out: rdn and qcknd wl to ld fnl 100yds: won gng away* **50/1**

3 **2** *1 ¼* **Winning Spirit (IRE)**[24] [1510] 2-9-3 .... TPQueally 7 75
(J Noseda) *slowly away: t.k.h and sn prom: led 1f out: edgd lft and hdd fnl 100yds* **4/11**[1]

0 **3** *1 ½* **High Style**[16] [1730] 2-9-3 .... RyanMoore 3 71
(R Hannon) *trckd ldr: led over 2f out: hdd 1f out: kpt on one pce* **12/1**[3]

0 **4** *½* **Cadeaux Du Monde**[21] [1595] 2-9-3 .... ChrisCatlin 1 69
(E J O'Neill) *led tl rdn and hdd over 2f out: kpt on ins fnl f* **16/1**

5 *¾* **Bodes Galaxy (IRE)** 2-8-12 .... JamesDoyle[(5)] 6 67
(N P Littmoden) *sltly bmpd s: in rr: r.o fnl f: nvr nrr* **25/1**

0 **6** *shd* **Napoleon Dynamite (IRE)**[24] [1510] 2-9-3 .... EddieAhern 2 67+
(J W Hills) *prom on ins: hung lft fr 2f out and nt persevered w ins fnl f* **16/1**

0 **7** *nk* **Just Oscar (GER)**[21] [1588] 2-9-3 .... DaneO'Neill 8 66
(W M Brisbourne) *chsd ldrs on outside: rdn 1/2-way: wknd wl over 1f out* **28/1**

34 **8** *7* **Calloff The Search**[28] [1420] 2-9-0 .... RobertMiles[(3)] 5 45
(W G M Turner) *led tl hdd over 2f out: wknd qckly* **10/1**[2]

69.78 secs (-0.32) **Going Correction** -0.15s/f (Firm) **8** Ran SP% **111.1**

Speed ratings (Par 93):96,94,92,91,90 90,90,80

CSF £66.47 TOTE £36.30: £5.80, £1.10, £2.30; EX 107.80.

Owner Michael T Lynch **Bred** Pier House Stud **Trained** East Ilsley, Berks

FOCUS

Not an easy race to rate with a disappointing favourite, and the form is not solid.

NOTEBOOK

Johannesburg Jack(IRE) appreciated the additional furlong and looks as if seven will suit him before long. There was no fluke, and his starting price was, with hindsight, an insult.

Winning Spirit(IRE) gave himself a difficult task by missing the break and then failing to settle. He can win similar races and, though he gave the impression he does just about get this trip at present, he has plenty of speed and a drop back to five furlongs would not be a problem. (op 4-9 tchd 1-2 in places)

High Style seemed to have improved a bit from his debut, and nurseries will be an obvious option after one more run.

Cadeaux Du Monde came on a bit for the experience of his first outing, and should improve again when the stable hits peak form. (op 11-1)

Bodes Galaxy(IRE), a Marju colt, will come into his own long term over seven furlongs and a mile. In the circumstances, he made a debut of some promise.

Napoleon Dynamite(IRE) has done better than his form figures suggest in two outings to date, and looks a nursery type after another outing.

Just Oscar(GER) showed more speed this time, but he needs to improve a bit more to become competitive at this level. (op 33-1)

2131 DJMT MAGNOTHERAPY HORSE RUG (S) STKS 1m 1f 209y

2:35 (2:37) (Class 6) 3-5-Y-O **£2,266** (£674; £337; £168) **Stalls High**

Form RPR

0000 **1** **Primed Up (IRE)**[140] 82 4-9-3 55 (b) RobynBrisland(5) 8 57
(G L Moore) *hld up on ins: hdwy 2f out: r.o to ld wl ins fnl f* **33/1**

0646 **2** *2* **Prince Valentine**[16] 1723 5-9-8 42 (be) RyanMoore 13 54
(G L Moore) *t.k.h: in tch: led over 2f out hdd 1f out: no ex ins fnl f* **7/1**

0000 **3** *nk* **Sunset Dreamer (USA)**[8] 1914 5-9-3 41 DaneO'Neill 4 48
(P Mitchell) *trckd ldrs: rdn to ld 1f out: hdd and lost 2nd wl ins fnl f* **25/1**

4500 **4** *1 ½* **Ringarooma**[6] 1958 4-9-9 49 (e[1]) OscarUrbina 7 51
(C N Allen) *slowly away: hdwy on outside 2f out: r.o ins fnl f: nvr nrr* **16/1**

30 **5** *3 ½* **Loriinae**[13] 1797 3-8-3 ChrisCatlin 5 39
(T G Mills) *in tch: kpt on one pce fnl 2f* **8/1**

5006 **6** *2 ½* **Just Tilly**[12] 1829 3-8-3 47 FrancisFerris 1 34
(P R Chamings) *led tl hdd over 2f out: wknd over 1f out* **20/1**

230 **7** *½* **Hillhall (IRE)**[16] 1729 4-9-8 47 GeorgeBaker 9 38
(W M Brisbourne) *chsd ldrs tl wknd over 1f out* **6/1**[2]

6 **8** *2* **Alwaysforsale (IRE)**[297] 4188 3-8-8 SteveDrowne 10 34
(J S Moore) *a towards rr* **16/1**

6400 **9** *3* **Mad Professor (IRE)**[23] 1547 3-8-8 62 (t) TQuinn 12 28
(D J S Ffrench Davis) *in tch tl lost action wl over 1f out: sn eased* **10/1**

6602 **10** *5* **Eijaaz (IRE)**[29] 1373 5-9-8 50 EddieAhern 6 19
(Mrs L Stubbs) *mid-div: bhd fnl 2f* **11/4**[1]

2310 **11** *2 ½* **Chookie Windsor**[70] 695 3-8-11 59 AdamKirby(3) 11 20
(M S Saunders) *in tch tl rdn and wknd over 2f out* **10/1**

3006 **12** *17* **Salinger (USA)**[116] 297 4-9-8 62 IanMongan 2 —
(Mrs L J Mongan) *hld up in rr: effrt over 3f out: sn btn* **13/2**[3]

P60 **13** *25* **African Blues**[226] 5947 3-8-9 ow1 (p) FergusSweeney 3 —
(M R Hoad) *trckd ldr to 4f out: wknd rapidly* **100/1**

2m 2.75s (0.15) **Going Correction** -0.15s/f (Firm)
WFA 3 from 4yo+ 14lb 13 Ran SP% **120.4**
Speed ratings (Par 101):93,91,91,89,87 85,84,83,80,76 74,61,41
CSF £246.19 TOTE £39.50: £8.40, £2.20, £10.40; EX 153.20.There was no bid for the winner.
Owner Prime Power GB Ltd **Bred** Fortbarrington Stud **Trained** Woodingdean, E Sussex

FOCUS
A poor seller run in a moderate time. The winner ran to last year's handicap form. Gary Moore saddled the first two.
Hillhall(IRE) Official explanation: jockey said gelding was unsuited by the track
Mad Professor(IRE) Official explanation: jockey said gelding hung left

2132 WEATHERBYS BANK H'CAP 1m 1f 209y

3:10 (3:11) (Class 6) (0-60,60) 4-Y-0+ **£2,590** (£770; £385; £192) **Stalls High**

Form RPR

0002 **1** **Asaateel (IRE)**[5] 1995 4-9-1 57 (p) RyanMoore 3 66
(G L Moore) *trckd ldrs: led 1f out: drvn out* **4/1**[1]

0061 **2** *½* **Christmas Truce (IRE)**[15] 1753 7-8-13 60 (v) JamesDoyle(5) 2 68
(Ms J S Doyle) *mid-div: hdwy and hanging lft whn plld out to outside: 1f out: fin strly to go 2nd wl ins fnl f* **8/1**[3]

0603 **3** *1* **Icannshift (IRE)**[23] 1541 6-8-4 46 ChrisCatlin 15 52
(T M Jones) *led tl rdn and hdd 1f out: lost 2nd wl ins fnl f* **10/1**

1245 **4** *2* **Wood Fern (UAE)**[2] 2075 6-7-11 46 oh1 LiamJones(7) 14 48
(W M Brisbourne) *s.i.s: sn mid-div: pushed along fr 4f out: kpt on one pce fnl 2f* **4/1**[1]

0001 **5** *½* **Zinging**[15] 1755 7-8-1 48 MarcHalford(5) 12 49
(J J Bridger) *sn trckd ldr: rdn 3f out: hung lft ins fnl 2f* **20/1**

4000 **6** *¾* **Megalala (IRE)**[15] 1753 5-8-6 48 AlanDaly 1 48
(J J Bridger) *prom: rdn 3f out: one pce ins fnl 2f* **66/1**

0060 **7** *1 ¼* **Jubilee Dream**[18] 1673 4-8-10 55 (t[1]) AmirQuinn(3) 8 52
(Mrs L J Mongan) *prom: rdn 4f out: one pce fnl 2f* **33/1**

0000 **8** *3* **Didnt Tell My Wife**[16] 1724 7-8-7 49 oh5 ow3 TQuinn 7 41
(G C H Chung) *hld up in rer: nvr on terms* **22/1**

4405 **9** *¾* **Thebestisyettocome**[100] 462 4-9-0 56 IanMongan 6 46
(T G Mills) *mid-div: wknd wl over 1f out* **6/1**[2]

0046 **10** *shd* **Lenwade**[15] 1755 5-8-1 46 oh3 DominicFox(3) 4 36
(G G Margarson) *s.i.s: sn mid-div: wknd 2f out* **9/1**

0130 **11** *1* **Miss Glory Be**[8] 1910 8-8-1 50 ow1 (p) JamieJones(7) 13 38
(Ernst Oertel) *chsd ldrs: rdn over 2f out: sn btn* **20/1**

3305 **12** *2* **Master'n Commander**[30] 1334 4-9-4 60 EddieAhern 11 44
(C A Cyzer) *slowly away: rdn 4f out: a bhd* **10/1**

0340 **13** *3* **Lucefer (IRE)**[146] 48 8-7-13 48 oh2 ow2 DeanWilliams(7) 10 26
(G C H Chung) *a bhd* **20/1**

0500 **P** **Halcyon Magic**[5] 1995 8-8-10 52 (b) HayleyTurner 5 —
(M Wigham) *a bhd: virtually p.u over 3f out: dismntd ins fnl f* **33/1**

2m 1.41s (-1.19) **Going Correction** -0.15s/f (Firm) 14 Ran SP% **119.6**
Speed ratings (Par 101):98,97,96,95,94 94,93,90,90,90 89,87,85,—
CSF £32.12 CT £304.61 TOTE £3.10: £2.00, £2.60, £3.60; EX 17.80.
Owner P R Iron **Bred** Shadwell Estate Company Limited **Trained** Woodingdean, E Sussex
■ Stewards' Enquiry : James Doyle three-day ban: carelesss riding (Jun 11-13); further two-day ban: used whip with excessive frequency and without giving gelding time to respond (Jun 14-15)

FOCUS
A modest handicap, not that strongly run. The winner was weighted to score.
Halcyon Magic Official explanation: jockey said gelding lost its action

2133 HARBEN'S EQUINE CARE CENTRE FILLIES' H'CAP 1m 3f 196y

3:45 (3:48) (Class 6) (0-65,65) 4-Y-0+ **£2,590** (£770; £385; £192) **Stalls High**

Form RPR

0064 **1** **Plain Champagne (IRE)**[8] 1911 4-8-4 51 oh8 RichardThomas 6 58
(Dr J R J Naylor) *hld up in tch: rdn to ld appr fnl f: drvn out* **50/1**

2440 **2** *2 ½* **Zaville**[13] 1809 4-9-4 65 PhilipRobinson 3 68+
(M A Jarvis) *in tch: hung lft and n.m.r 2f out: r.o to go 2nd fnl 50yds* **4/1**[1]

4132 **3** *1 ¾* **Ten-Cents**[15] 1754 4-9-0 61 GeorgeBaker 11 61
(C F Wall) *in rr: rdn and styd on fr over 1f out: nvr nrr* **4/1**[1]

3040 **4** *hd* **Ardea Brave (IRE)**[23] 1553 4-8-9 56 (p) EddieAhern 7 56
(M Botti) *led tl rdn and hdd appr fnl f: one pce after* **9/1**

6320 **5** *1 ¼* **Screen Test**[16] 1745 4-8-10 57 RyanMoore 9 55
(B G Powell) *trckd ldrs: rdn 4f out: wknd appr fnl f* **8/1**

4350 **6** *½* **Murrieta**[9] 1879 4-8-4 51 oh1 (v) ChrisCatlin 12 48
(Miss J R Gibney) *trckd ldrs: ev ch 2f out: rdn and wknd appr fnl f* **33/1**

000- **7** *3* **Bibi Helen**[568] 6602 4-7-11 51 oh1 LiamJones(7) 10 43
(W M Brisbourne) *trckd ldr tl wknd over 2f out* **33/1**

4331 **8** *3 ½* **Red Sail**[19] 1638 5-8-10 57 (b) OscarUrbina 8 43
(Dr J D Scargill) *hld up: nvr on terms* **5/1**[2]

4033 **9** *nk* **Kathryn Janeway (IRE)**[14] 1772 4-9-4 65 SteveDrowne 2 51
(W R Muir) *v.s.a: sn in tch: rdn over 2f out: sn wknd* **7/1**[3]

0100 **10** *3 ½* **Cantrip**[31] 1313 6-8-5 57 TravisBlock(5) 1 37
(Miss B Sanders) *a bhd* **8/1**

4663 **11** *nk* **Iamback**[15] 1766 6-7-11 51 oh13 (t) BRoper(7) 5 31
(Miss D A McHale) *slowly away: a struggling in rr* **25/1**

0005 **12** *120* **Time For You**[198] 5059 4-8-4 51 oh11 FrancisFerris 4 —
(J M Bradley) *broke wl but sn bhd: t.o fr 1/2-way* **50/1**

2m 32.01s (-0.19) **Going Correction** -0.15s/f (Firm) 12 Ran SP% **118.0**
Speed ratings (Par 98):94,92,91,91,90 89,87,85,85,83 82,—
CSF £237.38 CT £1012.38 TOTE £37.90: £6.80, £1.90, £1.50; EX 282.40.
Owner Cleeve Stables Racing Partnership **Bred** Mrs Marian Maguire **Trained** Shrewton, Wilts

FOCUS
A moderate race restricted to fillies. The winner showed big improvement but the form cannot be taken literally.
Kathryn Janeway(IRE) Official explanation: jockey said filly missed the break
Cantrip Official explanation: jockey said mare never travelled
Time For You Official explanation: jockey said filly moved badly

2134 MARTIN COLLINS H'CAP 5f 59y

4:20 (4:21) (Class 5) (0-75,71) 3-Y-0 **£3,886** (£1,156; £577; £288) **Stalls Low**

Form RPR

2306 **1** **Don't Tell Sue**[18] 1679 3-9-4 71 RyanMoore 1 85
(B W Hills) *mde all: shkn up and drew clr over 1f out: unchal* **10/3**[2]

5232 **2** *2 ½* **Light Mozart**[7] 1937 3-8-9 62 EddieAhern 6 67
(C E Brittain) *hld up: hdwy 2f out: hung lft but kpt on to go 2nd ins fnl f* **2/1**[1]

0445 **3** *1 ½* **Danny The Dip**[15] 1751 3-7-13 57 oh1 MarcHalford(5) 4 56
(J J Bridger) *sn trckd wnr: hung lft ins fnl 2f and lost 2nd ins last* **18/1**

0154 **4** *½* **Overwing (IRE)**[18] 1679 3-9-3 70 DaneO'Neill 3 67
(R M H Cowell) *tk keen hold: bhd and nvr on terms* **4/1**[3]

4053 **5** *3* **Ceredig**[29] 1378 3-8-13 66 TQuinn 5 52
(W R Muir) *t.k.h: a bhd* **9/2**

3062 **6** *nk* **Glenargo (USA)**[15] 1750 3-8-7 60 AdrianMcCarthy 2 45
(R A Harris) *chsd ldrs: rdn 1/2-way: sn btn* **9/1**

60.83 secs (-1.47) **Going Correction** -0.25s/f (Firm) 6 Ran SP% **109.9**
Speed ratings (Par 99):101,97,94,93,89 88
CSF £9.96 TOTE £3.90: £1.50, £1.60; EX 11.40.
Owner Mr & Mrs Peter Orton **Bred** Raffin Bloodstock **Trained** Lambourn, Berks

FOCUS
A moderate race comprising a sextet of horses who find it hard to win. Big improvement from the winner but the form is not all that strong.
Danny The Dip Official explanation: jockey said gelding hung left

2135 JOHN BLOOR MEMORIAL H'CAP 6f 209y

4:55 (4:56) (Class 6) (0-60,59) 4-Y-0+ **£2,590** (£770; £385; £192) **Stalls Low**

Form RPR

1240 **1** **Lord Chamberlain**[30] 1353 13-9-3 56 (b) SteveDrowne 1 65
(J M Bradley) *a in tch: rdn 2f out: swtchd rt over 1f out: rdn to ld fnl 75yds* **16/1**

2304 **2** *½* **Border Artist**[15] 1752 7-8-8 47 OscarUrbina 16 55
(B G Powell) *bhd tl hdwy and swtchd rt over 1f out: r.o to go 2nd ins fnl f* **20/1**

0045 **3** *nk* **Oh Boy (IRE)**[15] 1753 6-8-4 50 LiamJones(7) 3 57
(J M Bradley) *trckd ldr: rdn to ld 2f out: hdd 75yds out and lost 2nd cl home* **9/1**

0301 **4** *nk* **Iced Diamond (IRE)**[33] 1273 7-8-11 50 FergusSweeney 8 56
(W M Brisbourne) *towards rr: hdwy on ins over 1f out: r.o: nvr nrr* **16/1**

0600 **5** *2* **Trevian**[9] 1882 5-8-9 53 JamesDoyle(5) 9 54
(J M Bradley) *a in tch: effrt over 1f out: no ex* **14/1**

2040 **6** *shd* **Grezie**[30] 1348 4-8-10 52 RobertMiles(3) 15 53
(T D McCarthy) *racd wd: in tch: rdn and on pce fr over 1f out* **25/1**

0061 **7** *1 ¼* **Stamford Blue**[1] 2095 5-8-13 59 6ex (b) TolleyDean(7) 5 56+
(R A Harris) *v.s.a and wl bhd tl hdwy over 1f out: kpt on: nvr nrr* **6/1**[1]

2024 **8** *nk* **Hadath (IRE)**[8] 1923 9-9-0 53 ow1 (v) GeorgeBaker 14 50
(B G Powell) *bhd: rdn 2f out: kpt on one pce* **15/2**[2]

1330 **9** *hd* **Mister Elegant**[35] 1245 4-9-0 53 TQuinn 2 49
(J L Spearing) *led tl hdd 2f out: sn btn* **8/1**[3]

1516 **10** *1 ¾* **Attacca**[9] 1885 5-9-2 55 ChrisCatlin 12 47
(J R Weymes) *in tch: rdn over 2f out: sn btn* **15/2**[2]

0152 **11** *1* **Whatatodo**[15] 1753 4-9-2 55 HayleyTurner 13 44
(M L W Bell) *trckd ldrs tl wknd over 1f out* **6/1**[1]

-000 **12** *1 ¾* **Grand Place**[22] 1570 4-9-4 57 RyanMoore 6 41
(R Hannon) *chsd ldrs: rdn 2f out: sn wknd* **25/1**

0100 **13** *shd* **My Girl Pearl (IRE)**[88] 581 6-8-10 52 AdamKirby(3) 4 36
(M S Saunders) *mid-div tl wknd 2f out* **28/1**

0005 **14** *1 ½* **Postmaster**[16] 1725 4-8-10 49 (p) RobertHavlin 10 29
(R Ingram) *racd wd: in tch: rdn over 2f out: wknd* **20/1**

2023 **15** *2* **Contended (IRE)**[22] 1568 4-9-3 56 (p) DaneO'Neill 7 31
(Mrs L C Jewell) *chsd ldrs: rdn and wkng whn hampered over 1f out* **11/1**

1m 21.26s (-1.44) **Going Correction** -0.25s/f (Firm) 15 Ran SP% **120.6**
Speed ratings (Par 101):98,97,97,96,94 94,92,92,92,90 89,87,87,85,83
CSF £310.62 CT £3106.82 TOTE £17.30: £4.60, £7.70, £3.70; EX 139.30.
Owner W C Harries **Bred** Dragon's Stud **Trained** Sedbury, Gloucs

FOCUS
A routine and low-grade, but well-contested, Brighton handicap. Solid form for the grade.
Stamford Blue Official explanation: jockey said gelding missed the break

2136 REDMIRE STABLES & BUILDINGS H'CAP 5f 59y

5:25 (5:27) (Class 6) (0-65,65) 4-Y-0+ **£2,590** (£770; £385; £192) **Stalls Low**

Form RPR

1213 **1** **Forest Dane**[16] 1728 6-8-7 54 OscarUrbina 2 69
(Mrs N Smith) *mid-div: shkn up and hdwy over 1f out: led fnl 100yds: readily* **5/1**[3]

3530 **2** *1 ½* **Hello Roberto**[5] 1981 5-9-0 61 (p) AdrianMcCarthy 10 70
(R A Harris) *trckd ldr: led over 1f out: rdn and hdd fnl 100yds* **12/1**

2424 **3** *¾* **Hammer Of The Gods (IRE)**[19] 1645 6-8-11 58 (bt) TQuinn 9 64
(P S McEntee) *mid-div: hdwy over 1f out: r.o: nvr nrr* **11/4**[1]

0005 **4** *2* **Whistler**[4] 2027 9-9-4 65 (p) PaulFitzsimons 6 64
(Miss J R Tooth) *bhd: racd wd: hdwy and picked up appr fnl f: r.o: nvr nrr* **16/1**

0500 **5** *nk* **Limonia (GER)**[8] 1915 4-8-0 52 oh3 ow1 JamesDoyle(5) 12 50
(N P Littmoden) *chsd ldrs: rdn and wknd ins fnl f* **33/1**

0000 **6** *½* **Borzoi Maestro**[18] 1689 5-8-5 55 ow1 (v) AdamKirby(3) 3 51
(M Wellings) *led tl rdn and hdd over 1f out: fdd ins fnl f* **33/1**

0440 **7** *¾* **Imperium**[15] 1752 5-8-5 52 oh1 ow1 (p) RobertHavlin 1 45
(Stef Liddiard) *s.i.s: bhd tl mde mod late hdwy* **14/1**

5345 **8** *shd* **One Last Time**[152] [6693] 6-8-4 **51** oh8 .... RichardThomas 11 — 44
(Miss B Sanders) *bhd: effrt over 1f out: nvr on terms* **20/1**

0523 **9** *shd* **Enjoy The Buzz**[5] [1981] 7-8-5 **52** .... ChrisCatlin 4 — 44
(J M Bradley) *a towards rr* **4/1**[2]

4006 **10** *¾* **Campeon (IRE)**[11] [1846] 4-8-5 **59** .... LiamJones[(7)] 8 — 48
(J M Bradley) *chsd ldrs tl wknd over 1f out* **12/1**

2511 **11** *1* **Boanerges (IRE)**[31] [1310] 9-8-8 **55** .... RyanMoore 14 — 41
(J M Bradley) *hmpd s: a bhd* **10/1**

0045 **12** *2 ½* **Great Belief (IRE)**[27] [1430] 4-8-7 **57** .... RobertMiles[(3)] 13 — 33
(T D McCarthy) *wnt rt s: racd wd: a bhd* **14/1**

2400 **13** *5* **Millsy**[13] [1795] 4-8-9 **56** .... SteveDrowne 7 — 13
(J L Spearing) *chsd ldrs tl rdn and wknd 2f out* **16/1**

60.29 secs (-2.01) **Going Correction** -0.375s/f (Firm) — **13** Ran SP% **123.6**
Speed ratings (Par 101):101,98,97,94,93 92,91,91,91,90 88,84,76
CSF £64.89 CT £207.92 TOTE £4.90: £2.20, £4.10, £1.40; EX 66.20 Place 6 £ 596.74, Place 5 £ 491.28.
Owner The Ember Partnership **Bred** Loan And Development Corporation **Trained** Bury, W Sussex

FOCUS
A fair handicap, well contested by some proven performers. Solid form.
Hammer Of The Gods(IRE) Official explanation: jockey said gelding lost a shoe
One Last Time Official explanation: jockey said gelding lost a shoe
T/Plt: £936.80 to a £1 stake. Pool: £46,262.75. 36.05 winning tickets. T/Qpdt: £125.80 to a £1 stake. Pool: £3,825.00. 22.50 winning tickets. JS

[1762] SOUTHWELL (L-H)
Wednesday, May 31

OFFICIAL GOING: Standard
Wind: Almost nil Weather: Fine and sunny

2137 BBC RADIO NOTTINGHAM APPRENTICE H'CAP — 1m (F)
6:20 (6:22) (Class 6) (0-60,60) 4-Y-0+ — **£2,730** (£806; £403) **Stalls** Low

Form — RPR

0050 **1** **Dispol Peto**[13] [1795] 6-8-9 **50** .... (v) ChrisCavanagh 5 — 62
(R Johnson) *s.i.s: swtchd outside after 1f: hdwy over 2f out: hung lft and styd on to ld nr fin* **9/1**

5050 **2** *nk* **Shifty**[4] [2025] 7-9-5 **60** .... HeatherMcGee 9 — 71
(D Carroll) *trckd ldrs: led over 2f out: edgd lft: hdd nr fin* **8/1**

0000 **3** *7* **Preskani**[8] [1915] 4-8-9 **50** .... LukeMorris 10 — 47
(Mrs N Macauley) *w ldrs: outpcd over 4f out: rallied 3f out: one pce appr fnl f* **5/1**[1]

0060 **4** *nk* **Blue Empire (IRE)**[19] [1644] 5-9-2 **57** .... PatrickDonaghy 11 — 53
(C R Dore) *w ldrs: effrt 3f out: one pce appr fnl f* **5/1**[1]

2140 **5** *1* **El Palmar**[54] [906] 5-8-12 **53** .... MarkCoumbe 8 — 47
(M J Attwater) *chsd ldrs: wknd appr fnl f* **13/2**[3]

0512 **6** *1 ¾* **Kirkhammerton (IRE)**[15] [1765] 4-8-3 **49** ow1 .... (v) AdamCarter[(5)] 4 — 40
(M J Polglase) *hmpd sn after s: bhd tl styd on fnl 2f* **11/2**[2]

6024 **7** *3* **Quiet Reading (USA)**[34] [1257] 9-9-2 **57** .... (v) SophieDoyle 6 — 42
(M R Bosley) *in rr: edgd rt and bmpd over 4f out: hdwy on wd outside over 2f out: nvr nr ldrs* **12/1**

6566 **8** *3* **Ming Vase**[2] [2077] 4-8-5 **46** oh4 .... (p) VictoriaBehan 2 — 25
(P T Midgley) *chsd ldrs: wknd over 2f out* **20/1**

0 **9** *½* **First Boy (GER)**[34] [1257] 7-8-9 **55** .... FrankiePickard[(5)] 7 — 33
(D J Wintle) *sn wl bhd: kpt on fnl 2f: nvr a factor* **25/1**

0003 **10** *½* **Shannon Arms (USA)**[23] [1553] 5-9-2 **57** .... JosephWalsh 3 — 34
(R Brotherton) *led tl over 2f out: lost pl over 1f out* **11/1**

0600 **11** *3* **Savoy Chapel**[8] [1915] 4-8-7 **48** .... WilliamCarson 1 — 19
(D Carroll) *dwlt: nvr on terms* **16/1**

0060 **12** *9* **Active Account (USA)**[104] [423] 9-8-9 **50** .... (b) ChrisGlenister 13 — 3
(J R Holt) *racd wd: bhd fnl 2f* **25/1**

0060 **13** *1 ¼* **Inchloss (IRE)**[28] [1425] 5-9-2 **57** .... MarkWaite 14 — 7
(C N Kellett) *racd wd: bhd fnl 2f* **25/1**

0600 **14** *7* **Diamond Heritage**[15] [1764] 4-8-5 **46** oh7 .... (b[1]) JohnCavanagh 12 — —
(S Parr) *s.i.s: bmpd over 4f out: in rr whn hung lft over 2f out: sn bhd* **66/1**

1m 43.68s (-0.92) **Going Correction** -0.075s/f (Stan) — **14** Ran SP% **122.9**
Speed ratings (Par 101):101,100,93,93,92 90,87,84,84,83 80,71,70,63
CSF £75.85 CT £410.10 TOTE £10.00: £3.30, £2.90, £3.00; EX 113.10.
Owner Tim Forbes **Bred** B N And Mrs Toye **Trained** Newburn, Tyne & Wear
■ Stewards' Enquiry : Chris Glenister caution: used whip when out of contention
Mark Coumbe one-day ban: failed to ride to draw (Jun 11)

FOCUS
A low-grade handicap, no better than a seller, confined to inexperienced riders. The first two finished clear.

2138 DINE IN THE QUEEN MOTHER RESTAURANT CLAIMING STKS — 6f (F)
6:50 (6:53) (Class 6) 3-Y-0 — **£2,730** (£806; £403) **Stalls** Low

Form — RPR

3240 **1** **Hillbilly Cat (USA)**[13] [1792] 3-8-4 55 .... BenSwarbrick[(3)] 4 — 61
(T D Barron) *rrd and wnt rt s: sn trcking ldrs: led 2f out: styd on ins last* **11/4**[1]

0605 **2** *1 ½* **Mystic Queen (IRE)**[34] [1254] 3-8-8 35 .... FrankieMcDonald 6 — 57
(A P Jarvis) *w ldr: led 3f out: hdd 2f out: nt qckn ins fnl f* **20/1**

0506 **3** *2* **Miss Mujahid Times**[13] [1791] 3-7-13 41 .... (b) SilvestreDeSousa[(3)] 3 — 45
(A D Brown) *led tl 3f out: one pce appr fnl f* **33/1**

1220 **4** *¾* **Diktalex (IRE)**[40] [1109] 3-8-12 63 .... (t) NeilPollard 7 — 53
(C J Teague) *trckd ldrs: rdn and hung rt over 3f out: one pce fnl 2f* **4/1**[2]

052 **5** *nk* **Silvertown Sky (IRE)**[14] [1771] 3-7-11 42 .... NicolPolli[(7)] 5 — 44
(P L Gilligan) *bmpd s: lost pl over 4f out: kpt on appr fnl f* **7/1**[3]

0 **6** *1* **Apres Ski (IRE)**[275] [4816] 3-9-4 .... DeanCorby[(3)] 8 — 58
(J W Hills) *lost pl over 4f out: sme hdwy over 1f out: nvr a threat* **20/1**

5360 **7** *½* **Memphis Man**[20] [1617] 3-9-7 70 .... MickyFenton 2 — 56
(G C Bravery) *s.i.s: sn drvn along on outer: kpt on up wd outside fnl 2f: nvr on terms* **4/1**[2]

0300 **8** *2 ½* **Eskimo Nell**[11] [1859] 3-8-10 50 ow2 .... FergalLynch 1 — 38
(T D Easterby) *bhd and styd far side fnl 3f: nvr a factor* **8/1**

000 **9** *¾* **Par Excellence**[22] [1567] 3-7-11 50 .... DuranFentiman[(5)] 9 — 28
(W G M Turner) *w ldrs: lost pl over 1f out* **9/1**

1m 17.48s (0.58) **Going Correction** -0.075s/f (Stan) — **9** Ran SP% **112.7**
Speed ratings (Par 97):93,91,88,87,86 85,84,81,80
CSF £60.93 TOTE £3.30: £1.10, £6.30, £9.50; EX 87.50.The winner was subject to a friendly claim of £5,000.
Owner Laurence O'Kane **Bred** Adena Springs **Trained** Maunby, N Yorks

FOCUS
A low-grade claimer rated through the fourth.
Diktalex(IRE) Official explanation: trainer said filly was in season; vet said filly was lame post-race

2139 RACING THIS WEEKEND MAIDEN AUCTION STKS — 6f (F)
7:20 (7:24) (Class 6) 2-Y-O — **£2,730** (£604; £604) **Stalls** Low

Form — RPR

533 **1** **Ten Dollars More (IRE)**[12] [1811] 2-9-1 .... TPQueally 8 — 67
(J A Osborne) *chsd ldrs: outpcd 3f out: hdwy on wd outside over 2f out: styd on to ld last strides* **9/4**[2]

64 **2** *nk* **Flower Of Cork (IRE)**[16] [1743] 2-8-10 .... FergalLynch 7 — 61
(T D Easterby) *w ldrs: led 2f out: hdd and no ex nr fin* **15/2**[3]

2 *dht* **Intersky Sports (USA)** 2-9-1 .... DeanMcKeown 9 — 66
(K A Ryan) *rangy: unf: scope: chsd ldrs: rdn over 1f out: r.o ins last: no ex nr fin* **2/1**[1]

6 **4** *¾* **Tarif (IRE)**[32] [1284] 2-8-11 .... MickyFenton 2 — 60
(Mrs P Sly) *dwlt: sn drvn along and in tch: hdwy over 2f out: styd on ins last* **8/1**

60 **5** *shd* **Luscivious**[21] [1587] 2-9-3 .... J-PGuillambert 3 — 66
(M J Polglase) *w ldr: led 3f out: hdd 2f out: nt qckn ins last* **10/1**

6 *3* **Mickleberry (IRE)** 2-8-8 .... AdrianTNicholls 5 — 48
(J D Bethell) *lt-f: unf: s.i.s: sn in tch: rdn and hung rt over 1f out: sn wknd* **25/1**

630 **7** *1 ¼* **Our Toy Soldier**[32] [1284] 2-9-3 .... DerekMcGaffin 4 — 53
(B Smart) *led tl 3f out: wknd over 1f out* **14/1**

0 **7** *dht* **Dolly Coughdrop (IRE)**[30] [1342] 2-8-5 .... AndrewElliott[(5)] 1 — 46
(K R Burke) *dwlt: hdwy on inner to chse ldrs over 4f out: wknd 1f out* **16/1**

06 **9** *18* **Joella's Lad**[13] [1790] 2-8-13 .... SamHitchcott 10 — —
(Ms Deborah J Evans) *swvd rt s: sn chsng ldrs: hung rt and lost pl over 3f out: sn bhd: eased* **50/1**

10 *25* **Hair Of The Dog** 2-8-9 .... SebSanders 6 — —
(J G Given) *bkwd: s.i.s: sn in tch: rn wd and lost pl bnd over 3f out: hung bdly lft and sn bhd: virtually p.u* **14/1**

1m 18.11s (1.21) **Going Correction** -0.075s/f (Stan) — **10** Ran SP% **121.1**
Speed ratings (Par 91):88,87,87,86,86 82,80,80,56,23
TOTE £3.70: £1.50 TRIFECTA PL: Intersky Sports £1.30, Flower Of Cork £2.90; EX: IS £4.90, FOC £10.00; CSF: IS £3.75, FOC £10.42.
Owner A Taylor **Bred** Mrs L Hudson **Trained** Upper Lambourn, Berks

FOCUS
An average maiden auction event rated through the winner but one or two will improve for the outing.

NOTEBOOK
Ten Dollars More(IRE), who looked really well, stuck on after being tapped for toe and showed a willing attitude to get up near the line. He looks to be crying out for a seventh furlong.
Intersky Sports(USA), who stands over plenty of ground, has some furnishing to do. No stranger to his rider, he stuck on inside the last and will be wiser next time. (op 10-1 tchd 7-1)
Flower Of Cork(IRE), appreciating the extra furlong, worked hard to take a narrow lead but in the end she just missed out. She will improve again. (op 10-1 tchd 7-1)
Tarif(IRE), well supported, was edgy beforehand. He still looked very inexperienced, but to his credit kept staying on all the way to the line. This will have taught him plenty. (op 16-1 tchd 20-1)
Luscivious, making his all-weather bow, was in the thick of the action from the off and was only founmd wanting inside the last. He looks a likely nursery type. (op 9-1)
Mickleberry(IRE), lightly-made and narrow, was very inexperienced. (op 20-1)
Joella's Lad Official explanation: jockey said gelding had steering problems

2140 LADIES NIGHT IS 22ND JUNE H'CAP — 1m 6f (F)
7:50 (7:51) (Class 5) (0-75,72) 4-Y-0+ — **£3,238** (£963; £481; £240) **Stalls** Low

Form — RPR

3031 **1** **Eforetta (GER)**[15] [1766] 4-7-13 **53** .... EdwardCreighton[(3)] 5 — 68+
(D J Wintle) *trckd ldrs: led over 5f out: styd on wl: tk things easily towards fin* **8/1**

-001 **2** *nk* **Salut Saint Cloud**[25] [570] 5-8-9 **60** .... (p) TPQueally 8 — 71
(G L Moore) *mid-div: hdwy over 5f out: chsng 1st 2 3f out: wnt 2nd 1f out: styd on towards fin* **3/1**[2]

5634 **3** *4* **Cotton Eyed Joe (IRE)**[13] [1809] 5-9-7 **72** .... DeanMcKeown 10 — 77
(G A Swinbank) *hld up in tch: hdwy to join ldrs over 4f out: chal over 2f out: rdn and hung lft over 1f out: kpt on same pce* **11/4**[1]

1024 **4** *¾* **Romil Star (GER)**[22] [1560] 9-7-13 **55** .... (v) AndrewElliott[(5)] 9 — 59
(K R Burke) *chsd ldrs: outpcd over 3f out: kpt on wl fnl f* **6/1**[3]

2006 **5** *7* **Red Forest (IRE)**[172] [6540] 7-8-4 **55** .... (t) AdrianTNicholls 1 — 49
(J Mackie) *led tl over 5f out: outpcd on inner and n.m.r over 3f out: kpt on fnl 2f* **18/1**

3200 **6** *6* **Peak Park (USA)**[13] [1808] 6-9-3 **68** .... SamHitchcott 6 — 54
(P L Gilligan) *hld up in rr: hrd drvn over 5f out: nvr on terms* **14/1**

1520 **7** *hd* **Sand Repeal (IRE)**[11] [1847] 4-9-5 **70** .... J-PGuillambert 2 — 55
(Miss J Feilden) *trckd ldrs: drvn 7f out: lost pl 4f out* **12/1**

000- **8** *3 ½* **Chimes At Midnight (USA)**[585] [6369] 9-7-9 **53** oh11.(b) LukeMorris[(7)] 4 — 34
(Luke Comer, Ire) *hld up: hdwy on inner over 7f out: outpcd over 3f out: lost pl 2f out* **20/1**

1520 **9** *6* **Blue Hills**[77] [643] 5-8-9 **60** .... DarrenWilliams 3 — 32
(P W Hiatt) *trckd ldrs: drvn over 7f out: wknd 3f out* **14/1**

060/ **P** **Dawari (IRE)**[956] [5639] 8-8-11 **62** .... MickyFenton 11 — —
(R Ford) *sn trcking ldrs: hung rt and lost pl over 6f out: bhd whn p.u over 4f out* **20/1**

3m 6.76s (-2.84) **Going Correction** -0.075s/f (Stan) — **10** Ran SP% **112.9**
Speed ratings (Par 103):105,104,102,102,98 94,94,92,89,—
CSF £31.13 CT £82.38 TOTE £10.90: £1.90, £1.30, £1.70; EX 26.10.
Owner John W Egan **Bred** Gestut Rietberg **Trained** Naunton, Gloucs

FOCUS
A sound gallop and a cheeky winner. Rated through the placed horses and the form looks solid.
Dawari(IRE) Official explanation: vet said gelding was lame post-race

2141 SPONSOR A RACE AT SOUTHWELL H'CAP — 7f (F)
8:20 (8:23) (Class 6) (0-65,63) 4-Y-0+ — **£2,590** (£770; £385; £192) **Stalls** Low

Form — RPR

0150 **1** **Penel (IRE)**[15] [1764] 5-7-13 **49** .... (p) RoryMoore[(5)] 11 — 58
(P T Midgley) *trckd ldrs: outpcd over 3f out: gd hdwy and swtchd lft over 1f out: styd on to ld towards fin* **9/1**

0514 **2** *nk* **Feast Of Romance**[15] [1764] 9-8-5 **50** .... (b) DO'Donohoe 5 — 58
(G A Huffer) *trckd ldrs: led over 2f out: hung lft over 1f out: hdd nr fin* **13/2**[3]

0400 **3** *1 ¾* **Mister Benji**[33] [1276] 7-8-12 **57** .... DarrenWilliams 6 — 60
(B P J Baugh) *trckd ldrs: kpt on same pce fnl f* **7/1**

0213 **4** *1* **Bijou Dan**[6] [1947] 5-8-13 **63** .... (be) DuranFentiman[(5)] 9 — 64+
(W G Harrison) *sn drvn along in rr: bhd over 4f out: gd hdwy fnl 2f: fin strly* **11/2**[1]

0001 **5** *nk* **Downland (IRE)**[16] [1746] 10-9-0 **59** .... KimTinkler 3 — 59
(N Tinkler) *chsd ldrs: rdn over 2f out: one pce* **15/2**

6604 **6** *hd* **Priorina (IRE)**[22] [1574] 4-8-4 **49** oh3........................(v) FrankieMcDonald 7 49
(D Haydn Jones) *mid-div: outpcd over 3f out: hdwy on inner over 2f out: kpt on* **10/1**

000- **7** *½* **Benny The Ball (USA)**[590] [6279] 5-9-1 **60**...................... MickyFenton 12 58
(N P Littmoden) *chsd ldrs on outer: outpcd over 2f out: styd on same pce fnl f* **6/1**[2]

003/ **8** *1 ¼* **Love Academy**[1433] [2624] 11-7-11 **49** oh19................(b) LukeMorris(7) 10 44
(Luke Comer, Ire) *mid-div: outpcd over 4f out: hung rt and kpt on fnl f* **20/1**

5310 **9** *4* **Pawn In Life (IRE)**[19] [1644] 8-8-7 **57** ow1....................(b) DerekNolan(5) 2 42
(M J Polglase) *s.s: bhd tl sme hdwy fnl 2f* **8/1**

0500 **10** *1 ¼* **Italian Mist (FR)**[35] [1243] 7-8-9 **54**.. TPQueally 4 35
(R M H Cowell) *t.k.h: trckd ldrs on inner: led over 4f out: hdd over 2f out: hung lft and lost pl over 1f out* **22/1**

0000 **11** *nk* **Don Pasquale**[37] [1194] 4-8-4 **49** oh9.......................... AdrianTNicholls 13 30
(J T Stimpson) *s.i.s: sn drvn along: nvr on terms* **33/1**

4050 **12** *14* **Knickyknackienoo**[340] [2936] 5-8-7 **52** ow1....................... BrianReilly 14 —
(T T Clement) *s.i.s: hdwy on outer over 3f out: sn lost pl: eased* **14/1**

0040 **13** *40* **Christian Bendix**[19] [1645] 4-8-7 **52**................................. J-PGuillambert 8 —
(P Howling) *led tl over 4f out: lost pl over 2f out: virtually p.u fnl f: b.b.v: t.o: btn 40l* **11/1**

1m 30.07s (-0.73) **Going Correction** -0.075s/f (Stan) **13** Ran SP% **124.5**
Speed ratings (Par 101):101,100,98,97,97 96,96,94,90,88 88,72,26
CSF £67.75 CT £461.77 TOTE £9.50: £3.00, £4.20, £3.50; EX 120.10.
Owner M E Elsworthy **Bred** M Ervine **Trained** Westow, N Yorks

FOCUS
Another low-grade handicap no better than a seller but the time suggets the form, rated around the fifth, will prove reliable.
Pawn In Life(IRE) Official explanation: jockey said gelding was slowly away from stalls
Knickyknackienoo Official explanation: jockey said gelding was slowly away from stalls
Christian Bendix Official explanation: vet said gelding bled from the nose

2142 BOOK HOSPITALITY PACKAGES HERE H'CAP 1m (F)
8:50 (8:50) (Class 5) (0-75,75) 3-Y-O **£3,238** (£963; £481; £240) **Stalls** Low

Form RPR

4250 **1** **Makai**[21] [1599] 3-8-8 **65**.. StanleyChin 3 71
(M Johnston) *sn chsng ldrs: led 2f out: hld on towards fin* **16/1**

1 **2** *½* **Future's Dream**[5] [1984] 3-8-11 **73** 7ex......................... AndrewElliott(5) 6 81+
(K R Burke) *dwlt: sn pushed along: plld outside over 4f out: hdwy 2f out: styd on wl ins last: nt quite rch wnr* **6/5**[1]

646 **3** *¾* **Cindertrack**[219] [6072] 3-8-13 **70**.. TPQueally 5 74
(J A Osborne) *trckd ldrs: effrt on outer 2f out: styd on same pce ins last* **14/1**

4340 **4** *nk* **Keel (IRE)**[70] [695] 3-8-12 **74**.................................... RichardKingscote(5) 1 77
(J A Osborne) *restless in stalls: sn trcking ldrs: rdn over 2f out: styd on same pce fnl f* **6/1**[3]

4013 **5** *3 ½* **Secret Liaison**[6] [1948] 3-9-4 **75**.. SebSanders 2 71
(Sir Mark Prescott) *led: hdd 2f out: wknd fnl f* **2/1**[2]

6310 **6** *2* **Katie Lawson (IRE)**[106] [415] 3-8-4 **61** oh1...........(v) FrankieMcDonald 7 53
(D Haydn Jones) *s.i.s: sn chsng ldrs on outer: outpcd 3f out: wknd 1f out* **25/1**

3350 **7** *13* **Meantime (USA)**[20] [1613] 3-8-11 **68**...........................(b) AdrianTNicholls 4 34
(G Prodromou) *sn pushed along: lost pl over 4f out: sn bhd: eased ins last* **33/1**

1m 43.11s (-1.49) **Going Correction** -0.075s/f (Stan) **7** Ran SP% **112.4**
Speed ratings (Par 99):104,103,102,102,98 96,83
CSF £34.76 TOTE £13.10: £5.00, £1.80; EX 42.70 Place 6 £48.96, Place 5 £18.36.
Owner C H Greensit & W A Greensit **Bred** C H And W A Greensit **Trained** Middleham Moor, N Yorks

FOCUS
A steady gallop and a probably luckless runner-up. The form looks sound rated through the fourth.
Meantime(USA) Official explanation: jockey said gelding had no more to give
T/Plt: £111.20 to a £1 stake. Pool: £44,598.65. 292.70 winning tickets. T/Qpdt: £11.00 to a £1 stake. Pool: £4,168.80. 280.00 winning tickets. WG

1613 YARMOUTH (L-H)
Wednesday, May 31

OFFICIAL GOING: Good (good to firm in places)
Wind: Fresh, behind Weather: Overcast

2143 TOTETRIFECTA MAIDEN STKS (DIV I) 7f 3y
1:40 (1:40) (Class 5) 3-Y-O+ **£3,238** (£963; £481; £240) **Stalls** High

Form RPR

053 **1** **Hill Spirit**[18] [1680] 3-8-13 77... JohnEgan 2 83
(D R C Elsworth) *chsd ldrs: led over 1f out: rdn out* **4/1**[3]

023 **2** *2* **Another Genepi (USA)**[30] [1336] 3-8-8 77......................... MichaelHills 9 73
(J W Hills) *trckd ldrs: rdn and ev ch over 1f out: styd on same pce* **13/2**

43 **3** *1* **Mahrajaan (USA)**[39] [1135] 3-8-13 .... RHills 3 75
(J H M Gosden) *chsd ldrs: ev ch over 1f out: no ex ins fnl f* **5/2**[1]

3 **4** *nk* **Pearl's Girl**[214] [6143] 3-8-8 .... MartinDwyer 10 70
(W J Haggas) *s.i.s: hld up: hdwy over 2f out: styd on* **3/1**[2]

4340 **5** *hd* **Iwunder (IRE)**[247] [5505] 4-9-5 67.. AlanMunro 5 73
(Rae Guest) *led over 5f: no ex ins fnl f* **20/1**

63 **6** *5* **Swains Bridge (USA)**[328] [3287] 4-9-10 .... NickyMackay 11 65+
(L M Cumani) *hld up: nt clr run over 2f out: nvr trbld ldrs* **16/1**

0250 **7** *3* **Welcome Releaf**[7] [1941] 3-8-9 63 ow1................. StephenDonohoe(5) 8 54
(G C H Chung) *chsd ldrs over 5f* **100/1**

0 **8** *5* **Kartikeya (USA)**[186] [6435] 3-8-8 .... JamieSpencer 7 43+
(J R Fanshawe) *s.i.s: sn prom: shkn up and wknd over 1f out* **40/1**

9 *3* **Indian Sabre (IRE)** 3-8-13 .... ShaneKelly 4 32
(J Noseda) *s.s: outpcd* **25/1**

5000 **10** *2 ½* **Elli Lewtia**[6] [1960] 3-8-8 40.. DerekMcGaffin 6 21
(J Jay) *bhd fnl 4f* **100/1**

30 **11** *6* **Servillia (IRE)**[37] [1191] 3-8-8 .... SebSanders 1 5
(W R Swinburn) *hld up: rdn 1/2-way: sn wknd* **33/1**

1m 26.41s (-0.19) **Going Correction** +0.075s/f (Good)
WFA 3 from 4yo 11lb **11** Ran SP% **108.8**
Speed ratings (Par 103):104,101,100,100,100 94,90,85,81,78 72
CSF £25.42 TOTE £4.60: £1.40, £2.00, £1.50; EX 25.30 Trifecta £47.30 Pool £454.24 - 6.81 winning units.
Owner Chimera Racing **Bred** Gestut Goerlsdorf **Trained** Newmarket, Suffolk

FOCUS
A fair maiden for the course run fractionally quicker than the second division. The form is pretty solid, the fifth helping set the standard.
Elli Lewtia Official explanation: trainer said filly was in season

Servillia(IRE) Official explanation: jockey said filly hung left throughout

2144 TOTECOURSETOCOURSE EUROPEAN BREEDERS FUND NOVICE STKS 6f 3y
2:10 (2:11) (Class 5) 2-Y-O **£3,886** (£1,156; £577; £288) **Stalls** High

Form RPR

1 **Danebury Hill** 2-8-12 .... AlanMunro 4 83
(B J Meehan) *led early: w ldr: rdn over 1f: r.o to ld nr fin* **16/1**

31 **2** *hd* **Captain Marvelous (IRE)**[21] [1587] 2-9-5 .... MichaelHills 5 89
(B W Hills) *half-rrd s: sn led: rdn over 1f out: hdd nr fin* **11/8**[1]

3 *3 ½* **Malaaq** 2-8-7 .... RHills 3 67
(M A Jarvis) *prom: rdn over 1f out: edgd lft and styd on same pce* **8/1**

4 *hd* **Justy (USA)** 2-8-12 .... JamieSpencer 2 71
(M L W Bell) *chsd ldrs: rdn over 2f out: wknd ins fnl f* **9/2**[3]

5 *2* **Massenzio (IRE)** 2-8-12 .... JimmyFortune 1 65
(J H M Gosden) *s.s: hdwy over 2f out: sn rdn and ev ch: wknd ins fnl f* **12/1**

6 *1 ¾* **Gulf Express (USA)** 2-8-12 .... RobertWinston 6 65+
(Sir Michael Stoute) *s.i.s: sn in tch and racd green: shkn up over 2f out: edgd lft and wknd over 1f out* **7/2**[2]

1m 14.82s (1.12) **Going Correction** +0.075s/f (Good) **6** Ran SP% **107.2**
Speed ratings (Par 93):95,94,90,89,87 84
CSF £35.45 TOTE £23.90: £6.80, £1.10; EX 38.10.
Owner Britton House Stud Ltd **Bred** Britton House Stud Ltd **Trained** Manton, Wilts

FOCUS
Probably an above-average maiden for the course, with the first two coming nicely clear.

NOTEBOOK
Danebury Hill, who came into the race with a Phoenix Stakes entry, clearly has plenty of natural ability and strode away from the rest of the field along with the runner-up when asked to win his race. Plenty of top-class performers have won the race in recent history - Asset, Wilko and Imperial Stride have been the last three winners - and it would be very surprising if he was not capable of holding his own in a much higher grade.
Captain Marvelous(IRE) set a really good standard for the race and almost managed to defy a 7lb penalty for his success at Chester. However, the winner is probably going to prove to be very useful in the future and there is no guarantee he would swap form around if they met again on equal terms. (op 13-8 tchd 7-4)
Malaaq, whose dam was a smart sort as a juvenile, was the only filly in the race and acquitted herself well against the boys. A small sort, she pulled fairly hard early but kept on stoutly inside the final furlong, giving some mixed messages to what sort of trip will prove ideal. (op 10-1)
Justy(USA), who had been subject to some really decent gallop reports prior to his debut, has plenty of size and scope for improvement and was not given a really hard time when his chance had gone. He is sure to improve for the run and be of interest next time if making normal progression. (op 7-2)
Massenzio(IRE) has stamina in his pedigree on the dam side, as well as some speed from his sire, and will surely be better suited by further in time. (op 11-1)
Gulf Express(USA), the first two-year-old of 2006 to run for the stable, looked too inexperienced to do himself justice and will be wiser for the run. A horse with plenty of size and scope, his American pedigree suggests that, unltimately, a mile will be more up his street. (op 11-4)

2145 TOTEQUADPOT (S) STKS 6f 3y
2:45 (2:46) (Class 6) 2-Y-O **£2,266** (£674; £337; £168) **Stalls** High

Form RPR

0 **1** **Cheshire Prince**[21] [1587] 2-8-11 .... ShaneKelly 6 70+
(W M Brisbourne) *chsd ldrs: rdn to ld over 1f out: edgd lft: r.o* **13/2**

050 **2** *4* **Baytown Paikea**[34] [1248] 2-8-6 .... BrianReilly 3 53
(P S McEntee) *led 1f: chsd ldr: rdn to ld wl over 1f out: sn hdd: edgd rt and no ex ins fnl f* **20/1**

50 **3** *1 ¼* **Aggbag**[9] [1884] 2-8-11 .... JamieSpencer 5 56+
(M J Wallace) *hld up: hdwy over 2f out: rdn over 1f out: styng on same pce whn nt clr run ins fnl f* **15/8**[1]

0105 **4** *1 ¾* **Alittleriskie (IRE)**[2] [2064] 2-8-12 .... MartinDwyer 9 50
(J S Moore) *chsd ldrs: led over 2f out: rdn and hdd wl over 1f out: wknd ins fnl f* **8/1**

0 **5** *2 ½* **Put It On The Card**[16] [1744] 2-8-11 .... JimmyFortune 7 42
(P D Evans) *prom: rdn over 2f out: wknd over 1f out* **14/1**

0 **6** *2* **Champagne Perry**[23] [1535] 2-8-11 .... MichaelTebbutt 4 36
(V Smith) *chsd ldrs: lost pl over 4f out: rdn and wknd over 1f out* **33/1**

0 **7** *5* **Mum's Memories**[42] [1080] 2-8-11 .... PaulHanagan 8 21
(Jedd O'Keeffe) *led 5f out: rdn and hdd over 2f out: wknd over 1f out* **6/1**[3]

8 *3* **Marist Madame** 2-8-6 .... JohnEgan 2 7
(D K Ivory) *s.s: outpcd* **20/1**

9 *¾* **Heart And Hand (IRE)** 2-8-6 .... AlanMunro 1 —
(B J Meehan) *s.s: outpcd* **4/1**[2]

1m 15.6s (1.90) **Going Correction** +0.075s/f (Good) **9** Ran SP% **112.6**
Speed ratings (Par 91):90,84,83,80,77 74,68,64,63
CSF £123.14 TOTE £7.60: £1.60, £4.90, £1.30; EX 160.70 TRIFECTA Not won..The winner was bought in for 7,200gns
Owner D C Rutter & H Clewlow **Bred** The National Stud **Trained** Great Ness, Shropshire

FOCUS
A poor seller with the exception of the winner, who is above-average for the grade. The form is not likely to prove informative for future races.

NOTEBOOK
Cheshire Prince took full advantage of a drop in grade to win nicely. Still green under pressure and lugging into the centre of the track when making his challenge, he stretched away nicely and could prove to be a bit better than selling grade. (op 9-1)
Baytown Paikea had not shown a great deal of promise prior to the race and holds the form down for those that finished behind her. (op 16-1)
Aggbag does not look the most straightforward of characters, but essentially had every chance without being good enough. He does not look one to take a short price about. (tchd 6-4)
Alittleriskie(IRE) had every chance but again gave the impression that even six furlongs stretches her stamina. (op 5-1)
Put It On The Card never looked like getting involved and needs to find plenty of improvement to have a chance of troubling the judge in the near future. (tchd 16-1)
Heart And Hand(IRE) was slowly away from a moderate draw and never got into the race at any stage. (op 5-1 tchd 11-2)

2146 TOTETRIFECTA MAIDEN STKS (DIV II) 7f 3y
3:20 (3:21) (Class 5) 3-Y-O+ **£3,238** (£963; £481; £240) **Stalls** High

Form RPR

U4 **1** **Ahlawy (IRE)**[18] [1684] 3-8-13 .... NickyMackay 5 77
(L M Cumani) *hld up: hdwy over 2f out: r.o to ld post* **7/1**

0060 **2** *shd* **Madame Medusa (IRE)**[18] [1681] 3-8-8 72..................... KerrinMcEvoy 2 74+
(J A R Toller) *led: hdd over 5f out: led over 2f out: rdn and hung rt ins fnl f: nt run on and hdd post* **3/1**[1]

3 *½* **Wild Academy (IRE)** 3-8-8 .... MichaelHills 4 71
(G C Bravery) *chsd ldrs: rdn over 1f out: ev ch ins fnl f: styd on* **9/2**[3]

0 **4** *3* **Marajel (IRE)**[42] 1087 3-8-13 AlanMunro 7 68
(P W Chapple-Hyam) *s.i.s: hld up: styd on appr fnl f: nt trble ldrs* **9/2**[3]
0 **5** *3* **Hassaad**[11] 1844 3-8-13 RHills 6 60
(W J Haggas) *prom: rdn 1/2-way: wknd over 1f out* **10/3**[2]
0 **6** *9* **Stroll In The Park (IRE)**[42] 1087 3-8-11 ow1 AntonyProcter(3) 1 38
(D R C Elsworth) *prom over 4f* **12/1**
0 **7** *3* **Shoshoni**[19] 1640 3-8-8 MatthewHenry 10 24
(M A Jarvis) *led over 5f out: hdd over 2f out: wknd over 1f out* **25/1**
8 *1* **Wodhill Schnaps** 5-9-10 DerekMcGaffin 3 30
(D Morris) *s.i.s: hdwy over 2f out: sn wknd* **66/1**
00 **9** *3 1/2* **Cut Glass**[268] 5005 3-8-8 TedDurcan 11 12
(C E Brittain) *s.i.s: a in rr* **33/1**
0000 **10** *8* **Canary Girl**[169] 6569 3-8-1 40 KirstyMilczarek(7) 9 —
(Mrs C A Dunnett) *prom to 1/2-way* **66/1**
0 **11** *21* **Sansel**[7] 1940 3-8-1 DonnaCaldwell(7) 8 —
(J Ryan) *sn pushed along in rr: bhd fr 1/2-way* **100/1**

1m 26.5s (-0.10) **Going Correction** +0.075s/f (Good)
WFA 3 from 5yo 11lb **41** Ran SP% **115.4**
Speed ratings (Par 103):103,102,102,98,95 85,81,80,76,67 43
CSF £27.07 TOTE £6.20: £1.90, £1.80, £1.50; EX 33.00 Trifecta £153.40 Pool £695.89 - 3.22 winning units..
Owner Sheikh Mohammed Obaid Al Maktoum **Bred** Castlemartin Stud And Skymarc Farm **Trained** Newmarket, Suffolk

FOCUS
The slightly slower of the two maidens, which also looks less likely to produce as many winners although the form is quite solid.

2147 TOTESPORT.COM H'CAP 7f 3y
3:55 (3:55) (Class 4) (0-85,85) 4-Y-0+
£6,232 (£1,866; £933; £467; £233; £117) **Stalls** High

Form RPR
0022 **1** **Grey Boy (GER)**[15] 1760 5-8-6 **73** PaulHanagan 5 93
(R A Fahey) *w ldr: rdn to ld over 1f out: r.o* **7/4**[1]
1006 **2** *5* **Pintle**[28] 1407 6-8-12 **79** KerrinMcEvoy 7 86
(J L Spearing) *led: hdd over 4f out: rdn over 2f out: styng on same pce whn hung lft ins fnl f* **4/1**[2]
4006 **3** *3* **Fiefdom (IRE)**[19] 1629 4-9-4 **85** JohnEgan 1 84
(I W McInnes) *chsd ldrs: rdn over 2f out: wknd fnl f* **20/1**
1000 **4** *1/2* **H Harrison (IRE)**[34] 1262 6-8-1 **73** NataliaGemelova(5) 2 71
(I W McInnes) *w ldrs: led over 4f out: edgd rt and hdd over 2f out: wknd fnl f* **40/1**
5062 **5** *1 1/2* **Dispol Katie**[10] 1865 5-8-9 **76** JamieSpencer 6 70
(T D Barron) *trckd ldrs: led over 2f out: rdn and hdd over 1f out: wknd fnl f* **5/1**[3]
0500 **6** *1 1/4* **Capricho (IRE)**[25] 1474 9-8-6 **73** (p) PaulDoe 8 64
(J Akehurst) *hld up: hdwy over 2f: rdn and wknd over 1f out* **9/1**
6330 **7** *hd* **Bobski (IRE)**[18] 1692 4-9-2 **83** MartinDwyer 4 73
(G A Huffer) *s.s: hdwy 1/2-way: rdn and wknd over 1f out* **13/2**
0000 **8** *1/2* **Mineral Star (IRE)**[30] 1340 4-9-1 **85** SaleemGolam(3) 3 74
(M H Tompkins) *hld up: rdn 1/2-way: wknd 2f out* **10/1**

1m 26.2s (-0.40) **Going Correction** +0.075s/f (Good) **8** Ran SP% **112.7**
Speed ratings (Par 105):105,99,95,95,93 92,91,91
CSF £8.42 CT £98.88 TOTE £1.90: £1.10, £1.40, £5.80; EX 8.70 Trifecta £109.30 Pool £691.72 - 4.49 winning units..
Owner K & J **Bred** J Potempa **Trained** Musley Bank, N Yorks

FOCUS
The sort of winning time you would expect for a race like this, predictably faster than both divisions of the maiden. The winner could hardly have been more impressive but the form is not solid.
Fiefdom(IRE) Official explanation: jockey said gelding hung right throughout

2148 TOTEEXACTA H'CAP 1m 3y
4:30 (4:30) (Class 6) (0-65,65) 4-Y-0+ **£3,108** (£924; £462; £230) **Stalls** High

Form RPR
0333 **1** **Sol Rojo**[32] 1293 4-8-6 **53** ow1 (v) TedDurcan 7 65
(J Pearce) *s.i.s: hld up: hdwy over 1f out: r.o to ld wl ins fnl f* **12/1**
002 **2** *2* **Tuning Fork**[30] 1353 6-8-8 **55** AlanMunro 8 62
(T M Jones) *led: rdn over 2f out: hdd wl ins fnl f* **10/1**[3]
1130 **3** *1 1/4* **Redeye Special**[22] 1568 4-9-1 **62** JamieSpencer 9 66
(M L W Bell) *chsd ldrs: chal 2f over 2f out: sn rdn: hung lft over 1f out: no ex ins fnl f* **11/4**[1]
0603 **4** *1* **Kalani Star (IRE)**[10] 1462 6-7-13 **51** oh4 (vt) NataliaGemelova(5) 13 53
(I W McInnes) *mid-div: hdwy 5f out: outpcd over 3f out: styd on u.p fnl f* **33/1**
0040 **5** *3/4* **Angel River**[2] 2070 4-7-13 **51** oh12 (b) RoryMoore(5) 14 51
(J Ryan) *hld up: hdwy over 1f out: wknd ins fnl f* **100/1**
0303 **6** *1 1/2* **Motu (IRE)**[15] 1753 5-8-5 **52** oh1 ow1 (v) JohnEgan 1 49
(I W McInnes) *s.i.s: hld up: hdwy and swtchd lft 2f out: rdn over 1f out: hung lft ins fnl f: styd on same pce* **11/1**
2600 **7** *1 1/4* **Life's A Whirl**[29] 1382 4-8-11 **65** KirstyMilczarek(7) 2 59
(Mrs C A Dunnett) *hld up: hdwy over 2f out: wknd over 1f out* **33/1**
5022 **8** *shd* **Peace Lily**[18] 1683 4-8-11 **58** StephenCarson 3 52
(R F Johnson Houghton) *chsd ldrs: rdn over 2f out: wknd fnl f* **7/1**[2]
0032 **9** *hd* **King Of Meze (IRE)**[16] 1725 5-8-5 **52** (p) KerrinMcEvoy 12 45
(J S Wainwright) *chsd ldrs: rdn over 2f out: hung lft and wknd over 1f out* **12/1**
2040 **10** *1 1/4* **Collect**[226] 5940 4-8-12 **62** SaleemGolam(3) 16 52
(M H Tompkins) *hld up: rdn over 2f out: n.d* **14/1**
4005 **11** *6* **Rapid Flow**[11] 1852 4-8-5 **52** NickyMackay 10 28
(P D Evans) *chsd ldr to 1/2-way: wknd over 2f out* **25/1**
1550 **12** *1 1/4* **Saucy**[28] 1400 5-8-7 **54** ow1 ShaneKelly 4 28
(A W Carroll) *hld up: swtchd lft: rdn and wknd over 2f out* **18/1**
0405 **13** *nk* **Vibe**[154] 6680 5-8-4 **51** oh7 MartinDwyer 6 24
(A W Carroll) *mid-div: hdwy 1/2-way: rdn and wknd over 2f out* **25/1**
1001 **14** *13* **Wodhill Gold**[15] 1765 5-7-13 **51** oh5 (v) EmmettStack(5) 5 —
(D Morris) *mid-div: rdn 1/2-way: wknd over 2f out* **25/1**
0000 **15** *hd* **Bridegroom**[14] 1773 4-8-10 **57** PaulHanagan 15 —
(Lady Herries) *s.i.s: hld up: rdn 1/2-way: sn wknd* **10/1**[3]
2363 **16** *5* **Torquemada (IRE)**[18] 1665 5-9-1 **62** (p) PaulDoe 11 —
(W Jarvis) *s.i.s: sn prom: chsd ldr 1/2-way tl wknd over 2f out* **7/1**[2]

1m 40.63s (0.73) **Going Correction** +0.075s/f (Good) **16** Ran SP% **123.9**
Speed ratings (Par 101):99,97,95,94,94 92,91,91,90,89 83,82,82,69,68 63
CSF £120.51 CT £434.07 TOTE £13.50: £2.20, £2.50, £1.10, £11.70; EX 110.50 Trifecta £245.70 Part won. Pool £346.08 - 0.10 winning units..
Owner sportaracing.com **Bred** Mrs A Yearley **Trained** Newmarket, Suffolk

FOCUS
A big field, but a modest handicap and not that many ever got into it. The runners tended to stay mid-track throughout. Sound form.
Torquemada(IRE) Official explanation: trainer had no explanation for the poor form shown

2149 TOTESPORT 0800 221 221 H'CAP 1m 2f 21y
5:05 (5:07) (Class 6) (0-65,65) 4-Y-0+ **£3,108** (£924; £462; £230) **Stalls** Low

Form RPR
6260 **1** **Catskill**[38] 1164 4-9-4 **65** AlanMunro 7 77
(E F Vaughan) *trckd ldrs: rdn to ld over 1f out: all out* **16/1**
5612 **2** *shd* **Cottingham (IRE)**[16] 1723 5-8-4 **51** NickyMackay 1 63+
(T D Barron) *trckd ldrs: swtchd rt over 1f out: sn chsng wnr: r.o u.p* **3/1**[1]
0005 **3** *2 1/2* **Ariodante**[21] 1591 4-9-2 **63** ShaneKelly 10 70
(J M P Eustace) *led: rdn and hdd over 1f out: no ex ins fnl f* **12/1**
5000 **4** *1 3/4* **Street Life (IRE)**[21] 1591 8-9-3 **64** KerrinMcEvoy 8 68
(W J Musson) *hld up: hdwy over 1f out: nt rch ldrs* **5/1**[3]
0023 **5** *1/2* **Rotuma (IRE)**[11] 1850 7-8-8 **55** (b) JohnEgan 6 58
(M Dods) *hld up: hdwy over 2f out: styd on same pce fnl f* **9/2**[2]
0005 **6** *1 1/4* **Admiral Compton**[19] 1637 5-9-1 **62** MartinDwyer 2 62
(J R Boyle) *w ldr: rdn and ev ch over 1f out: wknd ins fnl f* **16/1**
0465 **7** *5* **Machinate (USA)**[170] 6567 4-8-8 **55** JamieSpencer 5 46
(W M Brisbourne) *s.i.s: hld up: hdwy over 3f out: stmbld over 2f out: sn rdn: wknd fnl f* **8/1**
1430 **8** *6* **Itcanbedone Again (IRE)**[39] 1152 7-8-8 **55** PaulHanagan 3 34
(Ian Williams) *prom: plld hrd: rdn and wknd over 1f out* **12/1**
0000 **9** *1/2* **Northside Lodge (IRE)**[109] 375 8-8-13 **63** SaleemGolam(3) 9 42
(W R Swinburn) *chsd ldrs 7f* **7/1**
5005 **10** *nk* **Panshir (FR)**[34] 1265 5-7-13 **51** oh1 RoryMoore(5) 11 29
(Mrs C A Dunnett) *dwlt: hld up: plld hrd: hdwy over 7f out: rdn: hung lft and wknd 2f out* **20/1**
0020 **11** *1/2* **Silver Court**[8] 1910 4-8-4 **51** oh3 StephenCarson 4 28
(A W Carroll) *hld up: plld hrd: wknd 3f out* **40/1**

2m 12.47s (4.37) **Going Correction** +0.475s/f (Yiel) **11** Ran SP% **117.8**
Speed ratings (Par 101):101,100,98,97,97 96,92,87,86,86 86
CSF £63.84 CT £618.18 TOTE £15.80: £3.10, £1.70, £3.00; EX 52.80 Trifecta £186.80 Part won. Pool £263.10 - 0.50 winning units..
Owner Mrs M E Domvile **Bred** London Thoroughbred Services Ltd **Trained** Newmarket, Suffolk

FOCUS
An ordinary handicap run at just an even pace. The first three were always prominent and the race has been rated through the third.
Machinate(USA) ◆ Official explanation: trainer said gelding had a breathing problem
Silver Court Official explanation: jockey said gelding hung right and bit slipped through its mouth

2150 TOTESPORTCASINO.COM H'CAP 1m 3f 101y
5:35 (5:35) (Class 6) (0-65,64) 4-Y-0+ **£3,108** (£924; £462; £230) **Stalls** Low

Form RPR
2320 **1** **Taxman (IRE)**[4] 2035 4-9-3 **63** (p) TedDurcan 4 75
(C E Brittain) *chsd ldr: led over 2f out: rdn out* **7/1**[3]
6043 **2** *nk* **Our Choice (IRE)**[3] 2044 4-9-1 **61** JamieSpencer 1 73
(N P Littmoden) *a.p: rdn to chse wnr over 1f out: r.o* **7/4**[1]
1004 **3** *3* **La Gessa**[44] 1058 4-8-7 **53** NickyMackay 8 60
(John Berry) *prom: lost pl 1/2-way: hdwy over 1f out: r.o* **12/1**
6501 **4** *nk* **Darghan (IRE)**[21] 1590 6-8-8 **59** StephenDonohoe(5) 11 69+
(W J Musson) *hld up: nt clr run over 2f out: hdwy over 1f out: r.o* **8/1**
0563 **5** *1 1/4* **Barbirolli**[19] 1637 4-9-4 **64** ShaneKelly 7 69
(W M Brisbourne) *hld up in tch: rdn over 2f out: no ex fnl f* **16/1**
0663 **6** *1* **Smoothie (IRE)**[28] 1415 8-8-3 **52** ow1 SaleemGolam(3) 3 55
(Ian Williams) *s.s: hld up: r.o ins fnl f: nvr nrr* **12/1**
P602 **7** *2* **Ferrando**[23] 1537 4-8-6 **52** AlanMunro 9 52
(D J Daly) *chsd ldrs: rdn over 2f out: wknd fnl f* **16/1**
1060 **8** *3/4* **Melvino**[15] 1756 4-9-2 **62** JimmyFortune 5 61
(T D Barron) *s.s: hld up: hdwy over 3f out: rdn 2f out: wknd over 1f out* **13/2**[2]
0300 **9** *1* **Wizard Looking**[28] 1425 5-9-2 **62** KerrinMcEvoy 6 59
(J S Wainwright) *hld up: plld hrd: hdwy over 2f out: rdn and wknd fnl f* **11/1**
1206 **10** *3 1/2* **Plenty Cried Wolf**[29] 1389 4-9-2 **62** PaulHanagan 2 53
(R A Fahey) *led: rdn and hdd over 2f out: wknd over 1f out* **33/1**
0500 **11** *13* **Native American**[12] 1821 4-9-4 **64** MartinDwyer 10 35
(T D McCarthy) *hld up in tch: wknd and eased over 1f out* **40/1**
3020 **12** *21* **Jackie Kiely**[28] 1415 5-9-1 **61** JohnEgan 12 —
(Stef Liddiard) *hld up: rdn over 3f out: wknd over 2f out* **20/1**

2m 32.46s (4.96) **Going Correction** +0.475s/f (Yiel) **12** Ran SP% **118.9**
Speed ratings (Par 101):100,99,97,97,96 95,94,93,93,90 81,65
CSF £19.19 CT £150.72 TOTE £7.60: £2.70, £1.50, £3.70; EX 21.60 Trifecta £229.00 Part won. Pool £322.67 - 0.67 winning units. Place 6 £ 16.69, Place 5 £ 11.13.
Owner C E Brittain **Bred** Darley **Trained** Newmarket, Suffolk

FOCUS
An ordinary handicap in which it seemed to be an advantage to race up with the pace. Improvement from the winner, with the second running to his turf best.
Native American Official explanation: jockey said gelding lost its action
Jackie Kiely Official explanation: jockey said gelding lost its action
T/Jkpt: Not won. T/Plt: £13.60 to a £1 stake. Pool: £49,929.75. 2,678.05 winning tickets. T/Qpdt: £5.60 to a £1 stake. Pool: £2,908.90. 383.90 winning tickets. CR

2151 - 2153a (Foreign Racing) - See Raceform Interactive

1705 LEOPARDSTOWN (L-H)
Wednesday, May 31

OFFICIAL GOING: Good

2154a SEAMUS MCGRATH MEMORIAL SAVAL BEG STKS (LISTED RACE) 1m 6f
7:30 (7:31) 4-Y-0+ **£26,937** (£7,903; £3,765; £1,282)

RPR
1 **Media Puzzle (USA)**[52] 932 9-9-1 101 (b) PJSmullen 4 107
(D K Weld, Ire) *trckd ldrs: 5th 1/2-way: 3rd early st: led 1f out: styd on wl u.p* **13/2**
2 *1* **Good Surprise**[3] 2056 5-9-1 106 (b) KJManning 5 106
(J S Bolger, Ire) *hld up in tch: tk clsr order appr st: 4th 2f out: 5th 1f out: r.o strly cl home* **4/1**[2]
3 *1/2* **Mkuzi**[256] 5331 7-9-6 107 FMBerry 1 110
(John M Oxx, Ire) *settled 3rd: 4th 1/2-way: 3rd and rdn appr st: 2nd under 2f out: no ex cl home* **9/2**[3]
4 *hd* **Cairdeas (IRE)**[31] 1324 5-9-1 107 TPO'Shea 6 105
(D K Weld, Ire) *hld up in rr: plld hrd early: prog 4f out: 5th over 1f out: 3rd ins fnl f: no ex cl home* **8/1**

5 2 ½ **Helena Molony (IRE)**[24] 1521 4-8-12 96 .... MJKinane 7 99
(John M Oxx, Ire) *hld up in tch: 7th 5f out: 5th and effrt early st: no imp fr over 1f out* **3/1**[1]

6 3 **Valentina Guest (IRE)**[17] 1707 5-8-12 94 .... JAHeffernan 3 95
(Peter Casey, Ire) *sn led: jnd appr 1/2-way: led again 4f out: rdn and strly pressed st: hdd 1f out: no ex* **16/1**

7 4 ½ **Virginia Woolf**[17] 1707 4-8-12 96 .... WSupple 2 90
(John M Oxx, Ire) *5th early: prog appr 1/2-way: disp ld 5f out: hdd 4f out: sn rdn: wknd ent st* **9/1**

8 3 ½ **Liss Ard (IRE)**[122] 6255 5-9-1 93 .... KFallon 8 89
(John Joseph Murphy, Ire) *sn 2nd: disp ld appr 1/2-way: 3rd u.p 5f out: wknd bef st* **14/1**

2m 57.8s **8** Ran SP% **110.2**
CSF £30.20 TOTE £5.60: £1.70, £1.80, £1.80; DF 31.40.
Owner Sir Michael Smurfit **Bred** Moyglare Stud Farm Ltd **Trained** The Curragh, Co Kildare
■ Another victory in this race for Dermot Weld whose previous winners include Vinnie Roe and Vintage Crop.

NOTEBOOK
Media Puzzle(USA), who has suffered leg problems since winning the 2002 Melbourne Cup, had not won in an abbreviated career since then, but was all the better for his return to the track over an inadequate trip at The Curragh last month. He won this in good style and provided all remains well, he will now head for the Ascot Gold Cup and in the longer term possibly a return to Flemington in the autumn. (op 6/1)

2155 - 2158a (Foreign Racing) - See Raceform Interactive

[1945]AYR (L-H)

Thursday, June 1

OFFICIAL GOING: Good (good to soft in places)
Wind: Breezy, half-against

2159 DM HALL EUROPEAN BREEDERS FUND MAIDEN STKS 6f
2:10 (2:10) (Class 4) 2-Y-O **£5,181** (£1,541; £770; £384) **Stalls** High

Form RPR

1 **Baltimore Jack (IRE)** 2-8-10 .... MichaelJStainton(7) 2 68
(R M Whitaker) *in tch: outpcd after 2f: rallied over 2f out: led and edgd rt over 1f out: pushed out fnl f* **33/1**

2 ½ **Waiheke Island** 2-8-12 .... DaleGibson 6 61
(B Mactaggart) *hld up: hdwy to chse wnr over 1f out: kpt on fnl f* **66/1**

6 3 3 **Howards Tipple**[20] 1632 2-9-3 .... TomEaves 7 57
(I Semple) *prom: effrt over 2f out: hung lft and no imp over 1f out* **33/1**

6 4 2 **Dubai's Touch**[15] 1780 2-9-3 .... JoeFanning 5 51
(M Johnston) *led to over 1f out: sn outpcd* **8/1**[3]

32 5 3 **Domino Dancer (IRE)**[22] 1588 2-9-3 .... PaulMulrennan 3 42+
(J Howard Johnson) *w ldrs tl wknd wl over 1f out* **9/4**[2]

6 11 **Evens And Odds (IRE)** 2-9-3 .... NCallan 4 9+
(K A Ryan) *w ldrs: rdn 2f out: sn wknd* **4/5**[1]

7 17 **Eldon Endeavour** 2-8-12 .... AndrewMullen(5) 1 —
(B Storey) *s.i.s: drvn and lost tch after 2f* **50/1**

1m 16.32s (2.65) **Going Correction** +0.25s/f (Good) **7** Ran SP% **106.8**
Speed ratings (Par 95):92,91,87,84,80 66,43
CSF £964.83 TOTE £19.70: £3.60, £8.40; EX 177.00.
Owner Clipper Group Holdings **Bred** P Monagnan And J Collins And G Dillon **Trained** Scarcroft, W Yorks

FOCUS
A mixed bag on looks but, with the three market leaders disappointing, this did not take as much winning as seemed likely beforehand. Difficult to rate, the fourth is the best guide.

NOTEBOOK
Baltimore Jack(IRE), a half-brother to a five-furlong juvenile winner, looked as though the race would do him good but turned in a fair effort on this racecourse debut. He has physical scope for improvement, should stay further and, although this bare form is ordinary, he is almost certainly capable of better. (op 25-1)
Waiheke Island, a leggy sort who looked as though the race would do her good, showed ability on this racecourse debut. She should have no problems staying seven furlongs plus and may be capable of better. (op 25-1)
Howards Tipple was again colty in the paddock and did not look straightforward in the race but left his debut form well behind. While he may do better in nurseries in due course, he is likely to continue to look vulnerable in this type of race. (op 20-1)
Dubai's Touch, a stocky colt, was again noisy in the paddock. He looked in good shape but, after enjoying the run of the race against the stands' rail, proved disappointing after his fair debut run. He may be better on a sound surface. (op 7-1)
Domino Dancer(IRE), a leggy sort who was on his toes throughout in the paddock, proved disappointing on ground that was softer than the official description. He will be suited by the return to a sound surface but is starting to look exposed.
Evens And Odds(IRE), the second foal of a juvenile mile winner, was the subject of favourable reports and looked plenty fit enough on this racecourse debut. He proved most disappointing on ground softer than the official but is worth another chance on a sound surface. (op 8-11 tchd 10-11 in places)

2160 DAWN GROUP RATING RELATED MAIDEN STKS 7f 50y
2:45 (2:45) (Class 5) 3-Y-O+ **£3,238** (£963; £481; £240) **Stalls** Low

Form RPR

3520 1 **Marmooq**[31] 1345 3-8-13 68 .... JoeFanning 4 76
(M Johnston) *prom: effrt over 2f out: led wl ins fnl f: all out* **9/2**[2]

3400 2 *shd* **Dream Rose (IRE)**[28] 1444 3-8-10 70 .... TonyCulhane 5 73
(M R Channon) *led: rdn over 1f out: hdd wl ins fnl f: rallied: jst hld* **9/2**[2]

000 3 11 **Lucky Lil**[37] 1217 4-8-13 41 .... MichaelJStainton(7) 3 44
(R M Whitaker) *trckd ldrs tl rdn and no ex fr 2f out* **33/1**

2225 4 2 ½ **Mina**[20] 1645 4-8-13 59 .... RobbieMills(7) 6 38
(Rae Guest) *prom on outside: effrt over 2f out: edgd lft and btn over 1f out* **7/2**[1]

0603 5 21 **Silk Merchant (IRE)**[31] 1344 3-8-13 61 .... PaulMulrennan 2 —
(J Howard Johnson) *keen: hld up ins: rdn 3f out: sn btn* **7/2**[1]

4365 6 6 **Pab Special (IRE)**[64] 795 3-8-13 68 .... NCallan 1 —
(K R Burke) *stmbld s: hld up in tch: wknd fr 3f out* **11/2**[3]

030 7 6 **Ocean Sunrise (IRE)**[208] 6251 3-8-5 68 .... GregFairley(5) 7 —
(M Johnston) *pressed ldr tl wknd fr 3f out* **7/1**

1m 35.04s (2.32) **Going Correction** +0.325s/f (Good)
WFA 3 from 4yo 10lb **7** Ran SP% **111.6**
Speed ratings (Par 103):99,98,86,83,59 52,45
CSF £23.63 TOTE £4.20: £1.90, £3.20; EX 10.10.
Owner Hamdan Al Maktoum **Bred** Matthews Breeding And Racing Ltd **Trained** Middleham Moor, N Yorks
■ Stewards' Enquiry : Tony Culhane one-day ban: used whip with excessive frequency (Jun 12)

FOCUS
Not a competitive race and few in-form runners. The pace was on the steady side and the 41-rated third confirms this bare form is modest.
Silk Merchant(IRE) Official explanation: trainer had no explanation for the poor form shown
Pab Special(IRE) Official explanation: jockey said gelding felt wrong behind

2161 MACKENZIE PARTNERSHIP H'CAP 5f
3:15 (3:15) (Class 5) (0-70,70) 3-Y-O **£3,368** (£1,002; £500; £250) **Stalls** High

Form RPR

4101 1 **Mormeatmic**[14] 1793 3-9-4 67 .... PaulMulrennan 7 77
(M W Easterby) *pressed ldr: led 1/2-way: rdn over 1f out: hld on wl whn hrd pressed wl ins fnl f* **11/4**[1]

550 2 *hd* **Dulce Sueno**[210] 6233 3-8-2 51 oh1 .... PaulHanagan 5 61+
(I Semple) *dwlt: sn pushed along in rr: hdwy over 1f out: ev ch wl ins fnl f: jst hld* **14/1**

2100 3 3 ½ **Rothesay Dancer**[28] 1448 3-9-7 70 .... TonyCulhane 3 67
(J S Goldie) *in tch: effrt and ev ch over 1f out: no ex ins fnl f* **7/1**

2213 4 ¾ **Toy Top (USA)**[27] 1453 3-9-5 68 ....(b) PhillipMakin 6 62
(M Dods) *cl up: effrt and ev ch whn hung lft over 1f out: no ex ins fnl f* **4/1**[2]

4002 5 1 ¼ **Newkeylets**[21] 1612 3-8-6 55 .... TomEaves 4 45
(I Semple) *hld up in tch: pushed along after 2f: effrt 2f out: sn no ex* **11/2**

402 6 ¾ **Mandarin Rocket (IRE)**[21] 1609 3-8-13 62 .... JoeFanning 2 49
(Miss L A Perratt) *in tch on outside: hung lft thrght: wknd fr 2f out* **15/2**

0340 7 10 **Mytton's Pride**[5] 2027 3-9-3 66 ....(p) NCallan 1 17
(A Bailey) *led to 1/2-way: wknd over 1f out* **5/1**[3]

61.51 secs (1.07) **Going Correction** +0.25s/f (Good) **7** Ran SP% **109.6**
Speed ratings (Par 99):101,100,95,93,91 90,74
CSF £37.69 TOTE £3.40: £2.00, £6.60; EX 47.30.
Owner M Broad & Mrs M E Attwood **Bred** A C Birkle **Trained** Sheriff Hutton, N Yorks

FOCUS
An ordinary handicap, run at a decent gallop and one in which things unfolded against the stands' rail. The race is rated through the third to his latest form.

2162 MACDONALDS LEGAL SERVICES H'CAP 1m 2f
3:45 (3:45) (Class 4) (0-85,84) 4-Y-O+ **£6,477** (£1,927; £963; £481) **Stalls** Low

Form RPR

1500 1 **Ryan's Future (IRE)**[208] 6254 6-8-10 78 .... GregFairley(5) 8 92
(Miss L A Perratt) *s.s: sn rcvrd and hld up: hdwy over 2f out: led 1f out: r.o strly* **20/1**

0312 2 2 **Trouble Mountain (USA)**[2] 2097 9-8-3 66 ....(t) DaleGibson 4 76
(M W Easterby) *hld up: hdwy 2f out: chsd wnr ins fnl f: r.o* **13/2**[3]

0632 3 3 ½ **Jordans Elect**[20] 1637 6-8-8 71 ow2 .... PhillipMakin 5 74
(P Monteith) *keen early: led tl hdd and no ex 1f out* **25/1**

0505 4 1 ¼ **Wigwam Willie (IRE)**[19] 1676 4-9-4 81 ....(p) NCallan 12 82
(K A Ryan) *prom: effrt over 2f out: no ex over 1f out* **7/1**

0325 5 *nk* **Hawkit (USA)**[5] 2025 5-8-1 69 .... AndrewMullen(5) 6 69
(A Bailey) *prom: effrt over 2f out: one pce over 1f out* **10/1**

3000 6 3 **Kames Park (IRE)**[22] 1585 4-9-7 84 .... TonyCulhane 1 79
(I Semple) *hld up: nt clr run over 2f out: sn rdn: kpt on: nvr rchd ldrs* **14/1**

4302 7 2 **Greenbelt**[6] 1987 5-8-4 67 .... JoeFanning 7 58
(G M Moore) *cl up: rdn 3f out: wknd over 1f out* **13/2**[3]

0505 8 3 **Regent's Secret (USA)**[27] 1456 6-8-12 75 .... FergalLynch 3 60
(J S Goldie) *hld up: pushed along over 2f out: n.d* **16/1**

2012 9 ½ **Press Express (IRE)**[20] 1651 4-8-7 77 .... LukeMorris(7) 11 61
(M L W Bell) *midfield: outpcd over 2f out: sn btn* **6/1**[2]

5200 10 20 **Emerald Bay (IRE)**[26] 1495 4-9-5 82 .... TomEaves 9 28
(I Semple) *trckd ldrs tl rdn and wknd over 2f out* **8/1**

2004 11 9 **Instructor**[33] 1281 5-9-1 78 .... PaulHanagan 2 7
(R A Fahey) *cl up tl wknd over 2f out: virtually p.u fnl f* **4/1**[1]

-000 12 5 **Buddy Brown**[11] 1864 4-8-13 76 .... PaulMulrennan 10 —
(J Howard Johnson) *towards rr: rdn and hung rt 3f out: sn lost tch* **50/1**

2m 11.2s (-0.52) **Going Correction** +0.075s/f (Good) **12** Ran SP% **116.8**
Speed ratings (Par 105):105,103,100,99,99 96,95,92,92,76 69,65
CSF £140.59 CT £3267.88 TOTE £19.80: £5.30, £2.40, £4.30; EX 242.00.
Owner Vimal Khosla **Bred** A F O'Callaghan **Trained** Ayr, S Ayrshire

FOCUS
A fair gallop to an ordinary handicap and those held up dominated in the closing stages. The pace was decent and the form looks solid.
Instructor Official explanation: jockey said gelding lost its action in straight
Buddy Brown Official explanation: jockey said gelding hung right-handed throughout

2163 PARADIGM H'CAP 7f 50y
4:20 (4:20) (Class 4) (0-85,82) 3-Y-O **£7,772** (£2,312; £1,155; £577) **Stalls** Low

Form RPR

6553 1 **The Osteopath (IRE)**[12] 1855 3-8-10 71 ....(p) PhillipMakin 3 79
(M Dods) *hld up in tch: smooth hdwy over 2f out: led over 1f out: carried hd awkwardly: pushed out fnl f* **3/1**[1]

0003 2 2 **Soto**[13] 1812 3-8-11 72 .... PaulMulrennan 7 75
(M W Easterby) *trckd ldrs: effrt and disp ld over 1f out: kpt on fnl f* **4/1**[3]

4330 3 *hd* **Great Chieftain (IRE)**[12] 1855 3-8-10 71 .... PaulHanagan 2 73
(R A Fahey) *keen: mde most to over 1f out: nt qckn* **6/1**

0004 4 5 **Tora Petcha (IRE)**[31] 1349 3-9-1 76 .... FergalLynch 5 65
(R Hollinshead) *hld up in tch: hdwy 1/2-way: effrt over 2f out: sn one pce* **9/2**

1025 5 2 ½ **John Keats**[13] 1812 3-9-7 82 .... TomEaves 4 65
(I Semple) *chsd ldrs: drvn along after 3f: no imp fnl 2f* **7/2**[2]

6 4 **Petross**[186] 3-8-4 65 .... StanleyChin 1 37
(R M Whitaker) *trckd ldrs: hung rt: hmpd and lost pl after 3f: no ch after* **14/1**

400 7 10 **Cole (IRE)**[229] 5888 3-7-13 65 oh8 ow2 .... AndrewMullen(5) 6 11
(J Howard Johnson) *keen: sn w ldr: rdn and wknd over 2f out* **20/1**

1m 35.23s (2.51) **Going Correction** +0.325s/f (Good) **7** Ran SP% **111.1**
Speed ratings (Par 101):98,95,95,89,86 82,70
CSF £14.31 TOTE £4.40: £2.30, £2.30; EX 14.30.
Owner Kevin Kirkup **Bred** Joe Rogers **Trained** Denton, Co Durham

FOCUS
An uncompetitive event in which the pace seemed sound and the runner-up sets the level, but the form is not strong.
Petross Official explanation: jockey said gelding suffered interference in running
Cole(IRE) Official explanation: jockey said gelding hung right-handed throughout

2164 MACDONALDS SOLICITORS H'CAP 7f 50y
4:50 (4:50) (Class 5) (0-75,73) 4-Y-0+ £5,181 (£1,541; £770; £384) Stalls Low

Form RPR
6551 1 **Bollin Edward**[19] [1683] 7-8-12 **64** NCallan 4 73
(K A Ryan) *keen: hld up: hdwy to ld ins fnl f: rdn out* **4/1**[2]
0005 2 1 **Linden's Lady**[31] [1348] 6-7-13 **56** oh1 ow2 (v) AndrewMullen(5) 7 62
(J R Weymes) *keen: hld up in tch: hdwy on outside to ld over 1f out: hdd ins fnl f: kpt on* **16/1**
0003 3 2 **Society Music (IRE)**[3] [2071] 4-9-7 **73** (p) FergalLynch 6 74
(M Dods) *hld up: rdn over 2f out: kpt on fnl f: nt rch ldrs* **8/1**
1213 4 nk **Stellite**[24] [1531] 6-8-12 **67** DanielTudhope(3) 3 67
(J S Goldie) *cl up: rdn over 2f out: no ex over 1f out* **11/4**[1]
4030 5 ½ **Alfonso**[33] [1280] 5-9-7 **73** (b) PaulHanagan 2 72
(I Semple) *keen: cl up: effrt over 2f out: no ex over 1f out* **9/2**[3]
0510 6 ¾ **George The Best (IRE)**[13] [1816] 5-8-10 **62** TonyCulhane 9 59
(Micky Hammond) *keen: led to over 1f out: sn btn* **20/1**
0000 7 ½ **Oddsmaker (IRE)**[5] [2020] 5-8-5 **62** (t) GregFairley(5) 5 57
(M A Barnes) *in tch outside: effrt and ch over 1f out: sn rdn and btn* **16/1**
0064 8 11 **Hansomelle (IRE)**[20] [1636] 4-8-9 **61** DaleGibson 8 28
(B Mactaggart) *prom tl rdn and wknd over 2f out: eased* **10/1**
5100 9 13 **Local Poet**[7] [1949] 5-9-7 **73** (bt) TomEaves 1 6
(I Semple) *in tch on ins tl wknd over 2f out* **8/1**

1m 33.63s (0.91) **Going Correction** +0.325s/f (Good) **9 Ran SP% 112.7**
Speed ratings (Par 103):107,105,103,103,102 101,101,88,73
CSF £63.03 CT £483.82 TOTE £5.20: £1.70, £4.40, £2.70; EX 64.60.
Owner N O'Brien,T Fawcett and J Ryan **Bred** Sir Neil And Lady Westbrook **Trained** Hambleton, N Yorks

FOCUS
Another ordinary handicap in which the pace was sound but the runner-up limits the form.

2165 WEDDINGS AT AYR RACECOURSE H'CAP 1m
5:20 (5:20) (Class 6) (0-60,60) 4-Y-0+ £3,238 (£963; £481; £240) Stalls Low

Form RPR
0000 1 **Tidy (IRE)**[6] [1996] 6-9-2 **60** GregFairley(5) 11 74+
(Micky Hammond) *hld up: hdwy to ld 2f out: rdn and r.o strly* **20/1**
1202 2 3½ **Mystical Ayr (IRE)**[7] [1947] 4-9-0 **58** AndrewMullen(5) 4 63
(Miss L A Perratt) *in tch: effrt and ev ch 2f out: kpt on fnl f: nt rch wnr* **6/1**
0061 3 nk **Inch High**[7] [1947] 8-8-12 **51** 6ex PaulHanagan 8 56
(J S Goldie) *keen: cl up: effrt and ev ch 2f out: one pce fnl f* **8/1**
0120 4 nk **Spanish Law**[35] [1253] 4-8-11 **53** (b) BenSwarbrick(3) 7 57
(M Dods) *hld up: effrt centre over 2f out: kpt on fnl f: nt rch ldrs* **16/1**
0045 5 2 **Queen's Echo**[16] [1761] 5-9-6 **59** PhillipMakin 5 58
(M Dods) *dwlt: hld up: effrt over 2f out: edgd lft over 1f out: no imp* **4/1**[1]
5010 6 1 **Jordans Spark**[7] [1947] 5-8-8 **47** PaulMulrennan 12 44+
(P Monteith) *bhd: rdn whn n.m.r over 2f out: kpt on fnl f: n.d* **20/1**
0602 7 3 **Tequila Sheila (IRE)**[22] [1594] 4-8-9 **48** NCallan 3 38
(K R Burke) *plld hrd: in tch tl rdn and wknd over 1f out* **5/1**[2]
U046 8 5 **Templet (USA)**[10] [1883] 6-8-6 **56** (b) DuranFentiman(5) 9 29
(W G Harrison) *s.i.s: sn wl bhd: nvr on terms* **40/1**
5062 9 hd **Fiddlers Creek (IRE)**[8] [1608] 7-9-0 **56** (tp) DanielTudhope(3) 6 34
(R Allan) *w ldr tl rdn and wknd wl over 1f out* **6/1**
5354 10 18 **Just Bond (IRE)**[35] [1253] 4-9-2 **55** TonyCulhane 2 —
(B Smart) *keen: led to 2f out: sn btn: eased whn no ch* **11/2**[3]
0040 11 ¾ **Red River Rock (IRE)**[22] [1591] 4-8-13 **52** TomEaves 1 —
(T J Fitzgerald) *chsd ldrs tl rdn and wknd over 2f out* **50/1**
340 12 11 **Stormy Love (IRE)**[13] [1814] 4-9-6 **59** JoeFanning 10 —
(M Johnston) *prom tl wknd qckly fr 3f out* **25/1**

1m 45.39s (1.90) **Going Correction** +0.325s/f (Good) **12 Ran SP% 115.4**
Speed ratings (Par 101):103,99,99,98,96 95,92,87,87,69 68,57
CSF £125.94 CT £1071.23 TOTE £29.90: £7.50, £2.80, £3.80; EX 154.30 Place 6 £6,440.29, Place 5 £189.42.
Owner P J Davies, J Donovan CBE, M D Hammond **Bred** Mick McGinn And James Waldron **Trained** Middleham Moor, N Yorks

FOCUS
Another handicap comprising mainly exposed sorts. The pace was sound and the form looks solid with those in the frame behind the winner close to their marks.
Tidy(IRE) Official explanation: trainer had no explanation for the apparent improvement in form
Jordans Spark Official explanation: jockey said gelding was denied a clear run
T/Plt: £7,730.90 to a £1 stake. Pool: £36,536.65. 3.45 winning tickets. T/Qpdt: £28.70 to a £1 stake. Pool: £4,149.20. 106.90 winning tickets. RY

1846 NOTTINGHAM (L-H)
Thursday, June 1

OFFICIAL GOING: Good (good to soft in places)
The going was described as ' good to soft in the back straight, easy side of good in the home straight'.
Wind: Light, half-behind Weather: Fine and sunny

2166 CARLTON MAIDEN AUCTION FILLIES' STKS 6f 15y
2:30 (2:37) (Class 4) 2-Y-0 £5,505 (£1,637; £818; £408) Stalls High

Form RPR
5 1 **Yerevan**[13] [1817] 2-8-8 SamHitchcott 13 74+
(M R Channon) *mde all stands' side: clr overall over 1f out: v easily* **11/1**
2 5 **Merry Moon (IRE)** 2-8-6 FergusSweeney 14 57
(M Dods) *cmpt: racd stands' side: chsd ldrs: wnt 2nd 2f out: no ch w wnr: 2nd of 6 that side* **40/1**
3 1¼ **Little Miss Wizzy** 2-8-4 HayleyTurner 17 51
(M L W Bell) *small: racd stands' side: sn outpcd: hdwy 2f out: styd on ins last: 3rd of 6 that gp* **25/1**
4 shd **Zanida (IRE)** 2-8-10 SebSanders 10 60+
(K R Burke) *unf: scope: racd far side: trckd ldrs: led that side over 1f out: no ch w stands' side: 1st of 10 that gp* **14/1**
2 5 ½ **Drifting Gold**[17] [1743] 2-8-1 EdwardCreighton(3) 15 49
(C G Cox) *racd stands' side: chsd ldrs: edgd lft over 1f out: kpt on same pce: 4th of 6 that gp* **15/2**[3]
6 1½ **Market Day** 2-8-10 KerrinMcEvoy 4 54+
(L M Cumani) *cmpt: unruly and uns rdr twice bef s: mid-div far side: kpt on fnl f: 2nd of 10 that gp* **10/1**
5 7 1½ **Whipchord (IRE)**[24] [1542] 2-8-3 RichardSmith(3) 7 45+
(R Hannon) *trckd ldrs far side: led over 2f out: hdd over 1f out: 3rd of 10 that gp* **6/1**[2]
8 ½ **Morinqua (IRE)** 2-8-6 DO'Donohoe 1 44+
(K A Ryan) *cmpt: unf: racd far side: chsd ldrs: edgd rt over 1f out: kpt on same pce: 4th of 10 that gp* **12/1**
0 9 3 **Cadi May**[45] [1046] 2-8-4 RobbieFitzpatrick 12 30
(W M Brisbourne) *racd stands' side: nvr wnt pce: 5th of 6 that gp* **50/1**
10 ½ **Dhanyata (IRE)** 2-8-7 ow1 SteveDrowne 3 34+
(B J Meehan) *leggy: unf: s.s: racd far side: nvr on terms: 5th of 10 that gp* **22/1**
11 1¼ **House Arrest** 2-8-0 ow1 JamesDoyle(5) 2 29+
(I A Wood) *unf: scope: awkward to ld: racd far side: chsd ldrs: wknd over 1f out: 6th of 10 that gp* **50/1**
12 ¾ **Sahara Dawn (IRE)** 2-8-10 PhilipRobinson 16 28
(C G Cox) *unf: scope: s.s: racd stands' side: nvr on terms: 6th of 6 that gp* **6/1**[2]
5 13 nk **Stormburst (IRE)**[38] [1181] 2-8-8 DaneO'Neill 11 29
(M Dods) *s.s: swtchd to r far side: nvr on terms: 7th of 10 that gp* **7/2**[1]
4 14 1½ **Moonlight Applause**[12] [1853] 2-8-10 DavidAllan 6 26
(T D Easterby) *led far side tl hdd & wknd over 2f out: 8th of 10 that gp* **20/1**
15 2½ **Tumblin Rosie** 2-8-4 FrancisNorton 5 13
(M Blanshard) *leggy: unf: racd far side: sn outpcd: 9th of 10 that gp* **33/1**
16 hd **Hester Brook (IRE)** 2-8-4 DavidKinsella 8 9
(J G M O'Shea) *lt-f: unf: s.i.s: a bhd on far side: 10th of 10 that gp* **66/1**

1m 15.57s (0.57) **Going Correction** -0.15s/f (Firm) **16 Ran SP% 118.1**
Speed ratings (Par 92):90,83,81,81,80 78,76,76,72,71 69,68,68,66,63 62
CSF £400.39 TOTE £15.70: £3.80, £14.90, £8.80; EX 837.00.
Owner Capital **Bred** Jenny Hall Bloodstock Ltd **Trained** West Ilsley, Berks

FOCUS
The stands' side proved a big advantage, six raced on that side including the first three home. It was a weak affair but the winner could hardly have scored any easier and the form could rate higher.

NOTEBOOK
Yerevan had clearly learnt plenty first time and turned this into a stroll in the park. She did not have much to beat but could hardly have done it any easier. (tchd 12-1)
Merry Moon(IRE), a close-coupled March foal, was her trainer's second string. Noisy in the paddock, she finished clear second best and the outing and the experience will not be lost on her. (op 50-1)
Little Miss Wizzy, a March foal, is well named. She stayed on from way off the pace and will be sharper for the outing. (op 22-1)
Zanida(IRE), a May foal, took charge on the far side but could only finish fourth overall. She clearly has ability. (tchd 16-1)
Drifting Gold, on turf this time, set off the the stands' side but tended to drift towards the middle on to the slowest ground of all. (op 8-1)
Market Day, a neat-looking February foal, was a handful on the way to the start. She was grasping the nettle late on and this will hopefully have settled down her pre-race nerves. (op 8-1)
Sahara Dawn(IRE) was handicapped by a slipping saddle and this debut effort if best ignored. Official explanation: jockey said saddle slipped (op 9-2 tchd 4-1)
Stormburst(IRE), on her toes and noisy in the paddock, was edgy in the stalls and her rider called the toss wrong leaving the traps after a sluggish start. (op 6-1)

2167 WEST BRIDGFORD MEDIAN AUCTION MAIDEN FILLIES' STKS 6f 15y
3:05 (3:08) (Class 5) 3-4-Y-0 £5,505 (£1,637; £818; £408) Stalls High

Form RPR
3 1 **Cape**[29] [1412] 3-9-0 OscarUrbina 5 81+
(J R Fanshawe) *trckd ldrs: edgd rt and led over 1f out: readily* **6/5**[1]
4402 2 ¾ **Bahhmirage (IRE)**[3] [2069] 3-9-0 50 (b) FrancisNorton 13 69
(Stef Liddiard) *chsd ldrs: wnt 2nd 1f out: comf hld* **14/1**[3]
3 2 **China Cherub** 3-9-0 DaneO'Neill 14 63+
(H Candy) *lengthy: bhd: hdwy and swtchd outside over 2f out: styd on fnl f* **16/1**
2322 4 hd **Namu**[211] [6225] 3-9-0 74 MichaelHills 10 62
(B W Hills) *led tl over 1f out: no ex whn n.m.r 1f out* **7/2**[2]
5 ½ **Tembladora (IRE)**[67] [752] 3-9-0 KerrinMcEvoy 7 61
(J W Hills) *mid-div: hdwy to chse ldrs over 2f out: kpt on same pce* **20/1**
50 6 1¾ **Some Diva**[20] [1641] 3-9-0 SebSanders 1 55
(W R Swinburn) *swtchd rt s: bhd tl kpt on fnl 2f* **33/1**
7 2 **Straight Gal (IRE)** 3-9-0 DO'Donohoe 4 49+
(G A Huffer) *leggy: unf: mid-div: kpt on fnl 2f: nvr a threat* **50/1**
0 8 nk **Cabriole**[25] [1513] 3-9-0 RichardHughes 12 49
(H R A Cecil) *chsd ldrs: wknd over 1f out* **14/1**[3]
50 9 1½ **Wendals**[20] [1646] 3-9-0 EddieAhern 8 44
(Rae Guest) *chsd ldrs: lost pl over 1f out* **28/1**
10 shd **Nightstrike (IRE)** 3-9-0 FergusSweeney 11 44+
(H Candy) *lengthy: sn in rr: sme hdwy 2f out: nvr on terms* **20/1**
0250 11 ¾ **Felin Gruvy (IRE)**[12] [1843] 3-9-0 73 StephenCarson 3 41
(R F Johnson Houghton) *chsd ldrs: drvn along 3f out: sn lost pl* **14/1**[3]
00 12 ½ **Malelane (IRE)**[229] [5888] 3-9-0 DavidAllan 9 40
(A Dickman) *chsd ldrs: lost pl 2f out* **100/1**
13 9 **Miss Ruby** 4-9-8 SteveDrowne 2 13
(Rae Guest) *dwlt: a in rr: bhd fnl 2f* **40/1**
14 1¼ **All Clued Up (IRE)** 3-9-0 HayleyTurner 6 9
(Rae Guest) *s.i.s: in rr: bhd fnl 2f* **50/1**

1m 15.12s (0.12) **Going Correction** -0.15s/f (Firm)
WFA 3 from 4yo 8lb **14 Ran SP% 116.8**
Speed ratings (Par 100):93,92,89,89,88 86,83,83,81,80 79,79,67,65
CSF £17.54 TOTE £2.10: £1.20, £3.50, £3.50; EX 26.00.
Owner Wyck Hall Stud **Bred** Wyck Hall Stud Ltd **Trained** Newmarket, Suffolk
■ Stewards' Enquiry : Oscar Urbina one-day ban: careless riding (Jun 12)

FOCUS
Lesson learnt, they all came down the stands' side. With the runner-up rated just 50, ahead of her much-improved effort at Leicester just three days earlier, it took no winning but the tidy winner has potential.

2168 ROBIN HOOD SPRINT H'CAP 5f 13y
3:35 (3:36) (Class 2) (0-100,93) 3-Y-0 £14,249 (£4,239; £2,118; £1,058) Stalls High

Form RPR
3214 1 **Glenviews Youngone (IRE)**[24] [1529] 3-8-4 **76** oh1 ow2 RobbieFitzpatrick 7 87
(Peter Grayson) *wnt lft s: hdwy on ins over 1f out: led jst ins last: hung lft: hld on towards fin* **20/1**
0104 2 ½ **Dark Missile**[12] [1857] 3-8-8 **80** RichardHughes 8 89
(A M Balding) *chsd ldrs: chalng whn carried lft ins last: no ex* **14/1**
1 3 1 **Lady Orpen (IRE)**[15] [1783] 3-9-7 **93** EddieAhern 6 102+
(Patrick Morris, Ire) *bmpd s: hdwy 2f out: styng on same pce whn sltly hmpd towards fin* **10/1**

3122 **4** *3/4* **Prince Tamino**[47] [1020] 3-8-13 **85**.................................... SteveDrowne 2 88+
(H Morrison) *trckd ldrs on outer: styng on same pce whn hmpd jst ins last* **10/3**[2]

0111 **5** *1* **Ripples Maid**[4] [2049] 3-9-0 **86** 6ex................................ RichardThomas 4 85
(J A Geake) *chsd ldrs: drvn over 2f out: kpt on same pce appr fnl f* **5/4**[1]

2334 **6** *1 1/4* **Scooby Dude (IRE)**[5] [2021] 3-8-8 **80**.............................. AdrianTNicholls 9 75
(Ms Deborah J Evans) *led: hung lft and hdd jst ins last: wknd towards fin* **15/2**[3]

4540 **7** *3/4* **Charles Darwin (IRE)**[25] [1512] 3-9-1 **87**...................... FergusSweeney 1 79+
(M Blanshard) *in rr: effrt and nt clr run over 1f out: swtchd rt: no threat after* **16/1**

0062 **8** *4* **Grazeon Gold Blend**[12] [1857] 3-9-0 **86**...................... GrahamGibbons 3 64
(J J Quinn) *trckd ldrs: hung lft over 2f out: wkng whn n.m.r over 1f out* **11/1**

4510 **9** *2 1/2* **Triskaidekaphobia**[21] [1604] 3-9-1 **87**.......................(b[1]) PaulFitzsimons 5 56
(Miss J R Tooth) *chsd ldrs: lost pl over 1f out* **33/1**

60.42 secs (-1.38) **Going Correction** -0.15s/f (Firm) **9** Ran SP% **117.0**
Speed ratings (Par 105):105,104,102,101,99 97,96,90,86
CSF £269.93 CT £2956.39 TOTE £26.70: £5.60, £3.10, £2.90; EX 322.80.
Owner Mrs M Shaughnessy and Mrs S Grayson **Bred** Leslie Young **Trained** Formby, Lancs
■ Stewards' Enquiry : Robbie Fitzpatrick caution: careless riding

FOCUS
£22,000 added money for this 76-93 sprint handicap but it was very messy late on. The third and fourth are the best guides to the form.

NOTEBOOK
Glenviews Youngone(IRE), having just her second outing on turf, made a forward move against the favoured stands' side rail but once in front, she hung left and impeded the runner-up near the line. (tchd 18-1 and 22-1)
Dark Missile, a potential improved, look in tip-top shape beforehand. She was almost upsides when carried left near the line and though beaten on merit, she deserves to go one better. (op 12-1)
Lady Orpen(IRE), a winner twice in Ireland since breaking her at Lingfield in February, swished her tail in the paddock and was awkward to post. After collecting a bump from the winner at the start, she was held when forced to take avoiding action near the finish. She seems better suited by six. (op 11-1)
Prince Tamino, 4lb higher than Kempton, really took the eye beforehand but he was racing widest of all on the slower ground and was going nowhere when knocked over just inside the last. This is best overlooked. (op 3-1 tchd 7-2)
Ripples Maid, under her 6lb penalty and dropped back in trip, was struggling soon after the halfway mark. This is best overlooked but when she reappears it will be from a much stiffer mark. (op 6-4 tchd 13-8 in a place)
Scooby Dude(IRE), who is being kept busy, showed bags of toe but hung away from the fence and contributed to the traffic problems in the final furlong. (op 7-1)
Charles Darwin(IRE), still 9lb higher than his last nursery win, never saw daylight. Official explanation: jockey said colt was denied a clear run (tchd 18-1)

2169 RACING UK ON CHANNEL 432 H'CAP — 1m 1f 213y
4:05 (4:06) (Class 3) (0-90,88) 4-Y-0+ **£9,456** (£2,813; £1,405; £702) **Stalls** Low

Form RPR

1345 **1** **Inchloch**[66] [6101] 4-8-5 **77**.. JamesDoyle(5) 9 85
(B G Powell) *hld up in rr: hdwy on outside 3f out: chal 1f out: hung lft: led nr fin* **16/1**

0 **2** *nk* **Kova Hall (IRE)**[73] [4801] 4-9-1 **82**.................................... GeorgeBaker 3 89
(B G Powell) *mde most: hdd towards fin* **80/1**

0112 **3** *1* **Blue Bajan (IRE)**[31] [1357] 4-9-1 **82**............................ AdrianTNicholls 14 93+
(Andrew Turnell) *swtchd rt s: t.k.h in rr: hdwy on inner over 3f out: nt clr run and swtchd rt over 2f out: styd on strly fnl f* **7/1**[2]

0500 **4** *1* **Torrens (IRE)**[15] [1775] 4-8-13 **80**.. GylesParkin 4 83+
(R A Fahey) *in tch on inner: effrt over 2f out: n.m.r kpt on same pce appr fnl f* **22/1**

5120 **5** *shd* **Prince Samos (IRE)**[19] [1678] 4-9-6 **87**.....................(b[1]) RichardHughes 6 90
(R Hannon) *trckd ldrs: effrt 4f out: kpt on same pce appr fnl f* **8/1**[3]

4440 **6** *nk* **Wiggy Smith**[15] [1779] 7-9-1 **82**.. EddieAhern 8 84
(O Sherwood) *chsd ldrs: chal over 3f out: kpt on one pce appr fnl f* **8/1**[3]

0005 **7** *1* **Sky Quest (IRE)**[235] [5757] 8-8-11 **78**............................(t) SebSanders 15 79+
(W R Swinburn) *hld up in rr: hdwy on inner and nt clr run 2f out: kpt on fnl f* **16/1**

3021 **8** *1/2* **Pagan Sword**[271] [4951] 4-9-7 **88**...................................... KerrinMcEvoy 2 88+
(Mrs A J Perrett) *t.k.h: sn trcking ldrs: one pce fnl 2f* **17/2**

535 **9** *1* **Resonate (IRE)**[148] [33] 8-8-11 **78**............................ FergusSweeney 10 76
(A G Newcombe) *mid-div: kpt on fnl 3f: nvr a real threat* **20/1**

3004 **10** *3/4* **Pevensey (IRE)**[31] [1357] 4-8-11 **83**...................... RichardKingscote(5) 11 79
(M A Buckley) *trckd ldrs: chal over 3f out: wknd 1f out* **9/1**

0640 **11** *1/2* **Gringo**[20] [1631] 4-8-7 **74**.. MichaelHills 7 69
(B W Hills) *hld up in rr: effrt over 2f out: no imp whn checked over 1f out* **5/1**[1]

3060 **12** *nk* **Evolution Ex (USA)**[24] [1544] 4-8-6 **78**....................... AndrewElliott(5) 12 73
(K R Burke) *w ldrs: wknd over 1f out* **20/1**

1300 **13** *1* **Blaise Hollow (USA)**[15] [1775] 4-9-7 **88**............................ SteveDrowne 1 81
(R Charlton) *s.i.s: hdwy into mid-div over 3f out: nvr nr ldrs* **12/1**

0600 **14** *9* **Shahzan House (IRE)**[26] [1484] 7-8-13 **80**....................(p) DaneO'Neill 16 56
(P G Murphy) *chsd ldrs: lost pl 3f out: sn bhd* **50/1**

2160 **15** *hd* **Underscore (USA)**[236] [5730] 4-8-5 **79**............................... TolleyDean(7) 5 54
(R A Harris) *mid-div: drvn 4f out: lost pl 3f out: sn bhd* **33/1**

3015 **16** *15* **Double Deputy (IRE)**[223] [6006] 5-9-3 **84**...................... GrahamGibbons 13 31
(J J Quinn) *hld up in rr: bhd fnl 3f: virtually p.u* **16/1**

2m 10.74s (1.04) **Going Correction** +0.30s/f (Good) **16** Ran SP% **117.3**
Speed ratings (Par 107):107,106,105,105,105 104,104,103,102,102 101,101,100,93,93 81
CSF £968.21 CT £9378.33 TOTE £20.20: £3.70, £7.80, £1.40, £4.70; EX 526.10.
Owner Jimmy & Rita Wenman **Bred** Lord Vestey **Trained** Morestead, Hants
■ Stewards' Enquiry : Adrian T Nicholls caution: careless riding

FOCUS
A tight-knit handicap with plenty meeting traffic problems. The first two are the best guides to the form, but it is not all that strong.

NOTEBOOK
Inchloch, out of luck in two starts over hurdles for Venetia Williams, was on his toes in the paddock. He hung fire inside the last but was persuaded to put his head in front near the line. (op 18-1)
Kova Hall(IRE), stablemate of the winner, had shown nothing in two starts over timber for Philip Hobbs. He took them along in his own time and was only just edged out. (op 66-1)
Blue Bajan(IRE), warm beforehand, was dropped in from his outside draw. Very keen, he had to pull wide to find room and was fast overhauling the first two at the line. He looks the best horse on the day and deserves to soon find compensation. (op 11-2)
Torrens(IRE), just 1lb higher than the last of his three wins last year, looked very fit and ran very well on ground a shade softer than he truly prefers. (tchd 20-1)
Prince Samos(IRE), 4lb higher than his Newbury, win had the blinkers on and seemed to need coaxing along.
Wiggy Smith showed a lot more than York on this much less-testing ground.
Sky Quest(IRE), absent since October and without the usual cheekpieces, is now 6lb than his last win less than two years ago. He met traffic problems trying to improve from the rear and did well to finish as close as he did.
Pagan Sword, without the visor, would not settle and was then messed about. Official explanation: jockey said gelding was denied a clear run (tchd 9-1)
Gringo, who needs to furnish, was dropped in at the start. He was going nowhere when nudged sideways by the winner. (op 11-2 tchd 6-1)

2170 RADCLIFFE ROAD H'CAP — 1m 54y
4:40 (4:40) (Class 5) (0-75,78) 4-Y-0+ **£5,505** (£1,637; £818; £408) **Stalls** Centre

Form RPR

0001 **1** **Rain Stops Play (IRE)**[6] [1993] 4-9-10 **78** 6ex.................... SebSanders 6 89
(M Quinn) *mde all: styd on fnl 2f: hld on wl* **11/4**[1]

0246 **2** *1 1/2* **Bond Diamond**[19] [1683] 9-8-5 **59**............................... RobbieFitzpatrick 5 67
(P T Midgley) *hld up in mid-div: hdwy on inner over 2f out: hung lft and wnt 2nd over 1f out: kpt on: no real imp* **12/1**

4404 **3** *2 1/2* **Libre**[13] [1821] 6-8-12 **66**.. PaulFitzsimons 7 68+
(F Jordan) *hld up off pce. hdwy over 2f out: n.m.r 1f out: styd on wl ins last* **9/1**

0031 **4** *shd* **Bridgewater Boys**[19] [1665] 5-9-1 **69**.............................(b) DO'Donohoe 4 71
(K A Ryan) *chsd ldrs: rdn and outpcd 3f out: kpt on fnl f* **17/2**

0053 **5** *nk* **Guildenstern (IRE)**[16] [1760] 4-9-7 **75**............................ SteveDrowne 2 76
(H Morrison) *trckd ldrs: keen: effrt 3f out: kpt on same pce* **7/1**[3]

0431 **6** *hd* **Parkview Love (USA)**[34] [1275] 5-8-12 **66**........................(v) DaneO'Neill 9 67
(D Shaw) *chsd ldrs: one pce fnl 2f* **11/1**

1065 **7** *3/4* **Barons Spy (IRE)**[132] [163] 5-8-0 **59** oh1 ow3............ JamesDoyle(5) 10 58
(R J Price) *hld up: hdwy to chse ldrs over 2f out: sn rdn: one pce* **10/1**

2011 **8** *4* **Commitment Lecture**[13] [1830] 6-9-1 **69**..........................(t) EddieAhern 1 59
(M Dods) *chsd ldrs: wknd 2f out* **5/1**[2]

0005 **9** *19* **Linda's Colin (IRE)**[14] [1802] 4-8-4 **65**............................... TolleyDean(7) 3 11
(R A Harris) *mid-div: effrt on outside 3f out: edgd lft and sn lost pl: eased* **12/1**

1066 **10** *16* **Following Flow (USA)**[13] [1830] 4-9-5 **73**......................(p) GeorgeBaker 8 —
(R Hollinshead) *s.i.s: in rr: swtchd lft 4f out and racd alone far side: sn lost pl and bhd: virtually p.u* **22/1**

1m 43.68s (-2.72) **Going Correction** -0.15s/f (Firm) **10** Ran SP% **113.5**
Speed ratings (Par 103):107,105,103,102,102 102,101,97,78,62
CSF £36.36 CT £259.85 TOTE £3.10: £1.40, £3.20, £3.10; EX 46.40.
Owner Paul Montgomery & Brian Morton **Bred** Lucayan Stud Ltd **Trained** Newmarket, Suffolk

FOCUS
All bar one elected to come down the favoured stands' side. The winner was in pole position throughout and the runner-up sets the standard.
Parkview Love(USA) Official explanation: jockey said gelding lost its action in last 50yds

2171 LADY BAY BRIDGE H'CAP — 1m 54y
5:10 (5:12) (Class 6) (0-65,65) 3-Y-0 **£3,238** (£963; £481; £240) **Stalls** Centre

Form RPR

0301 **1** **Punjabi**[22] [1593] 3-9-4 **62**.. J-PGuillambert 7 70
(Mrs G S Rees) *hld up towards rr: hdwy over 3f out: effrt over 2f out: led over 1f out: styd on strly: readily* **12/1**

000 **2** *1 1/4* **October Ben**[12] [1845] 3-9-2 **60**.. FergusSweeney 4 66
(M D I Usher) *hld up in rr: hdwy on outside over 2f out: styd on ins fnl f: no real imp* **40/1**

2440 **3** *shd* **Kasumi**[24] [1551] 3-9-1 **59**.. DaneO'Neill 8 64
(H Morrison) *trckd ldrs: t.k.h: kpt on same pce fnl f* **25/1**

0630 **4** *1* **Carloman**[12] [1859] 3-8-11 **58**...................................... NelsonDeSouza(3) 12 61
(R M Beckett) *uns rdr bef s: chsd ldrs: one pce appr fnl f* **14/1**

4463 **5** *1 1/4* **Stainley (IRE)**[12] [1851] 3-9-7 **65**................................ GrahamGibbons 1 65
(J D Bethell) *led tl over 1f out: fdd fnl f* **11/2**

503 **6** *1/2* **Aurora Jane (FR)**[71] [692] 3-9-7 **65**..................................... MichaelHills 3 64+
(B W Hills) *hld up in rr: effrt on outer over 3f out: kpt on: nvr rchd ldrs* **20/1**

6405 **7** *shd* **Pagan Crest**[33] [1291] 3-9-5 **63**.. KerrinMcEvoy 5 62+
(Mrs A J Perrett) *mid-div: kpt on fnl 2f: nvr rchd ldrs* **7/2**[1]

000 **8** *nk* **Noble Minstrel**[110] [380] 3-8-13 **57**........................(t) RobbieFitzpatrick 13 55
(S C Williams) *chsd ldrs: rdn and outpcd over 2f out: styd on fnl f* **7/1**

0006 **9** *1/2* **Million All Day (IRE)**[163] [6628] 3-8-11 **55**.................... SamHitchcott 11 52
(W R Muir) *hld up towards rr: kpt on fnl 2f: nvr on terms* **40/1**

5601 **10** *shd* **Queen Jean**[17] [1736] 3-8-11 **60**.................................... AndrewElliott(5) 9 57
(J G Given) *chsd ldr: chal over 2f out: wknd over 1f out* **9/2**[3]

060 **11** *shd* **Catabound (USA)**[25] [1513] 3-8-13 **57**.......................... PaulFitzsimons 16 53
(B R Millman) *in rr: hdwy on outer over 2f out: nvr a factor* **40/1**

6460 **12** *1 3/4* **Briery Blaze**[257] [5307] 3-9-5 **63**.................................... AdrianTNicholls 17 55
(Mrs K Walton) *prom: lost pl 3f out* **66/1**

005 **13** *nk* **Sanctity**[37] [1212] 3-9-0 **58**.. SebSanders 2 50
(J R Fanshawe) *in rr: effrt over 3f out: nvr a factor* **4/1**[2]

005 **14** *1/2* **Moon Melody (GER)**[19] [1691] 3-9-4 **62**........................ HayleyTurner 15 53
(M L W Bell) *chsd ldrs: lost pl over 2f out* **28/1**

000 **15** *21* **Lady Duxyana**[12] [1844] 3-9-2 **60**..................................... GeorgeBaker 10 2
(M D I Usher) *s.i.s: a in rr: bhd and eased 2f out* **50/1**

1m 44.96s (-1.44) **Going Correction** -0.15s/f (Firm) **15** Ran SP% **125.5**
Speed ratings (Par 97):101,99,99,98,97 96,96,96,96,95 95,94,93,93,72
CSF £439.53 CT £11210.71 TOTE £10.90: £3.10, £12.00, £7.30; EX 251.90 Place 6 £47,736.79, Place 5 £4,321.11.
Owner Capt James Wilson **Bred** Capt J H Wilson **Trained** Sollom, Lancs

FOCUS
A strong gallop and the winner quickened up well and scored in good style. The form looks pretty solid rated through the fourth.
T/Jkpt: Not won. T/Plt: £4,247.50 to a £1 stake. Pool: £53,531.00. 9.20 winning tickets. T/Qpdt: £284.00 to a £1 stake. Pool: £4,223.00. 11.00 winning tickets. WG

2113 SANDOWN (R-H)
Thursday, June 1

OFFICIAL GOING: Round course - good (good to soft in places); sprint course - good to soft
Wind: Virtually nil

2172 ESHER GREEN MAIDEN AUCTION STKS — 5f 6y
6:15 (6:23) (Class 5) 2-Y-0 **£3,886** (£1,156; £577; £288) **Stalls** High

Form RPR

32 **1** **Grand Prix**[15] [1770] 2-8-11 .... RyanMoore 8 83
(R Hannon) *broke wl: trckd ldrs: rdn to ld over 1f out: r.o wl* **10/11**[1]

0 **2** *3* **Dee Jay Wells**[14] 1796 2-8-11 .... MartinDwyer 4 72+
(R Hannon) *lw: prom: rdn and ev ch over 1f out: kpt on but nt pce of wnr* **25/1**
3 *3/4* **The King And I (IRE)** 2-8-13 .... PatDobbs 1 72+
(Miss E C Lavelle) *cmpt: str: bit bkwd: bhd: smooth prog fr 3f out: swtchd lft 2f out: n.m.r 1f out: r.o* **50/1**
4 *nk* **Billy Red** 2-8-11 .... KDarley 10 68
(J R Jenkins) *tall: bkwd: prom: led over 2f out: rdn and hdd over 1f out: kpt on same pce* **33/1**
5 *1* **The Jay Factor (IRE)** 2-8-4 .... EmmettStack(5) 11 67+
(Pat Eddery) *cmpt: bit bkwd: prom: hmpd and lost pl over 3f out: swtchd lft over 1f out: kpt on* **20/1**
6 *nk* **Land Ahoy** 2-8-11 .... FrankieMcDonald 6 64+
(D W P Arbuthnot) *neat: chsd ldrs: nt clr run and lost pl after 1f: in tch: kpt on fnl f* **33/1**
7 *hd* **Dubai Builder** 2-8-11 .... EddieAhern 15 63
(J S Moore) *rangy: scope: bit bkwd: chsd ldrs: swtchd lft 4f out: outpcd over 2f out: styd on fnl f* **4/1**[2]
8 *shd* **Lancaster's Quest** 2-8-9 .... RobertHavlin 12 61
(R Ingram) *unf: s.i.s: bhd: styd on fnl 2f: nvr trbld ldrs* **33/1**
9 *1 1/2* **Indian Song (IRE)** 2-8-4 .... JamieMackay 14 56+
(R F Johnson Houghton) *neat: bit bkwd: led for over 1f: chsd ldrs: nt clr run over 1f out: no ch after* **20/1**
54 **10** *1 1/2* **Weyba Downs (IRE)**[54] 912 2-8-11 .... TQuinn 7 62+
(J R Best) *lw: led after 1f: rdn and hdd over 1f out: cl 4th whn snatched up jst ins fnl f: eased whn btn* **20/1**
11 *4* **Up In Arms (IRE)** 2-8-11 .... JimCrowley 2 37
(P Winkworth) *cmpt: bkwd: slowly away and a in rr* **20/1**
12 *5* **Topic (IRE)** 2-8-8 .... RHills 9 16
(J W Hills) *lt-f: in tch: swtchd lft and effrt 2f out: wknd fnl f* **12/1**[3]
13 *6* **Red Hot Jazz (IRE)** 2-8-4 .... RoystonFfrench 3 —
(Mrs P N Dutfield) *w'like: bkwd: hmpd s: racd green and a bhd* **50/1**
14 *5* **Take My Turn** 2-8-9 .... TedDurcan 13 —
(M Blanshard) *w'like: bit bkwd: s.i.s and a bhd* **20/1**
3 **15** *nk* **Mogok Ruby**[41] 1107 2-8-11 .... SteveDrowne 5 —
(L Montague Hall) *prom tl wknd over 1f out* **14/1**

63.21 secs (1.00) **Going Correction** +0.025s/f (Good) **15** Ran SP% **127.1**
Speed ratings (Par 93):93,88,87,86,84 84,84,83,81,79 72,64,55,47,46
CSF £36.57 TOTE £1.90: £1.10, £5.10, £12.80; EX 22.40.
Owner Mrs J K Powell **Bred** Plantation Stud **Trained** East Everleigh, Wilts

FOCUS
In all probability this was just a modest juvenile maiden for the track, but the winner is full value for the winning margin and sets the standard, and the race ought to produce its share of future winners.

NOTEBOOK
Grand Prix, third and second respectively on his only two starts to date, put that previous experience to great advantage and got off the mark with a comfortable display. He quickened when asked to win his race, showing a decent attitude in the process, and was full value for the winning margin. Another furlong will be within his compass before the season's end, but his future ultimately lies with the Handicapper. (op 5-6 tchd Evens in places)
Dee Jay Wells, ninth on debut at Salisbury a fortnight previously, showed the clear benefit of that experience and duly posted a much-improved effort. He was no match for his winning stablemate over this trip, but left the impression he would come on again for this outing, and could benefit for a step-up to six furlongs now. (op 20-1)
The King And I(IRE) ◆, a 30,000gns purchase bred to be suited by farther in due course, posted a pleasing debut and must be rated better than the bare form. He was not helped by his outside draw, met trouble when trying to challenge nearing the final furlong, and kept on nicely when finally in the clear. This experience will not be lost on him and he looks capable of winning something similar in the coming weeks.
Billy Red, the first foal of a dual sprint winner, showed early speed before running green when the pressure was applied. He was helped by his high draw this time, but looks assured to improve for the experience nevertheless.
The Jay Factor(IRE), a half-brother to smart juvenile winners Crazee Mental and Sienna Gold amongst others, did well to finish as he did after being hampered nearing the halfway stage and losing vital momentum. He is better than his final position suggests and one to keep an eye on.
Land Ahoy, a half-brother to Secret Night and whose dam was herself a useful sprinter, showed ability and was another to shape better than the bare form suggests.
Dubai Builder, who cost 24,000gns as a two-year-old and is related to numerous winners at up to seven furlongs, was very well backed on course for this debut and, while ultimately never threatening, he still did more than enough to suggest he ought to really improve with this experience under his belt. He may already need another furlong, however. Official explanation: jockey said colt hung left (op 12-1)
Lancaster's Quest, bred for speed, lost all chance with a slow start yet was noted finishing his race well enough and can build on this. His stable are yet to have a winner this term.
Weyba Downs(IRE) Official explanation: jockey said colt hung right and left and became unbalanced
Topic(IRE), choicely-bred for speed, is from a yard whose juveniles often improve plenty as they gain experience and is one to keep on side when the market speaks in her favour. (op 11-1 tchd 10-1)
Red Hot Jazz(IRE) Official explanation: jockey said filly hung left out of stalls

2173 THE SPORTSMAN RACING H'CAP — 5f 6y
6:45 (6:56) (Class 4) (0-85,88) 3-Y-0+ **£5,505** (£1,637; £818; £408) **Stalls** High

Form RPR
2111 **1** **Cashel Mead**[6] 1981 6-8-11 **73** .... TravisBlock(5) 11 87+
(J L Spearing) *trckd ldr on far side: shkn up to ld jst over 1f out: r.o: pushed out* **15/8**[1]
0263 **2** *1 1/2* **Zarzu**[9] 1928 7-9-3 **74** .... RobertWinston 5 83
(C R Dore) *b: mid-div on far side: weaved his way through field fr over 2f out: wnt 2nd jst ins fnl f: kpt on* **16/1**
5015 **3** *1* **Auwitesweetheart**[31] 1338 4-9-12 **83** .... AlanMunro 6 88
(B R Millman) *in tch on far side: hdwy and drifted lft over 1f out: hung bdly rt ins fnl f: kpt on cl home* **25/1**
0555 **4** *nk* **Ingleton**[13] 1820 4-9-0 **71** .... RyanMoore 8 77+
(G L Moore) *chsd ldrs on far side: rdn and sltly outpcd over 2f out: styng on whn hmpd ins fnl f* **7/2**[2]
0200 **5** *1/2* **Bowness**[24] 1545 4-9-7 **78** .... KDarley 15 80
(J G Given) *s.i.s: sn rcvrd to chse ldrs on far side: kpt on same pce fnl f* **14/1**
6600 **6** *3/4* **Magic Glade**[50] 989 7-9-11 **82** .... RoystonFfrench 10 81
(R Brotherton) *lw: led on far side: rdn and hdd jst over 1f out: no ex* **25/1**
6300 **7** *3* **Logsdail**[13] 1820 6-9-4 **75** .... PatDobbs 7 64
(G L Moore) *b: bhd on far side: styd on fr 2f out: n.d* **12/1**
300 **8** *3/4* **Vague Star (ITY)**[10] 1899 4-8-9 **66** oh9 .... (b) RobertHavlin 9 52
(R Ingram) *b.nr hind: chsd ldrs on far side: rdn over 2f out: one pce fr 1f out* **66/1**
0040 **9** *1* **Extremely Rare (IRE)**[10] 1878 5-8-13 **70** .... JohnEgan 1 52
(M S Saunders) *lw: broke wl and disp ld on stands side: rdn and hdd whn drifted rt fr over 1f out* **25/1**
0000 **10** *hd* **Harrison's Flyer (IRE)**[167] 6590 5-9-6 **77** .... (p) TQuinn 13 59
(J M Bradley) *b: mid-div on far side tl hmpd 2f out: nt a danger after* **20/1**
4000 **11** *1 1/4* **Sentiero Rosso (USA)**[12] 1858 4-9-1 **72** .... (b) JamieMackay 12 49
(B Ellison) *lw: s.i.s and a in rr on far side* **11/1**[3]
0000 **12** *hd* **Mutawaqed (IRE)**[13] 1820 8-9-9 **80** .... (t) EddieAhern 3 56
(M A Magnusson) *lw: hld up and a in rr on far side* **14/1**
050- **13** *1 1/4* **Spliff**[614] 5786 5-10-0 **85** .... DeanMcKeown 2 57
(M S Saunders) *a bhd on stands side* **66/1**
1600 **14** *1/2* **Desperate Dan**[14] 1803 5-10-0 **85** .... (b) SteveDrowne 14 55
(J A Osborne) *mid-div on far side for over 3f* **16/1**
4001 **15** *5* **The Jobber (IRE)**[9] 1928 5-10-3 **88** 6ex .... TedDurcan 4 40
(M Blanshard) *lw: sn towards rr on far side* **12/1**

61.79 secs (-0.42) **Going Correction** +0.025s/f (Good) **15** Ran SP% **125.1**
Speed ratings (Par 105):104,101,100,99,98 97,92,91,89,89 87,87,85,84,76
CSF £33.88 CT £623.41 TOTE £2.60: £1.70, £3.10, £5.10; EX 30.70.
Owner Masonaires **Bred** D R Tucker **Trained** Kinnersley, Worcs
■ Stewards' Enquiry : Alan Munro caution: careless riding

FOCUS
A fair and competitive sprint for the class, which predictably saw those drawn high at an advantage, and the winner remains progressive. THe form looks solid rated around the placed horses.
Harrison's Flyer(IRE) Official explanation: jockey said gelding was hampered in straight

2174 IG INDEX H'CAP — 1m 2f 7y
7:20 (7:27) (Class 3) (0-90,89) 3-Y-0 **£8,096** (£2,408; £1,203; £601) **Stalls** High

Form RPR
0060 **1** **Salute Him (IRE)**[25] 1505 3-9-0 **82** .... TedDurcan 2 91
(M R Channon) *lw: mde all: rdn 2f out: sn hrd pressed: kpt on gamely to assert cl home: drvn out* **14/1**
10 **2** *1/2* **John Terry (IRE)**[329] 3269 3-9-1 **83** .... RyanMoore 1 91
(Mrs A J Perrett) *lw: v s.i.s: bhd: hdwy 3f out: rdn 2f out: styng on and ev ch ins fnl f: hld cl home* **5/1**[3]
11 **3** *1 3/4* **Crime Scene (IRE)**[28] 1440 3-9-7 **89** .... KDarley 3 94
(M Johnston) *trckd ldrs: rdn to chse wnr 2f out: kpt on same pce fnl f* **11/2**
2230 **4** *1/2* **Alhaitham (USA)**[20] 1640 3-9-3 **85** .... RHills 6 89
(J L Dunlop) *hld up: hdwy 3f out: sn rdn: ev ch 1f out: no ex* **7/1**
01 **5** *1 1/2* **Masterofthecourt (USA)**[17] 1741 3-8-13 **81** .... SteveDrowne 5 82+
(H Morrison) *lw: in tch: rdn 3f out: kpt on same pce fnl 2f* **9/2**[2]
61 **6** *8* **Grain Of Truth**[22] 1598 3-9-0 **82** .... RobertWinston 7 68
(Sir Michael Stoute) *in tch: rdn and effrt 2f out: wknd 1f out* **5/2**[1]
3421 **7** *4* **In Dubai (USA)**[223] 6007 3-9-5 **87** .... MartinDwyer 8 65
(M P Tregoning) *nt grwn: t.k.h early: trckd wnr: rdn 3f out: wknd 1f out* **13/2**
042 **8** *31* **Empire Dancer (IRE)**[24] 1552 3-8-6 **74** .... AlanMunro 4 —
(C N Allen) *plld hrd: trckd ldrs: hung lft fr 4f out: grad fdd* **20/1**

2m 11.75s (1.51) **Going Correction** +0.25s/f (Good) **8** Ran SP% **116.1**
Speed ratings (Par 103):103,102,101,100,99 93,90,52
CSF £83.29 CT £439.80 TOTE £19.50: £3.10, £2.30, £1.30; EX 143.70.
Owner Jaber Abdullah **Bred** Drumhass Stud **Trained** West Ilsley, Berks

FOCUS
A decent three-year-old handicap, but the race was run at an uneven pace, and although it seems sound, the form should be treated with caution.

NOTEBOOK
Salute Him(IRE) bounced back to his best and scored under a canny front-running ride. He showed decent attitude to knuckle down and repel the runner-up close home, with the longer trip clearly to his liking. A rise back up in the weights is now inevitable, however, and he still has to fully prove his effectiveness over this far when racing in a truly-run affair. (op 12-1)
John Terry(IRE), last seen trailing home behind Horatio Nelson in the Group 3 Superlative Stakes last year, was markedly upped in trip for this seasonal bow and confirmed he has trained on with a pleasing effort. However, he once again lost vital ground at the start and, while there are clearly races to be won with him this term, he must learn to break on terms if he is to progress as is hoped. Official explanation: jockey said colt missed the break (tchd 6-1 in a place)
Crime Scene(IRE), unbeaten in two previous outings to date, was not really suited by the tactical nature of the race and proved one paced when the race became serious nearing the two-furlong marker. He is capable of a little better and worth another try over this longer trip. (op 5-1 tchd 6-1)
Alhaitham(USA), popular in the betting ring for this handicap bow, had every chance yet failed to really get home over the longer trip, despite the race probably being run to suit. He remains a maiden after six outings, but really ought to get closer when reverting to a mile. (op 11-1)
Masterofthecourt(USA) ◆, whose trainer's previous runners in this event - Waverley and Odiham - were both successful, proved one paced from two out and was disappointingly well held on this handicap bow. He should certainly not be written off on the back of this effort, however, as he still has a lot of scope and would not have enjoyed the tactical nature of this event. It may also be that he needs genuinely fast ground. (tchd 4-1)
Grain Of Truth, off the mark on her seasonal bow at Ripon last time, failed to raise her game on this handicap bow and has to rate as disappointing. She may be in need of a stiffer test now - her dam won the Irish and Yorkshire Oaks - but on this evidence her current Group entries look ambitious. (tchd 3-1)
In Dubai(USA) paid for refusing to settle on this return from a 223-day break and is probably capable of leaving this form behind when faced with a stronger pace over this sort of trip.
Empire Dancer(IRE) Official explanation: jockey said gelding hung badly left having run free early

2175 STERLING MAIDEN STKS — 1m 2f 7y
7:55 (7:57) (Class 5) 3-Y-0 **£3,886** (£1,156; £577; £288) **Stalls** High

Form RPR
6233 **1** **Mashaahed**[21] 1603 3-9-3 102 .... RHills 4 93+
(B W Hills) *lw: a trav wl w ldr: led wl over 1f out: sn rdn and edged rt: kpt on wl* **8/13**[1]
052 **2** *1* **New Guinea**[26] 1483 3-9-3 84 .... PhilipRobinson 5 87+
(M A Jarvis) *lw: set stdy pce: qcknd pce over 3f out: hdd wl over 1f out: sn hmpd on rails and swtchd lft: styd on* **5/1**[2]
3 **3** *1 1/4* **Nosferatu (IRE)**[233] 5821 3-9-3 .... RyanMoore 2 83
(Mrs A J Perrett) *in tch: rdn to hold pl 4f out: wnt 3rd 1f out: styd on* **7/1**[3]
05 **4** *5* **Moohimm (IRE)**[41] 1120 3-9-3 .... MartinDwyer 7 73
(M P Tregoning) *lw: trckd ldrs: rdn and effrt 3f out: wknd ins fnl f* **14/1**
0 **5** *shd* **Brigadore (USA)**[245] 5574 3-9-3 .... SteveDrowne 9 73
(W R Muir) *mid-div: rdn over 3f out: styd on fnl f* **66/1**
6 *2* **Zirkel (IRE)** 3-9-3 .... EddieAhern 6 69
(Mrs A L M King) *rangy: unf: s.i.s: towards rr: hdwy over 3f out: sn rdn: no further imp fr 2f out* **100/1**
7 *shd* **Eastlands (IRE)** 3-9-3 .... JohnEgan 8 69?
(Jamie Poulton) *unf: scope: s.i.s: towards rr: rdn and no imp fr 3f out* **66/1**

44 **8** *1* **Archiestown (USA)**[19] 1680 3-9-3 .... TQuinn 3 67
(J L Dunlop) *lw: trckd ldrs and racd keenly: rdn over 3f out: sn outpcd* **8/1**

6 **9** *3/4* **Russian Dream (IRE)**[31] 1336 3-9-3 .... OscarUrbina 10 65
(W R Swinburn) *hld up and a towards rr* **50/1**

00 **10** *1 1/2* **Rada (IRE)**[29] 1418 3-8-12 .... KDarley 1 58?
(R Hannon) *hld up and a towards rr* **66/1**

2m 15.8s (5.56) **Going Correction** +0.25s/f (Good) **10** Ran SP% **116.3**
Speed ratings (Par 99):87,86,85,81,81 79,79,78,78,76
CSF £3.97 TOTE £1.50: £1.10, £1.80, £2.10; EX 5.90.
Owner Hamdan Al Maktoum **Bred** Lightbody Celebration Cakes **Trained** Lambourn, Berks
■ Stewards' Enquiry : John Egan £75 fine: passport irregularity

FOCUS
A very slow winning time - over four seconds slower than the preceding handicap - due to the tactical pace, and the first three came clear. The form appears to make sense but may not be that reliable.

2176 EXTRABET H'CAP 1m 6f
8:25 (8:30) (Class 4) (0-85,85) 4-Y-0+ **£5,505** (£1,637; £818; £408) **Stalls** Low

Form RPR

3035 **1** **Salute (IRE)**[8] 1931 7-8-13 **77** .... RobertHavlin 15 85
(P G Murphy) *trckd ldrs: rdn 3f out: tk narrow advantage ins fnl f: all out* **20/1**

2102 **2** *hd* **Michabo (IRE)**[25] 1517 5-9-7 **85** .... SteveDrowne 12 93
(H Morrison) *lw: led: rdn over 2f out: hdd narrowly ins fnl f: rallied gamely cl home: jst hld* **10/1**

4513 **3** *nk* **Tilt**[16] 1756 4-9-4 **82** .... FrancisNorton 10 90
(B Ellison) *t.k.h bhd ldrs: rdn over 2f out: ev ch over 1f out : kpt on cl home* **3/1**[1]

024/ **4** *3* **Full House (IRE)**[34] 3098 7-8-11 **75** .... RichardHughes 3 79
(P R Webber) *lw: mid-div: rdn and hdwy over 2f out: styd on* **16/1**

3641 **5** *1/2* **Tannenberg (IRE)**[6] 2000 5-8-12 **76** 6ex .... DeanMcKeown 16 79+
(G A Swinbank) *s.i.s: bhd: rdn and hdwy fr 3f out: styd on fnl f: nrst fin* **7/2**[2]

3210 **6** *2* **Velvet Heights (IRE)**[14] 1809 4-9-4 **82** .... KDarley 5 82
(J L Dunlop) *hld up towards rr: stdy hdwy fr 5f out: rdn and effrt 3f out: one pce fr 2f out* **14/1**

0562 **7** *nk* **Quizzene (USA)**[5] 2035 4-9-3 **81** .... RoystonFfrench 1 81
(M Johnston) *swtg: chsd ldrs: rdn and ev ch 3f out: one pce fr 2f out* **9/1**[3]

-430 **8** *3/4* **Stoop To Conquer**[14] 1808 6-9-1 **79** .... TQuinn 4 78
(J L Dunlop) *a mid-div* **12/1**

0220 **9** *1/2* **Self Respect (USA)**[15] 1779 4-9-6 **84** .... EddieAhern 11 82
(A King) *a mid-div* **25/1**

0020 **10** *1* **Isa'Af (IRE)**[14] 1808 7-8-7 **74** .... EdwardCreighton(3) 14 70
(P W Hiatt) *towards rr: sme late prog: n.d* **50/1**

4000 **11** *shd* **Heathcote**[14] 1808 4-8-4 **68** .... (p) StephenCarson 2 64
(G L Moore) *lw: hld up towards rr: rdn and sme hdwy over 2f out: no further imp fr over 1f out* **9/1**[3]

2404 **12** *2 1/2* **Master Cobbler (IRE)**[12] 1847 4-8-8 **72** .... (p) AlanMunro 9 65
(J Akehurst) *in tch: rdn and effrt over 3f out: grad fdd* **12/1**

1036 **13** *3* **Llamadas**[12] 1842 4-8-13 **77** .... RobertWinston 6 66
(C Roberts) *chsd ldrs: rdn 4f out: wknd 2f out* **50/1**

123- **14** *1 1/2* **Secret Pact (IRE)**[74] 6334 4-9-3 **81** .... RyanMoore 7 67
(A M Hales) *lw: prom early: grad lost pl: bhd fnl 3f* **33/1**

4460 **15** *4* **Yankeedoodledandy (IRE)**[8] 1943 5-8-9 **73** .... MartinDwyer 13 54
(C Roberts) *s.i.s: a towards rr* **66/1**

-060 **16** *3/4* **Anousa (IRE)**[377] 1866 5-9-7 **85** .... JimCrowley 8 65
(P Howling) *bit bkwd: a towards rr* **100/1**

3m 5.92s (1.41) **Going Correction** +0.25s/f (Good) **16** Ran SP% **122.2**
Speed ratings (Par 105):105,104,104,103,102 101,101,100,100,100 100,98,96,96,93 93
CSF £201.39 CT £784.75 TOTE £26.10: £4.00, £2.60, £1.40, £4.60; EX 369.80.
Owner The Golden Anorak Partnership **Bred** Ahmed M Foustok **Trained** East Garston, Berks

FOCUS
A decent staying handicap, run at a sound gallop, and the form looks solid for the grade with the first three coming clear.

2177 EXTRABET MILE H'CAP 1m 14y
8:55 (9:00) (Class 4) (0-80,80) 3-Y-0 **£6,477** (£1,927; £963; £481) **Stalls** High

Form RPR

0004 **1** **Debord (FR)**[6] 1978 3-8-2 **61** oh7 .... FrancisNorton 5 67
(Jamie Poulton) *s.i.s: bhd: rdn 3f out: swtchd lft to centre 2f out: styd on strly to ld wl ins fnl f* **25/1**

1033 **2** *1* **Robustian**[38] 1190 3-9-4 **77** .... StephenCarson 7 80
(R F Johnson Houghton) *keen towards rr: rdn and hdwy 4f out: swtchd lft to centre 3f out: styd on strly: ev ch ins fnl f: no ex* **15/2**

000 **3** *nk* **Barndeh (IRE)**[236] 5746 3-8-8 **67** .... (p) PhilipRobinson 10 70
(M A Jarvis) *lw: led for 2f: trckd ldr: rdn over 2f out: ev ch ins fnl f: no ex cl home* **12/1**

4215 **4** *1/2* **Acrobatic (USA)**[38] 1190 3-9-4 **77** .... RichardHughes 2 79
(R Charlton) *lw: hld up bhd: rdn and hdwy fr over 3f out: ev ch ins fnl f: no ex* **9/2**[1]

4446 **5** *2* **Crimson Flame (IRE)**[12] 1855 3-9-0 **73** .... TedDurcan 8 70
(M R Channon) *trckd ldrs: led narrowly over 2f out: sn rdn: no ex whn hdd ins fnl f* **12/1**

0263 **6** *1 1/2* **Isphahan**[41] 1115 3-9-4 **77** .... (v) RyanMoore 3 71
(A M Balding) *prom: led after 2f: rdn and narrowly hdd over 2f out: kpt on same pce fnl f* **6/1**[2]

314 **7** *3* **Herring (IRE)**[30] 1384 3-9-6 **79** .... AlanMunro 6 66
(D J Coakley) *chsd ldrs: rdn 3f out: one pce fnl 2f* **9/1**

0140 **8** *5* **Silver Chariot**[37] 1205 3-8-13 **72** .... RHills 9 47
(B W Hills) *chsd ldrs: rdn 3f out: wkng whn n.m.r over 1f out* **20/1**

0233 **9** *1/2* **Rose Of Inchinor**[239] 5695 3-8-10 **69** .... MartinDwyer 11 43
(M P Tregoning) *nt grwn: lw: plld hrd early: mid div: rdn 4f out: wknd over 1f out* **8/1**

054 **10** *7* **Italian Romance**[31] 1336 3-9-4 **77** .... RobertWinston 4 35
(M L W Bell) *lw: mid-div: rdn over 3f out: sn btn* **13/2**[3]

2135 **11** *1 3/4* **Bomber Command (USA)**[21] 1617 3-9-7 **80** .... EddieAhern 1 34
(J W Hills) *chsd ldrs: rdn 3f out: sn wknd* **7/1**

1m 45.74s (1.79) **Going Correction** +0.25s/f (Good) **11** Ran SP% **115.2**
Speed ratings (Par 101):101,100,99,99,97 95,92,87,87,80 78
CSF £198.19 CT £2413.24 TOTE £26.70: £5.10, £2.30, £3.30; EX 316.90 Place 6 £217.03, Place 5 £119.35.
Owner Eatonfield Racing Limited **Bred** Haras De Bernesq And Michel Henochsberg **Trained** Telscombe, E Sussex

FOCUS
A modest three-year-old handicap, run at a generous gallop, and those to be held up seemed at an advantage. The race is rated around the placed horses.

T/Plt: £53.10 to a £1 stake. Pool: £59,684.80. 819.30 winning tickets. T/Qpdt: £30.20 to a £1 stake. Pool: £3,634.40. 89.00 winning tickets. TM

2143 YARMOUTH (L-H)
Thursday, June 1

OFFICIAL GOING: Good
Wind: Light, behind Weather: Showers

2178 TOTEPLACEPOT EBF MEDIAN AUCTION MAIDEN STKS 6f 3y
2:20 (2:22) (Class 6) 2-Y-0 **£2,590** (£770; £385; £192) **Stalls** High

Form RPR

1 **Marmaida (IRE)** 2-8-12 .... PaulDoe 13 70
(W J Knight) *chsd ldrs: led over 1f out: edgd lft: rdn out* **50/1**

0 **2** *nk* **Straight Face (IRE)**[22] 1588 2-9-3 .... MickyFenton 15 74
(W J Knight) *a.p: rdn and ev ch over 1f out: edgd lft ins fnl f: r.o* **25/1**

0 **3** *2 1/2* **Proper (IRE)**[12] 1838 2-9-3 .... ChrisCatlin 9 67
(M R Channon) *led: racd keenly: hdd over 1f out: styd on same pce ins fnl f* **10/1**

4 *1* **Greyt Big Stuff (USA)** 2-9-3 .... TPQueally 2 64+
(B J Meehan) *hld up: hdwy over 1f out: nt rch ldrs* **8/1**[3]

3 **5** *shd* **Monkey Glas (IRE)**[47] 1019 2-9-3 .... JohnEgan 4 63
(K R Burke) *plld hrd and prom: rdn over 1f out: no ex ins fnl f* **5/1**[2]

6 *1 1/4* **Great Explorer (IRE)** 2-9-3 .... RichardMullen 5 60
(E J O'Neill) *chsd ldrs: outpcd over 2f out: styd on ins fnl f* **10/1**

3 **7** *nk* **Blue Monkey (IRE)**[33] 1284 2-9-3 .... JamieSpencer 1 59
(M L W Bell) *chsd ldrs: rdn and edgd lft over 1f out: wknd ins fnl f* **6/4**[1]

8 *5* **Spirited Speedfit (IRE)** 2-9-3 .... JimmyQuinn 10 44
(G G Margarson) *s.s: outpcd: nvr nrr* **33/1**

6 **9** *2* **Cyprus Rose**[31] 1347 2-8-10 ow1 .... RossStudholme(3) 7 34
(V Smith) *w ldr tl rdn 1/2-way: wknd 2f out* **14/1**

10 *1 1/2* **Sanbuch** 2-9-3 .... NickyMackay 14 33+
(L M Cumani) *dwlt: outpcd* **12/1**

00 **11** *hd* **Mum's Memories**[1] 2145 2-9-3 .... TonyHamilton 12 33
(Jedd O'Keeffe) *mid-div: rdn 1/2-way: sn wknd* **40/1**

12 *2 1/2* **My Sara** 2-8-12 .... ShaneKelly 6 20
(D J Daly) *hld up in tch: rdn and lost pl over 3f out: sn edgd lft and wknd* **33/1**

13 *2 1/2* **Rowan Venture** 2-9-0 .... SaleemGolam(3) 8 18
(M H Tompkins) *dwlt: outpcd* **33/1**

14 *1 1/2* **Raven Rascal** 2-8-5 .... StacyRenwick(7) 3 8
(J F Coupland) *s.s: outpcd* **100/1**

15 *2 1/2* **Hurricane Dennis** 2-9-3 .... DarryllHolland 11 6
(D K Ivory) *sn pushed along in rr: bhd fr 1/2-way* **33/1**

1m 15.94s (2.24) **Going Correction** +0.20s/f (Good) **15** Ran SP% **121.3**
Speed ratings (Par 91):93,92,89,87,87 86,85,79,76,74 74,70,67,65,62
CSF £973.52 TOTE £106.70: £23.10, £17.40, £3.00; EX 1535.70 TRIFECTA Not won..
Owner Lower Coombe Partnership **Bred** Tally-Ho Stud **Trained** Patching, W Sussex
■ A first winner for trainer William Knight, who was also responsible for the runner-up. The exacta paid £1,535.70 on the Tote.

FOCUS
Despite the size of the field, this did not look a strong contest and the form looks ordinary. The runners decided to come down the middle of the track and those that raced up with the pace held the advantage.

NOTEBOOK
Marmaida(IRE), a 17,000gns filly out of a winner at up to a mile, could be seen travelling really well towards the nearside of the leading group and found enough when asked to eventually hold off the late challenge of her stable-companion. She should improve and ought to find other opportunities.
Straight Face(IRE), unlike his stable-companion the winner, had the benefit of a previous run and stayed on well but could never quite get to her in time. He has a speedy pedigree, but shapes as though he could do with a bit further. (op 28-1)
Proper(IRE), as on his debut, made the running and lasted longer on this better ground and with that effort under his belt. There should be a small race in him and he may be worth a try over the minimum.
Greyt Big Stuff(USA) ◆, a 27,000gns half-brother to three winners, took a while to realise what was required, but was noted staying on well in the latter stages and did much of the best of those that tried to come from off the pace. He should come on for this and his pedigree suggests he will eventually come into his own over a bit further. (op 6-1)
Monkey Glas(IRE) pulled far too hard early over this extra furlong on this switch to grass. Not surprisingly, the response was very limited when he was eventually asked for his effort. (op 13-2)
Great Explorer(IRE), a 19,000gns half-brother to the ten-furlong winner Abbondanza, showed enough on this debut to suggest he has a future, but as his pedigree might suggest he probably needs a bit further. (op 9-1)
Blue Monkey(IRE) had given the impression on his Leicester debut that this extra furlong would be right up his street, but that is not how things worked out. He is surely better than this. (op 2-1)

2179 TOTESPORT 0800 221 221 (S) STKS 5f 43y
2:55 (2:56) (Class 6) 2-Y-0 **£2,266** (£674; £337; £168) **Stalls** High

Form RPR

0502 **1** **Baytown Paikea**[1] 2145 2-8-7 .... BrianReilly 2 56
(P S McEntee) *chsd clr ldr: led over 1f out: rdn out* **14/1**

2421 **2** *1/2* **Tokyo Jo (IRE)**[5] 2015 2-8-10 .... (v) SaleemGolam(3) 1 60
(K R Burke) *prom: rdn to chse wnr over 1f out: r.o* **1/1**[1]

503 **3** *3/4* **Aggbag**[1] 2145 2-8-12 .... JamieSpencer 6 57
(M J Wallace) *hld up: hdwy u.p over 1f out: styd on* **3/1**[2]

05 **4** *6* **Splendidio**[30] 1372 2-8-7 .... ChrisCatlin 3 30
(M R Channon) *sn pushed along in rr: hdwy 1/2-way: sn rdn: wknd fnl f* **9/2**[3]

05 **5** *1 1/2* **Mr Mini Scule**[37] 1223 2-8-12 .... JimmyQuinn 5 30
(A B Haynes) *hld up: effrt over 1f out: n.d* **8/1**

0006 **6** *8* **Sainara (IRE)**[3] 2073 2-8-7 .... (b[1]) ShaneKelly 7 —
(J M Bradley) *led and sn clr: rdn 2f out: sn hdd and wknd* **50/1**

65.03 secs (2.23) **Going Correction** +0.20s/f (Good) **6** Ran SP% **112.9**
Speed ratings (Par 91):90,89,88,78,76 63
CSF £29.28 TOTE £14.70: £3.40, £1.30; EX 27.80.There was no bid for the winner. Tokyo Jo was the subject of a friendly claim.
Owner Eventmaker Partnership **Bred** Launceston Stud **Trained** Newmarket, Suffolk
■ Stewards' Enquiry : Saleem Golam two-day ban: used whip with excessive frequency (Jun 12-13)

FOCUS
The field decided to stay against the stands' rail for this routine two-year-old seller. The front three pulled well clear and the future looks bleak for the others.

NOTEBOOK

Baytown Paikea was making a quick reappearance after finishing runner-up at a respectful distance in a similar event over an extra furlong here the previous day. After picking off the runaway leader, she showed plenty of determination to repel her two nearest challengers and beat Aggbag by exactly the same margin as she had 24 hours earlier. (op 9-1)

Tokyo Jo(IRE) stayed on well under some pretty severe pressure, but could never quite get to the winner. The drop in trip and quicker ground probably did not help her cause. (op 10-11 tchd 11-10 and 6-5 in places)

Aggbag, despite the best efforts of the champion jockey, was never getting there quickly enough and finished exactly the same distance behind Baytown Paikea as he had done here the previous day. Rather like the runner-up, the drop in trip probably did not help him, but even so he does still have a question mark against him. (op 9-2)

Splendidio, well beaten in her first two outings, fared no better here despite dropping into a seller for the first time. (op 11-2)

Mr Mini Scule, already well beaten in this sort of company, looks very moderate indeed. (op 9-1 tchd 12-1)

Sainara(IRE) set off like a scalded cat in the first-time blinkers, but her moment of glory only lasted until just after halfway.

2180 TOTEQUADPOT CLAIMING STKS — 1m 3f 101y

3:25 (3:26) (Class 6) 4-Y-0+ — **£2,590** (£770; £385; £192) **Stalls** Low

Form — RPR

3613 **1** **Oldenway**[10] 1887 7-9-7 72 .... TonyHamilton 1 — 66+
(R A Fahey) *s.i.s: sn led: shkn up over 1f out: r.o wl* **4/9**[1]

5416 **2** 3 **Starcross Maid**[23] 1560 4-8-8 48 .... JamieSpencer 2 — 48
(J F Coupland) *chsd wnr over 9f: rdn over 1f out: styd on same pce* **5/1**[2]

1204 **3** nk **Undeterred**[17] 1739 10-8-11 72 .... MickyFenton 3 — 51
(K J Burke) *a.p: chsd wnr 2f out: sn rdn: no ex ins fnl f* **5/1**[2]

4600 **4** 2 ½ **Tennessee Belle (IRE)**[64] 793 4-7-9 39 ow4 ....(e) KirstyMilczarek(7) 5 — 38
(C N Allen) *hld up in tch: plld hrd: rdn over 1f out: wknd ins fnl f* **33/1**[3]

0 **5** 26 **Gessecapade**[27] 1460 4-7-12 .... FrancisFerris 4 — —
(P S McEntee) *hld up: rdn over 3f out: sn wknd* **50/1**

2m 37.21s (9.71) **Going Correction** +0.575s/f (Yiel) — **5** Ran SP% **107.5**

Speed ratings (Par 101):87,84,84,82,63

CSF £2.87 TOTE £1.20: £1.10, £1.80; EX 2.20.The winner was the subject of a friendly claim.

Owner J J Staunton **Bred** Snailwell Stud Co Ltd **Trained** Musley Bank, N Yorks

FOCUS

A poor claimer run at a moderate pace resulting in a very slow winning time, even for a race like this. The fourth offers the best guide to the form.

2181 TOTESPORT.COM H'CAP — 1m 2f 21y

3:55 (3:56) (Class 6) (0-55,55) 4-Y-0+ — **£2,979** (£886; £442; £221) **Stalls** Low

Form — RPR

6122 **1** **Cottingham (IRE)**[1] 2149 5-9-4 51 .... JamieSpencer 6 — 64
(T D Barron) *a.p: led over 1f out: rdn out* **6/4**[1]

0000 **2** 1 ¾ **House Martin**[30] 1394 4-9-3 50 ....(p) BrianReilly 8 — 60
(C R Dore) *led: rdn and hdd over 1f out: staeyd on same pce* **33/1**

5064 **3** nk **Apache Point (IRE)**[12] 1850 9-9-7 54 .... KimTinkler 7 — 63
(N Tinkler) *mid-div: pushed along 1/2-way: hdwy 4f out: rdn and edgd lft over 1f out: styd on* **15/2**[3]

0235 **4** 1 ¾ **Rotuma (IRE)**[1] 2149 7-9-8 55 ....(b) ShaneKelly 3 — 61
(M Dods) *dwlt: hdwy 8f out: rdn over 1f out: edgd lft and no ex fnl f* **13/2**[2]

0050 **5** 1 ¼ **Tata Naka**[12] 1850 6-8-13 53 .... KirstyMilczarek(7) 10 — 56
(Mrs C A Dunnett) *hld up: hdwy u.p over 1f out: nt rch ldrs* **14/1**

0543 **6** 3 **Granary Girl**[24] 1537 4-9-5 52 .... JimmyQuinn 16 — 50
(J Pearce) *chsd ldr tl rdn over 2f out: wknd fnl f* **16/1**

4010 **7** hd **Dagola (IRE)**[9] 1911 5-9-1 51 .... SaleemGolam(3) 2 — 48
(C A Dwyer) *hld up: hdwy 3f out: nt trble ldrs* **16/1**

3000 **8** 2 **El Rey Royale**[29] 1425 4-9-1 53 .... DerekNolan(5) 15 — 46
(Micky Hammond) *prom: rdn over 2f out: wknd over 1f out* **33/1**

0230 **9** 4 **Eminence Gift**[35] 1249 4-9-5 52 .... RichardMullen 1 — 38
(K R Burke) *chsd ldrs: rdn over 3f out: wknd over 1f out* **12/1**

0500 **10** nk **Fuel Cell (IRE)**[6] 1996 5-9-0 54 ....(bt) JamesO'Reilly(7) 14 — 39
(J O'Reilly) *chsd ldrs: rdn whn stmbld over 2f out: sn wknd* **33/1**

3250 **11** 10 **Blue Hedges**[29] 1422 4-9-8 55 .... DarryllHolland 9 — 21
(H J Collingridge) *dwlt: hld up: effrt over 3f out: sn wknd* **14/1**

425 **12** 5 **At The Helm (IRE)**[24] 1553 4-9-4 51 .... ChrisCatlin 5 — 8
(W J Knight) *hld up: hmpd over 4f out: sn wknd* **14/1**

-565 **13** hd **Four Pleasure**[226] 5964 4-9-8 55 .... FrancisFerris 13 — 11
(A M Hales) *hld up: a in rr: wknd over 3f out* **40/1**

000 **14** 18 **Band Of Gold**[406] 1161 4-9-5 52 .... MickyFenton 12 — —
(J Pearce) *hld up: wknd over 4f out* **33/1**

1510 **15** 5 **Mad Maurice**[35] 1256 5-9-6 53 .... TPQueally 11 — —
(B J Curley) *mid-div: edgd lft over 4f out: sn rdn and wknd* **11/1**

2m 13.47s (5.37) **Going Correction** +0.575s/f (Yiel) — **15** Ran SP% **127.1**

Speed ratings (Par 101):101,99,99,97,96 94,94,92,89,89 81,77,77,62,58

CSF £75.87 CT £327.43 TOTE £2.70: £1.40, £12.60, £3.00; EX 98.90 Trifecta £239.40 Part won. Pool: £337.25 - 0.34 winning tickets..

Owner Twinacre Nurseries Ltd **Bred** B Kennedy **Trained** Maunby, N Yorks

FOCUS

A moderate handicap in which the well-supported favourite did the business. It is probably best rated through the fourth and backed up by the third and fifth, making it fairly reliable.

Blue Hedges Official explanation: trainer said colt was unsuited by the good ground

Mad Maurice Official explanation: trainer had no explanation for the poor form shown

2182 TOTEPOOL "A BETTER WAY TO BET" H'CAP — 5f 43y

4:30 (4:33) (Class 5) (0-75,75) 3-Y-0+ — **£3,886** (£1,156; £577; £288) **Stalls** High

Form — RPR

021 **1** **Taboor (IRE)**[13] 1816 8-9-2 63 .... RichardMullen 5 — 73
(R M H Cowell) *hld up in tch: rdn to ld ins fnl f: r.o* **8/1**

4036 **2** 1 ½ **Never Without Me**[23] 1563 6-8-12 59 .... MickyFenton 9 — 64
(J F Coupland) *w ldr: rdn and ev ch ins fnl f: unable qckn* **11/1**

5040 **3** 1 **Detonate**[9] 1913 4-8-9 56 oh8 .... AdrianMcCarthy 14 — 57
(Mrs C A Dunnett) *led: rdn and hdd ins fnl f: no ex* **25/1**

0420 **4** nk **Bluebok**[12] 1856 5-9-12 73 ....(t) JamieSpencer 7 — 73
(J M Bradley) *chsd ldrs: rdn and ev ch 1f out: no ex ins fnl f* **5/1**[1]

5064 **5** 1 ¼ **Russian Rocket (IRE)**[12] 1846 4-8-11 61 .... AdamKirby(3) 15 — 56
(Mrs C A Dunnett) *chsd ldrs: rdn over 1f out: styd on same pce* **11/2**[2]

0300 **6** hd **Gone'N'Dunnett (IRE)**[40] 1151 7-8-12 66 ....(v) KirstyMilczarek(7) 11 — 61
(Mrs C A Dunnett) *chsd ldrs: rdn over 1f out: styd on same pce* **14/1**

4003 **7** 1 **Henry Hall (IRE)**[33] 1297 10-9-8 69 .... KimTinkler 12 — 60
(N Tinkler) *chsd ldrs: sn pushed along: wknd ins fnl f* **7/1**[3]

0600 **8** hd **Fairgame Man**[236] 5738 8-8-2 56 oh9 .... LiamJones(7) 3 — 46
(J S Wainwright) *s.s: styd on ins fnl f: nvr nrr* **33/1**

3410 **9** ½ **Matsunosuke**[19] 1662 4-9-11 75 .... SaleemGolam(3) 10 — 64
(A B Coogan) *dwlt: styd on fnl f: nvr nrr* **14/1**

-000 **10** ¾ **Silver Prelude**[20] 1643 5-9-8 69 .... DarryllHolland 16 — 55
(D K Ivory) *chsd ldrs over 3f* **20/1**

6205 **11** 1 ¼ **Times Review (USA)**[30] 1383 5-9-3 64 ....(b) ShaneKelly 2 — 45
(C A Dwyer) *mid-div: rdn 1/2-way: wknd over 1f out* **20/1**

1036 **12** 1 ¾ **Silver Dane (IRE)**[9] 1928 4-10-0 75 ....(v) TPQueally 13 — 50
(Mrs C A Dunnett) *chsd ldrs to 1/2-way* **14/1**

0503 **13** ¾ **Kennington**[12] 1846 6-9-5 66 ....(b) ChrisCatlin 4 — 38
(Mrs C A Dunnett) *s.s: rdn 1/2-way: sn wknd* **7/1**[3]

4500 **14** 1 ½ **Majestical (IRE)**[40] 1151 4-9-2 63 ....(p) NickyMackay 8 — 30
(J M Bradley) *hld up in tch: plld hrd: rdn and wknd 2f out* **22/1**

00-6 **15** 3 **Red Apache (IRE)**[348] 2696 4-8-9 56 oh6 .... JimmyQuinn 1 — 12
(H J Collingridge) *s.i.s: a in rr* **66/1**

63.31 secs (0.51) **Going Correction** +0.20s/f (Good) — **15** Ran SP% **118.6**

Speed ratings (Par 103):103,100,99,98,96 96,94,94,93,92 90,87,86,83,79

CSF £82.18 CT £2152.01 TOTE £8.90: £2.30, £4.90, £7.10; EX 220.40 TRIFECTA Not won..

Owner T W Morley **Bred** Rathasker Stud **Trained** Six Mile Bottom, Cambs

FOCUS

A modest handicap and the form is pretty solid but held back slightly by the performance of the third, who was running from 8lb out of the weights.

Silver Prelude Official explanation: trainer said gelding was unsuited by the good ground

2183 TOTETRIFECTA H'CAP — 1m 3y

5:00 (5:00) (Class 4) (0-80,78) 4-Y-0+

£6,232 (£1,866; £933; £467; £233; £117) **Stalls** High

Form — RPR

6554 **1** **Boundless Prospect (USA)**[33] 1280 7-9-7 78 .... MickyFenton 6 — 89
(Miss Gay Kelleway) *hld up: hdwy over 2f out: led 1f out: edgd rt: rdn out* **5/1**[2]

5001 **2** 2 ½ **Habshan (USA)**[91] 559 6-9-6 77 .... DarryllHolland 4 — 82
(C F Wall) *chsd ldrs: rdn and ev ch over 1f out: styd on same pce ins fnl f* **15/2**

-P02 **3** 1 ¾ **Surwaki (USA)**[35] 1262 4-9-4 78 .... AdamKirby(3) 7 — 79
(C G Cox) *chsd ldr: rdn to ld 2f out: hdd over 1f out: no ex ins fnl f* **6/1**[3]

2232 **4** nk **Cross The Line (IRE)**[8] 1932 4-9-1 72 .... JamieSpencer 5 — 72
(A P Jarvis) *hld up: hdwy over 2f out: rdn and ev ch over 1f out: no ex ins fnl f* **1/1**[1]

3140 **5** ½ **Wester Lodge (IRE)**[277] 4795 4-9-2 73 .... ShaneKelly 8 — 72+
(J M P Eustace) *prom: outpcd over 2f out: styd on ins fnl f* **16/1**

6005 **6** 1 ½ **Zarabad (IRE)**[26] 1494 4-9-5 76 .... RichardMullen 3 — 72
(K R Burke) *trckd ldrs: rdn and ev ch over 1f out: wknd ins fnl f* **16/1**

0020 **7** 14 **Kabeer**[8] 1938 8-8-8 70 ....(t) StephenDonohoe(5) 1 — 33
(P S McEntee) *led: rdn and hdd 2f out: sn wknd* **16/1**

1m 41.04s (1.14) **Going Correction** +0.20s/f (Good) — **7** Ran SP% **110.4**

Speed ratings (Par 105):102,99,97,97,96 95,81

CSF £38.18 CT £215.14 TOTE £5.80: £2.90, £2.60; EX 36.10 Trifecta £309.40 Pool: £575.30 - 1.32 winning tickets..

Owner M M Foulger **Bred** Mrs Edgar Scott Jr & Mrs Lawrence Macelree **Trained** Exning, Suffolk

FOCUS

A fair little handicap in which the runners came down the middle of the course. The early pace was not strong and there were still five in a line across the track approaching the last furlong. The runner-up sets the standard for the form.

2184 TOTESPORTCASINO.COM H'CAP — 7f 3y

5:30 (5:32) (Class 5) (0-70,70) 3-Y-0+ — **£3,886** (£1,156; £577; £288) **Stalls** High

Form — RPR

2501 **1** **Joy And Pain**[20] 1645 5-8-9 58 ....(v) KevinGhunowa(7) 10 — 75+
(M J Attwater) *racd centre: chsd ldrs: rdn to ld and overall ldr over 1f out: sn clr: 1st of 8 in gp* **8/1**

600 **2** 4 **Poker Player (IRE)**[52] 949 4-9-11 67 .... MickyFenton 14 — 72
(G C Bravery) *racd stands' side: led that gp: rdn over 1f out: styng on same pce whn edgd lft ins fnl f: 1st of 5 in gp* **12/1**

0354 **3** 1 **Titinius (IRE)**[23] 1561 6-10-0 70 .... RichardMullen 2 — 72
(Micky Hammond) *racd centre: hld up: rdn over 3f out: hung lft over 2f out: hdwy over 1f out: styd on: 2nd of 8 in gp* **9/1**

422 **4** 2 **Generator**[77] 653 4-9-7 63 .... DarryllHolland 4 — 60
(Dr J D Scargill) *racd centre: chsd ldrs: rdn over 2f out: sn ev ch: wknd fnl f: 3rd of 8 in gp* **9/2**[1]

3000 **5** 1 **Zendaro**[230] 5880 4-9-6 62 .... ShaneKelly 5 — 56
(W M Brisbourne) *racd centre: overall ldr: rdn and hdd over 1f out: wknd fnl f: 4th of 8 in gp* **22/1**

0001 **6** 1 ¼ **Mugeba**[209] 6243 5-8-13 58 .... AdamKirby(3) 1 — 49
(Miss Gay Kelleway) *racd centre: hld up: hdwy over 2f out: rdn and ev ch over 1f out: wknd fnl f: 5th of 8 in gp* **13/2**[3]

2463 **7** ¾ **Meditation**[14] 1802 4-9-3 64 .... DerekNolan(5) 16 — 53
(I A Wood) *w ldr stands' side: over 4f: hung lft and wknd over 1f out: 2nd of 5 in gp* **6/1**[2]

0002 **8** 1 ¼ **Treasure House (IRE)**[14] 1802 5-9-4 67 .... LiamJones(7) 13 — 53
(M Blanshard) *racd stands' side: s.i.s: sn chsng ldrs: rdn over 3f out: edgd lft and wknd over 2f out: 3rd of 8 in gp* **13/2**[3]

5050 **9** 1 **Deep Sleep**[12] 1851 3-8-8 63 .... SaleemGolam(3) 3 — 46
(M H Tompkins) *racd centre: hld up in tch: rdn over 2f out: wknd over 1f out: 6th of 8 in gp* **14/1**

4452 **10** 2 **Rowan Warning**[104] 440 4-9-3 59 .... NickyMackay 15 — 37
(J R Boyle) *racd stands' side: hld up: a in rr: 4th of 5 in gp* **15/2**

0100 **11** 2 **Mandarin Spirit (IRE)**[34] 1275 6-9-13 69 .... ChrisCatlin 8 — 42
(G C H Chung) *racd centre: prom 5f: 7th of 8 in gp* **22/1**

5036 **12** 8 **Set Alight**[45] 1057 5-9-7 63 ....(v) TPQueally 12 — 15
(Mrs C A Dunnett) *racd stands' side: dwlt: rdn: hung lft and wknd 1/2-way: last of 5 in gp* **20/1**

0000 **13** 3 ½ **Princess Galadriel**[16] 1761 5-8-13 55 .... FrancisFerris 7 — —
(J M P Eustace) *racd centre: s.i.s: a in rr: bhd fr 1/2-way: last of 8 in gp* **22/1**

1m 27.61s (1.01) **Going Correction** +0.20s/f (Good)

WFA 3 from 4yo+ 10lb — **13** Ran SP% **124.2**

Speed ratings (Par 103):102,97,96,94,92 91,90,89,88,85 83,74,70

CSF £98.28 CT £906.65 TOTE £10.60: £2.60, £5.80, £2.30; EX 147.80 TRIFECTA Not won. Place 6 £987.90, Place 5 £73.29.

Owner Phones Direct Partnership **Bred** Jonathan Shack **Trained** Wysall, Notts

FOCUS

A modest handicap but a decisive success for Joy And Pain, who is improving for his new stable. Along with the third he helps sets the level for the form.

Deep Sleep Official explanation: jockey said gelding finished lame

T/Plt: £1,813.90 to a £1 stake. Pool: £44,727.30. 18.00 winning tickets. T/Qpdt: £44.40 to a £1 stake. Pool: £4,433.40. 73.80 winning tickets. CR

[1876]BATH (L-H)

Friday, June 2

OFFICIAL GOING: Good to firm

Wind: Slight against

2185 EUROPEAN BREEDERS FUND MAIDEN STKS 5f 161y

6:15 (6:18) (Class 5) 2-Y-O £3,886 (£1,156; £577; £288) Stalls Low

Form RPR

3 **1** **Apollo Five**[20] 1688 2-9-3 .... TPQueally 10 82
(D J Coakley) *s.i.s: hdwy over 2f out: rdn and r.o strly fnl f to ld last strides* **10/1**[3]

2 **2** hd **Dowlleh**[14] 1811 2-9-3 .... TonyCulhane 2 81
(M R Channon) *mde most: rdn over 1f out: hdd post* **5/1**[2]

42 **3** ¾ **Longquan (IRE)**[15] 1796 2-9-3 .... SebSanders 6 79
(P J Makin) *w ldr: rdn and ev ch ins fnl f: no ex nr fin* **7/4**[1]

30 **4** nk **Make Me An Offer (IRE)**[13] 1838 2-9-3 .... RHills 14 78
(B W Hills) *towards rr: hdwy 2f out: hdwy on outside 2f out: r.o fnl f* **18/1**

5 1 ¾ **Vaunt** 2-9-3 .... SteveDrowne 7 72+
(R Charlton) *s.i.s: sn chsd ldrs: one pce ins fnl 2f* **12/1**

0 **6** 2 ½ **Avery**[16] 1770 2-9-3 .... LPKeniry 5 64
(R J Hodges) *w ldrs: rdn over 2f out: wknd over 1f out* **100/1**

7 1 ½ **Piccolena Boy** 2-9-3 .... JimCrowley 13 59
(P Winkworth) *mid-div: effrt on outside: healfway: wknd over 1f out* **16/1**

8 ¾ **Farefield Lodge (IRE)** 2-9-0 .... AdamKirby(3) 9 56
(C G Cox) *s.i.s: sn in tch: wknd 2f out* **25/1**

9 2 **Pace Telecom Flyer (IRE)** 2-9-0 .... DeanCorby(3) 11 49
(J W Hills) *sn outpcd and a towards rr* **50/1**

0 **10** 4 **Queensgate**[21] 1639 2-8-12 .... FrancisNorton 3 31
(M Blanshard) *spd to 1/2-way* **66/1**

06 **11** 1 ¾ **Merlins Quest**[16] 1770 2-9-3 .... JohnEgan 8 31
(J M Bradley) *chsd ldrs tl wknd wl over 1f out* **50/1**

12 8 **Dancing Daisy (IRE)** 2-8-7 .... JamesDoyle(5) 1 —
(Mrs P N Dutfield) *slowly away: outpcd thrght* **100/1**

1m 12.72s (1.52) **Going Correction** -0.05s/f (Good) 12 Ran SP% **92.2**

Speed ratings (Par 93):87,86,85,85,83 79,77,76,74,68 66,55

CSF £35.25 TOTE £9.90: £2.60, £1.30, £1.10; EX 28.20.

Owner West Ilsley Racing **Bred** Llety Stud **Trained** West Ilsley, Berks

■ Siren's Gift (7/2) was withdrawn after proving unruly & injuring rider Martin Dwyer in the paddock. R4, deduct 20p in the £.

■ Stewards' Enquiry : Seb Sanders two-day ban: used whip with excessive force, and without giving colt time to respond (Jun 13-14)

FOCUS

This juvenile maiden included five making their debut but those with previous experience dominated the finish. The winning time was modest and the placed horses set the level for the form.

NOTEBOOK

Apollo Five gave the impression he is going to need in excess of this trip as he was flying at the finish. He will be aimed at nurseries next month so his future lies with the Handicapper. (op 12-1)

Dowlleh, runner up on his debut, filled the same spot. He has an ordinary affair such as this within his compass. (op 7-1)

Longquan(IRE) had every chance and this was another placed effort for him to add to his previous two tries. Now qualified for a handicap mark, he is another who will go the nursery route in due course. (op 2-1 tchd 9-4)

Make Me An Offer(IRE) was given a bit to do but did pick up as if he wants further. There is a little race in him. (op 20-1)

Vaunt fared best of the newcomers and is one to very much bear in mind for the future as he fell out of the stalls but made up the leeway. He was not knocked about in the closing stages and, with this race under his belt, he looks sure to win at some stage especially over another furlong or so. (tchd 14-1)

Farefield Lodge(IRE) Official explanation: jockey said colt was hampered in running

Queensgate Official explanation: jockey said filly was hampered in running

Dancing Daisy(IRE) Official explanation: jockey said filly was slowly away

2186 RACECOURSE VIDEO SERVICES H'CAP 1m 2f 46y

6:45 (6:46) (Class 5) (0-70,70) 4-Y-O+ £3,562 (£1,059; £529; £264) Stalls Low

Form RPR

5403 **1** **Smooth Jazz**[21] 1651 4-9-5 68 .... SebSanders 8 81
(R M Beckett) *in tch: rdn to ld over 1f out: r.o wl* **15/2**[2]

6000 **2** 2 ½ **Voice Mail**[38] 1207 7-9-7 70 .... (b) LPKeniry 11 78
(A M Balding) *a in tch: rdn and hdwy to chse wnr fnl f* **8/1**[3]

4432 **3** 1 ¾ **Hawridge King**[180] 5797 4-8-13 67 .... JamesDoyle(5) 13 72
(W S Kittow) *bhd: rdn and hdwy 2f out: kpt on u.p: nvr nrr* **8/1**[3]

0003 **4** 3 ½ **Gallego**[16] 1769 4-7-9 51 .... LiamJones(7) 2 49
(R J Price) *a in tch: rdn 3f out: n.m.r and swtchd rt over 1f out: no hdwy after* **11/2**[1]

6500 **5** nk **The Gaikwar (IRE)**[3] 2098 7-9-1 69 .... (b) RichardKingscote(5) 5 67
(R A Harris) *s.i.s: sn chsing ldrs: wkng whn hmpd over 1f out* **14/1**

3002 **6** ¾ **Aimee Vibert**[21] 1638 4-9-0 66 .... AdamKirby(3) 9 62
(W R Swinburn) *s.i.s: sn trckd ldrs: rdn 3f out: wknd over 1f out* **10/1**

2504 **7** 1 ½ **Velvet Waters**[22] 1614 5-9-4 67 .... StephenCarson 1 61
(R F Johnson Houghton) *trckd ldr tl rdn and wknd 2f out* **15/2**[2]

3000 **8** 3 **Arthurs Dream (IRE)**[16] 1772 4-8-3 52 .... FrancisNorton 15 40
(A W Carroll) *s.i.s: racd wd: nvr on terms* **10/1**

3310 **9** 2 **Jakarmi**[34] 1288 5-9-7 70 .... TonyCulhane 3 54
(B Palling) *led: rdn 3f out: hdd & wknd qckly over 1f out* **11/2**[1]

0000 **10** ½ **Veverka**[32] 1334 5-8-3 52 .... AdrianTNicholls 12 35
(J C Fox) *a towards rr* **50/1**

4400 **11** 2 **Seldemosa**[3] 2113 5-8-5 54 .... RobbieFitzpatrick 7 33
(M S Saunders) *mid-div: wknd over 2f out* **66/1**

365 **12** shd **Umlilo**[267] 5076 4-8-9 58 .... JimCrowley 6 37
(Mrs A J Perrett) *in tch tl wknd over 2f out* **25/1**

2560 **13** ¾ **Consonant (IRE)**[46] 1051 9-9-0 70 .... MarkCoumbe(7) 10 48
(D G Bridgwater) *in tch tl rdn 3f out: sn wknd* **20/1**

2120 **14** 6 **Montjeu Baby (IRE)**[10] 1926 4-8-12 61 .... JohnEgan 14 27
(S Kirk) *rrd s: a bhd* **14/1**

2m 8.59s (-2.41) **Going Correction** -0.05s/f (Good) 14 Ran SP% **120.1**

Speed ratings (Par 103):107,105,103,100,100 99,98,96,94,94 92,92,92,87

CSF £64.00 CT £501.67 TOTE £8.90: £2.20, £1.90, £2.90; EX 46.20.

Owner P D Savill **Bred** Stowell Hill Ltd **Trained** Whitsbury, Hants

FOCUS

A modest handicap run at a good gallop and the form looks solid rated around the third.

Aimee Vibert Official explanation: jockey said filly found nothing off bridle

2187 ABBA NIGHT SUPER 70S CLAIMING STKS 5f 11y

7:15 (7:16) (Class 6) 3-Y-O £2,266 (£674; £337; £168) Stalls Low

Form RPR

3500 **1** **Jucebabe**[14] 1825 3-8-1 60 ow1 .... FrancisNorton 2 47
(J L Spearing) *a in tch: rdn and edgd lft bef led ins fnl f* **14/1**

3133 **2** ¾ **Spirit Of Coniston**[17] 1751 3-8-13 62 .... (b[1]) RobbieFitzpatrick 4 57
(Peter Grayson) *led tl rdn and hdd ins fnl f* **5/2**[1]

3046 **3** ¾ **Danish Blues (IRE)**[9] 1937 3-8-8 65 .... (p) JamesDoyle(5) 12 54
(N P Littmoden) *s.i.s: rdn and hdwy 2f out: r.o ins fnl f: nvr nrr* **8/1**

0000 **4** ½ **Captain Torrance (IRE)**[21] 1646 3-9-5 48 .... SebSanders 1 63+
(P W Chapple-Hyam) *mid-div: rdn 1/2-way: hdwy on ins whn hmpd ins fnl f* **7/1**

4004 **5** 1 **Devon Ruby**[18] 1731 3-8-1 45 .... EmmettStack(5) 8 41
(C L Popham) *slowly away: bhd tl hdwy whn short of room 1f out* **33/1**

0203 **6** ¾ **Otis B Driftwood**[16] 1771 3-8-7 50 ow2 .... (b) ShaneKelly 7 40
(M Quinn) *trckd ldrs tl rdn and fdd ins fnl f* **9/2**[3]

6205 **7** shd **Safari**[16] 1771 3-7-9 41 .... LiamJones(7) 11 34
(R J Hodges) *a towards rr* **14/1**

0066 **8** 1 **First Among Equals**[16] 1771 3-8-8 50 .... (b) PaulFitzsimons 6 37
(Miss J R Tooth) *s.i.s: sn mid-div: wknd over 1f out* **33/1**

0164 **9** 1 ¼ **Twinned (IRE)**[9] 1937 3-8-9 65 .... (p) JohnEgan 9 33
(J S Moore) *w ldr tl rdn and wknd over 1f out* **7/2**[2]

000 **10** 1 ¾ **Balfour House**[101] 473 3-8-9 35 .... AdrianMcCarthy 10 27
(R A Harris) *t.k.h: a bhd* **50/1**

0600 **11** 4 **Jackie Francis (IRE)**[34] 1304 3-9-5 48 .... TonyCulhane 5 23
(R Brotherton) *in tch tl wknd wl over 1f out* **20/1**

62.79 secs (0.29) **Going Correction** -0.05s/f (Good) 11 Ran SP% **118.5**

Speed ratings (Par 97):95,93,92,91,90 89,88,87,85,82 76

CSF £48.03 TOTE £13.30: £3.10, £1.80, £2.90; EX 45.20.

Owner G M Eales **Bred** G M Eales **Trained** Kinnersley, Worcs

■ Stewards' Enquiry : Francis Norton five-day ban: careless riding (Jun 13-17)

FOCUS

An uncompetitive sprint claimer but the form appears reasonable.

Danish Blues(IRE) Official explanation: jockey said gelding was hanging left

Twinned(IRE) Official explanation: jockey said gelding had no more to give

2188 CLICK ONTO GREENCOPIERS.COM MEDIAN AUCTION MAIDEN STKS 1m 5y

7:45 (7:49) (Class 6) 3-Y-O £2,590 (£770; £385; £192) Stalls Low

Form RPR

052 **1** **Tasjeel (USA)**[23] 1598 3-8-12 79 .... RHills 6 71
(W J Haggas) *trckd ldr: rdn and edgd lft bef ld appr fnl f: jst hld on* **7/4**[1]

2 shd **Miss McGuire** 3-8-12 .... SteveDrowne 14 71
(G L Moore) *hld up: rdn over 2f out: r.o strly to go 2nd ins fnl f: jst failed* **33/1**

202 **3** 1 ¾ **Moonlight Music (IRE)**[17] 1759 3-8-12 79 .... RichardMullen 3 67
(E J O'Neill) *led tl rdn and hdd over 1f out: no ex whn hmpd ins fnl f* **9/4**[2]

3 **4** 1 **Moves Goodenough**[21] 1641 3-9-3 .... AdrianTNicholls 8 70
(Andrew Turnell) *t.k.h: mid-div: r.o one pce fnl f* **9/1**[3]

0 **5** 1 ¼ **Dab Hand (IRE)**[25] 1546 3-9-3 .... LPKeniry 9 67
(D M Simcock) *prom: rdn over 2f out: swtchd rt over 1f out: one pce* **40/1**

4 **6** ½ **Over Ice**[46] 1049 3-8-12 .... DarryllHolland 5 61
(Karen George) *s.i.s: sn mid-div: rdn 1/2-way: one pce ins fnl 2f* **16/1**

03 **7** nk **Even Bolder**[25] 1552 3-9-3 .... PatDobbs 10 65
(S Kirk) *trckd ldr: hung lft and one pce fr over 1f out* **33/1**

0 **8** nk **Highland Belle**[26] 1513 3-8-9 .... (v) NeilChalmers(3) 15 59
(A M Balding) *mid-div: hdwy 3f out: sn rdn: wknd over 1f out* **33/1**

30 **9** shd **Chasing A Dream**[39] 1191 3-8-12 .... TonyCulhane 11 59+
(B W Hills) *in tch: rdn over 2f out: n.m.r and no hdwy fr over 1f out* **16/1**

03 **10** 5 **Grateful**[21] 1640 3-8-12 .... SebSanders 13 48
(R M Beckett) *in rr: nvr on terms* **11/1**

11 ½ **Alevisia (FR)**[229] 3-8-12 .... VinceSlattery 1 46
(Noel T Chance) *v.s.a: nvr on terms* **100/1**

5040 **12** nk **Blue Army (IRE)**[32] 1352 3-9-3 52 .... AdrianMcCarthy 2 51?
(Jane Southcombe) *trckd ldrs tl wknd over 2f out: eased* **66/1**

13 1 ¾ **Piper's Song (IRE)** 3-9-3 .... DaneO'Neill 12 47
(H Candy) *slowly away: a bhd* **14/1**

0 **14** 3 **Jiminor Mack**[11] 1901 3-8-7 .... RichardKingscote(5) 4 35
(W J H Ratcliffe) *slowly away: a bhd* **40/1**

15 14 **Tyspane** 3-8-12 .... ShaneKelly 7 3
(S Kirk) *v.s.a: a bhd* **66/1**

1m 42.13s (1.03) **Going Correction** -0.05s/f (Good) 15 Ran SP% **121.6**

Speed ratings (Par 97):92,91,90,89,87 87,87,86,86,81 81,80,79,76,62

CSF £76.85 TOTE £2.60: £1.40, £9.50, £1.60; EX 114.70.

Owner Hamdan Al Maktoum **Bred** Shadwell Farm LLC **Trained** Newmarket, Suffolk

■ Stewards' Enquiry : R Hills one-day ban: careless riding (Jun 13)

FOCUS

Not a great maiden by any means with the 79 rated winner and third setting the standard and a modest winning time for the type of contest. The form looks shaky overall.

Chasing A Dream Official explanation: jockey said filly hung right-handed throughout

Jiminor Mack Official explanation: jockey said filly missed break

Tyspane Official explanation: jockey said, regarding running and riding, his orders were to give filly a good introduction, adding that filly got very upset going to post and in stalls, and was slow into stride, suffered interference early in race, and did not handle good to firm ground, so he felt it prudent to ease her in home straight

2189 BETFRED SPRINT SERIES H'CAP (QUALIFIER) 5f 161y

8:15 (8:18) (Class 4) (0-85,85) 3-Y-O+ £6,309 (£1,888; £944; £472; £235) Stalls Low

Form RPR

0120 **1** **Adantino**[9] 1939 7-8-6 70 .... (b) JamesMillman(7) 11 84+
(B R Millman) *hld up and bhd: rdn and hdwy fr 2f out: rdn and r.o to ld ins fnl f* **11/1**

3030 **2** 1 ¼ **Devon Flame**[25] 1545 7-9-7 78 .... DarryllHolland 1 86
(R J Hodges) *in tch: rdn and led over 1f out: hdd ins fnl f* **12/1**

0002 **3** ½ **Brigadore**[11] 1878 7-8-13 70 .... TPQueally 6 79+
(J G Given) *s.i.s: sn in tch: hdwy whn nt clr run and swtchd lft ins fnl f: r.o* **10/1**[3]

0502 **4** nk **Kingscross**[14] 1820 8-9-11 82 .... FergusSweeney 9 87
(M Blanshard) *hld up: hdwy 2f out: r.o ins fnl f* **12/1**

1150 **5** ½ **Holbeck Ghyll (IRE)**[20] 1662 4-8-12 72 .... NeilChalmers(3) 4 75
(A M Balding) *trckd ldrs: ev ch over 1f out: one pce ins fnl f* **7/1**[2]

0355 **6** 1 **Danehill Stroller (IRE)**[29] 1432 6-8-11 68 .... SebSanders 12 68
(R M Beckett) *bhd: rdn over 2f out: mde gd late hdwy* **10/1**[3]

6024 **7** nk **Cesar Manrique (IRE)**[11] 1878 4-8-10 **67** RHills 10 71+
(B W Hills) *in rr and sn rdn: sme hdwy whn nt clr run on rail 1f out: nt rcvr* 10/1[3]
1111 **8** hd **Cashel Mead**[1] 2173 6-9-3 **79** 6ex TravisBlock(5) 5 77
(J L Spearing) *s.i.s: sn in tch: edgd lft appr fnl f: wknd ins fnl f* 11/4[1]
0006 **9** 1 **Currency**[8] 1961 9-9-6 **77** SteveDrowne 14 72
(J M Bradley) *outpcd towards rr: nvr on terms* 33/1
3022 **10** 1 **Fizzlephut (IRE)**[27] 1475 4-9-6 **77** PaulFitzsimons 13 68
(Miss J R Tooth) *slowly away: t.k.h: rdn over 2f out: sme late hdwy* 20/1
1220 **11** 1 **Matterofact (IRE)**[20] 1672 3-8-10 **75** RichardThomas 3 61
(Mrs P N Dutfield) *chsd ldrs tl rdn and wknd 2f out* 66/1
3110 **12** 3 **Misaro (GER)**[29] 1432 5-8-10 **67** (b) AdrianMcCarthy 15 45
(R A Harris) *prom: led briefly 2f out: rdn and wknd ins fnl f* 25/1
0045 **13** shd **Smokin Beau**[9] 1936 9-9-9 **85** JamesDoyle(5) 8 62
(N P Littmoden) *prom: rdn 1/2-way: wknd wl over 1f out* 14/1
0000 **14** 1 ½ **Royal Orissa**[14] 1820 4-9-2 **73** (t) RobertHavlin 2 45
(D Haydn Jones) *slowly away: sn in mid-div: effrt 2f out: btn whn hmpd on ins over 1f out* 33/1
4020 **15** 2 ½ **Willhewiz**[34] 1285 6-9-5 **76** JohnEgan 7 40
(M S Saunders) *led tl rdn and hdd 2f out: wknd qckly* 20/1

1m 10.3s (-0.90) **Going Correction** -0.05s/f (Good)
WFA 3 from 4yo+ 8lb **15** Ran SP% **118.5**
Speed ratings (Par 105):104,102,101,101,100 99,98,98,97,95 94,90,90,88,85
CSF £121.26 CT £1399.03 TOTE £13.50: £4.00, £3.80, £4.30; EX 161.30.
Owner Tarka Two Racing **Bred** S D Bevan **Trained** Kentisbeare, Devon
FOCUS
A typically open sprint handicap and solid form, rated through the placed horses.
Royal Orissa Official explanation: jockey said gelding was unsuited by good to firm ground
Willhewiz Official explanation: jockey said gelding moved poorly

2190 VISIT GREENCOPIERS.COM FILLIES' H'CAP 5f 11y
8:45 (8:46) (Class 5) (0-70,68) 3-Y-O £3,886 (£1,156; £577; £288) Stalls Low

Form RPR
023 **1** **Loch Verdi**[20] 1687 3-9-7 **68** FergusSweeney 6 79+
(A M Balding) *mde all: qcknd clr fnl f: unchal* 6/5[1]
5140 **2** 2 **Indian Lady (IRE)**[236] 5755 3-8-10 **64** RussellKennemore(7) 2 64
(Mrs A L M King) *rrd s: hdwy 3f out: r.o to chse wnr fnl f* 22/1
0500 **3** nk **Musical Romance (IRE)**[9] 1937 3-9-2 **63** (b[1]) DarryllHolland 7 62
(B J Meehan) *hmpd sn after s: t.k.h: sn chsd ldrs: kpt on fnl f* 8/1[3]
0000 **4** 1 ¼ **Supreme Kiss**[9] 1937 3-9-4 **65** SebSanders 4 59
(Miss B Sanders) *bhd tl hdwy 1/2-way: kpt on fnl f: nvr nrr* 20/1
6400 **5** 3 **Divine White**[29] 1431 3-8-10 **57** JimCrowley 9 41
(Mrs A J Perrett) *sltly hmpd s: in tch: rdn and one pce fr over 1f out* 16/1
2004 **6** shd **Kellys Dream (IRE)**[29] 1431 3-9-0 **61** ShaneKelly 11 44
(M Quinn) *wnt lft fr wd draw sn after s: chsd wnr tl wknd fnl f* 11/1
6036 **7** ½ **Bermuda Beauty (IRE)**[123] 248 3-7-11 **51** LiamJones(7) 1 32
(J M Bradley) *broke wl: stmbld after 1f: sn bhd* 40/1
2420 **8** 1 ¾ **In Fashion**[16] 1771 3-8-2 **49** oh2 FrankieMcDonald 5 24
(R J Hodges) *t.k.h: trckd ldrs: rdn 1/2-way: wkng whn short of room on ins over 1f out* 50/1
5530 **9** 1 **Be My Charm**[247] 5540 3-9-2 **63** FrancisNorton 3 35
(M Blanshard) *in rr: effrt 1/2-way: wknd 1f out* 10/1
0003 **10** nk **Catherines Cafe (IRE)**[15] 1801 3-9-5 **66** RobertHavlin 8 36
(Mrs P N Dutfield) *hmpd sn after s: t.k.h in mid-div: rdn 1/2-way: sn wknd* 9/2[2]
6600 **11** 1 ½ **Baytown Lulu**[4] 2068 3-8-3 **55** EmmettStack(5) 10 20
(H S Howe) *racd wd: a in rr* 50/1

62.42 secs (-0.08) **Going Correction** -0.05s/f (Good) **11** Ran SP% **113.5**
Speed ratings (Par 96):98,94,94,92,87 87,86,83,82,81 79
CSF £37.07 CT £153.86 TOTE £2.00: £1.20, £6.60, £2.90; EX 38.00 Place 6 £67.37, Place 5 £57.26.
Owner J C Smith **Bred** Littleton Stud **Trained** Kingsclere, Hants
■ Stewards' Enquiry : Shane Kelly two-day ban: careless riding (Jun 13-14)
FOCUS
An ordinary fillies' handicap and only modest form, although the winner is open to improvement.
Bermuda Beauty(IRE) Official explanation: jockey said filly lost her action
T/Plt: £54.80 to a £1 stake. Pool: £56,727.65 - 754.75 winning units. T/Qpdt: £14.70 to a £1 stake. Pool: £3,396.50 - 170.10 winning units. JS

2015 CATTERICK (L-H)
Friday, June 2

OFFICIAL GOING: Good to firm
The ground was described as 'genuine good to firm, fast but no jar at all'.
Wind: Light; half against Weather: Fine and sunny

2191 EUROPEAN BREEDERS FUND NOVICE STKS 5f
1:50 (1:52) (Class 5) 2-Y-O £3,886 (£1,156; £577; £288) Stalls Low

Form RPR
1 **Aahayson** 2-8-12 PatCosgrave 4 68+
(K R Burke) *trckd ldrs: hdwy 2f out: rdn ins last: styd on to ld last 100 yds* 7/1[3]
25 **2** nk **My Valerina (IRE)**[6] 2026 2-8-7 DavidAllan 6 62+
(Mrs A Duffield) *cl up: led wl over 1f out: sn rdn: drvn ins last: hdd and nt qckn last 100 yds* 9/2[2]
1 **3** nk **Eliza May**[13] 1853 2-9-0 DO'Donohoe 5 68+
(K A Ryan) *dwlt: sn chsng ldrs: hdwy 2f out and sn rdn: ev ch tl drvn and no ex last 100 yds* 2/1[1]
4 1 ¼ **Whiffle (USA)** 2-8-7 KDarley 7 56
(M Johnston) *s.i.s and pushed along: hdwy on outer over 2f out: sn rdn and kpt on fnl f: nrst fin* 15/2
5 hd **Algol** 2-8-12 PaulMulrennan 2 60
(J Howard Johnson) *led: rdn 2f out: sn hdd and kpt on same pce* 7/1[3]
6 1 ¼ **Sweet Georgie Bee (IRE)** 2-8-12 TonyHamilton 3 56+
(R A Fahey) *sn outpcd towards rr: hdwy 2f out: kpt on ins last* 7/1[3]
0 **7** 2 ½ **Focus Star**[12] 1863 2-8-12 TomEaves 1 47
(J M Jefferson) *chsd ldrs: rdn along 2f out: sn wknd* 40/1
00 **8** nk **Devilfishpoker Com**[15] 1790 2-8-12 NeilPollard 8 45
(R C Guest) *keen: in tch tl rdn along and wknd 2f out* 100/1

62.18 secs (1.58) **Going Correction** -0.025s/f (Good) **8** Ran SP% **104.2**
Speed ratings (Par 93):86,85,85,83,82 80,76,75
CSF £31.68 TOTE £9.20: £1.90, £1.50, £1.10; EX 42.90.
Owner Mrs M Gittins **Bred** Whitsbury Manor Stud And Mrs M E Slade **Trained** Middleham Moor, N Yorks
FOCUS
A modest juvenile contest run 1.76sec slower than the later handicap over the same trip. The form could rate higher, but the slow time and proximity of the outsiders limits it.
NOTEBOOK
Aahayson, whose dam won on her juvenile debut, followed in her footsteps with a fine effort, getting up late on. He should come on for the run and can win again. He is entered in several of the sales races later in the season and, if going the right way, could prove worthy of taking his chance. (op 15-2)
My Valerina(IRE), runner-up to a fair sort on her debut, had failed to handle six furlongs on heavy ground last time. This was a better effort and she was only run down late on. She is more than capable of winning races. (tchd 11-2)
Eliza May, under a 7lb penalty for her win at Thirsk in heavy ground, missed the break but got into contention before having nothing left in reserve in the closing stages. This was still a creditable effort on very different ground from her debut, and this speedy sort looks the type for nurseries later in the year. (op 6-5)
Whiffle(USA) ◆ was the eyecatcher of the race. Not particularly bred for speed, she missed the break from her outside draw but was noted doing her best work at the finish. She should come on a good deal for this and will be winning races, possibly over longer trips, before long. (op 8-1 tchd 7-1)
Algol, another speedily-bred individual, showed plenty of it on this debut, taking the field along from his low draw before fading in the last quarter mile. He did not drop away once headed and should be better with this under his belt. (op 8-1)

2192 SCORTON CLAIMING STKS 7f
2:20 (2:21) (Class 6) 3-Y-O £2,730 (£806; £403) Stalls Low

Form RPR
3000 **1** **Next Ness (IRE)**[8] 1950 3-8-11 54 ow3 DNolan(3) 4 58
(R F Fisher) *sn in rr: hdwy on outside over 2f out: styd on to ld ins last: dismntd after line* 8/1
0000 **2** 1 ¾ **Nimble Star**[29] 1445 3-7-9 42 LeanneKershaw(5) 9 39
(C W Fairhurst) *t.k.h: w ldrs: upsides 1f out: no ex ins last* 20/1
0004 **3** shd **Sapphire Storm (IRE)**[15] 1791 3-7-13 42 ow2 AndrewMullen(5) 11 43
(P T Midgley) *w ldrs: led over 4f out: hdd and no ex ins last* 6/1[3]
0600 **4** nk **Mandarin Grand (IRE)**[26] 1501 3-7-9 36 (p) DuranFentiman(5) 6 38
(Miss L A Perratt) *chsd ldrs: outpcd over 3f out: hdwy on outer 2f out: styd on last* 40/1
00 **5** ½ **Roman History (IRE)**[44] 1073 3-8-8 58 ow1 PhillipMakin 2 45
(Miss Tracy Waggott) *led early: outpcd over 4f out: hdwy over 2f out: swtchd ins over 1f out: kpt on* 17/2
0006 **6** 1 ¾ **Dispol Valentine**[29] 1443 3-7-12 40 ow1 RoryMoore(5) 1 35
(P T Midgley) *trckd ldrs: effrt over 2f out: styd on same pce appr fnl f* 20/1
6000 **7** 2 ½ **Bold Love**[14] 1829 3-7-11 43 AndrewElliott(5) 12 27
(J D Bethell) *trckd ldrs: sn led: hdd over 4f out: wknd 1f out* 9/2[2]
0000 **8** 2 ½ **Cape Gold (IRE)**[13] 1855 3-8-5 62 TonyHamilton 5 24
(R A Fahey) *sn chsng ldrs: outpcd over 3f out: wknd over 1f out* 4/1[1]
0000 **9** nk **Pontefract Glory**[18] 1736 3-8-11 45 (p) TomEaves 10 29
(M Dods) *hdwy on outer to chse ldrs over 4f out: hung rt and lost pl over 3f out* 15/2
6004 **10** 6 **Moraadi**[24] 1576 3-8-0 35 (b) PaulQuinn 13 2
(D W Chapman) *s.i.s: a bhd* 20/1
000 **11** ¾ **Mandarin Dancer (IRE)**[26] 1501 3-8-0 36 (p) HayleyTurner 8 —
(Miss L A Perratt) *in tch: lost pl over 3f out* 25/1
2060 **12** 2 **Bertie Bear**[16] 1771 3-8-2 39 (bt) DominicFox(3) 7 —
(G G Margarson) *s.i.s: a bhd* 20/1
0006 **13** 8 **Millbrook Star (IRE)**[31] 1386 3-8-11 35 BrianReilly 3 —
(M C Chapman) *sn bhd* 40/1

1m 27.72s (0.36) **Going Correction** -0.025s/f (Good) **13** Ran SP% **113.6**
Speed ratings (Par 97):96,94,93,93,92 90,88,85,84,78 77,74,65
CSF £154.26 TOTE £9.10: £2.90, £5.70, £2.20; EX 268.00.
Owner Middleham Park Racing XLVI **Bred** Rathbarry Stud **Trained** Ulverston, Cumbria
FOCUS
A poor contest without a previous winner in the line-up and the slowest of the three races over the trip on the day. The form is weak with the runner-up the best guide.
Moraadi Official explanation: jockey said filly was unsuited by good to firm ground

2193 GREEN HAMMERTON H'CAP 1m 3f 214y
2:55 (2:55) (Class 5) (0-70,76) 4-Y-O+ £5,181 (£1,541; £770; £384) Stalls Low

Form RPR
2101 **1** **Mceldowney**[6] 2018 4-9-8 **76** 6ex GregFairley(5) 6 86
(M Johnston) *chsd ldng pair: pushed along 1/2-way: rdn over 4f out: styd on to ld jst ins last: r.o wl* 9/2[1]
6660 **2** 1 ¾ **San Deng**[23] 1591 4-8-12 **61** KDarley 1 68
(Micky Hammond) *hld up in rr: hdwy 4f out: rdn wl over 1f out: kpt on fnl f: nt rch wnr* 11/2[3]
0002 **3** nk **Toss The Caber (IRE)**[29] 1436 4-8-8 **57** (t) TomEaves 7 64
(K G Reveley) *trckd ldrs: hdwy 1/2-way: led wl over 2f out: rdn wl over 1f out: hdd jst ins last: kpt on same pce* 10/1
4045 **4** 1 ¾ **Silverhay**[21] 1631 5-9-7 **70** PhillipMakin 12 74
(T D Barron) *cl up: effrt to ld 4f out: rdn along 3f out: sn hdd: drvn and one pce fnl 2f* 5/1[2]
2353 **5** 2 **Rare Coincidence**[34] 975 5-8-1 **55** (p) DuranFentiman(5) 2 56
(R F Fisher) *led: rdn along and hdd 4f out: drvn and gradually wknd fnl 3f* 6/1
0506 **6** ¾ **Just Waz (USA)**[6] 2018 4-8-4 **53** HayleyTurner 9 53
(R M Whitaker) *chsd ldrs: rdn aloong 4f out: drvn and one pce over 2f out* 12/1
4654 **7** 1 ¼ **Royal Flynn**[4] 2075 4-8-11 **60** PatCosgrave 8 58
(M Dods) *stmbld bdly s: sn in midfield: hdwy to chse ldrs 4f out: rdn along wl over 2f out: sn no imp* 6/1
3400 **8** 3 ½ **Richtee (IRE)**[20] 1666 5-9-6 **69** TonyHamilton 3 61
(R A Fahey) *rrd s: sn in tch: pushed along 4f out: sn rdn and no hdwy* 16/1
0020 **9** ½ **Whitby Echo (IRE)**[58] 891 4-7-13 **53** AndrewElliott(5) 4 44
(R Hollinshead) *chsd ldrs: rdn along over 4f out: sn wknd* 20/1
0-60 **10** 9 **Rajam**[17] 1756 8-9-4 **67** PaulMulrennan 10 44
(G A Harker) *a rr* 25/1
0004 **11** 5 **Wolds Dancer**[7] 1997 4-8-4 **53** ow1 (b) DavidAllan 11 22
(T D Easterby) *hld up in rr: sme hdwy on outer over 3f out: sn rdn and wknd* 33/1

2m 37.28s (-1.72) **Going Correction** -0.025s/f (Good) **11** Ran SP% **113.0**
Speed ratings (Par 103):104,102,102,101,100 99,98,96,96,90 86
CSF £26.93 CT £231.79 TOTE £4.10: £2.20, £2.40, £2.80; EX 26.90.

Owner C G Maybury **Bred** St Clare Hall Stud **Trained** Middleham Moor, N Yorks
FOCUS
A modest handicap that appeared to be run at a decent gallop and the form appears reliable rated through the placed horses.

2194 LESLIE PETCH H'CAP 5f 212y
3:35 (3:36) (Class 4) (0-80,80) 4-Y-0+ **£7,772** (£2,312; £1,155; £577) **Stalls** Low

Form RPR
0404 **1** **Divine Spirit**[25] 1528 5-8-4 **63** DO'Donohoe 4 — 76
(M Dods) *hld up: hdwy over 2f out: led over 1f out: hung lft: hld on wl* **3/1**[1]
1605 **2** *nk* **Dhaular Dhar (IRE)**[41] 1143 4-9-4 **77** FergalLynch 9 — 89
(J S Goldie) *hld up: hdwy on inner 2f out: sn chsng ldrs: no ex ins last* **15/2**
6000 **3** *1* **Trojan Flight**[24] 1561 5-8-13 **72** PhillipMakin 10 — 81
(D W Chapman) *hld up: hdwy on outer over 2f out: kpt on same pce ins last* **6/1**[3]
0005 **4** *hd* **Bo McGinty (IRE)**[13] 1858 5-9-7 **80** (b) TonyHamilton 7 — 88
(R A Fahey) *trckd ldrs: nt qckn fnl f* **11/2**[2]
6000 **5** *2* **Loaderfun (IRE)**[13] 1858 4-9-2 **78** DNolan(3) 8 — 80
(N Wilson) *chsd ldrs: kpt on same pce fnl 2f* **33/1**
0500 **6** *3* **Melalchrist**[20] 1662 4-9-2 **75** (p) TomEaves 3 — 68
(J J Quinn) *s.i.s: hdwy to chse ldrs over 4f out: lost pl 2f out* **9/1**
1 **7** *hd* **Pick A Nice Name**[18] 1733 4-8-4 **70** MichaelJStainton(7) 1 — 63
(R M Whitaker) *s.i.s: hdwy on ins over 4f out: sn pushed along: no imp whn sltly hmpd on ins over 1f out* **9/1**
5410 **8** *½* **Bonne De Fleur**[20] 1662 5-9-4 **77** (b) KDarley 11 — 68
(B Smart) *swtchd lft after s: led tl hdd over 1f out: sn btn* **10/1**
0006 **9** *1 ½* **Ryedane (IRE)**[20] 1662 4-8-11 **70** (e) DavidAllan 5 — 57
(T D Easterby) *t.k.h: trckd ldrs: checked 3f out: lost pl 2f out* **13/2**

1m 13.56s (-0.44) **Going Correction** -0.025s/f (Good) **9** Ran SP% **111.8**
Speed ratings (Par 105):101,100,99,99,96 92,92,91,89
CSF £24.59 CT £123.97 TOTE £3.80: £1.20, £1.90, £2.90; EX 22.70.
Owner The Newcastle Racing Club **Bred** S R Hope And D Erwin Bloodstock **Trained** Denton, Co Durham
FOCUS
A fair sprint and an open race and the form is fair.
Pick A Nice Name Official explanation: jockey said filly was unsuited by good to firm ground

2195 ELLERY HILL RATING RELATED MAIDEN STKS (DIV I) 7f
4:15 (4:17) (Class 6) 3-Y-0+ **£2,388** (£705; £352) **Stalls** Low

Form RPR
0230 **1** **Confide (IRE)**[7] 1996 4-9-4 58 PatCosgrave 9 — 63
(G A Swinbank) *midfield: hdwy to trck ldrs 1/2-way: led wl over 1f out: clr ins last: comf* **5/2**[1]
4003 **2** *2 ½* **Ya Late Maite**[24] 1564 3-8-0 55 DuranFentiman(5) 11 — 49
(E S McMahon) *chsd ldrs: hdwy on outer over 2f out: sn rdn and kpt on ins last* **10/1**
2300 **3** *nk* **Margaret's Dream (IRE)**[10] 1914 5-9-1 42 FergalLynch 12 — 52
(D Carroll) *hld up: gd hdwy on inner over 2f out: rdn over 1f out: kpt on ins last* **25/1**
000 **4** *1 ¾* **Khetaab (IRE)**[31] 1390 4-9-4 55 (p) DavidAllan 6 — 50
(E J Alston) *chsd ldrs: rdn over 2f out: sn drvn and kpt on same pce* **15/2**[3]
3 **5** *2* **Ai Hawa (IRE)**[18] 1736 3-8-5 49 MCHussey 13 — 38
(Eamon Tyrrell, Ire) *towards rr: hdwy 3f out: rdn wl over 1f out: edgd lft and kpt on same pce* **11/2**[2]
5600 **6** *1* **Crusader's Gold (FR)**[13] 1859 3-8-8 57 TonyHamilton 3 — 38
(T D Easterby) *keen: trckd ldrs: hdwy on inner 3f out: chal and ev ch wl over 1f out: sn rdn and btn* **11/1**
0000 **7** *½* **Mighty Duel**[254] 5407 3-8-8 38 NeilPollard 2 — 37
(J R Norton) *bhd tl styd on fnl 2f* **100/1**
6000 **8** *1* **Champagne Rossini (IRE)**[23] 3 4-9-4 38 BrianReilly 1 — 38
(M C Chapman) *bhd tl sme late hdwy* **66/1**
2043 **9** *1 ½* **Cuesta Canyon (IRE)**[20] 1661 3-8-1 43 CharlotteKerton(7) 8 — 30
(M J Polglase) *chsd ldrs: rdn along 1/2-way: sn drvn and wknd* **33/1**
4005 **10** *1 ¼* **River Logic (IRE)**[37] 1232 3-8-8 53 PaulMulrennan 5 — 27
(J Howard Johnson) *chsd ldr: rdn along 2f out: sn wknd* **10/1**
0040 **11** *¾* **Moonlight Fantasy (IRE)**[29] 1433 3-8-8 50 KDarley 7 — 25
(N Tinkler) *prom on outer: rdn along wl over 2f out: drvn and wknd wl over 1f out* **14/1**
4423 **12** *nk* **Food For Thought**[216] 6150 3-8-5 57 DO'Donohoe 15 — 21
(J J Quinn) *a rr* **15/2**[3]
4000 **13** *½* **Madam Moschata**[6] 2019 3-8-0 60 AndrewMullen(5) 4 — 20
(D W Barker) *led: rdn along over 2f out: drvn and hdd wl over 1f out: wknd qckly* **33/1**
4000 **14** *5* **Gypsy Royal (IRE)**[248] 5537 4-9-1 48 PhillipMakin 14 — 10
(G Woodward) *a bhd* **25/1**
0500 **15** *1* **Frogs' Gift (IRE)**[24] 1577 4-9-1 40 TomEaves 10 — 7
(G M Moore) *a bhd* **50/1**

1m 26.53s (-0.83) **Going Correction** -0.025s/f (Good)
WFA 3 from 4yo+ 10lb **15** Ran SP% **118.7**
Speed ratings (Par 101):103,100,99,97,95 94,93,92,90,89 88,88,87,82,80
CSF £25.88 TOTE £2.70: £1.60, £3.90, £4.30; EX 46.00.
Owner Elsa Crankshaw & G Allan Ii **Bred** Kevin Foley **Trained** Melsonby, N Yorks
FOCUS
A moderate contest but the fastest of the three races over the trip on the day. The form is fairly weak but shopuld prove reliable.

2196 GO RACING IN YORKSHIRE H'CAP 1m 7f 177y
4:50 (4:51) (Class 5) (0-70,69) 4-Y-0+ **£5,181** (£1,541; £770; £384) **Stalls** Low

Form RPR
055 **1** **Industrial Star (IRE)**[13] 1854 5-9-5 **64** KDarley 1 — 72
(Micky Hammond) *s.i.s: hdwy 7f out: wnt 2nd 4f out: led over 2f out: hung lft: drvn out* **9/1**
224 **2** *2* **Calatagan (IRE)**[28] 1033 7-9-3 **67** AndrewMullen(5) 8 — 74+
(J M Jefferson) *w ldr: led after 2f: sn clr: hdd over 2f out: keeping on same pce whn crowded ins last* **7/1**
1051 **3** *nk* **Liberty Seeker (FR)**[27] 975 7-9-9 **68** PatCosgrave 11 — 74+
(G A Swinbank) *s.i.s: hld up in rr: stdy hdwy 3f out: wnt mod 3rd over 1f out: fin wl: too much to do* **5/2**[1]
3503 **4** *3* **College Rebel**[24] 1562 5-8-0 **50** oh2 AndrewElliott(5) 5 — 52
(J F Coupland) *chsd ldrs: drvn over 3f out: kpt on same pce* **12/1**
640 **5** *¾* **Ostfanni (IRE)**[9] 5747 6-8-9 **54** PaulMulrennan 10 — 55
(M Todhunter) *trckd ldrs: wnt 2nd over 5f out: one pce fnl 3f* **4/1**[2]
0050 **6** *½* **Siegfrieds Night (IRE)**[12] 1808 5-8-7 **52** (t) BrianReilly 7 — 53
(M C Chapman) *hld up in mid-div: kpt on fnl 2f: nvr trbld ldrs* **20/1**
0000 **7** *5* **Loves Travelling (IRE)**[20] 1666 6-9-3 **65** DNolan(3) 3 — 60
(N Wilson) *hld up in mid-div: kpt on fnl 2f: nvr on terms* **33/1**
4024 **8** *¾* **Singhalongtasveer**[24] 1562 4-8-4 **50** oh5 (tp) DO'Donohoe 6 — 44
(W Storey) *hld up and bhd: drvn 5f out: nvr a factor* **20/1**
4464 **9** *5* **Esquillon**[14] 1826 4-7-11 **50** oh3 LukeMorris(7) 2 — 38
(S Parr) *led 2f: chsd wnr: wnt lft and hit rail after 7f: lost pl over 3f out* **20/1**
00-0 **10** *nk* **Compton Commander**[6] 2018 8-9-10 **69** TonyHamilton 9 — 56
(E W Tuer) *mid-div: lost pl over 4f out* **33/1**
-000 **11** *¾* **October Mist (IRE)**[41] 869 12-8-13 **65** JamesReveley(7) 12 — 51
(K G Reveley) *hld up in rr: nvr a factor* **25/1**
4010 **12** *6* **Celtic Carisma**[17] 1758 4-8-10 **56** TomEaves 4 — 35
(K G Reveley) *trckd ldrs: lost pl 4f out: sn bhd* **5/1**[3]

3m 29.99s (-1.41) **Going Correction** -0.025s/f (Good)
WFA 4 from 5yo+ 1lb **12** Ran SP% **119.4**
Speed ratings (Par 103):102,101,100,99,98 98,96,95,93,93 92,89
CSF £63.47 CT £206.39 TOTE £8.70: £2.50, £2.90, £1.60; EX 89.10.
Owner Racing Management & Training Ltd **Bred** Emanuele Patruno **Trained** Middleham Moor, N Yorks
■ Stewards' Enquiry : Pat Cosgrave seven-day ban: in breach of Rule 156; making a positive move too late as a result of serious misjudgement (June 13-19)
FOCUS
A modest handicap and ordinary form, but run at a decent gallop and nothing got involved from off the pace apart from the third.
Industrial Star(IRE) Official explanation: trainer said, regarding the improved form shown, the gelding may have benefited from the step up in trip and today's better ground

2197 RACING HERE AGAIN NEXT FRIDAY APPRENTICE H'CAP 5f
5:25 (5:25) (Class 6) (0-65,64) 3-Y-0 **£2,730** (£806; £403) **Stalls** Low

Form RPR
0432 **1** **Hypnosis**[6] 2016 3-9-5 **59** MarkLawson 3 — 68
(D W Barker) *chsd ldng pair: swtchd rt and led 1½f out: sn rdn: drvn ins last and hld on wl* **7/2**[1]
5430 **2** *nk* **Northern Chorus (IRE)**[32] 1344 3-9-10 **64** MarcHalford 1 — 72
(A Dickman) *dwlt: sn trcking ldrs: hdwy wl over 2f out: swtchd rt and rdn to chse wnr entering last: sn drvn and kpt on* **4/1**[2]
0366 **3** *1 ½* **Trombone Tom**[32] 1344 3-9-7 **61** AndrewMullen 4 — 63
(J R Norton) *chsd ldrs: edgd rt over 2f out: hdwy to chse ldng pair over 1f out. sn rdn and kpt on same pce* **4/1**[2]
4051 **4** *¾* **Jakeini (IRE)**[6] 2016 3-9-7 **64** 6ex DuranFentiman(3) 5 — 63
(E S McMahon) *chsd ldrs: rdn along and sltly outpcd 1/2-way: styd on u.p appr last* **7/2**[1]
0366 **5** *4* **Obergurgl (IRE)**[15] 1793 3-9-9 **63** GregFairley 7 — 46
(Mrs A Duffield) *cl up: led after 2f: hung lft and hdd 1½f out: sn drvn and wknd* **11/1**
0411 **6** *¾* **Axis Shield (IRE)**[17] 1762 3-8-10 **53** DerekNolan(3) 2 — 33
(M C Chapman) *led 2f: cl up on inner and rdn and hmpd 1½f out: nt rcvr* **9/1**[3]
2500 **7** *1 ¼* **Miss Dixie**[34] 1304 3-9-4 **63** DawnRankin(5) 8 — 38
(Miss J A Camacho) *dwlt: racd wd: a rr* **14/1**

60.42 secs (-0.18) **Going Correction** -0.025s/f (Good) **7** Ran SP% **109.4**
Speed ratings (Par 97):100,99,97,95,89 88,86
CSF £16.06 CT £51.38 TOTE £3.60: £2.00, £2.70; EX 19.90.
Owner M Maloney J Rider R Snowden **Bred** Mrs V E Hughes **Trained** Scorton, N Yorks
FOCUS
A modest sprint but an overdue winner for the trainer. The form is fair with the third setting the level.

2198 ELLERY HILL RATING RELATED MAIDEN STKS (DIV II) 7f
5:55 (5:56) (Class 6) 3-Y-0+ **£2,388** (£705; £352) **Stalls** Low

Form RPR
0002 **1** **Jellytot (USA)**[14] 1829 3-8-0 59 AndrewMullen(5) 13 — 62
(K A Ryan) *towards rr: swtchd outside and gd hdwy 3f out: rdn to ld wl over 1f out: styd on* **4/1**[1]
050 **2** *2* **Panic Stations**[21] 1641 3-8-5 60 HayleyTurner 8 — 57
(M L W Bell) *chsd ldrs: rdn 2f out: kpt on same pce appr last* **4/1**[1]
4005 **3** *hd* **Coalite (IRE)**[24] 1564 3-8-5 59 (b[1]) SilvestreDeSousa(3) 9 — 59
(A D Brown) *led: rdn over 2f out: drvn: wandered and hdd wl over 1f out: kpt on same pce* **25/1**
0000 **4** *2 ½* **Whistleupthewind**[8] 1955 3-8-5 39 (b) DavidAllan 5 — 49
(J M P Eustace) *bhd: hdwy on outer wl over 2f out: sn rdn and kpt on u.p appr last: nrst fin* **66/1**
4504 **5** *2* **Ayam Jantan**[11] 1888 3-8-8 58 KDarley 3 — 47
(M Johnston) *prom: rdn along wl over 2f out: sn drvn and kpt on same pce* **5/1**[2]
0306 **6** *½* **Prince Duval (IRE)**[280] 4719 3-8-8 55 DO'Donohoe 7 — 46
(D Carroll) *in tch: hdwy over 2f out: sn rdn and no imp* **20/1**
0600 **7** *nk* **Grandos (IRE)**[3] 2112 4-9-4 55 FergalLynch 4 — 49
(T D Easterby) *in tch: hdwy over 2f out: sn rdn and kpt on same pce* **6/1**[3]
0523 **8** *1 ½* **Royal Pardon**[17] 1761 4-9-1 57 (p) NeilPollard 12 — 42
(R C Guest) *s.i.s and bhd tl styd on fnl 2f* **6/1**[3]
2200 **9** *1 ½* **Dark Champion**[3] 2112 6-9-4 58 (v) TomEaves 2 — 41
(R E Barr) *chsd ldrs: rdn along 2f out: sn drvn and no imp* **7/1**
6500 **10** *¾* **Bond Cruz**[26] 1501 3-8-8 48 (v[1]) PatCosgrave 14 — 35
(G R Oldroyd) *bhd tl sme late hdwy* **25/1**
3400 **11** *1 ¾* **Luke After Me (IRE)**[29] 1443 6-9-4 45 MichaelTebbutt 1 — 34
(Miss Tracy Waggott) *chsd ldrs on inner: rdn along wl over 2f out: grad wknd* **66/1**
4500 **12** *11* **Twilight Avenger (IRE)**[88] 594 3-8-1 55 (p) CharlotteKerton(7) 10 — —
(M J Polglase) *a rr: bhd fr 1/2-way* **40/1**
0050 **13** *¾* **Flaming Cat (IRE)**[15] 1792 3-8-8 54 TonyHamilton 6 — —
(J Wade) *midfield: rdn along 3f out and sn wknd* **100/1**
0044 **14** *2 ½* **Bottomless Wallet**[270] 5000 5-9-1 45 PaulMulrennan 11 — —
(F Watson) *midfield: rdn along 3f out: sn wknd* **66/1**

1m 27.1s (-0.26) **Going Correction** -0.025s/f (Good)
WFA 3 from 4yo+ 10lb **14** Ran SP% **118.1**
Speed ratings (Par 101):100,97,97,94,92 91,91,89,88,87 85,72,71,68
CSF £17.77 TOTE £3.90: £2.10, £2.10, £5.50; EX 22.10 Place 6 £49.39, Place 5 £33.89.
Owner David Fravigar, Kathy Dixon **Bred** Gallagher's Stud **Trained** Hambleton, N Yorks
FOCUS
The second division of this moderate maiden and, although slower than the first division, was quicker than the claimer over the same trip. The form is weak with the placed horses setting the standard.
Luke After Me(IRE) Official explanation: jockey said gelding ran too free

T/Plt: £69.20 to a £1 stake. Pool: £32,366.70. 341.35 winning tickets. T/Qpdt: £15.20 to a £1 stake. Pool: £2,159.40. 105.00 winning tickets. JR

1236 EPSOM (L-H)

Friday, June 2

OFFICIAL GOING: Good

Wind: Virtually nil

2199 PRINCESS ELIZABETH STKS (SPONSORED BY VODAFONE) (GROUP 3) (F&M) 1m 114y

1:40 (1:42) (Class 1) 3-Y-O+

£28,390 (£10,760; £5,385; £2,685; £1,345; £675) **Stalls** Low

Form RPR

1411 **1** **Echelon**[20] [1671] 4-9-9 103 .... KFallon 5 112+
(Sir Michael Stoute) *lw: hld up mid div: 5th ent st: nt clr run and swtchd rt 1f out: r.o wl to ld but drifted lft fnl 75yds: wnt rt nr fin* **15/8**[1]

1130 **2** ½ **Musicanna**[26] [1506] 5-9-6 106 .... (t) JamieSpencer 2 105
(J R Fanshawe) *in tch: hdwy 3f out: sn rdn: led jst over 1f out: no ex whn hdd wl ins fnl f* **5/1**[3]

5140 **3** ½ **Zayn Zen**[26] [1506] 4-9-6 95 .... PhilipRobinson 3 104
(M A Jarvis) *hld up mid div: rdn 3f out: drifted lft but styd on ins fnl f cl home* **25/1**

0465 **4** nk **Shersha (IRE)**[20] [1671] 7-9-6 .... JohnEgan 8 103
(Kevin F O'Donnell, Ire) *hld up bhd: rdn and hdwy fr 2f out: styd on to go 4th ins fnl f* **22/1**

4405 **5** ½ **Bahia Breeze**[26] [1506] 4-9-6 105 .... MJKinane 6 102
(Rae Guest) *hld up bhd: rdn and swtchd rt 2f out: no imp tl styd on fnl f: nrst fin* **10/1**

0045 **6** 1 **Coconut Squeak**[13] [1849] 4-9-6 98 .... (v) MickyFenton 9 100
(Stef Liddiard) *led after 1f: rdn over 2f out: hdd jst over 1f out: no ex* **50/1**

4544 **7** hd **Suzy Bliss**[27] [1472] 3-8-8 95 .... TedDurcan 7 96
(W R Swinburn) *hld up mid div: lost pl ent st: sn rdn: kpt on same pce fr 2f out* **25/1**

0264 **8** 1¼ **Saabiq (USA)**[26] [1509] 3-8-8 95 .... RyanMoore 10 94
(C E Brittain) *hld up bhd: rdn 3f out: no imp* **14/1**

115 **9** 1 **Tarfah (USA)**[352] [2600] 5-9-6 104 .... LDettori 1 95
(G A Butler) *lw: led for 1f: trckd ldr: rdn and ev ch 2f out: wknd ins fnl f: bbv* **4/1**[2]

3301 **10** 3½ **Nantyglo**[27] [1477] 3-8-8 103 .... TQuinn 4 84
(M L W Bell) *trckd ldrs: rdn and effrt 3f out: wkng whn n.m.r over 1f out* **13/2**

1m 45.59s (-0.15) **Going Correction** +0.175s/f (Good)
WFA 3 from 4yo+ 12lb **10** Ran SP% **114.5**
Speed ratings (Par 113):107,106,106,105,105 104,104,103,102,99
CSF £10.42 TOTE £2.70: £1.30, £2.00, £4.40; EX 11.90 Trifecta £511.00 Pool: £1,079.70 - 1.50 winning units.
Owner Cheveley Park Stud **Bred** Cheveley Park Stud Ltd **Trained** Newmarket, Suffolk
■ Stewards' Enquiry : Micky Fenton two-day ban: careless riding (Jun 13-14)

FOCUS

Just an ordinary Group 3 for fillies and mares and only around three lengths separated the first seven home, despite Coconut Squeak appearing to have set a reasonable pace. However, Echelon had to wait for a gap and did well to deny Musicanna - that one was returning to something like her best having disappointed on her reappearance - when finally in the clear. The winning time was not great, nearly a second slower than the following handicap, and the form overll is limited by the third and fourth..

NOTEBOOK

Echelon ◆ defied the penalty she picked up for winning a weak Group 3 over seven furlongs at Lingfield on her reappearance under a fine ride from the former champion. Settled a little way off the pace, she had to wait an age for a gap to appear, but Fallon did not panic in the slightest and she displayed a decent change of pace when finally in the clear. Although she only beat fourth-placed Shersha a similar margin to Lingfield, this did look a slightly better race and there should be plenty more to come. She will now be aimed at the Windsor Forest Stakes at Royal Ascot and she is worth having on your side. (op 7-4 tchd 9-4)

Musicanna, highly progressive last season but disappointing on her reappearance in the Group 3 Dahlia Stakes at Newmarket on her reappearance, left that effort well behind despite being unable to confirm last season's defeat of Echelon in a soft-ground Listed event. Although the winner won with more in hand than the official margin might suggest, this was still a smart performance and she should continue to go well at a similar level. (op 7-2)

Zayn Zen, just like the runner-up, was well below form in the Group 3 Dahlia Stakes at Newmarket on her reappearance, but this represented a return to her best form. Her effort is all the more creditable given she stays 11 furlongs, and there could be even more to come.

Shersha(IRE), around a length and a half behind Echelon in this grade over seven furlongs at Lingfield on her previous start, had little chance of reversing form but ran well. (op 25-1 tchd 33-1)

Bahia Breeze had looked a possible non stayer when fifth in the Group 3 Dahlia Stakes over nine furlongs at Newmarket on her previous start but, dropped back to a mile, she got going too late. She is smart at her best, but is just taking a little bit of working out at the moment. (op 12-1)

Coconut Squeak had never previously raced beyond seven furlongs, but she still went to the front and set a good pace and stayed there for longer than one might have expected. She is very game, and perhaps a little more talented than she often gets credit for, so it would be no surprise to see her add to last season's 50/1 Listed success if everything falls right for her at some stage.

Suzy Bliss was said to be warm before the race.

Tarfah(USA), a slightly below-par fifth in the Group 2 Windsor Forest Stakes when last seen nearly a year previously, proved disappointing on her return to action but had an excuse. Official explanation: vet said mare bled from nose (op 9-2)

2200 VODAFONE MILE (H'CAP) 1m 114y

2:10 (2:15) (Class 2) (0-105,102) 4-Y-O+

£21,812 (£6,531; £3,265; £1,634; £815; £409) **Stalls** Low

Form RPR

110 **1** **Hinterland (IRE)**[242] [5660] 4-9-2 94 .... PhilipRobinson 15 106+
(M A Jarvis) *swtg: trckd ldr: rdn over 2f out: led ins fnl f: r.o: drvn out* **7/1**[2]

2033 **2** 1½ **Skidrow**[7] [1985] 4-8-11 89 .... JamieSpencer 2 98
(M L W Bell) *chsd ldrs: rdn 3f out: kpt on to go 2nd wl ins fnl f* **10/1**

0025 **3** ½ **Shot To Fame (USA)**[9] [1935] 7-8-13 91 .... AdrianTNicholls 1 99
(D Nicholls) *led: rdn over 2f out: hdd ins fnl f: kpt on* **16/1**

2302 **4** hd **Flipando (IRE)**[27] [1495] 5-8-11 89 .... JimmyFortune 12 97+
(T D Barron) *swtg: s.i.s: hld up towards rr: rdn and swtchd rt over 2f out: styd on strly ins fnl f: nrst fin* **8/1**[3]

1214 **5** 1¼ **Akona Matata (USA)**[20] [1678] 4-8-13 91 .... RyanMoore 5 96
(C E Brittain) *swtg: in tch: rdn 3f out: kpt on same pce* **11/2**[1]

0121 **6** hd **Wavertree Warrior (IRE)**[9] [1932] 4-8-1 84 5ex .... JamesDoyle(5) 6 88
(N P Littmoden) *mid div: rdn over 3f out: styd on steadily fr 2f out* **8/1**[3]

0100 **7** ½ **Krugerrand (USA)**[32] [1357] 7-8-9 87 .... TPQueally 16 90+
(W J Musson) *hld up bhd: stdy hdwy fr 3f out: hung lft fr 2f out: swtchd rt whn nt clr run over 1f out: styd on: nt rch ldrs* **33/1**

000 **8** 1 **Humble Opinion**[32] [1357] 4-8-7 85 .... AlanMunro 11 86
(B J Meehan) *chsd ldrs: rdn 3f out: one pce fnl f* **16/1**

0225 **9** ½ **Granston (IRE)**[27] [1495] 5-8-9 87 .... TQuinn 7 87
(J D Bethell) *mid div: lost pl over 4f out: hung lft and kpt on same pce fr 2f out* **14/1**

56- **10** shd **Seulement (USA)**[282] 4-9-7 99 .... NickyMackay 3 99
(L M Cumani) *chsd ldrs: rdn over 2f out: wknd ins fnl f* **16/1**

0600 **11** nk **Thyolo (IRE)**[41] [1133] 5-8-4 85 ow2 .... (v) AdamKirby(3) 8 84
(C G Cox) *nvr bttr than mid div* **14/1**

0500 **12** ½ **Sky Crusader**[28] [1456] 4-8-9 87 .... RobertHavlin 4 85
(R Ingram) *in tch: hmpd on rails over 5f out: rdn 3f out: sn one pce* **25/1**

0200 **13** 3 **Royal Island (IRE)**[20] [1678] 4-9-10 102 .... JoeFanning 14 94+
(M Johnston) *mid div: rdn and no imp whn short of room over 1f out* **25/1**

6561 **14** hd **Trafalgar Square**[6] [1957] 4-8-5 83 5ex .... DavidKinsella 10 75
(J Akehurst) *plld hrd in rr: swtchd rt and hmpd 4f out: nvr a danger* **11/2**[1]

0000 **15** 1¼ **Johnny Jumpup (IRE)**[20] [1678] 4-9-1 96 .... NelsonDeSouza(3) 13 85
(R M Beckett) *rn wd ent st and a in rr* **33/1**

0050 **16** hd **Uhoomagoo**[27] [1495] 8-9-1 93 .... (b) NCallan 9 82
(K A Ryan) *a towards rr* **14/1**

1m 44.63s (-1.11) **Going Correction** +0.175s/f (Good) **16** Ran SP% **125.8**
Speed ratings (Par 109):111,109,109,109,107 107,107,106,105,105 105,105,102,102,101 101
CSF £74.78 CT £1144.93 TOTE £8.90: £2.30, £2.10, £5.00, £2.60; EX 118.40 Trifecta £1595.40 Pool: £2,247.07 - 0.10 winning units.
Owner Sheikh Mohammed **Bred** Gerald W Leigh **Trained** Newmarket, Suffolk

FOCUS

A good handicap, but Shot To Fame set just an ordinary pace having been allowed an easy lead, and it proved hard to make up ground from off the pace. Hinterland showed he retains all of his ability with a decisive success on his reappearance, and beat a reliable yardstick in Skidrow. Back on fourth, Flipando fared best of those held up and caught the eye running on late. Despite the apparent lack of pace, the winning time was still nearly a second faster than the earlier fillies/mares Group 3.

NOTEBOOK

Hinterland(IRE) showed very useful form to win his first two starts last season, but had not been seen since finishing down the field when favourite for a Pontefract handicap 242 days previously. According to his trainer he had two injuries to his right knee that needed operating on for chips. However, he showed he retains all of his ability with a decisive success, picking up well for pressure, having soon crossed over from his wide draw to grab a handy position. He is in the Royal Hunt Cup, but has picked up a 5lb penalty for that race and his connections also have a leading contender in Notability, so the ten-furlong Wolferton Stakes will also be considered. (op 8-1)

Skidrow was given every chance, but he does not seem to have a great deal in hand of the Handicapper at the moment and was no match for the winner. He is in good form, but will remain vulnerable. (op 12-1)

Shot To Fame(USA), stepped back up to a mile, was a bit edgy beforehand but got his own way out in front from the lowest stall of all and very nearly stole this. He is on a reasonable enough mark, but has not won since 2004 and things will not always fall so kindly. (tchd 18-1)

Flipando(IRE) ◆, 2lb higher than when second at Thirsk on his previous start, was given too much to do and ran out of time to catch the leaders. The best of those held up, he looks ready to end a losing run stretching back to 2004. (tchd 17-2)

Akona Matata(USA), dropped a furlong in trip, seemed to run his race but had no easy task off a career-high mark. (tchd 5-1 and 6-1)

Wavertree Warrior(IRE), racing off a career-high mark under the penalty he picked up following his recent win over seven furlongs at Goodwood, ran a creditable enough race but never really looked like picking up sufficiently. His rider suggested the track was not ideal. Official explanation: jockey said gelding was unsuited by track (op 17-2)

Krugerrand(USA), back a couple of furlongs in trip, did not look happy on the track and also met with some interference. He was running on and can do better on a more conventional course.

Seulement(USA) got warm before the race.

Trafalgar Square was 3lb well in under the penalty he picked up for winning at Goodwood on his previous start, but he pulled too hard and then met with trouble in running. Official explanation: vet said colt was injured on right front leg (tchd 6-1 in places)

2201 VODAFONE ROSE BOWL (HERITAGE H'CAP) 1m 2f 18y

2:45 (2:47) (Class 2) 4-Y-O+

£46,740 (£13,995; £6,997; £3,502; £1,747; £877) **Stalls** Low

Form RPR

5000 **1** **Chancellor (IRE)**[31] [1380] 8-8-3 87 ow3 .... (t) JohnEgan 13 102
(Ernst Oertel) *lw: hld up towards rr: 13th ent st: gd hdwy fr 3f out: led over 1f out: styd on gamely: drvn out* **40/1**

0622 **2** ¾ **Look Again**[16] [1775] 5-8-0 84 .... PaulHanagan 12 98
(R A Fahey) *mid div: hdwy 3f out: rdn and ev ch over 1f out: kpt on but no ex nr fin* **5/2**[1]

2101 **3** 1¼ **Star Of Light**[20] [1678] 5-8-13 97 4ex .... AlanMunro 4 109
(B J Meehan) *in tch: outpcd 3f out: styd on again fr 1f out: wnt 3rd fnl stride* **15/2**[3]

5003 **4** shd **Kings Quay**[27] [1495] 4-8-10 94 .... GrahamGibbons 2 105
(J J Quinn) *chsd ldrs: led over 2f out: sn rdn: hdd over 1f out: kpt on: lost 3rd fnl stride* **16/1**

0000 **5** ½ **Red Lancer**[209] [6254] 5-8-8 92 .... JamieSpencer 1 102
(R A Fahey) *s.i.s: sn mid div: rdn over 2f out: kpt on ins fnl f* **10/1**

242 **6** 1¼ **Putra Kuantan**[20] [1676] 6-8-5 89 .... PhilipRobinson 7 97
(M A Jarvis) *in tch: gng wl over 3f out: effrt 2f out: sn drifted lft: kpt on same pce* **12/1**

1321 **7** 1 **Chantaco (USA)**[4] [2079] 4-8-11 95 4ex .... MartinDwyer 8 101
(A M Balding) *hld up towards rr: hdwy over 3f out: sn rdn: nt clr run briefly 2f out: kpt on same pce fnl f* **15/2**[3]

3534 **8** shd **Crosspeace (IRE)**[13] [1839] 4-9-10 108 .... RoystonFfrench 9 114
(M Johnston) *mid div: outpcd over 3f out: styd on again ins fnl f* **16/1**

5020 **9** ½ **Impeller (IRE)**[27] [1484] 7-8-10 94 .... SteveDrowne 19 99
(W R Muir) *hld up towards rr: stdy prog fr 3f out: nt clr run 2f out: kpt on same pce fnl f* **22/1**

1433 **10** 1¼ **Profit's Reality (IRE)**[6] [2010] 4-9-2 100 .... RobbieFitzpatrick 3 103
(P A Blockley) *in tch: rdn over 3f out: swtchd rt and nt clr run over 2f out: no imp after* **33/1**

6604 **11** 1¾ **Nero's Return (IRE)**[4] [2086] 5-8-0 84 .... FrancisNorton 14 83
(M Johnston) *towards rr: sme late hdwy: nvr a danger* **25/1**

3300 **12** 2½ **Polygonal (FR)**[69] [728] 6-8-8 92 .... RyanMoore 15 87
(Ernst Oertel) *s.i.s: sn mid div: rdn 3f out: one pce fnl 2f* **50/1**

1330 **13** hd **Bobby Charles**[59] [867] 5-7-12 82 oh1 .... MatthewHenry 11 76
(Dr J D Scargill) *plld hrd early and a towards rr* **66/1**

1101 **14** *3* **All That And More (IRE)**[37] 1239 4-8-12 **96**..................... MichaelHills 5 85+
(B W Hills) *lw: led: rdn and hdd over 2f out: 5th and hld whn lost action and eased ins fnl f* **5/1**[2]

3052 **15** *10* **Counsel's Opinion (IRE)**[22] 1601 9-9-2 **100**................. GeorgeBaker 16 70+
(C F Wall) *lw: s.i.s and a bhd* **14/1**

1000 **16** *1 ½* **Gig Harbor**[328] 3344 7-7-12 **82** oh4................................ DavidKinsella 17 49
(Miss E C Lavelle) *chsd ldrs tl wknd over 2f out* **66/1**

6250 **17** *2* **Night Spot**[261] 5233 5-7-12 **82** oh2.................................... NickyMackay 6 45+
(B R Millman) *chsd ldrs: rdn over 2f out: hung lft and wknd over 1f out* **40/1**

2m 7.89s (-1.15) **Going Correction** +0.175s/f (Good) **17** Ran SP% **124.9**
Speed ratings (Par 109):111,110,109,109,108 107,107,107,106,105 104,102,102,99,91 90,88
CSF £135.36 CT £892.08 TOTE £54.50: £7.20, £1.50, £2.00, £3.80; EX 317.00 Trifecta £1275.90 Pool: £2,515.93 - 1.40 winning units.
Owner A S Reid **Bred** Norelands Bloodstock **Trained** Newmarket, Suffolk

FOCUS
A very good handicap and the form looks decent, despite the winner returning at 40/1. Chancellor had not been at his best for some time, but was 13lb lower than when third in this race last and took advantage to beat some other well-handicapped horses. There was some interference further back, but a worthy winner on the day.

NOTEBOOK
Chancellor(IRE), tenth to Galileo in the 2001 Derby, had not shown a great deal for his current yard since finishing third in this race last year off a mark 100 for Gerard Butler. However, he had looked a little unlucky on his reappearance at Lingfield and stepped up quite significantly on that effort to end a losing a run stretching back to his success in the Group 3 Gordon Richards Stakes at Sandown in 2004. He beat some well handicapped horses, but he was well in himself on old form and there was little fluke about this. (tchd 66-1 in a place and 50-1 in places)
Look Again was 9lb well in following his recent second to Blue Spinnaker at York, when he was no less than 13 lengths clear of the third, but that run came on easy ground and he could not take advantage on this quicker surface. This was still a very useful effort, though, especially considering the winner was very favourably handicapped on the pick of his form. (tchd 11-4 and 3-1 in places)
Star Of Light, 3lb well in under the penalty he picked up for winning at Newmarket on his previous start, was slightly hampered when just beginning to pick up and looked unlucky not have finished even closer. He remains progressive. (op 7-1)
Kings Quay, third in the Thirsk Hunt Cup on his previous start, travelled really well but found himself in front much sooner than was ideal, with All That And More quickly dropping away, and he could not sustain his effort. This was still a good run and he can do even better when ridden with more patience. (op 14-1)
Red Lancer ◆, eighth of 21 on his only previous start for this yard in the November Handicap last season, made a pleasing reappearance and could do even better with the benefit of this run - he was rated 110 in his prime. (op 16-1)
Putra Kuantan, back up in trip, ran well but could not quite build on the form he showed when a close second at Newmarket on his reappearance. (op 14-1)
Chantaco(USA), carrying a 4lb penalty for his recent success in the Zetland Gold Cup at Redcar, could not repeat that form and did not look totally happy on the track. (op 7-1 tchd 8-1 in places)
All That And More(IRE), 8lb higher than when winning over course and distance on his reappearance, can be forgiven this below-par effort as he lost his action. Official explanation: jockey said colt lost its action (op 11-2)
Counsel's Opinion(IRE) Official explanation: jockey said gelding ran flat

2202 VODAFONE CORONATION CUP (GROUP 1) 1m 4f 10y
3:25 (3:29) (Class 1) 4-Y-O+
£141,950 (£53,800; £26,925; £13,425; £6,725; £3,375) **Stalls** Centre

Form RPR

3411 **1** **Shirocco (GER)**[26] 1507 5-9-0 .... CSoumillon 5 124
(A Fabre, France) *lw: led for 3f: styd prom: led again 4f out: rdn and hrd pressed fr 2f out: styd on wl to assert ins fnl f* **8/11**[1]

5143 **2** *1 ¾* **Ouija Board**[40] 1180 5-8-11 117.. LDettori 2 118
(E A L Dunlop) *trckd ldng pair: rdn to chal 2f out: ev ch 1f out: no ex* **11/4**[2]

1645 **3** *½* **Enforcer**[26] 1507 4-9-0 109.. MartinDwyer 3 120
(W R Muir) *hld up bhd ldrs: 5th ent st: sn rdn: styd on fr 2f out: wnt 3rd and drifted lft ins fnl f* **66/1**

4422 **4** *2 ½* **Ace (IRE)**[32] 1365 5-9-0 .... KFallon 1 116
(A P O'Brien, Ire) *lw: plld hrd: trckd wnr: led 9f out: hdd 4f out: sn rdn to press wnr: kpt on same pce fr over 1f out* **11/2**[3]

0132 **5** *2 ½* **Notable Guest (USA)**[35] 1267 5-9-0 112..................... RichardHughes 6 112
(Sir Michael Stoute) *hld up bhd ldrs: rdn and effrt 3f out: wknd over 1f out* **14/1**

4536 **6** *9* **Something Exciting**[264] 5159 4-8-11 112................................. TQuinn 4 95
(D R C Elsworth) *hld up bhd ldrs tl outpcd ent the st* **50/1**

2m 37.64s (-1.09) **Going Correction** +0.175s/f (Good) **6** Ran SP% **110.1**
Speed ratings (Par 117):110,108,108,106,105 99
CSF £2.79 TOTE £1.80: £1.10, £1.60; EX 3.10.
Owner Baron G Von Ullmann **Bred** Baron G Von Ullmann **Trained** Chantilly, France
■ A sixth winner of the Coronation Cup for Andre Fabre, and a first-ever success round Epsom for Christophe Soumillon.

FOCUS
Only two previous winners at this level, but they are two of the best middle-distances horses in the world and it was a fascinating clash, although neither of them got the strong pace that suits them best and they were unable to produce Group 1 performances strictly on the figures. The winning time was very similar to that of the Oaks.

NOTEBOOK
Shirocco(GER) ◆ looked an absolute picture. He beat Enforcer by less than half the margin he managed to on easier ground in the Jockey Club Stakes on his reappearance/British debut, but was never going to be able to produce a high-class performance on the figures given how steady they went early, and his job was basically to see off his only realistic danger Ouija Board. He completed that task in style, finding plenty when strongly challenged around two furlongs out to gain a thoroughly professional success. All his best form previously had been on soft/testing ground, but this slightly better surface did not bother at all. He is now likely to be aimed at the King George, where he could face, among others, his stablemate and last year's top three-year-old Hurricane Run. (op 4-5 tchd 10-11)
Ouija Board, three times a Group 1 winner since taking the 2004 Oaks over course had distance, has not quite had things go her way this season - she was given too much to do off a steady pace in the Sheema Classic, before getting going too late in the Queen Elizabeth II Cup at Sha Tin on her previous start - and a steady pace again proved her undoing. One couldn't be sure she would have beaten Shirocco under any circumstances, but a stronger gallop would surely have seen her finish further clear of the likes of Enforcer. She may now go to Royal Ascot for either the Prince Of Wales's Stakes or the Hardwicke, and still has plenty more to offer. (op 9-4 tchd 3-1)
Enforcer ran a terrific race to take third, getting much closer to Shirocco than he managed in the Jockey Club Stakes at Newmarket on his previous start, but he must be flattered. Given he has good form over shorter, the steady pace would not have inconvenienced him as much as it did the front two, and he had also shown a liking for this track when winning a handicap at this meeting last year on his only previous start round here. Having said all that, he is a Group performer in his own right these days and could be found opportunities at a slightly lower level.
Ace(IRE), one and three quarter lengths behind Shirocco in the Breeders' Cup Turf last season, got badly worked up on the way to the start and pulled very hard in the race itself. In the circumstances it is surprising he finished so close, but that was probably down to the steady pace. (tchd 9-2)
Notable Guest(USA), back up to a mile and a half, never really figured and was below the form he showed to finish second to Day Flight in the Gordon Richard Stakes on his previous start. (op 16-1)
Something Exciting struggled a little after her second in last season's Oaks, and this reappearance effort offered little hope. (op 66-1)

2203 VODAFONE OAKS (GROUP 1) (FILLIES) 1m 4f 10y
4:05 (4:11) (Class 1) 3-Y-O
£250,626 (£94,989; £47,538; £23,703; £11,873; £5,958) **Stalls** Centre

Form RPR

6322 **1** **Alexandrova (IRE)**[16] 1777 3-9-0 .... KFallon 5 118+
(A P O'Brien, Ire) *lw: hld up bhd: 9th st: swtchd rt and smooth prog fr 3f out: led 2f out: sn qcknd clr and drifted lft: easily* **9/4**[1]

3651 **2** *6* **Rising Cross**[27] 1472 3-9-0 100.. GeorgeBaker 3 108
(J R Best) *mid div: 6th st: hdwy over 2f out: sn rdn: wnt 2nd over 1f out: stmbld bdly jst ins 1f out: nt pce of wnr* **33/1**

101 **3** *1 ¼* **Short Skirt**[16] 1777 3-9-0 99.. MJKinane 10 106+
(Sir Michael Stoute) *racd keenly: hld up: hdwy 5f out: disputing 3rd ent st:sn rdn: hung lft fr over 1f out: kpt on same pce* **9/2**[2]

3111 **4** *½* **Speciosa (IRE)**[26] 1508 3-9-0 114.................................... MickyFenton 4 105
(Mrs P Sly) *led: rdn and hdd 2f out: kpt on same pce: lost 3rd fnl stride* **5/1**[3]

12 **5** *2* **Guilia**[14] 1819 3-9-0 81.. AlanMunro 6 102
(Rae Guest) *chsd ldrs: disp 3rd ent st: sn rdn: one pce fnl 2f* **8/1**

0311 **6** *1 ¼* **Time On**[23] 1583 3-9-0 95.. LDettori 9 100
(J L Dunlop) *chsd ldr: rdn to chal ent st: wknd over 1f out* **7/1**

415 **7** *nk* **Kassiopeia (IRE)**[20] 1669 3-9-0 80.. TonyCulhane 7 99
(M R Channon) *hld up bhd: 10th and struggling ent st: sme late prog but nvr a threat* **66/1**

064 **8** *1 ½* **Kaylianni**[23] 1583 3-9-0 88... TedDurcan 11 97
(M R Channon) *hld up towards rr: 7th st: sn rdn: no imp* **100/1**

403 **9** *1 ¼* **Prowess (IRE)**[23] 1583 3-9-0 88.. MichaelHills 2 95
(B W Hills) *mid div: 8th st: wknd over 1f out* **33/1**

21 **10** *5* **Riyalma (IRE)**[26] 1509 3-9-0 102...................................... CSoumillon 8 87
(Sir Michael Stoute) *lw: in tch: disp 3rd ent st: sn rdn: hung lft over 2f out: wknd over 1f out* **9/2**[2]

2m 37.71s (-1.02) **Going Correction** +0.175s/f (Good) **10** Ran SP% **115.8**
Speed ratings (Par 110):110,106,105,104,103 102,102,101,100,97
CSF £87.39 CT £315.98 TOTE £3.30: £1.40, £6.70, £1.90; EX 112.80 Trifecta £684.90 Pool: £5,305.75 - 5.50 winning units.
Owner Mrs John Magnier, M Tabor & D Smith **Bred** Quay Bloodstock **Trained** Ballydoyle, Co Tipperary

FOCUS
Despite the presence of the 1000 Guineas winner, and many of the principals from some of the key 'trials', this was a very weak renewal of the Epsom Oaks. With Speciosa patently not staying, Alexandrova proved a class apart and finished well clear. They appeared to go a decent gallop through the first half mile or so, but the pace was then steadied. The winning time was only slightly slower than the Coronation Cup, but that was steadily run..

NOTEBOOK
Alexandrova(IRE) was not at her best and did not offer a great deal of Oaks promise when second to Short Skirt in the Musidora on her reappearance, but she was hampered soon after the start that day, and the race clearly brought her on significantly. Held up in a race ultimately run at just an ordinary gallop, she had plenty to do on the turn into the straight, but quickened up well down the outside and soon had the race won. While this was visually very impressive, and she could do no more than win, the bare form leaves a lot to be desired. She is a possible for the Irish Oaks, but John Magnier said "we'll be careful with her from now on", as this was very much her race, and it remains to be seen just how much more we will see of her. (tchd 5-2)
Rising Cross, who gained a deserved first success in pattern company at the tenth attempt when dead-heating for the Lupe at Goodwood on her previous start, fully justified the decision to supplement her for this race with a cracking run in second. Warm before the race, she was no match for the winner, who was well and truly in a different league, but deserves extra credit for holding on to second given how badly stumbled inside the last furlong. Her trainer said he had no plans for her at this stage and he is open to offers. (tchd 40-1)
Short Skirt, who got warm before the race, was a length and a quarter too good for Alexandrova in the Musidora at York on her reappearance, but could not confirm form with that rival on this better surface on a track her trainer felt she did not really handle. She also had a couple of extra furlongs to contend with, and was not guaranteed to get it strictly on breeding.
Speciosa(IRE), supplemented at a cost of £20,000, won the 1000 Guineas in the manner of a filly who had more to offer, but that form has taken some knocks since then and she had her stamina to prove over this extra half mile. Despite having got her own way out in front, and been able to very much steady the gallop, she quite clearly failed to last home. She will probably be dropped back to a mile next time and connections will consider races like the Coronation Stakes at Royal Ascot and the Falmouth Stakes at Newmarket. (tchd 11-2 and 6-1 in a place)
Guilia, the winner of a Thirsk maiden on her only start as a juvenile and just denied in the Swettenham Stakes on her reappearance, ran with credit in fifth but may just have been found out by her inexperience. (op 9-1)
Time On, a supplementary entry, could not dictate as she had done in the Cheshire Oaks, and this was a lot tougher in any case. (tchd 15-2)
Kassiopeia(IRE), rated just 80, helps give a guide to the strength of form. She should stay further. (tchd 80-1)
Riyalma(IRE) was well below the form she showed to win the Pretty Polly Stakes on her reappearance and was disappointing. Official explanation: trainer was unable to offer any explanation for poor form shown

2204 VODAFONE SURREY STKS (LISTED RACE) 7f
4:45 (4:48) (Class 1) 3-Y-O
£19,873 (£7,532; £3,769; £1,879; £941; £472) **Stalls** Low

Form RPR

1556 **1** **Racer Forever (USA)**[14] 1818 3-8-13 100..................... JimmyFortune 5 107
(J H M Gosden) *swtg: trckd ldrs: led wl over 1f out: r.o wl: readily* **8/1**

15 **2** *3* **Bouboulina**[43] 1094 3-8-8 87... JamieSpencer 4 95
(E A L Dunlop) *lw: hld up bhd ldrs: hdwy over 2f out: rdn to go 2nd jst over 1f out: kpt on but nt pce of wnr* **5/1**[2]

4221 **3** *hd* **Kingsgate Prince (IRE)**[14] 1818 3-9-3 108.................................... TQuinn 7 103
(J R Best) *racd keenly: led after 2f: rdn and hdd wl over 1f out: kpt on but nt pce of wnr* **6/4**[1]

1300 **4** *2* **Art Market (CAN)**[76] 665 3-8-13 100............................(b[1]) RyanMoore 1 94
(P F I Cole) *lw: chsd ldrs: rdn 3f out: kpt on same pce fnl 2f* **12/1**

1016 **5** *3* **Dingaan (IRE)**[10] 1924 3-8-13 94.. ChrisCatlin 2 86
(A M Balding) *swtg: hld up bhd ldrs: rdn and brief effrt 3f out* **12/1**

The Form Book, Raceform Ltd, Compton, RG20 6NL

6405 **6** *16* **Mutawajid (IRE)**[14] 1818 3-8-13 100............................ RichardHughes 3 44
(R Hannon) *led for 2f: chsd ldr: rdn 3f out: wknd over 1f out: eased* **11/2**[3]

1m 23.59s (-0.36) **Going Correction** +0.175s/f (Good) **6** Ran SP% **98.5**
Speed ratings (Par 107):109,105,105,103,99 81
CSF £34.79 TOTE £9.80: £3.50, £2.00; EX 43.00.

Owner Mohamed Obaida **Bred** Gainsborough Farm Llc **Trained** Newmarket, Suffolk

FOCUS
Not a very strong Listed race. The favourite, Kingsgate Prince, is better held up off a strong pace and Racer Forever took advantage to reverse recent Newbury form in no uncertain terms. The winning time was nearly a second slower than the following three-year-old handicap.

NOTEBOOK
Racer Forever(USA), an eye-catching sixth to Kingsgate Prince in a six-furlong Listed event at Newbury on his previous start, has clearly benefited quite significantly from that run and ran out a most decisive winner. With the favourite below form, this might not have been the strongest of Listed races, but he is progressing and deserves his chance in something like the Jersey Stakes at Royal Ascot. (op 6-1)

Bouboulina, who looked such a nice prospect when winning on her only start at two over this trip on Lingfield's Polytrack, stepped up on the form she showed when a disappointing fifth in a Newmarket conditions race on her reappearance. She picked up some valuable black type and could have more to offer. (op 6-1 tchd 9-2)

Kingsgate Prince(IRE) could not repeat the form he showed when winning a six-furlong Listed race at Newbury on his previous start (Racer Forever sixth), but appeared found out by the lack of early pace. After racing keenly, his rider let him get on with things, but he put up little resistance when challenged and seems much more effective when waited with. (op 13-8 tchd 7-4, 15-8 in a place)

Art Market(CAN), fitted with blinkers for the first time, was never dangerous on in his start in 76 days and did not offer much. (op 16-1 tchd 20-1)

Dingaan(IRE), a progressive sort on Polytrack in recent months, seemed to find this company a bit hot on his return to turf, but may have fared better off a stronger pace. (op 11-1 tchd 14-1)

Mutawajid(IRE) ran nowhere near the form he showed when fifth in a six-furlong Listed event at Newbury on his reappearance (one place in front of Racer Forever) and was a major disappointment. He was said to have not handled the track. Official explanation: jockey said colt did not handle track (op 5-1)

2205 VODAFONE GROUP SERVICES STKS (H'CAP) 7f
5:20 (5:20) (Class 2) (0-100,95) 3-Y-O

£18,696 (£5,598; £2,799; £1,401; £699; £351) **Stalls** Low

Form RPR

411 **1** **Song Of Passion (IRE)**[21] 1626 3-8-10 **84**........................ RyanMoore 3 99
(R Hannon) *lw: led for 1f: styd prom: led 3f out: r.o wl fnl f: rdn out* **3/1**[1]

5005 **2** *3 ½* **Mister Benedictine**[26] 1515 3-8-3 **77**.............................. NickyMackay 8 83
(W R Muir) *chsd ldrs: rdn and ev ch over 2f out: sn hung lft u.p: kpt on* **33/1**

5513 **3** *½* **King Of The Moors (USA)**[29] 1440 3-8-10 **84**............ JamieSpencer 12 89
(T D Barron) *lw: chsd ldrs: rdn and ev ch 2f out: sn edgd lft: kpt on* **8/1**[3]

5212 **4** *1 ½* **Spirit Of Arosa (IRE)**[13] 1843 3-8-4 **78**.............................. AlanMunro 4 79+
(J Akehurst) *mid div: hmpd over 4f out: rdn 3f out: kpt on same pce* **4/1**[2]

5100 **5** *shd* **Scarlet Flyer (USA)**[48] 1016 3-7-13 **76**................. NelsonDeSouza(3) 10 77
(G L Moore) *s.i.s: towards rr: gd hdwy 3f out: sn hung rt: no ex ins fnl f* **25/1**

4006 **6** *1* **Jeanmaire (IRE)**[26] 1512 3-8-13 **92**................................ TravisBlock(5) 9 90
(H Morrison) *chsd ldrs: rdn 3f out: kpt on same pce* **22/1**

4004 **7** *1 ½* **Tara Too (IRE)**[13] 1843 3-8-9 **83**.................................... KerrinMcEvoy 5 77
(D W P Arbuthnot) *lw: in tch: rdn 3f out: hung rt fr over 1f out: one pce after* **12/1**

2452 **8** *1* **Carmenero (GER)**[32] 1349 3-8-7 **81**............................. RichardHughes 7 72
(W R Muir) *hld up towards rr: sme late prog: n.d* **14/1**

144 **9** *2* **Dame Hester (IRE)**[36] 1250 3-8-7 **81**.................................. ChrisCatlin 1 67
(E J O'Neill) *in tch: lost action on bnd over 4f out: rdn 3f out: sn one pce* **12/1**

004 **10** *hd* **Guest Connections**[16] 1776 3-9-7 **95**.................................... TQuinn 2 81
(M R Channon) *lw: hmpd 4f out: a towards rr* **14/1**

0521 **11** *1 ½* **Royal Envoy (IRE)**[27] 1493 3-8-6 **80**................................ PaulHanagan 11 62
(B W Hills) *lw: a towards rr* **8/1**[3]

1030 **12** *2 ½* **Dubai Typhoon (USA)**[21] 1627 3-9-7 **95**...................... JimmyFortune 13 70
(C E Brittain) *lw: s.i.s: towards rr: hdwy 3f out: wknd over 1f out* **20/1**

4100 **13** *1 ¾* **River Kintyre**[268] 5043 3-8-11 **85**.................................... MichaelHills 6 56
(B W Hills) *led after 1f: rdn and hdd 3f out: sn btn* **25/1**

1m 22.74s (-1.21) **Going Correction** +0.175s/f (Good) **13** Ran SP% **115.7**
Speed ratings (Par 105):113,109,108,106,106 105,103,102,100,100 98,95,93
CSF £118.53 CT £746.57 TOTE £3.00: £1.70, £7.40, £2.20; EX 96.40 Place 6 £60.62, Place 5 £40.26.

Owner Thurloe Thoroughbreds XVI **Bred** Mrs Stephanie Hanly **Trained** East Everleigh, Wilts

FOCUS
The top weight was rated 5lb below the ceiling of 100 and this was perhaps not as strong a race as one might have expected for the grade. Also, very few of these could get involved from off the pace, despite the final time being nearly a second faster than the earlier Listed event.

NOTEBOOK
Song Of Passion(IRE) was only 3lb higher than when winning at Chester on her previous start and, always well placed, she followed up in good style. Now the winner of her last three starts, she is progressing into a very useful sort and may be aimed at a fillies' Listed event at Warwick. (op 9-4)

Mister Benedictine, dropped back from ten furlongs, was always handy and kept on to the line for his in-form yard. He looks on a fair mark.

King Of The Moors(USA), third over a mile on his handicap debut at Musselburgh, ran well in this tougher heat over a furlong shorter trip. (op 12-1)

Spirit Of Arosa(IRE) fared best of those to race off the pace and emerges with plenty of credit. She can do better again when she has the race run to suit. (op 9-2 tchd 5-1 in places)

Scarlet Flyer(USA) offered nothing on his reappearance at Kempton when last of 16 on the Polytrack, but this was much better. He may have been even closer had he not hung, and there could be more to come.

Jeanmaire(IRE), upped to seven furlongs for the first time, travelled well but did not find as much as had looked likely and can do better back over shorter. (op 16-1 tchd 25-1)

Royal Envoy(IRE), off the mark in a seven-furlong maiden at Thirsk on his previous start, would have found this tougher and did not pick up after racing a little keenly. (tchd 17-2)

T/Jkpt: Not won. T/Plt: £99.70 to a £1 stake. Pool: £151,975.00. 1,112.25 winning tickets. T/Qpdt: £23.90 to a £1 stake. Pool: £8,041.30. 248.60 winning tickets. TM

1743 WOLVERHAMPTON (A.W) (L-H)
Friday, June 2

OFFICIAL GOING: Standard
Wind: Moderate against Weather: Sunny

2206 ELECTRICAL CONTRACTORS ASSOCIATION CLIENT SPECIFIERS CHALLENGE CLAIMING STKS 1m 5f 194y(P)
2:00 (2:00) (Class 6) 4-Y-O+ **£2,730** (£806; £403) **Stalls** Low

Form RPR

-050 **1** **Lefonic**[41] 1138 4-9-3 50.. OscarUrbina 5 67
(G C H Chung) *w ldr: qcknd to ld over 5f out: rdn over 2f out: drvn out* **14/1**

1200 **2** *1 ¼* **He's A Star**[15] 1808 4-9-3 70... DarryllHolland 2 66
(Miss Gay Kelleway) *hld up in tch: rdn 4f out: chsd wnr over 1f out: nt qckn ins fnl f* **3/1**[2]

2255 **3** *nk* **York Cliff**[18] 1748 8-8-6 54.. LiamJones(7) 3 61
(W M Brisbourne) *s.i.s: hld up: rdn and hdwy 4f out: styd on same pce fnl f* **7/1**

4135 **4** *¾* **Champagne Shadow (IRE)**[40] 1167 5-9-3 80...............(b) EddieAhern 6 64
(G L Moore) *hld up: rdn and outpcd over 4f out: hdwy wl over 1f out: one pce fnl f* **8/11**[1]

4314 **5** *6* **Chater Knight (IRE)**[25] 1548 5-8-0 56........................(p) TolleyDean(7) 7 46
(R A Harris) *t.k.h: prom: chsd wnr over 4f out: rdn over 2f out: wknd fnl f* **13/2**[3]

0-06 **6** *7* **Jack Durrance (IRE)**[16] 771 6-8-9 37.............................. ShaneKelly 9 38
(G A Ham) *hld up: hdwy 4f out: sn rdn and wknd* **33/1**

7 *12* **King Georges (FR)**[72] 8-9-3 .... VinceSlattery 1 29
(J C Tuck) *s.i.s: sn chsng ldrs: rdn over 5f out: sn wknd* **16/1**

-000 **8** *18* **Grub Street**[73] 688 10-8-5 30 ow1............................... NeilChalmers(3) 4 —
(J Parkes) *set slow pl: hdd over 5f out: wknd 4f out* **50/1**

9 *41* **Kalawoun (FR)**[29] 4-8-7 .... SamHitchcott 8 —
(Ferdy Murphy) *bhd: reminders after 2f: pushed along over 7f out: lost tch over 5f out: t.o* **16/1**

3m 3.82s (-3.55) **Going Correction** -0.125s/f (Stan) **9** Ran SP% **132.1**
Speed ratings (Par 101):105,104,104,103,100 96,89,79,55
CSF £64.08 TOTE £16.60: £3.20, £1.60, £1.60; EX 120.70 TRIFECTA Not won..He's A Star was claimed by P. D. Evans for £10,000.

Owner Ian Pattle **Bred** Northmore Stud **Trained** Newmarket, Suffolk

FOCUS
This modest claimer was slowly-run for the first mile. The third is the best guide, although there are doubts over the form.
Jack Durrance(IRE) Official explanation: jockey said gelding hung left under pressure

2207 TAKE CONTROL WITH WBX.COM H'CAP 5f 20y(P)
2:30 (2:31) (Class 6) (0-60,60) 3-Y-O+ **£2,730** (£806; £403) **Stalls** Low

Form RPR

1261 **1** **Mystery Pips**[22] 1618 6-9-9 **55**..(v) KimTinkler 11 67
(N Tinkler) *a.p: rdn to ld over 1f out: r.o wl* **10/1**

0000 **2** *1 ¾* **Caustic Wit (IRE)**[3] 2095 8-9-9 **55**..............................(p) FergusSweeney 7 61
(M S Saunders) *mid-div: rdn and hdwy over 2f out: kpt on ins fnl f: nt trble wnr* **20/1**

0202 **3** *1* **Orchestration (IRE)**[36] 1255 5-9-2 **55**......................(v) StacyRenwick(7) 2 57
(M J Attwater) *chsd ldrs: rdn wl over 1f out: kpt on same pce fnl f* **8/1**

100 **4** *nk* **Auentraum (GER)**[7] 1981 6-10-0 **60**............................(p) DarryllHolland 1 61
(K McAuliffe) *hld up in mid-div: n.m.r on ins over 3f out: rdn and hdwy over 1f out: kpt on towards fin* **4/1**[1]

6200 **5** *shd* **Doctor's Cave**[11] 1878 4-9-7 **56**..............................(b) NeilChalmers(3) 8 57
(K O Cunningham-Brown) *sn led: rdn and hdd over 1f out: one pce* **16/1**

0006 **6** *nk* **Hard To Catch (IRE)**[30] 1402 8-9-7 **60**..................(b) JamesMillman(7) 13 60+
(D K Ivory) *bhd: c wd st: hdwy on outside fnl f: nvr nrr* **25/1**

6200 **7** *1 ½* **Piccleyes**[15] 1794 5-9-8 **54**...(b) EddieAhern 5 48
(M J Polglase) *chsd ldrs: rdn wl over 1f out: wknd ins fnl f* **10/1**

3603 **8** *nk* **Elvina**[193] 6407 5-9-10 **56**.. DaneO'Neill 3 49
(A G Newcombe) *s.i.s: nvr trbld ldrs* **6/1**[2]

3015 **9** *¾* **Henry Tun**[41] 1150 8-9-9 **58**..(b) JasonEdmunds(3) 6 48
(J Balding) *s.i.s: n.d* **7/1**[3]

6060 **10** *1 ¾* **Mind Alert**[15] 1795 5-9-9 **55**..(v) ShaneKelly 10 39
(D Shaw) *a bhd* **33/1**

0000 **11** *1* **El Potro**[13] 1846 4-9-13 **59**.. SebSanders 12 40
(E S McMahon) *outpcd* **25/1**

1320 **12** *nk* **Red Sovereign**[16] 1774 5-9-1 **54**.. MarkCoumbe(7) 4 33
(D G Bridgwater) *led early: rdn over 2f out: sn wknd* **10/1**

0035 **13** *5* **Clearing Sky (IRE)**[90] 580 5-9-5 **54**............................ SaleemGolam(3) 9 15+
(J R Boyle) *s.s: a in rr* **8/1**

62.17 secs (-0.65) **Going Correction** -0.125s/f (Stan) **13** Ran SP% **128.0**
Speed ratings (Par 101):100,97,95,95,94 94,92,91,90,87 86,85,77
CSF £207.37 CT £1754.91 TOTE £13.50: £3.20, £7.10, £3.90; EX 211.60 TRIFECTA Not won..

Owner Paglia & Fieno Racing **Bred** Michael Worton **Trained** Langton, N Yorks

FOCUS
A closely-knit low-grade affair that looks sound enough rated through the fourth.
Clearing Sky(IRE) Official explanation: jockey said mare was slowly away from stalls

2208 COMBINE BUSINESS WITH PLEASURE (S) STKS 5f 216y(P)
3:05 (3:06) (Class 6) 3-Y-O+ **£2,388** (£705; £352) **Stalls** Low

Form RPR

0013 **1** **Cd Europe (IRE)**[18] 1735 8-9-12 68........................... DeanMcKeown 13 73
(G A Swinbank) *hld up and bhd: hdwy 2f out: rdn to ld wl ins fnl f: r.o wl* **11/2**[3]

0250 **2** *1 ½* **Desert Opal**[6] 2020 6-9-12 63.. SebSanders 10 68
(D W Chapman) *hld up in tch: rdn over 2f out: led jst ins fnl f: sn hdd: nt qckn* **9/2**[2]

0035 **3** *1 ¼* **Aventura (IRE)**[31] 1387 6-9-4 54................................ BenSwarbrick(3) 8 59
(S R Bowring) *chsd ldrs: rdn over 2f out: r.o one pce fnl f* **14/1**

5020 **4** *1 ¼* **Mission Affirmed (USA)**[17] 1752 5-9-7 55.............(b) AdrianMcCarthy 6 56
(R A Harris) *s.i.s: sn mid-div: kpt on towards fin* **13/2**

0600 **5** *½* **Ockums Razor (IRE)**[10] 1923 3-9-4 77........................... DarryllHolland 4 57
(M J Polglase) *sn led: rdn wl over 1f out: hdd jst ins fnl f: fdd* **10/3**[1]

0653 **6** *nk* **Aswan (IRE)**[18] 1746 8-9-4 58...................................(t) AmirQuinn(3) 9 53
(S R Bowring) *led early: w ldr: rdn and ev ch 1f out: wknd ins fnl f* **8/1**

6362 **7** *1 ¼* **Global Achiever**[17] 1762 5-9-7 46...............................(p) OscarUrbina 11 49
(G C H Chung) *prom: rdn 2f out: wknd ins fnl f* **10/1**

0530 **8** *¾* **Smokincanon**[88] 602 4-9-4 50.. RobertMiles(3) 7 47
(W G M Turner) *t.k.h towards rr: rdn 2f out: nvr trbld ldrs* **33/1**

3002 **9** 2 1/2 **Mirasol Princess**[109] [397] 5-8-9 49 JamesMillman(7) 2 35
(D K Ivory) *towards rr whn hmpd on ins 4f out: n.d after* **8/1**
4531 **10** 1 1/2 **Wings Of Morning (IRE)**[17] [1764] 5-9-12 47 (v) EddieAhern 5 40
(D Carroll) *prom: edgd lft 4f out: rdn and wknd over 2f out* **10/1**
1420 **11** 3 **Laurel Dawn**[17] [1762] 8-9-12 47 (b) JimmyQuinn 3 31
(C N Kellett) *t.k.h in mid-div: bhd fnl 2f* **20/1**
160 **12** 3/4 **Magical Mimi**[31] [1397] 5-9-7 46 (t) DaneO'Neill 12 24
(K G Wingrove) *s.v.s: a in rr* **20/1**
2200 **13** 10 **Song Huntress**[16] [1771] 3-8-1 50 (p) MarkCoumbe(7) 1 —
(D G Bridgwater) *mid-div whn hmpd on ins and lost pl 4f out: sn bhd* **20/1**

1m 15.08s (-0.73) **Going Correction** -0.125s/f (Stan)
WFA 3 from 4yo+ 8lb **13** Ran SP% **134.3**
Speed ratings (Par 101):99,97,95,93,93 92,90,89,86,84 80,79,66
CSF £32.90 TOTE £6.10: £2.30, £1.80, £8.60; EX 35.20 Trifecta £252.10 Pool: £482.94 - 1.36 winning units.There was no bid for the winner. Desert Opal was claimed by Andrew Page for £6,000. Ockums Razor was claimed by Chris Dwyer for £6,000.
Owner Gary Flitcroft **Bred** Airlie Stud **Trained** Melsonby, N Yorks

FOCUS
This turned out to be quite a competitive seller with the first two setting a decent level.
Mirasol Princess Official explanation: jockey said mare suffered interference around 4f out
Song Huntress Official explanation: jockey said filly suffered interference around 4f out

2209 WBX.COM WORLD BET EXCHANGE H'CAP 1m 4f 50y(P)
3:45 (3:45) (Class 5) (0-70,70) 3-Y-O **£3,886** (£1,156; £577; £288) **Stalls** Low

Form RPR
4561 **1** **Spring Dream (IRE)**[32] [1350] 3-9-6 **69** SamHitchcott 11 77
(M R Channon) *s.i.s: rdn over 5f out: hdwy over 2f out: led over 1f out: r.o* **20/1**
5501 **2** 1 1/4 **Warsaw Pact (IRE)**[3] [2102] 3-9-3 **66** 6ex SebSanders 2 72
(Sir Mark Prescott) *hld up in tch: rdn over 3f out: ev ch over 1f out: nt qckn ins fnl f* **2/5**[1]
0355 **3** 2 1/2 **Archimboldo (USA)**[30] [1403] 3-9-7 **70** DaneO'Neill 7 72
(T Wall) *hld up and bhd: hdwy over 4f out: rdn and ev ch over 1f out: one pce* **25/1**
2164 **4** 1 **Dark Planet**[10] [1925] 3-8-12 **64** SaleemGolam(3) 8 64
(C E Brittain) *hld up in tch: led over 2f out: rdn and hdd over 1f out: no ex* **12/1**
000 **5** 3 1/2 **Valerie**[30] [1417] 3-9-0 **63** JimmyQuinn 5 58
(L M Cumani) *hld up towards rr: hdwy whn nt clr run and swtchd lft over 1f out: nvr trbld ldrs* **14/1**
0454 **6** 1/2 **Pukka Tique**[34] [1286] 3-8-11 **67** RussellKennemore(7) 1 61
(R Hollinshead) *led: rdn and hdd over 2f out: wknd 1f out* **16/1**
5206 **7** 1 1/4 **Blanc Visage**[41] [1153] 3-9-2 **65** IanMongan 12 57
(Mrs H Sweeting) *stdd s: hld up and bhd: nvr nr ldrs* **33/1**
4635 **8** 1 3/4 **Special Moment (IRE)**[30] [1424] 3-9-3 **66** (b[1]) DarryllHolland 10 55
(B W Hills) *t.k.h: sn chsng ldr: led 5f out: rdn and hdd over 2f out: wknd wl over 1f out* **14/1**
6601 **9** nk **Swayze (IRE)**[18] [1732] 3-9-5 **68** EddieAhern 9 57
(N P Littmoden) *hld up and bhd: hdwy 6f out: rdn over 4f out: wknd 2f out* **9/1**[3]
10 **10** 18 **Marmota (IRE)**[39] [1182] 3-9-4 **67** StanleyChin 6 27
(M Johnston) *hld up in tch: rdn 6f out: sn lost pl* **8/1**[2]
4500 **11** 1 **Russian Mist (IRE)**[23] [1599] 3-9-4 **67** ShaneKelly 3 25
(M J Wallace) *prom: rdn 5f out: wknd over 2f out* **16/1**
5250 **12** 4 **Reveur**[13] [1851] 3-9-3 **66** AdrianMcCarthy 4 18
(M Mullineaux) *s.i.s: a bhd* **25/1**

2m 41.81s (-0.61) **Going Correction** -0.125s/f (Stan) **12** Ran SP% **140.7**
Speed ratings (Par 99):97,96,94,93,91 91,90,89,88,76 76,73
CSF £32.57 CT £338.33 TOTE £20.20: £6.50, £1.30, £6.10; EX 39.50 Trifecta £285.20 Part won. Pool: £401.81 - 0.68 winning units..
Owner W H Ponsonby **Bred** R N Auld **Trained** West Ilsley, Berks

FOCUS
There were several unexposed sorts in this handicap but the form is rated at face value and looks sound, rated through the third, fourth and fifth.
Russian Mist(IRE) Official explanation: jockey said gelding had no more to give

2210 WORLD BET EXCHANGE WBX.COM H'CAP 1m 141y(P)
4:25 (4:26) (Class 6) (0-60,60) 3-Y-O **£2,730** (£806; £403) **Stalls** Low

Form RPR
0055 **1** **They All Laughed**[21] [1652] 3-8-13 **55** RobertMiles(3) 5 62
(P W Hiatt) *broke wl: stdd and lost pl after 1f: hdwy on outside 2f out: rdn to ld 1f out: sn hung lft: r.o wl* **14/1**
6500 **2** 3 1/2 **Almowj**[22] [1616] 3-8-9 **55** WilliamCarson(7) 11 55
(C E Brittain) *hld up in tch: lost pl over 3f out: sme hdwy 2f out: swtchd rt over 1f out: r.o ins fnl f: tk 2nd nr fin* **10/1**
0200 **3** 1/2 **Kissi Kissi**[21] [1649] 3-8-13 **55** BenSwarbrick(3) 3 54
(M J Attwater) *hld up and bhd: hdwy over 3f out: rdn over 2f out: one pce fnl f* **20/1**
5504 **4** 1 3/4 **Captain Bolsh**[29] [1433] 3-9-4 **57** (v[1]) JimmyQuinn 10 52
(J Pearce) *hld up towards rr: hdwy over 3f out: rdn over 2f out: swtchd rt ins fnl f: one pce* **10/3**[1]
0006 **5** nk **Dark Moon**[32] [1352] 3-9-3 **56** FergusSweeney 12 51
(A M Balding) *chsd ldr: rdn and ev ch 2f out: wknd ins fnl f* **10/1**
0000 **6** 3/4 **Sunny Parkes**[242] [5659] 3-9-2 **55** AdrianMcCarthy 8 48
(M Mullineaux) *prom: lost pl over 3f out: n.d after* **25/1**
040 **7** nk **Never Say Deya**[255] [5391] 3-9-5 **58** SamHitchcott 13 50
(M R Channon) *hld up: hdwy over 4f out: rdn and ev ch over 2f out: wknd over 1f out* **14/1**
2650 **8** hd **Halfwaytoparadise**[29] [1431] 3-9-7 **60** JamieMackay 4 52
(M L W Bell) *led: rdn over 2f out: hdd 1f out: wknd* **9/1**
0053 **9** 1 1/4 **Starboard Light**[18] [1747] 3-9-3 **56** EddieAhern 2 45
(R M Beckett) *hld up in tch: rdn and wknd over 2f out* **5/1**[3]
0000 **10** 1 1/2 **Mamichor**[37] [1241] 3-9-7 **60** IanMongan 6 46
(J R Boyle) *s.i.s: hld up and bhd: hdwy over 5f out: rdn and ev ch over 2f out: wknd over 1f out* **16/1**
0622 **11** 1 1/4 **Royal Embrace**[112] [364] 3-9-5 **58** (v) DaneO'Neill 1 42
(D Shaw) *a bhd* **9/2**[2]
0602 **12** 42 **Hand Of Destiny (USA)**[109] [406] 3-9-5 **58** (t) DarryllHolland 7 —
(N P Littmoden) *prom: rdn 3f out: sn wknd: virtually p.u fnl f* **5/1**[3]

1m 51.59s (-0.17) **Going Correction** -0.125s/f (Stan) **12** Ran SP% **130.6**
Speed ratings (Par 97):95,91,91,89,89 88,88,88,87,86 84,47
CSF £161.56 CT £2875.93 TOTE £18.00: £3.80, £4.40, £6.70; EX 122.00 TRIFECTA Not won..
Owner Clive Roberts **Bred** T G And B B Mills **Trained** Hook Norton, Oxon

FOCUS
A weak handicap rated around the first three to recent form.
They All Laughed Official explanation: trainer said, regarding the improved form shown, the gelding had failed to stay 1m 2f on its previous start and had benefited from today's drop in trip
Hand Of Destiny(USA) Official explanation: trainer said gelding was never travelling

2211 TIPPERS BUILDING MATERIALS H'CAP 7f 32y(P)
5:00 (5:02) (Class 6) (0-60,60) 4-Y-O+ **£2,730** (£806; £403) **Stalls** High

Form RPR
0000 **1** **African Gift**[30] [1413] 4-9-7 **60** EddieAhern 8 73
(J G Given) *hld up in tch: rdn to ld jst over 1f out: edgd lft ins fnl f: drvn out* **7/1**
0320 **2** 1 **Taranaki**[20] [1673] 8-9-5 **58** DarryllHolland 12 68
(P D Cundell) *hld up in mid-div: rdn over 2f out: hdwy wl over 1f out: kpt on ins fnl f* **5/2**[1]
5203 **3** 2 **Joshua's Gold (IRE)**[11] [1885] 5-9-0 **56** (v) DanielTudhope(3) 3 61
(D Carroll) *a.p: rdn to ld over 2f out: hdd jst over 1f out: no ex* **7/2**[2]
3014 **4** 2 1/2 **Iced Diamond (IRE)**[2] [2135] 7-9-7 **60** ShaneKelly 9 58
(W M Brisbourne) *s.i.s: sn swtchd lft: rdn over 2f out: hdwy over 1f out: nvr nr to chal* **4/1**[3]
5000 **5** shd **Burhaan (IRE)**[29] [1432] 4-9-4 **60** (t) AmirQuinn(3) 7 58
(J R Boyle) *hld up and bhd: rdn over 2f out: hdwy over 1f out: nvr trbld ldrs* **16/1**
3000 **6** 2 1/2 **Second Reef**[6] [2025] 4-9-3 **59** (b[1]) JasonEdmunds(3) 4 51
(E J Alston) *t.k.h: prom: rdn over 2f out: wknd wl over 1f out* **20/1**
1500 **7** nk **Scuba (IRE)**[20] [1673] 4-9-7 **60** (v) IanMongan 1 51
(H Morrison) *led: rdn and hdd over 2f out: wknd 1f out* **5/1**
0050 **8** nk **Out For A Stroll**[7] [1993] 7-9-7 **60** J-PGuillambert 5 50
(S C Williams) *bhd: c wd ent st: n.d* **10/1**
1300 **9** 5 **Distant Country (USA)**[20] [1665] 7-9-7 **60** (p) JimmyQuinn 11 37
(B D Leavy) *a bhd* **16/1**
3200 **10** 3 **Yorkie**[4] [2074] 7-9-5 **58** DeanMcKeown 6 27
(J Pearce) *bhd fnl 3f* **13/2**
2010 **11** 3 **Flying Edge (IRE)**[15] [1795] 6-9-6 **59** SamHitchcott 2 20
(E J Alston) *prom: rdn 4f out: wknd over 2f out* **8/1**

1m 29.46s (-0.94) **Going Correction** -0.125s/f (Stan) **11** Ran SP% **150.0**
Speed ratings (Par 101):100,98,96,93,93 90,90,90,84,80 77
CSF £32.16 CT £84.60 TOTE £12.60: £5.10, £1.10, £1.90; EX 47.70 Trifecta £531.00 Part won. Pool: £747.91 - 0.74 winning units. Place 6 £1,414.81, Place 5 £463.71.
Owner Mr & Mrs G Middlebrook **Bred** G And Mrs Middlebrook **Trained** Willoughton, Lincs

FOCUS
This low-grade contest was run at a fair pace and the form looks reliable rated around the third.
Scuba(IRE) Official explanation: jockey said gelding hung left throughout
T/Plt: £6,249.30 to a £1 stake. Pool: £33,386.85. 3.90 winning tickets. T/Qpdt: £104.30 to a £1 stake. Pool: £3,385.80. 24.00 winning tickets. KH

2212 - 2216a (Foreign Racing) - See Raceform Interactive

2043 SAN SIRO (R-H)
Friday, June 2

OFFICIAL GOING: Good to firm

2217a PREMIO EMILIO TURATI (GROUP 2) 1m
3:35 (3:48) 3-Y-O+ **£49,901** (£23,796; £13,519; £6,790)

RPR
1 **Ramonti (FR)**[20] 4-9-6 EBotti 6 114
(A Botti, Italy) *led after 2f, clear well over 1f out, ran on well* **30/100**[1]
2 2 1/2 **Ryono (USA)**[32] [1371] 7-9-6 TCastanheira 8 109
(S Smrczek, Germany) *hld up, 6th str, gd hdwy on outside fr wl over 1f out, tk 2nd ins fnl f, nvr reached wnr* **162/10**
3 snk **Bening (FR)**[19] [1712] 6-9-6 MDemuro 3 109
(O Pessi, Italy) *held up, 7th straight, headway on outside from well over 1f out, disp 2nd ins fnl f, stayed on same pace* **63/10**[3]
4 3 1/2 **Nordhal**[208] [6276] 7-9-6 DVargiu 1 102
(B Grizzetti, Italy) *always prominent, 2nd straight, weakening from over 1f out, lost 2nd inside final furlong* **20/1**
5 2 1/2 **Ceprin (IRE)**[208] [6276] 5-9-6 IRossi 2 97
(A & G Botti, Italy) *led 2f, 4th on inside straight, one pace final 2f* **30/100**[1]
6 nk **Igor Protti**[213] 4-9-6 EPedroza 4 96
(A Wohler, Germany) *always towards rear, not clear run when trying to make headway over 2f out, not recover* **113/10**
7 2 1/2 **Proudance (GER)**[85] [625] 4-9-6 WMongil 7 91
(R Suerland, Germany) *5th straight, headway to go 3rd over 2f out, soon ridden, weakened 1 1/2f out* **9/2**[2]
8 5 **Kill Cat (IRE)**[98] [508] 5-9-6 CColombi 5 81
(A Peraino, Italy) *prominent, 3rd straight, soon beaten* **37/1**

1m 38.7s **8** Ran SP% **207.1**
(Including 1 Euro stake): WIN 1.30 (coupled with Ceprin); PL 1.04, 1.60, 1.31; DF 8.94.
Owner Scuderia Antezzate **Bred** Scuderia Siba **Trained** Italy

2094 CHEPSTOW (L-H)
Saturday, June 3

OFFICIAL GOING: Good to firm
Wind: Virtually nil

2218 LETHEBY & CHRISTOPHER MAIDEN AUCTION STKS 6f 16y
6:40 (6:41) (Class 5) 2-Y-O **£3,368** (£1,002; £500; £250) **Stalls** High

Form RPR
5 **1** **Rainbow Mirage (IRE)**[24] [1595] 2-8-9 RobbieFitzpatrick 1 71
(E S McMahon) *trckd ldrs: hdwy on outer 2f out: rdn to ld ins last: kpt on* **6/1**[3]
2 nk **Southandwest (IRE)** 2-8-10 LPKeniry 8 71
(J S Moore) *chsd ldrs: hdwy over 2f out: rdn to ld and hung lft over 1f out: hdd and nt qckn ins last* **8/1**
3 1 1/2 **Simba Sun (IRE)** 2-8-9 AdamKirby(3) 7 69
(R M Beckett) *towards rr: hdwy over 2f out: rdn and kpt on ins last: nrst fin* **16/1**
4 nk **Slipasearcher (IRE)** 2-8-3 EdwardCreighton(3) 2 62
(P D Evans) *towards rr: hdwy 2f out: sn rdn and kpt on: nrst fin* **20/1**
0 **5** 1 **Cashcade (IRE)**[17] [1770] 2-8-7 NeilChalmers(3) 4 63
(A M Balding) *in tch: hdwy to chse ldrs over 2f out: sn rdn and one pce ent last* **40/1**
42 **6** 1/2 **Callisto Moon**[11] [1912] 2-8-9 ChrisCatlin 11 60
(R Curtis) *chsd ldrs on outer: rdn along over 2f out: kpt on same pce* **15/2**

7 1/2 **Disco Dan** 2-8-5 .... LiamJones(7) 9 62
(D M Simcock) *cl up: led wl over 2f out: sn rdn: drvn: hung lft and hdd over 1f out: wknd qckly* **12/1**
663 **8** 2 **Wrecking Crew (IRE)**[22] 1639 2-8-12 .... SteveDrowne 12 56
(B R Millman) *sn pushed along: a towards rr* **4/1**[2]
025 **9** 3 1/2 **Benllech**[16] 1796 2-8-11 .... FrankieMcDonald 6 44
(S Kirk) *led: rdn along 1/2-way: sn hdd and wkng whn sltly hmpd over 1f out* **7/4**[1]
10 10 **Oedipuss (IRE)** 2-8-6 .... EmmettStack(5) 5 14
(K J Burke) *prom: rdn along appr 1/2-way: sn lost pl and bhd fnl 2f* **33/1**
11 32 **Solis Obitus** 2-8-9 .... FrancisNorton 10 —
(B R Millman) *sn outpcd and a bhd* **40/1**

1m 12.21s (-0.19) **Going Correction** -0.075s/f (Good) **11** Ran SP% **119.7**
Speed ratings (Par 93):98,97,95,95,93 93,92,89,85,71 29
CSF £52.19 TOTE £8.40: £2.00, £4.70, £3.90; EX 112.50.
Owner R L Bedding **Bred** Neville O'Byrne And Roderick Ryan **Trained** Hopwas, Staffs

FOCUS
A fair winning time for a race like this, the form is difficult to assess with the winner the best guide for now.

NOTEBOOK
Rainbow Mirage(IRE) obviously benefited for his Ripon debut last time. His future lies in nurseries and he will not mind a step up in trip. (op 9-2)
Southandwest(IRE), an 8,000euros colt, did best of the newcomers and, although he is bred to be speedy, there must be a good chance he will get another furlong on this evidence. (op 16-1)
Simba Sun(IRE), a 21,000euros half-brother to the winning juvenile Damjanich, showed some promise on this debut and should come on for the run. (op 14-1)
Slipasearcher(IRE), a 16,000euros filly out of a dual-winner over the minimum trip as a juvenile, also showed some promise on this debut and should improve. (op 16-1)
Cashcade(IRE) again hinted at a modicum of ability and may be found opportunities in modest nurseries.
Callisto Moon again hinted at ability and may also be the type to find an opportunity in a nursery when they start next month. (op 13-2 tchd 6-1)
Benllech dropped away rather tamely and has questions to answer now. Official explanation: jockey said colt had breathing problem (op 15-8 tchd 2-1)
Solis Obitus Official explanation: jockey said filly lost her action

2219 LADBROKES SUPPORTS TY HAFEN H'CAP 2m 2f
7:10 (7:13) (Class 5) (0-75,74) 4-Y-0+ **£3,562** (£1,059; £529; £264) **Stalls** Low

Form RPR
6100 **1** **Our Monogram**[33] 1339 10-9-1 **67** .... AdamKirby(3) 6 74
(R M Beckett) *cl up: led after 3f: rdn along over 4f out: hdd over 2f out: sn drvn: rallied to ld again ins last: hld on gamely* **12/1**
0530 **2** *shd* **High Point (IRE)**[24] 1584 8-9-4 **72** .... RobynBrisland(5) 1 79
(G P Enright) *hld up and bhd: stdy hdwy over 4f out: rdn to chse ldng pair wl over 1f out: drvn ins last: styd on: jst failed* **14/1**
0455 **3** 1 **Arch Folly**[21] 1660 4-8-3 **57** oh4 ow2 .... NeilChalmers(3) 7 63
(J G Portman) *hld up in rr: hdwy over 5f out: str run on outer to ld over 2f out: sn rdn and edge lft: drvn and hdd ins last:no ex* **20/1**
3031 **4** 7 **Madiba**[18] 1758 7-8-6 **55** oh4 .... FrancisNorton 10 53
(P Howling) *hld up in midfield: hdwy 4f out: rdn to chse ldrs over 2f out: kpt on same pce* **10/1**
6326 **5** 1 1/4 **Theatre (USA)**[10] 1931 7-9-8 **71** .... SteveDrowne 14 67
(Jamie Poulton) *towards rr: hdwy on outer 1/2-way: effrt and in tch over 3f out: sn rdn and no imp* **6/1**[3]
-006 **6** 1/2 **Fiddlers Ford (IRE)**[16] 1808 5-8-13 **62** .... ChrisCatlin 11 58
(T Keddy) *prom: effrt to chse ldr 5f out: rdn along over 3 out: grad wknd* **11/2**[2]
4600 **7** 1 3/4 **Shingle Street (IRE)**[21] 1690 4-8-9 **60** .... (b) VinceSlattery 12 53
(Miss Venetia Williams) *chsd ldrs: rdn along on inner over 3f out: sn wknd* **25/1**
333/ **8** 4 **Cannon Fire (FR)**[23] 5-9-9 **72** .... DarryllHolland 13 61
(Evan Williams) *hld up in tch: hdwy over 4f out: swtchd ins and rdn over 3f out: sn btn* **11/4**[1]
006/ **9** 1 **Scratch The Dove**[28] 1054 9-7-13 **55** oh16 .... LiamJones(7) 2 42
(A E Price) *hld up: a towards rr* **66/1**
0546 **10** 3/4 **Bobsleigh**[21] 1690 7-8-4 **58** .... EmmettStack(5) 9 45
(H S Howe) *prom: rdn along 5f out: sn wknd* **11/1**
0000 **11** 38 **Cool Bathwick (IRE)**[4] 2099 7-8-3 **55** oh19 .... (b) EdwardCreighton(3) 8 —
(G H Yardley) *a rr* **100/1**
2006 **12** 11 **Moonshine Beach**[216] 6179 8-9-11 **74** .... ShaneKelly 4 2
(P W Hiatt) *led 3f: chsd ldrs tl rdn along over 5f out and sn wknd* **16/1**
0005 **13** 10 **Rule For Ever**[12] 1883 4-8-12 **63** .... (b[1]) RobertWinston 3 —
(M Johnston) *chsd ldrs: rdn along 7f out: sn wknd* **7/1**

3m 59.58s (-1.04) **Going Correction** -0.075s/f (Good)
WFA 4 from 5yo+ 2lb **13** Ran SP% **117.6**
Speed ratings (Par 103):99,98,98,95,94 94,93,92,91,91 74,69,65
CSF £161.41 CT £3305.13 TOTE £10.60: £2.70, £5.30, £7.50; EX 155.30.
Owner The Foxons Fillies Partnership **Bred** Astalon Ltd **Trained** Whitsbury, Hants
■ Stewards' Enquiry : Adam Kirby four-day ban: used whip with excessive frequency (Jun 14-17)

FOCUS
Not a great race by any means and some of them would have struggled with the trip. The proximity of te third limits the form.
Moonshine Beach Official explanation: jockey said gelding was unsuited by good to firm ground

2220 BATH ALES MAIDEN STKS 1m 2f 36y
7:40 (7:49) (Class 5) 3-Y-0+ **£3,368** (£1,002; £500; £250) **Stalls** Low

Form RPR
402 **1** **King Of Argos**[15] 1823 3-8-12 **80** .... SteveDrowne 15 79
(E A L Dunlop) *hld up in tch: smooth hdwy over 3f out: effrt and swtchd rt over 1f out: rdn and qcknd to ld 1f out: comf* **9/4**[2]
02 **2** 1 1/4 **Kerriemuir Lass (IRE)**[42] 1139 3-8-8 ow1 .... DarryllHolland 10 73
(M A Jarvis) *trckd ldrs: pushed along on outer and tk clsr order 4f out: rdn to chal 2f out: drvn and outpcd over 1f out: styd on nr fin* **2/1**[1]
26 **3** 1 1/4 **Mortarboard**[227] 5987 3-8-12 .... RichardMullen 1 74
(E J O'Neill) *prom: led over 6f out: rdn along 3f out: sn hdd: drvn and ev ch wl over 1f out: kpt on u.p ins last* **11/2**[3]
3 **4** 2 1/2 **River City (IRE)**[35] 566 9-9-11 .... VinceSlattery 16 70
(Noel T Chance) *bhd: pushed along 4f out: styd on wl fnl 2f: nrst fin* **15/2**
5 **5** *nk* **Quel Ange (FR)**[5] 2063 4-9-11 .... RichardThomas 6 69
(R J Hodges) *keen: hld up towards rr hdwy on inner 4f out: rdn to chse ldrs 2f out: kpt on same pce appr last* **100/1**
5- **6** 1 1/4 **King Kasyapa (IRE)**[623] 5666 4-9-11 .... RobertWinston 3 67
(P Bowen) *keen: chsd ldng pair: hdwy over 3f out: led over 2f out: sn rdn: drvn and hdd 1f out: wknd* **10/1**
6 **7** 7 **Dreams Jewel**[32] 1006 6-9-4 .... KevinGhunowa(7) 9 53
(C Roberts) *nvr nr ldrs* **33/1**

0-0 **8** 2 **Lake Imperial (IRE)**[8] 1290 5-9-11 .... HayleyTurner 5 49
(Heather Dalton) *a towards rr* **100/1**
6 **9** 3/4 **Secret Moment**[21] 1670 4-9-8 .... AdamKirby(3) 12 48
(C G Cox) *chsd ldrs: rdn along over 5f out: sn wknd* **66/1**
00 **10** *nk* **The Spread**[263] 5195 3-8-7 .... FrancisNorton 2 42
(M Blanshard) *a rr* **40/1**
0 **11** 1 1/2 **Ballymena**[5] 2063 5-8-13 .... TolleyDean(7) 13 40
(R A Harris) *in tch: hdwy on outer to chse ldrs 1/2-way: rdn along 4f out: sn wknd* **100/1**
00 **12** 1/2 **Kentuckian**[15] 1827 4-9-11 .... ShaneKelly 4 44
(P W Hiatt) *chsd ldrs on inner: rdn along 4f out: sn wknd* **100/1**
00 **13** 12 **Moonshine Creek**[15] 1826 4-9-11 .... LPKeniry 8 21
(P W Hiatt) *led 3f: prom tl rdn along over 4f out and sn wknd* **100/1**
14 35 **Elsie Alderman** 4-9-6 .... RobbieFitzpatrick 7 —
(J C Fox) *a rr* **66/1**

2m 9.65s (-0.25) **Going Correction** -0.075s/f (Good)
WFA 3 from 4yo+ 13lb **14** Ran SP% **113.7**
Speed ratings (Par 103):98,97,96,94,93 92,87,85,84,84 83,83,73,45
CSF £6.44 TOTE £2.80: £1.20, £1.50, £1.90; EX 7.70.
Owner P G Goulandris **Bred** Chippenham Lodge Stud Ltd **Trained** Newmarket, Suffolk

FOCUS
With Incidentally a non-runner this maiden appeared at the mercy of the other 80-rated horse in the line up, King Of Argos, and so it proved. The form behind looks mixed.
The Spread Official explanation: jockey said, regarding the apparent tender ride, his orders were to be midfield and make the best of his way home, adding that filly was outpaced early on and stayed on at one pace from 3f out; trainer said filly gets lit up and so he requested she was loaded last, and added she probably need in excess of 10f in future; vet said filly was slightly lame behind

2221 WESTCOUNTRYRACING.COM AFFORDABLE RACING H'CAP 1m 2f 36y
8:10 (8:17) (Class 6) (0-65,65) 4-Y-0+ **£2,914** (£867; £433; £216) **Stalls** Low

Form RPR
3024 **1** **Dove Cottage (IRE)**[38] 1244 4-9-2 **60** .... ChrisCatlin 4 70
(W S Kittow) *cl up: led after 2f: rdn along 3f out: drvn wl over 1f out: styd on strly* **9/2**[2]
2 2 **The Fonze (IRE)**[196] 2324 5-8-3 **47** .... TPO'Shea 12 53
(Eoin Doyle, Ire) *midfield: hdwy 1/2-way: chsd ldrs 3f out: rdn 2f out: kpt on u.p ins last* **9/4**[1]
0522 **3** *shd* **Mossmann Gorge**[4] 2099 4-8-9 **60** .... (b) KevinGhunowa(7) 3 66
(M Wellings) *trckd ldrs: hdwy on inner over 3f out: rdn along over 2f out: drvn wl over 1f out: kpt on* **11/2**[3]
0002 **4** *shd* **Finished Article (IRE)**[35] 1305 9-9-2 **65** .... StephenDonohoe(5) 10 71
(W J Musson) *hld up towards rr: hdwy on outer 3f out: rdn and str run over 1f out: nrst fin* **16/1**
0330 **5** 1/2 **Harare**[11] 1915 5-7-9 **46** .... (b[1]) LiamJones(7) 1 51
(R J Price) *hld up towards rr: gd hdwy on outer over 4f out: rdn to chal over 2f out: ev ch tl drvn and wknd over 1f out* **14/1**
2500 **6** 5 **Damburger Xpress**[24] 1591 4-8-13 **57** .... DarryllHolland 5 52
(D M Simcock) *a chsng ldrs: rdn along wl over 2f out: grad wknd* **8/1**
4255 **7** 3 1/2 **Financial Future**[4] 2099 6-8-5 **56** .... (p) LukeMorris(7) 14 45
(C Roberts) *midfield: hdwy to chse ldrs over 3f out: sn rdn and wknd 2f out* **12/1**
050 **8** *nk* **Kathleen Kennet**[16] 1797 6-9-5 **63** .... FergusSweeney 15 51
(Mrs H Sweeting) *a rr* **20/1**
3205 **9** *hd* **Majehar**[29] 1461 4-8-2 **46** oh1 .... FrancisNorton 13 34
(A G Newcombe) *a rr* **12/1**
1400 **10** *shd* **Summer Bounty**[19] 1729 10-9-3 **61** .... PaulFitzsimons 11 49
(F Jordan) *v.s.a: a bhd* **16/1**
0400 **11** 1 3/4 **Comeintothespace (IRE)**[25] 1560 4-8-12 **56** .... RobertWinston 2 40
(Miss Victoria Roberts) *keen: chsd ldrs: rdn along over 4f out: sn wknd* **33/1**
0000 **12** 9 **Sound That Alarm**[12] 1882 4-8-3 **47** .... RichardMullen 9 14
(P D Evans) *chsd ldrs: rdn along over 4f out: sn wknd* **40/1**
0000 **13** 2 1/2 **Arpetcheeo (USA)**[14] 1852 4-8-7 **51** ow1 .... ShaneKelly 8 13
(D Carroll) *prom: rdn along 4f out: sn drvn an d wknd 3f out* **100/1**
2230 **14** 3/4 **Optimum (IRE)**[39] 1222 4-9-6 **64** .... RobbieFitzpatrick 6 25
(J T Stimpson) *chsd ldrs: rdn along over 4f out: sn wknd* **40/1**
4-00 **15** 60 **Shibumi**[250] 5506 5-8-4 **48** .... HayleyTurner 16 —
(P A Trueman) *plld hrd: cl up tl wknd over 4f out* **100/1**

2m 9.79s (-0.11) **Going Correction** -0.075s/f (Good) **15** Ran SP% **123.8**
Speed ratings (Par 101):97,95,95,95,94 90,88,87,87,87 86,78,76,76,28
CSF £14.57 CT £59.53 TOTE £4.60: £1.50, £1.80, £2.00; EX 24.30.
Owner Reg Gifford **Bred** D R Tucker **Trained** Blackborough, Devon

FOCUS
A run-of-the-mill handicap and the winning time was fractionally slower than the preceding maiden. The form looks reasonable, rated through the third.
Kathleen Kennet Official explanation: jockey said mare was denied clear run
Summer Bounty Official explanation: jockey said gelding missed break and hung left-handed from 3f out
Arpetcheeo(USA) Official explanation: jockey said colt was unsuited by good to firm ground, and lost action in last 100yds
Shibumi Official explanation: jockey said mare bolted to post

2222 AVONBRIDGE AT WHITSBURY STUD H'CAP 5f 16y
8:40 (8:50) (Class 5) (0-75,77) 3-Y-0 **£3,886** (£1,156; £577; £288) **Stalls** High

Form RPR
3061 **1** **Don't Tell Sue**[3] 2134 3-9-11 **77** 6ex .... RyanMoore 1 89
(B W Hills) *mde all: rdn and qcknd wl over 1f out: kpt on* **5/6**[1]
3162 **2** 2 1/2 **Shes Minnie**[12] 1900 3-9-7 **73** .... RobertWinston 5 76
(J G M O'Shea) *chsd wnr: rdn 2f out: drvn and one pce ent last* **10/3**[2]
2100 **3** 3 **Egyptian Lord**[26] 1529 3-8-13 **65** .... (b) RobbieFitzpatrick 2 57
(Peter Grayson) *dwlt: hdwy on outer 1/2-way: rdn to chse ldng pair over 1f out: sn no imp* **12/1**
5364 **4** 1 3/4 **Arzaag**[24] 1589 3-9-4 **70** .... DarryllHolland 4 56
(D M Simcock) *chsd ldrs: rdn 2f out: sn one pce* **14/1**
2400 **5** 1 1/4 **Gwilym (GER)**[21] 1679 3-9-5 **71** .... SteveDrowne 8 52
(D Haydn Jones) *chsd ldrs: pushed along 1/2-way: sn wknd* **12/1**
1456 **6** *shd* **Bathwick Emma (IRE)**[25] 1569 3-9-6 **72** .... RichardMullen 7 53
(P D Evans) *chsd ldrs: rdn 1/2-way: sn wknd* **14/1**
002 **7** 2 **Hoh Wotanite**[112] 373 3-8-10 **62** .... ChrisCatlin 3 36
(A M Balding) *in tch: rdn along after 2f: outpcd and bhd fr 1/2-way* **11/1**[3]
4000 **8** 15 **Legal Call**[96] 533 3-7-10 **55** .... (p) LiamJones(7) 9 —
(M Appleby) *sn outpcd: a bhd* **40/1**

58.66 secs (-0.94) **Going Correction** -0.075s/f (Good) **8** Ran SP% **117.1**
Speed ratings (Par 99):104,100,95,92,90 90,87,63
CSF £3.84 CT £18.78 TOTE £1.90: £1.10, £1.20, £3.00; EX 3.80.

Owner Mr & Mrs Peter Orton **Bred** Raffin Bloodstock **Trained** Lambourn, Berks
FOCUS
A very one-sided affair for this sprint handicap and the winner looks progressive.
Bathwick Emma(IRE) Official explanation: jockey said filly was unsuited by good to firm ground

2223 LETHEBY & CHRISTOPHER H'CAP — 7f 16y

9:10 (9:20) (Class 5) (0-70,70) 4-Y-0+ — **£3,562** (£1,059; £529; £264) **Stalls** High

Form — RPR

2100 **1** **Top Mark**[43] [1112] 4-9-7 **70** ... SteveDrowne 12 — 81
(H Morrison) *trckd ldrs: hdwy to ld over 2f out: rdn wl over 1f out: drvn ins last: hld on wl* **4/1**[1]

4004 **2** ½ **Dvinsky (USA)**[7] [2020] 5-9-1 **64** ... RobbieFitzpatrick 16 — 74
(D Carroll) *in tch: hdwy 3f out: rdn to chal wl ov er 1f out: drvn and ev ch ins last: edgd lft and no ex towards fin* **13/2**[2]

0000 **3** 1 **Danielle's Lad**[36] [1273] 10-8-13 **62** ... FrancisFerris 8 — 69
(B Palling) *led: rdn along and hdd over 2f out: drvn over 1f out: kpt on wl u.p ins last* **14/1**

0302 **4** hd **Vienna's Boy (IRE)**[32] [1388] 5-8-13 **67** ... StephenDonohoe(5) 7 — 73
(W J Musson) *hld up: gd hdwy on wd outside 2f out: rdn to chse ldrs and edgd rt over 1f out: kpt on ins last* **8/1**

2535 **5** shd **Beneking**[4] [2095] 6-8-3 **55** ... (p) EdwardCreighton(3) 9 — 61
(D Burchell) *trckd ldrs: hdwy 3f out: rdn wl over 1f out: n.m.r ent last: kpt on* **14/1**

0004 **6** 1¼ **Measured Response**[25] [1568] 4-8-12 **61** ... RobertWinston 11 — 64
(J G M O'Shea) *hld up: gd hdwy over 2f out: rdn over 1f out: drvn and kpt on ins last* **12/1**

3506 **7** ¾ **What-A-Dancer (IRE)**[11] [1923] 9-9-4 **67** ... (p) DarryllHolland 10 — 68
(D J S Ffrench Davis) *towards rr: hdwy over 2f out: sn rdn: kpt on ins last: nt rch ldrs* **12/1**

0030 **8** ½ **Will The Till**[12] [1882] 4-8-6 **58** ow2 ... AdamKirby(3) 4 — 58
(J M Bradley) *in tch: rdn along over 2f out: grad wknd* **9/1**

0436 **9** 1¾ **Desert Lover (IRE)**[17] [1773] 4-8-11 **60** ... ShaneKelly 13 — 55
(R J Price) *towards rr: hdwy 2f out: sn rdn and no imp appr last* **7/1**[3]

-000 **10** ¾ **Willofcourse**[21] [1689] 5-8-10 **59** ... FergusSweeney 5 — 52
(H Candy) *cl up: rdn wl over 2f out: wkng whn n.m.r over 1f out* **28/1**

3000 **11** 2 **Pink Bay**[16] [1802] 4-8-4 **60** ... (v[1]) TolleyDean(7) 1 — 48
(W S Kittow) *in tch on outer: rdn along over 2f out: sn wknd* **20/1**

0100 **12** 3½ **Hawridge Sensation**[263] [5201] 4-8-9 **58** ... ChrisCatlin 14 — 37
(W S Kittow) *chsd ldrs: rdn along 3f out: sn wknd* **33/1**

3634 **13** ¾ **Mistral Sky**[42] [1151] 7-9-3 **66** ... (p) FrancisNorton 15 — 43
(Stef Liddiard) *a towards rr* **9/1**

1560 **14** shd **Sweetest Revenge (IRE)**[68] [761] 5-9-6 **69** ... HayleyTurner 6 — 46
(M D I Usher) *cl up: rdn along 3f out: sn wknd* **28/1**

0000 **15** 4 **Grand Place**[3] [2135] 4-8-8 **57** ... (t) RyanMoore 2 — 23
(R Hannon) *midfield: pushed along over 3f out: sn wknd* **20/1**

040- **16** 25 **Miss Sudbrook (IRE)**[609] [5953] 4-8-6 **55** ... RichardThomas 3 — —
(A W Carroll) *a outpcd and bhd* **33/1**

1m 22.24s (-1.06) **Going Correction** -0.075s/f (Good) **16** Ran SP% **128.0**
Speed ratings (Par 103):103,102,101,101,100 99,98,98,96,95 92,88,88,87,83 54
CSF £27.10 TOTE £4.30: £2.20, £2.70, £2.70, £2.80; EX 42.60 Place 6 £151.16, Place 5 £28.07.
Owner A J Richards **Bred** Ewar Stud Farms **Trained** East Ilsley, Berks
FOCUS
The vast majority of these had a very exposed look about them in an average 0-70 handicap. The form appears sound.
Vienna's Boy(IRE) Official explanation: jockey said gelding missed break
Desert Lover(IRE) Official explanation: jockey said gelding was unsuited by good to firm ground
Grand Place Official explanation: jockey said gelding lost its action
T/Plt: £104.00 to a £1 stake. Pool: £50,947.50. 357.60 winning tickets. T/Qpdt: £2.10 to a £1 stake. Pool: £4,356.60. 1,481.40 winning tickets. DO

2199 EPSOM (L-H)

Saturday, June 3

OFFICIAL GOING: Good to firm
Wind: Almost nil Weather: Sunny and very warm

2224 VODAFONE LIVE! STKS (HERITAGE H'CAP) — 1m 2f 18y

2:00 (2:03) (Class 2) (0-105,94) 3-Y-0 — **£46,740** (£13,995; £6,997; £3,502; £1,747; £877) **Stalls** Low

Form — RPR

3211 **1** **Stage Gift (IRE)**[23] [1615] 3-9-7 **94** ... RobertWinston 8 — 111+
(Sir Michael Stoute) *lw: hld up: 9th st: smooth prog to ld over 2f out: sn clr: pushed out: unchal* **5/2**[1]

1100 **2** 1¼ **Military Cross**[27] [1505] 3-9-3 **90** ... KFallon 11 — 102+
(W J Haggas) *plld hrd: hld up wl in rr: 14th st: prog on outer over 2f out: hung lft and bmpd rival over 1f out: chsd wnr: no imp* **10/1**

0521 **3** ½ **Lake Poet (IRE)**[6] [2046] 3-9-0 **87** 5ex ... KerrinMcEvoy 10 — 95
(C E Brittain) *trckd ldng pair: rdn over 2f out: outpcd whn sltly hmpd over 1f out: styd on ins fnl f* **16/1**

3161 **4** 1¼ **King's Head (IRE)**[36] [1268] 3-9-7 **94** ... PhilipRobinson 7 — 100
(M A Jarvis) *n.m.r over 8f out: settled midfield: 8th st: rdn over 2f out: styd on fr over 1f out: nrst fin* **5/1**[2]

6022 **5** 2½ **Burnbank (IRE)**[38] [1241] 3-8-0 **73** ow1 ... FrancisNorton 2 — 74
(W Jarvis) *prom: 4th st: sn rdn: outpcd over 2f out: kpt on same pce after* **25/1**

0013 **6** shd **Road To Love (IRE)**[225] [6005] 3-8-12 **85** ... KDarley 3 — 86
(M Johnston) *t.k.h: trckd ldr: upsides 3f out: outpcd and btn 2f out* **16/1**

2122 **7** shd **Salute The General**[14] [1841] 3-8-9 **82** ... MartinDwyer 4 — 83+
(W R Muir) *lw: trckd ldrs: 5th st: rdn and outpcd over 2f out: hmpd over 1f out: no ch after* **8/1**[3]

0110 **8** 1 **Gracechurch (IRE)**[17] [1781] 3-8-9 **82** ... ChrisCatlin 9 — 81
(M R Channon) *hld up wl in rr: 13th st: effrt on inner over 2f out: one pce and no prog* **50/1**

124 **9** shd **London Express (IRE)**[28] [1473] 3-9-5 **92** ... StanleyChin 15 — 91
(M Johnston) *chsd ldrs: 7th st: rdn and no prog over 2f out* **33/1**

6026 **10** ¾ **Charlie Tokyo (IRE)**[17] [1781] 3-8-5 **78** ... PaulHanagan 14 — 75+
(R A Fahey) *dwlt: hld up and racd wd: 11th st: effrt over 2f out: outpcd and btn whn bdly hmpd over 1f out* **10/1**

143 **11** ¾ **Merveilles**[23] [1615] 3-8-13 **86** ... JimmyFortune 6 — 82
(J H M Gosden) *hld up wl in rr: 12th st: brief effrt over 2f out: sn wknd* **17/2**

1002 **12** hd **Regal Royale**[28] [1490] 3-9-5 **92** ... MJKinane 13 — 87
(Sir Michael Stoute) *hld up last: plenty to do st: rdn on wd outside over 2f out: no ch* **9/1**

6156 **13** ½ **Punta Galera (IRE)**[9] [1951] 3-9-2 **89** ... RichardHughes 5 — 84
(R Hannon) *lw: settled midfield: 10th st: rdn and struggling wl over 2f out* **25/1**

1053 **14** 5 **Genari**[15] [1813] 3-9-3 **90** ... SteveDrowne 12 — 75
(P F I Cole) *led to over 2f out: wknd rapidly* **66/1**

1020 **15** nk **Nihal (IRE)**[23] [1615] 3-8-12 **85** ... JoeFanning 1 — 69
(M Johnston) *trckd ldrs: 6th st: wknd rapidly over 2f out* **66/1**

2m 6.57s (-2.47) **Going Correction** +0.05s/f (Good) **15** Ran SP% **122.4**
Speed ratings (Par 105):111,110,109,108,106 106,106,105,105,104 104,104,103,99,99
CSF £27.03 CT £343.68 TOTE £3.50: £1.70, £2.50, £4.90; EX 26.20 Trifecta £1484.10 Pool: £2,508.41 - 1.20 winning units.
Owner Ballymacoll Stud **Bred** Ballymacoll Stud Farm Ltd **Trained** Newmarket, Suffolk
FOCUS
A good competitive handicap run at a sound pace and won in emphatic style by the top weight. A race that tends to work out well, and no reason it shouldn't do so again as it's solid form..
NOTEBOOK
Stage Gift(IRE) ◆, a progressive colt who is maturing physically, was all the rage for this competitive handicap, despite have been raised 12lb for his Yarmouth stroll. He cruised to the front halfway up the straight and but for idling would have scored by a much bigger margin. He now looks on the verge of Pattern class and it would be no surprise to see him take his chance in the Hampton Court Stakes at Royal Ascot. (op 3-1)
Military Cross, stepping up in trip and back on a sound surface, ran much better despite being keen early. He came through in pursuit of the winner halfway up the straight, but in doing so hung markedly down the camber and caused major interference to Charlie Tokyo and hampered others. He is flattered by his proximity to the winner, but looks capable of winning similar races on fast ground this summer. (op 12-1)
Lake Poet(IRE), who had chased home the winner at Yarmouth, was carrying a penalty for his subsequent success at Newmarket but was still 4lb better off with that rival. He finished exactly the same distance behind as at Yarmouth but, despite the fact that he again performed with credit, the margin does not reflect the winner's superiority. (op 14-1)
King's Head(IRE), stepping up in trip after dead-heating in the Esher Cup, kept on in the closing stages without offering a threat to the winner. This was his first encounter with fast ground and he may be more effective on a stiffer track.
Burnbank(IRE), a maiden stepping up in trip and grade, had previous experience of this tricky course and ran as well as could have been expected. He is going the right way and should be able to get off the mark before too long on this evidence.
Road To Love(IRE), making his seasonal debut, ran well on ground faster than that which he showed his best form on as a juvenile. He should come on for the run and his style of racing suggests the drop back to a mile would not be a problem. (op 25-1)
Salute The General, who has been running well in similar races this season, was always close enough if good enough but appeared to be feeling the pinch when hampered as the runner-up drifted left entering the final furlong. He is a consistent sort and, although not especially well handicapped, should fare better back on a more conventional track.
Charlie Tokyo(IRE) ◆, who missed the break from his wide draw, settled in the slipstream of the eventual winner. Although unable to keep tabs on that rival, he was staying on down the outside and looked likely to finish in the frame when Military Cross came up his outside and cut across him, completely ending what chance he had. If he is dropped a few pounds he could be interesting in a slightly lower grade. (op 8-1)
Merveilles, who finished third to the winner at Yarmouth, could not build on that promise and never got into contention from off the pace. However, the combination of the unorthadox track and fast ground was probably against him, and he can be given another chance, especially on an easier surface. (op 8-1 tchd 9-1)
Regal Royale is a stable-mate of the winner and in the same ownership as the second. He was always one of the backmarkers but is worth another chance. (op 8-1 tchd 10-1)

2225 VODAFONE WOODCOTE STKS (LISTED RACE) — 6f

2:30 (2:33) (Class 1) 2-Y-0 — **£17,034** (£6,456; £3,231; £1,611; £807; £405) **Stalls** High

Form — RPR

1 **1** **Sadeek**[16] [1807] 2-9-0 ... NCallan 1 — 89+
(K A Ryan) *lw: stmbld s: trckd ldr: pushed into narrow ld 2f out: rdn to assert ins fnl f* **6/4**[1]

021 **2** ¾ **Going Straight (IRE)**[11] [1922] 2-8-9 ... RyanMoore 4 — 82
(I A Wood) *led: drvn and narrowly hdd 2f out: pressed wnr tl no ex ins fnl f* **20/1**

12 **3** nk **Always Fruitful**[8] [1998] 2-9-0 ... KDarley 2 — 86+
(M Johnston) *s.s: off the pce in last: rdn 1/2-way: no prog tl r.o strly fnl f: gaining fast at fin* **7/1**[3]

11 **4** 2 **Mubaashir (IRE)**[24] [1582] 2-9-5 ... LDettori 5 — 85
(E A L Dunlop) *lw: trckd ldng pair: rdn to chal 2f out: nt handling trck and nt qckn over 1f out: btn after* **7/4**[2]

40 **5** 1¾ **Loves Bidding**[17] [1770] 2-9-0 ... SteveDrowne 6 — 75
(R Ingram) *t.k.h: hld up in 5th: effrt over 2f out: no prog and btn over 1f out* **33/1**

1242 **6** 5 **Lord Charles**[12] [1897] 2-9-0 ... JohnEgan 3 — 60
(W G M Turner) *chsd ldng trio: rdn over 2f out: wknd wl over 1f out* **8/1**

1m 10.49s (-0.14) **Going Correction** -0.05s/f (Good) **6** Ran SP% **107.7**
Speed ratings (Par 101):98,97,96,93,91 84
CSF £27.07 TOTE £2.40: £1.50, £3.60; EX 35.10.
Owner John Browne **Bred** T K And Mrs P A Knox **Trained** Hambleton, N Yorks
FOCUS
Almost certainly an average renewal of this Listed contest, with the second, third and fifth having only ordinary form beforehand, although the winner may be capable of better.
NOTEBOOK
Sadeek, a game winner on soft ground on his debut, followed up on this much faster surface but had to work hard to get the better of the runner-up. He has proved himself a determined battler however, and he remains on course for the Coventry Stakes at Royal Ascot, where if he gets to the front it will take a good one to pass him. (op 6-5 tchd 13-8 in places)
Going Straight(IRE), who prior to this had shown just ordinary form on Polytrack, put up a fine effort from the front. Once headed by the winner she refused to give way and stuck to her task all the way to the line. Having earned black type for this connections can look for easier opportunities, although a race such as the Cherry Hinton next month might now figure in her programme. (op 33-1)
Always Fruitful looked the unlucky horse of the race. He missed the break badly and looked to be going nowhere halfway up the straight, but he picked up in such good style from that point that he was catching the first two hand over fist nearing the line. This was a decent boost for his Pontefract conqueror Hellvelyn, but along with the runner-up and fifth suggests this was an ordinary Woodcote. Official explanation: jockey said colt missed break (op 15-2)
Mubaashir(IRE), stepping up in trip, having taken the Lily Agnes last time, chased the leaders but did not look at home on the track and can be given a chance to prove he is better than this on a more conventional course. (op 2-1)
Loves Bidding, another stepping up in trip, finished closer to Mubaashir than on their respective debuts and may have improved for his first encounter with fast turf. However, his proximity to the principals limits the form. (op 50-1 tchd 66-1)

Lord Charles looked a non stayer and can do better when the emphasis is back on speed. Official explanation: trainer said colt failed to stay 6f (op 7-1)

2226 VODAFONE DIOMED STKS (GROUP 3) 1m 114y

3:00 (3:01) (Class 1) 3-Y-O+

£42,585 (£16,140; £8,077; £4,027; £2,017; £1,012) **Stalls** Low

Form				RPR
4134	**1**		**Nayyir**[49] 1018 8-9-4 110 LDettori 2 (G A Butler) *t.k.h: hld up: 7th st: stl same pl ins fnl 2f: weaved through after: r.o to ld last 75yds* **11/2**[3]	115+
4422	**2**	*nk*	**Boule D'Or (IRE)**[4] 2116 5-9-4 107 MichaelHills 5 (J Akehurst) *lw: hld up: last st: prog on outer 2f out: drvn to ld last 100yds: sn hdd: jst outpcd* **12/1**	112
4061	**3**	*½*	**Home Affairs**[19] 1739 4-9-4 111 RichardHughes 7 (Sir Michael Stoute) *lw: trckd ldng pair: gng strly but trapped on inner over 2f out tl last 100yds: r.o wl nr fin: no ch* **7/4**[1]	118+
1002	**4**	*shd*	**Momtic (IRE)**[19] 1739 5-9-4 105 KFallon 1 (W Jarvis) *chsd ldrs: 5th st: rdn wl over 2f out: prog to ld over 1f out: hdd and one pce last 100yds* **11/2**[3]	111
1401	**5**	*2*	**Zero Tolerance (IRE)**[16] 1806 6-9-4 106 JamieSpencer 4 (T D Barron) *trckd ldr: chal over 2f out: upsides over 1f out: btn whn n.m.r and hanging ins fnl f* **9/1**	107
6436	**6**	*¾*	**Kings Point (IRE)**[16] 1806 5-9-4 105 (p) PaulHanagan 3 (R A Fahey) *led to over 1f out: wknd fnl f* **14/1**	105
1030	**7**	*½*	**Chrysander**[16] 1806 4-9-4 102 (v[1]) TedDurcan 6 (M R Channon) *s.i.s: sn in tch: 6th st: rdn on outer over 2f out: no imp over 1f out: fdd* **50/1**	104
1161	**8**	*hd*	**Mulaqat**[28] 1488 3-8-6 104 MartinDwyer 8 (M P Tregoning) *lw: trckd ldng trio: rdn 3f out: effrt 2f out: wknd fnl f* **9/2**[2]	103

1m 43.48s (-2.26) **Going Correction** +0.05s/f (Good)
WFA 3 from 4yo+ 12lb **8** Ran SP% **111.6**
Speed ratings (Par 113):112,111,111,111,109 108,108,108
CSF £64.30 TOTE £6.70: £1.90, £3.00, £1.30; EX 83.30 Trifecta £248.30 Pool: £1,609.32 - 4.60 winning units.
Owner Abdulla Al Khalifa **Bred** Saeed Manana **Trained** Blewbury, Oxon

FOCUS
A rather messy renewal of this Group 3, producing an exciting finish and an unlucky loser. The winning time was about par for the type of race.

NOTEBOOK
Nayyir, who won this back in 2002 on his only previous visit here, was quite keen under restraint but was still in the rear although going well halfway up the straight before getting a dream run through, unlike the favourite, and putting his head in front close home. He has looked less of a force in the last year or two, which limits enthusiasm for the form, but he clearly likes this track. (op 6-1)
Boule D'Or(IRE) was finishing runner-up for the third successive time and has not scored since winning in Dubai on February 2005, but he did nothing wrong and, effective from a mile to ten furlongs and able to handle most ground, deserves to pick up a Group race somewhere this season. (tchd 14-1)
Home Affairs ◆, who won a Listed race last time but had been beaten in all his previous attempts at Group level, looked the unlucky horse of the race and a line through Momtic supports that view. He tracked the leaders but found himself with nowhere to go in the straight until it was too late. He finished strongly once finding an opening but was never going to catch the first two in time. He has been rated as if having won and should gain compensation before too long. (op 6-4)
Momtic(IRE), a course and distance winner, finished two and a half lengths behind the third at Windsor. He ran his race and along with the runner-up sets the standard for the form. He seems in good heart and has a good record at Sandown, so could be of interest in the valuable mile handicap on Eclipse day in which he finished runner-up last season. (op 5-1)
Zero Tolerance(IRE) is an admirable handicapper, but would not have been helped by the drying ground and the fact that he could not get to the front. Nevetheless this was a decent effort. (tchd 10-1)
Kings Point(IRE), back on more suitable ground and with the cheekpieces re-applied, was taken on up front by Zero Tolerance and that cost them both in the end.
Chrysander seems most effective on softer ground and the first-time visor failed to make a difference.
Mulaqat, the only three-year-old in the line-up, found this much tougher than the Listed race he won at Newmarket but did not look suited by the track. He will be better off back over ten furlongs against his own age group. (op 11-2)

2227 VODAFONE "DASH" STKS (HERITAGE H'CAP) 5f

3:30 (3:32) (Class 2) 3-Y-O+

£46,740 (£13,995; £6,997; £3,502; £1,747; £877) **Stalls** High

Form				RPR
3105	**1**		**Desert Lord**[23] 1602 6-8-8 **92** (b) DO'Donohoe 17 (K A Ryan) *led nr side gp over 3f out: def advantage over 1f out: clr fnl f: r.o wl* **12/1**[3]	107
6300	**2**	*1 ½*	**Bond City (IRE)**[269] 5044 4-9-1 **99** RobertWinston 8 (B Smart) *chsd nr side ldrs but nt on terms: drvn 2f out: hanging lft but r.o fnl f to take 2nd nr fin* **50/1**	108
0060	**3**	*nk*	**Continent**[15] 1835 9-8-8 **92** PaulHanagan 20 (D Nicholls) *taken down early: dwlt: wl in rr: prog against nr side rail over 1f out: r.o fnl f: nrst fin* **33/1**	100
4142	**4**	*¾*	**Sierra Vista**[21] 1663 6-9-3 **101** JohnEgan 5 (D W Barker) *lw: chsd ldng pair in centre: led gp 1f out: styd on but nt on terms ins fnl f* **16/1**	106
6132	**5**	*shd*	**Green Manalishi**[9] 1952 5-9-2 **100** LDettori 14 (D W P Arbuthnot) *lw: chsd nr side ldrs: rdn over 1f out: one pce fnl f* **10/1**[2]	105
0000	**6**	*1*	**Caribbean Coral**[23] 1602 7-7-13 **83** NickyMackay 18 (J J Quinn) *lw: off the pce in midfield nr side: drvn 1/2-way: styd on fnl f: unable to chal* **8/1**[1]	84
2013	**7**	*shd*	**Corridor Creeper (FR)**[9] 1952 9-10-0 **112** 4ex (p) ShaneKelly 9 (J M Bradley) *lw: prom on outer of nr side gp: outpcd wl over 1f out: styd on again u.p fnl f* **18/1**	112
0441	**8**	*nk*	**Merlin's Dancer**[23] 1602 6-8-9 **93** 4ex AdrianTNicholls 3 (D Nicholls) *lw: taken down early: led in centre: hdd 1f out: one pce fnl f: fin 2nd in that gp* **12/1**[3]	92
1011	**9**	*hd*	**Mutamared (USA)**[28] 1487 6-8-13 **97** NCallan 4 (K A Ryan) *hanging lft thrght: outpcd in centre: styd on u.p fr over 1f out: fin 3rd in gp* **8/1**[1]	95
0002	**10**	*nk*	**Night Prospector**[10] 1936 6-8-0 **84** AdrianMcCarthy 11 (G L Moore) *carried lft s: sn struggling towards rr of nr side gp: kpt on fr over 1f out* **12/1**[3]	81
4111	**11**	*shd*	**Empress Jain**[23] 1604 3-8-5 **96** 4ex PhilipRobinson 19 (M A Jarvis) *taken down early and walked to post: led nr side gp to over 3f out: fdd over 1f out* **8/1**[1]	93
3420	**12**	*½*	**Peace Offering (IRE)**[23] 1602 6-8-11 **95** JoeFanning 12 (D Nicholls) *hanging lft thrght: prom on outer of nr side gp: wknd jst over 1f out* **10/1**[2]	90
6660	**13**	*½*	**Intriguing Glimpse**[11] 1928 5-8-0 **84** FrankieMcDonald 1 (Miss B Sanders) *dwlt: wl off the pce in centre: nvr nr ldrs: fin 4th in gp* **40/1**	77
4056	**14**	*1*	**Jayanjay**[10] 1939 7-8-7 **91** RichardThomas 13 (Miss B Sanders) *sn outpcd and wl bhd nr side: nvr a factor: kpt on* **33/1**	80
0000	**15**	*nk*	**Texas Gold**[28] 1485 8-9-4 **102** MartinDwyer 7 (W R Muir) *lw: racd in centre: sn drvn and outpcd: nvr on terms: fin 5th in gp* **14/1**	89
2554	**16**	*½*	**Fromsong (IRE)**[16] 1803 8-9-0 **98** JimmyFortune 2 (D K Ivory) *chsd ldrs in centre tl wknd rapidly over 1f out: fin 6th in gp* **66/1**	83
1016	**17**	*nk*	**Zowington**[16] 1803 4-8-10 **94** AlanMunro 16 (C F Wall) *lw: squeezed out after 1f: wl bhd after: plugged on* **10/1**[2]	78
2005	**18**	*1*	**Cape Royal**[7] 2021 6-8-13 **97** (b[1]) RyanMoore 10 (J M Bradley) *s.v.s: wl bhd towards centre: plugged on* **33/1**	77
-200	**19**	*hd*	**Hoh Hoh Hoh**[21] 1663 4-8-4 **88** ChrisCatlin 15 (A M Balding) *hanging lft and sn struggling: a wl in rr* **40/1**	67
5004	**20**	*2 ½*	**Fire Up The Band**[9] 1952 7-9-9 **107** RichardHughes 6 (D Nicholls) *pressed ldr in centre to over 1f out: wkng whn heavily eased fnl f* **16/1**	76

54.49 secs (-1.19) **Going Correction** 0.0s/f (Good)
WFA 3 from 4yo+ 7lb **20** Ran SP% **124.5**
Speed ratings (Par 109):109,106,106,104,104 103,103,102,102,101 101,100,99,98,97 97,96,95,94,90
CSF £541.25 CT £17919.58 TOTE £19.20: £4.40, £8.60, £12.70, £4.20; EX 4003.30 TRIFECTA Not won..
Owner Bull & Bell Partnership **Bred** Cheveley Park Stud Ltd **Trained** Hambleton, N Yorks

FOCUS
A wide-open sprint with plenty of pace on, but those drawn high appeared to have a narrow advantage. A clean sweep of the places for northern-based trainers.

NOTEBOOK
Desert Lord ◆, who had not had the best of luck with the draw on his two most recent outings, had things work in his favour this time and made much of the running on the stands' side. He established a clear advantage as those in the centre began to falter and never looked like relinquishing it. He has been running really well since joining current connections this season, and having proven effective over further as well, will no doubt be taking his chance in many of the big sprint handicaps this summer (tchd 14-1 in a place)
Bond City(IRE) ◆, not seen since finishing unplaced in the Portland Handicap in September, has shown in the past that he handles this track and ran a fine race despite a moderate draw. He is a five-furlong specialist, so races such as the Gosforth Park Cup may be on his agenda, and that will give him four weeks to get over this.
Continent is not as good as he was but showed he is still capable of holding his own in these good handicaps. His best recent runs have been on fast ground and he looks a likely sort for the Wokingham at Royal Ascot.
Sierra Vista ◆, a prolific winner last season and from a stable just beginning to find its feet, ran a fine race from her low draw. She is another who should be winning soon and could well turn up at Newcastle's Plate meeting at the end of the month.
Green Manalishi is another who is holding his form well this season and was again not far away. He could be the sort for the Listed race at Sandown in two weeks' time.
Caribbean Coral, who won this race two years ago, has not won since following up in the Gosforth Park Cup later that month but is now rated 9lb lower. He was never able to land a blow this time, but there are signs that he is re-discovering some form. (tchd 15-2)
Corridor Creeper(FR), third in this last season, is a pretty consistent performer but never got in a blow at the leaders and appears to prefer easier ground than he encountered here. (op 16-1)
Merlin's Dancer, under a penalty for his Chester win, made a bold effort from his low draw but faded in the closing stages. He is in the Wokingham and with his trainer's record in big handicaps will be one to consider for that. (op 14-1)
Mutamared(USA) ◆, a stable companion of the winner, looked unhappy on the track and never got into contention. He will go for the Wokingham and the course will suit him much better. (op 7-1)
Empress Jain, on a four-timer, was 19lb higher than for her seasonal debut but this was her first encounter with the track and older rivals and she found it too much. She was not given too hard a time once beaten and can bounce back. (tchd 10-1 in a place)
Peace Offering(IRE) was another who found the camber difficult to cope with despite having been second in this race last year from a low draw. He has not won since taking the Cornwallis Stakes in October 2002, but that was at Ascot, which is where he is likely to be going next for the Wokingham.
Fire Up The Band was heavily eased and showed a lot more than first impressions suggest. (op 20-1)

2228 VODAFONE DERBY STKS (GROUP 1) (ENTIRE COLTS & FILLIES) 1m 4f 10y

4:20 (4:29) (Class 1) 3-Y-O

£740,695 (£280,728; £140,494; £70,051; £35,091; £17,610) **Stalls** Centre

Form				RPR
1112	**1**		**Sir Percy**[28] 1486 3-9-0 121 MartinDwyer 10 (M P Tregoning) *hld up in midfield: 11th st: gd prog and swtchd to inner 2f out: r.o wl and squeezed through fnl f to ld last 50yds* **6/1**[3]	121+
0322	**2**	*shd*	**Dragon Dancer**[23] 1603 3-9-0 104 DarryllHolland 11 (G Wragg) *pressed ldr after 4f: clr of rest over 3f out: persistent chal fnl 2f: styd on wl nr fin: jst hld* **66/1**	121
1261	**3**	*hd*	**Dylan Thomas (IRE)**[20] 1708 3-9-0 JMurtagh 18 (A P O'Brien, Ire) *prog to ld over 8f out: mde rest: hrd pressed by runner-up over 2f out and clr of rest: hdd last 50yds* **25/1**	120
1	**4**	*shd*	**Hala Bek (IRE)**[43] 1120 3-9-0 108 PhilipRobinson 5 (M A Jarvis) *lw: cl up: 6th st: chsd clr ldng pair over 2f out: clsd over 1f out: chalng whn veered bdly rt 100yds out: nt rcvr* **9/1**	121+
1	**5**	*2*	**Visindar**[19] 1749 3-9-0 CSoumillon 8 (A Fabre, France) *lw: lengthy: hld up towards rr: 10th and prog st: rdn to cl on ldrs fr 2f out: hanging lft but ch 1f out: nt qckn* **2/1**[1]	117
3142	**6**	*1*	**Best Alibi (IRE)**[16] 1805 3-9-0 103 RyanMoore 17 (Sir Michael Stoute) *lw: wl in rr: 14th st: hanging bdly lft but prog on outer fr over 2f out: nrst fin* **33/1**	115
61	**7**	*2*	**Sixties Icon**[26] 1546 3-9-0 90 ShaneKelly 4 (J Noseda) *trckd ldrs early: lost pl and 12th st: hanging lft but kpt on fnl 2f: nrst fin* **66/1**	112
442	**8**	*1 ¼*	**Mountain (IRE)**[20] 1708 3-9-0 JAHeffernan 13 (A P O'Brien, Ire) *w'like: scope: gd sort: wl in rr: 16th st: wl off the pce 3f out: styd on after: n.d* **50/1**	110
1141	**9**	*1 ¼*	**Linda's Lad**[21] 1668 3-9-0 LDettori 16 (A Fabre, France) *reluctant to go to post: hld up in midfield: 9th st: no prog over 2f out: wknd over 1f out* **9/1**	108

2111 **10** ¾ **Papal Bull**[23] 1603 3-9-0 .... RobertWinston 14 116+
(Sir Michael Stoute) *wl in rr and nt gng wl: 17th st: gd prog on inner 3f out: trying to cl whn bdly hmpd 2f out: nt rcvr* **11/1**

1121 **11** 1½ **Championship Point (IRE)**[28] 1473 3-9-0 110................ TedDurcan 7 109+
(M R Channon) *prom: 3rd st: sn rdn: wknd 2f out* **12/1**

1301 **12** 1¼ **Septimus (IRE)**[16] 1805 3-9-0 .... MJKinane 9 103
(A P O'Brien, Ire) *a wl in rr: last st: nvr a factor* **17/2**

2114 **13** 1¾ **Before You Go (IRE)**[21] 1668 3-9-0 104........................ IanMongan 3 100
(T G Mills) *hmpd after 4f: nvr beyond midfield: 15th and struggling st: no ch* **100/1**

1032 **14** ½ **Sienna Storm (IRE)**[28] 1473 3-9-0 96..........................(b[1]) MichaelHills 6 99
(M H Tompkins) *trckd ldrs: 8th and gng wl enough st: wknd rapidly over 2f out* **200/1**

151 **15** 4 **Atlantic Waves (IRE)**[44] 1093 3-9-0 100........................ JoeFanning 1 93
(M Johnston) *swtg: led to over 8f out: 5th and drvn st: sn wknd* **25/1**

4313 **16** 2½ **Snoqualmie Boy**[16] 1805 3-9-0 87.. JohnEgan 2 89
(D R C Elsworth) *t.k.h: prom: 4th st: wknd over 2f out* **150/1**

17 10 **Noddies Way** 3-9-0 .... RobertMiles 12 73
(J F Panvert) *w'like: dwlt: last tl brief effrt on outer 1/2-way: 13th and wkng st: sn bhd* **500/1**

1120 **P** **Horatio Nelson (IRE)**[28] 1486 3-9-0 .... KFallon 15 —
(A P O'Brien, Ire) *sn trckd ldrs: 7th st: drvn to cl over 2f out: 6th and hld whn broke down over 1f out: p.u: dead* **11/2**[2]

2m 35.23s (-3.50) **Going Correction** +0.05s/f (Good) **18** Ran SP% **127.5**
Speed ratings (Par 113):113,112,112,112,111 110,109,108,107,107 106,105,104,103,101 99,92,—
CSF £384.46 CT £9025.67 TOTE £7.40: £2.80, £10.50, £5.90; EX 500.40 Trifecta £11596.60 Pool: £63,700.17 - 3.90 winning units.
Owner A E Pakenham **Bred** The Old Suffolk Stud **Trained** Lambourn, Berks

FOCUS
An open renewal, but it was not run at the strongest of gallops and the time was just acceptable. It was something of a rough race and the fact that it produced a blanket finish indicates the principal middle-distance three-year-olds are much of a muchness at present. Sir Percy has been assessed as having run just a pound better than at Newmarket and can only be rated an average Derby winner. The second and fourth were big improvers, and the third, sixth and seventh stepped up on previous efforts too.

NOTEBOOK
Sir Percy, runner-up in the 2000 Guineas, was as usual edgy and sweating before hand and proved awkward to load. He took the brave route from off the pace and got through on the inside to score narrowly from the placed horses who had dominated virtually throughout. He had been jarred up after Newmarket and took a while to come right, but was clearly back to form and produced a turn of foot to snatch the race. He has several options now, with either the Irish Derby or the Eclipse the most likely alternatives providing he is none the worse for his exertions. (op 15-2 tchd 11-2)

Dragon Dancer ◆, bidding to become the first maiden for over a hundred years to win the Blue Riband, very nearly succeeded. Up with the pace from the start, he battled all the way up the straight but the winner's pace just got him there. Despite the fact that he has now been runner-up in his last three races, he is clearly progressing well and reversed form with both Hala Bek and Papal Bull, who had beaten him previously. He is in the King Edward VII at Royal Ascot and that could offer him a fine chance of compensation, providing Hala Bek does not re-oppose.

Dylan Thomas(IRE), who has done well over the winter and was the winner of the Derrinstown Derby Trial last time, was nevertheless third choice in the market of the four O'Brien runners. He ran a terrific race from the front, very much reminiscent of the stable's The Great Gatsby three years ago, and was only collared near the finish. He is another with the Royal Ascot option, but the Irish Derby looks a likely choice next, as he appears to be Coolmore's best option for that race at present. (op 28-1)

Hala Bek(IRE) ◆ ran a wonderful race for one so inexperienced, but in the end it was that lack of experience that cost him the race. Having been in the chasing group from the start, he went in pursuit of the leaders in the straight and was gradually wearing them down when swerving badly towards the paddock exit gate inside the final furlong. Robinson did well to stay aboard and then to rally his mount, but it was too late. He is in the King Edward VII and that could offer a chance of compensation, but connections may opt to give him more time in which case the Eclipse is a possible; however he would need to be supplemented for the Irish Derby. Wherever he goes, he does look the one in the frame most open to improvement, which should put him in pole position for the big middle-distance events later in the season. (op 10-1)

Visindar, bidding to give France their first Derby winner since 1976, was made favourite on the strength of three impressive performances. An athletic but not overly robust sort, he moved into contention early in the straight, came through with Hala Bek to have a chance, but faded in the closing stages. His connections blamed his inexperience, but he may also have stamina limitations, for while he is by a Derby winner there is a lot of speed on the dam's side of his pedigree, and his granddam was a sprinter. It will be interesting to see if he side-steps the Irish Derby now and goes for the ten-furlong Grand Prix de Paris instead. (op 11-4)

Best Alibi(IRE), a distant runner-up in the Dante on soft ground, appeared to put up an improved effort back on fast ground. He came from well back and was doing his best work late on, despite hanging badly. There looks to be more improvement to come from him.

Sixties Icon, by a Derby winner out of an Oaks winner, was having only his third outing, having won a Windsor maiden last time, and he was coltish before being saddled. He appeared to suffer in the rough and tumble of this race before running on past beaten horses once in line for home. He should benefit from this experience and may make up into a Group horse, and possibly a St Leger candidate, later in the season. (op 80-1 tchd 50-1)

Mountain(IRE), runner-up in the Derrinstown, was another doing his best work late, having been out the back for much of the way. With plenty of stamina in his pedigree, he is the type to make up into a St Leger horse.

Linda's Lad, who got very stirred up in the parade and was reluctant to go to post, was settled in mid-division in the race but did not pick up, although the trip should not have been a problem. He probably lost the race beforehand. Official explanation: jockey said colt hung left (op 12-1)

Papal Bull, a supplementary entry for £75,000, was never going from an early stage but had started to make inroads on the leaders when his passage was blocked halfway up the straight. Edgy before the race, his previous form with the runner-up entitled him to have finished in the frame, so he can be given another chance. (op 10-1 tchd 12-1)

Championship Point(IRE), a clear winner of the Predominate Stakes, should have had no problems with the trip and was ridden as if stamina was not an issue. However, he faded noticeably from the turn in and unless a problem surfaces it can only be assumed he was not good enough. (op 14-1)

Septimus(IRE), who appeared to be the stable's main contender until the ground dried out, was a market drifter and ran no sort of race on this fast ground. Like Mountain he may prove more of a St Leger horse in time. (op 9-1 tchd 10-1)

Atlantic Waves(IRE) should have had no problem with trip or ground and was up with the pace early. However, he was on the retreat before the home turn and this was disappointing. Official explanation: trainer said colt was lame post-race

Noddies Way was making his racecourse debut here, having moved stables when a former trainer recommended gelding him and preparing him for bumpers. Essentially jumps bred and facing an impossible task, he did remarkably well to finish only 30 lengths off the winner, but he was surely flattered.

Horatio Nelson(IRE) was the stable's number one, having worked very well at Ballydoyle earlier in the week, but his rider trotted him up and down at the start as if concerned something might be amiss. Having been checked over by the vet, he was settled just off the pace and travelled fine, but when asked for his effort the response was limited, and he was fading when he sadly broke down very badly. It was too severe an injury for him to be saved. (op 4-1)

2229 VODAFONE SIMPLY STKS (H'CAP) 1m 4f 10y
5:05 (5:07) (Class 2) (0-100,98) 4-Y-O+

£24,928 (£7,464; £3,732; £1,868; £932; £468) **Stalls** Centre

Form RPR

0053 **1** **Alfie Noakes**[10] 1933 4-8-8 **85**.. KerrinMcEvoy 10 93
(Mrs A J Perrett) *hld up: last st but wl in tch: stdy prog on outer 2f out: drvn and r.o wl to ld last strides* **12/1**

6301 **2** nk **Gavroche (IRE)**[10] 1933 5-9-7 **98**.. LDettori 12 106
(J R Boyle) *hld up: 10th st: prog on outer over 2f out: edgd lft and chalng whn bmpd 1f out: upsides nr fin: jst outpcd* **6/1**[3]

3060 **3** hd **Consular**[17] 1775 4-8-11 **88**.. PhilipRobinson 14 96
(M A Jarvis) *trckd ldng pair: led 2f out: edgd rt 1f out: hdd fnl strides* **11/2**[2]

4116 **4** 1 **Ameeq (USA)**[22] 1133 4-8-4 **81**.. AlanMunro 2 87
(G L Moore) *lw: trckd ldng trio: rdn 2f out: styd on fr over 1f out but nvr quite able to chal* **8/1**

4034 **5** 1¼ **Wingman (IRE)**[17] 1775 4-8-10 **87**.. EddieAhern 9 91+
(J W Hills) *hld up in rr: 12th st: nt clr run on inner over 2f out: last whn swtchd rt over 1f out: r.o fnl f: nt rcvr* **12/1**

5265 **6** hd **Glistening**[247] 5569 4-9-4 **95**.. NickyMackay 4 99+
(L M Cumani) *lw: hld up in rr: 11th st: effrt on inner whn hmpd 2f out: r.o wl fnl f: nt rcvr* **8/1**

5110 **7** shd **Top Seed (IRE)**[17] 1779 5-8-9 **86**.. TedDurcan 7 90+
(M R Channon) *wl in rr and trbld passage on inner: 13th st: nowhere to go over 2f out: plld wd and r.o fr over 1f out: nrst fin* **18/1**

55-1 **8** shd **Vengeance**[38] 1238 6-9-4 **95**.. PatDobbs 5 101+
(S Dow) *hld up in tch: 7th st: rdn to cl on ldrs 2f out: trying to chal whn squeezed out 1f out: nt rcvr* **11/1**

0-00 **9** ½ **Savannah Bay**[35] 1294 7-8-12 **89**.. NCallan 8 92
(B Ellison) *hld up towards rr: 9th st: shkn up and n.m.r 2f out: no prog after* **50/1**

1033 **10** ½ **Focus Group (USA)**[17] 1775 5-8-13 **90**..................... GrahamGibbons 6 92
(J J Quinn) *hld up: prog on outer and 6th st: rdn 3f out: wknd over 1f out* **8/1**

0151 **11** 1¼ **Solent (IRE)**[14] 1842 4-9-4 **95**.. RichardHughes 1 95
(R Hannon) *trckd ldrs: 5th st: no imp on ldrs 2f out: fdd over 1f out* **5/1**[1]

6030 **12** nk **Foodbroker Founder**[8] 1992 6-8-2 **79** oh1.................. MartinDwyer 13 78
(D R C Elsworth) *disp ld to 2f out: wknd fnl f* **50/1**

0004 **13** 6 **Massif Centrale**[10] 1933 5-9-3 **94**..............................(t) JohnEgan 3 84
(D R C Elsworth) *dwlt: sn in tch: 8th st: wknd rapidly 2f out* **20/1**

1102 **14** nk **Kinrande (IRE)**[237] 5757 4-8-9 **86**.............................. FergusSweeney 11 75
(P J Makin) *swtg: b.bkwd: disp ld to over 2f out: wknd rapidly* **25/1**

2m 36.6s (-2.13) **Going Correction** +0.05s/f (Good) **14** Ran SP% **121.2**
Speed ratings (Par 109):109,108,108,108,107 107,106,106,106,106 105,105,101,101
CSF £80.21 CT £450.50 TOTE £15.10: £3.90, £2.10, £2.50; EX 93.40 Trifecta £1170.50 Pool: £1,648.70 - 1 winning ticket.
Owner G C Stevens **Bred** Exors Of The Late Mrs Jill Rossdale **Trained** Pulborough, W Sussex

FOCUS
A decent handicap, but while it was run only 1.37sec slower than the Derby it lacked pace and there were several hard-luck stories. It produced another blanket finish, and the form is unlikely to be reliable, but there were nevertheless some promising efforts.

NOTEBOOK
Alfie Noakes, who had finished third to Gavroche at Goodwood, reversed that form on 4lb better terms. He was last of all turning in and the pace had not been strong, but he was brought with a long run down the outside and got his head in front virtually on the line. His previous win was on similar ground and, as he is elatively lightly raced, he looks to have more to offer. (op 10-1)

Gavroche(IRE), who beat today's winner at Goodwood, was 4lb worse off and only just failed to hold him off. He has done really well since being claimed last July, with two of his three successes coming on this track, but he will not find things easy when reassessed. Official explanation: jockey said horse hung left (op 10-1)

Consular ◆ made a bold bid to give jockey and trainer a measure of compensation after their unlucky defeat in the Derby. He was always in the right place and made his bid for home halfway up the straight, but despite battling well could not hold the late efforts of the first two. He looks reasonably handicapped now and connections may consider the Duke Of Edinburgh at Royal Ascot or possibly the Old Newton Cup at Haydock, where he gained his only previous success. (tchd 5-1)

Ameeq(USA), a dual All-Weather and hurdles winner since the turn of the year, was stepping back up in trip and ran well. He does not look quite as effective on turf as Polytrack, but a drop back to ten furlongs may help. (op 9-1)

Wingman(IRE), who has not won since September 2004, generally runs reasonably well and as a consequence has not been dropped much by the Handicapper. He got into a fair amount of trouble along the inside and never reached a challenging position.

Glistening ◆, lightly raced and dropped in trip for his seasonal debut, got no sort of run on the rail and had to be switched out, by which time the race was over. Noted to be coltish before having his saddle applied, this was a performance full of promise and he looks one to keep on the right side, with the Ebor a race that should be right up his street. (op 9-1)

Top Seed(IRE) ◆, back on a sounder surface, was another to suffer from trouble in running on more than one occasion. He has risen in the weights after a couple of wins earlier in the season, but was verging on Group class at one time so may not be finished winning yet. (tchd 16-1)

Vengeance, winner of the Great Metropolitan here after a spell over hurdles, was still in with a chance when getting squeezed out in the closing stages and, if none the worse may be able to bounce back. (tchd 12-1)

Focus Group(USA) has some decent form to his name but was another who did not look at home on this track. (op 13-2)

Solent(IRE) travelled well enough on the heels of the leaders but faded in the straight. He may be happier on a flatter track.

2230 VODAFONE SPRINT STKS (H'CAP) 6f
5:40 (5:40) (Class 2) (0-100,98) 4-Y-O+

£24,928 (£7,464; £3,732; £1,868; £932; £468) **Stalls** High

Form RPR

6330 **1** **Beaver Patrol (IRE)**[15] 1835 4-9-1 **89**.. KerrinMcEvoy 5 100
(R F Johnson Houghton) *trckd ldrs: 5th st: rdn over 2f out: prog over 1f out: drvn to ld last 75yds: jst hld on* **7/1**[2]

0151 **2** nk **Prince Namid**[7] 2021 4-9-2 **90**.. MichaelHills 17 100+
(Mrs A Duffield) *hld up wl off the pce: 14th st: rapid prog on wd outside over 1f out: fin strly: too much to do* **20/1**

0564 **3** *nk* **Bahamian Pirate (USA)**[7] 2038 11-9-9 **97**........................ EddieAhern 6 106
(D Nicholls) *hld up in midfield: 7th st: stdy prog 2f out: rdn to ld 100yds out: sn hdd and nt qckn* **25/1**

2042 **4** *1* **Idle Power (IRE)**[6] 2047 8-9-2 **90**.. LDettori 1 96
(J R Boyle) *led: hrd pressed fr 2f out: hdd & wknd last 100yds* **7/1**[2]

6060 **5** *¾* **Indian Trail**[45] 1086 6-9-6 **94**........................ RichardHughes 11 98
(D Nicholls) *lw: hld up in midfield: 10th st: gng wl 3f out: prog 2f out: trying to cl whn squeezed out jst over 1f out: nt rcvr* **9/2**[1]

0000 **6** *¾* **Fantasy Believer**[15] 1835 8-8-11 **85**........................ GrahamGibbons 10 87
(J J Quinn) *towards rr: 11th st: sn drvn: hanging lft but kpt on fnl 2f : nvr rchd ldrs* **22/1**

0000 **7** *shd* **Funfair Wane**[15] 1835 7-8-9 **86**.............................. SilvestreDeSousa(3) 3 87
(D Nicholls) *trckd ldrs: 6th st: effrt on inner over 2f out: hanging lft and nt qckn over 1f out: kpt on* **25/1**

0022 **8** *shd* **Rising Shadow (IRE)**[9] 1949 5-9-2 **90**........................ JamieSpencer 16 91
(T D Barron) *wl off the pce in rr: 15th st: sme prog 2f out: r.o last 150yds: no ch* **7/1**[2]

1010 **9** *¾* **Commando Scott (IRE)**[7] 2012 5-9-4 **92**........................ PaulHanagan 14 91
(I W McInnes) *a in midfield: 8th st: shkn up on outer over 2f out: no real prog* **16/1**

1250 **10** *nk* **Machinist (IRE)**[40] 1183 6-9-2 **90**................................ AdrianTNicholls 8 88
(D Nicholls) *racd on inner in midfield: 9th st: no real prog fnl 2f* **9/1**

3050 **11** *1¼* **Hidden Dragon (USA)**[107] 433 7-9-0 **88**.................... NickyMackay 15 82
(J Pearce) *wl in rr: 13th st and wl off the pce: sme prog 2f out: no ch whn hmpd 1f out: r.o wl last 100yds* **33/1**

0030 **12** *hd* **Gifted Gamble**[10] 1939 4-9-1 **89**..(b) NCallan 13 82
(K A Ryan) *prom: chsd ldr over 2f out to over 1f out: wknd* **33/1**

1410 **13** *shd* **Swinbrook (USA)**[16] 1803 5-9-0 **88**..........................(v) JimmyFortune 12 81
(J A R Toller) *s.s: detached and wl bhd: 16th st: kpt on fnl 2f: no ch* **11/1**

0161 **14** *1¼* **Fantaisiste**[38] 1246 4-8-13 **90**.................................. NelsonDeSouza(3) 2 79
(P F I Cole) *lw: trckd ldrs on inner: 4th st: wknd 2f out* **11/1**

0400 **15** *2½* **Joseph Henry**[291] 4457 4-9-1 **89**.. JoeFanning 4 71
(M Johnston) *chsd ldr to over 2f out: wknd* **33/1**

1604 **16** *3* **Mine Behind**[23] 1602 6-9-0 **88**.. AlanMunro 7 61
(J R Best) *towards rr: 12th st: effrt on inner over 2f out: swtchd rt over 1f out: sn eased* **8/1**[3]

0000 **17** *dist* **Just James**[16] 1803 7-9-10 **98**.. TedDurcan 9 —
(D Nicholls) *s.v.s: immediately t.o and allowed to amble around* **33/1**

68.49 secs (-2.14) **Going Correction** -0.05s/f (Good) **17** Ran SP% **127.9**
Speed ratings (Par 102):111,111,109,108 107,107,107,106,106 104,104,104,102,99 95,—
CSF £148.99 CT £3398.59 TOTE £9.00: £2.20, £5.00, £6.50, £1.50; EX 380.20 TRIFECTA Not won. Place 6 £765.44, Place 5 £320.36.
Owner G C Stevens **Bred** Kevin B Lynch **Trained** Blewbury, Oxon
■ Stewards' Enquiry : Eddie Ahern caution: careless riding

FOCUS
A good handicap run in a decent time, two seconds faster than the Woodcote, and another close finish. The proximity at the line of several soft ground performers suggest the going was not lightning fast.

NOTEBOOK
Beaver Patrol(IRE) ◆, who has been running well on soft of late but is suited by fast ground, sat just behind the leaders and picked up really well in the closing stages to hit the front and then just hold the late surge of the runner-up and complete a double for the owner and jockey. He has been in decent form this season after struggling for a good while after his successful juvenile campaign, and with this under his belt he could well be heading to Royal Ascot for the Wokingham. (op 10-1)
Prince Namid ◆, better known as a soft-ground performer and off his highest mark to date, came from well off the pace and very nearly caught the winner. He is clearly in very good heart and can gain compensation before long. (op 16-1)
Bahamian Pirate(USA), a veteran who has generally looked better on softer ground, is in decent form at present and ran a fine race, only being run out of it late on. He is on a reasonable mark nowadays and may be able to end a long losing run.
Idle Power(IRE), another whose best form has been with cut, made good use of his low draw and only gave best in the closing stages. He is one to watch for if returning to Goodwood, where he has such a fine record. (op 15-2 tchd 13-2)
Indian Trail, well backed for this before Fallon gave up the ride, came to deliver his challenge but got squeezed out at a vital point and was unable to pick up. He can be given another chance and he is yet another with a Wokingham entry. (tchd 5-1 in places)
Fantasy Believer, a previous course and distance winner, ran with credit and may well head to Newcastle for another crack at the Northern Sprint next. (op 20-1 tchd 25-1)
Funfair Wane has not won since taking the Ayr Gold Cup in 2004, but has not had that much racing in the meantime and this effort showed the ability is still there. He is also 4lb lower than for that last success. (op 33-1)
Rising Shadow(IRE), another who has been running well on soft ground, was doing his best work in the latter stages but never got into contention. (tchd 8-1)
Swinbrook(USA) Official explanation: jockey said gelding stumbled out of stalls
Just James Official explanation: jockey said gelding missed break
T/Jkpt: £161,466.00 to a £1 stake. Pool: £227,417.00. 1.00 winning ticket. T/Plt: £2,056.90 to a £1 stake. Pool: £229,640.30. 81.50 winning tickets. T/Qpdt: £393.80 to a £1 stake. Pool: £9,315.20. 17.50 winning tickets. JN

[1429]FOLKESTONE (R-H)

Saturday, June 3

OFFICIAL GOING: Good (good to firm in places)
Wind: Nil Weather: Sunny and warm

2231 INTERCASINO.CO.UK FOLKESTONE DERBY DAY H'CAP 1m 4f

2:05 (2:05) (Class 4) (0-85,89) 4-Y-0+ **£4,202** (£4,202; £963; £481) **Stalls** Low

Form RPR

1123 **1** **Blue Bajan (IRE)**[2] 2169 4-9-4 **82**.. DaneO'Neill 6 89
(Andrew Turnell) *keen: hld up in last: rdn and qckned to ld over 1f out: jnd on line* **5/4**[1]

0141 **1** *dht* **Finalmente**[7] 2035 4-9-11 **89**.. OscarUrbina 5 96
(N A Callaghan) *chsd ldr: rdn and ev ch over 2f out: rallied gamely fnl f to join ldr on line* **3/1**[2]

1421 **3** *4* **Polish Power (GER)**[18] 1756 6-8-13 **77**................................ LPKeniry 1 78
(J S Moore) *trckd ldrs: rdn over 2f out: outpcd fnl f* **4/1**[3]

2410 **4** *1* **Stolen Hours (USA)**[26] 1544 6-8-13 **77**........................... JimmyQuinn 2 76
(J Akehurst) *set stdy gallop: rdn and qcknd over 2f out: hdd over 1f out: sn outpcd* **9/1**

3520 **5** *nk* **Simonda**[10] 1931 5-9-6 **84**...(b) JimCrowley 7 83
(Mrs A J Perrett) *keen: trckd ldrs: rdn over 2f out: wl outpcd over 1f out* **13/2**

2m 39.28s (-1.22) **Going Correction** +0.05s/f (Good) **5** Ran SP% **112.8**
Speed ratings (Par 105):106,106,103,102,102
WIN: Finalmente £2.20, Blue Bajan £1.00; PL F £2.20, BB £1.10; EX: F/BB £2.40, BB/F £3.60, CSF: F/BB £3.71, BB/F £2.72.
Owner Dr John Hollowood **Bred** Dr J Hollowood **Trained** Broad Hinton, Wilts
Owner Edward M Kirtland **Bred** Helshaw Grange Stud Ltd **Trained** Newmarket, Suffolk

FOCUS
A decent enough handicap for the course, though lacking in numbers and run at a modest tempo until the final three furlongs.

2232 INTERCASINO.CO.UK H'CAP 7f (S)

2:35 (2:35) (Class 4) (0-85,85) 3-Y-0+ **£5,505** (£1,637; £818; £408) **Stalls** Low

Form RPR

0044 **1** **Ocean Pride (IRE)**[15] 1828 3-8-13 **80**............................(b[1]) DaneO'Neill 4 88
(R Hannon) *trckd ldrs stand side: led 2f out: clr fnl f: pushed out: comf* **15/2**

0300 **2** *1½* **Lord Of The East**[26] 1532 7-9-9 **85**........................ NataliaGemelova(5) 2 93
(I W McInnes) *led stands side gp: rdn and hdd 2f out: kpt on but no ch w wnr* **10/1**

6000 **3** *½* **Diamonds And Dust**[24] 1585 4-9-12 **83**................................(b[1]) RHills 1 90
(M H Tompkins) *s.i.s: sn rcvrd to press ldr stands side: ev ch tl onepced u.p fnl f* **7/1**

0066 **4** *2* **Grizedale (IRE)**[10] 1932 7-9-1 **72**......................................(t) TPQueally 10 74
(J Akehurst) *racd far side: rdn to ld far side pair and ev ch over 1f out: hung bdly lft and wknd fnl f* **9/1**

3230 **5** *1* **Outer Hebrides**[10] 1938 5-9-6 **82**..............................(vt) JamesDoyle(5) 5 81
(Stef Liddiard) *in tch stands side: effrt u.p over 2f out: wknd wl over 1f out* **13/2**

6000 **6** *¾* **Saxon Lil (IRE)**[9] 1962 4-8-12 **69**.................................... SamHitchcott 7 66
(J L Spearing) *chsd ldrs stand side: rdn over 2f out: wknd wl over 1f out* **6/1**[3]

3120 **7** *½* **Shogun Prince (IRE)**[15] 1828 3-8-10 **82**............. RichardKingscote(5) 8 74
(A King) *cl up on stands side: rdn over 2f out: sn wknd* **14/1**

0002 **8** *1¼* **Desert Dreamer (IRE)**[10] 1938 5-9-9 **80**...................... StephenCarson 3 73
(P R Chamings) *dwlt: hld up rr of stands side gp: rdn over 2f out: nvr trbld ldrs* **3/1**[1]

0210 **9** *7* **Pillars Of Wisdom**[39] 1207 4-9-6 **77**.. PaulDoe 9 51
(J L Dunlop) *led far side pair: hdd over 1f out: sn btn: eased fnl f* **9/2**[2]

1m 26.6s (-1.30) **Going Correction** -0.175s/f (Firm)
WFA 3 from 4yo+ 10lb **9** Ran SP% **120.8**
Speed ratings (Par 105):100,98,97,95,94 93,92,91,83
CSF £82.98 CT £557.26 TOTE £8.40: £2.60, £3.10, £2.70; EX 83.20 Trifecta £123.60 Part won. Pool: £174.10 - 0.35 winning units..
Owner D G Churston **Bred** Miss Laura Byrne **Trained** East Everleigh, Wilts

FOCUS
A moderate race with plenty of out-of-form runners. Two of them elected to race up the far side.

2233 INTERCASINO.CO.UK FILLIES' H'CAP 6f

3:05 (3:05) (Class 4) (0-85,84) 4-Y-0+ **£6,477** (£1,927; £963; £481) **Stalls** Low

Form RPR

4446 **1** **Golden Asha**[14] 1858 4-9-4 **81**... OscarUrbina 4 95
(N A Callaghan) *stdd s: hld up in rr: prog over 1f out: squeezed through to ld last 100 yds: readily* **9/4**[1]

0003 **2** *1* **Folga**[10] 1939 4-9-7 **84**.. RHills 3 95
(J G Given) *led: rdn 2f out: hdd last 100 yds: no ex* **4/1**[2]

4266 **3** *¾* **Rosapenna (IRE)**[40] 1188 4-8-9 **72**...................................... TPQueally 1 81
(C F Wall) *w.w in midfield: prog 2f out: sn ev ch: no ex u.p last 100 yds* **11/2**[3]

5610 **4** *½* **Daniella**[21] 1686 4-8-8 **71**..(p) FrancisFerris 5 78
(Rae Guest) *pressed ldr: rdn and ev ch 2f out: onepced wl ins fnl f* **10/1**

0012 **5** *shd* **Pippa's Dancer (IRE)**[9] 1961 4-8-7 **70**........................ RichardMullen 6 77
(W R Muir) *trckd ldrs: rdn 2f out: kpt on onepced* **6/1**

0300 **6** *5* **Highland Cascade**[40] 1183 4-8-8 **76**............................ JamesDoyle(5) 8 68
(J M P Eustace) *hld up: effrt u.p over 2f out: wknd fnl f* **12/1**

0016 **7** *½* **Mugeba**[2] 2184 5-7-9 **65** oh7..(t) LiamJones(7) 2 55
(Miss Gay Kelleway) *chsd ldrs: pushed along 3f out: effrt on outside 2f out: wknd fnl f* **9/1**

0400 **8** *2½* **Extremely Rare (IRE)**[2] 2173 5-8-4 **67**............................ JimmyQuinn 9 50
(M S Saunders) *chsd ldrs: rdn over 2f out: wknd wl over 1f out* **8/1**

1000 **9** *2* **My Girl Pearl (IRE)**[3] 2135 6-7-13 **65** oh13........... EdwardCreighton(3) 7 42
(M S Saunders) *hld up: rdn and effrt over 2f out: wknd wl over 1f out* **25/1**

1m 11.2s (-2.40) **Going Correction** -0.175s/f (Firm) **9** Ran SP% **122.2**
Speed ratings (Par 102):109,107,106,106,105 99,98,95,92
CSF £11.95 CT £46.18 TOTE £3.90: £1.80, £1.80, £1.90; EX 15.80 Trifecta £121.90 Pool: £180.30 - 1.05 winning units.
Owner Norcroft Park Stud **Bred** Norcroft Park Stud, And A J Hollis **Trained** Newmarket, Suffolk

FOCUS
A fair race, in which there was a good sprinting tempo, allowing the winner to come from last to first in the final two furlongs. The winning time was decent for the type of contest.

2234 INTERCASINO.CO.UK MAIDEN AUCTION STKS 6f

3:40 (3:40) (Class 5) 2-Y-0 **£3,886** (£1,156; £577; £288) **Stalls** Low

Form RPR

43 **1** **Hythe Bay**[9] 1959 2-8-0 ow1... JamesDoyle(5) 2 80
(R T Phillips) *mde all: rdn clr over 1f out: eased cl home: unchal* **7/1**[3]

2 *2½* **Go On Green (IRE)** 2-9-1 .... OscarUrbina 10 82
(E A L Dunlop) *cl up: chsd ldr 4f out: rdn over 1f out: no imp* **16/1**

2 **3** *1¼* **Buddies Girl (IRE)**[8] 1989 2-8-1 .... StephaneBreux(3) 5 68
(R Hannon) *dwlt: prog and swtchd rt 2f out: kpt on: nvr trbld ldrs* **11/10**[1]

2 **4** *½* **Caldra (IRE)**[8] 1980 2-8-9 .... DaneO'Neill 9 71+
(S Kirk) *in tch on outside: rdn 2f out: sn wknd* **2/1**[2]

5 *hd* **Part Timer (IRE)** 2-8-9 .... SamHitchcott 8 70
(M R Channon) *chsd ldrs: rdn 2f out: wknd fnl f* **14/1**

0 **6** *5* **Emma Jean Lad (IRE)**[43] 1107 2-8-9 .... FrancisFerris 4 55
(J S Moore) *chsd ldr tl 4f out: sn rdn and struggling* **33/1**

7 *3½* **Safari Sundowner (IRE)** 2-8-12 .... JimCrowley 7 48
(P Winkworth) *cl up tl 4f out: sn rdn and lost pl: no ch after* **22/1**

8 *3* **Danger Alley** 2-8-12 .... RichardMullen 3 39
(E J O'Neill) *dwlt: sn rdn to chse ldrs: outpcd 4f out: sn wl bhd* **16/1**

9 *1* **Linkslade Lad** 2-8-12 .... JimmyQuinn 1 36
(W R Muir) *slowly away: a wl bhd: t.o* **33/1**

10 *6* **Colonel Klink (IRE)** 2-8-9 .... JDSmith 6 15
(J S Moore) *s.s: a wl bhd: t.o* **40/1**

1m 12.88s (-0.72) **Going Correction** -0.175s/f (Firm) **10** Ran SP% **124.6**
Speed ratings (Par 93):97,93,92,91,91 84,79,75,74,66
CSF £111.37 TOTE £11.50: £2.30, £3.30, £1.10; EX 77.50 Trifecta £233.00 Part won. Pool: £328.18 - 0.69 winning units..

Owner Eastwell Manor Racing Ltd **Bred** C H Bothway **Trained** Adlestrop, Gloucs

FOCUS
Not a great maiden, but likely to contain several future winners at a sensible level. The winner won well, but it's hard to believe the two market leaders ran to their previous level.

NOTEBOOK
Hythe Bay had the rail to help her, but the speed she showed was no fluke, and she scored impressively. Ridden like this, she can put her pace to good use in nurseries. (op 5-1)

Go On Green(IRE), a 55,000gns son of former champion sprinter Kyllachy, made a solid debut and should have little problem going one better. He should then improve with racing. (op 14-1)

Buddies Girl(IRE), set plenty to do in midfield, never stopped running on but had too much ground to make up after switching wide into the centre of the track. She can do much better and should find a race soon. (op 5-4)

Caldra(IRE) did not live up to the promise of his debut, but was not helped by having to race in the middle of the course from his high draw. He deserves another chance, and should stay farther in due course. Official explanation: jockey said colt lost its action (op 11-4)

Part Timer(IRE) is bred to be speedy, and showed enough on this debut to suggest he has inherited some of his parents' ability. However, he is likely to be kept at a realistic level for the time being. (op 12-1 tchd 16-1)

Emma Jean Lad(IRE) showed a bit more speed this time, but will come into his own in nurseries and over an extra furlong or two.

2235 EBF INTERCASINO.CO.UK MAIDEN STKS 5f
4:10 (4:10) (Class 5) 3-Y-O+ **£3,886** (£1,156; £577; £288) **Stalls** Low

Form RPR

4452 **1** **Yellow Card**[18] [1751] 3-9-0 73 .... OscarUrbina 3 70
(N A Callaghan) *hld up: swtchd rt and prog over 1f out: led ins fnl f: wnt lft: pushed out* **2/1**[2]

2 *¾* **Prince Of Delphi** 3-9-0 .... DaneO'Neill 2 67
(H Candy) *led: rdn over 1f out: hdd 1f out: unable qck* **11/10**[1]

3 *1 ¼* **King Of Charm (IRE)** 3-9-0 .... GeorgeBaker 5 62
(G L Moore) *a.p: ev ch and rdn over 1f out: kpt on onepced* **20/1**

3023 **4** *shd* **Chanteuse Noire (USA)**[19] [1733] 3-8-9 63 .... (v) TPQueally 1 57
(J Noseda) *keen: trckd ldrs: swtchd rt and hdwy ins fnl f: nt rch ldrs* **8/1**[3]

0 **5** *hd* **Indian Ballet**[217] [6143] 3-8-9 .... RHills 9 56
(M A Jarvis) *cl up on outside: rdn to ld 1f out: hdd and hmpd ins fnl f: lost 3 pls cl home* **8/1**[3]

066 **6** *¾* **Silvanella (IRE)**[12] [1877] 3-8-9 40 .... FrancisFerris 6 54?
(M S Saunders) *bhd in last pair: rdn 3f out: kpt on fnl f: nt rch ldrs* **50/1**

50 **7** *nk* **Girandola**[200] [6351] 3-9-0 .... StephenCarson 4 58
(R F Johnson Houghton) *sn outpcd and wl bhd: styd on fnl f: nvr nrr* **33/1**

5043 **8** *3 ½* **Elusive Warrior (USA)**[18] [1750] 3-9-0 63 .... JimCrowley 7 45
(Mrs A J Perrett) *prom: rdn 2f out: wknd fnl f* **12/1**

0 **9** *1 ¾* **Maylea Gold (IRE)**[30] [1430] 3-8-9 .... JamesDoyle(5) 8 39
(Miss J Feilden) *chsd ldrs on outside: rdn 2f out: wkng whn bmpd over 1f out* **100/1**

0652 **10** *3* **Kahlua Bear**[19] [1728] 4-9-7 40 .... (b) SamHitchcott 10 28
(Miss K B Boutflower) *sn drvn along: chsd ldrs on outside: wkng whn bmpd over 1f out* **33/1**

60.61 secs (-0.19) **Going Correction** -0.175s/f (Firm)
WFA 3 from 4yo 7lb **10** Ran SP% **124.5**
Speed ratings (Par 103):94,92,90,90,90 89,88,83,80,75
CSF £4.73 TOTE £4.00: £1.10, £1.10, £5.00; EX 9.30 Trifecta £102.70 Pool: £302.51 - 2.09 winning units.

Owner John Livock Bloodstock Limited **Bred** Redmyre Bloodstock And S Hillen **Trained** Newmarket, Suffolk

■ Stewards' Enquiry : Oscar Urbina two-day ban: careless riding (Jun 14-15)

FOCUS
A fair maiden, though the time was modest, but a rough race in which several runners were hampered by the winner.

2236 INTERCASINO.CO.UK CONDITIONS STKS 1m 1f 149y
4:50 (4:50) (Class 3) 3-Y-O+ **£8,724** (£2,612; £1,306; £653) **Stalls** Low

Form RPR

5556 **1** **Weightless**[8] [1976] 6-9-2 108 .... JimCrowley 3 106
(Mrs A J Perrett) *mde all: rdn 2f out: r.o wl and a holding rivals after* **7/2**[3]

2153 **2** *1 ¼* **Take A Bow**[19] [1739] 5-9-2 105 .... JimmyQuinn 4 103
(P R Chamings) *chsd ldr for 2f: rdn 2f out: chsd ldr fnl f: no imp* **1/1**[1]

3130 **3** *2* **St Andrews (IRE)**[21] [1678] 6-10-0 106 .... RHills 1 111
(M A Jarvis) *chsd ldr after 2f: rdn 2f out: lost 2nd 1f out: onepced* **2/1**[2]

0500 **4** *7* **Pawan (IRE)**[21] [1663] 6-8-9 74 .... AnnStokell(7) 2 85?
(Miss A Stokell) *s.s: a last: rdn and lost tch wl over 2f out* **33/1**

2m 3.99s (-1.24) **Going Correction** +0.05s/f (Good) **4** Ran SP% **108.5**
Speed ratings (Par 107):106,105,103,97
CSF £7.54 TOTE £4.00; EX 8.50 Place 6 £85.85, Place 5 £69.57.

Owner M B Hawtin **Bred** Juddmonte Farms **Trained** Pulborough, W Sussex

FOCUS
A decent little race, though suffering from lack of runners. The winner dictated a modest tempo until quickening it up turning for home, so had the run of the race.

NOTEBOOK
Weightless was allowed to do his own thing in front, and that played straight into his hands. Under a well-judged ride, he never looked like being overhauled once the race began in earnest. (op 3-1)

Take A Bow, though failing to live up to favouritism, did not do badly considering that the winner has scored at Group 3 level, and had the race run to suit him. There will be other opportunities.

St Andrews(IRE) had a monumental task trying concede weight to the first two, so his starting price did seem rather short. However, he ran respectably in the circumstances. (op 15-8)

Pawan(IRE) was outclassed, but the modest early pace meant he kept in touch, travelling well enough, until the final bend.

T/Plt: £106.20 to a £1 stake. Pool: £41,628.55. 285.95 winning tickets. T/Qpdt: £13.20 to a £1 stake. Pool: £1,750.80. 97.50 winning tickets. SP

1883 MUSSELBURGH (R-H)
Saturday, June 3

OFFICIAL GOING: Good to firm (firm in places)
The ground was described as 'genuine good to firm, fast but no jar whatsoever'.
Wind: Moderate, half against Weather: Fine and sunny

2237 ARCHERFIELD HOUSE H'CAP 5f
2:20 (2:20) (Class 4) (0-85,80) 3-Y-O+ **£6,477** (£1,927; £963; £481) **Stalls** Low

Form RPR

000 **1** **Glencairn Star**[21] [1686] 5-8-10 65 .... DanielTudhope(3) 2 74+
(J S Goldie) *dwlt: hdwy and nt clr run over 1f out: burst through to ld ins last: r.o wl* **8/1**

5000 **2** *1* **Whinhill House**[21] [1686] 6-8-12 69 .... (p) MarkLawson(5) 9 74
(D W Barker) *chsd ldrs: led over 1f out: hdd and no ex ins last* **20/1**

0050 **3** *hd* **Ptarmigan Ridge**[14] [1856] 10-9-6 72 .... RoystonFfrench 1 76+
(Miss L A Perratt) *bhd: hdwy and n.m.r over 1f out: styd on ins last* **16/1**

0000 **4** *shd* **Colonel Cotton (IRE)**[134] [159] 7-9-6 72 .... (v) TonyHamilton 15 76+
(R A Fahey) *sn bhd: hdwy 2f out: kpt on wl ins last* **12/1**

6604 **5** *hd* **Angelofthenorth**[15] [1816] 4-8-4 61 oh4 .... GregFairley(5) 11 64
(C J Teague) *hmpd s: hdwy over 2f out: chsng ldrs 1f out: kpt on same pce* **25/1**

3062 **6** *hd* **Jun Fan (USA)**[12] [1886] 4-8-4 61 oh5 .... AndrewElliott(5) 6 63
(B Ellison) *chsd ldrs: edgd lft over 1f out: no ex ins last* **25/1**

2534 **7** *½* **Raccoon (IRE)**[25] [1563] 6-9-1 67 .... (v) MickyFenton 14 67
(T D Barron) *tubed; chsd ldrs on outer: kpt on same pce fnl f* **7/1**[3]

0130 **8** *¾* **Coconut Moon**[16] [1794] 4-8-9 61 oh6 .... DavidAllan 13 58
(E J Alston) *chsd ldrs on outer: kpt on same pce appr fnl f* **20/1**

4063 **9** *½* **Grigorovitch (IRE)**[21] [1662] 4-10-0 80 .... (p) TomEaves 4 75+
(I Semple) *t.k.h: trckd ldrs: nt clr run over 1f out: kpt on* **5/1**[1]

0041 **10** *nk* **Dizzy In The Head**[23] [1611] 7-8-13 65 .... (b) PaulMulrennan 8 59
(I Semple) *w ldrs: fdd appr fnl f* **9/1**

0600 **11** *1* **Malapropism**[15] [1820] 6-9-10 76 .... TonyCulhane 3 66
(M R Channon) *in rr on inner: nt clr run over 1f out: nvr on terms* **6/1**[2]

2003 **12** *½* **The Leather Wedge (IRE)**[15] [1816] 7-9-1 70 .... SaleemGolam(3) 7 58
(R Johnson) *led tl hdd and weakend over 1f out* **10/1**

3325 **13** *1* **Highland Song (IRE)**[16] [1793] 3-8-10 69 .... FergalLynch 10 53
(R F Fisher) *wnt rt s: sn in tch: lost pl over 1f out* **20/1**

0032 **14** *8* **Catch The Cat (IRE)**[23] [1611] 7-8-12 69 .... (v) AndrewMullen(5) 12 21
(Robert Gray) *swvd lft s: sn w ldrs: lost pl over 1f out: eased ins last* **9/1**

60.19 secs (-0.31) **Going Correction** -0.025s/f (Good)
WFA 3 from 4yo+ 7lb **14** Ran SP% **119.2**
Speed ratings (Par 105):101,99,99,98,98 98,97,96,95,95 93,92,91,78
CSF £163.80 CT £2535.33 TOTE £10.90: £3.40, £5.60, £4.60; EX 371.40.

Owner Frank Brady **Bred** Palm Tree Thoroughbreds **Trained** Uplawmoor, E Renfrews

FOCUS
An ordinary but competive sprint handicap in which they congregrated towards the stands' side.
Malapropism Official explanation: jockey said gelding was denied clear run
Catch The Cat(IRE) Official explanation: jockey said gelding finished lame

2238 ARCHERFIELD LINKS H'CAP 1m 6f
2:50 (2:50) (Class 3) (0-95,90) 4-Y-O+
£11,217 (£3,358; £1,679; £840; £419; £210) **Stalls** High

Form RPR

-111 **1** **Silvertown**[29] [1457] 11-8-10 79 .... TomEaves 5 88
(L Lungo) *led after 1f: edgd lft appr fnl f: hld on gamely* **9/2**[3]

0000 **2** *nk* **Ski Jump (USA)**[16] [1809] 6-8-6 75 .... (v) TonyHamilton 8 84
(R A Fahey) *led 1f: trckd wnr: effrt over 3f out: nt qckn ins last* **7/1**

5005 **3** *1 ¼* **Escayola (IRE)**[216] [6179] 6-9-0 83 .... (bt) FergalLynch 4 90
(W J Haggas) *hld up in rr: effrt on inner 2f out: styd on same pce ins last* **6/1**

1011 **4** *½* **Mceldowney**[1] [2193] 4-8-8 82 6ex .... GregFairley(5) 3 88
(M Johnston) *chsd ldrs: pushed along 7f out: kpt on same pce fnl f* **7/2**[1]

4360 **5** *1* **Most Definitely (IRE)**[17] [1779] 6-9-2 85 .... DavidAllan 7 90
(T D Easterby) *trckd ldrs gng wl: effrt on inner over 1f out: kpt on same pce* **4/1**[2]

2660 **6** *5* **Hiddensee (USA)**[24] [1584] 4-9-7 90 .... RoystonFfrench 2 88
(M Johnston) *hld up in tch: drvn along over 4f out: hung rt and lost pl over 1f out* **8/1**

4030 **7** *15* **Sand And Stars (IRE)**[32] [1376] 5-8-2 74 .... SaleemGolam(3) 6 51
(M H Tompkins) *w ldrs: effrt over 3f out: lost pl over 1f out: eased* **12/1**

11-0 **8** *dist* **Regal Setting (IRE)**[24] [4762] 5-9-1 84 .... PaulMulrennan 1 —
(J Howard Johnson) *swvd lft s: in rr: drvn 9f out: lost pl over 5f out: sn bhd: virtually p.u: t.o* **16/1**

3m 1.80s (-3.90) **Going Correction** -0.25s/f (Firm) **8** Ran SP% **111.9**
Speed ratings (Par 107):101,100,100,99,99 96,87,—
CSF £34.07 CT £186.46 TOTE £4.60: £1.40, £3.30, £1.70; EX 36.20.

Owner R J Gilbert & SW Group Logistics Limited **Bred** Juddmonte Farms **Trained** Carrutherstown, D'fries & G'way

FOCUS
A decent staying handicap, but it was run at just a steady gallop. The winner continues in terrific form and is very game, but the race was run to suit him much better than his hold-up rivals.

NOTEBOOK
Silvertown, 6lb higher, made it four Flat wins on the bounce. He dictated things from the front and simply would not be denied, but it was a close call in the end. (op 7-2)

Ski Jump(USA), 5lb lower than his last success, showed a return to form and in the end made the winner pull out all the stops. (op 8-1 tchd 9-1)

Escayola(IRE), absent since October, fought his rider due to the lack of serious pace. He was only found wanting inside the last and this was a sound effort over a trip that is his bare mimimum. (op 7-1)

Mceldowney, making a rapid return to action, was being niggled at turning into the back straight. He stuck to his guns but never looked a real threat. He is obviously as tough as old boots. (op 11-4)

Most Definitely(IRE), back to his last winning mark, travelled supremely well but when popped the question could only find the one pace. He could have done with a much stronger galloip and is well worth bearing in mind. (op 6-1)

Hiddensee(USA), in trouble turning in, hung fire as if feeling the ground. He has not been at his best so far this year.

Regal Setting(IRE) Official explanation: vet said gelding had a heart irregularity

2239 CALECO WASTE & SOUTHERN COMFORT H'CAP 1m
3:20 (3:20) (Class 4) (0-85,82) 3-Y-O **£6,477** (£1,927; £963; £481) **Stalls** Low

Form RPR
4351 **1** **Pressure Putt**[34] 1312 3-9-4 **79**.......... FergalLynch 3 89+
(W J Haggas) *trckd ldrs: smooth hdwy to ld 2f out: shkn up and styd on strly* **11/4**[1]
0506 **2** *3* **Zennerman (IRE)**[23] 1606 3-9-4 **82**.......... DanielTudhope(3) 1 85
(W M Brisbourne) *rrd s: hdwy over 2f out: hung rt and wnt 2nd over 1f out: no imp* **9/1**
3000 **3** *¾* **Luna Landing**[208] 6284 3-9-1 **76**.......... DaleGibson 7 77
(Jedd O'Keeffe) *chsd ldrs: outpcd over 3f out: styd on fnl f* **25/1**
2163 **4** *5* **Ahmedy (IRE)**[32] 1381 3-9-5 **80**.......... TonyCulhane 6 70
(M R Channon) *hld up: hdwy over 3f out: rdn and one pce fnl 2f* **7/2**[2]
5031 **5** *hd* **Methusaleh (IRE)**[30] 1444 3-9-4 **79**.......... DavidAllan 2 71+
(T D Easterby) *hld up: effrt over 2f out: one pce whn nt clr run over 1f out* **7/2**[2]
6361 **6** *1* **Stonehaugh (IRE)**[38] 1230 3-9-2 **77**..........(t) PaulMulrennan 4 64
(J Howard Johnson) *t.k.h: mde most tl 2f out: sn wknd* **14/1**
100 **7** *3 ½* **Coalpark (IRE)**[44] 1099 3-8-13 **79**.......... GregFairley(5) 8 58
(M Johnston) *w ldr: drvn over 3f out: lost pl over 1f out* **17/2**[3]
1 **8** *5* **Roscommon**[270] 5016 3-8-12 **73**.......... TomEaves 5 40
(I Semple) *in rr: sn pushed along: hung rt and bhd fnl 3f* **11/1**

1m 39.18s (-3.32) **Going Correction** -0.25s/f (Firm) **8** Ran SP% **110.5**
Speed ratings (Par 101):106,103,102,97,97 96,92,87
CSF £26.16 CT £476.10 TOTE £2.80: £1.20, £1.60, £5.20; EX 31.60.
Owner Lee Palmer **Bred** Mrs S Crompton **Trained** Newmarket, Suffolk

FOCUS
Ordinary form but the winner can progress further and the runner-up was back to something like his best juvenile form.
Zennerman(IRE) Official explanation: jockey said gelding reared as stalls opened

2240 HORSESHOE BAR & SMIRNOFF VODKA (S) STKS 1m
3:55 (3:56) (Class 5) 3-Y-O+ **£3,238** (£963; £481; £240) **Stalls** Low

Form RPR
0414 **1** **Ulysees (IRE)**[12] 1885 7-9-12 69.......... TomEaves 2 65
(I Semple) *trckd ldrs gng wl: chal 2f out: shkn up to ld post* **11/10**[1]
2250 **2** *shd* **Desert Lightning (IRE)**[5] 2077 4-9-7 55.......... PatCosgrave 3 60
(K R Burke) *s.i.s: sn trcking ldrs: led over 2f out: jst ct* **7/1**[3]
2430 **3** *3 ½* **High Swainston**[54] 940 5-9-4 45.......... DanielTudhope(3) 6 52
(R Craggs) *trckd ldrs: nt clr run and swtchd lft 2f out: hung rt and kpt on fnl f* **11/1**
0054 **4** *shd* **Proud Western (USA)**[11] 1914 8-9-7 42..........(t) RoystonFfrench 5 52
(B Ellison) *hld up: hdwy over 3f out: rdn over 1f out: edgd rt and kpt on same pce* **16/1**
0000 **5** *¾* **Aqua**[18] 1761 4-9-2 53.......... MickyFenton 1 45
(P T Midgley) *racd wd: in tch: outpcd over 3f out: kpt on fnl f* **33/1**
6061 **6** *¾* **Chateau (IRE)**[5] 2077 4-9-12 58.......... DeanMcKeown 7 56+
(G A Swinbank) *hld up in rr: hdwy on ins over 2f out: shkn up over 1f out: one pce whn hmpd ins last* **7/2**[2]
0436 **7** *¾* **Fit To Fly (IRE)**[18] 1757 5-9-7 41..........(p) JohnFortune 8 47
(R C Guest) *led tl over 2f out: lost pl over 1f out* **25/1**
1000 **8** *3 ½* **Mystified (IRE)**[33] 1345 3-9-1 61..........(b) TonyCulhane 9 43
(R F Fisher) *s.i.s: sn chsng ldrs: chal over 4f out: edgd lft 2f out: sn lost pl* **12/1**

1m 40.34s (-2.16) **Going Correction** -0.25s/f (Firm)
WFA 3 from 4yo+ 11lb **8** Ran SP% **111.0**
Speed ratings (Par 103):100,99,96,96,95 94,94,90
CSF £8.80 TOTE £1.80: £1.10, £1.80, £2.20; EX 8.40.There was no bid for the winner.
Owner The Farmer Boys (Jock, Danny & Ally) **Bred** Sweetmans Bloodstock **Trained** Carluke, S Lanarks
■ Cordage (14/1) was withdrawn; injured going to s. R4 applies, deduct 5p in the £.
■ Stewards' Enquiry : Royston Ffrench two-day ban: careless riding (Jun 14-15)

FOCUS
A run-of-the mill seller run at a strong gallop.

2241 ROSEBURN BAR & GORDONS GIN MAIDEN AUCTION STKS 5f
4:35 (4:41) (Class 5) 2-Y-O **£3,238** (£963; £481; £240) **Stalls** Low

Form RPR
1 **Holdin Foldin (IRE)** 2-8-11.......... PatCosgrave 2 85+
(K R Burke) *lengthy: unf: mde all: shkn up 1f out: sn qcknd wl clr: easily* **7/4**[1]
04 **2** *6* **The Mighty Ogmore**[16] 1790 2-8-7 ow2.......... MickyFenton 4 55
(R C Guest) *chsd wnr: rdn over 2f out: kpt on same pce fnl f* **8/1**
3 *nk* **Gap Princess (IRE)** 2-8-6.......... TonyHamilton 1 53
(R A Fahey) *rangy: unf: n.m.r on inner after 1f: chsd ldrs: kpt onf inal f* **7/1**
4 *2* **Persian Peril** 2-8-11.......... DeanMcKeown 5 51
(G A Swinbank) *lengthy: s.i.s: sn chsng ldrs: wknd fnl f* **6/1**[3]
634 **5** *7* **Esprit D'Amour (IRE)**[19] 1730 2-8-7.......... DavidAllan 3 22
(T D Easterby) *chsd ldrs: rdn over 2f out: lost pl over 1f out: sn bhd* **2/1**[2]

60.80 secs (0.30) **Going Correction** -0.025s/f (Good) **5** Ran SP% **107.6**
Speed ratings (Par 93):96,86,85,82,71
CSF £14.47 TOTE £2.40: £1.10, £3.40; EX 17.80.
Owner A Rhodes Haulage And P Timmins **Bred** Paul Starr **Trained** Middleham Moor, N Yorks

FOCUS
The two with previous experience had shown only moderate form, but no getting away from the ease with which newcomer Holdin Foldin scored, and he is going to hold his own in better company.

NOTEBOOK
Holdin Foldin(IRE) ◆, an April foal, knew his job. Dictating things from the front, he quickened right away when given the office. It took little winning but he looks a useful prospect. (op 6-4 tchd 2-1 in places)
The Mighty Ogmore, having her third run, tended to race wide. Her entry in a seller underlines the weakness of the race. (tchd 7-1)
Gap Princess(IRE), a February foal, stands over plenty of ground. Left short of room on the inner, she looked second best on the day and will be better suited by six furlongs. (tchd 11-2)
Persian Peril, a May foal, missed a beat at the start and did not get home. He looks as though he may need a little more time yet. (op 7-1)
Esprit D'Amour(IRE), having her fourth start, dropped right away and completed in her own time. She is certainly not progressing. (op 7-4)

2242 LOTHIAN DAF H'CAP 1m 4f
5:10 (5:10) (Class 6) (0-65,64) 4-Y-O+ **£3,238** (£963; £481; £240) **Stalls** High

Form RPR
5605 **1** **Acuzio**[40] 1194 5-8-5 **48**.......... DavidAllan 7 57
(W M Brisbourne) *in tch: effrt over 3f out: styd on up ins to ld ins last* **11/1**
0030 **2** *½* **Intavac Boy**[18] 1756 5-8-8 **54**.......... DanielTudhope(3) 5 62
(C W Thornton) *led: qcknd 4f out: wnt lft over 1f out: hdd and no ex ins last* **11/2**[2]
3600 **3** *nk* **Kyle Of Lochalsh**[17] 1201 6-7-13 **47**.......... AndrewElliott(5) 10 55
(J S Goldie) *hld up towards rr: hdwy over 5f out: chsng ldrs whn carried lft over 1f out: kpt on wl ins last* **13/2**[3]
1351 **4** *nk* **Crathorne (IRE)**[12] 1887 6-9-7 **64**.......... PaulMulrennan 2 71
(M Todhunter) *trckd ldrs: effrt 4f out: carried lft over 1f out: no ex ins last* **7/4**[1]
5045 **5** *5* **Colway Ritz**[17] 3490 12-7-13 **47** oh1 ow2.......... AndrewMullen(5) 6 46
(W Storey) *hld up in rr: hdwy over 3f out: one pce fnl 2f* **20/1**
6020 **6** *5* **Purple Dancer (FR)**[31] 1425 4-9-0 **57**.......... DeanMcKeown 3 48
(G A Swinbank) *swtchd rt s: hld up in rr: effrt 4f out: hung rt: kpt on fnl 2f: nvr on terms* **8/1**
0030 **7** *6* **Mary Gray**[19] 1748 4-8-6 **49**..........(b) RoystonFfrench 11 30
(M Johnston) *w ldr: lost pl 2f out* **11/1**
3106 **8** *¾* **Awaken**[37] 1249 5-8-5 **48**.......... DaleGibson 9 28
(Miss Tracy Waggott) *bhd: sme hdwy over 3f out: wknd 2f out* **20/1**
2460 **9** *4* **Grandma's Girl**[176] 6153 4-8-5 **51**.......... SaleemGolam(3) 8 25
(Robert Gray) *chsd ldrs: lost pl over 2f out* **33/1**
5205 **10** *18* **Blue Opal**[37] 1256 4-8-7 **50** ow5.......... MickyFenton 1 —
(Miss S E Hall) *in tch: drvn 5f out: hung lft and lost pl over 3f out: sn bhd* **16/1**

2m 35.41s (-1.49) **Going Correction** -0.25s/f (Firm) **10** Ran SP% **111.2**
Speed ratings (Par 101):94,93,93,93,89 86,82,82,79,67
CSF £65.16 CT £416.11 TOTE £16.10: £3.90, £2.70, £1.50; EX 147.70.
Owner Derek Hartland and Peter Gradwell **Bred** D W Hartland **Trained** Great Ness, Shropshire
■ Stewards' Enquiry : Daniel Tudhope one-day ban: careless riding (Jun 14)

FOCUS
A low-grade handicap run at a sound gallop but the placed horses got in each others way, leaving the door open for the winner.
Mary Gray Official explanation: jockey said filly hung left-handed throughout
Blue Opal Official explanation: jockey said filly was unsuited by good to firm/good in places going

2243 TYNECASTLE ARMS & TEACHER'S WHISKY H'CAP 1m 1f
5:45 (5:46) (Class 6) (0-65,65) 3-Y-O **£3,238** (£963; £481; £240) **Stalls** Low

Form RPR
3003 **1** **Apache Nation (IRE)**[14] 1859 3-9-0 **58**.......... PhillipMakin 2 64
(M Dods) *in tch: hdwy on outer over 2f out: styd on to ld ins last: jst hld on* **12/1**
001 **2** *hd* **English City (IRE)**[19] 1731 3-8-11 **55**.......... TonyCulhane 9 61
(B Smart) *s.i.s: sn mid-div: hdwy on outer over 3f out: styd on ins last: jst hld* **5/1**[2]
3565 **3** *½* **Touch Of Ivory (IRE)**[12] 1888 3-8-8 **52**.......... TonyHamilton 8 57
(R A Fahey) *hld up in mid-div: hdwy on inner over 3f out: kpt on wl fnl f* **12/1**
0245 **4** *nk* **Jaassey**[14] 1859 3-8-9 **58**.......... GregFairley(5) 16 62
(T D Walford) *trckd ldrs: led over 2f out: wnt lft over 1f out: hdd and no ex ins last* **9/1**
6000 **5** *1* **Gigs Magic (USA)**[26] 1533 3-8-4 **48**.......... RoystonFfrench 11 50
(M Johnston) *chsd ldrs: kpt on same pce fnl f* **16/1**
0001 **6** *shd* **The Great Delaney**[5] 2065 3-7-11 **44** 6ex.......... AndrewElliott(5) 5 48
(K McAuliffe) *w ldrs on outer: kpt on same pce fnl f* **3/1**[1]
2030 **7** *1* **Prince Evelith (GER)**[210] 6249 3-9-7 **65**.......... DeanMcKeown 7 65
(G A Swinbank) *bhd: hdwy and hung rt over 2f out: kpt on: nvr rchd ldrs* **15/2**[3]
4506 **8** *¾* **Hunting Haze**[237] 5769 3-9-6 **64**.......... MickyFenton 10 62
(Miss S E Hall) *w ldrs: fdd fnl f* **33/1**
0004 **9** *shd* **Alf Tupper**[40] 1182 3-9-4 **65**.......... SaleemGolam(3) 15 63
(M H Tompkins) *s.i.s: hdwy to chse ldrs over 5f out: kpt on same pce fnl 2f* **5/1**[2]
000 **10** *6* **Revolving World (IRE)**[13] 1866 3-9-1 **59**.......... PatCosgrave 1 45
(T J Fitzgerald) *mid-div: hdwy on outer 4f out: lost pl 2f out* **33/1**
505 **11** *1 ¼* **Kasarami (IRE)**[301] 4140 3-8-5 **52**.......... DanielTudhope(3) 3 36
(J S Goldie) *s.i.s: bhd: sme hdwy over 2f out: nvr on terms* **50/1**
000 **12** *1* **Dark Night (IRE)**[169] 6595 3-8-5 **49** ow1.......... TomEaves 12 31
(D W Barker) *hld up in rr: sme hdwy over 3f out: wknd 2f out* **25/1**
6000 **13** *4* **The Dunion**[9] 1950 3-7-13 **48** oh6 ow2.......... AndrewMullen(5) 4 22
(Miss L A Perratt) *a in rr* **40/1**
000 **14** *12* **Consent**[231] 5886 3-8-9 **53**.......... DavidAllan 13 —
(A Dickman) *in rr: sme hdwy over 3f out: lost pl over 2f out* **40/1**
5000 **15** *3 ½* **Lazzoom (IRE)**[24] 1593 3-8-6 **50**.......... DaleGibson 14 —
(Miss Tracy Waggott) *t.k.h in mid-field: lost pl 3f out: sn bhd* **100/1**
4005 **16** *1 ¾* **Boumsong (IRE)**[16] 1791 3-8-7 **51** oh4 ow5..........(v) PaulMulrennan 6 —
(R C Guest) *led: hdd over 2f out: sn lost pl: eased 1f out* **50/1**

1m 52.73s (-3.27) **Going Correction** -0.25s/f (Firm) **16** Ran SP% **120.9**
Speed ratings (Par 97):104,103,103,103,102 102,101,100,100,95 94,93,89,78,75 74
CSF £66.46 CT £786.86 TOTE £14.20: £2.60, £1.40, £2.60, £1.90; EX 48.60 Place 6 £279.70, Place 5 £43.79.
Owner Doug Graham **Bred** Crone Stud Farms Ltd **Trained** Denton, Co Durham

FOCUS
Another low-grade handicap, but it was run at a true pace.
T/Plt: £687.80 to a £1 stake. Pool: £45,323.20. 48.10 winning tickets. T/Qpdt: £42.00 to a £1 stake. Pool: £2,298.10. 40.40 winning tickets. WG

2137 SOUTHWELL (L-H)
Saturday, June 3

OFFICIAL GOING: Standard
Wind: Almost nil Weather: Fine and sunny

2244 SOUTHWELL-RACECOURSE.CO.UK MAIDEN STKS 1m (F)
6:20 (6:20) (Class 5) 3-Y-O **£3,238** (£963; £481; £240) **Stalls** Low

Form RPR
222 **1** **Speedy Sam**[13] 1866 3-9-3 77.......... DarrenWilliams 12 72
(K R Burke) *chsd ldrs: led over 2f out: sn rdn clr: hung lft over 1f out: eased ins fnl f* **5/2**[2]
020 **2** *5* **Digger Boy**[22] 1641 3-9-3 67.......... MatthewHenry 9 62
(M A Jarvis) *bhd: rdn over 2f out: r.o ins fnl f: nrst fin* **20/1**

02 **3** *2 ½* **Plush**[32] 1386 3-9-3 .... SebSanders 4 57
(Sir Mark Prescott) *sn led: hdd over 2f out: wknd fnl f* **6/1**[3]

43 **4** *1 ¼* **Lindenburgh Way (IRE)**[14] 1844 3-9-3 .... MichaelTebbutt 8 55
(B J Meehan) *mid-div: sn pushed along: rdn over 3f out: no imp* **5/6**[1]

6 **5** *1 ¼* **Xpres Maite**[30] 1445 3-9-0 .... AmirQuinn(3) 2 52
(S R Bowring) *prom over 4f* **40/1**

000 **6** *2* **Mighty Observer (IRE)**[233] 5847 3-9-3 49 .... JamieMackay 6 48
(M H Tompkins) *s.i.s: outpcd: nvr nrr* **40/1**

03 **7** *hd* **Ardent Prince**[215] 6199 3-9-3 .... DavidKinsella 10 48
(Heather Dalton) *chsd ldr 5f: sn rdn: wknd over 1f out* **33/1**

0645 **8** *5* **October Sun**[25] 1576 3-8-10 35 ....(b[1]) ChrisCavanagh(7) 7 38
(Miss D Mountain) *s.s: outpcd* **66/1**

0050 **9** *1 ¼* **Topflight Wildbird**[19] 1726 3-8-12 45 ....(b) J-PGuillambert 11 30
(Mrs G S Rees) *chsd ldrs over 4f* **100/1**

046 **10** *hd* **Veba (USA)**[299] 4220 3-8-10 69 .... SladeO'Hara(7) 1 35
(B W Hills) *prom over 4f* **20/1**

20 **11** *13* **Catherine Medici**[7] 2019 3-8-12 .... StanleyChin 5 —
(R M H Cowell) *mid-div: lost pl over 6f out: sn bhd* **25/1**

12 *43* **Diamondbanker** 3-9-3 .... LeeEnstone 3 —
(Jedd O'Keeffe) *s.i.s: outpcd* **66/1**

1m 43.31s (-1.29) **Going Correction** -0.175s/f (Stan) 12 Ran SP% **122.6**
Speed ratings (Par 99):99,94,91,90,89 87,86,81,80,80 67,24
CSF £54.51 TOTE £4.10: £1.10, £7.30, £2.10; EX 67.30.
Owner Mrs M Gittins **Bred** Cheveley Park Stud Ltd **Trained** Middleham Moor, N Yorks

FOCUS
An ordinary maiden. With the favourite Lindenbergh Way below form Speedy Sam was entitled to win in good style.
Lindenburgh Way(IRE) Official explanation: trainer's representative said colt was unsuited by fibresand surface
Xpres Maite Official explanation: jockey said gelding had no more to give

2245 PLAY GOLF AND COME RACING (S) STKS 1m (F)
6:50 (6:50) (Class 6) 4-Y-0+ **£2,388** (£705; £352) **Stalls** Low

Form RPR

0040 **1** **Resplendent Prince**[19] 1746 4-9-1 52 ....(v) DeanCorby(3) 14 58
(P Howling) *chsd ldrs: led over 2f out: rdn and hung lft over 1f out: edgd rt ins fnl f: r.o* **12/1**

6406 **2** *1 ¾* **Gem Bien (USA)**[9] 1947 8-8-12 54 ....(p) PaulQuinn 12 48
(D W Chapman) *in rr: hdwy over 3f out: rdn: hung lft and ev ch over 1f out: nt run on* **6/1**

4305 **3** *nk* **Paso Doble**[26] 1550 8-8-6 55 ow1 .... JamesMillman(7) 1 49
(B R Millman) *s.i.s: outpcd: hdwy over 1f out: r.o: nrst fin* **4/1**[2]

4152 **4** *nk* **Legal Lover (IRE)**[25] 1574 4-8-11 50 .... RussellKennemore(7) 5 53
(R Hollinshead) *a.p: chsd ldr over 4f out: led over 3f out: rdn and hdd over 2f out: no ex ins fnl f* **3/1**[1]

0460 **5** *1* **Gawrosz (POL)**[5] 2075 7-8-12 40 .... DavidKinsella 7 45
(G J Smith) *s.i.s: outpcd: hdwy and hung lft over 1f out: r.o: nrst fin* **33/1**

6046 **6** *2 ½* **Priorina (IRE)**[3] 2141 4-8-13 46 ....(v) RobertHavlin 9 41
(D Haydn Jones) *mid-div: outpcd over 4f out: hdwy u.p over 2f out: wknd fnl f* **13/2**

0000 **7** *6* **Duxford**[5] 2070 5-8-12 53 ....(p) JamieMackay 10 28
(D K Ivory) *s.i.s: outpcd: nvr nrr* **18/1**

U120 **8** *shd* **Musical Gift**[11] 1915 6-9-4 49 ....(v) J-PGuillambert 13 34
(P A Blockley) *mid-div: hdwy over 3f out: rdn and wknd over 1f out* **11/2**[3]

1000 **9** *nk* **Desert Fury**[24] 1591 9-9-4 50 ....(b) LeeEnstone 6 33
(R Bastiman) *s.i.s: hdwy over 3f out: rdn and wknd 2f out* **14/1**

00 **10** *5* **Galloping Gertie**[18] 1757 4-8-7 .... MatthewHenry 4 12
(J Hetherton) *s.i.s: outpcd* **66/1**

0604 **11** *2 ½* **Roko**[25] 1577 4-8-9 39 ....(bt) BenSwarbrick(3) 8 12
(S R Bowring) *led after 1f: rdn and hdd over 3f out: wknd 2f out* **66/1**

0600 **12** *1 ½* **Active Account (USA)**[3] 2137 9-8-5 50 ....(b) ChrisGlenister(7) 2 9
(J R Holt) *sn outpcd: effrt over 3f out: sn wknd* **50/1**

10/0 **13** *15* **Mujarad (USA)**[78] 285 6-8-5 ....(b) RDEgan(7) 11 —
(P M Mooney, Ire) *chsd ldrs over 4f* **66/1**

3135 **14** *24* **La Musique**[25] 1575 4-9-4 47 .... SebSanders 3 —
(P J McBride) *led 1f: wknd over 3f out* **8/1**

1m 43.55s (-1.05) **Going Correction** -0.175s/f (Stan) 14 Ran SP% **128.1**
Speed ratings (Par 101):98,96,95,95,94 92,86,86,85,80 78,76,61,37
CSF £86.58 TOTE £19.90: £6.20, £2.70, £1.70; EX 87.80.There was no bid for the winner.
Owner Mrs J P Howling **Bred** Miss K Rausing **Trained** Newmarket, Suffolk

FOCUS
If Gem Bien had been in a better mood on the day, he would have almost certainly won. Had Paso Doble got going a bit earlier he might have won, which, unfortunately, does not say much for the standard of the form.
Roko Official explanation: jockey said gelding stopped very quickly at approximately 4f marker
La Musique Official explanation: jockey said gelding moved poorly throughout

2246 PETER SIMM 18TH BIRTHDAY H'CAP 1m 3f (F)
7:20 (7:20) (Class 6) (0-65,62) 3-Y-0 **£2,590** (£770; £385; £192) **Stalls** Low

Form RPR

0000 **1** **Arsad (IRE)**[22] 1638 3-9-0 55 .... StanleyChin 7 63
(C E Brittain) *hld up: hdwy 1/2-way: rdn 3f out: styd on to ld nr fin* **40/1**

0041 **2** *¾* **Liberate**[3] 2124 3-9-6 61 6ex .... SebSanders 13 68+
(Sir Mark Prescott) *hld up: hmpd over 9f out: hdwy 6f out: rdn and hung lft over 2f out: led over 1f out: hdd u.p nr fin* **4/7**[1]

0504 **3** *1* **Citelle (IRE)**[22] 1652 3-8-13 54 ....(t) RobertHavlin 11 59
(Mrs P N Dutfield) *sn led: rdn and hdd over 1f out: no ex ins fnl f* **20/1**

000 **4** *7* **Trick Or Treat**[176] 6528 3-9-3 58 .... JamieMackay 2 52
(J G Given) *prom: rdn over 3f out: sn outpcd* **25/1**

0005 **5** *1* **Machhapuchhare**[19] 1732 3-8-13 54 .... JohnEgan 10 47
(W M Brisbourne) *chsd ldrs: edgd lft over 9f out: rdn over 3f out: hung lft and wknd over 1f out* **25/1**

0000 **6** *1* **Cragganmore Creek**[22] 1652 3-9-2 57 .... DerekMcGaffin 4 48
(D Morris) *hld up: effrt over 3f out: sn hung lft and no imp* **33/1**

0000 **7** *hd* **Dynamite Deano**[34] 1314 3-8-2 50 .... JamieJones(7) 6 41
(D K Ivory) *prom: rdn over 3f out: hung lft and wknd over 1f out* **33/1**

050 **8** *5* **Sahf London**[26] 1546 3-8-3 49 .... TravisBlock(5) 8 32
(G L Moore) *prom: hmpd and lost pl over 9f out: hdwy 6f out: rdn and wknd over 2f out* **16/1**[3]

4555 **9** *7* **Flashing Floozie**[34] 1314 3-8-10 51 .... DavidKinsella 12 22
(M F Harris) *chsd ldrs over 8f* **20/1**

0220 **10** *16* **Hits Only Life (USA)**[14] 1851 3-8-9 55 .... DerekNolan(5) 9 —
(J Pearce) *bhd whn hmpd over 9f out: n.d* **7/1**[2]

0045 **11** *5* **Mighty Kitchener (USA)**[78] 656 3-9-7 62 .... J-PGuillambert 3 —
(P Howling) *mid-divsion: lost pl 8f out: rdn and wknd 4f out* **16/1**[3]

4643 **F** **Impeccable Guest (IRE)**[5] 2082 3-8-6 52 .... LeanneKershaw(5) 14 —
(P C Haslam) *in rr whn hmpd and fell over 9f out* **7/1**[2]

000 **P** **Prophet Preacher (IRE)**[24] 1598 3-8-4 52 .... MarkCoumbe(7) 5 —
(M J Attwater) *in rr whn stmbld and rdr lost irons after 1f: sn bhd: p.u 1/2-way* **50/1**

2m 26.98s (-1.92) **Going Correction** -0.175s/f (Stan) 13 Ran SP% **127.9**
Speed ratings (Par 97):99,98,97,92,91 91,91,87,82,70 67,—,—
CSF £64.11 CT £640.37 TOTE £82.40: £17.70, £1.02, £5.80; EX 147.60.
Owner Sultan Ali **Bred** Barnane Stud **Trained** Newmarket, Suffolk
■ Stewards' Enquiry : Derek Nolan three-day ban: weighed in heavier than when weighed out (Jun 14-16)

FOCUS
A rough race early. Sahf London got a slight knock in the pack that caused him to hamper Liberate, who swerved out to his right, which caused the jock on Impeccable Guest to fall off. Given how narrowly he was beaten in the end, the favourite was probably unlucky not to have won.
Prophet Preacher(IRE) Official explanation: jockey said filly was hampered by loose horse, his saddle slipped, causing him to lose his stirrups

2247 CHESTERFIELD DAIRY SUPPLIES LIMITED H'CAP 6f (F)
7:50 (7:52) (Class 5) (0-70,70) 3-Y-0 **£3,238** (£963; £481; £240) **Stalls** Low

Form RPR

2401 **1** **Hillbilly Cat (USA)**[3] 2138 3-8-9 61 6ex .... BenSwarbrick(3) 7 66
(T D Barron) *chsd ldrs: rdn to ld over 1f out: r.o u.p* **9/4**[1]

0054 **2** *½* **Bold Argument (IRE)**[22] 1646 3-9-7 70 ....(t) RobertHavlin 6 73
(Mrs P N Dutfield) *dwlt: outpcd: hdwy over 1f out: rdn and hung lft ins fnl f: r.o* **11/2**[3]

0 **3** *2 ½* **Fikri**[42] 1153 3-9-0 63 .... JohnEgan 3 59
(T J Pitt) *trckd ldrs: led over 2f out: rdn and hdd over 1f out: no ex ins fnl f* **11/4**[2]

3001 **4** *½* **Mister Becks (IRE)**[18] 1768 3-7-13 51 oh1 .... JohnMcAuley(3) 5 45
(M C Chapman) *led: hdd over 3f out: sn rdn: styd on same pce appr fnl f* **10/1**

6336 **5** *hd* **Shopfitter**[15] 1825 3-7-11 51 oh11 ....(b) MarcHalford(5) 4 44
(Mrs C A Dunnett) *chsd ldrs: rdn over 1f out: styd on same pce* **25/1**

2510 **6** *½* **Smile For Us**[15] 1825 3-9-1 69 ....(b) JerryO'Dwyer(5) 1 61
(C Drew) *sn pushed along and prom: rdn to ld over 3f out: hdd over 2f out: styd on same pce appr fnl f* **6/1**

0100 **7** *hd* **Mujelle**[6] 2050 3-8-11 67 .... JamesMillman(7) 2 58
(D K Ivory) *s.i.s: outpcd: nvr nrr* **8/1**

8 *19* **Leonards Girl (IRE)**[289] 4517 3-8-0 56 .... RDEgan(7) 8 —
(P M Mooney, Ire) *plld hrd and prom: wknd 1/2-way: sn hung lft* **12/1**

1m 17.57s (0.67) **Going Correction** -0.175s/f (Stan) 8 Ran SP% **118.8**
Speed ratings (Par 99):88,87,84,83,83 82,82,56
CSF £15.91 CT £36.02 TOTE £3.00: £1.10, £1.20, £2.10; EX 22.70.
Owner Laurence O'Kane **Bred** Adena Springs **Trained** Maunby, N Yorks

FOCUS
A very ordinary handicap and the time was very slow. The form is held down by the proximity of the fourth and fifth.

2248 JOIN US ON LADIES NIGHT 22ND JUNE FILLIES' H'CAP 7f (F)
8:20 (8:20) (Class 6) (0-65,65) 4-Y-0+ **£2,730** (£806; £403) **Stalls** Low

Form RPR

4000 **1** **Rosein**[231] 5893 4-9-4 62 .... J-PGuillambert 2 75
(Mrs G S Rees) *chsd ldr: led over 4f out: rdn over 1f out: edgd lft ins fnl f: r.o* **11/1**

0106 **2** *2 ½* **Chickado (IRE)**[29] 1463 5-8-6 50 ow2 ....(p) RobertHavlin 6 56
(D Haydn Jones) *a.p: chsd wnr 3f out: rdn over 1f out: styd on same pce* **4/1**[3]

1164 **3** *3* **Sweet Pickle**[70] 732 5-9-3 64 ....(e) AmirQuinn(3) 8 62
(J R Boyle) *hld up: hdwy over 2f out: rdn over 1f out: no imp* **7/2**[2]

50-0 **4** *1 ¾* **Shosolosa (IRE)**[15] 1821 4-9-7 65 .... MichaelTebbutt 10 59
(B J Meehan) *mid-div: hdwy 1/2-way: rdn over 2f out: styd on same pce appr fnl f* **12/1**

3166 **5** *4* **Outrageous Flirt (IRE)**[247] 5566 4-8-2 51 .... MarcHalford(5) 9 34
(A Dickman) *sn outpcd: sme hdwy over 1f out: n.d* **15/2**

0130 **6** *1 ¾* **Tacid**[56] 917 4-8-5 49 .... JohnEgan 4 28
(Dr J D Scargill) *hld up in tch: nt clr run and lost pl 3f out: n.d after* **11/4**[1]

3000 **7** *1 ¼* **Wodhill Be**[26] 1538 6-8-2 46 oh2 .... DavidKinsella 7 21
(D Morris) *plld hrd and prom: rdn and wknd over 1f out* **11/1**

4000 **8** *6* **Hows That**[32] 1387 4-7-12 49 oh11 ow3 ....(e[1]) PatrickDonaghy(7) 3 9
(K R Burke) *led: hdd over 4f out: wknd over 2f out: sn hung rt* **16/1**

0005 **9** *3 ½* **Grandma Ryta**[29] 1460 4-8-2 46 oh11 .... PaulQuinn 5 —
(John Berry) *sn outpcd* **20/1**

3000 **10** *23* **Mansiya**[22] 1645 4-8-11 55 ....(b[1]) SebSanders 1 —
(C E Brittain) *chsd ldrs 4f: wknd qckly: eased over 1f out* **16/1**

1m 28.74s (-2.06) **Going Correction** -0.175s/f (Stan) 10 Ran SP% **121.5**
Speed ratings (Par 98):104,101,97,95,91 89,87,80,76,50
CSF £57.11 CT £196.84 TOTE £12.10: £4.00, £2.00, £1.60; EX 59.60.
Owner Mrs G S Rees **Bred** J Gittins And Capt J H Wilson **Trained** Sollom, Lancs

FOCUS
A low-grade handicap won by a filly who had not won since her racecourse debut. She looked fairly impressive in victory, but her overall record suggests she is one to take on next time. The time was the quickest of the night.

2249 EXPERIENCE NOTTINGHAMSHIRE H'CAP 7f (F)
8:50 (8:50) (Class 6) (0-60,57) 3-Y-0 **£2,730** (£806; £403) **Stalls** Low

Form RPR

005 **1** **Grand Palace (IRE)**[36] 1274 3-8-9 48 .... BenSwarbrick(3) 13 56
(D Shaw) *hld up: rdn 1/2-way: hdwy over 2f out: led and hung lft over 1f out : styd on u.p* **10/1**

0051 **2** *¾* **Markestino**[25] 1576 3-8-3 44 .... DuranFentiman(5) 12 50
(T D Easterby) *s.i.s: sn prom: rdn to chse wnr over 1f out: hung lft ins fnl f: styd on* **9/2**[1]

0000 **3** *3 ½* **Madam Mac (IRE)**[19] 1736 3-8-9 45 .... MichaelTebbutt 4 42
(B J Meehan) *chsd ldrs: led over 4f out: rdn and hdd over 2f out: no ex fnl f* **16/1**

0040 **4** *½* **Goodbye Girl (IRE)**[18] 1768 3-8-3 44 ....(p) MarcHalford(5) 11 40
(Mrs C A Dunnett) *chsd ldrs: led over 2f out: hung lft and hdd over 1f out: wknd ins fnl f* **20/1**

0525 **5** *1* **Silvertown Sky (IRE)**[3] 2138 3-8-3 42 .... DominicFox(3) 7 35
(P L Gilligan) *chsd ldrs: rdn over 2f out: wknd over 1f out* **9/1**

0026 **6** *1* **Fallal Parc**[16] 1799 3-8-7 43 .... RobertHavlin 6 34
(M F Harris) *led: hdd over 4f out: rdn and wknd over 1f out* **20/1**

0040 **7** *4* **Crush On You**[15] 1829 3-9-1 51 .... PaulQuinn 14 31
(R Hollinshead) *hld up: rdn 1/2-way: n.d* **7/1**[3]

0005 **8** *1 ¼* **Three Strings (USA)**[21] 1684 3-9-5 **55** .... JamieMackay 2 32
(P D Niven) *chsd ldrs over 4f* **15/2**
4320 **9** *2* **Chicherova (IRE)**[12] 1888 3-8-6 **49** .... DeanHeslop(7) 5 21
(T D Barron) *s.s: outpcd* **7/1**[3]
0600 **10** *1 ¼* **Samsouma (IRE)**[61] 859 3-9-2 **52** .... SebSanders 10 21
(C E Brittain) *hld up: rdn 1/2-way: wknd over 2f out* **7/1**[3]
1200 **11** *2* **Dylan (IRE)**[15] 1829 3-8-12 **48** .... KimTinkler 9 12
(N Tinkler) *s.i.s: sn outpcd* **6/1**[2]
660 **12** *11* **Dolly Brown**[210] 6251 3-9-3 **53** .... JohnEgan 8 —
(T D Easterby) *hld up in tch: rdn 1/2-way: sn wknd* **8/1**

1m 30.09s (-0.71) **Going Correction** -0.175s/f (Stan) 12 Ran SP% **127.3**
Speed ratings (Par 97):97,96,92,91,90 89,84,83,81,79 77,64
CSF £58.77 CT £747.90 TOTE £13.10: £3.80, £2.00, £10.50; EX 92.30 Place 6 £77.53, Place 5 £35.29.
Owner Simon Mapletoft Racing I **Bred** D McDonnell And Tower Bloodstock **Trained** Danethorpe, Notts

FOCUS
A very moderate race, but the first two might be a shade better than their current marks.
Grand Palace(IRE) Official explanation: trainer said, regarding the improved form shown, gelding was having its first run on fibresand
Dolly Brown Official explanation: jockey said filly was unsuited by kickback
T/Plt: £32.50 to a £1 stake. Pool: £38,747.00. 868.60 winning tickets. T/Qpdt: £5.00 to a £1 stake. Pool: £3,218.70. 469.70 winning tickets. CR

2250 - 2256a (Foreign Racing) - See Raceform Interactive

1600 CHANTILLY (R-H)
Saturday, June 3

OFFICIAL GOING: Good to soft

2257a PRIX DE ROYAUMONT (GROUP 3) (FILLIES) 1m 4f
2:20 (2:20) 3-Y-O **£27,586** (£11,034; £8,276; £5,517; £2,759)

RPR
1 **Minatlya (FR)**[39] 3-9-0 .... SPasquier 1 106
(A Fabre, France) *cl 3rd to str, looking for room bhd ldr fr over 2f out, pushed her way out wl over 1f out, led 1f out, rdn clr, ran on wl* **3/1**[2]
2 *nk* **Ponte Tresa (FR)**[30] 3-9-0 .... JVictoire 5 106
(Y De Nicolay, France) *raced in 5th to straight, stayed on from over 1f out, finished well but too late to worry winner* **15/1**
3 *2 ½* **Anna Mona (GER)**[24] 3-9-0 .... TThulliez 6 102
(N Clement, France) *hooded, raced in 4th to straight, stayed on final f to take 3rd last strides* **10/1**
4 *nk* **Penne (FR)**[33] 1370 3-9-0 .... IMendizabal 2 102
(J-C Rouget, France) *led to 1f out, lost 4th last strides* **11/1**
5 *2* **Wingspan (USA)**[33] 1370 3-9-0 .... OPeslier 7 99
(A Fabre, France) *raced in 6th to straight, ridden 2f out, never a factor* **41/10**[3]
6 *1 ½* **Penchee**[20] 1720 3-9-0 .... C-PLemaire 4 96
(Mme C Head-Maarek, France) *trckd ldr to str, still a cl 2nd whn carried lft by wnr wl over 1f out, lost place quickly and found nothing whn rdn* **6/5**[1]
7 *2* **Sister Trouble (FR)**[34] 1330 3-9-0 .... DBonilla 3 93
(F Head, France) *last throughout* **11/1**

2m 31.5s (-1.90) 7 Ran SP% **122.1**
PARI-MUTUEL: WIN 4.00; PL 2.80, 5.30; SF 27.60.
Owner H H Aga Khan **Bred** Snc Lagardere Elevage **Trained** Chantilly, France

NOTEBOOK
Minatlya(FR) was short of room when asked to make her move before the two-furlong marker. She then pushed her way through over a furlong out and ran on well to the line where she held on by a neck from the fast-finishing runner-up. She is likely to go to the Malleret next.
Ponte Tresa(FR) moved up takingly until being slightly hampered by the winner over a furlong out. She did quicken, but ultimately did not have the same speed as the winner. She is most likely to lock horns once more with the winner in the Malleret, her next intended target.
Anna Mona(GER) progressed up the centre of the track, making steady headway up the straight, and stayed on in the final furlong to just snatch third place on the line
Penne(FR) dictated the pace for much of the race. She accelerated at the two-furlong marker up the rail, but was headed at the furlong pole by the winner and was keeping on at the line where she was just beaten for third place.

2130 BRIGHTON (L-H)
Sunday, June 4

OFFICIAL GOING: Good to firm changing to firm after race 3 (3.20)
Wind: Moderate, half-against Weather: Warm and sunny

2258 BLUE CHIP ORIGINAL EBF NOVICE MEDIAN AUCTION STKS 5f 213y
2:20 (2:20) (Class 6) 2-Y-O **£3,238** (£963; £481) **Stalls** Low

Form RPR
1 **1** **Bahama Mama (IRE)**[22] 1675 2-9-1 .... ShaneKelly 4 80+
(J Noseda) *mde all: shkn up over 1f out: sn clr: comf* **1/6**[1]
2 *3 ½* **Pires** 2-8-12 .... SamHitchcott 5 66+
(M R Channon) *s.i.s: chsd wnr after 2f: rdn and no imp fr over 1f out but kpt on* **6/1**[2]
3 *6* **Daring You** 2-8-12 .... JosedeSouza 1 48
(P F I Cole) *trckd wnr for 2f: wknd over 1f out* **18/1**[3]

68.90 secs (-1.20) **Going Correction** -0.10s/f (Good) 3 Ran SP% **105.2**
Speed ratings (Par 91):104,99,91
CSF £1.47 TOTE £1.10; EX 1.50.
Owner Lucayan Stud **Bred** C J Foy **Trained** Newmarket, Suffolk

FOCUS
Newmarket maiden winner Bahama Mama only had a couple of newcomers to beat, and won comfortably. The winning time was very smart for a race like this, especially considering there were so few runners and the winner sets the standard for the form.

NOTEBOOK
Bahama Mama(IRE), off the mark on her debut in a five-furlong Newmarket maiden, would have found this much easier and followed up comfortably. She deserves her chance in better company. (op 2-13 tchd 2-11)
Pires, the first foal of an unraced half-sister to high-class jumps winner Queen Of Spades, attracted some market support and ran well, although he was no danger to the easy winner. (op 10-1)
Daring You, a 41,000gns half-brother to Genari, a dual six to eight-furlongs winner at two who was later Listed placed over 11 furlongs, was totally unfancied and finished up well beaten. (op 10-1)

2259 BRIGHTON & HOVE BUSES H'CAP 6f 209y
2:50 (2:51) (Class 5) (0-75,75) 4-Y-O+ **£3,886** (£1,156; £577; £288) **Stalls** Low

Form RPR
0060 **1** **Premier Fantasy**[164] 6657 4-9-0 **68** .... NickyMackay 4 75
(W J Haggas) *wnt rt leaving stalls and rdr unbalanced: settled in rr: rdn and hdwy over 1f out: r.o to ld fnl 100yds* **14/1**
0021 **2** *¾* **Franksalot (IRE)**[13] 1899 6-9-0 **68** .... RobertWinston 3 73
(I W McInnes) *a.p: ev ch over 1f out: r.o to go 2nd cl home* **7/2**[2]
0050 **3** *hd* **Regal Dream (IRE)**[33] 1382 4-9-5 **73** .... EddieAhern 1 77
(J W Hills) *a in tch on ins: rdn and led appr fnl f: hdd fnl 100yds: lost 2nd cl home* **8/1**
404 **4** *hd* **Vindication**[32] 1402 6-8-12 **66** .... (t) AlanMunro 6 69
(R M H Cowell) *s.i.s: t.k.h: sn prom: r.o one pce fnl f* **13/2**[3]
5003 **5** *hd* **Hurricane Coast**[5] 2098 7-8-13 **70** .... (b) AdamKirby(3) 7 73
(K McAuliffe) *hld up: hdwy whn hung lft over 1f out: r.o cl home* **12/1**
2042 **6** *1 ¾* **Aastral Magic**[10] 1962 4-9-6 **74** .... RyanMoore 8 72
(R Hannon) *prom: rdn 1/2-way: wknd wl over 1f out* **10/3**[1]
0500 **7** *½* **Big Bradford**[176] 6544 5-8-12 **66** .... ShaneKelly 5 63
(W R Muir) *led tl hdd & wknd over 1f out* **11/1**
4506 **8** *½* **Della Salute**[36] 1302 4-9-7 **75** .... MickyFenton 9 70
(Miss E C Lavelle) *sn trckd ldr: wknd qckly over 1f out* **8/1**
-004 **9** *hd* **A Woman In Love**[10] 1962 7-9-2 **70** .... SteveDrowne 2 65
(Miss B Sanders) *plld hrd: a bhd* **7/1**

1m 21.6s (-1.10) **Going Correction** -0.10s/f (Good) 9 Ran SP% **116.0**
Speed ratings (Par 103):102,101,100,100,100 98,97,97,97
CSF £62.98 CT £429.35 TOTE £22.90: £7.40, £1.70, £2.60; EX 124.10 TRIFECTA Not won..
Owner Cadell Overseas Ltd **Bred** P G Jacobs, J Osborne And A Briam **Trained** Newmarket, Suffolk

FOCUS
A modest handicap and just over a length separated the first five home. The third is the best guide to the level.

2260 BLUE CHIP BITES (S) STKS 6f 209y
3:20 (3:21) (Class 6) 3-Y-O+ **£2,266** (£674; £337; £168) **Stalls** Low

Form RPR
0300 **1** **Renegade (IRE)**[13] 1899 5-9-7 45 .... (b) IanMongan 13 50
(Mrs L J Mongan) *mde all: clr 2f out: rdn and wknd ins fnl f: jst hld on* **10/1**[3]
5006 **2** *nk* **Beau Marche**[19] 1752 4-9-7 45 .... (b) RyanMoore 10 50
(G G Margarson) *prom in chsng gp: chased wnr fr 2f out: clsng fast nr fin* **10/1**[3]
0000 **3** *1* **Great Composer (IRE)**[34] 1352 3-8-11 50 .... (b[1]) JimCrowley 14 43
(Mrs A J Perrett) *t.k.h in rr: r.o strly fnl f: nvr nrr* **9/2**[1]
6005 **4** *nk* **Indian Gem**[20] 1746 5-9-2 37 .... AlanDaly 4 41
(A J Chamberlain) *mid-div: hdwy over 2f out: r.o ins fnl f* **14/1**
0000 **5** *3* **Weet Watchers**[17] 442 6-9-2 35 .... StephanieHollinshead(5) 1 38
(T Wall) *in tch: rdn over 2f out: nt qckn fnl f* **33/1**
0302 **6** *nk* **Merdiff**[20] 1746 7-9-13 50 .... ShaneKelly 15 43
(W M Brisbourne) *bhd tl kpt on one pce fnl f* **5/1**[2]
0000 **7** *¾* **Tally (IRE)**[58] 904 6-9-0 41 .... MarkCoumbe(7) 5 35
(D G Bridgwater) *slowly away: bhd tl hdwy on outside over 1f out: nvr nr to chal* **20/1**
6500 **8** *shd* **Keresforth**[27] 1534 4-9-4 36 .... (b) AdamKirby(3) 9 35
(Mrs L C Jewell) *in rr: mde som late hdwy* **50/1**
0000 **9** *½* **Enchanting Times (IRE)**[26] 1567 3-8-1 55 .... (v) RoryMoore(5) 6 24
(D G Bridgwater) *chsd wnr to 2f out: sn wknd* **14/1**
10 *5* **Amisact** 4-9-2 .... MickyFenton 2 15
(D J S Ffrench Davis) *slowly away: a bhd* **22/1**
5400 **11** *3* **Tip Toes (IRE)**[172] 6575 4-9-2 42 .... J-PGuillambert 8 7
(P Howling) *a bhd* **16/1**
0500 **12** *5* **Zafarshah (IRE)**[5] 2098 7-9-0 45 .... (b) TolleyDean(7) 12 —
(R A Harris) *sddle slipped sn after s: in tch: rdn 1/2-way.wknd 2f out: eased* **9/2**[1]
0000 **13** *2* **Attishoe**[20] 1723 4-9-2 48 .... SteveDrowne 11 —
(Miss B Sanders) *prom to 1/2-way* **12/1**
-000 **14** *15* **Weet An Haul**[48] 1101 5-9-7 38 .... RobertWinston 7 —
(T Wall) *chsd ldrs: rdn 1/2-way: sn wknd* **20/1**
0500 **15** *49* **Frenchmans Lodge**[12] 1923 6-9-7 35 .... (b) EddieAhern 3 —
(L A Dace) *slowly away: a bhd: t.o fr 1/2-way* **33/1**

1m 22.7s **Going Correction** -0.10s/f (Good)
WFA 3 from 4yo+ 10lb 15 Ran SP% **119.8**
Speed ratings (Par 101):96,95,94,94,90 90,89,89,88,83 79,74,71,54,—
CSF £95.60 TOTE £14.20: £4.00, £3.70, £1.60; EX 92.50 Trifecta £88.70 Part won. Pool 125.06 - 0.10 winning units..There was no bid for the winner. Great Composer was claimed by M Attwater for £6,000.
Owner Mrs P J Sheen **Bred** Baronrath Stud **Trained** Epsom, Surrey

FOCUS
As is to be expected in a seller, moderate form and below average for the grade.
Zafarshah(IRE) Official explanation: jockey said saddle slipped

2261 BLUE CHIP DYNAMIC MAIDEN STKS 1m 3f 196y
3:50 (3:53) (Class 5) 3-Y-O+ **£3,886** (£1,156; £577; £288) **Stalls** High

Form RPR
065 **1** **Enjoy The Moment**[20] 1741 3-8-11 76 .... ShaneKelly 1 85
(J A Osborne) *led for 2f: wnt 2nd 4f out: led 2f out: rdn out fnl f* **11/1**
654 **2** *4* **Alasoun (IRE)**[24] 1613 3-8-11 81 .... RobertWinston 5 79
(Sir Michael Stoute) *hld up in tch: hung lft fr 2f out: chsd wnr fnl f* **13/8**[1]
543 **3** *3* **Monets Masterpiece (USA)**[11] 1940 3-8-11 84 ....(b) AlanMunro 2 74
(Mrs A J Perrett) *wnt 2nd after 2f: led 5f out: rdn and hdd 2f out: one pce after* **2/1**[2]
0 **4** *¾* **Artistic Lady**[254] 5428 3-8-6 .... MatthewHenry 4 68
(M A Jarvis) *chsd ldrs tl rdn and no hdwy fr over 1f out* **12/1**
03 **5** *hd* **Contra Mundum (USA)**[16] 1823 3-8-11 .... RyanMoore 6 72
(B J Meehan) *led after 2f: hdd 5f out: hung lft and wknd over 1f out* **7/2**[3]
6000 **6** *7* **Opera Belle**[12] 1911 4-9-0 43 .... LiamJones(7) 3 57?
(Miss Gay Kelleway) *prom tl wknd over 3f out* **40/1**
7 *6* **Fairlight Express (IRE)**[160] 6-9-12 .... SteveDrowne 8 53?
(Stef Liddiard) *slowly away: a bhd* **66/1**
8 *14* **Queen Of Song** 4-9-2 .... RobynBrisland(5) 9 25
(G L Moore) *slowly away: taken over to ins after s: a bhd* **33/1**
00 **9** *15* **Sansel**[4] 2146 3-8-1 .... RoryMoore(5) 7 —
(J Ryan) *a bhd: virtually t.o fr 1/2-way* **100/1**

2m 29.75s (-2.45) **Going Correction** -0.10s/f (Good)
WFA 3 from 4yo+ 15lb 9 Ran SP% **117.5**
Speed ratings (Par 103):104,101,99,98,98 94,90,80,70
CSF £29.79 TOTE £11.20: £2.40, £1.40, £1.10; EX 38.40 Trifecta £112.60 Pool: £380.70 - 2.40 winning units..

Owner Lynn Wilson And Martin Landau **Bred** Millsec Limited **Trained** Upper Lambourn, Berks
■ Stewards' Enquiry : Shane Kelly caution: used whip down the shoulder

FOCUS
This looked a reasonable maiden by Brighton's standards beforehand, but they came home well strung out and few of the principals gave their running. As a result the form is far from solid and limited by the sixth and seventh.

2262 MARTLETS HOSPICE SUMMER BALL H'CAP — 1m 1f 209y
4:20 (4:22) (Class 6) (0-60,60) 4-Y-0+ — **£2,590** (£770; £385; £192) Stalls High

Form				RPR
1560	**1**		**Diamond Dan (IRE)**[12] 1910 4-8-8 **47** ... ShaneKelly 6 (P D Evans) *a.p: led over 2f out: rdn out fnl f* **12/1**	56
0641	**2**	*2*	**Plain Champagne (IRE)**[4] 2133 4-8-9 **48** 6ex ... RichardThomas 5 (Dr J R J Naylor) *hld up: hdwy on outside 2f out: r.o fnl f to go 2nd nr fin* **3/1**[1]	53
0100	**3**	*½*	**Justcallmehandsome**[18] 1769 4-8-3 **49** ... DonnaCaldwell(7) 14 (D J S Ffrench Davis) *chsd ldr to 4f out: styd prom: styd on u.p fnl f* **33/1**	53
0006	**4**	*1 ¼*	**Megalala (IRE)**[4] 2132 5-8-4 **48** ... MarcHalford(5) 7 (J J Bridger) *in tch: rdn 3f out: kpt on one pce* **25/1**	50
6034	**5**	*½*	**Kalani Star (IRE)**[4] 2148 6-8-3 **47** ...(vt) NataliaGemelova(5) 10 (I W McInnes) *in rr: r.o fnl f: nvr nrr* **12/1**	48
0004	**6**	*1*	**Siena Star (IRE)**[19] 1757 8-9-7 **60** ... SteveDrowne 11 (Stef Liddiard) *wl in rr: mde sme late hdwy* **10/1**	59
6033	**7**	*1*	**Icannshift (IRE)**[4] 2132 6-8-7 **46** ... FergusSweeney 2 (T M Jones) *chsd ldrs on ins: rdn 1/2-way: wknd ins fnl f* **5/1**[2]	43
0050	**8**	*hd*	**Play Up Pompey**[32] 1400 4-8-13 **52** ... J-PGuillambert 8 (J J Bridger) *led tl hdd over 2f out: wknd over 1f out* **14/1**	48
5424	**9**	*1 ¾*	**Miss Monica (IRE)**[6] 2070 5-8-7 **46** ... HayleyTurner 4 (P W Hiatt) *a towards rr* **7/1**[3]	39
0004	**10**	*1 ¼*	**Southern Tide (USA)**[12] 1910 4-8-8 **47** ... JimmyQuinn 16 (J Pearce) *chsd ldrs: wkng whn n.m.r 1f out: eased* **14/1**	38
0030	**11**	*11*	**Agilete**[19] 1755 4-8-8 **47** ... AlanMunro 3 (J R Boyle) *a bhd* **14/1**	17
5000	**12**	*½*	**Didoe**[18] 1769 7-8-7 **49** ow2 ... RobertMiles(3) 15 (P W Hiatt) *racd wd: bhd fnl 3f* **28/1**	18
0320	**13**	*28*	**Golden Spectrum (IRE)**[19] 1753 7-8-11 **57** ...(p) TolleyDean(7) 9 (R A Harris) *racd on outside: rdn 1/2-way: sn bhd* **12/1**	—
3035	**P**		**Sailing Days**[277] 4864 4-9-7 **60** ... EddieAhern 1 (C A Cyzer) *wl bhd whn pu bef 1/2-way: b.b.v* **20/1**	—

2m 1.40s (-1.20) **Going Correction** -0.10s/f (Good) **14 Ran SP% 121.3**
Speed ratings (Par 101):100,98,98,97,96 95,95,94,93,92 83,83,60,—
CSF £46.10 CT £1203.50 TOTE £14.20: £3.90, £1.80, £6.50; EX 104.80 TRIFECTA Not won..
Owner Diamond Racing Ltd **Bred** Golden Vale Stud **Trained** Pandy, Abergavenny

FOCUS
A pretty moderate handicap and although the form is modest it appears sound enough.
Southern Tide(USA) Official explanation: jockey said colt had no more to give
Agilete Official explanation: jockey said gelding moved poorly
Didoe Official explanation: jockey said mare ran flat
Sailing Days Official explanation: vet said filly bled from nose

2263 ELITE RACING CLUB H'CAP — 5f 59y
4:50 (4:50) (Class 5) (0-70,70) 3-Y-0 — **£3,886** (£1,156; £577; £288) Stalls Low

Form				RPR
1620	**1**		**Lucayos**[19] 1751 3-9-1 **69** ...(b) RichardKingscote(5) 8 (Mrs H Sweeting) *racd wd: hung lft but wnt 2nd over 1f out: r.o to ld ins fnl f: won gng away* **11/4**[1]	75
366	**2**	*1*	**Piccostar**[31] 1431 3-9-1 **64** ... RyanMoore 6 (A B Haynes) *hld up in rr: hdwy over 1f out: r.o fnl f to go 2nd nr fin* **10/3**[2]	66
0251	**3**	*hd*	**Perfect Treasure (IRE)**[19] 1750 3-9-7 **70** ... AlanMunro 1 (J A R Toller) *led tl hdd 3f out: rdn and kpt on fnl f* **5/1**	71
0640	**4**	*1 ¾*	**Master Malarkey**[19] 1768 3-8-2 **51** oh9 ...(b) AdrianMcCarthy 7 (Mrs C A Dunnett) *trckd ldr: led 3f out: rdn: hdd and fdd ins fnl f* **25/1**	46
3500	**5**	*2*	**Thoughtsofstardom**[11] 1937 3-8-8 **57** ... HayleyTurner 9 (P S McEntee) *hld up: rdn 1/2-way: wknd wl over 1f out* **10/1**	44
0650	**6**	*½*	**Titus Maximus (IRE)**[49] 1036 3-9-7 **70** ... NickyMackay 5 (G A Butler) *slowly away: plld hrd and sn prom: wknd over 1f out* **11/2**	55
3410	**7**	*3 ½*	**Came Back (IRE)**[90] 601 3-9-6 **69** ... ShaneKelly 4 (J A Osborne) *chsd ldrs tl wknd 2f out* **9/2**[3]	41

62.00 secs (-0.30) **Going Correction** -0.10s/f (Good) **7 Ran SP% 112.9**
Speed ratings (Par 99):98,96,96,93,90 89,83
CSF £11.79 CT £41.66 TOTE £4.20: £2.10, £2.50; EX 12.00 Trifecta £83.20 Pool: £363.46 - 3.10 winning units. Place 6 £29.24, Place 5 £24.28.
Owner Alex Sweeting **Bred** P Sweeting **Trained** Lockeridge, Wilts

FOCUS
A modest sprint handicap but the form makes sense rated through the first two.
Came Back(IRE) Official explanation: jockey said colt was unsuited by firm going
T/Plt: £57.70 to a £1 stake. Pool: £56,905.90. 718.95 winning tickets. T/Qpdt: £27.40 to a £1 stake. Pool: £3,478.30. 93.80 winning tickets. JS

2264 - 2274a (Foreign Racing) - See Raceform Interactive

[2257] CHANTILLY (R-H)
Sunday, June 4

OFFICIAL GOING: Good

2275a PRIX DE SANDRINGHAM MITSUBISHI MOTORS (GROUP 2) (FILLIES) — 1m
2:10 (2:11) 3-Y-0 — **£51,103** (£19,724; £9,414; £6,276; £3,138)

			RPR
1		**Impressionnante**[21] 1719 3-8-11 ... OPeslier 1 (C Laffon-Parias, France) *raced in 4th, 3rd straight, pushed along to challenge 1 1/2f out, ridden to lead 150 yards out, ran on well* **11/8**[1]	111
2	*1 ½*	**Mostaqeleh (USA)**[47] 1068 3-8-11 ... RHills 3 (J L Dunlop) *raced in 3rd, 4th straight, ridden to press leaders 1 1/2f out, went 2nd close home, ran on* **12/1**[3]	108
3	*hd*	**New Girlfriend (IRE)**[21] 1719 3-8-11 ... C-PLemaire 5 (Robert Collet, France) *held up in last, pushed along and ran on 1 1/2f out, every chance final furlong, kept on* **5/1**[2]	108
4	*3*	**Phantom Rose (USA)**[18] 1789 3-8-11 ... CSoumillon 2 (A Fabre, France) *led, pushed along 2f out and ran on, joined 1 1/2f out, headed 150 yards out, no extra* **11/8**[1]	102
5	*4*	**Daaly Babet (FR)**[21] 1719 3-8-11 ... DBoeuf 4 (C Scandella, France) *raced in 2nd, pushed along 2f out, weakened 1 1/2f out* **33/1**	94

1m 35.6s **Going Correction** -0.325s/f (Firm) **5 Ran SP% 111.5**
Speed ratings: 110,108,108,105,101
PARI-MUTUEL: WIN 2.60; PL 1.50, 3.20; SF 13.20.
Owner Wertheimer Et Frere **Bred** Wertheimer Et Frere **Trained** Chantilly, France

NOTEBOOK
Impressionnante was a bit unlucky in the Pouliches and is a filly going from strength to strength. She settled well just behind the leader and then started a progressive run from the two-furlong marker. She then quickened and, having led with 150 yards left to run, she finally won in a convincing style. She appears to be on the upgrade still and acted well on the fastish ground. All being well she will go to Royal Ascot for the Coronation Stakes.
Mostaqeleh(USA) ran a decent race considering she had not been seen in public for nearly two months. Fourth early on, she quickened from halfway up the straight and battled on gamely for second place without threatening the winner. This outing will have brought her on and she is another possible for the Coronation Stakes. She enjoys this fastish ground.
New Girlfriend(IRE) was dropped out in last this time and brought with her run up the centre of the track. She looked dangerous halfway up the straight but did not quite go through with her effort. She will now be brought back in distance and targeted at the Prix Maurice de Gheest at Deauville.
Phantom Rose(USA), a good winner of both her previous races and the hot favourite, set out to make all the running but was in trouble soon after entering the straight. By the furlong marker she had given all. Strictly from a form point of view, this was a slight step up on previous efforts. However, she is thought capable of considerably better and possibly had an off day. She should not be written off for the future at this level.

2276a PRIX DU GROS-CHENE MITSUBISHI MOTORS (GROUP 2) — 5f
2:45 (2:44) 3-Y-0+ — **£51,103** (£19,724; £9,414; £6,276; £3,138)

			RPR
1		**Moss Vale (IRE)**[8] 2038 5-9-2 ... KFallon 7 (D Nicholls) *mid-division, 5th and pushed along half-way, ridden to lead over 1f out, ran on well final furlong* **13/2**[3]	122
2	*2*	**Benbaun (IRE)**[175] 6550 5-9-2 ...(v) JamieSpencer 6 (M J Wallace) *close 2nd, led narrowly half-way, headed over 1f out, kept on to hold 2nd* **15/2**	114
3	*½*	**Tax Free (IRE)**[29] 1485 4-9-2 ... AdrianTNicholls 9 (D Nicholls) *led, narrowly headed half-way, kept on under pressure final 1 1/2f* **5/2**[1]	113
4	*¾*	**Balthazaar's Gift (IRE)**[18] 1778 3-9-0 ... NCallan 2 (K A Ryan) *prominent, disputing 3rd half-way, every chance 1 1/2f out, stayed on til no extra close home* **16/1**	112
5	*snk*	**Pivotal Flame**[29] 1485 4-9-2 ...(p) GrahamGibbons 11 (E S McMahon) *prominent, disputing close 3rd half-way, ridden 1 1/2f out, one pace inside final furlong* **12/1**	109
6	*shd*	**Pivotal Point**[29] 1485 6-8-13 ... SebSanders 1 (P J Makin) *behind early, close 6th and running on half-way, no extra from 1 1/2f out* **12/1**	106
7	*1 ½*	**Tycoon's Hill (IRE)**[21] 1717 7-8-13 ... OPeslier 5 (Robert Collet, France) *mid-division, never dangerous* **14/1**	101
8	*hd*	**Mister Chocolate (IRE)**[13] 3-8-9 ... JAuge 3 (Robert Collet, France) *raced in last, never going pace* **33/1**	100
9	*½*	**Biniou (IRE)**[21] 1717 3-8-9 ... CSoumillon 8 (Robert Collet, France) *mid-division, ridden 2f out, no impression* **16/1**	98
10	*3*	**Latona (FR)**[21] 1717 4-8-13 ... TGillet 4 (J E Pease, France) *towards rear, 11th half-way, outpaced and beaten 2f out* **10/3**[2]	87
11	*6*	**Alyzea (IRE)**[21] 1717 3-8-6 ...(b) MBlancpain 12 (C Laffon-Parias, France) *prominent far side to half-way* **33/1**	63
12	*2*	**Ajigolo**[239] 5732 3-9-0 ... TedDurcan 10 (M R Channon) *towards rear, pushed along before half-way, never in contention* **25/1**	63

56.90 secs **Going Correction** -0.325s/f (Firm)
WFA 3 from 4yo+ 7lb **12 Ran SP% 120.3**
Speed ratings: 114,110,110,108,108 108,106,105,104,100 90,87
PARI-MUTUEL: WIN 7.00; PL 2.80, 3.40, 2.80; DF 22.70.
Owner Lady O'Reilly **Bred** Derek Veitch **Trained** Sessay, N Yorks

NOTEBOOK
Moss Vale(IRE), a recent winner in heavy ground at The Curragh, was settled in behind the leading group before changing directions a furlong and a half out. He then quickened like a classy sprinter and completely dominated the final stages. He looks very much on the upgrade following his change of stable and will now head for the King's Stand Stakes at Royal Ascot.
Benbaun(IRE), smartly out of the stalls, quickened well when the sprint warmed up but had nothing to offer when passed by the winner. This was a decent effort and he will now go to Royal Ascot for the King's Stand.
Tax Free(IRE) was smartly into his stride up the centre of the track. He ran on well but did not quicken as well as the first two past the post. This colt is still relatively inexperienced compared to the others and he may prove more effective over six furlongs. Like the winner, a stable-mate, he is entered for the King's Stand, but the Wokingham would be an attractive alternative.
Balthazaar's Gift(IRE) broke well near the stands' side and joined the leaders at the halfway stage. He kept up the good work until the end and, as he was a three-year-old carrying a Group Two penalty, his effort augurs well for the future.
Pivotal Flame was another to break quickly and he was always well up with the leading group. Given every chance, he just could not go the pace as the race came to an end.
Pivotal Point was towards the tail of the field early on before coming with a promising run a furlong and a half out. He never really looked like threatening the horses in the frame.
Latona(FR) had beaten a fair field of French sprinters over five furlongs at Longchamp on her latest start, but she had earlier won at up to seven furlongs, and on this quicker ground she could not live with these good British sprint specialists over the minimum.
Ajigolo was never going very well and was being urged along before the halfway stage.

2277a GRAND PRIX DE CHANTILLY MITSUBISHI MOTORS (GROUP 2) — 1m 4f
3:50 (3:49) 4-Y-0+ — **£51,103** (£19,724; £9,414; £6,276; £3,138)

			RPR
1		**Policy Maker (IRE)**[27] 1558 6-8-11 ... SPasquier 8 (E Lellouche, France) *help up, 9th and headway on outside straight, ran on to lead 1 1/2f out, ridden over 1f out, ridden out* **8/1**	119
2	*2*	**Salutino (GER)**[27] 1558 4-8-11 ... OPeslier 6 (A Fabre, France) *raced in 3rd, 2nd strght, led 2f out to 1 1/2f out,crossed by winner 1f out, jockey stopped riding briefly, ridden & kept o* **13/2**	116
3	*1 ½*	**Bellamy Cay**[27] 1558 4-8-11 ... CSoumillon 4 (A Fabre, France) *in touch, 3rd and pushed along straight, driven 2f out, kept on steadily* **10/3**[1]	114

4 ¾ **Geordieland (FR)**[56] 934 5-8-11 .... LDettori 3 113
(J-M Beguigne, France) *in touch, disputing 4th straight, pushed along 2f out, ran on from 1 1/2f out to take 4th, ran on* **14/1**

5 2 ½ **Hard Top (IRE)**[28] 1507 4-9-2 .... MJKinane 2 114
(Sir Michael Stoute) *mid-division, disputing 6th straight, ran on outside from over 1f out, never dangerous* **5/1**[3]

6 ¾ **Royal Highness (GER)**[35] 1331 4-8-8 .... TThulliez 5 105
(P Bary, France) *held up, disputing 6th straight, effort 1 1/2f out, stayed on but never in challenging position* **10/3**[1]

7 hd **Munsef**[28] 1507 4-8-11 .... RHills 7 107
(J L Dunlop) *mid-division, disputing 4th straight, pushed along over 2f out, ridden and not quicken 1 1/2f out* **9/2**[2]

8 2 **Marend (FR)**[27] 1558 5-9-2 .... DBoeuf 10 109
(D Sepulchre, France) *held up in last, ridden 1 1/2f out, never dangerous* **12/1**

9 10 **Petrograd (IRE)**[224] 6055 5-8-11 ....(b) GFaucon 9 89
(E Lellouche, France) *led to 2f out, eased when beaten* **100/1**

10 dist **Needle Rock (FR)**[78] 5-8-11 .... SCoffigny 1 —
(J-M Beguigne, France) *raced in 2nd til lost place approaching straight, eased over 2f out* **100/1**

2m 24.8s **Going Correction** -0.325s/f (Firm) **10** Ran SP% **121.8**
Speed ratings: 115,113,112,112,110 110,109,108,101,—
PARI-MUTUEL: WIN 7.60 (coupled with Petrograd); PL 1.70, 1.80, 1.30;DF 26.10.
Owner Ecurie Wildenstein **Bred** Dayton Investments Ltd **Trained** Lamorlaye, France

NOTEBOOK
Policy Maker(IRE) was winning the race for the second time in three years and did it in style. Settled towards the tail of the field early on, he was brought up the centre of the track with his run, took the lead one and a half out, and was then switched to the rail. He seems to be better than ever and now goes for the Grand Prix de Saint-Cloud.
Salutino(GER), always prominent, took second place early in the straight and led at the two-furlong marker. He was slightly hampered by the winner a little later and then stayed on again one-paced. He will probably be better suited to softer ground.
Bellamy Cay was given every possible chance and settled in third place in the early stages of the race. He came under pressure early in the straight and never really quickened, but he stayed on one-paced and held on well for third.
Geordieland(FR), never far from the leaders, was fourth when the field reached the straight and under pressure at the two-furlong marker. He was another who was one-paced throughout the final stages.
Hard Top(IRE), back on more suitable ground, was held up and given a fair bit to do. He ran on when brought up the centre of the track, and this was all together much more encouraging, especially as he was conceding a penalty to all of those who beat him.
Royal Highness(GER), in mid-division early on, was fourth into the straight and was soon being ridden. She just stayed on, and the ground was evidently considered too firm for her.
Munsef should have handled this quicker ground but failed to reproduce his Newmarket form.

2278a PRIX DU JOCKEY CLUB MITSUBISHI MOTORS (GROUP 1) (C&F) 1m 2f 110y
4:35 (4:41) 3-Y-O **£591,103** (£236,483; £118,241; £59,069; £29,586)

RPR

1 **Darsi (FR)**[33] 3-9-2 .... CSoumillon 7 117
(A De Royer-Dupre, France) *in tch, disp 5th early, 5th str, drvn to chase ldrs 2f out rdn to chal over 1f out, led 100 yds out, drvn out* **14/1**

2 ¾ **Best Name**[56] 935 3-9-2 .... C-PLemaire 12 115+
(Robert Collet, France) *held up, 11th straight, headway 2f out, ridden 1 1/2f out, finished well final furlong, took 2nd on line* **15/2**

3 snk **Arras (GER)**[33] 3-9-2 .... OPeslier 13 115
(A Fabre, France) *in tch, disp 5th early, 2nd and chal str, led over 2f out, rdn over 1 1/2f out and ran on, hdd 100 yds out, no ex* **7/1**[3]

4 shd **Art Deco (IRE)**[23] 1627 3-9-2 .... LDettori 9 115
(C R Egerton) *led 2f then disputing 3rd, 4th and pushed along straight, ran on under pressure 1 1/2f out, just missed 2nd* **12/1**

5 shd **Numide (FR)**[27] 1557 3-9-2 .... IMendizabal 2 115+
(J-C Rouget, France) *held up in last, driven 2f out, ran on from 1 1/2f out, finished strongly last 100 yards, nearest at finish* **9/1**

6 ½ **Irish Wells (FR)**[42] 1179 3-9-2 .... DBoeuf 8 114
(F Rohaut, France) *disputing 3rd early, 6th on rail straight, ridden to chase leaders 2f out, stayed on at one pace to line* **40/1**

7 1 ½ **Aussie Rules (USA)**[21] 1718 3-9-2 .... KFallon 1 111
(A P O'Brien, Ire) *held up, 9th towards inside straight, soon pushed along, under pressure 1 1/2f out, wknd appr fnl f* **11/4**[1]

8 1 **Hazeymm (IRE)**[22] 1668 3-9-2 .... TedDurcan 11 109
(M R Channon) *reluctant to lead, led after 2f, headed over 2f out, weakened inside final furlong* **25/1**

9 ¾ **Hello Sunday (FR)**[20] 1749 3-9-2 .... TJarnet 14 108
(Mme C Head-Maarek, France) *mid-division, disputing 7th straight, ridden and ran on 2f out til no extra from 1f out* **50/1**

10 1 **Champs Elysees**[31] 3-9-2 .... SPasquier 3 106
(A Fabre, France) *held up, 14th straight, ridden over 2f out, some headway til no extra inside final furlong* **22/1**

11 2 **Barastraight**[42] 1179 3-9-2 .... MJKinane 4 103
(J-C Rouget, France) *held up in 14th, 13th and driven straight, never a threat* **14/1**

12 shd **Olympian Odyssey**[29] 1486 3-9-2 .... JamieSpencer 6 102
(B W Hills) *mid-division, disputing 7th straight, pushed along 2f out, ridden 1 1/2f out, unable to quicken* **7/2**[2]

13 6 **Aspectus (IRE)**[21] 1715 3-9-2 .... ADeVries 10 92
(H Blume, Germany) *mid-division, pushed along 2f out, never dangerous* **20/1**

14 1 ½ **Fenice (IRE)**[11] 1944 3-9-2 .... JAuge 5 89
(Robert Collet, France) *held up, effort over 2f out, weakened over 1f out* **150/1**

15 8 **Hurricane Cat (USA)**[8] 2039 3-9-2 .... DavidMcCabe 15 75
(A P O'Brien, Ire) *prominent, 2nd after 2f, 3rd and ridden straight, soon lost place and eased* **33/1**

2m 5.80s **Going Correction** -0.325s/f (Firm) **15** Ran SP% **125.1**
Speed ratings: 104,103,103,103,103 102,101,101,100,99 98,98,93,92,86
PARI-MUTUEL: WIN 8.60; PL 3.00, 3.10, 2.80; DF 47.80.
Owner H H Aga Khan **Bred** H H The Aga Khans Studs S C **Trained** Chantilly, France

FOCUS
The second running of this race under its new shorter distance. A steady pace contributed to a blanket finish, with the pack closing fast at the finish and the first seven covered by little more than three lengths, but it was a similarly tight finish last year when the first two were Shamardal and Hurricane Run, so it is no reason to be negative. The first five went into the race unexposed and there is little solid to hang a level on, but the winner has provisionally been rated the same as last year. C. Soumillon was suspended 13-17th June (misuse of whip).

NOTEBOOK
Darsi(FR) raced behind the leading group and was beautifully placed in the straight. His attack began one and a half out and he led well inside the final furlong. He was put under considerable pressure and his jockey dropped his whip halfway through the final furlong. This was a fine effort from a colt who had previously won a small race over an extended mile and a half and he is now likely to be aimed at the Budweiser Irish Derby. His jockey was given a four-day ban for abusive use of the whip.
Best Name, having just his second race when a Listed winner at Longchamp on his reappearance, was settled towards the back of the field for the early part of this race and still only 11th into the straight. He made a forward move from the two-furlong marker and was closing fast at the finish. This was a cracking effort from an inexperienced colt who looks sure to stay further.
Arras(GER) had impressed in two minor races, most recently cantering up in a modest Provincial affair at Bordeaux-le-Bouscat, and he was quietly fancied to cope with this massive jump in class. Always well up there and a little free in the early part of the race, he was full of running when turning into the straight in second place and went for home early. He still looked like holding on at the furlong marker, but he just could not quicken in the final stages and he would have lost another couple of places in a few more strides. He is probably another who would have preferred a softer surface, but this was a very promising effort indeed from such an inexperienced colt.
Art Deco(IRE) broke smartly and led for the first couple of furlongs before dropping back to third place. He was fourth into the straight and ran on under pressure from one and a half out. He battled really well and was only narrowly beaten for third place. His trainer felt he needed softer ground and a longer trip.
Aussie Rules(USA) failed to reproduce his Poulains form, but Fallon said he fell asleep in the stalls while Hazeymm was delaying the start and that he is a lazy colt who proved hard to motivate.
Hazeymm(IRE) delayed the start considerably with his reluctance to go in the stalls, then broke smartly and ran free early on before taking the field along after the first two furlongs. He lost his lead over two out and then just stayed on one-paced as the race came to a close.
Olympian Odyssey, a fine third in the 2000 Guineas, was held up for the early part of this contest and, one but last coming into the straight, was slightly interfered with when trying to make a challenge. He weakened inside the final furlong and Spencer said that the colt felt flat.

1328 DUSSELDORF (R-H)
Sunday, June 4

OFFICIAL GOING: Soft

2279a HENKEL PREIS DER DIANA (DEUTSCHES STUTENDERBY - GERMAN OAKS) (GROUP 1) 1m 3f
3:35 (3:48) 3-Y-O **£98,276** (£39,310; £19,655; £10,000; £5,172)

RPR

1 **Almerita (GER)**[35] 1328 3-9-2 .... DarryllHolland 1 107
(W Hickst, Germany) *always close up, went 2nd over 3f out, led over 1f out, driven out* **34/10**[2]

2 nk **Karavel (GER)**[35] 1328 3-9-2 .... THellier 10 107
(P Schiergen, Germany) *always close up, 5th straight, ran on to take 2nd inside final f* **26/1**

3 1 ¼ **Nordtanzerin (GER)**[21] 1714 3-9-2 .... WMongil 3 105
(P Schiergen, Germany) *led after 2f, headed over 1f out, no extra inside final f* **9/5**[1]

4 ½ **Quelle Amore (GER)**[21] 1714 3-9-2 .... EPedroza 5 104
(A Wohler, Germany) *always close up, 3rd straight, one pace from over 1f out* **42/10**[3]

5 ½ **Ticinella (GER)**[10] 3-9-2 .... JimmyFortune 8 103
(C Brandstatter, Germany) *mid-division, headway under pressure from over 1f out, nearest at finish* **22/1**

6 ½ **Aramina (GER)** 3-9-2 .... ASuborics 14 103
(P Schiergen, Germany) *held-up in mid-division, headway 2f out, no extra inside final f* **86/10**

7 2 **Directa (GER)**[35] 1328 3-9-2 .... LHammer-Hansen 2 99
(Andreas Lowe, Germany) *always about same place* **104/10**

8 2 ½ **Mrs Snow**[21] 1713 3-9-2 .... AStarke 11 95
(Mario Hofer, Germany) *mid-division to straight, beaten well over 1f out* **20/1**

9 ½ **Auenprincess (GER)**[21] 1714 3-9-2 .... ABoschert 7 95
(U Ostmann, Germany) *some headway final 2f, never a factor* **16/1**

10 1 ¾ **Lasira (GER)**[35] 1328 3-9-2 .... FilipMinarik 9 92
(P Schiergen, Germany) *prominent, 7th straight on outside til beaten well over 1f out* **26/1**

11 nse **Nadine (GER)** 3-9-2 .... ABest 6 92
(H Hiller, Germany) *6th straight, soon beaten* **86/1**

12 hd **Donatessa (GER)**[48] 3-9-2 .... J-PCarvalho 12 91
(Mario Hofer, Germany) *always in rear* **37/1**

13 5 **Purity (GER)** 3-9-2 .... KKerekes 13 83
(Werner Glanz, Germany) *led 2f, tracked leader to over 3f out, 4th straight, weakened quickly* **20/1**

14 7 **Cocco (GER)** 3-9-2 .... MSautjeau 4 72
(M Rulec, Germany) *never nearer than mid-division, behind final 2f* **37/1**

15 dist **Messaia (GER)** 3-9-2 .... HGrewe 15 —
(S Smrczek, Germany) *started slowly, last throughout* **48/1**

2m 20.04s **15** Ran SP% **132.5**
(including 10 euro stakes): WIN 44.00; PL 17.00, 48.00, 14.00;SF 926.00.
Owner Dr C Berglar **Bred** B Fassbender **Trained** Germany

NOTEBOOK
Almerita(GER) dispelled stamina worries with a strong performance. It is unlikely she will run over a mile and a half though, and her big target is the Prix de l'Opera at the Arc meeting in October.
Nordtanzerin(GER), the well-fancied favourite, was a reluctant leader with no pace on early. She will no doubt be seen to better effect when held up in a more strongly-run race.

2217 SAN SIRO (R-H)
Sunday, June 4

OFFICIAL GOING: Good

2280a PREMIO PAOLO MEZZANOTTE (GROUP 3) (F&M) 1m 2f
3:50 (4:20) 4-Y-O+ **£29,663** (£13,588; £7,569; £3,785)

RPR

1 **Exhibit One (USA)**[43] 4-8-9 .... EBotti 12 102
(V Valiani, Italy) *always close up, 2nd straight, headway 2f out, driven to lead inside final furlong, soon in command, ran on* **705/100**

2 1 1/4 **Floriot (IRE)**[231] 4-8-9 ... IRossi 4 99
(Werner Glanz, Germany) *always prominent, 5th straight, led over 2f out to inside final furlong, tiring close home* **27/10**[2]
3 hd **La Vriga**[34] 1368 5-8-9 ... SMulas 1 99
(B Grizzetti, Italy) *held up, headway on outside from well over 1f out, ran on to just miss 2nd* **32/1**
4 1 1/2 **Smart Move (GER)**[238] 5786 4-8-9 ... APietsch 8 96
(H Blume, Germany) *mid-division, kept on steadily final 1 1/2f* **19/1**
5 shd **Wurfscheibe (GER)**[34] 1369 4-8-9 ... TMundry 3 96
(P Rau, Germany) *mid-division, outpaced 3f out, ran on well on outside final furlong to just miss 4th* **9/10**[1]
6 1 **Oligarchica (GER)**[742] 2341 5-8-9 ... MTellini 5 94
(R Rohne, Germany) *led to over 2f out, stayed on same pace* **20/1**
7 1/2 **Opatja**[34] 1368 4-8-9 ... SLandi 9 93
(L Camici, Italy) *tracked leader to half-way, 4th straight, beaten 2f out* **25/1**
8 1 **Sunsemperchi**[351] 2734 4-8-9 ... MMonteriso 11 92
(E Borromeo, Italy) *prominent, 3rd straight, weakened 2f out* **14/1**
9 8 **Love Money (IRE)**[372] 2100 4-8-9 ... MEsposito 2 77
(B Grizzetti, Italy) *always behind* **35/1**
10 8 **Vigata (IRE)**[287] 4620 5-8-9 ... CColombi 10 63
(V Valiani, Italy) *prominent to half-way* **22/1**
11 10 **Kykuit (IRE)**[34] 1368 4-8-12 ... MDemuro 6 48
(L Brogi, Italy) *held up in rear, brief effort 4f out, soon beaten, behind final 2f, eased* **63/10**[3]

2m 2.90s **11** Ran SP% **136.2**
(Including 1 Euro stake): WIN 8.05; PL 2.63, 1.80, 5.10; DF 16.23.
Owner Scuderia Diamante **Bred** Juddmonte Farms Inc **Trained** Italy

[1790] CARLISLE (R-H)

Monday, June 5

OFFICIAL GOING: Good to firm (firm in places)
Wind: Almost nil

2281 NORTHERN RACING DISCOUNT CARD MEDIAN AUCTION MAIDEN STKS 5f
2:20 (2:23) (Class 6) 2-Y-O **£2,590** (£770; £385; £192) **Stalls** High

Form RPR
1 **Russian Silk** 2-8-12 ... TomEaves 2 72
(Jedd O'Keeffe) *hld up bhd ldng gp: hdwy to ld 1f out: hung rt: kpt on wl* **22/1**
5 2 2 1/2 **Bollin Franny**[30] 1491 2-9-3 ... DavidAllan 4 71+
(T D Easterby) *cl up tl hmpd and outpcd after 1f: hdwy ins 2f out: kpt on wl fnl f: tk 2nd on line* **5/2**[2]
50 3 shd **Stepaside (IRE)**[10] 1982 2-9-3 ... RoystonFfrench 10 68
(M Johnston) *led: rdn 2f out: hdd 1f out: sn one pce* **9/1**
4 3/4 **Shotley Mac** 2-8-10 ... SuzzanneFrance(7) 7 65
(N Bycroft) *chsd ldrs tl edgd rt and no ex over 1f out* **33/1**
5 1/2 **Kindlelight Blue (IRE)** 2-8-12 ... JamesDoyle(5) 3 63+
(N P Littmoden) *s.i.s: outpcd tl hdwy 2f out: kpt on fnl f: nrst fin* **12/1**
6 6 **Valbenny (IRE)** 2-8-12 ... DeanMcKeown 8 37
(G A Swinbank) *s.i.s: sn in tch: rdn and wknd over 1f out* **14/1**
7 3/4 **Strathmore (IRE)** 2-9-3 ... RichardMullen 5 39
(E J O'Neill) *s.i.s: rn green in rr: nvr on terms* **9/1**
32 8 shd **Whiskey Junction**[11] 1959 2-9-3 ... AdrianTNicholls 1 38+
(A M Balding) *cl up on outside tl rdn and wknd over 1f out* **2/1**[1]
5 9 2 **Sophie's Dream**[21] 1730 2-9-3 ... DaleGibson 6 31
(J G Given) *chsd ldrs tl rdn and wknd over 1f out: eased whn no ch* **17/2**[3]
0 10 12 **Micky Mac (IRE)**[46] 1096 2-9-3 ... TonyHamilton 9 —
(I W McInnes) *chsd ldrs: hung bdly rt and wknd fr 1/2-way* **40/1**

62.21 secs (0.71) **Going Correction** -0.075s/f (Good) **10** Ran SP% **116.5**
Speed ratings (Par 91):91,87,86,85,84 75,74,73,70,51
CSF £75.74 TOTE £24.10: £4.70, £1.30, £2.20; EX 117.80.
Owner Only For Fun Partnership **Bred** Chippenham Lodge Stud Ltd **Trained** Middleham Moor, N Yorks

FOCUS
An ordinary bunch on looks and this form is unlikely to prove anything special. The pace was sound throughout and the race has been rated through the runner-up.

NOTEBOOK
Russian Silk, related to a six-furlong scorer and a winner up to a mile and a quarter, won an ordinary event in workmanlike fashion on this racecourse debut. She will stay at least six furlongs and may be capable of better. (op 25-1)
Bollin Franny is a consistent sort who is a bit better than this bare form suggests given he was squeezed out soon after the start. Although vulnerable to the better sorts in this type of event, he will be suited by six furlongs and should continue to give a good account. (op 7-2 tchd 9-4)
Stepaside(IRE), happier on this quicker ground, is now eleigible for handicaps. (op 15-2)
Shotley Mac, a colt lacking in physical presence, showed ability on this racecourse debut but, although open to improvement, is likely to continue to look vulnerable in this type of event.
Kindlelight Blue(IRE) showed ability at a modest level on this racecourse debut and left the impression that this experience and the step up to six furlongs plus will do him good. He is in good hands and may be able to pick up a modest event.
Valbenny(IRE), who is related to a multiple winner abroad, only hinted at ability on this racecourse debut but should improve for the experience.
Whiskey Junction, who lacks physical substance, got worked up at the start and proved a disappointment on this turf debut. He is capable of winning a small race but is not really one to be taking short odds about. Official explanation: jockey said colt hung left-handed throughout (tchd 5-2)
Micky Mac(IRE) Official explanation: jockey said saddle slipped

2282 VIACOM OUTDOOR CLAIMING STKS 7f 200y
2:50 (2:52) (Class 6) 3-Y-O+ **£2,730** (£806; £403) **Stalls** High

Form RPR
2230 1 **Art Elegant**[49] 1041 4-9-9 62 ... TonyHamilton 3 68
(G A Swinbank) *keen: trckd ldrs: rdn to ld appr fnl f: kpt on wl* **7/1**[3]
1000 2 1 **La Viola**[150] 56 4-9-0 56 ... (v) FrancisNorton 1 57
(K R Burke) *in tch: rdn over 2f out: rallied to chse wnr ins fnl f: kpt on* **14/1**
2000 3 1 **Distinctly Jim (IRE)**[26] 1593 3-8-12 57 ... DerekMcGaffin 5 61
(B Smart) *led to appr fnl f: kpt on same pce* **25/1**
3-13 4 1 **Le Chiffre (IRE)**[39] 5835 4-9-2 78 ... TolleyDean(7) 10 61
(R A Harris) *chsd ldrs: effrt and ev ch over 1f out: no ex ins fnl f* **5/1**[2]
0202 5 3/4 **Sawwaah (IRE)**[31] 1455 9-9-9 73 ... (v) AdrianTNicholls 7 60
(D Nicholls) *hld up: hdwy and swtchd rt 2f out: kpt on fnl f: no imp* **10/11**[1]
5000 6 1 1/4 **Ruby Legend**[20] 1757 8-8-10 46 ... JamesReveley(7) 4 51+
(K G Reveley) *bhd: pushed along over 3f out: kpt on fnl f: nvr rchd ldrs* **20/1**
0501 7 3/4 **Double Ransom**[25] 1608 7-9-4 49 ... (b) TomEaves 8 50
(Mrs L Stubbs) *in tch: outpcd over 3f out: n.d after* **7/1**[3]
400U 8 1 3/4 **Subsidise (IRE)**[6] 2107 3-8-4 54 ... (v) AndrewMullen(5) 2 48
(F P Murtagh) *hld up in tch: stdy hdwy after 3f: wknd over 2f out* **33/1**
0000 9 4 **Lazzoom (IRE)**[2] 2243 3-8-10 50 ... (t) GylesParkin 9 40
(Miss Tracy Waggott) *cl up tl rdn and wknd fr 2f out* **100/1**

1m 41.36s (1.27) **Going Correction** +0.025s/f (Good)
WFA 3 from 4yo+ 11lb **9** Ran SP% **113.3**
Speed ratings (Par 101):94,93,92,91,90 89,88,86,82
CSF £88.58 TOTE £8.70: £2.50, £3.60, £7.50; EX 73.00.
Owner M Sawers **Bred** Mrs S F Dibben **Trained** Melsonby, N Yorks

FOCUS
A race full of unreliable sorts in which the ordinary gallop favoured those racing prominently.
Lazzoom(IRE) Official explanation: jockey said gelding had a breathing problem

2283 VIACOM OUTDOOR FILLIES' H'CAP 1m 1f 61y
3:20 (3:23) (Class 5) (0-70,70) 3-Y-O **£3,886** (£1,156; £577; £288) **Stalls** High

Form RPR
0201 1 **Diamond De Triano (USA)**[16] 1851 3-9-4 70 ... DanielTudhope(3) 1 76+
(P W Chapple-Hyam) *cl up: led over 2f out: rdn and hung lft ins fnl f: hld on wl* **15/8**[1]
000 2 hd **Collette's Choice**[14] 1888 3-8-2 51 oh4 ... DaleGibson 5 57
(R A Fahey) *prom: drvn fr 3f out: no imp tl rallied over 1f out: chsd wnr ins last: kpt on: jst hld* **25/1**
3363 3 2 **Linton Dancer (IRE)**[14] 1888 3-7-13 53 ... AndrewMullen(5) 6 55
(J R Weymes) *cl up: ev ch and rdn over 2f out: kpt on same pce fnl f* **7/2**[2]
4000 4 1 1/4 **Dancing Flame**[16] 1851 3-8-6 55 ... FrancisNorton 9 55
(E J Alston) *led tl hdd over 2f out: one pce over 1f out* **11/2**
0250 5 2 **Lady Lochinver (IRE)**[33] 1416 3-8-5 54 ... DeanMcKeown 2 50
(Micky Hammond) *hld up in tch: effrt over 2f out: hung rt and outpcd over 1f out* **20/1**
4455 6 1/2 **Ellesappelle**[6] 2107 3-9-0 68 ... (v) AndrewElliott(5) 3 63
(K R Burke) *dwlt: rdn in rr 4f out: no imp fr 2f out* **5/1**[3]
0006 7 7 **Jenny Soba**[21] 1736 3-8-3 52 ... RoystonFfrench 8 33
(R M Whitaker) *in tch: rdn 3f out: sn btn* **11/1**

1m 57.65s (0.09) **Going Correction** +0.025s/f (Good) **7** Ran SP% **106.0**
Speed ratings (Par 96):100,99,98,96,95 94,88
CSF £42.09 CT £122.16 TOTE £2.70: £1.90, £7.00; EX 52.80.
Owner Diamond Racing Ltd **Bred** Swettenham Stud **Trained** Newmarket, Suffolk
■ Bollin Dolly was withdrawn (16/1, ref to enter stalls). R4 applies, deduct 5p in the £.

FOCUS
A fairly uncompetitive handicap in which the pace was only fair, but the form looks sound enough.

2284 CARLISLE CONFERENCE GROUP & WAVERLEY TBS H'CAP 5f 193y
3:50 (3:52) (Class 6) (0-60,60) 3-Y-O **£2,730** (£806; £403) **Stalls** High

Form RPR
0535 1 **Boy Dancer (IRE)**[11] 1950 3-8-13 52 ... FergalLynch 12 66+
(D W Barker) *hld up: nt clr run 1/2-way: swtchd lft and effrt 2f out: qcknd to ld ins fnl f: edgd rt: r.o wl* **5/1**[1]
4520 2 1 3/4 **Suhezy (IRE)**[26] 1594 3-8-10 49 ... TonyHamilton 2 52
(J S Wainwright) *cl up: led over 2f out to ins fnl f: kpt on: nt pce of wnr* **20/1**
0040 3 1 **Optical Seclusion (IRE)**[206] 6312 3-9-2 58 ... SaleemGolam(3) 7 58
(T J Etherington) *hld up: effrt outside over 1f out: edgd rt ins fnl f: kpt on* **25/1**
0063 4 nk **Drink To Me Only**[18] 1792 3-8-11 50 ... PhillipMakin 13 49
(J R Weymes) *prom: rdn over 2f out: one pce over 1f out* **10/1**
0600 5 1 **Inchmarlow (IRE)**[30] 1483 3-8-11 55 ... DuranFentiman(5) 9 51+
(T H Caldwell) *s.i.s: bhd tl hdwy over 1f out: kpt on fnl f: nrst fin* **33/1**
4000 6 1 **Casonova (IRE)**[21] 1736 3-8-10 49 ... FrancisNorton 16 42
(T D Easterby) *chsd ldrs: n.m.r briefly over 2f out: effrt over 1f out: sn no ex* **16/1**
3051 7 1 **Stanley Wolfe (IRE)**[18] 1792 3-8-5 49 ... AndrewMullen(5) 3 39
(James Moffatt) *led to over 2f out: no ex over 1f out* **14/1**
060 8 nk **Heads Turn (IRE)**[255] 5427 3-8-11 50 ... DavidAllan 8 39
(E J Alston) *bhd and outpcd: sme late hdwy: nvr on terms* **33/1**
0320 9 nk **The Grey One (IRE)**[16] 1859 3-9-2 55 ... (p) TonyCulhane 1 43
(J M Bradley) *sn rdn in midfield on outside: effrt 2f out: hung rt: no ex appr fnl f* **6/1**[2]
000 10 1/2 **Knickerless (IRE)**[272] 5032 3-8-10 54 ... JamesDoyle(5) 14 41
(N P Littmoden) *sn outpcd and rdn along: nvr rchd ldrs* **16/1**
0166 11 nk **Taras Tornado**[18] 1792 3-8-13 52 ... GrahamGibbons 11 38
(J J Quinn) *midfield: drvn and hung rt over 2f out: no imp* **9/1**
0042 12 nk **Quaker Boy**[18] 1792 3-9-5 58 ... TomEaves 5 43
(M Dods) *prom on outside: rdn over 2f out: n.m.r and sn lost pl* **7/1**[3]
000 13 1 3/4 **Megalo Maniac**[39] 1252 3-8-11 50 ... DeanMcKeown 4 30
(K G Reveley) *s.i.s: sn outpcd: nvr on terms* **33/1**
000 14 hd **Kings Cavalier (USA)**[20] 1752 3-9-2 55 ... (v) RoystonFfrench 10 34
(I W McInnes) *prom to 1/2-way: sn lost pl* **25/1**
0534 15 1/2 **Quadrophenia**[18] 1792 3-9-6 59 ... DaleGibson 6 37
(J G Given) *prom: effrt over 2f out: wknd over 1f out* **11/1**
1000 16 3 1/2 **Miltons Choice**[24] 1642 3-9-7 60 ... PatCosgrave 15 27
(J M Bradley) *s.i.s: nvr on terms* **12/1**
605 17 3 1/2 **Charming Princess**[9] 2019 3-8-8 50 ... DanielTudhope(3) 17 7
(J S Wainwright) *w ldrs tl rdn and wknd fr 2f out* **25/1**

1m 14.0s (0.39) **Going Correction** -0.075s/f (Good) **17** Ran SP% **122.1**
Speed ratings (Par 97):94,91,90,89,88 87,85,85,85,84 84,83,81,81,80 75,71
CSF £108.87 CT £2332.70 TOTE £5.90: £1.50, £5.50, £8.10, £2.60; EX 195.30.
Owner Break Dancer Partnership **Bred** Azienda Agricola Razza Emiliana **Trained** Scorton, N Yorks

FOCUS
A run-of-the-mill handicap judged on the performance of the runner-up, who has been ecposed in sellers, but the winner showed a good turn of foot and may well be capable of better.
Megalo Maniac Official explanation: jockey said gelding hung left-handed throughout

2285 VIACOM OUTDOOR H'CAP 5f
4:20 (4:20) (Class 6) (0-60,59) 3-Y-O **£2,730** (£806; £403) **Stalls** High

Form RPR
5064 1 **Bahamian Duke**[40] 1234 3-8-12 50 ... PatCosgrave 10 60
(K R Burke) *mde all: rdn 1/2-way: edgd lft ins fnl f: hld on wl* **8/1**
4321 2 1/2 **Hypnosis**[3] 2197 3-9-2 59 ... MarkLawson(5) 5 67
(D W Barker) *chsd ldrs: effrt 2f out: ev ch and hung lft ins fnl f: hld towards fin* **1/1**[1]

0025 **3** 1 3/4 **Newkeylets**[4] 2161 3-9-3 55 ....(p) TomEaves 2 56
(I Semple) *cl up tl rdn and nt qckn appr fnl f* **7/1**[3]

4005 **4** 1 **Sunset Ridge (IRE)**[34] 1378 3-9-3 55 .... DavidAllan 1 52
(Rae Guest) *in tch on outside: outpcd over 2f out: rallied over 1f out: kpt on: nrst fin* **12/1**

6600 **5** nk **Desert Hunter (IRE)**[23] 1687 3-8-12 50 .... DeanMcKeown 6 46
(Micky Hammond) *keen: hld up: hdwy over 2f out: rdn and no imp over 1f out* **20/1**

6204 **6** 3 1/2 **Laphonic (USA)**[25] 1612 3-8-11 52 .... SaleemGolam(3) 8 34
(T J Etherington) *dwlt: sn in tch: effrt over 2f out: no imp over 1f out* **4/1**[2]

0000 **7** 1 1/2 **Eldon Outlaw**[25] 1612 3-8-6 49 .... AndrewMullen(5) 4 25
(B Storey) *prom tl wknd over 1f out* **66/1**

6506 **8** 1/2 **Chunky Bell**[26] 1589 3-8-12 50 .... LeeEnstone 9 24
(P T Midgley) *dwlt: sn trcking ldrs: effrt over 2f out: sn wknd* **100/1**

0000 **9** 3/4 **Compton Flyer**[27] 1567 3-8-9 47 ....(p) TonyHamilton 7 18
(J M Bradley) *cl up tl rdn and wknd wl over 1f out* **16/1**

000 **10** 7 **Fashion Disaster**[44] 1147 3-8-1 46 ow2 .... JamieHamblett(7) 3 —
(A Crook) *racd wd: rdn and struggling fr 1/2-way* **50/1**

61.36 secs (-0.14) **Going Correction** -0.075s/f (Good) **10** Ran SP% **116.4**
Speed ratings (Par 97):98,97,94,92,92 86,84,83,82,71
CSF £16.14 CT £63.91 TOTE £9.10: £2.00, £1.10, £2.70; EX 18.40.
Owner Danum Racing **Bred** D R Tucker **Trained** Middleham Moor, N Yorks

FOCUS
A modest handicap but, although the pace was sound, this race favoured those racing prominently.

2286 BETFAIR APPRENTICE TRAINING SERIES H'CAP (PART OF THE "BETFAIR APPRENTICE TRAINING RACE" SERIES) 7f 200y
4:50 (4:54) (Class 6) (0-60,59) 4-Y-O+ **£2,730** (£806; £403) **Stalls** High

Form RPR

0500 **1** **Leighton Buzzard**[23] 1683 4-9-7 56 .... DonnaCaldwell 3 66+
(Mrs A Duffield) *bhd and sn outpcd: effrt whn nt clr run over 2f out: swtchd lft: led ins fnl f: r.o wl* **16/1**

0300 **2** 1 1/4 **Credential**[16] 1850 4-9-7 56 .... KevinGhunowa 6 63
(John A Harris) *hld up: hdwy over 2f out: ev ch ins fnl f: kpt on* **20/1**

6000 **3** nk **Son Of Thunder (IRE)**[49] 1045 5-9-1 55 .... WilliamCarson(5) 15 61
(M Dods) *keen: chsd ldrs: effrt over 2f out: ev ch ins fnl f: no ex* **7/1**[3]

6005 **4** 1 **Trevian**[5] 2135 5-8-8 50 .... BarrySavage(7) 5 54
(J M Bradley) *led: clr 1/2-way: hdd and no ex ins fnl f* **11/1**

5506 **5** 3/4 **Able Mind**[182] 6508 6-8-8 48 .... JamieHamblett(5) 10 50
(D W Thompson) *in tch: effrt over 2f out: one pce over 1f out* **16/1**

06/2 **6** 3/4 **Whittinghamvillage**[20] 1761 5-9-6 58 .... ChrisCavanagh(3) 2 58
(D W Whillans) *hld up outside: effrt over 2f out: hung rt: no imp over 1f out* **16/1**

6023 **7** 1/2 **Airedale Lad (IRE)**[16] 1852 5-9-1 50 .... MichaelJStainton 14 49
(R M Whitaker) *chsd ldrs: drvn over 2f out: no ex over 1f out* **7/1**[3]

0000 **8** shd **Pianoforte (USA)**[16] 1850 4-9-3 57 .... JamesRogers(5) 16 56
(E J Alston) *in tch: outpcd over 2f out: n.d after* **33/1**

1634 **9** nk **Thornaby Green**[11] 1947 5-8-5 45 .... DeanHeslop(5) 4 43
(T D Barron) *racd wd in midfield: effrt 3f out: edgd rt and no ex over 1f out* **13/2**[2]

0502 **10** 1 **Shifty**[5] 2137 7-9-4 58 .... HeatherMcGee(5) 13 56+
(D Carroll) *midfield: effrt over 2f out: sn no imp* **11/2**[1]

0000 **11** 1 3/4 **Anthemion (IRE)**[29] 1500 9-8-13 51 .... NeilBrown(3) 7 43
(Mrs J C McGregor) *midfield: effrt over 3f out: wknd over 2f out* **100/1**

3400 **12** 1/2 **Taminoula (IRE)**[35] 1353 5-8-10 50 .... LukeMorris(5) 12 41
(J G Given) *s.i.s: sn midfield: drvn over 3f out: sn btn* **20/1**

6500 **13** 1/2 **Nabir (FR)**[26] 1591 6-9-7 59 ....(tp) ThomasO'Brien(3) 11 49
(P D Niven) *prom: drvn over 3f out: wknd over 2f out* **20/1**

0040 **14** 1 **Wrenlane**[6] 2108 5-9-4 53 .... LiamJones 1 40
(J J Quinn) *unruly: uns rdr and loose bef s: keen: chsd ldrs tl wknd over 2f out* **14/1**

2002 **15** shd **Splodger Mac (IRE)**[23] 1665 7-9-4 53 ....(b) SuzzanneFrance 9 40
(N Bycroft) *towards rr: drvn 1/2-way: wknd over 2f out* **20/1**

0205 **U** **Grande Terre (IRE)**[24] 1636 5-9-3 57 .... JamesReveley(5) 8 —
(R A Fahey) *hld up: shkn up but no imp whn clipped heels of rival and uns rdr over 1f out* **8/1**

1m 40.09s **Going Correction** +0.025s/f (Good) **16** Ran SP% **120.5**
Speed ratings (Par 101):101,99,99,98,97 96,96,96,96,95 93,92,92,91,91 —
CSF £312.22 CT £2538.05 TOTE £17.00: £3.50, £2.60, £2.80, £3.10; EX 357.10 Place 6 £463.56, Place 5 £166.65.
Owner Diamond Racing Ltd **Bred** Mrs J A Rawding And Green Meadow Stud **Trained** Constable Burton, N Yorks
■ Stewards' Enquiry : Thomas O'Brien four-day ban: careless riding (Jun 16-19)

FOCUS
A modest event but a strong gallop favoured those coming from behind.
T/Jkpt: Not won. T/Plt: £874.70 to a £1 stake. Pool: £48,171.45. 40.20 winning tickets. T/Qpdt: £39.40 to a £1 stake. Pool: £4,275.50. 80.10 winning tickets. RY

2100 LEICESTER (R-H)
Monday, June 5

OFFICIAL GOING: Good to firm (firm in places)
Wind: Light, across Weather: Cloudy with sunny spells

2287 PYTCHLEY MAIDEN STKS 5f 218y
2:00 (2:04) (Class 4) 2-Y-O **£5,678** (£1,699; £849; £424; £211) **Stalls** Low

Form RPR

6 **1** **Soviet Palace (IRE)**[26] 1588 2-9-3 .... DO'Donohoe 7 82+
(K A Ryan) *chsd ldrs: led over 4f out: clr over 1f out: r.o* **10/3**[2]

2 1 1/4 **Folio (USA)** 2-9-3 .... RichardHughes 12 78+
(B W Hills) *s.i.s: hdwy over 4f out: rdn to chse wnr over 1f out : edgd rt ins fnl f: r.o* **12/1**

3 3 1/2 **Hunting Tower** 2-9-3 .... RyanMoore 1 68
(R Hannon) *hld up: hdwy over 2f out: sn rdn: styd on same pce fnl f* **16/1**

2 **4** 2 **Gremlin**[23] 1688 2-9-3 .... EddieAhern 6 62
(A King) *prom: rdn to chse wnr over 2f out: wknd over 1f out* **11/10**[1]

5 1 1/2 **Ghost Dancer** 2-9-3 .... NickyMackay 8 57+
(L M Cumani) *mid-div: outpcd over 2f out: nt clr run over 1f out: nvr trbld ldrs* **18/1**

45 **6** 1/2 **Carlitos Spirit (IRE)**[56] 944 2-9-3 .... DaneO'Neill 11 56
(B R Millman) *chsd ldrs: rdn over 2f out: hung lft and wknd over 1f out* **11/1**[3]

7 1 **Pertemps Networks** 2-9-3 .... PaulMulrennan 4 53+
(M W Easterby) *hmpd s: outpcd: sme hdwy over 2f out: nvr trbld ldrs* **40/1**

8 1 1/2 **Kat Act Two** 2-8-12 .... ShaneKelly 2 43
(J A Osborne) *s.s: outpcd* **25/1**

9 4 **Valley Observer (FR)** 2-9-3 .... TedDurcan 9 36
(W R Swinburn) *s.i.s: sn outpcd* **14/1**

10 1/2 **Kyshanty** 2-9-3 .... PatDobbs 3 35
(R Hannon) *sn outpcd* **40/1**

0 **11** 4 **Briarwood Bear**[18] 1796 2-9-3 .... FergusSweeney 5 23
(M Blanshard) *wnt lft s: sn prom: hung lft and wknd 1/2-way* **100/1**

030 **12** 5 **Piccolo Prezzo**[24] 1647 2-8-12 .... ChrisCatlin 10 3
(I A Wood) *led: hdd over 4f out: wknd over 2f out* **66/1**

1m 13.19s (-0.01) **Going Correction** 0.0s/f (Good) **12** Ran SP% **115.7**
Speed ratings (Par 95):100,98,93,91,89 88,87,85,79,79 73,67
CSF £40.17 TOTE £4.70: £1.60, £2.70, £2.90; EX 57.00 Trifecta £369.10 Pool: £743.43 - 1.43 winning tickets..
Owner David Reilly **Bred** Joe Rogers **Trained** Hambleton, N Yorks

FOCUS
A fairly decent maiden likely to produce winners and the winning time was smart for a race of its type.

NOTEBOOK
Soviet Palace(IRE), who showed up well for a long way from a bad draw on his debut at Newcastle, comes from a stable whose two-year-olds are thriving and he was never going to be caught inside the final furlong. Evidently a fair sort, he looks to have more to offer and should be up to landing a decent nursery, with further expected to suit in time. (op 4-1 tchd 9-2)
Folio(USA), bred to stay further in time, came out of the pack to chase the winner down, but he was never getting there in time. This was a highly pleasing initial effort and improvement is to be expected. (op 9-1)
Hunting Tower is extremely well bred, but not to be effective at around this sort of distance, being by Sadler's Wells out of a Machiavellian mare, so connections will no doubt have been delighted a the level of ability he was able to show at such an early stage. Improvement next time is to be expected with the experience under his belt, but it may not be until the seven-furlong juvenile races are introduced that he is able to win. (op 12-1)
Gremlin, who had a hard enough race when beaten by the draw on his debut at Warwick, was unable to confirm that promise in a better class of contest and it may well be that he is more of a nursery type. (op 5-4 after 11-8 in a place tchd Evens)
Ghost Dancer, whose stable's first juveniles of the season did not offer a great deal, is bred to need trips in excess of this, but he shaped well nonetheless, making some good late headway under tender handling. Many of his sire's progeny improve for a softer surface and he is definitely one to be interested in next time.
Carlitos Spirit(IRE) is not really progressing and looks more of a nursery sort. (tchd 12-1)
Pertemps Networks was done no favours at the start and shaped well considering. He should come on for the experience and will find easier opportunities. (op 33-1)
Kat Act Two comes from a stable which is capable of readying a juvenile, but he was slowly away and struggled for pace throughout. By a French Derby winner, he is going to improve with time and distance and there should be a deal of improvement to come. (op 20-1)
Valley Observer(FR), a half-brother to Kandidate, did not know what was required of him over what looked an inadequate distance and his stable's juveniles usually come on for the run. (op 12-1)

2288 HICKLING (S) STKS 5f 218y
2:30 (2:31) (Class 5) 3-5-Y-O **£3,238** (£963; £481; £240) **Stalls** Low

Form RPR

0062 **1** **Beau Marche**[1] 2260 4-8-12 45 ....(b) RyanMoore 9 50
(G G Margarson) *wnt rt s: sn pushed along in rr: hdwy over 2f out: styd on to ld wl ins fnl f* **8/1**

3000 **2** 1 1/4 **Von Wessex**[6] 2096 4-8-9 58 .... RobertMiles(3) 8 46
(W G M Turner) *chsd ldrs: led over 1f out: rdn and hdd wl ins fnl f* **28/1**

6423 **3** 1 3/4 **Drum Dance (IRE)**[7] 2077 4-9-10 49 .... KimTinkler 1 53
(N Tinkler) *s.i.s: sn pushed along in rr: hdwy 1/2-way: rdn over 1f out: styd on* **6/1**[2]

0366 **4** 3/4 **Beverley Beau**[13] 1909 4-9-3 44 .... KristinStubbs(7) 2 51
(Mrs L Stubbs) *prom: jnd ldrs over 2f out: rdn over 1f out: no ex fnl f* **28/1**

0205 **5** nk **Diamond Josh**[72] 732 4-9-2 61 .... DarryllHolland 7 42
(P D Evans) *chsd ldrs: rdn over 2f out: no ex fnl f* **7/2**[1]

0000 **6** hd **Revien (IRE)**[36] 1310 4-9-2 48 .... PaulFitzsimons 18 41
(Miss J R Tooth) *w ldrs: rdn over 1f out: styd on same pce* **40/1**

5100 **7** 1 1/2 **Mulberry Lad (IRE)**[20] 1752 4-9-7 48 .... ChrisCatlin 10 42
(P W Hiatt) *hmpd s: hdwy u.p over 2f out: wknd ins fnl f* **25/1**

0005 **8** hd **Hamaasy**[7] 2077 5-9-10 49 .... JoeFanning 6 44
(D Nicholls) *chsd ldrs: led over 3f out: rdn and hdd over 1f out: wknd ins fnl f* **15/2**

0000 **9** nk **Silver Visage (IRE)**[23] 1673 4-8-9 52 ....(p) AdamKirby(3) 5 31
(Miss J Feilden) *led: hdd over 3f out: wknd wl over 1f out* **9/1**

1000 **10** 3/4 **Dorn Hill**[26] 1594 4-9-5 45 ....(p) MickyFenton 17 36
(D G Bridgwater) *w ldrs 4f: wknd over 1f out* **50/1**

4400 **11** 3/4 **Imperium**[5] 2136 5-10-1 50 ....(p) SteveDrowne 14 44
(Stef Liddiard) *hld up: hdwy 1/2-way: wknd 2f out* **7/1**[3]

1600 **12** nk **Magical Mimi**[3] 2208 5-9-7 46 ....(bt[1]) NeilChalmers(3) 15 38
(K G Wingrove) *s.i.s: sn prom: rdn and wknd over 2f out* **33/1**

0060 **13** shd **Baytown Valentina**[31] 1464 3-8-11 47 ....(p) DaneO'Neill 4 33
(R Brotherton) *chsd ldrs 4f* **50/1**

02-0 **14** 5 **Beresford Boy**[24] 1645 5-8-12 50 .... FergusSweeney 3 11
(J A Pickering) *s.i.s: outpcd* **50/1**

4303 **15** 1 1/4 **Sister Gee (IRE)**[26] 1594 4-8-12 45 .... RussellKennemore(7) 12 14
(R Hollinshead) *mid-div: rdn 1/2-way: wknd 2f out* **14/1**

6004 **16** 15 **Macs All Heart (IRE)**[19] 1771 3-7-13 47 .... PaulHanagan 16 —
(A B Coogan) *s.s: outpcd* **16/1**

0000 **17** 4 **Be Like A Lion**[40] 1232 3-7-13 50 .... FrancisFerris 11 —
(B Palling) *dwlt: outpcd* **33/1**

1m 13.45s (0.25) **Going Correction** 0.0s/f (Good)
WFA 3 from 4yo+ 8lb **17** Ran SP% **119.4**
Speed ratings (Par 103):98,96,94,93,92 92,90,90,89,88 87,87,87,80,78 58,53
CSF £223.01 TOTE £10.60: £3.00, £7.10, £2.10; EX 210.10 TRIFECTA Not won..The winner was bought in for 6,000gns.
Owner E P Stibbe and D Brookes **Bred** Alan Spargo Ltd **Trained** Newmarket, Suffolk

FOCUS
Not the worst seller of all time, and the winner has been rated to his latest second at Brighton.
Silver Visage(IRE) Official explanation: jockey said gelding hung badly right
Sister Gee(IRE) Official explanation: jockey said filly lost her action

2289 ABBEY PARK CONDITIONS STKS 7f 9y
3:00 (3:00) (Class 4) 3-Y-O+ **£6,232** (£1,866; £933; £467; £233) **Stalls** Low

Form RPR

4563 **1** **Jedburgh**[49] 1050 5-9-4 102 ....(b) SebSanders 2 106
(J L Dunlop) *trckd ldrs: edgd lft over 1f out: hung rt 1f out: r.o to ld last strides* **9/2**

1220 **2** *nk* **Philharmonic**[19] [1778] 5-9-4 105 .... PaulHanagan 6 105
(R A Fahey) *chsd ldrs: led 1f out: rdn and hdd last strides* **3/1**[3]

0562 **3** *2* **Mac Love**[49] [1050] 5-9-4 105 .... SteveDrowne 5 100
(R Charlton) *plld hrd: led: hdd over 5f out: rdn to ld over 1f out: sn hdd: styd on same pce* **85/40**[1]

0531 **4** *1 1/4* **Polar Magic**[12] [1935] 5-9-4 99 .... JamieSpencer 1 96
(J R Fanshawe) *hld up: plld hrd: hdwy over 1f out: sn ev ch: no ex ins fnl f* **5/2**[2]

4131 **5** *shd* **Will He Wish**[31] [1456] 10-9-4 90 .... DarryllHolland 3 96
(S Gollings) *led over 5f out: rdn and hdd over 1f out: styd on same pce* **20/1**

1m 26.42s (0.32) **Going Correction** 0.0s/f (Good)
WFA 3 from 5yo+ 10lb 5 Ran SP% **108.5**
Speed ratings (Par 105):98,97,95,93,93
CSF £17.46 TOTE £5.60: £2.00, £1.30; EX 17.10.
Owner The Earl Cadogan **Bred** The Earl Cadogan **Trained** Arundel, W Sussex

FOCUS
A tight contest, not truly-run, and the winner has been rated 6lb off his best form.

2290 ROBERT POCHIN LTD PLUMBING & HEATING H'CAP 1m 1f 218y

3:30 (3:30) (Class 4) (0-85,85) 3-Y-O
£6,232 (£1,866; £933; £467; £233; £117) **Stalls** High

Form RPR

0331 **1** **Bandama (IRE)**[17] [1823] 3-9-7 **85** .... RyanMoore 5 93
(Mrs A J Perrett) *prom: chsd ldr 7f out: led over 2f out: rdn over 1f out: r.o* **3/1**[2]

0625 **2** *1 3/4* **Quince (IRE)**[8] [2046] 3-9-6 **84** .... (v[1]) JimmyQuinn 6 89
(J Pearce) *a.p: chsd wnr over 2f out: rdn over 1f out: styd on same pce fnl f* **6/1**

1440 **3** *1 1/2* **Auction Room (USA)**[26] [1583] 3-9-5 **83** .... RichardHughes 10 85
(B W Hills) *hld up in tch: outpcd over 3f out: r.o ins fnl f* **11/1**

01 **4** *nk* **Baizically (IRE)**[24] [1635] 3-9-7 **85** .... ShaneKelly 2 87
(J A Osborne) *hld up: hdwy over 2f out: rdn over 1f out: styd on* **5/2**[1]

025 **5** *3 1/2* **Zurbaran (IRE)**[10] [1984] 3-8-13 **77** .... MickyFenton 7 72
(K A Morgan) *chsd ldr 3f: rdn over 2f out: wknd ins fnl f* **50/1**

21 **6** *nk* **Sharplaw Autumn (USA)**[39] [1252] 3-9-2 **80** .... NickyMackay 1 74
(W J Haggas) *hld up: hdwy over 2f out: rdn and hung rt over 1f out: wknd ins fnl f* **5/1**[3]

2155 **7** *1/2* **Regal Connection (USA)**[17] [1837] 3-8-10 **74** .... KDarley 3 67
(M Johnston) *led over 7f: wknd fnl f* **12/1**

0010 **8** *shd* **Grey Paint (USA)**[27] [1569] 3-8-10 **74** .... (t) PatDobbs 9 67
(R Hannon) *chsd ldrs: rdn over 2f out: wknd over 1f out* **40/1**

326 **9** *1 3/4* **Brave Fight**[218] [6178] 3-8-11 **75** .... DaneO'Neill 4 65
(A King) *hld up in tch: rdn over 2f out: wknd over 1f out* **20/1**

0606 **10** *23* **Your Amount (IRE)**[17] [1828] 3-8-10 **74** .... JDSmith 8 20
(A King) *hld up: wknd over 2f out* **33/1**

4136 **11** *2 1/2* **Shaydreambeliever**[11] [1948] 3-8-6 **70** .... PaulHanagan 11 11
(R A Fahey) *hld up: rdn over 3f out: sn wknd* **20/1**

2m 6.66s (-1.64) **Going Correction** 0.0s/f (Good) 11 Ran SP% **117.4**
Speed ratings (Par 101):106,104,103,103,100 100,99,99,98,79 77
CSF £19.87 CT £175.86 TOTE £3.20: £1.40, £2.40, £2.10; EX 25.00 Trifecta £259.30 Pool: £1,051.95 - 2.88 winning tickets..
Owner Lady Clague **Bred** Newberry Stud Farm Ltd **Trained** Pulborough, W Sussex

FOCUS
Just a fair three-year-old handicap, and sound form rated through the second and third.
Your Amount(IRE) Official explanation: jockey said gelding was unsuited by the good to firm (firm in places) ground
Shaydreambeliever Official explanation: jockey said gelding lost its action

2291 HAPPY BIRTHDAY ROY WHEATLEY CLAIMING STKS 1m 60y

4:00 (4:02) (Class 5) 3-Y-O+ **£3,886** (£1,156; £577; £288) **Stalls** High

Form RPR

23 **1** **Grecian Gold (IRE)**[35] [1355] 4-10-0 .... PhilipRobinson 12 75
(C G Cox) *led: racd keenly: rdn and hdd over 1f out: edgd lft ins fnl f: rallied to ld post* **9/4**[1]

0036 **2** *shd* **Ask The Clerk (IRE)**[20] [1760] 5-9-10 68 .... MickyFenton 2 71
(Mrs P Sly) *hld up: hdwy over 2f: led over 1f out: hdd post* **7/2**[2]

4011 **3** *4* **Shrine Mountain (USA)**[27] [1574] 4-9-8 50 .... (v) EddieAhern 3 60
(J R Holt) *chsd ldrs: outpcd over 1f out: styd on ins fnl f* **7/2**[2]

0020 **4** *1 1/4* **Noorain**[21] [1725] 4-8-11 44 .... (t) SteveDrowne 4 46
(Stef Liddiard) *dwlt: hdwy over 6f out: rdn over 2f out: styd on same pce appr fnl f* **10/1**[3]

0003 **5** *3/4* **Fantasy Defender (IRE)**[13] [1915] 4-9-10 46 .... (v) KDarley 9 57
(Ernst Oertel) *hld up in tch: outpcd over 2f out: hdwy over 1f out: no imp ins fnl f* **14/1**

0000 **6** *3 1/2* **Ronnies Lad**[257] [5409] 4-8-9 42 .... ChrisHough(7) 7 41
(J R Norton) *sn outpcd: sme late hdwy: nvr nrr* **50/1**

0000 **7** *6* **Mytass**[7] [2070] 3-8-5 45 .... (b) ChrisCatlin 1 24
(J A Pickering) *prom: rdn over 2f out: sn wknd* **80/1**

2030 **8** *1/2* **Eddies Jewel**[233] [5897] 6-9-2 43 .... PaulHanagan 8 26
(H Alexander) *chsd wnr 3f: rdn and wknd over 1f out* **40/1**

U **9** *5* **Lucy Babe**[7] [2070] 3-8-6 .... FrancisFerris 14 12
(G Prodromou) *s.i.s: outpcd* **40/1**

00 **10** *1 3/4* **Alan The Aussie**[25] [1613] 3-8-4 .... KirstyMilczarek(7) 13 13
(G Prodromou) *hld up: rdn and wknd over 3f out* **66/1**

0400 **11** *11* **Fraternity**[28] [1553] 9-8-11 55 .... RussellKennemore(7) 6 —
(J A Pickering) *prom: chsd wnr over 5f out: rdn and wknd over 2f out* **16/1**

030- **12** *8* **Barbilyrifle (IRE)**[103] [1854] 5-9-2 55 .... JamieMackay 5 —
(N B King) *sn outpcd* **50/1**

1m 44.58s (-0.72) **Going Correction** 0.0s/f (Good)
WFA 3 from 4yo+ 11lb 12 Ran SP% **108.4**
Speed ratings (Par 103):103,102,98,97,96 93,87,86,81,80 69,61
CSF £7.94 TOTE £2.80: £1.30, £1.50, £1.80; EX 9.20 Trifecta £27.90 Pool: £297.15 - 7.58 winning tickets..The winner was claimed by Mustafa Khan for £12,000.
Owner Mike Watts And Steve Woodhams **Bred** Bloodstock Underwriting (ireland) Ltd **Trained** Lambourn, Berks

FOCUS
Probably a fair event for the grade, with two handicappers pulling clear. The form looks sound enough.

2292 COMPARE ODDS@GG-ODDS.COM MAIDEN STKS 1m 3f 183y

4:30 (4:31) (Class 5) 3-Y-O **£5,047** (£1,510; £755; £377; £188) **Stalls** High

Form RPR

5 **1** **Ivory Gala (FR)**[10] [1994] 3-8-12 .... JamieSpencer 6 79
(B J Meehan) *hld up in tch: hung rt and outpcd over 2f out: hdwy over 1f out: rdn to ld ins fnl f: hung rt: r.o* **2/1**[1]

0 **2** *2* **Karlovy**[17] [1819] 3-8-12 .... PhilipRobinson 2 75
(M A Jarvis) *racd wd but w ldrs over 3f: led over 2f out: rdn and hdd ins fnl f: styd on same pce* **4/1**[3]

3 **3** *1 3/4* **Moonshadow**[25] [1613] 3-8-12 .... EddieAhern 9 73
(H R A Cecil) *led over 10f: sn rdn: no ex ins fnl f* **11/4**[2]

3 **4** *3 1/2* **Sybella**[29] [1516] 3-8-12 .... IanMongan 4 67
(J L Dunlop) *w ldr over 3f: remained handy tl rdn and wknd over 1f out* **12/1**

4 **5** *1/2* **Artist's Muse (USA)**[29] [1516] 3-8-12 .... RichardHughes 1 66
(Mrs A J Perrett) *hld up: hdwy u.p 3f out: sn ev ch: hung rt over 1f out: wknd fnl f* **9/1**

55 **6** *1* **Riff Raff**[25] [1613] 3-8-12 .... PaulHanagan 7 65
(W Jarvis) *chsd ldrs 10f* **14/1**

30 **7** *1* **Bride To Be (USA)**[35] [1351] 3-8-12 .... SebSanders 3 63
(C E Brittain) *hld up: rdn over 2f out: sn wknd* **20/1**

8 *hd* **Cosmic Messenger (FR)** 3-9-0 .... StephaneBreux(3) 8 68?
(L A Dace) *s.s: hld up: rdn and wknd over 2f out* **66/1**

2m 32.31s (-2.19) **Going Correction** 0.0s/f (Good) 8 Ran SP% **110.6**
Speed ratings (Par 99):107,105,104,102,101 101,100,100
CSF £9.51 TOTE £3.50: £1.20, £2.10, £1.10; EX 14.20 Trifecta £100.90 Pool: £628.56 - 4.42 winning tickets..
Owner T W Bloodstock Ltd **Bred** T Wilson **Trained** Manton, Wilts

FOCUS
A fair maiden that is likely to produce winners, although the proximity of the final pair limits the level of the form.

2293 SHARNFORD FILLIES' H'CAP 7f 9y

5:00 (5:00) (Class 5) (0-70,67) 3-Y-O+ **£4,416** (£1,321; £660; £330; £164) **Stalls** Low

Form RPR

2053 **1** **Whitethorne**[233] [5893] 4-9-9 **67** .... GregFairley(5) 10 78
(R A Fahey) *racd centre: mde all: rdn and hung lft over 1f out: r.o* **8/1**[3]

3414 **2** *1* **Foreplay (IRE)**[28] [1551] 3-9-4 **67** .... KDarley 13 71
(E A L Dunlop) *racd stands' side: hld up: swtchd rt and hdwy over 1f out: r.o* **17/2**

4630 **3** *3/4* **Meditation**[4] [2184] 4-9-6 **64** .... DerekNolan(5) 6 70
(I A Wood) *led stands' side: rdn over 1f out: styd on* **5/1**[2]

0005 **4** *1/2* **Icecap**[13] [1914] 6-8-6 **48** oh7 .... StephaneBreux(3) 7 53
(W G M Turner) *racd stands' side: hld up: hdwy over 1f out: r.o* **33/1**

5012 **5** *hd* **Mon Petite Amour**[13] [1923] 3-8-1 **50** .... (p) FrankieMcDonald 4 50
(D W P Arbuthnot) *racd stands' side: chsd ldrs: rdn over 1f out: styd on same pce* **16/1**

5430 **6** *1 1/4* **Calamari (IRE)**[29] [1500] 4-9-3 **56** .... TPQueally 1 57
(Mrs A Duffield) *racd stands' side: s.i.s: sn mid-div: rdn over 1f out: nt trble ldrs* **16/1**

4041 **7** *nk* **Sweet Emily**[244] [5687] 4-10-0 **67** .... JamieSpencer 12 67
(J R Fanshawe) *racd stands' side: hld up: swtchd rt and hdwy over 2f out: eased whn btn ins fnl f* **9/4**[1]

035 **8** *hd* **Shamsalmaidan (IRE)**[251] [5534] 3-9-0 **63** .... MickyFenton 2 58
(C E Brittain) *racd stands' side: chsd ldrs: rdn over 2f out: styd on same pce fnl f* **22/1**

0066 **9** *6* **Baron Rhodes**[18] [1795] 5-9-12 **65** .... (p) GeorgeBaker 8 48
(J S Wainwright) *racd stands'side: prom over 5f: eased fnl f* **11/1**

0250 **10** *shd* **Linda Green**[6] [2095] 5-9-11 **64** .... TedDurcan 3 47
(M R Channon) *racd stands' side: hld up in tch: rdn over 2f out: wknd over 1f out: eased ins fnl f* **10/1**

2055 **11** *1 1/4* **Shinko (IRE)**[28] [1551] 3-8-10 **62** .... AdamKirby(3) 11 38
(Miss J Feilden) *racd centre: chsd wnr: rdn over 2f out: sn wknd* **22/1**

065 **12** *5* **Spanish Story**[43] [1165] 3-8-1 **50** .... ChrisCatlin 9 12
(A M Balding) *racd stands' side: prom over 4f* **12/1**

1m 26.5s (0.40) **Going Correction** 0.0s/f (Good)
WFA 3 from 4yo+ 10lb 12 Ran SP% **117.6**
Speed ratings (Par 100):97,95,95,94,94 92,92,92,85,85 83,78
CSF £71.89 CT £383.44 TOTE £10.50: £2.60, £2.50, £2.40; EX 68.60 Trifecta £215.50 Pool: £373.34 - 1.23 winning tickets. Place 6 £83.13, Place 5 £31.32.
Owner Mrs Doreen M Swinburn **Bred** Genesis Green Stud Ltd **Trained** Musley Bank, N Yorks

FOCUS
Modest handicap form and not solid based on the performance of the fourth from out of the handicap.
T/Plt: £51.10 to a £1 stake. Pool: £43,129.05. 615.25 winning tickets. T/Qpdt: £5.60 to a £1 stake. Pool: £3,321.10. 431.20 winning tickets. CR

1853 THIRSK (L-H)

Monday, June 5

OFFICIAL GOING: Good to firm (firm in places)
the ground was described as 'genuine good to firm, fast but no jar whatsoever'.
Wind: Almost nil Weather: Fine

2294 GREAT YORKSHIRE FILLIES' (S) STKS 6f

6:45 (6:45) (Class 5) 2-Y-O **£3,886** (£1,156; £577; £288) **Stalls** High

Form RPR

6033 **1** **Emma Told Lies**[9] [2015] 2-8-9 .... PaulMulrennan 5 55
(M W Easterby) *w ldr: led over 2f out: hung lft: hld on wl towards fin* **4/1**[2]

0466 **2** *1* **Minimum Fuss (IRE)**[15] [1862] 2-8-9 .... (b[1]) DaleGibson 3 52
(M W Easterby) *hld up: effrt over 2f out: hung lft and styd on fnl f: no ex towards fin* **12/1**

0 **3** *hd* **Ensign's Trick**[59] [908] 2-8-9 .... DavidAllan 9 51
(W M Brisbourne) *chsd ldrs: chal and hung lft 1f out: no ex ins last* **8/1**[3]

6 **4** *shd* **Dispol Truly (IRE)**[9] [2015] 2-8-6 .... BenSwarbrick(3) 4 51+
(P T Midgley) *s.i.s: wl bhd and reminders after 1f: hdwy: hung lft and hmpd over 1f out: styd on strly ins last* **14/1**

0 **5** *nk* **Heart And Hand (IRE)**[5] [2145] 2-8-9 .... (b[1]) JoeFanning 7 50
(B J Meehan) *sis: sn bhd and drvn along: hdwy over 1f out: kpt on ins last* **12/1**

52 **6** *1 1/2* **Burlington Fayr (IRE)**[9] [2015] 2-8-9 .... KimTinkler 2 46
(N Tinkler) *chsd ldrs: hung lft over 1f out: one pce* **7/2**[1]

41 **7** *7* **Mollyanko**[7] [2064] 2-8-9 .... MarcHalford(5) 8 30
(W G M Turner) *s.i.s: hung bdly lft thrght: sn detached: ended up racing far side* **4/1**[2]

0340 **8** *shd* **Minnie Magician**[15] [1862] 2-8-9 .... TonyHamilton 1 24
(C Grant) *chsd ldrs: wknd over 2f out* **9/1**

00 **9** ½ **Inch Forward**[9] 2015 2-8-9 .... TomEaves 6 23
(D W Barker) *led tl over 2f out: lost pl over 1f out* **14/1**

1m 15.96s (3.46) **Going Correction** +0.20s/f (Good) **9** Ran SP% **112.1**
Speed ratings (Par 90):84,82,82,82,81 79,70,70,69
CSF £48.65 TOTE £4.60: £1.40, £5.60, £3.90; EX 43.30.There was no bid for the winner. Dispol Truly was claimed by A G Newcombe for £6,000
Owner Nigel Gravett **Bred** M W Easterby **Trained** Sheriff Hutton, N Yorks

FOCUS
A weak fillies'-only race even by selling-race standards.

NOTEBOOK
Emma Told Lies appreciated the quicker ground and was persuaded to do just enough. As selling races go they do not come any weaker than this. (op 11-2)
Minimum Fuss(IRE), in first-time blinkers and racing on much quicker ground, travelled strongly but in the end had to settle for second best behind her stablemate.
Ensign's Trick, having just her second outing and her first on turf, was drawn against the stands'-side rail but she persisted in hanging left and, after having every chance, ended up racing towards the middle. (op 9-1)
Dispol Truly(IRE) was soon well off the pace. Hampered when starting to improve, she sprouted wings late on, sufficient for her to be claimed. She looked the best filly on the night.
Heart And Hand(IRE), in blinkers this time, looked reluctant on the way to post. Soon way off the pace, she stayed on when it was all over and will appreciate a step up to seven. (op 9-1)
Burlington Fayr(IRE), in front of the winner at Catterick, was drawn on the outer and did not look happy on this much quicker ground. Official explanation: jockey said filly was unsuited by the good to firm (firm in places) ground (op 10-3 tchd 4-1)
Mollyanko, the only previous winner in the line-up, did not take the eye in the paddock and moved moderately to post. A winner in heavy ground, she hung badly left throughout and ended up racing alone on the far side. Official explanation: jockey said filly was unsuited by the good to firm (firm in places) ground and hung left-handed throughout (op 3-1 tchd 9-2)

2295 JACK CALVERT FILLIES' H'CAP 5f
7:15 (7:15) (Class 4) (0-80,72) 3-Y-O+ **£6,477** (£1,927; £963; £481) **Stalls** High

Form RPR
5302 **1** **Hello Roberto**[5] 2136 5-9-2 **60**................................(p) AdrianMcCarthy 1 74
(R A Harris) *w ldrs: led 2f out: r.o wl fnl f* **7/2**[2]
202 **2** 1 ¼ **Millinsky (USA)**[32] 1448 5-9-7 **72**.................................. RobbieMills(7) 7 81
(Rae Guest) *hld up: hdwy over 2f out: chal over 1f out: nt qckn ins last* **5/2**[1]
1125 **3** 3 **Shrink**[343] 2977 5-10-0 **72**.. PhillipMakin 3 69
(M Dods) *trckd ldrs: nt clr run 2f out: kpt on same pce fnl f* **8/1**
6002 **4** 2 **Smiddy Hill**[25] 1618 4-9-4 **62**.. RoystonFfrench 2 51
(R Bastiman) *walked to post: dwlt: sn w ldrs: wknd fnl f* **11/2**
6004 **5** hd **Lyndalee (IRE)**[32] 1448 3-9-4 **69**.. DavidAllan 5 57
(T D Easterby) *led tl 2f out: wknd appr fnl f* **6/1**
0063 **6** 3 **Safranine (IRE)**[13] 1909 9-8-7 **58** oh3 ow5.................(p) AnnStokell(7) 4 34
(Miss A Stokell) *rrd s: hdwy on outside to chse ldrs over 2f out: edgd lft and wknd appr fnl f* **40/1**
1450 **7** 4 **True Magic**[23] 1686 5-9-12 **70**..................................(b[1]) GrahamGibbons 6 30
(J D Bethell) *w ldrs: wknd 2f out* **5/1**[3]

60.20 secs (0.10) **Going Correction** +0.20s/f (Good)
WFA 3 from 4yo+ 7lb **7** Ran SP% **110.7**
Speed ratings (Par 102):105,103,98,95,94 89,83
CSF £11.83 TOTE £4.30: £2.20, £1.80; EX 11.30.
Owner Peter A Price **Bred** I B Barker **Trained** Earlswood, Monmouths

FOCUS
A tight handicap and the form looks sound rated through the runner-up.
Safranine(IRE) Official explanation: jockey said mare reared and missed the break

2296 WEATHERBYS BANK H'CAP 1m 4f
7:45 (7:45) (Class 3) (0-90,82) 4-Y-O+ **£9,067** (£2,697; £1,348; £673) **Stalls** Low

Form RPR
0000 **1** **Nordwind (IRE)**[19] 1779 5-9-6 **81**.. FergalLynch 2 90
(W R Swinburn) *hld up in rr: effrt 4f out: hrd rdn and styd on ins last: led last strides* **7/1**
4360 **2** hd **Sualda (IRE)**[18] 1809 7-9-0 **75**.. PaulHanagan 5 84
(R A Fahey) *hld up in tch: smooth hdwy over 2f out: led over 1f out: jst collared* **11/4**[1]
0422 **3** 2 **Rocket Force (USA)**[10] 2000 6-8-11 **72**............................ DaleGibson 3 78
(N Wilson) *w ldrs: led over 2f out: hdd over 1f out: styd on same pce* **9/2**[2]
1512 **4** nk **Tarabut**[245] 5661 4-9-3 **78**... RHills 7 83
(E A L Dunlop) *trached ldrs: effrt over 2f out: kpt on same pce* **11/2**[3]
0300 **5** 4 **Sporting Gesture**[19] 1779 9-9-4 **79**................................ PaulMulrennan 4 78
(M W Easterby) *hld up in tch: drvn over 3f out: nvr trbld ldrs* **11/2**[3]
1010 **6** shd **Stretton (IRE)**[12] 1943 8-9-7 **82**... KDarley 6 81
(J D Bethell) *hld up in rr: effrt over 3f out: nvr trbld ldrs* **9/1**
4000 **7** 9 **Edas**[269] 5097 4-9-2 **77**.. GrahamGibbons 1 61
(J J Quinn) *t.k.h: trckd ldrs: lost pl over 2f out* **22/1**
6000 **8** nk **Dancer's Serenade (IRE)**[19] 1775 4-9-5 **80**.................. TonyCulhane 8 64
(T P Tate) *led: hdd over 2f out: lost pl over 1f out* **9/1**

2m 35.7s (0.50) **Going Correction** +0.20s/f (Good) **8** Ran SP% **112.5**
Speed ratings (Par 107):106,105,104,104,101 101,95,95
CSF £25.70 CT £95.56 TOTE £11.40: £3.80, £1.30, £1.40; EX 28.20.
Owner Mrs P W Harris **Bred** Christoph Berglar **Trained** Aldbury, Herts

FOCUS
A tactical event but in the end a true test. The runner-up ran right up to his mark.

NOTEBOOK
Nordwind(IRE), down 7lb after two outings this time, was a popular order on the morning line. Held together, he had everything thrown at him late on to just get there. His rider deserves full marks. Official explanation: trainer's rep had no explanation for the improved form shown (op 15-2)
Sualda(IRE), a winner three times in 2004, drew a blank last year. Back on a winning mark, he came there travelling easily best only to get mugged near the line. A fast-ground specialist, he deserves to go one better. (op 10-3 tchd 7-2)
Rocket Force(USA), 2lb higher, ran right up to his best. (op 11-2)
Tarabut, who looked very fit indeed, needs at least another couple of furlongs.
Sporting Gesture seems to be off the boil at present, mirrored by his slipping rating. (op 9-2)
Stretton(IRE) moved scratchily to post and never got competitive. (op 7-1)
Dancer's Serenade(IRE) dropped anchor in front but in the end dropped right away. He is hard to weigh up but may need much easier ground than he encountered here. (op 10-1 tchd 11-1)

2297 SHEPHERD HOMES H'CAP 7f
8:15 (8:15) (Class 4) (0-80,79) 3-Y-O **£6,477** (£1,927; £963; £481) **Stalls** Low

Form RPR
0100 **1** **Silver Dip**[16] 1843 3-9-6 **78**.. MichaelHills 4 87
(B W Hills) *hld up in tch: effrt over 3f out: hdwy to ld over 1f out: r.o wl: readily* **4/1**[2]
3303 **2** 2 ½ **Great Chieftain (IRE)**[4] 2163 3-8-13 **71**........................ PaulHanagan 6 73
(R A Fahey) *t.k.h: trckd ldrs: effrt over 2f out: styd on to take 2nd ins last* **6/1**
0025 **3** ¾ **Il Castagno (IRE)**[26] 1596 3-9-5 **77**.. KDarley 1 77
(B Smart) *led: hdd over 1f out: kpt on same pce* **9/2**[3]
0535 **4** 1 **Moonstreaker**[26] 1592 3-8-3 **68**..................... MichaelJStainton(7) 2 65
(R M Whitaker) *sn chsng ldrs: v ch and hung lft over 1f out: kpt on same pce* **15/2**
0163 **5** ½ **Viva Volta**[6] 2105 3-8-11 **69**.. DavidAllan 5 65
(T D Easterby) *hld up in rr: effrt 3f out: kpt on: nvr rchd ldrs* **5/1**
2200 **6** hd **Strong Approach (IRE)**[26] 1592 3-9-0 **72**........................ PhillipMakin 7 67
(T D Barron) *hld up in rr: effrt 3f out: kpt on: nvr trbld ldrs* **16/1**
3613 **7** ¾ **Abbey Cat (IRE)**[21] 1734 3-9-6 **78**................................ DeanMcKeown 3 71
(G A Swinbank) *sn chsng ldrs: effrt over 2f out: fdd fnl f* **7/2**[1]
3653 **8** 15 **Hotham**[226] 6024 3-8-11 **72**.. DNolan(3) 9 25
(N Wilson) *chsd ldrs on outer: drvn over 3f out: lost pl 2f out* **16/1**

1m 27.11s (0.01) **Going Correction** +0.20s/f (Good) **8** Ran SP% **114.9**
Speed ratings (Par 101):107,104,103,102,101 101,100,83
CSF £28.27 CT £112.50 TOTE £5.00: £1.80, £2.10, £1.40; EX 40.70.
Owner Burton Agnes Bloodstock **Bred** Mountgrange Stud Ltd **Trained** Lambourn, Berks
■ Buachaill Dona was withdrawn on vet's advice. R4 applies, deduct 10p in the £. New market formed.

FOCUS
Just a steady pace but the unexposed winner showed a good turn of foot and she should hold her own in stronger company than she met here. The form has a solid look about it.

2298 HERRIOT HAPPENING MAIDEN STKS 7f
8:45 (8:45) (Class 5) 3-Y-O+ **£5,181** (£1,541; £770; £384) **Stalls** Low

Form RPR
2033 **1** **First Approval**[11] 1956 3-8-9 74.. MichaelHills 2 69
(B W Hills) *trckd ldrs: led over 2f out: hld on* **5/4**[1]
5223 **2** hd **Lucksin (IRE)**[9] 2016 3-9-0 74.. JoeFanning 9 73
(N Tinkler) *trckd ldrs: chal over 1f out: no ex nr fin* **13/2**[3]
3 1 ½ **Conrad**[222] 6116 3-9-0 77.. PaulHanagan 10 69+
(R A Fahey) *hld up towards rr: hdwy over 2f out: styd on fnl f* **5/2**[2]
00 **4** 5 **Honor Me (IRE)**[10] 2001 3-8-9 .... GrahamGibbons 8 50
(J J Quinn) *t.k.h: chsd ldrs: one pce fnl 2f* **66/1**
04 **5** 1 ¼ **Shy Glance (USA)**[6] 2111 4-9-10 .... AdrianTNicholls 3 56+
(G A Swinbank) *s.i.s: hld up in rr: stdy hdwy over 2f out: shkn up over 1f out: nvr threatened ldrs* **20/1**
6 4 **Hill Billy Rock (IRE)** 3-9-0 .... DeanMcKeown 5 41+
(G A Swinbank) *s.i.s: in rr: kpt on fnl f* **7/1**
5660 **7** nk **Stormingmichaelori**[16] 1859 3-8-11 49................................ DNolan(3) 1 40
(N Wilson) *hdwy to ld after 1f: hdd over 2f out: sn btn* **66/1**
000 **8** 1 ¾ **Rainbow Prince**[39] 1252 3-8-11 35.............................. DanielTudhope(3) 7 36
(A Dickman) *trckd ldrs: wknd 2f out* **100/1**
0000 **9** 1 **Warren Place**[27] 1577 6-9-7 36..........................(b) SilvestreDeSousa(3) 4 37
(A D Brown) *chsd ldrs: drvn over 3f out: hung rt and lost pl 2f out* **150/1**
10 33 **Talbot Street** 3-8-9 ....(t) AndrewMullen(5) 6 —
(Robert Gray) *s.i.s: in rr whn hung rt bnd over 3f out: sn bhd: t.o: btn 33 l* **33/1**

1m 27.81s (0.71) **Going Correction** +0.20s/f (Good)
WFA 3 from 4yo+ 10lb **10** Ran SP% **111.2**
Speed ratings (Par 103):103,102,101,95,93 89,89,87,85,48
CSF £9.08 TOTE £2.30: £1.10, £1.60, £1.30; EX 9.10.
Owner Wickfield Stud And Hartshill Stud **Bred** Wickfield Stud And Hartshill Stud **Trained** Lambourn, Berks

FOCUS
An ordinary maiden. The first two looked fully exposed and the proximity of the lowly-rated eigth and ninth is of some concern.
Shy Glance(USA) ◆ Official explanation: jockey said gelding was denied a clear run
Talbot Street Official explanation: jockey said colt had a breathing problem

2299 BUCK INN THORNTON WATLASS H'CAP 1m
9:15 (9:16) (Class 5) (0-75,74) 3-Y-O+ **£3,886** (£1,156; £577; £288) **Stalls** Low

Form RPR
0313 **1** **Hula Ballew**[24] 1636 6-9-5 **65**.. PhillipMakin 5 74
(M Dods) *trckd ldrs: hefrt on ins over 2f out: styd on to ld last 75yds* **5/1**[2]
4600 **2** ½ **Go Solo**[30] 1494 5-10-0 **74**.. DeanMcKeown 13 82
(G A Swinbank) *sn chsng ldrs: wnt 2nd over 2f out: no ex wl ins last* **10/1**
0000 **3** ½ **Efidium**[239] 5774 8-9-1 **68**..................................... SuzzanneFrance(7) 15 75
(N Bycroft) *trckd ldr: led and qcknd 3f out: no ex and hdd wl ins last* **33/1**
2462 **4** 2 ½ **Bond Diamond**[4] 2170 9-8-13 **59**..................................... MickyFenton 10 60+
(P T Midgley) *t.k.h in rr: hdwy over 2f out: hung lft: styd on wl fnl f* **13/2**[3]
0000 **5** 1 ¼ **Capitalise (IRE)**[140] 123 3-7-8 **58** oh3 ow3.................. LiamJones(7) 4 53+
(V Smith) *hld up in rr: styd on fnl 2f: nvr rchd ldrs* **50/1**
0050 **6** nk **Tough Love**[30] 1494 7-9-11 **71**.. DavidAllan 1 69
(T D Easterby) *in rr: hdwy on inner over 2f out: nvr rchd ldrs* **12/1**
0004 **7** ½ **Kaymich Perfecto**[10] 1996 6-8-11 **64**.................. MichaelJStainton(7) 14 61
(R M Whitaker) *mid-div: effrt on outside over 2f out: nvr rchd ldrs* **9/1**
5455 **8** shd **Passion Fruit**[21] 1734 5-9-7 **67**.................................(b) PaulMulrennan 6 63
(C W Fairhurst) *hld up in rr: kpt on fnl 2f: nvr nrr* **11/1**
5616 **9** ½ **Major Magpie (IRE)**[31] 1455 4-9-9 **69**............................ FergalLynch 2 71+
(M Dods) *plld hrd in rr: hmpd after 1f: styd on fnl 2f: nvr on terms* **9/2**[1]
3000 **10** 6 **Bolton Hall (IRE)**[42] 1186 4-9-8 **68**................................ PaulHanagan 3 49
(R A Fahey) *hld up in rr: nvr on terms* **14/1**
6000 **11** ½ **Hypnotic**[34] 1380 4-9-11 **71**.. AdrianTNicholls 7 51
(D Nicholls) *chsd ldrs: lost pl over 2f out* **9/1**
0000 **12** 1 ½ **Terminate (GER)**[10] 1992 4-9-10 **70**.. KDarley 9 47
(N P Littmoden) *hld up in rr: sme hdwy on wd outside over 2f out: sn wknd* **9/1**
5006 **13** ¾ **Eliminator**[32] 1444 3-7-9 **57**................................ NataliaGemelova(5) 12 29
(I W McInnes) *in tch: lost pl over 2f out* **40/1**
0060 **14** 3 ½ **Wayward Shot (IRE)**[33] 1422 4-9-0 **60**............................ DaleGibson 11 27
(M W Easterby) *led tl 3f out: sn wknd* **33/1**

1m 40.43s (0.73) **Going Correction** +0.20s/f (Good)
WFA 3 from 4yo+ 11lb **14** Ran SP% **120.2**
Speed ratings (Par 103):104,103,103,100,99 98,98,98,97,91 91,89,89,85
CSF £52.93 CT £1549.23 TOTE £6.30: £1.90, £4.70, £9.70; EX 148.40 Place 6 £54.46, Place 5 £18.10.
Owner Mrs J W Hutchinson & Mrs P A Knox **Bred** T K & Mrs P A Knox **Trained** Denton, Co Durham
■ Stewards' Enquiry : Fergal Lynch caution: used whip down the shoulder in the forehand position

FOCUS
A steady gallop early on and Efidium's rider did her best to pinch it. The race has been rated through him.

T/Plt: £88.80 to a £1 stake. Pool: £52,079.50. 428.10 winning tickets. T/Qpdt: £28.60 to a £1 stake. Pool: £3,935.70. 101.70 winning tickets. WG

1896WINDSOR (R-H)

Monday, June 5

OFFICIAL GOING: Good to firm

Wind: Virtually nil

2300 INDEPENDENTAGE MOBILITY BUREAU EUROPEAN BREEDERS FUND NOVICE STKS 5f 10y

6:30 (6:30) (Class 5) 2-Y-O **£4,533** (£1,348; £674; £336) **Stalls High**

Form RPR

1 **Dutch Art** 2-8-12 ..... AlanMunro 5 99+
(P W Chapple-Hyam) *gd sort: strong: lw: in tch: led over 1f out: edgd to stands rail and qckd ins last: readily* **11/4**[2]

2 *1 ¾* **Simply Perfect** 2-8-7 ..... KFallon 6 90+
(J Noseda) *tall: unf: scope: bkwd: sn pshd along in rr but in tch: qckd 1/2-way and chal over 1f out: chsd wnr ins last but a readily* **5/2**[1]

2123 **3** *3 ½* **Spoof Master (IRE)**[35] [1354] 2-9-2 ..... RobertMiles(3) 9 87
(W G M Turner) *chsd ldrs:rdn 1/2-way: swtchd lft and kpt on over 1f out: one pce ins last* **8/1**

4 *¾* **Ripping** 2-8-7 ..... RichardHughes 8 72
(R Hannon) *in tch: hdwy to chse ldrs over 1f out: sn one pce* **8/1**

413 **5** *nk* **Fairfield Princess**[33] [1405] 2-9-0 ..... DaneO'Neill 3 78
(N A Callaghan) *chsd ldrs: rdn 1/2-way: wknd ins fnl f* **12/1**

6 *1 ½* **Siren's Gift** 2-8-7 ..... FergusSweeney 2 66
(A M Balding) *rr but in tch: rdn 1/2-way: nvr gng pce to be competitive but styd on fnl f* **7/1**[3]

1051 **7** *2 ½* **Il Palio (IRE)**[14] [1876] 2-9-2 ..... JamesMillman(7) 7 73
(B R Millman) *slt ld tl hdd over 1f out: sn wknd* **33/1**

13 **8** *1* **Bazroy (IRE)**[14] [1897] 2-9-0 ..... ShaneKelly 1 66+
(P D Evans) *s.i.s: sn in tch: effrt 1/2-way: edgd lft 2f out: sn wknd* **10/1**

15 **9** *7* **Best Woman**[14] [1897] 2-8-11 ..... IanMongan 4 32
(P Howling) *s.i.s: sn rdn: a bhd* **66/1**

60.50 secs (-0.60) **Going Correction** +0.025s/f (Good) 9 Ran SP% **111.2**

Speed ratings (Par 93):105,102,96,95,94 92,88,86,75

CSF £9.43 TOTE £4.30: £1.60, £1.50, £1.90; EX 9.90.

Owner Matthew Green **Bred** Cromlech Bloodstock **Trained** Newmarket, Suffolk

FOCUS

This should work out to be an above-average heat for the division and it saw two newcomers - the two market leaders - pull nicely clear at the finish. The winning time was very smart indeed for a race like this.

NOTEBOOK

Dutch Art, a 16,000gns purchase bred to make his mark this year, got his career off to a perfect start with a ready display. He was well-touted prior to this debut, certainly looked very fit, and acted well on the fast surface. Considering he is entitled to improve for this experience, he looks set for an exciting first season, and it was little surprise that connections cited the Norfolk Stakes at Royal Ascot as his most likely next port of call. (op 7-2)

Simply Perfect, a 220,000gns purchase whose dam was Group One placed over seven furlongs at two, could not live with the winner, yet still finished nicely clear of the remainder. She really ought to come on a bundle for this experience, looks capable of rating much higher before the season's end, and would have claims of reversing form with the winner in the future with this outing under her belt. (op 7-4)

Spoof Master(IRE) kept on inside the final furlong and ran an improved race in defeat. While he is more or less fully exposed over this trip under his penalty now, he has developed into a consistent performer, and is clearly versatile as regards underfoot conditions. He helps set the level of this form and looks worth trying over another furlong now. (op 10-1)

Ripping, related to plenty of winners at around this trip, looked a possible threat to the first two nearing the two-furlong marker, but she ultimately failed to sustain her effort and just got caught for third place late on. She enjoyed the fast surface and ought to benefit plenty for this debut experience.

Fairfield Princess, returning to turf, was firmly put in her place yet still ran very close to her recent level in defeat. She is another who helps to set the level of this form and could be worth trying over another furlong now.

Siren's Gift, a half-sister to her yard's former smart juvenile Speed Cop amongst others, proved easy to back ahead of this debut and shaped as though the experience was much needed. She ought to leave this form behind as she becomes more streetwise.

Bazroy(IRE) Official explanation: jockey said colt got upset in stalls and hung left-handed

2301 COLLYER BRISTOW SOLICITORS H'CAP 1m 67y

7:00 (7:00) (Class 5) (0-70,70) 3-Y-O **£3,238** (£963; £481; £240) **Stalls High**

Form RPR

0000 **1** **Bon Viveur**[7] [2065] 3-9-5 **68** ..... RichardHughes 10 76
(R Hannon) *chsd ldr: rdn 4f out: led over 1f out: hrd drvn ins last: jst hld on* **7/1**[1]

0054 **2** *nk* **Temperance (IRE)**[33] [1416] 3-9-6 **69** ..... JimmyFortune 12 76
(S Kirk) *chsd ldrs: hrd rdn and styd on strly to chse wnr ins last: gng on cl home: nt quite get up* **12/1**

0302 **3** *½* **Emily's Place (IRE)**[12] [1941] 3-9-5 **68** ..... DarryllHolland 1 74
(M H Tompkins) *hld up in rr: stl plenty to do over 2f out: hdwy on rails sn after and qckd to chse ldrs ins last: no ex cl home* **7/1**[1]

4665 **4** *2 ½* **Vodkatini**[17] [1828] 3-9-7 **70** ..... (v) SebSanders 8 70
(P J Makin) *in tch: rdn over 2f out: styd on one pce ins last* **7/1**[1]

4050 **5** *nk* **Bold Cross (IRE)**[16] [1851] 3-8-13 **65** ..... RobertMiles(3) 13 64
(E G Bevan) *led tl hdd over 1f out: wknd ins last* **12/1**

2010 **6** *3* **Magical Music**[23] [1681] 3-9-7 **70** ..... JimmyQuinn 5 62
(J Pearce) *in tch: n.m.r ins fnl 3f: styd on same pce fnl 2f* **16/1**

0205 **7** *2* **Orphina (IRE)**[7] [2065] 3-9-4 **67** ..... EddieAhern 4 55
(Pat Eddery) *bhd: rdn and hdwy over 2f out: chsd ldrs over 1f out: sn btn* **9/1**[3]

4550 **8** *1* **Endless Night**[34] [1375] 3-8-10 **64** ..... TravisBlock(5) 14 50
(H Morrison) *t.k.h: chsd ldrs: rdn over 2f out: wknd over 1f out* **7/1**[1]

006 **9** *½* **Ciccone**[24] [1649] 3-9-2 **65** ..... AlanMunro 9 49
(W Jarvis) *s.i.s: sn rcvrd to mid-div: rdn over 2f out: sn btn* **11/1**

3054 **10** *1 ¼* **Chia (IRE)**[73] [712] 3-9-2 **65** ..... (v[1]) KFallon 6 46
(D Haydn Jones) *broke wl: ken hold: stdd rr: sme hdwy 3f out: sn wknd* **8/1**[2]

2336 **11** *¾* **Rebellious Spirit**[10] [1999] 3-9-5 **68** ..... DarrenWilliams 3 48
(P W Hiatt) *bhd most of way* **12/1**

050 **12** *nk* **Rose Briar (IRE)**[11] [1956] 3-9-5 **68** ..... SteveDrowne 7 47
(R Charlton) *bhd most of way* **8/1**[2]

0040 **13** *13* **Atticus Trophies (IRE)**[8] [2050] 3-9-2 **65** ..... (b) DaneO'Neill 11 14
(K McAuliffe) *chsd ldrs: rdn 3f out: wknd over 2f out* **40/1**

0000 **14** *2* **Reviving (IRE)**[11] [1954] 3-9-5 **68** ..... StephenCarson 2 13
(R F Johnson Houghton) *chsd ldrs 5f* **25/1**

1m 44.85s (-0.75) **Going Correction** +0.025s/f (Good) 14 Ran SP% **125.8**

Speed ratings (Par 99):104,103,103,100,100 97,95,94,93,92 91,91,78,76

CSF £94.30 CT £643.60 TOTE £9.50: £3.50, £4.00, £2.10.

Owner Mrs J Wood **Bred** Khorshed And Ian Deane **Trained** East Everleigh, Wilts

■ Stewards' Enquiry : Richard Hughes two-day ban: used whip with excessive frequency (Jun 16-17)

FOCUS

A modest three-year-old handicap, run at a solid pace, and the form looks fair enough for the class.

Bon Viveur ◆ Official explanation: trainer said, regarding the improved form shown, the gelding is very lazy and may have benefited from today's faster ground

Emily's Place(IRE) Official explanation: jockey said filly had been hit across the face by another rider's whip

Rebellious Spirit Official explanation: jockey said gelding failed to handle the bend

Rose Briar(IRE) Official explanation: jockey said filly never travelled

Atticus Trophies(IRE) Official explanation: vet said gelding had bled from the nose

2302 INDEPENDENTAGE BANK OF SCOTLAND H'CAP 6f

7:30 (7:30) (Class 4) (0-80,79) 4-Y-O+ **£6,477** (£1,927; £963; £481) **Stalls High**

Form RPR

0355 **1** **Royal Challenge**[11] [1949] 5-9-3 **75** ..... DarryllHolland 11 88
(M H Tompkins) *in tch on stands rails: n.m.r 2f out: drvn and qcknd over 1f out to ld ins last: drvn out* **10/1**

1160 **2** *1 ¼* **Border Music**[27] [1561] 5-9-3 **78** ..... (b) NeilChalmers(3) 8 87
(A M Balding) *hld up mid-div: smooth hdwy to ld 1f out sn shkn up: hdd ins last and sn one pce* **15/2**[3]

0006 **3** *¾* **Oranmore Castle (IRE)**[17] [1820] 4-9-1 **73** ..... (t) TQuinn 14 80
(B W Hills) *hld up in rr: stl plenty to do whn swtchd lft to outside ins fnl 2f: qcknd to chal 1f out: styd on same pce* **9/1**

3350 **4** *2* **Rezzago (USA)**[12] [1939] 6-9-5 **77** ..... SebSanders 16 78
(W R Swinburn) *chsd ldrs on stands side: rdn 2f out: kpt on ins last but nvr gng pce to trble ldrs* **8/1**

0400 **5** *¾* **Born To Be Bold**[17] [1820] 4-8-12 **70** ..... RichardHughes 15 69
(R Hannon) *in tch: rdn over 2f out: edgd lft and styd on fnl f but nvr gng pce to trble ldrs* **14/1**

0101 **6** *½* **High Ridge**[11] [1961] 7-9-4 **76** ..... (p) LDettori 13 73
(J M Bradley) *bhd: rdn 2f out: hdwy over 1f out: kpt on but nvr gng pce to rch ldrs* **9/1**

0000 **7** *½* **Throw The Dice**[16] [1858] 4-9-3 **75** ..... RobertWinston 4 71
(D W Barker) *plld hrd: chsd ldrs tl wknd over 1f out* **20/1**

1002 **8** *½* **Harry Up**[32] [1438] 5-9-7 **79** ..... DO'Donohoe 3 73
(K A Ryan) *led tl hdd 1f out: sn wknd* **14/1**

0362 **9** *¾* **Resplendent Nova**[42] [1188] 4-8-12 **70** ..... IanMongan 12 62
(T G Mills) *chal for ld to 2f out: wknd over 1f out* **11/2**[1]

0000 **10** *hd* **European (ARG)**[37] [1280] 6-9-0 **75** ..... NelsonDeSouza(3) 9 66
(R M Beckett) *chsd ldrs over 4f* **50/1**

5020 **11** *nk* **Countdown**[23] [1662] 4-9-5 **77** ..... (v) KerrinMcEvoy 5 68
(Miss J A Camacho) *bhd tl sme late hdwy* **25/1**

1235 **12** *¾* **Effective**[70] [761] 6-9-5 **77** ..... KFallon 1 65
(A P Jarvis) *chsd ldrs: wkng whn hmpd ins fnl f* **20/1**

0401 **13** *½* **Greenwood**[23] [1673] 8-8-7 **72** ..... JosephWalsh(7) 2 59
(P G Murphy) *a outpcd* **20/1**

0201 **14** *shd* **Exmoor**[17] [1820] 4-9-7 **79** ..... SteveDrowne 6 65
(R Charlton) *s.i.s: nvr bttr than mid-div* **7/1**[2]

4500 **15** *shd* **Meikle Barfil**[28] [1545] 4-9-0 **72** ..... RyanMoore 7 58
(J M Bradley) *bhd: sme hdwy 1/2-way: sn wknd* **66/1**

0304 **16** *44* **Thurlestone Rock**[35] [1359] 6-9-4 **76** ..... (t) JimmyFortune 10 —
(B J Meehan) *a bhd: t.o* **16/1**

1m 13.3s (-0.37) **Going Correction** +0.025s/f (Good) 16 Ran SP% **120.7**

Speed ratings (Par 105):103,101,100,97,96 96,95,94,93,93 93,92,91,91,91 32

CSF £74.86 CT £712.82 TOTE £12.00: £3.90, £3.00, £3.00, £2.10; EX 156.40.

Owner Killarney Glen **Bred** Capt A L Smith-Maxwell **Trained** Newmarket, Suffolk

■ Stewards' Enquiry : Neil Chalmers two-day ban: careless riding (Jun 16-17)

Darryll Holland one-day ban: used whip down the shoulder in the forehand position (Jun 16)

FOCUS

A fair sprint, in which it paid to be drawn high, and the first three came nicely clear.

Thurlestone Rock Official explanation: jockey said gelding pulled up lame

2303 INDEPENDENTAGE PARTNERSHIP ASSURANCE STKS (REGISTERED AS THE LEISURE STAKES) (LISTED RACE) 6f

8:00 (8:01) (Class 1) 3-Y-O+

£15,898 (£6,025; £3,015; £1,503; £753; £378) **Stalls High**

Form RPR

2361 **1** **One Putra (IRE)**[30] [1481] 4-9-0 102 ..... (t) PhilipRobinson 10 111
(M A Jarvis) *trckd ldrs: led ins fnl 2f: hrd drvn and hld on wl cl home* **7/2**[1]

1120 **2** *hd* **Presto Shinko (IRE)**[48] [1069] 5-9-4 107 ..... RichardHughes 6 114
(R Hannon) *hld up in tch: n.m.r on rails 2f out: squeezed through to chse wnr jst ins last: fin strly: jst failed* **7/1**[2]

4200 **3** *2 ½* **Baltic King**[30] [1485] 6-9-0 106 ..... (t) JimmyFortune 4 103
(H Morrison) *chsd ldrs: rdn over 2f out: kpt on ins last but nvr gng pce to chal* **7/2**[1]

0310 **4** *2* **Celtic Mill**[30] [1485] 8-9-0 109 ..... (p) RobertWinston 8 97
(D W Barker) *led: hdd ins fnl 2f: one pce whn bmpd jst ins last: sn wknd* **8/1**[3]

2204 **5** *1 ¼* **Fayr Jag (IRE)**[19] [1778] 7-9-0 110 ..... TQuinn 7 93
(T D Easterby) *trckd ldrs tl tightened up and lost pl jst ins fnl 4f: kpt on fnl f but nvr in contention* **7/2**[1]

0000 **6** *hd* **The Kiddykid (IRE)**[19] [1778] 6-9-0 102 ..... JohnEgan 9 93
(P D Evans) *chsd ldr 4f: wknd over 1f out* **25/1**

0050 **7** *2 ½* **Connect**[235] [5853] 9-9-0 96 ..... (b) DarryllHolland 5 85
(M H Tompkins) *s.i.s: bhd: nvr gng pce to get comptetive* **66/1**

3600 **8** *¾* **Beckermet (IRE)**[19] [1778] 4-9-0 107 ..... SebSanders 1 83
(R F Fisher) *in tch: hdwy to chse ldrs fr 4f out to 3f out: wknd over 1f out* **14/1**

3312 **9** *3* **Assertive**[17] [1818] 3-8-10 108 ..... RyanMoore 3 78
(R Hannon) *hdwy to trck ldrs 1/2-way: hung lft and wknd over 1f out* **10/1**

5203 **10** *3 ½* **Andronikos**[10] [1979] 4-9-0 107 ..... (t) LDettori 2 63
(P F I Cole) *hld up in rr: effrt into mid-div 1/2-way: sn wknd* **20/1**

1m 12.52s (-1.15) **Going Correction** +0.025s/f (Good)

WFA 3 from 4yo+ 8lb 10 Ran SP% **116.1**

Speed ratings (Par 111):108,107,104,101,100 99,96,95,91,86

CSF £28.12 TOTE £4.70: £1.80, £2.80, £1.80; EX 40.40.

Owner H R H Sultan Ahmad Shah **Bred** Mount Coote Stud, Richard Pegum & M Bell Racing **Trained** Newmarket, Suffolk

FOCUS
A decent enough renewal of this Listed sprint rated around the sixth to his recent form.

NOTEBOOK
One Putra(IRE), the decisive winner of a reasonable conditions event at Haydock on his previous start, followed up in this better company with a game success. He had previously shown some of his best form when able to dominate, but is clearly just as effective when ridden with a little more patience. There is not much between the top sprinters and he will ultimately be worth a try in Group company. Before then, he has the option of taking up his entry in the Wokingham. (op 5-1)
Presto Shinko(IRE), a little disappointing in the Abernant Stakes at Newmarket on his previous start, returned to form with a smart effort in defeat considering he was conceding weight all round, and he may even have been unlucky not to win. Settled around mid-division, he had to wait for a gap against the stands'-side rail, and was just held after finally forcing his way through. He progressed well last season and clearly has plenty more to offer this term as well. Like the winner, he deserves a shot in Group company. (op 15-2 tchd 8-1)
Baltic King has not won since taking this race last year, but ran well in defeat behind a couple of smart sorts. He can have few excuses.
Celtic Mill, with the cheekpieces re-fitted, ran much better than in the Palace House on his previous start and gave the distinct impression he can do even better when returned to the minimum trip. (op 9-1 tchd 10-1)
Fayr Jag(IRE) had his ideal conditions, and had showed himself in good form when fourth in the Duke Of York Stakes on his reappearance, but he was hampered by Presto Shinko at about halfway and could not recover. Official explanation: jockey said gelding was hampered 2f out (op 11-4)
The Kiddykid(IRE) was again below the pick of his form. Official explanation: jockey said gelding had no more to give
Andronikos Official explanation: jockey said colt had no more to give

2304 INDEPENDENTAGE LIVE NATION (UK) MAIDEN STKS 1m 2f 7y
8:30 (8:32) (Class 5) 3-Y-O **£3,886** (£1,156; £577; £288) **Stalls** Low

Form RPR
03 **1** **Classic Punch (IRE)**[234] [5870] 3-9-3 .... JohnEgan 6 89
(D R C Elsworth) *mid-div: hdwy 5f out: edgd rt over 4f out: chsd ldrs sn after: drvn to ld last half f: hld on wl* **25/1**
3 **2** *nk* **Ask**[47] [1088] 3-9-3 .... KFallon 5 88
(Sir Michael Stoute) *chsd ldrs:rdn over 3f out:kpt on fr over 1f out:styng on whn n.m.r between horses ins last:fin wl:nt quite get up* **8/11**[1]
33 **3** *nk* **Montpellier (IRE)**[23] [1670] 3-9-3 .... SteveDrowne 3 88
(E A L Dunlop) *led after 2f: kpt on wl whn chal fr 3f out: hdd last half f but kpt on wl* **16/1**
4 **4** *4* **Millistar**[17] [1823] 3-8-12 .... PhilipRobinson 2 75
(M A Jarvis) *led 2f:styd chsng ldr: chal fr 3f out tl over 1f out: wknd fnl f* **10/1**[3]
243 **5** *5* **Star Crowned (USA)**[10] [1990] 3-9-3 93................................(t) LDettori 11 71
(B J Meehan) *chsd ldrs: rdn over 2f: sn btn* **10/3**[2]
0 **6** *1* **Stotsfold**[17] [1822] 3-9-3 .... TedDurcan 4 69
(W R Swinburn) *chsd ldrs: rdn over 2f out and sn wknd* **100/1**
0 **7** *nk* **Light Dreams**[34] [1374] 3-8-12 .... PaulDoe 8 63
(W J Knight) *mid-divison: racd on outer and wd into st 4f out: styd centre crse and nvr gng pce to rch ldrs* **100/1**
8 *5* **Detente** 3-8-12 .... OscarUrbina 16 54
(J R Fanshawe) *bhd: hday into mid-div over 3f out: n.d after* **50/1**
3 **9** *2 1/2* **Paraguay (USA)**[10] [1978] 3-9-0 .... EdwardCreighton[(3)] 13 54+
(M R Channon) *in tch whn bdly hmpd on rails over 4f out: kpt on again fnl 2f but nt rcvr* **33/1**
00 **10** *shd* **Atwirl**[8] [2048] 3-8-12 .... ShaneKelly 9 49
(D J Daly) *chsd ldrs tl wknd fr 3f out* **100/1**
0 **11** *1/2* **Brief History**[9] [2034] 3-9-3 .... DaneO'Neill 17 53+
(H Candy) *in tch whn carried rt to rails and hmpd over 4f out: n.d after* **66/1**
00 **12** *1/2* **Himba**[6] [2118] 3-9-3 .... JimCrowley 19 52+
(Mrs A J Perrett) *bhd whn bdly hmpd over 4f out: nt rcvr* **100/1**
6 **13** *1 1/4* **Electric Storm**[34] [1374] 3-9-3 .... RichardHughes 20 50
(R Charlton) *behin whn hmpd over 4f out: nt rcvr* **50/1**
14 *hd* **Greek Well (IRE)** 3-9-3 .... RobertWinston 18 49
(Sir Michael Stoute) *s.i.s: bhd: awkward bnd 5f out: bdly hmpd over 4f out: nt rcvr* **10/1**[3]
15 *8* **Klassen (USA)** 3-9-3 .... EddieAhern 10 34
(A King) *bhd whn hmpd over 4f out: nt rcvr* **100/1**
16 *7* **Montana Sky (IRE)** 3-9-3 .... JimmyFortune 15 21
(S Kirk) *bmpd s: bhd: bdly hmpd over 4f out: nt rcvr* **100/1**
0 **17** *1 3/4* **Command Respect**[284] [4690] 3-8-12 .... DarryllHolland 1 12
(E F Vaughan) *nvr bttr than mid-div: bhd fnl 3f* **100/1**
00 **18** *39* **Spinning Dancer (IRE)**[14] [1901] 3-8-12 .... IanMongan 12 —
(Ian Williams) *wnt rt s: chsd ldrs 6f: t.o* **100/1**

2m 8.84s (0.54) **Going Correction** +0.025s/f (Good) **18** Ran SP% **125.2**
Speed ratings (Par 99):98,97,97,94,90 89,89,85,83,83 82,82,81,81,74 69,67,36
CSF £44.14 TOTE £31.40: £4.90, £1.10, £3.20; EX 67.20.
Owner J C Smith **Bred** Granham Farm **Trained** Newmarket, Suffolk
■ Stewards' Enquiry : Dane O'Neill seven-day ban: careless riding (Jun 16-22)

FOCUS
A very good maiden that should produce plenty of winners, although they only went a steady pace for most of the way. It has been rated around the fourth.
Light Dreams Official explanation: jockey said filly hung left-handed

2305 INDEPENDENTAGE H'CAP 1m 3f 135y
9:00 (9:02) (Class 5) (0-70,74) 4-Y-O+ **£3,238** (£963; £481; £240) **Stalls** Low

Form RPR
41 **1** **Olimpo (FR)**[6] [2097] 5-9-11 **74** 6ex.................................... AlanMunro 10 81
(B R Millman) *stdd mid-div: gd hdwy fr 2f out: swtchd rt and styd on u.p to ld wl ins last* **9/2**[2]
1360 **2** *3/4* **Darling Deanie (IRE)**[247] [5610] 4-9-7 **70**............................ JohnEgan 16 75
(D R C Elsworth) *hld up in rr: swtchd to outside and stdy hdwy fr 2f out: qcknd to chal ins last: no ex cl home* **14/1**
5040 **3** *hd* **Velvet Waters**[3] [2186] 5-9-4 **67**...................................... StephenCarson 5 72
(R F Johnson Houghton) *sn led: rdn 2f out: hdd and no ex wl ins last* **10/1**
0005 **4** *nk* **Pittsburgh**[13] [1926] 4-8-10 **59**.. RichardHughes 12 64
(A M Balding) *hld up in rr: n.m.r fr 2f out tl 1f out: squeezed through and qcknd ins last: fin wl* **9/1**
0012 **5** *nk* **High Treason (USA)**[43] [1163] 4-9-2 **65**........................ PhilipRobinson 1 69
(W J Musson) *in tch: rdn and hdwy over 2f out: drvn to chal 1f out: one pce ins last* **4/1**[1]
000 **6** *3/4* **Eamon An Chnoic (IRE)**[139] [129] 5-8-0 **52**....... EdwardCreighton[(3)] 11 55
(B W Duke) *s.i.s: bhd: gd hdwy on outside 3f out: drvn to chal over 1f out: wknd ins last* **66/1**
1000 **7** *2* **Domenico (IRE)**[25] [1614] 8-8-10 **59**.................................. EddieAhern 3 59
(J R Jenkins) *mid-div: hdwy on outside to chse ldrs ins fnl 2f: wknd ins fnl f* **50/1**
0000 **8** *3* **Serramanna**[19] [1772] 5-8-3 **52**.. RichardThomas 8 47
(Dr J R J Naylor) *chsd ldrs: rdn 3f out: wknd 2f out* **16/1**
0000 **9** *hd* **Harcourt (USA)**[19] [1772] 6-8-13 **65**.............................. NeilChalmers[(3)] 2 60
(M Madgwick) *bhd whn hmpd on rails 5f out: kpt on fr 2f out but nvr in contention* **33/1**
1060 **10** *shd* **Lucky Leo**[310] [3955] 6-9-7 **70**... DarryllHolland 4 64
(Ian Williams) *chsd ldrs: drvn to chal 2f out: wknd appr fnl f* **20/1**
0504 **11** *8* **River Gypsy**[13] [1926] 5-8-4 **58** ow1.................. StephanieHollinshead[(5)] 9 40
(D R C Elsworth) *chsd ldrs tl over 2f out* **20/1**
2135 **12** *6* **Gramada (IRE)**[5] [2023] 4-9-7 **70**.................................... RobertWinston 6 42
(P A Blockley) *chsd ldrs tl wknd over 2f out* **11/1**
0031 **13** *3 1/2* **Gambling Spirit**[20] [1754] 4-9-2 **65**..................................... DaneO'Neill 13 31
(H Candy) *pressed ldrs 9f* **5/1**[3]
0150 **14** *2 1/2* **Liberty Run (IRE)**[19] [1769] 4-8-4 **53**......................(v[1]) FrankieMcDonald 7 15
(Mrs A J Hamilton-Fairley) *s.i.s:rr whn hung rt to rails over 5f out: nvr in contention* **66/1**
-060 **15** *1 1/4* **Come What Augustus**[8] [2314] 4-8-2 **51** oh1................. FrancisFerris 15 11
(R M Stronge) *a bhd* **66/1**
-600 **16** *2* **Mutamaasek (USA)**[37] [1288] 4-9-4 **67**...........................(t) SebSanders 14 24
(Lady Herries) *chsd ldrs a m* **12/1**

2m 29.93s (-0.17) **Going Correction** +0.025s/f (Good) **16** Ran SP% **121.4**
Speed ratings (Par 103):101,100,100,100,99 99,98,96,96,95 90,86,84,82,81 80
CSF £61.84 CT £605.45 TOTE £5.90: £2.00, £3.60, £3.50, £2.90; EX 123.00 Place 6 £59.71, Place 5 £48.37.
Owner Christine And Aubrey Loze **Bred** Ewar Stud Farm **Trained** Kentisbeare, Devon

FOCUS
A modest but competitive handicap with just over two lengths separating the first six home, and pretty straightforward form to rate.
Serramanna Official explanation: jockey said mare was denied a clear run
Gramada(IRE) Official explanation: jockey said filly had no more to give
Liberty Run(IRE) Official explanation: jockey said gelding did not handle the bend
T/Plt: £120.50 to a £1 stake. Pool: £81,297.65. 492.15 winning tickets. T/Qpdt: £23.60 to a £1 stake. Pool: £4,794.10. 150.10 winning tickets. ST

2306 - 2307a (Foreign Racing) - See Raceform Interactive

1782 NAAS (L-H)
Monday, June 5

OFFICIAL GOING: Good to firm

2308a NAAS SPRINT STKS (LISTED RACE) 5f
3:35 (3:35) 3-Y-O+ **£22,448** (£6,586; £3,137; £1,068)

RPR
1 **Osterhase (IRE)**[44] [1158] 7-9-12 111..................................(b) FMBerry 11 115
(J E Mulhern, Ire) *mde all: clr bef 1/2-way: drifted lft 1f out: styd on wl: eased cl home* **9/2**[1]
2 *1 1/2* **Moon Unit (IRE)**[9] [2038] 5-9-7 106.. WSupple 1 105
(H Rogers, Ire) *towards rr: prog into mod 6th 2f out: 3rd 1f out: kpt on wl wout troubling wnr* **9/2**[1]
3 *2* **Kingsdale Ocean (IRE)**[35] [1362] 3-9-0 97......................... TPO'Shea 10 97
(W M Roper, Ire) *chsd ldrs: mod 4th and rdn under 2f out: 2nd 1f out: kpt on same pce* **7/1**[3]
4 *1* **Fontanally Springs (IRE)**[31] [1469] 4-9-4 86........................ MJKinane 8 91
(H Rogers, Ire) *towards rr: styd on wl fr 1 1/2f out* **16/1**
5 *1* **Majestic Times (IRE)**[31] [1469] 6-9-10 103........................ VRDeSouza 6 93
(Liam McAteer, Ire) *chsd ldrs: no imp 2f out: kpt on ins fnl f* **6/1**[2]
6 *1/2* **Waterways (IRE)**[31] [1469] 3-8-11 106.............................. NGMcCullagh 9 85
(P J Prendergast, Ire) *chsd ldrs: mod 3rd 2f out: no ex fr over 1f out* **9/1**
7 *1 1/2* **Treasure Cay**[45] [1116] 5-9-7 ....(t) KJManning 7 83
(P W D'Arcy) *prom: mod 2nd 1/2-way: no ex fr over 1f out* **8/1**
8 *7* **Hidden Charm (IRE)**[239] [5777] 3-8-11 96.......................... PJSmullen 2 55
(D K Weld, Ire) *chsd ldrs on far rail: wknd fr 2f out* **10/1**
9 *1 1/2* **Gist (IRE)**[8] [2054] 3-8-11 85..(b) WMLordan 5 49
(W J Martin, Ire) *a bhd: trailing fr over 2f out* **33/1**
10 *hd* **Briland (IRE)**[314] [3826] 3-8-11 95...(t) JMurtagh 3 49
(M Halford, Ire) *chsd ldrs early: no ex fr 2f out* **12/1**
11 *shd* **Chained Emotion (IRE)**[31] [1469] 5-9-7 100................... DPMcDonogh 4 51
(Kevin Prendergast, Ire) *trailing fr 2f out* **20/1**

58.60 secs
WFA 3 from 4yo+ 7lb **11** Ran SP% **114.6**
CSF £23.02 TOTE £5.40: £2.10, £1.90, £2.70; DF 21.90.
Owner Michael Rosenfeld **Bred** E Kopica & M Rosenfeld **Trained** the Curragh, Co Kildare

FOCUS
A decent renewal of this Listed sprint, which contained proven Group performers Osterhase and Moon Unit as well as several other stakes winners.

NOTEBOOK
Osterhase(IRE), who relishes quick ground, was back to his best with an excellent front-running performance that saw him record the sixth Stakes-race success of his career. After showing his customary early dash, he was nicely clear of his rivals at halfway and, although drifting left, had the race in safe keeping heading into the final furlong. The seven-year-old was found to be lame on his return to action here in April but his performance here indicated that he remains as good as ever. He comes into his own at this time of year and will now head for a five-furlong Listed race at the Curragh on Derby weekend. He won this en route to taking that Curragh race two years ago. (op 4/1)
Moon Unit(IRE) ran another fine race. Ridden to deliver her challenge late on in customary style, she could not bridge the gap to the winner but did keep on well. She is in foal and it is likely that this was her final run. She has enjoyed a splendid career that has yielded five Stakes-race successes, highlighted by her victory in last year's Greenlands Stakes. (op 5/2)
Kingsdale Ocean(IRE) ran another good race and fared best of the three-year-olds. He could not match the winner's blistering early speed but stuck to his task well and ran to a similar level as when third to Moon Unit here in April. He is a smart colt and should be able to make his mark at Listed level this year.
Fontanally Springs(IRE), a stablemate of the runner-up, was staying on well on the outer over the final furlong and a half. She was stepping up considerably on the form of her comeback run behind Miss Sally at Cork last month. On this evidence, she would not need to progress much to pick up a valuable black-type placing.
Majestic Times(IRE) was never able to land a meaningful blow and was another that found it hard to cope with the early tempo set by the winner. He came here on the back of an encouraging run behind Miss Sally at Cork but probably did not match that level of form. He may do better back on easier ground.

Waterways(IRE), a very smart juvenile last term, improved on the form of her comeback run at Cork. She showed up well for a long way but had no more to give with over a furlong to run. She could be working her way back to form. (op 8/1)
Treasure Cay showed plenty of dash but had a tough task on the figures and had no more to give over the final furlong and a half.

2309a SWORDLESTOWN STUD SPRINT STKS (GROUP 3) (FILLIES) 6f
4:05 (4:05) 2-Y-O **£44,896** (£13,172; £6,275; £2,137)

RPR

1 **Brazilian Bride (IRE)**[44] 1157 2-8-12 .... DPMcDonogh 4 101+
(Kevin Prendergast, Ire) *sn 2nd: rdn to chal under 2f out: led over 1f out: styd on wl* **5/4**[1]

2 *2* **Gee Kel (IRE)**[19] 1782 2-8-12 .... WSupple 5 95
(Francis Ennis, Ire) *hld up in rr: hdwy 2f out: 2nd and rdn to chal 1f out: no ex wl ins fnl f* **14/1**

3 *hd* **Amber Valley**[17] 1831 2-8-12 .... NCallan 6 94
(K A Ryan) *led: clr early: rdn and strly pressed 2f out: hdd over 1f out: kpt on same pce* **2/1**[2]

4 *8* **New Spirit (IRE)**[9] 2037 2-8-12 .... DMGrant 3 70
(John Joseph Murphy, Ire) *chsd ldrs in 5th: rdn and no imp 2f out: one pce* **12/1**

5 *1 1/2* **Chanting (USA)** 2-8-12 .... WMLordan 1 66
(David Wachman, Ire) *4th to 1/2-way: rdn and wknd 2f out* **10/1**

6 *3/4* **Rose Of Battle**[57] 926 2-8-12 .... JMurtagh 2 64
(M Halford, Ire) *chsd ldrs in 3rd: rdn and wknd fr over 2f out* **9/1**[3]

69.80 secs **7 Ran SP% 111.2**
CSF £19.16 TOTE £2.50: £1.30, £4.30; DF 28.30.
Owner Lady O'Reilly **Bred** Skymarc Farms & Dr A J F O'Rei **Trained** Friarstown, Co Kildare

FOCUS
A race that has in the past been won by top-class juvenile fillies such as Damson and Rumplestiltskin. This year marked its first running as a Group Three and it looks to have thrown up another good winner.

NOTEBOOK
Brazilian Bride(IRE) had run out a very easy winner of a five-furlong maiden here in April and she comfortably bridged the gap to Group class. Settled in second behind Amber Valley, she improved to lead with over a furlong to run and stayed on strongly close home to make sure of victory. Clearly a talented filly, she may be even better suited by stepping up to seven furlongs. Kevin Prendergast has not made any definite plans for the daughter of Pivotal but he did outline a possible route that would take in the Phoenix Stakes followed by the Moyglare - both of which are run at The Curragh in August. (op 5/4 tchd 6/5)
Gee Kel(IRE) fared best of the maidens and produced a cracking effort on her third start. When the winner went to the front, she threw down her challenge on the far side of the runner-up but she was just unable to cope with Brazilian Bride inside the final furlong. Fourth to the unbeaten Drayton on her debut and then second to Gaudeamus over this course and distance last month, she showed enough to suggest that a Stakes-race success may come her way. (op 10/1)
Amber Valley acquitted herself well. A five-furlong maiden winner at Haydock in April, she ran second to the smart Gilded in a Listed race at York last month. She set a steady early pace and then kept on under pressure when the winner struck the front.
New Spirit(IRE) had previously run well in the two Listed races won by Drayton at The Curragh, but it looked as if the step up to six furlongs may have stretched her stamina. She should be able to win a maiden over the minimum distance. (op 14/1)
Chanting(USA) was not disgraced on her debut. Nearing the two-furlong marker it looked as if she might get involved, but she was unable to match the leaders when they quickened up. This run can be expected to bring her on considerably and she will be of interest if dropping back to maiden company for her next start. (op 7/1)
Rose Of Battle won a five-furlong maiden on heavy ground at The Curragh in April and was having her first run since then. She was the first under pressure and was starting to struggle with well over a furlong to run. She may do better back on an easier surface. (op 7/1)

2310 - 2312a (Foreign Racing) - See Raceform Interactive

2158 LONGCHAMP (R-H)
Monday, June 5

OFFICIAL GOING: Good

2313a PRIX DU PALAIS-ROYAL (GROUP 3) 7f
2:50 (2:49) 3-Y-O+ **£27,586** (£11,034; £8,276; £5,517; £2,759)

RPR

1 **Satri (IRE)**[34] 4-9-3 .... OPeslier 10 107
(J-M Beguigne, France) *raced in 3rd, 2nd and going well straight, led 2 1/2f out, found more when pressed 1f out, pushed out* **78/10**

2 *nk* **Helios Quercus (FR)**[15] 1873 4-9-3 .... TThulliez 9 106
(C Diard, France) *midfield, 4th straight, headway to press leader 2f out, stayed on* **34/10**[3]

3 *2 1/2* **Nid D'Abeilles (IRE)**[39] 1266 4-9-3 .... C-PLemaire 2 100
(P Bary, France) *held up, 8th straight, pushed along 2 1/2f out, took 3rd 1f out, kept on* **32/10**[1]

4 *3/4* **My Man (FR)**[11] 4-9-3 .... MBlancpain 3 98
(C Laffon-Parias, France) *raced in 2nd, 3rd straight, driven and lost place 2 1/2f out, stayed on again final f* **86/10**

5 *1/2* **Donatello (GER)**[11] 1973 5-9-3 .... JVictoire 6 96
(W Baltromei, Germany) *held up, last straight, driven on outside over 2f out, some headway 2f out to 1f out, no extra final f* **12/1**

6 *snk* **Together (FR)**[39] 1266 6-9-0 ....(b) SMaillot 1 93
(Mme C Vergne, France) *midfield, 6th straight, driven over 2f out, no extra* **18/1**

7 *2 1/2* **Saishu (IRE)**[34] 1398 4-9-0 .... CSoumillon 5 86
(E Libaud, France) *midfield, 5th straight, never dangerous* **12/1**

8 *3 1/2* **Poly Dance (FR)**[41] 5-9-3 .... IMendizabal 4 80
(J-C Rouget, France) *midfield, 7th straight, never a factor* **33/10**[2]

9 *5* **Choparlas (FR)**[16] 4-9-3 ....(b) FGeroux 7 67
(M Boutin, France) *led to 2 1/2f out, weakened* **10/1**

1m 20.1s **9 Ran SP% 121.3**
PARI-MUTUEL: WIN 8.80; PL 2.20, 1.70, 1.80; DF 18.90.
Owner E Ciampi **Bred** Petra Bloodstock Agency Ltd **Trained** France

NOTEBOOK
Satri(IRE), smartly into his stride on the outside, settled behind the leader and was then switched to the rail when he took the advantage at the two-furlong marker. Almost immediately joined by the eventual runner-up, the two had the race to themselves throughout the final furlong. A fast improving colt, he loved the firmish ground and has plenty of speed, and will now be aimed at the Prix Maurice de Gheest, with a possible run in the Prix Ris-Orangis beforehand.
Helios Quercus(FR), who looked extremely well, joined battle with the eventual winner at the two-furlong marker. He kept on really well but could not quicken to take the lead and was finally easily held at the finish. He was dropping back from nine furlongs so it was a decent effort, and he will back over the course and distance in the Prix de Porte Maillot at the end of the month.
Nid D'Abeilles(IRE), held up in the early stages, still had plenty to do in the straight. He slipped into top gear a furlong and a half out and finished best of all, but he never threatened the winner or the runner-up. He will come on for this outing and a longer trip could be an advantage.
My Man(FR) was given every possible chance and was always well up with the leaders. When things warmed up in the straight he could not quicken and just stayed on one-paced inside the final furlong. He is another who might be suited by a longer trip.

MUNICH (L-H)
Monday, June 5

OFFICIAL GOING: Soft

2314a PFERDEWETTEN.DE BAVARIAN CLASSIC (GROUP 3) 1m 2f
4:15 (4:34) 3-Y-O **£24,138** (£9,655; £4,828; £2,759)

RPR

1 **Imonso (GER)** 3-9-2 .... ASuborics 1 106
(P Schiergen, Germany) *4th early, 3rd halfway, ridden to press leader over 1 1/2f out, led 1f out, ridden out* **23/10**[2]

2 *3/4* **Dark Dancer (GER)** 3-9-2 .... CCzachary 7 105
(W Kelkel, Germany) *racd in 2nd, pushed along over 3f out, led 2f out, sn rdn and strongly pressed, hdd 1f out, one pace* **184/10**

3 *3/4* **Lateral**[26] 1600 3-9-2 .... WMongil 5 103
(P Schiergen, Germany) *hld up, 5th str, wnt 3rd but no impression on ldrs over 1f out, stayed on wl closing stages, nvr nrr* **9/10**[1]

4 *3* **Oriental Tiger (GER)**[43] 1176 3-9-2 ....(b) ABoschert 4 98
(U Ostmann, Germany) *3rd early, 4th halfway, headed on inside to go 3rd over 1 1/2f out, soon ridden and not quicken* **78/10**

5 *1 1/4* **Lucidor (GER)**[29] 1526 3-9-2 .... StanleyChin 3 96
(Frau E Mader, Germany) *always in rear* **78/10**

6 *14* **Sommertag (GER)**[29] 1526 3-9-2 .... THellier 6 71
(P Schiergen, Germany) *led, set slow pace, headed 2f out, weakened* **61/10**[3]

2m 16.24s **6 Ran SP% 124.9**
(including 10 Euro stake): WIN 33; PL 26, 39; SF 574.
Owner Gestut Schlenderhan **Bred** Gestut Schlenderhan **Trained** Germany

1958 LINGFIELD (L-H)
Tuesday, June 6

OFFICIAL GOING: Turf course - good to firm (firm in places); all-weather - standard
Wind: Almost nil Weather: Sunny and warm

2315 BRITISH CAR AUCTIONS MEDIAN AUCTION MAIDEN STKS 5f
2:30 (2:33) (Class 6) 2-Y-O **£3,238** (£963; £481; £240) **Stalls** High

Form RPR

42 1 **Scented Present**[22] 1737 2-9-3 .... LDettori 1 81+
(B J Meehan) *lw: mde all towards far side: clr of gp 1/2-way: shkn up 1f out: cleverly* **5/6**[1]

2 *1/2* **Impromptu** 2-9-3 .... SebSanders 14 73
(R M Beckett) *cmpt: bit bkwd: pressed nr side ldr: led gp 2f out: r.o fnl f: readily hld by wnr* **25/1**

3 *3/4* **Rebel Duke (IRE)** 2-9-3 .... TPQueally 11 70
(M G Quinlan) *str: lw: dwlt: sn chsd nr side ldrs: effrt and rn green 2f out: styd on fr over 1f out: nrst fin: 2nd of gp* **20/1**[3]

00 4 *1 1/2* **Pat Will (IRE)**[15] 1896 2-8-12 .... RobertWinston 15 60
(P D Evans) *racd nr side: off the pce in midfield: r.o fr over 1f out: nrst fin: 3rd of gp* **66/1**

4 5 *shd* **Vadinka**[20] 1770 2-9-3 .... JimCrowley 4 65+
(P Winkworth) *chsd wnr towards far side: nt on terms fr 1/2-way: one pce: 2nd of gp* **33/1**

6 *nk* **Party Best** 2-8-12 .... RyanMoore 10 58
(C E Brittain) *tall: str: bit bkwd: scope: racd nr side: off the pce in midfield: styd on fnl f: nvr nrr: 4th of gp* **50/1**

354 7 *nk* **Queen Of Narnia**[30] 1514 2-8-12 .... ChrisCatlin 18 57
(M R Channon) *lw: led nr side to 2f out: fdd fnl f: 5th of gp* **20/1**[3]

3 8 *nk* **Peggys Flower**[36] 1333 2-8-12 .... OscarUrbina 17 56
(N A Callaghan) *trckd nr side ldrs: cl up over 1f out: wknd ins fnl f: 6th of gp* **10/1**[2]

9 *3/4* **Sun Of The Sea** 2-9-3 .... GeorgeBaker 3 59
(N P Littmoden) *w'like: bit bkwd: s.s: last of those towards far side: prog 1/2-way: styd on fnl f: 3rd of gp* **33/1**

10 *1/2* **Lord Theo** 2-8-10 .... JamesMillman[(7)] 7 57
(D K Ivory) *tall: bkwd: dwlt: racd in middle tl jnd nr side gp 3f out: outpcd over 1f out: kpt on: 7th of gp* **25/1**

04 11 *nk* **Tom Paris**[38] 1284 2-9-3 .... SteveDrowne 8 56
(W R Muir) *lw: racd nr side: off the pce in midfield: one pce fnl 2f: fin 8th of gp* **50/1**

12 *2 1/2* **Marlyn Ridge** 2-9-3 .... DarryllHolland 16 47
(D K Ivory) *w'like: dwlt: racd nr side: outpcd and nvr on terms* **50/1**

3254 13 *1 1/2* **Pernomente (IRE)**[15] 1897 2-9-3 ....(t) JohnEgan 9 41
(J S Moore) *pressed nr side ldrs to over 1f out: wknd and eased* **25/1**

5 14 *1 1/2* **Ten For Tosca (IRE)**[28] 1559 2-9-3 .... ShaneKelly 6 36
(J A Osborne) *chsd far side ldrs: no imp 1/2-way: wknd over 1f out* **50/1**

0 15 *1/2* **Suzieblue (IRE)**[29] 1542 2-8-12 .... LPKeniry 5 29
(J S Moore) *racd towards far side: outpcd and nvr on terms* **100/1**

6 16 *1 1/2* **Bookiesindex Boy**[30] 1510 2-9-3 .... EddieAhern 2 29+
(J R Jenkins) *prom far side tl swvd bdly lft after 2f: sn struggling* **33/1**

17 *nk* **Ma Ridge** 2-9-3 .... RobertMiles 12 28
(T D McCarthy) *str: bit bkwd: dwlt: a bhd: hung fr nr side to far side rail fr 1/2-way* **80/1**

57.80 secs (-1.14) **Going Correction** -0.30s/f (Firm) **17 Ran SP% 105.1**
Speed ratings (Par 91):97,96,95,92,92 91,91,91,89,89 88,84,82,79,78 76,76
CSF £18.36 TOTE £1.70: £1.10, £4.50, £5.10; EX 24.00 Trifecta £107.80 Part won. Pool: £151.94 - 0.35 winning tickets..
Owner The Calvera Partnership **Bred** Mrs M Holdcroft And Mrs M Forsyth **Trained** Manton, Wilts
■ Nordic Light (5/1) was withdrawn on vet's advice. R4 applies, deduct 15p in £.

FOCUS
Hand timed. Not the most competitive of maidens, especially with the late withdrawal of the second favourite, but the winning time was very creditable for a race of its class and the form appears sound. The field split into two with the larger group racing stands' side and the smaller group coming down the middle. The evidence at the line was that there was little between the two groups.

NOTEBOOK

Scented Present, who had the best form but arguably the worst draw, bounded out of the stalls and Dettori decided to let him run straight rather than lose ground by joining the nearside bunch. The ploy paid off, if not by much, but it may be best to measure this effort by the margin he beat the others on his side, headed by Vadinka, rather than the distance to the runner-up. He may turn out at Royal Ascot, but will still need to improve a lot on this to figure there. (op Evens)

Impromptu ◆, 20,000gns colt out of a half-sister to Umistim, was always up with the pace against the nearside rail and ran on well to win the race on his side of the track. With this debut effort under his belt it should not take him long to go one better.

Rebel Duke(IRE) ◆, a half-brother to Your The Lady, Seihali and Major Faux Pas, stayed on very nicely over the last furlong or so and gave the impression he would come on a good deal for the experience. (op 12-1)

Pat Will(IRE), having her third run, seemed happier back on this faster surface and was noted putting in some good late work. She gives the impression another furlong would not come amiss and a modest event can be found.

Vadinka followed the favourite down the middle of the track and kept on to finish a clear second-best of those that raced that side. This is not the first time he has shown some ability.

Party Best ◆, a half-sister to a couple of winners including the useful Party Boss, is bred to need another couple of furlongs so it was no surprise that she could never get on terms with the principals despite staying on. There should be better to come from her in time.

Pernomente(IRE) Official explanation: jockey said gelding had a breathing problem

Ten For Tosca(IRE) Official explanation: jockey said colt lost a near front shoe

Bookiesindex Boy Official explanation: jockey said colt hung violently left 3f out

2316 CRIMESTOPPERS 0800 555 111 H'CAP — 6f

3:00 (3:03) (Class 6) (0-60,60) 3-Y-O — **£2,730** (£806; £403) **Stalls** High

Form — RPR

0004 **1** — **Just Down The Road (IRE)**[8] 2068 3-9-4 **57** — LDettori 5 — 65
(R A Harris) *racd towards centre: mde all: hrd rdn and hung lft fr over 1f out: hld on* — **20/1**

6632 **2** *nk* **Mr Cellophane**[9] 2050 3-9-7 **60** — EddieAhern 11 — 68
(J R Jenkins) *lw: hld up bhd ldrs: prog 2f out: chsd wnr over 1f out: str chal and carried lft ins fnl f: jst hld* — **4/1**[1]

3155 **3** *½* **Buzzin'Boyzee (IRE)**[18] 1825 3-9-1 **59** — StephenDonohoe(5) 18 — 65
(P D Evans) *b: hld up: last over 3f out: prog against nr side rail fr 2f out: r.o wl fnl f: gaining at fin* — **7/1**

5003 **4** *½* **Young Bertie**[40] 1263 3-9-7 **60** — SteveDrowne 6 — 65
(H Morrison) *lw: prom: drvn over 1f out: styd on fnl f: nvr quite able to chal* — **5/1**[2]

5655 **5** *2 ½* **Shannon House**[28] 1567 3-9-3 **56** — (p) ShaneKelly 12 — 53
(M J McGrath) *wl in rr: prog 2f out: kpt on fr over 1f out: n.d* — **16/1**

5005 **6** *hd* **Thoughtsofstardom**[2] 2263 3-9-4 **57** — BrianReilly 16 — 53
(P S McEntee) *towards rr against nr side rail: prog 1/2-way: one pce fr over 1f out* — **16/1**

2030 **7** *hd* **Pantomime Prince**[13] 1941 3-9-3 **56** — (p) JohnEgan 14 — 52+
(C A Dwyer) *hld up wl in rr: gng wl 1/2-way: nt clr run and swtchd lft over 1f out: styd on: no ch* — **20/1**

0050 **8** *¾* **North Fleet**[21] 1751 3-9-7 **60** — LPKeniry 1 — 54
(J M Bradley) *prom: chsd wnr briefly over 1f out: wknd fnl f* — **50/1**

066 **9** *2 ½* **Good Turn**[22] 1733 3-9-1 **54** — RichardHughes 10 — 40
(R Hannon) *dwlt: wl in rr: sme prog into midfield over 2f out: hrd rdn over 1f out: fdd* — **16/1**

0000 **10** *nk* **Bollywood (IRE)**[12] 1963 3-9-2 **60** — JamesDoyle(5) 13 — 45
(J J Bridger) *rdn in midfield over 3f out: outpcd and btn wl over 1f out* — **20/1**

0000 **11** *¾* **Forces Sweetheart**[40] 1263 3-9-5 **58** — HayleyTurner 2 — 41
(M L W Bell) *mostly pressed wnr to over 1f out: wknd rapidly* — **20/1**

5606 **12** *½* **Watch Out Jess**[21] 1751 3-8-12 **54** — EdwardCreighton(3) 7 — 35
(M Madgwick) *in tch on outer: rdn 2f out: sn btn* — **40/1**

0400 **13** *hd* **Whisper Inthe Wind (IRE)**[33] 1431 3-9-4 **60** — AdamKirby(3) 15 — 41
(Miss J Feilden) *racd nr side: chsd ldrs: wknd u.p 2f out* — **66/1**

0552 **14** *shd* **Arculinge**[19] 1801 3-9-4 **57** — TedDurcan 9 — 38
(M Blanshard) *b.nr fore: trckd ldng gp and racd on outer: rdn 2f out: sn wknd* — **6/1**[3]

000 **15** *1* **Task Complete**[249] 5581 3-9-2 **55** — VinceSlattery 4 — 33
(J A Osborne) *s.s: sme prog into midfield over 2f out: wknd wl over 1f out* — **40/1**

4000 **16** *shd* **Diktatorship (IRE)**[13] 1937 3-9-3 **56** — (v[1]) GeorgeBaker 3 — 33
(Miss Gay Kelleway) *racd on wd outside: in tch to over 2f out: sn struggling* — **20/1**

0030 **17** *2* **Creambiscuit**[29] 1549 3-9-4 **57** — RyanMoore 8 — 28
(N P Littmoden) *lw: cl up tl wknd rapidly 2f out: eased* — **9/1**

6650 **18** *½* **Vicky Pollard**[218] 6197 3-9-4 **57** — IanMongan 17 — 27
(P Howling) *pressed ldrs to wl over 1f out: wknd v rapidly* — **25/1**

1m 10.66s (-1.01) **Going Correction** -0.30s/f (Firm) — **18** Ran SP% **127.1**

Speed ratings (Par 97):94,93,92,92,88 88,88,87,84,83 82,82,81,81,80 80,77,76

CSF £91.58 CT £668.24 TOTE £17.30: £4.30, £1.60, £2.10, £1.70; EX 132.90 Trifecta £220.70 Part won. Pool: £310.85 - 0.20 winning tickets..

Owner Mrs D J Hughes **Bred** Stall Nerce **Trained** Earlswood, Monmouths

■ Stewards' Enquiry : L Dettori one-day ban: careless riding (Jun 17)

FOCUS

Hand timed. A modest handicap despite the size of the field. On this occasion all the runners bunched together centre to stands' side. The third sets the standard and the form could rate a little higher.

Good Turn Official explanation: jockey said filly missed the break

Bollywood(IRE) Official explanation: jockey said gelding was denied a clear run

Creambiscuit Official explanation: jockey said gelding had no more to give

2317 BARKER POLAND H'CAP — 7f

3:30 (3:32) (Class 6) (0-60,64) 4-Y-O+ — **£2,730** (£806; £403) **Stalls** High

Form — RPR

5011 **1** — **Joy And Pain**[5] 2184 5-9-4 **64** 6ex — (v) KevinGhunowa(7) 12 — 74
(M J Attwater) *lw: t.k.h: w ldrs: led over 2f out and c to nr side rail: rdn over 1f out: jst hld on* — **15/8**[1]

0125 **2** *nk* **Only If I Laugh**[50] 1057 5-8-13 **52** — RobbieFitzpatrick 13 — 61
(M J Attwater) *lw: trckd ldrs: effrt over 2f out: rdn to chse wnr fnl f: styd on: jst hld* — **7/1**[2]

4520 **3** *¾* **Rowan Warning**[5] 2184 4-9-6 **59** — LDettori 6 — 66
(J R Boyle) *hld up wl in rr and wl off the pce: prog 3f out: threaded through fnl 2f: fin strly: nt rch ldng pair* — **8/1**[3]

0550 **4** *¾* **Blue Line**[19] 1802 4-9-1 **54** — (v[1]) ChrisCatlin 11 — 59
(M Madgwick) *hld up in rr and racd on outer: prog and rdn over 2f out: styd on fnl f: nrst fin* — **33/1**

5015 **5** *½* **Charlie Bear**[28] 1570 5-9-5 **58** — AdrianMcCarthy 4 — 62
(Miss Z C Davison) *swtg: trckd ldng gp: prog on outer over 2f out: chsd wnr over 1f out to 1f out: one pce* — **16/1**

4440 **6** *1* **Arian's Lad**[7] 2095 5-9-0 **53** — FrancisFerris 9 — 54
(B Palling) *taken down early: w ldrs: drvn 2f out: fdd fnl f* — **20/1**

0603 **7** *¾* **Cherokee Nation**[14] 1923 5-9-4 **60** — AdamKirby(3) 16 — 59
(P W D'Arcy) *pressed ldrs: lost pl 1/2-way and sn struggling: styd on again fr over 1f out* — **20/1**

0003 **8** *1 ¾* **Moon Forest (IRE)**[21] 1752 4-8-12 **51** — (p) SteveDrowne 10 — 45
(J M Bradley) *lw: mde most to over 2f out: wknd jst over 1f out* — **20/1**

5160 **9** *1* **The Bonus King**[11] 1996 6-9-7 **60** — ShaneKelly 7 — 51
(J Jay) *hld up off the pce in midfield: effrt 3f out: wknd wl over 1f out* — **25/1**

3244 **10** *nk* **Neideen (IRE)**[241] 5734 4-9-7 **60** — SebSanders 17 — 51
(J Akehurst) *bit bkwd: w ldrs tl over 2f out: hanging and wknd wl over 1f out* — **10/1**

6450 **11** *½* **Hand Chime**[55] 985 9-9-1 **54** — JohnEgan 14 — 48+
(Ernst Oertel) *settled bhd ldng gp: nudged along and sme prog 2f out: nt on terms over 1f out: heavily eased ins fnl f* — **20/1**

0406 **12** *1 ¼* **Grezie**[6] 2135 4-8-13 **52** — RobertMiles 5 — 38
(T D McCarthy) *b: b.hind: racd on outer: in tch: prog and cl up over 1f out: sn wknd* — **20/1**

0350 **13** *2 ½* **Windy Prospect**[119] 334 4-9-2 **58** — EdwardCreighton(3) 3 — 37
(Miss Sheena West) *taken down early: a wl in rr: no prog fnl 2f* — **16/1**

0050 **14** *11* **Imtalkinggibberish**[41] 1245 5-8-13 **52** — EddieAhern 8 — 1
(J R Jenkins) *pressed ldrs to over 2f out: wknd rapidly* — **20/1**

5000 **15** *21* **Balerno**[76] 693 7-9-6 **59** — AlanMunro 18 — —
(R Ingram) *a wl in rr: t.o* — **25/1**

0000 **16** *1 ½* **Princess Galadriel**[5] 2184 5-9-2 **55** — TedDurcan 15 — —
(J M P Eustace) *a wl in rr: hanging bdly and wknd rapidly over 2f out: t.o* — **66/1**

0000 **P** — **Empty Gesture**[245] 5687 4-9-6 **59** — GeorgeBaker 1 — —
(J R Best) *lw: dwlt: a wl in rr: tailing off whn p.u over 1f out: dismntd* — **50/1**

6001 **P** — **Avenlea**[62] 890 5-8-13 **52** — RyanMoore 2 — —
(G L Moore) *lw: prom on outer: drvn over 2f out: stl chsng ldrs whn broke down jst over 1f out: p.u* — **20/1**

1m 22.04s (-2.17) **Going Correction** -0.30s/f (Firm) — **18** Ran SP% **126.7**

Speed ratings (Par 101):100,99,98,97,97 96,95,93,92,91 91,89,87,74,50 48,—,—

CSF £10.56 CT £96.82 TOTE £2.90: £1.40, £1.50, £2.10, £4.50; EX 13.70 Trifecta £179.20 Part won. Pool: £252.43 - 0.95 winning tickets..

Owner Phones Direct Partnership **Bred** Jonathan Shack **Trained** Wysall, Notts

■ A one-two for owners Phones Direct Partnership and trainer Michael Attwater.

FOCUS

Hand timed. Just a fair handicap despite the size of the field and, as in the previous race, they decided to race centre to stands' side. The form looks solid for the grade.

The Bonus King Official explanation: jockey said gelding lost its action

Hand Chime Official explanation: vet said gelding finished lame

Grezie Official explanation: jockey said filly had run flat

Imtalkinggibberish Official explanation: jockey said gelding lost its action; trainer said gelding had bled

Balerno Official explanation: jockey said gelding was unsuited by the good to firm (firm in places) going

Princess Galadriel Official explanation: jockey said mare hung badly left

Empty Gesture Official explanation: vet said gelding was lame

2318 HAYWARDS H'CAP — 7f

4:00 (4:01) (Class 5) (0-75,75) 3-Y-O — **£3,562** (£1,059; £529; £264) **Stalls** High

Form — RPR

5263 **1** — **Neardown Beauty (IRE)**[9] 2050 3-8-13 **67** — LDettori 7 — 80
(I A Wood) *hld up wl in rr: stdy prog on nr side fr over 2f out: chsd ldr over 1f out: carried hd high but pushed into ld last 75yds* — **3/1**[1]

6100 **2** *¾* **Kings Heir (IRE)**[28] 1569 3-9-7 **75** — SebSanders 4 — 86
(R M Beckett) *lw: pressed ldrs: led wl over 2f out: hrd rdn over 1f out: hdd last 75yds* — **12/1**

4401 **3** *3 ½* **Patavium Prince (IRE)**[19] 1801 3-9-1 **69** — TQuinn 9 — 70
(J R Best) *hld up bhd ldrs: plld out and effrt to chse ldr 2f out: hanging and nt qckn over 1f out: one pce after* — **6/1**[2]

0025 **4** *2* **Simpsons Ross (IRE)**[25] 1642 3-8-8 **62** — FergusSweeney 3 — 58
(R M Flower) *in tch: effrt over 2f out: chsd ldrs over 1f out: fdd* — **16/1**

5100 **5** *½* **Drawback (IRE)**[24] 1693 3-8-9 **70** — (p) TolleyDean(7) 6 — 65
(R A Harris) *sharp reminders sn after s: in tch: effrt u.p over 2f out: edgd rt and no imp* — **50/1**

0404 **6** *2 ½* **Goodbye Girl (IRE)**[3] 2249 3-7-11 **56** oh11 — (p) MarcHalford(5) 14 — 44
(Mrs C A Dunnett) *w ldrs to jst over 2f out: steadily wknd* — **33/1**

1006 **7** *nk* **Sigismundus (IRE)**[12] 1954 3-8-9 **66** — AmirQuinn(3) 2 — 53
(J R Boyle) *b.hind: s.s: hld up wl bhd: prog on wd outside over 2f out: hrd rdn and one pce over 1f out* — **25/1**

0042 **8** *1 ½* **The London Gang**[15] 1899 3-8-11 **65** — (v) RobertWinston 5 — 48
(P D Evans) *hld up in rr: effrt whn nt clr run and hmpd over 2f out: no prog after* — **6/1**[2]

352 **9** *9* **Five Two**[33] 1445 3-9-6 **74** — TedDurcan 1 — 33
(M R Channon) *b: trckd ldrs on outer: wknd over 2f out: eased* — **10/1**

3000 **10** *2 ½* **Mystic Roll**[24] 1681 3-9-2 **70** — (b[1]) JimmyFortune 8 — 22
(B J Meehan) *lw: w ldrs to over 2f out: wknd rapidly* — **20/1**

0240 **11** *1* **Laqataat (IRE)**[17] 1843 3-9-5 **73** — RHills 12 — 22
(J L Dunlop) *w ldrs: rdn and nt moving wl over 2f out: wknd and eased* — **10/1**

0500 **12** *¾* **Corrib (IRE)**[28] 1569 3-9-5 **73** — FrancisFerris 13 — 20
(B Palling) *s.v.s: a wl bhd* — **25/1**

0004 **13** *2 ½* **Squadron Leader (IRE)**[18] 1825 3-8-9 **63** — RyanMoore 11 — 4
(R Hannon) *hld up wl in rr: brief effrt 3f out: sn wknd* — **8/1**[3]

000 **14** *1* **Musical Chimes**[46] 1110 3-8-2 **56** oh3 — ChrisCatlin 15 — —
(C A Cyzer) *a wl bhd* — **40/1**

0430 **15** *6* **Desert Dust**[22] 1736 3-8-3 **57** ow1 — JohnEgan 10 — —
(R M H Cowell) *mde most to wl over 2f out: wknd rapidly and eased* — **20/1**

1m 21.85s (-2.36) **Going Correction** -0.30s/f (Firm) — **15** Ran SP% **121.0**

Speed ratings (Par 99):101,100,96,93,93 90,90,88,78,75 74,73,70,69,62

CSF £36.77 CT £210.60 TOTE £4.00: £1.70, £6.00, £2.40; EX 60.60 Trifecta £264.50 Part won. Pool: £372.56 - 0.20 winning tickets..

Owner Ramscove Ltd **Bred** Mrs Joan M Langmead **Trained** Upper Lambourn, Berks

FOCUS

Once again the field raced centre to stands' side for this quite competitive handicap though at the end the front pair pulled well clear. The winning time was fractionally faster than the preceding handicap for older horses, but the form is limited by the proximity of the sixth, who was racing from well out of the handicap.

Goodbye Girl(IRE) Official explanation: jockey said filly hung left

Sigismundus(IRE) Official explanation: trainer said gelding was unsuited by the good to firm (firm in places) ground

The London Gang Official explanation: jockey said colt was denied a clear run
Laqataat(IRE) Official explanation: jockey said filly lost her action
Corrib(IRE) Official explanation: jockey said filly missed the break
Desert Dust Official explanation: jockey said gelding lost its action

2319 STANLEY POWELL CLAIMING STKS 7f (P)
4:30 (4:31) (Class 6) 3-Y-O+ **£2,730** (£806; £403) **Stalls** Low

Form RPR

3122 **1** **Million Percent**[22] 1735 7-9-10 64 SebSanders 7 67
(K R Burke) *lw: b: trckd ldrs gng wl: effrt 2f out: drvn to ld last 150yds: sn clr* **7/2[2]**

0551 **2** *2* **Labelled With Love**[14] 1923 6-9-2 55 (t) LDettori 6 54
(J R Boyle) *lw: dwlt: hld up towards rr: prog over 2f out: drvn over 1f out: styd on fnl f to take 2nd nr fin* **9/4[1]**

2134 **3** *hd* **Fulvio (USA)**[81] 659 6-9-4 55 (v) J-PGuillambert 13 55
(P Howling) *lw: led: drvn over 2f out: hdd and one pce last 150yds: lost 2nd nr fin* **8/1**

4251 **4** *nk* **Dexileos (IRE)**[22] 1727 7-8-13 46 (t) ChrisCavanagh(7) 10 56
(David Pinder) *trckd ldrs on inner: effrt 2f out: rdn and nt qckn over 1f out: kpt on* **16/1**

5300 **5** *shd* **Smokincanon**[4] 2208 4-9-4 50 RobertMiles 3 54
(W G M Turner) *hld up in midfield: gng wl enough over 2f out: effrt over 1f out: sn nt qckn: kpt on last 100yds* **50/1**

5060 **6** *1* **What-A-Dancer (IRE)**[3] 2223 9-9-10 72 (p) DarryllHolland 9 57
(D J S Ffrench Davis) *hld up in last pair: stdy prog over 2f out: hanging and nt qckn over 1f out: kpt on* **6/1[3]**

4320 **7** *nk* **Gaudalpin (IRE)**[14] 1914 4-8-11 44 JohnEgan 1 44
(Ernst Oertel) *t.k.h: cl up: rdn and fnd nil over 1f out: wknd ins fnl f* **12/1**

0060 **8** *hd* **Salinger (USA)**[6] 2131 4-9-2 55 (p) ChrisCatlin 5 48
(Mrs L J Mongan) *taken down early: s.s: hld up in last: effrt 2f out: r.o last 150yds: nrst fin* **33/1**

0660 **9** *5* **Soviet Threat (IRE)**[18] 1830 5-9-4 62 (p) FergusSweeney 14 37
(A G Juckes) *mostly pressed ldr to 2f out: wknd rapidly over 1f out* **20/1**

0000 **10** *6* **Belrose (IRE)**[26] 1618 4-9-5 43 (v[1]) IanMongan 2 22
(Mrs C A Dunnett) *a towards rr: drvn 3f out: sn lost tch* **100/1**

664- **11** *3* **Rusky Dusky (USA)**[613] 5908 4-9-4 RyanMoore 4 14
(R Hannon) *a towards rr: lost tch wl over 2f out* **20/1**

5041 **12** *14* **Bellini Star**[36] 1622 3-8-10 60 (v) RobertWinston 12 —
(P D Evans) *lw: s.s: rousted along to chse ldrs 4f out: wknd 3f out: t.o* **7/1**

1m 26.67s (0.78) **Going Correction** +0.10s/f (Slow)
WFA 3 from 4yo+ 10lb 12 Ran SP% **119.9**
Speed ratings (Par 101):99,96,96,96,96 94,94,94,88,81 78,62
CSF £11.25 TOTE £3.80: £1.20, £2.40, £2.70; EX 16.70 Trifecta £41.30 Pool: £304.36 - 5.23 winning tickets..
Owner Spigot Lodge Partnership **Bred** D J And Mrs Deer **Trained** Middleham Moor, N Yorks

FOCUS
A routine claimer won by an in-form gelding with the third and fifth setting the standard, but the fourth anchoring the form.
Gaudalpin(IRE) Official explanation: jockey said filly had run too freely
Bellini Star Official explanation: jockey said saddle slipped

2320 GINGER MARSHALL LIFETIME IN RACING H'CAP 1m 4f (P)
5:00 (5:02) (Class 6) (0-60,60) 4-Y-O+ **£2,730** (£806; £403) **Stalls** Low

Form RPR

0530 **1** **Mostarsil (USA)**[12] 1958 8-9-3 **56** (p) RyanMoore 4 67
(G L Moore) *lw: trckd ldrs: prog and cl up 2f out: led on inner 1f out: rdn and in command fnl f* **9/2[1]**

2320 **2** *1* **Glendale**[34] 1400 5-9-4 **57** DarryllHolland 2 67
(D K Ivory) *lw: trckd ldrs: smooth run to ld on inner 2f out: drvn and hdd 1f out: edgd rt and nt qckn* **6/1[2]**

6400 **3** *2 ½* **Full Of Zest**[9] 2044 4-9-6 **59** (b) IanMongan 11 65
(Mrs L J Mongan) *sn trckd ldrs: gng wl 3f out: rdn to chal fr 2f out: nt qckn over 1f out: one pce after* **25/1**

0046 **4** *nk* **Siena Star (IRE)**[2] 2262 8-9-7 **60** SteveDrowne 16 65
(Stef Liddiard) *dwlt: hld up: prog to chse ldrs 3f out: sn hrd rdn: kpt on fr over 1f out: nvr able to chal* **20/1**

005 **5** *2* **Montage (IRE)**[24] 1670 4-9-1 **54** SebSanders 9 56
(J Akehurst) *lw: sn prom: effrt to ld 4f out: drvn and hdd 2f out: fdd* **20/1**

2320 **6** *½* **Larad (IRE)**[14] 1910 5-8-8 **47** (b) JohnEgan 13 48+
(J S Moore) *hld up wl in rr: sme prog 3f out: sn rdn: kpt on fnl 2f: nt rch ldrs* **10/1**

4263 **7** *nk* **Sudden Impulse**[14] 1911 5-8-3 **42** FrancisFerris 3 43+
(A D Brown) *hld up wl in rr: outpcd 3f out: prog on inner 2f out: styd on: nvr nrr* **25/1**

6452 **8** *hd* **Star Rising**[8] 2075 4-8-9 **48** TPQueally 12 48
(W J Musson) *hld up in rr: effrt 3f out: styd on fr over 1f out: nt rch ldrs* **7/1[3]**

6023 **9** *1 ¾* **Jomus**[34] 1400 5-9-3 **56** (p) RobertHavlin 6 54
(L Montague Hall) *taken down early: hld up: stdy prog on outer 5f out: gng wl 3f out: wknd wl over 1f out* **12/1**

5463 **10** *3* **Amwell Brave**[12] 1958 5-9-6 **59** EddieAhern 7 52
(J R Jenkins) *settled towards rr: drvn and sme prog over 2f out: wknd over 1f out* **9/2[1]**

3000 **11** *1 ¾* **Perfidious (USA)**[44] 1163 8-9-4 **60** (v) AmirQuinn(3) 15 50
(J R Boyle) *mostly chsd ldr to 4f out: sn u.p and btn* **16/1**

0234 **12** *hd* **Lysander's Quest (IRE)**[29] 1540 8-8-4 **43** ChrisCatlin 8 33
(R Ingram) *sn lost pl and in midfield: dropped to rr 3f out: no prog after* **12/1**

1066 **13** *1 ½* **Irish Ballad**[262] 5298 4-9-0 **56** SaleemGolam(3) 10 43
(W R Swinburn) *nvr beyond midfield: u.p and struggling over 4f out* **14/1**

3222 **14** *½* **Zaffeu**[22] 1748 5-8-11 **50** J-PGuillambert 5 36
(A G Juckes) *dwlt: a wl in rr: shkn up and no prog 4f out* **8/1**

400 **15** *6* **Volaire**[19] 1797 4-9-2 **55** (t) RichardThomas 1 32
(A J Lidderdale) *nvr beyond midfield: rdn on inner over 4f out: sn wknd* **66/1**

2420 **16** *19* **Sovereign Dreamer (USA)**[28] 1566 6-9-5 **58** ShaneKelly 14 4
(P F I Cole) *b.nr fore: mde most to 4f out: wknd rapidly: eased 2f out: t.o* **40/1**

2m 34.61s (0.22) **Going Correction** +0.10s/f (Slow) 16 Ran SP% **132.4**
Speed ratings (Par 101):103,102,100,100,99 98,98,98,97,95 94,94,93,92,88 76
CSF £30.63 CT £649.82 TOTE £5.70: £1.60, £1.90, £8.70, £4.20; EX 56.80 TRIFECTA Not won. Place 6 £18.97, Place 5 £14.54.
Owner G A Jackman **Bred** Shadwell Farm Inc **Trained** Woodingdean, E Sussex

FOCUS
A low-grade, but competitive handicap run at a sound pace and those that tracked the leaders seemed to be at an advantage. The form looks sound, rated around the placed horses.

Mostarsil(USA) Official explanation: trainer's representative said, regarding the improved form shown, gelding was unsuited by the way the race was run last time out
Larad(IRE) Official explanation: jockey said gelding did not face the kickback
Sovereign Dreamer(USA) Official explanation: vet said gelding finished lame
T/Jkpt: Not won. T/Plt: £30.80 to a £1 stake. Pool: £52,701.90. 1,248.95 winning tickets. T/Qpdt: £21.40 to a £1 stake. Pool: £2,751.10. 95.00 winning tickets. JN

1862 RIPON (R-H)
Tuesday, June 6

OFFICIAL GOING: Good to firm
Wind: Light, half-against

2321 E B F SPA WELTER MAIDEN STKS 5f
2:15 (2:16) (Class 5) 2-Y-O **£4,533** (£1,348; £674; £336) **Stalls** Low

Form RPR

223 **1** **Dimboola**[27] 1595 2-9-3 MichaelHills 3 74+
(B W Hills) *mde all stands rail: pushed along over 1f out: kpt on wl fnl f* **2/5[1]**

4 **2** *1 ¼* **Riotous (IRE)**[33] 1442 2-9-0 DanielTudhope(3) 8 70
(A Dickman) *chsd ldrs: effrt 2f out: chsd wnr ins fnl f: r.o* **10/1[3]**

54 **3** *nk* **Perlachy**[16] 1863 2-8-12 DuranFentiman(5) 4 68
(T D Easterby) *w wnr: rdn over 2f out: one pce fnl f* **20/1**

05 **4** *2 ½* **Amelie Brown (IRE)**[16] 1863 2-8-12 TonyCulhane 11 54
(N Tinkler) *sn drvn along bhd ldng gp: kpt on steadily fnl f: nrst fin* **33/1**

0 **5** *nk* **The Dandy Fox**[43] 1181 2-8-12 AdrianTNicholls 7 53
(D Nicholls) *in tch: drvn over 2f out: kpt on steadily fnl f* **100/1**

03 **6** *3 ½* **Seaton Snooks**[11] 1982 2-9-3 DavidAllan 2 46+
(T D Easterby) *sn outpcd and drvn along: sme late hdwy: nvr rchd ldrs* **9/1[2]**

5 **6** *dht* **Atheneum (IRE)**[18] 1811 2-9-3 JoeFanning 6 46
(M Johnston) *cl up tl edgd lft and outpcd fr 2f out* **14/1**

03 **8** *1* **Abdu**[8] 2072 2-9-3 DaleGibson 1 42
(M W Easterby) *chsd ldrs to 1/2-way: sn rdn and btn* **33/1**

0 **9** *1 ¾* **Providence Farm**[8] 2073 2-8-10 AdeleRothery(7) 9 36+
(M W Easterby) *s.i.s: nvr on terms* **100/1**

10 *nk* **Spence's Choice (IRE)** 2-9-3 JimmyQuinn 5 35
(M W Easterby) *coltish in paddock: missed break: nvr on terms* **50/1**

11 *26* **Jazzanova** 2-9-3 PaulMulrennan 10 —
(M W Easterby) *sn wl bhd: no ch fr 1/2-way* **50/1**

59.60 secs (-0.60) **Going Correction** -0.30s/f (Firm) 11 Ran SP% **113.7**
Speed ratings (Par 93):92,90,89,85,85 79,79,77,75,74 32
CSF £4.21 TOTE £1.40: £1.10, £2.20, £3.80; EX 5.10.
Owner Guy Reed And Mrs Ailsa Daniels **Bred** Guy Reed And Mrs A H Daniels **Trained** Lambourn, Berks

FOCUS
An ordinary bunch on looks and an uncompetitive race in which the field raced stands' side. The pace was fair and the form is rated around those in the frame behind the winner.

NOTEBOOK
Dimboola, who looked anything but straightforward in defeat over six here last time, did not have to improve to win an uncompetitive event having had the run of the race near the stands' rail. Life will be tougher from now on, though. (op 4-9)
Riotous(IRE) is not very big but looked in good shape and bettered the form of his debut at Redcar. He again shaped as though the step up to six furlongs would suit but is likely to remain vulnerable to the better types in this grade. (op 14-1)
Perlachy ran his best race on this first start on a sound surface but, although likely to remain vulnerable in this grade, left the impression that the return to six furlongs and the step into modest nursery company will suit in due course. (op 16-1)
Amelie Brown(IRE) proved suited by the return to a sound surface but was another in this race that shaped as though the step up to six furlongs and the switch into nursery company would see her in a better light. (op 40-1)
The Dandy Fox bettered the form of her racecourse debut at Pontefract but, although the step up to six furlongs will be more to her liking, she is likely to continue to look vulnerable in this type of event. (op 50-1)
Atheneum(IRE), dropped in trip, was not totally disgraced but he will have to do better if he is to make his mark in this grade in the near future. (tchd 12-1)
Providence Farm Official explanation: jockey said colt hung left and became unbalanced on the undulations
Spence's Choice(IRE), the nicest horse physically in the field, had his mind on other things in the paddock and was too green to do himself justice on this debut. He should leave this form behind in due course. Official explanation: jockey said gelding had run green (op 40-1)
Jazzanova Official explanation: jockey said gelding moved poorly throughout

2322 HOME SALE NETWORK H'CAP 1m 1f 170y
2:45 (2:45) (Class 5) (0-70,70) 4-Y-O+ **£3,886** (£1,156; £577; £288) **Stalls** High

Form RPR

3004 **1** **Bright Sun (IRE)**[7] 2108 5-9-3 **66** (t) KimTinkler 2 75
(N Tinkler) *keen: set stdy pce: mde all: rdn and r.o wl fr 2f out* **15/2**

4545 **2** *3 ½* **Top Spec (IRE)**[11] 1995 5-9-7 **70** JimmyQuinn 6 72+
(J Pearce) *s.i.s: hld up last: nt clr run over 2f out: hdwy over 1f out: kpt on to go 2nd towards fin: no ch w wnr* **5/1[3]**

0005 **3** *¾* **Wing Commander**[7] 2108 7-9-7 **70** (b) RoystonFfrench 5 71
(I W McInnes) *pressed ldr: rdn over 2f out: edgd rt: kpt on same pce fnl f: lost 2nd cl home* **17/2**

3044 **4** *nk* **Westcourt Dream**[40] 1249 6-8-2 **51** DaleGibson 7 51
(M W Easterby) *keen in tch: rdn over 3f out: one pce over 1f out* **8/1**

0062 **5** *¾* **Grande Roche (IRE)**[30] 1500 4-8-5 **54** DeanMcKeown 1 53
(G A Swinbank) *prom: effrt over 2f out: one pce over 1f out* **9/2[2]**

2336 **6** *nk* **Waterloo Corner**[145] 97 4-9-0 **66** DanielTudhope(3) 8 64
(R Craggs) *trckd ldrs: drvn over 3f out: no ex over 1f out* **25/1**

4300 **7** *3* **Qaasi (USA)**[25] 1651 4-9-0 **68** GregFairley(5) 10 61+
(Mrs K Walton) *hld up in tch: effrt whn nt clr run over 2f out: rdn and no imp over 1f out* **7/1**

0100 **8** *3 ½* **Cleaver**[8] 2088 5-9-1 **64** JamieSpencer 4 50+
(Lady Herries) *hld up: hdwy on outside over 2f out: edgd rt and wknd wl over 1f out: eased whn btn fnl f* **4/1[1]**

0200 **9** *11* **Almanshood (USA)**[11] 1992 4-9-7 **70** KDarley 3 35
(P L Gilligan) *hld up outside: hdwy over 3f out: hung rt and wknd over 2f out* **11/1**

0500 **10** *3 ½* **Fairy Monarch (IRE)**[35] 1395 7-8-2 **51** (b) JoeFanning 9 9
(P T Midgley) *keen: sn midfield: rdn over 3f out: sn btn: eased whn no ch fnl f* **50/1**

2m 1.21s (-3.79) **Going Correction** -0.30s/f (Firm) 10 Ran SP% **114.9**
Speed ratings (Par 103):103,100,99,99,98 98,96,93,84,81
CSF £44.15 CT £326.86 TOTE £8.00: £2.50, £1.90, £2.90; EX 55.90.

Owner Leeds Plywood And Doors Ltd **Bred** Terence McDonald **Trained** Langton, N Yorks

FOCUS

An ordinary bunch and the steady pace meant those racing close to the pace held the edge, which suggests the form may not prove reliable.

Westcourt Dream Official explanation: jockey said mare suffered interference in running

Waterloo Corner Official explanation: jockey said gelding was denied a clear run

Qaasi(USA) Official explanation: jockey said gelding denied a clear run

Cleaver Official explanation: jockey said gelding was unsuited by the good to firm ground

Almanshood(USA) Official explanation: jockey said gelding hung violently right

Fairy Monarch(IRE) Official explanation: jockey said gelding suffered interference in running

2323 RIPON, CATHEDRAL CITY OF DALES H'CAP — 6f

3:15 (3:15) (Class 3) (0-95,93) 3-Y-O+

£9,348 (£2,799; £1,399; £700; £349; £175) **Stalls** Low

Form — RPR

1-10 **1** **Desert Commander (IRE)**[19] 1803 4-9-10 **89** .... NCallan 4 — 107
(K A Ryan) *pressed ldr: led wl over 1f out: pushed clr: eased cl home* **6/1**[2]

1021 **2** 2½ **Zidane**[24] 1686 4-9-0 **79** .... JamieSpencer 1 — 90
(J R Fanshawe) *prom: rdn over 2f out: effrt over 1f out: chsd wnr ins fnl f: no imp* **7/4**[1]

6500 **3** ¾ **Pieter Brueghel (USA)**[10] 2017 7-9-10 **89** .... JoeFanning 3 — 98
(D Nicholls) *led tl hdd wl over 1f out: one pce fnl f* **17/2**

0400 **4** shd **Banjo Patterson**[9] 2047 4-9-7 **86** .... MichaelHills 5 — 94
(G A Huffer) *blkd s: sn outpcd: hdwy over 1f out: nrst fin* **15/2**[3]

0060 **5** ¾ **Don Pele (IRE)**[283] 4764 4-9-1 **85** .... AndrewMullen(5) 2 — 91
(K A Ryan) *prom tl rdn and nt qckn over 1f out* **28/1**

0001 **6** 1½ **Dazzling Bay**[27] 1597 6-9-13 **92** .... DavidAllan 10 — 94
(T D Easterby) *sn outpcd: hdwy over 1f out: kpt on fnl f: n.d* **17/2**

4200 **7** 1 **Prince Tum Tum (USA)**[10] 2017 6-9-5 **84** .... PaulMulrennan 6 — 83
(D W Barker) *hld up: effrt 2f out: no ex fnl f* **16/1**

0323 **8** 3 **Breaking Shadow (IRE)**[10] 2017 4-8-12 **80** .... BenSwarbrick(3) 12 — 70+
(T D Barron) *bhd and outpcd: nvr rchd ldrs* **8/1**

2340 **9** shd **Looks Could Kill (USA)**[29] 1532 4-9-1 **83** .... DanielTudhope(3) 11 — 72
(E J Alston) *hld up outside: effrt over 2f out: btn over 1f out* **33/1**

000- **10** 7 **Fremen (USA)**[599] 6193 6-9-1 **87** .... VictoriaBehan(7) 9 — 55
(D Nicholls) *sn towards rr: outpcd 1/2-way: nvr on terms* **100/1**

1611 **11** 8 **Niteowl Lad (IRE)**[295] 4427 4-8-12 **77** .... KDarley 7 — 21
(J Balding) *prom: shkn up briefly 2f out: eased* **33/1**

6010 **12** 33 **Kenmore**[31] 1487 4-10-0 **93** .... AdrianTNicholls 8 — —
(D Nicholls) *midfield: struggling 1/2-way: sn btn* **28/1**

1m 10.34s (-2.66) **Going Correction** -0.30s/f (Firm) **12** Ran SP% **114.2**

Speed ratings (Par 107):105,101,100,100,99 97,96,92,92,82 72,28

CSF £15.43 CT £89.04 TOTE £7.90: £2.40, £1.20, £3.20; EX 20.60.

Owner R J H Limited **Bred** Gainsborough Stud Management Ltd **Trained** Hambleton, N Yorks

FOCUS

A decent handicap but one in which those drawn low and those racing prominently came to the fore. The pace was sound and the form looks solid.

NOTEBOOK

Desert Commander(IRE) ◆, big and well but on his toes in the preliminaries, had the run of the race back on a sound surface but powered clear in the closing stages to win with more in hand than the margin suggests. He is only lightly raced and is capable of winning a decent handicap this term. Official explanation: trainer said, regarding the improved form shown, gelding may have bounced last time out (op 15-2 tchd 8-1)

Zidane ◆, ridden closer to the pace - at a track that suits prominent racers - than is usually the case, was well backed, looked in tremendous condition and ran creditably up in the weights and in grade. He has not had much racing and will surely be able to score again from his current mark. (op 15-8 tchd 2-1)

Pieter Brueghel(USA) really took the eye in the paddock and returned to something like his best returned to this trip and back on a sound surface. He had the run of the race next to the stands rail but does look to be coming to himself, and is one to keep an eye on away from progressive sorts when it looks as though he will be able to dominate. (tchd 8-1)

Banjo Patterson looked in good shape and fared the best of those attempting to come from off the pace. He is a bit better than this bare form and, on this evidence, will be suited by the return to seven furlongs. (op 13-2 tchd 8-1)

Don Pele(IRE) ◆, having his first start since August and his first for Kevin Ryan, was easy to back but shaped as though retaining plenty of ability. He has already slipped to a favourable mark and is the type to win races for this yard. Official explanation: jockey said gelding lost its action (tchd 33-1)

Dazzling Bay, an inconsistent sprinter who returned to form over course and distance last time when beating Prince Tum Tum, reproduced the form with the latter almost to the pound but was found out in this stronger event. (tchd 15-2)

Breaking Shadow(IRE) Official explanation: jockey said gelding was denied a clear run

Niteowl Lad(IRE) was well beaten but was not knocked about at any stage after showing plenty of early dash on this first run since August. He will be of much more interest back over five furlongs on a sound surface. Official explanation: jockey said gelding had a breathing problem

Kenmore Official explanation: jockey said colt lost its action

2324 WEATHERBYS BANK H'CAP — 1m 1f 170y

3:45 (3:46) (Class 4) (0-80,78) 3-Y-O **£6,309** (£1,888; £944; £472; £235) **Stalls** High

Form — RPR

560 **1** **Moon On A Spoon**[34] 1401 3-8-12 **69** .... JamieSpencer 10 — 82+
(J R Fanshawe) *hld up and bhd: effrt whn nt clr run over 2f out: qcknd to ld appr fnl f: readily* **12/1**

1310 **2** 1 **Fregate Island (IRE)**[20] 1781 3-9-7 **78** .... TonyCulhane 5 — 82
(W J Haggas) *trckd ldrs on outside: effrt and disp ld appr fnl f: kpt on: nt pce of wnr* **14/1**

2445 **3** ¾ **Markington**[26] 1605 3-8-13 **70** .... GrahamGibbons 11 — 74+
(J D Bethell) *midfield on ins: rdn over 3f out: effrt whn nt clr run 2f out: r.o fnl f* **10/1**

2152 **4** 1¼ **Flying Clarets (IRE)**[11] 1999 3-9-1 **72** .... TonyHamilton 13 — 72+
(R A Fahey) *hld up in tch: effrt whn n.m.r over 2f out: blkd wl over 1f out: kpt on fnl f* **11/2**[1]

2321 **5** ¾ **Just Observing**[33] 1434 3-9-6 **77** .... NickyMackay 3 — 76
(E A L Dunlop) *hld up: hdwy and prom over 2f out: outpcd over 1f out* **13/2**[3]

4150 **6** nk **Daaweitza**[18] 1828 3-8-10 **67** .... TomEaves 8 — 65
(B Ellison) *hld up: effrt over 2f out: hung lft wl over 1f out: kpt on fnl f: no imp* **18/1**

635 **7** 1 **Choreography**[41] 1230 3-8-7 **64** .... AdrianTNicholls 12 — 60
(D Nicholls) *keen: cl up: led over 2f out to appr fnl f: no ex* **16/1**

0464 **8** ¾ **Truly Fruitful (IRE)**[34] 1403 3-8-13 **70** .... PatCosgrave 9 — 65
(K R Burke) *hld up: effrt over 2f out: btn fnl f* **17/2**

531 **9** ½ **Sir Arthur (IRE)**[16] 1866 3-9-6 **77** .... KDarley 2 — 71
(M Johnston) *racd wd in midfield: effrt 3f out: edgd rt and btn over 1f out* **6/1**[2]

2150 **10** 8 **Manouche**[17] 1855 3-8-13 **70** .... (p) NCallan 6 — 49+
(K A Ryan) *led to over 2f out: no ex whn hmpd over 1f out: eased* **14/1**

01 **11** 4 **Teach To Preach (USA)**[56] 964 3-9-2 **73** .... MichaelHills 4 — 44+
(B W Hills) *chsd ldrs: effrt 3f out: no ex whn hmpd wl over 1f out* **6/1**[2]

0400 **12** 10 **Penny Glitters**[33] 1441 3-8-3 **60** .... FrancisNorton 7 — 12
(S Parr) *keen: cl up tl rdn and wknd fr 3f out* **33/1**

0100 **13** 12 **Razed**[54] 1005 3-9-2 **73** .... JoeFanning 1 — 2
(M Johnston) *bhd: rdn and lost tch fr 4f out* **33/1**

2m 0.84s (-4.16) **Going Correction** -0.30s/f (Firm) **13** Ran SP% **115.0**

Speed ratings (Par 101):104,103,102,101,101 100,99,99,98,92 89,81,71

CSF £163.38 CT £1728.30 TOTE £10.90: £2.70, £4.60, £3.40; EX 133.40.

Owner B McAllister **Bred** Chippenham Lodge Stud Ltd **Trained** Newmarket, Suffolk

■ Stewards' Enquiry : Jamie Spencer two-day ban: careless riding (Jun 17-18)

FOCUS

A run-of-the-mill handicap and an ordinary pace but an improved effort from the winner, who scored with plenty in hand and the form behind seems sound.

Moon On A Spoon ◆ Official explanation: trainer said, regarding the improved form shown, the fillys previous start was on the all-weather and she was better suited by today's turf

Flying Clarets(IRE) Official explanation: jockey said filly hung left throughout

Teach To Preach(USA) Official explanation: jockey said colt suffered interference in running

2325 GRANTLEY MAIDEN STKS — 1m

4:15 (4:21) (Class 5) 3-Y-O **£3,886** (£1,156; £577; £288) **Stalls** High

Form — RPR

4 **1** **It's Unbelievable (USA)**[279] 4871 3-9-3 .... NCallan 12 — 66
(B J Meehan) *trckd ldrs: led over 2f out: hld on wl fnl f* **15/2**

3660 **2** ½ **Nelsons Column (IRE)**[34] 1421 3-9-3 69 .... TomEaves 9 — 65
(G M Moore) *chsd ldrs: ev ch over 2f out: sn rdn: kpt on wl fnl f* **16/1**

0 **3** ¾ **Kinvara Lass (IRE)**[36] 1351 3-8-12 .... NickyMackay 2 — 57
(L M Cumani) *prom: rdn over 3f out: kpt on wl fnl f: nrst fin* **16/1**

0 **4** 1½ **Musical Magic**[48] 1085 3-8-12 .... KDarley 10 — 53+
(J Noseda) *midfield on ins: rdn over 3f out: rallied over 1f out: kpt on fnl f* **11/2**[3]

5 1 **Counterfactual (IRE)** 3-9-3 .... DerekMcGaffin 11 — 56
(B Smart) *prom: drvn over 2f out: one pce over 1f out* **66/1**

6 1 **Wind Star** 3-9-3 .... DeanMcKeown 14 — 53+
(G A Swinbank) *s.i.s: bhd: hdwy over 2f out: hung lft: no imp fnl f* **100/1**

060 **7** ¾ **Fadansil**[276] 4952 3-9-3 48 .... TonyHamilton 16 — 51
(J Wade) *led to over 2f out: sn no ex* **200/1**

4 **8** 2½ **Campanile**[236] 5850 3-8-12 .... JamieSpencer 5 — 46+
(J R Fanshawe) *hld up: hdwy over 2f out: btn over 1f out: eased ins fnl f* **5/1**[2]

5 **9** 2 **Stumped**[24] 1680 3-9-3 .... (t) TonyCulhane 15 — 39
(W J Haggas) *prom: effrt over 2f out: sn btn* **4/1**[1]

10 8 **Sweet Lavinia** 3-8-12 .... GrahamGibbons 7 — 12
(J D Bethell) *midfield: drvn over 3f out: sn btn* **66/1**

0000 **11** 2½ **Cape Courier (IRE)**[43] 1200 3-8-12 40 .... NataliaGemelova(5) 1 — 11
(I W McInnes) *midfield: rdn 4f out: sn btn* **200/1**

0 **12** 1¾ **Lillie Lou**[8] 2080 3-8-12 .... DavidAllan 4 — 1
(T D Easterby) *bhd: rdn 1/2-way: nvr on terms* **100/1**

00 **13** 3 **Soba Fella**[11] 2001 3-9-3 .... LeeEnstone 6 — —
(P T Midgley) *s.i.s: nvr on terms* **200/1**

06 **14** 34 **Orpen's Astaire (IRE)**[47] 1101 3-9-3 .... PaulMulrennan 8 — —
(Jedd O'Keeffe) *plld hrd: hld up: rdn 1/2-way: sn struggling* **100/1**

1m 38.89s (-2.21) **Going Correction** -0.30s/f (Firm) **14** Ran SP% **83.0**

Speed ratings (Par 99):99,98,97,96,95 94,93,91,89,81 78,76,73,39

CSF £56.94 TOTE £5.30: £2.10, £2.90, £3.60; EX 68.50.

Owner Stephen Dartnell **Bred** J Feins **Trained** Manton, Wilts

■ Benandonner (6/1) reared in stalls; and Zaif (7-2f) refused to enter stalls; withdrawn. Rule 4 deduction 30p in £.

FOCUS

A race lacking strength and one in which two market leaders were withdrawn at the start and two others disappointed. The pace was sound.

Wind Star Official explanation: jockey said gelding hung left throughout

Campanile Official explanation: jockey said filly became upset in stalls and had no more to give

Soba Fella Official explanation: jockey said gelding lost its action

Orpen's Astaire(IRE) Official explanation: jockey said gelding had a breathing problem

2326 STUDLEY ROYAL H'CAP — 1m 4f 10y

4:45 (4:48) (Class 5) (0-75,75) 4-Y-O+ **£4,533** (£1,348; £674; £336) **Stalls** High

Form — RPR

4630 **1** **Zarova (IRE)**[34] 1425 4-8-2 **56** .... JimmyQuinn 8 — 65+
(M W Easterby) *keen: hld up: nt clr run over 2f out: hdwy on ins over 1f out kpt on wl to ld cl home* **6/1**[3]

0605 **2** shd **Nessen Dorma (IRE)**[11] 2000 5-9-7 **75** .... (v) KDarley 5 — 84
(J G Given) *pressed ldr: led over 2f out: sn rdn: kpt on wl fnl f: hdd cl home* **7/2**[1]

5035 **3** 2 **Merrymaker**[10] 2018 6-9-6 **74** .... NCallan 6 — 80
(W M Brisbourne) *in tch: outpcd over 2f out: rallied over 1f out: nt rch first two* **6/1**[3]

2252 **4** 1¾ **Charlotte Vale**[10] 2018 5-9-2 **75** .... GregFairley(5) 2 — 78
(Micky Hammond) *hld up in tch: rdn over 2f out: rallied over 1f out: no imp fnl f* **7/2**[1]

1016 **5** 1¾ **Balwearie (IRE)**[15] 1887 5-8-5 **59** .... RoystonFfrench 7 — 59
(Miss L A Perratt) *led to over 2f out: no ex over 1f out* **11/2**[2]

6014 **6** shd **Aleron (IRE)**[10] 2018 8-9-5 **73** .... (p) GrahamGibbons 4 — 73
(J J Quinn) *keen: chsd ldrs tl wknd over 1f out* **9/1**

0004 **7** 2 **Kiama**[26] 1610 4-8-5 **59** .... JoeFanning 3 — 56
(M Johnston) *in tch: effrt over 2f out: wknd over 1f out* **12/1**

0060 **8** ½ **Mister Arjay (USA)**[21] 1756 6-8-6 **60** .... TomEaves 1 — 56
(B Ellison) *trckd ldrs: effrt over 2f out: wknd over 1f out* **16/1**

2m 35.54s (-1.46) **Going Correction** -0.30s/f (Firm) **8** Ran SP% **112.0**

Speed ratings (Par 103):92,91,90,89,88 88,86,86

CSF £26.11 CT £129.51 TOTE £8.10: £2.20, £1.50, £1.90; EX 34.00 Place 6 £269.70, Place 5 £229.08.

Owner Steve Hull **Bred** Mrs Clodagh McStay **Trained** Sheriff Hutton, N Yorks

FOCUS

A run-of-the-mill handicap in which the pace was only fair and the winning time was slow. The placed horses were close to their marks so the form may work out.

Charlotte Vale Official explanation: jockey said mare was unsuited by good to firm ground

Balwearie(IRE) Official explanation: jockey said gelding hung left throughout

T/Plt: £606.00 to a £1 stake. Pool: £55,710.50. 67.10 winning tickets. T/Qpdt: £481.60 to a £1 stake. Pool: £3,319.30. 5.10 winning tickets. RY

2300 WINDSOR (R-H)

Tuesday, June 6

OFFICIAL GOING: Good to firm

Wind: Nil Weather: Hot & sunny

2327 K&LNG INTERNATIONAL LAW FIRM H'CAP 1m 67y

6:30 (6:30) (Class 6) (0-65,70) 4-Y-O+ **£3,238** (£963; £481; £240) **Stalls** High

Form RPR

41 **1** **Full Victory (IRE)**[7] [2098] 4-9-12 **70** 6ex DaneO'Neill 2 82+
(R A Farrant) *in tch: gd hdwy 3f out: led ins fnl 2f: hrd drvn and edgd rt to stands rail ins last: r.o strly* **7/2**[1]

6000 **2** *1 ½* **Jools**[37] [1311] 8-9-0 **65** JamesMillman(7) 11 70
(D K Ivory) *s.i.s: bhd: hdwy 3f out: chsd wnr ins fnl f: kpt on same pce* **14/1**

0035 **3** *hd* **Lockstock (IRE)**[7] [2098] 8-8-11 **58** (p) AdamKirby(3) 6 63
(M S Saunders) *chsd ldrs: drvn to chal fr over 2f out unil over 1f out: kpt on same pce u.p ins last* **16/1**

0330 **4** *1* **Balearic Star (IRE)**[166] [6654] 5-8-12 **56** AlanMunro 9 59
(B R Millman) *bhd: swtchd to outside and hdwy over 2f out: rdn and kpt on fr over 1f out: gng on cl home but nvr gng pce to rch ldrs* **8/1**

5000 **5** *½* **Billy One Punch**[7] [2112] 4-9-2 **60** RobertWinston 8 62
(G G Margarson) *w ldr tl led appr fnl 4f: hdd ins fnl 2f: wknd fnl f* **16/1**

0612 **6** *½* **Christmas Truce (IRE)**[6] [2132] 7-8-11 **60** (v) JamesDoyle(5) 10 60
(Ms J S Doyle) *s.i.s: bhd: hdwy fr 4f out: drvn to chal ins fnl 2f: wknd fnl f* **11/2**[2]

0056 **7** *2 ½* **Admiral Compton**[6] [2149] 5-9-4 **62** (b) MartinDwyer 13 57
(J R Boyle) *chsd ldrs: rdn 3f out: wknd over 1f out* **11/1**

3331 **8** *1 ¼* **Sol Rojo**[6] [2148] 4-9-0 **58** 6ex (v) TedDurcan 5 50
(J Pearce) *s.i.s: bhd: hdwy 4f out: ev ch over 2f out: wknd over 1f out* **13/2**[3]

0006 **9** *½* **Border Edge**[7] [2114] 8-9-0 **63** (v) MarcHalford(5) 1 54
(J J Bridger) *rr: hdwy 4f out: chsd ldrs on outside over 2f out: sn rdn: wknd over 1f out* **20/1**

5040 **10** *1 ¾* **Oakley Absolute**[18] [1821] 4-9-7 **65** RichardHughes 3 52
(R Hannon) *chsd ldrs: rdn 3f out: wknd 2f out* **12/1**

0000 **11** *¾* **Final Promise**[18] [1821] 4-9-5 **63** StephenCarson 14 48
(J A Geake) *sn led: hdd over 4f out: wknd 3f out* **25/1**

0000 **12** *¾* **Rawaabet (IRE)**[40] [1257] 4-9-4 **62** LPKeniry 7 45
(P W Hiatt) *s.i.s: bhd: bhd most of way* **33/1**

4200 **P** **Barton Sands (IRE)**[36] [1334] 9-8-11 **55** (t) J-PGuillambert 4 —
(Ernst Oertel) *prom tl wknd qckly 1/2-way: t.o: p.u and dismntd 2f out* **12/1**

1m 46.49s (0.89) **Going Correction** +0.125s/f (Good) 13 Ran SP% **115.7**

Speed ratings (Par 101):100,98,98,97,96 96,93,92,92,90 89,88,—

CSF £51.31 CT £714.01 TOTE £4.10: £2.00, £4.60, £5.50; EX 42.20.

Owner Barnstaple Racing Club **Bred** Larry Ryan **Trained** Bampton, Devon

FOCUS

A modest handicap run at a good pace rated around the third and fifth to form.

Christmas Truce(IRE) Official explanation: jockey said gelding had no more to give

2328 KIRKPATRICK & LOCKHART NICHOLSON GRAHAM LLP MAIDEN FILLIES' STKS 6f

7:00 (7:01) (Class 4) 2-Y-O **£6,477** (£1,927; £963; £481) **Stalls** High

Form RPR

63 **1** **La Roca (IRE)**[13] [1930] 2-9-0 SebSanders 15 86
(R M Beckett) *led 1f: led again ins fnl fnl 3f: drvn and r.o strly fnl 2f* **5/1**[2]

2 *2* **Medley** 2-9-0 RichardHughes 2 80+
(R Hannon) *sn trcking ldrs: drvn over 2f out: chsd wnr fnl f but a hld* **7/2**[1]

3 **3** *3 ½* **Relkida**[15] [1896] 2-9-0 ChrisCatlin 11 70
(M R Channon) *led after 1f: hdd ins fnl 3f: sn rdn: styd pressing wnr tl wknd fnl f* **7/2**[1]

4 *2* **Russian Gift (IRE)** 2-8-11 AdamKirby(3) 5 64
(C G Cox) *bhd: hdwy 3f out: drvn over 2f out: kpt on same pce* **33/1**

5 *shd* **Tee Off (IRE)** 2-9-0 AlanMunro 7 63
(B W Hills) *s.i.s: bhd: swtchd lft to outside 3f out and hdwy sn after: one pce ins fnl 2f* **12/1**

6 *1* **Abunai** 2-9-0 SteveDrowne 6 60+
(R Charlton) *bhd: hdwy on outside whn n.m.r ins fnl 2f: kpt on fnl f but nvr in contention* **10/1**[3]

7 *hd* **Cheveme (IRE)** 2-9-0 DaneO'Neill 4 60
(B W Duke) *s.i.s: bhd: hdwy on outside over 2f out: sn rdn: wknd over 1f out* **40/1**

8 *1 ¼* **Easy Lover** 2-9-0 ShaneKelly 12 56+
(J A Osborne) *s.i.s: hdwy over 1f out but nvr in contention* **20/1**

9 *shd* **Seaflower Reef (IRE)** 2-8-11 NeilChalmers(3) 9 56
(A M Balding) *in tch: pushed along 1/2-way: wknd over 1f out* **16/1**

10 *shd* **Susanna's Prospect (IRE)** 2-9-0 JimmyFortune 3 55
(B J Meehan) *chsd ldrs: fdd fnl 2f* **16/1**

11 *¾* **Sparkling Eyes** 2-9-0 RyanMoore 14 53+
(C E Brittain) *chsd ldrs: rdn over 2f out: wknd sn after* **16/1**

12 *1* **Trickle (USA)** 2-9-0 RichardMullen 8 50+
(E A L Dunlop) *chsd ldrs: n.m.r 4f out: wknd 2f out* **20/1**

13 *5* **Goodwood Belle** 2-9-0 TQuinn 13 35
(J L Dunlop) *chsd ldrs over 3f* **25/1**

14 *¾* **Gib (IRE)** 2-9-0 MartinDwyer 10 33
(B W Hills) *chsd ldrs tl hmpd on rails 4f out: n.d after* **20/1**

15 *4* **Brave Amber** 2-9-0 TedDurcan 16 21
(M Blanshard) *early pce: bhd fr 1/2-way* **40/1**

U **16** *15* **Kaptain Kate**[8] [2072] 2-8-11 EdwardCreighton(3) 1 —
(R Brotherton) *slowly away: v geen and a wl bhd* **80/1**

1m 15.4s (1.73) **Going Correction** +0.125s/f (Good) 16 Ran SP% **122.7**

Speed ratings (Par 92):93,90,85,83,82 81,81,79,79,79 78,77,70,69,64 44

CSF £20.41 TOTE £5.70: £3.00, £2.70, £1.90; EX 21.50.

Owner P K Gardner **Bred** Ben Goldsmith, Mrs James Wigan And L T S **Trained** Whitsbury, Hants

FOCUS

A fair juvenile fillies' maiden that should produce a few winners, although the form is not easy to assess at this point.

NOTEBOOK

La Roca(IRE) ◆ confirmed the promise she showed on her two previous runs to win convincingly. There should be plenty more to come and it would be no surprise to see her try and pick up some black type at some stage. (op 7-1)

Medley, a half-sister to amongst others six-furlong juvenile winners Marching Song and Flower Market, out of a five-furlong two-year-old scorer, made a pleasing debut behind the convincing winner. (op 5-1)

Relkida did not really build on the form she showed when third over five furlongs here on her debut, but again showed plenty of ability and should be found an opening at some stage. (op 5-2 tchd 4-1)

Russian Gift(IRE) the first foal of an unraced half-sister to Border Subject, a multiple six to eight-furlong winner, and Toppling, a triple six to eight-furlong winner, made a pleasing introduction and is open to improvement.

Tee Off(IRE), a 140,000euros first foal of an unraced half-sister to French/Irish 2000 Guineas winner Bachir, made a respectable debut and is another capable of progressing.

Abunai, a half-brother to several middle-distance winners, out of a mile Listed winner, was continually denied a clear run and is better than she was able to show. (op 11-1)

2329 KLNG.COM H'CAP 5f 10y

7:30 (7:33) (Class 4) (0-85,85) 3-Y-O **£7,772** (£2,312; £1,155; £577) **Stalls** High

Form RPR

4362 **1** **Phantom Whisper**[17] [1848] 3-9-5 **83** AlanMunro 7 94
(B R Millman) *bhd: stl plenty to do 2f out: swtchd lft to centre of crse and rapid hdwy over 1f out: r.o strly to ld ins last:hld on wl* **16/1**

0231 **2** *1 ½* **Loch Verdi**[4] [2190] 3-8-10 **74** 6ex MartinDwyer 4 79
(A M Balding) *mde most tl hdd ins last: kpt on wl to hold 2nd but no ch w wnr* **10/1**

110 **3** *shd* **Matuza (IRE)**[10] [2014] 3-9-1 **79** KerrinMcEvoy 6 84
(W R Muir) *in tch: hdwy over 2f out: pressed ldrs 1f out: kpt on ins last to press for 2nd but no ch w wnr* **9/1**

106 **4** *shd* **Makabul**[15] [1900] 3-9-1 **79** DarryllHolland 5 83
(B R Millman) *s.i.s: bhd: hdwy in centre of crse fr 2f out: disp 2nd ins last but no imp on wnr* **40/1**

4213 **5** *hd* **Mannikko (IRE)**[24] [1672] 3-8-13 **77** (b[1]) TedDurcan 13 80
(G Wragg) *chsd ldrs: rdn and outpcd 1/2-way: styd on again fr over 1f out: kpt on wl cl home* **7/1**[3]

0354 **6** *1* **Brunelleschi**[24] [1672] 3-8-13 **77** (v[1]) ChrisCatlin 1 76
(P L Gilligan) *in tch in centre crse: hdwy 2f out: pressed ldrs ins last: sn one pce* **66/1**

0153 **7** *2 ½* **Blue Aura (IRE)**[24] [1679] 3-8-13 **77** SteveDrowne 3 66
(R Charlton) *chsd ldrs: rdn 1/2-way: wknd ins fnl f* **12/1**

1441 **8** *¾* **Rochdale**[24] [1679] 3-9-6 **84** PhilipRobinson 12 70+
(M A Jarvis) *broke wl: stdd into mid-div: pushed along 1/2-way: nvr gng pce to rch ldrs but kpt on ins last* **11/4**[2]

2002 **9** *1* **Fisola (IRE)**[40] [1264] 3-8-11 **78** AdamKirby(3) 8 60
(C G Cox) *s.i.s: bhd: drvn and hdwy over 2f out: nvr gng pce to rch ldrs* **28/1**

2000 **10** *shd* **Brandywell Boy (IRE)**[17] [1848] 3-9-4 **82** (b[1]) TQuinn 14 64
(D J S Ffrench Davis) *pushed rt after 1f: bhd: mod prog fnl f* **50/1**

1205 **11** *1 ¾* **Rag Tag (IRE)**[280] [4857] 3-9-7 **85** (t) LPKeniry 10 60
(A M Balding) *pressed ldr: stl ev ch over 1f out: sn wknd* **100/1**

0101 **12** *nk* **Devine Dancer**[21] [1751] 3-9-0 **78** DaneO'Neill 2 52
(H Candy) *pressed ldr: stl ev ch over 1f out: sn wknd* **33/1**

0300 **13** *nk* **Marriage Value (IRE)**[17] [1843] 3-9-0 **78** ShaneKelly 11 51
(J A Osborne) *edgd rt after 1f: a outpcd* **66/1**

1360 **14** *3 ½* **Saxon Saint**[248] [5601] 3-8-12 **76** HayleyTurner 16 35
(M D I Usher) *hmpd on rails after 1f: a bhd* **66/1**

0004 **15** *3 ½* **Supercast (IRE)**[15] [1900] 3-9-0 **78** (p) JohnEgan 9 23
(J S Moore) *chsd ldrs to 1/2-way* **50/1**

0611 **16** *98* **Don't Tell Sue**[3] [2222] 3-8-13 **77** 6ex RyanMoore 15 —
(B W Hills) *rrd stalls: veered lft off crse and virtually p.u* **5/2**[1]

61.52 secs (0.42) **Going Correction** +0.125s/f (Good) 16 Ran SP% **118.6**

Speed ratings (Par 101):101,98,98,98,97 96,92,91,89,89 86,86,85,80,74 —

CSF £155.06 CT £1541.72 TOTE £21.40: £4.00, £2.20, £2.60, £10.40; EX 244.20.

Owner Mrs Tina Ann Dormer **Bred** R Lawson **Trained** Kentisbeare, Devon

FOCUS

A good three-year-old sprint handicap and the form looks sound. They were spread out across the track at the line, with the eventual winner widest of all and closer to the far-side rail than the stands' side.

Brandywell Boy(IRE) Official explanation: jockey said colt suffered interference early stages

Don't Tell Sue Official explanation: jockey said colt reared up and hit its head on stalls, resulting in it tailing off

2330 K&LNG CHALLENGE US H'CAP 1m 67y

8:00 (8:05) (Class 3) (0-90,88) 3-Y-O**£10,725** (£3,209; £1,604; £802; £399) **Stalls** High

Form RPR

120 **1** **La Mottie**[234] [5904] 3-9-7 **88** TPQueally 5 107
(J Noseda) *s.i.s: hld up in rr: stdy hdwy 3f out: trckd ldrs 2f out: led over 1f out: pushed clr ins last: comf* **33/1**

21 **2** *2 ½* **Queen's Best**[221] [6128] 3-8-9 **76** RobertWinston 8 90
(Sir Michael Stoute) *s.i.s: t.k.h: sn trcking ldrs: rdn to ld 2f out: hdd over 1f out: kpt on but sn no ch w wnr* **5/2**[2]

0315 **3** *1* **Cactus King**[30] [1505] 3-9-2 **83** JimmyFortune 12 94
(J H M Gosden) *led: styd alone stands side and rdn 3f out: hdd 2f out: styd on same pce* **9/4**[1]

3311 **4** *shd* **Days Of My Life (IRE)**[12] [1954] 3-9-0 **81** SteveDrowne 11 92
(R Charlton) *prom tl outpcd over 3f out: kpt on fr over 1f out and styd on fnl f: nt rch ldrs* **4/1**[3]

2215 **5** *4* **Scot Love (IRE)**[20] [1781] 3-9-0 **81** ShaneKelly 2 83
(J Noseda) *bhd: hdwy 3f out: styd on same pce fnl 2f* **7/1**

4212 **6** *hd* **Lunar Express (USA)**[36] [1337] 3-9-2 **83** AlanMunro 10 85
(W J Haggas) *chsd ldrs: n.m.r 2f out and n.d after* **12/1**

0133 **7** *3* **Celebration Song (IRE)**[26] [1617] 3-9-3 **84** TedDurcan 4 79
(W R Swinburn) *chsd ldrs: rdn 3f out: wknd fr 2f out* **20/1**

0155 **8** *1 ½* **Pommes Frites**[168] [6627] 3-8-12 **79** MartinDwyer 6 70
(W R Muir) *chsd ldrs: rdn over 3f out: wknd over 2f out* **50/1**

2044 **9** *1* **Fire Two**[27] [1596] 3-8-13 **80** (v[1]) ChrisCatlin 7 69
(M R Channon) *bhd: sme hdwy 3f out: sn rdn and btn* **40/1**

5200 **10** *hd* **Charlton**[14] [1924] 3-9-4 **85** IanMongan 9 73
(T G Mills) *rdn over 4f out: a in rr* **50/1**

1151 **11** *5* **Orchard Supreme**[14] [1924] 3-9-7 **88** RichardHughes 3 65
(R Hannon) *bhd: sme hdwy fr 3f out but nvr in contention and sn bhd again* **20/1**

1m 44.99s (-0.61) **Going Correction** +0.125s/f (Good) 11 Ran SP% **118.4**

Speed ratings (Par 103):108,105,104,104,100 100,97,95,94,94 89

CSF £110.48 CT £279.47 TOTE £48.20: £10.10, £1.50, £1.50; EX 119.40.

Owner Lordship Stud **Bred** Tom Wilson **Trained** Newmarket, Suffolk

FOCUS

A very good handicap for the grade run at a decent pace; the form looks above average and should work out well. They all raced towards the middle of the track in the straight, apart from Cactus King, who stayed stands' side.

NOTEBOOK

La Mottie was runner-up in a six-furlong nursery off a mark of 83 after winning her maiden, was then down the field in the Rockfel Stakes and has since left Ralph Beckett's yard. Upped in trip and returned to handicap company off the back of a 234-day break, she made a successful debut for her new trainer in good style, foiling some much stronger-fancied opposition. There appeared little fluke about this success and it would be no surprise to eventually see her returned to Pattern company in search of black type. (tchd 40-1)

Queen's Best ◆, a six-furlong maiden winner at Newmarket on the second of her two runs as a juvenile, looked to have been given a very fair mark by the Handicapper, especially as connections thought her good enough to be entered in the Coronation Stakes at Royal Ascot. She has, though, reportedly taken a long time to come to hand and, upped in trip for her first run in 221 days, she very much gave the impression this run will put her just right. Her lenient-looking handicap mark can be exploited next time. Official explanation: jockey said filly ran without a front shoe (op 2-1 tchd 15-8)

Cactus King was well backed throughout the day to improve on the form he showed in a seven-furlong handicap on soft ground at Newmarket on his reappearance. However, his rider elected to race alone against the stands'-side rail in the straight (the others raced mid track) and the gamble went astray. It is impossible to say just how much of a disadvantage he was at, if at all, but he must be given another given just how much confidence there was behind him in the market. (op 5-2 tchd 11-4 and 3-1 in a place)

Days Of My Life(IRE), chasing the hat-trick off a 7lb higher than when winning at Goodwood on his previous start, was trying a mile for the first time, but is bred to stay this trip and may not have failed through lack of stamina. (op 5-1)

Scot Love(IRE), dropped back in trip and racing on ground with 'firm' in the description for the first time, failed to produce his best. The pick of his form has come on Polytrack and he may be suited by a return to that surface. (op 11-1)

2331 KIRKPATRICK & LOCKHART NICHOLSON GRAHAM LLP H'CAP — 6f

8:30 (8:32) (Class 6) (0-65,65) 4-Y-O+ — **£3,238** (£963; £481; £240) Stalls High

Form — RPR

1540 **1** **Bens Georgie (IRE)**[20] [1774] 4-9-2 **60** ... DaneO'Neill 15 — 73
(D K Ivory) *stdd s: hld up rr: stdy hdwy over 2f out: led over 1f out: drvn clr fnl f: readily* **10/1**

0645 **2** *2* **Russian Rocket (IRE)**[5] [2182] 4-9-3 **61** ... HayleyTurner 11 — 68
(Mrs C A Dunnett) *chsd ldrs: led appr fnl 2f: sn hrd drvn: hdd over 1f out: styd on but no ch w wnr* **8/1**[3]

2003 **3** *½* **Louphole**[24] [1689] 4-9-5 **63** ... SebSanders 9 — 69
(P J Makin) *chsd ldrs: rdn and ev ch 2f out: kpt on same pce ins last* **9/2**[1]

5640 **4** *½* **Full Spate**[43] [1188] 11-9-4 **62** ... RyanMoore 2 — 66
(J M Bradley) *stdd s: bhd: hdwy ins fnl 2f: sn hrd drvn: kpt on fnl f but nvr gng pce to rch ldrs* **25/1**

3040 **5** *1* **Savile's Delight (IRE)**[15] [1878] 7-9-5 **63** ...(bt) RobertWinston 12 — 64
(R Brotherton) *chsd ldrs: rdn 1/2-way: kpt on fnl f but nvr gng pce to chal* **12/1**

5013 **6** *shd* **Drumming Party (USA)**[25] [1645] 4-8-12 **59** ...(t) NeilChalmers(3) 16 — 60
(A M Balding) *bhd: hdwy over 2f out: rdn: hung lft fnl f and sn one pce* **7/1**[2]

0002 **7** *4* **Caustic Wit (IRE)**[4] [2207] 8-9-5 **63** ...(p) FergusSweeney 8 — 52
(M S Saunders) *chsd ldrs: rdn to chal over 2f out: wknd fnl f* **17/2**

0005 **8** *1* **Coranglais**[11] [1981] 6-8-12 **56** ...(b) SteveDrowne 13 — 42
(J M Bradley) *chsd ldrs: pushed along 1/2-way: wknd over 1f out* **8/1**[3]

1000 **9** *2½* **Mountain Pass (USA)**[42] [1211] 4-9-4 **62** ...(v) TedDurcan 14 — 40
(M J Wallace) *pressed ldrs: rdn over 3f out: wknd over 1f out* **25/1**

0050 **10** *1¼* **Chatshow (USA)**[15] [1878] 5-9-7 **65** ... ShaneKelly 4 — 39
(G F Bridgwater) *bhd: hdwy to press ldrs over 2f out: wknd wl over 1f out* **16/1**

1021 **11** *2½* **Blessed Place**[225] [6076] 6-9-2 **60** ...(t) TQuinn 10 — 27
(D J S Ffrench Davis) *led tl hdd over 2f out: sn btn* **16/1**

0066 **12** *¾* **Hard To Catch (IRE)**[4] [2207] 8-8-9 **60** ...(b) JamesMillman(7) 7 — 25
(D K Ivory) *chsd ldrs over 3f* **20/1**

3403 **13** *shd* **Hollow Jo**[25] [1644] 6-9-7 **65** ... EddieAhern 5 — 29
(J R Jenkins) *chsd ldrs: hrd rdn over 2f out: sn wknd* **10/1**

0100 **14** *nk* **Perfect Solution (IRE)**[35] [1383] 4-9-2 **60** ... KerrinMcEvoy 6 — 24
(J A R Toller) *a outpcd* **20/1**

1m 14.38s (0.71) **Going Correction** +0.125s/f (Good) — **14** Ran SP% **118.3**
Speed ratings (Par 101):100,97,96,96,94 94,89,87,84,82 79,78,78,78
CSF £81.33 CT £423.81 TOTE £7.50: £2.70, £3.70, £2.00; EX 105.20.
Owner Marcoe Electrical **Bred** Mrs Maureen Barbara Walsh **Trained** Radlett, Herts

FOCUS
A modest sprint handicap in which the form looks sound but ordinary. Despite the runners again coming towards the middle in the straight, those drawn high were at an advantage if the bare result is anything to go by, as eight of the first nine home were drawn eight or above.
Chatshow(USA) Official explanation: jockey said gelding lost its action
Hollow Jo Official explanation: jockey said gelding was unsuited by the good to firm ground, which he felt was loose on top

2332 K&LNG H'CAP — 1m 3f 135y

9:00 (9:02) (Class 5) (0-75,75) 3-Y-O — **£5,505** (£1,637; £818; £408) Stalls Low

Form — RPR

0060 **1** **Wannabe Posh (IRE)**[35] [1375] 3-8-7 **61** ... EddieAhern 1 — 72+
(J L Dunlop) *trckd ldrs: chal over 2f out: led wl over 1f out: pushed out ins last: readily* **9/1**

0104 **2** *1¾* **Risk Runner (IRE)**[15] [1881] 3-9-4 **72** ...(v) JDSmith 3 — 79
(A King) *t.k.h: hld up in rr: hdwy 4f out to chal ins fnl 3f: stl ev ch over 1f out: chsd wnr ins last but a hld* **14/1**

4060 **3** *1¼* **Urban Tiger (GER)**[31] [1476] 3-9-4 **72** ... TedDurcan 2 — 77
(A King) *bhd: hdwy 5f out: slt ld 2f out: hdd wl over 1f out: wknd ins last* **25/1**

0511 **4** *1¾* **La Via Ferrata (IRE)**[117] [349] 3-8-2 **59** ... NelsonDeSouza(3) 9 — 61
(P F I Cole) *bhd: hdwy 4f out: pushed along fr 3f out: styd on ins last and gng on cl home but nvr gng pce to rch ldrs* **20/1**

0553 **5** *shd* **Rajaall**[36] [1356] 3-9-6 **74** ... ChrisCatlin 5 — 76
(M R Channon) *chsd ldrs: rdn and slt ld 3f out: hdd 2f out: wknd over 1f out* **16/1**

0041 **6** *3* **Rahy's Crown (USA)**[50] [1052] 3-8-9 **63** ... RichardHughes 7 — 60
(R Hannon) *chsd ldrs: rdn 3f out: wknd ins fnl 2f* **11/2**[2]

022 **7** *1¼* **Brabazon (IRE)**[22] [1740] 3-9-4 **72** ... SteveDrowne 12 — 67
(R Charlton) *chsd ldrs: rdn 3f out: wknd over 2f out* **9/4**[1]

0036 **8** *¾* **Ritsi**[34] [1424] 3-9-2 **70** ...(t) RyanMoore 6 — 64
(Mrs A J Perrett) *bhd: kpt on fr over 2f out but nvr nr ldrs* **17/2**

006 **9** *1½* **Kaladin**[229] [5993] 3-8-6 **60** ... RichardMullen 4 — 52
(G L Moore) *t.k.h: in tch: rdn 3 out: hung bdly lft fr 2f out and sn bfn* **50/1**

2050 **10** *4* **Myrtle Bay (IRE)**[18] [1837] 3-9-5 **73** ... SebSanders 10 — 58
(K R Burke) *bhd: hdwy fr 4f out: nvr in contention* **16/1**

3000 **11** *shd* **Time Out (IRE)**[17] [1841] 3-9-5 **73** ... LPKeniry 11 — 58
(A M Balding) *t.k.h: stdd rr: hdwy 3f out: sn rdn and wknd* **33/1**

006 **12** *1¾* **Colinette**[19] [1797] 3-8-9 **63** ... DaneO'Neill 14 — 45
(H Candy) *bhd: hdwy 5f out: wknd 3f out* **20/1**

0031 **13** *3½* **Oporto (UAE)**[22] [1747] 3-9-2 **70** ... PhilipRobinson 8 — 47
(M A Jarvis) *led tl hdd 3f out: sn wknd* **8/1**[3]

0540 **14** *1¼* **Basiliko (USA)**[192] [6425] 3-9-7 **75** ... AlanMunro 13 — 50
(P W Chapple-Hyam) *chsd ldrs over a m* **16/1**

005 **15** *nk* **Karshaan (FR)**[230] [5970] 3-9-4 **72** ... JimCrowley 15 — 46
(P Winkworth) *bhd most of way* **33/1**

2m 31.71s (1.61) **Going Correction** +0.125s/f (Good) — **15** Ran SP% **123.3**
Speed ratings (Par 99):99,97,97,95,95 93,92,92,91,88 88,87,85,84,84
CSF £119.65 CT £3050.79 TOTE £9.20: £3.00, £3.80, £3.60; EX 257.60 Place 6 £743.58, Place 5 £246.75.
Owner Nicholas Cooper **Bred** Vizcaya Ag **Trained** Arundel, W Sussex

FOCUS
Just a modest handicap but solid enough rated through the fifth.
Wannabe Posh(IRE) Official explanation: trainer's rep said, regarding the improved form shown, the filly had been hampered on her last run at Bath and may have benefited from today's good to firm ground
Brabazon(IRE) Official explanation: jockey said colt was unsuited by the good to firm ground, which he felt was softer than reported
T/Plt: £573.80 to a £1 stake. Pool: £71,885.70. 91.45 winning tickets. T/Qpdt: £170.20 to a £1 stake. Pool: £5,382.50. 23.40 winning tickets. ST

2333 - 2339a (Foreign Racing) - See Raceform Interactive

1937 KEMPTON (A.W) (R-H)

Wednesday, June 7

OFFICIAL GOING: Standard
Wind: Virtually nil.

2340 V-DRINKS.COM TRANSYLVANIAN RED VODKA H'CAP — 5f (P)

7:00 (7:00) (Class 5) (0-75,80) 3-Y-O+ — **£3,238** (£963; £481; £240) Stalls High

Form — RPR

1332 **1** **Spirit Of Coniston**[5] [2187] 3-8-4 **57** ow2 ...(b) RobbieFitzpatrick 6 — 64
(Peter Grayson) *lw: trckd ldr: chal fnl f and drvn to ld fnl 50yds: kpt on wl* **10/3**[2]

2450 **2** *¾* **Summer Recluse (USA)**[25] [1686] 7-9-7 **67** ...(t) RyanMoore 5 — 74
(J M Bradley) *chsd ldrs: hdwy over 1f out: squeezed through ins last: stying on whn rdr dropped whip fnl 100yds: nt rch wnr* **11/2**

0340 **3** *hd* **Pride Of Joy**[36] [1378] 3-9-0 **67** ... DaneO'Neill 7 — 70
(D K Ivory) *lw: sn led: rdn 2f out: hdd fnl 50 yds: no ex and lost 2nd last strides* **14/1**

1110 **4** *hd* **Cashel Mead**[5] [2189] 6-10-1 **80** 6ex ... TravisBlock(5) 1 — 86
(J L Spearing) *stdd s: hld up in rr: hdwy over 1f out: kpt on wl fnl f and gng on cl home but nt rch ldrs* **4/1**[3]

1400 **5** *1¼* **Mambazo**[35] [1414] 4-9-8 **71** ...(e) AdamKirby(3) 4 — 72
(S C Williams) *lw: in tch: rdn over 2f out: styd on fnl f but nvr gng pce to rch ldrs* **8/1**

1263 **6** *1* **After The Show**[35] [1399] 5-9-13 **73** ... ChrisCatlin 2 — 70
(Rae Guest) *outpcd: drvn along 1/2-way: kpt on fnl f but nvr in contention* **9/4**[1]

0-04 **7** *5* **Canary Island (IRE)**[241] [5754] 4-9-13 **73** ... ShaneKelly 3 — 52
(J M Bradley) *a outpcd* **20/1**

60.82 secs (0.42) **Going Correction** +0.075s/f (Slow)
WFA 3 from 4yo+ 7lb — **7** Ran SP% **111.8**
Speed ratings (Par 103):99,97,97,97,95 93,85
CSF £20.76 TOTE £2.60: £1.30, £4.10; EX 16.60.
Owner Richard Teatum **Bred** Green Square Racing **Trained** Formby, Lancs

FOCUS
A strange race with those off the pace early on finding themselves unable to get into it. The form looks straightforward rated around the first two.
Canary Island(IRE) Official explanation: jockey said gelding hung left

2341 PEMBERTON GREENISH REDFERN H'CAP — 1m 2f (P)

7:28 (7:28) (Class 3) (0-95,95) 4-Y-O+
£7,790 (£2,332; £1,166; £583; £291; £146) Stalls High

Form — RPR

1000 **1** **Fairmile**[28] [1585] 4-8-9 **86** ... AdamKirby(3) 8 — 100+
(W R Swinburn) *hld up rr but in tch: rapid hdwy on outside over 1f out to ld fnl 75yds: readily* **16/1**

2510 **2** *1¼* **Tabadul (IRE)**[25] [1678] 5-9-7 **95** ... RHills 9 — 107
(E A L Dunlop) *lw: chsd ldr: led 2f out: sn hrd drvn: hdd and outpcd fnl 75yds* **5/1**[1]

2615 **3** *¾* **Obrigado (USA)**[53] [1017] 6-9-0 **88** ... DarryllHolland 12 — 98+
(W J Haggas) *swtg: t.k.h early: trckd ldrs: hday on rails and n.m.r over 1f out: kpt on u.p ins last but no imp cl home* **5/1**[1]

1232 **4** *hd* **Nice Tune**[28] [1585] 4-8-12 **86** ... RyanMoore 3 — 96
(C E Brittain) *chsd ldrs: wnt 2nd 2f out: sn rdn: kpt on same pce ins last* **11/2**[2]

3026 **5** *1* **Great Plains**[25] [1678] 4-9-2 **90** ... RichardHughes 5 — 98
(Mrs A J Perrett) *lw: hld up rr but in tch: stdy hdwa fr 5f out: to trck ldrs 3f out: rdn 2f out: no ex ins last* **5/1**[1]

234 **6** *4* **Young Mick**[32] [1484] 4-9-2 **90** ...(v) JimmyQuinn 4 — 91
(G G Margarson) *chsd ldrs: rdn over 2f out: wknd over 1f out* **6/1**[3]

1506 **7** *1¼* **Zamboozle (IRE)**[32] [1478] 4-8-4 **78** ... JohnEgan 7 — 76
(D R C Elsworth) *lw: rrd stalls: bhd: pushed along: drvn along 3f out: kpt on fr over 1f out but nvr in contention* **9/1**

1054 **8** *hd* **Glad Big (GER)**[14] [1938] 4-8-7 **81** ... ShaneKelly 10 — 79
(J A Osborne) *lw: bhd: rdn and sme hdwy 3f out: nvr in contention* **16/1**

0006 **9** *3* **Atlantic Quest (USA)**[25] [1692] 7-8-4 **85** ...(p) TolleyDean(7) 1 — 77
(R A Harris) *s.i.s: bhd most of way* **40/1**

6060 **10** *1¾* **King's Thought**[64] [865] 7-8-11 **85** ... IanMongan 6 — 74
(S Gollings) *b.bkwd: led tl hdd 2f out: sn wknd* **40/1**

100 **11** *5* **Barry Island**[46] [1133] 7-8-3 **77** ... JamieMackay 13 — 56
(D R C Elsworth) *in tch early: dropped rr 1/2-ways and nvr in contention after* **20/1**

0000 **12** *3½* **Lord Mayor**[11] [2012] 5-8-11 **85** ... EddieAhern 11 — 58
(R M H Cowell) *chsd ldrs tl wknd ins fnl 3f* **33/1**

010P **13** *3½* **El Tiger (GER)**[21] [1779] 5-8-12 **86** ...(p) TPQueally 2 — 52
(B J Curley) *swtg: rr thrght and nvr in contention* **33/1**

2m 7.40s (-1.60) **Going Correction** +0.075s/f (Slow) — **13** Ran SP% **117.0**
Speed ratings (Par 107):109,108,107,107,106 103,102,102,99,98 94,91,88
CSF £87.70 CT £465.43 TOTE £26.40: £6.00, £2.60, £2.00; EX 235.20.
Owner Mrs P W Harris **Bred** Pendley Farm **Trained** Aldbury, Herts

FOCUS
A good, competitive handicap likely to produce winners and rated fairly positively.

NOTEBOOK

Fairmile, who shaped a little better at Chester last time, was down 2lb and the switch to this forgiving surface enabled him to return to winning ways, finding a good change of gear late on to mow down Tabadul and maintain his 100% record with Kirby. Equally effective at 12 furlongs, he may yet be capable of further improvement and it is obviously worth bearing in mind his excellent relationship with the jockey. (op 20-1)

Tabadul(IRE) bolted up here on his reappearance, but was not seen to best effect when favourite for a handicap at Newmarket last time. The return to this surface brought about a better effort and he looked the likely winner at one point, but the winner soon cut him down. This was a fine effort off what was an 11lb higher mark than when winning on his seasonal debut. (op 11-2 tchd 6-1)

Obrigado(USA) has been running well over this course and distance and he may have been able to throw down more of a challenge had he not raced so keenly in the early stages, as it appeared to take its toll in the closing stages. (op 4-1 tchd 11-2)

Nice Tune is a tough and consistent sort who is rarely beaten far, but she continues to give the impression this sort of mark will continue to prevent her from winning. (op 5-1)

Great Plains was undoubtedly the most interesting runner on show, having run well in finishing ahead of Tabadul at Newmarket on his reappearance despite looking in need of the outing. A big, scopey sort he came through to have every chance in the straight, but having raced keenly early on he was unable to see his race out as strongly as hoped. He gave the impression he would be better suited to turf racing where he is more likely to get a true gallop and he deserves another chance. (op 9-2)

Young Mick, who was said to look dull in his coat before the race, has had a cracking year of it, winning six times, but this was not such a great effort and he may be in line for a break now. (tchd 13-2)

Zamboozle(IRE) Official explanation: jockey said colt reared on leaving stalls

King's Thought looked to be warm before the race. (tchd 50-1)

Barry Island was said to look dull in his coat prior to the off. (op 25-1)

2342 V REDVODKA TRANSYLVANIAN SUNSET COCKTAIL EBF NOVICE STKS — 6f (P)

7:56 (7:57) (Class 4) 2-Y-0 — **£5,181** (£1,541; £770; £384) **Stalls** High

Form				RPR
213	1		**Karayel (IRE)**[23] [1737] 2-9-2 ... RichardHughes 4 (R Hannon) *lw: trckd ldrs: drvn wnt 2nd ins last:qckd to ld fnl 75yds: readily* **7/2**[2]	88
	2	½	**Minaash (USA)** 2-8-12 ... ShaneKelly 2 (J Noseda) *w'like: chsd ldrs: led over 1f out: hrd drvn ins last: hdd and outpcd fnl 75yds* **6/1**	83
	3	5	**Dubai Magic (USA)** 2-8-12 ... SebSanders 6 (C E Brittain) *w'like: scope: lengthy: s.i.s: bhd: rdn over 2f out: hdwy on outside over 1f out: styd on wl to take 3rd last half f: nt tr* **5/1**[3]	68+
51	4	1	**Yerevan**[6] [2166] 2-9-0 ... ChrisCatlin 5 (M R Channon) *lw: disp ld tl slt advantage after 2f: rdn 3f out: hdd over 1f out and sn wknd* **11/4**[1]	67
015	5	1 ¾	**Down The Well (IRE)**[19] [1831] 2-8-11 ... TPQueally 8 (J A Osborne) *slt led for 2f: styd pressing ldr tl over 2f out: sn btn* **7/1**	58
0	6	1 ¼	**Global Traffic**[81] [663] 2-8-12 ... JosedeSouza 7 (P F I Cole) *swtg: bhd: n.m.r 3f out: sn drvn along: mod hdwy fr over 1f out* **33/1**	56
2510	7	1	**Camissa**[19] [1831] 2-8-11 ... DaneO'Neill 3 (D K Ivory) *outpcd most of way* **7/1**	52
53	8	5	**Aggresive**[15] [1912] 2-8-12 ... JohnEgan 1 (Ernst Oertel) *bhd: hdwy and wd bnd 3f out: sn wknd* **33/1**	38

1m 14.19s (0.49) **Going Correction** +0.075s/f (Slow) 8 Ran SP% **110.7**
Speed ratings (Par 95):99,98,91,90,88 86,85,78
CSF £23.06 TOTE £4.90: £1.50, £2.00, £2.70; EX 35.00.
Owner Kemal Kurt **Bred** Stall A And R **Trained** East Everleigh, Wilts

FOCUS

A good little novice event where the experience of Karayel won him the day and the form looks decent.

NOTEBOOK

Karayel(IRE) found things happening a little too quickly behind the potentially smart Hoh Mike at Windsor last month and this rise in distance looked certain to suit. Never far away, he found a good late burst to deny newcomer Minaash and looks a progressive sort who should do well in nurseries. (op 5-1 tchd 11-2 and 10-3 and 6-1 in places)

Minaash(USA), an athletic sort who holds an entry in the Group 2 Railway Stakes at the Curragh next month, is clearly held in high regard by connections and this was a highly satisfactory debut, simply being beaten by a more experienced rival. He should have little trouble shedding his maiden status before going on to better things. (op 7-2)

Dubai Magic(USA), related to several smart performers and on his toes in the paddock prior to the race, comes from a stable whose juveniles often improve a good deal for the run and he lacked the pace of the front pair. There should be significant improvement to come once tackling seven furlongs and he is worth watching out for in future. (op 6-1)

Yerevan, a very easy winner at Nottingham last week, found this tougher and failed to see her race out having taken them into the final quarter mile. This was disappointing, but she deserves another chance back on turf. (op 2-1)

Down The Well(IRE) ran as well as could have been expected and will find easier opportunities in nurseries. (op 10-1)

Aggresive Official explanation: jockey said gelding had no more to give

2343 V REDVODKA SPIRIT OF TRANSYLVANIA MAIDEN STKS — 7f (P)

8:24 (8:25) (Class 5) 3-Y-0+ — **£3,238** (£963; £481; £240) **Stalls** High

Form				RPR
2	1		**Third Set (IRE)**[18] [1844] 3-9-3 ... SteveDrowne 4 (R Charlton) *lw: t.k.h early: hld up in rr: plenty to do over 2f out: rapid hdwy ins fnl quarter m: led last half f: sn in command* **5/1**[2]	81+
32	2	1 ¼	**Mumaathel (IRE)**[32] [1476] 3-9-3 ... RHills 14 (M P Tregoning) *lw: led: rdn over 1f out: hdd and outpcd last half f* **5/6**[1]	78+
53	3	2 ½	**Local Spirit (USA)**[41] [1254] 3-8-12 ... RyanMoore 1 (C E Brittain) *bhd: hdwy over 3f out: chsd ldrs 2f out: styd on to take 3rd fnl f but nvr gng pce to chal* **14/1**	67
0	4	hd	**Imperial Harry**[229] [6013] 3-9-0 ... EdwardCreighton(3) 11 (M R Channon) *chsd ldrs: rdn over 2f out: styd on same pce fnl f* **25/1**	71
4	5	3	**Marbaa (IRE)**[25] [1674] 3-9-3 ... ShaneKelly 7 (E A L Dunlop) *chsd ldrs: pushed along over 2f out and styd on same pce* **8/1**	63
5	6	shd	**Dixie Storm (USA)**[49] [1087] 3-9-3 ... RichardHughes 9 (A M Balding) *lw: chsd ldrs: shkn up 2f out: fdd fnl f* **6/1**[3]	63
0	7	½	**Louise Dupin (IRE)**[26] [1650] 3-8-12 ... SebSanders 6 (R M Beckett) *chsd ldrs: wd bnd 3f out: hung lft over 2f out and n.d after* **50/1**	57
0	8	3 ½	**Humble Gift**[274] [5032] 3-8-12 ... IanMongan 12 (Mrs L J Mongan) *chsd ldr to 2f out: wknd over 1f out* **100/1**	48
	9	1 ¼	**Ticking** 3-9-3 ... ChrisCatlin 5 (T Keddy) *w'like: b.bkwd: str: s.i.s: bhd: kpt on fnl 2f but nvr in contntion* **66/1**	49+
	10	hd	**Blushing Light (USA)** 3-9-3 ... EddieAhern 2 (M A Magnusson) *w'like: b.bkwd: prom early but sn bhd* **25/1**	49+
	11	2 ½	**Seal Of Hope** 3-9-0 ... NelsonDeSouza(3) 8 (M P Tregoning) *w'like: b.bkwd: nvr bttr than mid-div* **50/1**	42
	12	nk	**Fluted Crystal** 3-8-12 ... DaneO'Neill 3 (H Candy) *slowly away: a in rr* **25/1**	36
	13	hd	**Wheelavit (IRE)** 3-9-3 ... GeorgeBaker 10 (B G Powell) *w'like: bkwd: s.i.s: hday to chse ldrs 1/2-way: wknd over 2f out* **66/1**	41
	14	1 ½	**Pronto Vende (IRE)** 3-9-0 ... AdamKirby(3) 13 (G A Butler) *rangy: chsd ldrs: wknd ins fnl 3f* **50/1**	37

1m 27.26s (0.46) **Going Correction** +0.075s/f (Slow) 14 Ran SP% **124.7**
Speed ratings (Par 103):100,98,95,95,92 91,91,87,85,85 82,82,82,80
CSF £9.27 TOTE £7.00: £2.30, £1.10, £4.00; EX 16.00.
Owner John Livock Bloodstock Limited **Bred** A Stroud And J Hanly **Trained** Beckhampton, Wilts

FOCUS

Just a fair maiden, but Third Set ran out a tidy winner. The form is rated through the runner-up but the third and fourth suggest it is not totally solid.

Louise Dupin(IRE) Official explanation: jockey said filly hung left

2344 PROVINCIAL LONDON MILE H'CAP (QUALIFIER) — 1m (P)

8:52 (8:54) (Class 4) (0-80,79) 3-Y-0 — **£5,699** (£1,695; £847; £423) **Stalls** High

Form				RPR
1110	1		**Royal Amnesty**[18] [1841] 3-9-2 **74** ... OscarUrbina 7 (G C H Chung) *rr but in tch: rapid hdwy fr 2f out to ld appr fnl f: hld on wl whn strly chal cl home* **9/2**[3]	80
0045	2	¾	**Mujood**[27] [1615] 3-9-5 **77** ... StephenCarson 4 (R F Johnson Houghton) *lw: chsd ldrs tl rdn and outpcd over 2f out: rallied and r.o strly fnl f: fin wl but nt rch wnr* **14/1**	81
2413	3	shd	**Illustrious Blue**[13] [1954] 3-9-7 **79** ... TPQueally 8 (J A Osborne) *s.i.s: rr: hdwy on outside over 2f out: r.o strly u.p fnl f: gng on cl home* **5/1**	83
3011	4	hd	**Punjabi**[6] [2171] 3-8-10 **68** 6ex ... J-PGuillambert 9 (Mrs G S Rees) *in tch: hdwy whn n.m.r over 2f out: str run ins fnl f: fin wl* **7/2**[1]	73+
6463	5	3 ½	**Cindertrack**[7] [2142] 3-8-12 **70** ... ShaneKelly 2 (J A Osborne) *led: rdn over 2f out and styd on wl to hold narrow advantage tl hdd appr fnl f: wknd ins last* **9/1**	65
3020	6	2	**Arabian Sea (IRE)**[18] [1841] 3-9-6 **78** ...(b[1]) RyanMoore 3 (C E Brittain) *lw: chsd ldr: str chal fr 3f out tl ins fnl 2f: wkng whn n.m.r sn after* **8/1**	69
13	7	½	**Wagtail**[35] [1419] 3-9-1 **73** ... SteveDrowne 5 (E A L Dunlop) *chsd ldrs to 2f out* **4/1**[2]	63
0400	8	9	**Lady Cree (IRE)**[267] [5209] 3-9-4 **76** ... RichardHughes 10 (W R Muir) *b.bkwd: bhd: nvr bttr than mid-div* **25/1**	45
000	9	nk	**Always Turn Left (IRE)**[272] [5071] 3-8-2 **60** oh5 ... DavidKinsella 1 (H S Howe) *a bhd* **33/1**	28
0053	10	13	**Local Fancy**[9] [2087] 3-9-3 **75** ... AlanMunro 6 (J M P Eustace) *in tch: pushed along 3f out: wknd over 2f out* **10/1**	13

1m 40.8s **Going Correction** +0.075s/f (Slow) 10 Ran SP% **120.7**
Speed ratings (Par 101):103,102,102,101,98 96,95,86,86,73
CSF £68.04 CT £333.47 TOTE £6.50: £1.60, £6.70, £2.00; EX 84.30.
Owner H C Chung **Bred** Brick Kiln Stud, Mrs L Hicks And Partners **Trained** Newmarket, Suffolk
■ Stewards' Enquiry : T P Queally four-day ban: used whip with excessive force and with whip arm above shoulder height (Jun 18-19,25-26)

FOCUS

A decent handicap run at a sound pace and the form looks solid.

Lady Cree(IRE) Official explanation: trainer said filly returned having swallowed sand

Local Fancy Official explanation: jockey said filly was unsuited by the surface

2345 WEATHERBYS PRINTING APPRENTICE H'CAP (ROUND 1) — 1m 4f (P)

9:20 (9:22) (Class 6) (0-65,65) 4-Y-0+ — **£2,388** (£705; £352) **Stalls** Centre

Form				RPR
0014	1		**Wild Pitch**[12] [1995] 5-9-9 **64** ...(b) MichaelJStainton 2 (P Mitchell) *stdd s: hld up in rr and confidently rdn: smooth hdwy on outside 2f out: led 1f out: sn clr: easily* **7/2**[1]	79+
0610	2	3 ½	**Birthday Star (IRE)**[46] [1138] 4-9-0 **60** ... AlanRutter(5) 5 (W J Musson) *hmpd on rails after 1f: sn chsng ldrs: wnt 2nd 2f out: drvn to chal over 1f out: kpt on but no ch w wnr sn after* **7/1**	66
0114	3	½	**Figaro's Quest (IRE)**[28] [1590] 4-9-3 **58** ...(b) DerekNolan 6 (P F I Cole) *sn led: hdd 1f out and sn outpcd* **9/2**[2]	63
6033	4	1 ½	**General Flumpa**[9] [2075] 5-8-9 **57** ... JonjoMilczarek(7) 13 (C F Wall) *hmpd on rails after 1f: bhd: hdwy 3f out: styd on fnl 2f but nvr gng pce to rch ldrs* **5/1**[3]	59
0000	5	1 ½	**Baileys Honour**[16] [1883] 4-8-0 **46** oh2 ... JosephWalsh(5) 10 (A G Newcombe) *hmpd on rails after 1f: bhd: rdn over 2f out: styd on u.p fnl f but nvr in contention* **20/1**	46
3526	6	1 ½	**Equilibria (USA)**[51] [891] 4-8-9 **50** ... RonanKeogh 11 (G L Moore) *chsd ldrs: rdn over 2f out: wknd over 1f out* **7/1**	48
6300	7	½	**Barnbrook Empire (IRE)**[36] [1392] 4-8-2 **46** oh4 ... TolleyDean(3) 8 (R A Harris) *chsd ldr to 2f out: sn btn* **25/1**	43
6000	8	nk	**Sharaab (USA)**[22] [4287] 5-8-7 **48** ...(t) DeanWilliams 3 (D E Cantillon) *in tch: rdn and effrt over 3f out but nvr in contention* **8/1**	44
5000	9	1 ¾	**Native American**[7] [2150] 4-9-9 **64** ... LiamJones 4 (T D McCarthy) *chsd ldrs: rdn 3f out: wknd 2f out* **33/1**	58
000/	10	6	**Mythological (USA)**[1746] [4356] 9-8-11 **55** ... RobbieMills(3) 14 (Luke Comer, Ire) *hmpd on rails after 1f: bhd most of way* **14/1**	39
0030	11	½	**Sorbiesharry (IRE)**[15] [1910] 7-8-0 **46** oh1 ... LukeMorris(5) 9 (Mrs N Macauley) *chsd ldrs tl wknd 3f out* **14/1**	29
0002	12	7	**Trysting Grove (IRE)**[64] [871] 5-8-2 **46** oh2 ... ThomasO'Brien(3) 7 (E G Bevan) *plld hrd: edgd rt after 1f: mid-div: rdn and effrt 4f out: sn wknd* **18/1**	18

2m 37.75s (0.85) **Going Correction** +0.075s/f (Slow) 12 Ran SP% **123.3**
Speed ratings (Par 101):100,97,97,96,95 94,94,93,92,88 88,83
CSF £28.68 CT £116.57 TOTE £5.20: £1.60, £3.20, £1.70 Place 6 £62.71, Place 5 £24.38.
Owner Mrs Julie Auletta **Bred** Wyck Hall Stud Ltd **Trained** Epsom, Surrey
■ Yenaled (14/1, vet's advice) was withdrawn. R4 applies, deduct 5p in the £.
■ Stewards' Enquiry : Derek Nolan four-day ban: careless riding (Jun 18-19,25-26)

FOCUS

A modest handicap won in great style by Wild Pitch and the form appears sound rated through the runner-up.

Baileys Honour Official explanation: jockey said filly was hampered early

Mythological(USA) Official explanation: trainer said gelding ran without tongue strap as it had come adrift and could not be re-fitted; jockey said gelding was hampered at start

Trysting Grove(IRE) Official explanation: trainer said mare was found to be in season post-race
T/Plt: £88.80 to a £1 stake. Pool: £50,329.70. 413.30 winning tickets. T/Qpdt: £10.30 to a £1 stake. Pool: £3,351.50. 240.40 winning tickets. ST

2315 LINGFIELD (L-H)

Wednesday, June 7

OFFICIAL GOING: Turf course - firm (good to firm in places); all-weather - standard

Wind: Virtually nil Weather: Sunny & fine

2346 FURLONGS & FAIRWAYS (S) STKS 5f (P)
1:50 (1:52) (Class 6) 2-Y-O **£2,388** (£705; £352) **Stalls** High

Form RPR

0415 **1** **Mrs Crossy (IRE)**[23] 1744 2-8-11 .... RichardHughes 7 60
(R Hannon) *hld up: prog fr 1/2-way: swtchd rt and r.o to chal 1f out: led ins fnl f: swished tail and drvn out* **9/2**[2]

054 **2** ½ **Splendidio**[6] 2179 2-8-6 .... ChrisCatlin 1 53
(M R Channon) *trckd ldrs: effrt 2f out: chal and upsides 1f out: nt qckn and jst hld last 100yds* **17/2**

5033 **3** 1 ¼ **Aggbag**[6] 2179 2-8-11 .... JamieSpencer 6 54
(M J Wallace) *chsd ldrs: rdn 2f out: nt qckn and outpcd over 1f out: styd on to take 3rd last stride* **7/2**[1]

5021 **4** *shd* **Baytown Paikea**[6] 2179 2-8-11 .... BrianReilly 2 53
(P S McEntee) *led for 1f: led again over 2f out and kicked on: hdd & wknd ins fnl f* **8/1**

3255 **5** *nk* **Diminuto**[36] 1379 2-8-6 .... HayleyTurner 3 47
(M D I Usher) *t.k.h: trckd ldrs: outpcd and nt qckn over 1f out: hanging but styd on ins fnl f* **7/1**[3]

5646 **6** 1 ¼ **All Talk**[23] 1744 2-8-7 ow1 .... DarryllHolland 9 44
(I A Wood) *trckd ldrs: rdn 2f out: wknd fnl f* **16/1**

0300 **7** 2 ½ **Piccolo Prezzo**[2] 2287 2-8-6 .... RyanMoore 8 34
(I A Wood) *outpcd and sn pushed along: nvr on terms* **12/1**

1054 **8** *hd* **Alittleriskie (IRE)**[7] 2145 2-8-11 .... LPKeniry 10 38
(J S Moore) *pushed up to ld after 1f: hdd over 2f out: wknd over 1f out* **25/1**

60 **9** 1 ¼ **Cyprus Rose**[6] 2178 2-8-6 .... JimmyQuinn 5 29
(V Smith) *sn restrained in last trio: nudged along briefly over 1f out: nvr nr ldrs: capable of bttr* **9/2**[2]

00 **10** 1 ½ **Gibsons**[36] 1372 2-8-11 .... RobertHavlin 4 28
(Mrs P N Dutfield) *s.v.s: a wl bhd* **50/1**

61.10 secs (1.32) **Going Correction** +0.05s/f (Slow) **10** Ran SP% **112.1**
Speed ratings (Par 91):91,90,88,88,87 85,81,81,79,76
CSF £40.71 TOTE £4.30: £1.90, £2.30, £1.70; EX 31.00 Trifecta £179.90 Pool: £438.54 - 1.73 winning units.The winner was bought in for 3,700gns. Aggbag was claimed by B.P.J Baugh for £6,000. Splendidio was claimed by Dean Ivory for £6,000.
Owner A C Pickford & N A Woodcock **Bred** Mrs C L Weld **Trained** East Everleigh, Wilts

FOCUS
A routine juvenile seller, with several of these having met each other before, and the form, limited by the sixth, will mean little outside this grade.

NOTEBOOK
Mrs Crossy(IRE), who had a couple of these rivals behind when making all at Kempton two starts back, confirmed the form despite utilising very contrasting tactics. She will continue to find life tough outside of this company, though when the nurseries start early next month that may provide her with a few more opportunities. (tchd 4-1)
Splendidio ran much better on this switch to Polytrack and reversed recent Yarmouth running with both Aggbag and Baytown Paikea. She had every chance and kept battling right to the line, so is well worth another go on this surface. (op 12-1)
Aggbag finally got the better of Baytown Paikea having finished behind her in his last two starts, but again gave the impression he ideally needs an extra furlong on a quick surface. (tchd 4-1)
Baytown Paikea was given a positive ride, but the attentions of Alittleriskie meant that she never had an easy time of it. She tried to nick a length or two out of her rivals off the final bend, but her earlier exertions must have taken their toll and she failed to see it out. (op 11-2)
Diminuto finished a length closer to Mrs Crossy than she did at Kempton on 7lb better terms, but she is not progressing and will need to find something even worse than this if she is to break her duck. (op 6-1)
Alittleriskie(IRE) was given a positive ride on this return to the minimum, but she got caught up in a speed duel with Baytown Paikea and she was the first of the pair to feel the pinch.
Cyprus Rose ◆, dropped into a seller for the first time in her third outing, broke well enough but was soon allowed to drift back through the field and only had the slow-starting Gibsons behind her for much of the way. Despite one crack of the whip soon after turning in, she did not receive the most vigorous of rides and it would be no surprise to see her do much better than this in due course. (op 4-1 tchd 5-1)
Gibsons Official explanation: jockey said gelding missed the break

2347 LADIES' EVENING SATURDAY JULY 22ND CLAIMING STKS 6f (P)
2:20 (2:22) (Class 6) 3-Y-O+ **£3,238** (£963; £481; £240) **Stalls** Low

Form RPR

0020 **1** **Mirasol Princess**[5] 2208 5-9-1 49 .... RyanMoore 3 60
(D K Ivory) *hld up wl in rr: effrt 2f out: stl only 8th 1f out: styd on strly on outer to ld fnl strides* **14/1**

1221 **2** ½ **Million Percent**[1] 2319 7-9-10 64 .... JamieSpencer 7 67
(K R Burke) *trckd ldrs: lost pl and trapped on ins 1/2-way: prog over 1f out: r.o to chal last 100yds: outpcd by wnr nr fin* **11/10**[1]

6030 **3** ½ **Cherokee Nation**[1] 2317 5-9-3 60 .... AdamKirby(3) 8 62
(P W D'Arcy) *lw: hld up in tch and gng wl: effrt 2f out: carried hd awkwardly over 1f out: styd on reluctantly ins fnl f* **11/2**[2]

5010 **4** ½ **Chantelle's Dream**[26] 1645 4-8-4 49 .... JamesDoyle(5) 5 49
(Ms J S Doyle) *snatched up and stmbld after 1f: trckd ldrs: effrt over 2f out: drvn to ld over 1f out: hdd & wknd fnl strides* **10/1**

0000 **5** 1 ¼ **Madrasee**[15] 1913 8-8-11 47 .... AmirQuinn(3) 2 50
(P G Murphy) *trckd ldrs: n.m.r on inner wl over 1f out: kpt on same pce fnl f* **25/1**

0000 **6** ¾ **Sergeant Lewis**[16] 1899 4-9-10 56 ....(bt) ShaneKelly 4 58
(R M Flower) *dwlt: hld up in last trio: sme prog 2f out: drvn and kpt on same pce fr over 1f out* **50/1**

000 **7** ½ **Pyramid**[20] 1794 4-9-8 48 .... BrianReilly 12 55
(P L Gilligan) *chsd ldr: drvn to ld over 2f out: hdd & wknd over 1f out* **66/1**

0002 **8** *hd* **Von Wessex**[2] 2288 4-9-0 58 .... RobertMiles 9 46
(W G M Turner) *prom: rdn 2f out: wknd fnl f* **14/1**

0000 **9** ½ **I Wish**[35] 1414 8-8-11 50 .... PaulFitzsimons 10 41
(Miss J R Tooth) *hld up in tch: rdn and no rspnse over 1f out: wknd* **25/1**

0005 **10** *hd* **Burhaan (IRE)**[5] 2211 4-9-6 60 ....(t) EddieAhern 6 50
(J R Boyle) *lw: hld up in last trio: shkn up over 2f out: no imp tl kpt on last 100yds* **12/1**

6643 **11** ¾ **Stagnite**[8] 2096 6-8-10 47 ....(b) KevinGhunowa(7) 11 45
(P A Blockley) *drvn to ld and set str pce: hdd over 2f out: wknd over 1f out* **9/1**[3]

06 **12** 16 **Apres Ski (IRE)**[7] 2138 3-8-13 .... DeanCorby(3) 1 4
(J W Hills) *bolted to post: a bhd: t.o fnl 2f* **50/1**

1m 13.3s (0.49) **Going Correction** +0.05s/f (Slow)
WFA 3 from 4yo+ 8lb **12** Ran SP% **116.2**
Speed ratings (Par 101):98,97,96,96,94 93,92,92,91,91 90,69
CSF £28.24 TOTE £18.60: £3.60, £1.10, £1.90; EX 40.20 Trifecta £104.40 Pool: £596.06 - 4.05 winning units.Million Percent was claimed by C. R. Dore for £10,000.
Owner Mrs D P Ivory **Bred** Bearstone Stud **Trained** Radlett, Herts
■ Stewards' Enquiry : Jamie Spencer caution: used whip with excessive frequency
Robert Miles two-day ban: careless riding (Jun 18-19)

FOCUS
A modest claimer and a rather messy contest in which a couple had valid excuses. The margins between the first four home demonstrate the quality of the contest and the form is anchored by the seventh.
Apres Ski(IRE) Official explanation: trainer said colt bolted to start

2348 GOLF AND GAMBLE AT LINGFIELD PARK H'CAP 1m (P)
2:50 (2:53) (Class 5) (0-70,70) 4-Y-O+ **£3,238** (£963; £481; £240) **Stalls** High

Form RPR

0002 **1** **Samuel Charles**[26] 1644 8-9-5 **68** .... RyanMoore 3 83
(C R Dore) *b.hind: trckd ldrs: effrt to ld over 1f out: sprinted clr fnl f* **7/2**[2]

2512 **2** 5 **Molem**[38] 1311 4-9-7 **70** ....(tp) JamieSpencer 11 73
(Lady Herries) *lw: led for 1f: trckd ldr: pushed into ld 2f out: hdd over 1f out: easily outpcd by wnr* **3/1**[1]

0235 **3** 1 ¼ **Naval Attache**[154] 42 4-8-2 **51** oh6 .... FrankieMcDonald 8 51
(B R Johnson) *t.k.h: trckd ldng pair: rdn 2f out: sn outpcd: plugged on* **20/1**

3425 **4** ½ **Island Rapture**[13] 1962 6-9-7 **70** .... EddieAhern 1 69
(J A R Toller) *trckd ldrs: prog 2f out: outpcd over 1f out: one pce after* **11/2**[3]

5300 **5** 1 ½ **Height Of Spirits**[12] 1996 4-8-8 **57** .... RobertMiles 10 53+
(T D McCarthy) *b: swtg: hld up in detached last: stl last over 2f out: nudged along and r.o fr over 1f out: hopeless task* **20/1**

6104 **6** ½ **Humility**[13] 1961 5-8-11 **60** .... ShaneKelly 6 54
(C A Cyzer) *lw: settled in midfield: effrt over 2f out: outpcd whn swtchd rt over 1f out: fdd* **14/1**

0005 **7** 1 **Elrafa Mujahid**[13] 1961 4-9-0 **63** ....(p) DarryllHolland 4 55
(Ernst Oertel) *chsd ldrs: rdn over 2f out: nt look keen and wl btn over 1f out* **11/1**

6506 **8** 1 ¾ **Piquet**[23] 1727 8-7-11 **51** oh10 .... MarcHalford(5) 5 39
(J J Bridger) *in tch: rdn 3f out: sn struggling and btn* **20/1**

060 **9** ½ **For Life (IRE)**[83] 654 4-8-8 **57** .... TPQueally 2 44
(A P Jarvis) *taken down early: led after 1f to 2f out: wknd rapidly fnl f* **33/1**

0600 **10** 1 ¼ **Elvina Hills (IRE)**[22] 1753 4-8-2 **51** oh1 .... JimmyQuinn 12 35
(P Mitchell) *hld up in last pair fr wd draw: brief effrt 2f out: sn wknd* **20/1**

0000 **11** 6 **Hey Presto**[25] 1673 6-8-6 **55** ....(p) PaulDoe 9 25
(R Rowe) *aggressively rdn to post: in tch: rdn over 3f out: sn btn* **20/1**

6356 **12** 1 ¾ **Mad**[30] 1537 5-8-3 **52** oh4 ow1 .... JohnEgan 7 18
(Ernst Oertel) *lw: nvr bttr than midfield: drvn in rr over 3f out: sn wknd* **13/2**

1m 38.78s (-0.65) **Going Correction** +0.05s/f (Slow) **12** Ran SP% **117.7**
Speed ratings (Par 103):105,100,98,98,96 96,95,93,93,91 85,84
CSF £12.33 CT £185.70 TOTE £4.80: £1.80, £1.50, £5.40; EX 16.10 Trifecta £382.50 Part won. Pool: £538.56 - 0.69 winning units..
Owner Chris Marsh **Bred** Sheikh Mohammed Obaid Al Maktoum **Trained** West Pinchbeck, Lincs

FOCUS
A decent handicap of its type run at a good pace. The winner was very impressive and although the placed horses were to form it may not prove that strong.
Height Of Spirits ◆ Official explanation: jockey said, regarding the running and riding, his orders were to drop the gelding out, and make his effort in home straight, adding that he felt the leaders went off too quickly and he was only running on through beaten horses; trainer said gelding had been held up in its race since winning a maiden over course and distance using such tactics
Mad Official explanation: jockey said mare had no more to give

2349 COME RACING AT LINGFIELD ON SATURDAY JUNE 10TH MAIDEN FILLIES' STKS (DIV I) 1m 2f
3:20 (3:23) (Class 5) 3-Y-O+ **£2,914** (£867; £433; £216) **Stalls** Low

Form RPR

43 **1** **And Again (USA)**[16] 1901 3-8-9 .... JamieSpencer 10 70
(J R Fanshawe) *trckd ldr: led 3f out: pushed along and in command ent fnl f: rdn out nr fin* **3/1**[2]

2 *nk* **Candle** 3-8-9 .... DaneO'Neill 7 70
(H Candy) *leggy: sn trckd ldrs: shkn up and effrt over 2f out: r.o fnl f to snatch 2nd nr fin* **16/1**

3 *shd* **Dawera (IRE)** 3-8-9 .... RyanMoore 11 73+
(Sir Michael Stoute) *w'like: b.bkwd: str: hld up in rr: sme prog fr 4f out: swtchd rt wl over 1f out : r.o wl fnl f: fin best of all* **6/1**[3]

44 **4** *shd* **Thumpers Dream**[12] 1994 3-8-9 .... EddieAhern 6 69
(H R A Cecil) *lw: trckd ldng pair: rdn over 2f out: styd on to cl fr over 1f out: a hld* **13/8**[1]

000 **5** 1 ¼ **In On The Act (IRE)**[8] 2118 3-8-9 .... JohnEgan 12 67
(Jamie Poulton) *prom: jnd wnr 3f out: sn rdn: stl upsides over 1f out: wknd ins fnl f* **16/1**

0 **6** 2 ½ **Muscari**[74] 720 4-9-8 .... TPQueally 14 62
(A P Jarvis) *t.k.h: hld up towards rr: sme prog 3f out: shkn up and one pce fnl 2f* **25/1**

7 *hd* **Izadore (IRE)** 3-8-9 .... ShaneKelly 2 62+
(E A L Dunlop) *leggy: dwlt: hld up in rr: sme prog fr 3f out: rn green but kpt on fnl f: nrst fin* **16/1**

5 **8** 2 **Dream Witness (FR)**[20] 1797 3-8-9 .... RichardHughes 13 58
(W R Muir) *w'like: led to 3f out: steadily wknd fnl 2f* **25/1**

35 **9** *hd* **Gates Of Eden (USA)**[304] 4194 3-8-9 .... KerrinMcEvoy 1 58
(M L W Bell) *hld up towards rr: shkn up 3f out: no real imp on ldrs* **7/1**

000 **10** 5 **Vinska (USA)**[249] 5611 3-8-7 53 ow1 .... DeanCorby(3) 9 49
(J W Hills) *chsd ldrs 10f: rdn 3f out: wknd 2f out* **50/1**

0 **11** 10 **Canvas (IRE)**[253] 5535 3-8-9 .... HayleyTurner 4 29
(Miss Z C Davison) *w'like: b.bkwd: nvr beyond midfield: wknd over 2f out* **66/1**

000 **12** 5 **Wild Lass**[37] 1351 5-9-8 38 .... RobbieFitzpatrick 8 20
(J C Fox) *t.k.h: hld up in rr: struggling fnl 3f* **100/1**

00 **13** *9* **Rockatorri**[13] 1955 3-8-9 ChrisCatlin 5 3
(M R Channon) *a wl in rr: struggling and detached fr 1/2-way* **66/1**

2m 12.37s (2.65) **Going Correction** -0.075s/f (Good)
WFA 3 from 4yo+ 13lb **13** Ran SP% **121.2**
Speed ratings (Par 100):86,85,85,85,84 82,82,80,80,76 68,64,57
CSF £48.26 TOTE £4.00: £1.40, £5.00, £2.70; EX 58.50 TRIFECTA Not won..
Owner Prince A A Faisal **Bred** Nawara Stud **Trained** Newmarket, Suffolk

FOCUS
A race full of decent types, slightly devalued by a poor time in comparison with the second division. That said, the race should produce its share of winners.

2350 COME RACING AT LINGFIELD ON SATURDAY JUNE 10TH MAIDEN FILLIES' STKS (DIV II) 1m 2f
3:50 (3:53) (Class 5) 3-Y-O+ **£2,914** (£867; £433; £216) **Stalls** Low

Form RPR

2 **1** **Quenched**[13] 1955 3-8-9 RichardHughes 13 92+
(J H M Gosden) *lw: reluctant to enter stalls: w ldr: led after 3f: mde rest: shkn up and asserted over 1f out: r.o wl: promising* **10/3**[3]

06 **2** *3 ½* **Green Room (FR)**[47] 1114 3-8-9 IanMongan 7 76+
(J L Dunlop) *hld up in midfield: nt on terms fr 5f out: stdy prog 3f out: pushed along and styd on to take 2nd nr fnish: quite promising* **33/1**

62 **3** *½* **Fleeting Memory**[30] 1546 3-8-9 RyanMoore 9 75
(Sir Michael Stoute) *lw: led for 3f: w wnr and clr of rest fr 1/2-way: rdn over 2f out: btn over 1f out: lost 2nd nr fin* **5/4**[1]

3 **4** *6* **Jewaar (USA)**[20] 1797 3-8-9 RHills 5 63+
(M A Jarvis) *w'like: s.i.s: hld up: rn wd bnd after 3f: rapid prog whn rn v wd bnd over 3f out: fdd fnl 2f* **11/4**[2]

5 *hd* **Matinee Idol** 3-8-9 DaneO'Neill 2 63
(H Candy) *leggy: w'like: s.i.s: hld up in last pair: prog 1/2-way but nvr on terms: kpt on steadily fnl 2f: nvr nrr* **66/1**

02 **6** *1 ¼* **With Style**[279] 4896 3-8-9 JamieSpencer 8 61
(E A L Dunlop) *lw: prom: chsd clr ldng pair 1/2-way: no imp over 2f out: wknd over 1f out* **12/1**

0 **7** *¾* **Boreana**[44] 1191 3-8-9 AlanMunro 1 59+
(P W Chapple-Hyam) *settled midfield: outpcd fr 1/2-way: pushed along and no prog after* **33/1**

8 *1 ¼* **Suzuki (IRE)** 3-8-9 RobertHavlin 3 57
(H Morrison) *w'like: scope: a towards rr: nt on terms fr 1/2-way: no ch fnl 3f* **100/1**

0306 **9** *2 ½* **Luciferous (USA)**[36] 1394 4-9-5 44 (v) AmirQuinn(3) 6 53?
(P G Murphy) *s.i.s: a wl in rr: no ch fnl 3f* **100/1**

000 **10** *4* **Kilmeena Magic**[37] 1351 4-9-8 40 RobbieFitzpatrick 10 45?
(J C Fox) *a wl in rr: no ch fr 4f out* **100/1**

40 **11** *1* **Al Dhahab (USA)**[229] 6007 3-8-9 KerrinMcEvoy 4 43
(C E Brittain) *chsd ldng pair to 1/2-way: wknd 3f out* **25/1**

6 **12** *9* **Raffiene (IRE)**[14] 1940 3-8-9 ChrisCatlin 12 25
(E J O'Neill) *a wl in rr: wknd 3f out* **100/1**

2m 7.73s (-1.99) **Going Correction** -0.075s/f (Good)
WFA 3 from 4yo 13lb **12** Ran SP% **117.1**
Speed ratings (Par 100):104,101,100,96,95 94,94,93,91,88 87,80
CSF £107.83 TOTE £4.40: £1.40, £4.10, £1.20; EX 82.30 Trifecta £360.20 Pool: £751.01 - 1.48 winning units.
Owner K Abdulla **Bred** Juddmonte Farms Ltd **Trained** Newmarket, Suffolk

FOCUS
A race that looked to have less well-bred sorts than the first division. However, it did contain two confirmed progressive fillies, which the first division did not. The time was much quicker, and the winner is clearly held in some regard.
Jewaar(USA) Official explanation: jockey said filly failed to handle track
Luciferous(USA) Official explanation: jockey said filly failed to handle track
Al Dhahab(USA) Official explanation: jockey said filly lost its action

2351 LINGFIELD PARK LEISURE CLUB H'CAP 1m 2f
4:20 (4:20) (Class 5) (0-75,75) 4-Y-O+ **£4,533** (£1,348; £674; £336) **Stalls** Low

Form RPR

0510 **1** **Secretary General (IRE)**[12] 1995 5-9-6 74 EddieAhern 6 84
(P F I Cole) *lw: prom in chsng gp: wnt 2nd over 4f out: led 3f out: rdn and kpt on steadily fnl 2f* **7/2**[1]

1-0 **2** *2 ½* **Inch Lodge**[12] 1993 4-8-6 67 ChrisCavanagh(7) 9 72
(Miss D Mountain) *led and rn wd bnd after 3f: sn clr: rn wd bnd over 3f out and sn hdd: chsd wnr after: no imp over 1f out* **20/1**

U5U0 **3** *1 ¼* **Chapter (IRE)**[247] 5662 4-9-2 70 RichardHughes 4 73
(Mrs A L M King) *prom 3f: styd prom in chsng gp: prog to chse ldng pair over 2f out: sn rdn: kpt on same pce* **25/1**

0150 **4** *nk* **Garibaldi (GER)**[106] 478 4-9-1 69 LPKeniry 1 71
(D R C Elsworth) *lw: hld up in last pair: wl off the pce 1/2-way: prog 4f out but nt on terms: rdn and kpt on: nvr rchd ldrs* **13/2**[3]

6500 **5** *1 ½* **Love Always**[43] 1206 4-9-7 75 PatDobbs 2 75
(S Dow) *hld up in last: wl off the pce 4f out: sme prog over 2f out: reminder over 1f out: styd on: nvr nr ldrs* **33/1**

3401 **6** *hd* **Count Kristo**[26] 1651 4-9-4 75 AdamKirby(3) 3 74
(C G Cox) *settled in midfield: off the pce fr 1/2-way: rdn and effrt over 2f out: one pce and no imp ldrs* **7/2**[1]

000 **7** *3* **Factual Lad**[22] 1754 8-9-0 68 DaneO'Neill 5 62
(B R Millman) *led for 3f: chsd ldr to over 4f out: wknd 2f out* **20/1**

0450 **8** *½* **Our Teddy (IRE)**[241] 5759 6-8-12 73 KevinGhunowa(7) 7 66
(P A Blockley) *a towards rr: off the pce 1/2-way: rdn and no prog over 2f out* **9/1**

4431 **9** *1 ¾* **Lisathedaddy**[15] 1926 4-9-2 70 GeorgeBaker 8 59
(B G Powell) *hld up towards rr: off the pce 1/2-way: brief effrt 3f out: sn shkn up and no prog* **5/1**[2]

0000 **10** *7* **Azizam**[32] 1478 4-9-7 75 AlanMunro 11 51
(P W Chapple-Hyam) *hld up in midfield: off the pce 1/2-way: rdn and effrt over 3f out: sn wknd* **7/1**

2m 8.17s (-1.55) **Going Correction** -0.075s/f (Good) **10** Ran SP% **113.3**
Speed ratings (Par 103):103,101,100,99,98 98,96,95,94,88
CSF £77.54 CT £1495.10 TOTE £4.60: £1.60, £5.70, £6.40; EX 98.80 Trifecta £614.20 Pool: £986.22 - 1.14 winning units..
Owner The Blenheim Partnership **Bred** Mrs C L Weld **Trained** Whatcombe, Oxon

FOCUS
A fair handicap won by a horse that clearly loves fast ground with the third the best guide to the form.

2352 LINGFIELD PARK GOLF CLUB H'CAP 1m 3f 106y
4:50 (4:50) (Class 6) (0-60,60) 3-Y-O **£2,730** (£806; £403) **Stalls** High

Form RPR

4014 **1** **Bob's Your Uncle**[43] 1221 3-9-4 57 RyanMoore 7 64
(J G Portman) *hld up in midfield: prog on inner over 3f out: led over 2f out: clr fnl f: rdn out* **7/2**[1]

000 **2** *2* **Travolta**[46] 1139 3-8-13 55 AdamKirby(3) 4 59
(C G Cox) *lw: chsd ldr to over 4f out: styd prom: rdn over 2f out: chsd wnr over 1f out: no imp* **13/2**[3]

0060 **3** *1 ¼* **Million All Day (IRE)**[6] 2171 3-9-2 55 JohnEgan 15 57
(W R Muir) *hld up in midfield: effrt 3f out: rdn and styd on same pce fnl 2f : tk 3rd ins fnl f* **11/1**

5060 **4** *1 ½* **Zizou (IRE)**[38] 1314 3-8-6 50 MarcHalford(5) 6 50
(J J Bridger) *led: wd bnd 7f out: wd again bnd over 3f out: hdd over 2f out: fdd over 1f out* **16/1**

560 **5** *2 ½* **Plemont Bay**[93] 590 3-9-7 60 IanMongan 14 56+
(M L W Bell) *hld up towards rr: off the pce and shkn up 3f out: kpt on steadily: nvr rchd ldrs* **16/1**

000 **6** *1 ¼* **Meohmy**[19] 1823 3-9-2 55 ChrisCatlin 11 49
(M R Channon) *wl in rr: hrd rdn over 3f out: plugged on fr over 2f out: n.d* **20/1**

0000 **7** *nk* **King's College (USA)**[38] 1314 3-8-11 50 (b) TPQueally 16 43
(G L Moore) *dwlt: hld up: prog to join ldrs over 4f out: upsides 3f out: wknd 2f out* **25/1**

5001 **8** *3 ½* **Unasuming (IRE)**[26] 1652 3-9-1 54 JimmyQuinn 1 42
(J Pearce) *prom: rdn 3f out: steadily wknd* **9/2**[2]

0000 **9** *3* **It's Basil**[38] 1314 3-8-11 50 (b[1]) FergusSweeney 2 33
(R M Flower) *prom: chsd ldr over 4f out to over 3f out: sn wknd* **14/1**

0020 **10** *1 ½* **Lovely Hidenka (USA)**[26] 1652 3-9-1 54 KerrinMcEvoy 8 34
(C E Brittain) *a wl in rr: off the pce and struggling 3f out* **17/2**

11 *2* **Bu-Ali (USA)**[38] 1327 3-8-11 50 DaneO'Neill 13 27
(B W Duke) *dwlt and rousted along early: wl in rr: brief effrt 3f out: sn wknd* **33/1**

0050 **12** *1 ¾* **Sweet Boulangere**[26] 1638 3-9-6 59 RichardHughes 12 33
(R Hannon) *lw: wl in rr: rdn and modest prog 3f out: wknd 2f out* **16/1**

000 **13** *8* **Bold Pioneer (USA)**[116] 372 3-9-3 56 GeorgeBaker 9 18
(C P Morlock) *hld up: a wl in rr: bhd fnl 2f* **33/1**

0000 **14** *7* **Hope's Eternal**[46] 1140 3-9-5 58 (b[1]) EddieAhern 5 8
(J L Dunlop) *prom tl wknd u.p 4f out: t.o* **7/1**

2m 30.19s (0.27) **Going Correction** -0.075s/f (Good) **14** Ran SP% **123.9**
Speed ratings (Par 97):96,94,93,92,90 89,89,87,84,83 82,81,75,70
CSF £25.37 CT £233.21 TOTE £3.10: £1.60, £1.70, £3.20; EX 36.00 Trifecta £147.00 Part won. Pool: £207.06 - 0.10 winning units. Place 6 £26.94, Place 5 £15.42.
Owner A S B Portman **Bred** Wheelersland Stud **Trained** Compton, Berks

FOCUS
A very moderate race, with Zizou probably the horse to rate the race through.
Zizou(IRE) Official explanation: jockey said gelding hung right
Unasuming(IRE) Official explanation: jockey said filly never travelled
Sweet Boulangere Official explanation: jockey said filly lost its action
Hope's Eternal Official explanation: jockey said colt hung left and was unsuited by the firm (good to firm in places) ground

T/Jkpt: Not won. T/Plt: £55.70 to a £1 stake. Pool: £44,464.60. 582.20 winning tickets. T/Qpdt: £22.30 to a £1 stake. Pool: £2,714.70. 89.90 winning tickets. JN

2166 NOTTINGHAM (L-H)
Wednesday, June 7

OFFICIAL GOING: Good to firm (good in places)
Wind: Almost nil Weather: Warm sunshine giving way to cloud later on

2353 VISITNOTTINGHAM.COM H'CAP 6f 15y
2:10 (2:10) (Class 5) (0-75,74) 3-Y-O **£3,886** (£1,156; £577; £288) **Stalls** High

Form RPR

0300 **1** **Charlie Delta**[32] 1482 3-9-4 74 DanielTudhope(3) 5 83
(D Carroll) *chsd ldrs: rdn to ld over 1f out: r.o* **9/1**

210 **2** *3* **Mary Delaney (USA)**[43] 1208 3-9-1 68 TedDurcan 9 68
(M J Wallace) *chsd ldrs: hung lft over 3f out: rdn and swtchd lft over 1f out : styd on same pce fnl f* **7/2**[1]

1006 **3** *nk* **Night In (IRE)**[8] 2110 3-9-7 74 (t) KimTinkler 8 73
(N Tinkler) *w ldr tl led over 3f out: rdn and hdd over 1f out: no ex ins fnl f* **25/1**

4610 **4** *1 ¼* **Valentino Swing (IRE)**[43] 1208 3-9-0 72 TravisBlock(5) 10 67
(J L Spearing) *hld up: hdwy over 2f out: rdn and bmpd over 1f out: wknd ins fnl f* **13/2**[2]

0256 **5** *1* **Myths And Verses**[46] 1137 3-8-8 61 RobertWinston 6 53
(T D Easterby) *dwlt: rdn over 1f out: nvr nrr* **16/1**

5204 **6** *nk* **Imperial Gain (USA)**[35] 1411 3-9-5 72 SebSanders 11 71+
(W R Swinburn) *hld up: nt clr run over 2f out: swtchd lft and hdwy over 1f out: hmpd 1f out: nvr trbld ldrs* **7/2**[1]

0400 **7** *nk* **Ochre Bay**[25] 1679 3-9-0 74 RussellKennemore(7) 2 65
(R Hollinshead) *sn pushed along in rr: nvr nrr* **11/1**

5165 **8** *1* **Tilly's Dream**[10] 2049 3-9-2 69 RichardMullen 1 57
(G C H Chung) *chsd ldrs: rdn and hung lft over 1f out: sn wknd* **12/1**

0046 **9** *10* **Good Companion (IRE)**[26] 1642 3-8-9 62 TQuinn 4 20
(J L Dunlop) *mid-div: sn drvn along: hung lft and wknd over 3f out* **7/1**[3]

0450 **10** *1 ¾* **Lyrical Blues (IRE)**[65] 852 3-8-10 70 JamesMillman(7) 7 22
(B R Millman) *led: hdd over 3f out: sn rdn: wknd 2f out* **14/1**

005 **11** *¾* **Buckle And Hyde**[242] 5737 3-8-6 59 KDarley 3 9
(Mrs A L M King) *chsd ldrs: hung lft over 3f out: wknd over 2f out* **40/1**

1m 14.5s (-0.50) **Going Correction** -0.25s/f (Firm) **11** Ran SP% **115.1**
Speed ratings (Par 99):93,89,88,86,85 85,84,83,70,67 66
CSF £39.62 CT £767.05 TOTE £11.20: £2.60, £2.10, £6.00; EX 70.50.
Owner Mrs B Ramsden **Bred** P K Gardner **Trained** Warthill, N Yorks

FOCUS
Just a fair sprint handicap but a clear-cut winner and the form is quite sound rated through the placed horses.
Good Companion(IRE) Official explanation: jockey said filly never travelled

2354 EUROPEAN BREEDERS FUND MAIDEN FILLIES' STKS (DIV I) 5f 13y
2:40 (2:41) (Class 5) 2-Y-O **£4,210** (£1,252; £625; £312) **Stalls** High

Form RPR

034 **1** **Bridge It Jo**[15] 1922 2-9-0 NCallan 8 82+
(Miss J Feilden) *trckd ldrs: led and hung lft over 1f out: sn rdn: edgd rt ins fnl f: r.o: eased nr fin* **9/2**[2]

2 3/4 **Turkus Quercus (USA)** 2-9-0 TQuinn 10 77
(J L Dunlop) *s.i.s: sn chsng ldrs: rdn and hung lft fr over 1f out: styd on* **7/1**

6 3 3 1/2 **Colchium (IRE)**[31] 1514 2-9-0 SteveDrowne 9 65
(H Morrison) *mde most over 3f: wknd ins fnl f* **7/2**[1]

4 1 1/4 **So Shy (IRE)** 2-9-0 FrancisNorton 4 60
(Stef Liddiard) *s.i.s: outpcd: hdwy over 1f out: nt trble ldrs* **33/1**

5 nk **Retaliate** 2-9-0 SebSanders 1 59
(M Quinn) *s.s: outpcd: hung lft 1/2-way: styd on appr fnl f: nt trble ldrs* **14/1**

6 1/2 **Shreddy Shrimpster** 2-8-9 DerekNolan(5) 7 57
(M J Wallace) *prom: rdn and hung lft 1/2-way: sn wknd* **16/1**

7 3 1/2 **Proud** 2-9-0 RobertWinston 2 51+
(M L W Bell) *wnt lft s: outpcd* **11/2**[3]

8 1 1/4 **Zahour Al Yasmeen** 2-9-0 TonyCulhane 5 40
(M R Channon) *s.i.s: sn outpcd: rdn and hung lft fr 1/2-way* **13/2**

9 1 1/4 **Spinning Crystal (IRE)** 2-9-0 MichaelHills 6 36
(B W Hills) *chsd ldrs: hung lft and lost pl 4f out: sn bhd* **6/1**

0 10 10 **Vizionary**[51] 1046 2-9-0 MickyFenton 3 —
(Mrs P Sly) *w ldr to 1/2-way: sn rdn and wknd* **20/1**

61.39 secs (-0.41) **Going Correction** -0.25s/f (Firm) **10** Ran SP% **116.2**
Speed ratings (Par 90):93,91,86,84,83 82,77,75,73,57
CSF £35.94 TOTE £4.70: £1.30, £2.00, £1.80; EX 26.70.
Owner Mrs P Jenner **Bred** A Parker **Trained** Exning, Suffolk

FOCUS
Seven of the ten runners were making their debuts, but they were an unexceptional group on looks and an open betting market suggested there were no potential stars among them. The time was slower than the second division and helps set the level for the form.

NOTEBOOK
Bridge It Jo, the most experienced runner in the line-up, settled behind the front pair before coming through to win cosily. She had gone off too fast at Lingfield last time, and the more patient tactics suited her better. She will bypass the Queen Mary and instead take her chance in a Listed race at Newmarket over six furlongs. (tchd 5-1)
Turkus Quercus(USA), who is related to several decent winners, ran best of the debutantes. She chased the front three before running on to follow home the winner and looks sure to benefit from the experience. (tchd 6-1)
Colchium(IRE) was again keen but put up an improved effort on this second start. Her future is likely to be in nurseries after one more run. (op 11-2)
So Shy(IRE), from the family of Flower Girl and Farmost, missed the break and could not go the early gallop, but found her feet in the second half of the race and was keeping on steadily in the closing stages.
Retaliate caught the eye, running on late having missed the break, and this cheaply-bought half-sister to a juvenile winner should improve with this run under her belt. (tchd 16-1)
Shreddy Shrimpsterrelated to several multiple winners, showed some ability before hanging into the centre of the track when pressure was applied.
Proud, from the family of Barathea and Gossamer, was easy to back, missed the break and never figured. (tchd 5-1 and 6-1)

2355 EUROPEAN BREEDERS FUND MAIDEN FILLIES' STKS (DIV II) 5f 13y
3:10 (3:15) (Class 5) 2-Y-O **£4,210** (£1,252; £625; £312) **Stalls** High

Form RPR

1 **Princess Iris (IRE)** 2-9-0 RichardMullen 2 84+
(E J O'Neill) *mde virtually all: swtchd rt over 3f out: hung lft 1f out: r.o wl* **22/1**

33 2 3 **Isobel Rose (IRE)**[37] 1347 2-9-0 JimmyFortune 3 71
(E A L Dunlop) *s.i.s: hld up: swtchd rt and hdwy over 1f out: hung lft ins fnl f: nt rch wnr* **4/1**[2]

4 3 nk **Lorena Wood (USA)**[16] 1896 2-9-0 LDettori 8 70
(B J Meehan) *chsd ldrs: rdn and nt clr run 1f out: no ex* **6/5**[1]

022 4 1 3/4 **Frisky Talk (IRE)**[26] 1647 2-9-0 MichaelHills 1 64
(B W Hills) *hung lft thrght: trckd wnr: rdn over 1f out: wknd ins fnl f* **11/2**

5 5 1 1/2 **Duskiness (FR)**[25] 1675 2-9-0 TedDurcan 6 58
(M J Wallace) *chsd ldrs: rdn 1/2-way: wknd fnl f* **9/2**[3]

0 6 1/2 **Fair 'n Square (IRE)**[30] 1542 2-9-0 FrancisNorton 10 57
(J L Spearing) *chsd ldrs: rdn 1/2-way: wknd over 1f out* **66/1**

00 7 5 **Springtime Parkes**[11] 2026 2-9-0 NCallan 9 39
(K A Ryan) *dwlt: outpcd* **33/1**

8 1 1/4 **Blakeshall Rose** 2-9-0 DeanMcKeown 5 34
(A J Chamberlain) *s.s: outpcd* **66/1**

05 9 5 **Delta Queen**[9] 2072 2-9-0 MickyFenton 4 16
(C N Kellett) *chsd ldrs to 1/2-way* **100/1**

61.23 secs (-0.57) **Going Correction** -0.25s/f (Firm) **9** Ran SP% **110.3**
Speed ratings (Par 90):94,89,88,85,83 82,74,72,64
CSF £100.51 TOTE £30.10: £3.70, £1.20, £1.20; EX 114.40.
Owner Miss A H Marshall **Bred** Frank Dunne **Trained** Averham Park, Notts

FOCUS
This second division of the maiden was run slightly faster than the first. The form is rated around the placed horses.

NOTEBOOK
Princess Iris(IRE) ◆ looks a potentially useful sort and managed to make all the running from her low draw. A market drifter, this daughter of the high-class juvenile Athlumney Lady really knew her job on her debut and was soon in front and on the rail after a quick start. She picked up really well when asked and drew away in the last furlong. Her trainer thinks a lot of her and she may well take her chance in the Albany Stakes at Royal Ascot over six furlongs, and the way she galloped on to the line suggests that trip will hold no fears for her. (op 16-1)
Isobel Rose(IRE) reversed Warwick form with Frisky Talk and seems to be going the right way. She was unable to lay up early but came through late to snatch the runner-up spot. She looks as though an extra furlong will suit and qualifies for nurseries after this run. (op 7-2 tchd 10-3)
Lorena Wood(USA), a well-backed favourite having shown promise on her debut, was unable to get the rail from her high draw and then did not really pick up in the closing stages. Her first run was on easy ground and this $90,000 daughter of the high-class Vilikaia possibly found this going too fast. (op 5-4 tchd 11-10 and 11-8 in places)
Frisky Talk(IRE) has had four chances now and, although she clearly has ability, she does not appear to be going the right way. (tchd 7-1)
Duskiness(FR) showed up well again and did best of the rest, but her future probably lies in handicaps. (op 6-1 tchd 13-2)
Blakeshall Rose Official explanation: jockey said filly jumped left and hung left

2356 LADIES NIGHT ON SATURDAY 8TH JULY MEDIAN AUCTION MAIDEN STKS 5f 13y
3:40 (3:42) (Class 5) 3-5-Y-O **£3,368** (£1,002; £500; £250) **Stalls** High

Form RPR

2 1 **Urbe Condita (IRE)**[34] 1437 3-9-0 KDarley 6 67+
(T J Etherington) *trckd ldr: racd keenly: led 1/2-way: drvn out* **11/8**[1]

3 2 shd **Libor (IRE)**[9] 2080 3-9-0 NickyMackay 2 67+
(L M Cumani) *hld up: swtchd lft and hdwy 1f out: nt clr run and swtchd rt ins fnl f: r.o wl* **11/4**[2]

335 3 1 1/4 **Charles Parnell (IRE)**[251] 5562 3-9-0 78 FergalLynch 1 62+
(M Dods) *hld up: r.o ins fnl f: nvr nr to chal* **4/1**[3]

P030 4 3/4 **Lord Mayfair (USA)**[20] 1791 4-9-0 37 (b) AnnStokell(7) 7 62?
(Miss A Stokell) *led to 1/2-way: sn rdn: styd on same pce fnl f* **150/1**

444 5 1/2 **Dragon Flame (IRE)**[16] 1877 3-9-0 64 SebSanders 4 57
(M Quinn) *chsd ldrs: hung lft thrght: rdn and ev ch 1f out: no ex* **8/1**

4000 6 2 1/2 **Hilltop Fantasy**[71] 778 5-9-2 42 LDettori 8 45
(V Smith) *chsd ldrs: rdn 1/2-way: wknd fnl f* **12/1**

0 7 1 3/4 **Orpenlina (IRE)**[11] 2016 3-8-9 TonyHamilton 3 35
(R A Fahey) *chsd ldrs to 1/2-way* **25/1**

60.72 secs (-1.08) **Going Correction** -0.25s/f (Firm)
WFA 3 from 4yo+ 7lb **7** Ran SP% **112.1**
Speed ratings (Par 103):98,97,95,94,93 89,87
CSF £5.08 TOTE £2.20: £1.50, £2.50; EX 4.90.
Owner Miss Z C Willis **Bred** Bryan Ryan **Trained** Norton, N Yorks

FOCUS
An ordinary maiden run just over half a second faster than the quicker of the two preceding juvenile events and resulting in a close finish. The form is rated through the fifth but limited by the fourth.

2357 NOTTINGHAM RACECOURSE CONFERENCE CENTRE H'CAP 1m 6f 15y
4:10 (4:10) (Class 5) (0-75,75) 4-Y-O+ **£3,238** (£963; £481; £240) **Stalls** Low

Form RPR

1666 1 **Ti Adora (IRE)**[20] 1800 4-9-3 71 FrancisNorton 12 79
(P W D'Arcy) *a.p: hmpd over 4f out: chsd ldr over 3f out: led 2f out: rdn out* **14/1**

5022 2 1 1/2 **Dhehdaah**[22] 1758 5-8-6 60 MickyFenton 6 66
(Mrs P Sly) *hld up in tch: rdn to chse wnr over 1f out: edgd lft: styd on same pce ins fnl f* **11/2**[3]

-630 3 1 1/2 **Indonesia**[20] 1809 4-9-1 69 KDarley 8 73
(T D Walford) *hld up and bhd: hdwy over 2f out: hung lft and rdr dropped reins ins fnl f: styd on* **66/1**

3055 4 hd **Tribe**[19] 1821 4-9-1 69 RobertWinston 3 75+
(Sir Michael Stoute) *hld up in tch: nt clr run and lost pl 3f out: hdwy over 1f out: styd on* **4/1**[1]

443 5 1 **Encrypt (IRE)**[19] 1827 4-7-13 56 oh8 EdwardCreighton(3) 2 58
(O Brennan) *led: rdn and hdd 2f out: no ex fnl f* **33/1**

4640 6 1 1/4 **The Grey Man**[18] 1847 5-8-11 65 RichardMullen 4 66
(E S McMahon) *prom: chsd ldr 8f out: rdn over 2f out: no ex fnl f* **33/1**

2063 7 nk **Dundry**[46] 1132 5-9-7 75 (p) JimmyFortune 13 75
(G L Moore) *hld up: hdwy over 3f out: no ex fnl f* **15/2**

0052 8 1/2 **Cripsey Brook**[9] 2078 8-9-0 75 JamesReveley(7) 1 74
(K G Reveley) *hld up: hdwy over 3f out: n.m.r and lost pl over 2f out: nvr trbld ldrs* **11/2**[3]

1200 9 2 1/2 **Whispering Death**[11] 2035 4-8-12 66 NickyMackay 5 62
(W J Haggas) *hld up: rdn over 2f out: n.d* **9/2**[2]

00-4 10 31 **Kristoffersen**[23] 1748 6-8-5 59 FrancisFerris 10 12
(Ian Williams) *hld up: rdn and wknd over 3f out* **12/1**

-060 11 26 **Halland**[20] 1808 8-9-2 70 (e) NCallan 11 —
(T J Fitzgerald) *s.i.s: hld up: effrt over 4f out: sn wknd* **20/1**

350 12 20 **Aylmer Road (IRE)**[46] 1132 4-8-11 65 TQuinn 7 —
(P F I Cole) *chsd ldr 6f: wknd 4f out* **14/1**

3m 3.27s (-3.83) **Going Correction** -0.125s/f (Firm) **12** Ran SP% **113.9**
Speed ratings (Par 103):105,104,103,103,102 101,101,101,100,82 67,56
CSF £82.87 CT £4850.53 TOTE £19.30: £2.80, £1.50, £8.50; EX 110.70.
Owner Mrs Jan Harris **Bred** Star Pointe Ltd **Trained** Newmarket, Suffolk

FOCUS
A fair staying handicap and an open race, with very few coming into this in top form. The third sets the standard but it is not rock solid.
Aylmer Road(IRE) Official explanation: jockey said colt lost its action

2358 VICTORIA ANTIQUES CONDITIONS STKS 1m 54y
4:40 (4:40) (Class 2) 3-Y-O+
£12,464 (£3,732; £1,866; £934; £466; £234) **Stalls** Centre

Form RPR

115- 1 **Librettist (USA)**[599] 6217 4-9-1 110 LDettori 5 114+
(Saeed Bin Suroor) *mde all: shkn up over 1f out: r.o: eased nr fin* **7/2**[3]

1 2 2 **Alfie Flits**[18] 1854 4-9-4 RobertWinston 2 110
(G A Swinbank) *chsd ldrs: rdn over 3f out: styd on ins fnl f: no ch w wnr* **11/2**

0035 3 4 **My Paris**[25] 1678 5-9-1 102 NCallan 8 98
(K A Ryan) *chsd wnr: rdn over 2f out: wknd fnl f* **11/4**[2]

4-40 4 2 1/2 **Iceman**[403] 1359 4-9-1 JimmyFortune 1 92
(J H M Gosden) *trckd ldrs, racd keenly: rdn over 3f out: wknd fnl f* **2/1**[1]

0441 5 1 3/4 **Indian Steppes (FR)**[11] 2011 7-8-10 89 TQuinn 6 83
(P S McEntee) *hld up in tch: rdn over 3f out: wknd over 1f out* **17/2**

5004 6 4 **Pawan (IRE)**[4] 2236 6-9-1 74 (b[1]) AnnStokell 4 79
(Miss A Stokell) *dwlt: hdwy 5f out: rdn over 2f out: sn wknd* **100/1**

5-00 7 1 **Propinquity**[355] 2676 4-9-1 97 TedDurcan 3 77
(W R Swinburn) *hld up: wknd over 2f out* **40/1**

6000 8 14 **Diamond Heritage**[7] 2137 4-9-1 39 (b) DeanMcKeown 7 45
(S Parr) *s.i.s: hld up: wknd over 3f out* **300/1**

1m 44.04s (-2.36) **Going Correction** -0.125s/f (Firm) **8** Ran SP% **111.9**
Speed ratings (Par 109):106,104,100,97,95 91,90,76
CSF £21.80 TOTE £3.60: £1.90, £1.40, £1.70; EX 24.50.
Owner Godolphin **Bred** Calumet Farm **Trained** Newmarket, Suffolk

FOCUS
An intriguing contest with smart horses returning from long absences and the form is not that solid. The runners came up the centre of the track in the straight.

NOTEBOOK
Librettist(USA) ◆, who was returning from a 20-month absence, made virtually all and, quickening up off a steady gallop shortly after halfway, soon had his rivals in trouble and ran on well to score. His trainer reported that the colt had done plenty of work, and he will try to find a Listed race next. (tchd 4-1 in a place)
Alfie Flits ◆, a former bumper winner dropping half a mile in trip from his Thirsk maiden win, tracked the leaders before keeping on really well in the closing stages. His trainer was pleased and felt that the gelding might have done better had he made the running. He is likely to be rated in the low 100s after this, which should enable him to take his chance in the Tote Ebor in August. (op 9-2 tchd 6-1)
My Paris, somewhat surprisingly, did not make the running, but appeared to run his race, although he does seem to prefer a little more cut in the ground. (op 5-2)
Iceman, another returning from a long absence, ran a little too freely in the early stages and could not pick up when the winner kicked for home. He should be better for the outing. (op 11-4)
Indian Steppes(FR), a progressive handicapper, had a fair bit to find judged on official ratings and probably ran as well as could be expected. (op 15-2)

Pawan(IRE) Official explanation: jockey said gelding ran too freely

2359 EUROPEAN BREEDERS FUND FILLIES' H'CAP — 1m 54y
5:10 (5:12) (Class 4) (0-85,85) 3-Y-O — **£6,477** (£1,927; £963; £481) **Stalls** Centre

Form	Pos	Dist	Horse / comment	Jockey	RPR
41	1		**Harvest Queen (IRE)**[35] 1417 3-9-5 **83** (P J Makin) *hld up in tch: led over 2f out: shkn up and hung lft over 1f out: r.o: eased towards fin* **11/2**[3]	SebSanders 6	99+
2113	2	2 ½	**Famcred**[13] 1962 3-9-4 **82** (L M Cumani) *hld up: hdwy 3f out: rdn to chse wnr and hung lft over 1f out: no imp* **9/4**[1]	NickyMackay 5	89
0454	3	2 ½	**Damelza (IRE)**[19] 1832 3-8-13 **77** (T D Easterby) *a.p: chsd ldr over 4f out: rdn over 2f out: styd on same pce appr fnl f* **16/1**	FergalLynch 8	78
4244	4	nk	**My Lovely Lady (IRE)**[13] 1946 3-8-4 **68** (M L W Bell) *s.i.s: hld up: hung lft fnl 3f: hdwy over 1f out: nrst fin* **20/1**	RichardMullen 11	68+
3601	5	4	**Zamala**[14] 1934 3-9-0 **78** (J L Dunlop) *hld up: hdwy 3f out: sn rdn: edgd lft and wknd wl over 1f out* **6/1**	MartinDwyer 13	69
1	6	½	**La Matanza**[34] 1445 3-8-11 **78** (T D Barron) *led 7f out: hdd over 2f out: wknd over 1f out* **18/1**	BenSwarbrick(3) 1	68
41	7	1	**Astrobella**[231] 5978 3-9-1 **82** (M H Tompkins) *dwlt: hld up: rdn over 3f out: n.d* **40/1**	SaleemGolam(3) 12	70
01	8	1	**Dansa Queen**[223] 6122 3-9-0 **78** (W R Swinburn) *hld up: hdwy over 4f out: sn rdn: wknd over 2f out* **14/1**	TedDurcan 3	63
2020	9	9	**Zaharath Al Bustan**[13] 1948 3-8-8 **72** (M R Channon) *led 1f: remained handy tl rdn and wknd over 2f out* **25/1**	TonyCulhane 4	37
0210	10	1 ½	**I'm In Love (USA)**[50] 1068 3-9-7 **85** (M A Magnusson) *s.i.s: sn prom: hmpd over 4f out: wknd 3f out* **20/1**	SteveDrowne 2	46
221	11	3 ½	**Magic Peak (IRE)**[16] 1901 3-8-11 **75** (Sir Michael Stoute) *chsd ldr 6f out to over 4f out: wknd over 3f out* **4/1**[2]	RobertWinston 7	28
0200	12	13	**Pairumani's Girl (IRE)**[29] 1569 3-8-11 **75** (J L Dunlop) *hld up: bhd fr 1/2-way* **50/1**	TQuinn 10	—

1m 44.55s (-1.85) **Going Correction** -0.125s/f (Firm) — **12** Ran SP% **116.0**
Speed ratings (Par 98):104,101,99,98,94 94,93,92,83,81 78,65
CSF £16.56 CT £187.47 TOTE £6.30: £2.20, £1.40, £3.50; EX 18.90.
Owner Bakewell Bloodstock Ltd **Bred** Bakewell Bloodstock **Trained** Ogbourne Maisey, Wilts

FOCUS
An interesting fillies' handicap featuring a number of unexposed sorts but this time they stuck to the inside rail in the straight. The form has been rated positively through the third and fourth.
Zaharath Al Bustan Official explanation: jockey said filly lost its action
Pairumani's Girl(IRE) Official explanation: jockey said filly lost its action

2360 TELETEXT RACING "HANDS AND HEELS" APPRENTICE SERIES H'CAP — 1m 1f 213y
5:40 (5:40) (Class 6) (0-65,63) 4-Y-0+ — **£3,071** (£906; £453) **Stalls** Low

Form	Pos	Dist	Horse / comment	Jockey	RPR
0505	1		**Tata Naka**[6] 2181 6-8-8 **53** (Mrs C A Dunnett) *hld up: hdwy over 3f out: led over 2f out: styd on* **9/1**	KirstyMilczarek(3) 11	60
0130	2	nk	**Fiore Di Bosco (IRE)**[23] 1729 5-8-3 **48** (T D Barron) *s.i.s: hld up: plld hrd: hdwy over 6f out: ev ch whn hung rt over 2f out: styd on* **13/2**[3]	DeanHeslop(3) 2	55
0000	3	2 ½	**Saluscraggie**[12] 1997 4-8-5 **50** (K G Reveley) *hld up: r.o ins fnl f: nrst fin* **25/1**	JamesReveley(3) 8	52
05	4	1 ¼	**Kickahead (USA)**[21] 1773 4-9-1 **60** (Ian Williams) *sn led: hdd over 2f out: no ex fnl f* **8/1**	StuartHaddon(3) 6	60
01	5	3 ½	**Boulevin (IRE)**[8] 2099 6-8-2 **43** 6ex (R J Price) *s.s: hdwy over 4f out: wknd over 1f out* **5/1**[2]	JamesRogers 9	37
5020	6	3 ½	**Shifty**[2] 2286 7-9-2 **58** (D Carroll) *trckd ldrs: racd keenly: wknd over 1f out* **13/2**[3]	HeatherMcGee 1	44
0053	7	2	**Ariodante**[7] 2149 4-9-7 **63** (J M P Eustace) *rdr lost iron leaving stalls: sn prom: wknd 2f out* **7/2**[1]	LukeMorris 3	46
0550	8	¾	**Norwegian**[259] 5400 5-8-5 **47** ow2 (Ian Williams) *plld hrd and prom: wknd over 1f out* **16/1**	RonanKeogh 10	28
0000	9	1	**Vandal**[15] 1911 6-8-2 **44** oh3 (M Appleby) *hld up: effrt over 3f out: n.d* **33/1**	JamieHamblett 7	23
5041	10	3	**Rudaki**[254] 5516 4-8-9 **51** (M E Sowersby) *chsd ldr over 6f: wknd over 2f out* **12/1**	NeilBrown 5	25
300	11	7	**Glory Be (ITY)**[18] 1852 4-8-3 **45** (J L Spearing) *sn pushed along in rr: bhd fnl 4f* **12/1**	JosephWalsh 4	5

2m 11.19s (1.49) **Going Correction** -0.125s/f (Firm) — **11** Ran SP% **114.7**
Speed ratings (Par 101):89,88,86,85,82 80,78,77,77,74 69
CSF £10.10 CT £2.49 TOTE £12.50: £3.30, £2.00, £11.30; EX 73.00 Place 6 £59.37, Place 5 £21.17.
Owner O Nugent **Bred** Ivyclose Ltd **Trained** Hingham, Norfolk

FOCUS
A moderate apprentices' handicap in which they again came up the centre in the straight, and a very slow winning time.
T/Plt: £102.20 to a £1 stake. Pool: £38,488.45. 274.70 winning tickets. T/Qpdt: £9.80 to a £1 stake. Pool: £2,665.90. 199.60 winning tickets. CR

2321 RIPON (R-H)
Wednesday, June 7

OFFICIAL GOING: Good to firm
21/2mm of water had been put on the track after racing the previous day. On a drying day the ground was described as 'very quick, bordering on firm'.
Wind: Light; half against Weather: Fine and sunny

2361 EURA AUDIT YORKSHIRE'S SMALL BUSINESS ACCOUNTANTS MAIDEN STKS — 6f
6:40 (6:40) (Class 5) 2-Y-O — **£3,886** (£1,156; £577; £288) **Stalls** Low

Form	Pos	Dist	Horse / comment	Jockey	RPR
2	1		**Prince Rossi (IRE)**[17] 1863 2-9-3 (J D Bethell) *mde all: hld on wl* **9/2**[3]	GrahamGibbons 8	75
0	2	¾	**Colditz (IRE)**[18] 1838 2-9-3 (M R Channon) *trckd ldrs: swtchd rt and effrt over 1f out: no ex wl ins last* **10/1**	JoeFanning 4	73
	3	shd	**Gweebarra** 2-9-3 (K A Ryan) *leggy: scope: s.s: hdwy and swtchd outside over 2f out: nt qckn ins last* **10/1**	DO'Donohoe 9	72+
3	4	nk	**Tombi (USA)**[12] 1998 2-9-3 (J Howard Johnson) *trckd ldrs: t.k.h: chal over 1f out: wknd towards fin* **6/4**[1]	JamieSpencer 10	72
64	5	2	**Rosbay (IRE)**[13] 1945 2-9-3 (T D Easterby) *w wnr: wknd fnl f* **7/2**[2]	DavidAllan 7	66
	6	shd	**Charlie Tipple** 2-9-3 (T D Easterby) *rangy: scope: s.i.s: sn drvn along: hdwy over 2f out: kpt on* **25/1**	MickyFenton 1	65
	7	5	**Ronnie Howe** 2-9-3 (M Dods) *leggy: s.v.s: sme hdwy over 2f out: lost pl over 1f out* **40/1**	TomEaves 5	50+
	8	1 ¾	**Bid For Gold** 2-9-3 (Jedd O'Keeffe) *cmpt: bit bkwd: s.s: sme hdwy over 2f out: wknd over 1f out* **25/1**	PaulMulrennan 11	45+
6	9	1 ½	**Skye But N Ben**[35] 1420 2-9-3 (T D Barron) *w ldrs: rdn over 2f out: sn lost pl* **12/1**	PhillipMakin 3	41

1m 13.42s (0.42) **Going Correction** -0.10s/f (Good) — **9** Ran SP% **116.4**
Speed ratings (Par 93):93,92,91,91,88 88,82,79,77
CSF £47.44 TOTE £5.80: £2.10, £2.50, £2.00; EX 53.30.
Owner Clarendon Thoroughbred Racing **Bred** Sir Eric Parker **Trained** Middleham Moor, N Yorks

FOCUS
A fair maiden with both the first two stepping up on their initial effort and the fourth setting the standard.

NOTEBOOK
Prince Rossi(IRE), who made his debut here on totally different ground, is all speed and showed a willing attitude when hotly pressed. A drop back to five will be no problem.
Colditz(IRE), who lacks size and scope, had clearly learnt a fair bit first time. He had to be switched to come between horses and in the end made the winner pull out all the stops. (op 9-1)
Gweebarra, a March foal, continually swished his tail in the paddock. After a sluggish start he ended up making his effort on the wide outside. In the end just found lacking, this initial outing will have taught him plenty. (tchd 8-1)
Tombi(USA), who looked very fit, was very keen to get on with it. After looking a real threat, he emptied near the line. A drop back to five looks on the cards. (op 13-8 tchd 9-4)
Rosbay(IRE), out of luck at Ayr, had no excuse this time but at least this third outing sets him up for a nursery campaign. (op 9-2)
Charlie Tipple, a big, well-made individual, took time to grasp what was required but there was much to like about the way he was going about his work late on. He looks a fine longer term prospect. (op 50-1)

2362 BOROUGHBRIDGE (S) H'CAP — 1m 4f 10y
7:10 (7:11) (Class 6) (0-60,55) 4-5-Y-O — **£2,914** (£867; £433; £216) **Stalls** High

Form	Pos	Dist	Horse / comment	Jockey	RPR
0060	1		**Hezaam (USA)**[22] 1758 5-9-2 **50** (Mrs A Duffield) *led after 1f: styd on wl fnl 2f: clr ins last: eased towards fin* **11/4**[1]	DO'Donohoe 9	63+
6000	2	3	**Bint Il Sultan (IRE)**[242] 5741 4-8-7 **41** (W M Brisbourne) *s.s: hdwy on ins and n.m.r over 2f out: wnt 2nd over 1f out: no ch w wnr* **14/1**	DavidAllan 8	47
000	3	2 ½	**Danzatrice**[18] 1850 4-9-7 **55** (C W Thornton) *in rr: hdwy 4f out: nt clr run over 2f out: styd on ins last* **28/1**	DeanMcKeown 1	57+
3160	4	¾	**Shaheer (IRE)**[3] 609 4-9-4 **52** (J Gallagher) *in rr: hdwy over 2f out: kpt on same pce* **12/1**	(t) KDarley 2	53
6606	5	1 ¼	**Pitsi Kahtoh**[9] 2075 4-8-2 **36** oh6 (P W Hiatt) *mid-div: effrt over 3f out: kpt on: nvr a threat* **15/2**	AdrianMcCarthy 3	35
0000	6	8	**Campbells Lad**[22] 1765 5-8-2 **36** oh1 (Mrs G S Rees) *led 1f: chsd ldrs: lost pl 2f out* **25/1**	DaleGibson 7	22
4162	7	13	**Starcross Maid**[6] 2180 4-9-0 **48** (J F Coupland) *chsd ldrs: effrt on outer over 3f out: wknd 2f out* **10/3**[2]	JamieSpencer 5	13
1000	8	1 ¾	**Dimashq**[28] 1590 4-8-8 **42** (Ronald Thompson) *chsd ldrs: lost pl 3f out* **7/1**	PhillipMakin 6	4
3020	9	27	**Ben Bacchus (IRE)**[8] 2099 4-9-0 **48** (P A Blockley) *s.i.s: sme hdwy 7f out: lost pl over 2f out: heavily eased* **6/1**[3]	(b) NCallan 10	—
0600	10	38	**Jenna Stannis**[7] 5697 4-8-11 **50** (W Storey) *chsd ldrs on outer: hung lft bnd over 5f out: sn lost pl and bhd: t.o* **25/1**	AndrewMullen(5) 4	—

2m 33.45s (-3.55) **Going Correction** -0.225s/f (Firm) — **10** Ran SP% **113.8**
Speed ratings: 102,100,98,97,97 91,83,81,63,38
CSF £40.32 CT £880.12 TOTE £3.20: £1.40, £3.60, £7.60; EX 47.20.The winner was bought in for 9,000gns.
Owner Six Iron Partnership **Bred** Shadwell Farm LLC **Trained** Constable Burton, N Yorks

FOCUS
A dire seller with the runner-up rated just 41 but the time was decent and the winner's confidence will have been boosted.
Danzatrice Official explanation: jockey said filly was denied a clear run
Starcross Maid Official explanation: jockey said filly was unsuited by the good to firm ground
Jenna Stannis Official explanation: jockey said filly hung left throughout

2363 SKY TELEVISION H'CAP — 6f
7:40 (7:41) (Class 4) (0-85,85) 3-Y-O — **£6,309** (£1,888; £944; £472; £235) **Stalls** Low

Form	Pos	Dist	Horse / comment	Jockey	RPR
4216	1		**Mr Sandicliffe**[19] 1836 3-9-5 **83** (B W Hills) *drvn along early: hdwy and nt clr run over 1f out: styd on to ld nr fin* **6/1**[2]	(p) MartinDwyer 4	93
115	2	½	**Damika (IRE)**[12] 1983 3-9-0 **78** (R M Whitaker) *trckd ldrs: led ins last: hdd nr fin* **11/4**[1]	DeanMcKeown 5	86
1400	3	1	**Mint**[249] 5601 3-8-3 **72** (D W Barker) *chsd ldrs: led over 1f out: hdd and no ex ins last* **25/1**	AndrewMullen(5) 1	77
0001	4	2	**Moorhouse Lad**[28] 1589 3-9-4 **82** (G Woodward) *led: hung rt and hdd over 1f out: wknd towards fin* **8/1**	RobertWinston 2	81
1240	5	1 ¼	**Peter Island (FR)**[8] 2105 3-8-13 **77** (J Gallagher) *chsd ldrs: wknd appr fnl f* **14/1**	NCallan 9	72
3334	6	½	**Mr Rooney (IRE)**[308] 4048 3-9-7 **85** (M Johnston) *w ldrs: wknd appr fnl f* **16/1**	KDarley 8	79+
0500	7	1 ¾	**Observatory Star (IRE)**[12] 1983 3-8-8 **72** (T D Easterby) *s.i.s: hdwy 2f out: styd on ins last* **20/1**	DavidAllan 3	61
1001	8	2 ½	**Greek Secret**[32] 1497 3-8-10 **74** (T D Easterby) *racd w one other far side: led that pair: no ch w stands' side fnl 2f* **7/1**[3]	FergalLynch 14	55+
1110	9	1	**Ocean Of Dreams (FR)**[144] 118 3-9-3 **81** (J D Bethell) *racd w other far side: w rival: eased whn no ch ins last* **20/1**	GrahamGibbons 12	59+
4416	10	hd	**Rainbow Bay**[19] 1812 3-8-13 **77** (R A Fahey) *sn chsng ldrs: lost pl over 1f out* **10/1**	TonyHamilton 6	54
3130	11	½	**Millfield (IRE)**[243] 5716 3-9-1 **79** (J Howard Johnson) *trckd ldrs on outer: effrt over 2f out: sn lost pl* **16/1**	JamieSpencer 10	55
0125	12	2 ½	**Crosby Hall**[249] 5613 3-9-4 **82** (N Tinkler) *s.i.s: swtchd lft after s: nvr on terms* **16/1**	(t) KimTinkler 13	50

0064 **13** ½ **Alugat (IRE)**[20] 1793 3-8-3 **67** RoystonFfrench 7 34
(Mrs A Duffield) *trckd ldrs: lost pl 2f out* **25/1**

1m 12.16s (-0.84) **Going Correction** -0.10s/f (Good) **13** Ran SP% **115.2**
Speed ratings (Par 101):101,100,99,96,94 94,91,88,87,86 86,82,82
CSF £20.48 CT £322.19 TOTE £5.90: £1.80, £2.40, £4.70.
Owner Henry Barton **Bred** Rosyground Stud **Trained** Lambourn, Berks
■ Stewards' Enquiry : Dean McKeown two-day ban: used whip with excessive frequency (Jun 18-19)

FOCUS
A competitive three-year-old sprint handicap rated fairly positively around the third and fourth. The two who went to the far side were swimming against the tide.

2364 DIRECTORS CUP (H'CAP) 1m
8:10 (8:10) (Class 3) (0-95,95) 4-Y-0+
£9,348 (£2,799; £1,399; £700; £349; £175) **Stalls** High

Form RPR

0221 **1** **Grey Boy (GER)**[7] 2147 5-8-5 **79** 6ex TonyHamilton 6 89
(R A Fahey) *w ldrs: chal over 2f out: led jst ins last: drvn out* **11/8**[1]

6-00 **2** *nk* **Bustan (IRE)**[9] 2079 7-9-7 **95** RobertWinston 9 104
(G C Bravery) *mde most: hdd over 2f out: kpt on wl fnl f: no ex towards fin* **40/1**

0000 **3** 1 ¾ **Tsaroxy (IRE)**[228] 6022 4-8-4 **78** JoeFanning 8 83
(J Howard Johnson) *w ldrs: slt ld over 2f out: hdd jst ins last: kpt on same pce* **33/1**

0011 **4** ¾ **Imperialistic (IRE)**[9] 2071 5-8-13 **92** 6ex AndrewElliott(5) 5 95
(K R Burke) *hld up: effrt on outer over 2f out: edgd lft: kpt on same pce appr fnl f* **8/1**

5162 **5** *nk* **Hartshead**[11] 2017 7-9-5 **93** DeanMcKeown 2 96
(G A Swinbank) *hld up: hdwy to chse ldrs over 2f out: wknd over 1f out* **4/1**[2]

1000 **6** ¾ **Bailieborough (IRE)**[214] 6248 7-8-2 **81** (v) AndrewMullen(5) 3 82
(Robert Gray) *s.i.s: kpt on fnl 2f: nt rch ldrs* **50/1**

5200 **7** ½ **Postgraduate (IRE)**[47] 1111 4-9-1 **89** (v[1]) NCallan 7 89
(W J Knight) *chsd ldrs: one pce fnl 2f* **12/1**

0361 **8** 5 **Vicious Warrior**[30] 1531 7-8-6 **80** ow1 MickyFenton 4 68
(R M Whitaker) *trckd ldrs: chal over 2f out: wknd over 1f out: eased ins last* **10/1**

-110 **9** 11 **River Royale**[49] 1086 4-9-4 **92** AdrianMcCarthy 1 55
(P W Chapple-Hyam) *in rr: rn wd bnd over 4f out: nvr on terms: eased ins fnl f* **11/2**[3]

1m 37.86s (-3.24) **Going Correction** -0.225s/f (Firm) **9** Ran SP% **112.7**
Speed ratings (Par 107):107,106,104,104,103 103,102,97,86
CSF £71.52 CT £1249.40 TOTE £2.00: £1.10, £7.90, £5.60; EX 51.90.
Owner K & J **Bred** J Potempa **Trained** Musley Bank, N Yorks

FOCUS
A decent handicap in which the first three were up there all the way. The third sets the standard.

NOTEBOOK
Grey Boy(GER), under his 6lb penalty, was stepping up a furlong in trip and had to battle hard to contain the renewed effort of the runner-up. He looked very straightforward here. (op 6-4 tchd 13-8)
Bustan(IRE), without a win for over four years, dictated things and deserves credit for the way he came back for more.
Tsaroxy(IRE), absent since October, has slipped to a handy mark. He took a narrow advantage halfway up the home straight but in the end did not see it out anywhere near as well as the first two. (op 40-1 tchd 50-1)
Imperialistic(IRE), who is in-foal, edged off a straight line as if feeling the fast ground. She is blooming and in top form. (op 7-1 tchd 13-2)
Hartshead, meeting Imperialistic on much better terms, was pulled out to mount a challenge but he never really looked a threat. He is well worth another chance. (tchd 9-2 in a place)
Bailieborough(IRE), absent since November, never got competietive though not beaten all that far in the end. (op 66-1)
Vicious Warrior was too keen for his own good and had nothing left in the tank at the business end. Official explanation: jockey said gelding ran too free early (op 11-1 tchd 12-1)
River Royale, absent since his return in April, never looked like making the turn for home. Official explanation: jockey said colt hung left round bend in home straight (op 5-1 tchd 9-2, 6-1 in a place)

2365 RIPON FARM SERVICES H'CAP 2m
8:40 (8:40) (Class 5) (0-75,72) 4-Y-0+ **£3,886** (£1,156; £577; £288) **Stalls** Low

Form RPR

0455 **1** **Mr Majestic**[9] 2078 4-8-7 **56** DeanMcKeown 4 66
(R M Whitaker) *trckd ldrs on inner: plld outside over 2f out: hung rt and led over 1f out: drvn out* **4/1**[2]

0305 **2** 2 ½ **Incursion**[16] 1887 5-9-10 **72** AdrianTNicholls 2 79
(D Nicholls) *set modest pce: qcknd 6f out: crowded and hdd over 1f out: no ex* **13/2**[3]

1330 **3** 3 **Paradise Flight (IRE)**[10] 2044 5-9-5 **67** (b) NCallan 7 70
(K A Ryan) *hld up in last: reminders over 5f out: styd on fnl 2f: nvr a threat* **7/2**[1]

S150 **4** 3 **Maneki Neko (IRE)**[20] 1809 4-9-9 **72** RobertWinston 1 72
(E W Tuer) *t.k.h: trckd ldr: chal 4f out: wknd over 1f out* **7/2**[1]

0204 **5** 11 **Classic Event (IRE)**[17] 3563 5-8-8 **56** DavidAllan 5 43
(T D Easterby) *s.s: t.k.h and hdwy to trck ldrs after 2f: outpcd over 3f out: sn lost pl: bhd whn eased fnl f* **7/2**[1]

0316 **6** 2 **Best Port (IRE)**[349] 2851 10-9-0 **62** TonyCulhane 6 46
(J Parkes) *hld up: effrt 4f out: wknd over 2f out: eased ins last* **8/1**

3m 33.07s (0.07) **Going Correction** -0.225s/f (Firm)
WFA 4 from 5yo+ 1lb **6** Ran SP% **111.1**
Speed ratings (Par 103):90,88,87,85,80 79
CSF £28.27 TOTE £5.70: £2.00, £2.40; EX 40.10.
Owner W M Ellis **Bred** Hellwood Stud Farm And G F Pemberton **Trained** Scarcroft, W Yorks

FOCUS
They went no gallop until the final three quarters of a mile resulting in a very slow winning time for a race like this. The form does not look that strong although the placed horses were close to their marks.
Classic Event(IRE) Official explanation: jockey said gelding was slowly away

2366 EURA AUDIT UK MAIDEN STKS 1m 1f 170y
9:10 (9:11) (Class 5) 3-Y-0+ **£3,886** (£1,156; £577; £288) **Stalls** High

Form RPR

23 **1** **Alcyon (IRE)**[23] 1741 3-8-11 JamieSpencer 8 88
(E A L Dunlop) *set mod pce: shkn up and qcknd over 4f out: hld on wl towards fin* **4/1**[2]

02 **2** ¾ **Thalberg**[39] 1289 3-8-11 PhilipRobinson 5 87
(M A Jarvis) *chsd ldrs: wnt 2nd over 2f out: styd on: no ex ins last* **5/4**[1]

3 5 **Kibara** 3-8-6 NickyMackay 6 79+
(L M Cumani) *rangy: s.i.s: bhd: hdwy on inner 2f out: n.m.r: styd on strly ins last: improve* **20/1**

3 **4** *shd* **My Arch**[19] 1814 4-9-10 NCallan 13 77
(K A Ryan) *trckd ldrs: wnt 2nd over 4f out: kpt on same pce fnl 3f* **6/1**

5 1 ¼ **Beldon Hill (USA)** 3-8-6 JoeFanning 7 70
(C E Brittain) *leggy: unf: rr-div: hdwy 3f out: styd on same pce: nvr nr ldrs* **40/1**

62 **6** 3 **Mustamad**[25] 1691 3-8-11 MartinDwyer 1 69+
(Sir Michael Stoute) *swtchd rt after s: mid-div: effrt on outer over 2f out: nvr trbld ldrs* **9/2**[3]

2 **7** ½ **Ten To The Dozen**[285] 4725 3-8-11 DarrenWilliams 9 68
(P W Hiatt) *mid-div: effrt over 3f out: nvr nr ldrs* **25/1**

8 4 **Marina Gamba (IRE)** 3-8-6 DO'Donohoe 12 55+
(E A L Dunlop) *rangy: s.i.s: bhd: sme hdwy over 2f out: nvr on terms* **25/1**

3 **9** 2 ½ **Knight Valliant**[291] 4579 3-8-11 PatCosgrave 10 56
(J Howard Johnson) *chsd ldrs: rdn over 3f out: lost pl over 1f out* **33/1**

0 **10** 2 **Moving Story**[22] 1759 3-8-11 MickyFenton 14 52+
(T J Fitzgerald) *hld up in rr: nvr a factor* **100/1**

6 **11** 3 **Midnight Diamond (IRE)**[22] 1759 3-8-11 TomEaves 2 46
(Mrs L Williamson) *sn drvn along: sn chsng ldr: lost pl 3f out* **100/1**

4400 **12** 46 **Chilsdown**[42] 1230 3-8-11 67 AdrianTNicholls 11 —
(Ronald Thompson) *in rr: hung bdly lft over 4f out: sn virtually p.u: t.o: btn 40l* **100/1**

13 5 **Angeline** 3-8-1 AndrewMullen(5) 3 —
(H Alexander) *awkward to load: s.s: hung lft thrght: sn bhd: t.o and virtually p.u over 3f out* **100/1**

2m 2.25s (-2.75) **Going Correction** -0.225s/f (Firm)
WFA 3 from 4yo 13lb **13** Ran SP% **118.7**
Speed ratings (Par 103):102,101,97,97,96 93,93,90,88,86 84,47,43
CSF £8.65 TOTE £5.50: £1.30, £1.40, £3.70; EX 15.80 Place 6 £238.48, Place 5 £54.15.
Owner Patrick Milmo Stuart Tilling Marc Milmo **Bred** Miss Ciara Eglington **Trained** Newmarket, Suffolk

FOCUS
A fair maiden in which the winner was given a masterful ride from the front by the champion. The form is rated around the fourth and seventh.
Chilsdown Official explanation: jockey said gelding hung left throughout
Angeline Official explanation: jockey said filly hung left throughout
T/Plt: £217.70 to a £1 stake. Pool: £59,169.50. 198.40 winning tickets. T/Qpdt: £16.40 to a £1 stake. Pool: £4,560.65. 205.15 winning tickets. WG

2367 - 2368a (Foreign Racing) - See Raceform Interactive

2151 LEOPARDSTOWN (L-H)
Wednesday, June 7

OFFICIAL GOING: Last 9 furlongs - good; remainder - good to firm

2369a BALLYOGAN STKS (GROUP 3) (F&M) 6f
7:00 (7:01) 3-Y-0+ **£31,379** (£9,172; £4,344; £1,448)

RPR

1 **Yomalo (IRE)**[36] 1377 6-9-6 PJSmullen 2 105
(Rae Guest) *settled 3rd: rdn st: chal wl ins fnl f: styd on wl to ld cl home* **9/1**

2 ½ **Noelani (IRE)**[33] 1469 4-9-9 105 MJKinane 3 106
(John M Oxx, Ire) *led: strly pressed early st: narrowly hdd under 1f out: regained ld 100 yds out: hdd cl home* **8/1**

3 *nk* **Mecca's Mate**[8] 2115 5-9-6 WSupple 5 102
(D W Barker) *trckd ldr in 2nd: chal travelling wl early st: narrow ld briefly under 1f out: hdd 100 yds out: kpt on* **9/2**[3]

4 *hd* **Miss Sally (IRE)**[11] 2038 4-9-11 111 (t) JMurtagh 6 107+
(M Halford, Ire) *trckd ldrs in 4th: rdn st: kpt on ins fnl f* **15/8**[1]

5 ¾ **Modeeroch (IRE)**[24] 1709 3-8-12 108 (b[1]) KJManning 4 97
(J S Bolger, Ire) *hld up in 5th: nt clr run early st: kpt on ins fnl f* **9/4**[2]

6 ¾ **Moone Cross (IRE)**[33] 1469 3-8-12 85 TPO'Shea 7 95
(Mrs John Harrington, Ire) *hld up in 6th: no imp st* **25/1**

7 5 ½ **Grandfield (IRE)**[5] 2213 4-9-6 64 NGMcCullagh 1 81?
(M J Grassick, Ire) *a bhd: trailing st* **66/1**

1m 14.3s **Going Correction** +0.40s/f (Good)
WFA 3 from 4yo+ 8lb **7** Ran SP% **110.2**
Speed ratings: 110,109,108,108,107 106,106
CSF £70.68 TOTE £13.40: £3.70, £2.80; DF 84.50.
Owner F Nowell **Bred** Ballyhane Stud **Trained** Newmarket, Suffolk

FOCUS
A race that has been dominated by British-trained runners, and Yomalo provided the raiders with their seventh win in the last eight years.

NOTEBOOK
Yomalo(IRE) held the third-lowest rating in the race and was looking for her first win for just over a year, but she came here on the back of quite an encouraging run in a five-furlong Listed race at Bath last month, in which she finished well to take sixth behind Indian Maiden. One of the first to come under pressure, she responded to her rider's urgings to go in pursuit of the front two with over a furlong to run and, although she still had plenty to do at that point, she ran on well to grab the lead in the final 50 yards. Rae Guest reported that his charge relishes a sound surface and felt that she was well suited by the stiff finish here. The Wokingham Handicap is now a possibility. (op 12/1)
Noelani(IRE) ran her best race since winning a Group Three at The Curragh last August. After setting off in front and dictating a steady pace, she lost the lead with a furlong to run but battled back to regain the initiative before the winner arrived on the scene. This was encouraging, and she can be placed to further advantage at Stakes level. (op 7/1)
Mecca's Mate came here off a fine third in the Temple Stakes. She was going well early in the straight and had a brief spell in the lead in the closing stages, before eventually having to settle for third. She may prefer easier ground and can certainly add to her Listed-race haul in the coming months.
Miss Sally(IRE) was found to be in season when third to Moss Vale in the Greenlands Stakes last time. She could not quite match the leaders when they quickened up in the straight, but was staying on towards the finish. She seems equally effective over six and seven furlongs but may just be better suited by an easier surface. (op 7/4 tchd 2/1)
Modeeroch(IRE), who was blinkered for the first time, did not enjoy the clearest of runs in the straight and was staying on quite well late on to finish a close fifth. Placed in a Group Three race over a mile here on her return to action last month, she will be worth another try at this trip. (op 2/1)

2371a JOCKEY CLUB OF TURKEY GLENCAIRN STKS (LISTED RACE) 1m
8:00 (8:01) 4-Y-0+ £22,448 (£6,586; £3,137; £1,068)

RPR

1 **Mustameet (USA)**[24] [1711] 5-9-4 109 .... DPMcDonogh 5 113
(Kevin Prendergast, Ire) *trckd ldrs: 4th 1/2-way: 2nd into st: sn chal: led wl ins fnl f: kpt on wl* **5/1**[3]

2 *nk* **Chelsea Rose (IRE)**[21] [1785] 4-9-1 112 .... WSupple 1 109
(C Collins, Ire) *sn led: strly pressed fr 2f out: hdd and no ex wl ins fnl f* **4/1**[2]

3 *½* **Lord Admiral (USA)**[10] [2053] 5-9-4 111 .... JMurtagh 3 111
(Charles O'Brien, Ire) *4th early: 3rd 1/2-way: rdn to chal early st: kpt on ins fnl f* **10/3**[1]

4 *nk* **Luas Line (IRE)**[221] [6164] 4-9-5 110 .... KFallon 6 112
(David Wachman, Ire) *hld up in tch: 5th into st: 4th and chal over 1f out: kpt on* **4/1**[2]

5 *4* **Fairy Of The Night (IRE)**[11] [2041] 4-9-1 101 .... MJKinane 4 100
(John M Oxx, Ire) *hld up in tch: outpcd over 3f out: rdn st: mod 5th and no imp fr over 1f out* **16/1**

6 *1* **Simple Exchange (IRE)**[37] [1365] 5-9-4 107 .... PJSmullen 2 101
(D K Weld, Ire) *settled 2nd: lost pl ent st: sn no ex* **7/1**

7 *¾* **Democratic Deficit (IRE)**[24] [1711] 4-9-6 106 .... KJManning 7 101
(J S Bolger, Ire) *trckd ldrs in 5th: 4th into st: sn no ex* **8/1**

1m 37.9s **Going Correction** -0.60s/f (Hard) 7 Ran SP% **109.2**
Speed ratings: 107,106,106,105,101 100,100
CSF £22.85 TOTE £6.10: £2.90, £2.00; DF 22.70.
Owner Hamdan Al Maktoum **Bred** Shadwell Farm LLC **Trained** Friarstown, Co Kildare

NOTEBOOK
Mustameet(USA) has now recorded four wins on ground ranging from good to firm to heavy, and he has maintained a good level of consistency. Runner-up in this race a year ago, he won a similar type of event over this course and distance in April, and trainer Kevin Prendergast may look for a Group Three contest for him in Italy or Germany now.
Chelsea Rose(IRE), a three-time Listed winner last season (twice here) from nine furlongs to a mile and a half, had finished fourth to the unbeaten Galatee on her first start of the year in a ten-furlong Group Three at Naas last month. She again performed creditably and will do better when she goes back up in distance with this run behind her. (op 7/2)
Lord Admiral(USA), winner of this event a year ago, was placed a couple of times in Dubai earlier this year and had the fast ground he relishes for the first time in three starts back home this season. He tracked the leaders and arrived with every chance from over a furlong out before finding no extra close home. (op 3/1 tchd 7/2)
Luas Line(IRE), a Listed winner over nine furlongs last year when she also landed a Grade One handicap at Belmont Park, made an encouraging return to action. She closed to look a possibility entering the final furlong before finding no extra late on. (op 7/2)
Fairy Of The Night(IRE) dropped to the rear after less than two furlongs and, although she made a forward move early in the straight, she was never able to get into serious contention. (op 14/1)
Simple Exchange(IRE), who was dropping in trip, was in second place on settling down but dropped out of contention early in the straight. (op 6/1)
Democratic Deficit(IRE) had a bit to do on official ratings thanks to a Group Three penalty. Even so, he ran disappointingly and dropped away early in the straight, having been ridden along in fifth before the turn in. (op 7/1 tchd 9/1)

2370 - 2373a (Foreign Racing) - See Raceform Interactive

FONTAINEBLEAU
Wednesday, June 7

OFFICIAL GOING: Good to soft

2374a PRIX MELISANDE (LISTED RACE) (FILLIES) 1m 2f
3:05 (3:05) 3-Y-0 £17,241 (£6,897; £5,172; £3,448; £1,724)

RPR

1 **Celebre Vadala (FR)**[24] [1720] 3-8-11 .... CSoumillon 6 102
(A Fabre, France) **11/10**[1]

2 *2* **Fantastic Santanyi** 3-8-11 .... (b) AStarke 7 98
(Mario Hofer, Germany)

3 *¾* **Nowisza (FR)**[6] 3-8-11 .... ACrastus 4 97
(Ron Caget, France)

4 *1* **Tonic Star (FR)**[21] 3-8-11 .... SPasquier 2 95
(E Lellouche, France)

5 *1½* **Private Dancer (FR)**[17] 3-8-11 .... TThulliez 1 92
(Y De Nicolay, France)

6 *½* **Folle Biche (FR)**[21] [1789] 3-8-11 .... RonanThomas 5 91
(Mme N Rossio, France)

7 *1* **In The Fashion (IRE)**[46] [1130] 3-8-11 .... OPeslier 3 90
(J Noseda) *soon led, under pressure 2f out, headed 1 1/2f out, weakened SP 10-1* **10/1**[2]

2m 2.80s 7 Ran SP% **56.7**
PARI-MUTUEL (Including 1 Euro stake): WIN 2.20; PL 1.80, 3.60;SF 11.60.
Owner H H Aga Khan **Bred** Snc Lagardere Elevage **Trained** Chantilly, France

NOTEBOOK
In The Fashion(IRE), well held in the Fred Darling last time out, is a daughter of In The Wings so this step up in trip might have been expected to suit, but she did not get home. The ground may have been softer than ideal but the impression she gives is that she is going to be difficult to place this season.

[1811] HAMILTON (R-H)
Thursday, June 8

OFFICIAL GOING: Good to firm (firm in places)
Wind: Breezy, across

2375 BEN RACEDAY MAIDEN AUCTION FILLIES' STKS (A QUALIFIER FOR THE HAMILTON PARK 2-Y-O SERIES FINAL) 6f 5y
2:00 (2:00) (Class 6) 2-Y-O £2,590 (£770; £385; £192) Stalls Low

Form RPR

0 1 **Majestic Roi (USA)**[15] [1930] 2-8-12 .... RobertWinston 6 79
(M R Channon) *wnt rt s: keen: trckd ldrs: rdn to ld ins fnl f: r.o wl* **4/5**[1]

2 *½* **Adaptation** 2-8-9 .... KDarley 2 74
(M Johnston) *hung rt thrght: pressed ldr: led over 1f out to ins fnl f: kpt on* **6/1**[3]

64 3 *4* **Top Tier**[32] [1499] 2-8-4 .... RoystonFfrench 5 57
(I Semple) *led to over 1f out: sn outpcd* **5/1**[2]

4 *1¼* **Cassie's Choice (IRE)** 2-8-8 .... DerekMcGaffin 3 57+
(B Smart) *hung rt thrght: outpcd: hdwy 2f out: no imp fnl f* **11/1**

003 5 *15* **Lovers Kiss**[19] [1853] 2-8-7 .... GrahamGibbons 1 11+
(N Wilson) *outpcd after 2f: eased whn no ch fnl f* **10/1**

0 6 *5* **Alavana (IRE)**[26] [1664] 2-8-11 ow1 .... FergalLynch 7 —
(D W Barker) *sn outpcd: no ch fr 1/2-way* **33/1**

1m 12.23s (-0.87) **Going Correction** -0.325s/f (Firm) 6 Ran SP% **106.9**
Speed ratings (Par 88):92,91,86,84,64 57
CSF £5.29 TOTE £1.70: £1.10, £2.60; EX 5.30.
Owner Jaber Abdullah **Bred** Gaines-Gentry Thoroughbreds **Trained** West Ilsley, Berks

FOCUS
Just an ordinary maiden and the form is nothing special, but the front two finished nicely clear.

NOTEBOOK
Majestic Roi(USA) was a beaten favourite on easy ground her debut at Goodwood, but still offered promise and showed the benefit of that run switched to a faster surface to win in determined fashion. There should be better to come. (op 10-11 tchd Evens in places)
Adaptation ◆, an 18,000gns half-sister to Razed, a mile juvenile winner, out of an 11-furlong scorer, made a pleasing debut behind the more experienced winner. She was well clear of the remainder and should soon find a similar race. (op 9-2)
Top Tier had shaped as though worth a step up to this trip, but was no match for the front two. (tchd 11-2 in a place)
Cassie's Choice(IRE), 16,500euros half-sister to Noora, a multiple mile to ten-furlong winner, and to Caitlin, a dual juvenile seven-furlong scorer, out of a fair six-furlong two-year-old winner who was later placed over ten furlongs, offered some promise and is open to improvement. (op 8-1)
Lovers Kiss looked of limited ability. Official explanation: jockey said filly was unsuited by the good to firm (firm in places) ground (op 12-1 tchd 14-1)

2376 HAMILTON PARK H'CAP 5f 4y
2:30 (2:30) (Class 6) (0-55,55) 3-Y-O+ £2,730 (£806; £403) Stalls Low

Form RPR

5110 1 **Boanerges (IRE)**[8] [2136] 9-10-0 55 .... DarrylHolland 6 66
(J M Bradley) *sn niggled in midfield in centre: hdwy to ld ins fnl f: kpt on wl* **9/1**

0305 2 *½* **Blue Maeve**[21] [1794] 6-9-6 50 .... SilvestreDeSousa(3) 7 59
(A D Brown) *overall ldr stands side to ins fnl f: kpt on towards fin* **10/1**

5230 3 *1* **Enjoy The Buzz**[8] [2136] 7-9-7 55 .... RonanKeogh(7) 8 60
(J M Bradley) *outpcd centre: hdwy 2f out: kpt on ins fnl f* **9/1**

0-05 4 *¾* **Haulage Man**[38] [1341] 8-9-5 46 .... (p) TonyHamilton 2 48
(Karen McLintock) *outpcd stands side: hung into centre and hdwy over 1f out: kpt on: nrst fin* **33/1**

0050 5 *nk* **Sir Loin**[253] [5552] 5-9-9 50 .... KDarley 4 51
(N Tinkler) *in tch stands side: effrt over 1f out: one pce* **16/1**

0322 6 *hd* **Rowanberry**[16] [1913] 4-9-7 48 .... RobertWinston 1 48
(R M H Cowell) *bhd stands side: effrt and swtchd over 1f out: no imp fnl f* **7/2**[1]

0000 7 *½* **Chairman Bobby**[21] [1794] 8-9-2 48 .... (p) MarkLawson(5) 10 46+
(D W Barker) *spd far side tl rdn and nt qckn over 1f out* **25/1**

2023 8 *½* **Orchestration (IRE)**[6] [2207] 5-9-7 48 .... (v) RobbieFitzpatrick 11 44+
(M J Attwater) *cl up far side tl rdn and no ex over 1f out* **5/1**[2]

3001 9 *1¼* **Jahia (NZ)**[37] [1391] 7-9-8 49 .... StanleyChin 3 40
(P T Midgley) *cl up stands side: edgd rt and outpcd fr 2f out* **16/1**

0646 10 *shd* **Muara**[43] [1235] 4-9-9 50 .... JoeFanning 9 41
(D W Barker) *racd centre: chsd ldrs tl wknd fr 2f out* **8/1**[3]

0-00 11 *hd* **Strawberry Patch (IRE)**[370] [2268] 7-9-12 53 .... FergalLynch 5 43
(J S Goldie) *trckd ldrs stands side tl wknd fr 2f out* **16/1**

4220 12 *nk* **He's A Rocket (IRE)**[21] [1794] 5-9-6 52 .... (b) AndrewElliott(5) 14 41+
(K R Burke) *spd far side tl rdn and outpcd fr 2f out* **9/1**

0056 13 *3½* **Prospect Court**[164] [6664] 4-9-9 55 .... GregFairley(5) 12 30+
(A C Whillans) *cl up far side: rdn 1/2-way: sn wknd* **20/1**

59.46 secs (-1.74) **Going Correction** -0.325s/f (Firm) 13 Ran SP% **118.3**
Speed ratings (Par 101):100,99,97,96,95 95,94,94,92,91 91,91,85
CSF £92.70 CT £841.31 TOTE £8.50: £2.70, £2.80, £3.50; EX 128.60.
Owner E A Hayward **Bred** Clare Dore Ltd **Trained** Sedbury, Gloucs

FOCUS
A very moderate sprint handicap but the form looks sound. They were spread across the track for much of the way, but those who raced centre to stands' side were at an advantage over Chairman Bobby, Orchestration, He's A Rocket and Prospect Court, who raced far side.
Rowanberry Official explanation: vet said filly had lost its front left shoe

2377 HAMILTON PARK CLAIMING STKS 6f 5y
3:00 (3:00) (Class 6) 3-4-Y-O £2,730 (£806; £403) Stalls Low

Form RPR

3664 1 **Beverley Beau**[3] [2288] 4-8-5 44 .... KristinStubbs(7) 6 51
(Mrs L Stubbs) *chsd ldrs: led over 1f out: edgd lft wl ins last: kpt on* **6/1**

0003 2 *nk* **Mostanad**[17] [1877] 4-9-2 50 .... (b[1]) DarryllHolland 4 55
(J M Bradley) *missed break: bhd and outpcd: gd hdwy on ins over 1f out: hmpd wl ins fnl f: r.o: jst hld* **8/1**

0000 3 *½* **Underthemistletoe (IRE)**[12] [2019] 4-8-2 44 ow2.. MichaelJStainton(7) 8 46
(R E Barr) *bhd: effrt over 2f out: kpt on ins fnl f* **33/1**

0000 4 *½* **The Keep**[222] [6154] 4-8-0 40 .... (b) DonnaCaldwell(7) 2 44+
(R E Barr) *chsd clr ldr: effrt over 2f out: no ex whn edgd lft and blkd wl ins fnl f* **40/1**

0000 5 *1* **Rockburst**[299] [4357] 4-8-11 68 .... AndrewElliott(5) 3 49
(K R Burke) *prom: outpcd 1/2-way: kpt on ins fnl f: no imp* **7/2**[2]

0000 5 *dht* **Shatin Leader**[17] [1886] 4-8-6 45 .... (p) StanleyChin 1 39
(Miss L A Perratt) *chsd ldr: rdn and edgd rt over 2f out: one pce fnl f* **20/1**

0001 7 *1* **Next Ness (IRE)**[6] [2192] 3-8-6 51 .... PaulMulrennan 9 42
(R F Fisher) *in tch on outside: drvn over 2f out: sn outpcd* **11/2**[3]

6200 8 *1½* **Sovereignty (JPN)**[23] [1760] 4-9-2 67 .... (v[1]) RobertWinston 5 41
(I Semple) *keen: led and sn clr: wknd and hdd over 1f out: hmpd and eased whn btn ins fnl f* **2/1**[1]

500 9 *2* **Nautico**[28] [1609] 3-8-1 50 ow2 .... RoystonFfrench 7 26
(Miss L A Perratt) *bhd: outpcd 1/2-way: nvr on terms* **20/1**

1m 11.9s (-1.20) **Going Correction** -0.325s/f (Firm)
WFA 3 from 4yo 8lb 9 Ran SP% **111.2**
Speed ratings (Par 101):95,94,93,93,91 91,90,88,85
CSF £47.38 TOTE £9.20: £1.80, £2.20, £11.50; EX 42.40.The winner was the subject of a friendly claim.
Owner Mrs L Stubbs **Bred** Mrs F A Veasey **Trained** Norton, N. Yorks
■ Stewards' Enquiry : Donna Caldwell two-day ban: careless riding (June 19,25)

FOCUS
A very moderate claimer with the poor third holding down the form and the winning (hand) time was only modest, even for such a low-grade race.
Next Ness(IRE) Official explanation: jockey said gelding hung right-handed

2378 DM HALL H'CAP (A QUALIFIER FOR THE HAMILTON PARK HANDICAP SERIES FINAL) 1m 65y
3:30 (3:30) (Class 5) (0-70,69) 4-Y-0+ **£3,886** (£1,156; £577; £288) **Stalls** High

Form RPR
0005 **1** **Nevada Desert (IRE)**[13] 1987 6-9-6 **68**........................ DeanMcKeown 2 75
(R M Whitaker) *in tch: effrt 3f out: led and edgd rt over 1f out: kpt on fnl f: jst lasted* **5/1**[2]
0500 **2** *shd* **Middlemarch (IRE)**[75] 726 6-9-5 **67**............................(p) FergalLynch 9 79+
(J S Goldie) *hld up: effrt whn nt clr run over 2f out: swtchd and hdwy over 1f out: r.o wl fnl f: jst failed* **7/1**
0000 **3** *nk* **Fair Shake (IRE)**[97] 567 6-9-6 **68**..(v) KDarley 1 74
(Karen McLintock) *hld up: hdwy outside over 2f out: kpt on fnl f: no ex towards fin* **22/1**
5000 **4** *1/2* **Fairy Monarch (IRE)**[2] 2322 7-8-3 **51**............................(b) JoeFanning 7 56
(P T Midgley) *hld up: hdwy over 2f out: ch over 1f out: one pce fnl f* **33/1**
5020 **5** *1/2* **Champain Sands (IRE)**[13] 1996 7-8-9 **57**..................... DarryllHolland 3 62+
(E J Alston) *hld up: effrt whn nt clr run over 2f and over 1f out: rdn and one pce fnl f* **7/1**
6323 **6** *3/4* **Jordans Elect**[7] 2162 6-9-7 **69**...................................... RoystonFfrench 8 71
(P Monteith) *trckd ldrs: n.m.r briefly over 2f out: rdn and one pce over 1f out* **9/2**[1]
0000 **7** *nk* **Anthemion (IRE)**[3] 2286 9-8-5 **53** ow2...................... PaulMulrennan 11 54
(Mrs J C McGregor) *led to over 2f out: no ex over 1f out* **20/1**
0640 **8** *hd* **Hansomelle (IRE)**[7] 2164 4-8-8 **61**................................ GregFairley(5) 6 62+
(B Mactaggart) *in tch ins: effrt whn n.m.r briefly 2f out: sn outpcd* **14/1**
3043 **9** *nk* **Defi (IRE)**[34] 1455 4-9-6 **68**..(b) RobertWinston 4 68
(I Semple) *cl up: led over 2f to over 1f out: sn btn* **13/2**
4003 **10** *1* **Mister Benji**[8] 2141 7-8-7 **55** ow4................................ GrahamGibbons 5 53
(B P J Baugh) *in tch: rdn over 2f out: sn outpcd* **10/1**
1405 **11** *shd* **El Palmar**[8] 2137 5-8-12 **60**....................................... RobbieFitzpatrick 10 58
(M J Attwater) *cl up: effrt over 2f out: wknd 1f out* **6/1**[3]

1m 44.78s (-4.52) **Going Correction** -0.45s/f (Firm) **11** Ran SP% **115.3**
Speed ratings (Par 103):104,103,103,103,102 101,101,101,101,100 99
CSF £37.97 CT £713.76 TOTE £6.50: £2.90, £1.40, £8.90; EX 56.30.
Owner J Barry Pemberton **Bred** Bryan Ryan **Trained** Scarcroft, W Yorks

FOCUS
A modest handicap rated around the fourth and fifth.
Hansomelle(IRE) Official explanation: jockey said filly was denied a clear run

2379 SAINTS AND SINNERS H'CAP 1m 3f 16y
4:00 (4:01) (Class 6) (0-60,61) 3-Y-0 **£3,071** (£906; £453) **Stalls** High

Form RPR
0412 **1** **Liberate**[5] 2246 3-9-9 **61** 6ex.. SebSanders 10 75+
(Sir Mark Prescott) *mde all: rdn over 3f out: drew clr fr 2f out: eased nr fin* **8/11**[1]
6146 **2** *4* **Hi Dancer**[19] 1859 3-9-0 **52**.. LeeEnstone 11 56
(P C Haslam) *hld up in tch: rdn over 3f out: rallied 2f out: chsd wnr ins fnl f: no imp* **14/1**
0545 **3** *1* **Bramcote Lorne**[8] 2124 3-9-6 **58**.................................... DarryllHolland 5 61
(S Parr) *cl up: ev ch over 3f out: no ex over 1f out: lost 2nd ins fnl f* **4/1**[2]
6606 **4** *3* **Dubai Around (IRE)**[52] 1044 3-9-4 **56**.......................... DeanMcKeown 6 54
(Micky Hammond) *trckd ldrs: effrt over 3f out: edgd rt and outpcd fr over 2f out* **20/1**
0500 **5** *1/2* **Hurry Up Helen (IRE)**[10] 2082 3-9-7 **59**...................... RobertWinston 8 56
(Mrs L Stubbs) *bhd: drvn and hdwy over 2f out: no imp fr over 1f out* **12/1**[3]
050 **6** *1/2* **Silver Mont (IRE)**[248] 5658 3-9-6 **58**.......................... RoystonFfrench 12 54
(Mrs A Duffield) *trckd ldrs: outpcd over 2f out: n.d after* **25/1**
0040 **7** *5* **Andorran (GER)**[38] 1345 3-9-1 **56**............................ DanielTudhope(3) 3 44
(A Dickman) *hld up: hdwy fr over 3f out: no imp fr 2f out* **20/1**
6054 **8** *1 1/4* **Wensleydale Star**[9] 2107 3-8-1 **46** ow1........................ DeanHeslop(7) 1 32
(T D Barron) *bhd: rdn centre over 3f out: nvr on terms* **25/1**
000P **9** *3/4* **Prophet Preacher (IRE)**[5] 2246 3-9-0 **52**................ RobbieFitzpatrick 7 37
(M J Attwater) *in tch tl rdn and wknd over 3f out* **50/1**
0000 **10** *3 1/2* **Mandarin Dancer (IRE)**[6] 2192 3-8-4 **42** oh4 ow2........... StanleyChin 2 22
(Miss L A Perratt) *sn bhd: struggling fr 4f out* **100/1**
4000 **11** *21* **Sparkbridge (IRE)**[14] 1946 3-9-3 **55**.. KDarley 9 —
(R F Fisher) *a bhd: struggling fnl 4f* **33/1**

2m 21.99s (-4.27) **Going Correction** -0.45s/f (Firm) **11** Ran SP% **115.4**
Speed ratings (Par 97):97,94,93,91,90 90,86,85,85,82 67
CSF £10.80 CT £28.42 TOTE £1.80: £1.10, £3.20, £1.60; EX 16.20.
Owner Eclipse Thoroughbreds-Osborne House III **Bred** Miss K Rausing **Trained** Newmarket, Suffolk

FOCUS
A moderate handicap run at just an ordinary pace, but the order changed little and very few ever got into it. The form is sound and the winner is value for more than the official margin.
Sparkbridge(IRE) Official explanation: jockey said gelding lost its action

2380 SAM COLLINGWOOD-CAMERON H'CAP 6f 5y
4:30 (4:30) (Class 5) (0-70,67) 3-Y-0+ **£4,857** (£1,445; £722; £360) **Stalls** Low

Form RPR
0410 **1** **Dizzy In The Head**[5] 2237 7-9-12 **65**.........................(b) RobertWinston 1 77
(I Semple) *mde all: clr 1/2-way: rdn and hung rt ins fnl f: kpt on wl* **5/1**[3]
0000 **2** *3/4* **Yorkshire Blue**[32] 1504 7-9-3 **56**....................................... FergalLynch 4 66+
(J S Goldie) *bhd and sn outpcd: gd hdwy over 1f out: chsd wnr ins fnl f: r.o* **9/2**[2]
5340 **3** *3/4* **Raccoon (IRE)**[5] 2237 6-10-0 **67**....................................(v) SebSanders 9 75
(T D Barron) *prom: outpcd 1/2-way: rallied over 1f out: kpt on fnl f* **4/1**[1]
0004 **4** *3/4* **Grey Cossack**[21] 1794 9-9-4 **57**.................................. RoystonFfrench 8 62
(Mrs L Stubbs) *s.i.s: effrt outside over 2f out: kpt on fnl f: nrst fin* **11/1**
3420 **5** *3/4* **Winthorpe (IRE)**[26] 1686 6-10-0 **67**.......................... GrahamGibbons 10 70
(J J Quinn) *chsd ldrs tl rdn and no ex over 1f out* **7/1**
0000 **6** *3/4* **Celtic Thunder**[85] 639 5-9-4 **57**.. KDarley 7 58
(T J Etherington) *sn outpcd: shortlived effrt 2f out: no imp fnl f* **12/1**
2020 **7** *nk* **Quantica (IRE)**[21] 1794 7-8-13 **52**...................................... JoeFanning 6 52
(N Tinkler) *cl up tl hung rt and wknd over 1f out* **8/1**
0345 **8** *1/2* **Aegean Dancer**[33] 1496 4-9-12 **65**.................................. GylesParkin 5 63
(B Smart) *hld up: effrt over 2f out: btn over 1f out* **6/1**
5000 **9** *4* **Snow Wolf**[19] 1846 5-8-13 **59**..................................(p) RonanKeogh(7) 3 45
(J M Bradley) *in tch tl wknd wl over 1f out* **25/1**

1m 11.48s (-1.62) **Going Correction** -0.325s/f (Firm) **9** Ran SP% **112.6**
Speed ratings (Par 103):97,96,95,94,93 92,91,90,85
CSF £26.92 CT £97.58 TOTE £4.00: £1.70, £1.90, £1.70; EX 32.80.
Owner Gordon McDowall **Bred** Bearstone Stud And T Herbert Jackson **Trained** Carluke, S Lanarks

FOCUS
An ordinary sprint handicap and a modest winning time for a race like this, but the form looks reasonable with the winner and third setting the level.
Quantica(IRE) Official explanation: jockey said gelding hing right-handed throughout

2381 HAMILTON PARK SUPER SIX H'CAP 1m 5f 9y
5:00 (5:01) (Class 5) (0-70,62) 4-Y-0+ **£3,886** (£1,156; £577; £288) **Stalls** High

Form RPR
2003 **1** **Shekan Star**[13] 1997 4-8-8 **49**.. KDarley 5 56
(K G Reveley) *hld up: stdy hdwy over 2f out: effrt over 1f out: kpt on wl to ld towards fin* **5/1**[2]
023 **2** *hd* **Bronze Dancer (IRE)**[12] 2018 4-9-6 **61**...................... RobertWinston 9 68
(G A Swinbank) *hld up in tch: effrt and rdn over 2f out: ev ch ins fnl f: kpt on: jst hld* **11/4**[1]
4610 **3** *shd* **Zeydnaa (IRE)**[190] 6472 6-8-8 **49**...................................... TonyHamilton 1 56
(C R Wilson) *trckd ldrs: rdn and led over 1f out: kpt on: hdd towards fin* **11/1**
3535 **4** *3* **Rare Coincidence**[6] 2193 5-8-11 **55**................................(p) DNolan(3) 3 58
(R F Fisher) *led after 2f: rdn over 2f out: hdd and no ex over 1f out* **5/1**[2]
0330 **5** *1* **Mr Maxim**[229] 5568 4-8-9 **50**.. StanleyChin 8 51
(R M Whitaker) *prom: effrt whn n.m.r briefly over 2f out: sn one pce* **9/1**
0140 **6** *5* **Reminiscent (IRE)**[40] 1308 7-8-13 **54**.......................(p) DarrenWilliams 2 48
(B P J Baugh) *s.i.s: hld up: effrt over 2f out: nvr rchd ldrs* **6/1**[3]
3205 **7** *3* **Millennium Hall**[120] 3342 7-9-2 **62**.................................. GregFairley(5) 4 52
(Miss Lucinda V Russell) *dwlt: bhd: rdn over 3f out: nvr on terms* **9/1**
0020 **8** *3/4* **Scurra**[79] 688 7-8-9 **50**.. RoystonFfrench 7 39
(A C Whillans) *prom: rdn over 3f out: wknd 2f out* **18/1**
P600 **9** *1 3/4* **Nakwa (IRE)**[29] 1590 8-8-11 **52**.................................... DeanMcKeown 6 39
(E J Alston) *led 2f: cl up tl rdn and wknd fr 2f out* **16/1**

2m 47.97s (-5.43) **Going Correction** -0.45s/f (Firm) **9** Ran SP% **113.8**
Speed ratings (Par 103):98,97,97,95,95 92,90,89,88
CSF £18.82 CT £142.60 TOTE £5.30: £1.60, £1.30, £5.00; EX 10.50 Place 6 £147.59, Place 5 £110.36.
Owner Star Alliance **Bred** The Welcome Alliance **Trained** Lingdale, Redcar & Cleveland

FOCUS
The early pace looked strong, but the leaders may have gone off too quick and set things up for the closers. The final winning time was modest for the type of contest but the first two ran to form.
Nakwa(IRE) Official explanation: jockey said gelding was unsuited by the good to firm (firm in places) ground and hung left-handed in straight
T/Plt: £185.70 to a £1 stake. Pool: £39,635.05. 155.75 winning tickets. T/Qpdt: £38.20 to a £1 stake. Pool: £2,640.50. 51.05 winning tickets. RY

2021 HAYDOCK (L-H)
Thursday, June 8

OFFICIAL GOING: Good to firm
Wind: Almost nil Weather: Hot and sunny

2382 PONTIN'S HOLIDAYS MAIDEN CLAIMING STKS 5f
2:20 (2:21) (Class 6) 2-Y-0 **£3,238** (£963; £481; £240) **Stalls** Centre

Form RPR
3323 **1** **Picture Frame**[17] 1884 2-8-12 .... TonyCulhane 4 65+
(N Tinkler) *sn pushed along in tch: impr to ld 2f out: r.o wl fnl f* **8/13**[1]
0 **2** *2 1/2* **Two Sips Sue**[21] 1796 2-8-5 .... PaulHanagan 1 49
(P D Evans) *in tch: effrt to take 2nd wl over 1f out: nt pce of wnr ins fnl f: eased whn hld cl home* **12/1**
00 **3** *2* **Pirner's Brig**[24] 1744 2-8-12 .... DaleGibson 5 49
(M W Easterby) *w ldr tl rdn 2f out: one pce fnl f* **26/1**
500 **4** *2* **Caj (IRE)**[24] 1743 2-8-10 .... ShaneKelly 6 40
(M Quinn) *in tch: sn prom: led over 2f out: sn hdd: wknd fnl f* **10/1**[3]
5 *2 1/2* **Inkjet (IRE)** 2-8-4 ow1.. JohnEgan 2 25
(Ms Deborah J Evans) *hld up: effrt over 2f out: no imp* **20/1**
6 *1/2* **Playing Games** 2-8-12 .... TomEaves 3 31+
(M W Easterby) *s.s: a outpcd* **20/1**
50 **7** *2* **Loch Clutha (IRE)**[17] 1884 2-8-7 .... NCallan 7 19
(K R Burke) *led: hdd over 2f out: sn rdn: wknd over 1f out* **7/2**[2]

62.94 secs (0.87) **Going Correction** +0.10s/f (Good) **7** Ran SP% **111.9**
Speed ratings (Par 91):97,93,89,86,82 81,78
CSF £8.83 TOTE £1.70: £1.30, £2.80; EX 9.10.The winner was claimed by J. T. Stimpson for £12,000. Two Sips Sue was claimed by Claes Bjorling for £10,000.
Owner P D Savill **Bred** A C M Spalding **Trained** Langton, N Yorks

FOCUS
An ordinary claimer and the winner did not have to be at his best to score.

NOTEBOOK
Picture Frame did not travel that well in the first half of the race but he was well on top at the finish, as his form entitled him to be. He found this company less taxing but a sixth furlong will suit in future. (op 4-6 tchd 8-11 in places)
Two Sips Sue, a cheap purchase at only 500gns, is a half-sister to Ligne d'Eau, a triple winner over six to seven furlongs, and to On The Waterline, a winner over six furlongs at two. She did not put up much of a show on her debut at Salisbury but, with that experience behind her and dropped in class, she improved on this second start. (op 10-1)
Pirner's Brig, well held in claimers on his previous two starts, ran his best race to date, but his performance anchors the form.
Caj(IRE) showed speed again but she is not getting home in her races. (op 8-1)
Inkjet(IRE), a half-sister to Ma Vielle Poque, a minor six-furlong winner at three, and Silver Instinct, a dual winner at three to four in Denmark, showed little on her debut.
Loch Clutha(IRE), dropping into a claimer for the first time, cut out the early running but dropped out disappointingly. (op 4-1)

2383 WIN £3MILLION @ WORLDCUPGAMES.COM MAIDEN STKS 6f
2:50 (2:52) (Class 5) 3-Y-0+ **£3,238** (£963; £481; £240) **Stalls** Centre

Form RPR
1 **Methaaly (IRE)** 3-9-0 .... MartinDwyer 3 73+
(W J Haggas) *hld up: rdn and hdwy over 2f out: led wl ins fnl f: r.o u.p* **6/1**[2]
30 **2** *shd* **Rogue**[32] 1513 4-9-3 .... AdrianMcCarthy 1 70
(Jane Southcombe) *chsd ldrs: rdn to ld 2f out: hdd wl ins fnl f: r.o u.p* **50/1**
3 *3* **Home Sweet Home (IRE)** 3-8-9 .... NCallan 9 59
(P D Evans) *prom: led over 2f out: sn hdd and rdn: nt qckn fnl f* **12/1**[3]
3456 **4** *3 1/2* **Opera Writer (IRE)**[13] 2001 3-9-0 **70**................................. DavidAllan 6 57+
(T D Easterby) *in tch: rdn 3f out: effrt whn n.m.r and hmpd over 1f out: nt trble ldrs* **16/1**

5 nk **Footstepsinthesnow (IRE)** 3-8-9 .... PaulHanagan 8 47
(M A Buckley) *s.i.s: in tch: effrt over 1f out: sn btn* **33/1**

44 **6** ½ **Dallma (IRE)**[27] [1630] 3-8-9 .... KerrinMcEvoy 4 46
(C E Brittain) *chsd ldrs: rdn over 2f out: sn wknd* **6/1**[2]

5 **7** 1¼ **Liskaveen Beauty**[13] [2001] 3-8-9 .... MickyFenton 5 42
(T J Fitzgerald) *racd keenly: hld up: rdn over 2f out: no imp* **20/1**

343 **8** ½ **Music By Mozart**[33] [1476] 3-9-0 .... AlanMunro 7 46
(P W Chapple-Hyam) *led: hdd over 2f out: rdn and wknd over 1f out* **8/11**[1]

9 7 **Im Ova Ere Dad (IRE)** 3-9-0 .... ShaneKelly 2 25
(D E Cantillon) *plld hrd: sn in tch: rdn and wknd qckly over 1f out: eased whn btn ins fnl f* **50/1**

10 79 **It's Gone** 3-9-0 .... DaleGibson 10 —
(J G Given) *wnt rt s: wl bhd: t.o* **33/1**

1m 15.08s (0.18) **Going Correction** +0.10s/f (Good)
WFA 3 from 4yo 8lb **10** Ran SP% **114.6**
Speed ratings (Par 103):102,101,97,93,92 92,90,89,80,—
CSF £268.80 TOTE £7.50: £1.90, £6.80, £2.80; EX 190.70.
Owner Hamdan Al Maktoum **Bred** Scuderia Golden Horse S R L **Trained** Newmarket, Suffolk

FOCUS
An ordinary maiden and the runner-up anchors the form, but the winner is bred to do better over further and could be better than the bare form suggests.
Music By Mozart Official explanation: trainer's rep had no explanation for the poor form shown
It's Gone Official explanation: jockey said gelding lost its action

2384 LOUIS TUSSAUD'S BLACKPOOL WAXWORKS H'CAP 6f
3:20 (3:22) (Class 5) (0-75,74) 4-Y-O+ **£3,238** (£963; £481; £240) **Stalls** Centre

Form RPR
6250 **1** **My Gacho (IRE)**[147] [100] 4-9-4 **71** ....(v) JimmyFortune 15 82
(T D Barron) *midfield: hdwy 1/2-way: led jst over 1f out: r.o* **16/1**

0000 **2** ½ **Lake Garda**[232] [5986] 5-9-3 **70** .... NCallan 13 80
(K A Ryan) *a.p: rdn to ld over 1f out: sn hdd: nt qckn towards fin* **15/2**[3]

0003 **3** shd **Trojan Flight**[6] [2194] 5-9-5 **72** .... TonyCulhane 10 81
(D W Chapman) *hld up: hdwy over 2f out: sn rdn: r.o ins fnl f* **13/2**[2]

5005 **4** 1¼ **No Grouse**[12] [2020] 6-8-11 **64** .... FrancisNorton 3 69
(E J Alston) *hld up: hdwy over 1f out: sn rdn: edgd rt ins fnl f: r.o towards fin* **16/1**

0023 **5** hd **Brigadore**[6] [2189] 7-9-3 **70** .... KerrinMcEvoy 8 75
(J G Given) *in rr: rdn and hdwy 2f out: styd on ins fnl f* **5/1**[1]

4060 **6** 3½ **Jilly Why (IRE)**[12] [2027] 5-8-10 **67** ow1 .... DerekNolan(5) 12 62
(Ms Deborah J Evans) *led: rdn 2f out: hdd over 1f out: wknd ins fnl f* **20/1**

0054 **7** hd **Apex**[21] [1795] 5-9-1 **68** .... KimTinkler 14 66+
(N Tinkler) *hmpd s: in rr: rdn whn nt clr run over 1f out: styd on ins fnl f: nt trble ldrs* **12/1**

0020 **8** nk **Distant Times**[10] [2074] 5-8-13 **66** ....(b) MJKinane 1 59
(T D Easterby) *chsd ldrs: rdn 2f out: wknd ins fnl f* **8/1**

0000 **9** 2½ **Royal Orissa**[6] [2189] 4-9-6 **73** ....(t) RobertHavlin 9 58
(D Haydn Jones) *in tch: rdn over 2f out: wknd 1f out* **50/1**

3556 **10** 1¼ **Danehill Stroller (IRE)**[6] [2189] 6-8-12 **68** ....(p) NelsonDeSouza(3) 7 50
(R M Beckett) *midfield: rdn and wknd over 1f out* **13/2**[2]

0066 **11** 3 **Who's Winning (IRE)**[38] [1359] 5-9-7 **74** ....(t) TQuinn 2 47
(B G Powell) *chsd ldrs: rdn over 2f out: wknd over 1f out* **8/1**

5305 **12** nk **Insubordinate**[17] [1885] 5-8-3 **56** .... MartinDwyer 11 28
(J S Goldie) *bhd: rdn 2f out: no imp* **14/1**

0000 **13** 1¼ **General Feeling (IRE)**[40] [1280] 5-9-5 **72** .... MickyFenton 5 40
(M Mullineaux) *a towards rr* **50/1**

4200 **14** shd **Hiccups**[29] [1597] 6-9-7 **74** ....(p) PaulQuinn 6 42
(D Nicholls) *midfield: rdn over 2f out: sn wknd* **12/1**

400 **15** ½ **Beyond The Clouds (IRE)**[357] [2615] 10-9-1 **68** .... DavidAllan 16 34
(J S Wainwright) *hld up: rdn 2f out: nvr on terms* **66/1**

30-0 **16** 3½ **Watching**[30] [1561] 9-9-7 **74** .... PaulHanagan 4 30
(R A Fahey) *prom: rdn over 2f out: wknd over 1f out* **28/1**

1m 14.76s (-0.14) **Going Correction** +0.10s/f (Good) **16** Ran SP% **124.8**
Speed ratings (Par 103):104,103,103,101,101 96,96,95,92,90 86,86,84,84,84 79
CSF £129.37 CT £882.92 TOTE £21.20: £4.00, £2.30, £1.90, £3.60; EX 197.20.
Owner Grant Mercer & R G Toes **Bred** Mount Coote Stud **Trained** Maunby, N Yorks

FOCUS
A modest handicap, but competitive enough, and the form looks pretty sound rated around the third and fourth.
General Feeling(IRE) Official explanation: jockey said gelding hung right-handed from halfway

2385 E B F BRANNIGAN'S BARS H'CAP 6f
3:50 (3:52) (Class 3) (0-95,90) 3-Y-O **£11,658** (£3,468; £1,733; £865) **Stalls** Centre

Form RPR
312 **1** **Tawaassol (USA)**[28] [1617] 3-9-1 **84** ....(t) MartinDwyer 11 96
(Sir Michael Stoute) *midfield: hdwy 1/2-way: led over 2f out: edgd lft ent fnl f: hung rt towards fin: r.o* **9/4**[2]

2412 **2** ½ **Imperial Sword**[13] [1986] 3-8-13 **82** .... JimmyFortune 6 93
(T D Barron) *stdd s: hld up: hdwy 2f out: ev ch ins fnl f: hung lft and hld towards fin* **8/1**[3]

5400 **3** 4 **Charles Darwin (IRE)**[7] [2168] 3-9-4 **87** .... FrancisNorton 4 86
(M Blanshard) *midfield: rdn over 2f out: hdwy over 1f out: kpt on ins fnl f: nt pce of ldrs* **25/1**

1506 **4** nk **Spearit (IRE)**[9] [2105] 3-8-7 **76** .... AlanMunro 8 74
(D R C Elsworth) *in rr: rdn over 1f out: styd on ins fnl f: nrst fin* **40/1**

0065 **5** 1 **Choysia**[20] [1836] 3-9-0 **83** .... NCallan 5 78
(D W Barker) *midfield: hdwy over 2f out: rdn and ev ch over 1f out: wknd ins fnl f* **14/1**

0005 **6** nk **Waterline Twenty (IRE)**[28] [1606] 3-8-11 **80** .... ShaneKelly 3 74
(P D Evans) *prom: rdn 1/2-way: wknd over 1f out* **33/1**

0313 **7** 1½ **Ooh Aah Camara (IRE)**[19] [1848] 3-9-2 **85** .... JohnEgan 2 75
(T J Pitt) *in tch: rdn over 2f out: wknd over 1f out* **14/1**

0334 **8** ¾ **Ryedale Ovation (IRE)**[19] [1848] 3-8-12 **81** .... DavidAllan 1 68
(T D Easterby) *prom: rdn and ev ch over 2f out: wknd over 1f out* **14/1**

1421 **9** ¾ **Westport**[7] [2109] 3-8-2 **76** 6ex .... AndrewMullen(5) 7 61
(K A Ryan) *midfield: rdn bef 1/2-way: wknd 2f out* **2/1**[1]

3000 **10** 3 **Colorus (IRE)**[28] [1606] 3-9-4 **87** .... PaulHanagan 12 63
(R A Fahey) *prom tl rdn and wknd over 1f out* **16/1**

0255 **11** 1 **John Keats**[7] [2163] 3-8-13 **82** ....(b) TomEaves 10 55
(I Semple) *led: rdn and hdd over 2f out: wknd over 1f out* **14/1**

2030 **12** 3½ **Figaro Flyer (IRE)**[12] [2014] 3-9-7 **90** .... TonyCulhane 9 53
(P Howling) *sn in rr: rdn over 2f out: n.d* **20/1**

1m 15.07s (0.17) **Going Correction** +0.10s/f (Good) **12** Ran SP% **121.8**
Speed ratings (Par 103):102,101,96,95,94 93,91,90,89,85 84,79
CSF £20.60 CT £378.03 TOTE £3.50: £1.50, £2.20, £8.50; EX 19.00 Trifecta £549.50 Part won. Pool: £774.04 - 0.20 winning tickets..

Owner Hamdan Al Maktoum **Bred** James T Gottwald **Trained** Newmarket, Suffolk

FOCUS
The market made this just about a three-horse race and two of those three came home clear of the rest. The form looks solid enough.

NOTEBOOK
Tawaassol(USA), tongue-tied for the first time, proved suited by the drop back to six furlongs and, while his main market rivals struggled to go the early pace, he did not. He showed signs of inexperience in the closing stages - this was only his fourth career start - by hanging right, and the chances are that there is even better to come. (op 5-2 tchd 11-4 in places)
Imperial Sword might not be at his best on ground this quick, and he did struggle to go the pace a bit in the early stages, but he saw his race out strongly, finishing clear of the rest, and he was probably unlucky to run into a lightly-raced and well-handicapped rival in Tawaassol. (op 10-1)
Charles Darwin(IRE) enjoyed a successful two-year-old campaign, and as a result he is now on a fairly high mark. He won the separate battle for third, but he is likely to remain vulnerable off this sort of rating. (op 33-1)
Spearit(IRE), who stayed on well from the back of the field, continues to look high in the handicap for what he has achieved. (op 50-1)
Choysia did not get home and will be happier back over the minimum trip. (op 12-1)
Waterline Twenty(IRE) probably needs a little more help from the Handicapper before she starts winning again.
Westport, saddled with a 6lb penalty and having his third run in two weeks, may have found this one outing too many. He was very disappointing and simply did not run his race. Official explanation: trainer said colt never travelled (op 9-4 tchd 5-2)

2386 BANK OF SCOTLAND CORPORATE STKS (LISTED RACE) (REGISTERED AS THE JOHN OF GAUNT STAKES) 7f 30y
4:20 (4:22) (Class 1) 4-Y-O+
£15,898 (£6,025; £3,015; £1,503; £753; £378) **Stalls** Low

Form RPR
2032 **1** **Quito (IRE)**[22] [1778] 9-8-12 **111** ....(b) TonyCulhane 5 110
(D W Chapman) *hld up in rr: rdn 2f out: hdwy over 1f out: hung lft whn str run to ld wl ins fnl f* **9/2**[3]

3050 **2** ½ **New Seeker**[19] [1840] 6-9-3 **110** ....(b) PhilipRobinson 2 114
(C G Cox) *led: rdn over 1f out: hdd wl ins fnl f: hld cl home* **2/1**[1]

4603 **3** 2 **Cape Columbine**[19] [1849] 4-8-7 **103** .... JohnEgan 3 99
(D R C Elsworth) *trckd ldrs: pushed along and outpcd 3f out: wnt lft whn styng on ins fnl f: no imp on front pair* **11/1**

0246 **4** nk **Excusez Moi (USA)**[11] [2047] 4-8-12 **99** ....(t) KerrinMcEvoy 4 103
(C E Brittain) *prom: rdn and ev ch over 1f out: no ex ins fnl f* **10/1**

4653 **5** 1¼ **Somnus**[22] [1778] 6-8-12 **110** .... MJKinane 7 100
(T D Easterby) *racd keenly: in tch: rdn 2f out: one pce fnl f* **11/4**[2]

2124 **6** ½ **Suggestive**[91] [619] 8-9-3 ....(b) NickyMackay 6 103
(W J Haggas) *in tch: effrt over 2f out: no ex fnl f* **11/2**

2432 **7** 4 **Appalachian Trail (IRE)**[110] [452] 5-8-12 **95** .... TomEaves 1 99+
(I Semple) *hld up: rdn 2f out: bmpd over 1f out: no imp whn n.m.r and hmpd ins fnl f: n.d after* **33/1**

1m 29.65s (-2.41) **Going Correction** -0.10s/f (Good) **7** Ran SP% **113.9**
Speed ratings (Par 111):109,108,106,105,104 103,99
CSF £13.85 TOTE £5.00: £2.20, £1.60; EX 16.40.
Owner Michael Hill **Bred** Sheikh Mohammed Bin Rashid Al Maktoum **Trained** Stillington, N Yorks
■ Stewards' Enquiry : John Egan two-day ban: careless riding (June 19-25)

FOCUS
A decent Listed contest but the early pace was not strong and the final time was ordinary for a race of this class. The fourth is the best guide to the form.

NOTEBOOK
Quito(IRE) found a tremendous turn of foot to run down the favourite inside the final furlong and get off the mark for the year. He deserves extra credit for winning despite the fact that the race was not run at a strong early gallop, and clearly at the age of nine he is as good as ever. The Golden Jubilee Stakes at Royal Ascot is his next target. (op 7-2)
New Seeker was a well-backed favourite as he had his conditions and it looked likely that, in the absence of another front-runner, he would be able to dominate this field, despite being saddled with a penalty. His rider set nothing like a break-neck gallop, reserving something for the sprint to the line, but he was still unable to hold off the fast-finishing winner. On paper he ran a good race giving 5lb to a higher-rated rival, but he did enjoy the run of the race. (op 9-4 tchd 5-2 in places)
Cape Columbine stayed on for an honourable third place and posted her best effort of the campaign to date. She is likely to remain difficult to place this season, though. (op 10-1 tchd 12-1)
Excusez Moi(USA), tongue tied for the first time, came there looking a real threat inside the final two furlongs, but he found little under pressure. In fairness, he had a stiff task on these terms. (op 12-1)
Somnus ran well in the Group Two Duke of York Stakes last time out and the weights were in his favour in this contest, but he needs to get his toe in to show his best and the ground on this occasion was just too quick. (op 7-2)
Suggestive, who won this race two years ago, did not find a lot at the business end and is not one to trust under pressure. (tchd 6-1)

2387 BLACKPOOL TOWER & CIRCUS H'CAP 1m 2f 120y
4:50 (4:53) (Class 4) (0-85,83) 4-Y-O+ **£6,477** (£1,927; £963; £481) **Stalls** High

Form RPR
3122 **1** **Trouble Mountain (USA)**[7] [2162] 9-8-4 **66** ....(t) DaleGibson 13 78
(M W Easterby) *in rr div: pushed along 5f out: hdwy over 1f out: r.o to ld towards fin* **9/1**

5305 **2** nk **Brief Goodbye**[40] [1302] 6-8-11 **73** .... MickyFenton 9 84
(John Berry) *in rr: rdn and hdwy over 2f out: led wl ins fnl f: hdd towards fin* **25/1**

0231 **3** 2 **Dragon Slayer (IRE)**[71] [800] 4-9-1 **77** .... TQuinn 7 84
(M J Attwater) *chsd ldrs: rdn over 1f out: led ins fnl f: sn hdd: no ex towards fin* **10/1**

0000 **4** nk **Oddsmaker (IRE)**[7] [2164] 5-8-2 **64** oh7 ....(t) FrancisNorton 8 71
(M A Barnes) *midfield: rdn and hdwy over 2f out: styd on ins fnl f* **66/1**

0300 **5** 1¾ **Little Jimbob**[18] [1864] 5-9-0 **76** .... PaulHanagan 14 80
(R A Fahey) *led: rdn and hdd ins fnl f: no ex* **11/1**

660 **6** nk **Motafarred (IRE)**[21] [1809] 4-8-13 **75** .... NCallan 15 78
(Micky Hammond) *prom: rdn and ev ch wl over 1f out: no ex ins fnl f* **50/1**

0026 **7** 2½ **Lucayan Dancer**[18] [1864] 6-8-13 **75** .... AdrianTNicholls 6 74
(D Nicholls) *hld up: rdn over 3f out: hdwy over 2f out: kpt on ins fnl f* **25/1**

0010 **8** nk **Mr Aitch (IRE)**[27] [1631] 4-8-8 **70** .... JohnEgan 12 68
(R T Phillips) *in rr: rdn over 3f out: hdwy over 1f out: styd on u.p ins fnl f: nt rch ldrs* **33/1**

1000 **9** hd **Rawdon (IRE)**[13] [1992] 5-9-7 **83** ....(v) HayleyTurner 1 81
(M L W Bell) *in tch: rdn 4f out: one pce fnl 2f* **20/1**

0160 **10** 1½ **Yakimov (USA)**[29] [1585] 7-9-7 **83** .... VinceSlattery 16 78
(D J Wintle) *hld up: rdn over 4f out: no imp* **20/1**

3526 **11** ¾ **Shape Up (IRE)**[40] [1281] 6-9-2 **78** ....(b) DavidAllan 5 72
(R Craggs) *chsd ldrs: rdn over 2f out: wknd over 1f out* **25/1**

0040 **12** 1½ **Pevensey (IRE)**[7] [2169] 4-9-7 **83** .... ShaneKelly 3 74
(M A Buckley) *midfield: rdn over 2f out: wknd over 1f out* **12/1**

0103 **13** *2* **Active Asset (IRE)**[10] 2079 4-9-2 **78**.............................. TonyCulhane 10 65
(M R Channon) *midfield: rdn and wknd over 3f out* **9/2**[2]
6000 **14** *shd* **Thyolo (IRE)**[6] 2200 5-9-7 **83**..................................(b) PhilipRobinson 11 70
(C G Cox) *a bhd* **7/1**[3]
4031 **15** *3* **Smooth Jazz**[6] 2186 4-8-12 **74** 6ex....................................... MJKinane 17 56
(R M Beckett) *midfield: rdn over 2f out: wknd over 1f out* **4/1**[1]
0010 **16** *4* **Cool Hunter**[18] 1864 5-9-7 **83**.. KerrinMcEvoy 4 58
(W R Swinburn) *in tch: rdn over 3f out: wknd over 1f out* **10/1**
000R **R** **Arabie**[27] 1651 8-8-10 **72**.. FrancisFerris 2 —
(Ian Williams) *ref to r: tk no part* **66/1**

2m 14.93s (-2.80) **Going Correction** -0.10s/f (Good) **17** Ran SP% **123.8**
Speed ratings (Par 105):106,105,104,104,102 102,100,100,100,99 98,97,96,96,94 91,—
CSF £225.76 CT £2302.37 TOTE £7.60: £1.70, £4.90, £2.50, £7.70; EX 168.70 Place 6 £368.06, Place 5 £257.44.
Owner Mrs Jean Turpin **Bred** Robert B Berger **Trained** Sheriff Hutton, N Yorks

FOCUS
A fair handicap, run at a strong early pace, and the first two came clear. The form looks sound.
Thyolo(IRE) Official explanation: trainer had no explanation for the poor form shown
Smooth Jazz Official explanation: trainer's rep said race came too soon for the gelding
T/Jkpt: Not won. T/Plt: £572.80 to a £1 stake. Pool: £59,595.15. 75.95 winning tickets. T/Qpdt: £32.60 to a £1 stake. Pool: £4,502.45. 102.15 winning tickets. DO

2258 BRIGHTON (L-H)
Friday, June 9

OFFICIAL GOING: Firm
Wind: Fresh, behind Weather: Sunny

2388 PRESS RED TO BACK ENGLAND ON ATR MEDIAN AUCTION MAIDEN STKS — 5f 213y
2:10 (2:11) (Class 6) 2-Y-O **£3,238** (£963; £481; £240) **Stalls** Low

Form RPR
05 **1** **Eddie Jock (IRE)**[15] 1945 2-9-3 .... RichardHughes 6 81
(M L W Bell) *s.i.s: outpcd after 2f: swtchd rt and hdwy on outside 2f out: r.o u.p to ld nr fin* **9/2**[3]
6 **2** *nk* **Lady Lily (IRE)**[14] 1989 2-8-12 .... EddieAhern 7 75
(H R A Cecil) *hld up in tch: swtchd rt over 3f out: led over 2f out: rdn over 1f out: hdd nr fin* **5/2**[1]
2 **3** *3* **Pires**[5] 2258 2-9-3 .... ChrisCatlin 8 71
(M R Channon) *a.p: carried rt over 3f out: sn rdn: one pce fnl f* **3/1**[2]
0 **4** *5* **Inflight (IRE)**[32] 1542 2-8-12 .... SebSanders 5 51
(R M Beckett) *led after 1f: rdn and hdd over 2f out: wknd fnl f* **8/1**
0 **5** *1 3/4* **Saxenberg**[63] 908 2-8-9 .... EdwardCreighton(3) 1 45
(Miss J R Gibney) *rdn over 4f out: sn outpcd* **100/1**
03 **6** *1 3/4* **Copper King**[10] 2094 2-9-3 .... MartinDwyer 2 45+
(A M Balding) *led 1f: rdn over 2f out: hung lft and wknd over 1f out: sn eased* **9/2**[3]
0 **7** *3/4* **Moist**[14] 1989 2-8-12 .... KerrinMcEvoy 3 38
(N A Callaghan) *s.i.s: sn outpcd* **12/1**

68.41 secs (-1.69) **Going Correction** -0.225s/f (Firm) **7** Ran SP% **109.7**
Speed ratings (Par 91):102,101,97,90,88 86,85
CSF £14.82 TOTE £6.10: £3.10, £1.40; EX 18.80 Trifecta £41.90 Pool: £394.81 - 6.68 winning units..
Owner C A Gershinson **Bred** J Egan, J Corcoran And J Judd **Trained** Newmarket, Suffolk

FOCUS
This was run at a good pace and the time was decent, 0.39 seconds faster than the later three-year-old handicap.

NOTEBOOK
Eddie Jock(IRE) appreciated the better ground and strong pace, and came home well to get up near the line. The form may not be that strong but he should pay his way in modest nursery company, and a step up to seven should not hurt. (tchd 4-1)
Lady Lily(IRE) improved for her debut effort and enjoyed this quicker ground. She looked the likeliest winner when hitting the front, but was eventually just pipped. A fillies' maiden at a similarly modest track should come her way. (tchd 11-4)
Pires, turning out again just five days after his debut over the course and distance, probably ran to a similar level. He is not bred to be effective over sprint distances and will appreciate a longer trip in time. (op 9-4)
Inflight(IRE) burnt herself out going too fast in front. (op 9-1)
Copper King did not handle the track and apparently lost his action on the firm ground. Official explanation: jockey said gelding lost its action (op 7-1)

2389 WORLD CUP BETTING WITH SKY BET H'CAP — 5f 59y
2:40 (2:42) (Class 4) (0-85,87) 3-Y-O+ **£6,477** (£1,927; £963; £481) **Stalls** Low

Form RPR
6600 **1** **Intriguing Glimpse**[6] 2227 5-10-0 **84**.................................. SebSanders 2 91
(Miss B Sanders) *hld up in tch: rdn to ld over 1f out: drvn out* **9/4**[1]
2305 **2** *3/4* **Quality Street**[60] 947 4-9-5 **75**....................................... KerrinMcEvoy 1 79
(P Butler) *chsd ldr: rdn over 1f out: r.o one pce fnl f* **13/2**[2]
2000 **3** *3/4* **One Way Ticket**[174] 6597 6-9-12 **82**.......................................(p) TQuinn 8 83
(J M Bradley) *led: rdn and hdd over 1f out: nt qckn ins fnl f* **20/1**
4461 **4** *3/4* **Golden Asha**[6] 2233 4-9-12 **87** 6ex................................ DerekNolan(5) 7 85
(N A Callaghan) *s.i.s: outpcd: rdn 3f out: hdwy and hung lft over 1f out: kpt on ins fnl f* **9/4**[1]
3000 **5** *hd* **Polish Emperor (USA)**[44] 1236 6-9-10 **83**..................(e) AdamKirby(3) 6 81
(W R Swinburn) *a.p: rdn over 2f out: one pce fnl f* **8/1**[3]
4100 **6** *3* **Laith (IRE)**[43] 1264 3-9-5 **82**...(b[1]) MartinDwyer 5 65
(B W Hills) *s.i.s: rdn and hdwy on outside over 2f out: wknd fnl f* **10/1**
-040 **7** *8* **Canary Island (IRE)**[2] 2340 4-8-10 **73**.......................... BarrySavage(7) 3 29
(J M Bradley) *wnt rt s: t.k.h: a bhd* **66/1**

60.37 secs (-1.93) **Going Correction** -0.225s/f (Firm)
WFA 3 from 4yo+ 7lb **7** Ran SP% **101.3**
Speed ratings (Par 105):106,104,103,102,102 97,84
CSF £13.44 CT £146.84 TOTE £2.90: £1.70, £4.00; EX 18.70 Trifecta £297.10 Pool: £556.66 - 1.33 winning units..
Owner Edward Hyde **Bred** Copy Xpress Ltd **Trained** Headley, Surrey
■ Redwood Star was withdrawn (6/1, refused to enter stalls). R4 applies, deduct 10p in the £.

FOCUS
A weakish handicap contested largely by hard-to-win-with types. The winner ws back to something like the form of last year's course and distance win.
Polish Emperor(USA) Official explanation: jockey said gelding was unsuited by the track

2390 SKY BET ENGLAND 3 PARAGUAY 0 10/1 - PRESS RED H'CAP — 6f 209y
3:10 (3:11) (Class 5) (0-70,68) 4-Y-O+ **£3,238** (£963; £481; £240) **Stalls** Low

Form RPR
0226 **1** **Ivory Lace**[36] 1432 5-9-0 **66**.. JamesDoyle(5) 5 76
(S Woodman) *chsd ldr: rdn over 3f out: led over 1f out: pushed out towards fin* **10/1**
3042 **2** *1/2* **Border Artist**[9] 2135 7-7-13 **49** oh2....................... EdwardCreighton(3) 10 58
(B G Powell) *hld up and bhd: hdwy over 3f out: rdn over 1f out: r.o ins fnl f: nt rch wnr* **13/2**[3]
3202 **3** *1/2* **Taranaki**[7] 2211 8-8-11 **58**... KerrinMcEvoy 2 66
(P D Cundell) *a.p: rdn 2f out: r.o ins fnl f* **4/1**[1]
0212 **4** *1 1/2* **Franksalot (IRE)**[5] 2259 6-9-7 **68**.................................... SebSanders 11 72
(I W McInnes) *hld up in mid-div: hdwy on outside over 3f out: ev ch over 2f out: sn rdn: nt qckn fnl f* **4/1**[1]
0453 **5** *1/2* **Oh Boy (IRE)**[9] 2135 6-8-3 **50**... ChrisCatlin 3 52
(J M Bradley) *led: rdn over 2f out: hdd over 1f out: no ex ins fnl f* **9/2**[2]
4252 **6** *1/2* **Green Pirate**[11] 2077 4-8-6 **53**... EddieAhern 9 54
(M Wellings) *hld up in tch: ev ch over 2f out: sn rdn: one pce* **15/2**
3036 **7** *3/4* **Motu (IRE)**[9] 2148 5-8-2 **52** ow2.............................(v) PatrickMathers(3) 4 51
(I W McInnes) *bhd: hdwy on ins over 1f out: n.d* **10/1**
4244 **8** *1 1/2* **Princely Vale (IRE)**[289] 4676 4-8-8 **62**......................... BarrySavage(7) 8 57
(W G M Turner) *hld up in mid-div: rdn 3f out: sn btn* **25/1**
6004 **9** *2* **Riolo (IRE)**[24] 1750 4-8-9 **59**... AdamKirby(3) 7 48
(K F Clutterbuck) *bhd: reminders after 2f: rdn 3f out: no rspnse* **20/1**

1m 20.49s (-2.21) **Going Correction** -0.225s/f (Firm) **9** Ran SP% **110.1**
Speed ratings (Par 103):103,102,101,100,99 99,98,96,94
CSF £67.97 CT £286.81 TOTE £12.90: £2.70, £2.70, £1.90; EX 52.90 Trifecta £265.20 Part won. Pool: £373.61 - 0.60 winning units..
Owner Christopher J Halpin **Bred** D R Tucker **Trained** East Lavant, W Sussex

FOCUS
They did not go a mad pace in this modest handicap. The form does not look strong, with the field made up mainly of horses who find winning difficult.
Green Pirate Official explanation: jockey said gelding failed to handle track
Riolo(IRE) Official explanation: jockey said gelding hung both ways

2391 SKY BET 12/1 HENRY WC TOP SCORER H'CAP — 1m 1f 209y
3:40 (3:45) (Class 5) (0-70,69) 3-Y-O **£3,238** (£963; £481; £240) **Stalls** High

Form RPR
036 **1** **Gower Song**[15] 1955 3-9-2 **64**.. TQuinn 9 71+
(D R C Elsworth) *hld up in mid-div: hdwy 6f out: led over 2f out: rdn out* **8/1**
0004 **2** *1/2* **Girardii**[39] 1350 3-9-0 **62**...(b) RichardHughes 4 65
(R Charlton) *led: rdn and hdd over 2f out: edgd lft over 1f out: kpt on ins fnl f* **11/2**[3]
500 **3** *3/4* **Kavachi (IRE)**[27] 1684 3-9-6 **68**.. EddieAhern 2 70
(E A L Dunlop) *a.p: wnt 2nd 5f out: rdn and ev ch over 2f out: nt qckn ins fnl f* **14/1**
4505 **4** *1 1/4* **Stellenbosch (USA)**[25] 1738 3-9-4 **66**............................... RyanMoore 12 66
(J W Hills) *hld up and bhd: rdn over 1f out: hdwy on outside fnl f: nrst fin* **7/1**
146 **5** *shd* **Samurai Jack (IRE)**[21] 1837 3-9-0 **69**.............................(t) SHunter(7) 11 68
(John A Quinn, Ire) *hld up and bhd: hdwy on outside over 4f out: rdn and ev ch over 2f out: one pce fnl f* **12/1**
3003 **6** *1* **Night Cru**[27] 1681 3-9-4 **66**.. KerrinMcEvoy 7 64
(C F Wall) *hld up in mid-div: rdn over 3f out: styd on same pce fnl f* **11/4**[1]
000 **7** *nk* **Polish Welcome**[39] 1351 3-8-5 **56** ow1........................... AdamKirby(3) 3 53
(S C Williams) *hld up in tch: lost pl 4f out: sn rdn: sme late prog* **25/1**
3322 **8** *nk* **Catbang (IRE)**[29] 1616 3-8-12 **65**.................................... DerekNolan(5) 6 61
(N A Callaghan) *chsd ldr 5f: rdn over 2f out: wknd fnl f* **4/1**[2]
0350 **9** *nk* **Shamsalmaidan (IRE)**[4] 2293 3-9-1 **63**........................... SebSanders 10 59
(C E Brittain) *hld up and bhd: hdwy on ins over 4f out: rdn over 2f out: wknd over 1f out* **16/1**
5550 **10** *8* **Flashing Floozie**[6] 2246 3-8-4 **52** ow1................................ JohnEgan 8 33
(M F Harris) *a towards rr* **33/1**

2m 1.03s (-1.53) **Going Correction** -0.225s/f (Firm) **10** Ran SP% **112.7**
Speed ratings (Par 99):97,96,96,95,94 94,93,93,93,87
CSF £49.77 CT £603.55 TOTE £6.80: £2.60, £2.30, £3.10; EX 37.30 Trifecta £534.70 Pool: £783.27 - 1.04 winning units..
Owner Usk Valley Stud **Bred** R E Crutchley **Trained** Newmarket, Suffolk

FOCUS
A modest handicap run at a steady early pace and very few got competitive. Slight improvement from the first three, and the potential for some more from the unexposed winner, who wasn't ridden as prominently as the second and third.

2392 SKY BET GERMANY 2 COSTA RICA 0 5/1 - PRESS RED CLAIMING STKS — 1m 1f 209y
4:10 (4:13) (Class 6) 4-Y-O+ **£2,266** (£674; £337; £168) **Stalls** High

Form RPR
4240 **1** **Miss Monica (IRE)**[5] 2262 5-8-2 46 ow2.............................. ChrisCatlin 2 49
(P W Hiatt) *hld up: hdwy on ins 4f out: rdn 2f out: led wl ins fnl f: drvn out* **5/2**[2]
6462 **2** *1 1/2* **Prince Valentine**[9] 2131 5-8-5 42....................................(b) RyanMoore 5 49
(G L Moore) *chsd ldr: rdn to ld 2f out: hdd and nt qckn wl ins fnl f* **9/4**[1]
00 **3** *3* **Return In Style (IRE)**[14] 1993 5-8-11 69...........................(p) EddieAhern 6 49
(J W Hills) *set slow pce: qckng 3f out: rdn and hdd 2f out: wknd ins fnl f* **9/2**
3500 **4** *2 1/2* **Shamwari Fire (IRE)**[200] 6394 6-8-2 45................... PatrickMathers(3) 3 39
(I W McInnes) *hld up: hdwy over 3f out: rdn over 2f out: edgd lft and wknd 1f out* **16/1**
5004 **5** *3* **Ringarooma**[9] 2131 4-8-5 49..(e) MartinDwyer 7 33
(C N Allen) *v rel to r: t.o tl hdwy 6f out: in tch 4f out: eased whn btn fnl f* **4/1**[3]
5505 **6** *1 1/2* **Elms Schoolboy**[25] 1723 4-8-8 45 ow1...........................(b) SebSanders 1 33
(P Howling) *hld up in tch: rdn over 3f out: sn wknd* **9/1**

2m 4.37s (1.77) **Going Correction** -0.225s/f (Firm) **6** Ran SP% **113.4**
Speed ratings (Par 101):83,81,79,77,75 73
CSF £8.74 TOTE £3.70: £2.00, £1.70; EX 9.10.
Owner P W Hiatt **Bred** Dr Karen Monica Sanderson **Trained** Hook Norton, Oxon

FOCUS
A poor contest run at a slow early pace, and extremely dubious form.

2393 WORLD CUP HAPPY HOUR WITH SKY BET H'CAP 5f 213y
4:40 (4:41) (Class 5) (0-75,74) 3-Y-O **£3,238** (£963; £481; £240) **Stalls** Low

Form RPR
2104 **1** **Mimiteh (USA)**[27] 1693 3-9-7 **74** .... SebSanders 1 78+
(R M Beckett) *a.p: rdn over 1f out: led ins fnl f: drvn out* **2/1**[1]
2113 **2** *1* **Sarah's Art (IRE)**[16] 1937 3-8-10 **63** ....(b) ChrisCatlin 2 64
(N A Callaghan) *hld up: hdwy over 2f out: ev ch over 1f out: edgd rt ent fnl f: kpt on* **11/4**[2]
0463 **3** *nk* **Danish Blues (IRE)**[7] 2187 3-8-5 **63** ....(p) JamesDoyle(5) 6 63
(N P Littmoden) *stdd s: in rr: rdn over 2f out: swtchd rt over 1f out: gd late hdwy on outside: nrst fin* **10/1**
060 **4** *shd* **Nahaar (IRE)**[28] 1641 3-8-10 **63** ....(p) MartinDwyer 5 63
(M P Tregoning) *led: rdn wl over 1f out: no ex towards fin* **11/2**
4020 **5** *½* **Picture Show (USA)**[67] 850 3-9-0 **67** .... RyanMoore 7 65
(C E Brittain) *chsd ldr 4f: rdn and kpt on same pce fnl 2f* **10/1**
0430 **6** *shd* **Elusive Warrior (USA)**[6] 2235 3-8-10 **63** ....(p) KerrinMcEvoy 4 61
(Mrs A J Perrett) *hld up in tch: rdn and one pce fnl 2f* **5/1**[3]

68.80 secs (-1.30) **Going Correction** -0.225s/f (Firm) **6** Ran SP% **110.2**
Speed ratings (Par 99):99,97,97,97,96 96
CSF £7.38 TOTE £3.00: £1.60, £1.60; EX 6.20 Place 6 £40.44, Place 5 £20.05.
Owner P K Gardner **Bred** Stonerside Stable **Trained** Whitsbury, Hants

FOCUS
A modest small-field handicap but it went largely as the market expected. With the second and third looking high enough in the weights the form probably doesn't amount to much, but the winner improved a couple of pounds and shaped as if she can do better again.
T/Plt: £98.00 to a £1 stake. Pool: £46,686.00. 347.50 winning tickets. T/Qpdt: £14.00 to a £1 stake. Pool: £3,214.40. 169.90 winning tickets. KH

2191 CATTERICK (L-H)
Friday, June 9

OFFICIAL GOING: Good to firm (firm in places)
9mm water had been put on the course over the previous four days. The ground was reckoned to be 'very firm, rough on the bends'.
Wind: Light, half-behind Weather: Fine and sunny

2394 STAPLETON MAIDEN AUCTION FILLIES' STKS 5f
2:20 (2:21) (Class 6) 2-Y-O **£2,730** (£806; £403) **Stalls** Low

Form RPR
2 **1** **Vale Of Belvoir (IRE)**[10] 2100 2-8-10 .... PatCosgrave 1 68+
(K R Burke) *sn trcking ldrs: led over 1f out: jst hld on* **1/1**[1]
0 **2** *shd* **La Vecchia Scuola (IRE)**[36] 1442 2-8-7 .... AdrianTNicholls 3 65
(D Nicholls) *led tl over 1f out: rallied ins fnl f: jst hld* **33/1**
3 *1 ¾* **Reem Al Fallah (IRE)** 2-8-7 .... RobertWinston 6 58
(M R Channon) *in tch: hdwy on outer over 2f out: sn chsng ldrs: nt qckn fnl f* **16/1**
00 **4** *1 ½* **Almora Guru**[13] 2026 2-8-4 .... PaulHanagan 8 50
(W M Brisbourne) *swtchd ins over 3f out: hdwy to join ldrs over 2f out: kpt on same pce fnl f* **50/1**
02 **5** *½* **The Italian Job**[31] 1559 2-8-7 .... DavidAllan 5 51
(T D Easterby) *w ldrs: kpt on one pce appr fnl f* **3/1**[2]
53 **6** *¾* **Ishibee (IRE)**[27] 1664 2-8-7 .... StephenCarson 9 48
(Mrs A Duffield) *trckd ldrs: lost pl over 1f out* **12/1**[3]

59.27 secs (-1.33) **Going Correction** -0.45s/f (Firm) **6** Ran SP% **93.5**
Speed ratings (Par 88):92,91,89,86,85 84
CSF £22.31 TOTE £1.50: £1.20, £3.90; EX 19.80.
Owner S Marley & Tweenhills Racing IX **Bred** Denis And Mrs Teresa Bergin **Trained** Middleham Moor, N Yorks
■ No Surprises was withdrawn (9/2, vet's advice.) R4 applies, deduct 15p in the £.

FOCUS
This was probably an ordinary maiden. It has been rated through the winner and fourth to previous marks, but it's not a race to be confident about.

NOTEBOOK
Vale Of Belvoir(IRE) had shown plenty of promise on her debut at Leicester, but she had to work hard to open her account this time, being pushed along early and needing plenty of driving to get on top. Her trainer felt that the track didn't really suit her and that she will prove better than this form in the long run. (op 10-11 tchd 11-10)
La Vecchia Scuola(IRE) improved on her debut run, showing up well all the way but just going down in a driving finish. She may find a small race.
Reem Al Fallah(IRE), related to juvenile winners, shaped quite well on this debut. (tchd 14-1)
Almora Guru, dropped in trip and on much faster ground, seemed to run better, particularly as she was drawn wide.
The Italian Job, who had run creditably here last time, dropped away from halfway and was disappointing. (op 10-3 tchd 9-2)

2395 NOEL & GEORGINA VERNON 10TH WEDDING ANNIVERSARY (S) STKS 1m 5f 175y
2:50 (2:50) (Class 6) 4-Y-O+ **£2,730** (£806; £403) **Stalls** Low

Form RPR
5005 **1** **Court Of Appeal**[31] 1560 9-8-12 60 ....(tp) TomEaves 2 54
(B Ellison) *trckd ldrs: chal over 5f out: led over 3f out: shkn up over 1f out: styd on wl* **8/13**[1]
25/0 **2** *2 ½* **Tipu Sultan**[33] 1500 6-8-12 48 .... RichardMullen 1 51
(Micky Hammond) *led 2f: trckd ldrs: wnt 2nd over 2f out: kpt on: no imp* **20/1**
0244 **3** *3 ½* **Romil Star (GER)**[9] 2140 9-8-13 45 ....(v) AndrewElliott(5) 4 52
(K R Burke) *trckd ldrs: led after 2f: qcknd over 6f out: hdd over 3f out: one pce* **9/4**[2]
000- **4** *21* **Protocol (IRE)**[61] 2851 12-8-12 ....(t) RobertWinston 3 17
(Mrs S Lamyman) *chsd ldrs: hrd drvn over 5f out: lost pl over 3f out: sn bhd and eased* **16/1**[3]
0460 **5** *14* **Cezzaro (IRE)**[281] 4885 8-8-12 37 .... DaleGibson 5 —
(T A K Cuthbert) *trckd ldrs: t.k.h: drvn over 4f out: sn lost pl and bhd: virtually p.u* **33/1**

3m 3.89s (-0.61) **Going Correction** -0.225s/f (Firm) **5** Ran SP% **106.3**
Speed ratings (Par 101):92,90,88,76,68
CSF £13.16 TOTE £1.40: £1.10, £6.00; EX 13.40.There was no bid for the winner.
Owner Spring Cottage Syndicate No 2 **Bred** John And Susan Davis **Trained** Norton, N Yorks

FOCUS
A slow time, even for a seller, but a relatively predictable result and rated through the third to recent course form.

2396 LIONWELD KENNEDY SPRINT H'CAP 5f
3:20 (3:21) (Class 5) (0-70,70) 3-Y-O+ **£3,886** (£1,156; £577; £288) **Stalls** Low

Form RPR
2300 **1** **Brut**[13] 2020 4-9-8 **64** .... FergalLynch 13 74
(D W Barker) *hld up: hdwy and swtchd outside over 1f out: r.o wl to ld last strides* **9/1**[3]
3060 **2** *½* **Strensall**[31] 1563 9-9-9 **65** .... PaulHanagan 4 73
(R E Barr) *chsd ldrs: r.o ins last: jst edgd out* **12/1**
0626 **3** *shd* **Jun Fan (USA)**[6] 2237 4-9-0 **56** .... PatCosgrave 12 64
(B Ellison) *sn chsng ldrs: no ex wl ins last* **8/1**[2]
0006 **4** *shd* **Borzoi Maestro**[9] 2136 5-8-12 **54** ....(p) JoeFanning 1 61
(M Wellings) *led: hdd and no ex nr fin* **14/1**
0003 **5** *½* **Atlantic Viking (IRE)**[18] 1886 11-9-10 **66** .... RobertWinston 3 71
(D Nicholls) *sn in rr and pushed along: swtchd rt over 1f out: styd on wl towards fin* **9/1**[3]
0030 **6** *½* **Henry Hall (IRE)**[8] 2182 10-9-13 **69** .... KimTinkler 11 72
(N Tinkler) *chsd ldrs: kpt on same pce fnl f* **9/1**[3]
0000 **7** *nk* **Law Maker**[37] 1399 6-9-1 **64** ....(v) MichaelJStainton(7) 2 66
(A Bailey) *chsd ldrs: kpt on same pce fnl f* **9/1**[3]
5000 **8** *1* **Unlimited**[13] 2027 4-9-1 **57** .... StephenCarson 6 57+
(Mrs A Duffield) *swtchd lft after s: hdwy on ins over 3f out: keeping on same pce whn nt clr run towards fin* **7/1**[1]
0403 **9** *¾* **Detonate**[8] 2182 4-8-9 **51** oh5 ....(p) TomEaves 9 46
(Mrs C A Dunnett) *sn chsng ldrs: one pce appr fnl f* **9/1**[3]
6006 **10** *1* **Disguise**[155] 47 4-9-9 **65** .... GrahamGibbons 7 56
(J J Quinn) *chsd ldrs: wknd over 1f out* **12/1**
0004 **11** *shd* **Rudi's Pet (IRE)**[18] 1886 12-10-0 **70** .... AdrianTNicholls 5 61
(D Nicholls) *chsd ldrs: wknd fnl f* **14/1**
0000 **12** *hd* **Special Gold**[20] 1846 4-9-6 **62** ....(b) DavidAllan 15 52
(T D Easterby) *in tch on outer: outpcd fnl 2f* **33/1**
0000 **13** *1 ½* **Mis Chicaf (IRE)**[20] 1846 5-8-11 **58** ....(t) AndrewMullen(5) 10 42
(Robert Gray) *sn drvn along and in rr* **25/1**
0000 **14** *7* **Jadan (IRE)**[13] 2027 5-9-4 **60** ....(p) KDarley 14 16
(E J Alston) *prom: wkng whn stmbld 2f out: sn eased* **12/1**
0000 **15** *1 ¼* **Grasslandik**[31] 1571 10-8-5 **54** oh11 ow3........................(p) AnnStokell(7) 8 5
(Miss A Stokell) *in tch: lost pl over 2f out: sn bhd* **125/1**

58.17 secs (-2.43) **Going Correction** -0.45s/f (Firm) **15** Ran SP% **117.6**
Speed ratings (Par 103):101,100,100,99,99 98,97,96,95,93 93,92,90,79,77
CSF £107.91 CT £924.27 TOTE £12.80: £3.20, £5.00, £2.40; EX 105.80.
Owner racingowners.co.uk **Bred** Mrs Deborah O'Brien **Trained** Scorton, N Yorks

FOCUS
A typical sprint handicap for the track with less than two lengths covering the first seven home, but the form looks rock solid.
Jadan(IRE) Official explanation: jockey said gelding stumbled 2f out

2397 SARAH LUNN MEMORIAL STKS (H'CAP) 5f 212y
3:50 (3:50) (Class 4) (0-85,85) 4-Y-O+ **£6,477** (£1,927; £963; £481) **Stalls** Low

Form RPR
3000 **1** **Mr Wolf**[36] 1438 5-9-3 **81** ....(p) FergalLynch 1 90
(D W Barker) *mde all: edgd rt fnl f: hld on towards fin* **9/2**[2]
0120 **2** *½* **Circuit Dancer (IRE)**[27] 1686 6-8-6 **70** .... AdrianTNicholls 4 78
(D Nicholls) *trckd ldrs on inner: effrt over 2f out: n.m.r over 1f out: r.o ins last: no ex towards fin* **9/2**[2]
0204 **3** *hd* **Knot In Wood (IRE)**[13] 2027 4-8-9 **73** .... PaulHanagan 10 80
(R A Fahey) *trckd ldrs: outpcd over 3f out: hdwy over 1f out: styd on wl towards fin* **15/2**
0023 **4** *hd* **Blackheath (IRE)**[27] 1686 10-8-3 **67** .... JoeFanning 2 73
(D Nicholls) *trckd wnr: kpt on same pce ins last* **11/2**[3]
0033 **5** *shd* **Trojan Flight**[1] 2384 5-8-8 **72** .... PhillipMakin 7 78
(D W Chapman) *hld up in rr: effrt on outer over 2f out: styd on fnl f: nt rch ldrs* **4/1**[1]
0004 **6** *½* **H Harrison (IRE)**[9] 2147 6-8-4 **73** .... AndrewElliott(5) 9 78
(I W McInnes) *chsd ldrs: rdn and hung lft over 1f out: kpt on one pce* **16/1**
0000 **7** *5* **Sir Don (IRE)**[281] 4882 7-8-2 **66** oh15........................ RichardMullen 6 56?
(E S McMahon) *rr-div: hdwy over 2f out: lost pl over 1f out* **100/1**
1336 **8** *nk* **Paris Bell**[15] 1949 4-8-12 **76** .... PaulQuinn 5 65
(T D Easterby) *s.i.s: hdwy on inner over 2f out: lost pl over 1f out* **6/1**
6160 **9** *3 ½* **Pomfret Lad**[20] 1856 8-8-13 **77** .... GrahamGibbons 3 55
(J J Quinn) *trckd ldrs: wknd over 1f out* **11/1**

1m 11.67s (-2.33) **Going Correction** -0.225s/f (Firm) **9** Ran SP% **113.0**
Speed ratings (Par 105):106,105,105,104,104 104,97,96,92
CSF £24.47 CT £147.06 TOTE £5.30: £1.90, £2.10, £2.40; EX 38.90.
Owner P Asquith **Bred** P Asquith **Trained** Scorton, N Yorks

FOCUS
Another sprint resulting in a blanket finish as just over a length covered the first six. The form is ordinary rated through the third.

2398 BARTON MAIDEN STKS 1m 3f 214y
4:20 (4:20) (Class 5) 3-Y-O+ **£3,886** (£1,156; £577; £288) **Stalls** Low

Form RPR
2223 **1** **Dream Champion**[11] 2081 3-8-11 75 .... KDarley 5 72+
(M R Channon) *chsd ldr: led 4f out: drvn clr over 1f out* **5/2**[2]
02 **2** *6* **Dayrose**[22] 1797 3-8-6 .... RobertWinston 1 60+
(Sir Michael Stoute) *trckd ldrs: drvn and 2nd over 3f out: nvr happy: rdr accepted defeat 1f out* **4/11**[1]
0606 **3** *2 ½* **True (IRE)**[149] 94 5-9-7 42 .... PaulHanagan 6 53?
(Mrs S Lamyman) *hld up: hdwy 7f out: wnt mod 3rd over 2f out: kpt on same pce* **33/1**[3]
6450 **4** *10* **Finnegans Rainbow**[11] 97 4-9-9 35 .... LeeVickers(3) 3 42
(M C Chapman) *hld up in last: drvn over 4f out: nvr a factor* **80/1**
0000 **5** *22* **Fox Flight (IRE)**[10] 2107 3-8-6 16 .... AndrewMullen(5) 2 7
(D W Barker) *prom early: pushed along after 2f: lost pl over 3f out: sn bhd* **200/1**
6 *25* **Talisker Rock (IRE)**[43] 6-9-12 .... TomEaves 7 —
(B Storey) *led tl 4f out: lost pl over 2f out: sn bhd: t.o* **100/1**

2m 34.72s (-4.28) **Going Correction** -0.225s/f (Firm)
WFA 3 from 4yo+ 15lb **6** Ran SP% **107.5**
Speed ratings (Par 103):105,101,99,92,78 61
CSF £3.54 TOTE £3.50: £2.00, £1.02; EX 4.80.
Owner Jaber Abdullah **Bred** G W Turner And Miss S J Turner **Trained** West Ilsley, Berks

FOCUS
An uncompetitive event and probably not much of a race, with the favourite running poorly and the 42-rated third setting a very modest level.

2399 PEN HILL H'CAP — 5f 212y
4:50 (4:51) (Class 6) (0-65,65) 3-Y-O — £2,730 (£806; £403) Stalls Low

Form — RPR

5321 **1** **Our Sheila**[13] 2019 3-9-7 **65** ... TomEaves 8 — 75
(B Smart) *led after 1f: edgd rt 2f out: hld on towards fin* **7/1**

4302 **2** *nk* **Northern Chorus (IRE)**[7] 2197 3-9-3 **64** ... DanielTudhope(3) 9 — 73
(A Dickman) *in tch: effrt over 2f out: hung lft and wnt 2nd over 1f out: no ex towards fin* **5/1**[2]

0204 **3** *1 1/2* **Butterfly Bud (IRE)**[243] 5768 3-9-0 **65** ... JamesO'Reilly(7) 7 — 70+
(J O'Reilly) *s.i.s: hdwy on inner and nt clr run 2f out: styd on wl fnl f* **20/1**

3036 **4** *1/2* **Esoterica (IRE)**[12] 2050 3-9-4 **62** ... (p) PhillipMakin 4 — 65
(T D Barron) *chsd ldrs: kpt on same pce appr fainl f* **11/2**[3]

4505 **5** *1 1/2* **Final Tune (IRE)**[39] 1344 3-9-7 **65** ... AdrianTNicholls 2 — 64
(D Nicholls) *rr-div: effrt on ins 3f out: kpt on: nvr rchd ldrs* **4/1**[1]

0053 **6** *1 1/2* **Coalite (IRE)**[7] 2198 3-8-12 **59** ... (b) SilvestreDeSousa(3) 10 — 53
(A D Brown) *chsd ldrs: one pce fnl 2f* **20/1**

3663 **7** *1* **Trombone Tom**[7] 2197 3-9-3 **61** ... DarrenWilliams 11 — 52
(J R Norton) *led 1f: chsd ldrs: wknd appr fnl f* **16/1**

2663 **8** *nk* **Rosita Mia (IRE)**[13] 2019 3-9-4 **62** ... RobertWinston 3 — 52
(D W Barker) *s.i.s: kpt on fnl 2f: nvr on terms* **8/1**

2344 **9** *3/4* **Bond Angel Eyes**[10] 2109 3-9-2 **65** ... GregFairley(5) 6 — 53
(G R Oldroyd) *chsd ldrs: effrt over 2f out: wknd over 1f out* **10/1**

530 **10** *1 1/4* **Josarty**[14] 2001 3-9-0 **58** ... GrahamGibbons 12 — 42
(J J Quinn) *prom on outer: outpcd fnl 2f* **28/1**

4050 **11** *1/2* **Eagle Eye**[16] 1941 3-9-4 **62** ... JDSmith 5 — 45
(G Wragg) *in rr: c wd over 2f out: shkn up over 1f out: nvr on terms: eased* **15/2**

0000 **12** *17* **Madam Moschata**[7] 2195 3-8-4 **53** ... AndrewMullen(5) 1 — —
(D W Barker) *s.i.s: hdwy on ins to chse ldrs over 4f out: lost pl 2f out: sn bhd and heavily eased* **66/1**

1m 12.59s (-1.41) **Going Correction** -0.225s/f (Firm) **12** Ran SP% **116.9**
Speed ratings (Par 97):100,99,97,96,94 92,91,91,90,88 87,65
CSF £39.40 CT £673.63 TOTE £6.20: £2.20, £2.00, £7.20; EX 26.00.
Owner Anthony D Gee **Bred** Mrs C R Philipson **Trained** Hambleton, N Yorks

FOCUS
A modest contest, but sound enough form with the runner-up, fourth and fifth close to recent form.

2400 CATTERICK FILLIES' H'CAP — 7f
5:20 (5:20) (Class 5) (0-75,73) 3-Y-O+ — £3,886 (£1,156; £577; £288) Stalls Low

Form — RPR

5254 **1** **Hazelhurst (IRE)**[233] 5976 3-8-7 **67** ... GregFairley(5) 7 — 75
(J Howard Johnson) *rr-div: effrt on outer over 3f out: edgd lft and styd on wl fnl f: led nr fin* **25/1**

2056 **2** *1* **Witchelle**[66] 864 5-8-11 **56** ... DavidAllan 12 — 65
(R Craggs) *swtchd lft after s: led: 4 l clr over 1f out: hdd nr fin* **7/1**

4001 **3** *1 1/4* **First Rhapsody (IRE)**[13] 2020 4-8-6 **56** ... AndrewElliott(5) 5 — 62
(T J Etherington) *mid-div: effrt on wd outside over 2f out: styd on fnl f* **9/1**

5101 **4** *nk* **Dispol Isle (IRE)**[18] 1885 4-9-6 **68** ... BenSwarbrick(3) 2 — 73
(T D Barron) *chsd ldrs: keeping on same pce whn hmpd ins last* **7/1**

0052 **5** *2* **Linden's Lady**[8] 2164 6-8-4 **54** oh1 ... (v) AndrewMullen(5) 4 — 54
(J R Weymes) *mid-div: effrt over 2f out: kpt on fnl f* **5/1**[2]

5000 **6** *3/4* **Frogs' Gift (IRE)**[7] 2195 4-8-9 **54** oh14 ... PaulQuinn 6 — 52?
(G M Moore) *s.i.s: hdwy 2f out: styd on ins last* **150/1**

0040 **7** *shd* **Lady Georgette (IRE)**[24] 1761 3-8-8 **63** ... RichardMullen 11 — 56
(E J O'Neill) *chsd ldrs: wknd fnl f* **20/1**

4002 **8** *3/4* **Dream Rose (IRE)**[8] 2160 3-9-1 **70** ... RobertWinston 8 — 64+
(M R Channon) *chsd ldrs: drvn over 3f out: wkng whn n.m.r jst ins last* **8/1**

00-0 **9** *1 1/4* **Algorithm**[10] 2112 4-8-4 **54** oh2 ... DuranFentiman(5) 1 — 46
(T D Easterby) *in rr: sme hdwy on inner over 2f out: nvr on terms* **80/1**

12 **10** *2 1/2* **Imperial Lucky (IRE)**[32] 1551 3-8-6 **61** ... KDarley 10 — 42
(M J Wallace) *chsd ldrs on outer: lost pl over 1f out* **11/4**[1]

0060 **11** *1 3/4* **Bint Royal (IRE)**[112] 440 8-8-10 **55** ... (v) JDSmith 9 — 36
(Miss V Haigh) *chsd ldrs: lost pl over 2f out* **50/1**

0466 **12** *6* **My Princess (IRE)**[14] 1993 4-10-0 **73** ... FergalLynch 3 — 37
(N A Callaghan) *slipped s: a in rr: bhd and eased over 1f out* **11/2**[3]

1m 25.68s (-1.68) **Going Correction** -0.225s/f (Firm)
WFA 3 from 4yo+ 10lb **12** Ran SP% **117.3**
Speed ratings (Par 100):100,98,97,97,94 93,93,92,91,88 86,79
CSF £184.57 CT £1737.61 TOTE £21.90: £3.90, £2.80, £3.20; EX 293.40 Place 6 £54.49, Place 5 £32.95.
Owner Transcend Bloodstock LLP **Bred** Martin Francis **Trained** Billy Row, Co Durham
■ Stewards' Enquiry : Greg Fairley one-day ban: careless riding (Jun 25)

FOCUS
Not many got into this fillies' handicap and the form looks shaky. It has been rated around those in the frame behind the winner.
My Princess(IRE) Official explanation: jockey said filly slipped shortly after start
T/Plt: £55.80 to a £1 stake. Pool: £36,806.55. 480.90 winning tickets. T/Qpdt: £16.60 to a £1 stake. Pool: £2,093.80. 93.20 winning tickets. WG

1975 GOODWOOD (R-H)
Friday, June 9

OFFICIAL GOING: Straight course - good; round course - good to firm
Wind: Virtually nil

2401 ELM FARM RESEARCH CENTRE STKS (H'CAP) — 1m 1f
6:25 (6:34) (Class 5) (0-70,70) 4-Y-O+ — £3,562 (£1,059; £529; £264) Stalls High

Form — RPR

5620 **1** **Night Storm**[17] 1926 5-9-0 **63** ... RyanMoore 12 — 78
(S Dow) *s.i.s: bhd: gd hdwy over 2f out: str run fnl f to ld cl home* **16/1**

0024 **2** *hd* **Alekhine (IRE)**[28] 1637 5-9-6 **69** ... (p) EddieAhern 6 — 84
(J R Boyle) *bhd: n.m.r over 3f out: hdwy sn after: chal over 1f out: led ins last: ct nr fin* **14/1**

4622 **3** *3* **Fasylitator (IRE)**[14] 1993 4-8-13 **67** ... RichardKingscote(5) 14 — 76
(D K Ivory) *chsd ldrs: led 2f out: sn hrd drvn: hdd ins last: sn wknd* **4/1**[2]

6160 **4** *7* **Danger Zone**[27] 1673 4-9-7 **70** ... (p) ShaneKelly 9 — 65+
(Mrs A J Perrett) *bhd: edgd rt 3f out: hdwy over 2f out: styd on but nvr gng pce to rch ldrs* **20/1**

5041 **5** *1* **Fantasy Crusader**[17] 1910 7-8-4 **56** ow4 ... NelsonDeSouza(3) 13 — 49
(R M H Cowell) *mid-div: hmpd on rails ins fnl 3f: swtchd lft and kpt on fnl f: nt rch ldrs* **11/1**

0000 **6** *hd* **Meelup (IRE)**[37] 1400 6-8-8 **57** ... (p) RobertHavlin 5 — 49
(P G Murphy) *in tch: rdn and kpt on fr over 1f out: nvr gng pce to rch ldrs* **40/1**

022 **7** *5* **Tuning Fork**[9] 2148 6-8-6 **55** ... PaulDoe 15 — 37
(T M Jones) *led tl hdd 2f out: sn wknd* **13/2**

0400 **8** *nk* **Oakley Absolute**[3] 2327 4-8-13 **65** ... (v1) AdamKirby(3) 11 — 47
(R Hannon) *chsd ldrs: rdn 3f out: wknd ins fnl 2f* **28/1**

0006 **9** *3/4* **Hallings Overture (USA)**[18] 1882 7-8-6 **55** ... FergusSweeney 3 — 35
(C A Horgan) *bhd: kpt n fnl 2f: nvr in contention* **40/1**

0500 **10** *2* **Play Up Pompey**[5] 2262 4-8-3 **52** ... FrankieMcDonald 4 — 28
(J J Bridger) *chsd ldrs: rdn 3f out: wknd over 2f out* **28/1**

0466 **11** *14* **Desert Reign**[21] 1821 5-9-3 **66** ... JamieSpencer 1 — 14+
(A P Jarvis) *lw: bhd most of way* **11/2**[3]

5060 **12** *11* **Piquet**[2] 2348 8-7-11 **51** oh11 ... MarcHalford(5) 7 — —+
(J J Bridger) *in tch 6f* **50/1**

0560 **13** *3/4* **Admiral Compton**[3] 2327 5-8-10 **62** ... AmirQuinn(3) 10 — —+
(J R Boyle) *chsd ldrs 6f* **20/1**

0004 **14** *5* **Monash Lad (IRE)**[37] 1425 4-9-4 **67** ... (b) DarryllHolland 2 — —
(M H Tompkins) *s.i.s: bhd most of way* **20/1**

3232 **15** *16* **Compton Court**[21] 1821 4-9-7 **70** ... RichardHughes 8 — —+
(A M Balding) *lw: chsd ldrs: rdn 3f out: sn wknd* **10/3**[1]

1m 54.27s (-2.59) **Going Correction** -0.15s/f (Firm) **15** Ran SP% **120.7**
Speed ratings (Par 103):105,104,102,95,95 94,90,90,89,87 75,65,64,60,55
CSF £198.28 CT £1104.25 TOTE £20.30: £4.20, £3.70, £1.90; EX 257.80.
Owner W Thornton & R E Anderson **Bred** The Lavington Stud **Trained** Epsom, Surrey
■ Stewards' Enquiry : Ryan Moore caution: used whip down the shoulder in the forehand position
Adam Kirby caution: used whip down the shoulder in the forehand position

FOCUS
An ordinary race for the track, but the pace was decent and the first three came clear, which suggests the form is sound..
Tuning Fork Official explanation: trainer said gelding lost a shoe
Desert Reign Official explanation: jockey said gelding was unsuited by the good to firm ground
Monash Lad(IRE) Official explanation: jockey said gelding was reluctant to race
Compton Court Official explanation: jockey said gelding moved poorly

2402 SOIL ASSOCIATION E B F MAIDEN STKS — 6f
6:55 (7:04) (Class 4) 2-Y-O — £4,695 (£1,397; £698; £348) Stalls Low

Form — RPR

5 **1** **Prince Of Elegance**[15] 1959 2-9-3 ... RyanMoore 11 — 88
(Mrs A J Perrett) *lw: scope: chsd ldrs: slt ld ins fnl 2f: hrd drvn and r.o strly fnl f* **13/2**[3]

2 *1 1/4* **Non Compliant** 2-9-3 ... EddieAhern 2 — 84
(J W Hills) *w'like: b.bkwd: chsd ldrs: drvn to chal 2f out: kpt on wl fnl f but no imp on wnr cl home* **33/1**

3 *1 1/4* **Kilburn** 2-9-0 ... AdamKirby(3) 7 — 81+
(C G Cox) *str: b.bkwd: in tch: rdn over 2f out: kpt on fnl f but nvr gng pce to rch ldrs* **20/1**

4 **4** *nk* **Endiamo (IRE)**[20] 1838 2-9-3 ... MartinDwyer 9 — 80
(M P Tregoning) *lw: chsd ldrs: rdn and one pce 2f out: kpt on u.p ins last but nvr gng pce to chal* **11/10**[1]

5 *1 3/4* **Sri Pekan Two** 2-9-3 ... JamieSpencer 6 — 74
(P F I Cole) *w'like: chsd ldrs: rdn to chal 2f out: wknd ins fnl f* **11/2**[2]

6 *1/2* **Baby Dordan (IRE)** 2-8-12 ... ShaneKelly 13 — 68
(D J Daly) *leggy: bhd: pushed along 2f out: kpt on wl fnl f but nvr nr ldrs* **66/1**

7 *1 1/4* **Stargazy** 2-8-12 ... RichardKingscote(5) 10 — 69
(R Charlton) *w'like: plld hrd: chsd ldrs: one pce whn n.m.r 1f out: sn wknd* **20/1**

8 *hd* **Rocker** 2-9-3 ... RobertHavlin 14 — 69
(P W Chapple-Hyam) *w'like: chsd ldrs: rdn 2f out: wknd ins fnl f* **10/1**

64 **9** *2* **Fort Worth (IRE)**[13] 2029 2-9-3 ... FergusSweeney 5 — 63
(B Gubby) *sprawled stalls but gd spd and sn ld: rdn 3f out: hdd ins fnl 2f and sn wknd* **33/1**

10 *nk* **Nur Tau (IRE)** 2-9-0 ... NelsonDeSouza(3) 1 — 62
(M P Tregoning) *leggy: sn pushed along and outpcd* **33/1**

11 *1 1/2* **Norisan** 2-9-3 ... RichardHughes 4 — 57
(R Hannon) *b.bkwd: hmpd s: in tch: pushed along 1/2-way: sn wknd* **16/1**

12 *1/2* **Numerical (IRE)** 2-9-3 ... SebSanders 12 — 56
(J L Dunlop) *w'like: b.bkwd: s.i.s: outpcd most of way* **25/1**

60 **13** *3 1/2* **Red Flare (IRE)**[15] 1945 2-9-3 ... ChrisCatlin 8 — 45
(M R Channon) *s.i.s: outpcd* **66/1**

14 *3* **Henry The Seventh** 2-9-3 ... FrankieMcDonald 3 — 36
(J W Hills) *w'like: b.bkwd: a outpcd* **50/1**

1m 11.36s (-1.49) **Going Correction** -0.35s/f (Firm) **14** Ran SP% **118.4**
Speed ratings (Par 95):95,93,91,91,88 88,86,86,83,83 81,80,75,75
CSF £207.40 TOTE £7.00: £1.80, £4.80, £5.20; EX 107.00.
Owner Mrs Gloria Cloran and Mrs Sue Whitehead **Bred** Platt Promotions Ltd **Trained** Pulborough, W Sussex

FOCUS
Plenty of well-bred debutants on display, so a maiden to keep in mind in the coming weeks.

NOTEBOOK
Prince Of Elegance stepped up on his Polytrack debut with a convincing victory over a good-sized field of unexposed rivals. He was still a bit green down the centre of the track, and can improve a bit more. (op 8-1 tchd 6-1)
Non Compliant, a 25,000 guinea athletic-looking son of Lujain out of a Selkirk mare, has a decent enough pedigree and did well considering his stable is not yet at its peak. An encouraging debut. (op 25-1)
Kilburn, a 52,000 guinea Grand Lodge colt whose dam stayed 1m2f, will be suited by longer trips in due course. In the circumstances, this was a pleasing debut, and he will improve as the season progresses.
Endiamo(IRE) was running on quicker ground this time and did not quite live up to the promise of his debut. However, he ran well enough and will come into his own over seven furlongs and a mile as he matures. (tchd Evens, 5-4 and 6-5 in places)
Sri Pekan Two, a 105,000 guinea son of Montjeu, will be at home over longer trips later in the season. However, he showed plenty of speed here and improvement is likely, so finding suitable races for him should not be hard. (op 4-1)
Baby Dordan(IRE)'s sire Desert Prince gets some speedy juveniles, and her dam has also produced a five furlong winner. She did not live up to that billing here, but she was going on well at the finish and it was it was still a decent debut against the colts. Improvement is likely.
Stargazy, an athletic sort, is bred to be a fast two-year-old, maybe staying a mile next year, and he showed plenty of pace on this debut. When he learns to settle, he will use it to better effect. (tchd 16-1)
Rocker, the first foal of the speedy Jessica's Dream, and by the superstar Rock Of Gibraltar, has plenty to live up to on breeding. Without setting the world alight, he made a satisfactory debut down the centre of the track, and can do better next time. (op 7-1)
Fort Worth(IRE) Official explanation: jockey said colt stumbled leaving stalls
Norisan is an athletic sort, but showed very little during the race. (op 20-1)
Numerical(IRE) got warm before the race.

2403 HILDON STKS (H'CAP) 1m
7:25 (7:35) (Class 5) (0-75,75) 3-Y-O £3,562 (£1,059; £529; £264) Stalls High

Form RPR

4050 **1** **Pagan Crest**[8] 2171 3-8-9 **63** .... KerrinMcEvoy 3 70
(Mrs A J Perrett) *mid-div: hdwy to take slt ld 1f out: hung bdly lft u.p to r alone stands side: jst hld on* **6/1**[2]

6540 **2** *shd* **Fratt'n Park (IRE)**[22] 1801 3-8-8 **62** .... SteveDrowne 4 69+
(J J Bridger) *bhd: hdwy 2f out: n.m.r sn after: str run fnl f: fin fast: jst failed* **33/1**

5503 **3** *nk* **Southport Star (IRE)**[15] 1963 3-9-6 **74** .... JamieSpencer 8 80
(J R Fanshawe) *s.i.s: hdwy 3f out: edgd lft over 2f out: chal fr wl over 1f out: stl disputing ld ins last: no ex cl home* **7/2**[1]

5506 **4** *shd* **High Class Problem (IRE)**[32] 1547 3-8-11 **65** .... ShaneKelly 14 71+
(P F I Cole) *s.i.s: sn rcvrd: chsng ldrs whn n.m.r and lost position wl over 1f out: str run ins last: fin wl* **9/1**

4210 **5** *2 1/2* **Deira (USA)**[20] 1843 3-9-4 **72** .... RyanMoore 7 72
(C E Brittain) *chsd ldrs: slt ld and hrd drvn 2f out: hdd 1f out: wknd ins last* **13/2**[3]

0041 **6** *nk* **Maidford (IRE)**[25] 1726 3-8-2 **56** oh4 .... ChrisCatlin 2 61+
(M Meade) *bhd: stdy hdwy whn bdly hmpd ins fnl 2f: rallied and r.o wl fnl f: nt rcvr* **20/1**

0000 **7** *3* **Zafantage**[39] 1348 3-8-13 **67** .... RichardHughes 15 60
(S Kirk) *chsd ldrs: drvn to chal 2f out: wknd fnl f* **20/1**

0010 **8** *nk* **Strife (IRE)**[25] 1736 3-8-0 **57** oh3 ow1 .... StephaneBreux(3) 12 49
(R Hannon) *slt ld tl narrowly hdd 4f out: slt ld again 3f out: hdd 2f out: wknd appr fnl f* **14/1**

3500 **9** *hd* **Giverny Spring**[32] 1552 3-9-0 **68** .... EddieAhern 9 59
(J W Hills) *in tch: hdwy to trck ldrs over 2f out: sn rdn: wknd over 1f out* **25/1**

4336 **10** *3* **Siakira**[192] 6467 3-8-10 **69** .... JamesDoyle(5) 13 53
(I A Wood) *bhd: nvr gng pce to rch ldrs* **25/1**

005 **11** *3/4* **Satin Doll**[39] 1335 3-9-4 **72** .... (p) MartinDwyer 11 55
(M P Tregoning) *chsd ldrs: rdn 3f out: wknd 2f out* **12/1**

0041 **12** *3/4* **Debord (FR)**[8] 2177 3-8-6 **60** 6ex .... JohnEgan 1 41
(Jamie Poulton) *lw: nvr really travelling: rdn over 3f out: a bhd* **8/1**

050 **13** *2 1/2* **Lord Laing (USA)**[121] 337 3-8-12 **66** .... DarryllHolland 6 41
(H J Collingridge) *bhd most of way* **25/1**

2065 **14** *nk* **Semi Detached (IRE)**[16] 1934 3-9-4 **75** .... AmirQuinn(3) 5 50
(J R Boyle) *lw: w ldr tl slt advantage 4f out: hdd 3f out: wkng whn n.m.r over 2f out* **9/1**

1m 39.21s (-1.06) **Going Correction** -0.15s/f (Firm) **14** Ran SP% **119.3**
Speed ratings (Par 99):99,98,98,98,96 95,92,92,92,89 88,87,85,84
CSF £201.67 CT £804.06 TOTE £7.50: £2.40, £9.70, £1.90; EX 288.20.
Owner The Gap Partnership **Bred** Fonthill Stud **Trained** Pulborough, W Sussex
■ Stewards' Enquiry : Steve Drowne two-day ban: careless riding (Jun 25-26)

FOCUS
A moderate race for the course, with plenty of traffic problems and a scrambling blanket finish.
Giverny Spring Official explanation: jockey said filly was unsuited by the good to firm ground

2404 CRIMBOURNE STUD STKS (H'CAP) 1m 1f 192y
7:55 (8:07) (Class 4) (0-85,84) 3-Y-O £7,124 (£2,119; £1,059; £529) Stalls High

Form RPR

1 **1** **Portal**[263] 5361 3-9-5 **82** .... JamieSpencer 7 97+
(J R Fanshawe) *s.i.s: hld up in rr: gd hdwy fr 2f out: drvn and str run fnl f: led cl home: readily* **11/2**[3]

3130 **2** *nk* **Babcary**[99] 558 3-8-7 **73** .... NelsonDeSouza(3) 1 79
(M P Tregoning) *led after 1f: kpt narrow ld: rdn fr 3f out: kpt on wl tl ct cl home* **33/1**

0021 **3** *1 1/2* **Mystic Storm**[17] 1925 3-8-9 **72** .... SebSanders 3 75
(Lady Herries) *lw: in tch: hdwy over 2f out: drvn to chse ldr over 1f out: no imp ins last and sn outpcd* **6/4**[1]

51 **4** *1 1/4* **Steppe Dancer (IRE)**[39] 1336 3-9-7 **84** .... AlanMunro 8 84+
(D J Coakley) *lw: s.i.s: bhd: hdwy 3f out: rdn and one pce 2f out: kpt on again ins last but nt pce to rch ldrs* **7/2**[2]

446 **5** *3/4* **Star Of The Desert (IRE)**[18] 1880 3-8-9 **75** .... AdamKirby(3) 2 74
(C G Cox) *chsd ldrs: rdn and effrt over 2f out: nt pce to chal: wknd ins fnl f* **25/1**

0150 **6** *shd* **Zilcash**[23] 1781 3-8-13 **76** .... DaneO'Neill 5 75
(A King) *chsd ldrs: rdn 3f out: kpt on same pce fnl 2f* **20/1**

001 **7** *1/2* **Oh Glory Be (USA)**[22] 1798 3-9-1 **78** .... RyanMoore 9 76+
(R Hannon) *bhd: stl plenty to do whn swtchd lft to outside 2f out: r.o wl fnl f but nt rch ldrs* **14/1**

0165 **8** *1 1/2* **Jebel Ali (IRE)**[39] 1356 3-8-9 **77** .... JamesDoyle(5) 4 72
(B Gubby) *led 1f: styd pressing ldr tl over 2f out: wknd over 1f out* **20/1**

2042 **9** *1/2* **Nikki Bea (IRE)**[17] 1925 3-8-4 **67** oh8 ow2 .... PaulDoe 12 64+
(Jamie Poulton) *chsd ldrs: rdn over 2f out: wkng on rails whn n.m.r appr fnl f* **33/1**

0106 **10** *1 1/2* **Kahlua Kiss**[15] 1963 3-8-12 **75** .... SteveDrowne 10 66
(W R Muir) *t.k.h: hld up in rr: rdn over 2f out and sn no prog* **33/1**

0350 **11** *5* **World In Action (IRE)**[27] 1684 3-8-6 **69** .... FrankieMcDonald 6 51
(A P Jarvis) *nver bttr than mid-div* **66/1**

624 **12** *11* **Amwaal (USA)**[258] 5455 3-9-2 **79** .... MartinDwyer 11 40
(J L Dunlop) *mid-div tl wknd 3f out* **7/1**

2m 8.44s (0.69) **Going Correction** -0.15s/f (Firm) **12** Ran SP% **120.5**
Speed ratings (Par 101):91,90,89,88,87 87,87,86,85,84 80,71
CSF £178.07 CT £408.10 TOTE £6.10: £2.70, £9.70, £1.30; EX 193.50.
Owner Cheveley Park Stud **Bred** Cheveley Park Stud Ltd **Trained** Newmarket, Suffolk

FOCUS
A fair handicap containing some relatively unexposed types who should improve, but there was no pace and the winning time was very moderate for a race of its type. Horses held up were at a disadvantage, and the winner, fourth and seventh in particular are better than the bare form.
Amwaal(USA) Official explanation: jockey said colt tired quickly 2f out; trainer later said colt was very stiff and sore morning after race

2405 ECOLOGIST STKS (H'CAP) 7f
8:25 (8:36) (Class 4) (0-85,85) 4-Y-O+ £6,800 (£2,023; £1,011; £505) Stalls High

Form RPR

1041 **1** **Waterside (IRE)**[39] 1340 7-9-2 **80** .... RyanMoore 3 89
(G L Moore) *lw: trckd ldrs: drvn to ld over 2f out: hld on wl thrght fnl f* **9/4**[1]

0020 **2** *1 1/4* **Desert Dreamer (IRE)**[6] 2232 5-9-2 **80** .... SebSanders 2 86
(P R Chamings) *bhd: hdwy and n.m.r ins fnl 2f: swtchd lft over 1f out: fin wl but nt rch wnr* **5/1**[2]

1600 **3** *shd* **Marko Jadeo (IRE)**[32] 1545 8-8-10 **74** .... DaneO'Neill 8 80
(S Dow) *s.i.s: t.k.h and hld up in rr:swtchd lft to outside over 1f out and kpt on ins last but nt pce to rch wnr* **8/1**

3156 **4** *hd* **Glencalvie (IRE)**[16] 1938 5-8-13 **77** .... (v) TQuinn 7 82
(J Akehurst) *in tch: rdn 3f out: hung lft over 2f out: n.m.r over 1f out: kpt on cl home* **10/1**

2000 **5** *1* **Doric (USA)**[21] 1835 5-9-6 **84** .... KerrinMcEvoy 4 86
(B Ellison) *in tch: rdn and hdwy on outside over 2f out: nvr gng pce to rch ldrs: wkng when n.m.r ins fnl f* **10/1**

24-0 **6** *3/4* **Optimus (USA)**[39] 1355 4-8-8 **72** .... RichardHughes 5 76+
(G A Butler) *s.i.s: bhd: effrt on rails whn nt clr run over 1f out: kpt on insde last but nvr in contention* **16/1**

2350 **7** *1/2* **Effective**[4] 2302 6-8-13 **77** .... JamieSpencer 1 76
(A P Jarvis) *trckd ldr tl led 4f out: narrowly hdd over 2f out: wknd ins fnl f* **8/1**

0055 **8** *5* **Purus (IRE)**[16] 1939 4-9-7 **85** .... DarryllHolland 9 70
(P Mitchell) *lw: chsd ldrs: pushed along 3f out: wknd fr 2f out* **13/2**[3]

0000 **9** *10* **Acomb**[38] 1382 6-9-3 **81** .... IanMongan 6 39
(Mrs L Richards) *plld hrd: led 3f: wknd 3f out* **16/1**

1m 25.99s (-2.05) **Going Correction** -0.15s/f (Firm) **9** Ran SP% **112.9**
Speed ratings (Par 105):105,103,103,103,102 101,100,94,83
CSF £12.76 CT £74.32 TOTE £2.40: £1.10, £2.10, £2.80; EX 14.10.
Owner Nigel Shields **Bred** Yeomanstown Stud **Trained** Woodingdean, E Sussex

FOCUS
A moderate handicap in which Waterside had lots going for him against rivals who had been largely out of form and was in charge after getting first run. Not form to betaken literally, though it has nominally been rated through the fourth.
Glencalvie(IRE) Official explanation: jockey said, regarding appearing to ease gelding shortly before winning post and losing third place by a head, had he kept riding he feared he would have struck the heels of the winner
Purus(IRE) Official explanation: jockey said gelding was unsuited by the good to firm ground

2406 GOODWOOD ORGANIC FARM MAIDEN FILLIES' STKS 1m
9:00 (9:11) (Class 5) 3-Y-O £3,562 (£1,059; £529; £264) Stalls High

Form RPR

30 **1** **Wasseema (USA)**[52] 1068 3-9-0 .... MartinDwyer 8 80+
(Sir Michael Stoute) *mde all: pushed along and qcknd fr 2f out: r.o strly fnl f: comf* **5/4**[1]

0 **2** *1 1/2* **Early Evening**[245] 5710 3-9-0 .... DaneO'Neill 3 76
(H Candy) *chsd wnr thrght: rdn fr 2f out: no ch ins fnl f but kpt on gamely to hold 2nd* **14/1**

02 **3** *shd* **Usk Poppy**[20] 1845 3-9-0 .... TQuinn 14 76
(D R C Elsworth) *lw: chsd ldrs: rdn and kpt on wl fnl f: gng on cl home but no ch w wnr* **4/1**[2]

34 **4** *shd* **Pearl's Girl**[9] 2143 3-9-0 .... DarryllHolland 6 76+
(W J Haggas) *in tch: drvn and hdwy over 1f out: r.o wl fnl f and gng on cl home to press for 2nd but no ch w wnr* **11/2**[3]

5 *2* **Spirit Of The Fen (IRE)** 3-9-0 .... RobertHavlin 16 71+
(J H M Gosden) *leggy: s.i.s: hdwy into mid-div 1/2-way: drvn and kpt on fnl f but nvr gng pce to trble ldrs* **33/1**

0 **6** *1* **Hanella (IRE)**[20] 1845 3-9-0 .... SebSanders 5 69
(R M Beckett) *b.hind: chsd ldrs tl one pce fnl f* **33/1**

6 **7** *hd* **Jabbara (IRE)**[23] 1777 3-9-0 .... KerrinMcEvoy 15 68
(C E Brittain) *in tch: rdn and kpt on fnl 2f: nt pace to rch ldrs* **28/1**

5 **8** *3 1/2* **Sessile (USA)**[225] 6122 3-9-0 .... RyanMoore 4 60+
(J H M Gosden) *bhd: pushed along and styd on fr over 1f out but nvr in contention* **16/1**

6 **9** *1 1/4* **Cape Maya**[21] 1822 3-9-0 .... JamieSpencer 12 57
(B J Meehan) *bhd: kpt on fr over 1f out: nvr in contention* **16/1**

04 **10** *1 1/2* **Shangazi (USA)**[15] 1956 3-9-0 .... RichardHughes 2 54+
(B W Hills) *chsd ldrs 6f* **25/1**

6 **11** *1* **Princess Danah (IRE)**[18] 1901 3-9-0 .... ShaneKelly 13 52
(W R Swinburn) *s.i.s: nvr in contention* **40/1**

03 **12** *nk* **Kineta (USA)**[291] 4630 3-9-0 .... SteveDrowne 1 51
(W R Muir) *bhd most of way* **33/1**

13 *1 1/2* **Clear Picture** 3-9-0 .... FrankieMcDonald 11 48
(A P Jarvis) *mid-div whn awkward bnd over 4f out: nvr in contention after* **100/1**

0 **14** *3/4* **Cunegonde**[239] 5850 3-9-0 .... IanMongan 9 46
(G L Moore) *in tch over 5f* **100/1**

20 **15** *2* **Rose Lady (IRE)**[20] 1844 3-8-11 .... EdwardCreighton(3) 7 41
(M R Channon) *bhd most of way* **33/1**

34 **16** *3* **Park Lane Princess (IRE)**[268] 5221 3-9-0 .... ChrisCatlin 10 34
(D M Simcock) *a in rr* **33/1**

1m 39.64s (-0.63) **Going Correction** -0.15s/f (Firm) **16** Ran SP% **124.7**
Speed ratings (Par 96):97,95,95,95,93 92,92,88,87,85 84,84,83,82,80 77
CSF £20.28 TOTE £2.20: £1.30, £4.40, £2.10; EX 31.80 Place 6 £110.51, Place 5 £24.62.
Owner Hamdan Al Maktoum **Bred** Swettenham Stud And Ben Sangster **Trained** Newmarket, Suffolk

FOCUS
Probably only an ordinary maiden behind the winner, who did not need to be at her best, but several reasonable performances.
Shangazi(USA) Official explanation: jockey said filly moved poorly on downhill section
T/Plt: £106.30 to a £1 stake. Pool: £50,762.65. 348.40 winning tickets. T/Qpdt: £5.00 to a £1 stake. Pool: £3,589.40. 529.60 winning tickets. ST

2382 HAYDOCK (L-H)
Friday, June 9

OFFICIAL GOING: Good to firm
Wind: Light, behind Weather: Hot and sunny

2407 WISH FM H'CAP (FOR LADY AMATEUR RIDERS) 1m 2f 120y
6:35 (6:35) (Class 6) (0-65,60) 4-Y-O+ £2,307 (£709; £354) Stalls High

Form RPR

0034 **1** **Gallego**[7] 2186 4-9-8 **51** .... MissABevan(7) 6 65
(R J Price) *s.i.s: bhd: hdwy over 3f out: chsd ldr 2f out: edgd lft and led ins fnl f: r.o* **7/1**[3]

0004 **2** *1 3/4* **Oddsmaker (IRE)**[1] 2387 5-10-2 **57** .... (t) MissAngelaBarnes(5) 11 68
(M A Barnes) *racd wd: led: clr 5f out: pushed along over 1f out: hdd ins fnl f: no ex cl home* **15/2**

6051 **3** *2 1/2* **Acuzio**[6] 2242 5-10-3 **53** 5ex .... MissEJJones 2 59
(W M Brisbourne) *chsd ldrs: wnt 2nd 3f out: sn rdn: lost 2nd 2f out: edgd lft ins fnl f: kpt on u.p* **5/1**[2]

5010 **4** *7* **Gala Sunday (USA)**[25] 1723 6-9-5 **46** .... MissKellyBurke(5) 5 39
(M W Easterby) *chsd ldrs: rdn and wknd over 2f out* **15/2**

1060 **5** *2 1/2* **Awaken**[6] 2242 5-9-10 **49** ow1 .... MissCMetcalfe(3) 3 38
(Miss Tracy Waggott) *bhd: hdwy 6f out: rdn and wknd over 2f out* **20/1**

2342 **6** ¾ **Dramatic Review (IRE)**[205] [6141] 4-9-13 **49**................(t) MrsCBartley 10 37
(P C Haslam) *chsd ldrs: rdn over 3f out: wknd over 2f out* **7/1**[3]

0444 **7** 2 **Westcourt Dream**[3] [2322] 6-9-8 **51**.............................. MissJCoward(7) 8 35
(M W Easterby) *s.s: rcvrd to sn chse ldr: lost 2nd 3f out: wknd 2f out* **3/1**[1]

0406 **8** 1 **Got To Be Cash**[230] [6033] 7-9-0 **41** oh6............. MissCarolineHurley(5) 9 23
(W M Brisbourne) *in tch: rdn over 3f out: wknd over 2f out* **25/1**

0000 **9** 10 **Mirage Prince (IRE)**[23] [1772] 4-9-11 **50**........................ MissLEllison(3) 4 14
(D Shaw) *hld up: rdn over 3f out: nvr on terms* **33/1**

0445 **10** 2 ½ **Phoenix Eye**[5] [1610] 5-9-5 **48**.................................. MissMMullineaux(7) 7 8
(M Mullineaux) *midfield tl rdn and wknd over 3f out* **12/1**

1030 **11** 2 ½ **Arctic Cove**[13] [597] 5-10-3 **60**.. MrsGHogg(7) 1 15
(Micky Hammond) *struggling 4f out: a bhd* **14/1**

2m 16.68s (-1.05) **Going Correction** -0.10s/f (Good) **11** Ran SP% **116.1**
Speed ratings (Par 101):99,97,95,90,89 88,87,86,79,77 75
CSF £56.38 CT £287.67 TOTE £8.30: £2.20, £2.60, £2.00; EX 60.30.
Owner My Left Foot Racing Syndicate **Bred** Mrs C C Regalado-Gonzalez **Trained** Ullingswick, H'fords
■ The first winner for Ally Bevan.

FOCUS
A modest handicap. The gallop seemed fair but very few got into the race. The winner was back to last year's course form.

2408 NORTHERN BRICKWORK H'CAP 1m 6f
7:05 (7:08) (Class 5) (0-70,66) 4-Y-0+ **£3,238** (£963; £481; £240) **Stalls** Low

Form RPR

6000 **1** **Sharp N Frosty**[11] [2075] 4-8-8 **53**.. JimCrowley 4 62
(W M Brisbourne) *midfield: rdn and hdwy 4f out: led over 2f out: jst hld on* **25/1**

0030 **2** hd **Primondo (IRE)**[37] [1415] 4-8-12 **57**... NCallan 6 66+
(J R Fanshawe) *midfield: hdwy 4f out: nt qckn 2f out: rdn and edgd lft wl over 1f out: sn edgd rt: edgd lft and wnt 2nd ins fnl f* **7/1**

0065 **3** 2 ½ **Red Forest (IRE)**[9] [2140] 7-8-13 **58**..................................(t) DaleGibson 7 63
(J Mackie) *chsd clr ldr: led over 4f out: hdd over 2f out: sn rdn: kpt on same pce ins fnl f* **11/2**[3]

3403 **4** 4 **My Legal Eagle (IRE)**[10] [2099] 12-8-5 **50**.................. AdrianMcCarthy 8 50
(E G Bevan) *hld up: rdn 3f out: hdwy over 1f out: one pce fnl f* **11/2**[3]

0004 **5** 5 **Let It Be**[11] [2078] 5-9-0 **59**... PaulHanagan 2 52
(K G Reveley) *chsd ldrs: rdn over 3f out: wknd over 1f out* **13/8**[1]

1236 **6** 7 **Lake Wakatipu**[20] [1847] 4-8-9 **54**.. JoeFanning 3 37
(M Mullineaux) *in rr: effrt and hdwy 3f out: wknd over 1f out* **14/1**

0106 **7** 10 **Duroob**[22] [1809] 4-9-7 **66**... PatCosgrave 9 35
(K R Burke) *chsd ldrs: rdn over 3f out: wknd over 2f out* **4/1**[2]

0400 **8** 60 **Fardi (IRE)**[11] [2078] 4-8-11 **56**.. PaulMulrennan 1 —
(K W Hogg) *led: sn clr: hdd over 4f out: wknd qckly: t.o* **100/1**

3m 2.61s (-3.68) **Going Correction** -0.10s/f (Good) **8** Ran SP% **112.9**
Speed ratings (Par 103):106,105,104,102,99 95,89,55
CSF £182.93 CT £1111.76 TOTE £27.80: £3.50, £2.20, £1.80; EX 196.10.
Owner Mark Wood **Bred** Wood And Hall **Trained** Great Ness, Shropshire

FOCUS
A modest event and, with the two market leaders disappointing it did not take as much winning as had seemed likely. It has been rated through the winner to last year's form.
Lake Wakatipu Official explanation: vet said filly pulled up lame

2409 EUROPEAN BREEDERS FUND WEAVER MAIDEN STKS 6f
7:40 (7:42) (Class 5) 2-Y-0 **£3,238** (£963; £481; £240) **Stalls** Centre

Form RPR

3 **1** **Alzerra (UAE)**[14] [1989] 2-8-12 .... TedDurcan 1 92+
(M R Channon) *wnt rt s: mde all: rdn over 1f out: r.o wl* **5/1**[2]

2 2 ½ **Cumin (USA)** 2-8-12 .... MichaelHills 4 85
(B W Hills) *midfield: hdwy over 2f out: wnt 2nd over 1f out: styd on ins fnl f: nt pce of wnr* **11/2**[3]

3 4 **Majounes Song** 2-8-12 .... JoeFanning 8 73
(M Johnston) *a.p: rdn over 1f out: outpcd fnl f* **10/1**

5 **4** 1 ¾ **Massenzio (IRE)**[9] [2144] 2-9-3 .... JimmyFortune 9 72
(J H M Gosden) *bmpd s: prom: rdn over 1f out: wknd fnl f* **5/2**[1]

5 2 ½ **Green Day Packer (IRE)** 2-9-3 .... LeeEnstone 2 65
(P C Haslam) *dwlt: chsd ldrs: pushed along 1/2-way: rdn 2f out: edgd lft and wknd over 1f out* **33/1**

6 1 ½ **Paint For Pleasure (IRE)** 2-9-3 .... AdrianMcCarthy 5 60
(P W Chapple-Hyam) *dwlt: in tch: rdn 2f out: wknd over 1f out* **10/1**

7 1 **Prix Masque (IRE)** 2-9-3 .... PhilipRobinson 10 57
(B Smart) *in tch: rdn over 2f out: wknd over 1f out* **7/1**

8 3 **Crow's Nest Lad** 2-9-3 .... DavidAllan 6 48
(T D Easterby) *dwlt: in rr: kpt on fr over 1f out: nvr trbld ldrs* **40/1**

9 1 ¾ **Moonwalking** 2-9-3 .... DaleGibson 14 43
(Jedd O'Keeffe) *towards rr: rdn 4f out: nvr rchd chalng position* **33/1**

10 1 ½ **Harry The Hawk** 2-9-3 .... TomEaves 13 39
(T D Walford) *midfield: rdn and wknd over 1f out* **100/1**

11 3 ½ **Soviet Sound (IRE)** 2-9-3 .... PaulHanagan 3 28
(Jedd O'Keeffe) *dwlt: sn pushed along in rr: nvr on terms* **50/1**

12 shd **Bollin Freddie** 2-9-3 .... FergalLynch 11 28
(T D Easterby) *s.s: a bhd* **40/1**

13 3 **Scarlet Baby** 2-9-3 .... NCallan 15 19
(K A Ryan) *hld up: pushed along 1/2-way: nvr on terms* **11/1**

14 ¾ **Cape Jasmine (IRE)** 2-8-12 .... PatCosgrave 7 11
(J Howard Johnson) *chsd ldrs to 1/2-way: sn struggling* **16/1**

1m 13.0s (-1.90) **Going Correction** -0.475s/f (Firm) **14** Ran SP% **119.2**
Speed ratings (Par 93):93,89,84,82,78 76,75,71,69,67 62,62,58,57
CSF £30.92 TOTE £6.10: £3.00, £2.20, £3.70; EX 22.60.
Owner Sheikh Ahmed Al Maktoum **Bred** Darley **Trained** West Ilsley, Berks
■ Stewards' Enquiry : Lee Enstone two-day ban: careless riding (Jun 25-26)

FOCUS
A fair maiden, run at a decent pace. The first two pulled clear of the remainder and the form could prove even better than it has initially been rated.

NOTEBOOK
Alzerra(UAE), who shaped well on soft on her debut, fully confirmed that promise with a much improved effort on this first run on fast ground. She should stay at least seven furlongs and may be able to hold her own in slightly better company. (op 9-2)
Cumin(USA) ◆, the second foal of a triple winner in Japan, shaped with a good deal of promise without being knocked about on this racecourse debut. She is open to plenty of improvement, especially over further, and is sure to win a similar event at the very least. (op 5-1)
Majounes Song, a half sister to fairly useful stayer Marias Magic and to middle distance all-weather winner Marias Magic, shaped well over what is likely to prove a most inadequate distance on this racecourse debut. She will be suited by further and is sure to win an ordinary event granted a more suitable test of stamina. (op 12-1)
Massenzio(IRE) failed to build on his debut effort, but he is in good hands and may well be suited by the step up to seven furlongs in due course, so he is not one to write off just yet. (op 3-1 tchd 7-2)
Green Day Packer(IRE), who is related to winners, shaped with a bit of promise on this racecourse debut and is entitled to improve for the experience.
Paint For Pleasure(IRE), who is related to several winners, was easy to back but not totally disgraced on this racecourse debut. He is in good hands and is likely to step up on this bare form in due course. Official explanation: vet said colt returned lame (op 8-1)
Cape Jasmine(IRE) Official explanation: vet said filly returned lame

2410 PAUL EDMONDSON DO A RUNNER NOW H'CAP 5f
8:10 (8:11) (Class 4) (0-80,77) 3-Y-0 **£6,477** (£1,927; £963; £481) **Stalls** Centre

Form RPR

0514 **1** **Jakeini (IRE)**[7] [2197] 3-8-9 **65**.. RichardMullen 2 77
(E S McMahon) *wnt lft s: a.p: rdn and edgd lft over 1f out: led ins fnl f: r.o* **8/1**

2524 **2** 2 **Blazing Heights**[10] [2110] 3-9-5 **75**...................................... FergalLynch 5 79
(J S Goldie) *n.m.r s: hld up: hdwy 1/2-way: rdn over 1f out: wnt 2nd ins fnl f: styd on* **9/2**[1]

2134 **3** 1 ¼ **Toy Top (USA)**[8] [2161] 3-8-12 **68**...................................(b) PhillipMakin 1 67
(M Dods) *led: rdn and edgd lft over 1f out: hdd ins fnl f: no ex* **10/1**

0055 **4** 1 **City For Conquest (IRE)**[10] [2110] 3-9-5 **75**.............(b) FrancisNorton 10 70
(K R Burke) *chsd ldrs: rdn over 1f out: edgd lft ins fnl f: kpt on same pce* **15/2**

1203 **5** 2 **Mulligan's Gold (IRE)**[10] [2110] 3-9-0 **70**............................. DavidAllan 8 57
(T D Easterby) *in tch: lugged lft whn rdn and outpcd 1/2-way: no imp after* **11/2**[3]

0412 **6** ¾ **Welcome Approach**[10] [2110] 3-9-0 **70**.......................... JimmyFortune 6 54
(J R Weymes) *in rr: rdn 1/2-way: hdwy whn carried lft over 1f out: one pce fnl f* **5/1**[2]

4005 **7** 3 **Gwilym (GER)**[6] [2222] 3-9-1 **71**.. NCallan 9 43
(D Haydn Jones) *a outpcd* **14/1**

1003 **8** 5 **Egyptian Lord**[6] [2222] 3-8-9 **65**.............................(b) RobbieFitzpatrick 4 17
(Peter Grayson) *in tch: rdn and edgd lft whn wknd over 1f out* **16/1**

3350 **9** 2 ½ **Smart Cassie**[43] [1264] 3-9-7 **77**....................................... RobertWinston 7 19
(D Shaw) *a in rr* **20/1**

1011 **10** nk **Mormeatmic**[8] [2161] 3-9-3 **73** 6ex................................ PaulMulrennan 3 14
(M W Easterby) *wnt rt s: chsd ldrs: rdn 1/2-way: sn wknd* **7/1**

59.49 secs (-2.58) **Going Correction** -0.475s/f (Firm) **10** Ran SP% **112.0**
Speed ratings (Par 101):101,97,95,94,91 89,85,77,73,72
CSF £42.08 CT £361.73 TOTE £12.30: £3.80, £2.50, £2.70; EX 75.70.
Owner Martin W Crane **Bred** Gestut Roemerhof **Trained** Hopwas, Staffs

FOCUS
An ordinary handicap run at a decent pace. The field raced in the centre, but the chief protaganists ended up towards the far side. Only the runner-up managed to come from the rear.
Mulligan's Gold(IRE) Official explanation: jockey said colt hung left throughout
Smart Cassie Official explanation: jockey said filly never travelled
Mormeatmic Official explanation: jockey said gelding never travelled

2411 OCS GROUP MAIDEN STKS 1m 30y
8:40 (8:44) (Class 5) 3-Y-0+ **£3,238** (£963; £481; £240) **Stalls** Low

Form RPR

0 **1** **Royal Oath (USA)**[20] [1844] 3-8-13 ....(t) JimmyFortune 3 87+
(J H M Gosden) *racd keenly: hld up: hdwy over 3f out: wnt 2nd over 2f out: led over 1f out: edgd lft ins fnl f: r.o* **9/4**[2]

3 **2** 1 ½ **Dukedom**[13] [2034] 3-8-13 .... RobertWinston 7 86+
(Sir Michael Stoute) *racd keenly: a.p: rdn and ev ch over 1f out: hld whn n.m.r ins fnl f: sn swtchd rt: nt qckn* **8/15**[1]

34 **3** 4 **Reflecting (IRE)**[28] [1649] 3-8-8 .... MichaelHills 8 65
(J W Hills) *led: rdn over 2f out: hdd over 1f out: wknd ins fnl f* **22/1**

6 **4** ¾ **Mexican Bob**[32] [1552] 3-8-13 .... LPKeniry 2 68
(Heather Dalton) *midfield: hdwy 4f out: rdn over 2f out: one pce over 1f out* **40/1**

4 **5** 1 ¼ **Gobi King**[14] [1984] 4-9-10 .... NickyMackay 4 68
(L M Cumani) *in tch: rdn and outpcd over 3f out: no imp after* **10/1**[3]

0500 **6** 3 ½ **Topflight Wildbird**[6] [2244] 3-8-8 45...........................(b) J-PGuillambert 1 52
(Mrs G S Rees) *hld up: pushed along and outpcd 3f out: nvr on terms* **200/1**

0 **7** 7 **Bold Medicean**[27] [1684] 3-8-13 .... DeanMcKeown 10 41
(T P Tate) *a bhd* **150/1**

-P00 **8** 13 **Come To Daddy (IRE)**[242] [5800] 4-9-10 40.................. PaulFitzsimons 6 14
(F Jordan) *racd keenly: prom tl rdn and wknd over 3f out* **200/1**

0 **9** nk **Hollie Dellamore**[102] [531] 4-9-5 .... FrancisNorton 5 —
(A P Jarvis) *racd keenly: midfield: hdwy 5f out: wknd over 3f out* **150/1**

1m 43.85s (-1.66) **Going Correction** -0.10s/f (Good)
WFA 3 from 4yo 11lb **9** Ran SP% **114.2**
Speed ratings (Par 103):104,102,98,97,96 93,86,73,72
CSF £3.73 TOTE £3.80: £1.10, £1.10, £2.20; EX 5.70.
Owner W S Farish & William S Farish Jnr **Bred** Farish And Farish Llc **Trained** Newmarket, Suffolk
■ Stewards' Enquiry : Jimmy Fortune two-day ban: careless riding (Jun 25-26)

FOCUS
A race lacking strength in depth, and teh form is held down by the proximity of the sixth. The gallop was only modest early on and so the first two didn't get the opportunity to show how good they are. The runner-up was well below his Newmarket form, but it was a fair performance nevertheless by the winner, who looks the sort to hold his own in better company.

2412 LLANGEDWYN MAIDEN STKS 1m 3f 200y
9:10 (9:13) (Class 5) 3-Y-0+ **£3,238** (£963; £481; £240) **Stalls** High

Form RPR

4046 **1** **Cresta Gold**[29] [1605] 3-8-4 70... DavidAllan 8 84+
(A Bailey) *mde virtually all: rdn over 1f out: r.o wl: eased cl home* **14/1**

022 **2** 2 ½ **Ermine Sea**[16] [1940] 3-8-9 86... JimmyFortune 11 84+
(J H M Gosden) *chsd wnr: rdn over 2f out: nt qckn ins fnl f* **5/6**[1]

3 2 ½ **Well Hidden** 3-8-5 ow1.. RobertWinston 1 75
(Sir Michael Stoute) *s.i.s: hld up: hdwy over 3f out: chsd ldrs over 2f out: no imp on ldrs* **7/2**[2]

4 **4** 3 ½ **Follow On**[39] [1343] 4-9-10 .... TPQueally 6 73
(A P Jarvis) *midfield: hdwy 3f out: hung lft fr over 2f out: one pce* **14/1**

6 **5** 8 **Forever Autumn**[34] [1483] 3-8-9 .... MichaelTebbutt 4 61
(B J Meehan) *trckd ldrs: rdn and hung lft 3f out: sn wknd* **20/1**

6 3 **Rainbow Zest** 3-8-9 .... AdrianMcCarthy 7 56
(P W Chapple-Hyam) *hld up: hdwy over 6f out: rdn and wknd over 1f out* **17/2**[3]

00 **7** 1 ¼ **Quintin**[19] [1866] 3-8-4 .... RichardMullen 5 49
(T D Easterby) *racd keenly: chsd ldrs tl rdn and wknd 4f out* **66/1**

04 8 3 ½ **Naval Hero (IRE)**[19] 1868 3-8-9 .... PaulHanagan 2 48
(Mrs L Williamson) *a bhd* **66/1**
0 9 *nk* **Triple Bluff**[14] 1994 3-8-9 .... JimCrowley 10 48
(Mrs A J Perrett) *racd keenly: chsd ldrs: rdn and edgd lft over 2f out: sn wknd* **12/1**
0 10 2 **Springwood Blues (IRE)**[293] 4579 3-8-4 .... PaulFitzsimons 3 40
(H Alexander) *s.i.s: a bhd* **100/1**

2m 34.12s (-0.87) **Going Correction** -0.10s/f (Good)
WFA 3 from 4yo 15lb **10** Ran SP% **117.1**
Speed ratings (Par 103):98,96,94,92,87 85,84,81,81,80
CSF £26.07 TOTE £22.10: £3.90, £1.10, £1.40; EX 50.90 Place 6 £78.77, Place 5 £34.35.
Owner P T Tellwright **Bred** P T Tellwright **Trained** Cotebrook, Cheshire

FOCUS
Another uncompetitive maiden and the ordinary gallop suited those closest to the pace. Enough horses appeared to run close to their best for the form to look sound, but it was such a big step up from the winner that there has to be a doubt.
Well Hidden Official explanation: jockey said filly hung left
T/Plt: £66.90 to a £1 stake. Pool: £41,750.35. 455.30 winning tickets. T/Qpdt: £7.20 to a £1 stake. Pool: £3,646.70. 372.40 winning tickets. DO

2206 WOLVERHAMPTON (A.W) (L-H)
Friday, June 9

OFFICIAL GOING: Standard
Wind: Light, against Weather: Fine and sunny

2413 TO SPONSOR A RACE CALL 0870 220 2442 (S) STKS 1m 141y(P)
2:30 (2:33) (Class 6) 3-Y-O+ **£2,388** (£705; £352) **Stalls** Low

Form RPR
3620 1 **Perez (IRE)**[41] 1288 4-9-2 72 .... (v[1]) EmmettStack(5) 13 73+
(Pat Eddery) *s.s: hdwy to chse ldr over 6f out: led on bit over 2f out : sn rdn clr* **3/1**[1]
3053 2 6 **Paso Doble**[6] 2245 8-9-0 55 .... (v[1]) JamesMillman(7) 7 59
(B R Millman) *mid-div: hdwy over 3f out: rdn over 1f out: no ch w wnr* **7/1**
2532 3 1 ½ **Frank's Quest (IRE)**[17] 1915 6-9-7 50 .... JamieSpencer 10 56
(A B Haynes) *hld up: hdwy over 2f out: rdn and hung lft over 1f out: nvr nrr* **4/1**[2]
3026 4 *shd* **Merdiff**[5] 2260 7-9-12 55 .... ShaneKelly 6 61
(W M Brisbourne) *mid-div: hdwy 1/2-way: rdn to chse wnr over 1f out: sn hung lft and no ex* **10/1**
4062 5 1 ½ **Gem Bien (USA)**[6] 2245 8-9-7 54 .... (p) JimmyQuinn 8 53
(D W Chapman) *rel to r: bhd: rdn and hung lft over 1f out: n.d* **5/1**[3]
4000 6 2 **Fraternity**[4] 2291 9-9-0 55 .... SladeO'Hara(7) 4 48
(J A Pickering) *led over 7f out: hdd over 2f out: wknd over 1f out* **20/1**
6200 7 1 **Bauhinia**[24] 1755 4-9-2 48 .... TPQueally 5 41
(J A R Toller) *s.s: rdn 1/2-way: n.d* **16/1**
1000 8 *shd* **Night Warrior (IRE)**[26] 549 6-9-12 51 .... (b) MickyFenton 9 51
(N P Littmoden) *hld up: hdwy over 2f out: wkng whn nt clr run over 1f out* **14/1**
2235 9 ¾ **Danum**[24] 1765 6-9-0 45 .... (p) RussellKennemore(7) 2 45
(R Hollinshead) *led 1f: chsd ldrs: rdn 1/2-way: wknd 2f out* **12/1**
0302 10 4 **Mujazaf**[26] 694 4-9-7 47 .... MichaelTebbutt 3 36
(D Burchell) *hld up: rdn over 3f out: a in rr* **25/1**
00 11 1 ¼ **Lets Be Lucky (IRE)**[38] 1387 4-9-7 .... PaulFitzsimons 1 34
(F Jordan) *hld up: effrt over 3f out: a in rr* **100/1**
30-0 12 33 **Barbilyrifle (IRE)**[4] 2291 5-9-7 55 .... JamieMackay 12 —
(N B King) *chsd ldrs to 1/2-way* **100/1**

1m 51.14s (-0.62) **Going Correction** 0.0s/f (Stan) **12** Ran SP% **114.1**
Speed ratings (Par 101):102,96,95,95,93 92,91,91,90,86 85,56
CSF £22.38 TOTE £3.90: £1.30, £3.10, £2.20; EX 28.90.The winner was sold to H. S. Hutchinson for 8,000gns.
Owner Pat Eddery Racing (Golden Fleece) **Bred** Calley House Syndicate **Trained** Nether Winchendon, Bucks

FOCUS
Basically an ordinary seller outside of the winner, but the pace was strong. Although the runner-up ran to his recent form, Perez did not need to run to his best.
Gem Bien(USA) Official explanation: jockey said gelding was reluctant to race

2414 WOLVERHAMPTON-RACECOURSE.CO.UK H'CAP 1m 1f 103y(P)
3:00 (3:02) (Class 6) (0-55,57) 4-Y-O+ **£2,730** (£806; £403) **Stalls** Low

Form RPR
1221 1 **Cottingham (IRE)**[8] 2181 5-9-10 **57** 6ex .... JamieSpencer 2 64
(T D Barron) *chsd ldrs: rdn over 2f out: styd on u.p to ld last strides* **4/5**[1]
5401 2 *shd* **Scamperdale**[35] 1460 4-9-5 **52** .... TPQueally 11 59
(B P J Baugh) *dwlt: sn chsng ldrs: rdn to ld and edgd lft ins fnl f: hdd last strides* **16/1**
5000 3 1 ½ **Zando**[13] 1553 4-9-3 **55** .... LiamTreadwell(5) 12 59
(E G Bevan) *chsd ldr: rdn to ld over 1f out: hdd ins fnl f: styng on same pce whn n.m.r sn after* **100/1**
2100 4 *nk* **Zoripp (IRE)**[11] 2075 4-9-2 **54** .... (b) StephenDonohoe(5) 6 57
(J G Given) *hld up: hdwy u.p over 2f out: styd on* **28/1**
0353 5 1 **Lockstock (IRE)**[3] 2327 8-9-5 **52** .... (p) RobbieFitzpatrick 10 54
(M S Saunders) *led: rdn and hdd over 1f out: no ex whn n.m.r ins fnl f* **7/1**[2]
2454 6 ½ **Wood Fern (UAE)**[9] 2132 6-9-5 **52** .... ShaneKelly 5 53+
(W M Brisbourne) *hld up: hmpd wl over 3f out: hdwy u.p over 1f out: nt rch ldrs* **8/1**[3]
0204 7 5 **Primeshade Promise**[10] 2098 5-9-5 **52** .... MichaelTebbutt 13 43
(D Burchell) *mid-div: hdwy and edgd lft wl over 3f out: rdn over 1f out: wknd fnl f* **16/1**
4020 8 1 ½ **Baby Barry**[214] 6287 9-9-5 **52** .... TonyHamilton 9 40
(R A Fahey) *hld up: hmpd wl over 3f out: n.d* **14/1**
0000 9 1 ¼ **Bubbling Fun**[148] 5824 5-9-1 **55** .... SladeO'Hara(7) 8 41
(T Wall) *hld up: hdwy 1/2-way: rdn and wknd over 1f out* **40/1**
0210 10 14 **Wanna Shout**[17] 1915 8-8-12 **52** .... JosephWalsh(7) 7 11
(R Dickin) *s.i.s: hld up: hdwy 1/2-way: rdn and wknd over 1f out* **25/1**
0000 11 39 **Armatore (USA)**[344] 3057 6-9-8 **55** .... (p) JimmyQuinn 1 —
(Ernst Oertel) *mid-div: wkng whn hmpd wl over 3f out* **40/1**
4250 12 ½ **At The Helm (IRE)**[8] 2181 4-9-4 **51** .... NCallan 4 —
(W J Knight) *mid-div: hmpd and wknd wl over 3f out: eased* **12/1**

2m 4.04s (1.42) **Going Correction** 0.0s/f (Stan) **12** Ran SP% **118.5**
Speed ratings (Par 101):93,92,91,91,90 89,85,84,83,70 35,35
CSF £15.14 CT £788.16 TOTE £1.60: £1.10, £3.10, £56.00; EX 15.10.
Owner Twinacre Nurseries Ltd **Bred** B Kennedy **Trained** Maunby, N Yorks

FOCUS
A dramatic race in which the favourite made very hard work of winning. Despite what looked a solid early gallop, the winning time was moderate for the grade, and the proximity of 100-1 chance Zando in third gives the form a shaky look.
Wood Fern(UAE) Official explanation: jockey said gelding was hampered 4f out
Armatore(USA) Official explanation: jockey said gelding lost its action end of back straight
At The Helm(IRE) Official explanation: jockey said filly lost its action going into final bend

2415 ENJOY EXECUTIVE HOSPITALITY AT WOLVERHAMPTON CLAIMING STKS 1m 141y(P)
3:30 (3:31) (Class 6) 3-Y-O **£2,730** (£806; £403) **Stalls** Low

Form RPR
1 **Odessa Star (USA)**[229] 6047 3-8-12 .... OscarUrbina 7 66
(J R Fanshawe) *hld up in tch: chsd ldr over 1f out: sn rdn and edgd lft: bmpd and led wl ins fnl f: r.o* **10/1**
2503 2 1 **Cape Win (IRE)**[10] 2101 3-9-3 72 .... (p) NCallan 9 68
(W J Haggas) *chsd ldrs: led over 2f out: rdn over 1f out: edgd rt and hdd wl ins fnl f* **3/1**[1]
6212 3 *hd* **Ruffie (IRE)**[25] 1747 3-8-11 67 .... StephenDonohoe(5) 11 67
(Miss Gay Kelleway) *s.i.s: hld up: hdwy 1/2-way: rdn over 1f out: r.o* **9/2**[3]
0056 4 7 **Lewis Lloyd (IRE)**[25] 1731 3-8-13 43 .... (t) JamieSpencer 5 49
(I A Wood) *chsd ldrs: hmpd over 7f out: rdn over 2f out: wknd over 1f out* **10/1**
0000 5 8 **Peak Seasons (IRE)**[13] 2034 3-8-11 52 .... MickyFenton 4 31
(W De Best-Turner) *chsd ldrs 6f* **66/1**
5620 6 1 ½ **Cecchetti (IRE)**[10] 2101 3-8-10 45 .... JimCrowley 1 26
(Mrs H Sweeting) *prom: rdn 1/2-way: sn lost pl* **20/1**
2400 7 3 **Mr Rigsby**[86] 646 3-8-12 62 .... DeanCorby(3) 10 25
(P Howling) *hld up: hdwy u.p over 2f out: sn wknd* **20/1**
0000 8 ½ **Mytass**[4] 2291 3-8-7 45 .... (b) DeanMcKeown 2 16
(J A Pickering) *chsd ldrs: wkng whn hmpd wl over 3f out* **50/1**
0000 9 *shd* **Cape Gold (IRE)**[7] 2192 3-8-7 62 .... (b[1]) TonyHamilton 12 16
(R A Fahey) *sn led: hdd over 2f out: wknd over 1f out* **20/1**
003 10 9 **Broughton Treasure**[342] 3134 3-8-2 46 .... JimmyQuinn 8 —
(W J Musson) *outpcd: hdwy over 2f out: sn wknd* **33/1**
4022 11 24 **Bahhmirage (IRE)**[8] 2167 3-8-11 50 .... (b) FrancisNorton 6 —
(Stef Liddiard) *hld up: pushed along 1/2-way: a in rr: wknd and eased fnl 2f: virtually p.u ins fnl f* **4/1**[2]

1m 52.59s (0.83) **Going Correction** 0.0s/f (Stan) **11** Ran SP% **102.0**
Speed ratings (Par 97):96,95,94,88,81 80,77,77,77,69 47
CSF £28.60 TOTE £9.50: £5.00, £1.80, £1.30; EX 66.70.The winner was claimed by Pump Technology Limited for £10,000.
Owner Deln Ltd & Howard Kaskel **Bred** Sugar Maple Farm **Trained** Newmarket, Suffolk
■ Mon Petite Amour was withdrawn (11/2, damaged stall.) R4 applies, deduct 10p in the £.

FOCUS
A poor claimer, run at just a fair pace, in which the front trio pulled a long way clear of the rest. Weak form, overall, but the unexposed winner was a big improver and the second and third ran close to their Wolverhampton handicap form.
Bahhmirage(IRE) Official explanation: jockey said filly ran flat

2416 EUROPEAN BREEDERS FUND MAIDEN STKS 5f 216y(P)
4:00 (4:04) (Class 5) 2-Y-O **£3,886** (£1,156; £577; £288) **Stalls** Low

Form RPR
340 1 **Hart Of Gold**[31] 1559 2-9-0 .... NCallan 4 79+
(M J Wallace) *chsd ldrs: rdn over 2f out: n.m.r over 1f out: styd on to ld nr fin* **12/1**[3]
0 2 *nk* **Not For Me (IRE)**[30] 1587 2-9-0 .... FrancisNorton 5 78+
(T J Pitt) *w ldr tl led over 2f out: sn rdn: hdd wl nr fin* **22/1**
00 3 6 **Just Oscar (GER)**[9] 2130 2-9-0 .... ShaneKelly 7 60
(W M Brisbourne) *chsd ldrs: rdn over 2f out: hung lft and wknd over 1f out* **28/1**
02 4 *nk* **Ebn Reem**[13] 2029 2-9-0 .... PhilipRobinson 9 59
(M A Jarvis) *led over 3f: wknd fnl f* **1/2**[1]
350 5 1 ½ **Everyman**[59] 961 2-8-9 .... (v[1]) StephenDonohoe(5) 6 55
(P D Evans) *s.i.s: outpcd: hung lft over 1f out: nvr nrr* **16/1**
6 6 16 **Generist**[45] 1223 2-8-9 .... FrancisFerris 1 —
(M J Attwater) *chsd ldrs: lost pl over 3f out: sn bhd* **80/1**
7 ½ **Little Tiny Tom** 2-9-0 .... AlanDaly 10 —
(C N Kellett) *s.i.s: outpcd* **100/1**
04 8 ½ **Cadeaux Du Monde**[9] 2130 2-9-0 .... JamieSpencer 3 —
(E J O'Neill) *s.s: outpcd* **9/2**[2]
9 1 ¼ **Head To Head (IRE)** 2-9-0 .... RobbieFitzpatrick 2 —
(Peter Grayson) *dwlt: outpcd* **40/1**
10 1 ¾ **Alevic (IRE)** 2-9-0 .... PaulMulrennan 8 —
(J R Norton) *s.i.s: outpcd* **66/1**

1m 16.51s (0.70) **Going Correction** 0.0s/f (Stan) **10** Ran SP% **112.4**
Speed ratings (Par 93):95,94,86,86,84 62,62,61,59,57
CSF £217.52 TOTE £13.20: £2.10, £6.90, £3.10; EX 129.40.
Owner Hartshead Mob **Bred** Bearstone Stud **Trained** Newmarket, Suffolk

FOCUS
A difficult race to assess with any confidence. Very few ever got involved, but with the red-hot favourite not performing to market expectations the form looks ordinary outside of the front pair, who pulled well clear.

NOTEBOOK
Hart Of Gold, who had shown ability on the Lingfield Polytrack on his debut before a couple of modest efforts on turf, bounced back to form having been gelded since his last run and the way he battled on the snatch the race shows that he found the extra furlong no problem. The form may not add up to much, but at least the evidence suggests this is his preferred surface. (op 10-1)
Not For Me(IRE) ◆, well beaten at the Chester May Meeting on his debut, was all the better for that experience but, after seeing off the favourite, he was unfortunate to get mugged near the line. His breeding suggested he would appreciate this extra furlong and it should not be long before he gets off the mark. (op 14-1 tchd 25-1)
Just Oscar(GER), as at Brighton last time, showed good speed for a long way before getting left behind by the front pair. He might be worth dropping to the minimum trip, but he may also need a drop in class or wait for the nurseries to start before he gets off the mark. (op 25-1 tchd 20-1)
Ebn Reem, switched to sand for the first time, was well backed to finally get off the mark but, after making much of the running, he was rather easily seen off from the home turn. This was disappointing and perhaps he needs soft ground on turf to show his best. (op 8-11)
Everyman, visored for the first time, was well behind early but plugged on down the home straight to finish miles clear of the others and earn a little credit. He is bred to stay much further than this and should do better in nurseries later in the season. (tchd 14-1 and 20-1)
Cadeaux Du Monde Official explanation: jockey said colt never travelled

2417 WEATHERBYS INSURANCE H'CAP 5f 216y(P)
4:30 (4:30) (Class 5) (0-70,70) 4-Y-0+ **£5,181** (£1,541; £770; £384) **Stalls** Low

Form RPR

0000 **1** **Prince Cyrano**[32] [1545] 7-9-6 **69** TPQueally 5 80+
(W J Musson) *a.p: rdn to ld 1f out: r.o* **33/1**

3100 **2** ¾ **Bahamian Ballet**[31] [1563] 4-9-4 **67** RobbieFitzpatrick 3 75
(E S McMahon) *chsd ldrs: rdn and ev ch 1f out: styd on* **14/1**

5401 **3** 1 **Bens Georgie (IRE)**[3] [2331] 4-9-5 **68** 6ex NCallan 12 73
(D K Ivory) *s.i.s: sn mid-div: hdwy 1/2-way: rdn and edgd lft over 1f out: styd on* **5/1**[2]

0023 **4** shd **Stoic Leader (IRE)**[31] [1561] 6-9-0 **70** SladeO'Hara(7) 4 76+
(R F Fisher) *hld up: hdwy over 1f out: nt clr run 1f out: r.o: nt rch ldrs* **13/2**[3]

1100 **5** shd **Misaro (GER)**[7] [2189] 5-9-4 **67** (b) AdrianMcCarthy 8 72
(R A Harris) *led 5f: no ex* **7/1**

1623 **6** shd **Gilded Cove**[13] [2027] 6-8-12 **68** RussellKennemore(7) 11 72
(R Hollinshead) *sn outpcd: hdwy over 2f out: rdn and edgd lft over 1f out: r.o: nt rch ldrs* **10/1**

4226 **7** 1¼ **Riquewihr**[23] [1774] 6-9-0 **63** (p) TonyHamilton 6 64
(J S Wainwright) *mid-div: rdn over 2f out: styd on ins fnl f: nvr trbld ldrs* **8/1**

3006 **8** hd **Gone'N'Dunnett (IRE)**[8] [2182] 7-8-10 **66** (v) KirstyMilczarek(7) 9 66
(Mrs C A Dunnett) *chsd ldrs: rdn over 2f out: edgd lft over 1f out: no ex fnl f* **25/1**

5030 **9** nk **Kennington**[8] [2182] 6-9-3 **66** (b) HayleyTurner 13 65
(Mrs C A Dunnett) *s.i.s: sn chsng ldrs: rdn over 2f out: styd on same pce appr fnl f* **33/1**

0063 **10** 3½ **Pamir (IRE)**[10] [2095] 4-9-0 **63** (b) FrancisNorton 10 52
(P R Chamings) *chsd ldrs: rdn 2f out: wknd fnl f* **11/1**

0000 **11** 5 **Elkhorn**[24] [1760] 4-9-3 **66** (v) DO'Donohoe 7 40
(Miss J A Camacho) *s.i.s: outpcd* **14/1**

0001 **12** 22 **Rosein**[6] [2248] 4-9-5 **68** 6ex J-PGuillambert 2 —
(Mrs G S Rees) *mid-div: wknd over 2f out* **10/1**

2156 **13** 1¾ **Seneschal**[18] [1878] 5-9-4 **67** JamieSpencer 1 —
(A B Haynes) *s.i.s: outpcd: rdn over 3f out: wknd over 2f out* **7/2**[1]

1m 15.12s (-0.69) **Going Correction** 0.0s/f (Stan) **13** Ran SP% **125.4**
Speed ratings (Par 103):104,103,101,101,101 101,99,99,98,94 87,58,55
CSF £453.81 CT £2799.97 TOTE £52.80: £14.80, £5.00, £3.10; EX 869.50.
Owner I Johnson **Bred** Helshaw Grange Stud Ltd **Trained** Newmarket, Suffolk
■ Stewards' Enquiry : Kirsty Milczarek caution: careless riding

FOCUS
A competitive handicap and the pace was decent without being breakneck, hence there being not much between the front nine at the post. Solid form.

2418 WOLVERHAMPTON HOLIDAY INN FILLIES' H'CAP 7f 32y(P)
5:00 (5:02) (Class 6) (0-60,59) 3-Y-0+ **£2,730** (£806; £403) **Stalls** High

Form RPR

4451 **1** **Free Angel (USA)**[228] [6082] 4-9-11 **55** FrancisNorton 6 71+
(M Wigham) *chsd ldrs: hung rt over 2f out: led over 1f out: r.o wl* **7/4**[1]

0050 **2** 3 **Sanctity**[8] [2171] 3-9-4 **58** OscarUrbina 10 62
(J R Fanshawe) *chsd ldrs: rdn and hung lft over 1f out: styd on same pce* **8/1**[3]

5100 **3** ¾ **Ektishaaf**[28] [1645] 4-9-13 **57** JamieMackay 11 65+
(C F Wall) *hld up: hdwy over 2f out: nt clr run over 1f out: styd on* **8/1**[3]

5040 **4** 2 **Guadaloup**[181] [6542] 4-9-10 **54** MickyFenton 8 55
(M Brittain) *led over 5f: wknd ins fnl f* **12/1**

1553 **5** 1 **Buzzin'Boyzee (IRE)**[3] [2316] 3-9-0 **59** StephenDonohoe(5) 9 57
(P D Evans) *hld up: hdwy over 2f out: rdn over 1f out: wknd ins fnl f* **9/4**[2]

4140 **6** 2 **Spark Up**[97] [586] 6-9-11 **55** (b) HayleyTurner 1 48
(J W Unett) *s.i.s: sn chsng ldrs: lost pl 4f out: n.d after* **12/1**

200 **7** 6 **Steady Rain**[27] [1670] 4-9-12 **56** (v[1]) DO'Donohoe 2 34
(P S McEntee) *s.i.s: hld up: nvr nrr* **25/1**

506 **8** 4 **Ailsa**[13] [2019] 4-9-6 **50** DeanMcKeown 5 17
(C W Thornton) *prom: nt clr run an dlost pl 3f out: n.d after* **25/1**

6010 **9** 3½ **Ellens Princess (IRE)**[27] [1683] 4-9-11 **58** DNolan(3) 7 16
(J S Wainwright) *chsd ldrs: ev ch over 2f out: sn wknd* **33/1**

006 **10** 2½ **Very Clear**[43] [1254] 4-9-7 **51** (p) TPQueally 12 3
(R M H Cowell) *s.i.s: hld up: a in rr* **33/1**

5020 **11** 3 **Glenviews Babalou (USA)**[25] [1725] 4-9-5 **49** RobbieFitzpatrick 3 —
(Peter Grayson) *bhd fnl 3f* **18/1**

0000 **12** 22 **Gypsy Royal (IRE)**[7] [2195] 4-9-4 **48** (t) J-PGuillambert 4 —
(G Woodward) *chsd ldrs over 4f* **66/1**

1m 30.72s (0.32) **Going Correction** 0.0s/f (Stan)
WFA 3 from 4yo+ 10lb **12** Ran SP% **125.1**
Speed ratings (Par 98):98,94,93,91,90 88,81,76,72,69 66,41
CSF £17.05 CT £99.40 TOTE £3.70: £2.10, £2.70, £2.50; EX 32.40 Place 6 £214.60, Place 5 £144.74.
Owner D Hassan **Bred** B D Gibbs Farm Llc, And William G Munn **Trained** Newmarket, Suffolk

FOCUS
An ordinary race of its type, but it was run at an even pace and the form is solid enough for the grade. The winner proved a class apart, but the unexposed second also deserves credit from her wide draw.
T/Jkpt: Not won. T/Plt: £777.30 to a £1 stake. Pool: £44,353.40. 41.65 winning tickets. T/Qpdt: £333.60 to a £1 stake. Pool: £2,299.50. 5.10 winning tickets. CR

2419 - 2428a (Foreign Racing) - See Raceform Interactive

2401 GOODWOOD (R-H)
Saturday, June 10

OFFICIAL GOING: Straight course - good (good to firm in places) changing to good to firm (good in places) after race 3 (3.30); round course - good to firm
Wind: Moderate, across Weather: Sunny & warm

2429 EMPIRE PROPERTY GROUP H'CAP 6f
2:20 (2:23) (Class 2) (0-100,100) 3-Y-0+
£16,514 (£4,944; £2,472; £1,237; £617; £310) **Stalls** Low

Form RPR

6303 **1** **Firenze**[13] [2047] 5-9-3 **89** LDettori 16 100+
(J R Fanshawe) *hld up and racd wd: stdy prog fr 1/2-way: led over 1f out: edgd lft and rdn out fnl f* **3/1**[1]

1602 **2** 1 **Border Music**[5] [2302] 5-8-9 **81** oh3 (b) RichardHughes 5 89
(A M Balding) *hld up wl in rr: prog 2f out: effrt to chse wnr ins fnl f: no real imp* **4/1**[2]

0000 **3** nk **Woodcote (IRE)**[35] [1487] 4-9-1 **90** AdamKirby(3) 12 97
(C G Cox) *pressed ldr: upsides 2f out: hanging rt and nt qckn over 1f out: styd on again ins fnl f* **20/1**

6040 **4** ¾ **Mine Behind**[7] [2230] 6-9-1 **87** JohnEgan 13 92
(J R Best) *hld up bhd ldng gp: prog on outer 2f out: drvn and looked dangerous ins fnl f: one pce last 100yds* **12/1**

4004 **5** 1 **Gloved Hand**[13] [2047] 4-8-10 **87** RoryMoore(5) 14 89
(J R Fanshawe) *pressed ldrs: poised to chal 2f out: shuffled along and hanging 1f out: nt qckn* **12/1**

14-5 **6** 1¼ **Seamus Shindig**[13] [2047] 4-8-11 **83** LPKeniry 9 81
(H Candy) *chsd ldng gp: shkn up 2f out: styd on same pce: no imp* **12/1**

351 **7** 2 **Sir Edwin Landseer (USA)**[85] 6-9-11 **100** EdwardCreighton(3) 8 92
(Christian Wroe, UAE) *stdd s: outpcd and wl bhd in last pair: styd on fr 2f out: nrst fin* **25/1**

0420 **8** ½ **Gallantry**[28] [1692] 4-9-1 **87** ChrisCatlin 1 78
(D W Barker) *led against nr side rail: hung rt fr 1/2-way: hdd & wknd over 1f out* **10/1**

0006 **9** ½ **Fantasy Believer**[7] [2230] 8-8-12 **84** GrahamGibbons 2 73
(J J Quinn) *chsd ldrs on nr side: drvn and cl up over 1f out: wknd* **8/1**[3]

0650 **10** 1¼ **Safari Sunset (IRE)**[233] [5999] 4-8-11 **83** JimCrowley 4 68
(P Winkworth) *prom to 2f out: steadily wknd* **20/1**

3154 **11** 2 **Angel Sprints**[17] [1936] 4-9-1 **87** AlanMunro 7 66
(B R Millman) *prom to 2f out: sn wknd* **9/1**

1420 **12** hd **Pic Up Sticks**[22] [1820] 7-8-13 **85** TQuinn 3 64
(B G Powell) *s.i.s: hld up in rr: rdn and no prog nr side over 1f out* **12/1**

6400 **13** 1¼ **Stagbury Hill (USA)**[17] [1935] 4-9-6 **92** RHills 11 67
(J W Hills) *outpcd and wl bhd: sn drvn: nvr a factor* **66/1**

0560 **14** hd **Jayanjay**[7] [2227] 7-9-3 **89** JimmyQuinn 6 63
(Miss B Sanders) *a towards rr: rdn over 2f out: n.d* **20/1**

69.83 secs (-3.02) **Going Correction** -0.25s/f (Firm) **14** Ran SP% **125.6**
Speed ratings (Par 109):110,108,108,107,105 104,101,100,100,98 95,95,94,93
CSF £13.73 CT £220.53 TOTE £3.30: £1.70, £1.90, £7.70; EX 21.20.
Owner Mrs Jan Hopper **Bred** Mrs J P Hopper **Trained** Newmarket, Suffolk

FOCUS
A solid-looking handicap, won in a good time by an improving and well-related filly.

NOTEBOOK
Firenze ◆ is improving as she gains experience, much like her illustrious sister Frizzante. With a moderate draw to overcome, she won in good style, travelling well, coming with a strong effort on the outer in mid-race, and pulling away nicely despite edging left. She picks up a 5lb penalty for the Wokingham Handicap at Royal Ascot but shapes as if there is more to come and would take plenty of stopping in that race if conditions suited her on the day.
Border Music, running from 3lb out of the handicap, does not look the easiest to win with on turf, and while it is most doubtful that he would have beaten the winner under any circumstances, his chance would have been made easier had he been able to come through horses and not around them. Goodwood suits him well, as he has run some of his best turf races there, and he would be of interest in a nice handicap at the 'Glorious' meeting under a specialist hold-up jockey. (op 5-1)
Woodcote(IRE), who has not won since making his racecourse debut, had been keeping good company recently, and was not been beaten far in his last three races despite some poor-looking form figures. He kept on nicely after initially hanging under pressure, and would not be without a chance in the Wokingham Handicap at Royal Ascot on his best form, if getting into the race.
Mine Behind is turning into a solid sprint handicapper and arguably ran up to his best. However, obvious winning opportunities are going to be tougher to come by if the Handicapper keeps raising him for his consistency. (tchd 14-1)
Gloved Hand finished behind her stablemate Firenze last time and could not find any way past her again. She is, however, making quiet progress and could still find further improvement when stepped up in trip again, as she appeared to just about stay a mile when with James Given last season. One would think that connections have a race in mind for her later in the season.
Seamus Shindig ◆ is making steady progress after his long absence and it is heartening to see that he did not regress from his last run. Held in some regard as a two-year-old, he caught the eye just in behind and looks capable of going close next time.

2430 EMPIRE PROPERTY GROUP CONDITIONS STKS 1m 4f
2:55 (2:57) (Class 3) 4-Y-0+
£9,815 (£2,938; £1,469; £735; £366; £184) **Stalls** Low

Form RPR

4142 **1** **Balkan Knight**[21] [1839] 6-8-9 105 LDettori 5 107+
(D R C Elsworth) *trckd ldr: clsd over 2f out: shkn up to ld 1f out: r.o wl: readily* **5/4**[1]

4164 **2** 1¾ **Art Eyes (USA)**[12] [2085] 4-9-0 105 JohnEgan 8 109
(D R C Elsworth) *led: 3l clr over 3f out: rdn and hdd 1f out: one pce* **10/3**[3]

0060 **3** 1½ **Wunderwood (USA)**[34] [1511] 7-8-9 98 AlanMunro 1 102
(Lady Herries) *chsd ldng pair: rdn over 2f out: kpt on same pce and nvr able to chal* **14/1**

-000 **4** 2½ **Orange Touch (GER)**[217] [6255] 6-8-9 103 RyanMoore 7 98
(Mrs A J Perrett) *a in 4th: shkn up 3f out: nt qckn and no imp fnl 2f* **10/1**

0232 **5** 6 **Camrose**[34] [1511] 5-8-9 99 (b) RichardHughes 2 88
(J L Dunlop) *hld up in 5th: shkn up and no rspnse wl over 2f out: no imp after and looked uneasy: wkng bdly nr fin* **11/4**[2]

1025 **6** nk **Littletown Bridge (USA)**[106] [510] 4-8-4 ChrisCatlin 6 83
(Christian Wroe, UAE) *a in 6th: rdn over 3f out: sn struggling* **33/1**

00 **7** 7 **Three Counties (IRE)**[29] [4899] 5-8-2 MarkCoumbe(7) 4 76?
(N I M Rossiter) *dwlt: a last: rdn 4f out: bhd fnl 2f* **100/1**

2m 36.0s (-2.92) **Going Correction** 0.0s/f (Good) **7** Ran SP% **113.9**
Speed ratings (Par 107):109,107,106,105,101 100,96
CSF £5.69 TOTE £2.00: £1.40, £2.10; EX 5.10.
Owner Raymond Tooth **Bred** Sheikh Mohammed Bin Rashid Al Maktoum **Trained** Newmarket, Suffolk

FOCUS
A decent little race, run at a good tempo. The first three look capable of going well again next time out.

NOTEBOOK
Balkan Knight showed a really nice turn of foot to get past his stablemate in the closing stages, and won going away. His handicap mark probably does not make him the easiest to place but when given a realistic chance, he is the sort to take it. Looking a long way into the future, his trainer believes he could be the ideal sort to take to Australia for the Melbourne Cup. (tchd 11-8 and 6-4 in places)
Art Eyes(USA) set the race up for her stable companion, but still emerges from the race with plenty of credit. Penalised 5lb and unable to claim the 3lb weight allowance that the others received, she beat the rest of her rivals nicely over a trip arguably short of her best. The trainer views her as a likely type for the Melbourne Cup, much like the winner, but another attempt at the Park Hill Stakes in September would seem a realistic target in the meantime. (op 3-1 tchd 7-2)
Wunderwood(USA) had seldom had the fast ground he needs since winning off 103 at Hamilton last summer, but conditions were much more to his liking here and he ran much better. With his stable generally in better form this season a repeat attempt at the Duke Of Edinburgh Stakes at the Royal meeting could well be on the horizon, as long as the Handicapper does not raise him much for the run.

Orange Touch(GER) ran a reasonable race on ground that would not have been totally ideal, and over a trip that could be argued is short of his best. He is already well handicapped on his best form, but has not recaptured his sparkle since a modest effort in the Irish St Leger back in 2004. As long as he does retain some of his old ability, he could be the sort to keep in mind for a decent handicap at the end of the season when the rain starts to fall again. (op 12-1)
Camrose was under pressure a long way from home and never became a realistic threat. His handicap mark is a touch high at the moment, which is probably forcing connections to run him in Listed company. (op 7-2)
Littletown Bridge(USA), once placed in the UAE Oaks, never threatened to get involved but did at least finish just behind a 99-rated horse. She was given a mark in the nineties in Dubai, so it will be interesting to see how the Handicapper assesses her. (op 25-1)

2431 EMPIRE PROPERTY GROUP ON THE HOUSE STKS (LISTED RACE) 1m
3:30 (3:30) (Class 1) 3-Y-0+ **£17,034** (£6,456; £3,231; £1,611; £807) **Stalls** High

Form RPR
14-0 **1** **Satchem (IRE)**[406] [1359] 4-9-5 106 ....(t) LDettori 5 116
(Saeed Bin Suroor) *hld up: prog 3f out: rdn to ld narrowly jst over 1f out: hdd wl ins fnl f: rallied to ld post* **10/3**[3]
1010 **2** *shd* **Stronghold**[23] [1806] 4-9-8 108 .... RichardHughes 4 119
(J H M Gosden) *trckd ldr after 3f: shkn up to ld over 1f out: sn hdd: rallied to ld wl ins fnl f: hdd post* **9/4**[2]
1532 **3** *7* **Take A Bow**[7] [2236] 5-9-5 105 .... AlanMunro 2 100
(P R Chamings) *hld up: rdn 3f out: sn struggling: no ch 2f out: tk modest 3rd wl ins fnl f* **8/1**
1214 **4** *1 1/4* **Mostashaar (FR)**[38] [1407] 4-9-5 109 .... RHills 1 97
(Sir Michael Stoute) *led: rdn and hdd over 1f out: wknd rapidly* **11/8**[1]
0606 **5** *36* **Chorus Beauty**[61] [941] 5-9-0 38 .... MarkCoombe 3 9
(N I M Rossiter) *chsd ldr for 3f: sn wknd: t.o* **200/1**
1m 37.37s (-2.90) **Going Correction** 0.0s/f (Good) **5** Ran SP% **107.6**
Speed ratings (Par 111):114,113,106,105,69
CSF £10.65 TOTE £4.00: £1.90, £1.70; EX 12.00.
Owner Godolphin **Bred** K Molloy **Trained** Newmarket, Suffolk

FOCUS
A small but select field for a Listed race that looks up to the required standard. The time was creditable for the grade and the first two showed improved form in pulling well clear.

NOTEBOOK
Satchem(IRE) ◆ provided further proof that Godolphin are making up for lost time, and quickly. Not seen since finishing ninth in last season's 2000 Guineas, he showed admirable battling qualities under pressure to hold off the race-fit Stronghold. Although there is a slight worry he may 'bounce' next time, he looks set for a good serason. He holds entries in the Hunt Cup, the Golden Jubilee and the July Cup. (op 3-1)
Stronghold ◆, back on his favoured fast ground after disappointing at York, is developing into a very smart performer and made Satchem battle all the way to the line. Although he could not make his fitness advantage tell, he would be 6lb better off if they met again in the Hunt Cup, and he has the class to be a big factor there if allowed his chance. (tchd 5-2)
Take A Bow has been in good form and gives the race a solid look. He rarely runs badly but cannot be easy to place. (op 10-1)
Mostashaar(FR) looked ill at ease on the track under pressure, and disappointed again. An impressive Royal Ascot at York winner, he deserves one more chance to redeem himself on a more galloping track, but is not looking the horse that landed the Britannia Stakes last season. (tchd 5-4)

2432 EMPIRE SCHIZOPHRENIA TRUST MAIDEN AUCTION STKS 6f
4:05 (4:08) (Class 5) 2-Y-0 **£3,400** (£1,011; £505; £252) **Stalls** Low

Form RPR
03 **1** **Proper (IRE)**[9] [2178] 2-8-9 .... ChrisCatlin 10 73+
(M R Channon) *led after 1f: mde rest: drvn and styd on wl fnl f* **9/2**[3]
2 *1* **Goodbye Cash (IRE)** 2-8-6 .... GrahamGibbons 5 67
(P D Evans) *led for 1f: mostly chsd wnr after: rdn 2f out: styd on ins fnl f: a hld* **25/1**
3 *1 1/4* **Den's Gift (IRE)** 2-8-13 .... AdamKirby(3) 9 73
(C G Cox) *chsd ldrs: rdn over 2f out: effrt u.p over 1f out: styd on* **14/1**
5 **4** *1/2* **Ioweyou**[18] [1922] 2-8-8 .... JohnEgan 2 64
(J S Moore) *in tch: rdn over 2f out: no prog tl r.o jst over 1f out: nrst fin* **15/2**
0 **5** *5* **Lancaster's Quest**[9] [2172] 2-8-11 .... RobertHavlin 11 52
(R Ingram) *dwlt: chsd ldrs: n.m.r over 3f out: outpcd and btn over 1f out* **16/1**
0 **6** *shd* **Recruit**[16] [1959] 2-9-2 .... RyanMoore 7 56
(R Hannon) *s.s: sn pushed along in rr: effrt on outer 1/2-way: outpcd u.p over 1f out* **3/1**[2]
7 *3/4* **Cheap Street** 2-8-11 .... TQuinn 1 49
(J G Portman) *dwlt: sn in tch but hanging: outpcd fr 2f out* **25/1**
8 *1 1/4* **Jack Oliver** 2-9-1 .... LDettori 13 49+
(B J Meehan) *prom: rdn and cl up 2f out: wknd jst over 1f out: eased nr fin* **5/2**[1]
4 **9** *shd* **Fiddlers Spirit (IRE)**[15] [1982] 2-8-9 .... JimmyQuinn 6 43
(J G M O'Shea) *wl in rr: outpcd and detached over 2f out: kpt on last 150yds* **33/1**
10 *2* **Tumble Jill (IRE)** 2-7-11 .... JosephWalsh(7) 3 32
(J S Moore) *dwlt: last and wl bhd over 3f out: nvr a factor* **50/1**
11 *1/2* **Storm Mission (USA)** 2-8-13 .... LPKeniry 4 40
(Miss V Haigh) *racd towards nr side: in tch to over 2f out: wknd* **40/1**
45 **12** *4* **Smirfy's Silver**[31] [1582] 2-8-11 .... RichardHughes 8 26
(W M Brisbourne) *chsd ldrs: hanging and wknd 2f out: eased fnl f* **7/1**
1m 12.24s (-0.61) **Going Correction** -0.25s/f (Firm) **12** Ran SP% **123.6**
Speed ratings (Par 93):94,92,91,90,83 83,82,80,80,78 77,72
CSF £121.87 TOTE £4.70: £1.80, £5.20, £3.70; EX 117.60.
Owner Billy Parish **Bred** Sean Finnegan **Trained** West Ilsley, Berks

FOCUS
A modest contest for the course, but the winner travelled quite well and a few in behind may make their mark in a lower grade.

NOTEBOOK
Proper(IRE) was noticeably weak in the market but won in good style after being up with the pace throughout. He looks to have a bit of scope about him, and he may have needed the first two runs to sharpen him up, so more improvement might be forthcoming. (op 7-2 tchd 5-1)
Goodbye Cash(IRE) is not overly big, but kept on stoutly for pressure all the way to the line. A race against her own sex would probably prove her best move next time. (tchd 33-1)
Den's Gift(IRE) was not given a hard time and kept plugging away under mostly hands and heels pressure. He looks sure to be suited by further than six furlongs.
Ioweyou, well supported in the market, did not look to handle the track very well, slightly hanging away from the stands'-side rail from halfway. She can be given another chance on a flatter track. (op 16-1)
Lancaster's Quest shaped like a horse that will need at least seven furlongs to have any sort of chance. Official explanation: jockey said colt was unsuited by the good to firm (good in places) ground (op 14-1)
Recruit had every chance but was nowhere near good enough against some modest opponents. Official explanation: jockey said colt hung left throughout (op 7-2)
Cheap Street shaped with some promise after starting slowly and failing to find room when needed at a crucial stage of the race. He is better than the bare form suggests. (tchd 33-1)
Jack Oliver looks like a horse that needs more time to grow into his frame. The jockey was looking downwards in the final stages, suggesting all may not have been right with him. Official explanation: jockey said gelding lost its action (op 11-4 tchd 3-1)
Storm Mission(USA) showed his inexperience under pressure but ran better than his final position suggests. There might be a race in him at a lower grade. (op 50-1)

2433 HITCHCOCK & KING STKS (H'CAP) 5f
4:40 (4:40) (Class 5) (0-70,75) 3-Y-0 **£3,562** (£1,059; £529; £264) **Stalls** Low

Form RPR
5003 **1** **Musical Romance (IRE)**[8] [2190] 3-9-1 63 .... (b) LDettori 6 71
(B J Meehan) *hld up bhd ldrs: effrt over 1f out: hanging and carried hd to one side: drvn ahd last 75yds* **4/1**[1]
0521 **2** *1/2* **Fantasy Explorer**[17] [1937] 3-9-4 66 .... GrahamGibbons 8 72
(J J Quinn) *stmbld s: pressed ldrs: led 2f out: rdn and pressed over 1f out : hdd last 75yds: kpt on* **9/2**[2]
6201 **3** *hd* **Lucayos**[6] [2263] 3-9-8 75 6ex .... (b) RichardKingscote(5) 3 80
(Mrs H Sweeting) *pressed ldng pair: upsides over 1f out: stl chalng ins fnl f: nt qckn last 100yds* **9/2**[2]
1544 **4** *1* **Overwing (IRE)**[10] [2134] 3-9-7 69 .... RyanMoore 2 70
(R M H Cowell) *racd towards nr side: disp ld to 2f out: nt qckn over 1f out: styd on again ins fnl f* **13/2**[3]
0004 **5** *3/4* **Supreme Kiss**[8] [2190] 3-9-0 62 .... JimmyQuinn 7 61
(Miss B Sanders) *s.s: t.k.h and hld up: effrt and swtchd rt 1f out: fnd nil* **12/1**
1030 **6** *1 1/4* **Miss Brush**[37] [1431] 3-9-1 63 .... ChrisCatlin 9 57
(J R Fanshawe) *racd on outer: in tch: hanging rt fr 1/2-way: wknd ins fnl f* **7/1**
0535 **7** *3/4* **Ceredig**[10] [2134] 3-9-2 64 .... TQuinn 4 55
(W R Muir) *disp ld to 2f out: wknd* **9/1**
4453 **8** *2 1/2* **Danny The Dip**[10] [2134] 3-8-2 55 .... MarcHalford(5) 5 36
(J J Bridger) *chsd ldrs for 3f: wknd u.p* **11/1**
5001 **9** *3/4* **Jucebabe**[8] [2187] 3-8-9 60 .... AdamKirby(3) 1 39
(J L Spearing) *a in rr: rdn and struggling 1/2-way* **10/1**
58.02 secs (-1.03) **Going Correction** -0.25s/f (Firm) **9** Ran SP% **117.3**
Speed ratings (Par 99):98,97,96,95,94 92,90,86,85
CSF £22.36 CT £85.08 TOTE £4.60: £1.70, £2.00, £1.90; EX 17.30.
Owner F C T Wilson **Bred** C H Wacker Iii **Trained** Manton, Wilts

FOCUS
A modest sprint in which the winner and third both looked fairly exposed.
Supreme Kiss Official explanation: jockey said filly missed the break

2434 ROBERT HOLMES & CO STKS (H'CAP) 1m 3f
5:15 (5:15) (Class 5) (0-70,75) 3-Y-0 **£3,562** (£1,059; £529; £264) **Stalls** Low

Form RPR
0001 **1** **Star Of Canterbury (IRE)**[68] [859] 3-9-7 70 .... LDettori 4 77
(A P Jarvis) *led after 1f and set stdy pce: kicked on over 4f out: rdn and hdd narrowly 2f out: rallied to ld ins fnl f* **3/1**[1]
0336 **2** *1 1/4* **Italic**[26] [1740] 3-9-6 69 .... (b[1]) RyanMoore 12 74
(Mrs A J Perrett) *led for 1f: trckd wnr after: effrt to ld narrowly 2f out: hdd u.p ins fnl f: no ex* **5/1**
034 **3** *hd* **Greenwich Village**[49] [1153] 3-9-5 68 .... RobertHavlin 9 73
(W J Knight) *trckd ldrs: rdn over 3f out: nt qckn and outpcd over 2f out: r.o again fnl f* **7/1**
3411 **4** *hd* **Black Beauty**[10] [2128] 3-9-7 75 .... JerryO'Dwyer(5) 10 79
(M G Quinlan) *trckd ldng pair: hrd rdn and nt qckn 3f out: styd on again fnl f* **7/2**[3]
0000 **5** *1 1/2* **Irish Whispers (IRE)**[245] [5733] 3-8-12 61 .... RHills 3 63
(B G Powell) *hld up in rr: prog on outer 3f out: swtchd rt and drifted rt fr 2f out: no imp after* **33/1**
0000 **6** *1/2* **Wings Of Dawn**[29] [1652] 3-8-6 55 .... AlanMunro 2 56
(M P Tregoning) *chsd ldrs: lost pl 5f out: rdn in rr over 3f out: plugged on* **25/1**
0505 **7** *3/4* **Roya**[19] [1880] 3-9-4 70 .... RichardSmith(3) 14 70
(R Hannon) *trckd ldrs: rdn and nt qckn 3f out: no imp after: fdd fnl f* **33/1**
0005 **8** *2* **Foreign Envoy (IRE)**[45] [1240] 3-9-1 64 .... JohnEgan 13 64+
(B W Hills) *hld up in rr: rdn 3f out: trying to stay on but no ch whn hmpd 2f out* **16/1**
0660 **9** *nk* **Bella Fiorella (IRE)**[81] [687] 3-7-13 51 oh4 .... DominicFox(3) 6 47
(Miss V Haigh) *hld up in rr: rdn 4f out: no rspnse and btn 3f out* **100/1**
0604 **10** *nk* **Zizou (IRE)**[3] [2352] 3-7-11 51 oh1 .... MarcHalford(5) 8 47
(J J Bridger) *hld up in tch: chsd ldrs gng wl enough over 2f out: hanging rt after: wknd rapidly over 1f out* **16/1**
000 **11** *1 1/4* **Warne's Way (IRE)**[50] [1120] 3-9-3 66 .... RichardHughes 1 60+
(R Hannon) *towards rr: rdn 4f out: trying to stay on whn hmpd over 2f out: no ch after* **10/1**
12 *38* **Rosalie**[314] 3-9-4 67 .... GrahamGibbons 5 —
(C F Wall) *in tch tl wknd over 3f out: bhd and eased 2f out: t.o* **20/1**
0342 **P** **Dimelight**[11] [2113] 3-9-7 70 .... TQuinn 7 —
(D R C Elsworth) *s.s: p.u and dismntd after 100yds* **10/3**[2]
2m 28.62s (1.41) **Going Correction** 0.0s/f (Good) **13** Ran SP% **135.8**
Speed ratings (Par 99):94,93,92,92,91 91,90,89,89,88 88,60,—
CSF £20.35 CT £108.54 TOTE £4.30: £1.80, £2.30, £3.10; EX 51.60.
Owner Eurostrait Ltd **Bred** Tally-Ho Stud **Trained** Twyford, Bucks
■ The final leg of a 779-1 five-timer for Frankie Dettori.
■ Stewards' Enquiry : Richard Smith two-day ban: careless riding (Jun 25-26)

FOCUS
A interesting handicap, but ruined as a reliable form guide by the slow early gallop. The time was very moderate indeed.
Foreign Envoy(IRE) Official explanation: jockey said gelding was denied a clear run
Zizou(IRE) Official explanation: jockey said gelding hung right
Dimelight Official explanation: jockey said filly stumbled leaving stalls causing tack to slip

2435 EMPIRE PROPERTY GROUP STKS (H'CAP) 1m
5:50 (5:50) (Class 2) (0-100,99) 4-Y-0+
£13,087 (£3,918; £1,470; £1,470; £489; £245) **Stalls** High

Form RPR
5200 **1** **Dansili Dancer**[49] [1129] 4-8-6 87 .... AdamKirby(3) 3 98
(C G Cox) *pressed ldng pair: shkn up over 2f out: led on outer over 1f out: drvn out* **10/1**
3424 **2** *1 1/4* **Red Spell (IRE)**[17] [1935] 5-9-1 93 .... RichardHughes 6 101
(R Hannon) *trckd ldrs gng wl: effrt over 1f out: rdn to chse wnr ins fnl f: no imp last 100yds* **10/3**[2]

3606 **3** *nk* **James Caird (IRE)**[175] 6601 6-8-10 **88** RHills 1 95+
(M H Tompkins) *hld up in last pair: effrt on outer 2f out: sltly checked over 1f out: styd on ins fnl f* **25/1**

0050 **3** *dht* **Tucker**[23] 1806 4-9-7 **99** TQuinn 5 106
(D R C Elsworth) *hld up in midfield: effrt on outer over 2f out: rdn and nt qckn over 1f out: kpt on ins fnl f* **7/2**[3]

6040 **5** *2* **Nero's Return (IRE)**[8] 2201 5-8-3 **81** StanleyChin 2 84
(M Johnston) *hld up in last trio: rdn over 2f out: outpcd wl over 1f out: styd on ins fnl f* **8/1**

0006 **6** *1 3/4* **Bahar Shumaal (IRE)**[21] 1839 4-9-7 **99** (t) RyanMoore 8 98
(C E Brittain) *dwlt: sn wl in tch: rdn 3f out: outpcd and btn wl over 1f out* **16/1**

3023 **7** *nk* **Binanti**[17] 1935 6-8-7 **85** AlanMunro 7 83
(P R Chamings) *pressed ldr gng wl: led 2f out: hdd over 1f out: edgd lft and fnd nil* **10/1**

0606 **8** *1* **Ettrick Water**[28] 1676 7-8-12 **90** (v) LDettori 9 86
(L M Cumani) *mde most to 2f out: sn btn* **11/8**[1]

4000 **9** *1/2* **Nashaab (USA)**[29] 1629 9-8-4 **82** ow2 (v) GrahamGibbons 4 77?
(P D Evans) *s.s: nvr gng wl and a in rr: rdn 1/2-way: struggling after* **25/1**

1m 38.93s (-1.34) **Going Correction** 0.0s/f (Good) **9** Ran SP% **130.3**
Speed ratings (Par 109):106,104,104,104,102 100,100,99,98
Place: Tucker £0.90, James Caird £2.10. Tricast: DD/RS/T £74.17; DD/RS/JC £429.37. CSF £49.16 TOTE £15.30: £3.30, £1.60; EX 82.80 Place 6 £64.16, Place 5 £38.01.
Owner The Troupers **Bred** The Magic Slipper Partnership **Trained** Lambourn, Berks

FOCUS
A solid handicap that should work out. They were spread across the track at the finish, with three of the first four among a quartet who ended up towards the stands' rail.

NOTEBOOK
Dansili Dancer, from a stable whose horses all seem to be running well, showed plenty of determination under his jockey to grind out a decisive victory. Still open to some improvement given his relative inexperience, he ought to give a good account of himself if he makes the cut for the Royal Hunt Cup at Royal Ascot, before, possibly, returning to Goodwood - a course he now has a two from three record at - for a handicap at the 'Glorious' meeting. (op 9-1)
Red Spell(IRE) had every chance and won 'his race' on the far side of the track. Well handicapped on his all-weather form, he may well need holding up for much longer in a strongly-run race, something that was not possible on this occasion, and the Hunt Cup at Royal Ascot may provide him with that opportunity. (op 7-2)
Tucker had every chance but failed to land a blow. Although he has run well at Goodwood before, his best efforts usually come at Newmarket. (op 9-2 tchd 5-1)
James Caird(IRE) ◆is still slightly high in the handicap on all of his winning form, but strongly suggested that he is capable of going close next time, possibly in the Royal Hunt Cup later in the month, after a thoroughly pleasing effort on his first run of the season. (op 9-2 tchd 5-1)
Nero's Return(IRE) is well handicapped on his best efforts of last season and looks to be steadily coming into form again after his stable's slow start to the season. He goes well here and will be of obvious interest if returned to the track for the 'Glorious' meeting in early August. (tchd 9-1)
Ettrick Water was a false price owing to his jockey's five winners earlier on the card, and he did not show a great deal off a fair handicap mark, despite having the run of the race. (op 6-4 tchd 13-8)
T/Plt: £61.80 to a £1 stake. Pool: £60,897.25. 719.30 winning tickets. T/Qpdt: £21.60 to a £1 stake. Pool: £2,285.80. 78.00 winning tickets. JN

2407 HAYDOCK (L-H)
Saturday, June 10

OFFICIAL GOING: Good to firm
Wind: Light, behind Weather: Hot and sunny

2436 NICHOLAS WHITTLE COMMUNICATIONS H'CAP 1m 3f 200y
2:10 (2:14) (Class 2) (0-100,91) 3-Y-O
£15,580 (£4,665; £2,332; £1,167; £582; £292) **Stalls** High

Form RPR

1212 **1** **Soapy Danger**[42] 1286 3-9-7 **91** KDarley 6 100
(M Johnston) *led after 1f: mde rest: rdn over 1f out: r.o* **4/1**[3]

11 **2** *1 3/4* **Hero Worship (IRE)**[42] 1286 3-9-4 **88** PhilipRobinson 2 94+
(M A Jarvis) *prom: pushed along and outpcd over 3f out: styd on ins fnl f to take 2nd towards fin* **5/2**[1]

531 **3** *1/2* **Salesin**[19] 1880 3-9-5 **89** NickyMackay 5 94
(L M Cumani) *hld up: clsd 3f out: rdn and hung lft over 2f out: rdr lost iron and styd on ins fnl f* **7/2**[2]

021 **4** *3/4* **Duty (IRE)**[30] 1613 3-9-3 **87** RobertWinston 1 91+
(Sir Michael Stoute) *s.i.s: in rr: rdn and hung lft 2 out: styd on ins fnl f: one pce cl home* **11/2**

2213 **5** *nk* **Barodine**[13] 2046 3-9-1 **85** EddieAhern 4 88
(H R A Cecil) *prom: rdn and hung lft over 1f out: no ex ins fnl f* **6/1**

2626 **6** *6* **Pinch Of Salt (IRE)**[21] 1841 3-8-9 **79** (t) MartinDwyer 3 73
(A M Balding) *hld up in tch: rdn 3f out: lft bhd fnl f* **10/1**

2m 32.63s (-2.36) **Going Correction** -0.30s/f (Firm) **6** Ran SP% **109.6**
Speed ratings (Par 105):95,93,93,93,92 88
CSF £13.67 TOTE £5.30: £1.80, £1.80; EX 10.20.
Owner Mrs R J Jacobs **Bred** Newsells Park Stud Limited **Trained** Middleham Moor, N Yorks

FOCUS
A decent handicap contested by progressive three-year-olds who are likely to win more races with the placed horses being the best guide to the form. The early pace was steady, though, resulting in a very modest winning time for a race like this.

NOTEBOOK
Soapy Danger, 2lb better off with Hero Worship for a length beating at Leicester last time, reversed the form on this quicker ground. He was more or less granted an uncontested lead, which is always a dangerous thing to give to a Johnston-trained horse, especially one with a progressive profile, and battled on well when challenged. The King George V Handicap at the Royal meeting looks the obvious target. (op 5-1)
Hero Worship(IRE) beat Soapy Danger at Leicester last time but was 2lb worse off at the weights with that rival here and the ground was quicker too. Unsuited by the way the race was run, he was outpaced as the tempo quickened in the straight but stayed on well towards the finish. A stronger pace would have suited him, and he might have the race run more to suit at Royal Ascot in the King George V Handicap. (op 3-1 tchd 10-3 in places)
Salesin won a soft-ground maiden at Bath last time and is by a German sire, so these quicker conditions were something of a concern. He hung left under pressure and perhaps he will need easier ground to be seen at his best in future.
Duty(IRE), a workmanlike winner of a Yarmouth maiden last time, was friendless in the market beforehand and did not have the race run to suit. Held up at the back of the field in a contest run at a steady gallop, he found himself in the wrong place when the sprint for home began. He did make up ground, but hung left when hit the whip, and is clearly still learning what this game is all about. There should be better to come from him. Official explanation: jockey said he lost an iron a furlong out (op 7-2 tchd 6-1)
Barodine looked a big threat as he loomed up alongside the eventual winner two furlongs out, but he was brushed aside when the battle began and dropped out inside the final furlong. The extra distance may have been against him, and a drop back to ten furlongs could be in his favour. (tchd 13-2)
Pinch Of Salt(IRE), who is still a maiden, did not find the necessary improvement to put that right on this step up in trip. (op 12-1)

2437 SHANK LANE STKS (H'CAP) 2m 45y
2:40 (2:41) (Class 2) (0-100,92) 4-Y-O+
£17,449 (£5,224; £2,612; £1,307; £652; £327) **Stalls** Low

Form RPR

2156 **1** **Bulwark (IRE)**[31] 1584 4-9-9 **92** (be) KerrinMcEvoy 1 101
(Mrs A J Perrett) *midfield: hdwy over 2f out: hung lft over 1f out: led ins fnl f: rdn out* **3/1**[2]

0110 **2** *1/2* **Colloquial**[14] 2013 5-9-6 **88** (v[1]) FergusSweeney 6 96
(H Candy) *led after 1f: hdd 3f out: sn rdn: regained ld over 1f out: hdd ins fnl f: r.o u.p* **14/1**

1612 **3** *shd* **Wing Collar**[23] 1809 5-9-3 **85** (p) DavidAllan 7 93
(T D Easterby) *hld up: pushed along over 3f out: hdwy over 2f out: lugged lft over 1f out: r.o ins fnl f* **17/2**[3]

0005 **4** *1 1/4* **Mirjan (IRE)**[24] 1779 10-9-8 **90** PaulHanagan 4 96
(L Lungo) *midfield: rdn over 4f out: hdwy 2f out: edgd lft and styd on ins fnl f* **12/1**

0451 **5** *3/4* **Toldo (IRE)**[14] 2013 4-9-3 **86** ShaneKelly 8 91
(G M Moore) *led for 1f: remained prom: regained ld 3f out: hdd over 1f out: no ex ins fnl f* **10/1**

010- **6** *5* **Dorothy's Friend**[661] 4858 6-9-8 **90** TedDurcan 11 89
(R Charlton) *hld up: rdn over 2f out: kpt on fnl f: nvr trbld ldrs* **16/1**

4321 **7** *1* **Numero Due**[28] 1685 4-9-0 **83** JamieSpencer 9 81
(G M Moore) *in tch: pushed along over 4f out: hung lft over 2f out: sn wknd* **5/2**[1]

-000 **8** *1 1/2* **Star Member (IRE)**[159] 4478 7-9-3 **85** EddieAhern 5 81
(Ian Williams) *in tch: rdn 3f out: wknd 2f out* **25/1**

6606 **9** *9* **Hiddensee (USA)**[7] 2238 4-9-2 **85** KDarley 3 71
(M Johnston) *trckd ldrs: rdn 4f out: wknd over 3f out* **16/1**

0600 **10** *1* **Anousa (IRE)**[9] 2176 5-8-12 **80** FrancisNorton 12 64
(P Howling) *a bhd* **100/1**

1062 **11** *18* **Valance (IRE)**[56] 1021 6-8-11 **79** RobertWinston 10 42
(C R Egerton) *racd keenly: midfield: hdwy over 6f out: rdn 3f out: wknd over 2f out* **11/1**

3m 29.56s (-8.34) **Going Correction** -0.30s/f (Firm)
WFA 4 from 5yo+ 1lb **11** Ran SP% **112.5**
Speed ratings (Par 109):108,107,107,107,106 104,103,102,98,97 88
CSF £42.65 CT £318.15 TOTE £3.90: £1.40, £3.90, £1.60; EX 48.10 Trifecta £229.20 Pool: £484.40. 1.50 winning tickets.
Owner Hesmonds Stud **Bred** Hesmonds Stud Ltd **Trained** Pulborough, W Sussex

FOCUS
A decent staying handicap and, despite the steady early pace, the form looks solid enough rated around second and fourth.

NOTEBOOK
Bulwark(IRE) is a tricky ride but he has plenty of ability, and he received a canny ride from McEvoy, who brought him with a well-timed challenge to get up in the closing stages. His form figures when ridden by McEvoy now read 111161, his only defeat coming when poorly drawn in the Chester Cup, and he has the ability to defy an even higher mark than this. The Northumberland Plate is apparently his next target, and a strong pace on the galloping track at Newcastle should suit him well. (op 10-3 tchd 7-2 in places)
Colloquial, visored for the first time, was allowed to set a steady pace in front and as a result he almost stole it. Headed early in the straight, he battled back well next to the rail to regain the lead, but could not hold off the winner. This was a solid effort, though, and he clearly stays well. (op 10-1)
Wing Collar, who was held up, was given a lot to do in a race not run at a great pace early on. He stayed on well, though, seeing out this longer trip well, and as he goes so well on fast ground he should be able to win a race of this nature off this sort of mark this summer. (op 10-1)
Mirjan(IRE) ran on well for fourth but his handicap mark remains stiff enough to make him vulnerable to sprightlier and less exposed rivals. (tchd 11-1)
Toldo(IRE), along with the eventual runner-up, benefited from racing at the front in a contest run at a steady early gallop, but he dropped out once headed inside the final two furlongs. While he is vulnerable to more progressive types, he is a consistent sort who seems to go on any ground. (tchd 11-1)
Dorothy's Friend, a very progressive performer back in 2004, was returning from a 661-day layoff and was entitled to need this. Not given a hard race to finish sixth, connections will no doubt have been greatly encouraged by this performance, and the ability appears to be still there.
Numero Due, raised 5lb for winning at Thirsk last time, found this a tougher assignment, although it was disappointing that he was unable to confirm form with his stablemate Toldo. Official explanation: jockey said gelding hung left (tchd 11-4 in places)

2438 TIMEFORM SILVER SALVER (REGISTERED AS THE CECIL FRAIL STKS) (LISTED RACE) (F&M) 6f
3:15 (3:20) (Class 1) 3-Y-O+
£15,898 (£6,025; £3,015; £1,503; £753; £378) **Stalls** Centre

Form RPR

1410 **1** **Paradise Isle**[35] 1485 5-9-4 103 KDarley 13 107
(C F Wall) *a.p: led over 2f out: rdn over 1f out: r.o* **6/1**

1215 **2** *1 1/4* **Nidhaal (IRE)**[254] 5571 3-8-6 107 MartinDwyer 12 97
(E A L Dunlop) *hld up: hdwy 1/2-way: rdn to chse wnr and edgd lft over 1f out: styd on ins fnl f* **7/2**[1]

1034 **3** *nk* **Clear Impression (IRE)**[21] 1849 4-9-0 94 J-PGuillambert 1 98+
(S C Williams) *trckd ldrs: nt clr run over 2f out: swtchd rt and rdn over 1f out: styd on ins fnl f* **16/1**

1302 **4** *3* **Dhekraa (IRE)**[39] 1377 3-8-6 97 PhilipRobinson 8 87
(M A Jarvis) *chsd ldrs: rdn 2f out: wknd ins fnl f* **5/1**[2]

2000 **5** *1* **Sweet Afton (IRE)**[39] 1377 3-8-6 KerrinMcEvoy 4 84
(Eamon Tyrrell, Ire) *in tch: outpcd over 2f out: kpt on fnl f: nt trble ldrs* **20/1**

1626 **6** *1/2* **Indian Maiden (IRE)**[11] 2115 6-9-4 104 TedDurcan 7 89
(M S Saunders) *towards rr: pushed along over 4f out: rdn and hdwy over 1f out: no imp fnl f* **7/1**

3436 **7** *1 1/4* **Strut**[14] 2032 3-8-6 99 (v[1]) PaulHanagan 11 79
(R Charlton) *in tch: rdn and wknd over 1f out* **11/2**[3]

2515 **8** *2 1/2* **Angus Newz**[14] 2022 3-8-10 100 (v) ShaneKelly 6 76
(M Quinn) *led: hdd over 3f out: rdn over 2f out: wknd 1f out* **20/1**

4154 **9** *hd* **Dixie Belle**[266] 5286 3-8-6 98 (t) TPQueally 3 71
(M G Quinlan) *w ldr: led over 3f out: hdd over 2f out: wknd 1f out* **33/1**

1610 **10** *2* **Fantaisiste**[7] 2230 4-9-0 90 NelsonDeSouza 10 67
(P F I Cole) *a bhd* **20/1**

0310 **11** *nk* **Bird Over**[22] [1820] 4-9-0 85 ... EddieAhern 9 66
(R M Beckett) *a bhd* **33/1**

1m 10.69s (-4.21) **Going Correction** -0.525s/f (Hard)
WFA 3 from 4yo+ 8lb **11** Ran SP% **107.1**
Speed ratings (Par 111):107,105,104,100,99 98,97,93,93,91 90
CSF £22.34 TOTE £7.50: £2.20, £1.80, £5.00; EX 32.90 Trifecta £445.60 Pool: £627.72. 0.10 winning tickets..
Owner The Equema Partnership **Bred** Jeremy Green And Sons **Trained** Newmarket, Suffolk
■ Coconut Squeak was withdrawn (16/1, refused to enter stalls).

FOCUS
A typically competitive fillies' Listed sprint and the form looks sound, although not strong for the grade.

NOTEBOOK
Paradise Isle, drawn nearest the stands' side, kept straight from her draw and raced more or less alone for most of the race. Her form figures over six furlongs on good ground or faster now read an impressive 22117110111, and connections appear to favour going for a Group Three race at York next over running her under a penalty in the Wokingham. (op 15-2)
Nidhaal(IRE), best in according to adjusted official ratings, looked a promising type for sprints this season, but she had suffered a stress fracture in the Cheveley Park Stakes on her final start at two and was fairly weak in the market for this reappearance. There was not a lot wrong with her performance in the race, though, as she beat those who raced up the middle of the track with her in decisive fashion. Normal improvement for this seasonal debut should see her off the mark in similar company. (op 11-4)
Clear Impression(IRE) came home first of the three that raced towards the far side of the track and ran a very good race at the weights. She is improving with every run and, on this evidence, could well win at this level this season. (op 20-1)
Dhekraa(IRE) finished a length in front of Clear Impression over five furlongs at Bath earlier this season, but this longer distance suited her rival better. A drop back to the minimum trip should pay dividends. (tchd 11-2)
Sweet Afton(IRE), a difficult filly to place off her current mark, was staying on at the finish and appreciated the return to six. (op 25-1)
Indian Maiden(IRE) does not really appreciate gound as quick as this. Official explanation: trainer said mare was unsuited by the good to firm ground (op 11-2 tchd 5-1)
Strut was well backed to bounce back to form on this quicker surface, but she never really gave her supporters much to shout about. (op 7-1)
Angus Newz did not appreciate being taken on for the lead on the far side. Official explanation: trainer said filly was unsuited by the good to firm ground (op 25-1)

2439 E B F GRUNDY FAMILY CELEBRATION MAIDEN STKS 5f
3:50 (3:54) (Class 5) 2-Y-O **£3,886** (£1,156; £577; £288) **Stalls** Centre

Form RPR
5 **1** **Part Timer (IRE)**[7] [2234] 2-9-3 ... TedDurcan 6 86
(M R Channon) *towards rr: pushed along 3f out: hdwy 2f out: edgd lft ins fnl f: r.o to ld towards fin* **9/1**
2 **2** ¾ **Invincible Force (IRE)**[15] [1982] 2-9-3 ... EddieAhern 5 83
(Ms Deborah J Evans) *a.p: led over 1f out: sn hung lft: hdd towards fin* **9/2**[3]
32 **3** 1 ½ **Winning Spirit (IRE)**[10] [2130] 2-9-3 ... ShaneKelly 10 78
(J Noseda) *hld up: hdwy gng wl 1/2-way: rdn and ev ch ins fnl f: no ex towards fin* **5/4**[1]
3 **4** 3 **Davaye**[23] [1790] 2-8-12 ... FrancisNorton 1 62
(K R Burke) *lugged rt and led: hdd over 1f out: wknd fnl f* **16/1**
5 3 **Blue Echo** 2-8-12 ... PhilipRobinson 3 51
(M A Jarvis) *prom: rdn over 1f out: sn wknd* **4/1**[2]
6 *nk* **Wanchai Night** 2-9-3 ... DavidAllan 11 55
(T D Easterby) *in tch: pushed along 2f out: wknd over 1f out* **20/1**
7 3 ½ **Tarraburn (USA)** 2-9-3 ... PaulHanagan 4 43
(J Howard Johnson) *in tch: pushed along and lost pl 3f out: bhd after* **16/1**
8 3 ½ **Imprimis Tagula (IRE)** 2-9-3 ... MartinDwyer 2 30
(A Bailey) *chsd ldrs to 1/2-way: bhd over 1f out* **20/1**
5 **9** 3 ½ **Daruma (IRE)**[38] [1405] 2-9-3 ... RobbieFitzpatrick 8 17
(Peter Grayson) *chsd ldrs: edgd lft 3f out: sn wknd* **50/1**
10 9 **Taran Tregarth** 2-8-12 ... MickyFenton 7 —
(A Bailey) *s.s: a outpcd and wl bhd* **50/1**

59.73 secs (-2.34) **Going Correction** -0.525s/f (Hard) **10** Ran SP% **117.8**
Speed ratings (Par 93):97,95,93,88,83 83,77,72,66,52
CSF £47.87 TOTE £9.10: £1.90, £1.50, £1.40; EX 57.00.
Owner Mrs T Burns **Bred** Rathasker Stud **Trained** West Ilsley, Berks

FOCUS
A modest-looking maiden that was dominated by horses with previous racing experience. It looks sound enough rated around the runner-up.

NOTEBOOK
Part Timer(IRE) showed the benefit of his debut, and the drop back to five did not count against this speedily-bred colt, although the way he was staying on at the finish suggests a return to six will suit in time. (op 12-1)
Invincible Force(IRE), runner-up in heavy ground here on his debut, had contrasting conditions to deal with this time but ran just as well. He is a half-brother to three winners over distances between six and ten furlongs, but he himself looks to be all speed. (op 6-1)
Winning Spirit(IRE) looked to have plenty in his favour dropped back to the minimum trip on fast ground against what looked average opposition, but he raced keenly in the early stages and found little off the bridle after coming through travelling strongly two furlongs out. A beaten favourite on all three starts to date, he is beginning to look like a disappointing sort and one to avoid. (op 11-10 tchd 6-4, 13-8 in places)
Davaye showed good speed but was seen off quite easily by the colts with a furlong to run.
Blue Echo, a half-sister to five winners, notably Putra Pekan, a very useful and prolific miler, did not appear to be starting off in the strongest of maidens so it was not a surprise to see some support for her, but in the end she was found wanting. She is entitled to improve for the experience, though. (op 5-1 tchd 11-2 in places)
Wanchai Night, whose dam was a useful multiple winning sprinter, hails from a stable whose juveniles invariably come on for their debut outings. (tchd 18-1)

2440 TILSTON FEARNALL H'CAP 1m 30y
4:25 (4:25) (Class 3) (0-90,90) 3-Y-0+ **£11,334** (£3,372; £1,685; £841) **Stalls** Low

Form RPR
000 **1** **Humble Opinion**[8] [2200] 4-9-7 83 ... TPQueally 14 93
(B J Meehan) *in tch: rdn to ld ins fnl f: r.o* **20/1**
1110 **2** 1 ¼ **Tyzack (IRE)**[15] [1985] 5-9-6 82 ... MickyFenton 5 89
(Stef Liddiard) *trckd ldrs: led over 2f out: hdd ins fnl f: no ex cl home* **20/1**
3024 **3** *nk* **Flipando (IRE)**[8] [2200] 5-9-13 89 ... JimmyFortune 15 95+
(T D Barron) *hld up: hdwy over 2f out: rdn over 1f out: r.o wl towards fin* **11/2**[2]
02 **4** 1 ½ **Kelucia (IRE)**[14] [2011] 5-9-6 85 ... NelsonDeSouza(3) 13 88+
(R M Beckett) *hld up: rdn and hdwy over 1f out: r.o ins fnl f: nt rch ldrs* **20/1**
0664 **5** 2 **Sew'N'So Character (IRE)**[15] [1985] 5-9-7 83 ... TedDurcan 7 81
(M Blanshard) *midfield: rdn over 3f out: styd on same pce fnl 2f* **20/1**
4033 **6** ½ **Kingdom Of Dreams (IRE)**[243] [5799] 4-9-5 81 ... ShaneKelly 3 78+
(J Noseda) *hld up: rdn and hdwy over 2f out: kpt on fnl f: nt trble ldrs* **16/1**
0062 **7** 1 **Pintle**[10] [2147] 6-9-3 79 ... KerrinMcEvoy 17 74
(J L Spearing) *cl up: rdn over 3f out: wknd ins fnl f* **25/1**
0156 **8** *shd* **Dr Thong**[183] [6533] 5-9-1 77 ... KDarley 10 72
(P F I Cole) *prom: rdn and ev ch over 2f out: wknd fnl f* **33/1**
5065 **9** 2 ½ **Freeloader (IRE)**[11] [2114] 6-9-2 78 ... PaulHanagan 11 67
(R A Fahey) *midfield: rdn over 2f out: wknd fnl f* **5/1**[1]
0011 **10** 4 **Rain Stops Play (IRE)**[9] [2170] 4-9-7 83 ... MartinDwyer 8 63
(M Quinn) *led: rdn and hdd over 2f out: wknd over 1f out* **10/1**
1012 **11** 2 **Along The Nile**[42] [1280] 4-9-2 78 ... JamieSpencer 16 53
(K G Reveley) *hld up: rdn over 2f out: no imp* **13/2**
6000 **12** *shd* **Liakoura (GER)**[33] [1544] 4-9-4 80 ... (t) EddieAhern 1 55
(Mrs A J Perrett) *midfield: hdwy 5f out: rdn over 2f out: edgd lft over 1f out: sn wknd* **16/1**
3500 **13** 7 **Calcutta**[49] [1129] 10-10-0 90 ... MichaelHills 12 49
(B W Hills) *pushed along 5f out: a bhd* **25/1**
2426 **14** 5 **Putra Kuantan**[8] [2201] 6-9-13 89 ... PhilipRobinson 6 36
(M A Jarvis) *midfield: rdn 3f out: sn wknd* **6/1**[3]
4044 **15** 3 **Very Wise**[274] [5095] 4-9-9 85 ... NickyMackay 2 25
(W J Haggas) *hld up: sddle slipped after 2f: hdwy 5f out: wknd over 2f out* **14/1**

1m 41.72s (-3.79) **Going Correction** -0.30s/f (Firm) **15** Ran SP% **116.9**
Speed ratings (Par 107):106,104,104,102,100 100,99,99,96,92 90,90,83,78,75
CSF £334.37 CT £2548.94 TOTE £30.10: £7.80, £6.10, £2.80; EX 576.20.
Owner Paul & Jenny Green **Bred** P C Green **Trained** Manton, Wilts

FOCUS
A competitive handicap featuring some useful performers, and the form looks pretty sound although not rock solid.

NOTEBOOK
Humble Opinion, held on easier ground in two previous starts this season, appreciated these quicker conditions and was travelling better than anything with two furlongs to run. It was just a question of what he would find off the bridle, and he delivered what he promised.
Tyzack(IRE) had got bogged down in heavy ground here on his last start, but he showed that form to be all wrong back on this quicker surface. He has clearly translated his All-Weather improvement back onto grass, and he should continue to go well off this sort of mark.
Flipando(IRE) again ran on well at the finish to post another consistent effort. The trouble is, he is beginning to look like one for each-way backers only, as he continues to find one or two too good.
Kelucia(IRE) was another running on late in the day. She is not the easiest of rides and her best chance of success off this sort of mark is likely to be back in a less-competitive handicap restricted to her own sex.
Sew'N'So Character(IRE) is desperately difficult to win with but he usually runs to a fair level, which results in little slippage of his handicap mark. (op 22-1 tchd 25-1)
Kingdom Of Dreams(IRE) is a son of Sadler's Wells, and he might well have found this ground on the fast side, especially over this shorter trip. His wins last season came over further on easier surfaces.
Pintle appeared to be found out by the extra furlong.
Dr Thong is entitled to come on for his first outing since December. (op 40-1)
Rain Stops Play(IRE) Official explanation: trainer said gelding was unsuited by the good to firm ground
Along The Nile Official explanation: jockey said gelding never travelled
Liakoura(GER) Official explanation: trainer said gelding was unsuited by the good to firm ground
Calcutta Official explanation: jockey said horse never travelled
Putra Kuantan Official explanation: jockey said gelding never travelled
Very Wise Official explanation: jockey said saddle slipped

2441 STARSKY H'CAP 1m 30y
5:00 (5:00) (Class 5) (0-75,71) 3-Y-0 **£3,238** (£963; £481; £240) **Stalls** Low

Form RPR
0060 **1** **Electric Warrior (IRE)**[21] [1855] 3-9-1 65 ... DarrenWilliams 9 72
(K R Burke) *racd keenly: hld up: hdwy 3f out: led jst over 2f out: sn hung lft: rdn out* **13/2**[3]
0003 **2** ½ **Barndeh (IRE)**[9] [2177] 3-9-4 68 ... (p) PhilipRobinson 6 73
(M A Jarvis) *stmbld s: a.p: ev ch fr 3f out: bmpd over 1f out: nt qckn cl home* **10/3**[2]
3600 **3** 1 ½ **Lady Disdain**[21] [1855] 3-9-0 64 ... JamieSpencer 7 66
(G M Moore) *hld up in midfield: rdn and nt qckn 3f out: styd on ins fnl f: gaining at fin* **12/1**
4120 **4** ½ **Musicmaestroplease (IRE)**[30] [1616] 3-8-12 62 ... FergusSweeney 2 63
(S Parr) *racd keenly: trckd ldrs: rdn and hung lft over 2f out: kpt on same pce fnl f* **13/2**[3]
0624 **5** 1 ½ **Royal Composer (IRE)**[10] [2126] 3-9-4 68 ... DavidAllan 3 65
(T D Easterby) *led: rdn and hdd jst over 2f out: hld whn bmpd over 1f out: no ex fnl f* **5/2**[1]
5633 **6** 1 **Spectacular Show (IRE)**[13] [2049] 3-9-7 71 ... ShaneKelly 8 66
(M Quinn) *trckd ldrs: rdn over 2f out: wknd over 1f out* **15/2**
5305 **7** 1 ½ **Pitbull**[250] [5659] 3-8-13 63 ... J-PGuillambert 4 55
(Mrs G S Rees) *racd keenly: lost pl after 1f: hld up: hdwy 3f out: rdn 2f out: wknd over 1f out* **16/1**
0516 **8** 9 **Zabeel Tower**[29] [1634] 3-8-6 63 ... GemmaAnderson(7) 5 34
(James Moffatt) *struggling 3f out: a bhd* **25/1**
525 **9** 9 **Prince Egor (IRE)**[25] [1759] 3-9-7 71 ... PaulHanagan 10 21
(M Dods) *a bhd* **12/1**

1m 43.54s (-1.97) **Going Correction** -0.30s/f (Firm) **9** Ran SP% **115.2**
Speed ratings (Par 99):97,96,95,94,93 92,90,81,72
CSF £28.38 CT £255.28 TOTE £7.30: £2.40, £1.80, £2.80; EX 29.70 Place 6 £102.20, Place 5 £56.91.
Owner Market Avenue Racing Club Ltd **Bred** Limestone Stud **Trained** Middleham Moor, N Yorks
■ Stewards' Enquiry : Darren Williams three-day ban: careless riding (Jun 25-27)

FOCUS
A modest handicap in which the early pace was steady and the form, rated through the third andf fourth, looks sound but ordinary.
Musicmaestroplease(IRE) Official explanation: jockey said colt lost a front shoe

T/Jkpt: Not won. T/Plt: £183.50 to a £1 stake. Pool: £85,116.70. 338.55 winning tickets. T/Qpdt: £45.10 to a £1 stake. Pool: £3,223.00. 52.80 winning tickets. DO

[2346]LINGFIELD (L-H)

Saturday, June 10

OFFICIAL GOING: Turf course - good to firm (firm in places); all-weather - standard

Wind: Moderate, behind Weather: Sunny & warm

2442 EUROPEAN BREEDERS FUND MAIDEN STKS 6f

1:55 (1:56) (Class 5) 2-Y-O **£3,886** (£1,156; £577; £288) **Stalls** High

Form				RPR
0	**1**		**Strike Force**[14] [2029] 2-9-3 .... RobertHavlin 1 (J H M Gosden) *led: rdn and hdd wl over 1f out: rallied u.p to ld last 50yds* **11/10**[1]	70
6	**2**	*nk*	**Foxy Games**[18] [1912] 2-8-7 .... JamesDoyle(5) 4 (D J S Ffrench Davis) *chsd ldr: rdn to ld wl over 1f out: hdd and no ex last 50yds* **33/1**	64
	3	*1*	**Diamond Light (USA)** 2-8-12 .... IanMongan 3 (J L Dunlop) *cl up: pushed along wl over 2f out: hung rt ins fnl f: one pce* **7/1**[3]	61
	4	*1 1/4*	**Ama De Casa (USA)** 2-8-12 .... SteveDrowne 2 (J Noseda) *hld up in tch: pushed along over 3f out: swtchd rt 1f out: no imp* **6/5**[2]	57

1m 11.9s (0.23) **Going Correction** -0.25s/f (Firm) 4 Ran SP% **108.5**

Speed ratings (Par 93):88,87,86,84

CSF £20.37 TOTE £3.20; EX 27.40.

Owner Cheveley Park Stud **Bred** Cheveley Park Stud Ltd **Trained** Newmarket, Suffolk

FOCUS

A tactical affair and a rather messy contest in which the four runners raced centre to stands' side. The pair with previous experience beat the two newcomers, but the winning time was modest so the form probably amounts to little.

NOTEBOOK

Strike Force, disappointing on soft ground on his debut, had different conditions and set a modest early pace, but still did not look happy and tended to hang left when put under pressure. Looking beaten once headed, fortunately for him the leader was not doing much in front and he somehow managed to grab victory from the jaws of defeat. To be fair six furlongs on fast ground on a sharp track like this is probably an insufficient test for him, but he will still need to improve from this if he is to win again. (op 7-4)

Foxy Games, all the better for her Kempton debut, looked like causing a surprise when moving to the front a furlong from home, but she did little once there and allowed the favourite to get back at her. This was an improvement, but this was an unsatisfactory contest in many ways so it would be unwise to get too carried away.

Diamond Light(USA), a $170,000 half-sister to a couple of smart performers in the US, looked very much in need of this initial experience and her breeding suggests she is going to need a stiffer test than this. (op 13-2)

Ama De Casa(USA), a $122,000 yearling but resold for $270,000 as a two-year-old, is a half-sister to a couple of winners in the US. Rather weaker in the market than the winner, she was held up last of the four but could never make any impression when asked for an effort. This race was probably not run to suit and it would be no surprise to see her leave this debut effort well behind. (op 4-5)

2443 WILLIAM HILL FOR WORLD CUP BETTING H'CAP 7f

2:25 (2:27) (Class 4) (0-85,83) 3-Y-O+

£6,232 (£1,866; £933; £467; £233; £117) **Stalls** High

Form				RPR
0063	**1**		**Fiefdom (IRE)**[10] [2147] 4-9-10 **82** .... PatrickMathers(3) 7 (I W McInnes) *chsd ldr: led over 1f out: styd on u.p* **16/1**	95
0310	**2**	*1 3/4*	**Goodenough Mover**[40] [1359] 10-10-0 **83** .... HayleyTurner 4 (Andrew Turnell) *racd midfield: rdn and hdwy over 2f out: chsd wnr ins fnl f: no imp* **16/1**	91
2221	**3**	*1 1/4*	**Storm On The Run (IRE)**[16] [1960] 3-9-3 **82** .... PatDobbs 1 (R Hannon) *hld up on outer: hrd rdn 2f out: hung rt and fnd little tl styd on last 100yds: nvr nrr* **5/1**[2]	83+
1030	**4**	*shd*	**Mina A Salem**[11] [2114] 4-8-12 **74** .... WilliamCarson(7) 5 (C E Brittain) *cl up: rdn over 2f out: hung lft and one pce after* **13/2**	78
0010	**5**	*1*	**Polish Index**[15] [1993] 4-8-12 **67** ....(p) RobertHavlin 3 (J R Jenkins) *led: rdn and hdd over 1f out: wknd wl ins fnl f* **15/2**	69
4044	**6**	*1/2*	**Vindication**[6] [2259] 6-8-6 **66** ....(t) JamesDoyle(5) 8 (R M H Cowell) *v.s.a: wl bhd: hdwy 2f out: rdn and no prog fnl f* **11/2**[3]	67
1001	**7**	*1 3/4*	**Top Mark**[7] [2223] 4-9-5 **74** .... SteveDrowne 6 (H Morrison) *cl up: rdn over 2f out: sn btn* **15/8**[1]	70
4333	**8**	*9*	**Goodwood Spirit**[245] [5730] 4-9-12 **81** .... DaneO'Neill 2 (J M Bradley) *plld hrd: hld up wl bhd: rdn over 2f out: n.d* **8/1**	54

1m 21.8s (-2.41) **Going Correction** -0.25s/f (Firm)

WFA 3 from 4yo+ 10lb 8 Ran SP% **114.8**

Speed ratings (Par 105):103,101,99,99,98 97,95,85

CSF £235.41 CT £1474.91 TOTE £11.50: £3.30, £2.00, £2.60; EX 40.00 Trifecta £369.80 Pool: £30,290.72. - 58.15 winning tickets.

Owner Stephen Hackney And Martin Higgins **Bred** Kildaragh Stud **Trained** Catwick, E Yorks

FOCUS

Just a fair handicap in which the pace looked ordinary and the form is fair rated through the runner-up. Again the field raced centre to stands' side, though slightly away from the rail. Nonetheless the winner was the one who raced closest to it.

Vindication Official explanation: jockey said gelding missed the break

Top Mark Official explanation: trainer said gelding ran flat

Goodwood Spirit Official explanation: jockey said gelding hung right

2444 BET ON ENGLAND @ WILLIAM HILL H'CAP 5f

3:00 (3:00) (Class 5) (0-70,70) 3-Y-O+ **£3,886** (£1,156; £577; £288) **Stalls** High

Form				RPR
0050	**1**		**Starduster**[15] [1981] 4-9-4 **60** .... SteveDrowne 6 (B R Millman) *chsd ldr: rdn over 1f out: led last 100yds: r.o wl* **6/1**[2]	71
0350	**2**	*1*	**Clearing Sky (IRE)**[8] [2207] 5-8-10 **52** .... IanMongan 1 (J R Boyle) *led on outer: rdn over 1f out: hdd and no ex last 100yds* **12/1**	59
6644	**3**	*3/4*	**Kempsey**[15] [1981] 4-9-8 **69** ....(v) StephenDonohoe(5) 9 (J J Bridger) *cl up on stands' side: rdn over 1f out: kpt on one pce* **6/1**[2]	73
0541	**4**	*1/2*	**Edged In Gold**[39] [1396] 4-8-9 **51** oh3 ....(e) HayleyTurner 10 (P J Makin) *hld up bhd: rdn and hdwy over 1f out: kpt on: nt rch ldrs* **8/1**	53
2020	**5**	*hd*	**Canadian Danehill (IRE)**[37] [1432] 4-10-0 **70** .... RichardMullen 2 (R M H Cowell) *chsd ldrs: rdn 2f out: kpt on one pce ins fnl f* **7/1**[3]	71
0000	**6**	*hd*	**Silver Prelude**[9] [2182] 5-9-11 **67** .... DaneO'Neill 5 (D K Ivory) *chsd ldrs: rdn over 1f out: unable qckn fnl f* **9/1**	67
1560	**7**	*1*	**Seneschal**[1] [2417] 5-9-11 **67** .... PatDobbs 3 (A B Haynes) *stdd s: hld up bhd: rdn 2f out: nvr pce to rch ldrs* **8/1**	63
0200	**8**	*shd*	**Whitbarrow (IRE)**[108] [480] 7-9-7 **70** .... JamesMillman(7) 7 (B R Millman) *taken down early: trckd ldrs: rdn 2f out: sn lost pl: no ch after* **11/2**[1]	66
3300	**9**	*nk*	**Parkside Pursuit**[28] [1689] 8-8-13 **62** .... KevinGhunowa(7) 8 (J M Bradley) *hld up: rdn over 1f out: fnd little* **12/1**	57
3041	**10**	*nk*	**Double M**[18] [1913] 9-8-9 **51** oh3 ....(v) RichardThomas 4 (Mrs L Richards) *hld up bhd: rdn over 1f out: no prog* **7/1**[3]	45

57.60 secs (-1.34) **Going Correction** -0.25s/f (Firm) **10** Ran SP% **116.6**

Speed ratings (Par 103):100,98,97,96,96 95,94,94,93,93

CSF £75.38 CT £463.07 TOTE £9.20: £2.70, £3.80, £2.00; EX 63.50 Trifecta £239.90 Part won. Pool: £338.01. - 0.34 winning tickets..

Owner Mrs Maureen Shenkin **Bred** Mrs M Shenkin **Trained** Kentisbeare, Devon

FOCUS

A modest sprint handicap in which the bulk of the field raced centre to stands' side, slightly away from Kempsey who raced against the rail throughout. The finish was fought out between two female greys and the winner along with the third sets the level for the form.

2445 BET ON GOALS @ WILLIAMHILL.CO.UK MEDIAN AUCTION MAIDEN STKS 5f

3:35 (3:36) (Class 5) 3-Y-O **£3,238** (£963; £481; £240) **Stalls** High

Form				RPR
4022	**1**		**Leopoldine**[16] [1960] 3-8-12 73 .... SteveDrowne 3 (H Morrison) *mde all: shkn up and drew clr over 1f out: v easily* **4/7**[1]	87
5633	**2**	*8*	**Discotheque (USA)**[50] [1109] 3-8-12 69 .... IanMongan 6 (P Howling) *chsd ldrs: rdn 3f out: tk 2nd ins fnl f: no ch w wnr* **3/1**[2]	55
0	**3**	*1 1/2*	**All Clued Up (IRE)**[9] [2167] 3-8-12 .... RichardMullen 4 (Rae Guest) *in tch: rdn to chse wnr over 2f out: rn green and no ch over 1f out* **40/1**	49
6	**4**	*6*	**Fly By Jove (IRE)**[395] [1629] 3-9-3 .... DaneO'Neill 1 (A M Balding) *s.s: a outpcd in rr: tk poor 4th nr fin* **17/2**[3]	30+
	5	*1/2*	**Decider (USA)** 3-8-10 .... KevinGhunowa(7) 2 (J M Bradley) *wnt lft s: sn rcvrd to chse wnr: rdn and hung lft over 2f out: sn wknd* **16/1**	28

57.30 secs (-1.64) **Going Correction** -0.25s/f (Firm) 5 Ran SP% **107.5**

Speed ratings (Par 99):103,90,87,78,77

CSF £2.34 TOTE £1.40: £1.10, £1.60; EX 2.70.

Owner R A Grossman & Normandie Stud Ltd **Bred** Mrs Dare Wigan **Trained** East Ilsley, Berks

FOCUS

The principals all raced pretty close to the stands' rail. This was as uncompetitive a maiden as one could imagine, but the winner recorded a faster time than in the preceding all-aged handicap so she should not be underestimated.

Fly By Jove(IRE) Official explanation: jockey said colt hung badly left

2446 WILLIAM HILL WORLD CUP WINNERS FILLIES' H'CAP 1m 2f (P)

4:10 (4:11) (Class 4) (0-85,80) 3-Y-O **£5,505** (£1,637; £818; £408) **Stalls** Low

Form				RPR
1	**1**		**Postage Stampe**[293] [4602] 3-9-7 **80** .... DaneO'Neill 5 (D M Simcock) *slowly away: hld up in tch: hdwy to chse ldr 3f out: rdn to ld 1f out: sn clr* **9/2**[3]	94+
4026	**2**	*4*	**Distinctive Look (IRE)**[38] [1423] 3-9-7 **80** ....(t) IanMongan 2 (B J Meehan) *led: rdn 2f out: hdd 1f out: sn outpcd* **10/1**	86
6010	**3**	*7*	**Lady Romanov (IRE)**[10] [2128] 3-8-3 **65** .... SaleemGolam(3) 6 (M H Tompkins) *hld up in last: rdn 4f out: sn outpcd: tk poor 3rd ins fnl f* **10/1**	58
21	**4**	*1 3/4*	**Whatizzit**[176] [6588] 3-9-3 **76** .... SteveDrowne 3 (E A L Dunlop) *hld up in tch: rdn and effrt 4f out: sn no ch w ldng pair: lost 3rd ins fnl f* **11/4**[2]	65
2023	**5**	*1 1/2*	**Moonlight Music (IRE)**[8] [2188] 3-9-4 **77** .... RichardMullen 4 (E J O'Neill) *chsd ldr: rdn 4f out: sn outpcd: no ch after* **5/1**	64
3232	**6**	*26*	**My Petra**[19] [1898] 3-9-2 **75** .... JDSmith 1 (A King) *t.k.h: trckd ldrs: rdn 4f out: sn wl bhd: eased last 2f: t.o* **2/1**[1]	12

2m 7.08s (-0.71) **Going Correction** +0.05s/f (Slow) 6 Ran SP% **113.0**

Speed ratings (Par 98):104,100,95,93,92 71

CSF £45.37 TOTE £5.80: £2.00, £5.20; EX 38.20.

Owner Trillium Place Racing **Bred** Blenheim Bloodstock **Trained** Newmarket, Suffolk

FOCUS

There was a very decent pace on in this fillies' handicap and the race only concerned the front pair from a long way out. The form looks solid rated through the runner-up.

My Petra Official explanation: trainer said filly was unsuited by a combination of the pace and trip on the AW

2447 EVENING RACING ON SATURDAY JUNE 17TH H'CAP 1m 4f (P)

4:45 (4:46) (Class 4) (0-85,84) 4-Y-O+ **£5,505** (£1,637; £818; £408) **Stalls** Low

Form				RPR
5265	**1**		**Chocolate Caramel (USA)**[21] [1842] 4-9-7 **84** .... JimCrowley 8 (Mrs A J Perrett) *trckd ldrs: rdn over 1f out: led ins fnl f: styd on wl* **7/1**[3]	92
0040	**2**	*3/4*	**Dower House**[17] [1943] 11-9-3 **80** ....(t) DaneO'Neill 5 (Andrew Turnell) *hld up: hdwy 4f out: rdn 2f out: ev ch fnl f: hld by wnr last 50yds* **14/1**	87
1333	**3**	*1 1/4*	**Nobelix (IRE)**[17] [1943] 4-8-8 **76** .... RoryMoore(5) 7 (J R Fanshawe) *chsd ldrs: rdn 2f out: led 1f out: edgd lft and sn hdd: no ex* **9/2**[2]	81
-531	**4**	*shd*	**Croon**[18] [1927] 4-8-12 **75** .... SteveDrowne 3 (H Morrison) *chsd ldr: upsides 4f out: led over 1f out: sn hdd: one pce* **11/4**[1]	80
0302	**5**	*2*	**Mandatum**[18] [1927] 5-9-3 **80** .... RichardMullen 6 (L M Cumani) *led: jnd and rdn 4f out: hdd over 1f out: wknd fnl f* **11/4**[1]	82
0005	**6**	*6*	**Berkhamsted (IRE)**[25] [1757] 4-8-8 **74** .... NeilChalmers(3) 10 (Tom Dascombe) *hld up in last: rdn 3f out: kpt on fnl f: n.d* **20/1**	66
2400	**7**	*nk*	**The Violin Player (USA)**[35] [1478] 5-9-2 **84** .... JamesDoyle(5) 1 (H J Collingridge) *hld up in rr: hrd drvn 3f out: sn no ch* **11/1**	76
0053	**8**	*5*	**Boot 'n Toot**[48] [1162] 5-8-12 **75** .... HayleyTurner 4 (C A Cyzer) *t.k.h: chsd ldrs: rdn and wknd over 2f out* **9/1**	59
0650	**9**	*15*	**Wait For The Will (USA)**[45] [1247] 10-8-1 **69** ....(b) RobynBrisland(5) 2 (G L Moore) *hld up: effrt 4f out: sn rdn and no ch: eased fnl f* **22/1**	29

2m 34.5s (0.11) **Going Correction** +0.05s/f (Slow) 9 Ran SP% **118.1**

Speed ratings (Par 105):101,100,99,99,98 94,94,90,80

CSF £100.72 CT £493.42 TOTE £8.20: £2.70, £3.80, £2.10; EX 73.90 Trifecta £505.30 Pool: £839.82. - 1.18 winning tickets. Place 6 £349.07, Place 5 £162.30.

Owner Mrs Priscilla Graham **Bred** Sierra Thoroughbreds **Trained** Pulborough, W Sussex

■ Stewards' Enquiry : Rory Moore one-day ban: used whip with excessive force (Jun 25)

FOCUS

Not a strong early pace in this, resulting in something of a sprint finish, and there were five in a line passing the furlong pole. The runner-up sets the standard.

The Violin Player(USA) Official explanation: jockey said gelding ran in snatches

T/Plt: £620.00 to a £1 stake. Pool: £32,787.25. 38.60 winning tickets. T/Qpdt: £64.30 to a £1 stake. Pool: £1,775.30. 20.40 winning tickets. SP

[2237] MUSSELBURGH (R-H)

Saturday, June 10

OFFICIAL GOING: Good to firm (firm in places on round course)

65mm water had been put on the track over the previous five days. The going on a fast drying day was described as 'hard, like a road'.

Wind: Moderate, half-behind Weather: Fine and sunny

2448 BALFOUR KILPATRICK SUPPLY CHAIN MAIDEN STKS — 1m
2:35 (2:35) (Class 5) 3-Y-0+ — £5,181 (£1,541; £770; £384) Stalls Low

Form				RPR
32-2	1		**Northern Boy (USA)**[15] [1984] 3-9-0 78 ... PhillipMakin 6 (T D Barron) *mde all: shkn up and wnt clr appr fnl f: unchal* **4/7**[1]	85
42	2	6	**Penzo (IRE)**[15] [2001] 3-9-0 ... DarryllHolland 1 (J Howard Johnson) *chsd wnr: drvn over 3f out: kpt on: no imp* **4/1**[2]	71
5	3	½	**Avelian (IRE)**[28] [1674] 3-9-0 ... TonyCulhane 5 (W J Haggas) *chsd ldrs: drvn over 3f out: kpt on same pce* **5/1**[3]	70
6	4	½	**Wind Star**[4] [2325] 3-9-0 ... DeanMcKeown 2 (G A Swinbank) *t.k.h: trckd ldrs: kpt on same pce fnl 2f* **14/1**	69
50-	5	2 ½	**Princess Of Aeneas (IRE)**[234] [5978] 3-8-9 ... TomEaves 4 (I Semple) *stdd s: t.k.h: sn wl in tch: outpcd over 2f out: kpt on fnl f* **33/1**	58
4	6	16	**Claudia May**[22] [1814] 5-9-1 ... GregFairley(5) 3 (Miss Lucinda V Russell) *s.i.s: lost pl 3f out: sn bhd* **100/1**	21

1m 40.69s (-1.81) **Going Correction** -0.25s/f (Firm)

WFA 3 from 5yo 11lb — 6 Ran SP% **110.9**

Speed ratings (Par 103):99,93,92,92,89 73

CSF £3.12 TOTE £1.60: £1.10, £1.80; EX 3.50.

Owner East Riding Horse Racing Syndicate Ltd **Bred** P Booker **Trained** Maunby, N Yorks

FOCUS

The betting suggested a one horse race, £25,000 was laid in one bet, and so it turned out with the winner given his own way in front. The form looks ordinary although the winner was impressive.

2449 GNER SPRINT TROPHY H'CAP — 5f
3:10 (3:11) (Class 3) 3-Y-0+ — £9,715 (£2,890; £1,444; £721) Stalls Low

Form				RPR
4204	1		**Bluebok**[9] [2182] 5-9-8 72 ... (t) TonyCulhane 12 (J M Bradley) *w ldrs: led over 2f out: styd on strly fnl f* **14/1**	89
-001	2	2	**Glencairn Star**[7] [2237] 5-9-3 70 ... DanielTudhope(3) 7 (J S Goldie) *squeezed for room after 100yds: hdwy on outer 2f out: styd on to go 2nd ins last: no imp* **9/2**[1]	79+
6304	3	1	**Bold Marc (IRE)**[21] [1856] 4-9-10 74 ... PatCosgrave 11 (K R Burke) *w ldrs: kpt on same pce fnl f* **8/1**	79
-503	4	hd	**Ptarmigan Ridge**[7] [2237] 10-9-8 72 ... TomEaves 10 (Miss L A Perratt) *rr-div: hdwy 2f out: kpt on fnl f* **11/1**	76
0002	5	1	**Whinhill House**[7] [2237] 6-9-1 70 ... (p) MarkLawson(5) 6 (D W Barker) *prom: kpt on same pce fnl 2f* **7/1**	70
3403	5	dht	**Raccoon (IRE)**[2] [2380] 6-8-13 66 ... BenSwarbrick(3) 5 (T D Barron) *chsd ldrs: one pce fnl 2f* **6/1**[3]	66
1262	7	½	**Compton Classic**[23] [1794] 4-7-9 50 ... (p) DuranFentiman(5) 9 (J S Goldie) *swtchd lft after s: bhd: styd on fnl 2f* **16/1**	48
-300	8	1	**Blue Tomato**[17] [1939] 5-9-8 72 ... DarryllHolland 4 (J M Bradley) *in rr: nt clr run over 1f out and ins last: swtchd rt: kpt on* **16/1**	66+
0-00	9	nk	**Betsen (IRE)**[31] [1597] 4-9-8 72 ... (t) AdrianTNicholls 8 (D Nicholls) *chsd ldrs: wknd fnl f* **40/1**	65
00-0	10	nk	**Harrison's Flyer (IRE)**[9] [2173] 5-9-5 74 ... (p) GregFairley(5) 2 (J M Bradley) *chsd ldrs: hmpd over 2f out: nt clr run over 1f out: no threat after* **16/1**	66
-003	11	8	**Rothesay Dancer**[9] [2161] 3-8-11 68 ... JoeFanning 1 (J S Goldie) *chsd ldrs: wkng whn n.m.r on inner over 1f out: sn lost pl and bhd* **20/1**	28
34-5	12	2	**Conjecture**[42] [1297] 4-9-3 72 ... AndrewMullen(5) 3 (R Bastiman) *led tl over 2f out: sn lost pl and bhd* **11/2**[2]	24

58.64 secs (-1.86) **Going Correction** -0.25s/f (Firm)

WFA 3 from 4yo+ 7lb — 12 Ran SP% **111.3**

Speed ratings (Par 107):104,100,99,98,97 97,96,94,94,93 81,77

CSF £71.25 CT £539.77 TOTE £15.60: £4.40, £2.00, £3.70; EX 58.50.

Owner E A Hayward **Bred** E Duggan And D Churchman **Trained** Sedbury, Gloucs

FOCUS

Not a strong event for the money on offer and the high-drawn horses in the end dominated. The form looks rock solid rated through the fourth with possibly even better to come from the first two.

NOTEBOOK

Bluebok, back on his favoured fast ground, overcame a double figure draw and was right on top in the end. Clearly at the top of his game, his trainer will be keen to pull him out under a penalty. (op 10-1)

Glencairn Star, 5lb higher, made his way to the outside. He went in pursuit of the winner inside the last but was never going to get near him. The way he runs a sixth furlong will surely suit him better. (op 5-1)

Bold Marc(IRE), without a win for over two years, was backed on the morning line but as it turned out the going was a fair bit faster than he truly prefers.

Ptarmigan Ridge stayed on from off the pace but the lightning fast ground was not to his liking. (op 10-1)

Whinhill House, renewing rivalry with Glencairn Star on 4lb better terms, was very weak on the exchanges and in the betting market. He never really fired. (tchd 7-1)

Raccoon(IRE), tubed, had the wind behind him but basically as last time, this is as good as he is now. (tchd 7-1)

Conjecture showed all his old toe to take them along but dropped out in a matter of strides as if something was badly wrong. Official explanation: trainer had no explanation for the poor form shown (op 5-1)

2450 GNER SCOTTISH SPRINT CUP (HERITAGE H'CAP) — 5f
3:45 (3:46) (Class 2) (0-105,101) 3-Y-0+

£31,160 (£9,330; £4,665; £2,335; £1,165; £585) Stalls Low

Form				RPR
0024	1		**Handsome Cross (IRE)**[28] [1662] 5-7-12 78 ... SilvestreDeSousa(3) 12 (D Nicholls) *led tl over 2f out: styd on wl to ld ins last: hld on wl* **20/1**	90
4200	2	nk	**Peace Offering (IRE)**[7] [2227] 6-9-2 93 ... PhillipMakin 16 (D Nicholls) *hld up: hdwy 2f out: kpt on wl ins last: no ex nr fin* **25/1**	104
2-12	3	½	**Judd Street**[30] [1602] 4-9-3 94 ... StephenCarson 1 (R F Johnson Houghton) *chsd ldrs on ins: kpt on wl fnl f: no ex last 50yds* **6/1**[1]	103
4410	4	½	**Merlin's Dancer**[7] [2227] 6-9-7 98 ... AdrianTNicholls 14 (D Nicholls) *w ldrs: led over 2f out tl ins last: no ex* **16/1**	105
-300	5	nk	**Fullandby (IRE)**[22] [1835] 4-8-4 86 ... AndrewElliott(5) 7 (T J Etherington) *mid-div: edgd rt and styd on wl fnl f: nt rch ldrs* **12/1**	92+
0-40	6	shd	**Chookie Heiton (IRE)**[28] [1663] 8-9-10 101 ... TomEaves 17 (I Semple) *racd wd: rr-div: hdwy 2f out: kpt on wl fnl f* **40/1**	106
6013	7	hd	**Bond Boy**[14] [2021] 9-8-5 85 ... (b) DanielTudhope(3) 15 (B Smart) *mid-div: styd on fnl 2f: nt rch ldrs* **20/1**	90
5-21	8	¾	**Highland Warrior**[37] [1438] 7-8-9 86 ... TonyCulhane 13 (J S Goldie) *in rr: hdwy and nt clr run over 2f out: styd on fnl f: nt rch ldrs* **9/1**	92+
5645	9	shd	**Plateau**[28] [1662] 7-8-1 78 ... JoeFanning 9 (D Nicholls) *chsd ldrs: kpt on same pce appr fnl f* **12/1**	79
0054	10	nk	**Bo McGinty (IRE)**[8] [2194] 5-7-12 80 ... (b) AndrewMullen(5) 8 (R A Fahey) *exited stalls awkwardly: hdwy over 2f out: kpt on: nvr rchd ldrs* **20/1**	80
00-2	11	1 ¼	**Bond City (IRE)**[7] [2227] 4-9-9 100 ... FergalLynch 5 (B Smart) *in rr: hdwy whn nt clr run over 1f out: nvr nr ldrs* **13/2**[2]	95+
1102	12	hd	**Spanish Ace**[28] [1662] 5-8-7 84 ... DarryllHolland 11 (J M Bradley) *mid-div: effrt over 2f out: nvr a factor* **7/1**[3]	78
0036	13	2	**Enchantment**[17] [1936] 5-8-11 88 ... (p) DeanMcKeown 4 (J M Bradley) *hmpd after 1f: nt clr run over 2f out: no threat* **25/1**	74
0110	14	hd	**Peopleton Brook**[17] [1936] 4-8-12 89 ... PatCosgrave 6 (J M Bradley) *n.m.r after 1f: sn prom: wkng whn sltly hmpd over 1f out* **16/1**	74
05-3	15	1 ½	**Mimi Mouse**[21] [1856] 4-8-2 84 ... DuranFentiman(5) 2 (T D Easterby) *chsd ldrs: wknd over 1f out* **9/1**	63
000-	16	3 ½	**Distinctly Game**[287] [4764] 4-9-4 95 ... NCallan 3 (K A Ryan) *towards rr: bdly hmpd over 1f out* **8/1**	60

58.27 secs (-2.23) **Going Correction** -0.25s/f (Firm) — 16 Ran SP% **122.8**

Speed ratings (Par 109):107,106,105,104,104 104,103,102,102,102 100,99,96,96,93 88

CSF £424.61 CT £3490.58 TOTE £24.80: £6.10, £7.60, £1.70, £5.40; EX 347.40 TRIFECTA Not won..

Owner Cereal Partners **Bred** Keith Wills **Trained** Sessay, N Yorks

■ Stewards' Enquiry : Pat Cosgrave one-day ban: careless riding (Jun 25)

FOCUS

A competitive line-up for this £50,000 handicap, the winner was one of four from David Nicholls yard. The high numbers again held sway. The race has been rated through the fourth and looks solid.

NOTEBOOK

Handsome Cross(IRE), 5lb lower than his last success, had the ground he likes and showing a willing attitude, his capable rider's claim in the end proved decisive.

Peace Offering(IRE), without a win for over three years, was fourth in this a year ago. In the end he was only just denied, doing best of those trying to come from off the pace, and surely the drought will end sooner rather than longer.

Judd Street ◆, his trainer's first runner here, did really well considering in both parts the high numbers held sway. He gave his all and deserves to find a nice consolation prize.

Merlin's Dancer, 8lb higher than Chester, had to work hard to get his head in front. Found out in the dash to the line, he lost nothing in defeat.

Fullandby(IRE) ◆, who has won at up to seven furlongs in the past, seemed to find this dash happening too quickly for him. Making his way to the outer, he was making serious inroads late on and is worth bearing in mind when faced with a slightly stiffer task.

Chookie Heiton(IRE), drawn widest of all, showed he is on the way back. A stiffer track plays more to his strengths.

Bond Boy took this a year ago from an 8lb lower mark but the ground was a whole lot faster this time.

Highland Warrior, trying to come from the back, saw no daylight and was knocked out of his stride at the elbow. Official explanation: jockey said gelding was denied a clear run (op 11-1 tchd 12-1)

Bond City(IRE), having his second outing in a week after an absence, found himself with no room at all when trying to improve. There will be other days. Official explanation: jockey said gelding never travelled (tchd 6-1)

Spanish Ace Official explanation: jockey said gelding was unsuited by the good to firm ground

2451 BENTLEY EDINBURGH (S) STKS — 5f
4:20 (4:28) (Class 4) 2-Y-0 — £6,232 (£1,866; £933; £467) Stalls Low

Form				RPR
042	1		**The Mighty Ogmore**[7] [2241] 2-8-6 ... JoeFanning 2 (R C Guest) *in tch in last: hdwy and swtchd rt over 2f out: led 1f out: r.o* **4/1**[3]	60
6	2	1 ½	**Me And Mine (USA)**[49] [1136] 2-8-11 ... PhillipMakin 5 (T D Barron) *carried rt s: trckd ldrs: led 2f out tl 1f out: no ex* **2/1**[2]	60
310	3	2	**Sunken Rags**[10] [2125] 2-8-11 ... PatCosgrave 3 (K R Burke) *w ldrs: rdn and wknd 1f out* **8/11**[1]	52
455	4	3 ½	**Argent Danseur**[14] [2015] 2-8-6 ... (v[1]) GregFairley(5) 4 (B S Rothwell) *wnt rt s: led tl 2f out: sn wknd* **14/1**	40

60.57 secs (0.07) **Going Correction** -0.25s/f (Firm) — 4 Ran SP% **117.9**

Speed ratings (Par 95):89,86,83,77

CSF £13.16 TOTE £5.60; EX 13.30.The winner was bought in for 12,000gns.

Owner Mrs Valerie Gorvin **Bred** Mrs J Gittins **Trained** Brancepeth, Co Durham

FOCUS

A poor turn out for a £10,000 added seller and the form is rated as average for the grade.

NOTEBOOK

The Mighty Ogmore, happy to sit last, switched to the favoured ground towards the centre. It cost connections dear to retain her. (old market op 6-1 tchd 7-1)

Me And Mine(USA), carried sideways at the start, took charge but in the end the winner proved the stronger. He can certainly take a run-of-the-mill seller. (old market op 11-2)

Sunken Rags, who contested a Listed race at Beverley, looked to have no excuse whatsoever on the day. (old market op 4-5 tchd 5-4, new market op 4-5)

Argent Danseur, in a first-time visor, exited the stalls sideways and did too much in front. (old market op 33-1)

2452 SMIRNOFF H'CAP — 1m 6f
4:55 (4:55) (Class 4) (0-85,83) 4-Y-0 **£7,478** (£2,239; £1,119; £560; £279) Stalls High

Form				RPR
-006	1		**Kames Park (IRE)**[9] [2162] 4-9-6 82 ... TomEaves 1 (I Semple) *stdd s: w.w in last: hdwy on ins and nt clr run over 1f out: swtchd outside: led last 75yds* **10/1**	93
0114	2	¾	**Mceldowney**[7] [2238] 4-9-2 83 ... GregFairley(5) 5 (M Johnston) *chsd ldr: sn pushed along: hrd drvn 6f out: plld out and led over 1f out: no ex and hdd wl ins last* **11/4**[2]	93
0030	3	4	**Double Obsession**[17] [1931] 6-9-6 82 ... (b) AdrianTNicholls 6 (D Nicholls) *led: hdd over 1f out: sn wknd* **13/2**	86
5-13	4	1 ¾	**Liberty Seeker (FR)**[8] [2196] 7-8-9 71 ... PatCosgrave 3 (G A Swinbank) *trckd ldrs: drvn and outpcd over 4f out: sn rdn: no real threat after* **11/8**[1]	73

0-05 **5** ½ **Balyan (IRE)**[15] 1991 5-9-6 82 .... DarryllHolland 2 83
(J Howard Johnson) *trckd ldrs: rdn over 3f out: wknd appr fnl f* **5/1**[3]

3m 1.56s (-4.14) **Going Correction** -0.25s/f (Firm) **5** Ran SP% **107.9**
Speed ratings (Par 105):101,100,98,97,97
CSF £35.41 TOTE £11.20: £2.60, £2.20; EX 48.20.

Owner Mrs June Delaney **Bred** Pat Beirne **Trained** Carluke, S Lanarks

■ Stewards' Enquiry : Greg Fairley one-day ban: careless riding (Jun 26)

FOCUS
Not a strong pace which played to the winner's strengths.

Balyan(IRE) Official explanation: jockey said gelding was unsuited by the good to firm (firm in places) ground

2453 DESIGNER CHRIS CLYNE & PAM JENKINS GRAND CUP STKS (LISTED RACE) 1m 6f
5:25 (5:25) (Class 1) 4-Y-0+
£17,034 (£6,456; £3,231; £1,611; £807; £405) **Stalls** High

Form RPR
-314 **1** **Sirce (IRE)**[14] 2013 4-8-9 92 ....(v) JoeFanning 6 101
(D J Coakley) *hld up: hdwy on inner over 2f out: r.o to ld ins last* **12/1**

11-2 **2** 1 **Ouninpohja (IRE)**[22] 1815 5-9-0 106 .... DeanMcKeown 3 104
(G A Swinbank) *sn trcking ldrs: effrt 3f out: hung lft and carried hd high: styd on ins last* **8/11**[1]

12-5 **3** nk **Foreign Affairs**[28] 1677 8-9-3 103 .... DarryllHolland 5 107
(Sir Mark Prescott) *led 1f: shkn up to ld over 8f out: rdn along over 3f out: edgd lft over 1f out: hdd and no ex ins last* **4/1**[2]

550- **4** 1½ **Astrocharm (IRE)**[259] 5458 7-8-9 98 .... NCallan 2 97
(M H Tompkins) *hld up: hdwy to trck ldrs over 5f out: kpt on same pce fnl 2f* **12/1**

0155 **5** 3 **Land 'n Stars**[93] 624 6-9-3 .... PaulDoe 4 101
(Jamie Poulton) *trckd ldrs: wknd fnl f* **7/1**[3]

115- **6** 63 **Im Spartacus**[335] 3386 4-9-0 105 .... FergalLynch 1 10
(D W Barker) *led after 1f: hdd over 8f out: lost pl over 3f out: sn bhd and eased: virtually p.u: btn 72l* **20/1**

2m 59.26s (-6.44) **Going Correction** -0.25s/f (Firm) **6** Ran SP% **110.6**
Speed ratings (Par 111):108,107,107,106,104 68
CSF £20.92 TOTE £17.20: £3.50, £1.30; EX 28.30.

Owner Dorothy & Ivan Topley **Bred** W P Churchward, D J Bloodstock And C Hue-Will **Trained** West Ilsley, Berks

FOCUS
A weak Listed race run at a muddling pace. Possibly Foreign Affairs is the key to the overall value of the form.

NOTEBOOK
Sirce(IRE), who had the least chance on official figures. came with a stealthy run up the inner to claim the prize inside the last. Her handicap mark will shoot up and quite what she achieved on the day is open to doubt. (tchd 14-1)

Ouninpohja(IRE) is a tricky cutsomer. When called on for an effort he carried his head high and to one side. He was persuaded to put his best foot foward inside the last but too late. Two miles will be within his reach but he does not want the ground as firm as this. (op 4-5 tchd 5-6 and evens in places)

Foreign Affairs, keen to dominate, went for glory once in line for home but edged away from the running rail, always looked highly vulnerable. This might be as good as he is now. (op 3-1)

Astrocharm(IRE), absent since September, likes fast ground but seems slightly better over two miles. She has never shone on her seasonal return so this was encouraging. (op 14-1 tchd 11-1)

Land 'n Stars, last seen in action at Nad Al Sheba in March, ran as if needing the blow out. (op 11-2)

Im Spartacus, dicing for the lead, dropped out in a matter of strides once in line for home and was allowed to complete in his own time. He arrived in this yard a sick horse last year and it remains to be seen how much ability he retains.

2454 STEPHEN HAY & ASSOCIATES LTD H'CAP 7f 30y
6:00 (6:01) (Class 4) (0-85,85) 4-Y-0+ **£6,477** (£1,927; £963; £481) **Stalls** Low

Form RPR
0010 **1** **Royal Dignitary (USA)**[29] 1629 6-8-13 80 .... SilvestreDeSousa(3) 4 91
(D Nicholls) *trckd ldrs: led over 1f out: hung bdly rt ins last: jst hld on* **15/2**

05-0 **2** hd **Imperial Echo (USA)**[31] 1597 5-8-6 73 .... BenSwarbrick(3) 8 83
(T D Barron) *hld up: hdwy and edgd lft over 2f out: styd on wl fnl f: jst hld* **10/1**

20-0 **3** ¾ **Red Romeo**[133] 220 5-9-5 83 .... NCallan 6 91
(G A Swinbank) *trckd ldrs: effrt over 2f out: styd on fnl f* **9/2**[1]

6355 **4** 1¼ **Serieux**[29] 1629 7-8-8 72 ....(v) AdrianTNicholls 7 80+
(D Nicholls) *trckd ldr: led over 5f out: hdd over 1f out: clinging on to 2nd whn bdly hmpd ins last* **6/1**[3]

0660 **5** ¾ **Pure Imagination (IRE)**[22] 1820 5-8-11 75 .... DarryllHolland 3 78
(J M Bradley) *in rr: hdwy on ins whn nt clr run over 2f out: swtchd lft and styd on fnl 2f* **6/1**[3]

2025 **6** 1¾ **Sawwaah (IRE)**[5] 2282 9-8-9 73 ....(v) TonyCulhane 5 71
(D Nicholls) *led to s: in rr: kpt on fnl 2f: nt rch ldrs* **7/1**

4/3 **7** 3 **Tajaathub (USA)**[20] 1865 4-9-7 85 .... JoeFanning 9 76
(M Johnston) *led over 1f: chsd ldrs: wknd appr fnl f* **10/1**

0625 **8** nk **Dispol Katie**[10] 2147 5-8-10 74 .... PhillipMakin 2 64
(T D Barron) *chsd ldrs: effrt over 3f out: wknd over 1f out* **10/1**

0-04 **9** 2½ **Primo Way**[14] 2017 5-9-2 80 ....(b) TomEaves 1 63
(I Semple) *in rr: effrt over 3f out: sn rdn and hung rt: nvr a factor* **11/2**[2]

1m 26.6s (-3.34) **Going Correction** -0.25s/f (Firm) **9** Ran SP% **113.7**
Speed ratings (Par 105):109,108,107,106,105 103,100,99,97
CSF £77.99 CT £378.40 TOTE £9.30: £2.60, £3.20, £1.90; EX 196.20 Place 6 £267.14, Place 5 £236.42.

Owner Middleham Park Racing XXXVI **Bred** Bentley Smith, J Michael O'Farrell Jr , Joan Thor **Trained** Sessay, N Yorks

FOCUS
A strongly-run handicap and the form looks solid and should prove reliable.

T/Plt: £292.40 to a £1 stake. Pool: £46,069.05. 115.00 winning tickets. T/Qpdt: £128.20 to a £1 stake. Pool: £2,252.60. 13.00 winning tickets. WG

1838 NEWBURY (L-H)
Saturday, June 10

OFFICIAL GOING: Good to firm
Wind: Slight, across

2455 BATHWICK TYRES LADY RIDERS' H'CAP 1m 2f 6y
6:30 (6:31) (Class 5) (0-70,70) 4-Y-0+ **£3,747** (£1,162; £580; £290) **Stalls** Centre

Form RPR
3-31 **1** **Great View (IRE)**[13] 2044 7-10-0 64 ....(p) MissLEllison(3) 14 72
(Mrs A L M King) *trckd ldrs: led over 2f out: drvn and kpt on wl fnl f* **7/1**[3]

0341 **2** ¾ **Gallego**[1] 2407 4-9-4 58 6ex ow3 .... MissABevan(7) 1 65
(R J Price) *plld hrd and stdd rr: wd into st and hdwy fr 2f out in centre: styd on to press wnr ins last but no ex nr fin* **11/2**[2]

30U **3** nk **Luis Melendez (USA)**[24] 1769 4-9-13 65 ....(t) MissMSowerby(5) 12 71
(Tom Dascombe) *lw: led tl narrowly hdd ins fnl 4f: styd chalng: kpt on u.p ins last: gng on again cl home* **20/1**

-606 **4** 1¼ **Hatch A Plan (IRE)**[25] 1754 5-10-1 62 .... MissEJJones 16 66
(Mrs A J Hamilton-Fairley) *in tch: hdwy to chse ldrs over 2f out: styd on fnl f: nt pce to rch ldrs nr fin* **20/1**

0000 **5** nk **Love You Always (USA)**[13] 2044 6-9-8 55 ....(t) MrsACooke 6 58+
(Miss J Feilden) *bhd: stl plenty to do over 2f out: sn styd on and r.o wl fnl f but nt rch ldrs* **33/1**

0612 **6** ½ **Cormorant Wharf (IRE)**[13] 2044 6-10-1 67 .... MissJPowell(5) 8 69
(G L Moore) *lw: mid-div: pushed along and sme hdwy 3f out: hung bdly rt to centre crse over 1f out: styd on nr fin* **5/1**[1]

6643 **7** ½ **Treetops Hotel (IRE)**[25] 1755 7-8-12 52 .... MissLBaldwin(7) 10 53+
(B R Johnson) *stdd rr and wl off pce: stl plenty to do 3f out: hdwy 2f out and hung rt to centre crse: styd on ins last: nt a danger* **12/1**

4006 **8** ¾ **Gingko**[24] 1769 9-8-12 52 .... MissVGraham(7) 7 52
(P R Webber) *chsd ldrs: rdn over 2f out: styd on same pce* **16/1**

0004 **9** ¾ **Blackmail (USA)**[25] 1754 8-9-6 60 ....(b) MissKarenPeippo(7) 5 58
(Miss B Sanders) *chsd ldrs: racd wd fr 7f out: wd into st and led ins fnl 4f: hdd over 2f out in centre crse: wknd fnl f* **16/1**

2100 **10** ¾ **Scottish River (USA)**[11] 2097 7-10-2 70 .... MissCNosworthy(7) 11 67
(M D I Usher) *bhd: hdwy and wd into centre crse: styd on fnl 2f but nvr rchd ldrs* **25/1**

0-01 **11** ½ **Primed Up (IRE)**[10] 2131 4-9-3 55 ....(b) MissHayleyMoore(5) 3 51
(G L Moore) *mid-div: hdwy 3f out: chsd ldrs 2f out: wakened fnl f* **12/1**

-010 **12** nk **Thorny Mandate**[18] 1926 4-10-3 64 .... MrsSBosley 13 59
(R F Johnson Houghton) *t.k.h: in tch: bmpd bnd 7f out: chsd ldrs 4f out: sn rdn: wknd over 1f out* **8/1**

0000 **13** 5 **Terminate (GER)**[5] 2299 4-10-5 66 ....(p) MrsEmmaLittmoden 4 52
(N P Littmoden) *slowly away: sn rcvrd to chse ldrs: wknd ins fnl 2f* **14/1**

2002 **14** 1¾ **He's A Star**[8] 2206 4-10-0 64 ....(p) MissEFolkes(3) 9 47
(P D Evans) *chsd ldrs: wd into st: wknd 2f out* **16/1**

260- **15** 6 **The Rip**[134] 5321 5-9-4 54 .... MrsLucindaCrowley(3) 2 25
(R M Stronge) *chsd ldrs over 6f* **25/1**

2m 10.05s (1.34) **Going Correction** -0.10s/f (Good) **15** Ran SP% **115.5**
Speed ratings (Par 103):90,89,89,88,87 87,87,86,85,85 84,84,80,79,74
CSF £39.28 CT £736.51 TOTE £6.70: £2.20, £3.00, £9.00; EX 54.30.

Owner All The Kings Horses **Bred** Terry McGrath **Trained** Wilmcote, Warwicks

FOCUS
This lady riders' handicap was run at a steady early gallop and the winner and third were flattered to extent after getting good rides.

Thorny Mandate Official explanation: jockey said gelding had a breathing problem

2456 ELITERACINGCLUB.COM MAIDEN AUCTION FILLIES' STKS 6f 8y
7:00 (7:03) (Class 4) 2-Y-0 **£5,181** (£1,541; £770; £384) **Stalls** High

Form RPR
0 **1** **Dhanyata (IRE)**[9] 2166 2-8-3 .... NelsonDeSouza(3) 10 86+
(B J Meehan) *w'like: scope: mde virtually all: def advantage over 2f out: rdn fnl f: hld on wl* **15/2**

54 **2** 1 **Harvest Joy (IRE)**[17] 1930 2-8-2 ow1 .... SaleemGolam(3) 2 82
(B R Millman) *rr but in tch: gd hdwy over 2f out: styd on u.p to go 2nd ins fnl f: kpt on but a hld by wnr* **5/1**[2]

3 nk **Love On Sight** 2-8-6 .... FrankieMcDonald 8 82
(A P Jarvis) *cmpt: bit bkwd: chsd ldrs: rdn fr 2f out: kpt on fnl f but nvr gng pce of wnr* **20/1**

23 **4** 6 **Buddies Girl (IRE)**[7] 2234 2-8-6 .... RyanMoore 15 64
(R Hannon) *pressed wnr 3f: styd chsng ldrs tl wknd fnl f* **11/4**[1]

0 **5** 1¼ **Red Hot Jazz (IRE)**[9] 2172 2-7-13 .... JamesDoyle(5) 5 58
(Mrs P N Dutfield) *bit bkwd: b.hind: bhd: rdn and hdwy fr 2f out but nvr gng pce to rch ldrs* **40/1**

4 **6** 2 **Rosie Cross (IRE)**[16] 1959 2-8-4 .... JimmyQuinn 3 52
(R F Johnson Houghton) *in tch: rdn and hdwy over 2f out: nt rch ldrs: wknd fnl f* **6/1**[3]

7 nk **Indian Ink (IRE)** 2-8-11 .... RichardHughes 7 58
(R Hannon) *str: bit bkwd: pressed ldrs over 3f: rdn over 2f out: wknd fnl f* **6/1**[3]

8 1 **Split Briefs (IRE)** 2-8-6 .... ShaneKelly 9 50
(D J Daly) *w'like: bit bkwd: chsd ldrs: rdn 1/2-way: wknd ins fnl 2f* **33/1**

0 **9** shd **Brierley Lil**[28] 1688 2-8-8 .... LPKeniry 11 52
(J L Spearing) *w'like: chsd ldrs 4f* **66/1**

10 hd **Princess Zada** 2-8-4 .... RichardThomas 1 48
(B R Millman) *w'like: tall: green and bhd: mod hday fnl f* **33/1**

11 1¾ **Swiftly Addicted (IRE)** 2-8-11 .... DaneO'Neill 6 49
(A King) *leggy: bit bkwd: scope: chsd ldrs 4f* **12/1**

12 nk **Sweet Lilly** 2-8-6 .... ChrisCatlin 12 43
(M R Channon) *w'like: scope: slowly away: bhd: mod prog fnl 2f* **12/1**

13 nk **Boogie Dancer** 2-7-13 .... EmmettStack(5) 14 41
(H S Howe) *w'like: bit bkwd: slowly away: v green an a in rr* **66/1**

14 9 **Chingford (IRE)** 2-8-6 .... HayleyTurner 13 16
(D W P Arbuthnot) *w'like: bit bkwd: chsd ldrs over 3f* **40/1**

15 12 **Bertrada (IRE)** 2-8-11 .... SteveDrowne 4 —
(H Morrison) *w'like: bit bkwd: in tch: rdn and sme hdwy 1/2-way: sn wknd* **16/1**

1m 11.98s (-2.34) **Going Correction** -0.45s/f (Firm) **15** Ran SP% **123.4**
Speed ratings (Par 92):97,95,95,87,85 82,82,81,81,80 78,78,77,65,49
CSF £43.32 TOTE £10.60: £3.30, £1.90, £10.30; EX 118.40.

Owner Mrs Sheila Tucker **Bred** Edmond And Richard Kent **Trained** Manton, Wilts

FOCUS
On paper this was not a great maiden for the track, but it was run in a fair time for a race of its nature, 0.84 seconds faster than the later three-year-old maiden, and the first three came clear.

NOTEBOOK

Dhanyata(IRE), who ran a bit better than the bare form suggests at Nottingham on her debut, showed good speed throughout and found more when challenged in the closing stages. A half-sister to sprint juvenile winners Three Star Rated, Hammer And Sickle and Guinea Hunter, she seemed well suited by the quick conditions. (op 8-1)

Harvest Joy(IRE), having her third outing, was perhaps at a slight disadvantage in having to race towards the outside of the pack, as the action developed nearer the stands'-side rail. Nurseries are on the horizon and will soon be an option for her. (tchd 4-1)

Love On Sight, whose dam won over seven furlongs at three, is bred to do better over further in time. This was a promising debut effort as she came well clear of the rest, and her stable's juveniles usually improve for their first run. (op 25-1)

Buddies Girl(IRE) showed early speed but she dropped away tamely and proved disappointing on this quicker ground. She is another for whom nurseries will soon become an option. (op 5-2 tchd 9-2)

Red Hot Jazz(IRE), who is out of a mare who won over six furlongs at three, is like the winner by Danetime. She looked in need of this debut and ran a fair race in the circumstances. She should come on for it.

Rosie Cross(IRE) looks one for nurseries after one more run. (op 5-1)

Sweet Lilly is an athletic type. (op 16-1)

Chingford(IRE) was very green in the paddock prior to the race.

Bertrada(IRE) unseated her jockey in the paddock prior to the race. Official explanation: jockey said he was unable to ride out (op 14-1)

2457 SPORTSMAN RACING FILLIES' H'CAP — 1m 2f 6y

7:30 (7:31) (Class 4) (0-80,77) 4-Y-0+ — £5,505 (£1,637; £818; £408) Stalls Centre

Form — RPR

34-0 **1** **Pine Cone (IRE)**[23] [1800] 4-9-7 **77** .... DaneO'Neill 1 — 87
(A King) *swtg: trckd ldrs: hrd drvn to chal 1f out: led last half f: kpt on wl* **6/1**

41-6 **2** *1* **Noora (IRE)**[85] [660] 5-9-2 **75** .... (v) AdamKirby(3) 7 — 83
(C G Cox) *trckd ldr tl slt ld ins fnl 4f: rdn over 2f out: hdd and one pce last half f* **6/1**

0042 **3** *1 3/4* **Sforzando**[11] [2108] 5-8-0 **63** .... KristinStubbs(7) 2 — 68
(Mrs L Stubbs) *bhd: hdwy over 2f out: shkn up and styd on fr over 1f out: tk 3rd ins last but nvr gng pce to rch ldrs* **11/2**[3]

-330 **4** *shd* **Kathryn Janeway (IRE)**[10] [2133] 4-8-8 **64** .... JohnEgan 4 — 68
(W R Muir) *bhd: hdwy 3f out: drvn to chse ldrs on rails 2f out: one pce fnl f* **14/1**

6344 **5** *1/2* **Rakata (USA)**[12] [2071] 4-8-13 **69** .... RichardHughes 6 — 73
(P F I Cole) *lw: sn led: hdd ins fnl 4f: styd pressing ldr tl over 1f out: wknd ins last* **12/1**

0121 **6** *1 1/2* **Summer Charm**[12] [2088] 4-8-12 **75** .... BRoper(7) 5 — 76
(W Jarvis) *rr but in tch: hdwy on outside over 2f out: sn rdn: edgd lft over 1f out and sn wknd* **4/1**[1]

15-0 **7** *3 1/2* **Golden Applause (FR)**[15] [1993] 4-9-0 **70** .... JimmyQuinn 8 — 64
(Mrs A L M King) *chsd ldrs: pushed along 3f out: n.m.r 2f out: sn wknd* **7/1**

-515 **8** *4* **Ma'Am (USA)**[23] [1804] 4-9-5 **75** .... RyanMoore 3 — 61
(I A Wood) *bhd: rdn: hung lft and no rspnse 2f out* **5/1**[2]

2m 6.80s (-1.91) **Going Correction** -0.10s/f (Good) — **8** Ran SP% **107.5**
Speed ratings (Par 102):103,102,100,100,100 99,96,93
CSF £36.52 CT £179.09 TOTE £7.10: £2.00, £1.70, £2.30; EX 24.90.
Owner Miss Janet Menzies **Bred** Lord Halifax **Trained** Barbury Castle, Wilts

FOCUS
An ordinary fillies' handicap and although the winner improved a touch and the runner-up ran to her best, the form overall is nothing special.
Ma'Am(USA) Official explanation: jockey said filly was unsuited by the good to firm ground

2458 CANTORSPREADFAIR.COM MAIDEN STKS — 6f 8y

8:00 (8:03) (Class 5) 3-Y-0 — £5,181 (£1,541; £770; £384) Stalls High

Form — RPR

1 **Bustin Justin (USA)** 3-9-3 .... ShaneKelly 9 — 83+
(J Noseda) *lw: unf: scope: lw: trckd ldr: led over 2f out: sn rdn: hdd jst ins fnl f: rallied u.p: hit over hd cl home: led last stride* **7/4**[1]

05 **2** *shd* **Disco Ball**[13] [2048] 3-8-12 .... ChrisCatlin 2 — 77
(G Wragg) *swtg: hld up in rr: stdy hdwy over 2f out: led jst ins last: sn rdn: ct last stride* **12/1**

0 **3** *5* **Kansas Gold**[16] [1960] 3-9-3 .... JohnEgan 4 — 67
(W R Muir) *lw: rr but in tch: hdwy 1/2-way: chsd ldrs and rdn 2f out: wknd fnl f* **100/1**

2 **4** *1* **Prince Of Delphi**[7] [2235] 3-9-3 .... DaneO'Neill 12 — 64
(H Candy) *w'like: lw: slt ld tl hdd over 2f out: wknd fnl f* **9/4**[2]

43-4 **5** *shd* **Aristofilia**[63] [916] 3-8-9 75 .... NelsonDeSouza(3) 7 — 59
(P F I Cole) *in tch: drvn to chse ldrs 2f out: sn outpcd* **10/1**

-600 **6** *3* **Miss Redactive**[23] [1801] 3-8-12 50 .... HayleyTurner 11 — 50
(M D I Usher) *slowly away: bhd: swtchd lft ins fnl 2f: kpt on fr over 1f out but nvr in contention* **100/1**

0- **7** *1 1/4* **It's Twilight Time**[386] [1850] 3-8-12 .... RyanMoore 1 — 46
(R Hannon) *bhd and outpcd most of way* **20/1**

40 **8** *nk* **Crafty Fox**[48] [1166] 3-9-3 .... FrankieMcDonald 5 — 50
(A P Jarvis) *lw: chsd ldrs: rdn over 2f out: sn wknd* **80/1**

9 *6* **Parthenope** 3-8-12 .... RichardThomas 8 — 27
(J A Geake) *unf: leggy: chsd ldrs over 3f* **100/1**

4-54 **10** *3 1/2* **You Call That Art (USA)**[34] [1513] 3-8-12 80 .... RichardHughes 10 — 17
(R Hannon) *lw: early spd: sn rdn: bhd fr 1/2-way* **9/2**[3]

1m 12.82s (-1.50) **Going Correction** -0.45s/f (Firm) — **10** Ran SP% **111.1**
Speed ratings (Par 99):92,91,85,83,83 79,78,77,69,65
CSF £22.17 TOTE £2.70: £1.10, £3.00, £7.10; EX 19.90.
Owner Zayat Stables Ltd **Bred** A U Jones & Marie D Jones **Trained** Newmarket, Suffolk

FOCUS
An ordinary maiden for the track and a modest winning time 0.84 seconds slower than the earlier two-year-old fillies' maiden. However, the well regarded winner and the unexposed runner-up came home clear.

2459 BBC RADIO BERKSHIRE FILLIES' H'CAP — 7f (S)

8:35 (8:36) (Class 5) (0-75,73) 3-Y-0+ — £3,238 (£963; £481; £240) Stalls High

Form — RPR

6303 **1** **Meditation**[5] [2293] 4-8-13 **63** .... JamesDoyle(5) 11 — 74
(I A Wood) *lw: mde all: drvn 3l clr over 1f out: r.o strly ins last* **6/1**[1]

0-00 **2** *1 3/4* **Way To The Stars**[21] [1844] 3-9-1 **70** .... RichardHughes 3 — 72+
(A M Balding) *lw: hld up in tch: hdwy over 2f out:drvn to chse wnr fnl f but a hld* **20/1**

4015 **3** *2* **La Fanciulla**[12] [2068] 3-8-8 **63** .... RyanMoore 6 — 60
(R Hannon) *hld up in rr: hdwy and n.m.r inside fnl 2f: styd on wl fnl f: kpt on cl home but nt rch ldrs* **8/1**[2]

-540 **4** *hd* **Palais Polaire**[11] [2095] 4-8-12 **57** .... RichardThomas 13 — 57
(J A Geake) *lw: chsd ldrs: rdn 2f out: one pce fnl f* **14/1**

3-52 **5** *1* **Chalentina**[29] [1649] 3-9-1 **70** .... JimmyQuinn 2 — 64
(H R A Cecil) *chsd ldrs: rdn and edgd rt ins fnl 2f: styd on same pce fnl f* **10/1**[3]

0-31 **6** *1/2* **Lii Najma**[17] [1941] 3-8-11 **66** .... JimmyFortune 15 — 58
(C E Brittain) *lw: chsd wnr: rdn over 2f out: wknd fnl f* **8/1**[2]

40-0 **7** *1/2* **Missed A Beat**[39] [1382] 4-9-9 **68** .... ChrisCatlin 12 — 63
(M Blanshard) *hld up in rr: hdwy whn nt clr run 2f out: swtchd lft to outside and kpt on wl fnl f but nvr gng pce to rch ldrs* **16/1**

-220 **8** *shd* **Peace Lily**[10] [2148] 4-8-12 **57** .... ShaneKelly 14 — 52+
(R F Johnson Houghton) *hld up: nt clr run fr over 2f out tl over 1f out: kpt on ins last but nt rcvr* **8/1**[2]

0000 **9** *nk* **Lady Duxyana**[9] [2171] 3-7-13 **54** oh1 .... HayleyTurner 8 — 44
(M D I Usher) *chsd ldrs: rdn and pushed rt 2f out: wknd fnl f* **66/1**

0006 **10** *hd* **Saxon Lil (IRE)**[7] [2232] 4-9-8 **67** .... LPKeniry 5 — 60+
(J L Spearing) *bhd: kpt fr over 1f out: styng on cl home but nvr in contention* **8/1**[2]

1-04 **11** *shd* **Toffee Vodka (IRE)**[14] [2011] 4-10-0 **73** .... FrankieMcDonald 4 — 66+
(J W Hills) *s.i.s: bhd: effrt on rails whn nt clr run fr 2f tl over 1f out: kpt on but nt rcvr* **6/1**[1]

5600 **12** *3 1/2* **Sweetest Revenge (IRE)**[7] [2223] 5-9-4 **66** .... RichardSmith(3) 1 — 50
(M D I Usher) *bhd: rdn and sme hdwy on outside 2f out: nt rch ldrs: sn wknd* **33/1**

10-6 **13** *1 1/2* **Nudrah**[28] [1672] 3-9-4 **73** .... DaneO'Neill 9 — 49
(J L Dunlop) *lw: bmpd s: sn chsng ldrs: wknd fr 2f out* **8/1**[2]

505 **14** *3* **Fleur A Lay (USA)**[48] [1166] 4-8-11 **56** .... JimCrowley 10 — 28
(Mrs A J Perrett) *t.k.h: chsd ldrs tl wknd and hmpd jst ins fnl 2f* **33/1**

1m 25.15s (-1.85) **Going Correction** -0.45s/f (Firm)
WFA 3 from 4yo+ 10lb — **14** Ran SP% **117.9**
Speed ratings (Par 100):92,90,87,87,86 85,85,85,84,84 84,80,78,75
CSF £128.42 CT £994.22 TOTE £7.60: £3.00, £4.40, £3.70; EX 154.50.
Owner Paddy Barrett **Bred** P E Barrett **Trained** Upper Lambourn, Berks

FOCUS
An average fillies' handicap, run at an ordinary gallop and in a modest time for the type of race. The winner was given a good ride and got the run of the race.
La Fanciulla Official explanation: jockey said filly was denied a clear run

2460 RELYON CLEANING NEWBURY H'CAP — 1m 5f 61y

9:05 (9:07) (Class 5) (0-75,73) 4-Y-0+ — £3,238 (£963; £481; £240) Stalls Centre

Form — RPR

6034 **1** **Mister Right (IRE)**[18] [1927] 5-9-4 **73** .... NelsonDeSouza(3) 1 — 82
(D J S Ffrench Davis) *plld hrd in rr: stl t.k.h 6f out: swtchd to outside over 4f out: chal fr 3f out: drvn to ld jst ins last: hld on wl* **8/1**

3201 **2** *1 1/4* **Taxman (IRE)**[10] [2150] 4-9-3 **69** .... (p) RyanMoore 6 — 77
(C E Brittain) *chsd ldrs: slt advantage fr 3f out: kpt on gamely whn strly chal tl hdd jst ins last: kpt on same pce* **11/2**[3]

251- **3** *1* **Mersey Sound (IRE)**[257] [5502] 8-8-12 **64** .... JohnEgan 5 — 70
(D R C Elsworth) *in tch: chsd ldrs 4f out: chal fr 3f out and stl upsides 1f out: one pce ins last* **7/1**

0250 **4** *3/4* **Nawow**[78] [628] 6-8-13 **65** .... DaneO'Neill 12 — 74+
(P D Cundell) *hld up in rr: hdwy whn hmpd and nt clr run over 2f out: styd on strly ins fnl f: gng on cl home* **14/1**

66-0 **5** *shd* **Boxhall (IRE)**[30] [1614] 4-9-4 **70** .... JimmyFortune 2 — 75
(W R Swinburn) *in tch: effrt whn hmpd 3f out: sn drvn along: hdwy over 1f out to chse ldrs: one pce last half f* **10/1**

04-6 **6** *nk* **Papeete (GER)**[40] [1339] 5-9-0 **66** .... JimmyQuinn 3 — 70
(Miss B Sanders) *chsd ldrs: n.m.r over 2f out and one pce: kpt on again ins fnl f* **12/1**

0-00 **7** *1* **Blue Away (IRE)**[28] [1690] 8-9-1 **67** .... FrankieMcDonald 4 — 70
(S Kirk) *lw: bhd: hdwy on outside over 3f out: chsd ldrs 2f out: kpt on same pce fnl f* **33/1**

0-43 **8** *3* **Queen Of Iceni**[23] [1800] 4-9-5 **71** .... (v) TQuinn 9 — 69
(J L Dunlop) *in tch: hdwy whn nt clr run 3f out: effrt sn after: wknd over 1f out* **5/1**[2]

00/0 **9** *18* **Chimes At Midnight (USA)**[10] [2140] 9-7-9 **54** oh12(b) LukeMorris(7) 11 — 25
(Luke Comer, Ire) *b.bkwd: chsd ldrs tl wknd ins fnl 3f* **50/1**

0432 **10** *hd* **Our Choice (IRE)**[10] [2150] 4-8-9 **66** .... JamesDoyle(5) 7 — 37
(N P Littmoden) *lw: led 1f: chsd ldrs to 3f out: sn wknd* **4/1**[1]

6220 **11** *3* **Eastborough (IRE)**[18] [1927] 7-9-7 **73** .... RichardHughes 10 — 39
(B G Powell) *swtg: led 10f out: hdd 3f out: wknd qckly over 2f out* **11/1**

/2-5 **12** *10* **Dalpe**[26] [1739] 5-8-8 **60** .... HayleyTurner 8 — 11
(A J Lidderdale) *lw: led after 1f: hdd 10f out: wknd 3f out* **66/1**

0060 **13** *2 1/2* **Romanova (IRE)**[24] [1772] 4-8-5 **57** .... RichardThomas 13 — 5
(Dr J R J Naylor) *s.i.s: bhd most of way* **66/1**

2m 51.47s (0.48) **Going Correction** -0.10s/f (Good) — **13** Ran SP% **115.3**
Speed ratings (Par 103):94,93,92,92,92 91,91,89,78,78 76,70,68
CSF £48.98 CT £323.64 TOTE £12.30: £3.30, £2.20, £2.40; EX 70.60 Place 6 £341.00, Place 5 £146.48.
Owner Miss A Jones **Bred** Joe Rogers **Trained** Lambourn, Berks

FOCUS
Just a modest staying handicap, but it was run at a fair gallop and the form looks sound enough.
Our Choice(IRE) Official explanation: jockey said gelding was unsuited by the good to firm ground
T/Plt: £1,193.50 to a £1 stake. Pool: £43,408.70. 26.55 winning tickets. T/Qpdt: £85.20 to a £1 stake. Pool: £3,028.30. 26.30 winning tickets. ST

2413 WOLVERHAMPTON (A.W) (L-H)

Saturday, June 10

OFFICIAL GOING: Standard to slow
Wind: Light, half-behind Weather: Hot and sunny

2461 EUROPEAN BREEDERS FUND MAIDEN FILLIES' STKS — 5f 216y(P)

6:15 (6:16) (Class 5) 2-Y-0 — £3,886 (£1,156; £577; £288) Stalls Low

Form — RPR

303 **1** **Three Decades (IRE)**[18] [1922] 2-9-0 .... EddieAhern 10 — 72+
(C A Cyzer) *chsd ldr: led 2f out: edgd rt over 1f out: pushed out* **11/4**[1]

2 *1 3/4* **Baldovina** 2-9-0 .... OscarUrbina 4 — 67
(M Botti) *a.p: rdn to chse wnr and edgd lft over 1f out: styd on* **9/1**

6 **3** *3* **Temtation (IRE)**[60] [968] 2-8-11 .... AmirQuinn(3) 7 — 58
(J R Boyle) *hld up in tch: outpcd 2f out: hdwy over 1f out: edgd lft: styd on* **11/1**

0 **4** *3/4* **Spanish Air**[17] [1930] 2-8-11 .... DeanCorby(3) 13 — 56
(J W Hills) *chsd ldrs: rdn over 1f out: no ex fnl f* **25/1**

The Form Book, Raceform Ltd, Compton, RG20 6NL

5 1 3/4 **Boogie Board** 2-9-0 .... RobbieFitzpatrick 11 50
(M J Attwater) *s.s: outpcd: r.o ins fnl f: nrst fin* **16/1**

6 *hd* **La Quinta (IRE)** 2-9-0 .... TedDurcan 8 50
(B J Meehan) *trckd ldrs: rdn over 2f out: edgd lft and wknd over 1f out* **11/2[3]**

0 7 1 1/4 **Up The Pole**[11] 2106 2-9-0 .... DaleGibson 12 46+
(M W Easterby) *s.s: hdwy over 2f out: rdn and wknd over 1f out* **10/1**

8 1 **Gorgeous Girl** 2-9-0 .... FrancisNorton 3 43
(P W D'Arcy) *s.s: nvr nrr* **14/1**

9 *nk* **Falimar** 2-9-0 .... PaulMulrennan 1 42
(Miss J A Camacho) *chsd ldrs over 4f* **14/1**

0 10 1 3/4 **Morinqua (IRE)**[9] 2166 2-9-0 .... DO'Donohoe 6 37+
(K A Ryan) *led 4f: wknd fnl f* **5/1[2]**

0 11 6 **Raven Rascal**[9] 2178 2-8-7 .... StacyRenwick(7) 5 19
(J F Coupland) *mid-div: hung rt and wknd over 3f out* **66/1**

12 14 **Pineapple Poll** 2-9-0 .... BrianReilly 2 —
(P L Gilligan) *s.s: outpcd* **25/1**

1m 17.5s (1.69) **Going Correction** +0.025s/f (Slow) 12 Ran SP% **114.5**
Speed ratings (Par 90):89,86,82,81,79 79,77,76,75,73 65,46
CSF £26.27 TOTE £3.70: £1.40, £2.30, £4.30; EX 42.20.
Owner Mrs Charles Cyzer **Bred** Michael Collins **Trained** Maplehurst, W Sussex

FOCUS
A modest juvenile fillies' maiden but the form has been rated positively and should work out.

NOTEBOOK
Three Decades(IRE) broke her maiden tag at the fourth time of asking with a straightforward success on this first attempt at a sixth furlong. She can be rated value for further than her winning margin - and is clearly right at home on this surface - but this was her easiest opportunity to date, and she will not prove easy to place now. (op 5-2)
Baldovina ◆, the first foal of a very smart triple ten-furlong winner in France, turned in a very pleasing debut effort and finished a clear second-best. She will no doubt need a stiffer test in time and clearly has a future. (op 11-1)
Temtation(IRE), sixth on debut at Folkestone 60 days previously, showed she is going the right way with a more encouraging display and again left the impression she would benefit for the experience. She also looked better suited by this longer trip.
Spanish Air ultimately paid for her early exertions in trying to get handy from the outside draw. This was a definite step in the right direction and she ought to do better as she becomes more streetwise. (op 22-1)
Boogie Board ◆, a half-sister to the modest miler Savoy Chapel, lost all chance at the start yet was noted finishing her race with gusto. She ought to be sharper for this experience and it would be no surprise were her up-and-coming yard to place her successfully in the not-too-distant future. (op 18-1)
La Quinta(IRE), who at a price of 150,000gns was by far the most expensive purchase in this line-up, did not find a great deal when push came to shove and looked in need of the experience. There is plenty to like about her pedigree and, like the majority of her yard's juveniles this season to date, she is likely get a deal closer next time. (op 6-1)
Up The Pole Official explanation: jockey said filly reared leaving stalls rendering her slowly away
Morinqua(IRE) showed decent early dash, but faded tamely nearing the final furlong and ran below the level of her debut at Nottingham nine days previously. On this evidence, she well may benefit for the drop back to five furlongs. Official explanation: jockey said filly lost her action (op 9-2)

2462 HOLIDAY INN GARDEN COURT WOLVERHAMPTON FILLIES' H'CAP 5f 20y(P)
6:45 (6:45) (Class 5) (0-70,70) 3-Y-0+ **£3,238** (£963; £481; £240) **Stalls Low**

Form RPR

3-00 1 **Coconut Moon**[7] 2237 4-8-10 **52** .... FrancisNorton 6 62+
(E J Alston) *chsd ldr: led over 1f out: rdn out* **7/2[1]**

2611 2 1 1/4 **Mystery Pips**[8] 2207 6-9-6 **62** ....(v) KimTinkler 3 67
(N Tinkler) *chsd ldrs: hmpd 2f out: sn rdn: styd on* **6/1**

3021 3 *nk* **Hello Roberto**[5] 2295 5-9-12 **68** 7ex................................(p) AdrianMcCarthy 7 72+
(R A Harris) *hld up in tch: swtchd rt and hmpd over 1f out: r.o ins fnl f: nt rch ldrs* **5/1[3]**

2020 4 *nk* **Sahara Silk (IRE)**[24] 1774 5-9-11 **70**................................(v) PatrickMathers(3) 5 73
(D Shaw) *sn pushed along in rr: hdwy over 1f out: running on whn nt clr run ins fnl f: nvr able to chal* **14/1**

0204 5 1/2 **Ashes (IRE)**[24] 1774 4-10-0 **70** .... PaulMulrennan 9 71
(K R Burke) *wnt lft s: mid-div: hdwy over 2f out: rdn and edgd lft over 1f out: styd on* **12/1**

0063 6 *hd* **Lady Bahia (IRE)**[45] 1243 5-9-4 **60**................................(b) RobbieFitzpatrick 1 60
(Peter Grayson) *chsd ldrs: rdn over 1f out: styd on same pce* **10/1**

0-62 7 *hd* **Lady Algarhoud (FR)**[38] 1414 4-9-6 **62** .... EddieAhern 8 62
(D K Ivory) *hmpd s: hdwy and hung lft over 1f out: nvr trbld ldrs* **4/1[2]**

140 8 1 1/2 **Sounds Simla (IRE)**[91] 626 3-8-2 **58**................................ StacyRenwick(7) 4 52
(J F Coupland) *hld up: nvr nrr* **40/1**

4000 9 *hd* **Extremely Rare (IRE)**[7] 2233 5-9-9 **65**................................ MickyFenton 2 58
(M S Saunders) *led over 3f: edgd lft and wknd ins fnl f* **8/1**

506- 10 1 1/2 **Queen Of Night**[263] 5379 6-9-2 **58** .... PaulQuinn 10 46
(D W Chapman) *s.s: outpcd* **33/1**

0636 11 5 **Safranine (IRE)**[5] 2295 9-8-4 **53** oh9 ow2................................(p) AnnStokell(7) 12 23
(Miss A Stokell) *chsd ldrs 3f* **66/1**

000- 12 10 **Plum Blossom**[231] 6030 3-8-2 **51** oh3................................ FrancisFerris 11 —
(S A Brookshaw) *dwlt: outpcd* **66/1**

63.02 secs (0.20) **Going Correction** +0.025s/f (Slow)
WFA 3 from 4yo+ 7lb 12 Ran SP% **116.1**
Speed ratings (Par 100):99,97,96,96,95 94,94,92,91,89 81,65
CSF £23.56 CT £103.79 TOTE £3.80: £1.80, £3.10, £2.10; EX 22.70.
Owner Valley Paddocks Racing Limited **Bred** Mrs R D Peacock **Trained** Longton, Lancs
■

FOCUS
A modest fillies' handicap, which saw those drawn low at an advantage, and the form looks fair and solid for the division.

2463 OWNERS SUPPORT RETRAINING OF RACEHORSES (S) STKS 1m 4f 50y(P)
7:15 (7:15) (Class 6) 3-Y-0 **£2,388** (£705; £352) **Stalls Low**

Form RPR

040- 1 **Gentian**[259] 5454 3-8-7 55................................ J-PGuillambert 6 58+
(Sir Mark Prescott) *chsd ldr: led over 3f out: sn rdn clr: eased ins fnl f* **7/2[1]**

0003 2 1 **Coffin Dodger**[12] 2070 3-8-0 42................................ KirstyMilczarek(7) 5 49
(C N Allen) *hld up: nt clr run 4f out: hdwy over 2f out: r.o: no ch w wnr* **8/1**

0454 3 1/2 **Macho Dancer (IRE)**[11] 2103 3-8-7 52................................ EddieAhern 10 48
(K J Burke) *plld hrd and prom: chsd wnr over 2f out: sn rdn and outpcd* **6/1[2]**

-000 4 1/2 **Dynamite Deano**[7] 2246 3-8-6 47 ow1................................ JamesMillman(7) 11 53
(D K Ivory) *hld up: hdwy 5f out: rdn over 2f out: styng on same pce whn hung lft fr over 1f out* **6/1[2]**

6400 5 10 **Cool Isle**[44] 1259 3-8-6 49 ow2................................(b) DeanCorby(3) 4 33
(P Howling) *prom: rdn over 2f out: sn wknd* **12/1**

-060 6 4 **Ten Commandments (IRE)**[25] 1768 3-8-7 37................................ FrancisFerris 8 25
(K J Burke) *s.i.s: hld up: rdn and hung lft over 1f out: nvr trbld ldrs* **50/1**

0601 7 1 1/4 **Shaika**[12] 2070 3-8-6 41................................ LiamJones(7) 2 29
(G Prodromou) *hld up: hdwy over 3f out: wknd over 2f out* **13/2[3]**

6450 8 14 **October Sun**[7] 2244 3-8-7 35 ow2................................ ChrisCavanagh(7) 9 7
(Miss D Mountain) *s.s: outpcd* **12/1**

6604 9 1 **Sahara Style**[28] 1661 3-8-8 43 ow3................................(b[1]) RussellKennemore(7) 7 7
(R Hollinshead) *led and sn clr: rdn over 4f out: hdd over 3f out: sn wknd* **11/1**

0066 10 13 **Just Tilly**[10] 2131 3-8-7 42................................ FrancisNorton 12 —
(P R Chamings) *hld up: rdn over 3f out: sn wknd* **14/1**

-004 11 19 **In The Fountain (IRE)**[127] 286 3-8-7 40................................ AdrianMcCarthy 3 —
(R A Harris) *chsd ldrs 8f* **25/1**

- 12 *dist* **Sea Sprite (IRE)** 3-8-12 .... FergusSweeney 1 —
(S Kirk) *s.s: outpcd: bhd whn hung rt over 7f out: virtually p.u fnl 2f* **14/1**

2m 43.18s (0.76) **Going Correction** +0.025s/f (Slow) 12 Ran SP% **118.1**
Speed ratings (Par 97):98,97,97,96,90 87,86,77,76,67 55,—
CSF £31.13 TOTE £4.40: £2.40, £2.70, £2.20; EX 33.00.The winner was sold to D. McCain for 10,000gns.
Owner Christopher Spence **Bred** Chieveley Manor Stud **Trained** Newmarket, Suffolk

FOCUS
A weak event, run at an average gallop, and the first four came clear. The winner is value for further and the placed horses set the level for the form.
Sea Sprite(IRE) Official explanation: jockey said gelding was never travelling

2464 SATURDAY NIGHT IS PARTY NIGHT AT WOLVERHAMPTON H'CAP 7f 32y(P)
7:45 (7:46) (Class 5) (0-75,74) 4-Y-0+ **£3,238** (£963; £481; £240) **Stalls High**

Form RPR

3024 1 **Vienna's Boy (IRE)**[7] 2223 5-9-0 **67**................................ TPQueally 10 76
(W J Musson) *s.i.s: hld up: hdwy over 1f out: r.o to ld wl ins fnl f* **10/1**

6340 2 1 1/4 **Mistral Sky**[7] 2223 7-8-11 **64**................................(v) FrancisNorton 5 70
(Stef Liddiard) *chsd ldrs: rdn to ld over 1f out: hdd wl ins fnl f* **10/1**

6600 3 *nk* **Silent Storm**[17] 1939 6-9-7 **74**................................ J-PGuillambert 8 79
(C A Cyzer) *chsd ldrs: rdn: hung lft and ev ch ins fnl f: unable qckn* **25/1**

-020 4 1 **Treasure House (IRE)**[9] 2184 5-8-6 **66**................................ LiamJones(7) 6 69
(M Blanshard) *hld up in tch: rdn and nt clr run over 1f out: styng on same pce whn n.m.r ins fnl f* **14/1**

1000 5 *shd* **Mandarin Spirit (IRE)**[9] 2184 6-9-1 **68**................................(p) OscarUrbina 12 70
(G C H Chung) *trckd ldrs: rdn over 1f out: no ex ins fnl f* **18/1**

0234 6 1 1/4 **Stoic Leader (IRE)**[1] 2417 6-9-0 **70**................................ DNolan(3) 2 69
(R F Fisher) *led: rdn: edgd rt: hdd and swished tail over 1f out: no ex ins fnl f* **4/1[2]**

0001 7 1/2 **African Gift**[8] 2211 4-8-12 **65**................................ EddieAhern 4 63
(J G Given) *chsd ldrs: rdn and nt clr run over 1f out: no ex ins fnl f* **5/1[3]**

0021 8 3/4 **Samuel Charles**[3] 2348 8-9-7 **74** 6ex................................ MickyFenton 1 70
(C R Dore) *s.i.s: sn chsng ldr: rdn over 2f out: no ex fnl f* **3/1[1]**

6040 9 1 1/2 **Lincolneurocruiser**[15] 1993 4-8-13 **66**................................ RobbieFitzpatrick 11 58
(Mrs N Macauley) *hld up: rdn over 1f out: nvr trbld ldrs* **12/1**

0000 10 1/2 **Connotation**[24] 1773 4-9-0 **67**................................ FergusSweeney 7 58
(A G Newcombe) *hld up: effrt over 1f out: n.d* **50/1**

1233 11 19 **White Bear (FR)**[48] 1164 4-9-0 **67**................................ PaulMulrennan 3 8
(C R Dore) *s.i.s: hld up: wknd 3f out* **8/1**

1m 30.37s (-0.03) **Going Correction** +0.025s/f (Slow) 11 Ran SP% **116.4**
Speed ratings (Par 103):101,99,99,98,97 96,95,95,93,92 71
CSF £104.84 CT £2419.27 TOTE £10.80: £3.40, £3.10, £5.00; EX 67.80.
Owner McGregor Bloodstock **Bred** Mark Commins **Trained** Newmarket, Suffolk
■

FOCUS
A modest handicap, run at a decent early pace, and the form looks ordinary but fair enough rated around the placed horses.

2465 HOTEL AND CONFERENCING AT DUNSTALL PARK MAIDEN STKS 1f 103y(P)
8:20 (8:21) (Class 5) 3-Y-0 **£3,238** (£963; £481; £240) **Stalls Low**

Form RPR

3-24 1 **Le Colombier (IRE)**[14] 2028 3-9-3 83................................ EddieAhern 10 82
(J W Hills) *hld up: hdwy over 6f out: rdn to ld and edgd lft wl ins fnl f: r.o* **11/4[1]**

02-3 2 1 **Montjeu Man**[28] 1684 3-9-3 80................................ DO'Donohoe 7 80
(E A L Dunlop) *chsd ldr 7f out: led 2f out: sn rdn and hung lft: hdd wl ins fnl f* **7/2[2]**

62-2 3 2 **Billich**[145] 124 3-9-3 77................................ RichardMullen 8 76
(E J O'Neill) *sn led: rdn and hdd 2f out: no ex fnl f* **4/1[3]**

6 4 2 1/2 **Regal Sunset (IRE)**[40] 1335 3-9-3 .... OscarUrbina 2 71
(W R Swinburn) *hmpd s: hld up: racd keenly: hdwy 1/2-way: rdn and hung lft over 1f out: wknd fnl f* **11/4[1]**

00 5 10 **Maria Antonia (IRE)**[26] 1733 3-8-8 ow1................................ DerekNolan(5) 3 48
(M J Wallace) *chsd ldrs 7f* **100/1**

6 1/2 **Inner Voice (USA)** 3-9-3 .... FrancisNorton 9 52
(Sir Michael Stoute) *dwlt: hld up: rdn over 3f out: a in rr* **7/1**

7 1 1/2 **Stockholder** 3-9-3 .... J-PGuillambert 6 49
(C A Cyzer) *dwlt: outpcd* **50/1**

00- 8 1 1/2 **Gypsy's Kiss**[299] 4421 3-9-3 .... FergusSweeney 1 46
(B P J Baugh) *wnt rt s: plld hrd and prom: wknd over 3f out* **100/1**

0400 9 1 1/2 **Blue Army (IRE)**[8] 2188 3-9-3 50................................ AdrianMcCarthy 5 43
(Jane Southcombe) *prom 6f* **66/1**

00 10 *shd* **Sa Nau**[14] 2028 3-9-3 .... MickyFenton 4 43
(T Keddy) *s.i.s: a in rr* **200/1**

2m 2.13s (-0.49) **Going Correction** +0.025s/f (Slow) 10 Ran SP% **114.0**
Speed ratings (Par 99):103,102,100,98,89 88,87,86,84,84
CSF £12.40 TOTE £4.40: £1.10, £1.70, £1.70; EX 12.10.
Owner Mrs Stevie Richards **Bred** Dermot Cantillon And Forenaghts Stud **Trained** Upper Lambourn, Berks

FOCUS
A fair maiden for the track, run at a solid pace, and the form makes sense and should prove sound.

2466 TO SPONSOR A RACE CALL 0870 220 2442 H'CAP 1m 1f 103y(P)
8:50 (8:50) (Class 6) (0-60,60) 3-Y-0 **£2,730** (£806; £403) **Stalls Low**

Form RPR

0-03 1 **Sarwin (USA)**[29] 1652 3-9-2 **55**................................ PhilipRobinson 7 65+
(W J Musson) *chsd ldrs: led 2f out: rdn and hung lft ins fnl f: r.o* **5/1[1]**

000- **2** 1 1/4 **Royal Curtsy**[260] 5427 3-9-3 **56** .... J-PGuillambert 4 66+
(Sir Mark Prescott) *chsd ldrs: rdn over 3f out: styng on same pce whn nt clr run wl ins fnl f* **11/2**[2]

6-00 **3** 1 **Teide Lady**[25] 1761 3-9-2 **55** .... FrancisFerris 12 61
(Rae Guest) *hld up: plld hrd: hdwy over 5f out: rdn over 2f out: ev ch over 1f out: sn hung lft: no ex ins fnl f* **20/1**

0500 **4** 3 1/2 **Smokey Blue**[17] 1941 3-9-1 **59** ....(v[1]) DerekNolan(5) 10 58
(M J Wallace) *s.i.s: hld up: hdwy over 2f out: wknd over 1f out* **40/1**

2-25 **5** 2 1/2 **Wee Charlie Castle (IRE)**[13] 2050 3-9-7 **60** .... OscarUrbina 1 54
(G C H Chung) *hld up in tch: lost pl over 5f out: swtchd rt and hdwy u.p over 1f out: edgd lft: nt trble ldrs* **11/2**[2]

0051 **6** nk **Grand Palace (IRE)**[7] 2249 3-8-12 **54** .... PatrickMathers(3) 11 48
(D Shaw) *hld up: plld hrd: hdwy over 2f out: rdn: hung lft and wknd over 1f out* **15/2**

0023 **7** 2 1/2 **Iberian Light (USA)**[29] 1634 3-9-2 **55** ....(p) DO'Donohoe 9 44
(N A Callaghan) *hld up: nvr trbld ldrs* **6/1**[3]

0-60 **8** 2 **Dzhani**[51] 1100 3-9-4 **57** .... MickyFenton 2 42
(Jedd O'Keeffe) *led over 7f: wknd over 1f out* **20/1**

4-22 **9** 1/2 **Wednesdays Boy (IRE)**[16] 1950 3-9-6 **59** .... PaulMulrennan 6 53+
(P D Niven) *chsd ldrs: hmpd and lost pl over 2f out: no ch whn hmpd 1f out* **6/1**[3]

0000 **10** hd **Earth Master (IRE)**[26] 1740 3-8-13 **55** ....(b) DNolan(3) 8 39
(S Kirk) *hdwy 7f out: wknd over 1f out* **50/1**

6-66 **11** 7 **Virginia Rose (IRE)**[15] 1984 3-9-4 **57** .... EddieAhern 5 28
(J G Given) *chsd ldr: rdn over 2f out: sn wknd* **10/1**

0-00 **12** 1 **Thomas A Beckett (IRE)**[12] 2065 3-9-2 **55** .... FrancisNorton 3 24
(P R Chamings) *hld up: bhd fnl 3f* **33/1**

4-04 **13** hd **Black Sea Pearl**[30] 1616 3-9-5 **58** .... RichardMullen 13 26
(P W D'Arcy) *hld up: rdn over 3f out: sn wknd* **11/1**

2m 2.85s (0.23) **Going Correction** +0.025s/f (Slow) 13 Ran SP% **122.1**
Speed ratings (Par 97):99,97,97,93,91 91,89,87,86,86 80,79,79
CSF £30.86 CT £520.32 TOTE £5.90: £2.40, £2.80, £4.00; EX 39.10 Place 6 £126.06, Place 5 £55.83.
Owner S Rudolf **Bred** Cynthia Knight **Trained** Newmarket, Suffolk
■ Stewards' Enquiry : Philip Robinson one-day ban: careless riding (Jun 25)

FOCUS
A moderate three-year-old handicap which saw the field finish fairly strung out behind the ready winner. The form looks sound for the class.
T/Plt: £272.70 to a £1 stake. Pool: £34,741.95. 93.00 winning tickets. T/Qpdt: £53.70 to a £1 stake. Pool: £2,456.90. 33.80 winning tickets. CR

2467 - 2470a (Foreign Racing) - See Raceform Interactive

2051 CURRAGH (R-H)
Saturday, June 10
OFFICIAL GOING: Good to firm

2471a PETER KEATLEY CURRAGH GROUNDCARE SILVER STKS (LISTED RACE) 1m 2f
7:25 (7:27) 3-Y-O+ **£24,693** (£7,244; £3,451; £1,175)

RPR

1 **Heliostatic (IRE)**[14] 2039 3-8-10 105 .... DJMoran 2 112
(J S Bolger, Ire) *settled 3rd: cl up ent st: rdn to ld 2f out: kpt on wl u.p fnl f* **9/2**[3]

2 1 **Cougar Bay (IRE)**[3] 2367 3-8-10 ....(b) KFallon 6 110
(David Wachman, Ire) *hld up in 5th: 4th and hdwy 2f out: 2nd and kpt on wl ins fnl f* **6/1**

3 3 **Reform Act (USA)**[10] 2155 3-8-7 95 .... PJSmullen 1 102
(D K Weld, Ire) *led: strly pressed ent st: rdn and hdd 2f out: 3rd and no ex ins fnl f* **4/1**[2]

4 2 1/2 **Helena Molony (IRE)**[10] 2154 4-9-6 96 .... MJKinane 5 98
(John M Oxx, Ire) *cl 2nd: rdn to chal early st: no ex fr 1 1/2f out* **9/2**[3]

5 1 1/2 **Akimbo (USA)**[336] 3345 5-9-9 107 .... WSupple 4 98
(James Leavy, Ire) *s.i.s and hld up in rr: prog into 5th under 2f out: kpt on same pce* **7/1**

6 7 **Davorin (JPN)**[237] 5929 5-9-9 93 .... JMurtagh 7 85
(R P Burns, Ire) *slt stumble leaving stalls: settled 4th: no ex early st* **14/1**

7 nk **Mon Michel (IRE)**[13] 2055 3-8-10 102 .... DPMcDonogh 3 85
(Kevin Prendergast, Ire) *hld up: 6th 1/2-way: no ex st* **7/2**[1]

2m 8.50s **Going Correction** +0.05s/f (Good)
WFA 3 from 4yo+ 13lb 7 Ran SP% **112.0**
Speed ratings: 105,104,101,99,98 93,92
CSF £29.80 TOTE £5.70: £2.70, £2.80; DF 47.10.
Owner Mrs J S Bolger **Bred** J S Bolger **Trained** Coolcullen, Co Carlow

FOCUS
A decent Listed contest with Heliostatic appreciating the drop in class and return to fast ground.

NOTEBOOK
Heliostatic(IRE), who ran much better in the Irish 2000 Guineas than he had in the Derrinstown, returned to form with a battling victory and the faster ground, on which he gained his only previous victory last season, was probably a major factor. By his trainer's own admission he is not that straightforward, but is still likely to take his chance in the Irish Derby nonetheless. (op 7/2)
Cougar Bay(IRE) battled on well, but could never quite get to the winner and shapes as though he needs a return to 12 furlongs.
Reform Act(USA) had a bit to find with a few of these at the weights, but emerged with credit after making much of the running. Much will depend on whether the Handicapper decides to raise her for this. (op 4/1 tchd 7/2)
Mon Michel(IRE) never got into the race and was disappointing, but this was his first try on fast ground and it obviously did not suit. Official explanation: vet said colt was clinically abnormal post race

2472 - 2473a (Foreign Racing) - See Raceform Interactive

2280 SAN SIRO (R-H)
Saturday, June 10
OFFICIAL GOING: Good

2474a PREMIO LUINO (UNRACED COLTS & GELDINGS) 7f
2:30 (2:33) 2-Y-O **£6,897** (£3,034; £1,655; £828)

RPR

1 **Notturno Di Chopin (IRE)** 2-9-0 .... WGambarota 6 76
(J Heloury, Italy)

2 hd **Sarabanda Heat** 2-9-0 .... DVargiu 9 75
(B Grizzetti, Italy)

3 3/4 **Depp (ITY)** 2-9-0 .... MDemuro 4 73
(L D'Auria, Italy)

4 nk **Lusolly** 2-9-0 .... EBotti 5 73
(M G Quinlan) *raced in 4th, headway 2f out to press leaders, stayed on same pace final furlong SP 1.01-1F* **101/100**[1]

5 1 1/2 **Tibroso (ITY)** 2-9-0 .... IRossi 2 69
(A & G Botti, Italy)

6 2 1/2 **Indio Sinedo (IRE)** 2-9-0 .... MTellini 1 62
(R Feligioni, Italy)

7 1/2 **Capitano Uncino (ITY)** 2-9-0 .... PConvertino 7 60
(M Marcialis, Italy)

8 5 **Cape Society (ITY)** 2-9-0 .... SMulas 3 47
(M Cicarelli, Italy)

9 12 **Royal Rumble (IRE)** 2-9-0 .... MEsposito 8 15
(G Miliani, Italy)

1m 28.9s 9 Ran SP% **49.8**
(Including 1 Euro stake): WIN 15.86; PL 3.40, 2.15, 1.75; DF 53.15.
Owner A Neri **Bred** Scuderia Pmz Sas **Trained** Italy

NOTEBOOK
Lusolly was sent off a warm favourite and was in the front rank throughout, but could not manage to match the principals' finishing speed in the final stages. It was a decent enough debut, but it is possible that there may not be too much more to come.

2475a PREMIO ARONA (UNRACED FILLIES) 7f
3:35 (3:46) 2-Y-O **£6,897** (£3,034; £1,655; £828)

RPR

1 **Finnic Girl (ITY)** 2-9-0 .... DVargiu 9 —
(B Grizzetti, Italy)

2 nk **Kilkenny (ITY)** 2-9-0 .... PConvertino 5 —
(A Marcialis, Italy)

3 1 1/4 **Maticochina** 2-9-0 .... DPorcu 4 —
(Laura Grizzetti, Italy)

4 5 **Lonesome Tonight** 2-9-0 .... MDemuro 12 —
(L D'Auria, Italy)

5 nk **Noverfancy (IRE)** 2-9-0 .... EBotti 2 —
(M Botti) *in touch, 6th straight, pushed along 3f out, never in contention SP 2.45-1* **49/20**[1]

6 1 **Shantell (ITY)** 2-9-0 .... FBranca 3 —
(M Guarnieri, Italy)

7 1/2 **Thathshan (ITY)** 2-9-0 .... GArena 11 —
(S Billeri, France)

8 5 **Tirzia (IRE)** 2-9-0 .... MTellini 7 —
(R Feligioni, Italy)

9 1/2 **Maxima (ITY)** 2-9-0 .... MPlanard 6 —
(M Bebbu, Italy)

10 1/2 **Mimita (IRE)** 2-9-0 .... SUrru 10 —
(M Cicarelli, Italy)

11 2 **Maona (IRE)** 2-9-0 .... SMulas 1 —
(G Miliani, Italy)

1m 30.2s 11 Ran SP% **29.0**
WIN 6.17; PL 2.53, 3.91, 3.86; DF 39.10.
Owner B Grizzetti **Bred** Azienda Agricola Razza Emiliana Srl **Trained** Italy

NOTEBOOK
Noverfancy(IRE) was given a considerate introduction on her debut and should benefit from the experience.

2093 BELMONT PARK (L-H)
Saturday, June 10
OFFICIAL GOING: Dirt course - fast; turf course - yielding

2476a MANHATTAN H'CAP (GRADE 1) (TURF) 1m 2f (T)
10:50 (10:55) 3-Y-O+ **£139,545** (£46,512; £25,582; £13,953; £6,977)

RPR

1 **Cacique (IRE)**[35] 5-8-8 .... EPrado 3 120
(R J Frankel, U.S.A) **22/10**[1]

2 hd **Relaxed Gesture (IRE)**[77] 741 5-8-7 .... KDesormeaux 1 119
(Christophe Clement, U.S.A) **4/1**

3 nk **Grey Swallow (IRE)**[28] 1721 5-8-10 .... ASolis 4 121
(D K Weld, Ire) *hld up in 6th on ins, swtchd outside and hdwy ent str, 3l 4th over 1f out, stayed on wl closing stages, nrst fin* **38/10**[3]

4 hd **English Channel (USA)**[35] 4-8-10 .... JRVelazquez 6 121
(T Pletcher, U.S.A) **47/20**[2]

5 3 3/4 **Silver Whistle (USA)**[70] 4-8-4 .... CVelasquez 5 108
(W Mott, U.S.A) **123/10**

6 6 1/4 **Sabre D'Argent (USA)**[21] 6-8-2 ....(b) ECoa 2 95
(T Albertrani, U.S.A) **32/1**

7 5 1/4 **Dreadnaught (USA)**[21] 6-8-3 .... GKGomez 7 86
(T Voss, U.S.A) **148/10**

2m 4.10s 7 Ran SP% **118.8**
PARI-MUTUEL: WIN 6.40; PL (1-2) 3.60, 4.30; SHOW (1-2-3) 3.00, 3.40, 4.00; SF 31.60.
Owner Juddmonte Farms **Bred** Juddmonte Farms **Trained** USA

NOTEBOOK
Grey Swallow(IRE) broke a bit slowly and was held up for a late run. He stayed on strongly in the straight to finish a never nearer third and, while fully effective over this trip, a return to 12 furlongs is likely to suit him.

2477a BELMONT STKS (GRADE 1) (DIRT) 1m 4f (D)
11:33 (11:35) 3-Y-O **£348,837** (£116,279; £63,953; £34,884; £17,442)

RPR

1 **Jazil (USA)**[35] 1498 3-9-0 .... FJara 8 121
(K McLaughlin, U.S.A) *rdr lost iron briefly leaving stalls, hld up & bhd, last after 2f, hdwy between rivals to ld 2 1/2f out, rdn 1 1/2f out, dr* **62/10**

2 1 1/4 **Bluegrass Cat (USA)**[35] 1498 3-9-0 .... JRVelazquez 9 119
(T Pletcher, U.S.A) *always prominent, pressing winner from 2 1/2f out to inside final f, no extra closing stages* **49/10**[3]

3 2 1/4 **Sunriver (USA)**[21] 3-9-0 .... RBejarano 2 116
(T Pletcher, U.S.A) *raced in 6th, ridden to go 3rd entering straight, stayed on at one pace* **6/1**

4 1 1/4 **Steppenwolfer (USA)**[35] 1498 3-9-0 .... RAlbarado 11 114
(D Peitz, U.S.A) *hld up, 11th 4f out, hdwy whn not clear run 3f out, n.m.r over 2f out, 4th str, sn rdn, stayed on at one pace* **48/10**[2]

5 5 **Oh So Awesome (USA)**[22] 3-9-0 ....(b) MESmith 6 106
(J Jerkens, U.S.A) *started slowly and behind, went 11th after 2f, 7th straight, one pace final 2f* **12/1**

6 2 **Hemingway's Key (USA)**[21] 1861 3-9-0 .... JRose 3 103
(N Zito, U.S.A) *raced in 10th, 8th straight, never a factor* **151/10**

7 4 1/2 **Platinum Couple (USA)**[21] 1861 3-9-0 ....(b) JLEspinoza 1 97
(J Lostritto, U.S.A) *midfield, went 5th 4f out, 6th straight, soon beaten* **38/1**

8 2 1/2 **Bob And John (USA)**[35] 1498 3-9-0 ....(b) GKGomez 4 93
(B Baffert, U.S.A) *led to 2 1/2f out, weakened* **47/10**[1]

9 4 1/4 **Sacred Light (USA)**[35] 3-9-0 ....(b) VEspinoza 12 86
(D Hofmans, U.S.A) *raced wide throughout, always towards rear* **265/10**

10 6 1/2 **High Finance (USA)**[37] 3-9-0 .... ECoa 5 77
(R Violette, U.S.A) *close up on inside til weakened 3f out* **104/10**

11 11 1/4 **Deputy Glitters (USA)**[35] 1498 3-9-0 .... EPrado 7 60
(T Albertrani, U.S.A) *prominent til weakened quickly 3f out* **122/10**

12 **Double Galore (USA)**[22] 3-9-0 ....(b) MLuzzi 10 60
(Myung Kwon Cho, U.S.A) *prominent til weakened 3f out, eased final f* **46/1**

2m 27.86s **12** Ran SP% **118.5**
PARI-MUTUEL: WIN 14.40; PL (1-2) 6.70, 6.40; SHOW (1-2-3) 4.70, 4.70, 6.10; SF 92.00.
Owner Shadwell Stable **Bred** Skara Glen Stables **Trained** USA

FOCUS
With neither the injured Barbaro nor impressive Preakness winner Bernardini on show the race lacked star quality, although the mid-race move Jazil made was impressive. The Kentucky Derby form dominated in this third leg of the Triple Crown.

NOTEBOOK
Jazil(USA), who came from well off the pace to dead-heat for fourth in the Kentucky Derby, appreciated this longer distance and made a powerful mid-race move to come through and lead turning in. A tough sort, he was given a 16-1 quote for the Breeders' Cup Classic by Coral, but he would need a very strong pace back over the shorter trip of ten furlongs as his forte is clearly stamina.
Bluegrass Cat(USA), runner-up in the Kentucky Derby, did best of those who raced towards the head of affairs but was no match for the winner. He is probably a bit better than the bare form suggests.
Sunriver(USA), winner of the Grade Two Peter Pan Stakes here over nine furlongs last month, was perhaps the most interesting runner on show and he posted a solid effort in third. He remains progressive.
Steppenwolfer(USA), third in the Kentucky Derby, did not enjoy the clearest of runs but finished clear of the rest, posting a sound effort in the circumstances.
Bob And John(USA), who never got involved in the Derby, was the disappointment of the race, dropping right away once headed.

2185 BATH (L-H)
Sunday, June 11

OFFICIAL GOING: Firm
Wind: Almost nil

2478 TOTEPLACEPOT MEDIAN AUCTION MAIDEN FILLIES' STKS 5f 161y
2:10 (2:11) (Class 6) 2-Y-O **£2,590** (£770; £385; £192) **Stalls** Low

Form RPR
4 **1** **Slipasearcher (IRE)**[8] 2218 2-9-0 .... ShaneKelly 3 73+
(P D Evans) *chsd ldrs: swtchd rt 1f out: led ins fnl f: kpt on wl: rdn out* **3/1**[2]

20 **2** 1 1/4 **Fly Time**[11] 2125 2-9-0 .... ChrisCatlin 1 69
(M R Channon) *led: rdn over 1f out: hdd ins fnl f: kpt on* **7/2**[3]

00 **3** 3 1/2 **Party Palace**[29] 1688 2-8-9 .... RichardKingscote(5) 7 57
(J A Osborne) *outpcd in rr early: styd on fnl f: nrst fin* **33/1**

002 **4** nk **Montemayorprincess (IRE)**[12] 2094 2-9-0 .... FrankieMcDonald 9 56
(D Haydn Jones) *trckd ldrs: pressed ldrs 3f out: sn rdn: kpt on same pce* **11/1**

6 **5** hd **Babylon Sister (IRE)**[20] 1896 2-9-0 .... RyanMoore 6 56
(R Hannon) *trckd ldrs: rdn ev ch over 1f out: sn one pce* **7/4**[1]

4 **6** 3 1/2 **Cleobury**[20] 1876 2-9-0 .... FergusSweeney 2 44
(M Meade) *prom: rdn over 2f out: sn btn* **66/1**

02 **7** 1/2 **La Marmotte (IRE)**[13] 2083 2-9-0 .... EddieAhern 8 43+
(J W Hills) *chsd ldrs: rdn over 2f out: sn one pce* **10/1**

8 2 **Abounding** 2-8-11 .... NelsonDeSouza(3) 4 36
(R M Beckett) *s.i.s: a outpcd in rr* **20/1**

1m 10.92s (-0.28) **Going Correction** -0.20s/f (Firm) **8** Ran SP% **110.2**
Speed ratings (Par 88):93,91,86,86,86 81,80,78
CSF £12.76 TOTE £4.20: £1.40, £1.30, £4.30; EX 16.70 Trifecta £225.60 Part won. Pool £317.75. - 0.70 winning units..
Owner Barry McCabe **Bred** Hugo Merry And Theo Waddington **Trained** Pandy, Abergavenny

FOCUS
Just a modest fillies' maiden rated around the runner-up.

NOTEBOOK
Slipasearcher(IRE), a pleasing fourth over six furlongs on her debut at Chepstow, improved on that effort to get off the mark at the second attempt. She may now be aimed at the Albany Stakes at Royal Ascot, although that company is likely to be a bit hot for her and she looks more of a nursery type for later in the season. (op 11-4 tchd 10-3)
Fly Time, second in a heavy-ground maiden at Thirsk on her debut before beating only one home in the Listed Hilary Needler at Beverley, seemed to have every chance returned to a more realistic grade. A modest race should come her way at some stage. (op 3-1)
Party Palace did her best work late on to grab third, and this represented improved form, but she was just passing beaten horses. She is likely to come into her own during the nursery season.
Montemayorprincess(IRE) may not have been ideally suited by ground this fast and just found a few too good. (op 10-1)
Babylon Sister(IRE) showed good early speed, but weakened rather tamely late on and failed to build on the encouragement she showed on her debut at Windsor. Official explanation: jockey said filly was unsuited by the firm going (op 9-4)

2479 TOTECOURSE TO COURSE H'CAP 1m 5y
2:40 (2:41) (Class 6) (0-60,62) 3-Y-O **£2,914** (£867; £433; £216) **Stalls** Low

Form RPR
0416 **1** **Maidford (IRE)**[2] 2403 3-8-13 **52** .... FergusSweeney 14 56+
(M Meade) *chsd ldrs: rdn 2f out: led narrowly 1f out: kpt on: rdn out* **5/1**[1]

0004 **2** nk **Whistleupthewind**[9] 2198 3-8-10 **49** ....(b) ShaneKelly 7 52
(J M P Eustace) *mid-div: rdn and no imp over 2f out: styd on wl fnl f: wnt 2nd fnl strides* **33/1**

06-0 **3** hd **Royal Agreement**[38] 1433 3-9-0 **53** .... TQuinn 6 56
(B G Powell) *led for 1f: prom: led over 3f out: rdn and hdd 1f out: kpt on* **16/1**

50-0 **4** hd **Benbrook**[46] 1241 3-9-6 **59** .... IanMongan 16 62
(J L Dunlop) *s.i.s: bhd: rdn and hdwy 2f out: styd on fnl f: nrst fin* **12/1**

-100 **5** 1 1/4 **Strife (IRE)**[2] 2403 3-9-0 **53** .... RichardHughes 10 55+
(R Hannon) *towards rr: rdn and swtchd rt over 1f out: styd on fnl f: nrst fin* **5/1**[1]

1350 **6** shd **Mid Valley**[20] 1888 3-9-0 **53** ....(p) RyanMoore 11 52
(J R Jenkins) *in tch: rdn and effrt 2f out: kpt on same pce* **12/1**

4403 **7** nk **Kasumi**[10] 2171 3-9-3 **61** .... TravisBlock(5) 13 60
(H Morrison) *t.k.h: prom: rdn 2f out: wknd ins fnl f* **15/2**[3]

0-05 **8** hd **Capitalise (IRE)**[6] 2299 3-8-13 **52** .... DarryllHolland 2 50
(V Smith) *towards rr: sme late prog: nvr a danger* **13/2**[2]

00-6 **9** nk **Emily's Pet (IRE)**[44] 1274 3-8-5 **47** .... EdwardCreighton(3) 8 45
(B W Duke) *nvr bttr than mid-div* **25/1**

0-00 **10** shd **Legal Call**[8] 2222 3-7-13 **45** ....(v[1]) LiamJones(7) 4 42
(M Appleby) *t.k.h trcking ldrs: rdn over 2f out: sn one pce* **100/1**

0551 **11** 2 **They All Laughed**[9] 2210 3-9-9 **62** .... RobertMiles 1 55
(P W Hiatt) *a towards rr* **8/1**

00-0 **12** nk **Khyber Knight (IRE)**[24] 1798 3-8-6 **45** .... AdrianMcCarthy 15 37
(Jane Southcombe) *led after 1f: hung rt on home bnd: hdd over 3f out: sn btn* **100/1**

4266 **13** shd **Murrumbidgee (IRE)**[18] 1941 3-9-7 **60** ....(v) EddieAhern 5 52
(J W Hills) *trckd ldrs: rdn whn tight of room 2f out: no imp after* **8/1**

00-0 **14** 5 **In Some Style (IRE)**[13] 2063 3-8-1 **47** .... TolleyDean(7) 3 27
(R A Harris) *mid-div tl wknd 2f out* **40/1**

306- **15** nk **Smoking Star**[215] 6290 3-9-5 **58** .... JohnEgan 12 38
(N I M Rossiter) *a towards rr* **66/1**

1m 40.63s (-0.47) **Going Correction** -0.20s/f (Firm) **15** Ran SP% **114.6**
Speed ratings (Par 97):94,93,93,93,92 91,91,91,91,91 89,88,88,83,83
CSF £178.94 CT £2474.10 TOTE £5.70: £2.10, £5.60, £4.80; EX 109.10 Trifecta £367.90 Part won. Pool £518.20 - 0.60 winning units..
Owner Ladyswood Stud **Bred** T Wada **Trained** Sherston,Wilts
■ Stewards' Enquiry : Eddie Ahern five-day ban (reduced from eight days on appeal; includes three deferred days): improper riding (Jun 25-29)

FOCUS
They finished well bunched in what was just a moderate handicap, and the form seems sound but limited.
Royal Agreement Official explanation: jockey said gelding hung right
Capitalise(IRE) Official explanation: jockey said gelding was denied a clear run
Murrumbidgee(IRE) Official explanation: jockey said gelding was denied a clear run

2480 TOTEQUADPOT H'CAP 1m 2f 46y
3:10 (3:13) (Class 6) (0-65,65) 3-Y-O **£2,914** (£867; £433; £216) **Stalls** Low

Form RPR
-363 **1** **Lester Leaps In (USA)**[19] 1925 3-9-7 **65** .... RyanMoore 6 73+
(R Hannon) *trckd ldrs: led 2f out: kpt on wl: rdn out* **5/2**[1]

30-0 **2** 2 1/2 **Golden Sprite**[18] 1941 3-9-3 **61** .... RobertHavlin 13 64
(B R Millman) *in tch: rdn to chal 2f out: ev ch over 1f out: kpt on* **16/1**

0200 **3** 1/2 **Mighty Dancer (IRE)**[12] 2101 3-9-2 **60** .... EddieAhern 9 62
(S Kirk) *hld up bhd: rdn and no imp over 2f out: styd on fr over 1f out: wnt 3rd fnl stride* **10/1**

006- **4** hd **French Opera**[198] 6424 3-9-3 **61** .... ShaneKelly 11 63+
(J A Osborne) *towards rr: outpcd over 3f out: styd on strly fnl f: nrst fin* **14/1**

0-36 **5** nk **Salvestro**[27] 1738 3-9-5 **63** .... IanMongan 7 64
(Mrs A J Perrett) *hld up bhd: hdwy over 3f out: sn rdn: kpt on same pce* **9/2**[3]

30-6 **6** hd **Snake Skin**[151] 85 3-8-11 **55** .... DavidKinsella 3 56
(J Gallagher) *led for 2f: prom: rdn and ev ch over 1f out: wknd* **20/1**

-220 **7** 2 **Tangarita**[19] 1925 3-9-1 **59** .... RichardHughes 12 56
(A M Balding) *hld up towards rr: sme late prog: nvr trbld ldrs* **4/1**[2]

3100 **8** 1 1/2 **Chookie Windsor**[11] 2131 3-8-11 **55** .... FergusSweeney 5 49
(M S Saunders) *trckd ldr: led after 2f: rdn and hdd 2f out: wknd fnl f* **20/1**

0400 **9** 3/4 **Lenoir (GER)**[46] 1241 3-9-6 **64** ....(v) ChrisCatlin 2 57
(V Smith) *s.i.s: a towards rr* **10/1**

000- **10** 2 1/2 **Tuscany Rose**[257] 5534 3-8-10 **54** ow1 .... DarryllHolland 8 42
(W R Muir) *mid-div tl wknd 1f out* **25/1**

00-0 **11** 5 **Gala Jackpot (USA)**[27] 1736 3-8-4 **48** oh1 ow2 .... JohnEgan 10 26
(W M Brisbourne) *chsd ldrs tl wknd 2f out* **33/1**

2m 8.01s (-2.99) **Going Correction** -0.20s/f (Firm) **11** Ran SP% **113.8**
Speed ratings (Par 97):103,101,100,100,100 100,98,97,96,94 90
CSF £41.13 CT £341.35 TOTE £3.60: £1.40, £3.50, £3.30; EX 50.50 TRIFECTA Not won..
Owner Bob Lalemant **Bred** Morgan's Ford Farm **Trained** East Everleigh, Wilts

FOCUS
A modest handicap, but the winning time was decent for the type of race and the form looks sound with those immediately behind the winner close to form.
Tuscany Rose Official explanation: jockey said filly hung right and did not handle bend

2481 TOTEPOOL "A BETTER WAY TO BET" H'CAP 1m 3f 144y
3:40 (3:41) (Class 6) (0-65,60) 4-Y-O+ **£2,914** (£867; £433; £216) **Stalls** Low

Form RPR
4004 **1** **Madhavi**[25] 1772 4-9-3 **56** .... RichardHughes 6 62
(R Hannon) *mde all: qcknd clr 2f out: kpt on wl: readily* **7/4**[1]

0510 **2** 2 **Ground Patrol**[111] 461 5-9-7 **60** .... RyanMoore 5 63
(G L Moore) *hld up: hdwy over 2f out: sn rdn: styd on to go 2nd fnl f: nt rch wnr* **5/2**[2]

0144 **3** 3/4 **Royal Axminster**[45] 1256 11-8-6 **45** .... RobertHavlin 2 47
(Mrs P N Dutfield) *w wnr: rdn 3f out: kpt on same pce fnl 2f* **5/1**[3]

6300 **4** 3 1/2 **Ulshaw**[13] 2075 9-8-2 **41** oh4 .... ChrisCatlin 4 37
(J M Bradley) *hld up: rdn 3f out: styd on fnl f: nvr trbld ldrs* **10/1**

6136 **5** 2 1/2 **Milk And Sultana**[76] 770 6-8-11 **50** .... EddieAhern 3 42
(G A Ham) *trckd ldrs: rdn 3f out: one pce fnl 2f* **7/1**

0000 **6** 1 **Vandal**[4] 2360 6-7-9 **41** .... LiamJones(7) 1 32
(M Appleby) *trckd ldrs: rdn 3f out: one pce fnl 2f* **14/1**

000- **7** 35 **Bold Arrow**[204] 6387 4-8-2 **41** oh11 .... DavidKinsella 7 —
(B J Llewellyn) *a bhd: t.o fnl 2f* **50/1**

2m 28.99s (-1.31) **Going Correction** -0.20s/f (Firm) **7** Ran SP% **111.8**
Speed ratings (Par 101):96,94,94,91,90 89,66
CSF £5.97 TOTE £2.50: £1.50, £2.00; EX 6.90.
Owner White Beech Farm **Bred** Elsdon Farms **Trained** East Everleigh, Wilts

FOCUS
A moderate handicap in which Madhavi very much enjoyed the run of the race. The form appears sound with the first three to their marks.

2482 TOTESPORT.COM H'CAP 1m 5y
4:10 (4:11) (Class 5) (0-70,72) 4-Y-0+ £4,533 (£1,348; £674; £336) Stalls Low

Form RPR
0-00 1 Bold Diktator[43] [1302] 4-9-5 68 ....(b) EddieAhern 8 78
(W R Muir) racd keenly: trckd ldrs: shkn up to ld 1f out: r.o wl: rdn out 5/1[2]
-650 2 1 1/4 Barons Spy (IRE)[10] [2170] 5-8-7 56 ow1 .... ShaneKelly 9 63
(R J Price) chsd ldrs: led 3f out: rdn and hdd 1f out: kpt on 15/2
-054 3 nk Trevian[6] [2286] 5-8-2 51 oh1 .... RichardThomas 6 57
(J M Bradley) trckd ldrs: rdn over 2f out: kpt on ins fnl f 13/2[3]
0-00 4 hd Adobe[139] [172] 11-8-7 56 .... JohnEgan 5 62
(W M Brisbourne) hld up: rdn over 2f out: hung lft 1f out: styd on ins fnl f 20/1
-002 5 1 1/2 Voice Mail[9] [2186] 7-9-9 72 ....(b) LPKeniry 3 74
(A M Balding) mid-div: rdn and effrt 2f out: kpt on same pce 5/2[1]
3-40 6 nk Prince Of The May[22] [1850] 4-8-5 54 .... ChrisCatlin 10 56
(H Morrison) led tl 3f out: sn one pce 16/1
4/46 7 1/2 Royal Indulgence[27] [1724] 6-7-9 51 oh8 .... LiamJones(7) 11 52
(W M Brisbourne) nvr bttr than mid div 20/1
0-04 8 5 Wind Chime (IRE)[25] [1769] 9-8-10 59 .... FergusSweeney 7 48
(A G Newcombe) in tch: brief effrt over 1f out: sn btn 9/1
0500 9 1/2 Monte Mayor Boy[12] [2098] 4-8-4 53 ....(p) FrankieMcDonald 4 41
(D Haydn Jones) towards rr: brief effrt 2f out 33/1
0-03 10 nk Louve Heureuse (IRE)[40] [1373] 5-8-5 54 .... TQuinn 1 41
(B G Powell) towards rr: rdn 3f out: no imp 16/1
5005 11 1 1/4 The Gaikwar (IRE)[9] [2186] 7-8-11 67 ....(b) TolleyDean(7) 2 51
(R A Harris) a towards rr 7/1

1m 38.87s (-2.23) **Going Correction** -0.20s/f (Firm) 11 Ran SP% 117.1
Speed ratings (Par 103):103,101,101,101,99 99,98,93,93,93 91
CSF £40.91 CT £248.14 TOTE £6.70: £2.00, £4.00, £1.90; EX 93.90 Trifecta £260.50 Pool £513.70. - 1.40 winning units.
Owner Kilmuir Partnership **Bred** T J And Mrs Heywood **Trained** Lambourn, Berks

FOCUS
A modest handicap that seems sound with the third to recent form.
The Gaikwar(IRE) Official explanation: vet said gelding lost a shoe

2483 TOTEEXACTA H'CAP 2m 1f 34y
4:40 (4:40) (Class 6) (0-60,61) 4-Y-0+ £2,914 (£867; £433; £216) Stalls Low

Form RPR
5301 1 Mostarsil (USA)[5] [2320] 8-10-0 61 5ex ....(p) RyanMoore 10 69+
(G L Moore) trckd ldrs: shkn up 3f out: led 2f out: styd on wl 15/8[1]
500- 2 1 1/2 Redspin (IRE)[26] [6612] 6-8-7 40 .... JohnEgan 2 46
(J S Moore) in tch: outpcd 3f out: styd on fr over 1f out: wnt 2nd cl home 13/2[3]
0-00 3 1 Barnbrook Empire (IRE)[4] [2345] 4-8-1 42 .... TolleyDean(7) 11 47
(R A Harris) hld up: hdwy 4f out: rdn to chse wnr 2f out: edgd lft u.p 1f out: no ex 16/1
-006 4 2 1/2 Eamon An Chnoic (IRE)[6] [2305] 5-9-2 52 .... EdwardCreighton(3) 4 54
(B W Duke) mid-div: effrt 3f out: kpt on same pce 10/1
0/05 5 2 1/2 Lets Try Again (IRE)[37] [1415] 9-9-4 51 .... RobertHavlin 7 50
(R A Farrant) trckd ldrs: rdn 3f out: one pce fnl 2f 14/1
5-00 6 2 1/2 Harlestone Linn[39] [1415] 4-9-2 50 .... IanMongan 1 46
(J L Dunlop) trckd ldr: led briefly over 2f out: sn rdn: wknd fnl f 7/1
3205 7 2 1/2 Screen Test[11] [2133] 4-9-7 55 .... EddieAhern 6 48
(B G Powell) slowly away: steadily rcvrd to ld 5f: rdn and hdd over 2f out: sn wknd 5/1[2]
-040 8 16 Gravardlax[26] [1767] 5-7-11 37 oh1 .... DonnaCaldwell(7) 3 11
(Miss D A McHale) a towards rr: lost tch 2f out 66/1
00-0 9 3/4 Paddys Tern[56] [194] 4-9-4 57 .... TravisBlock(5) 8 30
(N M Babbage) led for 5f: trckd ldrs tl wknd over 2f out 14/1
4-06 10 22 So Elegant (IRE)[110] [471] 4-9-4 52 .... ChrisCatlin 5 —
(J Jay) mid-div tl wknd over 2f out 10/1

3m 47.23s (-2.37) **Going Correction** -0.20s/f (Firm)
WFA 4 from 5yo+ 1lb 10 Ran SP% 116.2
Speed ratings (Par 101):97,96,95,94,93 92,91,83,83,72
CSF £14.07 CT £150.38 TOTE £3.00: £1.80, £2.70, £4.10; EX 14.50 Trifecta £143.20 Pool £520.66. - 2.58 winning units.
Owner G A Jackman **Bred** Shadwell Farm Inc **Trained** Woodingdean, E Sussex

FOCUS
A weak staying handicap, the winner being one of few with solid credentials and the form is not worth dwelling on.
So Elegant(IRE) Official explanation: trainer said filly was unsuited by the firm ground

2484 TOTESPORT 0800 221 221 H'CAP 5f 161y
5:10 (5:10) (Class 5) (0-70,70) 3-Y-0+ £3,886 (£1,156; £577; £288) Stalls Low

Form RPR
0020 1 Caustic Wit (IRE)[5] [2331] 8-9-7 63 ....(p) FergusSweeney 1 74
(M S Saunders) a.p: rdn 2f out: led ins fnl f: drvn out 8/1
0213 2 1 Hello Roberto[1] [2462] 5-9-12 68 7ex ....(p) AdrianMcCarthy 12 75
(R A Harris) led: rdn over 1f out: no ex whn hdd ins fnl f 4/1[1]
-400 3 1 Trace Clip[16] [1981] 8-8-10 52 .... JohnEgan 10 56
(N I M Rossiter) dwlt: bhd: rdn and swtchd rt 2f out: styd on to go 3rd cl home: nrst fin 7/1
54-0 4 nk Witchry[134] [224] 4-9-11 70 .... AdamKirby(3) 14 73
(A G Newcombe) prom: rdn 2f out: kpt on same pce fnl f 12/1
650- 5 1 1/4 Convince (USA)[247] [5719] 5-10-0 70 .... RyanMoore 7 69
(J M Bradley) mid-div: rdn 2f out: kpt on same pce: hld whn n.m.r cl home 9/2[2]
6506 6 1/2 Smirfys Party[36] [1481] 8-8-2 51 oh6 ....(p) LiamJones(7) 9 48
(W M Brisbourne) a mid-div 25/1
0050 7 3/4 Coranglais[5] [2331] 6-9-0 56 ....(p) ShaneKelly 5 50
(J M Bradley) a mid-div 5/1[3]
02-0 8 1 Arfinnit (IRE)[27] [1728] 5-8-9 51 oh3 ....(p) EddieAhern 13 42
(Mrs A L M King) mid-div: rdn over 2f out: wknd fnl f 22/1
5000 9 1 1/2 Majestical (IRE)[10] [2182] 4-9-4 60 ....(p) LPKeniry 4 46
(J M Bradley) s.i.s: a towards rr 16/1
000- 10 nk Zimbali[184] [6527] 4-8-10 52 .... ChrisCatlin 6 37
(J M Bradley) chsd ldrs: rdn 3f out: wknd over 1f out 25/1
0045 11 1/2 Devon Ruby[9] [2187] 3-7-10 51 oh6 .... EmmettStack(5) 2 34
(C L Popham) s.i.s and a in rr 33/1
0410 12 3/4 Double M[1] [2444] 9-8-9 51 oh3 ....(v) RichardThomas 3 32
(Mrs L Richards) mid-div tl 2f out 15/2

69.69 secs (-1.51) **Going Correction** -0.20s/f (Firm)
WFA 3 from 4yo+ 8lb 12 Ran SP% 117.8
Speed ratings (Par 103):102,100,99,98,97 96,95,94,92,91 91,90
CSF £37.89 CT £243.09 TOTE £6.90: £1.80, £1.80, £3.60; EX 43.40 Trifecta £447.80 Part won. Pool £630.73. - 0.54 winning units. Place 6 £77.28, Place 5 £28.38..
Owner Mrs Sandra Jones **Bred** Gainsborough Stud Management Ltd **Trained** Green Ore, Somerset

FOCUS
A modest sprint handicap run at a decent pace and the form looks sound.
Trace Clip Official explanation: jockey said gelding missed the break
T/Jkpt: £8,420.90 to a £1 stake. Pool: £100,814.00. 8.50 winning tickets. T/Plt: £141.30 to a £1 stake. Pool: £55,554.60. 286.85 winning tickets. T/Qpdt: £19.50 to a £1 stake. Pool: £3,126.80. 118.30 winning tickets. TM

2485 - 2488a (Foreign Racing) - See Raceform Interactive

2275 CHANTILLY (R-H)
Sunday, June 11

OFFICIAL GOING: Good

2489a PRIX PAUL DE MOUSSAC (EX PRIX DE LA JONCHERE) (GROUP 3) (C&G) 1m
2:10 (2:11) 3-Y-0 £27,586 (£11,034; £8,276; £5,517; £2,759)

RPR
1 Kentucky Dynamite (USA)[34] [1557] 3-8-10 .... C-PLemaire 8 111
(A De Royer-Dupre, France) raced in 2nd, ridden over 1f out, ran on gamely to lead last strides 7/2[1]
2 hd Kendargent (FR)[41] 3-8-10 .... RMarchelli 5 111
(Y Fouin, France) led, ridden approaching final f, headed last strides 20/1
3 1 Racinger (FR)[32] [1600] 3-8-10 .... DBonilla 2 109
(F Head, France) hld up, 6th str on ins, steadily taken to outside fr over 1 1/2f out, stayed on strongly fnl f to take 3rd cl home 6/1
4 1/2 Indianski (IRE)[18] [1944] 3-8-10 .... OPeslier 4 108
(C Laffon-Parias, France) raced in 4th, disputed 2nd 1 1/2f out to inside final f, one pace 9/2[3]
5 2 Beringoer (FR)[32] [1600] 3-8-10 .... TJarnet 3 104
(A Fabre, France) held up in 7th, some late headway to take 5th close home but never a factor 4/1[2]
6 shd Sovereign Dancer (GER)[28] [1715] 3-8-10 .... SPasquier 1 104
(Mario Hofer, Germany) raced in 3rd, one pace final 1 1/2f 7/1
7 1/2 Spirito Del Vento (FR)[24] [1810] 3-8-10 .... CSoumillon 7 103
(J-M Beguigne, France) held up, 6th straight, effort 1 1/2f out, unable to quicken 6/1
8 4 Salsalava (FR)[55] [1064] 3-8-10 .... DBoeuf 6 95
(P Demercastel, France) last throughout 12/1

1m 35.9s **Going Correction** -0.275s/f (Firm) 8 Ran SP% 113.9
Speed ratings: 111,110,109,109,107 107,106,102
PARI-MUTUEL: WIN 3.60; PL 1.50, 2.80, 2.00; DF 33.70.
Owner V Timoshenko **Bred** J S Carrion & Trustee Jr **Trained** Chantilly, France

NOTEBOOK
Kentucky Dynamite(USA) was a little caught for speed early in the straight but stayed on really well at the finish and took the advantage in the final ten yards. This was his first Group success and he is a horse who is very much suited by good or faster ground. A tough individual, the target now is the Prix Jean Prat back over the course and distance next month.
Kendargent(FR) ran a very brave race and tried to make every yard of the running. He quickened things up early in the straight and ran on tenaciously throughout the final furlong. A brave individual, he may well be suited to a softer surface, and he should be capable of taking a race of this category in the future. He is apparently not an easy individual to train, though.
Racinger(FR) settled behind the leaders and was not produced to challenge until halfway up the straight. He made up a lot of late ground, though, and took third place inside the final furlong.
Indianski(IRE) was given a waiting race and made his effort from the two-furlong marker. He still looked dangerous at the furlong pole but was then one-paced as the race drew to an end.

2490a PRIX DU CHEMIN DE FER DU NORD (GROUP 3) 1m
2:45 (2:44) 4-Y-0+ £27,586 (£11,034; £8,276; £5,517; £2,759)

RPR
1 Apsis[45] [1266] 5-8-12 .... CSoumillon 4 115
(A Fabre, France) close up in 4th, headway over 1f out, ridden to lead 130y out, driven out 11/4[2]
2 3/4 Turtle Bowl (IRE)[21] [1873] 4-8-12 .... OPeslier 8 113
(F Rohaut, France) hld up in rr, 6th str, hdwy down outside to disp 2nd with wnr 1f out, stayed on final f, tk 2nd last strides 7/2[3]
3 hd Early March[17] 4-8-12 .... KFallon 6 113
(Mme C Head-Maarek, France) led til headed 130y out, lost 2nd last strides 7/1
4 snk Doctor Dino (FR)[47] 4-8-12 .... TThulliez 7 112
(R Gibson, France) held up in 6th, 5th straight, 6th and not much room approaching final f, stayed on well closing stages 16/1
5 1 1/2 Svedov (FR)[41] [1371] 5-9-0 .... SPasquier 2 111
(E Lellouche, France) racd in 3rd on ins, angling out and n.m.r 1f out, switched back to inside and stayed on closing stages 7/1
6 3/4 Krataios (FR)[21] [1873] 6-9-2 .... MBlancpain 5 111
(C Laffon-Parias, France) raced in 2nd, ridden over 1f out, unable to quicken 9/4[1]
7 1 1/2 Here She Comes (FR)[19] 4-8-8 .... MJKinane 9 100
(Mme C Martens, France) started slowly and behind, went 7th over 2f out, never a factor 66/1
8 3 Quality Special (BRZ)[94] [623] 4-8-7 .... C-PLemaire 3 92
(P Bary, France) 5th halfway, 7th straight, soon beaten 33/1

1m 35.0s **Going Correction** -0.275s/f (Firm) 8 Ran SP% 115.0
Speed ratings: 115,114,114,113,112 111,110,107
PARI-MUTUEL: WIN 2.60 (coupled with Early March); PL 1.30, 1.40, 2.10; DF 5.10.
Owner K Abdulla **Bred** Juddmonte Farms **Trained** Chantilly, France

NOTEBOOK
Apsis, always well placed, progressed from a furlong and a half out up the centre of the track and quickened well inside the final furlong. When he is right this horse is a useful performer, and he will probably now be aimed at the Jacques le Marois at Deauville in August.
Turtle Bowl(IRE) is coming right back to his best form and this race will have put him spot on for the rest of the season. His challenge started from the two-furlong marker up the centre of the track and he was only run out of first place in the dying stages. Not given a hard time by his jockey, the Prix Messidor is now on the cards, followed by the Jacques le Marois.

Early March, who made a brave effort to lead from pillar to post, had a lead of several lengths coming into the straight and then quickened things up again. He rallied bravely on the far side after being headed.
Doctor Dino(FR) did not enjoy the best of runs in the straight. He was given a waiting race and appeared to be going easily halfway up the straight, but there was not much room for him to make his final challenge and he could only stay on when it was all over.

2491a PRIX DE DIANE HERMES (GROUP 1) (FILLIES) 1m 2f 110y

4:35 (4:36) 3-Y-O **£315,255** (£126,124; £36,062; £31,503; £15,779)

RPR

1 **Confidential Lady**[14] [2054] 3-9-0 .... SebSanders 3 116
(Sir Mark Prescott) *hld up, hdwy on ins to go 5th str, swtchd off rail over 2f out, rdn over 1 1/2f out, led 1f out, driven out* **8/1**

2 1 ½ **Germance (USA)**[21] [1874] 3-9-0 .... IMendizabal 15 113
(J-C Rouget, France) *close up on outside, 4th straight, smooth headway to lead 2f out, headed 1f out, one pace* **7/2**[1]

3 nse **Queen Cleopatra (IRE)**[14] [2054] 3-9-0 .... KFallon 4 113
(A P O'Brien, Ire) *midfield on inside, went 2nd entering straight, ridden to press leaders over 1 1/2f out, stayed on* **7/1**

4 2 **Mussoorie (FR)**[28] [1720] 3-9-0 .... TJarnet 8 109
(R Gibson, France) *held up, 9th straight, headway to dispute 3rd over 1 1/2f out, kept on at same pace* **22/1**

5 ¾ **Alix Road (FR)**[21] [1874] 3-9-0 .... OPeslier 5 108
(Mme M Bollack-Badel, France) *in rear early, 11th straight, headway on inside from over 2f out, stayed on at same pace final f* **16/1**

6 nk **Mauralakana (FR)**[28] [1719] 3-9-0 .... TGillet 16 107
(J-C Rouget, France) *held up, 10th straight, headway on outside over 2f out, one pace final f* **20/1**

7 3 **Heaven's Cause (USA)**[25] [1789] 3-9-0 .... TThulliez 1 102+
(N Clement, France) *in rear, 13th straight, not clear run over 1 1/2f out, stayed on from over 1f out but never near leaders* **20/1**

8 ½ **Chaibia (IRE)**[21] [1874] 3-9-0 .... DBoeuf 6 101
(D Smaga, France) *midfield, 8th straight, ridden and not quicken over 1 1/2f out* **66/1**

9 ½ **Grande Melody (IRE)**[28] [1720] 3-9-0 .... C-PLemaire 12 100
(P Bary, France) *in rear, 14th straight, some late headway* **33/1**

10 2 ½ **Alloway**[41] [1370] 3-9-0 .... SPasquier 10 96
(A Fabre, France) *in touch, 7th straight, ridden and beaten 2f out* **9/2**[3]

11 1 ½ **Pearl Sky (FR)**[25] 3-9-0 ....(b) DBonilla 13 93
(Y De Nicolay, France) *started slowly, 12th straight, ridden and edged right over 1/2f out, soon beaten* **50/1**

12 10 **Sanaya (IRE)**[21] [1874] 3-9-0 .... MJKinane 11 75
(A De Royer-Dupre, France) *in touch, 6th straight, beaten 2f out* **10/1**

13 2 ½ **Sirene Doloise (FR)**[42] [1330] 3-9-0 .... J-BEyquem 9 71
(A Bonin, France) *always in rear* **33/1**

14 ¾ **Daltaya (FR)**[28] [1719] 3-9-0 .... CSoumillon 14 69
(A De Royer-Dupre, France) *prominent, led 3f out to 2f out, weakened and eased* **4/1**[2]

15 dist **Danzon (USA)**[42] [1330] 3-9-0 .... MBlancpain 7 —
(J-C Rouget, France) *close up, 4th straight, soon weakened* **16/1**

16 dist **Keladora (USA)**[35] 3-9-0 .... J-RDubosc 2 —
(J-C Rouget, France) *led to 3f out, eased* **200/1**

2m 5.90s **Going Correction** -0.275s/f (Firm) **16** Ran SP% **128.6**
Speed ratings: 105,103,103,102,101 101,99,99,98,96 95,88,86,86,— —
PARI-MUTUEL: WIN 44.30; PL 9.20, 1.70, 4.80; DF 69.00.
Owner Cheveley Park Stud **Bred** Cheveley Park Stud Ltd **Trained** Newmarket, Suffolk
■ A first Classic winner after 36 years with a licence for big handicap specialist Sir Mark Prescott.
■ Stewards' Enquiry : Seb Sanders eight-day ban (June 20-27): excessive use of the whip.

NOTEBOOK

Confidential Lady, tucked in early in mid-division, came under pressure a furlong and a half out but picked up really well, led inside the final furlong, and won the race with a little in hand. After three quickish runs in Classics, she is now likely to be given a rest. Her jockey was suspended for eight days after being deemed to have hit her 32 times in the straight, but it looked nothing like as bad as that suggests.
Germance(USA) was quickly into her stride from her wide draw and it was not long before she settled behind her pacemaker. She hit the front running into the final two furlongs but just flattened as the race came to an end. It was a decent and brave effort, and she is now likely to given a rest. She will probably stay 12 furlongs in time.
Queen Cleopatra(IRE), another smartly out of the stalls, settled on the inside in third position early on. She lengthened her stride when things warmed up - nearly taking the lead a furlong and a half out - and battled on courageously to the line.
Mussoorie(FR), who had plenty to do when the field came into the straight, began her run from a furlong and a half out. Staying on up the centre of the track, she was a little one-paced in the latter stages.

DORTMUND (R-H)

Sunday, June 11

OFFICIAL GOING: Good

2492a GROSSER PREIS DER WIRTSCHAFT (GROUP 3) 1m 165y

4:15 (4:22) 3-Y-O+ **£22,069** (£6,897; £3,448; £2,069)

RPR

1 **Lord Of England (GER)**[28] [1715] 3-8-5 ow3........ AStarke 1 115
(Mario Hofer, Germany) *always close up, 3rd straight, led over 1f out, ran on strongly* **7/10**[1]

2 3 ½ **Lazio (GER)**[21] [1869] 5-9-2 .... ADeVries 5 107
(A Trybuhl, Germany) *hld up in rr, hdwy ent str, stayed on while hanging lft throughout fnl 2f to tk 2nd cl home* **5/1**[3]

3 nk **Willingly (GER)**[21] [1869] 7-9-2 .... FilipMinarik 7 106
(M Trybuhl, Germany) *raced in 5th, 4th straight, chased winner 1f out, lost 2nd close home* **33/10**[2]

4 5 **Billy Allen (IRE)**[30] [1659] 5-9-2 .... FSpanu 4 97
(F Chappet, France) *held up in 6th, stayed on at one pace final 2f but never near leaders* **61/10**

5 5 **Genios (GER)**[329] [3576] 5-9-2 .... ABoschert 3 87
(Dr A Bolte, Germany) *raced in 3rd, 5th straight, soon ridden and beaten* **9/1**

6 1 ½ **Marshall (FR)**[315] [3988] 6-9-0 .... MLarsen 8 83
(S Jensen, Denmark) *prominent til led 4f out, headed over 1f out, weakened quickly* **195/10**

7 2 **Last Action Hero (GER)**[210] 4-9-0 .... THellier 6 79
(N Sauer, Germany) *led to 4f out, 2nd straight, weakened 1 1/2f out* **183/10**

WFA 3 from 4yo+ 12lb **7** Ran SP% **132.9**
(including 10 euro stake): WIN 17.00; PL 11.00, 12.00, 12.00; SF 55.00.
Owner Stall Lucky Owner **Bred** Stall Pontresini **Trained** Germany

2474 SAN SIRO (R-H)

Sunday, June 11

OFFICIAL GOING: Good

2493a PREMIO BELGIRATE 5f 110y

5:10 (5:15) 3-Y-O **£6,897** (£3,034; £1,655; £828)

RPR

1 **My Sea Of Love**[274] [5143] 3-8-8 .... EBotti 8 101
(A & G Botti, Italy)

2 nse **Maturus Ardor (GER)** 3-8-8 .... J-PCarvalho 4 101
(Mario Hofer, Germany)

3 5 **Miss Lorella (IRE)**[28] [1713] 3-8-8 .... MMonteriso 5 84
(M Grassi, Italy)

4 ½ **My Mystic (USA)** 3-8-8 .... FBranca 1 82
(L Brogi, Italy)

5 3 **Miss Zoe** 3-8-8 .... MEsposito 11 72
(V Caruso, Italy)

6 1 ½ **Hosiva (GER)**[18] [1942] 3-8-13 .... APolli 2 73
(M G Quinlan) *always mid division (72/10)* **72/10**[1]

7 5 **Gamera (IRE)** 3-8-13 .... DPorcu 6 56
(Laura Grizzetti, Italy)

8 ¾ **Noble Twining (USA)**[347] [3033] 3-8-8 .... LManiezzi 3 49
(R Menichetti, Italy)

9 2 **Larione (IRE)** 3-8-5 .... DVargiu 7 39
(M Gasparini, Italy)

10 dist **Madan Di San Jore (IRE)** 3-8-8 .... PConvertino 12 —
(M Marcialis, Italy)

1m 33.8s **10** Ran SP% **12.2**
(including 1 Euro stake): WIN 11.28; PL 1.78, 1.23, 1.30; DF 14.48.
Owner Scuderia Dioscuri **Bred** Gainsborough Stud Management Ltd **Trained** Italy

NOTEBOOK

Hosiva(GER) could not raise her game in the final quarter mile and was well beaten.

2231 FOLKESTONE (R-H)

Monday, June 12

OFFICIAL GOING: Good to firm (firm in places)

Wind: Almost nil Weather: Sunny and very warm

2494 KMFM YOLANDE HEDGES H'CAP 5f

2:15 (2:17) (Class 6) (0-60,55) 3-Y-O+ **£2,730** (£806; £403) **Stalls** Low

Form RPR

005/ 1 **Millfields Dreams**[611] [6058] 7-9-0 **46** ow1........ JerryO'Dwyer[(5)] 8 58
(M G Quinlan) *trckd ldng pair: led wl over 1f out: rdn and styd on wl fnl f* **14/1**

1-06 2 1 ½ **Montillia (IRE)**[136] [216] 4-9-9 **50**........ AlanMunro 7 56
(C F Wall) *mde most to wl over 1f out: kpt on same pce u.p* **10/1**[3]

140- 3 shd **Flying Tackle**[274] [5147] 8-9-9 **50**........(v) RoystonFfrench 4 56
(I W McInnes) *cl up: rdn 2f out: nt qckn over 1f out: racd against nr side rail and styd on fnl f* **12/1**

0000 4 nk **Pro Tempore**[20] [1913] 4-9-2 **46**........ NeilChalmers[(3)] 3 51
(David Pinder) *chsd ldng gp: effrt over 1f out: kpt on same pce last 150yds* **10/1**[3]

50-0 5 ¾ **Heavens Walk**[40] [1414] 5-9-6 **50**........(t) AmirQuinn[(3)] 13 52+
(P J Makin) *s.s: wl in rr: swtchd to outer and effrt wl over 1f out : styd on: nrst fin* **12/1**

2303 6 ½ **Enjoy The Buzz**[4] [2376] 7-9-13 **54**........ RyanMoore 10 54+
(J M Bradley) *wl in rr: effrt towards outer fr 2f out: kpt on: nvr rchd ldrs* **11/4**[1]

-000 7 shd **Jasmine Pearl (IRE)**[35] [1534] 5-8-13 **40**........ HayleyTurner 2 40
(T M Jones) *trckd ldng gp and racd against nr side rail: nt clr run over 2f out to over 1f out: effrt sn after: one pce last 150yds* **28/1**

0104 8 1 ¼ **Chantelle's Dream**[5] [2347] 4-9-5 **49**........ AdamKirby[(3)] 11 44+
(Ms J S Doyle) *taken down early and fractious: dwlt: racd on outer and wl off the pce : plugged on fnl 2f: nvr able to chal* **14/1**

03-0 9 3 **Elvina**[10] [2207] 5-9-13 **54**........ LDettori 1 38
(A G Newcombe) *racd against nr side rail: w ldr for 2f: losing pl whn hmpd 2f out* **10/3**[2]

000/ 10 1 **Royal Supremacy (IRE)**[671] [4622] 5-9-1 **42**........ ChrisCatlin 5 22
(J M Bradley) *chsd ldrs: effrt and cl up 2f out: wknd rapidly fnl f* **25/1**

0-04 11 nk **Xaar Breeze**[76] [786] 3-8-2 **36**........ FrancisFerris 6 15
(Mrs P Townsley) *dwlt: wl in rr: effrt towards outer 2f out: hanging and sn wknd* **50/1**

-450 12 2 **Great Belief (IRE)**[12] [2136] 4-10-0 **55**........ TQuinn 12 27
(T D McCarthy) *wnt rt s: racd on outer and nvr on terms: wknd fnl f* **12/1**

0-00 13 shd **Italian Mist (FR)**[12] [2141] 7-8-9 **36** oh1........ EddieAhern 9 7
(R M H Cowell) *chsd ldng gp and racd towards outer: hanging bdly and wknd over 1f out* **28/1**

0000 14 nk **Enchanting Times (IRE)**[8] [2260] 3-9-7 **55**........(v) MickyFenton 14 25
(D G Bridgwater) *racd on wd outside: nvr on terms* **66/1**

60.19 secs (-0.61) **Going Correction** -0.225s/f (Firm)
WFA 3 from 4yo+ 7lb **14** Ran SP% **118.5**
Speed ratings (Par 101):95,92,92,91,90 89,89,87,83,81 80,77,77,77
CSF £138.50 CT £1740.71 TOTE £19.60: £6.80, £3.50, £3.30; EX 283.70 TRIFECTA Not won..
Owner R J King **Bred** T G Price **Trained** Newmarket, Suffolk
■ The frist winner in Britain for Jerry O'Dwyer, following 40 in Ireland.
■ Stewards' Enquiry : Amir Quinn one-day ban: careless riding (Jun 25)
Francis Ferris one-day ban: careless riding (Jun 25)

FOCUS

A poor handicap, but the form seems sound enough and it should produce the odd winner at a similar level.
Jasmine Pearl(IRE) Official explanation: jockey said mare lost its action
Chantelle's Dream Official explanation: trainer said filly was unsuited by the track

Elvina Official explanation: trainer said mare was unsuited by the track
Great Belief(IRE) Official explanation: jockey said gelding never travelled and hung right

2495 HOBBS PARKER TELECOM (S) STKS — 5f
2:45 (2:45) (Class 6) 2-Y-O — **£2,730** (£806; £403) **Stalls** Low

Form — RPR

3540 **1** **Queen Of Narnia**[6] [2315] 2-8-9 .... ChrisCatlin 4 — 61
(M R Channon) *racd against nr side rail: mde most: hrd pressed last 150yds: hld on wl* **5/2**[2]

30 **2** *nk* **Peggys Flower**[6] [2315] 2-8-9 .... LDettori 1 — 60
(N A Callaghan) *hld up in tch: effrt to chse wnr 1f out: str chal: a jst hld* **4/6**[1]

600 **3** *5* **Cyprus Rose**[5] [2346] 2-8-6 .... AdamKirby(3) 5 — 40
(V Smith) *w wnr to over 1f out: wknd fnl f* **16/1**

006 **4** *2 ½* **Lenard Frank (IRE)**[14] [2064] 2-9-0 .... (v) HayleyTurner 3 — 35
(M D I Usher) *t.k.h early: hld up bhd ldrs: wknd 2f out* **66/1**

0623 **5** *3 ½* **Circle Of Truth**[28] [1744] 2-9-0 .... RobertMiles 2 — 21
(W G M Turner) *dwlt: a last: wknd 2f out* **8/1**[3]

60.86 secs (0.06) **Going Correction** -0.225s/f (Firm) — 5 Ran SP% **107.0**
Speed ratings (Par 91):90,89,81,77,71
CSF £4.27 TOTE £3.60: £1.60, £1.20; EX 6.70.The winner was bought in for 5,000gns. Peggys Flower was the subject of a friendly claim.
Owner Capital **Bred** Peter Taplin **Trained** West Ilsley, Berks

FOCUS
Not a bad seller and the front two came clear.

NOTEBOOK
Queen Of Narnia has hardly been progressive and it was no surprise to see her dropped into this grade in a bid to get off the mark. Soon in front on the stands' side, she resisted the strong, persistent challenge of hot favourite Peggy's Flower and fully deserved the win. She and the favourite were clear of the third and there could be more to come from her in nurseries. (op 15-8)
Peggys Flower was solid in the market and expected to capitalise on this drop in grade, but she was unable to get by the winner having come through to challenge. She was clear of the third though and should have little trouble landing a race at this sort of level. (op 8-11)
Cyprus Rose had previously shown little and, although showing up well to a point here, she ended up being comfortably held. (op 20-1)
Lenard Frank(IRE) has not improved for a visor and he failed to get home having raced keenly. (op 100-1)
Circle Of Truth has looked better on the All-Weather to date and this was a poor effort, always struggling in last. (op 9-1)

2496 WILLIAM HILL FOR WORLD CUP BETTING H'CAP — 6f
3:15 (3:17) (Class 4) (0-85,83) 3-Y-O — **£6,477** (£1,927; £963; £481) **Stalls** Low

Form — RPR

2010 **1** **Didn't We (IRE)**[16] [2014] 3-9-7 **83** .... (v) IanMongan 2 — 87
(T G Mills) *racd against nr side rail: mde virtually all: hrd rdn fnl 2f: looked sure to be ct fnl f: kpt battling and jst hld on* **7/4**[1]

-521 **2** *shd* **Yellow Card**[9] [2235] 3-8-11 **73** .... LDettori 4 — 77
(N A Callaghan) *hld up in last: effrt 1f out: got through to press wnr last 75yds: jst failed* **11/4**[2]

013 **3** *nk* **Patavium Prince (IRE)**[6] [2318] 3-8-7 **69** .... TQuinn 1 — 75+
(J R Best) *trckd ldrs: cruising but nowhere to go fr wl over 1f out: swtchd rt and hmpd ins fnl f: nt qckn nr fin* **7/2**[3]

-334 **4** *nk* **Guilded Warrior**[25] [1801] 3-8-6 **68** .... (v[1]) AlanMunro 3 — 70
(W S Kittow) *chsd ldrs: pushed along over 2f out: chal u.p 1f out: upsides last 100yds: no ex nr fin* **11/2**

30-0 **5** *1* **Vegas Boys**[42] [1337] 3-9-0 **76** .... ChrisCatlin 5 — 75
(N A Callaghan) *w wnr: rdn over 1f out: stl upsides 100yds out: n.m.r and wknd* **10/1**

0360 **6** *8* **Smooch**[15] [2049] 3-9-3 **79** .... RyanMoore 6 — 54
(R M H Cowell) *racd on outer: in tch: rdn 1/2-way: wknd wl over 1f out* **16/1**

1m 11.96s (-1.64) **Going Correction** -0.225s/f (Firm) — 6 Ran SP% **115.6**
Speed ratings (Par 101):101,100,100,100,98 88
CSF £7.14 TOTE £2.70: £1.30, £1.40; EX 7.90.
Owner T G Mills **Bred** Mrs John McEnery **Trained** Headley, Surrey

FOCUS
A really competitive sprint handicap, despite the small field, and the average pace ensured it was a bunch finish. The first fivem were close to their pre-race marks.

2497 BET ON ENGLAND @ WILLIAM HILL H'CAP — 1m 4f
3:45 (3:45) (Class 6) (0-60,57) 4-Y-0+ — **£2,730** (£806; £403) **Stalls** Low

Form — RPR

0330 **1** **Icannshift (IRE)**[8] [2262] 6-8-9 **48** .... NeilChalmers(3) 11 — 56
(T M Jones) *trckd ldng pair: effrt 2f out: led on inner jst over 1f out: rdn out* **6/1**[3]

/00- **2** *¾* **Palace Walk (FR)**[9] [505] 4-9-7 **57** .... TQuinn 12 — 64
(B G Powell) *led: kicked on 3f out: rdn and hdd jst over 1f out: nt qckn* **5/1**[2]

0460 **3** *shd* **Lenwade**[12] [2132] 5-8-6 **42** .... JimmyQuinn 8 — 49
(G G Margarson) *chsd ldrs: rdn wl over 2f out: r.o fr over 1f out: gaining at fin* **6/1**[3]

0/00 **4** *2 ½* **Chimes At Midnight (USA)**[2] [2460] 9-8-6 **42** .... EddieAhern 6 — 45+
(Luke Comer, Ire) *hld up in last: stl in detached last pair 3f out: hrd rdn 2f out: r.o strly fnl f: hopeless task* **8/1**

0-00 **5** *½* **Cantrip**[12] [2133] 6-9-6 **56** .... StephenCarson 10 — 58
(Miss B Sanders) *trckd ldr: rdn to chal 2f out: wknd over 1f out* **13/2**

2340 **6** *¾* **Lysander's Quest (IRE)**[6] [2320] 8-8-7 **43** .... ChrisCatlin 5 — 44
(R Ingram) *trckd ldrs: rdn 3f out: nt qckn and outpcd sn after: kpt on* **9/2**[1]

00-0 **7** *5* **Expression Echo (IRE)**[140] [172] 4-8-9 **45** .... LPKeniry 9 — 38
(A G Newcombe) *hld up wl in rr: sme prog on inner over 2f out but nt on terms: flashed tail u.p and no hdwy over 1f out* **20/1**

000- **8** *½* **Liameliss**[265] [5389] 4-8-2 **45** .... JosephWalsh(7) 4 — 37
(M A Allen) *racd on outer in midfield: pushed along 5f out: struggling over 2f out* **40/1**

/00- **9** *hd* **Loitokitok**[267] [5173] 4-9-0 **50** .... TPQueally 1 — 42
(P D Cundell) *hld up wl in rr: shkn up briefly 1f out: nvr nr ldrs* **33/1**

000- **10** *1 ½* **Lasting Image**[296] [4583] 4-7-9 **38** oh4.......... LiamJones(7) 2 — 27
(S C Williams) *chsd ldrs: rdn 3f out: sn lost pl and btn* **25/1**

240- **11** *¾* **Tojoneski**[180] [6575] 7-8-10 **46** .... RoystonFfrench 3 — 34
(I W McInnes) *hld up in rr: nt clr run over 3f out: sme prog on inner 2f out but no ch: wknd fnl f* **16/1**

0000 **12** *1 ½* **My Boo**[34] [1562] 4-8-4 **40** .... (bt) AlanMunro 7 — 26
(T Keddy) *lost pl after 3f: nvr beyond midfield after: dropped to last pair and struggling 4f out* **16/1**

2m 37.89s (-2.61) **Going Correction** -0.225s/f (Firm) — 12 Ran SP% **113.6**
Speed ratings (Par 101):99,98,98,96,96 95,92,92,92,91 90,89
CSF £32.84 CT £186.89 TOTE £7.70: £2.60, £2.10, £2.70; EX 47.40 Trifecta £90.80 Pool: £307.22 - 2.40 winning tickets..
Owner Mrs R A Jennings **Bred** Piercetown Stud **Trained** Albury Heath, Surrey

FOCUS
Weak form but reasonable for the grade.
Tojoneski Official explanation: jockey said gelding hung right throughout

2498 BET ON GOALS @ WILLIAMHILL.CO.UK MEDIAN AUCTION MAIDEN STKS — 1m 1f 149y
4:15 (4:17) (Class 6) 3-4-Y-O — **£3,238** (£963; £481; £240) **Stalls** Low

Form — RPR

0064 **1** **Nefski Alexander (USA)**[13] [2118] 3-8-11 77.......... EddieAhern 9 — 73
(P F I Cole) *trckd ldrs: rdn to chse ldr over 2f out: styd on to ld last 100yds: hld on* **6/4**[1]

05 **2** *hd* **Art Man**[16] [2028] 3-8-11 .... JimCrowley 1 — 73
(Mrs A J Perrett) *trckd ldrs: rdn and effrt over 2f out: styd on fr over 1f out: tk 2nd nr fin: jst hld* **7/2**[3]

-022 **3** *½* **Apt To Run (USA)**[18] [1946] 3-8-11 72.......... (b) RichardMullen 3 — 72
(E A L Dunlop) *led for 2f: trckd ldr: led over 3f out and kicked 3 l clr: hrd rdn over 1f out: hdd last 100yds* **13/8**[2]

0 **4** *6* **Indian Pride**[21] [1901] 4-9-5 .... JimmyQuinn 5 — 57
(D J Coakley) *dwlt and rousted along s: sme prog fr rr 4f out: sn outpcd: chsd clr ldng trio 2f out: no imp* **16/1**

U0 **5** *½* **Lucy Babe**[7] [2291] 3-7-13 .... LiamJones(7) 2 — 55?
(G Prodromou) *settled off the pce in rr: outpcd over 3f out: shkn up 2f out: kpt on one pce* **66/1**

000- **6** *8* **Soviet Promise (IRE)**[279] [5029] 3-8-6 45.......... RoystonFfrench 7 — 39
(G G Margarson) *chsd ldrs: rdn 4f out: wknd wl over 2f out* **33/1**

7 *27* **Pinky** 3-8-6 .... TQuinn 10 — —
(B J McMath) *s.s: rn green: a bhd: lost tch 4f out: t.o* **40/1**

8 *40* **Flying Venture (IRE)** 4-9-5 .... MickyFenton 6 — —
(B J McMath) *t.k.h: led after 2f to over 3f out: wknd: virtually p.u over 1f out: lame* **66/1**

2m 3.23s (-2.00) **Going Correction** -0.225s/f (Firm)
WFA 3 from 4yo 13lb — 8 Ran SP% **114.6**
Speed ratings (Par 101):99,98,98,93,93 86,65,33
CSF £7.14 TOTE £2.60: £1.10, £1.50, £1.10; EX 8.60 Trifecta £13.30 Pool: £585.34 - 31.18 winning tickets..
Owner Lukis Joakim **Bred** Robert S Folsom **Trained** Whatcombe, Oxon

FOCUS
Only three ever really counted and they finished clear of the fourth. The winner and third set the standard.
Pinky Official explanation: jockey said filly was slowly away and never travelled
Flying Venture(IRE) Official explanation: jockey said filly hung badly left and had no steering

2499 WILLIAM HILL WORLD CUP WINNERS H'CAP — 1m 1f 149y
4:45 (4:46) (Class 5) (0-70,70) 4-Y-O+ — **£3,238** (£963; £481; £240) **Stalls** Low

Form — RPR

0005 **1** **Billy One Punch**[6] [2327] 4-8-7 **56** .... TQuinn 6 — 64
(G G Margarson) *trckd ldr after 3f: led over 5f out: in command fnl 2f: drvn out* **7/2**[2]

-415 **2** *1 ¼* **Fantasy Crusader**[3] [2401] 7-8-3 **52** .... RoystonFfrench 1 — 58
(R M H Cowell) *hld up in tch: effrt over 3f out: drvn to chse wnr 2f out: kpt on but no real imp* **9/2**[3]

6-01 **3** *1* **Catskill**[12] [2149] 4-9-7 **70** .... AlanMunro 4 — 74
(E F Vaughan) *trckd ldrs: rdn and hanging over 2f out: disp 2nd 2f out: one pce after* **5/2**[1]

-001 **4** *1* **Danish Monarch**[41] [1373] 5-8-5 **54** .... ChrisCatlin 3 — 56
(David Pinder) *led for 1f: chsd ldrs: drvn to dispute 2nd 2f out: nt qckn and no imp after* **12/1**

-050 **5** *nk* **Linda's Colin (IRE)**[11] [2170] 4-9-0 **63** .... AdrianMcCarthy 7 — 64
(R A Harris) *hld up in last trio: effrt 3f out: one pce u.p* **8/1**

0040 **6** *1* **Monash Lad (IRE)**[3] [2401] 4-8-11 **67** .... PatrickHills(7) 8 — 67
(M H Tompkins) *hld up in tch: lost pl 4f out: brought to wd outside 2f out: one pce* **14/1**

6126 **7** *¾* **Christmas Truce (IRE)**[6] [2327] 7-8-12 **64** .... (b[1]) AdamKirby(3) 2 — 62
(Ms J S Doyle) *led after 1f to over 5f out: chsd wnr to 2f out: wknd* **15/2**

5600 **8** *5* **Consonant (IRE)**[10] [2186] 9-9-3 **66** .... MickyFenton 5 — 55
(D G Bridgwater) *hld up in last: effrt over 3f out: wknd wl over 1f out* **10/1**

2m 1.49s (-3.74) **Going Correction** -0.225s/f (Firm) — 8 Ran SP% **115.3**
Speed ratings (Par 103):105,104,103,102,102 101,100,96
CSF £19.85 CT £45.42 TOTE £4.60: £1.80, £1.10, £1.40; EX 18.80 Trifecta £72.60 Pool: £447.34 - 4.37 winning tickets. Place 6 £18.84, Place 5 £2.45.
Owner Norcroft Park Stud **Bred** Norcroft Park Stud, And A J Hollis **Trained** Newmarket, Suffolk

FOCUS
Moderate handicap form and despite the decent time unlikely to prove solid.
Christmas Truce(IRE) Official explanation: jockey said gelding ran flat
T/Plt: £38.30 to a £1 stake. Pool: £38,092.20. 725.25 winning tickets. T/Qpdt: £3.60 to a £1 stake. Pool: £3,305.50. 673.40 winning tickets. JN

1996 PONTEFRACT (L-H)
Monday, June 12

OFFICIAL GOING: Good to firm
The running rail was again in place. The track had missed the thunder rain and the ground was reckoned to be ' quick, firm in places'.
Wind: Almost nil. Weather: Fine and sunny

2500 RENAULT VANS MAIDEN AUCTION FILLIES' STKS — 6f
6:45 (6:45) (Class 5) 2-Y-O — **£3,886** (£1,156; £577; £288) **Stalls** Low

Form — RPR

24 **1** **Pretty Majestic (IRE)**[13] [2106] 2-8-7 .... EdwardCreighton(3) 4 — 85+
(M R Channon) *trckd ldrs: shkn up and qcknd to ld 1f out: pushed clr* **2/1**[1]

043 **2** *3* **Angeletta**[16] [2026] 2-8-4 .... JoeFanning 10 — 70
(E S McMahon) *led tl 1f out: sn wl outpcd by wnr* **8/1**[3]

66 **3** *1 ¾* **Bahamian Love**[25] [1796] 2-8-4 .... JohnEgan 7 — 65
(B W Hills) *mid-div: hdwy and hung lft over 1f out: styd on fnl f* **5/2**[2]

6 **4** ½ **Mickleberry (IRE)**[12] 2139 2-8-5 ow1 GrahamGibbons 1 64
(J D Bethell) *w ldrs: led 2f out tl 1f out: fdd* **25/1**

5 3 **Namarian (IRE)** 2-8-6 DavidAllan 9 56+
(T D Easterby) *s.s: bhd: plld outside over 1f out: styd on steadily* **16/1**

6 3½ **Silver Appraisal** 2-8-6 PhilipRobinson 2 46
(B Smart) *sn outpcd and in rr: sme hdwy 2f out: nvr a factor* **10/1**

7 1¼ **Julatten (IRE)** 2-8-6 RobertWinston 6 42
(G A Swinbank) *trckd ldrs: stmbld 3f out: lost pl over 1f out* **17/2**

8 2 **Wakeys Wizzard** 2-8-5 ow1 NeilPollard 8 35
(M E Sowersby) *s.i.s: a bhd* **100/1**

9 6 **Mamora Reef** 2-8-4 PaulMulrennan 3 16
(J R Weymes) *w ldrs: wknd over 1f out* **20/1**

10 8 **Lady Toyah (IRE)** 2-8-4 PaulHanagan 5 —
(Mrs L Williamson) *s.i.s: a bhd* **50/1**

1m 16.55s (-0.85) **Going Correction** -0.20s/f (Firm) **10** Ran SP% **110.1**
Speed ratings (Par 90):97,93,90,90,86 81,79,77,69,58
CSF £16.70 TOTE £2.60: £1.20, £1.60, £1.70; EX 19.30.
Owner Jaber Abdullah **Bred** Peter Gibbons And Dermot Forde **Trained** West Ilsley, Berks

FOCUS
Almost certainly a weak maiden auction fillies' race but a ready winner and the second sets the standard.

NOTEBOOK
Pretty Majestic(IRE), who looked very fit indeed, floated across the firm ground on the way down. She travelled easily and lengthened well to go clear when given the office. (op 9-4 tchd 5-2 in a place)
Angeletta, who made little appeal in the paddock, found the totally different ground no problem but in the end she was left for dead by the winner. (tchd 17-2)
Bahamian Love looked to be feeling the ground when called on for an effort but she stayed on nicely at the end. This will set her up for a seven-furlong nursery. (tchd 11-4 and 3-1 in a place)
Mickleberry(IRE) took it up turning in but did not see it out up this uphill finish.
Namarian(IRE), a February foal, is on the leg and weak at present. After a slow break she turned in second last but, pulled wide, she came home in fine style and will improve a good deal in time.
Silver Appraisal, a February foal, was very green to post. Hopefully this will have taught her something. (op 7-1)
Julatten(IRE), a February foal, is on the leg and narrow. She lost her footing for a few strides around the halfway mark and dropped right away once in line for home. She will need more time yet. (op 12-1 tchd 8-1)

2501 TONY BETHELL MEMORIAL H'CAP 2m 1f 22y
7:15 (7:15) (Class 4) (0-80,75) 4-Y-0+ **£6,477** (£1,927; £963; £481) **Stalls** Low

Form RPR
24/4 **1** **Full House (IRE)**[11] 2176 7-9-11 **75** KDarley 8 81
(P R Webber) *hld up in tch: hdwy over 5f out: wnt 2nd 2f out: styd on gamely to ld nr fin* **11/4**[1]

0114 **2** nk **Prairie Sun (GER)**[27] 1758 5-9-5 **74** GregFairley(5) 7 80
(Mrs A Duffield) *trckd ldr: led 3f out: hdd nr fin* **9/2**[2]

6-00 **3** 2½ **Mister Arjay (USA)**[6] 2326 6-8-10 **60** PatCosgrave 9 63
(B Ellison) *chsd ldrs: hrd drvn 6f out: outpcd over 2f out: styd on fnl f* **16/1**

030 **4** ½ **Openide**[13] 2118 5-9-0 **67** EdwardCreighton(3) 2 69
(B W Duke) *t.k.h in rr: hdwy 6f out: kpt on same pce fnl 2f* **12/1**

5034 **5** 5 **College Rebel**[10] 2196 5-7-13 **56** oh8 KevinGhunowa(7) 3 52
(J F Coupland) *t.k.h: trckd ldrs: wknd over 1f out* **16/1**

0041 **6** shd **Haatmey**[14] 2078 4-9-6 **71** SamHitchcott 4 67
(M R Channon) *hld up in rr: hdwy u.p 5f out: sn chsng ldrs: wknd appr fnl f* **9/2**[2]

0215 **7** 16 **Linden Lime**[30] 1690 4-8-9 **60** JohnEgan 1 37
(Jamie Poulton) *hld up in rr: hdwy over 4f out: lost pl over 1f out* **9/2**[2]

06-0 **8** 11 **Moonshine Beach**[9] 2219 8-9-9 **73** DarrenWilliams 5 36
(P W Hiatt) *led: qcknd 6f out: hdd 3f out: sn lost pl* **10/1**[3]

030- **9** 45 **Piccolomini**[245] 5797 4-8-11 **62** TonyHamilton 6 —
(E W Tuer) *trckd ldrs: t.k.h: lost pl 5f out: t.o 2f out* **25/1**

3m 49.22s (-1.28) **Going Correction** -0.20s/f (Firm)
WFA 4 from 5yo+ 1lb **9** Ran SP% **113.6**
Speed ratings (Par 105):95,94,93,93,91 91,83,78,57
CSF £14.68 CT £162.31 TOTE £3.70: £1.60, £2.00, £2.80; EX 16.50.
Owner The Chamberlain Addiscott Partnership **Bred** Schwindibode Ag **Trained** Mollington, Oxon

FOCUS
A very steady gallop until the final three-quarters of a mile. The winner saw the trip out just the better under a strong ride, but the proximity of the fifth limits the form .

2502 DIXONS RENAULT H'CAP 1m 2f 6y
7:45 (7:45) (Class 4) (0-85,84) 3-Y-0 **£6,477** (£1,927; £963; £481) **Stalls** Low

Form RPR
3-21 **1** **Formal Decree (GER)**[17] 1999 3-9-1 **78** NCallan 7 98+
(G A Swinbank) *hld up: effrt on outside 4f out: hung lft and led wl over 1f out: sn wnt clr: eased towards fin* **9/4**[1]

13-6 **2** 6 **Road To Love (IRE)**[9] 2224 3-9-7 **84** KDarley 8 91
(M Johnston) *trckd ldrs: led briefly 2f out: kpt on: no ch w wnr* **7/2**[2]

0-02 **3** nk **Nesno (USA)**[14] 2081 3-8-11 **74** GrahamGibbons 6 80
(J D Bethell) *trckd ldrs: hdwy to chse ldrs whn hmpd 2f out: kpt on wl fnl f* **9/2**[3]

-640 **4** shd **Truly Fruitful (IRE)**[6] 2324 3-8-7 **70** PatCosgrave 3 76
(K R Burke) *trckd ldrs: styd on same pce appr fnl f* **18/1**

0315 **5** 5 **Methusaleh (IRE)**[9] 2239 3-9-2 **79** DavidAllan 4 76
(T D Easterby) *in rr: hrd drvn over 4f out: kpt on fnl f: nvr on terms* **20/1**

22-3 **6** 1¼ **Pigeon Island**[35] 1546 3-9-1 **78** FergusSweeney 5 72
(H Candy) *led tl hdd & wknd 2f out* **11/2**

1-10 **7** 28 **George's Flyer (IRE)**[128] 294 3-8-3 **66** (b) PaulHanagan 2 7
(R A Fahey) *hld up: hmpd bnd over 6f out: hrd drvn 3f out: sn lost pl and bhd: eased* **25/1**

4-1 **8** ½ **Oscillator**[44] 1306 3-9-0 **77** NickyMackay 1 17
(G A Butler) *in rr: pushed through on inner bnd over 6f out: hrd drvn over 4f out: lost pl over 2f out: sn bhd and eased* **8/1**

2m 9.55s (-4.53) **Going Correction** -0.20s/f (Firm) **8** Ran SP% **111.5**
Speed ratings (Par 101):110,105,104,104,100 99,77,77
CSF £9.57 CT £30.20 TOTE £3.30: £1.30, £1.40, £2.00; EX 9.10.
Owner Mrs Karen S Pratt **Bred** Gestut Olympia **Trained** Melsonby, N Yorks

FOCUS
A decent handicap for the grade and no hanging about, but in the end a wide-margin winner. Nesno looked second best on the night and the form appears solid, rated through the runner-up and fourth.
George's Flyer(IRE) Official explanation: vet said colt finished distressed
Oscillator Official explanation: jockey said colt was unsuited by the good to firm ground

2503 WEATHERBYS BANK PIPALONG STKS (LISTED RACE) (F&M) 1m 4y
8:15 (8:15) (Class 1) 4-Y-0+ **£19,631** (£7,472; £3,741; £1,869; £934) **Stalls** Low

Form RPR
-055 **1** **Bahia Breeze**[10] 2199 4-8-12 100 RobertWinston 1 96
(Rae Guest) *w ldr: led over 2f out: hld on towards fin* **5/4**[1]

11/6 **2** ½ **Mamela (GER)**[36] 1506 5-8-12 98 NickyMackay 2 94
(L M Cumani) *trckd ldrs: effrt over 2f out: styd on fnl f: no ex towards fin* **2/1**[2]

0114 **3** hd **Imperialistic (IRE)**[5] 2364 5-8-12 93 PhilipRobinson 3 94
(K R Burke) *hld up on ins: effrt over 2f out: sn chsng ldrs: no ex ins last* **7/2**[3]

6-05 **4** 4 **Gaelic Princess**[14] 2071 6-8-12 77 FergusSweeney 5 85?
(A G Newcombe) *trckd ldrs on outer: effrt over 2f out: hung lft over 1f out: sn wl outpcd* **28/1**

600- **5** nk **Malinsa Blue (IRE)**[233] 6022 4-8-12 77 PaulHanagan 4 84?
(S Parr) *reluctant ldr: shkn up 3f out: sn hdd: wl outpcd fnl f* **25/1**

1m 47.21s (1.51) **Going Correction** -0.20s/f (Firm) **5** Ran SP% **107.3**
Speed ratings (Par 111):84,83,83,79,79
CSF £3.76 TOTE £1.90: £1.10, £1.30; EX 3.20.
Owner S Balfour **Bred** P And Mrs Venner **Trained** Newmarket, Suffolk
■ Stewards' Enquiry : Philip Robinson two-day ban: used whip with excessive frequency and without giving time to respond (Jun 26-27)

FOCUS
An ordinary Listed race and no gallop at all until turning in, hence the proximity at the line of the lowly-rated fourth and fifth, who anchor the form.

NOTEBOOK
Bahia Breeze, with no one wanting to be there, took pole position going into the final turn. Kept right up to her work, she was always doing just enough. This taught us nothing more about her at all. (op 11-8 tchd 6-4 and 13-8 in a place)
Mamela(GER)showed the benefit of her first outing here and she deserves credit for the way she really battled all the way to the line. (op 7-4)
Imperialistic(IRE), in-foal to Lucky Story, is running out of time at the crease. With a bit to find with the first two and the ground plenty quick enough, she ran her heart out under a punishing ride. (tchd 3-1)
Gaelic Princess ran better than on her first two starts this time and, though highly flattered, she did at least pick up some valuable black type. (op 25-1)
Malinsa Blue(IRE), having her first outing for this trainer, dawdled in front and predictably was left behind in the sprint to the line. (op 28-1 tchd 22-1)

2504 SUNWIN RENAULT H'CAP 6f
8:45 (8:45) (Class 5) (0-70,69) 3-Y-0+ **£3,886** (£1,156; £577; £288) **Stalls** Low

Form RPR
0042 **1** **Dvinsky (USA)**[9] 2223 5-9-11 **66** RobbieFitzpatrick 12 77
(D Carroll) *trckd ldrs: edgd lft over 1f out: led ins last: styd on* **7/1**[2]

1012 **2** ¾ **Geojimali**[24] 1816 4-9-8 **63** FergalLynch 1 77+
(J S Goldie) *hld up in mid-div: hdwy on ins over 1f out: n.m.r: hmpd ins last: styd on wl towards fin* **11/4**[1]

1-00 **3** nk **Flying Edge (IRE)**[10] 2211 6-9-8 **63** JohnEgan 3 71
(E J Alston) *led: edgd rt over 1f out: hdd and no ex ins last* **10/1**

2501 **4** 1½ **Briery Lane (IRE)**[13] 2112 5-9-3 **63** (p) GregFairley(5) 9 66
(Mrs K Walton) *chsd ldrs: edgd rt over 1f out: styd on ins last* **8/1**[3]

0000 **5** 1 **Diamond Heritage**[5] 2358 4-8-4 **50** oh11 (b) AndrewElliott(5) 4 50+
(S Parr) *s.i.s: hdwy on ins 2f out: styd on ins last* **100/1**

41-0 **6** nk **Snow Bunting**[142] 171 8-8-12 **53** PaulHanagan 15 52
(Jedd O'Keeffe) *hld up: hdwy over 1f out: styd on strly ins last* **12/1**

460- **7** 1½ **Flur Na H Alba**[248] 5719 7-10-0 **69** (v) GrahamGibbons 5 64
(J J Quinn) *trckd ldrs: hmpd over 1f out: wknd and eased wl ins last* **20/1**

052- **8** 1½ **Our Mary (IRE)**[208] 6366 3-8-9 **63** AndrewMullen(5) 2 53
(Robert Gray) *chsd ldrs: fdd appr fnl f* **33/1**

0-05 **9** ½ **Inchmarlow (IRE)**[7] 2284 3-8-1 **55** DuranFentiman(5) 14 44
(T H Caldwell) *s.i.s: sme hdwy 2f out: nvr a factor* **25/1**

4-04 **10** ½ **Full Spate**[6] 2331 11-9-7 **62** NCallan 11 49+
(J M Bradley) *s.s: hdwy whn hmpd over 1f out: nt clr run ins last* **11/1**

0060 **11** shd **Ryedane (IRE)**[10] 2194 4-9-12 **67** (e) DavidAllan 7 54
(T D Easterby) *trckd ldrs: wknd over 1f out* **16/1**

0000 **12** 1¼ **Sentiero Rosso (USA)**[11] 2173 4-9-13 **68** (b) TomEaves 13 51
(B Ellison) *chsd ldrs on outer: wknd over 1f out* **12/1**

6500 **13** 4 **Salisbury World (IRE)**[17] 2001 3-7-13 **55** ow5 KevinGhunowa(7) 10 26
(J F Coupland) *t.k.h: trckd ldrs on outer: lost pl over 1f out* **50/1**

-350 **14** 3 **Mill By The Stream**[25] 1794 4-8-4 **50** oh5 (v) RoryMoore(5) 6 12
(P T Midgley) *chsd ldrs: wknd over 2f out* **20/1**

040- **15** 1¾ **Rectangle (IRE)**[329] 3583 6-9-3 **58** KDarley 8 15
(Micky Hammond) *hld up in mid-field: effrt 2f out: sn wknd* **14/1**

1m 16.67s (-0.73) **Going Correction** -0.20s/f (Firm)
WFA 3 from 4yo+ 8lb **15** Ran SP% **114.9**
Speed ratings (Par 103):96,95,94,92,91 90,88,86,86,85 85,83,78,74,72
CSF £22.87 CT £197.61 TOTE £8.10: £3.20, £1.10, £2.80; EX 15.40.
Owner Dennis Deacon **Bred** Eclipse Bloodstock And Tipperary Bloodstock **Trained** Warthill, N Yorks

FOCUS
A modest handicap that looks solid enough through the winner and third, but limited by the fifth.
Full Spate Official explanation: jockey said gelding was denied a clear run
Rectangle(IRE) Official explanation: trainer said gelding bled after race

2505 REG VARDY RENAULT H'CAP 5f
9:15 (9:15) (Class 6) (0-65,64) 4-Y-0+ **£3,238** (£963; £481; £240) **Stalls** Low

Form RPR
0056 **1** **Namir (IRE)**[40] 1414 4-8-13 **56** (vt) GrahamGibbons 12 66
(Stef Liddiard) *hld up in mid-div: hdwy on outside over 1f out: r.o to ld post* **12/1**

0000 **2** shd **Trick Cyclist**[35] 1528 5-9-3 **60** (b) DaleGibson 13 70
(M W Easterby) *chsd ldrs: styd on to ld last 75yds: hdd last stride* **8/1**[3]

0000 **3** ½ **Chairman Bobby**[4] 2376 8-8-5 **48** (p) NickyMackay 2 56
(D W Barker) *w ldrs: led over 1f out: hdd and no ex wl ins last* **10/1**

-006 **4** ¾ **Kings College Boy**[16] 2027 6-9-3 **60** (b) PaulHanagan 7 66+
(R A Fahey) *chsd ldrs: n.m.r 1f out: kpt on towards fin* **8/1**[3]

-362 **5** ½ **Never Without Me**[11] 2182 6-9-4 **61** DavidAllan 3 65
(J F Coupland) *chsd ldrs: kpt on fnl f* **15/2**[2]

3500 **6** hd **Seven No Trumps**[17] 1981 9-8-13 **56** NCallan 8 59+
(J M Bradley) *mid-div: hdwy on outer over 1f out: styd on ins last* **12/1**

0000 **7** 1 **Jadan (IRE)**[3] 2396 5-9-3 **60** (p) KDarley 14 59
(E J Alston) *mde most: hdd over 1f out: wknd ins last* **16/1**

64-0 **8** ¾ **Navigation (IRE)**[32] 1611 4-9-5 **62** TomEaves 1 59
(T J Etherington) *chsd ldrs on ins: kpt on same pce fnl 2f* **16/1**

0-46 **9** *hd* **Obe One**[38] [1459] 6-8-10 **53** ... RobertWinston 6 49+
(D Nicholls) *in rr: hdwy on inner whn hmpd over 1f out: swtchd ins: styd on ins last* **11/2**[1]
006 **10** *1* **Diamond Katie (IRE)**[37] [1496] 4-9-7 **64** ... KimTinkler 10 56
(N Tinkler) *chsd ldrs: fdd over 1f out* **16/1**
-000 **11** *nk* **Mis Chicaf (IRE)**[3] [2396] 5-8-10 **58** ... (t) AndrewMullen(5) 17 49
(Robert Gray) *in rr: sme hdwy over 1f out: nvr a factor* **33/1**
2050 **12** *1 ¼* **Times Review (USA)**[11] [2182] 5-9-6 **63** ... (b) JohnEgan 11 50
(C A Dwyer) *chsd ldrs: lost pl and n.m.r over 1f out* **25/1**
6045 **13** *1* **Angelofthenorth**[9] [2237] 4-8-13 **61** ... GregFairley(5) 4 44
(C J Teague) *chsd ldrs: lost pl over 1f out* **12/1**
0054 **14** *1 ¼* **Whistler**[12] [2136] 9-9-6 **63** ... (p) PaulFitzsimons 5 42
(Miss J R Tooth) *a in rr* **16/1**
-000 **15** *1* **Compton Plume**[16] [2020] 6-9-3 **60** ... PaulMulrennan 9 35
(M W Easterby) *rr-div: hmpd over 1f out* **16/1**
0045 **16** *¾* **Newsround**[20] [1913] 4-8-5 **48** ... (b) PaulQuinn 15 20
(D W Chapman) *s.i.s: a bhd* **50/1**

63.21 secs (-0.59) **Going Correction** -0.20s/f (Firm) **16** Ran SP% **119.7**
Speed ratings (Par 101):96,95,95,93,93 92,91,89,89,88 87,85,83,81,80 79
CSF £101.16 CT £1050.27 TOTE £17.00: £5.10, £2.20, £2.00, £1.50; EX 377.90 Place 6 £9.81, Place 5 £8.22.
Owner Simon Mapletoft Racing I **Bred** B Kennedy **Trained** Great Shefford, Berks

FOCUS
A modest handicap rated around the fifth and sixth to recent form.
Obe One Official explanation: jockey said gelding was denied a clear run
Angelofthenorth Official explanation: jockey said filly was unsuited by the good to firm ground
T/Plt: £14.00 to a £1 stake. Pool: £4,397.30. 2,097.60 winning tickets. T/Qpdt: £9.30 to a £1 stake. Pool: £2,726.30. 216.30 winning tickets. WG

2327 WINDSOR (R-H)
Monday, June 12
OFFICIAL GOING: Good to firm (firm in places)
Wind: Almost nil Weather: Sunny and warm

2506 COLIN JAVENS SPINAL INJURY TRUST EUROPEAN BREEDERS FUND MEDIAN AUCTION MAIDEN STKS 6f
6:35 (6:35) (Class 5) 2-Y-O **£3,886** (£1,156; £577; £288) **Stalls** High

Form RPR
0 **1** **Scarlet Runner**[17] [1989] 2-8-12 ... KerrinMcEvoy 14 89+
(J L Dunlop) *mde all: shkn up over 1f out: r.o wl* **10/1**
2 **2** *2 ½* **Spritza (IRE)**[16] [2026] 2-8-12 ... JamieSpencer 11 72
(M L W Bell) *chsd wnr: rdn over 1f out: styd on same pce* **2/1**[1]
4 **3** *shd* **Greyt Big Stuff (USA)**[11] [2178] 2-9-3 ... LDettori 3 77
(B J Meehan) *chsd ldrs: rdn over 1f out: styd on* **10/3**[2]
5 **4** *hd* **Vaunt**[10] [2185] 2-9-3 ... SteveDrowne 2 76+
(R Charlton) *hld up: hdwy 1/2-way: rdn over 1f out: styd on same pce fnl f* **9/2**[3]
5 *1 ¼* **Naayla (IRE)** 2-8-12 ... JimmyFortune 4 67
(B J Meehan) *chsd ldrs: swtchd lft over 1f out: styd on same pce* **25/1**
6 *½* **Pango's Legacy** 2-8-12 ... TravisBlock(5) 8 70+
(H Morrison) *hld up: hdwy over 2f out: rdn over 1f out: no ex ins fnl f* **33/1**
3 **7** *6* **Daring You**[8] [2258] 2-9-3 ... RyanMoore 6 48
(P F I Cole) *mid-div: sn drvn along: rdn and hung lft 2f out: n.d* **16/1**
8 *½* **Eager Igor (USA)** 2-9-3 ... StephenCarson 5 46+
(R F Johnson Houghton) *s.s: rdn and hung lft over 1f out: nvr nrr* **33/1**
9 *1* **Sunley Sovereign** 2-9-3 ... TedDurcan 9 43
(M R Channon) *s.s: rdn over 2f out: n.d* **33/1**
060 **10** *½* **Fasuby (IRE)**[48] [1203] 2-8-12 ... ShaneKelly 12 36
(P D Evans) *chsd ldrs: rdn over 2f out: sn wknd* **40/1**
11 *hd* **Okikoki** 2-9-3 ... DarryllHolland 15 40
(W R Muir) *mid-div: pushed along 1/2-way: nt clr run and wknd over 2f out* **20/1**
12 *1* **Converti** 2-9-0 ... NelsonDeSouza(3) 10 37
(P F I Cole) *sn outpcd* **33/1**
13 *1* **Our Herbie** 2-9-3 ... EddieAhern 13 33
(J W Hills) *s.s: outpcd* **20/1**
14 *14* **Trumps (IRE)** 2-9-3 ... FrancisNorton 16 —
(M Blanshard) *s.i.s: outpcd* **66/1**

1m 12.0s (-1.67) **Going Correction** -0.30s/f (Firm) **14** Ran SP% **118.6**
Speed ratings (Par 93):99,95,95,95,93 92,84,84,82,82 82,80,79,60
CSF £26.61 TOTE £11.30: £3.50, £1.60, £1.70; EX 34.30.
Owner Nicholas Jones **Bred** Coln Valley Stud **Trained** Arundel, W Sussex

FOCUS
A reasonable, typical Windsor maiden, rated around the second and fourth, that should produce a few winners.

NOTEBOOK
Scarlet Runner ◆ was down the field but did not shape badly on her debut at Newmarket and showed the benefit of that run to win convincingly. She looks ready for a step up in class and the Albany Stakes is a possible target. (tchd 11-1 in a place)
Spritza(IRE), runner-up on her debut in a heavy-ground maiden at Haydock, seemed to handle this faster surface well enough but was no match for the classy winner. A similar race should come her way. (tchd 15-8 and 9-4)
Greyt Big Stuff(USA), a promising fourth on her debut at Yarmouth, again showed ability and seems to be progressing along the right lines. (tchd 5-2 and 7-2)
Vaunt, an encouraging fifth on his debut at Bath, would have found this tougher but ran respectably. (op 11-2)
Naayla(IRE) ◆, a 75,000gns half-sister to useful German juvenile Medina, to six-furlong juvenile winners Contact and Motu, also winner over seven furlongs at four, and to Pike Bishop, a dual five-furlong winner at two, caught the eye travelling well for much of the way. She is open to improvement and could be one to keep in mind.
Pango's Legacy, a 22,000gns half-brother to Bagration, placed at two in Italy, made a respectable debut and should improve.
Fasuby(IRE) Official explanation: jockey said filly hung right

2507 MICHELMERSH BRICK HOLDINGS PLC CLAIMING STKS 1m 3f 135y
7:05 (7:06) (Class 5) 3-Y-O+ **£3,238** (£963; £481; £240) **Stalls** Low

Form RPR
3556 **1** **Ballybeg (IRE)**[28] [1732] 3-8-9 64 ... (b) RichardHughes 4 65
(R Hannon) *chsd clr ldr 4f: chal over 3f out: rdn to ld 2f out: sson edgd rt: styd on u.p* **7/1**
3000 **2** *1* **Ganymede**[23] [1690] 5-9-5 59 ... AdamKirby(3) 1 61
(J G M O'Shea) *hld up: hdwy u.p 2f out: edgd rt ins fnl f: styd on* **33/1**
-140 **3** *1 ¼* **Unique Moment**[24] [1837] 3-8-8 75 ... LDettori 7 60
(M Johnston) *hld up: hdwy to chse clr ldr over 7f out: rdn to ld over 3f out: hdd 2f out: edgd lft fnl f: styd on same pce* **15/8**[1]
0-51 **4** *1 ¾* **Ionian Spring (IRE)**[34] [1566] 11-9-11 81 ... DanielTudhope(3) 6 63
(D Carroll) *s.s: hld up: plld hrd: hdwy over 3f out: rdn over 1f out: no ex ins fnl f* **9/4**[2]
00 **5** *1* **Devonia Plains (IRE)**[13] [2118] 4-9-8 ... (v) RobertHavlin 5 55
(Mrs P N Dutfield) *chsd ldrs: rdn over 3f out: hung lft over 1f out: no ex* **66/1**
-005 **6** *3 ½* **Sky At Night (IRE)**[24] [1829] 3-8-3 51 ... JimmyQuinn 3 45
(P Mitchell) *hld up: rdn over 2f out: n.d* **25/1**
00-4 **7** *1 ½* **Arabian Moon (IRE)**[34] [1566] 10-9-6 48 ... DaneO'Neill 9 45
(R Brotherton) *hld up: hdwy u.p over 2f out: wknd over 1f out* **20/1**
5040 **8** *14* **River Gypsy**[7] [2305] 5-10-0 57 ... KFallon 8 31
(D R C Elsworth) *chsd ldrs 9f* **6/1**[3]
2-00 **9** *4* **Sovereign Dreamer (USA)**[6] [2320] 6-9-4 58 ... (b) RyanMoore 2 14
(P F I Cole) *led and sn clr: rdn and hdd over 3f out: sn wknd* **20/1**

2m 28.72s (-1.38) **Going Correction** -0.30s/f (Firm)
WFA 3 from 4yo+ 15lb **9** Ran SP% **110.1**
Speed ratings (Par 103):92,91,90,89,88 86,85,76,73
CSF £199.26 TOTE £7.40: £1.90, £4.80, £1.40; EX 146.20.Ballybeg (IRE) was claimed by Mr Bill Gavan for £12,000
Owner Des Kavanagh & Partners **Bred** Rathasker Stud **Trained** East Everleigh, Wilts

FOCUS
A modest claimer in which the first five home were separated by just five lengths, despite Sovereign Dream having gone fast enough to race into a clear lead early on. The form is muddling.
Ionian Spring(IRE) Official explanation: jockey said gelding missed the break
Sky At Night(IRE) Official explanation: jockey said gelding was unsuited by good to firm, firm in places ground

2508 SPINAL RESEARCH H'CAP 1m 2f 7y
7:35 (7:37) (Class 4) (0-80,80) 4-Y-O+ **£6,477** (£1,927; £963; £481) **Stalls** Low

Form RPR
0-06 **1** **Winners Delight**[17] [1992] 5-9-0 **73** ... RichardHughes 4 82
(C F Wall) *led: hdd over 8f out: chsd ldrs: rdn to ld 2f out: hung lft fr over 1f out: hdd ins fnl f: rallied to ld post* **14/1**
0-22 **2** *shd* **Folio (IRE)**[17] [1992] 6-9-5 **78** ... TPQueally 7 87
(W J Musson) *hld up: hdwy over 3f out: rdn to ld ins fnl f: hdd post* **4/1**[1]
1020 **3** *1 ¾* **Star Magnitude (USA)**[13] [2114] 5-9-4 **77** ... JimmyQuinn 12 83
(S Dow) *chsd ldrs: rdn over 3f out: styd on same pce fnl f* **10/1**
00-6 **4** *½* **Yo Pedro (IRE)**[39] [1435] 4-9-5 **78** ... JamieSpencer 8 83
(J R Fanshawe) *hld up: plld hrd: hdwy over 7f out: rdn over 1f out: styd on same pce* **5/1**[2]
05-0 **5** *nk* **Sky Quest (IRE)**[11] [2169] 8-9-5 **78** ... (t) TedDurcan 2 82
(W R Swinburn) *hld up: hdwy 2f out: sn rdn: one pce fnl f* **8/1**
0-00 **6** *¾* **Call Me Max**[19] [1938] 4-9-5 **78** ... JimmyFortune 5 81
(E A L Dunlop) *hld up in tch: rdn 2f out: no ex fnl f* **14/1**
3120 **7** *1* **Eloquent Knight (USA)**[44] [1281] 4-9-0 **73** ... KerrinMcEvoy 6 74
(W R Muir) *chsd ldrs: led over 8f out: hdd over 7f out: rdn to ld 3f out: hdd 2f out: no ex fnl f* **5/1**[2]
6-60 **8** *1 ¼* **Colinca's Lad (IRE)**[14] [2088] 4-8-6 **65** ... FrancisNorton 3 63
(J Ryan) *hld up: effrt over 2f out: swtchd rt 1f out: eased* **66/1**
-363 **9** *3 ½* **Feed The Meter (IRE)**[23] [1847] 6-8-10 **74** ... JerryO'Dwyer(5) 10 66
(J Ryan) *slwoly intos tride: hld up: rdn over 2f out: n.d* **7/1**[3]
1105 **10** *1* **Kylkenny**[13] [2097] 11-8-5 **71** ... (t) NBazeley(7) 1 61
(P D Cundell) *hld up: effrt over 2f out: sn wknd* **16/1**
4/0- **11** *shd* **Palatinate (FR)**[262] [5432] 4-9-4 **80** ... AdamKirby(3) 9 70
(C G Cox) *chsd ldrs: led over 7f out: hdd 3f out: wknd over 1f out* **20/1**
0-02 **12** *1* **Scutch Mill (IRE)**[20] [1926] 4-8-6 **67** ... (t) DarryllHolland 11 55
(Karen George) *hld up: plld hrd: a in rr* **12/1**

2m 7.20s (-1.10) **Going Correction** -0.30s/f (Firm) **12** Ran SP% **119.2**
Speed ratings (Par 105):92,91,90,90,89 89,88,87,84,83 83,83
CSF £69.64 CT £603.09 TOTE £20.30: £4.70, £1.90, £4.50; EX 101.20.
Owner Breckland Bingo **Bred** Peter Barclay **Trained** Newmarket, Suffolk

FOCUS
No more than a fair handicap and the form is ordinary, with the runner-up the best guide.
Yo Pedro(IRE) Official explanation: jockey said gelding ran too free

2509 CANACCORD H'CAP 5f 10y
8:05 (8:05) (Class 4) (0-85,85) 3-Y-O **£6,477** (£1,927; £722; £722) **Stalls** High

Form RPR
2-24 **1** **Prince Tamino**[11] [2168] 3-9-7 **85** ... SteveDrowne 2 97+
(H Morrison) *trckd ldrs: nt clr run over 1f out: swtchd lft: shkn up and qckned to ld towards fin* **9/4**[1]
1-03 **2** *¾* **Matuza (IRE)**[6] [2329] 3-9-1 **79** ... KerrinMcEvoy 1 85
(W R Muir) *chsd ldrs: rdn to ld ins fnl f: edgd rt and hdd towards fin* **5/2**[2]
0-21 **3** *1 ¼* **Cheney Hill**[21] [1877] 3-8-6 **70** ... DaneO'Neill 5 72
(H Candy) *w ldr: rdn and ev ch ins fnl f: styd on same pce* **7/2**[3]
-060 **3** *dht* **Azygous**[20] [1928] 3-9-2 **80** ... AlanMunro 3 82
(J Akehurst) *led: rdn and hdd ins fnl f: styng on same pce whn n.m.r towards fin* **12/1**
-320 **5** *2* **Tous Les Deux**[16] [2014] 3-8-13 **77** ... StephenCarson 7 71
(R F Johnson Houghton) *chsd ldrs: nt clr run over 1f out: sn outpcd* **6/1**
2-00 **6** *½* **Matterofact (IRE)**[10] [2189] 3-8-8 **72** ... RobertHavlin 4 65
(Mrs P N Dutfield) *prom: rdn and nt clr run over 1f out: wknd ins fnl f* **20/1**
0 **7** *5* **Lucky Lucioni (IRE)**[98] [592] 3-8-8 **75** ... AdamKirby(3) 6 50
(G A Butler) *hld up: outpcd fr 1/2-way* **25/1**

58.70 secs (-2.40) **Going Correction** -0.30s/f (Firm) **7** Ran SP% **112.1**
Speed ratings (Par 101):107,105,103,103,100 99,91
CSF £7.81 TOTE £3.50: £2.10, £1.90; EX 7.90.
Owner Thurloe Finsbury II **Bred** The National Stud **Trained** East Ilsley, Berks

FOCUS
A good little sprint handicap and the form looks solid rated around the placed horses.
Lucky Lucioni(IRE) Official explanation: jockey said gelding hung left throughout

2510 CMI PLC H'CAP 1m 67y
8:35 (8:35) (Class 5) (0-75,75) 4-Y-O+ **£3,238** (£963; £481; £240) **Stalls** High

Form RPR
2305 **1** **Aggravation**[31] [1644] 4-8-8 **62** ow2 ... KFallon 12 74
(D R C Elsworth) *hld up: hdwy and nt clr run over 1f out: r.o to ld and hung lft wl ins fnl f* **11/2**[3]
3-53 **2** *nk* **Bold Act (IRE)**[24] [1830] 4-9-3 **71** ... DaneO'Neill 13 82
(H Candy) *chsd ldrs: rdn to ld over 1f out: edgd rt: hdd wl ins fnl f* **9/1**
24-2 **3** *1 ½* **Cusoon**[30] [1673] 4-9-4 **72** ... (p) RyanMoore 6 82+
(G L Moore) *hld up: nt clr run 2f out: hdwy over 1f out: r.o: nt rch ldrs* **9/2**[1]

0203 **4** ½ **Selective**[19] [1932] 7-9-3 **71**....(t) JimmyFortune 5 77
(A W Carroll) *mid-div: hdwy and barged through over 1f out: sn rdn: styd on same pce ins fnl f* **16/1**

0002 **5** ½ **Jools**[6] [2327] 8-8-4 **65**.... JamesMillman(7) 11 70+
(D K Ivory) *hld up and bhd: hdwy on outside over 1f out: styd on same pce ins fnl f* **7/1**

3023 **6** 1½ **First Show**[18] [1957] 4-9-7 **75**.... ShaneKelly 14 77+
(J Noseda) *hld up: nt clr run fr over 2f out: nvr able to chal* **5/1**[2]

0/00 **7** *hd* **Personify**[31] [1651] 4-8-10 **67**....(p) AdamKirby(3) 7 68
(C G Cox) *chsd ldrs: rdn and hung lft over 2f out: hmpd over 1f out: no ex fnl f* **40/1**

-060 **8** 1¼ **Della Salute**[8] [2259] 4-9-7 **75**.... MickyFenton 3 73
(Miss E C Lavelle) *led: hdd 7f out: led over 3f out: rdn and hdd over 1f out: sn n.m.r: wknd ins fnl f* **66/1**

3504 **9** ¾ **Farewell Gift**[40] [1410] 5-9-5 **73**....(b) RichardHughes 9 70
(R Hannon) *chsd ldrs: rdn and n.m.r over 1f out: wknd ins fnl f* **14/1**

6606 **10** *hd* **Fabrian**[17] [1995] 8-9-0 **68**.... RobertMiles 4 64
(R J Price) *led 7f out: hdd over 3f out: wknd fnl f* **25/1**

0145 **11** ¾ **Boogie Magic**[20] [1910] 6-8-2 **56** oh5.... JimmyQuinn 8 51
(T Keddy) *hld up: n.d* **66/1**

-350 **12** 2 **Blue Trojan (IRE)**[13] [2114] 6-9-6 **74**.... JamieSpencer 1 64
(S Kirk) *hld up: effrt over 2f out: nt clr run and wknd over 1f out* **8/1**

3322 **13** 5 **Merrymadcap (IRE)**[21] [1882] 4-9-6 **74**....(b) FrancisNorton 2 52
(M Blanshard) *hld up: a in rr* **14/1**

0110 **14** 1½ **Raza Cab (IRE)**[19] [1938] 4-9-7 **75**.... DarryllHolland 10 50
(Karen George) *chsd ldrs: rdn over 3f out: n.m.r and wknd over 1f out* **14/1**

1m 42.1s (-3.50) **Going Correction** -0.30s/f (Firm) **14** Ran SP% **119.0**
Speed ratings (Par 103):105,104,103,102,102 100,100,99,98,98 97,95,90,89
CSF £52.57 CT £249.30 TOTE £6.70: £2.10, £3.20, £2.50; EX 47.30.
Owner Perry, Vivian & Elsworth **Bred** John Khan **Trained** Newmarket, Suffolk
■ Stewards' Enquiry : Jimmy Fortune two-day ban: careless riding (Jun 27-28)
Dane O'Neill caution: careless riding

FOCUS
A fair handicap for the grade and the form looks reliable enough through the principals, with the placed horses close to form.
Blue Trojan(IRE) Official explanation: jockey said gelding was unsuited by the good to firm (firm in places) ground
Merrymadcap(IRE) Official explanation: jockey said gelding ran free
Raza Cab(IRE) Official explanation: jockey said gelding was unsuited by the good to firm (firm in places) ground

2511 NEAR MISS CLUB FILLIES' H'CAP 6f
9:05 (9:07) (Class 5) (0-70,70) 3-Y-O **£3,886** (£1,156; £577; £288) **Stalls** High

Form RPR

0-00 **1** **Catspraddle (USA)**[40] [1411] 3-9-4 **67**.... RyanMoore 3 74
(R Hannon) *wnt lft s: led over 4f out: rdn out* **14/1**

-000 **2** *nk* **Xaluna Bay (IRE)**[15] [2049] 3-9-4 **67**.... KerrinMcEvoy 10 73
(W R Muir) *a.p: rdn to chse wnr over 1f out: r.o* **10/1**

-005 **3** 1¼ **Divine White**[10] [2190] 3-8-4 **53**.... AlanMunro 12 55
(Mrs A J Perrett) *chsd ldrs: rdn over 1f out: styd on same pce ins fnl f* **16/1**

0334 **4** *shd* **Wizby**[13] [2095] 3-8-4 **53**....(t) JimmyQuinn 15 55+
(P D Evans) *hld up: nt clr run over 1f out: swtchd lft and r.o ins fnl f: nt rch ldrs* **15/2**

5-41 **5** ¾ **Orange Dancer (IRE)**[14] [2068] 3-9-2 **70**.... TravisBlock(5) 8 69+
(H Morrison) *mid-div: hdwy over 2f out: rdn over 1f out: no ex ins fnl f* **11/2**[2]

0041 **6** *hd* **Just Down The Road (IRE)**[6] [2316] 3-8-10 **59** 6ex.... KFallon 14 58+
(R A Harris) *led: hdd over 4f out: rdn and nt clr run over 1f out: styd on same pce ins fnl f* **10/3**[1]

-60 **7** 4 **Bellabelini (IRE)**[62] [969] 3-8-11 **60**....(b[1]) JimmyFortune 1 47
(S Kirk) *hmpd s: outpcd: r.o u.p ins fnl f: nvr nrr* **33/1**

4-24 **8** ½ **Red Diadem**[41] [1386] 3-9-4 **67**.... MichaelHills 7 52+
(W J Haggas) *hld up: hdwy over 2f out: rdn over 1f out: wknd fnl f* **13/2**[3]

05-6 **9** ¾ **Athena's Dream**[31] [1646] 3-9-5 **68**.... RichardHughes 16 51
(C F Wall) *hld up: effrt over 2f out: wknd over 1f out* **15/2**

-030 **10** 2 **Catherines Cafe (IRE)**[10] [2190] 3-9-2 **65**.... RobertHavlin 13 42
(Mrs P N Dutfield) *a in rr* **16/1**

-325 **11** 2 **Sensuous**[27] [1750] 3-9-6 **69**.... DaneO'Neill 11 40
(R Hannon) *free to post: hld up: rdn 1/2-way: a in rr* **12/1**

00-0 **12** 1¼ **Bella Bertolini**[25] [1801] 3-9-2 **65**.... IanMongan 2 32
(T G Mills) *hmpd s: sn chsng ldrs: rdn and hung lft 2f out: sn wknd* **40/1**

30-0 **13** *hd* **Be My Charm**[10] [2190] 3-8-11 **60**.... FrancisNorton 5 27
(M Blanshard) *chsd ldrs over 3f* **33/1**

1m 11.75s (-1.92) **Going Correction** -0.30s/f (Firm) **13** Ran SP% **118.9**
Speed ratings (Par 96):100,99,97,97,96 96,91,90,89,86 84,82,82
CSF £144.43 CT £2346.94 TOTE £16.30: £4.10, £5.00, £4.80; EX 231.60 Place 6 £135.00, Place 5 £97.20.
Owner Mrs Suzanne Costello-Haloute **Bred** Clover Leaf Farms II Inc **Trained** East Everleigh, Wilts

FOCUS
A modest but competitive sprint handicap for fillies and the form looks sound overall, rated around those in the frame behind the winner.
T/Plt: £165.10 to a £1 stake. Pool: £60,440.20. 267.10 winning tickets. T/Qpdt: £108.00 to a £1 stake. Pool: £4,074.30. 27.90 winning tickets. CR

2512 - 2516a (Foreign Racing) - See Raceform Interactive

[1626] CHESTER (L-H)
Tuesday, June 13

OFFICIAL GOING: Good
Wind: almost nil Weather: overcast

2517 CHESTER CHRONICLE EBF MAIDEN STKS 5f 16y
6:45 (6:48) (Class 4) 2-Y-O **£5,181** (£1,541; £770; £384) **Stalls** Low

Form RPR

0 **1** **Northern Fling**[34] [1587] 2-9-3.... AdrianTNicholls 1 84+
(D Nicholls) *trckd ldrs: rdn over 1f out: edgd lft and qcknd to ld wl ins fnl f: r.o wl* **4/1**[1]

3 **2** 1¼ **Dress To Impress (IRE)**[15] [2084] 2-9-0.... AmirQuinn(3) 7 77
(J R Boyle) *led after 1f: rdn over 1f out: hdd wl ins fnl f: nt qckn cl home* **4/1**[1]

004 **3** 3½ **Pat Will (IRE)**[7] [2315] 2-8-12.... JohnEgan 2 59
(P D Evans) *trckd ldrs: rdn 2f out: no ex ins fnl f* **5/1**[3]

405 **4** 1 **Loves Bidding**[10] [2225] 2-9-3.... EddieAhern 9 60+
(R Ingram) *hld up: effrt and hdwy over 1f out: kpt on same pce ins fnl f: no imp on ldrs* **5/1**[3]

004 **5** ½ **Almora Guru**[4] [2394] 2-8-12.... DavidAllan 10 54
(W M Brisbourne) *towards rr: hdwy 2f out: rdn and hung lft over 1f out: swtchd rt ins fnl f: one pce* **33/1**

0 **6** ½ **Imprimis Tagula (IRE)**[3] [2439] 2-9-3.... SamHitchcott 5 57
(A Bailey) *led for 1f: remained prom: rdn 2f out: wknd ins fnl f* **33/1**

304 **7** 2 **Make Me An Offer (IRE)**[11] [2185] 2-9-3.... MichaelHills 8 50
(B W Hills) *midfield: rdn 2f out: wknd over 1f out* **9/2**[2]

8 *hd* **Rainbow Fox** 2-9-3.... PaulHanagan 3 49+
(R A Fahey) *s.i.s: a outpcd* **15/2**

0 **P** **Harriets Dream**[34] [1587] 2-8-12.... RobbieFitzpatrick 6 —
(Peter Grayson) *midfield: wnt wrong and lost pl qckly over 2f out: p.u over 1f out* **16/1**

61.94 secs (-0.11) **Going Correction** -0.025s/f (Good) **9** Ran SP% **115.0**
Speed ratings (Par 95):99,97,91,89,89 88,85,84,—
CSF £19.94 TOTE £3.60: £1.80, £1.50, £1.90; EX 17.70.
Owner Jim Dale/Jason Berry **Bred** Lady Juliet Tadgell **Trained** Sessay, N Yorks
■ Stewards' Enquiry : Adrian T Nicholls caution: careless riding

FOCUS
Just a moderate juvenile maiden, which saw the first two come nicely clear, and the form looks straightforward, although unexceptional.

NOTEBOOK
Northern Fling, seventh on his debut from a modest draw at this track in a better event 34 days previously, had the plum draw and, while lacking the early speed to take full advantage of that, he still had enough class to get off the mark in ready fashion. This showed the clear benefit of his debut experience, he shaped as though he ought to get another furlong in due course, and he clearly has a future.
Dress To Impress(IRE), third on heavy ground on debut in Listed company last time, showed decent early speed from his wide draw and held every chance. He seemed suited by this better ground and should not be too long in going one better on this evidence. (op 9-2 tchd 11-2)
Pat Will(IRE) ran a sound race - from her decent draw - and kept on under pressure in the final furlong. She helps set the level of this form and may find further improvement when stepping up to a sixth furlong. (op 11-2 tchd 9-2)
Loves Bidding was not disgraced from his wide draw and ran to his recent level in defeat. (op 13-2)
Almora Guru Official explanation: jockey said filly hung left throughout
Make Me An Offer(IRE) never got into serious contention from his unfavourable draw and failed to improve for this return to the minimum trip.

2518 ERNST & YOUNG H'CAP 1m 2f 75y
7:15 (7:16) (Class 5) (0-70,68) 3-Y-O **£3,562** (£1,059; £529; £264) **Stalls** High

Form RPR

-643 **1** **Princess Cocoa (IRE)**[13] [2124] 3-8-11 **58**.... PaulHanagan 12 66
(R A Fahey) *chsd ldrs: rdn over 2f out: led 1f out: r.o* **8/1**[3]

0-36 **2** 1½ **Aurora Jane (FR)**[12] [2171] 3-9-3 **64**.... MichaelHills 7 69
(B W Hills) *led: rdn under 2f out: hdd 1f out: no ex towards fin* **12/1**

-004 **3** *shd* **Dancing Flame**[8] [2283] 3-8-8 **55**.... DavidAllan 6 60
(E J Alston) *prom: rdn 3f out: styd on ins fnl f* **20/1**

012 **4** *shd* **English City (IRE)**[10] [2243] 3-8-9 **56**.... DerekMcGaffin 3 61
(B Smart) *hld up: rdn and edgd rt over 2f out: hdwy over 1f out: hung lft ins fnl f: r.o towards fin* **6/1**[2]

0-00 **5** 1¼ **Is It Me (USA)**[57] [1052] 3-8-11 **65**.... KevinGhunowa(7) 10 67
(P A Blockley) *hdwy to go prom after 2f: rdn over 3f out: rdr dropped whip over 2f out: styd on same pce fnl f* **66/1**

6333 **6** ½ **Alexian**[43] [1350] 3-9-7 **68**.... GeorgeBaker 5 69
(R Hollinshead) *hld up in rr: hdwy whn swtchd rt over 1f out: swtchd rt again ins fnl f: r.o* **8/1**[3]

0-03 **7** *hd* **Kavachi (IRE)**[4] [2391] 3-9-7 **68**.... EddieAhern 11 70+
(E A L Dunlop) *midfield: rdn over 2f out: hdwy over 1f out: eased whn no imp towards fin* **8/1**[3]

-233 **8** ¾ **Follow The Colours (IRE)**[20] [1934] 3-9-7 **68**.... ChrisCatlin 2 68+
(J W Hills) *hld up: nt clr run over 2f out: hdwy whn swtchd rt over 1f out: styd on ins fnl f* **3/1**[1]

0612 **9** 3½ **Keisha Kayleigh (IRE)**[18] [1997] 3-9-0 **61**.... NCallan 8 54
(B Ellison) *cl up: rdn 2f out: wknd ins fnl f* **10/1**

-046 **10** ¾ **Dream Of Paradise (USA)**[13] [2128] 3-9-1 **62**.... RoystonFfrench 1 54+
(Mrs L Williamson) *midfield: rdn over 2f out: hdwy over 1f out: keeping on one pce whn nt clr run ins fnl f: sn lost pl: n.d after* **14/1**

2500 **11** 2 **Reveur**[11] [2209] 3-8-13 **63**.... SilvestreDeSousa(3) 4 51
(M Mullineaux) *rdn over 2f out: a towards rr* **25/1**

4301 **12** 2½ **Mae Cigan (FR)**[22] [1881] 3-9-3 **64**.... TedDurcan 13 47
(M Blanshard) *midfield: rdn over 2f out: wknd over 1f out* **11/1**

100- **13** ¾ **Ditton Dancer**[221] [6244] 3-9-5 **66**.... GrahamGibbons 9 48
(J J Quinn) *racd keenly: n.m.r after s: hld up: pushed along over 4f out: n.d* **25/1**

2m 12.78s (-0.36) **Going Correction** -0.025s/f (Good) **13** Ran SP% **118.3**
Speed ratings (Par 99):100,98,98,98,97 97,97,96,93,93 91,89,88
CSF £94.92 CT £1856.13 TOTE £10.60: £2.50, £2.40, £6.40; EX 76.50.
Owner P Ashton **Bred** Corduff Stud **Trained** Musley Bank, N Yorks

FOCUS
A modest handicap, run at a decent early pace, and the winner scored readily from an unfavourable draw. The form looks solid rated around those just outside the frame.
Ditton Dancer Official explanation: trainer's rep said filly was unsuited by the good ground

2519 LIBERTY PROPERTIES PLC H'CAP 1m 2f 75y
7:45 (7:45) (Class 4) (0-85,79) 4-Y-O+ **£6,153** (£1,830; £914; £456) **Stalls** High

Form RPR

0260 **1** **Lucayan Dancer**[5] [2387] 6-9-3 **75**.... AdrianTNicholls 2 83
(D Nicholls) *hld up: hdwy over 2f out: rdn over 1f out: led ins fnl f: r.o* **5/1**[3]

3046 **2** *nk* **Prime Contender**[17] [2035] 4-8-10 **68**.... MichaelHills 6 75
(B W Hills) *sn led: rdn over 1f out: hdd ins fnl f: r.o u.p* **5/1**[3]

40-5 **3** 1¾ **Wester Lodge (IRE)**[12] [2183] 4-9-1 **73**.... NCallan 4 77
(J M P Eustace) *in tch: rdn over 2f out: styd on ins fnl f* **10/1**

1-00 **4** *hd* **Mr Aitch (IRE)**[5] [2387] 4-8-12 **70**.... JohnEgan 7 74
(R T Phillips) *hld up: rdn and hdwy whn nt clr run and swtchd rt over 1f out: styd on ins fnl f* **16/1**

0-04 **5** *hd* **Torrens (IRE)**[12] [2169] 4-9-7 **79**....(t) PaulHanagan 8 82
(R A Fahey) *in tch: hdwy over 2f out: rdn and ev ch ins fnl f: no ex towards fin* **4/1**[2]

3255 **6** 1¾ **Hawkit (USA)**[12] [2162] 5-8-10 **68**....(t) DavidAllan 5 68
(A Bailey) *hld up in rr: rdn and hdwy over 1f out: no imp on ldrs ins fnl f* **12/1**

0041 **7** ¾ **Bright Sun (IRE)**[7] [2322] 5-8-13 **71** 6ex....(t) KimTinkler 1 69
(N Tinkler) *t.k.h: prom: rdn 2f out: wknd ins fnl f* **11/2**

-453 **8** *5* **Transvestite (IRE)**[18] 1992 4-9-4 **76**.................................. EddieAhern 3 65
(J W Hills) *led early and n.m.r sn after s: remained prom: rdn over 2f out: wknd wl over 1f out* **7/2**[1]

2m 12.18s (-0.96) **Going Correction** -0.025s/f (Good) **8** Ran SP% **113.6**
Speed ratings (Par 105):102,101,100,100,100 98,98,94
CSF £29.68 CT £238.56 TOTE £5.80: £1.90, £1.70, £3.00; EX 18.80.
Owner James E Greaves **Bred** The National Stud Owner Breeders Club Ltd **Trained** Sessay, N Yorks

■ Stewards' Enquiry : Michael Hills one-day ban: careless riding (Jun 25)

FOCUS
A fair handicap, run at just a modest early pace, and the first two came clear. The form is ordinary but looks solid enough.

2520 BANK OF SCOTLAND CORPORATE H'CAP 7f 2y
8:15 (8:16) (Class 3) (0-95,90) 4-Y-O+ £10,094 (£3,020; £1,510; £755; £376) **Stalls** Low

Form RPR

6052 **1** **Dhaular Dhar (IRE)**[11] 2194 4-8-11 **80**.............................. FergalLynch 11 92
(J S Goldie) *hld up: hdwy 2f out: led 1f out: edgd lft ins fnl f: drvn out* **8/1**[3]

1-10 **2** *½* **Into The Breeze (IRE)**[31] 1667 6-9-2 **85**.......................... MichaelHills 4 95
(J W Hills) *midfield: hdwy over 2f out: nt clr run and swtchd rt over 1f out: wnt 2nd ins fnl f: styd on* **9/2**[1]

4-00 **3** *1 ¼* **Looks Could Kill (USA)**[7] 2323 4-9-0 **83**.......................... EddieAhern 9 90
(E J Alston) *midfield: hdwy whn nt clr run 2f out: sn swtchd rt: chalng 1f out: n.m.r ins fnl f: one pce cl home* **16/1**

0046 **4** *1 ¼* **H Harrison (IRE)**[4] 2397 6-7-11 **71**........................ NataliaGemelova(5) 7 75+
(I W McInnes) *in tch: nt clr run and lost pl 2f out: styd on ins fnl f: nt pce to trble ldrs* **10/1**

00-4 **5** *shd* **Mutawaffer**[25] 1835 5-9-4 **87**..(t) PaulHanagan 12 90+
(R A Fahey) *midfield: rdn 4f out: nt clr run 2f out: swtchd rt over 1f out: styd on ins fnl f: nt trble ldrs* **9/2**[1]

3002 **6** *½* **Lord Of The East**[10] 2232 7-8-13 **85**.......................... PatrickMathers(3) 2 87
(I W McInnes) *led: rdn and hdd 1f out: fdd ins fnl f* **7/1**[2]

0000 **7** *1* **General Feeling (IRE)**[5] 2384 5-8-0 **72**............... SilvestreDeSousa(3) 3 72
(M Mullineaux) *s.i.s: in rr: rdn over 1f out: kpt on ins fnl f: nvr trbld ldrs* **25/1**

00-0 **8** *¾* **Joseph Henry**[10] 2230 4-9-4 **87**.. JoeFanning 5 85
(M Johnston) *chsd ldrs: wnt 2nd over 3f out: lost 2nd over 1f out: wknd ins fnl f* **14/1**

000- **9** *2 ½* **The Crooked Ring**[269] 5285 4-8-10 **79**..............................(v) JohnEgan 1 75+
(P D Evans) *hld up: effrt and hdwy 2f out: eased whn btn ins fnl f* **12/1**

3230 **10** *½* **Breaking Shadow (IRE)**[7] 2323 4-8-11 **80**..................... PhillipMakin 10 70
(T D Barron) *midfield: effrt 2f out: wknd fnl f* **7/1**[2]

5024 **11** *shd* **Kingscross**[11] 2189 8-8-13 **82**... TedDurcan 6 72
(M Blanshard) *a bhd* **14/1**

0000 **12** *20* **Lake Andre (IRE)**[24] 1858 5-8-11 **80**.. NCallan 8 18
(K A Ryan) *prom: rdn 4f out: wknd over 2f out* **20/1**

1m 26.34s (-2.13) **Going Correction** -0.025s/f (Good) **12** Ran SP% **117.1**
Speed ratings (Par 107):111,110,109,107,107 106,105,104,102,101 101,78
CSF £43.27 CT £576.46 TOTE £8.00: £2.10, £2.10, £3.10; EX 37.20.
Owner J S Goldie **Bred** Gainsborough Stud Management Ltd **Trained** Uplawmoor, E Renfrews

FOCUS
A competitive handicap for the class, run at a strong early pace, and the form looks fair enough, rated through the third.

NOTEBOOK
Dhaular Dhar(IRE) ◆ relished the decent early pace and, after looking to have a fair amount to do approaching the final bend, he picked up strongly to mow on down his rivals and win going away. He is now coming good for his new connections, has now been successful on both his outings over course and distance, and strongly appeals as the type to defy a higher mark in the not-too-distant future. (op 7-1)
Into The Breeze(IRE) bounced back from a below-par effort at Lingfield last time, and was doing all of his best work towards the finish, having been denied a clear passage at the crucial stage. He is better than the bare form and looks back to very near his best again this year. (op 11-2)
Looks Could Kill(USA) turned in his best effort to date for his new yard and shaped slightly better than his finishing position suggests. He is probably at his best over six furlongs, and has a race within his compass from his current mark, but is not the easiest to catch right. (tchd 18-1)
H Harrison(IRE) must be rated better than the bare form, as he lost his place on the turn for home, and then finished his race well when recovering his momentum. This was a much more encouraging effort and he can find easier opportunities. (op 12-1)
Mutawaffer, popular in the betting ring despite his wide draw, did not get the best of passages when attempting to make his ground and is a shade better than his finishing position suggests. He is another who is probably happier over six furlongs, and is in the right hands at present, but really is a fiendishly hard horse to win with. (tchd 5-1)
The Crooked Ring Official explanation: trainer said gelding was unsuited by the good ground

2521 AKTIV KAPITAL UK LTD H'CAP 5f 16y
8:45 (8:45) (Class 4) (0-85,85) 3-Y-O+ £6,153 (£1,830; £914; £456) **Stalls** Low

Form RPR

6006 **1** **Magic Glade**[12] 2173 7-9-9 **79**....................................... RoystonFfrench 6 88
(R Brotherton) *chsd ldrs: led 1f out: drvn out* **12/1**

0241 **2** *nk* **Handsome Cross (IRE)**[3] 2450 5-9-11 **84** 6ex.... SilvestreDeSousa(3) 8 91
(D Nicholls) *in tch: rdn over 1f out: r.o ins fnl f...* **10/3**[1]

-001 **3** *hd* **Coconut Moon**[3] 2462 4-8-9 **64** 6ex....................................... DavidAllan 3 72+
(E J Alston) *hmpd s: midfield: lost pl over 3f out: hdwy 2f out: r.o wl towards fin* **9/2**[2]

-000 **4** *1 ¼* **Funfair Wane**[10] 2230 7-10-0 **84**................................... AdrianTNicholls 10 86+
(D Nicholls) *sn outpcd and bhd: hdwy over 1f out: r.o strly ins fnl f: nrst fin* **12/1**

0636 **5** *2* **Lady Bahia (IRE)**[3] 2462 5-8-9 **65** oh5...........................(b) JoeFanning 5 60
(Peter Grayson) *hmpd s: sn in midfield: effrt on wd outside over 2f out: no ex ins fnl f* **18/1**

0020 **6** *nk* **Harry Up**[8] 2302 5-9-9 **79**... NCallan 7 73
(K A Ryan) *w ldr: led over 3f out: rdn and hdd 1f out: wknd ins fnl f* **9/2**[2]

0000 **7** *2* **Law Maker**[4] 2396 6-8-9 **65** oh1....................................(v) SamHitchcott 9 52
(A Bailey) *towards rr: outpcd 3f out: kpt on ins fnl f: nvr trbld ldrs* **25/1**

0000 **8** *1* **Jadan (IRE)**[1] 2505 5-8-9 **65** oh5...(p) JohnEgan 1 48
(E J Alston) *led: hdd over 3f out: remained w ldr: rdn and ev ch over 1f out: wknd ins fnl f* **8/1**

3302 **9** *14* **Stoneacre Lad (IRE)**[17] 2021 3-9-8 **85**..................(b) RobbieFitzpatrick 4 18+
(Peter Grayson) *hmpd s: a outpcd* **6/1**[3]

3400 **10** *6* **Mytton's Pride**[12] 2161 3-8-2 **65** oh3.. ChrisCatlin 2 —
(A Bailey) *wnt rt s: midfield early: wknd 3f out* **12/1**

61.75 secs (-0.30) **Going Correction** -0.025s/f (Good)
WFA 3 from 4yo+ 7lb **10** Ran SP% **117.0**
Speed ratings (Par 105):101,100,100,98,95 94,91,89,67,57
CSF £52.11 CT £217.23 TOTE £17.00: £6.30, £1.50, £1.50; EX 217.10.
Owner Alan Solomon **Bred** Juddmonte Farms **Trained** Elmley Castle, Worcs

FOCUS
A decent enough sprint for the class, run at a strong early pace, and the first threewere in a tight finish but came clear.

2522 KEMIRA GROWHOW H'CAP (FOR LADY AMATEUR RIDERS) 1m 4f 66y
9:15 (9:16) (Class 5) (0-70,66) 4-Y-O+ £3,747 (£1,162; £580; £290) **Stalls** Low

Form RPR

2366 **1** **Lake Wakatipu**[4] 2408 4-9-4 **54**........................... MissMMullineaux(7) 11 62
(M Mullineaux) *hld up: hdwy 4f out: r.o to ld wl ins fnl f* **20/1**

0513 **2** *nk* **Acuzio**[4] 2407 5-9-6 **49**.. MrsSBosley 10 57
(W M Brisbourne) *prom: led over 5f out: rdn 2f out: hdd wl ins fnl f* **5/1**[1]

2553 **3** *½* **York Cliff**[11] 2206 8-9-11 **54**.. MissEJJones 9 61+
(W M Brisbourne) *midfield: lost pl 4f out: hdwy and swtchd rt ins fnl f: r.o strly towards fin* **11/1**

0051 **4** *¾* **Court Of Appeal**[4] 2395 9-10-6 **66** 6ex..................(tp) MissLEllison(3) 14 72
(B Ellison) *s.i.s: hdwy into midfield after 3f: trckd ldrs 6f out: rdn over 2f out: styd on ins fnl f* **8/1**[3]

6-00 **5** *¾* **Turner**[27] 1769 5-10-1 **58**.. MissNCarberry 12 64+
(W M Brisbourne) *hld up: hdwy whn nt clr run over 2f out: swtchd rt over 1f out: edgd lft ins fnl f: nt qckn towards fin* **13/2**[2]

4546 **6** *nk* **Wood Fern (UAE)**[4] 2414 6-9-0 **46** oh1.......... MrsLucindaCrowley(3) 13 50
(W M Brisbourne) *midfield: rdn and hdwy over 2f out: swtchd lft ins fnl f: styd on* **16/1**

1540 **7** *1 ¾* **Buscador (USA)**[18] 1987 7-9-2 **50**.................... MissCarolineHurley(5) 7 51
(W M Brisbourne) *led after 1f: hdd over 5f out: rdn and ev ch 2f out: fdd ins fnl f* **25/1**

4000 **8** *½* **Golden Boot**[52] 1138 7-10-3 **60**... MrsCBartley 2 60
(A Bailey) *s.s: in rr: gd hdwy 6f out: rdn over 1f out: one pce fnl f* **5/1**[1]

5100 **9** *nk* **Mustakhlas (USA)**[39] 1467 5-8-13 **47** ow1................. MissHGrissell(5) 4 47
(B P J Baugh) *led for 1f: remained prom tl rdn and outpcd over 2f out: no imp after* **25/1**

6-20 **10** *1 ½* **Dayoff (IRE)**[127] 318 5-9-6 **52**..................................(v) MissEFolkes(3) 6 50
(P D Evans) *bhd: niggled along over 7f out: nvr trbld ldrs* **14/1**

154- **11** *1 ½* **French Mannequin (IRE)**[292] 4695 7-9-7 **53**....(v) MissFayeBramley(3) 8 48
(P A Blockley) *midfield: lost pl 4f out: n.d after* **16/1**

2300 **12** *nk* **Hillhall (IRE)**[13] 2131 4-9-3 **46** oh1............................... MrsACooke 5 41
(W M Brisbourne) *handy after 3f: lost pl 3f out: n.d after* **33/1**

3206 **13** *hd* **Larad (IRE)**[7] 2320 5-9-4 **47**..(b) MrsSMoore 3 41
(J S Moore) *racd keenly: midfield: lost pl 6f out: n.d after* **10/1**

2216 **14** *24* **Desperation (IRE)**[94] 628 4-10-8 **65**.................. MrsEmmaLittmoden 1 21
(B D Leavy) *in tch: lost place 6f out: sn bhd* **13/2**[2]

2m 44.06s (3.41) **Going Correction** -0.025s/f (Good) **14** Ran SP% **122.4**
Speed ratings (Par 103):87,86,86,85,85 85,84,83,83,82 81,81,81,65
CSF £114.87 CT £1192.06 TOTE £33.10: £10.80, £2.50, £2.90; EX 293.20 Place 6 £377.49, Place 5 £223.81..
Owner Esprit De Corps Racing **Bred** T S And Mrs Wallace **Trained** Alpraham, Cheshire

■ Michelle Mullineaux's first Flat winner.

FOCUS
A moderate handicap for lady amateurs, run at a steady gallop, and the first six were closely bunched at the finish. The form is suspect and very ordinary.
Golden Boot Official explanation: jockey said gelding hung right-handed
T/Plt: £345.90 to a £1 stake. Pool: £63,525.35. 134.05 winning tickets. T/Qpdt: £54.70 to a £1 stake. Pool: £3,950.65. 53.40 winning tickets. DO

2106 REDCAR (L-H)
Tuesday, June 13

OFFICIAL GOING: Firm
Wind: Light, half-against

2523 SKYTIPS.CO.UK CALL 0845 86 88 371 MEDIAN AUCTION MAIDEN STKS 6f
2:30 (2:30) (Class 5) 2-Y-O £3,238 (£963; £481; £240) **Stalls** High

Form RPR

35 **1** **Monkey Glas (IRE)**[12] 2178 2-9-3 .... DarrenWilliams 3 73
(K R Burke) *keen: hld up in tch: rdn 2f out: led wl ins fnl f: hld on wl* **5/1**[3]

543 **2** *shd* **Perlachy**[7] 2321 2-9-3 .... DavidAllan 12 73
(T D Easterby) *led: rdn 2f out: hdd wl ins fnl f: rallied* **6/1**

26 **3** *nk* **Silca Soprano**[17] 2026 2-8-12 .... TonyCulhane 6 67+
(M R Channon) *prom: effrt 2f out: rdn and kpt on wl fnl f* **10/3**[2]

2 **4** *3* **Intersky Sports (USA)**[13] 2139 2-9-3 .... NCallan 10 63
(K A Ryan) *cl up: rdn and edgd lft wl over 1f out: no ex ins fnl f* **9/4**[1]

5 *3* **Ishetoo** 2-9-0 .... DanielTudhope(3) 5 54
(A Dickman) *towards rr: outpcd 1/2-way: rallied over 1f out: nvr rchd ldrs* **20/1**

00 **6** *1* **Focus Star**[11] 2191 2-9-3 .... TomEaves 2 51
(J M Jefferson) *chsd ldrs on outside tl rdn and outpcd fr 2f out* **80/1**

0 **7** *hd* **Umpa Loompa (IRE)**[34] 1595 2-9-3 .... AdrianTNicholls 1 50
(D Nicholls) *towards rr: rdn 1/2-way: wandered and no imp fr 2f out* **7/1**

8 *¾* **Averti Star** 2-9-3 .... RoystonFfrench 13 48
(Mrs A Duffield) *in tch on outside: rdn 1/2-way: no imp fr 2f out* **20/1**

0 **9** *1* **Rose Court**[53] 1121 2-8-5 .... JamesReveley(7) 4 40
(K G Reveley) *hld up: outpcd 1/2-way: n.d* **50/1**

10 *4* **Blissfully** 2-8-12 .... DeanMcKeown 7 28
(S Parr) *missed break: nvr on terms* **40/1**

0 **11** *2* **Hair Of The Dog**[13] 2139 2-9-3 .... RobertWinston 8 43+
(J G Given) *keen: chsd ldrs tl wknd wl over 1f out* **40/1**

12 *5* **Lady Davali** 2-8-12 .... DarryllHolland 11 7
(S Parr) *s.i.s: nvr on terms* **50/1**

1m 12.45s (0.75) **Going Correction** -0.075s/f (Good) **12** Ran SP% **116.9**
Speed ratings (Par 93):92,91,91,87,83 82,81,80,79,74 71,64
CSF £32.18 TOTE £6.70: £1.70, £1.60, £1.50; EX 52.40.
Owner Denis Fehan **Bred** D Bourke And Yuriy Meduedyev **Trained** Middleham Moor, N Yorks

FOCUS
An ordinary bunch on looks and this looked just ordinary form. The pace was fair and this form looks reliable, rated around the third.

NOTEBOOK
Monkey Glas(IRE) pulled far too hard at Yarmouth but, while still taking a tug, did settle better and showed a good attitude to get off the mark. He should stay seven furlongs and, although this bare form is ordinary, he may be capable of better. (op 6-1)
Perlachy, who turned in an improved effort last time, duly proved suited by the return to six furlongs and ran his best race yet. While vulnerable to the better types in this grade, he looks sure to pick up a minor event in due course. (op 7-1)

Silca Soprano put a below-par effort in testing ground at Haydock firmly behind her and, on this evidence, will be well suited by the step up to seven furlongs and she looks sure to win a similar event. (op 11-4)
Intersky Sports(USA) failed to build on his Fibresand debut on this first run on turf but left the impression that this trip on quick ground was too much of a test of speed. He will be suited by an extra furlong and possibly easier ground and is not one to write off yet. (op 15-8 tchd 5-2 in a place)
Ishetoo, the first foal of a juvenile five-furlong winner, showed ability without being knocked about on this racecourse debut. He is entitled to be better for this run and may do better. (op 33-1)
Focus Star again underlined his vulnerability in this type of event but may do better over further in modest handicap company in due course.
Hair Of The Dog, who took the eye in the paddock as a strong sort with plenty of scope, was again well beaten on this turf debut but showed up well for a long way and looks the sort physically to leave this form behind at some stage. Official explanation: jockey said colt spread a front plate

2524 RACING UK (S) STKS — 7f
3:00 (3:00) (Class 6) 2-Y-O — **£2,388** (£705; £352) **Stalls** High

Form — RPR
1 **Beau Sancy** 2-8-11 ... TomEaves 3 — 60+
(J Howard Johnson) *sn chsng ldrs: rdn 1/2-way: rn green and led appr fnl f: kpt on wl* **11/4**[3]
03 2 1 3/4 **Lansdown**[15] [2064] 2-8-6 ... KDarley 2 — 50
(M Meade) *chsd ldrs: led over 2f out to appr fnl f: kpt on same pce ins last* **2/1**[2]
4662 3 9 **Minimum Fuss (IRE)**[8] [2294] 2-8-6 ...(b) PaulMulrennan 4 — 26
(M W Easterby) *plld hrd: cl up tl rdn: wandered and wknd wl over 1f out* **7/4**[1]
00 4 5 **Mister Cricket (IRE)**[23] [1862] 2-8-11 ... NeilPollard 1 — 17
(M E Sowersby) *led to over 2f out: rdn and sn wknd* **22/1**
000 5 2 **Citoyen (IRE)**[47] [1248] 2-8-11 ... FergalLynch 5 — 12
(Ronald Thompson) *bhd: drvn over 2f out: sn btn* **10/1**

1m 26.3s (1.40) **Going Correction** -0.075s/f (Good) — 5 Ran SP% **109.8**
Speed ratings (Par 91):89,87,76,71,68
CSF £8.61 TOTE £3.20: £2.40, £1.10; EX 9.50.The winner was sold to Jeff Pearce for 11,000gns. Lansdown was claimed by Naughty Diesel Ltd for £6,000.
Owner Transcend Bloodstock LLP **Bred** Mrs J Keegan **Trained** Billy Row, Co Durham

FOCUS
A poor and uncompetitive event in which the pace was moderate.

NOTEBOOK
Beau Sancy, who looked fit for this racecourse debut, proved green once asked for an effort but knuckled down well to win going away. This bare form is weak but he should stay further and new connections saw enough promise to purchase him for 11,000gns. (op 3-1)
Lansdown, who achieved little when third in a heavy-ground seller on her previous start; turned in her best effort up in trip and back on a sound surface. She was claimed for £6000 and may be able to pick up a similarly uncompetitive event. (op 9-4)
Minimum Fuss(IRE) pulled far too hard to give herself any chance of lasting home over this longer trip and proved disappointing. The return to sprinting should suit but she is an exposed performer who is not one to be taking too short a price about. (op 13-8 tchd 9-4)
Mister Cricket(IRE), back on a sound surface, was again well beaten and, on the evidence of this run in a particularly weak event, is not going to be easy to place successfully. (op 20-1 tchd 16-1)
Citoyen(IRE), upped in trip, again showed nothing. (tchd 6-1)

2525 ANDERSON BARROWCLIFF H'CAP — 7f
3:30 (3:31) (Class 5) (0-75,75) 3-Y-O — **£3,238** (£963; £481; £240) **Stalls** High

Form — RPR
-040 1 **Queen's Composer (IRE)**[18] [1999] 3-9-4 **72** ... PhilipRobinson 4 — 78
(B Smart) *in tch: outpcd after 3f: rallied wl over 1f out: kpt on strly to ld towards fin* **9/2**[3]
50-0 2 1/2 **Ours (IRE)**[25] [1825] 3-8-6 **60** ... KDarley 8 — 65
(J D Bethell) *hld up: hdwy over 2f out: led ent fnl f: hdd towards fin* **20/1**
-201 3 1 1/2 **Marmooq**[12] [2160] 3-9-5 **73** ... JoeFanning 6 — 74
(M Johnston) *cl up: led over 1f out: edgd lft and hdd ent fnl f: one pce* **11/2**
0364 4 1 **Esoterica (IRE)**[4] [2399] 3-8-7 **61** ...(p) PhillipMakin 1 — 60
(T D Barron) *chsd ldrs: effrt and ch wl over 1f out: sn one pce* **7/2**[2]
303- 5 1 **Secret Assassin (IRE)**[241] [5889] 3-9-7 **75** ... KerrinMcEvoy 2 — 71
(W R Muir) *led to over 1f out: sn no ex* **13/2**
01-5 6 3/4 **Flylowflylong (IRE)**[115] [448] 3-9-2 **70** ... TomEaves 3 — 64
(I Semple) *keen: hld up in tch: rdn over 2f out: edgd lft and sn no ex* **9/1**
06-6 7 hd **Prince Duval (IRE)**[11] [2198] 3-7-12 **59** oh4 ow3 ... KellyHarrison(7) 7 — 52
(D Carroll) *in tch tl rdn and outpcd fr 2f out* **40/1**
0021 8 2 **Jellytot (USA)**[11] [2198] 3-8-0 **59** ... AndrewMullen(5) 5 — 47
(K A Ryan) *led to over 1f out: sn btn* **3/1**[1]
-500 9 24 **Rosthwaite (IRE)**[53] [1122] 3-8-12 **66** ... FergalLynch 9 — —
(Ronald Thompson) *hld up: rdn 1/2-way: sn lost tch* **33/1**

1m 23.2s (-12.37) **Going Correction** -0.075s/f (Good) — 9 Ran SP% **114.3**
Speed ratings (Par 99):106,105,103,102,101 100,100,98,70
CSF £87.57 CT £507.95 TOTE £6.70: £2.80, £4.50, £2.10; EX 91.60.
Owner Pinnacle Mozart Partnership **Bred** Saud Bin Saad And Thamer A Al-Kanhal **Trained** Hambleton, N Yorks

FOCUS
An ordinary handicap in which the gallop seemed sound and the field raced in the centre of the course. The form looks rock solid with the third, fourth and fifth to their marks.
Jellytot(USA) Official explanation: trainer had no explanation for the poor form shown

2526 REDCAR LIVE MEDIAN AUCTION MAIDEN STKS — 1m 3f
4:00 (4:01) (Class 6) 3-5-Y-O — **£2,388** (£705; £352) **Stalls** Low

Form — RPR
0-5 1 **Brigadore (USA)**[12] [2175] 3-8-10 ... KerrinMcEvoy 3 — 76
(W R Muir) *hld up in tch: stdy hdwy 1/2-way: outpcd over 3f out: rallied over 2f out: edgd lft and led ins fnl f: kpt on wl* **9/2**[3]
646 2 1 1/4 **Soulard (USA)**[25] [1827] 3-8-10 75 ... DarrylHolland 4 — 74
(J Noseda) *led after 3f: rdn over 2f out: hdd ins fnl f: r.o* **13/8**[2]
3-66 3 2 **Waterloo Corner**[7] [2322] 4-9-10 66 ... JoeFanning 5 — 71
(R Craggs) *trckd ldrs: ev ch 3f out: rdn and one pce appr fnl f* **9/1**
32-4 4 23 **Cheviot Heights**[34] [1598] 3-8-5 70 ... KDarley 1 — 53+
(Mrs A J Perrett) *keen: led 3f: sn hmpd: rdn 3f out: sn wknd: eased whn no ch fnl 2f* **6/4**[1]
0 5 11 **Cortina**[99] [590] 3-7-12 ... LiamJones(7) 2 — 12
(J Jay) *prom tl rdn and lost tch fr 4f out* **66/1**

2m 19.79s (-1.21) **Going Correction** -0.075s/f (Good)
WFA 3 from 4yo 14lb — 5 Ran SP% **107.8**
Speed ratings (Par 101):101,100,98,81,73
CSF £11.76 TOTE £4.60: £1.90, £1.70; EX 14.50.
Owner Mr & Mrs G Middlebrook/Mr & Mrs P Brain **Bred** And Mrs G Middlebrook & Brain International Lt **Trained** Lambourn, Berks

FOCUS
An uncompetitive event in which the gallop was only fair but the winner appeals as the type to progress again and the third sets the standard.
Cheviot Heights Official explanation: trainer's rep said filly suffered interference back straight and never travelled thereafter

2527 JOHN SMITH'S REDCAR STRAIGHT-MILE CHAMPIONSHIP (H'CAP) (QUALIFIER) — 1m
4:30 (4:30) (Class 3) (0-95,95) 3-Y-O+
£9,348 (£2,799; £1,399; £700; £349; £175) **Stalls** High

Form — RPR
-650 1 **Isidore Bonheur (IRE)**[38] [1495] 5-9-5 **80** ... RobertWinston 5 — 89
(G A Swinbank) *stdd last: stdy hdwy over 2f out: effrt over 1f out: ev ch ins fnl f: led cl home* **5/2**[1]
600- 2 hd **Desert Realm (IRE)**[288] [4832] 3-9-9 **95** ... JoeFanning 1 — 101
(M Johnston) *hld up in tch: hdwy to ld over 1f out: kpt on wl: hdd cl home* **9/1**
2201 3 2 1/2 **Kaveri (USA)**[19] [1962] 3-9-1 **87** ... KerrinMcEvoy 2 — 87
(C E Brittain) *prom: effrt and ev ch fr over 2f out tl one pce appr fnl f* **5/1**[3]
2346 4 2 1/2 **Stoic Leader (IRE)**[3] [2464] 6-9-7 **82** ... TonyCulhane 4 — 79
(R F Fisher) *hld up in tch: outpcd over 2f out: kpt on fnl f: nt rch first three* **9/2**[2]
00-3 5 hd **Efidium**[8] [2299] 8-8-2 **70** oh2 ... SuzzanneFrance(7) 9 — 67
(N Bycroft) *plld hrd: cl up: led over 2f to over 1f out: sn btn* **5/1**[3]
00-6 6 1 **Bailieborough (IRE)**[6] [2364] 7-9-1 **81** ...(v) GregFairley(5) 8 — 75
(Robert Gray) *in tch: outpcd over 2f out: n.d after* **9/1**
000- 7 1/2 **Lago D'Orta (IRE)**[352] [2957] 6-9-1 **83** ... VictoriaBehan(7) 6 — 76
(D Nicholls) *keen: sn chsng ldrs: ev ch over 2f out: wknd over 1f out* **20/1**
0010 8 1 1/4 **Baylaw Star**[17] [2017] 5-9-9 **89** ... AndrewMullen(5) 7 — 79
(K A Ryan) *led to over 2f out: wknd over 1f out* **11/1**

1m 35.8s (-2.00) **Going Correction** -0.075s/f (Good)
WFA 3 from 5yo+ 11lb — 8 Ran SP% **113.2**
Speed ratings (Par 107):107,106,104,101,101 100,100,98
CSF £25.47 CT £103.46 TOTE £3.60: £1.90, £3.20, £1.10; EX 33.90.
Owner John Mcaleese, Hubert Brown Kerr **Bred** Middle Park Stud Ltd **Trained** Melsonby, N Yorks

FOCUS
Mainly exposed performers but a decent gallop and this form should prove reliable, rated around the third.

NOTEBOOK
Isidore Bonheur(IRE) attracted support and did enough to register his best effort of the season under another excellent Winston ride. He should not be going up too much for this win but, given he is the type that needs things to fall right, may not be one to lump on at short odds next time. (op 11-4)
Desert Realm(IRE), making his reappearance and handicap debut, ran arguably his best race on his first run beyond sprint distances. He should prove equally effective over seven but may have little margin for error in more competitive company. (op 12-1)
Kaveri(USA), back up in trip and back on turf, ran creditably but seemed beaten on merit and may continue to look vulnerable against progressive or well-handicapped sorts in this type of event on turf. (tchd 4-1)
Stoic Leader(IRE), a consistent sort, has form on firm ground but was not at his best returned to turf and he will have to show more before he is worth a bet. (op 4-1)
Efidium had looked to be coming to hand at Thirsk on his reappearance earlier in the month but pulled too hard on this occasion and not surprisingly had little to offer in the closing stages. He is not one to write off yet, though. (op 7-1 tchd 15-2)
Bailieborough(IRE) was not disgraced at Ripon in a muddling event the previous week but proved a bit of a disappointment this time and he is another that will have to improve to win a similar handicap from his current mark. (op 6-1)
Baylaw Star Official explanation: jockey said gelding was unsuited by the firm ground

2528 REDCARRACING.CO.UK CLAIMING STKS — 2m 4y
5:00 (5:00) (Class 6) 4-Y-O+ — **£2,388** (£705; £352) **Stalls** Low

Form — RPR
1 **Mulligan's Pride (IRE)**[12] 5-9-4 ... RobertWinston 4 — 61
(G A Swinbank) *hld up: outpcd 6f out: rallied to ld over 2f out: hld on wl fnl f* **4/1**[2]
0501 2 nk **High Frequency (IRE)**[22] [1883] 5-7-13 50 ...(p) DeanHeslop(7) 2 — 48
(T D Barron) *cl up: led 5f to over 2f out: rallied: ev ch fnl f: hld cl home* **6/4**[1]
36-0 3 3 1/2 **Rouge Et Noir**[35] [1560] 8-9-0 45 ... DeanMcKeown 3 — 52
(K G Reveley) *hld up in tch: smooth hdwy to press ldrs whn n.m.r briefly 2f out: sn rdn and fnd little* **4/1**[2]
0-00 4 5 **Sahem (IRE)**[37] [1502] 9-9-5 70 ... AndrewMullen(5) 6 — 56
(Robert Gray) *hld up in tch: hdwy 1/2-way: rdn and wknd over 2f out* **9/1**
2443 5 1 1/2 **Romil Star (GER)**[4] [2395] 9-8-1 43 ...(v) PatrickDonaghy(7) 1 — 38
(K R Burke) *led to 5f out: wknd over 2f out* **11/2**[3]
5/0- 6 24 **Altitude Dancer (IRE)**[14] [581] 6-8-10 47 ... TonyHamilton 5 — 11
(A Crook) *chsd ldrs: sn pushed along: wknd fr over 4f out* **12/1**

3m 31.57s (0.07) **Going Correction** -0.075s/f (Good) — 6 Ran SP% **113.1**
Speed ratings (Par 101):96,95,94,91,90 78
CSF £10.63 TOTE £5.40: £2.20, £1.30; EX 14.00.High Frequency was claimed by A. Crook for £6,000. Rouge Et Noir was claimed by E. Nisbet for £10,000.
Owner Scotnorth Racing Ltd **Bred** Mrs J Norris **Trained** Melsonby, N Yorks

FOCUS
A weak event in which the gallop was only fair and best rated through the second.

2529 GO RACING AT BEVERLEY TOMORROW H'CAP — 1m 2f
5:30 (5:33) (Class 6) (0-55,55) 3-Y-O — **£2,388** (£705; £352) **Stalls** Low

Form — RPR
-653 1 **Touch Of Ivory (IRE)**[10] [2243] 3-9-5 **52** ...(p) TonyHamilton 6 — 58
(R A Fahey) *trckd ldrs on ins: led 3f out: kpt on wl fnl f* **6/1**[2]
0-00 2 nk **Osolomio (IRE)**[43] [1343] 3-9-8 **55** ... RobertWinston 11 — 60
(J G Given) *prom: drvn 3f out: rallied over 1f out: chsd wnr ent fnl f: r.o wl* **14/1**
-633 3 1 1/2 **William John**[36] [1533] 3-9-6 **53** ... TomEaves 3 — 56
(B Ellison) *sn rdn along towards rr: hdwy over 2f out: kpt on fnl f: nrst fin* **6/1**[2]
0-50 4 shd **Three Strings (USA)**[10] [2249] 3-9-0 **52** ...(p) AndrewMullen(5) 7 — 54
(P D Niven) *cl up: ev ch 3f out: sn rdn: one pce fnl f* **16/1**
-633 5 nk **Linton Dancer (IRE)**[8] [2283] 3-9-6 **53** ... DarrylHolland 9 — 55
(J R Weymes) *in tch on ins: effrt over 2f out: kpt on same pce fnl f* **9/1**
00-0 6 1 1/2 **Gettysburg (IRE)**[15] [2082] 3-8-12 **50** ... GregFairley(5) 14 — 49
(J Howard Johnson) *bhd: rdn 4f out: kpt on wl fnl 2f: nvr rchd ldrs* **25/1**

0-00 **7** ½ **Vice Admiral**[43] 1350 3-9-7 **54** (b[1]) PaulMulrennan 4 52
(M W Easterby) *led ins tl hdd 3f out: wknd over 1f out* **33/1**
000- **8** 2 **Taranis**[239] 5945 3-9-4 **51** J-PGuillambert 15 49+
(Sir Mark Prescott) *racd wd in tch: drvn over 4f out: effrt over 2f out: hung lft and sn outpcd: eased whn no ch ins fnl f* **2/1**[1]
-000 **9** *nk* **Samsouma (IRE)**[10] 2249 3-9-1 **48** KerrinMcEvoy 1 42
(C E Brittain) *bhd on ins: rdn over 3f out: kpt on fnl f: nvr on terms* **14/1**
00-2 **10** 1 **Elite Land**[29] 1731 3-8-12 **52** SuzzanneFrance(7) 5 44
(N Bycroft) *bhd on ins: shkn up 4f out: nvr on terms* **16/1**
0-00 **11** 2½ **The Preacher**[52] 1139 3-8-12 **50** StephenDonohoe(5) 10 37
(J G Given) *in tch tl rdn and wknd over 2f out* **66/1**
40-0 **12** 11 **Never Say Deya**[11] 2210 3-9-8 **55** TonyCulhane 8 21
(M R Channon) *midfield: drvn over 3f out: sn outpcd* **20/1**
0000 **13** 1½ **Megalo Maniac**[8] 2284 3-9-3 **50** DeanMcKeown 16 13
(K G Reveley) *s.i.s: a bhd* **50/1**
0-00 **14** 1 **Meddle**[62] 984 3-9-0 **50** BenSwarbrick(3) 12 11
(J Jay) *midfield: outpcd over 3f out: sn btn* **50/1**
-000 **15** 3 **Bond Cruz**[11] 2198 3-8-12 **48** (v) DanielTudhope(3) 2 4
(G R Oldroyd) *a bhd* **40/1**
326- **16** 2 **Olivair (IRE)**[346] 3114 3-9-6 **53** NeilPollard 17 5
(M E Sowersby) *racd wd: hld up: hung lft and wknd fr 4f out* **66/1**
-010 **17** ¾ **Unasuming (IRE)**[6] 2352 3-9-7 **54** KDarley 13 4
(J Pearce) *in tch on outside tl wknd 3f out: eased whn no ch fr 2f out* **8/1**[3]

2m 6.38s (-0.42) **Going Correction** -0.075s/f (Good) **17** Ran SP% **129.0**
Speed ratings (Par 97):98,97,96,96,96 95,94,93,92,92 90,81,80,79,76 75,74
CSF £86.07 CT £544.05 TOTE £8.80: £2.20, £4.40, £1.90, £3.30; EX 159.50 Place 6 £49.60, Place 5 £27.31.
Owner Colin Jarvis **Bred** John Hutchinson **Trained** Musley Bank, N Yorks

FOCUS
An ordinary event and one that did not take as much winning as seemed likely beforehand with the market leader disappointing. The form lookspretty reliable rated around the third, fifth and sixth.
Unasuming(IRE) Official explanation: jockey said filly lost its action
T/Plt: £55.30 to a £1 stake. Pool: £38,931.30. 513.25 winning tickets. T/Qpdt: £16.00 to a £1 stake. Pool: £2,417.20. 111.70 winning tickets. RY

[1796]SALISBURY (R-H)
Tuesday, June 13

OFFICIAL GOING: Good
Wind: Virtually nil

2530 GEORGE SMITH HORSEBOXES MAIDEN AUCTION STKS 6f
2:15 (2:17) (Class 5) 2-Y-O **£3,724** (£1,108; £553; £276) **Stalls High**

Form RPR
52 **1** **Sans Reward (IRE)**[21] 1922 2-8-8 ow1 SteveDrowne 6 74
(B J Meehan) *chsd ldrs: rdn over 2f out: r.o strly on rails to ld last strides* **13/8**[1]
0 **2** *nk* **Farefield Lodge (IRE)**[11] 2185 2-8-9 AdamKirby(3) 5 77
(C G Cox) *chsd ldrs: chal fr 2f out tl led ins fnl f: hdd and no ex last strides* **25/1**
6 **3** 1¾ **Land Ahoy**[12] 2172 2-9-2 FrankieMcDonald 15 76
(D W P Arbuthnot) *led: rdn 2f out: hdd ins last: wknd nr fin* **8/1**[3]
0 **4** 4 **Stagehand (IRE)**[50] 1189 2-8-9 AlanMunro 11 57
(B R Millman) *chsd ldrs: pushed along 1/2-way: kpt on same pce ins fnl f* **14/1**
02 **5** *nk* **Dee Jay Wells**[12] 2172 2-9-2 RichardHughes 12 63
(R Hannon) *chsd ldr tl over 2f out: wknd appr fnl f* **7/2**[2]
6 ½ **Ron In Ernest** 2-8-12 RichardThomas 9 57+
(J A Geake) *in tch: pushed along 1/2-way: kpt on fr over 1f out and styd on cl home: nt rch ldrs* **50/1**
0 **7** 1¼ **Red**[32] 1647 2-8-1 NelsonDeSouza(3) 8 46
(R M Beckett) *bhd: hdwy 2f out: kpt on ins last but n.d* **50/1**
05 **8** *hd* **Cashcade (IRE)**[10] 2218 2-8-6 NeilChalmers(3) 4 50
(A M Balding) *chsd ldrs: pushed along over 2f out: sn one pce* **8/1**[3]
9 *nk* **Masai Moon** 2-8-9 DaneO'Neill 16 49+
(B R Millman) *s.i.s: green in rr: hung rt over 2f out: hung lft over 1f out and kpt on: fin wl but nt a danger* **25/1**
10 *hd* **Blackwater Stream (IRE)** 2-8-9 RobertHavlin 7 49+
(Mrs P N Dutfield) *bhd: rdn and hung lft over 2f out: racd alone in centre crse and styd on fnl f: nvr in contention* **66/1**
0 **11** ½ **Gifted Heir (IRE)**[21] 1912 2-8-9 DavidKinsella 3 47
(I A Wood) *in tch: rdn over 2f out: sn one pce* **100/1**
0 **12** *nk* **Regal Ovation**[27] 1770 2-9-2 JimmyFortune 1 53
(W R Muir) *in tch: rdn over 2f out: n.d after* **18/1**
13 *shd* **Spiderback (IRE)** 2-9-2 RyanMoore 13 53+
(R Hannon) *s.i.s: sn pushed along in rr: styd on fnl 2f but nvr in contention* **12/1**
14 *nk* **Iced Tango** 2-8-9 PaulFitzsimons 14 45
(F Jordan) *nvr bttr than mid-div* **100/1**
15 ¾ **Fairly Honest** 2-8-13 AntonyProcter(3) 10 50
(D R C Elsworth) *s.i.s: nvr in contention* **33/1**
16 18 **Fade To Grey (IRE)** 2-8-9 RobertMiles 2 —
(W G M Turner) *s.i.s: green and a bhd* **66/1**

1m 16.02s (1.04) **Going Correction** +0.05s/f (Good) **16** Ran SP% **121.7**
Speed ratings (Par 93):95,94,92,86,86 85,84,83,83,83 82,82,82,81,80 56
CSF £55.43 TOTE £2.50: £1.30, £5.30, £3.60; EX 55.80.
Owner Sandy Briddon & Edward Butler **Bred** Rathbarry Stud **Trained** Manton, Wilts

FOCUS
Just an ordinary maiden and it proved hard to make up ground from off the pace. The time is the best guide to the level.

NOTEBOOK
Sans Reward(IRE), second to subsequent Woodcote runner-up Going Straight over five furlongs at Lingfield on her previous start, made hard work of this and seemed to need every yard of the sixth furlong. On this evidence she may already be in need of seven furlongs. (op 15-8 tchd 2-1)
Farefield Lodge(IRE) stepped up significantly on the form he showed on his debut at Bath and was just denied. He looks well up to finding a similar race. (op 22-1)
Land Ahoy shaped pleasingly on his debut at Sandown and confirmed that with another encouraging performance. Having shown good speed, he was ultimately no match for the front two but finished clear of the remainder and looks up to finding a similar race. (op 16-1)
Stagehand(IRE), who looked better than his finishing position suggested when down the field at Windsor on his debut, duly stepped up on that effort. He was under pressure some way out and shaped as though this run would bring him on again. (op 12-1)
Dee Jay Wells had shaped as though worth a step up in trip when second at Sandown on his previous start, but failed to confirm placings with Land Ahoy and was disappointing.
Ron In Ernest, a 14,000gns half-brother to Bod Groom Dancer, a triple sprinter/miler winner in Italy at two, offered promise and should improve.

2531 KEN COX "LIFETIME IN RACING" CLAIMING STKS 6f 212y
2:45 (2:47) (Class 5) 3-Y-O+ **£3,562** (£1,059; £529; £264) **Stalls High**

Form RPR
0000 **1** **Wild Lass**[6] 2349 5-8-11 38 (b[1]) LPKeniry 16 52
(J C Fox) *bhd: rdn 3f out: stl plenty to do 2f out: edgd lft and hdwy appr fnl f: fin strly: led cl home: readily* **100/1**
-000 **2** ½ **My Girl Pearl (IRE)**[10] 2233 6-8-13 49 FergusSweeney 11 53
(M S Saunders) *chsd ldrs: ev ch fr 2f out: stl chalng ins last tl ct cl home* **14/1**
6003 **3** *shd* **Marko Jadeo (IRE)**[4] 2405 8-9-9 74 DaneO'Neill 5 63
(S Dow) *s.i.s: bhd: hdwy on outside 3f out: slt ld ins fnl 2f: kpt narrow advantage tl hdd cl home* **13/2**
3005 **4** 3 **Smokincanon**[7] 2319 4-9-4 48 RobertMiles 14 50
(W G M Turner) *in tch: drvn 3f out: chal fr 2f out: wknd ins fnl f* **12/1**
13-4 **5** 1¼ **Le Chiffre (IRE)**[8] 2282 4-9-2 78 TolleyDean(7) 7 52
(R A Harris) *chsd ldrs: rdn 3f out: wknd fnl f* **6/1**[3]
0003 **6** 2 **Radius**[26] 1799 3-8-13 64 (t) SteveDrowne 3 42
(H Morrison) *in tch: pushed along and hdwy 3f out: rdn 2f out: sn btn* **13/2**
0-00 **7** 1¾ **European (ARG)**[8] 2302 6-9-2 75 NelsonDeSouza(3) 6 38
(R M Beckett) *chsd ldrs: slt ld over 3f out tl hdd over 2f out: sn wknd* **7/2**[1]
5050 **8** ¾ **Carcinetto (IRE)**[42] 1397 4-8-11 41 (p) FrancisFerris 12 28
(B Palling) *chsd ldrs: led over 2f out tl hdd ins fnl quarter m: sn wknd* **20/1**
0000 **9** 5 **Kilmeena Magic**[6] 2350 4-8-11 40 PatDobbs 8 15
(J C Fox) *sn led: hdd over 3f out: wknd over 2f out* **50/1**
0040 **10** 2½ **Squadron Leader (IRE)**[7] 2318 3-8-11 63 RyanMoore 15 14
(R Hannon) *in tch: rdn 3f out: wknd over 2f out* **4/1**[2]
00- **11** ½ **Exmoor Dancer (IRE)**[340] 3306 3-7-12 EmmettStack(5) 2 5
(H S Howe) *pressed ldrs over 4f* **50/1**
0000 **12** 5 **Awarding**[91] 638 6-8-9 43 (vt) SladeO'Hara(7) 10 —
(Dr J R J Naylor) *hdwy to chse ldrs 4f out: sn rdn: wknd 3f out* **25/1**
0-00 **13** 5 **Lucky Emerald (IRE)**[29] 1746 4-8-11 36 AlanMunro 13 —
(B Palling) *chsd ldrs 4f* **33/1**
00-4 **14** 7 **Sunny Haze**[28] 1768 3-8-11 33 RobertHavlin 1 —
(Mrs P N Dutfield) *a in rr* **100/1**
60-0 **15** *hd* **Just Bonnie**[22] 1877 4-9-2 32 (b[1]) PaulFitzsimons 9 —
(J M Bradley) *slowly away: a bhd* **100/1**
0-00 **16** *dist* **Frenchmans Lodge**[9] 2260 6-8-13 35 (b) EdwardCreighton(3) 4 —
(L A Dace) *slowly away: sn t.o* **66/1**

1m 29.39s (0.33) **Going Correction** +0.05s/f (Good)
WFA 3 from 4yo+ 10lb **16** Ran SP% **117.5**
Speed ratings (Par 103):100,99,99,95,94 92,90,89,83,80 80,74,68,60,60 —
CSF £1101.10 TOTE £77.60: £17.20, £4.20, £1.80; EX 1030.60.
Owner Mrs J A Cleary **Bred** Mrs J A Cleary **Trained** Collingbourne Ducis, Wilts

FOCUS
A very moderate claimer, but at least the pace was good. The second and fourth suggest the form is weak but solid, despite one or two disappointing.
Marko Jadeo(IRE) Official explanation: jockey said, regarding running and riding, his orders were to ride gelding as he had done in the past, adding that it is a hold-up horse, who is often slowly away; vet said gelding bled from the nose
Frenchmans Lodge Official explanation: vet said gelding bled from nose

2532 WISE CATERING MAIDEN STKS 6f 212y
3:15 (3:18) (Class 4) 3-Y-O **£5,181** (£1,541; £770; £384) **Stalls High**

Form RPR
1 **Sama Dubai (AUS)** 3-8-12 RyanMoore 2 82+
(Sir Michael Stoute) *hld up in rr: pushed along and hdwy fr 3f out: styd on to ld ins fnl f: r.o strly* **10/1**
4-34 **2** 1½ **Pirouetting**[24] 1844 3-8-12 85 RichardHughes 3 78
(B W Hills) *trckd ldrs: led ins fnl 2f: rdn over 1f out: heded and outpcd ins last* **6/4**[1]
4 **3** 3 **Greek Easter (IRE)**[53] 1119 3-8-12 JimmyFortune 15 73+
(B J Meehan) *chsd ldrs: n.m.r on rails over 1f out and sltly hmpd: kpt on same pce ins last* **7/2**[2]
00- **4** ¾ **King's Ransom**[213] 6319 3-9-3 FergusSweeney 10 73
(A M Balding) *hld up in rr: t.k.h early: hdwy fr 2f out: shkn up and no imp on ldrs fnl f* **16/1**
5 2½ **Amazing Charlie (IRE)** 3-8-12 JimCrowley 13 62
(Mrs A J Perrett) *bhd: pushed along 3f out: kpt on ins last but nvr gng pce to rch ldrs* **25/1**
0 **6** ¾ **Nightstrike (IRE)**[12] 2167 3-8-12 DaneO'Neill 14 60
(H Candy) *sn slt ld: hdd ins fnl 2f: wknd over 1f out* **25/1**
0 **7** 5 **Wheelavit (IRE)**[6] 2343 3-9-3 TQuinn 8 52
(B G Powell) *chsd ldrs tl wknd 2f out* **50/1**
0 **8** ½ **Little Miss Verity**[50] 1191 3-8-12 RichardThomas 12 45
(J A Geake) *chsd ldrs over 4f* **66/1**
0-0 **9** 1½ **Scrummage**[50] 1192 3-9-3 KFallon 6 46
(Sir Michael Stoute) *w ldr 4f: wknd fr 2f out* **5/1**[3]
0-6 **10** *nk* **Xenophile**[18] 1978 3-9-3 IanMongan 4 46
(J L Dunlop) *in tch: pushed along and wknd ins fnl 3f* **66/1**
0 **11** 1 **Burnt Orange (IRE)**[24] 1845 3-9-3 RobertMiles 5 43
(T D McCarthy) *chsd ldrs tl wknd over 2f out* **40/1**
0-0 **12** 9 **Ameliore (IRE)**[19] 1956 3-8-9 AdamKirby(3) 7 15
(S Woodman) *a in rr* **80/1**
13 6 **All About Him (USA)** 3-8-10 MarkCoumbe(7) 1 4
(N I M Rossiter) *slowly away: hdwy into mid-div 4f out: sn wknd* **100/1**

1m 28.13s (-0.93) **Going Correction** +0.05s/f (Good) **13** Ran SP% **111.2**
Speed ratings (Par 101):107,105,101,101,98 97,91,91,89,88 87,77,70
CSF £22.52 TOTE £10.00: £2.40, £1.50, £1.20; EX 28.10.
Owner Nasser Abdullah **Bred** Emirates Park Pty Ltd **Trained** Newmarket, Suffolk

FOCUS
A pretty ordinary maiden and the runner-up's official mark of 85 should not be used as a guide to the strength of the form, despite the fact the time was good. The third and fourth are better guides.

2533 E B F MARGADALE FILLIES' H'CAP 1m 1f 198y
3:45 (3:48) (Class 4) (0-85,80) 3-Y-O+ **£7,772** (£2,312; £1,155; £577) **Stalls High**

Form RPR
4-13 **1** **Island Odyssey**[22] 1898 3-9-10 **76** LDettori 4 89+
(E A L Dunlop) *mde all: set mod early gallop: drvn and qcknd over 2f out: unchal* **15/8**[1]
-42P **2** 3½ **Dimelight**[3] 2434 3-9-4 **70** TQuinn 3 74
(D R C Elsworth) *chsd wnr thrght: rdn and effrt 3f out: nvr gng pce to chal and sn outpcd* **7/2**[3]

The Form Book, Raceform Ltd, Compton, RG20 6NL

2-25 **3** *1* **Shamila**[32] 1635 3-9-6 **72** NickyMackay 1 74
(G A Butler) *sddle slipped sn after s: a in 3rd: rdn and one pce fnl 3f* **16/1**
00-0 **4** *5* **Generosia**[32] 1650 3-8-13 **65** (t) MartinDwyer 2 58
(A M Balding) *rr: pushed along and sme hdwy fr 3f out but nvr in contention* **14/1**
4 **5** *½* **Mawazeen (IRE)**[26] 1798 5-9-5 **65** MarkCoumbe(7) 5 59
(N I M Rossiter) *t.k.h in rr: rdn and no ch fnl 3f* **20/1**
4421 **6** *1* **Fann (USA)**[14] 2113 3-10-0 **80** RyanMoore 6 70
(C E Brittain) *rdn 4f out: a in rr* **2/1**[2]
2m 10.7s (2.24) **Going Correction** +0.05s/f (Good)
WFA 3 from 5yo 13lb **6** Ran SP% **107.6**
Speed ratings (Par 102):93,90,89,85,85 84
CSF £8.02 TOTE £2.70: £1.60, £2.00; EX 8.50.
Owner Mrs Janice Quy **Bred** Catridge Farm Stud Ltd **Trained** Newmarket, Suffolk

FOCUS
This did not look a bad fillies' handicap beforehand, but Island Odyssey had everything her own way up front - she went steady for the first half mile and was in a clear lead when increasing the pace - and the form should not be taken literally.
Fann(USA) Official explanation: trainer said filly was unsuited by way the race was run

2534 DUTTON GREGORY H'CAP 1m 4f
4:15 (4:16) (Class 5) (0-75,75) 4-Y-O+ **£3,562** (£1,059; £529; £264) **Stalls** High

Form RPR
321- **1** **Sir Monty (USA)**[225] 5760 4-9-5 **73** RyanMoore 9 81+
(Mrs A J Perrett) *trckd ldrs: hdwy to chal appr fnl f: r.o u.p to ld last strides* **6/1**[2]
-403 **2** *hd* **Velvet Waters**[8] 2305 5-8-12 **66** StephenCarson 7 74
(R F Johnson Houghton) *sn led: rdn 3f out: styd on u.p whn chal fr over 1f out: hdd and no ex last strides* **9/1**
0-20 **3** *1* **Ocean Avenue (IRE)**[20] 1943 7-9-7 **75** LDettori 5 81
(C A Horgan) *chsd ldrs: drvn to chal ins fnl 2f: stl upsides ins last: no ex nr fin* **6/1**[2]
1042 **4** *½* **Desert Island Disc**[15] 2067 9-8-11 **72** SladeO'Hara(7) 3 77
(Dr J R J Naylor) *hld up in rr: hdwy on outside fr 4f out: drvn to chse ldrs over 2f out: nt qckn ins last* **8/1**[3]
-000 **5** *3* **Takafu (USA)**[15] 2088 4-9-4 **72** FergusSweeney 10 72
(W S Kittow) *chsd ldrs: rdn 3f out: wknd over 1f out* **16/1**
-054 **6** *1¾* **Pittsburgh**[8] 2305 4-8-6 **60** ow1 RichardHughes 12 58
(A M Balding) *bhd: swtchd to outside 3f out and sn rdn: no imp and styd on one pce* **4/1**[1]
2-00 **7** *9* **Phoebe Woodstock (IRE)**[32] 1651 4-9-1 **72** (p) AdamKirby(3) 6 55
(W R Swinburn) *chsd ldrs: rdn 4f out: wknd over 1f out* **20/1**
-004 **8** *hd* **Eldorado**[15] 2088 5-8-13 **67** JimmyFortune 8 50
(S Kirk) *bhd: rdn and styd on into mid-div 3f out: nvr in contention and sn wknd* **6/1**[2]
666- **9** *2½* **Mexican Pete**[185] 6325 6-9-4 **72** MartinDwyer 4 51
(A W Carroll) *bhd: rdn and brief effrt over 3f out: nvr in contention and sn wknd* **10/1**
1-04 **10** *2* **Stolen Hours (USA)**[10] 2231 6-9-7 **75** JimmyQuinn 2 51
(J Akehurst) *rdn over 3f out: a bhd* **16/1**
0006 **11** *20* **Love Angel (USA)**[14] 2097 4-8-8 **62** SteveDrowne 1 6
(J J Bridger) *chsd ldrs 5f: sn bhd* **25/1**
2m 36.36s **Going Correction** +0.05s/f (Good) **11** Ran SP% **113.4**
Speed ratings (Par 103):102,101,101,100,98 97,91,91,89,88 75
CSF £56.84 CT £336.17 TOTE £7.50: £2.90, £2.70, £1.80; EX 58.40 Trifecta £344.90 Part won. Pool: £485.80 - 0.20 winning tickets..
Owner Lingfield Breakfast Club **Bred** D Holt And Dana Holt **Trained** Pulborough, W Sussex

FOCUS
A fair handicap, but despite the pace appearing quite reasonable, it proved hard to make up ground. The form looks solid enough though, rated around the runner-up and fourth.
Phoebe Woodstock(IRE) Official explanation: jockey said filly had no more to give
Stolen Hours(USA) Official explanation: jockey said horse was unsuited by the good ground
Love Angel(USA) Official explanation: jockey said gelding hung right

2535 TRETHOWANS SOLICITORS H'CAP 6f 212y
4:45 (4:50) (Class 6) (0-60,60) 3-Y-O **£3,238** (£963; £481; £240) **Stalls** High

Form RPR
000- **1** **Takitwo**[235] 6011 3-9-2 **55** DaneO'Neill 3 64
(P D Cundell) *s.i.s: sn in tch: hdwy to ld ins fnl 2f: drvn clr ins last* **33/1**
3054 **2** *2* **Davidia (IRE)**[20] 1941 3-9-7 **60** JimmyFortune 14 64+
(S Kirk) *chsd ldrs: rdn 3f out: styd on u.p to take 2nd cl home but no ch w wnr* **11/2**[2]
1300 **3** *nk* **Fateful Attraction**[16] 2050 3-9-2 **55** IanMongan 20 58
(I A Wood) *bhd: hdwy on outside fr 3f out: styd on u.p fnl 2f but nvr gng pce to trble wnr* **14/1**
60-4 **4** *shd* **Gift Aid**[45] 1304 3-8-12 **51** FergusSweeney 8 54
(P J Makin) *chsd ldrs: led appr fnl 3f: sn rdn: hdd ins fnl 2f: one pce ins last* **15/2**
-463 **5** *¾* **Mull Of Dubai**[15] 2065 3-9-4 **57** LPKeniry 17 58+
(J S Moore) *chsd ldrs: drvn and n.m.r 2f out: swtchd lft over 1f out: r.o ins last but nvr gng pce to trble ldrs* **5/1**[1]
5002 **6** *1¼* **Almowj**[11] 2210 3-9-2 **55** RyanMoore 15 53
(C E Brittain) *bhd: swtchd to outside and hdwy fr 2f out: styd on ins last but nvr in contention* **6/1**[3]
6006 **7** *¾* **Miss Redactive**[3] 2458 3-8-8 **50** DeanCorby(3) 6 46
(M D I Usher) *bhd: hdwy over 2f out: kpt on fr over 1f out but nvr in contention* **33/1**
0-65 **8** *½* **Dark Moon**[11] 2210 3-9-0 **53** RichardHughes 7 48
(A M Balding) *stdd s: bhd: hdwy 2f out: sn rdn: kpt on but n.d* **14/1**
0-40 **9** *½* **Welsh Cake**[33] 1616 3-9-7 **60** (bt[1]) TQuinn 4 53
(Mrs A J Perrett) *chsd ldrs: chal over 4f out to 2f out: wknd over 1f out* **12/1**
050 **10** *½* **March Gold (IRE)**[53] 1114 3-9-0 **53** SteveDrowne 18 45
(H Morrison) *s.i.s: bhd: pushed along on rails and n.m.r over 2f out: nvr in contention* **14/1**
-000 **11** *nk* **Montzando**[15] 2065 3-8-12 **58** JamesMillman(7) 13 49
(B R Millman) *chsd ldrs early: lost pl 1/2-way and n.d after* **12/1**
06-6 **12** *nk* **Sebaaq (USA)**[44] 1314 3-9-3 **56** (v) MartinDwyer 9 46
(M P Tregoning) *chsd ldrs: wknd 2f out: no ch whn n.m.r ins last* **10/1**
0000 **13** *½* **Lady Duxyana**[3] 2459 3-9-0 **53** HayleyTurner 2 42
(M D I Usher) *chsd ldrs: rdn 3f out: wknd 2f out* **33/1**
04-0 **14** *5* **Premier Cru**[35] 1567 3-8-13 **55** AdamKirby(3) 16 31
(Andrew Turnell) *chsd ldrs early: bhd fr 1/2-way* **25/1**
00-0 **15** *nk* **Task Complete**[7] 2316 3-9-2 **55** VinceSlattery 11 30
(J A Osborne) *sn ld: hdd over 3f out: sn btn* **66/1**
-005 **16** *6* **Valhar**[49] 1210 3-9-1 **54** PatDobbs 5 14
(J R Jenkins) *a in rr* **50/1**
5-00 **17** *17* **Waiting For Mary (IRE)**[35] 1567 3-9-5 **58** DavidKinsella 10 —
(J G M O'Shea) *pressed ldrs to 1/2-way* **28/1**
0 **18** *9* **Sarah's Prince (IRE)**[20] 1937 3-9-0 **53** JimmyQuinn 12 —
(D K Ivory) *bhd most of way* **33/1**
1m 29.55s (0.49) **Going Correction** +0.05s/f (Good) **18** Ran SP% **125.1**
Speed ratings (Par 97):99,96,96,96,95 93,93,92,91,91 91,90,90,84,84 77,57,47
CSF £199.11 CT £2796.11 TOTE £51.20: £11.80, £2.00, £3.70, £2.60; EX 626.10.
Owner Miss M C Fraser **Bred** Roden House Stud **Trained** Compton, Berks

FOCUS
Just a moderate handicap, but they went a strong pace and the form looks good and sound for the grade.
Takitwo ◆ Official explanation: trainer said, regarding the improved form shown, the gelding had strengthened up since running as a two-year-old
Valhar Official explanation: jockey said filly lost its action
Sarah's Prince(IRE) Official explanation: jockey said gelding stumbled and lost its action

2536 BATHWICK TYRES LADY RIDERS' SERIES H'CAP 6f
5:15 (5:16) (Class 5) (0-75,75) 4-Y-O+ **£3,591** (£1,113; £556; £278) **Stalls** High

Form RPR
0535 **1** **Guildenstern (IRE)**[12] 2170 4-10-1 **74** (t) MissVCartmel(7) 9 88
(H Morrison) *trckd ldrs: slt advantage over 1f out: shkn up and r.o strly ins fnl f* **5/1**[2]
0136 **2** *1* **Drumming Party (USA)**[7] 2331 4-9-2 **59** (t) MissMSowerby(5) 1 70
(A M Balding) *sn in tch: drvn to chse ldrs 1/2-way: chal appr fnl f: nt pce of wnr ins last* **11/2**[3]
5-02 **3** *3* **Summer Recluse (USA)**[6] 2340 7-9-8 **67** (t) MissSBradley(7) 5 69
(J M Bradley) *s.i.s: bhd: hmpd and stmbld over 3f out: kpt on fr over 1f out but nvr gng pce to rch ldrs* **7/1**
0200 **4** *½* **Willhewiz**[11] 2189 6-10-9 **75** MrsEmmaLittmoden 6 76
(M S Saunders) *slt ld: rdn over 2f out: hdd appr fnl f: wknd ins last* **6/1**
2324 **5** *nk* **Cross The Line (IRE)**[12] 2183 4-10-1 **72** MissKellyBurke(5) 8 72
(A P Jarvis) *s.i.s: bhd: pushed along and one pce over 2f out: sme prog fnl f* **3/1**[1]
4-04 **6** *¾* **Witchry**[2] 2484 4-10-4 **70** MissCHannaford 10 67
(A G Newcombe) *in tch: rdn 1/2-way: nvr gng pce to rch ldrs: wknd fnl f* **17/2**
3001 **7** *3* **Renegade (IRE)**[9] 2260 5-9-4 **58** 6ex ow7 (b) MissSSawyer(7) 7 51
(Mrs L J Mongan) *chsd ldrs: chal 3f out to 2f out: wknd over 1f out* **20/1**
0505 **8** *1¾* **Dancing Mystery**[49] 1211 12-9-10 **69** MissCNosworthy(7) 3 52
(E A Wheeler) *a outpcd* **12/1**
44-0 **9** *1½* **Princely Vale (IRE)**[4] 2390 4-9-10 **62** (p) MissEJJones 4 41
(W G M Turner) *chsd ldrs tl wknd ins fnl 2f* **14/1**
00-0 **10** *2½* **Tiffin Deano (IRE)**[14] 2096 4-8-13 **58** oh16 ow2 MissEJTuck(7) 2 29
(H J Manners) *sn bhd* **100/1**
1m 15.25s (0.27) **Going Correction** +0.05s/f (Good) **10** Ran SP% **114.5**
Speed ratings (Par 103):100,98,94,94,93 92,88,86,84,80
CSF £32.02 CT £196.49 TOTE £6.50: £2.80, £2.50, £2.00; EX 49.00 Place 6 £201.04, Place 5 £109.85.
Owner Scott-Barrett,Tufnell,Kerr-Dineen,Burley **Bred** Peter E Daly **Trained** East Ilsley, Berks
■ A first winner for Victoria Cartmel, on only her second ride.

FOCUS
Just an ordinary handicap restricted to lady riders, but the pace was sound enough and the form should prove reliable.
T/Jkpt: Not won. T/Plt: £64.00 to a £1 stake. Pool: £50,478.70. 575.75 winning tickets. T/Qpdt: £15.90 to a £1 stake. Pool: £2,886.50. 133.80 winning tickets. ST

LE LION-D'ANGERS (R-H)
Tuesday, June 13

OFFICIAL GOING: Good

2537a PRIX URBAN SEA (LISTED RACE) (FILLIES) 1m 3f 110y
3:05 (3:06) 3-Y-O **£17,241** (£6,897; £5,172; £3,448; £1,724)

RPR
1 **Mandesha (FR)**[15] 3-8-11 C-PLemaire 8 94
(A De Royer-Dupre, France)
2 *nk* **Flow Chart (UAE)**[31] 3-8-11 MAndrouin 5 94
(H-A Pantall, France)
3 *5* **Marachi Band (USA)**[25] 1837 3-8-11 (b) RichardMullen 11 86
(E J O'Neill) *prom, close 3rd on outside ½-way, drvn appr st, hrd rdn over 1f out & lost plce, gamely kpt on to retake 3rd cl hme (30-1)* **30/1**[1]
4 *½* **Song Of Kintyre (FR)**[27] 3-8-11 AClement 9 85
(A Couetil, France)
5 *½* **Snake Dancer (IRE)**[13] 3-8-11 TThulliez 2 85
(N Clement, France)
6 *nk* **Mademoiselle Louna (FR)**[81] 3-8-11 OPeslier 1 84
(J-M Beguigne, France)
7 *1½* **Pray For Sun (IRE)**[49] 3-8-11 SPasquier 3 82
(F Rohaut, France)
8 *3* **Fusaichi Dream (IRE)** 3-8-11 (b) FXBertras 7 77
(F Rohaut, France)
9 *¾* **Isobel Baillie**[31] 3-8-11 GToupel 4 76
(H-A Pantall, France)
10 *4* **Se La Vie (FR)**[35] 3-8-11 ACrastus 6 70
(P Demercastel, France)
2m 17.97s **10** Ran SP% **3.2**
PARI-MUTUEL (Including 1 Euro stake): WIN 3.20; PL 1.80, 3.10, 5.50;DF 11.30.
Owner Princess Zahra Aga Khan **Bred** Princes Zahra Aga Khan **Trained** Chantilly, France

NOTEBOOK
Marachi Band(USA), a 72-rated handicapper, rewarded connections' enterprise by earning some valuable black type. She has improved for the fitting of blinkers, but hopefully this will not damage her handicap mark too much.

2124 BEVERLEY (R-H)

Wednesday, June 14

OFFICIAL GOING: Good to firm

The ground was described as 'good, fast ground with no jar whatsoever'.
Wind: Moderate; half behind Weather: Fine and sunny

2538 RACING UK ON CHANNEL 432 CLAIMING STKS — 5f

2:10 (2:10) (Class 6) 2-Y-O — £3,238 (£963; £481; £240) Stalls High

Form — RPR

3211 **1** **Granny Peel (IRE)**[16] 2073 2-8-10 .... TonyHamilton 1 — 63
(K A Ryan) *chsd ldrs on outer: led 1f out: styd on wl* — 11/4[1]

506 **2** *3* **Bowl Em Over**[25] 1853 2-8-0 ....(p) PaulHanagan 4 — 41
(M E Sowersby) *led tl 2f out: kpt on same pce fnl f* — 20/1

0214 **3** *shd* **Baytown Paikea**[7] 2346 2-8-0 .... HayleyTurner 7 — 41
(P S McEntee) *swvd lft s: w ldrs: kpt on same pce fnl f* — 7/2[2]

66 **4** *nk* **Reflective Glory (IRE)**[32] 1664 2-9-0 .... GrahamGibbons 5 — 53
(J J Quinn) *chsd ldrs: kpt on same pce fnl 2f* — 11/2

01 **5** *3/4* **Spinning Game**[24] 1862 2-8-10 .... PaulQuinn 8 — 46+
(D W Chapman) *dwlt: sn in tch: keeping on same pce whn n.m.r ins last* — 7/1

403 **6** *1/2* **Elizabeth Garrett**[30] 1743 2-8-8 .... RobertWinston 2 — 42
(R M H Cowell) *sn chsng ldrs: wknd over 1f out* — 9/2[3]

7 *2* **Compton Verney** 2-8-11 .... PaulMulrennan 3 — 37
(M W Easterby) *s.s: sn detached in rr: styd on appr fnl f* — 33/1

150 **8** *1 1/2* **Best Woman**[9] 2300 2-8-11 .... DeanCorby(3) 6 — 34
(P Howling) *hmpd s: a outpcd and in rr* — 8/1

63.67 secs (-0.33) **Going Correction** -0.30s/f (Firm) — 8 Ran SP% **113.8**
Speed ratings (Par 91): 90,85,85,84,83 82,79,76
CSF £57.48 TOTE £3.00: £1.30, £4.80, £1.20; EX 43.90.The winner was the subject of a friendly claim.
Owner J Hopkinson and R Peel **Bred** Tally-Ho Stud **Trained** Hambleton, N Yorks

FOCUS
A run-of-the-mill claimer enabled the tough Granny Peel to record a fourth success. The race is rated negatively around the first two.

NOTEBOOK
Granny Peel(IRE) did not move at all well going down but on the way back it was a different story and she readily recorded her fourth win this time going right away at the end. She was retained at the ballot in the face of stiff opposition. (op 5-2 tchd 3-1, 9-4 in a place)
Bowl Em Over, in first-time cheekpieces, was keen to post. She gave the winner a lead but was readily brushed aside.
Baytown Paikea, having her seventh start, is now fully exposed. (tchd 4-1)
Reflective Glory(IRE), absent for a month, ran better than here last time and at least this opens up the nursery route for her. (op 6-1)
Spinning Game, who has changed stables, missed a beat at the start and was then going nowhere when running out of racing room inside the last. (op 13-2)
Elizabeth Garrett, awkward to load, had an outside draw to overcome this time. (op 6-1)
Compton Verney, a May foal, was noisy and inclined to be coltish in the paddock, the other seven runners were all fillies. He gave away many lengths at the start but at least showed he is not a hopeless case picking up nicely late on.
Best Woman, knocked over at the start, looks to be losing the plot. (op 9-1)

2539 WESTWOOD H'CAP — 1m 4f 16y

2:40 (2:40) (Class 6) (0-55,55) 3-Y-O — £3,238 (£963; £481; £240) Stalls High

Form — RPR

-022 **1** **Mister Fizzbomb (IRE)**[15] 2107 3-9-5 52 ....(v[1]) TonyHamilton 7 — 61
(J S Wainwright) *chsd ldr: led over 1f out: hld on wl* — 16/1

00-6 **2** *1* **Fonic Rock (IRE)**[44] 1350 3-9-7 54 .... JamieSpencer 6 — 61
(M L W Bell) *mid-div: hdwy on outer 3f out: chal 1f out: no ex* — 5/1[3]

0-02 **3** *1* **Collette's Choice**[9] 2283 3-9-0 47 .... PaulHanagan 1 — 56+
(R A Fahey) *hld up in rr: effrt over 3f out: styd on fnl f* — 4/1[2]

0-00 **4** *1* **Leo McGarry (IRE)**[44] 1352 3-9-2 49 .... NCallan 13 — 53
(S C Williams) *led tl over 1f out: styd on same pce* — 22/1

0-00 **5** *2* **Freeze The Flame (GER)**[25] 1851 3-9-5 55 .... NelsonDeSouza(3) 9 — 56
(C R Egerton) *chsd ldrs: one pce fnl 2f* — 9/1

000- **6** *1/2* **Alambic**[268] 5355 3-8-13 46 .... JamieMackay 4 — 46
(Sir Mark Prescott) *sn chsng ldrs: drvn 3f out: one pce fnl 2f* — 5/2[1]

-006 **7** *4* **Meohmy**[7] 2352 3-9-8 55 .... SamHitchcott 3 — 49
(M R Channon) *hld up towards rr: effrt over 3f out: nvr nr ldrs* — 14/1

-450 **8** *2 1/2* **El Dee (IRE)**[16] 2082 3-8-3 43 .... KellyHarrison(7) 11 — 33
(D Carroll) *t.k.h in mid-div: hdwy on inner 3f out: wknd over 1f out* — 20/1

0-00 **9** *1 1/4* **Sea Grain (IRE)**[30] 1736 3-9-5 55 .... SaleemGolam(3) 8 — 43
(Robert Gray) *stdd s: t.k.h in rr: sme hdwy 3f out: nvr a factor* — 25/1

5001 **10** *1/2* **Tallyhobye**[15] 2107 3-9-3 50 .... PaulMulrennan 10 — 37
(M E Sowersby) *t.k.h in rr: sme hdwy on outer 3f out: nvr on terms* — 14/1

606 **11** *3* **Every Inch (IRE)**[25] 1854 3-8-12 45 .... DavidAllan 14 — 27
(T D Easterby) *chsd ldrs: wkng whn n.m.r over 1f out* — 33/1

6000 **12** *1/2* **Tilen (IRE)**[41] 1441 3-9-0 47 ....(b) DeanMcKeown 2 — 28
(S Parr) *hld up in rr: drvn over 4f out: nvr a factor* — 66/1

000- **13** *51* **Fairytale Of York (IRE)**[180] 6588 3-8-7 40 .... GrahamGibbons 12 — —
(D Carroll) *rr-div: drvn 6f out: lost pl 3f out: sn bhd: virtually p.u: t.o: btn 51l* — 50/1

0-00 **14** *65* **Zingbat (IRE)**[19] 1984 3-9-3 50 .... RobertWinston 5 — —
(J G Given) *hung lft thrght: rn wd and lost pl bnd after 2f: m v wd and lost pl bnd over 4f out: sn virtually p.u: btn 65l* — 12/1

2m 39.91s (-0.30) **Going Correction** -0.30s/f (Firm) — 14 Ran SP% **121.5**
Speed ratings (Par 97): 89,88,87,87,85 85,82,81,80,79 77,77,43,—
CSF £88.70 CT £394.62 TOTE £14.70: £3.50, £2.00, £1.90; EX 83.10.
Owner S Enwright **Bred** Remora Bloodstock Ltd **Trained** Kennythorpe, N Yorks

FOCUS
A low-grade handicap, a seller in all but name. The pace was not strong and the race has been rated through the fifth.
Tallyhobye Official explanation: jockey said gelding ran too free in the early stages
Zingbat(IRE) Official explanation: trainer said gelding was kicked at the start and finished lame

2540 MCLEAN AND APPLETON H'CAP — 1m 1f 207y

3:10 (3:10) (Class 4) (0-80,80) 4-Y-O+ — £8,096 (£2,408; £1,203; £601) Stalls High

Form — RPR

0-00 **1** **Riley Boys (IRE)**[26] 1830 5-8-12 71 .... RobertWinston 2 — 82
(J G Given) *hld up in rr: hdwy on outer 3f out: swtchd ins over 1f out: led last 75yds: r.o wl* — 7/1

1323 **2** *1 3/4* **Augustine**[19] 2000 5-9-3 76 .... DarrenWilliams 8 — 83+
(P W Hiatt) *trckd ldrs: t.k.h: nt clr run over 2f out: styd on to take 2nd ins last* — 5/1[2]

0454 **3** *3/4* **Silverhay**[12] 2193 5-8-11 70 ....(p) JamieSpencer 5 — 76
(T D Barron) *chsd ldr: led after 2f: shkn up and qcknd over 3f out: hdd and no ex ins last* — 7/2[1]

-156 **4** *1* **Mount Usher**[18] 2020 4-8-2 61 .... AdrianTNicholls 1 — 72+
(G A Swinbank) *s.i.s: hld up in rr: hdwy 3f out: nt clr run and swtchd ins over 1f out: no room and swtchd outside: r.o wl* — 6/1

3300 **5** *hd* **Bobby Charles**[12] 2201 5-9-7 80 .... PaulHanagan 4 — 84
(Dr J D Scargill) *mid-div: hdwy on outer to chse ldrs over 2f out: kpt on same pce fnl f* — 9/1

-411 **6** *hd* **Dium Mac**[15] 2108 5-8-3 69 .... SuzzanneFrance(7) 7 — 72
(N Bycroft) *hld up in rr: hdwy on outer 6f out: chsng ldrs over 3f out: kpt on same pce appr fnl f* — 13/2

0-60 **7** *3 1/2* **Lysandra (IRE)**[28] 1779 4-9-1 74 .... KimTinkler 9 — 71
(N Tinkler) *in rr: hmpd and lost pl 3f out: kpt onf inal f* — 28/1

00-4 **8** *1 1/4* **Reaching Out (IRE)**[19] 1992 4-8-13 72 .... DarryllHolland 6 — 66
(N P Littmoden) *trckd ldrs: drvn over 3f out: wkng whn hmpd over 1f out* — 11/2[3]

0-03 **9** *11* **Viable**[15] 2104 4-8-5 64 .... DaleGibson 10 — 37
(Mrs P Sly) *led 2f: chsd ldrs: lost pl 2f out: eased ins last* — 11/1

000- **10** *2* **Apsara**[249] 5296 5-8-5 64 .... PaulMulrennan 3 — 34
(G M Moore) *chsd ldrs: wkng whn sltly hmpd 2f out: bhd whn eased ins last* — 33/1

2m 3.31s (-3.99) **Going Correction** -0.30s/f (Firm) — 10 Ran SP% **119.1**
Speed ratings (Par 105): 103,101,101,100,100 99,97,96,87,85
CSF £42.91 CT £145.92 TOTE £8.80: £2.80, £1.70, £1.30; EX 41.60.
Owner Paul Riley **Bred** P J Makin **Trained** Willoughton, Lincs
■ Stewards' Enquiry : Robert Winston two-day ban: careless riding (Jun 25-26)

FOCUS
A very rough race but sound enough on paper. Silverhay had no excuse from the front and the race has been rated through him, although with the runner-up.
Reaching Out(IRE) Official explanation: jockey said gelding hung right

2541 RED RUBY NIGHT HERE ON 22 JUNE H'CAP — 7f 100y

3:40 (3:40) (Class 5) (0-70,68) 4-Y-O+ — £5,181 (£1,541; £770; £384) Stalls High

Form — RPR

3012 **1** **Sake (IRE)**[19] 1996 4-9-7 68 .... KimTinkler 13 — 78
(N Tinkler) *chsd ldr: led over 2f out: styd on wl* — 9/2[2]

0604 **2** *1* **Blue Empire (IRE)**[14] 2137 5-8-8 55 .... HayleyTurner 14 — 63
(C R Dore) *t.k.h: led tl over 2f out: kpt on wl fnl f* — 17/2

2301 **3** *1* **Art Elegant**[9] 2282 4-9-7 68 6ex .... RobertWinston 8 — 73
(G A Swinbank) *in tch: hdwy over 2f out: kpt on same pce fnl f* — 6/1[3]

5-50 **4** *3/4* **Passion Fruit**[9] 2299 5-9-6 67 .... DeanMcKeown 6 — 70
(C W Fairhurst) *hld up in mid-div: hdwy on outer over 2f out: styd on same pce* — 14/1

0360 **5** *3/4* **Motu (IRE)**[5] 2390 5-8-2 52 ow2 ....(v) PatrickMathers(3) 10 — 53+
(I W McInnes) *s.i.s: hdwy over 2f out: kpt on wl fnl f* — 14/1

5-11 **6** *1/2* **Bollin Edward**[13] 2164 7-9-6 67 .... NCallan 1 — 67
(K A Ryan) *in rr: swtchd rt after s: hdwy over 2f out: kpt on fnl f: nvr rchd ldrs* — 4/1[1]

5-52 **7** *shd* **Sedge (USA)**[48] 1258 6-8-3 55 .... RoryMoore(5) 9 — 55
(P T Midgley) *hld up in mid-div: hdwy over 2f out: kpt on: nvr rchd ldrs* — 10/1

-500 **8** *1 1/2* **Windy Prospect**[8] 2317 4-8-11 58 .... DavidAllan 15 — 54
(Miss Sheena West) *chsd ldrs: wknd appr fnl f* — 20/1

-300 **9** *2* **Uhuru Peak**[32] 1665 5-8-7 54 ....(t) PaulMulrennan 3 — 45
(M W Easterby) *in rr: kpt on fnl 3f: nvr a factor* — 33/1

-620 **10** *1 1/4* **Flaxby**[15] 2112 4-8-4 51 ....(b) AdrianTNicholls 4 — 39
(J D Bethell) *hld up in rr: sme hdwy on outer over 2f out: sn wknd* — 10/1

00-0 **11** *1/2* **Peters Delite**[23] 1885 4-9-1 62 ....(p) PaulHanagan 11 — 49
(R A Fahey) *chsd ldrs: wknd over 1f out* — 16/1

-020 **12** *1/2* **Splodger Mac (IRE)**[9] 2286 7-7-13 53 .... SuzzanneFrance(7) 7 — 38
(N Bycroft) *chsd ldrs: effrt 3f out: lost pl over 1f out* — 22/1

0345 **13** *1 1/4* **Kalani Star (IRE)**[10] 2262 6-8-2 49 oh2 ....(vt) JamieMackay 12 — 31
(I W McInnes) *a in rr* — 16/1

6500 **14** *11* **Kingsmaite**[33] 1645 5-8-3 53 .... BenSwarbrick(3) 5 — 8
(S R Bowring) *mid-div: lost pl over 2f out: bhd whn eased ins last* — 20/1

1m 31.15s (-3.16) **Going Correction** -0.30s/f (Firm) — 14 Ran SP% **123.1**
Speed ratings (Par 103): 106,104,103,102,102 101,101,99,97,95 95,94,93,80
CSF £41.28 CT £244.71 TOTE £5.10: £2.00, £3.70, £1.90; EX 52.20 Trifecta £270.10 Part won. Pool: £380.44 - 0.40 winning units. Pool £228.26..
Owner Mrs Lara Dales **Bred** Illuminatus Investments **Trained** Langton, N Yorks

FOCUS
A moderate handicap run at a strong pace and the first two home had ideal draws. The form looks solid.

2542 THE COMMITMENTS PLAY LIVE ON 22 JUNE MAIDEN STKS — 7f 100y

4:10 (4:11) (Class 4) 3-Y-O+ — £5,181 (£1,541; £770; £384) Stalls High

Form — RPR

2 **1** **Robema**[14] 2129 3-8-6 .... GrahamGibbons 3 — 76
(J J Quinn) *trckd ldrs: led over 2f out: clr 1f out: readily* — 10/3[2]

32 **2** *5* **Dear Gracie (IRE)**[23] 1901 3-8-7 ow1 .... JamieSpencer 6 — 65
(J R Fanshawe) *hld up in midfield: effrt over 3f out: styd on u.p to go 2nd ins last: no ch w wnr* — 4/5[1]

3 *1 1/4* **Can Can Star** 3-8-11 .... NCallan 7 — 65
(J G Given) *chsd ldrs: kpt on fnl 2f* — 50/1

2-0 **4** *hd* **Ten To The Dozen**[7] 2366 3-8-11 .... DarrenWilliams 12 — 65
(P W Hiatt) *in tch: effrt over 2f out: kpt on same pce* — 11/1

65 **5** *3/4* **Xpres Maite**[11] 2244 3-8-11 .... PhillipMakin 1 — 63
(S R Bowring) *chsd ldrs: one pce fnl 2f* — 50/1

6 *1* **Silent Applause** 3-8-11 .... DarryllHolland 2 — 61
(Dr J D Scargill) *lost pl after 1f: bhd tl styd on appr fnl f* — 50/1

6 **7** *nk* **Hill Billy Rock (IRE)**[9] 2298 3-8-11 .... DeanMcKeown 9 — 60
(G A Swinbank) *in rr: effrt over 2f out: kpt on fnl f* — 40/1

8 *1 1/4* **Final Award (IRE)** 3-8-6 .... PaulMulrennan 10 — 52
(G M Moore) *chsd ldrs: outpcd over 2f out: wknd over 1f out* — 40/1

0-0 **9** *1 1/2* **Sand Sprite (IRE)**[18] 2028 3-8-6 .... RobertWinston 8 — 48
(Sir Michael Stoute) *s.s: bhd tl sme hdwy fnl 3f: nvr on terms* — 6/1[3]

10 *1* **Silk Topper (IRE)** 3-8-11 .... PaulHanagan 5 — 50
(R A Fahey) *s.i.s: bhd: sme hdwy over 2f out: nvr on terms* — 50/1

5-0 **11** *11* **Sharpe Image (IRE)**[33] 1649 3-8-6 .... AdrianTNicholls 4 — 18
(G Woodward) *mid-div: lost pl over 2f out: bhd whn eased ins last* — 66/1

0-06 **12** *1 1/2* **Vincent Vegas**[19] 1988 3-8-11 25 ....(p) TonyHamilton 11 — 19
(Mrs S Lamyman) *led tl over 2f out: sn lost pl: bhd whn eased ins last* — 100/1

1m 31.32s (-2.99) **Going Correction** -0.30s/f (Firm) — 12 Ran SP% **116.5**
Speed ratings (Par 105): 105,99,97,97,96 95,95,93,92,91 78,76
CSF £5.99 TOTE £4.50: £1.40, £1.10, £9.30; EX 8.20.

Owner Mrs J O'Connor **Bred** Newsells Park Stud Limited **Trained** Settrington, N Yorks
FOCUS
Just a steady pace and the progressive winner had flown the time Jamie Spencer woke up and found daylight.
Sand Sprite(IRE) Official explanation: jockey said filly missed the break

2543 WIN A RED RUBY HERE NEXT THURSDAY FILLIES' H'CAP 5f
4:40 (4:41) (Class 6) (0-55,59) 3-Y-O+ **£3,238** (£963; £481; £240) **Stalls** High

Form RPR
6460 **1** **Muara**[6] 2376 4-9-4 **50** ... MarkLawson(5) 14 60
(D W Barker) *chsd ldrs: styd on wl fnl f: led nr fin* **5/1**[1]
300- **2** *nk* **Slipperfoot**[215] 6311 3-9-7 **55** ... GrahamGibbons 18 61
(J J Quinn) *led: hdd and no ex towards fin* **8/1**[2]
0015 **3** *nk* **Estoille**[29] 1762 5-9-9 **50** ... PaulHanagan 8 58+
(Mrs S Lamyman) *chsd ldrs: kpt on wl ins last* **10/1**
60-6 **4** *1* **Cut Ridge (IRE)**[30] 1728 7-9-3 **44** ... PaulMulrennan 17 48
(J S Wainwright) *chsd ldrs: kpt on same pce ins last* **9/1**[3]
5202 **5** *hd* **Suhezy (IRE)**[9] 2284 3-9-1 **49** ... TonyHamilton 10 49+
(J S Wainwright) *mid-div: hdwy on outer over 1f out: styd on wl ins last* **5/1**[1]
-010 **6** *hd* **Jahia (NZ)**[6] 2376 7-9-8 **49** ... StanleyChin 9 51+
(P T Midgley) *stmbld s: hdwy on inner 3f out: styd on wl fnl f* **16/1**
63-0 **7** *½* **World At My Feet**[48] 1249 4-9-0 **48** ... SuzzanneFrance(7) 16 48
(N Bycroft) *chsd ldrs: kpt on same pce fnl f* **12/1**
0600 **8** *½* **Bint Royal (IRE)**[5] 2400 8-10-0 **55** ... (v) NCallan 6 53
(Miss V Haigh) *mid-div: hdwy over 1f out: kpt on* **25/1**
0416 **9** *nk* **Just Down The Road (IRE)**[2] 2511 3-9-4 **59** 6ex ... TolleyDean(7) 2 53
(R A Harris) *chsd ldrs on outer: one pce fnl 2f* **8/1**[2]
0600 **10** *1 ½* **Lady Palma Nova**[29] 1762 3-8-11 **45** ... JosedeSouza 19 33
(G P Kelly) *unruly s: chsd ldrs: fdd appr fnl f* **33/1**
0-06 **11** *1 ½* **Jinksonthehouse**[15] 2096 5-9-4 **45** ... HayleyTurner 4 30
(M D I Usher) *swtchd rt s: bhd: sme hdwy 2f out: nvr on terms* **33/1**
00-4 **12** *¾* **Yorke's Folly (USA)**[30] 1733 5-8-13 **45** ... (b) LeanneKershaw(5) 7 27
(C W Fairhurst) *in rr: sme hdwy 2f out: nvr a factor* **12/1**
0/00 **13** *1 ¼* **Nellie Gwyn**[30] 1733 4-8-13 **40** ... DeanMcKeown 1 17
(J G Given) *swtchd rt s: nvr on terms* **50/1**
60-0 **14** *hd* **Dolly Brown**[11] 2249 3-9-1 **49** ... DavidAllan 15 22
(T D Easterby) *dwlt: a in rr* **28/1**
5-61 **15** *1 ¼* **Limited Magician**[47] 1272 5-9-6 **47** ... (v) GylesParkin 11 18
(C Smith) *a in rr* **16/1**
0000 **16** *hd* **Value Plus (IRE)**[15] 2112 4-8-7 **41** ... JamieHamblett(7) 20 12
(S Parr) *sn bhd* **33/1**
-000 **17** *¾* **Lizzie Rocket**[129] 299 6-8-11 **45** ... (b) JamesO'Reilly(7) 12 13
(J O'Reilly) *mid-div: lost pl over 2f out* **33/1**
0060 **18** *shd* **Stephanie's Mind**[30] 1722 4-9-2 **43** ... JamieSpencer 5 10
(M Quinn) *sn towards rr* **11/1**
460- **19** *3 ½* **Martharum**[235] 6030 3-9-0 **48** ... PhillipMakin 13 —
(J J Quinn) *trckd ldrs: lost pl over 1f out: eased ins last* **33/1**

62.72 secs (-1.28) **Going Correction** -0.30s/f (Firm)
WFA 3 from 4yo+ 7lb **19** Ran SP% **134.1**
Speed ratings (Par 98):98,97,97,95,95 94,94,93,92,90 87,86,84,84,82 82,80,80,75
CSF £43.19 CT £421.19 TOTE £6.20: £1.90, £2.60, £3.00, £2.50; EX 45.10 Place 6 £42.91, Place 5 £23.83.
Owner W R Arblaster **Bred** W R And Mrs Arblaster **Trained** Scorton, N Yorks
FOCUS
A low-grade sprint handicap, a seller in all but name. As usual on fast ground here the high numbers held sway. The time was good for the grade and the form looks solid.
Jahia(NZ) Official explanation: trainer said mare stumbled at the start
Stephanie's Mind Official explanation: jockey said filly was never travelling
T/Jkpt: Not won. T/Plt: £12.60 to a £1 stake. Pool: £47,552.70. 2,748.90 winning tickets. T/Qpdt: £7.90 to a £1 stake. Pool: £2,206.20. 204.15 winning tickets. WG

2375 HAMILTON (R-H)
Wednesday, June 14
OFFICIAL GOING: Good to firm (firm in places)
Wind: Almost nil

2544 SAINTS AND SINNERS AMATEUR RIDERS' H'CAP 6f 5y
6:45 (6:45) (Class 6) (0-55,55) 4-Y-O+ **£3,296** (£1,014; £507) **Stalls** Low

Form RPR
66-5 **1** **Outrageous Flirt (IRE)**[11] 2248 4-11-0 **48** ... MissSBrotherton 7 57
(A Dickman) *hld up centre: hdwy over 1f out: led wl ins fnl f: r.o wl* **10/1**
-050 **2** *1* **Hamaasy**[9] 2288 5-10-13 **47** ... MrSDobson 13 53+
(D Nicholls) *overall ldr far side: hung bdly lft fr 1/2-way and ended up on stands rail over 1f out: hdd wl ins fnl f: r.o* **9/1**
610- **3** *1* **Smirfys Night**[200] 6429 7-10-11 **52** ... MissEGeorge(7) 2 55
(E S McMahon) *prom stands side: rdn and edgd rt over 2f out: kpt on ins fnl f* **12/1**
-544 **4** *¾* **Proud Western (USA)**[11] 2240 8-10-8 **45** ... (tp) MissLEllison(3) 10 46
(B Ellison) *sn wl outpcd far side: gd hdwy over 2f out: kpt on fnl f: no imp* **12/1**
0/03 **5** *shd* **Quicks The Word**[34] 1607 6-10-10 **49** ... MissHCuthbert(5) 8 49
(T A K Cuthbert) *prom centre: effrt over 2f out: one pce over 1f out* **16/1**
1003 **6** *nk* **Sundried Tomato**[36] 1577 7-10-12 **46** ... (p) MissADeniel 4 46
(D W Chapman) *chsd centre ldrs: rdn over 2f out: edgd rt and no ex over 1f out* **20/1**
00-0 **7** *shd* **Fairgame Man**[13] 2182 8-11-2 **50** ... MrsCBartley 14 49
(J S Wainwright) *prom far side: effrt and ev ch that gp over 1f out: kpt on same pce* **12/1**
3032 **8** *1 ½* **Weakest Link**[15] 2112 5-10-10 **49** ... MrSPearce(5) 5 44
(E J Alston) *in tch centre: outpcd over 2f out: no imp fnl f* **5/1**[1]
/054 **9** *hd* **Haulage Man**[6] 2376 8-10-12 **46** ... (p) MissPRobson 6 40
(Karen McLintock) *hld up: effrt over 2f out: no imp fnl f* **6/1**[2]
00-0 **10** *shd* **Strawberry Patch (IRE)**[6] 2376 7-11-0 **55** ow2 ... MrGGoldie(7) 11 49
(J S Goldie) *prom towards far side: effrt over 2f out: btn fnl f* **33/1**
0510 **11** *1 ¼* **Chairman Rick (IRE)**[35] 1594 4-10-6 **47** ... MissWGibson(7) 12 37
(D Nicholls) *missed break: sn outpcd: sme hdwy over 2f out: n.d* **16/1**
0006 **12** *nk* **Revien (IRE)**[9] 2288 4-10-7 **48** ... MrJDNolan(7) 3 37
(Miss J R Tooth) *chsd centre ldrs tl wknd over 1f out* **33/1**
6020 **13** *3* **Tequila Sheila (IRE)**[13] 2165 4-10-9 **48** ... MissKellyBurke(5) 1 28
(K R Burke) *racd stands side: prom tl wknd over 2f out* **13/2**[3]
5230 **14** *3* **Royal Pardon**[12] 2198 4-11-2 **55** ... (b[1]) MissJRiding(5) 9 26
(R C Guest) *keen: prom centre tl wknd over 2f out* **16/1**

1m 12.39s (-0.71) **Going Correction** -0.35s/f (Firm) **14** Ran SP% **114.7**
Speed ratings (Par 101):90,88,87,86,86 85,85,83,83,83 81,81,77,73
CSF £90.42 CT £1114.02 TOTE £6.40: £2.10, £3.70, £7.50; EX 131.40.
Owner Mrs D Hodgkinson **Bred** Mount Coote Stud **Trained** Sandhutton, N Yorks
FOCUS
A modest handicap in which the pace was sound and the field fanned across the course. There was no evidence of any draw bias and the form looks solid for the grade.
Sundried Tomato Official explanation: jockey said saddle slipped
Royal Pardon Official explanation: jockey said saddle slipped

2545 PERSIMMON PARTNERSHIPS CHAMPAGNE MAIDEN STKS (QUALIFIER FOR THE HAMILTON PARK 2-Y-O SERIES FINAL) 6f 5y
7:15 (7:15) (Class 4) 2-Y-O **£5,181** (£1,541; £770; £384) **Stalls** Low

Form RPR
1 **Narrjoo (USA)** 2-9-3 ... TonyCulhane 6 74+
(M R Channon) *keen: cl up: led over 2f out: rdn and r.o wl fnl f* **4/6**[1]
2 *½* **Vauquelin (IRE)** 2-9-3 ... RichardMullen 4 73+
(E S McMahon) *trckd ldrs: effrt over 1f out: sn chsng wnr: kpt on fnl f: improve* **9/2**[2]
3 *5* **Tobago Reef** 2-9-3 ... TomEaves 3 58
(Mrs L Stubbs) *s.i.s: hld up in tch: effrt over 2f out: outpcd over 1f out* **33/1**
4 *3* **Desert Soul** 2-9-3 ... JoeFanning 7 49
(M Johnston) *led to over 2f out: sn outpcd* **9/2**[2]
5 *1 ½* **Keep Your Distance** 2-9-3 ... JohnEgan 2 44
(K R Burke) *w ldrs tl wknd fr 2f out* **12/1**[3]

1m 12.72s (-0.38) **Going Correction** -0.35s/f (Firm) **5** Ran SP% **107.0**
Speed ratings (Par 95):88,87,80,76,74
CSF £3.71 TOTE £1.60: £1.10, £2.20; EX 2.90.
Owner Sheikh Ahmed Al Maktoum **Bred** Darley **Trained** West Ilsley, Berks
FOCUS
Few runners but this could prove a fair event for the track and the first two did well to pull clear in the last furlong and a half and could prove better than this.
NOTEBOOK
Narrjoo(USA), the first foal of a half-sister to a Nassau Stakes winner, proved green in the preliminaries and on the way to post but knew his job and justified the strong market support. Whether he would beat the runner-up next time remains to be seen but he is certainly open to improvement and should win more races. (op 4-5)
Vauquelin(IRE) ◆, who has winners over a variety of distances in his pedigree, took the eye in the paddock despite looking as though the race would do him good and shaped with a good deal of promise on this debut. He has plenty of physical scope, should have no problems with seven furlongs and is sure to pick up a similar event at the very least. (op 6-1 tchd 13-2 and 4-1)
Tobago Reef, out of a half-sister to several winners up to staying distances, showed ability on this racecourse debut and looks the type to improve granted a stiffer test and ordinary handicap company in due course. (op 20-1)
Desert Soul, the first foal of a smart winner over middle distances, took the eye in the paddock despite looking as though the race would do him good. He ran that way too, but is the type to leave this bare form behind in due course. (op 11-4)
Keep Your Distance, the first foal of a middle-distance winner, was not totally disgraced in what could turn out to be a fair event for the track and, although he may continue to look vulnerable in this grade, is likely to improve for the experience. (tchd 14-1)

2546 COFFEE EXPRESS (S) STKS 1m 65y
7:45 (7:46) (Class 5) 3-Y-O+ **£3,238** (£963; £481; £240) **Stalls** High

Form RPR
4141 **1** **Ulysees (IRE)**[11] 2240 7-10-1 69 ... PaulHanagan 3 62
(I Semple) *hld up: hdwy over 2f out: sn pushed along: led wl ins fnl f: comf* **9/4**[1]
4320 **2** *1 ¼* **Wiltshire (IRE)**[37] 1550 4-10-1 48 ... (v) TonyCulhane 12 59
(P A Blockley) *keen: led: rdn over 2f out: hdd and no ex wl ins fnl f* **11/1**
0-23 **3** *¾* **Alisdanza**[34] 1608 4-9-4 50 ... JoeFanning 1 46
(G A Swinbank) *hld up: hdwy over 2f out: rdn and kpt on ins fnl f* **7/1**[2]
3-34 **4** *hd* **Sarraaf (IRE)**[144] 170 10-10-1 63 ... TomEaves 2 57
(I Semple) *hld up: rdn over 3f out: hdwy and edgd rt over 1f out: kpt on fnl f* **8/1**[3]
3050 **5** *1 ½* **Insubordinate**[6] 2384 5-10-1 56 ... FergalLynch 14 53
(J S Goldie) *hld up: hdwy on ins over 1f out: nt clr run ins fnl f: no imp* **11/1**
1543 **6** *hd* **Donna's Double**[29] 1757 11-10-1 51 ... (p) TonyHamilton 13 53
(Karen McLintock) *prom tl rdn and nt qckn over 1f out* **9/1**
0004 **7** *¾* **Spring Time Girl**[16] 2077 4-9-10 43 ... (v) RobertWinston 9 46
(B Ellison) *bhd tl hdwy over 1f out: nvr rchd ldrs* **16/1**
0-00 **8** *shd* **Eccollo (IRE)**[69] 897 4-9-9 ... JohnEgan 6 47+
(T J Pitt) *dwlt: sn chsng ldr: effrt 3f out: wknd ent fnl f* **8/1**[3]
3534 **9** *3 ½* **Musiotal**[30] 1746 5-9-8 45 ... (p) SophieDoyle(7) 5 43
(P A Blockley) *in tch tl rdn and no ex fr 2f out* **25/1**
2502 **10** *½* **Desert Lightning (IRE)**[11] 2240 4-9-10 55 ... AndrewElliott(5) 8 41
(K R Burke) *prom tl edgd rt and outpcd fr over 2f out* **10/1**
1-06 **11** *15* **Jordans Spark**[13] 2165 5-10-1 46 ... PaulMulrennan 10 7
(P Monteith) *chsd ldrs: rdn over 3f out: wknd over 2f out* **33/1**
-000 **12** *6* **Lucky Largo (IRE)**[26] 1814 6-9-9 32 ... (v[1]) DerekMcGaffin 11 —
(D A Nolan) *chsd ldrs: rdn 4f out: sn wknd* **100/1**
550- **13** *1 ¼* **Happy Harry (IRE)**[248] 5769 3-8-7 44 ... (b[1]) AndrewMullen(5) 15 —
(B Storey) *chsd ldrs to 1/2-way: sn rdn and wknd* **100/1**
0/0- **14** *7* **Lion's Domane**[7] 605 9-9-8 35 ... NeilBrown(7) 4 —
(K W Hogg) *in tch on outside tl hung rt and wknd over 3f out* **100/1**

1m 45.43s (-3.87) **Going Correction** -0.425s/f (Firm)
WFA 3 from 4yo+ 11lb **14** Ran SP% **116.9**
Speed ratings (Par 103):102,100,100,99,98 98,97,97,93,93 78,72,71,64
CSF £26.60 TOTE £2.90: £1.70, £5.40, £2.30; EX 38.40.There was no bid for the winner.
Owner The Farmer Boys (Jock, Danny & Ally) **Bred** Sweetmans Bloodstock **Trained** Carluke, S Lanarks
FOCUS
A modest event but a race in which the pace was fair although the form looks shaky.
Insubordinate Official explanation: jockey said gelding was denied a clear run

2547 WALTER SCOTT SAINTS & SINNERS CHALLENGE CUP H'CAP 1m 65y
8:15 (8:16) (Class 4) (0-85,80) 4-Y-O+ **£8,096** (£2,408; £1,203; £601) **Stalls** High

Form RPR
-002 **1** **Go Solo**[9] 2299 5-9-1 **74** ... DeanMcKeown 8 83
(G A Swinbank) *pressed ldr: effrt 2f out: led ins fnl f: r.o wl* **5/2**[1]
006- **2** *½* **Toshi (USA)**[186] 6547 4-9-7 **80** ... TomEaves 4 88
(I Semple) *set stdy pce: led: rdn over 2f out: hdd ins fnl f: kpt on same pce* **16/1**

-050 **3** *nk* **Regent's Secret (USA)**[13] [2162] 6-9-0 **73**... FergalLynch 3 80
(J S Goldie) *hld up: effrt 3f out: hdwy over 1f out: kpt on wl fnl f: nrst fin* **3/1**[2]
0430 **4** *3* **Defi (IRE)**[6] [2378] 4-8-9 **68**...(p) TonyHamilton 9 68
(I Semple) *bhd: outpcd 1/2-way: hdwy over 1f out: nvr rchd ldrs* **11/1**
0601 **5** *hd* **Dark Charm (FR)**[18] [2025] 7-8-12 **71**...(p) PaulHanagan 1 71
(R A Fahey) *hld up in tch: outpcd 1/2-way: rallied over 2f out: no imp fnl f* **5/1**
3236 **6** *3* **Jordans Elect**[6] [2378] 6-8-10 **69**... RobertWinston 7 62
(P Monteith) *keen: prom tl rdn and wknd over 1f out* **9/2**[3]
00-0 **7** *3* **Red Chairman**[23] [1887] 4-8-7 **66**...(t) JoeFanning 5 52
(R Johnson) *chsd ldrs tl wknd fr 3f out* **50/1**
-000 **8** *1 ¼* **Happy As Larry (USA)**[106] [541] 4-9-4 **77**...(t) JohnEgan 2 60
(T J Pitt) *hld up in tch: effrt over 2f out: edgd rt and sn outpcd* **14/1**

1m 45.14s (-4.16) **Going Correction** -0.425s/f (Firm) **8** Ran SP% **111.3**
Speed ratings (Par 105):103,102,102,99,99 96,93,91
CSF £40.76 CT £120.10 TOTE £2.60: £1.10, £3.80, £1.90; EX 25.70.
Owner B Valentine **Bred** G Reed **Trained** Melsonby, N Yorks

FOCUS
An ordinary handicap in which the fairly steady early pace suited those racing close to the pace. The runner-up is the best guide to the form.

2548 PALL MALL CLAIMING STKS 1m 3f 16y
8:45 (8:45) (Class 5) 3-Y-O+ **£3,238** (£963; £481; £240) **Stalls** High

Form RPR
1403 **1** **Unique Moment**[2] [2507] 3-8-7 75... JoeFanning 5 65
(M Johnston) *pressed ldr: led over 2f out: rdn and edgd rt over 1f out: kpt on wl* **11/4**[2]
0625 **2** *3* **Grande Roche (IRE)**[8] [2322] 4-9-7 54...(b[1]) RobertWinston 7 60
(G A Swinbank) *prom: effrt and hd high over 2f out: chsd wnr ins fnl f: r.o* **4/1**[3]
6131 **3** *½* **Oldenway**[13] [2180] 7-9-12 71... PaulHanagan 11 64
(R A Fahey) *plld hrd: led: rdn and hdd over 2f out: one pce fnl f* **5/4**[1]
-500 **4** *2* **Myrtle Bay (IRE)**[8] [2332] 3-8-12 73... JohnEgan 6 61
(K R Burke) *hld up in tch: effrt over 2f out: no imp over 1f out* **11/1**
-460 **5** *2 ½* **Templet (USA)**[13] [2165] 6-9-2 46...(v) DuranFentiman[(5)] 4 52
(W G Harrison) *in tch: rdn and outpcd over 2f out: no imp after* **33/1**
4-00 **6** *2 ½* **Cordage (IRE)**[40] [1455] 4-9-10 60...(p) KDarley 1 51
(Karen McLintock) *hld up: rdn 3f out: nvr rchd ldrs* **20/1**
46 **7** *30* **Claudia May**[4] [2448] 5-9-4... PaulMulrennan 9 —
(Miss Lucinda V Russell) *bhd: rdn over 4f out: sn btn* **100/1**
046 **8** *16* **Now Tell Me This**[26] [1814] 3-8-3 42...(v) GregFairley[(5)] 8 —
(I Semple) *keen: in tch tl wknd fr 4f out* **40/1**
000- **9** *26* **Imperioli**[41] [6652] 4-9-4 30... TonyCulhane 3 —
(P A Blockley) *sn wl bhd: nvr on terms* **100/1**

2m 23.31s (-2.95) **Going Correction** -0.425s/f (Firm)
WFA 3 from 4yo+ 14lb **9** Ran SP% **111.6**
Speed ratings (Par 103):93,90,90,89,87 85,63,51,33
CSF £12.99 TOTE £3.30: £1.20, £1.90, £1.20; EX 15.70.
Owner J Shack **Bred** The Lavington Stud **Trained** Middleham Moor, N Yorks

FOCUS
An uncompetitive event in which the pace seemed fair but the form is limited by the proximity of the runner-up and fifth.
Imperioli Official explanation: jockey said gelding moved poorly throughout

2549 FIELD AND LAWN MARQUEES H'CAP 1m 4f 17y
9:15 (9:15) (Class 4) (0-80,80) 4-Y-O+ **£6,477** (£1,927; £963; £481) **Stalls** High

Form RPR
6-02 **1** **Sualda (IRE)**[9] [2296] 7-9-2 **75**... PaulHanagan 3 83
(R A Fahey) *in tch: hdwy and ev ch over 1f out: led wl ins fnl f: kpt on wl* **11/10**[1]
6200 **2** *hd* **Khanjar (USA)**[90] [652] 6-8-7 **71**... AndrewElliott[(5)] 6 79
(K R Burke) *led: rdn over 2f out: hrd pressed fr over 1f out: hdd wl ins fnl f: r.o* **16/1**
-602 **3** *3* **San Deng**[12] [2193] 4-8-5 **64**... KDarley 2 67
(Micky Hammond) *hld up: effrt over 2f out: kpt on fnl f: no imp* **7/2**[2]
0-34 **4** *½* **Easibet Dot Net**[23] [1887] 6-8-10 **69**...(p) TomEaves 4 71
(I Semple) *keen: chsd ldrs: effrt and edgd rt over 2f out: sn outpcd* **13/2**[3]
05 **5** *10* **Magnum Opus (IRE)**[26] [1827] 4-9-7 **80**... JohnEgan 5 66
(T J Pitt) *prom: rdn over 3f out: wknd over 2f out* **8/1**
3-00 **6** *½* **Andre Chenier (IRE)**[3] [1756] 5-8-3 **62**... JoeFanning 1 48
(P Monteith) *cl up tl rdn and wknd over 2f out* **11/1**

2m 34.11s (-5.07) **Going Correction** -0.425s/f (Firm) **6** Ran SP% **108.5**
Speed ratings (Par 105):99,98,96,96,89 89
CSF £18.64 TOTE £2.20: £1.40, £8.10; EX 19.10.
Owner J H Tattersall **Bred** St Simon Foundation **Trained** Musley Bank, N Yorks

FOCUS
An ordinary event in which the pace was fair and the form looks sound rated around the first two.

2550 SEE YOU AT GUYS AND DOLLS H'CAP 5f 4y
9:45 (9:47) (Class 5) (0-70,71) 3-Y-O+ **£3,886** (£1,156; £577; £288) **Stalls** Low

Form RPR
2045 **1** **Ashes (IRE)**[4] [2462] 4-10-0 **65**... PaulMulrennan 9 76
(K R Burke) *cl up: effrt 2f out: led ins fnl f: r.o wl* **10/1**[3]
0064 **2** *½* **Kings College Boy**[2] [2505] 6-9-9 **60**...(b) PaulHanagan 11 69+
(R A Fahey) *hld up: hdwy whn nt clr run briefly over 1f out: kpt on fnl f* **4/1**[1]
4101 **3** *nk* **Dizzy In The Head**[6] [2380] 7-10-6 **71** 6ex...(b) TomEaves 5 79
(I Semple) *led to ins fnl f: no ex towards fin* **4/1**[1]
0561 **4** *hd* **Namir (IRE)**[2] [2505] 4-9-11 **62** 6ex...(vt) GrahamGibbons 13 69
(Stef Liddiard) *prom on outside: effrt and ev ch over 1f out: one pce wl ins fnl f* **4/1**[1]
03 **5** *3* **Fikri**[11] [2247] 3-9-9 **67**...(bt[1]) JohnEgan 6 59
(T J Pitt) *prom tl rdn and nt qckn over 1f out* **14/1**
2620 **6** *¾* **Compton Classic**[4] [2449] 4-8-13 **50**...(p) FergalLynch 10 42
(J S Goldie) *in tch: drvn over 2f out: no imp over 1f out* **5/1**[2]
06-0 **7** *1* **Queen Of Night**[4] [2462] 6-9-7 **58**... TonyCulhane 4 46
(D W Chapman) *missed break: bhd tl sme late hdwy: nvr on terms* **25/1**
0-30 **8** *¾* **Tribute (IRE)**[23] [1878] 5-9-11 **62**... JoeFanning 2 47
(P A Blockley) *sn outpcd and drvn along: sme late hdwy: nvr on terms* **10/1**[3]
0540 **9** *nk* **Whistler**[2] [2505] 9-9-12 **63**...(p) PaulFitzsimons 7 47
(Miss J R Tooth) *sn outpcd: short-lived effrt on outside over 2f out: sn btn* **25/1**
0-05 **10** *1* **Shatin Leader**[6] [2377] 4-8-9 **46** oh1...(p) RobertWinston 1 26
(Miss L A Perratt) *trckd ldrs tl wknd appr fnl f* **16/1**

-000 **11** *1 ½* **Mister Marmaduke**[23] [1886] 5-8-13 **50**... DerekMcGaffin 8 24
(D A Nolan) *towards rr: outpcd 1/2-way: nvr on terms* **100/1**
000- **12** *nk* **Instinct**[198] [6446] 5-8-4 **46** oh4... AndrewElliott[(5)] 14 19
(Micky Hammond) *racd wd: midfield tl wknd fr 1/2-way* **66/1**
55-5 **13** *4* **She's Our Beauty (IRE)**[148] [128] 3-9-7 **65**... PaulQuinn 12 19
(D Nicholls) *towards rr: wknd over 2f out* **50/1**

59.04 secs (-2.16) **Going Correction** -0.35s/f (Firm)
WFA 3 from 4yo+ 7lb **13** Ran SP% **119.5**
Speed ratings (Par 103):103,102,101,101,96 95,93,92,92,90 88,87,81
CSF £48.28 CT £197.45 TOTE £15.00: £3.80, £2.10, £2.30; EX 78.70 Place 6 £18.85, Place 5 £3.12.
Owner Bryce, Dower, Morgan **Bred** E Campion **Trained** Middleham Moor, N Yorks
■ Stewards' Enquiry : Paul Mulrennan two-day ban: used whip with excessive frequency (Jun 25-26)

FOCUS
An ordinary handicap run at a decent pace and the field raced stands' side. The form looks solid with the winner and third to last year's best.
T/Plt: £25.70 to a £1 stake. Pool: £49,152.40. 1,391.30 winning tickets. T/Qpdt: £4.00 to a £1 stake. Pool: £3,232.30. 596.50 winning tickets. RY

2340 KEMPTON (A.W) (R-H)
Wednesday, June 14

OFFICIAL GOING: Standard
Wind: Moderate, behind

2551 WEATHERBYS INSURANCE APPRENTICE H'CAP (ROUND 2) 1m (P)
7:05 (7:06) (Class 5) (0-75,74) 4-Y-O+ **£3,238** (£963; £481; £240) **Stalls** High

Form RPR
0210 **1** **Samuel Charles**[4] [2464] 8-9-10 **74** 6ex... LiamJones 7 86
(C R Dore) *a in tch: led appr 2f out: in command fnl f* **11/4**[1]
444/ **2** *2* **Zangeal**[669] [4738] 5-8-12 **69**... JonjoMilczarek[(7)] 6 76
(C F Wall) *mid-div: rdn to trck wnr 2f out: no imp ins fnl f* **10/1**
5345 **3** *1* **Arctic Desert**[32] [1673] 6-9-5 **74**... JamesRogers[(5)] 8 79
(A M Balding) *t.k.h: hdwy on outside over 2f out: hung rt u.p and no hdwy fnl f* **9/2**[2]
-040 **4** *¾* **Play The Ball (USA)**[40] [1455] 4-9-6 **73**... JamesMillman[(3)] 2 76
(G A Butler) *hld up in rr: picked up appr fnl f: fin wl: nvr nrr* **8/1**
0-00 **5** *2 ½* **Sand Iron (IRE)**[15] [2098] 4-8-6 **56** oh3 ow1... RonanKeogh 11 53
(John Allen) *hld up in rr: mde sme late hdwy* **66/1**
1116 **6** *nk* **Indian Edge**[15] [2098] 5-9-3 **72**... JosephWalsh[(5)] 9 69
(B Palling) *led after 1f: rdn and hdd appr 2f out: sn wknd* **6/1**[3]
5600 **7** *hd* **Admiral Compton**[5] [2401] 5-8-13 **68**... WilliamCarson[(5)] 10 64
(J R Boyle) *hld up in rr: nvr on terms* **14/1**
0053 **8** *hd* **Peggys First**[22] [1913] 4-8-0 **55** oh10... LukeMorris[(5)] 5 51?
(D E Cantillon) *trckd ldrs: t.k.h: rdn over 2f out: sn wknd* **16/1**
0500 **9** *1* **Anduril**[10] [1651] 5-9-3 **70**... ThomasO'Brien[(3)] 3 63
(Miss M E Rowland) *mid-div: rdn 3f out: wknd wl over 1f out* **20/1**
00-0 **10** *1 ½* **Kareeb (FR)**[19] [1993] 9-8-10 **65**... AlanRutter[(5)] 12 55
(W J Musson) *hld up: a bhd* **6/1**[3]
00-0 **11** *½* **Robin Sharp**[102] [576] 8-8-5 **55** oh21...(p) RussellKennemore 4 44?
(J Akehurst) *led for 1f: rdn sn after 1/2-way: wknd 2f out* **66/1**
03/0 **12** *2 ½* **Love Academy**[14] [2141] 11-8-5 **55** oh13... SladeO'Hara 1 38
(Luke Comer, Ire) *chsd ldrs on ins tl rdn and wknd 2f out* **40/1**

1m 39.98s (-0.82) **Going Correction** +0.025s/f (Slow) **12** Ran SP% **116.4**
Speed ratings (Par 103):105,103,102,101,98 98,98,98,97,95 95,92
CSF £30.06 CT £119.93 TOTE £3.20: £1.80, £3.50, £2.80; EX 35.30.
Owner Chris Marsh **Bred** Sheikh Mohammed Obaid Al Maktoum **Trained** West Pinchbeck, Lincs

FOCUS
A modest apprentice handicap, but at least the pace was decent thanks to Indian Edge soon tearing off into a runaway lead. The form is not the most solid and is rated through the third for now.
Play The Ball(USA) Official explanation: jockey said gelding hung left
Love Academy Official explanation: jockey said saddle slipped

2552 123RACING.COM MAIDEN AUCTION STKS 6f (P)
7:35 (7:38) (Class 5) 2-Y-O **£3,238** (£963; £481; £240) **Stalls** High

Form RPR
0 **1** **Cavallo Di Ferro (IRE)**[20] [1959] 2-8-10... EddieAhern 12 68
(J R Boyle) *mde all: rdn clr ins fnl f* **12/1**
2 *2* **Grange Lili (IRE)** 2-8-7... RobbieFitzpatrick 6 59
(Peter Grayson) *s.i.s: sn in tch: hdwy over 1f out and r.o to go 2nd nr fin* **16/1**
3 *nk* **Clewer** 2-7-13 ow2... KevinGhunowa[(7)] 7 57
(P A Blockley) *chsd wnr: hung lft over 1f out: kpt on ins fnl f but lost 2nd cl home* **7/1**
4 *nk* **Vitznau (IRE)** 2-8-12... RichardHughes 1 62
(R Hannon) *a in tch on ins: rdn 2f out: one pce fnl f* **7/2**[1]
0 **5** *½* **Todwick Owl**[20] [1945] 2-8-10... TQuinn 3 59
(J G Given) *towards rr: hdwy over 3f out: hung lft and wknd over 1f out* **11/2**[3]
0 **6** *3* **House Arrest**[13] [2166] 2-8-4... NickyMackay 8 44
(I A Wood) *chsd ldrs: rdn over 2f out: wknd over 1f out* **16/1**
0 **7** *½* **My Sara**[13] [2178] 2-8-6... ChrisCatlin 5 44
(D J Daly) *mid-div: rdn 3f out: nvr on terms* **20/1**
0 **8** *1* **Take My Turn**[13] [2172] 2-8-10... TedDurcan 2 45
(M Blanshard) *s.i.s: sn in tch: hung lft 3f out: sn bhd* **25/1**
9 *½* **Tenterhooks (IRE)** 2-8-7... TPQueally 4 41+
(J A Osborne) *a towards rr* **7/1**
10 *1 ¾* **Having A Ball** 2-8-10... LPKeniry 11 38
(P D Cundell) *slowly away: a bhd* **25/1**
11 *¾* **Better Off Red (USA)** 2-8-6... AlanMunro 10 32
(B J Meehan) *slowly away: a bhd* **4/1**[2]
12 *10* **Flying Namid (IRE)** 2-8-4... FrancisFerris 9 —
(P A Blockley) *slowly away: a bhd* **20/1**

1m 14.96s (1.26) **Going Correction** +0.025s/f (Slow) **12** Ran SP% **119.3**
Speed ratings (Par 93):92,89,88,88,87 83,83,81,81,78 77,64
CSF £178.41 TOTE £15.10: £3.90, £6.40, £5.00; EX 170.40.
Owner John Hopkins, J-P Lim & keith Marsden **Bred** Michael Dalton **Trained** Epsom, Surrey

FOCUS
An ordinary juvenile maiden, but there should be a winner or two come out of it.

NOTEBOOK
Cavallo Di Ferro(IRE) made just about every yard from the inside draw. Reportedly green when last of ten on his Lingfield debut, admittedly in a race that has already produced a couple of winners, he was a different proposition here and there is no reason why he should not continue to progress. (op 8-1)

Grange Lili(IRE) ◆ ran a most eye-catching debut to snatch the runner-up spot. A nice-looking filly in the paddock, she is a half-sister to three winners in Italy and with improvement almost certain it should not be long before she emulates them.
Clewer ◆, a half-sister to winners abroad and from a yard that does well with its newcomers, was popular on the exchanges. She was very awkward at the start, but showed plenty in the race itself and had every chance. Tending to hang in the closing stages, she should have learnt plenty from this first outing. (op 8-1)
Vitznau(IRE) also showed ability on his debut from the widest draw, but he is a half-brother to three winners over longer trips which suggests he will appreciate further. (op 4-1 tchd 9-2)
Todwick Owl was not disgraced, but he did have the advantage of previous experience. (op 9-2)
Better Off Red(USA), a half-sister to seven winners including three smart performers in the US, never got into the race but is surely capable of better. (tchd 9-2)

2553 V-DRINKS.COM TRANSYLVANIAN RED VODKA H'CAP 6f (P)
8:05 (8:08) (Class 4) (0-80,79) 3-Y-O **£5,505** (£1,637; £818; £408) **Stalls** High

Form RPR
44-0 **1** **Finsbury**[48] 1261 3-8-12 **70** .... AlanMunro 8 75+
(C F Wall) *hld up in rr: hdwy over 1f out: drvn to ld last strides* **12/1**
0-20 **2** *shd* **Hoh Wotanite**[11] 2222 3-8-2 **60** oh1 .... ChrisCatlin 4 63
(A M Balding) *a in tch: rdn and outpcd wl over 1f out: rallied and kpt on to snatch 2nd cl home* **33/1**
20-4 **3** *shd* **And I**[25] 1845 3-8-13 **71** .... MartinDwyer 2 73
(M P Tregoning) *sn trckd ldr: hung lft over 1f out but led briefly ins fnl f: lost 2nd cl home* **13/2**
14-0 **4** *½* **What Do You Know**[32] 1672 3-9-3 **75** .... NickyMackay 6 76
(G A Butler) *trckd ldr for 1f: styd in tch: ev ch wl ins fnl f: no ex cl home* **14/1**
0-15 **5** *nk* **Spiritual Peace (IRE)**[25] 1848 3-9-7 **79** .... NCallan 5 79
(K A Ryan) *led tl rdn and hdd ins fnl f: no ex fnl 50yds* **4/1**[1]
3012 **6** *2* **Garstang**[19] 1983 3-9-3 **75** .... (b) RobbieFitzpatrick 9 69
(Peter Grayson) *slowly away: in rr tl mde sme late hdwy* **5/1**[3]
1622 **7** *1¼* **Shes Minnie**[11] 2222 3-9-1 **73** .... JamieSpencer 7 63
(J G M O'Shea) *s.i.s: sn in tch: rdn 2f out: wknd ins fnl f* **9/2**[2]
0060 **8** *3½* **Sigismundus (IRE)**[8] 2318 3-8-10 **71** .... AmirQuinn(3) 3 51
(J R Boyle) *slowly away: sn in tch: rdn 1/2-way: wknd over 1f out* **20/1**
2106 **9** *¾* **Cool Sting (IRE)**[42] 1411 3-9-1 **73** .... LDettori 10 51
(A M Balding) *a struggling in rr* **8/1**

1m 14.17s (0.47) **Going Correction** +0.025s/f (Slow) 9 Ran SP% **101.4**
Speed ratings (Par 101):97,96,96,96,95 93,91,86,85
CSF £258.22 CT £1986.50 TOTE £11.00: £3.30, £6.10, £2.00; EX 226.20.
Owner O Pointing **Bred** O Pointing **Trained** Newmarket, Suffolk

FOCUS
A tight sprint handicap, if weakened by the late withdrawal of Light Mozart, and a dramatic bunched finish. The form looks pretty ordinary rated through the runner-up and fifth.
Garstang Official explanation: jockey said gelding was hampered at the start

2554 TFM NETWORKS FILLIES' H'CAP 7f (P)
8:35 (8:38) (Class 5) (0-70,75) 3-Y-O **£3,238** (£963; £481; £240) **Stalls** High

Form RPR
1-00 **1** **Dancing Guest (IRE)**[17] 2050 3-9-5 **67** .... TQuinn 14 76
(G G Margarson) *slowly away: rdn and hdwy over 1f out: r.o to ld cl home* **20/1**
10-6 **2** *½* **Stormy Monday**[20] 1962 3-9-7 **69** .... EddieAhern 5 77
(J W Hills) *in tch: chsd winer over 2f out: led over 1f out: rdn and hdd cl home* **25/1**
-555 **3** *½* **Tabulate**[30] 1747 3-8-6 **54** .... ChrisCatlin 13 60
(P L Gilligan) *chsd ldrs: rdn and ev ch ins fnl f: no ex cl home* **25/1**
2631 **4** *nk* **Neardown Beauty (IRE)**[8] 2318 3-9-13 **75** 6ex .... JamieSpencer 3 81
(I A Wood) *s.i.s: in rr tl hdwy on outside over 1f out: kpt on: nvr nrr* **11/2**[3]
0435 **5** *2½* **Miss Wedge**[21] 1941 3-9-0 **62** .... (v[1]) IanMongan 12 61
(T G Mills) *led tl rdn and hdd over 1f out: wknd ins fnl f* **10/1**
4-14 **6** *1* **Pleasing**[25] 1851 3-9-4 **66** .... DaneO'Neill 4 62
(J L Dunlop) *in rr: rdn 2f out: mde sme late hdwy* **7/2**[2]
6-50 **7** *1¼* **Tilly's Dream**[7] 2353 3-9-7 **69** .... NCallan 8 62
(G C H Chung) *bhd: effrt on outside over 2f out: nvr on terms* **20/1**
1-42 **8** *2* **Foreplay (IRE)**[9] 2293 3-9-5 **67** .... LDettori 2 55
(E A L Dunlop) *t.k.h: in rr and effrt whn hmpd on ins over 2f out: nvr on terms* **11/4**[1]
4566 **9** *1½* **Bathwick Emma (IRE)**[11] 2222 3-9-5 **67** .... JimmyFortune 7 51
(P D Evans) *nvr bttr than mid-div* **33/1**
-565 **10** *1¾* **Alwariah**[41] 1433 3-8-4 **52** .... MartinDwyer 1 32
(C E Brittain) *slowly away: a bhd* **16/1**
-400 **11** *½* **Air Biscuit (IRE)**[17] 2050 3-9-0 **62** .... (t) AlanMunro 11 40
(C F Wall) *sn chsd ldr: rdn appr 2f out: sn wknd* **11/2**[3]
40-0 **12** *5* **Missdevina (IRE)**[14] 2129 3-9-2 **69** .... JerryO'Dwyer(5) 9 34
(M G Quinlan) *t.k.h: a in rr* **66/1**
00-0 **13** *4* **Cate Washington**[15] 2095 3-8-1 **52** .... SilvestreDeSousa(3) 6 7
(Mrs L Williamson) *chsd ldrs tl wknd 2f out* **50/1**
000- **14** *5* **Savannah Pride (IRE)**[215] 6312 3-8-10 **58** .... TedDurcan 10 —
(Ernst Oertel) *a towards rr: eased whn wl btn ins fnl f* **66/1**

1m 26.2s (-0.60) **Going Correction** +0.025s/f (Slow) 14 Ran SP% **119.7**
Speed ratings (Par 96):104,103,102,102,99 98,97,94,93,91 90,84,80,74
CSF £414.62 CT £12084.22 TOTE £30.10: £5.50, £8.80, £7.00; EX 375.00.
Owner John Guest **Bred** Kevin Foley **Trained** Newmarket, Suffolk
■ Stewards' Enquiry : Jamie Spencer caution: careless riding

FOCUS
A fair fillies' handicap and the time was very smart for a race like this, but a complete boil-over for punters. It has been rated positively around the fourth and fifth.
Foreplay(IRE) Official explanation: jockey said filly suffered interference

2555 V REDVODKA TRANSYLVANIAN SUNSET COCKTAIL H'CAP 7f (P)
9:05 (9:07) (Class 4) (0-85,83) 4-Y-O+ **£5,505** (£1,637; £818; £408) **Stalls** High

Form RPR
0-33 **1** **Irony (IRE)**[21] 1938 7-9-6 **82** .... LDettori 11 89
(A M Balding) *mde all: stdd in front over 2f out: rdn over 1f out: hld on* **4/1**[1]
3504 **2** *nk* **Rezzago (USA)**[9] 2302 6-9-1 **77** .... JimmyFortune 1 83
(W R Swinburn) *settled towards rr: rdn and hdwy over 1f out: r.o to go 2nd e cl home* **7/1**[3]
0-50 **3** *½* **Puya**[32] 1692 4-9-3 **79** .... DaneO'Neill 4 84
(H Candy) *a.p: rdn and chsd wnr ins fnl f: lost 2nd nr fin* **8/1**
-554 **4** *1¼* **Ingleton**[13] 2173 4-8-8 **70** .... (p) RyanMoore 13 72
(G L Moore) *chsd ldrs: ev ch appr fnl f: nt qckn ins* **5/1**[2]
00-2 **5** *1* **Material Witness (IRE)**[21] 1935 9-9-5 **81** .... MartinDwyer 2 80
(W R Muir) *trckd wnr tl rdn 1f out: one pce after* **11/1**
5455 **6** *nk* **Katiypour (IRE)**[109] 516 9-9-7 **83** .... RichardThomas 10 81
(Miss B Sanders) *mid-div: hdwy over 1f out: nvr nr to chal* **12/1**
50-0 **7** *hd* **Wrighty Almighty (IRE)**[26] 1820 4-9-4 **80** .... AlanMunro 5 78
(P R Chamings) *plld hrd: chsd ldrs: wknd 1f out* **33/1**
000- **8** *hd* **Overlord Way (GR)**[187] 6533 4-9-1 **77** .... IanMongan 12 74
(P R Chamings) *in rr: mde sme late hadway* **40/1**
3300 **9** *1¼* **Hits Only Heaven (IRE)**[39] 1494 4-9-4 **80** .... (e) RobbieFitzpatrick 6 74
(D Nicholls) *a towards rr* **12/1**
0202 **10** *nk* **Desert Dreamer (IRE)**[5] 2405 5-9-4 **80** .... NCallan 7 73
(P R Chamings) *hld up on ins: nvr on terms* **7/1**[3]
501- **11** *6* **Highest Regard**[300] 4506 4-9-3 **79** .... ChrisCatlin 9 57
(P L Gilligan) *t.k.h: a in rr* **20/1**
062- **12** *½* **Nor'Wester**[361] 2718 4-9-1 **77** .... JamieSpencer 14 53
(J R Fanshawe) *mid-div: wkng whn bdly hmpd ent fnl f* **9/1**
4410 **13** *2½* **Quantum Leap**[21] 1938 9-8-11 **73** .... (v) JimmyQuinn 3 43
(S Dow) *a bhd* **16/1**

1m 25.83s (-0.97) **Going Correction** +0.025s/f (Slow) 13 Ran SP% **122.5**
Speed ratings (Par 105):106,105,105,103,102 102,101,101,100,99 93,92,89
CSF £31.79 CT £227.79 TOTE £3.70: £1.90, £2.70, £2.80; EX 50.90.
Owner John Nicholls Ltd/mobley Homes **Bred** Mrs G Doyle **Trained** Kingsclere, Hants

FOCUS
A fair handicap but probably the most competitive contest of the evening. The form looks solid enough and could rate a little higher.
Ingleton Official explanation: jockey said colt hung left throughout
Nor'Wester Official explanation: jockey said gelding had no more to give

2556 TFM NETWORKS H'CAP 1m 4f (P)
9:35 (9:35) (Class 4) (0-85,85) 3-Y-O **£5,505** (£1,637; £818; £408) **Stalls** Centre

Form RPR
6310 **1** **Permanent Way (IRE)**[55] 1095 3-9-7 **85** .... JamieSpencer 3 91
(B J Meehan) *a in tch: shkn up over 2f out: r.o to ld over 1f out: comf* **13/2**[3]
00-4 **2** *½* **Phone In**[43] 1381 3-8-2 **66** oh1 .... JamieMackay 6 71
(Sir Mark Prescott) *t.k.h early: trckd ldrs: rdn to go 2nd over 1f out: no imp on wnr ins fianl f* **4/1**[2]
03-1 **3** *1* **Madroos**[19] 1975 3-9-2 **80** .... RHills 5 83
(J L Dunlop) *hld up in tch: outpcd on outside over 2f out: r.o wll fnl f: nvr nrr* **7/2**[1]
-264 **4** *1¾* **Raslan**[62] 1006 3-8-13 **77** .... StanleyChin 4 77
(M Johnston) *in rr: styd on fr over 1f out: nvr nrr* **10/1**
-113 **5** *hd* **Free To Air**[19] 1975 3-9-2 **80** .... LDettori 1 80
(A M Balding) *hld up in rr: rdn 2f out: nvr on terms* **4/1**[2]
34-0 **6** *2* **Wassfa**[35] 1583 3-8-13 **77** .... RyanMoore 2 74
(C E Brittain) *trckd ldr: rdn over 2f out: sn wknd* **16/1**
14 **7** *3* **Faversham**[47] 1270 3-9-1 **79** .... PhilipRobinson 8 71
(M A Jarvis) *led tl hdd over 2f out: rdn and sn wknd* **7/2**[1]

2m 37.29s (0.39) **Going Correction** +0.025s/f (Slow) 7 Ran SP% **112.8**
Speed ratings (Par 101):99,98,98,96,96 95,93
CSF £31.51 CT £104.77 TOTE £8.60: £3.20, £2.80; EX 20.30 Place 6 £17,297.86, Place 5 £9,272.35.
Owner Dr T A Ryan **Bred** Dr T A Ryan **Trained** Manton, Wilts

FOCUS
No great pace on for much of the way in this handicap which is rated through the fifth but the form might work out.
T/Plt: £26,994.40 to a £1 stake. Pool: £44,374.50. 1.20 winning tickets. T/Qpdt: £578.10 to a £1 stake. Pool: £3,672.20. 4.70 winning tickets. JS

2557 - 2558a (Foreign Racing) - See Raceform Interactive

2367 LEOPARDSTOWN (L-H)
Wednesday, June 14

OFFICIAL GOING: Good to firm

2559a BALLYCORUS STKS (GROUP 3) 7f
7:00 (7:01) 3-Y-O+ **£31,379** (£9,172; £4,344; £1,448)

RPR
1 **An Tadh (IRE)**[9] 2311 3-8-13 102 .... JMurtagh 4 111
(G M Lyons, Ire) *mde all: rdn and qcknd clr 1 1/2f out: styd on wl fnl f* **6/1**[3]
2 *1½* **Lord Admiral (USA)**[7] 2371 5-9-9 111 .... FMBerry 1 107
(Charles O'Brien, Ire) *hld up in rr: 3rd and smooth hdwy ent st: mod 2nd fnl f: kpt on wl* **11/4**[2]
3 *4½* **Misu Bond (IRE)**[39] 1486 3-8-13 .... PJSmullen 2 95
(B Smart) *trckd ldr in 2nd: tk clsr order 1/2-way: rdn appr st: no imp fr under 2f out: one pce* **8/11**[1]
4 *3* **Tiger Dance (USA)**[242] 5900 4-9-9 101 .... KFallon 3 88
(A P O'Brien, Ire) *s.i.s and hld up in 3rd: rdn bef st: one pce* **7/1**

1m 29.0s
WFA 3 from 4yo+ 10lb 4 Ran SP% **111.4**
CSF £21.81 TOTE £6.90; DF 28.50.
Owner Vincent Gaul **Bred** Gainsborough Stud Management L **Trained** Dunsany, Co. Meath

NOTEBOOK
An Tadh(IRE) benefited from a well-judged front running ride to score and gain his first win in Pattern company. He looks a true seven-furlong specialist. (op 11/2 tchd 13/2)
Lord Admiral(USA), dropped to this trip for the first time since he was a juvenile, travelled well enough but yet again found one too good to beat him. He is extremely frustrating. (op 9/4 tchd 3/1)
Misu Bond(IRE), fifth in the English 2000 Guineas, ran to nothing like that form and perhaps a tactical race in a small field like this does not suit him. Official explanation: jockey said colt did not like today's ground (op 8/11 tchd 4/5)
Tiger Dance(USA), off since October, never looked like landing a blow and has it to prove now. (op 6/1)

2563a THREE ROCK RACE 1m 6f
9:00 (9:00) 4-Y-O+ **£7,148** (£1,665; £734; £424)

RPR
1 **Kiswahili**[109] 523 4-9-4 .... DPMcDonogh 4 89+
(Sir Mark Prescott) *cl up in 2nd: led under 4f out: clr st: styd on wl: easily* **1/6**[1]
2 *13* **Boracay Dream (IRE)**[11] 999 4-9-2 66 .... TPO'Shea 1 62
(Patrick Michael Verling, Ire) *led: hdd under 4f out: outpcd appr st: kpt on same pce u.p fr 2f out* **16/1**[3]

3 *3* **Qasbah (GER)**[9] 2311 5-9-12 .... WSupple 3 68
(H Rogers, Ire) *hld up in tch: last appr st: mod 3rd and rdn 2f out: no ex fnl f* **7/1**[2]

4 *12* **Appiness (IRE)** 8-8-9 .... SHunter[(7)] 2 50
(John A Quinn, Ire) *slowly away: hld up in tch: 3rd and effrt 4f out: wknd ent st* **20/1**

2m 57.6s **4** Ran SP% **108.8**
CSF £4.16 TOTE £1.30; DF 4.20.
Owner Miss K Rausing **Bred** Miss K Rausing **Trained** Newmarket, Suffolk

NOTEBOOK
Kiswahili, already successful in one raid across the Irish Sea last autumn, had little to beat here and did it with the minimum of fuss. (op 1/7)
T/Jkpt: @1,178.80. Pool of @11,003.00 - 7 winning tickets. T/Plt: Not won. II

2560 - 2563a (Foreign Racing) - See Raceform Interactive

[2123]TABY (R-H)
Tuesday, June 13

OFFICIAL GOING: Firm

2564a TATTERSALLS DIANASLOPNING (FILLIES) 1m
7:43 (12:00) 3-Y-O
£21,742 (£10,000; £4,348; £3,045; £2,174; £1,303)

RPR
1 **Casata (IRE)**[301] 3-9-2 .... MMartinez 5 —
(F Reuterskiold, Sweden)
2 *½* **Auchroisk (SWE)** 3-9-2 .... MSvanberg 6 —
(Bruno Nilsson, Sweden)
3 *1 ½* **Negra Del Oro (GER)** 3-9-2 .... LHammer-Hansen 7 —
(A Lund, Norway)
4 *hd* **Will Be (IRE)**[240] 3-9-2 .... FJohansson 2 —
(R A Kvisla) *midfield, stayed on final 2f, nearest finish (62/10)* **62/10**[1]
5 *hd* **La Lula (IRE)**[320] 3-9-2 ....(b) KAndersen 10 —
(Kerstin Helander, Sweden)
6 *½* **Xaara (SWE)** 3-9-2 .... YvonneDurant 14 —
(M Kahn, Sweden)
7 *hd* **Hot Fudge (SWE)** 3-9-2 .... FDiaz 11 —
(L Reuterskiold, Sweden)
8 *1* **Est Est Est (IRE)** 3-9-2 .... SaraSlot 13 —
(Kerstin Helander, Sweden)
9 *hd* **Red Dress On (SWE)** 3-9-2 .... DDelgado 12 —
(T Gustafsson, Sweden)
10 *½* **Debbie (SWE)** 3-9-2 .... JJohansen 1 —
(Catharina Wenell, Sweden)
11 *2* **My Dock (IRE)** 3-9-2 .... DinaDanekilde 4 —
(Jan-Erik Pettersson, Sweden)
12 *1 ½* **Loreley (SWE)** 3-9-2 .... NCordrey 3 —
(P Wahl, Sweden)
13 *hd* **Definite Rose (SWE)** 3-9-2 ....(b) JLSanchez 9 —
(F Castro, Sweden)
14 *7* **Nashida (DEN)**[173] 3-9-2 .... MLarsen 8 —
(Eva Olofsson, Sweden)

1m 39.0s **14** Ran SP% **13.9**
(including 1kr stake): WIN 9.60; PL 4.08, 4.68, 1.54; DF 240.78.
Owner Stall Lambada Ab & Stig Hansson **Bred** William Shaugnessy **Trained** Sweden

NOTEBOOK
Will Be(IRE), whose trainer is now based in Lambourn, returned to his old haunts to contest the Swedish version of the 1000 Guineas with this filly, whose best form has been on the artificial surfaces. She was doing her best work late on.

[2493]SAN SIRO (R-H)
Wednesday, June 14

OFFICIAL GOING: Good to firm

2565a PREMIO INTRA (MAIDEN) (FILLIES) 6f
3:00 (3:06) 2-Y-O **£6,897** (£3,034; £1,655; £828)

RPR
1 **Vola Vola (IRE)** 2-8-11 .... MTellini 9 —
(R Feligioni, Italy)
2 *nse* **Tennessee Sun (IRE)** 2-9-0 .... LManiezzi 5 —
(R Menichetti, Italy)
3 *5* **Douby Douby (IRE)** 2-9-0 .... PConvertino 3 —
(P Paciello, Italy)
4 *5* **Fiore Di Marzo (IRE)** 2-8-11 .... MDemuro 6 —
(M Guarnieri, Italy)
5 *1 ¼* **Doraemon (ITY)** 2-8-11 .... SMulas 2 —
(Graziano Verricelli, Italy)
6 *6* **Tu Sei Romantica (IRE)** 2-8-11 .... DO'Donohoe 10 —
(K A Ryan) *started slowly and carried badly right, recovered to race in touch in 5th on outside, weakened over 2f out (4/5F)* **4/5**[1]
7 *5* **Superbisli (IRE)** 2-9-0 .... EBotti 1 —
(S Ibido, Italy)
8 *1 ¾* **Delitme (IRE)** 2-9-0 .... DPorcu 8 —
(M Gonnelli, Italy)
9 *10* **La Barrique (IRE)** 2-8-11 .... DVargiu 4 —
(B Grizzetti, Italy)

1m 12.6s **9** Ran SP% **55.6**
(including 1 Euro stake): WIN 8.52; PL 2.68, 2.80, 2.31; DF 35.10.
Owner Scuderia Zaro Snc **Bred** Scuderia Zaro Di Ornella Razzini **Trained** Italy

NOTEBOOK
Tu Sei Romantica(IRE), an Italian-owned daughter of Agnes World, was made odds-on favourite on this racecourse debut, but showed her inexperience by being slowly into her stride and was then hampered by the eventual winner. She did get into contention before fading in the last quarter mile and should have learnt from the experience.

[2388]BRIGHTON (L-H)
Thursday, June 15

OFFICIAL GOING: Firm

2566 THE SPORTSMAN NEWSPAPER APPRENTICE CLAIMING STKS 7f 214y
6:35 (6:35) (Class 6) 3-Y-O+ **£2,590** (£770; £385; £192) **Stalls** Low

Form RPR
-362 1 **Nuit Sombre (IRE)**[11] 1566 6-10-0 77........(v[1]) StephenDonohoe 1 57
(J G M O'Shea) *mde all: clr 1/2-way: tired ins fnl f: hld on* **13/8**[1]
0060 2 *1* **Croft (IRE)**[28] 1799 3-8-6 59 ow1........(v[1]) PatrickHills[(7)] 3 48
(J W Hills) *in tch: rdn and hdwy to chse wnr ins fnl f* **5/1**[3]
5000 3 *nk* **Zafarshah (IRE)**[11] 2260 7-9-4 45........(b) TolleyDean[(5)] 2 49
(R A Harris) *chsd wnr tl rdn and one pce ins fnl f* **15/2**
-000 4 *3 ½* **Legal Call**[4] 2479 3-8-6 45........(v) MarkCoumbe[(5)] 4 37
(M Appleby) *a abt same pl: no hdwy ins fnl 2f* **33/1**
3560 5 *2 ½* **Bhutan (IRE)**[38] 1541 11-9-2 40........ HarryPoulton[(5)] 5 34
(Jim Best) *hld up: no prog fnl 2f* **14/1**
0600 6 *9* **Tod Sloan (IRE)**[26] 1852 4-9-7 35........ MarcHalford 7 13
(J M Bradley) *in tch tl wknd over 2f out* **12/1**
0400 7 *2 ½* **Barachois Gaudy**[30] 1753 4-9-0 45........(b[1]) RichardKingscote 6 —
(Mrs N Smith) *t.k.h: a bhd* **16/1**
6040 8 *16* **Rock Of Cloonavery (IRE)**[16] 2101 3-8-11 48........(b[1]) TravisBlock 8 —
(S C Williams) *slowly away: a wl bhd* **7/2**[2]

1m 36.08s (1.04) **Going Correction** +0.05s/f (Good)
WFA 3 from 4yo+ 11lb **8** Ran SP% **111.9**
Speed ratings (Par 101):96,95,94,91,88 79,77,61
CSF £9.50 TOTE £1.80: £1.10, £2.10, £1.60; EX 8.30.The winner was the subject of a friendly claim.
Owner Pete Smith Car Sales **Bred** M P B Bloodstock Ltd **Trained** Elton, Gloucs
■ Stewards' Enquiry : Stephen Donohoe three-day ban: careless riding (Jun 26-28)

FOCUS
A very weak affair that saw the highest BHB-rated runner score, but still perform well below his official mark. The runner-up sets the standard.
Barachois Gaudy Official explanation: trainer said filly was in season

2567 THE SPORTSMAN H'CAP 6f 209y
7:05 (7:07) (Class 6) (0-65,62) 4-Y-O+ **£2,590** (£770; £385; £192) **Stalls** Low

Form RPR
0144 1 **Iced Diamond (IRE)**[13] 2211 7-8-9 **50**........ FergusSweeney 5 58
(W M Brisbourne) *hld up in rr: hdwy whn short of room over 1f out: swtchd rt: rdn and r.o to ld ins fnl f* **8/1**
600- 2 *½* **Keep Bacckinhit (IRE)**[231] 6126 4-9-5 **60**........ AdrianMcCarthy 10 67
(G L Moore) *t.k.h: prom whn bmpd ins fnl f: r.o to go 2nd nr fin* **16/1**
0610 3 *hd* **Stamford Blue**[15] 2135 5-8-10 **58**........(b) TolleyDean[(7)] 8 64
(R A Harris) *s.i.s: sn rdn in rr: hdwy on outside bef hung lft over 1f out: r.o ins fnl f: nvr nrr* **6/1**[3]
2023 4 *hd* **Taranaki**[6] 2390 8-9-5 **60**........ SebSanders 2 66
(P D Cundell) *t.k.h: prom tl bmpd jst ins fnl f: r.o* **7/2**[1]
-000 5 *1 ½* **Cree**[16] 2095 4-9-3 **58**........ LPKeniry 3 60
(W R Muir) *t.k.h: chsd ldrs: ev ch 2f out: hung lft and wknd ins fnl f* **25/1**
0054 6 *¾* **Icecap**[10] 2293 6-8-0 **44** oh2 ow1........ StephaneBreux[(3)] 7 44
(W G M Turner) *in rr: hdwy on outside 2f out: hung lft but kpt on fnl f: nvr on terms* **11/2**[2]
-355 7 *3* **Cayman Breeze**[127] 336 6-9-4 **59**........ TedDurcan 4 51
(J M Bradley) *in tch: hung lft and wknd over 1f out* **12/1**
5000 8 *hd* **Windy Prospect**[1] 2541 4-8-12 **58**........ RoryMoore[(5)] 1 49
(Miss Sheena West) *led tl rdn and hdd 2f out: hung lft and wknd over 1f out* **10/1**
0230 9 *2 ½* **Oneiro Way (IRE)**[16] 2095 4-9-7 **62**........ IanMongan 6 47
(P R Chamings) *prom: rdn 2f out: sn wknd* **20/1**
0046 10 *2* **Measured Response**[12] 2223 4-9-0 **60**........ StephenDonohoe[(5)] 9 40
(J G M O'Shea) *bhd: rdn 2f out and nvr on terms* **7/1**
0621 11 *5* **Beau Marche**[10] 2288 4-8-10 **51** 6ex........(b) ChrisCatlin 11 18
(G G Margarson) *a bhd* **12/1**

1m 22.1s (-0.60) **Going Correction** +0.05s/f (Good) **11** Ran SP% **114.5**
Speed ratings (Par 101):105,104,104,103,102 101,97,97,94,92 86
CSF £124.76 CT £835.29 TOTE £6.40: £2.10, £4.20, £3.70; EX 170.00.
Owner Gary Dewhurst **Bred** Mrs Kathleen McElroy **Trained** Great Ness, Shropshire

FOCUS
A moderate handicap, run at a generous early pace, and the form looks straightforward enough rated through the third and fourth.

2568 THE SPORTSMAN NEWSPAPER (S) STKS 1m 1f 209y
7:35 (7:36) (Class 6) 3-5-Y-O **£2,266** (£674; £337; £168) **Stalls** High

Form RPR
-060 1 **String Serenade (IRE)**[73] 854 5-8-13 41........ MichaelTebbutt 8 52
(V Smith) *hld up: hdwy on outside 2f out: hung lft but wnt 2nd over 1f out: led jst ins fnl f: sn clr* **14/1**
4622 2 *4* **Prince Valentine**[6] 2392 5-9-4 45........(b) RyanMoore 3 49
(G L Moore) *in tch: hdwy whn carried sltly lft ent fnl f: swtchd rt: r.o to go 2nd ins* **13/8**[1]
0-00 3 *½* **Kirkstall Lane**[17] 2066 3-8-5 45........(b[1]) ChrisCatlin 2 47
(R Hannon) *trckd ldr: led 1/2-way: clr 2f out: hrd rdn and hdd jst ins fnl f: sn btn* **14/1**
-000 4 *4* **Rosiella**[15] 501 4-8-13 43........(t) RobbieFitzpatrick 4 35
(M Appleby) *in rr: hdwy ins 2f out: styd on: nvr nr to chal* **16/1**
000 5 *7* **Edge Fund**[30] 1752 4-8-13 44........(p) StephenDonohoe[(5)] 6 27
(Miss Gay Kelleway) *led to 1/2-way: hrd rdn 2f out: sn wknd* **11/1**
-413 6 *3 ½* **Scuzme (IRE)**[27] 1829 3-8-6 53........ AndrewElliott[(5)] 5 26
(C J Gray) *v.s.a: a bhd* **15/8**[2]
6004 7 *2* **Tennessee Belle (IRE)**[14] 2180 4-8-13 39........(e) SebSanders 1 12
(C N Allen) *mid-div: rdn 1/2-way: sn btn* **9/1**[3]
3500 8 *12* **Count The Trees**[33] 1661 3-8-0 45........ AdrianMcCarthy 7 —
(W G M Turner) *chsd ldrs: rdn and wknd sn after 1/2-way* **14/1**

2m 2.75s (0.15) **Going Correction** +0.05s/f (Good)
WFA 3 from 4yo+ 13lb **8** Ran SP% **117.1**
Speed ratings (Par 101):101,97,97,94,88 85,84,74
CSF £38.24 TOTE £13.10: £3.70, £1.10, £5.80; EX 97.00.The winner was bought in for 6,200gns. Scuzme was claimed by Miss Sheena West for £6,000.
Owner Gerard Cashin **Bred** J C Harley And Evan Arkwright **Trained** Exning, Suffolk

FOCUS
A dire event, run at a strong early pace, and the form, rated through the runner-up to recent form, should be treated with a degree of caution.

Scuzme(IRE) Official explanation: jockey said gelding missed the break and was unsuited by the firm ground

2569 G & S MECHANICAL SERVICES H'CAP — 1m 3f 196y

8:05 (8:07) (Class 5) (0-70,60) 3-Y-O — **£3,886** (£1,156; £577; £288) **Stalls** High

Form				RPR
00-0	1		**Chess Board**[34] 1648 3-9-4 **57** .... SebSanders 6 (Sir Mark Prescott) *mde all: rdn 3f out: hld on wl fnl f* **9/4**[1]	68+
0230	2	2	**Iberian Light (USA)**[5] 2466 3-9-2 **55** .... (b[1]) ChrisCatlin 8 (N A Callaghan) *in tch: rdn to go 2nd over 1f out: no imp ins fnl f* **6/1**[3]	63
-114	3	2 ½	**La Via Ferrata (IRE)**[9] 2332 3-9-3 **59** .... NelsonDeSouza(3) 4 (P F I Cole) *in tch: rdn 2f out: kpt on one pce* **5/2**[2]	63
0-00	4	½	**Spaceman**[34] 1652 3-9-1 **54** .... (v[1]) NickyMackay 7 (L M Cumani) *trckd ldrs: chsd wnr 4f out tl rdn and wknd over 1f out* **14/1**	57
-040	5	2	**Constant Cheers (IRE)**[23] 1925 3-9-7 **60** .... (v[1]) TedDurcan 5 (W R Swinburn) *hld up: t.k.h: one pce fnl 2f* **7/1**	60
0-56	6	2 ½	**Being There**[122] 403 3-9-3 **56** .... JosedeSouza 2 (P F I Cole) *traked wnr to 4f out: wknd over 2f out* **20/1**	52
06-0	7	16	**Kaladin**[9] 2332 3-9-7 **60** .... RyanMoore 1 (G L Moore) *towards rr: rdn over 4f out: sn wl bhd* **8/1**	30
00-0	8	10	**South Hill**[44] 1375 3-8-3 **47** .... MarcHalford(5) 3 (M Blanshard) *rrd up s: brief effrt 5f out: sn btn* **25/1**	1

2m 31.31s (-0.89) **Going Correction** +0.05s/f (Good) — **8** Ran SP% **112.5**
Speed ratings (Par 99):104,102,101,100,99 97,87,80
CSF £15.70 CT £34.68 TOTE £3.30: £1.10, £1.80, £1.50; EX 12.50.
Owner Lord Derby **Bred** Stanley Estate And Stud Co **Trained** Newmarket, Suffolk

FOCUS
A moderate three-year-old handicap, but run at a sound pace and the form looks solid for the class.

Chess Board ◆ Official explanation: trainer's rep said, regarding the improved form shown, the colt had run a a bad race at Nottingham and may have benefited from today's 1m 4f trip

South Hill Official explanation: jockey said filly reared on leaving stalls

2570 THE SPORTSMAN KNOWS H'CAP — 5f 213y

8:35 (8:35) (Class 5) (0-70,75) 3-Y-O — **£3,886** (£1,156; £577; £288) **Stalls** Low

Form				RPR
1132	1		**Sarah's Art (IRE)**[6] 2393 3-9-1 **63** .... (b) ChrisCatlin 4 (N A Callaghan) *in tch: hdwy on outside 2f out: r.o fnl f to ld post* **11/4**[1]	66
662	2	hd	**Piccostar**[11] 2263 3-9-2 **64** .... RyanMoore 1 (A B Haynes) *trckd ldrs: led 2f out: rdn and hdd post* **7/2**[3]	66
0626	3	hd	**Glenargo (USA)**[15] 2134 3-8-10 **58** .... (p) AdrianMcCarthy 5 (R A Harris) *led tl hdd 2f out: rdn and ev ch fnl f: nt qckn cl home* **16/1**	59
0404	4	1 ¼	**Three Feathers**[31] 1726 3-8-4 **55** oh7 ow5 .... SaleemGolam(3) 2 (M Salaman) *chsd ldrs: rdn 2f out: kpt on one pce* **25/1**	53?
2013	5	shd	**Lucayos**[5] 2433 3-9-8 **75** 6ex .... (b) RichardKingscote(5) 3 (Mrs H Sweeting) *bmpd s: bhd: hdwy on ins 2f out but continuing to hang lft whn n.m.r ins fnl f* **7/2**[3]	76+
46-0	6	10	**Veba (USA)**[12] 2244 3-9-3 **65** .... TedDurcan 7 (B W Hills) *t.k.h: hld up: bhd fnl 2f* **14/1**	32
0004	7	nk	**Captain Torrance (IRE)**[13] 2187 3-8-7 **55** .... SebSanders 6 (P W Chapple-Hyam) *trckd ldrs on outside: rdn 1/2-way: sn hung lft: wknd 2f out* **3/1**[2]	21

1m 10.56s (0.46) **Going Correction** +0.05s/f (Good) — **7** Ran SP% **112.5**
Speed ratings (Par 99):98,97,97,95,95 82,81
CSF £12.28 TOTE £3.00: £2.00, £1.80; EX 10.90.
Owner Matthew Green **Bred** Newtownbarry House Stud **Trained** Newmarket, Suffolk

FOCUS
A modest three-year-old sprint, run at a fair pace, and although the first three came clear, the form is not totally solid.

Lucayos Official explanation: jockey said colt was denied a clear run

2571 THE SPORTSMAN NEWSPAPER H'CAP — 5f 59y

9:05 (9:08) (Class 6) (0-60,60) 3-Y-O+ — **£2,590** (£770; £385; £192) **Stalls** Low

Form				RPR
4000	1		**Imperium**[10] 2288 5-9-3 **49** .... (p) MickyFenton 5 (Stef Liddiard) *slowly away: in rr: hdwy and squeezed through ins fnl f to ld last strides* **13/2**[3]	56
-005	2	shd	**Princess Kai (IRE)**[30] 1752 5-8-9 **41** .... FergusSweeney 3 (R Ingram) *hld up: hdwy 2f out: r.o wl to go 2nd post* **12/1**	48
0505	3	shd	**Cosmic Destiny (IRE)**[35] 1618 4-9-11 **57** .... ChrisCatlin 11 (E F Vaughan) *a.p: led well over 1f out: rdn: hdd and lost 2nd post* **5/1**[1]	64
002-	4	¾	**Tomthevic**[243] 5898 8-8-10 **42** .... (p) RobbieFitzpatrick 4 (J M Bradley) *led tl hdd wl over 1f out: kpt on but no ex nr fin* **11/1**	46
0304	5	½	**Lord Mayfair (USA)**[8] 2356 4-8-6 **45** oh4 ow4 .... (b) AnnStokell(7) 6 (Miss A Stokell) *chsd ldr rdn 2f out: wknd ins fnl f* **12/1**	47
-000	6	nk	**Italian Mist (FR)**[3] 2494 7-8-6 **41** oh6 .... (e) SaleemGolam(3) 2 (R M H Cowell) *a in tch on ins: one pce ins fnl f* **20/1**	42
-000	7	nk	**Snow Wolf**[7] 2380 5-9-13 **59** .... (p) RyanMoore 10 (J M Bradley) *a in tch: rdn 2f out: fnd no ex ins fnl f* **11/2**[2]	59+
0000	8	½	**Majestical (IRE)**[4] 2484 4-10-0 **60** .... (b[1]) TedDurcan 8 (J M Bradley) *in tch: rdn 2f out: hung lft appr fnl f: no ex* **14/1**	58
0006	9	shd	**Hilltop Fantasy**[8] 2356 5-8-10 **42** .... SebSanders 1 (V Smith) *bhd: hdwy on ins whn n.m.r over 1f out: nvr on terms* **11/1**	39
50-0	10	½	**Ballybunion (IRE)**[33] 1689 7-9-7 **60** .... TolleyDean(7) 7 (R A Harris) *slowly away: racd wd: nvr on terms* **7/1**	55
0064	11	1	**Borzoi Maestro**[6] 2396 5-8-13 **52** .... (p) KevinGhunowa(7) 9 (M Wellings) *chsd ldrs tl hung bdly lft and wknd over 1f out* **11/2**[2]	44

62.71 secs (0.41) **Going Correction** +0.05s/f (Good) — **11** Ran SP% **116.7**
Speed ratings (Par 101):98,97,97,96,95 95,94,93,93,92 91
CSF £81.27 CT £431.71 TOTE £9.60: £2.10, £7.70, £1.80; EX 88.50 Place 6 £43.59, Place 5 £29.75.
Owner Mrs Stef Liddiard **Bred** Mrs H B Raw **Trained** Great Shefford, Berks

FOCUS
A moderate sprint which saw less than four lengths covering the entire field at the finish. The form is rated around the first two but looks far from solid.

Snow Wolf Official explanation: jockey said saddle slipped

Borzoi Maestro Official explanation: jockey said gelding hung left

T/Plt: £52.60 to a £1 stake. Pool: £37,846.85. 524.95 winning tickets. T/Qpdt: £7.90 to a £1 stake. Pool: £3,171.30. 296.20 winning tickets. JS

2442 LINGFIELD (L-H)

Thursday, June 15

OFFICIAL GOING: Standard
Wind: Almost nil Weather: Fine

2572 TRACKSIDE RESTAURANT MAIDEN STKS — 6f (P)

2:30 (2:41) (Class 5) 2-Y-O — **£3,238** (£963; £481; £240) **Stalls** Low

Form				RPR
0	1		**My Lovely Lesley (USA)**[15] 2125 2-8-12 .... IanMongan 9 (B J Meehan) *pressed ldng pair: rdn to ld narrowly jst over 1f out: hanging rt after: hld on* **2/1**[1]	74
	2	hd	**Danseuse** 2-8-12 .... J-PGuillambert 2 (C E Brittain) *pressed ldr: rdn to ld briefly over 1f out: pressed wnr after: jst hld* **16/1**	73
	3	nk	**Astronomic View** 2-9-3 .... DO'Donohoe 3 (E A L Dunlop) *dwlt: sn chsd ldrs: swtchd to inner over 1f out: chal fnl f: jst hld nr fin* **10/1**	78
5	4	1 ¼	**Bodes Galaxy (IRE)**[15] 2130 2-9-3 .... GeorgeBaker 11 (N P Littmoden) *chsd ldrs: rdn over 2f out: hanging rt but styd on fr over 1f out: nvr able to chal* **10/1**	74
	5	1 ¾	**Stoneacre Gareth (IRE)** 2-9-3 .... RobbieFitzpatrick 8 (Peter Grayson) *reluctant to enter stalls: s.s: sn chsd ldrs: rdn over 2f out: outpcd over 1f out: kpt on* **7/1**	69
0	6	2 ½	**Disco Dan**[12] 2218 2-9-3 .... DaneO'Neill 4 (D M Simcock) *trckd ldng trio: shkn up 2f out: cl up whn hmpd on inner jst over 1f out: no ch after* **5/1**[3]	64+
6	7	nk	**Candyland (IRE)**[27] 1817 2-8-12 .... TedDurcan 1 (M R Channon) *mde most to over 1f out: wknd rapidly fnl f* **9/2**[2]	55
	8	4	**Alnwick** 2-9-3 .... LPKeniry 7 (P D Cundell) *s.s: outpcd and a struggling* **33/1**	48
	9	hd	**Dawson Creek (IRE)** 2-9-3 .... FergusSweeney 10 (B Gubby) *nvr on terms w ldrs: struggling fr 1/2-way* **33/1**	48
	10	12	**Totally Free** 2-9-3 .... HayleyTurner 6 (M D I Usher) *s.s: bdly outpcd and a bhd* **25/1**	12

1m 14.62s (1.81) **Going Correction** +0.175s/f (Slow) — **10** Ran SP% **114.5**
Speed ratings (Par 93):94,93,93,91,89 86,85,80,80,64
CSF £36.56 TOTE £2.90: £1.10, £5.80, £2.30; EX 37.70.
Owner Gold Group International Ltd **Bred** John J Greely Iii **Trained** Manton, Wilts
■ Rowan Venture lost his rider on the way to the start, and was withdrawn due his jockey being unfit to ride.

FOCUS
An interesting juvenile maiden where all of the field were trying Polytrack for the first time, and a couple of participants appearing to be quite well regarded. The race ended up going off about ten minutes late waiting for the return of the ambulance.

NOTEBOOK

My Lovely Lesley(USA), who was looks a highly-strung type, is clearly held in some regard, as connections saw fit to introduce her in the Hilary Needler Trophy at Beverley. Not beaten far behind Queen Mary possible Roxan, she had a bit to do from her wide draw, but she battled on well, despite looking green in front, and landed the spoils narrowly. A step back up in class is now likely. (tchd 9-4)

Danseuse, whose dam was placed in Listed company at three, was one of only a couple that got a bit warm before the race. However, she was soon up the with the pace and was another to battle fairly well when asked to quicken.

Astronomic View ◆, who looked a nice sort in the paddock and was relaxed before her first run, has a lovely pedigree, boasting two Royal Ascot winners. Queen Mary winner On Tiptoes has already produced four winners, the Milton Bradley-trained Currency probably the most well known, and he looks certain to add to the family tally after a most promising effort. (op 12-1)

Bodes Galaxy(IRE) showed some promise on his debut, when a never-nearer fifth behind a 50/1 winner, but never really got in a serious blow, and hung left under pressure in the straight. (op 8-1)

Stoneacre Gareth(IRE) Stoneacre Garth, a half-brother to the Group-winning mare Innit, looked a bit leggy before his debut and was shouting to all his rivals entering the paddock. He was another that never really got into the race, after a slow start, and will definitely come on for the race. That said, he does look as if he will need more time. (tchd 15-2)

Disco Dan was starting to stay on when he was hampered just over a furlong from home, and lost any chance he had. (op 6-1)

Candyland(IRE), a Phoenix Stakes entry, weakened quickly in the straight after leading early. (op 3-1)

2573 FURLONGS AND FAIRWAYS (S) STKS — 7f (P)

3:05 (3:07) (Class 6) 3-Y-O+ — **£2,388** (£705; £352) **Stalls** Low

Form				RPR
0050	1		**Tuscany Queen (IRE)**[24] 1899 3-8-3 47 .... RichardSmith(3) 5 (R Hannon) *trckd ldr: rdn to ld 2f out: sn wl clr: drvn out* **8/1**[3]	60
0/00	2	5	**Watching**[7] 2384 9-9-7 74 .... (p) TonyHamilton 2 (R A Fahey) *cl up: rdn 3f out: outpcd 2f out: plugged on to take 2nd last 100yds* **11/2**[2]	55
00	3	¾	**Lucky Lucioni (IRE)**[3] 2509 3-8-8 75 .... NelsonDeSouza(3) 3 (G A Butler) *led to 2f out: sn outpcd by wnr: tired and lost 2nd last 100yds* **5/1**[1]	49
6200	4	½	**Mescalera (GER)**[23] 1914 5-9-2 41 .... FergusSweeney 14 (B G Powell) *sn chsd ldng pair: drvn and outpcd 2f out: one pce u.p* **16/1**	47
0034	5	nk	**Darker Than Blue**[16] 2101 3-8-7 42 ow1 .... (b) TedDurcan 11 (B J Meehan) *racd on outer: chsd ldrs: rdn 3f out: outpcd whn wd bnd 2f out: one pce after* **8/1**[3]	43
0000	6	nk	**Duxford**[12] 2245 5-9-7 48 .... (v[1]) DaneO'Neill 7 (D K Ivory) *dwlt: early reminders in rr: sme prog but u.p 1/2-way: plugged on fr over 1f out* **5/1**[1]	50
0-60	7	2	**Apres Ski (IRE)**[8] 2347 3-8-11 .... FrankieMcDonald 13 (J W Hills) *s.i.s: hld up in last pair: stl same pl 2f out: styd on over 1f out: rdn fnl f: nvr nrr* **50/1**	41+
0-00	8	4	**Tiptoeing**[21] 1950 3-8-3 58 .... SaleemGolam(3) 4 (M H Tompkins) *sn wl in rr: pushed along and struggling 1/2-way* **11/2**[2]	25
00	9	hd	**Bare Rambler**[34] 1646 3-8-11 .... (b[1]) HayleyTurner 8 (Stef Liddiard) *plld hrd early: hld up: wl in rr and struggling 3f out* **25/1**	30
000-	10	¾	**Bahama Reef (IRE)**[178] 6615 5-9-7 39 .... DavidKinsella 12 (B Gubby) *racd wd: sn in rr: struggling fr 3f out* **33/1**	32
00-	11	shd	**Bold Brownie**[260] 5543 4-9-2 .... AdrianMcCarthy 9 (Miss Z C Davison) *prom for 2f: wknd u.p fr 1/2-way* **50/1**	26
630	12	shd	**Postage (USA)**[21] 1950 3-8-11 55 .... (p) LPKeniry 1 (K A Morgan) *prom: drvn 1/2-way: sn wknd* **8/1**[3]	27

00-0 **13** *1 1/4* **Yorkies Boy**[28] [1802] 11-9-7 40 ....(p) AlanDaly 10 28
(N E Berry) *a wl in rr: nvr a factor* **20/1**
1m 26.77s (0.88) **Going Correction** +0.175s/f (Slow)
WFA 3 from 4yo+ 10lb **13** Ran SP% **118.8**
Speed ratings (Par 101):101,95,94,93,93 93,90,86,86,85 85,85,83
CSF £48.61 TOTE £12.70: £5.10, £2.30, £1.90; EX 67.80.The winner was bought in for 6,400gns.
Owner Mcdowell Racing **Bred** David Joseph Finnegan **Trained** East Everleigh, Wilts

FOCUS
An uncompetitive seller in which two of the runners were rated some 16lb higher than anything else in the race, so it is difficult to gauge with any certainty exactly how reliable this form will turn out to be. The form is best rated around the fourth to banded form.

2574 HENRY STREETER FILLIES' H'CAP 7f (P)
3:40 (3:41) (Class 6) (0-60,61) 3-Y-0+ **£2,730** (£806; £403) **Stalls** Low

Form RPR
-000 **1** **Moon Bird**[69] [902] 4-9-10 **56** .... TedDurcan 7 66
(C A Cyzer) *hld up wl in rr and racd on outer: rdn and gd prog fr wl over 1f out: sustained effrt to ld last 75yds* **25/1**
51-1 **2** *1/2* **Free Angel (USA)**[6] [2418] 4-10-1 **61** 6ex .... DaneO'Neill 9 69
(M Wigham) *s.i.s: sn trckd ldrs: rdn over 2f out: effrt u.p to ld 1f out: hdd last 75yds* **11/8**[1]
1046 **3** *1 1/4* **Humility**[8] [2348] 5-10-0 **60** .... IanMongan 13 65
(C A Cyzer) *dropped in bhd fr wd draw: wl in rr tl drvn and prog on outer fr over 1f out: r.o fnl f: nrst fin* **8/1**[3]
5504 **4** *1/2* **Blue Line**[9] [2317] 4-9-11 **57** ....(v) GeorgeBaker 2 61
(M Madgwick) *chsd ldrs: prog over 2f out: drvn and styd on same pce fr over 1f out* **7/1**[2]
4060 **5** *1/2* **Grezie**[9] [2317] 4-9-4 **50** .... MichaelTebbutt 8 52
(T D McCarthy) *restrained after s: wl in rr and racd wd: no prog tl r.o fnl f: nvr nrr* **11/1**
6500 **6** *nk* **Halfwaytoparadise**[13] [2210] 3-9-1 **57** .... HayleyTurner 11 58
(M L W Bell) *mde most: rdn 3f out: hdd & wknd 1f out* **33/1**
0041 **7** *3/4* **Jennverse**[31] [1728] 4-8-8 **47** .... JamesMillman[(7)] 1 46
(D K Ivory) *trckd ldng pair: rdn over 2f out: losing pl on inner whn n.m.r 1f out* **10/1**
-040 **8** *3/4* **A Woman In Love**[11] [2259] 7-9-12 **58** .... RichardThomas 12 55
(Miss B Sanders) *pressed ldr: upsides fr 3f out: stl disputing ld 1f out: gave up completely* **12/1**
346- **9** *shd* **Pearl Farm**[167] [6693] 5-9-3 **52** ....(t) NelsonDeSouza[(3)] 6 49
(C A Horgan) *chsd ldrs: rdn and effrt over 2f out: no prog over 1f out: wknd* **16/1**
3200 **10** *2* **Gaudalpin (IRE)**[9] [2319] 4-8-12 **44** ....(t) RobbieFitzpatrick 10 36
(Ernst Oertel) *in tch on outer: no prog 2f out: wknd over 1f out* **16/1**
0006 **11** *3* **Rancho Cucamonga (IRE)**[38] [1528] 4-9-13 **59** ....(b) J-PGuillambert 14 43
(T D Barron) *s.s: hld up in last: shkn up over 2f out: nvr a factor* **12/1**
0405 **12** *hd* **Angel River**[15] [2148] 4-8-8 **45** ....(b) RoryMoore[(5)] 3 28
(J Ryan) *cl up tl wknd rapidly wl over 1f out* **33/1**
5005 **13** *1/2* **Limonia (GER)**[15] [2136] 4-8-13 **48** .... SaleemGolam[(3)] 5 30
(N P Littmoden) *nvr beyond midfield: u.p and wkng over 2f out* **14/1**
5006 **14** *11* **Just Tallulah**[17] [2080] 3-8-10 **52** .... FergusSweeney 4 4
(N P Littmoden) *dwlt: a wl in rr: t.o* **33/1**
1m 27.37s (1.48) **Going Correction** +0.175s/f (Slow)
WFA 3 from 4yo+ 10lb **14** Ran SP% **129.6**
Speed ratings (Par 98):98,97,96,95,94 94,93,92,92,90 86,86,86,73
CSF £62.44 CT £347.97 TOTE £59.10: £16.70, £1.20, £3.30; EX 123.00.
Owner Mrs Charles Cyzer **Bred** C A Cyzer **Trained** Maplehurst, W Sussex

FOCUS
A moderate fillies' handicap and a surprise result, but the race time was slower than the seller, and does not suggest the form is that reliable, although the form appears sound enough on paper.
Jennverse Official explanation: jockey said filly was denied a clear run
Angel River Official explanation: jockey said filly was denied a clear run

2575 "WELL DONE VINCE" MEDIAN AUCTION MAIDEN STKS 7f (P)
4:15 (4:18) (Class 6) 3-4-Y-0 **£3,238** (£963; £481; £240) **Stalls** Low

Form RPR
1 **Ask No More** 3-9-0 .... BrianReilly 11 71
(P L Gilligan) *trckd ldrs: effrt to ld jst over 3f out: drvn and hrd pressed fnl f: jst hld on* **16/1**
6 **2** *shd* **Mcnairobi**[34] [1640] 3-8-9 .... LPKeniry 6 65
(P D Cundell) *trckd ldrs: rdn to chse wnr over 1f out: str chal fnl f: jst failed* **9/2**[3]
0- **3** *shd* **Distant Drums (IRE)**[245] [5850] 3-8-9 .... TedDurcan 8 65
(B W Hills) *pushed along in rr early: prog to midfield 1/2-way: rdn and gd hdwy on outer 2f out: chal fnl f: jst hld* **10/1**
432- **4** *5* **Desert Flair**[316] [4040] 3-8-9 77 .... DaneO'Neill 5 52
(R Hannon) *prom: chsd wnr 3f out to over 1f out: wknd tamely* **11/4**[1]
0000 **5** *1 3/4* **Musical Chimes**[9] [2318] 3-8-9 53 .... J-PGuillambert 10 47
(C A Cyzer) *chsd ldrs: hrd rdn fr over 2f out: outpcd and wl btn over 1f out* **25/1**
0 **6** *2 1/2* **Special Place**[58] [1065] 3-9-0 .... IanMongan 2 45
(J A R Toller) *towards rr and nvr on terms: shkn up over 2f out: no real prog* **20/1**
33- **7** *shd* **Turn Me On (IRE)**[377] [2263] 3-9-0 .... HayleyTurner 3 45
(M L W Bell) *cl up: rdn over 2f out: sn struggling: wknd over 1f out* **7/2**[2]
8 *1* **Meadow Floss** 3-8-9 .... PatDobbs 1 37
(S Kirk) *s.s: wl in rr: drvn and no imp fnl 2f* **14/1**
9 *2* **Pickwick Miss (USA)** 3-8-9 .... FergusSweeney 7 32
(D M Simcock) *dwlt: wl bhd: plugged on fr over 1f out: no ch* **25/1**
00- **10** *1* **Sham Ruby**[234] [6069] 4-9-5 ....(t) GeorgeBaker 4 29
(M R Bosley) *led to jst over 3f out: wknd 2f out* **66/1**
60-0 **11** *1 1/4* **Vixen Virago**[17] [2068] 3-8-9 49 .... AdrianMcCarthy 9 26
(Jane Southcombe) *nvr beyond midfield: u.p and struggling 3f out* **66/1**
12 *nk* **Demi Sec** 3-8-9 .... RichardThomas 12 25
(Dr J D Scargill) *dwlt: a wl in rr: wknd 2f out* **20/1**
00 **13** *7* **Hollie Dellamore**[6] [2411] 4-9-5 .... FrankieMcDonald 13 6
(A P Jarvis) *a wl in rr: bhd fnl 2f* **80/1**
2 **U** **Advancement**[17] [2080] 3-9-0 .... TonyHamilton 14 —
(R A Fahey) *rrd and uns rdr as stalls opened* **5/1**
1m 26.98s (1.09) **Going Correction** +0.175s/f (Slow)
WFA 3 from 4yo 10lb **14** Ran SP% **126.8**
Speed ratings (Par 101):100,99,99,94,92 89,89,87,85,84 83,82,74,—
CSF £86.11 TOTE £29.30: £8.40, £1.60, £4.00; EX 449.40.
Owner Harvey Bell **Bred** The Wayland Stud **Trained** Newmarket, Suffolk

FOCUS
This looked a very modest event beforehand, which was swiftly made even less competitive when Advancement reared up in the stalls and lost his jockey. The form looks shaky with the fifth probably the best guide for now.
Distant Drums(IRE) Official explanation: jockey said filly hung left in straight

2576 LINGFIELDPARK.CO.UK H'CAP 6f (P)
4:50 (4:53) (Class 5) (0-70,70) 3-Y-0 **£3,886** (£1,156; £577; £288) **Stalls** Low

Form RPR
2210 **1** **George The Second**[28] [1801] 3-8-6 **60** .... RichardKingscote[(5)] 5 67
(Mrs H Sweeting) *cl up: effrt 2f out: led over 1f out: jnd ins fnl f: kpt on wl nr fin* **3/1**[2]
3420 **2** *nk* **Bobby Rose**[16] [2095] 3-8-13 **62** .... DaneO'Neill 7 68
(D K Ivory) *t.k.h: hld up in rr: prog 2f out: swtchd to inner over 1f out: jnd wnr ins fnl f: no ex nr fin* **9/4**[1]
6012 **3** *3* **Red Vixen (IRE)**[41] [1464] 3-8-8 **57** .... HayleyTurner 1 54+
(C N Allen) *hld up in last pair: gng wl enough but stl in rr over 1f out: r.o to take 3rd ins fnl f: no ch of rching ldng pair* **7/1**
-052 **4** *1 1/2* **Mystic Queen (IRE)**[15] [2138] 3-8-5 **54** .... FrankieMcDonald 6 47
(A P Jarvis) *pressed ldr: led 3f out to over 1f out: wknd* **14/1**
150 **5** *1/2* **Boldinor**[55] [1122] 3-9-7 **70** .... AlanDaly 9 61
(N E Berry) *awkward in preliminaries: wnt lft s: chsd ldrs: nt qckn 2f out: n.d after* **10/1**
3644 **6** *hd* **Arzaag**[12] [2222] 3-9-2 **68** .... NelsonDeSouza[(3)] 3 59
(D M Simcock) *a midfield on inner: nt qckn 2f out: one pce after* **9/2**[3]
-000 **7** *5* **Mamichor**[13] [2210] 3-8-3 **55** ....(be[1]) SaleemGolam[(3)] 8 31
(J R Boyle) *s.s and hmpd sn after: t.k.h and in tch 4f out: wknd 2f out* **14/1**
06-0 **8** *1 3/4* **Hahns Peak**[74] [844] 3-8-2 **51** oh1 .... AdrianMcCarthy 4 21
(Mrs A L M King) *led to 3f out: wknd rapidly 2f out* **20/1**
000 **9** *5* **Terrys Alfie**[21] [1960] 3-7-9 **51** oh1 ....(b) CharlotteKerton[(7)] 2 6
(N P Littmoden) *prog fr rr to chse ldrs over 3f out: rdn whn rn v wd bnd 2f out and wknd* **25/1**
1m 13.99s (1.18) **Going Correction** +0.175s/f (Slow) **9** Ran SP% **117.5**
Speed ratings (Par 99):99,98,94,92,91 91,85,82,76
CSF £10.39 CT £43.23 TOTE £4.50: £1.50, £1.20, £1.40; EX 9.70.
Owner The Kennet Connection **Bred** R Withers **Trained** Lockeridge, Wilts
■ Stewards' Enquiry : Charlotte Kerton one-day ban: used whip when out of contention (Jun 26)

FOCUS
A modest handicap and the form looks relatively weak.

2577 VISIT US AT LINGFIELD PARK H'CAP 1m 4f (P)
5:25 (5:25) (Class 6) (0-55,55) 4-Y-0+ **£2,730** (£806; £403) **Stalls** Low

Form RPR
0000 **1** **Celtique**[85] [698] 4-9-8 **55** .... DO'Donohoe 12 69
(M Wigham) *broke on terms: prom: chsd ldr wl over 1f out: upsides fnl f: won on the nod* **5/1**[2]
0404 **2** *shd* **Ardea Brave (IRE)**[15] [2133] 4-9-8 **55** ....(p) TedDurcan 10 69
(M Botti) *led: drvn and jnd fnl f: jst pipped* **8/1**[3]
-000 **3** *5* **Serramanna**[10] [2305] 5-8-12 **52** .... SladeO'Hara[(7)] 6 58
(Dr J R J Naylor) *hld up towards rr: prog on outer fr 3f out: rdn and r.o to take 3rd fnl f: nt rch ldng pair* **12/1**
3-00 **4** *4* **Trials 'n Tribs**[38] [1540] 4-9-1 **48** .... J-PGuillambert 11 47
(C A Cyzer) *dwlt: hld up in last pair: prog 1/2-way: rdn to chse ldng trio 2f out: wknd fnl f* **16/1**
5-60 **5** *1/2* **Ocean Rock**[31] [1748] 5-9-4 **51** .... GeorgeBaker 13 50
(C A Horgan) *dwlt: hld up wl in rr: gng wl enough but off the pce over 4f out : sme prog 3f out: drvn and plugged on one pce* **14/1**
1004 **6** *3/4* **Zoripp (IRE)**[6] [2414] 4-9-1 **53** ....(b) StephenDonohoe[(5)] 2 50
(J G Given) *cl up: rdn and lost pl over 4f out: outpcd 3f out: kpt on again fr over 1f out* **14/1**
0-55 **7** *shd* **Montage (IRE)**[9] [2320] 4-9-7 **54** .... DaneO'Neill 16 51
(J Akehurst) *t.k.h: mostly pressed ldr to wl over 1f out: wknd rapidly fnl f* **14/1**
4220 **8** *3 1/2* **Good Article (IRE)**[52] [1201] 5-8-8 **48** .... JamesMillman[(7)] 3 40
(D K Ivory) *trckd ldrs: rdn over 2f out: grad wknd* **12/1**
-006 **9** *3/4* **Damburger Xpress**[12] [2221] 4-9-4 **54** .... SaleemGolam[(3)] 15 44
(D M Simcock) *prom: drvn 3f out: wknd 2f out* **12/1**
3331 **10** *1 1/2* **Twentytwosilver (IRE)**[9] [1729] 6-9-3 **50** .... MichaelTebbutt 1 38
(D B Feek) *hld up in last: gng wl enough but off the pce over 4f out: rdn 3f out: no ch of getting on terms* **7/2**[1]
4050 **11** *5* **Thebestisyettocome**[15] [2132] 4-9-7 **54** .... IanMongan 14 34
(T G Mills) *prom: drvn 5f out: wknd rapidly over 2f out* **8/1**[3]
0000 **12** *10* **Shakerattleandroll (IRE)**[17] [2088] 5-9-6 **53** .... RichardThomas 8 17
(Mrs L Richards) *nvr beyond midfield: rdn 5f out: wknd 3f out: sn bhd* **50/1**
200P **13** *15* **Barton Sands (IRE)**[9] [2327] 9-9-1 **55** ....(t) JamieJones[(7)] 4 —
(Ernst Oertel) *hld up wl in rr: rdn and losing tch 5f out: eased whn no ch 2f out: t.o* **25/1**
6000 **14** *1* **Elvina Hills (IRE)**[8] [2348] 4-9-3 **50** ....(p) FergusSweeney 9 —
(P Mitchell) *hld up wl in rr: rdn and wknd 5f out: t.o* **25/1**
0064 **15** *3* **Eamon An Chnoic (IRE)**[4] [2483] 5-9-5 **52** .... PatDobbs 5 —
(B W Duke) *trckd ldrs: rdn over 4f out: wknd rapidly: t.o whn eased 2f out* **8/1**[3]
2m 35.62s (1.23) **Going Correction** +0.175s/f (Slow) **15** Ran SP% **130.8**
Speed ratings (Par 101):102,101,98,95,95 95,95,92,92,91 87,81,71,70,68
CSF £47.96 CT £481.41 TOTE £5.20: £2.60, £3.40, £4.40; EX 86.10 Place 6 £101.35, Place 5 £45.35.
Owner D T L Limited **Bred** Wretham Stud **Trained** Newmarket, Suffolk

FOCUS
A very moderate event that could have easily had the words banded or selling in the race title. Apart from the first two they finished well spread out and the form should prove sound for the grade.
Zoripp(IRE) Official explanation: vet said gelding returned lame
Eamon An Chnoic(IRE) Official explanation: jockey said gelding banged its head on stalls and never travelled
T/Plt: £697.10 to a £1 stake. Pool: £33,709.35. 35.30 winning tickets. T/Qpdt: £538.90 to a £1 stake. Pool: £2,257.80. 3.10 winning tickets. JN

[2455]NEWBURY (L-H)

Thursday, June 15

OFFICIAL GOING: Good to firm

Race 9 charity race not under Rules, won by former smart performer Diktatorial.
Wind: Virtually nil

2578 CANTORSPREADFAIR.COM MAIDEN FILLIES' STKS (DIV I) 1m 2f 6y
1:40 (1:40) (Class 5) 3-Y-O £4,857 (£1,445; £722; £360) **Stalls Centre**

Form RPR
6-40 **1** **Kaylianni**[13] [2203] 3-9-0 88 ... TonyCulhane 8 80
(M R Channon) *chsd ldrs: chal 2f out: led wl over 1f out: hrd drvn ins last and kpt on wl cl home* **11/4**[2]

32 **2** *½* **Garafena**[28] [1798] 3-9-0 ... JamieSpencer 4 79
(Pat Eddery) *hld up in tch: hdwy and n.m.r 2f out: drvn and qcknd to chse wnr ins last: r.o u.p but a hld cl home* **6/1**[3]

0- **3** *1 ½* **Mabadi (USA)**[237] [6002] 3-9-0 ... RHills 7 76
(B W Hills) *hld up in rr: stdy hdwy on outside to trck ldrs 3f out: cl 3rd whn hung bdly rt ins last: kpt on again but nt rcvr* **20/1**

3 **4** *2* **Red Countess**[55] [1114] 3-9-0 ... RyanMoore 6 72
(Mrs A J Perrett) *chsd ldr: chal over 4f out tl led 3f out: rdn 2f out: hdd wl over 1f out: wknd ins last* **5/2**[1]

4- **5** *¾* **Adelfia (IRE)**[227] [6200] 3-9-0 ... NickyMackay 1 71
(Sir Michael Stoute) *chsd ldrs: rdn 3f out: outpcd 2f out: kpt on again ins last but nvr a danger* **9/1**

6 *2* **Kitabaat (IRE)** 3-9-0 ... MartinDwyer 9 67
(E A L Dunlop) *slowly away: sn rcvrd and rr but in tch: rdn over 2f out: styd on but nvr in contention* **16/1**

7 *3* **Jump Ship** 3-9-0 ... RichardHughes 2 61
(M P Tregoning) *hld up in rr: pushed along: effrt and rn green over 2f out: n.d after* **12/1**

2 **8** *½* **Sweet Spot**[10] [2307] 3-9-0 ... MCHussey 3 60
(Eamon Tyrrell, Ire) *led tl hdd 3f out: wknd fr 2f out* **8/1**

0- **9** *12* **Lihusn Al Haz (USA)**[254] [5692] 3-9-0 ... SebSanders 5 38
(C E Brittain) *pushed along in rr 7f out: a in rr* **50/1**

0 **10** *nk* **Helen Wood**[43] [1401] 3-8-7 ... FrankiePickard(7) 10 37
(M D I Usher) *t.k.h: chsd ldrs tl wknd fr 3f out* **100/1**

2m 9.57s (0.86) **Going Correction** -0.075s/f (Good) **10 Ran SP% 111.9**
Speed ratings (Par 96):93,92,91,89,89 87,85,84,75,74
CSF £18.50 TOTE £4.00: £1.50, £1.80, £7.10; EX 17.60.
Owner W A Harrison-Allan **Bred** Glebe Stud And Mrs F Woodd **Trained** West Ilsley, Berks

FOCUS
A moderately run contest and the winning time was 1.1 seconds slower than the second division. The race is rated around the runner-up and fourth.

2579 HIGHCLERE THOROUGHBRED RACING MAIDEN STKS (C&G) 6f 8y
2:10 (2:10) (Class 4) 2-Y-O £6,477 (£1,927; £963; £481) **Stalls Centre**

Form RPR
1 **Thousand Words** 2-9-0 ... RichardHughes 4 89+
(B W Hills) *hld up rr but in tch: hdwy 2f out: swtchd lft and qcknd 1f out to ld ins last: shkn up: green but sn clr: comf* **6/1**[3]

2 *1 ¼* **Charlie Farnsbarns (IRE)** 2-9-0 ... NCallan 8 82+
(B J Meehan) *slt advantage tl def ld whn rdn 2f out: hdd ins last: kpt on but nt pce of wnr* **9/1**

3 *2* **Golden Balls (IRE)** 2-9-0 ... RyanMoore 10 76
(R Hannon) *pressed ldr tl rdn 2f out: outpcd fnl f* **9/4**[1]

4 *nk* **Touch Of Style (IRE)** 2-8-11 ... AmirQuinn(3) 6 75
(J R Boyle) *chsd ldrs: rdn 2f out: wknd ins fnl f* **16/1**

5 **5** *2* **Mint State**[18] [2045] 2-9-0 ... JohnEgan 2 69
(D R C Elsworth) *s.i.s: plld hrd early: chsd ldrs: wknd fnl f* **6/1**[3]

6 *shd* **Ambrosiano** 2-9-0 ... MickyFenton 3 69+
(Miss E C Lavelle) *rr but in tch: hdwy 2f out: kpt on ins last but nvr gng pce to rch ldrs* **25/1**

7 *1 ¼* **Castara Bay** 2-9-0 ... PatDobbs 7 65
(R Hannon) *chsd ldrs: rdn over 2f out: wknd over 1f out* **40/1**

8 *hd* **Global Guest** 2-9-0 ... TonyCulhane 9 64
(M R Channon) *s.i.s: bhd: hdwy to chse ldrs 3f out: wknd fr 2f out: no ch whn n.m.r ins last* **25/1**

9 *3* **Mulvany (IRE)** 2-9-0 ... JamieSpencer 1 55
(B J Meehan) *a in rr and outpcd* **14/1**

10 *½* **Surrey Spinner** 2-9-0 ... KFallon 5 54
(Mrs A J Perrett) *s.i.s: bhd and outpcd most of way* **7/2**[2]

1m 14.21s (-0.11) **Going Correction** -0.075s/f (Good) **10 Ran SP% 114.2**
Speed ratings (Par 95):97,95,92,92,89 89,87,87,83,82
CSF £56.14 TOTE £8.00: £2.10, £2.60, £1.30; EX 56.40.
Owner K Abdulla **Bred** Juddmonte Farms Ltd **Trained** Lambourn, Berks

FOCUS
Just a fair maiden by the course's standards, but the winning time was creditable enough and the front three look above average.

NOTEBOOK
Thousand Words ◆, out of a winning half-sister to Exterior, was given a very patient ride early but found a decent turn of foot when asked to go and win his race. He gave the impression he would benefit from the outing so the future looks bright. (op 17-2 tchd 9-1)

Charlie Farnsbarns(IRE) ◆, a 105,000euros colt, ran a fine race from the front and kept on right to the line despite finding the winner too good. Given that the stable's debutants normally come on from the run, it should not be long before he goes one better and his breeding suggests he will really come into his own over further. (op 8-1)

Golden Balls(IRE) ◆, a 100,000gns half-brother to Morning Glow, may have been a beaten favourite on this debut but he did little wrong having raced close to the pace from the off and there should be a race in him before too long. (op 5-2 tchd 15-8)

Touch Of Style(IRE), a 52,000euros full-brother to Si Si Amiga plus a half-brother to four other winners, ran a very creditable debut. He should come on for this and, as a couple of his siblings proved very successful when sent to race in the US, he could be especially interesting if tried on sand. (op 14-1)

Mint State, the only colt in the field with previous experience, nonetheless did not help his chances by taking a good hold early and that told on him later on. He may need a bit more time and experience, whilst his breeding suggests he is likely to come into his own once handicapped and racing over further. (op 13-2 tchd 11-2)

Surrey Spinner, a 45,000gns half-brother to Oases and Paarl Rock, fluffed the start and never got into it thereafter. Given his solid position in the market, much better was presumably expected. (op 3-1 tchd 5-1)

2580 CANTORSPREADFAIR.COM MAIDEN FILLIES' STKS (DIV II) 1m 2f 6y
2:45 (2:45) (Class 5) 3-Y-O £4,857 (£1,445; £722; £360) **Stalls Centre**

Form RPR
2- **1** **Sandglass**[244] [5870] 3-9-0 ... RichardHughes 5 85+
(Mrs A J Perrett) *hld up in tch: hdwy 3f out: led 1f out: shkn up and edgd lft ins last: sn clr: easily* **15/8**[2]

-6 **2** *2 ½* **Acts Of Grace (USA)**[16] [2118] 3-9-0 ... SebSanders 2 80
(J L Dunlop) *chsd ldrs: drvn to ld 2f out: hdd 1f out: kpt on but nvr gng pce of wnr* **11/2**[3]

0-0 **3** *2 ½* **Reinstated (IRE)**[26] [1845] 3-9-0 ... MartinDwyer 4 75
(B W Hills) *t.k.h: trckd ldrs: drvn to chal 2f out: wknd fnl f* **50/1**

32-2 **4** *2 ½* **Edaara (IRE)**[57] [1085] 3-9-0 87 ... RHills 6 70
(W J Haggas) *rr but in tch: hdwy to trck ldrs over 2f out: wknd fnl f* **13/8**[1]

04 **5** *6* **Double Bay (USA)**[18] [2048] 3-9-0 ... JohnEgan 3 59
(Jane Chapple-Hyam) *led: rdn over 3f out and kpt slt advantage tl hdd 2f out: sn wknd* **22/1**

3- **6** *2* **Born Wild (GER)**[215] [6334] 3-9-0 ... KFallon 9 55
(Sir Michael Stoute) *chsd ldrs: pushed along 4f out: wknd over 2f out* **6/1**

0 **7** *1 ¼* **Lady Galadriel (USA)**[24] [1901] 3-9-0 ... NCallan 8 53
(J M P Eustace) *chsd ldr: chal over 3f out tl wknd qckly appr fnl 2f* **40/1**

8 *3* **Janaah** 3-9-0 ... RyanMoore 10 47
(C E Brittain) *a in rr* **40/1**

9 *9* **Midnight Moonlight** 3-9-0 ... TPQueally 7 30
(C F Wall) *s.i.s: bhd: sme hdwy over 3f out: sn wknd* **50/1**

2m 8.47s (-0.24) **Going Correction** -0.075s/f (Good) **9 Ran SP% 115.7**
Speed ratings (Par 96):97,95,93,91,86 84,83,81,74
CSF £11.99 TOTE £3.00: £1.20, £1.60, £6.80; EX 14.90.
Owner K Abdulla **Bred** Juddmonte Farms Ltd **Trained** Pulborough, W Sussex

FOCUS
A more solid pace than the first division and the winning time was 1.1 seconds faster. The fifth and seventh are the best guides to the form and the first two look above average.

2581 ALTOHIWAY ANNIVERSARY H'CAP 1m (S)
3:20 (3:22) (Class 4) (0-85,85) 3-Y-O £6,477 (£1,927; £963; £481) **Stalls Centre**

Form RPR
-126 **1** **Tempsford Flyer (IRE)**[27] [1832] 3-9-4 **82** ... KFallon 6 87
(J W Hills) *chsd ldrs: pushed along fr 3f out: ld appr fnl f: hung lft u.p last half f: hld on all out* **9/1**

3-32 **2** *hd* **Robustian**[14] [2177] 3-9-1 **79** ... StephenCarson 8 84+
(R F Johnson Houghton) *bhd: gd hdwy fr 2f out: chsd ldrs ins last: edgd lft and r.o wl cl home: nt quite get up* **7/1**

1- **3** *shd* **Alfie Tupper (IRE)**[290] [4839] 3-9-5 **83** ... RichardHughes 2 88+
(S Kirk) *plld hrd early and stdd rr: smooth hdwy over 2f out: qcknd to press ldrs ins last: struck over hd cl home: kpt on wl* **16/1**

2636 **4** *nk* **Isphahan**[14] [2177] 3-8-11 **75** ...(v) MartinDwyer 5 79
(A M Balding) *led: narrowly hdd appr fnl f: styd pressing ldrs: stl upsides whn carried lft: last half f: no ex last strides* **10/1**

2164 **5** *2* **Airbuss (IRE)**[21] [1951] 3-9-0 **78** ... ChrisCatlin 1 77
(M R Channon) *chsd ldrs: rdn 3f out: styd on over 1f out: wknd last half f* **6/1**[3]

61 **6** *3* **Tawaajud (USA)**[34] [1630] 3-9-2 **80** ... RHills 10 73
(B W Hills) *hld up in rr: hdwy over 3f out: nvr gng pce to rch ldrs: one pce fnl 2f* **5/1**[2]

-146 **7** *8* **Critic (IRE)**[29] [1776] 3-9-7 **85** ... JamieSpencer 7 73+
(M L W Bell) *bhd: hdwy over 3f out: pushed along and no imp 2f out: eased whn no ch ins last* **12/1**

-531 **8** *1 ½* **Hill Spirit**[15] [2143] 3-9-2 **80** ... JohnEgan 9 65+
(D R C Elsworth) *in tch: drvn to chse ldrs 3f out: wknd qckly appr fnl f* **11/4**[1]

030- **9** *1 ½* **Lopinot (IRE)**[259] [5570] 3-8-8 **72** ... NCallan 4 39
(B J Meehan) *chsd ldrs: rdn 3f out: stl ev ch over 2f out: sn btn* **66/1**

0-14 **10** *8* **Polliwilline (IRE)**[31] [1734] 3-9-4 **82** ... RyanMoore 3 31
(R Hannon) *chsd ldrs: rdn 3f out: ev ch 2f out: sn wknd: eased whn no ch ins last* **10/1**

1m 38.54s (-2.08) **Going Correction** -0.075s/f (Good) **10 Ran SP% 113.4**
Speed ratings (Par 101):107,106,106,106,104 101,93,91,90,82
CSF £68.55 CT £1011.70 TOTE £11.00: £3.20, £2.40, £3.80; EX 126.90.
Owner Mrs Brian Kingham **Bred** P Connolly **Trained** Upper Lambourn, Berks
■ Stewards' Enquiry : K Fallon one-day ban: careless riding (Jun 26)

FOCUS
This looks a decent handicap and was won in a reasonable time for the type of race. Things did become a little tight in the closing stages with the front four all edging over to the far rail and there was little between the quartet at the line. The form is rated through the fourth.

2582 LORD WEINSTOCK MEMORIAL STKS (REGISTERED AS THE BALLYMACOLL STUD STAKES) (LISTED RACE) (FILLIES) 1m 2f 6y
3:55 (3:56) (Class 1) 3-Y-O
£15,898 (£6,025; £3,015; £1,503; £753; £378) **Stalls Centre**

Form RPR
22-1 **1** **Princess Nada**[43] [1418] 3-8-9 83 ... NickyMackay 3 105+
(L M Cumani) *hld up rr: stdy hdwy over 2f out: drvn to ld jst ins last: kpt on strly* **11/2**[3]

3-54 **2** *1 ½* **Jaish (USA)**[27] [1819] 3-8-9 92 ... RHills 2 102
(J L Dunlop) *led: rdn over 2f out: hdd jst ins fnl f: kpt on but a hld by wnr* **16/1**

4-35 **3** *¾* **High Heel Sneakers**[29] [1777] 3-8-9 102 ... RyanMoore 8 101
(P F I Cole) *bhd: rdn and hdwy on outside fr 3f out: drvn to chal over 1f out: one pce ins last* **8/1**

1-2 **4** *1 ¼* **Star Cluster**[16] [2103] 3-8-9 93 ... RichardHughes 7 99
(H R A Cecil) *chsd ldr: rdn to chal over 2f out: stl wl there over 1f out: wknd ins last* **7/2**[2]

5-54 **5** *shd* **Cross Channel (USA)**[33] [1669] 3-8-9 95 ... SebSanders 4 98
(E A L Dunlop) *plld hrd: stdd towards rr 7f out but in tch: rdn over 2f out: chsd ldrs over 1f out but nvr gng pce to get competitive* **16/1**

1-21 **6** *hd* **Anna Pavlova**[19] [2024] 3-8-9 97 ... PaulHanagan 9 98
(R A Fahey) *towards rr but in tch: pushed along and sme hdwy over 2f out: nvr gng pce to rch ldrs and styd on same pce fnl f* **2/1**[1]

1 **7** *5* **Missisipi Star (IRE)**[34] [1650] 3-8-9 ... MCHussey 6 89
(Eamon Tyrrell, Ire) *keen hold: chsd ldrs: riven to chal over 2f out: wknd and hung lft ins last* **33/1**

00-3 **8** *2* **Queen Of Fire**[27] [1834] 3-8-9 97 ... JamieSpencer 1 85
(M R Channon) *chsd ldrs: pushed along 3f out: wknd ins fnl 2f* **16/1**

1- **9** *1 1/4* **Random Call (USA)**[233] [6097] 3-8-9 .... KFallon 5 82
(Sir Michael Stoute) *chsd ldrs tl wknd 2f out* **17/2**

2m 8.47s (-0.24) **Going Correction** -0.075s/f (Good) **9** Ran SP% **113.2**
Speed ratings (Par 104):97,95,95,94,94 93,89,88,87
CSF £85.83 TOTE £6.00: £1.80, £4.20, £2.20; EX 114.00.
Owner Sheikh Mohammed Obaid Al Maktoum **Bred** Darley **Trained** Newmarket, Suffolk

FOCUS
The early pace for this Listed race was very moderate and the field were still in a heap passing the two-furlong pole. The winning time was exactly the same as for the second division of the fillies' maiden, which is very moderate for a race of this stature. The form appears fair for the grade but may not prove that solid.

NOTEBOOK
Princess Nada was by some way the lowest-rated of the seven fillies in this race with an official mark, but she did not let that bother her. Held up in last place in a moderately-run race, she weaved her way through the field over the last couple of furlongs and eventually scored with a bit in hand. The modest winning time does put a question mark over the value of the form, but she is a progressive filly and now, that she has won a Listed race, that is unlikely to bother connections one iota. (op 8-1)
Jaish(USA), back on fast ground for the first time since her successful racecourse debut, was allowed an uncontested lead and that enabled her to conserve energy and keep going to hold all but the winner at bay. This was an improved effort, but the way the race was run does put a question mark over the true merit of the form.
High Heel Sneakers, back down from Group company, had every chance and it does seem as though this is her favoured surface, but as she had the highest official rating in the field it could be argued that she has run below form. (op 9-1)
Star Cluster, stepping up three furlongs in trip, should have progressed from last month's return from a lengthy absence and it was disappointing that she folded rather tamely in the closing stages, especially in such a moderately-run race. Perhaps she did not stay or her reappearance effort took more out of her than was thought, but she is still worth another chance. (op 10-3)
Cross Channel(USA) took a keen hold at the back of the field in this moderately-run contest and could never find the necessary speed when the sprint for the line started. This looks about as good as she is.
Anna Pavlova won three times on fast ground as a juvenile, so the return to this surface after her Haydock victory should not have been a problem. However, a combination of being held up in a slowly-run race and the step up in class did seem to find her out. (op 13-8)
Missisipi Star(IRE) Official explanation: vet said filly was in season

2583 CANTOR SPREADFAIR H'CAP 7f (S)
4:30 (4:31) (Class 5) (0-70,70) 3-Y-O £5,181 (£1,541; £770; £384) Stalls Centre

Form RPR
5402 **1** **Fratt'n Park (IRE)**[6] [2403] 3-8-13 **62** .... KFallon 2 69
(J J Bridger) *mid-div: rdn and hdwy fr 2f out to ld 1f out: hung lft and hit rail nr fin: drvn out* **6/1**[2]
464- **2** *3/4* **Antigoni (IRE)**[234] [6071] 3-9-4 **67** .... RichardHughes 9 72
(A M Balding) *s.i.s: bhd: hdwy over 2f out: drvn to chal over 1f ot: kpt on same pce ins last* **14/1**
5-00 **3** *hd* **Golden Alchemist**[33] [1681] 3-9-7 **70** .... JamieSpencer 3 74
(M D I Usher) *in tch: rdn and hdwy over 2f out: chal appr fnl f: kpt on same pce* **14/1**
4633 **4** *1 1/2* **Danish Blues (IRE)**[6] [2393] 3-8-11 **60** .... RyanMoore 14 60
(N P Littmoden) *chsd ldrs: rdn to chal over 1f out: no ex ins last* **11/1**
0-00 **5** *2* **Whisper Inthe Wind (IRE)**[9] [2316] 3-8-8 **60** .... DominicFox(3) 4 55
(Miss J Feilden) *chsd ldrs: rdn and ev ch over 1f out: wknd ins last* **80/1**
-022 **6** *1/2* **Mucho Loco (IRE)**[17] [2065] 3-8-13 **62** .... (b) NickyMackay 12 55
(J G Portman) *s.i.s: bhd: rdn and sltly hmpd 2f out: drvn and styd on ins last but nvr gng pce to rch ldrs* **15/2**
00-6 **7** *1/2* **Colton**[45] [1355] 3-8-12 **61** .... NCallan 6 53
(J M P Eustace) *in tch tl pushed along and outpcd 3f out: drvn and kpt on fnl f but nvr in contention* **11/1**
5230 **8** *1 1/2* **Musical Script (USA)**[18] [2050] 3-8-12 **61** .... TPQueally 8 49
(Mrs A J Hamilton-Fairley) *pressed ldrs tl slt ld 3f out: sn rdn: narrowly hdd 1f out: wknd sn after* **33/1**
2-24 **9** *1 1/4* **Royal Citadel (IRE)**[18] [2050] 3-9-6 **69** .... (v) PhilipRobinson 13 53
(C G Cox) *led 1f: rdn and ev ch over 1f out: sn wknd* **4/1**[1]
206- **10** *1 1/4* **Bee Seventeen (USA)**[298] [4602] 3-9-6 **69** .... TQuinn 5 50
(P F I Cole) *chsd ldrs: rdn over 2f out: wknd over 1f out* **40/1**
-446 **11** *hd* **Lisfannon**[35] [1616] 3-9-0 **63** .... MartinDwyer 16 44
(B W Hills) *racd stands side and led sole opponent that side but nvr gng pce to trble ldrs in main gp* **10/1**
3-36 **12** *shd* **Namoos (USA)**[21] [1956] 3-9-5 **68** .... RHills 15 48
(J L Dunlop) *racd stand side and chsd sole opponent that side: nvr gng pce to trble main gp* **7/1**[3]
0505 **13** *hd* **Bold Cross (IRE)**[10] [2301] 3-9-2 **65** .... TonyCulhane 7 45+
(E G Bevan) *chsd ldrs: rdn 3f out: wkng whn bdly hmpd 2f out* **14/1**
-300 **14** *1* **Dream Forest (IRE)**[21] [1963] 3-9-4 **67** .... JohnEgan 10 44+
(Mrs P N Dutfield) *chsd ldrs: wknd and hmpd 2f out* **40/1**
13-0 **15** *8* **Solicitude**[34] [1642] 3-9-0 **63** .... MickyFenton 11 18
(D Haydn Jones) *led after 1f: hdd 3f out: wknd and hung bdly rt u.p 2f out* **40/1**

1m 25.65s (-1.35) **Going Correction** -0.075s/f (Good) **15** Ran SP% **115.8**
Speed ratings (Par 99):104,103,102,101,98 98,97,96,94,93 92,92,92,91,82
CSF £80.17 CT £1145.89 TOTE £6.50: £2.20, £4.40, £5.70; EX 97.60.
Owner Double-R-Racing **Bred** P D Savill **Trained** Liphook, Hants

FOCUS
The field split into two with the much larger group coming down the centre, whilst the two highest-drawn horses raced up the stands' rail. The pace was good and resulted in a decent time for a race of its type and the form should prove sound.

2584 CANTORSPREADFAIR.COM H'CAP 1m 4f 5y
5:05 (5:05) (Class 4) (0-80,80) 3-Y-O £6,477 (£1,927; £963; £481) Stalls Centre

Form RPR
-012 **1** **Bauer (IRE)**[24] [1881] 3-8-6 **65** .... NickyMackay 6 78+
(L M Cumani) *hld up in rr: stdy hdwy over 2f out: led 1f out: pushed out: readily* **4/1**[2]
3-30 **2** *1 1/2* **Karlani (IRE)**[27] [1837] 3-8-7 **66** .... KFallon 2 77
(Sir Michael Stoute) *chsd ldrs: pushed along fr 5f out: drvn to chal over 1f out: kpt on same pce ins last but styd on to retain 2nd cl home* **8/1**
-601 **3** *hd* **Wannabe Posh (IRE)**[9] [2332] 3-8-8 **67** 6ex .... JamieSpencer 8 77
(J L Dunlop) *bhd: pushed along 6f out: hdwy on rails fr 3f out: kpt on u.p ins last but nt rch ldrs* **7/2**[1]
0-00 **4** *3/4* **Counting House (IRE)**[52] [1192] 3-8-13 **72** .... PhilipRobinson 14 81
(R Charlton) *chsd ldrs: led 3f out: sn rdn: hdd 1f out: wknd last half f* **33/1**
-042 **5** *6* **Risk Runner (IRE)**[9] [2332] 3-8-13 **72** .... (v) JDSmith 12 71
(A King) *bhd: stdy hdwy on outside over 3f out to chal fr 2f out: wknd 1f out* **7/1**
-614 **6** *1 1/2* **King's Revenge**[21] [1948] 3-9-2 **75** .... (b[1]) TQuinn 1 72
(T D Easterby) *pitched s: rr: hdwy 3f out: chsd ldrs and rdn over 2f out: wknd appr fnl f* **50/1**
31 **7** *3* **Aspasias Tizzy (USA)**[40] [1492] 3-9-5 **78** .... JoeFanning 3 70
(M Johnston) *led tl hdd 3f out: wknd over 1f out* **6/1**[3]
1-00 **8** *shd* **Grey Paint (USA)**[10] [2290] 3-9-1 **74** .... (t) RyanMoore 11 66
(R Hannon) *broke wl: stdd rr and sn bhd: pushed along and kpt on fnl f but nvr in contention* **40/1**
-040 **9** *3/4* **Floodlight Fantasy**[31] [1738] 3-8-7 **66** .... NCallan 10 57
(E S McMahon) *bhd: hdwy to chse ldrs 3f out: sn rdn: wknd fr 2f out* **16/1**
3044 **10** *1/2* **Feu D'Artifice (USA)**[31] [1738] 3-8-13 **72** .... RichardHughes 9 62
(R Hannon) *bhd: sme hdwy 4f out: nvr rchd ldrs: wknd 2f out* **12/1**
3-06 **11** *1 1/4* **Adage**[16] [2113] 3-8-7 **69** .... NeilChalmers(3) 4 57
(David Pinder) *in tch: rdn 3f out and sn wknd* **100/1**
1-40 **12** *shd* **Twill (IRE)**[29] [1781] 3-9-7 **80** .... MickyFenton 5 68
(H Morrison) *chsd ldrs: rdn 3f out: hung lft and wknd qckly 2f out* **40/1**
4-44 **13** *17* **Island Myth (IRE)**[20] [1975] 3-9-5 **78** .... MartinDwyer 15 39
(M P Tregoning) *chsd ldrs: rdn 5f out: wknd 4f out* **20/1**
004 **14** *3 1/2* **Ghallab**[33] [1691] 3-9-1 **74** .... RHills 7 29
(E A L Dunlop) *chsd ldrs tl wknd ins fnl 3f* **28/1**
6-34 **15** *6* **Ahmedy (IRE)**[12] [2239] 3-9-5 **78** .... TonyCulhane 13 23
(M R Channon) *chsd ldrs to 3f out* **33/1**

2m 32.77s (-3.22) **Going Correction** -0.075s/f (Good) **15** Ran SP% **115.6**
Speed ratings (Par 101):107,106,105,105,101 100,98,98,97,97 96,96,85,82,78
CSF £31.17 CT £122.36 TOTE £5.10: £1.90, £3.30, £2.00; EX 48.90.
Owner Aston House Stud **Bred** Aston House Stud **Trained** Newmarket, Suffolk

FOCUS
A fair handicap and the paced looked decent in this and ability to stay the trip was truly tested. A smart winning time for a race like this and the first four pulled well clear of the rest, and the form looks strong.
King's Revenge Official explanation: jockey said gelding slipped on leaving stalls
Island Myth(IRE) Official explanation: jockey said gelding was unsuited by the good to firm ground

2585 BOLLINGER CHAMPAGNE CHALLENGE SERIES H'CAP (FOR GENTLEMAN AMATEUR RIDERS) 1m 2f 6y
5:40 (5:40) (Class 5) (0-70,69) 4-Y-O+ £3,435 (£1,065; £532; £266) Stalls Centre

Form RPR
5-00 **1** **Forthright**[20] [1995] 5-11-5 **69** .... MrMJJSmith(5) 4 81
(A W Carroll) *chsd ldrs: led 4f out: drvn over 1f out: kpt on wl* **7/1**
6000 **2** *3* **Consonant (IRE)**[3] [2499] 9-11-0 **66** .... MrBAdams(7) 10 73
(D G Bridgwater) *prom: chsd wnr fr 3f out: kpt on but no imp fnl 2f* **20/1**
6321 **3** *shd* **Ramsgill (USA)**[31] [1748] 4-11-2 **66** .... MrSPearce(5) 2 73
(J Pearce) *bhd: hdwy fr 3f out: r.o fnl f to press for 2nd last strides but nvr nr wnr* **4/1**[2]
0005 **4** *shd* **Love You Always (USA)**[5] [2455] 6-10-3 **55** .... (t) MrRBirkett(7) 6 61
(Miss J Feilden) *bhd: hdwy 3f out: styd on to press for 2nd cl home but nvr gng pce to rch wnr* **7/1**
-141 **5** *1 1/2* **Wild Pitch**[8] [2345] 5-11-0 **64** .... (b) JackMitchell(5) 5 68
(P Mitchell) *bhd: swtchd to outside and hdwy over 2f out: styd on ins last but nvr gng pce to rch ldrs* **13/8**[1]
5056 **6** *5* **Elms Schoolboy**[6] [2392] 4-9-12 **50** oh5 .... (b) JPFeatherstone(7) 1 44
(P Howling) *bhd: sme hdwy fnl 2f: nvr in contention* **33/1**
4043 **7** *5* **Libre**[14] [2170] 6-11-1 **65** .... MrDanielChinn(5) 9 61+
(F Jordan) *bhd: sme hdwy over 2f out: nvr nr ldrs* **11/2**[3]
610- **8** *1 1/2* **Raffish**[87] [3747] 4-10-11 **63** .... MrMScudamore(7) 3 45
(M Scudamore) *bhd most of way* **40/1**
0015 **9** *1/2* **Zinging**[15] [2132] 7-10-0 **50** oh3 .... MrHHaynes(5) 8 31
(J J Bridger) *slt ld to 4f out: sn wknd* **20/1**
00-0 **10** *6* **Shortbread**[16] [2098] 4-10-9 **59** .... (p) MrNPearce(5) 7 28
(M Salaman) *disp ld to 4f out: sn wknd* **100/1**

2m 10.2s (1.49) **Going Correction** -0.075s/f (Good) **10** Ran SP% **114.4**
Speed ratings (Par 103):91,88,88,88,87 83,79,78,77,72
CSF £133.82 CT £633.72 TOTE £9.50: £3.20, £6.90, £1.70; EX 229.80 Place 6 £441.19, Place 5 £210.30.
Owner Mrs B Quinn **Bred** Wyck Hall Stud Ltd **Trained** Cropthorne, Worcs

FOCUS
A poor race, in which the leaders Shortbread and Zinging went off far too fast, plus some varied riding styles. Because of that, the form, rated around the third and fourth, may not be totally reliable.
Wild Pitch Official explanation: trainer said gelding coughed after race
T/Plt: £747.10 to a £1 stake. Pool: £44,115.10. 43.10 winning tickets. T/Qpdt: £96.40 to a £1 stake. Pool: £3,116.60. 23.90 winning tickets. ST

2178 YARMOUTH (L-H)
Thursday, June 15
OFFICIAL GOING: Good to firm (firm in places in back straight)
Wind: Fresh, behind Weather: Sunny

2586 EBF NOVICE MEDIAN AUCTION STKS 6f 3y
2:20 (2:21) (Class 6) 2-Y-O £2,590 (£770; £385; £192) Stalls High

Form RPR
1 **1** **Vital Equine (IRE)**[36] [1588] 2-9-2 .... RichardMullen 6 85
(E J O'Neill) *led: hdd over 4f out: sn pushed along: rdn to ld and hung lft over 1f out: r.o* **4/9**[1]
01 **2** *3* **Blue Madeira**[21] [1945] 2-9-6 .... TomEaves 2 80
(Mrs L Stubbs) *s.i.s: hdwy 1/2-way: rdn and hung rt over 1f out: styd on: no ch w wnr* **16/1**
514 **3** *3 1/2* **Yerevan**[8] [2342] 2-9-1 .... SamHitchcott 5 65
(M R Channon) *chsd ldr: led over 4f out: rdn and hdd over 1f out: wknd ins fnl f* **9/2**[2]
01 **4** *1 3/4* **Cheshire Prince**[15] [2145] 2-9-2 .... ShaneKelly 1 60
(W M Brisbourne) *chsd ldrs over 4f* **16/1**
5 *6* **Mastership (IRE)** 2-8-12 .... KerrinMcEvoy 4 38
(C E Brittain) *dwlt: outpcd* **14/1**[3]
4 **6** *22* **Breckland Boy**[18] [2045] 2-8-12 .... AdrianTNicholls 3 —
(Mrs C A Dunnett) *in rr: hung lft and wknd over 2f out* **33/1**

1m 12.68s (-1.02) **Going Correction** -0.20s/f (Firm) **6** Ran SP% **108.8**
Speed ratings (Par 91):98,94,89,87,79 49
CSF £8.55 TOTE £1.40: £1.20, £3.70; EX 7.00.
Owner Fasthandle Ltd **Bred** John Costello **Trained** Averham Park, Notts

FOCUS
A decent winning time for a race like this and the field finished strung out.

The Form Book, Raceform Ltd, Compton, RG20 6NL

NOTEBOOK
Vital Equine(IRE) followed up his win in a Newcastle race that has been working out well. He briefly looked in trouble when coming under pressure before halfway, but won well enough in the end despite appearing unsuited by this faster ground. Well regarded, he may go for the Richmond Stakes at Goodwood, a race his stable won last year with Always Hopeful. (op 1-2 tchd 8-15 in a place)
Blue Madeira, conceding weight all round, came through to take second inside the last but the winner was clear by that stage. He handled this faster ground and might be ready for a step up to seven furlongs.
Yerevan, a disappointment on sand last time, probably paid for going off too fast and setting it up for the favourite. Fading inside the last, she was run out of second spot.
Cheshire Prince, successful in a seller over course and distance, was not disgraced and looks a nursery type.
Mastership(IRE), whose dam was a winning daughter of high-class filly Warning Shadows, could never get involved after missing the break. (op 12-1)
Breckland Boy Official explanation: jockey said gelding hung both ways on the good to firm ground

2587 ULR NORWICH MAIDEN STKS 7f 3y
2:55 (2:56) (Class 5) 3-Y-O+ **£3,238** (£963; £481; £240) **Stalls** High

Form RPR
33 **1** **Stepping Stones**[34] 1650 3-8-9 .... EddieAhern 1 81
(H R A Cecil) *mde all: rdn clr fnl f* **11/1**
-602 **2** *3* **Madame Medusa (IRE)**[15] 2146 3-8-9 72........ AlanMunro 12 73
(J A R Toller) *chsd wnr: rdn over 1f out: styd on same pce* **8/1**
00 **3** *nk* **Boreana**[8] 2350 3-8-2 .... MCGeran(7) 13 72
(P W Chapple-Hyam) *chsd ldrs: rdn over 1f out: styd on same pce* **100/1**
04- **4** *1 ½* **Quantum (IRE)**[239] 5968 3-8-9 .... RobertHavlin 14 68
(J H M Gosden) *hld up in tch: rdn over 1f out: no ex fnl f* **50/1**
2-40 **5** *1 ¾* **Dama'A (IRE)**[32] 1719 3-8-9 82........ JimmyFortune 8 63
(J H M Gosden) *hld up: hdwy over 1f out: sn rdn: wknd ins fnl f* **7/2**[2]
60 **6** *nk* **Jabbara (IRE)**[6] 2406 3-8-9 .... KerrinMcEvoy 4 63
(C E Brittain) *chsd ldrs: rdn over 1f out: wknd fnl f* **33/1**
00 **7** *shd* **Esteem**[19] 2034 3-9-0 .... DarryllHolland 3 67+
(W Jarvis) *mid-div: hdwy and nt clr run over 1f out: nvr nr to chal* **66/1**
42-2 **8** *1* **Always Emirates (USA)**[39] 1513 3-9-0 82........(t) LDettori 16 65
(Saeed Bin Suroor) *trckd ldrs: rdn and nt clr run over 2f out: wknd fnl f* **7/4**[1]
06 **9** *1* **Nassar (IRE)**[33] 1674 3-8-7 .... LiamJones(7) 5 62
(G Prodromou) *sn outpcd: nvr nrr* **100/1**
10 *5* **Josie Marcus (USA)** 3-8-9 .... ShaneKelly 10 43
(J Noseda) *chsd ldrs over 5f* **9/2**[3]
3 **11** *nk* **Wild Academy (IRE)**[15] 2146 3-8-9 .... RichardMullen 9 43
(G C Bravery) *mid-div: rdn 1/2-way: wknd wl over 1f out* **9/1**
5 **12** *1* **Divo Nero (IRE)**[21] 1960 3-8-7 .... HeatherMcGee(7) 15 45
(L M Cumani) *hld up: a in rr* **100/1**
0 **13** *nk* **Miss Ruby**[14] 2167 4-9-5 .... JimmyQuinn 7 39
(Rae Guest) *sn outpcd* **125/1**
00 **14** *nk* **Maylea Gold (IRE)**[12] 2235 3-8-9 .... JerryO'Dwyer(5) 2 43
(Miss J Feilden) *s.i.s: plld hrd and sn prom: wknd 1/2-way* **200/1**
15 *3* **Fentastic** 3-8-2 .... RobbieMills(7) 6 30
(Rae Guest) *s.i.s: outpcd* **100/1**
0 **16** *15* **Genevieve**[33] 1684 4-9-5 .... TomEaves 11 —
(Mrs C A Dunnett) *sn outpcd* **200/1**

1m 24.85s (-1.75) **Going Correction** -0.20s/f (Firm)
WFA 3 from 4yo 10lb **16** Ran SP% **118.4**
Speed ratings (Par 103):102,98,98,96,94 94,94,92,91,86 85,84,84,83,80 63
CSF £93.07 TOTE £9.50: £2.30, £2.80, £51.00; EX 61.10 TRIFECTA Not won..
Owner K Abdulla **Bred** Juddmonte Farms Ltd **Trained** Newmarket, Suffolk

FOCUS
An ordinary maiden, not that strongly-run, with the first three prominent throughout. It is unlikely to prove solid form.
Esteem Official explanation: jockey said gelding was unsuited by good to firm ground
Always Emirates(USA) Official explanation: jockey said colt had a breathing problem
Wild Academy(IRE) Official explanation: trainer said filly finished lame

2588 NELSONS COUNTY (S) STKS 7f 3y
3:30 (3:31) (Class 6) 2-Y-O **£2,266** (£674; £337; £168) **Stalls** High

Form RPR
2405 **1** **Sad Times (IRE)**[25] 1862 2-7-13 ....(p) LiamJones(7) 2 58+
(W G M Turner) *chsd ldrs: rdn over 2f out: led 1f out: edgd rt: r.o* **7/1**
0 **2** *1 ¼* **Tumble Jill (IRE)**[5] 2432 2-8-6 .... SamHitchcott 6 55
(J S Moore) *chsd ldrs: rdn and ev ch over 1f out: styd on same pce ins fnl f* **8/1**
560 **3** *1* **Flying Lion**[65] 962 2-8-3 .... EdwardCreighton(3) 11 52
(M R Channon) *dwlt: hld up: hdwy over 2f out: rdn over 1f out: styd on* **10/1**
66 **4** *hd* **Generist**[6] 2416 2-7-13 .... StacyRenwick(7) 4 52
(M J Attwater) *led: plld hrd: hdd over 4f out: rdn to ld over 1f out: sn hdd: no ex ins fnl f* **20/1**
5 *1* **Three No Trumps** 2-8-6 .... RichardMullen 9 49
(D Morris) *s.i.s and hmpd s: sn prom: rdn over 1f out: styd on* **14/1**
00 **6** *1* **Moist**[6] 2388 2-8-6 .... KerrinMcEvoy 13 47
(N A Callaghan) *chsd ldrs: led over 2f out: rdn and hdd over 1f out: wknd ins fnl f* **7/2**[1]
06 **7** *11* **Champagne Perry**[15] 2145 2-8-9 ow1........ RossStudholme(3) 8 25
(V Smith) *wnt rt s: sn prom: wknd over 2f out* **50/1**
54 **8** *hd* **Little Hotpotch**[17] 2083 2-8-6 .... EddieAhern 7 19
(J R Jenkins) *chsd ldrs: led over 4f out: hdd over 2f out: wknd over 1f out* **8/1**
05 **9** *nk* **Heart And Hand (IRE)**[10] 2294 2-8-6 .... DarryllHolland 1 18
(B J Meehan) *chsd ldrs: rdn 1/2-way: wknd over 1f out* **13/2**[3]
0 **10** *8* **Fade To Grey (IRE)**[2] 2530 2-8-11 .... RobertMiles 10 3
(W G M Turner) *hld up: rdn over 2f out: a in rr* **66/1**
0 **11** *5* **Charlies Girl (IRE)**[72] 878 2-8-6 .... FrancisFerris 3 —
(M J Attwater) *chsd ldrs: rdn 1/2-way: wknd over 2f out* **25/1**
3 **12** *3 ½* **Feisty**[16] 2100 2-8-6 .... AlanMunro 12 —
(Rae Guest) *bhd fr 1/2-way* **11/2**[2]
0 **13** *3* **Hurricane Dennis**[14] 2178 2-8-11 .... JimmyFortune 5 —
(D K Ivory) *chsd ldrs: rdn over 4f out: wknd 1/2-way* **33/1**

1m 27.71s (1.11) **Going Correction** -0.20s/f (Firm) **13** Ran SP% **116.4**
Speed ratings (Par 91):85,83,82,82,81 79,67,67,66,57 51,47,44
CSF £57.07 TOTE £9.20: £2.80, £2.90, £2.40; EX 59.00 TRIFECTA Not won..There was no bid for the winner. Tumble Jill (IRE) was the subject of a friendly claim.
Owner Nutty Partners **Bred** John J Cosgrave **Trained** Sigwells, Somerset

FOCUS
A modest winning time, even for a race like this, and won by the most experienced runner in the line-up.

NOTEBOOK
Sad Times(IRE), the most experienced of these platers, got off the mark at the seventh attempt. The step up to seven furlongs and fitting of cheekpieces combined to good effect. (op 6-1)
Tumble Jill(IRE), down in grade and upped in trip for this second start, got away on terms this time and kept on for second. (op 9-1)
Flying Lion, whose first three runs were all over five furlongs on easy ground, the last twice finishing behind today's winner, was doing her best work at the end. (tchd 12-1)
Generist, making her debut on turf, had every chance but could not hold on to her narrow lead. She will stay this trip but needs to settle better.
Three No Trumps, a cheap yearling, is out of a mutiple middle-distance winner and will get further in time. (op 12-1)
Moist knew more this time on this drop in grade but did not quite see out the longer trip. (op 9-2 tchd 10-3)
Fade To Grey(IRE) Official explanation: jockey said colt was struck into
Feisty Official explanation: jockey said filly lost its action

2589 HKB WILTSHIRES FILLIES' H'CAP 1m 3y
4:05 (4:07) (Class 6) (0-65,64) 3-Y-O **£2,590** (£770; £385; £192) **Stalls** High

Form RPR
0042 **1** **Whistleupthewind**[4] 2479 3-8-6 49........(b) ShaneKelly 11 55
(J M P Eustace) *chsd ldrs: led over 3f out: r.o* **15/2**
5554 **2** *¾* **Al Rayanah**[25] 1867 3-8-12 62........ LiamJones(7) 1 66
(G Prodromou) *chsd wnr: rdn over 1f out: edgd rt ins fnl f: styd on* **15/2**
4000 **3** *¾* **Possessed**[33] 1681 3-9-6 63........ RobertHavlin 10 65
(T D McCarthy) *s.i.s: hdwy over 5f out: rdn over 1f out: styd on* **25/1**
1-20 **4** *½* **Imperial Lucky (IRE)**[6] 2400 3-9-4 61........ KerrinMcEvoy 12 62
(M J Wallace) *chsd ldrs: rdn over 1f out: kpt on* **9/2**[1]
4000 **5** *1 ¾* **Simplified**[27] 1829 3-8-7 50........ JimmyQuinn 6 47
(J Pearce) *s.i.s: hld up: hdwy u.p 2f out: sn edgd lft: no imp fnl f* **33/1**
5-02 **6** *2 ½* **Tender The Great (IRE)**[15] 2128 3-9-4 61........ DarryllHolland 4 52
(V Smith) *hld up: hmpd over 5f out: hdwy u.p and hung lft over 1f out: n.d* **6/1**[2]
-002 **7** *1* **October Ben**[14] 2171 3-9-5 62........ JimmyFortune 9 51
(M D I Usher) *s.i.s: hld up: hdwy uner press over 1f out: no imp fnl f* **13/2**[3]
0-00 **8** *1 ½* **Lambency (IRE)**[24] 1888 3-8-7 50........ EddieAhern 2 36
(J G Given) *hld up: n.d* **33/1**
5-00 **9** *hd* **Wendals**[14] 2167 3-9-7 64........ AlanMunro 8 49
(Rae Guest) *led over 4f: rdn and wknd over 1f out* **16/1**
4046 **10** *5* **Goodbye Girl (IRE)**[9] 2318 3-8-3 46 ow1........(p) AdrianTNicholls 13 20
(Mrs C A Dunnett) *prom over 4f* **16/1**
10- **11** *2* **Fun Time**[180] 6599 3-9-4 64........ EdwardCreighton(3) 7 33
(M R Channon) *hld up: rdn over 2f out: n.d* **14/1**
40-3 **12** *8* **Ravish**[17] 2069 3-9-2 59........(t) LDettori 3 10
(W J Haggas) *hld up in tch: plld hrd: rdn and wknd over 2f out* **13/2**[3]
0040 **13** *24* **Tilsworth Charlie**[45] 1352 3-8-7 50........ RichardMullen 5 —
(J R Jenkins) *chsd ldrs over 5f* **33/1**

1m 38.75s (-1.15) **Going Correction** -0.20s/f (Firm) **13** Ran SP% **113.8**
Speed ratings (Par 94):97,96,95,95,93 90,89,88,88,83 81,73,49
CSF £57.27 CT £1360.05 TOTE £6.70: £1.30, £3.60, £8.40; EX 84.10 Trifecta £526.70 Part won. Pool: £741.94 - 0.30 winning units..
Owner Blue Peter Racing 6 **Bred** Baydon House Stud **Trained** Newmarket, Suffolk

FOCUS
The field raced down the centre of the track in this low-grade handicap. The form looks sound enough with the fifth the best guide.
Tender The Great(IRE) Official explanation: trainer said filly ran too free in early stages
Ravish Official explanation: trainer's rep said filly was unsuited by good to firm ground

2590 BETFRED SPRINT SERIES QUALIFIER (H'CAP) 6f 3y
4:40 (4:40) (Class 5) (0-75,74) 3-Y-O+ **£3,562** (£1,059; £529; £264) **Stalls** High

Form RPR
6-63 **1** **Rosapenna (IRE)**[12] 2233 4-9-11 71........ EddieAhern 2 80
(C F Wall) *trckd ldrs: led over 1f out: hdd ins fnl f: edgd rt and r.o to ld nr fin* **3/1**[1]
3000 **2** *hd* **Blue Tomato**[5] 2449 5-9-7 72........ GregFairley(5) 5 80
(J M Bradley) *hld up: hdwy and nt clr run over 2f out: rdn to ld ins fnl f: hdd nr fin* **9/1**
0060 **3** *1 ¼* **Gone'N'Dunnett (IRE)**[6] 2417 7-8-10 63........(v) KirstyMilczarek(7) 11 67
(Mrs C A Dunnett) *led over 4f: styd on same pce ins fnl f* **11/1**
-446 **4** *nk* **Vindication**[5] 2443 6-9-6 66........(tp) RichardMullen 9 69
(R M H Cowell) *dwlt: hld up: hdwy 1/2-way: styd on same pce ins fnl f* **8/1**
0-06 **5** *¾* **Highland Cascade**[12] 2233 4-10-0 74........ ShaneKelly 7 75
(J M P Eustace) *chsd ldrs: rdn and ev ch over 1f out: styng on same pce whn n.m.r wl ins fnl f* **22/1**
0303 **6** *1* **Cherokee Nation**[8] 2347 5-9-0 60........ DarryllHolland 3 58
(P W D'Arcy) *hld up: hdwy over 1f out: rdn ins fnl f: nt run on* **12/1**
-023 **7** *shd* **Summer Recluse (USA)**[2] 2536 7-9-7 67........(t) KerrinMcEvoy 10 65
(J M Bradley) *chsd ldrs: rdn over 1f out: no ex ins fnl f* **11/2**[3]
0000 **8** *shd* **Bold Cheverak**[35] 1618 4-8-9 55 oh3........ SamHitchcott 6 53
(Mrs C A Dunnett) *chsd ldr: rdn and ev ch over 1f out: no ex* **22/1**
210/ **9** *4* **Kool Acclaim**[638] 5563 5-9-9 69........ AlanMunro 1 55
(S C Williams) *chsd ldrs over 4f* **22/1**
1-60 **10** *4* **Mugeba**[12] 2233 5-8-11 57........(t) LDettori 8 31
(Miss Gay Kelleway) *prom: nt clr run over 2f out: wknd over 1f out* **5/1**[2]
3100 **11** *18* **Norcroft**[33] 1686 4-9-10 70........(p) AdrianTNicholls 4 —
(Mrs C A Dunnett) *sn outpcd* **14/1**

1m 12.3s (-1.40) **Going Correction** -0.20s/f (Firm) **11** Ran SP% **113.9**
Speed ratings (Par 103):101,100,99,98,97 96,96,96,90,85 61
CSF £28.40 CT £259.96 TOTE £3.70: £1.50, £3.50, £2.90; EX 32.80 Trifecta £264.60 Part won. Pool: £372.71 - 0.50 winning units..
Owner Thoroughbred Farms Ltd **Bred** Epona Bloodstock Ltd **Trained** Newmarket, Suffolk

FOCUS
An ordinary handicap, and sound enough form ratd around the first two.
Kool Acclaim Official explanation: jockey said mare lost its action
Mugeba Official explanation: jockey said mare was unsuited by the good to firm ground
Norcroft Official explanation: jockey said gelding lost its action

2591 HALL FARM EQUINE CENTRE H'CAP 1m 3f 101y
5:15 (5:15) (Class 6) (0-60,59) 3-Y-O **£2,428** (£722; £361; £180) **Stalls** Low

Form RPR
000- **1** **El Alamein (IRE)**[212] 6360 3-9-4 56........ JamieMackay 4 65+
(Sir Mark Prescott) *led 1f: chsd ldrs: led over 2f out: rdn and hung rt over 1f out: styd on* **2/1**[1]

0032 **2** *1 ¼* **Coffin Dodger**[5] 2463 3-7-11 **42**................................ KirstyMilczarek(7) 5 49
(C N Allen) *s.i.s: hld up: hdwy and hung lft over 1f out: r.o ins fnl f: nt rch wnr* **9/1**[3]

60-0 **3** *1 ½* **Peas 'n Beans (IRE)**[17] 2082 3-9-0 **59**.......................... LukeMorris(7) 6 64
(M L W Bell) *hld up in tch: rdn and ev ch over 1f out: styd on same pce ins fnl f* **16/1**

0-00 **4** *3* **Delorain (IRE)**[31] 1741 3-9-3 **55**....................................(v¹) AlanMunro 12 55
(J A R Toller) *sn prom: outpcd 3f out: styd on u.p fr over 1f out* **40/1**

00-6 **5** *3 ½* **Mighty Observer (IRE)**[12] 2244 3-8-11 **49**.......................... LDettori 11 43
(M H Tompkins) *chsd ldrs: led 9f out: rdn and hdd over 2f out: wknd over 1f out* **12/1**

0-00 **6** *nk* **Dance A Daydream**[34] 1649 3-9-2 **54**......................... AdrianTNicholls 1 48
(J R Fanshawe) *hld up: rdn over 3f out: n.d* **14/1**

0-05 **7** *½* **Loch Awe**[20] 1997 3-9-3 **55**.. EddieAhern 2 48
(J G Given) *chsd ldrs 9f* **25/1**

06-0 **8** *nk* **That Look**[49] 1263 3-9-1 **53**.. ShaneKelly 8 45
(D E Cantillon) *hld up: nt clr run over 2f out: n.d* **20/1**

6010 **9** *½* **Shaika**[5] 2463 3-8-5 **50**.. LiamJones(7) 15 42
(G Prodromou) *dwlt: bhd: nrst fin* **18/1**

4532 **10** *nk* **Wise Choice**[17] 2082 3-9-4 **56**.. DarryllHolland 9 47
(N P Littmoden) *led after 1f: hdd 9f out: rdn over 2f out: wknd over 1f out* **4/1**[2]

-000 **11** *¾* **Boss Mak (IRE)**[36] 1599 3-8-12 **53**.......................... RossStudholme(3) 3 43
(V Smith) *hld up: hdwy over 3f out: wknd over 2f out* **40/1**

-000 **12** *7* **Go Amwell**[78] 797 3-8-10 **48**... RobertHavlin 7 27
(J R Jenkins) *hld up: a in rr* **40/1**

0-05 **13** *1 ¼* **Muckle**[23] 1925 3-9-6 **58**.. KerrinMcEvoy 14 35
(S C Williams) *chsd ldrs: rdn over 3f out: sn wknd* **12/1**

0-00 **14** *nk* **Woolfall King (IRE)**[49] 1263 2-8-7 **45**................................ JimmyQuinn 10 21
(G G Margarson) *plld hrd and prom: rdn and wknd 3f out* **66/1**

000 **15** *nk* **Rada (IRE)**[14] 2175 3-9-7 **59**.. JimmyFortune 13 35
(R Hannon) *hld up in tch: hmpd 6f out: rdn and wknd 3f out* **33/1**

0006 **16** *5* **Cragganmore Creek**[12] 2246 3-8-12 **50**.......................... RichardMullen 16 18
(D Morris) *hld up: a in rr* **33/1**

2m 27.51s (0.01) **Going Correction** -0.075s/f (Good) **16** Ran SP% **119.8**
Speed ratings (Par 97):96,95,94,91,89 89,88,88,88,87 87,82,81,81,80 77
CSF £17.74 CT £234.81 TOTE £2.90: £1.30, £2.20, £6.90, £6.00; EX 29.20 Trifecta £128.30 Pool: £321.75 - 1.18 winning units.
Owner Charles C Walker - Osborne House II **Bred** D Cantillon P Devlin And Forenaghts Stud Farm Lt **Trained** Newmarket, Suffolk

FOCUS
A modest handicap, but the form looks solid rated around the second and fifth, and the winner looks a typical Sir Mark Prescott improver.
El Alamein(IRE) ◆ Official explanation: trainer's rep said, regarding the improved form shown, the horse had been gelded over the winter and had also had a breathing operation since its last run
Coffin Dodger Official explanation: jockey said filly hung left in latter stages
That Look Official explanation: jockey said gelding was denied a clear run

2592 ORBIT TRAVEL SERVICES H'CAP — 1m 6f 17y
5:50 (5:51) (Class 5) (0-70,67) 3-Y-O — £3,400 (£1,011; £505; £252) Stalls High

Form RPR

0-60 **1** **Shore Thing (IRE)**[45] 1345 3-9-2 **62**.. LDettori 1 69
(M H Tompkins) *hld up: hdwy over 3f out: led over 2f out: rdn and hung lft fnl f: styd on* **7/1**

-061 **2** *shd* **Call Me George**[17] 2082 3-9-0 **65**.................................. GregFairley(5) 7 72
(M Johnston) *chsd ldrs: rdn 5f out: styd on u.p fnl f* **9/4**[1]

0-56 **3** *3* **Rivetting**[17] 2082 3-8-2 **48** oh2... JamieMackay 3 51
(Sir Mark Prescott) *chsd ldr tl led over 3f out: rdn and hdd over 2f out: no ex fnl f* **10/3**[2]

-416 **4** *5* **Rahy's Crown (USA)**[9] 2332 3-9-3 **63**.............................. JimmyFortune 6 59
(R Hannon) *chsd ldrs: rdn over 2f out: hung lft and wknd fnl f* **4/1**[3]

0-05 **5** *10* **Valerie**[13] 2209 3-9-2 **62**.. AlanMunro 4 44
(L M Cumani) *hld up: hdwy over 9f out: rdn and wknd 2f out* **9/1**

0-50 **6** *3* **Patavium (IRE)**[34] 1648 3-9-7 **67**.................................... RichardMullen 8 44
(E J O'Neill) *sn led: rdn and hdd over 3f out: wknd 2f out* **28/1**

-001 **7** *hd* **Arsad (IRE)**[12] 2246 3-9-2 **62**.. KerrinMcEvoy 2 39
(C E Brittain) *hld up: rdn 5f out: wknd over 3f out* **9/1**

000 **8** *34* **Vettori Dancer**[22] 1940 3-8-4 **50**... JimmyQuinn 5 —
(G G Margarson) *hld up: bhd fnl 5f* **28/1**

3m 4.00s (-1.30) **Going Correction** -0.075s/f (Good) **8** Ran SP% **113.2**
Speed ratings (Par 99):100,99,98,95,89 87,87,68
CSF £22.70 CT £61.41 TOTE £7.20: £1.60, £1.50, £1.70; EX 25.00 Trifecta £193.50 Place 6 £770.65, Place 5 £ 578.43.
Owner Roalco Limited **Bred** Airlie Stud And Sir Thomas Pilkington **Trained** Newmarket, Suffolk

FOCUS
This was run at a decent pace and the form, although not too solid, should work out. The winner improved around 10lb for this longer trip.
Shore Thing(IRE) Official explanation: trainer said, regarding the improved form shown, the colt may have benefited from ther step up in trip from 1m to today's 1m 6f
Vettori Dancer Official explanation: jockey said filly had no more to give
T/Jkpt: Not won. T/Plt: £1,400.10 to a £1 stake. Pool: £44,690.55. 23.30 winning tickets. T/Qpdt: £39.00 to a £1 stake. Pool: £3,163.40. 60.00 winning tickets. CR

2593 - 2596a (Foreign Racing) - See Raceform Interactive

2313 LONGCHAMP (R-H)
Thursday, June 15

OFFICIAL GOING: Good to soft

2597a LA COUPE (GROUP 3) — 1m 2f
2:20 (2:21) 4-Y-O+ — £27,586 (£11,034; £8,276; £5,517; £2,759)

RPR

1 **Blue Monday**[20] 1976 5-8-11 .... SteveDrowne 1 108
(R Charlton) *niggled early to track leader, 3rd straight, edged off rail and ridden 1½f out, stayed on under strong pressure to lead pos* **24/10**[2]

2 *hd* **Annenkov (IRE)**[22] 4-8-11 .... SPasquier 4 108
(E Lellouche, France) *set steady pace, ridden 1f out, headed post* **62/10**[3]

3 *nk* **Archange D'Or (IRE)**[25] 1873 4-8-11 .... TGillet 6 107
(A Fabre, France) *raced in 2nd, ridden over 1f out, stayed on at one pace, fin 4th, hd, 1l and nk; placed 3rd* **9/10**[1]

4 *¾* **Weightless**[12] 2236 6-8-11 .... JimCrowley 3 106
(Mrs A J Perrett) *raced in 5th on inside, kept to inside, stayed on at same pace final 2f, fin 5th, placed 4th* **16/1**

5 *1* **Mohandas (FR)**[83] 5-8-11 .... JVictoire 7 104
(W Hefter, Germany) *held up in last, switched outside and headway ½f out, staying on when squeezed up 100 yards out, fin 6th, placed 5th* **35/1**

6 *1* **Vatori (FR)**[6] 4-8-11 .... TThulliez 5 103
(P Demercastel, France) *held up in 6th, headway 1½f out, staying on when edged right inside final furlong, fin 3rd, hd and 1l; placed 6th* **84/10**

7 *1* **Gold Sound (FR)**[67] 934 4-8-11 .... OPeslier 2 101
(C Laffon-Parias, France) *raced in 4th, brief effort when not clear run 1 1/2f out* **11/1**

2m 10.5s **7** Ran SP% **123.6**
PARI-MUTUEL: WIN 3.40; PL 2.10, 3.00; SF 16.60.
Owner Mountgrange Stud **Bred** Darley **Trained** Beckhampton, Wilts

NOTEBOOK
Blue Monday gained his first success at Group level with a battling victory. Smartly out of the stalls, he was settled in second place on the rail behind the leader in a race run at a slow pace that developed into a sprint, and he gradually wore down the eventual second to get up on the line. He could make a quick reappearance at Royal Ascot next Friday in a Listed Handicap.
Annenkov(IRE) led the field at a slow pace until turning into the straight where he was asked to quicken, and halfway up the straight he looked like he was going to hold on but was eventually caught on the line.
Archange D'Or(IRE) was unsuited by the slow pace of the race. Positioned in mid-division throughout, he could not go with the first two when they accelerated after the last bend. He stayed on one paced to take fourth place but following a Stewards enquiry, he was moved up to third place.
Weightless, slowly out of the stalls, he was unable to take his normal front-running role. Positioned on the inside rail in mid-division, he made his move halfway up the straight but was a little short of room. He continued his run up the rail to eventually finish fifth but after the Stewards' enquiry he was placed fourth.

2218 CHEPSTOW (L-H)
Friday, June 16

OFFICIAL GOING: Good to firm
Wind: Almost nil Weather: Sunny

2598 TOTEPLACEPOT/E.B.F. NOVICE STKS — 6f 16y
6:30 (6:37) (Class 4) 2-Y-O — £4,533 (£1,348; £674; £336) Stalls High

Form RPR

321 **1** **Grand Prix**[15] 2172 2-9-2 .... PatDobbs 3 83+
(R Hannon) *w ldr: led 2f out: rdn out* **8/11**[1]

1 **2** *¾* **Marmaida (IRE)**[15] 2178 2-8-9 .... PaulDoe 2 74
(W J Knight) *a.p: rdn over 1f out: ev ch fnl f: nt qckn* **2/1**[2]

051 **3** *4* **Tom Tower (IRE)**[17] 2094 2-9-5 .... ChrisCatlin 1 72
(M R Channon) *led: rdn and hdd 2f out: wknd ins fnl f* **8/1**[3]

001 **4** *2* **Just Dust**[51] 1229 2-8-7 .... (p) LiamJones(7) 4 61
(W G M Turner) *hld up: hung lft after 1f: sn pushed along: rdn 3f out: wknd 2f out* **22/1**

5 *1 ¼* **Dansilver** 2-8-12 .... VinceSlattery 5 55
(D J Wintle) *outpcd* **100/1**

1m 11.85s (-0.55) **Going Correction** -0.025s/f (Good) **5** Ran SP% **107.7**
Speed ratings (Par 95):102,101,95,93,91
CSF £2.25 TOTE £1.90: £1.10, £1.30; EX 2.50.
Owner Mrs J K Powell **Bred** Plantation Stud **Trained** East Everleigh, Wilts

FOCUS
Not a great novice event with the first two having only won maiden auctions on their previous outings, but the winning time was good.
NOTEBOOK
Grand Prix did not mind the extra furlong on this faster ground and ran out a decisive winner with the help of the stands' rail. (tchd 4-6, 4-5 and 5-6 in places)
Marmaida(IRE) ran a sound race in defeat and it seems as if her shock debut win at Yarmouth was certainly no fluke. (tchd 9-4)
Tom Tower(IRE) did not appear to be suited by the step up to six back on a sounder surface. (tchd 7-1)
Just Dust, trying a longer trip, got found out on this step up in class. (op 33-1 tchd 18-1)
Dansilver, out of a 17-furlong winner at three, was always finding things happening too fast. (op 66-1 tchd 50-1)

2599 TOTESPORT 0800 221 221 CLAIMING STKS — 7f 16y
7:00 (7:06) (Class 6) 3-Y-O+ — £2,266 (£674; £337; £168) Stalls High

Form RPR

-040 **1** **Full Spate**[4] 2504 11-9-13 62... KFallon 7 68
(J M Bradley) *hld up and bhd: rdn and hdwy over 2f out: led jst ins fnl f: r.o wl* **7/1**

0003 **2** *1 ¼* **Danielle's Lad**[13] 2223 10-9-9 62.................................... FrancisFerris 11 63+
(B Palling) *w ldr: led over 3f out: rdn over 2f out: hdd jst ins fnl f: nt qckn* **7/2**[1]

0050 **3** *½* **Postmaster**[16] 2135 4-9-5 45... ChrisCatlin 10 56
(R Ingram) *bhd tl gd hdwy fnl f: fin wl* **14/1**

0400 **4** *¾* **Peruvian Style (IRE)**[34] 1683 5-8-12 50...................... JosephWalsh(7) 4 54
(J M Bradley) *hld up in tch: chal on bit 2f out: sn rdn: one pce fnl f* **16/1**

0002 **5** *nk* **My Girl Pearl (IRE)**[3] 2531 6-8-12 49...................... RobbieFitzpatrick 5 46
(M S Saunders) *hld up in mid-div: rdn and hdwy over 2f out: one pce fnl f* **11/2**[3]

-000 **6** *shd* **Dorn Hill**[11] 2288 4-8-8 45... (p) PaulDoe 9 41
(D G Bridgwater) *hld up in mid-div: hdwy over 3f out: sn rdn: hung lft over 1f out: one pce* **66/1**

240- **7** *1 ¾* **Wizard Quay**[239] 5994 3-8-3 50.................................... LiamJones(7) 14 45
(W K Goldsworthy) *sn prom: wknd 2f out* **50/1**

0030 **8** *1 ¾* **Fizzy Lizzy**[31] 1764 6-8-3 46.................................... AshleyHamblett(7) 1 34
(H E Haynes) *prom: rdn over 3f out: wknd over 2f out* **25/1**

4050 **9** *shd* **El Palmar**[3] 2378 5-8-8 57... KevinGhunowa(7) 3 39
(M J Attwater) *led over 3f: sn rdn: wknd 2f out* **9/2**[2]

3300 **10** *nk* **Mister Elegant**[16] 2135 4-9-5 51... VinceSlattery 8 42
(J L Spearing) *chsd ldrs: rdn over 3f out: sn wknd* **8/1**

64/0 **11** *1 ¾* **Rusky Dusky (USA)**[10] 2319 4-8-13 .... PatDobbs 12 31
(R Hannon) *prom: rdn over 2f out: sn wknd* **22/1**

-410 **12** *8* **Bellini Star**[10] 2319 3-7-13 60...................................(b) DonnaCaldwell(7) 6 9
(P D Evans) *a bhd: eased whn btn over 1f out* **16/1**

300- **13** *3 ½* **A One (IRE)**[161] 4497 7-9-0 60.................................... EmmettStack(5) 2 6
(H J Manners) *w ldr tl rdn and wknd over 3f out: eased whn no ch over 1f out* **16/1**

1m 23.38s (0.08) **Going Correction** -0.025s/f (Good)
WFA 3 from 4yo+ 9lb **13** Ran SP% **115.4**
Speed ratings (Par 101):98,96,96,95,94 94,92,90,90,90 88,79,75
CSF £29.45 TOTE £5.10: £2.50, £2.00, £6.00; EX 12.50.

Owner E A Hayward **Bred** Juddmonte Farms **Trained** Sedbury, Gloucs
■ Stewards' Enquiry : Emmett Stack one-day ban: failed to keep straight from stalls (Jun 27)
Kevin Ghunowa one-day ban: failed to keep straight from stalls (Jun 27)

FOCUS
A weakish claimer. The first two home, both veterans, were better than this last year but have not been so good this season.
My Girl Pearl(IRE) Official explanation: trainer said mare sustained a cut on its left fore

2600 TOTEQUADPOT MAIDEN FILLIES' STKS — 1m 4f 23y
7:30 (7:37) (Class 5) 3-Y-O — **£3,368** (£1,002; £500; £250) **Stalls** Low

Form				RPR
5-6	**1**		**Allegretto (IRE)**37 [1583] 3-9-0 .... KFallon 3 (Sir Michael Stoute) *led early: hld up in tch: rdn 3f out: led 1f out: styd on* **30/100**[1]	84+
26	**2**	1 1/2	**Nimra (USA)**34 [1669] 3-9-0 .... ChrisCatlin 6 (G A Butler) *a.p: rdn to ld 2f out: hdd 1f out: nt qckn* **7/1**[2]	82
6	**3**	7	**Miss Trinidad (USA)**21 [1994] 3-9-0 .... PatDobbs 5 (B J Meehan) *sn led: hdd over 5f out: rdn to ld briefly over 2f out: wknd 1f out* **12/1**	71
4	**4**	5	**Kentucky Warbler (IRE)**22 [1955] 3-9-0 .... JimCrowley 2 (H Morrison) *w ldrs: led over 5f out: rdn over 3f out: hdd over 2f out: wknd wl over 1f out* **10/1**[3]	63
00	**5**	12	**Virginia Plain**22 [1955] 3-9-0 .... FrancisFerris 1 (Miss Diana Weeden) *hld up and bhd: hdwy 4f out: sn rdn: wknd 2f out* **100/1**	44
	6	39	**Zah Reef** 3-8-7 .... KevinGhunowa(7) 4 (P A Blockley) *hld up in rr: pushed along over 5f out: struggling 4f out: t.o* **66/1**	—

2m 38.02s (-0.70) **Going Correction** +0.05s/f (Good) **6** Ran SP% **108.7**
Speed ratings (Par 96):104,103,98,95,87 61
CSF £2.69 TOTE £1.20: £1.10, £2.70; EX 2.10.
Owner Cheveley Park Stud **Bred** Miss K Rausing And Airlie Stud **Trained** Newmarket, Suffolk

FOCUS
An uncompetitive event, run at no great pace. The winner is likely to prove much the best of these.

2601 TOTESPORT.COM H'CAP — 1m 2f 36y
8:05 (8:11) (Class 5) (0-70,68) 4-Y-O+ — **£3,886** (£1,156; £577; £288) **Stalls** Low

Form				RPR
-241	**1**		**Dove Cottage (IRE)**13 [2221] 4-9-4 **65** .... ChrisCatlin 8 (W S Kittow) *led: hdd 5f out: w ldr: led over 3f out: clr 2f out: sn rdn: drvn out* **6/5**[1]	73+
005/	**2**	1 1/2	**Dareneur (IRE)**759 [2198] 6-8-3 **50** .... DavidKinsella 10 (J G M O'Shea) *hld up and bhd: hdwy on ins over 1f out: r.o to take 2nd nr fin: nt rch wnr* **50/1**	55
0200	**3**	nk	**Jackie Kiely**16 [2150] 5-8-13 **60** .... (t) RobbieFitzpatrick 2 (Stef Liddiard) *hld up towards rr: rdn and hdwy over 2f out: r.o one pce fnl f* **12/1**	64
4000	**4**	hd	**Summer Bounty**13 [2221] 10-8-13 **60** .... PaulFitzsimons 5 (F Jordan) *hld up: stdy hdwy over 3f out: chsd wnr and edgd lft over 1f out: nt qckn ins fnl f* **16/1**	64
2-00	**5**	1 1/2	**Montjeu Baby (IRE)**14 [2186] 4-8-13 **60** .... PatDobbs 1 (S Kirk) *hld up: hdwy on ins over 3f out: rdn 2f out: one pce fnl f* **11/1**	61
3000	**6**	3/4	**Yenaled**60 [1058] 9-8-3 **57** .... DonnaCaldwell(7) 3 (J M Bradley) *stdd s: hld up in rr: rdn and hdwy on outside over 2f out: no imp fnl f* **9/1**[3]	57
	7	2 1/2	**Wilderness Bay (IRE)**313 [4202] 4-9-7 **68** .... GeorgeBaker 7 (M R Bosley) *hld up in tch: rdn over 3f out: wknd 2f out* **12/1**	63
000/	**8**	3 1/2	**Heriot**30 [4144] 5-9-1 **62** .... VinceSlattery 6 (S C Burrough) *prom: rdn over 3f out: wknd over 2f out* **80/1**	50
0200	**9**	7	**Silver Court**16 [2149] 4-8-2 **49** oh3 .... FrancisFerris 9 (A W Carroll) *plld hrd: chsd ldr: led 5f out tl over 3f out: sn rdn: wknd over 1f out* **20/1**	24
0300	**10**	9	**Will The Till**13 [2223] 4-8-9 **56** .... KFallon 4 (J M Bradley) *prom: lost pl over 6f out: rdn over 3f out: sn bhd* **10/3**[2]	14

2m 10.68s (0.78) **Going Correction** +0.05s/f (Good) **10** Ran SP% **116.1**
Speed ratings (Par 103):98,96,96,96,95 94,92,89,84,77
CSF £90.50 CT £524.16 TOTE £2.20: £1.10, £11.20, £2.50; EX 84.20.
Owner Reg Gifford **Bred** D R Tucker **Trained** Blackborough, Devon

FOCUS
The leading pair went clear on the downhill run to the end of the back straight. The bare form is not convincing, with little recent form to go on.
Silver Court Official explanation: jockey said gelding ran too free and hung right
Will The Till Official explanation: jockey said, regarding easing gelding in closing stages, he thought something was wrong

2602 TOTEEXACTA MAIDEN H'CAP — 6f 16y
8:40 (8:47) (Class 5) (0-70,69) 3-Y-O+ — **£3,886** (£1,156; £577; £288) **Stalls** High

Form				RPR
05-0	**1**		**Vibe**16 [2148] 5-8-10 **44** .... RobbieFitzpatrick 8 (A W Carroll) *hld up and bhd: rdn and hdwy over 2f out: led ins fnl f: rdn out* **20/1**	54
4406	**2**	1	**Arian's Lad**10 [2317] 5-8-10 **51** .... TolleyDean(7) 12 (B Palling) *w ldr: led over 3f out: rdn and hdd over 2f out: rallied towards fin* **4/1**[2]	58
00-0	**3**	1 1/4	**Tamino (IRE)**29 [1801] 3-9-5 **60** .... JimCrowley 3 (H Morrison) *a.p: rdn and ev ch over 1f out: nt qckn ins fnl f* **8/1**	61
0-00	**4**	3/4	**Willofcourse**13 [2223] 5-9-9 **57** .... FergusSweeney 6 (H Candy) *hld up in tch: nt clr run fr 2f out: swtchd rt 1f out: kpt on towards fin* **11/1**	58+
0-62	**5**	nk	**Mannello**18 [2068] 3-9-2 **57** .... FrancisFerris 5 (B Palling) *a.p: led over 2f out: hrd rdn over 1f out: hdd and no ex ins fnl f* **9/1**	56+
6056	**6**	1 3/4	**Nazaaha (USA)**17 [2112] 4-9-2 **50** .... ChrisCatlin 7 (A G Newcombe) *hld up and bhd: hdwy over 2f out: one pce fnl f* **10/1**	45
-400	**7**	nk	**Tadlil**25 [1878] 4-9-7 **55** .... PatDobbs 9 (J M Bradley) *hld up: rdn 3f out: no hdwy fnl 2f* **8/1**	49
40-3	**8**	2 1/2	**Bellanora**38 [1565] 3-9-12 **67** .... StephenCarson 11 (R F Johnson Houghton) *w ldrs: rdn and ev ch 2f out: wkng whn hmpd 1f out* **7/1**[3]	51
0666	**9**	3/4	**Silvanella (IRE)**13 [2235] 3-8-9 **50** .... VinceSlattery 2 (M S Saunders) *nvr bttr than mid-div* **40/1**	32
-032	**10**	3/4	**Mostanad**8 [2377] 4-9-2 **50** .... (b) KFallon 1 (J M Bradley) *outpcd* **10/3**[1]	32
300	**11**	3	**Cape Of Storms**69 [916] 3-9-11 **69** .... EdwardCreighton(3) 14 (M R Channon) *led: hdd and rdn over 3f out: wknd 2f out* **16/1**	40
000-	**12**	3/4	**Aeronaut**202 [6433] 3-8-2 **43** oh5 .... DavidKinsella 13 (J M Bradley) *a bhd* **40/1**	12

1m 11.58s (-0.82) **Going Correction** -0.025s/f (Good)
WFA 3 from 4yo+ 7lb **12** Ran SP% **120.7**
Speed ratings (Par 103):104,102,101,100,99 97,96,93,92,91 87,86
CSF £98.91 CT £723.73 TOTE £35.50: £6.40, £2.80, £5.00; EX 194.70.
Owner Derek & Cheryl Holder **Bred** Cheveley Park Stud Ltd **Trained** Cropthorne, Worcs

FOCUS
This took little winning and the form is limited, although sound.
Willofcourse ◆ Official explanation: jockey said gelding was denied a clear run
Mannello Official explanation: jockey said, regarding easing filly shortly before winning post, the weight cloth had slipped and he had to stop riding
Mostanad Official explanation: jockey said gelding never travelled

2603 TOTEPOOL "A BETTER WAY TO BET" H'CAP — 7f 16y
9:15 (9:21) (Class 5) (0-75,75) 3-Y-O+ — **£3,886** (£1,156; £577; £288) **Stalls** High

Form				RPR
3500	**1**		**Blue Trojan (IRE)**4 [2510] 6-9-13 **74** .... GeorgeBaker 5 (S Kirk) *hld up and bhd: rdn and hdwy over 1f out: r.o to ld nr fin* **6/1**	83
0421	**2**	3/4	**Dvinsky (USA)**4 [2504] 5-9-11 **72** 6ex .... RobbieFitzpatrick 4 (D Carroll) *t.k.h: chsd ldr: rdn 2f out: led ins fnl f: hdd nr fin* **10/3**[2]	79
10-3	**3**	1 3/4	**Inka Dancer (IRE)**38 [1570] 4-8-11 **58** .... AdrianMcCarthy 9 (B Palling) *led: rdn over 1f out: hdd ins fnl f: no ex* **7/1**	61
6605	**4**	nk	**Pure Imagination (IRE)**6 [2454] 5-10-0 **75** .... KFallon 2 (J M Bradley) *hld up and bhd: rdn and hdwy over 2f out: nt qckn ins fnl f* **5/2**[1]	77
00-0	**5**	1 1/2	**Curtain Bluff**163 [36] 4-9-11 **75** .... EdwardCreighton(3) 8 (M R Channon) *hld up in mid-div: swtchd lft and hdwy 2f out: sn rdn: one pce fnl f* **25/1**	73
3453	**6**	nk	**Arctic Desert**2 [2551] 6-9-12 **73** .... ChrisCatlin 3 (A M Balding) *plld hrd in mid-div: rdn whn sltly hmpd 2f out: no hdwy* **4/1**[3]	70
-000	**7**	1 1/2	**Bow Wave**21 [1993] 4-9-4 **65** .... (v1) FergusSweeney 1 (H Candy) *racd wd: w ldr: rdn over 2f out: wknd ins fnl f* **14/1**	58
00-0	**8**	1 1/4	**Big Bradford**12 [2259] 5-9-5 **66** .... (v) PatDobbs 6 (W R Muir) *hld up in tch: rdn over 2f out: wknd 2f out* **16/1**	56
00-0	**9**	10	**Elidore**17 [2097] 6-9-5 **66** .... FrancisFerris 7 (B Palling) *rrd and s.s: hld up and plld hrd: rdn over 2f out: sn struggling* **33/1**	30

1m 22.61s (-0.69) **Going Correction** -0.025s/f (Good) **9** Ran SP% **117.8**
Speed ratings (Par 103):102,101,99,98,97 96,95,93,82
CSF £26.90 CT £146.41 TOTE £7.20: £3.10, £1.10, £2.20; EX 36.50 Place 6 £32.47, Place 5 £30.15.
Owner The Ex Katy Boys **Bred** Patrick Cassidy **Trained** Upper Lambourn, Berks

FOCUS
A moderate handicap in which the time did not compare too favourably with the claimer earlier on the card. The winner ran to this year's form.
T/Plt: £75.60 to a £1 stake. Pool: £46,517.75. 449.10 winning tickets. T/Qpdt: £44.20 to a £1 stake. Pool: £2,858.00. 47.80 winning tickets. KH

2429 GOODWOOD (R-H)
Friday, June 16

OFFICIAL GOING: Straight course - good; round course - good to firm
Wind: Moderate, against

2604 SOUTHERN DAILY ECHO EBF MEDIAN AUCTION MAIDEN STKS — 6f
6:15 (6:18) (Class 4) 2-Y-O — **£4,695** (£1,397; £698; £348) **Stalls** Low

Form				RPR
	1		**Divine Right** 2-8-12 .... JimmyFortune 2 (B J Meehan) *w'like: trckd ldr: led 1/2-way: pushed clr over 1f out: easily* **7/2**[1]	83+
	2	3 1/2	**Novista (IRE)** 2-9-0 .... SaleemGolam(3) 6 (M H Tompkins) *w'like: b.bkwd: hld up: hdwy to chse wnr over 2f out: kpt on but no imp fnl f* **20/1**	78
	3	2	**Follow The Flag (IRE)** 2-9-3 .... TedDurcan 3 (N P Littmoden) *str: prom: ev ch 2f out: kpt on at one pce after* **11/2**	72
	4	3/4	**Victory Spirit** 2-9-3 .... SebSanders 8 (J L Dunlop) *w'like: racd in tch on outside: rdn over 1f out: kpt on one pce* **11/2**	69
3	**5**	3/4	**Paymaster General (IRE)**21 [1980] 2-8-12 .... RoryMoore(5) 7 (M D I Usher) *lw: swvd rt s: sn in tch: rdn wl over 1f out: sn btn* **8/1**	67
	6	shd	**Pagan Rules (IRE)** 2-9-3 .... KerrinMcEvoy 4 (Mrs A J Perrett) *w'like: str: s.i.s: outpcd thrght* **4/1**[2]	67
	7	3	**Sepia Print (IRE)** 2-8-12 .... RHills 5 (W J Knight) *w'like: leggy: prom tl rdn 2f out: sn wknd* **14/1**	53
	8	2	**Inside Straight (IRE)** 2-9-3 .... RyanMoore 1 (R Hannon) *unf: b.bkwd: led to 1/2-way: rdn and dropped out qckly* **9/2**[3]	52

1m 14.18s (1.33) **Going Correction** +0.025s/f (Good) **8** Ran SP% **113.7**
Speed ratings (Par 95):92,87,84,83,82 82,78,75
CSF £70.25 TOTE £4.40: £1.60, £5.60, £2.10; EX 99.80.
Owner F C T Wilson **Bred** Countess De La Warr **Trained** Manton, Wilts

FOCUS
Hard to weigh up, with only Paymaster General having previous experience and a modest pace to halfway. However, there were some expensive newcomers on display, so the race may work out quite well. A hard race to assess but the winner should rate higher.

NOTEBOOK
Divine Right, a 100,000 guinea daughter of Observatory, is bred to be suited by a mile and beyond in due course. However, she trounced this field, all but one of which had never run before, and clearly has a future, with the Cherry Hinton on the agenda. (tchd 9-2)
Novista(IRE) ◆, a 20,000 guinea son of French Derby winner Anabaa Blue, and a Derby entry himself, made an encouraging debut given that he is bred to stay much farther than this sharp six furlongs. The winner looks useful, so he should be able to get off the mark soon.
Follow The Flag(IRE), a 75,000 guinea yearling, has plenty of speed in the pedigree, with trips around a mile looking likely to prove his maximum, and he showed enough early pace on this debut to give him every chance of getting off the mark. Official explanation: jockey said colt hung right throughout (op 7-1)
Victory Spirit has a winning pedigree, particularly at trips up to a mile, but fetched only 9,900 guineas as a yearling. In the circumstances, he did well on this debut against much pricier rivals. (op 10-1)
Paymaster General(IRE), the only one of these with a previous run behind him, seemed to be meeting better rivals this time and was firmly put in his place. His sights need to be kept relatively low for now. (tchd 17-2)
Pagan Rules(IRE), a 115,000 guinea son of Desert Prince, is bred to be high-class around a mile. Sent off second favourite, he never really got going, but improvement can be expected, especially when he tackles seven furlongs. (tchd 7-2)

2605 GABEM MAIDEN STKS 1m
6:45 (6:52) (Class 5) 3-Y-O **£3,562** (£1,059; £529; £264) **Stalls High**

Form RPR
322 **1** **Incidentally (IRE)**[23] 1934 3-9-3 80 RyanMoore 12 84
(R Hannon) *lw: led wl over 1f out: hrd rdn fnl f: all out* **9/4**[2]
-332 **2** *nk* **Multakka (IRE)**[22] 1951 3-9-3 85 RHills 10 83
(M P Tregoning) *hld up: hdwy over 2f out: swtchd lft over 1f out: rdn and pressed wnr fnl f* **5/4**[1]
05 **3** *5* **Press The Button (GER)**[21] 1978 3-9-0 AmirQuinn(3) 11 71
(J R Boyle) *mid-div: effrt on ins 2f out: one pce fnl f* **66/1**
0 **4** *hd* **Dance Spirit (IRE)**[28] 1822 3-9-3 JimmyFortune 7 71
(B J Meehan) *led tl hdd wl over 1f out: rdn and one pce after* **16/1**[3]
06 **5** *1 ½* **Stotsfold**[11] 2304 3-9-3 TedDurcan 6 71+
(W R Swinburn) *swtchd over to ins after s and bhd: hdwy 3f out: wknd over 1f out* **25/1**
00 **6** *3* **Mount Sinai**[34] 1684 3-9-3 SteveDrowne 8 61
(W J Knight) *bhd: effrt 3f out: nvr nr to chal* **100/1**
- **7** *nk* **Hot Agnes** 3-8-7 JamesDoyle(5) 5 55
(H J Collingridge) *w'like: b.bkwd: b.hind: a towards rr* **50/1**
0-0 **8** *7* **Cunegonde**[7] 2406 3-8-12 ShaneKelly 4 39
(G L Moore) *prom tl wknd over 2f out* **100/1**
0- **9** *1 ¾* **Stokesies Luck (IRE)**[249] 5796 3-9-3 RichardThomas 1 40
(J L Spearing) *unf: mid-div tl wknd 2f out* **100/1**
0 **10** *shd* **Seal Of Hope**[9] 2343 3-9-0 NelsonDeSouza(3) 3 40
(M P Tregoning) *bhd: rdn over 3f out: nvr on terms* **50/1**
0-0 **11** *8* **Canvas (IRE)**[9] 2349 3-8-9 SaleemGolam(3) 2 16
(Miss Z C Davison) *swtg: trckd ldrs to 3f out: wknd qckly* **100/1**

1m 40.74s (0.47) **Going Correction** -0.05s/f (Good) 11 Ran SP% **94.3**
Speed ratings (Par 99):95,94,89,89,88 85,84,77,75,75 67
CSF £3.32 TOTE £2.90: £1.20, £1.10, £4.90; EX 3.80.
Owner A J Ilsley & K T Ivory **Bred** D D And Mrs Jean P Clee **Trained** East Everleigh, Wilts

FOCUS
Two useful types dominated less talented rivals, but a number of those behind should improve enough to win. The form is not rock solid, rated around the fourth and fifth.
Press The Button(GER) Official explanation: jockey said gelding was unsuited by the good to firm ground

2606 FLORA ASTOR BIRTHDAY H'CAP 7f
7:15 (7:21) (Class 4) (0-80,80) 4-Y-0+ **£7,124** (£2,119; £1,059; £529) **Stalls High**

Form RPR
-214 **1** **Blue Java**[23] 1932 5-8-8 72 TravisBlock(5) 8 80
(H Morrison) *lw: trckd ldr: led over 2f out: rdn and jst hld on cl home* **11/4**[1]
-000 **2** *shd* **Dr Synn**[44] 1402 5-7-12 62 RoryMoore(5) 1 70
(J Akehurst) *hld up in rr: hdwy on outside 2f out: kpt on u.p but hung rt: jst failed* **9/1**
4010 **3** *1 ½* **Greenwood**[11] 2302 8-8-13 72 SteveDrowne 9 76
(P G Murphy) *trckd ldrs: rdn over 2f out: kpt on ins fnl f* **8/1**
-503 **4** *¾* **Regal Dream (IRE)**[12] 2259 4-9-0 73 RHills 3 79+
(J W Hills) *lw: hld up on ins: hdwy whn swtchd rt over 2f out: hmpd over 1f out: keeping on u.p whn checked again cl home* **8/1**
-100 **5** *1* **Deeper In Debt**[17] 2114 8-8-8 67 SebSanders 5 66
(J Akehurst) *swtg: bhd: effrt 2f out: styd on fnl f: nvr nr to chal* **8/1**
2261 **6** *1 ½* **Ivory Lace**[7] 2390 5-8-7 71 5ex JamesDoyle(5) 4 66
(S Woodman) *prom: ev ch over 1f out: hld whn squeezed out ins fnl f* **11/1**
-023 **7** *3* **Surwaki (USA)**[15] 2183 4-9-5 78 RyanMoore 6 66
(C G Cox) *swtg: hmpd s: sn mid-div: rdn over 2f out: no hdwy after* **4/1**[2]
36-0 **8** *5* **River Of Babylon**[20] 2011 5-9-6 79 JamieSpencer 2 54
(M L W Bell) *lw: a bhd* **7/1**[3]
0000 **9** *2 ½* **Acomb**[7] 2405 6-9-7 80 RichardThomas 7 48
(Mrs L Richards) *wnt lft s: plld hrd: led tl hdd over 2f out: wknd qckly: eased ins fnl f* **33/1**

1m 26.85s (-1.19) **Going Correction** -0.05s/f (Good) 9 Ran SP% **113.8**
Speed ratings (Par 105):104,103,102,101,100 98,95,89,86
CSF £27.83 CT £176.10 TOTE £3.90: £1.70, £2.70, £3.30; EX 28.30.
Owner Pangfield Partners **Bred** T J Billington **Trained** East Ilsley, Berks
■ Stewards' Enquiry : Rory Moore two-day ban: careless riding (Jun 27,30); further two-day ban: used whip with excessive frequency (Jul 1,2)

FOCUS
An ordinary handicap, but it looks solid enough at this level with several runners now reaching their peaks.

2607 PADDY DUDDY LIFETIME IN RACING MAIDEN STKS (H'CAP) 1m 6f
7:50 (7:52) (Class 5) (0-75,74) 3-Y-O **£3,562** (£1,059; £529; £264) **Stalls High**

Form RPR
4-33 **1** **Cape Secret (IRE)**[17] 2102 3-8-8 61 SebSanders 5 72
(R M Beckett) *mde all: rdn out fnl f and styd on wl* **9/2**[2]
5453 **2** *1 ½* **Bramcote Lorne**[8] 2379 3-8-5 58 KerrinMcEvoy 9 67
(S Parr) *hld up: hdwy 3f out: rdn to chse wnr fnl 2f* **9/1**
-360 **3** *1 ¼* **Ritsi**[10] 2332 3-9-3 70 (t) RyanMoore 2 77
(Mrs A J Perrett) *s.i.s: in rr tl rdn and hdwy over 2f out: styd on: nvr nrr* **12/1**
0-43 **4** *2 ½* **Great Tidings**[26] 1867 3-9-6 73 JoeFanning 11 76
(M Johnston) *tracked ldrs: rdn 2f out: one pce* **11/1**
00-3 **5** *1 ¾* **Picacho (IRE)**[18] 2066 3-8-9 62 TedDurcan 6 63
(J L Dunlop) *lw: bhd: effrt 3f out: nvr nr to chal* **14/1**
5-35 **6** *2 ½* **Rajaall**[10] 2332 3-9-7 74 SamHitchcott 7 72
(M R Channon) *lw: mid-div: rdn over 2f out: no further hdwy* **10/1**
0-45 **7** *shd* **Rehearsed (IRE)**[18] 2082 3-8-9 62 JimmyFortune 10 63+
(H Morrison) *lw: hld up: hdwy over 3f out: swtchd lft 2f out: hmpd over 1f out: no further prog* **12/1**
220 **8** *nk* **Brabazon (IRE)**[10] 2332 3-9-5 72 SteveDrowne 3 69
(R Charlton) *lw: in front rnk: rdn over 3f out: rdn and wknd over 1f out* **4/1**[1]
0-40 **9** *hd* **Kalantera (IRE)**[69] 918 3-8-7 60 (v[1]) LPKeniry 14 57
(A M Balding) *nvr bttr than mid-div* **40/1**
0000 **10** *shd* **Jack Absolute (IRE)**[18] 2082 3-8-11 64 ShaneKelly 13 61
(B J Meehan) *chsd eladers: n.m.r over 3f out: wknd over 2f out* **16/1**
0-00 **11** *17* **Billanroy (IRE)**[32] 1738 3-8-7 63 (b[1]) SaleemGolam(3) 8 36
(M H Tompkins) *a towards rr: eased ins fnl f* **50/1**
-005 **12** *12* **Hurry Up Helen (IRE)**[8] 2379 3-8-3 56 JamieMackay 4 12
(Mrs L Stubbs) *swtg: in tch tl wknd 3f out: eased whn btn ins fnl f* **12/1**
524 **13** *4* **Congestion Charge**[27] 1827 3-9-3 70 JamieSpencer 12 20
(E A L Dunlop) *trckd wnr tl wknd over 2f out: eased ins fnl f* **7/1**[3]
00-0 **14** *46* **Mighty Moon**[32] 1738 3-8-10 63 NickyMackay 1 —
(Lady Herries) *in rr: hdwy 7f out: wknd 5f out: sn wl bhd: t.o: 9.23s bhd 13th horse* **25/1**

3m 1.63s (-2.34) **Going Correction** -0.05s/f (Good) 14 Ran SP% **122.0**
Speed ratings (Par 99):104,103,102,101,100 98,98,98,98,98 88,81,79,53
CSF £44.92 CT £466.91 TOTE £5.30: £1.70, £4.70, £5.10; EX 75.70.
Owner Larkin, Legge And Milner **Bred** Declan And Catherine Macpartlin **Trained** Whitsbury, Hants

FOCUS
A fair handicap for the grade containing a number of runners attempting a longer trip, some with more success than others. The form should work out.
Congestion Charge Official explanation: vet said filly had been struck into

2608 CHARLIE CROCKER STKS (H'CAP) 1m 1f 192y
8:25 (8:27) (Class 4) (0-85,83) 3-Y-O **£7,124** (£2,119; £1,059; £529) **Stalls High**

Form RPR
1302 **1** **Babcary**[7] 2404 3-8-8 73 NelsonDeSouza(3) 1 85
(M P Tregoning) *lw: raced keenly: led for 1f: led again 3f out: pushed clr over 1f out: comf* **11/2**
0-23 **2** *1 ¾* **Midnight Traveller**[21] 1999 3-8-12 74 NickyMackay 3 83
(L M Cumani) *swtg: hld up: swtchd lft over 3f out: hdwy to go 2nd over 1f out: no imp fnl f* **3/1**[1]
-001 **3** *3 ½* **Bon Viveur**[11] 2301 3-8-8 70 5ex RyanMoore 2 72
(R Hannon) *chsd ldrs: rdn 3f out: one pce fnl 2f* **7/2**[2]
00-6 **4** *¾* **Haneen (USA)**[66] 963 3-8-3 65 KerrinMcEvoy 9 66
(J L Dunlop) *lw: chsd ldrs tl rdn and wknd over 1f out* **16/1**
4225 **5** *½* **Katchit (IRE)**[18] 2066 3-9-1 77 TedDurcan 7 77
(M R Channon) *swtg: t.k.h: hld up: effrt 2f out: wknd over 1f out* **10/1**
4114 **6** *shd* **Piano Player (IRE)**[43] 1444 3-8-11 73 ShaneKelly 6 73
(J A Osborne) *hld up in mid-div: rdn over 3f out: wknd over 1f out* **14/1**
4236 **7** *9* **Time For Life (USA)**[20] 2033 3-9-2 83 JamesDoyle(5) 4 66
(H J Collingridge) *a in rr* **16/1**
14-3 **8** *15* **Looker**[25] 1881 3-8-9 71 SebSanders 8 25
(R M Beckett) *lw: led after 1f: hdd 3f out: sn wknd* **5/1**[3]
-030 **9** *8* **Participation**[27] 1841 3-9-6 82 (p) JamieSpencer 5 21
(M J Wallace) *mid-div: wknd 2f out: eased ins fnl f* **8/1**

2m 6.62s (-1.13) **Going Correction** -0.05s/f (Good) 9 Ran SP% **117.9**
Speed ratings (Par 101):102,100,97,97,96 96,89,77,71
CSF £22.90 CT £66.88 TOTE £5.40: £2.20, £1.60, £1.80; EX 20.70.
Owner Major & Mrs R B Kennard And Partner **Bred** Stowell Hill Ltd And Major And Mrs R B Kennard **Trained** Lambourn, Berks

FOCUS
Not a bad little race, run at a good tempo and with improving horses filling the first four places.
Participation Official explanation: jockey said gelding had no more to give

2609 CHEVIOT ASSET MANAGEMENT STKS (H'CAP) 6f
9:00 (9:00) (Class 4) (0-80,78) 3-Y-O **£7,124** (£2,119; £1,059; £529) **Stalls Low**

Form RPR
5140 **1** **Roman Quest**[28] 1825 3-8-6 68 TravisBlock(5) 9 77
(H Morrison) *lw: hld up: hdwy over 1f out: shkn up to ld ins fnl f* **9/1**
1662 **2** *¾* **Mango Music**[19] 2049 3-9-4 75 TedDurcan 1 82
(M R Channon) *lw: prom: rdn to ld appr fnl f: hdd ins: nt qckn* **3/1**[1]
1144 **3** *2* **Hypocrisy**[19] 2049 3-9-6 77 J-PGuillambert 5 78+
(S C Williams) *b.hind: in tch: nt clr run fr over 2f out to over 1f out: r.o ins fnl f* **13/2**
-515 **4** *½* **Starlight Gazer**[20] 2014 3-9-6 77 RichardThomas 11 77
(J A Geake) *led tl rdn and hdd over 1f out: one pce fnl f* **4/1**[2]
-530 **5** *½* **Blue Aura (IRE)**[10] 2329 3-9-6 77 SteveDrowne 8 75
(R Charlton) *in tch: ev ch over 1f out: wknd ins fnl f* **6/1**[3]
4104 **6** *shd* **Rapsgate (IRE)**[17] 2105 3-9-2 73 (b) RyanMoore 10 71
(R Hannon) *lw: in tch: effrt on outside 2f out: wknd ins fnl f* **12/1**
0-00 **7** *½* **Tiber Tilly**[19] 2049 3-8-7 69 JamesDoyle(5) 7 65
(N P Littmoden) *chsd ldrs: rdn 2f out: one pce an no imp after* **16/1**
1-04 **8** *½* **Valentino Swing (IRE)**[9] 2353 3-9-1 72 KerrinMcEvoy 2 69+
(J L Spearing) *spd for 4f* **8/1**
0000 **9** *1 ¾* **Bollywood (IRE)**[10] 2316 3-7-12 60 MarcHalford(5) 6 49
(J J Bridger) *prom tl wknd wl over 1f out* **33/1**
10-0 **10** *9* **Pearly Poll**[27] 1843 3-9-5 76 SebSanders 3 38
(R M Beckett) *in tch tl wknd wl over 1f out* **25/1**
210- **11** *7* **Eversden (USA)**[269] 5395 3-9-7 78 JimmyFortune 4 19
(C G Cox) *towards rr: wl bhd fnl 2f* **12/1**

1m 12.27s (-0.58) **Going Correction** +0.025s/f (Good) 11 Ran SP% **121.8**
Speed ratings (Par 101):104,103,100,99,99 98,98,97,95,83 73
CSF £37.48 CT £198.83 TOTE £13.60: £3.70, £1.50, £2.10; EX 55.90 Place 6 £38.77, Place 5 £15.43.
Owner Scott-Barrett,Bryant,Dibb,Eavis,Morrison **Bred** Theakston Stud **Trained** East Ilsley, Berks

FOCUS
Some good formlines on show in this fair sprint handicap for three-year-olds, several of whom are still relatively unexposed and likely to improve. The second and third are closely matched on Newmarket running.
Tiber Tilly Official explanation: jockey said filly hung left
Valentino Swing(IRE) Official explanation: jockey said gelding was denied a clear run
Eversden(USA) Official explanation: jockey said colt moved poorly
T/Plt: £46.50. Pool £47,761.50, 749.00 winning tickets T/Qpdt: £12.70. Pool £3,331.00, 193.70 winning tickets JS

2353 NOTTINGHAM (L-H)
Friday, June 16

OFFICIAL GOING: Good to firm
Wind: Light, against Weather: Sunshine becoming overcast

2610 EUROPEAN BREEDERS FUND MAIDEN STKS 6f 15y
2:10 (2:13) (Class 5) 2-Y-O **£3,886** (£1,156; £577; £288) **Stalls High**

Form RPR
4 **1** **Whiffle (USA)**[14] 2191 2-8-12 KDarley 8 71+
(M Johnston) *chsd ldrs: rdn to ld and edgd rt over 1f out: r.o* **12/1**
2 *¾* **Gazboolou** 2-9-3 LDettori 10 74
(K R Burke) *chsd ldrs: rdn and nt clr run over 1f out: r.o* **3/1**[2]
3 *½* **Princess Georgina** 2-8-12 EddieAhern 11 67
(S C Williams) *hld up: hdwy and hmpd over 1f out: r.o* **12/1**
4 **4** *½* **Persian Peril**[13] 2241 2-9-3 DeanMcKeown 9 71
(G A Swinbank) *hld up: hdwy over 2f out: rdn and hung lft fr over 1f out: no ex ins fnl* **33/1**
0 **5** *3* **Spirited Speedfit (IRE)**[15] 2178 2-9-3 RobertWinston 1 62
(G G Margarson) *mid-div: hdwy over 1f out: no ex fnl f* **33/1**

0 **6** *1* **Danger Alley**[13] 2234 2-9-3 ......(v[1]) RichardMullen 3 59
(E J O'Neill) *led over 4f out: rdn and hdd over 1f out: wknd ins fnl f* **50/1**

7 *shd* **Musical Affair** 2-8-12 ...... RobbieFitzpatrick 2 53
(F Jordan) *prom: hung lft fr 1/2-way: wknd fnl f* **100/1**

02 **8** *3 1/2* **Colditz (IRE)**[9] 2361 2-9-3 ...... TonyCulhane 6 48
(M R Channon) *s.s and wnt lft start: outpcd* **9/2**[3]

9 *2 1/2* **Lordship (IRE)** 2-9-3 ...... PhilipRobinson 4 40
(M A Jarvis) *chsd ldrs over 4f* **9/2**[3]

2 **10** *6* **Orpen Prince (IRE)**[22] 1945 2-9-3 ...... NCallan 5 22+
(K A Ryan) *s.s and hmprd start: outpcd* **2/1**[1]

06 **11** *shd* **Joint Expectations (IRE)**[19] 2045 2-9-3 ...... JohnEgan 7 22
(Mrs C A Dunnett) *led: hdd over 4f out: wkng whn hmpd over 2f out* **100/1**

1m 15.08s (0.08) **Going Correction** -0.20s/f (Firm) **11** Ran SP% **119.9**
Speed ratings (Par 93):91,90,89,88,84 83,83,78,75,67 67
CSF £48.35 TOTE £9.70: £2.60, £3.00, £3.80; EX 42.60.
Owner Jumeirah Racing **Bred** Darley **Trained** Middleham Moor, N Yorks
■ Stewards' Enquiry : K Darley caution: careless riding

FOCUS
Just an ordinary maiden and, although difficult to race with certainty, it should produce a few winners.

NOTEBOOK
Whiffle(USA), an eye-catching fourth in a novice event over five furlongs at Catterick on her debut, made hard work of this. She is seemingly not a flashy type, but has the right attitude and will deserve her chance in a slightly higher grade. (op 18-1)
Gazboolou, a 42,000gns half-brother to Sound That Alarm, a five-furlong winner at three, out of a smart multiple sprint scorer, made a pleasing debut behind Whiffle, who had the benefit of previous experience. (op 7-2)
Princess Georgina, a sister to Mister Cosmi, a high-class six-furlong winner at two and later a useful miler, out of a winner over eight furlongs, was solid enough in the market showed plenty of ability. She met with some trouble in-running and could have been even closer. There is improvement in her and she should find a similar event. (op 11-1)
Persian Peril, fourth of five on his debut over five furlongs at Musselburgh, showed improved form stepped up to six furlongs. He should continue to progress.
Spirited Speedfit(IRE) seemed to step up on the form he showed on his debut at Yarmouth.
Colditz(IRE) started slowly and failed to confirm the improved form he showed at Ripon on his previous start and was disappointing. (op 7-2 tchd 5-1)
Lordship(IRE), a half-brother to King's Point, a smart triple winner over six to eight furlongs, out of a quite useful triple seven-furlong/miler, failed to show a great deal but attracted support in the market and can be given another chance. (op 13-2)
Orpen Prince(IRE) could not confirm the promise he showed when second on his debut at Ayr, but can be forgiven this as he got his nose stuck on the front of the starting stalls before the start.
Official explanation: jockey said colt was slowly away (tchd 5-2)

2611 BUY YOUR TICKETS ONLINE @NOTTINGHAMRACECOURSE.CO.UK H'CAP 6f 15y
2:40 (2:43) (Class 6) (0-65,65) 3-Y-0+ **£2,730** (£806; £403) **Stalls** High

Form RPR

6452 **1** **Russian Rocket (IRE)**[10] 2331 4-9-9 60 ...... JohnEgan 6 69
(Mrs C A Dunnett) *racd stands' side: chsd ldrs: rdn to ld over 1f out: r.o* **13/2**[1]

00-0 **2** *1/2* **Sir Don (IRE)**[7] 2397 7-9-0 51 ...... RichardMullen 11 59
(E S McMahon) *racd stands' side: s.i.s: hdwy over 3f out: rdn over 1f out: r.o: 2nd of 12 in gp* **20/1**

0300 **3** *nk* **Kennington**[7] 2417 6-10-0 65 ......(b) DarrenWilliams 12 72
(Mrs C A Dunnett) *racd stands' side: led: rdn over 2f out: hdd over 1f out: styd on: 3rd of 12 in gp* **9/1**[3]

0040 **4** *1/2* **Riolo (IRE)**[7] 2390 4-9-8 59 ......(b[1]) BrianReilly 8 65
(K F Clutterbuck) *racd stands' side: outpcd: rdn and hung lft over 2f out: hdwy over 1f out: r.o: 4th of 12 in gp* **66/1**

0030 **5** *hd* **Moon Forest (IRE)**[10] 2317 4-9-0 51 ......(p) LDettori 13 56
(J M Bradley) *racd stands' side: s.i.s: outpcd: hdwy u.p over 1f out: r.o: 5th of 12 in gp* **7/1**[2]

-000 **6** *1/2* **Yorkie**[14] 2211 7-9-4 55 ...... DeanMcKeown 16 59
(J Pearce) *racd stands' side: dwlt: outpcd: swtchd lft and hdwy over 1f out: nrst fin: 6th of 12 in gp* **16/1**

5021 **7** *nk* **King Egbert (FR)**[24] 1909 5-8-13 50 ...... TonyCulhane 9 53
(A W Carroll) *racd stands' side: sn prom: rdn over 1f out: no ex ins fnl f: 7th of 12 in gp* **7/1**[2]

3-04 **8** *1/2* **Mozakhraf (USA)**[43] 1437 4-9-11 62 ...... NCallan 7 63
(K A Ryan) *racd stands' side: chsd ldrs: rdn over 2f out: wknd ins fnl f: 8th of 12 in gp* **9/1**[3]

0-06 **9** *3* **Piddies Pride (IRE)**[25] 1899 4-9-4 60 ......(p) StephenDonohoe[(5)] 10 52
(Miss Gay Kelleway) *racd stands's ide: dwlt: outpcd: styd on ins fnl f: 9th of 12 in gp* **16/1**

0-00 **10** *1/2* **Waggledance (IRE)**[53] 1196 4-8-5 47 ...... DuranFentiman[(5)] 14 38
(D Carroll) *racd stands' side: w ldrs: rdn over 2f out: wknd fnl f: 10th of 12 in gp* **33/1**

3226 **11** *hd* **Rowanberry**[8] 2376 4-8-11 48 ...... EddieAhern 4 38+
(R M H Cowell) *racd far side: chsd ldr tl led that trio 1/2-way: wknd fnl f: 1st of 3 in gp* **7/1**[2]

444- **12** *5* **Sudden Edge**[256] 5666 4-9-9 60 ...... FergusSweeney 17 35
(H Candy) *w ldrs stands' side over 3f: wknd over 1f out: 11th of 12 in gp* **7/1**[2]

0461 **13** *nk* **Secret Vision (USA)**[39] 1534 5-8-9 46 ...... KDarley 2 20+
(R M H Cowell) *racd far side: led that trio to 1/2-way: wknd over 1f out: 2nd of 3 in gp* **14/1**

0000 **14** *2 1/2* **Mirage Prince (IRE)**[7] 2407 4-8-13 50 ...... RobbieFitzpatrick 15 17
(D Shaw) *racd stands' side: s.i.s: outpcd: last of 12 in gp* **66/1**

0043 **15** *8* **Monte Major (IRE)**[29] 1794 5-8-13 53 ......(v) PatrickMathers[(3)] 5 —+
(D Shaw) *racd far side: dwlt: hld up: wknd 1/2-way: last of 3 in gp* **14/1**

1m 13.41s (-1.59) **Going Correction** -0.20s/f (Firm)
WFA 3 from 4yo+ 7lb **15** Ran SP% **119.1**
Speed ratings (Par 101):102,101,100,100,100 99,98,98,94,93 93,86,86,82,72
CSF £136.92 CT £1199.04 TOTE £8.90: £2.50, £4.30, £3.10; EX 89.30.
Owner Mrs Christine Dunnett **Bred** Tally-Ho Stud **Trained** Hingham, Norfolk

FOCUS
A modest sprint handicap dominated by those on the near side of the track. Rowanberry, Secret Vision and Monte Major went far side, but had no chance. The form looks solid for the grade.
Yorkie Official explanation: jockey said gelding was denied a clear run
Rowanberry Official explanation: jockey said filly hung left
Monte Major(IRE) Official explanation: jockey said gelding suffered from a breathing problem

2612 MIDLANDS RACING - 10 GREAT VENUES - H'CAP 1m 1f 213y
3:15 (3:16) (Class 6) (0-60,60) 4-Y-0+ **£2,730** (£806; £403) **Stalls** Low

Form RPR

10-6 **1** **Fossgate**[17] 2108 5-9-6 **59** ...... LDettori 11 69
(J D Bethell) *a.p: rdn to ld 1f out: r.o* **8/1**[3]

0302 **2** *1 1/4* **Intavac Boy**[13] 2242 5-9-1 **54** ...... NCallan 2 62
(C W Thornton) *chsd ldrs: led over 2f out: rdn and hdd 1f out: edgd rt and unable qckn* **9/2**[1]

5223 **3** *1 1/4* **Mossmann Gorge**[13] 2221 4-9-7 **60** ......(b) EddieAhern 9 66
(M Wellings) *hld up: hdwy 1/2-way: rdn over 1f out: styd on* **8/1**[3]

0006 **4** *3/4* **Meelup (IRE)**[7] 2401 6-9-4 **57** ......(p) RobertHavlin 16 61
(P G Murphy) *chsd ldrs: rdn and ev ch over 2f out: edgd lft over 1f out: styd on same pce* **25/1**

0643 **5** *nk* **Apache Point (IRE)**[15] 2181 9-9-2 **55** ...... KimTinkler 6 59
(N Tinkler) *hld up: hdwy u.p over 1f out: hung rt ins fnl f: nt rch ldrs* **6/1**[2]

0464 **6** *3/4* **Siena Star (IRE)**[10] 2320 8-9-7 **60** ...... RobbieFitzpatrick 3 62
(Stef Liddiard) *dwlt: hld up: hdwy over 3f out: sn rdn: no imp fnl f* **14/1**

5-66 **7** *2* **Band**[21] 1996 6-9-1 **54** ...... RichardMullen 4 52
(E S McMahon) *chsd ldrs: rdn over 2f out: wknd over 1f out* **14/1**

0-36 **8** *2 1/2* **To Arms**[17] 2104 4-9-6 **59** ...... PhilipRobinson 8 53
(T D Easterby) *chsd ldrs: rdn over 2f out: wknd fnl f* **9/1**

2-06 **9** *nk* **Purple Dancer (FR)**[13] 2242 4-9-3 **56** ...... DeanMcKeown 7 49
(G A Swinbank) *hld up in tch: racd keenly: rdn and lost pl over 2f out: n.d after* **11/1**

0600 **10** *shd* **Melvino**[16] 2150 4-9-7 **60** ...... KDarley 15 53
(T D Barron) *s.i.s: hld up: rdn over 1f out: eased whn no ch ins fnl f* **8/1**[3]

00-0 **11** *nk* **Bubbling Fun**[7] 2414 5-9-2 **55** ...... RobertWinston 5 47
(T Wall) *hld up: effrt over 2f out: n.d* **40/1**

1004 **12** *3/4* **Migration**[19] 2044 10-8-12 **58** ...... JohnCavanagh[(7)] 10 49
(Mrs S Lamyman) *s.i.s: hld up: rdn and hung lft over 3f out: a in rr* **20/1**

0-00 **13** *shd* **Wizard Looking**[16] 2150 5-9-0 **60** ...... SladeO'Hara[(7)] 12 51
(J S Wainwright) *hld up: effrt and hmpd over 3f out: a in rr* **11/1**

65-0 **14** *3* **Machinate (USA)**[16] 2149 4-9-2 **55** ......(t) MartinDwyer 14 40
(W M Brisbourne) *hld up: rdn over 3f out: a in rr* **16/1**

0000 **15** *1 3/4* **Futoo (IRE)**[24] 1910 5-9-5 **58** ......(p) TonyCulhane 1 40
(D W Chapman) *sn led: rdn and hdd over 2f out: wknd over 1f out* **33/1**

2m 7.00s (-2.70) **Going Correction** -0.375s/f (Firm) **15** Ran SP% **125.7**
Speed ratings (Par 101):95,94,93,92,92 91,89,87,87,87 87,86,86,84,82
CSF £43.66 CT £311.04 TOTE £7.40: £3.50, £1.70, £3.10; EX 43.10.
Owner Mrs James Bethell **Bred** Mrs P A Clark **Trained** Middleham Moor, N Yorks

FOCUS
Just a moderate handicap but sound enough rated through the placed horses. They came middle to stands' side in the straight.

2613 JOHN SMITH'S EXTRA SMOOTH FILLIES' H'CAP 1m 1f 213y
3:50 (3:50) (Class 4) (0-85,82) 3-Y-0 **£6,477** (£1,927; £963; £481) **Stalls** Low

Form RPR

1- **1** **Reunite (IRE)**[226] 6227 3-9-5 **80** ...... LDettori 2 96+
(Saeed Bin Suroor) *chsd ldr: led over 3f out: shkn up over 1f out: r.o: eased ins fnl f* **10/11**[1]

26-1 **2** *3/4* **Solva**[44] 1419 3-9-3 **78** ...... EddieAhern 3 84
(B J Meehan) *chsd ldrs: lost pl over 7f out: hdwy over 5f out: wnt 2nd 3f out: rdn over 1f out: no ch w wnr* **13/8**[2]

410- **3** *6* **Persian Express (USA)**[258] 5604 3-9-0 **75** ...... MartinDwyer 4 70
(B W Hills) *hld up: outpcd over 3f out: nvr trbld ldrs* **10/1**[3]

232- **4** *3 1/2* **Munaa (IRE)**[230] 6158 3-8-9 **70** ...... NCallan 6 58
(K R Burke) *hld up: racd keenly: hdwy over 7f out: rdn and wknd over 1f out* **10/1**[3]

050- **5** *5* **Gamesters Lady**[258] 5605 3-9-7 **82** ...... DarrenWilliams 5 61
(W M Brisbourne) *sn led: rdn and hdd over 3f out: wknd 2f out* **22/1**

2m 8.24s (-1.46) **Going Correction** -0.375s/f (Firm) **5** Ran SP% **113.0**
Speed ratings (Par 98):90,89,84,81,77
CSF £2.74 TOTE £1.60: £1.10, £1.30; EX 2.40.
Owner Godolphin **Bred** Darley **Trained** Newmarket, Suffolk

FOCUS
Four of the five runners were making their seasonal reappearance and this did not look that strong a race for the grade, but Reunite won easily and is clearly significantly better than her current mark suggests with the third running to form. They raced down the centre of the track in the straight. The winning time was over a second slower than the previous race, an older-horse contest over the same trip, but they went just a steady pace early on.

2614 RACING UK ON CHANNEL 432 H'CAP 1m 54y
4:20 (4:21) (Class 3) (0-95,90) 3-Y-0+ **£9,067** (£2,697; £1,348; £673) **Stalls** Centre

Form RPR

2101 **1** **Samuel Charles**[2] 2551 8-8-12 **74** 6ex ...... RobertWinston 8 84
(C R Dore) *hld up: hdwy and hung lft fr over 1f out: r.o u.p to ld wl ins fnl f* **5/1**[3]

-000 **2** *1/2* **Calcutta**[6] 2440 10-10-0 **90** ...... MartinDwyer 6 99
(B W Hills) *hld up: hdwy over 1f out: rdn and ev ch ins fnl f: r.o* **10/1**

-003 **3** *1/2* **Diamonds And Dust**[13] 2232 4-9-7 **83** ......(b) NCallan 2 90
(M H Tompkins) *led: rdn over 2f out: hung lft fr over 1f out: hdd wl ins fnl f* **12/1**

0243 **4** *nk* **Flipando (IRE)**[6] 2440 5-9-13 **89** ...... KDarley 3 96
(T D Barron) *chsd ldrs: rdn and ev ch ins fnl f: nt run on* **1/1**[1]

-012 **5** *nk* **Habshan (USA)**[15] 2183 6-9-2 **78** ...... EddieAhern 5 84
(C F Wall) *chsd ldrs: rdn and hung lft fr over 1f out: styd on* **7/2**[2]

20-0 **6** *1 3/4* **Alchemist Master**[38] 1561 7-9-0 **76** ...... DeanMcKeown 1 78
(R M Whitaker) *chsd ldr: rdn over 2f out: styng on same pce whn hmpd ins fnl f* **25/1**

01/- **7** *17* **Russian Consort (IRE)**[583] 6611 4-9-12 **88** ...... TonyCulhane 4 51
(A King) *s.s: hld up: rdn over 2f out: wknd over 1f out* **16/1**

1m 42.17s (-4.23) **Going Correction** -0.375s/f (Firm) **7** Ran SP% **115.4**
Speed ratings (Par 107):106,105,105,104,104 102,85
CSF £52.65 CT £568.91 TOTE £7.10: £3.30, £4.10; EX 74.20.
Owner Chris Marsh **Bred** Sheikh Mohammed Obaid Al Maktoum **Trained** West Pinchbeck, Lincs

FOCUS
Not a great turnout for the prize money and the form looks ordinary for the grade, rated through the third. They went a good pace, but the winning time was nearly half a second slower than the following maiden, although it was still faster than the three-year-old handicap over the same trip. They raced middle to far side in the straight.

NOTEBOOK
Samuel Charles, the winner of two of his last three starts on Polytrack, including at Kempton two days earlier, continued his good run of form switched to turf to take advantage of a mark 4lb lower than in future. He was hanging when initially coming under pressure, but ultimately went through with his effort. There could yet be more to come, but he appeared to have a hard enough race and has been kept busy lately. He may be aimed at a Ladies' race at Ascot over seven furlongs, but the drop in trip is unlikely to suit. (tchd 11-2)
Calcutta, who is due to be dropped 3lb, returned to form with a good effort in defeat behind the well-handicapped winner. He is clearly still pretty useful at the age of ten. (op 8-1)
Diamonds And Dust, returned to a mile, made this a good test by appearing to race quite freely in front but was ultimately no match for the two held furthest off the pace. Still, he has found his form and could be ready to win when things fall right. (op 10-1)
Flipando(IRE), still 3lb higher than when last winning in 2004, was not beaten far but failed to inspire confidence. (op 11-8)
Habshan(USA) does not look that well handicapped on turf, but was not beaten far. (op 4-1 tchd 9-2)
Russian Consort(IRE), a really nice juvenile in 2004, has been off the track for 583 days and offered little on his return. (op 12-1)

2615 VISITNOTTINGHAM.COM MAIDEN STKS — 1m 54y
4:55 (4:58) (Class 5) 3-Y-O+ — **£3,238** (£963; £481; £240) **Stalls** Centre

Form			Horse	Jockey	RPR
23	1		**Minister Of State**[34] [1674] 3-9-0 (M A Jarvis) *mde all: rdn over 1f out: r.o* 9/4[2]	PhilipRobinson 10	86+
66-4	2	1 1/4	**Jihaaz (IRE)**[60] [1048] 3-9-0 73 (B W Hills) *chsd wnr: rdr dropped whip 2f out: styd on* 8/1	MartinDwyer 1	84
3-23	3	1/2	**Escape Clause (USA)**[21] [1984] 3-9-0 83 (Sir Michael Stoute) *hld up: plld hrd: hdwy over 1f out: hung lft: r.o: nt rch ldrs* 2/1[1]	RobertWinston 12	83+
3-2	4	1	**Villa Sonata**[19] [2048] 3-8-9 (J R Fanshawe) *chsd ldrs: rdn over 2f out: styd on same pce fnl f* 6/1[3]	OscarUrbina 3	76
23-	5	1	**Great Orator (USA)**[237] [6028] 4-9-10 (H Candy) *chsd ldrs: rdn over 2f out: no ex fnl f* 14/1	FergusSweeney 11	80
203-	6	7	**Sophie'Jo**[240] [5987] 3-8-9 72 (H R A Cecil) *hld up in tch: rdn over 3f out: wknd over 2f out* 8/1	EddieAhern 6	57
	7	3/4	**Naini Tal** 3-8-9 (D R C Elsworth) *s.s: bhd: rdn and swished tail over 3f out: r.o ins fnl f: nvr nrr* 50/1	JohnEgan 16	55
55	8	nk	**Quel Ange (FR)**[13] [2220] 4-9-10 70 (R J Hodges) *sn outpcd: effrt over 3f out: n.d* 66/1	FrankieMcDonald 17	62
	9	5	**Oasis Flower** 3-8-9 (J R Fanshawe) *s.i.s: rdn over 3f out: n.d* 33/1	NCallan 14	43
0	10	3/4	**Wodhill Schnaps**[16] [2146] 5-9-10 (D Morris) *hld up: rdn and edgd lft 3f out: sn wknd* 150/1	MichaelTebbutt 2	49
0	11	1 3/4	**Evening**[58] [1088] 3-8-9 (B W Hills) *hld up: plld hrd: wknd 3f out* 22/1	TonyCulhane 8	37
00	12	hd	**Flying Visitor**[31] [1759] 3-8-9 (J M P Eustace) *hld up: a in rr* 100/1	DeanMcKeown 13	37
44-0	13	10	**Bottomless Wallet**[14] [2198] 5-9-0 42 (F Watson) *hld up: nt clr run over 6f out: rdn over 3f out: sn wknd* 200/1	MarkLawson(5) 9	16
00-	14	2	**Riotous Assembly**[225] [6234] 3-9-0 (B Smart) *plld hrd and prom: rdn and wknd over 2f out* 100/1	DerekMcGaffin 5	14
00	15	1/2	**Whiston Lad (IRE)**[17] [2111] 3-9-0 (S R Bowring) *s.i.s: hld up: wknd over 3f out* 150/1	DarrenWilliams 7	13
00-0	16	3	**Mighty Duel**[14] [2195] 3-9-0 42 (J R Norton) *mid-div: wknd over 3f out* 150/1	NeilPollard 15	6

1m 41.74s (-4.66) **Going Correction** -0.375s/f (Firm)
WFA 3 from 4yo+ 10lb — 16 Ran SP% 122.5
Speed ratings (Par 103):108,106,106,105,104 97,96,96,91,90 88,88,78,76,76 73
CSF £20.47 TOTE £3.40: £2.00, £2.00, £1.70; EX 19.10.
Owner Cheveley Park Stud **Bred** Cheveley Park Stud Ltd **Trained** Newmarket, Suffolk

FOCUS
This looked a reasonable enough maiden for the time of year and the winning time was the fastest of the three races run over a mile on the card. The third and fourth set a decent standard. They stayed far side in the straight.

2616 BINGHAM H'CAP — 1m 54y
5:30 (5:31) (Class 5) (0-70,69) 3-Y-O — **£3,238** (£963; £481; £240) **Stalls** Centre

Form			Horse	Jockey	RPR
30-0	1		**Prince Evelith (GER)**[13] [2243] 3-9-1 63 (G A Swinbank) *mid-div: hdwy over 3f out: led over 2f out: sn rdn: all out* 6/1	DeanMcKeown 10	74
6630	2	shd	**Sgt Schultz (IRE)**[36] [1616] 3-9-1 63 (J S Moore) *hld up: hdwy over 3f out: r.o u.p ins fnl f* 11/1	RobertWinston 3	74
555	3	hd	**Rationale (IRE)**[52] [1218] 3-9-0 62 (S C Williams) *s.s: hld up: hdwy and hmpd over 3f out: rdn over 1f out: r.o* 11/2[3]	JohnEgan 1	73+
-542	4	1 1/2	**Temperance (IRE)**[11] [2301] 3-9-7 69 (S Kirk) *chsd ldrs: rdn and nt clr run over 1f out: styd on* 15/8[1]	LDettori 4	76
0-04	5	2 1/2	**Rainbow's Classic**[26] [1866] 3-9-7 69 (K A Ryan) *chsd ldrs: hmpd and lost pl over 3f out: hdwy u.p over 1f out: no ex ins fnl f* 5/1[2]	NCallan 9	70
5-01	6	3 1/2	**Makai**[16] [2142] 3-9-6 68 (M Johnston) *hld up: hdwy over 3f out: nt clr run and lost pl over 2f out: hdwy u.p over 1f out: wknd ins fnl f* 14/1	StanleyChin 2	61
1510	7	1/2	**Leamington Lad (IRE)**[19] [2050] 3-9-2 64 (J A Geake) *chsd ldrs: rdn over 2f out: wknd over 1f out* 5/1[2]	EddieAhern 13	56
-002	8	1	**Nimble Star**[14] [2192] 3-7-11 50 oh11 (C W Fairhurst) *led: plld hrd: hdd over 2f out: sn wknd* 66/1	LeanneKershaw(5) 6	40
0060	9	5	**Eliminator**[11] [2299] 3-8-6 57 (I W McInnes) *s.s: outpcd* 66/1	PatrickMathers(3) 5	35
3600	10	1 1/2	**Memphis Man**[16] [2138] 3-9-3 65 (G C Bravery) *s.s: hld up: wknd over 2f out* 66/1	MichaelTebbutt 7	40
000-	11	16	**Carrietau**[199] [6467] 3-9-1 63 (J G Given) *chsd ldrs: rdn and edgd lft over 3f out: wknd over 2f out* 33/1	MartinDwyer 11	1

1m 43.04s (-3.36) **Going Correction** -0.375s/f (Firm) — 11 Ran SP% 120.2
Speed ratings (Par 99):101,100,100,99,96 93,92,91,86,85 69
CSF £70.27 CT £390.32 TOTE £10.80: £2.00, £3.60, £1.50; EX 100.70 Place 6 £209.42, Place 5 £47.49.
Owner Allan Stennett **Bred** Gestut Etzean **Trained** Melsonby, N Yorks
■ Stewards' Enquiry : Martin Dwyer two-day ban: careless riding (Jun 27-28)

FOCUS
A modest but competitive handicap in which the fourth represents the best line to the form. The winning time was slower than both the earlier handicap won by Samuel Charles and the maiden won by Minister Of State.
Nimble Star Official explanation: jockey said filly ran too free early stages

T/Plt: £297.60 to a £1 stake. Pool: £34,806.05. 85.35 winning tickets. T/Qpdt: £21.50 to a £1 stake. Pool: £2,762.70. 94.90 winning tickets. CR

2172 SANDOWN (R-H)
Friday, June 16
OFFICIAL GOING: Good to firm (good in places)
Wind: Almost nil Weather: Sunny and warm

2617 BANK OF IRELAND EBF MAIDEN STKS — 5f 6y
2:20 (2:23) (Class 5) 2-Y-O — **£4,533** (£1,348; £674; £336) **Stalls** High

Form			Horse	Jockey	RPR
	1		**Special Day** 2-8-12 (B W Hills) *trckd ldrs: nt clr run fr 2f out tl squeezed through 1f out: sn led: rdn out* 7/4[1]	RHills 9	74+
	2	hd	**Gentleman Pirate** 2-9-3 (M H Tompkins) *s.i.s: hld up wl in rr: gd prog fr 2f out: chal 1f out: jst outpcd by wnr* 25/1	GeorgeBaker 4	74+
0	3	1	**Silver Hotspur**[40] [1510] 2-9-3 (P W Chapple-Hyam) *pressed ldrs: rdn to ld briefly 1f out: one pce last 100yds* 10/1	AlanMunro 2	71
0	4	1/2	**Sparkling Eyes**[10] [2328] 2-8-12 (C E Brittain) *racd on outer: hld up in tch: shkn up over 1f out: kpt on steadily: nvr rchd ldrs* 25/1	KerrinMcEvoy 1	64
5	5	3/4	**Road To Recovery**[32] [1737] 2-9-3 (A M Balding) *trckd ldrs: n.m.r and nt qckn over 1f out: one pce after* 9/2[2]	JamieSpencer 6	66
03	6	1 1/4	**High Style**[16] [2130] 2-9-3 (R Hannon) *mde most to 1f out: wknd* 13/2[3]	RyanMoore 8	62
	7	1 1/2	**El Bosque (IRE)** 2-9-3 (B R Millman) *dwlt: rn green in rr: nvr on terms* 20/1	SteveDrowne 10	56+
0250	8	1/2	**Benllech**[13] [2218] 2-9-3 (S Kirk) *w ldr tl over 1f out: wkng whn squeezed out jst ins fnl f: eased* 7/1	(t) JimmyFortune 3	61+
2	9	8	**Meru Camp (IRE)**[18] [2073] 2-9-3 (P Winkworth) *w ldrs to 1/2-way: wknd* 16/1	JimCrowley 7	26
	10	20	**King Of Tricks** 2-9-0 (M D I Usher) *outpcd and bhd 3f out: t.o* 50/1	RichardSmith(3) 11	—

62.05 secs (-0.16) **Going Correction** -0.15s/f (Firm) — 10 Ran SP% 109.8
Speed ratings (Par 93):95,94,93,92,91 89,86,85,73,41
CSF £52.16 TOTE £2.30: £1.20, £7.40, £2.90; EX 45.30.
Owner Suzanne & Nigel Williams **Bred** P And Mrs A G Venner **Trained** Lambourn, Berks
■ Sacre Coeur was withdrawn (14/1, unruly in stalls.) R4 applies, deduct 5p in the £.

FOCUS
A fair juvenile maiden, likely to produce winners.

NOTEBOOK
Special Day, a speedily-bred daughter of Fasliyev who was strongly supported in the market beforehand, weaved her way through under Hills and picked up in the style of a decent filly once in the clear. She was always holding the runner-up and looks well worth her place at a slighty higher level, with improvement anticipated. (op 15-8 tchd 2-1 in places)
Gentleman Pirate is bred to improve with time and distance and it was no surprise to see him disregarded in the betting considering his stable's moderate first-time-out record. However, having been in rear early, he made good headway on the outside threw down a challenge which failed only narrowly. He should be winning as soon as he tackles six furlongs.
Silver Hotspur, unable to cope with the soft ground on his debut at Newmarket, was always prominent on the outer, but lacked the pace of the front pair in the final furlong or so. This was a good effort and he should be winning in nurseries, if not beforehand. (op 8-1)
Sparkling Eyes showed more on this drop back in trip, but she should stay six furlongs and it may have been more a case of her just knowing more this time. Official explanation: jockey said filly hung left
Road To Recovery comes from a stable who have yet to really get going with their juveniles, but he has shown enough in two starts to suggest he will be winning once handicapped.
High Style does not really seem to be progressing, but he is now qualified for a handicap mark and should fare better in that sphere. (op 7-1)

2618 BRISTOL & WEST PROPERTY FINANCE H'CAP — 5f 6y
2:55 (2:57) (Class 4) (0-80,74) 4-Y-O+ — **£5,505** (£1,637; £818; £408) **Stalls** High

Form			Horse	Jockey	RPR
6000	1		**Malapropism**[13] [2237] 6-9-4 74 (M R Channon) *trckd ldr for 2f: styd prom: swtchd lft over 1f out: drvn and r.o to ld last stride* 8/1	EdwardCreighton(3) 5	82
0330	2	shd	**Chinalea (IRE)**[18] [2074] 4-9-4 71 (C G Cox) *led and sn crossed to far rail: drvn over 1f out: kpt on wl fnl f: hdd last stride* 6/1[3]	SteveDrowne 1	79
0-32	3	hd	**Endless Summer**[17] [2096] 9-8-4 62 (A W Carroll) *chsd ldrs: rdn and effrt over 1f out: r.o ins fnl f: jst pipped in blanket fin* 11/2[2]	JamesDoyle(5) 4	69
-041	4	shd	**Divine Spirit**[14] [2194] 5-9-0 67 (M Dods) *hld up in rr: prog 1/2-way: clsng whn nt clr run over 1f out tl ins fnl f: r.o nr fin: unlucky* 7/4[1]	JamieSpencer 9	77+
-600	5	1/2	**Salviati (USA)**[34] [1662] 9-9-1 68 (J M Bradley) *s.s: hld up in last pair: plenty to do over 1f out: plld out and r.o wl fnl f: nt rch ldrs* 12/1	RyanMoore 8	73+
5400	6	3/4	**Whistler**[2] [2550] 9-8-10 63 (Miss J R Tooth) *chsd ldrs: pushed along and lost pl 1/2-way: renewed effrt over 1f out: one pce last 100yds* 20/1	(p) RichardThomas 7	65
4100	7	3/4	**Matsunosuke**[15] [2182] 4-9-7 74 (A B Coogan) *pressed ldr after 2f: drvn over 1f out: hld ent fnl f: wknd last 100yds* 12/1	SebSanders 3	73
-000	8	1/2	**Logsdail**[15] [2173] 6-9-5 72 (G L Moore) *hld up in last: pushed along and no prog 1/2-way: n.d after* 10/1	PatDobbs 10	70
0-00	9	shd	**Harrison's Flyer (IRE)**[6] [2449] 5-9-7 74 (J M Bradley) *chsd ldng trio to over 1f out: wknd fnl f* 12/1	(p) TQuinn 6	71
0046	10	1	**Pawan (IRE)**[9] [2358] 6-9-0 74 (Miss A Stokell) *dwlt: rcvrd and in tch on outer: bmpd along 2f out: no prog whn rdr lost whip 1f out* 25/1	(b) AnnStokell(7) 2	68

61.01 secs (-1.20) **Going Correction** -0.15s/f (Firm) — 10 Ran SP% 117.9
Speed ratings (Par 105):103,102,102,102,101 100,99,98,98,96
CSF £56.06 CT £290.70 TOTE £10.40: £2.40, £2.40, £1.90; EX 71.10.
Owner Michael A Foy **Bred** Michael A Foy **Trained** West Ilsley, Berks

FOCUS
A tight sprint handicap, but contested largely by horses who find it hard to win these days. They finished well bunched, and the form is ordinary. Divine Spirit looked unlucky and has been rated the winner.

2619 BANK OF IRELAND BUSINESS & MID CORPORATE BANKING MAIDEN STKS 7f 16y

3:25 (3:27) (Class 4) 2-Y-O £5,181 (£1,541; £770; £384) Stalls High

Form	Pos	Dist	Horse / Details	RPR
	1		**Raincoat** 2-9-3 .... JimmyFortune 6 (J H M Gosden) *trckd ldrs: plld out and prog over 2f out: shkn up to ld 1f out: r.o wl* **10/3**[1]	86+
0	2	2 ½	**Miss Saafend Plaza (IRE)**[21] 1989 2-8-12 .... RyanMoore 4 (R Hannon) *led: kicked on 2f out: drvn and hdd 1f out: no ch w wnr but clr of remainder after* **10/1**	75
	3	2	**Tension Point** 2-9-3 .... ShaneKelly 8 (J A Osborne) *hld up in midfield: plld out and shkn up 2f out: styd on to take 3rd wl ins fnl f* **20/1**	75+
	4	¾	**Frosty Night (IRE)** 2-9-3 .... JoeFanning 10 (M Johnston) *dwlt: pushed along and sn cl up: shkn up over 2f out: kpt on same pce* **7/1**	73
	5	nk	**Grand Diamond (IRE)** 2-9-3 .... JimCrowley 3 (Mrs A J Perrett) *dwlt: hld up in rr: shuffled along on outer fr over 2f out: styd on steadily: nrst fin* **20/1**	72+
	6	¾	**Al Raahi** 2-9-3 .... TedDurcan 12 (M R Channon) *dwlt: wl in rr: pushed along and rn green over 2f out: prog over 1f out: one pce fnl f* **11/1**	70+
	7	shd	**Zelos (IRE)** 2-9-3 .... SteveDrowne 13 (J A Osborne) *hld up in rr: pushed along and nt clr run over 2f out to 1f out: kpt on steadily* **33/1**	70+
00	8	¾	**Venir Rouge**[20] 2009 2-9-3 .... GeorgeBaker 5 (M Salaman) *hld up in last pair: nt clr run 1f out: plld out and r.o fnl f: nvr nrr: do bttr* **40/1**	68+
3	9	½	**Dubai Magic (USA)**[9] 2342 2-9-3 .... KerrinMcEvoy 9 (C E Brittain) *t.k.h: trckd ldng pair: shkn up over 2f out: hld whn hmpd over 1f out: fdd* **9/2**[2]	67+
04	10	shd	**Alloro**[21] 1980 2-9-3 .... TQuinn 11 (D J S Ffrench Davis) *settled in midfield: pushed along over 2f out: one pce and no imp after* **16/1**	67+
50	11	2	**Right Option (IRE)**[27] 1838 2-9-3 .... JamieSpencer 1 (A P Jarvis) *pressed ldr: upsides 3f out to 2f out: hanging bdly rt and reluctant over 1f out: sn btn* **12/1**	62+
	12	2	**King Charles** 2-9-3 .... KFallon 7 (E A L Dunlop) *t.k.h: hld up in midfield: pushed along and hld whn hmpd over 1f out* **13/2**[3]	57+
	13	½	**Bobbish** 2-9-3 .... AlanMunro 2 (N A Callaghan) *s.s: a in last pair: pushed along and no prog 3f out* **25/1**	55

1m 31.08s (-0.01) **Going Correction** -0.25s/f (Firm) **13** Ran SP% **116.8**
Speed ratings (Par 95):90,87,84,84,83 82,82,81,81,81 78,76,76
CSF £33.41 TOTE £4.50: £1.90, £2.90, £8.10; EX 56.20.
Owner K Abdulla **Bred** Juddmonte Farms Ltd **Trained** Newmarket, Suffolk

FOCUS
A race capable of throwing up a decent performer and Raincoat provided Gosden with his fourth win in it in the last 12 years. With so little to go on one can only guess at what the form is worth and the time was ordinary, but there were some taking efforts, not least from the winner.

NOTEBOOK
Raincoat ◆, from a good middle-distance family, was representing his trainer in a race he has won three times in the last 11 years and he was able to improve that record in quite taking fashion. Never far off the leaders, he showed a nice change of gear once asked to go on and win the race and, considering he is bred to appreciate a little give in the ground, this has to go down as a decent effort. He will stay further in time and looks a useful prospect. (op 4-1)
Miss Saafend Plaza(IRE) put her experience to good use and tried to nick it from the front, but she was outclassed by the winner. She did hold on for second though and there may be further improvement to come back at six furlongs. (tchd 9-1)
Tension Point comes from a stable which can unearth the odd good juvenile and he made some late headway on the outside to claim third. This was a pleasing debut effort and he should have little trouble finding a maiden. (op 16-1)
Frosty Night(IRE) ◆, a Group I National Stakes entrant, comes from a stable who traditionally farm races such as this, but their juveniles have not been up to scratch thus far in 2006. Sluggish coming out of the stalls, he was unable to lead, but still raced prominently and held every chance without being able to muster a change of pace. He can be expected to improve for the outing however and should know a lot more next time. (tchd 15-2)
Grand Diamond(IRE) ◆ is bred for middle-distances and he made a highly encouraging debut under jump jockey Jim Crowley, staying on late having been outpaced. He, like Frosty Night, can be expected to come on a good deal for the outing and he will be winning once tackling a mile.
Al Raahi, bred to be effective at shorter, never really got into it, but he comes from a good stable so should have little trouble finding a race.
Zelos(IRE) never really got a crack at a clear run, but his stable's juvenile usually come on a good deal for their initial outing and he should find easier opportunities.
Venir Rouge had hinted at ability on his debut, and in coming from a hopeless position he again left the impression that there was a bit better to come. Official explanation: jockey said colt suffered interference in running
Dubai Magic(USA), third on his debut at Kempton, was unable to confirm that promise and failed to get home, having raced keenly. He is probably a bit better than this and should go on to show it in time. Official explanation: jockey said colt ran green (op 7-2)
Alloro Official explanation: jockey said colt suffered interference in running
Right Option(IRE) Official explanation: jockey said colt hung right
King Charles, a relation of Barathea and Gossamer, did not show a lot on this debut, but he would have been closer but for interference and a softer surface is going to help. He can leave this behind. Official explanation: jockey said gelding suffered interference in running (op 9-1)

2620 MOUSETRAP CHALLENGE CUP H'CAP 1m 14y

4:00 (4:03) (Class 4) (0-80,80) 3-Y-O £6,477 (£1,927; £963; £481) Stalls High

Form	Pos	Dist	Horse / Details	RPR
40-4	1		**Fantastisch (IRE)**[56] 1118 3-9-3 **76** .... JamieSpencer 10 (H R A Cecil) *trckd ldr: led wl over 2f out and kicked clr: drvn and flashed tail fnl f: in no real danger* **15/2**[3]	84
-063	2	1	**Rubenstar (IRE)**[16] 2126 3-9-6 **79** .... GeorgeBaker 12 (M H Tompkins) *dwlt: hld up in last trio: swtchd lft 2f out: rapid prog over 1f out: chsd wnr last 100yds: no ch to chal* **15/2**[3]	85+
-564	3	1 ¼	**Zabeel House**[22] 1954 3-9-7 **80** .... KFallon 11 (E A L Dunlop) *trckd ldrs: rdn to chse wnr 2f out: no imp 1f out: lost 2nd last 100yds* **11/2**[1]	83
16-0	4	1	**Right Ted (IRE)**[27] 1843 3-9-4 **77** .... RyanMoore 8 (R Hannon) *trckd ldrs: effrt over 2f out: rdn and styd on same pce fr over 1f out* **10/1**	78
54-0	5	nk	**Blu Manruna**[22] 1951 3-8-6 **65** ow1 ....(b) TQuinn 13 (J Akehurst) *rousted along on inner and sn led: hdd and nt qckn wl over 2f out: plugged on again fnl f* **25/1**	65
5-31	6	½	**The Osteopath (IRE)**[15] 2163 3-9-3 **76** ....(p) PhillipMakin 9 (M Dods) *plld hrd early: hld up towards rr: effrt and carried hd awkwardly 2f out: styd on: no ch* **7/1**[2]	75+
0-00	7	1	**Prince Zafonic**[34] 1680 3-8-9 **68** .... AlanMunro 3 (W Jarvis) *dwlt: hld up in last trio: rdn 3f out: hanging rt but styd on fr over 1f out: n.d* **20/1**	65
0-44	8	hd	**Aspen Falls (IRE)**[22] 1963 3-9-5 **78** .... SebSanders 4 (Sir Mark Prescott) *hld up in midfield: prog on outer 2f out: disp 3rd 1f out: no imp and eased last 75yds* **7/1**[2]	74
2-60	9	shd	**Kapellmeister (IRE)**[126] 365 3-9-2 **75** ....(p) SteveDrowne 14 (C R Egerton) *t.k.h: trckd ldng pair to 2f out: wknd fnl f* **25/1**	71
2-32	10	½	**Another Genepi (USA)**[16] 2143 3-9-1 **74** .... RHills 5 (J W Hills) *t.k.h: cl up: rdn over 2f out: disp 3rd 1f out: wknd* **15/2**[3]	69
0452	11	¾	**Mujood**[9] 2344 3-9-4 **77** .... StephenCarson 7 (R F Johnson Houghton) *plld hrd early: hld up in midfield: no imp 2f out: wknd* **14/1**	70
100-	12	3	**Sun Catcher (IRE)**[245] 5871 3-9-2 **78** .... RichardSmith[(3)] 6 (R Hannon) *hld up and sn detached in last: nvr in the hunt* **50/1**	64
6654	13	5	**Vodkatini**[11] 2301 3-8-11 **70** ....(v) JimmyFortune 1 (P J Makin) *hld up wl in rr: rdn and no prog whn bdly hmpd 2f out: no ch after* **11/1**	45
4465	14	nk	**Crimson Flame (IRE)**[15] 2177 3-8-12 **71** .... TedDurcan 2 (M R Channon) *trckd ldrs: rdn and wkng whn squeezed out jst over 1f out: eased* **12/1**	45

1m 41.46s (-2.49) **Going Correction** -0.25s/f (Firm) **14** Ran SP% **121.9**
Speed ratings (Par 101):102,101,99,98,98 97,96,96,96,96 95,92,87,87
CSF £60.88 CT £271.24 TOTE £8.60: £2.70, £3.60, £2.30; EX 80.40.
Owner Mrs M C Sweeney **Bred** Crone Stud Farms Ltd **Trained** Newmarket, Suffolk
■ Stewards' Enquiry : George Baker two-day ban: careless riding (Jun 27-28)

FOCUS
A fair handicap. The bare form is anchored somewhat by the fifth, but the winner is progressing and the second is going the right way.

2621 BANK OF IRELAND GLOBAL MARKETS H'CAP 1m 2f 7y

4:30 (4:35) (Class 4) (0-85,85) 4-Y-O+ £7,772 (£2,312; £1,155; £577) Stalls High

Form	Pos	Dist	Horse / Details	RPR
4/1	1		**Corran Ard (IRE)**[48] 1302 5-9-4 **82** .... RyanMoore 3 (Evan Williams) *hld up in rr: prog 3f out: drvn to ld ent fnl f: hld on wl nr fin* **8/1**[3]	91
56-6	2	hd	**Wellington Hall (GER)**[129] 325 8-9-0 **78** .... JimmyFortune 8 (P W Chapple-Hyam) *trckd ldrs: rdn and sltly outpcd wl over 1f out: rallied to chal u.str.p fnl f: jst hld* **12/1**	87
3032	3	½	**South O'The Border**[18] 2088 4-8-7 **76** .... JamesDoyle[(5)] 2 (T G Mills) *trckd ldrs: rdn to ld over 1f out: hdd ent fnl f: styd on* **5/1**[2]	84
-000	4	¾	**Coup D'Etat**[41] 1484 4-9-4 **82** .... TQuinn 11 (J L Dunlop) *hld up in rr: prog 2f out: rdn and styd on wl fnl f: nrst fin* **9/1**	89
35-0	5	nk	**Best Prospect (IRE)**[18] 2079 4-9-3 **81** .... PhillipMakin 1 (M Dods) *trckd ldr: led 3f out: drvn and hdd over 1f out: fdd last 100yds* **8/1**[3]	87
104-	6	3 ½	**Buster Hyvonen (IRE)**[275] 5235 4-8-8 **72** .... JamieSpencer 13 (J R Fanshawe) *hld up in rr: sme prog on inner over 2f out: shuffled along and styd on fr over 1f out: nt rch ldrs* **8/1**[3]	71+
4421	7	1 ¾	**Davenport (IRE)**[17] 2114 4-8-11 **82** .... JamesMillman[(7)] 10 (B R Millman) *s.s and lost 5 l: wl in rr: rdn 3f out: nt looking happy but kpt on fnl 2f: n.d* **8/1**[3]	78
0-2	8	hd	**Kova Hall (IRE)**[15] 2169 4-9-7 **85** .... GeorgeBaker 12 (B G Powell) *prom: rdn and outpcd 2f out: steadily wknd* **16/1**	81
6-00	9	½	**Evolution Ex (USA)**[15] 2169 4-8-11 **75** .... ShaneKelly 7 (K R Burke) *nvr beyond midfield: rdn over 2f out: grad wknd over 1f out* **20/1**	70
321-	10	2 ½	**Sacranun**[375] 2339 4-9-7 **85** .... NickyMackay 4 (L M Cumani) *hld up wl in rr: rdn over 2f out: no prog* **9/2**[1]	75
50-0	11	10	**Night Spot**[14] 2201 5-9-0 **78** .... AlanMunro 9 (B R Millman) *led to 3f out: wknd 2f out: t.o* **16/1**	49
0-00	12	6	**Mineral Star (IRE)**[16] 2147 4-9-4 **82** .... JoeFanning 6 (M H Tompkins) *t.k.h: hld up wl in rr: wknd over 2f out: t.o* **20/1**	42
00-0	13	14	**Gig Harbor**[14] 2201 7-8-11 **75** .... SebSanders 5 (Miss E C Lavelle) *t.k.h: trckd ldrs: wknd 2f out: heavily eased: t.o* **25/1**	8

2m 7.58s (-2.66) **Going Correction** -0.25s/f (Firm) **13** Ran SP% **122.1**
Speed ratings (Par 105):100,99,99,98,98 95,94,94,93,91 83,79,67
CSF £99.71 CT £538.61 TOTE £8.80: £2.90, £5.30, £2.10; EX 140.10.
Owner E Salmon **Bred** Eamon Salmon **Trained** Cowbridge, Vale Of Glamorgan

FOCUS
Ordinary stuff, but sound enough. The second and third set the level..
Gig Harbor Official explanation: jockey said gelding was unsuiited by the good to firm (good in places) ground

2622 IRISH TIMES H'CAP 1m 2f 7y

5:05 (5:07) (Class 5) (0-75,75) 3-Y-O £4,533 (£1,348; £674; £336) Stalls High

Form	Pos	Dist	Horse / Details	RPR
-603	1		**Urban Tiger (GER)**[10] 2332 3-9-4 **72** .... TedDurcan 4 (A King) *dwlt: hld up in last trio: plld out and rdn 2f out: gd prog to press ldr last 150yds: sustained chal to ld fnl stride* **9/2**[2]	83
4114	2	shd	**Black Beauty**[6] 2434 3-9-7 **75** .... RyanMoore 13 (M G Quinlan) *trckd ldrs: effrt to ld 2f out: drvn and styd on wl fnl f: hdd last stride* **5/1**[3]	86
4505	3	3	**Hill Of Almhuim (IRE)**[22] 1948 3-9-0 **68** ....(v) LPKeniry 12 (K R Burke) *led: pressed 3f out: hdd 2f out: kpt on same pce after* **20/1**	73
6-01	4	¾	**Moon On A Spoon**[10] 2324 3-9-6 **74** 5ex .... JamieSpencer 1 (J R Fanshawe) *hld up in rr: gd prog on outer to chal over 1f out and looked dangerous: edgd rt and wknd ins fnl f* **11/8**[1]	78
-503	5	2	**Cool Ebony**[17] 2111 3-9-2 **70** .... PhillipMakin 10 (M Dods) *trckd ldrs: effrt over 2f out: no imp over 1f out: fdd* **33/1**	70
-330	6	shd	**Synonymy**[46] 1350 3-8-9 **63** .... NickyMackay 8 (M Blanshard) *hld up in midfield: rdn on inner over 2f out: kpt on same pce: n.d* **28/1**	63
63-0	7	1	**Penmara**[16] 2124 3-8-4 **58** .... JamieMackay 9 (M H Tompkins) *s.i.s: hld up in last pair: shuffled along fr over 2f out: kpt on steadily: nvr nr ldrs* **28/1**	56
1644	8	1 ½	**Dark Planet**[14] 2209 3-8-8 **62** .... ShaneKelly 11 (C E Brittain) *chsd ldr for 2f: styd prom: rdn 3f out: stl cl up over 2f out: wknd over 1f out* **8/1**	57
00-0	9	1 ½	**Storm Of Arabia (IRE)**[23] 1941 3-8-11 **65** .... StephenCarson 3 (W R Swinburn) *settled towards rr: rdn over 2f out: no prog and sn btn* **66/1**	57

00-0 **10** *nk* **Pay On (IRE)**[19] [2048] 3-8-11 **65** .... AlanMunro 2 57
(W Jarvis) *hld up wl in rr: detached last and rdn 3f out: no prog tl kpt on fnl f* **16/1**

0-00 **11** *5* **Zafantage**[7] [2403] 3-8-13 **67** .... JimmyFortune 6 49
(S Kirk) *trckd ldrs: rdn over 2f out: wknd rapidly wl over 1f out* **25/1**

10-0 **12** *3* **Grandad Bill (IRE)**[43] [1444] 3-9-2 **70** .... TQuinn 7 47
(T D Easterby) *trckd ldrs: lost pl 3f out: wkng whn hmpd 2f out* **50/1**

3-66 **13** *hd* **Boquilobo**[18] [2081] 3-9-3 **71** .... JoeFanning 5 47
(M Johnston) *trckd ldr after 2f: upsides 3f out: wknd rapidly 2f out* **16/1**

2m 8.22s (-2.02) **Going Correction** -0.25s/f (Firm) **13** Ran SP% **121.7**
Speed ratings (Par 99):98,97,95,94,93 93,92,91,90,89 85,83,83
CSF £25.79 CT £420.01 TOTE £6.60: £2.30, £1.90, £6.20; EX 35.70 Place 6 £207.37, Place 5 £102.33.
Owner Four Mile Racing **Bred** Gestut Gorlsdorf **Trained** Barbury Castle, Wilts

FOCUS
A fair handicap, and the finish was dominated by the right horses. The first two are both improvers and the third has slipped to a decent mark.
Zafantage Official explanation: jockey said filly ran flat
T/Plt: £300.80 to a £1 stake. Pool: £49,534.70. 120.20 winning tickets. T/Qpdt: £73.10 to a £1 stake. Pool: £3,202.95. 32.40 winning tickets. JN

1831 YORK (L-H)
Friday, June 16

OFFICIAL GOING: Good to firm
Wind: Virtually nil

2623 HSS MAIDEN AUCTION STKS — 5f
2:30 (2:30) (Class 4) 2-Y-O — **£7,124** (£2,119; £1,059; £529) **Stalls** Centre

Form — RPR

1 **Wi Dud** 2-8-13 .... DO'Donohoe 3 91+
(K A Ryan) *dwlt: hdwy on outer 1/2-way: qcknd to ld wl over 1f out: comf* **5/1**[1]

252 **2** *1 1/4* **My Valerina (IRE)**[14] [2191] 2-8-5 .... RoystonFfrench 10 72
(Mrs A Duffield) *sn pushed along and outpcd towards rr: hdwy 2f out: rdn and styd on ins last* **13/2**[3]

465 **3** *1* **The Nifty Fox**[35] [1632] 2-8-10 .... DavidAllan 12 73
(T D Easterby) *cl up: rdn and ev ch 2f out: drvn and one pce ins last* **9/1**

0 **4** *hd* **Valley Of The Moon (IRE)**[17] [2106] 2-8-7 .... PaulHanagan 5 69
(R A Fahey) *in tch: pushed along and sltly outpcd 2f out: sn rdn and kpt on ins last: nrst fin* **11/1**

64 **5** *1* **Danum Dancer**[30] [1780] 2-8-9 .... TonyHamilton 8 68
(N Bycroft) *prom: rdn along 2f out: wknd appr last* **10/1**

6 *1/2* **Hurricane Spirit (IRE)** 2-8-11 .... GrahamGibbons 2 68
(J R Best) *led: rdn along 2f out: sn hdd and gradsually wknd appr last* **6/1**[2]

7 *hd* **Sir Charles** 2-8-9 .... FergalLynch 4 65
(M Dods) *towards rr tl styd on fnl 2f: nrst fin* **25/1**

8 *1* **Nordic Light (USA)** 2-8-13 .... AdrianMcCarthy 6 66
(P W Chapple-Hyam) *chsd ldrs: rdn 2f out: grad wknd* **8/1**

5 **9** *1/2* **Animated**[40] [1499] 2-9-0 .... AdrianTNicholls 7 65
(D Nicholls) *in tch: rdn along over 2f out: sn wknd* **10/1**

9 *dht* **Imperial Beach (USA)** 2-8-8 .... BenSwarbrick(3) 13 62
(T D Barron) *dwlt: towards rr: hdwy 2f out: sn rdn: edgd lft and wknd over 1f out* **25/1**

025 **11** *1 3/4* **Nota Liberata**[18] [2076] 2-8-7 .... DanielTudhope(3) 9 54
(G M Moore) *squeezed out s: a rr* **10/1**

12 *1 3/4* **Mambo Spirit (IRE)** 2-8-12 .... DaleGibson 1 50
(J G Given) *cl up: rdn along 2f out: sn wknd* **20/1**

13 *8* **Korty** 2-8-10 .... TPQueally 11 19
(W J Musson) *sn outpcd and bhd* **50/1**

60.29 secs (0.97) **Going Correction** +0.10s/f (Good) **13** Ran SP% **115.4**
Speed ratings (Par 95):96,94,92,92,90 89,89,87,86,86 84,81,68
CSF £33.37 TOTE £4.70: £2.00, £2.10, £2.60; EX 23.60.
Owner J Duddy,L Duddy,P Mcbride,E Duffy **Bred** D R Botterill **Trained** Hambleton, N Yorks

FOCUS
A modest juvenile maiden, run at a decent early pace, which produced a taking debut winner.

NOTEBOOK
Wi Dud, a 25,000gns purchase bred to make his mark at two, showed a neat turn of foot when asked to win his race and duly got his career off to a perfect start in ready fashion. He left the impression he would improve plenty for the experience, should get another furlong in due course, and rates another exciting juvenile prospect from his ever-improving yard. (op 10-3 tchd 11-2 in a place)
My Valerina(IRE) struggled to go the early pace, but kept responding to pressure and ultimately finished a clear second-best. She probably wants a stiffer test on this sort of ground and helps to set the level of this form. (op 7-1)
The Nifty Fox had every chance and posted an improved effort in defeat. It is not that long until the nurseries begin and he is likely to find his feet in when entering that sphere. (op 10-1)
Valley Of The Moon(IRE) ◆, who shaped slightly better than her finishing position suggests on debut last time, was doing all of her best work too late in the day on this drop back to the minimum trip. This was a definite step in the right direction, but she looks to be crying out for the return to a sixth furlong. (op 12-1)
Danum Dancer had his chance and, while only modest, he helps to set the level of this form. Official explanation: jockey said colt was unsuited by the good to firm ground (tchd 11-1 in a place)
Hurricane Spirit(IRE), who dam was a juvenile sprint winner and hails from a very fast family, was very well backed ahead of this racecourse debut. Having showed plenty of early dash, he ultimately paid for his early exertions, but still did enough to suggest he ought to have learnt a deal from the experience. (tchd 13-2)

2624 HSS.COM STKS (H'CAP) — 5f
3:05 (3:05) (Class 3) (0-95,95) 3-Y-0+ — **£8,290** (£2,466; £1,232; £615) **Stalls** Centre

Form — RPR

2600 **1** **Golden Dixie (USA)**[23] [1936] 7-9-3 **85** .... AdrianMcCarthy 3 98
(R A Harris) *midfield: gd hdwy on outer 2f out: rdn to ld 1f out: kpt on* **14/1**

-440 **2** *1 1/4* **Talbot Avenue**[113] [494] 8-9-13 **95** .... TPQueally 13 103
(M Mullineaux) *dwlt and hld up in rr: swtchd lft and hdwy over 1f out: sn rdn and styd on wl fnl f* **9/1**[3]

0220 **3** *nk* **Fizzlephut (IRE)**[14] [2189] 4-8-9 **77** .... PaulFitzsimons 12 84
(Miss J R Tooth) *in tch: hdwy 2f out: rdn to chse ldrs ent last: sn hung lft and kpt on same pce* **20/1**

0050 **4** *nk* **Cape Royal**[13] [2227] 6-9-7 **94** ....(b) GregFairley(5) 4 100
(J M Bradley) *sn prom: hdwy to ld over 2f out: rdn wl over 1f out: hdd 1f out and kpt on same pce* **12/1**

001- **5** *1/2* **Bold Minstrel (IRE)**[381] [2162] 4-8-12 **80** .... FergalLynch 10 84
(M Quinn) *cl up: rdn and ev ch over 1f out. wkng whn n.m.r wl ins last* **25/1**

0030 **6** *3/4* **Graze On**[27] [1858] 4-8-12 **87** ....(b) TolleyDean(7) 7 89
(R A Harris) *chsd ldrs: rdn along 2f out: kpt on u.p fnl f* **14/1**

-010 **7** *1/2* **The Jobber (IRE)**[15] [2173] 5-9-5 **87** .... PaulHanagan 16 87
(M Blanshard) *hld up towards rr: hdwy 2f out: rdn and edgd lft over 1f out and ins last: nrst fin* **16/1**

00-3 **8** *1 1/2* **One Way Ticket**[7] [2389] 6-9-0 **82** ....(p) TonyHamilton 1 76
(J M Bradley) *led: rdn along 1/2-way: sn hdd and grad wknd* **10/1**

5-30 **9** *nk* **Mimi Mouse**[6] [2450] 4-9-2 **84** .... DavidAllan 6 77
(T D Easterby) *in tch: hdwy to chse ldrs over 2f out: sn rdn and btn* **17/2**[2]

0-06 **10** *1 1/4* **Caribbean Coral**[13] [2227] 7-8-13 **81** .... GrahamGibbons 2 70
(J J Quinn) *s.i.s: a rr* **5/1**[1]

11-0 **11** *nk* **Niteowl Lad (IRE)**[10] [2323] 4-8-9 **77** .... RoystonFfrench 5 65
(J Balding) *cl up: rdn along and ev ch wl over 1f out: grad wknd* **10/1**

3000 **12** *1* **Wanchai Lad**[27] [1856] 5-8-12 **80** .... AdrianTNicholls 15 64
(D Nicholls) *chsd ldrs: rdn along 2f out: sn wknd* **9/1**[3]

-006 **13** *3/4* **Kay Two (IRE)**[42] [1469] 4-9-12 **94** .... DO'Donohoe 9 75
(R J Price) *chsd ldrs: pushed along over 2f out: wkng whn n.m.r over 1f out* **20/1**

00 **14** *hd* **Pachello (IRE)**[27] [1858] 4-9-0 **82** ....(t) PaulMulrennan 8 63
(J M Bradley) *dwlt: a rr* **50/1**

0025 **15** *1/2* **Whinhill House**[6] [2449] 6-8-8 **76** oh6 ....(p) TomEaves 14 55
(D W Barker) *wnt lft s: a rr* **10/1**

58.90 secs (-0.42) **Going Correction** +0.10s/f (Good) **15** Ran SP% **116.7**
Speed ratings (Par 107):107,105,104,104,103 102,101,98,98,96 95,94,93,92,91
CSF £123.51 CT £2563.98 TOTE £20.40: £11.20, £3.60, £5.80; EX 389.50 Trifecta £751.80 Part won. Pool: £1,058.92 - 0.20 winning tickets..
Owner Mrs Vicki Davies **Bred** G Strawbridge Jr **Trained** Earlswood, Monmouths

FOCUS
A decent enough sprint for the class and the form looks straightforward and fair with the fourth and fifth setting the standard.

NOTEBOOK
Golden Dixie(USA) settled much better this time and posted a personal-best effort to score a ready success. This proved him a very capable sprinter on his day and, while ultimately the Handicapper is going to raise him again for this, he would have to be of interest if turning out under a penalty. (op 12-1)
Talbot Avenue, returning from a 113-day break, finished all too late in the day under top weight. He has to rate a little unlucky, however, as he had to be switched to find the openings from off the pace, and would have no doubt given the winner more to think about with a clear passage. (op 8-1)
Fizzlephut(IRE) ran an improved race, despite hanging left under maximum pressure, and showed he is best kept to this trip. He can find easier assignments from his current mark, but is proving hard to catch right at present. (op 22-1)
Cape Royal was found wanting approaching the final furlong, but this was still his best effort for some time, and he may just have hit the front a little too soon. He still looks in need of a little further respite from the Handicapper, however.
Bold Minstrel(IRE) had his chance, yet appeared to blow-up on this first outing for 381 days, and looks sure to improve for the outing. He is one to look out for when the market speaks more in his favour.
Mimi Mouse Official explanation: jockey said filly had bled from the nose
Caribbean Coral, sixth in the Vodafone Dash last time, was never going from off the pace and turned in a tame effort. Official explanation: trainer had no explanation for the poor form shown (op 9-2)

2625 HSS HIRE STKS (H'CAP) — 2m 2f
3:40 (3:41) (Class 3) (0-95,95) 4-Y-0+ — **£11,658** (£3,468; £1,733; £865) **Stalls** Centre

Form — RPR

0002 **1** **Ski Jump (USA)**[13] [2238] 6-8-6 **79** ....(v) PaulHanagan 3 89+
(R A Fahey) *hld up in tch: smooth prog over 4f out: led over 3f out: rdn clr over 1f out: easily* **11/4**[2]

P-20 **2** *3* **The Nawab (IRE)**[37] [1584] 4-9-1 **89** .... IanMongan 6 94
(J L Dunlop) *hld up in rr: hdwy over 4f out: rdn to chse wnr 2f out: sn drvn and kpt on same pce* **10/11**[1]

60-2 **3** *7* **Overstrand (IRE)**[29] [1808] 7-7-13 **77** oh13 ow1 .... AndrewMullen(5) 4 74
(Robert Gray) *hld up in tch: hdwy over 4f out: rdn along to chse ldng pair over 2f out: sn drvn and outpcd wl over 1f out* **15/2**[3]

0-00 **4** *3/4* **Ten Carat**[20] [2013] 6-8-13 **86** ....(v) RoystonFfrench 1 82
(M Todhunter) *mde most tl rdn along and hdd over 3f out: sn wknd* **11/1**

004- **5** *13* **Darasim (IRE)**[49] [4348] 8-9-3 **95** ....(v) GregFairley(5) 2 77
(M Johnston) *cl up tl rdn along over 4f out: sn wknd* **10/1**

3m 57.34s (9.34)
WFA 4 from 6yo+ 1lb **5** Ran SP% **108.2**
CSF £5.46 TOTE £3.20: £1.40, £1.10; EX 4.30.
Owner P D Smith Holdings Ltd **Bred** Juddmonte Farms Inc **Trained** Musley Bank, N Yorks
■ Stewards' Enquiry : Ian Mongan one-day ban: careless riding (Jun 27)

FOCUS
A fair marathon handicap, run at a modest gallop, and the winner is value for at least double his winning margin.

NOTEBOOK
Ski Jump(USA), who signalled a return to form when second at Musselburgh last time, was given a confident ride and duly went one better with a most decisive success. The longer trip proved much to his liking and, while he can be expected to take a hike back up in the weights after this, his confidence should have been significantly boosted. (op 5-2 tchd 3-1)
The Nawab(IRE), well backed despite disappointing in the Chester Cup off this mark last time, could not match the finishing kick of the winner and must rate flattered by his proximity to that rival at the finish. He was a clear second-best, and may prefer softer ground, but he does look in need of respite from the Handicapper on this evidence. (op 11-10)
Overstrand(IRE), racing from 13lb out of the handicap, produced another sound effort - on a track he clearly enjoys - yet ultimately got found out by the drop back in trip. He can expect to go up again in the weights now, but that will clearly be deserved. (op 8-1)
Ten Carat dropped out after doing most of the donkey work, but still managed to improve a touch on his previous efforts this term. (tchd 10-1)
Darasim(IRE), having his first run back on the Flat - and for his former trainer - after a mixed spell over hurdles during the winter, threw in the towel when push came to shove and really is regressing fast. (op 9-1 tchd 11-1)

2626 SKF ROUS (S) STKS — 6f
4:10 (4:10) (Class 4) 2-Y-O — **£6,800** (£2,023; £1,011; £505) **Stalls** Centre

Form — RPR

003 **1** **Party Palace**[5] [2478] 2-8-1 .... RichardKingscote(5) 1 54
(J A Osborne) *in tch: hdwy to chse ldrs 2f out: rdn over 1f out: chal ent last: drvn and kpt on to ld on line* **6/1**[3]

05 **2** *shd* **Put It On The Card**[16] 2145 2-8-11 ....(v[1]) GrahamGibbons 5 59
(P D Evans) *chsd ldrs: hdwy 2f out: rdn to ld over 1f out: drvn and hdd briefly wl ins last: rallied to ld last 50 yds: hdd online* **33/1**

4212 **3** *1 ½* **Tokyo Jo (IRE)**[15] 2179 2-8-1 ....(v) AndrewElliott(5) 14 49
(K R Burke) *cl up gng wl: effrt and hung bdly lft ent last: rdn to ld briefly wl ins last: sn hdd and no ex last 50 yds* **4/1**[2]

00 **4** *¾* **Providence Farm**[10] 2321 2-8-4 .... AdeleRothery(7) 11 52
(M W Easterby) *dwlt: sn pushed along in rr: hdwy 2f out: rdn and hung lft over 1f out: kpt on ins last: nrst fin* **100/1**

06 **5** *½* **Global Traffic**[9] 2342 2-8-11 .... JosedeSouza 8 50
(P F I Cole) *chsd ldrs: rdn and edgd lft fr wl over 1f out: kpt on same pce ins last* **7/1**

015 **6** *3 ½* **Spinning Game**[2] 2538 2-8-6 .... PaulQuinn 6 35
(D W Chapman) *chsd ldrs: rdn along 2f out: drvn and wknd fr over 1f out* **13/2**

7 *¾* **Roxy Singer** 2-8-6 .... TPQueally 2 33
(W J Musson) *sn rdn along: outpcd and bhd: hdwy 2f out: styd on appr last* **25/1**

0 **8** *1 ¼* **Dispol Moonlight (IRE)**[18] 2076 2-8-8 .... BenSwarbrick(3) 3 34
(T D Barron) *sn rdn along and outpcd in rr tl sme late hdwy* **20/1**

42 **9** *2* **Jord (IRE)**[50] 1248 2-8-6 .... MickyFenton 9 23
(J A Osborne) *led: rdn along and hdd over 2f out: sn wknd* **7/2**[1]

0 **10** *shd* **Don't Try It On**[34] 1682 2-8-11 .... PaulMulrennan 7 28
(M W Easterby) *sn rdn along and outpcd: a towards rr* **100/1**

6 **11** *1 ¾* **Playing Games**[8] 2382 2-8-11 .... TomEaves 13 22
(M W Easterby) *dwlt and wnt lft s: a rr* **100/1**

6623 **12** *nk* **Minimum Fuss (IRE)**[3] 2524 2-8-6 ....(b) DaleGibson 12 17
(M W Easterby) *cl up: rdn along over 2f out: drvn wl over 1f out and sn wknd* **16/1**

5502 **13** *1 ½* **Readyforone**[18] 2064 2-8-11 ....(b) PaulHanagan 4 17
(P D Evans) *cl up: led over 2f out: sn rdn: hdd over 1f out and sn wknd* **10/1**

00 **14** *7* **Fath And Furiouth (IRE)**[34] 1682 2-8-11 .... LeeEnstone 10 —
(P C Haslam) *a rr* **80/1**

1m 14.46s (1.90) **Going Correction** +0.10s/f (Good) **14** Ran SP% **113.1**
Speed ratings (Par 95):91,90,88,87,87 82,81,79,77,77 74,74,72,63
CSF £190.91 TOTE £8.30: £2.60, £7.90, £1.90; EX 222.00.The winner was bought in for 9,800gns.
Owner Elaine and Martyn Booth **Bred** Llety Stud **Trained** Upper Lambourn, Berks
■ Stewards' Enquiry : Jose de Souza caution: careless riding

FOCUS
A modest juvenile seller although possibly not as strong as some past renewals, and the first two came clear in a thrilling finish.

NOTEBOOK
Party Palace just did enough to repel the runner-up in a bobbing finish and register her first success at the third attempt. She has clearly now found her level and is well suited by quick ground. (op 4-1)
Put It On The Card was only just denied and turned in his best effort to date in the first-time visor. This is his grade, but he was a clear second-best, and has been improved since stepping up to this trip. (op 40-1)
Tokyo Jo(IRE) had every chance under a positive ride, but had no more to offer when pressed inside the final furlong. She probably found this ground plenty fast enough and helps set the level of this form. (tchd 9-2 in places)
Providence Farm was doing all of his best work at the finish, having made a sluggish start, and struggled to go the early pace. This was his best effort to date and he is one to bear in mind when faced with a stiffer test at this sort of level.
Jord(IRE) dropped out tamely nearing two out, having shown decent early dash, and was well beaten before her stamina for this extra furlong came into question. (op 4-1)
Fath And Furiouth(IRE) Official explanation: jockey said gelding hung left-handed throughout

2627 PRINCE OF WALES'S OWN REGIMENT OF YORKSHIRE H'CAP 1m 208y
4:45 (4:45) (Class 4) (0-80,80) 4-Y-0+ **£6,800** (£2,023; £1,011; £505) **Stalls** Low

Form RPR

5-24 **1** **Topatoo**[28] 1830 4-9-2 **75** .... TPQueally 9 91+
(M H Tompkins) *hld up in rr: smooth hdwy 3f out: led ent last and sn rdn clr* **11/2**[1]

00-0 **2** *2 ½* **She's Our Lass (IRE)**[31] 1761 5-7-11 **63** ow1 .... KellyHarrison(7) 10 72+
(D Carroll) *hld up: hdwy 3f out: nt clr run and swtchd rt over 1f out: sn rdn and styd on wl fnl f* **16/1**

0040 **3** *½* **Instructor**[15] 2162 5-9-5 **78** .... PaulHanagan 1 83
(R A Fahey) *led: rdn along over 2f out: drvn and hdd ent last: kpt on same pce* **7/1**[2]

000- **4** *¾* **Tedsdale Mac**[238] 6008 7-7-11 **63** oh8 ow2 .... SuzzanneFrance(7) 6 66
(N Bycroft) *towards rr: hdwy on inner over 2f out: sn rdn and styd on fnl f* **50/1**

0053 **5** *½* **Wing Commander**[10] 2322 7-8-10 **69** ....(b) RoystonFfrench 7 71
(I W McInnes) *chsd ldrs: rdn along wl over 2f out: drvn over 1f out and kpt on same pce* **12/1**

6-60 **6** *nk* **Flighty Fellow (IRE)**[48] 1280 6-9-2 **75** ....(v[1]) TomEaves 3 76
(Miss J A Camacho) *trckd ldng pair: hdwy to chse ldr 3f out: rdn and ev ch 2f out: drvn and one pce appr last* **16/1**

0314 **7** *¾* **Bridgewater Boys**[15] 2170 5-8-4 **68** ....(b) AndrewMullen(5) 4 68
(K A Ryan) *chsd ldr: rdn along over 2f out: drvn and wknd wl over 1f out* **8/1**

6160 **8** *nk* **Major Magpie (IRE)**[11] 2299 4-8-10 **69** .... FergalLynch 15 74+
(M Dods) *hld up in rr: hdwy 3f out: nt clr run and swtchd rt 2f out and again over 1f out: swtchd lft and hmpd ins last: eased* **15/2**[3]

0051 **9** *nk* **Nevada Desert (IRE)**[8] 2378 6-8-8 **74** 6ex .... MichaelJStainton(7) 14 73
(R M Whitaker) *chsd ldrs: rdn along over 2f out: sn drvn and grad wknd* **11/1**

50-0 **10** *½* **Typhoon Ginger (IRE)**[26] 1864 11-7-12 **62** oh2 ow1 AndrewElliott(5) 17 60
(G Woodward) *bhd: hdwy 3f out: styd on ins last: nt rch ldrs* **25/1**

60-1 **11** *½* **Mistress Twister**[35] 1636 5-8-9 **71** .... BenSwarbrick(3) 16 68
(T D Barron) *in tch on outer: hdwy to chse ldrs 3f out: rdn over 2f out and grad wknd* **10/1**

4400 **12** *¾* **Harvest Warrior**[21] 1985 4-9-4 **77** ....(b) DavidAllan 5 72
(T D Easterby) *chsd ldrs: rdn along over 2f out: sn btn* **16/1**

-003 **13** *½* **Fair Shake (IRE)**[8] 2378 6-8-9 **68** ....(v) TonyHamilton 11 62
(Karen McLintock) *a midfield* **33/1**

00-1 **14** *1 ½* **Epicurean**[21] 1997 4-8-8 **67** .... MickyFenton 8 58
(Mrs K Walton) *in tch: rdn along 3f out: sn wknd* **25/1**

4624 **15** *1 ¼* **Bond Diamond**[11] 2299 9-8-2 **61** .... DaleGibson 12 50
(P T Midgley) *hld up: a towards rr* **12/1**

0-00 **16** *nk* **Nashaab (USA)**[6] 2435 9-9-7 **80** ....(v) IanMongan 2 68
(P D Evans) *chsd ldrs on inner: rdn along 3f out: drvn 2f out and sn wknd* **25/1**

-000 **17** *9* **Qaasi (USA)**[10] 2322 4-8-9 **68** .... PaulMulrennan 13 38
(Mrs K Walton) *bhd fr 1/2-way* **25/1**

1m 51.38s (0.39) **Going Correction** +0.275s/f (Good) **17** Ran SP% **121.5**
Speed ratings (Par 105):109,106,106,105,105 104,104,104,103,103 102,102,101,100,99 99,91
CSF £85.20 CT £655.74 TOTE £6.30: £1.80, £4.60, £2.50, £11.60; EX 128.90.
Owner Mrs P R Bowring **Bred** M P Bowring **Trained** Newmarket, Suffolk

FOCUS
A fair handicap for the class, run at a sound gallop in a good time, and the ready winner is value for further. The form behind looks solid with the fourth and seventh the best guides.
Major Magpie(IRE) Official explanation: jockey said gelding was denied a clear run

2628 BOLLINGER CHAMPAGNE CHALLENGE SERIES H'CAP (FOR GENTLEMAN AMATEUR RIDERS) 1m 4f
5:20 (5:21) (Class 4) (0-80,77) 4-Y-0+ **£6,246** (£1,937; £968; £484) **Stalls** Centre

Form RPR

0-00 **1** **Richtee (IRE)**[14] 2193 5-10-5 **65** .... MrBMcHugh(7) 10 76
(R A Fahey) *trckd ldrs: hdwy over 4f out: led over 2f out and wnt lft: sn rdn: drvn and hdd ins last: styd on to ld nr fin* **9/1**

5325 **2** *¾* **Dovedon Hero**[23] 1943 6-10-9 **67** ....(b) MrPCollington(5) 4 79+
(P J McBride) *dwlt: hld up and bhd: hdwy 3f out: n.m.r 2f out: chal on bit ent last: sn led: rdn: faltered and hdd nr fin* **9/1**

05-0 **3** *3 ½* **Almizan (IRE)**[19] 2044 6-10-7 **65** ....(b) MrDHutchison(5) 5 69
(G L Moore) *hld up towards rr: hdwy 3f out: rdn wl over 1f out: styd on* **11/1**

5452 **4** *nk* **Top Spec (IRE)**[10] 2322 5-10-12 **70** .... MrSPearce(5) 1 74
(J Pearce) *hld up towards rr: hdwy 3f out: rdn wl over 1f out: kpt on ins last* **4/1**[1]

62-0 **5** *½* **El Chaparral (IRE)**[163] 33 6-10-9 **67** .... CJCallow(5) 3 70
(F P Murtagh) *hld up: hdwy 3f out: rdn to chse ldrs 2f out: sn one pce* **25/1**

6-00 **6** *nk* **Rajam**[14] 2193 8-10-4 **62** .... MrSFMagee(5) 7 64
(G A Harker) *hld up towards rr: hdwy on outer over 2f out: sn rdn and kpt on same pce* **50/1**

2-42 **7** *1 ½* **Calatagan (IRE)**[14] 2196 7-10-10 **68** .... MrOWilliams(5) 11 68
(J M Jefferson) *led 5f: chsd ldr tl led again over 3f out: rdn and hdd over 2f out: sn drvn and wknd wl over 1f out* **11/2**[2]

2/0- **8** *½* **Beat The Heat (IRE)**[17] 1192 8-11-3 **70** .... MrSDobson 2 69
(Jedd O'Keeffe) *chsd ldrs: rdn along 3f out: drvn 2f out: wkng whn n.m.r wl over 1f out* **8/1**

3-00 **9** *½* **Sand And Stars (IRE)**[13] 2238 5-10-12 **70** .... MrSPJones(5) 9 68
(M H Tompkins) *a rr* **9/1**

3-12 **10** *4* **Caraman (IRE)**[95] 168 8-10-11 **69** .... MrRTierney(5) 6 61
(J J Quinn) *trckd ldrs: effrt 3f out: sn rdn along and btn* **6/1**[3]

0040 **11** *18* **Akritas**[21] 1991 5-11-5 **77** .... MrOCole(5) 8 40
(P F I Cole) *chsd ldr: led after 5f: rdn along and hdd over 3f out: wknd qckly* **9/1**

2m 35.11s (2.71) **Going Correction** +0.275s/f (Good) **11** Ran SP% **114.9**
Speed ratings (Par 105):101,100,98,97,97 97,96,96,95,93 81
CSF £85.41 CT £901.38 TOTE £11.40: £2.70, £3.10, £4.50; EX 101.90 Place 6 £398.76, Place 5 £190.23.
Owner Terence Elsey and Richard Mustill **Bred** Niall Farrell **Trained** Musley Bank, N Yorks
■ The first winner for Barry McHugh.
■ Stewards' Enquiry : Mr P Collington one-day ban: careless riding (Jun 30)

FOCUS
A modest event of its type which saw the first two come clear. The form is ordinary and is worth treating with a degree of caution.
T/Jkpt: Not won. T/Plt: £424.70 to a £1 stake. Pool: £68,053.15. 116.95 winning tickets. T/Qpdt: £24.20 to a £1 stake. Pool: £3,641.70. 111.20 winning tickets. JR

2629 - (Foreign Racing) - See Raceform Interactive

2478 BATH (L-H)
Saturday, June 17

OFFICIAL GOING: Firm
Wind: Almost nil.

2630 E B F / BATHWICK TYRES NOVICE STKS 5f 11y
2:10 (2:10) (Class 4) 2-Y-0 **£4,533** (£1,348; £674; £336) **Stalls** Low

Form RPR

6 **1** **Resignation (IRE)**[60] 1066 2-8-12 .... PatDobbs 3 93+
(R Hannon) *travelled wl bhd ldng pair: led jst over 1f out: r.o wl: comf* **2/1**[1]

4135 **2** *3* **Fairfield Princess**[12] 2300 2-8-9 .... GregFairley(5) 1 81
(N A Callaghan) *led: drifted rt 2f out: rdn and hdd jst over 1f out: no ex* **9/2**

415 **3** *½* **King's Bastion (IRE)**[21] 2009 2-9-5 .... HayleyTurner 4 84
(M L W Bell) *chsd ldng trio: rdn over 2f out: wnt 3rd over 1f out: kpt on same pce* **5/2**[2]

031 **4** *5* **Proper (IRE)**[7] 2432 2-9-2 .... SamHitchcott 5 63
(M R Channon) *w ldr: rdn 3f out: wknd ent fnl f* **11/4**[3]

61.12 secs (-1.38) **Going Correction** -0.25s/f (Firm) **4** Ran SP% **106.8**
Speed ratings (Par 95):101,96,95,87
CSF £10.26 TOTE £2.80; EX 14.90.
Owner Richard Morecombe **Bred** Luke O'Reilly **Trained** East Everleigh, Wilts

FOCUS
A fair little novice event, run at a sound pace in a good time, and the winner is capable of rating higher.

NOTEBOOK
Resignation(IRE) ◆ got off the mark at the second time of asking with an impressive display. He showed the clear benefit of his recent debut in a hotter contest at Newmarket, travelled takingly this time before putting the race to bed nearing the final furlong, and looks sure to improve again for this experience. He is due to be aimed at the Super Sprint at Newbury next month in a bid to enhance his trainer's already decent record in that event. (op 9-4 tchd 15-8)
Fairfield Princess had her chance from the front, but was eventually firmly put in her place when the winner asserted. She is fully exposed over this trip now, but still rates as a fair benchmark for this form. (op 7-2)
King's Bastion(IRE), fifth at Ascot over six furlongs last time, did not look suited by this drop back in trip and was well held. (op 9-4 tchd 3-1)
Proper(IRE), off the mark at Goodwood a week previously, found it all too hot nearing the final furlong and failed to improve for the drop to this trip. (op 3-1)

2631 BATHWICK TYRES MAIDEN AUCTION STKS — 5f 11y
2:45 (2:46) (Class 6) 2-Y-O — £2,590 (£770; £385; £192) Stalls Low

Form — RPR

2 **1** **Southandwest (IRE)**^{14} [2218] 2-8-9 .... JohnEgan 8 — 87
(J S Moore) *mde all: shkn up 2f out: r.o wl: readily* — **9/4**^{2}

23 **2** *2 ½* **Lipocco**^{31} [1770] 2-8-11 .... SebSanders 7 — 80
(R M Beckett) *chsd ldrs: rdn to go 2nd over 1f out: no further imp on wnr ins fnl f* — **8/11**^{1}

0 **3** *3* **Hester Brook (IRE)**^{16} [2166] 2-8-1 .... DominicFox(3) 10 — 62
(J G M O'Shea) *chsd wnr tl over 1f out: kpt on same pce fnl f* — **100/1**

0 **4** *3* **Star Strider**^{53} [1203] 2-8-13 .... AdrianTNicholls 9 — 60
(A M Balding) *s.i.s: sn rcvrd to chse ldrs: rdn over 2f out: fdd fnl f* — **16/1**

0 **5** *1* **Dancing Daisy (IRE)**^{15} [2185] 2-8-4 .... FrankieMcDonald 2 — 48
(Mrs P N Dutfield) *in tch: rdn over 3f out: edgd rt 2f out: sn wknd* — **100/1**

06 **6** *hd* **Fair 'n Square (IRE)**^{10} [2355] 2-8-4 .... FrancisFerris 3 — 47
(J L Spearing) *chsd ldrs: rdn over 2f out: wknd jst over 1f out* — **50/1**

46 **7** *½* **Cleobury**^{6} [2478] 2-8-7 ow1 .... FergusSweeney 11 — 48
(M Meade) *nvr bttr than mid div* — **50/1**

50 **8** *1 ½* **Whipchord (IRE)**^{16} [2166] 2-8-6 .... PatDobbs 4 — 42
(R Hannon) *tight of room 2f out: a towards rr* — **9/1**^{3}

9 *1 ¼* **Fongalong** 2-8-1 .... EdwardCreighton(3) 1 — 35
(Tom Dascombe) *s.i.s: a towards rr* — **28/1**

04 **10** *nk* **Spirit Rising**^{19} [2072] 2-8-4 .... GregFairley(5) 5 — 39
(J M Bradley) *s.i.s: sn mid-div: wknd over 1f out* — **50/1**

11 *3 ½* **The Light Fandango** 2-8-11 .... AdrianMcCarthy 6 — 29
(R A Harris) *mid-div: rdn 3f out: steadily fdd* — **25/1**

61.59 secs (-0.91) **Going Correction** -0.25s/f (Firm) — 11 Ran SP% **119.7**
Speed ratings (Par 91):97,93,88,83,81 81,80,78,76,75 70
CSF £4.11 TOTE £3.30: £1.20, £1.10, £15.20; EX 5.70 Trifecta £103.00 Part won. Pool: £145.10 - 0.20 winning units..
Owner B McNicholas & M Feehan **Bred** Paul Hardy **Trained** Upper Lambourn, Berks

FOCUS
This was probably just a modest juvenile maiden, but the form looks sound rated through the runner-up, and the winner did the job in good style.

NOTEBOOK
Southandwest(IRE), runner-up on debut a fortnight previously, never saw another rival from the front and duly went one better on this drop to the minimum trip. He is clearly progressive and, with his versatility as regards trip sure to be of advantage, he looks capable of rating higher before the season's end. (op 6-4 tchd 5-2 in places)
Lipocco, whose two previous outings have been over course and distance and was very well backed for this, again managed to find one too good, yet appeared to do nothing wrong in defeat. He is now eligible for nursery mark, and was a clear second-best this time, but he may just be ready to tackle a sixth furlong now. (op 5-4)
Hester Brook(IRE), who lost all chance with a slow start on debut 16 days previously, broke much better this time and posted a sound effort in defeat as a result. She can build on this and looks the type to find her feet when the nurseries begin.
Star Strider ultimately paid for using up too much energy in trying to recover from a sluggish start. This was still an improved effort, however, and this well-related colt should come on again for the experience. Another furlong is also sure to be to his liking in due course. (op 18-1 tchd 12-1)

2632 BATHWICK TYRES (S) STKS — 5f 161y
3:20 (3:21) (Class 6) 3-Y-O+ — £2,266 (£674; £337; £168) Stalls Low

Form — RPR

2055 **1** **Diamond Josh**^{12} [2288] 4-8-13 58 .... StephenDonohoe(5) 5 — 60
(P D Evans) *chsd ldrs: outpcd over 3f out: r.o strly fnl f: led fnl strides* — **4/1**^{1}

1040 **2** *½* **Chantelle's Dream**^{5} [2494] 4-8-12 48 .... SophieDoyle(7) 9 — 59
(Ms J S Doyle) *prom: led over 2f out: sn rdn: edgd lft ins fnl f: ct fnl strides* — **16/1**

-040 **3** *½* **Xaar Breeze**^{5} [2494] 3-8-6 36 .... FrancisFerris 10 — 49
(Mrs P Townsley) *s.i.s: bhd: swtchd rt and hdwy 2f out: styd on wl fnl f: wnt 3rd fnl strides: nrst fin* — **66/1**

0005 **4** *½* **Madrasee**^{10} [2347] 8-8-10 46 .... AmirQuinn(3) 12 — 50
(P G Murphy) *bhd: hdwy over 3f out: sn rdn: styd on fnl f* — **16/1**

0000 **5** *¾* **Snow Wolf**^{2} [2571] 5-8-13 54 .... (p) GregFairley(5) 7 — 52
(J M Bradley) *chsd ldrs: rdn 2f out: wnt 2nd briefly jst ins fnl f: no ex cl home* — **6/1**^{3}

0201 **6** *¾* **Mirasol Princess**^{10} [2347] 5-8-12 50 .... JamesMillman(7) 13 — 51
(D K Ivory) *bhd: hdwy over 2f out: sn rdn: kpt on same pce* — **5/1**^{2}

0-00 **7** *2* **Ballybunion (IRE)**^{2} [2571] 7-9-4 60 .... AdrianMcCarthy 6 — 43
(R A Harris) *sn led: rdn and hdd over 2f out: one pce fnl f* — **4/1**^{1}

-020 **8** *nk* **Von Wessex**^{10} [2347] 4-8-11 50 .... LiamJones(7) 11 — 42
(W G M Turner) *nvr bttr than mid-div* — **12/1**

00-0 **9** *hd* **Ms Polly Garter**^{45} [1413] 4-8-6 35 .... BarrySavage(7) 4 — 37
(J M Bradley) *towards rr: rdn 3f out: hdwy 2f out: no further imp fnl f* — **100/1**

6065 **10** *1* **Chorus Beauty**^{7} [2431] 5-8-6 38 .... MarkCoumbe(7) 16 — 34
(N I M Rossiter) *s.i.s: bhd: sme late prog: n.d* — **50/1**

2200 **11** *¾* **He's A Rocket (IRE)**^{9} [2376] 5-9-4 50 .... (b) DarrenWilliams 2 — 36
(K R Burke) *chsd ldrs: rdn over 3f out: wknd fnl f* — **7/1**

0-05 **12** *2 ½* **Weet Watchers**^{13} [2260] 6-8-13 36 .... StephanieHollinshead(5) 8 — 28
(T Wall) *mid-div tl over 1f out* — **66/1**

0-05 **13** *6* **Dolce Maria (IRE)**^{117} [466] 3-8-6 47 .... (t) HayleyTurner 14 — —
(M R Bosley) *mid-div on outer: bhd fnl 2f* — **33/1**

0600 **14** *1 ½* **Baytown Valentina**^{12} [2288] 3-8-7 42 ow1 .... (v) FergusSweeney 3 — —
(R Brotherton) *mid-div tl wknd 2f out* — **80/1**

4200 **15** *10* **In Fashion**^{15} [2190] 3-8-6 46 .... (b^{1}) JimCrowley 1 — —
(R J Hodges) *chsd ldrs tl wknd over 2f out* — **50/1**

-000 **16** *7* **Kiss The Rain**^{131} [315] 6-8-13 41 .... (b) AdrianTNicholls 15 — —
(R Brotherton) *chsd ldrs on outer tl wknd 2f out* — **20/1**

1m 10.54s (-0.66) **Going Correction** -0.25s/f (Firm)
WFA 3 from 4yo+ 7lb — 16 Ran SP% **119.7**
Speed ratings (Par 101):94,93,92,92,91 90,87,86,86,85 84,81,73,71,57 48
CSF £66.47 TOTE £5.50: £2.20, £5.20, £15.10; EX 94.30 TRIFECTA Not won..There was no bid for the winner. Madrasee was claimed by Mr Norman Berry for £6,000.
Owner Diamond Racing Ltd **Bred** J W Ford **Trained** Pandy, Abergavenny

FOCUS
A dire sprint, which saw the first six fairly closely covered at the finish, and the form is far from solid.
Ballybunion(IRE) Official explanation: jockey said gelding lost a shoe
Baytown Valentina Official explanation: jockey said filly was hampered 1f out
Kiss The Rain Official explanation: jockey said mare had no more to give

2633 BOB HOUSE MEMORIAL H'CAP — 1m 3f 144y
3:50 (3:51) (Class 5) (0-75,75) 3-Y-O — £3,886 (£1,156; £577; £288) Stalls Low

Form — RPR

5054 **1** **Stellenbosch (USA)**^{8} [2391] 3-8-12 66 .... PatDobbs 4 — 75
(J W Hills) *chsd ldrs: rdn 2f out: styd on to ld 1f out: rdn out* — **16/1**

3012 **2** *¾* **Winds Of Change**^{17} [2124] 3-8-7 66 .... GregFairley(5) 7 — 74+
(M Johnston) *w ldr: rdn to ld 2f out: hdd 1f out: kpt on but no ex cl home* — **3/1**^{2}

00-1 **3** *2* **El Alamein (IRE)**^{2} [2591] 3-8-8 62 6ex .... SebSanders 1 — 67+
(Sir Mark Prescott) *led: rdn and hdd 2f out: rallied and ev ch 1f out: kpt on same pce* — **4/6**^{1}

5043 **4** *4* **Citelle (IRE)**^{14} [2246] 3-8-3 57 .... (t) FrankieMcDonald 2 — 55
(Mrs P N Dutfield) *chsd ldrs: rdn 3f out: one pce fnl 2f* — **25/1**

3220 **5** *3* **Mambo Sun**^{17} [2124] 3-8-4 65 .... KevinGhunowa(7) 3 — 59
(P A Blockley) *in tch: outpcd 3f out: nt a danger after* — **16/1**

3553 **6** *7* **Archimboldo (USA)**^{15} [2209] 3-9-4 75 .... EdwardCreighton(3) 5 — 57
(T Wall) *hld up: short-lived effrt over 2f out* — **25/1**

1465 **7** *6* **Samurai Jack (IRE)**^{8} [2391] 3-8-12 69 .... (t) NelsonDeSouza(3) 6 — 42
(John A Quinn, Ire) *hld up: brief effrt 3f out* — **12/1**^{3}

2m 26.99s (-3.31) **Going Correction** -0.20s/f (Firm) — 7 Ran SP% **112.1**
Speed ratings (Par 99):103,102,101,98,96 91,87
CSF £61.14 TOTE £17.40: £3.90, £1.50; EX 50.90.
Owner Ray Empson, Nick Hubbard, Gary Woodward **Bred** Hermitage Farm Llc **Trained** Upper Lambourn, Berks

FOCUS
A modest three-year-old handicap, run at a solid pace, and the form looks sound for the class.

2634 BATHWICK TYRES FILLIES' H'CAP — 1m 5y
4:25 (4:25) (Class 5) (0-70,70) 3-Y-O+ — £3,886 (£1,156; £577; £288) Stalls Low

Form — RPR

6201 **1** **Night Storm**^{8} [2401] 5-10-0 69 .... SebSanders 1 — 77+
(S Dow) *slowly away: bhd: gd hdwy over 2f out: led wl over 1f out: drifted lft fnl f: pushed out* — **6/4**^{1}

5-30 **2** *1* **Starboard Light**^{15} [2210] 3-8-1 55 .... NelsonDeSouza(3) 7 — 59
(R M Beckett) *led tl 5f out: led again over 2f out: rdn and hdd wl over 1f out : kpt on* — **14/1**

0/04 **3** *1 ½* **Shosolosa (IRE)**^{14} [2248] 4-9-8 63 .... MichaelTebbutt 5 — 65
(B J Meehan) *chsd ldrs: rdn over 2f out: kpt on same pce* — **16/1**

5-20 **4** *2* **Whatatodo**^{17} [2135] 4-8-13 54 .... HayleyTurner 4 — 51
(M L W Bell) *chsd ldrs: rdn over 3f out: one pce fnl 2f* — **7/2**^{3}

054- **5** *1* **Emphasis**^{233} [6120] 3-9-5 70 .... JimCrowley 3 — 63
(Mrs A J Perrett) *s.i.s: racd in 5th: outpcd over 2f out: nvr trbld ldrs* — **7/1**

1-04 **6** *8* **Ignition**^{18} [2113] 4-9-9 64 .... DarrenWilliams 6 — 41
(W M Brisbourne) *prom: led 5f out tl over 2f out: wknd over 1f out* — **10/3**^{2}

1m 38.8s (-2.30) **Going Correction** -0.20s/f (Firm)
WFA 3 from 4yo+ 10lb — 6 Ran SP% **110.3**
Speed ratings (Par 100):103,102,100,98,97 89
CSF £22.59 TOTE £2.20: £1.50, £4.60; EX 15.00.
Owner W Thornton & R E Anderson **Bred** The Lavington Stud **Trained** Epsom, Surrey

FOCUS
A modest fillies handicap, run at a decent pace, and the in-form winner is value for further with the race rated through the placed horses.
Ignition Official explanation: trainer said filly was unsuited by firm ground

2635 BATHWICK TYRES H'CAP — 5f 161y
5:00 (5:00) (Class 4) (0-85,91) 3-Y-O+ £6,309 (£1,888; £944; £472; £235) Stalls Low

Form — RPR

-302 **1** **Devon Flame**^{15} [2189] 7-9-8 79 .... JimCrowley 6 — 86
(R J Hodges) *cl up: rdn 3f out: tk narrow advantage ins fnl f:all out* — **2/1**^{2}

2004 **2** *hd* **Willhewiz**^{4} [2536] 6-9-4 75 .... SebSanders 7 — 81
(M S Saunders) *prom: led over 2f out: rdn and narrowly hdd ins fnl f : kpt on* — **7/1**

6000 **3** *2* **Desperate Dan**^{16} [2173] 5-9-5 83 .... FrankiePickard(7) 5 — 83
(J A Osborne) *hld up: rdn to chse ldrs 2f out: kpt on ins fnl f* — **25/1**

606- **4** *1 ½* **Inch By Inch**^{231} [6161] 7-8-13 73 .... (b) AmirQuinn(3) 3 — 68
(P J Makin) *chsd ldrs: rdn over 3f out: hld whn hmpd ins fnl f : wnt 4th cl home* — **20/1**

2041 **5** *2* **Bluebok**^{7} [2449] 5-9-2 78 .... (t) GregFairley(5) 1 — 66
(J M Bradley) *led for over 2f: sn rdn: wknd ins fnl f* — **7/4**^{1}

0660 **6** *13* **Who's Winning(IRE)**^{9} [2384] 5-9-0 71 .... GeorgeBaker 2 — 17
(B G Powell) *reminders sn after s: prom for 3f: eased ins fnl f* — **4/1**^{3}

1m 10.53s (-0.67) **Going Correction** -0.25s/f (Firm) — 6 Ran SP% **110.8**
Speed ratings (Par 105):94,93,91,89,86 69
CSF £15.56 TOTE £3.50: £2.10, £2.40; EX 13.70.
Owner R J Hodges **Bred** W C Tincknell And Mrs A Tincknell **Trained** Charlton Adam, Somerset

FOCUS
A fair sprint, which saw the first two come clear, and the form appears sound, although not that strong.
Inch By Inch Official explanation: jockey said mare was denied a clear run
Bluebok Official explanation: jockey said gelding had no more to give
Who's Winning(IRE) Official explanation: vet said gelding bled from nose

2636 BATHWICK TYRES LADY RIDERS' H'CAP — 1m 2f 46y
5:35 (5:38) (Class 6) (0-55,55) 4-Y-O+ — £2,810 (£871; £435; £217) Stalls Low

Form — RPR

2436 **1** **Another Con (IRE)**^{89} [684] 5-9-2 38 .... MrsMarieKing(5) 2 — 47
(P A Blockley) *hld up bhd: hdwy 2f out: styd on strly fnl f: led fnl strides* — **16/1**

0060 **2** *1* **Gingko**^{7} [2455] 9-9-11 49 .... MissVGraham(7) 7 — 57
(P R Webber) *towards rr: wnt wd on bnd 4f out: hdwy over 2f out: styd on wl to go 2nd fnl strides* — **9/1**

-022 **3** *nk* **Friends Hope**^{127} [363] 5-10-7 55 .... MissFayeBramley(3) 10 — 62
(P A Blockley) *hld up towards rr: stdy prog on rails fr over 2f out: ev ch ins fnl f: kpt on* — **6/1**^{2}

5466 **4** *½* **Wood Fern (UAE)**^{4} [2522] 6-9-13 44 .... MissEJJones 3 — 50
(W M Brisbourne) *mid-div: hdwy on rails over 3f out: rdn to ld jst ins fnl f: sn hdd: no ex* — **7/1**^{3}

5601 **5** *1 ½* **Diamond Dan (IRE)**^{13} [2262] 4-10-5 53 .... MissEFolkes(3) 14 — 56
(P D Evans) *s.i.s: towards rr: hdwy on outer 5f out: rdn to ld 2f out: hdd ins fnl f: no ex* — **9/2**^{1}

4444 **6** *3* **Queue Up**^{43} [1460] 4-9-7 38 .... MissCHannaford 4 — 35
(A G Newcombe) *chsd ldrs: rdn over 2f out: sn one pce* — **12/1**

1365 **7** *1 ¼* **Milk And Sultana**^{6} [2481] 6-9-12 50 .... MissEJTuck(7) 1 — 45
(G A Ham) *chsd ldrs: rdn and ev ch 2f out: wknd fnl f* — **12/1**

-400 **8** *nk* **Ruling Reef**[25] 1910 4-9-12 **48**.......................... MissAshleighHorton(5) 12 43
(M D I Usher) *chsd ldrs tl lost pl over 5f out: n.d after* **20/1**

20-0 **9** *hd* **Danzare**[103] 596 4-10-5 **55**.. MissVCartmel(5) 9 49
(Mrs A J Hamilton-Fairley) *led tl 2f out: sn one pce* **20/1**

0055 **10** *nk* **Guadiana (GER)**[19] 2070 4-9-5 **39**...........................(v^1) MissLEllison(3) 8 33
(A W Carroll) *towards rr: sme late late prog: n.d* **14/1**

0006 **11** *nk* **Vandal**[6] 2481 6-9-3 **41** ow1.. MrsDButler(7) 6 34
(M Appleby) *nvr bttr than mid-div* **33/1**

5241 **12** *nk* **Opera Knight**[25] 1911 6-10-0 **45**..................................... MrsSBosley 15 37
(A W Carroll) *mid-div: hdwy 5f out: rdn over 2f out: sn btn* **9/2**[1]

3060 **13** *2* **Luciferous (USA)**[10] 2350 4-9-8 **44**....................(v) MissMSowerby(5) 13 33
(P G Murphy) *a towards rr* **11/1**

-603 **14** *9* **Escobar (POL)**[11] 853 5-9-11 **47**........................(p) MrsCThompson(5) 5 19
(Mrs P Townsley) *mid-div tl wknd over 2f out* **16/1**

500- **15** *5* **Knead The Dough**[341] 3401 5-9-2 **40**........................ MissIPickard(7) 11 2
(A E Price) *prom tl wknd 3f out* **50/1**

30/0 **16** *3* **Canni Thinkaar (IRE)**[20] 235 5-9-7 **45**..................(p) MissZoeLilly(7) 16 1
(P Butler) *prom for 4f: bhd fnl 3f* **50/1**

2m 10.78s (-0.22) **Going Correction** -0.20s/f (Firm) **16** Ran SP% **131.7**
Speed ratings (Par 101):92,91,90,90,89 86,85,85,85,85 85,84,83,76,72 69
CSF £157.40 CT £992.03 TOTE £25.60: £4.00, £2.90, £3.30, £1.70; EX 195.90 Trifecta £278.80 Part won. Pool: £392.79 - 0.10 winning units. Place 6 £137.62, Place 5 £47.66.
Owner Market Avenue Racing Club Ltd **Bred** Matthew Tynan **Trained** Lambourn, Berks
FOCUS
A weak event of its type, run at a fair gallop, and the form seems sound rated through the fourth and fifth but should be treated with a degree of caution.
T/Plt: £209.00 to a £1 stake. Pool: £44,526.10. 155.50 winning tickets. T/Qpdt: £94.80 to a £1 stake. Pool: £2,051.50. 16.00 winning tickets. TM

2287 LEICESTER (R-H)
Saturday, June 17

OFFICIAL GOING: Good to firm
Wind: Light, behind Weather: Fine and sunny

2637 E.H. SMITH BUILDERS MERCHANTS FILLIES' H'CAP 5f 218y
6:45 (6:45) (Class 5) (0-70,70) 3-Y-O+ **£5,047** (£1,510; £755; £377; £188) **Stalls** Low

Form RPR

0125 **1** **Pippa's Dancer (IRE)**[14] 2233 4-9-13 **69**........................ RichardMullen 4 79
(W R Muir) *chsd ldrs: rdn to ld over 1f out: r.o* **7/2**[2]

2260 **2** *½* **Riquewihr**[8] 2417 6-10-0 **70**..(p) AlanMunro 6 78
(J S Wainwright) *chsd ldrs: rdn over 1f out: edgd rt ins fnl f: r.o* **11/2**[3]

1643 **3** *shd* **Sweet Pickle**[14] 2248 5-9-7 **63**..(e) EddieAhern 5 71
(J R Boyle) *s.i.s: hld up: hdwy u.p over 1f out: r.o* **6/1**

4500 **4** *1 ¼* **True Magic**[12] 2295 5-9-12 **68**.................................. GrahamGibbons 10 72
(J D Bethell) *s.i.s: sn prom: rdn over 1f out: no ex towards fin* **16/1**

0004 **5** *1* **Pro Tempore**[5] 2494 4-8-9 **51** oh5...................................... ChrisCatlin 9 52
(David Pinder) *chsd ldr: rdn and ev ch over 1f out: wknd wl ins fnl f* **14/1**

-562 **6** *1 ¼* **Witchelle**[8] 2400 5-9-0 **59**... DanielTudhope(3) 7 57
(R Craggs) *led: rdn: hung lft and hdd over 1f out: wknd ins fnl f* **10/3**[1]

0100 **7** *6* **Missperon (IRE)**[102] 608 4-8-11 **58**......................... AndrewMullen(5) 1 38
(K A Ryan) *chsd ldrs over 3f* **12/1**

5003 **8** *2 ½* **Depressed**[23] 1961 4-9-9 **65**...(p) JohnEgan 3 37
(Ernst Oertel) *hld up: hdwy over 2f out: wknd over 1f out* **6/1**

043/ **9** *10* **Scrunch**[708] 3711 5-9-9 **65**..(p) PaulFitzsimons 2 7
(Miss J R Tooth) *s.i.s: sn outpcd* **66/1**

1m 11.05s (-2.15) **Going Correction** -0.325s/f (Firm) **9** Ran SP% **111.0**
Speed ratings (Par 100):101,100,100,98,97 95,87,84,70
CSF £21.69 CT £105.33 TOTE £4.50: £1.20, £2.00, £2.40; EX 21.80.
Owner Perspicacious Punters Racing Club **Bred** Clody Norton And Mrs Con Collins **Trained** Lambourn, Berks
■ Stewards' Enquiry : Eddie Ahern two-day ban: used whip with excessive frequency (Jun 28-29)
FOCUS
A modest fillies' handicap, run at a decent pace, and the form looks fair enough for the class.

2638 LAWSON WEST SOLICITORS MAIDEN FILLIES' STKS 5f 218y
7:15 (7:20) (Class 4) 2-Y-O
£6,232 (£1,866; £933; £467; £233; £117) **Stalls** Low

Form RPR

1 **Hope'N'Charity (USA)** 2-9-0 .... PhilipRobinson 15 81+
(C G Cox) *chsd ldrs: led over 1f out: r.o wl* **16/1**

2 **2** *3* **Baldovina**[7] 2461 2-9-0 .... OscarUrbina 14 69
(M Botti) *dwlt: sn prom: rdn and ev ch over 1f out: sn outpcd* **16/1**

4 **3** *¾* **Capannina**[33] 1737 2-9-0 .... TPQueally 1 66+
(J Noseda) *chsd ldrs: outpcd over 1f out: edgd rt and r.o ins fnl f* **7/2**[2]

332 **4** *¾* **Isobel Rose (IRE)**[10] 2355 2-9-0 .... RichardMullen 5 64
(E A L Dunlop) *chsd ldrs: rdn over 1f out: edgd rt and no ex fnl f* **4/1**[3]

6 **5** *½* **La Quinta (IRE)**[7] 2461 2-9-0 .... ChrisCatlin 2 63
(B J Meehan) *chsd ldr: led 1/2-way: rdn and hdd over 1f out: no ex ins fnl f* **25/1**

6 *¾* **Roclette (USA)** 2-9-0 .... MichaelHills 16 60
(B W Hills) *s.s: hdwy over 1f out: nt trble ldrs* **2/1**[1]

7 *3* **Addictive** 2-9-0 .... GrahamGibbons 3 51
(S C Williams) *mid-div: rdn over 2f out: wknd over 1f out* **20/1**

8 *¾* **Millestan (IRE)** 2-9-0 .... EddieAhern 12 55+
(H R A Cecil) *s.s: hdwy over 2f out: wknd over 1f out* **14/1**

0 **9** *½* **Silver Flame**[22] 1989 2-9-0 .... JohnEgan 9 48
(B J Meehan) *chsd ldrs over 4f* **33/1**

10 *hd* **Bay Of Light** 2-9-0 .... AlanMunro 4 47
(P W Chapple-Hyam) *dwlt: outpcd: styd on ins fnl f: nrst fin* **14/1**

11 *hd* **Xaar Too Busy** 2-9-0 .... RoystonFfrench 13 46
(Mrs A Duffield) *s.s: outpcd: nvr nrr* **66/1**

12 *1 ¾* **Poor Nelly** 2-9-0 .... TQuinn 6 41
(J L Dunlop) *mid-div: wknd 1/2-way* **33/1**

13 *nk* **Perfect Style (IRE)** 2-9-0 .... FergusSweeney 7 46+
(M Blanshard) *chsd ldrs over 3f* **66/1**

14 *nk* **Tranquility** 2-9-0 .... JimmyQuinn 10 39
(J Pearce) *s.s: sn prom: wknd over 1f out* **25/1**

15 *1 ¼* **Hemispear** 2-9-0 .... PaulFitzsimons 11 36
(Miss J R Tooth) *led to 1/2-way: wknd wl over 1f out* **100/1**

16 *¾* **Astroangel** 2-8-11 .... SaleemGolam(3) 8 33
(M H Tompkins) *s.i.s: outpcd* **66/1**

1m 11.86s (-1.34) **Going Correction** -0.325s/f (Firm) **16** Ran SP% **124.5**
Speed ratings (Par 92):95,91,90,89,88 87,83,82,81,81 81,78,78,78,76 75
CSF £233.48 TOTE £20.60: £5.90, £3.50, £2.00; EX 417.70.
Owner S R Hope And S W Barrow **Bred** D Brown And Lendy Brown **Trained** Lambourn, Berks
FOCUS
A fair juvenile fillies' maiden, run at a solid pace, and it produced a taking debut winner. The form should work out.
NOTEBOOK
Hope'N'Charity(USA) ♦, who has a North American pedigree and whose dam is closely related to such top-class performers as Agnes World and Hishi Akebono, got her career off to a perfect start with a taking success. She clearly knew her job as she was handy from the start, stayed every yard of this trip, and is entitled to improve for the experience. It will be interesting to see where she is pitched in for her next assignment as she looks capable of rating plenty higher before the season's end.
Baldovina confirmed the promise of her recent Wolverhampton debut with another solid effort in defeat. Granted she had the advantage of previous experience this time, but she has done little wrong in her two outings to date, and certainly did enough to suggest she can find a race in the coming weeks. In the longer term, however, a longer trip is sure to suit. (op 22-1)
Capannina, whose Windsor debut effort last time has worked out particularly well, proved relatively easy to back on this step-up in trip and again left the impression the experience was needed. She saw out the longer trip well and will no doubt be placed to strike during the summer. (op 10-3 tchd 4-1)
Isobel Rose(IRE), popular in the betting ring on this first attempt at a sixth furlong, ran below her recent level in defeat and was well held. This was the first occasion she has finished out of the frame in her four career starts. (op 13-2)
La Quinta(IRE), behind the runner-up on debut at Wolverhampton a week previously, was found wanting approaching the final furlong yet still posted an improved effort all the same. She is likely to do better as she becomes more streetwise.
Roclette(USA), a $250,000 purchase related to several winners at up to a mile, must have been giving all the right signs at home as she was a popular choice in the betting ahead of this racecourse debut. However, she spoilt any chance she may have had by losing ground with a sluggish start and never seriously threatened thereafter. Improvement can now be expected. Official explanation: jockey said filly was slowly away (tchd 15-8, 7-4 and 9-4 in places)
Bay Of Light, whose dam was a ten-furlong winner at three yet has herself produced winning sprinters, proved clueless at the start and was doing all of her best work when the race was over. She will most likely come into her own when eligible for a handicap mark and upped in trip in due course. (op 12-1)

2639 CASTLES PEUGEOT 207 H'CAP 5f 2y
7:45 (7:47) (Class 3) (0-95,90) 3-Y-O
£11,217 (£3,358; £1,679; £840; £419; £210) **Stalls** Low

Form RPR

3020 **1** **Stoneacre Lad (IRE)**[4] 2521 3-9-2 **85**....................(b) RobbieFitzpatrick 1 93
(Peter Grayson) *s.i.s: outpcd: racd alone stands' side: hdwy over 1f out : r.o to ld towards fin* **14/1**

0-20 **2** *1 ¾* **Fisola (IRE)**[11] 2329 3-8-8 **77**... PhilipRobinson 3 79
(C G Cox) *wnt rt s: racd centre: chsd ldrs: rdn and hung rt over 1f out: led ins fnl f: hdd towards fin: 1st of 10 in gp* **10/1**

0000 **3** *½* **Brandywell Boy (IRE)**[11] 2329 3-8-10 **79**.............................(b) TQuinn 2 79
(D J S Ffrench Davis) *racd centre: chsd ldrs: rdn over 1f out: r.o: 2nd of 10 in gp* **28/1**

-014 **4** *shd* **Moorhouse Lad**[10] 2363 3-8-12 **81**................................... ShaneKelly 10 81
(G Woodward) *led centre to 1/2-way: led over 1f out: hdd and unable qckn ins fnl f: 3rd of 10 in gp* **11/1**

1-11 **5** *shd* **Terentia**[26] 1900 3-9-6 **89**... RichardMullen 9 88
(E S McMahon) *racd centre: chsd ldrs: rdn over 1f out: r.o: 4th of 10 in gp* **5/1**[2]

1-4 **6** *nk* **Bajan Parkes**[21] 2014 3-9-1 **84**.................................... FergusSweeney 7 82+
(H Candy) *hmpd s and sn outpcd: racd centre: r.o ins fnl f : nt trble ldrs: 5th of 10 in gp* **3/1**[1]

-620 **7** *hd* **Grazeon Gold Blend**[16] 2168 3-9-2 **85**.................(v^1) GrahamGibbons 4 83
(J J Quinn) *hmpd s: racd center: chsd ldrs: rdn over 1f out: styd on same pce ins fnl f: 6th of 10 in gp* **18/1**

6110 **8** *nk* **Don't Tell Sue**[11] 2329 3-9-2 **85**...................................... MichaelHills 11 82
(B W Hills) *racd centre: chsd ldr tl led 1/2-way: rdn: hung rt and hdd over 1f out: no ex ins fnl f: 7th of 10 in gp* **15/2**[3]

10-0 **9** *nk* **Qusoor (IRE)**[58] 1091 3-9-4 **87**... EddieAhern 8 83
(J L Dunlop) *racd centre: chsd ldrs: rdn over 1f out: styd on same pce ins fnl f: 8th of 10 in gp* **16/1**

-546 **10** *hd* **Brunelleschi**[11] 2329 3-8-6 **75**..(v) ChrisCatlin 6 70
(P L Gilligan) *racd centre: hmpd s: chsd ldrs: outpcd 1/2-way: r.o ins fnl f: 9th of 10 in gp* **16/1**

3621 **11** *2* **Phantom Whisper**[11] 2329 3-9-7 **90**.................................... AlanMunro 5 78
(B R Millman) *hmpd s: racd centre: outpcd: last of 10 in gp* **5/1**[2]

58.86 secs (-2.04) **Going Correction** -0.325s/f (Firm) **11** Ran SP% **114.7**
Speed ratings (Par 103):103,100,99,99,99 98,98,97,97,97 93
CSF £143.04 CT £2384.24 TOTE £12.20: £2.80, £3.30, £11.10; EX 155.60.
Owner Richard Teatum **Bred** Mrs Annie Hughes **Trained** Formby, Lancs
FOCUS
A decent enough sprint for the class, but it produced an unsatisfactory result, as several were hampered at the start and the winner raced alone against the stands' side rail. The race is rated around the placed horses.
NOTEBOOK
Stoneacre Lad(IRE), who lost his chance at the start at Chester four days previously, missed the break and struggled to go the early pace, but his rider's decision to stay stands' side paid great dividends, and he ultmately ran out a ready winner. He may well have been flattered by this, but it still proved him capable on his day, and it was his first success to date on turf. (op 12-1)
Fisola(IRE) came out on top of the remaining ten who raced down the middle of the track and, reversing recent Windsor form with a number of rivals, she showed her true colours with a much-improved effort. She remains lightly-raced, but is likely to edge back up in the weights again after this. (op 12-1)
Brandywell Boy(IRE) showed much his best form for quite some time and has slipped back to a fair mark now. On this evidence he is running back into form now and could build on this. (op 33-1)
Moorhouse Lad ran a solid race in defeat, back over his optimum trip, but ultimately looked to go off too fast for his own good. He is developing into a consistent sprinter. (op 12-1)
Terentia, bidding for her fourth consecutive success, had her chance yet was eventually found out by her latest 9lb hike in the weights. This was the quickest ground she has raced on to date and she may be capable of getting closer from this mark when reverting to an easier surface. (tchd 11-2)
Bajan Parkes, having his first outing over the minimum trip, was done no favours at the start and, by the time he fully recovered his momentum, the race was all but over. He is well worth another chance. (op 5-2)
Don't Tell Sue, who lost all chance at the start at Windsor last time, had every chance on this occasion and it looks as if the Handicapper now has his measure. (op 8-1)
Phantom Whisper, raised 7lb for resuming winning ways at Windsor 11 days previously, was another who got hampered at the start and is most probably best off forgiven this form. (op 6-1 tchd 9-2)

2640 SPORTINGCHRONICLE.COM H'CAP 1m 1f 218y

8:15 (8:16) (Class 5) (0-75,81) 4-Y-0+ **£5,362** (£1,604; £802; £401; £199) **Stalls** High

Form RPR

-230 **1** **Snowed Under**[19] 2088 5-9-5 **73** TQuinn 2 88
(J D Bethell) *chsd ldrs: led over 7f out: rdn clr fnl f* **7/2**[1]

0051 **2** 3 ½ **Billy One Punch**[5] 2499 4-8-8 **62** 5ex AlanMunro 8 70
(G G Margarson) *led: plld hrd: stdd and hdd over 7f out: chsd wnr 2f out: sn rdn and edgd rt: styd on same pce* **4/1**[2]

4543 **3** 1 **Silverhay**[3] 2540 5-9-2 **70** (p) PhillipMakin 11 76
(T D Barron) *chsd ldrs. rdn over 2f out: styd on same pce appr fnl f* **9/2**[3]

5101 **4** 1 ¾ **Secretary General (IRE)**[10] 2351 5-9-13 **81** EddieAhern 10 84
(P F I Cole) *dwlt: hdwy over 8f out: outpcd over 2f out: nt clr run over 1f out: n.d after* **9/2**[3]

50-0 **5** hd **Our Teddy (IRE)**[10] 2351 6-9-3 **71** RobbieFitzpatrick 7 73
(P A Blockley) *hld up: hdwy u.p over 1f out: nvr trbld ldrs* **33/1**

-000 **6** shd **Magic Sting**[19] 2079 5-9-7 **75** MickyFenton 1 77
(M L W Bell) *hld up in tch: rdn over 2f out: styd on same pce appr fnl f* **14/1**

6-35 **7** ¾ **Barbirolli**[17] 2150 4-8-9 **63** ShaneKelly 4 64
(W M Brisbourne) *hld up: effrt over 2f out: n.d* **14/1**

0025 **8** 1 ¼ **Voice Mail**[6] 2482 7-9-4 **72** (v) ChrisCatlin 3 70
(A M Balding) *hld up: rdn over 2f out: n.d* **14/1**

-000 **9** 5 **Bolton Hall (IRE)**[12] 2299 4-8-12 **66** TonyHamilton 5 55
(R A Fahey) *chsd ldrs tl rdn and wknd over 1f out* **14/1**

U0-3 **10** nk **Chapter (IRE)**[10] 2351 4-9-2 **70** PatDobbs 6 58
(Mrs A L M King) *hld up: rdn over 2f out: sn wknd* **16/1**

2m 4.04s (-4.26) **Going Correction** -0.325s/f (Firm) 10 Ran SP% **114.1**
Speed ratings (Par 103):104,101,100,99,98 98,98,97,93,92
CSF £16.95 CT £62.75 TOTE £4.30: £1.90, £1.50, £2.00; EX 21.70.
Owner Mrs G Fane **Bred** Mrs G Fane **Trained** Middleham Moor, N Yorks

FOCUS
A fair handicap, run at a strong early pace, and the form looks solid for the class.
Secretary General(IRE) Official explanation: jockey said gelding missed the break

2641 POTTERS CARPETS AND KITCHENS H'CAP 1m 60y

8:45 (8:45) (Class 6) (0-60,60) 3-Y-0+ **£3,238** (£963; £481; £240) **Stalls** High

Form RPR

2124 **1** **Magic Warrior**[32] 1753 6-9-7 **53** PatDobbs 14 61
(J C Fox) *chsd ldrs: rdn over 1f out: r.o to ld wl ins fnl f* **12/1**

2-04 **2** 1 **Spanish Law**[16] 2165 4-9-7 **53** (b) PhillipMakin 3 59
(M Dods) *chsd ldr: led 3f out: rdn over 1f out: hdd wl ins fnl f* **8/1**

5052 **3** hd **Foolish Groom**[18] 2098 5-9-12 **58** (v) FergusSweeney 7 64
(R Hollinshead) *hld up: hdwy over 2f out: r.o* **11/2**[1]

0113 **4** ½ **Shrine Mountain (USA)**[12] 2291 4-9-7 **53** (v) RichardMullen 2 57
(J R Holt) *dwlt: rcvrd to ld 7f out: hdd 3f out: rdn and ev ch fr over 1f out tl no ex wl ins fnl f* **9/1**

-001 **5** nk **Leighton Buzzard**[12] 2286 4-9-11 **60** DanielTudhope(3) 13 64+
(Mrs A Duffield) *hld up: hdwy over 1f out: nt rch ldrs* **11/2**[1]

205U **6** nk **Grande Terre (IRE)**[12] 2286 5-9-11 **57** TonyHamilton 11 60
(R A Fahey) *hld up: hdwy over 1f out: styd on same pce towards fin* **11/1**

1-00 **7** 1 ¾ **Ellens Princess (IRE)**[8] 2418 4-9-5 **54** DNolan(3) 8 53
(J S Wainwright) *hld up: hdwy over 1f out: nt rch ldrs* **50/1**

6350 **8** shd **Choristar**[50] 1276 5-9-4 **50** DaleGibson 6 49
(J Mackie) *hld up: hdwy over 1f out: nt rch ldrs* **20/1**

6361 **9** ½ **Peephole**[29] 1829 3-9-3 **59** MickyFenton 12 54
(A Bailey) *led 1f: chsd ldrs: rdn over 1f out: wknd ins fnl f* **16/1**

-002 **10** ¾ **Credential**[12] 2286 4-9-5 **56** AndrewElliott(5) 10 52
(John A Harris) *prom: rdn over 2f out: n.m.r and wknd ins fnl f* **7/1**[3]

30-4 **11** ¾ **Balearic Star (IRE)**[11] 2327 5-9-3 **56** JamesMillman(7) 5 50
(B R Millman) *hld up: swtchd rt and hdwy over 1f out: n.d* **13/2**[2]

3605 **12** 7 **Motu (IRE)**[3] 2541 5-9-0 **49** (v) PatrickMathers(3) 4 27
(I W McInnes) *hld up: a in rr* **9/1**

0/00 **13** 3 **Lawood (IRE)**[31] 1772 6-10-0 **60** (v) VinceSlattery 1 31
(L P Grassick) *chsd ldrs: rdn over 3f out: wknd 2f out* **66/1**

0-40 **14** 5 **Zantero**[18] 2112 4-9-1 **47** RobbieFitzpatrick 9 7
(W M Brisbourne) *s.i.s: hld up: plld hrd: rn wd bnd 1/2-way: wknd over 3f out* **66/1**

1m 44.38s (-0.92) **Going Correction** -0.325s/f (Firm)
WFA 3 from 4yo+ 10lb 14 Ran SP% **119.3**
Speed ratings (Par 101):91,90,89,89,89 88,86,86,86,85 84,77,74,69
CSF £101.71 CT £609.77 TOTE £19.90: £5.50, £4.20, £3.30; EX 119.10.
Owner Miss H J Flower **Bred** Patrick Eddery Ltd **Trained** Collingbourne Ducis, Wilts

FOCUS
A moderate winning time for the grade and the form is just ordinary with the third the best guide.
Magic Warrior Official explanation: jockey said gelding slipped on bend

2642 SANDICLIFFE MOTOR GROUP H'CAP 7f 9y

9:15 (9:16) (Class 4) (0-80,79) 3-Y-0

£6,232 (£1,866; £933; £467; £233; £117) **Stalls** Low

Form RPR

06-0 **1** **Lyrical Sound (IRE)**[52] 1241 3-9-1 **73** MichaelHills 5 82+
(B W Hills) *racd centre: s.i.s: outpcd: hdwy u.p over 1f out: r.o to ld wl ins fnl f* **10/1**

4652 **2** 1 **Creative Mind (IRE)**[17] 2126 3-9-5 **77** RichardMullen 11 83
(E J O'Neill) *led centre: overall ldr 3f out: rdn and edgd rt over 1f out: hdd wl ins fnl f* **15/2**[3]

-602 **3** 2 ½ **Dune Melody (IRE)**[23] 1954 3-9-7 **79** JohnEgan 10 79
(J S Moore) *racd centre: hld up in tch: rdn over 1f out: styd on same pce ins fnl f* **16/1**

4035 **4** ½ **Bathwick Alice**[19] 2087 3-8-6 **71** JamesMillman(7) 2 69
(B R Millman) *racd stands' side: led that duo and overall ldr over 4f out: hdd 3f out: hung rt fr over 1f out: styd on* **16/1**

10-0 **5** ½ **Cinematic (IRE)**[29] 1828 3-9-4 **79** SaleemGolam(3) 9 76
(M H Tompkins) *racd centre: hld up in tch: plld hrd: rdn over 1f out: styd on same pce* **17/2**

-052 **6** 1 **Mister Benedictine**[15] 2205 3-9-6 **78** EddieAhern 4 73+
(W R Muir) *racd centre: hld up in tch: rdn over 1f out: styng on same pce whn nt clr run ins fnl f* **5/2**[1]

0-13 **7** 1 ½ **Lavenham (IRE)**[28] 1843 3-9-5 **77** PatDobbs 7 67
(R Hannon) *racd centre: s.s: hld up: rdn over 1f out: nt trble ldrs* **5/1**[2]

24-6 **8** 3 ½ **Woodcote Place**[28] 1845 3-8-13 **71** AlanMunro 8 52
(P R Chamings) *dwlt and hmpd s: racd centre: plld hrd and sn prom: wknd over 1f out* **15/2**[3]

16 **9** 4 **La Matanza**[10] 2359 3-9-1 **76** BenSwarbrick(3) 1 47
(T D Barron) *led stands' side and overall ldr: hdd over 4f out: wknd over 1f out* **11/1**

0-44 **10** 1 **Tora Petcha (IRE)**[16] 2163 3-9-3 **75** GrahamGibbons 6 43
(R Hollinshead) *racd centre: chsd ldrs over 4f* **14/1**

1m 24.34s (-1.76) **Going Correction** -0.325s/f (Firm) 10 Ran SP% **115.1**
Speed ratings (Par 101):97,95,93,92,91 90,89,85,80,79
CSF £81.76 CT £1219.98 TOTE £12.90: £2.80, £1.70, £2.70; EX 70.90 Place 6 £1,508.21, Place 5 £829.94.
Owner Gryffindor (www.racingtours.co.uk) **Bred** Musaid Abo Salim **Trained** Lambourn, Berks

FOCUS
A fair three-year-old handicap, run at a decent early pace, and the form looks sound enough rated through the runner-up.
T/Plt: £1,383.20 to a £1 stake. Pool: £46,138.55. 24.35 winning tickets. T/Qpdt: £244.20 to a £1 stake. Pool: £3,003.80. 9.10 winning tickets. CR

[2572] LINGFIELD (L-H)

Saturday, June 17

OFFICIAL GOING: Turf course - good to firm; all-weather - standard
Wind: Nil Weather: Sunny and warm

2643 PREMIER PENSIONS MANAGEMENT CONSULTANCY MEDIAN AUCTION MAIDEN FILLIES' STKS 5f

6:35 (6:36) (Class 6) 2-Y-0 **£3,238** (£963; £481; £240) **Stalls** High

Form RPR

466 **1** **Autumn Storm**[25] 1922 2-9-0 StephenCarson 7 60
(R Ingram) *racd against nr side rail: mde most: rdn over 1f out: kpt on wl fnl f* **66/1**

2 ¾ **Centreboard (USA)** 2-9-0 SteveDrowne 4 57+
(R Charlton) *trckd ldrs: hanging lft fr 2f out and rn green: effrt over 1f out : nt qckn and hld last 100yds* **4/6**[1]

6 **3** hd **Shreddy Shrimpster**[10] 2354 2-8-9 DerekNolan(5) 3 57
(M J Wallace) *w wnr: rdn 2f out: edgd rt over 1f out: no ex last 150yds* **25/1**

00 **4** 2 ½ **Sunstroke (IRE)**[44] 1429 2-8-9 JerryO'Dwyer(5) 5 48
(M G Quinlan) *chsd ldrs: rdn 3f out: outpcd wl over 1f out: n.d after: uns rdr after fin* **50/1**

202 **5** ½ **Fly Time**[6] 2478 2-9-0 SamHitchcott 1 46
(M R Channon) *dwlt: sn chsd ldrs: rdn 1/2-way: wknd jst over 1f out* **9/4**[2]

6 1 ¼ **Rowan River** 2-9-0 PaulDoe 6 41
(M H Tompkins) *s.v.s: rn green and bhd: nvr a factor* **20/1**

6434 **7** 3 **She Wont Wait**[36] 1639 2-8-9 MarcHalford(5) 2 30
(T M Jones) *dwlt: racd on outer: nvr on terms w ldrs: wknd over 1f out* **14/1**[3]

58.20 secs (-0.74) **Going Correction** -0.35s/f (Firm) 7 Ran SP% **109.5**
Speed ratings (Par 88):91,89,89,85,84 82,77
CSF £104.98 TOTE £54.50: £13.40, £1.20; EX 129.30.
Owner Coyne, O'Connell, Plowman **Bred** Llety Stud **Trained** Epsom, Surrey

FOCUS
A shock result with Autumn Storm making all on the stands' rail to deny the inexperienced favourite. The form is difficult to rate with confidence at this stage.

NOTEBOOK
Autumn Storm had shown only modest form in three attempts on the All-Weather, but the switch to turf was clearly key for the filly and she made the most of her stands' rail draw. The hot favourite would no doubt have won but for running green, but she stuck on well under pressure and fully deserved the win. Nurseries are likely to present her with her best chance of winning again, but that does depend on what sort of mark she is given. (op 50-1)
Centreboard(USA), a non-runner because of firm ground the previous week, was allowed to take her chance on this surface and was rightly made a short-priced favourite in what looked a weak contest. However, she showed distinct signs of greenness and was hanging on the ground, in the end proving unable to get by the winner. She should find a maiden on this evidence and improve for a slower surface, but it remains to be seen how good she is. Official explanation: jockey said filly ran very green (op 4-5 tchd 5-6 in places)
Shreddy Shrimpster stepped up on her debut effort, showing a lot of speed, and she will be qualified for handicaps after one more outing. (op 20-1 tchd 18-1)
Sunstroke(IRE) has gradually progressed with each run and she is another for whom modest nurseries later in the season will represent her best winning chance.
Fly Time came into this as the one to beat, having twice finished second in three previous attempts, but she was unable to reproduce either of those efforts and looks one to have reservations about. (op 15-8 tchd 5-2)
Rowan River, whose stable's juveniles often benefit from a run, was too green to do herself any real justice and could never get into it. It is likely, however, that she will improve with time and distance. (op 25-1)
She Wont Wait is well exposed and may need dropping in grade. (op 16-1)

2644 PREMIER PENSIONS MANAGEMENT ACTUARIAL H'CAP 6f

7:05 (7:06) (Class 6) (0-65,64) 3-Y-0 **£3,071** (£906; £453) **Stalls** High

Form RPR

0043 **1** **Sapphire Storm (IRE)**[15] 2192 3-7-12 **46** oh3 ow1 RoryMoore(5) 7 49
(P T Midgley) *trckd ldrs: rdn and effrt over 1f out: styd on fnl f to ld last 50yds* **11/2**[1]

0-06 **2** hd **Double Valentine**[44] 1433 3-8-8 **51** ow1 SteveDrowne 9 53
(R Ingram) *trckd ldr: led 2f out: drvn and hanging lft fnl f: hdd last 50yds* **8/1**[3]

400- **3** 3 ½ **Make My Dream**[190] 6529 3-9-7 **64** J-PGuillambert 10 56
(J Gallagher) *trckd ldrs: shkn up 2f out: outpcd over 1f out: kpt on ins fnl f* **17/2**

0600 **4** ½ **Batchworth Fleur**[36] 1640 3-8-2 **45** StephenCarson 5 35
(E A Wheeler) *prom: rdn 2f out: fdd fnl f and lost 3rd nr fin* **11/1**

2500 **5** 1 **Welcome Releaf**[17] 2143 3-8-12 **60** DerekNolan(5) 6 47
(G C H Chung) *towards rr: rdn 1/2-way: effrt u.p over 1f out: sn btn* **9/1**

4-60 **6** ¾ **Good Companion (IRE)**[10] 2353 3-9-1 **58** (b[1]) IanMongan 3 43
(J L Dunlop) *swtchd fr outside draw: wl in rr and sn struggling: reminders 4f out: nvr on terms* **11/2**[1]

4300 **7** 4 **Desert Dust**[11] 2318 3-8-7 **50** (p) LPKeniry 12 23
(R M H Cowell) *taken down early: led to 2f out: wknd rapidly* **9/1**

3365 **8** 3 **Shopfitter**[14] 2247 3-7-11 **45** (b) MarcHalford(5) 4 9
(Mrs C A Dunnett) *chsd ldrs on outer: rdn 1/2-way: wknd 2f out: eased over 1f out* **11/1**

0000 **9** 2 **Mamichor**[2] 2576 3-8-12 **55** (be) PaulDoe 8 13
(J R Boyle) *hld up: a in last pair: rdn and no prog over 2f out: wknd* **15/2**[2]

6404 **10** ½ **Master Malarkey**[13] 2263 3-8-5 **48** (b) AdrianMcCarthy 1 5
(Mrs C A Dunnett) *chsd ldrs on outer for 2f: wknd 2f out: sn bhd* **10/1**

6-00 **11** *1 1/2* **Hahns Peak**[2] 2576 3-8-7 **50**.......... SamHitchcott 2 — 2
(Mrs A L M King) *dwlt: hld up in last pair: rdn 1/2-way: wknd 2f out: eased* **25/1**

69.89 secs (-1.78) **Going Correction** -0.35s/f (Firm) 11 Ran SP% **113.8**
Speed ratings (Par 97):97,96,92,91,90 89,83,79,77,76 74
CSF £46.97 CT £368.16 TOTE £4.90: £1.70, £4.00, £5.30; EX 50.40.
Owner J F Wright **Bred** Dermot Farrington **Trained** Westow, N Yorks
■ Stewards' Enquiry : Rory Moore three-day ban: used whip with excessive frequency and without giving filly time to respond (Jul 3-5)

FOCUS
Dire stuff and the form rated through the winner to her plating form with little else solid to go on.
Hahns Peak Official explanation: jockey said gelding was unsuited by good to firm ground

2645 PREMIER PENSIONS MANAGEMENT ADMINISTRATION H'CAP — 7f
7:35 (7:37) (Class 6) (0-65,60) 3-Y-O+ **£3,071** (£906; £453) **Stalls** High

Form — RPR

3630 **1** **Torquemada (IRE)**[17] 2148 5-10-0 **60**.......... PaulDoe 1 — 69
(W Jarvis) *stdd s: hld up wl in rr: stdy prog on outer over 2f out: rdn to ld over 1f out and sn in command: idled and drvn out* **9/1**

6-00 **2** *1/2* **For Life (IRE)**[10] 2348 4-9-7 **53**..........(p) FrankieMcDonald 9 — 61
(A P Jarvis) *taken down early: t.k.h: mde most: hdd and nt qckn over 1f out: kpt on again ins fnl f* **33/1**

6/55 **3** *nk* **Limit Down (IRE)**[33] 1727 5-8-5 **42**.......... RoryMoore(5) 14 — 49
(John Berry) *dwlt: sn pressed ldrs: chal 2f out: nt qckn over 1f out: kpt on ins fnl f* **20/1**

0155 **4** *1 3/4* **Charlie Bear**[11] 2317 5-9-12 **58**.......... AdrianMcCarthy 12 — 60
(Miss Z C Davison) *dwlt: hld up in rr: prog over 2f out: chsd ldrs over 1f out: sn rdn and nt qckn: kpt on same pce* **17/2**

0006 **5** *nk* **Miss Madame (IRE)**[32] 1753 5-9-8 **54**.......... IanMongan 7 — 56
(T G Mills) *dwlt: rcvrd to join ldr 4f out: rdn and outpcd wl over 1f out: plugged on* **11/2**[1]

1252 **6** *nk* **Only If I Laugh**[11] 2317 5-9-2 **55**.......... KevinGhunowa(7) 10 — 56
(M J Attwater) *in tch on outer: rdn and ch 2f out: fdd fnl f* **6/1**[2]

0026 **7** *1 1/2* **Almowj**[4] 2535 3-9-0 **55**.......... RyanMoore 13 — 52+
(C E Brittain) *chsd ldrs for 3f: lost pl and sn pushed along: renewed effrt over 1f out: nt rch ldrs: eased last 75yds* **13/2**[3]

0500 **8** *1 1/2* **Out For A Stroll**[15] 2211 7-9-11 **57**.......... J-PGuillambert 5 — 50
(S C Williams) *racd on outer and sn last: effrt u.p over 2f out: nt pce to rch ldrs* **12/1**

-000 **9** *hd* **Life's A Whirl**[17] 2148 4-9-12 **58**..........(p) SteveDrowne 4 — 50
(Mrs C A Dunnett) *chsd ldrs: rdn over 2f out: wknd over 1f out* **20/1**

5203 **10** *2 1/2* **Rowan Warning**[11] 2317 4-10-0 **60**.......... KerrinMcEvoy 11 — 46
(J R Boyle) *taken down early: wl in rr: shkn up and effrt 2f out: sn no prog and btn* **11/2**[1]

0-30 **11** *5* **King's Charter (USA)**[36] 1652 3-8-9 **50**..........(v[1]) SamHitchcott 15 — 20
(S Dow) *prom on nr side: rdn over 2f out: wknd wl over 1f out* **40/1**

00-0 **12** *5* **Canary Girl**[17] 2146 3-7-9 **43** oh1 ow2.......... LiamJones(7) 8 — —
(Mrs C A Dunnett) *w ldrs for 3f: wknd rapidly* **80/1**

65-0 **13** *8* **Four Pleasure**[16] 2181 4-9-7 **53**.......... LPKeniry 3 — —
(A M Hales) *chsd ldrs on outer to 1/2-way: wknd rapidly* **66/1**

45-0 **14** *13* **One Last Time**[17] 2136 6-8-11 **43**.......... SebSanders 16 — —
(Miss B Sanders) *hld up in tch: rdn over 2f out: wknd rapidly and eased: t.o* **11/2**[1]

1m 22.84s (-1.37) **Going Correction** -0.35s/f (Firm)
WFA 3 from 4yo+ 9lb 14 Ran SP% **119.6**
Speed ratings (Par 101):93,92,92,90,89 89,87,85,85,82 77,71,62,47
CSF £289.05 CT £5810.92 TOTE £12.00: £4.60, £10.10, £9.50; EX 393.60.
Owner Canisbay Bloodstock **Bred** Oak Lodge Stud/hamford Stud/lileagh Fox **Trained** Newmarket, Suffolk

FOCUS
Moderate stuff and a slow time, although the form appears sound enough on paper.
One Last Time Official explanation: trainer said gelding had bled

2646 PREMIER PENSIONS MANAGEMENT TRUSTEESHIP MEDIAN AUCTION MAIDEN STKS — 1m 4f (P)
8:05 (8:05) (Class 6) 3-4-Y-O **£3,238** (£963; £481; £240) **Stalls** Low

Form — RPR

-252 **1** **Chronomatic**[23] 1948 3-8-10 73.......... PaulDoe 5 — 60
(M H Tompkins) *t.k.h: sn settled bhd ldrs: rdn and outpcd over 2f out: r.o over 1f out: led last 100yds* **3/1**[3]

0000 **2** *1 1/4* **It's Basil**[10] 2352 3-8-10 47..........(b) IanMongan 1 — 58
(R M Flower) *cl up: led 3f out: drvn 4 l clr over 1f out: wknd and hdd last 100yds* **25/1**

2 **3** *3/4* **Hernando Royal**[74] 863 3-8-10.......... SteveDrowne 3 — 56
(H Morrison) *restless stalls: s.s: mostly in last pair and nt gng that wl: drvn 4f out: sn outpcd: styd on fnl 2f: nrst fin* **13/8**[1]

3-3 **4** *1 1/2* **Gouranga**[30] 1798 3-8-5.......... LPKeniry 6 — 49
(H Candy) *mostly chsd ldr to 3f out: drvn to chse new ldr 2f out: no imp and btn jst over 1f out* **5/2**[2]

0005 **5** *1 1/4* **Peak Seasons (IRE)**[8] 2415 3-8-10 48.......... AdrianMcCarthy 4 — 52
(W De Best-Turner) *led to 3f out: chsd ldr to 2f out: fdd* **66/1**

0606 **6** *2 1/2* **Ten Commandments (IRE)**[7] 2463 3-8-0 35.......... EmmettStack(5) 2 — 43
(K J Burke) *hld up in tch: outpcd and rdn wl over 2f out: sn no ch* **66/1**

0 **7** *2 1/2* **Gavanello**[33] 1741 3-8-10.......... JimmyFortune 8 — 44
(W R Swinburn) *dwlt: hld up in last: pushed along 4f out: outpcd 3f out: no ch after* **20/1**

50 **8** *9* **Dream Witness (FR)**[10] 2349 3-8-5.......... KerrinMcEvoy 7 — 25
(W R Muir) *hld up: prog 1/2-way: rdn over 4f out: wknd 3f out* **12/1**

2m 35.98s (1.59) **Going Correction** +0.10s/f (Slow) 8 Ran SP% **111.0**
Speed ratings (Par 101):98,97,96,95,94 93,91,85
CSF £68.65 TOTE £3.90: £1.10, £2.50, £1.40; EX 91.30.
Owner Ms C L C Bourke-Jones **Bred** Pigeon House Stud **Trained** Newmarket, Suffolk

FOCUS
A modest maiden run at a sedate gallop and the form looks suspect with banded-class performers close up.
Hernando Royal Official explanation: jockey said colt never travelled

2647 PREMIER PENSIONS MANAGEMENT ADVISER REVIEW H'CAP — 1m 2f (P)
8:35 (8:35) (Class 5) (0-70,70) 4-Y-O+ **£3,238** (£963; £481; £240) **Stalls** Low

Form — RPR

2 **1** **The Fonze (IRE)**[14] 2221 5-7-13 **51** oh4.......... DominicFox(3) 14 — 63+
(Eoin Doyle, Ire) *hld up bhd ldrs: prog 2f out: rdn to ld 1f out: sn in command* **9/2**[1]

3050 **2** *2* **Master'n Commander**[17] 2132 4-8-9 **58**.......... J-PGuillambert 4 — 66
(C A Cyzer) *settled in rr: rdn over 3f out: prog to press ldrs 2f out: outpcd 1f out: styd on to take 2nd last stride* **14/1**

1604 **3** *shd* **Danger Zone**[8] 2401 4-9-6 **69**..........(p) IanMongan 8 — 77
(Mrs A J Perrett) *cl up: effrt over 2f out: hrd rdn to chal 1f out: sn outpcd by wnr: lost 2nd last stride* **13/2**[3]

1/02 **4** *3/4* **Inch Lodge**[10] 2351 4-8-13 **69**.......... ChrisCavanagh(7) 9 — 75
(Miss D Mountain) *racd wd: in tch: prog to trck ldr over 4f out: rdn to ld wl over 1f out: hdd and btn 1f out* **10/1**

4032 **5** *2* **Santando**[23] 1958 6-9-5 **68**..........(b) RyanMoore 5 — 71
(C E Brittain) *led for 2f: chsd ldr to over 4f out: rdn 3f out: cl up u.p 2f out: fdd fnl f* **5/1**[2]

320/ **6** *1* **Sir Laughalot**[484] 5615 6-8-11 **60**.......... KerrinMcEvoy 1 — 61
(Miss E C Lavelle) *t.k.h early: prom: lost pl 3f out: shuffled along and kpt on same pce fr over 1f out* **14/1**

1260 **7** *shd* **Christmas Truce (IRE)**[5] 2499 7-8-8 **62**..........(b) JamesDoyle(5) 2 — 62
(Ms J S Doyle) *rousted along in rr 7f out: rn in snatches after: kpt on u.p fnl 2f: no ch* **16/1**

0000 **8** *1/2* **Connotation**[7] 2464 4-8-13 **62**.......... LPKeniry 3 — 62
(A G Newcombe) *settled rr of main gp: prog on inner wl over 1f out: shkn up and flashed tail ins fnl f: nvr nr ldrs* **33/1**

/004 **9** *9* **Three Welshmen**[13] 1882 5-8-4 **53**.......... FrankieMcDonald 12 — 35
(D Burchell) *prom: rdn and lost pl over 3f out: sn no ch* **25/1**

2000 **10** *3/4* **Almanshood (USA)**[11] 2322 4-9-0 **68**.......... RichardKingscote(5) 6 — 49
(P L Gilligan) *led after 2f: drvn 4f out: hdd wl over 1f out: wknd rapidly and eased fnl f* **25/1**

6005 **11** *15* **Burgundy**[23] 1958 9-9-5 **68**..........(b) GeorgeBaker 7 — 21
(P Mitchell) *dwlt: hld up last of main gp: sme prog on outer 3f out: sn lost tch: t.o* **8/1**

0500 **12** *18* **Kathleen Kennet**[14] 2221 6-8-11 **60**.......... SteveDrowne 13 — —
(Mrs H Sweeting) *rcd v wd: in tch to 1/2-way: t.o over 3f out* **33/1**

-604 **13** *nk* **Mixing**[22] 1987 4-8-5 **61**.......... BRoper(7) 11 — —
(W Jarvis) *rel to r and lft 100yds: t.o thrght* **20/1**

-122 **14** *6* **Molem**[10] 2348 4-9-7 **70**..........(tp) SebSanders 10 — —
(Lady Herries) *hld up in tch: wknd rapidly 4f out: t.o over 2f out: eased* **9/2**[1]

2m 7.18s (-0.61) **Going Correction** +0.10s/f (Slow) 14 Ran SP% **124.1**
Speed ratings (Par 103):106,104,104,103,102 101,101,100,93,93 81,66,66,61
CSF £65.81 CT £417.34 TOTE £5.60: £2.40, £3.30, £1.90; EX 103.20.
Owner J A Dunphy **Bred** Mrs Olivia Farrell **Trained** Mooncoin, Co. Kilkenny
■ Dominic Fox's first winner for over a year.
■ Stewards' Enquiry : J-P Guillambert two-day ban: used whip with excessive force (Jun 28-29)

FOCUS
A modest heat but the race looks sound with the placed horses to form.
Christmas Truce(IRE) Official explanation: jockey said gelding never travelled
Almanshood(USA) Official explanation: jockey said gelding got its tongue over the bit
Burgundy Official explanation: jockey said gelding stopped very quickly
Kathleen Kennet Official explanation: jockey said mare suffered erratic steering problems
Molem Official explanation: trainer had no explanation for the poor form shown

2648 LAURA SARJEANT MEMORIAL H'CAP — 1m (P)
9:05 (9:05) (Class 6) (0-60,60) 3-Y-O **£3,071** (£906; £453) **Stalls** High

Form — RPR

0420 **1** **Nikki Bea (IRE)**[8] 2404 3-9-4 **57**.......... PaulDoe 11 — 64
(Jamie Poulton) *t.k.h: trckd ldr for 3f: styd cl up: effrt to ld over 2f out: hrd rdn over 1f out: hld on wl* **7/2**[2]

3-04 **2** *nk* **Carloman**[16] 2171 3-9-5 **58**.......... SebSanders 2 — 64
(R M Beckett) *s.i.s: hld up: prog over 2f out: hrd rdn and hanging lft over 1f out: hung fire but drvn into 2nd last stride* **7/2**[2]

0542 **3** *shd* **Davidia (IRE)**[4] 2535 3-9-7 **60**.......... JimmyFortune 6 — 66
(S Kirk) *cl up: rdn to chse wnr over 1f out: chal fnl f: nt qckn last 100yds: lost 2nd fnl stride* **9/4**[1]

0502 **4** *1 1/4* **Panic Stations**[15] 2198 3-9-5 **58**.......... HayleyTurner 3 — 61
(M L W Bell) *hld up in tch: chsd ldrs 2f out: n.m.r on inner 1f out: nt qckn after* **11/2**[3]

0-03 **5** *2 1/2* **Hogan's Heroes**[52] 1232 3-9-2 **55**.......... KerrinMcEvoy 12 — 52
(G A Butler) *t.k.h: trckd ldr after 3f: led over 3f out to over 2f out: cl up and n.m.r on inner jst over 1f out: wknd* **10/1**

30-0 **6** *19* **Night Rainbow (IRE)**[139] 234 3-9-7 **60**.......... SteveDrowne 7 — 14
(C Tinkler) *plld hrd early: hld up: wknd rapidly over 2f out: t.o* **33/1**

-355 **7** *1 1/2* **Royal Tavira Girl (IRE)**[51] 1263 3-9-0 **58**.......... JerryO'Dwyer(5) 8 — 8
(M G Quinlan) *sn in rr: rdn 1/2-way: wknd over 3f out: t.o* **16/1**

050 **8** *hd* **Deserted Prince (IRE)**[67] 969 3-8-13 **57**..........(b[1]) DerekNolan(5) 10 — 7
(M J Wallace) *led to over 3f out: gave up and sn t.o* **16/1**

1m 40.78s (1.35) **Going Correction** +0.10s/f (Slow) 8 Ran SP% **114.4**
Speed ratings (Par 97):97,96,96,95,92 73,72,72
CSF £16.21 CT £32.58 TOTE £5.20: £1.40, £1.90, £1.60; EX 22.40 Place 6 £125.09, Place 5 £78.41.
Owner Nikki Beach Partnership **Bred** Dr Paschal Carmody **Trained** Telscombe, E Sussex

FOCUS
A moderately-run affair but sound enough form rated around the first three.
Night Rainbow(IRE) Official explanation: jockey said filly had no more to give
T/Plt: £577.80 to a £1 stake. Pool: £44,328.60. 56.00 winning tickets. T/Qpdt: £62.80 to a £1 stake. Pool: £3,218.20. 37.90 winning tickets. JN

2617 SANDOWN (R-H)
Saturday, June 17

OFFICIAL GOING: Good to firm (firm in places in back straight)
Wind: Slight, across

2649 RBS H'CAP — 7f 16y
2:20 (2:24) (Class 2) (0-100,97) 3-Y-O+
£12,464 (£3,732; £1,866; £934; £466; £234) **Stalls** High

Form — RPR

1216 **1** **Wavertree Warrior (IRE)**[15] 2200 4-9-0 **83**.......... JimmyFortune 9 — 95
(N P Littmoden) *trckd ldr: led wl over 1f out: rdn out and in command fnl f* **5/1**[1]

0411 **2** *1 1/2* **Waterside (IRE)**[8] 2405 7-9-0 **83**.......... RyanMoore 6 — 91
(G L Moore) *a.p: rdn and styd on to go 2nd wl ins fnl f* **5/1**[1]

-010 **3** *3/4* **King's Caprice**[21] 2012 5-9-7 **90**..........(t) DarryllHolland 13 — 96
(J A Geake) *led tl rdn and hung lft wl over 1f out: lost 2nd wl ins fnl f* **17/2**[3]

0631 **4** *1 3/4* **Fiefdom (IRE)**[7] 2443 4-9-1 **87**.......... PatrickMathers(3) 7 — 88
(I W McInnes) *t.k.h in mid-div: styd on one pce ins fnl 2f* **7/1**[2]

0-06 **5** *1/2* **Landucci**[47] 1340 5-8-13 **82**.......... MichaelHills 12 — 82
(J W Hills) *mid-div: styd on one pce fnl 2f* **16/1**

0000 **6** *nk* **Jalamid (IRE)**[21] 2012 4-9-12 **95**..........(t) MartinDwyer 5 — 94
(J H M Gosden) *t.k.h early: hld up: effrt over 2f out: nt qckn* **5/1**[1]

-000 **7** ½ **Sky Crusader**^{15} [2200] 4-9-2 **85** .... RobertHavlin 1 83
(R Ingram) *towards rr: mde sme late hdwy* **11/1**

0-U0 **8** ¾ **Coeur Courageux (FR)**^{29} [1835] 4-10-0 **97** .... TomEaves 11 93
(D Nicholls) *t.k.h: rdn over 3f out: sn btn* **14/1**

6000 **9** 2½ **Moayed**^{20} [2047] 7-8-13 **82** ....(b) KerrinMcEvoy 8 72
(N P Littmoden) *bhd whn n.m.r fr over 2f out: nvr nr to chal* **10/1**

-315 **10** 2 **Will He Wish**^{12} [2289] 10-9-7 **90** .... IanMongan 4 74
(S Gollings) *racd wd: rdn 3f out: sn btn* **14/1**

0-00 **11** 1 **Intoxicating**^{42} [1487] 4-10-0 **97** .... StephenCarson 2 79
(R F Johnson Houghton) *a bhd* **25/1**

05- **12** 1 **Emilio**^{233} 5-9-10 **93** ....(t) FJohansson 10 72
(R A Kvisla) *t.k.h in mid-div: rdn over 2f out: sn wknd* **33/1**

-040 **13** 66 **Guest Connections**^{15} [2205] 3-9-1 **93** .... TedDurcan 3 —
(M R Channon) *rrd up bdly leaving stalls: t.o fr 1/2-way* **25/1**

1m 27.19s (-3.90) **Going Correction** -0.35s/f (Firm)
WFA 3 from 4yo+ 9lb **13** Ran SP% **120.3**
Speed ratings (Par 109):108,106,105,103,102 102,101,101,98,95 94,93,18
CSF £27.87 CT £220.19 TOTE £6.70: £2.20, £2.30, £4.10; EX 16.90 Trifecta £576.50 Pool: £1,055.71 - 1.30 winning units..

Owner Wavertree Racing Partnership C **Bred** Liam Queally **Trained** Newmarket, Suffolk

FOCUS

A fair handicap, but it was not strongly-run and hold-up horses were at a clear disadvantage. The form has been rated through the third.

NOTEBOOK

Wavertree Warrior(IRE), back down in trip, was happier on this more conventional track and gained his third win in five starts. He was always in the first two and won decisively. (op 6-1)

Waterside(IRE) was 3lb higher than when winning at Goodwood earlier in the month and 9lb above the mark off which he won this event two years ago. Delivering another solid effort, he was never far away and moved into second place near the finish. (op 9-2 tchd 11-2)

King's Caprice, down the field in the Victoria Cup on his latest start, tried to make all from his draw against the rail but was unable to repel the winner's challenge. (op 10-1 tchd 12-1 in places)

Fiefdom(IRE), raised 5lb for his win at Lingfield, could never get into the action but this was a race dominated by those who raced prominently. (op 13-2 tchd 6-1)

Landucci, whose last five wins have all come at Brighton, was never able to get in a blow on this first turf outing of the year.

Jalamid(IRE), another 2lb lower, was well backed on this occasion but could never get to the leaders in a race where it paid to be prominent. (op 11-2)

Moayed was short of room when first trying to improve from the back of the field but was in the clear in sufficient time had he been good enough. (op 14-1)

Will He Wish Official explanation: jockey said gelding ran flat

Guest Connections Official explanation: jockey said gelding reared as stalls opened

2650 PADDYPOWERCASINO.COM H'CAP 7f 16y

2:55 (2:58) (Class 3) (0-90,87) 3-Y-O **£8,096** (£2,408; £1,203; £601) **Stalls High**

Form RPR

-460 **1** **Louie Louie (IRE)**^{21} [2033] 3-9-2 **82** .... KerrinMcEvoy 8 89
(N A Callaghan) *a.p: rdn over 1f out: r.o to ld nr fin* **11/2**^{2}

5502 **2** nk **Jimmy The Guesser**^{23} [1963] 3-8-12 **78** .... TedDurcan 10 84
(N P Littmoden) *a.p: drvn and r.o to go 2nd last strides* **14/1**

1 **3** nk **Against The Grain**^{20} [2048] 3-9-4 **84** .... JoeFanning 12 89
(M Johnston) *trckd ldr: rdn and led 2f out: edgd lft run-in: hdd and lost 2nd cl home* **4/1**^{1}

0-05 **4** ½ **Scarlet Flyer (USA)**^{15} [2205] 3-8-9 **75** .... IanMongan 6 79
(G L Moore) *hld up: swtchd rt and hdwy on outside over 2f out: styd on fnl f: nvr nrr* **12/1**

5-20 **5** ½ **Carmenero (GER)**^{15} [2205] 3-9-0 **80** .... RichardMullen 14 83
(W R Muir) *t.k.h in mid-div: kpt on one pce* **16/1**

014 **6** 1¼ **Stanley Goodspeed**^{19} [2087] 3-8-7 **76** ow1........ DeanCorby$^{(3)}$ 15 75
(J W Hills) *mid-div: hdwy on ins over 1f out: n.m.r ins fnl f* **20/1**

0-40 **7** ½ **Tara Too (IRE)**^{15} [2205] 3-9-1 **81** .... EddieAhern 9 79
(D W P Arbuthnot) *trckd ldrs: rdn and wknd 2f out* **16/1**

0-01 **8** 1¼ **Silver Dip**^{12} [2297] 3-9-4 **84** .... MichaelHills 2 79
(B W Hills) *hld up on outside: rdn over 2f out: no further hdwy* **6/1**^{3}

0441 **9** ½ **Ocean Pride (IRE)**^{14} [2232] 3-9-5 **85** ....(b) RyanMoore 3 79
(R Hannon) *slowly away: swtchd to ins: in rr and nvr on terms* **8/1**

431- **10** ¾ **Judraan**^{251} [5752] 3-9-6 **86** ....(t) MartinDwyer 7 78
(M A Jarvis) *t.k.h: prom tl wknd qckly 2f out* **7/1**

0000 **11** shd **Sleeping Storm (IRE)**^{26} [1900] 3-8-1 **74** .... KMay$^{(7)}$ 13 65+
(B J Meehan) *a in rr* **33/1**

535- **12** 1 **Rembrandt Quality (USA)**^{182} [6599] 3-8-10 **76** .... JamieMackay 11 65
(Mrs A J Perrett) *led tl hdd 2f out: rdn and sn wknd* **12/1**

402- **13** 3½ **Blades Girl**^{261} [5570] 3-9-4 **84** .... DO'Donohoe 5 64
(K A Ryan) *veered lft leaving stalls: a bhd* **20/1**

-542 **14** ¾ **Bold Argument (IRE)**^{14} [2247] 3-8-6 **72** .... RobertHavlin 4 50
(Mrs P N Dutfield) *hld up: a bhd* **40/1**

1m 27.8s (-3.29) **Going Correction** -0.35s/f (Firm) **14** Ran SP% **122.0**
Speed ratings (Par 103):104,103,103,102,102 100,100,98,98,97 97,96,92,91
CSF £77.58 CT £348.54 TOTE £6.80: £2.50, £4.30, £1.70; EX 115.10.

Owner Jack Banks Racing **Bred** Mark Commins **Trained** Newmarket, Suffolk

■ Stewards' Enquiry : Ted Durcan caution: careless riding

FOCUS

As in the opener over the same trip, horses trying to come from behind seemed at a disadvantage. The first five were all close to their best, however, and the level of the form looks sound.

NOTEBOOK

Louie Louie(IRE), racing off a career-low mark, was suited by the return to fast ground and got on top near the line. He should not go up too much for this. (op 13-2)

Jimmy The Guesser was 3lb lower than when runner-up on sand last time, his first attempt at this trip. Prominent all the way, he saw out the seven furlongs on this stiff track well. (tchd 16-1)

Against The Grain, unexposed after winning his only start, made a bold bid to follow up but, after going a couple of lengths to the good, he was worn down near the finish. A return to easier ground should suit him and he can land a decent handicap. (op 5-1 tchd 11-2)

Scarlet Flyer(USA) ◆ was staying on stoutly down the outside but the effort was always coming too late. He did best of those trying to come from behind and is running into form.

Carmenero(GER) made progress up the far rail without ever getting to the principals. Official explanation: jockey said gelding suffered interference in running (op 14-1)

Stanley Goodspeed was held when short of room against the rail in the final furlong. This was only his fourth run and there could be a bit more improvement in him.

Ocean Pride(IRE), racing from a 5lb higher mark, could never get into the hunt after going out to his left exiting the stalls but did not do too badly in the end. Official explanation: jockey said colt missed the break (tchd 15-2)

2651 PADDYPOWERPOKER.COM SCURRY STKS (LISTED RACE) 5f 6y

3:25 (3:30) (Class 1) 3-Y-O

£15,898 (£6,025; £3,015; £1,503; £753; £378) **Stalls High**

Form RPR

5150 **1** **Angus Newz**^{7} [2438] 3-8-11 100........ DarryllHolland 2 100
(M Quinn) *hld up: hdwy 2f out: led 1f out: r.o strly* **10/1**

54-0 **2** 2 **Dixie Belle**^{7} [2438] 3-8-11 98........(t) JimmyFortune 5 93
(M G Quinlan) *s.i.s: hdwy 1/2-way: rdn to chse wnr ins fnl f* **12/1**

2406 **3** hd **Gamble In Gold (IRE)**^{21} [2022] 3-8-8 85........ RyanMoore 7 89
(R Hannon) *bhd tl swtchd lft over 1f out: r.o wl fnl f* **12/1**

2-21 **4** ¾ **Leopoldine**^{7} [2445] 3-8-8 73........ EddieAhern 6 87
(H Morrison) *a.p: chsd ldr 2f out tl fdd ins fnl f* **5/1**^{3}

6-05 **5** nk **Clare Hills (IRE)**^{45} [1408] 3-8-11 95........(p) RichardMullen 3 89
(K R Burke) *led tl rdn and hdd 1f out: no ex ins fnl f* **20/1**

0213 **6** 1¾ **Green Park (IRE)**^{21} [2022] 3-8-13 96........ TonyHamilton 4 84
(R A Fahey) *prom tl wknd over 1f out* **4/1**^{2}

143- **7** ½ **Curtail (IRE)**^{228} [6220] 3-9-2 105........ TomEaves 9 85
(I Semple) *s.i.s: outpcd thrght* **6/1**

-102 **8** ¾ **Guto**^{21} [2022] 3-8-13 99........ DO'Donohoe 8 91+
(K A Ryan) *prom on ins: hld whn hmpd ins fnl f* **5/2**^{1}

2141 **9** 2 **Glenviews Youngone (IRE)**^{16} [2168] 3-8-8 83...... RobbieFitzpatrick 10 77+
(Peter Grayson) *hld up on ins making hdwy whn twice hmpd over 1f out: nt rcvr* **12/1**

31-1 **10** ½ **Rare Breed**^{18} [2110] 3-8-13 86........ MickyFenton 1 71
(Mrs L Stubbs) *racd wd: hung rt fr 2f out: sn btn* **16/1**

60.76 secs (-1.45) **Going Correction** -0.175s/f (Firm) **10** Ran SP% **122.3**
Speed ratings (Par 107):104,100,100,99,98 96,95,94,90,90
CSF £129.02 TOTE £13.90: £2.60, £3.40, £3.40; EX 141.90 TRIFECTA Not won..

Owner J G Dooley **Bred** Henry And Mrs Rosemary Moszkowicz **Trained** Newmarket, Suffolk

FOCUS

Not strong form for the grade. The leaders went very quick and the first three came from off the pace. The race has been rated through the principals, with the unexposed fourth a big improver.

NOTEBOOK

Angus Newz, without the usual visor, gained her second win of the season at this level. She does not look straightforward but has a bright turn of foot which was seen to good effect here, and this could be the way to ride her. Official explanation: trainer said, regarding the improved form shown, filly was unsuited last time by the good to firm ground and, though the going was the same here, in his opinion this was better ground than was encountered last time

Dixie Belle was sharper for her recent return to action but the drop to five furlongs for the first time in her career found her out as, after a slow start, she was doing her best work at the end.

Gamble In Gold(IRE), who faced a stiff task at the weights, had to be switched for a run prior to coming home in good style. This was a decent effort. (op 14-1)

Leopoldine, who had plenty on at the weights, did best of those to race prominently from the outset. She is an improving filly but this will not have done her handicap mark any good. (op 13-2)

Clare Hills(IRE) showed decent pace on this drop back in trip but after getting over to the rail she could not hold on inside the last. This was more encouraging.

Guto was already feeling the pinch when he was hampered against the rail and eased inside the last. Official explanation: jockey said gelding was denied a clear run (op 3-1)

Glenviews Youngone(IRE) could never get a gap when trying to improve up the rail and this run should be forgotten. (tchd 14-1)

Rare Breed Official explanation: jockey said gelding hung right

2652 LOMBARD H'CAP 5f 6y

4:00 (4:02) (Class 5) (0-75,75) 3-Y-O **£4,533** (£1,348; £674; £336) **Stalls High**

Form RPR

-044 **1** **Glasshoughton**^{22} [1983] 3-9-3 **71** .... PhillipMakin 9 79
(M Dods) *a.p: led over 1f out: drvn out* **8/1**^{3}

0-00 **2** 1 **Balian**^{18} [2105] 3-8-9 **63** ....(p) IanMongan 3 67
(G L Moore) *bhd: hdwy over 1f out: c through on ins to go 2nd post* **40/1**

5212 **3** shd **Yellow Card**^{7} [2496] 3-9-5 **73** .... KerrinMcEvoy 1 77+
(N A Callaghan) *in rr: hdwy whn short of room 2f out: swtchd rt appr fnl f: chsd wnr ins fnl f tl lost 2nd post* **3/1**^{1}

0031 **4** ½ **Musical Romance (IRE)**^{7} [2433] 3-8-12 **66** ....(b) JimmyFortune 7 74+
(B J Meehan) *s.i.s: hdwy over 1f out: fin fast: nvr nrr* **7/1**^{2}

0050 **5** nk **Gwilym (GER)**^{8} [2410] 3-8-11 **65** .... RobertHavlin 6 66
(D Haydn Jones) *bhd tl mde mod late hdwy* **25/1**

4-04 **6** 1½ **What Do You Know**^{3} [2553] 3-9-7 **75** .... MartinDwyer 11 70
(G A Butler) *prom: chsd ldr 2f out tl started to hang lft: wknd fnl f* **8/1**^{3}

32-0 **7** ½ **Cativo Cavallino**^{161} [60] 3-9-0 **68** .... PaulDoe 4 62
(Jamie Poulton) *hld up: rdn 2f out: sn btn* **66/1**

66-5 **8** 1¾ **Mouchoir**^{49} [1279] 3-9-4 **72** ....(b) EddieAhern 10 59
(P J Makin) *a bhd* **16/1**

00-3 **9** ¾ **Mint**^{10} [2363] 3-9-5 **73** .... TomEaves 5 58
(D W Barker) *chsd ldr to 2f out: sn wknd* **7/1**^{2}

40-2 **10** ¾ **Indian Lady (IRE)**^{15} [2190] 3-8-4 **65** .... RussellKennemore$^{(7)}$ 13 47
(Mrs A L M King) *s.i.s: sn mid-div: wknd 2f out* **9/1**

-001 **11** ¾ **Catspraddle (USA)**^{5} [2511] 3-9-5 **73** 6ex........ RyanMoore 2 52
(R Hannon) *in tch tl rdn and wknd 1/2-way* **7/1**^{2}

-045 **12** 2½ **Supreme Kiss**^{7} [2433] 3-8-7 **61** .... JimmyQuinn 8 31
(Miss B Sanders) *chsd ldrs tl rdn and wknd qckly 1/2-way* **14/1**

-350 **13** nk **Ceredig**^{7} [2433] 3-8-7 **61** ow1........(b^{1}) DarryllHolland 12 30
(W R Muir) *led tl hdd wl over 1f out: wknd qckly* **16/1**

60.98 secs (-1.23) **Going Correction** -0.175s/f (Firm) **13** Ran SP% **120.9**
Speed ratings (Par 99):102,100,100,99,98 96,95,92,91,90 89,85,84
CSF £301.09 CT £1219.92 TOTE £10.20: £4.20, £14.10, £1.70; EX 483.80.

Owner J N Blackburn **Bred** Theakston Stud **Trained** Denton, Co Durham

FOCUS

Fairly ordinary form despite the time comparing well with the previous race. The winner looked fairly exposed and it was a bit messy immediately behind him, with several not enjoying the best of runs.

Yellow Card Official explanation: jockey said gelding was denied a clear run

What Do You Know Official explanation: jockey said gelding hung left

Supreme Kiss Official explanation: jockey said filly hung left

Ceredig Official explanation: jockey said gelding had a breathing problem

2653 COUTTS H'CAP 1m 6f

4:35 (4:35) (Class 4) (0-85,85) 4-Y-O+ **£5,505** (£1,637; £818; £408) **Stalls Centre**

Form RPR

6-61 **1** **Ti Adora (IRE)**^{10} [2357] 4-8-12 **76** .... DarryllHolland 10 82
(P W D'Arcy) *t.k.h: nvr far away: led appr fnl f: rdn: all out* **15/8**^{1}

B-6P **2** nk **Tender Trap (IRE)**^{98} [628] 8-9-4 **82** .... IanMongan 6 88
(T G Mills) *t.k.h: hld up in rr: hdwy over 1f out: squeezed through to go 2nd ins fnl f: jst failed* **9/1**

4-66 **3** 2 **Papeete (GER)**^{7} [2460] 5-8-2 **66** oh1........ JimmyQuinn 3 69
(Miss B Sanders) *led after 3f: rdn and hdd appr fnl f: one pce* **5/2**^{2}

0124 **4** ½ **Maystock**[19] 2067 6-8-6 **70** TedDurcan 1 72
(B G Powell) *led for 3f: rdn and outpcd 3f out: styd on again fnl f* **9/2**[3]

0600 **5** *nk* **Global Challenge (IRE)**[24] 1931 7-8-2 **66** oh1 DavidKinsella 9 68
(P G Murphy) *in rr: outpcd and rdn 3f out: styd on fnl f: nvr nr to chal* **12/1**

6 ½ **Bauhaus (IRE)**[34] 6180 5-8-6 **70** MickyFenton 7 71
(R T Phillips) *in tch: rdn over 2f out: one pce after* **7/1**

3m 6.22s (1.71) **Going Correction** -0.35s/f (Firm) **6** Ran SP% **111.7**
Speed ratings (Par 105):81,80,79,79,79 78
CSF £18.81 CT £41.22 TOTE £2.30: £1.60, £3.90; EX 25.10.

Owner Mrs Jan Harris **Bred** Star Pointe Ltd **Trained** Newmarket, Suffolk

FOCUS
A pedestrian winning time for a race of its class. They went no pace and the form cannot be considered strong.

2654 PADDYPOWER.COM H'CAP 1m 1f
5:10 (5:11) (Class 3) (0-90,90) 3-Y-O **£8,096** (£2,408; £1,203; £601) **Stalls** High

Form RPR

10- **1** **Count Trevisio (IRE)**[247] 5852 3-9-7 **90** KerrinMcEvoy 7 99
(Saeed Bin Suroor) *led for 3f: led again over 1f out: flashed tail u.p: all out* **5/1**[3]

31-1 **2** *nk* **Heaven Knows**[28] 1855 3-9-0 **83** DarryllHolland 4 91
(W J Haggas) *hld up in tch: hdwy 2f out: rdn and pressed wnr thrght fnl f* **11/8**[1]

1-0 **3** 1¼ **Salt Man**[58] 1093 3-9-4 **87** MartinDwyer 8 93
(M P Tregoning) *trck ldr: led 6f out: hung bdly lft and hdd over 1f out: kpt on one pce fnl f* **16/1**

10-2 **4** 1½ **John Terry (IRE)**[16] 2174 3-9-5 **88** RyanMoore 2 91
(Mrs A J Perrett) *hld up in rr: rdn 3f out: kpt on one pce fnl 2f* **5/2**[2]

-530 **5** *shd* **Tumbleweed Glory (IRE)**[23] 1951 3-8-8 **77** TedDurcan 3 79
(B J Meehan) *hld up: effrt on outside 2f out: nvr nr to chal* **33/1**

1- **6** ¾ **In Full Cry**[398] 1723 3-9-1 **84** JoeFanning 6 85
(M Johnston) *chsd ldrs: rdn 3f out: one pce fr over 1f out* **9/1**

0-63 **7** *11* **Velvet Valley (USA)**[51] 1252 3-8-3 **72** DO'Donohoe 1 63+
(Sir Michael Stoute) *trckd ldrs: wnt 2nd 1/2-way: wknd over 1f out: eased ins fnl f* **16/1**

1m 52.66s (-3.45) **Going Correction** -0.35s/f (Firm) **7** Ran SP% **112.0**
Speed ratings (Par 103):101,100,99,98,98 97,87
CSF £11.81 CT £98.03 TOTE £6.10: £3.60, £1.70; EX 18.00.

Owner Godolphin **Bred** Quay Bloodstock **Trained** Newmarket, Suffolk

FOCUS
A useful handicap contested mainly by progressive three-year-olds and it should work out, although the fifth does limit the form.

NOTEBOOK
Count Trevisio(IRE) made a winning debut at two but disappointed on his second run back in October. He took advantage of an inviting gap up the rail to show ahead for a second time before edging left under pressure and giving a flash of the tail. (op 4-1)

Heaven Knows, who went up 5lb for his Thirsk success, could never get by the winner on this very different ground. The return to an easier surface will suit him. (op 13-8 tchd 7-4 and 15-8 in places)

Salt Man, down in grade after reappearing in a Listed race, tried to quicken from the front in the straight but hung badly away from the rail under pressure. He is not straightforward. (op 20-1)

John Terry(IRE) broke on terms this time. He ran his race but was found out by a 5lb rise on this first encounter with fast ground. (op 9-4 tchd 2-1)

Tumbleweed Glory(IRE) ran a better race with the blinkers omitted but is likely to remain vulnerable from this sort of mark. (op 25-1)

In Full Cry, off the track for over a year since his winning debut, could never land a telling blow. His win came on fast ground but easier conditions, and a further step up in trip, could be what he needs. (op 11-1)

2655 J C APOLLO MAIDEN STKS 1m 2f 7y
5:45 (5:52) (Class 5) 3-Y-O **£4,533** (£1,348; £674; £336) **Stalls** High

Form RPR

0- **1** **Corum (IRE)**[231] 6142 3-9-3 JimmyFortune 14 82
(J H M Gosden) *trckd ldrs: wnt 2nd over 2f out: led wl over 1f out: rdn clr* **6/1**[2]

-332 **2** *4* **Alhaajes (USA)**[22] 1994 3-9-3 97 MartinDwyer 11 74
(B W Hills) *led tl rdn and hdd wl over 1f out: styd on one pce* **8/13**[1]

00 **3** 1¼ **Gaze**[22] 1994 3-8-12 JoeFanning 13 67
(W Jarvis) *t.k.h: slowly away: sn mid-div: hdwy on ins 2f out: kpt on one pce* **40/1**

6 **4** *1* **Zirkel (IRE)**[16] 2175 3-9-3 DO'Donohoe 2 70
(Mrs A L M King) *towards rr: hdwy on outside over 2f out: styd on one pce* **33/1**

5 ½ **Majaales (USA)** 3-9-3 DarryllHolland 8 69+
(M P Tregoning) *hld up: styd on fnl f: nvr nrr* **12/1**

-60 **6** ½ **Cape Maya**[8] 2406 3-8-5 KMay[(7)] 5 63
(B J Meehan) *bhd: styd on ins fnl 2f: nvr nr to chal* **25/1**

0 **7** *3* **Mr Wiseguy**[21] 2028 3-9-3 MickyFenton 1 63
(G C Bravery) *trckd ldrs: rdn over 2f out: sn wknd* **16/1**

8 *5* **Triple Bend** 3-9-3 RyanMoore 10 53
(Mrs A J Perrett) *trckd ldr: rdn 3f out: wknd 2f out* **10/1**

9 *9* **Hensting House** 3-9-3 AlanDaly 12 36
(Dr J R J Naylor) *in tch: rdn 3f out: sn wknd* **66/1**

10 *24* **Songmaster (USA)** 3-9-3 KerrinMcEvoy 7 —
(Mrs A J Perrett) *a towards rr* **9/1**[3]

2m 10.12s (-0.12) **Going Correction** -0.35s/f (Firm) **10** Ran SP% **119.6**
Speed ratings (Par 99):86,82,81,81,80 80,77,73,66,47
CSF £10.08 TOTE £7.80: £1.70, £1.10, £7.90; EX 14.50 Place 6 £193.63, Place 5 £96.34.

Owner H R H Princess Haya Of Jordan **Bred** The Vallee Des Reves Syndicate **Trained** Newmarket, Suffolk

■ Noddies Way and Rifaat were withdrawn after giving trouble in the stalls.

FOCUS
A very slow winning time indeed. Little depth to this maiden and the level of the form is shaky, with the favourite well below par. The winner was quite impressive all the same.

T/Plt: £360.90 to a £1 stake. Pool: £85,755.95. 173.45 winning tickets. T/Qpdt: £89.30 to a £1 stake. Pool: £3,150.30. 26.10 winning tickets. JS

2623 YORK (L-H)
Saturday, June 17

OFFICIAL GOING: Good to firm
5mm of water had been put on the track overnight. The ground was described as 'better than Friday, basically just on the fast side of good'.
Wind: Almost nil. Weather: Fine and sunny.

2656 QUEEN MOTHER'S CUP (LADY AMATEUR RIDERS) (H'CAP) 1m 4f
2:05 (2:05) (Class 3) (0-95,94) 3-Y-O+ **£9,993** (£3,099; £1,548; £774) **Stalls** Centre

Form RPR

312- **1** **Soulacroix**[247] 5848 5-10-6 **91** MissFCumani[(3)] 3 102+
(L M Cumani) *trckd ldrs: hdwy 3f out: rdn to ld ent last: edgd lft and styd on wl* **11/4**[1]

0000 **2** *2* **Thyolo (IRE)**[9] 2387 5-9-9 **80** MissJFerguson[(3)] 5 88
(C G Cox) *hld up: gd hdwy over 2f out: rdn over 1f out: styd on ins last* **14/1**

6-20 **3** ½ **Dunaskin (IRE)**[63] 1017 6-10-7 **92** MissHCuthbert[(3)] 1 99
(Karen McLintock) *led: rdn along over 2f out: drvn over 1f out: hdd ent last: no ex last 100 yds* **50/1**

3422 **4** 2½ **Nawamees (IRE)**[24] 1933 8-10-5 **90** (p) MissHayleyMoore[(3)] 4 93
(G L Moore) *hld up: hdwy 5f out: rdn to chse ldrs 2f out: sn drvn and kpt on same pce* **8/1**

-211 **5** 2½ **Saif Sareea**[42] 1439 6-9-9 **77** MissRDavidson 6 76
(N G Richards) *chsd ldrs: rdn along over 2f out: grad wknd* **9/2**[2]

3005 **6** 1¾ **Sporting Gesture**[12] 2296 9-9-8 **76** MissSBrotherton 9 72
(M W Easterby) *towards rr: hdwy over 3f out: rdn and kpt on fnl 2f: nt rch ldrs* **6/1**[3]

-600 **7** *6* **Crow Wood**[19] 2079 7-10-12 **94** MissADeniel 10 81
(J J Quinn) *a rr* **15/2**

-062 **8** *19* **Given A Choice (IRE)**[24] 1943 4-10-4 **86** MrsCBartley 2 42
(J G Given) *chsd ldrs: rdn along over 3f out: sn wknd* **9/1**

4213 **9** 2½ **Polish Power (GER)**[14] 2231 6-9-9 **77** MrsSMoore 8 29
(J S Moore) *hld up in tch: hdwy on outer 3f out: rdn along 2f out and sn no imp* **12/1**

2-04 **10** *28* **Daring Affair**[155] 109 5-9-4 **75** oh4 MissKellyBurke[(3)] 7 —
(K R Burke) *racd wd: in tch: pushed along 1/2-way: sn lost pl and bhd fnl 4f* **40/1**

055 **11** *8* **Magnum Opus (IRE)**[3] 2549 4-9-12 **80** (v[1]) MrsEmmaLittmoden 11 —
(T J Pitt) *chsd ldrs: rdn along 1/2-way: wknd 4f out* **33/1**

2m 33.08s (0.68) **Going Correction** +0.225s/f (Good) **11** Ran SP% **113.7**
Speed ratings (Par 107):106,104,104,102,101 99,95,83,81,62 57
CSF £41.86 CT £1542.86 TOTE £4.00: £1.60, £6.60; EX 54.50 TRIFECTA Not won..
Owner P Makin **Bred** D Bunn **Trained** Newmarket, Suffolk
■ Luca Cumani's third successive win in this rich prize for lady amateur riders.

FOCUS
A decent handicap and the form looks straightforward with the time good.

NOTEBOOK
Soulacroix, who changed hands for 90,0000gns, floated to post. He took charge entering the final furlong and was firmly in command at the line. He stays much further and could be set for a good season. (op 3-1 tchd 7-2)

Thyolo(IRE), third at the Royal meeting here a year ago, has lost his way since and has tumbled down the ratings. Trying a longer trip than usual and with the headgear discarded, he ran much better. (op 10-1)

Dunaskin(IRE) took them along at a sensible pace but in the end did not see out the trip as well as the first two. He is still 3lb higher than his last winning mark. (op 40-1)

Nawamees(IRE), without a win on the Flat since 2001, was asked to race from a career-high mark.

Saif Sareea, who recently changed hands for 50,000gns, was much too free for his own good. A much stronger pace would have suited him a lot better. (op 4-1)

Sporting Gesture, who took this in 2003, was lining-up for the fifth consecutive time. He never got competitive and time seems to be taking its toll on him. (op 9-1)

Polish Power(GER) Official explanation: jockey said horse would not let itself down on the good to firm ground

2657 CADOGAN SILVER SALVER H'CAP 1m 208y
2:35 (2:35) (Class 2) (0-105,96) 3-Y-O+ **£16,840** (£5,010; £2,503; £1,250) **Stalls** Low

Form RPR

0120 **1** **Goodbye Mr Bond**[19] 2079 6-9-4 **86** KDarley 1 97
(E J Alston) *hld up in midfield: hdwy on inner over 3f out: nt clr run 2f out: swtchd rt and rdn ent last: kpt on to ld nr fin* **6/1**[2]

2250 **2** *hd* **Granston (IRE)**[15] 2200 5-9-3 **85** TQuinn 6 96
(J D Bethell) *led: rdn along over 2f out: drvn over 1f out: hdd and no ex nr fin* **11/1**

-000 **3** 1¼ **Krugerrand (USA)**[15] 2200 7-9-4 **86** TPQueally 4 94
(W J Musson) *trckd ldrs: hdwy on bit 2f out and ev ch tl rdn and nt qckn ins last* **6/1**[2]

-004 **4** 1¾ **El Coto**[19] 2079 6-9-10 **92** NCallan 2 97
(K A Ryan) *towards rr: pushed along 4f out: swtchd rt and rdn 2f out: styd on wl fnl f: nrst fin* **7/1**[3]

-115 **5** *shd* **Dancing Lyra**[19] 2079 5-9-0 **82** PaulHanagan 9 88+
(R A Fahey) *rr: pushed along 1/2-way: rdn along 3f out: hdwy and nt clr run 2f out: swtchd ins and styd on strly* **8/1**

6/5- **6** *nk* **Premier Dane (IRE)**[38] 4405 4-9-8 **90** RobertWinston 8 94
(N G Richards) *cl up: rdn along over 2f out: grad wknd* **16/1**

5060 **7** *nk* **Go Tech**[19] 2079 6-9-2 **84** DavidAllan 3 87
(T D Easterby) *trckd ldrs: hdwy 3f out: rdn 2f out and sn one pce* **16/1**

44-0 **8** *1* **Very Wise**[7] 2440 4-9-3 **85** TonyCulhane 10 86
(W J Haggas) *hld up in rr: hdwy 3f out: rdn 2f out and no imp* **33/1**

-625 **9** 3½ **Hartshead**[10] 2364 7-9-10 **92** DeanMcKeown 5 86
(G A Swinbank) *midfield: rdn along 3f out: edgd lft 2f out and sn btn* **14/1**

0333 **10** *4* **Speed Dial Harry (IRE)**[27] 1864 4-8-5 **78** (v) AndrewElliott[(5)] 12 64
(K R Burke) *prom: rdn along 3f out: sn wknd* **33/1**

22-2 **11** *1* **Master Of The Race**[18] 2114 4-9-0 **82** KFallon 11 66
(Sir Michael Stoute) *puleld hrd: in tch on outer: rdn along 3f out: sn btn* **9/2**[1]

14-1 **12** *hd* **Rio Riva**[61] 1043 4-10-0 **96** PhilipRobinson 7 80
(Miss J A Camacho) *keen: chsd ldrs: rdn along 3f out: wknd over 2f out* **7/1**[3]

1m 51.83s (0.84) **Going Correction** +0.225s/f (Good) **12** Ran SP% **115.5**
Speed ratings (Par 109):105,104,103,102,102 101,101,100,97,93 93,92
CSF £68.56 CT £414.94 TOTE £7.10: £2.20, £3.30, £2.00; EX 84.20 Trifecta £682.60 Part won. Pool £961.50 - 0.10 winning units..

Owner Peter J Davies **Bred** Michael Ng **Trained** Longton, Lancs

FOCUS

Another good handicap that appeared to be run at just a steady gallop, but the overall time was reasonable. The form looks sound rated around the third.

NOTEBOOK

Goodbye Mr Bond made up for his Redcar misfortune. Handling the fast ground, he had to switch for a run but proved very willing and put his head in front near the line.

Granston(IRE) dictated things from the front. He looked as though he had pinched it but was found out near the line. This trip stretches him to the very limit. (tchd 12-1)

Krugerrand(USA), who has won this twice before, travelled supremely well and his rider was looking round for dangers at one stage. The ground was plenty fast enough for him though and when called on for a final effort he simply could not reel in the first two. (tchd 13-2 in places)

El Coto, caught flat-footed when the pace increased, stayed on strongly after being switched. He would have preferred an end-to-end gallop. (op 13-2)

Dancing Lyra, quite keen in the rear, found himself outpaced turning in. His rider had to search for racing room and, eventually switching him to the inner, he finished best of all. He can certainly find another race. (op 9-1)

Premier Dane(IRE), who made up into a smart juvenile hurdler, ran well but is another who could have done with a more evenly-run race. (op 22-1)

Master Of The Race, fitted with a sheepskin noseband, took a fierce grip. He was one of the first in trouble and the ground was plenty quick enough for this luckless maiden. Official explanation: jockey said colt was unsuited by the good to firm ground (tchd 5-1 in a place)

Rio Riva, now a gelding, was awash with sweat in the paddock and was well below his best. He is a horse who runs fresh but he would not want the ground any quicker than he encountered here. After a short break he will hopefully bounce back. (op 15-2)

2658 WILLIAM HILL TROPHY (HERITAGE H'CAP) 6f

3:10 (3:10) (Class 2) (0-105,100) 3-Y-O **£55,054** (£16,379; £8,185; £4,088) **Stalls** Centre

Form				RPR
-241	1		**Prince Tamino**[5] [2509] 3-8-13 **92** 7ex SteveDrowne 16 (H Morrison) *in tch on outer: smooth hdwy 2f out: rdn to ld 1f out: r.o wl* **9/1**	106
-121	2	1 ½	**Tawaassol (USA)**[9] [2385] 3-8-11 **90** (t) RHills 9 (Sir Michael Stoute) *trckd ldrs: hdwy 2f out: rdn over 1f out: kpt on ins last* **13/2**[2]	100
0-02	3	hd	**High Curragh**[49] [1292] 3-8-1 **85** AndrewMullen(5) 11 (K A Ryan) *lw: cl up: rdn and edgd lft 2f out: led briefly and hung lft over 1f out: sn hdd and kpt on same pce* **9/1**	94
3-20	4	nk	**Orpsie Boy (IRE)**[21] [2032] 3-8-0 **84** JamesDoyle(5) 14 (N P Littmoden) *hld up: hdwy 2f out: sn rdn and kpt on ins last: nrst fin* **40/1**	92
1-31	5	1 ¾	**Trafalgar Bay (IRE)**[21] [2014] 3-9-3 **96** ShaneKelly 13 (S Kirk) *hld up towards rr: hdwy 2f out: sn rdn and styd on strly ins last: nrst fin* **14/1**	99+
1115	6	1 ¼	**Ripples Maid**[16] [2168] 3-8-10 **89** RichardThomas 2 (J A Geake) *slipped bdly s and bhd: hdwy 1/2-way: rdn 2f out and kpt on: nrst fin* **20/1**	88
4-31	7	nk	**Sunrise Safari (IRE)**[37] [1609] 3-8-3 **82** (v) RoystonFfrench 12 (I Semple) *chsd ldrs: rdn along 2f out: sn one pce* **25/1**	80
4122	8	¾	**Imperial Sword**[9] [2385] 3-8-7 **86** RobertWinston 20 (T D Barron) *bhd tl styd on fnl 2f* **25/1**	82+
-350	9	shd	**King Orchisios (IRE)**[21] [2032] 3-8-12 **91** NCallan 1 (K A Ryan) *led: rdn along 2f out: edgd rt: bmpd and hdd over 1f out: sn wknd* **20/1**	87
-000	10	1 ¼	**Calypso King**[28] [1848] 3-8-8 **87** TQuinn 17 (J W Hills) *towards rr tl styd on fnl 2f* **66/1**	79
2-40	11	½	**Gallery Girl (IRE)**[21] [2022] 3-9-0 **93** DavidAllan 3 (T D Easterby) *trckd ldrs: hdwy 2f out: sn rdn and ev ch tl drvn and wknd ent last* **50/1**	84
2161	12	¾	**Mr Sandicliffe**[10] [2363] 3-8-10 **89** (p) TonyCulhane 10 (B W Hills) *towards rr: hdwy 2f out: sn rdn and no imp* **25/1**	77
122	13	shd	**Pearly Wey**[21] [2014] 3-9-2 **95** KDarley 7 (C G Cox) *hmpd s: sn in tch: hdwy to chse ldrs 2f out: sn rdn and wknd* **7/1**[3]	83
25-0	14	4	**Crosby Hall**[10] [2363] 3-8-1 **80** (t) KimTinkler 15 (N Tinkler) *slipepd s: a towards rr* **100/1**	56
51-1	15	1	**River Bravo (IRE)**[22] [1986] 3-9-1 **94** AlanMunro 18 (P W Chapple-Hyam) *stdd s and swtchd lft to far side: effrt and sme hdwy over 2f out: nvr a factor* **12/1**	67
4-11	16	25	**Ingleby Arch (USA)**[36] [1633] 3-9-5 **98** KFallon 5 (T D Barron) *lw: slipped s: sn rdn along in rr: a bhd and virtually p.u fnl f* **5/1**[1]	—
3	17	3	**Conrad**[12] [2298] 3-7-12 **77** oh2 (p) PaulHanagan 8 (R A Fahey) *slipped bdly s: a rr* **50/1**	—
-111	18	1 ¼	**Borehan**[21] [2032] 3-9-7 **100** PhilipRobinson 6 (M A Jarvis) *lw: cl up: rdn along 2f out: sn wknd: lost action and virtually p.u fnl f* **7/1**[3]	—

1m 11.89s (-0.67) **Going Correction** +0.10s/f (Good) **18** Ran SP% **119.3**

Speed ratings (Par 105):108,106,105,105,103 101,100,99,99,98 97,96,96,91,89 56,52,50

CSF £57.17 CT £566.59 TOTE £11.70: £3.00, £1.80, £2.40, £8.70; EX 77.70 Trifecta £1166.80 Pool: £14,626.49 - 8.90 winning units..

Owner Thurloe Finsbury II **Bred** The National Stud **Trained** East Ilsley, Berks

FOCUS

A high-class renewal of this rich handicap. Several for one reason or another lost their chance at the start, Ripples Maid was the worst away. The form has been rated positively.

NOTEBOOK

Prince Tamino, under his penalty for his Windsor success, travelled strongly down the wide outside. He showed a nice turn of foot to win going away and looks highly progressive. After three races in quick succession he deserves a short break. (op 8-1)

Tawaassol(USA), 6lb higher, was tightened up at a vital stage. He stayed on to snatch second spot near the line and at some stage must be worth another try over seven furlongs.

High Curragh, gelded since Ripon, looked full of condition. He kept close tabs on his stablemate at the head of affairs but gave that horse a nudge as he took the lead. Only run out of it near the line, he should continue to give a good account of himself. (op 10-1)

Orpsie Boy(IRE), narrowly beaten in a blanket finish at Chester first time, must have been unsuited by the soft at Newmarket. He was putting in all his best work at the finish and must be worth a try over seven furlongs. (tchd 50-1)

Trafalgar Bay(IRE), taken down early and led to post, stayed on when it was all over and basically at this level, needs a stiffer test.

Ripples Maid, 9lb higher than her last success, slipped badly leaving the stalls and did amazingly well to finish so close. Official explanation: jockey said filly slipped leaving stalls

Sunrise Safari(IRE) lacks substance and after a busy juvenile career, already looks fully exposed. (op 20-1)

King Orchisios(IRE), who has a long stride, took them along but was fast coming to the end of his tether when his stablemate High Curragh gave him a bump. He has yet to fulfill expectations this time but must surely be worth another try over the minimum trip.

Pearly Wey still lacks experience. After collecting a bump at the start, in the end he dropped right away and may not be mature enough mentally for such a stiff test at this stage of his career. (tchd 15-2)

River Bravo(IRE) was switched to race towards the far side. His Haydock win was over seven on much easier ground.

Ingleby Arch(USA), who really took the eye in the paddock, was taken gingerly to post. He slipped leaving the stalls and was then taken out of his stride after the first furlong. Never figuring, in the end he simply completed in his own time. This is best overlooked. Official explanation: trainer had no explanation for the poor form shown (op 11-2)

Conrad Official explanation: jockey said colt lost its action 2f out

Borehan looked a picture but his action does not suggest he wants fast ground. After racing up with the pace, he faltered and seemed to lose his action. In the end he virtually walked over the line. He will be back in time. Official explanation: jockey said colt lost its action 2f out (tchd 8-1)

2659 DANIEL PRENN ROYAL YORKSHIRE H'CAP 1m 2f 88y

3:40 (3:40) (Class 2) (0-100,94) 3-Y-O **£14,249** (£4,239; £2,118; £1,058) **Stalls** Low

Form				RPR
2-11	1		**Reem Three**[31] [1781] 3-9-0 **87** NickyMackay 5 (L M Cumani) *hld up in rr: hdwy 3f out: n.m.r 2f out: effrt and nt clr run over 1f out: swtchd lft and rdn ent last: led last 100 yds* **9/2**[3]	95+
1-13	2	shd	**Crime Scene (IRE)**[16] [2174] 3-9-3 **90** KDarley 7 (M Johnston) *trckd ldrs: hdwy 3f out: rdn to chal 2f out: styd on to ld jst ins last: hdd last 100 yds: kpt on* **11/2**	98
6-14	3	shd	**King's Head (IRE)**[14] [2224] 3-9-7 **94** PhilipRobinson 8 (M A Jarvis) *hld up in rr: hdwy 3f out: effrt on outer 2f out: rdn to chal over 1f out: ev ch tl drvn and no ex towards fin* **9/4**[1]	102
6214	4	1 ½	**Bin Rahy (IRE)**[21] [2024] 3-8-9 **82** ChrisCatlin 4 (M R Channon) *chsd ldr: hdwy to ld over 2f out: rdn wl over 1f out: drvn and hdd jst ins last. wknd* **12/1**	87
014	5	3	**Great Hawk (USA)**[20] [2046] 3-9-0 **87** KFallon 1 (Sir Michael Stoute) *lw: trckd ldrs: hdwy 3f out: rdn 2f out and ch tl drvn and wknd over 1f out* **5/2**[2]	88+
4-64	6	9	**Doctor Scott**[37] [1615] 3-8-8 **81** StanleyChin 6 (M Johnston) *prom: rdn along 3f out: wknd over 2f out* **16/1**	63
0461	7	shd	**Norman Beckett**[23] [1948] 3-8-2 **75** oh1 PaulHanagan 3 (I Semple) *a towards rr* **20/1**	57
36-1	8	5	**Abbondanza (IRE)**[47] [1343] 3-8-13 **86** PaulMulrennan 2 (J Howard Johnson) *led: rdn along 3f out: sn hdd & wknd* **25/1**	59

2m 11.12s (0.64) **Going Correction** +0.225s/f (Good) **8** Ran SP% **115.1**

Speed ratings (Par 105):106,105,105,104,102 95,94,90

CSF £29.56 CT £69.29 TOTE £4.50: £1.80, £1.60, £1.30; EX 25.30 Trifecta £84.50 Pool: £833.10 - 7.00 winning units..

Owner Sheikh Mohammed Obaid Al Maktoum **Bred** Darley **Trained** Newmarket, Suffolk

FOCUS

A good handicap run at just a steady gallop until the final half-mile and should work out with the fourth setting the standard. The winner had to overcame severe traffic problems and is clearly still on the up.

NOTEBOOK

Reem Three, 9lb higher than when winning in the soft here in May, was keen towards the rear. She had to search long and hard for an opening and showed a nice turn of foot to get up near the line, clearly to her rider's relief. She is clearly improving at a rate of knots. (op 7-2)

Crime Scene(IRE), very warm beforehand, was very well backed. He settled better than on some occasions in the past and, after working hard to take a narrow advantage inside the last, in the end he only just missed out. (op 9-1)

King's Head(IRE), put to sleep at the back, made his effort on the wide outside. In the end he only just missed out and is progressing nicely. (tchd 11-4)

Bin Rahy(IRE), on his toes beforehand, was stepping up in trip and encountering fast ground for the first time. He went for home halfway up the straight but in the end was not quite up to it. (op 10-1 tchd 16-1 in a place)

Great Hawk(USA) really took the eye in the paddock. He flattered on the inner but in the end Fallon threw in the towel. This may be as good as he is. (op 11-4 tchd 3-1)

2660 LEONARD SAINER EBF MAIDEN STKS 6f

4:15 (4:18) (Class 4) 2-Y-O **£6,541** (£1,946; £972; £485) **Stalls** Centre

Form				RPR
	1		**Alderney (USA)** 2-8-12 PhilipRobinson 6 (M A Jarvis) *gd sort: trckd ldrs: swtchd lft and smooth hdwy to ld over 1f out: sn clr* **11/4**[2]	92+
22	2	4	**Dowlleh**[15] [2185] 2-9-3 TonyCulhane 7 (M R Channon) *swtg: cl up: rdn along over 2f out: drvn over 1f out: kpt on u.p ins last: no ch w wnr* **5/1**[3]	82
3	3	shd	**Majounes Song**[8] [2409] 2-8-12 KDarley 1 (M Johnston) *led: rdn along 2f out: hdd over 1f out: kpt on same pce* **17/2**	77
2	4	½	**Minaash (USA)**[10] [2342] 2-9-3 ShaneKelly 5 (J Noseda) *cl up: ev ch over 1f out: sn one pce* **7/4**[1]	80
	5	11	**Farleigh House (USA)** 2-9-3 RHills 2 (M H Tompkins) *w'like: v.s.a: a bhd* **25/1**	47
0	6	28	**Seriously Lucky (IRE)**[45] [1420] 2-9-3 KFallon 4 (D Nicholls) *prom: pushed along 1/2-way: sn lost pl and eased* **5/1**[3]	—

1m 12.73s (0.17) **Going Correction** +0.10s/f (Good) **6** Ran SP% **110.7**

Speed ratings (Par 95):102,96,96,95,81 43

CSF £16.12 TOTE £3.80: £2.10, £2.70; EX 19.70.

Owner Sheikh Mohammed **Bred** Darley **Trained** Newmarket, Suffolk

FOCUS

A weak turnout for a maiden race carrying £10,000 added money, but in the end a most impressive winner and the time was decent.

NOTEBOOK

Alderney(USA) ◆, a quality filly, has apparently been quite keen at home and she was very free to post. Skilfully settled in behind horses, she made her way to the outside and when given the office quickened right away. She is clearly very useful and deserves to take her chance in something like the Cherrry Hinton. (tchd 3-1 and 100-30 in a place)

Dowlleh ◆, haing his third run, was awash with sweat. Hard at work two furlongs out, he stuck on grimly to claim second spot in the last stride. A seventh furlong will be very much in his favour. (op 11-2)

Majounes Song, a good-topped filly, took them along but she was swept aside by the winner and lost second spot on the line. She will greatly appreciate a seventh furlong and seems sure to make her mark. (op 7-1 tchd 9-1)

Minaash(USA), runner-up on the All-Weather on his debut, travelled strongly but he was always doing too much and he had nothing at all left to give inside the last and was fading near the line. (tchd 9-4)

Farleigh House(USA), a well-made newcomer, was clueless and trailed throughout. (tchd 20-1)

Seriously Lucky(IRE) dropped out in matter of strides. Having lost his action, he was allowed to complete in his own time. Official explanation: jockey said colt lost its action (op 9-1)

The Form Book, Raceform Ltd, Compton, RG20 6NL

2661 CHARLES HENRY MEMORIAL H'CAP 6f
4:50 (4:50) (Class 4) (0-80,80) 3-Y-O+ **£7,124** (£2,119; £1,059; £529) **Stalls** Centre

Form RPR
0234 **1** **Blackheath (IRE)**[8] 2397 10-8-12 **67**.................... SilvestreDeSousa(3) 20 82
(D Nicholls) *racd alone stands side: a.p: led 2f out: rdn clr over 1f out: styd on* **22/1**
-063 **2** 1 1/4 **Oranmore Castle (IRE)**[12] 2302 4-9-7 **73**..............................(t) TQuinn 1 85
(B W Hills) *trckd ldrs centre gng wl: smooth hdwy 2f out: rdn to chse wnr ins last: kpt on* **8/1**[3]
0-43 **3** 1/2 **Knot In Wood (IRE)**[8] 2397 4-9-7 **73**................................ StanleyChin 12 83
(R A Fahey) *in tch: hdwy to chse ldrs 1/2-way: rdn wl over 1f out: styd on ins last* **7/1**[2]
0506 **4** 1 1/4 **Steel Blue**[21] 2017 6-9-4 **77**.................................... MichaelJStainton(7) 11 83
(R M Whitaker) *cl up centre: led that gp 2f out: sn rdn and wknd ent last* **12/1**
0-54 **5** *hd* **No Grouse**[9] 2384 6-8-11 **63**.. DavidAllan 18 69
(E J Alston) *towards rr: hdwy 2f out. sn rdn: kpt on u.p ins last: nrst fin* **14/1**
0-31 **6** *shd* **Petite Mac**[30] 1794 6-8-2 **61** oh1.............................. SuzzanneFrance(7) 8 66
(N Bycroft) *chsd ldrs: rdn along 2f out: wknd over 1f out* **16/1**
3551 **7** *hd* **Royal Challenge**[12] 2302 5-10-0 **80**....................................... NCallan 7 85
(M H Tompkins) *midfield: hmpd and outpcd 1/2-way: rdn and kpt on fnl 2f* **8/1**[3]
3360 **8** 1 1/4 **Paris Bell**[8] 2397 4-9-10 **76**.. PaulQuinn 2 77
(T D Easterby) *dwlt and bhd tl styd on fnl 2f* **40/1**
3-14 **9** 3/4 **Indian Spark**[23] 1949 12-9-4 **70**...................................... FergalLynch 4 69
(J S Goldie) *towards rr: hdwy 2f out: sn rdn and kpt on fnl f* **14/1**
1016 **10** *nk* **High Ridge**[12] 2302 7-9-10 **76**...(p) RHills 10 74
(J M Bradley) *cl up: rdn along over 2f out: wknd over 1f out* **25/1**
0440 **11** *hd* **Danzig River (IRE)**[29] 1820 5-9-9 **75**................................. ShaneKelly 13 72
(D Nicholls) *chsd ldrs: rdn along over 2f out: wkng whn bmpd over 1f out* **28/1**
0200 **12** 1 1/4 **Distant Times**[9] 2384 5-8-12 **64**...............................(b) DeanMcKeown 16 58
(T D Easterby) *chsd ldrs: rdn and hung lft and rt over 1f out: sn wknd* **50/1**
0032 **13** 1/2 **Soto**[16] 2163 3-8-13 **72**... DaleGibson 5 64
(M W Easterby) *a midfield* **33/1**
0335 **14** *1* **Trojan Flight**[8] 2397 5-9-9 **75**.. TonyCulhane 6 64
(D W Chapman) *hld up towards rr: hdwy whn hmpd over 1f out: nvr a factor* **12/1**
4-00 **15** 2 1/2 **Navigation (IRE)**[5] 2505 4-8-10 **62**................................ NickyMackay 15 44
(T J Etherington) *chsd ldrs: rdn along over 2f out: grad wknd* **33/1**
0451 **16** 1 1/2 **Ashes (IRE)**[3] 2550 4-9-5 **71** 7ex..................................... PaulMulrennan 9 48
(K R Burke) *overall ldr centre: rdn along and hdd 2f out: sn wknd and eased* **16/1**
-060 **17** 3/4 **Currency**[15] 2189 9-9-9 **75**... KDarley 3 50
(J M Bradley) *chsd ldrs 2f: sn lost pl and bhd* **20/1**
0005 **18** *5* **Loaderfun (IRE)**[15] 2194 4-9-7 **76**...............................(b[1]) DNolan(3) 14 36
(N Wilson) *chsd ldrs: rdn along 1/2-way: sn wknd* **33/1**
400- **19** *5* **Bold Haze**[231] 6140 4-9-0 **66**.. RobertWinston 19 11
(Miss S E Hall) *blindfold removed late: slowly away and a bhd* **25/1**
5-01 **20** *40* **My Gacho (IRE)**[9] 2384 4-9-10 **76**.......................................(v) KFallon 17 —
(T D Barron) *rrd bdly and lft many lengths: a t.o* **5/1**[1]

1m 12.4s (-0.16) **Going Correction** +0.10s/f (Good)
WFA 3 from 4yo+ 7lb **20** Ran SP% **125.3**
Speed ratings (Par 105):105,103,102,101,100 100,100,98,97,97 97,95,94,93,90 88,87,80,73,20
CSF £173.29 CT £1419.14 TOTE £25.40: £4.10, £2.90, £1.60, £3.70; EX 266.20.
Owner Middleham Park Racing Xx & Streamhill **Bred** John McKay **Trained** Sessay, N Yorks

FOCUS
A maximum field for this 61-80 handicap. A competitive contest and the form looks solid rated around the runner-up and fifth. The winner raced alone down the stands' side.
Trojan Flight Official explanation: jockey said gelding suffered interference

2662 MICHAEL SOBELL MAIDEN STKS 1m
5:25 (5:29) (Class 4) 3-Y-O **£6,541** (£1,946; £972; £485) **Stalls** Low

Form RPR
3-22 **1** **Safqa**[36] 1650 3-8-12 79.. RHills 2 79
(B W Hills) *mde all: rdn over 2f out: styd on wl fnl f* **11/4**[2]
2-32 **2** 1 3/4 **O'Tara (IRE)**[29] 1814 3-9-3 80... NCallan 5 80
(M H Tompkins) *trckd wnr: effrt 2f out: sn rdn and ch over 1f out tl drvn and one pce ins last* **4/1**[3]
-3 **3** 2 1/2 **Mighty**[21] 2028 3-9-3 .... KFallon 7 74+
(Sir Michael Stoute) *s.i.s: sn chsng ldng pair: rdn along 3f out and kpt on same pce* **6/4**[1]
0 **4** *nk* **Mambonow (USA)**[28] 1844 3-9-3 .... ShaneKelly 1 74+
(J Noseda) *bhd tl hdwy 3f out: styd on fnl 2f: nrst fin* **20/1**
5 *18* **Musical Giant (USA)** 3-9-3 .... PaulMulrennan 3 32
(J Howard Johnson) *chsd ldrs: rdn along 4f out and sn wknd* **25/1**
6 *2* **Strong Survivor (USA)** 3-9-3 .... NickyMackay 6 28
(L M Cumani) *s.i.s: a rr* **11/1**
04 **7** 1 3/4 **Regal Raider (IRE)**[42] 1493 3-9-3 .... TonyCulhane 4 24
(I Semple) *in tch: rdn along over 4f out: sn wknd* **33/1**

1m 40.61s (1.11) **Going Correction** +0.225s/f (Good) **7** Ran SP% **106.5**
Speed ratings (Par 101):103,101,99,98,80 78,77
CSF £11.88 TOTE £3.60: £2.00, £2.10; EX 13.20 Place 6 £185.80, Place 5 £65.06.
Owner Hamdan Al Maktoum **Bred** Shadwell Estate Company Limited **Trained** Lambourn, Berks
■ Wind Shuffle was withdrawn (12/1, unruly in stalls). R4 applies, deduct 5p in the £.

FOCUS
An ordinary maiden, Safqa had her own way in front and had 4lb in hand of the exposed runner-up on official ratings and those two set the standard.
Musical Giant(USA) Official explanation: jockey said colt hung right throughout
Regal Raider(IRE) Official explanation: jockey said gelding lost its action; trainer said gelding was found to be lame left fore

T/Jkpt: Not won. T/Plt: £206.00 to a £1 stake. Pool: £140,780.16. 498.85 winning tickets. T/Qpdt: £18.30 to a £1 stake. Pool: £5,884.40. 237.60 winning tickets. JR

[2565] SAN SIRO (R-H)
Saturday, June 17
OFFICIAL GOING: Good to firm

2670a PRIMI PASSI (GROUP 3) 6f
3:30 (3:35) 2-Y-O **£29,467** (£13,270; £7,472; £3,736)

RPR
1 **Golden Titus (IRE)**[20] 2-8-11 .... SLandi 7 104
(A Renzoni, Italy) *tracked leaders, challenged 1 1/2f out, led 1f out, pushed out* **277/100**[1]
2 1 1/4 **Xenes** 2-8-11 .... CFiocchi 1 101
(R Menichetti, Italy) *led, narrowly headed half-way, led again 2f out to 1f out, kept on* **178/10**
3 *hd* **Docksil**[20] 2062 2-8-8 .... DVargiu 6 97
(B Grizzetti, Italy) *close up, close 3rd half-way, pushed along 2f out, ran on at one pace* **4/1**[3]
4 *2* **Amante Latino** 2-8-11 .... MEsposito 2 94
(V Caruso, Italy) *towards rear, ran on from 2f out to take 4th* **105/10**
5 1 3/4 **Ladak**[20] 2-8-11 .... SMulas 3 89
(B Grizzetti, Italy) *always mid-division* **27/1**
6 *12* **Recoaro (IRE)** 2-8-11 .... MDemuro 4 53
(B Grizzetti, Italy) *prominent, led narrowly half-way to 2f out, no extra from over 1f out* **36/10**[2]
7 *nse* **Golden Surfside (USA)** 2-8-11 .... MTellini 5 53
(M Fratini, Italy) *towards rear, never in contention* **38/1**
8 1 1/4 **Diamond Fire (IRE)**[20] 2060 2-8-11 .... EPedroza 8 49
(A Wohler, Germany) *behind, never a factor* **107/10**

1m 10.8s **8** Ran SP% **97.0**
(Including 1 Euro stake): WIN 3.77; PL 1.82, 3.82, 2.03; DF 36.83.
Owner Scuderia Millenium **Bred** Scuderia Golden Horse Srl **Trained** Italy

2671a GRAN PREMIO D'ITALIA (LISTED RACE) 1m 2f
4:40 (4:40) 3-Y-O **£21,724** (£9,559; £5,214; £2,607)

RPR
1 **Primary (USA)**[37] 1603 3-9-7 .... MDemuro 3 110
(W J Haggas) *held up, 10th straight, headway on outside 2f out, led approaching final furlong, ran on well, pushed out SP 11-10F* **11/10**[1]
2 2 1/2 **Fa A Mezz**[41] 3-9-2 .... EBotti 1 101
(A & G Botti, Italy)
3 2 1/2 **Pressing (IRE)**[27] 1872 3-9-2 .... MTellini 11 96
(R Feligioni, Italy)
4 1 1/4 **Miles Gloriosus (USA)**[27] 1872 3-9-2 .... CFiocchi 9 94
(R Menichetti, Italy)
5 *nse* **Arpino (GER)**[47] 3-9-4 .... WMongil 2 96
(P Schiergen, Germany)
6 *1* **Chacotero (IRE)** 3-9-2 .... KKerekes 6 92
(Werner Glanz, Germany)
7 *3* **Fanzago (FR)**[41] 3-9-2 .... MMonteriso 10 86
(O Pessi, Italy)
8 3 1/4 **Hands Clean (IRE)**[34] 1713 3-8-11 .... FBranca 7 76
(A Candi, Italy)
9 1 1/2 **Fringuell** 3-9-2 .... WGambarota 12 78
(S Iacobelli)
10 *6* **Diarius (GER)**[27] 1872 3-9-2 .... ADeVries 4 67
(H Blume, Germany)
11 *18* **Golden Stud (IRE)**[27] 1872 3-9-2 .... DVargiu 5 35
(M Fratini, Italy)
12 *12* **Scipione Borghese** 3-9-2 .... SLandi 8 13
(L Camici, Italy)

2m 0.30s **12** Ran SP% **47.6**
WIN 2.10; PL 1.45, 1.82, 2.32; DF 7.97.
Owner Highclere Thoroughbred Racing XXVI **Bred** G W Humphrey & Louise I Humphrey **Trained** Newmarket, Suffolk

NOTEBOOK
Primary(USA) looked to have been found a good opportunity by connections and won with plenty in hand. He was given a confident hold-up ride which proved much too potent for his rivals.

[2530] SALISBURY (R-H)
Sunday, June 18
OFFICIAL GOING: Good to firm (firm in places)
Wind: Virtually nil

2672 DOUGLAS THOMAS 70TH BIRTHDAY "CITY BOWL" H'CAP 1m 4f
2:00 (2:00) (Class 4) (0-85,85) 4-Y-O+ **£6,477** (£1,927; £963; £481) **Stalls** High

Form RPR
0-05 **1** **Love Always**[11] 2351 4-8-8 **72**.. PatDobbs 6 78+
(S Dow) *trckd ldrs: lost position 6f out: nt clr run and swtchd lft over 1f out: r.o wl to ld cl home: rdn out* **14/1**
1600 **2** 1/2 **Yakimov (USA)**[10] 2387 7-9-0 **81**........................... EdwardCreighton(3) 4 85
(D J Wintle) *s.i.s: bhd: hdwy over 2f out: sn rdn: styd on wl ins fnl f to go 2nd cl home* **12/1**
4032 **3** *nk* **Velvet Waters**[5] 2534 5-8-4 **68**.. StephenCarson 3 71
(R F Johnson Houghton) *led for 3f: prom: rdn 2f out: ev ch ins fnl f: no ex cl home* **7/2**[2]
5334 **4** *shd* **Modaffaa**[25] 1943 6-9-0 **78**.. JimmyFortune 2 81
(P R Webber) *trckd ldr: led after 3f: qcknd pce 3f out: hrd pressed fr 2f out: no ex whn ct cl home* **7/2**[2]
3232 **5** *hd* **Augustine**[4] 2540 5-8-12 **76**.. DarrenWilliams 7 79
(P W Hiatt) *in tch: hdwy 4f out: rdn to chal 2f out: ev ch ins fnl f: no ex cl home* **10/3**[1]
0424 **6** *2* **Desert Island Disc**[5] 2534 9-8-4 **75** ow3........................ SladeO'Hara(7) 5 74
(Dr J R J Naylor) *trckd ldrs: rdn 3f out: one pce fnl 2f* **15/2**
0-40 **7** *8* **Solo Flight**[23] 1992 9-9-7 **85**... RyanMoore 8 72
(H Morrison) *hld up: effrt over 1f out: sn wknd* **6/1**[3]

2m 35.49s (-0.87) **Going Correction** +0.025s/f (Good) **7** Ran SP% **107.9**
Speed ratings (Par 105):103,102,102,102,102 100,95
CSF £142.87 CT £637.31 TOTE £15.10: £4.60, £6.30; EX 60.90.

Owner T Staplehurst **Bred** T Staplehurst **Trained** Epsom, Surrey
FOCUS
A competitive handicap despite the smallish field, but the pace was modest for the first mile.
Solo Flight Official explanation: jockey said gelding was unsuited by the good (good to firm places) ground

2673 CHAS H. BAKER MAIDEN FILLIES' STKS 1m
2:30 (2:33) (Class 5) 3-Y-O £5,181 (£1,541; £770; £384) Stalls High

Form				RPR
55	1		**Gelder**[55] 1191 3-9-0 ... JimmyFortune 7 (H Morrison) *mde virtually all: kpt on wl fnl f: rdn out* 10/1	68
0-5	2	3/4	**Royal Fantasy (IRE)**[48] 1351 3-8-11 ... AdamKirby(3) 4 (J R Fanshawe) *in tch: hdwy 2f out: rdn and ev ch over 1f out: kpt on cl home* 9/2[3]	67+
2	3	3/4	**Majestic Halo**[22] 2028 3-9-0 ... SteveDrowne 11 (E A L Dunlop) *trckd ldrs: rdn and ev ch over 1f out: kpt on* 9/4[1]	65
23-0	4	1/2	**Tawaafud**[46] 1418 3-9-0 82 ... RHills 3 (B W Hills) *trckd ldrs: rdn to chal 2f out: no ex ins fnl f* 7/2[2]	64
00-0	5	2 1/2	**Always Turn Left (IRE)**[11] 2344 3-8-9 55 ... EmmettStack(5) 9 (H S Howe) *in tch: rdn over 2f out: kpt on same pce fnl f* 100/1	58?
0	6	3 1/2	**Don't Mind Me**[21] 2048 3-9-0 ... TQuinn 1 (T Keddy) *in tch: rdn and effrt 2f out: one pce fnl f* 33/1	50
	7	1 1/2	**Desert Joy** 3-9-0 ... LPKeniry 5 (D R C Elsworth) *s.i.s: towards rr: sme late prog: n.d* 20/1	47+
-4	8	shd	**Valdemosa**[27] 1901 3-9-0 ... ChrisCatlin 12 (B I Case) *towards rr: rdn over 2f out: no imp* 25/1	46
06-0	9	hd	**Smoking Star**[7] 2479 3-8-7 58 ... MarkCoumbe(7) 8 (N I M Rossiter) *prom: led briefly over 3f out: sn rdn: wknd over 1f out* 100/1	46
	10	1/2	**Useful** 3-9-0 ... TedDurcan 10 (A W Carroll) *s.i.s: a towards rr* 100/1	45
	11	3/4	**Primrose Queen** 3-9-0 ... JDSmith 2 (D R C Elsworth) *hld up towards rr: brief effrt over 2f out* 40/1	43
5	12	5	**Sajaaya (AUS)**[24] 1956 3-9-0 ... (t) RyanMoore 13 (Sir Michael Stoute) *s.i.s: sn mid div: wknd over 1f out* 7/1	31
	13	5	**Format** 3-9-0 ... SebSanders 6 (A W Carroll) *s.i.s: a towards rr* 66/1	20

1m 43.5s (0.41) **Going Correction** +0.025s/f (Good) 13 Ran SP% **111.2**
Speed ratings (Par 96):98,97,96,96,93 90,88,88,88,87 86,81,76
CSF £47.89 TOTE £13.30: £2.50, £1.70, £1.30; EX 59.20.
Owner The Queen **Bred** The Queen **Trained** East Ilsley, Berks
FOCUS
Probably a modest maiden, with the newcomers all well beaten.

2674 HAPPY FATHERS DAY TO VERNON EELES H'CAP 5f
3:00 (3:01) (Class 4) (0-85,91) 3-Y-O+ £6,477 (£1,927; £963; £481) Stalls Centre

Form				RPR
6001	1		**Intriguing Glimpse**[9] 2389 5-10-1 86 ... SebSanders 12 (Miss B Sanders) *trckd ldrs: qcknd up wl to ld jst over 1f out: r.o wl: rdn out* 6/1[3]	99
06-2	2	1 1/2	**Our Fugitive (IRE)**[29] 1856 4-9-6 77 ... JoeFanning 11 (A W Carroll) *led: rdn: hdd and drifted lft jst over 1f out: nt pce of wnr* 5/1[2]	85
21-0	3	1 3/4	**Blessed Place**[12] 2331 6-8-4 66 oh10 ... (t) JamesDoyle(5) 4 (D J S Ffrench Davis) *prom: rdn over 2f out: kpt on same pce fnl f* 28/1	67
0001	4	3/4	**Malapropism**[2] 2618 6-9-6 80 6ex ... EdwardCreighton(3) 10 (M R Channon) *chsd ldrs: rdn over 2f out: kpt on same pce* 6/1[3]	78
-200	5	1 3/4	**Pic Up Sticks**[8] 2429 7-9-13 84 ... TQuinn 5 (B G Powell) *chsd ldrs: rdn over 1f out: sn wknd* 7/1	76
0-00	6	1	**Hornpipe**[43] 1475 4-10-0 85 ... TedDurcan 3 (M S Saunders) *a mid div* 20/1	73+
1020	7	3/4	**Spanish Ace**[8] 2450 5-9-13 84 ... RyanMoore 6 (J M Bradley) *s.i.s: a towards rr* 9/2[1]	69
0-00	8	1 1/4	**Meikle Barfil**[13] 2302 4-8-11 68 ... SteveDrowne 8 (J M Bradley) *a towards rr* 25/1	48
0-05	9	3	**Polish Emperor (USA)**[9] 2389 6-9-10 81 ... (e) JimmyFortune 9 (W R Swinburn) *chsd ldrs: rdn over 2f out: wknd over 1f out* 6/1[3]	50
4306	10	nk	**Lindbergh**[43] 1475 4-9-13 84 ... PatDobbs 2 (R Hannon) *a towards rr* 9/1	52

60.23 secs (-1.36) **Going Correction** +0.025s/f (Good) 10 Ran SP% **112.3**
Speed ratings (Par 105):111,108,105,104,101 100,99,97,92,91
CSF £33.64 CT £785.69 TOTE £8.90: £2.80, £2.10, £4.60; EX 38.20.
Owner Edward Hyde **Bred** Copy Xpress Ltd **Trained** Headley, Surrey
FOCUS
A typical Salisbury sprint handicap, well contested and of a fair standard for the money.
Polish Emperor(USA) Official explanation: jockey said gelding never travelled

2675 AXMINSTER CARPETS CATHEDRAL STKS (LISTED RACE) 6f
3:30 (3:30) (Class 1) 3-Y-O+
£18,169 (£6,886; £3,446; £1,718; £860; £432) Stalls High

Form				RPR
-110	1		**Etlaala**[32] 1778 4-9-7 110 ... RHills 6 (B W Hills) *s.i.s: hld up and keen: tk clsr order and nt clr run over 1f out: shkn up to ld ins fnl f: r.o wl: readily* 4/1[2]	118
2202	2	1 3/4	**Philharmonic**[13] 2289 5-9-3 105 ... SebSanders 1 (R A Fahey) *hld up: hdwy 2f out: sn rdn: ev ch jst ins fnl f: nt pce of wnr fnl 50yds* 7/1	109
4425	3	hd	**Pivotal Flame**[14] 2276 4-9-3 106 ... GrahamGibbons 2 (E S McMahon) *travelled wl: prom: led over 3f out: swtchd to far rails over 2f out: rdn 1f out: no ex whn hdd sn after* 9/2[3]	108+
-202	4	2	**Presto Shinko (IRE)**[13] 2303 5-9-7 107 ... RyanMoore 5 (R Hannon) *chsd ldrs: rdn 2f out: edgd lft ins fnl f: kpt on same pce* 10/3[1]	106
20-0	5	3/4	**Balmont (USA)**[19] 2115 5-9-3 109 ... JimmyFortune 4 (J Noseda) *led for 3f: chsd ldr: hmpd on rails over 2f out: sn rdn: one pce fnl f* 5/1	100+
5140	6	2 1/2	**Loyal Royal (IRE)**[22] 2032 3-8-10 93 ... LPKeniry 3 (D R C Elsworth) *w ldr: rdn whn hmpd over 2f out: sn hung rt: wknd fnl f* 20/1	92
-030	7	hd	**Out After Dark**[19] 2115 5-9-3 102 ... (b) AdamKirby 7 (C G Cox) *chsd ldrs: rdn over 2f out: wknd over 1f out* 7/1	92

1m 12.98s (-2.00) **Going Correction** +0.025s/f (Good)
WFA 3 from 4yo+ 7lb 7 Ran SP% **107.7**
Speed ratings (Par 111):114,111,111,108,107 104,104
CSF £27.68 TOTE £5.10: £2.80, £3.40; EX 28.00.
Owner Hamdan Al Maktoum **Bred** Matthews Breeding And Racing Ltd **Trained** Lambourn, Berks
■ Stewards' Enquiry : Graham Gibbons three-day ban: careless riding (Jun 29-30, Jul 1)

FOCUS
A Listed race of reasonable quality, with the winner having landed a Group 2 as a juvenile. A very acceptable winning time for a race like this.
NOTEBOOK
Etlaala was suited by the faster ground and is now back on course to have a good summer. He has a touch of class and can be placed to use it. (op 7-2)
Philharmonic ran with great credit against a smart winner, continuing his fine form of recent weeks. (op 12-1)
Pivotal Flame continues to run well, only to find one or two too good. He is a useful sprinter, and will be placed to advantage in the coming months. (tchd 5-1)
Presto Shinko(IRE) had a bit to find on official figures, so more or less ran his race. He has trained on well, but falls a bit short of the best. (op 3-1 tchd 11-4)
Balmont(USA) has not won for three years but hinted at better to come here, so should not be quickly dismissed even in smart company from now on. (op 7-2)
Loyal Royal(IRE) had a lot to find at the weights, so did well in the circumstances. (op 28-1)
Out After Dark was not beaten far, and can find better opportunities when returned to handicaps. (op 8-1 tchd 9-1)

2676 ALBERT SAMUEL FILLIES' H'CAP 6f 212y
4:00 (4:03) (Class 5) (0-70,65) 3-Y-O+ £3,562 (£1,059; £529; £264) Stalls High

Form				RPR
2200	1		**Peace Lily**[8] 2459 4-9-5 56 ... StephenCarson 5 (R F Johnson Houghton) *trckd ldrs: nt clr run on rails 2f out: sn swtchd lft: led jst ins fnl f: qcknd up wl: rdn out* 3/1[2]	67
0153	2	2	**La Fanciulla**[8] 2459 3-9-3 63 ... RyanMoore 2 (R Hannon) *w ldrs: led wl over 1f out: sn rdn: hdd jst ins fnl f: nt pce of wnr* 11/4[1]	66
-650	3	3	**Dark Moon**[5] 2535 3-8-7 53 ... ChrisCatlin 3 (A M Balding) *led tl over 2f out: rdn and remained cl up: kpt on same pce fnl f* 8/1	48
-000	4	1 3/4	**Pink Bay**[15] 2223 4-9-4 55 ... (v) FergusSweeney 1 (W S Kittow) *sn prom: led over 2f out tl wl over 1f out: sn rdn: one pce fnl f* 7/1	48
5050	5	1 3/4	**Fleur A Lay (USA)**[8] 2459 4-9-1 52 ... (p) JimCrowley 6 (Mrs A J Perrett) *hld up bhd ldrs: rdn over 3f out: one pce fnl 2f* 12/1	41
00-6	6	3	**Lady Edge (IRE)**[48] 1348 4-9-5 56 ... JimmyFortune 4 (A W Carroll) *chsd ldrs: rdn and edgd rt over 1f out: sn wknd* 14/1	37
3344	U		**Wizby**[6] 2511 3-8-10 56 ow3 ... (t) GrahamGibbons 7 (P D Evans) *hmpd and uns rdr after 1f* 4/1[3]	—

1m 29.36s (0.30) **Going Correction** +0.025s/f (Good)
WFA 3 from 4yo 9lb 7 Ran SP% **109.6**
Speed ratings (Par 100):99,96,93,91,89 85,—
CSF £10.66 CT £51.68 TOTE £4.00: £2.00, £1.60; EX 9.60.
Owner Mrs R F Johnson Houghton **Bred** Mrs R F Johnson Houghton **Trained** Blewbury, Oxon
FOCUS
A moderate race, with the winner breaking her maiden at the 13th attempt.

2677 LEVY BOARD H'CAP 1m 6f 15y
4:30 (4:31) (Class 4) (0-85,79) 3-Y-O £5,505 (£1,637; £818; £408) Stalls Far side

Form				RPR
3424	1		**Som Tala**[19] 2117 3-9-4 76 ... TedDurcan 5 (M R Channon) *led: rdn and narrowly hdd 3f out: rallied gamely u.p: led again ins fnl f: styd on strly* 11/1	87
4121	2	1	**Liberate**[10] 2379 3-9-0 72 ... SebSanders 2 (Sir Mark Prescott) *trckd ldrs: jnd ldr after 4f: rdn into narrow advantage 3f out: no ex whn hdd ins fnl f* 5/4[1]	82
2212	3	1 1/4	**Meadow Mischief (FR)**[37] 1648 3-9-7 79 ... JimmyFortune 4 (E A L Dunlop) *w wnr for 4f: trckd ldrs: rdn to chal 3f out: ev ch 1f out: no ex and edgd rt nr fin* 3/1[3]	88+
0612	4	1 1/4	**Call Me George**[3] 2592 3-8-7 65 ... JoeFanning 1 (M Johnston) *trckd ldrs: pushed along over 5f out: rdn over 3f out: swtchd lft over 1f out: no imp* 9/4[2]	71

3m 6.80s (0.57) **Going Correction** +0.025s/f (Good) 4 Ran SP% **108.5**
Speed ratings (Par 101):99,98,97,97
CSF £25.35 TOTE £8.70; EX 26.20.
Owner Sheikh Ahmed Al Maktoum **Bred** Usk Valley Stud **Trained** West Ilsley, Berks
FOCUS
A decent little race, with some good stables represented, but disappointingly low on numbers.

2678 TELETEXT "HANDS AND HEELS" SERIES APPRENTICE H'CAP 1m
5:00 (5:01) (Class 6) (0-65,65) 3-Y-O £3,238 (£963; £481; £240) Stalls High

Form				RPR
0-00	1		**Jill Dawson (IRE)**[22] 2034 3-8-9 52 ... KirstyMilczarek 1 (John Berry) *trckd ldrs: led wl over 1f out: sn drifted lft: kpt on wl* 16/1	61
2660	2	3	**Murrumbidgee (IRE)**[7] 2479 3-8-12 60 ... PatrickHills(5) 3 (J W Hills) *trckd ldrs: led over 2f out: hdd wl over 1f out: kpt on same pce* 13/2[3]	63
2-05	3	1 1/4	**Ollie George (IRE)**[20] 2069 3-9-5 65 ... (v[1]) JamesRogers(3) 11 (A M Balding) *rdr lost iron briefly leaving stalls: mid div: lost pl 4f out: styd on fr over 1f out: wnt 3rd ins fnl f* 5/1[2]	65
5510	4	2 1/2	**They All Laughed**[7] 2479 3-9-5 62 ... LukeMorris 8 (P W Hiatt) *prom: rdn over 2f out: one pce fnl f* 7/1	56
00-0	5	1 1/4	**Forest Lodge (IRE)**[24] 1955 3-8-6 49 ... NBazeley 4 (D R C Elsworth) *towards rr: hdwy 5f out: rdn and drifted lft over 3f out: no further imp* 14/1	40
000-	6	1 1/4	**Moyoko (IRE)**[285] 5029 3-8-6 52 ... LauraReynolds(3) 2 (M Blanshard) *in tch: rdn and drifted lft over 3f out: one pce fnl 2f* 28/1	40
0-00	7	1/2	**Baytown Lulu**[16] 2190 3-8-7 50 ... JamieHamblett 10 (H S Howe) *nvr bttr than mid div* 50/1	37
00-1	8	1/2	**Takitwo**[5] 2535 3-9-4 61 6ex ... ChrisCavanagh 7 (P D Cundell) *led tl over 2f out: grad fdd* 15/8[1]	47
-030	9	2 1/2	**Oasis Sun (IRE)**[81] 797 3-8-7 53 ow4 ... KylieManser(3) 5 (J R Best) *in tch: rdn over 3f out: wknd 2f out* 14/1	33
-000	10	1	**Mujelle**[15] 2247 3-9-4 64 ... JamesMillman(3) 9 (D K Ivory) *a towards rr* 20/1	42
0-00	11	15	**In Some Style (IRE)**[7] 2479 3-8-1 47 ... (p) TolleyDean(3) 13 (R A Harris) *a towards rr: eased fnl f* 40/1	—
6000	12	1/2	**Mr Cheers**[30] 1829 3-8-7 50 ... (p) RonanKeogh 6 (R A Harris) *mid div tl wknd 2f out: eased fnl f* 18/1	—

1m 43.78s (0.69) **Going Correction** +0.025s/f (Good) 12 Ran SP% **114.4**
Speed ratings (Par 97):97,94,92,90,89 87,87,86,84,83 68,67
CSF £108.52 CT £612.91 TOTE £13.50: £3.10, £2.50, £2.20; EX 103.80 Place 6 £7,081.46, Place 5 £242.89.
Owner Joe McCarthy & Friends **Bred** Sean Burke **Trained** Newmarket, Suffolk
FOCUS
A typically modest line-up for a race of this type, made worse by the complete flop of what appeared to be a solid favourite.

Jill Dawson(IRE) Official explanation: trainer sais, regarding the improved form shown, the filly may have benefited from the drop in class and today's faster ground
Takitwo Official explanation: jockey said he lost an iron at the start
T/Plt: £6,173.00 to a £1 stake. Pool: £45,663.65. 5.40 winning tickets. T/Qpdt: £260.90 to a £1 stake. Pool: £3,209.00. 9.10 winning tickets. TM

2656 YORK (L-H)
Sunday, June 18

OFFICIAL GOING: Good to firm
2.5mm water was put on the track since the previous day. The ground was reckoned to be just on the quick side of good.
Wind: Light, half-behind Weather: Light rain, mainly fine but overcast

2679 CONSTANT SECURITY FILLIES' H'CAP — 1m 2f 88y
2:20 (2:21) (Class 4) (0-85,85) 3-Y-0 — **£6,477** (£1,927; £963; £481) **Stalls** Low

Form				RPR
1524	1		**Flying Clarets (IRE)**[12] 2324 3-8-8 **72** PaulHanagan 4 (R A Fahey) *trckd ldrs: t.k.h: effrt over 3f out: nt clr run 2f out: styd on wl to ld last 150yds* **5/1**[2]	78
6-16	2	1 ¼	**Grain Of Truth**[17] 2174 3-9-4 **82** RobertWinston 8 (Sir Michael Stoute) *hld up in last: smooth hdwy 3f out: led 1f out: sn hdd and nt qckn* **8/1**	86
5-21	3	½	**Tasjeel (USA)**[16] 2188 3-9-1 **79** MichaelHills 1 (W J Haggas) *upset and uns rdr in paddock: trckd ldrs: outpcd 3f out: c outside over 1f out: styd on strly ins last* **9/1**	82
-003	4	2	**Lady Disdain**[8] 2441 3-8-2 **66** oh2 NickyMackay 6 (G M Moore) *trckd ldr: chal 3f out: led 2f out: hdd 1f out: one pce* **25/1**	65
66-1	5	1	**Abhisheka (IRE)**[37] 1649 3-9-7 **85** LDettori 2 (Saeed Bin Suroor) *trckd ldrs: effrt over 3f out: kpt on same pce fnl 2f* **6/5**[1]	82
5-50	6	shd	**Regal Connection (USA)**[13] 2290 3-8-8 **72** KDarley 5 (M Johnston) *chsd ldrs: drvn 4f out: one pce fnl 2f* **20/1**	69
41-0	7	2 ½	**Astrobella**[11] 2359 3-9-2 **80** NCallan 7 (M H Tompkins) *swtchd lft s: hld up in rr: hdwy on outside to chse ldrs 7f out: lost pl over 1f out* **33/1**	72
4-03	8	3	**Auction Room (USA)**[13] 2290 3-9-5 **83** RichardHughes 3 (B W Hills) *drvn to ld: set mod pce: qcknd over 4f out: hdd 2f out: sn lost pl* **13/2**[3]	70

2m 13.83s (3.35) **Going Correction** +0.35s/f (Good) **8** Ran SP% **108.1**
Speed ratings (Par 98):100,99,98,97,96 96,94,91
CSF £38.36 CT £304.95 TOTE £6.50: £1.50, £2.10, £2.00; EX 48.00.
Owner The Matthewman Partnership **Bred** Gabriel Bell **Trained** Musley Bank, N Yorks

FOCUS
A fair handicap in which the first two did well making ground from behind after what was not a strong pace. The placed horses set the standard.

2680 BATHROOMS BY DESIGN E B F MEDIAN AUCTION MAIDEN STKS — 6f
2:50 (2:50) (Class 4) 2-Y-0 — **£6,541** (£1,946; £972; £485) **Stalls** Centre

Form				RPR
	1		**Ela Aleka Mou** 2-8-12 PhilipRobinson 8 (M A Jarvis) *w'like: cmpt: racd alone stands' side: chsd ldrs: led over 2f out: hung lft: styd on wl ins last* **8/1**[3]	77+
2	2	1 ½	**Folio (USA)**[13] 2287 2-9-3 RichardHughes 6 (B W Hills) *stdd s: sn trcking ldrs: shkn up and chal appr fnl f: no ex ins last* **8/13**[1]	78
	3	1 ¾	**Aviva** 2-9-3 TomEaves 1 (J Howard Johnson) *w'like: rangy: chsd ldrs: kpt on same pce appr fnl f* **18/1**	72
	4	½	**Fourfoot Bay (IRE)** 2-9-3 LDettori 7 (J D Bethell) *rangy: scope: s.s: hdwy to trck ldrs over 3f out: outpcd 2f out: styd on ins last* **7/1**[2]	71
056	5	5	**First Valentini**[20] 2076 2-8-12 TonyHamilton 5 (N Bycroft) *led tl over 2f out: wknd fnl f* **40/1**	51
	6	hd	**Darfour** 2-9-3 RoystonFfrench 3 (M Johnston) *w'like: angular: scope: dwlt: in tch on outer: rn green and hung lft over 2f out: wandered and wnt rt fnl f: kpt on* **18/1**	55
	7	4	**Oscarshall (IRE)** 2-9-3 MichaelHills 9 (M H Tompkins) *w'like: angular: s.s: sme hdwy over 2f out: hung rt and wknd over 1f out* **20/1**	43
5	8	1 ½	**Gallows Hill (USA)**[31] 1807 2-9-3 PaulHanagan 4 (R A Fahey) *chsd ldrs: rdn over 2f out: sn lost pl* **16/1**	39
06	9	31	**Only A Grand**[28] 1863 2-8-12 PaulMulrennan 2 (R Bastiman) *prom 2f: sn lost pl and bhd: t.o: btn 31l* **100/1**	—

1m 13.4s (0.84) **Going Correction** +0.10s/f (Good) **9** Ran SP% **110.1**
Speed ratings (Par 95):98,96,93,93,86 86,80,78,37
CSF £12.30 TOTE £8.50: £1.80, £1.10, £4.00; EX 14.20.
Owner John Davies (stonehill) **Bred** Brook Stud Bloodstock Ltd **Trained** Newmarket, Suffolk

FOCUS
Probably just an ordinary median maiden auction event with the runner-up and fifth setting the standard.

NOTEBOOK
Ela Aleka Mou, a March foal, is a solid-looking filly. She went to post best and kept to the favoured stands' side, after going on soon after halfway she was right on top at the finish. (op 5-1)
Folio(USA), who lacks scope, looked very fit. He moved up on the bridle but in the end was very definitely second best. (op 5-6 tchd 10-11 and evens in places)
Aviva, a January foal, is a good-bodied individual who holds an Epsom Derby entry. Never far away, he kept changing his legs and the experience will not be lost on him. Seven furlongs and less-quick ground will be in his favour. (op 20-1 tchd 16-1)
Fourfoot Bay(IRE), who stands over plenty of ground, was restless in the stalls and started slowly. He showed plenty of ability but will benefit from being given more time. (op 8-1 tchd 13-2)
First Valentini, upset in the paddock, showed bags of toe but may not be the type to progress. (op 33-1)
Darfour, an immature type, was clueless but is the type to do better over further as he gains experience. (op 12-1 tchd 20-1)

2681 RACINGUK.TV H'CAP — 7f
3:20 (3:20) (Class 4) (0-85,85) 3-Y-0+ — **£8,096** (£2,408; £1,203; £601) **Stalls** Low

Form				RPR
5-02	1		**Imperial Echo (USA)**[8] 2454 5-9-1 **75** BenSwarbrick(3) 7 (T D Barron) *in tch: hdwy to ld over 2f out: hld on wl* **15/2**[2]	88
60-6	2	¾	**Marshman (IRE)**[25] 1935 7-9-11 **85** SaleemGolam(3) 5 (M H Tompkins) *hld up: hdwy over 2f out: chal jst ins last: no ex towards fin* **6/1**[1]	96
0-66	3	2	**Bailieborough (IRE)**[5] 2527 7-9-3 **79** (v) AndrewMullen(5) 8 (Robert Gray) *s.i.s: hdwy 2f out: styd on ins last* **20/1**	85
62-0	4	hd	**Top Dirham**[57] 1143 8-9-7 **78** DaleGibson 6 (M W Easterby) *hld up in rr: hdwy on stands' side over 2f out: hung lft and kpt on same pce fnl f* **8/1**[3]	83
0-35	5	2 ½	**Efidium**[5] 2527 8-8-6 **70** SuzzanneFrance(7) 10 (N Bycroft) *s.i.s: hdwy on outer over 2f out: kpt on wl ins last* **11/1**	69
-506	6	¾	**Tough Love**[13] 2299 7-8-12 **69** DavidAllan 1 (T D Easterby) *hld up in mid-div: hdwy over 3f out: sn chsng ldrs: kpt on same pce appr fnl f* **12/1**	66
6250	7	1 ¼	**Dispol Katie**[8] 2454 5-9-1 **72** PhillipMakin 12 (T D Barron) *trckd ldrs: c stands' side 4f out: kpt on same pce fnl 2f* **14/1**	66
300-	8	½	**Neon Blue**[215] 6354 5-9-1 **72** (v) HayleyTurner 11 (R M Whitaker) *chsd ldrs: one pce fnl 2f* **14/1**	64
603-	9	¾	**Ali D**[247] 5884 8-8-9 **66** oh4 TomEaves 9 (G Woodward) *chsd ldrs on inner: wknd appr fnl f* **33/1**	56
2000	10	1 ½	**Prince Tum Tum (USA)**[12] 2323 6-9-11 **82** EddieAhern 14 (D W Barker) *w ldrs: wknd over 1f out* **9/1**	68
0026	11	¾	**Lord Of The East**[5] 2520 7-9-11 **85** PatrickMathers(3) 2 (I W McInnes) *chsd ldrs: lost pl over 1f out* **16/1**	70
1045	12	3 ½	**Bessemer (JPN)**[40] 1561 5-9-4 **78** DanielTudhope(3) 4 (D Carroll) *hld up in rr: hdwy over 3f out: hung lft and lost pl over 1f out* **10/1**	53
000-	13	4	**Passionately Royal**[314] 4218 4-8-9 **66** oh1 PaulHanagan 3 (R A Fahey) *in tch: drvn over 4f out: lost pl over 2f out* **25/1**	31
0-06	14	shd	**King Harson**[40] 1561 7-9-2 **73** (v) LDettori 15 (J D Bethell) *racd wd 1st 2f: led on outer: hdd over 2f out: sn wknd* **6/1**[1]	38

1m 24.62s (-0.78) **Going Correction** +0.10s/f (Good) **14** Ran SP% **117.3**
Speed ratings (Par 105):108,107,104,104,101 100,99,98,98,96 95,91,86,86
CSF £49.34 CT £871.31 TOTE £7.00: £2.40, £2.30, £8.00; EX 21.90.
Owner J Stephenson **Bred** Derby Lane Farm **Trained** Maunby, N Yorks
■ Stewards' Enquiry : Andrew Mullen two-day ban: used whip with excessive frequency (Jun 29-30)

FOCUS
A competitive handicap for the grade and the form looks sound. The winner was back to his very best, likewise the fourth.
King Harson Official explanation: jockey said gelding lost its action

2682 PRESS MAIDEN STKS — 1m 4f
3:50 (3:50) (Class 4) 3-Y-0+ — **£6,477** (£1,927; £963; £481) **Stalls** Centre

Form				RPR
0-30	1		**Prowess (IRE)**[16] 2203 3-8-8 **88** MichaelHills 7 (B W Hills) *mde all: set mod pce: qcknd 4f out: styd on strly fnl f* **9/4**[2]	90+
3-24	2	3 ½	**Spell Casting (USA)**[30] 1813 3-8-13 **85** NCallan 2 (M H Tompkins) *trckd ldrs: chal over 2f out: hung lft over 1f out: kpt on same pce* **12/1**	89
-522	3	2 ½	**New Guinea**[17] 2175 3-8-13 **86** PhilipRobinson 6 (M A Jarvis) *trckd ldrs: one pce whn hit over hd by rdr of runner-up's whip over 1f out* **5/2**[3]	87+
4	4	4	**Greyside (USA)**[37] 1635 3-8-8 GregFairley(5) 5 (J Howard Johnson) *s.i.s: sn trckng ldrs: outpcd and hung lft over 2f out: kpt on fnl f* **25/1**	79
24-3	5	2	**Dan Dare (USA)**[23] 1994 3-8-13 **94** RobertWinston 1 (Sir Michael Stoute) *trckd ldrs: outpcd over 3f out: wknd over 1f out* **13/8**[1]	75
	6	19	**Talpour (IRE)**[14] 6-9-10 LeeVickers(3) 4 (M C Chapman) *hld up in last: wl in tch: outpcd over 3f out: lost pl over 2f out: sn bhd* **200/1**	45

2m 34.83s (2.43) **Going Correction** +0.35s/f (Good)
WFA 3 from 4yo+ 14lb **6** Ran SP% **109.5**
Speed ratings (Par 105):105,102,101,98,97 84
CSF £25.76 TOTE £3.20: £1.60, £3.40; EX 40.20.
Owner M H Dixon **Bred** M H Dixon **Trained** Lambourn, Berks

FOCUS
Oaks also-ran Prowess opened her account under a positive ride. The placed horses seemed to run to their pre-race marks.
Dan Dare(USA) Official explanation: jockey said colt was unsuited by the good to firm ground

2683 SMITH BROTHERS H'CAP — 6f
4:20 (4:20) (Class 2) (0-100,96) 4-Y-0+ — **£12,954** (£3,854; £1,926; £962) **Stalls** Centre

Form				RPR
60-5	1		**Don Pele (IRE)**[12] 2323 4-8-9 **84** NCallan 2 (K A Ryan) *trckd ldr far side: led that gp and overall over 1f out: jst hld on* **9/1**	96+
0540	2	hd	**Bo McGinty (IRE)**[8] 2450 5-8-4 **79** (b) PaulHanagan 5 (R A Fahey) *trckd ldrs stands' side: led that gp over 1f out: styd on wl fnl f: jst hld* **6/1**[3]	90
1512	3	1 ¾	**Prince Namid**[15] 2230 4-9-4 **93** MichaelHills 7 (Mrs A Duffield) *dwlt: racd stands' side: hdwy and hung lft 2f out: styd on fnl f* **3/1**[1]	99
0032	4	nk	**Folga**[15] 2233 4-8-9 **84** EddieAhern 6 (J G Given) *s.i.s: racd stands' side: sn chsng ldrs: kpt on fnl f* **17/2**	89
50-0	5	nk	**Connect**[13] 2303 9-9-4 **96** (b) SaleemGolam(3) 9 (M H Tompkins) *racd stands' side: hld up: n.m.r on inner 2f out: kpt on fnl f* **11/1**	100
026-	6	2 ½	**Tony The Tap**[231] 6180 5-8-13 **88** FrancisFerris 3 (B Palling) *racd far side: trckd ldrs: effrt over 2f out: kpt on same pce* **25/1**	84
0001	7	¾	**Mr Wolf**[9] 2397 5-8-9 **84** (p) FergalLynch 1 (D W Barker) *led far side tl over 1f out: wknd fnl f* **15/2**	78
5540	8	4	**Fromsong (IRE)**[15] 2227 8-9-7 **96** PhilipRobinson 8 (D K Ivory) *racd stands' side: trckd ldrs: wknd over 1f out* **16/1**	78
0-00	9	½	**Joseph Henry**[5] 2520 4-8-7 **87** GregFairley(5) 10 (M Johnston) *led stands' side tl hdd & wknd over 1f out* **16/1**	68
3005	10	1	**Fullandby (IRE)**[8] 2450 4-8-11 **86** KDarley 4 (T J Etherington) *swtchd lft after s and racd far side: chsd ldrs: rdn and edgd rt 2f out: wknd and eased appr fnl f* **9/2**[2]	64

1m 11.7s (-0.86) **Going Correction** +0.10s/f (Good) **10** Ran SP% **113.7**
Speed ratings (Par 109):109,108,106,106,105 102,101,95,95,93
CSF £60.53 CT £205.52 TOTE £11.00: £2.70, £2.20, £1.40; EX 82.50 Trifecta £163.90 Pool £969.90, 4.20 winning units.
Owner Pedro Rosas **Bred** John J Cosgrave **Trained** Hambleton, N Yorks
■ Stewards' Enquiry : Paul Hanagan one-day ban: used whip with excessive frequency (Jun 29)

FOCUS
They split into two distinct groups. The winner was once rated 21lb higher and his new handler has plenty of leeway to play with and the runner-up sets the standard.

NOTEBOOK

Don Pele(IRE), a Listed winner at two, has plummetted down the ratings. He took command on the far side but in the end the post came just in time. He should continue to give a good account of himself. (op 10-1)

Bo McGinty(IRE), with just one win in his last 27 starts, is not easy to predict. He took charge on the stands' side, and really powering home, in the end was just denied. However, will he perform as well next time? (op 13-2)

Prince Namid, 3lb higher, made a sluggish start. He hung as if feeling the fast ground but to his credit kept going all the way to the line. He will bounce back when he gets the give underfoot he relishes. (op 5-2)

Folga sat down when the stalls opened. If anything she seems to need the sixth furlong now. (op 8-1)

Connect likes it here and he showed enough to suggest that he is close to his best after making his return in Listed company. (op 10-1)

Tony The Tap, who made little appeal in the paddock, returned on a career high-mark despite failing to hit the target last term for another yard. (op 33-1)

Fullandby(IRE) is not easy to predict and here he simply did not look in the mood. (op 11-2 tchd 6-1)

2684 FOUR HIGH PETERGATE HOTEL AND SAWFISH SOFTWARE APPRENTICE H'CAP — 1m 5f 197y

4:50 (4:50) (Class 5) (0-70,69) 4-Y-O+ — **£5,505** (£1,637; £818; £408) **Stalls** Low

Form — RPR

-002 **1** **Compton Eclaire (IRE)**[27] 1883 6-8-4 **52**............(v) AndrewMullen(3) 11 — 63
(B Ellison) *s.i.s: hdwy 4f out: styd on to ld last 75 yds: kpt on strly* **12/1**

-000 **2** *2* **Whispering Death**[11] 2357 4-9-0 **64**............(v1) LiamJones(5) 6 — 72
(W J Haggas) *trckd ldrs: wnt 2nd over 4f out: led over 2f out: hdd and no ex wl ins last* **15/2**[3]

3-03 **3** *3/4* **Indonesia**[11] 2357 4-9-10 **69**............ DanielTudhope 4 — 76
(T D Walford) *sn trcking ldrs: effrt over 3f out: styd on same pce fnl furlog* **9/1**

-001 **4** *1* **Dark Parade (ARG)**[24] 1958 5-8-6 **56**............(b) JamieJones(5) 12 — 62
(G L Moore) *hld up in rr: hdwy 3f out: sn rdn: kpt on: nvr able chal* **6/1**[1]

4520 **5** *1 1/4* **Star Rising**[12] 2320 4-8-7 **52**............ PatrickMathers 2 — 56
(W J Musson) *hld up in rr: hdwy on outside over 3f out: kpt on: nvr rchd ldrs* **7/1**[2]

30-5 **6** *5* **Mr Maxim**[10] 2381 4-8-0 **50** oh2............ MichaelJStainton(5) 13 — 47
(R M Whitaker) *chsd ldrs: one pce fnl 3f* **20/1**

0042 **7** *4* **Oddsmaker (IRE)**[9] 2407 5-9-1 **63**............(t) GregFairley(3) 10 — 54
(M A Barnes) *trckd ldrs: t.k.h: led 6f out tl over 2f out: wknd qckly fnl f* **8/1**

10-3 **8** *4* **Zeydnaa (IRE)**[10] 2381 6-8-6 **51**............ SaleemGolam 5 — 37
(C R Wilson) *chsd ldrs: wknd over 1f out* **6/1**[1]

0-03 **9** *1/2* **Danzatrice**[11] 2362 4-8-9 **54**............ BenSwarbrick 8 — 39
(C W Thornton) *in tch: effrt 4f out: lost pl over 1f out* **25/1**

16-6 **10** *6* **Best Port (IRE)**[11] 2365 10-9-1 **60**............ DominicFox 3 — 37
(J Parkes) *hld up in mid-field: effrt 4f out: sn wknd* **25/1**

0-00 **11** *1 3/4* **Perfect Punch**[22] 1138 7-8-10 **60**............ JamesReveley(5) 9 — 34
(K G Reveley) *hld up towards rr: effrt on wd outside 4f out: sn btn* **40/1**

406 **12** *3* **Reminiscent (IRE)**[10] 2381 7-7-12 **50**............(p) SoniaEaton(7) 1 — 20
(B P J Baugh) *hld up in rr: drvn over 3f out: nvr on terms* **25/1**

-301 **13** *11* **Zarova (IRE)**[12] 2326 4-9-1 **60**............ PaulMulrennan 14 — 15
(M W Easterby) *hld up in rr: drvn over 3f out: no rspnse* **8/1**

0-44 **14** *1 1/4* **Transit**[100] 570 7-8-8 **56** ow1............ MarkLawson(5) 7 — 9
(B Ellison) *led tl 6f out: lost pl over 3f out* **25/1**

3m 2.25s (3.81) **Going Correction** +0.35s/f (Good) — **14** Ran SP% **115.3**
Speed ratings (Par 103):103,101,101,100,100 97,95,92,92,89 88,86,80,79
CSF £85.73 CT £854.18 TOTE £12.10: £3.10, £2.10, £3.50; EX 69.90 Place 6 £192.60, Place 5 £57.75.
Owner S V Rutter **Bred** Declan And Catherine Macpartlin **Trained** Norton, N Yorks
■ Stewards' Enquiry : Jamie Jones one-day ban: used whip with excessive frequency (Jun 29)

FOCUS

No gallop in the early stages so the winner deserves credit for coming from off the pace but it was basically a case of the runner-up turning up his nose at what looked a first-class winning opportunity. The form is rated as average for the grade.

Zarova(IRE) Official explanation: jockey said colt lost its action

T/Jkpt: Not won. T/Plt: £174.70. Pool £75,882. 317 winning tickets T/Qpdt: £39.00. Pool £3,920. 74.25 winning tickets WG

2685 - (Foreign Racing) - See Raceform Interactive

1468 CORK (R-H)

Sunday, June 18

OFFICIAL GOING: Firm (good to firm in places)

2686a KERRY SPRING WATER ROCHESTOWN STKS (LISTED RACE) — 6f

3:05 (3:07) 2-Y-O — **£24,693** (£7,244; £3,451; £1,175)

RPR

1 **He's A Decoy (IRE)**[18] 2152 2-9-1............ MJKinane 5 — 100+
(David Wachman, Ire) *sn trckd ldr in 2nd: rdn 2f out: chal and led fr 1f out: sn clr: styd on wl: comf* **6/4**[1]

2 *2* **Varsity Blues (IRE)**[9] 2419 2-9-1............ WJLee 2 — 91
(T Stack, Ire) *prom: mainly 3rd: 2nd and no imp u.p fr under 1f out: kpt on same pce* **9/2**[3]

3 *1* **Howya Now Kid (IRE)**[9] 2419 2-9-1............ JMurtagh 3 — 88
(G M Lyons, Ire) *racd mainly 4th: 3rd and no imp u.p ins fnl f: kpt on same pce* **3/1**[2]

4 *1* **Saint Andrew (IRE)**[14] 2268 2-9-1............ PJSmullen 4 — 85
(Peter Casey, Ire) *sn led: sltly hmpd and lost action over 1f out: sn hdd and dropped to 4th: kpt on same pce* **8/1**

5 *5* **Musthav (IRE)**[16] 2212 2-8-12............(b1) WMLordan 1 — 67
(T Stack, Ire) *in tch in rr: no imp u.p and bhd fnl f* **5/1**

1m 11.5s — **5** Ran SP% **111.0**
CSF £8.64 TOTE £1.80: £1.20, £2.10; DF 4.30.
Owner Joseph Joyce **Bred** Holborn Trust Co **Trained** Goolds Cross, Co Tipperary

NOTEBOOK

He's A Decoy(IRE), a winner over seven furlongs on his debut, handled the shorter trip and faster ground well enough, despite the steady pace. His trainer will now look at the Superlative Stakes at Newmarket's July meeting next. (op 6/4 tchd 5/4)

Varsity Blues(IRE), a dual previous winner, chased the winner home but was never able to reduce the deficit. (op 7/2)

Howya Now Kid(IRE), who was narrowly beaten by today's runner-up at Fairyhouse, was further behind having been held up in a steadily-run race. (op 5/2)

2689a KERRY GROUP EUROPEAN BREEDERS FUND NOBLESSE STKS (GROUP 3) (FILLIES) — 1m 4f

4:35 (4:40) 3-Y-O+ — **£44,827** (£13,103; £6,206; £2,068)

RPR

1 **Sina Cova (IRE)**[14] 2273 4-9-9 97............ JMurtagh 6 — 107
(Peter Casey, Ire) *sn trckd ldr in 2nd: led over 5f out: travelling wl st: rdn clr fr over 1 1/2f out: styd on wl: easily* **16/1**

2 *4 1/2* **Kushnarenkovo**[14] 2273 3-8-9 97............ JAHeffernan 3 — 100
(A P O'Brien, Ire) *dwlt: sn chsd ldrs in 5th: rdn in 3rd over 4f out: 2nd and no imp u.p fr under 2f out: kpt on same pce* **7/1**

3 *2* **Allexina**[32] 1785 4-9-9 106............ FMBerry 2 — 97
(John M Oxx, Ire) *in rr: clsr in 5th bef st: rdn in 4th 2f out: sn 3rd and no imp: kpt on one pce* **9/2**[3]

4 *1/2* **Hovering (IRE)**[7] 2488 3-8-9 94............(bt1) KJManning 4 — 96
(J S Bolger, Ire) *trckd ldrs in 4th: clsr in 2nd and rdn over 4f out: hung towards rail and no imp fr 2f out: sn dropped to 4th and kpt on on* **10/1**

5 *9* **Perfect Hedge**[64] 1026 4-9-9 107............ MJKinane 7 — 82
(John M Oxx, Ire) *trckd ldrs: mainly 3rd: lost pl over 4f out: dropped to 6th bef st: sn no imp u.p* **7/2**[2]

6 *9* **Kiswahili**[4] 2563 4-9-9............ DPMcDonogh 8 — 67
(Sir Mark Prescott) *led: hdd over 5f out: lost pl qckly: trailing in rr and n.d fr bef st* **10/3**[1]

P **Dancing Sky (IRE)**[14] 2273 3-8-9 100............ PJSmullen 5 — —
(D K Weld, Ire) *broke out of stalls: reloaded: racd in 6th: 4th over 4f out: rdn st: no imp and eased fr under 2f out: p.u lame ins fnl f* **7/2**[2]

2m 32.7s
WFA 3 from 4yo+ 14lb — **8** Ran SP% **113.2**
CSF £117.11 TOTE £24.50: £5.20, £4.00; DF 139.30.
Owner Basil Brindley **Bred** Basil Brindley **Trained** Stamullen, Co Meath

NOTEBOOK

Kiswahili, winner of a minor race at Leopardstown four days earlier, tried to make very yard in this better company but faded very tamely after losing the advantage just after halfway. She does not look up to this level at this stage. (op 3/1 tchd 7/2)

Dancing Sky(IRE) Official explanation: jockey said filly lost her action in the closing stages

2690 - 2691a (Foreign Racing) - See Raceform Interactive

1714 COLOGNE (R-H)

Sunday, June 18

OFFICIAL GOING: Good

2692a PFERDEWETTEN.DE-TROPHY (GROUP 2) — 1m

3:50 (3:57) 4-Y-O+ — **£27,586** (£10,345; £4,138; £2,759)

RPR

1 **Arcadio (GER)**[21] 2061 4-9-6............ ASuborics 2 — 114
(P Schiergen, Germany) *held up in 5th, 4th straight, headway down outside from over 1 1/2f out, strong run final f to lead close home* **1/2**[1]

2 *nk* **Soldier Hollow**[35] 1712 6-9-6............ THellier 4 — 113
(P Schiergen, Germany) *raced in 2nd behind slow pace, led over 1f out, caught close home* **23/10**[2]

3 *1 1/2* **Lazio (GER)**[7] 2492 5-9-6............ OPeslier 6 — 110
(A Trybuhl, Germany) *raced in 4th, 5th straight, stayed on under pressure final 1 1/2f* **49/10**[3]

4 *3/4* **Apeiron (GER)**[28] 1869 5-9-6............(b) J-PCarvalho 7 — 109
(Mario Hofer, Germany) *started slowly and behind, stayed on final 2f but nver a factor* **18/1**

5 *1 1/2* **Willingly (GER)**[7] 2492 7-9-6............ JVictoire 1 — 106
(M Trybuhl, Germany) *pulled hard tracking leader in 3rd, one pace final 1 1/2f* **111/10**

6 *1 1/4* **Madresal (GER)**[231] 6190 7-9-6............ AGoritz 5 — 103
(P Schiergen, Germany) *set slow pace, headed over 1f out, weakened* **174/10**

1m 40.68s (2.29) — **6** Ran SP% **132.9**
(including 10 euro stake): WIN 15; PL 12, 15; SF 34.
Owner Gestut Schlenderhan **Bred** *unknown **Trained** Germany

2670 SAN SIRO (R-H)

Sunday, June 18

OFFICIAL GOING: Good to firm

2693a GRAN PREMIO DI MILANO (GROUP 1) — 1m 4f

3:05 (3:05) 3-Y-O+ — **£140,028** (£70,814; £41,324; £20,662)

RPR

1 **Shamdala (IRE)**[28] 1875 4-9-3............ CSoumillon 3 — 115
(A De Royer-Dupre, France) *raced in 3rd, went 2nd 1 1/2f out, led 1f out, ran on well* **9/20**[1]

2 *1 1/2* **Groom Tesse**[28] 1870 5-9-6............(b) SLandi 6 — 116
(L Camici, Italy) *led after 2f, set steady pace, headed 1f out, kept on* **56/10**[3]

3 *1 1/4* **Vol De Nuit**[23] 1976 5-9-3............ MDemuro 5 — 111
(L M Cumani) *led 2f then raced in 2nd, stayed on at same pace final 2f* **32/10**[2]

4 *3 1/2* **Hattan (IRE)**[19] 2116 4-9-6............ KerrinMcEvoy 2 — 109
(C E Brittain) *saddled slipped forward leaving stalls, raced in 4th throughout but unable to be ridden final 2f* **105/10**

5 *1/2* **Montalegre (IRE)**[14] 4-9-6............ EBotti 4 — 108
(A & G Botti, Italy) *held up in last, never a factor* **25/1**

6 *hd* **Nicaron (GER)**[48] 1369 4-9-6............ DBonilla 1 — 108
(H Steinmetz, Germany) *raced in 5th, never a factor* **101/10**

2m 28.7s — **6** Ran SP% **129.5**
TOTE (including 1 euro stake): WIN 1.44; PL 1.19, 1.71; SF 3.13.
Owner H H Aga Khan **Bred** His Highness The Aga Khan's Studs S C **Trained** Chantilly, France

NOTEBOOK

Shamdala(IRE) thrives on fast ground and, despite the kind of pedestrian pace which would have counted against a filly proven over much further, she did not need to be given a hard race to score with some comfort. The Yorkshire Oaks is her next port of call, followed by an end-of-season tour of the Far East.

Vol De Nuit had pole position sitting in behind the leader for most of the trip, but was unable to raise his game when the tempo finally quickened.

Hattan(IRE) was virtually unrideable from the moment his saddle slipped leaving the stalls and this run is best forgotten.

2694a OAKS D'ITALIA (GROUP 1) (FILLIES) 1m 3f
4:15 (4:15) 3-Y-O £201,269 (£108,193; £64,772; £32,386)

RPR

1 **Dionisia (USA)**[22] 2043 3-8-11 .... CSoumillon 14 115
(R Menichetti, Italy) *always prominent, 3rd straight, led 2f out, quickened clear, easily* 19/4[3]

2 *6* **Twardowska (ITY)** 3-8-11 .... C-PLemaire 7 105
(F Losani, Italy) *10th straight, headway over 3f out, 5th 2f out, stayed on final f* 23/1

3 *¾* **Souvenance**[35] 1714 3-8-11 .... MDemuro 16 104
(Sir Mark Prescott) *disputed lead to 2f out, stayed on at one pace* 3/1[2]

4 *nk* **Sabana Perdida (IRE)**[35] 1713 3-8-11 .... MTellini 10 104
(R Feligioni, Italy) *in touch, 5th straight, one pace final 2f* 138/10

5 *snk* **Mara Spectrum (IRE)**[42] 3-8-11 .... DVargiu 11 103
(B Grizzetti, Italy) *raced in 7th or 8th, close up 2f out, no extra final f* 118/10

6 *5* **Veronica Franco (ITY)** 3-8-11 .... MMonteriso 9 95
(E Borromeo, Italy) *held up in rear, stayed on steadily final 2f* 118/10

7 *hd* **La Bandera**[22] 2043 3-8-11 .... MEsposito 12 95
(B Grizzetti, Italy) *never near leaders* 67/1

8 *1 ¾* **Rising Cross**[16] 2203 3-8-11 .... GeorgeBaker 4 79
(J R Best) *held up in rear, 11th straight, hung left 4f out, ridden 3f out, little response* 11/10[1]

9 *5* **Damascena (GER)** 3-8-11 .... WMongil 15 79
(P Schiergen, Germany) *prominent, 4th straight, weakened quickly 2f out* 84/10

10 *½* **Turning Light (GER)**[35] 1714 3-8-11 .... EPedroza 3 78
(Mario Hofer, Germany) *made no show* 169/10

11 *1 ¼* **Wickwing**[22] 2043 3-8-11 .... EBotti 8 76
(A & G Botti, Italy) *disputed lead to 2f out, weakened quickly* 27/1

12 *5* **Samerous (FR)**[35] 1714 3-8-11 .... ADeVries 13 68
(H Blume, Germany) *always in rear* 179/10

13 *½* **Ekagra**[22] 2043 3-8-11 .... SLandi 2 67
(F & L Camici, Italy) *never a factor* 51/1

14 *11* **Musa Golosa**[35] 1713 3-8-11 .... SMulas 1 50
(B Grizzetti, Italy) *never a factor* 40/1

15 *dist* **Black Profusion (IRE)**[22] 2043 3-8-11 .... FBranca 6 —
(P Martometti, Italy) *always behind* 48/1

2m 14.5s 15 Ran SP% 149.5
WIN 5.74; PL 2.14, 4.10, 1.80; DF 174.83.
Owner Scuderia Razza Dell'Olmo **Bred** E H B Lane III **Trained** Italy

NOTEBOOK
Dionisia(USA) proved her disappointing effort in the Italian 1,000 Guineas all wrong with a dominant display, shooting clear at the quarter-mile pole and soon putting the issue beyond doubt.
Souvenance posted a gutsy effort, sharing the pace-setting duties and keeping on gamely once the winner swept past. Now placed in Group Three, then Group Two, then Group One company, she will have her sights lowered and try to win a Listed event.
Rising Cross was among the backmarkers in the early stages and, despite momentarily being short of room when switching to the outside early in the home straight, never looked like justifying favouritism. This may have come too soon after Epsom.

2281 CARLISLE (R-H)
Monday, June 19

OFFICIAL GOING: Home straight - good to firm (good in places); far side - good (good to firm in places)
Wind: Fairly strong; half against

2695 CARLISLE LVA NOVICE AUCTION STKS 5f
2:15 (2:16) (Class 5) 2-Y-O £3,238 (£963; £481; £240) Stalls High

Form RPR

2522 1 **My Valerina (IRE)**[3] 2623 2-8-4 .... RoystonFfrench 3 73
(Mrs A Duffield) *pressed ldr: rdn 1/2-way: led ins fnl f: kpt on wl* 11/8[1]

42 2 *3* **Riotous (IRE)**[13] 2321 2-8-9 .... DanielTudhope(3) 6 70
(A Dickman) *led: rdn 2f out: hdd ins fnl f: no ex* 11/8[1]

3 *2* **La Esperanza** 2-8-2 .... JoeFanning 1 53
(T D Barron) *chsd ldrs: effrt 2f out: one pce fnl f* 6/1[2]

4 *2 ½* **Dispol Splendid (IRE)** 2-8-2 .... DaleGibson 2 44
(T D Barron) *prom: rdn over 2f out: outpcd over 1f out* 16/1[3]

5 *½* **Violet's Pride** 2-7-11 .... AndrewElliott(5) 4 42
(S Parr) *in tch: niggled 1/2-way: effrt and hung lft over 2f out: outpcd whn hung rt ins fnl f* 25/1

00 6 *9* **Hair Of The Dog**[6] 2523 2-8-7 .... RobertWinston 5 15
(J G Given) *sn chsng ldrs: rdn and wknd wl over 1f out* 33/1

62.91 secs (1.41) **Going Correction** -0.05s/f (Good) 6 Ran SP% 111.2
Speed ratings (Par 93):86,81,78,74,73 58
CSF £3.25 TOTE £2.30: £1.10, £1.50; EX 3.40.
Owner V Hubbard D Clinton S Gale & M Milns **Bred** C H Wacker Iii **Trained** Constable Burton, N Yorks

FOCUS
A moderate winning time for this uncompetitive race that went to the form horses. The form is straightforward, rated around the first two.

NOTEBOOK
My Valerina(IRE) is not very big but has plenty of courage and again showed a good attitude turned out quickly after her York run to get off the mark. However, given her lack of physical scope she is going to be vulnerable under a penalty to the better types and may not be easy to place from now on. (op 5-4 tchd 6-4)
Riotous(IRE), a reliable sort, had the run of the race and ran creditably to chase home an exposed sort, but he is likely to remain vulnerable in this type of event. (op 6-4 tchd 13-8)
La Esperanza, out of a dual winner up to seven furlongs, was not disgraced in this ordinary event against a couple of exposed but reliable yardsticks and looks the sort to do better in ordinary handicaps over further in due course. (op 8-1)
Dispol Splendid(IRE) from a stable that has been in good form, looked fit enough for this debut and showed ability. She may do better over further once handicapped. (op 12-1)
Violet's Pride, out of a five-furlong winner, hinted at ability despite being green and looking ill-at-ease on the very quick ground. She may be capable of better but will have to improve a fair bit to win a race in this grade.
Hair Of The Dog again took the eye in the preliminaries but proved a big disappointment in this uncompetitive event. He will have to show more before he is worth a bet.

2696 CROSBY CLAIMING STKS 1m 1f 61y
2:45 (2:45) (Class 6) 3-Y-O+ £2,730 (£806; £403) Stalls High

Form RPR

-605 1 **Awaken**[10] 2407 5-9-0 45 .... PhillipMakin 3 57
(Miss Tracy Waggott) *hld up: effrt whn nt clr run 2f out: swtchd and rdn to ld ins fnl f: r.o* 7/1[3]

6600 2 *1* **Bella Fiorella (IRE)**[9] 2434 3-8-1 47 .... DominicFox(3) 2 55
(Miss V Haigh) *hld up: effrt outside to ld over 1f out: hdd ins fnl f: r.o* 20/1

0406 3 *3 ½* **Monash Lad (IRE)**[7] 2499 4-9-3 65 .... SaleemGolam(3) 5 54
(M H Tompkins) *prom on outside: effrt and ev ch wl over 1f out: one pce fnl f* 10/3[1]

0256 4 *2* **Sawwaah (IRE)**[9] 2454 9-9-6 71 ....(v) AdrianTNicholls 11 50
(D Nicholls) *hld up in tch on ins: effrt 2f out: one pce appr fnl f* 10/3[1]

0-06 5 *1* **Campbells Lad**[12] 2362 5-9-0 35 .... PatrickMathers(3) 10 45
(Mrs G S Rees) *led tl hdd over 1f out: sn outpcd* 20/1

05 6 *1 ¼* **Roman History (IRE)**[17] 2192 3-8-4 48 ow2 .... BenSwarbrick(3) 7 44
(Miss Tracy Waggott) *chsd ldrs: effrt 2f out: sn outpcd* 16/1

3-00 7 *3* **Eminence Gift**[18] 2181 4-8-13 50 .... FrancisNorton 6 33
(K R Burke) *trckd ldrs: rdn 3f out: outpcd whn n.m.r wl over 1f out* 15/2

00-0 8 *1* **Loaded Gun**[19] 1560 6-8-10 46 .... AndrewElliott(5) 8 33
(W Storey) *in tch: outpcd 1/2-way: n.d after* 33/1

4303 9 *1 ¼* **High Swainston**[16] 2240 5-9-0 45 .... DanielTudhope(3) 9 32
(R Craggs) *trckd ldrs tl rdn and wknd fr 2f out* 5/1[2]

0-06 10 *1* **Ruby Legend**[14] 2282 8-8-13 46 .... JamesReveley(7) 12 33
(K G Reveley) *hld up: rdn over 3f out: nvr rchd ldrs* 16/1

00-0 11 *1 ¼* **Jenna Stannis**[12] 2362 4-8-10 47 .... JoeFanning 1 21
(W Storey) *chsd ldrs tl wknd fr 2f out* 66/1

12 *24* **Bamalam** 3-8-6 ow2 .... TonyHamilton 4 —
(C R Wilson) *s.i.s: nvr on terms* 40/1

1m 59.41s (1.85) **Going Correction** +0.175s/f (Good)
WFA 3 from 4yo+ 11lb 12 Ran SP% 115.3
Speed ratings (Par 101):98,97,94,92,91 90,87,86,85,84 83,62
CSF £141.47 TOTE £7.40: £2.60, £11.40, £1.40; EX 218.20.
Owner Miss T Waggott **Bred** Juddmonte Farms **Trained** Spennymoor, Co Durham

FOCUS
A modest event in which the gallop was fair and a race that did not take as much winning as seemed likely with several market leaders disappointing. The form is weak with the winner the best guide.

2697 BORDER CONSTRUCTION H'CAP 7f 200y
3:15 (3:17) (Class 5) (0-70,70) 4-Y-O+ £3,886 (£1,156; £577; £288) Stalls High

Form RPR

/460 1 **Royal Indulgence**[8] 2482 6-7-11 51 oh8 .... LiamJones(5) 7 60
(W M Brisbourne) *bhd: rdn over 3f out: kpt on wl to ld towards fin* 25/1

-301 2 *nk* **Confide (IRE)**[17] 2195 4-8-12 61 .... RobertWinston 4 71+
(G A Swinbank) *hld up outside: rdn to ld over 1f out: rdr looked rnd and stopped riding briefly ins last: shkn up last 50yds: hdd cl home* 3/1[1]

40-5 3 *1 ¾* **Gifted Flame**[37] 1665 7-9-7 70 .... PaulHanagan 8 74
(J J Quinn) *hld up: hdwy over 3f out: rdn over 2f out: kpt on ins fnl f* 6/1[3]

0205 4 *1* **Champain Sands (IRE)**[11] 2378 7-8-8 57 .... DavidAllan 3 59
(E J Alston) *hld up: hdwy over 3f out: edgd rt and no imp fr 2f out* 9/1

00-4 5 *1* **Tedsdale Mac**[3] 2627 7-7-12 54 ow1 .... SuzzanneFrance(7) 2 54
(N Bycroft) *bhd: rdn 3f out: edgd rt and kpt on fnl f: no imp* 11/2[2]

0-03 6 *2* **Son Of Thunder (IRE)**[14] 2286 5-8-6 55 .... TomEaves 1 50+
(M Dods) *chsd ldrs: rdn over 3f out: no ex over 1f out* 11/2[2]

-605 7 *nk* **Abstract Folly (IRE)**[24] 1996 4-8-7 56 ....(b) AdrianTNicholls 6 50
(J D Bethell) *hld up in tch: rdn 3f out: btn over 1f out* 7/1

-004 8 *½* **Fairy Monarch (IRE)**[11] 2378 7-8-2 51 oh1 ....(b) JoeFanning 10 44
(P T Midgley) *in tch: effrt 3f out: wknd over 1f out* 25/1

-525 9 *shd* **Linden's Lady**[10] 2400 6-8-7 56 ....(v) TonyHamilton 11 49
(J R Weymes) *taken early to post: hld up: rdn 3f out: nvr on terms* 16/1

-000 10 *5* **Anthemion (IRE)**[11] 2378 9-8-0 54 ow3 .... AndrewMullen(5) 5 36
(Mrs J C McGregor) *pressed ldr tl wknd fr 2f out* 25/1

0060 11 *1 ½* **Redwood Rocks (IRE)**[64] 1035 5-9-7 70 .... DerekMcGaffin 9 48
(B Smart) *led to over 1f out: sn wknd* 14/1

0005 12 *6* **Aqua**[16] 2240 4-7-13 53 oh4 ow2 .... RoryMoore(5) 12 17
(P T Midgley) *prom tl rdn and wknd over 2f out: eased whn btn* 100/1

1m 41.0s (0.91) **Going Correction** +0.175s/f (Good) 12 Ran SP% 117.6
Speed ratings (Par 103):102,101,99,98,97 95,95,95,95,90 88,82
CSF £95.90 CT £530.46 TOTE £36.60: £9.50, £1.60, £1.70; EX 200.30 TRIFECTA Not won..
Owner P G Evans **Bred** P V And J P Jackson **Trained** Great Ness, Shropshire
■ Stewards' Enquiry : Robert Winston 28-day ban: failed to ride for first place (Jun 30 - Jul 27)

FOCUS
An ordinary race but a controversial finish with the rider of the runner-up (banned for 28 days) taking things easy when in a clear lead in the last furlong and getting collared in the closing stages. The form may not prove solid with the fourth the solid guide.

2698 HAPPY RETIREMENT RON BARRY H'CAP 7f 200y
3:45 (3:46) (Class 5) (0-75,71) 3-Y-O £3,238 (£963; £481; £240) Stalls High

Form RPR

65-5 1 **Decree Nisi**[29] 1868 3-8-12 62 .... RoystonFfrench 4 69
(Mrs A Duffield) *prom: rdn over 3f out: rallied to ld ins fnl f: styd on wl* 10/1

1204 2 *1 ¼* **Musicmaestroplease (IRE)**[9] 2441 3-8-6 61 .... AndrewElliott(5) 1 65
(S Parr) *cl up: led over 2f out: hdd ins fnl f: r.o* 11/4[2]

3032 3 *2* **Great Chieftain (IRE)**[14] 2297 3-9-7 71 .... PaulHanagan 6 70
(R A Fahey) *keen: led to over 2f out: edgd rt and no ex over 1f out* 7/4[1]

-540 4 *2 ½* **Mister Maq**[19] 2128 3-8-9 59 ....(p) TomEaves 2 53
(M Dods) *hld up in tch: rdn over 3f out: no imp over 1f out* 6/1

5045 5 *3 ½* **Ayam Jantan**[17] 2198 3-8-6 56 .... JoeFanning 8 42
(M Johnston) *trckd ldrs: rdn 3f out: wknd over 1f out* 7/2[3]

3-00 6 *26* **Sinner Or Saint (IRE)**[30] 1855 3-9-6 70 .... FergalLynch 5 —
(T D Easterby) *hld up: rdn 3f out: sn btn* 16/1

1m 41.4s (1.31) **Going Correction** +0.175s/f (Good) 6 Ran SP% 114.5
Speed ratings (Par 99):100,98,96,94,90 64
CSF £38.49 CT £71.81 TOTE £10.30: £3.80, £1.60; EX 41.30.
Owner RSJ Partnership **Bred** A Perry And N McLoughlin **Trained** Constable Burton, N Yorks

FOCUS
An uncompetitive handicap in which the pace was just fair and the third sets the standard.
Decree Nisi Official explanation: trainer said, regarding the improved form shown, the gelding had strengthened up in the winter and may have benefited from today's quicker ground
Sinner Or Saint(IRE) Official explanation: jockey said colt lost its action

2699 CARRIER TRANSICOLD FILLIES' H'CAP 6f 192y
4:15 (4:18) (Class 5) (0-70,70) 3-Y-O **£3,238** (£963; £481; £240) **Stalls High**

Form RPR
0141 **1** **Inaminute (IRE)**[22] 2050 3-8-10 **64**.............................. AndrewElliott(5) 6 76
(K R Burke) *prom: effrt over 2f out: led wl over 1f out: edgd lft: kpt on wl fnl f* **3/1**[2]
4000 **2** *2* **Penny Glitters**[13] 2324 3-8-5 **57**................................ DanielTudhope(3) 1 63
(S Parr) *prom: effrt and ev ch over 2f out: kpt on ins fnl f: nt rch wnr* **12/1**
-023 **3** *½* **Emily's Place (IRE)**[14] 2301 3-9-3 **69**.................... SaleemGolam(3) 4 74
(M H Tompkins) *midfield: effrt over 2f out: wandered fr over 1f out: no imp fnl f* **15/8**[1]
4-60 **4** *2 ½* **Fortress**[23] 2016 3-8-8 **57**..(b[1]) DavidAllan 3 55
(E J Alston) *chsd ldrs: led over 3f out to wl over 1f out: one pce* **16/1**
0-06 **5** *3 ½* **Eurana**[28] 1888 3-8-2 **51** oh4.. JoeFanning 12 39
(Jedd O'Keeffe) *keen: cl up tl rdn and no ex fr 2f out* **25/1**
300- **6** *½* **Ruby Rubble**[257] 5695 3-7-13 **55**............................. PatrickDonaghy(7) 7 41
(K R Burke) *dwlt: bhd and rdn over 3f out: hung rt over 1f out: nvr rchd ldrs* **20/1**
60-0 **7** *nk* **Briery Blaze**[18] 2171 3-8-11 **60**................................. RobertWinston 2 46
(Mrs K Walton) *hld up: rdn over 2f out: n.d* **10/1**
0-33 **8** *1 ½* **Takanewa (IRE)**[19] 2129 3-9-2 **70**.............................. AndrewMullen(5) 5 51
(J Howard Johnson) *keen: led to over 3f out: wknd over 1f out* **7/1**[3]
500- **9** *4* **Silver Sail**[253] 5768 3-8-2 **51**...................................... RoystonFfrench 11 21
(J S Wainwright) *in tch tl rdn and wknd over 2f out* **33/1**
0020 **10** *8* **Nimble Star**[3] 2616 3-8-2 **51** oh12.................................. PaulHanagan 8 —
(C W Fairhurst) *hld up: rdn over 3f out: nvr on terms* **20/1**
36-0 **11** *6* **Lucidity Light (IRE)**[35] 1747 3-9-2 **65**........................... FrancisNorton 9 —
(J D Bethell) *midfield: rdn over 3f out: sn btn* **25/1**
0066 **12** *4* **Dispol Valentine**[17] 2192 3-7-13 **53** oh13 ow2............. RoryMoore(5) 10 —
(P T Midgley) *bhd: rdn over 3f out: sn btn* **66/1**

1m 27.52s (0.42) **Going Correction** +0.175s/f (Good) 12 Ran SP% **116.6**
Speed ratings (Par 96):104,101,101,98,94 93,93,91,87,77 71,66
CSF £33.55 CT £85.78 TOTE £3.70: £1.70, £3.20, £1.30; EX 46.80.
Owner Ray Bailey **Bred** R Bailey **Trained** Middleham Moor, N Yorks

FOCUS
A modest event in which the pace was sound but those racing up with the pace held the edge. The form looks pretty solid rated around the placed horses.
Briery Blaze Official explanation: jockey said filly had no more to give
Takanewa(IRE) Official explanation: jockey said filly ran too free

2700 WARWICK BRIDGE H'CAP 5f 193y
4:45 (4:46) (Class 6) (0-60,60) 3-Y-O+ **£2,730** (£806; £403) **Stalls High**

Form RPR
0220 **1** **Bodden Bay**[114] 514 4-9-3 **52**................................... DanielTudhope(3) 2 61
(D Carroll) *cl up: led over 2f out: hld on gamely fnl f* **12/1**[3]
0003 **2** *½* **Chairman Bobby**[7] 2505 8-8-9 **46**..........................(p) MarkLawson(5) 15 54
(D W Barker) *led to over 2f out: rallied: kpt on u.p fnl f* **6/1**[2]
0540 **3** *nk* **Haulage Man**[5] 2544 8-8-13 **45**....................................(p) PaulHanagan 1 52
(Karen McLintock) *bhd: hdwy stands side over 1f out: kpt on wl fnl f* **14/1**
460- **4** *nk* **The Old Soldier**[297] 4711 8-9-5 **51**.. DavidAllan 6 57
(A Dickman) *bhd: edgd rt and hdwy over 1f out: kpt on wl fnl f: nrst fin* **12/1**[3]
-316 **5** *hd* **Petite Mac**[2] 2661 6-9-7 **60**...................................... SuzzanneFrance(7) 16 65
(N Bycroft) *bhd tl hdwy far side over 1f out: nrst fin* **4/1**[1]
004- **6** *½* **Paddywack (IRE)**[170] 6695 9-8-13 **45**..................................(b) PaulQuinn 9 49
(D W Chapman) *midfield: effrt whn n.m.r over 2f out: one pce fr over 1f out* **25/1**
-460 **7** *1* **Obe One**[7] 2505 6-9-7 **53**.. RobertWinston 14 54+
(D Nicholls) *s.i.s: hld up: effrt over 2f out: no imp* **4/1**[1]
006- **8** *½* **Frimley's Matterry**[287] 4999 6-8-13 **45**................................. TomEaves 11 44
(R E Barr) *prom tl rdn and no ex wl over 1f out* **22/1**
06-4 **9** *¾* **Attila The Hun**[48] 1391 7-8-12 **44**............................... AdrianTNicholls 8 41
(F Watson) *stdd towards rr: effrt stands side over 1f out: no imp* **33/1**
3500 **10** *hd* **Mill By The Stream**[7] 2504 4-8-13 **45**................................ JoeFanning 4 42
(P T Midgley) *in tch: effrt over 2f out: wknd over 1f out* **16/1**
0-00 **11** *nk* **Fairgame Man**[5] 2544 8-9-4 **50**..................................... TonyHamilton 13 46
(J S Wainwright) *in tch towards far side tl wknd wl over 1f out* **14/1**
6000 **12** *1* **Bint Royal (IRE)**[5] 2543 8-9-3 **52**..............................(v) DominicFox(3) 10 45+
(Miss V Haigh) *midfield: rdn over 2f out: outpcd whn hmpd over 1f out* **25/1**
0454 **13** *1 ¾* **Sharp Hat**[27] 1909 12-8-12 **44**.. DaleGibson 5 31
(D W Chapman) *chsd ldrs tl wknd wl over 1f out* **25/1**
000- **14** *1 ½* **Drury Lane (IRE)**[203] 6445 6-8-7 **44**....................(p) AndrewElliott(5) 17 27
(D W Chapman) *chsd ldrs to 2f out: sn rdn and btn* **16/1**
0036 **15** *hd* **Sundried Tomato**[5] 2544 7-9-0 **46**..............................(p) PhillipMakin 7 28
(D W Chapman) *cl up tl rdn and wknd over 1f out* **14/1**
00-0 **16** *2* **Instinct**[5] 2550 5-8-10 **42**.. FergalLynch 12 18+
(Micky Hammond) *s.i.s: keen in rr: rdn over 2f out: no imp whn hmpd over 1f out* **66/1**
00-0 **17** *4* **Maluti**[35] 1722 5-8-8 **43**..(b[1]) SaleemGolam(3) 3 7
(Rae Guest) *s.i.s: a bhd* **33/1**

1m 14.54s (0.93) **Going Correction** -0.05s/f (Good) 17 Ran SP% **124.7**
Speed ratings (Par 101):91,90,89,89,89 88,87,86,85,85 84,83,81,79,79 76,71
CSF £77.42 CT £1079.94 TOTE £15.00: £2.40, £2.10, £3.50, £3.80; EX 118.40.
Owner Andy Franks & Steve Franks **Bred** Gary Middlemiss **Trained** Warthill, N Yorks
■ Stewards' Enquiry : David Allan one-day ban: careless riding (Jun 30)

FOCUS
A good early gallop and a race in which it paid to race prominently but a very moderate winning time for a race like this. The form looks solid enough rated around those in the frame.
Instinct Official explanation: jockey said gelding was denied a clear run

2701 HEADS NOOK H'CAP 5f
5:15 (5:15) (Class 5) (0-70,68) 3-Y-O **£3,238** (£963; £481; £240) **Stalls High**

Form RPR
-641 **1** **Bahamian Duke**[14] 2285 3-8-10 **57**................................. FrancisNorton 8 67
(K R Burke) *mde all: rdn over 2f out: hld on wl fnl f* **4/1**[3]
3022 **2** *hd* **Northern Chorus (IRE)**[10] 2399 3-9-2 **66**............... DanielTudhope(3) 2 75
(A Dickman) *keen: trckd ldrs: effrt and ev ch over 1f out: kpt on ins fnl f* **3/1**[1]
0-05 **3** *½* **Desert Hunter (IRE)**[14] 2285 3-8-2 **49** oh1...................... PaulHanagan 5 56
(Micky Hammond) *prom: effrt over 2f out: kpt on ins fnl f* **11/2**
00-2 **4** *½* **Slipperfoot**[5] 2543 3-8-8 **55**..................................... RobertWinston 10 60+
(J J Quinn) *in tch: effrt 2f out: kpt on u.p fnl f* **7/2**[2]
40-3 **5** *2 ½* **Optical Seclusion (IRE)**[14] 2284 3-8-7 **57**................. SaleemGolam(3) 1 53
(T J Etherington) *towards rr: rdn over 2f out: checked over 1f out: no imp fnl f* **9/1**
0510 **6** *½* **Stanley Wolfe (IRE)**[14] 2284 3-8-0 **52** ow3............... AndrewMullen(5) 7 46
(James Moffatt) *keen: cl up tl rdn and no ex over 1f out* **11/1**
6-40 **7** *2* **Alugat (IRE)**[12] 2363 3-9-2 **63**.................................... RoystonFfrench 9 49
(Mrs A Duffield) *prom: effrt over 2f out: no ex over 1f out* **9/1**
0-45 **8** *1 ½* **Lyndalee (IRE)**[14] 2295 3-9-7 **68**.. DavidAllan 6 48
(T D Easterby) *plld hrd: cl up tl wknd wl over 1f out* **12/1**
5-50 **9** *5* **She's Our Beauty (IRE)**[5] 2550 3-9-4 **65**............................ PaulQuinn 4 26
(D Nicholls) *bhd: hung lft bnd over 3f out: nvr on terms* **50/1**

61.34 secs (-0.16) **Going Correction** -0.05s/f (Good) 9 Ran SP% **120.6**
Speed ratings (Par 99):99,98,97,97,93 92,89,86,78
CSF £17.28 CT £68.24 TOTE £5.60: £2.00, £1.80, £1.50; EX 24.80 Place 6 £64.67, Place 5 £58.13.
Owner Danum Racing **Bred** D R Tucker **Trained** Middleham Moor, N Yorks

FOCUS
Another ordinary handicap but one in which the pace was sound and this bare form should prove reliable. The placed horses are the best guides to the form.
Lyndalee(IRE) Official explanation: jockey said filly ran too free
T/Jkpt: Not won. T/Plt: £155.30 to a £1 stake. Pool: £53,846.70. 253.00 winning tickets. T/Qpdt: £43.70 to a £1 stake. Pool: £2,739.00. 46.30 winning tickets. RY

[1688]WARWICK (L-H)
Monday, June 19

OFFICIAL GOING: Good to firm (firm in places)
Wind: Light, behind. Weather: Overcast.

2702 RACING UK AMATEUR RIDERS' H'CAP 1m 22y
6:45 (6:48) (Class 6) (0-60,60) 4-Y-O+ **£2,307** (£709; £354) **Stalls Low**

Form RPR
-004 **1** **Adobe**[8] 2482 11-10-10 **56**....................................... MrBenBrisbourne(7) 15 63
(W M Brisbourne) *hld up: hdwy over 3f out: led ins fnl f: r.o* **25/1**
0035 **2** *1 ¼* **Fantasy Defender (IRE)**[14] 2291 4-10-2 **46**..........(v) MrDavidTurner(5) 2 50
(Ernst Oertel) *a.p: chsd ldr 3f out: led over 1f out: rdr sn dropped whip: hdd and unable qck ins fnl f* **8/1**[3]
2401 **3** *2 ½* **Lord Chamberlain**[19] 2135 13-10-13 **59**................(b) MissSBradley(7) 12 57
(J M Bradley) *hld up: swtchd lft and hdwy over 1f out: styd on same pce ins fnl f* **14/1**
-104 **4** *½* **Gala Sunday (USA)**[10] 2407 6-10-7 **46**........................ MissSBrotherton 4 43
(M W Easterby) *mid-div: hit rails over 3f out: hdwy over 1f out: r.o* **9/1**
0-31 **5** *2* **Terenzium (IRE)**[27] 1915 4-10-8 **52**............................ MissFCumani(5) 10 44
(L M Cumani) *stmbld s and bhd: hdwy over 1f out: nt clr run ins fnl f: nt rch ldrs* **9/4**[1]
0-66 **6** *1* **Lady Edge (IRE)**[1] 2676 4-10-12 **56**................................. MrMJJSmith(5) 7 46
(A W Carroll) *chsd ldrs: rdn over 2f out: wknd fnl f* **28/1**
0030 **7** *½* **Shannon Arms (USA)**[19] 2137 5-11-4 **57**................................ MrSWalker 6 46
(R Brotherton) *led: rdn and hdd over 1f out: wknd fnl f* **14/1**
3310 **8** *shd* **Sol Rojo**[13] 2327 4-10-13 **57**...(v) MrSPearce(5) 16 46
(J Pearce) *s.i.s: hld up: nvr trbld ldrs* **7/1**[2]
0336 **9** *1 ¼* **Drumroll (IRE)**[30] 1852 4-11-1 **57**........................... MrMatthewSmith(3) 1 43
(Miss J Feilden) *hld up: hdwy over 3f out: rdn and wknd over 1f out* **16/1**
0560 **10** *shd* **Carpet Ride**[20] 2099 4-10-9 **55**.. MrElliott(7) 8 40
(B G Powell) *chsd ldr 5f: wknd over 1f out* **25/1**
5510 **11** *1 ¼* **Welsh Whisper**[20] 2098 7-10-4 **46**........................... MissFayeBramley(3) 5 29
(S A Brookshaw) *hld up: nvr nrr* **33/1**
1000 **12** *½* **Mulberry Lad (IRE)**[14] 2288 4-10-0 **46**........ MissDawnBridgewater(7) 14 27
(P W Hiatt) *chsd ldrs over 5f* **40/1**
0206 **13** *½* **Shifty**[12] 2360 7-11-0 **58**... MissDAllman(5) 13 38
(D Carroll) *chsd ldrs 5f* **18/1**
0-03 **14** *1 ¼* **Hill Of Clare (IRE)**[27] 1910 4-10-1 **47**............................ MrJGoss(7) 9 24
(P R Webber) *chsd ldrs over 5f* **18/1**
100/ **15** *½* **Dartanian**[75] 5314 4-10-4 **50**...................................... MrMScudamore(7) 3 26
(M Scudamore) *s.i.s: outpcd* **100/1**
00-0 **16** *hd* **Emperor's Well**[37] 1666 7-11-0 **60**.............................. MissJCoward(7) 17 36
(M W Easterby) *chsd ldrs over 5f* **40/1**
000- **17** *11* **Shaaban (IRE)**[246] 5371 5-10-4 **50**...................................... MrMPrice(7) 11 1
(R J Price) *s.i.s: outpcd* **125/1**

1m 39.75s (0.15) **Going Correction** -0.20s/f (Firm) 17 Ran SP% **114.9**
Speed ratings (Par 101):91,89,87,86,84 83,83,83,81,81 80,80,79,78,77 77,66
CSF £192.18 CT £3014.18 TOTE £17.40: £4.00, £2.20, £2.30, £1.70; EX 129.60.
Owner P R Kirk **Bred** Sheikh Mohammed Bin Rashid Al Maktoum **Trained** Great Ness, Shropshire
■ The first winner for Ben Brisbourne, son of Mark.

FOCUS
A weak event of its type, run at a fair pace, and the form looks sound enough for the class.
Terenzium(IRE) Official explanation: jockey said colt was slowly away from stalls

2703 EUROPEAN BREEDERS FUND MAIDEN FILLIES' STKS 5f
7:15 (7:19) (Class 5) 2-Y-O **£3,886** (£1,156; £577; £288) **Stalls Low**

Form RPR
0224 **1** **Frisky Talk (IRE)**[12] 2355 2-9-0 .... TonyCulhane 2 74
(B W Hills) *led: hdd and j. path over 1f out: rallied to ld nr fin* **4/1**[2]
2 *hd* **Abby Road (IRE)** 2-9-0 .... LDettori 4 73
(B J Meehan) *s.i.s: sn chsng ldrs: led over 1f out: rdn and hdd nr fin* **4/6**[1]
3 *1 ½* **Chervil** 2-9-0 .... RichardHughes 6 68
(Mrs A J Perrett) *s.i.s: sn chsng ldrs: outpcd 3f out: hdwy over 1f out: styd on same pce ins fnl f* **9/1**
3 **4** *½* **Reem Al Fallah (IRE)**[10] 2394 2-9-0 .... JamieSpencer 3 66
(M R Channon) *chsd wnr 3f: sn edgd rt: hung lft and no ex ins fnl f* **6/1**[3]
5 *3 ½* **Pusey Street Lady** 2-9-0 .... J-PGuillambert 5 53
(J Gallagher) *s.i.s: outpcd: hdwy and hung rt over 1f out: wknd ins fnl f* **40/1**
6 *nk* **Damhsoir (IRE)** 2-8-9 .... EmmettStack(5) 1 52
(H S Howe) *s.i.s: outpcd* **66/1**
7 *27* **Laurels Lady** 2-8-9 .... NataliaGemelova(5) 7 —
(I W McInnes) *swvd rt s: outpcd* **50/1**

59.42 secs (-0.78) **Going Correction** -0.325s/f (Firm) 7 Ran SP% **110.2**
Speed ratings (Par 90):93,92,90,89,83 83,40
CSF £6.53 TOTE £6.20: £1.90, £1.10; EX 10.40.
Owner Paul McNamara **Bred** Yeomanstown Stud **Trained** Lambourn, Berks

FOCUS
A fair fillies' juvenile maiden, which saw the first two come clear, and it should produce its share of future winners.

The Form Book, Raceform Ltd, Compton, RG20 6NL

NOTEBOOK

Frisky Talk(IRE) belatedly opened her account at the fifth time of asking with a battling success. She had to fight to get back at the eventual runner-up, having jumped a path entering the final furlong, but she probably did not have to be quite at her best to take this and it remains to be seen just how much progression she has left in her. (op 3-1)

Abby Road(IRE) ◆, by far the highest-priced of these at the sales and very well backed to make a winning debut, overcame a sluggish start and looked the most likely winner on entering the final furlong. However, she failed to sustain her effort thereafter and ultimately failed to cope with the renewed challenge of the winner near the line. She is clearly well-regarded - as her Irish Group 1 entry implies - and in keeping with the majority of her yard's juvenile team so far this term, she ought to improve a bundle for the experience. (op 4-5 tchd 10-11 in places)

Chervil, a half-sister to numerous winners from a mile to ten furlongs, took time to find her stride and was not surprisingly outpaced when it mattered. This still must rate a pleasing debut effort, however, and she ought to have little trouble in breaking her duck when upped to a sixth furlong in due course (op 11-1 tchd 17-2)

Reem Al Fallah(IRE), third on her recent Catterick debut, showed slightly-improved form and looks the type to do better when qualified for a nursery mark. (op 7-1 tchd 8-1)

Laurels Lady Official explanation: jockey said filly veered right at start

2704 FORESTERS ARMS FILLIES' H'CAP — 6f 21y

7:45 (7:47) (Class 6) (0-60,60) 3-Y-O — **£2,730** (£806; £403) Stalls Low

Form — RPR

0 **1** **Bakhoor (IRE)**[116] 3-8-11 **50** .... AlanMunro 1 — 59
(W Jarvis) *hld up in tch: led over 1f out: sn edgd rt: rdn clr* **7/2**[1]

5-06 **2** *2* **Some Diva**[18] 2167 3-9-5 **58** .... JamieSpencer 3 — 60
(W R Swinburn) *chsd ldr: led over 2f out: rdn and hdd over 1f out: styd on same pce* **7/2**[1]

0-60 **3** *½* **The Lady Caster**[21] 2068 3-8-13 **52** .... (v[1]) SebSanders 6 — 53
(R M Beckett) *led: hdd over 2f out: rdn and ev ch over 1f out: styd on same pce fnl f* **22/1**

0053 **4** *nk* **Divine White**[7] 2511 3-9-0 **53** .... JimCrowley 4 — 53
(Mrs A J Perrett) *chsd ldrs: rdn and nt clr run 1f out: styd on same pce* **4/1**[2]

0-60 **5** *nk* **Free Silver (IRE)**[47] 1412 3-9-4 **57** .... RichardMullen 2 — 56
(Miss K B Boutflower) *hld up: plld hrd: hdwy over 2f out: rdn over 1f out: styd on* **20/1**

-062 **6** *½* **Double Valentine**[2] 2644 3-8-11 **50** .... MickyFenton 11 — 48
(R Ingram) *chsd ldrs: rdn over 1f out: no ex fnl f* **5/1**[3]

0360 **7** *1½* **Bermuda Beauty (IRE)**[17] 2190 3-8-10 **49** .... TonyCulhane 5 — 42
(J M Bradley) *hld up: rdn over 1f out: nt trble ldrs* **20/1**

0-00 **8** *shd* **Task Complete**[6] 2535 3-8-13 **52** .... VinceSlattery 13 — 45
(J A Osborne) *prom: rdn over 2f out: edgd lft over 1f out: styd on same pce* **66/1**

05-0 **9** *½* **Buckle And Hyde**[12] 2353 3-9-2 **55** .... RichardHughes 10 — 46
(Mrs A L M King) *hld up: rdn over 1f out: n.d* **33/1**

-066 **10** *hd* **Reality Time (IRE)**[145] 189 3-8-10 **54** .... RichardKingscote(5) 9 — 45
(J A Osborne) *hld up: rdn over 2f out: n.d* **40/1**

0-04 **11** *nk* **Honor Me (IRE)**[14] 2298 3-9-3 **56** .... JimmyQuinn 8 — 46
(J J Quinn) *s.i.s: a in rr* **14/1**

365- **12** *9* **Wig Wam Bam (IRE)**[301] 4624 3-9-2 **60** .... GregFairley(5) 7 — 23
(R A Fahey) *prom: lost pl over 3f out: sn bhd* **18/1**

660 **13** *11* **Lady Becks (IRE)**[55] 1218 3-8-4 **50** .... TolleyDean(7) 12 — —
(R A Harris) *mid-div: lost pl 4f out: sn bhd* **50/1**

1m 10.99s (-1.11) **Going Correction** -0.20s/f (Firm) — 13 Ran SP% **115.7**
Speed ratings (Par 94):99,96,95,95,94 94,92,92,91,91 90,78,64
CSF £13.62 CT £231.65 TOTE £4.90: £1.50, £1.40, £5.20; EX 27.10.
Owner Ziad A Galadari **Bred** Galadari Sons Stud Company Limited **Trained** Newmarket, Suffolk

FOCUS

A moderate fillies' handicap, which saw two unexposed types fill the first two places, and the form looks fair and solid enough.

Bakhoor(IRE) Official explanation: trainer's rep said, regarding the improved form shown, the filly was having her first run for the yard and her first run on turf

Buckle And Hyde Official explanation: jockey said filly was unsuited by the firm ground

Honor Me(IRE) Official explanation: jockey said filly jumped awkwardly leaving stalls

2705 PRICEWATERHOUSECOOPERS H'CAP — 7f 26y

8:15 (8:16) (Class 4) (0-80,78) 4-Y-O+ — **£6,477** (£1,927; £963; £481) Stalls Low

Form — RPR

3031 **1** **Meditation**[9] 2459 4-8-7 **69** .... JamesDoyle(5) 7 — 78
(I A Wood) *led: hdd over 4f out: rdn to ld over 1f out: r.o* **13/2**

53-1 **2** *¾* **Whitethorne**[14] 2293 4-8-10 **72** .... GregFairley(5) 4 — 79+
(R A Fahey) *hld up: nt clr run 1/2-way: hdwy over 1f out: r.o* **5/1**

0464 **3** *½* **H Harrison (IRE)**[6] 2520 6-8-10 **72** .... NataliaGemelova(5) 1 — 78
(I W McInnes) *chsd ldr: led over 4f out: rdn and hdd over 1f out: styd on same pce ins fnl f* **9/2**[3]

2034 **4** *1* **Selective**[7] 2510 7-9-0 **71** .... (v[1]) SebSanders 6 — 74
(A W Carroll) *hld up: hdwy u.p over 1f out: nt rch ldrs* **4/1**[2]

60-0 **5** *nk* **Underscore (USA)**[18] 2169 4-9-5 **76** .... AdrianMcCarthy 3 — 78
(R A Harris) *chsd ldrs: rdn over 2f out: styd on same pce fnl f* **20/1**

0400 **6** *3* **Hayyani (IRE)**[78] 843 4-9-6 **77** .... RichardMullen 2 — 72
(K McAuliffe) *chsd ldrs over 5f* **16/1**

0100 **7** *1* **Lizarazu (GER)**[26] 1932 7-9-0 **78** .... (p) TolleyDean(7) 5 — 70
(R A Harris) *s.i.s: hld up: rdn over 1f out: sn hung lft and wknd* **9/1**

60-1 **8** *31* **Premier Fantasy**[15] 2259 4-8-13 **70** .... NickyMackay 8 — —
(W J Haggas) *s.s: a bhd: rdn over 2f out: eased fnl f* **7/2**[1]

1m 22.27s (-2.73) **Going Correction** -0.20s/f (Firm) — 8 Ran SP% **111.0**
Speed ratings (Par 105):107,106,105,104,104 100,99,64
CSF £36.52 CT £156.04 TOTE £7.00: £1.80, £1.70, £1.30; EX 24.00.
Owner Paddy Barrett **Bred** P E Barrett **Trained** Upper Lambourn, Berks

FOCUS

A competitive handicap for the class, run at an uneven pace, and the form should be treated with a degree of caution.

2706 TWEENHILLS FARM AND STUD WARWICKSHIRE OAKS STKS (LISTED RACE) — 1m 2f 188y

8:45 (8:45) (Class 1) 4-Y-O+

£15,898 (£6,025; £3,015; £1,503; £753; £378) Stalls Low

Form — RPR

053- **1** **Power Girl (GER)**[232] 6192 4-8-9 94 .... JamieSpencer 2 — 95
(P F I Cole) *chsd ldrs: shkn up to ld wl ins fnl f: edgd lft: r.o* **14/1**

4-32 **2** *shd* **Mango Mischief (IRE)**[32] 1804 5-8-9 105 .... SebSanders 1 — 95
(J L Dunlop) *led: qcknd over 2f out: rdn over 1f out: hdd wl ins fnl f: edgd lft: r.o* **4/6**[1]

301- **3** *1* **Play Me**[257] 5700 4-8-9 85 .... AlanMunro 5 — 93
(P W Chapple-Hyam) *chsd ldrs: rdn and n.m.r over 1f out: styd on* **12/1**[3]

4-01 **4** *nk* **Pine Cone (IRE)**[9] 2457 4-8-9 82 .... RichardHughes 6 — 92
(A King) *hld up in tch: rdn over 2f out: unable qckn towards fin* **12/1**[3]

50-5 **5** *¾* **Idealistic (IRE)**[43] 1511 5-8-9 92 .... NickyMackay 3 — 91
(L M Cumani) *dwlt: sn prom: rdn over 1f out: edgd rt: no ex ins fnl f* **10/3**[2]

0530 **6** *8* **Boot 'n Toot**[5] 2447 5-8-9 72 .... J-PGuillambert 4 — 77
(C A Cyzer) *s.i.s: hld up: hdwy over 3f out: wknd over 1f out* **33/1**

2m 16.64s (-2.76) **Going Correction** -0.20s/f (Firm) — 6 Ran SP% **108.1**
Speed ratings (Par 111):102,101,101,100,100 94
CSF £22.50 TOTE £15.30: £4.40, £1.10; EX 21.30.
Owner D Bass **Bred** Carlton Consultants Ltd **Trained** Whatcombe, Oxon

FOCUS

A modest winning time for a race like this, due to the uneven pace, and the form looks just ordinary for the class with the third the best guide.

NOTEBOOK

Power Girl(GER), making her British debut for her new yard, dug deep in the closing stages and just did enough to repel the runner-up when it mattered. She had never raced on ground this fast before, but it proved to be no problem, and she clearly stays well. Entitled to improve a deal for the outing, she has now significantly boosted her paddock value, and promises to do even better when racing on an easier surface once again. (op 16-1)

Mango Mischief(IRE), by far the highest of these on BHB ratings, had every chance from the front, and was only denied by the smallest of margins, yet did not look overly happy on the fast ground late on. This must rate as disappointing, but time may tell she was not disgraced in defeat, and she should prove happier when reverting to slightly easier ground. (op 8-11 tchd 4-5 in places)

Play Me could not match the speed of the first two, but was staying on well enough towards the finish, and posted an encouraging return from a 257-day break. This will have blown her handicap mark now, but she is a big filly, and should improve a bundle for the outing. (op 8-1)

Pine Cone(IRE), who won a fillies' handicap from a mark of 77 nine days previously, turned in a pleasing enough first effort at this much higher level and would have ideally preferred a stronger overall gallop. She will most likely face another rise in the weights now. (tchd 11-1)

Idealistic(IRE) proved disappointing and failed to raise her game for this return to faster ground. She was another who would have ideally preferred a stonger overall pace, however. (op 7-2)

2707 RACING UK H'CAP — 1m 2f 188y

9:15 (9:16) (Class 6) (0-65,63) 4-Y-O+ — **£2,730** (£806; £403) Stalls Low

Form — RPR

4646 **1** **Siena Star (IRE)**[3] 2612 8-9-2 **58** .... MickyFenton 2 — 66
(Stef Liddiard) *hld up in tch: led over 1f out:: edgd lft ins fnl f: drvn out* **6/1**[3]

6430 **2** *¾* **Treetops Hotel (IRE)**[9] 2455 7-8-9 **51** .... SebSanders 4 — 58
(B R Johnson) *hld up: hdwy over 2f out: rdn and swtchd rt 1f out: r.o* **9/2**[2]

-305 **3** *shd* **Harare**[16] 2221 5-8-0 **47** ow2 .... (b) JamesDoyle(5) 12 — 54
(R J Price) *trckd ldrs: ev ch over 1f out: sn rdn: nt run on* **6/1**[3]

0100 **4** *2½* **Thorny Mandate**[9] 2455 4-9-7 **63** .... AlanMunro 10 — 65
(R F Johnson Houghton) *plld hrd and prom: rdn and hung lft over 1f out: styd on* **15/2**

0300 **5** *1* **Agilete**[15] 2262 4-8-0 **45** .... NelsonDeSouza(3) 3 — 46
(J R Boyle) *s.i.s: hld up: plld hrd: styd on ins fnl f: nvr nrr* **18/1**

/02- **6** *nk* **Master Nimbus**[18] 4565 6-8-3 **45** .... JimmyQuinn 1 — 45
(J J Quinn) *chsd ldrs: rdn over 1f out: wknd ins fnl f* **3/1**[1]

-030 **7** *1¼* **Louve Heureuse (IRE)**[8] 2482 5-8-12 **54** .... JamieSpencer 8 — 52
(B G Powell) *led: rdn and hdd over 1f out: wknd ins fnl f* **12/1**

0050 **8** *3½* **Mccormack (IRE)**[20] 2108 4-8-7 **49** .... RichardMullen 11 — 40
(Micky Hammond) *hld up: nvr nrr* **16/1**

000 **9** *4* **Kentuckian**[16] 2220 4-8-5 **47** .... FrancisFerris 9 — 31
(P W Hiatt) *s.i.s: hld up: rdn over 2f out: n.d* **50/1**

05-0 **10** *¾* **Time For You**[19] 2133 4-8-2 **44** oh4 .... NickyMackay 6 — 27
(J M Bradley) *prom: rdn and lost pl over 2f out: sn wknd* **66/1**

0-60 **11** *11* **Skelligs Rock (IRE)**[107] 582 6-8-9 **51** ow1 .... TonyCulhane 5 — 14
(A W Carroll) *hld up: racd keenly: wknd 3f out* **16/1**

160- **12** *21* **Ben Kenobi**[254] 5740 8-8-4 **51** oh2 ow7 .... GregFairley(5) 13 — —
(Mrs P Ford) *s.i.s: plld hrd: hdwy 9f out: wknd 3f out* **33/1**

2m 18.14s (-1.26) **Going Correction** -0.20s/f (Firm) — 12 Ran SP% **114.6**
Speed ratings (Par 101):96,95,95,93,92 92,91,89,86,85 77,62
CSF £31.65 CT £169.00 TOTE £6.20: £2.20, £1.60, £2.20; EX 34.40 Place 6 £43.91, Place 5 £12.27 .
Owner ownaracehorse.co.uk (Shefford) **Bred** Mrs A J Brudenell **Trained** Great Shefford, Berks

FOCUS

A poor handicap, run at an average pace, and the form looks very modest but sound enough.

Skelligs Rock(IRE) Official explanation: jockey said gelding slipped on first bend

T/Plt: £37.20 to a £1 stake. Pool: £46,110.65. 903.55 winning tickets. T/Qpdt: £13.30 to a £1 stake. Pool: £2,660.40. 147.70 winning tickets. CR

2506 WINDSOR (R-H)

Monday, June 19

OFFICIAL GOING: Good to firm

Wind: Light, across. Weather: Fine becoming cloudy.

2708 CHG-MERIDIAN H'CAP — 1m 67y

6:35 (6:36) (Class 5) (0-75,75) 4-Y-O+ — **£3,238** (£963; £481; £240) Stalls High

Form — RPR

3051 **1** **Aggravation**[7] 2510 4-8-12 **66** 6ex .... KFallon 5 — 77
(D R C Elsworth) *hld up in last trio: prog fr 3f out: pressed ldr over 1f out: urged along to ld ins fnl f: styd on* **9/4**[1]

4/06 **2** *½* **Optimus (USA)**[10] 2405 4-9-0 **71** .... AdamKirby(3) 1 — 81
(G A Butler) *hld up wl in rr: prog on outer wl over 2f out: drvn to press wnr ins fnl f: a hld* **25/1**

-015 **3** *nk* **Phluke**[37] 1692 5-9-7 **75** .... StephenCarson 6 — 84
(R F Johnson Houghton) *led: rdn over 2f out against nr side rail: hdd ins fnl f: kpt on* **14/1**

6223 **4** *2½* **Fasylitator (IRE)**[10] 2401 4-8-13 **67** .... JimmyFortune 9 — 70
(D K Ivory) *hld up in midfield: effrt over 2f out: swtchd lft over 1f out: kpt on same pce* **9/2**[2]

6624 **5** *½* **Ermine Grey**[23] 2025 5-8-9 **63** ow1 .... NCallan 4 — 65
(A W Carroll) *wl in tch: drvn over 2f out: effrt and cl up bhd ldng trio ent fnl f: wknd* **9/1**

0025 **6** *1¼* **Jools**[7] 2510 8-8-4 **65** .... JamesMillman(7) 12 — 64+
(D K Ivory) *t.k.h: hld up in midfield: n.m.r over 2f out: one pce after* **15/2**

7 *½* **Kilimandscharo (USA)**[30] 4-8-2 **56** oh6 .... FrankieMcDonald 2 — 54
(Miss Victoria Roberts) *chsd ldrs: rdn on outer 3f out: steadily outpcd fnl 2f* **100/1**

6060 **8** *½* **Fabrian**[7] 2510 8-9-0 **68** .... ShaneKelly 14 — 65+
(R J Price) *trckd ldrs: shkn up and nt qckn 2f out: hmpd on inner over 1f out and lost all ch: running on again at fin* **20/1**

1000 **9** ¾ **Scottish River (USA)**[9] [2455] 7-8-12 **66**........................ MartinDwyer 13 61+
(M D I Usher) *customary sluggish s and lft 12l: latched on to main gp 4f out: kpt on fr over 1f out: no ch* **33/1**

0006 **10** ½ **Simplify**[32] [1802] 4-7-11 **56** oh2....................................(p) MarcHalford(5) 7 50
(T M Jones) *prom: chsd ldr over 3f out and racd towards outer: wknd over 1f out* **33/1**

0000 **11** *hd* **Rawaabet (IRE)**[13] [2327] 4-8-6 **60** ow1................................ LPKeniry 11 54
(P W Hiatt) *chsd ldr for 3f: wknd u.p 2f out* **50/1**

56-0 **12** 1¾ **Dr Thong**[9] [2440] 5-9-7 **75**.. EddieAhern 8 65
(P F I Cole) *trckd ldrs: rdn whn hmpd 2f out: no ch after* **13/2**[3]

00-0 **13** 1½ **Hawridge Sensation**[16] [2223] 4-7-13 **60** oh1 ow4......... JamieJones(7) 3 46+
(W S Kittow) *dwlt: wl in rr: effrt whn n.m.r 2f out: no ch after* **66/1**

0426 **14** 5 **Aastral Magic**[15] [2259] 4-9-4 **72**.. RyanMoore 10 47
(R Hannon) *prom: chsd ldr after 3f to over 3f out: wkng whn squeezed out 2f out* **16/1**

1m 44.19s (-1.41) **Going Correction** -0.10s/f (Good) **14** Ran SP% **115.5**
Speed ratings (Par 103):103,102,102,99,99 97,97,96,96,95 95,93,92,87
CSF £69.44 CT £649.74 TOTE £3.20: £1.90, £4.00, £3.60; EX 24.90.
Owner Perry, Vivian & Elsworth **Bred** John Khan **Trained** Newmarket, Suffolk

FOCUS
A fair pace for this handicap and almost a carbon copy of the race Aggravation won here seven days earlier. The third sets the standard.
Fabrian Official explanation: jockey said gelding ran too free
Scottish River(USA) Official explanation: jockey said gelding missed the break
Aastral Magic Official explanation: jockey said filly ran out of room approaching final furlong

2709 SIMCORP DIMENSION SOFTWARE FOR ASSET MANAGERS (S) STKS 6f
7:05 (7:06) (Class 5) 2-Y-O **£3,238** (£963; £481; £240) **Stalls** High

Form RPR

302 **1** **Peggys Flower**[7] [2495] 2-8-6 .... DO'Donohoe 2 53
(N A Callaghan) *cl up: led wl over 1f out and sn 2 l clr: carried hd high fnl f: hld on to dwindling advantage nr fin* **11/8**[1]

4151 **2** *nk* **Mrs Crossy (IRE)**[12] [2346] 2-8-11 .... RyanMoore 11 57
(R Hannon) *w ldrs: rdn 1/2-way: struggling to hold pl 2f out: rallied fnl f and gaining on wnr fin* **10/3**[2]

2555 **3** 1 **Diminuto**[12] [2346] 2-8-6 .... HayleyTurner 9 49
(M D I Usher) *pressed ldrs: rdn over 2f out: nt qckn wl over 1f out: styd on again fnl f* **12/1**

0600 **4** 2 **Fasuby (IRE)**[7] [2506] 2-8-7 ow1.. ShaneKelly 8 44
(P D Evans) *chsd ldrs but nvr quite on terms: rdn wl over 2f out: one pce and no imp* **10/1**

6466 **5** *nk* **All Talk**[12] [2346] 2-8-6 .... ChrisCatlin 5 42
(I A Wood) *walked to post: settled wl in rr: pushed along over 3f out: sn off pce: styd on u.p fr over 1f out: n.d* **33/1**

00 **6** 3 **Suzieblue (IRE)**[13] [2315] 2-8-6 .... LPKeniry 1 33
(J S Moore) *racd on outer: chsd ldrs but nvr on terms: no imp u.p over 2f out: wknd fnl f* **20/1**

0542 **7** ½ **Splendidio**[12] [2346] 2-7-13 .... JamieJones(7) 6 32
(D K Ivory) *led: hanging and hdd wl over 1f out: wknd rapidly* **7/1**[3]

3564 **8** 8 **Afric Star**[21] [2064] 2-8-6 .... MartinDwyer 3 8
(P D Evans) *outpcd and a wl bhd* **25/1**

0064 **9** 3 **Lenard Frank (IRE)**[7] [2495] 2-8-4 ....(v) FrankiePickard(7) 7 4
(M D I Usher) *sn struggling in rr: wknd 1/2-way* **100/1**

1500 **10** ¾ **Best Woman**[5] [2538] 2-8-11 .... IanMongan 4 1
(P Howling) *nvr beyond midfield: wknd 1/2-way* **20/1**

000 **11** ½ **Gibsons**[12] [2346] 2-8-6 .... TravisBlock(5) 10 —
(Mrs P N Dutfield) *rdn in rr after 2f: wknd over 2f out* **100/1**

12 18 **Corrucaseco** 2-8-3 .... RichardSmith(3) 12 —
(M D I Usher) *s.v.s: a t.o* **33/1**

1m 13.38s (-0.29) **Going Correction** -0.20s/f (Firm) **12** Ran SP% **115.7**
Speed ratings (Par 93):93,92,91,88,88 84,83,72,68,67 67,43
CSF £4.90 TOTE £2.80: £1.40, £1.60, £2.70; EX 6.00.The winner was bought in for 9,400gns. Mrs Crossy was claimed by Mr Nigel Coulson-Stephens for £6,000.
Owner M O'Donovan **Bred** F O'Brien **Trained** Newmarket, Suffolk

FOCUS
Basically a fillies' seller with the two geldings starting at 100-1 and finishing at the back. Few ever got into it and the form looks about par for the grade.

NOTEBOOK
Peggys Flower, up a furlong, probably only needed repeat her Folkestone effort from the previous week to land this, but having gone clear of her rivals she seemed to think she had done enough and at the line she had nothing to spare. She does not look one to place maximum faith in. (tchd 6-4)
Mrs Crossy(IRE), like the winner trying this trip for the first time, seemed to hit a flat spot at halfway but then came back for more and gave the favourite a bit of a fright near the line. She is a consistent sort at this level. (op 7-2)
Diminuto, another trying an extra furlong and racing on turf for the very first time after six outings on sand, kept on trying but ended up with a rear view of Mrs Crossy for the third consecutive race. She has nothing in the way of scope.
Fasuby(IRE), unplaced in four maidens, ran better on this drop in class and may improve a bit more over an extra furlong. (op 11-1)
All Talk did best of those that were held up, though that is not saying much and she went one better than Diminuto by finishing behind Mrs Crossy for the fourth consecutive time.
Splendidio, just half a length behind Mrs Crossy at Lingfield last time, failed to see out this extra furlong and perhaps she is better suited by Polytrack. (op 8-1)

2710 TRAILFINDERS EUROPEAN BREEDERS FUND MAIDEN STKS 5f 10y
7:35 (7:36) (Class 4) 2-Y-O **£5,181** (£1,541; £770; £384) **Stalls** High

Form RPR

23 **1** **Racing Stripes (IRE)**[46] [1429] 2-9-3 .... PatDobbs 8 75+
(A B Haynes) *mde all: clr over 1f out: pushed out: readily* **10/3**[2]

6 **2** 1½ **Abunai**[13] [2328] 2-8-12 .... SteveDrowne 2 68+
(R Charlton) *carried lft s: prog fr rr 1/2-way: rdn and styd on to take 2nd ins fnl f: no ch w wnr* **9/2**[3]

3 *nk* **Callwood Dancer (IRE)** 2-8-12 .... MichaelHills 5 64
(B W Hills) *dwlt: sn chsd ldrs: rdn and jinked lft over 1f out: kpt on to take 3rd ins fnl f* **6/1**

00 **4** 1 **Queensgate**[17] [2185] 2-8-12 .... MartinDwyer 6 60
(M Blanshard) *pressed wnr: hung lft 1/2-way: rdn and hld 2f out: wknd ins fnl f* **50/1**

0 **5** *nk* **Sunley Sovereign**[7] [2506] 2-9-3 .... TedDurcan 1 64
(M R Channon) *s.i.s: rn green and outpcd after 2f: detached last 2f out: rdn and styd on steadily fr over 1f out* **33/1**

6 1¾ **Tracer** 2-9-3 .... RyanMoore 7 64+
(R Hannon) *dwlt: sn trckd ldng pair: rn green whn pushed along 2f out: eased whn btn ins fnl f* **5/2**[1]

540 **7** 3 **Weyba Downs (IRE)**[18] [2172] 2-9-3 .... TQuinn 4 47
(J R Best) *chsd ldrs tl wknd wl over 1f out* **16/1**

4 **8** ½ **Billy Red**[18] [2172] 2-9-3 .... EddieAhern 3 45
(J R Jenkins) *veered sharply lft sn after s: rn green on outer: in tch tl wknd wl over 1f out* **9/2**[3]

60.65 secs (-0.45) **Going Correction** -0.10s/f (Good) **8** Ran SP% **113.1**
Speed ratings (Par 95):99,96,96,94,94 91,86,85
CSF £18.30 TOTE £4.10: £1.30, £2.00, £1.90; EX 18.00.
Owner Mrs L Bloxsome & T Wilkinson **Bred** J F O'Malley **Trained** Collingbourne Ducis, Wilts

FOCUS
A bit of a messy race, but the time was fair and the winner deserved it.

NOTEBOOK
Racing Stripes(IRE), probably unlucky not to win a four-runner Folkestone maiden on his debut, hit the gates running and made full use of his rails draw, showing none of the waywardness that he showed at the Kent track. The form is probably ordinary, but at least he is going the right way and his early speed should continue to prove an asset. (op 9-2)
Abunai who encountered traffic problems on her debut, was done no favours by the wayward Billy Red soon after the start. She came home strongly enough, but it would be very hard to suggest that her earlier problems cost her the race. The drop in trip was probably a bigger problem and she should go one better before too long if put back over further. Official explanation: jockey said filly suffered interference at start (op 10-3 tchd 5-1)
Callwood Dancer(IRE), a 100,000euros half-sister to Walklikeanegyptian out of a half-sister to Maroof, showed a fair amount of ability on this debut and gave the impression she would come on for the run. (op 8-1)
Queensgate again showed early speed, but is not finishing her races at present. She is at least now qualified for nurseries which are now just a couple of weeks away. (tchd 66-1)
Sunley Sovereign does not seem to have learnt anything from his debut and did not get into gear until it was far too late. To be fair his relatives all needed much more time, so there could be better to come from him some way down the line. (op 28-1)
Tracer ◆, a 92,000gns half-brother to the very smart German stayer Western Devil and winning two-year-olds Pemba and Just One Look, looked badly in need of this debut. His dam won at up to 12 furlongs, so a longer trip and a bit more experience should see him leave this debut well behind. (op 11-4 tchd 9-4)
Billy Red dived violently out to his left after breaking from the stalls and that was his chance ended. Official explanation: jockey said colt hung badly left leaving stalls (tchd 5-1)

2711 SLOUGH TRADING ESTATES H'CAP 6f
8:05 (8:05) (Class 4) (0-80,79) 4-Y-O+ **£6,477** (£1,927; £963; £481) **Stalls** High

Form RPR

0201 **1** **Caustic Wit (IRE)**[8] [2484] 8-8-8 **66** 6ex.....................(p) FergusSweeney 3 76
(M S Saunders) *taken down early: trckd ldrs: led wl over 1f out: drvn and hrd pressed fnl f: hld on wl* **6/1**[3]

1323 **2** *nk* **Nautical**[31] [1820] 8-9-5 **77**... JimmyFortune 6 86
(A W Carroll) *settled in midfield: urged along and effrt 2f out: plld out to press wnr fnl f: r.o but a jst hld* **7/2**[1]

0033 **3** ¾ **Louphole**[13] [2331] 4-8-4 **62**... ChrisCatlin 4 69
(P J Makin) *hld up in rr: gng wl sn after 1/2-way: prog over 1f out: drvn and styd on fnl f: nvr able to chal* **5/1**[2]

-005 **4** 1¼ **Born To Be Bold**[14] [2302] 4-8-10 **68**.................................... RyanMoore 5 71
(R Hannon) *pushed along off the pce over 3f out: no real imp tl rdn and styd on fnl f: nrst fin* **5/1**[2]

0-00 **5** *nk* **Buy On The Red**[31] [1820] 5-9-3 **75**...................................(b) MartinDwyer 8 77
(W R Muir) *w ldr: rdn over 2f out: nt qckn and hld over 1f out: plugged on* **16/1**

0360 **6** *shd* **Silver Dane (IRE)**[18] [2182] 4-9-1 **73**...............................(v) HayleyTurner 1 75
(Mrs C A Dunnett) *racd on outer in midfield: effrt 2f out: clsd on ldrs over 1f out: fdd u.p ins fnl f* **25/1**

3302 **7** ½ **Chinalea (IRE)**[3] [2618] 4-8-10 **71**....................................... AdamKirby(3) 7 71
(C G Cox) *mde most: urged along and hdd wl over 1f out: grad wknd* **7/2**[1]

50/0 **8** 7 **Spliff**[18] [2173] 5-9-7 **79**.. TedDurcan 2 58
(M S Saunders) *sn off the pce in last: nvr a factor* **33/1**

6443 **9** ¾ **Kempsey**[9] [2444] 4-8-6 **69**...(v) StephenDonohoe(5) 9 46
(J J Bridger) *w ldrs for 2f: sn lost pl and struggling* **12/1**

40-0 **10** 9 **Elgin Marbles**[56] [1188] 4-8-12 **70**...(t) PatDobbs 10 20
(A B Haynes) *s.s: brief rcvry after 2f: bhd sn after 1/2-way* **50/1**

1m 11.7s (-1.97) **Going Correction** -0.20s/f (Firm) **10** Ran SP% **114.4**
Speed ratings (Par 105):105,104,103,101,101 101,100,91,90,78
CSF £26.31 CT £112.57 TOTE £5.90: £1.90, £1.40, £2.60; EX 15.80.
Owner Mrs Sandra Jones **Bred** Gainsborough Stud Management Ltd **Trained** Green Ore, Somerset

FOCUS
A competitive sprint handicap run at a good pace and the form looks solid rated around the first three.

2712 FINSPREADS MAIDEN STKS 1m 2f 7y
8:35 (8:38) (Class 5) 3-Y-O+ **£3,886** (£1,156; £577; £288) **Stalls** Low

Form RPR

5 **1** **Imperial Star (IRE)**[23] [2034] 3-8-13 .... JimmyFortune 12 88+
(J H M Gosden) *trckd ldrs: pushed along 3f out: prog to ld wl over 1f out: sn clr: comf* **3/1**[1]

-4 **2** 5 **Sabah**[49] [1358] 3-8-5 .... NeilChalmers(3) 2 67
(A M Balding) *prom: trckd ldr 1/2-way: led wl over 2f out to wl over 1f out: kpt on but no ch w wnr* **33/1**

55- **3** *shd* **Silken Act (CAN)**[272] [5391] 3-8-8 .... PhilipRobinson 17 67
(Mrs A J Perrett) *wnt rt s: chsd ldr to 1/2-way: styd prom: drvn and nt qckn 2f out: styd on again fnl f* **3/1**[1]

0-30 **4** *nk* **Hunting Party (IRE)**[47] [1421] 3-8-13 73.........................(t) MichaelHills 11 71
(B W Hills) *led: narrowly hdd wl over 2f out: styd pressing ldr to wl over 1f out: one pce after* **16/1**

0 **5** 1½ **Wizards Dream**[23] [2028] 3-8-13 .... LPKeniry 15 69+
(D R C Elsworth) *wnt lft s: off the pce in midfield: shuffled along 3f out: kpt on steadily fnl 2f: nrst fin* **40/1**

205- **6** ½ **Ned Ludd (IRE)**[259] [5665] 3-8-13 80.................................... RyanMoore 16 68
(R Hannon) *chsd ldrs: rdn and cl up 2f out: fdd* **7/1**[2]

06 **7** *nk* **Muscari**[12] [2349] 4-9-6 .... FrankieMcDonald 14 62
(A P Jarvis) *dwlt and hmpd s: sn chsd ldrs: rdn 4f out: outpcd and struggling over 2f out: plugged on* **100/1**

0 **8** 1¼ **Samarinda (USA)**[23] [2034] 3-8-13 .... EddieAhern 8 65
(E A L Dunlop) *dwlt: sn in ldng gp: shkn up 3f out: grad wknd fnl 2f* **66/1**

0 **9** ½ **Greek Well (IRE)**[14] [2304] 3-8-13 .... KFallon 9 66+
(Sir Michael Stoute) *prom: pushed along over 3f out: struggling whn n.m.r 2f out: btn after and eased ins fnl f* **3/1**[1]

44 **10** 1 **Follow On**[10] [2412] 4-9-11 .... TQuinn 1 62
(A P Jarvis) *wl in rr: bustled along over 4f out: no prog tl styd on fnl 2f: n.d* **50/1**

11 *nk* **Indian Girl** 3-8-5 .... EdwardCreighton(3) 13 56
(M R Channon) *wl in rr: pushed along 4f out: sme prog over 2f out but nvr on terms: eased ins fnl f* **100/1**
12 *shd* **Diamond Shower (USA)** 3-8-13 .... SteveDrowne 3 61+
(E A L Dunlop) *s.s: a in rr and rn green: kpt on fnl 2f* **66/1**
04 13 *3* **Musical Magic**[13] 2325 3-8-8 .... ShaneKelly 4 50+
(J Noseda) *a wl in rr: last 1/2-way: no ch fnl 3f* **11/1**[3]
65 14 *1 1/2* **Forever Autumn**[10] 2412 3-8-13 .... TedDurcan 5 53
(B J Meehan) *settled off the pce in midfield: pushed along and no prog 3f out: wknd* **80/1**
60 15 *6* **Russian Dream (IRE)**[18] 2175 3-8-13 .... OscarUrbina 7 41
(W R Swinburn) *a wl in rr: wknd 3f out* **50/1**
0 16 *2* **Camp Attack**[35] 1741 3-8-13 .... StephenCarson 6 37
(S Dow) *nvr beyond midfield and nvr on terms: wknd and eased fnl 2f* **100/1**

2m 7.83s (-0.47) **Going Correction** -0.10s/f (Good)
WFA 3 from 4yo 12lb **16** Ran SP% **118.2**
Speed ratings (Par 103):97,93,92,92,91 91,90,89,89,88 88,88,85,84,79 78
CSF £119.87 TOTE £3.80: £1.60, £4.70, £1.60; EX 94.40.
Owner H R H Princess Haya Of Jordan **Bred** Deerfield Farm **Trained** Newmarket, Suffolk
■ King Kasyapa was withdrawn (bolted on way to s; 14/1.) R4 applies, deduct 5p in the £.

FOCUS
Probably an ordinary maiden and the winning time was 0.38 seconds slower than the following three-year-old handicap, but the winner was very impressive and can probably hold his own in better company. The fourth and seventh suggest the form is sound enough.
Greek Well(IRE) Official explanation: jockey said colt had no more to give
Camp Attack Official explanation: jockey said gelding hung right

2713 VC CASINO.COM H'CAP 1m 2f 7y
9:05 (9:06) (Class 5) (0-70,71) 3-Y-O **£3,238** (£963; £481; £240) **Stalls** Low

Form RPR
3-61 1 **Gower Song**[10] 2391 3-9-7 **68** .... TQuinn 7 80+
(D R C Elsworth) *hld up in last pair: prog wl over 3f out: led over 2f out: shkn up and drew clr fnl f* **11/2**
-501 2 *3 1/2* **Pagan Crest**[10] 2403 3-9-3 **64** .... KerrinMcEvoy 9 70
(Mrs A J Perrett) *trckd ldrs: effrt to chal wl over 2f out: outpcd by wnr fr over 1f out* **7/2**[2]
2302 3 *3/4* **Iberian Light (USA)**[4] 2569 3-8-7 **54** .... (b) OscarUrbina 2 58
(N A Callaghan) *prom: effrt to ld over 4f out: hung bdly lft 3f out: hdd over 2f out: one pce after* **7/1**
-444 4 *shd* **Emilion**[35] 1747 3-9-2 **63** .... EddieAhern 1 67
(W J Haggas) *settled in rr: pushed along 4f out: effrt on outer over 2f out: kpt on same pce u.p* **20/1**
00-1 5 *1* **Indigo Dancer**[55] 1226 3-8-2 **49** oh2 .... ChrisCatlin 8 51
(C F Wall) *hld up in last: detached and urged along over 4f out: styd on u.p fnl 2f: no ch of rching ldrs* **7/1**
-031 6 *3 1/2* **Sarwin (USA)**[9] 2466 3-9-0 **61** .... PhilipRobinson 5 59+
(W J Musson) *awkward s: in tch: rdn 3f out: wknd 2f out* **5/1**[3]
3631 7 *4* **Lester Leaps In (USA)**[8] 2480 3-9-10 **71** 6ex .... RyanMoore 3 59
(R Hannon) *w ldr to 1/2-way: sn rdn: nrly upsides wl over 2f out: sn wknd* **3/1**[1]
6040 8 *16* **Zizou (IRE)**[9] 2434 3-7-11 **49** oh1 .... MarcHalford(5) 4 6
(J J Bridger) *w ldr for 4f: rdn over 4f out: wknd over 3f out: t.o* **33/1**
0-50 9 *2 1/2* **Maximix**[86] 720 3-9-1 **62** .... MichaelHills 6 15
(B W Hills) *mde most to over 4f out: reluctant 3f out: t.o* **22/1**

2m 7.45s (-0.85) **Going Correction** -0.10s/f (Good) **9** Ran SP% **116.3**
Speed ratings (Par 99):99,96,95,95,94 91,88,75,73
CSF £24.63 CT £137.34 TOTE £5.70: £1.90, £1.60, £1.90; EX 14.40 Place 6 £41.06, Place 5 £17.76.
Owner Usk Valley Stud **Bred** R E Crutchley **Trained** Newmarket, Suffolk

FOCUS
A fair little handicap and the time was slightly quicker than the preceding all-aged maiden, but the form is pretty ordinary.
Iberian Light(USA) Official explanation: jockey said gelding hung both ways
T/Plt: £19.80 to a £1 stake. Pool: £68,576.30. 2,527.65 winning tickets. T/Qpdt: £5.20 to a £1 stake. Pool: £3,826.60. 541.80 winning tickets. JN

2714 - 2716a (Foreign Racing) - See Raceform Interactive

FRAUENFELD (R-H)
Sunday, June 18

OFFICIAL GOING: Good

2717a DAVIDOFF 26. SWISS DERBY (ENTIRE COLTS & FILLIES) 1m 4f
2:35 (2:48) 3-Y-O **£21,239** (£8,496; £6,372; £4,248)

RPR
1 **Majofils (FR)** 3-9-2 .... RobertHavlin 2 —
(M Weiss, Switzerland)
2 *1 1/2* **Befon (FR)**[86] 3-9-2 .... MBlancpain 8 —
(K Schafflutzel, Switzerland)
3 *2 1/2* **Romanoff (GER)** 3-9-2 .... PConvertino 4 —
(M Weiss, Switzerland)
4 *2 1/2* **Aspecto (FR)**[27] 3-9-2 .... MAndrouin 7 —
(H-A Pantall, France)
5 *nk* **Remember Ramon (USA)**[39] 1586 3-9-2 .... DO'Donohoe 1 —
(M J Wallace) *led tl headed and ridden just over 1 1/2f out, weakened, lost 4th last strides (11/2)* **11/2**[1]
6 *1 1/2* **Milord Du Bourg (FR)**[92] 672 3-9-2 .... OPlacais 3 —
(K Schafflutzel, Switzerland)
7 *2* **Queen Of Saba**[252] 5787 3-8-13 .... BrigitteRenk 5 —
(M Weiss, Switzerland)
8 **Yokoran (SWI)** 3-9-2 .... TCastanheira 9 —
(Karin Suter, Switzerland)
9 **Jerry Lee (IRE)** 3-9-2 .... MKolb 6 —
(M Weiss, Switzerland)

2m 37.1s **9** Ran SP% **15.4**
(including 1SFr stake): WIN 6.70; PL 1.60, 1.90, 1.30; SF 19.70.
Owner Appapays Racing Club **Bred** Sas Haras De La Huderie & Jean-Pierre Deroubaix **Trained** Switzerland

NOTEBOOK
Remember Ramon(USA) raced keenly in front around these sharp bends and was quickly left behind as the field entered the short home straight.

2718 - (Foreign Racing) - See Raceform Interactive

2009 ASCOT (R-H)
Tuesday, June 20

OFFICIAL GOING: Good to firm
Wind: Almost nil Weather: Fine

2719 COVENTRY STKS (GROUP 2) 6f
2:35 (2:37) (Class 1) 2-Y-O
£45,424 (£17,216; £8,616; £4,296; £2,152; £1,080) **Stalls** Low

Form RPR
11 1 **Hellvelyn**[25] 1998 2-9-1 .... TedDurcan 6 105+
(B Smart) *lw: prom nr side: effrt to ld wl over 1f out: rdn and styd on wl fnl f* **4/1**[1]
1 2 *3/4* **Major Cadeaux**[31] 1838 2-9-1 .... RichardHughes 2 103+
(R Hannon) *lw: racd nr side: mde most: rdn and hdd wl over 1f out: styd on wl fnl f: a hld* **11/2**[2]
1 3 *1* **Tariq**[24] 2029 2-9-1 .... AlanMunro 15 100+
(P W Chapple-Hyam) *lw: racd in centre for over 1f: nt on terms on outer after: rdn and prog over 2f out: styd on wl fnl f: nrst fin* **12/1**
5 4 *1/2* **Kalgoorlie (USA)**[24] 2029 2-9-1 .... ShaneKelly 18 98+
(J Noseda) *lw: sn outpcd and struggling: last of main gp over 2f out: swtchd lft over 1f out: r.o strly fnl f: fin best of all* **66/1**
2 5 *nk* **Jo'Burg (USA)**[31] 1838 2-9-1 .... MJKinane 20 97+
(Mrs A J Perrett) *trckd other pair in centre: led trio over 2f out: styd on but nvr quite on terms* **12/1**
12 6 *nk* **La Neige**[24] 2009 2-9-1 .... TonyCulhane 5 96
(M R Channon) *lw: hld up in tch nr side: rdn and effrt 2f out: styd on same pce and nvr rchd ldrs* **25/1**
114 7 *hd* **Mubaashir (IRE)**[17] 2225 2-9-1 .... LDettori 9 96
(E A L Dunlop) *lw: chsd nr side ldrs: rdn over 2f out: kpt on same pce: n.d* **20/1**
11 8 *1/2* **Sadeek**[17] 2225 2-9-1 .... NCallan 17 94
(K A Ryan) *lw: racd in centre for over 1f: prom whn c across to nr side: rdn over 2f out: fdd jst over 1f out* **10/1**[3]
41 9 *hd* **Prince Golan (IRE)**[30] 1863 2-9-1 .... DO'Donohoe 3 94+
(K A Ryan) *w ldr over 3f: rdn whn n.m.r 2f out: steadily wknd* **50/1**
11 10 *1* **Baby Strange**[24] 2009 2-9-1 .... RobbieFitzpatrick 1 91
(P A Blockley) *swtg: chsd nr side ldrs: rdn over 2f out: no imp over 1f out: wknd fnl f* **10/1**[3]
312 11 *hd* **Captain Marvelous (IRE)**[20] 2144 2-9-1 .... MichaelHills 14 90
(B W Hills) *dwlt: racd in centre over 1f: hld up: rdn and prog 2f out: one pce and no hdwy fnl f* **33/1**
121 12 *1* **Everymanforhimself (IRE)**[20] 2127 2-9-1 .... EddieAhern 7 87
(J G Given) *lw: chsd ldrs nr side: rdn 1/2-way: no imp 2f out: wknd* **20/1**
01 13 *nk* **Johannesburg Jack (IRE)**[20] 2130 2-9-1 .... SteveDrowne 10 86
(H Morrison) *dwlt: hld up nr side: rdn and no real prog fnl 2f* **66/1**
1 14 *1 3/4* **Carson's Spirit (USA)**[70] 961 2-9-1 .... ChrisCatlin 4 81
(W S Kittow) *chsd nr side ldrs over 2f: sn lost pl and struggling* **66/1**
15 *hd* **Holy Roman Emperor (IRE)**[13] 2368 2-9-1 .... KFallon 13 80+
(A P O'Brien, Ire) *cmpt: str: lw: racd in centre for over 1f: racd on outer after: nvr on terms w ldrs: edgd rt over 1f out: eased whn no ch f* **4/1**[1]
41 16 *1 3/4* **Deadshot Keen (IRE)**[49] 1372 2-9-1 .... JamieSpencer 8 75
(B J Meehan) *lw: dwlt: racd nr side: a wl in rr* **33/1**
13 17 *3* **Chjimes (IRE)**[24] 2009 2-9-1 .... PJSmullen 21 66
(K R Burke) *lw: led trio in centre to over 2f out: sn no ch* **33/1**
1 18 *1/2* **Baltimore Jack (IRE)**[19] 2159 2-9-1 .... DeanMcKeown 16 65
(R M Whitaker) *lw: dwlt: racd in centre for over 1f: struggling on outer fr 1/2-way* **66/1**
19 *hd* **Hammers Boy (IRE)**[14] 2336 2-9-1 .... WMLordan 12 64
(T Stack, Ire) *racd in centre for over 1f: chsd ldrs on outer: rdn 1/2-way: wknd 2f out* **25/1**
03 20 *9* **Tudor Prince (IRE)**[24] 2029 2-9-1 .... JimmyFortune 19 37
(B J Meehan) *w ldr in centre trio to 1/2-way: wknd* **100/1**
31 21 *5* **Zafonical Storm (USA)**[84] 775 2-9-1 .... KerrinMcEvoy 11 22
(B W Duke) *racd in centre for over 1f: rdn and struggling on outer over 3f out: sn wknd: t.o* **100/1**

1m 14.51s (-1.49) **Going Correction** 0.0s/f (Good) **21** Ran SP% **124.9**
Speed ratings (Par 105):109,108,106,106,105 105,104,104,104,102 102,101,100,98,98 95,91,91,90,78 72
CSF £21.22 TOTE £5.40: £2.20, £2.60, £4.20; EX 29.00 Trifecta £516.40 W/U.
Owner H E Sheikh Rashid Bin Mohammed **Bred** N E and Mrs Poole and Trickledown Stud **Trained** Hambleton, N Yorks
■ A record-sized field for the Coventry Stakes, which dates back to 1890.

FOCUS
The field initially raced in three groups before the eight down the centre joined the main body of the field, leaving three to race in isolation centre-to-far-side. The stands' side appeared favoured. Not a great deal of solid quality form going into this and with the first nine covered by under 4l this was not a strong renewal, rated 3lb off the race average. Note: In order that one of the premier meetings of the Flat season is not left without any information regarding race times, provisional speed figures have been calculated using a combination of updated versions of the existing median times and projected median times where race distances have changed. Once more data is available for the new Ascot, the median times will be revised.

NOTEBOOK
Hellvelyn, never far from the action towards the near side, travelled well before taking it up but was in front plenty soon enough and idled before holding the runner-up. Unbeaten in three starts now, this progressive colt will stay further than this and could be a 2000 Guineas candidate next season. (op 9-2)
Major Cadeaux, a winner in soft ground on his debut, was soon in front but once headed by the winner was always just being held, the pair having it between them from some way out. He should progress and another furlong ought not to trouble him. (op 6-1 tchd 13-2)
Tariq ◆ gained his debut victory in soft ground but had no problem at all with this sound surface. One of a group of eight to initially race down the centre, he then raced down the outer of the main body of the field and ran on in good style in the latter stages. His draw cost him here and there should be a nice race to be won with him. (op 11-1)
Kalgoorlie(USA) ◆, who was also behind today's third on his debut in soft ground, ran quite a race. Tacking over to race with the main bunch, he was still at the rear of the field going to the two pole and then had to be switched for a run before finishing really strongly. He should progress again for this effort.
Jo'Burg(USA) ran to his debut form with Major Cadeaux and emerges with plenty of credit as he was one of three to race in isolation out in the centre of the track. This was his first run on a sound surface and he handled it well. (tchd 14-1)
La Neige, better away this time, was keeping on at the end without quite getting to the leaders. He should stay a seventh furlong.
Mubaashir(IRE), keeping on well at the end but never quite able to get in a blow, was more suited by this track than Epsom and certainly stayed the six furlongs.

Sadeek showed good speed after tacking over to the near side but could not go with the principals when the pace lifted.
Prince Golan(IRE) showed plenty of speed on this quicker ground but was put in his place in the final two furlongs, finishing up just a head behind his better-fanced stablemate.
Baby Strange, winner of the first race at the 'new' Ascot, once again became stirred up in the preliminaries and needs to relax before his races. This ground was not ideal for him. (op 12-1)
Holy Roman Emperor(IRE), impressive winner of a Leopardstown maiden first time out and the only entry from the powerful Ballydoyle yard, was a market drifter. Racing on the outside of the main group, he hung to his right when brought under pressure and was eased down with his chance gone. (op 7-2 tchd 9-2 in places)

2720 KING'S STAND STKS (BRITISH LEG OF THE GLOBAL SPRINT CHALLENGE) (GROUP 2) 5f

3:10 (3:15) (Class 1) 3-Y-O+

£113,560 (£43,040; £21,540; £8,060; £8,060; £2,700) **Stalls** Low

Form				RPR
1		**Takeover Target (AUS)**[101] 7-9-7 .... JayFord 17 (J Janiak, Australia) *cmpt: str: racd stands' side: in tch: led overall over 1f out: r.o ins fnl f: hld on gamely* **7/1**[2]	124
06-2	**2**	*shd*	**Benbaun (IRE)**[16] 2276 5-9-2 111 ....(v) JamieSpencer 12 (M J Wallace) *racd stands' side: midfield: hdwy over 1f out: hung rt ins fnl f: r.o strly towards fin* **16/1**	119+
0-06	**3**	*½*	**Pivotal Point**[16] 2276 6-9-2 110 .... LDettori 5 (P J Makin) *racd stands' side: hld up: hdwy 2f out: r.o ins fnl f: 3rd of 18 in gp* **25/1**	117
4	*nk*	**Falkirk (NZ)**[44] 6-9-2 ....(bt) JMurtagh 9 (Lee Freedman, Australia) *tall: lw: racd stands' side: towards rr: swtchd lft and hdwy over 1f out: fin wl: 4th of 18 in gp* **14/1**	116+
-21	**4**	*dht*	**Dandy Man (IRE)**[45] 1485 3-8-10 .... NGMcCullagh 22 (C Collins, Ire) *lw: racd far side: prom: led gp 3f out: r.o u.p: hld towards fin: 1st of 10 in gp* **10/1**[3]	114+
-003	**6**	*hd*	**Baltic King**[15] 2303 6-9-2 106 ....(t) JimmyFortune 2 (H Morrison) *swtg: racd stands' side: chsd ldrs: hdwy over 2f out: nt qckn ins fnl f: 5th of 18 in gp* **16/1**	115
7	*hd*	**Glamour Puss (NZ)**[66] 6-9-4 ....(b) StevenKing 18 (Danny O'Brien, Australia) *w'like: lw: racd stands' side: midfield: rdn 2f out: styd on ins fnl f: 6th of 18 in gp* **16/1**	116
0011	**8**	*hd*	**Moss Vale (IRE)**[16] 2276 5-9-5 109 .... KFallon 7 (D Nicholls) *lw: racd stands' side: s.i.s: towards rr: hdwy over 2f out: r.o ins fnl f: fin 7th of 18 in gp* **5/1**[1]	117+
112-	**9**	*nk*	**La Cucaracha**[290] 4940 5-8-13 112 .... MichaelHills 25 (B W Hills) *lw: racd far side: midfield: effrt and hdwy 2f out: kpt on ins fnl f: 2nd of 10 in gp* **7/1**[2]	109
0540	**10**	*hd*	**The Tatling (IRE)**[21] 2115 9-9-2 113 .... RyanMoore 26 (J M Bradley) *racd far side: towards rr: hdwy over 1f out: styd on ins fnl f: 3rd of 10 in gp* **20/1**	112
1120	**11**	*shd*	**Les Arcs (USA)**[21] 2115 6-9-2 111 .... JohnEgan 15 (T J Pitt) *lw: racd stands' side: chsd ldrs: rdn over 1f out: no ex ins fnl f: 8th of 18 in gp* **33/1**	111
10-0	**12**	*nk*	**Ashdown Express (IRE)**[63] 1069 7-9-2 111 .... AlanMunro 14 (C F Wall) *racd stands' side: towards rr: hdwy 2f out: styd on ins fnl f: nt pce to trble ldrs: 9th of 18 in gp* **50/1**	110
42-0	**13**	*¾*	**La Chunga (USA)**[44] 1508 3-8-7 111 .... DarryllHolland 16 (J Noseda) *racd stands' side: s.i.s: towards rr: rdn and hdwy over 1f out: nvr trbld ldrs: 10th of 18 in gp* **33/1**	103
-033	**14**	*1 ¼*	**Mecca's Mate**[13] 2369 5-8-13 100 .... NCallan 11 (D W Barker) *lw: racd stands' side: midfield: rdn and wknd over 1f out: 11th of 18 in gp* **100/1**	100
1-33	**15**	*1*	**Tax Free (IRE)**[16] 2276 4-9-2 104 .... AdrianTNicholls 19 (D Nicholls) *racd far side: chsd ldrs: rdn 2f out: wknd ins fnl f: 4th of 10 in gp* **12/1**	100
3141	**16**	*hd*	**Reverence**[21] 2115 5-9-5 108 .... KDarley 27 (E J Alston) *racd far side: midfield: rdn over 2f out: wknd over 1f out: 5th of 10 in gp* **16/1**	102
11-0	**17**	*½*	**Resplendent Glory (IRE)**[21] 2115 4-9-2 110 .... IanMongan 1 (T G Mills) *racd stands' side: hung rt thrght: w ldr tl rdn and wknd over 1f out: 12th of 18 in gp* **40/1**	97
20-0	**18**	*2*	**Majestic Missile (IRE)**[45] 1485 5-9-2 112 ....(vt[1]) TonyCulhane 4 (W J Haggas) *racd stands' side: a towards rr: 13th of 18 in gp* **20/1**	90
0-00	**19**	*shd*	**Texas Gold**[17] 2227 8-9-2 102 .... MartinDwyer 24 (W R Muir) *racd far side: chsd ldrs: rdn over 2f out: wknd over 1f out: 6th of 10 in gp* **100/1**	89
1-04	**20**	*½*	**Celtic Mill**[15] 2303 8-9-2 109 ....(p) EddieAhern 23 (D W Barker) *racd far side: led gp for 2f: wknd over 1f out: 7th of 10 that side* **100/1**	88
0130	**21**	*shd*	**Corridor Creeper (FR)**[17] 2227 9-9-2 108 ....(p) ShaneKelly 28 (J M Bradley) *racd far side: chsd ldrs tl rdn and wknd over 1f out: 8th of 10 in gp* **66/1**	87
0-02	**22**	*1 ½*	**The Trader (IRE)**[21] 2115 8-9-2 110 ....(b) TedDurcan 20 (M Blanshard) *racd far side: a bhd: 9th of 10 in gp* **33/1**	82
10-0	**23**	*1*	**Godfrey Street**[21] 2115 3-8-13 107 .... PatDobbs 21 (R Hannon) *racd far side: midfield to 1/2-way: sn bhd: last of 10 in gp* **100/1**	79
0040	**24**	*nk*	**Fire Up The Band**[17] 2227 7-9-2 104 .... WSupple 13 (D Nicholls) *racd stands' side: chsd ldrs tl rdn and wknd over 1f out: 14th of 18 in gp* **100/1**	77
0-20	**25**	*6*	**Bond City (IRE)**[10] 2450 4-9-2 99 .... RobertWinston 8 (B Smart) *racd stands' side: midfield: rdn over 2f out: wknd over 1f out: 15th of 18 in gp* **100/1**	56
31-0	**26**	*5*	**Boogie Street**[45] 1485 5-9-2 109 .... RichardHughes 3 (R Hannon) *lw: racd stands' side: a bhd: last of finishers in gp* **22/1**	38
6424	**B**		**Orientor**[21] 2115 8-9-2 102 .... ChrisCatlin 6 (J S Goldie) *racd stands' side: towards rr: effrt over 2f out: no real imp whn b.d over 1f out* **100/1**	—
13-0	**F**		**Tabaret**[45] 1485 3-8-10 103 .... DeanMcKeown 10 (R M Whitaker) *lw: led stands' side gp: hdd wl over 1f out: wkng whn clipped heels and fell sn after* **100/1**	—

59.79 secs (-2.13) **Going Correction** 0.0s/f (Good)
WFA 3 from 4yo+ 6lb **28** Ran SP% **129.0**
Speed ratings (Par 115):112,111,111,110,110 110,109,109,109,108 108,108,106,104,103 103,102,99,98,98 97,95,93,93,83 7
CSF £97.81 TOTE £5.70: £2.80, £7.60, £5.20; EX 218.10 Trifecta £3325.00 Pool: £7.961.80 - 1.70 winning units..
Owner J & B Janiak **Bred** Meringo Stud Farm **Trained** Australia
■ The first winner in Britain for Joe Janiak and Jay Ford, & the second in this race for Australian raiders following Choisir in 2003.
■ Stewards' Enquiry : Ian Mongan two-day ban: careless riding (Jul 1-2)

FOCUS
A typically competitive Group sprint and very little covering the first dozen at the line. The field split into two, with the larger group of 18 coming stands' side whilst the other ten went far side. The first four all raced in the stands'-side group, but three of the first ten raced on the other flank and were not beaten far, suggesting there was not a major bias. A comparison with the later Windsor Castle Stakes for two-year-olds suggests the time was nothing special, backed up by the distances covering the first 12 home and the form does not look particularly strong, although sound enough.

NOTEBOOK
Takeover Target(AUS), who cost just £500 and is trained by a part-time taxi driver, was always close to the pace in the stands'-side group and showed plenty of guts to battle his way to a famous if narrow victory. Although not as authoritative as his compatriot Choisir three years ago, this was still a fine effort under a Group 1 penalty and he obviously had no problems with the track. He will now bid to emulate Choisir by following up in the Golden Jubilee on Saturday. (op 6-1)
Benbaun(IRE) is as hard as nails and finished with a real flourish in the stands'-side group, but the winner had got first run and he just failed to peg him back. He did at least reverse recent Chantilly form with Moss Vale and deserves to win again at Group level before too long. (tchd 14-1 in places)
Pivotal Point came from some way off the pace and finished with a real rattle against the stands'-side rail. This was his best effort in an abbreviated career since winning the Diadem here in September 2004, but he may be a bit better over six these days and probably needs easier ground over this trip at this level.
Dandy Man(IRE) ◆ showed that his Palace House victory was no fluke and emerged the clear-cut winner of the separate race on the far side. It is impossible to judge how disadvantaged those on the far side were, if at all, but one thing that is for certain is that being only a three-year-old he has the potential to make a name for himself in top-class sprints for a few years to come. (tchd 16-1 in places)
Falkirk(NZ) ◆ was racing over a shorter trip than he is used to in Australia and it showed as he came from near last to finish in great style despite getting into a barging match with Baltic King near the line. Connections can only have been encouraged by this. (tchd 16-1 in places)
Baltic King, who is yet to win above Listed company, had every chance in the stands'-side group and this was probably one of his very best efforts. He did have a good record at the old Ascot.
Glamour Puss(NZ) was brought over to race in the stands'-side group despite being drawn closer to the far rail. All her wins in Australia have been over further, so it was no surprise to see her doing her best work late. (op 14-1)
Moss Vale(IRE), well backed, lost crucial ground at the start, and his finishing effort was a case of too little too late. He may well have found this trip on a sound surface a little too sharp for him. (op 13-2 tchd 7-1)
La Cucaracha ◆ has a fine record fresh, so the nine-month break was a positive as much as anything else. She kept on to finish second in the far-side group and can hardly have been said to have run below form despite only finishing ninth. There will be other days.
The Tatling(IRE), winner of this race two years ago, finished well and nearly got up to finish second in the far-side group. Despite his age he still has what it takes to win in Group company when things fall right.
Reverence always seemed to be struggling to go the pace in the far-side group and probably found the ground too quick. (op 14-1)
Resplendent Glory(IRE) Official explanation: jockey said colt hung right throughout
Celtic Mill blazed a trail in the far-side group until around halfway. (op 66-1)
Orientor was already beaten when tripped up by the prostrate Tabaret a furlong out. (op 66-1)
Tabaret showed good early speed in the stands'-side group, but was already on the retreat when clipping a rival's heels a furlong out and crashing to the ground. (op 66-1)

2721 ST JAMES'S PALACE STKS (GROUP 1) (ENTIRE COLTS) 1m (R)

3:50 (3:57) (Class 1) 3-Y-O

£141,950 (£53,800; £26,925; £13,425; £6,725; £3,375) **Stalls** High

Form				RPR
3-41	**1**		**Araafa (IRE)**[24] 2039 3-9-0 116 .... AlanMunro 2 (J Noseda) *sn trckd clr ldr: clsd to ld over 2f out: clr wl over 1f out: r.o wl: unchal* **2/1**[1]	121+
2-13	**2**	*2*	**Stormy River (FR)**[37] 1718 3-9-0 .... OPeslier 4 (N Clement, France) *w'like: lw: hld up last: detached and pushed along over 3f: rapid prog 2f out: chsd wnr jst ins fnl f: r.o: no ch* **7/2**[2]	117+
0-00	**3**	*1 ¾*	**Ivan Denisovich (IRE)**[37] 1718 3-9-0 .... KFallon 9 (A P O'Brien, Ire) *lw: settled in midfield: rdn over 2f out: prog over 1f out: styd on to take 3rd ins fnl f* **13/2**[3]	112
4-22	**4**	*¾*	**Marcus Andronicus (USA)**[37] 1718 3-9-0 .... JMurtagh 10 (A P O'Brien, Ire) *lw: hld up wl in rr: prog on outer over 2f out: rdn to dispute 2nd 1f out: wknd ins fnl f* **9/1**	110
5-22	**5**	*1 ½*	**Metropolitan Man**[25] 1990 3-9-0 103 .... KerrinMcEvoy 3 (D M Simcock) *wl in rr: rdn over 2f out: kpt on same pce fr over 1f out: n.d* **40/1**	106
-104	**6**	*hd*	**Yasoodd**[24] 2039 3-9-0 108 .... ChrisCatlin 5 (M R Channon) *lw: racd wd: hld up towards rr: rdn and prog over 2f out: chsng ldrs over 1f out: wknd fnl f* **16/1**	106
-221	**7**	*1*	**Royal Power (IRE)**[37] 1715 3-9-0 107 .... LDettori 8 (M R Channon) *lw: prom: chsd wnr 2f out: no imp: wknd rapidly jst ins fnl f* **12/1**	104
6146	**8**	*7*	**Yarqus**[30] 1872 3-9-0 100 .... RyanMoore 11 (C E Brittain) *chsd ldrs: lost pl over 3f out: wknd 2f out* **66/1**	88
113	**9**	*nk*	**Decado (IRE)**[24] 2039 3-9-0 .... DPMcDonogh 7 (Kevin Prendergast, Ire) *neat: lw: s.i.s: pushed up to chse ldrs: rdn wl over 2f out: wknd rapidly over 1f out* **7/1**	87
2-14	**10**	*4*	**Aeroplane**[24] 2031 3-9-0 100 .... EddieAhern 6 (P W Chapple-Hyam) *lw: prom tl wknd rapidly over 2f out: eased* **16/1**	78
35-0	**11**	*5*	**Arabian Prince (USA)**[24] 2039 3-9-0 .... CO'Donoghue 1 (A P O'Brien, Ire) *led and sn clr: c wd bnd over 2f out: sn hdd and btn: eased over 1f out* **66/1**	66

1m 39.59s (-3.30) **Going Correction** +0.05s/f (Good) **11** Ran SP% **116.3**
Speed ratings (Par 113):114,112,110,109,108 107,106,99,99,95 90
CSF £8.45 TOTE £2.70: £1.40, £1.60, £2.30; EX 10.60 Trifecta £53.20 Pool: £5,940.98 - 79.24 winning units.
Owner Saleh Al Homaizi & Imad Al Sagar **Bred** Sweetmans Bloodstock **Trained** Newmarket, Suffolk
■ Alan Munro's first Royal Ascot winner since 1994.

FOCUS
Not a strong renewal, George Washington being a notable absentee, and Araafa had a straightforward task to confirm his Curragh improvement. The runner-up may well be better than this and the race has been rated through the seventh.

NOTEBOOK
Araafa(IRE) has improved with each race and he gained his second Group 1 victory in comfortable style. Always well placed, he moved to the front early in the home straight and was never seriously threatened after that, although the second was cutting into his lead in the latter stages. A class act who is effective on both fast and testing ground, he will go for races like the Sussex and the Queen Elizabeth II now and connections are relishing a possible rematch with George Washington. (op 7-4 tchd 9-4 in places and 13-8 in places)

The Form Book, Raceform Ltd, Compton, RG20 6NL

Stormy River(FR) ◆, ridden differently, was in last place and not going too well at halfway and was still at the back of the field turning for home. Running on strongly against the rail, he made rapid progress to move into second but Peslier was not hard on him when it was obvious he could not reach the winner. His trainer believed that the work done at home to get him to settle better had been too successful and that he had over-relaxed here. There is better to come from him. (tchd 4-1 in places)

Ivan Denisovich(IRE), chosen by Fallon in preference to Marcus Andronicus, who finished ahead of him at Longchamp, stayed on in the straight without ever looking likely to threaten the winner. He is a smart colt but has now been beaten on all five starts at this level. (op 7-1)

Marcus Andronicus(USA) finished in front of both Stormy River and Ivan Denisovich when runner-up to stablemate Aussie Rules in the French Guineas. He ran his race but, after disputing second spot briefly in the straight, he weakened inside the last. (op 12-1 tchd 14-1 in places)

Metropolitan Man ◆, back on fast ground, ran on from the rear of the field without ever reaching a challenging position. This was a personal best and he should be placed to win a decent race at a slightly lower level. (op 50-1)

Yasoodd, having his first run on fast ground, was beaten a bit further than he had been at either Longchamp or the Curragh and is going to remain tricky to place.

Royal Power(IRE), successful in the German Guineas on his latest start, went after the winner with two furlongs to run but faded quickly out of the picture inside the last.

Yarqus, whose last two runs were over a mile and a half, was out of his depth. Ten furlongs could turn out to be his trip.

Decado(IRE) finished only three lengths behind Araafa in the Irish Guineas, but that was on heavy ground and he could not come close to confirming the form on this different surface.

Aeroplane, in the same ownership as the winner, ran here rather than in the Jersey over a furlong shorter. With hindsight, that race would have proved the better option. (tchd 20-1)

Arabian Prince(USA) got across from his number one stall to take up pacemaking duties, but ran wide off the home turn, allowing the winner through, and was soon back-pedalling. (tchd 80-1)

2722 QUEEN ANNE STKS (GROUP 1) — 1m (S)

4:25 (4:33) (Class 1) 4-Y-0+

£141,950 (£53,800; £26,925; £13,425; £6,725; £3,375) **Stalls** Low

Form — RPR

60-6 **1** **Ad Valorem (USA)**^{72} [930] 4-9-0 .... KFallon 2 — 123
(A P O'Brien, Ire) *lw: wnt rt s: trckd ldrs: pushed along and outpcd 4f out: swtchd rt and rallied over 2f out: edgd lft ins fnl f: drvn out* **13/2**

5-63 **2** *1 ½* **Court Masterpiece**^{31} [1840] 6-9-0 114 .... JamieSpencer 3 — 123+
(E A L Dunlop) *lw: s.i.s: hld up: hdwy over 2f out and gng wl:: swtchd lft over 1f out: clsng abt 1l down whn n.m.r and hmpd ins fnl f* **11/2**^{3}

110- **3** *nk* **Proclamation (IRE)**^{290} [4940] 4-9-0 122 .... LDettori 9 — 119
(Saeed Bin Suroor) *lw: s.i.s: hld up: hdwy over 2f out: rdn to chse ldrs over 1f out: nt qckn ins fnl f* **2/1**^{2}

14-1 **4** *1 ¾* **Peeress**^{31} [1840] 5-8-11 118 .... MJKinane 8 — 118+
(Sir Michael Stoute) *lw: b.hind: racd keenly: trckd ldrs: led over 2f out: rdn over 1f out: hdd whn n.m.r and hmpd ins fnl f: nt rcvr* **7/4**^{1}

20-2 **5** *7* **Vortex**^{48} [1407] 7-9-0 109 .... (t) MartinDwyer 5 — 99
(Miss Gay Kelleway) *lw: b.hind: trckd ldrs: led 3f out: hdd over 2f out: wknd over 1f out* **20/1**

0115 **6** *4* **Kandidate**^{31} [1840] 4-9-0 110 .... (t) RyanMoore 6 — 90
(C E Brittain) *lw: racd keenly: led: hdd over 3f out: rdn and wknd 2f out* **16/1**

50-5 **7** *4* **Akimbo (USA)**^{10} [2471] 5-9-0 107 .... WSupple 4 — 80
(James Leavy, Ire) *w ldr: led over 3f out: sn hdd: wknd over 2f out* **66/1**

1m 40.0s (-1.86) **Going Correction** 0.0s/f (Good) — **7** Ran SP% **110.6**

Speed ratings (Par 117):109,107,107,105,98 94,90

CSF £38.63 TOTE £8.00: £2.60, £3.20; EX 50.50 Trifecta £166.70 w/u.

Owner Mrs John Magnier & R W Ingham **Bred** Calumet Farm **Trained** Ballydoyle, Co Tipperary

■ Stewards' Enquiry : K Fallon four-day ban: careless riding (Jul 1-4)

FOCUS

A race with a rich history, but this year's renewal was spoilt to a degree by a pedestrian early pace which might have been avoided had Godolphin's other runner Belenus not been withdrawn. The steady pace arguably contributed to the controversial outcome, which saw the winner Ad Valorem hanging badly away from the whip and causing a knock-on effect involving Peeress and Court Masterpiece. The form looks messy, but the winner has been rated to his previous best.

NOTEBOOK

Ad Valorem(USA), winless last season, having been unbeaten as a juvenile including a victory in the Middle Park, bounced back to winning form and the better ground was probably a major factor. However, after hitting the front he hung badly away to his left under a right-hand drive and caused major problems for his two nearest pursuers. He probably only kept the race thanks to the winning margin, but would not have won by anything like as far had the trouble not taken place and the way this race was run does put a big question mark over the true value of the form. (op 8-1)

Court Masterpiece did have a question mark over his ability to stay this trip, as the majority of his wins have been over shorter and his two wins over this distance have both been over the easy Goodwood Mile. Ridden with stamina apparently in mind, the moderate pace was a big help to him and his rider was swinging away on the bridle for much of the way. Once asked for his effort, he did not exactly engage the afterburner, but was still staying on when the winner pushed Peeress onto him and he got badly squeezed against the stands' rail. He ran on again once in the clear, but the damage had been done and it is anyone's guess how much ground he lost as a result. (op 6-1 tchd 13-2 and 5-1)

Proclamation(IRE), not seen since disappointing in the William Hill Sprint Cup over a trip too short at Haydock last September, was held up in the early stages on this debut for Godolphin before making a move on the outside a quarter of a mile out, but he could only plug on at one pace from that point. The problems his stable has endured this spring give him a ready-made excuse for this performance, but he is probably worth another chance as a few from the yard are starting to win again and he may be happier on an easier surface than this. (op 7-4 tchd 9-4 in places)

Peeress was totally unsuited by the way this race was run as she was doing far too much early. It was only her class that kept her in the race for as long as she did and she was still in there battling when badly hampered by the winner entering the last furlong. She would not have won otherwise, but may have held on to a place. (tchd 15-8 in places)

Vortex has run some fine races on this track in the past, but he had a mountain to climb at this level and found it all too much. (tchd 22-1, 25-1 in places)

Kandidate probably did too much too soon and paid the penalty. (op 25-1)

2723 ASCOT STKS (H'CAP) — 2m 4f

4:55 (5:08) (Class 2) (0-95,93) 4-Y-0+

£34,276 (£10,263; £5,131; £2,568; £1,281; £643) **Stalls** High

Form — RPR

-050 **1** **Baddam**^{24} [2013] 4-9-2 87 .... IanMongan 15 — 104+
(M R Channon) *lw: hld up wl in rr: stdy prog on outer fr 6f out: led jst ins fnl 2f: sn drvn clr* **33/1**

102- **2** *5* **Top The Charts**^{15} [5875] 4-8-12 83 .... FMBerry 27 — 95
(A J Martin, Ire) *lw: t.k.h: hld up bhd ldrs: prog 3f out: chsd wnr wl over 1f out to jst over 1f out: kpt on to take 2nd again last stride* **5/1**^{1}

3 *hd* **Shamayoun (FR)**^{59} 4-8-2 73 .... (p) NickyMackay 22 — 85
(C R Egerton) *hld up wl in rr: gd prog on outer fr 5f out: rdn to chse wnr jst over 1f out: hung lft ins fnl f: lost 2nd fin* **10/1**^{3}

4/41 **4** *3 ½* **Full House (IRE)**^{8} [2501] 7-8-9 78 3ex .... KDarley 6 — 86
(P R Webber) *lw: hld up wl in rr: prog over 4f out: styd on same pce fr over 2f out* **16/1**

1142 **5** *2* **Mceldowney**^{10} [2452] 4-8-10 86 .... GregFairley$^{(5)}$ 7 — 92+
(M Johnston) *chsd ldrs for 7f: lost pl and midfield after: prog over 3f out: drvn to chse ldrs 2f out: fdd fnl f* **33/1**

0341 **6** *2 ½* **Mister Right (IRE)**^{10} [2460] 5-8-8 77 .... TQuinn 11 — 81+
(D J S Ffrench Davis) *hld up in last trio: gd prog on wd outside 3f out: clsd on ldrs over 1f out: sn wknd* **66/1**

3-02 **7** *½* **Elusive Dream**^{24} [2013] 5-9-9 92 .... JamieMackay 8 — 95
(Sir Mark Prescott) *lw: rn in snatches: trckd ldrs: prog gng strly to ld over 4f out: hdd jst ins fnl 2f: wknd* **12/1**

05-3 **8** *½* **Escayola (IRE)**^{17} [2238] 6-9-2 85 .... (b) TonyCulhane 14 — 88
(W J Haggas) *lw: b: hld up in midfield: no real prog 4f out: kpt on fnl 2f: no ch* **8/1**^{2}

0303 **9** *4* **Double Obsession**^{10} [2452] 6-8-11 80 .... (v) KerrinMcEvoy 25 — 79
(D Nicholls) *prom: rdn 3f out: stl chsng ldrs 2f out: wknd* **20/1**

5302 **10** *1 ¼* **High Point (IRE)**^{17} [2219] 8-8-1 75 .... RobynBrisland$^{(5)}$ 5 — 72
(G P Enright) *t.k.h: hld up midfield: sme prog 4f out: nt clr run 2f out: one pce after* **66/1**

000/ **11** *1 ¼* **Tikram**^{74} [5639] 9-8-11 80 .... (b) JimmyFortune 17 — 76
(G L Moore) *lw: hld up in midfield: rdn over 6f out: effrt u.p 3f out: one pce* **50/1**

040- **12** *nk* **Distant Prospect (IRE)**^{83} [5903] 9-9-2 85 .... MartinDwyer 26 — 86+
(A M Balding) *hld up wl in rr: stl at bk of main gp 5f out: prog on inner whn hmpd 2f out: nt rcvr* **66/1**

4-05 **13** *½* **Casual Glance**^{48} [1409] 4-9-2 87 .... MJKinane 1 — 82
(A M Balding) *hld up wl in rr: stl wl in rr over 3f out: modest prog on wd outside fr over 2f out* **40/1**

1443 **14** *½* **Establishment**^{27} [1931] 9-8-8 77 .... LDettori 29 — 72
(C A Cyzer) *hld up in midfield: pushed along and n.m.r 5f out: no prog over 2f out: wknd over 1f out* **16/1**

2103 **15** *½* **Trance (IRE)**^{24} [2035] 6-8-12 81 .... (p) NCallan 12 — 75
(T D Barron) *lw: s.s: hld up wl in rr: hmpd on inner 9f out: n.m.r 5f out: effrt whn hmpd 2f out: no ch* **28/1**

6- **16** *½* **Pacolet (IRE)**^{13} [2372] 7-8-3 75 .... DMGrant$^{(3)}$ 28 — 69
(Patrick J Flynn, Ire) *hld up wl in rr: modest effrt on outer over 3f out: sn no prog* **20/1**

0-24 **17** *3* **Archduke Ferdinand (FR)**^{38} [1690] 8-8-11 80 .... EddieAhern 21 — 71
(A King) *lw: trckd ldrs: prog 6f out: trckd ldr 4f out: wknd rapidly over 2f out* **33/1**

03/1 **18** *18* **Prins Willem (IRE)**^{97} [420] 7-9-4 87 .... (t) JamieSpencer 24 — 60+
(J R Fanshawe) *lw: hld up in midfield: lost pl after 7f: n.m.r on inner 5f out: hmpd 2f out: no ch* **14/1**

-022 **19** *nk* **Michabo (IRE)**^{19} [2176] 5-9-6 89 .... SteveDrowne 19 — 61
(H Morrison) *led to over 4f out: wknd wl over 2f out* **20/1**

2 **20** *12* **Irish Wolf (FR)**^{52} [966] 6-8-6 75 .... (p) RobertWinston 13 — 35
(P Bowen) *hld up in midfield: wknd over 3f out: sn bhd* **33/1**

12-4 **21** *23* **Tarabut**^{15} [2296] 4-8-7 78 .... RHills 16 — 15
(E A L Dunlop) *prom: pressed ldrs 5f out: wknd rapidly 3f out: t.o* **20/1**

0/2- **22** *1* **Football Crazy (IRE)**^{269} [4030] 7-8-11 80 .... RyanMoore 9 — 16
(P Bowen) *hld up in midfield: wknd 4f out: t.o* **40/1**

110- **23** *7* **Afrad (FR)**^{59} [5903] 5-9-10 93 .... RichardHughes 4 — 22
(N J Henderson) *lw: prom tl wknd rapidly 4f out: t.o* **25/1**

3210 **24** *5* **Numero Due**^{10} [2437] 4-8-11 82 .... ChrisCatlin 2 — 6
(G M Moore) *hld up wl in rr: lost tch over 4f out: t.o* **25/1**

/000 **25** *14* **Savannah Bay**^{17} [2229] 7-9-4 87 .... KFallon 3 — —
(B Ellison) *lw: racd wd in midfield: wknd and eased 4f out: t.o* **20/1**

2200 **26** *3* **Eastborough (IRE)**^{10} [2460] 7-8-2 71 .... HayleyTurner 20 — —
(B G Powell) *t.k.h: hld up in last trio: rapid prog 12f out to join ldng pair 9f out: wknd rapidly 5f out: t.o* **100/1**

3052 **27** *8* **Incursion**^{13} [2365] 5-8-3 72 .... AdrianTNicholls 23 — —
(D Nicholls) *a wl in rr: t.o* **66/1**

0-16 **28** *7* **Admiral (IRE)**^{24} [2013] 5-9-5 88 .... JohnEgan 18 — —
(T J Pitt) *b: trckd ldr tl wknd rapidly 5f out: t.o: lame* **16/1**

29 *10* **Burntoakboy**^{16} [2267] 8-8-5 74 .... WMLordan 10 — —
(Michael Cunningham, Ire) *w'like: lw: chsd ldng gp: wknd 7f out: t.o* **25/1**

4m 22.04s (-1.86) **Going Correction** +0.05s/f (Good)

WFA 4 from 5yo+ 2lb — **29** Ran SP% **133.2**

Speed ratings (Par 109):107,105,104,103,102 101,101,101,99,99 98,98,98,98,98 97,96,89,89,84 75,74,72,70,64 63,60,57,5

CSF £154.25 CT £1853.38 TOTE £41.20: £7.50, £2.20, £3.10, £4.60; EX 216.80 Trifecta £1916.70 Pool: £5,669.24 - 2.10 winning units..

Owner N Martin **Bred** Mrs V Rapkins **Trained** West Ilsley, Berks

■ A first success at the Royal meeting for Ian Mongan, who was unseated when Baddam jinked after the line.

FOCUS

A big field, but not too many of them were seen with a serious chance. Probably sound form, rated around the fourth and fifth, although the extreme distance means it is only strictly relevant to a handful of other handicaps all year..

NOTEBOOK

Baddam, who was having his first run at this marathon trip, travelled very well and, in front with two furlongs to run, came clear to win in good style. Progressive last year, when trained by John Dunlop, he has become well handicapped after failing to fire this season.

Top The Charts had not run on the Flat since October, when trained by Richard Hannon, but was a winner over hurdles earlier this month. Representing the yard which won this event last year at York with Leg Spinner, he was taking a big step up in trip but was never far away. He gave chase to the winner in the straight but could never get to him. (tchd 6-1 in places and 7-1 in a place)

Shamayoun(FR), who won two of his three races on the Flat in France last year, was a winner over hurdles at the Cheltenham Festival this spring. Improving down the outside of the pack, he could not get to the winner but would have been second had he not hung into the centre of the track. (op 12-1)

Full House(IRE), under a 3lb penalty for his win at Pontefract earlier in the month, was held up off the pace before staying on steadily from out of the pack in the final half-mile.

Mceldowney, upped in trip and raised a further 3lb, ran another decent race but it does look as if the Handicapper is in charge now.

Mister Right(IRE) ◆, 4lb higher than at Newbury, improved nicely from the back of the field to look a threat but did not quite see out this longer trip. There is probably more to come from him back over shorter.

Elusive Dream, up 2lb to a career-high mark for finishing second at the last meeting here, ran well for a long way but was another for whom the trip proved just too much. (tchd 14-1)

Escayola(IRE), who shaped well on his reappearance at Musselburgh, stayed the trip but was never able to get into the contest. (op 10-1)

Double Obsession, successful in this event two years ago when trained by Mark Johnston, ran a creditable race with the visor back on but could never quite land a blow.

Distant Prospect(IRE), having his first run on the Flat since last year's Cesarewitch, encountered more than his share of traffic problems when attempting to stay on in the straight and Dwyer eventually had to accept the situation. (op 50-1)

Archduke Ferdinand(FR) should have stayed, but after turning into the home straight in second place his stamina gave out.

2724 WINDSOR CASTLE STKS (LISTED RACE) 5f

5:30 (5:45) (Class 1) 2-Y-O

£31,229 (£11,836; £5,923; £2,953; £1,479; £742) **Stalls** Low

Form RPR

16 **1** **Elhamri**[25] [1977] 2-9-3 .... DPMcDonogh 15 104
(S Kirk) *lw: mde all: rdn over 1f out: r.o gamely* **20/1**

25 **2** *nk* **Conquest (IRE)**[31] [1838] 2-9-3 ....(b[1]) JimmyFortune 2 103
(W J Haggas) *lw: t.k.h: hld up: hdwy 2f out: chsd wnr 1f out: ev ch ins fnl f: hld cl home* **8/1**

4 **3** *1 ½* **The Old Fella**[24] [2009] 2-9-3 .... KFallon 4 98+
(R Hannon) *dwlt: outpcd and bhd: hdwy over 1f out: fin wll: nrst fin* **12/1**

5 **4** *½* **Snaefell (IRE)**[18] [2212] 2-9-3 ....(t) JMurtagh 11 96
(M Halford, Ire) *lengthy: str: scope: lw: hld up: rdn and hdwy over 2f out: r.o ins fnl f* **14/1**

31 **5** *hd* **Dazed And Amazed**[23] [2045] 2-9-3 .... RichardHughes 3 95
(R Hannon) *lw: b.hind: wnt rt s: a.p: rdn and ev ch over 1f out: styd on: no ex cl home* **13/2**[2]

21 **6** *1* **We'll Confer**[26] [1959] 2-9-3 .... NCallan 12 91
(K A Ryan) *lw: prom: rdn and ev ch over 1f out: no ex ins fnl f* **7/1**[3]

7 *shd* **Rabatash (USA)**[14] [2333] 2-9-3 .... MJKinane 14 91+
(David Wachman, Ire) *leggy: scope: lw: hmpd s: towards rr: hdwy and edgd rt over 2f out: styd on ins fnl f: nt pce to chal* **13/2**[2]

11 **8** *1* **Espartano**[50] [1354] 2-9-3 .... JamieSpencer 1 87
(M J Wallace) *lw: hld up: rdn over 2f out: hdwy over 1f out: kpt on ins fnl f: no imp on ldrs* **4/1**[1]

140 **9** *½* **Stolt (IRE)**[20] [2127] 2-9-3 .... DNolan 8 86
(N Wilson) *chsd ldrs: rdn over 2f out: ev ch over 1f out: wknd ins fnl f* **100/1**

2231 **10** *½* **Dimboola**[14] [2321] 2-9-3 ....(p) MichaelHills 7 84
(B W Hills) *towards rr: rdn and hdwy over 1f out: sn edgd rt: kpt on: nvr trbld ldrs* **16/1**

12 **11** *1 ¼* **Fathom Five (IRE)**[22] [2076] 2-9-3 .... KDarley 5 82+
(B Smart) *midfield: rdn over 1f out: no imp* **66/1**

222 **12** *2 ½* **See In The Dark (IRE)**[39] [1639] 2-9-3 .... AlanMunro 10 70
(B J Meehan) *bhd: kpt on fnl f: nt pce to trble ldrs* **66/1**

1 **13** *½* **Aahayson**[18] [2191] 2-9-3 .... PatCosgrave 9 69
(K R Burke) *midfield: rdn over 2f out: wknd over 1f out* **50/1**

6126 **14** *2 ½* **Avertuoso**[20] [2127] 2-9-3 .... RobertWinston 6 60
(B Smart) *bmpd s: midfield: rdn 2f out: edgd rt fr over 1f out: wknd fnl f* **50/1**

130 **15** *nk* **Bazroy (IRE)**[15] [2300] 2-9-3 ....(v[1]) ShaneKelly 16 58
(P D Evans) *midfield: rdn over 2f out: hmpd whn wkng over 1f out* **100/1**

2426 **16** *¾* **Lord Charles**[17] [2225] 2-9-3 .... TonyCulhane 17 56
(W G M Turner) *midfield: rdn whn bmpd over 2f out: wknd over 1f out* **33/1**

421 **17** *2 ½* **Scented Present**[14] [2315] 2-9-3 .... LDettori 13 47+
(B J Meehan) *prom tl rdn and wknd over 1f out* **13/2**[2]

0 **18** *nk* **Stargazy**[11] [2402] 2-9-3 .... SteveDrowne 18 46
(R Charlton) *midfield: outpcd after 2f* **66/1**

60.82 secs (-1.10) **Going Correction** 0.0s/f (Good) **18** Ran SP% **121.9**

Speed ratings (Par 101):104,103,101,100,100 98,98,96,95,95 93,89,88,84,83 82,78,78

CSF £165.94 TOTE £54.30: £11.80, £3.70, £2.10; EX 649.70 Trifecta £3159.70 Part won. Pool: £4,450.34 - 0.20 winning units. Place 6 £699.65, Place 5 £356.14.

Owner Norman Ormiston **Bred** Highfield Stud Ltd **Trained** Upper Lambourn, Berks

FOCUS

A race that has been considered a bit of a sideshow over the years, but this looked a good renewal and the winning time compared favourably with the earlier King's Stand and the form looks solid. The whole field decided to race centre to stands' side.

NOTEBOOK

Elhamri ◆, all at sea on soft ground at Goodwood last time, was a reformed character back on this sounder surface. Always up with the pace towards the centre of the track, he looked likely to be swallowed up by the runner-up throughout the last furlong but kept on pulling out a bit more. He should continue to do well given the right conditions and should stay a bit further.

Conquest(IRE), whose two previous outings had both been on soft ground, was sporting first-time blinkers but was still keen enough and throwing his head about in the early stages. Nevertheless, he was produced with what looked a race-winning challenge up the stands' rail only to find the leader was not prepared to give in. He has the ability, but does not look straightforward so backing him carries a certain risk. (op 9-1)

The Old Fella ◆ ran a remarkable race, struggling to go the early pace before making up so much late ground that he may even have won in another 20 yards. He made his debut over an extra furlong here, and it is not hard to see why judged on this effort, so when he goes back up in trip he looks one to follow. He may well turn out to be the best of these. (op 11-1)

Snaefell(IRE), who got off the mark when encountering fast ground for the first time in his most recent outing, was staying on nicely at the line and looks in need of an extra furlong. (op 16-1 tchd 20-1 in a place)

Dazed And Amazed, on fast ground for the first time, did not look completely happy on it and was inclined to hang away to his right in the closing stages when holding every chance. There are other races to be won with him under suitable conditions. (op 6-1)

We'll Confer was by no means disgraced, but the drop back to the minimum trip did not appear to suit him. He should be placed to advantage in the coming weeks. (tchd 15-2 in places)

Espartano never really managed to get into the race from the stands' rail draw and perhaps the faster ground did not suit him. Official explanation: jockey said colt never travelled (tchd 9-2 in places)

Bazroy(IRE) Official explanation: jockey said colt hung right

Scented Present should have had no problem with this ground and was a bit disappointing. Official explanation: jockey said colt ran flat (op 6-1 tchd 7-1 in places)

T/Jkpt: Not won. T/Plt: £3,152.70 to a £1 stake. Pool: £320,027.66. 74.10 winning tickets. T/Qpdt: £142.60 to a £1 stake. Pool: £13,418.25. 69.60 winning tickets. JN

2566 BRIGHTON (L-H)

Tuesday, June 20

OFFICIAL GOING: Firm

Wind: Fresh; half-against

2725 3663 FIRST FOR FOOD SERVICE APPRENTICE H'CAP 1m 1f 209y

6:35 (6:35) (Class 6) (0-60,60) 4-Y-0+ **£2,590** (£770; £385; £192) **Stalls** High

Form RPR

2425 **1** **Seattle Robber**[23] [2044] 4-9-2 **60** ....(b) KevinGhunowa[(5)] 8 67
(P A Blockley) *in tch: wnt 2nd over 2f out: hung lft bef led appr fnl f: r.o ins fnl f: hld on* **7/2**[1]

2003 **2** *hd* **Jackie Kiely**[4] [2601] 5-9-7 **60** ....(t) AdamKirby 4 67+
(Stef Liddiard) *hld up in rr: hdwy over 2f out: styd on to press wnr wl ins fnl f* **7/2**[1]

2401 **3** *3* **Miss Monica (IRE)**[11] [2392] 5-8-2 **46** .... TolleyDean[(5)] 7 47
(P W Hiatt) *in rr: hdwy 3f out: styd on one pce fnl f* **11/2**[2]

0-00 **4** *¾* **Danzare**[3] [2636] 4-9-2 **55** .... NeilChalmers 2 54
(Mrs A J Hamilton-Fairley) *led clr over 2f out: rdn and hdd over 1f out: sn btn* **16/1**

4343 **5** *2 ½* **Heathyards Joy**[46] [1460] 5-7-11 **41** ....(p) LiamJones[(5)] 1 36
(R Hollinshead) *bhd and nvr on terms* **8/1**

0014 **6** *1 ¾* **Danish Monarch**[8] [2499] 5-8-10 **54** .... ChrisCavanagh[(5)] 6 45
(David Pinder) *trckd ldr tl rdn and wknd over 2f out* **13/2**[3]

0003 **7** *7* **Sunset Dreamer (USA)**[20] [2131] 5-8-2 **41** oh1 .... SaleemGolam 3 19
(P Mitchell) *in tch to 1/2-way* **8/1**

-010 **8** *5* **Primed Up (IRE)**[10] [2455] 4-8-11 **57** ow4 ....(b) KatieOrchin[(7)] 5 26
(G L Moore) *chsd ldrs tl wknd 4f out* **15/2**

2m 4.15s (1.55) **Going Correction** +0.25s/f (Good) **8** Ran SP% **113.0**

Speed ratings (Par 101):103,102,100,99,97 96,90,86

CSF £15.00 CT £64.16 TOTE £4.50: £2.30, £1.20, £2.10; EX 14.90.

Owner J T Billson **Bred** Littleton Stud **Trained** Lambourn, Berks

FOCUS

A moderate handicap, run at a generous early pace, and the form looks solid with the two market leaders coming clear.

2726 BLAKES BUTCHERS MAIDEN AUCTION STKS 5f 59y

7:05 (7:05) (Class 6) 2-Y-O **£2,590** (£770; £385; £192) **Stalls** Low

Form RPR

066 **1** **Fair 'n Square (IRE)**[3] [2631] 2-8-5 .... FrancisNorton 4 63
(J L Spearing) *hld up: hdwy and swtchd rt over 1f out: r.o to ld ins fnl f: won gng away* **8/1**

04 **2** *1* **Inflight (IRE)**[11] [2388] 2-8-5 .... NelsonDeSouza[(3)] 2 63
(R M Beckett) *led for 1f: wnt 2nd over 1f out: rdn and passed by wnr ins fnl f* **9/2**[3]

045 **3** *hd* **Nicada (IRE)**[25] [1980] 2-8-6 .... JamesDoyle[(5)] 3 65
(Miss Gay Kelleway) *outpcd tl hdwy appr fnl f: nvr nrr* **10/1**

6 **4** *½* **Gold Spirit (IRE)**[36] [1730] 2-8-13 .... LPKeniry 6 65
(E J O'Neill) *led after 1f: rdn: hdd and no ex ins fnl f* **7/4**[1]

45 **5** *1 ½* **Vadinka**[14] [2315] 2-8-13 .... JimCrowley 1 60
(P Winkworth) *w ldrs after 1f: wknd appr fnl f* **2/1**[2]

6 *4* **City Bhoy** 2-8-12 .... RobertHavlin 5 45
(Tom Dascombe) *slowly away: sn outpcd* **16/1**

64.35 secs (2.05) **Going Correction** +0.25s/f (Good) **6** Ran SP% **114.0**

Speed ratings (Par 91):93,91,91,90,87 81

CSF £43.62 TOTE £7.70: £3.10, £1.90; EX 38.30.

Owner The Square Milers **Bred** Liam Phelan **Trained** Kinnersley, Worcs

FOCUS

A moderate juvenile maiden, run at a fair pace. The form is weak although the winner is value for slightly further.

NOTEBOOK

Fair 'n Square(IRE) showed a decent turn of foot to mow down her rivals and get off the mark at the fourth attempt in fairly taking style. She had shown promise on her second outing at Nottingham, but showed very little last time out, and the switch to this undulating course clearly proved to her liking. Her future lies with the Handicapper now. (op 9-1 tchd 7-1)

Inflight(IRE) tried to make it a test on this slight drop back in trip, and held every chance entering the final furlong, yet was ultimately firmly put in her place by the winner's turn of foot. She may be better off reverting to the minimum trip and now qualifies for a nursery mark. (op 11-2)

Nicada(IRE) did not look at all suited by the drop to this slightly shorter trip, but enjoyed this much faster surface, and turned in a more encouraging effort in defeat.

Gold Spirit(IRE), sixth on debut at Redcar 36 days previously, dropped out when push came to shove and proved disappointing. (tchd 2-1)

Vadinka ran below expectations and may have found this ground too fast for his liking. He has it to prove now nevertheless. (op 15-8)

2727 JOHN SMITH'S NO NONSENSE RACING MAIDEN H'CAP 6f 209y

7:35 (7:35) (Class 5) (0-70,67) 3-Y-O **£3,238** (£963; £481; £240) **Stalls** Low

Form RPR

4306 **1** **Elusive Warrior (USA)**[11] [2393] 3-9-0 **60** ....(p) JimCrowley 7 64
(Mrs A J Perrett) *t.k.h: hld up: hdwy on outside over 1f out: led ins fnl f: rdn out* **7/1**[3]

0-32 **2** *1 ¼* **Cape Win (IRE)**[11] [2415] 3-9-2 **67** ....(p) LiamJones[(5)] 5 68
(W J Haggas) *hld up: rdn and r.o to go 2nd ins fnl f* **10/3**[1]

-550 **3** *½* **Shinko (IRE)**[15] [2293] 3-8-9 **58** ....(p) DeanCorby[(3)] 2 58
(Miss J Feilden) *trckd ldr: rdn to ld appr fnl f: hdd ins last and lost 2nd nr fin* **10/1**

3-45 **4** *1* **Aristofilia**[10] [2458] 3-9-2 **65** .... NelsonDeSouza[(3)] 4 62
(P F I Cole) *s.i.s: hmpd over 4f out: rdn and sme hdwy over 1f out: kpt on* **10/3**[1]

3200 **5** *nk* **The Grey One (IRE)**[15] [2284] 3-8-7 **53** ....(p) RyanMoore 6 49
(J M Bradley) *trckd ldr: led over 2f out: hdd appr fnl f: no ex* **10/3**[1]

0040 **6** *4* **Perfect Order (USA)**[77] [879] 3-8-7 **53** ....(p) ChrisCatlin 1 38
(N A Callaghan) *led tl hdd over 2f out: hung lft and sn wknd* **7/2**[2]

1m 24.94s (2.24) **Going Correction** +0.25s/f (Good) **6** Ran SP% **113.0**

Speed ratings (Par 99):97,95,95,93,93 88

CSF £30.64 TOTE £8.00: £3.30, £2.30; EX 35.40.

Owner John Connolly **Bred** Steve Peskoff **Trained** Pulborough, W Sussex

FOCUS

A moderate handicap, made up of largely disappointing sorts, and the form, rated through the runner-up, should be treated with caution.

Elusive Warrior(USA) Official explanation: trainer's representative said, regarding the improved form shown, this was a step up in trip and gelding was more settled

2728 HARDINGSCATERING.CO.UK (S) STKS — 7f 214y
8:05 (8:06) (Class 6) 3-Y-O+ £2,266 (£674; £337; £168) Stalls Low

Form RPR

6222 1 **Prince Valentine**[5] 2568 5-9-5 45 ....(p) RyanMoore 1 50
(G L Moore) *hld up in tch: rdn and hdwy to ld 2f out: rdn out fnl f* 4/1[2]

0-00 2 1 **Love's Design (IRE)**[28] 1923 9-9-2 40 ....(v) DeanCorby[(3)] 9 48
(Miss J Feilden) *hld up: hdwy over 1f out: rdn and r.o to go 2nd ins fnl f* 25/1

0-00 3 1 1/4 **Khyber Knight (IRE)**[9] 2479 3-8-4 45 .... AdrianMcCarthy 5 38
(Jane Southcombe) *bhd: hdwy over 1f out: r.o wl fnl f: nvr nrr* 25/1

0204 4 3/4 **Noorain**[15] 2291 4-9-0 42 ....(t) FrancisNorton 3 38
(Stef Liddiard) *prom: rdn and ev ch appr fnl f: one pce fnl f* 4/1[2]

0000 5 nk **Windy Prospect**[5] 2567 4-8-12 53 .... AshleyHamblett[(7)] 8 43
(Miss Sheena West) *in tch: effrt on outside 2ff out: no exsra appr fnl f* 11/2

5436 6 hd **Granary Girl**[19] 2181 4-9-0 49 .... JimmyQuinn 4 37
(J Pearce) *in tch on outside: rdn and wknd appr fnl f* 5/1[3]

0400 7 nk **Super Dominion**[57] 1197 9-9-5 41 .... LPKeniry 6 42
(R Hollinshead) *hld up: rdn over 2f out: no further hdwy* 20/1

3202 8 6 **Wiltshire (IRE)**[6] 2546 4-8-12 48 ....(v) KevinGhunowa[(7)] 10 28
(P A Blockley) *led until 2f out: wknd over 1f out* 2/1[1]

0000 9 9 **Kussharro**[28] 1923 5-9-5 32 .... HayleyTurner 2 7
(Mrs L J Young) *trckd ldr tl rdn and wknd over 2f out* 33/1

1m 37.83s (2.79) **Going Correction** +0.25s/f (Good)
WFA 3 from 4yo+ 10lb — 9 Ran SP% **120.8**
Speed ratings (Par 101):96,95,93,93,92 92,92,86,77
CSF £102.51 TOTE £5.20: £1.30, £7.80, £5.30; EX 72.80.There was no bid for the winner. Windy Prospect was claimed by P. A. Blockley for £6000.

Owner D R Hunnisett **Bred** Mrs E Y Hunnisett **Trained** Woodingdean, E Sussex

FOCUS
A moderate affair, even by selling standards, that was run at a decent early pace despite which the form is not solid.

Kussharro Official explanation: jockey said gelding bled from the nose

2729 THE SPORTSMAN NEWSPAPER FILLIES' H'CAP — 7f 214y
8:35 (8:35) (Class 5) (0-70,68) 3-Y-O+ £3,886 (£1,156; £577; £288) Stalls Low

Form RPR

2444 1 **My Lovely Lady (IRE)**[13] 2359 3-9-11 **67** .... HayleyTurner 4 73
(M L W Bell) *t.k.h: trckd ldrs: led over 1f out: drvn out fnl f* 7/2[2]

00-2 2 3/4 **Keep Baccknhit (IRE)**[5] 2567 4-10-0 **60** .... RyanMoore 3 67
(G L Moore) *trckd ldrs: rdn to chse wnr fr over 1f out: kpt on ins fnl f* 5/2[1]

1 3 hd **Odessa Star (USA)**[11] 2415 3-9-9 **65** .... OscarUrbina 6 69+
(J G Portman) *bhd: hdwy over 1f out: nvr nrr* 8/1

65-0 4 1 **Umlilo**[18] 2186 4-9-9 **55** .... JimCrowley 7 59
(Mrs A J Perrett) *in tch: rdn and hung lft over 1f out: r.o ins fnl f* 11/1

0546 5 1 **Icecap**[5] 2567 6-8-12 **47** .... SaleemGolam[(3)] 5 49
(W G M Turner) *in tch: led over 2f out: hdd over 1f out: sn wknd* 4/1[3]

0054 6 4 **Indian Gem**[16] 2260 5-8-2 **41** oh4 .... KevinGhunowa[(7)] 2 34
(A J Chamberlain) *led tl hdd over 2f out: wknd over 1f out* 14/1

0310 7 23 **Oporto (UAE)**[14] 2332 3-9-12 **68** .... MatthewHenry 1 6+
(M A Jarvis) *trckd ldr: wkng whn hmpd over 1f out: nt rcvr and eased* 9/2

1m 37.57s (2.53) **Going Correction** +0.25s/f (Good)
WFA 3 from 4yo+ 10lb — 7 Ran SP% **115.1**
Speed ratings (Par 100):97,96,96,95,94 90,67
CSF £12.89 TOTE £5.50: £1.40, £2.10; EX 21.20.

Owner Mrs Moira Gershinson **Bred** J C Fagan **Trained** Newmarket, Suffolk

FOCUS
A moderate fillies' handicap that saw the first three come clear and the form looks straighforward with the runner-up to recent form.

2730 THE SPORTSMAN NEWSPAPER H'CAP — 5f 213y
9:05 (9:06) (Class 6) (0-65,69) 3-Y-O £2,590 (£770; £385; £192) Stalls Low

Form RPR

622 1 **Piccostar**[5] 2570 3-9-7 **65** .... RyanMoore 7 70
(A B Haynes) *chsd ldrs: rdn to ld ins fnl f: hld on nr fin* 9/4[1]

1321 2 nk **Sarah's Art (IRE)**[5] 2570 3-9-11 **69** 6ex ....(b) ChrisCatlin 9 73
(N A Callaghan) *a.p on outside: led 1/2-way: rdn and hdd ins fnl f: kpt on* 9/4[1]

4044 3 1 **Three Feathers**[5] 2570 3-7-11 **46** oh3 .... LiamJones[(5)] 4 47
(M Salaman) *in tch: hung lft over 1f out: r.o ins fnl f* 7/1[3]

0-60 4 nk **Watch Out Jess**[14] 2316 3-8-8 **52** .... LPKeniry 8 52
(M Madgwick) *bhd tl hdwy over 1f out: r.o fnl f: nvr nrr* 16/1

6555 5 2 **Shannon House**[14] 2316 3-8-10 **54** ....(v[1]) FrankieMcDonald 1 48
(M J McGrath) *t.k.h: in tch: no hdwy fr over 1f out* 8/1

-300 6 5 **Pantomime Prince**[14] 2316 3-8-8 **55** ....(p) SaleemGolam[(3)] 5 34
(C A Dwyer) *s.i.s: outpcd: nvr on terms* 5/1[2]

00-0 7 4 **Pink Pyjamas**[43] 1549 3-8-2 **46** oh5 ....(v[1]) JimmyQuinn 6 13
(J A R Toller) *trckd ldrs tl wknd 2f out* 25/1

00-0 8 2 **New Blood (IRE)**[39] 1640 3-8-2 **49** oh11 ow3 ....(t) NelsonDeSouza[(3)] 3 10
(J M Bradley) *bhd: rdn over 2f out: nvr on terms* 50/1

060- 9 4 **Young Flavio**[207] 6420 3-9-4 **65** ....(p) AdamKirby[(3)] 2 14
(J M Bradley) *led tl hdd 1/2-way: wknd qckly 2f out* 9/1

1m 11.44s (1.34) **Going Correction** +0.25s/f (Good) — 9 Ran SP% **123.5**
Speed ratings (Par 97):101,100,99,98,96 89,84,81,76
CSF £7.53 CT £31.99 TOTE £5.20: £2.40, £1.10, £1.70; EX 5.30 Place 6 £207.32, Place 5 £159.87..

Owner K Corke & M L Brett **Bred** Catridge Farm Stud Ltd **Trained** Collingbourne Ducis, Wilts

FOCUS
Another moderate affair, run at a decent clip, and the form looks straightforward.

Young Flavio Official explanation: jockey said gelding was unsuited by the firm ground

T/Plt: £43.50 to a £1 stake. Pool £40,804.25 - 683.35 winning units. T/Qpdt: £9.50 to a £1 stake. Pool £2,644.20 - 204.10 winning units. JS

2294 THIRSK (L-H)
Tuesday, June 20

OFFICIAL GOING: Good to firm (firm in places)
The ground was described as 'on the quick side but no jar whatsoever'.
Wind: Fresh, half-behind Weather: Fine but overcast and breezy

2731 ESK (S) STKS — 6f
2:20 (2:20) (Class 5) 2-Y-O £3,886 (£1,156; £577; £288) Stalls High

Form RPR

0331 1 **Emma Told Lies**[15] 2294 2-8-13 .... PaulMulrennan 9 59
(M W Easterby) *mde all: hung lft thrght: styd on wl fnl f* 8/1

64 2 1 1/2 **Dispol Truly (IRE)**[15] 2294 2-8-6 .... FergusSweeney 10 48
(A G Newcombe) *dwlt: swtchd lft and hdwy over 1f out: wandered and styd on fnl f* 10/1

035 3 shd **Flamestone**[28] 1912 2-8-11 .... PhilipRobinson 5 52
(J D Bethell) *w ldrs: kpt on same pce ins last* 4/1[2]

664 4 1/2 **Reflective Glory (IRE)**[6] 2538 2-8-6 .... GrahamGibbons 8 46
(J J Quinn) *chsd ldrs: outpcd 2f out: kpt on wl fnl 150yds* 7/2[1]

0 5 3 **Compton Verney**[6] 2538 2-8-11 .... TomEaves 6 42
(M W Easterby) *s.i.s: hdwy over 1f out: nvr nr ldrs* 33/1

00 6 2 1/2 **Don't Try It On**[4] 2626 2-8-11 .... DaleGibson 7 34
(M W Easterby) *drvn along and outpcd after 2f: no threat after* 80/1

050 7 3 **Delta Queen**[13] 2355 2-8-7 ow1 .... MickyFenton 4 21
(C N Kellett) *mid-div: drvn over 2f out: nvr on terms* 50/1

032 8 hd **Lansdown**[7] 2524 2-8-1 .... AndrewMullen[(5)] 3 20
(Robert Gray) *chsd ldrs on outer: lost pl over 1f out* 15/2

23U3 9 7 **Go On Jessica (IRE)**[22] 2073 2-8-6 .... JoeFanning 2 —
(A G Juckes) *chsd ldrs on outer: wknd over 1f out* 7/1

03 10 10 **Ensign's Trick**[15] 2294 2-8-6 .... DavidAllan 1 —
(W M Brisbourne) *mid-div on wd outside: wknd and eased 2f out* 20/1

11 24 **Eastern Premium** 2-8-6 .... PaulHanagan 11 —
(R A Fahey) *slowly away: hung bdly lft thrght: t.o 2f out: virtually p.u* 9/2[3]

1m 12.75s (0.25) **Going Correction** -0.175s/f (Firm) — 11 Ran SP% **115.8**
Speed ratings (Par 93):91,89,88,88,84 80,76,76,67,53 21
CSF £80.87 TOTE £6.20: £2.20, £2.50, £2.20; EX 40.70.There was no bid for the winner.
Owner Nigel Gravett **Bred** M W Easterby **Trained** Sheriff Hutton, N Yorks

FOCUS
An ordinary seller but an improved effort from both the winner and the runner-up and the form looks strong for the grade. The stands' side rail seemed an advantage.

NOTEBOOK
Emma Told Lies made every yard and despite a marked tendency to hang left, always looked like carrying the day. She should hold her own in modest nursery company. (op 15-2)
Dispol Truly(IRE), behind the winner on her two previous starts, seemed to run better. Trapped on the rails, she had to switch wide but, tending to wander, in the end was just found wanting. (tchd 9-1)
Flamestone, back on turf and dropped in class, was in the thick of things from start to finish. (op 9-2)
Reflective Glory(IRE), dropped to plating level, stayed on after getting outpaced and will appreciate a slightly stiffer test. (op 5-1)
Compton Verney, better behaved in the paddock, was again putting in his best work at the finish and is crying out for a seventh furlong.
Lansdown Official explanation: trainer said filly was in season
Eastern Premium, who is narrow and not very big, walked out of the traps and wanting to do nothing but hang badly left, was soon hopelessly placed. (op 5-1)

2732 DOVE H'CAP — 6f
2:55 (2:55) (Class 4) (0-85,85) 3-Y-O+ £6,477 (£1,927; £963; £481) Stalls High

Form RPR

-010 1 **My Gacho (IRE)**[3] 2661 4-9-5 **76** ....(v) PhillipMakin 10 88
(T D Barron) *mde all: rdn and kpt on wl fnl f* 8/1

00-2 2 1/2 **Lake Garda**[12] 2384 5-8-11 **73** .... AndrewMullen[(5)] 9 84
(K A Ryan) *w wnr: rdn and hung lft over 1f out: no ex wl ins last* 7/2[1]

1202 3 1/2 **Circuit Dancer (IRE)**[11] 2397 6-8-11 **71** .... SilvestreDeSousa[(3)] 8 80
(D Nicholls) *w ldrs: nt qckn ins last* 11/2[2]

0004 4 1 **Inter Vision (USA)**[31] 1858 6-9-11 **85** .... DanielTudhope[(3)] 4 91+
(A Dickman) *hld up: hdwy over 2f out: rdn and edgd lft over 1f out: nvr able chal* 15/2

30-0 5 3/4 **Millfield (IRE)**[13] 2363 3-8-13 **77** .... TomEaves 3 79
(J Howard Johnson) *dwlt: swtchd rt after s: sn drvn along: styd on fnl 2f: nvr nr ldrs* 66/1

4004 6 1/2 **Banjo Patterson**[14] 2323 4-10-0 **85** .... PhilipRobinson 6 87
(G A Huffer) *chsd ldrs: effrt over 2f out: kpt on same pce* 7/2[1]

6022 7 1/2 **Border Music**[10] 2429 5-9-12 **83** ....(b) FergusSweeney 1 84
(A M Balding) *hld up: effrt on outer over 2f out: kpt on: nvr trbld ldrs* 6/1[3]

-200 8 4 **Gallantry**[10] 2429 4-9-9 **85** .... MarkLawson[(5)] 7 74
(D W Barker) *chsd ldrs: wknd fnl f* 10/1

2000 9 nk **Hiccups**[12] 2384 6-9-0 **71** ....(v[1]) PaulHanagan 5 59
(D Nicholls) *unruly stalls: rrd s: sme hdwy over 2f out: wknd over 1f out* 25/1

1000 10 5 **Norcroft**[5] 2590 4-8-13 **70** ....(p) J-PGuillambert 2 43
(Mrs C A Dunnett) *chsd ldrs on outer: lost pl over 2f out: sn bhd* 50/1

1m 10.34s (-2.16) **Going Correction** -0.175s/f (Firm)
WFA 3 from 4yo+ 7lb — 10 Ran SP% **113.4**
Speed ratings (Par 105):107,106,105,104,103 102,102,96,96,89
CSF £34.73 CT £150.54 TOTE £7.40: £3.60, £1.40, £1.70; EX 25.00.
Owner Grant Mercer & R G Toes **Bred** Mount Coote Stud **Trained** Maunby, N Yorks

FOCUS
The stands'-side rail was the place to be and the first three home had the highest draws which suggests the form may not be that strong.

2733 MIDDLEHAM CASTLE MEDIAN AUCTION MAIDEN STKS — 7f
3:30 (3:30) (Class 5) 2-Y-O £3,886 (£1,156; £577; £288) Stalls Low

Form RPR

0 1 **Jane Of Arc (FR)**[21] 2106 2-8-12 .... DavidAllan 5 72
(T D Easterby) *led tl 3f out: rallied and led towards fin* 20/1

2 hd **Kirklees (IRE)** 2-9-3 .... JoeFanning 11 76
(M Johnston) *mid-div: hdwy over 2f out: styd on strly ins last: jst failed: improve* 20/1

43 3 shd **Greyt Big Stuff (USA)**[8] 2506 2-9-3 .... PhilipRobinson 8 76
(B J Meehan) *sn trcking ldrs: slt ld 3f out: hung fire ins last: hdd nr fin* 1/1[1]

250 4 1 3/4 **Suhayl Star (IRE)**[52] 1284 2-9-0 .... EdwardCreighton(3) 12 72
(M R Channon) *chsd ldrs: kpt on same pce appr fnl f* **16/1**[3]

5 2 1/2 **Centenary (IRE)** 2-9-3 .... TomEaves 2 65
(J Howard Johnson) *sn in rr and pushed along: hdwy over 1f out: edgd rt: styd on* **25/1**

02 6 3/4 **Straight Face (IRE)**[19] 2178 2-9-3 .... MickyFenton 13 63+
(W J Knight) *chsd ldrs: fdd fnl f* **9/2**[2]

7 1/2 **Meridian Grey (USA)** 2-8-12 .... AndrewMullen(5) 7 62
(K A Ryan) *s.i.s: hdwy to chse ldrs after 2f: one pce fnl 2f* **9/2**[2]

8 1 **Smugglers Bay (IRE)** 2-9-3 .... FergalLynch 4 59
(T D Easterby) *dwlt: hdwa and in tch over 4f out: one pce fnl 2f* **40/1**

9 3 **Go Red** 2-9-3 .... PaulMulrennan 3 52
(M W Easterby) *t.k.h: trckd ldrs on inner: wknd fnl 2f* **80/1**

10 4 **My Monna** 2-8-12 .... SamHitchcott 10 36
(M R Channon) *in rr and sn drvn along: nvr on terms* **25/1**

6 11 shd **Denton Hawk**[42] 1559 2-9-3 .... PhillipMakin 6 41
(M Dods) *chsd ldrs: wknd 2f out* **50/1**

00 12 23 **Up The Pole**[10] 2461 2-8-5 .... AdeleRothery(7) 9 —
(M W Easterby) *unruly in stalls: lost pl after 1f: sn bhd: virtually p.u* **100/1**

0 13 20 **Cicada (IRE)**[30] 1863 2-9-3 .... PaulHanagan 1 —
(J R Weymes) *s.i.s: sn detached in rr: t.o 2f out: virtually p.u* **100/1**

1m 27.52s (0.42) **Going Correction** -0.025s/f (Good) **13** Ran SP% **117.1**
Speed ratings (Par 93):96,95,95,93,90 89,89,88,84,80 80,53,30
CSF £325.40 TOTE £19.70: £3.00, £3.80, £1.20; EX 290.90.

Owner Cressington Park Farms **Bred** P Locke & Jill Locke **Trained** Great Habton, N Yorks

FOCUS
Probably a very ordinary median auction maiden run at just a steady pace. The favourite looked somewhat reluctant, the runner-up looks the big improver.

NOTEBOOK
Jane Of Arc(FR), on the leg and narrow, took them along and battled back to worry the favourite out of it. It now depends on what nursery mark she receives. (op 14-1)
Kirklees(IRE) ◆, a February foal, has a lot more size and substance than many of these. He took time to find full stride but would have made it with a little further to go. He should improve a good deal for the outing and the experience. (op 14-1)
Greyt Big Stuff(USA) is well named. He went on three furlongs out but tended to hang left and carry his head high. He hung fire inside the last and was just worried out of it. He needs some sort of headgear. (op 5-4 tchd 11-8 in a place)
Suhayl Star(IRE), drawn on the outside, ran better but this may be as good as he is, on turf at least. (op 14-1)
Centenary(IRE), on the leg and lightly-made, looked very fit. He struggled to keep up but was going on nicely at the finish. He may not be seen at his best until he tackles middle-distances at three.
Straight Face(IRE) had the worst of the draw and seemed to struggle to see out the seventh furlong. Official explanation: jockey said colt hung left throughout (op 4-1 tchd 7-2)
Meridian Grey(USA), a February foal, stands over plenty of ground. He was half asleep in the paddock and is the type to improve a fair bit in time. (op 6-1)
Smugglers Bay(IRE) Official explanation: jockey said colt's bit slipped through its mouth
Up The Pole Official explanation: jockey said filly was unsuited by the good to firm (firm in places) ground

2734 GO RACING IN YORKSHIRE MAIDEN STKS 7f
4:05 (4:05) (Class 5) 3-Y-O **£5,181** (£1,541; £770; £384) **Stalls** Low

Form RPR

2-00 1 **Aamaaq**[45] 1490 3-9-3 85 .... PhilipRobinson 12 75+
(J L Dunlop) *trckd ldrs: led on outer 2f out: pushed clr fnl f: readily* **8/11**[1]

64 2 2 1/2 **Wind Star**[10] 2448 3-9-3 .... MickyFenton 4 61+
(G A Swinbank) *in rr: hdwy: nt clr run and swtchd rt over 1f out: styd on to take 2nd nr line* **14/1**

3 1 **Shiitake** 3-8-12 .... TomEaves 2 53
(Miss L A Perratt) *s.i.s: bhd tl hdwy on wd outside over 2f out: kpt on wl fnl f* **66/1**

-564 4 shd **Opera Writer (IRE)**[12] 2383 3-9-3 66 .... DavidAllan 5 61+
(T D Easterby) *trckd ldrs: kpt on same pce fnl 2f* **12/1**[3]

65 5 1 3/4 **Cordelia**[39] 1630 3-8-12 .... SamHitchcott 7 48
(B W Hills) *chsd ldrs: rdn over 2f out: one pce* **4/1**[2]

5 6 nk **Counterfactual (IRE)**[14] 2325 3-9-3 .... DerekMcGaffin 3 56+
(B Smart) *dwlt: sn chsng ldrs: kpt on same pce fnl 2f: completed another circ after being being p.u* **14/1**

7 2 1/2 **Beautiful Summer (IRE)** 3-8-12 .... PaulHanagan 11 41+
(R A Fahey) *mid-divsion: one pce whn hmpd over 1f out* **18/1**

0000 8 1 **Rainbow Prince**[15] 2298 3-9-0 38 .... DanielTudhope(3) 1 43
(A Dickman) *led: qcknd over 3f out: hdd 2f out: wknd fnl f* **200/1**

0-05 9 1 1/4 **Coronation Flight**[32] 1814 3-8-7 41 .... AndrewMullen(5) 9 35
(F P Murtagh) *chsd ldrs: hung lft over 1f out: sn lost pl* **150/1**

060- 10 3/4 **Considerthelilies (IRE)**[244] 5976 3-8-12 57 .... RoystonFfrench 6 33
(Miss L A Perratt) *chsd ldrs: lost pl 2f out* **66/1**

11 1 **Kings Confession (IRE)** 3-8-10 .... KellyHarrison(7) 10 35
(D Carroll) *s.i.s: sn detached in rr* **40/1**

12 1 1/4 **Rigat** 3-9-3 .... PhillipMakin 8 32
(T D Barron) *plld hrd in mid-field on outer: lost pl over 2f out* **18/1**

1m 26.54s (-0.56) **Going Correction** -0.025s/f (Good) **12** Ran SP% **116.0**
Speed ratings (Par 99):102,99,98,97,95 95,92,91,90,89 88,86
CSF £12.87 TOTE £1.70: £1.10, £3.10, £6.90; EX 18.20.

Owner Hamdan Al Maktoum **Bred** Shadwell Estate Company Limited **Trained** Arundel, W Sussex
■ Stewards' Enquiry : Micky Fenton two-day ban: careless riding (Jul 1-2)
Daniel Tudhope two-day ban: careless riding (Jul 1-2)

FOCUS
A weak maiden run at just a steady pace and in the end a one-sided contest. The form does not look strong.

2735 LADIES EVENING 4TH JULY FILLIES' H'CAP 1m
4:40 (4:40) (Class 3) (0-90,83) 3-Y-O+ **£9,067** (£2,697; £1,348; £673) **Stalls** Low

Form RPR

3131 1 **Hula Ballew**[15] 2299 6-9-6 69 .... PhillipMakin 2 76
(M Dods) *w ldr: led 2f out: hung lft: hld on towards fin* **7/2**[2]

-054 2 1/2 **Gaelic Princess**[8] 2503 6-10-0 77 .... FergusSweeney 5 83
(A G Newcombe) *hld up: hdwy on ins over 2f out: wnt 2nd over 1f out: no ex wl ins last* **10/1**

1332 3 1/2 **Tour D'Amour (IRE)**[36] 1734 3-8-9 68 .... MickyFenton 4 71
(R Craggs) *chsd ldrs: drvn 3f out: styd on wl ins last* **8/1**

122- 4 2 **Commentary**[242] 6010 3-9-10 83 .... PhilipRobinson 3 81
(W J Haggas) *stdd s: hld up: hdwy to go hand 3rd over 3f out: rdn 2f out: kpt on same pce* **15/8**[1]

-002 5 shd **Way To The Stars**[10] 2459 3-8-13 72 .... PaulHanagan 6 70
(A M Balding) *hld up: effrt over 2f out: nvr able chal* **5/1**

4543 6 1 3/4 **Damelza (IRE)**[13] 2359 3-9-3 76 .... DavidAllan 1 70
(T D Easterby) *led tl 2f out: wknd fnl f* **4/1**[3]

1m 39.3s (-0.40) **Going Correction** -0.025s/f (Good)
WFA 3 from 6yo 10lb **6** Ran SP% **113.9**
Speed ratings (Par 104):101,100,100,98,97 96
CSF £36.18 TOTE £4.30: £1.70, £3.70; EX 24.50.

Owner Mrs J W Hutchinson & Mrs P A Knox **Bred** T K & Mrs P A Knox **Trained** Denton, Co Durham

FOCUS
A 90 top limit but the three-year-old Commentary was the highest-rated on just 83. The only two older fillies in the line-up finished one-two and the form appears sound enough.

NOTEBOOK
Hula Ballew kept close tabs on the leader and despite coming off a straight line under pressure, always looked like doing just enough. It was her third success in her last four starts. (op 10-3)
Gaelic Princess, back in her right grade, sneeked through on the inner to throw down the gauntlet but she always looked like being just held.
Tour D'Amour(IRE), given a five-week break, seemed to be ridden to conserve her stamina in this falsely-run race. She was coming back for more inside the last and best after an absence, deserves to be ridden more positively next time. (op 17-2 tchd 15-2)
Commentary, a keen type, went in pursuit of the two leaders but when called on for a serious effort was never doing anything like enough. It remains to be seen how much she has progressed from two to three, if at all. (tchd 9-4)
Way To The Stars, tucked in, tried to improve from off what was not a strong pace and she never looked like doing so. Official explanation: jockey said filly was unsuited by the good to firm (firm in places) ground (op 11-2 tchd 9-2)
Damelza(IRE) took them along in her own time but in the end seemed to have no excuse whatsover. (op 11-2)

2736 WHITE SWAN AMPLEFORTH H'CAP 1m 4f
5:10 (5:10) (Class 4) (0-80,77) 4-Y-O+ **£6,477** (£1,927; £963; £481) **Stalls** Low

Form RPR

1504 1 **Maneki Neko (IRE)**[13] 2365 4-9-0 70 .... TonyHamilton 7 78
(E W Tuer) *led: set mod pce: qcknd over 3f out: hld on wl* **5/1**[3]

6023 2 1 **San Deng**[6] 2549 4-8-8 64 .... PhilipRobinson 6 70
(Micky Hammond) *sn trcking ldr: chal over 2f out: no ex ins last* **9/4**[1]

0420 3 1/2 **Oddsmaker (IRE)**[2] 2684 5-8-0 63 ....(t) JamieJones(7) 5 68
(M A Barnes) *rrd s: tk fierce hold in rr: hdwy over 2f out: styd on ins last* **13/2**

2-00 4 nk **Sharp Reply (USA)**[22] 2079 4-9-0 77 .... MichaelJStainton(7) 8 82
(R M Whitaker) *trckd ldrs: effrt over 2f out: styd on same pce fnl f* **4/1**[2]

6000 5 2 **Melvino**[4] 2612 4-8-4 60 .... JoeFanning 3 62
(T D Barron) *stdd s: t.k.h in rr: effrt over 2f out: kpt on: nvr rchd ldrs* **11/2**

0146 6 1 **Aleron (IRE)**[14] 2326 8-9-2 72 ....(v) GrahamGibbons 4 72
(J J Quinn) *trckd ldrs: hung rt and outrpced over 3f out: swtchd ins over 1f out: nvr able chal* **9/1**

5-60 7 1 1/2 **Bowled Out (GER)**[25] 2000 4-8-10 66 .... PaulHanagan 2 64
(P J McBride) *t.k.h: hdwy over 3f out: wknd over 1f out* **14/1**

2m 37.89s (2.69) **Going Correction** -0.025s/f (Good) **7** Ran SP% **112.8**
Speed ratings (Par 105):90,89,89,88,87 86,85
CSF £16.23 CT £72.22 TOTE £5.00: £2.50, £1.80; EX 16.20.

Owner Mr & Mrs C Tompkins & E Tuer **Bred** Miss Orlagh Sherry **Trained** Great Smeaton, N Yorks

FOCUS
A tactical affair and the winner was given a masterful ride from the front. The time was very slow and the form looks paper thin.

Bowled Out(GER) Official explanation: trainer said filly was unsuited by the good to firm (firm in places) ground

2737 THIRSK RACE FOR LIFE 9TH JULY H'CAP 7f
5:45 (5:45) (Class 5) (0-75,78) 3-Y-O+ **£3,886** (£1,156; £577; £288) **Stalls** Low

Form RPR

5066 1 **Tough Love**[2] 2681 7-9-8 69 ....(p) DavidAllan 5 79+
(T D Easterby) *hld up in rr: hdwy over 2f out: nt clr run and swtchd ins over 1f out: led last 100yds: styd on* **9/1**[3]

3554 2 1/2 **Serieux**[10] 2454 7-9-8 72 ....(v) SilvestreDeSousa(3) 4 81
(D Nicholls) *trckd ldrs: led over 1f out: hung lft and hdd ins last: no ex* **11/2**[2]

6-16 3 1 1/4 **Stonehaugh (IRE)**[17] 2239 3-9-5 75 ....(t) TomEaves 2 78
(J Howard Johnson) *w ldrs: chal 2f out: kpt on same pce ins last* **25/1**

3012 4 hd **Confide (IRE)**[1] 2697 4-8-9 61 .... AndrewElliott(5) 3 66
(G A Swinbank) *trckd ldrs: chal 2f out: kpt on same pce fnl 150yds* **11/8**[1]

0400 5 4 **Lincolneurocruiser**[10] 2464 4-9-3 64 .... GrahamGibbons 1 59
(Mrs N Macauley) *hld up: sn in mid-field: effrt over 2f out: one pce* **18/1**

30-0 6 nk **Tom Forest**[32] 1830 4-9-2 68 .... AndrewMullen(5) 11 62+
(K A Ryan) *lost pl after 1f: sn in rr and drvn along. hdwy over 2f out: edgd rt 1f out: kpt on* **25/1**

002 7 nk **Poker Player (IRE)**[19] 2184 4-9-7 68 .... MickyFenton 13 61
(G C Bravery) *drvn to ld on outer: hdd over 1f out: sn wknd* **11/1**

-414 8 1/2 **Merlins Profit**[49] 1394 6-9-0 61 .... TonyHamilton 9 53+
(G A Swinbank) *s.i.s: sme hdwy over 2f out: nvr a factor* **16/1**

1014 9 1/2 **Dispol Isle (IRE)**[11] 2400 4-9-4 68 .... BenSwarbrick(3) 8 58
(T D Barron) *in tch: effrt on outer over 2f out: edgd lft and wknd over 1f out* **22/1**

00-5 10 3 1/2 **Rockburst**[12] 2377 4-9-2 63 .... NeilPollard 6 44
(K R Burke) *in rr: effrt on outer over 2f out: nvr on terms: hmpd over 1f out* **100/1**

210- 11 3 1/2 **Sparkwell**[276] 5313 4-9-9 75 .... MarkLawson(5) 12 47
(D W Barker) *s.i.s: t.k.h in rr: hung rt over 2f out: nvr on terms* **9/1**[3]

5014 12 5 **Briery Lane (IRE)**[8] 2504 5-9-2 63 ....(p) PaulHanagan 10 22
(Mrs K Walton) *t.k.h: lost pl after 2f: n.d after* **16/1**

1m 25.77s (-1.33) **Going Correction** -0.025s/f (Good)
WFA 3 from 4yo+ 9lb **12** Ran SP% **115.9**
Speed ratings (Par 103):106,105,104,103,99 98,98,97,97,93 89,83
CSF £54.38 CT £1199.63 TOTE £12.00: £2.60, £2.60, £6.60; EX 54.90 Place 6 £82.09, Place 5 £19.38.

Owner D A West **Bred** Branston Stud Ltd **Trained** Great Habton, N Yorks

FOCUS
An end-to-end gallop and overall the form looks sound with the runner-up the best guide.
T/Plt: £39.80 to a £1 stake. Pool: £40,256.55. 737.45 winning tickets. T/Qpdt: £7.70 to a £1 stake. Pool: £2,038.10. 195.75 winning tickets. WG

2596 LONGCHAMP (R-H)

Tuesday, June 20

OFFICIAL GOING: Good

2738a PRIX DU LYS (GROUP 3) (C&G) 1m 4f

2:50 (2:52) 3-Y-O **£27,586** (£11,034; £8,276; £5,517; £2,759)

			RPR
1		**Rail Link**[22] 3-8-12 CSoumillon 4 (A Fabre, France) *held up, 3rd straight, smooth headway to lead over 1f out, pushed out, easily* **7/10**[1]	113
2	2 ½	**Sudan (IRE)**[20] 2158 3-8-12 SPasquier 2 (E Lellouche, France) *tracked his pacemaker in 2nd til led over 2 1/2f out, ridden over 1 1/2f out, headed over 1f out, one pace* **24/10**[2]	109
3	2	**Britannic**[20] 2158 3-8-12 TJarnet 6 (A Fabre, France) *raced in 3rd on outside, 2nd straight, stayed on at same pace final 2f* **72/10**[3]	106
4	5	**Prince Flori (GER)**[44] 1526 3-9-1 HGrewe 1 (S Smrczek, Germany) *held up, 4th straight, ridden over 2f out, soon beaten* **73/10**	101
5	4	**Spicy Wings (FR)**[22] 3-8-12 C-PLemaire 5 (P Bary, France) *held up, 5th straight, never a factor* **74/10**	91
6	dist	**Batian (FR)**[292] 3-8-12 (b) OPlacais 3 (E Lellouche, France) *given reminder leaving stalls, led to over 2 1/2f out, eased* **24/10**[2]	—

2m 32.2s **6** Ran SP% **153.8**

PARI-MUTUEL: WIN 1.70; PL 1.20, 1.30; SF 3.30.

Owner K Abdulla **Bred** Juddmonte Farms Ltd **Trained** Chantilly, France

NOTEBOOK

Rail Link was held up and sat patiently behind the leaders until the turn into the straight. He was brought from off the rail and asked to quicken, then easily put distance between himself and the rest of the fields. Eased down before the line for a very easy win. The jockey reported he could go to the Grand Prix de Paris.

Sudan(IRE) sat in behind his pacemaker in second position. As the field turned into the straight he was asked to quicken. He took the lead over two and a half out, but had nothing to give when the winner swept past him before the furlong pole and he stayed on one paced.

BritannicRaced up with the pace in third position, he moved up to second on the turn into the straight but stayed on one paced over the last two furlongs

Prince Flori(GER) was held up out the back. Turning into the straight he moved up to fourth position and was being ridden over two furlongs out without posing any danger to the first three.

2719 ASCOT (R-H)

Wednesday, June 21

OFFICIAL GOING: Good to firm

Wind: Moderate, half-against Weather: Fine

2739 JERSEY STKS (GROUP 3) 7f

2:35 (2:36) (Class 1) 3-Y-O

£36,907 (£13,988; £7,000; £3,490; £1,748; £877) **Stalls** Low

Form				RPR
2-21	1		**Jeremy (USA)**[25] 2031 3-9-1 109 MJKinane 9 (Sir Michael Stoute) *lw: hld up: hdwy and swtchd rt over 2f out: r.o to ld ins fnl f: rdn out* **9/2**[2]	115+
3-10	2	2	**Asset (IRE)**[46] 1486 3-9-1 107 RichardHughes 1 (R Hannon) *lw: in tch: rdn over 2f out: led 1f out: edgd rt and hdd ins fnl f: nt qckn* **5/1**[3]	109
2213	3	hd	**Kingsgate Prince (IRE)**[19] 2204 3-9-1 107 GeorgeBaker 4 (J R Best) *hld up: nt clr run over 2f out: edgd rt and hdwy over 1f out: swtchd lft ins fnl f: r.o: nrst fin* **25/1**	109+
3120	4	nk	**Assertive**[16] 2303 3-9-1 106 RyanMoore 8 (R Hannon) *hld up: pushed along and hdwy over 2f out: rdn to chse ldrs over 1f out: styd on ins fnl f* **33/1**	108
1	5	½	**Secret World (IRE)**[63] 1087 3-9-1 LDettori 2 (J Noseda) *s.i.s: hld up: rdn and hdwy whn n.m.r over 2f out: styng on whn lugged rt ins fnl f: one pce cl home* **11/4**[1]	107
4-10	6	½	**Red Clubs (IRE)**[46] 1486 3-9-6 117 MichaelHills 10 (B W Hills) *hld up in midfield: hdwy over 3f out: ev ch ins fnl f: no ex towards fin* **10/1**	110
5251	7	½	**Cousteau**[25] 2028 3-9-1 97 EddieAhern 12 (P W Chapple-Hyam) *w ldr: led 4f out: rdn over 1f out: sn hdd: fdd ins fnl f* **40/1**	104
5-61	8	5	**Racer Forever (USA)**[19] 2204 3-9-1 108 JimmyFortune 13 (J H M Gosden) *lw: hld up: hdwy 3f out: rdn whn bmpd over 2f out: wknd ins fnl f* **11/1**	90
20-1	9	nk	**Saville Road**[62] 1094 3-9-1 97 ShaneKelly 6 (D J Daly) *midfield: n.m.r and hmpd over 2f out: sn rdn: no imp after* **20/1**	90
31	10	9	**Rydal Mount (IRE)**[27] 1956 3-8-12 82 FergusSweeney 11 (W S Kittow) *trckd ldrs: rdn whn n.m.r and hmpd over 2f out: sn wknd* **100/1**	62
0-31	11	2	**Proud Killer**[43] 1565 3-9-1 75 JohnEgan 3 (J R Jenkins) *lw: led: hdd 4f out: rdn 3f out: wknd over 2f out* **100/1**	60
2-	12	½	**Mednaya (IRE)**[34] 1810 3-8-12 FSpanu 5 (R Gibson, France) *unf: racd keenly: trckd ldrs: rdn 2f out: wkng whn hung rt over 1f out* **50/1**	56
-560	13	9	**Manston (IRE)**[33] 1818 3-9-1 99 PJSmullen 14 (B J Meehan) *a bhd* **66/1**	34
-111	14	46	**Levera**[35] 1776 3-9-1 107 JamieSpencer 7 (A King) *in tch: rdn whn nt much and hmpd over 2f out: sn lost pl: eased over 1f out: t.o* **5/1**[3]	—

1m 27.54s (-1.46) **Going Correction** +0.15s/f (Good) **14** Ran SP% **115.0**

Speed ratings (Par 109):114,111,111,111,110 110,109,103,103,93 90,90,79,27

CSF £24.14 TOTE £4.40: £1.60, £2.10, £7.00; EX 26.90 Trifecta £271.00 Pool: £5,615.81 - 14.71 winning tickets..

Owner Mrs Elizabeth Moran **Bred** Brookdale **Trained** Newmarket, Suffolk

■ Stewards' Enquiry : F Spanu one-day ban: careless riding (Jul 2)

FOCUS

A fair renewal of this Group 3 for three-year-olds, run at a strong early pace in what looked a decent time, and it proved an advantage to come from off the pace. The form looks solid, rated through the third and fourth horses, and the winner is capable of rating higher.

NOTEBOOK

Jeremy(USA) ◆, who just got up in a Listed event on soft ground at Newmarket last time, took this rise to Group company in his stride and followed-up under a patient ride by Kinane, being full value for his winning margin. He looked to have plenty to do on passing halfway, but once switched mid-track for his effort he responded strongly, and showed a brave attitude when squeezing through rivals nearing the two-furlong marker. He has yet to finish out of the first two places in his seven outings to date, his versatility as regards underfoot conditions is a real advantage, and it would come as little surprise to see him upped to a mile in the not-too-distant future. It is unlikely we have seen the best of him just yet. (tchd 5-1 in places)

Asset(IRE), who ran too freely when finishing ninth in the 2000 Guineas last time, showed his true colours on this drop back to seven furlongs with a solid effort in defeat. He travelled sweetly on the stands' rail, and responded kindly when asked to win his race, but ultimately lacked the finishing kick of the winner. Granted he had the best of the draw this time, but there is little doubt he can be placed to strike in Group company, and this really does appear to be his optimum trip. (tchd 11-2)

Kingsgate Prince(IRE) endured a toubled passage from off the pace, but was motoring when in the clear late on, and produced a career-best effort in defeat - narrowly confirming his Newbury Listed form with Assertive in the process. He appreciated reverting to more patient tactics and really has been a revelation for connections since starting his winning spree on the Polytrack early this year. He deserves to find a race at this level.

Assertive, disappointing against his elders over six furlongs at Windsor last time, bounced back to his best on this return to racing against his own age group and was another who prospered from a patient ride. He showed a willing attitude throughout and, along with Kingsgate Prince, helps to set the level of this form. (op 50-1)

Secret World(IRE), impressive when taking the Wood Ditton over a mile on debut 63 days previously and whose trainer had won this twice in the past four years, was bidding to become the first since Zilzal in 1989 to land this prize directly from a maiden success. However, he reportedly endured a nightmare journey to the track, suffering numerous grazes to his legs, and his participation was still in doubt as he was being taken very quietly to post. He was sluggish from the gates - thus forcing Dettori into a hold-up ride - but still emerged to have his chance before meeting a little trouble two out and then hanging towards the stands' rail and finding only the same pace when it mattered. It is very hard to know just how much his pre-race troubles cost him, but he looked a colt with a big future when winning last time, and must be given the benefit of doubt. (op 3-1 tchd 10-3 in places and 5-2 in places)

Red Clubs(IRE), who flopped in the 2000 Guineas when last seen 46 days previously, bounced back to form over this shorter trip and turned in a very brave effort under his 5lb penalty. He may have just been better off with a more patient ride, but he emerges with real credit all the same, and it would not be the biggest surprise to see him drop back to six furlongs after this, given he does hold an entry in the July Cup next month.

Cousteau, finally off the mark when making all in maiden company on soft ground 25 days previously, failed to really get home in this company under very a positive ride over this shorter trip. He still turned in a career-best effort, however, and the drop to Listed company can see him get closer once again on this evidence.

Racer Forever(USA), who beat Kingsgate Prince when winning in Listed company at Epsom last time, had his chance and his fate was already sealed prior to meeting a little trouble nearing the two-furlong pole. He is slightly better than the bare form, but still has to prove he is up to Group level. (tchd 12-1 in places)

Saville Road, last seen winning a conditions race on his seasonal bow at Newmarket in April, lost any chance when he bumped into Secret World approaching two out and must be rated better than his finishing position suggests. The drop into Listed company can see him in a much better light. Official explanation: jockey said colt suffered interference in running (tchd 25-1 in places)

Levera, who impressed when landing his fourth consecutive success in a Listed Handicap at York 35 days previously, was starting to look laboured prior to being hampered before two out, and thus losing any chance. This was obviously very disappointing, and it remains to be seen how much his confidence will now have been dented, plus he was later found to be lame on his near-fore Official explanation: vet said colt was lame (op 9-2)

2740 WINDSOR FOREST STKS (GROUP 2) (F&M) 1m (S)

3:10 (3:12) (Class 1) 4-Y-O+

£73,814 (£27,976; £14,001; £6,981; £3,497; £1,755) **Stalls** Low

Form				RPR
12-4	1		**Soviet Song (IRE)**[32] 1840 6-8-12 119 JamieSpencer 4 (J R Fanshawe) *s.i.s: hld up in last pair: gd prog on outer jst over 2f out: swept into ld over 1f out and sn clr: in n.d after* **11/8**[1]	119+
1-11	2	2	**Echelon**[19] 2199 4-8-12 103 MJKinane 6 (Sir Michael Stoute) *lw: settled in rr: pushed along over 2f out: prog over 1f out: styd on to chse wnr ins fnl f: no imp* **3/1**[2]	111
-123	3	1 ¾	**Royal Alchemist**[25] 2041 4-8-12 102 MartinDwyer 3 (M D I Usher) *lw: led: rdn 2f out: hdd over 1f out: outpcd but kpt on fnl f* **33/1**	107
4-03	4	¾	**Zayn Zen**[19] 2199 4-8-12 95 PhilipRobinson 9 (M A Jarvis) *hld up in midfield: effrt over 2f out: rdn and hanging over 1f out: kpt on same pce* **25/1**	105
60-4	5	nk	**Luas Line (IRE)**[14] 2371 4-9-3 KFallon 5 (David Wachman, Ire) *lw: hld up in rr: prog on outer over 2f out: chal over 1f out: sn outpcd: fdd* **7/1**[3]	110
2-21	6	nk	**Violet Park**[45] 1506 5-8-12 103 RichardHughes 7 (B J Meehan) *stdd s: hld up in last: stl last but gng easily 2f out: shkn up and no rspnse over 1f out* **14/1**	104
0-04	7	¾	**Bon Nuit (IRE)**[45] 1506 4-8-12 102 AlanMunro 1 (G Wragg) *trckd ldng pair: rdn 2f out: edgd rt and grad fdd fr over 1f out* **25/1**	102
00-2	8	1 ¾	**Chantilly Beauty (FR)**[39] 1671 4-8-12 (b) TJarnet 2 (R Pritchard-Gordon, France) *trckd ldng trio: rdn and losing pl whn sltly hmpd over 1f out* **20/1**	98
246-	9	7	**Shapira (GER)**[249] 5915 5-8-12 OPeslier 8 (Andreas Lowe, Germany) *trckd ldr to over 2f out: wknd rapidly* **14/1**	82
5	10	6	**Astronomia (NZ)**[25] 2011 4-8-11 103 LDettori 10 (Saeed Bin Suroor) *trckd ldrs: shkn up over 2f out: sn wknd rapidly* **12/1**	67

1m 40.67s (-1.13) **Going Correction** +0.15s/f (Good) **10** Ran SP% **116.0**

Speed ratings (Par 115):111,109,107,106,106 105,105,103,96,90

CSF £4.92 TOTE £2.50: £1.20, £1.60, £3.80; EX 4.80 Trifecta £67.50 Pool: £5,126.28 - 53.90 winning tickets..

Owner Elite Racing Club **Bred** Elite Racing Club **Trained** Newmarket, Suffolk

FOCUS

Two horses dominated the market prior to the race, but it turned into a one-horse affair as Soviet Song stamped her mark on the race. The first two apart, there was little strength in depth for a Group 2 race at Royal Ascot although the winning time looked about right for the grade.

NOTEBOOK

Soviet Song(IRE), running in the race without the Group 1 penalty she carried last season, bounced back to her brilliant best, showing an awesome turn of foot when asked to quicken down the middle of the track. There was a stage of the race where her pilot looked to be taking a very risky route down the stands-side rail, but, possibly remembering what happened the day before on Court Masterpiece, he steered her to the outside and a clear path. Her record at the Royal meeting (including York last season) reads 2231, and she looks to be the best of her sex at a mile in Europe when on her game. She won in such good style that connections may be slightly disappointed now that they did not go for the Group 1 Queen Anne Stakes the previous day, but she has plenty of options to look forward to during the season, with the Falmouth Stakes at Newmarket the most likely next port of call, before taking on the boys again in the Sussex Stakes. (op 6-4 tchd 13-8 and 7-4 in a place)

Echelon was never really travelling with any fluency in the early stages and, at one point looked to be going nowhere. However, she responded to pressure, staying on well to the line, without having any chance with Soviet Song. She gave the strong impression that she would be suited by further in top-flight company, a view confirmed by connections after the race. (op 5-2 tchd 10-3 in places)

Royal Alchemist, who filled the same position in a Group Two in Ireland last time, made a bold bid for victory with two furlongs to go, after setting only a medium pace in front, but was predictably put in her place by the classy winner. She has an entry in the Eclipse at Sandown, which does look a bit optimistic unless that race cuts up badly, but connections are no doubt delighted by the efforts of their filly, who is semingly improved at the age of four and is a fine flag-bearer for her small stable. The Prix de L'Opera, run on Arc weekend at Longchamp, is reported to be the main plan for her later in the season. (tchd 25-1 in places)

Zayn Zen, 3lb worse off for a length beating by Echelon last time at Epsom, was another in the race who gave the impression that she needed further in top-class company. On the balance of her form she had no right to beat an in-form Soviet Song, and probably ran right up to her best. If connections are to continue in such a high grade with her, a step up in trip is almost certainly required.

Luas Line(IRE), nicely supported in the market prior to the off, had it to do giving weight away for winning a Group One handicap in America last year. She moved into contention with the winner but could not pick up once that rival quickened. (op 10-1)

Violet Park, who was deliberately restrained as the gates flew open, could never get on terms with the principals despite weaving her way through runners towards the end of the race. A Group Three winner last time and a regular opponent of Royal Alchemist during the current season, it is no secret that she is much happier on a softer surface. (tchd 16-1 in places)

Bon Nuit(IRE), who beat Echelon in July of last season, has been a bit disappointing in 2006 and did not show any immediate signs of a return to form. Her previous form was below the required class to win a normal Group Two, having been regularly beaten in Listed and Group Three company, and she probably ran as well as she was entitled to.

Chantilly Beauty(FR) had looked a bit unlucky when beaten by Echelon at Lingfield earlier in the season, but was firmly put in her place on ground that may have been a bit quick for her. (tchd 25-1)

Shapira(GER), who has always looked to need her first run of the season, and can be expected to improve for the run, although it is difficult to believe she came into such a prestigious race without being fit. Unimpressive in the paddock before the race, some of her best form suggested she should have performed much better. (op 12-1)

Astronomia(NZ), placed in Group Two company in Australia, disappointed badly again and is running well below her best form. She stayed a bit further than a mile in her homeland but, at this stage, she does not seem to have brought any of her classy form with her, and she has it all to prove now. Official explanation: jockey said filly hung left (op 14-1)

2741 PRINCE OF WALES'S STKS (GROUP 1) — 1m 2f

3:50 (3:50) (Class 1) 4-Y-O+

£211,207 (£80,049; £40,061; £19,975; £10,006; £5,021) **Stalls** High

Form — RPR

-432 **1** — **Ouija Board**[19] 2202 5-8-11 117 ... OPeslier 5 — 123+
(E A L Dunlop) *lw: hld up in tch: swtchd lft and hdwy over 1f out: r.o to ld ins fnl f and edgd rt: pushed out cl home* **8/1**[3]

4-11 **2** *½* **Electrocutionist (USA)**[88] 743 5-9-0 124 ... LDettori 4 — 124
(Saeed Bin Suroor) *h.d.w: lw: set stdy pce: qcknd tempo over 2f out: hdd ins fnl f: hld cl home* **9/4**[2]

-132 **3** *¾* **Manduro (GER)**[31] 1873 4-9-0 ... CSoumillon 6 — 123
(A Fabre, France) *w'like: lw: trckd ldr to over 4f out: remained prom: rdn over 1f out: nt qckn ins fnl f* **12/1**

11-1 **4** *¾* **David Junior (USA)**[88] 742 4-9-0 123 ... JamieSpencer 3 — 121
(B J Meehan) *lw: hld up: tk clsr order 5f out: effrt 2f out: sn lugged rt: ev ch ins fnl f: r.o same pce cl home* **11/8**[1]

1-11 **5** *shd* **Notnowcato**[22] 2116 4-9-0 112 ... MJKinane 1 — 121
(Sir Michael Stoute) *cl up: wnt 2nd over 4f out: rdn over 1f out: ev ch ins fnl f: no ex cl home* **12/1**

-215 **6** *1* **Corre Caminos (FR)**[31] 1873 4-9-0 ... TJarnet 2 — 119+
(M Delzangles, France) *w'like: t.k.h: hld up in rr: rdn over 1f out: sn hung rt: nvr able to chal* **33/1**

2-24 **7** *1 ¼* **Ace (IRE)**[19] 2202 5-9-0 ... (v) KFallon 7 — 117
(A P O'Brien, Ire) *swtg: took t.k.h: hld up: rdn over 2f out: no impresson on ldrs* **9/1**

2m 6.92s (-1.08) **Going Correction** +0.20s/f (Good) — **7** Ran SP% **112.3**
Speed ratings (Par 117):112,111,111,110,110 109,108
CSF £25.46 TOTE £6.40: £2.40, £1.80; EX 22.50.

Owner Lord Derby **Bred** Stanley Estate & Stud Co **Trained** Newmarket, Suffolk

FOCUS

A tremendous renewal of the Prince Of Wales's Stakes. Four of the seven runners had previously won at the highest level, gaining a total of 11 Group 1s between them, and the other three had won in either Group 2 or Group 3 company. However, rather disappointingly, there were no confirmed front-runners in the line so, with Electrocutionist setting just a steady pace for much of the way, it turned into a comparative sprint in the straight and the entire field was separated by just over four lengths at the line. The fifth appeared to run his race and is the best guide to the form.

NOTEBOOK

Ouija Board was not at her best off a steady pace behind Shirocco in the Coronation Cup at Epsom on her previous start, but it did not inconvenience her this time and she produced an effort right up there with her very best. Held up a little way off the ordinary gallop, she still had a few lengths to find when switched out with her run inside the final two furlongs, but displayed a taking turn of foot to ultimately win going away. She was due to be given a summer break, but it would be hard to put her away whilst in this sort of form and connections will now consider both the Eclipse Stakes at Sandown and the King George back here over a mile and a half, although she would have to be supplemented for the latter. Her main aim, though, is a trip to the US later in the year for another Breeders' Cup. The Filly & Mare Turf would seem the most likely option at this stage, but given she has proven herself against the colts, it would not be a total surprise to see her line up in the Turf. (op 7-1 tchd 17-2 in places and 9-1 in a place)

Electrocutionist(USA), a really game winner of the Dubai World Cup nearly three months previously, had not exactly had an ideal preparation for this given his stable had to be shut down for a couple of weeks less than a month previously, but he was still quite well fancied by connections. With no confirmed front-runner in the line up, he was forced to make his own running but was able to dictate very much on his own terms and had every chance. This performance proved he has recovered well from his exertions in the desert and he is likely to remain a major force in many of the top-middle distances races in Europe and beyond. He may be stepped back up to a mile and a half for the King George, but will have to be at his very best to beat Hurricane Run. (op 5-2)

Manduro(GER), supplemented for this off the back of his close second to Laverock in the Group 1 Prix d'Ispahan, ran a tremendous race in third and fully justified his connections' decision to run. Andre Fabre has an unbelievable amount of talent at his disposal in the middle-distance department, and this one is yet another who will be worth utmost respect in future. (op 10-1)

David Junior(USA), last year's Champion Stakes winner, and so impressive when winning the Dubai Duty Free Stakes at Nad Al Sheba, failed to show his customary turn of foot and was said by his jockey to have been unsuited by the lack of early pace. He seems to have bundles of natural speed, so it was disappointing he could not cope with the way this race was run, but it would be folly to write him off following one below-par showing, and he can be given a chance to redeem himself in the Eclipse. (tchd 6-4 in places)

Notnowcato, who has progressed from handicap company to win a couple of ordinary Group 3 contests this term, was coltish in the paddock and ran a cracker against some of the best middle-distance horses around. He is clearly still improving, but one cannot help but think he is a touch flattered by the margin of defeat given the lack of early pace. (op 11-1)

Corre Caminos(FR), a five-length winner of the Group 1 Prix Ganay before running fifth in the Prix d'Ispahan (Manduro second), raced keenly off the steady gallop and never really posed a threat. He can do better in a stronger-run race.

Ace(IRE), who boiled over badly prior to his fourth in the Coronation Cup (Ouija Board second) at Epsom last time, again got himself in a bit of a state and offered little in the race itself. He appears to be losing his way quite seriously and looks best watched until he showing signs of a revival. (op 12-1)

2742 ROYAL HUNT CUP (HERITAGE H'CAP) — 1m (S)

4:25 (4:29) (Class 2) 3-Y-O+

£62,320 (£18,660; £9,330; £4,670; £2,330; £1,170) **Stalls** Low

Form — RPR

13-0 **1** — **Cesare**[88] 728 5-8-8 **94** ... JamieSpencer 3 — 108+
(J R Fanshawe) *racd nr side: hld up in rr: nt clr run 2f out: prog over 1f out: chsd ldr ins fnl f: r.o wl to ld nr fin* **14/1**

-102 **2** *nk* **Stronghold**[11] 2431 4-9-8 **108** ... RichardHughes 2 — 121
(J H M Gosden) *lw: hld up nr side: nt clr run over 2f out: prog to ld overall over 1f out: r.o fnl f: collared nr fin: 2nd of 18 in gp* **14/1**

2145 **3** *1 ¾* **Akona Matata (USA)**[19] 2200 4-8-5 **91** ... KerrinMcEvoy 11 — 100+
(C E Brittain) *lw: hld up nr side: squeezed through over 1f out: r.o fnl f: no imp ldng pair: 3rd of 18 in gp* **16/1**

10-1 **4** *2 ½* **Hinterland (IRE)**[19] 2200 4-8-13 **99** 5ex ... PhilipRobinson 8 — 102
(M A Jarvis) *trckd nr side ldr: led overall over 3f out: hdd and outpcd over 1f out: 4th of 18 in gp* **15/2**[2]

3100 **5** *1* **Pentecost**[34] 1806 7-9-3 **103** ... MartinDwyer 9 — 104+
(A M Balding) *lw: t.k.h: hld up last of nr side gp: n.m.r 4f out: effrt 2f out: styd on fr over 1f out: 5th of 18 in gp* **66/1**

51-4 **6** *½* **Pinpoint (IRE)**[25] 2012 4-8-8 **94** ... TedDurcan 4 — 94
(W R Swinburn) *trckd nr side ldrs: outpcd fr 2f out: one pce after: 6th of 18 in gp* **9/1**

6-41 **7** *¾* **Forgery (IRE)**[60] 1129 4-8-7 **93** ... KFallon 5 — 91+
(G A Butler) *hld up in rr of nr side gp: swtchd to wd outside and rdn 2f out: kpt on: nvr on terms: 7th of 18 in gp* **11/1**

-000 **8** *1* **Mine (IRE)**[25] 2012 8-9-2 **102** ... (v) TQuinn 30 — 98+
(J D Bethell) *hld up rr of far side gp: prog 2f out: styd on to ld last strides: no ch: 1st of 12 in gp* **20/1**

1300 **9** *shd* **Capable Guest (IRE)**[46] 1495 4-8-7 **93** ... ChrisCatlin 28 — 89+
(M R Channon) *hld up far side: prog on outer to ld gp wl over 1f out: hdd last strides: no ch: 2nd of 12 in gp* **50/1**

4242 **10** *nk* **Red Spell (IRE)**[11] 2435 5-8-7 **93** ... (b[1]) RyanMoore 21 — 88+
(R Hannon) *hld up in rr far side: prog 2f out: drvn to chal ins fnl f: kpt on: no ch: 3rd of 12 in gp* **40/1**

20-3 **11** *½* **Langford**[39] 1678 6-8-11 **97** ... LDettori 25 — 91+
(M H Tompkins) *dwlt: hld up last of far side gp: effrt 2f out: styd on fnl f: no ch: 4th of 12 in gp* **25/1**

3113 **12** *shd* **Dabbers Ridge (IRE)**[34] 1806 4-8-11 **97** ... MichaelHills 10 — 90
(B W Hills) *dwlt: hld up nr side: prog on wd outside over 2f out: outpcd and btn over 1f out: 8th of 18 in gp* **33/1**

1-11 **13** *¾* **Pride Of Nation (IRE)**[26] 1985 4-8-10 **96** ... NickyMackay 27 — 88+
(L M Cumani) *lw: trckd far side ldrs: cl up and nt clr run 2f out: kpt on same pce after: no ch: 5th of 12 in gp* **11/2**[1]

-002 **14** *1* **Ace Of Hearts**[23] 2079 7-9-1 **101** ... EddieAhern 6 — 90
(C F Wall) *prom nr side: chsd ldr over 3f out to 2f out: wknd: 9th of 18 in gp* **20/1**

21-1 **15** *½* **Minority Report**[46] 1495 6-8-6 **92** ... C-PLemaire 1 — 80
(L M Cumani) *hld up in tch nr side: trckd ldrs against nr side rail 2f out: wknd over 1f out: 10th of 18 in gp* **8/1**[3]

0200 **16** *3* **Impeller (IRE)**[19] 2201 7-8-8 **94** ... DarryllHolland 26 — 75+
(W R Muir) *t.k.h: hld up in rr far side: effrt 2f out: no prog over 1f out: 6th of 12 in gp* **66/1**

214- **17** *1 ½* **Unshakable (IRE)**[193] 5876 7-8-5 **91** ... FrancisNorton 14 — 69
(Bob Jones) *trckd nr side ldrs to 2f out: steadily wknd: 11th of 18 in gp* **66/1**

-503 **18** *1 ¼* **Tucker**[11] 2435 4-8-13 **99** ... (v[1]) JohnEgan 15 — 74
(D R C Elsworth) *hld up towards rr nr side: rdn and losing pl whn bmpd over 1f out: 12th of 18 in gp* **33/1**

/002 **19** *1 ½* **Bustan (IRE)**[14] 2364 7-8-9 **95** ... MJKinane 22 — 67
(G C Bravery) *prom far side: stl cl up 2f out: wknd over 1f out: 7th of 12 in gp* **66/1**

/11- **20** *nk* **Stagelight (IRE)**[496] 342 4-9-4 **104** ... ShaneKelly 20 — 75
(J Noseda) *lw: ldng trio on far side to 2f out: wknd: 8th of 12 in gp* **50/1**

-622 **21** *2* **Babodana**[34] 1806 6-9-10 **110** ... RHills 18 — 76
(M H Tompkins) *racd on outer of nr side gp: nvr on terms: struggling fnl 2f: 13th of 18 in gp* **40/1**

-023 **22** *5* **Prince Of Thebes (IRE)**[25] 2012 5-8-8 **94** ... PaulDoe 23 — 49+
(J Akehurst) *edgy: prom far side: led gp 1/2-way to wl over 1f out: wknd rapidly : 9th of 12 in gp* **33/1**

0044 **23** *1* **El Coto**[4] 2657 6-8-6 **92** ... (p) DO'Donohoe 24 — 45+
(K A Ryan) *trckd far side ldrs: rdn wl over 2f out: wknd over 1f out: 10th of 12 in gp* **33/1**

2031 **24** *1 ¼* **Divine Gift**[42] 1585 5-8-11 **97** ... (b[1]) NCallan 29 — 47+
(K A Ryan) *w far side ldrs: rdn whn no room against rail 2f out: wknd: 11th of 12 in gp* **50/1**

The Form Book, Raceform Ltd, Compton, RG20 6NL

1-00 **25** *nk* **River Royale**[14] [2364] 4-8-6 **92** .... AlanMunro 12 41
(P W Chapple-Hyam) *hld up nr side: nvr on terms: wl bhd over 1f out: 14th of 18 in gp* **100/1**

-001 **26** *nk* **Dansili Dancer**[11] [2435] 4-8-3 **92** 5ex........ (p) AdamKirby(3) 16 40
(C G Cox) *trckd nr side ldrs to over 2f out: wknd rapidly: 15th of 18 in gp* **50/1**

00-4 **27** *shd* **Another Bottle (IRE)**[60] [1129] 5-8-12 **98**........ SteveDrowne 13 46
(R Charlton) *trckd nr side ldrs: wknd and eased fnl 2f: 16th of 18 in gp* **10/1**

0-00 **28** *7* **Spanish Don**[39] [1678] 8-8-9 **95**........ LPKeniry 17 27
(D R C Elsworth) *b: racd on outer of nr side: chsd ldrs over 5f: wknd rapidly: 17th of 18 in gp* **100/1**

1034 **29** *18* **Blythe Knight (IRE)**[34] [1806] 6-9-1 **101**........ GrahamGibbons 19 —
(J J Quinn) *led far side to 1/2-way: wknd rapidly: t.o: last of 12 in gp* **100/1**

0253 **30** *19* **Shot To Fame (USA)**[19] [2200] 7-8-4 **90**........ AdrianTNicholls 7 —
(D Nicholls) *led nr side to over 3f out: wknd rapidly: t.o: last of gp* **33/1**

1m 40.62s (-1.18) **Going Correction** +0.15s/f (Good) **30** Ran SP% **134.6**
Speed ratings (Par 109):111,110,108,106,105 104,104,103,103,102 102,102,101,100,99 96,95,94,92,92 90,85,84,83,82 82,8
CSF £171.58 CT £3223.25 TOTE £21.00: £4.70, £5.30, £5.50, £2.00; EX 218.60 Trifecta £6157.90 Pool: £12,142.40 - 1.40 winning tickets..

Owner Cheveley Park Stud **Bred** Cheveley Park Stud Ltd **Trained** Newmarket, Suffolk

FOCUS
It is very disappointing that as important a handicap as this should be marred by such an obvious draw bias. Mine ran his heart out again, but won nothing for finishing first on his side. All of the action unfolded on the near-side rail, with Cesare just getting past Stronghold, who was giving away 14lb to the runner-up, in the dying strides. The winning time was a solid one when compared with the earlier Windsor Forest and the runner-up sets a good standard.

NOTEBOOK
Cesare ◆, not seen since being well beaten when strongly fancied for the Lincoln Handicap back in March, came with a late, late effort to pick off the gallant Stronghold close to the line.Spencer gave him a very brave ride, holding him up just off the pace along the inside rail, having every chance of finding no room if weakening runners came back on him. However, he was extricated from his inside position with perfection and got there just in time. Appearing to go on any ground, he should be capable of holding in his own in a slightly higher grade but, in the short-term, a return to Ascot for the Totesport International Stakes in July looks the mostly likely next port of call. (tchd 16-1 in places)

Stronghold almost pulled off a brilliant weight-carrying performance. Setting sail for home at the furlong pole, he appeared to have all his rivals covered until Cesare swooped from the clouds. Undoubtedly the 14lb he had to give the eventual winner made a difference, and possibly the length of time he was left in front did not help either, but he emerges from the race with plenty of credit and looks ready for a step up in grade. (op 12-1)

Akona Matata(USA), the first home of those drawn in a double-digit stall, is making up into a decent sort, reversing Epsom form with Hinterland, albeit on much better terms, in the process, despite not getting the best of passages during the race. Much like the winner, the Totesport International, over the same course, looks the logical race for him. (op 20-1)

Hinterland(IRE) ◆, who yet again gave trouble at the start, looked to be going strongly in front two furlongs from home before slightly weakening in the latter stages. He clearly has a bit of a mind of his own, but talent to go with it, and is the sort who might benefit from being gelded. Still open to plenty of improvement, he might be the right type for the Bunbury Cup next time, before having his sights raised. (op 8-1 tchd 17-2 in a place)

Pentecost, a winner is Dubai back in March, went off a massive price for a horse that seems to adore Ascot , and more importantly the Royal Meeting - he won the Britannia in 2002 and was 4th in the Hunt Cup in 2003. He ran a screamer off a very high handicap mark and is on to keep in mind for the Totesport International next time, although the Totescoopsix Stakes at Sandown, a race he has won before, could be a target in the interim.

Pinpoint(IRE), arguably a bit unlucky last time over course and distance, is steadily making up into a decent handicapper, and put up another fine performance for one so inexperienced. He did not get home as well as the horses in front of him, and appeared to lose concentration a bit inside the final furlong, drifting ever so slightly both ways under pressure, so a drop in trip for the Bunbury Cup could ideally suit him. (tchd 10-1 in places)

Forgery(IRE), not seen since landing the Spring Cup at Newbury back in April, became outpaced when the tempo was increased just over two furlongs from home, and could never get on terms with the leading players. He has well documented leg problems, and may well need ground with much more ease in it. (tchd 12-1)

Mine(IRE), a previous winner of the race, in some respects might as well have stayed in his box at home, as he had absolutely no chance of winning from his draw. 3lb lower in the handicap than when winning the race in 2004, he emerges with plenty of credit, but one has no idea how he would have fared with a lower, and more advantageous, draw. The Bunbury Cup, in which he has a fantastic record, is probably his next target. (op 22-1 tchd 25-1 in places)

Capable Guest(IRE), well behind Minority Report last time at Thirsk, ran some fair races in the spring, and bounced back to something like his best, despite having no chance of winning from his stalls position. Third in the Coventry Stakes in 2004, his run behind Forgery in the Spring Cup was deemed to be slightly unlucky given his draw, something he again suffered with again, and he was not that far behind that rival again, although they were split by the width of the track. He is probably going to turn out to be a solid mile handicapper during the season and there are plenty of races for him.

Red Spell(IRE) ◆, much like in his last race, was on the wrong side of the track, and never had a chance of winning. On the positive side, he came to win 'his race' on the far side inside the final furlong, and just got run out of things in the last 100 yards. Given a level playing field next time, he ought to go close, with the Bunbury Cup a realistic option for his next race.

Langford ◆ ran much better than his final position suggests, even though it was on the 'wrong' side of the track. Held up off the pace, he finished really strongly in the final stages and may well have won the race on his side of the track had he not momentarily been stopped by the wall of three horses in front of him just inside in the final furlong. There was a lot to like about the run and should be followed where ever he runs next. (op 33-1)

Dabbers Ridge(IRE) did not see out the trip after briefly looking to have a chance two furlongs from home.

Pride Of Nation(IRE) ◆, so impressive in two runs prior to the race, was drawn on the wrong side of the track, and punters who forced him into favouritism, after all the evidence of the previous day, had clearly not done their homework. He is almost certainly much better than the run suggests, as he again travelled powerfully for much of the race, but the ground may have been a bit too lively for him in any case given the evidence of the Form Book. With the going much more likely to be in his favour, the Cambridgeshire, run in the autumn at Newmarket, could easily turn out to be his big handicap this season, and he remains a very interesting prospect. (tchd 6-1)

Minority Report, who had much the best stalls position of the Cumani-trained pair in the field, came into the race on the back of an impressive performance at Thirsk. Pushed along over two furlongs from home, he never really weakened, but stayed on at the one pace all the way to the line, giving the impression that he was not up to the grade. (op 9-1 tchd 10-1 in places)

Stagelight(IRE) shaped well in the early stages of the races, and was entitled to have needed the run after such a long absence. (op 66-1)

Another Bottle(IRE), who was a massive ante-post plunge in the weeks running up to the race, did not show a great deal during the race and dropped out tamely when the race took shape. The trainer reported that he had been found to have heat in his leg on the morning of the race, but his jockey was given instructions to pull him out at the start if he was not sound. Given that he did take his chance, it is not easy to use the 'possible' injury as an excuse, although all credit must go to the trainer for telling punters before the race of the problem. Official explanation: jockey said gelding was never travelling (op 9-1 tchd 8-1 in places)

Spanish Don, a former Cambridgehire winner, seems to have completely lost the plot.

Blythe Knight(IRE), winner of the Lincoln at the start of the season, ran a really poor race and was beaten a long way from home.

Shot To Fame(USA) Official explanation: jockey said gelding had no more to give

2743 QUEEN MARY STKS (GROUP 2) (FILLIES) 5f
4:55 (5:04) (Class 1) 2-Y-O

£39,746 (£15,064; £7,539; £3,759; £1,883; £945) **Stalls** Low

Form RPR

1111 **1** **Gilded (IRE)**[33] [1831] 2-8-12 .... RichardHughes 12 96
(R Hannon) *lw: in tch: rdn to ld over 1f out: r.o* **11/2**[3]

2 **2** *1* **Simply Perfect**[16] [2300] 2-8-12 .... KFallon 14 92
(J Noseda) *athletic: lw: midfield: hdwy 2f out: wnt 2nd over 1f out: r.o towards fin* **9/2**[2]

61 **3** *½* **Nina Blini**[51] [1347] 2-8-12 .... LDettori 13 91
(B J Meehan) *w'like: hld up: hdwy on outside 2f out: rdn to chse ldrs over 1f out: edgd lft ins fnl f: nt qckn cl home* **12/1**

04 **4** *¾* **Sparkling Eyes**[5] [2617] 2-8-12 .... KerrinMcEvoy 4 88
(C E Brittain) *midfield: hdwy over 1f out: sn rdn: styd on ins fnl f: nt pce to rch ldrs* **66/1**

41 **5** *1 ¼* **Slipasearcher (IRE)**[10] [2478] 2-8-12 .... ShaneKelly 1 83+
(P D Evans) *w'like: leggy: in rr: hmpd after 1f: rdn and hdwy whn nt clr run and swtchd rt over 1f out: styd on ins fnl f* **40/1**

42 **6** *¾* **Vital Statistics**[24] [2045] 2-8-12 .... TQuinn 8 81
(D R C Elsworth) *midfield: rdn and hdwy over 1f out: kpt on ins fnl f: nt pce to trble ldrs* **50/1**

441 **7** *½* **Christmas Tart (IRE)**[23] [2083] 2-8-12 .... ChrisCatlin 6 79?
(V Smith) *s.s: racd keenly in rr: nt clr run 2f out: edgd rt whn rdn and hdwy over 1f out: nt rch ldrs: no ex cl home* **50/1**

24 **8** *3* **Tarkamara (IRE)**[39] [1675] 2-8-12 .... JimmyFortune 7 68
(P F I Cole) *w ldr: led 2f out: rdn and hdd over 1f out: wknd fnl f* **33/1**

3 **9** *1 ¼* **Su Doku (USA)**[23] [2083] 2-8-12 .... CSoumillon 3 67+
(N P Littmoden) *s.s: in rr: hdwy over 1f out: no imp on ldrs: eased whn btn ins fnl f* **16/1**

4 **10** *¾* **Ripping**[16] [2300] 2-8-12 .... RyanMoore 2 61+
(R Hannon) *w'like: midfield: rdn 2f out: nt clr run over 1f out: sn swtchd rt: nvr a danger* **16/1**

1 **11** *hd* **Roxan (IRE)**[21] [2125] 2-8-12 .... NCallan 9 60+
(K A Ryan) *w'like: scope: lw: midfield: nt clr run ent fnl 2f: sn swtchd rt: nvr a danger* **6/4**[1]

2363 **12** *shd* **Feelin Foxy**[26] [1977] 2-8-12 .... JamieSpencer 10 60+
(D Shaw) *racd keenly: hld up: effrt 2f out: n.m.r over 1f out: sn btn: eased fnl f* **66/1**

1 **13** *nk* **Princess Iris (IRE)**[14] [2355] 2-8-12 .... RichardMullen 5 59
(E J O'Neill) *str: led: rdn and hdd 2f out: wknd 1f out* **8/1**

431 **14** *¾* **Hythe Bay**[18] [2234] 2-8-12 .... SteveDrowne 15 56+
(R T Phillips) *cl up: rdn and wkng whn hmpd over 1f out* **50/1**

1 **15** *2* **Sunley Gift**[33] [1817] 2-8-12 .... SamHitchcott 11 49+
(M R Channon) *prom: rdn over 2f out: wkng whn hmpd over 1f out* **16/1**

63.06 secs (1.66) **Going Correction** +0.15s/f (Good) **15** Ran SP% **124.3**
Speed ratings (Par 102):92,90,89,88,86 85,84,79,77,76 76,75,75,74,71
CSF £30.33 TOTE £6.30: £2.20, £1.60, £3.00; EX 21.60 Trifecta £245.60 Pool: £6,306.84 - 18.23 winning tickets..

Owner Mrs J Wood **Bred** Tally-Ho Stud **Trained** East Everleigh, Wilts

■ Stewards' Enquiry : Jimmy Fortune one-day ban: careless riding (Jul 2)
Chris Catlin one-day ban: careless riding (Jul 3)

FOCUS
This did not look like a very strong renewal of the Queen Mary and the winning time was over two seconds slower than the previous day's Windsor Castle, but there was a very worthy winner in Gilded, who was completing a five-timer.

NOTEBOOK
Gilded(IRE) ◆, the winner of her last four starts, including in Listed company at York on her previous start, continued her tremendous run of form with her best effort to date. She was far from ideally drawn in stall 12, but showed bags of early pace to take up a handy position and nothing could live with her once Hughes asked her to extend. There was talk of stepping her up to six furlongs for the Cherry Hinton, but she is so good at this trip it would make sense to aim for the Super Sprint at Newbury and it will take a very fast one indeed to stop her there, even though she will have to shoulder a stiff penalty. Interestingly, Richard Hannon's last two Queen Mary winners, Lyric Fantasy and Risky both went on to take the Super Sprint. (op 5-1 tchd 6-1 in places)

Simply Perfect, who ran second to a potentially smart sort in a very good maiden at Windsor on her debut, ran a terrific race upped significantly in grade. She is bred to get a little further and looks a smart sort in the making. (op 7-2)

Nina Blini, a narrow winner of a Warwick maiden 51 days previously, ran a fine race stepped up significantly in class, and her effort is all the more creditable given she came widest of all with her challenge. (op 14-1)

Sparkling Eyes, who showed just fair form when fourth over this trip in maiden company at Sandown on her previous start, ran a huge race stepped up in class and there was plenty to like about effort. She should win when returned to maiden company before stepping back up in class.

Slipasearcher(IRE) improved on the form of her maiden win at Bath and was unlucky not to have finished even closer, as she was hampered early on and then denied a clear run when beginning to pick up. (tchd 50-1)

Vital Statistics, who failed to confirm her debut promise when second in an uncompetitive maiden at Newmarket on her previous start, ran better this time. On this evidence, it will be a major disappointment if she cannot find a maiden.

Christmas Tart(IRE), off the mark in a four-runner maiden on heavy ground at Sandown on her previous start, would have found this tougher but ran well and may have been closer with a clearer run. (op 66-1)

Su Doku(USA), who did not seem to enjoy heavy ground when third of four behind Christmas Tart on her debut, ran respectably in this much better contest for one so inexperienced. (op 50-1)

Roxan(IRE), the winner of the Listed Hilary Needler at Beverley on her debut, was the one they all had to beat on that form but she failed to give her running. Hampered and short of room just as the race began to get serious, she could not recover and looks to be found out by her inexperience. She was later reported to have returned lame, and that is obviously another valid excuse. She can be given another chance. Official explanation: vet said filly was lame (op 7-4 tchd 2-1)

Feelin Foxy Official explanation: jockey said filly hung left throughout

Princess Iris(IRE), who showed good speed to make a winning debut at Nottingham, again showed pace but weakened out of contention rather disappointingly. (tchd 9-1 in places)

2744 SANDRINGHAM H'CAP (LISTED RACE) (FILLIES) 1m (S)
5:30 (5:43) (Class 1) (0-110,105) 3-Y-O

£31,229 (£11,836; £5,923; £2,953; £1,479; £742) Stalls Low

Form RPR

1111 1 **Red Evie (IRE)**[22] [2103] 3-8-12 **96** JamieSpencer 4 111+
(M L W Bell) *hld up wl in rr: nt clr run over 2f out: swtchd sharply rt sn after: rapid prog over 1f out: r.o to ld last stride* **5/1**[1]

20-1 2 *hd* **La Mottie**[15] [2330] 3-8-12 **96** LDettori 2 108
(J Noseda) *hld up: smooth prog fr 3f out: rdn to ld jst over 1f out: r.o fnl f: hdd last stride* **5/1**[1]

3-13 3 *1 ½* **Makderah (IRE)**[33] [1819] 3-8-12 **96** RHills 19 105+
(M P Tregoning) *lw: hld up in tch: smooth prog 3f out: led jst over 2f out: rdn and hdd jst over 1f out: one pce ins fnl f* **5/1**[1]

1-10 4 *1 ¼* **Shortest Day**[39] [1669] 3-8-11 **95** (t) RichardHughes 7 101
(Sir Michael Stoute) *lw: s.s: hld up in rr gng wl: prog over 2f out: sn rdn: styd on same pce fr over 1f out* **16/1**

4-11 5 *2* **Harvest Queen (IRE)**[14] [2359] 3-8-10 **94** DarryllHolland 1 95
(P J Makin) *racd against nr side rail: trckd ldrs: rdn and outpcd fr 2f out: kpt on: no ch* **8/1**[3]

5-15 6 *3* **Illuminise (IRE)**[26] [1990] 3-8-7 **91** oh3 KFallon 20 85+
(E A L Dunlop) *swtchd fr wd draw to nr side rail and hld up in rr: nt clr run briefly over 2f out: rdn and kpt on fr over 1f out: no ch* **25/1**

110- 7 *2 ½* **Expensive**[249] [5904] 3-9-7 **105** EddieAhern 16 93
(C F Wall) *hld up towards outer: prog fr 2f out: keeping on but no ch whn bmpd over 1f out* **50/1**

254- 8 *2 ½* **Psychic Star**[275] [5367] 3-8-10 **94** KerrinMcEvoy 14 77
(W R Swinburn) *settled in midfield: u.p and struggling in rr wl over 2f out: plugged on* **50/1**

0-66 9 *3* **Jeanmaire (IRE)**[19] [2205] 3-8-7 **91** oh2 TravisBlock 18 67
(H Morrison) *led: kicked clr 3f out: hdd & wknd jst over 2f out* **50/1**

0-05 10 *6* **Sweet Afton (IRE)**[11] [2438] 3-8-13 **97** MJKinane 17 59
(Eamon Tyrrell, Ire) *hld up in last trio: swtchd to wd outside and prog over 2f out: no ch w ldrs over 1f out: wknd* **50/1**

4 11 *3* **Polished Gem (IRE)**[51] [1363] 3-8-9 **93** PJSmullen 5 48+
(D K Weld, Ire) *trckd ldrs: rdn and losing pl whn bdly hmpd over 1f out* **8/1**[3]

\- 12 *1* **Sharapova (IRE)**[51] [1367] 3-8-7 **91** oh3 NGMcCullagh 21 44
(M J Grassick, Ire) *racd on wd outside: trckd ldrs: rdn wl over 2f out: sn wknd* **22/1**

2640 13 *1 ½* **Saabiq (USA)**[19] [2199] 3-8-10 **94** (p) TedDurcan 9 43
(C E Brittain) *t.k.h: prom: rdn and wknd rapidly jst over 2f out* **33/1**

14-5 14 *2* **Stage Flight**[45] [1509] 3-9-4 **102** JimmyFortune 6 47
(B J Meehan) *hld up wl in rr: effrt but nowhere nr ldrs whn hmpd over 1f out* **50/1**

50- 15 *½* **Ciao (IRE)**[26] [2006] 3-8-7 **91** oh9 DMGrant 13 35
(John Joseph Murphy, Ire) *prom on outer over 4f: sn wknd rapidly and last 2f out* **66/1**

1-51 16 *1* **After You**[26] [1990] 3-9-2 **100** MichaelHills 3 41
(B W Hills) *lw: prom against nr side rail over 5f: wknd rapidly* **16/1**

-510 17 *1 ¼* **Adeje Park (IRE)**[38] [1713] 3-8-7 **91** oh2 AlanMunro 11 29
(P W Chapple-Hyam) *lw: prom: wkng rapidly whn sltly hmpd 2f out* **50/1**

1-33 18 *1 ¼* **Nyarhini**[46] [1472] 3-8-11 **95** SteveDrowne 8 31
(G Wragg) *t.k.h: prom tl wknd rapidly over 2f out* **16/1**

1-11 19 *14* **Song Of Passion (IRE)**[19] [2205] 3-8-9 **93** RyanMoore 12 —
(R Hannon) *t.k.h: chsd ldrs: rdn 3f out: wknd rapidly 2f out: t.o* **13/2**[2]

1m 41.35s (-0.45) **Going Correction** +0.15s/f (Good) **19** Ran SP% **127.6**
Speed ratings (Par 104):108,107,106,105,103 100,97,95,92,86 83,82,80,78,78 77,75,74,60
CSF £25.98 CT £124.65 TOTE £5.10: £2.00, £1.50, £1.90, £3.40; EX 17.80 Trifecta £67.70 Pool: £6,085.34 - 63.73 winning tickets. Place 6 £119.00, Place 5 £48.14.

Owner Terry Neill **Bred** Dermot Cantillon And Forenaghts Stud **Trained** Newmarket, Suffolk

■ Wasseema was withdrawn (14/1, ref to enter stalls). R4 applies, deduct 5p in the £.

■ Stewards' Enquiry : Jamie Spencer four-day ban: careless riding (Jul 2-5)

FOCUS

A hot renewal of this fillies' Listed handicap, run at a sound early pace - the time was decent when compared with earlier events - and the field came home strung out. The form looks rock-solid for the division and the highly-progressive winner is value for further.

NOTEBOOK

Red Evie(IRE) ◆, highly-progressive and raised just 2lb for winning her third consecutive handicap at Leicester 22 days previously, ultimately just got up in the dying strides to record her fifth straight success in remarkable fashion and is value for further than the narrow winning margin. Having been held-up early from her decent draw, she was continually denied a clear passage when attempting to make-up ground, but once eventually in the clear she flew home from an impossible-looking position to mow her down rivals and score. She is clearly a Group-class filly in the making, and has gone from strength-to-stength since winning her maiden back in March, with all ground seemingly coming alike to her. Her connections did not rule out the possibility of a tilt at the Group 1 Falmouth Stakes next month and, while that may still seem a little ambitious, it is assured that have yet to see the best of her. (op 9-2)

La Mottie ◆, a winner on her seasonal debut for her new yard at Windsor 15 days previously, was only pipped in the final strides and did nothing wrong in defeat. She travelled takingly in midfield through the early parts, found plenty when asked to improve and, after finally getting the better of Makderah, looked most likely to collect until the eventual winner mugged her close home. This must rate a personal-best effort, she has improved since joining Jeremy Noseda, and can be placed to gain compensation at this level before too long. (op 11-2 tchd 6-1 and 13-2 in places)

Makderah(IRE), third at Newbury behind Scottish Stage in the last of the Oaks trials 33 days previously, shaped better than her finishing position suggests on this drop back to a mile. She was quickly covered up from her wide draw, and there was a lot to like about the manner in which she swept to the front passing the two-furlong marker, but that move ultimately took its toll and she had no more to offer when it really mattered inside the final furlong. This would appear to be her optimum trip, and while she may well have been better off with a slightly more patient ride, there is little doubt she is up to winning in Listed company in the not-too-distant future. (op 6-1 tchd 13-2 in places)

Shortest Day, who flopped as a beaten joint-favourite in the Lingfield Oak's trial last time, was doing all of her best work towards the finish on this drop back in trip and posted a clear personal-best effort in defeat. The application of a tongue tie had a positive effect and she left the definite impression she is capable of picking up some valuable black type when returned to a stiffer test in due course.

Harvest Queen(IRE), winner of her two previous outings this term, was ultimately found out by her latest 11lb rise in the weights on this step-up in class yet was not at all disgraced in defeat. She remains in great heart and helps to set the standard of this form. (tchd 9-1 in places)

Illuminise(IRE), whose trainer has won this race with two of his three previous runners, was immediately switched to the stands'-side rail from her outside draw, losing ground in the process, and would have been closer at the finish but for enduring a troubled passage nearing the two-furlong pole. She is clearly more at home on this faster ground and remains capable of a little more improvement.

Expensive, making her three-year-old debut after a 249-day break, posted a very pleasing return to action and was not disgraced under top weight. She is better than the bare form and ought to improve a deal for the outing. (tchd 66-1 and 33-1 in places)

Polished Gem(IRE), who beat Sharapova on her final outing at two and making her handicap bow having disappointed in Group 3 on her three-year-old debut 51 days previously, was starting to beat a retreat prior to losing any chance when being hampered by the winner approaching the final furlong. She is clearly better than her finishing position suggests. (tchd 9-1 and 10-1 in places)

Sharapova(IRE), a maiden winner on her reappearance at the Curragh in May, got no cover through the race from her outside stall and should not be totally written off on the back of this display. (op 25-1)

Stage Flight Official explanation: jockey said filly suffered interference in running

Nyarhini, last seen finishing third in the Lupe 46 days previously, proved far too keen on this handicap bow and ultimately paid the price when dropping out tamely before the two-furlong pole. She has it to prove now, but is capable of much better when consenting to settle.

Song Of Passion(IRE), who landed a hat-trick when producing a career-best to win at Epsom 19 days previously, was another who ultimately paid for refusing to settle and ran well below expectations. It remains to be seen just how much progression she has left in her. (op 6-1 tchd 7-1)

T/Jkpt: £43,015.00 to a £1 stake. Pool: £272,630.50. 4.00 winning tickets. T/Plt: £68.50 to a £1 stake. Pool: £348,825.09. 3,715.55 winning tickets. T/Qpdt: £27.00 to a £1 stake. Pool: £11,714.90. 319.95 winning tickets. DO

2544 HAMILTON (R-H)

Wednesday, June 21

OFFICIAL GOING: Good (good to soft in places) changing to good to soft after race 3 (3.25)

Persistent rain soon turned the ground, good at the start of the day, to soft especially on the round course.

Wind: Strong, half-behind Weather: Cold, wet and windy

2745 LANARKSHIRE CHAMBER OF COMMERCE MEDIAN AUCTION MAIDEN STKS (HAMILTON PARK 2-Y-O SERIES QUALIFIER) 6f 5y
2:15 (2:15) (Class 6) 2-Y-O £2,590 (£770; £385; £192) Stalls Centre

Form RPR

1 **Hinton Admiral** 2-9-3 JoeFanning 5 79+
(M Johnston) *rangy: scope: mde all: hung bdly lft over 1f out: r.o wl towards fin* **10/11**[1]

2 *½* **Wait Watcher (IRE)** 2-8-12 PaulHanagan 1 67
(P A Blockley) *rangy: unf: scope: s.i.s: sn chsng ldrs: swtchd rt jst ins last: kpt on wl* **9/2**[2]

63 3 *½* **Howards Tipple**[20] [2159] 2-9-3 TomEaves 3 70
(I Semple) *w wnr: edgd lft 1f out: kpt on same pce* **12/1**

0 4 *12* **Prix Masque (IRE)**[12] [2409] 2-9-3 RobertWinston 4 34+
(B Smart) *chsd ldrs: drvn over 3f out: lost pl over 1f out* **7/1**

5 5 *1* **Ocean Of Champagne**[22] [2106] 2-8-9 DanielTudhope(3) 2 26+
(A Dickman) *s.s: sn drvn along in last: bhd fnl 2f* **6/1**[3]

1m 13.27s (0.17) **Going Correction** -0.175s/f (Firm) **5** Ran SP% **105.0**
Speed ratings (Par 91):91,90,89,73,72
CSF £4.63 TOTE £1.60: £1.10, £2.10; EX 4.60.

Owner Gainsborough Stud **Bred** Gainsborough Stud Management Ltd **Trained** Middleham Moor, N Yorks

FOCUS

A weak maiden and the bare form is not up to much but the winner has any amount of potential.

NOTEBOOK

Hinton Admiral ◆, whose dam has produced several winners over a variety of trips including the Queen's Vase winner Shanty Star, is an April foal with plenty of size and scope. He travlled strongly in front but no doubt through greeness hung right across the track. Right on top at the line, he can go a long way. (op 4-5 after Evens in places, tchd 11-10 in a place)

Wait Watcher(IRE), not foaled until mid-May, has a fair amount of size and scope. She stuck on when switched inside but is flattered by her proximity to the winner. It was a fair first run and she deserves to find a race. (op 5-1 tchd 11-2, 6-1 in a place)

Howards Tipple, a bag of nerves, was taken to post ahead of the others. The most experienced in the field, this may be as good as he is and he must learn to settle down. (op 11-1 tchd 14-1)

Prix Masque(IRE), a moderate walker, still looked to be carrying condition and he will need plenty more time yet. (op 11-2)

Ocean Of Champagne never went a yard and perhaps the ground was starting to turn against her. (op 5-1)

2746 GEORGE WIMPEY H'CAP 1m 65y
2:50 (2:51) (Class 6) (0-60,60) 3-Y-O £3,238 (£963; £481; £240) Stalls High

Form RPR

0005 1 **Gigs Magic (USA)**[18] [2243] 3-8-7 **46** JoeFanning 8 51
(M Johnston) *trckd ldrs: led 1f out: edgd lft: hld on wl* **15/2**

35 2 *½* **Ai Hawa (IRE)**[19] [2195] 3-8-9 **48** MCHussey 12 52
(Eamon Tyrrell, Ire) *trckd ldrs: effrt over 3f out: styd on to chal ins last: no ex* **9/1**

-220 3 *1* **Wednesdays Boy (IRE)**[11] [2466] 3-8-13 **52** PaulMulrennan 15 54
(P D Niven) *hld up: effrt over 3f out: nt clr run over 2f out: styd on fnl* **13/2**[3]

3610 4 *nk* **Peephole**[4] [2641] 3-9-6 **59** (v) MickyFenton 14 60
(A Bailey) *chsd ldrs: drvn over 3f out: kpt on same pce appr fnl f* **5/1**[1]

00-0 5 *shd* **Dark Night (IRE)**[18] [2243] 3-8-7 **46** ow1 TomEaves 11 47
(D W Barker) *hld up towards rr: rdn and lost pl over 3f out: hdwy on outside 2f out: styd on wl fnl f* **40/1**

3100 6 *1 ¾* **Beginners Luck (IRE)**[43] [1576] 3-7-10 **42** ow1 KellyHarrison(7) 4 39
(D Carroll) *hld up: hdwy and nt clr run 2f out: edgd rt and kpt on fnl f* **50/1**

5-50 7 *shd* **Inchdhuaig (IRE)**[21] [2128] 3-9-4 **57** RobertWinston 3 54
(P C Haslam) *hld up on outer: effrt 3f out: kpt on: nvr rchd ldrs* **8/1**

-005 8 *nk* **Cape Sydney (IRE)**[34] [1792] 3-8-3 **42** RoystonFfrench 10 38
(D W Barker) *led 1f: trckd ldrs: led over 2f out: hdd 1f out: one pce* **20/1**

05-0 9 *2* **Kasarami (IRE)**[18] [2243] 3-8-8 **50** DanielTudhope(3) 1 42
(J S Goldie) *s.i.s: hdwy over 4f out: nvr rchd ldrs* **25/1**

5-12 10 *nk* **Markestino**[18] [2249] 3-8-9 **48** DavidAllan 6 39
(T D Easterby) *trckd ldrs: effrt 3f out: wknd fnl f* **5/1**[1]

0-10 11 *10* **Queen Jean**[20] [2171] 3-9-7 **60** FergalLynch 13 28
(J G Given) *led after 1f: hdd over 2f out: wknd over 1f out* **6/1**[2]

-000 12 *4* **The Dunion**[18] [2243] 3-8-0 **44** oh1 ow3 AndrewMullen(5) 5 3
(Miss L A Perratt) *in tch: lost pl 2f out: sn bhd and eased* **66/1**

000 13 *1 ½* **Prince Marju (IRE)**[65] [1049] 3-8-9 **48** PatCosgrave 9 3
(P A Blockley) *rrd s: sme hdwy on wd outside over 4f out: wknd 3f out: sn bhd: eased* **25/1**

1m 50.04s (0.74) **Going Correction** +0.075s/f (Good) **13** Ran SP% **112.2**
Speed ratings (Par 97):99,98,97,97,97 95,95,94,92,92 82,78,77
CSF £62.97 CT £473.71 TOTE £9.60: £2.60, £2.10, £2.50; EX 76.80.

Owner J Barson **Bred** R McDonald **Trained** Middleham Moor, N Yorks
■ Stewards' Enquiry : M C Hussey one-day ban: used whip with excessive frequency (Jul 2)
FOCUS
A very modest handicap run at just a steady pace and they seemed to get in each others' way. However, the form appears sound at face value rated through the runner-up, fourth and sixth.
Markestino Official explanation: jockey said gelding was unsuited by good, good to soft in places, ground

2747 KINGS SECURITY FILLIES' H'CAP — 1m 1f 36y
3:25 (3:26) (Class 5) (0-70,69) 3-Y-0+ — **£4,533** (£1,348; £674; £336) **Stalls** High

Form — RPR
-006 **1** — **Topflight Wildbird**[12] [2411] 3-7-12 **55** oh7 ow5........(b) AndrewElliott(5) 2 — 68
(Mrs G S Rees) *chsd ldrs: hdwy on outside to ld over 2f out: clr 1f out: eased nr fin* **33/1**
-400 **2** 5 **Hansomelle (IRE)**[13] [2378] 4-9-2 **57**.................................. DaleGibson 4 — 61
(B Mactaggart) *in rr: styd on fnl 3f: wnt 2nd ins last: no ch w wnr* **12/1**
5160 **3** 1 ½ **Dispol Veleta**[31] [1864] 5-9-11 **69**.................................. BenSwarbrick(3) 9 — 70
(T D Barron) *sn in tch: effrt 3f out: kpt on same pce* **4/1**[2]
0-63 **4** ¾ **Lauro**[22] [2108] 6-9-4 **59**.. TomEaves 6 — 58
(Miss J A Camacho) *in tch: wnt 2nd over 1f out: no ex* **4/1**[2]
-233 **5** 1 ½ **Alisdanza**[7] [2546] 4-8-9 **50**.................................. RobertWinston 5 — 46
(G A Swinbank) *hld up in last: hdwy over 3f out: kpt on: nvr trbld ldrs* **3/1**[1]
-306 **6** 5 **Calamari (IRE)**[16] [2293] 4-9-0 **55**.................................. RoystonFfrench 8 — 41
(Mrs A Duffield) *trckd ldrs: led 3f out: sn hdd: wknd fnl f* **8/1**
6/26 **7** 3 ½ **Whittinghamvillage**[16] [2286] 5-8-12 **58**.................. GregFairley(5) 7 — 37
(D W Whillans) *w ldrs: chal over 3f out: wknd over 1f out* **6/1**[3]
0060 **8** nk **Ballycroy Girl (IRE)**[58] [1201] 4-9-0 **55**.................................. MickyFenton 1 — 33
(A Bailey) *led tl 3f out: lost pl over 1f out* **33/1**
4 **9** ½ **Ship Mate (IRE)**[28] [1940] 3-9-2 **68**.................................. MCHussey 10 — 44
(Eamon Tyrrell, Ire) *trckd ldrs: effrt over 3f out: lost pl over 1f out* **12/1**

2m 0.20s (0.54) **Going Correction** +0.075s/f (Good)
WFA 3 from 4yo+ 11lb — **9** Ran SP% **111.7**
Speed ratings (Par 100):100,95,94,93,92 87,84,84,83
CSF £362.80 CT £1914.39 TOTE £40.30: £6.80, £3.40, £2.10; EX 445.20.
Owner P Bamford **Bred** Dandy's Farm **Trained** Sollom, Lancs
FOCUS
A sound gallop in the deteriorating conditions and a much-improved effort from the wide-margin winner. The runner-up and fourth are rated to recent form.
Topflight Wildbird Official explanation: trainer had no explanation for the improved form shown

2748 HAMILTON PARK CLAIMING STKS — 5f 4y
4:00 (4:00) (Class 6) 3-Y-0+ — **£2,590** (£770; £385; £192) **Stalls** Centre

Form — RPR
-041 **1** — **Further Outlook (USA)**[30] [1886] 12-8-13 68............ DanielTudhope(3) 2 — 76
(D Carroll) *mde all: hung rt over 1f out: hld on wl* **3/1**[1]
0000 **2** 1 ½ **Unlimited**[12] [2396] 4-8-12 56.................................. RoystonFfrench 7 — 67
(Mrs A Duffield) *w ldrs: chal over 2f out: kpt on same pce ins last* **5/1**[3]
0-35 **3** nk **Atlantic Viking (IRE)**[12] [2396] 11-9-6 66...................... RobertWinston 3 — 74
(D Nicholls) *sn in rr: hdwy and hung rt over 1f out: kpt on ins last* **4/1**[2]
-000 **4** nk **Sovereignty (JPN)**[13] [2377] 4-8-7 62...................... StephenCairns(7) 4 — 67
(I Semple) *trckd ldrs: kpt on fnl f* **12/1**
0-40 **5** hd **Rudi's Pet (IRE)**[12] [2396] 12-8-13 65...................... VictoriaBehan(7) 1 — 72
(D Nicholls) *chsd ldrs on ins: kpt on same pce fnl f* **10/1**
4035 **6** 1 ¼ **Raccoon (IRE)**[11] [2449] 6-9-7 66..............................(v) BenSwarbrick(3) 6 — 72
(T D Barron) *chsd ldrs: outpcd over 2f out: no threat after* **5/1**[3]
0-00 **7** 2 ½ **Viewforth**[33] [1816] 8-9-0 57..(b) TomEaves 8 — 54
(I Semple) *chsd ldrs: wknd appr fnl f* **7/1**
00-0 **8** 9 **Northern Svengali (IRE)**[30] [1886] 10-8-10 41.........(t) DerekMcGaffin 11 — 19
(D A Nolan) *w ldrs on outside: lost pl over 1f out: sn bhd* **100/1**

60.03 secs (-1.17) **Going Correction** -0.125s/f (Firm) — **8** Ran SP% **108.6**
Speed ratings (Par 101):104,101,101,100,100 98,94,79
CSF £16.22 TOTE £3.20: £1.70, £2.00, £1.50; EX 16.00.Rudi's Pet was the subject of a friendly claim. Atlantic Viking was the subject of a friendly claim.
Owner Diamond Racing Ltd **Bred** Gainsborough Farm Inc **Trained** Warthill, N Yorks
FOCUS
The winner was entitled to take this claimer and always looked in charge. The form is straightforward and looks sound overall.

2749 CLYDESDALE BANK H'CAP — 6f 5y
4:35 (4:35) (Class 5) (0-75,70) 3-Y-0+ — **£4,533** (£1,348; £674; £336) **Stalls** Centre

Form — RPR
0002 **1** — **Yorkshire Blue**[13] [2380] 7-9-2 **58**.................................. FergalLynch 3 — 71
(J S Goldie) *in rr: sn drvn along: hdwy 2f out: styd on strly to ld last 75yds* **4/1**[2]
3-00 **2** 1 ¼ **Bundy**[34] [1795] 10-8-7 **52**.................................. BenSwarbrick(3) 9 — 61
(M Dods) *w ldrs on outside: led over 2f out: hdd and no ex ins last* **12/1**
02-5 **3** 2 **Howards Princess**[31] [1865] 4-10-0 **70**.................................. TomEaves 2 — 73
(I Semple) *w ldrs on inner: chal over 1f out: kpt on same pce* **14/1**
0500 **4** shd **Ellens Academy (IRE)**[25] [2027] 11-9-13 **69**.................. RobertHavlin 6 — 72
(E J Alston) *hld up: smooth hdwy over 2f out: sn trcking ldrs: one pce fnl f* **9/1**
3543 **5** nk **Titinius (IRE)**[20] [2184] 6-9-9 **70**.................................. GregFairley(5) 5 — 72
(Micky Hammond) *in rr: sn drvn along: kpt on fnl 2f: nvr able chal* **7/2**[1]
0000 **6** 1 ½ **Elkhorn**[21] [2417] 4-9-6 **62**..(p) PaulMulrennan 4 — 60
(Miss J A Camacho) *trckd ldrs: wknd fnl f* **20/1**
1000 **7** 1 ¼ **Local Poet**[20] [2164] 5-9-12 **68**..(b) TonyHamilton 1 — 62
(I Semple) *trckd ldrs on inner: wknd over 1f out* **9/1**
0611 **8** 4 **Obe Bold (IRE)**[41] [1607] 5-8-8 **57**.................................. KevinGhunowa(7) 7 — 39
(A Berry) *led tl over 2f out: sn lost pl* **11/2**[3]
4206 **9** 8 **Beowulf**[22] [2109] 3-8-13 **62**.................................. JoeFanning 8 — 20
(M Johnston) *trckd ldrs on outer: wknd over 1f out* **11/2**[3]

1m 12.5s (-0.60) **Going Correction** -0.125s/f (Firm)
WFA 3 from 4yo+ 7lb — **9** Ran SP% **112.1**
Speed ratings (Par 103):99,97,94,94,94 92,90,85,74
CSF £48.71 CT £605.44 TOTE £4.20: £1.50, £3.50, £2.20; EX 76.20.
Owner Thoroughbred Leisure Racing Club 2 **Bred** R T And Mrs Watson **Trained** Uplawmoor, E Renfrews
FOCUS
They went a strong pace and the form looks sound. The winner came from last to first, being firmly in command at the line.

2750 SCOTTISH RACING MEDIAN AUCTION MAIDEN STKS — 1m 3f 16y
5:10 (5:10) (Class 6) 3-4-Y-0 — **£2,730** (£806; £403) **Stalls** High

Form — RPR
2 **1** — **Riodan (IRE)**[32] [1854] 4-9-4 .... DNolan(3) 5 — 64+
(J J Quinn) *trckd ldrs: led over 1f out: styd on* **7/4**[1]
50-2 **2** 1 ½ **Minthare (IRE)**[26] [1988] 3-8-13 59.................................. TonyHamilton 3 — 67
(C Grant) *trckd ldrs: led 3f out: hung rt and hdd over 1f out: no ex* **14/1**
0-2 **3** 7 **Riverhill (IRE)**[31] [1868] 3-8-13 .... TomEaves 1 — 55
(J Howard Johnson) *s.i.s: hdwy on ins to chse ldrs 4f out: wknd over 1f out* **5/2**[2]
646 **4** 2 **Luck In Running (USA)**[45] [1503] 3-8-13 72.................. JoeFanning 4 — 52
(M Johnston) *chsd ldrs: edgd lft 3f out: lost pl 2f out* **8/1**
0043 **5** 5 **Dancing Flame**[8] [2518] 3-8-8 53.................................. RobertHavlin 2 — 39
(E J Alston) *t.k.h: led: hdd 3f out: wknd 2f out* **7/2**[3]

2m 28.86s (2.60) **Going Correction** +0.20s/f (Good)
WFA 3 from 4yo 13lb — **5** Ran SP% **104.9**
Speed ratings (Par 101):98,96,91,90,86
CSF £21.25 TOTE £2.20: £1.10, £4.80; EX 19.40.
Owner Lawrence Mullaney & John Marson **Bred** Geoffrey Thompson And Crystal Bloodstock **Trained** Settrington, N Yorks
FOCUS
A very weak maiden and the winner's stamina seemed to carry the day in the end. The runner-up is the best guide to the level.

2751 GUYS AND DOLLS APPRENTICE SERIES H'CAP (ROUND 1) — 1m 5f 9y
5:40 (5:40) (Class 6) (0-60,60) 4-Y-0+ — **£2,730** (£806; £403) **Stalls** High

Form — RPR
5354 **1** — **Rare Coincidence**[13] [2381] 5-9-2 **52**..............................(p) AndrewElliott 2 — 61
(R F Fisher) *t.k.h: led: hdd 4f out: led 2f out: styd on* **4/1**[3]
0300 **2** 1 ¾ **Mary Gray**[18] [2242] 4-8-10 **46**..(v[1]) SladeO'Hara 3 — 53
(M Johnston) *trckd ldrs: hmpd 4f out: hung lft: styd on fnl 2f: tk 2nd post* **6/1**
05-0 **3** shd **Millennium Hall**[13] [2381] 7-9-10 **60**.................................. PJMcDonald 5 — 66
(Miss Lucinda V Russell) *dwlt: hdwy over 5f out: led and edgd rt 4f out: hdd 2f out: kpt on same pce* **8/1**
0323 **4** 1 ¾ **Caymans Gift**[23] [2078] 6-9-4 **57**.................................. NeilBrown(3) 4 — 61
(A C Whillans) *hld up in rr: effrt over 3f out: kpt on: nvr able chal* **3/1**[2]
000- **5** 1 **Regal Fantasy (IRE)**[50] [6555] 6-8-5 **41** oh11.................. KevinGhunowa 6 — 44?
(P A Blockley) *chsd ldrs: outpcd over 3f out: one pce fnl 2f* **14/1**
005- **6** 13 **Acca Larentia (IRE)**[28] [3183] 5-8-5 **41** oh10.................. KellyHarrison 7 — 25
(Mrs H O Graham) *chsd ldrs: outpcd over 5f out: lost pl over 3f out: sn bhd* **40/1**
0-02 **7** 4 **Rafelite**[30] [1879] 4-9-8 **58**.................................. RussellKennemore 8 — 37
(Lady Herries) *trckd ldrs: wknd qckly over 3f out: sn bhd* **11/4**[1]

2m 59.11s (5.71) **Going Correction** +0.20s/f (Good) — **7** Ran SP% **106.2**
Speed ratings (Par 101):90,88,88,87,87 79,76
CSF £23.73 CT £147.38 TOTE £5.00: £2.50, £3.30; EX 34.40 Place 6 £187.93, Place 5 £159.08.
Owner A Kerr **Bred** D R Tucker **Trained** Ulverston, Cumbria
FOCUS
A very modest event in which the winner was not scoring out of turn. The winning time was slow and the form looks shaky.
T/Plt: £259.90 to a £1 stake. Pool: £29,203.10. 82.00 winning tickets. T/Qpdt: £36.90 to a £1 stake. Pool: £1,731.70. 34.70 winning tickets. WG

2551 KEMPTON (A.W) (R-H)
Wednesday, June 21

OFFICIAL GOING: Standard
Wind: Fresh across

2752 WEATHERBYS BANK APPRENTICE H'CAP (ROUND 3) — 1m 2f (P)
7:00 (7:00) (Class 4) (0-80,80) 4-Y-0+ — **£5,505** (£1,637; £818; £408) **Stalls** High

Form — RPR
0050 **1** — **Burgundy**[4] [2647] 9-8-9 **68**..(b) AshleyHamblett(3) 5 — 78
(P Mitchell) *s.i.s: hld up: hdwy 4f out: carried wd on bnd over 2f out: forcefully rdn and r.o to ld fnl 50yds* **7/1**
-103 **2** ¾ **Let Slip**[22] [2113] 4-8-13 **74**.................................. BRoper(5) 7 — 83
(W Jarvis) *t.k.h: chsd ldrs: rdn to ld over 1f out: hdd fnl 50yds* **3/1**[1]
6-00 **3** 4 **King's Thought**[14] [2341] 7-9-10 **80**.................................. LiamJones 2 — 81
(S Gollings) *led for 4f: styd prom: led again 2f out: hdd over 1f out: wknd ins fnl f* **5/1**[3]
-040 **4** 3 ½ **Red Contact (USA)**[30] [1882] 5-9-1 **74**......................(p) HarryPoulton(3) 6 — 69
(J R Best) *t.k.h: led after 4f: hdd 2f out: rdn and wknd ent fnl f* **12/1**
-401 **5** 3 ½ **Charlie Kennet**[22] [2104] 8-8-12 **71**.................................. KylieManser(3) 3 — 59
(Mrs H Sweeting) *rrd up s and v.s.a: hdwy 4f out: racd wd bnd over 2f out: sn btn* **9/2**[2]
4316 **6** ½ **Parkview Love (USA)**[20] [2170] 5-9-2 **72**..........................(v) DerekNolan 8 — 59
(D Shaw) *mid-div: wknd 2f out* **5/1**[3]
6000 **7** 1 ¼ **Admiral Compton**[7] [2551] 5-8-7 **68**.................................. WilliamCarson(5) 4 — 53
(J R Boyle) *prom tl wknd over 2f out* **8/1**
5005 **8** 39 **Glenviews Oldport (USA)**[86] [771] 4-8-5 **61** oh19.......(b) RonanKeogh 1 — —
(Peter Grayson) *a bhd: eased over 1f out: t.o* **33/1**

2m 10.63s (1.63) **Going Correction** +0.125s/f (Slow) — **8** Ran SP% **110.8**
Speed ratings (Par 105):98,97,94,91,88 88,87,56
CSF £26.50 CT £108.93 TOTE £7.50: £2.70, £1.10, £3.30; EX 28.50.
Owner Mrs S Sheldon **Bred** Cheveley Park Stud Ltd **Trained** Epsom, Surrey
■ Stewards' Enquiry : Ashley Hamblett caution: used whip down the shoulder in the forehand position
FOCUS
A modest handicap and weak form for the grade with the time modest.

2753 FITZPATRICK CIVIL ENGINEERING MAIDEN FILLIES' STKS — 1m 2f (P)
7:28 (7:33) (Class 5) 3-Y-0+ — **£3,238** (£963; £481; £240) **Stalls** High

Form — RPR
2 **1** — **Candle**[14] [2349] 3-8-12 .... FergusSweeney 4 — 81
(H Candy) *trckd ldr: led 4f out: rdn appr fnl f: jst hld on* **4/1**[2]
43 **2** shd **Greek Easter (IRE)**[8] [2532] 3-8-12 .... LDettori 6 — 81
(B J Meehan) *a.p: rdn to go 2nd over 1f out: pressed wnr clly thrght fnl f* **4/1**[2]
54 **3** 2 ½ **Regent's Park**[40] [1650] 3-8-12 .... SteveDrowne 13 — 76
(R Charlton) *chsd ldrs: wnt 2nd 2f out to over 1f out: no ex ins fnl f* **3/1**[1]
0 **4** 1 ½ **Dream Shared**[27] [1955] 3-8-12 .... RichardMullen 2 — 73
(E A L Dunlop) *in tch: rdn over 3f out: kpt on one pce ins fnl 2f* **16/1**
5 2 ½ **Aegean Pearl (USA)** 3-8-12 .... JimmyFortune 12 — 69+
(J H M Gosden) *in tch: rdn over 1f out: wknd ins fnl f* **6/1**[3]
6 5 **Maud's Cat (IRE)** 3-8-12 .... FrankieMcDonald 14 — 59
(A P Jarvis) *t.k.h: led to 4f out: rdn and wknd wl over 1f out* **10/1**
7 10 **Moon Empress (FR)** 3-8-12 .... MartinDwyer 8 — 40
(W R Muir) *slowly away: nvr on terms* **16/1**

8 ½ **Mezzo** 3-8-12 .... NickyMackay 11 39
(L M Cumani) *a bhd* **12/1**
00 9 3 **Helen Wood**[6] 2578 3-8-12 .... HayleyTurner 3 34
(M D I Usher) *slowly away: nvr got into r* **66/1**
10 5 **Chifney Rush (IRE)** 3-8-12 .... MichaelHills 7 24
(B W Hills) *mid-div: sn pushed along: wknd over 3f out* **20/1**
46 11 ½ **Over Ice**[19] 2188 3-8-12 .... DarryllHolland 9 23
(Karen George) *mid-div: rdn 1/2-way: sn bhd* **18/1**
0 12 1 ½ **Fluted Crystal**[14] 2343 3-8-12 .... ChrisCatlin 1 20
(H Candy) *s.i.s: a bhd* **50/1**
13 4 **Niza D'Alm (FR)**[52] 5-9-10 .... SamHitchcott 5 13
(Miss Suzy Smith) *v.s.a: a bhd* **66/1**
0 14 15 **Silk Purse**[30] 1901 3-8-12 .... FrancisFerris 10 —
(Rae Guest) *s.i.s: sn mid-div: rdn 1/2-way: sn wl bhd* **66/1**

2m 8.32s (-0.68) **Going Correction** +0.125s/f (Slow)
WFA 3 from 5yo 12lb **14** Ran SP% **124.3**
Speed ratings (Par 100):107,106,104,103,101 97,89,89,86,82 82,81,78,66
CSF £20.53 TOTE £5.20: £1.70, £1.50, £1.70; EX 17.00.
Owner Mrs David Blackburn **Bred** Mrs M J Blackburn **Trained** Kingston Warren, Oxon

FOCUS
A race with a definite wide range of abilities, as the first six home were well clear of the rest of the field. The time was the fastest of the three over the trip at the meeting and the form could prove above average with the principals clear.
Over Ice Official explanation: jockey said filly hung right throughout

2754 FITZPATRICK STREETSCAPE H'CAP 1m 2f (P)
7:56 (7:59) (Class 4) (0-85,84) 3-Y-0 **£5,505** (£1,637; £818; £408) **Stalls** High

Form RPR
-154 1 **Acrobatic (USA)**[20] 2177 3-9-0 77 .... RichardHughes 6 85
(R Charlton) *led for 1f: styd prom: rdn over 1f out: kpt on to ld fnl 75yds* **6/1**[3]
61 2 nk **Celtic Spirit (IRE)**[23] 2063 3-8-6 72 .... NelsonDeSouza(3) 5 80
(R M Beckett) *a in tch: rdn over 1f out: edgd lft but r.o to go 2nd cl home* **10/1**
0-60 3 ½ **Kahlua Kiss**[12] 2404 3-8-10 73 .... MartinDwyer 8 80
(W R Muir) *t.k.h: trckd ldr after 2f: hrd rdn to ld 1f out: hdd wl ins fnl f and lost 2nd cl home* **40/1**
011- 4 1 **Faith And Reason (USA)**[274] 5393 3-9-7 84 .... LDettori 1 89
(Saeed Bin Suroor) *led after 1f: rdn and hdd 1f out: edgd leaft and one pce ins fnl f* **11/4**[1]
-133 5 1 ¾ **Illustrious Blue**[14] 2344 3-9-3 80 .... TPQueally 3 82
(J A Osborne) *hld up: hmpd on ins 1/2-way: hdwy on outside over 3f out: rdn and wknd over 1f out* **6/1**[3]
441- 6 2 **Los Cabos (IRE)**[245] 5970 3-9-3 80 .... JimmyFortune 7 78
(J H M Gosden) *s.i.s: sn mid-div: rdn over 2f out: sn btn* **13/2**
1101 7 ½ **Royal Amnesty**[14] 2344 3-9-1 78 .... OscarUrbina 2 75
(G C H Chung) *hld up: hdwy on outside over 3f out: wknd over 1f out* **3/1**[2]
023 8 5 **Plush**[18] 2244 3-8-2 65 .... JamieMackay 4 52
(Sir Mark Prescott) *t.k.h: hld up: no hdwy fnl 2f* **12/1**

2m 8.74s (-0.26) **Going Correction** +0.125s/f (Slow) **8** Ran SP% **112.8**
Speed ratings (Par 101):106,105,105,104,103 101,101,97
CSF £61.36 CT £2165.15 TOTE £7.30: £2.20, £2.90, £14.80; EX 94.20.
Owner K Abdulla **Bred** Juddmonte Farms Inc **Trained** Beckhampton, Wilts
■ Stewards' Enquiry : Jamie Mackay two-day ban: careless riding (Jul 2-3)

FOCUS
A fair handicap but the form may prove ordinary with the fourth to form.
Illustrious Blue Official explanation: jockey said colt suffered interference in running

2755 FITZPATRICK CONTRACTORS EBF MAIDEN FILLIES' STKS 7f (P)
8:24 (8:25) (Class 5) 2-Y-0 **£3,886** (£1,156; £577; £288) **Stalls** High

Form RPR
0 1 **Easy Lover**[15] 2328 2-9-0 .... ShaneKelly 5 76+
(J A Osborne) *hld up in tch: wnt 2nd wl over 1f out: led briefly jst ins fnl f: rallied u.p to ld again last stride* **5/1**
6 2 shd **Market Day**[20] 2166 2-9-0 .... NickyMackay 4 76+
(L M Cumani) *chsd ldrs: outpcd 1/2-way: rallied 2f out: led jst ins fnl f: hrd rdn and hdd last stride* **7/2**[3]
3 3 **Party (IRE)** 2-9-0 .... RichardHughes 6 69
(R Hannon) *sn led: hdd 1/2-way: led again 2f out: rdn and hdd again jst ins fnl f: wknd* **7/4**[1]
0 4 3 ½ **Kat Act Two**[16] 2287 2-9-0 .... TPQueally 1 60
(J A Osborne) *in tch on outside: hdwy 1/2-way: wknd over 1f out* **20/1**
2 5 1 ½ **Grange Lili (IRE)**[7] 2552 2-9-0 .... RobbieFitzpatrick 3 56
(Peter Grayson) *t.k.h: prom: nt clr run over 2f out to over 1f out: sn btn* **3/1**[2]
04 6 2 ½ **Spanish Air**[11] 2461 2-9-0 .... EddieAhern 2 50
(J W Hills) *led 1/2-way: hdd 2f out: sn wknd* **12/1**

1m 30.26s (3.46) **Going Correction** +0.125s/f (Slow) **6** Ran SP% **112.7**
Speed ratings (Par 90):85,84,81,77,75 72
CSF £22.76 TOTE £7.70: £2.50, £1.70; EX 38.90.
Owner Mountgrange Stud **Bred** Lordship Stud **Trained** Upper Lambourn, Berks

FOCUS
A fair fillies' maiden, run at a steady early gallop, and the first two came clear. However, the form behind looks shaky.

NOTEBOOK
Easy Lover, eighth on debut at Windsor 15 days previously, got off the mark at the second attempt with a game success. She looked held when the runner-up came alongside in the final furlong, but she knuckled down for pressure, and ultimately proved resolute near the finish. The extra furlong proved much to her liking, indeed she will get further in due course, and remains open to further improvement. (op 7-1)
Market Day, sixth on debut at Nottingham 20 days previously after provng troublesome at the start, looked all over the winner when hitting the front late on, but she ultimately did nothing in front, and was hauled back in the final strides. It may be that she was not quite ready for this step-up in trip, but she was still clear of the rest at the finish, and can be placed to get off the mark before too long. (op 2-1)
Party(IRE), a 55,000gns purchase related to winners at around this trip, was well backed for this racecourse debut and clearly knew her job. She just failed to see out the trip as well as the first two, and may well be better off dropping to six furlongs in the short term, but clearly she has a future. (op 9-4)
Kat Act Two, eighth on debut at Leicester 16 days previously, did not shape as though the extra furlong was really ideal and never seriously figured. She looks much more of a nursery type.
Grange Lili(IRE), runner-up on debut at this venue over six furlongs a week previously, ran freely through the early parts and then met trouble on the rail at the top of the home straight. She is better than this. (op 7-2)
Spanish Air ran below-par on this first attempt at a seventh furlong and dropped out tamely when headed. She now qualifies for a nursery mark, however. (op 14-1)

2756 FITZPATRICK HIGHWAY SERVICES H'CAP 6f (P)
8:52 (8:54) (Class 4) (0-85,85) 3-Y-0 **£5,505** (£1,637; £818; £408) **Stalls** High

Form RPR
0002 1 **Xaluna Bay (IRE)**[9] 2511 3-8-3 67 .... RichardMullen 4 79
(W R Muir) *mid-div: rdn and gd hdwy to go 2nd 1f out: drvn clr fnl f* **9/1**
-042 2 1 ¼ **Dark Missile**[20] 2168 3-9-7 85 .... RichardHughes 8 93
(A M Balding) *hmpd sn after s: in rr: hdwy whn nt clr run over 2f out: r.o wl fnl f to go 2nd nr fin: nvr nrr* **11/2**[3]
-420 3 nk **Woodnook**[24] 2049 3-8-11 75 .... JimmyFortune 6 82
(J A R Toller) *chsd leaders: wnt 2nd over 1f out: no ex ins fnl f* **7/1**
2405 4 ½ **Peter Island (FR)**[14] 2363 3-8-11 75 .... ChrisCatlin 2 81
(J Gallagher) *led for 1f: led again over 2f out: hdd 1f out: no ex ins fnl f* **11/1**
3110 5 4 **Blushing Thief (USA)**[62] 1091 3-9-1 79 .... AlanMunro 7 73
(W Jarvis) *nvr bttr than mid-div* **9/2**[1]
2511 6 1 ¾ **Gavarnie Beau (IRE)**[22] 2105 3-8-13 77 .... FrancisNorton 11 65
(M Blanshard) *chsd ldrs: rdn whn n.m.r on ins over 1f out: no ex* **11/2**[3]
0-06 7 ¾ **Laith (IRE)**[12] 2389 3-9-1 79 .... MartinDwyer 9 65
(B W Hills) *led after 1f: hdd over 2f out: wknd over 1f out* **9/1**
3000 8 ½ **Marriage Value (IRE)**[15] 2329 3-8-11 75 ....(b[1]) ShaneKelly 1 60
(J A Osborne) *s.i.s: sn in mid-div on outside but nvr on terms* **25/1**
1-00 9 2 ½ **Ocean Of Dreams (FR)**[14] 2363 3-9-3 81 .... GrahamGibbons 3 58
(J D Bethell) *a towards rr* **12/1**
1504 10 5 **Stoneacre Boy (IRE)**[29] 1928 3-9-2 80 ....(b) RobbieFitzpatrick 5 42
(Peter Grayson) *chsd ldrs: wkng whn jinked rt over 1f out* **5/1**[2]
60-0 11 3 ½ **Saxon Saint**[15] 2329 3-8-9 73 .... HayleyTurner 10 25
(M D I Usher) *outpcd: a bhd* **33/1**

1m 14.08s (0.38) **Going Correction** +0.125s/f (Slow) **11** Ran SP% **120.9**
Speed ratings (Par 101):102,100,99,99,93 91,90,89,86,79 75
CSF £59.62 CT £376.28 TOTE £6.30: £1.80, £2.30, £2.30; EX 49.40.
Owner The Parkside Partnership **Bred** Deer Forest Stud Ltd **Trained** Lambourn, Berks

FOCUS
A fair sprint, run at a sound pace, and the first four came clear. The form is solid rated around the third.
Gavarnie Beau(IRE) Official explanation: jockey said gelding suffered interference
Laith(IRE) Official explanation: jockey said gelding hung right
Ocean Of Dreams(FR) Official explanation: jockey said colt lost its action
Saxon Saint Official explanation: jockey said gelding suffered interference on final bend

2757 MEWS ELECTRICAL H'CAP 7f (P)
9:20 (9:22) (Class 4) (0-85,85) 3-Y-0+ **£5,505** (£1,637; £818; £408) **Stalls** High

Form RPR
0550 1 **Purus (IRE)**[12] 2405 4-9-11 80 .... DarryllHolland 3 89
(P Mitchell) *mde all: drvn out fnl f: r.o wl* **20/1**
2305 2 ¾ **Outer Hebrides**[18] 2232 5-9-13 82 ....(vt) EddieAhern 1 89
(Stef Liddiard) *hld up on outside: hdwy to go 2nd jst ins fnl f: kpt on u.p* **11/1**
024- 3 shd **Killena Boy (IRE)**[263] 5599 4-9-12 81 .... AlanMunro 8 88+
(W Jarvis) *in tch: hdwy 2f out: edgd lft bef swtchd rt ins fnl f: r.o* **9/1**[3]
303 4 3 **Titian Dancer**[27] 1960 3-8-11 75 .... TedDurcan 9 71
(W R Swinburn) *a.p: rdn over 1f out: one pce fnl f* **4/1**[2]
21 5 nk **Third Set (IRE)**[14] 2343 3-9-7 85 .... SteveDrowne 6 89+
(R Charlton) *in tch: rdn and hld whe hmpd ins fnl f* **11/4**[1]
4556 6 5 **Katiypour (IRE)**[7] 2555 9-10-0 83 .... RichardThomas 10 68
(Miss B Sanders) *bhd: effrt over 1f out: nvr on terms* **12/1**
6003 7 2 **Silent Storm**[11] 2464 6-9-5 74 .... J-PGuillambert 7 54
(C A Cyzer) *chsd ldrs: rdn over 2f out: wknd over 1f out* **14/1**
0404 8 ½ **Play The Ball (USA)**[7] 2551 4-9-4 73 ....(b[1]) NickyMackay 5 52
(G A Butler) *a towards rr* **16/1**
2155 9 ½ **Scot Love (IRE)**[15] 2330 3-9-3 81 .... ShaneKelly 4 55
(J Noseda) *sn chsd ldrs: rdn and wknd qckly 2f out* **11/4**[1]
0005 10 16 **Chateau Nicol**[28] 1932 7-9-11 80 ....(v) TQuinn 2 16
(B G Powell) *a outpcd in rr* **16/1**

1m 26.87s (0.07) **Going Correction** +0.125s/f (Slow)
WFA 3 from 4yo+ 9lb **10** Ran SP% **122.6**
Speed ratings (Par 105):104,103,103,99,99 93,91,90,90,71
CSF £232.70 CT £2190.81 TOTE £24.30: £8.60, £3.70, £2.80; EX 437.20 Place 6 £909.23, Place 5 £497.15.
Owner J Morton **Bred** K Nercessian **Trained** Epsom, Surrey
■ Stewards' Enquiry : Eddie Ahern two-day ban: careless riding (Jul 2-3)

FOCUS
A fair handicap, run at a sound pace, and the first three came clear. The form looks straightforward, rated around the placed horses.
Scot Love(IRE) Official explanation: jockey said colt lost its action on final bend and was eased
Chateau Nicol Official explanation: jockey said gelding was never travelling
T/Plt: £823.20 to a £1 stake. Pool: £39,020.20. 34.60 winning tickets. T/Qpdt: £73.80 to a £1 stake. Pool: £2,166.90. 21.70 winning tickets. JS

2361 RIPON (R-H)
Wednesday, June 21

OFFICIAL GOING: Good to firm
Wind: Moderate across

2758 HIGH MOOR APPRENTICE (S) STKS 6f
6:40 (6:40) (Class 6) 3-4-Y-0 **£2,590** (£770; £385; £192) **Stalls** Low

Form RPR
0551 1 **Diamond Josh**[4] 2632 4-9-12 58 .... JamieHamblett 7 61+
(P D Evans) *chsd ldr stands side: hdwy to ld over 3f out: clr wl over 1f out: kpt on* **7/2**[1]
0000 2 1 ¼ **Dematraf (IRE)**[43] 1577 4-9-2 40 .... JohnCavanagh 20 47
(Ms Deborah J Evans) *led far side gpod: rdn along over 2f out: hung lft appr last: kpt on* **12/1**
0000 3 1 ¾ **Hows That**[18] 2248 4-9-2 35 ....(p) PatrickDonaghy 17 42
(K R Burke) *in tch far side: hdwy 2f out: sn rdn and kpt on ins last* **33/1**
400 4 ½ **Sounds Simla (IRE)**[11] 2462 3-9-0 74 .... JemmaMarshall 16 44
(J F Coupland) *chsd ldr far side: rdn along 2f out: kpt on same pce* **11/1**
-000 5 nk **Pontefract Glory**[19] 2192 3-9-0 39 ....(p) KMay 5 43
(M Dods) *towards rr stands side: hdwy over 2f out: sn rdn and kpt on fnl f: nrst fin* **25/1**
-630 6 nk **Rosita Mia (IRE)**[12] 2399 3-8-9 60 .... LukeMorris 15 37
(D W Barker) *dwlt: sn chsng ldrs far side: rdn along 2f out: sn one pce* **5/1**[2]

-466 **7** 2 **Desertina (IRE)**[42] 1594 4-9-2 49 LauraReynolds 2 33
(R M Whitaker) *chsd ldrs stands side: rdn along 2f out: sn no imp* **11/2**[3]

0400 **8** 1 **Moonlight Fantasy (IRE)**[19] 2195 3-9-0 49 DanielleMcCreery 3 33
(N Tinkler) *bhd stands side tl styd on fnl 2f* **20/1**

0660 **9** nk **Dispol Valentine**[2] 2699 3-8-4 38 (p) PaulPickard(5) 19 27
(P T Midgley) *dwlt: sn chsng ldrs far side: rdn along over 2f out and sn btn* **50/1**

-003 **10** 1 3/4 **Underthemistletoe (IRE)**[13] 2377 4-9-2 42 MarkCoumbe 11 24
(R E Barr) *in tch stands side: rdn along 1/2-way: n.d* **33/1**

6040 **11** shd **Roko**[18] 2245 4-9-2 37 (bt) GaryEdwards(5) 8 28
(S R Bowring) *chsd ldr stands side: rdn along wl over 2f out: sn wknd* **100/1**

0530 **12** 1 1/2 **Peggys First**[7] 2551 4-9-7 45 JamesRogers 14 24
(D E Cantillon) *in tch on outer of stands side: gp: rdn along over 2f out: sn wknd* **12/1**

0-00 **13** 1 1/4 **Graceful Flight**[50] 1391 4-8-11 39 FrankiePickard(5) 10 15
(P T Midgley) *a towards rr stands side* **100/1**

5100 **14** hd **Chairman Rick (IRE)**[7] 2544 4-9-12 47 LanceBetts 18 24
(D Nicholls) *a rr far side* **16/1**

0000 **15** shd **Kings Cavalier (USA)**[16] 2284 3-9-0 50 (v) AdeleRothery 9 17
(I W McInnes) *racd stands side: bhd fr 1/2-way* **25/1**

0-00 **16** 2 **Ms Polly Garter**[4] 2632 4-8-11 35 BarrySavage(5) 12 8
(J M Bradley) *racd stands side: bhd fr 1/2-way* **100/1**

500- **17** 2 **Inherit (IRE)**[7] 6541 4-9-7 50 MarkWaite 1 7
(B S Rothwell) *overall ldr stands side: hdd over 3f out: sn rdn and wknd over 2f out* **33/1**

3-00 **18** 1 1/2 **World At My Feet**[7] 2543 4-9-2 48 DeanHeslop 4 —
(N Bycroft) *towards rr stands side: swtchd rt and hdwy 1/2-way: sn rdn and wknd 2f out* **7/1**

0-00 **19** 11 **Just Bonnie**[8] 2531 4-9-2 32 (b) PietroRomeo(5) 13 —
(J M Bradley) *racd on outer of stands side gp: a towards rr* **100/1**

1m 12.64s (-0.36) **Going Correction** -0.175s/f (Firm)
WFA 3 from 4yo 7lb **19** Ran SP% **123.6**
Speed ratings (Par 101):95,93,91,90,89 89,86,85,85,82 82,80,79,78,78 75,73,71,56
CSF £42.02 TOTE £4.30: £2.20, £3.40, £6.50; EX 53.90.The winner was bought in for 5,200gns.
Owner Diamond Racing Ltd **Bred** J W Ford **Trained** Pandy, Abergavenny

FOCUS
This was a weak seller. They split into two, a smaller group of seven racing on the far side although the groups merged in the latter stages. Not many got into it.
Chairman Rick(IRE) Official explanation: jockey said gelding missed break
World At My Feet Official explanation: trainer said filly was badly struck into

2759 IHT FREE INVESTMENTS MEDIAN AUCTION MAIDEN STKS 5f
7:10 (7:10) (Class 5) 2-Y-O **£3,886** (£1,156; £577; £288) **Stalls** Low

Form RPR

52 **1** **Bollin Franny**[16] 2281 2-9-3 DavidAllan 9 72
(T D Easterby) *cl up: effrt over 1f out: sn rdn and kpt on to ld last 100 yds* **5/4**[1]

0 **2** nk **Ronnie Howe**[14] 2361 2-9-3 PhillipMakin 7 71
(M Dods) *cl up: led over 2f out: rdn wl over 1f out: drvn ins last: hdd and no ex last 100 yds* **11/1**

3 **3** hd **Bush Breakfast**[30] 1876 2-9-3 JimCrowley 5 70
(P Winkworth) *chsd ldrs: hdwy 2f out: rdn to chal on outer ent last and ev ch tl drvn and no ex last 100 yds* **10/1**[3]

00 **4** 1 1/2 **Dolly Coughdrop (IRE)**[21] 2139 2-8-12 PatCosgrave 4 60
(K R Burke) *chsd ldrs: hdwy 2f out: rdn and n.m.r ins last: kpt on* **18/1**

2025 **5** 3 1/2 **Fly Time**[4] 2643 2-8-12 TonyCulhane 3 47
(M R Channon) *led: rdn along 1/2-way: sn hdd & wknd over 1f out* **3/1**[2]

6 3 **Ask Yer Dad** 2-9-3 MickyFenton 10 41
(Mrs P Sly) *v s.i.s and bhd: sn pushed along: styd on appr last* **10/1**[3]

7 nk **Nomoreblondes** 2-8-12 LeeEnstone 1 35
(P T Midgley) *a towards rr* **33/1**

8 1 1/2 **The Brat** 2-8-9 PatrickMathers(3) 6 30
(James Moffatt) *in tch: rdn along 2f out: sn wknd* **20/1**

9 1 **Charleys Spirit** 2-8-12 PaulFessey 8 26
(T D Barron) *a rr* **12/1**

00 **10** 1 **Raven Rascal**[11] 2461 2-8-5 StacyRenwick(7) 2 23
(J F Coupland) *s.i.s: a rr* **100/1**

60.29 secs (0.09) **Going Correction** -0.175s/f (Firm) **10** Ran SP% **117.6**
Speed ratings (Par 93):92,91,91,88,83 78,77,75,73,72
CSF £16.88 TOTE £2.30: £1.10, £2.70, £2.70; EX 20.60.
Owner Sir Neil Westbrook **Bred** Sir & Exors Of Late Lady Westbrook **Trained** Great Habton, N Yorks

FOCUS
Shaky form, rated through the winner, with the time not backing the level up.

NOTEBOOK
Bollin Franny got off the mark at the third time of asking, hanging left a little under pressure but just getting the best of a three-sided tussle. This was a moderate race but there could be a bit more to come from him over an extra furlong. (op 2-1)
Ronnie Howe, a half-brother to two winners out of a successful sprinter, fell out of the stalls on his debut here but knew more this time. He went on with over two furlongs to run and was able to secure the rail, but after being tackled he could not quite hold on. (op 12-1)
Bush Breakfast was being pushed along before halfway but came through to hold every chance before giving best in the last half-furlong. He had no problem with this faster ground. (op 11-1)
Dolly Coughdrop(IRE) ran her best race to date on this third run but was just held when short of room behind the leading trio entering the last. (op 16-1)
Fly Time was smartly away to lead, but she did not last much beyond halfway and is not progressing. (op 5-2 tchd 10-3 in a place)
Ask Yer Dad, whose dam was a winning sister to top-class juvenile filly Pharaoh's Delight, completely missed the break and ran green in rear but did stay on past several rivals in the final furlong. He can improve for the experience. (op 9-1 tchd 8-1)

2760 NORMAN WELLS MEMORIAL CHALLENGE TROPHY H'CAP 6f
7:40 (7:40) (Class 3) (0-95,84) 3-Y-O
£9,348 (£2,799; £1,399; £700; £349; £175) **Stalls** Low

Form RPR

3-00 **1** **Mutamarres**[49] 1404 3-9-3 80 (v1) RobertWinston 2 95
(Sir Michael Stoute) *qckly away: mde all: shkn up over 1f out and styd on wl* **11/2**[3]

1152 **2** 2 1/2 **Damika (IRE)**[14] 2363 3-9-5 82 DeanMcKeown 7 89
(R M Whitaker) *a.p: effrt to chal 2f out: sn rdn and one pce appr last* **7/2**[1]

-526 **3** 4 **Call My Number (IRE)**[21] 2126 3-9-5 82 TonyCulhane 1 77
(M R Channon) *trckd ldrs: hung bdly rt frn 1/2-way: rdn wl over 1f out: styd on ins last* **5/1**[2]

0-01 **4** shd **Charlie Delta**[14] 2353 3-9-4 84 DanielTudhope(3) 4 79
(D Carroll) *in tch: hmpd 1/2-way and sn rdn along: styd on to chse ldrs over 1f out: sn drvn and one pce* **7/1**

0655 **5** 1/2 **Choysia**[13] 2385 3-9-3 80 PaulHanagan 5 73
(D W Barker) *chsd ldrs: rdn along 2f out: grad wknd* **14/1**

00-0 **6** 3 **River Kintyre**[19] 2205 3-9-5 82 MickyFenton 8 66
(B W Hills) *a rr* **25/1**

0-10 **7** nk **Greek Secret**[14] 2363 3-8-11 74 (p) DavidAllan 6 57
(T D Easterby) *in tch: rdn along over 2f out: sn wknd* **8/1**

34-6 **8** 1/2 **Mr Rooney (IRE)**[14] 2363 3-9-6 83 KDarley 3 65
(M Johnston) *cl up: rdn along wl over 2f out: sn wknd* **11/2**[3]

-006 **9** 5 **Surely Truly (IRE)**[24] 2049 3-8-7 70 (p) PatCosgrave 9 37
(K R Burke) *dwlt: sn chsng ldrs: rdn along 1/2-way: sn wknd* **12/1**

1m 11.05s (-1.95) **Going Correction** -0.175s/f (Firm) **9** Ran SP% **111.5**
Speed ratings (Par 103):106,102,97,97,96 92,92,91,84
CSF £23.79 CT £99.33 TOTE £5.70: £2.50, £1.50, £2.10; EX 17.80.
Owner Hamdan Al Maktoum **Bred** Shadwell Estate Company Limited **Trained** Newmarket, Suffolk

FOCUS
A fair handicap with improved showings from the first two.

NOTEBOOK
Mutamarres, well beaten in two runs on Kempton's Polytrack this spring, was dropping to six furlongs for the first time on this return to turf. Sharpened up by the visor, he made all on the stands' side, coming away when challenged with two furlongs to run. (op 9-2)
Damika(IRE), another 4lb higher, looked a danger at the two pole but was unable to quicken with the winner. This was a fair effort from his draw and he is still going the right way. (op 10-3)
Call My Number(IRE) tracked the leaders near the stands' rail but hung into the centre of the track under pressure. Keeping on, he will be best served by a return to seven furlongs. (op 11-2)
Charlie Delta, raised 10lb after Nottingham, was found wanting off this career-high mark. He was hampered when Call My Number began hanging, but for which he would have finished a bit closer. (op 8-1)
Choysia again shaped as if a drop back to five furlongs might be required. (op 11-1)

2761 PRICEWATERHOUSECOOPERS H'CAP 1m 1f 170y
8:10 (8:10) (Class 4) (0-85,79) 4-Y-O+ **£6,309** (£1,888; £944; £472; £235) **Stalls** High

Form RPR

-222 **1** **Folio (IRE)**[9] 2508 6-9-1 78 StephenDonohoe(5) 9 90+
(W J Musson) *hld up in rr: smooth hdwy on inner wl over 2f out: chal 1f out: shkn up to ld wl ins last* **7/2**[2]

3005 **2** nk **Little Jimbob**[13] 2387 5-9-2 74 PaulHanagan 7 86
(R A Fahey) *led: rdn along over 2f out: edgd lft and jnd 1f out: sn drvn and hdd wl ins last: kpt on* **11/4**[1]

1030 **3** 3 1/2 **Active Asset (IRE)**[13] 2387 4-9-7 79 TonyCulhane 8 84
(M R Channon) *trckd ldrs: hdwy over 2f out: rdn wl over 1f out: kpt on same pce* **5/1**[3]

0-53 **4** 1 1/4 **Wester Lodge (IRE)**[8] 2519 4-9-1 73 DavidAllan 6 76
(J M P Eustace) *in tch: hdwy 3f out: rdn along 2f out and sn one pce* **15/2**

46-5 **5** 2 **Thistle**[48] 1439 5-8-12 70 PatCosgrave 4 69
(J Howard Johnson) *trckd ldrs: effrt 3f out: rdn along 2f out and sn one pce* **22/1**

0410 **6** 1/2 **Bright Sun (IRE)**[8] 2519 5-9-0 72 (t) KimTinkler 2 70
(N Tinkler) *chsd ldr: rdn along over 2f out: sn wknd* **8/1**

00-0 **7** nk **Apsara**[7] 2540 5-8-6 64 PaulQuinn 5 61
(G M Moore) *keen: hld up: a rr* **33/1**

60-5 **8** 5 **Low Cloud**[135] 319 6-8-7 65 (p) JimmyQuinn 3 53
(J J Quinn) *a rr* **20/1**

-000 **9** 6 **Dancer's Serenade (IRE)**[16] 2296 4-9-3 75 RobertWinston 1 51
(T P Tate) *dwlt: sn in tch: effrt on outer over 3f out: sn rdn and btn* **7/1**

2m 2.45s (-2.55) **Going Correction** -0.10s/f (Good) **9** Ran SP% **113.0**
Speed ratings (Par 105):106,105,102,101,100 99,99,95,90
CSF £12.83 CT £46.14 TOTE £4.50: £1.50, £1.90, £1.60; EX 14.00.
Owner Goodey and Broughton **Bred** Lord Rothschild **Trained** Newmarket, Suffolk

FOCUS
An ordinary handicap, although one or two went into the race on nice marks. The third is the best guide to the form.

2762 NORTHGATE INFORMATION SOLUTIONS H'CAP 1m 4f 10y
8:40 (8:40) (Class 5) (0-75,74) 4-Y-O+ **£3,886** (£1,156; £577; £288) **Stalls** High

Form RPR

0601 **1** **Hezaam (USA)**[14] 2362 5-8-3 56 PaulFessey 6 63+
(Mrs A Duffield) *set stdy pce: rdn along over 2f out: drvn and edgd lft over 1f out: styd on gamely ins last* **7/2**[2]

3022 **2** 3/4 **Intavac Boy**[5] 2612 5-8-2 55 oh1 JoeFanning 3 61
(C W Thornton) *trckd wnr: effrt to chal over 2f out: sn rdn: drvn and ev ch ins last: no ex towards fin* **9/4**[1]

0-00 **3** 1 **Leslingtaylor (IRE)**[25] 2018 4-8-12 65 TomEaves 7 69
(J J Quinn) *trckd ldng pair: effrt 3f out: rdn along 2f out and kpt on same pce appr last* **12/1**

5-00 **4** nk **Estrelle (GER)**[45] 1502 4-9-3 70 JimmyQuinn 5 74
(H R A Cecil) *trckd ldrs: hdwy 3f out: rdn 2f out: kpt on same pce* **4/1**[3]

-360 **5** 1 1/2 **To Arms**[5] 2612 4-8-6 59 DavidAllan 2 61+
(T D Easterby) *hld up towards rr: effrt 3f out: sn rdn and no imp appr last* **10/1**

-353 **6** 3 **Merrymaker**[15] 2326 6-9-7 74 KDarley 1 71
(W M Brisbourne) *hld up: a rr* **9/2**

-200 **7** nk **Dayoff (IRE)**[8] 2522 5-8-2 55 oh3 (v) PaulHanagan 4 51
(P D Evans) *in tch: rdn along 3f out: wknd fnl 2f* **16/1**

2m 35.34s (-1.66) **Going Correction** -0.10s/f (Good) **7** Ran SP% **113.8**
Speed ratings (Par 103):101,100,99,99,98 96,96
CSF £11.71 TOTE £3.60: £1.70, £2.30; EX 8.10.
Owner Six Iron Partnership **Bred** Shadwell Farm LLC **Trained** Constable Burton, N Yorks

FOCUS
A modest handicap run at a steady pace and the first four raced in the same order virtually throughout. The winner has become well handicapped and the second and third ran to form.
Dayoff(IRE) Official explanation: jockey said mare was unsuited by undulating track

2763 COVERDALE MAIDEN STKS 6f
9:10 (9:10) (Class 5) 3-Y-O **£3,886** (£1,156; £577; £288) **Stalls** Low

Form RPR

3 **1** **Home Sweet Home (IRE)**[13] 2383 3-8-12 RobertWinston 4 76
(P D Evans) *a.p: hdwy to ld wl over 1f out: rdn clr ent last* **7/2**[3]

32 **2** 4 **Libor (IRE)**[14] 2356 3-9-3 KDarley 12 69+
(L M Cumani) *chsd ldrs: rdn along over 2f out: drvn and kpt on same pce appr last* **15/8**[1]

00 **3** nk **Cabriole**[20] 2167 3-8-12 JimmyQuinn 3 63
(H R A Cecil) *in tch: hdwy over 2f out: swtchd rt and rdn over 1f out: kpt on same pce appr last* **9/1**

22-4 **4** *nk* **Namu**[20] 2167 3-8-12 72 TonyCulhane 2 62
(B W Hills) *led: rdn along over 2f out: hdd wl over 1f out and grad wknd* **11/4**[2]

5 *5* **Question (USA)** 3-8-12 JimCrowley 5 47
(J M Bradley) *midfield: hdwy to chse ldrs 2f out: swtchd rt and rdn over 1f out: wknd ent last* **66/1**

0 **6** *½* **Im Ova Ere Dad (IRE)**[13] 2383 3-9-3 DaleGibson 15 51
(D E Cantillon) *bhd tl styd on fnl 2f* **50/1**

5-5 **7** *1¼* **Mujeak (IRE)**[61] 1127 3-9-3 PaulHanagan 11 47
(J J Quinn) *chsd ldrs: rdn along over 2f out: sn wknd* **18/1**

50 **8** *½* **Liskaveen Beauty**[13] 2383 3-8-12 MickyFenton 10 40
(T J Fitzgerald) *bhd tl sme late hdwy* **40/1**

00 **9** *4* **Wilmas Gal**[31] 1868 3-8-12 (t) RoystonFfrench 1 28
(R Bastiman) *a rr* **100/1**

000- **10** *hd* **Beverley Hills (IRE)**[250] 5881 3-8-7 40 GregFairley(5) 16 28
(J Howard Johnson) *a towards rr* **100/1**

11 *5* **One More Than Ten** 3-9-3 DavidAllan 9 18+
(T D Easterby) *s.i.s: a rr* **66/1**

04 **12** *5* **Mandarin Lady**[23] 2080 3-8-12 TomEaves 8 —+
(Miss J A Camacho) *dwlt: a rr* **14/1**

0-0 **13** *¾* **Automation**[21] 2129 3-8-9 DanielTudhope(3) 14 —
(C W Thornton) *a towards rr* **100/1**

5 **14** *4* **Decider (USA)**[11] 2445 3-9-0 EdwardCreighton(3) 7 —
(J M Bradley) *chsd ldrs to 1/2-way: sn wknd and eased over 1f out* **66/1**

1m 12.16s (-0.84) **Going Correction** -0.175s/f (Firm) **14 Ran SP% 117.4**
Speed ratings (Par 99):98,92,92,91,85 84,82,82,76,76 69,63,62,56
CSF £9.97 TOTE £4.70: £1.90, £1.30, £3.10; EX 8.50 Place 6 £9.62, Place 5 £3.46.
Owner John P Jones **Bred** Western Bloodstock **Trained** Pandy, Abergavenny

FOCUS
Probably an ordinary maiden, with the time on a par with the seller. The sixth and tenth limit the form.
Liskaveen Beauty Official explanation: jockey said filly was unsuited by undulating track
One More Than Ten Official explanation: jockey said gelding ran green
Decider(USA) Official explanation: jockey said colt bolted to post and hung left-handed during race
T/Plt: £6.60 to a £1 stake. Pool: £44,938.65 - 4,935.85 winning units T/Qpdt: £2.30 to a £1 stake. Pool: £2,988.60 - 950.65 winning units JR

2739 ASCOT (R-H)
Thursday, June 22

OFFICIAL GOING: Good to firm
Wind: Moderate; half against Weather: Fine

2771 NORFOLK STKS (GROUP 2) 5f
2:35 (2:35) (Class 1) 2-Y-O

£39,746 (£15,064; £7,539; £3,759; £1,883; £945) **Stalls** Low

Form RPR

1 **1** **Dutch Art**[17] 2300 2-9-1 AlanMunro 3 106+
(P W Chapple-Hyam) *lw: hld up: swtchd rt and effrt 2f out: prog over 1f out: hanging rt but led ent fnl f: r.o wl* **11/4**[2]

211 **2** *1¾* **Hoh Mike (IRE)**[31] 1897 2-9-1 JamieSpencer 4 106+
(M L W Bell) *lw: hld up in rr: effrt against nr side rail over 1f out and nowhere to go: swtchd rt and r.o wl to take 2nd last 100yds: n* **2/1**[1]

122 **3** *1* **Cav Okay (IRE)**[24] 2084 2-9-1 RyanMoore 5 96
(R Hannon) *lw: w ldr: led wl over 1f out: hdd and outpcd ent fnl f* **22/1**

11 **4** *2* **Sonny Red (IRE)**[27] 1977 2-9-1 RichardHughes 1 89
(R Hannon) *lw: trckd ldrs: effrt against nr side rail over 1f out: kpt on same pce fnl f* **9/2**[3]

1 **5** *2½* **Strategic Prince**[35] 1796 2-9-1 LDettori 10 80
(P F I Cole) *lw: racd on outer: in tch: rdn bef 1/2-way: hanging rt and outpcd over 1f out* **12/1**

212 **6** *½* **Mood Music**[22] 2127 2-9-1 RichardMullen 2 78
(E J O'Neill) *trckd ldrs: n.m.r jst over 2f out: rdn and edgd rt 1f out: wknd* **40/1**

1 **7** *1½* **Holdin Foldin (IRE)**[19] 2241 2-9-1 PatCosgrave 7 73
(K R Burke) *lw: trckd ldrs: rdn wl over 1f out: wknd fnl f* **12/1**

8 *2* **City Of Tribes (IRE)**[16] 2333 2-9-1 JMurtagh 11 66
(G M Lyons, Ire) *neat: prom on outer: rdn over 1f out: wknd* **11/1**

4210 **9** *1¼* **Scented Present**[2] 2724 2-9-1 (b[1]) PJSmullen 9 61
(B J Meehan) *lw: led to wl over 1f out: wknd and eased* **66/1**

10 *3½* **Take To The Skies (IRE)** 2-9-1 KFallon 6 48
(A P Jarvis) *rangy: scope: lw: s.s: outpcd and detached in last: nvr a factor* **25/1**

4054 **11** *5* **Loves Bidding**[9] 2517 2-9-1 SteveDrowne 8 30
(R Ingram) *in tch tl wknd rapidly jst over 2f out* **100/1**

61.03 secs (-0.37) **Going Correction** +0.025s/f (Good) **11 Ran SP% 115.0**
Speed ratings (Par 105):103,100,98,95,91 90,88,85,83,77 69
CSF £8.02 TOTE £3.80: £1.60, £1.40, £5.80; EX 6.20 Trifecta £105.90 Pool: £6,274.59 - 42.06 winning units.
Owner Mrs Susan Roy **Bred** Cromlech Bloodstock **Trained** Newmarket, Suffolk

FOCUS
The fast ground made this a real test of speed. Dutch Art confirmed the big impression he made on his Windsor debut, but Hoh Mike would have given him more to do with a clear run and has been rated upsides him. The winning time was about par for a race like this.

NOTEBOOK
Dutch Art has been sold since his debut win at Windsor over subsequent Queen Mary Stakes runner-up Simply Perfect. He followed up in good style, coming wide for a clear run and keeping on for a comfortable victory, and while the favourite did not get the best of runs he won on merit. He should continue to improve. (op 5-2 tchd 3-1 in places)
Hoh Mike(IRE) ◆ suffered his only previous defeat at the hands of Elhamri, who won the Windsor Castle this week. Held up in the rear, he tried for a run up the fence but was shut off by Sonny Red. Switched, he was only ninth passing the final furlong but finished well, if too late to trouble the winner. He can make amends. (op 9-4 tchd 5-2)
Cav Okay(IRE) appreciated this much quicker surface and ran his best race since his taking debut at Newbury, showing plenty of dash and keeping on, only losing out on second in the last half-furlong. The Molecomb at Goodwood could be the race for him. (tchd 20-1 and 25-1)
Sonny Red(IRE), unbeaten in two starts in soft ground, did not prove quite as effective on this sound surface. (op 4-1)
Strategic Prince ran here rather than in the Coventry Stakes following a mix-up with the entries. Hanging when under pressure, he really could have done with the sixth furlong.
Mood Music ran as well as could be expected against this better class of opponent. (op 33-1)
Holdin Foldin(IRE), who beat a subsequent selling winner on his debut at Musselburgh, was not disgraced in this very different company. (op 16-1)
City Of Tribes(IRE), who made a winning debut at Tipperary, faded after showing pace on the outside of the bunch. (op 10-1)
Scented Present, who beat only one home in the Windsor Castle on the second day of the meeting, showed pace in the first-time blinkers before dropping away.

2772 RIBBLESDALE STKS (GROUP 2) (FILLIES) 1m 4f
3:10 (3:11) (Class 1) 3-Y-O

£79,543 (£30,147; £15,087; £7,522; £3,768; £1,891) **Stalls** High

Form RPR

5-12 **1** **Mont Etoile (IRE)**[43] 1583 3-8-12 88 MichaelHills 1 112+
(W J Haggas) *b.hind: lw: swtchd rt s: hld up in rr: nt clr run under 2f out and again whn hdwy over 1f out: str run wl ins fnl f to ld nr fin* **25/1**

12-1 **2** *nk* **Scottish Stage (IRE)**[34] 1819 3-8-12 101 KFallon 10 111+
(Sir Michael Stoute) *lw: midfield: hdwy whn nt clr run over 2f out: running on whn nt clr run and swtchd rt to ld briefly wl ins fnl f: nt qckn* **5/2**[1]

5-23 **3** *¾* **Maroussies Wings (IRE)**[36] 1777 3-8-12 91 KDarley 8 108
(P C Haslam) *racd keenly: trckd ldrs: rdn to ld over 1f out: edgd lft ins fnl f: sn hdd: hld cl home* **25/1**

-353 **4** *½* **High Heel Sneakers**[7] 2582 3-8-12 102 RyanMoore 2 107
(P F I Cole) *lw: hld up: pushed along and hdwy on outside 2f out: edgd rt whn chsd ldrs over 1f out: ch ins fnl f: nt qckn cl hme* **14/1**

1-1 **5** *nk* **Reunite (IRE)**[6] 2613 3-8-12 80 LDettori 7 107
(Saeed Bin Suroor) *lw: midfield: effrt whn nt clr run 2f out: hdwy to chse ldrs over 1f out: ch ins fnl f: no ex cl home* **7/1**

21 **6** *nk* **Quenched**[15] 2350 3-8-12 RichardHughes 3 106
(J H M Gosden) *lw: prom: led over 2f out: rdn and hdd over 1f out: stl cl up but hld whn bmpd wl ins fnl f* **6/1**[3]

-440 **7** *1¼* **Suzy Bliss**[20] 2199 3-8-12 95 KerrinMcEvoy 11 104
(W R Swinburn) *hld up: nt clr run over 1f out: sn rdn and swtchd lft: kpt on ins fnl f: nvr able to chal* **33/1**

1 **8** *shd* **Novellara**[35] 1797 3-8-12 88 EddieAhern 6 104
(H R A Cecil) *midfield: rdn and hdwy 2f out: sn chsd ldrs: no ex ins fnl f* **11/1**

32 **9** *3* **Park Esteem (IRE)**[29] 1942 3-8-12 DarryllHolland 4 99
(J Noseda) *b.hind: led: pushed along over 3f out: hdd over 2f out: wknd over 1f out* **20/1**

1-1 **10** *2½* **Alessandria**[29] 1942 3-8-12 98 JamieSpencer 5 95
(E A L Dunlop) *lw: hld up in midfield: effrt 2f out: no imp whn faltered over 1f out: sn wknd* **4/1**[2]

14-1 **11** *3* **Sindirana (IRE)**[40] 1669 3-8-12 92 CSoumillon 9 99+
(Sir Michael Stoute) *lw: racd keenly: trckd ldrs: rdn and ch whn nt clr run and swtchd lft over 1f out: sn wknd: eased fnl f* **6/1**[3]

2m 30.23s (-2.77) **Going Correction** +0.05s/f (Good) **11 Ran SP% 120.0**
Speed ratings (Par 108):111,110,110,109,109 109,108,108,106,105 103
CSF £85.83 TOTE £35.50: £7.20, £1.50, £7.50; EX 141.40 Trifecta £1671.60 Pool: £6,121.46 - 2.60 winning units.
Owner Tony Hirschfeld Des Scott L K Piggott **Bred** Paget Bloodstock **Trained** Newmarket, Suffolk

FOCUS
Just an ordinary renewal of this Group 2, with the best previous form being at Listed level. It was a somewhat rough race, and there was a 15-minute enquiry befor the result was made official. The gallop was sound enough and the time up to par for the type of contest.

NOTEBOOK
Mont Etoile(IRE), who is beautifully bred, has really come to herself this season since stepping up to middle-distances. She was switched in behind her field from her outside draw, followed the favourite through, and despite trouble in running, produced the best turn of foot to get up close home. She is going the right way and the Irish Oaks could be on the agenda, although she will need to be supplemented. Races such as the Yorkshire Oaks and Park Hill are alternatives. (tchd 33-1)
Scottish Stage(IRE) ◆, who missed the Oaks, like the winner did not get the best of luck in running but looked to be coming to win her race when the winner pounced. She is still quite inexperienced and did not look entirely happy on the fast ground, but is still progressing and the Irish Oaks could give her an opportunity to gain compensation, especially as the track may suit her better. (op 3-1 tchd 10-3 in places)
Maroussies Wings(IRE) ◆, who finished third, with the subsequent Oaks winner in second, in the Musidora last time, proved that was no fluke with another fine display. She made a bold bid for home halfway up the straight only to be collared by the fast finishers late on. She deserves to win a Pattern race and the Lancashire Oaks in a couple of weeks represents a suitable opportunity.
High Heel Sneakers, stepping up in trip, is a pretty consistent sort at Pattern level and ran her race again, having had only the winner behind her turning in. She just seems to lack the extra gear that could win her races in this company but the Listed Galtres Stakes at York may represent a decent opportunity for her. (op 25-1)
Reunite(IRE), a previously unbeaten half-sister to the French Derby winner Anabaa Blue, was stepping up in trip and grade having easily won a handicap off a mark of 80 last time. She arguably limits the form, but she has plenty of potential and was another who did not get the best of runs. With her effort having flattened out in the closing stages, it would be no surprise to see her dropped back in trip next time. (op 6-1)
Quenched, another stepping up in trip and grade, ran a fine race, having been prominent throughout. She took the lead early in the straight and stuck to her task once headed, but suffered a little in the scrimmaging as the first two came through. She looks capable of winning in Pattern company if continuing to go the right way after this. (op 5-1 tchd 13-2)
Suzy Bliss was another who ran a bit better than the bare facts suggest in this messy race.
Alessandria, held up off the pace, appeared to be travelling well turning in but dropped away as if something was amiss. Official explanation: jockey said filly never travelled (tchd 9-2 and 5-1 in places)
Sindirana(IRE) was close enough for much of the way, but got hampered and faded in the straight and was allowed to come home in her own time. (tchd 13-2 and 7-1 in places)

2773 GOLD CUP (GROUP 1) 2m 4f
3:50 (3:51) (Class 1) 4-Y-O+

£136,953 (£51,906; £25,977; £12,952; £6,488; £3,256) **Stalls** High

Form RPR

046- **1** **Yeats (IRE)**[242] 6059 5-9-2 KFallon 8 123+
(A P O'Brien, Ire) *sn settled in 4th: effrt over 3f out: led over 2f out: rdn clr and in n.d over 1f out* **7/1**

6-33 **2** *4* **Reefscape**[32] 1875 5-9-2 CSoumillon 2 119+
(A Fabre, France) *lw: sn settled in 7th: lost pl and 9th 4f out: effrt whn forced wd and bmpd bnd over 2f out: kpt on fnl 2f to take 2nd nr fin* **10/3**[2]

60-1 **3** *hd* **Distinction (IRE)**[33] 1839 7-9-2 117 MJKinane 4 117
(Sir Michael Stoute) *lw: sn settled in 5th: effrt 3f out: rdn to chse wnr wl over 1f out : no imp: lost 2nd nr fin* **5/2**[1]

40-5 **4** *3* **High Action (USA)**[33] 1839 6-9-2 101 RichardHughes 3 114
(Ian Williams) *lw: sn led: rdn and hdd over 2f out: one pce after* **100/1**

1-42 **5** *1½* **Sergeant Cecil**[34] 1833 7-9-2 111 AlanMunro 11 112
(B R Millman) *lw: keen early: hld up in 10th: prog 4f out: bmpd bnd over 2f out: rdn and no imp ldrs fnl 2f* **5/1**[3]

/23- **6** *¾* **Guadalajara (GER)**[264] 5639 5-8-13 108 LDettori 12 109+
(Saeed Bin Suroor) *w'like: lw: keen early: hld up in 8th: prog to 5th 4f out: bmpd bnd over 2f out: nt qckn and btn sn after: fdd* **12/1**

30-3 **7** *5* **Barolo**[24] 2085 7-9-2 109 .... JMurtagh 7 106
(W R Swinburn) *sn restrained into 6th: rdn over 4f out: struggling whn bmpd bnd over 2f out: wknd* **25/1**

2-21 **8** *nk* **Tungsten Strike (USA)**[24] 2085 5-9-2 106 .... RyanMoore 6 106
(Mrs A J Perrett) *lw: s.s: sn trckd ldng pair: chsd ldr 8f out: rdn over 4f out: wknd 2f out* **8/1**

0502 **9** *19* **Winged D'Argent (IRE)**[24] 2085 5-9-2 108 .... JoeFanning 5 85
(M Johnston) *sn trckd ldr: lost 2nd 8f out: rdn over 4f out: struggling whn jinked lft and set off chain reaction bnd over 2f out: t.o* **33/1**

-511 **10** *3* **Akarem**[26] 2010 5-9-2 .... PatCosgrave 10 81
(K R Burke) *lw: settled in 11th: brief effrt 4f out: wknd over 2f out: t.o* **40/1**

-606 **11** *129* **Motafarred (IRE)**[14] 2387 4-9-0 75 .... NCallan 9 —
(Micky Hammond) *last after 6f: struggling 6f out: wknd 3f out: t.o and walked last f* **200/1**

3/51 **P** **Media Puzzle (USA)**[22] 2154 9-9-2 .... (b) PJSmullen 1 —
(D K Weld, Ire) *settled in 9th: rdn 5f out: sn btn: poor 11th whn broke down and p.u nr fin: dead* **16/1**

4m 20.45s (-4.15) **Going Correction** +0.05s/f (Good)
WFA 4 from 5yo+ 2lb **12** Ran SP% **116.2**
Speed ratings (Par 117):110,108,108,107,106 106,104,104,96,95 —,—
CSF £29.17 TOTE £8.80: £2.60, £1.50, £1.40; EX 37.30 Trifecta £69.80 Pool: £8,374.70 - 85.07 winning units.
Owner Mrs John Magnier & Mrs David Nagle **Bred** Barronstown Stud & Orpendale **Trained** Ballydoyle, Co Tipperary
■ Stewards' Enquiry : L Dettori two-day ban: careless riding (Jul 3-4)

FOCUS
The pace was sound, but this was by no means a strong renewal, and the proximity of fourth-placed High Action is an obvious concern. Yeats has been rated to last year's Coronation Cup level.

NOTEBOOK
Yeats(IRE), last year's Coronation Cup winner, had been off the track since October. Unproven over this far, but ridden as if the trip would not be a problem, he quickened to the front approaching the final quarter-mile and drew clear to win very comfortably. A class act in this division, he has the Melbourne Cup as his principal target. (op 13-2)
Reefscape has plenty of form in easy ground but is also well at home on a sound surface. After losing his pitch with half a mile to run, he was then caught up in the trouble on the home turn before staying on to take second near the line, never posing a threat to the winner. He is a most consistent performer. (op 7-2 tchd 4-1 in places and 3-1 in places)
Distinction(IRE) was runner-up to Westerner in this event a year ago at York. He ran a solid race but, after chasing the winner to no avail through the last couple of furlongs, he was just run out of second. The Goodwood Cup, a race he won last year, is his next target. (tchd 11-4)
High Action(USA), who set a decent pace, came back to his field from Swinley Bottom and was headed by the winner early in the straight, but stuck on well to see out this marathon trip. This was a career-best effort.
Sergeant Cecil, trying this trip for the first time, was involved in the scrimmaging turning in and could make no further progress. As admirable a performer as he is, he is unlikely to have too much improvement in him at seven and may be a little hard to place successfully. (op 9-2 tchd 11-2 in places)
Guadalajara(GER) was formerly with Peter Schiergen in Germany then Jean-Claude Rouget in France. Having her first run of the year and stepping up a mile in trip, she was another involved in the trouble on the home turn - her rider was judged to be at fault - and she did not really get home. (op 20-1)
Barolo had to prove himself at this trip but was in trouble before stamina became an issue. (op 40-1)
Tungsten Strike(USA) had been in good form and looked sure to give a good acount of himself, but he was feeling the pace on the turn and surprisingly didn't get home. Official explanation: jockey said gelding had no more to give (tchd 9-1 in places)
Winged D'Argent(IRE) was already struggling when deemed to have been pushed against the rail on the home turn.
Akarem never looked like justifying the outlay on his supplementary entry. (op 50-1)
Media Puzzle(USA), only the second European horse to win the Melbourne Cup, sadly suffered a fatal injury to his near-fore close to the line. (op 20-1)

2774 BRITANNIA STKS (HERITAGE H'CAP) (C&G) 1m (S)
4:25 (4:33) (Class 2) (0-105,100) 3-Y-O
£34,276 (£10,263; £5,131; £2,568; £1,281; £643) **Stalls** Low

Form RPR

1-12 **1** **Sir Gerard**[26] 2024 3-8-12 **91** .... JamieSpencer 2 106+
(J R Fanshawe) *lw: racd nr side: hld up: hdwy whn nt clr run and swtchd rt over 2f out: r.o to ld ins fnl f: rdn out* **9/2**[1]

-142 **2** *2* **Easy Air**[30] 1924 3-8-11 **90** .... LDettori 5 101+
(E A L Dunlop) *lw: racd nr side: midfield: rdn and hdwy whn nt clr run over 2f out: r.o ins fnl f: nt rch wnr* **14/1**

-413 **3** *nk* **Upper Hand**[36] 1776 3-9-6 **99** .... TonyCulhane 21 109
(M R Channon) *lw: unruly in stalls: racd nr side: midfield: hdwy over 2f out: rdn to ld overall over 1f out: hdd ins fnl f: no ex cl h* **66/1**

0-21 **4** *hd* **Smart Enough**[27] 1978 3-8-7 **86** .... KerrinMcEvoy 14 96
(M A Magnusson) *racd nr side: led overall: rdn and hdd over 1f out: styd on same pce ins fnl f* **16/1**

-020 **5** *shd* **Regal Royale**[19] 2224 3-8-12 **91** .... MJKinane 8 100+
(Sir Michael Stoute) *lw: racd nr side: hld up: hdwy whn nt clr run and swtchd rt 2f out: r.o ins fnl f: nt rch ldrs* **20/1**

12-3 **6** *1 ½* **Jumbajukiba**[26] 2033 3-8-10 **89** ow1 .... JMurtagh 6 94+
(Mrs A J Perrett) *racd nr side: hld up: rdn 2f out: hdwy wl over 1f out: styd on ins fnl f* **25/1**

1213 **7** *shd* **Kalankari (IRE)**[26] 2024 3-9-0 **93** .... PaulHanagan 10 99
(A M Balding) *lw: racd nr side: trckd ldrs: effrt to chal over 2f out: kpt on same pce ins fnl f* **22/1**

02-1 **8** *nk* **Supaseus**[40] 1680 3-8-8 **87** .... SteveDrowne 19 92
(H Morrison) *lw: racd nr side: in tch: rdn over 1f out: kpt on same pce ins fnl f* **14/1**

02-1 **9** *nk* **Master Pegasus**[33] 1845 3-8-7 **86** .... AlanMunro 1 90
(C F Wall) *lw: racd nr side: hld up: hdwy 2f out: swtchd rt over 1f out: kpt on ins fnl f: nt rch ldrs* **33/1**

-23 **10** *1 ¾* **Dark Islander (IRE)**[30] 1924 3-9-1 **94** .... EddieAhern 4 94
(J W Hills) *racd nr side: in tch: rdn to chse ldrs 2f out: no ex ins fnl f* **20/1**

0400 **11** *1 ½* **Guest Connections**[5] 2649 3-9-0 **93** .... CraigAWilliams 13 90
(M R Channon) *racd nr side: midfield: rdn 2f out: one pce fnl f* **100/1**

1-31 **12** *hd* **Dunelight (IRE)**[47] 1490 3-9-1 **94** .... PhilipRobinson 18 90
(C G Cox) *lw: racd nr side: prom: rdn and ev ch 2f out: fdd ins fnl f* **12/1**[3]

-120 **13** *½* **Porters (USA)**[50] 1404 3-8-10 **89** .... RichardHughes 17 84
(R Hannon) *s.s: qckly swtchd lft to r nr side: towards rr: hdwy 2f out: edgd rt over 1f out: nvr trbld ldrs* **100/1**

-221 **14** *2 ½* **Plum Pudding (IRE)**[40] 1681 3-8-11 **90** .... RyanMoore 3 80
(R Hannon) *lw; racd nr side: prom: rdn 2f out: wknd fnl f* **15/2**[2]

-132 **15** *2* **Crime Scene (IRE)**[5] 2659 3-8-11 **90** .... DarryllHolland 16 75
(M Johnston) *racd nr side: hld up: rdn over 1f out: no imp* **16/1**

0165 **16** *5* **Dingaan (IRE)**[20] 2204 3-9-0 **93** .... (p) ChrisCatlin 22 66
(A M Balding) *lw: s.s: racd nr side: midfield: rdn 2f out: nvr on terms* **100/1**

-521 **17** *1* **Layazaal (IRE)**[28] 1951 3-9-3 **96** .... RHills 11 67
(J L Dunlop) *racd nr side: midfield: rdn over 2f out: sn bmpd: n.d* **20/1**

15-1 **18** *¾* **Archerfield Links (USA)**[68] 1016 3-8-11 **90** .... CSoumillon 12 59
(N A Callaghan) *lw: racd nr side: hld up: effrt and sme hdwy over 2f out: eased whn no imp over 1f out* **12/1**[3]

3-35 **19** *1* **Zato (IRE)**[61] 1131 3-9-7 **100** .... TedDurcan 28 67
(M R Channon) *swtchd qckly lft to r nr side: hld up: rdn and sme hdwy over 1f out: wknd fnl f* **100/1**

6-55 **20** *shd* **Champions Gallery**[28] 1951 3-8-11 **90** .... TQuinn 30 57
(D R C Elsworth) *qckly swtchd lft to r nr side: hld up: rdn over 2f out: wl btn fnl f* **33/1**

0-02 **21** *1* **Military Cross**[19] 2224 3-9-2 **95** .... KFallon 15 60
(W J Haggas) *lw: racd nr side: hld up: nt clr run and hmpd over 2f out: eased whn n.d over 1f out* **12/1**[3]

61-3 **22** *2 ½* **Giganticus (USA)**[65] 1067 3-9-1 **94** .... MichaelHills 29 53+
(B W Hills) *racd far side: trckd ldr: led sole rival on that side 3f out: nvr on terms w nr side gp: 1st of 2 in gp* **12/1**[3]

0-16 **23** *1 ½* **Gandor (IRE)**[41] 1627 3-8-10 **89** .... JimmyFortune 25 44
(J H M Gosden) *racd nr side: rdn over 2f out: wknd over 1f out* **20/1**

-115 **24** *¾* **Peppertree Lane (IRE)**[26] 2024 3-8-12 **91** .... KDarley 26 45
(M Johnston) *racd nr side: midfield: rdn over 2f out: wknd over 1f out* **20/1**

1232 **25** *¾* **Direct Debit (IRE)**[49] 1440 3-8-9 **88** .... RobertWinston 9 40
(M L W Bell) *racd nr side: midfield: rdn over 2f out: wknd and eased over 1f out* **33/1**

512 **26** *5* **Motaraqeb**[26] 2033 3-8-8 **87** .... (t) MartinDwyer 7 27
(Sir Michael Stoute) *lw: racd nr side: s.i.s: a bhd* **14/1**

-300 **27** *3 ½* **Dubai Typhoon (USA)**[20] 2205 3-8-13 **92** .... RichardMullen 20 24
(C E Brittain) *racd nr side: hld up: pushed along 1/2-way: nvr on terms* **100/1**

0-04 **28** *6* **Art Market (CAN)**[20] 2204 3-9-4 **97** .... (b) NCallan 24 16
(P F I Cole) *lw: racd nr side: prom: rdn over 3f out: wknd over 2f out* **100/1**

00-2 **29** *1 ¾* **Desert Realm (IRE)**[9] 2527 3-9-2 **95** .... JoeFanning 23 10
(M Johnston) *racd nr side: midfield: rdn over 3f out: wknd over 2f out* **33/1**

4-45 **30** *¾* **Bonnie Prince Blue**[34] 1832 3-8-7 **86** .... WSupple 27 —+
(B W Hills) *racd far side: led sole rival on that side to 3f out: bhd after: 2nd of 2 in gp* **100/1**

1m 39.87s (-1.93) **Going Correction** +0.025s/f (Good) **30** Ran SP% **144.7**
Speed ratings (Par 105):110,108,107,107,107 105,105,105,105,103 101,101,101,98,96 91,90,90,89,88 87,85,83,83,82 77,73
CSF £60.54 CT £3876.18 TOTE £4.50: £1.50, £3.60, £12.70, £4.70; EX 74.30 Trifecta £6077.20 Part won. Pool: £8,559.50 - 0.20 winning units..
Owner Miss Rose-Anne Galligan **Bred** Whitsbury Manor Stud And Stowell Hill Ltd **Trained** Newmarket, Suffolk

FOCUS
The winning time was decent for a race like this. All bar two of the field raced on the stands' side. This is usually a strong handicap, and a positive view has been taken of the form, with the first six all improving.

NOTEBOOK
Sir Gerard ◆, put up 5lb after his unlucky second at Haydock, was held up at the rear of the pack. Switched out and making rapid headway, he led inside the last for a ready victory. He can rate higher still. (op 11-2 tchd 6-1)
Easy Air was experiencing a sound surface for the first time on only his second run on turf. Well drawn, he had to wait for a run but was finishing well along the rail. There should be a good handicap in him.
Upper Hand played up in the stalls again. Returning to a mile, he showed narrowly in front going to the furlong pole but could not hold on. This was a fine effort at the weights. (tchd 100-1)
Smart Enough needed the help of a Monty Roberts rug to enter the stalls. On his handicap debut, he made the running and stuck on surprisingly well when headed. (tchd 18-1)
Regal Royale was running on strongly at the end and just missed the frame. A step back up to ten furlongs should suit him.
Jumbajukiba ◆, back on fast ground, made up a lot of ground from the rear near the rail but was a little short of room inside the last and his rider was not too hard on him from then on.
Kalankari(IRE), up another 3lb, ran a decent race without being able to turn around Haydock form with Sir Gerard. (op 25-1)
Supaseus ran a decent race on this handicap debut and can be placed to advantage at a slightly lesser level. (tchd 16-1)
Master Pegasus was keeping on at the finish and by no means disgraced.
Dunelight(IRE), racing prominently but never able to get to the front, could not defy a 6lb higher mark in this stronger grade. (tchd 14-1 in places)
Porters(USA), whose last seven races had been on Polytrack, did well to reach his final position after fluffing the start.
Plum Pudding(IRE), who went up 10lb for winning at Newmarket, might have found this ground too fast. (op 10-1)
Military Cross shaped better than his finishing position suggests as the breaks never came. Official explanation: jockey said gelding was denied a clear run (op 11-1)
Giganticus(USA) found himself racing down the far side with only his stablemate for company and this is best ignored.

2775 HAMPTON COURT STKS (LISTED RACE) 1m 2f
4:55 (5:10) (Class 1) 3-Y-O
£31,229 (£11,836; £5,923; £2,953; £1,479; £742) **Stalls** High

Form RPR

3130 **1** **Snoqualmie Boy**[19] 2228 3-8-11 90 .... JohnEgan 10 109
(D R C Elsworth) *lw: trckd ldng quartet: rdn and effrt 2f out: led 1f out: drvn out* **33/1**

1 **2** *½* **Petrovich (USA)**[64] 1088 3-8-11 .... KFallon 14 108+
(J Noseda) *lw: trckd ldng pair: shkn up and nt qckn 2f out: rallied to chse wnr ins fnl f: gaining at fin* **7/2**[2]

-120 **3** *1* **Hazeymm (IRE)**[18] 2278 3-8-11 107 .... TedDurcan 12 106
(M R Channon) *t.k.h: led at stdy pce: kicked on 3f out: hdd 1f out: kpt on fnl f but a jst outpcd* **11/1**

-610 **4** *nk* **Mulaqat**[19] 2226 3-9-2 104 .... MartinDwyer 6 111+
(M P Tregoning) *lw: swtchd to inner after s and hld up in rr: hmpd after 1f: nt clr run over 2f out: r.o wl fr over 1f out: nrst fin* **16/1**

-331 **5** *nk* **Mashaahed**[21] 2175 3-8-11 102 .... RHills 13 105
(B W Hills) *sn trckd ldr: chal 2f out and upsides to 1f out: one pce fnl f* **16/1**

112 **6** ¾ **Ivy Creek (USA)**[41] 1627 3-8-11 109 SteveDrowne 3 103+
(G Wragg) *lw: swtg: t.k.h: forced to r wd early: trckd ldrs: rdn and effrt 2f out: one pce* **9/4**[1]

3-41 **7** 1 **Hopeful Purchase (IRE)**[23] 2111 3-8-11 95 TonyCulhane 4 101
(W J Haggas) *hld up in midfield: rdn and effrt 2f out: kpt on same pce and no imp on ldrs* **25/1**

2-12 **8** ½ **Deepwater Bay (USA)**[28] 1953 3-8-11 102 CSoumillon 1 100
(A M Balding) *dropped in fr wd draw and hld up in rr: effrt over 2f out: styd on fr over 1f out on wd outside: n.d* **25/1**

-346 **9** 1¼ **Silver Blue (IRE)**[47] 1488 3-8-11 95 RyanMoore 11 98
(R Hannon) *lw: trckd ldrs on inner: rdn over 2f out: no prog* **100/1**

12 **10** hd **Purple Moon (IRE)**[47] 1488 3-8-11 99 MJKinane 8 98
(Sir Michael Stoute) *lw: t.k.h early: hld up in midfield: rdn and effrt over 2f out: one pce and no imp* **9/1**

-431 **11** 2½ **Senor Dali (IRE)**[23] 2118 3-8-11 95 TQuinn 15 93
(J L Dunlop) *t.k.h: hld up: bdly hmpd after 1f and last after: rdn and no real prog over 2f out* **50/1**

14 **12** 2 **Leningrad (IRE)**[35] 1805 3-8-11 JamieSpencer 5 89
(M L W Bell) *t.k.h: hld up in rr: rdn over 2f out: hanging and reluctant: no prog* **16/1**

2-26 **13** 1 **Tell**[26] 2030 3-8-11 102 LDettori 2 87
(J L Dunlop) *lw: forced to r v wd in rr: rdn and no prog over 2f out* **14/1**

0-0 **14** ¾ **Crookhaven**[11] 2487 3-8-11 DMGrant 9 86
(John Joseph Murphy, Ire) *rangy: scope: t.k.h: pressed ldrs: wknd over 2f out* **50/1**

61 **15** nk **Invention (USA)**[27] 1994 3-8-11 97 RichardHughes 7 85
(J H M Gosden) *lw: t.k.h: hld up in rr: rdn and no prog over 2f out* **13/2**[3]

2m 6.73s (-1.27) **Going Correction** +0.05s/f (Good) **15** Ran SP% **124.5**
Speed ratings (Par 107):107,106,105,105,105 104,103,103,102,102 100,98,97,97,97
CSF £145.12 TOTE £57.60: £10.20, £2.00, £3.90; EX 423.10 TRIFECTA Not won..
Owner J C Smith **Bred** Littleton Stud **Trained** Newmarket, Suffolk

FOCUS
A decent renewal of this Listed contest. The pace was not that strong early and nothing managed to come from behind, but the form makes sense and is of a good standard for the grade.

NOTEBOOK
Snoqualmie Boy, who was well beaten in the Derby on his previous run, was more at home at this level and had track and trip to suit. He made a decisive move early in the straight and once in front held on tenaciously. He looks capable of winning more races at around this trip. (op 40-1)
Petrovich(USA) ◆, an expensive colt who won a division of the Wood Ditton on his sole previous start, travelled well in the slipstream of the leaders, but appeared to hit a flat spot early in the straight before running on well in the final furlong. It looked as if his inexperience contributed to his defeat and he will know a lot more next time. He has some big-race entries, looks one to follow and should be winning at Pattern level before long. (op 4-1 tchd 9-2)
Hazeymm(IRE), who ran quite well from the front in the Prix du Jockey-Club, was again keen but ran his race, keeping on well once headed. He sets the standard for the form. (op 12-1)
Mulaqat ◆, stepping back up in trip, adopted similar tactics to the winner of the Ribblesdale, trying to come through on the inside having been held up in the rear. He did not get a clear passage and was doing his best work late, so this was a good effort under his penalty. (tchd 14-1 and 18-1 in a place)
Mashaahed, who won his maiden over this trip having finished third in the Chester Vase previously, appeared to have every chance and ran as well as could have been expected. (op 14-1)
Ivy Creek(USA) ◆, who was sweating up in the paddock and was free on the way to post, was not that well drawn and did not help himself in the race by taking a hold and racing on the outside of the field. He did settle eventually but it was not the biggest surprise that he had little in reserve for the business end. He is better than the bare result indicates, and can be given another chance, but has some maturing to do if he is to fully realise his potential. (tchd 5-2)
Hopeful Purchase(IRE) got closer to Ivy Creek than he had at Sandown earlier in the season, but that colt appeared to run a little below par.
Deepwater Bay(USA), stepping up in trip, was held up from his outside draw but had to come around his field to make a challenge and never got into contention.
Invention(USA), whose maiden win was on easy ground, was quite keen under restraint and could not pick up in the straight. (op 7-1 tchd 15-2, 8-1 in places and 9-1 in a place)

2776 BUCKINGHAM PALACE STKS (HERITAGE H'CAP) 7f
5:30 (5:47) (Class 2) (0-105,105) 3-Y-O+

£34,276 (£10,263; £5,131; £2,568; £1,281; £643) **Stalls** Low

Form RPR

0500 **1** **Uhoomagoo**[20] 2200 8-8-9 90 (b) NCallan 7 102
(K A Ryan) *hld up: hdwy over 3f out: rdn over 2f out: led over 1f out: edgd rt ins fnl f: r.o* **25/1**

4320 **2** nk **Appalachian Trail (IRE)**[14] 2386 5-9-0 95 (b) TomEaves 28 106
(I Semple) *hld up: hdwy 3f out: rdn over 1f out: ev ch ins fnl f: hld last strides* **50/1**

0230 **3** 1 **Binanti**[12] 2435 6-8-3 84 WSupple 2 93
(P R Chamings) *lw: in tch: effrt whn nt clr run over 1f out: rn on towards fin: nt rch front pair* **33/1**

3110 **4** 1 **Bayeux (USA)**[47] 1487 5-8-13 94 KFallon 24 100
(G A Butler) *midfield: hdwy over 2f out: edgd lft whn rdn and chsd ldrs over 1f out: no ex towards fin* **14/1**

40-5 **5** nk **Eden Rock (IRE)**[61] 1129 5-8-13 94 LDettori 21 99+
(Pat Eddery) *lw: hld up: hdwy whn nt clr run 2f out: r.o towards fin* **10/1**

6-31 **6** ½ **Jedburgh**[17] 2289 5-9-10 105 (b) MJKinane 6 109
(J L Dunlop) *lw: hld up: nt clr run 2f out: rdn and hdwy over 1f out: styd on ins fnl f* **13/2**[1]

5610 **7** nk **Trafalgar Square**[20] 2200 4-8-5 86 AlanMunro 16 89+
(J Akehurst) *b: hld up: nt clr run over 2f out: rdn and hdwy whn nt clr run again and swtchd rt over 1f out: styd on wl fnl f* **20/1**

0-52 **8** 2½ **Marching Song**[26] 2012 4-8-13 94 RichardHughes 8 91+
(R Hannon) *hld up: hdwy whn nt clr run 2f out: rdn whn nt clr run again and swtchd rt over 1f out: kpt on ins fnl f: nt trble ldrs* **10/1**

0000 **9** ¾ **Moayed**[5] 2649 7-8-1 82 (bt) AdrianMcCarthy 11 77
(N P Littmoden) *swtg: dwlt: midfield: hdwy over 2f out: ev ch wl over 1f out: wknd ins fnl f* **33/1**

0-20 **10** ½ **Munaddam (USA)**[26] 2012 4-9-2 97 RHills 10 90
(E A L Dunlop) *racd keenly: midfield: effrt and hdwy 2f out: one pce fnl f* **20/1**

4415 **11** ½ **Indian Steppes (FR)**[15] 2358 7-8-8 89 TQuinn 18 81
(P S McEntee) *in tch: rdn and nt clr run 2f out: sn swtchd rt: one pce fnl f* **66/1**

2211 **12** 1 **Grey Boy (GER)**[15] 2364 5-8-2 83 PaulHanagan 3 73
(R A Fahey) *lw: prom: rdn over 2f out: losing pl whn n.m.r over 1f out: no imp after* **15/2**[3]

0-00 **13** ¾ **Stagbury Hill (USA)**[12] 2429 4-8-7 88 EddieAhern 13 76
(J W Hills) *b: hld up: hmpd whn nt clr run over 2f out: styd on fnl f: nvr trbld ldrs* **100/1**

4654 **14** hd **Shersha (IRE)**[20] 2199 7-9-3 98 JohnEgan 4 85
(Kevin F O'Donnell, Ire) *lw: in tch: rdn over 2f out: sn losing pl whn n.m.r: no imp after* **22/1**

0000 **15** nk **Sky Crusader**[5] 2649 4-8-4 85 RichardMullen 12 71
(R Ingram) *lw: hld up: rdn over 2f out: nvr trbld ldrs* **40/1**

3000 **16** ½ **Millennium Force**[64] 1086 8-8-8 89 ChrisCatlin 23 74
(M R Channon) *in rr: rdn over 2f out: hdwy over 1f out: no imp ins fnl f* **66/1**

4-64 **17** 3½ **Excusez Moi (USA)**[14] 2386 4-9-3 98 (tp) KerrinMcEvoy 27 74
(C E Brittain) *cl up: rdn 2f out: wknd over 1f out* **33/1**

4-05 **18** ¾ **Paper Talk (USA)**[26] 2012 4-8-12 93 MichaelHills 1 67
(B W Hills) *led: hdd wl over 1f out: sn hung rt: wknd fnl f* **9/1**

20-6 **19** 1¼ **Notability (IRE)**[26] 2012 4-9-5 100 PhilipRobinson 22 71
(M A Jarvis) *cl up: rdn over 2f out: wknd over 1f out* **7/1**[2]

4400 **20** ¾ **Compton's Eleven**[26] 2012 5-9-2 97 CraigAWilliams 20 66
(M R Channon) *prom: rdn and ev ch over 2f out: wknd over 1f out* **50/1**

6314 **21** 2 **Fiefdom (IRE)**[5] 2649 4-8-3 87 PatrickMathers(3) 14 51
(I W McInnes) *prom: rdn over 2f out: wknd over 1f out* **33/1**

-331 **22** 1 **Irony (IRE)**[8] 2555 7-8-6 87 5ex MartinDwyer 17 48
(A M Balding) *prom tl rdn and wknd qckly 3f out: n.m.r over 2f out* **33/1**

0-25 **23** 1 **Material Witness (IRE)**[8] 2555 9-8-7 88 DarryllHolland 9 46
(W R Muir) *lw: midfield: rdn and lost palce 3f out: bhd after* **50/1**

0/ **24** 3 **Desert Gold (IRE)**[17] 2312 5-8-7 88 ow1 JamieSpencer 15 39
(A J Martin, Ire) *str: lw: s.v.s: a bhd* **15/2**[3]

126- **25** 5 **Senator's Alibi**[88] 754 8-8-6 87 NGMcCullagh 26 25
(T J O'Mara, Ire) *cl up: rdn over 2f out: sn wknd* **100/1**

0-30 **26** 2½ **High Reach**[47] 1487 6-8-12 93 SteveDrowne 19 24
(W R Muir) *midfield: rdn over 2f out: wknd over 1f out* **100/1**

1-02 **27** 2½ **Goodenough Mover**[12] 2443 10-7-12 84 EmmettStack(5) 5 9
(Andrew Turnell) *wnt rt s: prom: rdn over 2f out: n.m.r whn sn wknd* **25/1**

1m 27.45s (-1.55) **Going Correction** +0.025s/f (Good) **27** Ran SP% **134.8**
Speed ratings (Par 109):109,108,107,106,106 105,105,102,101,100 100,99,98,98,97 97,93,92,90,89 87,86,85,81,76 73,70
CSF £962.18 CT £33462.53 TOTE £28.00: £5.10, £11.60, £17.30, £4.30; EX 1230.20 Trifecta £4062.60 Part won. Pool: £5,722 - 0.10 winning units. Place 6 £2,010.01, Place 5 £1,321.32.
Owner J Duddy & T Fawcett **Bred** C Mason & Mrs Nt Pope **Trained** Hambleton, N Yorks
■ Stewards' Enquiry : Darryll Holland one-day ban: used whip when out of contention (Jul 3)

FOCUS
A decent, competitive handicap run at a sound pace in which all the runners raced towards the stands' side. Straightforward form, with the first two both to last year's best.

NOTEBOOK
Uhoomagoo ◆ is a useful performer when he gets his favoured conditions - seven furlongs and a sound surface - and often hits form around this time of year. He settled in behind the leaders on the stands' rail and picked up well to take the lead below the distance. However, he had to dig deep to resist the determined challenge of the runner-up in the last furlong. He has often followed up a win in the past and it would be no surprise to see him take his chance in the Journal 'Good Morning' Handicap at Newcastle, which he has won in the past.
Appalachian Trail(IRE) ◆, who was out of his depth on his recent return from a break following an All-Weather campaign, is well suited by fast ground on turf and ran a terrific race from his high draw. He is not especially well handicapped, being 3lb higher than for his last win, but a repeat of this performance should see him picking up a good handicap before too long.
Binanti, whose last three wins have been on Polytrack, was another to run well on conditions that have suited him well in the past. He does not win that often, but he could be one to bear in mind, especially if connections choose to re-apply the headgear.
Bayeux(USA) ◆, who rediscovered his form for new connections when dropped to sprint trips during the winter, was another who ran well from his high draw but flattened out in the last furlong and may be better back at six.
Eden Rock(IRE) ◆, formerly with Sir Michael Stoute, ran on nicely in the latter stages, having not had the best of passages. This was his second good effort for new connections and, relatively lightly raced, he may yet be able to fulfill his early promise. (op 12-1)
Jedburgh, winner of this race last year when it took place at York, was settled on the rail behind the winner and, although keeping on, had too much ground to make up. He looks as if the Handicapper has his measure now, and he may have to contest conditions and Listed events again in future. (op 7-1 tchd 8-1 in places)
Trafalgar Square is another who looks high enough in the weights at present, but he ran well, having suffered an uninterrupted passage. (op 22-1)
Marching Song, runner-up in the Victoria Cup over course and distance last month, was unable to build on that off a 2lb higher mark, but was another to suffer traffic problems. (tchd 11-1 in a place)
Moayed, who has been below-par since early in the year, showed a bit more fire this time and is dropping to a competitive mark. (tchd 40-1 in places)
Shersha(IRE) Official explanation: jockey said mare was denied a clear run
Paper Talk(USA) had the rail draw and set the pace as he likes to do, but folded rather tamely and may be better suited by the undulations at Newmarket. (op 10-1 tchd 12-1 in places)
Notability(IRE), who looked unlucky in the Victoria Cup here last month, was not helped by the draw but appeared to have every chance before fading. Connections had been concerned beforehand about his effectiveness on the drying ground. (tchd 6-1 and 15-2 in a place)
Desert Gold(IRE), who drifted in the market despite some big bets, lost all chance with a very slow start. Official explanation: jockey said mare was difficult in stalls and missed break (op 11-2 tchd 8-1)
High Reach Official explanation: jockey said gelding lost a front shoe
T/Jkpt: Not won. T/Plt: £615.70 to a £1 stake. Pool: £345,500.19. 409.60 winning tickets. T/Qpdt: £404.30 to a £1 stake. Pool: £12,293.85. 22.50 winning tickets. JN

2538 BEVERLEY (R-H)
Thursday, June 22

OFFICIAL GOING: Good to firm
Wind: Slight, half-against

2777 BETFAIR APPRENTICE TRAINING SERIES FILLIES' H'CAP 1m 1f 207y
6:50 (6:50) (Class 5) (0-75,74) 4-Y-O+ **£5,505** (£1,637; £818; £408) **Stalls** High

Form RPR

006- **1** **The Pen**[28] 5001 4-8-2 55 oh3 DeanWilliams 2 57
(C W Fairhurst) *cl up: led 2f out: rdn and hdd ins last: rallied to ld nr line* **7/1**

-600 **2** shd **Lysandra (IRE)**[8] 2540 4-9-2 74 DanielleMcCreery(5) 1 76
(N Tinkler) *trckd ldrs: hdwy on outer over 2f out: led isndie last: hdd and no ex nr line* **3/1**[2]

1620 **3** 2½ **Starcross Maid**[15] 2362 4-7-11 55 oh7 LukeMorris(5) 3 52
(J F Coupland) *trckd ldrs: hdwy 2f out: rdn over 1f out: kpt on same pce ins last* **5/1**

0423 **4** ½ **Sforzando**[12] 2457 5-8-10 63 KristinStubbs 4 59
(Mrs L Stubbs) *hld up in tch: hdwy on outer 2f out: rdn and one pce ent last* **15/8**[1]

00-2 **5** *6* **Bint Il Sultan (IRE)**[15] 2362 4-8-2 **55** oh14.................. KevinGhunowa 5 40
(W M Brisbourne) *trckd ldrs: rdn along 2f out: wknd over 1f out* **4/1**[3]

500- **6** *1 3/4* **Ivana Illyich (IRE)**[8] 5409 4-8-2 **55** oh18......................(p) KellyHarrison 7 36
(J S Wainwright) *led: rdn along over 2f out: sn hdd & wknd appr last* **20/1**

2m 7.05s (-0.25) **Going Correction** -0.35s/f (Firm) **6** Ran SP% **113.7**
Speed ratings (Par 100):87,86,84,84,79 78
CSF £28.64 TOTE £8.10: £2.70, £2.70; EX 42.80.
Owner William Hill **Bred** Mrs R D Peacock **Trained** Middleham Moor, N Yorks

FOCUS
A very moderate fillies' handicap restricted to apprentices who had not ridden more than 20 winners. They went an ordinary pace and the winning time was very slow, 3.37 seconds slower than the later three-year-old handicap over the same trip. The form looks poor, limited by the third.

2778 RON PEACHEY 60TH BIRTHDAY MAIDEN AUCTION STKS 7f 100y
7:20 (7:20) (Class 4) 2-Y-O **£5,505** (£1,637; £818; £408) **Stalls High**

Form RPR
1 **Drumfire (IRE)** 2-9-1 .... RoystonFfrench 3 86+
(M Johnston) *trckd ldr: hdwy to ld 3f out: rdn wl over 1f out: styd on strly* **8/11**[1]

2 *6* **Armigerent (IRE)** 2-8-13 .... NickyMackay 4 70+
(M Johnston) *trckd ldrs: hdwy 3f out: chal 2f out: sn rdn and one pce appr last* **11/2**[3]

0 **3** *1* **Global Guest**[7] 2579 2-9-0 .... SamHitchcott 5 69
(M R Channon) *trckd ldng pair: hdwy 3f out: rdn 2f out and sn one pce* **7/2**[2]

0 **4** *17* **Wakeys Wizzard**[10] 2500 2-8-4 .... NeilPollard 2 18
(M E Sowersby) *rrd s: a rr* **33/1**

5 *3/4* **Munster Mountain (IRE)** 2-8-3 .... KevinGhunowa(7) 6 22
(P A Blockley) *keen: led: rdn along and hdd 3f out: sn wknd* **7/1**

1m 32.28s (-2.03) **Going Correction** -0.35s/f (Firm) **5** Ran SP% **111.0**
Speed ratings (Par 95):97,90,89,69,68
CSF £5.34 TOTE £1.60: £1.10, £3.00; EX 5.20.
Owner Kennet Valley Thoroughbreds Iv **Bred** Epona Bloodstock Ltd **Trained** Middleham Moor, N Yorks

FOCUS
A maiden that lacked strength in depth, but Mark Johnston introduced a couple of nice types, not least Drumfire, who really powered away when getting the hang of things late on.

NOTEBOOK
Drumfire(IRE) ◆, a 43,000euros half-brother to useful juvenile Ho Choi, a dual winner at six/seven furlongs out of a quite smart dual six/seven-furlong winner at two, has been given an entry in the Group 1 National Stakes and justified his short starting price with quite an impressive debut success. Never far away, he took a little bit of encouragement from the saddle to get going, but really hit full stride in the last furlong to draw right away. There was loads to like about this performance, not least because he gave the impression he is open to plenty of improvement, and he looks a likeable type. He is worth his place in better company. (op 10-11 tchd evens in places)
Armigerent(IRE), a 27,000euros purchase out of a half-sister to Kutub, a top-class multiple nine to 12-furlong winner at two to four, seemed to travel that bit better than his winning stablemate, but was found wanting somewhat when let down. Time may show he bumped into quite a nice type and he can do better with the benefit of this outing.
Global Guest, well beaten on his debut in just a fair six-furlong Newbury maiden on his debut, ran creditably upped in trip but was no match for either of the Johnston horses late on. He gives the impression he has a bit of improvement in him, and he could do better when handicapped in nurseries later in the season. (op 11-4)
Wakeys Wizzard, upped in trip, reared as the stalls opened and offered little. (op 16-1)
Munster Mountain(IRE), an 8,000gns first foal of a triple mile winner at three and four in Italy, showed up well early on but dropped out tamely.

2779 GUEST AND PHILIPS H'CAP 1m 100y
7:50 (7:51) (Class 3) (0-90,88) 3-Y-O **£11,217** (£3,358; £1,679; £840; £419) **Stalls High**

Form RPR
3114 **1** **Days Of My Life (IRE)**[16] 2330 3-9-0 **81**......................... NickyMackay 1 101+
(R Charlton) *chsd clr ldr: hdwy to ld over 2f out: sn clr: easily* **4/5**[1]

-440 **2** *9* **Fire Two**[16] 2330 3-8-11 **78**.. SamHitchcott 3 79
(M R Channon) *chsd ldrs: pushed along 1/2-way: rdn 3f out: styd on appr last: no ch w wnr* **9/1**

00-3 **3** *2* **Luna Landing**[19] 2239 3-8-9 **76**... DaleGibson 2 73
(Jedd O'Keeffe) *chsd ldrs: rdn along 3f out: no imp fr wl over 1f out* **14/1**

5-13 **4** *2* **Kinsya**[34] 1832 3-8-10 **80**... SaleemGolam(3) 5 73
(M H Tompkins) *hld up in tch: effrt 3f out: sn rdn and nvr a factor* **11/4**[2]

12-6 **5** *3/4* **Silidan**[41] 1626 3-9-7 **88**.. MickyFenton 4 79
(T P Tate) *led and sn wl clr at fast pce: rdn and hdd over 2f out: wknd qckly* **8/1**[3]

1m 42.51s (-4.89) **Going Correction** -0.35s/f (Firm) **5** Ran SP% **110.0**
Speed ratings (Par 103):110,101,99,97,96
CSF £8.79 TOTE £1.80: £1.10, £3.30; EX 8.10.
Owner Mountgrange Stud **Bred** Sir E J Loder **Trained** Beckhampton, Wilts

FOCUS
A really uncompetitive handicap for the grade, but they went a strong pace and the form is rated at face value.

NOTEBOOK
Days Of My Life(IRE) seemingly found this much easier than the Windsor handicap he was only fourth in on his previous start and came home alone. At one point it looked as though Silidan would take quite a bit of catching when that one was clear in front, but full credit to Mackay for not panicking. This was clearly an uncompetitive race, so one will hope the Handicapper does not overreact. (op 11-10 tchd 6-5 in a place)
Fire Two, without the visor, was just being niggled some way out and only confirmed second place once Days Of My Life was long gone. (op 6-1)
Luna Landing may be open to improvement when he steps up in trip. (op 8-1)
Kinsya could not repeat the form he showed when third behind two very useful sorts on soft ground at York on his previous start. (op 3-1 tchd 10-3)
Silidan was given an enterprising ride, but offered little when challenged and was disappointing. (op 6-1)

2780 BP SALTEND H'CAP 5f
8:20 (8:21) (Class 6) (0-65,63) 3-Y-O+ **£3,238** (£963; £481; £240) **Stalls High**

Form RPR
0642 **1** **Kings College Boy**[8] 2550 6-9-11 **60**.........................(b) TonyHamilton 7 73
(R A Fahey) *trckd ldrs: hdwy 2f out: rdn to ld appr last: drvn out* **9/2**[1]

0006 **2** *3/4* **Celtic Thunder**[14] 2380 5-9-5 **54**...................................(b) NickyMackay 8 64+
(T J Etherington) *dwlt and bhd: hdwy 2f out: swtchd lft and rdn over 1f out: styd on strly ins last: edgd rt and nt qckn towards fin* **11/1**

0-06 **3** *1* **Rosie's Result**[31] 1886 6-8-4 **44** oh1..................... AndrewMullen(5) 15 50
(M Todhunter) *prom: rdn along wl over 1f out: kpt on u.p ins last* **12/1**

000 **4** *shd* **Waggledance (IRE)**[6] 2611 4-8-5 **47**........................... KellyHarrison(7) 16 53
(D Carroll) *chsd ldrs: rdn along 2f out: drvn and kpt on ins last* **15/2**[3]

3302 **5** *shd* **St Ivian**[51] 1391 6-8-9 **44**.. JimmyQuinn 17 49
(Mrs N Macauley) *in tch on inner: hdwy 2f out: sn rdn and kpt on ins last: nrst fin* **8/1**

444 **6** *1/2* **Proud Western (USA)**[8] 2544 8-8-10 **45**..................(tp) SamHitchcott 13 48
(B Ellison) *outpcd and sn pushed along in rr: hdwy 2f out: rdn and styng on whn n.m.r ent last: kpt on towards fin* **8/1**

40-3 **7** *nk* **Flying Tackle**[10] 2494 8-9-1 **50**...............................(v) RoystonFfrench 9 52+
(I W McInnes) *chsd ldrs: rdn along wl over 1f out: drvn and one pce appr last* **5/1**[2]

40-0 **8** *1* **Rectangle (IRE)**[10] 2504 6-9-9 **58**...................................(t) ShaneKelly 11 56
(Micky Hammond) *towards rr: hdwy 2f out: sn rdn and kpt on ins last: nt rch ldrs* **20/1**

00-0 **9** *nk* **Beyond The Clouds (IRE)**[14] 2384 10-10-0 **63**............ FergalLynch 10 63+
(J S Wainwright) *towards rr: hdwy 2f out: sn rdn and no imp appr last* **16/1**

6112 **10** *1/2* **Mystery Pips**[12] 2462 6-10-0 **63**..................................(v) KimTinkler 12 58
(N Tinkler) *led: rdn along 2f out: drvn and hdd appr last: sn wknd* **8/1**

0000 **11** *3/4* **Blue Knight (IRE)**[46] 1504 7-9-10 **62**....................(vt) DanielTudhope(3) 1 55
(D Carroll) *racd wd: a towards rr* **33/1**

-300 **12** *2 1/2* **Tribute (IRE)**[8] 2550 5-9-6 **62**................................ KevinGhunowa(7) 6 45
(P A Blockley) *midfield: rdn along 2f out: no hdwy* **33/1**

0106 **13** *1/2* **Jahia (NZ)**[8] 2543 7-9-0 **49**.. MickyFenton 5 30
(P T Midgley) *a towards rr* **20/1**

0000 **14** *6* **Lizzie Rocket**[8] 2543 6-8-7 **45**...........................(v) BenSwarbrick(3) 2 3
(J O'Reilly) *in tch on outer: rdn along 1/2-way: sn wknd* **50/1**

0660 **15** *1 3/4* **Baron Rhodes**[17] 2293 5-10-0 **63**...........................(p) PaulMulrennan 3 15
(J S Wainwright) *chsd ldrs to 1/2-way: sn wknd* **20/1**

63.82 secs (-0.18) **Going Correction** 0.0s/f (Good) **15** Ran SP% **124.0**
Speed ratings (Par 101):101,99,98,98,97 97,96,95,94,93 92,88,87,78,75
CSF £50.16 CT £587.07 TOTE £5.30: £1.90, £5.40, £4.70; EX 62.90.
Owner The Cosmic Cases **Bred** Lady Jennifer Green **Trained** Musley Bank, N Yorks

FOCUS
A moderate sprint handicap but the level is not rock solid.

2781 COTTINGHAM PARK GOLF AND COUNTRY CLUB H'CAP 1m 1f 207y
8:50 (8:50) (Class 4) (0-80,79) 3-Y-O **£8,096** (£2,408; £1,203; £601) **Stalls High**

Form RPR
-310 **1** **Sir Arthur (IRE)**[16] 2324 3-9-5 **77**.............................. RoystonFfrench 6 82
(M Johnston) *cl up: led after 2f: rdn 2f out: edgd lft and drvn over 1f out: hdd ins last: rallied to ld nr line* **8/1**

6431 **2** *shd* **Princess Cocoa (IRE)**[9] 2518 3-8-6 **64** 6ex.................. TonyHamilton 7 69
(R A Fahey) *led 2f: prom: hdwy on inenr 2f out: rdn to ld ins last: sn drvn: hdd and no ex nr line* **8/1**

-322 **3** *nk* **Robustian**[7] 2581 3-9-7 **79**.. StephenCarson 2 83
(R F Johnson Houghton) *hld up: hdwy 3f out: swtchd wd and effrt 2f out: rdn and styd on wl fnl f* **9/2**[2]

06-0 **4** *1* **Hunting Haze**[19] 2243 3-8-4 **62**.. JimmyQuinn 10 64
(Miss S E Hall) *in tch: hdwy over 2f out: rdn over 1f out: kpt on ins last: nrst fin* **20/1**

4-31 **5** *hd* **And Again (USA)**[15] 2349 3-9-2 **74**................................. OscarUrbina 9 76
(J R Fanshawe) *hld up in tch: hdwy 3f out: rdn and ch over 1f out: drvn and one pce ins last* **7/2**[1]

U41 **6** *3/4* **Ahlawy (IRE)**[22] 2146 3-9-6 **78**.. NickyMackay 5 78
(L M Cumani) *hld up in tch: hdwy 3f out: swtchd lft and rdn wl over 1f out: sn drvn and kpt on same pce* **7/2**[1]

1-02 **7** *1* **Fregate Island (IRE)**[16] 2324 3-9-7 **79**............................. ShaneKelly 1 77
(W J Haggas) *trckd ldrs: effrt over 2f out: sn rdn and one pce appr last* **6/1**[3]

-603 **8** *1* **Suits Me**[49] 1444 3-9-1 **73**.. GrahamGibbons 3 69
(J J Quinn) *dwlt and in rr tl styd on fnl 2f: nt rch ldrs* **16/1**

30 **9** *2* **Paraguay (USA)**[17] 2304 3-9-0 **75**........................ EdwardCreighton(3) 8 68
(M R Channon) *a rr* **16/1**

300 **10** *9* **Bride To Be (USA)**[17] 2292 3-8-12 **70**............................ MickyFenton 4 46
(C E Brittain) *cl up: rdn along wl over 2f out: sn wknd* **33/1**

2m 3.68s (-3.62) **Going Correction** -0.35s/f (Firm) **10** Ran SP% **118.6**
Speed ratings (Par 101):100,99,99,98,98 98,97,96,94,87
CSF £71.65 CT £327.69 TOTE £10.60: £3.00, £1.60, £1.60; EX 78.40.
Owner Mrs Mary Keaney **Bred** Lodge Park Stud **Trained** Middleham Moor, N Yorks
■ Stewards' Enquiry : Royston Ffrench one-day ban: used whip with excessive frequency (Jul 3)

FOCUS
A fair handicap in which Sir Arthur proved good enough, despite not appearing totally happy on the fast ground. The form is fair and rated positively.

2782 LARARDS RESIDENTIAL SALES H'CAP 7f 100y
9:20 (9:21) (Class 6) (0-60,59) 3-Y-O **£3,238** (£963; £481; £240) **Stalls High**

Form RPR
40-0 **1** **Walnut Grove**[33] 1859 3-8-8 **49**.............................. BenSwarbrick(3) 15 57+
(T D Barron) *chsd ldrs: hdwy over 2f out: rdn to ld 1f out: styd on* **9/1**

4-54 **2** *2* **Jaassey**[19] 2243 3-9-1 **58**.. AndrewMullen(5) 9 61
(T D Walford) *hld up towards rr: hdwy over 2f out: sn rdn: styd on ins last* **7/2**[1]

5504 **3** *3/4* **Carr Hall (IRE)**[22] 2128 3-9-2 **54**...................................... DavidAllan 3 55+
(T D Easterby) *cl up: rdn over 2f out: drvn to ld briefly over 1f out: sn hdd and kpt on same pce* **7/1**[2]

3-00 **4** *1/2* **Farne Island**[33] 1859 3-9-7 **59**.................................. GrahamGibbons 6 59
(J J Quinn) *bmpd s: keen and hld up in rr: hdwy on inner 2f out: styd on ins last: nrst fin* **14/1**

5000 **5** *1 1/4* **Salisbury World (IRE)**[10] 2504 3-8-12 **50**.................... DarrenWilliams 7 47
(J F Coupland) *hmpd s and bhd: hdwy over 4f out: rdn to chse ldrs on inner 2f out: drvn and one pce ent last* **33/1**

0-00 **6** *nk* **Gala Jackpot (USA)**[11] 2480 3-8-7 **45**.............................. ShaneKelly 10 41
(W M Brisbourne) *hld up towards rr: hdwy over 2f out: sn rdn: swtchd rt over 1f out: styd on strly ins last: nrst fin* **22/1**

0-03 **7** *1 1/2* **Distinctly Jim (IRE)**[17] 2282 3-9-6 **58**......................... DerekMcGaffin 11 50
(B Smart) *chsd ldrs: rdn along wl over 2f out: kpt on same pce fr over 1f out* **15/2**[3]

2025 **8** *nk* **Suhezy (IRE)**[8] 2543 3-8-12 **50**..................................... TonyHamilton 5 41
(J S Wainwright) *wnt lft s: sn led: rdn along and hdd over 2f out: grad wknd* **8/1**

3040 **9** *1* **Noble Nova**[24] 2065 3-8-12 **53**........................ EdwardCreighton(3) 13 42
(M R Channon) *midfield: effrt and sme hdwy 3f out: sn rdn and no imp fnl 2f* **8/1**

0000 **10** *shd* **Kings Cavalier (USA)**[1] 2758 3-8-12 **50**........................(v) JimmyQuinn 16 39
(I W McInnes) *chsd ldrs: rdn along wl over 2f out and sn wknd* **20/1**

00-4 **11** *shd* **Thornton Princess**[26] 2019 3-8-9 **52**........................ GregFairley(5) 12 40
(B S Rothwell) *a towards rr* **14/1**

6-00 **12** *nk* **Stormingmichaelori**[17] 2298 3-8-8 **49**.................... DanielTudhope(3) 8 37
(N Wilson) *a towards rr* **33/1**
0536 **13** *½* **Coalite (IRE)**[13] 2399 3-9-2 **57**...........................(p) SilvestreDeSousa(3) 2 43
(A D Brown) *cl up: rdn to ld over 2f out: sn drvn and hdd over 1f out: wknd* **20/1**
0006 **14** *1 ½* **Casonova (IRE)**[17] 2284 3-8-9 **47**.................................. MickyFenton 14 30
(T D Easterby) *a towards rr* **9/1**
0600 **15** *¾* **Eliminator**[5] 2616 3-9-0 **52**.......................................(b[1]) RoystonFfrench 1 33
(I W McInnes) *a rr* **33/1**

1m 32.53s (-1.78) **Going Correction** -0.35s/f (Firm) **15** Ran SP% **124.7**
Speed ratings (Par 97):96,93,92,92,90 90,88,88,87,87 87,86,86,84,83
CSF £37.92 CT £245.10 TOTE £15.10: £3.70, £2.20, £2.70; EX 87.00 Place 6 £93.10, Place 5 £22.38 .
Owner Mrs M West **Bred** Mrs M West **Trained** Maunby, N Yorks

FOCUS
A moderate handicap, but they went a strong pace and the form looks reliable enough for the level rated through the third.
Kings Cavalier(USA) Official explanation: jockey said gelding bled from the nose
T/Plt: £115.60 to a £1 stake. Pool: £34,560.20. 218.15 winning tickets. T/Qpdt: £22.80 to a £1 stake. Pool: £2,979.00. 96.30 winning tickets. JR

2758 RIPON (R-H)

Thursday, June 22

OFFICIAL GOING: Good to firm
The ground was described as 'on the fast side of good with a very good cover of grass'.
Wind: Fresh; half behind Weather: Overcast but dry

2783 E B F GO RACING IN YORKSHIRE MAIDEN STKS 6f
2:15 (2:15) (Class 5) 2-Y-O **£4,533** (£1,348; £674; £336) **Stalls** Low

Form RPR
64 **1** **Dubai's Touch**[21] 2159 2-9-3 .... RoystonFfrench 9 84+
(M Johnston) *trckd ldrs: led over 2f out: rdn clr fnl f* **4/1**[3]
5 **2** *7* **Ghost Dancer**[17] 2287 2-9-3 .... NickyMackay 8 63
(L M Cumani) *t.k.h: trckd ldrs: kpt on same pce* **3/1**[1]
6 **3** *1 ¼* **Silver Appraisal**[10] 2500 2-8-12 .... IanMongan 1 54
(B Smart) *chsd ldrs: kpt on fnl f* **6/1**
0 **4** *¾* **Spence's Choice (IRE)**[16] 2321 2-9-3 .... PaulMulrennan 5 57
(M W Easterby) *t.k.h: lost pl after 1f: hdwy 2f out: kpt on ins last* **66/1**
5 *1 ¼* **Lemon Silk (IRE)** 2-9-3 .... MickyFenton 7 53
(T P Tate) *w'like: unf: s.i.s: outpcd and bhd: kpt on fnl f* **9/1**
6 **6** *1* **Windjammer**[27] 1982 2-9-3 .... DavidAllan 3 50
(T D Easterby) *led tl over 2f out: lost pl over 1f out* **7/1**
0 **7** *½* **Averti Star**[9] 2523 2-9-3 .... TPQueally 4 49
(Mrs A Duffield) *hmpd s: outpcd and bhd: sme late hdwy* **16/1**
8 *¾* **Movethegoalposts** 2-8-12 .... GregFairley(5) 2 47
(M Johnston) *rangy: sn chsng ldrs: hung rt over 2f out: lost pl over 1f out* **7/2**[2]

1m 12.0s (-1.00) **Going Correction** -0.25s/f (Firm) **8** Ran SP% **111.4**
Speed ratings (Par 93):96,86,85,84,82 81,80,79
CSF £15.52 TOTE £4.30: £1.60, £1.20, £2.10; EX 12.30.
Owner Salem Suhail **Bred** Miss S N Ralphs **Trained** Middleham Moor, N Yorks

FOCUS
A modest maiden but an improved effort from the progressive winner, although those behind look modest.

NOTEBOOK
Dubai's Touch, who has plenty of size and scope, really took the eye in the paddock. Kept up to his work, he came right away and the stable is back on the right track now.
Ghost Dancer, who looked very fit, pulled too hard for his own good and was left flat-footed when the winner engaged top gear. (op 2-1)
Silver Appraisal, who continually swished her tail in the paddock, improved on her debut effort and a seventh furlong will not come amiss. (op 7-1)
Spence's Choice(IRE), who looked very fit, stayed on after getting outpaced and will need another outing before he can compete in nurseries. (op 50-1)
Lemon Silk(IRE), a March foal, took time to grasp the nettle but put in some pleasing late work. This will have opened his eyes. (op 11-1)
Windjammer, racing on totally different ground, took them along but at this stage the sixth furlong looked beyond him. (op 9-1 tchd 10-1)
Movethegoalposts, a March foal, stands over plenty of ground. Very green to post, he hung as if possibly feeling the fast ground before dropping right away. He will leave this debut effort behind in due course. (op 4-1)

2784 ADLER & ALLAN H'CAP 5f
2:50 (2:51) (Class 5) (0-75,70) 3-Y-O+ **£3,886** (£1,156; £577; £288) **Stalls** Low

Form RPR
3625 **1** **Never Without Me**[10] 2505 6-9-5 **61**................................ FergalLynch 2 72
(J F Coupland) *trckd ldrs on inner: led over 1f out: edgd rt: r.o* **6/1**[2]
3450 **2** *nk* **Aegean Dancer**[14] 2380 4-9-7 **63**.. IanMongan 12 73
(B Smart) *swtchd rt and racd far side: trckd that pair: led that side ins last: r.o: 1st of 3 that gp* **9/1**
0603 **3** *1* **Gone'N'Dunnett(IRE)**[7] 2590 7-9-6 **62**...................(v) J-PGuillambert 13 68
(Mrs C A Dunnett) *w ldr far side: kpt on same pce ins last: 2nd of 3 that gp* **11/1**
0606 **4** *nk* **Jilly Why (IRE)**[14] 2384 5-9-4 **65**...............................(v[1]) DerekNolan(5) 11 70
(Ms Deborah J Evans) *w ldrs on outer: styd on same pce fnl f* **14/1**
0306 **5** *1* **Henry Hall (IRE)**[13] 2396 10-9-12 **68**................................. KimTinkler 7 69
(N Tinkler) *chsd ldrs: kpt on same pce appr fnl f* **8/1**
6-02 **6** *hd* **Strensall**[13] 2396 9-9-11 **67**.. DavidAllan 9 67
(R E Barr) *w ldrs: led over 2f out tl over 1f out: kpt on same pce* **14/1**
6005 **7** *hd* **Salviati (USA)**[6] 2618 9-9-12 **68**... TPQueally 8 68
(J M Bradley) *s.s: hdwy on outer over 2f out: kpt on same pce fnl f* **9/1**
46-3 **8** *nk* **Fayr Sky (IRE)**[61] 1137 3-9-6 **68**...................................... MickyFenton 14 66
(J J Quinn) *led other pair far side tl hdd and no ex ins last: 3rd of 3 that gp* **18/1**
60-0 **9** *hd* **Flur Na H Alba**[10] 2504 7-9-13 **69**............................(v) GrahamGibbons 5 67
(J J Quinn) *chsd ldrs: kpt on same pce fnl 2f* **11/1**
40-0 **10** *¾* **Flaran**[42] 1618 6-8-12 **54**.. RoystonFfrench 3 49
(J A R Toller) *in rr: kpt on fnl 2f: nvr a threat* **16/1**
25-3 **11** *4* **Shrink**[17] 2295 5-10-0 **70**.. PhillipMakin 6 50
(M Dods) *mid-div: wknd and eased over 1f out* **7/1**[3]
0000 **12** *¾* **Oceanico Dot Com (IRE)**[33] 1846 4-8-8 **57**........(tp) KevinGhunowa(7) 4 34
(A Berry) *led tl over 2f out: lost pl over 1f out* **25/1**
3003 **13** *3* **Kennington**[6] 2611 6-9-8 **64**...(b) HayleyTurner 1 29
(Mrs C A Dunnett) *s.s: a detached in rr* **11/2**[1]

58.86 secs (-1.34) **Going Correction** -0.25s/f (Firm)
WFA 3 from 4yo+ 6lb **13** Ran SP% **118.3**
Speed ratings (Par 103):100,99,97,97,95 95,95,94,94,93 86,85,80
CSF £58.59 CT £605.26 TOTE £7.10: £2.30, £3.40, £3.80; EX 91.20.
Owner J F Coupland **Bred** Miss Nathalie Lismonde **Trained** Grimsby, Lincs
■

FOCUS
Three, including the second and third, went to race on the far side from their outside draws. In the end there was precious little between the two sides and the form looks sound.
Shrink Official explanation: jockey said mare failed to handle track
Kennington Official explanation: jockey said gelding was slow into stride

2785 RICHMOND CLAIMING STKS 6f
3:25 (3:25) (Class 5) 3-Y-O+ **£3,886** (£1,156; £577; £288) **Stalls** Low

Form RPR
1600 **1** **Pomfret Lad**[13] 2397 8-9-6 76.................................... GrahamGibbons 15 73
(J J Quinn) *led far side 1f: trckd ldr: led that gp 2f out: r.o wl: 1st of 6 that gp* **7/2**[1]
4004 **2** *1 ¼* **Peruvian Style (IRE)**[6] 2599 5-8-9 50..................... NelsonDeSouza(3) 6 61
(J M Bradley) *racd stands' side: chsd ldrs: led that side over 2f out: r.o fnl f* **9/1**[3]
-000 **3** *1 ¾* **Special Gold**[13] 2396 4-9-0 57...(b) DavidAllan 4 58
(T D Easterby) *racd stands' side: chsd ldrs: kpt on same pce appr fnl f* **14/1**
0002 **4** *hd* **Unlimited**[1] 2748 4-8-10 56... TPQueally 9 53
(Mrs A Duffield) *racd stands' side: chsd ldrs: hrd drvn over 2f out: kpt on same pce* **4/1**[2]
5000 **5** *2 ½* **Mill By The Stream**[3] 2700 4-8-11 45.............................. MickyFenton 13 46
(P T Midgley) *racd far side: chsd ldrs: one pce fnl 2f: 2nd of 6 that gp* **33/1**
-000 **6** *½* **Tuscan Flyer**[30] 1914 8-8-10 41...............................(b) RoystonFfrench 14 44
(R Bastiman) *racd far side: trckd ldrs: one pce fnl 2f: 3rd of 6 that gp* **33/1**
0054 **7** *nk* **Smokincanon**[9] 2531 4-8-11 48.. RobertMiles 11 44
(W G M Turner) *racd far side: sn chsng ldrs: one pce fnl 2f* **14/1**
6/00 **8** *nk* **Shank On Fourteen (IRE)**[47] 1496 5-8-12 73........ PatrickDonaghy(7) 8 51
(K R Burke) *dwlt: racd stands' side: effrt and swtchd outside over 2f out: nvr nr ldrs* **20/1**
6-40 **9** *2 ½* **Attila The Hun**[3] 2700 7-8-12 44...................................... FergalLynch 7 36
(F Watson) *racd stands' side: in rr: outpcd fnl 2f* **66/1**
-200 **10** *¾* **Quantica (IRE)**[14] 2380 7-8-11 50...................................... KimTinkler 10 33
(N Tinkler) *swtchd rt and racd far side: led that side after 1f: hdd 2f out: sn wknd: 5th of 6 that gp* **10/1**
0000 **11** *shd* **Compton Plume**[10] 2505 6-9-0 60....................................... DaleGibson 12 35
(M W Easterby) *racd far side: chsd ldrs: outpcd fnl 2f: 6th of 6 that gp* **14/1**
0065 **12** *nk* **Zap Attack**[38] 1735 6-8-10 41...................................(tp) TonyHamilton 2 30
(J Parkes) *led stands' side tl over 2f out: lost pl over 1f out* **40/1**
4000 **13** *8* **Victoriana**[42] 1618 5-8-0 37...(p) RoryMoore(5) 5 1
(H J Collingridge) *racd stands' side: prom: lost pl over 2f out: sn bhd* **150/1**
0-04 **14** *nk* **Pitch Up (IRE)**[41] 1643 4-9-8 72.. IanMongan 3 17
(T G Mills) *racd stands' side: prom: rdn 3f out: lost pl and eased over 1f out* **7/2**[1]

1m 11.32s (-1.68) **Going Correction** -0.25s/f (Firm) **14** Ran SP% **118.8**
Speed ratings (Par 103):101,99,97,96,93 92,92,91,88,87 87,87,76,76
CSF £33.13 TOTE £4.40: £1.70, £3.40, £3.60; EX 37.60.
Owner Maxilead Limited **Bred** R G Percival And Miss S M Rhodes **Trained** Settrington, N Yorks
■ Stewards' Enquiry : Graham Gibbons one-day ban: not riding to draw (3 Jul)

FOCUS
Six chose to go to the far side headed by the winner with the fifth next home of that group. An ordinary claimer but the form looks sound enough rated through the runner-up.
Smokincanon Official explanation: jockey said gelding ran flat
Pitch Up(IRE) Official explanation: jockey said gelding was sore behind saddle

2786 TOTAL BUTLER H'CAP 1m 4f 10y
4:00 (4:00) (Class 4) (0-85,85) 3-Y-O **£6,309** (£1,888; £944; £472) **Stalls** High

Form RPR
442 **1** **Scotland Yard (UAE)**[54] 1306 3-8-11 **75**.................... RoystonFfrench 1 85
(M Johnston) *led after 1f: set mod pce: qcknd 5f out: hdd over 2f out: led over 1f out: styd on wl* **5/2**[2]
0-04 **2** *2* **Baltic Princess (FR)**[54] 1283 3-8-3 **67**........................... NickyMackay 4 73+
(M Johnston) *trckd ldrs: effrt over 3f out: styd on on ins to snatch 2nd wl ins last* **5/1**
4453 **3** *nk* **Markington**[16] 2324 3-8-6 **70**....................................... GrahamGibbons 2 76
(J D Bethell) *led 1f: trckd wnr: slt ld over 2f out: hdd over 1f out: kpt on same pce* **3/1**[3]
4-30 **4** *1 ¼* **Merveilles**[19] 2224 3-9-7 **85**.. RobertHavlin 3 89
(J H M Gosden) *hld up in last: hdwy over 4f out: rdn 2f out: one pce* **7/4**[1]

2m 37.43s (0.43) **Going Correction** -0.175s/f (Firm) **4** Ran SP% **106.6**
Speed ratings (Par 101):91,89,89,88
CSF £13.19 TOTE £2.80; EX 9.30.
Owner Jumeirah Racing **Bred** Darley **Trained** Middleham Moor, N Yorks

FOCUS
A tactical affair resulting in a very moderate winning time for a race like this and not a race to draw firm conclusions from.

2787 LADIES' DAY H'CAP 1m
4:35 (4:36) (Class 3) (0-90,90) 4-Y-O+
£9,348 (£2,799; £1,399; £700; £349; £175) **Stalls** High

Form RPR
0033 **1** **Diamonds And Dust**[6] 2614 4-9-0 **83**.................................(b) TPQueally 3 91
(M H Tompkins) *led: hdd over 2f out: rallied to ld ins last* **4/1**[2]
0332 **2** *½* **Skidrow**[20] 2200 4-9-7 **90**... HayleyTurner 5 97
(M L W Bell) *trckd ldrs: effrt over 3f out: chal 2f out: edgd lft and no ex wl ins last* **3/1**[1]
-003 **3** *½* **Barathea Dreams (IRE)**[23] 2114 5-8-9 **78**...................... JimmyQuinn 1 84
(J S Moore) *trckd ldrs: sltl ld over 2f out: hdd and no ex ins last* **9/2**[3]
-314 **4** *½* **Jubilee Street (IRE)**[45] 1532 7-8-12 **81**........................ RoystonFfrench 6 86+
(Mrs A Duffield) *trckd ldrs: drvn 4f out: kpt on and n.m.r on ins last 100yds* **3/1**[1]

0-06 **5** ½ **Alchemist Master**[6] 2614 7-8-2 **78** ow2 MichaelJStainton(7) 4 82
(R M Whitaker) *hld up in rr: slipped bnd over 5f out: hdwy to chse ldrs 4f out: one pce appr fnl f* **12/1**

6 5 **Starnevees (FR)**[279] 5-9-6 **89** NickyMackay 2 81
(L M Cumani) *hld up: bmpd bnd over 5f out: hdwy over 3f out: rdn 2f out: nvr able chal: wknd over 1f out* **9/2**[3]

1m 37.91s (-3.19) **Going Correction** -0.175s/f (Firm) **6** Ran SP% **114.1**
Speed ratings (Par 107):108,107,107,106,106 101
CSF £16.74 TOTE £5.70: £2.50, £1.90; EX 12.40.
Owner Mrs S Ashby **Bred** Whitsbury Manor Stud **Trained** Newmarket, Suffolk

FOCUS
A decent handicap run at a sound gallop but a blanket finish and despite the first two being close to form, the may be best not taken literally.

NOTEBOOK
Diamonds And Dust, 5lb lower than his last success, took them along but his goose looked cooked when headed. However, his rider was at his strongest and, refusing to accept defeat, forced his head back in front inside the last. (op 5-1)
Skidrow, 8lb higher than his last success, made his effort on the outside of the pack. Tending to edge left, in the end the winning combination proved just too strong. (op 11-4 tchd 7-2)
Barathea Dreams(IRE) went on travelling best but on this quick ground he was run out of it inside the last. This was a sound effect on this quick going away from his beloved Sandown. (op 5-1)
Jubilee Street(IRE), absent for six weeks, was the first to come under serious pressure. He kept chiselling away but was held when running out of racing room inside the last. He should be spot-on next time. (op 10-3)
Alchemist Master, 7lb higher than his last win, had trouble making the bend exiting the back straight. He stuck on in willing fashion in the final two furlongs and looks right back to his very best. (op 9-1)
Starnevees(FR), without a win for nearly two years and having his first run in Britain, took a bump leaving the back straight. He never really threatened and in the end was allowed to complete in his own time. The outing will bring him on and he will appreciate a return to further.

2788 BEAUMONT ROBINSON LADIES' DERBY H'CAP (LADY AMATEUR RIDERS) 1m 4f 10y
5:10 (5:11) (Class 6) (0-65,62) 4-Y-0+ **£3,123** (£968; £484; £242) **Stalls** High

Form RPR
0514 **1** **Court Of Appeal**[9] 2522 9-10-4 **60** (tp) MissLEllison(3) 10 69
(B Ellison) *trckd ldr: led over 6f out: drvn and styd on wl fnl 2f* **7/2**[1]
45-5 **2** 1 **Colway Ritz**[19] 2242 12-9-4 **43** MissPRobson 9 50
(W Storey) *chsd ldrs: wnt 2nd over 3f out: kpt on: no real imp* **12/1**
3661 **3** ½ **Lake Wakatipu**[9] 2522 4-10-1 **59** 5ex MissMMullineaux(5) 11 65
(M Mullineaux) *hld up in rr: hdwy 4f out: styd on fnl 2f: nt qckn fnl f* **15/2**
0050 **4** 1½ **Three Boars**[49] 1436 4-9-11 **50** (b) MissSBrotherton 7 54
(S Gollings) *s.i.s: sn trcking ldrs: effrt over 2f out: kpt on same pce* **9/1**
5132 **5** 1¼ **Acuzio**[9] 2522 5-10-2 **55** MissEJJones 1 57
(W M Brisbourne) *mid-div: effrt 4f out: kpt on: nvr rchd ldrs* **7/2**[1]
2460 **6** 3 **Platinum Charmer (IRE)**[36] 1769 6-10-2 **60** (p) MissKellyBurke(5) 12 57
(K R Burke) *led tl over 6f out: wknd over 1f out* **13/2**[2]
1000 **7** 1½ **Mustakhlas (USA)**[9] 2522 5-9-4 **46** MissFayeBramley(3) 4 41
(B P J Baugh) *in rr: effrt over 3f out: kpt on fnl f* **12/1**
1541 **8** 2½ **Scotty's Future(IRE)**[40] 1666 8-10-9 **62** MrsCBartley 6 53
(A Berry) *hld up in rr: effrt 4f out: nvr a factor* **7/1**[3]
000- **9** 4 **Little Task**[18] 5683 8-8-13 **43** oh17 MissAWallace(5) 3 27
(J S Wainwright) *racd wd: a towards rr* **50/1**
0-40 **10** hd **Red River Rebel**[43] 1590 8-9-5 **49** MissJRiding(5) 8 33
(J R Norton) *trckd ldrs: drvn over 4f out: lost pl 3f out* **14/1**

2m 36.58s (-0.42) **Going Correction** -0.175s/f (Firm) **10** Ran SP% **116.1**
Speed ratings (Par 101):94,93,93,92,91 89,88,86,83,83
CSF £48.16 CT £298.08 TOTE £4.30: £1.70, £3.80, £2.30; EX 20.50.
Owner Spring Cottage Syndicate No 2 **Bred** John And Susan Davis **Trained** Norton, N Yorks

FOCUS
A low-grade lady riders' handicap although the form looks reasonable with the first three close to their marks.
Scotty's Future(IRE) Official explanation: jockey said gelding was unsuited by the good to firm ground

2789 REETH H'CAP 1m
5:45 (5:45) (Class 6) (0-65,62) 4-Y-0+ **£2,590** (£770; £385; £192) **Stalls** High

Form RPR
0543 **1** **Trevian**[11] 2482 5-8-8 **49** TPQueally 18 61+
(J M Bradley) *hld up in mid-div: smooth hdwy over 2f out: nt clr run over 1f out: squeezed through and led ins last: hld on towards fin* **4/1**[1]
0015 **2** ½ **Leighton Buzzard**[5] 2641 4-9-2 **60** DanielTudhope(3) 3 68+
(Mrs A Duffield) *s.i.s: bhd: hdwy over 2f out: edgd rt ins last: r.o towards fin* **7/1**[3]
-520 **3** 1¼ **Sedge (USA)**[8] 2541 6-8-9 **55** (p) RoryMoore(5) 1 60
(P T Midgley) *in tch: effrt over 2f out: styng on same pce whn hmpd ins last* **20/1**
-340 **4** shd **Thornaby Green**[17] 2286 5-7-12 **44** AndrewMullen(5) 9 49
(T D Barron) *led after 1f: edgd lft: hdd and hmpd ins last* **8/1**
03-0 **5** 1¾ **Ali D**[4] 2681 8-9-7 **62** J-PGuillambert 13 65+
(G Woodward) *mid-div: hdwy over 3f out: nt clr run over 1f out: styd on same pce ins last* **10/1**
0050 **6** nk **Panshir (FR)**[22] 2149 5-8-5 **46** HayleyTurner 11 46
(Mrs C A Dunnett) *chsd ldrs: styd on same pce finbal f* **16/1**
6200 **7** 1 **Flaxby**[8] 2541 4-8-10 **51** (b) GrahamGibbons 8 55+
(J D Bethell) *trckd ldrs: keeping on same pce whn hmpd ins last* **12/1**
-006 **8** 2½ **Cordage (IRE)**[8] 2548 4-9-5 **60** (v[1]) TonyHamilton 17 52
(Karen McLintock) *ld 1f: chsd ldrs: wknd ins last* **25/1**
-006 **9** 2½ **Frogs' Gift (IRE)**[13] 2400 4-8-4 **45** JimmyQuinn 15 31
(G M Moore) *chsd ldrs on inner: effrt over 2f out: wknd appr fnl f* **33/1**
6602 **10** 4 **Orpen Quest (IRE)**[33] 1852 4-7-13 **45** (v) MarcHalford(5) 19 22
(M J Attwater) *s.i.s: kpt on fnl 3f: nvr nr ldrs* **15/2**
41-0 **11** 1¼ **Rudaki**[15] 2360 4-8-5 **51** GregFairley(5) 5 25
(M E Sowersby) *in rr: sme hdwy on outside over 3f out: nvr a factor* **25/1**
00-4 **12** 1¼ **Shamwari Fire (IRE)**[13] 2392 6-7-12 **44** NataliaGemelova(5) 7 15
(I W McInnes) *mid-div:effrt 3f out: edgd lft: nvr a factor* **33/1**
4601 **13** ½ **Royal Indulgence**[3] 2697 6-8-3 **49** 6ex LiamJones(5) 4 19
(W M Brisbourne) *s.i.s: sme hdwy on outside 3f out: edgd rt: nvr a factor* **6/1**[2]
3450 **14** ½ **Kalani Star (IRE)**[8] 2541 6-8-6 **47** (v) PaulMulrennan 6 16
(I W McInnes) *chsd ldrs: outpcd fnl 2f* **20/1**
00-0 **15** 1 **Red Lantern**[33] 1852 5-7-13 **43** oh7 JohnMcAuley(3) 12 10
(M J Attwater) *mid-div: drvn 4f out: nvr a factot* **66/1**
000 **16** 1¼ **Galloping Gertie**[19] 2245 4-8-2 **43** oh13 DaleGibson 16 7
(J Hetherton) *nvr on terms* **100/1**

650- **17** nk **Keyalzao (IRE)**[253] 5187 4-8-1 **45** oh11 ow2 (v[1]) NelsonDeSouza(3) 10 8
(A Crook) *a in rr* **100/1**
15-0 **18** 2 **Star Fern**[150] 172 5-8-0 **44** DominicFox(3) 14 3
(M J Attwater) *s.s: a bhd* **14/1**

1m 38.49s (-2.61) **Going Correction** -0.175s/f (Firm) **18** Ran SP% **125.6**
Speed ratings (Par 101):106,105,104,104,102 102,101,98,96,92 90,89,89,88,87 86,86,84
CSF £27.96 CT £533.48 TOTE £3.90: £1.40, £1.90, £5.20, £2.70; EX 17.50 Place 6 £215.64, Place 5 £130.39.
Owner Folly Road Racing Partners (1996) **Bred** L A C Ashby **Trained** Sedbury, Gloucs
■ Stewards' Enquiry : Andrew Mullen two-day ban: careless riding (Jul 3-4)

FOCUS
A fair winning time for the class of contest. It was like dodgem cars in the closing stages and therefore the form is somewhat messy, with the third and fourth setting the standard.
Ali D Official explanation: jockey said gelding was denied a clear run
T/Plt: £331.50 to a £1 stake. Pool: £35,538.35. 78.25 winning tickets. T/Qpdt: £52.20 to a £1 stake. Pool: £1,693.20. 24.00 winning tickets. WG

2461 WOLVERHAMPTON (A.W) (L-H)
Thursday, June 22

OFFICIAL GOING: Standard
Wind: Fresh; half behind Weather: Fine

2790 WBX.COM WORLD BET EXCHANGE CLAIMING STKS 1m 4f 50y(P)
2:25 (2:25) (Class 5) 3-Y-0+ **£3,412** (£1,007; £504) **Stalls** Low

Form RPR
2101 **1** **Zalkani (IRE)**[45] 1548 6-9-11 70 DeanMcKeown 11 57
(J Pearce) *hld up towards rr: hdwy 4f out: rdn 2f out: styd on to ld nr fin* **9/4**[1]
/460 **2** hd **High Hope (FR)**[57] 1247 8-9-4 64 (b) RobynBrisland(5) 6 54
(G L Moore) *hld up towards rr: hdwy over 4f out: led 2f out: rdn clr over 1f out: ct nr fin* **5/1**[3]
6630 **3** 1 **Iamback**[22] 2133 6-8-11 38 (t) AdamKirby(3) 9 44
(Miss D A McHale) *prom: rdn over 5f out: sltly outpcd over 2f out: styd on fnl f* **11/1**
4454 **4** 1 **Ice And Fire**[7] 1766 7-9-2 42 (b) AshleyHamblett(7) 5 51
(J T Stimpson) *hld up towards rr: hdwy over 2f out: rdn and edgd rt over 1f out: edgd lft ins fnl f: styd on* **12/1**
3145 **5** 5 **Chater Knight (IRE)**[20] 2206 5-8-11 55 (p) TolleyDean(7) 4 38
(R A Harris) *led early: hld up in tch: led over 4f out: rdn and hdd over 2f out: wknd ins fnl f* **3/1**[2]
6000 **6** 1½ **Nakwa (IRE)**[14] 2381 8-9-9 50 FrancisNorton 8 41
(E J Alston) *sn led: hdd over 5f out: lost pl and n.m.r on ins 4f out: n.d after* **16/1**
0400 **7** 5 **Gravardlax**[11] 2483 5-9-4 36 (tp) JamieMackay 2 28
(Miss D A McHale) *nvr nr ldrs* **66/1**
-006 **8** 8 **Moonlight (GER)**[24] 2070 3-8-4 44 ow1 AlanDaly 1 15
(Dr J R J Naylor) *hld up in mid-div: rdn over 3f out: sn bhd* **28/1**
0-10 **9** 2½ **Mobane Flyer**[23] 2108 6-9-5 60 ShaneKelly 10 12
(R A Fahey) *w ldr: led over 5f out tl over 4f out: rdn and wknd wl over 2f out* **6/1**
00-0 **10** 3½ **Armatore (USA)**[13] 2414 6-8-13 52 (p) JamieJones(7) 7 7
(Ernst Oertel) *a bhd* **50/1**

2m 40.1s (-2.32) **Going Correction** -0.225s/f (Stan)
WFA 3 from 4yo+ 14lb **10** Ran SP% **115.5**
Speed ratings (Par 103):98,97,97,96,93 92,88,83,81,79
CSF £13.49 TOTE £2.50: £1.10, £3.40, £3.70; EX 11.00.
Owner Jeff Pearce **Bred** His Highness The Aga Khan's Studs S C **Trained** Newmarket, Suffolk

FOCUS
This turned out to be a competitive claimer, but the form is modest and limited by the fourth.

2791 WBX.COM WORLD BET EXCHANGE MAIDEN AUCTION FILLIES' STKS 5f 20y(P)
3:00 (3:00) (Class 5) 2-Y-0 **£3,238** (£963; £481; £240) **Stalls** Low

Form RPR
4 **1** **Hucking Hope (IRE)**[54] 1295 2-8-6 LPKeniry 10 68
(J R Best) *a.p: rdn to ld 1f out: wandered ins fnl f: r.o* **12/1**
25 **2** nk **Drifting Gold**[21] 2166 2-8-4 ow3 AdamKirby(3) 1 68
(C G Cox) *led after 1f: rdn and hdd 1f out: r.o* **11/4**[2]
2 **3** nk **Princess Ileana (IRE)**[45] 1542 2-8-8 FrancisNorton 8 68
(K R Burke) *led 1f: w ldr: rdn and ev ch 1f out: nt qckn* **5/4**[1]
5 **4** 5 **Galaxy Of Stars**[54] 1278 2-8-8 ShaneKelly 2 53+
(D Shaw) *s.i.s: hdwy and edgd lft over 1f out: nt rch ldrs* **16/1**
5 shd **Fine Leg** 2-7-13 JamesDoyle(5) 7 46
(P J McBride) *chsd ldrs: rdn 2f out: wknd fnl f* **16/1**
6 1¼ **Bert's Memory** 2-8-8 DO'Donohoe 5 45
(K A Ryan) *s.i.s: nvr nr ldrs* **11/2**[3]
5 **7** nk **Inkjet (IRE)**[14] 2382 2-8-4 AdrianTNicholls 4 40
(Ms Deborah J Evans) *s.i.s: sme hdwy whn hung lft over 1f out: n.d* **50/1**
00 **8** 1 **Charlies Girl (IRE)**[7] 2588 2-8-6 ow2 RobbieFitzpatrick 3 38
(M J Attwater) *a bhd* **25/1**
9 ½ **Sister Etienne (IRE)** 2-8-4 PaulFessey 6 35
(T D Barron) *dwlt: sn chsng ldrs: hung rt over 3f out: rdn 2f out: wknd fnl f* **8/1**
10 9 **Piccolini** 2-8-8 (b[1]) DeanMcKeown 9 6
(Mrs G S Rees) *prom: n.m.r over 2f out: sn wknd* **22/1**
11 6 **Kyoto City** 2-8-4 PaulQuinn 11 —
(D W Chapman) *s.s: a in rr* **66/1**

62.30 secs (-0.52) **Going Correction** -0.225s/f (Stan) **11** Ran SP% **128.7**
Speed ratings (Par 90):95,94,94,86,85 83,83,81,81,66 57
CSF £48.38 TOTE £13.00: £4.00, £1.30, £1.10; EX 66.60.
Owner Hucking Horses **Bred** Gerry O'Sullivan **Trained** Hucking, Kent

FOCUS
It paid to be close to the pace in this modest event run at a decent clip and the form is best rated around the placed horses.

NOTEBOOK
Hucking Hope(IRE), given time to get over her Ripon debut, proved good enough despite still showing signs of inexperience.
Drifting Gold was reverting to the minimum trip having been just touched off over course and distance on her debut. She lost little in defeat and deserves to take a similar event. (op 5-2 tchd 3-1)
Princess Ileana(IRE) had no excuses on what was a totally different surface to the soft ground at Windsor. (op 6-4 tchd 15-8)
Galaxy Of Stars again gave the impression that an extra furlong may help after losing ground at the start. (op 20-1 tchd 25-1)
Fine Leg showed ability on her debut but eventually paid the penalty for trying to go the pace.

Sister Etienne(IRE) Official explanation: jockey said filly did not handle the bend
Piccolini Official explanation: jockey said filly hung to the left and to the right

2792 TAKE CONTROL WITH WBX.COM H'CAP 5f 216y(P)
3:35 (3:35) (Class 6) (0-60,61) 3-Y-0+ **£2,730** (£806; £403) **Stalls** Low

Form				RPR
5000	1		**Scuba (IRE)**[20] 2211 4-9-7 **58**....(b[1]) TravisBlock(5) 2 (H Morrison) *a.p: rdn over 2f out: hung lft over 1f out: led ent fnl f: r.o* **6/1**[3]	68
6-33	2	1 1/4	**Gracie's Gift (IRE)**[31] 1878 4-9-12 **58**.... DeanMcKeown 4 (A G Newcombe) *outpcd: gd hdwy on outside and edgd lft fnl f: nt rch wnr* **13/2**	64
-000	3	nk	**Bond Playboy**[26] 2020 6-10-0 **60**....(p) DarrenWilliams 6 (G R Oldroyd) *chsd ldrs: lost plcd over 3f out: sn rdn: rallied over 1f out: kpt on ins fnl f* **12/1**	65
0000	4	1/2	**Mountain Pass (USA)**[16] 2331 4-9-12 **58**....(v) PaulDoe 12 (M J Wallace) *prom: rdn over 2f out: hung lft over 1f out: led briefly 1f out: no ex towards fin* **25/1**	62
1101	5	shd	**Boanerges (IRE)**[14] 2376 9-10-0 **60**.... ShaneKelly 8 (J M Bradley) *hld up in mid-div: rdn over 2f out: hdwy 1f out: nvr able to chal* **12/1**	63
03-5	6	1	**California Laws**[23] 2112 4-9-9 **55**.... PaulFessey 7 (T D Barron) *s.i.s: rdn over 2f out: hdwy fnl f: nvr nrr* **9/2**[2]	55
0230	7	3/4	**Orchestration (IRE)**[14] 2376 5-9-9 **55**....(v) RobbieFitzpatrick 11 (M J Attwater) *a.p: rdn 3f out: no hdwy fnl 2f* **14/1**	53
2005	8	shd	**Doctor's Cave**[20] 2207 4-9-6 **55**....(b) NeilChalmers(3) 10 (K O Cunningham-Brown) *no hdwy fnl 2f* **16/1**	53
2011	9	1	**Caustic Wit (IRE)**[3] 2711 8-10-1 **61** 6ex....(p) FergusSweeney 3 (M S Saunders) *sn bhd: nt clr run 3f out: swtchd rt over 1f out: n.d* **3/1**[1]	56
405	10	1 1/2	**Savile's Delight (IRE)**[16] 2331 7-9-8 **57**....(bt) DNolan(3) 9 (R Brotherton) *w ldr: led over 2f out: sn rdn: hdd 1f out: wknd* **11/1**	47
0006	11	1 3/4	**Second Reef**[20] 2211 4-9-8 **54**....(p) FrancisNorton 5 (E J Alston) *led: hdd and n.m.r on ins over 2f out: wknd over 1f out* **9/1**	39
4-50	12	13	**Val De Maal (IRE)**[41] 1645 6-9-6 **59**....(v) DawnRankin(7) 1 (Miss J A Camacho) *s.i.s: a bhd* **25/1**	5

1m 14.55s (-1.26) **Going Correction** -0.225s/f (Stan) 12 Ran SP% **124.8**
Speed ratings (Par 101):99,97,96,96,96 94,93,93,92,90 88,70
CSF £47.38 CT £463.47 TOTE £9.10: £2.80, £1.20, £4.60; EX 71.70.
Owner Graham Doyle and Applause PR **Bred** Mountarmstrong Stud **Trained** East Ilsley, Berks
■ Stewards' Enquiry : D Nolan one-day ban: careless riding (Jul 3)
Francis Norton one-day ban: careless riding (Jul 3)

FOCUS
A typically competitive low-grade sprint handicap rated around the runner-up.
California Laws Official explanation: jockey said gelding missed the break

2793 WBX.COM WORLD BET EXCHANGE (S) H'CAP 7f 32y(P)
4:10 (4:11) (Class 6) (0-60,60) 3-Y-0+ **£2,388** (£705; £352) **Stalls** High

Form				RPR
3000	1		**Mister Elegant**[6] 2599 4-9-10 **51**.... AdrianTNicholls 6 (J L Spearing) *hld up in tch: rdn over 3f out: led ins fnl f: drvn out* **10/1**	63
0401	2	nk	**Resplendent Prince**[19] 2245 4-9-13 **54**....(v) PaulDoe 11 (P Howling) *a.p: rdn to ld 2f out: hdd ins fnl f: r.o* **9/1**	65
5512	3	1 1/4	**Labelled With Love**[16] 2319 6-9-13 **54**....(t) FergusSweeney 3 (J R Boyle) *t.k.h in rr: hdwy over 2f out: rdn wl over 1f out: nt qckn ins fnl f* **9/2**[1]	62
10-0	4	3/4	**Writ (IRE)**[138] 297 4-10-0 **55**.... LPKeniry 5 (Ernst Oertel) *hld up in tch: rdn over 2f out: one pce fnl f* **33/1**	61
-353	5	1	**Aventura (IRE)**[20] 2208 6-9-6 **54**.... MSemple(7) 8 (S R Bowring) *s.i.s: sn mid-div: rdn over 3f out: hdwy over 2f out: one pce fnl f* **10/1**	57
-002	6	nk	**Bundy**[1] 2749 10-9-8 **52**.... BenSwarbrick(3) 2 (M Dods) *hld up and bhd: hdwy fnl f: nvr nr to chal* **9/1**	54
0204	7	shd	**Mission Affirmed (USA)**[20] 2208 5-9-5 **53**....(p) TolleyDean(7) 10 (R A Harris) *racd wd: hld up and bhd: rdn over 3f out: hdwy fnl f: nt rch ldrs* **7/1**[3]	55
0264	8	3/4	**Merdiff**[13] 2413 7-10-0 **55**.... ShaneKelly 9 (W M Brisbourne) *anticipated s: s.i.s: rdn over 2f out: sme hdwy fnl f: n.d* **9/1**	55
6536	9	1 3/4	**Aswan (IRE)**[20] 2208 8-9-11 **55**....(t) AmirQuinn(3) 12 (S R Bowring) *led: rdn and hdd 2f out: wknd ins fnl f* **16/1**	51
0050	10	2	**Burhaan (IRE)**[15] 2347 4-10-0 **55**....(t) DarrenWilliams 4 (J R Boyle) *rdn over 2f out: a towards rr* **10/1**	45
0014	11	hd	**Haroldini (IRE)**[30] 1913 4-9-9 **50**....(p) GeorgeBaker 1 (J Balding) *prom over 3f* **6/1**[2]	40
4000	12	1 1/2	**Mr Rigsby**[13] 2415 3-9-7 **60**.... DeanCorby(3) 7 (P Howling) *prom: rdn 3f out: wknd 2f out* **33/1**	46

1m 29.09s (-1.31) **Going Correction** -0.225s/f (Stan)
WFA 3 from 4yo+ 9lb 12 Ran SP% **114.0**
Speed ratings (Par 101):98,97,96,95,94 93,93,92,90,88 88,86
CSF £93.23 CT £465.76 TOTE £18.90: £6.70, £4.00, £2.00; EX 135.10.There was no bid for the winner.
Owner M Lawrence & W Cooper **Bred** J Spearing And Kate Ive **Trained** Kinnersley, Worcs

FOCUS
A tightly-knit seller but the form looks sound enough, rated through those in the frame behind the winner.
Merdiff Official explanation: jockey said gelding missed the break

2794 WBX.COM WORLD BET EXCHANGE H'CAP 1m 141y(P)
4:45 (4:45) (Class 5) (0-70,69) 4-Y-0+ **£3,886** (£1,156; £577; £288) **Stalls** Low

Form				RPR
2134	1		**Bijou Dan**[22] 2141 5-8-12 **63**....(b) AdamKirby(3) 7 (W G Harrison) *hld up and bhd: rdn and hdwy on ins 2f out: led wl ins fnl f: drvn out* **5/1**[1]	72
0-02	2	nk	**La Viola**[17] 2282 4-8-0 **53**....(b) AndrewElliott(5) 8 (K R Burke) *hld up in mid-div: hdwy 5f out: rdn over 2f out: led briefly ins fnl f: r.o* **9/1**	61
0204	3	1/2	**Treasure House (IRE)**[12] 2464 5-9-4 **66**.... FrancisNorton 4 (M Blanshard) *hld up: nt clr run over 1f out: hdwy fnl f: r.o* **8/1**	73
3464	4	1	**Stoic Leader (IRE)**[9] 2527 6-9-4 **69**.... DNolan(3) 13 (R F Fisher) *swtchd lft s: hld up and bhd: hdwy 3f out: sn rdn: swtchd rt over 1f out: edgd lft ins fnl f: kpt on* **6/1**[2]	74
0-03	5	1/2	**Zando**[13] 2414 4-8-7 **55**.... PaulDoe 1 (E G Bevan) *hld up in mid-div: rdn and hdwy over 2f out: ev ch ins fnl f: nt qckn* **12/1**	59
1406	6	shd	**Spark Up**[13] 2418 6-8-0 **53**....(b) JamesDoyle(5) 5 (J W Unett) *hld up in mid-div: hdwy over 3f out: rdn to ld over 1f out: hdd and no ex ins fnl f* **9/1**	57
1100	7	2 1/2	**Lord Of Dreams (IRE)**[36] 1773 4-9-3 **65**.... FrankieMcDonald 10 (D W P Arbuthnot) *hld up and bhd: rdn over 2f out: late hdwy on ins: n.d* **12/1**	63
0030	8	1 1/2	**Mister Benji**[14] 2378 7-8-9 **57**.... DarrenWilliams 11 (B P J Baugh) *t.k.h: prom: rdn and ev ch over 2f out: wknd ins fnl f* **16/1**	52
3100	9	1 1/2	**Jakarmi**[20] 2186 5-9-7 **69**.... FrancisFerris 9 (B Palling) *w ldr: led over 5f out: rdn over 2f out: hdd over 1f out: wknd ins fnl f* **6/1**[2]	61
0510	10	shd	**Bollin Michael**[26] 2025 4-8-12 **65**....(b) DuranFentiman(5) 12 (T D Easterby) *prom: chal gng wl 2f out: sn rdn: wknd ins fnl f* **7/1**[3]	57
0455	11	21	**Queen's Echo**[21] 2165 5-8-10 **58**.... ShaneKelly 3 (M Dods) *a bhd: eased whn no ch fnl 2f* **8/1**	6
-000	12	3 1/2	**Eathie**[24] 2075 4-8-6 **54** ow3.... RobbieFitzpatrick 6 (M J Attwater) *chsd ldrs: wknd over 4f out: eased whn no ch fnl 2f* **50/1**	—
4000	13	25	**Comeintothespace (IRE)**[19] 2221 4-8-5 **53**.... AdrianTNicholls 2 (Miss Victoria Roberts) *led: hdd over 5f out: rdn 4f out: sn wknd: eased whn no ch fnl 2f* **25/1**	—

1m 49.12s (-2.64) **Going Correction** -0.225s/f (Stan) **13** Ran SP% **127.0**
Speed ratings (Par 103):102,101,101,100,99 99,97,96,94,94 76,73,50
CSF £53.30 CT £370.06 TOTE £4.10: £1.40, £1.60, £4.50; EX 37.00.
Owner Bert Markey **Bred** James Thom And Sons **Trained** Lesmahagow, S Lanarks
■ Stewards' Enquiry : Francis Ferris two-day ban: careless riding (Jul 3-4)

FOCUS
This wide-open handicap was just as competitive as expected and the form is solid rated through the placed horses and the fifth.
Lord Of Dreams(IRE) Official explanation: jockey said colt was hampered on the first bend
Queen's Echo Official explanation: jockey said mare was hampered on the first bend
Comeintothespace(IRE) Official explanation: jockey said gelding lost its action

2795 WORLD BET EXCHANGE WBX.COM H'CAP 1m 4f 50y(P)
5:20 (5:25) (Class 6) (0-65,65) 3-Y-0 **£2,730** (£806; £403) **Stalls** Low

Form				RPR
0-00	1		**Desert Sea (IRE)**[24] 2065 3-9-2 **60**.... FergusSweeney 2 (C Tinkler) *led early: a.p: rdn 3f out: led 2f out: drvn out* **16/1**	72
0-42	2	1 1/4	**Phone In**[8] 2556 3-9-7 **65**.... JamieMackay 5 (Sir Mark Prescott) *a.p: led 3f out: rdn and hdd 2f out: nt qckn ins fnl f* **4/6**[1]	75
-405	3	8	**Bolckow**[22] 2128 3-9-7 **65**.... DO'Donohoe 11 (K A Ryan) *hld up and bhd: rdn and hdwy over 3f out: edgd lft over 1f out: one pce* **20/1**	67+
0124	4	5	**English City (IRE)**[9] 2518 3-8-12 **56**.... DerekMcGaffin 6 (B Smart) *t.k.h in mid-div: rdn over 3f out: no hdwy* **9/2**[2]	45
0000	5	nk	**Mystified (IRE)**[19] 2240 3-9-4 **65**....(b) DNolan(3) 9 (R F Fisher) *hmpd s: hld up: hdwy over 5f out: rdn over 3f out: sn wknd* **33/1**	54
3005	6	shd	**Sunbolt (IRE)**[32] 1867 3-9-7 **65**.... PaulFessey 7 (T D Barron) *prom: led over 4f out: rdn and hdd 3f out: wknd 2f out* **20/1**	54
00-0	7	3	**Archivist (IRE)**[122] 460 3-9-0 **58**.... FrancisNorton 4 (M Blanshard) *hld up: hdwy 5f out: wknd over 3f out* **20/1**	42
2003	8	5	**Mighty Dancer (IRE)**[11] 2480 3-9-2 **60**.... FrankieMcDonald 12 (S Kirk) *hld up and bhd: nt clr run on ins 4f out: nvr nr ldrs* **10/1**[3]	36
3406	9	nk	**Zed Candy (FR)**[24] 2065 3-9-0 **65**.... AshleyHamblett(7) 3 (J T Stimpson) *t.k.h: sn led: hdd over 4f out: rdn and wknd 3f out* **20/1**	40
2060	10	15	**Blanc Visage**[20] 2209 3-9-4 **62**.... GeorgeBaker 10 (Mrs H Sweeting) *wnt lft s: hld up and bhd: hdwy 5f out: wknd 3f out* **14/1**	13
000-	11	nk	**Nona**[246] 5978 3-8-13 **62**.... JamesDoyle(5) 1 (Jedd O'Keeffe) *uns rdr bef s: hld up in tch: lost pl whn n.m.r on ins 6f out: rdn over 4f out: sn bhd* **20/1**	13
0-30	12	17	**Cartoonist (IRE)**[22] 2124 3-8-13 **57**.... RichardThomas 8 (A King) *bmpd s: a bhd: t.o* **20/1**	—

2m 38.22s (-4.20) **Going Correction** -0.225s/f (Stan) 12 Ran SP% **131.3**
Speed ratings (Par 97):105,104,98,95,95 95,93,89,89,79 79,68
CSF £27.38 CT £283.00 TOTE £30.10: £5.70, £1.10, £3.40; EX 137.60 Place 6 £56.14, Place 5 £32.33.
Owner Bonusprint **Bred** Peter McGlynn **Trained** Compton, Berks

FOCUS
A very decent winning time for a race like this, 1.88 seconds quicker than the earlier claimer for older horses and rated positively through the runner-up.
Mighty Dancer(IRE) Official explanation: jockey said gelding was denied a clear run
T/Plt: £48.30 to a £1 stake. Pool: £29,327.25. 443.10 winning tickets. T/Qpdt: £37.40 to a £1 stake. Pool: £1,896.90. 37.50 winning tickets. KH

2796 - 2798a (Foreign Racing) - See Raceform Interactive

2489 CHANTILLY (R-H)
Thursday, June 22

OFFICIAL GOING: Good

2799a PRIX HAMPTON (LISTED RACE) 5f
3:25 (3:25) 3-Y-0+ **£17,241** (£6,897; £5,172; £3,448; £1,724)

			RPR
1		**Tycoon's Hill (IRE)**[18] 2276 7-9-2.... OPeslier 5 (Robert Collet, France)	104
2	3/4	**Treasure Cay**[17] 2308 5-9-2.... IMendizabal 11 (P W D'Arcy) *close up towards outside, stayed on under pressure final f to take 2nd last strides (20/1)* **20/1**[1]	101
3	snk	**Alyzea (IRE)**[18] 2276 3-8-10.... MBlancpain 10 (C Laffon-Parias, France)	98
4	shd	**Omasheriff (IRE)**[28] 1973 4-9-5....(b) YLerner 6 (Bruce Hellier, Germany)	103
5	1 1/2	**Mister Chocolate (IRE)**[18] 2276 3-8-10.... JAuge 12 (Robert Collet, France) **36/1**[2]	93
6	snk	**Priere**[19] 4-8-12.... TThulliez 4 (N Clement, France)	90
7	1/2	**Stormiano (GER)**[46] 4-9-2.... ADeVries 7 (Dr A Bolte, Germany)	92
8	snk	**Ratio**[258] 5729 8-9-5.... TGillet 14 (J E Hammond, France)	95
9	3/4	**Karlo Guitar (BRZ)**[97] 6-9-5.... C-PLemaire 3 (M Delzangles, France)	92
10	snk	**Matrix (GER)**[28] 1973 5-9-5.... JVictoire 1 (W Baltromei, Germany)	92
11		**Arizona Sun (IRE)**[31] 3-8-7.... MGuyon 13 (A Fabre, France)	84

The Form Book, Raceform Ltd, Compton, RG20 6NL

12 **Shoeshine Boy (IRE)**[632] 8-9-2 .... GBraem 8 89
(Mlle A De Clerck, France)

13 **Meliksah (IRE)**[39] 1717 12-9-2 .... TRicher 9 89
(Mrs D Smith, Germany) **42/1**[3]

58.70 secs
WFA 3 from 4yo+ 6lb **13** Ran SP% **9.8**
PARI-MUTUEL: WIN 6.20 (coupled with Mister Chocolate): PL 2.90, 5.30,3.60; DF 77.90.
Owner R C Strauss **Bred** Kilfrush Stud Ltd **Trained** Chantilly, France

NOTEBOOK
Treasure Cay, who is unable to race in Britain at the moment due to a stalls ban, ran a fine race from a disadvantageous high draw and may well return to France for the Goup 3 Prix du Cercle at Deauville on August 3rd.

2771 ASCOT (R-H)
Friday, June 23

OFFICIAL GOING: Good to firm
Wind: Almost nil Weather: Sunny & warm

2800 ALBANY STKS (GROUP 3) (FILLIES) 6f
2:35 (2:35) (Class 1) 2-Y-O

£34,068 (£12,912; £6,462; £3,222; £1,614; £810) **Stalls** Low

Form RPR

4 **1** **Sander Camillo (USA)**[28] 1989 2-8-12 .... LDettori 7 104+
(J Noseda) *lw: racd nr side: mde virtually all: shkn up and drew clr jst over 1f out: edgd rt but wl in command fnl f* **4/1**[1]

1 **2** 1 ½ **Silk Blossom (IRE)**[65] 1082 2-8-12 .... MichaelHills 16 100
(B W Hills) *lw: hld up and racd towards outer: prog 2f out: r.o fnl f to take 2nd last 75yds: no ch of rching wnr* **7/1**

01 **3** ½ **Scarlet Runner**[11] 2506 2-8-12 .... KerrinMcEvoy 17 98
(J L Dunlop) *racd on outside and hld up in midfield: prog over 2f out: r.o to chse wnr ins fnl f: no imp: lost 2nd last 75yds* **20/1**

2 **4** 2 ½ **Medley**[17] 2328 2-8-12 .... RichardHughes 6 91+
(R Hannon) *lw: dwlt: hld up wl in rr: swtchd rt and effrt over 2f out: styd on fr over 1f out: nrst fin* **8/1**

31 **5** shd **Satulagi (USA)**[53] 1360 2-8-12 .... JohnEgan 8 90
(J S Moore) *dwlt: sn chsd ldrs: rdn over 2f out: kpt on same pce: nvr able to chal* **100/1**

11 **6** shd **Bahama Mama (IRE)**[19] 2258 2-8-12 .... KFallon 13 90
(J Noseda) *lw: w ldrs: pressed wnr 2f out to over 1f out: wknd fnl f* **6/1**[2]

41 **7** 3 **Riverside Dancer (USA)**[55] 1295 2-8-12 .... NCallan 20 81
(K A Ryan) *racd towards outer: cl up bhd ldrs: rdn 2f out: grad fdd fr over 1f out* **20/1**

32 **8** ¾ **Baltic Belle (IRE)**[30] 1930 2-8-12 .... RyanMoore 4 79
(R Hannon) *lw: dwlt: wl in rr: rdn over 2f out: effrt u.p over 1f out: no real prog after* **16/1**

631 **9** 1 **La Roca (IRE)**[17] 2328 2-8-12 .... MJKinane 10 76
(R M Beckett) *hld up in rr: swtchd to outer and effrt over 2f out: no prog over 1f out* **20/1**

2 **10** ¾ **Danseuse**[8] 2572 2-8-12 .... MartinDwyer 3 73
(C E Brittain) *outpcd and struggling on nr side over 3f out: effrt u.p over 1f out: no imp* **50/1**

3436 **11** ½ **Cassiara**[23] 2125 2-8-12 .... JimmyQuinn 14 72+
(J Pearce) *stmbld s: nvr beyond midfield: rdn whn hmpd jst over 2f out: no ch after* **33/1**

2 **12** 4 **Goodbye Cash (IRE)**[13] 2432 2-8-12 .... ShaneKelly 9 60
(P D Evans) *trckd ldrs: rdn and wknd 2f out* **66/1**

4123 **13** nk **Amber Valley**[18] 2309 2-8-12 .... RobertWinston 15 59
(K A Ryan) *lw: w ldrs tl wknd rapidly jst over 2f out* **12/1**

1 **14** ½ **Emma's Surprise**[24] 2106 2-8-12 .... DO'Donohoe 19 58
(K A Ryan) *dwlt: racd on outer and sn struggling: u.p and btn 1/2-way* **25/1**

3 **15** nk **Elizabeth Street (USA)**[47] 1514 2-8-12 .... EddieAhern 5 57
(P F I Cole) *cl up on inner tl wknd rapidly 2f out* **20/1**

12 **16** shd **Just Joey**[23] 2125 2-8-12 .... DarryllHolland 12 56
(J R Weymes) *w ldrs to 1/2-way: wknd rapidly* **25/1**

21 **17** ½ **Bicoastal (USA)**[28] 1989 2-8-12 .... JimmyFortune 11 55
(B J Meehan) *lw: hld up bhd ldrs: rdn whn hmpd jst over 2f out: wknd rapidly* **13/2**[3]

0 **18** 1 ¼ **Cheveme (IRE)**[17] 2328 2-8-12 .... OPeslier 1 51
(B W Duke) *s.s: a wl in rr: nvr a factor* **100/1**

1m 14.27s (-1.73) **Going Correction** -0.20s/f (Firm) **18** Ran SP% **119.9**
Speed ratings (Par 100):103,101,100,97,96 96,92,91,90,89 88,83,83,82,81 81,81,79
CSF £25.16 TOTE £5.30: £2.10, £2.70, £5.60; EX 42.10 Trifecta £945.40 Pool: £4,660.80 - 3.50 winning units.
Owner Sir Robert Ogden **Bred** P Robertson And Brenda Robertson **Trained** Newmarket, Suffolk

FOCUS
This was run in the sort of winning time you would expect for a race of its type, and it has been rated an average renewal. It does not look rock solid, with the fifth a bit of a concern, but Sander Camillo has been rated only a length behind her stable's 2005 winner of the corresponding race, La Chunga.

NOTEBOOK
Sander Camillo(USA) ◆ fully made up for her debut defeat, on ground that was far too soft for her, with a solid-looking and classy performance. Always to the fore, travelling well, she stretched away from the field just before the two-furlong marker and kept on strongly. Quotes as high as 33/1 for next season's 1000 Guineas do not seem unreasonable, and her pedigree suggests she has every chance of staying a mile, as her sire Dixie Union won a Grade 1 in America over nine furlongs and the dam was high-class there from six furlongs to a mile. The Princess Margaret Stakes and the Lowther are options, and she also holds an entry for the Group 1 Moyglare Stud Stakes. (op 9-2 tchd 5-1 in places)
Silk Blossom(IRE) , who was not helped by a moderate draw, was touted as a Queen Mary type after her winning debut, but she was under strong pressure three furlongs from home, before switching to the middle of the track and coming home strongly in the final furlong. There was nothing in the effort to suggest that she would have been suited by the minimum trip at this level and, indeed, she looks as though she may get a seventh furlongs in time. The Princess Margaret Stakes would seem the ideal next race for her, as long as Sander Camillo does not turn up. (op 6-1)
Scarlet Runner, who finished behind Sander Camillo on her debut before winning at Windsor last time, had every chance but was not quite in the same class as the winner on the day. She looks sure to keep on improving, and has the Goffs Million as a possible target later in the season, but there is no obvious reason why she should reverse form with the winner in the foreseeable future.
Medley, who was behind La Roca on her debut, took a while to get organised and only managed to keep on at the one pace after finding room from behind a wall of horses. She made her challenge at the same time as Silk Blossom, but had nowhere near the same turn-of-foot that filly had, and is likely to struggle in similar company over six furlongs. That said, she ought to win her maiden without too much fuss and, ultimately, may benefit from a bit further. (op 11-1)
Satulagi(USA) was the surprise package in the race, as although she had won a race, which has produced winners, it was at a fairly low-level. Outpaced in Ireland last time over five furlongs, she enjoyed the step back up in trip and ran her heart out for her small stable. She has a few nice entries already and should do her yard proud.
Bahama Mama(IRE), who ran a really quick time in a three-runner race at Brighton last time, was upsides the winner with a furlong and a half to go, but did not seem to see out the trip - although she did have to do plenty of early work to get over from a high draw. A less-demanding six furlongs or even five will probably be ideal for her in the future, although it would not be the biggest surprise to see her return for a crack at the Princess Margaret next, which is run over the same trip. (op 11-2 tchd 13-2 and 7-1 in places)
Riverside Dancer(USA) showed plenty of pace from her wide draw and gave the strong impression that a drop down to five furlongs is required, especially if tried in similar company again. (op 25-1)
Baltic Belle(IRE), a filly who appears to have plenty of size about her, struggled to go the early pace and was going nowhere three furlongs from home. However, she picked up fairly well, as others weakened around her, and already looks in need of further, and possibly more time to mature. (op 20-1)
La Roca(IRE) never got into the race and was beaten a long way from home. She looked a long way below the required class for a Group 3. (op 16-1)
Amber Valley, a close second to Queen Mary winner Gilded earlier in the season, ran a long way below her recent best and gave the impression that five furlongs is more likely to suit her. Official explanation: trainer's representative said filly had been unsuited by the good to firm going
Bicoastal(USA), who won the Newmarket race in which Sander Camillo made her debut, travelled nicely for a lot of the race before being hampered quite badly twice, especially on the second occasion by Just Joey, and was not given a hard time afterwards. One suspects she would have been involved in the shake-up otherwise, and she can easily be given another chance. Official explanation: jockey said filly had run flat (tchd 6-1 and 7-1 in places)

2801 KING EDWARD VII STKS (GROUP 2) (C&G) 1m 4f
3:10 (3:11) (Class 1) 3-Y-O

£122,394 (£46,388; £23,215; £11,575; £5,798; £2,910) **Stalls** High

Form RPR

-110 **1** **Papal Bull**[20] 2228 3-8-12 106 .... KFallon 4 116+
(Sir Michael Stoute) *lw: racd keenly: trckd ldrs: effrt over 2f out: rdn to ld over 1f out: edgd rt and r.o ins fnl f: in command last strides* **5/4**[1]

2-11 **2** nk **Red Rocks (IRE)**[27] 2030 3-8-12 107 .... LDettori 9 115
(B J Meehan) *lw: led at stdy pce: rdn and hdd over 1f out: stl ev ch and r.o u.p ins fnl f: hld last strides* **3/1**[2]

610 **3** 2 ½ **Sixties Icon**[20] 2228 3-8-12 90 .... ShaneKelly 2 111
(J Noseda) *hld up: rdn and hdwy 2f out: styd on ins fnl f: nt rch front pair* **8/1**[3]

-212 **4** 2 **Degas Art (IRE)**[27] 2030 3-8-12 .... JohnEgan 1 108
(D R C Elsworth) *racd keenly: prom: rdn over 2f out: outpcd over 1f out* **14/1**

11 **5** 1 **Tam Lin**[35] 1813 3-8-12 97 .... RobertWinston 5 106
(Sir Michael Stoute) *lw: s.i.s: racd keenly: hld up: sn in midfield: effrt and hung rt fr over 2f out: tail flashed u.p: one pce fnl* **14/1**

1-63 **6** 4 **Morghim (IRE)**[48] 1488 3-8-12 96 .... RHills 6 100
(J L Dunlop) *lw: hld up in rr: rdn and rn wd bnd wl over 2f out: sn hung rt: no imp on ldrs* **50/1**

-633 **7** 1 **Baan (USA)**[41] 1668 3-8-12 102 .... MartinDwyer 8 98
(M Johnston) *in tch: pushed along 4f out: rdn over 2f out: edgd rt and wknd over 1f out* **33/1**

5-14 **8** 2 **Steppe Dancer (IRE)**[14] 2404 3-8-12 84 .... JamieSpencer 7 95
(D J Coakley) *lw: s.i.s: sn trckd ldrs: rdn over 2f out: wknd over 1f out* **33/1**

1-13 **9** 7 **Youmzain (IRE)**[40] 1708 3-8-12 106 .... TonyCulhane 3 84
(M R Channon) *hld up: stmbld on bnd wl over 2f out: sn rdn: nvr a danger* **8/1**[3]

2m 28.02s (-4.98) **Going Correction** -0.125s/f (Firm) **9** Ran SP% **112.8**
Speed ratings (Par 111):111,110,109,107,107 104,103,102,97
CSF £4.65 TOTE £2.20: £1.20, £1.30, £2.00; EX 4.40 Trifecta £25.10 Pool: £6,474.95 - 182.94 winning units.
Owner Mrs J Magnier, D Smith & M Tabor **Bred** B H And C F D Simpson **Trained** Newmarket, Suffolk
■ Stewards' Enquiry : Shane Kelly caution: careless riding
L Dettori six-day ban: used whip with excessive frequency and without giving time to respond (Jul 5-10)

FOCUS
A decent renewal of this contest, featuring some progressive types and a couple that finished in mid field in the Derby. The early pace was not strong, resulting in a few pulling for their heads early and it suited those that raced handily. Even so, the winning time was about par for the type of contest, despite being 0.78 seconds slower than the King George V Handicap, and the form looks sound enough..

NOTEBOOK
Papal Bull ◆, tenth in the Derby when not getting the clearest of runs, bounced back to winning form despite not much going right for him in the race itself. Firstly, he was caught out wide running down to Swinley Bottom and took a fierce hold as a result, and even when the field raced up the hill towards the home straight he found little cover. One of the first off the bridle, he could have been excused for having little left in the tank, but in fact he kept on responding to pressure and despite hanging into the runner-up as ranged alongside a furlong out, he ground out a well-deserved victory. This was a splendid effort under the circumstances and he strikes as the type to carry on improving with racing. (op 11-8 tchd 6-4 and 6-5 and 13-8 in places and 11-10 in places)
Red Rocks(IRE) ◆, stepping up an extra two furlongs in trip, was given a canny ride from the front by Dettori who set his own tempo for much of the way before quickening soon after the field turned for home. He did nothing wrong and certainly saw out the extra distance, but just ran into very determined and talented rival on the day. He seems a versatile sort when it comes to ground conditions and on this evidence he looks well up to winning in Group company. (op 5-2 tchd 10-3)
Sixties Icon ◆, who finished three places in front of Papal Bull in the Derby, was given a patient ride in a race run to suit those that raced closer to the pace. He stayed on well once in line for home, but the front two had gone beyond recall and, as at Epsom, he gave the impression this trip is barely far enough, especially if the pace is not strong. Given his relative lack of experience this was still a very creditable effort and the St Leger could be just the type of race for him. (op 7-1)
Degas Art(IRE) looks a stayer, so the modest early tempo did not help him at all, and like a few of the others, he pulled too hard early. Once the pace increased, he was found wanting but he still finished about the same distance behind Red Rocks as he had at Newmarket last time, which does suggest he ran to form. He looks well up to winning a Listed contest at least given a truly run race. (op 16-1 tchd 20-1 in places)
Tam Lin, the least-experienced in the field and winner of a four-runner Hamilton Listed event last time, found this rather different. He was close enough turning in, but still looked green in the home straight and was never doing enough. He may well be the type that improves with racing. (op 12-1)

Morghim(IRE) faced a very difficult task in trying to come from so far back given the way the race panned out and being forced so wide on the home bend was the last thing he needed. He does not look up to this level, but this was only his third outing so there is time.
Baan(USA) looks well and truly exposed now and was out of his depth here.
Steppe Dancer(IRE), having only his second start on turf after two outings on Polytrack, pulled very hard early and that made an already stiff task virtually impossible. (tchd 40-1)
Youmzain(IRE), taking a huge step up in class, already had a mountain to climb when getting unbalanced on the crown of the home bend. (op 9-1)

2802 CORONATION STKS (GROUP 1) (FILLIES) 1m (R)

3:50 (3:51) (Class 1) 3-Y-O

£152,170 (£57,673; £28,863; £14,391; £7,209; £3,618) **Stalls** High

Form				RPR
11-0	**1**		**Nannina**[47] [1508] 3-9-0 113 ... JimmyFortune 13 (J H M Gosden) *lw: hld up in midfield: 8th st: prog on inner over 2f out: led over 1f out and sn drvn 3 l clr: styd on wl* **6/1**[1]	118+
23-0	**2**	*2*	**Flashy Wings**[47] [1508] 3-9-0 115 ... JamieSpencer 9 (M R Channon) *lw: settled in rr: rdn and 10th st: prog on outer 2f out: styd on to take 2nd ins fnl f: no ch w wnr* **13/2**[2]	112
-130	**3**	*3/4*	**Nasheej (USA)**[26] [2054] 3-9-0 107 ... RyanMoore 15 (R Hannon) *lw: trckd ldrs: 5th st: rdn and nt qckn over 2f out: styd on again fnl f to snatch 3rd last stride* **20/1**	110
1-04	**4**	*shd*	**Race For The Stars (USA)**[26] [2054] 3-9-0 ... KFallon 5 (A P O'Brien, Ire) *lw: settled in rr: 12th st: drvn and prog on outer 2f out: disp 2nd ins fnl f: one pce nr fin* **7/1**[3]	110
-050	**5**	*1*	**Rajeem**[54] [1328] 3-9-0 96 ... KerrinMcEvoy 14 (C E Brittain) *hld up wl in rr: 11th and prog on inner st: nt clr run over 1f out: styd on: nrst fin* **150/1**	108
11-4	**6**	*shd*	**Silca's Sister**[47] [1508] 3-9-0 115 ... LDettori 7 (Saeed Bin Suroor) *lw: mostly chsd ldr to 2f out: rdn and steadily fdd* **7/1**[3]	108
4-11	**7**	*1*	**Vague (USA)**[127] [436] 3-9-0 108 ... MJKinane 11 (J Noseda) *lw: hld up in rr: 14th and rdn st: kpt on fr over 1f out: n.d* **20/1**	105
5-31	**8**	*3/4*	**Price Tag**[40] [1719] 3-9-0 ... TThulliez 12 (P Bary, France) *lengthy: lw: dwlt: hld up wl in rr: 13th st: effrt on outer whn nt clr run 2f out: no ch after* **6/1**[1]	103
-114	**9**	*1/2*	**Speciosa (IRE)**[21] [2203] 3-9-0 114 ... MickyFenton 1 (Mrs P Sly) *lw: led and crossed fr wd draw to rail: hdd & wknd over 1f out* **9/1**	102
2-52	**10**	*1/2*	**Wake Up Maggie (IRE)**[27] [2031] 3-9-0 108 ... AlanMunro 10 (C F Wall) *hld up in midfield: 9th st: rdn over 2f out: sn no prog and btn* **14/1**	101
11	**11**	*2*	**Lolita (GER)**[54] [1328] 3-9-0 ... OPeslier 8 (Andreas Lowe, Germany) *rangy: unf: scope: racd on outer: prog fr rr 5f out: 8th st: rdn over 2f out : wknd over 1f out* **12/1**	97
0-10	**12**	*1 1/4*	**Nantyglo**[21] [2199] 3-9-0 103 ... TQuinn 2 (M L W Bell) *lw: dwlt: swtchd fr wd draw to inner and hld up in last: rdn over 2f out: no rspnse* **150/1**	94
11-0	**13**	*1 3/4*	**Donna Blini**[47] [1508] 3-9-0 114 ... RichardHughes 6 (B J Meehan) *trckd ldrs: 6th st: rdn over 2f out: sn wknd* **33/1**	90
1-52	**14**	*2*	**Mostaqeleh (USA)**[19] [2275] 3-9-0 98 ... RHills 4 (J L Dunlop) *lw: prom: 4th st: rdn to dispute 2nd 2f out: sn wknd rapidly* **50/1**	85
0-1	**15**	*9*	**Nightime (IRE)**[26] [2054] 3-9-0 ... PJSmullen 3 (D K Weld, Ire) *prom: 3rd st: wknd rapidly 2f out: eased* **7/1**[3]	64

1m 39.14s (-2.96) **Going Correction** -0.125s/f (Firm) **15** Ran SP% **119.5**
Speed ratings (Par 110):109,107,106,106,105 105,104,103,102,102 100,99,97,95,86
CSF £41.05 TOTE £7.80: £3.10, £2.70, £9.10; EX 30.10 Trifecta £533.10 Pool: £8,328.23 - 11.09 winning units. Nannina failed dope test but B sample proved negative and she kept race.
Owner Cheveley Park Stud **Bred** Cheveley Park Stud Ltd **Trained** Newmarket, Suffolk

FOCUS

A fantastic renewal, with no fewer than five Guineas winners from around Europe and Dubai taking part, plus the winners of several of the key fillies' races of 2005. Some of those down the field behind Speciosa at Newmarket were much happier on this ground, so no great surprise that they reversed the form. It was an acceptable winning time for such a prestigious contest.

NOTEBOOK

Nannina ◆, not seen since finishing down the field in the 1000 Guineas back in May, returned to her very best under an excellent ride. Not much had gone right for her in the spring, well documented niggles and soft ground proving a nuisance to her preparation, but she had the form in the book as a two-year-old to prove she was a top-class filly - a defeat of Oaks winner Alexandova bares testament to that. Always tracking the pace on the inside rail, she came with a really strong run just over a furlong from home and simply had too much class in hand to be caught after getting to the front. Connections have plenty of options, but nominated the Sussex Stakes at Goodwood as her next target, where she will take on the boys for the first time. She can make up into one of the stars of the season. (op 13-2 tchd 7-1 in places)
Flashy Wings, who like the winner had run down the field in the 1000 Guineas on soft ground, confirmed that she had trained on, finishing strongly down the middle of the track in the final furlong. It is possible to argue that she was given a shade too much to do, from an awkward position, but to say she would have beaten the winner with a similar run down the inside of the track would be stretching the imagination a bit. However, it must be noted that she only had three rivals behind her off the final turn, one of them being the fourth home. Connections believe that she needed the run after an absence, so more improvement can be expected. (op 7-1 tchd 15-2 in places)
Nasheej(USA), who has run in plenty of the top fillies' races already, ran almost to the pound with Nannina on Fillies' Mile form as a two-year-old, and battled on bravely to the line after becoming slightly outpaced in the home straight. A step up in trip might prove ideal for her, with a race like the Sun Chariot towards the end of the season a reasonable target. However, that is not to say she cannot mix it with the best of the milers of her sex, as she finished in front of plenty of good horses with top-class form at the trip.
Race For The Stars(USA), back on her favoured fast surface, looked to be given too much ground to make up after settling at the rear of the pack early. Not for the first time, she took a while to get going, but still managed to come with a promising-looking effort down the middle of the track in the straight. She appeared not to get home, and might not be quite up to Group 1 company. However, things could have been different if she had been closer to the pace throughout, and had not been forced fairly wide of the home bend. She is entitled to one more chance.
Rajeem, who lost 27 kilos while travelling to Germany last time, ran by far her best race to date, and can be counted as slightly unlucky not to have finished a bit closer, after meeting Speciosa going backwards late on. She will need to prove the run is no fluke, and one will have a better idea of her true ability after her next run. She holds an entry in the Group 1 Pretty Polly Stakes at the Curragh, which seems a sensible next target. (op 100-1)
Silca's Sisterwas ridden to get the trip but did not seem to fully stay a mile - despite having finished fourth in the English 1000 Guineas. However, after the race it transpired that she had been struck into. Official explanation: vet said filly had been struck into behind (op 13-2 tchd 15-2 in places)
Vague(USA) had plenty to do in the straight and did well to finish as close as she did. Having her first run since landing the UAE 1000 Guineas in February, she is entitled to come on for the run.
Price Tag, demoted to second after winning the French 1000 Guineas, did not get the best of runs up the home straight, but probably would not have troubled the winner even with a totally clear passage, given the way her effort flattened out when finding space. She may want ten furlongs. (tchd 13-2 in places)
Speciosa(IRE) overcame her outside draw and led for much of the race, but having handled the turn perfectly well she had nothing left when they closed on her and weakened through the field. She has had plenty of racing already during 2006 at the top level, and it is not a massive surprise to see those who finished behind her in the 1000 Guineas comprehensively reverse form on ground they all would have preferred back in May. She will be given a break now until the autumn. (tchd 10-1)
Wake Up Maggie(IRE), who was forced to weave from left to right down the home straight in an attempt to find room, gave the strong impression that a mile stretches her stamina in top-class company. (op 16-1 tchd 20-1 in places)
Lolita(GER), the winner of the German 1000 Guineas and suppemented for this, almost certainly found conditions too quick for her, given all the evidence in the Form Book. She had finished miles in front of fifth-placed Rajeem in Germany, and one suspects she will be a totally different proposition on ground with ease.
Donna Blini did not get home after racing prominently. A return to sprinting looks in order.
Nightime(IRE), such an impressive winner of the Irish 1000 Guineas on soft ground, dropped out very tamely and one can only presume that the ground was too quick for her. Official explanation: jockey said filly was unsuited by the good to firm ground (op 13-2 tchd 15-2 and 8-1 in places)

2803 WOLFERTON H'CAP (LISTED RACE) 1m 2f

4:25 (4:28) (Class 1) (0-110,113) 4-Y-0+

£31,229 (£11,836; £5,923; £2,953; £1,479; £742) **Stalls** High

Form				RPR
5-55	**1**		**I'm So Lucky**[35] [1815] 4-8-7 **96** ... JoeFanning 11 (M Johnston) *lw: mde all: rdn 2f out: abt 3 l clr over 1f out: kpt on wl* **16/1**	107
23-1	**2**	*1 1/4*	**Wild Savannah**[48] [1484] 4-9-0 **103** ... JimmyFortune 16 (J H M Gosden) *lw: trckd ldrs: nt clr run over 2f out: rdn and swtchd lft wl over 1f out: sn wnt 2nd: r.o and edgd rt ins fnl f: nt* **9/2**[2]	112+
5340	**3**	*1/2*	**Crosspeace (IRE)**[21] [2201] 4-9-3 **106** ... RoystonFfrench 9 (M Johnston) *lw: midfield: niggled along over 4f out: sn lost pl: rdn and hdwy 2f out: nt clr run and swtchd lft ins fnl f: r.o wl* **20/1**	114
-211	**4**	*1 1/2*	**Blue Monday**[8] [2597] 5-9-10 **113** 3ex ... SteveDrowne 8 (R Charlton) *lw: midfield: niggled along over 4f out: rdn whn hdwy and nt clr run over 1f out: styd on wl towards fin* **15/2**	118+
0-13	**5**	*nk*	**Star Of Light**[21] [2201] 5-8-11 **100** ... AlanMunro 3 (B J Meehan) *racd keenly: prom: rdn over 2f out: styd on same pce fnl f* **6/1**[3]	105
4222	**6**	*hd*	**Boule D'Or (IRE)**[20] [2226] 5-9-4 **107** ... MichaelHills 2 (J Akehurst) *lw: dwlt: racd keenly: hld up: rdn and hdwy on outside 2f out: styd on and edgd rt ins fnl f: one pce cl home* **16/1**	111
-536	**7**	*3/4*	**Salamanca**[27] [2011] 4-8-8 **97** ... JamieSpencer 7 (S Kirk) *lw: hld up: pushed along 4f out: rdn and hdwy 2f out: styd on ins fnl f: nt rch ldrs* **25/1**	100
0-50	**8**	*3/4*	**Courageous Duke (USA)**[134] [356] 7-8-11 **100** ... OPeslier 10 (J Noseda) *s.s: hld up: hdwy on outside 3f out: rdn 2f out: one pce fnl f* **33/1**	101
100-	**9**	*1/2*	**Forward Move (IRE)**[266] [5590] 4-9-5 **108** ... RyanMoore 13 (R Hannon) *bit bkwd: tracked ldrs: rdn over 2f out: wknd fnl f* **50/1**	108
-031	**10**	*1/2*	**Blue Spinnaker (IRE)**[37] [1775] 7-8-10 **99** ... PaulMulrennan 5 (M W Easterby) *midfield: rdn 2f out: nt clr run over 1f out: sn lost pl: no imp after* **12/1**	98
-024	**11**	*1 3/4*	**Momtic (IRE)**[20] [2226] 5-9-3 **106** ... KFallon 15 (W Jarvis) *midfield: rdn whn nt clr run over 1f out: outpcd after* **10/1**	102
/1-1	**12**	*1*	**Public Forum**[55] [1301] 4-8-7 **96** ... RichardHughes 14 (Sir Michael Stoute) *swtg: w wnr to 4f out: rdn over 2f out: wknd over 1f out* **7/2**[1]	90
0034	**13**	*2*	**Kings Quay**[21] [2201] 4-8-7 **96** ... GrahamGibbons 1 (J J Quinn) *lw: hld up: nt clr run 3f out and again over 2f out: nvr on terms* **20/1**	86
0004	**14**	*2*	**Compton Bolter (IRE)**[42] [1628] 9-9-2 **105** ... (b) LDettori 6 (G A Butler) *hld up: pushed along over 4f out: rdn and sme hdwy over 2f out: wknd over 1f out: eased whn btn ins fnl f* **33/1**	92
0223	**15**	*3/4*	**Kew Green (USA)**[43] [1601] 8-9-6 **109** ... DaneO'Neill 12 (P R Webber) *in tch: rdn over 2f out: wknd over 1f out* **33/1**	94
1245	**16**	*10*	**Grand Passion (IRE)**[24] [2116] 6-9-1 **104** ... TedDurcan 4 (G Wragg) *midfield: rdn over 2f out: sn nt clr run and lost pl: bhd after* **33/1**	70

2m 4.15s (-3.85) **Going Correction** -0.125s/f (Firm) **16** Ran SP% **122.1**
Speed ratings (Par 111):110,109,108,107,107 107,106,105,105,105 103,102,101,99,99 91
CSF £78.51 CT £1490.13 TOTE £21.90: £3.40, £1.50, £5.50, £2.10; EX 115.10 Trifecta £1729.90 Pool: £7,065.96 - 2.90 winning units.
Owner Mrs S J Brookhouse **Bred** Leydens Farm Stud **Trained** Middleham Moor, N Yorks

FOCUS

A very decent handicap run at a solid pace and about the sort of winning time as you would expect for a race like this. Despite that, very few ever got into it and the winner had the race in the bag from some way out. The draw played its part too, with the front four coming from the highest-drawn half of the field.

NOTEBOOK

I'm So Lucky had plenty going for him, being back over his best trip and, probably more relevantly, back on the same mark as for his last victory. Given the sort of positive ride for which the stable's representatives are so renowned, he set a decent early pace but still kept enough in the tank to quicken into what became an unassailable lead soon after turning in. His stable have endured a rather stuttering early part of the season, but this was a trademark victory by one of their inmates in a red-hot race, so they may well have turned the corner.
Wild Savannah ◆, who had I'm So Lucky nearly six lengths behind him when winning at Newmarket last time, was 6lb worse off with him here. Taking a handy position from the rails draw, he did find himself trapped in a pocket approaching the last two furlongs and took a while to get out. Given how well he finished once in the clear, he would probably have given the winner plenty to think about with a clear run and deserves compensation in a similarly competitive event. A race like the John Smiths' Cup could be the sort of race for him. (tchd 5-1 in places)
Crosspeace(IRE) rather found himself trapped in amongst horses soon after turning for home, but stayed on very well once seeing daylight. This was an encouraging effort and he is gradually dropping back to a fair mark, but a return to 12 furlongs may be needed.
Blue Monday may technically have been dropping in class, having won a Group 3 at Longchamp just eight days previously, but he still faced a stiff task in conceding weight to this talented field. As he did not enjoy the clearest of runs before finishing to some purpose, he still emerges with a lot of credit. (op 8-1)
Star Of Light did well to stick on and finish where he did as he found himself trapped out wide from his low draw in the early stages and raced very keenly as a result. There are more races to be won with him given the rub of the green. (op 11-2 tchd 13-2 in places)
Boule D'Or(IRE), down from Group 3 company, was held up from his wide draw but faced a stiff task in trying to come from so far back given the way the contest panned out, especially as he was forced very wide on the home bend. He is a talented performer, but is putting together a lengthy losing run. (op 20-1)

Salamanca ◆, trying this trip for the first time, was given a patient ride before making her effort tight against the inside rail once in line for home. She appeared to get a clear run and was staying on nicely at the line, so as far as her stamina is concerned this was encouraging. Official explanation: jockey said filly was unsuited by the good to firm ground

Courageous Duke(USA) Official explanation: jockey said gelding missed the break

Public Forum, unbeaten in three well spaced-out previous efforts, appeared to hold the ideal position just behind the leader against the inside rail for most of the way, but once asked for his effort the response was very disappointing. He has questions to answer now. (tchd 4-1)

Kings Quay Official explanation: jockey said gelding hung left throughout

2804 QUEEN'S VASE (GROUP 3) 2m

4:55 (4:59) (Class 1) 3-Y-O

£34,068 (£12,912; £6,462; £3,222; £1,614; £810) **Stalls** High

Form RPR

2121 **1** **Soapy Danger**[13] [2436] 3-9-1 96 ..... KDarley 10 103
(M Johnston) *lw: dwlt: rousted along to go prom: rn in snatches after: drvn to ld over 2f out: hung rt over 1f out: styd on wl* **4/1**[3]

0-11 **2** 1 ¼ **Galient (IRE)**[44] [1586] 3-9-1 93 ..... PhilipRobinson 9 101
(M A Jarvis) *lw: led: rdn and hdd over 2f out: hld whn hmpd on inner over 1f out : edgd lft but styd on fnl f* **11/4**[1]

-222 **3** ½ **Ermine Sea**[14] [2412] 3-9-1 85 ..... JimmyFortune 5 100
(J H M Gosden) *trckd ldng pair: rdn and nt qckn over 2f out: styd on fr over 1f out: unable to chal* **33/1**

4 1 ¾ **Road To Mandalay (IRE)**[19] [2274] 3-9-1 ..... KFallon 3 98
(A P O'Brien, Ire) *neat: lw: t.k.h early: hld up in rr: nt clr run 3f out: rdn and one pce fnl 2f* **7/2**[2]

1124 **5** shd **Lightning Strike (GER)**[32] [1898] 3-9-1 83 ..... IanMongan 4 98
(T G Mills) *lw: hld up wl in rr: taken to outer and drvn over 2f out: kpt on but nvr gng pce to rch ldrs* **66/1**

5-21 **6** ½ **Shipmaster**[35] [1826] 3-9-1 78 ..... EddieAhern 11 98
(A King) *lw: trckd ldrs: rdn over 2f out: one pce and no imp after* **33/1**

34-4 **7** 1 ½ **Private Business (USA)**[55] [1300] 3-9-1 104 ..... RichardHughes 2 96
(B W Hills) *racd on outer: hld up in midfield: rdn 3f out: no prog after* **11/1**

61 **8** nk **Mount Kilimanjaro (IRE)**[25] [2066] 3-9-1 78 ..... MJKinane 8 95
(J L Dunlop) *lw: hld up in last pair: rdn over 3f out: one pce and no ch fnl 2f* **14/1**

-150 **9** 1 ½ **Kassiopeia (IRE)**[21] [2203] 3-8-12 90 ..... TonyCulhane 6 91
(M R Channon) *t.k.h: hld up in rr: rdn and no prog over 2f out* **16/1**

-311 **10** nk **Ogee**[32] [1898] 3-9-1 91 ..... RyanMoore 7 93
(Sir Michael Stoute) *lw: hld up in last: gng wl enough 4f out: rdn and no prog over 2f out* **15/2**

4-4 **11** 1 **Blue Ksar (FR)**[48] [1488] 3-9-1 102 ..... (t) LDettori 1 92
(Saeed Bin Suroor) *lw: mostly trckd ldr: rdn to chal over 2f out: wknd wl over 1f out* **12/1**

3m 25.6s (-10.90) **11** Ran SP% **116.6**

CSF £15.05 TOTE £5.40: £1.90, £1.80, £7.60; EX 11.70 Trifecta £347.80 Pool: £5,850.10 - 11.94 winning units.

Owner Mrs R J Jacobs **Bred** Newsells Park Stud Limited **Trained** Middleham Moor, N Yorks

■ Stewards' Enquiry : K Darley one-day ban: careless riding (Jul 4)

FOCUS

On paper a decent staying contest, but it seemed to develop into a sprint from off the home bend. Despite that, not many seemed to appreciate the two-mile trip and the form behind the front two is slightly questionable.

NOTEBOOK

Soapy Danger, who holds an entry in the King George VI And Queen Elizabeth Diamond Stakes, won in the style typical of his stable, battling hard when getting to the front and doing enough to hold on. There is no doubt that he hampered the runner-up as he drifted over to the inside rail, but he looked the winner on merit and will surely keep on improving. It would seem highly unlikely that he will come back to the course to take up the King George engagement, as two miles appeared to suit him well and races over that trip, or just slightly shorter, would seem the logical route to take with him. (op 7-2 tchd 9-2 in places)

Galient(IRE) came with a renewed effort after being headed, and hampered, over a furlong from home, staying on strongly all the way to the line. A race such as the Bahrain Trophy, run at Newmarket in July, might be within his compass before we have a better idea if he could make up into a St Leger horse. (op 5-2 tchd 3-1 and 10-3 in places)

Ermine Sea stuck to his task well and looked to be going better the further he went. He has yet to win a race of any description, so could probably now do with a nice maiden victory to enhance his confidence.

Road To Mandalay(IRE), who holds Group 1 entries in Ireland over varying trips, was still travelling nicely coming into the straight, but appeared to be outstayed in the final three furlongs. He has plenty of scope for more improvement, but may need to be dropped in trip slightly to be seen at his best. (op 9-2 tchd 5-1 in places)

Lightning Strike(GER), who looked to be almost twice the size of any of his rivals, just kept galloping away down the middle of the track after being held up early. The trip looked to suit, so the chances are that he was probably flying a bit too high in Group 3 company.

Shipmaster only has a rating of 78, so ran above himself, despite never posing a threat at any stage. (tchd 40-1 in places)

Private Business(USA), who had only been tried at up to ten furlongs before the race, did not get home and probably could do with going down in trip by at least half a mile. (op 12-1)

Mount Kilimanjaro(IRE) was always towards the rear and never got into the race. He is better than the effort suggests and would have been better suited by racing closer to the pace. (tchd 16-1 in places)

Ogee was always at the back of the field and never threatened to get involved. He did not seem to see out the two-mile trip. (op 8-1)

Blue Ksar(FR) dropped out very tamely after racing prominently. He did not see out the trip at all.

2805 KING GEORGE V STKS (HERITAGE H'CAP) 1m 4f

5:30 (5:32) (Class 2) (0-105,102) 3-Y-O

£34,276 (£10,263; £5,131; £2,568; £1,281; £643) **Stalls** High

Form RPR

1-21 **1** **Linas Selection**[56] [1270] 3-8-9 90 ..... KDarley 7 107+
(M Johnston) *lw: midfield: hdwy 6f out: led over 2f out: rdn and edgd rt over 1f out: r.o wl fnl f: wl in command* **9/2**[2]

6-51 **2** 3 ½ **Enjoy The Moment**[19] [2261] 3-8-3 84 ..... CraigAWilliams 3 96
(J A Osborne) *hld up in midfield: rdn and hdwy on outside over 2f out: wnt 2nd ins fnl f: styd on: nt trble wnr* **50/1**

-311 **3** 1 ¾ **Bandama (IRE)**[18] [2290] 3-8-10 91 ..... RyanMoore 11 100
(Mrs A J Perrett) *lw: in tch: effrt and wnt rt over 2f out: styd on ins fnl f* **7/1**[3]

5213 **4** ½ **Lake Poet (IRE)**[20] [2224] 3-8-8 89 ..... KerrinMcEvoy 14 97
(C E Brittain) *trckd ldrs: rdn 2f out: wnt 2nd over 1f out tl ins fnl f: kpt on same pce after* **9/1**

1240 **5** ½ **London Express (IRE)**[20] [2224] 3-8-9 90 ..... RobertWinston 13 97
(M Johnston) *in tch: lost pl 4f out: nt clr run under 3f: sn rdn: hdwy over 1f out: styd on ins fnl f* **25/1**

-646 **6** ¾ **Doctor Scott**[6] [2659] 3-8-0 81 ..... RoystonFfrench 5 87+
(M Johnston) *hld up: pushed along 3f out: hdwy over 2f out: swtchd rt wl over 1f out and again ins fnl f: fin wl* **33/1**

-111 **7** 1 ¼ **Pearly King (USA)**[34] [1841] 3-9-2 97 ..... KFallon 2 101+
(Sir Michael Stoute) *swtg: midfield on outside: hdwy 3f out: effrt to chse wnr 2f out: sn edgd rt: lost 2nd over 1f out: wknd and eased ins fnl* **4/1**[1]

-220 **8** nk **Salute The General**[20] [2224] 3-8-1 82 ..... RichardMullen 10 86
(W R Muir) *midfield: pushed along over 5f out: rdn 3f out: one pce fnl f* **12/1**

-414 **9** ¾ **Numeric (GER)**[34] [1841] 3-8-2 83 ..... MartinDwyer 4 85+
(J H M Gosden) *swtchd qckly lft s: towards rr: rdn over 2f out: hdwy whn edgd rt over 1f out: kpt on ins fnl f: nvr able to challe* **8/1**

1401 **10** shd **Prince Charlemagne (IRE)**[25] [2081] 3-7-12 84 ..... JamesDoyle(5) 9 86
(N P Littmoden) *racd keenly: midfield: rdn 3f out: sme hdwy over 1f out: no imp fnl f* **20/1**

616 **11** 2 **Balanced Budget**[26] [2046] 3-8-11 92 ..... ShaneKelly 1 91
(J Noseda) *hld up: effrt 3f out: no imp* **25/1**

1100 **12** ½ **Gracechurch (IRE)**[20] [2224] 3-7-11 81 ..... EdwardCreighton(3) 17 79
(M R Channon) *midfield: rdn over 2f out: wknd over 1f out* **40/1**

1-20 **13** 3 ½ **Hard To Explain (IRE)**[26] [2046] 3-9-0 95 ..... NickyMackay 12 88
(L M Cumani) *trckd ldrs: rdn and ev ch over 2f out: wknd over 1f out* **25/1**

3-62 **14** 7 **Road To Love (IRE)**[11] [2502] 3-8-3 84 ..... JoeFanning 8 65
(M Johnston) *led: rdn and hdd over 2f out: wkng whn n.m.r and hmpd wl over 1f out* **20/1**

-523 **15** 1 **Beckett Hall (IRE)**[35] [1822] 3-7-13 80 ..... FrankieMcDonald 18 60
(R Hannon) *w ldr to 6f out: rdn 4f out: wknd over 2f out* **100/1**

0-55 **16** shd **Beau Nash (USA)**[34] [1841] 3-8-8 89 ..... AlanMunro 19 69
(P W Chapple-Hyam) *lw: a towards rr: eased whn n.d over 1f out* **20/1**

-125 **17** 9 **The Last Drop (IRE)**[36] [1805] 3-9-7 102 ..... MichaelHills 15 67
(B W Hills) *hld up: lft bhd fnl 2f* **33/1**

5450 **18** 5 **Fiddlers Wood**[29] [1951] 3-8-2 83 ow1 ..... (p) AdrianTNicholls 6 40
(V Smith) *sn rdn: a bhd* **100/1**

1-12 **19** hd **Idarah (USA)**[26] [2046] 3-8-10 91 ..... RHills 16 48
(W J Haggas) *s.i.s: midfield: rdn 3f out: sn wknd* **14/1**

2m 27.24s (-5.76) **Going Correction** -0.125s/f (Firm) **19** Ran SP% **124.2**

Speed ratings (Par 105):114,111,110,110,109 109,108,108,107,107 106,106,103,99,98 98,92,89,88

CSF £227.77 CT £1588.81 TOTE £5.80: £1.70, £6.00, £1.80, £2.10; EX 535.60 Trifecta £2816.90 Pool: £6,506.85 - 1.64 winning units. Place 6 £85.65, Place 5 £34.24.

Owner Mrs R J Jacobs **Bred** Newsells Park Stud Limited **Trained** Middleham Moor, N Yorks

■ Linas Selection completed a 466.5-1 hat-trick for trainer Mark Johnston.

FOCUS

A cracking handicap, run at a scorching gallop thanks to Road To Love and Beckett Hall, and a very smart winning time indeed for a race of its type, 0.78 seconds faster than the earlier Group 2 over the same trip. Solid form, and a race that is sure to produce winners.

NOTEBOOK

Linas Selection ◆, whose effort behind Papal Bull at Newmarket in April looks wonderful form now, did his bit for the form of that contest with his second victory in the meantime, and he could hardly have been more impressive in achieving it. Powering his way to the front soon after turning in, he gradually forged further and further clear to win in style. The winning time backs up the positive visual impression of this race and he looks well up to winning something even better before the season is out. (tchd 5-1 in places and 4-1 in places)

Enjoy The Moment ◆ was taking on rather better company on this handicap debut compared to the field he beat in a Brighton maiden last time, but he covered himself in glory by finishing in great style despite being forced very wide from the home turn. He is still relatively lightly raced and looks capable of winning a very nice prize over this trip given a sound surface. (tchd 40-1 in places)

Bandama(IRE) raised 6lb and stepping up two furlongs in trip, lost little in defeat in his bid for a hat-trick and finished in pleasing style against the inside rail. There will be other days. (op 8-1)

Lake Poet(IRE), trying this trip for the first time, was arguably unfortunate to be raised 2lb for only finishing third at Epsom. He had every chance and did not appear to fail through lack of stamina, but he does lack the scope of a few of the others. (tchd 10-1 and 11-1 in places)

London Express(IRE) ◆ ran much better than he did at Epsom last time, reversing the form with several who finished ahead of him that day and narrowing the gap considerably with Lake Poet. He does not necessarily strike as a progressive type, but with his stable now hitting top gear it will be a surprise if he does not find another opportunity before too long.

Doctor Scott ◆, below form in three previous efforts this season but on a decent mark now, put up a really eye-catching performance over this longer trip and was noted finishing as well as anything. The stable look to be well and truly back now, so he is definitely one to look out for next time, especially if upped in trip another furlong or two.

Pearly King(USA), bidding for a four-timer, seemed to hold every chance but did not see the race out as well as the others. He seemed to find this longer trip beyond him, let alone the 7lb higher mark. (op 3-1 tchd 9-2 in places and 5-1 in a place)

Salute The General, whose only previous victory came when long odds-on for a Fibresand maiden, is rather better than that and ran another creditable race in this exalted company. He deserves to win another race, but is more exposed than most of these and looks handicapped to the hilt. (op 11-1)

Numeric(GER) did not enjoy the clearest of passages and stayed on pretty well to finish closer to both Pearly King and Salute The General than he did at Newbury last time. That said, all three of them were found lacking in this better contest. (tchd 9-1 in places)

T/Jkpt: Not won. T/Plt: £95.00 to a £1 stake. Pool: £333,918.90 - 2,563.60 winning units. T/Qpdt: £30.50 to a £1 stake. Pool: £14,532.45 - 351.90 winning units. JN

2159 AYR (L-H)

Friday, June 23

OFFICIAL GOING: Good

Wind: Breezy, against

2806 SAGA 105.2FM MAIDEN AUCTION STKS 5f

2:25 (2:26) (Class 5) 2-Y-O **£3,238** (£963; £481; £240) **Stalls** Low

Form RPR

4 **1** **Zanida (IRE)**[22] [2166] 2-8-11 ..... PatCosgrave 3 78+
(K R Burke) *mde all: pushed clr fr over 1f out: edgd rt wl ins fnl f: easily* **5/4**[1]

6 **2** 5 **Valbenny (IRE)**[18] [2281] 2-8-7 ..... DeanMcKeown 4 56
(G A Swinbank) *s.i.s: hld up: hdwy and edgd lft fr 2f out: wnt 2nd wl ins fnl f: no ch w wnr* **10/1**

3 ½ **Spectacular Joy (IRE)** 2-8-8 ..... SaleemGolam(3) 5 58
(Mrs A Duffield) *s.i.s: hld up in tch: hdwy to chse wnr appr fnl f to wl ins last: no ex* **8/1**

62 **4** ¾ **Me And Mine (USA)**[13] [2451] 2-8-12 ..... PhillipMakin 7 57
(T D Barron) *cl up tl edgd lft and no ex over 1f out* **7/2**[2]

5 **5** *3* **Retaliate**[16] [2354] 2-8-5 .... FrancisNorton 6 39
(M Quinn) *cl up tl rdn and wknd over 1f out* **5/1**[3]
0035 **6** *3 ½* **Lovers Kiss**[15] [2375] 2-8-7 .... DaleGibson 2 28
(N Wilson) *chsd ldrs: outpcd 1/2-way: n.d after* **16/1**
000 **7** *2 ½* **Devilfishpoker Com**[21] [2191] 2-9-0 .... NeilPollard 1 26
(R C Guest) *sn outpcd: no ch fr 1/2-way* **66/1**

60.77 secs (0.33) **Going Correction** -0.05s/f (Good) **7** Ran SP% **110.9**
Speed ratings (Par 93):95,87,86,85,80 74,70
CSF £14.23 TOTE £2.00: £1.50, £6.50; EX 17.70.
Owner Clipper Group Holdings **Bred** Sean Beston **Trained** Middleham Moor, N Yorks

FOCUS
An uncompetitive event but a decent gallop and a ready winner, who should be able to hold her own in a bit better company.

NOTEBOOK
Zanida(IRE) ◆, related to several winners, fully confirmed debut promise and won with a good deal to spare. She is a speedy type who looked in good shape and looks the sort to hold her own in slightly stronger company. (op 11-8 tchd 6-4 in places and 13-8 in a place)
Valbenny(IRE) bettered her debut effort and left the strong impression that the step up to six furlongs and beyond would see her in a better light in due course. She is in good hands and is the type to win a small event.
Spectacular Joy(IRE), the first foal of a fairly useful sprint winner in Germany, looked fit and showed ability on this racecourse debut. Although this bare form is only ordinary, he should improve for the experience. (op 11-1)
Me And Mine(USA) again had his limitations exposed in this type of event and he will be of more interest in low-grade nursery company around this trip. (tchd 4-1)
Retaliate proved easy to back and failed to build on the bit of promise shown on her debut. She will have to show more before she is worth a bet in this type of event. (op 7-2)
Lovers Kiss has had plenty of chances and again underlined her vulnerability in this type of event.

2807 CLYDE PROPERTY MAIDEN AUCTION STKS 6f
3:00 (3:00) (Class 5) 2-Y-O **£3,886** (£1,156; £577; £288) **Stalls** Low

Form RPR
0 **1** **Moonwalking**[14] [2409] 2-9-1 .... DaleGibson 9 77
(Jedd O'Keeffe) *bhd and sn outpcd: hdwy 2f out: kpt on wl to ld cl home* **50/1**
44 **2** *nk* **Persian Peril**[7] [2610] 2-8-12 .... DeanMcKeown 8 73
(G A Swinbank) *led: rdn and edgd lft over 1f out: kpt on fnl f: hdd cl home* **11/2**
4 **3** *nk* **Cassie's Choice (IRE)**[15] [2375] 2-8-10 .... DerekMcGaffin 4 70
(B Smart) *chsd ldrs: drvn 1/2-way: rallied fnl f: kpt on* **25/1**
3 **4** *1* **Princess Palatine (IRE)**[24] [2106] 2-8-7 .... PatCosgrave 1 64
(K R Burke) *chsd ldrs: rdn 1/2-way: effrt and ev ch 1f out: no ex wl ins fnl f* **13/8**[1]
43 **5** *3 ½* **Fongs Gazelle**[33] [1863] 2-8-10 .... J-PGuillambert 2 57
(M Johnston) *in tch: outpcd over 2f out: kpt on fnl f: no imp* **7/2**[2]
6 *1 ¾* **Stay Active (USA)** 2-9-1 .... PaulHanagan 3 61+
(I Semple) *s.i.s: rn green in rr: effrt 2f out: sn no imp* **14/1**
2 **7** *½* **Merry Moon (IRE)**[22] [2166] 2-8-10 .... PhillipMakin 7 50
(M Dods) *chsd ldrs tl rdn and wknd over 1f out* **5/1**[3]
0 **8** *2 ½* **Vanatina (IRE)**[53] [1347] 2-8-10 .... FrancisNorton 6 42
(A Bailey) *chsd ldrs tl edgd rt and wknd wl over 1f out* **100/1**
450 **9** *hd* **Smirfy's Silver**[13] [2432] 2-9-1 .... FergalLynch 5 47
(W M Brisbourne) *in tch: rdn over 2f out: sn btn* **20/1**

1m 14.6s (0.93) **Going Correction** -0.05s/f (Good) **9** Ran SP% **110.6**
Speed ratings (Par 93):91,90,90,88,84 81,81,77,77
CSF £286.82 TOTE £80.00: £11.00, £1.20, £5.60; EX 370.30.
Owner W R B Racing 38 (wrbracing.com) **Bred** Chippenham Lodge Stud Ltd **Trained** Middleham Moor, N Yorks

FOCUS
A modest event in which the pace was sound.

NOTEBOOK
Moonwalking improved a good deal on his debut effort and, although the bare form of this race is modest at best, he is the type to improve again when upped to seven furlongs and he may be capable of better.
Persian Peril ran creditably having enjoyed the run of the race and this represented his best effort yet. Although vulnerable to the better types in this grade, he may pick up a small race once handicapped. (op 17-2)
Cassie's Choice(IRE) bettered her debut effort and left the impression that the step up to seven furlongs would be in her favour. She looks capable of winning a small event granted a suitable test in due course. (op 20-1)
Princess Palatine(IRE), a leggy type, failed to build on the form shown at Redcar on her debut and, on this evidence, is likely to continue to look vulnerable in this type of event. (op 7-4 tchd 2-1 in places)
Fongs Gazelle, from a stable back among the winners, was not totally disgraced and is likely to continue to look vulnerable in this type of event but again left the impression that the step up to seven furlongs would suit. (op 3-1)
Stay Active(USA), out of a fairly useful sprint winner in the States, hinted at ability after a tardy start on this racecourse debut and is entitled to improve for the experience. (op 12-1)

2808 RENAULT VANS H'CAP 1m 2f
3:35 (3:35) (Class 6) (0-55,55) 4-Y-0+ **£3,238** (£963; £481; £240) **Stalls** Low

Form RPR
65 **1** **Brief Statement (IRE)**[28] [1988] 4-9-3 **55** .... LiamJones(5) 6 65
(W M Brisbourne) *hld up: pushed along over 3f out: hdwy wd 2f out: kpt on wl fnl f to ld cl home* **9/1**[3]
0505 **2** *shd* **Insubordinate**[9] [2546] 5-9-7 **54** .... FergalLynch 9 64
(J S Goldie) *s.i.s: bhd tl hdwy 2f out: kpt on wl fnl f: jst failed* **9/1**[3]
1302 **3** *nk* **Fiore Di Bosco (IRE)**[16] [2360] 5-9-3 **50** .... PhillipMakin 4 59
(T D Barron) *keen in midfield: hdwy to ld ent fnl f: kpt on: hdd cl home* **5/1**[1]
1-00 **4** *1 ½* **Heartcrusher (IRE)**[27] [2020] 4-9-8 **55** .... DeanMcKeown 1 61
(G A Swinbank) *hld up: hdwy over 2f out: edgd lft and prom over 1f out: no ex ins fnl f* **16/1**
00-0 **5** *¾* **Woolly Back (IRE)**[44] [1591] 5-9-7 **54** .... FrancisNorton 14 59
(A C Whillans) *plld hrd: stdd rr: hdwy fr 2f out: nrst fin* **16/1**
42-6 **6** *1* **Dramatic Review (IRE)**[14] [2407] 4-8-10 **48** ....(bt[1]) GregFairley(5) 10 51
(P C Haslam) *chsd ldrs tl rdn and no ex over 1f out* **10/1**
0-00 **7** *shd* **El Rey Royale**[22] [2181] 4-9-3 **50** .... J-PGuillambert 8 53
(Micky Hammond) *w ldr: led 4f out to ent fnl f: sn btn* **8/1**[2]
0-03 **8** *½* **Saluscraggie**[16] [2360] 4-8-9 **49** .... NeilBrown(7) 3 51
(K G Reveley) *bhd: rdn over 3f out: kpt on fnl f: nvr rchd ldrs* **9/1**[3]
606- **9** *½* **Kristiansand**[343] [3501] 6-9-8 **55** .... PaulHanagan 11 56
(P Monteith) *keen: chsd ldrs tl wknd over 1f out* **12/1**
20-0 **10** *nk* **Montara (IRE)**[42] [1653] 7-9-3 **53** ....(p) SaleemGolam(3) 2 53
(Barry Potts, Ire) *midfield: outpcd 3f out: n.d after* **12/1**

2354 **11** *½* **Rotuma (IRE)**[22] [2181] 7-9-6 **53** ....(b) TomEaves 13 52
(M Dods) *in tch: rdn 3f out: wknd over 1f out* **5/1**[1]
-000 **12** *1 ¼* **Eminence Gift**[4] [2696] 4-9-3 **50** ....(p) PatCosgrave 12 47
(K R Burke) *keen: mde most to 4f out: wknd 2f out* **12/1**
100- **13** *32* **Argent**[302] [4698] 5-8-10 **48** .... AndrewMullen(5) 5 —
(Miss L A Perratt) *chsd ldrs: rdn 4f out: wknd over 2f out: t.o* **50/1**

2m 9.91s (-1.81) **Going Correction** -0.10s/f (Good) **13** Ran SP% **120.3**
Speed ratings (Par 101):103,102,102,101,100 100,100,99,99,98 98,97,71
CSF £88.33 CT £457.83 TOTE £11.30: £3.10, £3.50, £2.30; EX 163.80.
Owner Midland Racing Partnership **Bred** S Ross **Trained** Great Ness, Shropshire

FOCUS
A low-grade event in which the pace was sound and the form looks solid with the time decent.
Brief Statement(IRE) ◆ Official explanation: trainer said, regarding the improved form shown, the gelding had been unsuited by the heavy ground on its previous start at Haydock

2809 RENAULT TRAFIC H'CAP 1m
4:10 (4:11) (Class 4) (0-80,80) 3-Y-O **£6,477** (£1,927; £963; £481) **Stalls** Low

Form RPR
0114 **1** **Punjabi**[16] [2344] 3-8-10 **69** .... J-PGuillambert 4 79+
(Mrs G S Rees) *keen: hld up in tch: smooth hdwy outside over 2f out: shkn up to ld appr fnl f: readily* **13/2**
1506 **2** *1 ¼* **Daaweitza**[17] [2324] 3-8-7 **66** .... PaulHanagan 8 73
(B Ellison) *hld up in tch: effrt over 2f out: ev ch over 1f out: hung lft and kpt on ins fnl f* **10/1**
1- **3** *1* **Just Intersky (USA)**[324] [4053] 3-9-6 **79** .... DeanMcKeown 9 84+
(G A Swinbank) *swtchd lft s: hld up: effrt whn nt clr run over 2f out: hdwy over 1f out: kpt on fnl f* **6/1**[3]
1112 **4** *nk* **Moody Tunes**[25] [2087] 3-9-7 **80** .... PatCosgrave 1 84
(K R Burke) *trckd ldrs: effrt and ev ch over 1f out: kpt on same pce ins fnl f* **9/2**[2]
0632 **5** *1 ¼* **Rubenstar (IRE)**[7] [2620] 3-9-3 **79** .... SaleemGolam(3) 6 80
(M H Tompkins) *keen: trckd ldrs: effrt 2f out: one pce whn checked ent fnl f* **7/2**[1]
0-44 **6** *nk* **Heureux (USA)**[28] [1999] 3-9-6 **79** .... TomEaves 5 79
(J Howard Johnson) *w ldr: led briefly over 1f out: sn no ex* **12/1**
0-06 **7** *1 ½* **Strong Approach (IRE)**[18] [2297] 3-8-8 **70** .... BenSwarbrick(3) 3 67
(T D Barron) *hld up: effrt over 2f out: sn no imp* **18/1**
324 **8** *shd* **Airbound (USA)**[129] [409] 3-8-5 **69** .... GregFairley(5) 2 66
(M Johnston) *led to over 1f out: sn wknd* **13/2**
4120 **9** *1 ¼* **Stolen Glance**[23] [2128] 3-8-11 **70** .... DaleGibson 7 64
(M W Easterby) *chsd ldrs tl wknd fr 2f out* **12/1**

1m 42.56s (-0.93) **Going Correction** -0.10s/f (Good) **9** Ran SP% **111.1**
Speed ratings (Par 101):100,98,97,97,96 95,94,94,93
CSF £65.23 CT £398.07 TOTE £9.00: £2.50, £2.50, £2.90; EX 44.50.
Owner Capt James Wilson **Bred** Capt J H Wilson **Trained** Sollom, Lancs

FOCUS
A fair event in which the pace seemed sound and the race has been rated fairly positively.

2810 RENAULT MASTER H'CAP 1m
4:45 (4:45) (Class 4) (0-85,83) 4-Y-O+ **£6,477** (£1,927; £963; £481) **Stalls** Low

Form RPR
010- **1** **Namroud (USA)**[223] [6322] 7-9-5 **81** .... PaulHanagan 8 91
(R A Fahey) *prom: effrt and disp ld over 1f out: asserted wl ins last* **9/1**
-134 **2** *nk* **Stellite**[22] [2164] 6-8-5 **67** .... DaleGibson 3 76
(J S Goldie) *trckd ldrs: effrt and disp ld over 1f out: hld wl ins fnl f* **7/1**[2]
0001 **3** *1 ¾* **Tidy (IRE)**[22] [2165] 6-8-0 **67** .... AndrewMullen(5) 4 72
(Micky Hammond) *hld up in tch: rdn over 2f out: no imp tl kpt on fnl f: nt rch first two* **10/1**
4-05 **4** *nk* **Chief Scout**[28] [1985] 4-8-12 **74** .... TomEaves 7 79
(I Semple) *pressed ldr: ev ch tl one pce appr fnl f* **12/1**
0033 **5** *1* **Society Music (IRE)**[22] [2164] 4-8-10 **72** .... PhillipMakin 5 74
(M Dods) *hld up in tch: effrt over 2f out: no imp fnl f* **14/1**
00-3 **6** *1* **Tsaroxy (IRE)**[16] [2364] 4-9-2 **78** .... PatCosgrave 6 78
(J Howard Johnson) *s.i.s: hld up outside: effrt over 2f out: nvr rchd ldrs* **11/1**
0110 **7** *nk* **Rain Stops Play (IRE)**[13] [2440] 4-9-7 **83** .... FrancisNorton 1 82
(M Quinn) *led to over 1f out: sn wknd* **15/2**[3]
-241 **8** *½* **Topatoo**[7] [2627] 4-9-2 **81** 6ex .... SaleemGolam(3) 2 79
(M H Tompkins) *keen: hld up in tch: effrt over 2f out: wknd over 1f out* **11/10**[1]

1m 40.48s (-3.01) **Going Correction** -0.10s/f (Good) **8** Ran SP% **113.7**
Speed ratings (Par 105):111,110,108,108,107 106,106,105
CSF £68.84 CT £646.71 TOTE £11.20: £1.90, £1.90, £2.30; EX 74.60.
Owner The Yorkshire Lancashire Alliance **Bred** Audley Farm Inc **Trained** Musley Bank, N Yorks

FOCUS
An ordinary event and one that did not take as much winning as seemed likely beforehand but a decent winning time, over two seconds quicker than the preceding three-year-old handicap, and the form looks solid rated around the first three.

2811 ARNOLD CLARK RENAULT H'CAP 7f 50y
5:20 (5:22) (Class 6) (0-55,56) 4-Y-O+ **£3,238** (£963; £481; £240) **Stalls** Low

Form RPR
1-06 **1** **Snow Bunting**[11] [2504] 8-9-6 **53** .... PaulHanagan 10 62+
(Jedd O'Keeffe) *hld up: rdn 3f out: hdwy to ld ins fnl f: r.o wl* **11/2**[2]
0450 **2** *1 ¼* **Newsround**[11] [2505] 4-8-12 **48** ....(b) BenSwarbrick(3) 4 53
(D W Chapman) *dwlt: sn prom: effrt and ev ch ent fnl f: no ch w wnr* **40/1**
0-05 **3** *nk* **Pride Of Kinloch**[29] [1947] 6-9-2 **52** ....(p) DNolan(3) 3 57
(N Wilson) *trckd ldrs: effrt and led over 2f out: hdd ins fnl f: one pce* **10/1**
1441 **4** *hd* **Iced Diamond (IRE)**[8] [2567] 7-9-9 **56** 6ex .... FergalLynch 13 60
(W M Brisbourne) *hld up: hdwy 2f out: rdn and r.o fnl f: nrst fin* **7/1**
-613 **5** *¾* **Inch High**[22] [2165] 8-9-1 **51** .... SaleemGolam(3) 8 53
(J S Goldie) *midfield: hmpd after 2f: hdwy over 1f out: kpt on fnl f: no imp* **13/2**[3]
-042 **6** *½* **Spanish Law**[6] [2641] 4-9-6 **53** ....(b) PhillipMakin 6 54
(M Dods) *in tch: sn lost pl: rdn over 2f out: kpt on wl fnl f: nvr nrr* **4/1**[1]
3003 **7** *1 ¼* **Margaret's Dream (IRE)**[21] [2195] 5-9-3 **50** .... J-PGuillambert 5 48
(D Carroll) *chsd ldrs: effrt over 2f out: wknd over 1f out* **20/1**
0006 **8** *nk* **Yorkie**[7] [2611] 7-9-8 **55** .... DeanMcKeown 1 52
(J Pearce) *hld up: hdwy 3f out: outpcd over 1f out* **10/1**
014 **9** *½* **Bahrain Gold (IRE)**[81] [862] 6-9-6 **53** ....(b) DaleGibson 9 48
(N P McCormack) *cl up: ev ch over 2f out: outpcd over 1f out* **25/1**
56-0 **10** *1* **Prospect Court**[15] [2376] 4-8-12 **50** .... AndrewMullen(5) 11 43
(A C Whillans) *keen: towards rr: effrt over 2f out: btn over 1f out* **33/1**
0200 **11** *5* **Tequila Sheila (IRE)**[9] [2544] 4-9-1 **48** .... PatCosgrave 14 28
(K R Burke) *hld up: rdn 3f out: nvr on terms* **20/1**

0000 **12** *nk* **Bint Royal (IRE)**[4] 2700 8-9-0 **52**................................(v) LiamJones(5) 12 31
(Miss V Haigh) *racd wd in midfield: struggling over 2f out: sn btn* **22/1**

0320 **13** *nk* **King Of Meze (IRE)**[23] 2148 5-9-1 **48**..............................(p) TomEaves 2 26
(J S Wainwright) *keen: chsd ldrs tl wknd over 2f out* **12/1**

1200 **14** *5* **Ariesanne (IRE)**[94] 691 5-8-7 **45**.................................... GregFairley(5) 7 10
(A C Whillans) *led to over 2f out: wknd over 1f out* **33/1**

1m 32.3s (-0.42) **Going Correction** -0.10s/f (Good) **14** Ran SP% **113.1**

Speed ratings (Par 101):98,96,96,96,95 94,93,92,92,91 85,85,84,78

CSF £209.62 CT £2174.15 TOTE £7.20: £3.10, £12.00, £2.00; EX 278.50.

Owner W R B Racing 49 (wrbracingcom) **Bred** The Queen **Trained** Middleham Moor, N Yorks

FOCUS

An ordinary event in which the pace was sound, although the form is not rock solid, with the fifth and sixth the best guides.

2812 AYR FAMILY DAY ON 9TH JULY APPRENTICE H'CAP 1m 5f 13y

5:55 (5:55) (Class 5) (0-70,67) 4-Y-0+ **£3,238** (£963; £481; £240) **Stalls** Low

Form RPR

5533 **1** **York Cliff**[10] 2522 8-8-11 **54**.. LiamJones 2 62+
(W M Brisbourne) *hld up in tch: effrt over 2f out: no imp tl kpt on wl fnl f: led towards fin* **11/4**[1]

-165 **2** *nk* **Balwearie (IRE)**[17] 2326 5-9-1 **58**.................................(p) PJMcDonald 6 66
(Miss L A Perratt) *trckd ldrs: effrt and led over 1f out: rdn and edgd lft: kpt on: hdd towards fin* **9/2**[2]

0360 **3** *2* **Ego Trip**[25] 2075 5-8-7 **55**..(b) AdeleRothery(5) 3 60
(M W Easterby) *keen: led to over 1f out: kpt on same pce fnl f* **9/2**[2]

-006 **4** *1* **Andre Chenier (IRE)**[9] 2549 5-9-2 **62**.............................. PJBenson(3) 8 66
(P Monteith) *hld up in tch: effrt over 2f out: edgd lft and no ex over 1f out* **9/1**

-600 **5** *2 ½* **Halland**[16] 2357 8-9-7 **67**.. NeilBrown(3) 4 67+
(T J Fitzgerald) *hld up: sme hdwy over 4f out: rdn over 2f out: sn outpcd: kpt on fnl f: no imp* **16/1**

060 **6** *2 ½* **Duroob**[14] 2408 4-9-3 **65**.. PatrickDonaghy(5) 5 61
(K R Burke) *hld up: struggling over 2f out: sn n.d* **11/2**[3]

60/3 **7** *2* **Copplestone (IRE)**[32] 1883 10-8-0 **48** oh3......................(p) NSLawes(5) 7 41
(A C Whillans) *keen: cl up tl wknd over 2f out* **14/1**

0-00 **8** *11* **Bramantino (IRE)**[53] 1346 6-9-7 **64**.............................(b) KellyHarrison 1 41
(T A K Cuthbert) *hld up: rdn 3f out: sn btn* **16/1**

2m 55.62s (-0.99) **Going Correction** -0.10s/f (Good) **8** Ran SP% **106.8**

Speed ratings (Par 103):99,98,97,96,95 93,92,85

CSF £12.88 CT £42.88 TOTE £3.10: £1.30, £1.70, £1.70; EX 5.10 Place 6 £1,249.92, Place 5 £703.02.

Owner P Wright-Bevans **Bred** F Hinojosa **Trained** Great Ness, Shropshire

FOCUS

A modest event in which the pace was only fair and the form does not look strong rated around the principals.

T/Plt: £13,593.60 to a £1 stake. Pool: £35,380.85. 1.90 winning tickets. T/Qpdt: £274.40 to a £1 stake. Pool: £2,559.30. 6.90 winning tickets. RY

2604 GOODWOOD (R-H)

Friday, June 23

OFFICIAL GOING: Straight course - good; round course - good to firm

Wind: Moderate, half-against

2813 TAURUS WASTE RECYCLING APPRENTICE STKS (H'CAP) 6f

5:45 (5:50) (Class 5) (0-70,70) 3-Y-0+ **£3,562** (£1,059; £529; £264) **Stalls** Low

Form RPR

0002 **1** **Blue Tomato**[8] 2590 5-10-0 **70**.................................... LiamTreadwell 11 81+
(J M Bradley) *s.i.s: sn mid-div: hrd rdn to ld ins fnl f: kpt on* **7/2**[1]

2020 **2** *½* **Zazous**[24] 2095 5-8-13 **55**.. MarcHalford 12 65
(J J Bridger) *a.p: led over 1f out: edgd sharply lef and hd ins fnl f: r.o cl home* **9/1**

2131 **3** *1 ½* **Forest Dane**[23] 2136 6-9-4 **60**.................................. RichardKingscote 10 65
(Mrs N Smith) *sn prom on outside: rdn over 1f out: kpt on fnl f* **4/1**[2]

-520 **4** *2 ½* **Kahlua Bear**[20] 2235 4-8-6 **51** oh11...........................(b) SladeO'Hara(3) 4 49
(Miss K B Boutflower) *s.i.s: sn mid-div: swtchd rt over 1f out: r.o but nvr nr to chal* **66/1**

05/1 **5** *½* **Millfields Dreams**[11] 2494 7-8-10 **52** 7ex....................... JerryO'Dwyer 1 48
(M G Quinlan) *chsd ldrs: rdn and no ex appr fnl f* **9/2**[3]

2000 **6** *shd* **Whitbarrow (IRE)**[13] 2444 7-9-7 **68**.......................... JamesMillman(5) 5 64
(B R Millman) *led tl rdn and hdd over 1f out: sn btn* **7/1**

6000 **7** *1 ¼* **Sweetest Revenge (IRE)**[13] 2459 5-9-1 **64**............. FrankiePickard(7) 6 56
(M D I Usher) *chsd ldrs tl wknd over 1f out* **20/1**

0402 **8** *½* **Chantelle's Dream**[6] 2632 4-8-4 **51** oh3...................... SophieDoyle(5) 9 41
(Ms J S Doyle) *gave trble bef s: t.k.h: prom tl wknd wl over 1f out* **8/1**

40-0 **9** *3* **Wizard Quay**[7] 2599 3-7-11 **51** oh1................................ LukeMorris(5) 3 32
(W K Goldsworthy) *a towards rr* **25/1**

4003 **10** *½* **Trace Clip**[12] 2484 8-8-5 **52**...................................... MarkCoumbe(5) 2 32
(N I M Rossiter) *s.i.s: a bhd* **10/1**

2006 **11** *1* **Aintnecessarilyso**[117] 529 8-8-2 **51** oh4.................(p) PietroRomeo(7) 8 28
(J M Bradley) *a bhd* **20/1**

50-5 **12** *½* **Piper Lily**[49] 1466 4-8-4 **51** oh7.................................. LauraReynolds(5) 7 26
(M Blanshard) *a struggling in rr* **20/1**

1m 11.73s (-1.12) **Going Correction** -0.15s/f (Firm)

WFA 3 from 4yo+ 7lb **12** Ran SP% **122.7**

Speed ratings (Par 103):101,100,98,95,94 94,92,91,87,87 85,85

CSF £34.12 CT £125.89 TOTE £3.40: £1.80, £3.00, £2.10; EX 45.70.

Owner Dab Hand Racing **Bred** Bearstone Stud **Trained** Sedbury, Gloucs

■ Liam Treadwell's first winner on the Flat.

■ Stewards' Enquiry : Liam Treadwell caution: careless riding

FOCUS

A moderate but competitive handicap, rated around the placed horses, and the form should prove sound.

Chantelle's Dream Official explanation: trainer said filly was found to be in season

2814 GOLF AT GOODWOOD STKS (H'CAP) 1m 1f 192y

6:15 (6:21) (Class 6) (0-60,60) 3-Y-0 **£3,238** (£963; £481; £240) **Stalls** High

Form RPR

6002 **1** **Bella Fiorella (IRE)**[4] 2696 3-8-5 **47**.............................. DominicFox(3) 5 56
(Miss V Haigh) *mid-div: rdn and hdwy wl over 1f out: kpt on to ld nr fin* **12/1**

4635 **2** *nk* **Mull Of Dubai**[10] 2535 3-9-4 **57**..................................... SamHitchcott 14 65
(J S Moore) *trckd ldrs: wnt 2nd 2f out: ev ch ins fnl f: passed by wnr nr fin* **7/1**[2]

-600 **3** *½* **Haiti Dancer**[42] 1652 3-8-12 **54**.. AdamKirby(3) 6 61
(C G Cox) *led tl rdn and edgd rt ins fnl f: hdd and lost 2nd nr fin* **10/1**

-002 **4** *3 ½* **Osolomio (IRE)**[10] 2529 3-8-10 **56** ow1....................... JamesMillman(7) 4 56
(J G Given) *towards rr: rdn and hdwy fr 2f out: one pce fnl f* **11/2**[1]

0000 **5** *2* **Go Amwell**[8] 2591 3-8-9 **48**.. PaulDoe 12 45
(J R Jenkins) *s.i.s: hdwy 3f out: rdn and one pce ins fnl 2f* **40/1**

-050 **6** *shd* **Capitalise (IRE)**[12] 2479 3-9-2 **55**.................................... DarryllHolland 11 51
(V Smith) *chsd ldrs: rdn 3f out: no hdwy sn after* **15/2**[3]

000- **7** *½* **Lolla's Spirit (IRE)**[239] 6120 3-9-5 **58**............................ MickyFenton 1 53
(M L W Bell) *mid-div: lost pl 6f out: nvr on terms after* **25/1**

00-0 **8** *½* **Vinska (USA)**[16] 2349 3-8-11 **53**.................................... DeanCorby(3) 16 48
(J W Hills) *nvr bttr than mid-div* **40/1**

00-0 **9** *2* **Sirbrit**[62] 1141 3-8-13 **52**.. JDSmith 13 43+
(W J Musson) *slowly away: a bhd* **16/1**

0-55 **10** *3 ½* **Machhapuchhare**[20] 2246 3-8-13 **52**................................ JimCrowley 15 36
(W M Brisbourne) *slowly away: short-lived effrt on ins 3f out: nvr on terms* **16/1**

0-04 **11** *nk* **Benbrook**[12] 2479 3-9-6 **59**.. MichaelTebbutt 3 42
(J L Dunlop) *a towards rr* **7/1**[2]

0602 **12** *1 ½* **Croft (IRE)**[8] 2566 3-9-5 **58**....................................... FergusSweeney 8 39
(R M Stronge) *in tch: effrt over 2f out: sn wknd* **14/1**

-000 **13** *5* **Bold Pioneer (USA)**[16] 2352 3-9-0 **53**........................ StephenCarson 7 24
(C P Morlock) *a bhd* **50/1**

5423 **14** *2 ½* **Davidia (IRE)**[6] 2648 3-9-7 **60**.......................................(b[1]) PatDobbs 10 26
(S Kirk) *trckd ldr to 5f out: rdn 3f out: hung lft and sn btn* **7/1**[2]

6-00 **15** *2 ½* **Catabound (USA)**[22] 2171 3-9-2 **55**................................ RobertHavlin 2 17
(B R Millman) *prom: chsd ldr 5f out tl wknd rapidly 2f out* **16/1**

2m 7.72s (-0.03) **Going Correction** 0.0s/f (Good) **15** Ran SP% **116.4**

Speed ratings (Par 97):100,99,99,96,94 94,94,94,92,89 89,88,84,82,80

CSF £83.44 CT £766.20 TOTE £16.50: £3.40, £2.60, £3.70; EX 141.60.

Owner R J Budge **Bred** Jack Ronan And Des Vere Hunt Farm Co **Trained** Wiseton, Notts

■ Grateful (12/1, refused to enter stalls) was withdrawn. R4 applies, deduct 5p in the £.

■ Stewards' Enquiry : Sam Hitchcott three-day ban: used whip with excessive force (Jul 4-6)

FOCUS

A modest race, run at a better pace that other races on the round track at this meeting and the form looks sound.

Croft(IRE) Official explanation: jockey said gelding hung right throughout

2815 RENAULT TRAFIC MAIDEN STKS 1m 1f

6:45 (6:54) (Class 5) 3-Y-0+ **£3,400** (£1,011; £505; £252) **Stalls** High

Form RPR

-262 **1** **Distinctive Look (IRE)**[13] 2446 3-8-7 82.........................(t) RyanMoore 3 72
(B J Meehan) *chsd ldrs: short of room 2f out: swtchd to ins and rdn to ld jst ins fnl f: drew clr* **9/2**[3]

03 **2** *3 ½* **Muntada**[29] 1955 3-8-7 .... DarryllHolland 7 65
(M P Tregoning) *led after 1f: rdn and hdd jst ins fnl f: nt pce of wnr* **5/1**

0-22 **3** *2* **Thalberg**[16] 2366 3-8-12 86.. PhilipRobinson 4 66
(M A Jarvis) *led for 1f: prom tl rdn and wknd ent fnl f* **7/4**[1]

4 *nk* **Valuta (USA)** 3-8-12 ....(t) FJohansson 5 65
(R A Kvisla) *hld up: mde mod late prog: nvr on terms* **50/1**

0 **5** *3 ½* **Monsignor Fred**[24] 2118 4-9-9 .... DaneO'Neill 8 59
(H Candy) *s.i.s: hld up: nvr got into r* **20/1**

00 **6** *1 ¾* **Seal Of Hope**[7] 2605 3-8-9 .... NelsonDeSouza(3) 6 55
(M P Tregoning) *a struggling in rr* **33/1**

00 **7** *½* **Triple Bluff**[14] 2412 3-8-12 .... JimCrowley 2 54
(Mrs A J Perrett) *plld hrd: mid-div: bhd fr over 2f out* **20/1**

-304 **8** *1 ¼* **Alhaitham (USA)**[22] 2174 3-8-12 85................................ MartinDwyer 1 51
(J L Dunlop) *in tch: swtchd lft over 2f out: wknd wl over 1f out* **2/1**[2]

1m 55.7s (-1.16) **Going Correction** 0.0s/f (Good)

WFA 3 from 4yo 11lb **8** Ran SP% **119.0**

Speed ratings (Par 103):105,101,100,99,96 95,94,93

CSF £26.64 TOTE £4.90: £1.30, £1.70, £1.30; EX 26.30.

Owner Sangster Family **Bred** Swettenham Stud **Trained** Manton, Wilts

FOCUS

Hard to weigh up, but shaky and nothing special for a maiden race at this track.

Alhaitham(USA) Official explanation: jockey said saddle slipped

2816 RENAULT VANS MAIDEN AUCTION FILLIES' STKS 6f

7:15 (7:22) (Class 4) 2-Y-0 **£6,800** (£2,023; £1,011; £505) **Stalls** Low

Form RPR

223 **1** **Crystal Gazer (FR)**[35] 1817 2-8-8 .... RyanMoore 9 73
(R Hannon) *a.p: led 1/2-way: drvn out fnl f* **2/1**[1]

6 **2** *hd* **Cosmopolitan Lady**[65] 1082 2-8-7 .... MartinDwyer 4 71+
(D M Simcock) *wnt lft s: sn prom: pressed wnr wl ins fnl f* **9/4**[2]

3 *1 ¼* **Mason Ette** 2-8-5 .... PhilipRobinson 1 66
(C G Cox) *led to 1/2-way: hung lft fr 2f out but r.o ins fnl f* **11/2**[3]

0 **4** *1 ¾* **Kerswell**[31] 1912 2-8-5 ow1... RobertHavlin 8 60
(B R Millman) *in tch: rdn and ev ch 1f out: hung lft and no ex* **66/1**

5 *1 ¾* **Dora Explora** 2-8-4 .... AdrianMcCarthy 12 54
(P W Chapple-Hyam) *outpcd: made sme late hdwy* **10/1**

0 **6** *1* **Maid Of Ale (IRE)**[32] 1896 2-8-11 .... MichaelTebbutt 10 58
(B J Meehan) *chsd ldrs: rdn 2f out: no further hdwy* **20/1**

7 *hd* **World's Heroine (IRE)** 2-8-8 .... AdamKirby(3) 11 58
(G A Butler) *swtchd lft s: outpcd: styd on appr fnl f* **14/1**

8 *shd* **My Tiger Lilly** 2-8-6 .... PaulDoe 7 52+
(W J Knight) *hmpd s: outpcd but kpt on towards fin* **20/1**

9 *2* **Lapina (IRE)** 2-8-1 .... EmmettStack(5) 2 46+
(Pat Eddery) *a outpcd in rr* **20/1**

0 **10** *1 ¼* **Inflagranti**[77] 908 2-8-4 .... NelsonDeSouza(3) 6 44+
(J G Portman) *prom: rdn over 2f out: wknd over 1f out* **100/1**

0 **11** *shd* **Gib (IRE)**[17] 2328 2-8-9 .... DarryllHolland 3 45
(B W Hills) *carried lft s: prom tl wknd wl over 1f out* **16/1**

00 **12** *hd* **Brierley Lil**[13] 2456 2-8-8 .... SamHitchcott 5 44
(J L Spearing) *prom tl wknd 2f out* **33/1**

1m 12.52s (-0.33) **Going Correction** -0.15s/f (Firm) **12** Ran SP% **120.8**

Speed ratings (Par 92):96,95,94,91,89 88,87,87,85,83 83,82

CSF £6.12 TOTE £3.00: £1.50, £1.50, £2.30; EX 6.20.

Owner A F Merritt **Bred** Cheik Sultan B K B Z Al Nahyan **Trained** East Everleigh, Wilts

FOCUS

A routine maiden which probably contained several future winners, but there is unlikely to be anything special in the line-up.

NOTEBOOK

Crystal Gazer(FR) got the extra furlong well, and her consistency cannot be faulted. Now she has won her maiden, she will probably make the switch to nurseries and, being a reliable type, should hold her own for the time being. (op 13-8 tchd 6-4 and 9-4)

Cosmopolitan Lady had obviously been doing well since her debut to be such a short price, and compensation looks likely after going so close against a more experienced rival. (op 7-2)

Mason Ette, a Grand Lodge filly with middle-distance stamina on her dam's side, should improve with experience and longer trips, so this was an encouraging debut. Official explanation: jockey said filly hung right early stages (op 13-2)

Kerswell had an unfortunate experience in the stalls on her debut, but seems to have put it behind her. This was a fair effort, and she should settle down to make her mark around seven furlongs or a mile. (op 40-1)

Dora Explora, a well-bred Vettori filly, but incredibly cheap, did enough on this debut to suggest she has inherited some ability. If she goes on from here, she would be one of racing's all-time bargains and, while she is unlikely to be anything special, a win is not out of the question.

Maid Of Ale(IRE), a 40,000 guinea Barathea filly, stepped up a bit on her debut effort, but looks a nursery type in the making. (op 16-1)

World's Heroine(IRE), a 40,000 guinea Spinning World filly, made a satisfactory debut, and should come on for the run. (op 12-1 tchd 16-1)

My Tiger Lilly was a relatively cheap purchase, but showed enough on this debut to give connections some hope. She should stay at least ten furlongs next year. (op 25-1)

Lapina(IRE) Official explanation: jockey said filly missed the break

2817 RENAULT MASTER STKS (H'CAP) 1m 6f
7:50 (7:51) (Class 2) (0-100,98) 4-Y-0+ £12,954 (£3,854; £1,926; £962) Stalls High

Form RPR

-603 **1** **Wunderwood (USA)**[13] 2430 7-9-7 98 RyanMoore 7 110+
(Lady Herries) *trckd ldr: led 3f out: rdn clr over 1f out: v comf* 9/2[2]

-510 **2** 2 1/2 **Solent (IRE)**[20] 2229 4-9-4 95 DaneO'Neill 6 103
(R Hannon) *in tch: chsd wnr over 2f out: no imp fnl f* 11/2

3601 **3** 2 **Mudawin (IRE)**[30] 1943 5-8-9 86 DarrylHolland 4 91
(Jane Chapple-Hyam) *trckd ldrs: rdn 3f out: one pce ins fnl 2f* 9/1

0/40 **4** 3 1/2 **Pretty Star (GER)**[30] 1931 6-8-8 85 MartinDwyer 1 85
(A King) *bhd: effrt on ins 3f out: sn n.m.r and no hdwy after* 7/1

-345 **5** 1 1/4 **Wingman (IRE)**[20] 2229 4-8-10 87 PhilipRobinson 2 85
(J W Hills) *hld up in tch: rdn 3f out: sn btn* 3/1[1]

2-00 **6** 1 **Fortune Island (IRE)**[27] 2013 7-8-10 90 (vt) NelsonDeSouza(3) 8 87
(D E Pipe) *led tl rdn and hdd 3f out: sn btn* 20/1

0351 **7** nk **Salute (IRE)**[22] 2176 7-8-5 82 RobertHavlin 3 79
(P G Murphy) *hld up: effrt 3f out: sn btn* 8/1

6-51 **8** 2 1/2 **Chocolate Caramel (USA)**[13] 2447 4-8-11 88 JimCrowley 5 81
(Mrs A J Perrett) *hld up in tch: wknd over 2f out* 5/1[3]

3m 1.85s (-2.12) **Going Correction** 0.0s/f (Good) 8 Ran SP% **113.6**
Speed ratings (Par 109):106,104,103,101,100 100,99,98
CSF £28.93 CT £211.40 TOTE £5.20: £1.70, £2.70, £2.50; EX 45.40.
Owner Tony Perkins **Bred** Darley Stud Management, L L C **Trained** Patching, W Sussex

FOCUS
Not a bad handicap and the form reads quite well, with the winner possessing a touch of class, though the pace was modest until the home straight. Wunderwood was the only runner to track the front-running Fortune Island; the others always had a just a little too much to do once the race hotted up.

NOTEBOOK
Wunderwood(USA) got a nice tow from the leader, and completed the job with aplomb. He stayed the trip well, and is worth campaigning at these longer distances from now on. (op 5-1 tchd 4-1 and 7-2 in a place)

Solent(IRE) ran into a rival who was primed to run a big race here, so did well in the circumstances. In doing so, he ran his best race ever at Goodwood, proving he does act on the course. (tchd 6-1)

Mudawin(IRE) won on Polytrack last time, and this was a fair effort on turf. He is is good form at present, and threatening to recapture his form of two seasons ago. (tchd 10-1)

Pretty Star(GER) looked as if this trip would be ideal, but he was just short of what was required. He may be worth another chance at this distance in less-competitive company.

Wingman(IRE) was trying a longer trip, and the way he failed to pick up hinted at a return to a mile and a half. (op 7-2)

Fortune Island(IRE) tried to control things from the front, but was easily picked off. However, he is capable of finding improvement when least expected if past form is any guide. (op 14-1)

Salute(IRE) failed to reproduce his battling Sandown win. He is more at home in slightly lower company. (op 15-2)

2818 PETERS PLC FILLIES' STKS (H'CAP) 7f
8:25 (8:26) (Class 4) (0-85,82) 3-Y-0+ £6,800 (£2,023; £1,011; £505) Stalls High

Form RPR

-104 **1** **Daniella**[20] 2233 4-9-11 70 (p) FrancisFerris 2 81
(Rae Guest) *mde all: rdn over 1f out: in command fnl f* 11/2

0060 **2** 1 **Saxon Lil (IRE)**[13] 2459 4-9-6 65 SamHitchcott 8 73
(J L Spearing) *trckd ldrs: wnt 2nd wl over 1f out: no imp ins fnl f* 13/2

-140 **3** 4 **Polliwilline (IRE)**[8] 2581 3-10-0 82 RyanMoore 7 76
(R Hannon) *trckd wnr tl rdn wl over 1f out: sn outpcd* 9/2[3]

0-41 **4** 1 **Mimiteh (USA)**[14] 2393 3-9-7 78 NelsonDeSouza(3) 4 73
(R M Beckett) *in rr: mde sme late hdwy* 7/2[1]

40-1 **5** 4 **Oceancookie (IRE)**[53] 1348 4-9-8 70 (t) NeilChalmers(3) 1 55
(A M Balding) *v.s.a: nvr on terms* 4/1[2]

00-0 **6** 3 **Lady Cree (IRE)**[16] 2344 3-9-6 74 (t) MartinDwyer 6 48
(W R Muir) *a towards rr* 16/1

6023 **7** 20 **Dune Melody (IRE)**[6] 2642 3-9-11 79 MickyFenton 3 —
(J S Moore) *chsd ldrs: rdn 2f out: wknd qckly: eased ins fnl f* 4/1[2]

1m 26.87s (-1.17) **Going Correction** 0.0s/f (Good)
WFA 3 from 4yo 9lb 7 Ran SP% **115.0**
Speed ratings (Par 102):106,104,100,99,94 91,68
CSF £40.64 CT £174.16 TOTE £6.00: £2.50, £3.30; EX 53.00.
Owner Ms E Reffo & B Cooper **Bred** Amethyst Stud **Trained** Newmarket, Suffolk

FOCUS
A fair fillies' handicap in which the winner was allowed to do her own thing in front and sets the standard for the form.
Oceancookie(IRE) Official explanation: jockey said filly missed the break

2819 GRANNIES 50TH CELEBRATION STKS (H'CAP) 1m
8:55 (8:55) (Class 4) (0-85,85) 4-Y-0+ £6,800 (£2,023; £1,011; £505) Stalls High

Form RPR

4112 **1** **Waterside (IRE)**[6] 2649 7-9-5 83 RyanMoore 3 91
(G L Moore) *mde all: shkn up to go clr appr fnl f: comf* 9/4[1]

5-40 **2** 1 1/4 **Dry Ice (IRE)**[51] 1410 4-9-1 79 FergusSweeney 1 84+
(H Candy) *hld up in rr: swtchd lft ent fnl f: r.o stongly to snatch 2nd cl home* 10/1[3]

5006 **3** shd **Capricho (IRE)**[23] 2147 9-8-6 70 PaulDoe 7 75+
(J Akehurst) *bhd: hdwy on ins 3f out: n.m.r fr wl over 1f out: rdn and r.o ins fnl f* 14/1

5040 **4** nk **Farewell Gift**[11] 2510 5-8-6 73 (b) StephaneBreux(3) 5 77
(R Hannon) *trckd wnr to 4f out: sn rdn: nt qckn fnl f* 10/1[3]

5541 **5** 1/2 **Boundless Prospect (USA)**[22] 2183 7-9-6 84 MickyFenton 4 87
(Miss Gay Kelleway) *in tch: hdwy 3f out: rdn 2f out: nt qckn fr over 1f out* 11/2[2]

4-00 **6** 1/2 **Diktatorial**[63] 1111 4-9-4 85 (t) AdamKirby(3) 2 87
(G A Butler) *trckd ldrs: rdn wl over 1f out: nt qckn* 10/1[3]

411 **7** 2 **Full Victory (IRE)**[17] 2327 4-8-11 75 DaneO'Neill 6 72
(R A Farrant) *t.k.h: trckd wnr to 4f out: sn rdn: wknd wl over 1f out* 9/4[1]

1m 39.98s (-0.29) **Going Correction** 0.0s/f (Good) 7 Ran SP% **110.9**
Speed ratings (Par 105):101,99,99,99,98 98,96
CSF £24.78 TOTE £2.70: £1.60, £2.90; EX 29.40 Place 6 £283.71, Place 5 £158.68.
Owner Nigel Shields **Bred** Yeomanstown Stud **Trained** Woodingdean, E Sussex
■ A four-timer at the meeting for jockey Ryan Moore.

FOCUS
A decent little handicap in which Waterside was allowed an uncontested lead at a soft pace and is rated to his best.
Full Victory(IRE) Official explanation: jockey said gelding hung right and was unsuited by the good to firm ground
T/Plt: £184.50 to a £1 stake. Pool: £36,752.45. 145.35 winning tickets. T/Qpdt: £22.70 to a £1 stake. Pool: £3,466.55. 112.80 winning tickets. JS

2044 **NEWMARKET (JULY)** (R-H)
Friday, June 23

OFFICIAL GOING: Good to firm
Wind: Light, across Weather: Fine and sunny

2820 THESPORTSMAN.COM APPRENTICE H'CAP 1m
6:00 (6:06) (Class 5) (0-70,70) 3-Y-0+ £3,886 (£1,156; £577; £288) Stalls Low

Form RPR

-026 **1** **Tender The Great (IRE)**[8] 2589 3-8-4 61 ThomasO'Brien(5) 12 69
(V Smith) *racd stands' side: hld up: hdwy over 2f out: sn rdn and hung lft: led 1f out: sn hdd: styd on to ld post* 18/1

-044 **2** nk **Tiber Tiger (IRE)**[28] 1993 6-9-2 63 (b) JemmaMarshall(5) 3 74+
(N P Littmoden) *racd far side: hld up: hdwy 1/2-way: led ins fnl f: idled and hdd post* 11/2[2]

1134 **3** 1 3/4 **Shrine Mountain (USA)**[6] 2641 4-8-8 53 DonnaCaldwell(5) 6 60+
(J R Holt) *racd far side: chsd clr ldr 6f out: rdn and nt clr run over 1f out: styd on* 8/1

4005 **4** 1/2 **Lincolneurocruiser**[3] 2737 4-9-5 64 RussellKennemore(3) 9 68
(Mrs N Macauley) *racd stands' side: chsd ldrs: led and hung lft over 1f out: sn hdd: styd on same pce* 11/1

1252 **5** 3 **Favouring (IRE)**[38] 1764 4-8-4 51 oh1 (v) ChrisHough(5) 4 48
(M C Chapman) *racd far side: overall ldr and sn clr: hdd 3f out: rdn: edgd rt and ev ch over 1f out: wknd ins fnl f* 12/1

0352 **6** 1 1/2 **Fantasy Defender (IRE)**[4] 2702 4-8-4 51 oh5 (v) TolleyDean(5) 8 45
(Ernst Oertel) *racd stands' side: hld up: hdwy over 2f out: rdn and hung lft over 1f out: nt rch ldrs* 8/1

0P-0 **7** 1 1/4 **Cavan Gael (FR)**[130] 405 4-8-10 57 RobbieMills(5) 7 48
(P Howling) *racd stands' side: hld up: rdn and hung lft fr over 2f out: nt trble ldrs* 33/1

0404 **8** 3 **Riolo (IRE)**[7] 2611 4-8-12 57 (b) KevinGhunowa(3) 14 41
(K F Clutterbuck) *racd stands' side: chsd ldrs: rdn and hung lft over 1f out: sn wknd* 50/1

3000 **9** 3/4 **Orpen Wide (IRE)**[25] 1123 4-9-7 63 StephenDonohoe 1 45
(M C Chapman) *chsd ldr far side: 2f: sn lost pl: n.d after* 15/2[3]

0200 **10** 2 **Kabeer**[22] 2183 8-9-8 67 (t) DerekNolan(3) 10 44
(P S McEntee) *racd stands' side: led that gp: overall ldr 3f out: rdn: hung lft and hdd over 1f out: sn wknd* 33/1

5060 **11** 1 3/4 **Lygeton Lad**[115] 542 8-9-1 60 (t) RonanKeogh(3) 5 33
(Miss Gay Kelleway) *racd stands' side: hld up: effrt over 2f out: sn hung lft and wknd* 12/1

0131 **12** 1/2 **Takes Tutu (USA)**[48] 1480 7-10-0 70 TravisBlock 2 42
(C R Dore) *racd far side: dwlt: hdwy 1/2-way: wknd 2f out* 5/1[1]

4050 **13** 2 **Angel River**[8] 2574 4-8-9 51 oh6 (b) RoryMoore 16 19
(J Ryan) *racd stands' side: mid-div: rdn and wknd over 2f out* 50/1

0-00 **14** 1 1/4 **Burning Moon**[24] 2104 5-9-6 65 JamieJones(3) 11 30
(J Ryan) *racd stands' side: mid-div: rdn 1/2-way: hung lft and wknd over 2f out* 50/1

0-40 **15** 1 1/2 **Southern Tide (USA)**[19] 2262 4-8-3 52 oh5 ow1 StevenCorrigan(7) 15 13
(J Pearce) *racd stands' side: chsd ldrs 5f* 20/1

5104 **16** shd **Abbeygate**[39] 1725 5-8-4 51 oh6 BRoper(5) 13 12
(T Keddy) *racd stands' side: sn outpcd* 12/1

1m 39.09s (-1.34) **Going Correction** -0.075s/f (Good)
WFA 3 from 4yo+ 10lb 16 Ran SP% **119.2**
Speed ratings (Par 103):103,102,100,100,97 95,94,91,90,88 87,86,84,83,81 81
CSF £105.61 CT £900.83 TOTE £16.00: £2.80, £1.50, £1.80, £3.70; EX 84.40.
Owner Miss Kwok-Mei Ada Yip **Bred** Y Wai Kwan **Trained** Exning, Suffolk
■ Stewards' Enquiry : Ronan Keogh three-day ban: used whip with excessive frequency (July 4-6)

FOCUS
A competitive if modest apprentice handicap and a somewhat messy contest. The field split into two early, with the larger group coming stands' side. However, as the leaders in the nearside group eventually started to hang left the two groups had basically merged by the time the field reached the two-furlong pole. The principals all finished towards the far side of the track and three of the first five had raced on that side throughout. The form looks sound rated through the third.
Shrine Mountain(USA) Official explanation: jockey said gelding suffered interference in running
Burning Moon Official explanation: jockey said gelding was unsuited by the good to firm ground

2821 NGK SPARK PLUGS MAIDEN STKS 6f
6:30 (6:31) (Class 4) 2-Y-0 £4,533 (£1,348; £674; £336) Stalls Low

Form RPR

2 **1** **Charlie Farnsbarns (IRE)**[8] 2579 2-9-3 LDettori 4 84+
(B J Meehan) *led: hdd over 3f out: led over 1f out: r.o wl* 13/8[1]

3 **2** 3 **Kay Gee Be (IRE)**[29] 1945 2-9-3 JamieSpencer 9 75
(D J Daly) *trckd ldrs: rdn over 1f out: styd on same pce* 3/1[2]

3 1 **Froissee** 2-8-12 JimmyFortune 6 67+
(N A Callaghan) *sn outpcd: hdwy over 1f out: r.o* 25/1

3 **4** nk **Rebel Duke (IRE)**[17] 2315 2-9-3 TPQueally 2 71
(M G Quinlan) *w ldr tl led over 3f out: rdn and hdd over 1f out: no ex ins fnl f* 11/2[3]

5 2 1/2 **River Tarrant** 2-8-12 NCallan 1 59
(P W Chapple-Hyam) *s.s: hld up: hdwy over 2f out: wknd ins fnl f* 20/1

6 1 **Timber Treasure (USA)** 2-9-3 EddieAhern 7 61
(H R A Cecil) *chsd ldrs over 4f* 7/1

7 shd **Tobosa** 2-9-3 LPKeniry 3 60
(W Jarvis) *chsd ldrs: rdn over 1f out: sn wknd* 50/1

8 3 **King Joshua (IRE)** 2-9-3 .... ChrisCatlin 5 51
(G A Butler) *s.i.s: hld up: wknd over 1f out* **16/1**
9 1 3/4 **Botham (USA)** 2-9-3 .... JohnEgan 8 46
(T J Pitt) *plld hrd and prom: wknd over 1f out* **12/1**
1m 12.6s (-0.75) **Going Correction** -0.075s/f (Good) 9 Ran SP% **115.1**
Speed ratings (Par 95):102,98,96,96,92 91,91,87,85
CSF £6.24 TOTE £2.30: £1.10, £1.50, £3.50; EX 5.00.
Owner The English Girls **Bred** Tinnakill Partnership I **Trained** Manton, Wilts

FOCUS
Probably a fair maiden contest in which the field tended to edge towards the middle of the track, despite the stalls being on the far side. The winning time was very decent for a race like this.

NOTEBOOK
Charlie Farnsbarns(IRE) ◆, given a positive ride, duly confirmed the favourable impression he made on his recent Newbury debut. The way he grabbed the ground up the final hill was another indication that he will get at least another furlong without too much bother. (op 7-4)
Kay Gee Be(IRE) ◆ was on very different ground compared with his Ayr debut, but ran another creditable race and just ran into an above-average sort. There is a maiden waiting for him. (op 10-3 tchd 7-2)
Froissee ◆, a 19,000gns half-sister to Mr Sandicliffe, took a while to get into gear but was noted putting in some eye-catching late work up the final hill. She is one to watch out for.
Rebel Duke(IRE), up a furlong from his debut, showed up prominently for a long way and should be up to winning an ordinary maiden. (op 15-2)
River Tarrant, who cost just 2,000gns as a foal, is a half-sister to a two-year-old winner over the minimum trip. The market did not suggest much was expected on this debut, but she did show a little ability. (op 16-1)
Timber Treasure(USA), who cost $340,000 as a two-year-old, is a half-brother to the Irish-trained Listed-winner Lord Admiral. He showed some ability in the early stages of this debut and will hopefully improve enough to start justifying his price tag. (tchd 13-2 in a place)

2822 READ KIEREN IN THE SPORTSMAN H'CAP 1m 4f
7:00 (7:02) (Class 5) (0-75,72) 4-Y-0+ **£3,886** (£1,156; £577; £288) **Stalls** Centre

Form RPR
-400 **1** **Gringo**[22] 2169 4-9-7 **72** .... OscarUrbina 5 84
(B W Hills) *s.s: hld up: hdwy and edgd rt over 1f out: led and hung rt ins fnl f: r.o* **7/1**
-022 **2** 3/4 **Soufah (IRE)**[24] 2104 4-8-13 **64** .... LDettori 1 75
(J L Dunlop) *a.p: chsd ldr 5f out: rdn to ld over 1f out: sn edgd lft and hdd: styd on* **3/1**[1]
0-60 **3** *nk* **Tayman (IRE)**[51] 1400 4-8-8 **59** .... SteveDrowne 11 69
(G Wragg) *hld up: hdwy 5f out: rdn to ld 1f out: hdd and nt clr run ins fnl f: unable qckn* **6/1**[3]
0530 **4** 2 **Ariodante**[16] 2360 4-8-12 **63** .... TPQueally 7 70
(J M P Eustace) *hld up: nt clr run over 2f out: hdwy and nt clr run over 1f out: rdn and hung lft ins fnl f: nt trble ldrs* **20/1**
24-3 **5** *hd* **Bouquet**[24] 2104 4-9-2 **67** .... JamieSpencer 3 75+
(J R Fanshawe) *hld up in tch: racd keenly: nt clr run and lost pl over 2f out: hdwy and swtchd lft over 1f out: no imp ins fnl f* **9/2**[2]
6412 **6** 3 **Plain Champagne (IRE)**[19] 2262 4-8-4 **55** .... RichardThomas 10 57
(Dr J R J Naylor) *hld up: hmpd over 2f out: n.d* **12/1**
4-02 **7** *hd* **Zaville**[23] 2133 4-9-2 **67** ....(p) NCallan 6 69
(M A Jarvis) *sn led: rdn and hdd over 1f out: wknd ins fnl f* **8/1**
-005 **8** *hd* **Cantrip**[11] 2497 6-8-5 **56** .... JimmyQuinn 8 57
(Miss B Sanders) *chsd ldr 7f: rdn over 1f out: wknd fnl f* **16/1**
/004 **9** 4 **Chimes At Midnight (USA)**[11] 2497 9-8-2 **53** oh11 .... ChrisCatlin 9 48
(Luke Comer, Ire) *hld up: rdn and wknd over 1f out* **33/1**
1323 **10** 7 **Ten-Cents**[23] 2133 4-8-9 **60** .... EddieAhern 2 44
(C F Wall) *plld hrd and prom: rdn over 2f out: wkng whn hmpd over 1f out* **10/1**
4320 **11** *nk* **Our Choice (IRE)**[13] 2460 4-9-0 **65** .... TedDurcan 4 48
(N P Littmoden) *chsd ldrs: rdn over 3f out: wknd over 1f out* **10/1**
2m 31.08s (-1.83) **Going Correction** -0.075s/f (Good) 11 Ran SP% **120.5**
Speed ratings (Par 103):103,102,102,100,100 98,98,98,95,91 91
CSF £28.99 CT £138.24 TOTE £8.90: £2.80, £1.90, £2.50; EX 42.10.
Owner Guy Reed **Bred** Guy Reed **Trained** Lambourn, Berks
■ Stewards' Enquiry : Oscar Urbina one-day ban: careless riding (Jul 4)

FOCUS
An ordinary handicap run at an average pace in which the winner scored comfortably despite giving his rivals a start. The form appears sound enough, rated through the fourth and fifth.

2823 RWSLTD.CO.UK GALLOPING GEEGEES H'CAP 1m
7:30 (7:33) (Class 5) (0-75,75) 3-Y-0 **£3,886** (£1,156; £577; £288) **Stalls** Low

Form RPR
521- **1** **Starship (IRE)**[174] 6699 3-9-7 **75** .... KFallon 6 82+
(W J Haggas) *hld up: hdwy over 2f out: rdn to ld wl ins fnl f* **9/2**[2]
-255 **2** 1/2 **Wee Charlie Castle (IRE)**[13] 2466 3-8-13 **67** .... OscarUrbina 2 73
(G C H Chung) *a.p: led over 1f out: sn rdn: edgd rt and hdd wl ins fnl f* **14/1**
-035 **3** 1/2 **Hogan's Heroes**[6] 2648 3-8-4 **58** oh1 ow2 .... JohnEgan 5 63+
(G A Butler) *hld up: plld hrd: hdwy and nt clr run over 1f out: hung lft and r.o ins fnl f: nt rch ldrs* **25/1**
3303 **4** 3 **Blacktoft (USA)**[23] 2128 3-8-12 **66** .... EddieAhern 1 64
(E A L Dunlop) *led over 6f out: rdn: edgd rt and hdd over 1f out: wknd ins fnl f* **7/1**
-033 **5** *nk* **Southport Star (IRE)**[14] 2403 3-9-6 **74** .... JamieSpencer 9 73+
(J R Fanshawe) *s.i.s: hld up: hdwy over 1f out: sn rdn: wkng whn hmpd ins fnl f* **10/3**[1]
-011 **6** 3/4 **Diamond De Triano (USA)**[18] 2283 3-9-4 **75** .... DanielTudhope(3) 11 71
(P W Chapple-Hyam) *chsd ldrs: rdn and ev ch over 1f out: wknd ins fnl f* **11/2**[3]
-003 **7** *hd* **Golden Alchemist**[8] 2583 3-9-2 **70** .... HayleyTurner 10 65
(M D I Usher) *led: hdd over 6f out: rdn over 2f out: wknd ins fnl f* **12/1**
00-0 **8** 5 **Macs Ransom (USA)**[26] 2050 3-8-6 **60** .... ChrisCatlin 3 44
(N A Callaghan) *plld hrd and prom: rdn over 3f out: wknd over 1f out* **12/1**
0106 **9** 1/2 **Magical Music**[18] 2301 3-8-13 **67** .... JimmyQuinn 8 49
(J Pearce) *hld up: rdn and wknd over 1f out* **20/1**
-510 **10** 2 **Luckylover**[41] 1681 3-9-3 **71** .... TPQueally 12 49
(M G Quinlan) *hld up: hdwy over 3f out: rdn and wknd over 1f out* **11/1**
060- **11** 13 **Bitter Chill**[185] 6628 3-9-4 **72** .... SteveDrowne 7 20
(H Morrison) *prom: rdn over 2f out: sn wknd* **14/1**
1m 40.04s (-0.39) **Going Correction** -0.075s/f (Good) 11 Ran SP% **114.8**
Speed ratings (Par 99):98,97,97,94,93 92,92,87,87,85 72
CSF £64.24 CT £1405.98 TOTE £3.50: £1.60, £5.00, £5.70; EX 41.10.
Owner Mrs Magnier/Scott/Hirschfeld & Piggott **Bred** L K Piggott And A Hirschfeld **Trained** Newmarket, Suffolk

FOCUS
A competitive little handicap in which the field stayed against the far rail until fanning out starting the final climb. The early pace was not that strong and the race developed into a sprint over the last couple of furlongs. The runner-up sets the standard.

2824 THE SPORTSMAN RACING H'CAP 7f
8:05 (8:06) (Class 3) (0-95,86) 3-Y-0+ **£8,096** (£2,408; £1,203; £601) **Stalls** Low

Form RPR
12-0 **1** **Red Cape (FR)**[66] 1067 3-9-5 **86** .... LDettori 8 93+
(N A Callaghan) *chsd ldrs: led over 4f out: edgd lft over 1f out: rdn out* **8/1**
0130 **2** 1 1/4 **Romany Nights (IRE)**[26] 2047 6-9-13 **85** ....(b) JohnEgan 3 91
(Miss Gay Kelleway) *hld up: hdwy over 2f out: rdn over 1f out: styd on* **15/2**
-005 **3** 1/2 **Ans Bach**[27] 2033 3-9-5 **86** ....(p) NCallan 4 90+
(M A Jarvis) *prom: hmpd and lost pl over 2f out: hdwy over 1f out: nt clr run ins fnl f: r.o* **7/1**[3]
2200 **4** 1 **Namroc (IRE)**[28] 1992 5-9-10 **82** .... OscarUrbina 9 84
(N A Callaghan) *chsd ldrs: rdn over 1f out: styd on same pce ins fnl f* **11/2**[2]
0060 **5** *hd* **Fantasy Believer**[13] 2429 8-9-11 **83** .... KFallon 1 85
(J J Quinn) *hld up: hdwy over 2f out: rdn over 1f out: edgd lft and no ex ins fnl f* **7/1**[3]
0056 **6** 2 **Waterline Twenty (IRE)**[15] 2385 3-8-11 **78** .... ShaneKelly 6 71
(P D Evans) *hld up: effrt over 1f out: nvr trbld ldrs* **25/1**
050- **7** 1 **Poetical (IRE)**[240] 6119 5-9-7 **79** .... JimmyFortune 5 73
(D J Daly) *led: hdd over 4f out: rdn over 1f out: wknd ins fnl f* **20/1**
1- **8** 1/2 **Queen's Pudding (IRE)**[269] 5531 3-9-4 **85** .... JamieSpencer 2 83+
(J R Fanshawe) *dwlt: hld up: effrt over 1f out: n.d: eased ins fnl f* **13/8**[1]
-300 **9** 8 **Jonny Ebeneezer**[26] 2047 7-10-0 **86** ....(b) EddieAhern 7 58
(M Wellings) *plld hrd and prom: rdn and wknd over 1f out* **16/1**
1m 27.78s (1.00) **Going Correction** -0.075s/f (Good)
WFA 3 from 5yo+ 9lb 9 Ran SP% **115.8**
Speed ratings (Par 107):91,89,89,87,87 85,84,83,74
CSF £66.56 CT £444.91 TOTE £7.20: £1.90, £2.40, £2.70; EX 59.10.
Owner Franconson Partners **Bred** G And Mrs Forien **Trained** Newmarket, Suffolk

FOCUS
A decent handicap, but spoilt to a degree by a pedestrian early pace which played into the hands of the eventual winner. Not surprisingly the winning time was very moderate for the grade, and the runner-up is probably the best guide to the level.

NOTEBOOK
Red Cape(FR), tailed off in his only previous outing this season when apparently hitting his head on the stalls, showed that effort to be all wrong. However, this victory boiled down to a well-judged piece of riding by Dettori, who dictated things perfectly from the front after taking it up before halfway. Despite the slow time and the way the race was run, it may be worth giving him the benefit of the doubt as he did look a nice type in three runs on Polytrack last winter.
Romany Nights(IRE), yet to win beyond six furlongs and making a rare appearance over this trip, had every chance and the slow early pace would have been a help to him. He is certainly more exposed than the pair that finished either side of him. (op 8-1)
Ans Bach ◆ was done no favours at all by the moderate early pace and could never get a run until it was too late. This looks to be more his trip and compensation surely awaits.
Namroc(IRE), beaten 14 times since a successful racecourse debut, was given every chance but he stays much further than this and apart from the trip being too short, a pedestrian early pace was the last thing he needed. It was no great surprise that he was lacking for foot over the last furlong or so. (op 15-2 tchd 8-1)
Fantasy Believer ◆ is a winner over this trip, though most of his recent efforts have been over shorter. He could never land a blow in this messy race, but is now 17lb lower than at the start of last season and 4lb below his last winning mark, so he is worth keeping in mind for when the money is down. (op 6-1)
Queen's Pudding(IRE), winner of her only previous outing, a Nottingham maiden fillies' event last autumn that worked out extremely well afterwards, never threatened to land a blow on this belated return. There are several possibilities for this disappointing effort, one of which is that she has not trained on. In any case her next outing should tell us a lot more. (op 7-4)

2825 THE SPORTSMAN RACING MAIDEN STKS 1m 2f
8:40 (8:42) (Class 5) 3-Y-0 **£5,181** (£1,541; £770; £384) **Stalls** Centre

Form RPR
5-0 **1** **Rhinebird**[60] 1192 3-9-3 .... OscarUrbina 4 85+
(J R Fanshawe) *hld up: hdwy over 2f out: led over 1f out: r.o wl* **16/1**
6- **2** 3 1/2 **Dubai Melody (USA)**[268] 5554 3-8-12 .... DavidKinsella 8 73
(J H M Gosden) *chsd ldrs: edgd rt and led over 1f out: sn hdd and outpcd* **22/1**
3 3/4 **Road Home** 3-9-3 .... SteveDrowne 11 77+
(G Wragg) *hld up: effrt and hmpd 1f out: styd on: nt trble ldrs* **33/1**
4-33 **4** 3 **Monets Masterpiece (USA)**[19] 2261 3-9-3 80 ....(t) AlanMunro 9 71
(Mrs A J Perrett) *prom: rdn and ev ch over 1f out: sn hmpd and wknd* **7/1**[3]
5 3/4 **January** 3-9-3 .... LDettori 1 70
(Saeed Bin Suroor) *s.i.s: hld up: hdwy over 3f out: rdn: edgd rt and ev ch over 1f out: sn wknd* **13/8**[1]
-304 **6** 3/4 **Hunting Party (IRE)**[4] 2712 3-9-3 73 ....(t) JohnEgan 6 68
(B W Hills) *led: rdn: edgd lft and hdd over 1f out: wknd ins fnl f* **13/2**[2]
03- **7** 7 **India Run (IRE)**[294] 4908 3-9-3 .... EddieAhern 2 55+
(J L Dunlop) *hld up: nvr nr to chal* **12/1**
05 **8** 4 **Queen Isabella**[35] 1822 3-8-12 .... JamieSpencer 5 56+
(J R Fanshawe) *chsd ldrs: rdn and ev ch over 1f out: sn hmpd and wknd* **8/1**
9 5 **Manipulate** 3-9-3 .... NickyMackay 10 38
(L M Cumani) *hld up: rdn and wknd over 2f out* **16/1**
0- **10** 19 **Sonny Mac**[237] 6142 3-9-3 ....(t) NCallan 3 —
(B J Meehan) *s.i.s: hld up: rdn and wknd over 2f out* **50/1**
11 13 **Nanosecond (USA)** 3-9-3 .... JimmyFortune 7 —
(J H M Gosden) *s.i.s: sn prom: rdn over 3f out: sn hung lft and wknd* **7/1**[3]
2m 4.25s (-2.19) **Going Correction** -0.075s/f (Good) 11 Ran SP% **116.2**
Speed ratings (Par 99):105,102,101,99,98 98,92,89,85,70 59
CSF £318.71 TOTE £23.30: £5.80, £6.20, £7.00; EX 441.30.
Owner Chris Van Hoorn **Bred** Hascombe And Valiant Studs **Trained** Newmarket, Suffolk

FOCUS
Probably not a bad maiden as there were some interesting types from big yards and the fourth sets the level. The pace looked fair enough and although there were some traffic problems late on it made no difference to the result.

2826 THESPORTSMAN.COM H'CAP 5f

9:10 (9:12) (Class 5) (0-75,74) 3-Y-O **£3,886** (£1,156; £577; £288) **Stalls** Low

Form RPR

-212 **1** **Fantasy Explorer**[13] 2433 3-9-0 **67** KFallon 7 84+
(J J Quinn) *chsd ldr: led 2f out: sn rdn clr* **5/2**[1]

0133 **2** *2* **Patavium Prince (IRE)**[11] 2496 3-9-2 **69** GeorgeBaker 1 76
(J R Best) *a.p: rdn to chse wnr fnl f: no imp* **4/1**[3]

5444 **3** *1 ¼* **Overwing (IRE)**[13] 2433 3-9-1 **68** EddieAhern 6 71
(R M H Cowell) *trckd ldrs: plld hrd: n.m.r over 3f out: rdn over 1f out : styd on same pce* **12/1**

0123 **4** *½* **Red Vixen (IRE)**[8] 2576 3-7-11 **57** KirstyMilczarek(7) 3 58
(C N Allen) *chsd ldrs: rdn over 1f out: styd on same pce* **20/1**

0056 **5** *shd* **Thoughtsofstardom**[17] 2316 3-7-12 **56** oh1 ow1 (p) JamesDoyle(5) 8 56
(P S McEntee) *hld up: rdn over 1f out: nt rch ldrs* **22/1**

2123 **6** *½* **Yellow Card**[6] 2652 3-9-6 **73** OscarUrbina 9 72
(N A Callaghan) *hld up: nvr nrr* **7/2**[2]

0314 **7** *nk* **Musical Romance (IRE)**[6] 2652 3-8-13 **66** (b) LDettori 2 63+
(B J Meehan) *s.i.s: hld up: racd keenly: nt clr run fr over 1f out: nvr able to chal* **7/2**[2]

50-0 **8** *3* **Sofinella (IRE)**[32] 1900 3-8-13 **66** JimmyFortune 4 53
(A W Carroll) *led 3f: wknd fnl f* **16/1**

5-00 **9** *3* **Smart Cassie**[14] 2410 3-9-7 **74** SteveDrowne 5 50
(D Shaw) *hld up: plld hrd: hdwy 1/2-way: wknd over 1f out* **20/1**

60.07 secs (0.51) **Going Correction** -0.075s/f (Good) 9 Ran SP% **120.5**
Speed ratings (Par 99):92,88,86,86,85 85,84,79,74
CSF £12.94 CT £103.78 TOTE £3.20: £1.30, £1.80, £3.90; EX 15.30 Place 6 £2,724.57, Place 5 £1,031.94.

Owner The Fantasy Fellowship E **Bred** Sexton Enterprises **Trained** Settrington, N Yorks

FOCUS
Despite this being a sprint handicap, the early pace was surprisingy moderate and a few were pulling for their heads. As a result the winning time was pretty modest for the class of contest but the form appears sound enough rated through the placed horses.

Musical Romance(IRE) Official explanation: jockey filly was denied a clear run

T/Plt: £2,558.40 to a £1 stake. Pool: £40,305.00. 11.50 winning tickets. T/Qpdt: £1,378.20 to a £1 stake. Pool: £3,166.35. 1.70 winning tickets. CR

2523 REDCAR (L-H)

Friday, June 23

OFFICIAL GOING: Firm (good to firm in places)

The ground was described as 'on the quick side but no jar and a good covering of grass'.

Wind: Light half behind Weather: Fine and dry

2827 DAVID BOSOMWORTH CHAMPAGNE MAIDEN STKS 5f

2:15 (2:16) (Class 5) 2-Y-O **£3,238** (£963; £481; £240) **Stalls** Centre

Form RPR

323 **1** **Winning Spirit (IRE)**[13] 2439 2-9-3 TPQueally 4 81
(J Noseda) *mde all: shkn up and wnt clr over 1f out: readily* **2/1**[1]

32 **2** *2* **Dress To Impress (IRE)**[10] 2517 2-9-0 AmirQuinn(3) 3 74
(J R Boyle) *trckd ldrs: wnt 2nd 2f out: kpt on: no imp* **2/1**[1]

5 **3** *1 ¼* **Algol**[21] 2191 2-9-3 TonyHamilton 5 69
(J Howard Johnson) *chsd ldrs: rdn 2f out: kpt on same pce* **14/1**[3]

536 **4** *1 ¼* **Ishibee (IRE)**[14] 2394 2-8-12 PaulFessey 1 60
(Mrs A Duffield) *chsd ldrs on outer: styd on same pce fnl 2f* **20/1**

5 *¾* **Durova (IRE)** 2-8-12 DavidAllan 2 57
(T D Easterby) *neat: dwlt: hdwy over 2f out: kpt on same pce* **33/1**

44 **6** *3 ½* **Nufoudh (IRE)**[24] 2094 2-9-3 StanleyChin 7 50
(M Johnston) *chsd ldrs: edgd rt over 2f out: outpcd and hung lft* **10/3**[2]

7 *5* **Grazie Mille** 2-8-7 DuranFentiman(5) 6 27
(T D Easterby) *leggy: unf: dwlt: a detached in last* **33/1**

58.25 secs (-0.45) **Going Correction** +0.025s/f (Good) 7 Ran SP% **107.1**
Speed ratings (Par 93):104,100,98,96,95 90,82
CSF £5.19 TOTE £2.90: £1.50, £1.70; EX 6.30.

Owner Saeed Suhail **Bred** Mountarmstrong Stud **Trained** Newmarket, Suffolk

FOCUS
A very smart winning time for a race like this, 0.37 seconds faster than the later maiden handicap for older horses.

NOTEBOOK
Winning Spirit(IRE), beaten favourite on every previous run, enjoyed the change of tactics to lead from start to finish. Always going well in front, he kept on resolutely and saw the trip out well, to win with plenty in hand. Making the running had a positive effect on the horse, and he could well be a decent sprinting juvenile, as his debut effort, on ground he probably did not like, has worked out nicely. He holds plenty of entries, including one for the Group One National Stakes, and is clearly rated above average by his stable. (op 7-4 tchd 9-4 in places)
Dress To Impress(IRE) had shown more than enough in his first two runs to make him of serious interest in what looked to be ordinary maiden company. Held up off the pace, he could never get to the easy winner and probably bumped into a fair sort. His turn should not be far away. (tchd 7-4)
Algol showed some decent early pace on his debut before tying up in the final stages. Weak in the market prior to the off and giving trouble at the start, he never got to the head of affairs and gives the impression he may need more time. (op 9-1)
Ishibee(IRE), who was sweating before the race, showed only mild promise again, staying on reasonably well after being behind early. Her future will probably be in the forthcoming nurseries.
Durova(IRE) never got involved, after missing the break, and found things happening too quickly for her. (op 20-1)
Nufoudh(IRE) raced with plenty of zest early in the race, but found very little again off the bridle, hanging left under pressure, and looks one to avoid in the short-term. (op 7-2 tchd 4-1)
Grazie Mille, a Bertolini half-sister to winners Percy Douglas and Billy Allen, was slowly away from the stalls and never looked like catching the main body of the field at any stage. She will need to make dramatic improvement to get involved next time.

2828 JACKSONS-CPL SOLICITORS WE-CAN-WORK-IT-OUT H'CAP 2m 4y

2:50 (2:52) (Class 5) (0-75,75) 4-Y-O+ **£4,857** (£1,445; £722; £360) **Stalls** Low

Form RPR

421- **1** **Key Time (IRE)**[300] 4748 4-8-7 **61** JamieMackay 2 69+
(Sir Mark Prescott) *trckd ldrs: led 3f out: styd on wl* **10/3**[1]

4551 **2** *1* **Mr Majestic**[16] 2365 4-8-5 **59** DavidAllan 4 66
(R M Whitaker) *trckd ldrs: drvn over 3f out: styd on to take 2nd ins last: no real imp* **10/3**[1]

-003 **3** *1* **Mister Arjay (USA)**[11] 2501 6-8-5 **59** TonyHamilton 7 65
(B Ellison) *sn led: qcknd 6f out: hdd 3f out: kpt on same pce* **6/1**

0520 **4** *1 ½* **Cripsey Brook**[16] 2357 8-9-0 **75** JamesReveley(7) 5 79
(K G Reveley) *hld up in last: in tch: effrt over 2f out: styd on fnl f: nt rch ldrs* **5/1**[3]

-232 **5** *shd* **Bronze Dancer (IRE)**[15] 2381 4-8-4 **63** AndrewElliott(5) 1 67
(G A Swinbank) *hld up: hdwy 4f out: rdn and hung lft over 2f out: kpt on: nvr trbld ldrs* **4/1**[2]

-501 **6** *8* **Lefonic**[21] 2206 4-8-7 **61** StanleyChin 6 55
(G C H Chung) *restless in stalls: stmbld s: sn trcking ldrs: lost pl over 2f out* **14/1**

06-0 **7** *hd* **Thewhirlingdervish (IRE)**[27] 2018 8-8-11 **70** DuranFentiman(5) 3 64
(T D Easterby) *hld up in tch: stmbld bnd 5f out: wknd over 2f out* **14/1**

3m 31.26s (-0.24) **Going Correction** +0.075s/f (Good) 7 Ran SP% **110.4**
Speed ratings (Par 103):103,102,102,101,101 97,97
CSF £13.50 TOTE £2.80: £2.50, £3.10; EX 15.60.

Owner G Moore - Osborne House **Bred** Airlie Stud **Trained** Newmarket, Suffolk

FOCUS
A modest staying handicap. There was not a great deal of pace from the outset, but it was not run at a crawl. The form is rated through the runner-up backed up by the third.

Thewhirlingdervish(IRE) Official explanation: jockey said gelding stumbled on the bend

2829 PERTEMPS MAIDEN STKS 1m 3f

3:25 (3:25) (Class 5) 3-Y-O+ **£3,238** (£963; £481; £240) **Stalls** Low

Form RPR

1 **Eta Draconis (IRE)** 3-8-11 TPQueally 3 73+
(Saeed Bin Suroor) *lengthy: unf: trckd ldrs: pushed along over 5f out: nt clr run and swtchd over 2f out: wnt 2nd 1f out: styd on to ld last s* **10/3**[2]

2 *nk* **Hyperalert (USA)** 3-8-11 StanleyChin 7 73+
(M Johnston) *rangy: scope: led: set modest pce: hdd after 2f: drvn to ld 3f out: hung lft: 3l clr 1f out: rdr put whip down ins last: hd* **6/1**[3]

32 **3** *3 ½* **Mobaasher (USA)**[43] 1605 3-8-11 JamieMackay 6 67
(Sir Michael Stoute) *trckd ldrs: effrt and hung lft 3f out: kpt on same pce: nvr able chal* **4/5**[1]

4 *¾* **Barton Belle**[19] 4-9-5 TonyHamilton 2 61
(G A Swinbank) *dwlt: in tch: pushed along over 4f out: carried rt over 2f out: kpt on* **13/2**

5 *nk* **Chrisjen** 4-9-0 MarkLawson(5) 1 60?
(M W Easterby) *dwlt: hdwy on ins 4f out: wnt rt over 2f out: kpt on* **100/1**

00 **6** *10* **Bold Medicean**[14] 2411 3-8-11 PaulFessey 4 49
(T P Tate) *hld up in tch: drvn and outpcd over 4f out: sn lost pl* **100/1**

535- **7** *14* **Rockpiler**[229] 5019 4-9-10 **50** DarrenWilliams 5 27
(D W Thompson) *led after 2f: set modest pce: qcknd over 5f out: hdd 3f out: lost pl over 1f out: sn bhd and eased* **100/1**

2m 23.03s (2.03) **Going Correction** +0.075s/f (Good)
WFA 3 from 4yo 13lb 7 Ran SP% **109.2**
Speed ratings (Par 103):95,94,92,91,91 84,74
CSF £20.77 TOTE £3.60: £2.40, £2.40; EX 23.10.

Owner Godolphin **Bred** Southern Bloodstock **Trained** Newmarket, Suffolk

■ Stewards' Enquiry : Stanley Chin 28-day ban: dropped hands and lost first place (Jul 4-31)

FOCUS
A modest winning time for a thoroughly unsatisfactory race. The race is rated through the third at face value, but the proximity of the fifth casts a little doubt on the reliability of the form, as she was an unraced four-year-old that was clearly not fancied to go close. The first two home were also unraced, but from stables you would expect to see a prominent showing from first-time out.

2830 JACKSONS-CPL SOLICITORS ELEANOR RIGBY H'CAP 6f

4:00 (4:00) (Class 3) (0-95,84) 3-Y-O+ **£9,715** (£2,890; £1,444; £721) **Stalls** Centre

Form RPR

0324 **1** **Folga**[5] 2683 4-10-0 **84** JamieMackay 5 95
(J G Given) *trckd ldrs: keen early: effrt over 2f out: edgd rt and led ins last: jst hld on* **9/2**[1]

0101 **2** *shd* **My Gacho (IRE)**[3] 2732 4-9-12 **82** 6ex (v) PaulFessey 7 93
(T D Barron) *trckd ldrs: led over 1f out: hdd ins last: rallied and jst hld* **5/1**[2]

-060 **3** *1 ½* **Caribbean Coral**[7] 2624 7-9-11 **81** DarrenWilliams 1 87
(J J Quinn) *hld up: hdwy over 2f out: chsng ldrs over 1f out: unable qckn* **9/2**[1]

0-03 **4** *2 ½* **Red Romeo**[13] 2454 5-9-13 **83** TonyHamilton 4 82
(G A Swinbank) *sn pushed along: hdwy 2f out: styd on ins last* **9/2**[1]

3600 **5** *2* **Paris Bell**[6] 2661 4-9-6 **76** PaulQuinn 8 69
(T D Easterby) *hld up: effrt over 2f out: nvr nr to chal* **7/1**[3]

1013 **6** *½* **Dizzy In The Head**[9] 2550 7-8-9 **70** (b) DuranFentiman(5) 3 61
(I Semple) *sn w ldrs: rdn over 2f out: wknd jst ins last* **15/2**

0010 **7** *hd* **Mr Wolf**[5] 2683 5-9-9 **84** (p) MarkLawson(5) 6 75
(D W Barker) *set str pce: hdd over 1f out: sn wknd* **7/1**[3]

1m 10.68s (-1.02) **Going Correction** +0.025s/f (Good) 7 Ran SP% **108.0**
Speed ratings (Par 107):107,106,104,101,98 98,97
CSF £23.79 CT £91.58 TOTE £6.10: £3.20, £2.60; EX 25.10.

Owner The Thrill Seekers **Bred** P Onslow **Trained** Willoughton, Lincs

■ Stewards' Enquiry : Paul Fessey three-day ban: used whip with excessive frequency and without allowing time to respond (Jul 4-6)

FOCUS
A solid-looking handicap run at a strong pace and the form looks solid with the fourth the best guide.

NOTEBOOK
Folga, who was content to sit off the early pace, battled really well under pressure to just hang on as the line approached. She is a tough and mainly consistent sprinting filly. (op 11-2)
My Gacho(IRE), carrying a 6lb penalty, is in the form of his life at the moment and only narrowly went down to Folga in a driving finish. However, and on the minus side, he is very high in the weights now and it will take another big effort from him to win again in the short-term. (op 9-2)
Caribbean Coralpulled very hard, despite the generous-looking gallop, and failed to get home after moving up to the leaders stylishly. He is well handicapped at the moment and is one to bear in mind. (op 4-1)
Red Romeo was never really travelling on the bridle from an early stage, but kept on respectably in the final furlong to finish just behind the places. He has winning form at up to seven furlongs and would be on real interest if stepped up to that trip soon, and had Fallon booked for the ride, as his form figures on the horse are 11120. (tchd 5-1)
Dizzy In The Head helped to set the pace and had little chance of seeing out the trip, given how quickly he went early. (op 5-1)
Mr Wolf, who bounced back to form last time, had no chance of sustaining the gallop he helped to set in front. High in the handicap after his last win, he does like to lead, but definitely appeared to go off too quickly in front. (tchd 15-2)

2831 JOHN SMITH'S REDCAR STRAIGHT-MILE CHAMPIONSHIP STKS (H'CAP) (QUALIFIER) 1m

4:35 (4:35) (Class 5) (0-75,73) 3-Y-O+ £3,238 (£963; £481; £240) Stalls Centre

Form				RPR
-040	1		Kaymich Perfecto[18] 2299 6-8-13 62 MichaelJStainton(7) 6 (R M Whitaker) hld up: effrt over 3f out: led over 2f out: r.o wl 3/1[2]	76
6240	2	3 1/2	Bond Diamond[7] 2627 9-9-5 61 RobbieFitzpatrick 4 (P T Midgley) hld up: hdwy over 2f out: wnt 2nd over 1f out: no imp 7/2[3]	67
-355	3	3/4	Efidium[5] 2681 8-9-7 70 SuzzanneFrance(7) 1 (N Bycroft) led after 2f: hdd over 2f out: styd on fnl f 7/2[3]	74
0035	4	2	Hurricane Coast[19] 2259 7-9-13 69 (b) TonyHamilton 3 (C R Dore) hld up: smooth hdwy over 2f out: sn rdn and fnd little 15/2	69
2013	5	3 1/2	Marmooq[10] 2525 3-9-7 73 StanleyChin 5 (M Johnston) led 2f: w ldr: drvn 4f out: hung rt over 2f out: sn lost pl 5/2[1]	65
-000	6	12	Born For Diamonds (IRE)[27] 2019 4-8-4 51 oh9 AndrewElliott(5) 2 (R E Barr) t.k.h: trckd ldrs: lost pl over 2f out: sn bhd 50/1	15

1m 37.46s (-0.34) **Going Correction** +0.025s/f (Good)
WFA 3 from 4yo+ 10lb 6 Ran SP% 111.7
Speed ratings (Par 103):102,98,97,95,92 80
CSF £13.69 TOTE £5.90: £1.50, £2.70; EX 18.00.
Owner G B Bedford **Bred** Mrs F S Williams **Trained** Scarcroft, W Yorks

FOCUS
A very ordinary handicap and the pace was just average, but the form looks sound.

2832 PERTEMPS EMPLOYMENT ALLIANCE CLAIMING STKS 1m 2f

5:10 (5:10) (Class 6) 3-Y-O+ £2,388 (£705; £352) Stalls Low

Form				RPR
0-63	1		True (IRE)[14] 2398 5-8-13 45 PaulFessey 7 (Mrs S Lamyman) hld up: hdwy 4f out: styd on to ld over 1f out: drvn out 6/1[2]	48
-060	2	1 3/4	Ruby Legend[4] 2696 8-9-5 46 JamesReveley(7) 5 (K G Reveley) hld up in mid-div: hdwy on outer over 4f out: hung lft and styd on to take 2nd nr line 20/1	58
6-00	3	shd	Parchment (IRE)[28] 1996 4-8-13 50 MarkLawson(5) 3 (A J Lockwood) chsd ldrs: led 3f out tl over 1f out: kpt on same pce 13/2[3]	49
1-00	4	1 3/4	Rudaki[1] 2789 4-9-11 51 JasonEdmunds(3) 2 (M E Sowersby) chsd ldrs: effrt over 3f out: one pce fnl 2f 14/1	56
0010	5	1 1/4	Tallyhobye[9] 2539 3-8-8 50 RobbieFitzpatrick 1 (M E Sowersby) s.i.s: hdwy 3f out: kpt on fnl f 13/2[3]	46
6020	6	1	Eijaaz (IRE)[23] 2131 5-8-13 49 KristinStubbs(7) 9 (Mrs L Stubbs) dwlt: hld up in rr: hdwy on ins over 3f out: chal over 1f out: sn wknd 5/1[1]	44
0-00	7	1 1/4	Jenna Stannis[4] 2696 4-8-6 47 (t) AndrewElliott(5) 4 (W Storey) chsd ldrs: wknd over 1f out 20/1	33
60-0	8	1 3/4	Azahara[23] 1293 4-8-11 41 (b[1]) DavidAllan 11 (K G Reveley) hld up in rr: effrt 3f out: nvr nr ldrs 10/1	29
30-0	9	3	Piccolomini[11] 2501 4-10-0 62 TonyHamilton 10 (E W Tuer) led tl 3f out: lost pl over 1f out 11/1	40
00-6	10	2	Ronnies Lad[18] 2291 4-9-1 42 DuranFentiman(5) 8 (J R Norton) trckd ldrs on outer: rdn over 3f out: sn btn 20/1	29
600	11	nk	For No One (IRE)[24] 2111 3-8-10 65 StanleyChin 6 (M Johnston) trckd ldrs: drvn over 4f out: lost pl over 1f out 7/1	30
-300	12	5	Charlie Tango (IRE)[16] 1947 5-9-11 55 PatrickMathers(3) 12 (D W Thompson) sn trcking ldrs on outer: drvn over 3f out: wknd over 2f out 17/2	27

2m 6.84s (0.04) **Going Correction** +0.075s/f (Good)
WFA 3 from 4yo+ 12lb 12 Ran SP% 119.0
Speed ratings (Par 101):102,100,100,99,98 97,96,94,92,90 90,86
CSF £123.38 TOTE £8.40: £2.10, £4.40, £1.80; EX 192.30.
Owner The Underlaws **Bred** Philip Newton **Trained** Ruckland, Lincs

FOCUS
A routine claimer and the pace was no more than ordinary. The form is sound but limited.

2833 JOAN & ERNEST OXLEY GOLDEN WEDDING ANNIVERSARY MAIDEN H'CAP 5f

5:45 (5:45) (Class 5) (0-70,67) 3-Y-O+ £3,238 (£963; £481; £240) Stalls Centre

Form				RPR
0-00	1		Dark Champion[21] 2198 6-9-7 54 (b[1]) DavidAllan 2 (R E Barr) trckd ldrs: led 2f out: hld on towards fin 7/2[1]	61
035	2	nk	Fikri[9] 2550 3-9-7 67 (bt) JamesO'Reilly(7) 4 (T J Pitt) squeezed out s: in rr and sn drvn along: hdwy 2f out: wnt 2nd jst ins last: no ex nr fin 6/1	71
00-5	3	2	Shunkawakhan (IRE)[30] 1937 3-9-10 63 StanleyChin 5 (G C H Chung) trckd ldrs: effrt 2f out: kpt on same pce 8/1	60
-000	4	1	Dysonic (USA)[38] 1764 4-8-6 42 oh7 (p) JasonEdmunds(3) 7 (J Balding) chsd ldrs: kpt on same pce fnl 2f 14/1	37
3045	5	nk	Lord Mayfair (USA)[8] 2571 4-8-10 50 (b) AnnStokell(7) 6 (Miss A Stokell) led: edgd lft and hdd 2f out: kpt on fnl f 8/1	44
36-5	6	shd	Mullady Penelope[39] 1733 3-9-2 55 PaulFessey 10 (Mrs A Duffield) trckd ldrs: rdn over 2f out: kpt on fnl f 6/1	47
-050	7	1	Montana[24] 2112 6-9-1 48 LeeEnstone 3 (C W Fairhurst) chsd ldrs: hung lft and hmpd over 1f out: no threat after 11/2[3]	38
0566	8	nk	Nazaaha (USA)[7] 2602 4-9-3 50 (p) TonyHamilton 1 (A G Newcombe) wnt rt s: in rr and sn drvn along: nvr on terms 9/2[2]	39
/000	9	nk	Nellie Gwyn[9] 2543 4-8-9 42 oh2 JamieMackay 9 (J G Given) s.i.s: a in rr and sn drvn along 16/1	30

58.62 secs (-0.08) **Going Correction** +0.025s/f (Good)
WFA 3 from 4yo+ 6lb 9 Ran SP% 119.1
Speed ratings (Par 103):101,100,97,95,95 95,93,93,92
CSF £25.58 CT £159.85 TOTE £4.80: £1.60, £1.40, £4.40; EX 40.40 Place 6 £78.43, Place 5 £64.29.
Owner A Suddes **Bred** R G Percival **Trained** Seamer, N Yorks

■ Stewards' Enquiry : Ann Stokell caution: careless riding
James O'Reilly seven-day ban: used whip with excessive frequency and above shoulder height (Jul 4-10)

FOCUS
Races do not come much worse than this, with the nine runners having failed to win from 128 attempts between them, 47 of those by the eventual winner. The form is sound enough, but cannot be rated positively.
T/Plt: £366.30 to a £1 stake. Pool: £32,617.25. 65.00 winning tickets. T/Qpdt: £138.60 to a £1 stake. Pool: £1,573.70. 8.40 winning tickets. WG

2834 - 2839a (Foreign Racing) - See Raceform Interactive

2718 LIMERICK (R-H)

Friday, June 23

OFFICIAL GOING: Good to firm

2840a MCINERNEY HOMES MARTIN MOLONY STKS (LISTED RACE) 1m 3f 70y

7:20 (7:21) 3-Y-O+ £24,693 (£7,244; £3,451; £1,175)

			RPR
1		Foreign Affairs[13] 2453 8-9-12 DPMcDonogh 4 (Sir Mark Prescott) sn prom: led bef 1/2-way: drvn along fr 5f out: strly pressed fr 1 1/2f out: styd on wl u.p fnl f 7/4[1]	95
2	3/4	Ask Carol (IRE)[12] 2486 5-9-6 67 (p) JAHeffernan 6 (Joseph G Murphy, Ire) hld up: 8th u.p 3f out: hdwy on outer over 1f out: styd on wl: nrest at fin 33/1	88
3	shd	Helena Molony (IRE)[13] 2471 4-9-6 96 FMBerry 9 (John M Oxx, Ire) settled 3rd: 4th 1/2-way: hdwy appr st: 2nd and chal 1 1/2f out: ev ch: no imp ins fnl f: kpt on u.p 7/1	88
4	1/2	Reform Act (USA)[13] 2471 3-8-7 95 TPO'Shea 5 (D K Weld, Ire) sn led: hdd bef 1/2-way: 2nd and drvn along over 3f out: 4th 1 1/2f out: kpt on u.p 5/1[3]	87
5	hd	Gavroche (IRE)[20] 2229 5-9-9 KJManning 3 (J R Boyle) s.i.s and hld up in rr: hdwy over 4f out: 4th 3f out: 3rd and chal 1 1/2f out: no ex ins fnl f 7/2[2]	90
6	1	Ice Princess (IRE)[47] 1521 3-8-7 84 WSupple 1 (David Wachman, Ire) trckd ldrs in 5th: rdn st: kpt on fnl f 33/1	85
7	1/2	Sable D'Olonne (IRE)[18] 2307 3-8-7 90 WJLee 2 (T Stack, Ire) hld up towards rr: kpt on fr 1 1/2f out 20/1	84
8	1 1/2	Dapple Grey (IRE)[23] 2157 3-8-7 83 WMLordan 8 (T Stack, Ire) mid-div: 6th 1/2-way: kpt on same pce fr 3f out 9/1	82
9	1 1/2	Subtle Affair (IRE)[41] 1703 4-9-6 84 JMurtagh 10 (P F Cashman, Ire) chsd ldrs: 3rd 1/2-way: 4th u.p 4f out: sn no ex 16/1	79
10	4	The Carbon Unit (USA)[75] 4-9-12 PShanahan 7 (C Collins, Ire) a towards rr: no imp fr 3f out 16/1	79

2m 24.0s
WFA 3 from 4yo+ 13lb 10 Ran SP% 120.2
CSF £78.42 TOTE £2.60: £1.70, £5.80, £1.80; DF 197.00.
Owner Charles C Walker - Osborne House **Bred** Miss K Rausing **Trained** Newmarket, Suffolk

NOTEBOOK
Foreign Affairs, who came here chasing his sixth Listed victory, went to the front at an early stage. Over what is probably his minimum trip, he was driven along with half a mile to run but, to his credit, answered his jockey's every call. An admirable campaigner, he has been a thorough credit to connections and will be capable of adding to his stakes-race haul as the season goes on. (op 5/4)
Ask Carol(IRE) was the surprise package of the race as she came into this with a rating of 67 and had earlier this month won a seven-furlong Down Royal handicap off a 7lb lower mark. Given a patient ride, she stormed home over the final furlong and was gaining on the leader with every stride, thoroughly vindicating her connections' decision to pitch her in at this level.
Helena Molony(IRE) ran quite well having stuck to the pace from the outset. She has run several good races in defeat at Listed level, including when second to Galatee at Gowran in May, and could be able to make her mark at this level. She may appreciate a slightly easier surface. (op 6/1)
Reform Act(USA), who won a ten-furlong handicap off a mark of 89 last month, came here on the back of a creditable third in the Silver Stakes at The Curragh. She ran a solid race but possibly did not match the form of her previous effort. (op 4/1)
Gavroche(IRE) is a very smart handicapper and, having been ridden patiently, he started a forward move nearing the end of the back straight. He looked a possible danger to the winner at one stage in the straight but had no more to offer inside the final furlong. (op 4/1)
Ice Princess(IRE), who won her maiden here last year, ran quite well and looked as if she might reach the frame nearing the furlong pole. She has now posted two solid efforts at Listed level this year and may be able to reach the frame in a Listed race.
Sable D'Olonne(IRE) was taking a rise in class after winning a ten-furlong maiden at Naas on her debut earlier this month. She was under pressure some way from home but was putting in her best work at the finish and will be of interest when she steps up in trip.

2841 - 2843a (Foreign Racing) - See Raceform Interactive

2800 ASCOT (R-H)

Saturday, June 24

OFFICIAL GOING: Good to firm (firm in places)
Wind: Almost nil Weather: Sunny and warm

2844 CHESHAM STKS (LISTED RACE) 7f

2:30 (2:33) (Class 1) 2-Y-O

£31,229 (£11,836; £5,923; £2,953; £1,479; £742) Stalls Low

Form				RPR
3	1		Champlain[35] 1838 2-9-3 PhilipRobinson 11 (M A Jarvis) hld up: hdwy over 3f out: led over 1f out: r.o wl 7/2[2]	101+
	2	2	Country Song (USA)[18] 2336 2-9-5 KFallon 10 (David Wachman, Ire) w'like: s.i.s: hld up: nt clr run over 2f out: hdwy over 1f out: sn ev ch: edgd lft and nt qckn ins fnl f 5/1[3]	98
510	3	hd	Middleham (IRE)[24] 2127 2-9-3 JoeFanning 2 (M Johnston) led: rdn and hdd over 2f out: kpt on u.p ins fnl f 12/1	96
23	4	1	Pires[15] 2388 2-9-3 SamHitchcott 7 (M R Channon) unf: scope: racd keenly: cl up: led over 2f out: hung rt and hdd over 1f out: styd on same pce ins fnl f 33/1	93
3	5	3/4	Gweebarra[17] 2361 2-9-3 NCallan 3 (K A Ryan) unf: racd keenly: trckd ldrs: nt clr run over 3f out: nt qckn 2f out: kpt on ins fnl f: nt pce to chal 12/1	91
2	6	nk	Cumin (USA)[15] 2409 2-8-12 MichaelHills 8 (B W Hills) w'like: leggy: lw: hld up: rdn whn nt clr run and hmpd over 2f out: sme hdwy over 1f out: nt trble ldrs 11/2	85+
123	7	1 3/4	Always Fruitful[21] 2225 2-9-3 KDarley 4 (M Johnston) in tch: rdn over 2f out: edgd rt over 1f out: no ex ins fnl f 9/4[1]	86
0	8	13	Montalembert (USA)[35] 1838 2-9-3 JohnEgan 5 (J S Moore) s.i.s: midfield: hdwy over 3f out: rdn over 2f out: wknd over 1f out 100/1	54
5	9	10	Kindlelight Blue (IRE)[19] 2281 2-9-3 RyanMoore 6 (N P Littmoden) hld up: struggling whn n.m.r over 2f out: nvr on terms 50/1	29
5	10	8	Green Day Packer (IRE)[15] 2409 2-9-3 LDettori 9 (P C Haslam) cl up tl hmpd whn wkng over 2f out 18/1	9

3 **11** *15* **Tension Point**[8] [2619] 2-9-3 .... ShaneKelly 1 —
(J A Osborne) *w ldr tl rdn and wknd over 2f out* **25/1**

1m 27.9s (-1.10) **Going Correction** -0.175s/f (Firm) **11** Ran SP% **115.4**
Speed ratings (Par 101):99,96,96,95,94 94,92,77,65,56 39
CSF £20.42 TOTE £4.80: £1.90, £1.90, £3.60; EX 16.60 Trifecta £258.50 Pool: £6,794.32 - 18.66 winning tickets..
Owner Sheikh Mohammed **Bred** Darley **Trained** Newmarket, Suffolk

FOCUS
The winning time was nothing special for a race of this type, but it looked a decent renewal of the Chesham and four of the first five have been rated big improvers.

NOTEBOOK
Champlain ◆ had finished third on his debut behind Major Cadeaux and Jo'Burg, who were second and fifth in the Coventry Stakes on the first day of the Royal meeting. Tackling faster ground, which his breeding suggested he would appreciate, he was well suited by the extra furlong and stayed on strongly once in front. The Superlative Stakes at Newmarket could be next. (op 3-1 tchd 9-2, 5-1 in places)
Country Song(USA), an athletic and attractive type, was giving weight all round following his two wins at Tipperary. He did not travel as well as some and came with his effort deep on the track, before edging left under pressure and proving unable to go with the winner inside the last. (op 4-1)
Middleham(IRE), a stablemate of the beaten favourite, made the running and stayed on when headed. He saw out this longer trip well and is progressing nicely with racing. (op 14-1)
Pires, never far away, showed a lot more than he had in a pair of Brighton maidens over a furlong shorter. If he can reproduce this form he will have no problem getting off the mark. (op 50-1)
Gweebarra, upped in both trip and class for this seond outing, showed a big step up in form and a maiden success should be a formality. (op 14-1 tchd 11-1 in places)
Cumin(USA), an attractive filly, did well to finish as close as she did after being hampered by the runner-up. This looks her trip. (op 5-1 tchd 6-1)
Always Fruitful had a troubled passage in the Woodcote last time but there were no excuses here. He was never really going and could not pick up in the latter stages. (op 11-4 tchd 3-1 in places)
Tension Point Official explanation: jockey said colt lost its action

2845 HARDWICKE STKS (GROUP 2) 1m 4f
3:05 (3:05) (Class 1) 4-Y-0+

£79,492 (£30,128; £15,078; £7,518; £3,766; £1,890) **Stalls** High

Form RPR
-031 **1** **Maraahel (IRE)**[44] [1601] 5-9-0 120 ....(v) RHills 6 121
(Sir Michael Stoute) *lw: dwlt: hld up in midfield: prog 2f out: rdn to ld narrowly ins fnl f: hld on wl* **9/2**[3]
0-12 **2** *hd* **Mountain High (IRE)**[29] [1976] 4-9-0 110 .... KFallon 8 121
(Sir Michael Stoute) *lw: trckd ldng pair: effrt over 2f out: drvn to ld over 1f out: narrowly hdd ins fnl f: kpt on wl: jst hld* **7/2**[1]
6453 **3** *1 ½* **Enforcer**[22] [2202] 4-9-0 109 .... KerrinMcEvoy 1 118
(W R Muir) *lw: hld up in last pair: rdn 3f out: prog on outer 2f out: chsd ldng pair ins fnl f: no imp last 100yds* **8/1**
2-12 **4** *¾* **Day Flight**[27] [2061] 5-9-0 115 .... RichardHughes 9 119+
(J H M Gosden) *lw: hld up in midfield: effrt over 2f out: trying to cl whn squeezed out over 1f out: kpt on same pce after* **5/1**
5-05 **5** *2* **Hard Top (IRE)**[20] [2277] 4-9-0 115 .... MJKinane 5 114
(Sir Michael Stoute) *swtg: t.k.h: led for 2f: trckd ldr: led over 2f out to over 1f out: wknd ins fnl f* **4/1**[2]
2-45 **6** *½* **Self Defense**[28] [2010] 9-9-0 108 .... AlanMunro 2 113
(Miss E C Lavelle) *hld up in last pair: rdn 4f out: struggling and no prog 3f out: kpt on fnl f* **50/1**
1-62 **7** *nk* **Collier Hill**[91] [741] 8-9-5 116 .... DeanMcKeown 7 118
(G A Swinbank) *trckd ldng pair: rdn over 2f out: grad wknd fr over 1f out* **9/1**
4-36 **8** *3* **Bandari (IRE)**[25] [2116] 7-9-0 118 .... MartinDwyer 3 108
(M Johnston) *reluctant to post: led after 2f to over 2f out: wknd wl over 1f out* **17/2**

2m 29.25s (-3.75) **Going Correction** +0.025s/f (Good) **8** Ran SP% **110.7**
Speed ratings (Par 115):113,112,111,111,110 109,109,107
CSF £19.23 TOTE £5.20: £1.70, £1.60, £2.50; EX 18.70 Trifecta £170.90 Pool: £4,188.67 - 17.40 winning tickets..
Owner Hamdan Al Maktoum **Bred** Shadwell Estate Company Limited **Trained** Newmarket, Suffolk
■ Sir Michael Stoute was responsible for first and second.

FOCUS
An ordinary winning time for a Group 2, just 0.72 seconds faster than the later handicap. Although not out of the top drawer, the form looks pretty sound.

NOTEBOOK
Maraahel(IRE) has been placed three times at Group 1 level but this was his biggest victory to date. Upped in trip and patiently ridden, he came with a strong run to edge ahead of his stablemate early in the final furlong and was always holding him from then on. (op 4-1 tchd 5-1 in places)
Mountain High(IRE) ◆ had ground conditions to suit. After taking a narrow lead he was headed by his stable companion inside the last but kept battling to the line. This was his best run to date and there is better still to come from this lightly-raced colt. (op 10-3 tchd 4-1 in places)
Enforcer, who ran a similar race behind Shirocco and Ouija Board in the Coronation Cup, ran on strongly down the outside in the straight without getting to the front pair. He is capable of landing a big one and is likely to be seen next in the Princess of Wales's Stakes at Newmarket.
Day Flight, having the first run of his career on fast ground, would have been a little closer had his passage not been interrupted. He is most consistent and has never finished out of the frame. (tchd 11-2)
Hard Top(IRE), from the same yard as the first and second, had ground conditions to suit, but refused to settle as he tracked the leader and his exertions ultimately told.
Self Defense, who had a good bit to find at the weights, made late progress from the rear of the field but was never really a factor.
Collier Hill faced a stiff task under the Group 1 penalty for last year's Irish St Leger win. (op 11-1 tchd 12-1 in places)
Bandari(IRE) beat Maraahel into second in last year's renewal at York, but he has not sparkled this term and he had no answers when headed early in the straight. (op 15-2 tchd 9-1)

2846 GOLDEN JUBILEE STKS (BRITISH LEG OF THE GLOBAL SPRINT CHALLENGE) (GROUP 1) 6f
3:45 (3:46) (Class 1) 3-Y-0+

£198,730 (£75,320; £37,695; £18,795; £9,415; £4,725) **Stalls** Low

Form RPR
1200 **1** **Les Arcs (USA)**[4] [2720] 6-9-4 111 .... JohnEgan 4 122
(T J Pitt) *lw: midfield: hdwy over 2f out: led over 1f out: all out towards fin* **33/1**
1-04 **2** *nk* **Balthazaar's Gift (IRE)**[20] [2276] 3-8-11 111 .... JamieSpencer 14 120
(K A Ryan) *bhd: rdn and hdwy to burst through small gap over 1f out: r.o strly and lugged rt ins fnl f: gaining cl home* **50/1**
1 **3** *2* **Takeover Target (AUS)**[4] [2720] 7-9-4 .... JayFord 13 116
(J Janiak, Australia) *w ldr: led over 2f out: hdd over 1f out: hung rt ins fnl f: no ex cl home* **7/2**[1]
0-00 **4** *½* **Ashdown Express (IRE)**[4] [2720] 7-9-4 111 .... AlanMunro 5 114
(C F Wall) *towards rr: wnt lft whn rdn and hdwy over 1f out: r.o ins fnl f: nvr nrr* **50/1**
11-0 **5** *nk* **Amadeus Wolf**[49] [1486] 3-8-11 120 .... NCallan 9 111
(K A Ryan) *trckd ldrs: rdn and edgd rt fr over 2f out: styd on ins fnl f* **7/1**
5400 **6** *1 ¼* **The Tatling (IRE)**[4] [2720] 9-9-4 113 .... RyanMoore 2 109
(J M Bradley) *lw: swtchd rt s: hld up: rdn and hdwy over 1f out: styd on ins fnl f: nt rch ldrs* **20/1**
010- **7** *hd* **Iffraaj**[266] [5638] 5-9-4 114 .... LDettori 15 109+
(Saeed Bin Suroor) *in tch: rdn over 2f out: no ex ins fnl f* **6/1**[2]
-365 **8** *1* **Eisteddfod**[25] [2115] 5-9-4 109 .... JimmyFortune 1 106+
(P F I Cole) *hld up: rdn 2f out: n.m.r and hmpd over 1f out: styd on ins fnl f: nt rch ldrs* **33/1**
0-02 **9** *shd* **Noelani (IRE)**[17] [2369] 4-9-1 .... MJKinane 6 102
(John M Oxx, Ire) *leggy: angular: midfield: rdn whn n.m.r and hmpd over 1f out: kpt on ins fnl f but n.d* **33/1**
0 **10** *¾* **Glamour Puss (NZ)**[4] [2720] 6-9-1 ....(b) StevenKing 10 100
(Danny O'Brien, Australia) *lw: trckd ldrs: n.m.r and hmpd over 2f out: sn lost pl: no imp after* **13/2**[3]
-063 **11** *½* **Pivotal Point**[4] [2720] 6-9-4 110 .... DarryllHolland 11 102
(P J Makin) *prom: rdn 2f out: edgd rt over 1f out: wknd ins fnl f* **16/1**
62-0 **12** *1 ¼* **Ajigolo**[20] [2276] 3-8-11 111 .... SamHitchcott 8 96
(M R Channon) *led: rdn and hdd over 2f out: wknd over 1f out: edgd rt ins fnl f* **100/1**
10-5 **13** *2* **Gift Horse**[38] [1778] 6-9-4 106 .... KFallon 3 92
(D Nicholls) *lw: swtchd rt s: hld up: swtchd rt and hdwy 2f out: nt rch ldrs: wknd ins fnl f* **7/1**
1101 **14** *1 ½* **Etlaala**[6] [2675] 4-9-4 110 .... RHills 19 87
(B W Hills) *hld up: hdwy over 2f out: rdn over 1f out: wknd and eased ins fnl f* **14/1**
0-45 **15** *½* **Fayr Jag (IRE)**[19] [2303] 7-9-4 110 .... TQuinn 7 86
(T D Easterby) *midfield: rdn and hdwy whn nt clr run over 1f out: sn btn* **14/1**
4500 **16** *5* **Royal Storm (IRE)**[49] [1487] 7-9-4 99 .... RichardHughes 12 71
(Mrs A J Perrett) *midfield tl wknd wl over 1f out* **150/1**
0321 **17** *1 ¼* **Quito (IRE)**[16] [2386] 9-9-4 111 ....(b) TonyCulhane 18 67
(D W Chapman) *lw: midfield: rdn over 2f out: wknd wl over 1f out* **20/1**
6000 **18** *3* **Beckermet (IRE)**[19] [2303] 4-9-4 107 .... MartinDwyer 16 58
(R F Fisher) *racd alone in centre: in tch tl over 2f out: sn bhd* **125/1**

1m 13.12s (-2.88) **Going Correction** -0.175s/f (Firm)
WFA 3 from 4yo+ 7lb **18** Ran SP% **118.8**
Speed ratings (Par 117):112,111,108,108,107 106,105,104,104,103 102,101,98,96,95 89,87,83
CSF £1142.62 TOTE £48.70: £11.30, £11.80, £1.60; EX 3498.00 Trifecta £9819.40 Pool: £67,767.99 - 4.90 winning tickets..
Owner Willie McKay **Bred** Elk Manor Farm **Trained** Bawtry, S Yorks
■ Stewards' Enquiry : Alan Munro two-day ban: careless riding (Jul 5-6)

FOCUS
The winning time was almost identical to the Wokingham, and therefore modest for a Group 1. All bar Beckermet raced up the stands' side, with the first two coming up the rail. The race has been rated around the fourth, but the form is shaky and unlikely to stand up.

NOTEBOOK
Les Arcs(USA) has taken a circuitous route to Group 1-winning sprinter, having begun his career over ten furlongs and even run once over hurdles. He made rapid strides during the winter but had only finished eleventh in the King's Stand on Tuesday and had plenty to find here with Takeover Target. Held up close to the rail, he came with a good run to head the favourite going to the final furlong and show improved form, but his lead was being reduced by the fast-finishing runner-up close home. The July Cup at Newmarket is next on the agenda, and connections also now have an eye on the Breeders' Cup Mile. (tchd 40-1)
Balthazaar's Gift(IRE) was drawn high but ended up on the stands' rail. He was still at the rear of the field approaching the final furlong, but produced a strong burst inside the last and would have caught the winner in a couple more strides. His wins at two came on easy ground but he is clearly well at home on a sound surface. (tchd 66-1)
Takeover Target(AUS), who had Les Arcs behind when landing the King's Stand under a penalty earlier in the week, was unable to follow up despite racing over his optimum trip. He showed with a definite lead not long after halfway, but could not repel the winner and was also run out of second close home. His running here has provisionally been rated 8lb below his King's Stand form and connections felt the race had probably come too quickly for him. They are optimistic of better again in the July Cup at Newmarket next. (op 11-4)
Ashdown Express(IRE), another to have run in the King's Stand, was doing his best work at the end but his trainer thought that the watered ground did not suit him.
Amadeus Wolf, a stablemate of the runner-up, was reverting to sprinting after failing to stay when seventh in the 2000 Guineas. Always prominent, he was relegated two places inside the last. (op 15-2 tchd 8-1 in places and 13-2 in places)
The Tatling(IRE), the King's Stand tenth, was switched away from the rail to make his effort out wide and was another keeping on late.
Iffraaj, who took the Wokingham at York a year ago for Michael Jarvis, ran a decent first race for Godolphin and there is better to come from him when the yard is firing again. (op 7-1)
Eisteddfod produced a decent effort considering that he was racing on unfavourable ground as well as being hampered.
Noelani(IRE), tackling her fastest conditions to date, ran an encouraging race despite being caught up in some trouble. (tchd 40-1 in places)
Glamour Puss(NZ), expected to be sharper for her run earlier in the week, was never really going and was held when hampered by Amadeus Wolf. (tchd 15-2 in places and 7-1 in places)
Pivotal Point, third in the King's Stand, with today's winner behind, was unable to reproduce that form over this longer trip.
Gift Horse was drawn two, but was switched to make his effort on the outside where he was arguably at a disadvantage. (tchd 15-2)
Etlaala, who got warm before the race, was obliged to race deep on the track and could never get into the action. (op 16-1)
Fayr Jag(IRE) had his conditions but has not won since taking this race two years ago. (tchd 16-1)

2847 WOKINGHAM STKS (HERITAGE H'CAP) 6f
4:25 (4:25) (Class 2) (0-110,108) 3-Y-0+

£49,856 (£14,928; £7,464; £3,736; £1,864; £936) **Stalls** Low

Form RPR
0036 **1** **Baltic King**[4] [2720] 6-9-10 **106** ....(t) JimmyFortune 6 120
(H Morrison) *lw: racd nr side: hld up in rr: gng wl but plenty to do 2f out: gd prog over 1f out: str burst to ld last 100yds: sn clr* **10/1**[3]
0-31 **2** *1 ½* **Firenze**[14] [2429] 5-8-11 **93** 5ex .... JamieSpencer 1 105+
(J R Fanshawe) *hld up wl in rr: taken to outer and prog 1/2-way: rdn to ld over 1f out: hdd and outpcd last 100yds* **5/1**[1]
5643 **3** *1 ½* **Bahamian Pirate (USA)**[21] [2230] 11-9-1 **97** .... EddieAhern 8 102
(D Nicholls) *hld up towards rr nr side: nt clr run briefly over 2f out: prog wl over 1f out: styd on to take 3rd wl ins fnl f* **33/1**

31-1 **4** ½ **Borderlescott**[36] 1835 4-9-6 **102**................................ RoystonFfrench 19 106
(R Bastiman) *cl up: effrt to ld briefly wl over 1f out: one pce fnl f* **14/1**

-261 **5** 1 ¼ **Yomalo (IRE)**[17] 2369 6-9-3 **99** 5ex.. TQuinn 4 99
(Rae Guest) *dwlt: wl in rr and pushed along early: prog fr wl over 1f out: styd on fnl f: nt pce to chal* **14/1**

-605 **6** *hd* **Indian Trail**[21] 2230 6-8-12 **94**.. KFallon 20 93+
(D Nicholls) *hld up: hmpd 4f out: wl in rr after: n.m.r over 1f out: gd prog fnl f: nrst fin* **11/1**

2-21 **7** *hd* **Kostar**[42] 1667 5-8-9 **94**.. AdamKirby(3) 12 93
(C G Cox) *taken to post 15 mins early: trckd ldng gp: rdn and nt qckn 2f out: styd on fr over 1f out: nt pce to trble ldrs* **12/1**

0-05 **8** *shd* **Connect**[6] 2683 9-9-0 **96**..(b) MichaelHills 13 95
(M H Tompkins) *hld up wl in rr: taken to wd outside and prog fr 2f out: kpt on same pce fnl f* **100/1**

-301 **9** *nk* **Beaver Patrol (IRE)**[21] 2230 4-8-12 **94** 5ex................. KerrinMcEvoy 11 92
(R F Johnson Houghton) *lw: trckd ldrs: rdn and nt qckn 2f out: kpt on same pce after* **12/1**

20-6 **10** ½ **Intrepid Jack**[36] 1835 4-9-1 **97**...................................... SteveDrowne 15 93+
(H Morrison) *hld up in midfield: outpcd 2f out: styd on again fnl f: no ch* **8/1**[2]

0-00 **11** *hd* **Just James**[21] 2230 7-9-2 **98**.. AlanMunro 7 94
(D Nicholls) *hld up wl in rr: prog on wd outside over 2f out: kpt on same pce fnl f* **50/1**

-123 **12** ¾ **Judd Street**[14] 2450 4-8-12 **94**.................................... StephenCarson 25 87
(R F Johnson Houghton) *w ldrs: led over 2f out gng strly: hdd wl over 1f out: wknd fnl f* **40/1**

-611 **13** ½ **One Putra (IRE)**[19] 2303 4-9-11 **107** 5ex...................(t) PhilipRobinson 10 99
(M A Jarvis) *pressed nr side ldrs: rdn to dispute ld 2f out: fdd fnl f* **14/1**

2002 **14** *shd* **Peace Offering (IRE)**[14] 2450 6-8-13 **95**.................... RichardHughes 5 86+
(D Nicholls) *taken down early: hld up in rr: gng wl 2f out but plenty to do: one pce fr over 1f out* **22/1**

-033 **15** 1 ½ **Strike Up The Band**[36] 1818 3-9-5 **108**...................... AdrianTNicholls 21 95
(D Nicholls) *racd on outer: gd spd and wl on terms over 4f: fdd fnl f* **40/1**

1605 **16** *1* **Obe Gold**[84] 830 4-9-8 **104**.. JohnEgan 18 88
(M R Channon) *hld up in midfield: rdn and hanging 2f out: lost pl bdly: kpt on again fnl f* **100/1**

4104 **17** *shd* **Merlin's Dancer**[14] 2450 6-9-2 **98**.................................... TonyCulhane 9 82
(D Nicholls) *lw: trckd nr side ldrs: nt clr run briefly over 2f out: fdd over 1f out* **50/1**

3203 **18** *nk* **Bahiano (IRE)**[49] 1487 5-9-5 **101**.. RyanMoore 17 84
(C E Brittain) *racd on outer in midfield: effrt on wd outside 2f out: wknd fnl f* **16/1**

-000 **19** ½ **Texas Gold**[4] 2720 8-9-6 **102**.. MartinDwyer 3 83
(W R Muir) *dwlt: hld up wl in rr: effrt 2f out: one pce and no real prog* **33/1**

0100 **20** ¾ **Commando Scott (IRE)**[21] 2230 5-8-7 **92**............. PatrickMathers(3) 22 71
(I W McInnes) *n.m.r after 1f: racd on outer in midfield: struggling fr 2f out* **100/1**

-406 **21** *nk* **Chookie Heiton (IRE)**[14] 2450 8-9-5 **101**............................. MJKinane 2 79
(I Semple) *wl in rr: last and struggling 2f out: kpt on fnl f* **20/1**

0-01 **22** 1 ¾ **Greenslades**[27] 2047 7-9-3 **99** 5ex............................... DarryllHolland 14 72
(P J Makin) *taken down early: buffeted abt in midfield early: chsd ldrs: stl cl up 2f out: wknd over 1f out* **33/1**

-010 **23** ½ **Zomerlust**[28] 2012 4-8-13 **95**...................................... GrahamGibbons 28 66
(J J Quinn) *prom on outer: slipped over 4f out: stl cl up 2f out: wknd* **33/1**

510 **24** ¾ **Sir Edwin Landseer (USA)**[14] 2429 6-9-1 **100**....(p) SaleemGolam(3) 24 69
(Christian Wroe, UAE) *t.k.h on outer: chsd ldrs for 4f: wknd* **100/1**

-110 **25** *hd* **Mutamared (USA)**[21] 2227 6-9-1 **97**...................................... NCallan 27 66
(K A Ryan) *lw: taken down early: racd on outer in midfield: wknd over 1f out* **14/1**

-300 **26** 2 ½ **High Reach**[2] 2776 6-8-11 **93**... NickyMackay 26 54
(W R Muir) *spd on outer for 4f: wkng whn bmpd jst over 1f out* **100/1**

0400 **27** 2 ½ **Fire Up The Band**[4] 2720 7-9-8 **104**................................(v) PatDobbs 16 58
(D Nicholls) *w ldrs nr side: disp ld over 2f out: sn rdn and wknd rapidly* **100/1**

00-0 **28** *5* **Distinctly Game**[14] 2450 4-8-13 **95**...............................(b[1]) JoeFanning 23 34
(K A Ryan) *lw: mde most to over 2f out: wknd rapidly* **100/1**

1m 13.15s (-2.85) **Going Correction** -0.175s/f (Firm)
WFA 3 from 4yo+ 7lb **28** Ran SP% **129.7**
Speed ratings (Par 109):112,110,108,107,105 105,105,105,104,103 103,102,102,101,99 98,98,98,97,96 95,93,92,91,91 88,8
CSF £52.23 CT £1644.51 TOTE £16.90: £4.60, £1.60, £9.00, £3.50; EX 87.60 Trifecta £3543.30 Pool: £9,482.20 - 1.90 winning tickets..
Owner Thurloe Thoroughbreds Viii **Bred** R F And Mrs Knipe **Trained** East Ilsley, Berks

FOCUS
A strong handicap which demonstrated how little there is between the top sprinters and leading handicappers. A low draw proved to be an advantage. The winning time was just 3/100ths of a second slower than the Golden Jubilee, but although this time was creditable for the grade, enthusiasm is slightly tempered by the time of the other contest being below-par for a race of its class.

NOTEBOOK
Baltic King finished sixth in Tuesday's King's Stand Stakes, five places ahead of Golden Jubilee winner Les Arcs. Taking full advantage of his draw, he produced a strong run near the rail to cut down the favourite in the last half-furlong. He is better than ever and would be well worth his place in the July Cup, where the big field and strong pace would play to his strengths. (op 12-1 tchd 14-1)
Firenze ◆ appeared ideally drawn on the rail but there was a good deal of congestion with the whole field coming over and Spencer took her to the outer of the field while making progress from the rear. After striking the front, she edged to her left and could not hold the winner's strong run. She would very likely have won had she taken a more direct route, and can gain compensation. (tchd 11-2 and 6-1 in places)
Bahamian Pirate(USA) retains plenty of enthusiasm despite his advancing years and stayed on well into third. He has now run two successive decent races on fast ground and should continue to give a good account.
Borderlescott has been very well placed and this was another sound effort off a career-high mark, although a bit more ease in the ground might have suited him. He is now ready for a crack at Pattern races. (op 12-1)
Yomalo(IRE), a Group 3 winner last time, was officially 4lb well in. Slowly away as usual, leaving herself with a lot to do, she finished strongly without getting to the leaders.
Indian Trail ◆, who got warm beforehand, was the unlucky horse of the race. Fortunate to stay on his feet when hampered after two furlongs, he did not get a clear run when beginning to keep on and reached his final position without Fallon being too hard on him. A big handicap can come his way.
Kostar, taken to post early and away on terms, ran a solid race back down in trip without being able to go with the leaders at the two pole. (op 11-1 tchd 14-1 in places)
Connect belied his big price with a creditable effort. (op 66-1)
Beaver Patrol(IRE) had underfoot conditions to suit and ran a decent race from a 5lb higher mark.
Intrepid Jack ◆, from the same stable as the winner, found himself a little outpaced with a quarter of a mile to run but was coming home strongly at the end. There is a decent prize to be won with him. (op 7-1)
Peace Offering(IRE) travelled well on the bridle for a long way but was slightly hampered with two furlongs to run and his rider was not hard on him from then on. He remains on a reasonable mark. (op 20-1)

2848 DUKE OF EDINBURGH STKS (HERITAGE H'CAP) 1m 4f
4:55 (5:00) (Class 2) (0-105,105) 3-Y-0+
£34,276 (£10,263; £5,131; £2,568; £1,281; £643) **Stalls** High

Form RPR

346 **1** **Young Mick**[17] 2341 4-8-8 **89**..(v) TQuinn 4 98
(G G Margarson) *in tch: rdn 2f out: r.o to ld over 1f out: edgd rt ins fnl f: all out* **28/1**

65-6 **2** *hd* **Glistening**[21] 2229 4-9-0 **95**.. NickyMackay 6 103+
(L M Cumani) *lw: midfield: hdwy whn nt clr run and swtchd lft over 2f out: r.o strly ins fnl f: jst failed* **4/1**[1]

-220 **3** ½ **Palomar (USA)**[28] 2013 4-9-5 **100**.................................... SteveDrowne 13 108
(R Charlton) *midfield: nt clr run on bnd wl over 2f out: rdn and hdwy over 1f out: r.o ins fnl f: hld cl home* **16/1**

3000 **4** ½ **Polygonal (FR)**[22] 2201 6-8-9 **90**.. JohnEgan 11 97
(Ernst Oertel) *midfield: rdn and hdwy 2f out: forced lft over 1f out: r.o ins fnl f: nt qckn fnl strides* **50/1**

13-3 **5** *nk* **Thunder Rock (IRE)**[49] 1484 4-8-8 **89**...................................... KFallon 2 97+
(Sir Michael Stoute) *chsd ldrs: rdn over 2f out: swtchd lft over 1f out: running on whn nt clr run and snatched up wl ins fnl f: nt rcvr* **9/2**[2]

-244 **6** *hd* **Rehearsal**[36] 1815 5-8-11 **92**.. JamieSpencer 12 98
(L Lungo) *trckd ldr: rdn to ld over 2f out: hdd over 1f out: r.o same pce ins fnl f* **16/1**

6-03 **7** *shd* **Consular**[21] 2229 4-8-9 **90**.. PhilipRobinson 14 96
(M A Jarvis) *racd keenly: trckd ldrs: rdn and ch 2f out: nt qckn ins fnl f* **10/1**[3]

3210 **8** *hd* **Chantaco (USA)**[22] 2201 4-8-13 **94**.................................. MartinDwyer 1 100
(A M Balding) *plld hrd: led: rdn and hdd over 2f out: r.o same pce ins fnl f* **16/1**

5406 **9** 1 ¼ **Bravo Maestro (USA)**[26] 2079 5-8-9 **90**.......................... RyanMoore 18 96+
(N P Littmoden) *hld up: rdn and hdwy whn nt clr run over 1f out: eased whn denied run ins fnl f* **25/1**

-531 **10** ½ **Alfie Noakes**[21] 2229 4-8-7 **88**.. KerrinMcEvoy 8 91
(Mrs A J Perrett) *lw: midfield: rdn 3f out: nt clr run over 2f out: kpt on ins fnl f: nt rch ldrs* **12/1**

-421 **11** *shd* **Balkan Knight**[14] 2430 6-9-10 **105**.. LDettori 15 108
(D R C Elsworth) *lw: midfield: sltly hmpd on bnd over 2f out: sn rdn: n.m.r over 1f out: kpt on ins fnl f: nvr able to chal* **9/2**[2]

6153 **12** 1 ¼ **Obrigado (USA)**[17] 2341 6-8-7 **88**.................................. DarryllHolland 19 89
(W J Haggas) *stdd s: hld up: rdn and hdwy over 1f out: kpt on tl one pce ins fnl f* **20/1**

5/10 **13** *hd* **Vengeance**[21] 2229 6-9-0 **95**.. PatDobbs 9 95
(S Dow) *in tch: settled in midfield after 3f: rdn over 2f out: kpt on same pce after* **25/1**

6000 **14** *1* **Crow Wood**[7] 2656 7-8-11 **92**.................................... GrahamGibbons 16 91
(J J Quinn) *midfield: hmpd on bnd over 2f out: sn rdn: no imp fr over 1f out* **33/1**

0-64 **15** *6* **Cruise Director**[35] 1842 6-8-5 **86**.. KDarley 17 75
(Ian Williams) *hld up: rdn over 2f out: nvr on terms* **66/1**

00-0 **16** ¾ **Temple Place (IRE)**[35] 1585 5-8-8 **89**....................(t) RoystonFfrench 10 77
(D McCain Jnr) *s.i.s: hld up: effrt over 2f out: nvr trbld ldrs* **100/1**

-110 **17** *26* **Arturius (IRE)**[27] 2056 4-9-7 **102**.. NCallan 7 48
(P J Rothwell, Ire) *qckly swtchd rt after s: racd keenly: in tch: tk clsr order after 3f: rdn over 2f out: sn wkd* **66/1**

21-0 **18** 1 ½ **Pagan Sword**[23] 2169 4-8-7 **88**...(v) MJKinane 5 32
(Mrs A J Perrett) *bmpd s: hld up: pushed along over 3f out: nvr on terms* **14/1**

0-10 **19** *1* **All That And More (IRE)**[22] 2201 4-9-0 **95**...................... MichaelHills 3 37
(B W Hills) *a bhd* **20/1**

2m 29.97s (-3.03) **Going Correction** +0.025s/f (Good) **19** Ran SP% **127.0**
Speed ratings (Par 109):111,110,110,110,110 109,109,109,108,108 108,107,107,106,102 102,84,83,83
CSF £130.56 CT £1936.82 TOTE £29.50: £4.50, £2.00, £5.70, £12.10; EX 286.70 Trifecta £4079.70 Pool: £5,746.08 - 1.00 winning ticket..
Owner M F Kentish **Bred** M F Kentish **Trained** Newmarket, Suffolk
■ A winner on his final ride for Richard Quinn. He rode over 2,100 winners in Britain, the first in 1981.
■ Stewards' Enquiry : T Quinn one-day ban: careless riding (Jul 5); further five-day ban: used whip with excessive frequency and without giving gelding time to respond (Jul 6-10)

FOCUS
A solid winning time for a race like this, just 0.72 seconds slower than the Hardwicke. Solid handicap form, despite the fact that the field was so closely packed at the line.

NOTEBOOK
Young Mick, a former banded performer, has made enormous strides since those days and just held on to a dwindling advantage to record his seventh win of the year. He has retained his form very well and this represented further improvement. (op 25-1)
Glistening ◆ had been unfortunate at Epsom and again things did not really go for him. After being switched to the outside, he still had about eight opponents ahead of him entering the last but he ran on strongly and would have got there in a couple more strides. He can make amends, perhaps over a little further, and looks an obvious type for the Ebor. (tchd 9-2 in places)
Palomar(USA), back down in trip and fitted with earplugs, ran his best race since arriving from France. He handles this fast ground and was keeping on strongly against the rail.
Polygonal(FR) had been well held in two previous outings on turf this year but these were his conditions and he was running on at the end. (op 40-1)
Thunder Rock(IRE) ◆, having his first run over a trip this far, was never far away but failed to get a clear passage in the latter stages. It did not cost him the race but he would have finished that bit closer. (tchd 5-1 and 11-2 in a place)
Rehearsal, third in this at York last year, showed in front early in the straight but could not hold on. This was a solid run but he remains a little high in the weights.
Consular was right in there fighting at the two pole and lost little in defeat. (op 9-1)
Chantaco(USA), whose best form is at ten furlongs, made the running and to his credit did not fold when headed.
Bravo Maestro(USA), running over this far for the first time, ran out of room on the approach to the final furlong and his rider had to ease him down. (tchd 33-1 in places)
Alfie Noakes, 3lb higher than at Epsom, did not get the breaks this time but should not be written off.
Balkan Knight could never quite get involved after meeting with a bit of trouble but this was a good effort at the weights. (op 8-1)
All That And More(IRE) had shown improved form front running this year and had the worst of the draw.

2849 QUEEN ALEXANDRA STKS (CONDITIONS RACE) 2m 5f 159y
5:30 (5:34) (Class 2) 4-Y-0+

£34,276 (£10,263; £5,131; £2,568; £1,281; £643) **Stalls** High

Form RPR

0501 **1** **Baddam**[4] [2723] 4-9-0 87 .... IanMongan 4 82
(M R Channon) *hld up: last to 1/2-way: prog 5f out: wd bnd 3f out: clsd on ldrs 1f out: drvn and qcknd to ld nr fin* **11/2**

1-10 **2** *nk* **Cover Up (IRE)**[26] [2085] 9-9-12 108 .... KFallon 13 92
(Sir Michael Stoute) *lw: hld up in rr: prog to ld after 6f: kicked on 3f out: drvn and hdd jst over 1f out: rallied to ld last 100yds: hdd nr fi* **3/1**[1]

2-25 **3** *¾* **Vinando**[26] [2085] 5-9-2 103 ....(bt) LDettori 9 81
(C R Egerton) *lw: trckd ldrs: prog over 2f out: drvn to ld jst over 1f out: hdd and no ex last 100yds* **4/1**[2]

-415 **4** *1 ½* **Ebtikaar (IRE)**[28] [2013] 4-9-0 95 .... RHills 12 79+
(J L Dunlop) *lw: hld up wl in rr: stl in last pair 3f out: nt clr run 2f out: plld out over 1f out: r.o fnl f: hopeless task* **9/2**[3]

052- **5** *hd* **Corrib Eclipse**[35] [5248] 7-9-2 99 .... RyanMoore 2 79
(Ian Williams) *prom: chsd ldr 4f out to 2f out: hld whn n.m.r 1f out: one pce* **9/1**

4-24 **6** *½* **Dancing Bay**[45] [1584] 9-9-2 104 .... JamieSpencer 11 79
(N J Henderson) *t.k.h: hld up in rr: effrt 3f out: chsng ldrs 2f out: sn rdn and nt qckn: one pce after* **13/2**

4430 **7** *4* **Establishment**[4] [2723] 9-9-2 77 .... MartinDwyer 10 75
(C A Cyzer) *t.k.h: hld up towards rr: effrt over 2f out: rdn and wknd over 1f out* **33/1**

200- **8** *¾* **Considine (USA)**[10] [5903] 5-9-2 55 .... TonyCulhane 1 74?
(C J Mann) *lw: trckd ldrs: rdn over 2f out: wknd u.p jst over 1f out* **150/1**

3252 **9** *11* **Dovedon Hero**[8] [2628] 6-9-2 67 ....(b) JimmyFortune 7 63
(P J McBride) *t.k.h: hld up in rr: last 3f out: brief effrt over 2f out: sn btn and eased* **66/1**

00-0 **10** *6* **Three Counties (IRE)**[14] [2430] 5-9-2 65 .... MarkCoumbe 5 57
(N I M Rossiter) *chsd ldrs tl wknd u.p 3f out* **200/1**

34-3 **11** *7* **Avalon**[35] [1839] 4-9-0 108 .... MJKinane 3 50
(Jonjo O'Neill) *lw: led for 6f: chsd ldr to 5f out: wknd rapidly over 2f out* **11/1**

30 **12** *7* **Dubai Sunday (JPN)**[34] [1006] 5-9-2 ....(bt[1]) BrianReilly 8 43
(P S McEntee) *plld hrd: hld up: prog to chse ldrs 5f out: wknd rapidly over 2f out* **100/1**

04-0 **13** *49* **Brendan's Surprise**[5] [1461] 4-9-0 40 .... NCallan 6 —
(K J Burke) *hld up in tch: prog to chse ldr 5f out to 4f out: wknd rapidly and sn t.o* **200/1**

5m 4.06s (15.86)
WFA 4 from 5yo+ 2lb **13** Ran SP% **117.3**
CSF £21.97 TOTE £7.20: £2.30, £1.80, £1.90; EX 28.60 Trifecta £149.90 Pool: £6,392.27 - 30.26 winning tickets. Place 6 £101.93, Place 5 £38.22.
Owner N Martin **Bred** Mrs V Rapkins **Trained** West Ilsley, Berks
■ Baddam is the first horse since Mountain Cross in 1978 to complete the Ascot Stakes-Queen Alexandra double.

FOCUS
They went no pace and it resulted in a sprint finish, relatively speaking. The seventh and eighth were too close to the classier first six for comfort, and not too much can be read into the form.

NOTEBOOK
Baddam, comfortable winner of the Ascot Stakes on the meeting's opening day, completed a rare double. The slow pace suited him and, after making progress from the back of the field, he ran on to get on top close home. The bare form flatters him but he is a progressive stayer. (op 6-1 tchd 13-2)
Cover Up(IRE) came very close to landing his third win in this unique event and his fourth at Royal Ascot all told. Attempting to give away 10lb or more, he was brought through to lead after three-quarters of a mile but did not wind up the pace until the last three furlongs. Headed going to the last, he rallied bravely but was just held. (tchd 11-4 and 7-2 in places)
Vinando showed with a narrow advantage in the straight but could not quite hold on, despite battling hard. He is usually thereabouts but is without a win since October 2004. (tchd 9-2 in places and 7-2 in places)
Ebtikaar(IRE) had only had one behind him turning into the straight and, after finding trouble at the two pole, he had too much to do to make up the leeway off this steady pace. He is capable of making amends. (op 11-2 tchd 6-1 in places)
Corrib Eclipse, winner of this event two years, was successful over hurdles last month. He turned for home in second spot but could soon find only the one pace. (op 11-1)
Dancing Bay, in the frame in the last two runnings of this race, was held in the final quarter of a mile and well below form. (op 9-2)
Establishment Official explanation: jockey said gelding ran too free
Avalon has not lived up to expectations and has become one to be wary of. (op 10-1)
T/Jkpt: Not won. T/Plt: £126.50 to a £1 stake. Pool: £307,508.59. 1,774.45 winning tickets. T/Qpdt: £21.30 to a £1 stake. Pool: £14,828.20. 514.45 winning tickets. DO

2806 AYR (L-H)
Saturday, June 24
OFFICIAL GOING: Good (good to firm in places)

2850 CORAL "BOOKMAKER OF THE YEAR" H'CAP 1m 5f 13y
2:25 (2:26) (Class 3) (0-95,90) 4-Y-0+ **£9,067** (£2,697; £1,348; £673) **Stalls** Low

Form RPR

-113 **1** **Greenwich Meantime**[45] [1584] 6-9-2 85 .... PaulHanagan 4 101+
(R A Fahey) *in tch: smooth hdwy to ld 2f out: sn clr* **6/4**[1]

6523 **2** *4* **Lets Roll**[29] [1991] 5-9-0 90 .... KevinGhunowa[(7)] 3 96
(C W Thornton) *cl up: effrt and ev ch over 2f out: kpt on fnl f: nt rch wnr* **11/2**[2]

0061 **3** *hd* **Kames Park (IRE)**[14] [2452] 4-9-4 87 .... TomEaves 11 93
(I Semple) *hld up: rdn over 3f out: hdwy over 1f out: kpt on: nrst fin* **16/1**

2 **4** *nk* **Castle Howard (IRE)**[35] [1842] 4-9-1 89 .... StephenDonohoe[(5)] 10 94
(W J Musson) *hld up: rdn over 3f out: kpt on fnl f: no imp* **7/1**[3]

1-11 **5** *2* **Silvertown**[21] [2238] 11-9-1 84 .... PatCosgrave 2 87
(L Lungo) *led to 2f out: outpcd fnl f* **11/1**

-605 **6** *2 ½* **Most Definitely (IRE)**[21] [2238] 6-9-2 85 .... FergalLynch 8 84
(T D Easterby) *hld up: rdn over 3f out: rallied over 1f out: n.d* **12/1**

2524 **7** *1* **Charlotte Vale**[18] [2326] 5-8-5 74 .... PaulMulrennan 1 72
(Micky Hammond) *midfield: rdn 4f out: shortlived effrt over 2f out: sn no imp* **25/1**

3536 **8** *1 ¾* **Merrymaker**[3] [2762] 6-8-5 74 .... PaulFessey 7 69
(W M Brisbourne) *hld up: rdn over 3f out: n.d* **22/1**

4223 **9** *2* **Rocket Force (USA)**[19] [2296] 6-8-3 72 .... DaleGibson 5 64
(N Wilson) *chsd ldrs tl rdn and wknd fr 2f out* **18/1**

0620 **10** *34* **Given A Choice (IRE)**[7] [2656] 4-8-11 80 .... RobertWinston 6 25
(J G Given) *chsd ldrs: rdn and hung lft 3f out: sn wknd* **12/1**

2m 50.82s (-5.79) **Going Correction** -0.20s/f (Firm) **10** Ran SP% **110.9**
Speed ratings (Par 107):109,106,106,106,105 103,102,101,100,79
CSF £8.69 CT £85.96 TOTE £2.30: £1.90, £1.90, £2.30; EX 6.10.
Owner K Lee D Barlow B Crumbley & L Rutherford **Bred** Juddmonte Farms **Trained** Musley Bank, N Yorks

FOCUS
A decent handicap but a mainly exposed bunch with another improved performance from the one progressive sort. The pace was fair and the form appears sound enough through the placed horses.

NOTEBOOK
Greenwich Meantime ◆, who looked better than the bare form of his Chester Cup run, turned in his best effort yet over this shorter trip. He has done nothing but improve for current connections and will be interesting at fair odds back over two miles in the Northumberland Plate. (op 13-8 tchd 11-8)
Lets Rollhas a good record at this track and ran creditably in a race that suited racing close to the pace. He is a consistent sort who should continue to give a good account but this showed his vulnerability to progressive sorts from his current mark. (op 6-1 tchd 5-1)
Kames Park(IRE), 5lb higher than for his Musselburgh win, was not disgraced in a moderately-run race given that this contest suited those racing close to the pace. A more end-to-end gallop will suit and he is the type to win again for his current stable. (op 14-1)
Castle Howard(IRE), a mile and seven furlong winner in France, was inconvenienced by the way this race panned out and he left the impression that the return to further in a more truly-run race would be in his favour. (op 5-1)
Silvertown, who has been in tremendous form, was again allowed the run of the race but was found out by his latest rise in the weights. He is best when allowed to dominate but looks vulnerable from this mark. (op 9-1 tchd 12-1)
Most Definitely(IRE), back on the same mark as when last successful, is another that may be a bit better than the bare form given the way things panned out. A truly-run race over middle distances suits and he is not one to write off yet. (op 11-1 tchd 10-1)

2851 CORAL FILLIES' STKS (HERITAGE H'CAP) 7f 50y
2:55 (2:56) (Class 2) 3-Y-0+

£28,044 (£8,397; £4,198; £2,101; £1,048; £526) **Stalls** Low

Form RPR

3010 **1** **Tagula Sunrise (IRE)**[28] [2017] 4-9-2 85 .... PaulHanagan 1 98
(R A Fahey) *in tch: effrt over 2f out: led 1f out: edgd lft: kpt on strly* **15/2**

2500 **2** *2 ½* **Dispol Katie**[6] [2681] 5-8-3 72 .... PaulFessey 3 79
(T D Barron) *cl up: rdn over 2f out: kpt on fnl f: nt rch wnr* **16/1**

0-01 **3** *1* **Miss Meggy**[40] [1734] 4-8-10 79 ....(b) TomEaves 4 83
(Miss J A Camacho) *midfield: rdn over 2f out: kpt on fnl f: no imp* **10/1**

1143 **4** *nk* **Imperialistic (IRE)**[12] [2503] 5-9-5 93 .... AndrewElliott[(5)] 9 96+
(K R Burke) *hld up: hdwy outside 2f out: kpt on fnl f: no imp* **7/1**[3]

1311 **5** *1 ¾* **Hula Ballew**[4] [2735] 6-8-6 75 6ex .... PaulMulrennan 10 74
(M Dods) *set decent gallop: hdd and no ex 1f out* **7/1**[3]

3-15 **6** *hd* **Heaven Sent**[36] [1834] 3-8-5 83 ow1 .... RobertWinston 8 78
(Sir Michael Stoute) *hld up: effrt outside over 2f out: hung lft: no imp fnl f* **2/1**[1]

5/ **7** *nk* **Nebraska Lady (IRE)**[258] [5778] 4-8-10 79 .... PatCosgrave 2 76
(E J O'Neill) *s.i.s: bhd tl sme late hdwy: n.d* **25/1**

3-12 **8** *1 ¼* **Whitethorne**[5] [2705] 4-8-3 72 .... DaleGibson 6 66
(R A Fahey) *cl up tl rdn and wknd appr fnl f* **4/1**[2]

4/30 **9** *¾* **Tajaathub (USA)**[14] [2454] 4-8-13 82 .... StanleyChin 7 74
(M Johnston) *hld up in midfield: outpcd whn n.m.r 2f out: sn btn* **22/1**

26-0 **10** *8* **Siena Gold**[53] [1377] 4-9-1 89 .... StephenDonohoe[(5)] 5 60
(J G Given) *in tch tl wknd over 2f out* **100/1**

1m 30.2s (-2.52) **Going Correction** -0.20s/f (Firm)
WFA 3 from 4yo+ 9lb **10** Ran SP% **114.3**
Speed ratings (Par 96):106,103,102,101,99 99,99,97,96,87
CSF £113.54 CT £840.27 TOTE £10.30: £2.50, £3.00, £3.60; EX 99.60.
Owner David M Knaggs & Mel Roberts **Bred** Thomas Doherty **Trained** Musley Bank, N Yorks
■ Stewards' Enquiry : Andrew Elliott two-day ban: careless riding (Jul 5,20)

FOCUS
Not the most competitive of races for the money on offer but a decent gallop and this form should stand up at a similar level with the third, fourth and fifth all close to form.

NOTEBOOK
Tagula Sunrise(IRE) appreciated the decent gallop and showed he is as effective on a sound surface as he is on a testing one. She is a fair sort in this grade but she did have things teed up for her to a certain extent and will find things tougher in more competitive company after reassessment. (op 8-1)
Dispol Katie ◆ has slipped to a handy mark and showed clear-cut signs of a return to form. She may be a bit better than the bare form given she fared the best of those to race up with the strong gallop and is one to keep a close eye on in similar company.
Miss Meggy, 5lb higher than at Redcar, ran equally as well in defeat and looks a good guide to the worth of this form. On this evidence she looks worth another try over a mile. (tchd 9-1)
Imperialistic(IRE) has risen a fair way in the weights but showed herself to be in good heart. She is arguably more effective with a bit more cut in the ground, but she is likely to remain vulnerable from her current mark in this type of event.
Hula Ballew has been in tremendous form this year and is a bit better than this bare form given she set a strong gallop (new tactics). She is worth another chance in similar company ridden with a bit more restraint. (op 6-1)
Heaven Sent, a lightly-raced sort who looked to have fair prospects in this company, had a decent gallop but looked anything but happy on the fast ground and proved a disappointment. Easier ground may suit and she is worth another chance. (op 9-4 tchd 5-2 in places)

2852 CORAL "BET FREE BY PHONE ON 0800 242 232" H'CAP 5f
3:25 (3:25) (Class 4) (0-85,78) 4-Y-0+ **£6,477** (£1,927; £963; £481) **Stalls** Low

Form RPR

0012 **1** **Glencairn Star**[14] [2449] 5-9-0 71 .... J-PGuillambert 4 80+
(J S Goldie) *hld up: swtchd rt 1/2-way: qcknd to ld wl ins fnl f: r.o wl* **4/1**[1]

5034 **2** *½* **Ptarmigan Ridge**[14] [2449] 10-9-1 72 .... PaulHanagan 7 79
(Miss L A Perratt) *cl up: effrt over 1f out to wl ins fnl f: kpt on* **11/1**

0414 **3** *nk* **Divine Spirit**[8] [2618] 5-8-11 68 .... FergalLynch 8 74
(M Dods) *prom: effrt over 1f out: kpt on ins fnl f* **9/2**[2]

0002 **4** *nk* **Trick Cyclist**[12] [2505] 5-8-5 62 ....(b) DaleGibson 5 67
(M W Easterby) *keen: sn led: hdd over 1f out: rallied: no ex wl ins fnl f* **7/1**

3001 **5** *shd* **Brut**[15] [2396] 4-8-11 68 .... PhillipMakin 1 73
(D W Barker) *dwlt: sn prom: effrt over 1f out: kpt on fnl f: no imp* **7/1**

0235 **6** *¾* **Brigadore**[16] [2384] 7-8-13 70 .... RobertWinston 6 76+
(J G Given) *s.i.s: hld up in tch: effrt whn nt clr run over 1f out: keeping on whn no room wl ins fnl f* **11/2**[3]

0630 **7** *nk* **Grigorovitch (IRE)**[21] [2237] 4-9-7 78 ....(p) TomEaves 3 79+
(I Semple) *plld hrd: chsd ldrs: nt clr run 1/2-way: rdn over 1f out no room last half f: nt rcvr* **7/1**

The Form Book, Raceform Ltd, Compton, RG20 6NL

3043 **8** 1 **Bold Marc (IRE)**[14] 2449 4-9-3 **74** .... PatCosgrave 2 71
(K R Burke) *early ldr: cl up tl rdn and outpcd fnl f* **6/1**

59.61 secs (-0.83) **Going Correction** -0.125s/f (Firm) **8** Ran SP% **113.7**
Speed ratings (Par 105):101,100,99,99,99 97,97,95
CSF £46.98 CT £205.73 TOTE £3.60: £2.50, £2.20, £1.80; EX 27.30.
Owner Frank Brady **Bred** Palm Tree Thoroughbreds **Trained** Uplawmoor, E Renfrews

FOCUS
Only eight runners but a very messy race and best rated around the third and fifth. The winner showed a good turn of foot, though, and remains capable of better.

2853 CORAL BACKING CHILDREN 1ST H'CAP 1m 1f 20y
4:00 (4:03) (Class 5) (0-75,71) 4-Y-0+ **£5,181** (£1,541; £770; £384) **Stalls** Low

Form RPR
2556 **1** **Hawkit (USA)**[11] 2519 5-9-2 **66** .... RobertWinston 2 78
(A Bailey) *hld up: hdwy over 2f out: led over 1f out: rdn out* **11/2**[3]
0-02 **2** 1 1/4 **Middlemarch (IRE)**[16] 2378 6-9-4 **68** .... DaleGibson 7 78
(J S Goldie) *chsd ldrs: effrt over 2f out: chsd wnr fnl f: kpt on* **5/2**[1]
4203 **3** 1 1/4 **Oddsmaker (IRE)**[4] 2736 5-8-6 **63** ....(t) JamieJones(7) 4 70
(M A Barnes) *plld hrd: hld up: hdwy over 1f out: kpt on fnl f* **11/2**[3]
2366 **4** 1 **Jordans Elect**[10] 2547 6-9-2 **66** .... PaulMulrennan 8 71
(P Monteith) *cl up: led over 2f to over 1f out: no ex* **12/1**
6015 **5** shd **Dark Charm (FR)**[10] 2547 7-9-7 **71** ....(p) PaulHanagan 6 76
(R A Fahey) *keen in tch: effrt over 2f out: no imp over 1f out* **6/1**
1411 **6** 1 1/4 **Ulysees (IRE)**[10] 2546 7-9-5 **69** .... TomEaves 1 71
(I Semple) *hld up in tch: rdn over 2f out: sn one pce* **5/1**[2]
-110 **7** nk **Commitment Lecture**[23] 2170 6-9-5 **69** ....(t) PhillipMakin 5 71
(M Dods) *hld up: rdn over 3f out: nvr on terms* **10/1**
00-5 **8** 7 **Zendaro**[23] 2184 4-8-10 **60** .... FergalLynch 9 48
(W M Brisbourne) *led to over 2f out: wknd over 1f out* **16/1**

1m 55.56s (-0.28) **Going Correction** -0.20s/f (Firm) **8** Ran SP% **113.0**
Speed ratings (Par 103):93,91,90,89,89 88,88,82
CSF £19.16 CT £78.01 TOTE £6.80: £1.70, £1.30, £2.30; EX 29.00.
Owner Phil Buchanan **Bred** Hargus Sexton And Sandra Sexton **Trained** Cotebrook, Cheshire

FOCUS
An ordinary event and only a fair pace resulted in a very moderate winning time for a race of its class. The form is not strong rated through the third.
Zendaro Official explanation: jockey said saddle slipped

2854 CORAL IN SCOTLAND EUROPEAN BREEDERS FUND MAIDEN STKS 7f 50y
4:30 (4:31) (Class 5) 2-Y-0 **£3,886** (£1,156; £577; £288) **Stalls** Low

Form RPR
1 **Silent Waves (USA)** 2-9-3 .... J-PGuillambert 1 81+
(M Johnston) *chsd ldrs: rdn over 2f out: rallied and led ent fnl f: styd on wl* **8/15**[1]
2 1 1/2 **Musca (IRE)** 2-9-3 .... TomEaves 5 74
(J Howard Johnson) *trckd ldrs: led over 1f out: edgd lft: hdd ent fnl f: one pce* **8/1**[3]
3 7 **Cape Dancer (IRE)** 2-8-12 .... PaulMulrennan 3 52
(J S Wainwright) *s.i.s: bhd: rdn 1/2-way: sme late hdwy: no ch w first two* **28/1**
4 nk **Fleetwood Image** 2-9-3 .... PaulHanagan 2 56
(J R Weymes) *hld up in tch: rdn over 3f out: no imp fr 2f out* **20/1**
5 **5** shd **Muncaster Castle (IRE)**[37] 1790 2-9-3 .... RobertWinston 4 56
(R F Fisher) *cl up: ev ch over 2f out: wknd over 1f out* **14/1**
2 **6** 1/2 **Waiheke Island**[23] 2159 2-8-12 .... DaleGibson 7 49
(B Mactaggart) *keen: led to over 1f out: wknd* **5/1**[2]
7 2 1/2 **Salto Chico** 2-9-3 .... FergalLynch 6 48
(W M Brisbourne) *bhd: rdn 1/2-way: nvr on terms* **28/1**

1m 33.44s (0.72) **Going Correction** -0.20s/f (Firm) **7** Ran SP% **111.3**
Speed ratings (Par 93):87,85,77,76,76 76,73
CSF £4.99 TOTE £1.60: £1.20, £3.70; EX 4.30.
Owner Salem Suhail **Bred** M375 Thoroughbreds, R Murphy & Dr S Price-Murphy **Trained** Middleham Moor, N Yorks
■

FOCUS
A race lacking strength and an ordinary gallop meant a moderate winning time for a race like this. The first two were clear and so the form has been rated fairly positively.

NOTEBOOK
Silent Waves(USA) ◆, an expensive brother to a high-class winner at up to nine furlongs in the States, looked as though the race would do him good and turned in a workmanlike display on this racecourse debut. He looked green when asked for his effort and, given his physique, is the sort to leave this bare form a long way behind in due course. (op 4-7 tchd 4-6 in a place and 1-2 in places)
Musca(IRE), related to a couple of winners, looked fit enough to do himself justice and ran creditably on this racecourse debut. He pulled clear of the remainder and looks sure to win a modest event. (op 10-1)
Cape Dancer(IRE), a sister to a triple winner up to seven furlongs, hinted at ability on this racecourse debut and, although she should improve for the run, may do better over further once handicapped.
Fleetwood Image, the first foal of a ten-furlong winner, hinted at ability on this racecourse debut but left the impression that a step up in trip would suit and he may do better once handicapped.
Muncaster Castle(IRE) had the run of the race and was not totally disgraced but left the strong impression that he is likely to remain vulnerable in this type of event. (tchd 16-1)
Waiheke Island proved too keen and failed by a long chalk to build on her debut effort on this quicker ground and over this longer trip. She lacks much in the way of physical scope and is likely to remain vulnerable in this type of event. (op 9-2 tchd 6-1)

2855 CORAL.CO.UK H'CAP 5f
5:05 (5:05) (Class 4) (0-85,77) 3-Y-0 **£6,477** (£1,927; £963; £481) **Stalls** Low

Form RPR
0110 **1** **Mormeatmic**[15] 2410 3-9-4 **74** .... PaulMulrennan 6 80
(M W Easterby) *cl up: rdn to ld appr fnl f: kpt on: all out* **12/1**
5242 **2** shd **Blazing Heights**[15] 2410 3-9-5 **75** .... FergalLynch 7 84+
(J S Goldie) *hld up in tch: n.m.r fr 1/2-way: effrt whn hmpd ins fnl f: kpt on wl towards fin: jst failed* **10/3**[2]
3250 **3** 3/4 **Highland Song (IRE)**[21] 2237 3-8-10 **66** .... RobertWinston 3 69
(R F Fisher) *chsd ldrs: effrt 1/2-way: edgd lft fr over 1f out: one pce ins fnl f* **5/1**
0-65 **4** 1 1/2 **Howards Prince**[50] 1453 3-8-9 **65** ....(p) TomEaves 5 63
(I Semple) *led tl hdd appr fnl f: kpt on same pce ins last* **20/1**
0441 **5** 1/2 **Glasshoughton**[7] 2652 3-9-5 **75** .... PhillipMakin 1 71+
(M Dods) *prom: effrt whn n.m.r over 1f out: hmpd twice ins fnl f: nt rcvr* **11/4**[1]
50-2 **6** 5 **Dulce Sueno**[23] 2161 3-8-2 **58** oh1 .... PaulHanagan 2 36
(I Semple) *dwlt: sn chsng ldrs: rdn and wknd over 1f out* **7/2**[3]
4-10 **7** 3/4 **Rondo**[49] 1482 3-9-7 **77** .... PaulFessey 4 52
(T D Barron) *in tch on outside: rdn over 2f out: btn over 1f out* **10/1**

59.53 secs (-0.91) **Going Correction** -0.125s/f (Firm) **7** Ran SP% **110.2**
Speed ratings (Par 101):102,101,100,98,97 89,88
CSF £47.92 TOTE £8.40: £2.80, £2.30; EX 27.00.
Owner M Broad & Mrs M E Attwood **Bred** A C Birkle **Trained** Sheriff Hutton, N Yorks
■ Stewards' Enquiry : Fergal Lynch one-day ban: careless riding (Jul 5)

FOCUS
Another single-figure field but, although the pace was sound, another race in which several met trouble and this bare form does not look entirely reliable.
Rondo Official explanation: jockey said gelding hung right-handed throughout

2856 CORALPOKER.COM FILLIES' H'CAP 6f
5:40 (5:40) (Class 5) (0-70,65) 3-Y-0+ **£3,368** (£1,002; £500; £250) **Stalls** Low

Form RPR
0010 **1** **African Gift**[14] 2464 4-10-0 **65** .... RobertWinston 3 80
(J G Given) *hld up: hdwy over 2f out: led 1f out: rdn and r.o strly* **4/1**[1]
0060 **2** 3 **Rancho Cucamonga (IRE)**[9] 2574 4-9-2 **53** ....(v) J-PGuillambert 8 59
(T D Barron) *hld up: hdwy outside over 2f out: hung lft over 1f out: kpt on ins fnl f: no ch w wnr* **6/1**[2]
000- **3** hd **Aahgowangowan (IRE)**[275] 5420 7-9-9 **60** ....(t) PhillipMakin 2 66
(M Dods) *led to 1f out: edgd rt and kpt on same pce fnl f* **10/1**
0055 **4** 1 1/4 **Electron Pulse**[25] 2109 3-9-3 **61** .... FergalLynch 6 61
(J S Goldie) *bhd and sn outpcd: rdn and hdwy over 1f out: kpt on fnl f* **16/1**
004- **5** 2 **Monda**[210] 6438 4-9-7 **58** .... PaulMulrennan 4 54
(Miss J A Camacho) *chsd ldrs tl rdn and no ex over 1f out* **20/1**
060 **6** 2 **Diamond Katie (IRE)**[12] 2505 4-9-8 **59** .... PaulHanagan 7 49
(N Tinkler) *towards rr: outpcd 1/2-way: no imp over 1f out* **4/1**[1]
0253 **7** nk **Newkeylets**[19] 2285 3-8-10 **54** ....(p) TomEaves 1 43
(I Semple) *prom tl rdn and wknd over 1f out* **12/1**
0013 **8** 1 1/2 **First Rhapsody (IRE)**[15] 2400 4-9-0 **56** .... AndrewElliott(5) 10 41
(T J Etherington) *in tch tl wknd fr 2f out* **4/1**[1]
60-0 **9** 3 1/2 **Considerthelilies (IRE)**[4] 2734 3-8-13 **57** ....(p) PaulFessey 9 31
(Miss L A Perratt) *chsd ldrs to 2f out: sn rdn and btn* **66/1**
-531 **10** 3 **Miss Lopez (IRE)**[100] 653 3-9-6 **64** .... PatCosgrave 5 29
(K R Burke) *keen: in tch: rdn over 2f out: sn btn* **7/1**[3]

1m 12.54s (-1.13) **Going Correction** -0.125s/f (Firm)
WFA 3 from 4yo+ 7lb **10** Ran SP% **115.7**
Speed ratings (Par 100):102,98,97,96,93 90,90,88,83,79
CSF £27.75 CT £228.64 TOTE £6.00: £2.50, £2.80, £2.80; EX 24.10 Place 6 £113.65, Place 5 £76.44.
Owner Mr & Mrs G Middlebrook **Bred** G And Mrs Middlebrook **Trained** Willoughton, Lincs

FOCUS
An ordinary event in which the pace was sound and no hard-luck stories this time. The fourth and fifth were to form and set the standard.
T/Plt: £152.80 to a £1 stake. Pool: £46,246.65. 220.80 winning tickets. T/Qpdt: £11.00 to a £1 stake. Pool: £2,542.40. 170.60 winning tickets. RY

2643 LINGFIELD (L-H)
Saturday, June 24

OFFICIAL GOING: Turf course - good to firm; all-weather - standard
Wind: Moderate, behind

2857 LINGFIELDPARK.CO.UK MAIDEN AUCTION STKS 7f
6:30 (6:31) (Class 5) 2-Y-0 **£3,238** (£963; £481; £240) **Stalls** High

Form RPR
3 **1** **Simba Sun (IRE)**[21] 2218 2-8-11 .... NelsonDeSouza(3) 6 85+
(R M Beckett) *w'like: lw: mde all: shkn up over 1f out: drew clr: eased cl home* **4/6**[1]
04 **2** 7 **Stagehand (IRE)**[11] 2530 2-8-11 .... AlanMunro 1 65
(B R Millman) *t.k.h: chsd wnr wl over 1f out: readily outpcd fnl f* **4/1**[2]
06 **3** 2 1/2 **House Arrest**[10] 2552 2-8-1 .... EdwardCreighton(3) 2 51
(I A Wood) *trckd wnr tl rdn and wknd wl over 1f out* **22/1**
4 1 **The Skerret** 2-8-9 .... JimCrowley 5 54
(P Winkworth) *w'like: plld hrd: trckd ldrs: wknd wl over 1f out* **18/1**
64 **5** 5 **Tarif (IRE)**[24] 2139 2-8-10 .... MickyFenton 3 42
(Mrs P Sly) *w'like: in tch: rdn 4f out: bhd fr 1/2-way* **5/1**[3]
0 **6** 6 **Colonel Klink (IRE)**[21] 2234 2-8-10 .... JDSmith 4 27
(J S Moore) *leggy: slowly away: a outpcd in rr* **66/1**

1m 22.4s (-1.81) **Going Correction** -0.225s/f (Firm) **6** Ran SP% **107.8**
Speed ratings (Par 93):101,93,90,89,83 76
CSF £3.24 TOTE £1.70: £1.10, £2.30; EX 3.20.
Owner The Calvera Partnership **Bred** T Ward **Trained** Whitsbury, Hants

FOCUS
A moderate juvenile maiden, yet the winner was impressive and looks capable of rating higher.

NOTEBOOK
Simba Sun(IRE) ◆, third at Chepstow on debut 21 days previously, relished the step up to this extra furlong and made all up the stands' rail for an impressive first success. He is clearly progressive and enjoyed the decent ground. While he got all of the seven furlongs, he does possess his share of early speed, and his trainer is reportedly very keen to send him to Ireland for the valuable Tattersalls Sales Race at the Curragh next month. (tchd 8-13, 8-11 in a place)
Stagehand(IRE) spoilt his chances of really getting home over the extra furlong by refusing to settle through the early stages. This was still his best effort to date, and he still looks to be very much learning the ropes, so may fare better as he becomes more streetwise in due course. He is also now eligible for a nursery mark. (op 9-2)
House Arrest did not appear to really see out the extra furlong and proved very one paced from two out. She should find her feet in due course, and is now eligible for a handicap mark, but may be better off sticking to six furlongs in the short term. (op 25-1)
The Skerret, a cheap purchase whose dam won over this trip at two, ultimately paid for running too freely, yet still shaped with a degree of promise and is entitled to improve for the experience. (op 14-1)
Tarif(IRE) failed to raise his game for the step-up to this longer trip and never really figured. He is in danger of going the wrong way. (op 4-1)

2858 LINGFIELD PARK GOLF COURSE H'CAP 5f

7:00 (7:01) (Class 5) (0-75,76) 3-Y-0+ £3,238 (£963; £481; £240) Stalls High

Form RPR

1005 1 Misaro (GER)[15] 2417 5-9-5 66 (b) AdrianMcCarthy 10 79
(R A Harris) *lw: mde all: rdn over 1f out: in command fnl f* 4/1[2]

0014 2 1 3/4 Malapropism[6] 2674 6-9-12 76 EdwardCreighton(3) 7 83
(M R Channon) *a.p: chsd wnr 2f out: edgd lft and no imp ins fnl f* 5/1

3502 3 1 1/4 Clearing Sky (IRE)[14] 2444 5-8-6 56 oh2 SaleemGolam(3) 8 58
(J R Boyle) *in tch on ins: t.k.h: n.m.r over 1f out: r.o ins fnl f* 8/1

0-22 4 1 3/4 Millinsky (USA)[19] 2295 5-9-6 74 RobbieMills(7) 1 70
(Rae Guest) *trckd ldr to wl over 1f out: fdd ins fnl f* 3/1[1]

0-52 5 hd Quality Street[15] 2389 4-10-0 75 RyanMoore 4 70
(P Butler) *lw: mid-division: rdn 1/2-way: kpt on one pce fnl fnl f* 9/2[3]

-060 6 1 Jinksonthehouse[10] 2543 5-8-6 56 oh16 DeanCorby(3) 6 47?
(M D I Usher) *nvr bttr than mid-div* 33/1

0000 7 1 1/2 Majestical (IRE)[9] 2571 4-8-9 56 oh1 (p) SteveDrowne 2 42
(J M Bradley) *in rr: outpcd fr over 2f out* 14/1

5050 8 1/2 Dancing Mystery[11] 2536 12-9-4 65 (b) StephenCarson 5 49
(E A Wheeler) *t.k.h: rdn wl over 1f out: sn wknd* 8/1

00-0 9 1/2 Zimbali[13] 2484 4-8-9 56 oh9 JimCrowley 3 38
(J M Bradley) *in tch on outside tl wknd over 1f out* 25/1

-060 10 3 Wise Wager (IRE)[43] 1643 4-9-2 63 TPQueally 9 35
(Miss Z C Davison) *s.i.s: hmpd after 1f: nt clr run 2f out: sn eased* 20/1

56.90 secs (-2.04) **Going Correction** -0.225s/f (Firm) 10 Ran SP% **120.3**
Speed ratings (Par 103):107,104,102,99,99 97,95,94,93,88
CSF £24.63 CT £139.20 TOTE £4.40: £1.90, £1.60, £2.20; EX 33.80.
Owner C Waters **Bred** Wilhelm Fasching **Trained** Earlswood, Monmouths

FOCUS
Am ordinary sprint handicap, but run at a decent clip and the form looks fair enough, although the proximity of the sixth is a slight worry.
Millinsky(USA) Official explanation: jockey said mare ran flat
Wise Wager(IRE) Official explanation: jockey said filly never travelled and was unsuited by the good to firm ground

2859 RESTRUCTURING MAIDEN STKS 6f

7:30 (7:31) (Class 5) 3-Y-0+ £3,886 (£1,156; £577; £288) Stalls High

Form RPR

3 1 China Cherub[23] 2167 3-8-9 DaneO'Neill 9 75+
(H Candy) *in tch: nt clr run whn swtchd lft 2f out: swtchd rt over 1f out: drvn to ld nr fin* 9/4[1]

03 2 nk Kansas Gold[14] 2458 3-9-0 DarryllHolland 8 70
(W R Muir) *lw: led: rdn 2f out: hdd and kpt on: hdd nr fin* 10/1

4-0 3 1/2 Bijli (IRE)[35] 1845 3-9-0 TPQueally 6 68
(J Noseda) *lw: a.p: ev ch ins fnl f: no ex cl home* 8/1

6 4 1 1/4 Benandonner (USA)[42] 1680 3-9-0 SteveDrowne 3 64
(E A L Dunlop) *in tch: effrt over 2f out: nt qckn ins fnl f* 7/2[2]

0 5 nk Blushing Light (USA)[17] 2343 3-9-0 FJohansson 12 63
(M A Magnusson) *in tch: rdn over 2f out: kpt on one pce* 33/1

6 nk Mail Express (IRE) 3-8-9 NickyMackay 10 57+
(L M Cumani) *w'like: scope: lengthy: lw: slowly away: in rr whn nt clr run fr wl over 1f out: nvr on terms* 5/1

0 7 1 1/2 Indian Sabre (IRE)[24] 2143 3-9-0 ShaneKelly 4 58
(J Noseda) *unf: lw: in tch on outside tl rdn and wknd over 1f out* 16/1

40 8 1 3/4 Neardown Queen[38] 1771 3-8-4 JamesDoyle(5) 7 48
(I A Wood) *slowly away: sn prom: rdn over 2f out: carried lft sn after: wknd* 50/1

0- 9 4 Patitiri (USA)[291] 5032 3-8-9 AdrianMcCarthy 11 36
(M G Quinlan) *t.k.h: a bhd* 40/1

3 10 11 King Of Charm (IRE)[21] 2235 3-9-0 RyanMoore 5 8
(G L Moore) *w'like: leggy: s.i.s: effrt 1/2-way: sn bhd* 4/1[3]

1m 10.46s (-1.21) **Going Correction** -0.225s/f (Firm) 10 Ran SP% **123.1**
Speed ratings (Par 103):99,98,97,96,95 95,93,91,85,71
CSF £28.23 TOTE £4.20: £1.30, £2.40, £3.60; EX 28.10.
Owner Wayne And Hilary Thornton **Bred** Wayne And Hilary Thornton **Trained** Kingston Warren, Oxon

FOCUS
A modest three-year-old maiden. The form has not been rated positively overall, although the winner did well and can go on to better things.
Mail Express(IRE) ◆ Official explanation: jockey said filly was denied a clear run

2860 ALAN CROWDER MEMORIAL H'CAP 7f 140y

8:00 (8:01) (Class 5) (0-75,75) 3-Y-0+ £3,238 (£963; £481; £240) Stalls Centre

Form RPR

-001 1 Bold Diktator[13] 2482 4-9-12 71 (b) SteveDrowne 1 80
(W R Muir) *a in tch on outside: rdn 2f out: led over 1f out: all out* 3/1[2]

0664 2 hd Grizedale (IRE)[21] 2232 7-9-12 71 (t) PaulDoe 7 79
(J Akehurst) *stdd s: hdwy over 2f out: wnt 2nd 1f out and rdn to press wnr cl home* 7/1

20-6 3 1 3/4 Mythical Charm[164] 86 7-8-13 58 (t) RyanMoore 6 62
(J J Bridger) *a in tch: rdn over 1f out: nt qckn ins fnl f* 14/1

6103 4 1 Stamford Blue[9] 2567 5-8-13 58 (b) AdrianMcCarthy 8 60
(R A Harris) *t.k.h: prom tl one pce appr fnl f* 5/1[3]

0-05 5 1/2 Curtain Bluff[6] 2603 4-9-11 73 EdwardCreighton(3) 5 73
(M R Channon) *bhd: rdn over 2f out: nvr nr to chal* 8/1

0311 6 3 Meditation[5] 2705 4-9-11 75 6ex JamesDoyle(5) 2 72+
(I A Wood) *trckd ldr: rdn 2f out: wknd over 1f out* 2/1[1]

000- 7 3/4 Parisi Princess[367] 2807 5-8-6 54 oh23 NelsonDeSouza(3) 4 45?
(D L Williams) *led tl rdn and hdd over 1f out: wknd ins fnl f* 66/1

0000 8 3 Hey Presto[17] 2348 6-8-12 60 SaleemGolam(3) 3 43
(R Rowe) *in rr and a bhd* 16/1

1m 31.2s (-0.26) **Going Correction** -0.225s/f (Firm) 8 Ran SP% **112.7**
Speed ratings (Par 103):92,91,90,89,88 85,84,81
CSF £23.46 CT £250.24 TOTE £4.90: £1.40, £1.90, £3.20; EX 25.60.
Owner Kilmuir Partnership **Bred** T J And Mrs Heywood **Trained** Lambourn, Berks

FOCUS
A very moderate winning time for a race of its class. The first two came clear, but the form is far from solid.
Meditation Official explanation: jockey said filly ran flat

2861 CLEVER CLOGS DAY NURSERY, BRENTWOOD, ESSEX (S) STKS 1m 4f (P)

8:30 (8:31) (Class 6) 3-Y-0+ £2,388 (£705; £352) Stalls Low

Form RPR

1354 1 Champagne Shadow (IRE)[22] 2206 5-9-13 78 (b) RyanMoore 3 66+
(G L Moore) *trckd ldrs: led wl over 1f out: sn clr: easily* 8/13[1]

6-0 2 6 Alwaysforsale (IRE)[24] 2131 3-8-5 EdwardCreighton(3) 4 51
(J S Moore) *t.k.h in mid-div: rdn over 2f out: styd on to go 2nd nr fin: no ch w wnr* 33/1

2200 3 nk Good Article (IRE)[9] 2577 5-9-8 46 DarryllHolland 7 51
(D K Ivory) *hld up on outside: hdwy over 3f out: chsd clr wnr over 1f out tl tired and lost 2nd cl home* 8/1[2]

00-0 4 1 1/2 Tip Toes (IRE)[20] 2260 4-9-0 37 DeanCorby(3) 6 43
(P Howling) *mid-div: kpt on one pce ins fnl 2f* 66/1

0056 5 1 1/2 Sky At Night (IRE)[12] 2507 3-8-8 51 (b[1]) DaneO'Neill 9 47+
(P Mitchell) *racd on outside in mid-div: effrt whn nt clr run 3f out: no hdwy fnl 2f* 10/1[3]

0600 6 1/2 Salinger (USA)[18] 2319 4-9-3 60 JamesDoyle(5) 5 45
(Mrs L J Mongan) *mid-div: rdn 4f out: outpcd fr over 2f out* 10/1[3]

4005 7 1 Cool Isle[14] 2463 3-8-3 46 (b) JimmyQuinn 8 38
(P Howling) *prom: rdn to ld over 2f out: hdd & wknd wl over 1f out* 16/1

3020 8 8 Mujazaf[15] 2413 4-9-5 45 (p) NeilChalmers(3) 11 31
(D Burchell) *trckd ldr: rdn 4f out: sn wknd* 14/1

066 9 shd Ten Commandments (IRE)[7] 2646 3-8-3 39 AdrianMcCarthy 1 25
(K J Burke) *led tl rdn and hdd over 2f out: wknd qckly* 33/1

0040 10 hd Tennessee Belle (IRE)[9] 2568 4-8-10 35 (e) KirstyMilczarek(7) 10 25
(C N Allen) *a in rr* 33/1

00-0 11 5 Our Glenard[47] 1541 7-9-5 37 SaleemGolam(3) 13 22
(J E Long) *slowly away: a bhd* 33/1

0 12 3/4 Fentastic[9] 2587 3-8-3 FrancisFerris 12 16
(Rae Guest) *leggy: a wl in rr* 33/1

000- 13 1 3/4 Fosroc (USA)[277] 5388 4-9-5 52 NelsonDeSouza(3) 14 18
(B R Johnson) *a bhd* 33/1

600- 14 3 1/2 Fitzsimons (IRE)[199] 6521 3-8-8 45 SteveDrowne 2 12
(A M Hales) *trckd ldrs tl rdn and wknd over 3f out* 28/1

2m 33.82s (-0.57) **Going Correction** +0.025s/f (Slow)
WFA 3 from 4yo+ 14lb 14 Ran SP% **126.3**
Speed ratings (Par 101):102,98,97,96,95 95,94,89,89,89 85,85,84,81
CSF £40.22 TOTE £1.60: £1.10, £7.30, £3.90; EX 41.90.There was no bid for the winner. Alwaysforsale was the subject of a friendly claim.
Owner D R Hunnisett **Bred** Mrs Kate Watson **Trained** Woodingdean, E Sussex
■ Stewards' Enquiry : Ryan Moore one-day ban: careless riding (Jul 5)

FOCUS
A dire event, even by selling standards. Champagne Shadow was different class and won as he was entitled to.
Good Article(IRE) Official explanation: jockey said gelding hung left

2862 LINGFIELD PARK LEISURE CLUB H'CAP 1m 2f (P)

9:00 (9:00) (Class 6) (0-60,61) 4-Y-0+ £2,730 (£806; £403) Stalls Low

Form RPR

21 1 The Fonze (IRE)[7] 2647 5-8-12 56 JerryO'Dwyer(5) 4 67+
(Eoin Doyle, Ire) *hld up in mid-div: rdn over 1f out: qcknd to ld fnl 50yds: won gng away* 5/4[1]

3202 2 1 Glendale[18] 2320 5-9-6 59 JimmyQuinn 12 68
(D K Ivory) *trckd ldrs: t.k.h: r.o to go 2nd ins fnl f* 6/1[2]

1241 3 1 1/4 Magic Warrior[7] 2641 6-9-7 60 PatDobbs 1 67
(J C Fox) *mid-div: rdn 3f out: hdwy whn hmpd on ins over 2f out: rallied to ld briefly ins fnl f: no ex nr fin* 9/1[3]

0230 4 shd Jomus[18] 2320 5-9-2 55 (p) RobertHavlin 7 61
(L Montague Hall) *towards rr: racd wd: hdwy over 3f out: kpt on fnl f: nvr nrr* 14/1

330- 5 hd Bienheureux[175] 6701 5-9-3 56 (v[1]) DarryllHolland 10 62+
(Miss Gay Kelleway) *hld up in rr: hdwy on ins fr over 1f out: nt qckn ins fnl f* 14/1

0064 6 3/4 Meelup (IRE)[8] 2612 6-9-0 56 (p) AmirQuinn(3) 5 61
(P G Murphy) *led: rdn over 2f out: hdd & wknd ins fnl f* 16/1

5102 7 2 Ground Patrol[13] 2481 5-9-8 61 RyanMoore 11 62
(G L Moore) *s.i.s: sn in tch: ev ch tl fdd ent fnl f* 10/1

3005 8 1/2 Height Of Spirits[17] 2348 4-9-4 57 NickyMackay 2 60+
(T D McCarthy) *b: t.k.h: hld up in rr: hdwy on ins over 2f out: hmpd 1f out: nt rcvr* 16/1

4003 9 1 1/4 Full Of Zest[18] 2320 4-9-4 57 (b) IanMongan 3 55
(Mrs L J Mongan) *in tch: rdn to chse ldr 3f out: edgd lft and wknd fnl f* 16/1

0006 10 nk Yenaled[8] 2601 9-9-3 56 SteveDrowne 6 53
(J M Bradley) *in tch: rdn 3f out: wknd over 1f out* 25/1

0400 11 3/4 Bishops Finger[32] 1926 6-9-6 59 (b) PaulDoe 8 55
(Jamie Poulton) *b: bhd: rdn over 1f out: sn btn* 16/1

0-50 12 3/4 Smoothly Does It[25] 2098 5-9-3 59 NeilChalmers(3) 9 53
(Mrs A J Bowlby) *a bhd* 25/1

003 13 nk Return In Style (IRE)[15] 2392 5-8-13 59 (p) PatrickHills(7) 13 53
(J W Hills) *bhd: hdwy over 4f out: wknd over 2f out* 33/1

3-00 14 5 Optimum (IRE)[21] 2221 4-9-7 60 MickyFenton 14 44
(J T Stimpson) *in tch tl wknd over 3f out* 66/1

2m 7.94s (0.15) **Going Correction** +0.025s/f (Slow) 14 Ran SP% **126.8**
Speed ratings (Par 101):100,99,98,98,97 97,95,95,94,94 93,92,92,88
CSF £8.56 CT £54.91 TOTE £2.20: £1.70, £2.50, £2.90; EX 12.00 Place 6 £26.33, Place 5 £23.18.
Owner J A Dunphy **Bred** Mrs Olivia Farrell **Trained** Mooncoin, Co. Kilkenny

FOCUS
A modest handicap, but run at a sound pace and the form looks solid for the class.
T/Plt: £25.40 to a £1 stake. Pool: £34,501.30. 988.35 winning tickets. T/Qpdt: £9.10 to a £1 stake. Pool: £2,892.80. 232.85 winning tickets. JS

2820 NEWMARKET (JULY) (R-H)

Saturday, June 24

OFFICIAL GOING: Good to firm

The surface was much the same as the previous meeting on Friday night - good fast ground with an excellent covering of lush grass.
Wind: Light, across Weather: Fine and sunny

2863 VC CASINO.COM H'CAP 7f

2:10 (2:11) (Class 4) (0-85,85) 3-Y-0 £6,477 (£1,927; £963; £481) Stalls High

Form RPR

0-60 1 Cape Of Luck (IRE)[67] 1067 3-9-7 85 GeorgeBaker 3 89
(P Mitchell) *hld up: hdwy over 2f out: led and hung rt over 1f out: rdn and swvd lft ins fnl f: styd on* 25/1

-205 2 nk Carmenero (GER)[7] 2650 3-9-2 80 RichardMullen 9 83
(W R Muir) *hld up in tch: rdn and hung lft 1f out: r.o* 11/1

4003 **3** ½ **Charles Darwin (IRE)**[16] 2385 3-9-6 **84**........................ FrancisNorton 1 86
(M Blanshard) *trckd ldrs: rdn and ev ch over 1f out: sn bmpd: styd on* **20/1**

1060 **4** *nk* **Cool Sting (IRE)**[10] 2553 3-8-5 **72** ow2........................ NeilChalmers(3) 5 73
(A M Balding) *prom: outpcd over 2f out: hdwy over 1f out: styd on u.p* **50/1**

-155 **5** *4* **Sir Orpen (IRE)**[28] 2032 3-8-13 **77**.................................... ChrisCatlin 10 67
(T D Barron) *trckd ldrs: plld hrd: led over 2f out: rdn and hdd over 1f out: hmpd and wknd 1f out* **13/2**[2]

1-53 **6** ½ **Cactus King**[18] 2330 3-9-5 **83**.. RobertHavlin 11 72
(J H M Gosden) *dwlt: rcvrd to ld 6f out: rdn and hdd over 2f out: edgd lft over 1f out: sn wknd* **1/1**[1]

165 **7** *1* **Sir Douglas**[30] 1963 3-8-12 **76**.. TPQueally 7 62
(J A Osborne) *hld up: effrt over 1f out: nvr trbld ldrs* **25/1**

600 **8** *1* **Littledodayno (IRE)**[54] 1337 3-8-6 **70**........................... JamieMackay 8 54
(M Wigham) *hld up: nt clr run fr over 2f out: nvr trbld ldrs* **66/1**

-210 **9** ¾ **Royal Envoy (IRE)**[22] 2205 3-9-0 **78**..................................... TedDurcan 2 60
(B W Hills) *chsd ldrs: rdn over 2f out: wknd over 1f out* **14/1**

35-0 **10** ¾ **Rembrandt Quality (USA)**[7] 2650 3-8-10 **74**.................. JimCrowley 6 54
(Mrs A J Perrett) *hld up: hdwy 1/2-way: nt clr run and lost pl over 2f out: n.d after* **16/1**

-130 **11** *3* **Lavenham (IRE)**[7] 2642 3-8-12 **76**...................................... DaneO'Neill 12 47
(R Hannon) *chsd ldrs over 5f* **10/1**[3]

4410 **12** ½ **Sands Of Barra (IRE)**[35] 1855 3-8-10 **77**............... NelsonDeSouza(3) 4 47
(N A Callaghan) *led 1f: remained w ldrs: rdn over 2f out: sn wknd* **12/1**

1m 24.94s (-1.84) **Going Correction** -0.125s/f (Firm) **12** Ran SP% **116.9**
Speed ratings (Par 101):105,104,104,103,99 98,97,96,95,94 91,90
CSF £261.76 CT £5581.57 TOTE £28.40: £4.00, £3.70, £3.80; EX 247.90.
Owner Champions Gallery **Bred** Colm And Miss Orla McCourt **Trained** Epsom, Surrey

FOCUS
A fair handicap but there was little in the way of solid recent form to go on.

2864 PLAY 24/7 AT VC CASINO.COM H'CAP 6f
2:40 (2:44) (Class 4) (0-80,80) 3-Y-0+ **£6,477** (£1,927; £963; £481) **Stalls** High

Form RPR

0212 **1** **Zidane**[18] 2323 4-10-0 **80**.. OscarUrbina 11 96+
(J R Fanshawe) *hld up: swtchd lft 1f out: shkn up and r.o to ld wl ins fnl f: readily* **2/1**[1]

10 **2** *2* **Pick A Nice Name**[22] 2194 4-8-10 **69**.................. MichaelJStainton(7) 9 75
(R M Whitaker) *s.i.s: hld up: plld hrd: swtchd lft over 2f out: rdn and hung lft over 1f out: styd on* **25/1**

0205 **3** *shd* **Canadian Danehill (IRE)**[14] 2444 4-8-11 **68**............... JamesDoyle(5) 2 74
(R M H Cowell) *disp ld tl led over 3f out: rdn and hdd over 1f out: styd on* **14/1**

0111 **4** *hd* **Joy And Pain**[18] 2317 5-9-3 **69**.......................................(v) DaneO'Neill 10 74
(M J Attwater) *chsd ldrs: rdn to ld and edgd rt over 1f out: hdd and unable qck wl ins fnl f* **15/2**[3]

-001 **5** *nk* **Prince Cyrano**[15] 2417 7-9-7 **73**.. TPQueally 6 78
(W J Musson) *hld up in tch: rdn and ev ch over 1f out: edgd rt: styd on same pce* **16/1**

4212 **6** ½ **Dvinsky (USA)**[8] 2603 5-9-7 **73**................................ RobbieFitzpatrick 15 76
(D Carroll) *chsd ldrs: nt clr run over 1f out: swtchd lft and nt clr run ins fnl f: nvr able to chal* **8/1**

241- **7** ¾ **Lipizza (IRE)**[234] 6226 3-9-3 **76**.. DO'Donohoe 8 77+
(N A Callaghan) *hld up: hdwy over 2f out: nt clr run ins fnl f: nt trble ldrs* **25/1**

0103 **8** 1 ¼ **Greenwood**[8] 2606 8-9-6 **72**... RobertHavlin 13 69
(P G Murphy) *hld up: nt clr run over 1f out: swtchd lft and styd on ins fnl f: nt rch ldrs* **20/1**

0632 **9** 1 ¼ **Oranmore Castle (IRE)**[7] 2661 4-9-9 **75**..........................(t) TedDurcan 4 68
(B W Hills) *s.i.s: hld up: nt clr run over 2f out: hdwy over 1f out: wknd ins fnl f* **10/3**[2]

013- **10** *nk* **Balik Pearls**[225] 6312 3-9-3 **76**.. FrancisNorton 1 68
(N A Callaghan) *hld up: rdn over 1f out: n.d* **33/1**

2464 **11** *1* **Royal Bandit**[44] 1609 3-8-8 **67**... RichardMullen 3 56
(N A Callaghan) *s.i.s: outpcd: nvr nrr* **50/1**

0000 **12** ½ **Bucharest**[27] 2050 3-8-2 **61** oh1.. JamieMackay 7 49
(M Wigham) *stmbld s: racd keenly and sn prom: rdn over 2f out: wkng whn hmpd over 1f out and 1f out* **50/1**

50-0 **13** *shd* **Me**[66] 1085 3-8-11 **70**... ChrisCatlin 14 58
(P W Chapple-Hyam) *chsd ldrs: wkng when hmpd ins fnl f* **16/1**

10/0 **14** 1 ¾ **Kool Acclaim**[9] 2590 5-8-13 **65**... MickyFenton 12 47
(S C Williams) *led: hdd over 3f out: rdn and edgd rt over 1f out: wkng whn hmpd ins fnl f* **50/1**

-630 **15** ¾ **Polar Force**[147] 224 6-9-1 **70**...................................... NelsonDeSouza(3) 5 50
(Mrs C A Dunnett) *chsd ldrs: rdn over 1f out: sn wknd* **25/1**

1m 11.44s (-1.91) **Going Correction** -0.125s/f (Firm)
WFA 3 from 4yo+ 7lb **15** Ran SP% **122.8**
Speed ratings (Par 105):107,104,104,103,103 102,101,100,98,98 96,96,96,93,92
CSF £65.67 CT £588.02 TOTE £2.40: £1.40, £7.10, £3.40; EX 77.10.
Owner Mrs Jan Hopper **Bred** Mrs J P Hopper And Mrs E M Grundy **Trained** Newmarket, Suffolk
■ Stewards' Enquiry : Robbie Fitzpatrick one-day ban: careless riding (Jul 5)
D O'Donohoe caution: careless riding

FOCUS
A fair, competitive handicap on paper that was turned into a one-horse show. The form looks solid through the placed horses and should prove reliable.

2865 VC CASINO.COM E B F FILLIES' H'CAP 1m
3:15 (3:20) (Class 4) (0-85,78) 3-Y-0+ **£6,477** (£1,927; £963; £481) **Stalls** High

Form RPR

-21 **1** **Caressed**[24] 2129 3-9-9 **78**... OscarUrbina 5 85+
(J R Fanshawe) *hld up: swtchd lft over 2f out: hdwy over 1f out: rdn to ld ins fnl f: r.o* **1/1**[1]

-214 **2** *1* **Lucky Token (IRE)**[31] 1934 3-9-4 **73**.............................. RichardMullen 2 78
(E A L Dunlop) *led: racd keenly: rdn over 1f out: edgd lft and hdd ins fnl f: styd on* **8/1**

01-0 **3** ½ **Dansa Queen**[17] 2359 3-9-7 **76**.. TedDurcan 7 80
(W R Swinburn) *wnt rt s: chsd ldr: rdn over 1f out: styd on* **22/1**

2011 **4** ½ **Night Storm**[7] 2634 5-10-0 **73**... JimmyQuinn 6 78
(S Dow) *hld up: hdwy and nt clr run over 1f out: nt clr run ins fnl f: styd on* **4/1**[2]

0-00 **5** *hd* **Missed A Beat**[14] 2459 4-9-7 **66**...................................... FrancisNorton 4 71+
(M Blanshard) *prom: nt clr run and lost pl over 1f out: styd on ins fnl f* **12/1**

4660 **6** *3* **My Princess (IRE)**[15] 2400 4-10-0 **73**............................... MickyFenton 1 70
(N A Callaghan) *chsd ldrs: rdn over 2f out: wknd fnl f* **18/1**

1-33 **7** *2* **Sant Elena**[68] 1056 3-9-6 **75**.. ChrisCatlin 3 66
(G Wragg) *prom: rdn over 2f out: wknd fnl f* **13/2**[3]

1m 39.02s (-1.41) **Going Correction** -0.125s/f (Firm)
WFA 3 from 4yo+ 10lb **7** Ran SP% **111.7**
Speed ratings (Par 102):102,101,100,100,99 96,94
CSF £9.36 TOTE £1.80: £1.50, £3.00; EX 10.60.
Owner Cheveley Park Stud **Bred** Cheveley Park Stud Ltd **Trained** Newmarket, Suffolk

FOCUS
A fair fillies' handicap in which the three-year-olds dominated. The winner looks porgressive and the second and fourth sets a reasonable standard.
Night Storm Official explanation: jockey said mare missed the break
Missed A Beat Official explanation: jockey said filly hung to the left

2866 PLAY VC CASINO.COM H'CAP 5f
3:50 (3:50) (Class 2) (0-100,89) 3-Y-0
£12,464 (£3,732; £1,866; £934; £466; £234) **Stalls** High

Form RPR

0144 **1** **Moorhouse Lad**[7] 2639 3-8-12 **80**...................................... JimmyQuinn 5 87
(G Woodward) *a.p: rdn to ld ins fnl f: r.o* **9/1**

3500 **2** ½ **King Orchisios (IRE)**[7] 2658 3-9-7 **89**.............................. DO'Donohoe 2 94
(K A Ryan) *racd stands' side: mid-div: hdwy over 1f out: sn rdn: r.o* **3/1**[1]

-410 **3** *hd* **Rochdale**[18] 2329 3-9-1 **83**... RichardMullen 7 88
(M A Jarvis) *racd stands' side: sn pushed along in rr: rdn over 1f out: r.o wl ins fnl f* **3/1**[1]

1154 **4** *hd* **Total Impact**[32] 1924 3-9-5 **87**.. ChrisCatlin 3 91
(C A Cyzer) *racd stands' side: s.i.s: outpcd: r.o u.p ins fnl f: nrst fin* **5/1**[2]

1010 **5** *1* **Devine Dancer**[18] 2329 3-8-9 **77**.. DaneO'Neill 8 77
(H Candy) *racd stands' side: chsd ldr: rdn and ev ch 1f out: no ex wl ins fnl f* **9/1**

0003 **6** 1 ¼ **Brandywell Boy (IRE)**[7] 2639 3-8-7 **78**..................(b) NelsonDeSouza(3) 6 74
(D J S Ffrench Davis) *racd stands' side: chsd ldrs: outpcd over 3f out: styd on ins fnl f* **13/2**[3]

310- **7** *hd* **Gilt Linked**[242] 6098 3-9-2 **84**... TedDurcan 4 79
(B W Hills) *racd stands' side: led and overall ldr 4f out: rdn over 1f out: hdd & wknd ins fnl f* **16/1**

0300 **8** 2 ½ **Figaro Flyer (IRE)**[16] 2385 3-9-6 **88**.. PaulDoe 9 74
(P Howling) *racd stands' side: chsd ldrs: rdn over 1f out: wknd ins fnl f* **12/1**

10-0 **9** 3 ½ **Titian Saga (IRE)**[27] 2049 3-8-10 **78**.................................. MickyFenton 1 52
(C N Allen) *racd alone centre: led 1f: hung rt and wknd over 1f out* **25/1**

58.29 secs (-1.27) **Going Correction** -0.125s/f (Firm) **9** Ran SP% **117.4**
Speed ratings (Par 105):105,104,103,103,101 99,99,95,90
CSF £36.86 CT £103.16 TOTE £9.40: £2.30, £1.50, £1.70; EX 48.20.
Owner Ron Hull **Bred** P Onslow **Trained** Conisbrough, S Yorks

FOCUS
The top weight was rated 11lb lower than the ceiling for this event and the form looks ordinary for the grade, but the winning time was perfectly acceptable for a race of its type.

NOTEBOOK
Moorhouse Lad, never far off what looked a fair early gallop, was shaken up after the leaders had passed the two-furlong pole and quickened to the front where he was able to hold off the late challengers down the middle of the track. This was the first time he had got himself into the frame in five starts on ground faster than good, but more is now required and connections are considering bringing him back here next Friday evening under a penalty. (op 10-1 tchd 11-1 in a place)
King Orchisios(IRE) would have found this much easier than at York last week. On that evidence the return to this trip looked an obvious move, but he could not go the early pace and although staying on at the death, looks as though he may be a difficult horse to place. (tchd 10-3 in places)
Rochdale made gradual late headway, but has not gone on from his Rowley Mile success back in May. (op 7-2)
Total Impact stayed on widest of all, but appears to be a much better horse on sand. (tchd 11-2)
Devine Dancer proved a touch one-paced after racing close to the pace throughout. (op 8-1)
Brandywell Boy(IRE) made late headway, but failed to reproduce his latest Leicester effort. (op 7-1)
Gilt Linked Official explanation: jockey said filly had no more to give

2867 PLAY VC CASINO.COM MAIDEN STKS 7f
4:20 (4:21) (Class 4) 2-Y-0 **£2,941** (£2,941; £674; £336) **Stalls** High

Form RPR

0 **1** **Norisan**[15] 2402 2-9-3 .... DaneO'Neill 7 85
(R Hannon) *led: rdn over 1f out: edgd lft and hdd ins fnl f: rallied to join wnr post* **9/2**[3]

1 *dht* **Halicarnassus (IRE)** 2-9-3 .... TedDurcan 6 85
(M R Channon) *chsd ldr: rdn to ld ins fnl f: jnd post* **7/2**[2]

3 *2* **Costume** 2-8-12 .... RobertHavlin 8 75
(J H M Gosden) *s.i.s: sn chsng ldrs: nt clr run over 1f out: styd on same pce ins fnl f* **3/1**[1]

4 1 ½ **Emerald Wilderness (IRE)** 2-9-3 .... ChrisCatlin 5 76
(M R Channon) *s.i.s: hdwy over 2f out: styd on same pce fnl f* **13/2**

5 *hd* **Guacamole** 2-8-12 .... OscarUrbina 1 71+
(B W Hills) *hld up: hdwy over 1f out: nt trble ldrs* **5/1**

6 *7* **Downbeat** 2-9-3 .... JimmyQuinn 2 58
(J L Dunlop) *hld up:: wknd 2f out* **12/1**

7 ½ **Grand Heights (IRE)** 2-9-3 .... TPQueally 4 60+
(J L Dunlop) *chsd ldrs over 5f* **10/1**

8 2 ½ **Present** 2-8-12 .... MichaelTebbutt 3 46
(D Morris) *dwlt: plld hrd and sn prom: rdn and wknd wl over 1f out* **25/1**

1m 27.14s (0.36) **Going Correction** -0.125s/f (Firm) **8** Ran SP% **116.0**
Speed ratings (Par 95):92,92,89,88,87 79,79,76
WIN: Halicarnassus £2.60, Norisan £3.50. PL: Halicarnassus £1.60, Norisan £2.00, £1.60. EX: H/N £17.10, N/H £18.00. CSF: H/N £10.00, N/H £10.50..
Owner Box 41 **Bred** Yeomanstown Lodge Stud **Trained** West Ilsley, Berks
Owner The Waney Racing Group Inc **Bred** The National Stud Owner Breeders Club Ltd **Trained** East Everleigh, Wilts

FOCUS
An ordinary maiden in which only one of these had previous experience. The winning time was ordinary, which suggests none of them are likely to be world-beaters.

NOTEBOOK
Norisan, the only one with previous experience, looked as though he would come on plenty for his debut run in what looked a decent Goodwood maiden and so he did, making virtually all the running up the stands' rail and showing a likeable attitude to rally when hard pressed inside the closing stages. (op 6-1)
Halicarnassus(IRE), a 35,000gns half-brother to Follow My Lead and also to three winners in the US, was up with the pace throughout and looked to have the race won at one stage, but had to share the spoils in the end. He looked plenty fit enough beforehand, but still has a bit of filling out to do and this was a promising first effort. (op 6-1)

Costume, out of a high-class triple winner over ten furlongs in France, did not look particularly forward in the paddock. She travelled nicely for much of the way, but was unable to quicken once the opening arrived. (op 7-4)
Emerald Wilderness(IRE), a 135,000gns half-brother to Ooh Aah Camara, was therefore the highest priced of these at auction but he could only keep on at one pace when asked to quicken and can only improve for the experience. (op 8-1)
Guacamole, out of a half-sister to three winners, was another that was clearly not fully wound up but he also made some late headway to indicate better was to come next time. (op 8-1)

2868 PLAY ROULETTE AT VC CASINO.COM MAIDEN STKS 1m
4:50 (4:53) (Class 5) 3-Y-O **£5,181** (£1,541; £770; £384) **Stalls** High

Form RPR
1 **Multidimensional (IRE)** 3-9-3 .... TedDurcan 6 94
(H R A Cecil) *hld up in tch: rdn to ld ins fnl f: r.o wl: hung rt towards fin* **10/1**
34 2 3½ **Jewaar (USA)**[17] [2350] 3-8-12 .... RichardMullen 5 81
(M A Jarvis) *plld hrd and prom: rdn and ev ch 1f out: styng on same pce whn hung rt wl ins fnl f* **5/1**[3]
62 3 nk **Uno**[28] [2034] 3-8-12 .... OscarUrbina 7 80
(B W Hills) *led: rdn and edgd lft over 1f out: hdd and unable qck ins fnl f: bmpd towards fin* **11/4**[1]
3-6 4 2½ **Alsadaa (USA)**[28] [2028] 3-9-3 ....(t) RobertHavlin 9 79
(J H M Gosden) *chsd ldr: rdn and ev ch whn hung lft over 1f out: nt run on* **3/1**[2]
03- 5 1¼ **Trimlestown (IRE)**[185] [6642] 3-9-3 .... DaneO'Neill 4 76
(H Candy) *hld up: rdn over 1f out: nvr trbld ldrs* **33/1**
6 5 **Al Qasi (IRE)** 3-9-3 .... AdrianMcCarthy 2 65
(P W Chapple-Hyam) *plld hrd and prom: edgd lft thrght: rdn and wknd over 1f out* **11/4**[1]
0- 7 1¼ **Gold Express**[255] [5833] 3-9-3 .... FrancisNorton 8 62
(W A O'Gorman) *hld up plld hrd: wknd over 1f out* **33/1**
8 4 **Sasetti (IRE)** 3-8-7 .... RoryMoore(5) 1 48
(J R Fanshawe) *s.i.s: outpcd* **25/1**
030- 9 2 **El Capitan (FR)**[250] [5949] 3-9-3 73........ RobbieFitzpatrick 3 48
(Miss Gay Kelleway) *hld up: wknd over 2f out* **50/1**

1m 37.19s (-3.24) **Going Correction** -0.125s/f (Firm) **9** Ran SP% **115.8**
Speed ratings (Par 99):111,107,107,104,103 98,97,93,91
CSF £57.18 TOTE £8.00: £2.40, £1.90, £1.40; EX 33.40.
Owner Niarchos Family **Bred** The Niarchos Family **Trained** Newmarket, Suffolk

FOCUS
A competitive-looking maiden. Those that had run had shown a fair level of form and there were strong words on track for Al Qasi, but he looked in need of the experience. A very smart winning time for a race like this, 2.2 seconds faster than the earlier fillies' handicap over the same trip.
Sasetti(IRE) Official explanation: jockey said filly missed the break

2869 PLAY BLACKJACK AT VC CASINO.COM H'CAP 1m 6f 175y
5:25 (5:26) (Class 5) (0-75,75) 4-Y-O+ **£3,886** (£1,156; £577; £288) **Stalls** Centre

Form RPR
0416 1 **Haatmey**[12] [2501] 4-9-2 70........(v1) ChrisCatlin 9 79
(M R Channon) *hld up: nt clr run over 2f out: swtchd lft: hdwy over 1f out: styd on u.p to ld wl ins fnl f* **4/1**[1]
2205 2 hd **Dubai Ace (USA)**[13] [545] 5-8-5 62........ NeilChalmers(3) 4 71
(Miss Sheena West) *chsd ldr: rdn to ld over 1f out: hdd wl ins fnl f* **7/1**
0-40 3 3 **Annambo**[69] [1033] 6-9-6 74........ TedDurcan 7 79
(D Morris) *chsd ldrs: rdn and ev ch over 1f out: no ex ins fnl f* **6/1**[3]
3421 4 ¾ **Senor Set (GER)**[40] [1745] 5-8-2 56 oh3........ JimmyQuinn 5 59
(J Pearce) *hld up in tch: rdn ad hmpd 2f out: styd on same pce fnl f* **4/1**[1]
-006 5 1¾ **Spinning Coin**[53] [1376] 4-9-7 75........ RichardMullen 8 76
(J G Portman) *led: rdn and hdd over 1f out: wknd ins fnl f* **9/1**
-000 6 8 **Spanish Ridge (IRE)**[26] [2078] 4-9-3 71........ JamieMackay 2 61+
(J L Dunlop) *dwlt: hld up: swtchd lft and hmpd over 2f out: n.d* **11/1**
3600 7 9 **Jadeeron**[53] [1392] 7-8-4 58 oh11 ow2........(p) AlanDaly 6 35
(Miss D A McHale) *hld up: hdwy over 2f out: sn rdn and wknd* **33/1**
1143 8 9 **Figaro's Quest (IRE)**[17] [2345] 4-8-4 58........(b) PaulDoe 1 23
(P F I Cole) *hld up: plld hrd: hdwy over 7f out: sn edgd rt: rdn and wknd wl over 1f out* **11/2**[2]
-302 9 22 **Keshya**[138] [318] 5-8-4 63........ JamesDoyle(5) 3 —
(N P Littmoden) *trckd ldrs: plld hrd: hmpd 7f out: wknd over 2f out* **17/2**

3m 9.56s (-1.48) **Going Correction** -0.125s/f (Firm) **9** Ran SP% **114.0**
Speed ratings (Par 103):98,97,96,95,94 90,85,81,69
CSF £31.74 CT £164.94 TOTE £4.90: £1.70, £2.90, £2.20; EX 53.80 Place 6 £111.08, Place 5 £7.01.
Owner M Channon **Bred** Darley **Trained** West Ilsley, Berks
■ Stewards' Enquiry : Paul Doe two-day ban: careless riding (Jul 11,12)
Chris Catlin five-day ban; used whip with excessive force (Jul 5-9)

FOCUS
The early pace was not strong and the winning time was modest for the grade. They still finished well strung out and the form has a very ordinary look to it.
Spanish Ridge(IRE) Official explanation: jockey said gelding was denied a clear run
Keshya Official explanation: jockey said mare ran too free early
T/Plt: £121.00 to a £1 stake. Pool: £57,177.85. 344.90 winning tickets. T/Qpdt: £4.70 to a £1 stake. Pool: £3,591.00. 564.60 winning tickets. CR

2827 REDCAR (L-H)
Saturday, June 24

OFFICIAL GOING: Firm
Wind: Almost nil

2870 MARKET CROSS JEWELLERS SALE NOW ON (S) STKS 7f
2:20 (2:20) (Class 6) 2-Y-O **£2,590** (£770; £385; £192) **Stalls** Centre

Form RPR
5603 1 **Flying Lion**[9] [2588] 2-8-0 ow1........ ThomasO'Brien(7) 9 58+
(M R Channon) *dwlt: sn in tch: hdwy on outer over 2f out: led wl over 1f out: rdn clr and kpt on* **11/2**
0320 2 2 **Lansdown**[4] [2731] 2-8-1 .... AndrewMullen(5) 4 52
(Robert Gray) *prom: rdn to ld briefly 2f out: sn hdd and kpt on same pce u.p fnl f* **10/1**
4051 3 shd **Sad Times (IRE)**[9] [2588] 2-8-7 ....(p) LiamJones(5) 6 58
(W G M Turner) *dwlt: sn pushed along in rr: swtchd lft and hdwy 2f out: sn rdn and kpt on u.p fnl f* **5/1**[3]
6644 4 5 **Reflective Glory (IRE)**[4] [2731] 2-8-6 .... TonyHamilton 3 39
(J J Quinn) *trckd ldrs: pushed along: lost pl and rdn along 1/2-way: hdwy 2f out: styd on u.p ins last: nt rch ldrs* **10/3**[1]
02 5 3 **Tumble Jill (IRE)**[9] [2588] 2-8-6 .... LPKeniry 7 32
(J S Moore) *prom: pushed along over 2f out: sn rdn and btn wl over 1f out* **9/2**[2]
05 6 nk **Compton Verney**[4] [2731] 2-8-11 .... DavidAllan 5 36
(M W Easterby) *cl up: rdn along over 2f out and sn wknd* **5/1**[3]
00 7 nk **Fade To Grey (IRE)**[9] [2588] 2-8-6 .... MarcHalford(5) 2 35
(W G M Turner) *trckd ldrs: hdwy 3f out: cl up tl rdn 2f out and sn wknd* **50/1**
00 8 9 **Dispol Moonlight (IRE)**[8] [2626] 2-8-8 ....(b1) BenSwarbrick(3) 8 13
(T D Barron) *prom on outer: rdn along wl over 2f out: sn wknd* **9/1**
004 9 7 **Mister Cricket (IRE)**[11] [2524] 2-8-11 ....(p) NeilPollard 1 —
(M E Sowersby) *led: rdn along and hdd 2f out: sn wknd* **66/1**

1m 24.79s (-0.11) **Going Correction** -0.20s/f (Firm) **9** Ran SP% **112.5**
Speed ratings (Par 91):92,89,89,83,80 80,79,69,61
CSF £56.99 TOTE £5.20: £1.90, £4.00, £1.80; EX 72.00.The winner was sold to S Pearson for 8,000gns.
Owner Stephen Roots **Bred** Mike Channon Bloodstock Ltd & M Bishop **Trained** West Ilsley, Berks

FOCUS
An average seller rated around the winner and third.

NOTEBOOK
Flying Lion, whose stable won the race the previous season, appears to have improved for the step up in trip, staying on well throughout the final furlong to win with a little bit in hand. She would have a chance in an early seven-furlong nursery before they start getting really competitive.
Lansdown seems suited by the trip but was never going to trouble the winner at any stage. (op 12-1)
Sad Times(IRE) was under strong pressure from a very early stage and did really well to finish as close as she did. A mile looks within her range at a low-grade.
Reflective Glory(IRE) kept going for pressure but does not look like a horse that is about to win a race of any description in the near future. (op 9-4)
Tumble Jill(IRE) had every chance but failed by a long way to reproduce her last effort. There did not seem to be any obvious reason for the regressive effort.
Fade To Grey(IRE) Official explanation: jockey said colt hung right last 2f

2871 "THE HOUSE" YARM H'CAP 1m 6f 19y
3:00 (3:00) (Class 6) (0-60,60) 4-Y-O+ **£3,238** (£963; £481; £240) **Stalls** Low

Form RPR
0045 1 **Let It Be**[15] [2408] 5-9-4 57........ DavidAllan 8 65
(K G Reveley) *trckd ldrs: hdwy 4f out: rdn 2f out: styd on to ld wl ins last: drvn and jst hld on* **5/1**[2]
0021 2 shd **Compton Eclaire (IRE)**[6] [2684] 6-8-8 52........(v) AndrewMullen(5) 2 60
(B Ellison) *hld up towards rr: gd hdwy on outer 3f out: led 2f out: sn rdn and edgd lft: drvn and hddd wl ins last: rallied and jst hld* **11/4**[1]
6-53 3 3½ **Red Forest (IRE)**[15] [2408] 7-8-12 56........(t) GregFairley(5) 3 59
(J Mackie) *trckd ldr: hdwy to ld over 3f out: rdn and hdd 2f out: sn drvn and one pce appr last* **5/1**[2]
420- 4 nk **Lodgician (IRE)**[25] [5550] 4-8-11 53........ DanielTudhope(3) 12 56
(J J Quinn) *chsd ldrs: hdwy 4f out: rdn along over 2f out: sn drvn and kpt on same pce* **17/2**
0100 5 2 **Celtic Carisma**[22] [2196] 4-9-2 55........ TonyHamilton 4 55
(K G Reveley) *hld up in midfield: hdwy over 4f out: rdn along wl over 2f out: drvn and no imp fr wl over 1f out* **12/1**
-440 6 nk **Transit**[6] [2684] 7-8-11 55........ MarkLawson(5) 5 55
(B Ellison) *hld up: hdwy over 3f out: sn rdn along and no imp fnl 2f* **20/1**
3-00 7 nk **Arctic Cove**[15] [2407] 5-9-5 58........ DarrenWilliams 1 57
(Micky Hammond) *in tch: hdwy 4f out: rdn along over 2f out and no further prog* **33/1**
00-2 8 nk **Redspin (IRE)**[13] [2483] 6-7-13 41 oh1........ SilvestreDeSousa(3) 9 40
(J S Moore) *hld up: hdwy to chse ldrs 1/2-way: rdn along 3f out: sn btn* **8/1**[3]
-000 9 1 **Perfect Punch**[6] [2684] 7-9-0 60........ JamesReveley(7) 7 58
(K G Reveley) *hld up in rr: hdwy on outer 3f out: rdn along 2f out and nvr nr ldrs* **66/1**
0/00 10 nk **Compton Commander**[22] [2196] 8-9-2 60........ PJMcDonald(5) 14 57
(E W Tuer) *nvr bttr than midfield* **20/1**
5-52 11 2½ **Colway Ritz**[2] [2788] 12-8-5 44 ow1........ NeilPollard 10 38
(W Storey) *trckd ldrs: hdwy 4f out: rdn along 3f out: sn wknd* **10/1**
6/00 12 ¾ **Garston Star**[39] [1754] 5-8-13 52........ LPKeniry 13 45
(J S Moore) *led: rdn along 4f out: sn hdd & wknd* **25/1**
030- 13 ¾ **Bargain Hunt (IRE)**[7] [5186] 5-8-3 42........ HayleyTurner 6 34
(W Storey) *midfield: rdn along over 4f out: sn wknd* **25/1**
666/ 14 16 **Alpha Juliet (IRE)**[214] [5196] 5-8-3 42........ PaulQuinn 11 11
(C J Teague) *s.i.s: a rr* **100/1**

3m 2.52s (-2.50) **Going Correction** -0.125s/f (Firm) **14** Ran SP% **121.1**
Speed ratings (Par 101):102,101,99,99,98 98,98,98,97,97 95,95,95,85
CSF £17.68 CT £74.73 TOTE £5.20: £1.90, £2.40, £2.20; EX 15.00.
Owner A Frame **Bred** Sir Eric Parker **Trained** Lingdale, Redcar & Cleveland
■ Stewards' Enquiry : Mark Lawson two-day ban: used whip down the shoulder in forehand position (Jul 5-6)

FOCUS
A very moderate staying race, in which many horses were out of form, maidens or too high in the handicap. That said the form looks straightforward.
Let It Be Official explanation: trainer had no explanation for the improvement in form

2872 32RED.COM H'CAP 1m 2f
3:35 (3:35) (Class 2) (0-100,100) 4-Y-O+ **£11,658** (£3,468; £1,733; £865) **Stalls** Low

Form RPR
0600 1 **Go Tech**[7] [2657] 6-8-4 83 ow1........ DavidAllan 3 91
(T D Easterby) *set stdy pce: qcknd 3f out: rdn and edgd rt wl over 1f out sn drvn and kpt on wl fnl f* **15/8**[1]
6501 2 nk **Isidore Bonheur (IRE)**[11] [2527] 5-8-6 85........ TonyHamilton 4 93
(G A Swinbank) *trckd ldng pair: hdwy 3f out: rdn to chal wl over 1f out and ev chr tl drvn and no ex wl ins last* **11/4**[2]
06-2 3 2½ **Toshi (USA)**[10] [2547] 4-7-12 82 ow1........ AndrewMullen(5) 2 85
(I Semple) *trckd ldng pair: hdwy 3f out: rdn: n.m.r and swtchd lft wl over 1f out: sn one pce* **4/1**[3]
0403 4 1¾ **Instructor**[8] [2627] 5-8-2 81 oh3........ HayleyTurner 5 81
(R A Fahey) *cl up: rdn along 3f out: ev ch tl wknd over 1f out* **4/1**[3]
15-6 5 10 **Im Spartacus**[14] [2453] 4-9-2 100........ MarkLawson(5) 1 81
(D W Barker) *s.i.s: a rr* **12/1**

2m 3.55s (-3.25) **Going Correction** -0.125s/f (Firm) **5** Ran SP% **109.1**
Speed ratings (Par 109):108,107,105,104,96
CSF £7.13 TOTE £2.10: £1.40, £1.70; EX 6.50.
Owner Ryedale Partners No 4 **Bred** A G Nicholson **Trained** Great Habton, N Yorks
■ Stewards' Enquiry : David Allan one-day ban: used whip with excessive frequency (Jul 5)

FOCUS
A decent, if small, handicap run at a modest-early pace and not the most solid, but rated at face value for now.

The Form Book, Raceform Ltd, Compton, RG20 6NL

NOTEBOOK

Go Tech set the race up for himself perfectly from the front, and had just enough in hand to hold off Isidore Bonheur throughout the final furlong. A winner over course and distance at the meeting last year off a 3lb higher mark, it seems sensible to believe that connections will plot a similar path to the one they took with him last season, meaning the next stop will be the John Smiths Cup at York in July. (op 2-1 tchd 9-4 in a place)

Isidore Bonheur(IRE), stepping back up in trip, ran right up to his recent best, but the jury is still out to whether he is effective off a handicap mark in the mid-eighties. (op 5-2 tchd 3-1)

Toshi(USA), who was receiving upwards of 6lb from the front two, had every chance given the way the race was run, but was not good enough on the day. He only has a maiden victory to his name and it might be that he is at his very best on ground with ease in it. (op 7-2)

Instructor was fairly keen early and could not muster a serious challenge when the race took shape. He needs to come down the weights a touch to have an obvious chance. (op 9-2)

Im Spartacus showed very little again but is entitled to need time after the problems he has had. (tchd 11-1)

2873 32RED.COM H'CAP 6f

4:10 (4:10) (Class 5) (0-70,68) 3-Y-O **£3,238** (£963; £481; £240) **Stalls** Centre

Form RPR

3211 **1** **Our Sheila**[15] 2399 3-9-2 **68** MarkLawson(5) 8 73
(B Smart) *cl up: led after 2f: rdn 2f out: drvn and hung rt ins last: kpt on* **9/4**[1]

-012 **2** ½ **Maison Dieu**[25] 2109 3-8-11 **61** DanielTudhope(3) 5 64
(E J Alston) *in tch: effrt and n.m.r 2f out: swtchd rt and rdn to chal 1f out: ev ch whn sltl hmpd ins last: kpt on* **10/3**[2]

52-0 **3** 3½ **Our Mary (IRE)**[12] 2504 3-8-8 **60** AndrewMullen(5) 1 53
(Robert Gray) *a cl up: rdn 2f out: kpt on same pce* **12/1**

050- **4** 2 **Stanley Bay (IRE)**[273] 5465 3-8-11 **58** DavidAllan 4 45
(T D Easterby) *towards rr tl styd on fnl 2f* **22/1**

3-54 **5** nk **Moonstreaker**[19] 2297 3-9-0 **66** GregFairley(5) 3 52
(R M Whitaker) *towards rr tl styd on fnl 2f* **4/1**[3]

0634 **6** 2½ **Drink To Me Only**[19] 2284 3-7-12 **50** EmmettStack(5) 6 29
(J R Weymes) *chsd ldrs: rdn over 2f out: wkng whn hmpd over 1f out* **8/1**

0-35 **7** nk **Optical Seclusion (IRE)**[5] 2701 3-8-10 **57** TonyHamilton 2 35
(T J Etherington) *led 2f. cl up tl rdn along and wknd 2f out* **7/1**

0-00 **8** 8 **Miss Dixie**[22] 2197 3-8-10 **57** NeilPollard 7 11
(Miss J A Camacho) *chsd ldrs: rdn over 2f out: sn wknd* **20/1**

1m 10.11s (-1.59) **Going Correction** -0.20s/f (Firm) 8 Ran SP% **114.3**

Speed ratings (Par 99):102,101,96,94,93 90,89,79

CSF £9.77 CT £71.23 TOTE £2.40: £1.40, £1.70, £2.70; EX 8.00.

Owner Anthony D Gee **Bred** Mrs C R Philipson **Trained** Hambleton, N Yorks

■ Stewards' Enquiry : Daniel Tudhope two-day ban: careless riding (Jul 5-6)

FOCUS

A very modest sprint, as the runner-up had only won a seller and the third's best effort was when beaten in a claimer. However, the form looks sound enough at a low level.

2874 WEDDINGS AT REDCAR RACECOURSE CLAIMING STKS 7f

4:40 (4:40) (Class 5) 3-Y-O+ **£4,533** (£1,348; £674; £336) **Stalls** Centre

Form RPR

2564 **1** **Sawwaah (IRE)**[5] 2696 9-9-0 71 (p) SilvestreDeSousa(3) 8 69+
(D Nicholls) *midfield: swtchd outside and hdwy 1/2-way: led over 2f out: rdn clr over 1f out: styd on on* **3/1**[2]

000- **2** 1¼ **Pay Time**[280] 5299 7-8-1 41 DonnaCaldwell(7) 10 54
(R E Barr) *in tch: hdwy to ld 3f out: sn rdn and hdd over 2f out: kpt on same pce* **66/1**

60-4 **3** nk **The Old Soldier**[5] 2700 8-8-13 51 DavidAllan 7 58
(A Dickman) *s.i.s and bhd: hdwy over 2f out: rdn and styd on ins last: nrst fin* **11/2**

-000 **4** 2 **Inside Story (IRE)**[39] 1757 4-9-1 62 (b[1]) DarrenWilliams 2 55
(M W Easterby) *prom: rdn along over 2f out: sn drvn and one pce* **4/1**[3]

06-0 **5** 1 **Frimley's Matterry**[5] 2700 6-8-11 45 DanielTudhope(3) 9 51
(R E Barr) *bhd: hdwy over 2f out: styd on appr last: nrst fin* **16/1**

3013 **6** 3½ **Art Elegant**[10] 2541 4-9-3 68 TonyHamilton 1 45
(G A Swinbank) *in tch: hdwy to chse ldrs over 2f out: sn rdn and btn* **11/4**[1]

0015 **7** hd **Downland (IRE)**[24] 2141 10-9-0 52 KimTinkler 5 42
(N Tinkler) *keen: hld up in midfield: swtchd outside and hdwy 3f out: rdn 2f out and sn wknd* **9/1**

000 **8** 2½ **Centreofattention**[29] 2001 3-7-9 44 DuranFentiman(5) 12 30
(Mrs A Duffield) *chsd ldrs whn squeezed out sn after s: a towards rr* **25/1**

0-00 **9** 1¾ **Our Serendipity**[39] 1761 3-7-13 43 PaulQuinn 13 25
(K G Reveley) *prom: rdn along 3f out: sn wknd* **33/1**

6504 **10** 5 **Fayrz Please (IRE)**[39] 1763 5-8-9 37 JohnMcAuley(3) 4 16
(M C Chapman) *cl up: rdn along 3f out: wknd 2f out* **66/1**

30-0 **11** 2½ **Eddies Jewel**[19] 2291 6-8-12 41 PaulFitzsimons 11 9
(H Alexander) *keen: chsd ldrs: rdn along over 3f out: sn wknd* **50/1**

26-0 **12** 4 **Olivair (IRE)**[11] 2529 3-8-0 51 ow6 AndrewMullen(5) 6 1
(M E Sowersby) *a rr* **33/1**

00-0 **13** 3½ **Inherit (IRE)**[3] 2758 4-8-7 50 (t) GregFairley(5) 14 —
(B S Rothwell) *led: rdn along 1/2-way: hdd 3f out and sn wknd* **33/1**

00-0 **14** 9 **Ronnie From Donny (IRE)**[39] 1762 6-8-10 35 JohnCavanagh(7) 3 —
(C J Teague) *chsd ldrs: rdn along and lost pl 1/2-way: sn bhd* **80/1**

1m 23.03s (-1.87) **Going Correction** -0.20s/f (Firm)

WFA 3 from 4yo+ 9lb 14 Ran SP% **121.8**

Speed ratings (Par 103):102,100,100,97,96 92,92,89,87,82 79,74,70,60

CSF £210.49 TOTE £3.60: £2.60, £12.10, £1.70; EX 337.10.

Owner Fayzad Thoroughbred Limited **Bred** Shadwell Estate Company Limited **Trained** Sessay, N Yorks

FOCUS

A very ordinary claimer and not a race to be confident about. Sawwaah often runs well in these types of races, but was still a bit below form on adjusted figures.

Frimley's Matterry Official explanation: jockey said gelding hung left last 2f

Fayrz Please(IRE) Official explanation: jockey said gelding was unsuited by the firm ground

2875 ARYM FLOWERS OF REDCAR MAIDEN STKS 6f

5:15 (5:15) (Class 5) 3-Y-O+ **£3,238** (£963; £481; £240) **Stalls** Centre

Form RPR

35-3 **1** **Charles Parnell (IRE)**[17] 2356 3-9-0 74 DarrenWilliams 7 67
(M Dods) *hld up: gd hdwy 2f out: rdn to chal ent last: edgd rt and led last 100 yds* **15/8**[2]

2232 **2** ¾ **Lucksin (IRE)**[19] 2298 3-9-0 75 DavidAllan 3 65
(N Tinkler) *cl up: led over 3f out: rdn wl over 1f out: drvn ent last: hdd and no ex last 100 yds* **5/4**[1]

-335 **3** 5 **Primarily**[36] 1816 4-9-7 62 (p) TonyHamilton 4 52
(A Berry) *cl up: effrt over 2f out: sn rdn and ev ch tl wknd over 1f out* **7/1**

0005 **4** ½ **Diamond Heritage**[12] 2504 4-9-2 45 (b) AndrewMullen(5) 2 50
(S Parr) *cl up: rdn along over 2f out: grad wknd* **25/1**

0004 **5** 1¼ **Khetaab (IRE)**[22] 2195 4-9-4 53 (b[1]) DanielTudhope(3) 6 46
(E J Alston) *dwlt: in tch: hdwy ½-way: rdn 2f out and sn wknd* **5/1**[3]

00/ **6** 8 **Villa Chigi (IRE)**[590] 6619 4-9-2 GregFairley(5) 1 22
(G R Oldroyd) *led: pushed along and hdd over 3f out: sn rdn and wknd* **100/1**

000- **7** 21 **Lady Luisa (IRE)**[292] 4997 4-8-9 40 (bt[1]) AnnStokell(7) 5 —
(Miss A Stokell) *s.i.s: a rr: hung lft and bhd fr 1/2-way* **50/1**

1m 10.63s (-1.07) **Going Correction** -0.20s/f (Firm)

WFA 3 from 4yo 7lb 7 Ran SP% **115.2**

Speed ratings (Par 103):99,98,91,90,89 78,50

CSF £4.66 TOTE £2.80: £1.80, £1.10; EX 3.40.

Owner C A Lynch **Bred** R And Mrs R Hodgins **Trained** Denton, Co Durham

FOCUS

An ordinary maiden won by a horse with a bit of scope and the form looks sound enough with the fourth setting the standard.

2876 BEST DRESSED LADY H'CAP 5f

5:50 (5:50) (Class 6) (0-60,55) 3-Y-O **£2,730** (£806; £403) **Stalls** Centre

Form RPR

060 **1** **Money Mate (IRE)**[40] 1736 3-8-11 **52** JamesO'Reilly(7) 2 58
(J O'Reilly) *prom: hdwy to ld 2f out: rdn over 1f out: drvn ins last and kpt on wl* **11/2**[2]

6-56 **2** nk **Mullady Penelope**[1] 2833 3-9-2 **55** GregFairley(5) 1 59
(Mrs A Duffield) *in tch on outer: hdwy 2f out: rdn to chal ent last and ev ch tl no ex nr fin* **11/2**[2]

00-0 **3** 2 **Malelane (IRE)**[23] 2167 3-8-10 **44** DavidAllan 9 44+
(A Dickman) *hld up: hdwy 2f out: nt clr run and hmpd over 1f out: swtchd lft and rdn ent last: styd on strly* **17/2**[3]

-116 **4** shd **Axis Shield (IRE)**[22] 2197 3-9-0 **53** EmmettStack(5) 7 49
(M C Chapman) *led: pushed along and hdd over 2f out: sn rdn and kpt on same pce appr last* **5/1**[1]

-060 **5** shd **Signor Whippee**[37] 1792 3-8-11 **45** TonyHamilton 3 41
(A Berry) *cl up: led brifely over 2f out: sn hdd: drvn and kpt on same pce* **9/1**

6-06 **6** 1 **Musette (IRE)**[102] 637 3-8-4 **43** AndrewMullen(5) 4 35
(R E Barr) *prom: rdn along and edgd rt over 1f out: sn drvn and one pce* **14/1**

0-60 **7** nk **Networker**[44] 1612 3-8-3 **44** ow4 JamesReveley(7) 10 34
(K G Reveley) *cl up on outer: rdn along 2f out: edgd lft over 1f out and kpt on same pce* **25/1**

3000 **8** 1¾ **Desert Dust**[7] 2644 3-8-11 **45** (p) LPKeniry 6 28
(R M H Cowell) *hld up: hdwy over 2f out: sn rdn: edgd lft and wknd over 1f out* **11/2**[2]

0014 **9** nk **Mister Becks (IRE)**[21] 2247 3-8-13 **50** JohnMcAuley(3) 8 32
(M C Chapman) *prom: rdn along 2f out: sn wknd* **5/1**[1]

-050 **10** shd **Charming Princess**[19] 2284 3-8-11 **48** DanielTudhope(3) 5 30
(J S Wainwright) *squeezed out s: a rr* **12/1**

58.60 secs (-0.10) **Going Correction** -0.20s/f (Firm) 10 Ran SP% **118.2**

Speed ratings (Par 97):92,91,88,88,88 86,85,83,82,82

CSF £36.40 CT £263.66 TOTE £10.80: £2.90, £1.80, £2.50; EX 69.40 Place 6 £25.04, Place 5 £5.33.

Owner A Skelton **Bred** Mrs Anne Marie Burns **Trained** Doncaster, S Yorks

FOCUS

A modest winning time, even for a moderate contest like this and the form is limited, rated around the fourth and fifth.

Charming Princess Official explanation: jockey said filly suffered interference at start

T/Plt: £13.50 to a £1 stake. Pool: £36,202.50. 1,948.00 winning tickets. T/Qpdt: £4.80 to a £1 stake. Pool: £1,964.20. 300.45 winning tickets. JR

2702 WARWICK (L-H)

Saturday, June 24

OFFICIAL GOING: Good to firm (good in places)

Wind: Nil Weather: Fine

2877 PSA PEUGEOT CITROEN APPRENTICE H'CAP 1m 22y

6:45 (6:47) (Class 6) (0-60,58) 3-Y-O **£2,730** (£806; £403) **Stalls** Low

Form RPR

6001 **1** **Emotive**[25] 2101 3-9-7 **58** AshleyHamblett(3) 8 66+
(I A Wood) *hld up in mid-div: hdwy over 2f out: rdn to ld and hung rt fr over 1f out: r.o* **7/2**[1]

0400 **2** 1½ **Crush On You**[21] 2249 3-9-1 **49** RussellKennemore 11 54
(R Hollinshead) *hld up towards rr: rdn and hdwy over 1f out: r.o ins fnl f: nt trble wnr* **12/1**

-003 **3** 3 **Madam Mac (IRE)**[21] 2249 3-8-5 **44** KMay(5) 10 42
(B J Meehan) *chsd ldrs: led 2f out tl over 1f out: one pce* **9/1**[3]

-000 **4** 1 **Under Fire (IRE)**[26] 2069 3-9-0 **48** RobertMiles 7 44
(A W Carroll) *s.i.s: bhd tl hdwy over 1f out: swtchd lft ins fnl f: nt rch ldrs* **33/1**

2003 **5** 2 **Kissi Kissi**[22] 2210 3-9-3 **51** BenSwarbrick 16 42
(M J Attwater) *hld up towards rr: c wd st: rdn and hdwy over 2f out: one pce fnl f* **14/1**

0004 **6** ½ **Legal Call**[9] 2566 3-8-9 **43** (v) LiamJones 9 33
(M Appleby) *led early: chsd ldrs: led over 3f out: rdn and hdd over 2f out: wknd ins fnl f* **16/1**

5500 **7** ½ **Flashing Floozie**[15] 2391 3-8-12 **46** (v[1]) TravisBlock 15 35
(M F Harris) *t.k.h in mid-div: rdn and hdwy over 2f out: wkng whn bmpd over 1f out* **12/1**

6-03 **8** ½ **Royal Agreement**[13] 2479 3-9-6 **54** AdamKirby 6 42
(B G Powell) *sn led: hdd over 3f out: ev ch 2f out: wkng whn edgd lft ins fnl f* **5/1**[2]

00-0 **9** shd **Tuscany Rose**[13] 2480 3-9-5 **53** RichardKingscote 3 40
(W R Muir) *prom: ev ch 2f out: wknd over 1f out* **16/1**

600 **10** 1½ **Bellabelini (IRE)**[12] 2511 3-9-7 **55** RonanKeogh 13 39
(S Kirk) *hld up in mid-div: rdn and no hdwy fnl 2f* **9/1**[3]

6600 **11** hd **Lady Becks (IRE)**[5] 2704 3-8-13 **50** (p) TolleyDean(3) 12 34
(R A Harris) *n.d* **33/1**

0564 **12** ½ **Lewis Lloyd (IRE)**[15] 2415 3-8-10 **49** (b[1]) JamieHamblett(5) 14 31
(I A Wood) *nvr nr ldrs* **14/1**

0063 **13** 2½ **Boucheen**[46] 1576 3-8-4 **45** GaryWales(7) 4 22
(Ms Deborah J Evans) *s.s: sn mid-div: wknd 3f out* **22/1**

0500 **14** 10 **Xpres Boy (IRE)**[36] 1825 3-9-4 **52** MarcHalford 2 6
(S R Bowring) *prom tl wknd wl over 1f out* **14/1**

-000 **15** *2* **Jessica Wigmo**[141] [287] 3-8-7 **48** .... JackDean(7) 5 —
(A W Carroll) *hld up in tch: rdn over 2f out: wknd wl over 1f out* **20/1**

1m 39.68s (0.08) **Going Correction** -0.05s/f (Good) **15** Ran SP% **121.0**
Speed ratings (Par 97):97,95,92,91,89 89,88,88,87,86 86,85,83,73,71
CSF £43.64 CT £354.12 TOTE £4.60: £2.40, £5.10, £3.20; EX 79.10.
Owner Christopher Shankland **Bred** Mrs J Mitchell **Trained** Upper Lambourn, Berks

FOCUS
A poor handicap rated through the placed horses to form.
Royal Agreement Official explanation: jockey said gelding hung badly right

2878 SEE MORE ON RACING UK MAIDEN AUCTION STKS 5f

7:15 (7:17) (Class 5) 2-Y-O £3,238 (£963; £481; £240) **Stalls** Low

Form RPR
22 **1** **Invincible Force (IRE)**[14] [2439] 2-8-9 .... EddieAhern 5 79+
(Ms Deborah J Evans) *w ldr: led on bit jst over 1f out: shkn up ins fnl f: comf* **30/100**[1]
03 **2** *1 3/4* **Hester Brook (IRE)**[7] [2631] 2-8-1 .... DominicFox(3) 2 62+
(J G M O'Shea) *w ldr: rdn and hdd jst over 1f out: nt qckn* **14/1**[3]
0 **3** *3 1/2* **Bonny Scotland (IRE)**[66] [1082] 2-7-13 .... LiamJones(5) 6 49
(Miss V Haigh) *wnt rt s: sn chsng ldrs: rdn over 1f out: one pce* **33/1**
4 *1* **Equal And Approved** 2-8-10 ow1 .... RichardHughes 1 52+
(R Hannon) *played up in stalls: s.s: bhd tl late hdwy: nrst fin* **13/2**[2]
60 **5** *3/4* **Bookiesindex Boy**[18] [2315] 2-8-12 .... RobbieFitzpatrick 7 51+
(J R Jenkins) *carried rt s: sn prom: lost action briefly over 3f out: hung bdly lft fnl 2f: eased whn btn towards fin* **14/1**[3]
6 *1* **Back In The Red (IRE)** 2-8-12 .... AdamKirby(3) 4 50
(M Wellings) *sn outpcd: hung bdly rt jst over 1f out: a in rr* **25/1**

59.80 secs (-0.40) **Going Correction** -0.25s/f (Firm) **6** Ran SP% **110.4**
Speed ratings (Par 93):93,90,84,83,81 80
CSF £5.67 TOTE £1.40: £1.10, £2.40; EX 3.80.
Owner Terry Cummins **Bred** Robert Wilson **Trained** Lydiate, Merseyside

FOCUS
A weak affair rated around time.

NOTEBOOK
Invincible Force(IRE) had less to do this time and made it third time lucky in pretty smooth fashion. (op 2-5 tchd 4-9)
Hester Brook(IRE) produced another solid display but was clearly playing second fiddle in the closing stages. (op 12-1)
Bonny Scotland(IRE), a half-sister to the sprinter No Time, had been quite highly tried when trailing in after a slow start on her Newmarket debut. (op 25-1)
Equal And Approved is quite speedily-bred and connections will be hoping that she comes on for the experience. (op 11-2)
Bookiesindex Boy may well have done himself a mischief when taking a false step after a furlong and a half. Official explanation: jockey said colt hung left (op 12-1)

2879 WBX.COM WORLD BET EXCHANGE H'CAP (PART OF THE WARWICK STAYERS SERIES) 1m 6f 213y

7:45 (7:46) (Class 4) (0-85,85) 4-Y-O+ £6,477 (£1,927; £963; £481) **Stalls** Low

Form RPR
403- **1** **Pseudonym (IRE)**[12] [4573] 4-8-2 **66** oh4 .... FrancisNorton 8 61
(M F Harris) *led early: hld up in mid-div: rdn whn swtchd rt and hdwy 2f out: led ins fnl f: r.o wl: fin 1st, 2½l: disq. (prohibited substance)* **5/1**[3]
6060 **2** *2 1/2* **Hiddensee (USA)**[14] [2437] 4-9-5 **83** ....(b[1]) JoeFanning 6 75
(M Johnston) *sn led: hdd after 1f: a.p: rdn over 2f out: ev ch ins fnl f: nt qckn: fin 2nd, 2½l: awrdd r* **11/4**[1]
6350 **3** *1/2* **Kristensen**[45] [1584] 7-8-6 **70** ....(v) FrankieMcDonald 7 62
(Karen McLintock) *hld up in mid-div: hdwy over 6f out: rdn 3f out: styd on ins fnl f fin 3rd, pl 2nd* **9/2**[2]
2000 **4** *1* **Eastborough (IRE)**[4] [2723] 7-8-8 **72** ow1 .... EddieAhern 4 62
(B G Powell) *hld up and bhd: hdwy 3f out: sn rdn: styd on one pce fnl f fin 4th, plcd 3rd* **11/4**[1]
0044 **5** *2 1/2* **Delta Force**[25] [2099] 7-7-13 **68** oh21 ow2 .... RoryMoore(5) 3 55?
(P A Blockley) *prom: led over 4f out: rdn wl over 1f out: hdd & wknd ins fnl f: fin 5th, plcd 4th* **12/1**
04-0 **6** *18* **Top Trees**[4] [1541] 8-8-2 **66** oh26 .... DavidKinsella 1 30
(W S Kittow) *led after 1f tl over 4f out: wknd 3f out: fin 6th, plcd 5th* **25/1**
000- **7** *19* **Pawn Broker**[62] [5421] 9-9-7 **85** ....(b) GeorgeBaker 5 24
(Miss J R Tooth) *hld up in rr: hdwy over 5f out: wknd 3f out: eased whn no ch fnl f: fin 7th, plcd 6th* **20/1**
501- **8** *18* **Legally Fast (USA)**[44] [5822] 4-8-4 **68** oh7 ow2 .... AdrianTNicholls 2 —
(S C Burrough) *hld up and bhd: rdn 9f out: eased whn no ch fnl 2f* **10/1**

3m 14.73s (-1.17) **Going Correction** -0.05s/f (Good) **8** Ran SP% **113.6**
Speed ratings (Par 105):101,99,99,98,97 87,77,68
CSF £18.89 CT £65.29 TOTE £5.30: £1.60, £1.40, £1.60; EX 23.70.
Owner Mrs D J Brown **Bred** Ballymacoll Stud Farm Ltd **Trained** Edgcote, Northants
■ Stewards' Enquiry : Rory Moore one-day ban: using whip with excessive force (Jul 5)

FOCUS
It may turn out that this staying handicap was won by a progressive sort, but the form looks dubious and is limited by the fifth. Pseudonym subs. disq. (morphine in post-race sample).
Pawn Broker Official explanation: jockey said gelding was unsuited by the good to firm ground
Legally Fast(USA) Official explanation: jockey said gelding had no more to give

2880 PLANET FASHION ETERNAL STKS (LISTED RACE) (FILLIES) 7f 26y

8:15 (8:19) (Class 1) 3-Y-O

£15,898 (£6,025; £3,015; £1,503; £753; £378) **Stalls** Low

Form RPR
-263 **1** **Spinning Queen**[28] [2031] 3-8-11 103 .... MichaelHills 1 96
(B W Hills) *hld up: hdwy and swtchd rt over 1f out: sn led: r.o wl* **10/11**[1]
4435 **2** *3* **Secret Night**[32] [1924] 3-8-11 84 .... RoystonFfrench 7 88
(J A R Toller) *hld up: rdn and hdwy over 1f out: 2nd whn edgd lft ins fnl f: one pce* **22/1**
3130 **3** *1 1/4* **Ooh Aah Camara (IRE)**[16] [2385] 3-8-11 84 .... FrancisNorton 2 85
(T J Pitt) *a.p: rdn over 2f out: one pce fnl f* **20/1**
-400 **4** *hd* **Tara Too (IRE)**[7] [2650] 3-8-11 81 .... JoeFanning 6 84
(D W P Arbuthnot) *hld up in tch: rdn 3f out: one pce fnl f* **25/1**
1440 **5** *nk* **Dame Hester (IRE)**[22] [2205] 3-8-11 79 ....(b[1]) RichardMullen 4 83
(E J O'Neill) *hld up and bhd: late hdwy: nvr able to chal* **25/1**
6314 **6** *hd* **Neardown Beauty (IRE)**[10] [2554] 3-8-11 73 .... AdamKirby 8 83?
(I A Wood) *s.i.s: sn swtchd lft: rdn 2f out: kpt on ins fnl f: nt rch ldrs* **33/1**
015- **7** *hd* **Oceans Apart**[296] [4898] 3-8-11 91 .... KDarley 5 82
(P F I Cole) *w ldr: edgd lft and led briefly over 1f out: wknd wl ins fnl f* **14/1**[3]
1-52 **8** *7* **Bouboulina**[22] [2204] 3-8-11 96 .... RHills 3 63
(E A L Dunlop) *led: rdn and hdd over 1f out: sn wknd* **7/2**[2]
4063 **9** *2* **Gamble In Gold (IRE)**[7] [2651] 3-8-11 85 .... RichardHughes 10 58
(R Hannon) *prom: rdn 2f out: sn wknd: eased fnl f* **14/1**[3]

1m 21.62s (-3.38) **Going Correction** -0.30s/f (Firm) **9** Ran SP% **107.7**
Speed ratings (Par 104):107,103,102,101,101 101,101,93,90
CSF £25.16 TOTE £1.80: £1.10, £4.10, £3.10; EX 35.10.
Owner Marston Stud & Cavendish Investing Ltd **Bred** R A Bonnycastle And Marston Stud **Trained** Lambourn, Berks

FOCUS
This was not the strongest of Listed events although the form looks pretty sound, with the runner-up and sixth close to their marks.

NOTEBOOK
Spinning Queen had the form in the book to win this and did not mind a return to fast ground. (op 11-10 tchd 5-6, 6-5 in places and early 5-4 in places)
Secret Night had plenty on her plate on this return to turf and was making no impression on the winner when shifting left on the closing stages. (op 20-1)
Ooh Aah Camara(IRE) was up in grade and back over a longer trip but did not appear to be beaten for stamina. (tchd 22-1)
Tara Too(IRE) was another to run respectably on a step up from handicap company. (op 20-1)
Dame Hester(IRE) got going too late in the first-time blinkers and perhaps a return to a mile is needed. (op 20-1)
Neardown Beauty(IRE) is another who seems ready for another crack at a mile. (tchd 40-1)
Oceans Apart seemed to get found out by the extra furlong but she may have just been in need of the run. (op 12-1)
Bouboulina folded up tamely after making the running. (op 4-1 tchd 9-2)

2881 WROXALL ABBEY MAIDEN STKS 7f 26y

8:45 (8:46) (Class 5) 3-Y-O+ £3,238 (£963; £481; £240) **Stalls** Low

Form RPR
4-33 **1** **Mahrajaan (USA)**[24] [2143] 3-9-0 79 .... RHills 5 69+
(J H M Gosden) *sn chsng ldr: rdn to ld over 1f out: r.o* **7/4**[2]
-342 **2** *1 1/4* **Pirouetting**[11] [2532] 3-8-9 80 .... MichaelHills 4 60+
(B W Hills) *led: rdn and hdd over 1f out: nt qckn ins fnl f* **1/1**[1]
6-35 **3** *1 1/4* **Cindertrack**[17] [2344] 3-9-0 75 .... EddieAhern 2 62+
(J A Osborne) *a.p: rdn over 1f out: r.o one pce fnl f* **6/1**[3]
4- **4** *3* **Zalzaar (IRE)**[263] [5693] 4-9-6 .... AdamKirby(3) 3 54
(C G Cox) *s.i.s: sn mid-div: rdn 3f out: no real prog fnl 2f* **9/1**
0-0P **5** *2 1/2* **Look Here's May**[53] [1387] 4-8-11 40 .... RussellKennemore(7) 1 42
(R Hollinshead) *t.k.h in mid-div: rdn and hung lft over 2f out: wknd fnl f* **100/1**
-0 **6** *shd* **Weet For Ever (USA)**[34] [1868] 3-9-0 .... RobbieFitzpatrick 7 47
(P A Blockley) *wnt rt s: t.k.h in rr: nvr trbld ldrs* **40/1**
-400 **7** *1/2* **Zantero**[7] [2641] 4-9-9 42 .... FergusSweeney 6 46
(W M Brisbourne) *plld hrd in rr: n.d* **66/1**
0-0 **8** *9* **Stokesies Luck (IRE)**[8] [2605] 3-9-0 .... RichardThomas 8 21
(J L Spearing) *wnt rt s: rdn over 3f out: a bhd* **66/1**

1m 23.98s (-1.02) **Going Correction** -0.30s/f (Firm)
WFA 3 from 4yo 9lb **8** Ran SP% **117.1**
Speed ratings (Par 103):93,91,90,86,83 83,83,72
CSF £3.95 TOTE £2.90: £1.10, £1.10, £2.30; EX 3.20.
Owner Hamdan Al Maktoum **Bred** Farfellow Farms Ltd **Trained** Newmarket, Suffolk

FOCUS
A moderate winning time, 2.38 seconds slower than the preceding Listed race. The form is limited by the proximity of the fifth.
Zantero Official explanation: jockey said gelding ran too free early stages
Stokesies Luck(IRE) Official explanation: jockey said colt was unsuited by the good to firm (firm in places) ground

2882 WEST MIDLANDS RACING CLUB H'CAP 1m 2f 188y

9:15 (9:17) (Class 5) (0-75,72) 3-Y-O £3,238 (£963; £481; £240) **Stalls** Low

Form RPR
50-0 **1** **Fear To Tread (USA)**[60] [1205] 3-9-6 **71** .... EddieAhern 1 78+
(J L Dunlop) *hld up in tch: rdn to ld jst over 1f out: sn hung lft: r.o* **4/1**[2]
-005 **2** *1/2* **Is It Me (USA)**[11] [2518] 3-9-0 **65** .... RobbieFitzpatrick 4 71
(P A Blockley) *led: rdn over 2f out: hdd jst over 1f out: kpt on* **9/1**
-100 **3** *3* **Lucky Lark**[30] [1948] 3-9-7 **72** .... JoeFanning 6 73
(M Johnston) *chsd ldr: rdn 3f out: one pce fnl f* **11/2**[3]
3336 **4** *hd* **Alexian**[11] [2518] 3-9-2 **67** .... FergusSweeney 7 67
(R Hollinshead) *hld up in rr: rdn and hdwy 2f out: one pce fnl f* **4/1**[2]
6535 **5** *hd* **Coda Agency**[53] [1375] 3-8-10 **61** .... KDarley 5 61
(D W P Arbuthnot) *hld up in tch: rdn and one pce fnl 3f* **7/2**[1]
-050 **6** *2 1/2* **Foreign Envoy (IRE)**[14] [2434] 3-8-12 **63** .... MichaelHills 3 58
(B W Hills) *hld up in rr: rdn 4f out: no rspnse* **8/1**

2m 18.25s (-1.15) **Going Correction** -0.05s/f (Good) **6** Ran SP% **98.7**
Speed ratings (Par 99):102,101,99,99,99 97
CSF £28.25 TOTE £5.40: £3.00, £4.60; EX 88.90 Place 6 £16.09, Place 5 £7.09.
Owner Robin F Scully **Bred** Clovelly Farms **Trained** Arundel, W Sussex

FOCUS
A modest little handicap but sound enough form, rated around the runner-up, fourth and fifth.
Fear To Tread(USA) Official explanation: trainer's rep said, regarding the improved form shown, the filly had benefited from the step up in trip and today's firmer ground
T/Plt: £52.20 to a £1 stake. Pool: £36,543.80. 510.50 winning tickets. T/Qpdt: £12.50 to a £1 stake. Pool: £2,227.60. 131.20 winning tickets. KH

2883 - 2889a (Foreign Racing) - See Raceform Interactive

2500 PONTEFRACT (L-H)

Sunday, June 25

OFFICIAL GOING: Good to firm

Wind: Moderate half against Weather: Fine

2890 E B F TOTEPLACEPOT MAIDEN FILLIES' STKS 6f

2:10 (2:10) (Class 5) 2-Y-O £4,533 (£1,348; £674; £336) **Stalls** Low

Form RPR
5 **1** **Precocious Star (IRE)**[80] [892] 2-9-0 .... PaulHanagan 4 76+
(K R Burke) *trckd ldrs: hdwy 2f out: swtchd rt and effrt over 1f out: rdn to ld ins last: styd on* **8/1**
2 *1* **Weekend Fling (USA)** 2-9-0 .... KDarley 5 70
(M Johnston) *led: rdn along and hdd over 1f out: rallied ins last: kpt on wl* **11/2**[3]
3 *1/2* **Blithe** 2-9-0 .... NickyMackay 9 72+
(W J Haggas) *carried bdly rt s: sn rr green and bhd tl hdwy wl over 1f out: styd on strly ins last* **14/1**
3 **4** *hd* **Malaaq**[25] [2144] 2-9-0 .... RHills 8 68
(M A Jarvis) *carried rt s: sn trcking ldrs: hdwy to ld over 1f out: sn rdn and edgd lft: hdd and drvn ins last: no ex* **5/6**[1]

440 **5** *1* **Onenightinlisbon (IRE)**[25] 2125 2-8-11 .... DanielTudhope(3) 2 67+
(P T Midgley) *trckd ldrs on inner: effrt whn n.m.r and hmpd 2f out: swtchd rt and rdn over 1f out: kpt on* **16/1**
263 **6** *1 ½* **Silca Soprano**[12] 2523 2-9-0 .... TonyCulhane 3 60
(M R Channon) *trckd ldrs: hdwy to chse ldng pair over 2f out: sn rdn and edgd lft: drvn and wknd appr last* **9/2**[2]
06 **7** *2* **Alavana (IRE)**[17] 2375 2-8-9 .... MarkLawson(5) 7 54
(D W Barker) *wnt rt s: sn cl up: rdn along 2f out: grad wknd* **100/1**
000 **8** *5* **Soundasapound**[26] 2106 2-8-11 .... PatrickMathers(3) 6 39
(I W McInnes) *in tch: rdn along 1/2-way: sn outpcd* **100/1**
9 *32* **Littlemadgebob** 2-9-0 .... TomEaves 1 —
(J R Norton) *a outpcd and bhd fr 1/2-way* **50/1**

1m 18.01s (0.61) **Going Correction** 0.0s/f (Good) 9 Ran SP% **115.7**
Speed ratings (Par 90):95,93,93,92,91 89,86,80,37
CSF £51.39 TOTE £9.50: £2.20, £2.10, £3.30; EX 45.80.
Owner Market Avenue Racing Club Ltd **Bred** Tom Twomey **Trained** Middleham Moor, N Yorks

FOCUS
A fair maiden won by subsequent Group One winner Nannina 12 months earlier. An improved effort by the winner and the race has been rated positively.

NOTEBOOK
Precocious Star(IRE), troubled with sore shins after her debut at Leicester in April, was edgy and tended to swish her tail in the paddock. She stayed on in willing fashion to master the runner-up inside the last and should improve again. (tchd 9-1)
Weekend Fling(USA), a March foal, is on the leg and narrow. She certainly knew her job and stuck on in grim fashion when headed. She looks a ready-made winner. (op 5-1)
Blithe ♦, a February born daughter of Pivotal, carried the same colours as Nannina a year ago. Carried almost off the track at the start, she made ground hand over fist and would have prevailed with a bit further to go. She looks a big improver and must be followed.
Malaaq, a good walker, really took the eye in the paddock. Making her effort on the outer, she edged left in front and looked to have no excuse. Official explanation: jockey said, regarding appearing drop hands shortly before the line, filly became unbalanced when passed by a rival in closing stages and changed her legs several times (op 10-11 tchd Evens in places and 4-5)
Onenightinlisbon(IRE), a short-backed filly, was left short of room turning in. She was staying on at the finish and clearly relished the step up to six furlongs.
Silca Soprano lacks size and scope and seems not to be progressing. (op 5-1)

2891 TOTESPORT 0800 221 221 FILLIES' H'CAP 1m 4y
2:40 (2:40) (Class 5) (0-70,71) 3-Y-0+ **£3,886** (£1,156; £577; £288) **Stalls** Low

Form RPR
4604 **1** **Burton Ash**[36] 1852 4-9-5 **54** .... KDarley 2 64
(J G Given) *trckd ldr: effrt 2f out: sn rdn: drvn to chal ins last: styd on wl to ld nr line* **7/2**[1]
-440 **2** *shd* **Westcourt Dream**[16] 2407 6-9-1 **50** .... DaleGibson 1 60
(M W Easterby) *led: rdn along 2f out: drvn ent last: hdd and no ex nr line* **4/1**[2]
-001 **3** *1* **Dancing Guest (IRE)**[11] 2554 3-9-12 **71** .... NCallan 5 77+
(G G Margarson) *keen: hld up in tch: hdwy 2f out: rdn over 1f out: styd on ins last: nrst fin* **11/2**
6120 **4** *1* **Keisha Kayleigh (IRE)**[12] 2518 3-9-1 **60** .... TomEaves 4 64
(B Ellison) *chsd ldrs: rdn along 2f out: drvn and kpt on same pce fnl f* **5/1**[3]
0-50 **5** *2* **Rockburst**[5] 2737 4-9-9 **63** .... AndrewElliott(5) 7 64
(K R Burke) *chsd ldrs: rdn along over 2f out: sn no imp* **16/1**
2100 **6** *1* **Wanna Shout**[16] 2414 8-9-1 **50** .... TonyCulhane 6 49
(R Dickin) *hld up: a rr* **12/1**
-000 **7** *1* **Ellens Princess (IRE)**[8] 2641 4-9-1 **53** .... DNolan(3) 8 49
(J S Wainwright) *in tch: hdwy to chse ldrs 3f out: sn rdn and wknd* **16/1**
2300 **8** *1* **Royal Pardon**[11] 2544 4-9-4 **53** ....(p) JohnFortune 9 47
(R C Guest) *a towards rr* **18/1**
0-00 **9** *1 ½* **Typhoon Ginger (IRE)**[9] 2627 11-9-10 **59** .... HayleyTurner 3 50
(G Woodward) *hld up: hdwy on inner 3f out: rdn to chse ldrs wl over 1f out sn wknd* **6/1**

1m 46.29s (-1.41) **Going Correction** 0.0s/f (Good)
WFA 3 from 4yo+ 10lb 9 Ran SP% **113.3**
Speed ratings (Par 100):97,96,95,94,92 91,90,89,88
CSF £17.09 CT £74.19 TOTE £4.30: £1.70, £1.70, £1.60; EX 17.40.
Owner Mrs Susan M Lee **Bred** Mrs S M Lee **Trained** Willoughton, Lincs

FOCUS
A modest handicap run at a strong pace and the form looks sound rated around the next three outside the places and should prove reliable.

2892 TOTEPOOL FILLIES' STKS (HERITAGE H'CAP) 1m 2f 6y
3:10 (3:10) (Class 2) 3-Y-0+
£28,044 (£8,397; £4,198; £2,101; £1,048; £526) **Stalls** Low

Form RPR
0-10 **1** **Mistress Twister**[9] 2627 5-8-4 **70** .... PaulFessey 3 78
(T D Barron) *hld up: hdwy over 2f out: rdn to ld ins last: drvn and hld on wl* **5/1**[3]
0542 **2** *nk* **Gaelic Princess**[5] 2735 6-8-11 **77** .... FergusSweeney 6 84
(A G Newcombe) *hld up in rr: hdwy 2f out: swtchd lft and rdn ent last: styd on strly: jst hld* **15/2**
1-15 **3** *1 ¼* **Miss Provvidence (IRE)**[39] 1775 4-9-10 **90** .... NCallan 2 95
(W R Swinburn) *led: rdn along and edgd rt over 1f out: drvn and hdd jst ins last: kpt on same pce* **2/1**[1]
5241 **4** *1 ½* **Flying Clarets (IRE)**[7] 2679 3-8-0 **78** 6ex .... PaulHanagan 4 80
(R A Fahey) *cl up: chal 2f out: sn rdn: hmpd and hit in face w opponents whip over 1f out: wknd* **9/4**[2]
1-62 **5** *hd* **Noora (IRE)**[15] 2457 5-8-9 **78** ....(v) AdamKirby(3) 5 80
(C G Cox) *trckd ldng pair: rdn along wl over 1f out: wknd ent last* **7/1**
0-62 **6** *1* **Danehill Dazzler (IRE)**[27] 2071 4-8-12 **78** .... ChrisCatlin 1 78
(Ian Williams) *trckd ldrs: rdn along wl over 1f out: sn drvn and wknd 1f out* **16/1**

2m 12.1s (-1.98) **Going Correction** 0.0s/f (Good)
WFA 3 from 4yo+ 12lb 6 Ran SP% **110.9**
Speed ratings (Par 96):107,106,105,104,104 103
CSF £38.84 TOTE £7.70: £3.40, £3.40; EX 42.00.
Owner Dave Scott **Bred** Mrs F A Veasey **Trained** Maunby, N Yorks

FOCUS
A poor turn-out for a £45,000 Heritage Fillies' Handicap on the back of Royal Ascot. The pace was very steady with no one wanting to go on and overall the form does not look strong, although the winner, second and fourth were close to form.

NOTEBOOK
Mistress Twister, just 2lb higher than Hamilton, showed the right sort of spirit to land this valuable prize. (tchd 11-2)
Gaelic Princess, waited with in a tactical affair, had to switch to find room but in the end just missed out. (tchd 8-1)
Miss Provvidence(IRE), winner of four of her last six starts, was the reluctant leader. This trip looks her bare minimum now and she is surely better than she showed on the day. (op 9-4)
Flying Clarets(IRE), keen due to the lack of pace, was making very hard work of it when struck across the face by a rival rider's whip. (tchd 5-2)
Noora(IRE), 3lb higher, has a poor strike rate on turf. (op 11-2)
Danehill Dazzler(IRE) was only beaten about four lengths in the end but it was only a two-furlong dash and this probably flattters her. (op 14-1)

2893 TOTESPORT.COM PONTEFRACT CASTLE STKS (LISTED RACE) 1m 4f 8y
3:40 (3:40) (Class 1) 4-Y-0+ **£19,631** (£7,472; £3,741; £1,869) **Stalls** Low

Form RPR
12 **1** **Alfie Flits**[18] 2358 4-8-12 107 .... DeanMcKeown 3 113+
(G A Swinbank) *trckd ldng pair: hdwy 3f out: led over 1f out and sn clr* **5/6**[1]
3-25 **2** *2 ½* **Camrose**[15] 2430 5-8-12 99 ....(b) KDarley 5 105
(J L Dunlop) *set stdy pce: qcknd 1/2-way: rdn along 2f out: hdd over 1f out and kpt on same pce* **8/1**
630- **3** *¾* **Lost Soldier Three (IRE)**[274] 5458 5-8-12 105 .... NickyMackay 1 104
(L M Cumani) *trckd ldr: effrt 3f out: sn rdn along and one pce fnl 2f* **3/1**[2]
50-4 **4** *23* **Astrocharm (IRE)**[15] 2453 7-8-7 99 .... NCallan 2 75+
(M H Tompkins) *hld up: a rr* **5/1**[3]

2m 45.15s (4.85) **Going Correction** 0.0s/f (Good) 4 Ran SP% **107.3**
Speed ratings (Par 111):83,81,80,65
CSF £7.48 TOTE £1.70; EX 6.30.
Owner Dom Flit **Bred** Shadwell Estate Company Limited **Trained** Melsonby, N Yorks

FOCUS
A tactical affair resulting in a pedestrian winning time for a Listed race, 6.2 seconds slower than the later three-year-old maiden. The runner-up is the best guide to the form.

NOTEBOOK
Alfie Flits, turned out in tip-top condition, has a powerful, long stride. He made his effort three wide turning in but the further they went the further he drew clear. It was another step up the ladder and he can climb a fair bit higher yet. (tchd 10-11 and 4-5 in places)
Camrose, a lot cooler and much more settled beforehand, had 8lb to find with the winner on official figures. He wound up the gallop from the front in the final five furlongs but in the end the winner was simply too good. (op 13-2)
Lost Soldier Three(IRE) looked in good trim on his return but he is essentially a stayer and could have done with a much stronger gallop. He will be back. (op 7-2)
Astrocharm(IRE), a close third in this a year ago, ran poorly this time and never looked like taking a hand. Official explanation: trainer said mare was found to be in season

2894 TOTEEXACTA PONTEFRACT CUP (H'CAP) 2m 1f 216y
4:10 (4:10) (Class 4) (0-85,80) 4-Y-0+ **£6,477** (£1,927; £963; £481) **Stalls** Low

Form RPR
/5-3 **1** **Monolith**[38] 1808 8-9-10 **80** .... PaulHanagan 5 89
(L Lungo) *hld up: hdwy 6f out: rdn along to chse clr ldng pair 3f out: drvn ent last: styd on wl to ld last 50 yds* **9/2**[2]
0-01 **2** *½* **Our Monogram**[22] 2219 10-8-11 **70** .... NelsonDeSouza(3) 3 78
(R M Beckett) *led: pushed along 1/2-way: rdn clr 3f out: drvn 2f out: hdd and no ex last 50 yds* **11/2**[3]
6660 **3** *4* **John Forbes**[27] 2078 4-8-13 **70** .... TomEaves 7 74
(B Ellison) *hld up and bhd: hdwy 4f out: rdn along 2f out: styd on appr last: nrst fin* **16/1**
0304 **4** *3 ½* **Openide**[13] 2501 5-8-6 **65** .... EdwardCreighton(3) 6 65
(B W Duke) *chsd ldr: rdn along over 4f out: drvn over 2f out and sn wknd* **11/1**
-121 **5** *11* **Kayf Aramis**[38] 1808 4-8-8 **65** .... PaulQuinn 2 53
(J L Spearing) *hld up in rr: effrt and sme hdwy 3f out: sn rdn along and nvr a factor* **3/1**[1]
0-23 **6** *4* **Overstrand (IRE)**[9] 2625 7-8-4 **65** .... AndrewMullen(5) 1 49
(Robert Gray) *hld up: effrt and hdwy 4f out: rdn along wl over 2f out: sn btn* **7/1**
3-03 **7** *30* **Paradise Flight (IRE)**[18] 2365 5-8-9 **65** ....(b) NCallan 4 16
(K A Ryan) *hld up: hdwy over 4f out: rdn along over 2f out and sn wknd: eased fnl f* **3/1**[1]

3m 59.93s (-3.07) **Going Correction** 0.0s/f (Good)
WFA 4 from 5yo+ 1lb 7 Ran SP% **110.3**
Speed ratings (Par 105):106,105,104,102,97 95,82
CSF £26.92 TOTE £5.40: £3.30, £2.30; EX 21.10.
Owner Elite Racing Club **Bred** Juddmonte Farms **Trained** Carrutherstown, D'fries & G'way

FOCUS
An end-to-end gallop with the game runner-up returning a personal best at the age of ten. The form is rated at face value.
Kayf Aramis Official explanation: jockey said gelding had no more to give
Paradise Flight(IRE) Official explanation: jockey said mare had no more to give

2895 TOTECOURSE TO COURSE MAIDEN STKS 1m 4f 8y
4:40 (4:42) (Class 5) 3-Y-0 **£4,533** (£1,348; £674; £336) **Stalls** Low

Form RPR
2-2 **1** **Fyvie**[73] 1006 3-8-12 .... DO'Donohoe 7 77
(E A L Dunlop) *trckd ldr: led wl over 2f out: sn rdn clr: drvn and kpt on fnl f* **9/4**[1]
2 *2 ½* **Yemen Desert (IRE)** 3-8-12 .... KDarley 2 73+
(M Johnston) *towards rr: hdwy 1/2-way: rdn along 3f out: hdwy to chse wnr ins last: sn drvn and kpt on* **7/2**[2]
0 **3** *1* **Grave Matters (USA)**[60] 1240 3-9-3 .... RoystonFfrench 4 76
(M Johnston) *chsd ldrs: rdn along 3f out: drvn to chse wnr 2f out: sn one pce* **12/1**
5 **4** *10* **Anasena**[26] 2111 3-8-12 .... PaulHanagan 6 55
(G G Margarson) *hld up towards rr: hdwy over 3f out: sn rdn and nvr nr ldrs* **20/1**
0-4 **5** *5* **Artistic Lady**[21] 2261 3-8-12 .... NCallan 5 47
(M A Jarvis) *prom: rdn along 4f out: wknd 3f out* **5/1**
45 **6** *2* **Artist's Muse (USA)**[20] 2292 3-8-12 .... RichardHughes 8 44
(Mrs A J Perrett) *led: rdn along over 3f out: hdd wl over 2f out: sn wknd* **4/1**[3]
0450 **7** *3 ½* **Mighty Kitchener (USA)**[22] 2246 3-9-3 60 .... TonyCulhane 10 44
(P Howling) *nvr a factor* **25/1**
0-0 **8** *17* **Springwood Blues (IRE)**[16] 2412 3-8-12 .... ChrisCatlin 1 11
(H Alexander) *a rr* **100/1**
30 **9** *37* **Dawn Spirit**[37] 1827 3-8-12 .... PhillipMakin 9 —
(J R Weymes) *chsd ldrs: rdn along over 4f out: sn wknd* **33/1**
0 **10** *½* **Diamondbanker**[22] 2244 3-9-3 .... TomEaves 3 —
(Jedd O'Keeffe) *a rr* **66/1**

2m 38.95s (-1.35) **Going Correction** 0.0s/f (Good) 10 Ran SP% **111.4**
Speed ratings (Par 99):104,102,101,95,91 90,88,76,52,51
CSF £9.03 TOTE £2.90: £1.20, £1.60, £3.10; EX 11.40.

Owner Gainsborough Stud **Bred** Gainsborough Stud Management Ltd **Trained** Newmarket, Suffolk

FOCUS

A fair winning time for a race like this, 6.2 seconds quicker than the immediately preceding slowly-run Listed event. The first three finished a long way ahead and it was probably a fair maiden.

2896 TOTESPORTCASINO.COM H'CAP 6f

5:10 (5:11) (Class 5) (0-75,74) 3-Y-O **£4,533** (£1,348; £674; £336) **Stalls** Low

Form RPR

0601 **1** **Electric Warrior (IRE)**[15] 2441 3-9-2 **69**........................ PaulHanagan 13 79+
(K R Burke) *in tch: hdwy on inner 2f out: swtchd rt and rdn to ld ins last: drvn out* **9/2**[2]

6322 **2** 1 ¼ **Mr Cellophane**[19] 2316 3-8-9 **62**.. KDarley 7 68
(J R Jenkins) *trckd ldrs: hdwy 2f out and sn rdn:drvn ent last and kpt on same pce* **9/2**[2]

0-46 **3** shd **Imperial Gain (USA)**[18] 2353 3-9-3 **70**..................................(p) NCallan 5 76
(W R Swinburn) *prom: effrt 2f out: sn rdn along and kpt on same pce ins last* **5/1**[3]

5106 **4** nk **Smile For Us**[22] 2247 3-8-10 **68**..................................(b) JerryO'Dwyer(5) 2 73
(C Drew) *led to 1/2-way: cl up tl rdn and one pce fnl 2f* **22/1**

05-0 **5** ½ **Pitbull**[15] 2441 3-8-3 **61**.. AndrewElliott(5) 8 65
(Mrs G S Rees) *chsd ldrs on outer: rdn along 2f out: drvn and kpt on same pce appr last* **12/1**

5300 **6** 2 **Josarty**[16] 2399 3-8-2 **55**.. ChrisCatlin 12 53
(J J Quinn) *bhd: hdwy 2f out: sn rdn and kpt on wl fnl f: nrst fin* **66/1**

-321 **7** ½ **Bel Cantor**[30] 2001 3-9-2 **74**.. RichardKingscote(5) 4 70
(W J H Ratcliffe) *cl up: led 1/2-way: rdn clr wl over 1f out: drvn and hdd ins last: wknd* **13/2**

-000 **8** 1 ½ **Ochre Bay**[18] 2353 3-9-4 **71**.. GrahamGibbons 15 63
(R Hollinshead) *s.i.s and bhd: hdwy 2f out: styd on ins last: nrst fin* **25/1**

5351 **9** ¾ **Boy Dancer (IRE)**[20] 2284 3-8-7 **60**........................... RichardHughes 11 49
(D W Barker) *towards rr: rdn along 1/2-way: nvr nr ldrs* **4/1**[1]

3000 **10** hd **Cape Of Storms**[9] 2602 3-8-13 **66**................................... TonyCulhane 14 55
(M R Channon) *chsd ldrs on outer: rdn along over 2f out: grad wknd* **25/1**

6-50 **11** 2 **English Archer**[26] 2109 3-8-9 **62** ow3................................ PhillipMakin 9 45
(J R Weymes) *a rr* **66/1**

5340 **12** ¾ **Quadrophenia**[20] 2284 3-8-4 **57**....................................... DaleGibson 10 37
(J G Given) *in tch: rdn along over 2f out: sn wknd* **25/1**

4-40 **13** 3 **Bond Angel Eyes**[16] 2399 3-8-9 **62**..................................... TomEaves 1 33
(G R Oldroyd) *a towards rr* **33/1**

6 **14** 2 ½ **Petross**[24] 2163 3-8-10 **63**... DeanMcKeown 3 27
(R M Whitaker) *chsd ldrs on inner: rdn along over 2f out: sn wknd* **40/1**

-660 **15** 6 **Immaculate Red**[37] 1825 3-8-5 **58**................................ RoystonFfrench 6 4
(R Bastiman) *a towards rr* **50/1**

1m 17.11s (-0.29) **Going Correction** 0.0s/f (Good) **15** Ran SP% **120.3**

Speed ratings (Par 99):101,99,99,98,98 95,94,92,91,91 88,87,83,80,72

CSF £22.19 CT £108.71 TOTE £6.10: £2.70, £1.60, £2.70; EX 30.60 Place 6 £393.96, Place 5 £102.08.

Owner Market Avenue Racing Club Ltd **Bred** Limestone Stud **Trained** Middleham Moor, N Yorks

FOCUS

A strong gallop and the form looks sound with those in the frame behind the winner to form.

Bel Cantor Official explanation: jockey said colt ran too freely

Immaculate Red Official explanation: jockey said gelding was hampered when jumping out of stalls

T/Plt: £466.50 to a £1 stake. Pool: £44,542.25. 69.70 winning tickets. T/Qpdt: £93.30 to a £1 stake. Pool: £3,519.20. 27.90 winning tickets. JR

2877 WARWICK (L-H)

Sunday, June 25

OFFICIAL GOING: Firm (good to firm in places)

Wind: Nil Weather: Cloudy with sunny spells

2897 HAROLD AND PETER CLARKE 60TH BIRTHDAY H'CAP 5f

2:30 (2:30) (Class 5) (0-70,68) 3-Y-O+ **£3,238** (£963; £481; £240) **Stalls** Low

Form RPR

0-00 **1** **Parkside Pursuit**[15] 2444 8-9-5 **59**.................................. JimCrowley 16 72
(J M Bradley) *hld up: hdwy over 1f out: hung lft and r.o to ld wl ins fnl f* **20/1**

0013 **2** 1 **Coconut Moon**[12] 2521 4-9-12 **66**................................... FrancisNorton 2 76
(E J Alston) *led: rdn and hdd wl ins fnl f* **5/2**[1]

0000 **3** 1 ¼ **Ruby's Dream**[39] 1774 4-8-10 **50**................................(p) JoeFanning 4 55
(J M Bradley) *s.i.s: sn prom: rdn over 1f out: r.o* **20/1**

2132 **4** nk **Hello Roberto**[14] 2484 5-9-7 **68**................................(p) TolleyDean(7) 1 72
(R A Harris) *chsd ldr: rdn over 1f out: unable qckn ins fnl f* **7/2**[2]

0000 **5** shd **Law Maker**[12] 2521 6-9-8 **62**...(v) LPKeniry 8 66
(A Bailey) *chsd ldrs: n.m.r and outpcd over 1f out: styd on towards fin* **14/1**

5053 **6** nk **Cosmic Destiny (IRE)**[10] 2571 4-9-3 **57**........................ DaneO'Neill 13 60
(E F Vaughan) *hld up in tch: rdn and edgd lft fr over 1f out: styd on same pce* **7/1**[3]

0500 **7** ½ **Chatshow (USA)**[19] 2331 5-9-6 **60**.................................... ShaneKelly 10 61
(G F Bridgwater) *hld up: nt clr run fr over 1f out: nvr able to chal* **14/1**

6360 **8** nk **Safranine (IRE)**[15] 2462 9-8-3 **50**............................(p) AnnStokell(7) 11 50
(Miss A Stokell) *s.i.s: hdwy over 1f out: no imp ins fnl f* **40/1**

0-00 **9** 1 ¼ **Grand Parrot**[27] 2080 3-8-6 **52**.................................... AdrianMcCarthy 7 47
(W De Best-Turner) *chsd ldrs: rdn over 1f out: wknd ins fnl f* **33/1**

50-5 **10** 1 ¾ **Convince (USA)**[14] 2484 5-9-13 **67**................................... RyanMoore 5 56
(J M Bradley) *mid-div: rdn 1/2-way: wknd fnl f* **7/2**[2]

2315 **11** 5 **Katie Killane**[33] 1909 4-8-9 **49** oh4..............................(v) MickyFenton 17 20
(M Wellings) *wnt rt s: outpcd* **20/1**

59.40 secs (-0.80) **Going Correction** -0.075s/f (Good)

WFA 3 from 4yo+ 6lb **11** Ran SP% **118.5**

Speed ratings (Par 103):103,101,99,98,98 98,97,97,95,92 84

CSF £66.71 CT £1075.53 TOTE £24.20: £6.20, £1.70, £4.90; EX 195.20.

Owner J M Bradley **Bred** J K Keegan **Trained** Sedbury, Gloucs

FOCUS

A typically competitive sprint handicap run at a good pace with the fourth the best guide to the level.

Coconut Moon Official explanation: jockey said saddle slipped

Chatshow(USA) Official explanation: jockey said gelding was denied a clear run

2898 SEE MORE ON RACING UK H'CAP 6f 21y

3:00 (3:02) (Class 5) (0-75,73) 3-Y-O+ **£3,238** (£963; £481; £240) **Stalls** Low

Form RPR

1251 **1** **Pippa's Dancer (IRE)**[8] 2637 4-10-0 **73**........................ RichardMullen 7 83
(W R Muir) *chsd ldr 5f out: rdn to ld 1f out: jst hld on* **4/1**[3]

0460 **2** hd **Pawan (IRE)**[9] 2618 6-9-4 **70**...(b) AnnStokell(7) 8 79
(Miss A Stokell) *s.i.s: hld up: hdwy over 1f out: edgd lft: r.o* **9/1**

0230 **3** nk **Summer Recluse (USA)**[10] 2590 7-9-8 **67**........................(t) RyanMoore 3 75
(J M Bradley) *s.i.s: hld up: hdwy over 1f out: r.o u.p* **7/2**[2]

-003 **4** ¾ **Flying Edge (IRE)**[13] 2504 6-9-6 **65**................................ FrancisNorton 6 71
(E J Alston) *led: rdn and hdd 1f out: unable qckn ins fnl f* **4/1**[3]

3550 **5** 2 ½ **Cayman Breeze**[10] 2567 6-8-10 **55**.................................... TedDurcan 5 54
(J M Bradley) *prom: rdn over 1f out: wknd ins fnl f* **7/1**

0005 **6** nk **Cree**[10] 2567 4-8-11 **56**.. JamieSpencer 1 54
(W R Muir) *hld up in tch: plld hrd: rdn over 1f out: edgd lft and wknd ins fnl f* **3/1**[1]

-050 **7** 5 **Inca Soldier (FR)**[26] 2109 3-8-8 **60**.................................... NeilPollard 2 41
(R C Guest) *s.s: outpcd* **33/1**

0-00 **8** 4 **Beau Jazz**[26] 2112 5-8-9 **54** oh13................................ AdrianMcCarthy 4 25
(W De Best-Turner) *chsd ldrs over 4f* **66/1**

1m 11.04s (-1.06) **Going Correction** -0.15s/f (Firm)

WFA 3 from 4yo+ 7lb **8** Ran SP% **114.2**

Speed ratings (Par 103):101,100,100,99,96 95,88,83

CSF £39.11 CT £137.34 TOTE £4.90: £1.70, £2.00, £1.60; EX 24.20.

Owner Perspicacious Punters Racing Club **Bred** Clody Norton And Mrs Con Collins **Trained** Lambourn, Berks

FOCUS

A tight little handicap with four horses separated by around a length at the line. The form is ordinary but straightforward, rated around the third and fourth to form.

Beau Jazz Official explanation: jockey said gelding finished lame behind

2899 RACING UK MAIDEN STKS 7f 26y

3:30 (3:32) (Class 5) 2-Y-O **£3,238** (£963; £481; £240) **Stalls** Low

Form RPR

1 **Monachello (USA)** 2-9-3 .... RyanMoore 5 75+
(Mrs A J Perrett) *sn pushed along and prom: rdn and hung lft fr over 1f out: led ins fnl f: r.o* **9/1**

2 1 ¼ **Spanish Hidalgo (IRE)** 2-9-3 .... IanMongan 6 72+
(J L Dunlop) *sn outpcd: hdwy over 1f out: nt clr run ins fnl f: r.o* **11/1**

3 nk **Hurlingham** 2-9-3 .... JoeFanning 3 71+
(M Johnston) *chsd ldr over 4f out: rdn to ld over 1f out: sn edgd lft: hdd ins fnl f: hung rt towards fin* **2/1**[1]

664 **4** 5 **Generist**[10] 2588 2-8-12 .... RobbieFitzpatrick 7 54
(M J Attwater) *led over 5f: wknd ins fnl f* **33/1**

6 **5** 2 **Zeeuw (IRE)**[31] 1959 2-9-3 .... DarryllHolland 4 54
(D J Coakley) *hld up in tch: racd keenly: nt clr run over 4f out: wknd over 1f out* **7/2**[2]

020 **6** 1 **Colditz (IRE)**[9] 2610 2-9-3 .... TedDurcan 8 51
(M R Channon) *sn outpcd* **7/2**[2]

7 2 ½ **Miss Silver Spurs** 2-8-12 .... J-PGuillambert 2 40
(M D I Usher) *dwlt: outpcd* **25/1**

30 **8** 3 **Daring You**[13] 2506 2-9-3 .... JamieSpencer 1 37
(P F I Cole) *chsd ldr over 2f: wknd 2f out* **7/1**[3]

1m 24.93s (-0.07) **Going Correction** -0.15s/f (Firm) **8** Ran SP% **115.4**

Speed ratings (Par 93):94,92,92,86,84 83,80,76

CSF £101.58 TOTE £11.00: £3.30, £3.00, £1.30; EX 50.60.

Owner Mark Tracey **Bred** Calumet Farm **Trained** Pulborough, W Sussex

FOCUS

A decent juvenile event in which the front three drew clear with the fourth to form.

NOTEBOOK

Monachello(USA), whose dam was a high-class US sprinter, does have stamina in his pedigree and he overcame distinct greeness to make a winning debut and provide his trainer with her second juvenile winner of the season. He hung to his left having come through to take it up, but was always doing enough under Moore and won a shade comfortably. He holds a precautionary entry in next year's Derby, but any future success is likely to come at handicap level and it would not surprise to see him go on to a conditions race following this. (op 8-1)

Spanish Hidalgo(IRE), like many in this ownership bred to come into his own over middle-distances, comes from a stable not normally associated with first time up winners, so the fact he was able to show so much bodes well for his future. Having been outpaced early he came with a strong run in the straight and would have pressed the winner hard had he not been halted in him run. He can pick up a maiden on this evidence. (op 8-1)

Hurlingham ◆, representing a re-invigorated Johnston team, is going to require further in time and he was ultimately done for a turn of speed having shown up well early. Like so many debutants from his stable, greeness was also a major contributor in his defeat - jumping the path and hanging - and he should have learned a good deal from this. A maiden should be his for the taking. (op 7-4 tchd 9-4)

Generist showed up well for a long way and is going to find life easier in low-grade nurseries.

Zeeuw(IRE), a never-nearer sixth on his debut at Lingfield back in May, failed to last out having raced keenly and is probably best off back at six furlongs for the time being. He will soon be qualified for nurseries. Official explanation: jockey said colt ran too free (op 5-1)

Colditz(IRE) is not progressing and the sooner nurseries arrive the better.

Daring You Official explanation: jockey said colt hung right

2900 WENHAM MAJOR EBENEZER CUP (H'CAP) 1m 22y

4:00 (4:03) (Class 4) (0-85,83) 4-Y-O+ **£6,477** (£1,927; £963; £481) **Stalls** Low

Form RPR

-620 **1** **Pintle**[15] 2440 6-9-3 **79**.. FrancisNorton 7 90
(J L Spearing) *mde all: rdn over 1f out: styd on* **13/2**[3]

0114 **2** 1 ¼ **Night Storm**[1] 2865 5-8-11 **73**.. RyanMoore 5 81
(S Dow) *s.i.s: hld up: hdwy over 2f out: rdn and hung lft fr over 1f out: ev ch ins fnl f: nt qckn* **11/4**[2]

0-64 **3** 2 ½ **Yo Pedro (IRE)**[13] 2508 4-9-2 **78**...................................... JamieSpencer 1 80
(J R Fanshawe) *hld up: hdwy 1/2-way: rdn over 2f out: hung lft over 1f out: styd on same pce* **5/2**[1]

1102 **4** 1 **Tyzack (IRE)**[15] 2440 5-9-7 **83**.. MickyFenton 2 83
(Stef Liddiard) *hld up in tch: rdn over 2f out: no ex fnl f* **5/2**[1]

0060 **5** 2 **Atlantic Quest (USA)**[18] 2341 7-9-1 **82** ow1..........(p) LiamTreadwell(5) 6 77
(R A Harris) *s.i.s: hdwy 1/2-way: rdn and edgd lft 2f out: wknd fnl f* **16/1**

0-05 **6** 2 **Underscore (USA)**[6] 2705 4-8-7 **76**................................ TolleyDean(7) 4 67
(R A Harris) *chsd wnr 6f out: rdn 2f out: wknd fnl f* **16/1**

6-30 **7** 3 ½ **Dakota Rain (IRE)**[48] 1532 4-9-0 **76**................................ NeilPollard 3 59
(R C Guest) *chsd wnr 2f: rdn and wknd over 1f out* **28/1**

00-0 **8** *4* **Beltane**[26] 2108 8-8-2 **64** oh27 .... AdrianMcCarthy 8 38
(W De Best-Turner) *hld up: bhd fnl 5f* **100/1**

1m 38.34s (-1.26) **Going Correction** -0.025s/f (Good) **8** Ran SP% **113.3**
Speed ratings (Par 105):105,103,101,100,98 96,92,88
CSF £24.30 CT £56.68 TOTE £9.70: £2.40, £1.20, £1.30; EX 33.50.
Owner Robert Heathcote **Bred** R And Mrs Heathcote **Trained** Kinnersley, Worcs

FOCUS
Only the four ever mattered in a tactical affair. The first two were to form but it does not look that strong behind.
Night Storm Official explanation: jockey said mare hung left-handed
Beltane Official explanation: jockey said gelding never travelled

2901 WARWICK INTERNATIONAL FESTIVAL MAIDEN STKS 1m 2f 188y
4:30 (4:30) (Class 5) 3-Y-0+ **£3,886** (£1,156; £577; £288) **Stalls** Low

Form RPR

0-62 **1** **Green Room (FR)**[18] 2350 3-8-8 82 .... IanMongan 2 60
(J L Dunlop) *chsd ldrs: rdn to ld and hung lft fr over 1f out: styd on* **2/5**[1]

2 *½* **Particle (IRE)** 3-8-13 .... JoeFanning 1 64+
(M Johnston) *dwlt: hld up: hdwy over 2f out: n.m.r over 1f out: hmpd ins fnl f: r.o* **3/1**[2]

3 *nk* **Primitive Academy**[60] 4-9-12 .... TedDurcan 7 64
(H R A Cecil) *chsd ldr: hung rt 3f out: led 2f out: sn rdn and hdd: styd on* **14/1**[3]

0055 **4** *7* **Peak Seasons (IRE)**[8] 2646 3-8-13 48 .... AdrianMcCarthy 5 51
(W De Best-Turner) *led: rdn and hdd 2f out: wkng whn nt clr run over 1f out* **28/1**

4543 **5** *1* **Macho Dancer (IRE)**[15] 2463 3-8-8 46 .... J-PGuillambert 4 44
(K J Burke) *plld hrd and prom: rdn over 2f out: wknd over 1f out* **16/1**

0/ **6** *1 ½* **Tanmeya**[8] 3204 5-9-7 .... NeilPollard 6 42
(R C Guest) *s.i.s: hld up: n.d* **50/1**

7 *16* **Precious Lucy (FR)**[6] 7-9-7 .... VinceSlattery 3 13
(G F Bridgwater) *hld up: hdwy over 6f out: wknd over 3f out* **50/1**

2m 19.46s (0.06) **Going Correction** -0.025s/f (Good)
WFA 3 from 4yo+ 13lb **7** Ran SP% **116.3**
Speed ratings (Par 103):98,97,97,92,91 90,78
CSF £1.96 TOTE £1.40: £1.10, £2.20; EX 2.90.
Owner Nigel & Carolyn Elwes **Bred** Aylesfield Farms Stud Ltd **Trained** Arundel, W Sussex
■ Stewards' Enquiry : Ian Mongan three-day ban: careless riding (Jul 6,7-9)

FOCUS
A weak maiden and an important victory for the well-bred but scopeless Green Room, although the result would have been different had she not hampered the unlucky runner-up. Those just behind the first three are the best guides to the form.
Tanmeya Official explanation: jockey said mare was unsuited by the firm ground

2902 WARWICKRACECOURSE.CO.UK H'CAP 1m 4f 134y
5:00 (5:01) (Class 5) (0-70,68) 4-Y-0+ **£3,238** (£963; £481; £240) **Stalls** Low

Form RPR

0043 **1** **La Gessa**[25] 2150 4-7-13 **53** .... KirstyMilczarek(7) 5 65
(John Berry) *hld up: hdwy over 2f out: rdn to ld 1f out: r.o* **8/1**

60-0 **2** *1* **Lucky Leo**[20] 2305 6-9-7 **68** .... DarryllHolland 12 78
(Ian Williams) *hld up: hdwy over 4f out: rdn to ld and edgd lft over 1f out: sn hdd: styd on same pce* **7/2**[1]

5014 **3** *5* **Darghan (IRE)**[25] 2150 6-8-7 **59** .... StephenDonohoe(5) 1 61
(W J Musson) *hld up in tch: rdn over 1f out: wknd ins fnl f* **4/1**[2]

00-2 **4** *hd* **Palace Walk (FR)**[13] 2497 4-8-11 **58** .... TedDurcan 8 60
(B G Powell) *led over 11f out: rdn and hdd over 1f out: wknd fnl f* **9/1**

-326 **5** *shd* **Nina Fontenail (FR)**[39] 1772 5-8-13 **60** .... FrancisNorton 3 62
(B R Millman) *hld up: swtchd lft and hdwy over 1f out: nt clr run 1f out: swtchd rt and no ex fnl f* **9/2**[3]

0002 **6** *½* **Ganymede**[13] 2507 5-8-12 **59** .... DaneO'Neill 11 60
(J G M O'Shea) *hld up: hdwy over 4f out: rdn and hung lft 2f out: sn btn* **16/1**

1604 **7** *1 ½* **Shaheer (IRE)**[18] 2362 4-8-2 **49** .... DavidKinsella 9 47
(J Gallagher) *led 1f: remained handy: rdn and ev ch over 1f out: sn wknd* **25/1**

200- **8** *2 ½* **Laurollie**[310] 4555 4-8-6 **53** .... RichardThomas 10 47
(Dr J R J Naylor) *hld up in tch: chsd ldr 5f out: rdn over 2f out: wknd over 1f out* **40/1**

-005 **9** *2* **Turner**[12] 2522 5-8-10 **57** .... RyanMoore 13 48
(W M Brisbourne) *hld up: a in rr* **7/1**

3064 **10** *3* **Beauchamp Trump**[51] 1457 4-9-1 **62** ....(t) JamieSpencer 2 48
(G A Butler) *hld up: rdn over 3f out: a in rr* **8/1**

5-00 **11** *7* **Aylmer Road (IRE)**[18] 2357 4-9-2 **63** .... JoeFanning 6 38
(P F I Cole) *chsd ldrs: rdn 7f out: wknd over 2f out* **12/1**

000/ **12** *30* **Didifon**[29] 4216 11-8-8 **55** ....(b) LPKeniry 4 —
(Mrs L J Young) *sn chsng ldr: rdn 7f out: wknd 1/2-way* **66/1**

2m 41.19s (-2.41) **Going Correction** -0.025s/f (Good) **12** Ran SP% **126.5**
Speed ratings (Par 103):106,105,102,102,102 101,100,99,98,96 91,73
CSF £38.25 CT £135.96 TOTE £11.20: £3.00, £2.00, £1.90; EX 68.50 Place 6 £25.23, Place 5 £8.51.
Owner Mrs Rosemary Moszkowicz **Bred** Henry And Mrs Rosemary Moszkowicz **Trained** Newmarket, Suffolk

FOCUS
The front two pulled clear in what was a moderate handicap. The pace was not strong and the form was ordinary rated through the runner-up.
T/Plt: £46.40 to a £1 stake. Pool: £42,804.90. 672.40 winning tickets. T/Qpdt: £11.20 to a £1 stake. Pool: £2,682.70. 176.90 winning tickets. CR

2903 - 2915a (Foreign Racing) - See Raceform Interactive

2279 DUSSELDORF (R-H)
Sunday, June 25

OFFICIAL GOING: Good

2910a DEUTSCHLAND-PREIS DER FREUNDE UND FORDERER (GROUP 1) 1m 4f
3:15 (3:20) 3-Y-0+ **£62,069** (£24,138; £11,724; £5,862; £3,103)

RPR

1 **Donaldson (GER)**[50] 4-9-6 .... TMundry 7 113
(P Rau, Germany) *made all, set slow pace, ridden 1 1/2f out, driven out* **94/10**

2 *¾* **Schiaparelli (GER)**[20] 3-8-4 .... FilipMinarik 3 110
(P Schiergen, Germany) *raced in 3rd tracking leader, ridden & n.m.r against inside rail 1f out, stayed on closing stages, not rch wnr* **6/4**[2]

3 *1 ¾* **Salutino (GER)**[21] 2277 4-9-6 .... ASuborics 6 109
(A Fabre, France) *pressed leader in 2nd, ridden 1 1/2f out, one pace* **9/10**[1]

4 *1 ¾* **El Tango (GER)**[28] 2061 4-9-6 .... WMongil 5 106
(P Schiergen, Germany) *raced in 4th, stayed on at one pace under pressure final 1 1/2f* **131/10**

5 *2* **Simonas (IRE)**[245] 6059 7-9-6 .... EPedroza 1 103
(A Wohler, Germany) *raced in 5th on inside, effort when slightly hampered over 1 1/2f out, unable to quicken* **59/10**[3]

6 *6* **Bailamos (GER)**[36] 1860 6-9-6 .... ADeVries 2 93
(P Schiergen, Germany) *raced in 7th, never a factor* **287/10**

7 *8* **All Spirit (GER)**[55] 1369 4-9-6 .... J-PCarvalho 4 80
(N Sauer, Germany) *raced in 6th, never a factor* **17/1**

2m 33.06s
WFA 3 from 4yo+ 14lb **7** Ran SP% **132.8**
TOTE (including ten euro stakes): WIN 104; PL 11, 10, 10; SF 437.
Owner Gestut Ittlingen **Bred** Gestut Hof Ittlingen **Trained** Germany

NOTEBOOK
Donaldson(GER) caused a bit of a surprise and this victory was down to him being gifted an easy lead and totally dictating matters from the front. He has looked held in two previous outings in Group company so this form should be treated with some caution.
Schiaparelli(GER) did not enjoy the run of the race and would almost certainly have preferred a stronger pace. He was probably the best horse on the day.
Salutino(GER) would probably have preferred easier ground and could never find the necessary turn of foot at the end of this moderately run contest.

2314 MUNICH (L-H)
Sunday, June 25

OFFICIAL GOING: Good

2912a PREIS DES BANKHAUSES HSBC RIEMER STUTEN MEILE (LISTED RACE) (F&M) 1m
3:35 (3:40) 3-Y-0+ **£8,276** (£3,034; £1,655; £828)

RPR

1 **Norwegian Pride (FR)**[31] 1974 4-9-6 .... AGoritz 5 106
(P Schiergen, Germany) **157/10**

2 *1* **Molly Art (GER)**[31] 1974 4-9-6 ....(b) ABoschert 9 104
(U Ostmann, Germany) **39/10**[3]

3 *shd* **Aurea (GER)**[245] 6051 3-8-5 .... KKerekes 10 98
(A Trybuhl, Germany) **26/1**

4 *½* **New Inspiration (GER)**[31] 1974 5-9-3 .... WPanov 6 99
(W Kujath, Germany) **18/1**

5 *½* **Flor Y Nata (USA)**[29] 2059 3-8-5 .... JamieMackay 2 96
(Sir Mark Prescott) *on her toes in paddock, missed break, in rear, last straight, headway between horses to go 4th inside final f, one pace* **29/10**[2]

6 *1 ½* **Deauville (GER)** 3-8-5 ....(b) JVictoire 4 93
(Frau E Mader, Germany) **27/10**[1]

7 *2* **Imperia (GER)**[29] 2059 3-8-5 .... NRichter 7 88
(W Hickst, Germany) **49/10**

8 *2* **Sissy So Lucky (GER)** 3-8-8 .... FGeroux 8 86
(A Trybuhl, Germany) **20/1**

9 *10* **To Green (GER)**[250] 5967 3-8-8 .... JBojko 1 63
(Mario Hofer, Germany) **114/10**

10 *3* **Manda Honor (GER)**[56] 1328 3-8-5 .... AStarke 3 53
(Mario Hofer, Germany) **48/10**

1m 37.57s
WFA 3 from 4yo+ 10lb **10** Ran SP% **135.0**
TOTE (including ten euro stakes): WIN 167; PL 34, 24, 53; SF 1611.
Owner Stall Vio **Bred** Haseg S A **Trained** Germany

NOTEBOOK
Flor Y Nata(USA) as usual was quite wound up in the preliminaries and the crucial moment came when she missed the break. She stayed on well from last place turning for home and, although at one stage it looked like she might pinch third, her run petered out in the last 100 yards.

2629 SAINT-CLOUD (L-H)
Sunday, June 25

OFFICIAL GOING: Good to soft

2913a PRIX DE MALLERET (GROUP 2) (FILLIES) 1m 4f
2:50 (2:50) 3-Y-0 **£51,103** (£19,724; £9,414; £6,276; £3,138)

RPR

1 **Time On**[23] 2203 3-8-9 .... OPeslier 7 111+
(J L Dunlop) *led over 10f out, ridden clear 1 1/2f out, 3 lengths clear inside final f, eased closing stages* **11/4**[2]

2 *1 ½* **Lahudood**[17] 3-8-9 .... FSpanu 1 106
(J E Hammond, France) *held up, 6th straight, headway to go 2nd 1 1/2f out, ran on closing stages (winner eased)* **14/1**

3 *4* **Litalia (IRE)**[31] 3-8-9 .... C-PLemaire 4 99
(P Schiergen, Germany) *disputed 3rd, 4th straight, one pace final 1 1/2f* **7/1**

4 *hd* **Penchee**[22] 2257 3-8-9 .... SPasquier 6 99
(Mme C Head-Maarek, France) *led 1 1/2f, tracked winner til weakening 1 1/2f out* **6/1**[3]

5 *2* **Minatlya (FR)**[22] 2257 3-8-9 .... CSoumillon 2 96
(A Fabre, France) *held up disputing 5th, close last straight, effort on outside 1 1/2f out, one pace final f, unseated rider after finish* **11/10**[1]

6 *3* **Histoire De Moeurs (FR)**[32] 3-8-9 .... TThulliez 3 91
(Y De Nicolay, France) *held up in rear til headway over 5f out, 3rd straight, weakened well over 1f out* **14/1**

7 *8* **Mrs Backshoe (IRE)**[9] 3-8-9 .... SHamel 5 78
(F Poulsen, France) *disputed 3rd, 4th straight, soon weakened* **33/1**

2m 38.8s **Going Correction** +0.10s/f (Good) **7** Ran SP% **117.3**
Speed ratings: 109,108,105,105,103 101,96
PARI-MUTUEL: WIN 3.60; PL 2.30, 3.60; SF 28.40.
Owner R Barnett **Bred** W And R Barnett Ltd **Trained** Arundel, W Sussex

NOTEBOOK

Time On, sixth in the Epsom Oaks last time, redeemed her reputation with a clear-cut success. She is clearly at her best when allowed to dictate, she revelled on the soft ground, and still appears to be improving. The Yorkshire Oaks and the Prix Vermeille now look on the cards.

Lahudood, still a maiden, was waited with early on and eventually brought with a late challenge in the straight, but the winner had gone beyond recall. She will now have a break and be brought back again for a race in Deauville.

Litalia(IRE), another given a patient ride, made a forward move early in the straight and battled on gamely to take third place.

Penchee was settled behind the leader and got outpaced when things were quickened up early in the straight. She then had a ding-dong battle and only missed third place by a head.

2914a GRAND PRIX DE SAINT-CLOUD (GROUP 1) — 1m 4f

3:25 (3:25) 4-Y-0+ **£157,628** (£63,062; £31,531; £15,752; £7,890)

Pos	Dist	Horse	Jockey	RPR
1		**Pride (FR)**[27] [2092] 6-8-13 (A De Royer-Dupre, France) *held up, close 5th straight, headway 2f out, driven to lead last stride* **7/1**[3]	C-PLemaire 1	123
2	*hd*	**Hurricane Run (IRE)**[28] [2053] 4-9-2 (A Fabre, France) *raced in 3rd, led and reminder 2 1/2f out, 1 1/2 lengths up over 1f out, hard ridden final f, caught last stride* **2/9**[1]	KFallon 4	126
3	*2*	**Laverock (IRE)**[35] [1873] 4-9-2 (C Laffon-Parias, France) *held up in rear to straight, headway well over 1f out, stayed on one pace under pressure final f, took 3rd 100 yds out* **14/1**	DBonilla 3	122
4	*2*	**Policy Maker (IRE)**[21] [2277] 6-9-2 (E Lellouche, France) *raced in 4th, 3rd straight, soon chasing leader, ridden & 1 1/2 lengths behind 1f out, weakened gradually* **6/1**[2]	SPasquier 2	119
5	*20*	**Petrograd (IRE)**[21] [2277] 5-9-2 (E Lellouche, France) *led to 2 1/2f out, weakened 2f out* **250/1**	GFaucon 6	87
6	*8*	**Near Honor (GER)**[56] [1331] 8-9-2 (A Fabre, France) *raced in 2nd, joined leader 7f out, 4th & weakening quickly straight* **200/1**	MSautjeau 5	74

2m 35.9s **Going Correction** +0.10s/f (Good) **6** Ran SP% **116.2**

Speed ratings: 119,118,117,116,102 97

PARI-MUTUEL: WIN 7.60; PL 1.10, 1.10; SF 16.70.

Owner N P Bloodstock **Bred** N P Bloodstock Ltd **Trained** Chantilly, France

NOTEBOOK

Pride(FR) looked a picture in the paddock and ran the race of her life. For much of the 12 furlongs the mare was settled in fifth position and she didn't begin her final run to the line until half way up the straight. Brought up the centre of the track, she took the advantage 20 yards from the post and battled gamely in the final stages. Her likely programme now is the Yorkshire Oaks and then a race during Arc weekend before another campaign outside France.

Hurricane Run(IRE) looked in great shape in the paddock and had a beautiful action on the way to the start. Dropped in behind the two pacemakers, he was being niggled at soon after the stalls opened. He took the advantage early in the straight and fended off all challenges until the dying stages. For whatever reason he was not at his best, but he is still an intended runner in the King George at the end of next month.

Laverock(IRE) made up a lot of late ground and was last until the home straight. He tried to follow the winner, but could not quicken in the same way. This distance might just stretch his stamina.

Policy Maker(IRE) raced in fourth place and just behind the odds-on favourite. He quickened well early in the straight, and looked dangerous, but his run came to an end inside the final furlong.

2598 CHEPSTOW (L-H)

Monday, June 26

OFFICIAL GOING: Good to soft

Wind: Almost nil Weather: Rain for first two races.

2916 BETFRED (S) STKS — 5f 16y

6:50 (6:50) (Class 6) 2-Y-0 **£2,266** (£674; £337; £168) **Stalls** High

Form	Pos	Dist	Horse	Jockey	RPR
006	1		**Suzieblue (IRE)**[7] [2709] 2-8-6 (J S Moore) *a.p: rdn to ld jst over 1f out: drvn out* **4/1**[2]	(p) LPKeniry 1	48
63	2	*1 ¾*	**Shreddy Shrimpster**[9] [2643] 2-8-7 ow1 (M J Wallace) *w ldr: led 2f out: rdn whn edgd rt and bmpd over 1f out: sn n.m.r and hdd: nt qckn ins fnl f* **4/6**[1]	NCallan 3	43
0540	3	*1*	**Alittleriskie (IRE)**[19] [2346] 2-8-11 (J S Moore) *led 3f: rdn and ev ch whn bmpd over 1f out: nt qckn fnl f* **8/1**[3]	(b[1]) PatDobbs 8	43
0640	4	*1 ¼*	**Lenard Frank (IRE)**[7] [2709] 2-8-11 (M D I Usher) *trckd ldrs: edgd rt over 3f out: rdn and one pce fnl 2f* **50/1**	(v) FergusSweeney 4	39
	5	*3 ½*	**Ladas Lad** 2-8-11 (W G M Turner) *s.s: outpcd: nvr nrr* **12/1**	RobertMiles 9	26
U0	6	*shd*	**Kaptain Kate**[20] [2328] 2-8-3 (R Brotherton) *s.s: sn chsng ldrs: rdn over 2f out: hung lft and wknd over 1f out* **25/1**	EdwardCreighton(3) 2	21
	7	*hd*	**Bronco's Filly (IRE)** 2-8-6 (J G M O'Shea) *dwlt: sn in tch: hmpd over 3f out: hung lft 2f out: sn bhd* **25/1**	FrankieMcDonald 6	20

63.08 secs (3.48) **Going Correction** +0.325s/f (Good) **7** Ran SP% **108.4**

Speed ratings (Par 91):85,82,80,78,73 72,72

CSF £6.28 TOTE £6.00: £2.70, £1.10; EX 14.30.There was no bid for the winner. Shreddy Shrimpster was claimed by A. B. Haynes for £6,000.

Owner A D Crook **Bred** Tally-Ho Stud **Trained** Upper Lambourn, Berks

FOCUS

A moderate time, even for a race like this. A weak event with the favourite not running to form.

NOTEBOOK

Suzieblue(IRE), fitted with cheekpieces for the first time, got on top inside the last to land a few decent bets. With the favourite below par this did not take much winning. (op 8-1)

Shreddy Shrimpster, third in a weak maiden last time, could not capitalise on this drop in grade. She seemed to be beaten on merit, although she did not enjoy the clearest of passages and this easy ground was probably against her. (op 4-9)

Alittleriskie(IRE), a stablemate of the winner, wore blinkers for the first time. She was right in the action when taking a bump from the favourite and could soon produce no more. (tchd 9-1)

Lenard Frank(IRE), exposed as a poor plater, did not shape as if the drop back to five furlongs was ideal. (op 33-1)

Ladas Lad, out of a middle-distance winner, was slowly away on this debut and trailed until passing a couple of rivals late on. (op 14-1 tchd 11-1)

Kaptain Kate Official explanation: jockey said bit slipped through filly's mouth

Bronco's Filly(IRE) Official explanation: jockey said filly hung left-handed

2917 AVONMOUTH & PORTBURY OCCUPATIONAL HEALTH MAIDEN STKS — 1m 4f 23y

7:20 (7:22) (Class 5) 3-Y-0+ **£3,238** (£963; £481; £240) **Stalls** Low

Form	Pos	Dist	Horse	Jockey	RPR
32	1		**Ask**[21] [2304] 3-8-12 (Sir Michael Stoute) *sn led: hdd after 2f: chsd ldr: shkn up to ld 2f out: sn clr: easily* **2/9**[1]	DaneO'Neill 2	91+
-326	2	*7*	**My Petra**[16] [2446] 3-8-8 74 ow1 (A King) *led after 2f: rdn and hdd 2f out: eased whn btn ins fnl f* **10/1**[2]	JDSmith 8	74+
0	3	*3 ½*	**Fairlight Express (IRE)**[22] [2261] 6-9-12 (Stef Liddiard) *s.i.s: bhd tl styd on fnl 3f: nvr nrr* **200/1**	FrancisNorton 5	59?
0	4	*12*	**Izadore (IRE)**[19] [2349] 3-8-7 (E A L Dunlop) *hld up: hdwy on ins 5f out: wknd over 2f out* **25/1**	ShaneKelly 1	35
5/6	5	*2 ½*	**King Kasyapa (IRE)**[23] [2220] 4-9-12 (P Bowen) *hld up and bhd: hdwy on ins over 3f out: wknd over 2f out* **22/1**[3]	VinceSlattery 3	36
00	6	*6*	**Ballymena**[23] [2220] 5-9-0 (R A Harris) *hld up: rdn and hdwy over 4f out: wknd 3f out* **200/1**	TolleyDean(7) 4	21
0	7	*34*	**Montana Sky (IRE)**[21] [2304] 3-8-12 (S Kirk) *plld hrd: led early: prom: rdn over 5f out: wknd over 3f out* **100/1**	MickyFenton 7	—
00	8	*55*	**Light Dreams**[21] [2304] 3-8-7 (W J Knight) *hld up in tch: rdn 4f out: sn wknd* **50/1**	NCallan 6	—

2m 41.06s (2.34) **Going Correction** +0.325s/f (Good)

WFA 3 from 4yo+ 14lb **8** Ran SP% **103.1**

Speed ratings (Par 103):105,100,98,90,88 84,61,25

CSF £1.43 TOTE £1.20: £1.02, £1.10, £18.70; EX 1.90.

Owner The Duke Of Devonshire & Mrs J Magnier **Bred** Side Hill Stud **Trained** Newmarket, Suffolk

■ Stewards' Enquiry : Tolley Dean caution: used whip without giving mare time to respond

FOCUS

A decent winning time for the type of contest, but this was generally a weak maiden in which the first two would have finished further clear but for being eased.

Light Dreams Official explanation: jockey said filly hung left in straight

2918 WEATHERBYS BANK H'CAP — 1m 2f 36y

7:50 (7:51) (Class 5) (0-75,75) 4-Y-0+ **£3,368** (£1,002; £500; £250) **Stalls** Low

Form	Pos	Dist	Horse	Jockey	RPR
06-0	1		**Tashkandi (IRE)**[164] [107] 6-9-7 75 (P Bowen) *mde all: rdn clr over 1f out: drvn out* **50/1**	VinceSlattery 6	84
550	2	*1 ½*	**Quel Ange (FR)**[10] [2615] 4-9-1 69 (R J Hodges) *a.p: rdn to chse wnr 1f out: kpt on same pce* **12/1**	JimCrowley 4	75
32-3	3	*1*	**Hawridge King**[24] [2186] 4-8-13 67 (W S Kittow) *t.k.h: a.p: rdn over 2f out: kpt on ins fnl f* **4/1**[1]	MickyFenton 8	71
060-	4	*¾*	**Proprioception (IRE)**[42] [5998] 4-7-9 56 oh3 (W K Goldsworthy) *hld up in mid-div: hdwy on ins over 4f out: rdn over 3f out: outpcd over 2f out: styd on fnl f* **50/1**	LukeMorris(7) 2	59
3412	5	*shd*	**Gallego**[16] [2455] 4-8-2 61 (R J Price) *hld up and bhd: hdwy over 2f out: one pce fnl f* **13/2**	JamesDoyle(5) 1	63
0-00	6	*nk*	**Night Spot**[10] [2621] 5-9-7 75 (B R Millman) *t.k.h in tch: chsd wnr over 2f out to 1f out: no ex* **11/1**	GeorgeBaker 5	77
4530	7	*nk*	**Transvestite (IRE)**[13] [2519] 4-9-7 75 (J W Hills) *swtchd lft sn after s: hld up and bhd: sme late hdwy* **5/1**[2]	RHills 12	76+
0032	8	*1 ½*	**Jackie Kiely**[6] [2725] 5-8-6 60 (Stef Liddiard) *hld up in mid-div: rdn 2f out: nvr trbld ldrs* **4/1**[1]	(t) FrancisNorton 10	58+
	9	*5*	**Otranto (USA)**[115] 4-8-8 62 (M Johnston) *prom: rdn 4f out: wknd wl over 1f out* **6/1**[3]	RoystonFfrench 11	51
-115	10	*7*	**Brave Dane (IRE)**[40] [1769] 8-8-8 62 (A W Carroll) *s.v.s: hdwy over 4f out: eased whn btn over 1f out* **10/1**	ShaneKelly 7	38

2m 17.72s (7.82) **Going Correction** +0.325s/f (Good) **10** Ran SP% **113.3**

Speed ratings (Par 103):81,79,79,78,78 78,77,76,72,67

CSF £547.31 CT £2940.22 TOTE £41.80: £7.70, £4.40, £1.60; EX 589.90.

Owner P Bowen **Bred** His Highness The Aga Khan's Studs S C **Trained** Little Newcastle, Pembrokes

FOCUS

The winner set a very modest pace, resulting in a pedestrian winning time for a race of its type. The first three were always prominent. Thewinner has rated a lot higher in the past and the third and fourth ran to form.

Transvestite(IRE) Official explanation: jockey said gelding was unsuited by the good to soft ground

Brave Dane(IRE) Official explanation: jockey said gelding was unsuited by the good to soft ground

2919 WESTERN DAILY PRESS MAIDEN STKS — 1m 14y

8:20 (8:21) (Class 5) 3-Y-0+ **£3,238** (£963; £481; £240) **Stalls** High

Form	Pos	Dist	Horse	Jockey	RPR
6-42	1		**Jihaaz (IRE)**[10] [2615] 3-9-0 79 (B W Hills) *keen early: mde all: rdn clr over 1f out: readily* **1/1**[1]	RHills 7	87+
06	2	*6*	**Hanella (IRE)**[17] [2406] 3-8-9 (R M Beckett) *a.p: chsd wnr over 2f out: sn rdn: no imp* **6/1**[3]	NCallan 5	66
0-4	3	*2 ½*	**Imperial Harry**[19] [2343] 3-8-11 (M R Channon) *t.k.h: a.p: rdn 3f out: no ex fnl f* **7/1**	EdwardCreighton(3) 1	65
0	4	*4*	**Piper's Song (IRE)**[24] [2188] 3-9-0 (H Candy) *fly-jmpd s: sn in tch: rdn 3f out: wknd 2f out* **25/1**	DaneO'Neill 6	56
45	5	*2*	**Marbaa (IRE)**[19] [2343] 3-9-0 (E A L Dunlop) *hld up and bhd: rdn over 2f out: nvr trbld ldrs* **9/2**[2]	ShaneKelly 4	51
64	6	*1 ½*	**Mexican Bob**[17] [2411] 3-9-0 (Heather Dalton) *plld hrd in rr: rdn over 2f out: no rspnse* **33/1**	LPKeniry 2	48
34	7	*1 ¼*	**Moves Goodenough**[24] [2188] 3-9-0 (Andrew Turnell) *hld up in mid-div: rdn over 3f out: bhd fnl 2f* **12/1**	FrancisNorton 8	45
0	P		**Flying Venture (IRE)**[14] [2498] 4-9-2 (B J McMath) *in tch tl p.u over 4f out: b.b.v* **200/1**	JohnMcAuley(3) 3	—

1m 37.04s (1.04) **Going Correction** +0.325s/f (Good)

WFA 3 from 4yo 10lb **8** Ran SP% **109.9**

Speed ratings (Par 103):107,101,98,94,92 91,89,—

CSF £6.68 TOTE £2.00: £1.10, £3.50, £1.30; EX 10.70.

Owner Hamdan Al Maktoum **Bred** Gazar Partnership **Trained** Lambourn, Berks

FOCUS

The field raced down the centre. A weakish maiden, but another improved showing from the winner and the winning time was decent, over two seconds faster than the later handicap. The runner-up was roughly to form.

Flying Venture(IRE) Official explanation: jockey said filly bled from the nose

2920 BETFRED H'CAP STKS (QUALIFIER) — 6f 16y

8:50 (9:02) (Class 5) (0-70,70) 3-Y-0 **£3,886** (£1,156; £577; £288) **Stalls** High

Form	Pos	Dist	Horse	Jockey	RPR
1034	1		**Stamford Blue**[2] [2860] 5-8-9 58 (R A Harris) *bhd: rdn over 3f out: hdwy 2f out: led ins fnl f: r.o* **5/1**[2]	(b) TolleyDean(7) 5	69

5/15 **2** *1* **Millfields Dreams**[3] 2813 7-8-9 **51** .... PatDobbs 7 59
(M G Quinlan) *led: rdn wl over 1f out: hdd ins fnl f: nt qckn* **4/1**[1]

203 **3** *2* **Ten Shun**[33] 1941 3-9-0 **63** .... NCallan 12 63
(P D Evans) *trckd ldrs: rdn and ev ch 2f out: one pce fnl f* **20/1**

5-01 **4** *3* **Vibe**[10] 2602 5-8-4 **51** oh1 .... JamesDoyle(5) 3 44
(A W Carroll) *hld up towards rr: hdwy 3f out: sn rdn: one pce fnl 2f* **15/2**

4060 **5** *2 1/2* **Crystal Mystic (IRE)**[27] 2095 4-8-9 **51** oh1 .... RobertMiles 14 37
(B Palling) *w ldr: ev ch over 2f out: sn rdn: wknd over 1f out* **8/1**

040- **6** *1/2* **Stokesies Wish**[265] 5686 6-9-3 **59** .... FrancisNorton 10 43
(J L Spearing) *t.k.h: trckd ldrs: rdn over 2f out: wknd fnl f* **20/1**

0-00 **7** *3/4* **Wizard Quay**[3] 2813 3-7-9 **51** oh2 .... (b[1]) LukeMorris(7) 15 31
(W K Goldsworthy) *bhd: effrt whn hung lft over 3f out: n.d* **66/1**

-004 **8** *1/2* **Willofcourse**[10] 2602 5-9-1 **57** .... DaneO'Neill 8 37
(H Candy) *hld up: hdwy 3f out: rdn wl over 1f out: wknd fnl f* **11/2**[3]

0103 **9** *6* **Dunn Deal (IRE)**[28] 2074 6-10-0 **70** .... ShaneKelly 16 32
(W M Brisbourne) *t.k.h: a bhd* **15/2**

0-00 **10** *26* **Elgin Marbles**[7] 2711 4-10-0 **70** .... SamHitchcott 2 —
(A B Haynes) *prom: rdn 3f out: sn wknd: t.o* **66/1**

1m 13.19s (0.79) **Going Correction** +0.325s/f (Good)
WFA 3 from 4yo+ 7lb **10** Ran SP% **99.2**
Speed ratings (Par 103):107,105,103,99,95 95,94,93,85,50
CSF £18.47 CT £230.30 TOTE £4.90: £1.70, £2.10, £3.10; EX 26.40.
Owner Brian Hicks **Bred** Mrs Wendy Miller **Trained** Earlswood, Monmouths
■ Guilded Warrior (8/1) and Binty (66/1) were both withdrawn after bolting before the start. R4 applies, deduct 10p in the £.

FOCUS
A race that was delayed when two horses got loose beforehand. The runners again came up the centre of the track. A modest handicap, but the time was creditable so the form looks solid.
Vibe Official explanation: jockey said gelding hung left-handed
Dunn Deal(IRE) Official explanation: jockey said gelding stumbled shortly after start

2921 LETHEBY & CHRISTOPHER FILLIES' H'CAP 1m 14y
9:20 (9:29) (Class 5) (0-70,69) 3-Y-O **£3,368** (£1,002; £500; £250) **Stalls** High

Form RPR

344U **1** **Wizby**[8] 2676 3-7-12 **53** .... DonnaCaldwell(7) 5 58
(P D Evans) *sltly hmpd s: sn led: hdd over 2f out: led nr fin: r.o* **6/1**[2]

-204 **2** *hd* **Imperial Lucky (IRE)**[11] 2589 3-8-12 **60** .... NCallan 8 64
(M J Wallace) *hld up: hdwy 5f out: rdn over 1f out: led cl home: hdd nr fin* **10/3**[1]

4161 **3** *hd* **Maidford (IRE)**[15] 2479 3-8-7 **55** .... FergusSweeney 2 59+
(M Meade) *carried lft s: sn prom: led over 2f out: rdn over 1f out: hdd cl home* **10/3**[1]

-000 **4** *1 1/4* **Zafantage**[10] 2622 3-9-2 **64** .... GeorgeBaker 9 65
(S Kirk) *led early: lost pl over 5f out: rallied over 2f out: kpt on ins fnl f* **13/2**[3]

03-0 **5** *9* **Kineta (USA)**[17] 2406 3-9-7 **69** .... FrancisNorton 3 49+
(W R Muir) *carried lft s: sn chsng ldrs: rdn over 2f out: sn wknd* **16/1**

13 **6** *shd* **Odessa Star (USA)**[6] 2729 3-9-0 **65** .... NeilChalmers(3) 4 45+
(J G Portman) *carried lft s: sn prom: rdn and wknd 2f out* **10/3**[1]

0540 **7** *5* **Chia (IRE)**[21] 2301 3-9-0 **62** .... (p) FrankieMcDonald 7 31
(D Haydn Jones) *swvd bdly lft s: rdn 4f out: a in rr* **14/1**

1m 39.33s (3.33) **Going Correction** +0.325s/f (Good) **7** Ran SP% **109.4**
Speed ratings (Par 96):96,95,95,94,85 85,80
CSF £23.92 CT £70.12 TOTE £7.50: £3.50, £1.90; EX 33.70 Place 6 £11.83, Place 5 £10.71.
Owner Miss D L Wisbey & R J Viney **Bred** Miss Deborah Wisbey **Trained** Pandy, Abergavenny

FOCUS
This was run in fading light. Far from solid form, with four runners inconvenienced to various degrees at the start. The winner ran to her juvenile best.
T/Plt: £33.00 to a £1 stake. Pool: £48,849.90. 1,080.00 winning tickets. T/Qpdt: £19.60 to a £1 stake. Pool: £2,642.60. 99.40 winning tickets. KH

2448 MUSSELBURGH (R-H)
Monday, June 26

OFFICIAL GOING: Firm (good to firm in places)
Wind: Virtually nil

2922 RACING UK ON CHANNEL 432 (S) STKS 5f
2:30 (2:30) (Class 6) 2-Y-O **£2,730** (£806; £403) **Stalls** Low

Form RPR

643 **1** **Top Tier**[18] 2375 2-8-6 .... TomEaves 7 53+
(I Semple) *cl up: rdn to ld over 1f out: styd on* **5/2**[1]

3 **2** *1* **La Esperanza**[7] 2695 2-8-6 .... PaulFessey 6 49
(T D Barron) *chsd ldrs: rdn along 1/2-way: drvn and wandered wl over 1f out: edgd rt and styd on ins last* **3/1**[2]

60 **3** *shd* **Denton Hawk**[6] 2733 2-8-11 .... PhillipMakin 3 54
(M Dods) *dwlt: towards rr: hdwy 1/2-way: rdn wl over 1f out: styd on ent last* **6/1**[3]

5062 **4** *3/4* **Bowl Em Over**[12] 2538 2-8-6 .... PaulHanagan 2 46
(M E Sowersby) *led: rdn along 2f out: drvn and hdd over 1f out: wknd ins last* **13/2**

50 **5** *3/4* **Daruma (IRE)**[16] 2439 2-8-11 .... (b[1]) RobbieFitzpatrick 5 49
(Peter Grayson) *chsd ldrs: rdn along and outpcd over 2f out: styd on u.p ins last* **8/1**

500 **6** *1/2* **Loch Clutha (IRE)**[18] 2382 2-8-7 ow1 .... (p) DarryllHolland 4 43+
(K R Burke) *sn pushed along towards rr: rdn and hdwy 2f out: drvn and kpt on same pce appr last* **8/1**

7 *dist* **Wrynoes Pass (IRE)** 2-8-11 .... GylesParkin 1 —
(R F Fisher) *s.i.s: soon outpcd and wl bhd* **22/1**

60.19 secs (-0.31) **Going Correction** -0.325s/f (Firm) **7** Ran SP% **107.8**
Speed ratings (Par 91):89,87,87,86,84 84,—
CSF £8.88 TOTE £2.80: £1.50, £1.80; EX 6.70.There was no bid for the winner.
Owner Bernard Bargh, Jeff Hamer, Steve Henshaw **Bred** B Bargh **Trained** Carluke, S Lanarks

FOCUS
A modest seller, rated around the fourth and fifth.

NOTEBOOK
Top Tier, a cheap purchase at 1,200gns, had showed up well in better races on her two most recent outings and the drop back to five furlongs looked to hold no fears. Well supported beforehand, she edged ahead over a furlong out and stayed on strongly to win with a bit to spare. This looks about her level, but it is not an impossibility she could pick up a small nursery at one of the lesser tracks. (op 4-1)
La Esperanza, a real drifter in the market beforehand, shaped well on her debut at Carlisle without suggesting she has the speed to win at the minimum distance and that was again the case here. Unable to capitalise on the drop in grade, she should improve for a sixth furlong and can win at this level. (op 6-4)
Denton Hawk, a non-stayer over seven furlongs at Thirsk last week, was helped by the drop in trip/grade and he kept on well into third. There is a race for him at this level. (op 8-1)
Bowl Em Over showed up well to a furlong out, at which point she was done for a finishing kick, but she kept on to the line and looks worth a try at six furlongs. (op 7-1)
Daruma(IRE) showed a bit more in the blinkers, but the headgear cannot be guaranteed to have the same effect in future. (op 10-1)

2923 NO NONSENSE SCOTTISH BREWERS H'CAP 1m
3:00 (3:00) (Class 6) (0-65,63) 3-Y-O **£3,412** (£1,007; £504) **Stalls** Low

Form RPR

3644 **1** **Esoterica (IRE)**[13] 2525 3-9-3 **59** .... (b[1]) PaulFessey 10 69
(T D Barron) *trckd ldrs: hdwy 2f out: swtchd lft and rdn to ld ent last: hung rt and sn clr* **5/1**[3]

0036 **2** *3* **Azurine (IRE)**[32] 1946 3-9-7 **63** .... JoeFanning 12 66
(M Johnston) *dwlt: hdwy to chse ldrs after 1f: effrt 2f out: sn rdn and kpt on ins last* **12/1**

002 **3** *hd* **Feelin Irie (IRE)**[35] 1888 3-9-7 **63** .... KimTinkler 8 66
(N Tinkler) *led: rdn along 2f out: drvn and hdd entereing last: kpt on same pce* **9/2**[2]

0460 **4** *1* **Dream Of Paradise (USA)**[13] 2518 3-9-3 **59** .... PaulHanagan 1 60
(Mrs L Williamson) *hld up towards rr: hdwy on inner 3f out: rdn to chse ldrs over 1f ouyt: drvn and no imp fnl f* **12/1**

6335 **5** *1 1/4* **Linton Dancer (IRE)**[13] 2529 3-8-11 **53** .... DarryllHolland 3 51
(J R Weymes) *cl up: rdn along over 2f out: drvn wl over 1f out and grad wknd* **6/1**

0-26 **6** *hd* **Mandarin Rocket (IRE)**[25] 2161 3-9-4 **60** .... TomEaves 4 57?
(Miss L A Perratt) *towards rr: hdwy on outer over 2f oiut: sn rdn and kpt on appr last: nrst fin* **25/1**

-031 **7** *hd* **Apache Nation (IRE)**[23] 2243 3-9-4 **60** .... PhillipMakin 11 57
(M Dods) *hld up in rr: effrt 3f out and sn pushed along: rdn 2f out: styd on appr last: nrst fin* **5/2**[1]

1006 **8** *2 1/2* **Beginners Luck (IRE)**[5] 2746 3-8-2 **44** oh3 .... DaleGibson 9 35
(D Carroll) *in tch: rdn along wl over 2f out: sn wknd* **25/1**

-030 **9** *2* **Distinctly Jim (IRE)**[4] 2782 3-9-2 **58** .... DerekMcGaffin 6 45
(B Smart) *midfield: rdn along 3f: sn wknd* **12/1**

0443 **10** *8* **Augustus Livius(IRE)**[50] 1501 3-8-3 **45** .... JimmyQuinn 2 13
(W Storey) *chsd ldrs: rdn along 3f out: sn wknd* **20/1**

0-50 **11** *25* **Boumsong (IRE)**[23] 2243 3-8-3 **45** oh2 ow1 .... AdrianTNicholls 7 —
(R C Guest) *s.i.s: a rr* **100/1**

1m 39.11s (-3.39) **Going Correction** -0.325s/f (Firm) **11** Ran SP% **114.2**
Speed ratings (Par 97):103,100,99,98,97 97,97,94,92,84 59
CSF £58.26 CT £287.97 TOTE £5.70: £2.10, £2.90, £1.60; EX 52.40.
Owner J Stephenson **Bred** A Lyons Bloodstock **Trained** Maunby, N Yorks
■ Stewards' Enquiry : Adrian T Nicholls two-day ban: jabbed and punched gelding after race (Jul 7, 9)

FOCUS
A modest handicap and pretty ordinary form, rated through the third, with the favourite disappointing. The winner improved for the blinkers.
Augustus Livius(IRE) Official explanation: jockey said gelding was unsuited by the firm (good to firm in places) ground

2924 BETTINGSITE.CO.UK NOVICE AUCTION STKS 7f 30y
3:30 (3:31) (Class 5) 2-Y-O **£3,886** (£1,156; £577; £288) **Stalls** Low

Form RPR

1 **1** **Ingleby Princess**[56] 1342 2-8-6 .... PaulFessey 3 66+
(T D Barron) *trckd ldng pair: hdwy 3f out: led over 2f out: rdn wl over 1f out: edgd rt and styd on ins last* **5/4**[1]

3401 **2** *1/2* **Hart Of Gold**[17] 2416 2-9-1 .... PaulHanagan 5 74
(M J Wallace) *plld hrd: cl up: effrt over 2f out: rdn and ev ch over 1f out: kpt on ins last* **11/4**[2]

3 *3/4* **Karma Llama (IRE)** 2-8-7 .... GylesParkin 4 64
(B Smart) *dwlt: sn trckd ldrs: pushed along on outer 3f out: hdwy 2f out: sn rdn and ev over 1f out: edgd rt and kpt on fnl f* **8/1**

4 *3/4* **Musical Land (IRE)** 2-8-12 .... DarryllHolland 1 67
(J R Weymes) *s.i.s: sn trcking ldrs: effrt over 2f out: kpt on under hand riding appr last: bttr for r* **14/1**

60 **5** *3 1/2* **Dee Cee Elle**[30] 2026 2-8-4 .... KDarley 2 50+
(M Johnston) *set stdy pce: qcknd 1/2-way: rdn along wl over 2f out: sn hdd: drvn and wknd wl over 1f out* **9/2**[3]

1m 31.16s (1.22) **Going Correction** -0.325s/f (Firm) **5** Ran SP% **107.1**
Speed ratings (Par 93):80,79,78,77,73
CSF £4.56 TOTE £2.10: £1.10, £1.50; EX 4.20.
Owner Dave Scott **Bred** Wheelersland Stud **Trained** Maunby, N Yorks

FOCUS
A modest juvenile event and the time was not the best. Muddling form, rated through the first two to their pre-race marks.

NOTEBOOK
Ingleby Princess, who showed plenty of pace to make a winning debut at Newcastle over five furlongs, is bred to stay this sort of distance and she pulled out more close home to thwart the challenge of the well-supported Hart Of Gold. Evidently a fair sort, she remains open to further improvement, but completing the hat-trick is going to be an awful lot harder. (op 10-11 tchd 6-4 in a place and 11-8 in places)
Hart Of Gold, a winner over six furlongs at Wolverhampton last time, faced a stiff task giving 9lb to the winner and, although beaten, he emerges as the best horse at the weights. There may be more to come from him. (op 4-1 tchd 5-1 in places and 6-1 in a place)
Karma Llama(IRE), whose stable have an admirable record here with their juveniles, was struggling in rear early on, but she made a good forward move as they raced inside the final quarter mile and momentarily looked the winner a furlong out, but her lack of experience told in the end. This was a highly promising debut and she should have little trouble finding a maiden if going the right way from this. (op 7-1)
Musical Land(IRE), bred to be effective at this distance, shaped with considerable promise and still looked as though the experience would do him good. His stable's juveniles usually benefit from a run and he is one to keep on side in future. (op 12-1 tchd 10-1)
Dee Cee Elle ran well to a point, but she is more of a handicap type and can be expected to improve in that sphere. (op 5-1 tchd 4-1 in places)

2925 EDINBURGH EVENING NEWS FILLIES' H'CAP 5f
4:00 (4:01) (Class 5) (0-75,69) 3-Y-O+ **£4,533** (£1,348; £674; £336) **Stalls** Low

Form RPR

6365 **1** **Lady Bahia (IRE)**[13] 2521 5-9-4 **59** .... (b) RobbieFitzpatrick 4 69
(Peter Grayson) *trckd ldr: hdwy to chal wl over 1f out: rdn to ld ent last: styd on* **8/1**

3212 **2** *1 1/4* **Hypnosis**[21] 2285 3-9-2 **63** .... TomEaves 2 67
(D W Barker) *chsd ldrs: rdn along 2f out: styd on u.p ins last* **11/4**[1]

4-11 **3** ¾ **Our Little Secret (IRE)**[48] 1563 4-9-7 **69**................. KevinGhunowa(7) 5 72
(A Berry) *led: rdn along and joiuned wl over 1f out: hdd ent last: no ex* **10/3**[2]

1120 **4** *nk* **Mystery Pips**[4] 2780 6-9-8 **63**.......................................(v) KimTinkler 3 65
(N Tinkler) *chsd ldr: rdn along 2f out: edgd rt and sn drvn and one pce appr last* **11/2**[3]

0030 **5** *2* **Rothesay Dancer**[16] 2449 3-9-6 **67**................................ PaulHanagan 9 60
(J S Goldie) *in tch: rdn along and hdwy 2f out: sn drvn and no imp* **7/1**

-300 **6** *hd* **Champagne Cracker**[46] 1611 5-9-8 **63**......................... TonyHamilton 1 57+
(I Semple) *s.i.s and bhd: hdway 2f out: styd on appr last: nt rch ldrs* **6/1**

6-00 **7** *14* **Queen Of Night**[12] 2550 6-9-0 **55**.................................... TonyCulhane 8 —
(D W Chapman) *v slwoly into stride: a behin d* **14/1**

58.42 secs (-2.08) **Going Correction** -0.325s/f (Firm)
WFA 3 from 4yo+ 6lb **7** Ran SP% **109.7**
Speed ratings (Par 100):103,101,99,99,96 95,73
CSF £27.80 CT £80.93 TOTE £7.20: £3.80, £1.60; EX 32.00.
Owner Peter Grayson Racing Clubs Limited **Bred** Piercetown Stud **Trained** Formby, Lancs

FOCUS
A modest sprint in which both Champagne Cracker and Queen Of Night lost their chances at the start. Ordinary form, with the winner pretty exposed.
Rothesay Dancer Official explanation: jockey said saddle slipped
Champagne Cracker Official explanation: jockey said blindfold got stuck on bridle and mare was slowly away

2926 WATCH LIVE RACING ON RACING UK H'CAP 7f 30y
4:30 (4:34) (Class 6) (0-55,54) 3-Y-0+ **£2,730** (£806; £403) **Stalls** Low

Form RPR

025- **1** **Carnivore**[223] 6363 4-10-0 **54**... PaulFessey 2 68+
(T D Barron) *cl up: effrt 2f out: swtchd lft and rdn to ld over 1f out: styd on wl* **4/1**[1]

300- **2** 2½ **Bandos**[274] 5491 6-9-13 **53**...(t) TomEaves 12 61
(I Semple) *led: rdn along 2f out: drvn and hdd over 1f out: kpt on* **11/1**

5160 **3** *nk* **Attacca**[26] 2135 5-10-0 **54**.. DarryllHolland 9 61
(J R Weymes) *chsd ldrs: hdwy over 2f out: sn rdn and kpt on same pce fnl f* **7/1**[3]

0060 **4** *1* **Second Reef**[4] 2792 4-10-0 **54**.. DavidAllan 8 59+
(E J Alston) *towards rr: hdwy over 2f out: rdn and kpt on appr last: nrst fin* **12/1**

0426 **5** *shd* **Spanish Law**[3] 2811 4-9-13 **53**.......................................(b) PhillipMakin 10 57
(M Dods) *midfield: effrt over 2f out: sn rdn along and no imp* **9/2**[2]

6-51 **6** ½ **Outrageous Flirt (IRE)**[12] 2544 4-10-0 **54**..................... PaulHanagan 6 57
(A Dickman) *in tch: rdn to chse ldrs 2f out: sn drvn and no imp* **4/1**[1]

0/00 **7** *5* **Algorithm**[17] 2400 4-9-7 **47**.. FergalLynch 3 37
(T D Easterby) *nvr nr ldrs* **20/1**

0200 **8** ¾ **Glenviews Babalou (USA)**[17] 2418 4-9-7 **47**.....(b) RobbieFitzpatrick 13 35
(Peter Grayson) *dwedlt: sn in tch: rdn along 3f out: sn wknd* **33/1**

4446 **9** ½ **Proud Western (USA)**[4] 2780 8-9-5 **45**....................(tp) PatCosgrave 14 32
(B Ellison) *dwlt: midfield: rdn alonga nd sme hdwy 3f out: sn drvn and btn* **10/1**

0010 **10** ½ **Next Ness (IRE)**[18] 2377 3-9-5 **54**.................................... GylesParkin 1 39
(R F Fisher) *stdd s: a rr* **25/1**

-000 **11** *6* **Jenna Stannis**[3] 2832 4-9-2 **47**....................................(t) AndrewElliott(5) 5 17
(W Storey) *a rr* **33/1**

0/0- **12** *1* **Loyalty Lodge (IRE)**[441] 971 4-9-5 **45**............................ DaleGibson 4 12
(M W Easterby) *a bhd* **66/1**

000 **13** *9* **Spirit Guide (FR)**[15] 1422 4-9-10 **50**................................ JohnFortune 11 —
(R C Guest) *dwlt: a rr* **100/1**

0-00 **14** *5* **Geordie Dancer (IRE)**[59] 1273 4-10-0 **54**.......................(p) JoeFanning 7 —
(A Berry) *prom: n.m.r after 1f: rdn along 3f out and sn wknd* **33/1**

1m 26.51s (-3.43) **Going Correction** -0.325s/f (Firm)
WFA 3 from 4yo+ 9lb **14** Ran SP% **115.7**
Speed ratings (Par 101):106,103,102,101,101 100,95,94,93,93 86,85,74,69
CSF £43.26 CT £307.98 TOTE £4.50: £1.60, £5.40, £2.80; EX 75.60.
Owner The Meat Eaters **Bred** Lord Halifax **Trained** Maunby, N Yorks

FOCUS
Solid form for the grade, and it should prove reliable. The winner can probably do better.
Next Ness(IRE) Official explanation: trainer said gelding finished lame right fore

2927 RECTANGLE GROUP H'CAP 1m 4f
5:00 (5:00) (Class 6) (0-60,60) 4-Y-0+ **£3,071** (£906; £453) **Stalls** High

Form RPR

0-03 **1** **Kyle Of Lochalsh**[15] 2242 6-8-8 **47**.................................... FergalLynch 9 59
(J S Goldie) *hld up in midfield: hdwy 3f out: rdn to ld and hung bdly lft appr last: sn clr* **5/2**[1]

2630 **2** 3½ **Sudden Impulse**[20] 2320 5-7-13 **41**...................... SilvestreDeSousa(3) 5 47
(A D Brown) *a.p: effrt 3f out: rdn to ld over 2f out: drvn and hdd over 1f out: kpt on same pce* **20/1**

0006 **3** 2½ **Nakwa (IRE)**[4] 2790 8-8-11 **50**.. DavidAllan 11 52
(E J Alston) *towards rr: hdwy 3f out: rdn 2f out: kpt on appr last: nrst fin* **20/1**

3010 **4** *nk* **Zarova (IRE)**[8] 2684 4-9-7 **60**.. JimmyQuinn 7 62
(M W Easterby) *hld up in tch: hdwy 3f out: rdn to chse ldrs over 1f out: drvn and wknd ent last* **12/1**

0005 **5** ¾ **Melvino**[6] 2736 4-9-6 **59**.. PhillipMakin 6 60
(T D Barron) *hld up in midfield: hdwy 3f out: rdn 2f out and sn no imp* **13/2**

3002 **6** *3* **Mary Gray**[5] 2751 4-8-7 **46**..(v) JoeFanning 2 42
(M Johnston) *cl up: led after 2f: rdn along 3f out: sn hdd & wknd* **4/1**[2]

40-0 **7** *3* **Tojoneski**[14] 2497 7-8-6 **45**.. PaulHanagan 8 36
(I W McInnes) *hld up: a towards rr* **16/1**

50-0 **8** *4* **Safe Shot**[77] 939 7-8-0 **44** oh6 ow3.........................(p) AndrewMullen(5) 1 29
(Mrs J C McGregor) *a towards rr* **100/1**

-023 **9** *2* **Toss The Caber (IRE)**[24] 2193 4-9-7 **60**.........................(t) TomEaves 10 42
(K G Reveley) *trckd ldrs: hdwy 3f out: sn rdn and wknd fnl 2f* **9/2**[3]

504- **10** *shd* **Full As A Rocket (IRE)**[384] 2362 5-9-0 **53**................ AdrianTNicholls 4 34
(D Nicholls) *led 2f: prom tl rdn along over 3f out and sn wknd* **12/1**

0000 **11** *19* **Lucky Largo (IRE)**[12] 2546 6-7-12 **42** oh9 ow1........(v) AndrewElliott(5) 3 —
(D A Nolan) *prom: rdn along over 3f out and sn wknd* **100/1**

2m 33.81s (-3.09) **Going Correction** -0.325s/f (Firm) **11** Ran SP% **112.9**
Speed ratings (Par 101):97,94,93,92,92 90,88,85,84,84 71
CSF £58.35 CT £805.16 TOTE £3.50: £1.50, £4.80, £6.40; EX 63.60.
Owner Loch Ness Racing Club **Bred** Terry Minahan **Trained** Uplawmoor, E Renfrews
■ Stewards' Enquiry : Andrew Elliott ten-day ban: improper riding - continued riding when gelding appeared lame (Jul 7-16)

FOCUS
A moderate handicap won in good style by Kyle Of Lochalsh.
Full As A Rocket(IRE) Official explanation: jockey said gelding hung right-handed throughout
Lucky Largo(IRE) Official explanation: vet said gelding was lame

2928 BOOK ON-LINE ON MUSSELBURGH-RACECOURSE.CO.UK H'CAP 5f
5:30 (5:31) (Class 6) (0-55,53) 3-Y-0+ **£2,730** (£806; £403) **Stalls** Low

Form RPR

4540 **1** **Sharp Hat**[7] 2700 12-9-5 **44**.. TonyCulhane 4 58
(D W Chapman) *cl up stands rail: hdwy to ld over 1f out: sn rdn and clr ins last* **10/1**

-062 **2** 2½ **Montillia (IRE)**[14] 2494 4-9-11 **50**.................................. DarryllHolland 16 55
(C F Wall) *cl up centre: rdn and ev ch over 1f out: drvn and kpt on same pce ins last* **9/2**[1]

000- **3** *shd* **Bond Becks (IRE)**[296] 4959 6-10-0 **53**.............................. TomEaves 15 58
(B Smart) *chsd ldrs centre: hdwy 2f out: sn rdn and ev ch over 1f out: drvn and one pce ins last* **11/1**

6641 **4** *hd* **Beverley Beau**[18] 2377 4-9-1 **47**.................................. KristinStubbs(7) 6 51
(Mrs L Stubbs) *chsd ldrs towards stands rail: rdn along 2f out: kpt on u.p ins last* **8/1**[3]

0-00 **5** *shd* **Strawberry Patch (IRE)**[12] 2544 7-9-9 **48**....................... FergalLynch 9 52
(J S Goldie) *in tch centre: hdwy 2f out: sn rdn and kpt on ins last* **12/1**

3052 **6** *hd* **Blue Maeve**[18] 2376 6-9-11 **53**............................... SilvestreDeSousa(3) 10 59+
(A D Brown) *chsd ldrs centre: rdn and styng on whn nt clr run ent last: kpt on towards fin* **11/2**[2]

2000 **7** *1* **Percy Douglas**[39] 1794 6-9-6 **52**..............................(bt) AnnStokell(7) 11 51
(Miss A Stokell) *overall ldr centre: rdn along 2f out: hdd over 1f out: wknd ins last* **20/1**

-063 **8** *hd* **Rosie's Result**[4] 2780 6-8-13 **43**................................ AndrewMullen(5) 14 42
(M Todhunter) *prom centre: rdn along wl over 1f out: kpt on same pce ins last* **8/1**[3]

0000 **9** *nk* **Mister Marmaduke**[12] 2550 5-9-1 **40**.............................(p) DavidAllan 13 37
(D A Nolan) *bhd: hdwy wl over 1f out: sn rdn and kpt on ins last: nrst fin* **100/1**

2300 **10** ½ **New Options**[34] 1909 9-9-5 **44**.................................(b) RobbieFitzpatrick 2 40
(Peter Grayson) *bhd tl styd on appr last: nrst fin* **8/1**[3]

0000 **11** *nk* **Fox Covert (IRE)**[55] 1391 5-8-11 **41**..........................(p) MarkLawson(5) 8 36
(D W Barker) *chsd ldrs on stands raiul: rdn along wl over 1f out: grad wknd* **14/1**

-050 **12** *3* **Shatin Leader**[12] 2550 4-9-2 **41**......................................(p) PaulHanagan 7 25
(Miss L A Perratt) *a towards rr* **33/1**

0-00 **13** *nk* **Northern Svengali (IRE)**[5] 2748 10-9-2 **41**..............(t) DerekMcGaffin 17 24
(D A Nolan) *bhd fr 1/2-way* **100/1**

60-0 **14** *nk* **Mutayam**[46] 1611 6-9-8 **47**...(t) NeilPollard 5 29
(D A Nolan) *dwlt: a rr* **66/1**

000- **15** *nk* **Alfie Lee (IRE)**[273] 5508 9-9-1 **40**..................................(tp) JimmyQuinn 1 21
(D A Nolan) *a rr* **33/1**

00-0 **16** *15* **Liberation Square**[46] 1612 3-8-12 **43**..........................(p) TonyHamilton 3 —
(J S Goldie) *a rr* **40/1**

006- **17** *69* **Seallarain**[389] 2224 3-8-9 **40**.. JoeFanning 12 —
(A Berry) *in tch: sn lost pl: bhd and lost action 1/2-way: virtually p.u over 1f out* **100/1**

58.53 secs (-1.97) **Going Correction** -0.325s/f (Firm)
WFA 3 from 4yo+ 6lb **17** Ran SP% **116.2**
Speed ratings (Par 101):102,98,97,97,97 97,95,95,94,93 93,88,88,87,87 63,—
CSF £48.86 CT £524.90 TOTE £13.80: £2.70, £1.20, £4.20, £2.80; EX 37.80 Place 6 £37.18, Place 5 £25.93.
Owner Miss N F Thesiger **Bred** Littleton Stud **Trained** Stillington, N Yorks

FOCUS
A grand performance by old-timer Sharp Hat in this modest handicap, his best run since late 2004. Solid-looking form.
Mister Marmaduke Official explanation: jockey said gelding was denied a clear run
Seallarain Official explanation: jockey said filly lost its action
T/Jkpt: £19,031.70 to a £1 stake. Pool: £522,703.00. 19.50 winning tickets. T/Plt: £105.90 to a £1 stake. Pool: £64,440.15. 444.20 winning tickets. T/Qpdt: £35.50 to a £1 stake. Pool: £2,995.95. 62.30 winning tickets. JR

2708 WINDSOR (R-H)
Monday, June 26

OFFICIAL GOING: Good to soft (good in places)
Wind: Nil Weather: Overcast

2929 MCGEE GROUP FILLIES' H'CAP 1m 2f 7y
6:40 (6:41) (Class 5) (0-70,74) 3-Y-0 **£3,238** (£963; £481; £240) **Stalls** Low

Form RPR

-611 **1** **Gower Song**[7] 2713 3-9-11 **74** 6ex.. JohnEgan 5 91+
(D R C Elsworth) *hld up in rr: prog over 3f out: led 2f out: rdn and strly pressed 1f out: styd on wl* **9/4**[1]

5424 **2** 1¼ **Temperance (IRE)**[10] 2616 3-9-7 **70**................................... RyanMoore 10 82
(S Kirk) *trckd ldrs: rdn over 2f out: effrt to press wnr over 1f out: sustained chal fnl f tl no ex nr fin* **3/1**[2]

0-04 **3** *5* **Generosia**[13] 2533 3-8-13 **62**...(t) RichardHughes 2 64
(A M Balding) *hld up in rr: pushed along and prog to press ldrs 3f out: nt qckn and btn over 1f out* **20/1**

0-66 **4** *hd* **Snake Skin**[15] 2480 3-8-5 **54**... DavidKinsella 1 56
(J Gallagher) *cl up: rdn to chal and upsides 2f out: sn one pce and lft bhd* **28/1**

055- **5** 3½ **Lunar River (FR)**[250] 5976 3-9-2 **65**.............................(t) KerrinMcEvoy 7 60
(E A L Dunlop) *hld up: last over 4f out: pushed along and prog over 3f out: outpcd by ldrs 2f out: plugged on* **14/1**

36-0 **6** *1* **Siakira**[17] 2403 3-9-2 **65**.. IanMongan 9 58
(I A Wood) *hld up wl in rr: brought wd over 4f out and prog to join ldrs: wknd 2f out* **50/1**

35-0 **7** ¾ **Gates Of Eden (USA)**[19] 2349 3-9-5 **68**......................... JamieSpencer 14 60
(M L W Bell) *prom: lft in ld over 4f out: hdd & wknd 2f out* **14/1**

34-0 **8** 1½ **Park Lane Princess (IRE)**[17] 2406 3-8-11 **60**............... MartinDwyer 12 49
(D M Simcock) *hld up wl in rr: last and rdn 4f out: nvr on terms after: plugged on fr over 2f out* **40/1**

4201 **9** *nk* **Nikki Bea (IRE)**[9] 2648 3-8-10 **59**..................................... PaulDoe 13 48
(Jamie Poulton) *hld up in midfield: rdn and effrt over 2f out: no ch w ldrs: wknd fnl f* **9/1**[3]

0-00 **10** *5* **Cunegonde**[10] 2605 3-8-2 **51**.. RichardMullen 4 30
(G L Moore) *hld up in rr: sme prog over 4f out: wknd over 2f out* **66/1**

5542 **11** 1¾ **Al Rayanah**[11] 2589 3-9-0 **63**.. NKNicolaou 15 39
(G Prodromou) *s.i.s: plld hrd and led after 1f: rn wd bnd 5f out and sn hdd: wknd 3f out: eased 2f out* **20/1**

3-43 **12** 3/4 **Reflecting (IRE)**[17] 2411 3-9-6 **69** .... AlanMunro 6 43
(J W Hills) *led for 1f: styd prom: upsides over 3f out: sn wknd* **12/1**
3-00 **13** 3 1/2 **Penmara**[10] 2622 3-8-8 **57** .... NickyMackay 11 25
(M H Tompkins) *s.i.s: nvr beyond midfield: wknd over 2f out* **10/1**
0500 **14** 17 **March Gold (IRE)**[13] 2535 3-8-2 **51** oh1 .... JamieMackay 3 —
(H Morrison) *chsd ldrs tl wknd over 3f out: t.o* **20/1**
2m 10.23s (1.93) **Going Correction** +0.20s/f (Good) **14** Ran SP% **119.5**
Speed ratings (Par 96):100,99,95,94,92 91,90,89,89,85 83,83,80,66
CSF £7.61 CT £108.09 TOTE £3.00: £1.50, £1.80, £4.20; EX 9.00.
Owner Usk Valley Stud **Bred** R E Crutchley **Trained** Newmarket, Suffolk

FOCUS
A reasonable enough fillies' handicap for the grade, but they went just a steady pace for much of the way. They all raced far side in the straight. The first two finished clear, with the third and fourth to form.

2930 SLATER MAIDMENT CENTENARY MAIDEN AUCTION STKS 6f
7:10 (7:12) (Class 5) 2-Y-O **£3,886** (£1,156; £577; £288) **Stalls** High

Form RPR
3 **1** **Oi Vay Joe (IRE)**[77] 944 2-8-13 .... KerrinMcEvoy 8 78
(W Jarvis) *w ldrs: rdn 2f out: narrow ld ins fnl f: drvn and jst hld on* **11/4**[2]
0 **2** hd **Okikoki**[14] 2506 2-8-11 .... MartinDwyer 4 75
(W R Muir) *racd against far side rail: mde most: hdd ins fnl f: kpt on wl: jst hld* **25/1**
3 nk **Smokey Oakey (IRE)** 2-8-11 .... NickyMackay 16 75
(M H Tompkins) *dwlt: sn in tch on outer: prog 2f out: rdn and styd on wl last 100yds: nrst fin* **25/1**
4 nk **Transpique (IRE)** 2-8-13 .... AdamKirby(3) 1 81+
(C G Cox) *trckd ldrs: cl up whn nt clr run over 1f out: styd on ins fnl f: jst unable to chal* **16/1**
35 **5** 1 **Paymaster General (IRE)**[10] 2604 2-8-9 .... HayleyTurner 9 69
(M D I Usher) *chsd ldrs: hrd rdn 2f out: struggling over 1f out: styd on again ins fnl f* **14/1**
6 1/2 **Billy Dane (IRE)** 2-9-2 .... JamieSpencer 5 74
(B J Meehan) *trckd ldrs: cl up whn nt clr run over 1f out: hanging lft and kpt on same pce fnl f* **12/1**
0 **7** nk **Susanna's Prospect (IRE)**[20] 2328 2-8-4 .... JohnEgan 12 64+
(B J Meehan) *dwlt: sn in tch in midfield: clsng whn nt clr run over 1f out: stl cl up whn nowhere to go ins fnl f and eased* **10/1**[3]
4 **8** nk **Vitznau (IRE)**[12] 2552 2-8-13 .... RichardHughes 6 69
(R Hannon) *w ldr: drvn 2f out: upsides 1f out: wknd last 150yds* **9/4**[1]
9 nk **Ede's Dot Com (IRE)** 2-8-11 .... PaulDoe 7 66
(W J Knight) *w ldrs: drvn 2f out: fdd fnl f* **66/1**
0 **10** 3/4 **Spiderback (IRE)**[13] 2530 2-8-13 .... RyanMoore 13 66
(R Hannon) *racd on outer and towards rr: rdn and sme prog 2f out: rn green 1f out: no hdwy after* **14/1**
0 **11** nk **King Charles**[10] 2619 2-8-13 .... RichardMullen 14 71+
(E A L Dunlop) *dwlt: pushed along in last pair and wl off the pce: prog 2f out: styng on whn rn out of room last 100yds and snatched up* **12/1**
0 **12** 1 3/4 **Safari Sundowner (IRE)**[23] 2234 2-8-13 .... IanMongan 15 60
(P Winkworth) *spd on outer to press ldrs: rdn over 2f out: fdd over 1f out* **50/1**
13 2 **Oh So Saucy** 2-8-6 .... AlanMunro 3 47+
(C F Wall) *s.s: wl off the pce in last pair: shuffled along 2f out: nvr nr ldrs* **16/1**
14 4 **Cavendish** 2-8-9 .... ChrisCatlin 10 38
(J M P Eustace) *a wl in rr: n.d fnl 2f* **33/1**
15 hd **Wool Mart** 2-8-9 .... TedDurcan 2 37
(M Blanshard) *s.s: a wl in rr* **50/1**
16 1 1/4 **Respect My Wishes** 2-8-4 .... StephenCarson 11 29+
(R Ingram) *sn wl in rr: struggling over 2f out* **66/1**
1m 15.15s (1.48) **Going Correction** +0.20s/f (Good) **16** Ran SP% **124.5**
Speed ratings (Par 93):98,97,97,96,95 94,94,94,93,92 92,90,87,82,81 80
CSF £81.11 TOTE £3.80: £1.30, £6.10, £7.80; EX 56.00.
Owner The Oi Vay Joe Partnership **Bred** Lars Pearson **Trained** Newmarket, Suffolk

FOCUS
They finished in a bunch and this was probably just an ordinary maiden. Again, they all raced far side in the straight.

NOTEBOOK
Oi Vay Joe(IRE), third in a fair five-furlong maiden round here on his debut 77 days previously, showed no ill effects of his little break and just proved good enough on this step up in trip. He did not have much in hand, but should make a reasonable nursery type. (op 2-1 tchd 3-1 in places)
Okikoki was well beaten on his debut over course and distance, but showed the benefit of that run and was just held. There should be a similar race in him.
Smokey Oakey(IRE), a 13,500euros half-brother to six winners, including useful dual ten-furlong winner El Bueno out of a three-year-old scorer in the US, belied his big odds with a very pleasing introduction. He should improve plenty for this and can find a similar event.
Transpique(IRE), a 29,000gns half-brother to Give A Whistle, a dual five-furlong winner at three and four, as well as Roman Mistress, a triple five- to six-furlong scorer, out of a useful six- to seven-furlong winner at three, was one of a handful who was denied a clear run in the bunch finish and was a little unlucky. Official explanation: jockey said colt was denied a clear run
Paymaster General(IRE), who showed a modest level of ability in two runs at Goodwood, ran well and was not beaten far. (op 16-1)
Billy Dane(IRE), a 30,000gns half-brother to Princely Vale, a triple six- to seven-furlong winner at two, and Mr Hullabalou, a six-furlong winner at three, did not enjoy a clear run and can improve on this. (op 10-1)
Susanna's Prospect(IRE) ◆, well held on her debut over course and distance, stepped up on that effort and is much better than her finishing position suggests, as she was continually denied a clear run against the fair rail. She looks one to keep an eye out for. Official explanation: jockey said filly was denied a clear run (op 12-1)
Vitznau(IRE), a beaten favourite when fourth on his debut at Kempton, was really strongly supported in the market but finished up well held. He showed good speed and may be capable of better on good ground. (op 5-1)
King Charles Official explanation: jockey said gelding was denied a clear run closing stages

2931 CHEVAL PROPERTY H'CAP 6f
7:40 (7:42) (Class 4) (0-85,84) 3-Y-O **£6,477** (£1,927; £963; £481) **Stalls** High

Form RPR
6223 **1** **Burning Incense (IRE)**[30] 2014 3-9-1 **78** .... RichardHughes 1 93+
(R Charlton) *hld up in rr: nt clr run over 1f out: threaded through fnl f to ld last 75yds: cleverly* **11/4**[1]
-040 **2** 1/2 **Valentino Swing (IRE)**[10] 2609 3-8-7 **70** .... (p) KerrinMcEvoy 10 74
(J L Spearing) *w ldrs thrght: upsides u.p fnl f: outpcd nr fin* **16/1**
0135 **3** nk **Lucayos**[11] 2570 3-8-7 **75** .... (b) RichardKingscote(5) 3 78
(Mrs H Sweeting) *pressed ldr: led 2f out: drvn fnl f: hdd last 75yds* **20/1**
1332 **4** nk **Patavium Prince (IRE)**[3] 2826 3-8-6 **69** .... StephenCarson 9 71
(J R Best) *hld up: rdn and prog on outer fr 2f out: tried to chal fnl f: one pce last 75yds* **15/2**
-064 **5** 1/2 **Spearit (IRE)**[18] 2385 3-8-10 **73** .... JohnEgan 11 74
(D R C Elsworth) *hld up: nt clr run 2f out and swtchd to outer: drvn and styd on fnl f: nrst fin* **12/1**
-205 **6** 1 1/2 **Danawi (IRE)**[48] 1565 3-8-4 **67** .... MartinDwyer 6 63
(R Hannon) *dwlt: hld up: shkn up 2f out: one pce and no imp ldrs fnl f* **16/1**
3212 **7** 1 1/4 **Sarah's Art (IRE)**[6] 2730 3-8-2 **65** .... (b) ChrisCatlin 5 57
(N A Callaghan) *pressed ldrs: hrd rdn over 1f out: wknd fnl f* **8/1**
0-05 **8** 1/2 **Cinematic (IRE)**[9] 2642 3-9-0 **77** .... JamieSpencer 2 68
(M H Tompkins) *towards rr: last and rdn whn nt clr run over 1f out and swtchd sharply rt: plugged on* **12/1**
-064 **9** 2 **Makabul**[20] 2329 3-9-3 **80** .... AlanMunro 8 65
(B R Millman) *dwlt: hld up in rr: gng wl enough whn bdly hmpd over 1f out: nt rcvr* **7/1**[3]
6622 **10** 1 1/4 **Mango Music**[10] 2609 3-9-1 **78** .... TedDurcan 7 59
(M R Channon) *pressed ldrs for 4f: steadily wknd* **5/1**[2]
1100 **11** 1 **Don't Tell Sue**[9] 2639 3-9-7 **84** .... RyanMoore 4 62
(B W Hills) *bmpd sn after s: mde most to 2f out: sn eased* **12/1**
1m 14.02s (0.35) **Going Correction** +0.20s/f (Good) **11** Ran SP% **118.3**
Speed ratings (Par 101):105,104,103,103,102 100,99,98,95,94 92
CSF £51.16 CT £762.53 TOTE £3.80: £1.50, £4.90, £7.30; EX 74.50.
Owner Thurloe Thoroughbreds XV **Bred** Pier House Stud **Trained** Beckhampton, Wilts
■ Stewards' Enquiry : Richard Kingscote one-day ban: used whip with excessive frequency (Jul 7)
Richard Hughes two-day ban: careless riding (Jul 7, 9)

FOCUS
Just a fair sprint handicap, but a good effort from Burning Incense, who overcame trouble in-running. Solid-enough form.

2932 CLIC SARGENT H'CAP 1m 67y
8:10 (8:11) (Class 4) (0-80,80) 3-Y-O **£5,829** (£1,734; £866; £432) **Stalls** High

Form RPR
0-30 **1** **Sicilian (IRE)**[47] 1596 3-8-13 **72** .... JohnEgan 11 83
(B W Hills) *reminders sn after s: led after 2f: mde rest: rdn over 2f out: clr and in command over 1f out* **10/1**
2-00 **2** 2 1/2 **Shogun Prince (IRE)**[23] 2232 3-9-2 **80** .... RichardKingscote(5) 13 85
(A King) *hld up bhd ldrs: rdn over 2f out: chsd wnr over 1f out: no impression* **16/1**
36-6 **3** shd **Theatre Royal**[29] 2048 3-8-3 **62** .... MartinDwyer 4 67
(A M Balding) *settled in rr: prog over 2f out: drvn and styd on fr over 1f out: nrst fin* **11/1**
0000 **4** 1 3/4 **Sleeping Storm (IRE)**[9] 2650 3-8-5 **71** .... KMay(7) 12 72
(B J Meehan) *prom: chsd wnr 2f out to over 1f out: one pce* **20/1**
6-04 **5** 1 1/2 **Right Ted (IRE)**[10] 2620 3-9-3 **76** .... RyanMoore 6 73
(R Hannon) *sn restrained bhd ldrs: rdn and effrt over 2f out: fdd fnl f* **5/1**[2]
3020 **6** nk **Cantabilly (IRE)**[28] 2065 3-8-11 **70** .... ChrisCatlin 1 67
(M R Channon) *towards rr: rdn 3f out: struggling 2f out: plugged on* **14/1**
21 **7** 2 **Don Pietro**[28] 2069 3-9-2 **75** .... TedDurcan 9 70+
(D J Coakley) *led for 2f: chsd wnr to 2f out: wknd: eased last 100yds* **3/1**[1]
060 **8** 1/2 **Nassar (IRE)**[11] 2587 3-8-10 **69** .... (v[1]) NKNicolaou 3 60
(G Prodromou) *hld up in last pair: brief effrt u.p 2f out: sn no prog* **66/1**
2000 **9** hd **Charlton**[20] 2330 3-9-7 **80** .... IanMongan 8 70
(T G Mills) *dwlt: a wl in rr: rdn and struggling over 2f out* **20/1**
-220 **10** 3 **Catbang (IRE)**[17] 2391 3-8-6 **65** .... KerrinMcEvoy 7 48+
(N A Callaghan) *t.k.h: hld up in midfield: styd alone on nr side in st: nvr on terms* **7/1**[3]
5643 **11** 2 1/2 **Zabeel House**[10] 2620 3-9-7 **80** .... JamieSpencer 2 58
(E A L Dunlop) *hld up in last pair: drvn and no real prog over 2f out: wknd fnl f* **5/1**[2]
053 **12** 13 **Press The Button (GER)**[10] 2605 3-8-12 **74** .... AmirQuinn(3) 10 22
(J R Boyle) *t.k.h: prom tl wknd 3f out: t.o* **16/1**
1m 46.73s (1.13) **Going Correction** +0.20s/f (Good) **12** Ran SP% **117.7**
Speed ratings (Par 101):102,99,99,97,96 95,93,93,93,90 87,74
CSF £154.16 CT £1822.44 TOTE £15.10: £3.70, £6.30, £3.10; EX 201.10.
Owner J R Fleming **Bred** J Fleming And Abbey Bloodstock **Trained** Lambourn, Berks

FOCUS
A fair handicap run at what appeared quite a good pace, and the time compared favourably with that for the maiden. Only Catbang tried his luck near side, and he was beaten a mile.

2933 TIGER DEVELOPMENTS H'CAP 1m 3f 135y
8:40 (8:41) (Class 5) (0-70,70) 3-Y-O **£3,238** (£963; £481; £240) **Stalls** Low

Form RPR
0141 **1** **Bob's Your Uncle**[19] 2352 3-8-12 **61** .... AlanMunro 7 68
(J G Portman) *hld up in midfield: stdy prog against far rail over 2f out: drvn to ld last 150 yds: styd on wl* **11/2**[2]
0-00 **2** 1 1/4 **Storm Of Arabia (IRE)**[10] 2622 3-8-13 **62** .... TedDurcan 9 67
(W R Swinburn) *hld up towards rr: rdn and prog on outer fr over 2f out: r.o to take 2nd nr fin* **16/1**
-036 **3** hd **Kalatime (IRE)**[31] 1997 3-9-4 **67** .... MartinDwyer 10 71
(A M Balding) *racd freely: led: rdn 2f out: hdd and one pce last 150yds* **8/1**
0400 **4** 1 1/2 **Floodlight Fantasy**[11] 2584 3-9-1 **64** .... RichardMullen 5 66
(E S McMahon) *t.k.h: trckd ldrs: rdn and disp 2nd over 1f out: one pce* **5/1**[1]
6-15 **5** 1/2 **High Seasons**[42] 1740 3-9-2 **68** .... SaleemGolam(3) 3 69
(B R Millman) *t.k.h early: prom: rdn over 2f out: one pce fr over 1f out* **6/1**[3]
-500 **6** nk **Maximix**[7] 2713 3-8-13 **62** .... OscarUrbina 14 63+
(B W Hills) *hld up in midfield: hmpd bnd over 6f out: prog to trck ldrs 2f out and gng wl enough: shkn up and no rspnse over 1f out* **20/1**
-000 **7** 2 **Grey Paint (USA)**[11] 2584 3-9-7 **70** .... (t) RyanMoore 4 68
(R Hannon) *trckd ldrs: effrt 3f out: no imp over 1f out: fdd* **8/1**
-500 **8** 3 1/2 **Meantime (USA)**[26] 2142 3-9-2 **65** .... NKNicolaou 12 59+
(G Prodromou) *hld up in last pair: urged along and effrt fr wl off the pce over 2f out: no ch: eased last 100yds whn stl styng on* **50/1**
000 **9** 1 3/4 **Sa Nau**[16] 2465 3-8-2 **51** oh1 .... ChrisCatlin 8 40
(T Keddy) *dwlt: wl in rr: rdn 4f out: nvr on terms* **50/1**
-030 **10** 1 1/4 **Kavachi (IRE)**[13] 2518 3-9-5 **68** .... JamieSpencer 2 63+
(E A L Dunlop) *dwlt: sn chsd ldr: hrd rdn over 2f out: wknd over 1f out: heavily eased ins fnl f* **11/2**[2]
0 **11** 5 **Bu-Ali (USA)**[19] 2352 3-7-9 **51** oh3 .... SophieDoyle(7) 15 30
(B W Duke) *chsd ldr tl over 2f out: wknd rapidly* **66/1**
54-5 **12** 7 **Find It Out (USA)**[36] 1866 3-8-11 **63** .... BenSwarbrick(3) 6 31
(T D Barron) *a wl in rr: wknd 3f out* **8/1**

621- **13** *45* **Pip's Baby**[240] 6150 3-9-1 **64** .... JohnEgan 13 —
(S Kirk) *t.k.h: hld up in midfield: wknd 4f out: t.o* **9/1**

2m 34.32s (4.22) **Going Correction** +0.20s/f (Good) **13** Ran SP% **121.1**
Speed ratings (Par 99):93,92,92,91,90 90,89,86,85,84 81,76,46
CSF £88.87 CT £713.46 TOTE £3.60: £1.40, £5.40, £4.10; EX 112.10.
Owner A S B Portman **Bred** Wheelersland Stud **Trained** Compton, Berks

FOCUS
A modest handicap, not all that strong for the track, but sound-enough form. With not much pace on early, the winning time was moderate for the type of race. They all raced far side in the straight.

2934 CLAREVILLE CAPITAL MAIDEN STKS — 1m 67y
9:10 (9:13) (Class 5) 3-Y-O — **£3,886** (£1,156; £577; £288) **Stalls** High

Form — RPR

3 **1** **Our Putra**[31] 2001 3-9-3 .... (t) RichardHughes 2 78+
(M A Jarvis) *led: narrowly hdd over 3f out to 2f out: drvn into def advantage over 1f out: styd on wl* **3/1**[1]

5-3 **2** *1 1/4* **Wulimaster (USA)**[35] 1880 3-9-3 .... KerrinMcEvoy 6 75+
(Sir Michael Stoute) *settled midfield: shkn up wl over 1f out: r.o fnl f to take 2nd nr fin* **10/3**[2]

0 **3** *nk* **Bordello**[69] 1065 3-9-3 .... MartinDwyer 13 74
(B W Hills) *t.k.h: trckd ldng pair: hrd rdn over 2f out: chsd wnr over 1f out: no imp: lost 2nd nr fin* **6/1**

64 **4** *2 1/2* **Regal Sunset (IRE)**[16] 2465 3-9-3 .... TedDurcan 1 68
(W R Swinburn) *w wnr: led narrowly over 3f out to 2f out: wknd fnl f* **6/1**

0 **5** *1/2* **Medfae (KSA)**[100] 669 3-9-3 .... AlanMunro 3 67
(C F Wall) *t.k.h: trckd ldrs: rdn over 2f out: no imp after* **66/1**

00 **6** *1/2* **Wheelavit (IRE)**[13] 2532 3-9-0 .... AdamKirby(3) 14 66
(B G Powell) *t.k.h: trckd ldrs: rdn and cl up 2f out: fdd* **66/1**

6- **7** *3/4* **Hazelnut**[248] 6002 3-8-12 .... JamieSpencer 10 59+
(J R Fanshawe) *dwlt: hld up in last pair: pushed along over 2f out: kpt on steadily: nvr nrr* **11/2**[3]

8 *1/2* **Dream Dance** 3-8-12 .... RichardMullen 9 59+
(H Morrison) *dwlt: hld up in midfield: shkn up over 2f out: no prog over 1f out: eased ins fnl f* **18/1**

9 *nk* **Hooplah** 3-8-12 .... RyanMoore 4 57+
(J H M Gosden) *hld up in midfield: pushed along whn stmbld over 3f out: no real prog after* **8/1**

-0 **10** *3/4* **Eastlands (IRE)**[25] 2175 3-9-3 .... JohnEgan 8 61
(Jamie Poulton) *dwlt: a in rr: rdn 3f out: one pce and no prog* **20/1**

00 **11** *6* **Lady Galadriel (USA)**[11] 2580 3-8-12 .... HayleyTurner 12 42
(J M P Eustace) *reluctant to enter stalls: a wl in rr: bhd fnl 2f* **50/1**

0 **12** *14* **Ticking**[19] 2343 3-9-3 .... ChrisCatlin 11 15
(T Keddy) *a last: t.o fnl 2f* **50/1**

1m 49.88s (4.28) **Going Correction** +0.20s/f (Good) **12** Ran SP% **120.1**
Speed ratings (Par 99):86,84,84,81,81 80,80,79,79,78 72,58
CSF £12.77 TOTE £2.80: £2.10, £1.60, £3.00; EX 9.10 Place 6 £358.34, Place 5 £245.52.
Owner H R H Sultan Ahmad Shah **Bred** Lady Juliet Tadgell **Trained** Newmarket, Suffolk

FOCUS
An ordinary maiden and a very moderate winning time for the type of race, 3.15 seconds slower than the earlier handicap over the same trip. The bare form is not strong. They all raced far side in the straight.
Lady Galadriel(USA) Official explanation: trainer said filly was in season
Ticking Official explanation: jockey said gelding hung badly right
T/Plt: £839.60 to a £1 stake. Pool: £67,976.15. 59.10 winning tickets. T/Qpdt: £209.80 to a £1 stake. Pool: £3,714.10. 13.10 winning tickets. JN

2790 WOLVERHAMPTON (A.W) (L-H)
Monday, June 26

OFFICIAL GOING: Standard
Wind: Light, against Weather: Overcast

2935 STAY AT WOLVERHAMPTON HOLIDAY INN AMATEUR RIDERS' (S) STKS — 1m 4f 50y(P)
2:15 (2:15) (Class 6) 4-Y-O+ — **£2,307** (£709; £354) **Stalls** Low

Form — RPR

54-0 **1** **French Mannequin (IRE)**[13] 2522 7-10-6 52 .... (v) MissFayeBramley(3) 9 50+
(P A Blockley) *chsd ldrs: outpcd and n.m.r over 2f out: hdwy to chse ldr over 1f out: r.o to ld wl ins fnl f* **11/4**[1]

4366 **2** *3* **Granary Girl**[6] 2728 4-10-4 46 .... MrSPearce(5) 12 45
(J Pearce) *led: pushed clr 2f out: edgd rt over 1f out: hdd and no ex ins fnl f* **11/2**[3]

000- **3** *2 1/2* **Ashstanza**[317] 4353 5-10-7 45 .... MrOPestryy(7) 6 46
(R D E Woodhouse) *chsd ldr: rdn over 2f out: styd on same pce appr fnl f* **66/1**

0-04 **4** *2 1/2* **Beaumont Girl (IRE)**[98] 442 4-10-2 40 .... (t) MrsKLDarmody(7) 2 37+
(Miss M E Rowland) *hld up: hdwy over 1f out: nrst fin* **11/1**

5-00 **5** *3/4* **Bolshoi Ballet**[9] 414 8-10-9 55 .... MrBMcHugh(5) 4 41
(R A Fahey) *mid-div: hdwy 3f out: sn rdn: no imp appr fnl f* **9/2**[2]

0566 **6** *3/4* **Elms Schoolboy**[11] 2585 4-10-12 45 .... JPFeatherstone(7) 3 45
(P Howling) *s.s: hld up: hdwy and swtchd lft over 1f out: nvr nrr* **8/1**

30-6 **7** *1 3/4* **Stolen Song**[176] 5 6-10-7 53 .... (b) MrJBurdon(7) 10 37
(J Ryan) *prom: rdn over 3f out: wknd wl over 1f out* **14/1**

-000 **8** *1/2* **Tilla**[12] 973 6-10-4 53 .... (v) MrSPJones(5) 7 31
(Mrs A J Hamilton-Fairley) *s.i.s: hdwy 10f out: rdn and wknd over 1f out* **11/1**

5605 **9** *4* **Bhutan (IRE)**[11] 2566 11-10-11 42 .... MrJJBest(3) 5 30
(Jim Best) *hld up: n.d* **14/1**

0200 **10** *14* **Mi Odds**[55] 1389 10-11-0 61 .... MrsMMorris 1 7
(Mrs N Macauley) *hld up: a bhd* **6/1**

006- **11** *nk* **Mel's Moment (USA)**[358] 3163 4-10-7 58 .... (b) MrMPrice(7) 8 7
(R J Price) *hld up: wknd 4f out* **10/1**

000- **12** *19* **Royal Sailor (IRE)**[167] 6576 4-10-7 45 .... MrAChahal(7) 11 —
(J Ryan) *s.i.s: hld up: wknd over 3f out* **40/1**

2m 45.26s (2.84) **Going Correction** -0.225s/f (Stan) **12** Ran SP% **128.7**
Speed ratings (Par 101):81,79,77,75,75 74,73,73,70,61 60,48
CSF £19.41 TOTE £4.70: £1.40, £1.60, £38.30; EX 21.30 Trifecta £162.10 Part won. Pool: £228.32 - 0.69 winning tickets..There was no bid for the winner.
Owner J T Billson **Bred** Limestone Stud **Trained** Lambourn, Berks

FOCUS
A bad race, rated through the poor third, and a moderate early pace resulted in a slow time, even for a contest like this. Very few ever got into it thanks to the way the race was run.
Mi Odds Official explanation: jockey said gelding never travelled

2936 WORLD BET EXCHANGE WBX.COM H'CAP — 7f 32y(P)
2:45 (2:46) (Class 6) (0-60,60) 3-Y-O+ — **£2,730** (£806; £403) **Stalls** High

Form — RPR

2033 **1** **Joshua's Gold (IRE)**[24] 2211 5-9-6 **55** .... (v) DanielTudhope(3) 8 70
(D Carroll) *hld up in tch: rdn to ld and edgd lft over 1f out: r.o* **6/1**

0234 **2** *3 1/2* **Taranaki**[11] 2567 8-10-0 **60** .... DaneO'Neill 1 66
(P D Cundell) *s.i.s: sn prom: n.m.r 2f out: sn rdn: styd on: nt trble wnr* **5/1**[3]

1343 **3** *nk* **Fulvio (USA)**[20] 2319 6-9-9 **55** .... (v) J-PGuillambert 7 60
(P Howling) *chsd ldrs: led and edgd lft over 2f out: rdn and hdd over 1f out: no ex fnl f* **12/1**

5535 **4** *nk* **Go Garuda**[96] 693 5-9-11 **60** .... AdamKirby(3) 10 64
(Miss Gay Kelleway) *s.i.s: outpcd: r.o u.p ins fnl f: nrst fin* **15/2**

2526 **5** *1* **Only If I Laugh**[9] 2645 5-9-8 **54** .... GrahamGibbons 5 56
(M J Attwater) *chsd ldrs: rdn and edgd lft over 1f out: styd on same pce* **7/2**[1]

4414 **6** *nk* **Iced Diamond (IRE)**[3] 2811 7-10-0 **60** .... JamieSpencer 12 64+
(W M Brisbourne) *s.i.s: hld up: nt clr run 2f out: hdwy over 1f out: no imp fnl f* **9/2**[2]

4030 **7** *1/2* **Edin Burgher (FR)**[45] 1644 5-9-9 **55** .... (p) SamHitchcott 9 55
(T T Clement) *sn outpcd: rdn over 1f out: n.d* **7/1**

0050 **8** *3 1/2* **Elrafa Mujahid**[19] 2348 4-9-11 **60** .... (p) SaleemGolam(3) 2 51
(Ernst Oertel) *led: hung rt and hdd over 2f out: wknd over 1f out* **6/1**

0000 **9** *1/2* **Connotation**[9] 2647 4-10-0 **60** .... FergusSweeney 11 49
(A G Newcombe) *s.s: a in rr* **33/1**

2640 **10** *3 1/2* **Merdiff**[4] 2793 7-9-9 **55** .... ShaneKelly 4 35
(W M Brisbourne) *hld up: rdn over 2f out: wknd over 1f out* **12/1**

00/0 **11** *1 1/4* **Benny The Ball (USA)**[26] 2141 5-9-11 **57** .... MickyFenton 3 34
(N P Littmoden) *chsd ldr: rdn and ev ch whn hung rt over 2f out: sn n.m.r and wknd* **14/1**

3200 **12** *15* **Golden Spectrum (IRE)**[22] 2262 7-9-3 **56** .... (b) TolleyDean(7) 6 —
(R A Harris) *s.i.s: hdwy 4f out: rdn and wknd over 2f out* **25/1**

1m 29.08s (-1.32) **Going Correction** -0.225s/f (Stan) **12** Ran SP% **138.7**
Speed ratings (Par 101):98,94,93,93,92 91,91,87,86,82 81,64
CSF £42.78 CT £384.21 TOTE £8.00: £2.00, £1.40, £2.80; EX 55.90 Trifecta £226.70 Part won. Pool: £319.37 - 0.65 winning tickets..
Owner Simon Bean, David Jones **Bred** M G Masterson **Trained** Warthill, N Yorks

FOCUS
A modest handicap run at just an average pace and not many got into it. The winner is rated to his turf best and the form is sound.

2937 VERSION ONE'S BE A WINNER CLAIMING STKS — 5f 216y(P)
3:15 (3:16) (Class 6) 3-Y-O — **£3,238** (£963; £481; £240) **Stalls** Low

Form — RPR

6446 **1** **Arzaag**[11] 2576 3-9-1 65 .... (b[1]) RyanMoore 1 61+
(D M Simcock) *s.s: hdwy and nt clr run over 1f out: shkn up to ld wl ins fnl f: r.o* **3/1**[2]

00 **2** *1 3/4* **Sarah's Prince (IRE)**[13] 2535 3-9-1 50 .... DaneO'Neill 8 56
(D K Ivory) *dwlt: outpcd: hdwy u.p over 2f out: rdn to ld and edgd lft ins fnl f: sn hdd and unable qck* **25/1**

4011 **3** *2* **Hillbilly Cat (USA)**[23] 2247 3-8-6 65 .... BenSwarbrick(3) 6 44
(T D Barron) *chsd ldrs: led 2f out: sn rdn: hdd and no ex ins fnl f* **13/8**[1]

243 **4** *2* **In Hope**[82] 890 3-8-0 48 .... HayleyTurner 3 29
(Ernst Oertel) *chsd ldrs: rdn over 1f out: wknd ins fnl f* **12/1**

6630 **5** *2 1/2* **Trombone Tom**[17] 2399 3-9-1 58 .... ShaneKelly 4 37
(J R Norton) *led 1f: remained handy: rdn and ev ch over 1f out: wknd ins fnl f* **9/2**

0-10 **6** *3 1/2* **Charley's Aunt (IRE)**[164] 105 3-8-2 63 .... ChrisCatlin 2 13
(Mrs C A Dunnett) *prom over 4f* **4/1**[3]

6263 **7** *3 1/2* **Glenargo (USA)**[11] 2570 3-9-1 54 .... (p) AdrianMcCarthy 7 16
(R A Harris) *sddle slipped sn after s: led 5f out: hdd 2f out: eased ins fnl f* **15/2**

0-00 **8** *10* **Canvas (IRE)**[10] 2605 3-8-1 48 ow1 .... FrancisNorton 9 —
(Miss Z C Davison) *sn outpcd* **33/1**

1m 15.1s (-0.71) **Going Correction** -0.225s/f (Stan) **8** Ran SP% **127.5**
Speed ratings (Par 97):95,92,90,87,84 79,74,61
CSF £78.58 TOTE £3.60: £1.90, £10.10, £1.10; EX 89.50 Trifecta £390.10 Part won. Pool: £549.57 - 0.10 winning tickets..The winner was subject to a friendly claim. Hillbilly Cat was claimed by Roger Ingram for £7,000.
Owner Fawzi Abdulla Nass **Bred** Millsec Limited **Trained** Newmarket, Suffolk

FOCUS
A weakish claimer and the winning time was 0.2 seconds slower than the following two-year-old maiden. It is doubtful if the winner had to improve.
Glenargo(USA) Official explanation: jockey said saddle slipped

2938 EUROPEAN BREEDERS FUND MAIDEN STKS — 5f 216y(P)
3:45 (3:46) (Class 5) 2-Y-O — **£3,886** (£1,156; £577; £288) **Stalls** Low

Form — RPR

02 **1** **Not For Me (IRE)**[17] 2416 2-9-3 .... JohnEgan 10 78
(T J Pitt) *mde all: rdn over 1f out: jst hld on* **13/8**[2]

2 **2** *hd* **Non Compliant**[17] 2402 2-9-3 .... MichaelHills 12 77
(J W Hills) *hld up in tch: chsd wnr and hung rt over 3f out: rdn over 1f out: r.o* **6/4**[1]

0 **3** *1 1/4* **Lord Theo**[20] 2315 2-8-10 .... JamesMillman(7) 2 74
(D K Ivory) *chsd ldrs: outpcd 2f out: r.o ins fnl f* **7/1**[3]

00 **4** *8* **My Sara**[12] 2552 2-8-12 .... ShaneKelly 11 45
(D J Daly) *sn outpcd: styd on ins fnl f: nrst fin* **14/1**

0 **5** *2* **Having A Ball**[12] 2552 2-9-3 .... LPKeniry 4 44
(P D Cundell) *sn pushed along and prom: wknd wl over 1f out* **25/1**

6 *2 1/2* **Foxies Firstglance** 2-8-12 .... DO'Donohoe 5 31
(R D E Woodhouse) *s.i.s: outpcd* **66/1**

7 *6* **Kastan** 2-9-3 .... FergusSweeney 3 18
(B Palling) *sn outpcd* **10/1**

0 **8** *8* **Head To Head (IRE)**[17] 2416 2-9-3 .... MickyFenton 7 —
(Peter Grayson) *s.i.s: outpcd* **14/1**

0 **9** *1 1/4* **Taran Tregarth**[16] 2439 2-8-12 .... SamHitchcott 6 —
(A Bailey) *slowly into stride: outpcd* **66/1**

46 **10** *1/2* **Breckland Boy**[11] 2586 2-9-3 .... ChrisCatlin 8 —
(Mrs C A Dunnett) *chsd ldrs 4f* **20/1**

0 **11** *3* **Little Tiny Tom**[17] 2416 2-9-3 .... VinceSlattery 1 —
(C N Kellett) *chsd ldrs to 1/2-way* **50/1**

1m 14.9s (-0.91) **Going Correction** -0.225s/f (Stan) **11** Ran SP% **126.6**
Speed ratings (Par 93):97,96,95,84,81 78,70,59,58,57 53
CSF £4.67 TOTE £3.50: £1.10, £1.10, £1.70; EX 5.00 Trifecta £26.10 Pool: £475.93 - 12.93 winning tickets.

Owner Ms K O'Hare **Bred** Floral Partnership **Trained** Bawtry, S Yorks

FOCUS

A two-horse race according to the market and that is how it worked out, despite both not being well drawn, with the pair filling the first two places. The form should prove sound enough. The winning time was fair for a race like this, 0.2 seconds faster than the preceding three-year-old claimer.

NOTEBOOK

Not For Me(IRE) confirmed the promise of his improved effort over course and distance last time with a game front-running victory. He did not have much to spare at the line, but is entitled to progress a bit more and the nurseries are not that far away which should widen his opportunities. (op 6-4 tchd 7-4)

Non Compliant was not well drawn, but still arrived to hold every chance and just found the winner too determined. He is nothing special, but should find a maiden. (op 11-10)

Lord Theo ◆ improved a good deal from his debut and was snapping at the heels of the principals all the way up the home straight. The distance back to the third suggests he should be able to find an opportunity. (tchd 8-1)

My Sara emerged to finish very much best of the rest and despite her sprinting pedigree she shapes as though she will appreciate further.

Having A Ball, halved the distance he finished behind My Sara at Kempton last time, but that was about as much as he achieved. The best of him will probably not be seen until he is handicapped and racing over further.

2939 WBX.COM WORLD BET EXCHANGE H'CAP — 5f 20y(P)

4:15 (4:15) (Class 5) (0-70,70) 3-Y-O **£3,238** (£963; £481; £240) **Stalls** Low

Form				RPR
0-05	**1**		**Steel City Boy (IRE)**[30] 2016 3-8-6 **58** .... DanielTudhope(3) 11 (D Carroll) *s.i.s: sn chsng ldrs: led 2f out: pushed clr fnl f* **20/1**	73+
504	**2**	*4*	**Artie's Son (IRE)**[30] 2016 3-8-6 **60** .... DuranFentiman(5) 8 (T D Easterby) *sn pushed along in rr: hdwy u.p over 1f out: edgd lft: no ch w wnr* **7/1**	60+
-006	**3**	*1 3/4*	**Crusader's Gold (FR)**[24] 2195 3-8-3 **52** .... ChrisCatlin 7 (T D Easterby) *s.i.s: outpcd: r.o ins fnl f: nrst fin* **10/1**	46
4000	**4**	*1 1/4*	**Mytton's Pride**[13] 2521 3-8-11 **60** .... SamHitchcott 9 (A Bailey) *disp ld 3f: sn rdn: styd on same pce* **25/1**	50
3403	**5**	*3/4*	**Pride Of Joy**[19] 2340 3-9-4 **67** .... DaneO'Neill 1 (D K Ivory) *led 3f: rdn and swtchd rt over 1f out: no ex* **4/1**[1]	54
0030	**6**	*nk*	**Egyptian Lord**[17] 2410 3-9-6 **69** ....(b) MickyFenton 2 (Peter Grayson) *chsd ldrs: rdn 2f out: styd on same pce* **9/2**[2]	55
6-65	**7**	*1/2*	**Obergurgl (IRE)**[24] 2197 3-8-11 **60** .... DO'Donohoe 5 (Mrs A Duffield) *chsd ldrs: rdn and edgd lft over 1f out: wknd ins fnl f* **14/1**	44
6615	**8**	*nk*	**Phinerine**[27] 2096 3-8-12 **68** ....(b) TolleyDean(7) 4 (R A Harris) *in rr: hdwy and nt clr run 1/2-way: rdn and nt clr run over 1f out: sn wknd* **6/1**[3]	51
5005	**9**	*hd*	**Hits Only Jude (IRE)**[35] 1900 3-9-7 **70** .... DeanMcKeown 12 (J Pearce) *racd wd: prom: lost pl over 3f out: n.d after* **7/1**	52
0605	**10**	*1 1/2*	**Signor Whippee**[2] 2876 3-8-2 **51** oh1........(b1) FrancisNorton 3 (A Berry) *hmpd sn after s: outpcd* **10/1**	28
0046	**11**	*6*	**Kellys Dream (IRE)**[24] 2190 3-8-9 **58** .... RyanMoore 6 (M Quinn) *chsd ldrs: rdn 1/2-way: sn wknd* **6/1**[3]	13

61.17 secs (-1.65) **Going Correction** -0.225s/f (Stan) **11** Ran SP% **125.2**

Speed ratings (Par 99):104,97,94,92,91 91,90,89,89,87 77

CSF £163.46 CT £1521.11 TOTE £36.40: £22.00, £2.90, £5.30; EX 203.20 TRIFECTA Not won..

Owner Ninerus **Bred** Mrs A B McDonnell **Trained** Warthill, N Yorks

■ Stewards' Enquiry : Dane O'Neill caution: careless riding

FOCUS

This turned out to be a case of the winner first, the rest nowhere. The winning time was decent for a race like this, and the form should prove sound.

Obergurgl(IRE) Official explanation: jockey said gelding lost its action

Hits Only Jude(IRE) Official explanation: jockey said gelding was denied a clear run

Signor Whippee Official explanation: jockey said gelding was hampered on leaving stalls

2940 MOORCROFT RACEHORSE WELFARE CENTRE MEDIAN AUCTION MAIDEN STKS — 1m 141y(P)

4:45 (4:45) (Class 6) 3-Y-O **£2,590** (£770; £385; £192) **Stalls** Low

Form				RPR
-420	**1**		**Empire Dancer (IRE)**[25] 2174 3-8-10 70........ KirstyMilczarek(7) 11 (C N Allen) *led: hdd 7f out: w ldr tl led over 3f out: clr over 1f out: comf* **13/2**	73
0	**2**	*3*	**Kings Confession (IRE)**[6] 2734 3-8-10 .... KellyHarrison(7) 3 (D Carroll) *n.m.r sn after s: outpcd: hdwy over 1f out: nt trble wnr* **50/1**	67+
4-0	**3**	*2*	**Campanile**[20] 2325 3-8-12 .... JamieSpencer 10 (J R Fanshawe) *hld up: hdwy over 5f out: rdn to chse wnr and hung lft over 1f out: wknd fnl f* **9/4**[2]	58
05	**4**	*4*	**Dab Hand (IRE)**[24] 2188 3-9-3 .... RyanMoore 5 (D M Simcock) *prom: rdn to chse wnr over 2f out: hung lft and wknd over 1f out* **3/1**[3]	54
4000	**5**	*10*	**Blue Army (IRE)**[16] 2465 3-9-3 50........(b1) SamHitchcott 4 (Jane Southcombe) *mid-div: effrt over 3f out: sn wknd* **50/1**	33
5-0	**6**	*2 1/2*	**Jenise (IRE)**[53] 1445 3-8-7 .... DuranFentiman(5) 7 (Mark Campion) *w ldr: led 7f out: hdd over 3f out: wknd 2f out* **25/1**	23
2	**7**	*3*	**Vampyrus**[28] 2063 3-9-3 .... DaneO'Neill 2 (H Candy) *chsd ldrs: rdn over 3f out: wknd over 2f out* **7/4**[1]	22
00	**8**	*12*	**Moving Story**[19] 2366 3-9-3 .... MickyFenton 6 (T J Fitzgerald) *sn outpcd* **25/1**	—
000-	**9**	*11*	**Chillipetals**[324] 4153 3-8-9 48........ JasonEdmunds(3) 9 (J Balding) *sn outpcd* **66/1**	—
0-00	**10**	*6*	**Canary Girl**[9] 2645 3-8-12 38........ BrianReilly 8 (Mrs C A Dunnett) *prom: hung rt and wknd over 4f out* **100/1**	—

1m 50.15s (-1.61) **Going Correction** -0.225s/f (Stan) **10** Ran SP% **119.6**

Speed ratings (Par 97):98,95,93,90,81 78,76,65,55,50

CSF £273.59 TOTE £6.60: £1.60, £32.90, £1.50; EX 433.70 Trifecta £402.90 Part won. Pool: £567.50 - 0.35 winning tickets. Place 6 £219.51, Place 5 £107.35.

Owner Golfers Dream Syndicate **Bred** Golden Vale Stud **Trained** Newmarket, Suffolk

FOCUS

Not a strong maiden with less than half the field holding a realistic chance, but the winner scored with some authority, though it is doubtful if he had to improve.

Canary Girl Official explanation: jockey said filly hung right

T/Plt: £228.00 to a £1 stake. Pool: £43,998.15. 140.85 winning tickets. T/Qpdt: £30.90 to a £1 stake. Pool: £3,178.90. 76.00 winning tickets. CR

2738 LONGCHAMP (R-H)

Monday, June 26

OFFICIAL GOING: Soft

2941a PRIX DE LA PORTE MAILLOT (GROUP 3) — 7f

2:05 (2:07) 3-Y-O+ **£27,586** (£11,034; £8,276; £4,138; £4,138)

			RPR
1		**Marchand D'Or (FR)**[39] 1810 3-8-7 .... DBonilla 11 (F Head, France) *made all, gd early speed to get across to ins rail after 1f from outside draw, qcknd 3l clr over 1f out, rdn out* **5/1**[3]	113
2	*3*	**Ridaar (FR)**[60] 1266 6-9-2 .... YGourraud 4 (J-P Gallorini, France) *disp 2nd on ins, 3rd str, effort and unable to qckn over 1 1/2f out, rallied against ins rail to tk 2nd fnl 30 yards* **9/1**	108
3	*snk*	**Together (FR)**[21] 2313 6-8-12 ....(b) SMaillot 8 (Mme C Vergne, France) *last to under 2f out, stayed on down outside to take 3rd on line, nrst fin* **20/1**	104
4	*nk*	**Helios Quercus (FR)**[21] 2313 4-9-2 .... TThulliez 12 (C Diard, France) *hld up in rr, 9th str, hdwy towards outside fr under 2f out, styd on wl fnl f, dead-heated for 5th, plcd dh 4th* **9/2**[2]	107
4	*dht*	**Biniou (IRE)**[5] 3-8-7 .... OPeslier 1 (Robert Collet, France) *hmpd on ins after 1f, plld hrd towards rr, 8th str, hdwy on ins to disp 4th 1f out, one pce, dead-heated for 5th, plcd dht 4th* **14/1**	104
6	*hd*	**Lucky Strike**[32] 1973 8-9-2 .... ADeVries 9 (A Trybuhl, Germany) *3rd whn edgd rt bnd after 1f, disp 2nd, 2nd st, outpcd by wnr 1 1/2f out, lost 2nd last 30y, fin 4th, disq, plcd 6th* **13/2**	106
7	*1*	**Marabout Directa (GER)**[46] 5-9-2 .... AHelfenbein 6 (Andreas Lowe, Germany) *raced in 4th, 5th straight on inside, effort over 1 1/2f out, one pace* **10/1**	104
8	*1/2*	**Rageman**[56] 1371 6-9-5 .... SPasquier 10 (M Cheno, France) *raced in 6th on outside, ridden 1 1/2f out, unable to quicken* **20/1**	106
9	*2*	**Donatello (GER)**[21] 2313 5-9-2 .... JVictoire 3 (W Baltromei, Germany) *raced in 7th, never a factor* **20/1**	98
10	*10*	**Early March**[15] 2490 4-9-2 .... CSoumillon 7 (Mme C Head-Maarek, France) *raced in 5th, 4th straight, brief effort over 1 1/2f out, soon beaten and eased* **7/4**[1]	73

1m 22.0s

WFA 3 from 4yo+ 9lb **10** Ran SP% **124.6**

PARI-MUTUEL: WIN 7.20; PL 2.80, 3.40, 8.20; DF 23.20.

Owner Mme J-L Giral **Bred** Mme J-L Giral **Trained** France

NOTEBOOK

Marchand D'Or(FR) dominated this Group 3 race from the moment the stalls opened. He was immediately taken into the lead from his outside draw, quickened one and a half furlongs out, and the race was at his mercy from that point. He passed the post alone and was highly impressive. Connections are now looking at the Group 1 Maurice de Gheest at Deauville in August.

Ridaar(FR) did his very best and followed the winner throughout. He quickened half way up the straight and battled on gamely to take second place in the closing places, but was found to have sustained a knock after the race.

Together(FR), held up for a late challenge, was brought up the centre of the track and started to improve from one and half out. She ran on well and only missed second place by a narrow margin.

Biniou(IRE) was badly hampered turning into the straight and had to be settled before making his challenge. He is another that was running on at the end.

Helios Quercus(FR) still had plenty to do coming into the straight. He made up late ground and was involved in a little bit of argy bargy around the furlong marker.

Lucky Strike finished fourth, but was demoted for causing problems to several other runners in the early part of the race. His rider was suspended for four days.

2942a PRIX DAPHNIS (GROUP 3) (C&G) — 1m 1f

2:35 (2:37) 3-Y-O **£27,586** (£11,034; £8,276; £5,517; £2,759)

			RPR
1		**Dilek (FR)**[17] 3-8-11 .... CSoumillon 6 (A De Royer-Dupre, France) *reluctant ldr tl hdd 5 1/2f out, 2md str, shaken up to ld again over 1 1/2f out, qcknd clr, pushed out, eased cl home* **5/4**[1]	113+
2	*2*	**Champs Elysees**[22] 2278 3-8-11 .... SPasquier 2 (A Fabre, France) *hld up, 3rd str, sn pushed along and slightly outpcd, rdn to tk 2nd ins fnl f, stayed on wl closing stages* **7/2**[2]	109
3	*2 1/2*	**Hello Sunday (FR)**[22] 2278 3-8-11 .... C-PLemaire 1 (Mme C Head-Maarek, France) *tracked leader in 3rd early, 4th straight, kept on under pressure to take 3rd final 50 yards* **11/2**	104
4	*1/2*	**Salsalava (FR)**[15] 2489 3-8-11 .... TJarnet 5 (P Demercastel, France) *raced in 2nd off slow pace til quickened to lead 5 1/2f out, headed over 1 1/2f out, weakened* **14/1**	103
5	*snk*	**Moon Prospect (IRE)**[64] 1179 3-8-11 .... OPeslier 3 (F Head, France) *held up in rear, 6th straight, never a factor* **4/1**[3]	103
6	*1 1/2*	**Nice Applause (IRE)**[52] 3-8-11 .... TThulliez 4 (Mme J Laurent-Joye Rossi, France) *held up in rear, 6th straight, never a factor* **14/1**	100

1m 55.7s **6** Ran SP% **115.4**

PARI-MUTUEL: WIN 1.80; PL 1.40, 1.80; SF 4.20.

Owner H H Aga Khan **Bred** His Highness The Aga Khan's Stud S C **Trained** Chantilly, France

NOTEBOOK

Dilek(FR) looks a champion in the making judging by the way he took this event. Leading early on before settling in second place, he quickened impressively from one and half out and his jockey spent most of the final furlong looking over his shoulders. Connections could be tempted by the Prix Jean Prat, whilst the Jacques Le Marois has also been mentioned as a future target.

Champs Elysees never had a chance with the winner, but still ran a sound race. He spend most of his time in third position before making his effort half way up the straight.

Hello Sunday(FR), fourth rounding the turn before the straight, was outpaced shortly after and then ran on again to take third place inside the final furlong.

Salsalava(FR), smartly out of the stalls, took up the running after a furlong but was completely outpaced when things quickened up in the straight.

2777 BEVERLEY (R-H)

Tuesday, June 27

OFFICIAL GOING: Good to firm (firm in places)

The ground was reckoned to be 'on the quick side of good'.

Wind: Moderate half behind Weather: Fine

2943 PADDOCK BAR MAIDEN AUCTION FILLIES' STKS 7f 100y

2:15 (2:15) (Class 5) 2-Y-O £3,886 (£1,156; £577; £288) Stalls High

Form				RPR
263	1		**Hucking Hot**[27] 2125 2-8-4 ... JohnEgan 3 (J R Best) *plld hrd: trckd ldrs: hdwy whn n.m.r and stmbld over 3f out: rdn to chse ldr wl over 1f out: kpt on to ld inslast* **11/8**[1]	73+
	2	1/2	**Dollar Chick (IRE)** 2-8-13 ... JoeFanning 6 (M Johnston) *sn led: stmbld over 4f out: pushed along 2f out: sn rdn: hung bdly lft ent last: sn hdd: kpt on u.p* **2/1**[2]	79+
	3	2 1/2	**Dancing Granny** 2-8-13 ... HayleyTurner 2 (M L W Bell) *trckd ldng pair: hdwy to chse ldr over 2f out: sn rdn and kpt on same pce fnl f* **10/1**	73
54	4	5	**Ioweyou**[17] 2432 2-8-7 ... DarryllHolland 5 (J S Moore) *keen: sn chsng ldr: rdn along over 2f out: sn wknd* **7/2**[3]	55
	5	1 1/4	**Chip N Pin** 2-7-13 ... DuranFentiman(5) 4 (T D Easterby) *s.i.s: a rr* **28/1**	49
0	6	18	**Lady Davali**[14] 2523 2-8-4 ... PaulHanagan 1 (S Parr) *chsd ldrs: hung lft and rn wd 1/2-way: sn rdn along and bhd fnl 2f* **66/1**	7+

1m 34.42s (0.11) **Going Correction** -0.30s/f (Firm) **6** Ran SP% **111.7**

Speed ratings (Par 90):87,86,83,77,76 55

CSF £4.33 TOTE £2.60: £1.60, £1.30; EX 5.10.

Owner Hucking Horses **Bred** Taker Bloodstock **Trained** Hucking, Kent

FOCUS

A very steady gallop. The winner had finished third in a Listed race here over five furlongs last time and followed in the footsteps of stablemate Rising Cross a year ago. She was in receipt of 9lb from the placed horses, both newcomers.

NOTEBOOK

Hucking Hot, very keen, met trouble coming off the home turn. She hung left and made very hard work of it in the end. A drop back in trip and less firm ground should enable her to show her true potential. (op Evens tchd 7-4)

Dollar Chick(IRE) ◆, an April foal, is a good-bodied type. She set her own pace and jumped a path leaving the back straight. Setting sail for home three furlongs out, her inexperience showed and she hung badly left. Coming back for more at the line, she was giving the winner 9lb and this must go down as a very good first effort. (op 3-1)

Dancing Granny, not born until mid-May, is on the leg and narrow. Forced to switch inside the runner-up, she stuck on in her own time and the experience will not be lost on her. (op 12-1 tchd 9-1)

Ioweyou, on her toes and continually swishing her tail, was very keen and hung right before fading. This was her third start and she does not impress as the type to progress. (op 9-2 tchd 3-1)

Chip N Pin, cheaply bought, is a good-bodied filly and after a tardy start she showed a glimmer of ability on her first start. (op 33-1 tchd 25-1)

2944 RACING UK ON SKY 432 CLAIMING STKS 1m 4f 16y

2:45 (2:46) (Class 5) 3-Y-O+ £3,238 (£963; £481; £240) Stalls High

Form				RPR
4031	1		**Unique Moment**[13] 2548 3-8-8 70 ... JoeFanning 3 (M Johnston) *mde all: rdn along over 2f out: drvn ent last and styd on strly* **5/4**[1]	62
0265	2	1	**Fort Churchill (IRE)**[31] 2035 5-9-10 66 ...(bt) TomEaves 6 (B Ellison) *trac ked ldrs: hdwy to chse wnr over 1f out: sn rdn and no imp wl ins last* **11/2**[3]	62
0-56	3	2 1/2	**Mr Maxim**[9] 2684 4-9-1 48 ...(v[1]) MichaelJStainton(7) 8 (R M Whitaker) *a promiennt: rdn along 2f out: kpt on same pce* **10/1**	56
1313	4	1/2	**Oldenway**[13] 2548 7-9-6 70 ... JamesReveley(7) 9 (R A Fahey) *trckd ldrs: swtchd lft and effrt over 1f out: sn no imp* **9/4**[2]	60+
-003	5	5	**Barnbrook Empire (IRE)**[16] 2483 4-8-7 41 ... TolleyDean(7) 7 (R A Harris) *hld up towards rr: sme hdwy over 2f out: nvr nr ldrs* **20/1**	39
06-0	6	9	**Starmix**[76] 975 5-9-3 46 ...(b) PaulMulrennan 1 (G A Harker) *a rr* **100/1**	28
122/	7	shd	**Whaleef**[30] 5006 8-9-6 70 ...(tp) NCallan 4 (B J Llewellyn) *in tch: rdn along over 3f out: sn wknd* **10/1**	31
000-	8	hd	**Perfectionist**[252] 5963 4-9-0 45 ... HayleyTurner 2 (Mrs C A Dunnett) *cl up: rdn along 3f out: sn wknd* **50/1**	24
000	9	39	**Soba Fella**[21] 2325 3-8-6 28 ... RobbieFitzpatrick 5 (P T Midgley) *a rr* **200/1**	—

2m 37.82s (-2.39) **Going Correction** -0.30s/f (Firm)

WFA 3 from 4yo+ 14lb **9** Ran SP% **117.0**

Speed ratings (Par 103):95,94,92,92,89 83,82,82,56

CSF £8.87 TOTE £2.20: £1.10, £1.80, £2.60; EX 12.10.The winner was claimed by D J French Davis for £15,000.

Owner J Shack **Bred** The Lavington Stud **Trained** Middleham Moor, N Yorks

FOCUS

Only four with a realistic chance at the weights beforehand and the winning time was moderate, even for a claimer. The exciteable winner had the run of the race.

Soba Fella Official explanation: jockey said gelding had a breathing problem

2945 HAPPY BIRTHDAY JANE H'CAP 1m 1f 207y

3:15 (3:20) (Class 4) (0-85,77) 4-Y-O+ £6,477 (£1,927; £963; £481) Stalls High

Form				RPR
-001	1		**Riley Boys (IRE)**[13] 2540 5-9-7 77 ... RobertWinston 2 (J G Given) *hld up in rr: hdwy over 2f out: rdn to ld ins last: jst hld on* **9/4**[2]	83
0-45	2	shd	**Tedsdale Mac**[8] 2697 7-7-13 62 ... SuzzanneFrance(7) 3 (N Bycroft) *trckd ldrs: hdwy 3f out: rdn wl over 1f out: styd on wl fnl f: jst failed* **16/1**	68
0535	3	1 1/2	**Wing Commander**[11] 2627 7-8-12 68 ...(b) RoystonFfrench 5 (I W McInnes) *cl up: rdn to ld wl over 1f out: drvn and hdd ins last: one pce* **6/1**	71
5-05	4	1/2	**Sky Quest (IRE)**[15] 2508 8-9-4 77 ...(tp) AdamKirby(3) 4 (W R Swinburn) *hld up: hdwy over 2f out: sn rdn and one pce ent last* **4/1**[3]	79
0052	5	5	**Little Jimbob**[6] 2761 5-9-4 74 ... PaulHanagan 1 (R A Fahey) *cl up: led after 2f: rdn along over 2f out: hdd over 1f out: sn drvn and wknd* **6/4**[1]	67
00-0	6	6	**Edas**[22] 2296 4-9-5 75 ... GrahamGibbons 6 (J J Quinn) *led 2f: cl up tl rdn along 3f out and sn wknd* **20/1**	56

2m 2.53s (-4.77) **Going Correction** -0.30s/f (Firm) **6** Ran SP% **115.7**

Speed ratings (Par 105):107,106,105,105,101 96

CSF £35.21 TOTE £2.90: £1.80, £4.00; EX 38.60.

Owner Paul Riley **Bred** P J Makin **Trained** Willoughton, Lincs

FOCUS

The top-weight was 8lb below the race ceiling and the early pace was just steady.

2946 HBLB H'CAP 5f

3:45 (3:45) (Class 3) (0-95,93) 3-Y-O+ £8,096 (£2,408; £1,203; £601) Stalls High

Form				RPR
5402	1		**Bo McGinty (IRE)**[9] 2683 5-9-0 79 ...(b) PaulHanagan 7 (R A Fahey) *trckd ldrs: swtchd rt over 1f out: swtchd lft and rdn ent last: styd on wl to ld last 100 yds* **4/1**[2]	92
01	2	1 1/4	**Golden Dixie (USA)**[11] 2624 7-9-11 90 ... AdrianMcCarthy 10 (R A Harris) *midfield: hdwy 2f out: sn rdn and styd on wl fnl f* **6/1**[3]	99
0504	3	hd	**Cape Royal**[11] 2624 6-10-0 93 ...(b) TPQueally 9 (J M Bradley) *sn led: rdn wl over 1f out: hdd and no ex last 100 yds* **10/1**	101
125-	4	nk	**Wyatt Earp (IRE)**[213] 6431 5-9-5 84 ... TonyHamilton 12 (R A Fahey) *in tch: rdn along 2f out: styd on wl fnl f: nrst fin* **7/1**	91+
4602	5	1 1/2	**Pawan (IRE)**[2] 2898 6-8-2 74 oh4 ...(b) AnnStokell(7) 4 (Miss A Stokell) *bhd: rdn along 2f out: kpt on ins last: nrst fin* **25/1**	75
0-03	6	hd	**Woodcote (IRE)**[17] 2429 4-9-9 91 ...(p) AdamKirby(3) 1 (C G Cox) *wnt lft s: sn chsng ldrs: rdn along 2f out: one pce ent last* **9/1**	92+
0306	7	hd	**Graze On**[11] 2624 4-9-0 86 ...(b) TolleyDean(7) 11 (R A Harris) *prom: rdn along and edgd lft over 1f out: sn drvn and one pce ent last* **10/1**	86
0105	8	5	**Wicked Uncle**[35] 1928 7-9-0 79 ...(b) DarryllHolland 5 (S Gollings) *rdn along 1/2-way and a rr* **33/1**	61
4643	9	3	**H Harrison (IRE)**[8] 2705 6-8-9 74 oh2 ... RoystonFfrench 2 (I W McInnes) *a rr* **33/1**	45
0004	10	3/4	**Funfair Wane**[14] 2521 7-9-5 84 ... AdrianTNicholls 14 (D Nicholls) *chsd ldrs on inner: rdn along 2f out: wkng whn n.m.r over 1f out* **7/2**[1]	52
1100	11	5	**Peopleton Brook**[17] 2450 4-9-9 88 ... NCallan 8 (J M Bradley) *chsd ldr: rdn along over 2f out: sn wknd* **14/1**	38

60.61 secs (-3.39) **Going Correction** -0.425s/f (Firm) **11** Ran SP% **113.6**

Speed ratings (Par 107):110,108,107,107,104 104,104,96,91,90 82

CSF £26.62 CT £219.27 TOTE £4.80: £1.80, £2.00, £3.20; EX 31.90.

Owner Paddy McGinty & Bo Turnbull **Bred** Stephen Breen **Trained** Musley Bank, N Yorks

■ Stewards' Enquiry : Paul Hanagan caution: careless riding

FOCUS

As usual the low drawn horses were at a disadvantage.

NOTEBOOK

Bo McGinty(IRE), raised 3lb after York, was able to run from his old mark here. Switched inside, in the end he won going away ending his lengthy losing run. (op 7-2)

Golden Dixie(USA), 5lb higher, was running from a career-high mark. He finished with quite a flourish and is a credit to his trainer.

Cape Royal, with the blinkers fitted again, showed blinding speed but on this uphill track could not last out. (op 11-1)

Wyatt Earp(IRE), absent since November, was putting in some fine late work and can add to his record when stepped back up in trip. (op 9-1)

Pawan(IRE), making a quick return from 4lb out of the handicap, ran a blinder from his outside draw but the fact remains he has not tasted success for over a year now. (op 20-1)

Woodcote(IRE), worst drawn, travelled strongly but could never take a serious hand. At least this shows he is in very good heart.

Wicked Uncle Official explanation: jockey said gelding was unsuited by the good to firm (firm in places) ground

Funfair Wane, without a win since his 2004 Ayr Gold Cup success, was cool and calm beforehand for once. He could not get his head in front and his chance had long gone when left short of room and eased over a furlong out. He lost a shoe and may not relish such quick ground these days. Official explanation: jockey said gelding lost a shoe and was unsuited by the good to firm (firm in places) ground

2947 Y.W.M. WASTE H'CAP 7f 100y

4:15 (4:16) (Class 5) (0-70,69) 3-Y-O+ £5,181 (£1,541; £770; £384) Stalls High

Form				RPR
0000	1		**Orpen Wide (IRE)**[4] 2820 4-9-7 64 ow1 ...(b[1]) LeeVickers(3) 2 (M C Chapman) *hld up and bhd: hdwy 3f out: str run on outer appr last: sn rdn: edgd rt and styd on to ld nr line* **50/1**	73
2525	2	nk	**Favouring (IRE)**[4] 2820 4-8-10 50 ...(v) DarryllHolland 3 (M C Chapman) *led: rdn 2f out: drvn over 1f out: hdd and no ex nr line* **12/1**	58
6042	3	hd	**Blue Empire (IRE)**[13] 2541 5-9-3 57 ... HayleyTurner 9 (C R Dore) *trckd ldrs: hdwy 2f out: swtchd ins and rdn to have ev ch ins last: kpt on* **7/1**[3]	65
0226	4	2	**Dudley Docker (IRE)**[75] 1002 4-9-6 63 ... DanielTudhope(3) 6 (D Carroll) *dwlt: hld up in rr: hdwy over 2f out: rdn to chse ldrs over 1f out: n.m.r ins last: kpt on* **10/1**	66+
-016	5	1/2	**Makai**[11] 2616 3-9-3 66 ... StanleyChin 14 (M Johnston) *chsd ldrs: hdwy 3f out: rdn to chal and ev ch over 1f out: drvn and hld whn n.m.r room wl ins last* **16/1**	68+
0602	6	1	**Saxon Lil (IRE)**[4] 2818 4-9-11 65 ... FrancisNorton 11 (J L Spearing) *chsd ldrs: hdwy 3f out: rdn to chal on outer over 1f out and ev ch tl edgd rt and wknd ins last* **7/2**[1]	64
-116	7	1 1/4	**Bollin Edward**[13] 2541 7-9-13 67 ... NCallan 10 (K A Ryan) *in tch: hdwy to chse ldrs over 2f out: sn rdn and one pce* **7/2**[1]	63
0002	8	1 3/4	**Penny Glitters**[8] 2699 3-8-8 57 ... DeanMcKeown 1 (S Parr) *cl up: rdn along over 2f out: grad wknd appr last* **33/1**	46
3-45	9	shd	**Le Chiffre (IRE)**[14] 2531 4-9-7 68 ...(p) TolleyDean(7) 4 (R A Harris) *hld up towards rr: hdwy on inner oevr 2f out: sn rdn and no imp* **28/1**	59
0-00	10	1/2	**Peters Delite**[13] 2541 4-9-3 57 ... TonyHamilton 8 (R A Fahey) *a rr* **33/1**	47
0000	11	nk	**Qaasi (USA)**[11] 2627 4-9-9 63 ... JoeFanning 5 (Mrs K Walton) *chsd ldrs: rdn along over 2f out: grad wknd* **25/1**	52
0-00	12	1 1/2	**Observatory Star (IRE)**[20] 2363 3-9-6 69 ... DavidAllan 7 (T D Easterby) *midfield: rdn along 3f out: sn wknd* **20/1**	52
0000	13	1	**Bolton Hall (IRE)**[10] 2640 4-9-10 64 ... PaulHanagan 12 (R A Fahey) *midfield: pushed along 1/2-way: sn wknd* **11/2**[2]	47+
00-0	14	3/4	**Kudbeme**[43] 1734 4-9-4 65 ... SuzzanneFrance(7) 15 (N Bycroft) *s.i.s: a rr* **33/1**	46

0000 **15** *5* **General Feeling (IRE)**[14] [2520] 5-10-0 **68** ... TPQueally 13 37
(M Mullineaux) *s.i.s: a rr* **22/1**

1m 31.1s (-3.21) **Going Correction** -0.30s/f (Firm)
WFA 3 from 4yo+ 9lb **15** Ran SP% **122.2**
Speed ratings (Par 103):106,105,105,103,102 101,100,98,97,97 96,95,94,93,87
CSF £533.28 CT £4799.30 TOTE £40.40: £10.60, £4.30, £2.60; EX 389.50.
Owner Andy & Bev Wright **Bred** Mrs Marian Maguire **Trained** Market Rasen, Lincs
■ Stewards' Enquiry : Tolley Dean two-day ban: careless riding (Jul 9-10)
Stanley Chin caution: careless riding

FOCUS
Fast and furious stuff with the first two both overcoming outside draws.
Orpen Wide(IRE) Official explanation: trainer said, regarding apparent improvement in form, gelding was suited by the first time blinkers
Makai Official explanation: jockey said gelding suffered interference in running
Observatory Star(IRE) Official explanation: jockey said gelding did not face the ear plugs
Kudbeme Official explanation: jockey said filly missed the break

2948 RACING UK MAIDEN STKS 1m 100y
4:45 (4:46) (Class 5) 3-Y-O **£5,181** (£1,541; £770; £384) **Stalls** High

Form RPR
1 **Ceremonial Jade (UAE)** 3-9-3 ... NCallan 5 77
(M Botti) *trckd ldr on inner: hdwy 2f out: swtchd lft and rdn to ld over 1f out: hung bdly lft ins last: drvn out* **33/1**
-523 **2** *1 3/4* **Madaares (USA)**[48] [1596] 3-9-3 78 ... RHills 1 73
(M Johnston) *hld up: hdwy on outer over 2f out: rdn to chse wnr ent last sn edgd rt and one pce* **2/7**[1]
0 **3** *5* **Final Award (IRE)**[13] [2542] 3-8-12 ... TomEaves 8 57
(G M Moore) *led: rdn along over 2f out: hdd over 1f out: wknd ins last* **25/1**
5 **4** *hd* **Just Lille (IRE)**[52] [1493] 3-8-12 ... PaulFessey 7 57
(Mrs A Duffield) *chsd ldrs: rdn along over 2f out: sn one pce* **11/1**[3]
0 **5** *4* **Oasis Flower**[11] [2615] 3-8-12 ... OscarUrbina 2 49
(J R Fanshawe) *hld up in tch: effrt and sme hdwy over 2f out: sn rdn and btn* **6/1**[2]
0 **6** *3/4* **Silk Topper (IRE)**[13] [2542] 3-9-3 ... PaulHanagan 6 52
(R A Fahey) *chsd ldrs: rdn along 3f out: wknd 2f out* **25/1**
7 *3/4* **Golden Groom** 3-9-3 ... LeeEnstone 3 50
(C W Fairhurst) *a rr* **80/1**
8 *13* **Height Of Esteem** 3-9-3 ... TPQueally 4 23
(M Mullineaux) *hld up: hdwy on outer to chse ldrs over 3f out: rdn along over 2f out and sn wknd* **50/1**

1m 45.45s (-1.95) **Going Correction** -0.30s/f (Firm) **8** Ran SP% **114.2**
Speed ratings (Par 99):97,95,90,90,86 85,84,71
CSF £43.45 TOTE £25.90: £5.50, £1.02, £5.00; EX 45.40.
Owner Giuliano Manfredini **Bred** Darley **Trained** Newmarket, Suffolk
■ A first training success for Newmarket-based Italian Marco Botti.

FOCUS
25/1 bar three. A moderate pace and a surprise winner, but it looked no fluke.

2949 RACING HERE AGAIN ON 7TH JULY APPRENTICE H'CAP 5f
5:15 (5:16) (Class 6) (0-55,55) 3-Y-O+ **£3,238** (£963; £481; £240) **Stalls** High

Form RPR
04-6 **1** **Paddywack (IRE)**[8] [2700] 9-9-4 **45** ...(b) JamesMillman 14 57
(D W Chapman) *towards rr: gd hdwy 2f out: str run to ld ins last: kpt on strly* **11/2**[1]
0-40 **2** *1* **Yorke's Folly (USA)**[13] [2543] 5-9-4 **45** ...(b) PJBenson 10 53
(C W Fairhurst) *in tch: hdwy and n.m.r wl over 1f out: sn rdn and styd on strly ins last* **25/1**
5006 **3** *shd* **Seven No Trumps**[15] [2505] 9-9-10 **55** ...(p) BarrySavage[(4)] 3 63+
(J M Bradley) *hld up: gd hdwy on outer over 1f out: rdn and ev ch ent last: sn drvn: edgd rt and nt qckn* **16/1**
1164 **4** *3* **Axis Shield (IRE)**[3] [2876] 3-9-6 **53** ... ChrisHough 18 47
(M C Chapman) *led: rdn along and hdd wl over 1f out: kpt on same pce u.p ins last* **10/1**
4030 **5** *1/2* **Detonate**[18] [2396] 4-9-13 **54** ... KirstyMilczarek 19 48
(Mrs C A Dunnett) *cl up: rdn to ld wl over 1f out: drvn and hdd ins last: wknd* **8/1**
0526 **5** *dht* **Blue Maeve**[1] [2928] 6-9-12 **53** ... VictoriaBehan 8 47+
(A D Brown) *chsd ldrs: rdn wl over 1f out: kpt on same pce* **9/1**
520- **7** *hd* **Sholto**[225] [6345] 8-9-3 **48** ...(b) PaulPickard[(4)] 12 42
(J O'Reilly) *in tch: hdwy 2f out: rdn and ch over 1f out: wknd ent last* **20/1**
-000 **8** *1/2* **Fairgame Man**[8] [2700] 8-9-7 **48** ...(p) JamieHamblett 15 42+
(J S Wainwright) *in tch: hdwy 2f out: rdn: n.m.r and bmpd over 1f out: kpt on ins last* **9/1**
0-30 **9** *shd* **Flying Tackle**[5] [2780] 8-9-9 **50** ...(v) PatrickDonaghy 17 41
(I W McInnes) *towards rr: hdwy wl over 1f out: sn rdn and kpt on ins last: nt rch ldrs* **13/2**[2]
-000 **10** *1/2* **Ballybunion (IRE)**[10] [2632] 7-10-0 **55** ... TolleyDean 11 49+
(R A Harris) *cl up: rdn along 2f out: sn wknd* **12/1**
0-00 **11** *3/4* **Zimbali**[3] [2858] 4-9-2 **47** ... PietroRomeo[(4)] 4 34
(J M Bradley) *midfield: rdn along 2f out: sn no imp* **66/1**
-000 **12** *1 1/4* **College Queen**[64] [1195] 8-9-5 **46** ... BRoper 13 28
(S Gollings) *a rr* **33/1**
-660 **13** *1/2* **Wolfman**[56] [1397] 4-9-4 **45** ...(p) LukeMorris 9 25
(D W Barker) *a rr* **40/1**
50-5 **14** *shd* **Sir Loin**[19] [2376] 5-9-7 **48** ... DanielleMcCreery 20 28
(N Tinkler) *chsd ldrs on inner: rdn along and bmpd over 1f out: sn wknd* **7/1**[3]
0502 **15** *2* **Hamaasy**[13] [2544] 5-9-9 **50** ... LanceBetts 6 22+
(D Nicholls) *cl up: disp ld 1/2-way: sn rdn along and wknd* **16/1**
4200 **16** *3/4* **Laurel Dawn**[25] [2208] 8-9-5 **46** ...(b) MarkWaite 16 15
(C N Kellett) *sn outpcd and a bhd* **20/1**

62.15 secs (-1.85) **Going Correction** -0.425s/f (Firm) **16** Ran SP% **121.1**
WFA 3 from 4yo+ 6lb
Speed ratings (Par 101):97,95,95,90,89 89,89,88,88,87 86,84,83,83,80 79
CSF £151.87 CT £2170.45 TOTE £4.40: £1.70, £4.70, £4.60, £2.40; EX 281.80 Place 6 £88.40, Place 5 £74.03.
Owner David W Chapman **Bred** Colm McEvoy **Trained** Stillington, N Yorks

FOCUS
A low-grade seller in all but name with the draw crucial as usual on fast ground here.
T/Jkpt: Not won. T/Plt: £88.10 to a £1 stake. Pool: £48,661.70. 402.85 winning tickets. T/Qpdt: £43.80 to a £1 stake. Pool: £2,460.40. 41.50 winning tickets. JR

2725 BRIGHTON (L-H)
Tuesday, June 27

OFFICIAL GOING: Firm (good to firm in places)
The runners mainly came to the centre of the track, though the final race winner made it all the way over to the stands' rail.
Wind: Moderate; half behind.

2950 WEATHERBYS BANK MAIDEN AUCTION STKS 5f 213y
2:30 (2:31) (Class 5) 2-Y-O **£3,238** (£963; £481; £240) **Stalls** Low

Form RPR
06 **1** **Disco Dan**[12] [2572] 2-8-12 ... RyanMoore 4 70+
(D M Simcock) *trckd ldr: shkn up to ld ent fnl f: sn in command* **11/8**[1]
4 **2** *2* **Early Promise (IRE)**[50] [1535] 2-8-5 ow1 ... BrianReilly 3 57
(P L Gilligan) *t.k.h: led tl rdn and hdd ent fnl f: kpt on one pce* **8/1**
00 **3** *2 1/2* **Regal Ovation**[14] [2530] 2-9-0 ... SteveDrowne 1 58
(W R Muir) *chsd ldrs: rdn over 2f out: one pce fr over 1f out* **4/1**[2]
0453 **4** *3/4* **Nicada (IRE)**[7] [2726] 2-8-5 ...(p) JamesDoyle[(5)] 6 52
(Miss Gay Kelleway) *racd wd: effrt over 2f out: one pce fr over 1f out* **4/1**[2]
3000 **5** *10* **Piccolo Prezzo**[20] [2346] 2-8-4 ... ChrisCatlin 5 15
(I A Wood) *t.k.h on outside: wknd wl over 1f out* **25/1**
06 **6** *3* **Crystal Ice (IRE)**[48] [1587] 2-8-4 ... RichardMullen 2 5
(Mrs L Williamson) *a bhd: sn rdn and outpcd* **9/2**[3]

1m 11.35s (1.25) **Going Correction** +0.025s/f (Good) **6** Ran SP% **115.2**
Speed ratings (Par 93):92,89,86,85,71 67
CSF £13.97 TOTE £2.10: £1.50, £3.50; EX 17.10.
Owner David Cohen **Bred** T G And B B Mills **Trained** Newmarket, Suffolk

FOCUS
A modest race, though the first three home are relatively lightly-raced.

NOTEBOOK
Disco Dan would have finished closer but for being hampered last time, and this time he was always in the perfect position. Connections believe he will be even better on a more galloping track. (tchd 2-1, 9-4 in a place)
Early Promise(IRE) seemed to stay the extra furlong alright, though she would help herself if she settled a bit better. She would not be without hope in low-quality maidens like this. (tchd 10-1)
Regal Ovation is now qualified for nurseries and can hardly be overburdened on his efforts so far. He is of limited ability, but was badly drawn in his first two races, and does seem to be improving a bit. (op 5-1 tchd 7-2)
Nicada(IRE) has not shown the pace to win at five furlongs, or the stamina to succeed at six in maiden company. However, he is consistent, and should be lightly-weighted in nurseries from now on, with either trip an option. (op 11-2 tchd 6-1)
Piccolo Prezzo looks very moderate, and will be more at home back in selling compnay. (op 33-1)
Crystal Ice(IRE) was very disappointing, and may not have been suited by the track. (op 7-2 tchd 10-3)

2951 WEATHERBYS INSURANCE MEDIAN AUCTION MAIDEN STKS 7f 214y
3:00 (3:02) (Class 6) 3-4-Y-O **£2,590** (£770; £385; £192) **Stalls** Low

Form RPR
-2 **1** **Miss McGuire**[25] [2188] 3-8-9 ... RyanMoore 5 65+
(G L Moore) *a in tch: led over 1f out: r.o wl: comf* **4/6**[1]
600- **2** *3* **Snow Symphony (IRE)**[288] [5177] 3-9-0 63 ... ChrisCatlin 4 63
(D M Simcock) *sn led: hdd over 1f out: nt pce of wnr* **17/2**
5503 **3** *3 1/2* **Shinko (IRE)**[7] [2727] 3-8-6 58 ...(p) DeanCorby[(3)] 7 50
(Miss J Feilden) *hld up: styd on fr over 1f out: nvr nr to chal* **15/2**[3]
0220 **4** *nk* **Bahhmirage (IRE)**[18] [2415] 3-8-9 65 ...(b) SteveDrowne 6 49
(Stef Liddiard) *t.k.h: prom: rdn 3f out: no hdwy ins fnl 2f* **10/3**[2]
000- **5** *5* **Annies Valentine**[342] [3638] 3-8-9 40 ... J-PGuillambert 2 38
(J Gallagher) *hld up: rdn 1/2-way. wknd over 2f out* **50/1**
0- **6** *2 1/2* **Highband**[283] [5300] 3-8-9 ... LPKeniry 1 32
(M Madgwick) *a bhd* **66/1**
0-0 **7** *1/2* **Command Respect**[22] [2304] 3-8-9 ... RichardMullen 3 31
(E F Vaughan) *t.k.h: prom: rdn 3f out: sn btn* **25/1**

1m 37.0s (1.96) **Going Correction** +0.025s/f (Good) **7** Ran SP% **112.7**
Speed ratings (Par 101):91,88,84,84,79 76,76
CSF £7.11 TOTE £1.50: £1.20, £2.80; EX 7.70.
Owner D J Deer **Bred** D J And Mrs Deer **Trained** Woodingdean, E Sussex

FOCUS
A moderate winning time and a weakly-contested race with the exception of the winner, an unexposed filly who should prove to be a cut above these.

2952 CLASSIC EVENT MARQUEES CLAIMING STKS 1m 1f 209y
3:30 (3:31) (Class 6) 3-Y-O+ **£2,266** (£674; £337; £168) **Stalls** High

Form RPR
5045 **1** **Fortune Point (IRE)**[58] [648] 8-9-11 50 ...(v) ShaneKelly 9 63
(A W Carroll) *mde all: rdn 1f out: r.o fnl f* **15/2**
4013 **2** *1 1/4* **Miss Monica (IRE)**[7] [2725] 5-8-10 46 ... ChrisCatlin 6 46
(P W Hiatt) *hld up: rdn and hdwy to chse wnr fr over 1f out* **11/4**[1]
0601 **3** *1 3/4* **String Serenade (IRE)**[12] [2568] 5-9-2 47 ... DManning 1 49
(V Smith) *hld up in mid-div: hdwy over 1f out: styd on fnl f: nvr nrr* **9/2**[3]
0-40 **4** *1* **Arabian Moon (IRE)**[15] [2507] 10-9-5 45 ... RichardHughes 4 50
(R Brotherton) *in tch: briefly wnt 2nd wl over 1f out: sn one pce* **15/2**
005 **5** *2* **Edge Fund**[12] [2568] 4-8-10 40 ... JamesDoyle[(5)] 10 42
(Miss Gay Kelleway) *in rr: rdn 2f out: mde sme late hdwy* **16/1**
-002 **6** *1 1/2* **Love's Design (IRE)**[7] [2728] 9-8-12 40 ...(v) DeanCorby[(3)] 8 39
(Miss J Feilden) *chsd wnr tl wl over 1f out: sn wknd* **14/1**
00-0 **7** *nk* **Gran Clicquot**[50] [1541] 11-9-3 37 ... RobynBrisland[(5)] 2 46
(G P Enright) *chsd ldrs tl rdn and wknd over 2f out* **33/1**
0-00 **8** *11* **Big Bradford**[11] [2603] 5-9-7 62 ... SteveDrowne 3 24
(W R Muir) *a bhd: lost tch 3f out* **7/2**[2]
6065 **9** *17* **Pitsi Kahtoh**[20] [2362] 4-8-10 36 ... RobertMiles 7 —
(P W Hiatt) *hld up: a bhd: lost tch over 3f out* **11/1**

2m 3.44s (0.84) **Going Correction** +0.025s/f (Good)
WFA 3 from 4yo+ 12lb **9** Ran SP% **114.4**
Speed ratings (Par 101):97,96,94,93,92 91,90,81,68
CSF £28.17 TOTE £8.40: £2.60, £1.10, £2.50; EX 40.10 Trifecta £129.50 Pool: £543.95 - 2.98 winning units.Big Bradford was claimed by S. L. Walker for £8,000.
Owner The T J Racing Partnership **Bred** Dr A J O'Reilly And Skymarc Farm **Trained** Cropthorne, Worcs

FOCUS
A weak race, though with course specialists finishing second and third, it should hold up round here.
Pitsi Kahtoh Official explanation: jockey said filly ran too free to post

2953 WBX.COM WORLD BET EXCHANGE H'CAP — 1m 3f 196y
4:00 (4:01) (Class 5) (0-70,70) 4-Y-0+ £3,886 (£1,156; £577; £288) Stalls High

Form RPR
3011 1 **Mostarsil (USA)**[16] 2483 8-9-1 64.....(p) RyanMoore 4 77+
(G L Moore) *mde all: rdn over 2f out: r.o and in command fnl f* 5/2[1]
0041 2 3 1/2 **Madhavi**[16] 2481 4-8-11 60..... RichardHughes 3 67
(R Hannon) *chsd ldr thrght: rdn over 2f out: kpt on for 2nd fnl f* 7/2[2]
66-0 3 1/2 **Mexican Pete**[14] 2534 6-9-2 70..... JamesDoyle(5) 5 76
(A W Carroll) *hld up: rdn and hdwy to dispute 2nd over 1f out: no ex ins fnl f* 5/1
0040 4 nk **Blackmail (USA)**[17] 2455 8-8-10 59.....(b) FrankieMcDonald 1 65
(Miss B Sanders) *hld up: hmpd on ins 4f out: sn swtchd rt: styd on fnl f but nvr nr to chal* 9/2[3]
0320 5 6 **Jackie Kiely**[1] 2918 5-8-11 60.....(t) MickyFenton 2 56
(Stef Liddiard) *chsd ldrs: rdn over 2f out: wknd over 1f out* 7/2[2]
2m 30.48s (-1.72) **Going Correction** +0.025s/f (Good) 5 Ran SP% **107.9**
Speed ratings (Par 103):106,103,103,103,99
CSF £10.86 TOTE £2.60: £1.50, £2.00; EX 5.80.
Owner G A Jackman **Bred** Shadwell Farm Inc **Trained** Woodingdean, E Sussex

FOCUS
A typical Brighton handicap, though lacking in numbers.
Jackie Kiely Official explanation: jockey said gelding had a breathing problem

2954 THE LORD'S TAVERNERS H'CAP — 6f 209y
4:30 (4:30) (Class 5) (0-75,75) 3-Y-0+ £3,238 (£963; £481; £240) Stalls Low

Form RPR
2616 1 **Ivory Lace**[11] 2606 5-9-3 69..... JamesDoyle(5) 2 83+
(S Woodman) *hld up in tch: rdn to ld over 1f out: r.o wl fnl f* 13/2[3]
0153 2 1 1/4 **Phluke**[8] 2708 5-10-0 75..... StephenCarson 4 84
(R F Johnson Houghton) *trckd ldr: led over 2f out: hdd over 1f out: kpt on but nt qckn fnl f* 3/1[2]
0-22 3 2 1/2 **Keep Baccknhit (IRE)**[7] 2729 4-8-13 60..... RyanMoore 6 63
(G L Moore) *plld hrd: sn restrained in rr: effrt on on outside over 1f out: r.o ins fnl f but nvr nr to chal* 2/1[1]
4260 4 1 **Aastral Magic**[8] 2708 4-9-11 72..... RichardHughes 3 72
(R Hannon) *prom tl rdn and lost pl over 1f out* 9/1
5034 5 1 1/4 **Regal Dream (IRE)**[11] 2606 4-9-12 73..... ShaneKelly 5 70
(J W Hills) *s.i.s: nvr got into r* 3/1[2]
0000 6 3/4 **Acomb**[11] 2606 6-10-0 75..... RichardThomas 1 70
(Mrs L Richards) *led tl hdd over 2f out: wknd rapidly over 1f out* 25/1
1m 22.21s (-0.49) **Going Correction** +0.025s/f (Good) 6 Ran SP% **110.5**
Speed ratings (Par 103):103,101,98,97,96 95
CSF £25.29 TOTE £8.50: £4.20, £1.80; EX 32.50.
Owner Christopher J Halpin **Bred** D R Tucker **Trained** East Lavant, W Sussex

FOCUS
An ordinary handicap with a small field.
Keep Baccknhit(IRE) Official explanation: jockey said filly ran too free
Acomb Official explanation: trainer said gelding lost a shoe

2955 WORLD BET EXCHANGE WBX.COM H'CAP — 5f 59y
5:00 (5:03) (Class 6) (0-65,65) 3-Y-0+ £2,590 (£770; £385; £192) Stalls Low

Form RPR
04-0 1 **Multahab**[43] 1727 7-8-9 46 oh5.....(t) BrianReilly 6 69
(Miss D A McHale) *mde all: c stands' side over 3f out: clr fr wl over 1f out: v easily* 12/1
0001 2 5 **Imperium**[12] 2571 5-9-0 51.....(p) MickyFenton 8 56
(Stef Liddiard) *s.i.s: hdwy over 1f out: wnt 2nd ins fnl f* 5/1[2]
0-05 3 hd **Heavens Walk**[15] 2494 5-8-10 50.....(t) AmirQuinn(3) 5 54
(P J Makin) *s.i.s: hdwy to go 2nd briefly ent fnl f: lost 2nd ins last* 5/1[2]
1015 4 1 3/4 **Boanerges (IRE)**[5] 2792 9-9-9 60..... RyanMoore 10 58
(J M Bradley) *mid-div: rdn and kpt on appr fnl f: one pce* 4/1[1]
4100 5 1 1/2 **Double M**[16] 2484 9-8-9 46 oh2.....(v) RichardThomas 3 39
(Mrs L Richards) *hld up in rr: mde sme late hdwy* 14/1
0052 6 hd **Princess Kai (IRE)**[12] 2571 5-8-9 46 oh5..... FergusSweeney 2 38
(R Ingram) *bhd: sme late hdwy but nvr on terms* 7/1[3]
4-00 7 3/4 **Princely Vale (IRE)**[14] 2536 4-9-4 55.....(v) RobertMiles 7 44
(W G M Turner) *prom on ins tl wknd over 1f out* 12/1
0054 8 hd **Madrasee**[10] 2632 8-8-9 46 oh3..... AlanDaly 11 34
(N E Berry) *chsd ldrs tl wknd over 1f out* 12/1
-000 9 1 1/2 **Reviving (IRE)**[22] 2301 3-9-3 60..... StephenCarson 1 41
(R F Johnson Houghton) *chsd ldrs tl wknd wl over 1f out* 10/1
0006 10 1/2 **Italian Mist (FR)**[12] 2571 7-8-4 46 oh9.....(e) JamesDoyle(5) 4 27
(R M H Cowell) *a bhd* 18/1
0060 11 nk **Hilltop Fantasy**[12] 2571 5-8-9 46 oh9..... ChrisCatlin 9 26
(V Smith) *a bhd* 25/1
4-00 12 12 **Canary Island (IRE)**[18] 2389 4-10-0 65..... ShaneKelly 12 —
(J M Bradley) *chsd wnr to 1/2-way: sn bhd* 25/1
61.42 secs (-0.88) **Going Correction** +0.025s/f (Good)
WFA 3 from 4yo+ 6lb 12 Ran SP% **117.6**
Speed ratings (Par 101):108,100,99,96,94 94,92,92,90,89 88,69
CSF £70.43 CT £342.51 TOTE £13.50: £4.20, £1.90, £2.10; EX 103.90 Trifecta £437.60 Part won. Pool of £616.43 - 0.45 winning units. Place 6 £45.97, Place 5 £21.88.
Owner P J Burke and Dave Anderson **Bred** Shadwell Estate Company Limited **Trained** Newmarket, Suffolk

FOCUS
Weak in quality, but well contested and the winning time was decent. However, unsatisfactory in so far as the winner was the only runner to come all the way to the stands' rail - the others were near the middle.
Madrasee Official explanation: trainer said mare lost a near-fore shoe
T/Plt: £62.00 to a £1 stake. Pool: £46,708.20. 549.65 winning tickets. T/Qpdt: £16.30 to a £1 stake. Pool: £2,929.10. 132.60 winning tickets. JS

2578 NEWBURY (L-H)
Tuesday, June 27

OFFICIAL GOING: Good (good to firm in places)
Wind: Virtually nil

2956 WEATHERBYS APPRENTICE H'CAP — 1m 3f 5y
5:55 (5:57) (Class 5) (0-70,70) 4-Y-0+ £3,238 (£963; £481; £240) Stalls Centre

Form RPR
-125 1 **High Treason (USA)**[22] 2305 4-9-0 65..... AlanRutter(5) 5 77+
(W J Musson) *hld up in rr: hdwy and nt clr run ins fnl 3f: qcknd fr 2f out to ld jst ins fnl f: pushed out* 10/3[1]
325- 2 2 **Looks The Business (IRE)**[247] 4573 5-8-11 60..... LiamJones(3) 12 69
(W G M Turner) *sn led: rdn over 2f out: hdd and nt qckn jst ins fnl f* 16/1
0003 3 1 **Serramanna**[12] 2577 5-8-3 52 oh2 ow1..... SladeO'Hara(3) 2 59
(Dr J R J Naylor) *chsd ldrs: ev ch 2f out: sn rdn: one pce ins last* 8/1
0334 4 5 **General Flumpa**[20] 2345 5-8-4 57 ow1..... JonjoMilczarek(7) 9 56
(C F Wall) *swtg: bhd: hdwy on outside over 2f out: rdn to chse ldrs over 1f out: hung lft and wknd fnl f* 7/1
1050 5 1 1/4 **Kylkenny**[15] 2508 11-9-10 70.....(t) TravisBlock 11 67
(P D Cundell) *chsd ldrs: rdn and ev ch ins fnl 2f: wknd fnl f* 12/1
5000 6 1/2 **Play Up Pompey**[18] 2401 4-8-4 53 ow1..... RussellKennemore(3) 1 49
(J J Bridger) *in tch: rdn and effrt over 2f out: wknd over 1f out* 33/1
0546 7 nk **Pittsburgh**[14] 2534 4-8-8 59..... JamesRogers(5) 10 45
(A M Balding) *in tch: rdn 3f out: sn btn: fin 8th: plcd 7th* 6/1[2]
2233 8 1/2 **Mossmann Gorge**[11] 2612 4-9-0 60.....(b) AndrewElliott 7 45
(M Wellings) *lw: chsd ldrs: rdn 3f out: wknd qckly 2f out: fin 9th: plcd 8th* 8/1
0/00 9 7 **Lake Imperial (IRE)**[12] 2220 5-8-10 56..... GregFairley 6 30
(Heather Dalton) *bmpd sn after s: rdn over 3f out: a in rr: fin 10th: plcd 9th* 8/1
0-35 10 14 **Double Spectre (IRE)**[29] 2088 4-9-5 65..... RichardKingscote 3 16
(Jean-Rene Auvray) *lw: bmpd sn after s: t.k.h and sddle slipped after 1f: effrt 3f out: n.d and sn wknd: fin 11th: plcd 10th* 13/2[3]
0064 D 6 **Megalala (IRE)**[23] 2262 5-8-5 51 oh4..... MarcHalford 8 37
(J J Bridger) *t.k.h: chsd ldrs: rdn and effrt over 2f out: sn wknd: fin 7th, disq: plcd last* 40/1
2m 21.84s (-0.43) **Going Correction** -0.025s/f (Good) 11 Ran SP% **115.5**
Speed ratings (Par 103):100,98,97,94,93 92,88,87,82,72 88
CSF £60.03 CT £396.89 TOTE £3.90: £1.60, £2.70, £2.50; EX 30.90.
Owner S Rudolf **Bred** Helmut Von Finck **Trained** Newmarket, Suffolk
■ Stewards' Enquiry : Jonjo Milczarek one-day ban: careless riding (Jul 9). Marc Halford one-day ban: used whip down the shoulder in forehand position (Jul 9). Megalala disq. (weighed in light)

FOCUS
A modest handicap contested by mostly exposed performers. Ordinary form, but probably sound.
Mossmann Gorge Official explanation: trainer said gelding had been struck into behind
Double Spectre(IRE) Official explanation: jockey said saddle slipped

2957 E B F PELICAN MAIDEN FILLIES' STKS — 6f 8y
6:25 (6:30) (Class 4) 2-Y-0 £6,477 (£1,927; £963; £481) Stalls High

Form RPR
0 1 **Indian Ink (IRE)**[17] 2456 2-9-0..... RichardHughes 13 88+
(R Hannon) *mde all: shkn up and qcknd over 1f out: comf* 5/1[3]
5 2 2 1/2 **Naayla (IRE)**[15] 2506 2-9-0..... LDettori 7 81+
(B J Meehan) *w'like: str: chsd wnr thrght: rdn over 2f out: nt qcknd fr over 1f out* 15/8[1]
5 3 3 **Tee Off (IRE)**[21] 2328 2-9-0..... MichaelHills 1 72+
(B W Hills) *lw: chsd ldrs in centre crse in 3rd thrght: rdn over 2f out: wknd ins fnl f* 4/1[2]
4 1 1/4 **Lakshmi (IRE)** 2-9-0..... TedDurcan 2 68
(M R Channon) *w'like: str: b.bkwd: s.i.s: hld up mid-div: pushed along 2f out: kpt on fnl f but nvr gng pce to rch ldrs* 33/1
5 3 1/2 **Splendored Love (USA)** 2-9-0..... RyanMoore 10 57
(R Hannon) *w'like: b.bkwd: s.i.s: sn rcvrd to chse ldrs: rdn over 2f out: sn outpcd* 16/1
3 6 nk **Diamond Light (USA)**[17] 2442 2-9-0..... DaneO'Neill 16 56
(J L Dunlop) *chsd ldrs tl rdn and outpcd over 2f out: kpt on again ins last* 16/1
7 nk **Rubilini** 2-8-7..... ThomasO'Brien(7) 6 55+
(M R Channon) *unf: scope: b.bkwd: slowly away: bhd: pushed along over 3f out: kpt on fnl f but nver gng pce to rch ldrs* 25/1
8 shd **Blue Bamboo** 2-9-0..... JimCrowley 3 55
(Mrs A J Perrett) *w'like: s.i.s: sn rcvrd and in tch: rdn over 2f out: n.d after* 20/1
9 1/2 **Look Who's Dancing** 2-9-0..... KerrinMcEvoy 11 54
(J L Dunlop) *w'like: b.bkwd: chsd ldrs: pushed along 1/2-way: sn outpcd and n.d after* 14/1
10 2 **Apache Dream (IRE)** 2-9-0..... SteveDrowne 14 48+
(B J Meehan) *leggy: lw: s.i.s: sn rcvrd to chse ldrs: rdn over 2f out: sn wknd* 17/2
11 2 **Blue Mistral (IRE)** 2-9-0..... PaulDoe 4 42
(W J Knight) *w'like: leggy: b.bkwd: nvr bttr than mid-div* 50/1
12 shd **Bright Moon** 2-9-0..... PatDobbs 15 41
(R Hannon) *w'like: b.bkwd: chsd ldrs over 3f* 33/1
13 nk **Ocean Blaze** 2-9-0..... AlanMunro 8 40
(B R Millman) *str: b.bkwd: s.i.s: sn chsng ldrs: rdn 3f out: sn bhd* 22/1
1m 12.32s (-2.00) **Going Correction** -0.30s/f (Firm) 13 Ran SP% **121.2**
Speed ratings (Par 92):101,97,93,92,87 86,86,86,85,83 80,80,79
CSF £13.67 TOTE £6.90: £2.50, £1.40, £1.70; EX 22.10.
Owner Raymond Tooth **Bred** Killeen Castle Stud **Trained** East Everleigh, Wilts

FOCUS
Experience proved to be all important in this fillies' maiden as only four had run before and they provided the first three home. The winning time was the fastest of the three races over the trip on the day, including one for older horses, and the race has been rated positively, but time will tell if it proves this good.

NOTEBOOK
Indian Ink(IRE), who was backed in from 12-1 to 6-1 on her debut here earlier in the month, was clearly expected to do better than seventh, but her trainer said that she had blown up that day and she put the experience to good use on this second start, running out a ready winner. It is questionable what she beat, but there should be improvement to come. (op 11-2)
Naayla(IRE) ran with promise on her debut at Windsor and improved on that performance here. The winner had the benefit of the rail and won comfortably, but this was still a solid effort, and the pair were nicely clear of the rest. (op 2-1 tchd 7-4 and 9-4 in places)
Tee Off(IRE), stuck out wide from her low draw, could not go with the first two in the closing stages but posted a solid effort. She is a likely type for nurseries after one more run. (op 9-2)
Lakshmi(IRE), whose dam is an unraced half-sister to useful dual seven-furlong juvenile winner Kootenay, was unfancied on her debut but shaped with promise from her low draw. Softer ground may suit her in time.
Splendored Love(USA), whose dam is an unraced half-sister to five winners, including quite useful Billy Sue's Rib, a multiple winning sprinter in the US, is another who can improve for this intitial outing. (op 12-1)
Diamond Light(USA) was the other runner in the line-up apart from the first three home who had the benefit of previous racing experience, but she is bred to need further and will not come into her own until stepped up to middle distances next year.

2958 MOUNTGRANGE STUD MAIDEN FILLIES' STKS 7f (S)
6:55 (7:00) (Class 4) 2-Y-O £6,477 (£1,927; £963; £481) Stalls High

Form RPR

1 **Sudoor** 2-9-0 .... SteveDrowne 6 87+
(J L Dunlop) *unf: scope: t.k.h: hld up in tch: pushed along 2f out: qcknd to ld jst ins fnl f: sn in command: easily* **16/1**

2 1 ¾ **Cast In Gold (USA)** 2-9-0 .... KFallon 5 83+
(B J Meehan) *unf: scope: gd sort: chsd ldrs: rdn to ld 2f out: hdd jst ins last: kpt on but sn no ch w wnr* **7/1[3]**

3 1 ¼ **Circle Of Love** 2-9-0 .... KerrinMcEvoy 2 80+
(J L Dunlop) *leggy: scope: s.i.s: sn rcvrd to trck ldrs: ev ch 2f out: kpt on to hold 3rd cl home but nvr a danger to 1st or 2nd* **25/1**

6 4 nk **Roclette (USA)**[10] 2638 2-9-0 .... MichaelHills 12 79
(B W Hills) *w'like: lw: b.hind: t.k.h early: hdwy over 2f out: drvn to chse ldrs over 1f out: one pce ins last* **5/4[1]**

5 shd **Nicomedia (IRE)** 2-9-0 .... PatDobbs 1 79+
(R Hannon) *w'like: b.bkwd: chsd ldrs: rdn over 2f out: styd on same pce fr over 1f out* **66/1**

02 6 3 ½ **Miss Saafend Plaza (IRE)**[11] 2619 2-9-0 .... RichardHughes 4 70
(R Hannon) *lw: led tl hdd 2f out: wknd fnl f* **7/2[2]**

0 7 shd **Bay Of Light**[10] 2638 2-9-0 .... AlanMunro 11 70
(P W Chapple-Hyam) *w'like: in tch: rdn and outpcd over 3f out: styd on again fnl f but nvr gng pce to rch ldrs* **20/1**

8 2 **Molly Pitcher (IRE)** 2-9-0 .... LDettori 10 65+
(M A Jarvis) *w'like: b.bkwd: chsd ldrs: rdn over 2f out: wknd over 1f out* **7/1[3]**

9 nk **Anthea** 2-9-0 .... DaneO'Neill 13 64+
(B R Millman) *leggy: b.bkwd: s.i.s: bhd: effrt 3f out: nvr nr ldrs: hung lft and wknd over 1f out* **50/1**

10 2 ½ **Niqaab** 2-9-0 .... TonyCulhane 9 58+
(B W Hills) *lw: lengthy: sn chsng ldrs: wknd fr 2f out* **25/1**

11 1 **Security Tiger (IRE)** 2-9-0 .... SamHitchcott 3 55
(M R Channon) *w'like: leggy: s.i.s: bhd and sn rdn: sme hdwy over 2f out: wkng whn hit over hd over 1f out* **40/1**

12 nk **Treat** 2-9-0 .... TedDurcan 7 54
(M R Channon) *unf: scope: b.bkwd: slowly away: a in rr* **20/1**

1m 25.46s (-1.54) **Going Correction** -0.30s/f (Firm) 12 Ran SP% **120.7**
Speed ratings (Par 92):96,94,92,92,92 88,88,85,85,82 81,81
CSF £116.06 TOTE £20.00: £6.80, £2.30, £4.10; EX 225.90.
Owner Hamdan Al Maktoum **Bred** Shadwell Estate Company Limited **Trained** Arundel, W Sussex

FOCUS
This looked a fairly decent maiden, which was backed up by paddock inspection, and the form is likely to work out and throw up plenty of winners. The sixth sets the standard for now.

NOTEBOOK
Sudoor, whose dam is an unraced sister to high-class juvenile Bahhare, is by Fantastic Light and bred to be smart. A winning debut was perhaps not expected, though, given her starting price, and she can only improve for this comfortable success. She looks well worth her place in better grade and looks a nice prospect. (op 9-1)
Cast In Gold(USA) ◆, closely related to St Leger winner Rule Of Law, has a Moyglare Stud Stakes entry. She could not cope with the comfortable winner but ran with plenty of promise of better to come, and hails from a stable whose juveniles invariably improve for an outing. (op 6-1 tchd 15-2)
Circle Of Love, a half-sister to Cassydora, a seven-furlong winner at two and later high-class over middle distances at three, is bred to be decent, but once again the betting suggested that little was expected from her on her debut. She ran well, though, and can only get better as she gains experience and steps up in distance. (op 16-1)
Roclette(USA), again made favourite, is becoming an expensive filly to follow. The extra furlong should have suited her but, having raced a touch keenly early on, she could not even hang on to third place in the closing stages. She has the ability to win an average maiden, but nurseries may be more her thing after one more run. (op 7-4)
Nicomedia(IRE), whose dam was a six-furlong winner at two, unexpectedly got the better of her much more fancied stable companion, and is another who looks likely to be suited by nurseries in time. (op 50-1)
Miss Saafend Plaza(IRE) brought solid placed form to the table but did not get home after setting the pace. She ran well enough for the race to be rated around her, though, and nurseries will soon be an option. (op 9-2)

2959 COOLMORE ORATORIO CONDITIONS STKS 6f 8y
7:30 (7:31) (Class 4) 3-Y-O £7,772 (£2,312; £1,155; £577) Stalls High

Form RPR

00-0 1 **Lady Livius (IRE)**[31] 2032 3-9-0 87 .... DaneO'Neill 1 97
(R Hannon) *stdd s: sn trcking ldr: led over 1f out: drvn and r.o strly ins last* **20/1**

21-0 2 1 ¼ **Murfreesboro**[39] 1818 3-9-5 98 .... RyanMoore 4 98
(J H M Gosden) *t.k.h: trckd ldrs: shkn up and hung lft fr 2f out: chsd wnr and continued to hang lft fnl f: nt rcvr* **7/2[3]**

2-40 3 1 **Johannes (IRE)**[55] 1404 3-9-1 100 .... KFallon 2 91
(D Nicholls) *lw: stdd s: drvn along over 3f out: styd on to chse ldrs ins fnl f but nvr gng pce to chal* **9/4[2]**

12-4 4 2 ½ **Northern Empire (IRE)**[55] 1408 3-9-1 107 .... LDettori 5 84
(B J Meehan) *lw: t.k.h: trckd ldrs: n.m.r 2f out: sn rdn: nvr gng pce to get competitive and sn btn fnl f* **13/8[1]**

0-56 5 5 **Mutawajid (IRE)**[25] 2204 3-9-1 98 .... RichardHughes 3 69
(R Hannon) *led tl hdd over 1f out: sn btn* **6/1**

1m 12.49s (-1.83) **Going Correction** -0.30s/f (Firm) 5 Ran SP% **110.1**
Speed ratings (Par 101):100,98,97,93,87
CSF £84.82 TOTE £13.40: £2.20, £2.10; EX 60.80.
Owner Mrs John Lee **Bred** W Maxwell Ervine **Trained** East Everleigh, Wilts

FOCUS
A race made up of twilight horses who are difficult to place, and who were attempting to bounce back from a poor run on their previous start. It is doubtful if the form is reliable.
Northern Empire(IRE) Official explanation: jockey said colt ran too free early

2960 LADBROKESPOKER.COM ROSE BOWL STKS (LISTED RACE) 6f 8y
8:00 (8:00) (Class 1) 2-Y-O
£13,343 (£5,057; £2,530; £1,261; £632; £317) Stalls High

Form RPR

315 1 **Dazed And Amazed**[7] 2724 2-9-0 .... RichardHughes 8 95
(R Hannon) *lw: b.hind: trckd ldrs: drvn to chal fr 1f out: qcknd to ld fnl 50yds: readily* **5/1[3]**

2 2 nk **Vauquelin (IRE)**[13] 2545 2-9-0 .... RichardMullen 5 94
(E S McMahon) *w'like: str: lw: led over 4f out: rdn and styd on wl to keep slt advantage fr over 1f out tl hdd and no ex fnl 50yds* **7/1**

51 3 1 ¼ **Prince Of Elegance**[18] 2402 2-9-0 .... RyanMoore 2 90
(Mrs A J Perrett) *lw: bmpd s: sn chsng ldrs: rdn 2f out: styd on same pce fnl f* **9/2[2]**

126 4 nk **La Neige**[7] 2719 2-9-0 .... TonyCulhane 1 89+
(M R Channon) *lw: chsd ldrs: rdn and effrt to press ldrs 2f out: one pce fnl f* **2/1[1]**

410 5 2 **Deadshot Keen (IRE)**[7] 2719 2-9-0 .... LDettori 4 83
(B J Meehan) *wnt lft s: sn pressing ldrs: rdn 2f out: wknd ins fnl f* **10/1**

3 6 ½ **Golden Balls (IRE)**[12] 2579 2-9-0 .... KFallon 3 82+
(R Hannon) *hmpd s: bhd: drvn and hdwy to chse ldrs over 2f out: nvr gng pce to chal: one pce fr over 1f out* **6/1**

4 7 hd **Touch Of Style (IRE)**[12] 2579 2-9-0 .... AmirQuinn 6 81
(J R Boyle) *lw: hld up in rr: hdwy whn nt clr run ins fnl 2f: effrt and green ins last: keeping on whn hung rt cl home* **33/1**

21 8 1 **Prince Rossi (IRE)**[20] 2361 2-9-0 .... GrahamGibbons 7 78
(J D Bethell) *lerd tl hdd over 4f out: rdn 3f out: wknd over 1f out: no ch whn hmpd cl home* **20/1**

514 9 30 **Dickie Le Davoir**[27] 2127 2-9-0 .... RobertWinston 9 —
(K R Burke) *swtg: s.i.s: bhd: effrt whn n.m.r 2f out: nvr in contention and eased fnl f* **12/1**

1m 12.95s (-1.37) **Going Correction** -0.30s/f (Firm) 9 Ran SP% **119.5**
Speed ratings (Par 101):97,96,94,94,91 91,90,89,49
CSF £41.29 TOTE £6.60: £2.20, £2.60, £2.20; EX 50.40.
Owner Mrs R Ablett **Bred** Whitsbury Manor Stud And Pigeon House Stud **Trained** East Everleigh, Wilts
■ Stewards' Enquiry : Amir Quinn caution: careless riding

FOCUS
Not a great Listed race but sound enough rated around the fourth being two lengths off his Coventry Stakes effort.

NOTEBOOK
Dazed And Amazed, fifth in the Windsor Castle Stakes on his previous start, may well have been a gallop short there according to his trainer, hence the quick reappearance. He won more comfortably than the winning margin suggests, got the sixth furlong well, and deserves a crack at a Group race now. (op 4-1)
Vauquelin(IRE), runner-up at Hamilton on his debut, was well backed from double-figure prices and justified the decision to bump him up in grade despite still being a maiden. Clearly he has plenty of ability, and a maiden win should be a formality on the way to better things. (op 14-1)
Prince Of Elegance, a winner at Goodwood on his previous start, had more to do in this company but ran a solid race. He should get a bit further in time. (op 13-2)
La Neige, sixth in the Coventry Stakes a week earlier, ran below that form, but not by a huge amount. He might have done better had he enjoyed more cover, but due to his low draw he was stuck on the outside. (op 15-8 tchd 9-4)
Deadshot Keen(IRE), well beaten in the Coventry, showed that bare form to be wrong, finishing much closer to La Neige than he did at Ascot. Official explanation: jockey said gelding jumped left leaving stalls (op 12-1)
Golden Balls(IRE), taking his chance in Listed company on only his second start, was another hampered by having to race towards the outside while the action developed near the rail. He still looked green and can do better in time. Official explanation: jockey said colt was hampered leaving stalls (op 9-2)
Dickie Le Davoir Official explanation: jockey said colt ran flat

2961 HEATHERWOLD STUD FILLIES' H'CAP 1m 2f 6y
8:30 (8:31) (Class 4) (0-85,82) 3-Y-O £6,477 (£1,927; £963; £481) Stalls Centre

Form RPR

-603 1 **Kahlua Kiss**[6] 2754 3-8-12 73 .... RichardMullen 4 80
(W R Muir) *rr but in tch: rdn over 2f out: hdwy over 1f out: r.o ins last and qcknd wl u.p to ld last stride* **14/1**

6-12 2 hd **Solva**[11] 2613 3-9-3 78 .... LDettori 8 85
(B J Meehan) *chsd ldr: rdn to take slt ld 2f out: kpt on wl fnl f: ct last stride* **9/4[1]**

3021 3 1 ¼ **Babcary**[11] 2608 3-9-4 82 .... NelsonDeSouza(3) 7 87+
(M P Tregoning) *led: keen early: rdn and hdd 2f out: styd pressing tl outpcd ins last* **4/1[3]**

44-1 4 1 ½ **Balloura (USA)**[57] 1351 3-9-0 75 .... MichaelHills 5 77
(W J Haggas) *chsd ldrs: rdn over 2f out: wknd ins fnl f* **13/2**

103 5 2 **Off Message (IRE)**[34] 1942 3-9-5 80 .... SteveDrowne 6 78
(E A L Dunlop) *bhd: pushed along and sme hdwy ins fnl 2f: nvr gng pce to be competitive* **12/1**

-1 6 4 **Divine River**[67] 1118 3-9-7 82 .... KFallon 3 72
(A P Jarvis) *bhd: sme hdwy over 2f out: sn wknd* **3/1[2]**

0-63 7 1 ¼ **Canyouwin**[127] 460 3-8-2 63 .... DavidKinsella 2 51
(J H M Gosden) *chsd ldrs tl wknd ins fnl 3f* **20/1**

2m 7.43s (-1.28) **Going Correction** -0.025s/f (Good) 7 Ran SP% **108.2**
Speed ratings (Par 98):104,103,102,101,100 96,95
CSF £40.88 CT £132.27 TOTE £10.50: £2.70, £2.10; EX 43.70.
Owner M J Caddy **Bred** Whitsbury Manor Stud **Trained** Lambourn, Berks
■ Elise was withdrawn (11/1, refused to enter stalls). R4 applies, deduct 5p in the £.

FOCUS
A fair fillies' handicap run at a sound pace, and the form looks fairly straightforward rated around the second and fourth.

2962 BHG BUSINESS ADVISERS H'CAP 5f 34y
9:00 (9:01) (Class 5) (0-70,69) 3-Y-O+ £3,886 (£1,156; £577; £288) Stalls High

Form RPR

1362 1 **Drumming Party (USA)**[14] 2536 4-9-4 59 .... (t) LPKeniry 2 69+
(A M Balding) *trckd ldrs: led over 1f out: rdn and veered bdly rt last half f: hld on wl* **8/1[3]**

-240 2 ½ **Cesar Manrique (IRE)**[25] 2189 4-9-11 66 .... MichaelHills 10 73
(B W Hills) *bhd: hdwy on rails over 1f out: swtchd lft last half f: r.o wl but nt rch wnr* **9/2[2]**

-000 3 ¾ **Harrison's Flyer (IRE)**[11] 2618 5-10-0 69 .... (p) RyanMoore 6 73
(J M Bradley) *lw: b: in tch: hdwy to chal over 1f out: kpt on wl cl home* **9/1**

4530 4 shd **Danny The Dip**[17] 2433 3-8-2 54 .... MarcHalford(5) 7 56
(J J Bridger) *chsd ldrs: rdn over 1f out: styd on wl cl home* **33/1**

12-3 5 ½ **Dance To The Blues (IRE)**[58] 1315 5-9-11 69 .... (p) AdamKirby(3) 5 71
(B De Haan) *chsd ldrs: rdn 2f out: kpt on wl fnl f: gng on cl home* **8/1[3]**

-620 6 shd **Lady Algarhoud (FR)**[17] 2462 4-9-2 57 .... AlanMunro 1 59
(D K Ivory) *lw: chsd ldrs: chal fr over 1f out: styd on same pce fnl f* **9/1**

1-03 7 shd **Blessed Place**[9] 2674 6-9-1 56 .... LDettori 3 57
(D J S Ffrench Davis) *led tl hdd over 1f out: styd on same pce ins last* **7/2[1]**

0050 8 1 **Salviati (USA)**[5] 2784 9-9-13 68 .... JimCrowley 9 66
(J M Bradley) *lw: b: slowly away: rdn and sme hdwy fnl f: nvr gng pce to rch ldrs* **10/1**

5022 9 1 **Cerulean Rose**[28] 2095 7-9-2 62 .... JamesDoyle(5) 8 56
(A W Carroll) *nvr gng pce to rch ldrs* **9/2[2]**

0030 **10** 1 ¼ **Trace Clip**[4] 2813 8-8-4 **52** ...... MarkCoumbe(7) 4 42
(N I M Rossiter) *lw: slowly away: outpcd most of way* **25/1**

61.72 secs (-0.84) **Going Correction** -0.30s/f (Firm)
WFA 3 from 4yo+ 6lb **10** Ran SP% **116.7**
Speed ratings (Par 103):94,93,92,91,91 90,90,89,87,85
CSF £43.96 CT £342.28 TOTE £7.70: £2.20, £3.50, £3.10; EX 82.20 Place 6 £594.68, Place 5 £226.07.
Owner Mrs P Hastings **Bred** R N Clay, Et Al **Trained** Kingsclere, Hants

FOCUS
A modest sprint for the track rated around the third and fourth. The winning time was very moderate for the grade and only two lengths covered the first seven at the line.
Blessed Place Official explanation: jockey said, regarding the running and riding, he had tried to make all, as when successful at Yarmouth previously, adding that gelding responds more to being pushed than being hit and did not appear to like being crowded
Trace Clip Official explanation: jockey said gelding missed the break
T/Plt: £1,782.10 to a £1 stake. Pool: £49,925.90. 20.45 winning tickets. T/Qpdt: £279.70 to a £1 stake. Pool: £3,554.20. 9.40 winning tickets. ST

2963 - 2965a (Foreign Racing) - See Raceform Interactive

2630 BATH (L-H)
Wednesday, June 28

OFFICIAL GOING: Good to firm
Wind: Nil Weather: Cloudy

2966 BATHWICK TYRES LADY RIDERS' H'CAP — 1m 2f 46y
6:40 (6:41) (Class 6) (0-65,65) 4-Y-0+ **£2,498** (£774; £387; £193) Stalls Low

Form — RPR
4361 **1** **Another Con (IRE)**[11] 2636 5-9-0 **46** oh5 ...... MissFayeBramley(3) 4 56
(P A Blockley) *hld up in mid-div: swtchd rt and hdwy on wd outside 2f out: led ins fnl f: r.o* **7/1**[2]
4664 **2** 1 **Wood Fern (UAE)**[11] 2636 6-8-12 **46** oh2 ...... MissMSowerby(5) 3 54
(W M Brisbourne) *hld up and bhd: swtchd rt and gd hdwy over 1f out: r.o ins fnl f* **7/1**[2]
-000 **3** 2 **Didoe**[24] 2262 7-8-13 **47** ow1 ...... MrsMarieKing(5) 1 51
(P W Hiatt) *chsd ldr: led over 3f out: hdd and no ex ins fnl f* **22/1**
3053 **4** 1 **Harare**[9] 2707 5-9-3 **51** oh1 ow5 ...... (b) MissABevan(5) 9 53
(R J Price) *hld up in mid-div: hdwy on outside 4f out: one pce fnl f* **10/1**
0-22 **5** 1 ¼ **Expected Bonus (USA)**[36] 1911 7-9-3 **46** oh2 ...... MissSBrotherton 12 46
(Jamie Poulton) *hld up: hdwy over 2f out: no imp fnl f* **17/2**
0602 **6** 1 **Gingko**[11] 2636 9-9-0 **50** ...... MissVGraham(7) 2 48
(P R Webber) *s.i.s: hdwy 8f out: one pce fnl 2f* **6/1**[1]
26-0 **7** 2 **Ile Michel**[86] 854 9-10-3 **65** ...... MissRachelD'Arcy(5) 11 59
(Lady Herries) *s.i.s: plld hrd: hdwy on ins 8f out: wknd fnl f* **22/1**
0040 **8** nk **Spring Time Girl**[14] 2546 4-9-3 **46** oh3 ...... (v) MissLEllison 6 40
(B Ellison) *hld up: hdwy over 7f out: lost pl 4f out: n.d after* **16/1**
2060 **9** 4 **Larad (IRE)**[15] 2522 5-9-3 **46** oh3 ...... (b) MrsSMoore 8 32
(J S Moore) *hld up and bhd: hdwy on ins over 5f out: wknd fnl f* **16/1**
06-5 **10** ½ **Able Mind**[23] 2286 6-9-0 **48** ...... MissHCuthbert(5) 10 33
(D W Thompson) *t.k.h: prom tl wknd wl over 1f out* **8/1**[3]
6015 **11** nk **Diamond Dan (IRE)**[11] 2636 4-9-7 **53** ...... MissEFolkes(3) 15 38
(P D Evans) *prom tl wknd 2f out* **7/1**[2]
00/0 **12** 6 **Didifon**[3] 2902 11-9-7 **57** ow2 ...... MissJBuck(7) 14 30
(Mrs L J Young) *prom 4f* **100/1**
006- **13** 2 ½ **Mabella (IRE)**[334] 2522 4-9-4 **54** oh4 ow8 ...... (t) MissIsabelTompsett(7) 5 22
(B J Llewellyn) *led: hdd over 3f out: wknd over 2f out* **100/1**
000/ **14** 1 ½ **Imperial Rocket (USA)**[24] 4774 9-9-6 **54** ow2(t) MissHayleyMoore(5) 16 20
(W K Goldsworthy) *prom: jnd ldr 8f out: wknd over 2f out* **40/1**
6064 **U** **Hatch A Plan (IRE)**[18] 2455 5-10-5 **62** ...... MissEJJones 7 —
(Mrs A J Hamilton-Fairley) *bhd whn clipped heels and uns rdr over 8f out* **11/1**

2m 10.19s (-0.81) **Going Correction** -0.15s/f (Firm) **15** Ran SP% **115.7**
Speed ratings (Par 101):97,96,94,93,92 92,90,90,86,86 86,81,79,78,—
CSF £50.41 CT £1021.37 TOTE £8.00: £2.80, £2.90, £4.90; EX 73.70.
Owner Market Avenue Racing Club Ltd **Bred** Matthew Tynan **Trained** Lambourn, Berks
■ Stewards' Enquiry : Miss J Buck three-day ban: used whip when out of contention (Jul 9,15,18)

FOCUS
A typically moderate lady riders' event. The form seems sound enough overall.

2967 M. J. CHURCH MAIDEN STKS — 5f 161y
7:10 (7:12) (Class 5) 2-Y-0 **£3,238** (£963; £481; £240) Stalls Low

Form — RPR
54 **1** **Bodes Galaxy (IRE)**[13] 2572 2-9-3 ...... MickyFenton 1 78
(N P Littmoden) *mde all: rdn 2f out: drvn out* **9/1**[3]
54 **2** ½ **Vaunt**[16] 2506 2-9-3 ...... SteveDrowne 8 76
(R Charlton) *a.p: wnt 2nd over 2f out: rdn and ev ch over 1f out: nt qckn ins fnl f* **1/1**[1]
0 **3** ½ **Cheap Street**[18] 2432 2-9-3 ...... StephenCarson 2 78+
(J G Portman) *chsd ldrs on ins: rdn over 2f out: nt clr run ins fnl f and cl home: nt rcvr* **25/1**
0 **4** 5 **Piccolena Boy**[26] 2185 2-9-3 ...... JimCrowley 5 58
(P Winkworth) *w ldrs: rdn over 2f out: wknd over 1f out* **18/1**
0 **5** nk **Totally Free**[13] 2572 2-9-3 ...... HayleyTurner 9 57
(M D I Usher) *sn outpcd: sme late hdwy: nvr nr ldrs* **100/1**
50 **6** nk **It's No Problem (IRE)**[85] 878 2-8-12 ...... FergusSweeney 6 51
(Jean-Rene Auvray) *bhd: rdn 3f out: nvr trbld ldrs* **20/1**
64 **7** 4 **Mac Gille Eoin**[68] 1107 2-9-3 ...... LPKeniry 4 43
(J Gallagher) *w ldrs tl wknd over 2f out* **40/1**
0 **8** 1 **Cryptic Clue (USA)**[32] 2029 2-9-3 ...... RichardHughes 1 40
(Mrs A J Perrett) *prom: rdn over 2f out: wknd over 1f out* **15/8**[2]
9 2 ½ **Fun In The Sun** 2-9-3 ...... AdrianMcCarthy 3 31
(Jane Southcombe) *s.i.s: outpcd* **100/1**

1m 11.1s (-0.10) **Going Correction** -0.15s/f (Firm) **9** Ran SP% **113.1**
Speed ratings (Par 93):94,93,92,86,85 85,79,78,75
CSF £17.72 TOTE £10.80: £2.40, £1.10, £4.70; EX 23.10.
Owner Mark Harniman **Bred** T Stewart **Trained** Newmarket, Suffolk

FOCUS
Just an average juvenile maiden, although the front three did draw five lengths clear of the remainder and the form looks sound. Cheap Street finished full of running and would have won had he been able to get into the clear.

NOTEBOOK
Bodes Galaxy(IRE), a keeping-on fourth on Lingfield's Polytrack last time, appreciated the positive tactics and was always holding the persistent challenge of favourite Vaunt, although he would surely have been beaten had Cheap Street got a run. Evidently effective at this trip, seven furlongs is going to suit in time and he could be the type to do well in nurseries. (tchd 8-1 and 10-1)
Vaunt, who ran well from a bad draw at Windsor most recently, was forced to race wide here but still looked the likeliest winner racing inside the final quarter mile. However, Bodes Galaxy pulled out extra and he was unable to get by. Now qualified for nurseries, that may be the way for him to go. (op 8-11)
Cheap Street, well held on his debut at Goodwood, was always going well on the inside and he picked up well when asked, but soon found himself with nowhere to go and he was forced to go past the line in third full of running. He would have won had he got out into the clear and he can surely pick up a maiden. Official explanation: jockey said colt was denied a clear run (tchd 20-1)
Piccolena Boy stepped up on his recent course debut effort and he looks a likely type for nurseries. (op 14-1)
Totally Free made a little late headway having been outpaced early on and he too may be one for low-grade nurseries later in the season.
Cryptic Clue(USA), who failed to shine in soft ground on his debut at Newmarket, was a well-supported second favourite with the faster surface clearly expected to suit, but having shown some early pace, he dropped away in particularly tame fashion. He is clearly believed to have ability, but has yet to show it. (op 7-2)

2968 KLEENEZE IN TO EUROPE (S) H'CAP — 1m 5y
7:40 (7:42) (Class 6) (0-60,58) 3-Y-0 **£2,266** (£674; £337; £168) Stalls Low

Form — RPR
000- **1** **Thornfield Clo (IRE)**[328] 4092 3-8-10 **47** ...... RichardHughes 2 54
(R Hannon) *s.i.s: sn led: rdn over 2f out: r.o wl* **8/1**
1030 **2** 2 ½ **Penang Cinta**[49] 1593 3-9-4 **58** ...... AdamKirby(3) 13 59
(G A Butler) *s.i.s: bhd: swtchd rt over 4f out: rdn over 3f out: swtchd rt over 2f out: hdwy over 1f out: edgd rt and tk 2nd* **4/1**[1]
6243 **3** hd **The Jailer**[44] 1726 3-8-5 **42** ...... (p) DavidKinsella 5 43
(J G M O'Shea) *led early: chsd wnr: rdn over 2f out: nt qckn fnl f* **11/2**[3]
-003 **4** 1 **Khyber Knight (IRE)**[8] 2728 3-8-5 **42** ...... AdrianMcCarthy 16 41
(Jane Southcombe) *bhd tl rdn and hdwy over 2f out: kpt on same pce fnl f* **16/1**
0-45 **5** ¾ **Joy In The Guild (IRE)**[44] 1726 3-8-6 **43** ...... LPKeniry 10 40
(W S Kittow) *bhd tl hdwy on ins over 1f out: r.o* **11/1**
1000 **6** shd **Chookie Windsor**[17] 2480 3-9-2 **53** ...... FergusSweeney 11 50
(M S Saunders) *a.p: rdn over 2f out: one pce* **8/1**
-600 **7** 2 ½ **Apres Ski (IRE)**[13] 2573 3-9-4 **55** ...... FrankieMcDonald 9 46
(J W Hills) *t.k.h in mid-div: hdwy over 3f out: wknd over 2f out* **16/1**
5260 **8** shd **Saxon Star (IRE)**[65] 1200 3-8-6 **43** ...... HayleyTurner 3 34
(M D I Usher) *hld up in tch: rdn and wknd over 2f out* **20/1**
5640 **9** 4 **Lewis Lloyd (IRE)**[4] 2877 3-8-12 **49** ...... SebSanders 14 31
(I A Wood) *hld up in tch: rdn 3f out: wknd over 1f out* **13/2**
0-00 **10** shd **Is**[99] 687 3-8-6 **50** ...... RobbieMills(7) 6 31
(Rae Guest) *s.i.s: nvr nr ldrs* **22/1**
6-00 **11** 1 ¼ **Smoking Star**[10] 2673 3-8-11 **55** ...... MarkCoumbe(7) 4 33
(N I M Rossiter) *hld up in mid-div: rdn 3f out: no rspnse* **33/1**
0005 **12** 1 ½ **Simplified**[13] 2589 3-8-11 **48** ...... JimmyQuinn 1 23
(J Pearce) *s.i.s: sn rcvrd: t.k.h in mid-div: hdwy on ins over 4f out: rdn 3f out: sn wknd* **5/1**[2]
0-00 **13** 2 ½ **Forever Rocky**[44] 1726 3-8-4 **41** ow1 ...... (b[1]) PaulFitzsimons 7 10
(F Jordan) *rdn over 3f out: a bhd* **33/1**
000 **14** 14 **Silvabella (IRE)**[56] 1417 3-8-9 **46** ow1 ...... (v) SteveDrowne 15 —
(D Haydn Jones) *mid-div: rdn over 3f out: sn bhd* **16/1**

1m 40.47s (-0.63) **Going Correction** -0.15s/f (Firm) **14** Ran SP% **128.6**
Speed ratings (Par 97):97,94,94,93,92 92,89,89,85,85 84,83,80,66
CSF £41.02 CT £204.60 TOTE £10.70: £3.70, £1.50, £1.70; EX 57.80.The winner was bought in for 7,200gns.
Owner Dr Michael Dunleavy **Bred** Denis O'Flynn **Trained** East Everleigh, Wilts

FOCUS
Comfortable winner Thornfield Clo is likely to prove a little better than selling grade, but this was a very poor race.
Thornfield Clo(IRE) Official explanation: trainer said, regarding the improved form shown, the filly had strengthened up over the winter

2969 BRISTOL PORT COMPANY H'CAP — 1m 5y
8:10 (8:12) (Class 5) (0-70,70) 4-Y-0+ **£3,886** (£1,156; £577; £288) Stalls Low

Form — RPR
/000 **1** **Personify**[16] 2510 4-8-13 **65** ...... (p) AdamKirby(3) 13 75
(C G Cox) *hld up in tch: rdn 4f out: led over 1f out: edgd lft ins fnl f: drvn out* **8/1**[3]
0422 **2** 1 **Border Artist**[19] 2390 7-7-13 **51** oh1 ...... EdwardCreighton(3) 14 59
(B G Powell) *hld up in mid-div: hdwy wl over 1f out: sn rdn: r.o ins fnl f* **10/1**
0050 **3** hd **The Gaikwar (IRE)**[17] 2482 7-8-13 **65** ...... (b) AmirQuinn(3) 5 73
(R A Harris) *stdd s: plld hrd: hdwy over 2f out: rdn over 1f out: r.o ins fnl f* **11/1**
1005 **4** 1 **Deeper In Debt**[12] 2606 8-9-2 **65** ...... SebSanders 6 70
(J Akehurst) *hld up in mid-div: hdwy over 2f out: rdn and ev ch over 1f out: nt qckn ins fnl f* **5/1**[2]
220 **5** shd **Tuning Fork**[19] 2401 6-8-6 **55** ...... FergusSweeney 12 60
(T M Jones) *led: rdn and hdd over 1f out: no ex ins fnl f* **17/2**
-004 **6** hd **Danzare**[8] 2725 4-8-4 **53** ...... JimmyQuinn 4 58
(Mrs A J Hamilton-Fairley) *a.p: rdn over 1f out: kpt on ins fnl f* **20/1**
0-00 **7** 1 **Hawridge Sensation**[9] 2708 4-8-7 **56** ow1 ...... MickyFenton 2 58
(W S Kittow) *s.i.s: rdn and hdwy on outside over 1f out: nvr trbld ldrs* **33/1**
0250 **8** shd **Voice Mail**[11] 2640 7-9-7 **70** ...... (b) LPKeniry 1 79+
(A M Balding) *hld up and bhd: stdy hdwy on ins over 4f out: nt clr run ins fnl f: nt rcvr* **4/1**[1]
-040 **9** ¾ **Wind Chime (IRE)**[17] 2482 9-8-0 **56** ...... JosephWalsh(7) 8 56
(A G Newcombe) *nvr nrr* **20/1**
3535 **10** 3 **Lockstock (IRE)**[19] 2414 8-8-9 **58** ...... (p) RichardHughes 11 51
(M S Saunders) *prom: rdn over 2f out: ev ch over 1f out: wknd ins fnl f* **9/1**
000- **11** ¾ **Lifted Way**[292] 5094 7-9-6 **69** ...... SteveDrowne 3 61
(P R Chamings) *hld up: hdwy on ins 5f out: wknd over 2f out* **33/1**
-03P **12** ½ **Storm Centre**[92] 777 4-8-10 **64** ...... JamesDoyle(5) 7 55
(Miss J S Davis) *hld up and bhd: rdn whn nt clr run over 2f out: n.d* **33/1**
0041 **13** shd **Adobe**[9] 2702 11-8-12 **61** 6ex ...... SamHitchcott 9 51
(W M Brisbourne) *a towards rr* **8/1**[3]
0-33 **14** hd **Start Of Authority**[36] 1914 5-8-2 **51** oh8 ...... DavidKinsella 15 41
(J Gallagher) *a bhd* **20/1**
0-00 **15** 5 **Elidore**[12] 2603 6-9-1 **64** ...... FrancisFerris 10 42
(B Palling) *chsd ldr: rdn and ev ch 2f out: sn wknd: eased whn btn wl ins fnl f* **50/1**

1m 39.52s (-1.58) **Going Correction** -0.15s/f (Firm) **15** Ran SP% **121.9**
Speed ratings (Par 103):101,100,99,98,98 98,97,97,96,93 92,92,92,92,87
CSF £78.50 CT £915.05 TOTE £9.60: £2.90, £3.10, £5.30; EX 112.50.
Owner Courtenay Club **Bred** Darley **Trained** Lambourn, Berks

FOCUS
A very ordinary handicap, in which the early pace was sound. The runner-up looks a sound guide.

Voice Mail Official explanation: jockey said gelding was denied a clear run
Start Of Authority Official explanation: jockey said gelding lost its action on the bend

2970 WITHY KING SOLICITORS MAIDEN STKS 1m 3f 144y
8:40 (8:42) (Class 5) 3-Y-O+ **£3,238** (£963; £481; £240) **Stalls** Low

Form RPR
3424 **1** **Strategic Mount**[30] 2066 3-8-11 76 .... SteveDrowne 1 84+
(P F I Cole) *chsd ldr: led gng wl over 2f out: shkn up and wnt clr ins fnl f: comf* **9/4**[2]
0052 **2** *4* **Is It Me (USA)**[4] 2882 3-8-11 65 .... RobbieFitzpatrick 4 78
(P A Blockley) *led: rdn and hdd over 2f out: one pce* **13/2**
0-03 **3** *nk* **Reinstated (IRE)**[13] 2580 3-8-6 82 .... SamHitchcott 7 72
(B W Hills) *a.p: rdn over 4f out: one pce fnl 2f* **5/1**[3]
4- **4** *2 ½* **Gordonsville**[273] 5554 3-8-11 .... SebSanders 3 73
(A M Balding) *s.i.s: hld up: hdwy over 5f out: rdn and outpcd 4f out: rallied over 2f out: sn no imp* **2/1**[1]
5 **5** *15* **Matinee Idol**[21] 2350 3-8-6 .... FergusSweeney 2 44+
(H Candy) *hld up: rdn 4f out: struggling 3f out* **12/1**
60 **6** *6* **Electric Storm**[23] 2304 3-8-11 .... RichardHughes 6 40+
(R Charlton) *hld up: dropped rr 4f out: sn rdn and struggling* **9/1**
7 *52* **Peachy Pear** 3-8-6 .... LPKeniry 5 —
(Mrs L J Young) *s.i.s: sn wl bhd: t.o* **50/1**

2m 26.57s (-3.73) **Going Correction** -0.15s/f (Firm) **7** Ran SP% **113.8**
Speed ratings (Par 103): 106,103,103,101,91 87,52
CSF £17.04 TOTE £3.50: £2.10, £2.60; EX 13.00.
Owner Ben & Sir Martyn Arbib **Bred** Arbib Bloodstock Partnership **Trained** Whatcombe, Oxon

FOCUS
A decent winning time for a race like this. Only a fair maiden but the form should prove more reliable than most.

2971 AVONBRIDGE AT WHITSBURY STUD H'CAP 5f 161y
9:10 (9:10) (Class 5) (0-70,72) 3-Y-O+ **£3,886** (£1,156; £577; £288) **Stalls** Low

Form RPR
0333 **1** **Louphole**[9] 2711 4-9-5 62 .... AmirQuinn(3) 1 75
(P J Makin) *hld up in tch: hdwy on ins over 1f out: rdn and rdr dropped whip ins fnl f: sn led: r.o* **9/2**[1]
-030 **2** *½* **Blessed Place**[1] 2962 6-8-11 56 .... JamesDoyle(5) 8 67
(D J S Ffrench Davis) *led: rdn over 1f out: hdd wl ins fnl f: kpt on* **6/1**[3]
-046 **3** *½* **Witchry**[15] 2536 4-10-0 68 .... LPKeniry 5 77
(A G Newcombe) *hld up: hdwy over 2f out: rdn over 1f out: kpt on ins fnl f* **12/1**
2303 **4** *nk* **Summer Recluse (USA)**[3] 2898 7-9-13 67 .... SteveDrowne 6 75
(J M Bradley) *hld up: hdwy over 2f out: rdn over 1f out: kpt on ins fnl f* **9/2**[1]
-560 **5** *½* **Danehill Stroller (IRE)**[20] 2384 6-9-11 65 .... (p) SebSanders 9 72+
(R M Beckett) *swtchd lft sn after s: hld up and bhd: rdn and hdwy on ins fnl f: nt rch ldrs* **5/1**[2]
0500 **6** *nk* **Coranglais**[17] 2484 6-8-12 52 .... (p) JimCrowley 10 58
(J M Bradley) *hld up and bhd: rdn and hdwy over 1f out: swtchd lft jst ins fnl f: nt qckn* **15/2**
0110 **7** *1* **Caustic Wit (IRE)**[6] 2792 8-10-4 72 6ex .... (p) FergusSweeney 11 74
(M S Saunders) *prom: chsd ldr over 2f out: sn rdn: no ex wl ins fnl f* **7/1**
5600 **8** *2* **Seneschal**[18] 2444 5-9-10 64 .... RichardHughes 3 59
(A B Haynes) *hld up and bhd: hdwy 2f out: swtchd lft jst over 1f out: sn rdn: wknd ins fnl f* **9/1**
00-0 **9** *7* **Firework**[46] 1689 8-8-13 53 .... StephenCarson 2 25
(E A Wheeler) *w ldr tl wknd over 2f out: eased whn no ch ins fnl f* **25/1**
00-0 **10** *1 ¼* **Knead The Dough**[11] 2636 5-8-2 49 oh10 .... SophieDoyle(7) 12 16
(A E Price) *hld up in tch: rdn over 2f out: wknd wl over 1f out* **100/1**
00-0 **11** *1 ½* **Miracle Baby**[64] 1225 4-8-4 49 oh13 .... MarcHalford(5) 7 11
(A J Chamberlain) *prom: rdn 3f out: sn wknd* **40/1**

1m 10.34s (-0.86) **Going Correction** -0.15s/f (Firm) **11** Ran SP% **116.5**
Speed ratings (Par 103): 99,98,97,97,96 96,94,92,82,81 79
CSF £30.77 CT £309.92 TOTE £6.20: £1.90, £2.60, £2.90; EX 30.30 Place 6 £218.38, Place 5 £73.31.
Owner Ten Of Hearts **Bred** Mrs P Harford **Trained** Ogbourne Maisey, Wilts

FOCUS
An ordinary handicap, and sound form for the grade.
Firework Official explanation: jockey said gelding hung right-handed
T/Plt: £87.60 to a £1 stake. Pool: £57,873.15. 482.25 winning tickets. T/Qpdt: £15.40 to a £1 stake. Pool: £4,720.60. 225.40 winning tickets. KH

2695 CARLISLE (R-H)
Wednesday, June 28

OFFICIAL GOING: Good (good to soft in places)
Wind: Breezy, half-against

2972 EUROPEAN BREEDERS FUND MAIDEN STKS 5f 193y
2:20 (2:21) (Class 5) 2-Y-O **£3,886** (£1,156; £577; £288) **Stalls** High

Form RPR
325 **1** **Domino Dancer (IRE)**[27] 2159 2-9-3 .... DarryllHolland 10 88+
(J Howard Johnson) *mde virtually all: drew clr fr wl over 1f out: easily* **3/1**[1]
20 **2** *8* **Orpen Prince (IRE)**[12] 2610 2-9-3 .... NCallan 4 64
(K A Ryan) *awkward s: sn prom: effrt and chsd wnr appr fnl f: no imp* **3/1**[1]
0 **3** *½* **Autour Du Monde**[39] 1853 2-8-12 .... LeeEnstone 7 58
(P C Haslam) *cl up tl edgd rt and no ex fr 2f out* **66/1**
4 *4* **White Deer (USA)** 2-9-3 .... KDarley 5 51
(M Johnston) *sn outpcd: effrt u.p over 2f out: nvr rchd ldrs* **3/1**[1]
6 **5** *3* **Wanchai Night**[18] 2439 2-9-3 .... DavidAllan 3 42
(T D Easterby) *plld hrd: disp ld to 1/2-way: wknd wl over 1f out* **10/1**[2]
6 *3 ½* **Mazin Lady** 2-8-12 .... TomEaves 8 26
(Miss J A Camacho) *s.i.s: hdwy and prom on ins over 3f out: wknd 2f out* **16/1**[3]
7 *3 ½* **Dee Valley Boy (IRE)** 2-9-3 .... GrahamGibbons 6 21
(J D Bethell) *towards rr: faltered after 1f: sn outpcd: n.d after* **33/1**
8 *9* **Packers Hill (IRE)** 2-9-3 .... DeanMcKeown 1 —
(G A Swinbank) *s.i.s: hung lft thrght: nvr on terms* **25/1**
0 **9** *¾* **Eldon Endeavour**[27] 2159 2-8-12 .... AndrewMullen(5) 2 —
(B Storey) *chsd ldrs on outside tl wknd over 2f out* **150/1**

1m 14.52s (0.91) **Going Correction** +0.05s/f (Good) **9** Ran SP% **98.9**
Speed ratings (Par 93): 95,84,83,78,74 69,65,53,52
CSF £8.38 TOTE £3.30: £1.10, £1.20, £11.40; EX 6.50.
Owner Transcend Bloodstock LLP **Bred** D And Mrs D Veitch **Trained** Billy Row, Co Durham
■ Fishforcompliments was withdrawn (7/1, refused to enter stalls). R4 applies, deduct 10p in the £.

FOCUS
A mixed bag but a much-improved effort from Domino Dancer, who is the type to hold his own in stronger company. Not an easy race to rate with the runner-up well off form.

NOTEBOOK
Domino Dancer(IRE), who disappointed on ground softer than the official description last time, turned in his best effort yet back on a sound surface. Although he had the run of the race he won with some authority, he should stay seven and can hold his own in stronger company. (tchd 10-3)
Orpen Prince(IRE), who disappointed on fast ground last time, fared better back on this good surface. He has plenty of physical scope and, although his form so far is nothing special, appeals as the type to win an ordinary nursery, especially when upped to seven furlongs. (op 2-1)
Autour Du Monde, well beaten in heavy ground on her debut last month, fared much better this time but looks the type to do better in ordinary nursery company once qualified for a handicap mark.
White Deer(USA), a half brother to a dual hurdle winner and out of a mile and a half winner, proved green in the paddock and in the race. This debut form is modest and he left the impression a much stiffer test of stamina would be in his favour. (op 10-3 tchd 4-1)
Wanchai Night failed to build on his debut effort and, although he is likely to remain vulnerable in this type of event, he will have to settle better if he is to progress. (op 12-1)
Mazin Lady, who has several winners in her pedigree, hinted at ability on this racecourse debut and is entitled to come on for the experience, but she will have to improve a good deal to win a similar event in this grade. (op 20-1)
Packers Hill(IRE), related to a couple of winners abroad, took the eye in the paddock as a strong sort who looked very much in need of the race. Although he showed little, he is the type physically to leave this bare form behind in due course.

2973 ST JAMES SECURITY MAIDEN AUCTION STKS 5f
2:50 (2:51) (Class 5) 2-Y-O **£3,886** (£1,156; £577; £288) **Stalls** High

Form RPR
2 **1** **Ponty Rossa (IRE)**[29] 2106 2-8-6 .... DavidAllan 15 71+
(T D Easterby) *in tch: effrt over 1f out: styd on to ld cl home* **10/3**[1]
0 **2** *hd* **Rainbow Fox**[15] 2517 2-8-13 .... PaulHanagan 11 76
(R A Fahey) *rn green early in rr: hdwy ins 2f out: styd on wl fnl f: jst hld* **9/1**
0 **3** *shd* **Mamora Reef**[16] 2500 2-8-9 ow5 .... DarryllHolland 14 71
(J R Weymes) *cl up: led over 1f out: kpt on: hdd towards fin* **50/1**
0 **4** *nk* **Bid For Gold**[21] 2361 2-9-2 .... RobertWinston 8 77
(Jedd O'Keeffe) *chsd ldrs: effrt and ev ch over 1f out: kpt on: hld cl home* **11/1**
5 *1 ¼* **Pavlovia** 2-8-11 .... FergalLynch 10 68
(T D Easterby) *s.i.s: bhd tl gd hdwy over 1f out: kpt on fnl f: nvr nrr* **25/1**
02 **6** *3 ½* **La Vecchia Scuola (IRE)**[19] 2394 2-8-6 .... AdrianTNicholls 9 50
(D Nicholls) *led tl hdd over 1f out: sn outpcd* **5/1**[2]
3 **7** *nk* **Tobago Reef**[14] 2545 2-8-9 .... TomEaves 5 52
(Mrs L Stubbs) *prom on outside tl rdn and outpcd over 1f out* **8/1**[3]
8 *½* **Ice Mountain** 2-8-11 .... PhilipRobinson 13 52+
(B Smart) *trckd ldrs tl wknd over 1f out* **10/3**[1]
9 *½* **Rue Soleil** 2-8-0 ow1 .... AndrewMullen(5) 2 44
(J R Weymes) *outpcd tl hdwy over 1f out: nvr able to chal* **66/1**
10 *2* **Nanny State (IRE)** 2-8-4 .... JoeFanning 6 36
(P C Haslam) *racd wd: hld up: effrt over 2f out: hung lft and wknd over 1f out* **40/1**
00 **11** *2* **Vodkat**[33] 1982 2-8-6 .... KimTinkler 12 31
(N Tinkler) *in tch tl wknd fr 2f out* **25/1**
12 *3 ½* **Misaine (IRE)** 2-8-9 .... KDarley 3 21
(T J Etherington) *sn outpcd and drvn along: nvr on terms* **25/1**
13 *1 ½* **West Warning** 2-8-9 .... (b[1]) PaulMulrennan 7 16
(M W Easterby) *s.v.s: nvr on terms* **66/1**
14 *4* **Yungaburra (IRE)** 2-8-11 .... DeanMcKeown 4 4
(G A Swinbank) *towards rr: shkn up 2f out: sn btn* **20/1**

62.23 secs (0.73) **Going Correction** +0.05s/f (Good) **14** Ran SP% **116.0**
Speed ratings (Par 93): 96,95,95,95,93 87,86,86,85,82 78,73,70,64
CSF £29.82 TOTE £2.90: £1.30, £3.20, £10.90; EX 25.60.
Owner The Lapin Blanc Racing Partnership **Bred** Jim McDonald **Trained** Great Habton, N Yorks

FOCUS
An ordinary bunch on looks and, with less than a half a length covering the first four home, this bare form looks ordinary as well. That said, the second, third and fourth were all big improvers while the winner should do a bit better.

NOTEBOOK
Ponty Rossa(IRE), who showed ability over six furlongs on her debut in a race that has thrown up winners, successfully negotiated the drop to this trip at this stiff course and showed a willing attitude. The return to further will suit and she may do better in ordinary nursery company. (op 3-1 tchd 11-4)
Rainbow Fox, who is related to several winners over sprint distances, looked in need of the race in the paddock and proved green early on but showed enough in the second half of the contest to suggest that he can win a similar event. (op 17-2 tchd 10-1)
Mamora Reef, well beaten on her debut at Pontefract, had the run of the race and turned in a much-improved effort over this shorter trip. She would have won in theory had her rider not posted 5lb of overweight and she looks capable of making amends in ordinary company. (op 66-1)
Bid For Gold, from a stable going well at present, bettered his debut effort by some way and, given he has physical scope for further improvement, may be capable of winning a modest event in due course. (op 14-1)
Pavlovia, the first foal of a dual mile and a quarter winner, is not very big but showed clear signs of ability on this racecourse debut and, although this bare form is nothing special, she appeals as the type to win a minor event granted a suitable test.
La Vecchia Scuola(IRE), edgy in the preliminaries, failed to build on her improved Catterick run at this stiffer course and, although vulnerable to the better types in this grade, she may be the type that appreciates more of a test of speed. (op 9-2)
Ice Mountain, related to several winners up to middle distances, looked in need of the run on this racecourse debut but showed enough to suggest he possesses ability and he is the type to improve. (op 11-4)
Nanny State(IRE) Official explanation: jockey said filly hung left-handed from halfway

2974 CARLING CARLISLE BELL (H'CAP) 7f 200y
3:20 (3:22) (Class 4) (0-80,82) 3-Y-O+ **£19,431** (£5,781; £2,889; £1,443) **Stalls** High

Form RPR
0503 **1** **Regent's Secret (USA)**[14] 2547 6-9-3 73 .... FergalLynch 12 86
(J S Goldie) *hld up: rdn 3f out: hdwy centre to ld wl ins fnl f: kpt on wl* **11/1**
0011 **2** *1 ¼* **Riley Boys (IRE)**[1] 2945 5-9-12 82 5ex .... RobertWinston 14 92
(J G Given) *towards rr: rdn and hdwy fr 2f out: led briefly ins fnl f: kpt on* **8/1**[3]
3115 **3** *¾* **Hula Ballew**[4] 2851 6-9-4 74 5ex .... PhillipMakin 7 82
(M Dods) *in tch: effrt over 2f out: kpt on fnl f* **9/1**

6-10 **4** *hd* **Vicious Warrior**[21] [2364] 7-9-9 **79**.................................. DeanMcKeown 9 87
(R M Whitaker) *cl up: led over 1f out to ins fnl f: nt qckn* **20/1**
-606 **5** *3 ½* **Flighty Fellow (IRE)**[12] [2627] 6-9-4 **74**.................................. TomEaves 10 74
(Miss J A Camacho) *in tch: effrt 3f out: one pce fr over 1f out* **14/1**
5054 **6** *hd* **Wigwam Willie (IRE)**[27] [2162] 4-9-9 **79**..............................(p) NCallan 15 78
(K A Ryan) *in tch: effrt and rdn over 2f out: one pce over 1f out* **13/2**[2]
0650 **7** *nk* **Freeloader (IRE)**[18] [2440] 6-9-6 **76**.................................. PaulHanagan 4 75
(R A Fahey) *prom: rdn over 2f out: one pce over 1f out* **9/2**[1]
00-0 **8** *½* **Lago D'Orta (IRE)**[15] [2527] 6-9-10 **80**.......................... AdrianTNicholls 2 78+
(D Nicholls) *missed break: bhd tl hdwy over 1f out: nvr nrr* **66/1**
3-50 **9** *¾* **Resonate (IRE)**[27] [2169] 8-9-7 **77**.................................. KDarley 11 73
(A G Newcombe) *midfield: effrt over 2f out: nvr able to chal* **14/1**
1326 **10** *1 ¼* **Latif (USA)**[33] [1987] 5-8-12 **73**.................................. DerekNolan(5) 13 66
(Ms Deborah J Evans) *towards rr: effrt and rdn over 2f out: edgd rt and sn no imp* **20/1**
0661 **11** *1 ¼* **Tough Love**[8] [2737] 7-9-4 **74** 5ex..(p) DavidAllan 1 64
(T D Easterby) *bhd: rdn over 2f out: nvr on terms* **20/1**
2-00 **12** *hd* **Thunderwing (IRE)**[72] [1043] 4-9-9 **79**.................................. PatCosgrave 8 69
(K R Burke) *in tch: drvn 1/2-way: outpcd fr over 2f out* **33/1**
-150 **13** *nk* **Wahoo Sam (USA)**[113] [611] 6-9-5 **75**.................................. JoeFanning 5 64
(K A Ryan) *set decent pce to over 1f out: sn btn* **16/1**
0121 **14** *1 ½* **Sake (IRE)**[14] [2541] 4-9-3 **73**.................................. KimTinkler 6 59
(N Tinkler) *cl up tl edgd rt and wknd fr 2f out* **10/1**
-065 **15** *½* **Alchemist Master**[8] [2787] 7-8-12 **75**.................................. MichaelJStainton(7) 3 59
(R M Whitaker) *racd wd in midfield: edgd rt and wknd fr over 2f out* **25/1**
-000 **16** *5* **Mineral Star (IRE)**[12] [2621] 4-9-10 **80**.......................... DarrylHolland 17 53
(M H Tompkins) *wnt rt s: nvr on terms* **20/1**
2-04 **17** *½* **Top Dirham**[10] [2681] 8-9-8 **78**..(p) DaleGibson 16 50
(M W Easterby) *hld up: rdn over 2f out: sn btn* **11/1**

1m 39.06s (-1.03) **Going Correction** +0.05s/f (Good) **17** Ran SP% **124.9**
Speed ratings (Par 105):107,105,105,104,101 101,100,100,99,98 97,96,96,95,94 89,89
CSF £88.70 CT £873.65 TOTE £13.80: £3.10, £2.10, £2.40, £7.00; EX 143.60.
Owner Mrs M Craig **Bred** Adena Springs **Trained** Uplawmoor, E Renfrews

FOCUS
A competitive handicap in which the sound gallop teed things up for those coming from off the pace. Strong, solid form for the grade, which should pay to follow.

2975 GROLSCH CUMBERLAND PLATE (H'CAP) 1m 3f 107y
3:50 (3:52) (Class 4) (0-80,80) 3-Y-0+ **£19,431** (£5,781; £2,889; £1,443) **Stalls** Low

Form RPR
4-61 **1** **Cresta Gold**[19] [2412] 3-8-9 **78**.................................. DavidAllan 16 96+
(A Bailey) *chsd ldrs: led 2f out: sn clr* **12/1**
2601 **2** *5* **Lucayan Dancer**[15] [2519] 6-9-8 **78**.................................. AdrianTNicholls 15 86
(D Nicholls) *hld up: hdwy ins 2f out: chsd wnr ins fnl f: kpt on: no imp* **20/1**
0021 **3** *2* **Go Solo**[14] [2547] 5-9-7 **77**.................................. DeanMcKeown 11 82
(G A Swinbank) *hld up: hdwy centre 2f out: kpt on fnl f: no imp* **9/1**[3]
6343 **4** *shd* **Cotton Eyed Joe (IRE)**[28] [2140] 5-9-0 **70**.................................. PatCosgrave 12 74
(G A Swinbank) *in tch: effrt and rdn 3f out: kpt on same pce fr 2f out* **8/1**[2]
2002 **5** *nk* **Khanjar (USA)**[14] [2549] 6-9-0 **75**.................................. AndrewElliott(5) 5 79
(K R Burke) *cl up: effrt and ev ch 2f out: outpcd fnl f* **20/1**
4116 **6** *nk* **Dium Mac**[14] [2540] 5-8-6 **69**.................................. SuzzanneFrance(7) 1 73
(N Bycroft) *hld up: hdwy outside over 2f out: hung rt: kpt on: no imp* **25/1**
0056 **7** *hd* **Sporting Gesture**[11] [2656] 9-9-4 **74**.................................. PaulMulrennan 8 77
(M W Easterby) *midfield: outpcd over 3f out: no imp fr over 1f out* **20/1**
-004 **8** *1 ¼* **Sharp Reply (USA)**[8] [2736] 4-9-7 **77**..........................(v) PhilipRobinson 13 78
(R M Whitaker) *keen: led to 2f out: wknd fnl f* **14/1**
-021 **9** *nk* **Sualda (IRE)**[14] [2549] 7-9-10 **80**.................................. PaulHanagan 3 81
(R A Fahey) *in tch: effrt over 2f out: hung rt: no ex over 1f out* **10/1**
-434 **10** *1 ½* **Tcherina (IRE)**[33] [2000] 4-9-9 **79**.................................. FergalLynch 14 77
(T D Easterby) *trckd ldrs: effrt 3f out: no ex over 1f out* **11/1**
10-0 **11** *1 ¾* **Karlu (GER)**[64] [1206] 4-9-10 **80**.................................. RobertWinston 17 76
(Pat Eddery) *hld up: effrt centre over 2f out: nvr on terms* **12/1**
4421 **12** *¾* **Scotland Yard (UAE)**[6] [2786] 3-8-11 **80** 5ex.......................... RoystonFfrench 9 74
(M Johnston) *chsd ldrs: rdn over 3f out: wknd 2f out* **9/2**[1]
2-30 **13** *1 ½* **Tedstale (USA)**[163] [125] 8-9-10 **80**..(b) NCallan 10 72
(K A Ryan) *hld up: rdn over 3f out: edgd rt and nvr on terms* **16/1**
-055 **14** *6* **Balyan (IRE)**[18] [2452] 5-9-10 **80**..(p) DarrylHolland 7 62
(J Howard Johnson) *hld up: rdn over 3f out: nvr on terms* **20/1**
6052 **15** *3* **Nessen Dorma (IRE)**[22] [2326] 5-9-8 **78**..(p) KDarley 2 56
(J G Given) *prom tl wknd fr 3f out* **8/1**[2]
-663 **16** *34* **Waterloo Corner**[15] [2526] 4-8-12 **68**.................................. JoeFanning 6 —
(R Craggs) *hld up: struggling over 3f out: eased whn no ch* **66/1**

2m 23.15s (-4.90) **Going Correction** +0.05s/f (Good)
WFA 3 from 4yo+ 13lb **16** Ran SP% **120.1**
Speed ratings (Par 105):101,97,95,95,95 95,95,94,94,93 91,91,90,85,83 58
CSF £239.58 CT £2265.01 TOTE £11.80: £4.60, £5.70, £2.80, £2.20; EX 393.40.
Owner P T Tellwright **Bred** P T Tellwright **Trained** Cotebrook, Cheshire

FOCUS
Strong form for the grade and solid too, with the second to sixth inclusive all within a pound of recent form. An improved performance from the winner, who won with a good deal in hand.

2976 PERSIMMON HOMES H'CAP 5f
4:20 (4:20) (Class 4) (0-85,77) 3-Y-0 **£6,477** (£1,927; £963; £481) **Stalls** High

Form RPR
4415 **1** **Glasshoughton**[4] [2855] 3-9-5 **75**.................................. PhillipMakin 4 84
(M Dods) *cl up: led over 1f out: edgd rt: drvn out* **3/1**[1]
4126 **2** *½* **Welcome Approach**[19] [2410] 3-8-13 **69**.................................. DarrylHolland 5 76
(J R Weymes) *hld up in tch: rdn and hdwy over 1f out: kpt on fnl f* **7/1**
6411 **3** *¾* **Bahamian Duke**[9] [2701] 3-8-7 **63** 6ex.................................. PatCosgrave 3 67
(K R Burke) *led to over 1f out: nt qckn fnl f* **5/1**[3]
2035 **4** *shd* **Mulligan's Gold (IRE)**[19] [2410] 3-8-13 **69**.................................. FergalLynch 6 73
(T D Easterby) *hld up in tch: hdwy 2f out: no imp fnl f* **6/1**
402 **5** *4* **The History Man (IRE)**[29] [2105] 3-9-7 **77**..........................(b) DaleGibson 7 67
(M W Easterby) *keen: prom tl rdn and wknd over 1f out* **7/1**
-100 **6** *1 ½* **Rondo**[4] [2855] 3-9-7 **77**.................................. PaulFessey 2 61
(T D Barron) *chsd ldrs tl edgd lft and wknd fr 2f out* **20/1**
0122 **7** *2 ½* **Maison Dieu**[4] [2873] 3-8-5 **61**.................................. DavidAllan 8 36
(E J Alston) *chsd ldrs tl edgd rt and wknd fr 2f out* **7/2**[2]
5-00 **8** *½* **Crosby Hall**[11] [2658] 3-9-7 **77**..(t) KimTinkler 1 50
(N Tinkler) *chsd ldrs: outpcd whn n.m.r and wknd fr 2f out* **20/1**

61.67 secs (0.17) **Going Correction** +0.05s/f (Good) **8** Ran SP% **112.7**
Speed ratings (Par 101):100,99,98,97,91 89,85,84
CSF £23.65 CT £99.18 TOTE £3.60: £1.90, £2.40, £1.90; EX 30.20.

Owner J N Blackburn **Bred** Theakston Stud **Trained** Denton, Co Durham

FOCUS
A run of the mill sprint handicap in which the pace was sound, and this form should stand up at a similar level. The winner is progressing.

2977 EUROPEAN BREEDERS FUND FILLIES' H'CAP 6f 192y
4:50 (4:50) (Class 4) (0-85,77) 3-Y-0+ **£6,477** (£1,927; £963; £481) **Stalls** High

Form RPR
-504 **1** **Passion Fruit**[14] [2541] 5-9-2 **65**.................................. DeanMcKeown 5 82
(C W Fairhurst) *hld up in tch: c stands side ent st: shkn up and overall ldr over 1f out: sn clr* **4/1**[2]
3165 **2** *5* **Petite Mac**[9] [2700] 6-8-4 **60**.................................. SuzzanneFrance(7) 1 64
(N Bycroft) *prom: c stands side ent st: ev ch that gp over 1f out: kpt on: no ch w wnr: 2nd in gp* **15/2**
3323 **3** *¾* **Tour D'Amour (IRE)**[8] [2735] 3-8-10 **68**.................................. DavidAllan 4 67
(R Craggs) *chsd ldrs: c stands side ent st: outpcd over 2f out: kpt on fnl f: no imp: 3rd in gp* **6/1**
2602 **4** *4* **Riquewihr**[11] [2637] 6-9-9 **72**..(p) RobertWinston 3 64
(J S Wainwright) *hld up: c stands side and effrt over 2f out: no imp: 4th in gp* **10/1**
021- **5** *½* **Scotland The Brave**[242] [6139] 6-9-2 **65**..........................(v) GrahamGibbons 7 55+
(J D Bethell) *chsd ldrs: styd far side in st: rdn and no ch w stands side fr 2f out: 1st in that gp* **15/2**
5002 **6** *1* **Dispol Katie**[4] [2851] 5-9-9 **72**.................................. PaulFessey 6 60
(T D Barron) *led: c stands side in st: hdd over 1f out: sn btn: last of five that gp* **10/3**[1]
1-56 **7** *3* **Flylowflylong (IRE)**[15] [2525] 3-8-11 **69**.................................. TomEaves 2 46+
(I Semple) *bhd: struggling 1/2-way: styd towards far side in st: hung rt: no imp: 2nd in gp* **14/1**
54-1 **8** *6* **Hazelhurst (IRE)**[19] [2400] 3-8-9 **72**.................................. GregFairley(5) 8 33+
(J Howard Johnson) *hld up in tch: effrt in far side gp over 2f out: sn btn: 3rd in gp* **11/2**[3]
00-5 **9** *5* **Malinsa Blue (IRE)**[16] [2503] 4-10-0 **77**.................................. PaulHanagan 9 28+
(S Parr) *in tch: styd far side in st: rdn and btn over 1f out: last of four in gp* **20/1**

1m 27.42s (0.32) **Going Correction** +0.05s/f (Good)
WFA 3 from 4yo+ 9lb **9** Ran SP% **116.8**
Speed ratings (Par 102):100,94,93,88,88 87,83,76,71
CSF £34.46 CT £180.86 TOTE £6.70: £1.60, £3.50, £2.00; EX 79.40 Place 6 £204.18, Place 5 £119.41.
Owner G H & S Leggott **Bred** G H And Simon Leggott **Trained** Middleham Moor, N Yorks

FOCUS
An ordinary handicap but, although there was an even divide in the straight, those that came to the stands' side held a big advantage. The form is not the strongest.
Dispol Katie Official explanation: jockey said filly hung right-handed from halfway
T/Plt: £176.60 to a £1 stake. Pool: £43,569.45. 180.05 winning tickets. T/Qpdt: £55.30 to a £1 stake. Pool: £2,945.20. 39.40 winning tickets. RY

2752 KEMPTON (A.W) (R-H)
Wednesday, June 28

OFFICIAL GOING: Standard
Wind: Light behind Weather: Fine

2978 WEATHERBYS PRINTING APPRENTICE H'CAP (ROUND 4) 1m (P)
7:00 (7:00) (Class 6) (0-65,63) 3-Y-0+ **£3,238** (£963; £481; £240) **Stalls** High

Form RPR
0020 **1** **October Ben**[13] [2589] 3-8-9 **61**.................................. FrankiePickard(7) 1 69
(M D I Usher) *hld up in last: rapid prog on wd outside fr 2f out: sustained run to ld last 50yds* **20/1**
-315 **2** *½* **Terenzium (IRE)**[9] [2702] 4-8-12 **52**.................................. HeatherMcGee(5) 3 61
(L M Cumani) *trckd ldrs: gng wl 2f out: shuffled along and r.o to ld last 150yds: hdd and outpcd last 50yds* **5/2**[1]
0060 **3** *1* **Damburger Xpress**[13] [2577] 4-8-13 **51**.................................. KirstyMilczarek(3) 11 58
(D M Simcock) *settled in midfield: clsd on ldrs and nt clr run over 2f out: swtchd to inner fnl f: r.o to take 3rd nr fin* **13/2**[2]
-005 **4** *nk* **Sand Iron (IRE)**[14] [2551] 4-9-3 **52**.................................. SladeO'Hara 7 58
(John Allen) *prom: rdn to chal 2f out: led briefly 1f out: wknd last 75yds* **25/1**
0254 **5** *hd* **Simpsons Ross (IRE)**[22] [2318] 3-9-1 **60**.................................. JamieJones 8 64
(R M Flower) *towards rr: rdn 1/2-way: styd on u.p fr over 2f out: nvr quite pce to chal* **14/1**
4013 **6** *1 ½* **Lord Chamberlain**[9] [2702] 13-10-0 **63**..(b) LiamJones 10 65
(J M Bradley) *off the pce and rdn in rr 1/2-way: effrt u.p over 2f out: kpt on but no imp fnl f* **7/1**[3]
1003 **7** *¾* **Justcallmehandsome**[24] [2262] 4-9-1 **50**..........................(v) DonnaCaldwell 5 50
(D J S Ffrench Davis) *pressed ldr: led over 2f out to 1f out: wknd* **11/1**
2514 **8** *¾* **Dexileos (IRE)**[22] [2319] 7-9-1 **50**..(t) KevinGhunowa 13 49
(David Pinder) *led: rdn and hdd over 2f out: wknd fnl f* **8/1**
0006 **9** *hd* **Duxford**[13] [2573] 5-8-11 **46**..(be) RussellKennemore 9 44
(D K Ivory) *chsd ldrs: hrd rdn 3f out: grad wknd fr over 1f out* **16/1**
0-40 **10** *¾* **Balearic Star (IRE)**[11] [2641] 5-9-2 **54**.................................. JamesMillman(3) 6 50
(B R Millman) *hld up in last pair: rdn over 3f out: clsd on main gp 2f out: plugging on one pce whn nt clr run ins fnl f* **9/1**
0000 **11** *6* **Jazrawy**[63] [1244] 4-9-5 **54**.................................. AshleyHamblett 2 37
(Miss Gay Kelleway) *a wl in rr: struggling 1/2-way: bhd fnl 2f* **8/1**
0-00 **12** *nk* **Perfect Solution (IRE)**[22] [2331] 4-9-9 **58**.................................. RonanKeogh 4 40
(J A R Toller) *a towards rr: rdn and wknd 3f out* **33/1**
00-0 **P** **Shibumi**[25] [2221] 5-8-5 **45**.................................. NBazeley(5) 12 —
(P A Trueman) *bmpd s and rdr lost irons: nt rcvr: p.u 1/2-way* **66/1**

1m 40.87s (0.07) **Going Correction** +0.05s/f (Slow)
WFA 3 from 4yo+ 10lb **13** Ran SP% **120.6**
Speed ratings (Par 101):101,100,99,99,99 97,96,96,95,95 89,88,—
CSF £68.40 CT £393.77 TOTE £25.20: £6.60, £1.30, £4.70; EX 83.60.
Owner Wayne Kearns **Bred** R S Cole **Trained** Upper Lambourn, Berks

FOCUS
A moderate apprentice riders' handicap, run at a strong early gallop, and the form looks fair rated through the runner-up.
Balearic Star(IRE) Official explanation: jockey said gelding never travelled

2979 V-DRINKS.COM TRANSYLVANIAN RED VODKA MAIDEN STKS 7f (P)
7:28 (7:30) (Class 4) 2-Y-O £4,533 (£1,348; £674; £336) Stalls High

Form				RPR
0	1		**Sanbuch**[27] 2178 2-9-3 ... NickyMackay 8 (L M Cumani) *in rr: rdn whn n.m.r 1/2-way: gd prog u.p over 1f out: led ins fnl f: hung rt but won gng away* **12/1**	81+
	2	1 1/4	**Cape Schanck** 2-9-3 ... JohnEgan 6 (Jane Chapple-Hyam) *dwlt: sn in midfield: rdn wl over 2f out: prog wl over 1f out : upsides ent fnl f: outpcd by wnr* **14/1**	78
026	3	1 1/4	**Straight Face (IRE)**[8] 2733 2-9-3 ... PaulDoe 4 (W J Knight) *trckd ldrs: rdn to chal 2f out: led 1f out: hdd and outpcd ins fnl f* **5/1**[1]	75
	4	2 1/2	**Obstructive** 2-9-0 ... NelsonDeSouza[(3)] 12 (Ernst Oertel) *led: rn green whn rdn over 2f out: hdd & wknd 1f out* **25/1**	69
5	5	1/2	**Mastership (IRE)**[13] 2586 2-9-3 ... KerrinMcEvoy 9 (C E Brittain) *dwlt: sn in midfield: rdn over 2f out: kpt on fnl f: n.d* **12/1**	67
426	6	1 3/4	**Callisto Moon**[25] 2218 2-9-3 ... DaneO'Neill 2 (R Curtis) *stmbld s: sn chsd ldrs: rdn over 2f out: no imp and no ch after* **13/2**[3]	63
	7	nk	**Bed Fellow (IRE)** 2-9-3 ... JamieSpencer 14 (A P Jarvis) *trckd ldrs: shkn up on inner over 2f out: one pce over 1f out: wknd fnl f* **6/1**[2]	62+
0	8	1 1/2	**Lordship (IRE)**[12] 2610 2-9-3 ... MatthewHenry 10 (M A Jarvis) *chsd ldr to 2f out: wknd rapidly fnl f* **16/1**	59
	9	1/2	**Golden Desert (IRE)** 2-9-3 ... IanMongan 3 (T G Mills) *dwlt: wl in rr and pushed along: prog 1/2-way into midfield: wknd over 1f out* **11/1**	57
	10	2 1/2	**Heywood** 2-9-3 ... TedDurcan 13 (M R Channon) *v s.i.s: a wl in rr and struggling* **13/2**[3]	51
	11	nk	**Color Man** 2-9-3 ... ShaneKelly 5 (Mrs A J Perrett) *dwlt: sn pushed along: a detached in rr* **10/1**	50
	12	2 1/2	**Grimes Glory** 2-9-3 ... RyanMoore 7 (R Hannon) *dwlt: sn rdn and struggling in last trio* **7/1**	44
0	13	1 1/2	**Rowan Venture**[27] 2178 2-9-3 ... AlanMunro 11 (M H Tompkins) *chsd ldrs for 4f: wknd* **25/1**	40

1m 28.53s (1.73) **Going Correction** +0.05s/f (Slow) 13 Ran SP% **123.2**
Speed ratings (Par 95):92,90,89,86,85 83,83,81,81,78 77,75,73
CSF £174.79 TOTE £15.50: £5.30, £3.20, £1.50; EX 528.30.
Owner Scuderia Rencati Srl **Bred** The Lavington Stud **Trained** Newmarket, Suffolk
■ Stewards' Enquiry : Ian Mongan caution: careless riding

FOCUS
A potentially fair juvenile maiden, run at a decent early pace, and the form should work out. The winner can rate higher.

NOTEBOOK
Sanbuch showed the clear benefit of his recent Yarmouth debut and, after looking held when being ridden at halfway, he sprouted wings passing two out and ultimately won comfortably. The extra furlong was clearly needed, indeed he shaped as though he may already need a mile, and he should improve again mentally for the experience. It will be interesting to see where he is pitched in next. (tchd 11-1)
Cape Schanck, a 12,000gns gelding whose dam won over this trip as a juvenile, ran green through the early parts, but gradually the penny dropped as the race developed, and he was eventually only put in his place by the winner inside the final furlong. This was a pleasing debut effort and he really ought to find a maiden in the coming weeks. (op 12-1)
Straight Face(IRE) showed his true colours on this All-Weather bow and only lacked the pace of the front pair late on. He fared best of those to race prominently, and helps to set the level of this form, as he is starting to look exposed now. Official explanation: jockey said saddle slipped (op 9-2)
Obstructive, related to winners over a mile plus, was well away from his decent draw yet ultimately paid for his early exertions at the head of affairs. He shaped as though the experience would be of real benefit and is entitled to get closer next time.
Mastership(IRE), as on his recent Yarmouth debut, was none too smart from the gates, yet still posted a much-improved effort in defeat. He ultimately shaped as though he needed all of this trip, and looks to be going the right way, but he must learn to break on terms.
Heywood, who cost 72,000gns as a foal and is related to most notably smart 5f-1m winner Ratio, was always playing catch-up after losing ground at the start. He was nibbled at in the betting ring and is best forgiven this effort. (op 9-1 tchd 10-1)

2980 E B F SUNRISE RADIO MAIDEN FILLIES' STKS 6f (P)
7:56 (8:00) (Class 5) 2-Y-O £3,886 (£1,156; £577; £288) Stalls High

Form				RPR
0	1		**Zahour Al Yasmeen**[21] 2354 2-9-0 ... TedDurcan 8 (M R Channon) *disp ld tl led 1/2-way: hrd pressed and drvn over 1f out: styd on wl fnl f* **16/1**	72
	2	1 1/4	**To Party (IRE)** 2-8-11 ... NelsonDeSouza[(3)] 1 (M P Tregoning) *wnt lft s: racd wd towards rr: prog over 2f out: chsd wnr over 1f out: one pce fnl f* **9/2**[2]	68
	3	nk	**Laureldean Express** 2-9-0 ... RichardMullen 4 (E J O'Neill) *in tch: shkn up over 2f out: nt qckn over 1f out: styd on ins fnl f* **6/1**	67
	4	1	**First Princess (IRE)** 2-9-0 ... ChrisCatlin 6 (C Tinkler) *s.s: last and struggling to 2f out: styd on fr over 1f out: nrst fin* **16/1**	64+
	5	nk	**Bronte's Hope** 2-9-0 ... DaneO'Neill 5 (M P Tregoning) *dwlt: in tch in rr: prog over 2f out: disp 2nd over 1f out: fdd fnl f* **7/2**[1]	63
	6	1	**Ronaldsay** 2-9-0 ... RyanMoore 10 (R Hannon) *dwlt: struggling in last pair: effrt over 2f out: nt clr run and swtchd lft over 1f out: kpt on* **11/1**	60+
020	7	1/2	**Peppin's Gold (IRE)**[58] 1347 2-9-0 ... AlanMunro 3 (B R Millman) *w wnr to 1/2-way: chsd to over 1f out: wknd fnl f* **11/2**[3]	59
3	8	3 1/2	**Clewer**[14] 2552 2-8-7 ... KevinGhunowa[(7)] 9 (P A Blockley) *chsd ldrs: rdn wl over 3f out: wknd wl over 1f out* **11/2**[3]	48
04	9	3	**Kat Act Two**[7] 2755 2-9-0 ... ShaneKelly 2 (J A Osborne) *cl up tl wknd wl over 2f out* **8/1**	39

1m 14.8s (1.10) **Going Correction** +0.05s/f (Slow) 9 Ran SP% **116.7**
Speed ratings (Par 90):94,92,91,90,90 88,88,83,79
CSF £87.41 TOTE £18.10: £4.80, £1.70, £3.80; EX 87.20.
Owner Jaber Abdullah **Bred** Gainsborough Stud Management Ltd **Trained** West Ilsley, Berks

FOCUS
A fair fillies' maiden, run at a sound enough pace, and it should produce its share of future winners.

NOTEBOOK
Zahour Al Yasmeen, eighth on her debut at Nottingham three weeks previously, stepped up greatly on that effort and ran out a ready winner on this All-Weather bow. The step up to this longer trip proved more to her liking, she showed a decent attitude under pressure, and it would be a surprise were she not to have more to offer now her confidence will have been boosted. (op 20-1 tchd 25-1)
To Party(IRE), whose dam was a useful five-furlong winner as a juvenile, was unable to get any cover through the race and shaped as though the experience was much needed. She can be expected to be sharper next time. (op 7-1 tchd 4-1)
Laureldean Express ◆, a 40,000euros purchase whose dam was a ten-furlong winner at three and later won over hurdles, shaped with a deal of promise considering this trip would have been plenty sharp enough for her. She has a future and is one to be with when faced with a suitably stiffer test in due course. (op 7-1)
First Princess(IRE) ◆, a 19,000gns half-sister to most notably top-class US/British middle-distance performer Storming Home, was done few favours at the start and was always playing catch-up thereafter. The manner in which she finished her race was most encouraging, however, and connections look to have a very interesting prospect on their hands. She ought to relish the step up to a seventh furlong. (tchd 20-1)
Bronte's Hope, a cheaply-purchased first foal of a dam who was placed over five furlongs at two, was rather surprisingly the shorter-priced of her yard's two runners. She ultimately looked greatly in need of this experience, but is bred to made her mark as a sprinter, and is entitled to improve. (op 4-1)
Clewer, easy to back, dropped out rather tamely when push came to shove and failed to improve on her recent debut over course and distance. She may be more of a nursery type, but this could also have been a hotter event, and it is possible she may not have all that much more to offer. (op 7-2 tchd 6-1)

2981 PREMIER BANQUETING H'CAP 6f (P)
8:24 (8:27) (Class 4) (0-85,81) 3-Y-O+ £5,505 (£1,637; £818; £408) Stalls High

Form				RPR
5544	1		**Ingleton**[14] 2555 4-9-3 **69** ... (p) RyanMoore 10 (G L Moore) *settled midfield: drvn and effrt 2f out: hanging but r.o to ld last 75yds* **9/2**[2]	79
1105	2	3/4	**Blushing Thief (USA)**[7] 2756 3-9-6 **79** ... (b[1]) AlanMunro 5 (W Jarvis) *prom: trckd ldr over 2f out: rdn and hung fire over 1f out: forced ahd 1f out: idled and hdd last 75yds* **14/1**	85
0-32	3	hd	**Signor Peltro**[32] 2032 3-9-8 **81** ... DaneO'Neill 6 (H Candy) *dwlt: towards rr: prog over 2f out: drvn and nt qckn over 1f out: styd on ins fnl f* **11/4**[1]	86
3232	4	nk	**Nautical**[9] 2711 8-9-4 **70** ... GylesParkin 3 (A W Carroll) *led: hrd rdn over 2f out: hdd and one pce 1f out* **7/1**	76
1201	5	2	**Adantino**[26] 2189 7-9-3 **76** ... (b) JamesMillman[(7)] 4 (B R Millman) *trckd ldrs: gng wl enough 2f out: sn rdn and no rspnse* **8/1**	76
0000	6	3/4	**Norcroft**[8] 2732 4-9-4 **70** ... (p) JohnEgan 9 (Mrs C A Dunnett) *trckd ldrs: rdn whn n.m.r and lost pl wl over 1f out: kpt on fnl f* **33/1**	68
0160	7	1	**High Ridge**[11] 2661 7-9-9 **75** ... (p) JamieSpencer 7 (J M Bradley) *wl in rr: lft cheekpiece hanging off and reluctant over 2f out: modest late prog* **14/1**	70
012-	8	nk	**Nistaki (USA)**[305] 4767 5-9-3 **72** ... PatrickMathers[(3)] 2 (D Shaw) *stdd s: wl in rr: rdn and hanging over 2f out: no real prog* **25/1**	66
1552	9	nk	**Financial Times (USA)**[36] 1928 4-9-9 **75** ... FrancisNorton 1 (Stef Liddiard) *chsd ldr to over 2f out: hanging lft and sn wknd* **11/1**	68
2356	10	hd	**Brigadore**[4] 2852 7-9-4 **70** ... KerrinMcEvoy 8 (J G Given) *a in rr: drvn on inner over 2f out: no real prog* **13/2**[3]	62
0302	11	5	**Hits Only Cash**[30] 2074 4-9-6 **72** ... RichardMullen 12 (J Pearce) *dwlt: drvn in last: a bhd* **12/1**	49
0050	12	3 1/2	**Chateau Nicol**[7] 2757 7-10-0 **80** ... (v) TedDurcan 11 (B G Powell) *prom tl wknd rapidly 2f out* **25/1**	47

1m 13.0s (-0.70) **Going Correction** +0.05s/f (Slow)
WFA 3 from 4yo+ 7lb 12 Ran SP% **121.8**
Speed ratings (Par 105):106,105,104,104,101 100,99,98,98,98 91,86
CSF £66.50 CT £212.55 TOTE £6.60: £3.00, £5.00, £1.30; EX 107.40.
Owner Gillespie Brothers **Bred** Thomas Trafford **Trained** Woodingdean, E Sussex

FOCUS
A competitive handicap run at a true pace and the winning time was well up to par. Solid form, the first three showing improvement.
High Ridge Official explanation: jockey said gelding resented the kickback
Nistaki(USA) Official explanation: jockey said gelding hung left
Financial Times(USA) Official explanation: jockey said gelding hung left in home straight

2982 SUNRISE RADIO H'CAP 1m 4f (P)
8:52 (8:55) (Class 4) (0-80,76) 4-Y-O+ £5,505 (£1,637; £818; £408) Stalls Centre

Form				RPR
0511	1		**Prime Powered (IRE)**[33] 1995 5-9-7 **76** ... RyanMoore 7 (G L Moore) *jnd ldr 8f out: disp tl drvn to ld 3f out: 2 l clr 2f out: hld on nr fin: stole r* **4/1**[2]	82
-043	2	nk	**St Savarin (FR)**[93] 763 5-9-7 **76** ... JamieSpencer 5 (R A Fahey) *led at stdy pce: jnd 8f out: hdd 3f out: rdn over 1f out: reeling in wnr nr fin but too much to do* **7/1**	82
6-21	3	1/2	**Dinner Date**[58] 1334 4-8-7 **62** ... ShaneKelly 4 (T Keddy) *hld up in last pair: lost grnd whn pce qcknd 3f out: prog and swtchd rt over 1f out: clsd fnl f: too much to do* **6/1**[3]	67+
-000	4	1/2	**Cleaver**[22] 2322 5-8-8 **63** ... AlanMunro 6 (Lady Herries) *hld up in 5th/6th: outpcd 3f out: drvn on outer and styd on fr over 1f out: nrst fin* **8/1**	67
1200	5	3/4	**Eloquent Knight (USA)**[16] 2508 4-9-6 **75** ... (t) RichardMullen 8 (W R Muir) *trckd ldng pair: rdn whn pce qcknd 3f out: outpcd 2f out: kpt on* **13/2**	78
-663	6	1 1/2	**Papeete (GER)**[11] 2653 5-8-10 **65** ... DarryllHolland 1 (Miss B Sanders) *t.k.h: hld up in 5th/6th: outpcd over 2f out: one pce and no imp after* **15/2**	66
2621	7	shd	**Sabbiosa (IRE)**[30] 2067 4-9-0 **69** ... KerrinMcEvoy 2 (J L Dunlop) *hld up bhd ldng pair after 4f: rdn over 3f out: outpcd over 2f out: one pce after* **11/4**[1]	70
6006	8	4	**African Sahara (USA)**[30] 2088 7-8-3 **65** ... (t) KirstyMilczarek[(7)] 3 (Miss D Mountain) *hld up in last pair: outpcd and detached over 2f out but gng wl enough: no ch after* **16/1**	59

2m 38.32s (1.42) **Going Correction** +0.05s/f (Slow) 8 Ran SP% **115.5**
Speed ratings (Par 105):97,96,96,96,95 94,94,91
CSF £32.27 CT £166.31 TOTE £5.20: £1.30, £2.40, £2.60; EX 35.40.
Owner Prime Power GB Ltd **Bred** Caribbean Quest Partnership **Trained** Woodingdean, E Sussex

FOCUS
A messy contest, run at an early dawdle, and as a result a moderate winning time for the grade. The place to be was at the front as the front pair held those positions throughout, but because of the way the race was run the form looks suspect.
African Sahara(USA) Official explanation: jockey said horse was struck into

2983 MARTIN COLLINS ENTERPRISES H'CAP (LONDON MILE QUALIFIER) 1m (P)

9:20 (9:24) (Class 4) (0-85,84) 3-Y-0+ **£5,505** (£1,637; £818; £408) **Stalls** High

Form				RPR
3000	**1**		**Hits Only Heaven (IRE)**[14] 2555 4-9-5 **78**........(e) SilvestreDeSousa(3) 4 (D Nicholls) *mde virtually all: bowled along after 2f: urged along over 1f out: kpt on wl fnl f* **14/1**	92
-564	**2**	*1 1/4*	**Glencalvie (IRE)**[19] 2405 5-9-6 **76**............................(v) KerrinMcEvoy 10 (J Akehurst) *prom: chsd wnr over 4f out: rdn 2f out: clr of rest fnl f but a hld* **8/1**	87
4210	**3**	*3*	**Davenport (IRE)**[12] 2621 4-9-5 **82**.............................. JamesMillman(7) 5 (B R Millman) *dwlt: last trio tl prog on inner over 2f out: styd on to take 3rd nr fin: no ch* **10/1**	86
05-3	**4**	*nk*	**Rowan Lodge (IRE)**[60] 1302 4-9-6 **76**.....................(b1) NickyMackay 11 (M H Tompkins) *prom: chsd ldng pair over 2f out: no imp over 1f out: fdd and lost 3rd nr fin* **16/1**	79
3052	**5**	*3*	**Outer Hebrides**[7] 2757 5-9-12 **82**...............................(vt) FrancisNorton 2 (Stef Liddiard) *hld up in rr: rdn wl over 2f out: kpt on one pce and n.d* **8/1**	79
2005	**6**	*shd*	**Pic Up Sticks**[10] 2674 7-10-0 **84**....................................... RyanMoore 12 (B G Powell) *hld up in last trio: prog 2f out: no ch w ldrs fnl f* **16/1**	80
-503	**7**	*1 1/4*	**Puya**[14] 2555 4-9-10 **80**.. DaneO'Neill 6 (H Candy) *t.k.h: prom: drvn over 2f out: wknd over 1f out* **13/2**[2]	73
00-0	**8**	*1 1/4*	**Overlord Way (GR)**[14] 2555 4-9-5 **75**................................ IanMongan 3 (P R Chamings) *hld up in last trio: hrd rdn 3f out: sn outpcd and btn* **20/1**	66
24-3	**9**	*3/4*	**Killena Boy (IRE)**[7] 2757 4-9-11 **81**.................................... AlanMunro 7 (W Jarvis) *racd on outer: chsd ldrs: u.p and hanging over 2f out: sn btn* **3/1**[1]	70
0404	**10**	*4*	**Red Contact (USA)**[7] 2752 5-9-4 **74**................................(p) JohnEgan 8 (J R Best) *settled midfield: hrd rdn and no rspnse 3f out: wknd 2f out* **14/1**	54
-006	**11**	*1/2*	**Call Me Max**[16] 2508 4-9-7 **77**.......................................(v) JamieSpencer 9 (E A L Dunlop) *nvr beyond midfield: wknd 2f out* **7/1**[3]	55
1100	**12**	*1 1/4*	**Raza Cab (IRE)**[16] 2510 4-9-6 **76**.................................... DarryllHolland 13 (Karen George) *chsd ldrs: rdn wl over 2f out: wknd rapidly wl over 1f out* **10/1**	52
000-	**13**	*8*	**Jay Gee's Choice**[337] 3829 6-9-11 **81**................................ TedDurcan 1 (B G Powell) *a in rr: lost tch 3f out: wl bhd after* **40/1**	38
	14	*92*	**Bianca Sforza**[293] 4-9-9 **82**.....................................(t) PatrickMathers(3) 14 (D Shaw) *plld hrd: chsd wnr to over 4f out: wknd v rapidly: t.o over 2f out: virtually p.u over 1f out* **50/1**	—

1m 38.76s (-2.04) **Going Correction** +0.05s/f (Slow) **14** Ran SP% **125.5**
Speed ratings (Par 105):112,110,107,107,104 104,103,101,101,97 96,95,87,—
CSF £125.13 CT £1235.06 TOTE £15.70: £4.10, £2.50, £3.90; EX 155.70 Place 6 £399.71, Place 5 £205.17.
Owner Lilly Hall Racing **Bred** Waterside Stud **Trained** Sessay, N Yorks

FOCUS
A smart winning time for a race like this, over two seconds quicker than the opening apprentice handicap over the same trip. Despite a sizzling gallop, the front pair were always at the sharp end and the winner made all. The form looks rock solid.
Killena Boy(IRE) Official explanation: jockey said gelding felt wrong behind
Bianca Sforza Official explanation: jockey said filly had a bad breathing problem
T/Plt: £613.60 to a £1 stake. Pool: £45,557.90 - 54.20 winning units T/Qpdt: £79.70 to a £1 stake. Pool: £3,653.30 - 33.90 winning units JN

2672 SALISBURY (R-H)

Wednesday, June 28

OFFICIAL GOING: Good
Wind: Virtually nil

2984 EUROPEAN BREEDERS FUND MAIDEN FILLIES' STKS 5f

2:30 (2:32) (Class 4) 2-Y-0 **£4,857** (£1,445; £722; £360) **Stalls** High

Form				RPR
	1		**Enticing (IRE)** 2-9-0 .... MichaelHills 9 (W J Haggas) *str: scope: stdd s: hld up in tch: smooth hdwy fr 2f out: swtchd rt 1f out: qcknd to ld sn after: easily* **8/1**	84+
6	**2**	*1 1/2*	**Siren's Gift**[23] 2300 2-9-0 .... FergusSweeney 7 (A M Balding) *w'like: sn led: rdn 2f out: hdd ins fnl f: sn outpcd* **6/1**[3]	75
40	**3**	*2*	**Ripping**[7] 2743 2-9-0 .... RyanMoore 3 (R Hannon) *lw: chsd ldr: rdn and effrt over 2f out: nvr gng pce to chal: wknd last half f* **9/4**[1]	68
0	**4**	*nk*	**Indian Song (IRE)**[27] 2172 2-9-0 .... StephenCarson 6 (R F Johnson Houghton) *chsd ldrs: rdn 2f out: one pce whn sltly hmpd on rail 1f out* **20/1**	67
	5	*1 1/4*	**Ms Victoria (IRE)** 2-9-0 .... RichardHughes 2 (B J Meehan) *unf: scope: s.i.s: sn rcvrd to chse ldrs: rdn 1/2-way: wknd fnl f* **5/1**[2]	62+
0	**6**	*6*	**Chingford (IRE)**[18] 2456 2-9-0 .... FrankieMcDonald 1 (D W P Arbuthnot) *s.i.s: rdn 1/2-way: a outpcd* **66/1**	41
	7	*3*	**Countyourblessings** 2-9-0 .... NickyMackay 4 (J G Portman) *w'like: leggy: chsd ldrs 3f* **33/1**	30
	8	*2*	**The Grey Bam Bam** 2-9-0 .... JimCrowley 8 (R J Hodges) *w'like: b.bkwd: s.i.s: sn outpcd* **66/1**	23

61.07 secs (-0.52) **Going Correction** -0.075s/f (Good) **8** Ran SP% **83.5**
Speed ratings (Par 92):101,98,95,94,92 83,78,75
CSF £26.50 TOTE £7.30: £2.10, £1.80, £1.10; EX 22.00.
Owner Lael Stable **Bred** Lael Stables **Trained** Newmarket, Suffolk
■ Turkus Quercus was withdrawn (9/4JF, refused to enter stalls). R4 applies, deduct 30p in the £.
■ Stewards' Enquiry : Michael Hills caution: careless riding

FOCUS
Not a bad little sprint maiden for fillies, run in a very decent time, and quite a taking performance from Enticing. The form looks sound.

NOTEBOOK
Enticing(IRE), the second foal of the stable's smart sprinting juvenile Superstar Leo, is bred to be pretty fast and made the ideal introduction. Settled just off the pace in the early stages, she basically seemed to be taking the first half of the race to learn what it was all about, but she responded well in the latter stages to hands-and-heels riding to ultimately win going away. She ought to improve plenty for this experience and deserves to step up in class. Her dam was worth following during her juvenile career, and on this evidence one will not go far wrong keeping this one on side. (op 15-2 tchd 13-2)
Siren's Gift, who was withdrawn after playing up in the preliminaries on her intended debut, made it on to the course three days later and showed ability when sixth at Windsor. This was another sound effort behind the potentially useful winner and she seems to be going the right way now. (op 5-1 tchd 13-2)
Ripping finished in front of today's runner-up when fourth on her debut at Windsor, but had since finished down the field in the Queen Mary at Royal Ascot. Turned out quickly, this was a respectable effort and a maiden should come her way. (op 5-2 tchd 11-4)
Indian Song(IRE), who was unlucky not to have finished a little closer on her debut over this trip at Sandown, showed the benefit of that run and emerges with credit. (tchd 22-1)
Ms Victoria(IRE), the second foal of a mare placed in sprints in Italy, gave the impression she can do better with the benefit of this run. (op 6-1 tchd 9-2)

2985 SMITH & WILLIAMSON MAIDEN FILLIES' STKS 6f 212y

3:00 (3:05) (Class 4) 3-Y-0 **£5,505** (£1,637; £818; £408) **Stalls** Centre

Form				RPR
0-23	**1**		**Usk Poppy**[19] 2406 3-9-0 77... JohnEgan 10 (D R C Elsworth) *chsd ldrs: drvn to ld 2f out: styd on strly fnl f* **5/2**[1]	75+
03	**2**	*3/4*	**Lilac Star**[47] 1649 3-8-9 .... EmmettStack(5) 6 (Pat Eddery) *lw: chsd ldrs: rdn over 2f out: chsd wnr ins last: kpt on but no imp cl home* **8/1**	73
0-4	**3**	*2*	**Vino**[58] 1351 3-9-0 .... MichaelHills 9 (B W Hills) *chsd ldr 4f out: slt led over 2f out: sn hdd: outpcd ins last* **16/1**	68
	4	*nk*	**Tilbury** 3-9-0 .... TedDurcan 2 (H R A Cecil) *w'like: lw: mid-div:hdwy 3f out:pushed along 2f out:rdn and styng on whn nt clr run and swtchd lft jst ins last:kpt on agai* **8/1**	70+
63	**5**	*1 3/4*	**Scylla Cadeaux (IRE)**[30] 2063 3-9-0 .... RyanMoore 12 (Sir Michael Stoute) *sn ld: narrowly hdd over 2f out: styd pressing ldrs tl wknd fnl f* **4/1**[2]	63
0	**6**	*3 1/2*	**Miswadah (IRE)**[68] 1119 3-9-0 .... RHills 5 (E A L Dunlop) *chsd ldrs: pushed along 3f out: outpcd fnl 2f* **10/1**	53
32-4	**7**	*nk*	**Desert Flair**[13] 2575 3-9-0 74.. RichardHughes 7 (R Hannon) *chsd ldrs: rdn 3f out: wknd over 1f out* **7/1**[3]	53
0	**8**	*1/2*	**Useful**[10] 2673 3-8-7 .... WilliamCarson(7) 1 (A W Carroll) *w'like: bhd: pushed along 3f out: r.o wl fnl f but nvr gng pce to be competitive* **100/1**	51+
	9	*2 1/2*	**Warden Rose** 3-9-0 .... LPKeniry 15 (D R C Elsworth) *leggy: b.hind: slowly away: bhd: kpt on fr over 1f out: nvr in contention* **20/1**	45
	10	*shd*	**Cosmic Girl** 3-9-0 .... DaneO'Neill 3 (H Candy) *s.i.s: bhd: sme hdwy fnl 2f* **33/1**	45
0	**11**	*1 1/4*	**Parthenope**[18] 2458 3-9-0 .... RichardThomas 11 (J A Geake) *chsd ldrs: rdn over 3f out: wknd 2f out* **100/1**	41
	12	*1 1/4*	**Sprinkle** 3-9-0 .... SebSanders 14 (R M Beckett) *w'like: b.bkwd: s.i.s: bhd: pushed along 1/2-way: nvr in contention* **20/1**	38
0-0	**13**	*nk*	**It's Twilight Time**[18] 2458 3-9-0 .... PatDobbs 4 (R Hannon) *chsd ldrs over 4f* **66/1**	37
	14	*shd*	**Norakit** 3-8-11 .... EdwardCreighton(3) 13 (M R Channon) *w'like: b.bkwd: slowly away: a in rr* **33/1**	37
0	**15**	*15*	**Format**[10] 2673 3-9-0 .... JimmyQuinn 8 (A W Carroll) *unf: slowly away: a bhd* **100/1**	—
	16	*dist*	**Petite Boulangere (IRE)** 3-9-0 .... ShaneKelly 16 (S Kirk) *unf: scope: w ldr 2f: sn wknd: eased whn lost tch 1/2-way: t.o* **40/1**	—

1m 27.88s (-1.18) **Going Correction** -0.075s/f (Good) **16** Ran SP% **120.6**
Speed ratings (Par 98):103,102,99,99,97 93,93,92,89,89 88,86,86,86,69 —
CSF £20.61 TOTE £3.30: £1.40, £3.10, £3.60; EX 28.00.
Owner Usk Valley Stud **Bred** Usk Valley Stud **Trained** Newmarket, Suffolk

FOCUS
This looked a reasonable enough fillies' maiden for the time of year, the winner showing slight improvement.
Useful Official explanation: jockey said, regarding the running and riding, his orders had been to drop in behind, as he was drawn 1, and let filly run through horses and finish as close as possible; vet said filly was having a good blow post race
Petite Boulangere(IRE) Official explanation: jockey said filly ran too freely to post

2986 GOADSBY BIBURY CUP (H'CAP) 1m 4f

3:30 (3:31) (Class 3) (0-95,92) 3-Y-0

£11,217 (£3,358; £1,679; £840; £419; £210) **Stalls** High

Form				RPR
0-10	**1**		**Oh Glory Be (USA)**[19] 2404 3-8-7 **78**.......................... RichardHughes 9 (R Hannon) *stdd s: hld up in rr: hdwy on rails 3f out: rdn to ld wl over 1f out: sn in command: readily* **20/1**	89+
2231	**2**	*2 1/2*	**Dream Champion**[19] 2398 3-8-3 **74**............................... JohnEgan 12 (M R Channon) *lw: led: rdn 3f out: hdd wl over 1f out: kpt on wl to hold 2nd but no ch w wnr fnl f* **7/1**[3]	81
0-24	**3**	*nk*	**John Terry (IRE)**[11] 2654 3-9-2 **87**.................................... RyanMoore 7 (Mrs A J Perrett) *mid-div: rdn along 3f out: styd on fr over 1f out: kpt on to press for 2nd ins last: nvr gng pce to trble wnr* **5/1**[2]	94
24-1	**4**	*hd*	**Kyoto Summit**[67] 1139 3-9-5 **90**...................................... NickyMackay 8 (L M Cumani) *chsd ldrs: rdn 3f out: styd on same pce fr over 1f out* **5/1**[2]	97
551-	**5**	*1 1/4*	**Sin City**[286] 5252 3-8-2 **73**... FrancisNorton 10 (R A Fahey) *bhd: stl plenty to do over 2f out: drvn and hdwy fr 2f out: hung lft over 1f out: r.o cl home but nvr in contention* **11/4**[1]	78+
3-13	**6**	*1 1/4*	**Madroos**[14] 2556 3-8-10 **81**... RHills 5 (J L Dunlop) *chsd ldr over 7f out: rdn along 3f out: wknd over 1f out* **10/1**	84
1	**7**	*1 3/4*	**Simondiun**[40] 1822 3-9-7 **92**.. JimCrowley 2 (Mrs A J Perrett) *bhd: rdn and sme hdwy fr 3f out: nvr nr ldrs and hung lft u.p over 1f out* **25/1**	92
1135	**8**	*1*	**Free To Air**[14] 2556 3-8-9 **80**.. LDettori 6 (A M Balding) *stedaied rr after 1f: rdn and sme hdwy fr 3f out: nvr gng pce to rch ldrs* **14/1**	78
-241	**9**	*10*	**Le Colombier (IRE)**[18] 2465 3-8-12 **83**............................. MichaelHills 3 (J W Hills) *in tch: drvn to chse ldrs 4f out: wknd fr 3f out* **16/1**	65
5230	**10**	*3*	**Beckett Hall (IRE)**[5] 2805 3-8-9 **80**.................................... SebSanders 1 (R Hannon) *rdn 5f out: a in rr* **40/1**	57
051	**11**	*11*	**Alqaab (USA)**[46] 1670 3-9-2 **87**.. AlanMunro 11 (M P Tregoning) *lw: chsd ldrs: rdn over 4f out: wknd over 3f out* **7/1**[3]	47

2m 35.72s (-0.64) **Going Correction** +0.025s/f (Good) **11** Ran SP% **117.7**
Speed ratings (Par 103):103,101,101,101,100 99,98,97,90,88 81
CSF £151.32 CT £822.50 TOTE £25.30: £5.00, £2.00, £2.80; EX 188.20.
Owner I A N Wight **Bred** W S Farish **Trained** East Everleigh, Wilts

FOCUS
This looked a strong renewal of the Bibury Cup on paper, but the bare form did not look up to that assessement, with only a steady pace and the runner-up looking quite exposed. The winner is progressive, however.

The Form Book, Raceform Ltd, Compton, RG20 6NL

NOTEBOOK

Oh Glory Be(USA) ◆, the only filly in the field, showed improved form for the step up to a mile and a half and ran out a most emphatic winner. Although only seventh over ten furlongs at Goodwood on her previous start, she had finished to good effect and her trainer was sure she would do better over this longer trip. Hannon will wait and see what the Handicapper does with her, but thinks she is not far off Listed class. (op 16-1)

Dream Champion enjoyed the run of the race out in front and found only the impressive winner too good. He is a consistent sort and should continue to go well. (op 10-1)

John Terry(IRE), upped to a mile and a half for the first time, seemed to get this longer trip quite well without ever quite looking likely to win. (tchd 6-1)

Kyoto Summit, not seen since hacking up in a ten-furlong maiden at Nottingham over two months previously, ran well in this better contest and gave the impression there could be a bit more to come yet. (op 11-2)

Sin City ◆, sold out of Luca Cumani's yard for 80,000gns after winning a mile nursery at Yarmouth off a mark of 66, was returning from a 286-day break. Held up out the back, he got no sort of run when the race got serious and stayed on far too late to pose a threat. Things did not go his way this time, but it would be unwise to give up on him just yet. (tchd 3-1)

Madroos seemed well enough placed but did not pick up when it mattered. Official explanation: jockey said colt had been struck into (op 14-1)

Simondiun, forced to carry top weight following a six-length debut success over ten furlongs at Newbury, hung under pressure and never really featured. (op 20-1)

Alqaab(USA), who outstayed the highly-rated Areyoutalkingtome when off the mark over ten furlongs at Lingfield on his previous start, represented the trainer who won this race last year with Magic Instinct, but he was well beaten.

2987 GOADSBY FILLIES' H'CAP — 6f

4:00 (4:03) (Class 5) (0-70,71) 3-Y-O — **£3,724** (£1,108; £553; £276) Stalls High

Form — RPR

4160 **1** **Just Down The Road (IRE)**[14] 2543 3-8-11 **60**......... AdrianMcCarthy 6 — 66
(R A Harris) *mde all: edgd lft fr ins fnl 2f: r.o wl u.p fnl f* **14/1**

-625 **2** 1 ¼ **Mannello**[12] 2602 3-8-8 **57**......... FrancisFerris 10 — 59
(B Palling) *chsd ldrs: rdn 1/2-way: styd on wl to chse wnr fnl f but a hld* **11/1**[3]

-062 **3** shd **Some Diva**[9] 2704 3-8-9 **58**......... SebSanders 15 — 60+
(W R Swinburn) *s.i.s: sn rcvrd: drvn and effrt to press ldrs over 2f out: kpt on same pce fnl f* **5/1**[1]

221 **4** nk **Piccostar**[8] 2730 3-9-8 **71** 6ex......... JamieSpencer 13 — 72
(A B Haynes) *in tch: rdn and hdwy over 1f out: kpt on ins last but nvr gng pce to chal* **10/1**[2]

5520 **5** nk **Arculinge**[22] 2316 3-8-7 **56**......... NickyMackay 3 — 56
(M Blanshard) *b.hind: bhd: n.m.r ins fnl 2f: swtchd lft over 1f out: r.o strly ins last: gng on cl home* **14/1**

-006 **6** ½ **Matterofact (IRE)**[16] 2509 3-9-0 **68**......... TravisBlock(5) 16 — 67
(Mrs P N Dutfield) *chsd ldr: styng on whn crossed ins fnl 2f: kpt on but nvr gng pce to chal after* **12/1**

5553 **7** shd **Tabulate**[14] 2554 3-8-6 **55**......... ChrisCatlin 8 — 53
(P L Gilligan) *bhd: rdn and hday on outside over 1f out: kpt on wl fnl f: nt raech ldrs* **12/1**

-240 **8** nk **Red Diadem**[16] 2511 3-9-2 **65**......... TonyCulhane 12 — 62+
(W J Haggas) *keen hold: stdd mid-div: drvn and kpt on fr over 1f out: nvr gng pce to trble ldrs* **12/1**

3250 **9** ½ **Sensuous**[16] 2511 3-9-2 **65**......... RichardHughes 9 — 61
(R Hannon) *lw: stdd s: rr: hday 2f out: kpt on fnl f but nvr gng pce to rch ldrs* **16/1**

1234 **10** nk **Red Vixen (IRE)**[5] 2826 3-8-1 **57**......... KirstyMilczarek(7) 4 — 52
(C N Allen) *bhd: hdwy 2f out: drvn and kpt on wl on outside fr over 1f out but nvr in contention* **14/1**

0-30 **11** ¾ **Diamond World**[35] 1937 3-8-9 **58**......... ShaneKelly 7 — 51
(C A Horgan) *chsd ldrs: rdn 3f out: wknd fnl f* **50/1**

1532 **12** 1 ¼ **La Fanciulla**[10] 2676 3-9-0 **63**......... RyanMoore 5 — 52
(R Hannon) *lw: bhd: n.m.r ins fnl 2f and 1f out: nt rcvr and nvr in contention* **5/1**[1]

-605 **13** ½ **Free Silver (IRE)**[9] 2704 3-8-8 **57**......... JohnEgan 2 — 45
(Miss K B Boutflower) *outpcd most of way* **20/1**

06-0 **14** nk **Bee Seventeen (USA)**[13] 2583 3-9-4 **67**......... LDettori 1 — 54
(P F I Cole) *stdd s: swtchd to far side rail: rdn 3f out: nvr gng pce to be competitive* **20/1**

-513 **15** shd **Perfect Treasure (IRE)**[24] 2263 3-9-7 **70**......... AlanMunro 11 — 56
(J A R Toller) *nvr bttr than mid-div* **10/1**[2]

1m 14.94s (-0.04) **Going Correction** -0.075s/f (Good) — **15** Ran SP% **120.3**

Speed ratings (Par 96):97,95,95,94,94 93,93,93,92,92 91,89,88,88,88

CSF £155.24 CT £906.47 TOTE £23.50: £6.10, £3.50, £2.00; EX 422.00.

Owner Mrs D J Hughes **Bred** Stall Nerce **Trained** Earlswood, Monmouths

FOCUS

Just a modest fillies' handicap, but very competitive and the form looks reasonable for the grade. The winner was back to her juvenile best with the second and third running to recent form.

Tabulate Official explanation: vet said filly was in season

2988 NOEL CANNON MEMORIAL TROPHY H'CAP — 1m

4:30 (4:34) (Class 2) (0-100,97) 3-Y-0+

£13,398 (£4,011; £2,005; £1,004; £500; £251) Stalls High

Form — RPR

6645 **1** **Sew'N'So Character (IRE)**[18] 2440 5-8-12 **81**......... TedDurcan 15 — 92
(M Blanshard) *bhd: hdwy 2f out: str run on rails fr over 1f out to ld last half f: kpt on wl* **14/1**

-024 **2** ¾ **Kelucia (IRE)**[18] 2440 5-9-2 **85**......... SebSanders 2 — 94
(R M Beckett) *bhd: hday and n.m.r ins fnl 2f: swtchd to rail: hrd drvn and r.o fnl f: kpt on but nt rch wnr* **8/1**

5003 **3** hd **Audience**[30] 2086 6-9-3 **86**.........(p) PaulDoe 14 — 95
(J Akehurst) *swtg: stdd s: bhd: swtchd to outside and hdwy fr 2f out: r.o u.p fnl f: kpt on cl home* **13/2**[3]

0002 **4** 1 **Calcutta**[12] 2614 10-9-7 **90**......... MichaelHills 4 — 96
(B W Hills) *bhd: rdn on outside fr 3f out: r.o u.p fr over 1f out: no ex nr fin* **16/1**

3322 **5** 1 ¼ **Skidrow**[6] 2787 4-9-7 **90**......... JamieSpencer 11 — 93
(M L W Bell) *chsd ldr: led jst ins fnl 2f: sn hrd drvn: hdd & wknd last half f* **5/1**[1]

-000 **6** hd **Sekula Pata (NZ)**[103] 7-8-8 **80**.........(b) SaleemGolam(3) 1 — 83
(Christian Wroe, UAE) *led tl hdd jst ins fnl 2f: wknd fnl f* **100/1**

5-05 **7** 1 **Norton (IRE)**[30] 2086 9-9-5 **88**......... IanMongan 5 — 89
(T G Mills) *bhd: hdwy fr 2f out: kpt on ins last but nvr gng pce to rch ldrs* **25/1**

2420 **8** nk **Red Spell (IRE)**[7] 2742 5-9-10 **93**.........(b) RichardHughes 10 — 93
(R Hannon) *lw: chsd ldrs: rdn and one pce fnl 2f* **11/2**[2]

3460 **9** ½ **Silver Blue (IRE)**[6] 2775 3-9-2 **95**......... RyanMoore 16 — 92
(R Hannon) *bhd: sme hdwy on ins 2f out but nvr gng pce to rch ldrs* **16/1**

2-01 **10** ¾ **Red Cape (FR)**[5] 2824 3-8-13 **92** 6ex......... LDettori 13 — 87
(N A Callaghan) *chsd ldrs: rdn over 2f out: wknd fnl f* **13/2**[3]

-105 **11** nk **South Cape**[42] 1776 3-9-1 **94**......... TonyCulhane 12 — 88
(M R Channon) *bhd: kpt on fr over 1f out: nvr in contention* **33/1**

103- **12** 1 **Salinja (USA)**[270] 5608 4-9-11 **94**......... AlanMunro 8 — 88
(Mrs A J Perrett) *chsd ldrs: rdn over 2f out: wknd fnl f* **20/1**

5120 **13** ¾ **Motaraqeb**[6] 2774 3-8-8 **87**.........(t) RHills 7 — 77
(Sir Michael Stoute) *lw: chsd ldrs: rdn 3f out: wknd over 1f out* **10/1**

535- **14** shd **Cape Greko**[337] 3824 4-10-0 **97**......... DaneO'Neill 9 — 89
(A M Balding) *s.i.s: sn in tch: wknd over 2f out* **66/1**

-530 **15** nk **Genari**[25] 2224 3-8-9 **88**......... SteveDrowne 3 — 77
(P F I Cole) *chsd ldrs: rdn 3f out: wknd fr 2f out* **25/1**

31-0 **16** 1 ½ **Judraan**[11] 2650 3-8-6 **85**.........(t) RichardMullen 6 — 71
(M A Jarvis) *chsd ldrs 5f* **28/1**

1m 42.43s (-0.66) **Going Correction** -0.075s/f (Good)

WFA 3 from 4yo+ 10lb — **16** Ran SP% **118.7**

Speed ratings (Par 109):100,99,99,98,96 96,95,95,94,94 93,92,92,91,91 90

CSF £110.56 CT £841.79 TOTE £16.00: £3.20, £2.70, £2.40, £2.60; EX 133.60 Trifecta £526.40 Part won. Pool: £741.50 - 0.30 winning tickets..

Owner Aykroyd And Sons Ltd **Bred** R C Snaith **Trained** Upper Lambourn, Berks

FOCUS

The richest race on the card and a reasonable renewal of this valuable handicap, featuring two previous winners of the race in last year's shock winner Audience and the 2002 scorer Calcutta. The principals came from off the pace, suggesting they went a sound gallop, but the winning time was very moderate. The form should prove sound.

NOTEBOOK

Sew'N'So Character(IRE) was winless since May of last year and had had a few chances this term, but his trainer was of the opinion that basically nothing had gone his way so far this season. Able to race off a mark 6lb lower than when gaining that last success, he responded gamely to pressure to win in determined fashion. Now he has got his head back in front, this could have boosted his confidence, and he should not look on too bad a mark when the Handicapper has his say.

Kelucia(IRE) had finished one place in front of today's winner at Haydock on her previous start, but could not confirm placings after having to be switched with her challenge. She has been in quite good form since joining her current connections and can surely find a race at some stage this season, possibly in fillies-only company.

Audience ◆, 7lb lower than when winning this race last year, had shaped as though coming to hand when third at Sandown on his previous start and again ran well. He looks ready to exploit his current mark. (tchd 7-1)

Calcutta, just 2lb lower than when winning this race in 2002, had returned to form when second at Nottingham on his previous start, and again ran well in what was a better contest. (tchd 18-1)

Skidrow, who has been in cracking form in defeat in recent starts, including when second at Epsom and Ripon on his two most recent runs, seemed to have his chance. He looks high enough in the weights and may benefit from having a few pounds taken off his back by an apprentice.

Sekula Pata(NZ), a winner in South Africa but not in much form when last seen in Dubai, offered promise at a huge price off the back of a 103-day break.

Norton(IRE) did not enjoy the best of runs and could do better.

Red Spell(IRE), tenth of 30 in the Hunt Cup at Royal Ascot just a week previously (and third of 12 on the unfavoured far side of the track), may have been feeling the effects of that run. (op 6-1)

Red Cape(FR), 2lb 'wrong' under the penalty he picked up for winning over seven furlongs at Newmarket on his previous start, was not at his best this time. (op 5-1)

Genari Official explanation: vet said colt finished lame behind

2989 KINGS SALISBURY H'CAP — 1m 1f 198y

5:00 (5:03) (Class 3) (0-95,93) 4-Y-0+ — **£8,096** (£2,408; £1,203; £601) Stalls High

Form — RPR

2-65 **1** **Great Plains**[21] 2341 4-9-3 **89**......... RichardHughes 4 — 103
(Mrs A J Perrett) *lw: hld up mid-div: rdn 3f out: led jst ins fnl 2f: drvn out* **9/2**[1]

-001 **2** 1 **Fairmile**[21] 2341 4-9-2 **91**......... AdamKirby(3) 5 — 104
(W R Swinburn) *lw: bhd: swtchd to outside 3f out: styd on u.p to chse wnr over 1f out: kpt on but a hld* **11/2**[2]

0203 **3** 5 **Star Magnitude (USA)**[16] 2508 5-8-5 **77**......... JimmyQuinn 7 — 80
(S Dow) *lw: chsd ldrs: drvn along over 4f out: styng on whn hmpd by wkng horse 1f out and sn outpcd* **14/1**

1/-0 **4** nk **Russian Consort (IRE)**[12] 2614 4-8-11 **83**......... DaneO'Neill 10 — 85
(A King) *slowly away: bhd: stl plenty to do over 2f out: r.o fnl f: gng on cl home but nvr gng pce to be a danger* **50/1**

2000 **5** 1 ½ **Impeller (IRE)**[7] 2742 7-9-7 **93**......... SteveDrowne 8 — 93
(W R Muir) *bhd: pushed along 3f out: no much room and styd on fr 2f out but nvr in contention* **7/1**

-001 **6** 2 **The Composer**[33] 1987 4-8-2 **74** oh2......... FrancisNorton 12 — 70
(M Blanshard) *t.k.h in rr: hdwy and n.m.r 3f out: sn pushed along: n.d* **9/1**

2325 **7** 1 ¾ **Augustine**[10] 2672 5-8-5 **77**......... ChrisCatlin 6 — 69
(P W Hiatt) *sn in tch: rdn 4f out: wknd over 2f out* **12/1**

3-00 **8** 2 **Foodbroker Founder**[10] 2229 6-8-4 **76**......... JohnEgan 9 — 65
(D R C Elsworth) *in tch: pushed along 3f out: wkng whn n.m.r 2f out* **6/1**[3]

5-05 **9** 1 ¼ **Best Prospect (IRE)**[12] 2621 4-8-9 **81**......... TonyCulhane 1 — 67+
(M Dods) *chsd ldrs: drvn and slt ld 2f out: sn hdd: wknd and eased fnl f* **8/1**

030- **10** 1 **Cavallini (USA)**[294] 5048 4-8-12 **84**......... RyanMoore 3 — 68
(G L Moore) *sn led: hdd 4f out: wknd 2f out* **20/1**

1-10 **11** 1 ½ **Fortunate Isle (USA)**[60] 1301 4-9-5 **91**......... RHills 11 — 73
(B W Hills) *chsd ldrs tl wknd over 2f out* **13/2**

0-20 **12** 2 **Kova Hall (IRE)**[12] 2621 4-8-13 **85**......... TedDurcan 2 — 63+
(B G Powell) *chsd ldr: led 4f out: hdd & wknd qckly 2f out* **33/1**

2m 7.35s (-1.11) **Going Correction** +0.025s/f (Good) — **12** Ran SP% **118.8**

Speed ratings (Par 107):105,104,100,99,98 97,95,94,93,92 91,89

CSF £28.09 CT £325.47 TOTE £5.40: £1.80, £2.70, £4.50; EX 21.80.

Owner K Abdulla **Bred** Juddmonte Farms Ltd **Trained** Pulborough, W Sussex

■ Stewards' Enquiry : Adam Kirby one-day ban: careless riding (Jul 9)

FOCUS

Quite a good handicap, but the early pace seemed just steady. The front two pulled well clear and are both progressive.

NOTEBOOK

Great Plains ◆ was 6lb better off with Fairmile for around three lengths on his latest running at Kempton and that proved decisive. There was plenty to like about the way he ran on when asked and there may be even more to come - connections think he should be able to get a mile and a half.

Fairmile, 5lb higher than when winning over this trip on Kempton's Polytrack on his previous start, could not confirm form with the winner on 6lb worse terms. Still, he pulled well clear of the remainder and this was another fine effort. (op 5-1)

Star Magnitude(USA) met with some trouble, but he still would have had little chance with the front two and was basically third best. This was a creditable effort. (tchd 16-1)

Russian Consort(IRE) looked a really useful type as a juvenile but missed all of last year and offered little on his return. However, this was a lot better and he clearly retains plenty of ability. He was very slowly away, but made up the lost ground easily enough thanks to the steady early pace, and kept on quite well in the latter stages.
Impeller(IRE) ran a respectable enough race off top weight. (op 15-2 tchd 8-1)
The Composer, from 2lb out of the handicap, was 9lb higher than when winning on heavy ground at Haydock on his previous start, and this was tougher. (op 14-1 tchd 16-1)
Foodbroker Founder, a winner over hurdles at Stratford on his previous start, was not at his best returned to the Flat.
Best Prospect(IRE) Official explanation: jockey said gelding lost its action
Fortunate Isle(USA) offered little on his return from a two-month break. (op 7-1 tchd 6-1)

2990 CONGRATULATIONS TO SALISBURY CITY FC "CHAMPIONS" H'CAP — 1m 1f 198y

5:30 (5:31) (Class 5) (0-75,75) 3-Y-O — **£3,562** (£1,059; £529; £264) **Stalls** High

Form	Pos	Dist	Horse	RPR
2255	**1**		**Katchit (IRE)**[12] [2608] 3-9-7 **75** .... TonyCulhane 8 (M R Channon) *bhd: hdwy 3f out: drvn to ld appr fnl f: kpt on wl* **12/1**	83
-053	**2**	2	**Ollie George (IRE)**[10] [2678] 3-8-11 **65** .... (v) JamieSpencer 1 (A M Balding) *lw: rdn after s and sn chsng ldr: led 4f out: rdn 2f out: hdd appr fnl f: kpt on for 2nd: no ch w wnr* **8/1**	69
3005	**3**	*shd*	**Sky High Guy (IRE)**[37] [1898] 3-8-13 **67** .... ShaneKelly 7 (S Kirk) *bhd: rdn 3f out: hdwy over 2f out: styd on strly fnl f: pressed for 2nd cl hom but no imp on wnr* **16/1**	71
0223	**4**	*hd*	**Apt To Run (USA)**[16] [2498] 3-9-4 **72** .... (b) RichardMullen 9 (E A L Dunlop) *in tch: rdn and hdwy 3f out: styd on fr over 1f out but nvr gng pce to chal* **9/1**	75
06-0	**5**	2	**Height Of Fury (IRE)**[46] [1681] 3-9-2 **70** .... LDettori 5 (J L Dunlop) *bhd: pushed along 3f out: styd on fr over 1f out but nvr in contention* **6/1**[2]	70+
-600	**6**	1 ½	**Kapellmeister (IRE)**[12] [2620] 3-9-5 **73** .... (p) AlanMunro 6 (C R Egerton) *bhd: drvn 3f out: styd on fnl 2f but nvr nr ldrs* **25/1**	70
4534	**7**	¾	**Merchant Bankes**[30] [2065] 3-8-12 **69** .... SaleemGolam(3) 4 (W G M Turner) *bhd:rdn and hdwy 3f out: nvr rchd ldrs and one pce fnl 2f* **22/1**	64
0440	**8**	3	**Feu D'Artifice (USA)**[13] [2584] 3-9-2 **70** .... (b[1]) RyanMoore 14 (R Hannon) *lw: chsd ldrs: rdn and effrt over 2f out: wknd over 1f out* **7/1**[3]	60
0410	**9**	2	**Debord (FR)**[19] [2403] 3-8-11 **65** .... FrancisNorton 3 (Jamie Poulton) *lw: bhd: rdn 5f out: nvr gng pce to get competitive* **20/1**	51
4-30	**10**	3	**Looker**[12] [2608] 3-9-2 **70** .... SebSanders 12 (R M Beckett) *led tl hdd 4f out: wknd over 2f out* **14/1**	50
42P2	**11**	3 ½	**Dimelight**[15] [2533] 3-9-2 **70** .... JohnEgan 2 (D R C Elsworth) *sn chsng ldrs: rdn over 3f out: wknd qckly fr 2f out* **5/1**[1]	44
046	**12**	5	**Tranos (USA)**[30] [2063] 3-9-1 **69** .... NickyMackay 11 (L M Cumani) *chsd ldrs: rdn 3f out: wknd 2f out: eased whn btn fnl f* **8/1**	33
03-6	**13**	20	**Sophie'Jo**[12] [2615] 3-9-2 **70** .... TedDurcan 10 (H R A Cecil) *chsd ldrs: rdn 4f out: sn wknd: eased and virtually p.u fnl f* **9/1**	—

2m 8.87s (0.41) **Going Correction** +0.025s/f (Good) 13 Ran SP% **118.9**
Speed ratings (Par 99):99,97,97,97,95 94,93,91,89,87 84,80,64
CSF £101.43 CT £1554.56 TOTE £13.40: £3.30, £2.60, £6.00; EX 117.20 Place 6 £156.72, Place 5 £112.46.
Owner Tim Corby **Bred** D J Burke **Trained** West Ilsley, Berks

FOCUS
A modest handicap, but they went a decent pace and the form looks good enough for the grade.
Height Of Fury(IRE) Official explanation: jockey said colt had run too freely
Looker Official explanation: jockey said filly had no more to give
Tranos(USA) Official explanation: jockey said colt had run too freely
Sophie'Jo Official explanation: jockey said filly had no more to give
T/Jkpt: Not won. T/Plt: £164.50 to a £1 stake. Pool: £51,586.10. 228.85 winning tickets. T/Qpdt: £51.90 to a £1 stake. Pool: £2,761.60. 39.30 winning tickets. ST

2991 - 2997a (Foreign Racing) - See Raceform Interactive

[2745]HAMILTON (R-H)

Thursday, June 29

OFFICIAL GOING: Good to firm
Wind: almost nil

2998 SCOTTISH WOMAN MAGAZINE LADY AMATEUR H'CAP — 1m 5f 9y

7:00 (7:00) (Class 6) (0-65,60) 4-Y-O+ — **£3,296** (£1,014; £507) **Stalls** High

Form	Pos	Dist	Horse	RPR
6613	**1**		**Lake Wakatipu**[7] [2788] 4-9-13 **56** .... MissMMullineaux(5) 8 (M Mullineaux) *chsd ldrs: led over 2f out: pushed out* **7/1**[3]	64
/30-	**2**	1 ¼	**Front Rank (IRE)**[18] [1344] 6-10-3 **60** .... MissJSayer(5) 13 (Mrs Dianne Sayer) *prom: c wd st: pushed along over 2f out: kpt on fnl f: nt rch wiinner* **11/1**	66
5331	**3**	½	**York Cliff**[6] [2812] 8-10-2 **54** .... MissEJJones 11 (W M Brisbourne) *hld up: hdwy over 2f out: kpt on fnl f: nrst fin* **10/3**[1]	59
0620	**4**	¾	**Fiddlers Creek (IRE)**[18] [2165] 7-9-12 **55** .... (t) MissARyan(5) 1 (R Allan) *hld up midfield: hdwy 3f out: kpt on fnl f: no imp* **14/1**	59
0031	**5**	*shd*	**Shekan Star**[21] [2381] 4-10-0 **52** .... MissPRobson 5 (K G Reveley) *keen: hld up: hdwy over 2f out: no ex wl ins fnl f* **5/1**[2]	56
-005	**6**	1 ¼	**Baileys Honour**[22] [2345] 4-9-6 **44** .... MissCHannaford 3 (A G Newcombe) *bhd: pushed along and hdwy 3f out: kpt on: nrst fin* **16/1**	46
3234	**7**	7	**Caymans Gift**[8] [2751] 6-10-0 **57** .... MissHCuthbert(5) 10 (A C Whillans) *midfield: stmbld 1/2-way: rdn and outpcd fr 2f out* **8/1**	49
10-0	**8**	¾	**Cyber Santa**[55] [1467] 8-9-7 **45** .... MissADeniel 4 (J Hetherton) *led to over 2f out: wknd over 1f out* **50/1**	35
10/0	**9**	½	**Tom Bell (IRE)**[10] [2099] 6-10-1 **53** .... (v) MissRDavidson 9 (J G M O'Shea) *keen: in tch tl rdn and wknd fr over 2f out* **7/1**[3]	43
5-03	**10**	5	**Millennium Hall**[8] [2751] 7-10-8 **60** .... MissSBrotherton 6 (Miss Lucinda V Russell) *hld up: shortlived effrt 4f out: sn btn* **9/1**	42
06-0	**11**	2	**Paint The Lily (IRE)**[12] [2111] 5-8-10 **41** oh6...... MissVictoriaCasey(7) 12 (F Watson) *bhd: rdn 4f out: nvr on terms* **100/1**	20
550-	**12**	½	**Peter's Imp (IRE)**[60] [5890] 11-8-12 **43** .... MissWGibson(7) 7 (A Berry) *chsd ldrs tl wknd over 3f out* **50/1**	21
520-	**13**	35	**Green Falcon**[364] [3059] 5-8-12 **41** oh3......... MissJRiding(5) 2 (Miss S E Forster) *cl up tl wknd over 3f out* **33/1**	—

2m 51.86s (-1.54) **Going Correction** -0.40s/f (Firm) 13 Ran SP% **114.6**
Speed ratings (Par 101):88,87,86,86,86 85,81,80,80,77 76,75,54
CSF £76.87 CT £302.91 TOTE £9.20: £2.40, £4.30, £1.80; EX 172.90.
Owner Esprit De Corps Racing **Bred** T S And Mrs Wallace **Trained** Alpraham, Cheshire

FOCUS
A modest handicap in which the lack of pace in the first half of the race suited those racing prominently. Straightforward to rate with the winner to form.

2999 CRUISE EBF MAIDEN STKS (A QUALIFIER FOR THE HAMILTON PARK 2-Y-O SERIES FINAL) — 6f 5y

7:30 (7:30) (Class 5) 2-Y-O — **£3,886** (£1,156; £577; £288) **Stalls** Low

Form	Pos	Dist	Horse	RPR
2	**1**		**Adaptation**[21] [2375] 2-8-12 .... KDarley 1 (M Johnston) *mde most: drew clr fr over 1f out: easily* **1/8**[1]	78+
6300	**2**	5	**Our Toy Soldier**[29] [2139] 2-9-3 .... DerekMcGaffin 3 (B Smart) *wnt rt s: plld hrd and sn cl up: outpcd fr 2f out* **12/1**[2]	56
0	**3**	1 ¼	**Mr Wall Street**[71] [1080] 2-9-3 .... TomEaves 4 (Mrs L Williamson) *dwlt: sn in tch: effrt over 2f out: sn outpcd* **16/1**[3]	52+
0	**4**	23	**Perfect Reflection**[55] [1454] 2-8-12 .... FergalLynch 2 (A Berry) *cl up tl hung rt and lost tch fr 1/2-way* **66/1**	—

1m 12.61s (-0.49) **Going Correction** -0.50s/f (Hard) 4 Ran SP% **104.0**
Speed ratings (Par 93):83,76,74,44
CSF £1.90 TOTE £1.10; EX 2.00.
Owner J Shack **Bred** Newsells Park Stud Limited **Trained** Middleham Moor, N Yorks

FOCUS
A very-one sided event with the favourite not needing to improve to win with plenty to spare. The winning time was very slow.

NOTEBOOK
Adaptation did not have to build on debut form to win a most uncompetitive event with plenty in hand. Life will be tougher from now on but she is open to improvement, especially over further and, given her scratchy action, she may prefer more cut in the ground. (op 1-7 tchd 1-6 in a place)
Our Toy Soldier, returned to turf, again had his limitations exposed in this type of event. He looked anything but straightforward and looks one to continue to field against in this type of event. (op 8-1)
Mr Wall Street again showed ability at a modest level but is going to continue to look vulnerable in this type of event. (op 14-1)
Perfect Reflection, soundly beaten on her debut at Musselburgh over five furlongs, again showed nothing. Official explanation: jockey said filly hung right-handed throughout (op 50-1)

3000 THOROUGHBRED BREEDERS' ASSOCIATION GOLF DAY SPRINT FILLIES' H'CAP — 5f 4y

8:00 (8:00) (Class 4) (0-80,80) 3-Y-O — **£7,772** (£2,312; £1,155; £577) **Stalls** Low

Form	Pos	Dist	Horse	RPR
-312	**1**		**Loch Verdi**[23] [2329] 3-9-3 **76** .... DarryllHolland 8 (A M Balding) *cl up: led over 1f out: rdn and r.o wl* **4/6**[1]	90+
6220	**2**	1	**Shes Minnie**[15] [2553] 3-8-13 **72** .... RobertWinston 7 (J G M O'Shea) *prom: effrt over 1f out: chsd wnr ins fnl f: kpt on* **11/2**[2]	82
0305	**3**	1 ¾	**Rothesay Dancer**[3] [2925] 3-8-5 **67** .... (p) DanielTudhope(3) 5 (J S Goldie) *led to over 1f out: nt qckn ins fnl f* **9/1**[3]	71
0554	**4**	1	**City For Conquest (IRE)**[20] [2410] 3-9-1 **74** .... (b) RoystonFfrench 4 (K R Burke) *chsd ldrs tl rdn: hung rt and no ex over 1f out* **9/1**[3]	74
-226	**5**	3 ½	**Best Double**[83] [901] 3-8-9 **68** .... KDarley 3 (G A Butler) *in tch: outpcd and hung rt 1/2-way: nvr rchd ldrs* **9/1**[3]	56
3606	**6**	2	**Smooch**[17] [2496] 3-9-3 **76** .... (v[1]) TomEaves 2 (R M H Cowell) *cl up tl put hd in air and wknd fr 2f out* **25/1**	57
5-06	**7**	18	**Christa Bee**[40] [1849] 3-9-7 **80** .... (p) FergalLynch 1 (A Berry) *virtually ref to r: t.o thrght* **33/1**	—

58.28 secs (-2.92) **Going Correction** -0.50s/f (Hard) 7 Ran SP% **112.2**
Speed ratings (Par 98):103,101,98,97,91 88,59
CSF £4.51 CT £16.52 TOTE £1.40: £1.10, £3.10; EX 6.70.
Owner J C Smith **Bred** Littleton Stud **Trained** Kingsclere, Hants

FOCUS
A run-of-the-mill handicap but another step in the right direction for the steadily progressive winner. The form is not all that strong, but sound.
Christa Bee Official explanation: jockey said filly froze in stalls and missed break

3001 NESSCO TELECOMS MAIDEN STKS — 1m 1f 36y

8:30 (8:30) (Class 5) 3-4-Y-O — **£3,238** (£963; £481; £240) **Stalls** High

Form	Pos	Dist	Horse	RPR
0-22	**1**		**Otelcaliforni (USA)**[55] [1458] 3-8-9 75 .... DarryllHolland 10 (J Noseda) *trckd ldrs: rdn to ld over 1f out: kpt on wl fnl f* **11/10**[1]	74
0-	**2**	*nk*	**White Lightening (IRE)**[265] [5718] 3-8-9 .... GregFairley(5) 1 (J Howard Johnson) *midfield: effrt over 2f out: chsd wnr ins fnl f: kpt on towards fin* **16/1**	78
	3	3 ½	**Hayden Grace** 3-8-9 .... KDarley 8 (M Johnston) *pressed ldr: ev ch and rdn over 3f out: rallied: one pce over 1f out* **6/1**[3]	66
-334	**4**	¾	**Blushing Hilary (IRE)**[29] [2124] 3-8-9 70 .... (v) TomEaves 5 (Miss J A Camacho) *led tl edgd rt and hdd over 1f out: sn outpcd* **2/1**[2]	64
0	**5**	1 ½	**Final Esteem**[74] [1034] 3-9-0 .... RobertWinston 3 (I Semple) *s.i.s: bhd tl hdwy on outside over 2f out: nvr rchd ldrs* **33/1**	66
5	**6**	12	**Musical Giant (USA)**[12] [2662] 3-9-0 .... PaulMulrennan 2 (J Howard Johnson) *in tch: outpcd 3f out: sn btn* **33/1**	42
000-	**7**	*hd*	**Allouette**[227] [6342] 3-8-6 46 .... DanielTudhope(3) 7 (W J H Ratcliffe) *s.i.s: rdn in rr over 3f out: sn btn* **100/1**	37
	8	2 ½	**Carabinieri (IRE)** 3-9-0 .... RoystonFfrench 6 (J Barclay) *missed break: nvr on terms* **100/1**	37
00-0	**9**	8	**Kristalchen**[78] [974] 4-9-6 50 .... GylesParkin 4 (D W Thompson) *keen: chsd ldrs to 4f out: sn rdn and btn* **150/1**	16
00-	**10**	½	**Beacon Rambler**[258] [5883] 4-9-11 .... FergalLynch 9 (F Watson) *s.i.s: nvr on terms* **150/1**	20

1m 55.88s (-3.78) **Going Correction** -0.40s/f (Firm)
WFA 3 from 4yo 11lb 10 Ran SP% **110.3**
Speed ratings (Par 103):100,99,96,95,94 83,83,81,74,74
CSF £18.84 TOTE £2.10: £1.10, £3.40, £2.50; EX 19.20.
Owner Sir Robert Ogden **Bred** Grange Con Stud **Trained** Newmarket, Suffolk

FOCUS
A race lacking strength and a race run at just an ordinary gallop. The winner had little to beat and the form looks a bit shaky at this stage.

3002 EUROPEAN BREEDERS FUND FILLIES' CONDITIONS STKS — 1m 65y

9:00 (9:00) (Class 3) 3-Y-O+
£11,217 (£3,358; £1,679; £840; £419; £210) **Stalls** High

Form	Pos	Dist	Horse	RPR
25-4	**1**		**Squaw Dance**[34] [1979] 4-8-9 97 .... DarryllHolland 6 (W J Haggas) *led after 2f: shkn up 2f out: edgd lft and kpt on wl fnl f* **11/4**[3]	104
0-44	**2**	3 ½	**Little Miss Gracie**[33] [2041] 4-8-9 98 .... RobertWinston 2 (A B Haynes) *trckd ldrs: effrt and ev ch over 2f out: kpt on same pce fnl f* **6/5**[1]	96

1434 **3** *1* **Imperialistic (IRE)**[5] 2851 5-8-9 93 FergalLynch 4 94
(K R Burke) *s.s: hld up: hdwy 3f out: rdn and wandered fr 2f out: no imp fnl f* **9/4**[2]
000- **4** *27* **Vondova**[279] 5440 4-8-9 77 TomEaves 7 32
(D A Nolan) *prom tl rdn and wknd over 3f out* **100/1**
500/ **5** *13* **Lady Tilly**[607] 6465 9-8-9 PaulMulrennan 3 2
(W G Harrison) *led 2f: cl up tl rdn and wknd fr 3f out* **200/1**
00- **6** *17* **Renee Lard (IRE)**[256] 5921 3-7-13 PaulFessey 1 —
(A Berry) *hld up in tch: wknd 5f out: t.o* **200/1**
1m 44.52s (-4.78) **Going Correction** -0.40s/f (Firm)
WFA 3 from 4yo+ 10lb **6** Ran SP% **104.9**
Speed ratings (Par 104):107,103,102,75,62 45
CSF £5.59 TOTE £3.30: £1.70, £1.10; EX 6.90.
Owner Tony Hirschfeld Des Scott L K Piggott **Bred** M L Page **Trained** Newmarket, Suffolk
FOCUS
Not a strong race for the money and, given the winner was allowed her own way in front, this bare form may not prove entirely reliable.
NOTEBOOK
Squaw Dance, who is in foal to Dubawi, had the run of the race back on a sound surface and, although a convincing winner of an uncompetitive event, would be no good thing to follow up in stronger company next time. (op 10-3 tchd 4-1 in a place)
Little Miss Gracie, the winner of this race last year, was ideally placed in a race run at a muddling gallop and did not do too much wrong. She too has not been the easiest to place successfully, though. (op 5-6)
Imperialistic(IRE), back over a mile, was not disgraced given that this race suited those racing up with the pace and she left the impression that easier ground would have suited. Life will be tough back in handicaps from her current mark. Official explanation: jockey said mare missed break (op 11-4)
Vondova, very lightly raced in recent times, offered no immediate promise on this first run for the stable.
Lady Tilly had a stiff task at the weights and was well beaten on this first run since October 2004.
Renee Lard(IRE), who has shown no worthwhile form, faced an impossible task. (op 150-1)

3003 TONY SCHOLES 40TH BIRTHDAY H'CAP 6f 5y
9:30 (9:30) (Class 6) (0-65,64) 4-Y-0+ **£2,730** (£806; £403) **Stalls** Low

Form RPR
0021 **1** **Yorkshire Blue**[8] 2749 7-9-9 64 6ex FergalLynch 7 76
(J S Goldie) *outpcd and bhd: gd hdwy and swtchd rt over 1f out: led ins fnl f: r.o wl* **11/4**[1]
5066 **2** *1 ¾* **Smirfys Party**[18] 2484 8-8-4 45 (v) RoystonFfrench 12 52
(W M Brisbourne) *bhd: hdwy centre over 1f out: chsd wnr ins fnl f: kpt on fin* **16/1**
4601 **3** *½* **Muara**[15] 2543 4-8-9 55 MarkLawson(5) 10 61
(D W Barker) *in tch: effrt 2f out: ev ch ins fnl f: kpt on same pce* **8/1**
0000 **4** *1 ¼* **Blue Knight (IRE)**[7] 2780 7-9-4 62 (vt) DanielTudhope(3) 1 64
(D Carroll) *midfield: rdn 1/2-way: hdwy over 1f out: nrst fin* **10/1**
0032 **5** *shd* **Chairman Bobby**[10] 2700 8-8-7 48 (p) RobertWinston 11 49
(D W Barker) *led to ins fnl f: kpt on same pce* **4/1**[2]
-400 **6** *2* **Attila The Hun**[7] 2785 7-8-3 44 AdrianTNicholls 13 39
(F Watson) *w ldr tl wknd ins fnl f* **66/1**
5106 **7** *2 ½* **George The Best (IRE)**[28] 2164 5-9-2 62 GregFairley(5) 5 50
(Micky Hammond) *dwlt: bhd: effrt centre over 1f out: nvr rchd ldrs* **5/1**[3]
0000 **8** *hd* **Fox Covert (IRE)**[3] 2928 5-7-11 43 oh2 (p) AndrewElliott(5) 9 30
(D W Barker) *chsd ldr tl wknd wl over 1f out* **14/1**
3353 **9** *¾* **Primarily**[5] 2875 4-9-7 62 (p) KDarley 8 47
(A Berry) *midfield: drvn 1/2-way: outpcd fr 2f out* **8/1**
0000 **10** *2 ½* **Mister Marmaduke**[3] 2928 5-8-2 43 oh3 (p) PaulFessey 4 21
(D A Nolan) *outpcd and bhd: nvr on terms* **33/1**
-000 **11** *1 ¼* **Northern Svengali (IRE)**[3] 2928 10-8-9 50 oh2 ow7(t) PaulMulrennan 2 24
(D A Nolan) *chsd ldrs tl hung rt and wknd fr 2f out* **100/1**
1m 10.52s (-2.58) **Going Correction** -0.50s/f (Hard) **11** Ran SP% **112.6**
Speed ratings (Par 101):97,94,94,92,92 89,86,85,84,81 79
CSF £47.35 CT £317.62 TOTE £3.00: £2.30, £4.60, £2.20; EX 48.30 Place 6 £6.65, Place 5 £3.28..
Owner Thoroughbred Leisure Racing Club 2 **Bred** R T And Mrs Watson **Trained** Uplawmoor, E Renfrews
FOCUS
An ordinary handicap but one in which the strong pace helped tee things up for a finisher. The race unfolded centre-to-stands' side. The form seems sound enough, with another step up from the winner.
Northern Svengali(IRE) Official explanation: jockey said gelding hung right throughout
T/Plt: £4.90 to a £1 stake. Pool: £50,264.70. 7,477.45 winning tickets. T/Qpdt: £3.40 to a £1 stake. Pool: £3,479.50. 754.35 winning tickets. RY

2637 LEICESTER (R-H)
Thursday, June 29

OFFICIAL GOING: Good to firm
Wind: Light; behind Weather: Cloudy with sunny periods

3004 KOMMERLING GOLD LADIES H'CAP (LADY AMATEUR RIDERS) 5f 2y
6:45 (6:46) (Class 5) (0-70,70) 3-Y-0+ **£3,646** (£1,138; £569; £284; £142) **Stalls** Low

Form RPR
0003 **1** **Ruby's Dream**[4] 2897 4-9-6 51 oh1 (p) MissFayeBramley(3) 3 60
(J M Bradley) *hld up: hdwy 1/2-way: r.o to ld wl ins fnl f* **9/1**
2053 **2** *nk* **Canadian Danehill (IRE)**[5] 2864 4-10-7 68 MissHayleyMoore(5) 2 76
(R M H Cowell) *hld up: hdwy 1/2-way: rdn and hung rt over 1f out: r.o* **4/1**[1]
4-50 **3** *nk* **Conjecture**[19] 2449 4-10-9 70 MissRBastiman(5) 9 77
(R Bastiman) *led: rdn over 1f out: hdd wl ins fnl f* **16/1**
3324 **4** *1 ¼* **Patavium Prince (IRE)**[3] 2931 3-10-0 69 MissKFerguson(7) 10 69
(J R Best) *mid-div: hdwy 2f out: styd on* **6/1**[2]
0060 **5** *1* **Town House**[55] 1466 4-9-2 51 oh6 MissEJTuck(7) 6 50
(B P J Baugh) *chsd ldr: rdn and ev ch over 1f out: no ex ins fnl f* **100/1**
0000 **6** *hd* **El Potro**[27] 2207 4-9-7 56 MissEGeorge(7) 13 54
(J R Holt) *chsd ldrs: rdn over 1f out: styd on same pce fnl f* **20/1**
0500 **7** *hd* **Salviati (USA)**[2] 2962 9-10-5 68 MissSBradley(7) 14 65
(J M Bradley) *dwlt: hdwy and edgd lft over 1f out: nt rch ldrs* **10/1**
5614 **8** *1 ¾* **Namir (IRE)**[15] 2550 4-10-4 60 (vt) MrsMMorris 12 51
(S R Bowring) *chsd ldrs: rdn 1/2-way: no ex fnl f* **8/1**
2-00 **9** *nk* **Arfinnit (IRE)**[18] 2484 5-9-9 51 oh6 (p) MissLEllison 4 41
(Mrs A L M King) *wnt rt s: hld up: rdn 1/2-way: hdwy over 1f out: hung rt and no imp ins fnl furlong* **25/1**
3036 **10** *nk* **Cherokee Nation**[14] 2590 5-9-9 56 MissRachelD'Arcy(5) 11 45
(P W D'Arcy) *hld up: stmbld 1/2-way: rdn and hung lft over 1f out: nt trble ldrs* **8/1**
2000 **11** *2 ½* **Laurel Dawn**[2] 2949 8-9-2 51 oh5 (b) MissSusannahWileman(7) 7 31
(C N Kellett) *s.i.s: sn prom: hung rt and wknd over 1f out* **50/1**
0-20 **12** *½* **Indian Lady (IRE)**[12] 2652 3-10-2 64 MissNCarberry 1 40
(Mrs A L M King) *hld up: hdwy 1/2-way: rdn and wknd over 1f out* **15/2**[3]
6110 **13** *1 ¼* **Obe Bold (IRE)**[8] 2749 5-10-1 57 MrsCBartley 5 31
(A Berry) *prom: lost pl 4f out: bhd fr 1/2-way* **12/1**
0606 **14** *¾* **Jinksonthehouse**[5] 2858 5-9-4 51 oh11 MissAshleighHorton(5) 8 22
(M D I Usher) *prom: rdn 1/2-way: hung lft and wknd over 1f out* **50/1**
59.92 secs (-0.98) **Going Correction** -0.25s/f (Firm)
WFA 3 from 4yo+ 6lb **14** Ran SP% **114.5**
Speed ratings (Par 103):97,96,96,94,92 92,91,89,88,88 84,83,81,80
CSF £40.67 CT £583.38 TOTE £10.20: £3.70, £1.30, £5.80; EX 39.70.
Owner Gwilym Fry **Bred** Miss J Chaplin **Trained** Sedbury, Gloucs
FOCUS
Those drawn low had the edge. A modest handicap, but pretty sound form.

3005 KOMMERLING CONNOISSEUR MAIDEN AUCTION STKS 5f 218y
7:15 (7:17) (Class 5) 2-Y-0 **£3,886** (£1,156; £577; £288) **Stalls** Low

Form RPR
1 **Chin Wag (IRE)** 2-8-13 RichardMullen 1 81+
(E S McMahon) *chsd ldrs: led over 2f out: edgd lft over 1f out: hung rt ins fnl f: r.o strly* **11/2**[3]
2 *4* **Beautiful Madness (IRE)** 2-8-1 DominicFox(3) 2 57+
(M G Quinlan) *s.i.s: sn prom: rdn to chse wnr over 1f out: sn outpcd* **16/1**
0 **3** *4* **Tres Hombres**[53] 1510 2-8-9 SteveDrowne 6 47
(Tom Dascombe) *chsd ldrs: n.m.r and outpcd over 2f out: n.d after* **6/1**
0 **4** *shd* **Pas De Trois**[42] 1796 2-8-9 StephenCarson 5 46
(R F Johnson Houghton) *s.i.s: hld up: hdwy over 2f out: sn rdn and outpcd* **14/1**
40 **5** *1 ½* **Fiddlers Spirit (IRE)**[19] 2432 2-8-7 ow3 StephenDonohoe(5) 3 45
(J G M O'Shea) *led over 3f: wknd fnl f* **20/1**
6 *¾* **Teen Ager (FR)** 2-8-11 JohnEgan 7 41+
(J S Moore) *s.s: outpcd: swtchd lft over 2f out: n.d* **5/1**[2]
0 **7** *1 ¼* **Elle's Angel (IRE)**[87] 849 2-8-4 PaulFitzsimons 8 31
(B R Millman) *prom: rdn over 2f out: wknd fnl f* **66/1**
4 **8** *shd* **Victory Spirit**[13] 2604 2-8-9 SebSanders 4 35
(J L Dunlop) *chsd ldr: rdn over 2f out: wknd fnl f* **1/1**[1]
1m 12.05s (-1.15) **Going Correction** -0.25s/f (Firm) **8** Ran SP% **115.1**
Speed ratings (Par 93):97,91,86,86,84 83,81,81
CSF £86.17 TOTE £8.00: £1.90, £3.90, £2.10; EX 124.10.
Owner J C Fretwell **Bred** R N Auld **Trained** Hopwas, Staffs
FOCUS
They raced down the centre. Not much previous form to go on, particularly with the favourite below par, but the winner looks likely to be at least this good.
NOTEBOOK
Chin Wag(IRE) ◆, whose granddam is the smart French middle-distance filly Fly Me, made an impressive start to his career. He was notably green and did not really know how to gallop, but there was no denying the turn of foot he showed to leave his rivals toiling. This was not a strong race but he can go on to better things. (op 5-1 tchd 9-2 and 8-1)
Beautiful Madness(IRE), a cheap buy as a foal, moved into second place approaching the final furlong but then had only a rear view of the winner. (tchd 20-1)
Tres Hombres, whose debut run was on soft ground, was unable to step up on that over an extra furlong. He needs one more run to be eligible for nurseries. (op 7-2 tchd 13-2)
Pas De Trois, again slow to find his stride, showed a bit of ability and is another who looks a nursery type. (op 12-1)
Fiddlers Spirit(IRE) showed a bit more dash on this occasion but was well held in the end. (tchd 25-1)
Teen Ager(FR), a half-brother to multiple middle-distance winner Tarwila, was somewhat green on this debut and can be expected to improve for the experience. Official explanation: jockey said colt missed the break and hung left throughout (op 14-1 tchd 7-2)
Elle's Angel(IRE) Official explanation: jockey said filly hung left
Victory Spirit was under pressure not long after halfway and this was not his running. (op 6-5 tchd 11-8)

3006 KOMMERLING CLASSIC (S) STKS 7f 9y
7:45 (7:46) (Class 5) 3-Y-0 **£3,238** (£963; £481; £240) **Stalls** Low

Form RPR
000- **1** **Maid In England**[255] 5947 3-8-6 45 NelsonDeSouza(3) 10 45
(M P Tregoning) *chsd ldrs: led over 2f out: rdn and hung rt over 1f out: r.o* **11/1**
0005 **2** *3* **Pontefract Glory**[8] 2758 3-8-9 39 (p) LiamJones(5) 7 43
(M Dods) *chsd ldrs: rdn and swtchd rt 2f out: styd on same pce fnl f* **13/2**[3]
0600 **3** *hd* **Bertie Bear**[27] 2192 3-9-0 35 (v) BrianReilly 2 42
(G G Margarson) *prom: rdn and lost pl over 4f out: hdwy u.p and swtchd rt over 1f out: styd on* **66/1**
1050 **4** *1* **Joking John**[41] 1825 3-9-5 39 LeeEnstone 14 44
(C W Fairhurst) *hld up: hdwy 1/2-way: rdn over 1f out: styd on same pce* **25/1**
4000 **5** *shd* **Moonlight Fantasy (IRE)**[8] 2758 3-9-0 49 (p) JoeFanning 17 39
(N Tinkler) *chsd ldrs: ev ch over 2f out: sn rdn: no ex fnl f* **14/1**
0443 **6** *hd* **Three Feathers**[9] 2730 3-8-7 52 JamesMillman(7) 11 39
(M Salaman) *hld up: hdwy u.p over 1f out: nt rch ldrs* **8/1**
0000 **7** *2 ½* **Mytass**[20] 2415 3-9-0 37 (b) MickyFenton 8 32
(J A Pickering) *led over 4f: wknd fnl f* **50/1**
00-6 **8** *1 ¼* **Soviet Promise (IRE)**[17] 2498 3-8-6 45 DominicFox(3) 3 24
(G G Margarson) *mid-div: rdn 1/2-way: wknd fnl f* **20/1**
5022 **9** *2* **Lucys Lady**[30] 2101 3-8-9 47 RichardMullen 13 26+
(K R Burke) *s.i.s: hld up: hdwy over 2f out: sn rdn: wknd and eased fnl f* **5/2**[1]
000 **10** *1* **Island Green (USA)**[126] 487 3-9-0 45 TPQueally 12 21
(B J Curley) *hld up: hdwy over 1f out: n.d* **14/1**
-000 **11** *2 ½* **Balfour House**[27] 2187 3-9-0 35 PaulFitzsimons 9 15
(R A Harris) *mid-div: rdn over 2f out: wknd and eased fnl f* **66/1**
0 **12** *3 ½* **Straight Gal (IRE)**[28] 2167 3-8-9 DO'Donohoe 6 —
(G A Huffer) *s.i.s: hld up: hdwy 1/2-way: wknd and eased over 1f out* **5/1**[2]
0-00 **13** *shd* **New Blood (IRE)**[9] 2730 3-8-9 35 StephenDonohoe(5) 1 5
(J M Bradley) *sn outpcd* **66/1**
000 **14** *2 ½* **Wilmas Gal**[8] 2763 3-8-9 (t) SebSanders 5 —
(R Bastiman) *s.i.s: hld up: a in rr* **66/1**
60-0 **15** *17* **African Blues**[29] 2131 3-9-0 10 (p) SteveDrowne 4 —
(M R Hoad) *chsd ldrs to 1/2-way* **150/1**

-400 **16** *3* **Dream Factor (IRE)**^{153} [211] 3-8-9 60........................ JohnEgan 15 —
(J O'Reilly) *chsd ldrs over 4f* **14/1**

0-00 **17** *18* **At The Bar**^{45} [1746] 3-8-9 45........................ DerekNolan(5) 16 —
(A J Chamberlain) *sn outpcd* **100/1**

1m 25.19s (-0.91) **Going Correction** -0.25s/f (Firm) **17** Ran SP% **116.2**
Speed ratings (Par 99):95,91,91,90,90 89,87,85,83,82 79,75,75,72,52 49,28
CSF £72.59 TOTE £13.20: £4.10, £2.30, £9.90; EX 98.10.The winner was bought in for 9,000gns.

Owner The Holmes Office **Bred** S J And Mrs Pembroke **Trained** Lambourn, Berks

FOCUS
A weak seller, rated around the third and fourth.
Lucys Lady Official explanation: jockey said filly hung left throughout
Straight Gal(IRE) Official explanation: jockey said filly bled from the nose

3007 KOMMERLING DETLEF BECKER H'CAP 1m 60y
8:15 (8:15) (Class 4) (0-85,86) 3-Y-O
£6,232 (£1,866; £933; £467; £233; £117) **Stalls** High

Form RPR

1141 **1** **Days Of My Life (IRE)**^{7} [2779] 3-9-3 **86** 5ex........ RichardKingscote(5) 5 96+
(R Charlton) *chsd ldr 3f: shkn up to ld over 1f out: readily* **4/9**^{1}

2-16 **2** *2* **Sharplaw Autumn (USA)**^{24} [2290] 3-9-0 **78**.................. TonyCulhane 1 84
(W J Haggas) *led: rdn and hdd over 1f out: sn outpcd* **11/2**^{2}

-602 **3** *2* **Nelsons Column (IRE)**^{23} [2325] 3-8-9 **73**........................ JoeFanning 6 74
(G M Moore) *hld up in tch: rdn over 2f out: styd on same pce appr fnl f* **12/1**

1460 **4** *2 1/2* **Critic (IRE)**^{14} [2581] 3-9-4 **82**........................ SteveDrowne 3 77
(M L W Bell) *hld up: rdn over 2f out: nt clr run over 1f out: n.d* **9/1**^{3}

-005 **5** *1* **Renderoc (USA)**^{35} [1953] 3-9-7 **85**........................ JohnEgan 7 78
(J S Moore) *hld up: rdn over 3f out: n.d* **16/1**

0- **6** *6* **Westering Home (IRE)**^{307} [4741] 3-8-9 **73**..................(b) MickyFenton 2 52
(J Mackie) *prom: chsd ldr 5f out tl rdn and wknd over 1f out* **33/1**

1m 45.58s (0.28) **Going Correction** -0.15s/f (Firm) **6** Ran SP% **111.2**
Speed ratings (Par 101):92,90,88,85,84 78
CSF £3.24 TOTE £1.40: £1.10, £2.70; EX 3.40.

Owner Mountgrange Stud **Bred** Sir E J Loder **Trained** Beckhampton, Wilts

FOCUS
A slowly-run race and a very moderate winning time for a race like this. A straighforward task for the well-in winner, and the form is not all that strong.

3008 KOMMERLING HANS PABST H'CAP 1m 1f 218y
8:45 (8:45) (Class 4) (0-80,77) 3-Y-O **£5,362** (£1,604; £802; £401; £199) **Stalls** High

Form RPR

5012 **1** **Pagan Crest**^{10} [2713] 3-8-9 **65**........................ KerrinMcEvoy 8 73+
(Mrs A J Perrett) *led 8f out: rdn and hung lft fr over 2f out: hdd over 1f out: r.o to ld post* **15/8**^{1}

5305 **2** *shd* **Tumbleweed Glory (IRE)**^{12} [2654] 3-9-6 **76**........................ TedDurcan 5 84
(B J Meehan) *hld up: plld hrd: hdwy over 3f out: led over 1f out: rdn and hdd post* **5/1**^{2}

0-32 **3** *1 1/4* **Barndeh (IRE)**^{19} [2441] 3-9-1 **71**........................(p) PhilipRobinson 3 77
(M A Jarvis) *led: hdd 8f out: swtchd centre over 3f out: sn rdn: hung lft over 1f out: styd on* **15/8**^{1}

-040 **4** *4* **On Air (USA)**^{48} [1648] 3-8-11 **67**........................ JoeFanning 2 65
(M Johnston) *hld up in tch: rdn over 2f out: wknd fnl f* **14/1**

-440 **5** *3/4* **Tora Petcha (IRE)**^{12} [2642] 3-8-9 **72**.................. RussellKennemore(7) 7 69
(R Hollinshead) *trckd ldrs: racd keenly: rdn over 2f out: styd on same pce appr fnl f* **40/1**

-100 **6** *1 3/4* **George's Flyer (IRE)**^{17} [2502] 3-8-10 **66**..................(b) TonyHamilton 6 59
(R A Fahey) *prom: rdn over 2f out: wknd fnl f* **20/1**

0641 **7** *1* **Nefski Alexander (USA)**^{17} [2498] 3-9-7 **77**........................ SebSanders 1 68
(P F I Cole) *hld up: hdwy 3f out: rdn and wknd over 1f out* **8/1**^{3}

2m 6.47s (-1.83) **Going Correction** -0.15s/f (Firm) **7** Ran SP% **111.2**
Speed ratings (Par 101):101,100,99,96,96 94,93
CSF £11.21 CT £17.93 TOTE £2.60: £1.50, £2.40; EX 11.20.

Owner The Gap Partnership **Bred** Fonthill Stud **Trained** Pulborough, W Sussex

FOCUS
They went no great gallop. A fairly ordinary handicap, but the first three are going the right way with the winner possibly worth a bit more than the bare form.

3009 JARVIS SIX FOOT INJURED JOCKEYS FUND H'CAP 1m 3f 183y
9:15 (9:15) (Class 5) (0-75,72) 4-Y-O+ **£5,181** (£1,541; £770; £384) **Stalls** High

Form RPR

-004 **1** **Mr Aitch (IRE)**^{16} [2519] 4-9-4 **69**........................ JohnEgan 3 78
(R T Phillips) *chsd ldr over 10f out: led over 1f out: rdn out* **5/1**

4524 **2** *1 1/2* **Top Spec (IRE)**^{13} [2628] 5-9-4 **69**........................ JimmyQuinn 2 76
(J Pearce) *s.i.s: hld up: hdwy over 2f out: rdn to chse wnr over 1f out: styd on* **10/3**^{2}

0323 **3** *2* **Velvet Waters**^{11} [2672] 5-9-3 **68**........................ StephenCarson 4 72
(R F Johnson Houghton) *led: rdn and hdd over 1f out: no ex ins fnl f* **11/4**^{1}

-600 **4** *1 1/2* **Bowled Out (GER)**^{9} [2736] 4-9-1 **66**........................ TPQueally 8 67
(P J McBride) *hld up: hdwy over 1f out: nt rch ldrs* **14/1**

345- **5** *1 1/4* **Foursquare Flyer (IRE)**^{316} [4474] 4-9-7 **72**.................. MickyFenton 5 71
(J Mackie) *s.i.s: hld up: pushed along 5f out: rdn over 2f out: hung rt and styd on ins fnl f: nt trble ldrs* **28/1**

-630 **6** *2 1/2* **Magic Amigo**^{31} [2088] 5-9-7 **72**........................ TonyCulhane 7 67
(J R Jenkins) *trckd ldrs: plld hrd: rdn over 2f out: wknd over 1f out* **12/1**

-001 **7** *1/2* **Richtee (IRE)**^{13} [2628] 5-9-4 **69**........................ TonyHamilton 6 64
(R A Fahey) *s.i.s: sn prom: rdn over 2f out: wknd over 1f out* **9/2**^{3}

640- **8** *3* **Authenticate**^{236} [6266] 4-8-11 **62**........................ RichardMullen 1 52
(E J O'Neill) *hld up in tch: rdn over 3f out: wknd over 1f out* **12/1**

2m 33.77s (-0.73) **Going Correction** -0.15s/f (Firm) **8** Ran SP% **110.1**
Speed ratings (Par 103):96,95,93,92,91 90,89,87
CSF £20.33 CT £50.21 TOTE £4.70: £1.10, £1.50, £1.80; EX 21.80 Place 6 £104.71, Place 5 £41.71..

Owner Bellflower Racing Ltd **Bred** Mount Coote Stud **Trained** Adlestrop, Gloucs

FOCUS
The third set only a steady pace and the winning time was moderate. It is doubtful if this form will prove solid given the messy nature of the race.
T/Plt: £275.10 to a £1 stake. Pool: £55,727.40. 147.85 winning tickets. T/Qpdt: £25.30 to a £1 stake. Pool: £4,505.50. 131.50 winning tickets. CR

2857 LINGFIELD (L-H)
Thursday, June 29

OFFICIAL GOING: Standard
Wind: Almost nil Weather: Sunny and very warm

3010 CHRIS WOTTON CUP MEDIAN AUCTION MAIDEN FILLIES' STKS 7f (P)
2:00 (2:01) (Class 5) 2-Y-O **£3,238** (£963; £481; £240) **Stalls** Low

Form RPR

65 **1** **Babylon Sister (IRE)**^{18} [2478] 2-9-0........................ PatDobbs 8 64+
(R Hannon) *mde all: set v stdy pce tl qcknd over 2f out: wl clr over 1f out: unchal* **7/2**^{2}

0 **2** *4* **Tenterhooks (IRE)**^{15} [2552] 2-9-0........................ ShaneKelly 9 54
(J A Osborne) *pressed wnr: drvn and nt qckn 2f out: n.d after: hld on for 2nd* **8/1**

0 **3** *nk* **Abounding**^{18} [2478] 2-9-0........................ SebSanders 4 53
(R M Beckett) *trckd ldrs: rdn and wl outpcd 2f out: kpt on fnl f to press for 2nd nr fin* **33/1**

0 **4** *1 1/4* **Bertrada (IRE)**^{19} [2456] 2-9-0........................ SteveDrowne 6 50
(H Morrison) *trckd ldrs: rdn and outpcd over 2f out: no ch after* **14/1**

3 **5** *1 3/4* **Little Miss Wizzy**^{28} [2166] 2-9-0........................ JamieSpencer 5 45
(M L W Bell) *hld up in last: rdn and struggling whn pce increased over 2f out: no ch after* **13/8**^{1}

0 **6** *nk* **Gorgeous Girl**^{19} [2461] 2-9-0........................ FrancisNorton 1 45
(P W D'Arcy) *sn pushed up to chse ldng pair: rdn wl over 2f out: sn outpcd: wknd fnl f* **12/1**

0255 **7** *3* **Fly Time**^{8} [2759] 2-9-0........................ ChrisCatlin 3 37
(M R Channon) *t.k.h: hld up in rr: last and struggling 3f out: wknd 2f out* **11/2**^{3}

00 **8** *1/2* **River Rosie (IRE)**^{37} [1922] 2-9-0........................ AlanMunro 7 36
(J G Portman) *racd wd: in tch: effrt over 2f out: sn rdn and wknd* **10/1**

1m 29.05s (3.16) **Going Correction** +0.075s/f (Slow) **8** Ran SP% **113.2**
Speed ratings (Par 90):84,79,79,77,75 75,71,71
CSF £30.67 TOTE £4.20: £1.10, £2.80, £6.10; EX 32.40.

Owner Michael Pescod **Bred** Oak Lodge Stud And Liscullen Stud **Trained** East Everleigh, Wilts

FOCUS
A slow pace resulted in a moderate winning time, even for a weak race like this. Very few ever got into it and the form should be treated with a degree of caution.

NOTEBOOK
Babylon Sister(IRE), who may have found the ground too quick when disappointing at Bath last time, was gifted a soft lead over this longer trip and a decisive injection of speed rounding the home turn netted her the race. Given the way the contest was run and the slow time, the form may not add up to much, and her stamina for the trip has not yet been truly proven. (op 9-2 tchd 5-1)
Tenterhooks(IRE), another tackling an extra furlong, took a handy position but could not go with the winner when she quickened things up rounding the home bend. This was an improvement on her debut effort, but she will need to progress a fair amount again if she is to win a race. (op 17-2 tchd 9-1 and 7-1)
Abounding, who finished six lengths behind Babylon Sister on her Bath debut, ran very close to that form on this different surface. To be fair her pedigree is all about stamina so the best of her is unlikely to be seen before next season. (op 25-1)
Bertrada(IRE), stone last on her Newbury debut, has a middle-distance pedigree so a slowly-run race over this trip was never going to play to her strengths. She is another likely to show her best in the longer term. (op 16-1)
Little Miss Wizzy had the best previous form coming into this, but found herself out the back in a slowly-run race and could never get involved. Things did not pan out for her here, but she is worth another chance to confirm the promise of her Nottingham debut. (op 11-8 tchd 15-8 in places)

3011 MGM FACILITIES H'CAP 7f (P)
2:30 (2:31) (Class 6) (0-65,65) 3-Y-O **£3,238** (£963; £481; £240) **Stalls** Low

Form RPR

006- **1** **Mataram (USA)**^{287} [5255] 3-9-4 **62**........................ AlanMunro 5 70
(W Jarvis) *trckd ldrs: effrt on inner over 1f out: r.o to ld ins fnl f: sn drvn clr* **20/1**

2-00 **2** *1 3/4* **High Octave (IRE)**^{48} [1642] 3-9-6 **64**........................ JamieSpencer 4 67+
(B G Powell) *hld up in last trio: gng wl but plenty to do over 2f out: swtchd to outside and r.o strly fnl f: no ch of catching wnr* **14/1**

5500 **3** *shd* **Endless Night**^{24} [2301] 3-9-3 **61**........................ SteveDrowne 7 64
(H Morrison) *towards rr: pushed along 3f out: prog on inner over 1f out: styd on to take 3rd nr fin* **7/1**^{2}

3000 **4** *1/2* **Dream Forest (IRE)**^{14} [2583] 3-9-7 **65**........................ RobertHavlin 8 67
(Mrs P N Dutfield) *racd on outer in midfield: pushed along 1/2-way: no prog tl hrd rdn and styd on fr over 1f out: nrst fin* **33/1**

54-0 **5** *shd* **Musical Echo**^{38} [1901] 3-9-7 **65**........................ KerrinMcEvoy 10 66+
(G C H Chung) *hld up in midfield: gng easily over 2f out: trapped bhd rivals wl over 1f out to ins fnl f: kpt on one pce after* **14/1**

5210 **6** *1/2* **Titus Lumpus (IRE)**^{36} [1941] 3-9-3 **61**........................ JimmyQuinn 6 61
(R M Flower) *mde most: drvn on 2f out: hdd ins fnl f: wknd rapidly and lost 4 pls nr fin* **20/1**

1400 **7** *1 1/4* **Super Frank (IRE)**^{49} [1616] 3-9-3 **64**..................(t) AdamKirby(3) 13 61
(G A Butler) *dropped in fr wd draw and hld up in last trio: rdn and struggling over 2f out: styd on fr over 1f out: n.d* **8/1**^{3}

-205 **8** *3/4* **Picture Show (USA)**^{20} [2393] 3-9-6 **64**........................ SebSanders 14 59
(C E Brittain) *racd wd: pressed ldrs: upsides over 2f out: fdd u.p fnl f* **12/1**

00-3 **9** *3/4* **Make My Dream**^{12} [2644] 3-9-3 **61**........................ JimCrowley 12 54
(J Gallagher) *pressed ldng pair: drvn 2f out: stl cl up 1f out: wknd ins fnl f* **16/1**

-050 **10** *1/2* **Orphina (IRE)**^{24} [2301] 3-9-6 **64**........................(v^{1}) ShaneKelly 3 55
(Pat Eddery) *hld up in last trio: pushed along 3f out: swtchd rt over 2f out: kpt on fnl f: nvr a ch* **10/1**

0-10 **11** *1 1/4* **Takitwo**^{11} [2678] 3-9-3 **61**........................ ChrisCatlin 2 49
(P D Cundell) *hld up in rr: effrt 2f out: drvn to chse main gp 1f out: sn wknd* **10/1**

4202 **12** *1 1/2* **Bobby Rose**^{14} [2576] 3-9-7 **65**........................ DaneO'Neill 9 49
(D K Ivory) *racd towards outer: w ldrs: upsides wl over 2f out: btn over 1f out: wknd rapidly ins fnl f* **9/2**^{1}

2101 **13** *nk* **George The Second**^{14} [2576] 3-9-1 **64**.............. RichardKingscote(5) 11 47
(Mrs H Sweeting) *w ldr to 2f out: wknd over 1f out* **9/2**^{1}

00-0 **14** *6* **Milton's Keen**^{32} [2048] 3-9-7 **65**........................ BrianReilly 1 32
(P S McEntee) *chsd ldrs to 1/2-way: wknd u.p wl over 2f out* **50/1**

1m 26.83s (0.94) **Going Correction** +0.075s/f (Slow) **14** Ran SP% **119.5**
Speed ratings (Par 97):97,95,94,94,94 93,92,91,90,89 88,86,86,79
CSF £265.56 CT £2165.51 TOTE £25.10: £6.70, £4.80, £2.60; EX 220.50.

Owner Sales Race 2001 Syndicate **Bred** B P Walden Jr And James Anthony **Trained** Newmarket, Suffolk

FOCUS

A modest if competitive handicap and sound-enough form. The winning time was about right for a race like this, despite being 2.22 seconds faster than the opener. A typical race for Lingfield with several finishing strongly.

Mataram(USA) ◆ Official explanation: trainer's rep said, regarding the improved form shown, the gelding had been a weak two-year-old which had strengthened up and was also having its first run on the all-weather

Musical Echo ◆ Official explanation: jockey said filly was denied clear run

George The Second Official explanation: jockey said colt ran flat

3012 TINDLE NEWSPAPERS H'CAP — 6f (P)
3:00 (3:00) (Class 4) (0-85,85) 3-Y-0+ **£7,772** (£2,312; £1,155; £577) **Stalls** Low

Form | RPR

4243 **1** **Hammer Of The Gods (IRE)**[29] [2136] 6-9-2 **73**.......(bt) JamieSpencer 3 — 85
(P S McEntee) *mde all: set generous pce: kicked on again over 1f out: hung rt but styd on wl* **15/8**[1]

0630 **2** 2 ½ **Roman Quintet (IRE)**[31] [2074] 6-9-1 **72**.......... KerrinMcEvoy 9 — 76
(D W P Arbuthnot) *trckd ldng pair: gng wl enough over 2f out: rdn and edgd rt over 1f out: fnd little but tk 2nd ins fnl f* **7/1**[3]

4/56 **3** hd **Seamus Shindig**[19] [2429] 4-9-10 **81**.......... DaneO'Neill 1 — 84
(H Candy) *chsd ldrs: rdn over 2f out and struggling: effrt on inner over 1f out: kpt on same pce* **10/3**[2]

-005 **4** ½ **Buy On The Red**[10] [2711] 5-10-0 **85**..........(b) SteveDrowne 4 — 87
(W R Muir) *pressed wnr: rdn over 2f out: nt qckn over 1f out: fdd* **9/1**

4005 **5** 1 ½ **Mambazo**[22] [2340] 4-8-10 **70**..........(e) AdamKirby[(3)] 6 — 67
(S C Williams) *t.k.h: hld up in last: stl last over 2f out: drvn and limited rspnse over 1f out: kpt on fnl f: no ch* **20/1**

-065 **6** 2 **Landucci**[12] [2649] 5-9-5 **76**.......... MichaelHills 8 — 67
(J W Hills) *hld up: prog on outer over 3f out: rdn and nt qckn over 2f out: no real prog after* **8/1**

1113 **7** 1 ½ **Up Tempo (IRE)**[34] [1993] 8-8-11 **68**..........(b) JimmyQuinn 5 — 55
(C R Dore) *chsd ldrs: rdn bef 1/2-way: struggling over 2f out* **7/1**[3]

2632 **8** 3 **Zarzu**[28] [2173] 7-9-12 **83**.......... HayleyTurner 2 — 61
(C R Dore) *settled in rr: rdn and no prog over 2f out: wl btn over 1f out* **14/1**

1m 12.66s (-0.15) **Going Correction** +0.075s/f (Slow) 8 Ran SP% **115.4**

Speed ratings (Par 105):104,100,100,99,97 95,93,89

CSF £15.89 CT £41.37 TOTE £2.40: £1.20, £1.80, £1.80; EX 15.90.

Owner Graham Newton & Russell Reed **Bred** Kilfrush Stud Ltd **Trained** Newmarket, Suffolk

FOCUS

A decent spring handicap run at a solid pace. Few got into the race and the consistent winner was very impressive. The overall form may not be too strong, with the second, third and fourth not having been at their best recently.

Mambazo Official explanation: jockey said gelding ran too free

3013 SURREY VETERANS CLAIMING STKS — 2m (P)
3:30 (3:31) (Class 6) 4-Y-0+ **£3,071** (£906; £453) **Stalls** Low

Form | RPR

5016 **1** **Lefonic**[6] [2828] 4-9-6 61.......... OscarUrbina 8 — 63
(G C H Chung) *trckd ldr: led 5f out: kicked 4 l clr over 2f out: kpt on steadily after* **9/2**[3]

6303 **2** 2 **Iamback**[7] [2790] 6-8-1 38..........(t) JamieMackay 5 — 42
(Miss D A McHale) *chsd ldrs: pushed along over 4f out: effrt but outpcd over 2f out: kpt on to take 2nd ins fnl f: unable to chal* **8/1**

4602 **3** 3 ½ **High Hope (FR)**[7] [2790] 8-8-5 64..........(b) RobynBrisland[(5)] 10 — 47
(G L Moore) *hld up midfield: prog over 4f out: chsd wnr wl over 2f out: fnd nil and no imp: lost 2nd ins fnl f* **11/4**[1]

0400 **4** shd **Akritas**[13] [2628] 5-9-10 75..........(t) JamieSpencer 1 — 61
(P F I Cole) *dwlt: hld up in last pair: prog on outer over 4f out: chsd ldrs but outpcd over 2f out: hanging bdly over 1f out: plugged o* **4/1**[2]

4000 **5** 3 **Gravardlax**[7] [2790] 5-8-6 35 ow2.......... BrianReilly 4 — 39
(Miss D A McHale) *in tch in rr: pushed along over 4f out: outpcd over 3f out: kpt on but n.d after* **33/1**

4140 **6** 9 **Montosari**[59] [1339] 7-9-2 67.......... GeorgeBaker 9 — 38
(P Mitchell) *cl up: chsd wnr over 4f out to wl over 2f out: sn wknd u.p* **11/4**[1]

005 **7** 1 ¼ **Devonia Plains (IRE)**[17] [2507] 4-9-0 65..........(v) RobertHavlin 2 — 35
(Mrs P N Dutfield) *chsd ldrs: rdn 5f out: sn lost tch* **33/1**

0 **8** ½ **All Square (IRE)**[23] [1911] 6-9-0 42.......... SteveDrowne 6 — 34
(R A Farrant) *led to 5f out: sn wknd and bhd* **28/1**

0000 **9** 2 ½ **My Boo**[17] [2497] 4-8-0 36 ow1..........(tp) HayleyTurner 7 — 17
(T Keddy) *in tch: drvn over 6f out: bhd fnl 4f* **25/1**

003- **10** 14 **Mr Dip**[8] [6571] 6-8-7 32.......... ChrisCatlin 3 — 7
(L A Dace) *hld up last pair: rdn 5f out: sn bhd: t.o* **40/1**

3m 29.25s (0.46) **Going Correction** +0.075s/f (Slow) 10 Ran SP% **118.2**

Speed ratings (Par 101):101,100,98,98,96 92,91,91,90,83

CSF £37.80 TOTE £5.40: £2.10, £2.40, £1.30; EX 48.30.

Owner Ian Pattle **Bred** Northmore Stud **Trained** Newmarket, Suffolk

FOCUS

A modest staying claimer, but the time was about as you would expect for a race of its class suggesting that the pace was honest and stamina for the trip was truly tested. Weak form.

Akritas Official explanation: jockey said gelding hung left

3014 VIC BARFOOT HALF CENTURY H'CAP — 1m (P)
4:00 (4:00) (Class 6) (0-65,62) 4-Y-0+ **£3,238** (£963; £481; £240) **Stalls** High

Form | RPR

0-04 **1** **Writ (IRE)**[7] [2793] 4-9-0 **55**.......... HayleyTurner 12 — 68
(Ernst Oertel) *led for 2f: trckd ldr: rdn to ld again jst over 1f out: steadily drew clr* **25/1**

1303 **2** 3 **Redeye Special**[29] [2148] 4-9-7 **62**.......... JamieSpencer 4 — 68
(M L W Bell) *hld up in midfield: rdn wl over 2f out: prog on inner over 1f out : styd on to take 2nd last 50yds* **9/4**[1]

3-53 **3** ½ **Naval Attache**[22] [2348] 4-8-9 **50**.......... JimmyQuinn 9 — 55
(B R Johnson) *led after 2f: drvn and hdd jst over 1f out: no ch w wnr after: lost 2nd last 50yds* **9/1**

05-0 **4** 2 **Future Deal**[48] [1638] 5-9-6 **61**.......... OscarUrbina 3 — 61
(C A Horgan) *trckd ldrs: rdn to chse ldng pair 2f out: no imp: fdd fnl f* **16/1**

6030 **5** nk **Busy Man (IRE)**[64] [1244] 7-8-11 **52**.......... PaulDoe 1 — 52+
(J R Jenkins) *dwlt: t.k.h: hld up in last trio: last whn nt clr run over 2f out: pushed along on inner and styd on wl fr over 1f out* **16/1**

0060 **6** ½ **Simplify**[10] [2708] 4-8-13 **54**..........(p) AlanMunro 11 — 53
(T M Jones) *hld up in midfield: rdn over 2f out: nt qckn and btn sn after* **10/1**

4152 **7** ½ **Fantasy Crusader**[17] [2499] 7-8-13 **54**.......... DaneO'Neill 7 — 51
(R M H Cowell) *trckd ldng pair: rdn wl over 2f out: fdd over 1f out* **5/1**[2]

20/6 **8** 1 **Sir Laughalot**[12] [2647] 6-9-5 **60**.......... SebSanders 2 — 55
(Miss E C Lavelle) *lost pl and in rr over 5f out: drvn over 2f out: one pce and no prog* **15/2**

-000 **9** ¾ **Balerno**[23] [2317] 7-8-13 **54**.......... JDSmith 8 — 47
(R Ingram) *hld up in last: effrt on wd outside 3f out: no real prog* **20/1**

0463 **10** hd **Humility**[14] [2574] 5-9-5 **60**.......... ShaneKelly 10 — 53
(C A Cyzer) *plld hrd early: hld up in rr: prog on outer to chse ldrs over 2f out: wknd over 1f out* **13/2**[3]

0230 **11** nk **Contented (IRE)**[29] [2135] 4-8-13 **54**..........(p) SteveDrowne 6 — 46
(Mrs L C Jewell) *trckd ldrs: rdn over 2f out: steadily wknd* **14/1**

0505 **12** 3 **Fleur A Lay (USA)**[11] [2676] 4-8-11 **52**..........(p) JimCrowley 5 — 37
(Mrs A J Perrett) *a towards rr: rdn 3f out: sn wknd* **33/1**

1m 39.92s (0.49) **Going Correction** +0.075s/f (Slow) 12 Ran SP% **121.6**

Speed ratings (Par 101):100,97,96,94,94 93,93,92,91,91 90,87

CSF £81.52 CT £590.84 TOTE £31.80: £8.50, £1.30, £2.70; EX 117.80.

Owner A S Reid **Bred** Sean Collins **Trained** Newmarket, Suffolk

FOCUS

A reasonably competitive little handicap run at a fair pace. The form seems sound enough.

Busy Man(IRE) Official explanation: vet said gelding was lame

3015 ALLEN BALL MEMORIAL H'CAP — 1m 2f (P)
4:30 (4:30) (Class 4) (0-85,85) 3-Y-0 **£7,772** (£2,312; £1,155; £577) **Stalls** Low

Form | RPR

065 **1** **Stotsfold**[13] [2605] 3-8-9 **73**.......... AlanMunro 6 — 81+
(W R Swinburn) *hld up in tch: prog over 2f out: effrt on inner over 1f out: drvn to ld last 150yds: hung rt but kpt on* **9/1**

11-4 **2** 1 ¼ **Faith And Reason (USA)**[8] [2754] 3-9-6 **84**.......... KerrinMcEvoy 8 — 89
(Saeed Bin Suroor) *pressed ldng pair: shkn up over 2f out: led over 1f out: fnd nthing in front and edgd rt: hdd last 150yds* **5/4**[1]

-140 **3** 1 ½ **Herring (IRE)**[28] [2177] 3-8-13 **77**.......... SebSanders 7 — 79
(D J Coakley) *restless stalls: hld up in tch: prog on outer 3f out: rdn and nt qckn over 1f out: kpt on fnl f* **15/2**[3]

0-54 **4** ¾ **Moohimm (IRE)**[28] [2175] 3-8-12 **76**.......... DaneO'Neill 1 — 77
(M P Tregoning) *mde most: rdn over 2f out: hdd over 1f out: fdd* **9/1**

6050 **5** ½ **Scarlet Knight**[33] [2014] 3-9-7 **85**.......... GeorgeBaker 2 — 85
(P Mitchell) *hld up last: clsd steadily on ldrs 2f out: rdn and nt qckn over 1f out: one pce after* **20/1**

1650 **6** 6 **Jebel Ali (IRE)**[20] [2404] 3-8-8 **77**.......... JamesDoyle[(5)] 4 — 65
(B Gubby) *w ldr: hrd rdn wl over 2f out: wknd rapidly jst over 1f out* **9/1**

-060 **7** 5 **Your Amount (IRE)**[24] [2290] 3-8-8 **72** ow2.......... JDSmith 5 — 51
(A King) *trckd ldrs: rdn wl over 2f out: sn wknd* **25/1**

-215 **8** nk **Just Observing**[23] [2324] 3-8-13 **77**..........(v[1]) JamieSpencer 3 — 55
(E A L Dunlop) *trckd ldrs: rdn and lost pl whn hmpd on inner 3f out: no ch after* **4/1**[2]

2m 7.44s (-0.35) **Going Correction** +0.075s/f (Slow) 8 Ran SP% **114.8**

Speed ratings (Par 101):104,103,101,101,100 96,92,91

CSF £20.84 CT £91.78 TOTE £9.30: £1.70, £1.20, £3.60; EX 31.20.

Owner Mrs P W Harris **Bred** Pendley Farm **Trained** Aldbury, Herts

FOCUS

A decent three-year-old handicap and the winning time was almost three seconds quicker than the following contest over the same trip. The form looks sound, with the first four showing improvement.

Stotsfold ◆ Official explanation: trainer's rep said, regarding the improved form shown, the gelding was very green and had improved with every run

3016 SURREY ROYAL BRITISH LEGION H'CAP — 1m 2f (P)
5:00 (5:04) (Class 6) (0-55,55) 3-Y-0 **£2,388** (£705; £352) **Stalls** Low

Form | RPR

-006 **1** **Dance A Daydream**[14] [2591] 3-9-6 **53**.......... JamieSpencer 8 — 61+
(J R Fanshawe) *settled midfield: rdn over 3f out: prog over 2f out: drvn to ld last 150yds: immediately hung rt, idled and hmpd runner-up:* **11/2**[2]

0-13 **2** ¾ **Carlton Scroop (FR)**[65] [1221] 3-9-6 **53**..........(b) ShaneKelly 9 — 58+
(J Jay) *reluctant to enter stalls: settled midfield: effrt on outer over 2f out: str run to cl on wnr whn hmpd 100yds out: nt rcvr* **11/2**[2]

6-03 **3** 1 ½ **Million All Day (IRE)**[22] [2352] 3-9-6 **53**.......... SteveDrowne 7 — 53
(W R Muir) *trckd ldrs: rdn over 2f out: nt qckn over 1f out: styd on same pce fnl f* **4/1**[1]

-000 **4** hd **Polish Welcome**[20] [2391] 3-9-7 **54**.......... SebSanders 4 — 54
(S C Williams) *hld up midfield: prog to trck ldrs over 2f out: rdn and effrt over 1f out: kpt on same pce* **10/1**

0565 **5** ½ **Sky At Night (IRE)**[5] [2861] 3-9-4 **51**..........(v[1]) DaneO'Neill 2 — 50
(P Mitchell) *dwlt: towards rr: drvn and effrt on inner over 2f out: styd on fr over 1f out: nt pce to threaten* **10/1**

-005 **6** ½ **Pactolos Way**[63] [1269] 3-9-8 **55**.......... GeorgeBaker 10 — 53
(P R Chamings) *pressed ldrs: rdn over 3f out: effrt u.p to ld over 1f out: hdd & wknd last 150yds* **10/1**

0000 **7** ½ **Mamichor**[12] [2644] 3-9-3 **50**.......... FergusSweeney 12 — 47
(J R Boyle) *hld up in rr: rdn and effrt whn nt clr run over 2f out: keeping on whn nt clr run 1f out: nt rch ldrs* **33/1**

0000 **8** 1 **Earth Master (IRE)**[19] [2466] 3-9-3 **50**..........(b) PatDobbs 3 — 45
(S Kirk) *mde most to over 1f out: stl nrly upsides ent fnl f: wknd rapidly* **33/1**

0406 **9** 3 **Perfect Order (USA)**[9] [2727] 3-9-6 **53**..........(p) OscarUrbina 11 — 43
(N A Callaghan) *s.s: hld up in last: shkn up over 2f out: nvr on terms* **14/1**

00-6 **10** 3 ½ **Moyoko (IRE)**[11] [2678] 3-9-5 **52**.......... FrancisNorton 1 — 35
(M Blanshard) *racd midfield: drvn on inner wl over 2f out: no imp and hld whn hmpd 1f out* **20/1**

0002 **11** 1 **It's Basil**[12] [2646] 3-9-6 **53**..........(b) JimmyQuinn 5 — 34
(R M Flower) *t.k.h: w ldr: drvn over 2f out: wknd rapidly over 1f out* **8/1**[3]

5555 **12** 1 ¾ **Shannon House**[9] [2730] 3-9-7 **54**.......... VinceSlattery 6 — 32
(M J McGrath) *hld up wl in rr: hrd rdn and no prog over 2f out* **14/1**

0005 **13** 17 **Musical Chimes**[14] [2575] 3-9-3 **50**.......... HayleyTurner 14 — —
(C A Cyzer) *t.k.h: pressed ldr to over 3f out: wkng rapidly whn hmpd over 2f out: t.o* **33/1**

0-00 **14** 1 ¾ **Vinska (USA)**[6] [2814] 3-9-6 **53**.......... AlanMunro 13 — —
(J W Hills) *restrained s: hld up in rr: brief effrt on outer 4f out: wknd 3f out: t.o* **25/1**

2m 10.35s (2.56) **Going Correction** +0.075s/f (Slow) 14 Ran SP% **119.9**

Speed ratings (Par 97):92,91,90,90,89 89,88,88,85,82 82,80,67,65

CSF £33.29 CT £133.38 TOTE £5.30: £2.10, £1.80, £2.10; EX 37.10.

Owner Cheveley Park Stud **Bred** Cheveley Park Stud Ltd **Trained** Newmarket, Suffolk

FOCUS

A modest winning time for the type of race, almost three seconds slower than the preceding handicap over the same trip. A modest race in which the form looks sound with both the first two capable of better.

Dance A Daydream Official explanation: trainer's rep said, regarding the improved form shown, the filly may have benefited from running on an all-weather surface
Mamichor Official explanation: jockey said gelding was denied clear run
It's Basil Official explanation: jockey said gelding had no more to give
Vinska(USA) Official explanation: jockey said saddle slipped

3017 POPPY SUPORT H'CAP — 1m 4f (P)
5:30 (5:32) (Class 6) (0-60,66) 3-Y-O — **£3,238** (£963; £481; £240) **Stalls** Low

Form — RPR
4164 **1** **Rahy's Crown (USA)**[14] 2592 3-9-7 **60** PatDobbs 13 — 71
(R Hannon) *dwlt: hld up wl in rr: prog over 4f out: rdn to chse clr ldr over 2f out: clsd to ld last 100yds* **6/1**[3]
-001 **2** *1 1/4* **Desert Sea (IRE)**[7] 2795 3-9-13 **66** 6ex FergusSweeney 8 — 75+
(C Tinkler) *rrd stalls and dwlt: sn trckd ldrs: led gng easily wl over 3f out: clr over 2f out: hdd & wknd last 100yds* **9/4**[1]
5605 **3** *1/2* **Plemont Bay**[22] 2352 3-9-4 **57** JamieSpencer 16 — 66
(M L W Bell) *hld up wl in rr: prog on outer over 3f out: drvn to chse ldng pair 2f out: tried to cl but nt qckn fnl f* **12/1**
5006 **4** *3 1/2* **Life Peer**[37] 1925 3-9-0 **56** (p) NeilChalmers(3) 15 — 59
(J G Portman) *hld up wl in rr: plenty to do over 3f out: drvn and styd on wl after: no ch of rching ldng trio* **20/1**
00-0 **5** *5* **The Spread**[26] 2220 3-9-4 **57** FrancisNorton 2 — 52
(M Blanshard) *dwlt: settled towards rr: lost tch w ldrs over 3f out: plugged on* **33/1**
-002 **6** *1/2* **Travolta**[22] 2352 3-8-13 **55** AdamKirby(3) 7 — 49
(C G Cox) *led for 3f: pressed ldr tl led over 4f out to wl over 3f out: sn hrd rdn and wknd* **4/1**[2]
0405 **7** *2* **Constant Cheers (IRE)**[14] 2569 3-9-6 **59** (p) AlanMunro 5 — 50
(W R Swinburn) *trckd ldrs: rdn over 3f out: steadily wknd fr over 2f out* **10/1**
0-00 **8** *3 1/2* **The Struie**[37] 1925 3-9-7 **60** (p) ChrisCatlin 14 — 45
(E F Vaughan) *hld up wl in rr: sme prog on outer over 4f out: lost tch w ldrs over 3f out: no ch after* **25/1**
3023 **9** *1/2* **Iberian Light (USA)**[10] 2713 3-9-1 **59** (b) JerryO'Dwyer(5) 9 — 44
(N A Callaghan) *prom: chsd ldng pair wl over 3f out to wl over 2f out: wknd u.p* **15/2**
-050 **10** *20* **Muckle**[14] 2591 3-9-2 **55** ShaneKelly 1 — 8
(S C Williams) *hld up in midfield: lost tch over 3f out: eased over 1f out: t.o* **20/1**
-200 **11** *4* **Left Hand Drive**[59] 1350 3-8-9 **55** (t) KevinGhunowa(7) 3 — 1
(B W Duke) *sn drvn in last: nvr gng wl: t.o* **33/1**
0-00 **12** *hd* **Hope's Eternal**[22] 2352 3-9-3 **56** JamieMackay 6 — 2
(J L Dunlop) *trckd ldrs: rdn 5f out: sn wknd: t.o* **33/1**
-300 **13** *3* **Cartoonist (IRE)**[7] 2795 3-9-4 **57** DaneO'Neill 4 — —
(A King) *rousted along sn after s: led after 3f to over 4f out: wknd rapidly: t.o* **25/1**
0 **14** *10* **Alevisia (FR)**[27] 2188 3-9-2 **55** VinceSlattery 11 — —
(Noel T Chance) *nvr beyond midfield: wknd 5f out: t.o* **66/1**
40-0 **15** *3* **Al Dhahab (USA)**[22] 2350 3-9-6 **59** OscarUrbina 12 — —
(C E Brittain) *t.k.h: cl up tl wknd rapidly over 4f out: t.o* **25/1**

2m 34.12s (-0.27) **Going Correction** +0.075s/f (Slow) **15** Ran SP% **125.0**
Speed ratings (Par 97):103,102,101,99,96 95,94,92,91,78 75,75,73,67,65
CSF £17.91 CT £167.41 TOTE £7.60: £2.30, £1.70, £2.70; EX 22.20 Place 6 £117.52, Place 5 £28.26.
Owner Jaber Abdullah **Bred** Gainsborough Stud Management Llc **Trained** East Everleigh, Wilts

FOCUS
A competitive middle-distance handicap for the grade and the winning time was decent for a race of its type. The form should prove reliable at this level.
Al Dhahab(USA) Official explanation: jockey said filly lost a front shoe
T/Plt: £498.10 to a £1 stake. Pool: £36,713.15. 53.80 winning tickets. T/Qpdt: £7.90 to a £1 stake. Pool: £3,967.40. 368.00 winning tickets. JN

1756 NEWCASTLE (L-H)
Thursday, June 29
OFFICIAL GOING: Good to firm (good in places)
Wind: Slight, behind

3018 NEXENT MAIDEN AUCTION STKS — 6f
2:20 (2:21) (Class 5) 2-Y-O — **£4,533** (£1,348; £674; £336) **Stalls** High

Form — RPR
6 **1** **Charlie Tipple**[22] 2361 2-8-11 MickyFenton 10 — 70
(T D Easterby) *chsd ldrs stands side: hdwy over 2f out: rdn to ld wl over 1f out: kpt on* **10/3**[1]
0 **2** *2 1/2* **Sir Charles**[13] 2623 2-8-10 ow1 FergalLynch 8 — 62
(M Dods) *in tch: stands side: hdwy wl over 2f out: sn rdn and styd on fnl f* **7/1**[3]
0 **3** *hd* **Storm Mission (USA)**[19] 2432 2-8-13 DominicFox(3) 13 — 67
(Miss V Haigh) *prom stands side: hdwy to ld that gp and overall ldr 2f out: sn rdn and hdd: kpt on same pce fnl f* **33/1**
24 **4** *1 1/2* **Intersky Sports (USA)**[16] 2523 2-8-11 NCallan 14 — 57
(K A Ryan) *overall ldr stands side: rdn along and hdd 2f out: sn drvn and wknd appr last* **9/2**[2]
5 *1/2* **Grand Art (IRE)** 2-8-13 LDettori 5 — 58+
(M H Tompkins) *trckd ldng pair far side: hdwy 1/2-way: rdn to ld that gp wl over 1f out: sn one pce* **7/1**[3]
5 **6** *1/2* **Ishetoo**[16] 2523 2-8-8 DanielTudhope(3) 9 — 54
(A Dickman) *chsd ldrs stands side: rdn along wl over 2f out: sn one pce* **16/1**
7 *1/2* **Mandy's Maestro (USA)** 2-8-9 MichaelJStainton(7) 16 — 58
(R M Whitaker) *in tch stands side: rdn along 1/2-way: no imp fnl 2f* **15/2**
0 **8** *nk* **Imperial Beach (USA)**[13] 2623 2-8-13 PaulFessey 12 — 54
(T D Barron) *s.i.s and towards rr stands side tl sme late hdwy* **10/1**
0 **9** *2* **Soviet Sound (IRE)**[20] 2409 2-8-13 PaulMulrennan 2 — 48+
(Jedd O'Keeffe) *chsd ldr far side: hdwy to ld that gp b riefly 2f out: sn hdd & wknd* **40/1**
0 **10** *4* **Fire Alarm**[47] 1664 2-8-9 TonyHamilton 7 — 32
(J J Quinn) *a towards rr stands side* **20/1**
0 **11** *1 1/2* **Ruthles Philly**[47] 1664 2-8-8 RobertWinston 6 — 27+
(D W Barker) *led far side gp: rdn along and hdd 2f out: sn wknd* **40/1**
12 *6* **Artificial** 2-8-11 DaleGibson 3 — 12+
(T D Easterby) *a towards rr far side* **20/1**
13 *1 3/4* **Finlay's Footsteps** 2-8-11 TomEaves 1 — 6+
(G M Moore) *a towards rr far side* **33/1**
14 *3* **Darcy's Pride (IRE)** 2-8-4 RoystonFfrench 15 — —
(D W Barker) *s.i.s: a bhd stands side* **33/1**
15 *15* **Hesaguru (IRE)** 2-8-13 DeanMcKeown 4 — —
(J R Norton) *in tch far side: pushed along and wknd 1/2-way: sn bhd* **50/1**

1m 14.51s (-0.58) **Going Correction** -0.25s/f (Firm) **15** Ran SP% **118.2**
Speed ratings (Par 93):93,89,89,87,86 86,85,85,82,77 75,67,64,60,40
CSF £22.90 TOTE £3.80: £1.60, £2.50, £15.50; EX 16.00 TRIFECTA Not won..
Owner Norman Jackson **Bred** P Wyatt And Ranby Hall **Trained** Great Habton, N Yorks

FOCUS
An ordinary maiden in which the field split in two and those who raced stands' side held the call. Not easy to set the level of the form, but the winner stepped up from his debut.

NOTEBOOK
Charlie Tipple took the eye on his debut despite only finishing sixth of nine, and he was nicely backed to go in second time up. His stable's juveniles invariably improve for their debut outings and he ran out a clear winner. He can do better again in time. (op 9-2 tchd 5-1 in a place)
Sir Charles, staying on at the end of his race over five furlongs on his debut, appreciated this longer trip and looks one for modest nurseries after one more run. (op 9-2)
Storm Mission(USA), who is a half-brother to several winners, notably Oaks winner Jet Ski Lady, ran better than his market position suggested he would. He is progressing along the right lines.
Intersky Sports(USA) showed good speed but once again found a few too strong. He will soon be able to run in nursery company and that avenue may prove more suitable. (op 5-1)
Grand Art(IRE), whose dam is a half-sister to six winners, was first home from the group which raced on the far side. He did best of the newcomers and is entitled to improve. (op 11-2)
Ishetoo did not really build on the modest promise he showed on his debut.

3019 KNOWLEDGE I.T. SILVER ANNIVERSARY H'CAP — 2m 19y
2:50 (2:50) (Class 4) (0-80,74) 4-Y-O+
£6,232 (£1,866; £933; £467; £233; £117) **Stalls** Centre

Form
0033 **1** **Mister Arjay (USA)**[6] 2828 6-8-6 **59** TomEaves 7 — 68
(B Ellison) *chsd clr ldr: hdwy over 4f out: rdn over 2f out: styd on to ld appr last: drvn and kpt on wl* **9/2**[2]
2033 **2** *1/2* **Oddsmaker (IRE)**[5] 2853 5-8-10 **63** (t) NCallan 8 — 71
(M A Barnes) *hld up in rr: hdwy on inner 4f out: swtchd rt and effrt 2f out: rdn to chse wnr ent last: sn drvn and kpt on* **10/1**
3 *1* **Behlaya (IRE)**[64] 931 5-9-7 **74** DavidAllan 3 — 81
(T D Easterby) *hld up: hdwy 4f out: effrt and n.m.r over 2f out: sn rdn and hdwy over 1f out: styd on ins last: nrst fin* **20/1**
4-36 **4** *2* **Lady Misha**[147] 270 4-8-5 **58** DaleGibson 5 — 62
(Jedd O'Keeffe) *chsd ldng pair: hdwy 4f out: rdn over 2f out: drvn over 1f out and kpt on same pce* **33/1**
0050 **5** *4* **Rule For Ever**[26] 2219 4-8-8 **61** (v[1]) JoeFanning 2 — 61
(M Johnston) *led and sn clr: rdn along 5f out: drvn over 2f out: hdd over 1f out and sn wknd* **14/1**
1 **6** *2 1/2* **Mulligan's Pride (IRE)**[16] 2528 5-8-8 **61** DeanMcKeown 6 — 58
(G A Swinbank) *hld up towards rr: hdwy over 5f out: rdn along wl over 2f out: sn btn* **12/1**
003- **7** *2* **Double Vodka (IRE)**[41] 5792 5-9-1 **68** TonyHamilton 1 — 62
(C Grant) *a towards rr* **12/1**
1005 **8** *1 3/4* **Celtic Carisma**[5] 2871 4-8-2 **55** PaulFessey 9 — 47
(K G Reveley) *chsd ldrs: rdn along over 3f out: sn wknd* **7/1**[3]
432 **9** *54* **Accordello (IRE)**[41] 1827 5-8-7 **60** RobertWinston 4 — —
(K G Reveley) *trckd ldrs: hdwy over 5f out: rdn along 3f out: lost action and wknd over 2f out: virtually p.u* **5/4**[1]

3m 32.17s (-3.03) **Going Correction** -0.15s/f (Firm) **9** Ran SP% **114.0**
Speed ratings (Par 105):101,100,100,99,97 96,95,94,67
CSF £47.86 CT £809.60 TOTE £5.50: £1.50, £3.10, £5.80; EX 56.60 Trifecta £301.60 Part won. Pool: £424.85 - 0.10 winning tickets..
Owner Keith Middleton **Bred** Barbara Hunter **Trained** Norton, N Yorks

FOCUS
A 0-80 staying handicap but the top-weight raced off just 74 and, with the favourite failing to run her race, it proved a modest affair. It has been rated through the runner-up.
Accordello(IRE) Official explanation: jockey said mare lost her action

3020 GNER 10TH BIRTHDAY SEATON DELAVAL TROPHY H'CAP — 1m 3y(S)
3:20 (3:23) (Class 2) (0-100,97) 4-Y-O+
£18,696 (£5,598; £2,799; £1,401; £699; £351) **Stalls** High

Form — RPR
2434 **1** **Flipando (IRE)**[13] 2614 5-8-13 **89** PaulFessey 1 — 99
(T D Barron) *hld up towards rr: gd hdwy on inner 2f out: rdn ent last: qcknd wl to ld last 100 yds* **9/2**[2]
166- **2** *1* **Bolodenka (IRE)**[264] 5743 4-8-5 **81** TonyHamilton 5 — 89
(R A Fahey) *hld up: gd hdwy over 2f out: swtchd lft and rdn to chal over 1f out: ev ch ins last: nt qckn towards fin* **7/1**
6250 **3** *shd* **Hartshead**[12] 2657 7-8-9 **90** AndrewElliott(5) 6 — 98
(G A Swinbank) *trckd ldng pair: effrt 2f out: swtchd lft and rdn over 1f out: led ins last: drvn: hdd and nt qckn last 100 yds* **8/1**
5001 **4** *1 1/2* **Blue Trojan (IRE)**[13] 2603 6-8-2 **78** NickyMackay 7 — 82
(S Kirk) *trckd ldr: hdwy 2f out: sn rdn and ch over 1f out: drvn and one pce ins last* **15/2**
0-30 **5** *hd* **Langford**[8] 2742 6-9-7 **97** LDettori 8 — 101
(M H Tompkins) *led: qcknd 3f out: rdn 2f out: edgd lft over 1f out: hdd & wknd ins last* **11/4**[1]
4-10 **6** *1 1/4* **Rio Riva**[12] 2657 4-9-5 **95** RobertWinston 9 — 96
(Miss J A Camacho) *hld up in rr: hdwy over 2f out: rdn and n.m.r over 1f out: wknd* **6/1**[3]
-005 **7** *1 1/4* **Doric (USA)**[20] 2405 5-8-7 **83** PatCosgrave 4 — 81
(B Ellison) *hld up towards rr: hdwy 2f out: rdn over 1f out: wknd ent last* **11/1**
5422 **8** *5* **Gaelic Princess**[4] 2892 6-8-2 **78** oh1 JoeFanning 2 — 65
(A G Newcombe) *hld up towards rr: hdwy on outer over 2f out: rdn wl over 1f out: sn btn* **12/1**
-000 **9** *nk* **Artistic Style**[31] 2079 6-9-0 **90** TomEaves 3 — 76
(B Ellison) *chsd ldrs: rdn along over 2fr out: sn wknd* **25/1**

1m 40.27s (-1.63) **Going Correction** -0.25s/f (Firm) **9** Ran SP% **114.4**
Speed ratings (Par 109):98,97,96,95,95 93,92,87,87
CSF £35.56 CT £244.74 TOTE £6.40: £1.60, £3.00, £3.40; EX 50.50 Trifecta £172.70 Pool: £520.59 - 2.14 winning tickets..
Owner Mrs J Hazell **Bred** Denis McDonnell **Trained** Maunby, N Yorks

FOCUS
A decent handicap and the form looks sound enough. The winner has been very consistent and deserved this.

NOTEBOOK
Flipando(IRE) finally broke a 14-race losing streak and picked up well when the gap opened up next to the rail in the final furlong. He is the type who needs everything to drop right, though, and he remains more of an each-way bet than a win-only type. (op 6-1)
Bolodenka(IRE) is another who likes the race to fall into his lap late off a good pace. A winner first time out last season, he was having his first start for Richard Fahey on this seasonal reappearance and again showed he can go well fresh. (op 6-1)
Hartshead has slipped slightly in the handicap but he remains on a mark which leaves him vulnerable. This was a solid effort in defeat, though. (op 9-1)
Blue Trojan(IRE) normally competes in lower grade than this and he found the competition tougher than at Chepstow earlier in the month. (tchd 8-1)
Langford, who ran well on the wrong side in the Royal Hunt Cup, may have found this race coming too soon after that big effort eight days earlier. (op 3-1)
Rio Riva settled better this time but he was still below the form he showed on his reappearance, albeit he is now on a 7lb higher mark. (op 15-2)

3021 EUROPEAN BREEDERS FUND/GNER GO RACING HOPPINGS STKS (LISTED RACE) (F&M) 1m 2f 32y
3:50 (3:51) (Class 1) 3-Y-O+ **£17,034** (£6,456; £3,231; £1,611; £807) **Stalls** Centre

Form RPR
322- **1** **Pictavia (IRE)**[284] 5347 4-9-5 107 LDettori 1 105+
(Saeed Bin Suroor) *mde all: qcknd over 2f out: rdn wl over 1f out: styd on strly fnl f* **10/11**[1]
-111 **2** *1 ¼* **Reem Three**[12] 2659 3-8-7 91 NickyMackay 5 101
(L M Cumani) *keen: trckd ldng pair: effrt over 2f out: swtchd rt and rdn over 1f out: kpt on u.p ins last* **11/8**[2]
10 **3** *6* **Missisipi Star (IRE)**[14] 2582 3-8-7 MCHussey 2 89
(Eamon Tyrrell, Ire) *hld up: hdwy over 3f out: rdn to chse ldng pair and edgd lft over 1f out: sn one pce* **33/1**
20-0 **4** *5* **Whazzat**[126] 4-9-5 RobertWinston 4 80
(P W Chapple-Hyam) *dwlt: sn chsng wnr: rdn along wl over 2f out: drvn and wknd wl over 1f out* **9/1**[3]
4 **5** *2 ½* **Penfection (IRE)**[33] 2043 3-8-8 89 ow1 (t) NCallan 3 76
(M Botti) *hld up: effrt and hdwy to chse ldrs over 2f out: sn rdn and wknd fr wl over 1f out* **40/1**

2m 7.95s (-3.85) **Going Correction** -0.15s/f (Firm)
WFA 3 from 4yo 12lb 5 Ran SP% **109.9**
Speed ratings (Par 111):109,108,103,99,97
CSF £2.38 TOTE £1.70: £1.30, £1.20; EX 2.90.
Owner Godolphin **Bred** Gainsborough Stud Management L **Trained** Newmarket, Suffolk

FOCUS
Not the most competitive Listed race ever seen, but a welcome return to the winner's enclosure for last year's Oaks third Pictavia. The runner-up continues to progress.

NOTEBOOK
Pictavia(IRE), third in the 2005 Oaks, was having her first start for Godolphin and missing the headgear she wore for the second half of last year. She had easily the best form on offer and won as the adjusted ratings suggested she would. This should have done her confidence some good and connections will now be keen to get her back competing in Group company. (op 11-10 tchd 6-5)
Reem Three, a progressive filly who notched the last of a hat-trick of wins in a handicap off 87 last time, earned some well-deserved black type on her first outing in Listed company. She had 16lb to find with the favourite on adjusted official ratings, but she kept her up to her work and, as a comparatively lightly-raced three-year-old, she can improve further. (op 5-4 tchd 6-4)
Missisipi Star(IRE) did not seem to get this trip last time out but she was later reported to have been in season so that may have been misleading. She ran a fair race this time given that she was up against it at the weights. (op 20-1)
Whazzat was a smart two-year-old but decent performances since have been few and far between. Having her first outing for four months and making her debut for her new stable, she once again ran below her best. (op 10-1 tchd 8-1)
Penfection(IRE), tongue tied for the first time on her first start outside Italy, was out of her depth. (op 33-1)

3022 PIMMS CLAIMING STKS 1m 4f 93y
4:20 (4:20) (Class 6) 3-Y-O+ **£2,590** (£770; £385; £192) **Stalls** Low

Form RPR
2652 **1** **Fort Churchill (IRE)**[2] 2944 5-9-10 66 (bt) TomEaves 10 74+
(B Ellison) *trckd ldng pair: smooth hdwy 3f out: led on bit 2f out: qcknd clr over 1f out: easily* **9/4**[1]
5436 **2** *6* **Donna's Double**[15] 2546 11-9-4 51 (p) PaulFessey 4 58
(Karen McLintock) *hld up: hdwy over 4f out: rdn over 2f out: kpt on ins last* **14/1**
3134 **3** *½* **Oldenway**[2] 2944 7-9-13 70 TonyHamilton 9 66
(R A Fahey) *cl up: effrt to ld wl over 2f out: sn rdn and hdd 2f out: one pce* **5/2**[2]
0-00 **4** *5* **Loaded Gun**[10] 2696 6-8-12 46 AndrewElliott(5) 6 48
(W Storey) *chsd ldrs: rdn along over 3f out: sn drvn and outpcd fnl 2f* **66/1**
00-0 **5** *3* **Sun King**[18] 1562 9-9-5 54 (t) JamesReveley(7) 5 52
(K G Reveley) *hld up towards rr: sme hdwy on outer over 3f out: nvr a factor* **16/1**
4063 **6** *4* **Monash Lad (IRE)**[10] 2696 4-9-8 64 LDettori 2 42
(M H Tompkins) *hld up: a towards rr* **8/1**
0025 **7** *12* **Khanjar (USA)**[1] 2975 6-9-13 75 (p) PatCosgrave 7 28
(K R Burke) *led: rdn along over 3f out: hdd wl over 2f out: sn wknd* **11/4**[3]
0-60 **8** *hd* **Ronnies Lad**[6] 2832 4-9-0 42 DuranFentiman(5) 8 19
(J R Norton) *midfield: rdn along over 4f out and sn wknd* **100/1**
0 **9** *15* **Auburndale**[59] 1343 4-9-9 PJMcDonald(5) 1 4
(A Crook) *a rr* **150/1**
-005 **10** *36* **Fox Flight (IRE)**[20] 2398 3-8-3 17 (p) RoystonFfrench 3 —
(D W Barker) *chsd ldrs 4f: sn lost pl and bhd fr 1/2-way* **200/1**

2m 40.11s (-3.44) **Going Correction** -0.15s/f (Firm)
WFA 3 from 4yo+ 14lb 10 Ran SP% **113.3**
Speed ratings (Par 101):105,101,100,97,95 92,84,84,74,50
CSF £34.06 TOTE £3.50: £1.50, £2.90, £1.20; EX 26.50 Trifecta £105.60 Pool: £464.35 - 3.12 winning tickets..The winner was the subject of a friendly claim.
Owner Benton And Partners **Bred** P H Betts **Trained** Norton, N Yorks

FOCUS
Very few could be fancied in this fair claimer, which has been rated through the runner-up.

3023 WOODFORD GROUP PLC H'CAP 7f
4:50 (4:50) (Class 5) (0-75,75) 3-Y-O **£4,857** (£1,445; £722; £360) **Stalls** High

Form RPR
6011 **1** **Electric Warrior (IRE)**[4] 2896 3-9-8 75 6ex PatCosgrave 6 85+
(K R Burke) *hld up in tch: smooth hdwy on inner over 2f out: rdn to chal ent last: sn led: drvn and kpt on wl towards fin* **15/8**[1]
1635 **2** *nk* **Viva Volta**[24] 2297 3-9-1 68 DavidAllan 3 77
(T D Easterby) *led after 1f: pushed along 2f out: rdn and edgd lft ent last: sn hdd: drvn and ev ch tl no ex towards fin* **11/2**
6-30 **3** *3* **The Terrier**[41] 1812 3-9-5 72 NCallan 2 73
(G A Swinbank) *hld up: hdwy over 2f out: sn rdn and kpt on same pce fnl f* **12/1**
0420 **4** *nk* **Quaker Boy**[24] 2284 3-8-4 57 PaulFessey 5 57
(M Dods) *trckd ldrs: hdwy to chse ldr 2f out: sn rdn and wknd ent last* **12/1**
160 **5** *¾* **La Matanza**[12] 2642 3-9-4 74 BenSwarbrick(3) 7 72
(T D Barron) *hld up in rr: hdwy 2f out: rdn and kpt on ins last: nrst fin* **16/1**
0-02 **6** *shd* **Ours (IRE)**[16] 2525 3-8-10 63 LDettori 4 61
(J D Bethell) *hld up in rr: hdwy over 2f out: sn rdn and no imp* **7/2**[2]
4-52 **7** *nk* **Superior Star**[59] 1345 3-8-9 62 TonyHamilton 8 59
(R A Fahey) *led 1f: chsd ldr tl rdn along over 2f out and grad wknd* **4/1**[3]
0-00 **8** *4* **Roonah (FR)**[153] 211 3-8-4 57 RoystonFfrench 1 44
(Karen McLintock) *chsd ldrs: pushed along 1/2-way: sn rdn and wknd wl over 2f out* **66/1**

1m 25.31s (-4.69) **Going Correction** -0.25s/f (Firm) 8 Ran SP% **115.1**
Speed ratings (Par 99):105,104,101,100,100 99,99,95
CSF £12.84 CT £96.39 TOTE £2.70: £1.40, £1.50, £2.10; EX 19.90 Trifecta £77.00 Pool: £459.32 - 4.23 winning tickets. Place 6 £59.56, Place 5 £27.23.
Owner Market Avenue Racing Club Ltd **Bred** Limestone Stud **Trained** Middleham Moor, N Yorks

FOCUS
An ordinary handicap but the winner is a progressive three-year-old and the form looks solid.
T/Plt: £76.80 to a £1 stake. Pool: £51,090.15. 485.40 winning tickets. T/Qpdt: £5.80 to a £1 stake. Pool: £4,035.00. 509.40 winning tickets. JR

2984 SALISBURY (R-H)
Thursday, June 29

OFFICIAL GOING: Good (good to firm in places; good to firm on the loop)
Wind: Virtually nil

3024 GAMEBOOKER.COM H'CAP 1m 1f 198y
2:10 (2:10) (Class 5) (0-70,70) 4-Y-O+ **£3,562** (£1,059; £529; £264) **Stalls** High

Form RPR
0040 **1** **Eldorado**[16] 2534 5-9-2 65 JimmyFortune 7 75
(S Kirk) *chsd ldrs: hrd rdn to ld but hung lft over 1f out: kpt on: drvn out* **5/1**[2]
6043 **2** *1* **Danger Zone**[12] 2647 4-9-6 69 (p) IanMongan 8 77
(Mrs A J Perrett) *hld up in last trio: sltly outpcd 3f out: styd on fr over 1f out: wnt 2nd fnl strides* **5/1**[2]
0002 **3** *hd* **Consonant (IRE)**[14] 2585 9-9-0 66 DNolan(3) 6 74
(D G Bridgwater) *in tch: rdn over 2f out: chsd wnr jst ins fnl f: kpt on but no ex whn ct for 2nd fnl strides* **9/1**
1004 **4** *1 ¾* **Thorny Mandate**[10] 2707 4-9-0 63 StephenCarson 2 67
(R F Johnson Houghton) *s.i.s: sn in tch: rdn over 3f out: wnt 2nd briefly 1f out: kpt on same pce* **10/1**
-430 **5** *4* **Queen Of Iceni**[19] 2460 4-9-7 70 (v) TedDurcan 9 67
(J L Dunlop) *trckd ldr: led 3f out: sn rdn: edgd lft and hdd over 1f out: wknd* **4/1**[1]
-020 **6** *½* **Scutch Mill (IRE)**[17] 2508 4-9-1 64 (t) RyanMoore 3 60
(Karen George) *hld up in last pair: rdn wl over 2f out: one pce fnl f* **15/2**[3]
0004 **7** *1* **Rosiella**[14] 2568 4-7-11 51 oh10 (t) LiamJones(5) 4 45
(M Appleby) *s.i.s: hld up last: rdn over 4f out: no imp* **66/1**
-504 **8** *1 ½* **Garibaldi (GER)**[11] 2351 4-9-5 68 LPKeniry 5 59
(D R C Elsworth) *chsd ldrs on outer: rdn over 3f out: wknd over 1f out* **5/1**[2]
4000 **9** *¾* **Oakley Absolute**[20] 2401 4-8-13 62 RichardHughes 1 52
(R Hannon) *reminders and sn swtchd rt to ld: rdn over 3f out: sn hdd and edgd lft: wknd over 1f out* **9/1**

2m 9.42s (0.96) **Going Correction** -0.05s/f (Good) 9 Ran SP% **112.3**
Speed ratings (Par 103):94,93,93,91,88 88,87,86,85
CSF £29.13 CT £215.47 TOTE £6.70: £1.70, £1.70, £2.90; EX 40.70.
Owner S J McCay **Bred** Miss K Rausing **Trained** Upper Lambourn, Berks

FOCUS
A modest handicap, run at no more than a fair pace, and the first four came clear. The form is not strong and might not work out.
Eldorado Official explanation: trainer's representative had no explanation for the improved form shown

3025 HERBERT AND GWEN BLAGRAVE EBF MAIDEN STKS (C&G) 6f 212y
2:40 (2:42) (Class 4) 2-Y-O **£6,477** (£1,927; £963; £481) **Stalls** Centre

Form RPR
30 **1** **Dubai Magic (USA)**[13] 2619 2-9-0 RichardMullen 8 76
(C E Brittain) *set stdy pce: hdd over 2f out: sn rdn: r.o again to ld fnl 75yds: rdn out* **13/2**[3]
2 *nk* **Spring Is Here (FR)** 2-9-0 RyanMoore 3 76+
(R Hannon) *prom: led over 2f out and qcknd pce: sn rdn: flyj. path 100yds out: sn hdd: no ex* **8/1**
3 *3* **Raffaas** 2-9-0 MartinDwyer 6 68
(M P Tregoning) *s.i.s: blkd after 50yds: towards rr: rdn 3f out: styd on fr over 1f out: wnt 3rd jst ins fnl f* **9/4**[1]
4 *3* **Princeton (IRE)** 2-8-11 EdwardCreighton(3) 5 60
(M R Channon) *trckd ldrs: rdn over 2f out: kpt on same pce* **16/1**
5 *½* **Eglevski (IRE)** 2-9-0 IanMongan 4 59
(J L Dunlop) *unruly stalls: trckd ldrs: rdn over 2f out: kpt on same pce* **20/1**
6 *2 ½* **Altar (IRE)** 2-9-0 RichardHughes 11 52
(R Hannon) *s.i.s: sltly hmpd after 50yds: hld up: rdn over 2f out: wknd fnl f* **4/1**[2]
7 *¾* **Love Brothers** 2-9-0 TedDurcan 1 50+
(M R Channon) *w ldr: n.m.r over 2f out: sn rdn: wknd fnl f* **10/1**
6 **8** *shd* **Ron In Ernest**[16] 2530 2-9-0 RichardThomas 7 50
(J A Geake) *prom: rdn over 2f out: wknd 1f out* **12/1**
0 **9** *¾* **Numerical (IRE)**[20] 2402 2-9-0 TPQueally 12 48
(J L Dunlop) *in tch: rdn over 2f out: hung lft over 1f out: wknd* **12/1**
10 *1 ¼* **Nightinshining (IRE)** 2-9-0 TonyCulhane 2 45+
(A King) *s.i.s: stmbld after 4f: a towards rr* **16/1**
11 *13* **Bathwick Breeze** 2-9-0 PaulFitzsimons 10 11
(B R Millman) *rn green: sn drvn along: bhd fnl 3f* **33/1**

1m 30.97s (1.91) **Going Correction** -0.05s/f (Good) 11 Ran SP% **119.2**
Speed ratings (Par 95):87,86,83,79,79 76,75,75,74,73 58
CSF £58.54 TOTE £8.80: £2.30, £2.00, £1.60; EX 57.30.

Owner Mohamed Obaida **Bred** Gainsborough Farm Llc **Trained** Newmarket, Suffolk

FOCUS

The form of this juvenile maiden is hard to accurately assess, with just four previous runners in the field, and the first two came clear. The winning time was moderate for the type of race.

NOTEBOOK

Dubai Magic(USA) showed a decent attitude to get back on top inside the final furlong and just did enough to break his duck at the third time of asking. He may have been fortunate that the winner fly-jumped when in front entering the final furlong, but this was still a much-improved effort, and he looks the type to progress as he becomes more streetwise. His future lies with the Handicapper, however. (op 5-1)

Spring Is Here(FR) ◆, who cost 42,000gns as a foal and is related to winners at up to ten furlongs, looked to have the race in safe keeping prior to fly-jumping when in front passing the furlong marker and losing vital momentum. However, this must still rate as a very pleasing debut effort, he was nicely clear of the rest at the finish, and granted the normal improvement he really ought to be placed to strike in the coming weeks. (op 15-2)

Raffaas, whose dam won over ten furlongs at three and was placed in the 1000 Guineas, was all the rage in the betting ahead of this racecourse debut. However, he was always playing catch-up after a sluggish start and never really looked like justifying the strong support. With this experience under his belt, however, he looks assured to go plenty closer next time out. (op 4-1)

Princeton(IRE), whose full-brother Blue Grouse won over this trip at two and whose dam was herself a smart juvenile, looked in need of the run and he emerges with credit in the circumstances.

Altar(IRE), a 44,000gns purchase related to modest winners at up to ten furlongs, proved easy to back and was never really in the hunt following a slow start. He was not given a hard time when his chance evaporated, however, and the fact he holds a Group 1 entry suggests he is thought capable of much better than this. (op 6-1)

3026 AXMINSTER CARPETS AUCTION STKS (CONDITIONS RACE) 6f

3:10 (3:14) (Class 2) 2-Y-0

£14,022 (£4,198; £2,099; £1,050; £524; £263) **Stalls** Centre

Form			Horse	RPR
51	**1**		**Rainbow Mirage (IRE)**[26] 2218 2-8-3 ... RichardMullen 4 (E S McMahon) *chsd ldrs: pushed along over 3f out: rdn to ld ins fnl f: sn hung lft: drvn out* **4/1**[3]	87+
2131	**2**	*1 ¼*	**Karayel (IRE)**[22] 2342 2-8-9 ... RichardHughes 2 (R Hannon) *trckd ldrs: swtchd lft to chal over 1f out: drifted sltly rt jst ins fnl f: no ex* **5/2**[1]	89
62	**3**	*1*	**Cosmopolitan Lady**[6] 2816 2-8-2 ow1 ... MartinDwyer 5 (D M Simcock) *led: rdn over 2f out: hdd ins fnl f: sn swtchd rt: kpt on* **7/1**	79
3211	**4**	*1*	**Grand Prix**[13] 2598 2-8-9 ... RyanMoore 9 (R Hannon) *trckd ldrs: rdn to chal 2f out: cl 4th but hld whn n.m.r fnl 75yds* **11/4**[2]	83
10	**5**	*1*	**Prospect Place**[29] 2127 2-8-9 ow1 ... TonyCulhane 6 (M Dods) *t.k.h bhd ldrs: rdn over 2f out: kpt on same pce fr over 1f out* **25/1**	80
021	**6**	*½*	**Cavort (IRE)**[36] 1930 2-8-3 ... EmmettStack 7 (Pat Eddery) *hld up but in tch: rdn and effrt over 2f out: kpt on same pce fnl f* **10/1**	73
0	**7**	*nk*	**Fongalong**[12] 2631 2-7-13 ... EdwardCreighton 8 (Tom Dascombe) *stdd s but in tch: rdn 2f out: no imp* **125/1**	68?
1233	**8**	*½*	**Spoof Master (IRE)**[24] 2300 2-8-8 ... RobertMiles 1 (W G M Turner) *wnt lft s: sn prom: rdn 2f out: one pce fnl f* **7/1**	75

1m 15.52s (0.54) **Going Correction** -0.05s/f (Good) 8 Ran SP% **114.0**

Speed ratings (Par 99):94,92,91,89,88 87,87,86

CSF £14.33 TOTE £5.50: £1.80, £1.40, £2.00; EX 18.80.

Owner R L Bedding **Bred** Neville O'Byrne And Roderick Ryan **Trained** Hopwas, Staffs

■ Stewards' Enquiry : Martin Dwyer caution: careless riding

FOCUS

A decent conditions event - featuring six previous winners - and the field came home in indian file behind the ready winner. The winner and runner-up's recent wins have worked out well.

NOTEBOOK

Rainbow Mirage(IRE), off the mark at Chepstow 26 days previously, followed up under a fairly confident ride by Mullen. He arrived on the scene full of running approaching the final furlong and, despite hanging when in front late on, ultimately won with authority. He is evidently well thought of by connections, ought to get another furlong in due course, and deserves a crack at a higher grade now. (op 6-1)

Karayel(IRE) ran a solid race in defeat, but had no chance in giving 6lb to the winner. He has done little wrong in his career to date, may be ready to tackle a stiffer test now, and helps to set the standard for this form. (op 3-1)

Cosmopolitan Lady had her chance from the front, yet ultimately proved a sitting duck for the winner. She has ability and may fare better now she is eligible for a nursery mark. (op 15-2 tchd 13-2)

Grand Prix, bidding for the hat-trick, had his limitations exposed at the weights and was not disgraced. (op 9-4 tchd 10-3)

Prospect Place pulled too hard for his own good and failed to quicken on this ground. He would most likely appreciate the return to easier ground and looks more of a nursery type. (op 20-1)

Cavort(IRE), off the mark at Goodwood last month, struggled to go the early pace and was never a serious factor. She is another who would have found this ground plenty quick enough. (op 12-1)

Spoof Master(IRE) dropped out rather tamely when push came to shove and this was the first time he has finished out of the frame in six career outings. (op 11-2)

3027 ALAN BLENCOWE MOTOR RACING SPRINT H'CAP 5f

3:40 (3:41) (Class 4) (0-85,83) 3-Y-0+ **£6,477** (£1,927; £963; £481) **Stalls** Centre

Form			Horse	RPR
1324	**1**		**Hello Roberto**[4] 2897 5-8-13 **68** ... (p) AdrianMcCarthy 10 (R A Harris) *mde all: kpt on gamely: rdn out* **9/1**	80
0142	**2**	*¾*	**Malapropism**[5] 2858 6-9-7 **76** ... TedDurcan 11 (M R Channon) *cl up: rdn over 2f out: kpt on to go 2nd jst ins fnl f: hld fnl 50yds* **11/2**[2]	86
3020	**3**	*nk*	**Chinalea (IRE)**[10] 2711 4-9-3 **72** ... RichardHughes 9 (C G Cox) *chsd ldrs: rdn over 2f out: kpt on ins fnl f* **5/1**[1]	81
0415	**4**	*nk*	**Bluebok**[12] 2635 5-9-9 **78** ... TonyCulhane 5 (J M Bradley) *pushed along in tch: rdn over 2f out: styd on ins fnl f* **8/1**	85
0042	**5**	*1 ½*	**Willhewiz**[12] 2635 6-9-6 **75** ... JohnEgan 6 (M S Saunders) *chsd ldrs: rdn over 2f out: one pce fr ove 1f out* **6/1**[3]	77
2203	**6**	*nk*	**Fizzlephut (IRE)**[13] 2624 4-9-8 **77** ... PaulFitzsimons 1 (Miss J R Tooth) *cl up: rdn over 2f out: sn one pce* **10/1**	78
0061	**7**	*½*	**Magic Glade**[16] 2521 7-9-12 **81** ... TPQueally 2 (R Brotherton) *w wnr: rdn 2f out: wknd fnl f* **12/1**	80
05-0	**8**	*1 ¾*	**Rag Tag (IRE)**[23] 2329 3-9-7 **82** ... (t) LPKeniry 4 (A M Balding) *hld up: rdn and effrt over 1f out: fnd little* **33/1**	75
0020	**9**	*shd*	**Night Prospector**[26] 2227 6-10-0 **83** ... RyanMoore 12 (G L Moore) *bhd: swtchd lft 3f out: sn rdn: no imp* **5/1**[1]	76
0003	**10**	*½*	**Desperate Dan**[12] 2635 5-9-6 **82** ... FrankiePickard(7) 3 (J A Osborne) *a towards rr* **14/1**	73
-450	**11**	*¾*	**Smokin Beau**[27] 2189 9-9-13 **82** ... JimmyFortune 7 (N P Littmoden) *a in rr* **20/1**	70

60.50 secs (-1.09) **Going Correction** -0.05s/f (Good)

WFA 3 from 4yo+ 6lb 11 Ran SP% **115.3**

Speed ratings (Par 105):106,104,104,103,101 100,100,97,97,96 95

CSF £56.70 CT £231.63 TOTE £9.60: £2.80, £1.60, £2.30; EX 32.30.

Owner Peter A Price **Bred** I B Barker **Trained** Earlswood, Monmouths

FOCUS

A fair sprint, run at a strong pace, and the first four came clear. The form should prove sound.

Night Prospector Official explanation: jockey said gelding hung right-handed

3028 H S LESTER MEMORIAL H'CAP 1m 6f 15y

4:10 (4:10) (Class 4) (0-85,85) 4-Y-0+ **£6,477** (£1,927; £963; £481) **Stalls** Far side

Form			Horse	RPR
0-40	**1**		**Master Cobbler (IRE)**[28] 2176 4-8-6 **70** ... (p) TPQueally 11 (J Akehurst) *hld up towards rr: swtchd to outer over 5f out: stdy prog fr 3f out: rdn to ld over 1f out: styd on wl* **14/1**	81
0005	**2**	*2*	**Takafu (USA)**[16] 2534 4-8-6 **70** ... FrankieMcDonald 12 (W S Kittow) *mid div: tk clsr order 6f out: led narrowly over 2f out: sn rdn: hdd over 1f out: kpt on* **14/1**	78
1244	**3**	*½*	**Maystock**[12] 2653 6-8-6 **70** ow1 ... TedDurcan 13 (B G Powell) *trckd ldrs: rdn over 3f out: styd on to regain 3rd ins fnl f* **20/1**	77
-314	**4**	*¾*	**Croon**[19] 2447 4-8-6 **75** ... TravisBlock(5) 1 (H Morrison) *trckd ldrs: wnt 2nd over 6f out: led over 3f out: rdn and hdd over 2f out: no ex ins fnl f* **4/1**[2]	81
60-2	**5**	*2*	**Darling Deanie (IRE)**[24] 2305 4-8-7 **71** ... JohnEgan 8 (D R C Elsworth) *hld up towards rr: hdwy wl over 3f out: ev ch over 1f out: one pce fnl f* **7/1**	74
2-23	**6**	*1*	**Prince Vector**[37] 1927 4-9-5 **83** ... RichardHughes 4 (A King) *mid div: rdn and hdwy over 3f out: effrt over 2f out: kpt on same pce* **6/1**[3]	85
5306	**7**	*2*	**Boot 'n Toot**[10] 2706 5-8-8 **72** ... MartinDwyer 6 (C A Cyzer) *hld up towards rr: hdwy 3f out: sn rdn: one pce fr over 1f out* **33/1**	71
-6P2	**8**	*2 ½*	**Tender Trap (IRE)**[12] 2653 8-9-6 **84** ... IanMongan 7 (T G Mills) *hld up towards rr: n.m.r on rails and snatched up over 5f out: sme hdwy into mid div 3f out: no further imp fr 2f out* **16/1**	79
00-2	**9**	*½*	**San Hernando**[36] 1931 6-8-4 **71** ... (v) SaleemGolam(3) 5 (Miss E C Lavelle) *in tch tl lost pl 6f out: nvr a danger after* **12/1**	66
0200	**10**	*2 ½*	**Isa'Af (IRE)**[28] 2176 7-7-13 **70** ... LukeMorris(7) 10 (P W Hiatt) *hld up towards rr: hdwy 5f out: wknd 2f out* **40/1**	61
0-00	**11**	*½*	**Jeepstar**[33] 2013 6-9-3 **81** ... RichardThomas 3 (S C Williams) *led tl over 3f out: grad fdd* **20/1**	72
04/0	**12**	*14*	**Wavertree Boy (IRE)**[34] 1991 6-9-7 **85** ... LPKeniry 9 (D R C Elsworth) *a towards rr* **33/1**	56
21-1	**13**	*nk*	**Sir Monty (USA)**[16] 2534 4-8-13 **77** ... RyanMoore 2 (Mrs A J Perrett) *trckd ldrs: rdn over 3f out: sn btn: eased over 1f out* **5/2**[1]	48+

3m 5.68s (-0.55) **Going Correction** -0.05s/f (Good) 13 Ran SP% **120.1**

Speed ratings (Par 105):99,97,97,97,96 95,94,92,92,91 90,82,82

CSF £183.35 CT £3888.64 TOTE £20.30: £4.90, £5.40, £4.00; EX 266.00.

Owner A D Spence **Bred** A Butler **Trained** Epsom, Surrey

FOCUS

A modest winning time for the grade and the form is worth treating with a degree of caution.

Darling Deanie(IRE) Official explanation: jockey said filly hung right-handed

Isa'Af(IRE) Official explanation: jockey said gelding was unsuited by good to firm ground

Wavertree Boy(IRE) Official explanation: vet said gelding was distressed

Sir Monty(USA) Official explanation: jockey said gelding had no more to give

3029 POSHCHATEAUX.COM MAIDEN STKS 1m 1f 198y

4:40 (4:43) (Class 4) 3-Y-0+ **£5,505** (£1,637; £818; £408) **Stalls** High

Form			Horse	RPR
5	**1**		**Majaales (USA)**[12] 2655 3-8-12 ... RHills 3 (M P Tregoning) *in tch: tk clsr over 3f out: edgd lft over 2f out: rdn to ld 1f out: styd on strly* **5/2**[2]	77+
0	**2**	*2*	**Diamond Shower (USA)**[10] 2712 3-8-12 ... JimmyFortune 10 (E A L Dunlop) *led tl over 3f out: sn rdn and remained cl up: kpt on ins fnl f to regain 2nd cl home* **25/1**	74
55-3	**3**	*¾*	**Silken Act (CAN)**[10] 2712 3-8-7 ... RyanMoore 2 (Mrs A J Perrett) *chsd ldrs: led over 3f out: rdn over 2f out: hdd 1f out: lost 2nd cl home* **6/4**[1]	67
0-0	**4**	*1 ½*	**Mohtarres (USA)**[34] 1994 3-8-12 ... MartinDwyer 11 (M A Jarvis) *chsd ldrs: rdn 3f out: kpt on same pce fnl 2f* **22/1**	69
	5	*nk*	**Valart** 3-8-7 ... AlanDaly 5 (C Tinkler) *mid div: rdn over 3f out: styd on fnl f* **66/1**	64
0-0	**6**	*2*	**Sonny Mac**[6] 2825 3-8-12 ... (t) TedDurcan 7 (B J Meehan) *a mid div* **80/1**	65
	7	*1 ½*	**Somersault** 3-8-0 ... JamieHamblett(7) 4 (Sir Michael Stoute) *hld up towards rr: hdwy into mid div 5f out: rdn 3f out: no further imp* **12/1**	57+
0	**8**	*½*	**Naini Tal**[13] 2615 3-8-7 ... JohnEgan 1 (D R C Elsworth) *hld up towards rr: rdn 3f out: no imp tl styd on fnl f* **9/1**[3]	56
60	**9**	*1 ¼*	**Secret Moment**[26] 2220 4-9-10 ... RichardThomas 12 (C G Cox) *in tch: effrt over 3f out: one pce fnl 2f* **50/1**	59
40	**10**	*1*	**Soubriquet (IRE)**[30] 2118 3-8-12 ... IanMongan 13 (T G Mills) *mid div: rdn 3f out: wknd 1f out* **10/1**	57
0	**11**	*1*	**Klassen (USA)**[24] 2304 3-8-9 ... EdwardCreighton(3) 14 (A King) *hld up towards rr: hdwy 4f out: sn rdn: wknd over 1f out* **66/1**	55
00	**12**	*1*	**Woolsey**[31] 2063 3-8-12 ... TonyCulhane 6 (M Blanshard) *hld up towards rr: short lived effrt 3f out* **66/1**	53
	13	*19*	**Silken Dance (IRE)** 3-8-12 ... AdrianMcCarthy 8 (G L Moore) *a towards rr: t.o fr over 1f out* **50/1**	17
	14	*69*	**Biggin Hill (IRE)** 3-8-12 ... RichardHughes 9 (H R A Cecil) *s.i.s: a bhd: eased fnl 2f: btn 112 1/2 l* **10/1**	—

2m 11.96s (3.50) **Going Correction** -0.05s/f (Good)

WFA 3 from 4yo 12lb 14 Ran SP% **122.3**

Speed ratings (Par 105):84,82,81,80,80 78,77,77,76,75 74,73,58,3

CSF £73.28 TOTE £3.60: £1.50, £5.10, £1.20; EX 88.90.

Owner Hamdan Al Maktoum **Bred** Shadwell Farm LLC **Trained** Lambourn, Berks

FOCUS

A pedestrian winning time, 2.54 seconds slower than the opening handicap, and an ordinary maiden which probably took little winning. The form looks shaky.

The Form Book, Raceform Ltd, Compton, RG20 6NL

3030 AXMINSTER CARPETS APPRENTICE H'CAP — 1m

5:10 (5:11) (Class 5) (0-70,70) 3-Y-O — **£3,562** (£1,059; £529; £264) **Stalls** Centre

Form	Pos	Dist	Horse / Trainer / Comment	Jockey & draw	Odds	RPR
6602	**1**		**Murrumbidgee (IRE)**[11] [2678] 3-8-5 **58** (J W Hills) *mid div: hdwy over 2f out: led over 1f out: sn drifted rt: r.o wl: pushed out*	PatrickHills(5) 3	**15/2**	66
-001	**2**	*3*	**Jill Dawson (IRE)**[11] [2678] 3-8-10 **58** 6ex (John Berry) *prom: rdn over 2f out: kpt on same pce fr over 1f out: tk 2nd fnl stride*	KirstyMilczarek 7	**5/2**[1]	59
3000	**3**	*hd*	**Bride To Be (USA)**[7] [2781] 3-9-5 **70** (C E Brittain) *s.i.s: towards rr: hdwy 4f out: chsd wnr 1f out: kpt on same pce: lost 2nd fnl stride*	WilliamCarson(3) 4	**40/1**	71
5035	**4**	*nk*	**Cool Ebony**[13] [2622] 3-9-7 **69** (M Dods) *chsd ldrs: outpcd and hmpd over 2f out: swtchd lft and styd on strly fnl f*	PJBenson 6	**9/2**[2]	69+
2033	**5**	*2*	**Ten Shun**[3] [2920] 3-9-1 **63** (P D Evans) *hld up: smooth hdwy over 2f out: led briefly over 1f out: wknd ins fnl f*	RobbieMills 1	**6/1**[3]	58
0-06	**6**	*1 3/4*	**Gizmondo**[91] [802] 3-8-4 **55** (M L W Bell) *chsd ldrs: rdn over 3f out: hung lft over 2f out: one pce after*	LukeMorris(3) 12	**50/1**	46
006	**7**	*2 1/2*	**Mount Sinai**[13] [2605] 3-9-6 **68** (W J Knight) *a mid div*	JamieHamblett 11	**20/1**	54
5104	**8**	*1 1/4*	**They All Laughed**[11] [2678] 3-8-12 **60** (P W Hiatt) *towards rr: sme late hdwy: nvr a factor*	ChrisHough 13	**14/1**	43
-000	**9**	*3/4*	**Time Out (IRE)**[23] [2332] 3-9-5 **70** (A M Balding) *led tl over 3f out: sn hung lft and wknd*	JamesRogers(3) 2	**20/1**	51
1005	**10**	*1 1/4*	**Drawback (IRE)**[23] [2318] 3-9-2 **67** (R A Harris) *t.k.h: prom: led over 3f out tl over 1f out: wknd*	(b1) TolleyDean(3) 10	**33/1**	45
4650	**11**	*nk*	**Crimson Flame (IRE)**[13] [2620] 3-9-7 **69** (M R Channon) *prom tl wknd 2f out*	(v1) AlanRutter 8	**7/1**	46
0-20	**12**	*19*	**Hand Of Destiny (USA)**[27] [2210] 3-8-7 **58** (N P Littmoden) *s.i.s: a in rr*	(bt1) JemmaMarshall(3) 5	**25/1**	—
0-00	**13**	*27*	**Misterbianco (IRE)**[59] [1336] 3-8-9 **60** (B J Meehan) *hmpd s: prom after 1f: wkng whn hmpd over 2f out*	KMay(3) 9	**16/1**	—

1m 43.77s (0.68) **Going Correction** -0.05s/f (Good) **13** Ran SP% **118.6**

Speed ratings (Par 99):94,91,90,90,88 86,84,83,82,81 80,61,34

CSF £24.13 CT £722.94 TOTE £9.70: £2.80, £1.50, £7.90; EX 30.30 Place 6 £148.77, Place 5 £46.75.

Owner Abbott Racing Partners **Bred** R Warren **Trained** Upper Lambourn, Berks

■ The first winner for Patrick Hills, son of Richard who won the previous race and nephew of winning trainer John.

■ Stewards' Enquiry : Luke Morris two-day ban: careless riding (Jul 10,11)

FOCUS

A modest apprentice riders' handicap, run at a fair pace, and the form looks sound enough without being strong.

Hand Of Destiny(USA) Official explanation: jockey said gelding was never travelling

T/Jkpt: Not won. T/Plt: £402.90 to a £1 stake. Pool: £44,354.80. 80.35 winning tickets. T/Qpdt: £40.40 to a £1 stake. Pool: £3,248.70. 59.50 winning tickets. TM

[2494] FOLKESTONE (R-H)

Friday, June 30

OFFICIAL GOING: Good to firm (firm in places)

Wind: Slight, half-against

3031 MAKITA LITHIUM-ION MEDIAN AUCTION MAIDEN STKS — 7f (S)

2:30 (2:31) (Class 5) 2-Y-O — **£3,238** (£963; £481; £240) **Stalls** Low

Form	Pos	Dist	Horse / Trainer / Comment	Jockey & draw	Odds	RPR
	1		**Fuji (IRE)** 2-9-3 (M L W Bell) *hdwy whn lost action and swtchd rt over 2f out: led over 1f out: drvn: jst hld on*	JimmyQuinn 6	**7/2**[2]	66
0	**2**	*nk*	**Law Of The Land (IRE)**[41] [1838] 2-9-3 (W R Muir) *t.k.h: hld up: rdn and hdwy over 1f out: fin strly to go 2nd ins fnl f: clsng fast on wnr post*	MartinDwyer 2	**7/1**[3]	65+
03	**3**	*3*	**Global Guest**[8] [2778] 2-9-3 (M R Channon) *trckd ldr tl rdn and one pce ins fnl f*	SamHitchcott 8	**7/2**[2]	57
5	**4**	*1 1/2*	**Three No Trumps**[15] [2588] 2-8-12 (D Morris) *in tch: hmpd 2f out: kpt on one pce*	ShaneKelly 5	**12/1**	49
	5	*1 3/4*	**Hocinail (FR)** 2-9-3 (P Winkworth) *prom tl outpcd over 2f out*	JimCrowley 7	**16/1**	49+
0	**6**	*2 1/2*	**Linkslade Lad**[27] [2234] 2-9-3 (W R Muir) *prom for 4f*	(b1) IanMongan 9	**33/1**	42
	7	*3*	**Glorious Prince (IRE)** 2-9-3 (M G Quinlan) *s.i.s: hld up in tch: no hdwy fnl 2f*	RyanMoore 1	**11/4**[1]	35
6	**8**	*shd*	**City Bhoy**[10] [2726] 2-9-3 (Tom Dascombe) *led tl rdn and hdd wl over 1f out: wknd qckly*	FergusSweeney 4	**25/1**	34
060	**9**	*24*	**Merlins Quest**[28] [2185] 2-9-3 (J M Bradley) *in tch to 1/2-way: sn wl bhd*	TPQueally 3	**10/1**	—

1m 28.8s (0.90) **Going Correction** -0.05s/f (Good) **9** Ran SP% **113.1**

Speed ratings (Par 93):92,91,88,86,84 81,78,78,50

CSF £27.57 TOTE £4.70: £1.60, £2.00, £1.60; EX 30.80 Trifecta £57.40 Pool: £569.59 - 7.04 winning tickets..

Owner Tweenhills Racing IX & Michael Lynch **Bred** Golden Vale Stud **Trained** Newmarket, Suffolk

■ Stewards' Enquiry : Jimmy Quinn one day ban: careless riding (Jul 11)

FOCUS

A modest maiden, run at no more than a fair pace, and the first two came clear. Difficult to be confident about the level of the form, and it could be rated higher.

NOTEBOOK

Fuji(IRE), who cost 82,000gns, ultimately did just enough to prevail from the fast-finishing runner-up and get his head in front at the first time of asking. He ran very green when switched wide for his effort, but he sealed the race when showing a neat turn of foot to lead and go clear nearing the final furlong, and was always going to hang on. This was his yard's first juvenile debutant winner of the current campaign and he looks sure to stay a mile before the season's end. (op 11-4 tchd 5-2)

Law Of The Land(IRE), supported in the betting ring, was checked momentarily when beginning his effort on the rail but flew home once in the clear. The winner had just gone beyond recall, but this was a big step up on the form of his debut and he can be placed to go one better before long while his yard remains in decent form. (op 12-1)

Global Guest ran his race, with no apparent excuses, and helps to set the level of this form. He now qualifies for a nursery mark and it would not be a surprise to see him fare better in that sphere. (op 2-1)

Three No Trumps was done no favours when the winner came across her nearing two out and can be rated slightly better than the bare form. She will be qualified for nurseries after her next assignment and is going the right way. Official explanation: trainer said filly was struck into (op 11-1)

Hocinail(FR), bred to be suited by farther in due course, ran green when the race became serious and not surprisingly shaped as though he is in need of a stiffer test. (op 14-1 tchd 20-1)

Glorious Prince(IRE), the first foal of an unplaced sister to Fillies' Mile winner Gloriosa, was all the rage in the betting beforehand and was clearly expected to go close. However, after being given time to find his feet following a sluggish start, he found nothing when switched and asked for his effort. It later emerged that he had suffered an overreach. He is evidently quite well thought of and is worth another chance. Official explanation: vet said colt suffered an overreach (op 6-1)

3032 TKM PLUMBERS MERCHANTS LTD MEDIAN AUCTION MAIDEN STKS — 7f (S)

3:00 (3:04) (Class 6) 3-5-Y-O — **£2,730** (£806; £403) **Stalls** Low

Form	Pos	Dist	Horse / Trainer / Comment	Jockey & draw	Odds	RPR
	1		**Baleegh (USA)** 3-9-0 (M P Tregoning) *sn chsd ldr: rdn over 1f out: led fnl 100yds: drvn out*	MartinDwyer 8	**5/2**[2]	73
-525	**2**	*3/4*	**Chalentina**[20] [2459] 3-8-9 69 (H R A Cecil) *sn led: rdn over 1f out: no ex and hdd fnl 100yds*	JimmyQuinn 4	**9/4**[1]	66
0	**3**	*3*	**Meadow Floss**[15] [2575] 3-8-9 (S Kirk) *a in tch: rdn wl over 1f out: kpt on one pce*	LPKeniry 1	**20/1**	58+
00	**4**	*nk*	**Wodhill Schnaps**[14] [2615] 5-9-9 (D Morris) *in rr: styd on fr over 1f out: nvr nrr*	ShaneKelly 7	**33/1**	65
5	**5**	*1 1/2*	**Amazing Charlie (IRE)**[17] [2532] 3-8-9 (Mrs A J Perrett) *prom: rdn 2f out: one pce fr over 1f out*	JimCrowley 2	**7/2**[3]	53
	6	*5*	**Lady's Law** 3-8-9 (G G Margarson) *in rr: sme hdwy over 1f out: nvr nr to chal*	RyanMoore 9	**12/1**	40
0-00	**7**	*6*	**Astronova**[143] [333] 3-8-2 45 (M H Tompkins) *prom on outside tl wknd over 2f out*	PatrickHills(7) 10	**40/1**	23
000-	**8**	*nk*	**Ello Lucky (IRE)**[416] [1601] 4-8-11 35 (J M Bradley) *in tch tl rdn and wknd over 2f out*	BarrySavage(7) 3	**66/1**	26
00-0	**9**	*16*	**Lady Luisa (IRE)**[6] [2875] 4-8-11 40 (Miss A Stokell) *plld hrd: prom tl wknd rapidly 3f out*	(t) AnnStokell(7) 5	**100/1**	—

1m 27.07s (-0.83) **Going Correction** -0.05s/f (Good)

WFA 3 from 4yo+ 9lb **9** Ran SP% **101.9**

Speed ratings (Par 101):102,101,97,97,95 89,83,82,64

CSF £6.44 TOTE £3.40: £1.20, £1.10, £5.40; EX 7.70 Trifecta £44.40 Pool: £412,18 - 6.58 winning tickets..

Owner Hamdan Al Maktoum **Bred** Shadwell Farm LLC **Trained** Lambourn, Berks

■ Barney McGrew withdrawn (8/1, refused to enter stalls). R4 applies, deduct 10p in the £.

FOCUS

A modest maiden, with little strength in depth, and the first two came clear.

Meadow Floss Official explanation: jockey said saddle slipped

3033 SCRUFFS HARDWEAR ITS GONNA GET DIRTY CLAIMING STKS — 6f

3:30 (3:30) (Class 5) 3-Y-O+ — **£3,238** (£963; £481; £240) **Stalls** Low

Form	Pos	Dist	Horse / Trainer / Comment	Jockey & draw	Odds	RPR
0411	**1**		**Further Outlook (USA)**[9] [2748] 12-9-1 68 (D Carroll) *racd stands' side: mde all rdn out: hld on gamely*	DanielTudhope(3) 1	**9/2**[3]	65
6433	**2**	*hd*	**Sweet Pickle**[13] [2637] 5-9-0 65 (J R Boyle) *slowly away and carried rt after s: sn swtchd to stands' side: in rr tl swtchd rt and gd hdwy over 1f out: r.o wl*	(e) AmirQuinn(3) 8	**11/4**[2]	63
0025	**3**	*1/2*	**My Girl Pearl (IRE)**[14] [2599] 6-8-9 49 (M S Saunders) *a.p on stands' side: rdn over 2f out: kpt on fnl f*	FergusSweeney 2	**10/1**	54
5511	**4**	*1 1/2*	**Diamond Josh**[9] [2758] 4-8-7 58 (P D Evans) *racd stands' side: chsd wnr tl wknd ins fnl f*	StephenDonohoe(5) 7	**9/4**[1]	52
0005	**5**	*1/2*	**Snow Wolf**[13] [2632] 5-9-0 54 (J M Bradley) *sn trckd ldr far side: led that gp 1f out and kpt on one pce*	(p) RyanMoore 11	**15/2**	53
0010	**6**	*3/4*	**Renegade (IRE)**[17] [2536] 5-9-2 46 (Mrs L J Mongan) *wnt rt s: led far side gp after 1f: hdd 1f out: no ex*	(b) IanMongan 5	**16/1**	53
0200	**7**	*1 1/2*	**Von Wessex**[13] [2632] 4-9-0 45 (W G M Turner) *racd on outside of stands' side gp: in tch tl wknd fnl f*	RobertMiles 6	**28/1**	46
0403	**8**	*hd*	**Xaar Breeze**[13] [2632] 3-8-10 43 (Mrs P Townsley) *in tch on stands' side for 4f*	SamHitchcott 4	**20/1**	47
5000	**9**	*1*	**Keresforth**[26] [2260] 4-8-10 36 (Mrs L C Jewell) *in rr on far side: hung lft to centre over 1f out: nvr on terms*	(p) ShaneKelly 9	**100/1**	39
0000	**10**	*3/4*	**Silver Visage (IRE)**[25] [2288] 4-8-12 49 (Miss J Feilden) *led far side gp for 1f: bhd fnl 2f*	LPKeniry 10	**33/1**	38
60-0	**11**	*7*	**Ballyhooligan (IRE)**[170] [83] 3-8-9 50 (Jamie Poulton) *chsd ldrs stands' side tl wknd 2f out*	RobertHavlin 3	**50/1**	19

1m 12.68s (-0.92) **Going Correction** -0.05s/f (Good)

WFA 3 from 4yo+ 7lb **11** Ran SP% **116.5**

Speed ratings (Par 103):104,103,103,101,100 99,97,97,95,94 85

CSF £16.30 TOTE £4.60: £1.30, £1.70, £2.70 Trifecta £61.60 Pool: £405.26 - 4.67 winning tickets..

Owner Diamond Racing Ltd **Bred** Gainsborough Farm Inc **Trained** Warthill, N Yorks

■ Stewards' Enquiry : Ian Mongan three-day ban: careless riding (Jul 11,13,15)

FOCUS

An ordinary claimer, but featuring some in-form sprinters. The four who raced on the far side at a disadvantage, and the runner-up was unfortunate not to score after being hampered at the start. My Girl Pearl sets the standard on last year's course and distance second.

3034 JEWSONS BUILDERS MERCHANTS MAIDEN STKS — 5f

4:00 (4:00) (Class 5) 3-Y-O+ — **£3,886** (£1,156; £577; £288) **Stalls** Low

Form	Pos	Dist	Horse / Trainer / Comment	Jockey & draw	Odds	RPR
506-	**1**		**Safari Mischief**[363] [3142] 3-9-0 67 (P Winkworth) *trckd ldr: led wl over 1f out: rdn out*	JimCrowley 4	**5/2**[2]	63
000-	**2**	*1 1/4*	**Epineuse**[284] [5362] 3-8-9 40 (J R Best) *s.i.s: sn in tch: hrd rdn and hdwy over 1f out to chse wnr wl ins fnl f*	LPKeniry 6	**18/1**	54
03	**3**	*1/2*	**All Clued Up (IRE)**[20] [2445] 3-8-9 (Rae Guest) *a.p: rdn to chse wnr over 1f out tl wl ins fnl f*	MartinDwyer 2	**11/2**[3]	52
50-0	**4**	*1/2*	**Vicky Pollard**[24] [2316] 3-8-6 52 (P Howling) *led tl rdn and hdd wl over 1f out: kpt on one pce ins fnl f*	DeanCorby(3) 1	**16/1**	50
30	**5**	*nk*	**King Of Charm (IRE)**[6] [2859] 3-9-0 (G L Moore) *hld up: rdn 2f out: n.m.r and swtchd rt over 1f out: nvr quite nr enough to chal*	RyanMoore 7	**2/1**[1]	57+
00	**6**	*1*	**Burnt Orange (IRE)**[17] [2532] 3-9-0 (T D McCarthy) *in tch on outside: rdn 1/2-way: no hdwy fr over 1f out*	RobertHavlin 8	**7/1**	51

0455 **7** *shd* **Lord Mayfair (USA)**[7] 2833 4-8-13 44..........................(b) AnnStokell(7) 5 52?
(Miss A Stokell) *chsd ldrs: rdn 2f out: one pce fnl f* **8/1**

60.49 secs (-0.31) **Going Correction** -0.05s/f (Good)
WFA 3 from 4yo 6lb **7** Ran SP% **112.0**
Speed ratings (Par 103):100,98,97,96,95 94,94
CSF £41.70 TOTE £3.70: £1.80, £6.30; EX 67.10 Trifecta £299.30 Part won. Pool: £421.64 - 0.34 winnign tickets..
Owner P Winkworth **Bred** Bearstone Stud **Trained** Chiddingfold, Surrey
■ Stewards' Enquiry : L P Keniry one-day ban: careless riding (Jul 11)

FOCUS
A weak maiden, which saw the first five fairly closely covered at the finish, and the form is worth treating with a degree of caution.

3035 "NEW" SKIL CLASSIC H'CAP — 1m 4f
4:30 (4:30) (Class 6) (0-60,60) 4-Y-0+ **£2,730** (£806; £403) **Stalls** Low

Form RPR

5214 **1** **Rose Bien**[46] 1745 4-8-10 **52**..........................(p) EdwardCreighton(3) 3 61
(P J McBride) *hld up towards rr: hdwy on outside over 2f out: rdn and styd on to ld wl ins fnl f* **7/1**[2]

3301 **2** *3/4* **Icannshift (IRE)**[18] 2497 6-8-11 **50**.......................... FergusSweeney 7 57
(T M Jones) *led: clr 3f out: shkn up over 1f out: r.o but hdd wl ins fnl f* **12/1**

1045 **3** *hd* **Missie Baileys**[100] 697 4-9-3 **56**.......................... IanMongan 11 63
(Mrs L J Mongan) *hld up in rr: hdwy 2f out: styd on wl fnl f: nvr nrr* **16/1**

3005 **4** *1 1/2* **Agilete**[11] 2707 4-8-6 **45**.......................... MartinDwyer 2 50
(J R Boyle) *bhd: hdwy on outside 2f out: styd on: nvr nrr* **18/1**

04-3 **5** *nk* **Tavalu (USA)**[24] 966 4-9-7 **60**.......................... RyanMoore 6 64
(G L Moore) *mid-div: rdn 2f out: kpt on one pce* **11/4**[1]

4603 **6** *1 3/4* **Lenwade**[18] 2497 5-8-4 **43**.......................... JimmyQuinn 10 44
(G G Margarson) *s.i.s: bhd: rdn over 2f out: styd on but nvr nr to chal* **8/1**[3]

3406 **7** *shd* **Lysander's Quest (IRE)**[18] 2497 8-8-2 **41**..........................(v) NickyMackay 4 42
(R Ingram) *trckd ldr: rdn 3f out: wknd over 1f out* **10/1**

-605 **8** *3/4* **Bullseye**[58] 1400 4-8-5 **47**.......................... DanielTudhope(3) 14 47
(J R Boyle) *in tch: effrt over 2f out: no hdwy fr over 1f out* **8/1**[3]

66-0 **9** *nk* **Irish Ballad**[24] 2320 4-9-3 **56**..........................(t) StephenCarson 9 55
(W R Swinburn) *hld up: a towards rr* **16/1**

0000 **10** *shd* **Native American**[23] 2345 4-9-7 **60**.......................... RobertHavlin 13 59
(T D McCarthy) *prom: rdn over 2f out: sn btn* **66/1**

2000 **11** *2 1/2* **Dayoff (IRE)**[9] 2762 5-8-6 **50**..........................(b) StephenDonohoe(5) 12 45
(P D Evans) *a towards rr* **25/1**

0-00 **12** *1 1/4* **Domenico (IRE)**[25] 2305 8-9-5 **58**.......................... ShaneKelly 1 51
(J R Jenkins) *a bhd* **25/1**

0-30 **13** *1 1/2* **Coppermalt (USA)**[24] 574 8-8-6 **45** ow1.......................... LPKeniry 5 36
(R Curtis) *mid-div tl wknd over 2f out* **28/1**

0-24 **14** *11* **Palace Walk (FR)**[5] 2902 4-9-5 **58**.......................... JimCrowley 8 31
(B G Powell) *prom: rdn over 3f out: wknd over 2f out* **7/1**[2]

2m 36.02s (-4.48) **Going Correction** -0.25s/f (Firm) **14** Ran SP% **120.3**
Speed ratings (Par 101):104,103,103,102,102 101,100,100,100,100 98,97,96,89
CSF £85.05 CT £1310.34 TOTE £9.90: £3.10, £3.60, £4.40; EX 78.20 Trifecta £250.10 Part won. Pool: £352.27 - 0.77 winning tickets..
Owner P J Pateman **Bred** Mrs J F Budgett **Trained** Newmarket, Suffolk

FOCUS
A moderate handicap, but run at a sound pace, and solid enough form of its type.
Lenwade Official explanation: jockey said gelding missed the break
Domenico(IRE) Official explanation: jockey said gelding was unsuited by the good to firm (firm in places) ground and the track

3036 INVICTA MOTORS TRANSIT FILLIES' H'CAP — 1m 1f 149y
5:00 (5:02) (Class 5) (0-75,71) 3-Y-0+ **£3,238** (£963; £481; £240) **Stalls** Low

Form RPR

5-00 **1** **Golden Applause (FR)**[20] 2457 4-10-0 **68**.......................... SamHitchcott 2 77
(Mrs A L M King) *hld up on outside: hdwy 1/2-way: wnt 2nd over 2f out: sn led: rdn out fnl f* **13/2**

-253 **2** *2* **Shamila**[17] 2533 3-9-5 **71**.......................... NickyMackay 1 76
(G A Butler) *led after 2f: rdn and headed wl over 1f out: nt qckn ins fnl f* **7/2**[2]

3310 **3** *1/2* **Red Sail**[30] 2133 5-9-1 **55**..........................(b) ShaneKelly 4 59
(Dr J D Scargill) *hld up in rr: hdwy on outside fr 2f out to stay on fnl f: nvr nrr* **9/2**[3]

0-00 **4** *3/4* **Greenmeadow**[31] 2113 4-9-4 **58**.......................... LPKeniry 5 61
(S Kirk) *hld up in tch: rdn 2f out: styd on one pce* **11/1**

5-04 **5** *1 1/4* **Umlilo**[10] 2729 4-9-1 **55**.......................... JimCrowley 8 55
(Mrs A J Perrett) *prom: rdn 2f out: no further hdwy* **8/1**

40-0 **6** *1/2* **Collect**[30] 2148 4-8-12 **59**..........................(b[1]) PatrickHills(7) 7 59
(M H Tompkins) *slowly away: nvr on terms* **12/1**

0300 **7** *5* **Louve Heureuse (IRE)**[11] 2707 5-8-7 **50**.......................... EdwardCreighton(3) 6 40
(B G Powell) *led for 2f: wknd over 2f out* **16/1**

-362 **8** *16* **Aurora Jane (FR)**[17] 2518 3-8-12 **64**.......................... MartinDwyer 3 24
(B W Hills) *plld hrd: chsd ldr after 2f: wknd over 2f out* **11/4**[1]

2m 2.88s (-2.35) **Going Correction** -0.25s/f (Firm)
WFA 3 from 4yo+ 12lb **8** Ran SP% **113.4**
Speed ratings (Par 100):99,97,97,96,95 95,91,78
CSF £29.00 CT £112.42 TOTE £9.40: £2.90, £1.60, £1.80; EX 40.50 Trifecta £93.70 Pool: £588.63 - 4.46 winningt tickets. Place 6 £84.88, Place 5 £51.03.
Owner Lesley And Russell Field **Bred** Ecurie Skymarc Farm **Trained** Wilmcote, Warwicks
■ Stewards' Enquiry : Nicky Mackay two-day ban: careless riding (Jul 11,13)

FOCUS
A modest fillies' handicap, run at an uneven pace, but the winner was possibly value for slightly further.
Aurora Jane(FR) Official explanation: jockey said filly suffered interference in running
T/Plt: £169.00 to a £1 stake. Pool: £48,301.40. 208.60 winning tickets. T/Qpdt: £61.40 to a £1 stake. Pool: £3,090.90. 37.20 winning tickets. JS

3018 NEWCASTLE (L-H)
Friday, June 30

OFFICIAL GOING: Good to firm (good in places)
Wind: Light, half-against

3037 ASPERS CASINO H'CAP — 1m 2f 32y
6:45 (6:45) (Class 5) (0-75,75) 4-Y-0+ **£3,562** (£1,059; £529; £264) **Stalls** Centre

Form RPR

1564 **1** **Mount Usher**[16] 2540 4-8-7 **61**.......................... DeanMcKeown 8 71+
(G A Swinbank) *keen: hld up in tch: hdwy outside to ld over 1f out: rdn and r.o fnl f* **2/1**[1]

5204 **2** *1* **Cripsey Brook**[7] 2828 8-9-0 **75**..........................(t) JamesReveley(7) 3 83+
(K G Reveley) *hld up in tch: effrt over 2f out: nt clr run over 1f out: rallied and chsd wnr ins fnl f: r.o* **6/1**[3]

6540 **3** *1 1/4* **Royal Flynn**[28] 2193 4-8-3 **57**.......................... PaulFessey 4 63
(M Dods) *prom: rdn to ld briefly over 1f out: nt qckn ins fnl f* **7/1**

0-61 **4** *1/2* **Fossgate**[14] 2612 5-8-10 **64**.......................... KDarley 7 69
(J D Bethell) *w ldr: rdn over 3f out: rallied: one pce ins fnl f* **4/1**[2]

4234 **5** *3/4* **Sforzando**[8] 2777 5-8-2 **63**.......................... KristinStubbs(7) 2 67
(Mrs L Stubbs) *missed break: keen in rr: rdn 4f out: hdwy over 1f out: nrst fin* **16/1**

60-0 **6** *1 1/4* **Compton Dragon (USA)**[19] 1500 7-7-12 **57**..........................(b) AndrewElliott(5) 5 58
(R Johnson) *dwlt: sn cl up: rdn over 2f out: outpcd over 1f out* **12/1**

-534 **7** *1 1/2* **Wester Lodge (IRE)**[9] 2761 4-9-5 **73**.......................... NCallan 6 71
(J M P Eustace) *set stdy pce: rdn over 2f out: hdd over 1f out: sn no ex* **15/2**

6002 **8** *hd* **Lysandra (IRE)**[8] 2777 4-9-4 **72**.......................... KimTinkler 1 70
(N Tinkler) *chsd ldrs: rdn 3f out: wknd fnl f* **12/1**

2m 10.21s (-1.59) **Going Correction** -0.075s/f (Good) **8** Ran SP% **113.2**
Speed ratings (Par 103):103,102,101,100,100 99,98,97
CSF £13.97 CT £68.62 TOTE £2.90: £2.00, £1.40, £2.10; EX 18.00.
Owner Mrs F H Crone **Bred** Juddmonte Farms **Trained** Melsonby, N Yorks

FOCUS
Exposed performers and a steady pace, but the first four were all very close to form.

3038 NORTHERN ROCK GOSFORTH PARK CUP (H'CAP) — 5f
7:15 (7:17) (Class 2) (0-105,103) 3-Y-0+
£18,696 (£5,598; £2,799; £1,401; £699; £351) **Stalls** High

Form RPR

0020 **1** **Peace Offering (IRE)**[6] 2847 6-8-12 **95**.......................... VictoriaBehan(7) 2 106
(D Nicholls) *prom centre: effrt over 2f out: led ins fnl f: kpt on wl* **14/1**

6300 **2** *1 1/4* **Grigorovitch (IRE)**[6] 2852 4-8-8 **84** oh6.......................... TomEaves 13 90
(I Semple) *stdd stands side: hdwy over 1f out: kpt on fnl f: nt rch wnr* **11/1**

-424 **3** *nk* **Sierra Vista**[27] 2227 6-9-6 **101**.......................... MarkLawson(5) 14 106
(D W Barker) *cl up: led stands side over 2f out: hdd ins fnl f: no ex* **11/2**[1]

0603 **4** *1/2* **Continent**[27] 2227 9-9-2 **92**.......................... FrancisNorton 12 95
(D Nicholls) *prom stands side: effrt 2f out: nt qckn fnl f* **14/1**

0050 **5** *3/4* **Fullandby (IRE)**[12] 2683 4-8-10 **86**.......................... RoystonFfrench 1 87
(T J Etherington) *outpcd centre: hdwy over 1f out: edgd rt ins fnl f: kpt on: nrst fin* **20/1**

5043 **6** *hd* **Cape Royal**[3] 2946 6-9-3 **93**.......................... KDarley 6 93
(J M Bradley) *sn racd alone towards far side: gd spd tl no ex ins fnl f* **11/1**

5003 **7** *nk* **Pieter Brueghel (USA)**[24] 2323 7-8-13 **89**.......................... PhillipMakin 16 88
(D Nicholls) *w stands side ldrs tl rdn and nt qckn over 1f out* **6/1**[2]

0-51 **8** *1/2* **Don Pele (IRE)**[12] 2683 4-8-11 **87** 3ex.......................... NCallan 8 84
(K A Ryan) *in tch stands side: drvn over 2f out: no imp fnl f* **11/2**[1]

2120 **9** *1/2* **Fyodor (IRE)**[70] 1116 5-9-13 **103**.......................... TonyCulhane 7 98
(W J Haggas) *hld up stands side: hdwy over 1f out: nvr rchd ldrs* **10/1**[3]

-210 **10** *shd* **Highland Warrior**[20] 2450 7-8-10 **86**.......................... J-PGuillambert 5 81
(J S Goldie) *bhd: rdn over 2f out: hdwy centre over 1f out: n.d* **11/1**

0360 **11** *3/4* **Enchantment**[20] 2450 5-8-6 **87**..........................(p) GregFairley(5) 10 79
(J M Bradley) *hld up stands side: rdn and effrt 2f out: btn ins fnl f* **25/1**

000- **12** *6* **Matty Tun**[251] 6021 7-8-8 **84** oh3.......................... DeanMcKeown 11 54
(J Balding) *rrd s: keen and sn prom: rdn and wknd 2f out* **40/1**

2136 **13** *3 1/2* **Green Park (IRE)**[13] 2651 3-8-13 **95**.......................... PaulHanagan 4 53
(R A Fahey) *racd outside of stands side gp: sn outpcd: nvr on terms* **14/1**

00-5 **14** *6* **Titus Alone (IRE)**[49] 1633 3-9-1 **97**.......................... DO'Donohoe 3 33
(B Smart) *sn outpcd centre: nvr on terms* **33/1**

1040 **15** *5* **Merlin's Dancer**[6] 2847 6-9-8 **98**.......................... AdrianTNicholls 15 16
(D Nicholls) *led stands side to over 2f out: sn wknd* **10/1**[3]

59.44 secs (-2.06) **Going Correction** -0.25s/f (Firm)
WFA 3 from 4yo+ 6lb **15** Ran SP% **122.2**
Speed ratings (Par 109):106,104,103,102,101 101,100,99,99,98 97,88,82,72,64
CSF £154.99 CT £985.76 TOTE £17.50: £5.60, £3.60, £1.90; EX 371.60.
Owner Lady O'Reilly **Bred** Chevington Stud **Trained** Sessay, N Yorks
■ This valuable handicap provided Victoria Behan with her first winner in nearly a year.

FOCUS
A competitive handicap in which all bar one raced centre to stands' side. The pace was sound and this form should prove reliable.

NOTEBOOK
Peace Offering(IRE), who had shaped as though better than the bare form at Royal Ascot, looked in tremendous shape and showed a good attitude to win his first race since 2002. Now he has got his head in front where it matters, he may be able to go on from here. (op 12-1 tchd 16-1)
Grigorovitch(IRE), who would have finished much closer with a clear run at Ayr last time, showed what he could do when getting the breaks and deserves credit given he was 6lb out of the handicap. He is the type that needs things to fall right but is one to keep an eye on. (op 12-1)
Sierra Vista has been in good form this year and ran another solid race in defeat. She is a good guide to the worth of this form and, although vulnerable to progressive or well handicapped sorts in this type of event, should continue to give a good account. (op 6-1 tchd 5-1)
Continent had the run of the race and ran creditably but, given he is not the most reliable around and has not won for nearly two years, he does not really appeal as one to place maximum faith in.
Fullandby(IRE)'s going days have not been easy to predict this year but he turned in a creditable run having been taken off his feet in the early stages. He left the impression that easier ground may be more to his liking.
Cape Royalgets little respite for his consistency and he again showed his customary dash on his own on the far side. However he is likely to remain vulnerable to progressive or well handicapped types from his current mark. (op 10-1)
Pieter Brueghel(USA) looked in good shape and ran creditably against the stands side rail but, although on a fair mark at present, left the impression that the return to six furlongs would be more to his liking. (op 7-1)
Don Pele(IRE), under a penalty for his York success, failed to build on that effort but he did not really seem to appreciate the drop to the minimum distance and he will be seen to better effect back over six furlongs. (op 5-1 tchd 6-1 in a place)
Merlin's Dancer Official explanation: jockey said gelding bled from the nose

3039 GUINNESS MAIDEN FILLIES' STKS — 7f
7:45 (7:47) (Class 5) 3-Y-0+ **£3,886** (£1,156; £577; £288) **Stalls** High

Form RPR

324- **1** **Amy Louise (IRE)**[281] 5418 3-8-12 78.......................... NCallan 6 62+
(T D Barron) *mde all: drew clr fr 2f out: easily* **4/11**[1]

0050 **2** *6* **Cape Sydney (IRE)**[9] 2746 3-8-12 42.......................... PaulHanagan 8 46
(D W Barker) *prom: effrt over 2f out: chsd wnr over 1f out: no imp* **8/1**[2]

66- **3** *6* **Distant Vision (IRE)**[289] 5221 3-8-12.......................... FergalLynch 7 30
(A Berry) *cl up: effrt over 2f out: outpcd over 1f out* **33/1**

4 *5* **Mrs Quince** 4-9-7.......................... AdrianTNicholls 4 19
(F Watson) *dwlt: hld up: hdwy 3f out: wknd 2f out* **33/1**

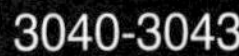

0030 **5** *3* **Underthemistletoe (IRE)**[9] 2758 4-9-7 42 .... TomEaves 2 11
(R E Barr) *keen: prom tl wknd fr 2f out* **14/1**

6 *2* **Altessa (IRE)** 3-8-12 .... FrancisNorton 3 3
(E J Alston) *in tch: outpcd 3f out: sn btn* **10/1**[3]

030- **7** *13* **Montrachet Belle**[331] 4056 4-9-2 45 .... DeclanMcGann(5) 5 —
(R Johnson) *racd wd: in tch 3f: sn wknd* **66/1**

1m 26.4s (-3.60) **Going Correction** -0.25s/f (Firm)
WFA 3 from 4yo 9lb **7** Ran SP% **107.6**
Speed ratings (Par 100):99,92,85,79,76 73,59
CSF £3.07 TOTE £1.30: £1.10, £2.10; EX 2.70.
Owner P D Savill **Bred** P D Savill **Trained** Maunby, N Yorks

FOCUS
A most uncompetitive event in which the favourite did not have to run to her best to win with plenty in hand. The form has been rated according to the best view of the runner-up.

3040 WEATHERBYS BANK H'CAP 1m 3y(S)
8:20 (8:20) (Class 4) (0-85,87) 3-Y-0+

£6,232 (£1,866; £933; £467; £233; £117) **Stalls** High

Form RPR

1-20 **1** **Along The Nile**[20] 2440 4-9-12 78 .... (t) TonyCulhane 5 87
(K G Reveley) *trckd ldrs: rdn to ld 1f out: kpt on wl* **7/1**[2]

6050 **2** *½* **Claret And Amber**[133] 444 4-9-8 74 .... PaulHanagan 1 82
(R A Fahey) *hld up: hdwy over 1f out: kpt on fnl f* **12/1**

-626 **3** *½* **Everest (IRE)**[97] 726 9-10-0 80 .... RoystonFfrench 4 86
(B Ellison) *trckd ldrs: effrt 2f out: kpt on ins fnl f* **16/1**

0030 **4** *hd* **Fair Shake (IRE)**[14] 2627 6-9-2 68 .... (v) TonyHamilton 7 74
(Karen McLintock) *bhd: rdn 1/2-way: hdwy and swtchd to outside over 1f out: kpt on: hld wl ins fnl f* **25/1**

-663 **5** *¾* **Bailieborough (IRE)**[12] 2681 7-9-13 79 .... (v) NCallan 3 83
(Robert Gray) *dwlt: bhd: effrt outside over 1f out: no imp ins fnl f* **9/1**[3]

1411 **6** *¾* **Days Of My Life (IRE)**[1] 3007 3-9-6 87 6ex .... RichardKingscote(5) 2 90
(R Charlton) *cl up: led briefly over 1f out: no ex ins last* **4/7**[1]

4304 **7** *½* **Defi (IRE)**[16] 2547 4-8-13 65 .... (b) TomEaves 8 66
(I Semple) *hld up in tch: effrt over 1f out: no imp fnl f* **9/1**[3]

1006 **8** *5* **Mezuzah**[35] 1985 6-9-9 75 .... PaulMulrennan 6 65
(M W Easterby) *cl up tl rdn and no ex wl over 1f out* **25/1**

520- **9** *¾* **Vanadium**[274] 5567 4-10-0 80 .... JamieMackay 9 68
(J G Given) *led to over 1f out: sn btn* **33/1**

1m 39.85s (-2.05) **Going Correction** -0.25s/f (Firm)
WFA 3 from 4yo+ 10lb **9** Ran SP% **120.4**
Speed ratings (Par 105):100,99,99,98,98 97,96,91,91
CSF £86.96 CT £1318.05 TOTE £8.60: £1.50, £3.00, £2.90; EX 111.50.
Owner J Musgrave **Bred** Lucayan Stud Ltd And Whatton Manor Stud **Trained** Lingdale, Redcar & Cleveland

FOCUS
A bunch finish following a steady pace, and the form is far from solid. With the favourite disappointing it did not take as much winning as seemed likely.

3041 BETFRED POKER SPRINT SERIES H'CAP (QUALIFIER) 6f
8:50 (8:51) (Class 5) (0-75,75) 3-Y-0+ **£4,857** (£1,445; £722; £360) **Stalls** High

Form RPR

0021 **1** **Blue Tomato**[7] 2813 5-9-8 74 .... LiamTreadwell(5) 11 88
(J M Bradley) *hld up stands side: hdwy to ld that gp over 1f out: kpt on wl fnl f: 1st of 11 stands side* **17/2**

0211 **2** *1 ½* **Yorkshire Blue**[1] 3003 7-9-3 64 6ex .... FergalLynch 9 74
(J S Goldie) *swtchd to stands side s: bhd and rdn along: hdwy over 1f out: chsd wnr ins fnl f: r.o: 2nd of 11 in gp* **11/2**[1]

6403 **3** *2 ½* **Dorn Dancer (IRE)**[34] 2020 4-9-3 64 .... RoystonFfrench 18 66
(D W Barker) *prom stands side: effrt over 2f out: kpt on same pce fnl f: 3rd of 11 in gp* **16/1**

5004 **4** *1 ¾* **Ellens Academy (IRE)**[9] 2749 11-9-8 69 .... FrancisNorton 6 66+
(E J Alston) *hld up far side: gd hdwy over 1f out: led that gp ins fnl f: no ch w stands side: 1st of 8 in gp* **12/1**

0600 **5** *1* **Currency**[13] 2661 9-9-11 72 .... KDarley 10 66+
(J M Bradley) *hld up outside of far side gp: effrt over 2f out: drifted over to stands side over 1f out: kpt on: 4th of 11 in gp* **25/1**

-065 **6** *nk* **Highland Cascade**[15] 2590 4-9-12 73 .... NCallan 12 66
(J M P Eustace) *racd on outside of stands side gp: effrt over 2f out: kpt on fnl f: no imp: 5th of 11 in gp* **25/1**

0320 **7** *½* **Soto**[13] 2661 3-9-4 72 .... PaulMulrennan 15 63
(M W Easterby) *chsd stands side ldrs: effrt over 2f out: no ex over 1f out: 6th of 11 in gp* **50/1**

4143 **8** *nk* **Divine Spirit**[6] 2852 5-9-7 68 .... DO'Donohoe 7 58+
(M Dods) *hld up in tch far side: hdwy and ev ch that gp ins fnl f: nt qckn: 2nd of 8 that gp* **15/2**[3]

0000 **9** *hd* **Sentiero Rosso (USA)**[18] 2504 4-9-2 63 .... (t) TomEaves 4 53+
(B Ellison) *chsd far side ldrs: effrt over 2f out: one pce fnl f: 3rd of 8 in gp* **20/1**

0004 **10** *shd* **Colonel Cotton (IRE)**[27] 2237 7-9-11 72 .... (v) PaulHanagan 1 62+
(R A Fahey) *keen: in tch far side: hdwy to ld that gp briefly ins fnl f: 4th of 8 in gp* **13/2**[2]

3350 **11** *½* **Trojan Flight**[13] 2661 5-9-13 74 .... TonyCulhane 5 67+
(D W Chapman) *hld up far side: hdwy and cl up that gp whn nt clr run ent fnl f: nt rcvr: 5th of 8 in gp* **12/1**

0050 **12** *½* **Loaderfun (IRE)**[13] 2661 4-9-9 73 .... DNolan(3) 17 60
(N Wilson) *cl up stands side: rdn over 2f out: wknd over 1f out: 7th of 11 in gp* **66/1**

-140 **13** *1* **Indian Spark**[13] 2661 12-9-7 68 .... J-PGuillambert 3 52+
(J S Goldie) *cl up far side: drvn over 2f out: no ex fr over 1f out: 6th of 8 in gp* **12/1**

0101 **14** *nk* **African Gift**[6] 2856 4-9-10 71 6ex .... DeanMcKeown 16 54
(J G Given) *hld up stands side: effrt over 2f out: sn no imp: 8th of 11 in gp* **10/1**

10-0 **15** *nk* **Sparkwell**[10] 2737 4-10-0 75 .... AdrianTNicholls 20 57
(D W Barker) *sn led stands side: hdd over 1f out: sn btn: 9th of 11 in gp* **33/1**

41-0 **16** *3* **Kool Ovation**[48] 1686 4-9-2 68 .... GregFairley(5) 8 41+
(A Dickman) *chsd far side ldrs tl wknd over 1f out: 7th of 8 in gp* **50/1**

0015 **17** *¾* **Brut**[6] 2852 4-9-2 68 .... MarkLawson(5) 2 39+
(D W Barker) *led far side: hung rt over 1f out: hdd ins fnl f: wknd: last of 8 in gp* **25/1**

0-02 **18** *2* **Bahamian Ballet**[21] 2417 4-9-7 68 .... JamieMackay 13 33
(E S McMahon) *racd on outside of stands side gp: hld up: rdn over 2f out: wknd over 1f out: 10th of 11 in gp* **20/1**

0000 **19** *1 ½* **Throw The Dice**[25] 2302 4-9-11 72 .... PhillipMakin 14 32
(D W Barker) *hld up stands side: rdn and wknd over 2f out: last of 11 in gp* **12/1**

1m 12.5s (-2.59) **Going Correction** -0.25s/f (Firm)
WFA 3 from 4yo+ 7lb **19** Ran SP% **126.2**
Speed ratings (Par 103):107,105,101,99,98 97,96,96,96,96 95,94,93,93,92 88,87,85,83
CSF £49.08 CT £779.59 TOTE £7.70: £2.00, £2.30, £3.60, £2.80; EX 53.60.
Owner Dab Hand Racing **Bred** Bearstone Stud **Trained** Sedbury, Gloucs
■ Stewards' Enquiry : Paul Hanagan two-day ban: careless riding (Jul 11,13)

FOCUS
A competitive sprint in which the stands side group held the edge over those that raced on the far side. Solid form.
Highland Cascade Official explanation: trainer said filly bled from the nose

3042 WEATHERBYS INSURANCE H'CAP 5f
9:20 (9:20) (Class 5) (0-75,73) 3-Y-0 **£4,857** (£1,445; £722; £360) **Stalls** High

Form RPR

1343 **1** **Toy Top (USA)**[21] 2410 3-9-1 67 .... (b) PhillipMakin 2 75
(M Dods) *trckd ldrs: rdn to ld 1f out: kpt on strly* **8/1**

2122 **2** *1 ½* **Hypnosis**[4] 2925 3-8-11 63 .... TomEaves 6 66
(D W Barker) *disp ld to 1f out: kpt on ins fnl f* **5/1**[3]

0023 **3** *nk* **Making Music**[31] 2109 3-9-1 67 .... (p) TonyCulhane 9 69
(T D Easterby) *midfield: outpcd over 2f out: kpt on fnl f: nrst fin* **10/1**

0222 **4** *½* **Northern Chorus (IRE)**[11] 2701 3-9-0 66 .... (v[1]) PaulHanagan 5 66
(A Dickman) *keen in tch: rdn 2f out: kpt on fnl f: no imp* **10/3**[2]

5141 **5** *½* **Jakeini (IRE)**[21] 2410 3-9-5 71 .... FergalLynch 3 69
(E S McMahon) *in tch: drvn 1/2-way: kpt on ins fnl f* **11/4**[1]

0-30 **6** *½* **Mint**[13] 2652 3-9-7 73 .... NCallan 8 70
(D W Barker) *led tl edgd lft and hdd appr fnl f: sn outpcd* **12/1**

-000 **7** *shd* **The Thrifty Bear**[31] 2109 3-8-12 64 .... LeeEnstone 10 60
(C W Fairhurst) *prom: rdn and outpcd over 2f out: no imp fnl f* **22/1**

6-30 **8** *½* **Fayr Sky (IRE)**[8] 2784 3-9-2 68 .... KDarley 7 62
(J J Quinn) *outpcd and bhd tl sme late hdwy: nvr on terms* **7/1**

0063 **9** *¾* **Night In (IRE)**[23] 2353 3-9-5 71 .... (t) KimTinkler 1 63
(N Tinkler) *racd wd in midfield: struggling fr 1/2-way* **16/1**

53-0 **10** *¾* **Hotham**[25] 2297 3-9-1 70 .... DNolan(3) 4 59
(N Wilson) *sn outpcd: nvr on terms* **25/1**

60.02 secs (-1.48) **Going Correction** -0.25s/f (Firm) **10** Ran SP% **120.9**
Speed ratings (Par 99):101,98,98,97,96 95,95,94,93,92
CSF £49.62 CT £425.76 TOTE £12.20: £2.40, £2.00, £2.50 Place 6 £216.06, Place 5 £146.29.
Owner D Vic Roper **Bred** L Kengye **Trained** Denton, Co Durham

FOCUS
An ordinary handicap contested by relatively exposed three-year-olds, but one in which the pace was sound throughout and those racing right up with the pace held the edge. An improved effort from the winner, while the second and third were pretty much to form.
Jakeini(IRE) Official explanation: jockey said colt ran flat
T/Plt: £274.50 to a £1 stake. Pool: £63,021.10. 167.55 winning tickets. T/Qpdt: £33.70 to a £1 stake. Pool: £4,811.20. 105.40 winning tickets. RY

2863

NEWMARKET (JULY) (R-H)
Friday, June 30

OFFICIAL GOING: Good to firm
Wind: Light, across

3043 HILLS DRINKS DISTRIBUTORS EBF MAIDEN FILLIES' STKS 6f
6:00 (6:02) (Class 4) 2-Y-0 **£4,533** (£1,348; £674; £336) **Stalls** Low

Form RPR

1 **Wid (USA)** 2-9-0 .... JimmyFortune 1 84
(J L Dunlop) *w'like: scope: chsd ldrs: swtchd rt over 1f out: rdn to ld wl ins fnl f: edgd lft: r.o* **16/1**

2 *½* **Light Shift (USA)** 2-9-0 .... TedDurcan 11 83+
(H R A Cecil) *leggy: scope: lw: trckd ldrs: rdn over 1f out: r.o* **7/1**[3]

3 *hd* **Yaqeen** 2-9-0 .... RHills 2 82+
(M A Jarvis) *gd sort: hld up: nt clr run fr over 1f out tl r.o wl ins fnl f* **5/2**[1]

426 **4** *shd* **Vital Statistics**[9] 2743 2-9-0 .... JohnEgan 9 82
(D R C Elsworth) *lw: w ldrs: rdn to ld 1f out: edgd lft and hdd wl ins fnl f* **5/2**[1]

5 *1 ¼* **Onida (IRE)** 2-9-0 .... PhilipRobinson 12 78
(C G Cox) *w'like: unf: w ldrs: rdn and ev ch over 1f out: styd on same pce fnl f* **14/1**

3 **6** *1* **Party (IRE)**[9] 2755 2-9-0 .... RichardHughes 8 78+
(R Hannon) *led: rdn over 2f out: hdd 1f out: styng on same pce whn hmpd wl ins fnl f* **11/2**[2]

7 *2* **Zonta Zitkala** 2-9-0 .... SebSanders 5 69
(R M Beckett) *gd sort: hld up: effrt and edgd lft over 1f out: nt trble ldrs* **16/1**

8 *3 ½* **Keidas (FR)** 2-9-0 .... GeorgeBaker 7 59
(C F Wall) *w'like: bkwd: s.i.s: hld up: n.d* **33/1**

9 *1 ¾* **Wickedish** 2-9-0 .... JoeFanning 4 54
(P Howling) *gd sort: bkwd: hld up: hmpd over 4f out: n.d* **66/1**

10 *3 ½* **Majolica** 2-8-9 .... JamesDoyle(5) 6 43
(N P Littmoden) *cmpt: b.bkwd: prom: lost pl 4f out: n.d after* **33/1**

11 *½* **Call Me Rosy (IRE)** 2-9-0 .... AlanMunro 10 42
(C F Wall) *cmpt: s.i.s: sn mid-div: wknd 2f out* **25/1**

0 **12** *11* **Pineapple Poll**[20] 2461 2-9-0 .... ChrisCatlin 3 9
(P L Gilligan) *swtg: mid-div: lost pl 1/2-way: sn bhd* **100/1**

1m 14.3s (0.95) **Going Correction** +0.025s/f (Good) **12** Ran SP% **115.7**
Speed ratings (Par 92):94,93,93,92,91 89,87,82,80,75 74,60
CSF £116.59 TOTE £18.40: £5.30, £2.60, £1.70; EX 115.40.
Owner Hamdan Al Maktoum **Bred** Shadwell Farm LLC **Trained** Arundel, W Sussex
■ Stewards' Enquiry : Jimmy Fortune caution: careless riding

FOCUS
A useful looking field of maiden fillies, and the form looks sound, although Vital Statistics probably did not quite reproduce her Queen Mary sixth in fourth.

NOTEBOOK
Wid(USA), whose stable scored with 16-1 shot Sudoor in a fillies' maiden at Newbury three days earlier, repeated the trick with this similarly unfancied filly. Her dam was a Listed winner at two and it would not be a surprise to see her move up into that sort of company in due course as she won a shade comfortably here from what looked a fair field. Her stable's juveniles invariably improve for a run. (op 14-1)
Light Shift(USA), a sister to Erewhon, a winner at two in the US and stakes placed over a mile, is also closely related to the high-class middle-distance pair Shiva and Limnos. Her Moyglare Stud Stakes entry suggested she had been showing plenty at home and she duly posted an encouraging display on her debut. She can only improve with time and when stepped up in trip. (tchd 13-2)

Yaqeen, who cost $400,000, was easily the most expensive of these at the sales. A half-sister to middle-distance winners Grand Couturier and Sir Edward Elgar, she was the rider's pick of the Hamdan Al Maktoum pair, in preference to the winner. Hills got it wrong this time but she was staying on well at the finish and will not have a problem getting off the mark. (tchd 9-4)
Vital Statistics, sixth in the Queen Mary on her previous start and stepping up in trip, brought a solid level of form to the race and her performance is probably a good guide to the level of the form. She had every chance but was beaten by some promising newcomers. Official explanation: jockey said saddle slipped (op 9-4)
Onida(IRE), who cost 100,000euros and is entered in the Phoenix Stakes, is out of a mare who won over 12 furlongs. She ran a promising race on her debut and clearly has more speed than the dam's side of her pedigree would suggest. (op 16-1)
Party(IRE), dropping back in trip having shown speed on her debut, again led the field. She could win a fair nursery after one more run. (op 13-2, 7-1 in places)

3044 SMIRNOFF H'CAP — 1m
6:30 (6:33) (Class 5) (0-75,74) 3-Y-0+ — **£3,886** (£1,156; £577; £288) **Stalls** Low

Form — RPR
/062 **1** **Optimus (USA)**[11] 2708 4-9-8 **71** ... AdamKirby(3) 1 — 85
(G A Butler) *b: hld up in tch: rdn to ld and edgd lft 1f out: r.o* **8/1**
0523 **2** *2* **Foolish Groom**[13] 2641 5-8-12 **58** ...(v) TedDurcan 14 — 67
(R Hollinshead) *s.i.s: hld up: nt clr run over 2f out: hdwy over 1f out: r.o: nt rch wnr* **16/1**
3-05 **3** *1 ¼* **Ali D**[8] 2789 8-8-11 **62** ... JamesDoyle(5) 7 — 68
(G Woodward) *lw: hld up: r.o ins fnl f: nrst fin* **12/1**
0054 **4** *nk* **Lincolneurocruiser**[7] 2820 4-8-11 **64** ... RussellKennemore(7) 3 — 69
(Mrs N Macauley) *lw: plld hrd and prom: rdn over 1f out: styd on same pce* **25/1**
-001 **5** *1* **Forthright**[15] 2585 5-10-0 **74** ... JimmyFortune 5 — 77
(A W Carroll) *chsd ldrs: rdn over 1f out: no ex* **8/1**
36-0 **6** *½* **Sonny Parkin**[177] 33 4-9-12 **72** ...(v) JayFord 9 — 74
(G A Huffer) *hld up in tch: rdn over 1f out: fnd nil* **25/1**
0065 **7** *hd* **Miss Madame (IRE)**[13] 2645 5-8-4 **55** oh3... LiamJones(5) 10 — 57
(T G Mills) *lw: plld hrd: mde most 7f: no ex* **16/1**
0000 **8** *1* **Logsdail**[14] 2618 6-9-10 **70** ...(p) RyanMoore 15 — 69
(G L Moore) *b: hld up: hdwy over 1f out: eased whn btn ins fnl f* **7/2**[1]
0261 **9** *nk* **Tender The Great (IRE)**[7] 2820 3-8-5 **61** ... ChrisCatlin 13 — 60
(V Smith) *hld up: hdwy over 1f out: no imp fnl f* **10/1**
0442 **10** *hd* **Tiber Tiger (IRE)**[7] 2820 6-9-3 **63** ...(b) DarryllHolland 4 — 61
(N P Littmoden) *hld up: effrt over 1f out: n.d* **9/2**[2]
0511 **11** *½* **Aggravation**[11] 2708 4-9-13 **73** 6ex... JohnEgan 2 — 70
(D R C Elsworth) *b.hind: lw: mid-div: hdwy 2f out: rdn and hung lft over 1f out: sn wknd* **7/1**[3]
500P **12** *1 ¼* **Halcyon Magic**[30] 2132 8-8-6 **55** oh5...(b) DominicFox(3) 12 — 49
(M Wigham) *chsd ldrs: rdn 1/2-way: wknd over 1f out* **100/1**
003 **13** *8* **Boreana**[15] 2587 3-9-3 **73** ... AlanMunro 11 — 49
(P W Chapple-Hyam) *lw: prom over 5f* **20/1**
00-0 **14** *2* **Paradise Street (IRE)**[73] 1070 3-9-0 **70** ... OscarUrbina 8 — 41
(J R Fanshawe) *plld hrd and prom: wknd over 2f out* **33/1**
100- **15** *3* **Oh Danny Boy**[193] 6622 5-9-10 **70** ... SebSanders 6 — 34
(Jane Chapple-Hyam) *bkwd: chsd ldrs: rdn over 3f out: wknd 2f out* **25/1**

1m 39.98s (-0.45) **Going Correction** +0.025s/f (Good)
WFA 3 from 4yo+ 10lb — **15** Ran SP% **123.9**
Speed ratings (Par 103):103,101,99,99,98 97,97,96,96,96 95,94,86,84,81
CSF £121.32 CT £1577.34 TOTE £12.30: £4.10, £5.00, £4.90; EX 174.70.
Owner Andrew P Wyer **Bred** Strategy Bloodstock **Trained** Blewbury, Oxon
FOCUS
A relatively low level handicap, but a competitive one, although the early pace was nothing special.

3045 STELLA ARTOIS CLAIMING STKS — 1m
7:00 (7:03) (Class 5) 3-Y-0 — **£3,886** (£1,156; £577; £288) **Stalls** Low

Form — RPR
300 **1** **Paraguay (USA)**[8] 2781 3-9-3 75 ... TedDurcan 1 — 78
(M R Channon) *lw: chsd ldrs: swtchd rt 2f out: rdn to ld ins fnl f: r.o* **9/1**
2 *shd* **Medieval Maiden** 3-8-9 ... TPQueally 6 — 70
(W J Musson) *w'like: hld up: hdwy over 1f out: r.o* **25/1**
0300 **3** *shd* **Participation**[14] 2608 3-9-0 79 ...(p) JimmyFortune 8 — 75
(M J Wallace) *b.hind: hld up: swtchd rt over 2f out: hdwy over 1f out: rdn and edgd lft ins fnl f: r.o* **6/1**
4-00 **4** *1 ¼* **Envision**[34] 2024 3-9-5 85 ... RyanMoore 4 — 77
(R Hannon) *chsd ldr: rdn to ld over 2f out: hung rt over 1f out: hdd and no ex ins fnl f* **9/4**[1]
2552 **5** *3* **Wee Charlie Castle (IRE)**[7] 2823 3-9-0 67 ... OscarUrbina 7 — 65
(G C H Chung) *led over 5f: rdn and hung rt over 1f out: no ex ins fnl f* **9/2**[3]
-322 **6** *nk* **Cape Win (IRE)**[10] 2727 3-8-4 67 ...(p) LiamJones(5) 5 — 59
(W J Haggas) *lw: hld up in tch: racd keenly: rdn over 1f out: wknd ins fnl f* **11/4**[2]
500 **7** *8* **Deserted Prince (IRE)**[13] 2648 3-8-9 57 ... JohnEgan 3 — 41
(M J Wallace) *hld up in tch: rdn over 1f out: sn wknd* **20/1**
-003 **8** *½* **Carpeting**[50] 1616 3-8-11 58 ...(v) ChrisCatlin 9 — 42
(D Morris) *hld up: rdn over 2f out: sn hung lft and wknd* **16/1**
000 **9** *24* **Maylea Gold (IRE)**[15] 2587 3-8-9 53 ... MickyFenton 2 — —
(Miss J Feilden) *plld hrd and prom: wknd wl over 2f out* **66/1**

1m 40.97s (0.54) **Going Correction** +0.025s/f (Good) — **9** Ran SP% **115.9**
Speed ratings (Par 99):98,97,97,96,93 93,85,84,60
CSF £203.05 TOTE £10.90: £3.00, £3.40, £2.10; EX 234.40.Paraguay (USA) was claimed by Miss V. Haigh for £18,000.
Owner Jumeirah Racing **Bred** Nutbush Farm **Trained** West Ilsley, Berks
FOCUS
This claimer featured three horses officially rated 75 or higher, but they were joined in a tight finish by an unfancied newcomer and the form is suspect.

3046 ROUTE COLCHESTER H'CAP — 1m 4f
7:35 (7:38) (Class 4) (0-80,77) 3-Y-0 — **£5,505** (£1,637; £818; £408) **Stalls** Centre

Form — RPR
6111 **1** **Gower Song**[4] 2929 3-9-4 **74** 6ex... JohnEgan 10 — 88
(D R C Elsworth) *hld up: hdwy over 3f out: rdn to ld over 1f out: hung rt ins fnl f: styd on* **15/8**[1]
-004 **2** *2* **Counting House (IRE)**[15] 2584 3-9-4 **74** ... SteveDrowne 9 — 85
(R Charlton) *lw: chsd ldrs: nt clr run over 2f out: sn rdn: styd on and hung lft ins fnl f: no imp* **11/2**[2]
0122 **3** *3* **Winds Of Change**[13] 2633 3-9-0 **70** ... JoeFanning 5 — 76
(M Johnston) *chsd ldr tl led over 3f out: rdn and hdd over 1f out: wknd ins fnl f* **8/1**
0541 **4** *¾* **Stellenbosch (USA)**[13] 2633 3-9-1 **71** ... RHills 6 — 76
(J W Hills) *hld up: hdwy over 2f out: styd on same pce fnl f* **12/1**
1-03 **5** *1 ¼* **Snark (IRE)**[46] 1738 3-9-6 **76** ... SebSanders 7 — 79
(P J Makin) *led: rdn over 4f out: hdd over 3f out: hung lft and wknd over 1f out* **6/1**[3]
5-15 **6** *1 ¾* **Power Of Future (GER)**[31] 2117 3-9-7 **77** ... RichardHughes 2 — 77
(H R A Cecil) *hmpd s: sn prom: rdn over 2f out: wknd fnl f* **7/1**
0-51 **7** *3* **Brigadore (USA)**[17] 2526 3-9-7 **77** ... JimmyFortune 11 — 72
(W R Muir) *lw: hld up: rdn and swtchd lft over 2f out: wknd over 1f out* **20/1**
31-0 **8** *1 ¼* **Altilhar (USA)**[53] 1547 3-9-2 **72** ... RyanMoore 8 — 65
(G L Moore) *hld up: n.d* **16/1**
0506 **9** *3* **Foreign Envoy (IRE)**[6] 2882 3-8-7 **63** ... OscarUrbina 1 — 52
(B W Hills) *hld up in tch: rdn over 2f out: sn hung lft and wknd* **25/1**
10-3 **10** *19* **Persian Express (USA)**[14] 2613 3-9-4 **74** ... MichaelHills 4 — 32
(B W Hills) *chsd ldrs over 9f* **33/1**
40-0 **11** *1 ¾* **Basiliko (USA)**[24] 2332 3-8-10 **73** ...(b[1]) MCGeran(7) 3 — 28
(P W Chapple-Hyam) *dwlt and wnt lft s: hld up: rdn over 4f out: wknd 3f out* **66/1**

2m 30.68s (-2.23) **Going Correction** +0.025s/f (Good) — **11** Ran SP% **114.7**
Speed ratings (Par 101):108,106,104,104,103 102,100,99,97,84 83
CSF £10.91 CT £65.91 TOTE £2.60: £1.40, £2.60, £1.70; EX 13.80.
Owner Usk Valley Stud **Bred** R E Crutchley **Trained** Newmarket, Suffolk
FOCUS
A fair handicap and solid form for the grade. A race worth treating positively, with the winner continuing to progress, the runner-up showing improved form, and the third and fourth pretty much to their Bath level..

3047 EBF JBR LEISURE LIMITED FILLIES' CONDITIONS STKS — 6f
8:05 (8:07) (Class 3) 3-Y-0+ — **£8,096** (£2,408; £1,203; £601) **Stalls** Low

Form — RPR
/3-0 **1** **Jewel In The Sand (IRE)**[59] 1377 4-8-7 101... RichardHughes 2 — 81
(R Hannon) *lw: chsd ldrs: rdn to ld over 1f out: r.o u.p* **11/2**
0-45 **2** *nk* **Gloved Hand**[20] 2429 4-8-7 86... OscarUrbina 7 — 81
(J R Fanshawe) *hld up: hdwy over 1f out: sn rdn: r.o* **11/4**[1]
01-6 **3** *1 ½* **Gimasha**[134] 433 4-8-10 ... AlanMunro 4 — 79
(W Jarvis) *trckd ldrs: led 2f out: sn rdn: hdd over 1f out: no ex ins fnl f* **3/1**[2]
6336 **4** *1* **Spectacular Show (IRE)**[20] 2441 3-8-3 70... ChrisCatlin 6 — 74
(M Quinn) *lw: hld up: hdwy over 1f out: sn rdn: no ex ins fnl f* **33/1**
0060 **5** *5* **Shifty Night (IRE)**[41] 1849 5-8-7 48... JohnEgan 5 — 58?
(Mrs C A Dunnett) *chsd ldrs 4f* **100/1**
-110 **6** *¾* **Empress Jain**[27] 2227 3-8-3 99 ow3... PhilipRobinson 1 — 57
(M A Jarvis) *led: hung rt and hdd 2f out: sn wknd* **10/3**[3]
331 **7** *9* **Stepping Stones**[15] 2587 3-8-3 82... JoeFanning 3 — 30+
(H R A Cecil) *lw: trckd ldr: hung rt fr 1/2-way: wknd 2f out* **13/2**

1m 12.8s (-0.55) **Going Correction** +0.025s/f (Good)
WFA 3 from 4yo+ 7lb — **7** Ran SP% **107.4**
Speed ratings (Par 104):104,103,101,100,93 92,80
CSF £18.40 TOTE £6.10: £2.40, £2.20; EX 24.50.
Owner Sand Associates **Bred** Gerrardstown House Stud **Trained** East Everleigh, Wilts
FOCUS
A messy conditions race, the form of which is held down by the fourth and fifth. No telling how good Jewel In The Sand is these days, but she was a long way off her official mark of 101 here.
NOTEBOOK
Jewel In The Sand(IRE), very lightly raced since winning the Cherry Hinton over the course and distance back in 2004, was best in at the weights for this conditions race and won for the first time since. She did not show much on her seasonal return but proved that she retains ability here, although a narrow success over a filly rated 15lb her inferior suggests her three-figure rating flatters her considerably. (tchd 5-1)
Gloved Hand, well backed into favouritism despite having a bit to find at the weights with one or two of her rivals, narrowly failed to justify the support. It is to be hoped that the Handicapper does not take this form literally as she has been held in handicap company recently off marks in the mid to high 80s, and it is probably more a case of the winner running well below her current mark. (op 10-3 tchd 7-2 in a place)
Gimasha was entitled to need this first outing since February, but she only finished a length in front of a filly rated 70 and she will have to improve a good deal if she is going to be winning soon off a mark in the 90s. (op 5-2 tchd 7-2)
Spectacular Show(IRE) is fully exposed, prefers softer ground and was out of her depth in this company. She did not run badly in the circumstances.
Shifty Night(IRE), who had the headgear left off this time, is a plating-class mare, so her relative proximity at the finish does not say a lot for the value of the form.
Empress Jain is all speed and plenty doubted whether she would get home over this extra furlong. Those doubts were confirmed. Official explanation: jockey said filly hung right (op 3-1)
Stepping Stones disappointed on this drop in trip, once again hanging right from some way out. When she won at Yarmouth she had a right-hand rail to race against, and that might be the key to future success with her as she is clearly not straightforward. Official explanation: jockey said saddle slipped

3048 TALK THE NIGHTCLUB H'CAP — 1m 2f
8:40 (8:41) (Class 4) (0-85,82) 3-Y-0+
£5,297 (£1,586; £793; £396; £198; £99) **Stalls** Centre

Form — RPR
2313 **1** **Dragon Slayer (IRE)**[22] 2387 4-9-9 **77** ... RyanMoore 1 — 85
(M J Attwater) *hld up: hdwy over 1f out: rdn to ld ins fnl f: edgd rt: r.o* **5/1**[2]
-532 **2** *shd* **Bold Act (IRE)**[18] 2510 4-9-6 **74** ... DaneO'Neill 3 — 82
(H Candy) *lw: hld up: hdwy over 3f out: rdn to ld over 1f out: hdd ins fnl f: r.o* **6/1**[3]
30-6 **3** *hd* **Sweet Indulgence (IRE)**[35] 1991 5-9-4 **77**... StephenDonohoe(5) 6 — 85
(W J Musson) *lw: hld up: hdwy over 1f out: r.o* **12/1**
-310 **4** *1* **Smooth Jazz**[22] 2387 4-9-7 **75** ... SebSanders 9 — 81
(R M Beckett) *chsd ldrs: rdn and ev ch over 1f out: styd on same pce* **7/1**
6-62 **5** *1 ¼* **Wellington Hall (GER)**[14] 2621 8-9-12 **80**... JimmyFortune 8 — 84
(P W Chapple-Hyam) *lw: hld up: hdwy over 1f out: no imp ins fnl f* **7/1**
-000 **6** *¾* **Rawdon (IRE)**[22] 2387 5-9-13 **81** ...(v) HayleyTurner 11 — 83
(M L W Bell) *chsd ldrs: rdn and ev ch over 1f out: styd on same pce* **16/1**
0-52 **7** *1* **Brief Goodbye**[22] 2387 6-9-8 **76** ... MickyFenton 12 — 76
(John Berry) *prom: rdn over 1f out: no ex* **9/2**[1]
-061 **8** *nk* **Winners Delight**[18] 2508 5-9-8 **76** ... RichardHughes 10 — 76
(C F Wall) *led: racd keenly: hdd and hmpd over 8f out: remained handy tl wknd ins fnl f* **7/1**
1000 **9** *nk* **Barry Island**[23] 2341 7-9-6 **74** ... JohnEgan 7 — 73
(D R C Elsworth) *s.i.s: hld up: rdn over 1f out: n.d* **12/1**
4006 **10** *½* **Hayyani (IRE)**[11] 2705 4-9-9 **77** ... RichardMullen 5 — 75
(K McAuliffe) *lw: s.i.s: hld up: rdn over 1f out: n.d* **40/1**

0-40 **11** *1* **Reaching Out (IRE)**[16] 2540 4-9-2 **70** .... DarryllHolland 4 66
(N P Littmoden) *racd keenly: led over 8f out: rdn and hdd over 1f out: wknd ins fnl f* **25/1**

2m 7.16s (0.72) **Going Correction** +0.025s/f (Good) **11** Ran SP% **114.2**
Speed ratings (Par 105):98,97,97,96,95 95,94,94,94,93 92
CSF £34.00 CT £339.47 TOTE £4.60: £1.70, £2.50, £3.70; EX 29.00.
Owner Carl Would **Bred** Arandora Star Syndicate **Trained** Wysall, Notts

FOCUS
A bunch finish and a modest time, so impossible to rate the form that highly.
Barry Island Official explanation: jockey said gelding was struck into behind

3049 ANTICA CLASSIC SAMBUCA H'CAP 5f
9:10 (9:10) (Class 4) (0-85,84) 3-Y-O **£5,505** (£1,637; £818; £408) **Stalls** Low

Form RPR
2121 **1** **Fantasy Explorer**[7] 2826 3-8-11 **74** 7ex .... DarryllHolland 2 89
(J J Quinn) *a.p: chsd ldr over 3f out: led over 1f out: rdn out* **11/8**[1]
2120 **2** *1 3/4* **Sarah's Art (IRE)**[4] 2931 3-8-2 **65** ....(b) ChrisCatlin 6 74
(N A Callaghan) *hld up: swtchd lft and hdwy over 1f out: r.o* **6/1**[3]
0603 **3** *1 1/4* **Azygous**[18] 2509 3-9-2 **79** .... AlanMunro 3 84
(J Akehurst) *chsd ldrs: outpcd over 3f out: hdwy over 1f out: r.o* **15/2**
4443 **4** *1 3/4* **Overwing (IRE)**[7] 2826 3-8-5 **68** .... RichardMullen 7 66
(R M H Cowell) *chsd ldrs: rdn 1/2-way: styd on same pce appr fnl f* **14/1**
5460 **5** *3/4* **Brunelleschi**[13] 2639 3-8-10 **73** ....(v) BrianReilly 1 69
(P L Gilligan) *chsd ldr over 1f: remained handy: swtchd lft 3f out: styd on same pce appr fnl f* **16/1**
0036 **6** *3/4* **Brandywell Boy (IRE)**[6] 2866 3-9-1 **78** .... SebSanders 8 71
(D J S Ffrench Davis) *lw: sn outpcd: rdn and hung lft over 1f out: nvr nrr* **9/1**
-202 **7** *1/2* **Fisola (IRE)**[13] 2639 3-9-0 **77** .... PhilipRobinson 5 68
(C G Cox) *sn outpcd* **9/2**[2]
10-0 **8** *3/4* **Gilt Linked**[6] 2866 3-9-7 **84** .... RyanMoore 4 72
(B W Hills) *led over 3f: wknd ins fnl f* **12/1**

59.09 secs (-0.47) **Going Correction** +0.025s/f (Good) **8** Ran SP% **116.6**
Speed ratings (Par 101):104,101,99,96,95 94,93,92
CSF £10.30 CT £46.90 TOTE £2.40: £1.10, £1.50, £2.40; EX 8.60 Place 6 £529.79, Place 5 £232.98.
Owner The Fantasy Fellowship E **Bred** Sexton Enterprises **Trained** Settrington, N Yorks

FOCUS
They went fast early in this sprint handicap and the improving winner did well to quicken as he did. Sound form, with the first two standing out at the weights beforehand.
Fisola(IRE) Official explanation: jockey said filly was slowly away
T/Plt: £1,177.60 to a £1 stake. Pool: £49,202.00. 30.50 winning tickets. T/Qpdt: £53.50 to a £1 stake. Pool: £4,649.90. 64.30 winning tickets. CR

2935 WOLVERHAMPTON (A.W) (L-H)
Friday, June 30

OFFICIAL GOING: Standard
Wind: Light, behind Weather: Fine and warm

3050 SPONSOR A RACE BY CALLING 0870 220 2442 MAIDEN STKS (DIV I) 5f 216y(P)
1:50 (1:51) (Class 5) 3-Y-O+ **£2,914** (£867; £433; £216) **Stalls** Low

Form RPR
-302 **1** **Elegant Times (IRE)**[34] 2019 3-8-10 63 ow1 .... SebSanders 8 64
(T D Easterby) *a.p: rdn to ld wl over 1f out: r.o* **11/2**[3]
0-43 **2** *1* **And I**[16] 2553 3-8-9 72 ....(p) DarryllHolland 7 60
(M P Tregoning) *led early: w ldr: led 4f out: rdn whn edgd rt and hdd wl over 1f out: edgd lft wl ins fnl f: nt qckn* **4/6**[1]
05 **3** *1* **Blushing Light (USA)**[6] 2859 3-9-0 .... FJohansson 10 62
(M A Magnusson) *chsd ldrs: rdn over 2f out: kpt on one pce fnl f* **20/1**
4 *5* **Bayberry King (USA)** 3-9-0 .... DaneO'Neill 1 47
(J S Goldie) *s.i.s: hdwy over 2f out: rdn and wkng whn edgd lft wl over 1f out* **5/1**[2]
00 **5** *1 1/2* **Mister Jingles**[32] 2080 3-8-7 .... MichaelJStainton(7) 9 43
(R M Whitaker) *broke wl: hld up and sn lost pl: nvr nr ldrs* **40/1**
0-40 **6** *nk* **Kirstys Lad**[45] 1764 4-9-7 36 ....(b) HayleyTurner 4 44?
(M Mullineaux) *sn chsng ldrs: wknd over 2f out* **40/1**
7 *1/2* **Whistle Away** 3-8-11 .... SaleemGolam(3) 2 41
(W R Swinburn) *s.i.s: sn mid-div: rdn over 2f out: btn whn swtchd rt over 1f out* **14/1**
0 **8** *nk* **Pronto Vende (IRE)**[23] 2343 3-8-11 .... AdamKirby(3) 3 40
(G A Butler) *outpcd* **20/1**
0000 **9** *2* **Warren Place**[25] 2298 6-9-7 36 ....(v) MickyFenton 5 36?
(A D Brown) *sn led: hdd 4f out: rdn whn n.m.r on ins over 2f out: sn wknd* **66/1**

1m 15.28s (-0.53) **Going Correction** -0.025s/f (Stan)
WFA 3 from 4yo+ 7lb **9** Ran SP% **114.6**
Speed ratings (Par 103):102,100,99,92,90 90,89,89,86
CSF £9.09 TOTE £5.30: £1.30, £1.10, £4.30; EX 10.80.
Owner Times Of Wigan **Bred** Times Of Wigan Ltd **Trained** Great Habton, N Yorks

FOCUS
This weak maiden was virtually a second slower than the other division. The favourite was below-par and the sixth and ninth limit the form.
Kirstys Lad Official explanation: jockey said gelding jumped left from stalls and suffered interference
Pronto Vende(IRE) Official explanation: jockey said gelding was outpaced and hung left

3051 RINGSIDE SUITE 700 THEATRE STYLE CONFERENCE CLAIMING STKS 1m 4f 50y(P)
2:20 (2:20) (Class 6) 4-Y-O+ **£3,238** (£963; £481; £240) **Stalls** Low

Form RPR
1011 **1** **Zalkani (IRE)**[8] 2790 6-9-4 70 .... DeanMcKeown 2 64
(J Pearce) *hld up: hdwy 6f out: led wl over 2f out: rdn and hdd wl over 1f out: styd on to ld nr fin* **1/2**[1]
0400 **2** *nk* **Tennessee Belle (IRE)**[6] 2861 4-7-9 35 ow3 .... KirstyMilczarek(7) 4 48
(C N Allen) *hld up in rr: hdwy 6f out: led wl over 1f out: rdr sn dropped whip: edgd lft ins fnl f: hdd nr fin* **25/1**
00-0 **3** *23* **Shaaban (IRE)**[11] 2702 5-8-6 58 ow1 .... AdamKirby(3) 5 18
(R J Price) *rn in snatches: in tch: jnd ldrs over 3f out: wknd qckly over 2f out* **16/1**[3]
160- **4** *14* **Gallery Breeze**[256] 5948 7-8-9 64 .... RobbieFitzpatrick 3 —
(P A Blockley) *led after 1f tl wl over 2f out: wknd qckly: fin lame* **9/4**[2]
50-0 **5** *1 1/2* **Keyalzao (IRE)**[8] 2789 4-7-10 32 ....(v) DominicFox(3) 6 —
(A Crook) *hld up in tch: wnt 2nd 9f out: rdn and wknd qckly 3f out* **50/1**
00/0 **6** *dist* **Dartanian**[11] 2702 4-8-4 50 .... FrancisFerris 1 —
(M Scudamore) *led 1f: rdn and lost pl 8f out: virtually p.u 5f out: t.o* **25/1**

2m 43.88s (1.46) **Going Correction** -0.025s/f (Stan) **6** Ran SP% **113.0**
Speed ratings (Par 101):94,93,78,69,68 —
CSF £18.42 TOTE £1.30: £1.10, £8.00; EX 9.90.
Owner Jeff Pearce **Bred** His Highness The Aga Khan's Studs S C **Trained** Newmarket, Suffolk

FOCUS
A very uncompetitive event run in a slow time, and worthless form.
Gallery Breeze Official explanation: vet said mare finished lame
Dartanian Official explanation: jockey said mare moved badly throughout

3052 INFORMRACING.COM FLAT RACING SPEED RATINGS H'CAP 5f 216y(P)
2:50 (2:50) (Class 6) (0-60,60) 3-Y-O+ **£3,071** (£906; £453) **Stalls** Low

Form RPR
0000 **1** **Joyeaux**[34] 2020 4-10-0 **60** ....(v[1]) DerekMcGaffin 12 68
(J Hetherton) *bhd: rdn 3f out: hdwy over 1f out: r.o wl u.p to ld nr fin* **20/1**
0003 **2** *1/2* **Bond Playboy**[8] 2792 6-10-0 **60** ....(p) DarrenWilliams 4 67
(G R Oldroyd) *a.p: rdn to ld over 1f out: edgd lft ins fnl f: hdd nr fin* **5/1**[1]
-500 **3** *hd* **Val De Maal (IRE)**[8] 2792 6-9-13 **59** ....(b[1]) DaneO'Neill 3 65
(Miss J A Camacho) *s.i.s: rdn and hdwy wl over 1f out: ev ch whn n.m.r on ins wl ins fnl f: r.o* **20/1**
0140 **4** *nk* **Bahrain Gold (IRE)**[7] 2811 6-9-4 **53** ....(b) AdamKirby(3) 10 58
(N P McCormack) *led early: a.p: rdn over 1f out: edgd lft ent fnl f: r.o* **10/1**
0600 **5** *2* **Mind Alert**[28] 2207 5-9-4 **53** ....(v) PatrickMathers(3) 5 52+
(D Shaw) *hld up in mid-div: hdwy on ins 2f out: rdn over 1f out: n.m.r ins fnl f: no ex* **20/1**
0004 **6** *shd* **Mountain Pass (USA)**[8] 2792 4-9-7 **58** ....(v) DerekNolan(5) 1 57
(M J Wallace) *chsd ldrs: rdn to ld wl over 1f out: sn hdd: hld whn nt clr run and swtchd rt ins fnl f: one pce* **5/1**[1]
2106 **7** *nk* **Ruman (IRE)**[134] 428 4-9-12 **58** .... RobbieFitzpatrick 9 56+
(M J Attwater) *bhd: hmpd over 3f out: nt clr run over 1f out: swtchd lft ent fnl f: nrst fin* **8/1**[3]
0-00 **8** *nk* **White Ledger (IRE)**[160] 164 7-9-9 **55** .... PatDobbs 13 52
(R E Peacock) *in rr: c wd st: rdn over 1f out: nvr nrr* **50/1**
2526 **9** *hd* **Green Pirate**[21] 2390 4-9-0 **53** ....(p) MichaelJStainton(7) 6 49
(M Wellings) *hld up in mid-div: rdn 1f out: no rspnse* **5/1**[1]
0300 **10** *1/2* **Edin Burgher (FR)**[4] 2936 5-9-4 **55** .... MarcHalford(5) 11 50
(T T Clement) *in tch: lost pl 4f out: sn rdn: c v wd st: n.d* **10/1**
0530 **11** *1 1/2* **Far Note (USA)**[136] 410 8-9-0 **53** ....(bt) MSemple(7) 2 43
(S R Bowring) *prom: led over 3f out: hung rt and hdd wl over 1f out: wknd ent fnl f* **20/1**
0050 **12** *5* **Doctor's Cave**[8] 2792 4-9-9 **55** ....(b) SebSanders 8 30
(K O Cunningham-Brown) *chsd ldrs: rdn over 2f out: wknd wl over 1f out* **12/1**
1004 **13** *3 1/2* **Auentraum (GER)**[28] 2207 6-9-12 **58** ....(p) DarryllHolland 7 23
(C R Dore) *sn led: hdd over 3f out: rdn and wknd over 1f out* **7/1**[2]

1m 15.01s (-0.80) **Going Correction** -0.025s/f (Stan) **13** Ran SP% **120.5**
Speed ratings (Par 101):104,103,103,102,100 99,99,99,98,98 96,89,84
CSF £111.15 CT £2139.83 TOTE £31.20: £6.80, £1.80, £8.20; EX 127.60.
Owner PSB Holdings Ltd **Bred** Mrs Ann Jarvis **Trained** Norton, N Yorks
■ Stewards' Enquiry : Darren Williams one-day ban: careless riding (Jul 11)

FOCUS
There was quite a bit of trouble in running in this typically wide-open low-grade sprint handicap. Solid form.
Bond Playboy Official explanation: jockey said gelding hung left
Ruman(IRE) ◆ Official explanation: jockey said gelding was unlucky in running
Auentraum(GER) Official explanation: jockey said gelding hung right

3053 SPONSOR A RACE BY CALLING 0870 220 2442 MAIDEN STKS (DIV II) 5f 216y(P)
3:20 (3:20) (Class 5) 3-Y-O+ **£2,914** (£867; £433; £216) **Stalls** Low

Form RPR
0-6 **1** **Greek Renaissance (IRE)**[41] 1844 3-9-0 .... DarryllHolland 1 87+
(M P Tregoning) *hld up in tch: nt clr run over 1f out: led on bit ins fnl f: easily* **4/5**[1]
33 **2** *3* **Evident Pride (USA)**[66] 1212 3-8-11 .... NeilChalmers(3) 4 69
(B R Johnson) *s.i.s: hdwy on ins over 3f out: outpcd 2f out: rallying whn edgd lft jst ins fnl f: r.o to snatch 2nd* **7/2**[2]
06 **3** *shd* **Nightstrike (IRE)**[17] 2532 3-8-9 .... DaneO'Neill 6 64
(H Candy) *a.p: rdn and ev ch over 1f out: nt qckn ins fnl f* **12/1**
0-5 **4** *hd* **Indian Ballet**[27] 2235 3-8-9 .... SebSanders 3 63
(M A Jarvis) *led: rdn wl over 1f out: hdd and no ex ins fnl f* **4/1**[3]
-0 **5** *2 1/2* **Hot Agnes**[14] 2605 3-8-9 .... MichaelTebbutt 9 56+
(H J Collingridge) *hld up and bhd: hdwy wl over 1f out: sn pushed along: nvr trbld ldrs* **33/1**
-060 **6** *6* **Harrington Bates**[31] 2112 5-9-7 43 .... VHalliday 5 45
(R M Whitaker) *hld up in tch: hung rt over 2f out: sn wknd* **25/1**
0 **7** *nk* **One More Than Ten**[9] 2763 3-8-9 .... DuranFentiman(5) 10 42
(T D Easterby) *s.i.s: a bhd* **66/1**
8 *8* **Miss Imperious** 3-8-9 .... DerekMcGaffin 7 13
(B Smart) *s.i.s: a bhd* **33/1**
0000 **9** *7* **Pyramid**[23] 2347 4-9-7 48 .... BrianReilly 2 —
(P L Gilligan) *w ldr over 2f: sn rdn: wknd 2f out* **20/1**
050- **10** *1 3/4* **Kamari Gold**[240] 6224 3-9-0 43 .... DarrenWilliams 8 —
(M Mullineaux) *sn bhd* **66/1**

1m 14.31s (-1.50) **Going Correction** -0.025s/f (Stan)
WFA 3 from 4yo+ 7lb **10** Ran SP% **122.9**
Speed ratings (Par 103):109,105,104,104,101 93,92,82,72,70
CSF £3.83 TOTE £1.90: £1.10, £1.20, £2.80; EX 6.00.
Owner Ballymacoll Stud **Bred** Ballymacoll Stud Farm Ltd **Trained** Lambourn, Berks

FOCUS
This was almost a second quicker than the first division and faster than the Class 6 handicap. Quite sound, with the runner-up to form. The winner could be on a fair mark after this.
Miss Imperious Official explanation: jockey said filly was slowly away and ran green

3054 ENJOY EXECUTIVE HOSPITALITY AT WOLVERHAMPTON (S) STKS 7f 32y(P)
3:50 (3:52) (Class 6) 2-Y-O **£2,388** (£705; £352) **Stalls** Low

Form RPR
30 **1** **Feisty**[15] 2588 2-8-6 .... FrancisFerris 6 56
(Rae Guest) *sn chsng ldr: rdn 3f out: led jst ins fnl f: edgd lft: r.o* **14/1**
063 **2** *1/2* **House Arrest**[6] 2857 2-8-6 .... DarryllHolland 2 55
(I A Wood) *led: rdn over 1f out: hdd jst ins fnl f: nt qckn* **9/4**[1]
006 **3** *2* **Moist**[15] 2588 2-8-3 .... NelsonDeSouza(3) 7 50
(N A Callaghan) *dwlt: hld up: hdwy over 3f out: rdn over 2f out: sn outpcd: kpt on ins fnl f* **11/4**[2]

	4	nk	**The Slider** 2-7-13 .... KevinGhunowa(7) 3 (P A Blockley) *hld up: outpcd over 2f out: styd on ins fnl f* **12/1**	49
0	5	10	**Moody Goose**[59] [1379] 2-8-6 .... RobbieFitzpatrick 5 (M Meade) *s.i.s: t.k.h: sn in tch: bhd fnl 3f* **14/1**	24
410	6	shd	**Mollyanko**[25] [2294] 2-8-7 .... MarcHalford(5) 4 (W G M Turner) *s.s: a bhd* **7/2**[3]	30
0	7	shd	**Corrucaseco**[11] [2709] 2-8-6 .... HayleyTurner 1 (M D I Usher) *prom over 3f* **28/1**	24

1m 32.58s (2.18) **Going Correction** -0.025s/f (Stan) **7** Ran SP% **104.1**
Speed ratings (Par 91):86,85,83,82,71 71,71
CSF £36.76 TOTE £16.50: £4.20, £1.70; EX 41.70.There was no bid for the winner.
Owner Rae Guest **Bred** Miss Rachel E Flynn **Trained** Newmarket, Suffolk
■ Roxy Singer was withdrawn (11/2, refused to enter stalls). R4 applies, deduct 15p in the £.

FOCUS
A poor seller, the time and those with form confirming that assessment.

NOTEBOOK
Feisty lived up to her name after being supported in a similar event at Yarmouth last time when she finished a long way behind Moist after losing her action.
House Arrest got the trip well in this lower grade but did not find as much off the bridle as the winner. (tchd 5-2)
Moist had finished well ahead of the winner at Yarmouth but Feisty lost her action that day. (op 7-2)
The Slider, despite being a half-sister to course-and-distance maiden winner Actuality, is bred to need further. Beginning her career in the basement, it does look as though she will improve when stepped up in distance. (op 8-1)

3055 YELL H'CAP — 7f 32y(P)
4:20 (4:22) (Class 5) (0-70,70) 3-Y-0 **£3,886** (£1,156; £577; £288) **Stalls** High

Form				RPR
2200	1		**Catbang (IRE)**[4] [2932] 3-9-2 **65** .... MickyFenton 3 (N A Callaghan) *s.i.s: t.k.h in mid-div: hdwy over 3f out: rdn and swtchd rt over 1f out: led ins fnl f: edgd lft: r.o* **3/1**[1]	75
0-00	2	1 ¾	**Corrib (IRE)**[24] [2318] 3-9-7 **70** .... FrancisFerris 10 (B Palling) *s.i.s: sn chsng ldrs: rdn over 2f out: led over 1f out: hdd and nt qckn ins fnl f* **33/1**	75
1	3	nk	**Ask No More**[15] [2575] 3-9-6 **69** .... BrianReilly 12 (P L Gilligan) *hld up in mid-div: rdn over 3f out: hdwy over 2f out: kpt on ins fnl f* **12/1**	73
2042	4	1 ¼	**Imperial Lucky (IRE)**[4] [2921] 3-9-1 **69** .... DerekNolan(5) 4 (M J Wallace) *s.i.s: rdn and hdwy over 2f out: kpt on same pce fnl f* **3/1**[1]	70
5644	5	shd	**Opera Writer (IRE)**[10] [2734] 3-8-12 **66** ....(e) DuranFentiman(5) 11 (T D Easterby) *s.i.s: bhd: rdn over 2f out: late hdwy: nrst fin* **14/1**	67
-316	6	1 ½	**Lii Najma**[20] [2459] 3-8-10 **66** .... WilliamCarson(7) 1 (C E Brittain) *prom: n.m.r on ins and lost pl after 1f: plld out wl over 1f out: sme late prog* **15/2**[3]	63
030	7	1	**Even Bolder**[28] [2188] 3-9-7 **70** .... PatDobbs 9 (S Kirk) *led 1f: led over 2f out: rdn and hdd over 1f out: wknd ins fnl f* **16/1**	64
1505	8	1 ¾	**Boldinor**[15] [2576] 3-9-4 **67** .... AlanDaly 2 (N E Berry) *hld up: sn in tch: rdn over 2f out: wknd wl over 1f out* **14/1**	57
0-06	9	8	**Henchman**[41] [1851] 3-9-0 **66** .... NelsonDeSouza(3) 7 (Lady Herries) *prom over 3f* **8/1**	35
6005	10	hd	**Ockums Razor (IRE)**[28] [2208] 3-9-4 **70** .... JohnMcAuley(3) 5 (C A Dwyer) *prom: led over 4f out: rdn and hdd over 2f out: wknd wl over 1f out* **12/1**	38
6-50	11	2	**Mouchoir**[13] [2652] 3-9-7 **70** ....(b) DarryllHolland 6 (P J Makin) *a bhd* **10/1**	33
33-0	12	18	**Rose Of Inchinor**[29] [2177] 3-9-4 **67** .... DaneO'Neill 8 (M P Tregoning) *led after 1f tl over 4f out: wknd over 3f out* **13/2**[2]	—

1m 29.11s (-1.29) **Going Correction** -0.025s/f (Stan) **12** Ran SP% **132.8**
Speed ratings (Par 99):106,104,103,102,102 100,99,97,88,87 85,65
CSF £143.95 CT £1140.23 TOTE £4.50: £2.10, £9.70, £3.80; EX 197.90.
Owner R K Carvill **Bred** Addison Racing Ltd Inc **Trained** Newmarket, Suffolk

FOCUS
A fair handicap, and sound enough form.
Mouchoir Official explanation: jockey said gelding would not face the kickback

3056 HOLD YOUR CHRISTMAS PARTY AT WOLVERHAMPTON AMATEUR RIDERS' H'CAP — 1m 141y(P)
4:50 (4:50) (Class 6) (0-60,60) 4-Y-0+ **£2,637** (£811; £405) **Stalls** Low

Form				RPR
3100	1		**Sol Rojo**[11] [2702] 4-11-1 **59** ....(v) MrSPearce(5) 8 (J Pearce) *hld up in mid-div: hdwy 2f out: rdn to ld ins fnl f: jst hld on* **11/2**[2]	69
-660	2	shd	**Band**[14] [2612] 6-10-7 **53** .... MissEGeorge(7) 4 (E S McMahon) *a.p: wnt 2nd 3f out: rdn to ld 1f out: hdd ins fnl f: r.o* **9/2**[1]	63
3433	3	2 ½	**Fulvio (USA)**[4] [2936] 6-10-9 **55** ....(v) MissFGuillambert(7) 13 (P Howling) *s.i.s: hld up and bhd: hdwy over 2f out: c wd st: ev ch ins fnl f: nt qckn* **8/1**	60
-000	4	1 ¼	**Cantarna (IRE)**[34] [2025] 5-10-13 **57** .... MrStephenHarrison(5) 11 (J Mackie) *hld up in mid-div: rdn and hdwy over 2f out: one pce fnl f* **11/2**[2]	59
0300	5	nk	**Shannon Arms (USA)**[11] [2702] 5-10-11 **57** .... MrCMartin(7) 3 (R Brotherton) *t.k.h: led over 6f out: rdn and hdd 1f out: wknd wl ins fnl f* **15/2**[3]	58
0-00	6	½	**Bridegroom**[30] [2148] 4-11-5 **58** ....(p) MrSWalker 2 (Lady Herries) *a.p: rdn over 3f out: btn whn swtchd lft wl ins fnl f* **8/1**	58
0-00	7	2 ½	**Emperor's Well**[11] [2702] 7-11-0 **60** ....(b) MissJCoward(7) 1 (M W Easterby) *led: hdd over 6f out: chsd ldr to 3f out: rdn and ev ch over 1f out: wknd fnl f* **14/1**	55
000	8	3	**Samson Quest**[60] [1353] 4-10-11 **55** ....(v) MrMJJSmith(5) 9 (A W Carroll) *bhd: sme hdwy on ins wl over 1f out: n.d* **15/2**[3]	44
100/	9	6	**Oh Golly Gosh**[179] [6064] 5-11-4 **57** .... MrsEmmaLittmoden 10 (N P Littmoden) *s.i.s: a bhd* **25/1**	33
-035	10	1 ¼	**Zando**[8] [2794] 4-10-9 **55** ....(v[1]) MissIPickard(7) 6 (E G Bevan) *s.i.s: bhd tl hdwy on outside over 2f out: c wd st: sn wknd* **8/1**	28
3360	11	4	**Drumroll (IRE)**[11] [2702] 4-10-11 **57** ....(b[1]) MrRBirkett(7) 7 (Miss J Feilden) *towards rr: rdn 4f out: no rspnse* **16/1**	22
404-	12	16	**Monashee Express (IRE)**[333] [3991] 4-10-11 **55** .... MrNPearce(5) 12 (G H Yardley) *a in rr: rdn over 3f out: eased whn no ch fnl 2f* **28/1**	—

1m 52.03s (0.27) **Going Correction** -0.025s/f (Stan) **12** Ran SP% **125.7**
Speed ratings (Par 101):97,96,94,93,93 92,90,87,82,81 77,63
CSF £32.47 CT £209.48 TOTE £6.40: £2.80, £2.10, £2.40; EX 36.80 Place 6 £31.72, Place 5 £24.09.
Owner sportaracing.com **Bred** Mrs A Yearley **Trained** Newmarket, Suffolk

FOCUS
They went a strong gallop which is often the case in these amateur events. The form looks solid and should prove reliable.
T/Plt: £33.70 to a £1 stake. Pool: £33,904.50. 734.40 winning tickets. T/Qpdt: £51.50 to a £1 stake. Pool: £2,013.00. 28.90 winning tickets. KH

3057 - 3059a (Foreign Racing) - See Raceform Interactive

2467 CURRAGH (R-H)
Friday, June 30

OFFICIAL GOING: Good

3060a WOODPARK & BALLYSHEEHAN STUDS STKS (LISTED RACE) (FILLIES) — 7f
7:30 (7:31) 2-Y-O **£24,693** (£7,244; £3,451; £1,175)

			RPR
1		**Gaudeamus (USA)**[24] [2336] 2-8-12 .... KJManning 2 (J S Bolger, Ire) *hld up in tch: 4th and smooth hdwy 2f out: led 1 1/2f out: clr whn edgd rt u.p ins fnl f: styd on wl* **10/3**[2]	94+
2	2	**The Real Thing (IRE)**[20] [2467] 2-8-12 .... PShanahan 5 (C Collins, Ire) *hld up in tch: 6th after 1/2-way: 4th and rdn over 1f out: 2nd and kpt on wl ins fnl f* **4/1**[3]	89
3	¾	**Simonetta (IRE)**[26] [2264] 2-8-12 ....(p) DJMoran 6 (J S Bolger, Ire) *led: rdn and strly pressed 2f out: hdd 1 1/2f out: 3rd and no ex ins fnl f* **12/1**	87
4	hd	**Pelican Waters (IRE)**[9] [2764] 2-8-12 .... MJKinane 3 (Mrs John Harrington, Ire) *prom early: settled towards rr: 7th under 2f out: kpt on u.p fnl f* **12/1**	87
5	2	**Liscanna (IRE)** 2-8-12 .... KFallon 8 (David Wachman, Ire) *s.i.s: sn trckd ldrs: 4th appr 1/2-way: 6th and no imp whn sltly checked 1f out: kpt on same pce* **7/1**	82
6	nk	**Evening Rushour (IRE)**[16] [2557] 2-8-12 .... JAHeffernan 4 (Brian Nolan, Ire) *prom: 2nd 1/2-way: 3rd u.p 2f out: no ex fr over 1f out* **25/1**	81
7	2 ½	**Miss Beatrix (IRE)**[16] [2557] 2-8-12 .... DPMcDonogh 1 (Kevin Prendergast, Ire) *settled 3rd: 2nd and rdn to chal 2f out: no ex over 1f out: eased cl home* **9/4**[1]	75
8	4 ½	**Moverra (IRE)**[13] [2665] 2-8-12 .... NGMcCullagh 7 (M J Grassick, Ire) *chsd ldrs early: rdn and wknd over 2f out: eased ins fnl f* **14/1**	63

1m 27.7s **Going Correction** 0.0s/f (Good) **8** Ran SP% **112.2**
Speed ratings: 98,95,94,94,92 92,89,84
CSF £16.42 TOTE £4.60: £1.50, £1.40, £3.30; DF 18.60.
Owner Mrs J S Bolger **Bred** Manganard LLC **Trained** Coolcullen, Co Carlow

FOCUS
It is very hard to rate this much higher than it has been as there was little decent form on offer pre-race.

NOTEBOOK
Gaudeamus(USA) ran out a ready winner on this debut in Listed company and appreciated the return to an easier surface. She is clearly progressing nicely, left the impression she will enjoy the step up to a mile in due course, and should be high on confidence now. Her trainer later indicated that the Group 1 Moyglare Stud Stakes was her main target this term. (op 3/1)
The Real Thing(IRE), a course maiden winner over six furlongs last time, picked up nicely approaching the final furlong only to find the winner gone beyond recall. She got the extra furlong well and is capable of finding a race in this class before the season's end. (op 4/1 tchd 9/2)
Simonetta(IRE), in first-time cheekpieces, kept to her task when headed by her winning stablemate, but did not appear totally suited by the drop back to this trip. (op 12/1 tchd 14/1)
Pelican Waters(IRE), whose yard won this event last season, posted a much-improved effort and stayed the extra furlong well enough. She failed to seriously threaten, however.
Miss Beatrix(IRE), easily off the mark at Leopardstown last time, looked a threat two from home, yet ultimately found much less than anticipated when push came to shove. She has it to prove now.

3061 - 3063a (Foreign Racing) - See Raceform Interactive

2517 CHESTER (L-H)
Saturday, July 1

OFFICIAL GOING: Good to firm changing to good to firm (firm in places) after race 3 (3.15pm)
Wind: Light, behind. Weather: Hot & sunny.

3064 WARWICK INTERNATIONAL NOVICE STKS — 5f 16y
2:05 (2:05) (Class 4) 2-Y-O **£4,728** (£1,406; £702; £351) **Stalls** Low

Form				RPR
221	1		**Invincible Force (IRE)**[7] [2878] 2-9-2 .... FrancisNorton 2 (Ms Deborah J Evans) *mde all: rdn ins fnl f: r.o* **11/4**[2]	87
2310	2	1	**Dimboola**[11] [2724] 2-9-5 .... MichaelHills 1 (B W Hills) *sn chsd ldrs: rdn and edgd lft over 1f out: r.o to take 2nd fnl strides* **5/2**[1]	86
1400	3	shd	**Stolt (IRE)**[11] [2724] 2-9-2 .... DNolan(3) 5 (N Wilson) *a.p: rdn and ev ch over 1f out: nt qckn ins fnl f* **10/1**	86
01	4	1	**Northern Fling**[18] [2517] 2-9-5 .... AdrianTNicholls 3 (D Nicholls) *chsd ldrs: drew upsides ldng pair wl over 2f out: sn hung rt: lost grnd ent fnl 2f: kpt on after tl one pce fnl st* **5/2**[1]	85+
2135	5	3 ½	**Mind The Style**[36] [1977] 2-9-0 .... LiamJones(5) 4 (W G M Turner) *pushed along and outpcd after 1f: nvr trbld ldrs* **7/1**[3]	70

61.75 secs (-0.30) **Going Correction** -0.15s/f (Firm) **5** Ran SP% **105.4**
Speed ratings (Par 96):96,94,94,92,87
CSF £9.06 TOTE £3.60: £1.70, £1.70; EX 13.60.
Owner Terry Cummins **Bred** Robert Wilson **Trained** Lydiate, Merseyside

FOCUS
A fair novice event in which they went a good gallop. The winner got the run of the race. Not much to choose between the first four, with the second and third rated close to their pre-race marks.

NOTEBOOK
Invincible Force(IRE), who received weight from the rest of the field, got out of the stalls quickly and grabbed the rail. Hugging it throughout, he was always holding his pursuers and, having shown ability on heavy ground and fast ground, he is clearly a versatile sort. (op 3-1)
Dimboola, who finished in mid-division in the Windsor Castle Stakes, had the best draw but he was not as fast away as the eventual winner and was denied the lead next to the rail. He ran well enough but his form appears to have plateaued and he looks likely to remain vulnerable to more progressive rivals. (tchd 9-4)
Stolt(IRE), who finished one place in front of Dimboola at Royal Ascot when an unconsidered 100-1 shot, again finished close to the Barry Hills-trained colt. Both he and the runner-up help set the level of the form. (op 8-1)

Northern Fling, who won his maiden over the course and distance last time, ran green and came wide into the straight. Inexperience cost him here but he is likely to improve with time. Official explanation: jockey said colt was unsuited by the good to firm ground (op 9-4)

Mind The Style was expected to appreciate this quicker ground but he struggled to go the early pace and was never really a threat.

3065 BRYN THOMAS CRANE HIRE H'CAP — 1m 4f 66y

2:40 (2:40) (Class 4) (0-85,79) 3-Y-O **£5,829** (£1,734; £866; £432) **Stalls** Low

Form	Pos	Dist	Horse / (Trainer) comment	Jockey	SP	RPR
2312	**1**		**Dream Champion**[3] 2986 3-9-2 **74** (M R Channon) *a.p: led over 3f out: rdn clr over 2f out: styd on wl*	FergalLynch 5	**1/1**[1]	80+
4610	**2**	*5*	**Norman Beckett**[14] 2659 3-8-12 **73** (I Semple) *trckd ldrs: rdn over 5f out: wnt 2nd 3f out: one pce and no imp on wnr fnl 2f*	(p) DNolan(3) 1	**5/1**[3]	71
000-	**3**	*1 1/2*	**Trafalgar Day**[249] 6102 3-8-7 **65** (W M Brisbourne) *hld up: rdn 5f out: nt clr run 3f out: swtchd rt over 2f out: sn wnt 3rd: one pce after*	RichardMullen 2	**10/1**	61
50-5	**4**	*15*	**Gamesters Lady**[15] 2613 3-9-7 **79** (W M Brisbourne) *trckd ldrs: pushed along wl over 7f out: outpcd over 5f out: hung rt whn bhd over 4f out: n.d after*	DarrenWilliams 4	**14/1**	51
0-10	**5**	*7*	**Teach To Preach (USA)**[25] 2324 3-9-1 **73** (B W Hills) *led: rdn and hdd over 3f out: wknd over 2f out*	MichaelHills 3	**11/4**[2]	33

2m 38.59s (-2.06) **Going Correction** -0.15s/f (Firm) **5** Ran SP% **109.1**

Speed ratings (Par 102):100,96,95,85,81

CSF £6.29 TOTE £1.90: £1.20, £2.50; EX 4.60.

Owner Jaber Abdullah **Bred** G W Turner And Miss S J Turner **Trained** West Ilsley, Berks

FOCUS

An uncompetitive handicap and ordinary form for the grade. The winner confirmed his improved Salisbury running.

Teach To Preach(USA) Official explanation: jockey said colt was unsuited by the good to firm ground

3066 WARWICK INTERNATIONAL MAIDEN STKS — 1m 2f 75y

3:15 (3:15) (Class 4) 3-Y-O+ **£5,829** (£1,734; £866; £432) **Stalls** High

Form	Pos	Dist	Horse / (Trainer) comment	Jockey	SP	RPR
0-3	**1**		**Mabadi (USA)**[16] 2578 3-8-11 (B W Hills) *racd keenly: chsd ldr: led over 1f out: sn lugged lft: drvn out*	MichaelHills 5	**4/9**[1]	69
53	**2**	*1*	**Avelian (IRE)**[21] 2448 3-9-2 (W J Haggas) *hld up: hdwy over 4f out: rdn over 3f out: edgd lft over 1f out: r.o cl home*	FergalLynch 1	**11/4**[2]	73
5435	**3**	*nk*	**Macho Dancer (IRE)**[6] 2901 3-8-8 46 (K J Burke) *led: rdn and hdd over 1f out: no ex cl home*	EdwardCreighton(3) 4	**16/1**[3]	67?
0-0	**4**	*18*	**Skit**[51] 1605 3-9-2 (W M Brisbourne) *chsd ldrs: rdn and wknd over 4f out*	DarrenWilliams 3	**25/1**	38
00	**5**	*8*	**Smoke It (IRE)**[36] 1984 3-9-2 (A Berry) *sn bhd: rdn after 2f: nvr a danger*	FrancisNorton 2	**25/1**	23

2m 11.76s (-1.38) **Going Correction** -0.15s/f (Firm) **5** Ran SP% **109.5**

Speed ratings (Par 105):99,98,97,83,77

CSF £1.88 TOTE £1.50: £1.10, £1.60; EX 1.60.

Owner Hamdan Al Maktoum **Bred** Shadwell Farm LLC **Trained** Lambourn, Berks

FOCUS

A modest maiden judged by the prominent performance of the 46-rated Macho Dancer in third.

3067 WARWICK INTERNATIONAL H'CAP — 7f 2y

3:50 (3:50) (Class 3) (0-90,84) 3-Y-O£10,094 (£3,020; £1,510; £755; £376) **Stalls** Low

Form	Pos	Dist	Horse / (Trainer) comment	Jockey	SP	RPR
0566	**1**		**Waterline Twenty (IRE)**[8] 2824 3-8-13 **76** (P D Evans) *trckd ldrs: led over 1f out: r.o*	FrancisNorton 4	**9/1**	84
1-26	**2**	*1 1/4*	**Lunar Express (USA)**[25] 2330 3-8-13 **81** (W J Haggas) *in tch: rdn over 2f out: styd on to take 2nd towards fin: nt trble wnr*	LiamJones(5) 1	**4/1**[2]	86
02-0	**3**	*3/4*	**Blades Girl**[14] 2650 3-9-0 **82** (K A Ryan) *sn led: rdn over 2f out: hdd over 1f out: no ex towards fin*	(p) AndrewMullen(5) 10	**20/1**	85
0-62	**4**	*1*	**Zennerman (IRE)**[28] 2239 3-9-4 **81** (W M Brisbourne) *hld up: rdn 2f out: hdwy over 1f out: swtchd lft ins fnl f: styd on*	FergalLynch 9	**11/1**	81
5022	**5**	*1/2*	**Jimmy The Guesser**[14] 2650 3-9-3 **80** (N P Littmoden) *in tch: rdn 2f out: hung lft over 1f out: kpt on same pce ins fnl f*	RichardThomas 5	**4/1**[2]	79
0100	**6**	*nk*	**Fangorn Forest (IRE)**[38] 1934 3-8-10 **73** (R A Harris) *midfield: rdn over 2f out: one pce fnl f*	(p) AdrianMcCarthy 11	**25/1**	71
0000	**7**	*1 1/2*	**Calypso King**[14] 2658 3-9-7 **84** (J W Hills) *racd keenly: hld up: hdwy over 2f out: hung lft over 1f out: fdd ins fnl f*	FrankieMcDonald 6	**17/2**	78
0253	**8**	*4*	**Il Castagno (IRE)**[26] 2297 3-8-13 **76** (B Smart) *led early: remained prom: rdn and ev ch over 1f out: wknd and eased fnl f*	DerekMcGaffin 3	**8/1**[3]	60
6-01	**9**	*5*	**Lyrical Sound (IRE)**[14] 2642 3-9-1 **78** (B W Hills) *midfield tl wknd 3f out*	MichaelHills 2	**10/3**[1]	49
-060	**10**	*3*	**Bellsbank (IRE)**[117] 601 3-8-6 **72** (A Bailey) *s.s: a bhd*	EdwardCreighton(3) 7	**33/1**	35

1m 26.38s (-2.09) **Going Correction** -0.15s/f (Firm) **10** Ran SP% **114.6**

Speed ratings (Par 104):105,103,102,101,101 100,98,94,88,85

CSF £43.09 CT £723.57 TOTE £13.00: £3.80, £1.80, £5.90; EX 63.50.

Owner Waterline Racing Club **Bred** Mountarmstrong Stud **Trained** Pandy, Abergavenny

FOCUS

A fairly competitive handicap, albeit not the classiest for the grade. They went a good pace, though, and the form looks sound enough.

NOTEBOOK

Waterline Twenty(IRE), blessed with a good low draw, chased the fast early pace and was in the ideal position to capitalise when they turned into the straight. She was running off a career-low mark and, for the first time, proved that she stays seven furlongs.

Lunar Express(USA) had the best draw and also bagged a good position on the rail, but she was a bit short of room early in the straight when her rider wanted to go for home and the eventual winner got first run on her. There is a race to be won with her off this sort of mark when things fall more kindly. (op 7-2)

Blades Girl was not well drawn but her early speed got her to the front where she raced one off the rail in dispute of the lead. Given how fast she went in the early stages it is to her credit that she hung on for third - her fellow pace-setter Il Castagno dropped back to a well-held eighth. She would appear to have the ability to win a similar race when granted a less-contested lead.

Zennerman(IRE) did not have the best of draws and struggled to get into it from off the pace. Perhaps he needs a mile these days over a track as sharp as this. (op 10-1)

Jimmy The Guesser ran well on fast ground at Sandown last time but all his previous best efforts on turf had come with some juice. He hung left here and might have found this second run in a row on fast ground too much. Official explanation: jockey said gelding was unsuited by the track (op 5-1)

Fangorn Forest(IRE) had the worst of the draw and did not run badly in the circumstances. (op 20-1)

Lyrical Sound(IRE) appears to be an inconsistent sort and she threw in another poor performance here. One could blame the track again, as was done at Epsom on her seasonal reappearance but, whatever the reason was, she is better than this. Official explanation: jockey said filly was unsuited by the track (op 4-1)

Bellsbank(IRE) Official explanation: jockey said filly was restless in stalls and slowly away

3068 BRYN THOMAS CRANE HIRE CLAIMING STKS — 1m 2f 75y

4:20 (4:22) (Class 5) 3-Y-O+ **£3,432** (£1,021; £510; £254) **Stalls** High

Form	Pos	Dist	Horse / (Trainer) comment	Jockey	SP	RPR
054-	**1**		**Vale De Lobo**[181] 4380 4-8-11 77 (W J Haggas) *hld up: hdwy over 4f out: rdn to ld over 1f out: r.o*	LiamJones(5) 3	**5/1**[3]	77
5561	**2**	*2*	**Hawkit (USA)**[7] 2853 5-9-5 71 (A Bailey) *midfield: hdwy over 6f out: rdn over 2f out: styd on ins fnl f*	RichardMullen 6	**9/2**[2]	77
-514	**3**	*1*	**Ionian Spring (IRE)**[19] 2507 11-8-13 80 (D Carroll) *midfield: hdwy to chse ldrs over 6f out: led over 2f out: hdd over 1f out: no ex ins fnl f*	DNolan(3) 8	**9/4**[1]	72
-000	**4**	*nk*	**Nashaab (USA)**[15] 2627 9-9-2 75 (P D Evans) *bhd: rdn and hdwy 2f out: r.o ins fnl f*	(v) FrancisNorton 2	**7/1**	71
3000	**5**	*9*	**Hillhall (IRE)**[18] 2522 4-8-9 43 (W M Brisbourne) *a towards rr*	WilliamCarson(7) 1	**33/1**	54
100-	**6**	*3*	**Tetragon (IRE)**[313] 4647 6-8-9 64 (D Carroll) *chsd ldrs tl rdn and wknd over 5f out*	KellyHarrison(7) 9	**33/1**	48
0200	**7**	*2*	**Cardinal Venture (IRE)**[45] 1775 8-8-13 85 (K A Ryan) *w ldr: led 4f out: hdd over 2f out: wknd over 1f out*	(p) AndrewMullen(5) 10	**13/2**	47
3621	**8**	*35*	**Nuit Sombre (IRE)**[16] 2566 6-9-4 75 (J G M O'Shea) *led: hdd 4f out: wknd over 2f out: eased over 1f out: t.o*	(p) AdrianTNicholls 7	**15/2**	—

2m 10.39s (-2.75) **Going Correction** -0.15s/f (Firm) **8** Ran SP% **109.1**

Speed ratings (Par 103):105,103,102,102,95 92,91,63

CSF £25.07 TOTE £6.90: £1.90, £2.00, £1.40; EX 31.30.Vale de Lobo was claimed by Mr B. R. Millman for £25,000

Owner Mrs M Findlay **Bred** J B Haggas **Trained** Newmarket, Suffolk

FOCUS

A fair claimer and they went a decent pace thanks to Cardinal Venture and Nuit Sombre taking each other on for the lead. The runner-up ran to form and helps set the level.

Nuit Sombre(IRE) Official explanation: jockey said gelding had no more to give

3069 WARWICK INTERNATIONAL GROUP H'CAP — 5f 16y

4:50 (4:50) (Class 3) (0-90,90) 3-Y-O£10,094 (£3,020; £1,510; £755; £376) **Stalls** Low

Form	Pos	Dist	Horse / (Trainer) comment	Jockey	SP	RPR
3060	**1**		**Graze On**[4] 2946 4-9-10 **86** (R A Harris) *a.p: rdn to ld ent fnl f: r.o*	(b) AdrianMcCarthy 1	**6/1**	96
6450	**2**	*1*	**Plateau**[21] 2450 7-9-0 **76** (D Nicholls) *in tch: rdn 2f out: chsd wnr ins fnl f: r.o: a hld*	DerekMcGaffin 5	**7/2**[2]	82
4023	**3**	*1/2*	**Raymond's Pride**[37] 1949 6-9-1 **82** (K A Ryan) *bhd: rdn over 1f out: r.o ins fnl f: nrst fin*	(b) AndrewMullen(5) 8	**10/1**	87+
2412	**4**	*nk*	**Handsome Cross (IRE)**[18] 2521 5-9-9 **85** (D Nicholls) *a.p: led 2f out: rdn and hdd ent fnl f: sn no ex*	AdrianTNicholls 4	**5/2**[1]	89
0132	**5**	*shd*	**Coconut Moon**[6] 2897 4-8-9 **71** oh5 (E J Alston) *midfield: rdn and hdd over 1f out: styd on ins fnl f*	FrancisNorton 6	**5/1**[3]	74
0060	**6**	*3/4*	**Kay Two (IRE)**[15] 2624 4-10-0 **90** (R J Price) *hld up: rdn and hdwy over 1f out: styd on ins fnl f: no ex cl home*	DarrenWilliams 9	**25/1**	90
4500	**7**	*nk*	**Smokin Beau**[2] 3027 9-9-6 **82** (N P Littmoden) *midfield: rdn over 1f out: kpt on ins fnl f: nt pce to chal*	RichardThomas 10	**16/1**	81
00-0	**8**	*7*	**The Crooked Ring**[18] 2520 4-9-1 **77** (P D Evans) *a outpcd*	RichardMullen 7	**16/1**	51
2/0-	**9**	*3 1/2*	**Signor Panettiere**[258] 5938 5-9-11 **90** (R J Smith, Spain) *led: rdn and hdd 2f out: wknd over 1f out*	(t) EdwardCreighton(3) 2	**16/1**	52
000-	**10**	*3/4*	**Prince Of Blues (IRE)**[371] 2910 8-8-4 **71** oh23 (M Mullineaux) *in tch tl rdn and wknd over 1f out*	(e1) LiamJones(5) 3	**50/1**	30

60.47 secs (-1.58) **Going Correction** -0.15s/f (Firm) **10** Ran SP% **114.3**

Speed ratings (Par 107):106,104,103,103,102 101,101,90,84,83

CSF £26.70 CT £212.08 TOTE £8.40: £2.90, £2.30, £2.90; EX 40.30 Place 6 £25.15, Place 5 £14.76.

Owner Tom Tuohy Paraic Gaffney **Bred** Mrs Sandra Cooper **Trained** Earlswood, Monmouths

FOCUS

A typical sprint handicap around this tight track, in which a low draw once again proved all-important. Sound form.

NOTEBOOK

Graze On, drawn best of all and well positioned on the rail just behind the pace for most of the race, enjoyed a dream run. His performance once again demonstrated how, in a competitive sprint handicap around here, a good draw and a trouble-free trip count for so much. (op 9-2)

Plateau, whose only win in his previous 30 starts had come over this course and distance last summer, was on a mark 4lb lower than for that success. He had his chance but could not get to the winner, who saw the trip out well, and he remains one to oppose at short odds purely because of his poor strike-rate. (tchd 9-2)

Raymond's Pride had a poor draw and was dropped in as a result. On ground much quicker than ideal, he finished his race strongly, and is clearly on good terms with himself. He has the ability to win off his current mark when conditions allow. (op 11-1)

Handsome Cross(IRE), who won this race last year off a 2lb lower mark, was up with the pace throughout and was the first to kick for home in the straight. He could not hold off the closing pack, though, and probably used up too much energy in the first half of the race. (op 3-1)

Coconut Moon, racing in better company than she is used to, ran well from 5lb out of the handicap, but her improvement is being kept in check by the assessor. (tchd 9-2)

Kay Two(IRE) won in Listed company in Ireland at two, but he has struggled in that sort of grade and in handicaps since. This was his second start for his new stable and it looks as though he will have to drop a bit more in the ratings before he wins again. (op 33-1)

The Crooked Ring Official explanation: jockey said gelding moved poorly throughout

Signor Panettiere Official explanation: jockey said gelding hung right

Prince Of Blues(IRE) Official explanation: vet said gelding was lame

T/Plt: £23.80 to a £1 stake. Pool: £45,362.70. 1,386,75 winning tickets. T/Qpdt: £11.10 to a £1 stake. Pool: £2,386.60. 157.70 winning tickets. DO

3010 **LINGFIELD** (L-H)
Saturday, July 1

OFFICIAL GOING: Turf course - good to firm; all-weather - standard
Wind: Nil Weather: Sunny and warm

3070 EUROPEAN BREEDERS FUND MAIDEN STKS 5f
6:30 (6:30) (Class 5) 2-Y-O £3,886 (£1,156; £577; £288) Stalls High

Form RPR
24 1 **Minaash (USA)**[14] 2660 2-9-3 ShaneKelly 5 84+
(J Noseda) *mde all: shkn up over 1f out: hanging but wl in command fnl f* **4/7**[1]
03 2 3 ½ **Silver Hotspur**[15] 2617 2-9-3 JimmyFortune 3 71
(P W Chapple-Hyam) *s.i.s: t.k.h and hld up: rdn to chse wnr wl over 1f out: no impresssion* **5/2**[2]
33 3 hd **Bush Breakfast**[10] 2759 2-9-3 JimCrowley 4 70
(P Winkworth) *prom: outpcd and rdn 1/2-way: styd on again ins fnl f* **16/1**
65 4 3 ½ **La Quinta (IRE)**[14] 2638 2-8-5 KMay(7) 2 53
(B J Meehan) *mostly chsd wnr to wl over 1f out: wknd fnl f* **12/1**[3]
4340 5 6 **She Wont Wait**[14] 2643 2-8-12 FergusSweeney 1 31
(T M Jones) *in tch to 2f out: wknd rapidly* **40/1**
59.61 secs (0.67) **Going Correction** +0.05s/f (Good) 5 Ran SP% **108.2**
Speed ratings (Par 94):96,90,90,84,74
CSF £2.10 TOTE £1.50: £1.10, £1.80; EX 2.10.
Owner Sultan Ali **Bred** G Watts Humphrey Jr **Trained** Newmarket, Suffolk

FOCUS
Not that competitive a maiden, but a good effort from Minaash to pull so far clear of a fair yardstick in Silver Hotspur.

NOTEBOOK
Minaash(USA) did not really build on his debut promise when only fourth at York on his previous start but, dropped in trip, he only had one serious rival in the form of Silver Hotspur, and won readily despite hanging. He deserves to step up in class. (op 4-6)
Silver Hotspur, an improved third at Sandown on his previous start, seemed to run his race but was no match for the useful winner. (op 2-1)
Bush Breakfast confirmed the ability he showed on his first two starts and just found a couple too good. He should make a fair nursery type. (tchd 14-1)
La Quinta(IRE), dropped a furlong in trip, was well beaten and needed this run to qualify for nurseries. She could do better yet. (op 10-1 tchd 14-1)
She Wont Wait will find things easier in a lower grade. (tchd 50-1)

3071 LINGFIELD PARK LEISURE CLUB H'CAP 5f
7:00 (7:00) (Class 5) (0-70,65) 3-Y-O+ £3,238 (£963; £481; £240) Stalls High

Form RPR
-053 1 **Heavens Walk**[4] 2955 5-8-13 **50** (t) SebSanders 7 68+
(P J Makin) *dwlt: hld up off the pce: prog 2f out: burst through against nr side rail to ld jst over 1f out: sn wl clr* **9/2**[2]
0006 2 4 **Whitbarrow (IRE)**[8] 2813 7-9-7 **65** JamesMillman(7) 9 69
(B R Millman) *chsd ldrs: effrt 2f out: swtchd lft to chal over 1f out: sn outpcd by wnr* **5/1**[3]
0536 3 ½ **Cosmic Destiny (IRE)**[6] 2897 4-9-6 **57** DaneO'Neill 2 59
(E F Vaughan) *dwlt: racd on outer: prog 1/2-way: clsd on ldrs over 1f out: one pce fnl f* **7/1**
0210 4 ¾ **King Egbert (FR)**[15] 2611 5-8-6 **50** TolleyDean(7) 4 50
(A W Carroll) *hld up in rr and off the pce: effrt 2f out: n.m.r over 1f out: sn outpcd* **8/1**
02-4 5 nk **Tomthevic**[16] 2571 8-8-2 **46** oh5 (p) BarrySavage(7) 8 44
(J M Bradley) *led at fast pce: hdd jst over 1f out: pushed along and wknd* **25/1**
-001 6 nk **Parkside Pursuit**[6] 2897 8-10-0 **65** 6ex JimCrowley 6 62
(J M Bradley) *hld up in last: effrt 2f out: nvr on terms and n.d* **5/1**[3]
5023 7 2 **Clearing Sky (IRE)**[7] 2858 5-9-3 **54** MartinDwyer 1 44
(J R Boyle) *chsd ldr: rdn 1/2-way: clsd over 1f out: sn wknd* **13/2**
0202 8 ¾ **Zazous**[8] 2813 5-9-5 **56** RyanMoore 3 43
(J J Bridger) *chsd ldng pair: rdn 1/2-way: wknd over 1f out* **4/1**[1]
4500 9 10 **Great Belief (IRE)**[19] 2494 4-9-1 **52** ShaneKelly 5 —
(T D McCarthy) *restless stalls: dwlt: a struggling: rdn after 2f: wknd 2f out* **16/1**
58.76 secs (-0.18) **Going Correction** +0.05s/f (Good) 9 Ran SP% **118.2**
Speed ratings (Par 103):103,96,95,94,94 93,90,89,73
CSF £28.01 CT £158.19 TOTE £6.10: £1.50, £2.50, £4.80; EX 34.70.
Owner Mrs P J Makin **Bred** Mrs P J Makin **Trained** Ogbourne Maisey, Wilts
■ Stewards' Enquiry : James Millman one-day ban: careless riding (Jul 13)

FOCUS
A moderate sprint handicap, but a clear-cut winner in Heavens Walk, who showed improved form.

3072 VERITAS DGC FILLIES' H'CAP 7f
7:30 (7:30) (Class 5) (0-75,70) 3-Y-O £3,238 (£963; £481; £240) Stalls High

Form RPR
0421 1 **Whistleupthewind**[16] 2589 3-8-6 **55** ow1 (b) ShaneKelly 12 63
(J M P Eustace) *racd against nr side rail: mde all: clr over 1f out: hung lft after : kpt on and nvr in any real danger* **7/2**[1]
3550 2 1 **Royal Tavira Girl (IRE)**[14] 2648 3-8-3 **55** DominicFox(3) 10 60
(M G Quinlan) *hld up in rr: prog towards nr side fr 2f out: chsd wnr fnl f: clsd but nvr able to chal* **16/1**
0-60 3 nk **Ciccone**[26] 2301 3-8-13 **62** LPKeniry 11 66
(W Jarvis) *racd against nr side rail: hld up in tch: effrt to dispute 2nd over 1f out: edgd lft after and nt qckn* **12/1**
0400 4 3 **Lady Georgette (IRE)**[22] 2400 3-8-11 **60** ChrisCatlin 1 56
(E J O'Neill) *hld up in rr: prog wl over 1f out: kpt on same pce fnl f* **20/1**
2105 5 2 **Deira (USA)**[22] 2403 3-9-7 **70** RyanMoore 2 61
(C E Brittain) *racd on outer: in tch: chsd wnr briefly wl over 1f out: wknd fnl f* **4/1**[2]
4460 6 1 ¼ **Lisfannon**[16] 2583 3-9-0 **63** DarryllHolland 7 50
(B W Hills) *cl up: trckd wnr 1/2-way and gng wl: rdn over 2f out: wknd wl over 1f out* **6/1**[3]
-005 7 1 **Whisper Inthe Wind (IRE)**[16] 2583 3-8-8 **57** JimCrowley 4 42
(Miss J Feilden) *t.k.h: hld up and racd on outer: rdn over 2f out: no rspnse* **16/1**
4021 8 3 ½ **Fratt'n Park (IRE)**[16] 2583 3-9-5 **68** JimmyFortune 5 43
(J J Bridger) *t.k.h: hld up and racd on outer: rdn over 2f out: wknd over 1f out* **4/1**[2]
0060 9 2 **Miss Redactive**[18] 2535 3-8-2 **51** oh2 HayleyTurner 8 21
(M D I Usher) *lost pl after 2f: struggling in rr 4f out: sn btn* **25/1**
4-00 10 4 **Laqataat (IRE)**[25] 2318 3-9-7 **70** (t) MartinDwyer 3 29
(J L Dunlop) *plld hrd: chsd wnr to 1/2-way: sn wknd rapidly* **10/1**
1m 24.71s (0.50) **Going Correction** +0.05s/f (Good) 10 Ran SP% **113.7**
Speed ratings (Par 97):99,97,97,94,91 90,89,85,82,78
CSF £58.98 CT £469.96 TOTE £3.60: £1.20, £5.90, £3.00; EX 41.60.
Owner Blue Peter Racing 6 **Bred** Baydon House Stud **Trained** Newmarket, Suffolk

FOCUS
A pretty weak handicap in which a high draw was an advantage. The first three all improved a little but the form does not look all that strong.
Fratt'n Park(IRE) Official explanation: jockey said filly ran too free early

3073 LINDA & STEVE PEPPER'S WEDDING CELEBRATION MEDIAN AUCTION MAIDEN STKS 1m 2f (P)
8:00 (8:00) (Class 5) 3-4-Y-O £3,238 (£963; £481; £240) Stalls Low

Form RPR
5-33 1 **Local Spirit (USA)**[24] 2343 3-8-12 69 RyanMoore 10 73
(C E Brittain) *trckd ldrs: prog over 2f out: led wl over 1f out: swished tail repeatedly and drvn out* **6/4**[1]
0 2 2 ½ **Midnight Moonlight**[16] 2580 3-8-12 TPQueally 4 69
(C F Wall) *dwlt: hld up wl in rr: rapid prog on outer over 2f out: chsd wnr over 1f out: drvn and nt qckn* **25/1**
-235 3 2 ½ **Moonlight Music (IRE)**[21] 2446 3-8-12 74 ChrisCatlin 6 64
(E J O'Neill) *led for 1f: trckd ldr to 6f out: rdn over 2f out: outpcd over 1f out: kpt on* **11/4**[2]
00 4 2 **Mr Wiseguy**[14] 2655 3-9-3 JimmyFortune 7 65
(G C Bravery) *sn chsng ldrs: rdn over 2f out: outpcd wl over 1f out: one pce* **9/1**
00 5 nk **Mrs Solese (IRE)**[32] 2118 3-8-12 FergusSweeney 8 59
(J R Boyle) *prom: chsd ldr 6f out: rdn to ld jst over 2f out: hdd & wknd wl over 1f out* **20/1**
00 6 ½ **Salonga (IRE)**[32] 2118 3-8-12 SebSanders 1 58
(C F Wall) *settled towards rr: pushed along over 4f out: no prog over 2f out: hanging and wl btn over 1f out* **10/1**
0-50 7 2 **Satin Doll**[22] 2403 3-8-12 72 MartinDwyer 3 55
(M P Tregoning) *stmbld s: sltly hmpd after 100yds: settled midfield: rdn 3f out: no rspnse* **5/1**[3]
8 3 **Maseem** 3-9-3 FrancisFerris 9 54
(Rae Guest) *s.s: rn green and drvn along in rr: nvr a factor* **40/1**
0-0 9 8 **Prima Markova**[59] 1417 3-8-12 DaneO'Neill 11 34
(D J Daly) *a wl in rr: rdn and struggling over 4f out* **66/1**
000 10 2 ½ **Maya's Prince**[46] 1753 4-10-0 47 HayleyTurner 5 34
(M D I Usher) *led after 1f and sn clr: hdd & wknd rapidly jst over 2f out* **66/1**
0000 11 dist **Smart Golden Boy (IRE)**[58] 1433 3-9-3 45 (p) ShaneKelly 2 —
(Mrs L C Jewell) *a in rr: t.o over 4f out: btn over 1f by 10th horse* **66/1**
2m 8.73s (0.94) **Going Correction** +0.05s/f (Slow)
WFA 3 from 4yo 11lb 11 Ran SP% **117.9**
Speed ratings (Par 103):98,96,94,92,92 91,90,87,81,79 —
CSF £50.70 TOTE £2.40: £1.10, £6.30, £1.30; EX 59.80.
Owner Sheikh Marwan Al Maktoum **Bred** Darley **Trained** Newmarket, Suffolk

FOCUS
A pretty ordinary maiden, rated through the fifth.
Maya's Prince Official explanation: jockey said gelding ran too free throughout
Smart Golden Boy(IRE) Official explanation: jockey said gelding had a breathing problem

3074 BROOKE EQUINE WELFARE CHARITY (S) STKS 1m 4f (P)
8:30 (8:30) (Class 6) 3-Y-O+ £2,388 (£705; £352) Stalls Low

Form RPR
2003 1 **Good Article (IRE)**[7] 2861 5-9-8 46 DarryllHolland 7 64
(D K Ivory) *settled in last: prog over 4f out: swept into ld over 2f out and sn clr: kpt on steadily fnl f* **12/1**[2]
3541 2 3 **Champagne Shadow (IRE)**[7] 2861 5-9-13 78 (b) RyanMoore 4 64
(G L Moore) *trckd ldrs: poised to chal over 2f out but sn outpcd by wnr: unavailing chse after* **2/11**[1]
0-04 3 10 **Tip Toes (IRE)**[7] 2861 4-9-3 39 ShaneKelly 6 38
(P Howling) *led after 1f to 6f out: trckd ldr tl led 3f out to over 2f out: sn outpcd and btn: wandering fnl f* **33/1**
-450 4 3 ½ **Ambersong**[46] 1541 8-9-8 39 (v) JimmyFortune 5 38
(A W Carroll) *s.s: hld up in tch: rdn over 4f out: wl outpcd over 2f out: plugged on slowly* **16/1**[3]
6006 5 1 ¼ **Salinger (USA)**[7] 2861 4-9-3 47 (b) JamesDoyle(5) 9 36
(Mrs L J Mongan) *plld hrd: hld up tl led 6f out to 3f out: wknd over 2f out* **33/1**
00 6 7 **Fentastic**[7] 2861 3-8-4 FrancisFerris 3 19
(Rae Guest) *prom: upsides 3f out: wknd rapidly over 2f out* **100/1**
0 7 5 **Amisact**[27] 2260 4-9-3 SebSanders 2 11
(D J S Ffrench Davis) *a in rr: struggling in last 5f out* **80/1**
00-0 8 11 **Maraval**[50] 1652 3-8-2 52 (v[1]) KevinGhunowa(7) 1 —
(M Wellings) *led for 1f: prom: wkng whn barged into rail 5f out: sn bhd* **50/1**
2m 34.47s (0.08) **Going Correction** +0.05s/f (Slow)
WFA 3 from 4yo+ 13lb 8 Ran SP% **108.2**
Speed ratings (Par 101):101,99,92,90,89 84,81,73
CSF £13.65 TOTE £9.70: £1.10, £1.02, £2.80; EX 18.40.There was no bid for the winner. Champagne Shadow was claimed by K. A. Ryan for £6,000.
Owner T G N Burrage **Bred** T G N Burrage **Trained** Radlett, Herts

FOCUS
With Champagne Shdow well below his official mark of 78, this was a very moderate race, even by selling standards.
Salinger(USA) Official explanation: jockey said gelding hung right
Maraval Official explanation: jockey said gelding lost its action

3075 ARENA LEISURE PLC H'CAP 1m 4f (P)
9:00 (9:00) (Class 6) (0-65,63) 3-Y-O £2,388 (£705; £352) Stalls Low

Form RPR
1-03 1 **Lady Romanov (IRE)**[21] 2446 3-9-7 **63** GeorgeBaker 3 79
(M H Tompkins) *trckd ldrs: rdn over 3f out: effrt over 2f out: led 1f out and drvn clr* **12/1**
1143 2 3 ½ **La Via Ferrata (IRE)**[16] 2569 3-9-3 **59** JosedeSouza 5 69
(P F I Cole) *hld up midfield: prog to join ldrs 4f out: gng easily 3f out: rdn to ld over 1f out: hdd and one pce 1f out* **10/1**
0400 3 5 **Zizou (IRE)**[12] 2713 3-8-4 **46** HayleyTurner 9 48
(J J Bridger) *settled in midfield: rdn over 3f out: outpcd over 2f out: kpt on to take 3rd nr fin* **25/1**
6440 4 hd **Dark Planet**[15] 2622 3-9-4 **60** RyanMoore 6 62
(C E Brittain) *trckd ldr after 4f to 3f out: sn hrd rdn: outpcd fnl 2f* **13/2**[3]

00-0 **5** ½ **Taranis**[18] [2529] 3-8-8 **50** ...... SebSanders 8 51
(Sir Mark Prescott) *led at stdy pce: drvn over 3f out: hdd over 1f out: wknd rapidly ins fnl f* **9/4**[1]

5320 **6** ¾ **Wise Choice**[16] [2591] 3-8-11 **58** ...... JamesDoyle(5) 2 58
(N P Littmoden) *trckd ldr for 4f: styd prom: hrd rdn and chalng over 2f out: sn btn* **16/1**

0322 **7** 1 ½ **Coffin Dodger**[16] [2591] 3-7-11 **46** ...... KirstyMilczarek(7) 11 43
(C N Allen) *s.s: hld up in rr: lost tch w ldrs over 3f out: shuffled along and no ch after* **8/1**

0-44 **8** ¾ **Newport Boy (IRE)**[86] [894] 3-9-6 **62** ...... JimmyFortune 12 58
(S Kirk) *a wl in rr: struggling over 4f out: sn lost tch* **10/1**

06-4 **9** 2 **French Opera**[20] [2480] 3-9-5 **61** ...... ShaneKelly 4 54
(J A Osborne) *hld up in rr: pushed along over 4f out: lost tch over 3f out: no ch* **9/1**

0-15 **10** 6 **Indigo Dancer**[12] [2713] 3-8-5 **47** ...... MartinDwyer 1 30
(C F Wall) *t.k.h: hld up in midfield: outpcd 3f out: eased whn no ch over 1f out* **9/2**[2]

3306 **11** 3 ½ **Synonymy**[15] [2622] 3-9-6 **62** ...... ChrisCatlin 7 40
(M Blanshard) *a wl in rr: rdn and struggling over 4f out: sn lost tch* **20/1**

5004 **12** 21 **Smokey Blue**[21] [2466] 3-9-2 **58** ......(v) DarryllHolland 13 —
(M J Wallace) *a in last pair: bhd fr over 3f out: t.o* **33/1**

2m 34.13s (-0.26) **Going Correction** +0.05s/f (Slow) **12** Ran SP% **126.7**
Speed ratings (Par 98):102,99,96,96,95 95,94,93,92,88 86,72
CSF £132.20 CT £2981.76 TOTE £14.70: £4.60, £3.10, £5.50; EX 65.90 Place 6 £106.73, Place 5 £100.14.
Owner P Heath, K Bowry, K Chapman **Bred** Rory Mathews **Trained** Newmarket, Suffolk

FOCUS
A modest handicap in which the first two have a good record on this surface and look improved.
Smokey Blue Official explanation: jockey said gelding did not face the kickback
T/Plt: £41.50 to a £1 stake. Pool: £29,390.05. 516.75 winning tickets. T/Qpdt: £9.10 to a £1 stake. Pool: £2,472.30. 200.10 winning tickets. JN

3037 NEWCASTLE (L-H)
Saturday, July 1

OFFICIAL GOING: Good to firm
Wind: Breezy, behind

3076 JOHN SMITH'S "EXTRA COLD" CHIPCHASE STKS (GROUP 3) 6f
2:10 (2:10) (Class 1) 3-Y-O+
£28,390 (£10,760; £5,385; £2,685; £1,345; £675) **Stalls** High

Form RPR

-450 **1** **Fayr Jag (IRE)**[7] [2846] 7-9-2 109 ...... DavidAllan 3 115
(T D Easterby) *cl up: led over 1f out: rdn and hld on wl fnl f* **5/2**[1]

0000 **2** ½ **Beckermet (IRE)**[7] [2846] 4-9-2 105 ...... SteveDrowne 5 113
(R F Fisher) *trckd ldrs: effrt 2f out: kpt on fnl f to take 2nd cl home* **7/1**

-040 **3** ½ **Celtic Mill**[11] [2720] 8-9-2 107 ......(p) KerrinMcEvoy 2 112
(D W Barker) *led: rdn and hdd over 1f out: kpt on fnl f: lost 2nd cl home* **8/1**

2022 **4** 4 **Philharmonic**[13] [2675] 5-9-2 104 ...... PaulHanagan 1 100
(R A Fahey) *prom: effrt outside over 1f out: outpcd fnl f* **3/1**[2]

002- **5** ¾ **Masta Plasta (IRE)**[266] [5742] 3-8-10 109 ...... TomEaves 6 97
(J Howard Johnson) *keen in tch: rdn 1/2-way: btn over 1f out* **6/1**[3]

0330 **6** shd **Mecca's Mate**[11] [2720] 5-8-13 101 ...... DO'Donohoe 7 94
(D W Barker) *keen: hld up in tch: effrt and swtchd lft over 2f out: no imp over 1f out* **13/2**

6-00 **7** 6 **Royal Millennium (IRE)**[45] [1778] 8-9-2 100 ...... TonyCulhane 4 79
(M R Channon) *in tch: rdn over 2f out: sn btn* **12/1**

1m 10.92s (-4.17) **Going Correction** -0.375s/f (Firm)
WFA 3 from 4yo+ 6lb **7** Ran SP% **112.5**
Speed ratings (Par 113):112,111,110,105,104 104,96
CSF £19.66 TOTE £3.80: £2.40, £4.80; EX 22.40.
Owner Jonathan Gill **Bred** Canice M Farrell Jnr **Trained** Great Habton, N Yorks

FOCUS
An uncompetitive Group 3 in which the early pace was only fair. Those racing close to the pace held the edge and this bare form may not prove reliable. Ordinary form for the grade, but sound enough amongst the principals.

NOTEBOOK
Fayr Jag(IRE) had the run of this uncompetitive Group 3 event and did enough to win his first race in over two years. However this form does not look entirely reliable and he is likely to have his limitations exposed in the July Cup later in the month. (op 3-1)
Beckermet(IRE) had conditions to suit and ran his best race since his reappearance run. He shaped as though a stiffer test of stamina would have been in his favour but, given his record this year, may be one to take on in more competitive company next time. (op 8-1)
Celtic Mill was allowed an easy lead and ran creditably against the stands' rail. The return to five furlongs will not be an inconvenience and he looks capable of winning a similar event when the emphasis is on speed.
Philharmonic had his limitations exposed back in Group company - even in an ordinary race - and left the impression that a stronger overall gallop on easier ground would have been more to his liking. (op 11-4)
Masta Plasta(IRE), a fair juvenile last year when allowed to stride on, was below his best ridden with more restraint on this first start since October. He will have to settle better than he did here if he is to progress in similar company this term. (op 13-2)
Mecca's Mate, much improved last year, has yet to score this term but, although she has shown she retains all ability, she was not seen to best effect in a muddling race. A strong pace on slower ground suits ideally and she is not one to write off. (op 6-1)

3077 TOTESCOOP6 NORTHERN SPRINT (H'CAP) 6f
2:45 (2:45) (Class 2) (0-100,98) 3-Y-O+
£18,696 (£5,598; £2,799; £1,401; £699; £351) **Stalls** High

Form RPR

6056 **1** **Indian Trail**[7] [2847] 6-9-12 **94** ...... TonyCulhane 15 111+
(D Nicholls) *hld up in tch: hdwy stands rail to ld appr fnl f: rdn and r.o strly* **11/4**[1]

-036 **2** 2 **Woodcote (IRE)**[4] [2946] 4-9-6 **91** ......(p) AdamKirby(3) 9 102
(C G Cox) *led tl hdd appr fnl f: kpt on ins last* **12/1**

-425 **3** 2 ½ **Ice Planet**[43] [1835] 5-9-9 **91** ...... TomEaves 13 95
(D Nicholls) *bhd: rdn 1/2-way: hdwy over 1f out: nrst fin* **5/1**[2]

1012 **4** hd **My Gacho (IRE)**[8] [2830] 4-9-2 **84** ......(v) PhillipMakin 2 87+
(T D Barron) *racd alone centre: cl up tl rdn and nt qckn fnl f* **10/1**

-110 **5** ½ **Ingleby Arch (USA)**[14] [2658] 3-9-10 **98** ...... PaulFessey 8 98
(T D Barron) *in tch: effrt 2f out: kpt on same pce fnl f* **12/1**

0044 **6** ¾ **Ellens Academy (IRE)**[1] [3041] 11-8-3 **76** oh8 ...... TravisBlock(5) 14 75
(E J Alston) *hld up: hdwy over 1f out: kpt on fnl f: nrst fin* **20/1**

5016 **7** shd **Johnston's Diamond (IRE)**[35] [2021] 8-9-2 **84** ...... SteveDrowne 10 83
(E J Alston) *trckd ldrs: rdn over 2f out: one pce over 1f out* **40/1**

-050 **8** shd **Connect**[7] [2847] 9-9-10 **95** ......(b) SaleemGolam(3) 7 94
(M H Tompkins) *in tch on outside: effrt 2f out: sn one pce* **18/1**

-003 **9** nk **Looks Could Kill (USA)**[18] [2520] 4-9-1 **83** ...... DavidAllan 3 81
(E J Alston) *hld up: rdn 1/2-way: effrt on outside over 1f out: sn no imp* **25/1**

0605 **10** hd **Fantasy Believer**[8] [2824] 8-9-0 **82** ...... AlanMunro 11 79
(J J Quinn) *hld up midfield: effrt over 1f out: sn no ex* **12/1**

46-1 **11** 1 ¾ **Algharb**[38] [1939] 4-9-6 **88** ...... RHills 12 87+
(W J Haggas) *hld up: rdn and effrt 2f out: nvr able to chal* **11/2**[3]

0521 **12** 5 **Dhaular Dhar (IRE)**[18] [2520] 4-9-2 **84** ...... KerrinMcEvoy 5 61
(J S Goldie) *midfield on outside: rdn over 2f out: btn over 1f out* **11/1**

0500 **13** 2 **Hidden Dragon (USA)**[28] [2230] 7-9-5 **87** ...... KDarley 4 58
(J Pearce) *racd on outside: hld up: hung bdly lft fr 1/2-way: sn btn* **22/1**

1m 10.98s (-4.11) **Going Correction** -0.375s/f (Firm)
WFA 3 from 4yo+ 6lb **13** Ran SP% **119.9**
Speed ratings (Par 109):112,109,106,105,105 104,103,103,103,103 100,94,91
CSF £35.75 CT £166.82 TOTE £3.70: £1.90, £4.80, £2.60; EX 53.00 Trifecta £350.30 Pool £710.56 - 1.44 winning units.
Owner Martin Love **Bred** Whitsbury Manor Stud **Trained** Sessay, N Yorks
■ Stewards' Enquiry : Steve Drowne two-day ban: dropped hands and lost sixth place (Jul 13,15)

FOCUS
A strong handicap, rated positively around the second and third, in which the majority raced towards the stands' side. The early pace was not overly strong and those held up were at a disadvantage.

NOTEBOOK
Indian Trail ◆ was well supported and confirmed the favourable impression he created in the Wokingham at Royal Ascot the previous week. Although he had the run of the race, the manner in which he went about his business suggested strongly that he can win again in similar company. (tchd 3-1, 10-3 in a place)
Woodcote(IRE), who did not have a chance to show what he was capable of from a bad draw at Beverley, had the run of the race and fared much better this time. He pulled clear of the remainder and, although without a win for some time, looks capable of landing a similar event.
Ice Planet, 11lb higher than his last win, ran creditably and fared the best of those that attempted to come from off the pace. He should continue to give a good account but looks vulnerable to progressive sorts from his current mark. (tchd 11-2, 6-1 in a place)
My Gacho(IRE), upped in the weights and in grade, was another at this meeting to show that racing in the centre of the course was no disadvantage. He should continue to give a good account, especially back in a lesser grade. (op 14-1)
Ingleby Arch(USA) confirmed that his last run at York had not done him justice and he ran creditably. However he again shaped as though the return to seven furlongs would see him in a better light and he is worth another chance.
Ellens Academy(IRE), turned out quickly after a decent effort at this course the previous evening, was not disgraced in a race that favoured those racing prominently. However his losing run confirms he is not one to place maximum faith in. (op 18-1)
Algharb, free to post, was not seen to best effect back on turf but may not be one to write off just yet. (op 5-1 tchd 6-1)

3078 JOHN SMITH'S NORTHUMBERLAND PLATE (HERITAGE H'CAP) 2m 19y
3:20 (3:21) (Class 2) 3-Y-O+
£123,320 (£37,120; £18,560; £9,260; £4,640; £2,340) **Stalls** Centre

Form RPR

4515 **1** **Toldo (IRE)**[21] [2437] 4-8-2 **86** ...... NelsonDeSouza(3) 16 97
(G M Moore) *led 6f: led again over 2f out: hrd pressed fnl f: hld on gamely* **33/1**

-242 **2** nk **River Alhaarth (IRE)**[36] [1991] 4-8-6 **87** ...... AlanMunro 19 98
(P W Chapple-Hyam) *chsd ldrs: rdn and outpcd over 3f out: rallied over 1f out: kpt on fnl f to take 2nd cl home* **20/1**

1131 **3** shd **Greenwich Meantime**[7] [2850] 6-8-9 **90** 5ex ...... PaulHanagan 18 101
(R A Fahey) *hld up midfield: hdwy to chse wnr over 1f out: ch ins fnl f: kpt on: hld cl home* **9/2**[1]

10/6 **4** 3 ½ **Dorothy's Friend**[21] [2437] 6-8-9 **90** ...... SteveDrowne 5 97
(R Charlton) *prom: drvn fr over 4f out: rallied: one pce over 1f out* **15/2**[2]

0-64 **5** ½ **Tarandot (IRE)**[35] [2023] 5-8-12 **93** ...... TonyCulhane 2 99
(G G Margarson) *hld up: effrt whn n.m.r over 4f and over 2f out: kpt on fnl f: no imp* **40/1**

5-30 **6** ½ **Escayola (IRE)**[11] [2723] 6-8-4 **85** ......(bt) RHills 1 90
(W J Haggas) *hld up: hdwy whn n.m.r over 2f out: kpt on fnl f: no imp* **9/1**

0000 **7** hd **Savannah Bay**[11] [2723] 7-8-6 **87** ......(b) TonyHamilton 6 92
(B Ellison) *bhd: hdwy over 2f out: kpt on fnl f: nvr rchd ldrs* **40/1**

0-54 **8** hd **Mirjan (IRE)**[21] [2437] 10-8-10 **91** ......(b) TomEaves 13 96
(L Lungo) *hld up in tch: hdwy and prom over 2f out: no ex over 1f out* **25/1**

-561 **9** nk **Bulwark (IRE)**[21] [2437] 4-9-1 **96** ......(be) KerrinMcEvoy 9 101
(Mrs A J Perrett) *hld up: hdwy over 2f out: no imp whn n.m.r ins fnl f* **9/2**[1]

5133 **10** ¾ **Tilt**[30] [2176] 4-8-5 **86** ...... PaulFessey 14 90
(B Ellison) *racd wd in midfield: hdwy to chse ldrs 3f out: wknd over 1f out* **25/1**

-411 **11** nk **Finalmente**[28] [2231] 4-8-12 **93** ...... OscarUrbina 10 96
(N A Callaghan) *keen: in tch: effrt and drvn whn nt clr run over 2f out: sn n.d* **11/1**

1-23 **12** 1 ¼ **Wing Collar**[21] [2437] 5-8-6 **87** ......(p) DavidAllan 8 89
(T D Easterby) *towards rr: drvn over 4f out: nvr rchd ldrs* **8/1**[3]

244/ **13** ¾ **Swing Wing**[671] [5170] 7-9-5 **105** ...... MarcHalford(5) 4 106
(P F I Cole) *towards rr: rdn 4f out: nvr on terms* **50/1**

1-10 **14** 2 **Mikao (IRE)**[52] [1584] 5-8-6 **87** ...... KDarley 3 86
(M H Tompkins) *in tch: drvn over 4f out: outpcd fr 2f out* **9/1**

50-3 **15** nk **Odiham**[35] [2013] 5-8-8 **94** ......(b[1]) TravisBlock(5) 17 92
(H Morrison) *racd wd: hld up: rdn 3f out: edgd lft and sn no imp* **12/1**

-004 **16** 5 **Ten Carat**[15] [2625] 6-8-5 **86** ......(v) RoystonFfrench 15 78
(M Todhunter) *hld up: pushed along 4f out: nvr on terms* **100/1**

45-0 **17** 1 **Acropolis (IRE)**[35] [2010] 5-9-4 **104** ...... GregFairley(5) 11 95
(J Howard Johnson) *cl up: led after 6f: sn clr: hdd over 2f out: sn btn* **50/1**

0-44 **18** 2 ½ **Astrocharm (IRE)**[6] [2893] 7-9-1 **99** ...... SaleemGolam(3) 12 87
(M H Tompkins) *hld up: shortlived effrt 3f out: sn btn* **50/1**

0/4- **19** 13 **Tiyoun (IRE)**[426] [1387] 8-8-4 **85** ...... DaleGibson 20 57
(Jedd O'Keeffe) *keen: cl up tl rdn and wknd fr over 4f out* **100/1**

6056 **20** 12 **Most Definitely (IRE)**[7] [2850] 6-8-4 **85** ......(p) PaulQuinn 7 43
(T D Easterby) *keen in tch: rdn whn n.m.r over 4f out: sn btn* **33/1**

3m 27.48s (-7.72) **Going Correction** -0.20s/f (Firm) **20** Ran SP% **126.3**
Speed ratings (Par 109):111,110,110,109,108 108,108,108,108,107 107,107,106,105,105 103,102,101,94,88
CSF £584.35 CT £3535.91 TOTE £41.70: £6.40, £6.30, £1.80, £1.50; EX 589.50 Trifecta £9631.40 Part won. Pool £13,565.37 - 0.40 winning units..

Owner J W Armstrong **Bred** Mrs C A Moore **Trained** Middleham Moor, N Yorks
■ Stewards' Enquiry : Nelson De Souza two-day ban: using whip with excessive frequency (Jul 13,15)
Alan Munro one-day ban: careless riding (Jul 13)

FOCUS
Few progressive performers for this valuable handicap but this looks sound form. Although the pace was sound, those held up were at a disadvantage. The first three home overcame the supposed bias against those drawn high.

NOTEBOOK
Toldo(IRE), who had the rub of a steadily-run race when behind Bulwark at Haydock last time, appreciated the better gallop and turned in a career-best effort. He displayed a very willing attitude and, although he is likely to be vulnerable to progressive or well handicapped sorts after reassessment, should continue to give a good account.
River Alhaarth(IRE), a steadily progressive sort, turned in his best effort yet on his first outing over this longer trip. This stiffer test of stamina seemed to suit and he could be a long-range option for the Cesarewitch at Newmarket in autumn.
Greenwich Meantime has thrived for current connections and, although beaten this time, ran up to his best under a penalty. He will reportedly be campaigned for the Ebor at York next month but, given he is due to go up a further 5lb, may be vulnerable to the lightly-raced and more progressive types. (op 11-2 tchd 6-1 in a place)
Dorothy's Friend, just behind Toldo after a lengthy break at Haydock last time, was one of the first off the bridle but kept responding. An even stiffer test of stamina will be in his favour and his campaign is likely to be geared towards the Cesarewitch in October.
Tarandot(IRE), upped to this trip for the first time in two years, fared the best of those to come from off the pace and looks a bit better than the bare form given she was short of room on a couple of occasions. She handles much softer ground but her record suggests she is not sure to put it all in next time.
Escayola(IRE), with the tongue-tie refitted, was not disgraced given he met trouble and that this race was against those held up. He is back on a fair mark and is one to keep an eye on in a race that looks likely to be run at an end-to-end gallop. (op 17-2)
Savannah Bay ran his best race for current connections with the blinkers refitted and may be a bit better than the bare form given he had a fair bit of ground to make up turning for home. He will also be interesting back over obstacles for this yard.
Bulwark(IRE), a progressive stayer who goes best for Kerrin McEvoy, shaped as though a bit better than the bare form given the way this race panned out and that he met trouble late on. He is worth another chance in similar company. Official explanation: jockey said colt was denied a clear run
Tilt, up in the weights and in grade, ran well for a long way and will be of more interest back over shorter in a lesser grade. He is the type to win more races for his current stable.
Finalmente, a lightly-raced and progressive sort, was just being asked for his effort when meeting trouble and this final placing is best ignored. He is well worth another chance over this trip and in a similar grade. (op 10-1)

3079 DOUG MOSCROP JOURNAL "GOOD MORNING" H'CAP — 7f
3:55 (3:57) (Class 2) (0-100,98) 3-Y-O+

£12,464 (£3,732; £1,866; £934; £466; £234) **Stalls** High

Form				RPR
-021	**1**		**Imperial Echo (USA)**[13] 2681 5-8-12 **80** ... PaulFessey 11	91
			(T D Barron) *hld up: hdwy 2f out: kpt on wl to ld cl home* **7/1**[3]	
4000	**2**	*nk*	**Compton's Eleven**[9] 2776 5-9-13 **95** ... TonyCulhane 15	105
			(M R Channon) *in tch: rdn to ld ent fnl f: kpt on: hdd cl home* **16/1**	
-210	**3**	*½*	**Malcheek (IRE)**[50] 1629 4-9-3 **85** ... DavidAllan 14	94
			(T D Easterby) *led tl hdd ent fnl f: kpt on same pce* **16/1**	
2300	**4**	*1 ¼*	**Breaking Shadow (IRE)**[18] 2520 4-8-10 **78** ... PhillipMakin 1	83
			(T D Barron) *hld up: hdwy over 1f out: kpt on fnl f: nrst fin* **20/1**	
2000	**5**	*½*	**Gallantry**[11] 2732 4-9-1 **83** ... SteveDrowne 3	87
			(D W Barker) *hld up: hdwy over 1f out: kpt on fnl f: nrst fin* **25/1**	
0101	**6**	*shd*	**Royal Dignitary (USA)**[21] 2454 6-8-12 **83** ... SilvestreDeSousa(3) 12	87
			(D Nicholls) *cl up: rdn over 2f out: outpcd fnl f* **13/2**[2]	
4644	**7**	*shd*	**Stoic Leader (IRE)**[9] 2794 6-8-12 **80** ... PaulMulrennan 13	83
			(R F Fisher) *prom: effrt 2f out: one pce fnl f* **16/1**	
-000	**8**	*shd*	**Just James**[7] 2847 7-10-0 **96** ... AlanMunro 7	99+
			(D Nicholls) *bhd and outpcd tl gd hdwy centre appr fnl f: nrst fin* **12/1**	
0-62	**9**	*3 ½*	**Marshman (IRE)**[13] 2681 7-9-3 **88** ... SaleemGolam(3) 6	82
			(M H Tompkins) *hld up: effrt over 1f out: nvr rchd ldrs* **13/2**[2]	
13	**10**	*nk*	**Against The Grain**[14] 2650 3-8-9 **85** ... RoystonFfrench 5	75
			(M Johnston) *cl up centre: rdn 3f out: wknd over 1f out* **10/3**[1]	
0000	**11**	*1 ¾*	**Traytonic**[44] 1806 5-9-6 **88** ... PaulQuinn 2	76
			(D Nicholls) *racd centre: prom tl wknd over 2f out* **25/1**	
0050	**12**	*hd*	**Doric (USA)**[2] 3020 5-9-1 **83** ... (p) KerrinMcEvoy 4	71
			(B Ellison) *chsd centre ldrs tl wknd over 2f out* **11/1**	
2-65	**13**	*1 ¼*	**Silidan**[9] 2779 3-8-10 **86** ... KDarley 9	67
			(T P Tate) *cl up centre tl wknd fr 2f out* **25/1**	
0-35	**14**	*9*	**Pacific Pride**[35] 2031 3-9-8 **98** ... PaulHanagan 10	55
			(J Howard Johnson) *prom tl rdn and wknd over 2f out* **14/1**	
-U00	**15**	*12*	**Coeur Courageux (FR)**[14] 2649 4-9-12 **94** ... TomEaves 8	22
			(D Nicholls) *in tch to 3f out: sn wknd* **25/1**	

1m 23.94s (-6.06) **Going Correction** -0.375s/f (Firm)
WFA 3 from 4yo+ 8lb — **15** Ran SP% **122.7**
Speed ratings (Par 109):108,107,107,105,105 104,104,104,100,100 98,98,96,86,72
CSF £106.29 CT £1095.08 TOTE £8.60: £3.00, £6.40, £5.40; EX 178.40 Trifecta £370.10 Part won. Pool £521.34 - 0.50 winning units..
Owner J Stephenson **Bred** Derby Lane Farm **Trained** Maunby, N Yorks

FOCUS
Mainly exposed types in this fair handicap but a decent gallop and this bare form should stand up at a similar level.

NOTEBOOK
Imperial Echo(USA) is better than ever this year and turned in a career-best performance from this 5lb higher mark. A decent gallop over this trip seems to suit and, given he should not be going up too much for this win, he should continue to give a good account. (tchd 15-2)
Compton's Eleven had the run of the race and ran his best race on turf since a solid fourth in the UAE in February. He has slipped to a fair mark and is capable of winning a race of this nature but may not be one to place maximum faith in.
Malcheek(IRE), having his first run for nearly two months, had the run of the race against the stands' rail and returned to form back on his favoured sound surface. He has little margin for error from his current mark but should continue to give a good account when he gets his ground.
Breaking Shadow(IRE), a stable companion of the winner, ran a typical race and was anything but disgraced but, given his losing run and the fact that he needs things to fall right, would not be one to place too much faith in.
Gallantry is edging down in the weights and ran creditably. He may have to come down a few more pounds before regaining the winning thread but is certainly not one to write off just yet. (op 22-1)
Royal Dignitary(USA), up in the weights and in grade after his Musselburgh win, kept fairly straight this time and ran to a similar level. He had the run of the race though and is likely to remain vulnerable in this type of event. (op 7-1)
Just James ran a typical race but, although he has slipped in the weights, he has not won for nearly three years and remains one to tread very carefully with. (op 14-1)

Against The Grain, the least experienced member of this field, proved a disappointment, especially given the current form of his stable, but he will be worth another chance in this type of event granted easier ground. (op 4-1 tchd 3-1)

3080 JOHN SMITH'S NO NONSENSE EBF MAIDEN STKS — 6f
4:25 (4:26) (Class 4) 2-Y-O

£6,232 (£1,866; £933; £467; £233; £117) **Stalls** High

Form				RPR
	1		**Champery (USA)** 2-9-3 ... KDarley 6	83+
			(M Johnston) *cl up: drvn over 2f out: rallied and led ins fnl f: r.o strly* **5/2**[1]	
53	**2**	*2*	**Algol**[8] 2827 2-9-3 ... TomEaves 7	74
			(J Howard Johnson) *chsd ldrs: effrt over 2f out: kpt on to chse wnr wl ins fnl f: no imp* **11/1**	
05	**3**	*1 ½*	**Hawaii Prince**[40] 1884 2-9-0 ... SilvestreDeSousa(3) 4	70
			(D Nicholls) *led tl hdd and no ex ins fnl f* **16/1**	
	4	*hd*	**Snowflight** 2-9-3 ... PaulHanagan 5	69+
			(R A Fahey) *in tch: outpcd and hung lft after 3f: gd hdwy over 1f out: kpt on fnl f* **14/1**	
222	**5**	*3*	**Dowlleh**[14] 2660 2-9-3 ... TonyCulhane 2	60+
			(M R Channon) *prom: effrt over 2f out: outpcd fnl f* **11/4**[2]	
	6	*6*	**Oh Gracious Me (IRE)** 2-9-3 ... AlanMunro 8	42+
			(P A Blockley) *in tch: rdn and effrt over 1f out: edgd lft and sn btn* **4/1**[3]	
	7	*3 ½*	**Mambomoon** 2-9-3 ... DavidAllan 1	31+
			(T D Easterby) *bhd and sn outpcd: nvr on terms* **25/1**	
	8	*2*	**Stevie Gee (IRE)** 2-9-3 ... KerrinMcEvoy 3	25+
			(G A Swinbank) *sn bhd: no ch fr 1/2-way* **13/2**	

1m 12.59s (-2.50) **Going Correction** -0.375s/f (Firm) 2y crse rec — **8** Ran SP% **113.3**
Speed ratings (Par 96):101,98,96,96,92 84,79,76
CSF £29.98 TOTE £4.10: £1.90, £2.90, £3.60; EX 46.00.
Owner Jumeirah Racing **Bred** Darley **Trained** Middleham Moor, N Yorks
■ Stewards' Enquiry : K Darley caution: careless riding

FOCUS
A fair gallop and in all probability ordinary form on the face of it, especially with the market leader disappointing, but the winner is a decent type with the scope to hold his own in better company.

NOTEBOOK
Champery(USA) ◆, a Derby entry who has several winners up to middle distances in his pedigree, took the eye in the preliminaries and created a favourable impression on this racecourse debut. He will stay further and appeals strongly as the type to win more races. (op 9-2)
Algol again ran creditably upped to this trip for the first time and looks a decent guide to the worth of this form. On this evidence he should stay seven furlongs and looks capable of picking up a small race in the north. (op 14-1)
Hawaii Prince has improved with every outing and turned in his best effort yet. Although he is likely to remain vulnerable to the better types in this grade, he will be interesting up to this trip in ordinary nursery company.
Snowflight showed ability on this racecourse debut, despite being either very green or ill-at-ease on the ground (or both). He should stay further than six furlongs and is sure to be placed to best advantage in due course. (op 20-1)
Dowlleh looked the one to beat judged on his three previous efforts but he was very easy to back and proved a disappointment. He is worth another chance but given he is starting to look exposed, may remain vulnerable to the more progressive sorts in this type of event. (op 11-8)
Oh Gracious Me(IRE), who is related to a couple of winners, hinted at ability on this racecourse debut and is entitled to improve for the experience. (tchd 9-2)

3081 TOTESPORT.COM H'CAP — 1m 2f 32y
4:55 (4:57) (Class 4) (0-85,83) 3-Y-O+

£6,232 (£1,866; £933; £467; £233; £117) **Stalls** Centre

Form				RPR
0303	**1**		**Active Asset (IRE)**[10] 2761 4-9-10 **78** ... TonyCulhane 4	87
			(M R Channon) *hld up in tch: hdwy over 2f out: led ins fnl f: r.o wl* **9/2**[3]	
1-6	**2**	*1 ¼*	**In Full Cry**[14] 2654 3-9-4 **83** ... KDarley 7	90
			(M Johnston) *chsd ldrs: rdn over 4f out: rallied to ld over 1f out: edgd lft: hdd ins fnl f: kpt on* **11/4**[1]	
1221	**3**	*2 ½*	**Trouble Mountain (USA)**[23] 2387 9-9-2 **70** ... (t) DaleGibson 6	72
			(M W Easterby) *hld up in tch: outpcd over 2f out: kpt on fnl f: nt rch first two* **9/2**[3]	
	4	*½*	**Dzesmin (POL)**[272] 4-10-0 **82** ... SteveDrowne 3	83
			(R C Guest) *hld up: hdwy over 1f out: no imp fnl f* **12/1**	
0-00	**5**	*shd*	**Red Chairman**[17] 2547 4-8-9 **63** oh1 ... (t) TomEaves 1	64
			(R Johnson) *plld hrd in rr: rdn over 2f out: kpt on fnl f: n.d* **33/1**	
1466	**6**	*2 ½*	**Aleron (IRE)**[11] 2736 8-9-3 **71** ... AlanMunro 2	67
			(J J Quinn) *hld up in tch: effrt over 2f out: no imp over 1f out* **10/1**	
1030	**7**	*3*	**Ransom Strip (USA)**[37] 1948 3-8-4 **69** ... RoystonFfrench 9	59
			(M Johnston) *cl up tl rdn and wknd fr 2f out* **16/1**	
4034	**8**	*hd*	**Instructor**[7] 2872 5-9-10 **78** ... PaulHanagan 5	68+
			(R A Fahey) *trckd ldrs: rdn over 2f out: sn wknd* **7/2**[2]	
	9	*nk*	**Best Of The Lot (USA)**[322] 4-9-8 **76** ... KerrinMcEvoy 8	65
			(T J Fitzgerald) *led to over 1f out: sn wknd* **14/1**	

2m 8.92s (-2.88) **Going Correction** -0.20s/f (Firm)
WFA 3 from 4yo+ 11lb — **9** Ran SP% **117.5**
Speed ratings (Par 105):103,102,100,99,99 97,95,94,94
CSF £17.64 CT £59.29 TOTE £6.50: £2.20, £1.70, £1.70; EX 23.20.
Owner aAIM Racing Syndicate **Bred** Rathasker Stud **Trained** West Ilsley, Berks

FOCUS
An ordinary event, rated through the first two. The bare form may not prove very strong.

3082 MILLER UK H'CAP — 1m (R)
5:25 (5:31) (Class 4) (0-80,80) 3-Y-O

£6,232 (£1,866; £933; £467; £233; £117) **Stalls** Centre

Form				RPR
0-01	**1**		**Prince Evelith (GER)**[15] 2616 3-8-7 **66** ... KerrinMcEvoy 9	77+
			(G A Swinbank) *hld up: hdwy 2f out: led wl ins fnl f: r.o* **11/4**[1]	
5062	**2**	*¾*	**Daaweitza**[8] 2809 3-8-8 **67** ... TomEaves 6	76
			(B Ellison) *chsd ldrs: effrt over 2f out: edgd lft and led briefly ins fnl f: r.o* **7/1**	
1645	**3**	*1 ½*	**Airbuss (IRE)**[16] 2581 3-9-4 **77** ... TonyCulhane 8	85+
			(M R Channon) *hld up in tch: effrt on ins over 2f out: nt clr run ins fnl f: r.o* **11/2**[3]	
023	**4**	*1*	**Feelin Irie (IRE)**[5] 2923 3-8-4 **63** ... KimTinkler 4	66
			(N Tinkler) *led: rdn over 2f out: hdd and no ex ins fnl f* **12/1**	
1433	**5**	*hd*	**European Dream (IRE)**[43] 1828 3-9-7 **80** ... JohnFortune 3	83
			(R C Guest) *hld up: hdwy over 1f out: nvr rchd ldrs* **9/2**[2]	
5-51	**6**	*1 ½*	**Decree Nisi**[12] 2698 3-8-6 **65** ... RoystonFfrench 2	64
			(Mrs A Duffield) *in tch: outpcd over 2f out: no imp after* **8/1**	
-045	**7**	*1 ¼*	**Rainbow's Classic**[15] 2616 3-8-8 **67** ... DO'Donohoe 1	68+
			(K A Ryan) *prom: effrt over 2f out: no ex whn hmpd ins fnl f* **10/1**	

51-0 **8** 7 **Vanilla Delight (IRE)**[31] 2126 3-9-2 75............................ PaulHanagan 7 55
(J Howard Johnson) *chsd ldrs: rdn over 2f out: sn btn* **16/1**

1m 40.98s (-2.50) **Going Correction** -0.20s/f (Firm) **8** Ran SP% **106.5**
Speed ratings (Par 102):104,103,101,100,100 99,97,90
CSF £18.89 CT £72.06 TOTE £3.80: £1.50, £2.50, £2.00; EX 24.40 Place 6 £130.52, Place 5 £53.32.
Owner Allan Stennett **Bred** Gestut Etzean **Trained** Melsonby, N Yorks
■ Categorical was withdrawn (9/1, unruly in stalls). R4 applies, deduct 10p in the £.

FOCUS
A run-of-the-mill handicap but a fair pace and an improved effort from the winner, who took this with more in hand than the official margin suggests. The second and third ran to form.
T/Jkpt: Not won. T/Plt: £245.80 to a £1 stake. Pool: £114,926.15. 341.30 winning tickets. T/Qpdt: £46.10 to a £1 stake. Pool: £5,363.20. 86.00 winning tickets. RY

3043 NEWMARKET (JULY) (R-H)

Saturday, July 1

OFFICIAL GOING: Firm
Wind: Light, across Weather: Hot and sunny

3083 NEWMARKETRACECOURSES.CO.UK MAIDEN STKS 7f
1:50 (1:52) (Class 4) 2-Y-O **£4,533** (£1,348; £674; £336) **Stalls** High

Form RPR

1 **Rallying Cry (USA)** 2-9-3 .... JimmyFortune 3 88+
(J H M Gosden) *w'like: scope: b.bkwd: hld up: racd keenly: swtchd lft and hdwy over 1f out: led ins fnl f: edgd rt: r.o wl* **7/1**[3]

5 **2** 2 ½ **Farleigh House (USA)**[14] 2660 2-9-3 .... TPQueally 9 74
(M H Tompkins) *trckd ldrs: nt clr run over 1f out: r.o ins fnl f: no ch w wnr* **20/1**

0 **3** *hd* **Castara Bay**[16] 2579 2-9-3 .... RichardHughes 6 73
(R Hannon) *s.i.s: sn trcking ldrs: rdn over 1f out: styd on same pce ins fnl f* **15/2**

4 *1* **Mesbaah (IRE)** 2-9-3 .... MartinDwyer 8 70
(M A Jarvis) *w'like: scope: bkwd: chsd ldr: led over 1f out: sn rdn and hdd: edgd rt and no ex ins fnl f* **11/2**[2]

6 **5** *nk* **Al Raahi**[15] 2619 2-9-3 .... TedDurcan 10 70
(M R Channon) *led: rdn and hdd over 1f out: styd on same pce* **4/1**[1]

6 *nk* **Iron Fist (IRE)** 2-9-3 .... RobbieFitzpatrick 1 69
(E J O'Neill) *leggy: rangy: lw: chsd ldrs: rdn to ld 1f out: hdd and no ex ins fnl f* **12/1**

000 **7** ½ **Venir Rouge**[15] 2619 2-9-3 .... AlanDaly 12 68+
(M Salaman) *swtg: hld up: nt clr run over 1f out: styng on whn hmpd ins fnl f: nvr able to chal* **25/1**

55 **8** *1* **Mint State**[16] 2579 2-9-3 .... JohnEgan 7 65+
(D R C Elsworth) *swtg: hld up: plld hrd: swtchd lft over 2f out: sn rdn and no imp* **7/1**[3]

0 **9** 1 ½ **Fairly Honest**[18] 2530 2-9-0 .... AntonyProcter(3) 2 61
(D R C Elsworth) *hld up in tch: racd keenly: hung lft fr 1/2-way: rdn and ev ch 2f out: wknd fnl f* **50/1**

10 1 ½ **Shmookh (USA)** 2-9-3 .... PhilipRobinson 5 57
(J L Dunlop) *leggy: scope: chsd ldrs: rdn over 2f out: wknd over 1f out* **4/1**[1]

11 *25* **Diverse Forecast (IRE)** 2-9-3 .... JamieSpencer 11 —
(Mrs P Sly) *cmpt: swtg: s.s: outpcd* **16/1**

1m 27.89s (1.11) **Going Correction** +0.025s/f (Good) **11** Ran SP% **116.3**
Speed ratings (Par 96):94,91,90,89,89 89,88,87,85,83 55
CSF £138.01 TOTE £8.30: £3.10, £3.00, £2.50; EX 254.70.
Owner H R H Princess Haya Of Jordan **Bred** Flaxman Holdings Ltd **Trained** Newmarket, Suffolk

FOCUS
A potentially above-average juvenile maiden, run at a solid pace, and the winner looks capable of rating higher.

NOTEBOOK
Rallying Cry(USA) ♦, a $95,000 purchase whose dam was a high-class ten furlong performer at 3-4, got his career off to a perfect start with a taking debut success. He proved keen under restraint through the early parts, but once the penny dropped he picked up strongly when asked to win his race, and looked better the further he went. He is obviously entitled to improve for the experience, and his trainer indicated his next target would probably be the Solario Stakes at Sandown in August, in which his yard has a decent record. (op 13-2)
Farleigh House(USA), fifth on debut at York last time, met trouble nearing the final furlong yet it made little difference to the overall result. This was a much-improved effort, he clearly enjoyed the step up to this extra furlong, and can be placed to get off the mark before long.
Castara Bay, seventh on debut at Newbury 16 days previously, was doing his best work towards the finish on this step up in trip and would have been a little closer but for missing the break. He is going the right way and clearly appreciated the stiffer test. (op 7-1 tchd 8-1)
Mesbaah(IRE), a half-brother to some usefuls winner at up to ten furlongs, showed up well for a fair way and left the impression he ought to improve a deal for this debut experience. He will stay further in time. (op 5-1)
Al Raahi ultimately paid for his exertions at the head of affairs and improved marginally on his debut at Sandown last time. He looks more of a nursery type. (op 5-1 tchd 11-2 in a place)
Mint State rather spoilt his chances by refusing to settle under restraint, but he was still noted as finishing his race well enough, under a considerate ride. It would be a surprise if he were not to better this when qualified for nurseries.
Shmookh(USA), closely related to high-class performer Mujahid and whose dam was a sprint winner, left the impression he would benefit a deal from this debut experience and can be expected to get closer next time. Official explanation: jockey said colt ran very green (op 7-2)

3084 WALKER TRANSPORT EMPRESS STKS (LISTED RACE) (FILLIES) 6f
2:25 (2:26) (Class 1) 2-Y-O
£13,343 (£5,057; £2,530; £1,261; £632; £317) **Stalls** High

Form RPR

1 **1** **Hope'N'Charity (USA)**[14] 2638 2-8-12 .... PhilipRobinson 10 93
(C G Cox) *sn led: hld over 4f out: led over 1f out: sn rdn and edgd lft: r.o* **5/4**[1]

315 **2** *1* **Satulagi (USA)**[8] 2800 2-8-12 .... JohnEgan 3 90
(J S Moore) *chsd ldrs: rdn and ev ch 2f out: styd on* **5/1**[2]

01 **3** *nk* **My Lovely Lesley (USA)**[16] 2572 2-8-12 .... DarryllHolland 9 89
(B J Meehan) *lw: s.i.s: hld up: swtchd lft and hdwy over 1f out: hung lft ins fnl f: r.o* **14/1**

3031 **4** ¾ **Three Decades (IRE)**[21] 2461 2-8-12 .... MartinDwyer 11 87
(C A Cyzer) *plld hrd and prom: nt clr run over 1f out: styd on ins fnl f* **25/1**

0341 **5** ½ **Bridge It Jo**[24] 2354 2-8-12 .... TPQueally 8 85
(Miss J Feilden) *trckd ldrs: swtchd lft over 2f out: rdn and ev ch over 1f out: no ex ins fnl f* **16/1**

13 **6** ½ **Eliza May**[29] 2191 2-8-12 .... NCallan 12 84
(K A Ryan) *b.hind: s.i.s: sn prom: rdn and nt clr run over 1f out: styd on* **14/1**

12 **7** ½ **Marmaida (IRE)**[15] 2598 2-8-12 .... PaulDoe 7 82
(W J Knight) *chsd ldr: led over 4f out: rdn and hdd over 1f out: wknd ins fnl f* **16/1**

1352 **8** ¾ **Fairfield Princess**[14] 2630 2-8-12 .... PaulFitzsimons 6 80
(N A Callaghan) *hld up: plld hrd: rdn over 1f out: nvr trbld ldrs* **14/1**

3 **9** ½ **Princess Georgina**[15] 2610 2-8-12 .... JamieSpencer 5 79+
(S C Williams) *hld up: nt clr run over 1f out: hmpd ins fnl f: nvr trbld ldrs* **9/1**

10 *nk* **El Toreador (USA)** 2-8-12 .... NickyMackay 1 78
(G A Butler) *w'like: hld up: effrt over 2f out: wknd fnl f* **33/1**

4410 **11** ¾ **Christmas Tart (IRE)**[10] 2743 2-8-12 .... JimmyFortune 4 75
(V Smith) *s.i.s: hld up: a in rr* **8/1**[3]

1m 12.76s (-0.59) **Going Correction** +0.025s/f (Good) **11** Ran SP% **120.8**
Speed ratings (Par 99):104,102,102,101,100 99,99,98,97,97 96
CSF £7.51 TOTE £2.20: £1.30, £1.90, £3.10; EX 8.80.
Owner S R Hope And S W Barrow **Bred** D Brown And Lendy Brown **Trained** Lambourn, Berks

FOCUS
Traditionally one of the weakest Listed races in the calendar, but this looks a relatively competitive renewal, with the winner's rating bettered only by Slip Dance (2004) in recent years. Sound form by the look of it.

NOTEBOOK
Hope'N'Charity(USA) ♦, an impressive debut winner at Leicester a fortnight previously, followed up under a positive ride from Robinson and showed a decent attitude when asked to win her race. She is clearly useful and she is well suited by a quick surface. It would be surprising if there isn't more to come, and she could return for the Group 2 Cherry Hinton later this month. (op 6-4)
Satulagi(USA), fifth in the Albany Stakes at Royal Ascot eight days previously, confirmed that effort was no fluke with another solid effort in defeat. She is evidently improving, enjoys a quick surface, and left the impression she would get another furlong. (tchd 11-2)
My Lovely Lesley(USA), off the mark in a Lingfield maiden last time, posted a career-best effort in defeat on this step back up in class and would have been closer but for losing ground with a sluggish start. She remains open to further improvement and will get another furlong on this evidence. Official explanation: jockey said filly hung awkwardly left leaving stalls
Three Decades(IRE) did well to finish as close as she did, having refused to settle through the early parts, and ran her best race to date in defeat. She has done most of her racing on the All-Weather so far, but this proves she is just as effective on turf.
Bridge It Jo held every chance on this step up in class, yet failed to really get home over this stiff six furlongs. She can better this when reverting to the minimum trip and remains in decent form.
Eliza May ran a shade better than her finishing position suggests and appreciated the step up to this trip. This was her best effort to date, but she probably still requires an easier surface. (op 12-1)

3085 FRED ARCHER STKS (LISTED RACE) 1m 4f
3:00 (3:03) (Class 1) 4-Y-O+ **£15,898** (£6,025; £3,015; £1,503; £753) **Stalls** High

Form RPR

-614 **1** **Admiral's Cruise (USA)**[35] 2010 4-9-0 107.................. JimmyFortune 5 80
(B J Meehan) *hld up: hdwy to ld over 1f out: sn clr* **13/2**

1-22 **2** *4* **Ouninpohja (IRE)**[21] 2453 5-9-0 106.................................. NCallan 6 79+
(G A Swinbank) *lw: trckd ldrs: nt clr run and lost pl over 1f out: r.o ins fnl f: no ch w wnr* **7/2**[2]

4630 **3** *5* **Amwell Brave**[25] 2320 5-9-0 49.. PaulDoe 2 66?
(J R Jenkins) *hld up: hdwy u.p over 1f out: wknd fnl f* **100/1**

-055 **4** 3 ½ **Hard Top (IRE)**[7] 2845 4-9-0 114...................................... JamieSpencer 1 60
(Sir Michael Stoute) *lw: trckd ldr: rdn and ev ch over 1f out: wknd fnl f* **4/5**[1]

6-42 **5** 1 ½ **Art Eyes (USA)**[21] 2430 4-8-12 105...................................... JohnEgan 3 56
(D R C Elsworth) *led: rdn and hdd over 1f out: wknd fnl f* **5/1**[3]

2m 30.7s (-2.21) **Going Correction** +0.025s/f (Good) **5** Ran SP% **108.8**
Speed ratings (Par 111):108,105,102,99,98
CSF £27.72 TOTE £6.80: £3.10, £2.20; EX 39.70.
Owner Joe L Allbritton **Bred** Lazy Lane Stables Inc **Trained** Manton, Wilts

FOCUS
A fair Listed event, run at a modest pace, but the form looks highly suspect, with odds-on Hard Top and Art Eyes finishing behind a 49-rated third.

NOTEBOOK
Admiral's Cruise(USA), rather disappointing at Ascot 35 days previously, bounced back to his best on this return to a quick surface and was full value for his winning margin. He proved better suited by the switch to more patient tactics over this trip and showed a neat turn of foot when asked to win his race. He looks a Group performer in the making, even if this form may not be the strongest for the class. (op 8-1)
Ouninpohja(IRE) once again endured a luckless passage when it mattered and, by the time he was in clear, the winner had gone beyond recall. He can be rated better than the bare form, and most probably wants a stiffer test on slightly easier ground, but he is still proving rather frustating this term. (tchd 10-3 and 4-1 in a place)
Amwell Brave ran a huge race at the weights on this big step up in class and only gave way nearing the final furlong. His proximity at the finish clearly holds the form down, and it is hard to know just what to make of this apparent career-best effort, as he had looked fully exposed previously.
Hard Top(IRE), who proved too keen in the Hardwicke Stakes a week previously, once again ran too freely on this drop in class and has to rate bitterly disappointing. He has it all to prove now, even allowing for the fact he may have found this coming too soon. Official explanation: trainer's representative said colt had run too keenly (op 8-11 tchd 5-6)
Art Eyes(USA) was another to run way below her previous best and looked moody when pressed for the lead approaching the final furlong. Official explanation: jockey said filly was struck into from behind (op 11-2 tchd 6-1)

3086 WOODFORD RESERVE CRITERION STKS (GROUP 3) 7f
3:35 (3:36) (Class 1) 3-Y-O+
£28,390 (£10,760; £5,385; £2,685; £1,345; £675) **Stalls** High

Form RPR

-246 **1** **Suggestive**[23] 2386 8-9-2 108.......................................(b) NickyMackay 7 111
(W J Haggas) *trckd ldrs: rdn to ld wl ins fnl f: r.o* **10/1**

6-23 **2** *hd* **Mac Love**[26] 2289 5-9-2 102.................................... RichardHughes 4 110
(R Charlton) *hld up in tch: n.m.r over 1f out: rdn to ld 1f out: hdd wl ins fnl f: edgd rt: r.o* **6/1**[3]

-502 **3** *1* **New Seeker**[23] 2386 6-9-2 110.....................................(b) PhilipRobinson 3 108
(C G Cox) *lw: sn led: rdn and swished tail over 1f out: sn hdd: styd on same pce* **5/4**[1]

1341 **4** *hd* **Nayyir**[28] 2226 8-9-7 110.. NCallan 5 115+
(G A Butler) *lw: hld up: hdwy and nt clr run over 1f out: swtchd lft and running on whn nt clr run wl ins fnl f: nvr able to chal* **7/2**[2]

2-02 **5** 3 1/2 **Sir Xaar (IRE)**[61] [1362] 3-8-8 109.................................... DarryllHolland 2 95
(B Smart) *chsd ldr over 5f out: rdn and ev ch over 1f out: wknd ins fnl f* **6/1**[3]

0551 **6** *hd* **Bahia Breeze**[19] [2503] 4-8-13 100.................................... SebSanders 1 95
(Rae Guest) *prom: rdn over 1f out: wknd ins fnl f* **16/1**

1m 24.16s (-2.62) **Going Correction** +0.025s/f (Good)
WFA 3 from 4yo+ 8lb **6** Ran SP% **110.2**
Speed ratings (Par 113):115,114,113,113,109 109
CSF £63.20 TOTE £13.40: £3.60, £3.30; EX 53.20.
Owner Mrs Barbara Bassett **Bred** Keith Freeman **Trained** Newmarket, Suffolk

FOCUS
A bit of a muddling contest and just an ordinary renewal of this Group 3, rated around the winner and runner-up to the balance of their form.

NOTEBOOK
Suggestive dug deep when it mattered and ultimately just did enough to record a first success in Group company. He was disappointing at Haydock last time, but that effort came after a break, and he was fully entitled to have needed that run. Capable of holding his form well, he shows no signs of decline, and is likely have another crack at the Lennox Stakes at Goodwood next month. (op 8-1)
Mac Love ran his best race in a long while and was only just denied. He settled better this time and, while he is not one in which to place maximum faith, he is worth persevering with in this class. (op 11-2)
New Seeker, well backed, had his chance yet could not match the finishing kick of the first two. He remains in good heart, and helps to set the level of this form, but he continues hard to place in this class. (op 13-8)
Nayyir ◆ ran much better than his finishing position suggests, as he endured a nightmare passage when it mattered, and has to rate unfortunate. He could be expected to reverse this form in the future and should go very close if turning up in the Lennox Stakes next month - a race he won back in 2003. (tchd 4-1 in places)
Sir Xaar(IRE) was not at all disgraced racing against his elders for the first time, but his fate was still sealed entering the final furlong. Official explanation: jockey said colt was unsuited by the firm ground

3087 THE HOME OF HORSE RACING H'CAP 6f
4:05 (4:06) (Class 4) (0-80,77) 3-Y-O **£5,505** (£1,637; £818; £408) **Stalls** High

Form RPR

-000 **1** **Savernake Blue**[43] [1812] 3-9-0 77.................................... ThomasO'Brien(7) 3 81
(M R Channon) *lw: s.i.s: hld up: hdwy over 1f out: led ins fnl f: r.o* **10/1**

1046 **2** 1 3/4 **Rapsgate (IRE)**[15] [2609] 3-9-2 72....................................(b) RichardHughes 7 71
(R Hannon) *trckd ldrs: rdn over 1f out: r.o* **8/1**

400 **3** *hd* **Crafty Fox**[21] [2458] 3-7-13 60.................................... AndrewElliott(5) 8 58
(A P Jarvis) *lw: chsd ldrs: rdn and ev ch over 1f out: styd on same pce ins fnl f* **16/1**

1555 **4** 1 1/4 **Sir Orpen (IRE)**[7] [2863] 3-9-6 76.................................... JimmyFortune 4 70
(T D Barron) *chsd ldrs: rdn and ev ch over 1f out: no ex ins fnl f* **5/2**[1]

2165 **5** 3 **Danetime Lord (IRE)**[56] [1497] 3-8-11 67....................................(p) NCallan 6 52
(K A Ryan) *chsd ldrs: led 2f out: hdd & wknd ins fnl f* **7/2**[2]

4605 **6** *nk* **Brunelleschi**[1] [3049] 3-9-3 73.................................... BrianReilly 5 58
(P L Gilligan) *lw: chsd ldrs: rdn over 2f out: wknd fnl f* **11/2**[3]

5005 **7** 2 **Welcome Releaf**[14] [2644] 3-8-3 59 oh1 ow1....................................(v1) MartinDwyer 2 38
(G C H Chung) *hld up: rdn over 2f out: n.d* **20/1**

0-00 **8** 1 **Titian Saga (IRE)**[7] [2866] 3-9-5 75.................................... DarryllHolland 9 51
(C N Allen) *led 4f: wkng whn hmpd over 1f out* **12/1**

0-04 **9** 6 **Princess Cleo**[41] [1865] 3-9-5 75.................................... TedDurcan 1 33
(T D Easterby) *swtg: hld up: rdn over 2f out: wknd over 1f out* **8/1**

1m 13.02s (-0.33) **Going Correction** +0.025s/f (Good) **9** Ran SP% **115.8**
Speed ratings (Par 102):103,100,100,98,94 94,91,90,82
CSF £87.14 CT £1285.22 TOTE £14.20: £3.60, £1.90, £3.10; EX 44.00.
Owner Michael A Foy **Bred** Michael A Foy **Trained** West Ilsley, Berks

FOCUS
A modest sprint, run at a generous early pace, and the winner won nicely under top weight.
Welcome Releaf Official explanation: jockey said gelding was unsuited by the firm ground

3088 EUROPEAN BREEDERS FUND FILLIES' H'CAP 1m
4:35 (4:38) (Class 3) (0-90,87) 3-Y-O+ **£9,067** (£2,697; £1,348; £673) **Stalls** High

Form RPR

0242 **1** **Kelucia (IRE)**[3] [2988] 5-10-0 85.................................... SebSanders 9 96
(R M Beckett) *s.i.s: hld up: hdwy to ld 1f out: rdn out* **4/1**[2]

1 **2** 1 **Bosset (USA)**[42] [1844] 3-9-5 85.................................... TPQueally 7 91+
(J Noseda) *lw: a.p: swtchd lft over 1f out: sn ev ch: hung lft ins fnl f: styd on same pce* **5/1**[3]

4441 **3** 1 1/2 **My Lovely Lady (IRE)**[11] [2729] 3-8-3 69.................................... JohnEgan 4 72
(M L W Bell) *chsd ldrs: swtchd lft over 1f out: styd on same pce fnl f* **7/1**

-210 **4** *shd* **Magic Peak (IRE)**[24] [2359] 3-8-9 75.................................... DarryllHolland 1 78+
(Sir Michael Stoute) *hld up: hdwy over 1f out: styd on same pce fnl f* **16/1**

0-41 **5** 2 1/2 **Fantastisch (IRE)**[15] [2620] 3-9-1 81.................................... TedDurcan 3 78
(H R A Cecil) *led 1f: chsd ldr: rdn and ev ch fr 2f out tl wknd ins fnl f* **7/2**[1]

2235 **6** *hd* **Spring Goddess (IRE)**[71] [1112] 5-9-5 81.................................... AndrewElliott(5) 5 80
(A P Jarvis) *lw: hld up: nvr trbld ldrs* **10/1**

2013 **7** *nk* **Kaveri (USA)**[18] [2527] 3-9-7 87.................................... JimmyFortune 8 83
(C E Brittain) *led 7f out: rdn and hdd 1f out: sn wknd* **16/1**

1-32 **8** 1 3/4 **Famcred**[24] [2359] 3-9-5 85.................................... NickyMackay 2 77
(L M Cumani) *chsd ldrs: rdn over 2f out: wknd over 1f out* **7/2**[1]

1m 40.61s (0.18) **Going Correction** +0.025s/f (Good)
WFA 3 from 4yo+ 9lb **8** Ran SP% **114.5**
Speed ratings (Par 104):100,99,97,97,94 94,94,92
CSF £24.32 CT £135.35 TOTE £5.40: £1.60, £2.20, £2.00; EX 36.00.
Owner B Scanlon & F Brady **Bred** Fernando Bermudez **Trained** Whitsbury, Hants

FOCUS
A fair fillies' handicap, but run at just a modest pace. The winner confirmed her Salisbury improvement.

NOTEBOOK
Kelucia(IRE), second at Salisbury three days previously, defied top weight and opened her account for the current campaign at the fifth attempt. This return to racing against her own sex obviously helped, but she did well to quicken off the modest early pace, and is clearly back at the top of her game again now.
Bosset(USA), off the mark on debut at Newbury 42 days previously, had every chance to follow up on this handicap debut over this extra furlong. She was by far the least experienced filly in the race and this has to rate a pleasing effort. She can be placed to strike again. (op 9-2)
My Lovely Lady(IRE), up 2lb for winning at Brighton 11 days previously, had her chance and posted a solid effort in defeat. She should continue to pay her way in such events. (op 9-1)
Magic Peak(IRE) posted an improved effort and would probably have been seen to even better effect off a stronger early gallop. She can build on this, although at present is very much one of her leading yard's lesser lights.
Fantastisch(IRE), off the mark on her handicap bow at Sandown last time, had the run of the race but seemed to be found out by her 5lb higher mark, although the modest pace possibly contributed too.

Famcred proved very disappointing, finishing out of the frame for the first time in her career. She is better than this, but has questions to answer now all the same. (tchd 4-1)

3089 NEWMARKETEXPERIENCE.CO.UK APPRENTICE H'CAP 7f
5:10 (5:10) (Class 5) (0-70,70) 3-Y-O+ **£3,886** (£1,156; £577; £288) **Stalls** High

Form RPR

0544 **1** **Lincolneurocruiser**[1] [3044] 4-9-2 63.................... RussellKennemore(5) 8 75
(Mrs N Macauley) *lw: racd stands' side: hld up: hdwy 1/2-way: led over 2f out: rdn out* **10/1**

2042 **2** 3/4 **Musicmaestroplease (IRE)**[12] [2698] 3-8-4 61....... JamieHamblett(7) 12 70+
(S Parr) *racd stands' side: chsd ldrs: nt clr run and swtchd rt over 1f out: hung lft and styd on ins fnl f* **14/1**

6502 **3** 3/4 **Barons Spy (IRE)**[20] [2482] 5-9-0 56.................................... RobertMiles 5 64
(R J Price) *racd stands' side: hld up: hdwy over 2f out: sn rdn: styd on* **13/2**[2]

0000 **4** 1 **Life's A Whirl**[14] [2645] 4-8-7 54....................................(p) KirstyMilczarek(5) 13 59
(Mrs C A Dunnett) *racd stands' side: hld up: hdwy and swtchd lft over 1f out: nt rch ldrs* **25/1**

002 **5** 4 **For Life (IRE)**[14] [2645] 4-8-9 54....................................(p) AndrewElliott(3) 15 49
(A P Jarvis) *lw: racd stands' side dwlt: sn chsng ldrs: rdn and ev ch 2f out: sn rdn: hung lft and nt run on* **16/1**

1064 **6** 1/2 **Smile For Us**[6] [2896] 3-9-1 68....................................(b) JerryO'Dwyer(3) 17 58
(C Drew) *taced stands' side: chsd ldrs: rdn over 2f out: wknd over 1f out* **33/1**

6301 **7** *nk* **Torquemada (IRE)**[14] [2645] 5-9-7 63.................................... NeilChalmers 11 55
(W Jarvis) *racd stands' side: hld up: hdwy over 2f out: wknd fnl f* **8/1**

1335 **8** 1 1/2 **Ballare (IRE)**[60] [1394] 7-8-9 51 oh5....................................(v) AmirQuinn 7 39
(P J Makin) *racd stands' side: hld up: styd on ins fnl f: nvr nrr* **20/1**

0-00 **9** 3 1/2 **Kareeb (FR)**[17] [2551] 9-8-13 62.................................... AlanRutter(7) 2 41+
(W J Musson) *racd far side: chsd ldr: led that gp over 2f out: no ch w stands' side: 1st of 4 in gp* **7/1**[3]

0140 **10** *hd* **Dispol Isle (IRE)**[11] [2737] 4-9-12 68.................................... BenSwarbrick 18 46
(T D Barron) *lw: racd stands' side: chsd ldrs: rdn over 2f out: wknd over 1f out* **16/1**

4464 **11** *nk* **Vindication**[16] [2590] 6-9-6 65....................................(tp) RichardKingscote(3) 1 42+
(R M H Cowell) *trckd ldrs far side: rdn over 1f out: no ex: 2nd of 4 in gp* **10/1**

000- **12** 1 **Commander Wish**[232] [6309] 3-8-4 61 ow2.................... JPFeatherstone(7) 9 35
(P Howling) *lw: racd stands's ide: dwlt: hld up: hdwy over 2f out: wknd over 1f out* **33/1**

0-60 **13** 2 1/2 **Middle Eastern**[128] [489] 4-8-2 51 oh1.................................... SophieDoyle(7) 16 19
(P A Blockley) *racd stands' side: led that gp over 4f: rdn and wknd over 1f out* **25/1**

3025 **14** 1/2 **St Ivian**[9] [2780] 6-8-6 51 oh7.................................... DuranFentiman(3) 6 18
(Mrs N Macauley) *b: racd stands' side: hld up: rdn over 2f out: sn wknd* **40/1**

020 **15** 3 1/2 **Poker Player (IRE)**[11] [2737] 4-9-6 67.................................... AshleyHamblett(5) 3 24+
(G C Bravery) *racd far side: chsd ldrs: swtchd rt over 2f out: sn wknd: 3rd of 4 in gp* **12/1**

0-60 **16** 1 3/4 **Tantien**[42] [1852] 4-8-2 51 oh14.................................... PatrickDonaghy(7) 14 4
(John A Harris) *b: racd stands' side: sn outpcd* **100/1**

-000 **17** 1 3/4 **Warden Warren**[156] [200] 8-8-13 60....................................(b) ThomasO'Brien(5) 4 8+
(Mrs C A Dunnett) *led far side over 4f: sn wknd: last of 4 in gp* **12/1**

1114 **18** 5 **Joy And Pain**[7] [2864] 5-9-9 70....................................(v) KevinGhunowa(5) 10 4
(M J Attwater) *racd stands' side: chsd ldrs over 5f* **11/2**[1]

1m 25.5s (-1.28) **Going Correction** +0.025s/f (Good)
WFA 3 from 4yo+ 8lb **18** Ran SP% **126.1**
Speed ratings (Par 103):108,107,106,105,100 100,99,97,93,93 93,92,89,88,84 82,80,75
CSF £136.04 CT £1028.10 TOTE £12.40: £2.60, £3.00, £2.40, £6.80; EX 222.10 Place 6 £2,532.81, Place 5 £425.19.
Owner Peter Smith P C Coaches Limited **Bred** David Brown, Slatch Farm Stud And G B Turnbull L **Trained** Sproxton, Leics
■ Stewards' Enquiry : Kevin Ghunowa one-day ban: careless riding (Jul 13); one-day ban: failed to keep straight from stalls (Jul 15)

FOCUS
A modest handicap, which saw the four racing on the far side at a distinct disadvantage. The first four came clear. Sound form which should prove reliable.
T/Plt: £664.80 to a £1 stake. Pool: £61,524.25. 67.55 winning tickets. T/Qpdt: £88.00 to a £1 stake. Pool: £4,308.30. 36.20 winning tickets. CR

2929 WINDSOR (R-H)
Saturday, July 1

OFFICIAL GOING: Good to firm
Wind: Virtually nil. Weather: Hot & sunny.

3090 TOTEPLACEPOT MAIDEN STKS 6f
2:00 (2:00) (Class 5) 3-4-Y-O **£3,238** (£963; £481; £240) **Stalls** High

Form RPR

44 **1** **Falmassim**[49] [1687] 3-9-3 .... LDettori 16 63+
(L M Cumani) *trckd ldrs: led 2f out: shkn up and hld on wl whn chal ins fnl f* **11/4**[1]

-606 **2** 3/4 **Good Companion (IRE)**[14] [2644] 3-9-3 55.................... JimmyQuinn 12 61
(J L Dunlop) *in tch: n.m.r 2f out: hung bdly lft over 1f out: fin wl u.p but nt pce of wnr* **14/1**

3-02 **3** *nk* **Rogue**[23] [2383] 4-9-4 63.................................... GeorgeBaker 13 55+
(Jane Southcombe) *in tch: hdwy whn carried bdly lft over 1f out: rallied and r.o ins last: fin wl but nt rch wnr* **3/1**[2]

0 **4** 1/2 **Royal Senga**[37] [1960] 3-8-12 .... FergusSweeney 8 53+
(C A Horgan) *bhd: swtchd lft to outside ins fnl 2f: r.o wl fnl f: no ex cl home* **66/1**

2056 **5** 1 1/2 **Danawi (IRE)**[5] [2931] 3-9-3 67....................................(v1) RyanMoore 7 54
(R Hannon) *bhd: hdwy on outside fr 2f out: chsd ldrs 1f out: kpt on same pce ins last* **9/2**[3]

6 1/2 **Monaco Prince (IRE)** 3-9-3 .... JayFord 3 52
(G A Huffer) *s.i.s: sn recovrd to ld after 1f: hdd 2f out: styd chalng tl wknd last half f* **12/1**

5 **7** *shd* **Footstepsinthesnow (IRE)**[23] [2383] 3-8-12 .... ShaneKelly 2 47
(M A Buckley) *chsd ldrs: rdn to chal 1f out: wknd last half f* **16/1**

06 **8** 3 **Im Ova Ere Dad (IRE)**[10] [2763] 3-9-3 .... ChrisCatlin 9 43
(D E Cantillon) *s.i.s: bhd: styd on fr over 1f out: nvr gng pce to be competitive* **33/1**

5 **9** 1 1/4 **Question (USA)**[10] [2763] 3-8-12 .... JimCrowley 14 34
(J M Bradley) *chsd ldrs 1/2-way: n.m.r 2f out: sn wknd* **20/1**

The Form Book, Raceform Ltd, Compton, RG20 6NL

50-0 **10** *nk* **Girandola**[28] 2235 3-9-3 64 .... StephenCarson 15 38
(R F Johnson Houghton) *chsd ldrs: rdn and one pce whn n.m.r on rail 2f out: n.d after* **16/1**

0- **11** *hd* **Wolf Pack**[453] 877 4-9-9 .... SamHitchcott 1 38
(R W Price) *bhd: sn rdn: sme hdwy fnl f* **50/1**

00- **12** *½* **Martian Mystery**[325] 4255 3-8-12 .... LPKeniry 6 31
(M Madgwick) *outpcd most of way* **66/1**

44-0 **13** *2* **Sudden Edge**[15] 2611 4-9-9 59 .... DaneO'Neill 10 30
(H Candy) *bhd: sme hdwy whn n.m.r over 1f out: nvr in contention* **14/1**

0 **14** *1 ¾* **All About Him (USA)**[18] 2532 3-8-10 .... MarkCoumbe(7) 4 25
(N I M Rossiter) *chsd ldrs over 4f* **100/1**

15 *5* **Boysie Brigador (USA)**[338] 3-9-3 .... (t) FJohansson 5 10
(R A Kvisla) *a in rr* **20/1**

50 **16** *½* **Decider (USA)**[10] 2763 3-8-10 .... BarrySavage(7) 11 9
(J M Bradley) *led 1f: wknd qckly 2f out* **80/1**

1m 13.32s (-0.35) **Going Correction** -0.15s/f (Firm)
WFA 3 from 4yo 6lb 16 Ran SP% 122.3
Speed ratings (Par 103):96,95,94,93,91 91,91,87,85,85 84,84,81,79,72 71
CSF £39.94 TOTE £3.20: £1.60, £3.00, £2.00; EX 58.50 Trifecta £122.10 Part won. Pool £172.09 - 0.20 winning units..
Owner Scuderia Rencati Srl **Bred** Azienda Agricola Francesca **Trained** Newmarket, Suffolk
■ Stewards' Enquiry : Jimmy Quinn three-day ban: careless riding (July 13,15-16)

FOCUS
A big field, but no strength in depth and the runner-up has an official mark of just 55.

3091 TOTEPOOL MIDSUMMER STKS (LISTED RACE) 1m 67y
2:35 (2:36) (Class 1) 3-Y-O+ **£15,898** (£6,025; £3,015; £1,503; £753) **Stalls** High

Form RPR

15/1 **1** **Librettist (USA)**[24] 2358 4-9-3 110 .... LDettori 1 113+
(Saeed Bin Suroor) *hld up in tch: qcknd to chal 3f out: led sn after: shkn up fnl f: sn in command: easily* **2/5**[1]

115- **2** *1 ¼* **Prince Of Light (IRE)**[274] 5591 3-8-13 106 .... JoeFanning 4 111
(M Johnston) *disp ld 1f: trckd ldrs: chsd wnr fr 2f out: styd on u.p but a wl hld fnl f* **6/1**[3]

16-0 **3** *3 ½* **Humungous (IRE)**[105] 665 3-8-8 102 .... DaneO'Neill 5 98
(C R Egerton) *t.k.h: disp ld tl slt advantage 5f out: narrowly hdd 3f out: wknd over 1f out* **25/1**

00-0 **4** *½* **Forward Move (IRE)**[8] 2803 4-9-3 108 .... RyanMoore 2 99
(R Hannon) *sn slt ld: hdd 5f out: styd chalng tl slt ld 3f out: sn hdd: wknd over 1f out* **9/2**[2]

1- **5** *1 ¾* **Akram (IRE)**[97] 3892 4-9-3 95 .... GeorgeBaker 3 95
(Jonjo O'Neill) *rr but in tch: rdn over 2f: nvr gng pce to rch ldrs: eased ins fnl f* **40/1**

1m 40.27s (-5.33) **Going Correction** -0.425s/f (Firm) course record
WFA 3 from 4yo 9lb 5 Ran SP% 110.2
Speed ratings (Par 111):109,107,104,103,102
CSF £3.39 TOTE £1.40: £1.10, £2.20; EX 2.00.
Owner Godolphin **Bred** Calumet Farm **Trained** Newmarket, Suffolk

FOCUS
Three of these wanted to make the pace and as a result they went a good gallop in the early stages, which set it up for Librettist, who was ridden patiently.

NOTEBOOK
Librettist(USA), who was best in at the weights, sat off the fast early gallop and had the race fall into his lap. He won easily and was value for further than the winning margin, and deserves to return to Group company now. (op 1-2)
Prince Of Light(IRE) had suffered foot problems in the spring which was the reason for this belated seasonal reappearance. His rider wisely gave up the fight for the early lead after a furlong which allowed him to throw down a determined challenge to Librettist in the straight, but unfortunately for him Dettori had plenty in hand on the favourite. Nevertheless, this was a decent seasonal return and improvement for the outing could well see him win in similar company. He did, however, apparently return very foot sore, which would be a concern. (op 7-2)
Humungous(IRE), having his first run since March, raced keenly and helped set a strong early pace. That cost him in the second half of the race. (op 20-1)
Forward Move(IRE), a disappointing sort who is not an easy ride, used up too much energy in the early stages trying to grab the lead, and he too paid for that effort in the straight. (op 11-2 tchd 6-1)
Akram(IRE) had a tough task at the weights and was having his first outing on the level for almost a year. He was always at the back of the field but did not run too badly. He likes this sort of ground. (op 33-1)

3092 TOTESPORT STKS (HERITAGE H'CAP) 6f
3:10 (3:10) (Class 2) (0-105,100) 3-Y-O+
£31,160 (£9,330; £4,665; £2,335; £1,165; £585) **Stalls** High

Form RPR

0000 **1** **One More Round (USA)**[35] 2012 8-8-11 92 .... (b) JamesDoyle(5) 1 102
(N P Littmoden) *hld up in rr: n.m.r over 2f out: qcknd over 1f out: styd on strly to ld wl ins last: drvn out* **25/1**

-006 **2** *hd* **The Kiddykid (IRE)**[26] 2303 6-9-5 100 .... StephenDonohoe(5) 9 110
(P D Evans) *chsd ldrs: rdn and slt ld 1f out: hdd and no ex wl ins last* **12/1**

0103 **3** *½* **King's Caprice**[14] 2649 5-9-0 90 .... (t) SamHitchcott 6 98
(J A Geake) *sn slt ld: rdn 2f out: hung lft over 1f out: sn hdd: styd chalng tl no ex wl ins last* **12/1**

6050 **4** *1 ¼* **Obe Gold**[7] 2847 4-9-10 100 .... ChrisCatlin 10 104
(M R Channon) *bhd: hdwy on outside 1/2-way: drvn to chse ldrs 1f out: sn one pce* **12/1**

002 **5** *shd* **First Order**[38] 1939 5-8-11 87 .... J-PGuillambert 8 91
(Ernst Oertel) *t.k.h: sn in tch: drvn to chal 1f out: outpcd ins last* **16/1**

4100 **6** *hd* **Swinbrook (USA)**[28] 2230 5-8-12 88 .... (v) JoeFanning 16 96+
(J A R Toller) *bhd: hdwy and nt clr run ins fnl 2f: styng on whn hmpd ins last: kpt on cl home but nt rcvr* **11/2**[2]

26-6 **7** *nk* **Tony The Tap**[13] 2683 5-8-11 87 .... FrancisFerris 7 89
(B Palling) *chsd ldrs: hrd rdn to chal over 1f out: outpcd ins last* **20/1**

0424 **8** *½* **Idle Power (IRE)**[28] 2230 8-9-0 90 .... LDettori 14 91+
(J R Boyle) *hld up mid-div: effrt whn nt clr run ins fnl 2f: kpt on fnl f but nvr in contention* **9/2**[1]

1230 **9** *nk* **Judd Street**[7] 2847 4-9-5 95 .... StephenCarson 2 95
(R F Johnson Houghton) *chsd ldrs: drvn to chal over 1f out: wknd last half f* **8/1**

-404 **10** *1 ½* **Mine Behind**[21] 2429 6-8-11 87 .... LPKeniry 12 83
(J R Best) *mid-div: rdn and effrt 2f out: nvr gng pce to chal and styd on same pce* **6/1**[3]

/60- **11** *1 ¾* **Cyclical**[266] 5745 4-9-0 90 .... ShaneKelly 11 80
(G A Butler) *bhd: rdn over 2f out: kpt on fnl f but nvr gng pce to rch ldrs* **16/1**

0100 **12** *nk* **The Jobber (IRE)**[15] 2624 5-8-10 86 .... JimmyQuinn 13 75
(M Blanshard) *chsd ldrs: rdn 3f out: wknd over 1f out* **33/1**

6030 **13** *¾* **If Paradise**[35] 2021 5-9-6 96 .... RyanMoore 15 83
(R Hannon) *chsd ldrs tl wknd over 1f out* **20/1**

-160 **14** *1 ¾* **Zowington**[28] 2227 4-9-3 93 .... GeorgeBaker 4 75
(C F Wall) *sn pressing ldrs: rdn and ev ch fr 2f out: wknd appr fnl f* **12/1**

05-0 **15** *1 ¾* **Emilio**[14] 2649 5-9-0 90 .... (t) FJohansson 5 67
(R A Kvisla) *chsd ldrs 4f* **66/1**

00-0 **16** *5* **Russian Symphony (USA)**[176] 54 5-8-10 86 .... (b) DaneO'Neill 3 48
(C R Egerton) *chsd ldrs over 3f* **16/1**

1m 11.35s (-2.32) **Going Correction** -0.15s/f (Firm) 16 Ran SP% 125.2
Speed ratings (Par 109):109,108,108,106,106 106,105,104,104,102 100,99,98,96,94 87
CSF £293.77 CT £3928.39 TOTE £32.80: £7.60, £3.60, £4.40, £3.10; EX 701.20 TRIFECTA Not won..
Owner Nigel Shields **Bred** Kenneth L Ramsey And Sarah K Ramsey **Trained** Newmarket, Suffolk
■ Stewards' Enquiry : Stephen Donohoe one-day ban: failed to keep straight from stalls (Jul 13)

FOCUS
A competitive handicap and a tight finish, but despite its value it lacked any unexposed or clearly progressive performers. The first two used to be better than this, but the exposed third holds the form down and it's not that strong for the grade.

NOTEBOOK
One More Round(USA) has always had the ability to win a race off this sort but he is a tricky ride who needs to be produced late, and all too often he finishes well but fails to get up. Everything fell into place this time and he won for the first time in almost four years, but he would hardly be one to back to repeat the trick next time.
The Kiddykid(IRE), who usually competes in Pattern grade, has seen his rating drop this year and was running in handicap company for the first time in three years. Only beaten narrowly, he ran well, especially as a bit of cut would have suited him better. (op 14-1)
King's Caprice, who normally races over further, showed plenty of speed to lead the field next to the stands' rail. He kept on well once headed, as befits a dual seven-furlong winner, and is clearly in good form.
Obe Gold, who did not run badly in the Wokingham on his return from almost three months off last time, built on that effort and stayed on well for fourth. He won handicaps in Dubai off three-figure marks earlier this year so it would be dangerous to assume he is held by the Handicapper.
First Order is on a mark he should be able to win off and he had every chance, but the rise in grade perhaps found him out. (op 14-1)
Swinbrook(USA) ◆ had the best of the draw but did not enjoy the smoothest of passages in the race itself. He would have gone close with a clear run and the Handicapper may not have his measure yet. Official explanation: jockey said gelding was denied a clear run (op 6-1)
Tony The Tap, who placed five times but failed to win last year, has seen his handicap mark remain stubbornly high as a result. Now with a new stable, he remains one to oppose for the time being.
Idle Power(IRE) could not find a way through a packed field and his effort is probably best ignored. Official explanation: jockey said gelding missed the break (tchd 5-1)
Cyclical ran a bit better than his finishing position suggests and is entitled to come on for this seasonal reappearance.
Russian Symphony(USA) Official explanation: jockey said gelding hung left

3093 TOTECOURSE TO COURSE H'CAP 1m 3f 135y
3:45 (3:45) (Class 2) (0-100,98) 3-Y-O+
£12,464 (£3,732; £1,866; £934; £466; £234) **Stalls** Low

Form RPR

0-54 **1** **Luberon**[71] 1117 3-8-6 89 .... JoeFanning 3 104+
(M Johnston) *sn led: narrowly hdd 7f out: styd chalng tl led again wl over 3f out: drvn clr appr fnl f: comf* **8/1**

0400 **2** *3* **Pevensey (IRE)**[23] 2387 4-8-11 81 oh1 .... ShaneKelly 9 89
(M A Buckley) *bhd: hdwy 3f out: rdn over 2f out: styd on u.p to chse wnr ins last but no ch* **11/1**

33-1 **3** *1 ¼* **Millville**[45] 1779 6-9-12 96 .... LDettori 5 102
(M A Jarvis) *chsd ldrs: rdn 3f out: chsd wnr 2f out: sn no imp: weakned and lost 2nd ins last* **7/2**[1]

1100 **4** *1 ¼* **Top Seed (IRE)**[28] 2229 5-9-2 86 .... SamHitchcott 10 90
(M R Channon) *rr: plld way to ld 7f out: narrowly hdd wl over 3f out: styd pressing wnr to 2f out: wknd appr fnl f* **6/1**

-231 **5** *1 ¼* **Blue Bajan (IRE)**[28] 2231 4-9-2 86 .... ChrisCatlin 6 88
(Andrew Turnell) *s.i.s: rr but in tch: hdwy 3f out: sn rdn: chsd ldrs 2f out: wknd over 1f out* **9/2**[2]

1164 **6** *2* **Ameeq (USA)**[28] 2229 4-8-11 81 .... RyanMoore 8 80
(G L Moore) *in tch: hdwy to chse ldrs 3f out: sn rdn: wknd 2f out* **7/2**[1]

7 *4* **Montevideo**[144] 5522 6-8-11 81 oh1 .... JimCrowley 7 73?
(Jonjo O'Neill) *stdd rr after 2f: rdn over 3f out and nvr in contention* **33/1**

0002 **8** *2 ½* **Thyolo (IRE)**[14] 2656 5-8-12 82 .... DaneO'Neill 1 70
(C G Cox) *in tch: hdwy to chse ldrs whn carried lft 3f out: sn wknd* **5/1**[3]

9 *1 ½* **Freddy (ARG)**[461] 7-9-1 85 .... (t) HayleyTurner 2 71
(Ernst Oertel) *chsd ldrs: rdn: hung lft and wknd 3f out* **25/1**

2m 24.92s (-5.18) **Going Correction** -0.425s/f (Firm)
WFA 3 from 4yo+ 13lb 9 Ran SP% 119.8
Speed ratings (Par 109):100,98,97,96,95 94,91,89,88
CSF £94.79 CT £368.84 TOTE £10.50: £2.30, £5.20, £2.30; EX 164.70 TRIFECTA Not won..
Owner Brian Yeardley Continental Ltd **Bred** Card Bloodstock **Trained** Middleham Moor, N Yorks

FOCUS
They did not go a great gallop here and the form is not all that strong. This was easily Luberon's best effort, but he benefited from racing prominently.

NOTEBOOK
Luberon, out of form earlier in the season, had been given a break since he last ran and came back stronger than ever. Up there throughout in a race not run at a mad gallop, he pulled nicely clear of the rest a furlong out and won easily. He got the longer trip well and can improve again. Official explanation: trainer's representative had no explanation for the improved form shown (op 17-2 tchd 11-1, 12-1 in places)
Pevensey(IRE) ran a better race than of late and was a shade unlucky to run into a well-handicapped three-year-old. (op 12-1)
Millville, who is arguably better on easier ground, ran a fair race, but he stays further than this and would have preferred a stronger-run race over this trip. (tchd 4-1)
Top Seed(IRE), at his best coming with a late run from off a decent pace, was not suited by the modest early gallop, pulled his way to the front and failed to run to his best. (op 11-2)
Blue Bajan(IRE) is a similar type to Top Seed and was another who would have preferred a sounder all-round gallop. (op 5-1 tchd 11-2 in places)
Ameeq(USA) remains on a 4lb higher mark than when last successful on the All-Weather, but he has still to win on turf in 11 starts on turf. (tchd 4-1)
Thyolo(IRE) was carried left on the turn into the straight and early in the straight by the hanging Freddy, but he did not look much of a threat at the time anyway. Official explanation: jockey said gelding suffered interference in running (tchd 11-2)
Freddy(ARG) was a triple Grade 1 winner in his native Argentina in 2002 but has been lightly raced and unsuccessful since. Having his first start in more than a year and making his debut in this country, he hung away his chance but was not going well in any case. Official explanation: jockey said horse hung left

3094 SARACEN-PROMOTIONS.CO.UK H'CAP 6f

4:15 (4:16) (Class 5) (0-70,70) 3-Y-O+ £3,238 (£963; £481; £240) Stalls High

Form RPR

2500 1 **Linda Green**[26] 2293 5-9-5 62 ChrisCatlin 15 73
(M R Channon) *hld up in rr: hdwy and swtchd lft 1f out: r.o strly to ld ins last* 7/1[2]

1100 2 1 1/4 **Caustic Wit (IRE)**[3] 2971 8-9-6 70 (p) TolleyDean(7) 9 77
(M S Saunders) *chsd ldrs: chal fr 2f out: stl ev ch ins last: kpt on but nt pce of wnr* 9/1

2300 3 nk **Musical Script (USA)**[16] 2583 3-8-9 58 JimmyQuinn 12 63
(Mrs A J Hamilton-Fairley) *chsd ldrs: rdn over 2f out: styd on same pce ins last* 25/1

300 4 hd **Kitchen Sink (IRE)**[40] 1899 4-8-8 51 oh4 (e) FergusSweeney 3 57
(P J Makin) *chsd ldrs: led 1f out: hdd ins last and sn one pce* 20/1

4013 5 1 1/4 **Bens Georgie (IRE)**[22] 2417 4-9-10 67 DaneO'Neill 2 69
(D K Ivory) *bhd: hdwy 2f out: chsd ldrs and bmpd jst ins last: one pce* 8/1[3]

2124 6 hd **Franksalot (IRE)**[22] 2390 6-9-8 68 PatrickMathers(3) 14 69
(I W McInnes) *in tch on rails: n.m.r over 2f out: styd on fnl f but nvr gng pce to rch ldrs* 4/1[1]

0000 7 1 **Sweetest Revenge (IRE)**[8] 2813 5-9-1 61 RichardSmith(3) 5 59
(M D I Usher) *bhd: hdwy on outside over 2f out: nvr gng pce to chal and kpt on same pce ins last* 25/1

-550 8 1 **Marker**[56] 1474 6-9-7 69 EmmettStack(5) 10 64+
(J A Geake) *bhd: nt clr run fr over 2f out: styd on fnl f but nvr in contention* 14/1

0253 9 nk **My Girl Pearl (IRE)**[1] 3033 6-8-8 51 oh2 StephenCarson 11 45
(M S Saunders) *led tl hdd 1f out: sn wknd* 12/1

5006 10 1 **Coranglais**[3] 2971 6-8-9 52 (p) JimCrowley 1 43
(J M Bradley) *sn chsng ldrs on outside: rdn 1/2-way: wknd appr fnl f* 9/1

4521 11 shd **Russian Rocket (IRE)**[15] 2611 4-9-7 64 HayleyTurner 7 55
(Mrs C A Dunnett) *chsd ldrs: rdn 3f out: wknd over 1f out* 7/1[2]

2-00 12 1/2 **Cativo Cavallino**[14] 2652 3-9-3 66 LPKeniry 13 54
(Jamie Poulton) *chsd ldrs 4f* 33/1

0401 13 1/2 **Full Spate**[15] 2599 11-9-8 65 RyanMoore 6 53
(J M Bradley) *bhd and outpcd most of way* 8/1[3]

6033 14 3 1/2 **Gone'N'Dunnett (IRE)**[9] 2784 7-9-5 62 (v) J-PGuillambert 8 39
(Mrs C A Dunnett) *chsd ldrs 4f* 10/1

0-00 15 4 **Gavioli (IRE)**[49] 1689 4-8-9 52 (p) ShaneKelly 4 17
(J M Bradley) *chsd ldrs: wkng whn hmpd ins fnl 2f* 40/1

1m 12.17s (-1.50) **Going Correction** -0.15s/f (Firm)
WFA 3 from 4yo+ 6lb 15 Ran SP% **128.5**
Speed ratings (Par 103):104,102,101,101,100 99,98,97,96,95 95,94,93,89,83
CSF £68.64 CT £1569.06 TOTE £8.30: £3.20, £4.80, £8.90; EX 82.90 TRIFECTA Not won..
Owner Stephen Roots **Bred** Colin Tinkler **Trained** West Ilsley, Berks
■ Stewards' Enquiry : Chris Catlin two-day ban: careless riding (Jul 13,15)

FOCUS
An ordinary sprint handicap contested by mainly exposed performers. The form should prove reliable.
Russian Rocket(IRE) Official explanation: jockey said gelding was denied a clear run

3095 SIMON HUNT LAST WEEKEND OF FREEDOM FILLIES' H'CAP 1m 2f 7y

4:45 (4:46) (Class 5) (0-75,75) 3-Y-O+ £3,886 (£1,156; £577; £288) Stalls High

Form RPR

0600 1 **Della Salute**[19] 2510 4-10-0 72 SamHitchcott 2 81
(Miss E C Lavelle) *hld up in rr: hdwy 2f out: chsd ldr ins fnl 2f: hrd drvn to ld lst half f: hld on wl* 9/1

21-4 2 nk **Whatizzit**[21] 2446 3-9-6 75 LDettori 8 83
(E A L Dunlop) *sn led: rdn over 2f out: hdd last half f: kpt on u.p but no ex cl home* 11/4[1]

316- 3 1 1/2 **Bracklinn**[264] 5808 4-9-8 66 DaneO'Neill 4 72
(J R Fanshawe) *chsd ldrs: rdn to go 2nd 3f out: nvr gng pce to chal and styd on same pce fr over 1f out* 4/1[2]

0030 4 nk **Depressed**[14] 2637 4-9-1 64 (p) JamesDoyle(5) 9 69
(Ernst Oertel) *hld up in rr: hdwy 3f out: chsd ldrs over 2f out: kpt on same pce fr over 1f out* 12/1

-000 5 1 1/2 **Phoebe Woodstock (IRE)**[18] 2534 4-9-12 70 (p) ShaneKelly 5 72+
(W R Swinburn) *chsd ldrs tl rdn and lost pl 3f out: hmpd over 2f out: drvn and styd on again fnl f: nvr a danger* 8/1

5051 6 1 **Tata Naka**[24] 2360 6-8-13 57 HayleyTurner 6 57
(Mrs C A Dunnett) *chsd ldrs: rdn 3f out: wknd appr fnl f* 8/1

2500 7 1 1/2 **At The Helm (IRE)**[22] 2414 4-8-9 53 oh3 ChrisCatlin 3 50
(W J Knight) *rr but in tch: keen early: rdn and effrt 3f out: nvr gng pce to rch ldrs: wknd appr fnl f* 25/1

5044 8 2 1/2 **Blue Line**[16] 2574 4-8-10 54 LPKeniry 7 47
(M Madgwick) *in tch: rdn 4f out: nvr in contention after* 13/2[3]

045 9 10 **Double Bay (USA)**[16] 2580 3-9-1 70 RyanMoore 1 44+
(Jane Chapple-Hyam) *chsd ldr: rdn 4f out: wknd 3f out: bhd whn hmpd over 2f out: eased whn no ch fnl f* 7/1

2m 5.10s (-3.20) **Going Correction** -0.425s/f (Firm)
WFA 3 from 4yo+ 11lb 9 Ran SP% **116.3**
Speed ratings (Par 100):95,94,93,93,92 91,90,88,80
CSF £34.26 CT £117.28 TOTE £13.50: £4.00, £1.20, £2.50; EX 39.30 Trifecta £54.10 Pool: £152.60 - 2.00 winning tickets. Place 6 £208.86, Place 5 £109.16.
Owner Webster Partnership **Bred** Blackdown Stud **Trained** Wildhern, Hants

FOCUS
Ordinary form but it should be reliable.
Double Bay(USA) Official explanation: jockey said filly hung right
T/Plt: £254.60 to a £1 stake. Pool: £48,567.20. 139.25 winning tickets. T/Qpdt: £116.00 to a £1 stake. Pool: £2,509.70. 16.00 winning tickets. ST

3050 WOLVERHAMPTON (A.W) (L-H)

Saturday, July 1

OFFICIAL GOING: Standard
Wind: Nil Weather: Warm

3096 EUROPEAN BREEDERS FUND MAIDEN FILLIES' STKS 5f 216y(P)

6:45 (6:48) (Class 5) 2-Y-O £3,886 (£1,156; £577; £288) Stalls Low

Form RPR

62 1 **Market Day**[10] 2755 2-9-0 NickyMackay 3 83+
(L M Cumani) *a gng wl: rdn to ld 1f out: pushed out* 4/5[1]

2 1 **Queen Noverre (IRE)** 2-9-0 RichardMullen 2 77+
(E J O'Neill) *w ldr: led over 2f out: sn rdn: hdd 1f out: nt qckn* 5/1[2]

5364 3 9 **Ishibee (IRE)**[8] 2827 2-9-0 JoeFanning 8 50
(Mrs A Duffield) *w ldrs: ev ch over 2f out: sn rdn: wknd over 1f out* 7/1[3]

4 4 **Newport Lass (IRE)** 2-9-0 NCallan 5 38
(K R Burke) *s.i.s: hdwy on ins over 2f out: sn wknd* 10/1

0 5 3 1/2 **Musical Affair**[15] 2610 2-9-0 BrianReilly 1 28
(F Jordan) *sn led: rdn and hdd over 2f out: wknd wl over 1f out* 25/1

02 6 2 **Tenterhooks (IRE)**[2] 3010 2-9-0 VinceSlattery 6 22
(J A Osborne) *sn bhd: short-lived effrt on outside over 2f out* 9/1

7 2 **Wachiwi (IRE)** 2-9-0 FrankieMcDonald 4 16
(A P Jarvis) *led early: chsd ldrs tl rdn and wknd over 2f out* 20/1

00 8 14 **Vanatina (IRE)**[8] 2807 2-9-0 RobbieFitzpatrick 7 —
(A Bailey) *s.s: outpcd* 25/1

1m 15.02s (-0.79) **Going Correction** -0.05s/f (Stan) 8 Ran SP% **116.3**
Speed ratings (Par 91):103,101,89,84,79 77,74,55
CSF £5.01 TOTE £1.60: £1.02, £1.10, £4.50; EX 6.70.
Owner Allevamento Gialloblu **Bred** Biddestone Stud **Trained** Newmarket, Suffolk

FOCUS
Decent form from the front two, who finished nine lengths clear.

NOTEBOOK
Market Day, pipped on the post over seven at Kempton last time, was always travelling like an odds-on shot. She was nicely on top of the only remaining danger at the end. (op 8-13)
Queen Noverre(IRE) ◆ probably came up against an above-average sort for this type of contest on her debut. Finishing well clear of the others, normal improvement should see her go one better. (op 9-2)
Ishibee(IRE) did not find the extra furlong combined with a switch to sand the answer. (tchd 5-1)
Newport Lass(IRE), half-sister to a couple of winners, came in for a little support in the market but did not show a great deal on her debut. (op 14-1)
Wachiwi(IRE) Official explanation: jockey said filly was slowly away and never travelling
Vanatina(IRE) Official explanation: jockey said filly lost its action

3097 SPONSOR A RACE BY CALLING 0870 220 2442 H'CAP 5f 216y(P)

7:15 (7:16) (Class 4) (0-85,79) 3-Y-O+ £6,477 (£1,927; £963; £481) Stalls Low

Form RPR

0206 1 **Harry Up**[18] 2521 5-9-13 78 NCallan 8 90
(K A Ryan) *mde all: rdn wl over 1f out: rdn out* 5/1[3]

0122 2 1/2 **Geojimali**[19] 2504 4-9-2 67 FergalLynch 3 78
(J S Goldie) *a.p: rdn over 2f out: chsd wnr and edgd lft over 1f out: r.o ins fnl f* 9/4[1]

12-0 3 1 1/4 **Portmeirion**[59] 1413 5-8-12 63 J-PGuillambert 1 70
(S C Williams) *hld up in tch: rdn over 1f out: kpt on ins fnl f* 9/2[2]

6236 4 1 1/2 **Gilded Cove**[22] 2417 6-8-9 67 RussellKennemore(7) 4 70
(R Hollinshead) *broke wl: sn stdd: rdn over 2f out: hdwy wl over 1f out: nvr able to chal* 5/1[3]

0450 5 3 **Bessemer (JPN)**[13] 2681 5-9-13 78 (v[1]) JoeFanning 6 72
(D Carroll) *sn chsng wnr: rdn over 2f out: lost 2nd over 1f out: wknd fnl f* 11/1

5006 6 8 **Melalchrist**[29] 2194 4-9-7 72 (p) FrancisNorton 2 42
(J J Quinn) *s.s: nvr nr ldrs* 8/1

5040 7 7 **Stoneacre Boy (IRE)**[10] 2756 3-9-8 79 (b) RobbieFitzpatrick 7 28
(Peter Grayson) *hld up in tch: hung rt and lost pl over 3f out: sn bhd* 16/1

5004 8 dist **True Magic**[14] 2637 5-9-2 67 TedDurcan 5 —
(J D Bethell) *rdr failed to remove blindfold: v.s.a: completed crse in own time* 18/1

1m 14.65s (-1.16) **Going Correction** -0.05s/f (Stan)
WFA 3 from 4yo+ 6lb 8 Ran SP% **112.9**
Speed ratings (Par 105):105,104,102,100,96 86,76,—
CSF £16.22 CT £53.32 TOTE £6.70: £2.90, £1.10, £2.20; EX 25.10.
Owner The Fishermen **Bred** J E Rose **Trained** Hambleton, N Yorks

FOCUS
An ordinary handicap, but sound form for the grade.
Stoneacre Boy(IRE) Official explanation: jockey said gelding hung right and lost its action
True Magic Official explanation: jockey said mare ducked her head down as stalls opened making it impossible for him to reach the blindfold until the other horses were half a furlong down the track

3098 REMEMBER FAMILY FUN DAYS AT WOLVERHAMPTON STAYERS' H'CAP 1m 5f 194y(P)

7:45 (7:45) (Class 4) (0-85,85) 4-Y-O+ £6,477 (£1,927; £963; £481) Stalls Low

Form RPR

2012 1 **Taxman (IRE)**[21] 2460 4-8-7 71 (p) TedDurcan 3 77
(C E Brittain) *a.p: rdn over 2f out: sustained chal fnl f: led last stride* 6/1[3]

-120 2 shd **Caraman (IRE)**[15] 2628 8-8-5 69 FrancisNorton 9 75
(J J Quinn) *chsd ldr: disp ld 8f out tl def advantage over 4f out: rdn wl over 1f out: hdd last stride* 16/1

06-2 3 shd **Gandalf**[70] 1132 4-9-0 78 RichardHughes 1 84+
(J R Fanshawe) *hld up and bhd: swtchd rt over 3f out: rdn and hdwy over 2f out: ev ch ins fnl f: r.o* 13/8[1]

0014 4 3 1/2 **Dark Parade (ARG)**[13] 2684 5-7-13 70 oh1 ow4 JamieJones(7) 8 71
(G L Moore) *hld up in rr: rdn and hdwy over 2f out: wknd ins fnl f* 5/1[2]

0602 5 3 **Hiddensee (USA)**[7] 2879 4-9-5 83 (v[1]) JoeFanning 4 80
(M Johnston) *set stdy pce: hdd over 4f out: rdn over 2f out: wknd ins fnl f* 7/1

6612 6 2 1/2 **Wise Owl**[96] 765 4-9-7 85 JimmyQuinn 5 78
(J Pearce) *hld up and bhd: rdn over 2f out: nvr trbld ldrs* 5/1[2]

2155 7 5 **Shaunas Vision (IRE)**[39] 1927 7-9-1 79 NCallan 2 65
(D K Ivory) *hld up in tch: rdn 3f out: wknd wl over 1f out* 20/1

2160 8 6 **Desperation (IRE)**[18] 2522 4-8-10 74 (b[1]) J-PGuillambert 6 52
(B D Leavy) *hld up: sn in tch: rdn 4f out: wknd 3f out* 25/1

125- 9 31 **Fisby**[16] 6029 5-8-3 72 EmmettStack(5) 7 6
(K J Burke) *hld up in tch: lost pl over 4f out: nt clr run 3f out: sn bhd: t.o* 25/1

3m 5.32s (-3.05) **Going Correction** -0.05s/f (Stan) 9 Ran SP% **116.6**
Speed ratings (Par 105):103,102,102,100,99 97,94,91,73
CSF £91.50 CT £223.83 TOTE £7.00: £2.50, £4.00, £1.10; EX 110.40.
Owner C E Brittain **Bred** Darley **Trained** Newmarket, Suffolk
■ Stewards' Enquiry : Richard Hughes caution (reduced from one-day ban on appeal): careless riding

FOCUS
An exciting finish to an ordinary staying handicap run at a steady pace. The form is not strong.

3099 GRAHAM BONEHILL 60TH BIRTHDAY CELEBRATION FILLIES' H'CAP 7f 32y(P)
8:15 (8:16) (Class 5) (0-70,69) 3-Y-O+ £3,886 (£1,156; £577; £288) Stalls High

Form RPR
3106 1 **Katie Lawson (IRE)**[31] 2142 3-8-11 58........................(v) FrancisNorton 8 67
(D Haydn Jones) *hld up and bhd: rdn 4f out: hdwy over 1f out: r.o wl to ld nr fin* **33/1**
5024 2 ½ **Panic Stations**[14] 2648 3-8-3 57........................ LukeMorris(7) 7 64
(M L W Bell) *chsd ldrs: rdn over 2f out: squeezed through and hit repeatedly by rival jockey's whip over 1f out: led jst ins fnl f: hdd* **12/1**
-420 3 ½ **Foreplay (IRE)**[17] 2554 3-9-8 69........................ RichardMullen 11 75
(E A L Dunlop) *hld up in mid-div: rdn and hdwy 3f out: ev ch ins fnl f: nt qckn* **12/1**
4066 4 ½ **Spark Up**[9] 2794 6-8-9 53........................(b) StephenDonohoe(5) 12 60
(J W Unett) *swtchd lft sn after s: hld up in rr: hdwy on ins wl over 1f out: sn rdn: swtchd rt ins fnl f: nrst fin* **9/1**
1411 5 1 ¼ **Inaminute (IRE)**[12] 2699 3-9-3 69........................ AndrewElliott(5) 10 70
(K R Burke) *sn prom: swtchd lft wl over 1f out: kpt on ins fnl f* **4/1**[2]
0310 6 1 **Tamora**[47] 1727 4-8-11 50........................(v) FrankieMcDonald 2 51
(A P Jarvis) *led: rdn and hdd 2f out: no ex towards fin* **11/1**
41-0 7 1 **Sweet Emily**[26] 2293 4-10-0 67........................ RichardHughes 3 74+
(J R Fanshawe) *prom: lost pl over 3f out: rallying on ins whn hmpd over 1f out: nt rcvr* **7/2**[1]
5530 8 nk **Tabulate**[3] 2987 3-8-3 55........................ RichardKingscote(5) 1 53+
(P L Gilligan) *w ldr: led 2f out: hrd rdn over 1f out: hdd jst ins fnl f: eased whn btn towards fin* **4/1**[2]
0000 9 5 **Lady Duxyana**[18] 2535 3-8-1 48........................ DavidKinsella 4 30
(M D I Usher) *s.i.s: a bhd* **33/1**
0001 10 nk **Moon Bird**[16] 2574 4-9-8 61........................ TedDurcan 9 45
(C A Cyzer) *a bhd* **8/1**[3]
0-0P 11 shd **Shibumi**[3] 2978 5-8-9 48 oh3........................ SamHitchcott 5 32
(P A Trueman) *a towards rr* **100/1**
226- 12 1 ¼ **Sincerely**[234] 6298 4-9-2 60........................ AurelioMedeiros(5) 6 40+
(B W Hills) *hmpd and rdr lost irons sn after s: sn prom: 3rd whn nrly uns rdr bnd after 1f: lost pl over 2f out* **25/1**

1m 29.44s (-0.96) **Going Correction** -0.05s/f (Stan)
WFA 3 from 4yo+ 8lb 12 Ran SP% **117.8**
Speed ratings (Par 100):103,102,101,101,99 98,97,97,91,91 91,89
CSF £376.97 CT £4970.68 TOTE £58.40: £6.70, £2.90, £2.60; EX 532.10.
Owner Monolithic Refractories Ltd **Bred** J Kilpatrick **Trained** Efail Isaf, Rhondda C Taff

FOCUS
This competitive handicap for the grade appeared to be run at a decent pace. The first three all showed improved form, with the fourth a fair guide.
Sincerely Official explanation: jockey said he lost his irons shortly after the start

3100 WOLVERHAMPTON RACECOURSE CONFERENCE CENTRE MAIDEN STKS 1m 1f 103y(P)
8:45 (8:46) (Class 4) 3-Y-O+ £6,477 (£1,927; £963; £481) Stalls Low

Form RPR
2 1 **Armada**[61] 1336 3-9-3........................ J-PGuillambert 12 77+
(Sir Michael Stoute) *hld up in mid-div: rdn over 3f out: hdwy over 2f out: led ins fnl f: r.o* **10/11**[1]
5 2 1 **Beldon Hill (USA)**[24] 2366 3-8-12........................ TedDurcan 8 70
(C E Brittain) *chsd ldr: led over 3f out: rdn over 1f out: hdd and nt qckn ins fnl f* **13/2**[2]
0202 3 3 **Digger Boy**[28] 2244 3-9-3 68........................ MatthewHenry 4 69
(M A Jarvis) *hld up towards rr: stdy hdwy over 4f out: rdn whn swtchd rt over 2f out: forced wd ent st: edgd lft 1f out: styd on* **12/1**
00 4 1 **Samarinda (USA)**[12] 2712 3-9-3........................ NCallan 3 67
(E A L Dunlop) *prom: rdn over 2f out: swtchd lft wl over 1f out: sn wknd* **22/1**
45 5 ½ **Gobi King**[22] 2411 4-9-13........................ NickyMackay 11 66+
(L M Cumani) *hld up towards rr: hdwy 2f out: nvr trbld ldrs* **12/1**
6 2 **Aphorism** 3-8-12........................ JoeFanning 2 57
(J R Fanshawe) *hld up towards rr: hdwy over 4f out: rn sltly wd ent st: sn hung lft and wknd* **14/1**
7 6 **Cankara (IRE)** 3-8-5........................ KellyHarrison(7) 10 45
(D Carroll) *s.s: nvr nr ldrs* **50/1**
00-6 8 ¾ **Sunny Parkes**[29] 2210 3-8-12 52........................ JimmyQuinn 1 44
(M Mullineaux) *hld up in mid-div: rdn 4f out: sn lost pl* **50/1**
6- 9 2 ½ **Satisfaction (IRE)**[383] 2543 3-9-3........................ RichardMullen 9 44
(E J O'Neill) *prom: rdn over 3f out: wknd over 2f out* **20/1**
34 10 2 **River City (IRE)**[13] 2220 9-9-13........................ VinceSlattery 5 40
(Noel T Chance) *a bhd* **17/2**[3]
60 11 ½ **Raffiene (IRE)**[24] 2350 3-8-12........................ RobbieFitzpatrick 7 34
(E J O'Neill) *led: rdn and hdd over 3f out: wknd over 2f out* **50/1**
12 5 **The Combo** 3-9-3........................ FrancisNorton 6 29
(M Blanshard) *s.i.s: a bhd* **33/1**

2m 1.51s (-1.11) **Going Correction** -0.05s/f (Stan)
WFA 3 from 4yo+ 10lb 12 Ran SP% **116.2**
Speed ratings (Par 105):102,101,98,97,97 95,90,89,87,85 84,80
CSF £5.87 TOTE £2.10: £1.10, £2.90, £1.10; EX 6.10.
Owner Highclere Thoroughbred Racing XXVIII **Bred** Itchen Valley Stud **Trained** Newmarket, Suffolk

FOCUS
They went no pace in what did not appear to be a great maiden. The form looks quite sound and there should be better to come from the winner.

3101 THE RED DEVILS DISPLAY AT WOLVERHAMPTON 17TH JULY H'CAP 1m 141y(P)
9:15 (9:16) (Class 4) (0-80,80) 3-Y-O+ £6,477 (£1,927; £963; £481) Stalls Low

Form RPR
1341 1 **Bijou Dan**[9] 2794 5-8-10 67........................(b) DuranFentiman(5) 4 76
(W G Harrison) *t.k.h in tch: rdn over 1f out: led ins fnl f: r.o* **7/1**[3]
6464 2 ¾ **Luck In Running (USA)**[10] 2750 3-8-7 69........................ JoeFanning 1 76
(M Johnston) *a.p: rdn over 1f out: ev ch ins fnl f: nt qckn* **12/1**
2234 3 nk **Fasylitator (IRE)**[12] 2708 4-9-11 77........................ NCallan 12 84+
(D K Ivory) *hld up and bhd: rdn 2f out: hdwy 1f out: r.o* **11/2**[2]
4110 4 hd **Full Victory (IRE)**[8] 2819 4-9-9 75........................ SamHitchcott 10 82
(R A Farrant) *hld up in mid-div: rdn and hdwy over 1f out: hung lft and struck on hd by rival jockey's whip jst ins fnl f: kpt on* **14/1**
6054 5 1 **Pure Imagination (IRE)**[15] 2603 5-9-2 73........................ StephenDonohoe(5) 5 77
(J M Bradley) *hld up in mid-div: rdn 3f out: hdwy wl over 1f out: ev ch ins fnl f: no ex towards fin* **16/1**
1342 6 ¾ **Stellite**[8] 2810 6-9-4 70........................ TedDurcan 8 73+
(J S Goldie) *hld up and bhd: rdn and hdwy 1f out: nt rch ldrs* **4/1**[1]
2043 7 hd **Treasure House (IRE)**[9] 2794 5-9-2 68........................ FrancisNorton 11 70
(M Blanshard) *hld up and bhd: rdn over 2f out: c wd st: nvr nrr* **7/1**[3]
0033 8 shd **Barathea Dreams (IRE)**[9] 2787 5-9-6 72........................ JimmyQuinn 7 74
(J S Moore) *prom: led over 6f out: hrd rdn over 1f out: hdd ins fnl f: fdd* **11/2**[2]
0540 9 1 ½ **Glad Big (GER)**[24] 2341 4-10-0 80........................ VinceSlattery 9 79
(J A Osborne) *hld up in tch: rdn 2f out: wknd over 1f out* **11/1**
3-00 10 1 ¾ **Solicitude**[16] 2583 3-8-5 67........................ FrankieMcDonald 2 61
(D Haydn Jones) *led: hdd over 6f out: prom tl rdn and wknd 1f out* **33/1**
62-0 11 1 ¼ **Nor'Wester**[17] 2555 4-9-9 75........................ RichardHughes 6 68
(J R Fanshawe) *hld up and bhd: rdn 3f out: no rspnse* **14/1**
01-0 12 2 ½ **Highest Regard**[17] 2555 4-9-12 78........................ BrianReilly 3 66
(P L Gilligan) *hld up in mid-div: rdn whn sltly hmpd on ins over 1f out: sn bhd* **16/1**

1m 50.28s (-1.48) **Going Correction** -0.05s/f (Stan)
WFA 3 from 4yo+ 10lb 12 Ran SP% **119.8**
Speed ratings (Par 105):104,103,103,102,102 101,101,101,99,98 97,94
CSF £89.23 CT £509.82 TOTE £12.40: £3.90, £3.10, £2.50; EX 137.60 Place 6 £101.87, Place 5 £88.36 .
Owner Bert Markey **Bred** James Thom And Sons **Trained** Lesmahagow, S Lanarks

FOCUS
The pace was only modest in this competitive handicap and the form does not look too sound.
T/Plt: £48.60 to a £1 stake. Pool: £28,074.45. 421.15 winning tickets. T/Qpdt: £24.50 to a £1 stake. Pool: £2,821.30. 85.20 winning tickets. KH

3102 - 3104a (Foreign Racing) - See Raceform Interactive

3057 CURRAGH (R-H)
Saturday, July 1

OFFICIAL GOING: Good

3105a AUDI PRETTY POLLY STKS (GROUP 1) (F&M) 1m 2f
3:40 (3:44) 3-Y-O+
£103,448 (£32,758; £15,517; £5,172; £3,448; £1,724)

RPR
1 **Alexander Goldrun (IRE)**[34] 2053 5-9-8 116........................ KJManning 1 118
(J S Bolger, Ire) *settled 4th: 3rd early st: chal 2f out: led over 1f out: strly pressed cl home: all out* **11/8**[1]
2 nk **Chelsea Rose (IRE)**[24] 2371 4-9-8 110........................ PShanahan 4 117
(C Collins, Ire) *cl 2nd: rdn to ld under 2f out: hdd over 1f out: rallied u.p: jst failed* **6/1**
3 2 **Red Bloom**[44] 1804 5-9-8........................ JMurtagh 2 113
(Sir Michael Stoute) *led: rdn and hdd under 2f out: kpt on same pce* **7/2**[2]
4 shd **Tropical Lady (IRE)**[61] 1365 6-9-8 109........................ DJMoran 3 113
(J S Bolger, Ire) *hld up towards rr: 5th and prog 1/2-way: 4th early st: kpt on fr over 1f out* **16/1**
5 6 **Queen Cleopatra (IRE)**[20] 2491 3-8-11 110........................ KFallon 5 102
(A P O'Brien, Ire) *5th early: 6th 1/2-way: rdn ent st: no imp fr 2f out* **11/2**[3]
6 3 ½ **Ardbrae Lady**[34] 2054 3-8-11 105........................ FMBerry 7 96
(Joseph G Murphy, Ire) *slowly away and hld up in rr: no imp st* **20/1**
7 9 **Perfect Hedge**[13] 2689 4-9-8 105........................ MJKinane 6 80
(John M Oxx, Ire) *trckd ldrs in 3rd: 5th early st: sn no ex* **50/1**

2m 4.80s **Going Correction** -0.10s/f (Good)
WFA 3 from 4yo+ 11lb 7 Ran SP% **106.6**
Speed ratings: 114,113,112,112,107 104,97
CSF £8.58 TOTE £2.10: £1.30, £3.20; DF 12.80.
Owner Mrs N O'Callaghan **Bred** Dermot Cantillon **Trained** Coolcullen, Co Carlow

FOCUS
A truly run contest and a second consecutive victory in this race for Alexander Goldrun. Solid form, the winner not far off her best.

NOTEBOOK
Alexander Goldrun(IRE) was always in a good position and quickened up well to confirm last year's running with Red Bloom, but had to dig deep to repel the rallying runner-up. She is now likely to try and repeat last year's victory in the Nassau. (op 5/4)
Chelsea Rose(IRE), always close to the pace, picked off Red Bloom with a quarter of a mile left to run and, with her stamina not in doubt, battled back in game style after the favourite had gone past her. She has not won at Group level since taking the 2004 Moyglare Stud Stakes, but there are plenty more opportunities to put that right. (op 4/1)
Red Bloom was given a very positive ride in a bid to reverse last year's form in this race with Alexander Goldrun, but she failed to get home. (op 7/2 tchd 4/1)
Tropical Lady(IRE) ran a good deal better than on her reappearance and she showed her best form of last year at around this time.
Queen Cleopatra(IRE) reversed Irish 1,000 Guineas form with Ardbrae Lady, but that is all she achieved against her elders and this does not bode well for the Classic generation on the distaff side. (op 6/1 tchd 7/1)
Ardbrae Lady Official explanation: trainer said filly was found to be in season post race

3107a AT THE RACES CURRAGH CUP (GROUP 3) 1m 6f
4:45 (4:45) 3-Y-O+
£31,034 (£9,827; £4,655; £1,551; £1,034; £517)

RPR
1 **Kastoria (IRE)**[43] 1833 5-9-8 108........................(t) MJKinane 3 112
(John M Oxx, Ire) *hld up in rr: pushed along 5f out: hdwy on outer early st: cl 3rd and chal over 1f out: led ins fnl f: styd on wl* **9/4**[1]
2 hd **Collier Hill**[7] 2845 8-10-0........................ DeanMcKeown 2 118
(G A Swinbank) *trckd ldrs in 4th: 5th into st: hdwy 2f out: 2nd and chal over 1f out: ever ch: jst failed* **5/2**[2]
3 1 ½ **Mkuzi**[31] 2154 7-9-11 107........................ FMBerry 7 113
(John M Oxx, Ire) *trckd ldr in 2nd: led over 2f out: rdn and strly pressed over 1f out: hdd ins fnl f: no ex cl home* **5/1**[3]
4 3 ½ **Akarem**[9] 2773 5-9-11........................ PatCosgrave 5 108
(K R Burke) *settled 3rd: 4th and drvn along ent st: kpt on same pce fr 2f out* **12/1**
5 4 **Good Surprise**[31] 2154 5-9-11 106........................(b) KJManning 1 102
(J S Bolger, Ire) *hld up towards rr: hdwy over 4f out: 3rd into st: sn no ex* **13/2**
6 1 **Virginia Woolf**[6] 2909 4-9-8 98........................ CatherineGannon 4 85
(John M Oxx, Ire) *sn drvn into ld: clr bef 1/2-way: strly pressed ent st: hdd & wknd over 2f out* **16/1**
7 10 **Mutakarrim**[34] 2056 9-9-11 106........................ PJSmullen 6 —
(D K Weld, Ire) *chsd ldrs in 5th: dropped to rr and rdn appr st: sn no ex* **10/1**

2m 58.64s **Going Correction** -0.10s/f (Good) 7 Ran SP% **112.0**
Speed ratings: 112,111,111,109,106 101,101
CSF £7.75 TOTE £2.70: £1.50, £2.30; DF 5.40.

Owner H H Aga Khan **Bred** H H Aga Khan's Stud's S C **Trained** Currabeg, Co Kildare

FOCUS

A decent pace for this staying event thanks to Kastoria's pacemaker Virginia Woolf. The principals were generally very close to form.

NOTEBOOK

Kastoria(IRE) appreciated the strong pace set by her stablemate and showed real grit to get the better of the runner-up in a dour battle to the line. This sounder surface probably suited her better than the soft ground she encountered at York and her consistency should enable her to find other opportunities in Pattern company. The Park Hill, in which she was narrowly beaten last year, would seem the ideal target once again. (op 5/2)

Collier Hill, back at the scene of his famous victory in last year's Irish St Leger, did little wrong but could not quite contain the mare under his penalty. He should be cherry-ripe now. (op 9/4)

Mkuzi, bidding for a hat-trick in this contest, did little wrong and kept on battling but the impression was that this was a stronger renewal than those he has been successful in. (op 9/2)

Akarem finished about the same distance behind Mkuzi as he did in this race last year when trained by Kevin Prendergast, which backs up the impression that this was a stronger heat. He looks better over shorter in any case. (op 8/1)

Good Surprise is yet to win beyond 12 furlongs and failed to confirm earlier Leopardstown form with Mkuzi. (op 7/1)

3106 - 3108a (Foreign Racing) - See Raceform Interactive

1721 HOLLYWOOD PARK (L-H)

Saturday, July 1

OFFICIAL GOING: Turf course - firm; dirt course - fast

3109a CASHCALL MILE (GRADE 3) (F&M) (TURF) 1m (T)

10:43 (10:46) 3-Y-0+

£232,558 (£87,209; £52,326; £31,977; £20,349; £11,628)

RPR

1 **Dance In The Mood (JPN)**[27] 5-8-11 ..... VEspinoza 8 118
(Kazuo Fujisawa, Japan) **26/10**[1]

2 1 ¾ **Sweet Talker (USA)**[33] 4-8-11 ..... RADominguez 5 114
(H G Motion, U.S.A) **34/10**[2]

3 ½ **Luas Line (IRE)**[10] 2740 4-8-11 ..... AGryder 7 113
(David Wachman, Ire) *always in touch, came wide entering straight, ran on final f to take 3rd last strides* **132/10**

4 nk **Dancing Edie (USA)**[33] 4-8-7 ..... PValenzuela 4 108
(Craig Dollase, U.S.A) **14/1**

5 hd **Cambiocorsa (USA)**[76] 4-8-7 ..... JKCourt 1 108
(Doug O'Neill, U.S.A) **47/10**[3]

6 nk **Shining Energy (USA)**[33] 4-8-11 .....(b) CNakatani 3 111
(J Canani, U.S.A) **26/10**[1]

7 3 **Toupie**[131] 4-8-7 ..... TBaze 2 100
(C B Greely, U.S.A) **142/10**

8 14 **Flying Glitter (USA)**[252] 4-8-7 ..... ASolis 6 68
(R Werner, U.S.A) **303/10**

1m 33.33s **8** Ran SP% **119.3**

PARI-MUTUEL (including $2 stakes): WIN 7.20; PL (1-2) 4.40, 5.00; SHOW (1-2-3) 3.40, 3.80, 7.00 DF 19.00; SF 32.80.

Owner Shadai Race Horse Co Ltd **Bred** Shadai Farm **Trained** Japan

2897 WARWICK (L-H)

Sunday, July 2

OFFICIAL GOING: Firm (good to firm in places)

Wind: Nil

3110 WARWICK SCHOOL MEDIAN AUCTION MAIDEN STKS 5f

2:20 (2:20) (Class 5) 2-Y-0 **£3,238** (£963; £481; £240) **Stalls** Low

Form RPR

0 1 **Compton Fields**[45] 1796 2-8-12 ..... RichardKingscote[(5)] 4 75+
(R Charlton) *s.i.s: hld up: hdwy over 1f out: r.o to ld wl ins fnl f* **2/1**[2]

2 2 ½ **Impromptu**[26] 2315 2-9-3 ..... SebSanders 2 73
(R M Beckett) *w ldrs: hmpd 2f out: lft in ld over 1f out: rdn and hdd wl ins fnl f* **4/6**[1]

06 3 2 ½ **Danger Alley**[16] 2610 2-9-3 .....(b[1]) RichardMullen 1 63
(E J O'Neill) *w ldrs: rdn and ev ch over 1f out: no ex ins fnl f* **12/1**[3]

06 4 ½ **Avery**[30] 2185 2-9-3 ..... JimCrowley 3 61
(R J Hodges) *chsd ldrs: rdn over 3f out: outpcd fr 1/2-way* **20/1**

5 R **Violet's Pride**[13] 2695 2-8-5 ..... CharlotteKerton[(7)] 6 47+
(S Parr) *led: hung lft 2f out: rdn: hung rt: hdd and rn out through rails over 1f out* **40/1**

60.46 secs (0.26) **Going Correction** -0.025s/f (Good) **5** Ran SP% **108.2**

Speed ratings (Par 94):96,95,91,90,—

CSF £3.53 TOTE £3.50: £1.30, £1.10; EX 5.10.

Owner Exors Of The Late D A Shirley **Bred** Exors Of The Late D Shirley **Trained** Beckhampton, Wilts

FOCUS

A modest maiden with a small turnout. The first two home are of a fair standard but all told this is not a race to be too positive about.

NOTEBOOK

Compton Fields showed the benefit of his debut run to turn over the odds-on favourite. He looks as if an extra furlong would suit, and should improve quite a bit more. (tchd 15-8)

Impromptu failed to justify the odds, but the winner is probably a fair type in the making. Now runner-up in both his races, he can go one better. (op 4-5)

Danger Alley has the pace for this trip but was beaten late on by two reasonable sorts. He will be at home in nurseries now he is qualified. (op 8-1)

Avery, having his third race, is a nursery type, and should appreciate an extra furlong. (op 14-1)

Violet's Pride showed a lot of pace until veering and crashing off the track at the paddock exit – something which is becoming a regular occurrence here. (op 33-1)

3111 MATTERSONS TRADE PRODUCTS MAIDEN STKS 6f 21y

2:50 (2:50) (Class 5) 3-Y-0+ **£3,238** (£963; £481; £240) **Stalls** Low

Form RPR

2-44 1 **Namu**[11] 2763 3-8-12 63 ..... MichaelHills 2 75
(B W Hills) *mde all: rdn clr over 1f out* **11/8**[1]

032 2 3 **Kansas Gold**[8] 2859 3-9-3 70 ..... RichardMullen 1 71
(W R Muir) *a.p: chsd wnr 1/2-way: rdn 2f out: no imp* **11/8**[1]

4040 3 5 **Riolo (IRE)**[9] 2820 4-9-4 57 .....(b) JamesDoyle[(5)] 6 57+
(K F Clutterbuck) *chsd ldrs: rdn and hung rt over 3f out: sn outpcd: no ch whn hung lft over 1f out* **9/1**[3]

00 4 12 **Shoshoni**[32] 2146 3-8-12 ..... PhilipRobinson 3 15
(M A Jarvis) *chsd wnr to 1/2-way: sn wknd* **15/2**[2]

0000 5 5 **Prince Marju (IRE)**[11] 2746 3-9-3 44 ..... RobbieFitzpatrick 5 5
(P A Blockley) *sn outpcd* **50/1**

0000 P **Value Plus (IRE)**[18] 2543 4-8-11 36 ..... JamieHamblett[(7)] 4 —
(S Parr) *chsd ldr: rdn and wkng whn broke down over 2f out: sn p.u* **100/1**

1m 11.3s (-0.80) **Going Correction** -0.025s/f (Good)

WFA 3 from 4yo 6lb **6** Ran SP% **108.9**

Speed ratings (Par 103):104,100,93,77,70 —

CSF £3.10 TOTE £2.40: £1.10, £1.40; EX 3.40.

Owner Philip G Harvey **Bred** Philip Graham Harvey **Trained** Lambourn, Berks

FOCUS

An ordinary maiden, rated through the runner-up. The winner had the run of the race from the front.

Riolo(IRE) Official explanation: jockey said gelding hung both ways

Shoshoni Official explanation: jockey said filly lost its action on bend

3112 MATTERSONS STEEL SERVICES CRAIG MITCHELL MEMORIAL MEDIAN AUCTION MAIDEN STKS 7f 26y

3:25 (3:27) (Class 5) 3-5-Y-0 **£3,238** (£963; £481; £240) **Stalls** Low

Form RPR

6020 1 **Orpen Quest (IRE)**[10] 2789 4-9-4 45 .....(v) KevinGhunowa[(7)] 13 63
(M J Attwater) *chsd ldrs: led over 2f out: edgd lft and hdd over 1f out: rdn to ld ins fnl f: r.o* **14/1**

03-5 2 nk **Secret Assassin (IRE)**[19] 2525 3-9-3 74 ..... NCallan 8 59
(W R Muir) *chsd ldrs: rdn and hung rt over 1f out: led 1f out: sn hdd: r.o* **9/4**[2]

2322 3 ¾ **Lucksin (IRE)**[8] 2875 3-9-3 74 ..... JoeFanning 10 57
(N Tinkler) *chsd ldrs: rdn to ld over 1f out: sn hdd: no ex ins fnl f* **2/1**[1]

4 shd **Casual Affair** 3-9-3 ..... RichardMullen 14 57+
(E J O'Neill) *s.i.s: hld up: hdwy and hmpd over 1f out: r.o: nt rch ldrs* **14/1**

5 2 ½ **Kilgary (USA)** 3-8-12 ..... TPQueally 2 46+
(J Noseda) *s.i.s: hld up: hdwy over 1f out: nt rch ldrs* **6/1**[3]

00 6 3 ½ **Louise Dupin (IRE)**[25] 2343 3-8-12 ..... SebSanders 7 36
(R M Beckett) *s.i.s: hld up: effrt and nt clr run over 1f out: nvr nrr* **8/1**

0054 7 ½ **Diamond Heritage**[8] 2875 4-9-4 50 ..... JamieHamblett[(7)] 1 43
(S Parr) *prom: rdn over 2f out: sn wknd* **33/1**

6 8 3 **Tajjree**[38] 1960 3-8-12 .....(p) LPKeniry 6 27
(Miss K B Boutflower) *s.i.s: plld hrd: hdwy over 5f out: ev ch over 2f out: wkng whn hmpd over 1f out* **33/1**

9 nk **Goodenough Prince** 3-8-12 ..... RichardKingscote[(5)] 12 32
(Andrew Turnell) *sn outpcd* **25/1**

0000 10 2 **Eathie**[10] 2794 4-9-11 47 .....(v[1]) FrancisFerris 5 29
(M J Attwater) *led over 4f: wknd fnl f* **50/1**

11 8 **Winning Connection (IRE)** 3-9-3 ..... RobbieFitzpatrick 9 —
(P A Blockley) *dwlt: outpcd* **28/1**

1m 24.65s (-0.35) **Going Correction** -0.025s/f (Good)

WFA 3 from 4yo 8lb **11** Ran SP% **118.0**

Speed ratings (Par 103):101,100,99,99,96 92,92,88,88,86 77

CSF £44.00 TOTE £18.90: £4.70, £1.40, £1.30; EX 83.10.

Owner Mrs J Osbaldeston **Bred** Pursuit Of Truth Syndicate **Trained** Wysall, Notts

FOCUS

A weak race, with the first three home having had many opportunities in the past. A much-improved effort from the winner at face value, but the form may well not stand up.

Tajjree Official explanation: jockey said filly was struck into

3113 SPIRIT VOLKSWAGEN H'CAP 1m 22y

4:00 (4:01) (Class 4) (0-80,80) 3-Y-0+ **£6,477** (£1,927; £963; £481) **Stalls** Low

Form RPR

0125 1 **Habshan (USA)**[16] 2614 6-10-0 77 ..... SebSanders 3 86
(C F Wall) *hld up: hdwy to chse ldr over 1f out: styd on u.p to ld wl ins fnl f* **4/1**[3]

-330 2 1 **Jaad**[32] 2126 3-9-8 **80** ..... RHills 6 85
(M Johnston) *led over 6f out: rdn clr over 1f out: hdd wl ins fnl f* **9/2**

0401 3 2 ½ **Queen's Composer (IRE)**[19] 2525 3-9-5 **77** ..... PhilipRobinson 7 76
(B Smart) *chsd ldrs: rdn over 1f out: styd on same pce* **3/1**[1]

1000 4 hd **Lizarazu (GER)**[13] 2705 7-9-7 **77** .....(p) TolleyDean[(7)] 5 77
(R A Harris) *hld up: hdwy over 1f out: no imp fnl f* **12/1**

6-00 5 ¾ **River Of Babylon**[16] 2606 5-10-0 **77** ..... RichardMullen 1 76
(M L W Bell) *chsd ldrs: rdn over 1f out: no ex fnl f* **16/1**

0011 6 2 ½ **Bold Diktator**[8] 2860 4-9-12 **75** .....(b) NCallan 2 68
(W R Muir) *led: hdd over 6f out: trckd ldr: plld hrd: rdn over 2f out: wknd fnl f* **11/2**

-053 7 5 **Ali D**[2] 3044 8-8-13 **62** ..... FergusSweeney 4 44
(G Woodward) *hld up: rdn over 2f out: sn outpcd* **7/2**[2]

1m 38.44s (-1.16) **Going Correction** -0.025s/f (Good)

WFA 3 from 4yo+ 9lb **7** Ran SP% **114.4**

Speed ratings (Par 105):104,103,100,100,99 97,92

CSF £22.21 TOTE £5.00: £2.00, £2.30; EX 25.80.

Owner Alan & Jill Smith **Bred** Darley Stud Management, L L C **Trained** Newmarket, Suffolk

FOCUS

A fair handicap, with the winner the best guide to the form, which looks sound enough. Hills controlled the pace on Jaad, only to be picked off by the winner.

Bold Diktator Official explanation: jockey said gelding ran too free

3114 WBX.COM WORLD BET EXCHANGE H'CAP (PART OF THE WARWICK STAYERS SERIES) 2m 39y

4:35 (4:36) (Class 4) (0-80,73) 3-Y-0+ **£6,477** (£1,927; £963; £481) **Stalls** Low

Form RPR

2644 1 **Raslan**[18] 2556 3-8-10 **73** ..... RoystonFfrench 5 87+
(M Johnston) *a.p: chsd ldr over 3f out: rdn to ld 1f out: styd on: edgd lft towards fin* **7/1**

21-1 2 2 **Key Time (IRE)**[9] 2828 4-9-7 **65** ..... SebSanders 9 76
(Sir Mark Prescott) *led: rdn and hdd 1f out: styd on same pce* **5/4**[1]

51-3 3 3 **Mersey Sound (IRE)**[22] 2460 8-9-6 **64** ..... LPKeniry 4 72
(D R C Elsworth) *prom: rdn over 3f out: styd on same pce fnl 2f* **4/1**[3]

0212 4 1 ¼ **Compton Eclaire (IRE)**[8] 2871 6-8-8 **57** .....(v) AndrewMullen[(5)] 2 63
(B Ellison) *hld up: rdn over 2f out: nvr nrr* **5/2**[2]

0050 5 13 **Turner**[7] 2902 5-8-8 **57** ..... LiamJones[(5)] 7 47
(W M Brisbourne) *hld up in tch: rdn over 2f out: hung lft and wknd over 1f out* **10/1**

366/ 6 14 **Blackcomb Mountain (USA)**[28] 6240 4-9-2 **60** ..... RichardThomas 6 34
(M F Harris) *s.s: a bhd* **50/1**

0-00 **7** ¾ **Three Counties (IRE)**[8] 2849 5-9-0 **65**........................ MarkCoumbe(7) 1 38
(N I M Rossiter) *trckd ldr: racd keenly: rdn over 3f out: sn wknd* **50/1**

3m 29.6s (-3.10) **Going Correction** -0.025s/f (Good)
WFA 3 from 4yo+ 19lb 7 Ran SP% **118.5**
Speed ratings (Par 105):106,105,103,102,96 89,89
CSF £17.13 CT £41.09 TOTE £8.40: £3.30, £1.40; EX 20.90.
Owner Jumeirah Racing **Bred** Darley **Trained** Middleham Moor, N Yorks

FOCUS
A decent little stayers' race, run at a fair pace, controlled by Sanders on the runner-up. The bare form does not look all that strong but the first two are progressive.

3115 GODIVA METAL CENTRE LTD NON FERROUS H'CAP 1m 2f 188y
5:05 (5:08) (Class 6) (0-60,61) 3-Y-0+ **£2,730** (£806; £403) **Stalls** Low

Form RPR
3611 **1** **Another Con (IRE)**[4] 2966 5-9-1 **47** 6ex.................... RobbieFitzpatrick 1 53
(P A Blockley) *hld up: hdwy on outside over 1f out: r.o u.p to ld post* **10/3**[1]
0646 **2** *hd* **Meelup (IRE)**[8] 2862 6-9-7 **56**..(p) AmirQuinn(3) 6 62
(P G Murphy) *chsd ldrs: led 2f out: rdn clr over 1f out: hdd post* **8/1**
3650 **3** *nk* **Milk And Sultana**[15] 2636 6-9-2 **48**.. TPQueally 3 53
(G A Ham) *hld up: hdwy over 2f out: sn rdn: styd on* **12/1**
5000 **4** 1 ½ **Flashing Floozie**[8] 2877 3-8-2 **46** ow2.......................... RichardThomas 15 48
(M F Harris) *plld hrd and prom: rdn over 2f out: styd on* **28/1**
352 **5** ½ **Ai Hawa (IRE)**[11] 2746 3-8-7 **51**... NCallan 12 52
(Eamon Tyrrell, Ire) *plld hrd and prom: rdn over 2f out: hung lft ins fnl f: styd on* **5/1**[2]
0-03 **6** *nk* **Peas 'n Beans (IRE)**[17] 2591 3-8-9 **60**............................ LukeMorris(7) 9 61+
(M L W Bell) *hld up: hdwy u.p over 2f out: nt rch ldrs* **6/1**[3]
6461 **7** *nk* **Siena Star (IRE)**[13] 2707 8-10-1 **61**................................. RobertHavlin 10 61
(Stef Liddiard) *hld up in tch: rdn and edgd lft over 1f out: styd on* **7/1**
-000 **8** ¾ **Typhoon Ginger (IRE)**[7] 2891 11-9-8 **59**.......... RichardKingscote(5) 14 60+
(G Woodward) *hld up: hdwy over 1f out: hmpd ins fnl f: nvr trble ldrs* **14/1**
005 **9** 2 ½ **Virginia Plain**[16] 2600 3-7-13 **48**................................ EmmettStack(5) 17 42
(Miss Diana Weeden) *chsd ldrs: led 3f out: sn rdn and hdd: wknd fnl f* **50/1**
-225 **10** 1 ¼ **Expected Bonus (USA)**[4] 2966 7-8-12 **44**.............................. PaulDoe 7 36
(Jamie Poulton) *hld up in tch: racd keenly: rdn over 3f out: wknd fnl f* **15/2**
/000 **11** 7 **Lawood (IRE)**[15] 2641 6-9-9 **55**..(v) VinceSlattery 16 35
(L P Grassick) *hld up: in rr whn hmpd over 3f out: n.d* **100/1**
0-00 **12** 1 **Bubbling Fun**[16] 2612 5-9-6 **52**.................................. RoystonFfrench 2 30
(T Wall) *hld up: hdwy over 3f out: rdn and wknd over 1f out* **25/1**
0000 **13** 6 **Tilen (IRE)**[18] 2539 3-7-12 **47** ow2..................................(b) LiamJones(5) 8 14
(S Parr) *led 8f: sn wknd* **50/1**
026- **P** **Truman**[270] 5700 5-9-4 **55**.. LiamTreadwell(5) 5 —
(John A Harris) *hld up: effrt whn broke down over 3f out: sn p.u* **16/1**
0000 **U** **Compton Flyer**[27] 2285 3-7-13 **43**.. FrancisFerris 4 —
(J M Bradley) *prom: lost pl 7f out: t.o whn swvd rt and uns rdr 1f out* **33/1**

2m 18.51s (-0.89) **Going Correction** -0.025s/f (Good)
WFA 3 from 5yo+ 12lb 15 Ran SP% **124.8**
Speed ratings (Par 101):102,101,101,100,100 99,99,99,97,96 91,90,86,—,—
CSF £29.61 CT £299.66 TOTE £3.00: £1.70, £3.20, £3.00; EX 50.00.
Owner Market Avenue Racing Club Ltd **Bred** Matthew Tynan **Trained** Lambourn, Berks

FOCUS
A modest, but competitive handicap in which the winner was completing a hat-trick, although she did not quite reproduce the level of her previous win. Fairly sound form, limited by the fourth.
Bubbling Fun Official explanation: jockey said mare stopped quickly

3116 BOLLINGER CHAMPAGNE CHALLENGE SERIES H'CAP (IN ASSOCIATION WITH THE DAILY TELEGRAPH) 1m 4f 134y
5:40 (5:40) (Class 5) (0-70,70) 4-Y-0+ **£3,123** (£968; £484; £242) **Stalls** Low

Form RPR
6-03 **1** **Mexican Pete**[5] 2953 6-11-5 **70**....................................... MrMJJSmith(5) 10 83
(A W Carroll) *a.p: chsd ldr over 3f out: led over 1f out: rdn clr* **4/1**[3]
2520 **2** 3 **Dovedon Hero**[8] 2849 6-11-5 **70**..............................(b) MrPCollington(5) 2 78
(P J McBride) *s.s: hld up: hdwy over 1f out: nt rch wnr* **7/2**[2]
0054 **3** 1 ¼ **Love You Always (USA)**[17] 2585 6-10-2 **55**..................(t) MrRBirkett(7) 4 61
(Miss J Feilden) *dwlt: hld up: hdwy over 1f out: nrst fin* **12/1**
3213 **4** 1 ½ **Ramsgill (USA)**[17] 2585 4-11-1 **66**.................................... MrSPearce(5) 5 70
(J Pearce) *chsd ldrs: rdn over 2f out: styd on same pce appr fnl f* **3/1**[1]
5141 **5** ¾ **Court Of Appeal**[10] 2788 9-11-5 **65**.................................(tp) MrSDobson 3 68
(B Ellison) *led: rdn and hdd over 1f out: edgd rt and no ex fnl f* **6/1**
5-03 **6** 1 ¼ **Almizan (IRE)**[16] 2628 6-10-13 **64**............................(b) MrDHutchison(5) 9 65
(G L Moore) *chsd ldrs: rdn over 2f out: wknd over 1f out* **4/1**[3]
130/ **7** 15 **Davoski**[350] 4383 12-9-11 **50**... MrJGoss(7) 6 27
(Dr P Pritchard) *hld up: rdn: hung lft and wknd over 2f out* **40/1**
06-0 **8** 23 **Mel's Moment (USA)**[6] 2935 4-10-5 **58**............................(b) MrCHughes(7) 8 —
(R J Price) *chsd ldr tl rdn over 3f out: wknd over 2f out* **33/1**

2m 45.68s (2.08) **Going Correction** -0.025s/f (Good) 8 Ran SP% **114.6**
Speed ratings (Par 103):92,90,89,88,88 87,78,63
CSF £18.47 CT £152.40 TOTE £4.50: £2.40, £1.20, £2.90; EX 17.20 Place 6 £14.90, Place 5 £14.08..
Owner First Chance Racing **Bred** First Chance Racing **Trained** Cropthorne, Worcs

FOCUS
A low-grade contest, in which the winner showed a fine turn of foot and now looks back in top form. Ordinary form, but sound.
T/Plt: £17.80 to a £1 stake. Pool: £36,156.50. 1,477.90 winning tickets. T/Qpdt: £17.20 to a £1 stake. Pool: £2,436.20. 104.30 winning tickets. CR

3090 WINDSOR (R-H)
Sunday, July 2

OFFICIAL GOING: Good to firm (firm in places)
Wind: Nil

3117 TOTEJACKPOT NURSERY 6f
2:30 (2:31) (Class 5) 2-Y-0 **£3,886** (£1,156; £577; £288) **Stalls** High

Form RPR
2220 **1** **See In The Dark (IRE)**[12] 2724 2-9-7 **77**.................................. LDettori 2 79
(B J Meehan) *bhd: hdwy in centre crse over 2f out: chal 1f out: led ins last: hld on all out* **9/2**[1]
004 **2** *shd* **Dolly Coughdrop (IRE)**[11] 2759 2-8-10 **66**.......................... ChrisCatlin 7 68
(K R Burke) *s.i.s: bhd: stl plenty to do 1/2-way: hdwy in centre crse over 1f out: str chal last half f: jst failed* **20/1**
040 **3** *shd* **Tom Paris**[26] 2315 2-8-10 **66**...(b[1]) MartinDwyer 14 67
(W R Muir) *slt ld on stands rail: rdn over 2f out:kpt slt advantage tl hdd ins last:styd on gamely:nt quite pce to ld again cl home* **14/1**
036 **4** *hd* **High Style**[16] 2617 2-9-3 **73**.. RyanMoore 5 74
(R Hannon) *s.i.s: t.k.h: hdwy fr 2f out: str run ins last: chal cl home but nt quite get up* **8/1**
310 **5** *hd* **Stir Crazy (IRE)**[75] 1066 2-8-12 **71**....................... EdwardCreighton(3) 13 71
(M R Channon) *bhd: hdwy fr 2f out: str run u.p and fin wl fnl f: gng on cl home* **5/1**[2]
0024 **6** *shd* **Montemayorprincess (IRE)**[21] 2478 2-8-4 **60**........ FrankieMcDonald 8 60
(D Haydn Jones) *chsd ldrs: chal in centre crse over 1f out: kpt on and styd chalng ins last: no ex cl home* **10/1**
613 **7** 1 **Beckenham's Secret**[44] 1824 2-9-7 **77**................................ AlanMunro 1 74
(B R Millman) *sn w ldr: stl chalng over 1f out: outpcd last half f* **11/1**
456 **8** *nk* **Carlitos Spirit (IRE)**[27] 2287 2-8-12 **68**............................ SteveDrowne 3 64
(B R Millman) *hdwy to chse ldrs in centre crse 1/2-way: ev ch 1f out: one pce last half f* **10/1**
036 **9** ½ **Copper King**[23] 2388 2-8-4 **63**.................................... NeilChalmers(3) 10 58
(A M Balding) *chsd ldrs on stands side:rdn over 2f out: wknd last half f* **16/1**
0043 **10** 5 **Pat Will (IRE)**[19] 2517 2-8-9 **65**.. ShaneKelly 4 45
(P D Evans) *ken hold: wnt rt after 1f: chsd ldrs: wknd fnl f* **16/1**
5553 **11** 2 **Diminuto**[13] 2709 2-7-13 **55** ow1.. HayleyTurner 11 29+
(M D I Usher) *t.k.h: chsd ldrs: rdn over 2f out: wknd over 1f out* **7/1**[3]
316 **12** 8 **Auction Time**[50] 1682 2-8-3 **59**.. FrancisNorton 12 9
(J L Spearing) *chsd ldrs over 3f* **11/1**
6404 **13** 1 **Lenard Frank (IRE)**[6] 2916 2-7-12 **54** oh11.................(v) DavidKinsella 9 1
(M D I Usher) *s.i.s: bhd: swtchd lft and brief effrt over 2f out: nvr in contention and sn bhd* **50/1**

1m 12.54s (-1.13) **Going Correction** -0.20s/f (Firm) 13 Ran SP% **118.5**
Speed ratings (Par 94):99,98,98,98,98 98,96,96,95,89 86,75,74
CSF £94.93 CT £1210.02 TOTE £4.40: £2.20, £3.00, £2.80; EX 106.60 TRIFECTA Not won..
Owner N Attenborough,Mrs L Mann,Mrs L Way **Bred** Thomas F Hannon **Trained** Manton, Wilts

FOCUS
The first nursery of the current season, run at a sound pace, and it produced a blanket finish between the first six. The official ratings shown next to each horse are estimated and for information purposes only.

NOTEBOOK
See In The Dark(IRE), outclassed in the Windsor Castle at Royal Ascot last time, just got up in a blanket finish to register his first success at the fifth attempt. He took time to find his full stride, suggesting this trip is on the sharp-side now, and deserves credit as he defied top weight from a moderate draw. The step up to a seventh furlong can see him find further improvement in this sphere. (op 4-1)
Dolly Coughdrop(IRE) looks to have begun nursery life on a decent enough mark on this evidence, as she was slow to break, and only really got going approaching the final furlong. She was eventually beaten by the smallest of margins, enjoyed the step back-up to six furlongs, and can soon be placed to gain compensation. (tchd 25-1)
Tom Paris, equipped with first-time blinkers, was quick to bag the stands' side rail and showed a decent attitude when put under maximum pressure in the final furlong. He stayed the trip well enough, but the early speed he showed this time suggests he may be better off dropping back to the minimum trip in the short term.
High Style made a sluggish start, before refusing to settle through the early parts, but he still finished his race with purpose and was only just beaten. He can be rated better than the bare form and is clearly happiest over this trip.
Stir Crazy(IRE), stepping up to this trip for the first time, was another doing his best work towards the finish and posted a much more encouraging effort. He can find a race of this nature when ridden more prominently over this trip. (tchd 11-2 in places)
Montemayorprincess(IRE) put in a career-best effort in defeat and was another not beaten at all far. She probably needs easier ground and is going the right way. (op 8-1)
Diminuto Official explanation: jockey said filly was denied a clear run

3118 TOTEEXACTA H'CAP 5f 10y
3:00 (3:02) (Class 5) (0-70,66) 3-Y-0 **£3,238** (£963; £481; £240) **Stalls** High

Form RPR
3140 **1** **Musical Romance (IRE)**[9] 2826 3-9-7 **66**............................(b) LDettori 9 72
(B J Meehan) *s.i.s: hld up rr but in tch: drvn and qcknd over 1f out: led last half f: drvn out* **3/1**[1]
-002 **2** *nk* **Balian**[15] 2652 3-9-5 **64**...(p) RyanMoore 13 69
(G L Moore) *early speed: outpcd after 2f but styd in tch: drvn and hdwy over 1f out: styd on strly ins last: nt pce to rch wnr* **4/1**[2]
0000 **3** 1 **Montzando**[19] 2535 3-8-10 **55**...(v[1]) AlanMunro 11 56
(B R Millman) *pressed ldr tl slt ld 1f out: hdd last half frulong: outpcd cl home* **9/1**
0505 **4** *shd* **Gwilym (GER)**[15] 2652 3-9-5 **64**.. RobertHavlin 12 65
(D Haydn Jones) *slt ld tl hdd 1f out: styd chalng tl outpcd last half f* **7/1**[3]
-010 **5** *nk* **Jucebabe**[22] 2433 3-8-10 **55**.. FrancisNorton 7 55
(J L Spearing) *chsd ldrs: str chal appr fnl f: no ex last half f* **16/1**
0-03 **6** 2 **Tamino (IRE)**[16] 2602 3-9-1 **60**.. SteveDrowne 4 53
(H Morrison) *in tch: hdwy to press ldrs and rdn ins fnl 2f: wknd fnl f* **4/1**[2]
0-00 **7** 3 ½ **Bella Bertolini**[20] 2511 3-9-1 **60**... ShaneKelly 8 40
(T G Mills) *chsd ldrs: effrt 2f out: wknd fnl f* **33/1**
5304 **8** 1 **Danny The Dip**[5] 2962 3-8-4 **54**.. MarcHalford(5) 1 31+
(J J Bridger) *s.i.s: hung bdly lft and racd alone far side after 2f: no ch w stands side fr over 1f out* **12/1**
6150 **9** 7 **Phinerine**[6] 2939 3-9-5 **64**.......................................(b) AdrianMcCarthy 6 15
(R A Harris) *chsd ldrs 3f* **18/1**
0-00 **10** 2 ½ **Ameliore (IRE)**[19] 2532 3-8-2 **47** oh2........................... HayleyTurner 5 —
(S Woodman) *a outpcd* **50/1**
0626 **11** 1 ¼ **Double Valentine**[13] 2704 3-8-8 **53**.. ChrisCatlin 3 —
(R Ingram) *spd to 1/2-way* **14/1**
6004 **12** 5 **Batchworth Fleur**[15] 2644 3-7-13 **47** oh5........ EdwardCreighton(3) 2 —
(E A Wheeler) *pressed ldrs to 1/2-way* **33/1**

59.76 secs (-1.34) **Going Correction** -0.20s/f (Firm) 12 Ran SP% **120.8**
Speed ratings (Par 100):102,101,99,99,99 96,90,88,77,73 71,63
CSF £14.70 CT £94.85 TOTE £3.90: £2.10, £1.80, £3.20; EX 7.70 Trifecta £181.40 Part won. Pool £255.50 - 0.60 winning units..
Owner F C T Wilson **Bred** C H Wacker Iii **Trained** Manton, Wilts

FOCUS
A moderate sprint, run at a strong early pace, and the first two came clear late on.
Danny The Dip Official explanation: jockey said gelding hung left
Batchworth Fleur Official explanation: jockey said filly bled from the nose

3119 TOTEQUADPOT H'CAP 1m 2f 7y
3:35 (3:35) (Class 2) (0-100,94) 3-Y-O

£12,464 (£3,732; £1,866; £934; £466; £234) Stalls Low

Form				RPR
51	1		**Imperial Star (IRE)**[13] 2712 3-9-5 92 ... RichardHughes 4 (J H M Gosden) *hld up rr but in tch: stdy hdwy fr 3f out: shkn up to ld appr fnl f: sn in command: easily* 13/8[1]	105+
0601	2	1 1/4	**Salute Him (IRE)**[31] 2174 3-9-0 87 ... TedDurcan 8 (M R Channon) *led after 1f: rdn over 2f out: hdd appr fnl f: styd on for 2nd but no ch w wnr* 14/1	95
10-1	3	1/2	**Count Trevisio (IRE)**[15] 2654 3-9-7 94 ... LDettori 5 (Saeed Bin Suroor) *led 1f: styd trcking ldr: drvn to chal over 2f out: stl upsides over 1f out: one pce u.p sn after* 2/1[2]	101
3223	4	3/4	**Robustian**[10] 2781 3-8-7 80 ... StephenCarson 6 (R F Johnson Houghton) *chsd ldrs: rdn and effrt over 2f out: nvr quite gng pce to chal: outpcd fnl f* 15/2	86
54-0	5	8	**Psychic Star**[11] 2744 3-9-5 92 ... KerrinMcEvoy 2 (W R Swinburn) *sn in rr: rdn over 4f out: sn lost tch* 16/1	82+
2135	6	4	**Barodine**[22] 2436 3-8-12 85 ... AlanMunro 7 (H R A Cecil) *chsd ldrs: rdn over 3f out: sn btn* 11/2[3]	68+

2m 3.69s (-4.61) **Going Correction** -0.45s/f (Firm) 6 Ran SP% **111.1**
Speed ratings (Par 106):100,99,98,98,91 88
CSF £23.49 CT £45.28 TOTE £2.10: £1.80, £3.50; EX 37.60 Trifecta £59.60 Pool £159.70 - 1.90 winning units..
Owner H R H Princess Haya Of Jordan **Bred** Deerfield Farm **Trained** Newmarket, Suffolk

FOCUS
A decent three-year-old handicap, run at a fair pace, and the progressive winner is value for further.

NOTEBOOK
Imperial Star(IRE) ◆, impressive when getting off the mark in a course-and-distance maiden last time, maintained his progression by following-up to make a winning handicap debut with another taking success. He was given a very patient ride by Hughes, before emerging full of running before two out, and ultimately quickened to win with authority. Considering he still looked green this time, he seems sure to improve again for the experience, and he does look a Pattern performer in the making. However, his trainer afterwards declared that he is likely to have another outing in a three-year-old handicap next time. (op 7-4 tchd 2-1 in a place)
Salute Him(IRE), who dictated when winning at Sandown last time off a 5lb lower mark, stuck to his task gamely once headed late on and proved he gets all of this trip. He is a tough sort, remains in good heart, and helps to set the level of this form. (op 16-1)
Count Trevisio(IRE), raised 4lb for winning on his seasonal return at Sandown 15 days previously, had his chance under a prominent ride and just failed to see out this slightly longer trip as well as the front pair. (op 9-4)
Robustian again appeared to do little wrong in defeat, but was found wanting at the business end of the race. He is a most consistent performer, and stayed this trip well, but probably faces another rise in the weights now. (op 7-1)
Barodine Official explanation: jockey said colt lost its action

3120 EBF TOTESPORT.COM FILLIES' CONDITIONS STKS 5f 10y
4:10 (4:10) (Class 2) 2-Y-O

£12,464 (£3,732; £1,866; £934; £466; £234) Stalls High

Form				RPR
	1		**Pelican Key (IRE)** 2-8-6 ... RyanMoore 2 (D M Simcock) *s.i.s: sn in tch: hdwy 1/2-way: led appr fnl f: drvn and kpt on strly* 13/2[3]	80+
23	2	1	**Princess Ileana (IRE)**[10] 2791 2-8-8 ... FrancisNorton 4 (K R Burke) *chsd ldrs: drvn to chal fr ins fnl 2f: stl ev chance 1f out: outpcd by wnr ins last* 7/1	78
415	3	1/2	**Slipasearcher (IRE)**[11] 2743 2-8-8 ... ShaneKelly 5 (P D Evans) *in tch: drvn along 1/2-way: swtchd lft and hdwy over 1f out: hung lft u.p and one pce ins last* 1/1[1]	77
10	4	1 1/4	**Miss Otis**[32] 2125 2-8-11 ... TonyCulhane 1 (P Winkworth) *sn slt ld: hdd appr fnl f: wknd ins last* 9/2[2]	75
0	5	1 1/2	**Seaflower Reef (IRE)**[26] 2328 2-8-8 ... MartinDwyer 3 (A M Balding) *chsd ldrs: hampred over 3f out: sn rdn: nveer gng pce to rch ldrs after* 16/1	67
661	6	8	**Autumn Storm**[15] 2643 2-8-8 ... StephenCarson 6 (R Ingram) *s.i.s: bhd: sme hdwy 1/2-way: nvr gng pce to rch ldrs: wknd over 1f out* 28/1	38
41	7	21	**Hucking Hope (IRE)**[10] 2791 2-8-8 ... KerrinMcEvoy 7 (J R Best) *sn outpcd: eased whn no ch fnl f* 9/1	—

60.41 secs (-0.69) **Going Correction** -0.20s/f (Firm) 7 Ran SP% **113.3**
Speed ratings (Par 97):97,95,94,92,90 77,43
CSF £49.13 TOTE £7.30: £2.80, £2.90; EX 37.00.
Owner Khalifa Dasmal **Bred** Patrick Gleeson **Trained** Newmarket, Suffolk

FOCUS
A fair juvenile fillies' conditions event, run at a sound pace, and the debutante winner looks capable of rating higher.

NOTEBOOK
Pelican Key(IRE), a 130,000gns half-sister to a useful juvenile sprinter in Italy, overcame a sluggish start and showed a great attitude in the final furlong to repel the runner-up and make a winning debut. She was well backed for this, so is clearly well regarded by connections, and looked at home on the fast surface. Her connections stated that she would not be rushed this term, but hoped she would take in a Listed event before the season's end. (op 12-1 tchd 14-1 in places)
Princess Ileana(IRE) once again did little wrong in defeat and posted a personal-best effort. She would have found this ground plenty fast enough and really ought to be placed to get off the mark before too long. (tchd 15-2)
Slipasearcher(IRE), a slightly unlucky fifth in the Queen Mary 11 days previously, ran well below that level of form and never seriously threatened. She may have found this coming too soon. (tchd 6-5)
Miss Otis had her chance, but faded when push came to shove, and did not look totally happy on the quick ground. Time will most likely tell she faced an impossible task in giving away weight this time. (op 7-2 tchd 5-1)
Hucking Hope(IRE) Official explanation: jockey said filly was unsuited by the good to firm (firm in places) ground

3121 TOTETRIFECTA H'CAP 1m 67y
4:45 (4:45) (Class 3) (0-90,90) 3-Y-O+

£8,724 (£2,612; £1,306; £653; £326; £163) Stalls High

Form				RPR
30-1	1		**Bee Stinger**[51] 1644 4-8-11 73 ... ChrisCatlin 2 (I A Wood) *t.k.h: trckd ldr: drvn to chal fr 2f out: edgd rt u.p last half f: led cl home* 13/2	81
6201	2	hd	**Pintle**[7] 2900 6-9-9 85 6ex ... KerrinMcEvoy 8 (J L Spearing) *led: rdn over 2f out: kpt slt advantage tl hdd an no ex cl home* 4/1[2]	93
3-05	3	1 1/4	**All Quiet**[92] 826 5-9-2 78 ... RichardHughes 9 (R Hannon) *rr but in tch: hdwy over 2f out: swtchd to stands rail and effrt ins last: hld whn n.m.r cl home* 6/1	83
5-10	4	1	**Archerfield Links (USA)**[10] 2774 3-9-3 88 ... RyanMoore 6 (N A Callaghan) *hld up rr but in tch: hdwy and drvn along 3f out: chsd ldrs 2f out: sn one pce and no imp: wknd last half f* 3/1[1]	89
30-4	5	1 3/4	**Percy's Pearl (USA)**[33] 2114 4-8-13 78 ... AntonyProcter(3) 1 (D R C Elsworth) *slowly away: sn in tch: hdwy 3f out: chsd ldrs 2f out: wknd ins last* 11/2[3]	77
3150	6	2	**Will He Wish**[15] 2649 10-10-0 90 ... TonyCulhane 7 (S Gollings) *t.k.h in rr: mod prog fnl 2f: nvr in contention* 16/1	84
4466	7	6	**San Antonio**[34] 2086 6-9-5 81 ... AlanMunro 10 (Mrs P Sly) *chsd ldrs: rdn 3f out: wknd fr 2f out* 13/2	61
/0-0	8	1 1/4	**Palatinate (FR)**[20] 2508 4-8-13 78 ... AdamKirby(3) 3 (C G Cox) *chsd ldrs: rdn over 3f out: wknd qckly 2f out* 25/1	55
0-	9	1 1/2	**Mohawk Star (IRE)**[398] 1048 5-8-13 75 ... SteveDrowne 4 (I A Wood) *nvr in contention* 33/1	49

1m 40.69s (-4.91) **Going Correction** -0.45s/f (Firm)
WFA 3 from 4yo+ 9lb 9 Ran SP% **114.0**
Speed ratings (Par 107):106,105,104,103,101 99,93,92,91
CSF £32.23 CT £164.82 TOTE £8.80: £2.10, £2.10, £2.00; EX 50.20 Trifecta £215.60 Part won. Pool £303.70 - 0.90 winning units..
Owner Sporting Occasions No 11 **Bred** Templeton Stud **Trained** Upper Lambourn, Berks

FOCUS
A fair handicap, which was run at an uneven pace, yet the form still looks sound for the class.

NOTEBOOK
Bee Stinger, 10lb higher than when winning on the Polytrack at Lingfield when last seen 51 days previously, proved free through the early stages on this return to action, but that was still not enough to stop him following up with a last-gasp success. He proved well suited by the quick surface and this has to rate as career-best display. It will be interesting to see how the Handicapper reacts, but he has improved from three to four and is open to further improvement at this distance. (op 8-1)
Pintle, under a penalty for making all at Warwick a week previously, soon adopted her favoured position at the head of affairs and very nearly followed up. She had the run of the race, but is clearly back in decent heart again now, and may just prefer dropping back to seven furlongs.
All Quiet fared the best of those to come from off the pace, but she found just the same pace under pressure and never looked a serious threat to the leaders. She is entitled to improve a touch for the outing, but probably needs further respite from the Handicapper. (tchd 11-2)
Archerfield Links(USA), well below-par in the Britannia Handicap at Royal Ascot ten days previously, was always making heavy weather of it from off the pace and probably found this coming too soon. His rider later reported that his saddle had slipped. Official explanation: jockey said saddle slipped (op 11-4 tchd 10-3 in a place)
Percy's Pearl(USA) proved disappointing and was never in the hunt at any stage. He is capable of better and looks well worth a try over further now. (tchd 6-1)
Mohawk Star(IRE) Official explanation: jockey said gelding was unsuited by the good to firm (firm in places) ground

3122 AT THE RACES MAIDEN STKS 1m 3f 135y
5:20 (5:20) (Class 5) 3-5-Y-O £3,238 (£963; £481; £240) Stalls Low

Form				RPR
6	1		**Peppertree**[51] 1650 3-8-9 ... OscarUrbina 9 (J R Fanshawe) *trckd ldrs: led wl over 1f out: drvn and hld on wl fnl f* 4/1[3]	85
34	2	1 1/2	**Sybella**[27] 2292 3-8-9 ... RyanMoore 8 (J L Dunlop) *bhd: drvn along over 3f out: hdwy over 2f out: chsd wnr ins last but no imp u.p* 7/1	83
262	3	1/2	**Nimra (USA)**[16] 2600 3-8-6 80 ... AdamKirby(3) 6 (G A Butler) *chsd ldrs: rdn to take slt ld 2f out: hdd wl over 1f out: one pce fnl f* 2/1[1]	82
	4	1 1/2	**Last Warrior** 3-9-0 ... RichardHughes 10 (J H M Gosden) *chsd ldrs: rdn fr 3f oit: styd on same pce fr over 1f out* 9/2	85
03	5	3 1/2	**Grave Matters (USA)**[7] 2895 3-9-0 ... JoeFanning 1 (M Johnston) *chsd ldr tl led jst ins fnl 3f: hdd 2f out: sn btn* 7/2[2]	79
450-	6	9	**Acknowledgement**[415] 1673 4-9-10 72 ... AntonyProcter(3) 3 (D R C Elsworth) *bhd: hdwy over 3f out: no imp on ldrs fnl 2f* 33/1	65
	7	3 1/2	**William's Way**[24] 4-9-13 ... ChrisCatlin 2 (I A Wood) *sn led: hdd jst ins fnl 3f: sn btn* 40/1	59
	8	5	**Rowe Park** 3-8-11 ... EdwardCreighton(3) 7 (Mrs L C Jewell) *s.i.s: a bhd* 66/1	51
0	9	48	**Queen Of Song**[28] 2261 4-9-8 ... ShaneKelly 5 (G L Moore) *s.i.s: a bhd: eased fnl 3f: t.o* 50/1	—

2m 24.52s (-5.58) **Going Correction** -0.45s/f (Firm)
WFA 3 from 4yo 13lb 9 Ran SP% **115.1**
Speed ratings (Par 103):100,99,98,97,95 89,87,83,51
CSF £30.82 TOTE £4.80: £1.50, £2.90, £1.30; EX 17.40 Trifecta £89.80 Pool £328.90 - 2.60 winning units. Place 6 £214.45, Place 5 £56.55..
Owner Wood Hall Stud Limited **Bred** Wood Hall Stud **Trained** Newmarket, Suffolk

FOCUS
A modest maiden, run at a sound enough pace, and the field came home fairly strung out.
T/Jkpt: Not won. T/Plt: £211.40 to a £1 stake. Pool: £61,305.70 - 211.65 winning units T/Qpdt: £30.90 to a £1 stake. Pool:£4,173.50 - 99.70 winning units ST

3102 CURRAGH (R-H)
Sunday, July 2

OFFICIAL GOING: Straight course - good to firm; round course - good

3123a BUDWEISER GUINNESS H'CAP (PREMIER HANDICAP) 1m
1:30 (1:31) 3-Y-O+ £35,917 (£10,537; £5,020; £1,710)

			RPR
1		**Bush Maiden (IRE)**[18] 2560 6-9-2 90 ... TPO'Shea 24 (Mrs Seamus Hayes, Ire) *mid-div: clsr in 4th over 2f out: rdn to chal and ld 1 1/2f out: styd on wl u.p ins fnl f* 11/1[2]	100
2	3/4	**Absolute Image (IRE)**[36] 2040 4-9-1 89 ... PJSmullen 23 (D K Weld, Ire) *chsd ldrs: 3rd and checked sltly under 2f out: 2nd fr over 1f out: kpt on wl u.p ins fnl f* 14/1	97
3	2 1/2	**Mombassa (IRE)**[63] 1325 6-9-3 91 ... FMBerry 20 (Edward Lynam, Ire) *mid-div: clsr in 5th over 2f out: no imp u.p in 3rd and kpt on same pce fnl f* 14/1	94
4	2	**Peculiar Prince (IRE)**[18] 2560 4-8-1 78 ... RPCleary(3) 18 (Liam McAteer, Ire) *prom: rdn to chal and on terms fr 2f out: hdd over 1 1/2f out: sn no imp u.p: kpt on same pce* 20/1	76

5 ½ **Keen Look (IRE)**[7] 2907 7-8-6 80 ow1 JohnEgan 21 77
(Gerard Keane, Ire) *towards rr: rdn and kpt on wl wout threatening fr under 2f out* **12/1**[3]

6 1 ½ **Master Marvel (IRE)**[36] 2040 5-8-3 84 MACleere(7) 12 78+
(T J O'Mara, Ire) *towards rr: swtchd to outer over 1f out: rdn and kpt on wl wout threatening* **12/1**[3]

7 shd **Zacharova (IRE)**[11] 2769 3-8-2 90 DJMoran(5) 15 83
(J S Bolger, Ire) *sn led: rdn over 2f out: strly pressed and hdd over 1 1/2f out: sn no imp u.p: kpt on same pce* **11/1**[2]

8 nk **Mooretown Boy (IRE)**[30] 2216 6-8-8 82 WMLordan 16 75
(F Oakes, Ire) *towards rr: rdn and kpt on wout threatening fr under 2f out* **12/1**[3]

9 2 **Sheer Tenby (IRE)**[27] 2312 9-8-13 87 (t) KJManning 19 75
(Paul A Roche, Ire) *rr of mid-div: rdn and kpt on wout threatening fr 2f out* **25/1**

10 hd **Tanzanite (IRE)**[34] 2086 4-9-5 93 KFallon 10 81
(D W P Arbuthnot) *towards rr: prog into 8th 2f out: sn no imp u.p: kpt on same pce* **12/1**[3]

11 1 ½ **Dream Catch (IRE)**[36] 2040 6-8-8 82 RMBurke 22 67
(Lester Winters, Ire) *rr of mid-div: swtchd over 1f out: kpt on same pce u.p* **20/1**

12 ½ **Fairy Of The Night (IRE)**[25] 2371 4-9-11 99 MJKinane 4 83+
(John M Oxx, Ire) *towards rr: no imp and kpt on same pce u.p fr 2f out* **16/1**

13 nk **Skyscape**[23] 2424 4-8-12 86 JAHeffernan 14 69
(Thomas Cooper, Ire) *mid-div: clsr in 6th over 2f out: sn no imp u.p* **14/1**

14 2 ½ **Deerpark (IRE)**[14] 2688 4-8-13 90 CDHayes(3) 5 67+
(John F Gleeson, Ire) *mid-div: no imp u.p fr 2f out* **10/1**[1]

15 ½ **Shayrazan (IRE)**[36] 2040 5-9-0 88 (t) MCHussey 7 64+
(James Leavy, Ire) *mid-div: no imp u.p and kpt on same pce fr 2f out* **14/1**

16 2 **Zero Tolerance (IRE)**[29] 2226 6-10-4 106 PaulFessey 9 78+
(T D Barron) *trckd ldrs: no ex u.p fr 2f out* **11/1**[2]

17 hd **Bricks And Porter (IRE)**[27] 2312 6-8-9 90 (t) SHunter(7) 11 61
(John A Quinn, Ire) *prom: no ex u.p fr 2f out* **20/1**

18 4 **Portant Fella**[23] 2424 7-8-9 83 (b) CatherineGannon 13 46
(Ms Joanna Morgan, Ire) *cl up: rdn fr 3f out: wknd and bhd fr under 2f out* **20/1**

19 nk **Amourallis (IRE)**[27] 2311 5-9-4 92 WSupple 1 54+
(H Rogers, Ire) *dwlt and towards rr thrght* **25/1**

20 ¾ **Snap**[36] 2040 5-7-13 78 SMGorey(5) 6 38+
(Liam McAteer, Ire) *chsd ldrs: no ex u.p and bhd fr under 2f out* **33/1**

21 shd **Rockazar**[18] 2560 5-9-1 89 JMurtagh 2 49+
(G M Lyons, Ire) *chsd ldrs: no ex u.p fr 2f out* **12/1**[3]

22 2 ½ **Andramad (IRE)**[32] 2153 3-7-13 87 PBBeggy(5) 17 42
(Kevin Prendergast, Ire) *chsd ldrs: no ex u.p fr under 3f out: bhd fr under 2f out* **25/1**

23 9 **Due Respect (IRE)**[12] 2312 6-8-7 81 WJO'Connor 3 16+
(D T Hughes, Ire) *mid-div: no ex u.p fr over 2f out* **20/1**

1m 37.4s **Going Correction** -0.375s/f (Firm)
WFA 3 from 4yo+ 9lb **24** Ran SP% **143.4**
Speed ratings: 108,107,104,102,102 100,100,100,98,98 96,96,95,93,92 90,90,86,86,85 85,83,74
CSF £151.74 CT £1333.33 TOTE £13.40: £3.50, £3.70, £6.60, £5.40; DF 175.10.
Owner Mrs Seamus Hayes **Bred** Pheopotstown Stud **Trained** Curragh, Co Kildare

NOTEBOOK
Tanzanite(IRE), 7lb higher than when scoring at Sandown 34 days previously, was never a threat from off the pace and ran below her new mark. She ideally needs softer ground. (op 14/1)
Zero Tolerance(IRE) was unable to get to the lead from his unfavourable draw and failed to run his race. This was a very stiff task under top weight and he ideally wants an easier surface. (op 10/1)

3124a KING OF BEERS STKS (REGISTERED AS THE RICHARD H FAUGHT MEMORIAL) (LISTED RACE) 5f

2:05 (2:05) 3-Y-0+ **£44,896** (£13,172; £6,275; £2,137)

RPR

1 **Dandy Man (IRE)**[12] 2720 3-9-6 110 PShanahan 4 117
(C Collins, Ire) *trckd ldr in 2nd: rdn to ld under 1f out: styd on wl u.p* **5/4**[1]

2 1 **Benbaun (IRE)**[12] 2720 5-9-11 (b) PJSmullen 8 115
(M J Wallace) *trckd ldrs: mainly 4th: no imp u.p and kpt on into 2nd wout troubling wnr fnl f* **5/2**[2]

3 ½ **Osterhase (IRE)**[27] 2308 7-9-11 111 (b) FMBerry 5 113
(J E Mulhern, Ire) *led: strly pressed and hdd under 1f out: kpt on and dropped to 3rd wl ins fnl f* **13/2**[3]

4 ½ **Majestic Times (IRE)**[27] 2308 6-9-9 101 VRDeSouza 6 109
(Liam McAteer, Ire) *sn pushed along in mid-div: mod 6th over 1f out: kpt on without threatening* **25/1**

5 ½ **Tournedos (IRE)**[72] 1116 4-9-9 KFallon 2 108
(R Charlton) *chsd ldrs: mod 5th and kpt on same pce u.p fr over 1f out* **10/1**

6 hd **Green Manalishi**[29] 2227 5-9-6 MJKinane 7 104
(D W P Arbuthnot) *trckd ldrs: mainly 3rd: no imp and kpt on same pce fnl f* **10/1**

7 2 **Kingsdale Ocean (IRE)**[27] 2308 3-9-1 97 TPO'Shea 3 95
(W M Roper, Ire) *towards rr: no imp u.p fr under 2f out* **20/1**

8 shd **Fontanally Springs (IRE)**[27] 2308 4-9-3 88 WSupple 1 93
(H Rogers, Ire) *towards rr: no imp u.p fr under 2f out* **66/1**

58.40 secs **Going Correction** -0.20s/f (Firm)
WFA 3 from 4yo+ 5lb **8** Ran SP% **114.6**
Speed ratings: 115,113,112,111,111 110,107,107
CSF £4.34 TOTE £1.70: £1.10, £1.20, £1.50; DF 3.30.
Owner Exors of the late A McLean **Bred** Mountarmstrong Stud **Trained** The Curragh, Co Kildare

FOCUS
Solid form. The proximity of the fourth is a slight worry, but he had one run that was arguably of this level last year.

NOTEBOOK
Dandy Man(IRE) ◆, who looked unlucky when drawn on the far side in the King's Stand at Royal Ascot, reversed placings with the runner-up there and gained compensation with a clear-cut success on this drop into Listed company. He has developed into a high-class sprinter this year, and considering he is only three, he should still be on an upward curve. He will now be aimed at the Nunthorpe in August and possibly then a crack at the Prix de l'Abbaye at Longchamp in October. (op 6/4)
Benbaun(IRE), just pipped by Takeover Target and narrowly in front of the badly drawn Dandy Man in the King's Stand last time, had blinkers replacing the visor. He won this last year but never quite looked like repeating the feat this time and was a bit below his best. That said, time will probably tell he faced an impossible task against the winner, and he could be open to further improvement when reverting to a sixth furlong. (op 2/1)
Osterhase(IRE), runner-up to Benbaun in this event last year, came into this back at the top of his game after winning at Naas last time. Having shown his customary early dash, he had no answer when the winner swept past him, but stuck to his task bravely and rates a decent benchmark for this form. (op 9/2)
Majestic Times(IRE), despite not looking totally in love with the faster surface, still managed to get a lot closer to Osterhase than had been the case at Naas last time and turned in a personal-best effort in defeat. When returning to softer ground, he can get closer again in this class. (op 20/1)
Tournedos(IRE) ran right up to his best, despite never looking a threat. He is proving hard to place. (op 8/1)
Green Manalishi was ridden slightly more prominently than is often the case and performed close to his recent level.

3125a JOHN ROARTY MEMORIAL SCURRY H'CAP (PREMIER HANDICAP) 6f 63y

2:40 (2:41) 3-Y-0+ **£35,917** (£10,537; £5,020; £1,710)

RPR

1 **Taqseem (IRE)**[63] 1318 3-9-3 93 DPMcDonogh 17 103
(Kevin Prendergast, Ire) *a.p: cl 2nd fr 1f out: styd on wl u.p to edge ahd ins fnl f* **14/1**[3]

2 hd **Bonus (IRE)**[50] 1667 6-9-7 91 KFallon 5 102
(G A Butler) *mid-div: prog into 4th under 2f out: rdn to chal and ld over 1f out: narrowly hdd ins fnl f: kpt on wl* **7/1**[1]

3 2 **Baggio (IRE)**[28] 2269 5-9-7 91 FMBerry 8 96
(Charles O'Brien, Ire) *mid-div: rdn and styd on wl into 3rd without threatening fnl f* **7/1**[1]

4 ½ **Orpailleur**[36] 2040 5-9-1 85 KJManning 9 89
(Ms Joanna Morgan, Ire) *sn led: strly pressed and hdd 2f out: no imp and kpt on same pce u.p fr over 1f out* **25/1**

5 shd **Tiffany Gardens (IRE)**[22] 2470 4-8-1 74 (p) CDHayes(3) 1 77
(T Hogan, Ire) *a.p: rdn to ld fr 2f out: strly pressed and hdd over 1f out: sn no imp u.p: kpt on same pce* **20/1**

6 shd **Ocean Gift**[14] 2691 4-8-9 79 JohnEgan 2 82
(Patrick J Flynn, Ire) *mid-div: rdn and kpt on without threatening fr over 1f out* **20/1**

7 2 **Chained Emotion (IRE)**[27] 2308 5-9-9 98 PBBeggy(5) 23 95
(Kevin Prendergast, Ire) *chsd ldrs: no imp u.p and kpt on same pce fr over 1f out* **25/1**

8 ½ **Basra (IRE)**[11] 2765 3-8-4 85 (b[1]) DJMoran(5) 6 79
(J S Bolger, Ire) *rr of mid-div: rdn and kpt on without threatening fr over 1f out* **14/1**[3]

9 ½ **Benwilt Breeze (IRE)**[15] 2664 4-9-8 92 WSupple 7 86
(G M Lyons, Ire) *prom: no imp u.p and kpt on same pce fr under 2f out* **16/1**

10 nk **Libras Child (IRE)**[2] 3059 7-7-13 74 SMGorey(5) 19 68
(P Delaney, Ire) *s.i.s: rdn and kpt on without threatening fr under 2f out* **25/1**

11 nk **Point Calimere (IRE)**[15] 2664 5-8-12 82 NGMcCullagh 11 75
(Liam McAteer, Ire) *rrd up leaving stalls: sn mid-div: kpt on same pce u.p fr 2f out* **25/1**

12 nk **Moone Cross (IRE)**[25] 2369 3-9-2 92 C-PLemaire 15 82
(Mrs John Harrington, Ire) *mid-div: kpt on same pce u.p fr 2f out* **20/1**

13 nk **Senator's Alibi**[10] 2776 8-8-8 85 MACleere(7) 10 76
(T J O'Mara, Ire) *mid-div: no imp and kpt on same pce u.p fr 2f out* **20/1**

14 ¾ **Delphie Queen (IRE)**[71] 1156 5-8-11 88 EMButterly(7) 14 77
(M Halford, Ire) *chsd ldrs: no imp and kpt on same pce u.p fr 2f out* **16/1**

15 ½ **Rising Shadow (IRE)**[29] 2230 5-9-5 89 PaulFessey 12 76
(T D Barron) *mid-div: kpt on same pce u.p fr 2f out* **12/1**[2]

16 ½ **Kid Creole (IRE)**[15] 2664 8-8-8 78 PatCosgrave 24 64
(T M Walsh, Ire) *s.i.s and nvr a factor* **16/1**

17 hd **Mist And Stone (IRE)**[23] 2420 3-8-13 89 JMurtagh 25 72
(G M Lyons, Ire) *prom: 5th under 2f out: sn no imp u.p* **14/1**[3]

18 shd **Crooked Throw (IRE)**[1] 3104 7-8-9 83 5ex TPO'Shea 20 64
(C F Swan, Ire) *mid-div best: nvr a factor* **12/1**[2]

19 1 **Golden Legacy (IRE)**[382] 2604 4-9-10 94 PJSmullen 21 76
(D K Weld, Ire) *mid-div: no imp u.p and kpt on same pce fr 2f out* **16/1**

20 1 ½ **Tiger Royal (IRE)**[252] 6043 10-9-2 86 (b) CO'Donoghue 16 64
(C A Murphy, Ire) *mid-div: no imp u.p fr 2f out* **20/1**

21 1 ½ **Alone He Stands (IRE)**[36] 2040 6-10-0 98 DarryllHolland 3 71
(J C Hayden, Ire) *towards rr thrght: nvr a factor* **20/1**

22 hd **Lady Orpen (IRE)**[31] 2168 3-9-5 95 CSoumillon 4 66+
(Patrick Morris, Ire) *chsd ldrs: no imp u.p fr 2f out: wknd and eased ins fnl f* **14/1**[3]

23 ½ **That's Hot (IRE)**[23] 2420 3-9-3 93 MJKinane 13 62
(G M Lyons, Ire) *mid-div best: nvr a factor* **12/1**[2]

24 2 ½ **Enfield Chase (IRE)**[27] 2312 5-8-12 82 WMLordan 22 46
(T Stack, Ire) *chsd ldrs: no ex u.p fr 2f out* **25/1**

25 2 ½ **Sanfrancullinan (IRE)**[98] 751 4-8-7 80 (b) RPCleary(3) 18 37
(M Halford, Ire) *mid-div best: bhd and n.d fr over 1f out* **16/1**

1m 15.6s **Going Correction** -0.20s/f (Firm)
WFA 3 from 4yo+ 6lb **25** Ran SP% **152.0**
Speed ratings: 104,103,101,100,100 100,97,96,96,95 95,94,94,93,92 92,91,91,90,88 86,86,85,82,78
CSF £107.76 CT £788.67 TOTE £31.60: £7.30, £2.10, £1.50, £7.40; DF 121.60.
Owner Hamdan Al Maktoum **Bred** Shadwell Estate Company Ltd **Trained** Friarstown, Co Kildare

NOTEBOOK
Bonus(IRE), returning from a 50-day break, gave his all in defeat and was only just denied. He had a better draw than the winner, however, and continues to run below his previous best and All-Weather form. (op 6/1)

3126a ANHEUSER-BUSCH ADVENTURE PARKS RAILWAY STKS (GROUP 2) 6f

3:10 (3:11) 2-Y-0

£51,724 (£16,379; £7,758; £2,586; £1,724; £862)

RPR

1 **Holy Roman Emperor (IRE)**[12] 2719 2-9-1 KFallon 1 107
(A P O'Brien, Ire) *chsd ldrs: clsr in 3rd over 1f out: styd on wl u.p to ld wl ins fnl f* **4/1**[2]

2 ¾ **Drayton (IRE)**[36] 2037 2-9-1 WMLordan 6 105
(T Stack, Ire) *sn led: qcknd clr fr over 2f out: kpt on same pce and hdd wl ins fnl f* **9/2**[3]

3 1 ½ **Excellent Art**[34] 2084 2-9-1 MJKinane 5 101
(N A Callaghan) *trckd ldrs: 2nd fr 2f out: no imp u.p and dropped to 3rd ins fnl f: kpt on same pce* **11/8**[1]

4 1 1/2 **Creachadoir (IRE)**[35] 2052 2-9-1 .... KJManning 2 96
(J S Bolger, Ire) *towards rr: prog into 4th 1 1/2f out: no imp and kpt on same pce u.p fnl f* **11/1**

5 nk **Emerald Hill (IRE)**[46] 1784 2-9-1 .... JMurtagh 7 95
(M Halford, Ire) *mid-div: mainly 7th: no imp and kpt on without threatening u.p fr over 1f out* **14/1**

6 1 **Fabrigas (IRE)**[28] 2268 2-9-1 .... DPMcDonogh 9 92
(Kevin Prendergast, Ire) *trckd ldrs: rdn 2f out: sn no imp u.p: kpt on same pce* **16/1**

7 1/2 **Zafonical Storm (USA)**[12] 2719 2-9-1 .... JohnEgan 4 91
(B W Duke) *chsd ldrs: no imp u.p and kpt on same pce fr under 2f out* **66/1**

8 4 **Chjimes (IRE)**[12] 2719 2-9-1 .... PJSmullen 3 79
(K R Burke) *towards rr: no imp u.p fr under 2f out* **16/1**

9 4 **Espartano**[12] 2724 2-9-1 .... CSoumillon 8 67+
(M J Wallace) *cl up: no ex u.p fr 2f out: eased fr over 1f out* **9/1**

1m 12.5s **Going Correction** -0.20s/f (Firm) **9** Ran SP% **118.5**
Speed ratings: 105,104,102,100,99 98,97,92,86
CSF £23.08 TOTE £4.60: £1.50, £1.60, £1.20; DF 29.30.
Owner Mrs John Magnier **Bred** Tower Bloodstock **Trained** Ballydoyle, Co Tipperary
■ Holy Roman Emperor was Aidan O'Brien's eighth winner of this race since 1997.

FOCUS
A decent renewal. It has been rated around the second and third, with the winner finishing the race well and confirming the good impression he made on his debut. The proximity of the seventh is the only worry.

NOTEBOOK
Holy Roman Emperor(IRE), disappointing in the Coventry Stakes at Royal Ascot, left that effort firmly behind and showed his true colours with a ready success. He had to wait for his run nearing two out, but once in the clear Fallon made up his mind, and he was always going to get up inside the final furlong. This effort puts him up there with the best of the juveniles to have run thus far this term and he looks sure to enjoy another furlong before too long. It would be little surprise to see him now follow a similar path to last year's winner - and subsequent 2000 Guineas hero - George Washington. (op 3/1)
Drayton(IRE), having his first outing over six furlongs, showed his now customary early dash and only gave way to the winner inside the final furlong. While he stayed the trip well enough, and fully proved his versatility as regards underfoot conditions, he may be happiest over the minimum trip at present. He would likely prove very hard to reel in if travelling to Goodwood for the Molecomb Stakes next month. (op 9/2 tchd 5/1)
Excellent Art, unbeaten in two previous outings, was all the rage in the betting to complete the hat-trick on this debut in Group company. However, having run a little freely through the early parts, he never really looked that happy and was ultimately well held. It would be wrong to write him off on the back of this display - after all, he ran to his highest RPR yet, albeit narrowly - and this form is much more solid than the Sandown win - but he may be more effective back on easier ground in the future. (op 7/4)
Creachadoir(IRE), third on his debut at this venue 35 days previously, is clearly well thought of by connections and ran a big race in defeat for one so inexperienced. A maiden should be a formality on this evidence. (op 10/1)
Zafonical Storm(USA) appeared to show much-improved form but should be given the benefit of doubt for now.
Chjimes(IRE) was never a serious threat and has now been below-par on his last two outings. He is in danger of going the wrong way. (op 14/1)
Espartano, a beaten favourite in the Windsor Castle at Royal Ascot last time, failed to see out the extra furlong and was not given a hard time when his chance had gone. (op 7/1)

3127a BUDWEISER IRISH DERBY (GROUP 1) (ENTIRE COLTS & FILLIES) 1m 4f
3:50 (3:51) 3-Y-O
£584,482 (£198,620; £95,172; £33,103; £22,758; £12,413)

RPR

1 **Dylan Thomas (IRE)**[29] 2228 3-9-0 119 .... KFallon 9 124+
(A P O'Brien, Ire) *sn settled mid-div: 6th early st: clsr in 3rd under 2f out: rdn to ld over 1f out: qckly clr: styd on wl: impressive* **9/2**[1]

2 3 1/2 **Gentlewave (IRE)**[42] 1872 3-9-0 .... JMurtagh 8 118
(A Fabre, France) *mid-div: 10th bef st: rdn in 6th over 1f out: styd on wl wout threatening wnr fnl f* **11/2**[3]

3 1 1/2 **Best Alibi (IRE)**[29] 2228 3-9-0 .... MJKinane 7 116
(Sir Michael Stoute) *trckd ldrs: 3rd fr 1/2-way: no imp u.p and kpt on same pce fr over 1f out* **9/1**

4 1 1/2 **Dragon Dancer**[29] 2228 3-9-0 .... DarryllHolland 12 113
(G Wragg) *led: t.k.h: hdd after 3f: chsd ldrs after: 5th appr st: sn 4th: no imp and kpt on same pce u.p fr over 1f out* **7/1**

5 1/2 **Darsi (FR)**[28] 2278 3-9-0 .... CSoumillon 2 112
(A De Royer-Dupre, France) *parted company w rdr on way to s: mid-div: 7th early st: no imp and kpt on same pce u.p fr under 2f out* **5/1**[2]

6 shd **Mountain (IRE)**[29] 2228 3-9-0 109 .... JAHeffernan 11 113+
(A P O'Brien, Ire) *cl up: mainly 2nd: no imp u.p and kpt on same pce fr 1 1/2f out: no ex whn checked sltly ins fnl f* **14/1**

7 shd **Heliostatic (IRE)**[22] 2471 3-9-0 105 .... KJManning 10 112
(J S Bolger, Ire) *prom: led after 3f: rdn clr st: strly pressed under 2f out: hdd over 1f out: sn no ex* **25/1**

8 1 **Best Name**[28] 2278 3-9-0 .... C-PLemaire 4 110
(Robert Collet, France) *mid-div: clsr in 5th early st: no imp u.p and kpt on same pce fr under 2f out* **13/2**

9 4 **Classic Punch (IRE)**[27] 2304 3-9-0 .... JohnEgan 5 104
(D R C Elsworth) *towards rr: no imp u.p and kpt on same pce st* **22/1**

10 2 **Puerto Rico (IRE)**[35] 2055 3-9-0 109 .... CO'Donoghue 1 101
(A P O'Brien, Ire) *towards rr: thrght: no imp u.p st* **12/1**

11 3/4 **Monsieur Henri (USA)**[18] 2562 3-9-0 79 .... NGMcCullagh 13 100?
(J C Hayden, Ire) *towards rr: no imp u.p fr wl bef st* **400/1**

12 2 1/2 **Cougar Bay (IRE)**[22] 2471 3-9-0 103 ....(b) WMLordan 3 96
(David Wachman, Ire) *mid-div: clsr in 4th appr st: sn no imp u.p* **28/1**

13 20 **Land Before Time (IRE)**[32] 2153 3-9-0 78 .... RMBurke 6 64
(R J Osborne, Ire) *cl up: plld hrd: rdn over 4f out: sn lost pl and wknd* **200/1**

2m 29.7s **Going Correction** -0.375s/f (Firm) **13** Ran SP% **112.8**
Speed ratings: 115,112,111,110,110 110,110,109,106,105 105,103,90
CSF £25.91 TOTE £3.70: £1.80, £1.60, £4.80; DF 27.00.
Owner Mrs John Magnier **Bred** Tower Bloodstock **Trained** Ballydoyle, Co Tipperary
■ Aidan O'Brien's fourth Irish Derby and Kieren Fallon's second.

FOCUS
A solid renewal in which the Epsom form put that of the Prix du Jockey Club in the shade, with three of the Epsom runners reaching the first four, the Chantilly winner only fifth, and the Chantilly runner-up a disappointing eighth. The race has primarily been rated around the third, sixth and seventh.

NOTEBOOK
Dylan Thomas(IRE), involved in a dramatic finish at Epsom, produced a performance of stunning authority to leave a strong field for dead in a Classic that ties together the form of the three other major European Derbys that prefaced it. The narrowness of the margins in the Vodafone Derby left many questions unanswered, but Dylan Thomas rose to the occasion in tremendous fashion. Several factors contributed to this triumph, and first and foremost it was a big help that Kieren Fallon was able to ride him with more restraint than had been the case at Epsom, where the shape of the race committed Johnny Murtagh a long way from home. However, Fallon was categorical that going right-handed at a more orthodox track made the essential difference. Stamina is clearly no longer an issue in regard to the colt, but his trainer indicated that he would not be averse to bringing him back to ten furlongs to contest the Irish Champion Stakes. (op 9/2 tchd 5/1)
Gentlewave(IRE), wide-margin winner of the Italian Derby and supplemented for this for 100,000 euros, confirmed that he gets the trip really well. Having had three behind him on the approach to the straight, he was still only sixth over a furlong out before responding resolutely in the closing stages. A line of form involving Numide had indicated that the principals from the Prix du Jockey Club might prove too strong for him, but that was misleading. The reduced distance of the French Classic is a factor that perhaps should have been given greater attention in pre-race assessments. (op 5/1 tchd 6/1)
Best Alibi(IRE) did his bit for Epsom form with an honest display to take third place. No match for Septimus in the Dante, he had looked very much unsuited by the Epsom track before staying on to finish a close-up sixth. A son of King's Best, whose career ended in this race, he is developing into a high-class performer and a drop back to ten furlongs could pay dividends. (op 8/1)
Dragon Dancer failed to settle effectively, which damaged his chance, and he performed quite creditably in the circumstances without confirming Epsom running with Dylan Thomas. The tag of best maiden in training is a millstone that he deserves to lose. (op 6/1)
Darsi(FR) was a supplementary entry after landing the Prix du Jockey Club. He might have run a bit flat, but his jockey offered no excuses, and it looks as if the French version may not have been up to scratch, a view endorsed by Best Name's inability to impose his presence. (op 9/2)
Mountain(IRE), eighth at Epsom, managed a couple of places better this time and might have been just a bit closer but for meeting interference inside the last furlong. Second to Dylan Thomas in the Derrinstown Stud Derby Trial, he has enough ability to pick up a Group 3 race. (op 12/1)
Heliostatic(IRE), stepping up to a mile and a half for the first time, took over in the lead after less than half a mile had been covered and made an early bid for glory before the straight. It looked as if he simply did not stay, and a return to ten furlongs would seem to be the logical next step.
Best Name, who finished a bit further behind Darsi than he had at Chantilly, might not have seen out this longer trip. (op 11/2)
Classic Punch(IRE), winner of a maiden last time, was unable to handle the step up in class. (op 20/1)
Puerto Rico(IRE), back up in trip, failed to build on the promise of his Gallinule victory.

3128a ARTHUR GUINNESS EUROPEAN BREEDERS FUND H'CAP (PREMIER HANDICAP) 1m 4f
4:35 (4:37) 3-Y-O+ **£35,917** (£10,537; £5,020; £1,710)

RPR

1 **Telemachus**[2] 3058 6-8-10 84 5ex ....(b) JohnEgan 16 94
(Noel Meade, Ire) *mid-div: 9th appr st: rdn and clsd fr under 2f out: 2nd on inner fr 1f out: sn led: styd on wl* **11/2**[1]

2 nk **The Last Hurrah (IRE)**[67] 5929 6-8-11 85 ....(b) TPO'Shea 1 95
(Mrs John Harrington, Ire) *chsd ldrs: 7th appr st: 3rd under 2f out: rdn to chal and ld over 1f out: hdd and kpt on same pce ins fnl f* **16/1**

3 1 1/2 **Day To Remember**[37] 1992 5-9-3 91 ....(t) KFallon 4 98
(E F Vaughan) *mid-div: 8th appr st: rdn to chal in 4th fr under 2f out: 3rd and kpt on same pce u.p fr 1f out* **8/1**[3]

4 2 **Dashing Home (IRE)**[8] 2886 7-9-3 91 .... DPMcDonogh 14 95
(Noel Meade, Ire) *led: rdn clr early st: sn reduced ld: strly pressed and hdd over 1f out: sn no imp: kpt on same pce u.p* **14/1**

5 3/4 **Visit Wexford (IRE)**[11] 2769 5-8-12 86 ....(b) PJSmullen 9 89
(John E Kiely, Ire) *mid-div: 11th bef 1/2-way: rdn in 8th over 1f out: kpt on wout threatening* **9/1**

6 shd **The God Of Love (USA)**[32] 2155 3-8-4 91 .... NGMcCullagh 11 94
(G M Lyons, Ire) *chsd ldrs: 6th appr st: no imp u.p and kpt on same pce fr over 1f out* **10/1**

7 3/4 **Princess Nala (IRE)**[35] 2056 4-9-7 95 .... JMurtagh 8 97
(M Halford, Ire) *trckd ldrs: rdn to chal fr 2f out: no imp and kpt on same pce fr over 1f out* **11/2**[1]

8 nk **Davorin (JPN)**[22] 2471 5-9-5 93 .... KJManning 6 94+
(R P Burns, Ire) *trckd ldrs: 5th appr st: rdn to chal under 2f out: hmpd 1f out: sn no ex* **16/1**

9 1 1/2 **Uva Fragola**[14] 2690 3-7-13 91 .... DJMoran(5) 15 90
(J S Bolger, Ire) *chsd ldrs: 4th appr st: no imp u.p and kpt on same pce fr 1 1/2f out* **11/1**

10 2 **Mutadarek**[36] 2042 5-8-5 82 .... RPCleary(3) 2 78
(Eoin Griffin, Ire) *dwlt: towards rr: no imp u.p and kpt on same pce st* **12/1**

11 shd **Artistic Lad**[259] 5414 6-9-1 89 .... JAHeffernan 7 85
(Mrs John Harrington, Ire) *towards rr: no imp u.p st* **33/1**

12 hd **Emmpat (IRE)**[21] 2488 8-8-12 86 .... FMBerry 12 82
(C F Swan, Ire) *s.i.s: towards rr: sme prog appr st: sn no imp u.p* **13/2**[2]

13 2 1/2 **Gift Range (IRE)**[46] 1785 4-9-13 101 .... MJKinane 3 93
(John M Oxx, Ire) *prom: mainly 2nd: rdn in 3rd appr st: sn no ex* **12/1**

14 1 **Articulation**[67] 1019 5-8-8 82 ....(p) WMLordan 10 73
(C Byrnes, Ire) *rr of mid-div best: no imp u.p st* **16/1**

15 10 **Fire Finch**[9] 2841 5-8-1 78 ....(tp) CDHayes(3) 5 54
(T Hogan, Ire) *mid-div: towards rr and no ex u.p fr over 2f out* **25/1**

2m 32.0s **Going Correction** -0.375s/f (Firm)
WFA 3 from 4yo+ 13lb **16** Ran SP% **129.1**
Speed ratings: 108,107,106,105,104 104,104,104,103,101 101,101,100,99,92
CSF £101.08 CT £729.15 TOTE £7.20: £2.60, £7.90, £2.30; DF 173.50.
Owner A J Kerr **Bred** Cheveley Park Stud Ltd **Trained** Castletown, Co Meath
■ Stewards' Enquiry : T P O'Shea three-day ban: careless riding (Jul 11-13)

NOTEBOOK
Day To Remember, 8lb higher than when scoring at Newmarket 37 days previously, emerged from off the pace to have his chance and ran again very close to his recent level. He ideally needs an easier surface. (op 7/1)

3129a NETJETS CELEBRATION STKS (LISTED RACE) 1m
5:10 (5:11) 3-Y-O+ **£44,896** (£13,172; £6,275; £2,137)

RPR

1 **Mustameet (USA)**[25] 2371 5-9-12 111 .... DPMcDonogh 4 121+
(Kevin Prendergast, Ire) *chsd ldrs: 6th bef st: prog travelling wl into 4th under 2f out: rdn to chal and ld over 1f out: sn clr: styd on wl: comf* **9/2**[2]

2 4 **Arch Rebel (USA)**[49] 1711 5-9-12 110 .... FMBerry 6 111
(Noel Meade, Ire) *mid-div: pushed along in 5th appr st: rdn to chal in 6th over 1f out: kpt on into 2nd wout troubling wnr fnl f* **6/1**

3 nk **Albertinelli (IRE)**[15] [2666] 3-9-0 .... JAHeffernan 2 105
(A P O'Brien, Ire) *trckd ldr in 2nd: rdn to chal st: no imp and kpt on same pce fnl f* **8/1**

4 nk **Golden Arrow (IRE)**[36] [2039] 3-9-0 108........ (b) PJSmullen 3 105
(D K Weld, Ire) *trckd ldr in 3rd: rdn to chal fr 2f out: no imp and kpt on same pce fr over 1f out* **10/3**[1]

5 nk **An Tadh (IRE)**[18] [2559] 3-9-5 107........ JMurtagh 7 109
(G M Lyons, Ire) *led: strly pressed fr 2f out: hdd over 1f out: sn no ex: kpt on same pce* **11/2**[3]

6 nk **Abigail Pett**[35] [2054] 3-9-2 108........ (b) KJManning 1 105
(J S Bolger, Ire) *dwlt: towards rr: rdn in cl 7th over 1f out: no imp and kpt on same pce fnl f* **8/1**

7 nk **Akimbo (USA)**[12] [2722] 5-9-9 104........ RMBurke 8 105
(James Leavy, Ire) *dwlt: towards rr: no imp u.p and kpt on same pce fr under 2f out* **25/1**

8 3 **Arabian Prince (USA)**[12] [2721] 3-9-0 101........ KFallon 9 96
(A P O'Brien, Ire) *trckd ldrs: pushed along in 4th appr st: attempted to chal and nt clr run fr over 1f out: sn eased* **8/1**

9 5 **Elusive Double (IRE)**[252] [6048] 4-9-9 94........ MJKinane 5 86
(Daniel William O'Sullivan, Ire) *towards rr thrght: bhd and no ex u.p fr 2f out* **40/1**

1m 36.2s **Going Correction** -0.375s/f (Firm)
WFA 3 from 4yo+ 9lb **10** Ran SP% **110.5**
Speed ratings: 114,110,109,109,109 108,108,105,100
CSF £29.46 TOTE £3.50: £1.50, £2.70, £2.50; DF 23.20.
Owner Hamdan Al Maktoum **Bred** Shadwell Farm LLC **Trained** Friarstown, Co Kildare

NOTEBOOK
Mustameet(USA), who beat Chelsea Rose at Leopardstown last time, came right away from his rivals in the final furlong to score in great fashion. This was his third success at this level from his last four outings, it must be rated as a personal-best effort, and he is evidently still on an upwards curve. He certainly deserves another crack at Group company now. (op 4/1)
Arch Rebel(USA) was firmly put in his place by the winner this time, yet still ran close to his official rating in defeat. He has done little wrong since returning from his spell over hurdles and ideally requires a softer surface. (op 4/1)
Albertinelli(IRE), unbeaten in two previous outings, stuck to his task under pressure and left the impression he may need a stiffer test. He is an imposing colt, enjoys a quick surface, and remains progressive. (op 7/1)
Golden Arrow(IRE), very well backed, had finished behind Arafaa in the 2000 Guineas on heavy ground last time. He never really threatened on this return to quicker ground is just struggling to find his form at present. (op 9/2)
Arabian Prince(USA) was tight for room at various stages in the home straight and is better than his finishing position suggests. He is proving hard to catch right, however. (op 7/1)

3130 - (Foreign Racing) - See Raceform Interactive

[2692] COLOGNE (R-H)

Sunday, July 2

OFFICIAL GOING: Good

3131a OPPENHEIM-UNION-RENNEN (GROUP 2) 1m 3f
4:10 (4:20) 3-Y-O **£41,379** (£15,862; £8,276; £3,448)

RPR

1 **Aspectus (IRE)**[28] [2278] 3-9-2 .... AStarke 4 108
(H Blume, Germany) *first to show, settled in 3rd to straight, led over 2f out, ridden 1f out, ran on well* **34/10**[2]

2 1 **Lauro (GER)**[32] [2158] 3-9-2 .... WMongil 5 106
(P Schiergen, Germany) *tracked leader, 2nd straight, every chance over 1f out, ran on same pace* **3/5**[1]

3 4 1/2 **Oriental Tiger (GER)**[27] [2314] 3-9-2 .... ABoschert 6 99
(U Ostmann, Germany) *raced in 4th to straight, kept on one pace final 2f* **21/2**

4 3 **Imonso (GER)**[27] [2314] 3-9-2 .... ASuborics 1 94
(P Schiergen, Germany) *raced in 5th to straight, never able to challenge* **46/10**[3]

5 1 **Dwilano (GER)**[17] 3-9-2 .... AHelfenbein 2 93
(P Remmert, Germany) *6th straight, ridden over 2f out, reached 4th 2f out, one pace* **15/1**

6 3 **Sommertag (GER)**[27] [2314] 3-9-2 .... (b) THellier 3 88
(P Schiergen, Germany) *last to straight, always behind* **12/1**

7 10 **Lucky Galic (GER)** 3-9-2 .... (b) ADeVries 7 72
(A Trybuhl, Germany) *led after 1f, headed over 2f out, soon weakened* **22/1**

2m 13.92s **7** Ran SP% **130.1**
(including 10 euro stakes): WIN 44; PL 13, 11, 15; SF 65.
Owner Gestut Rottgen **Bred** Gestut Roettgen **Trained** Germany

[1789] MAISONS-LAFFITTE (R-H)

Sunday, July 2

OFFICIAL GOING: Good

3132a PRIX DU BOIS (GROUP 3) 5f
2:50 (2:51) 2-Y-O **£27,586** (£11,034; £8,276; £5,517; £2,759)

RPR

1 **Sandwaki (USA)**[17] [2596] 2-8-11 .... OPeslier 2 106
(C Laffon-Parias, France) *made all, pushed out, ran on well* **3/5**[1]

2 1 1/2 **Boccassini (GER)**[35] [2060] 2-8-8 .... JVictoire 4 98
(M Rulec, Germany) *held up, headway to go 3rd 1f out, kept on under pressure to take 2nd close home* **16/1**

3 nk **Palin**[37] 2-8-11 .... FBranca 5 100
(F Folco, Italy) *disputed 3rd on outside, went 2nd 1f out, soon ridden, rider hit over hand by jockey of 2nd & lost his whip close home* **11/1**

4 1 **Take Blood (FR)**[17] [2596] 2-8-8 .... TJarnet 1 93
(Mlle S-V Tarrou, France) *tracked winner on rails, ridden & one pace from over 1f out* **16/1**

5 snk **Poltava (FR)**[17] [2596] 2-8-8 .... DBoeuf 6 92
(D Smaga, France) *reluctant to load, held up in rear, hard ridden & disputed 4th final f, never nearer* **81/10**[3]

6 1 **Magic America (USA)**[45] 2-8-8 .... (b) SPasquier 3 89
(Mme C Head-Maarek, France) *chased winner, ridden well over 1f out, weakened quickly 1f out* **26/10**[2]

59.80 secs **6** Ran SP% **121.4**
PARI-MUTUEL: WIN 1.60; PL 1.20, 3.90; SF 18.10.
Owner Wertheimer Et Frere **Bred** *unknown **Trained** Chantilly, France

NOTEBOOK
Sandwaki(USA), always at the head of affairs, set a fair pace before accelerating away from his rivals one and a half furlongs out. He was always in control and ran out an easy winner.
Boccassini(GER), held up in fifth position, made his move at the furlong marker where he progressed up the inside to take second place.
Palin was settled in fourth until produced at the furlong pole. He moved into second place, but in the final 100 yards the jockey lost his whip and he was caught by the eventual second.
Take Blood(FR), who tracked the eventual winner on the inside rail, was hard ridden at the furlong pole where he stayed on at one pace.

3133a PRIX CHLOE (GROUP 3) (FILLIES) 1m 1f
3:25 (3:25) 3-Y-O **£27,586** (£11,034; £8,276; £5,517; £2,759)

RPR

1 **Sexy Lady (GER)**[36] [2059] 3-8-11 .... TMundry 5 106
(P Rau, Germany) *held up, in rear til over 1f out, ridden & ran on to take 2nd inside final f, fin 2nd, 1½l: awrdd r* **99/10**

2 3 **Grigorieva (IRE)**[20] [2516] 3-8-11 .... MSautjeau 2 103
(A Fabre, France) *held up in rear, last 2f out, headway under strong press on outside to take 3rd close home, fin 3rd, 1½l & 1½l plcd 2nd* **36/10**[3]

3 1 1/2 **Summer's Eve**[38] [1955] 3-8-11 .... DaneO'Neill 1 100
(H Candy) *always in touch, challenged over 1f out, every chance when squeezed up just inside final f, no extra, fin 4th, plcd 3rd* **16/1**

4 1 1/2 **Heaven's Cause (USA)**[21] [2491] 3-8-11 .... TThulliez 4 97
(N Clement, France) *tracked leaders, one pace final 2f, fin 5th, plcd 4th* **7/2**[2]

5 1/2 **Galma (FR)**[20] [2516] 3-8-11 .... SPasquier 3 96
(E Lellouche, France) *a prom, led over 2f out to appr fnl f, still ev ch whn squeezed up just ins fnl f, eased, fin 6th, plcd 5th* **10/1**

6 2 **Private Dancer (FR)**[25] [2374] 3-8-11 .... DBonilla 8 92
(Y De Nicolay, France) *set slow pace to half-way, behind final 2f, fin 7th, plcd 6th* **18/1**

7 snk **Karavel (GER)**[28] [2279] 3-8-11 .... OPeslier 7 92
(P Schiergen, Germany) *led half-way to over 2f out, disputing 2nd on rails when badly hampered just inside final f, eased, fin 8th, plcd 7th* **22/10**[1]

D **Mandesha (FR)**[19] [2537] 3-8-11 .... DBoeuf 6 109
(A De Royer-Dupre, France) *hld up in rr on outside, pulling hard early, qcknd to ld over 1f out, edged left jst ins fnl f, ran on wl, fin 1st, 1½l: disq* **48/10**

1m 54.7s **8** Ran SP% **121.9**
PARI-MUTUEL: WIN 10.90; PL 3.10, 1.70, 3.80; DF 17.00.
Owner Gestut Ittlingen **Bred** Gestut Hof Ittlingen **Trained** Germany

NOTEBOOK
Sexy Lady(GER) was held up in the rear until over a furlong out where she was asked to quicken. She produced a good effort, but was overpowered by Mandesha and was not able to quicken. She was lucky to be awarded the race in the Stewards' room.
Grigorieva(IRE) raced in last position until two furlongs out where she made her move up the outside under strong pressure. She showed good acceleration and battled on to take third place, but was later awarded second.
Summer's Eve, held up mid division in a slowly run race, was switched to the outside and made her challenge a furlong out, but was then hampered by Mandesha. She found nothing more and stayed on one pace to take fourth before being awarded third in the Stewards' room
Heaven's Cause(USA) soon in a prominent position, the slow pace did not do her any favours and when the pace quickened one and a half furlongs out she could only stay on one pace.
Mandesha(FR) was held up in the rear on the outside where she took a fierce hold. When asked to make her move, she quickened up to join the leaders and subsequently drifted towards the rail, impeding the run of the favourite Karavel. She was unlucky to lose the race in the Stewards room.

[3109] HOLLYWOOD PARK (L-H)

Sunday, July 2

OFFICIAL GOING: Turf course - firm; dirt course - fast

3134a TRIPLE BEND INVITATIONAL H'CAP (GRADE 1) (DIRT) 7f
12:21 (12:48) 3-Y-O+ **£104,651** (£34,884; £20,930; £10,465; £3,488)

RPR

1 **Siren Lure (USA)**[50] 5-8-9 .... ASolis 6 123
(Art Sherman, U.S.A) **33/10**[2]

2 1 1/2 **Battle Won (USA)**[57] 6-8-3 .... VEspinoza 5 113
(M Mitchell, U.S.A) **42/10**

3 1 **Unfurl The Flag (USA)**[274] 6-8-4 .... JKCourt 7 111
(D Bernstein, U.S.A) **71/10**

4 2 1/4 **Publication (USA)**[792] 7-8-6 .... (b) DFlores 3 108
(V Cerin, U.S.A) **39/10**[3]

5 1 1/2 **Areyoutalkintome (USA)**[28] 5-8-4 .... (b) DCohen 1 102
(Doug O'Neill, U.S.A) **122/10**

6 4 **Vortex**[12] [2722] 7-8-3 .... (b) TBaze 9 90
(Miss Gay Kelleway) *held up towards outside, effort over 2f out, driven and 5th straight, unable to quicken* **27/1**

7 hd **Seattle Buddy (USA)**[71] 4-8-1 .... (b) JOchoa 10 88
(George P Frousiakis, U.S.A) **337/10**

8 1 1/4 **Prorunner (USA)**[22] 4-8-1 .... GKGomez 8 84
(Molly Pearson, U.S.A) **239/10**

9 2 1/2 **Trickey Trevor (USA)**[28] 7-8-7 .... RBaze 4 84
(J Hollendorfer, U.S.A) **31/10**[1]

10 5 3/4 **Thunder Touch (USA)**[22] 5-8-0 .... NArroyoJr 2 62
(V Cerin, U.S.A) **556/10**

1m 21.29s **10** Ran SP% **119.4**
PARI-MUTUEL: WIN 8.60; PL (1-2) 4.00, 5.80; SHOW (1-2-3) 3.20, 4.00,5.80; SF 55.60.
Owner Stuart Kesselman, Tony & Marilyn Melkonian **Bred** Desperado Stables **Trained** USA

NOTEBOOK
Vortex ran a solid race, and looked like he might make the frame when moving up from the rear to go fifth over a furlong out, but his effort petered out in the closing stages.

2922 MUSSELBURGH (R-H)
Monday, July 3

OFFICIAL GOING: Good (good to soft in places)
Wind: Virtually nil

3135 BOLLINGER CHAMPAGNE CHALLENGE SERIES H'CAP (FOR GENTLEMAN AMATEUR RIDERS) 2m
6:55 (6:56) (Class 6) (0-55,52) 4-Y-0+ £3,123 (£968; £484; £242) Stalls Low

Form RPR
40-5 1 **Ostfanni (IRE)**[11] 2196 6-11-5 52 CJCallow(5) 9 71
(M Todhunter) *hld up towards rr: hdwy 5f out: chsd ldrs 3f out: styd on to ld appr last: sn wl clr* 9/2[1]
-005 2 14 **Bolshoi Ballet**[7] 2935 8-10-12 45 (v) MrBMcHugh(5) 5 47
(R A Fahey) *midfield: pushed along 1/2-way: rdn over 4f out: styd on fnl 2f: too 2nd ins last: no ch w wnr* 22/1
4406 3 1 1/4 **Transit**[9] 2871 7-11-7 52 (p) MrDEngland(3) 12 53
(B Ellison) *in tch: hdwyu to chse ldrs over 5f out: rdn along to chse ldr over 2f out: sn drvn and kpt on same pce* 7/1[3]
-120 4 3 **Smart Boy Prince (IRE)**[33] 1766 5-10-13 46 MrMJJSmith(5) 2 43
(C Smith) *cl up: led after 7f: hdd 7f out: rdn along over 4f out: drvn and plugged on same pce fr over 2f out* 6/1[2]
0026 5 3 **Mary Gray**[7] 2927 4-11-4 46 (v) MrWHogg 10 39
(M Johnston) *trckd ldng pair: hdwy to ld 7f out: pushed clr 5f out: rdn 3f out: sn drvn: hdd & wknd qckly over 1f out* 9/2[1]
000/ 6 6 **Kings Square**[51] 5229 6-10-7 40 TjadeCollier(5) 1 26
(M W Easterby) *hld up: hdwy and in tch over 5f out: rdn along wl over 3f out: sn no imp* 25/1
6-03 7 7 **Rouge Et Noir**[20] 2528 8-11-3 50 MrDHutchison(5) 11 28
(P Monteith) *in tch: hdwy to chse ldng pair 7f out: rdn along to chse clr ldr 4f out: wknd wl over 2f out* 12/1
0/30 8 5 **Copplestone (IRE)**[10] 2812 10-10-8 43 (p) MrCWhillans(7) 3 15
(A C Whillans) *led 7f: rdn along over 7f out and sn wknd* 20/1
-424 9 4 **Teutonic (IRE)**[35] 1883 5-10-8 43 MrGGilbertson(7) 4 10
(R F Fisher) *v.s.a: a bhd* 10/1
05-6 10 1 1/2 **Acca Larentia (IRE)**[12] 2751 5-9-12 33 oh2 ow1 (p) MrCMcGaffin(7) 6 —
(Mrs H O Graham) *chsd ldrs: rdn along over 7f out: sn wknd* 100/1
020- 11 7 **Court One**[8] 2317 8-10-12 40 MrSDobson 7 —
(R E Barr) *s.i.s and bhd: hdwy and in tch 1/2-way: rdn along over 3f out and sn wknd* 7/1[3]
0-06 12 11 **Minivet**[8] 1436 11-10-9 42 MrSFMagee(5) 8 —
(R Allan) *a rr* 20/1

3m 36.11s (2.21) **Going Correction** +0.05s/f (Good) 12 Ran SP% 111.1
Speed ratings (Par 101):96,89,88,86,85 82,78,76,74,73 70,64
CSF £107.32 CT £657.79 TOTE £7.20: £1.90, £5.30, £3.20; EX 123.40.
Owner Ian Hall Racing **Bred** Mrs Brigitte Schlueter **Trained** Orton, Cumbria
■ The first Flat winner for Chris Callow.

FOCUS
A modest staying handicap, run at a strong pace. Winning hurdler Ostfanni relished every yard of the trip and came home alone. The second and third ran to form.
Rouge Et Noir Official explanation: jockey said gelding lost right fore shoe

3136 WILKINSON CORR NURSERY 5f
7:25 (7:25) (Class 4) 2-Y-0 £5,181 (£1,541; £770; £384) Stalls Low

Form RPR
6431 1 **Top Tier**[7] 2922 2-8-12 62 7ex RobbieFitzpatrick 3 60
(Peter Grayson) *keen: in tch: swtchd rt and hdwy over 1f out: rdn to ld ins last: kpt on wl* 12/1
2111 2 1 **Granny Peel (IRE)**[19] 2538 2-9-3 67 PaulFessey 5 61
(K A Ryan) *cl up: effrt 2f out: sn rdn and ev ch tl drvn and no ex wl ins last* 7/2[2]
0421 3 1/2 **The Mighty Ogmore**[23] 2451 2-8-11 66 NataliaGemelova(5) 1 59
(R C Guest) *dwlt: in tyouch and pushed along 1/2-way: rdn wl over 1f out: styd on ins last: nrst fin* 6/1
3105 4 hd **Stir Crazy (IRE)**[1] 3117 2-9-7 71 J-PGuillambert 2 63
(M R Channon) *chased ldng pair: pushed along and sltly outrpced 1/2-way: kpt on u.p ins last* 3/1[1]
3311 5 shd **Emma Told Lies**[13] 2731 2-8-10 60 PaulMulrennan 4 52
(M W Easterby) *led: rdn along 2f out: drvn and hdd ins last: kpt on same pce* 4/1[3]
610 6 hd **Major Third (IRE)**[35] 2076 2-9-6 70 DavidAllan 6 61
(T D Easterby) *trckd ldrs: hdwy 2f out: sn rdn and ev ch ent last: sn drvn and kpt on same pce* 13/2
0002 7 6 **Emergency Services**[42] 1876 2-8-2 57 (b[1]) JamesDoyle(5) 7 26
(Tom Dascombe) *sn rdn along and outpcd: a rr* 10/1

61.24 secs (0.74) **Going Correction** +0.05s/f (Good) 7 Ran SP% 111.6
Speed ratings (Par 96):96,94,93,93,93 92,83
CSF £50.96 TOTE £15.10: £6.40, £1.50; EX 58.10.
Owner Bernard Bargh, Jeff Hamer, Steve Henshaw **Bred** B Bargh **Trained** Formby, Lancs

FOCUS
A competitive nursery, but four of the first five home had been doing their winning in claiming/selling company and the form looks nothing special, if sound enough. The official ratings shown next to each horse are estimated and for information purposes only.

NOTEBOOK
Top Tier, winner of a seller at this course last week, handled the step back up in grade and made a successful nursery debut, this time being ridden with a little more restraint and coming with a strong late run. Ultimately a cosy winner, she looks progressive and should have every chance of completing a hat-trick. (op 9-1)
Granny Peel(IRE), on a four-timer following three comfortable wins in claiming company, came through to have every chance inside the final quarter-mile, but she lacked the winner's finishing kick. She is clearly up to winning a nursery. (op 3-1)
The Mighty Ogmore, retained for 12,000gns after winning a seller here last month, kept on having been outpaced and shaped very much like a filly who needs a sixth furlong. (op 5-1)
Stir Crazy(IRE), a close-up fifth at Windsor 24 hours earlier, was again doing his best work late and the drop back down to five furlongs ultimately proved against him. (tchd 7-2)
Emma Told Lies, a dual winner in six-furlong sellers last month, was made plenty of use of on this return to five furlongs and had the rail to race against, but she was in trouble over a furlong out and ultimately dropped away. (op 11-2 tchd 6-1 in a place)
Major Third(IRE) could have done without the rain and really looks in need of further. (op 15-2 tchd 8-1)
Emergency Services was always struggling to go the gallop, the first-time blinkers evidently failing to make a difference. (op 12-1)

3137 RACING UK CHANNEL 432 H'CAP 7f 30y
7:55 (7:56) (Class 6) (0-65,63) 3-Y-0+ £3,238 (£963; £481; £240) Stalls Low

Form RPR
00-2 1 **Pay Time**[9] 2874 7-8-10 46 DonnaCaldwell(7) 9 56
(R E Barr) *sn led: rdn along over 2f out: hung lft wl over 1f out: styd on wl towards fin* 9/1
0604 2 nk **Second Reef**[7] 2926 4-9-8 51 DavidAllan 3 60
(E J Alston) *hld up and bhd: gd hdwy on inner 3f out: rdn over 1f out and sn ev ch: drvn ins last and kpt on* 4/1[1]
6-00 3 nk **Prospect Court**[10] 2811 4-9-4 47 PaulFessey 4 55
(A C Whillans) *a.p: rdn along on inner over 2f out: drvn over 1f out and ev ch tl no ex wl ins last* 12/1
-055 4 1/2 **Final Tune (IRE)**[24] 2399 3-9-9 63 SilvestreDeSousa(3) 11 67
(D Nicholls) *hld up towards rr: hdwy on outer wl over 2f out: rdn to chse ldrs over 1f out: kpt on ins last: nrst fin* 9/2[2]
4-61 5 3 **Paddywack (IRE)**[6] 2949 9-9-2 45 (b) PaulQuinn 7 44
(D W Chapman) *towards rr: hdwy 3f out: rdn over 2f out: drvn and no imp fr wl over 1f out* 5/1[3]
/260 6 3 **Whittinghamvillage**[12] 2747 5-10-0 57 PatCosgrave 2 48
(D W Whillans) *chsd ldrs: rdn along 3f out: kpt on same pce fnl 2f* 9/1
5250 7 3/4 **Linden's Lady**[14] 2697 6-9-6 54 (v) JamesDoyle(5) 1 43
(J R Weymes) *chsd ldrs on outer: rdn along 3f out: sn wknd* 13/2
6-05 8 3 1/2 **Frimley's Mattery**[9] 2874 6-9-2 45 RobbieFitzpatrick 10 25
(R E Barr) *chsd ldrs: rdn wl over 2f out: sn drvn and wknd* 8/1
000- 9 4 **Troodos Jet**[40] 4824 5-8-10 42 BenSwarbrick(3) 8 12
(K W Hogg) *chsd ldrs to 1/2-way: sn wknd* 33/1
00-0 10 3 1/2 **Cut Glass**[33] 2146 3-9-9 60 J-PGuillambert 6 18
(C E Brittain) *prominet: rdn along over 3f out and sn wknd* 16/1
00-0 11 31 **Wood Dalling (USA)**[52] 1637 8-8-12 41 PaulMulrennan 5 —
(Mrs J C McGregor) *a rr* 66/1

1m 29.72s (-0.22) **Going Correction** +0.05s/f (Good)
WFA 3 from 4yo+ 8lb 11 Ran SP% 117.3
Speed ratings (Par 101):103,102,102,101,98 94,94,90,85,81 46
CSF £44.78 CT £448.58 TOTE £8.90: £1.70, £2.10, £3.50; EX 54.70.
Owner Mrs R E Barr **Bred** M Paver And M D M Racing Thoroughbreds Ltd **Trained** Seamer, N Yorks

FOCUS
A modest handicap, but solid form which looks reliable for the grade.

3138 WILKINSONCORR.COM H'CAP 7f 30y
8:25 (8:25) (Class 6) (0-60,65) 3-Y-0 £3,071 (£906; £453) Stalls Low

Form RPR
6346 1 **Drink To Me Only**[9] 2873 3-8-9 48 PaulHanagan 11 56
(J R Weymes) *dwlt: sn in midfield: hdwy on inner over 2f out: rdn over 1f out: sn drvn and styd on to ld last 50 yds* 13/2[3]
6441 2 hd **Esoterica (IRE)**[7] 2923 3-9-12 65 6ex (b) PaulFessey 4 72
(T D Barron) *trckd ldrs: hdwy over 2f out: rdn to ld ent last: sn drvn: hdd and no ex last 50 yds* 2/1[1]
5-65 3 3 **Myths And Verses**[26] 2353 3-9-1 59 JamesDoyle(5) 8 59
(K A Ryan) *chsd ldrs: hdwy over 2f out: sn rdn: drvn over 1f out: kpt on same pce* 13/2[3]
0504 4 1/2 **Joking John**[4] 3006 3-8-2 41 oh2 PaulQuinn 1 39
(C W Fairhurst) *midfield: hdwy on outer over 2f out: rdn and ch whn edgd rt over 1f out: styd on u.p ins last* 8/1
6-00 5 2 **Bold Tiger (IRE)**[58] 1497 3-9-0 53 GylesParkin 12 46
(Miss Tracy Waggott) *sn led: rdn along over 2f out: drvn and edgd lft over 1f out: hdd ent last and sn wknd* 33/1
-266 6 2 1/2 **Mandarin Rocket (IRE)**[7] 2923 3-9-7 60 DavidAllan 6 47
(Miss L A Perratt) *bhd: hdwy over 2f out: styd on appr last: nrst fin* 8/1
00-0 7 nk **Silver Sail**[14] 2699 3-8-7 46 NeilPollard 5 32
(J S Wainwright) *in tch: hdwy 3f out: sn rdn and kpt on same pce fnl 2f* 50/1
0260 8 2 **Almowj**[16] 2645 3-9-1 54 J-PGuillambert 3 35
(C E Brittain) *a towards rr* 11/2[2]
0-40 9 nk **Thornton Princess**[11] 2782 3-8-10 49 PaulMulrennan 9 29
(B S Rothwell) *prom: rdn along 3f out: wknd over 2f out* 16/1
60-0 10 1 3/4 **Fadansil**[27] 2325 3-8-13 52 PatCosgrave 7 27
(J Wade) *sn rdn along: a towards rr* 16/1
0-00 11 17 **Eldon Outlaw**[28] 2285 3-8-7 46 ow1 RobbieFitzpatrick 2 —
(B Storey) *cl up: rdn along 1/2-way: sn wknd* 50/1

1m 30.21s (0.27) **Going Correction** +0.05s/f (Good) 11 Ran SP% 116.2
Speed ratings (Par 98):100,99,96,95,93 90,90,88,87,85 66
CSF £19.38 CT £89.45 TOTE £8.90: £2.00, £1.10, £2.70; EX 35.10.
Owner Lovely Bubbly Racing **Bred** Mrs Deborah O'Brien **Trained** Middleham Moor, N Yorks

FOCUS
The front two pulled three lengths clear in what was a pretty ordinary handicap. The winner ran to his previous turf best.
Thornton Princess Official explanation: jockey said filly lost its action

3139 WATCH LIVE ON THEBETTINGSITE.CO.UK CLAIMING STKS 1m 1f
8:55 (8:56) (Class 5) 3-Y-0+ £3,238 (£963; £481; £240) Stalls Low

Form RPR
00/0 1 **Fremen (USA)**[27] 2323 6-9-11 82 SilvestreDeSousa(3) 11 75+
(D Nicholls) *trckd ldrs gng wl: smooth hdwy to ld 2f out: rdn clr appr last: comfortably* 5/1[3]
0065 2 7 **Burnley Al (IRE)**[58] 1480 4-9-8 57 (p) PaulHanagan 10 55
(R A Fahey) *led: rdn along and edgd lft over 2f out: sn hdd: drvn and one pce over 1f out* 7/2[2]
-444 3 3 **Ballyhurry (USA)**[22] 1455 9-9-10 67 TonyCulhane 7 51
(J S Goldie) *towards rr: hdwy 3f out: swtchd rt over 2f out: sn rdn and kpt on fnl f* 7/2[2]
-065 4 1 1/4 **Campbells Lad**[14] 2696 5-9-7 40 PaulFessey 3 45
(Mrs G S Rees) *prom: effrt to challenge 3f out and ev ch tl rdn 2f out and sn wknd* 33/1
0U3 5 1 1/2 **Luis Melendez (USA)**[23] 2455 4-9-7 67 (t) JamesDoyle(5) 8 47
(Tom Dascombe) *prom: rdn along over 3f out and sn btn* 3/1[1]
0206 6 2 1/2 **Eijaaz (IRE)**[10] 2832 5-9-0 49 KristinStubbs(7) 9 37
(Mrs L Stubbs) *dwlt: sn rdn along in rr: styd on fnl 2f: nvr a factor* 7/1
00-0 7 11 **Slavonic (USA)**[37] 2020 5-9-6 57 (p) RobbieFitzpatrick 5 14
(B Storey) *a rr* 11/1
0-06 8 1/2 **Cashema (IRE)**[40] 1530 5-9-3 36 (vt[1]) GylesParkin 4 10
(D R MacLeod) *cl up: rdn along over 3f out and sn wknd* 100/1
6/ 9 10 **Panfield Belle (IRE)**[726] 3635 5-9-2 PatCosgrave 6 —
(R Allan) *a rr* 66/1

The Form Book, Raceform Ltd, Compton, RG20 6NL

10 13 **Noble Tiger (IRE)**[8] 5-9-2 .... PaulMulrennan 2 —
(Mrs S C Bradburne) *a rr* **66/1**

1m 54.69s (-1.31) **Going Correction** +0.05s/f (Good) 10 Ran SP% **113.9**
Speed ratings (Par 103):107,100,98,97,95 93,83,83,74,62
CSF £22.07 TOTE £5.80: £1.70, £2.30, £1.10; EX 30.40.
Owner Miss C King Mrs A Seed Ms Finola Devaney **Bred** Flaxman Holdings Ltd **Trained** Sessay, N Yorks

FOCUS
The formerly very useful Fremen turned this ordinary claimer into a procession. His form rivals were not at their best.

3140 WILKINSON & CORR LTD "SPECIALISTS" H'CAP 1m 4f
9:25 (9:27) (Class 6) (0-55,55) 3-Y-0+ **£2,730** (£806; £403) **Stalls** High

Form RPR

6302 **1** **Sudden Impulse**[7] 2927 5-8-11 **41** .... SilvestreDeSousa(3) 10 55
(A D Brown) *in tch: hdwy over 4f out: led wl over 2f out: rdn and edgd rt wl over 1f out: styd on* **6/1**

00-6 **2** 2 **Alambic**[19] 2539 3-8-6 **46** .... J-PGuillambert 4 57
(Sir Mark Prescott) *a.p: led over 3f out: rdn and hdd wl over 2f out: sn drvn and kpt on same pce* **7/2**[2]

-031 **3** 5 **Kyle Of Lochalsh**[7] 2927 6-9-12 **53** 6ex......................... TonyCulhane 12 56
(J S Goldie) *midfield: hdwy over 3f out: rdn over 2f out: kpt on same pce* **3/1**[1]

0063 **4** nk **Nakwa (IRE)**[7] 2927 8-9-4 **45** .... DavidAllan 8 47
(E J Alston) *towards rr: hdwy over 2f out: sn rdn and styd on appr last: nrst fin* **6/1**

3541 **5** 4 **Rare Coincidence**[12] 2751 5-10-0 **55** ....(p) PaulMulrennan 3 51
(R F Fisher) *led: rdn along ov er 4f out: hdd over 3f out and sn wknd* **5/1**[3]

06-0 **6** hd **Kristiansand**[10] 2808 6-9-8 **54** .... PJMcDonald(5) 14 50
(P Monteith) *hld up: hdwy over 2f out: sn rdn: and no imp* **16/1**

000- **7** 4 **Monashee Grey (IRE)**[296] 5122 3-8-0 **40** .... PaulHanagan 2 29
(R A Fahey) *nvr bttr than midfield* **33/1**

0-00 **8** 8 **Safe Shot**[7] 2927 7-8-6 **38** oh3......................................(p) JamesDoyle(5) 6 14
(Mrs J C McGregor) *chsd ldr: rdn along over 4f out: sn wknd* **50/1**

6-06 **9** 5 **Starmix**[6] 2944 5-9-5 **46** ....(b) PaulFessey 7 14
(G A Harker) *a bhd* **50/1**

0-25 **10** 1 ½ **Bint Il Sultan (IRE)**[11] 2777 4-9-0 **41** .... RobbieFitzpatrick 11 7
(W M Brisbourne) *s.i.s: a bhd* **10/1**

4000 **11** 8 **Fardi (IRE)**[24] 2408 4-9-6 **50** .... BenSwarbrick(3) 1 —
(K W Hogg) *chsd ldrs: rdn along 1/2-way: wknd over 4f out* **50/1**

2m 38.83s (1.93) **Going Correction** +0.05s/f (Good)
WFA 3 from 4yo+ 13lb 11 Ran SP% **116.3**
Speed ratings (Par 101):95,93,90,90,87 87,84,79,76,75 69
CSF £26.47 CT £74.22 TOTE £8.60: £1.70, £1.70, £1.50; EX 38.70 Place 6 £81.96, Place 5 £34.15..
Owner Mrs S L Salt **Bred** Sagittarius Bloodstock Associates Ltd **Trained** Pickering, York
■ Alan Brown's first winner since resuming his training career.

FOCUS
A good test and the front two pulled clear in this modest handicap. Quite sound form overall.
T/Plt: £57.00 to a £1 stake. Pool: £53,297.65. 682.50 winning tickets. T/Qpdt: £6.30 to a £1 stake. Pool: £3,877.40. 454.30 winning tickets. JR

2890 PONTEFRACT (L-H)
Monday, July 3

OFFICIAL GOING: Good to firm
The running rail from the 6f bend to the winning post was again in place. After 7mm overnight rain the ground was described as 'genuine firm'.
Wind: Light; half-against Weather: Sunny and hot

3141 SOUTHDALE / CIRCA LADIES H'CAP (LADY AMATEUR RIDERS) 1m 2f 6y
2:15 (2:15) (Class 5) (0-70,70) 3-Y-0+ **£3,747** (£1,162; £580; £290) **Stalls** Low

Form RPR

5433 **1** **Silverhay**[16] 2640 5-10-9 **70** ....(p) MrsCBartley 1 79
(T D Barron) *w ldr: led 6f out: edgd rt 1f out: hld on towards fin* **9/2**[1]

6126 **2** ½ **Cormorant Wharf (IRE)**[23] 2455 6-10-1 **67** .... MissJPowell(5) 10 75
(G L Moore) *swtchd lft after s: hld up in rr: hdwy on outside over 4f out: chal ins last: no ex towards fin* **6/1**[2]

4251 **3** 1 ¾ **Seattle Robber**[13] 2725 4-9-13 **63** ....(b) MissFayeBramley(3) 12 68
(P A Blockley) *swtchd lft after s: hld up in rr: hdwy over 2f out: styd on wl fnl f* **13/2**[3]

-311 **4** shd **Great View (IRE)**[23] 2455 7-10-8 **69** ....(p) MissLEllison 7 74
(Mrs A L M King) *chsd ldrs: pushed along 5f out: styd on same pce fnl f* **9/2**[1]

-300 **5** shd **Iberus (GER)**[43] 405 8-9-11 **58** ....(v) MissSBrotherton 2 62
(S Gollings) *trckd ldrs: wnt 2nd over 2f out: one pce fnl f* **28/1**

06-1 **6** 5 **The Pen**[11] 2777 4-9-9 **56** .... MrsSBosley 5 51
(C W Fairhurst) *chsd ldrs: one pce fnl 2f* **9/1**

-030 **7** 3 ½ **Viable**[19] 2540 4-9-11 **63** .... MissLAllan(5) 9 51
(Mrs P Sly) *sn trcking ldrs: t.k.h: lost pl over 1f out* **12/1**

0-10 **8** 2 ½ **Epicurean**[17] 2627 4-10-1 **67** .... MissHWragg(5) 4 50
(Mrs K Walton) *mid-div: effrt 3f out: wknd 2f out* **11/1**

2-05 **9** ½ **El Chaparral (IRE)**[17] 2628 6-10-6 **67** .... MissRDavidson 13 49
(F P Murtagh) *hld up in rr: hdwy and in tch 6f out: lost pl over 1f out* **14/1**

-513 **10** 10 **Nicozetto (FR)**[18] 939 6-8-11 **51** ....(b) MissWGibson(7) 6 14
(N Wilson) *dwlt: hld up in rr: effrt 3f out: sn wknd* **14/1**

010- **11** 1 **Wahchi (IRE)**[357] 3388 7-9-8 **62** ow1 .... MissJCoward(7) 8 24
(M W Easterby) *hld up in rr: bhd fnl 4f* **16/1**

0/0- **12** dist **Attack Minded**[415] 1709 5-8-13 **51** oh27 .... MissAWallace(5) 11 —
(L R James) *t.k.h: led tl 6f out: sn lost pl: t.o fnl 2f: virtually p.u* **100/1**

060- **13** dist **Blissphilly**[503] 388 4-8-13 **51** oh25 ....(b[1]) MissCarolineHurley(5) 3 —
(M Mullineaux) *mid-div: lost pl 6f out: sn bhd: t.o 3f out: virtually p.u* **100/1**

2m 13.28s (-0.80) **Going Correction** -0.025s/f (Good) 13 Ran SP% **114.7**
Speed ratings (Par 103):102,101,100,100,100 96,93,91,90,82 82,—,—
CSF £28.90 CT £173.17 TOTE £5.40: £1.90, £2.00, £2.90; EX 32.00.
Owner D C Rutter P J Huntbach **Bred** Major W R Hern And W H Carson **Trained** Maunby, N Yorks

FOCUS
An end-to-end gallop and in the end Carol Bartley's strength in the saddle swayed the issue. Not bad form for the grade, and pretty solid too.

3142 AEDAS ARCHITECTS FILLIES' H'CAP 1m 4y
2:45 (2:46) (Class 5) (0-70,69) 3-Y-0+ **£4,533** (£1,348; £674; £336) **Stalls** Low

Form RPR

0020 **1** **Dream Rose (IRE)**[24] 2400 3-9-12 **69** .... TonyCulhane 13 78
(M R Channon) *rr-div: hdwy on wd outside over 4f out: led 1f out: styd on wl* **14/1**

-060 **2** 1 ½ **Jenny Soba**[28] 2283 3-7-12 **48** .... LukeMorris(7) 12 54
(R M Whitaker) *bhd: hdwy over 1f out: swtchd rt and styd on wl ins last* **40/1**

05U6 **3** nk **Grande Terre (IRE)**[16] 2641 5-9-8 **56** .... PaulHanagan 5 63
(R A Fahey) *mid-div: drvn and hdwy over 3f out: kpt on same pce ins last* **6/1**[2]

4402 **4** 1 **Westcourt Dream**[8] 2891 6-9-2 **50** .... DaleGibson 2 55
(M W Easterby) *chsd ldrs: edgd rt and kpt on same pce appr fnl f* **4/1**[1]

0020 **5** 5 **Penny Glitters**[6] 2947 3-9-0 **57** .... KerrinMcEvoy 8 49
(S Parr) *chsd ldrs: outpcd fnl 2f* **9/1**

0362 **6** shd **Azurine (IRE)**[7] 2923 3-9-6 **63** .... JoeFanning 3 54
(M Johnston) *chsd ldrs: wknd over 1f out* **6/1**[2]

/043 **7** 3 **Shosolosa (IRE)**[16] 2634 4-10-0 **62** .... KDarley 9 48
(B J Meehan) *w ldrs: led over 2f out: hdd 1f out: sn wknd* **8/1**[3]

0-00 **8** nk **Giverny Spring**[24] 2403 3-9-8 **65** .... EddieAhern 6 49
(J W Hills) *mid-div: drvn 3f out: wknd over 1f out* **16/1**

0000 **9** 1 **Ellens Princess (IRE)**[8] 2891 4-9-5 **53** ....(p) TonyHamilton 7 36
(J S Wainwright) *lost pl after 2f: sn drvn along: nvr a threat* **25/1**

/000 **10** 2 **Algorithm**[7] 2926 4-8-8 **47** .... DuranFentiman(5) 1 26
(T D Easterby) *chsd ldrs: lost pl over 1f out* **25/1**

1006 **11** 25 **Wanna Shout**[8] 2891 8-9-2 **50** .... PhillipMakin 11 —
(R Dickin) *s.i.s: a in rr: bhd whn eased ins last* **25/1**

3066 **12** 2 ½ **Calamari (IRE)**[12] 2747 4-9-6 **54** ....(t) DO'Donohoe 10 —
(Mrs A Duffield) *in rr: drvn over 2f out: sn lost pl: bhd whn eased ins last* **12/1**

5626 **13** 22 **Witchelle**[16] 2637 5-9-11 **59** .... AdrianTNicholls 4 —
(R Craggs) *led tl over 2f out: sn lost pl: bhd whn heavily eased ins last* **8/1**[3]

1m 46.28s (0.58) **Going Correction** -0.025s/f (Good)
WFA 3 from 4yo+ 9lb 13 Ran SP% **115.0**
Speed ratings (Par 100):96,94,94,93,88 88,85,84,83,81 56,54,32
CSF £486.43 CT £3784.56 TOTE £14.40: £3.80, £11.00, £2.00; EX 600.90.
Owner Jaber Abdullah **Bred** Gainsborough Stud Management Ltd **Trained** West Ilsley, Berks

FOCUS
They tended to race wide away from the running rail and the first two both had outside draws. Pretty ordinary, the first two coming back to something like their two-year-old form.
Witchelle Official explanation: jockey said mare lost her action

3143 SPINDRIFTER CONDITIONS STKS 6f
3:15 (3:19) (Class 3) 2-Y-0 **£7,478** (£2,239; £1,119; £560) **Stalls** Low

Form RPR

641 **1** **Dubai's Touch**[11] 2783 2-9-2 .... JoeFanning 2 91
(M Johnston) *trckd ldr: effrt over 2f out: styd on fnl f: led post* **4/7**[1]

2 **2** shd **Armigerent (IRE)**[11] 2778 2-8-10 .... KDarley 1 85
(M Johnston) *led: edgd rt and racd dentre: rdn and hung lft over 1f out: r.o: hdd last stride* **6/1**[3]

51 **3** 1 ½ **As One Does**[45] 1811 2-9-2 .... DO'Donohoe 4 86
(K A Ryan) *trckd ldrs: effrt over 2f out: kpt on same pce appr fnl f* **5/2**[2]

4 72 **Craig Y Nos** 2-8-3 ow1 .... AdrianTNicholls 3 —
(A Berry) *dwlt: sn outpcd and pushed along: bhd fnl 2f: virtually p.u: t.o: btn 72 l* **66/1**

1m 17.76s (0.36) **Going Correction** -0.025s/f (Good) 4 Ran SP% **108.0**
Speed ratings (Par 98):96,95,93,—
CSF £4.50 TOTE £1.50; EX 4.00.
Owner Salem Suhail **Bred** Miss S N Ralphs **Trained** Middleham Moor, N Yorks

FOCUS
A disapointing turnout considering the race carried £500 appearance money. The form is not worth a great deal and it is not a race to put much faith in.

NOTEBOOK
Dubai's Touch, who really took the eye beforehand, made very hard work of it and it was only in the very last stride that he put his head in front. He may benefit from a short break. (op 8-13 tchd 8-15 and 4-6 in places)
Armigerent(IRE), a well-made type, is not the most fluent of movers. He edged away from the running rail and took them along towards the centre. Hanging left when sent two or three lengths clear coming to the final furlong, he was pipped by his stablemate on the line. He had made his debut over further and his trainer regards him as more of a stayer than a sprinter. (op 11-2 tchd 7-1)
As One Does, a good-bodied type, was encountering much quicker ground and gave a good account of himself. (op 11-4)
Craig Y Nos, the biggest in the field, was clueless yet by completing in her own time she picked up a total of £987. It could turn out to be her biggest pay-day.

3144 EBF PARK SUITE FILLIES' H'CAP 6f
3:45 (3:45) (Class 3) (0-95,87) 3-Y-0+
£11,217 (£3,358; £1,679; £840; £419; £210) **Stalls** Low

Form RPR

3241 **1** **Folga**[10] 2830 4-9-13 **87** .... KDarley 6 99
(J G Given) *wnt lft s: w ldr: hung lft and led 1f out: r.o strly* **5/2**[1]

6024 **2** 1 ¾ **Riquewihr**[5] 2977 6-8-12 **72** ....(p) TonyHamilton 3 79
(J S Wainwright) *led tl 1f out: no ex* **15/2**

6022 **3** 2 ½ **Madame Medusa (IRE)**[18] 2587 3-8-7 **73** ....(v[1]) KerrinMcEvoy 4 71
(J A R Toller) *wnt rt s: chsd ldrs: effrt over 2f out: kpt on fnl f* **9/2**

0-00 **4** ½ **Qusoor (IRE)**[16] 2639 3-9-5 **85** .... RHills 2 81
(J L Dunlop) *hld up in tch: effrt over 2f out: kpt on same pce* **10/1**

6100 **5** 3 ½ **Fantaisiste**[23] 2438 4-9-9 **86** ....(b[1]) NelsonDeSouza(3) 1 74
(P F I Cole) *racd on inner: chsd ldrs: edgd rt and wknd over 1f out* **4/1**[3]

1303 **6** 6 **Ooh Aah Camara (IRE)**[9] 2880 3-9-4 **84** .... JimmyFortune 5 52
(T J Pitt) *squeezed out s: sn chsng ldrs on outer: sn drvn along: lost pl over 1f out: eased ins last* **7/2**[2]

1m 16.22s (-1.18) **Going Correction** -0.025s/f (Good)
WFA 3 from 4yo+ 6lb 6 Ran SP% **109.8**
Speed ratings (Par 104):106,103,100,99,95 87
CSF £20.30 TOTE £2.70: £1.40, £4.00; EX 19.30.
Owner The Thrill Seekers **Bred** P Onslow **Trained** Willoughton, Lincs

FOCUS
Not strong form, but another improved run from the winner and the runner-up is consistent.

NOTEBOOK
Folga, who looked in tip-top condition, was racing from a 3lb higher mark over a stiffer six. She bounced off the fast ground and is in the form of her life.

Riquewihr looks another in good form at present, and after taking them along she did not go down without a fight. (op 9-1)
Madame Medusa(IRE), in a first-time visor, basically did nothing wrong on the day but in the past she has looked a tricky type and she is now a maiden after seven outings. (op 5-1)
Qusoor(IRE), down 3lb after two previous outings this year, does not look to have grown at all from two to three and she seems likely to continue to struggle. (op 7-1)
Fantaisiste, who is in foal, was tried in blinkers but to little effect. Kempton looks her second home. (op 9-2)
Ooh Aah Camara(IRE) was the meat in the sandwich at the start and she was never happy thereafter. Something of a character, this is best overlooked. Official explanation: jockey said filly suffered interference at start

3145 THIRSK ARE RACING TOMORROW H'CAP — 1m 4f 8y
4:15 (4:15) (Class 6) (0-60,60) 3-Y-O — **£3,238** (£963; £481; £240) **Stalls** Low

Form — RPR
-023 **1** **Collette's Choice**[19] 2539 3-9-0 **53** PaulHanagan 8 — 66
(R A Fahey) *in tch: effrt and hmpd 3f out: hdwy to ld 2f out: edgd rt over 1f out: styd on strly* **6/1**[2]
-000 **2** *4* **Vice Admiral**[20] 2529 3-8-12 **51** DaleGibson 11 — 57
(M W Easterby) *drvn to ld 1f: chsd ldrs: kpt on to take 2nd towards fin* **40/1**
0-06 **3** *1 1/4* **Wings Of Dawn**[23] 2434 3-8-13 **52** KDarley 12 — 56
(M P Tregoning) *chsd ldrs: drvn over 4f out: one pce fnl f* **10/1**
0221 **4** *hd* **Mister Fizzbomb (IRE)**[19] 2539 3-9-5 **58** (b) TonyHamilton 1 — 62
(J S Wainwright) *led after 1f: hdd 2f out: one pce* **15/2**
-005 **5** *hd* **Freeze The Flame (GER)**[19] 2539 3-9-0 **53** (b[1]) JimmyFortune 13 — 56
(C R Egerton) *sn trcking ldrs on outer: kpt on same pce appr fnl f* **10/1**
-004 **6** *1/2* **Leo McGarry (IRE)**[19] 2539 3-8-10 **49** EddieAhern 17 — 52
(S C Williams) *chsd ldrs on outer: one pce fnl 2f* **33/1**
6333 **7** *4* **William John**[20] 2529 3-8-9 **53** StephenDonohoe[(5)] 6 — 49
(B Ellison) *prom: effrt 3f out: wknd over 1f out* **13/2**[3]
4532 **8** *3/4* **Bramcote Lorne**[17] 2607 3-9-7 **60** KerrinMcEvoy 2 — 55
(S Parr) *mid-div: hdwy to chse ldrs 3f out: wknd appr fnl f* **4/1**[1]
0-00 **9** *2 1/2* **Sirbrit**[10] 2814 3-8-12 **51** PhilipRobinson 9 — 42
(W J Musson) *bhd: hdwy on inner over 2f out: kpt on: nvr nr ldrs* **12/1**
0060 **10** *5* **Meohmy**[19] 2539 3-8-11 **50** (v[1]) TonyCulhane 4 — 33
(M R Channon) *hld up in mid-field: drvn over 3f out: nvr on terms* **22/1**
0-62 **11** *3 1/2* **Fonic Rock (IRE)**[19] 2539 3-8-11 **57** LukeMorris[(7)] 16 — 34
(M L W Bell) *chsd ldrs: lost pl over 1f out* **14/1**
3450 **12** *nk* **King's Fable (USA)**[63] 1350 3-9-3 **56** JoeFanning 10 — 33
(M Johnston) *in tch: drvn over 2f out: sn lost pl* **10/1**
00-0 **13** *9* **Navajo Warrior (IRE)**[62] 1386 3-8-3 **49** oh1 ow8.. MichaelJStainton[(7)] 3 — 11
(T D Easterby) *chsd ldrs: lost pl 3f out* **80/1**
6060 **14** *7* **Every Inch (IRE)**[19] 2539 3-7-12 **42** DuranFentiman[(5)] 7 — —
(T D Easterby) *a in rr: bhd fnl 3f* **40/1**
0-05 **15** *1/2* **Dark Night (IRE)**[12] 2746 3-8-7 **46** RHills 14 — —
(D W Barker) *s.i.s: swtchd lft after s: in rr: rdn and hung bdly rt 3f out: sn wknd* **14/1**
0-00 **16** *2 1/2* **Intavac Girl**[44] 1854 3-7-13 **41** oh11 JohnMcAuley[(3)] 5 — —
(C W Thornton) *a in rr: bhd fnl 3f* **100/1**
5-00 **17** *dist* **Sharpe Image (IRE)**[19] 2542 3-9-1 **54** AdrianTNicholls 15 — —
(G Woodward) *prom: lost pl over 5f out: t.o 3f out: virtually p.u* **66/1**

2m 38.78s (-1.52) **Going Correction** -0.025s/f (Good) 17 Ran SP% **123.6**
Speed ratings (Par 98):104,101,100,100,100 99,97,96,95,91 89,89,83,78,78 76,—
CSF £243.65 CT £2385.96 TOTE £6.80: £1.80, £10.00, £3.00, £1.80; EX 575.00.
Owner P D Smith Holdings Ltd **Bred** Highclere Stud Ltd **Trained** Musley Bank, N Yorks

FOCUS
An end-to-end gallop resulting in a decent winning time for a race like this. Not bad form for the grade, and quite solid rated through the fourth, fifth and sixth. There could be more to come from the winner.
Sirbrit Official explanation: jockey said gelding was unsuited by good to firm ground
Fonic Rock(IRE) Official explanation: jockey said filly had no more to give
Dark Night(IRE) Official explanation: jockey said gelding lost its action on final bend
Sharpe Image(IRE) Official explanation: jockey said filly had no more to give

3146 WILFRED UNDERWOOD MEMORIAL MAIDEN FILLIES' STKS — 1m 2f 6y
4:45 (4:46) (Class 5) 3-4-Y-O — **£5,181** (£1,541; £770; £384) **Stalls** Low

Form — RPR
-62 **1** **Acts Of Grace (USA)**[18] 2580 3-9-0 KerrinMcEvoy 6 — 85
(J L Dunlop) *chsd ldrs: styd on to ld 1f out: kpt on strly: readily* **5/2**[1]
2- **2** *2* **Piety (IRE)**[257] 5978 3-9-0 JoeFanning 10 — 81
(M Johnston) *chsd ldrs: kpt on wl to take 2nd ins last: improve* **8/1**
4-44 **3** *1/2* **Thumpers Dream**[26] 2349 3-9-0 **85** EddieAhern 5 — 80
(H R A Cecil) *trckd ldrs: rdn to ld over 2f out: hdd 1f out: kpt on same pce* **5/1**
0 **4** *11* **Beautiful Summer (IRE)**[13] 2734 3-9-0 TonyHamilton 4 — 59
(R A Fahey) *hld up in tch: effrt 3f out: sn wl outpcd* **50/1**
2 **5** *hd* **Yemen Desert (IRE)**[8] 2895 3-9-0 KDarley 8 — 59
(M Johnston) *trckd ldrs: hmpd over 2f out: wknd over 1f out* **7/2**[3]
6 *2 1/2* **Pochard** 3-8-9 StephenDonohoe[(5)] 3 — 54
(J M P Eustace) *in rr: drvn over 4f out: nvr on terms* **50/1**
05 **7** *1 1/4* **Consuelita**[46] 1798 3-9-0 RHills 2 — 52
(B J Meehan) *chsd ldrs: effrt 3f out: sn btn* **20/1**
6-2 **8** *8* **Dubai Melody (USA)**[10] 2825 3-9-0 JimmyFortune 9 — 36+
(J H M Gosden) *led tl over 2f out: mod 4th and wl btn whn heavily eased over 1f out* **3/1**[2]
00-5 **9** *12* **Xenia**[173] 93 3-8-11 **42** JohnMcAuley[(3)] 1 — 14
(T J Etherington) *in rr: sme hdwy on inner over 4f out: sn lost pl and bhd* **100/1**

2m 12.43s (-1.65) **Going Correction** -0.025s/f (Good) 9 Ran SP% **113.2**
Speed ratings (Par 100):105,103,103,94,94 92,91,84,75
CSF £22.07 TOTE £3.30: £1.40, £2.30, £1.60; EX 28.10.
Owner Prince A A Faisal **Bred** Nawara Stud **Trained** Arundel, W Sussex

FOCUS
Not a bad maiden, the first three finishing clear with the third probably a fair guide.
Dubai Melody(USA) Official explanation: jockey said filly lost her action

3147 WRAGBY H'CAP — 1m 4y
5:15 (5:15) (Class 5) (0-75,75) 3-Y-O+ — **£4,533** (£1,348; £674; £336) **Stalls** Low

Form — RPR
0401 **1** **Kaymich Perfecto**[10] 2831 6-9-6 **69** MichaelJStainton[(7)] 11 — 82
(R M Whitaker) *hld up towards rr: gd hdwy over 2f out: led over 1f out: drvn clr* **11/2**[2]
0-53 **2** *2 1/2* **Gifted Flame**[14] 2697 7-10-0 **70** TonyHamilton 8 — 77
(J J Quinn) *trckd ldrs on outer: styd on to take 2nd ins last: no ch w wnr* **10/1**
1310 **3** *1/2* **Takes Tutu (USA)**[10] 2820 7-10-0 **70** PhilipRobinson 4 — 76
(C R Dore) *t.k.h in rr: drvn 3f out: styd on wl appr fnl f* **7/1**
0040 **4** *nk* **Fairy Monarch (IRE)**[14] 2697 7-8-9 **51** oh1 (b) JoeFanning 6 — 56
(P T Midgley) *hld up in rr: hdwy over 2f out: kpt on appr fnl f* **25/1**
5353 **5** *2* **Wing Commander**[6] 2945 7-9-9 **68** (b) LeeVickers[(3)] 2 — 68
(I W McInnes) *chsd ldrs: n.m.r and swtchd rt over 1f out: kpt on* **7/1**
000- **6** *2* **Jumeirah Scarer**[354] 3474 5-9-6 **62** EddieAhern 1 — 58
(K A Ryan) *chsd ldrs: outpcd fnl 2f* **16/1**
1600 **7** *1 1/4* **Major Magpie (IRE)**[17] 2627 4-9-13 **69** PhillipMakin 3 — 62
(M Dods) *hld up in mid-field: effrt on inner over 2f out: wknd over 1f out* **3/1**[1]
-000 **8** *4* **Hypnotic**[28] 2299 4-9-11 **67** AdrianTNicholls 10 — 51
(D Nicholls) *t.k.h: w ldrs: wknd over 1f out* **20/1**
0600 **9** *nk* **Wayward Shot (IRE)**[28] 2299 4-9-2 **58** DaleGibson 12 — 41
(M W Easterby) *led tl over 2f out: sn wknd* **40/1**
3520 **10** *1/2* **Five Two**[27] 2318 3-9-7 **72** TonyCulhane 9 — 52
(M R Channon) *sn chsng ldrs on outer: led over 2f out: hdd & wknd over 1f out* **12/1**
0-30 **11** *1/2* **Chapter (IRE)**[16] 2640 4-9-5 **68** (p) LukeMorris[(7)] 5 — 49
(Mrs A L M King) *rrd s: a in rr and sn drvn along* **16/1**
005- **12** *6* **Dream Mountain**[195] 6634 3-9-2 **67** KDarley 7 — 32
(M Johnston) *chsd ldrs: lost pl over 1f out: eased ins last* **13/2**[3]

1m 44.9s (-0.80) **Going Correction** -0.025s/f (Good)
WFA 3 from 4yo+ 9lb 12 Ran SP% **118.3**
Speed ratings (Par 103):103,100,100,99,97 95,94,90,90,89 89,83
CSF £58.01 CT £398.93 TOTE £7.90: £2.80, £2.70, £2.10; EX 54.60 Place 6 £180.76, Place 5 £92.39..
Owner G B Bedford **Bred** Mrs F S Williams **Trained** Scarcroft, W Yorks

FOCUS
A strong gallop and a progressive winner of this ordinary handicap. The form should prove reliable.
Five Two Official explanation: jockey said gelding had no more to give
T/Jkpt: £14,715.70 to a £1 stake. Pool: £82,905.50. 4.00 winning tickets. T/Plt: £155.90 to a £1 stake. Pool: £57,998.95. 271.45 winning tickets. T/Qpdt: £15.70 to a £1 stake. Pool: £3,263.50. 153.20 winning tickets. WG

3117 WINDSOR (R-H)
Monday, July 3

OFFICIAL GOING: Good to firm (firm in places)
Wind: Nil Weather: Sunny, hot

3148 TOTEPLACEPOT FILLIES' MEDIAN AUCTION MAIDEN STKS — 5f 10y
6:40 (6:40) (Class 5) 2-Y-O — **£3,886** (£1,156; £577; £288) **Stalls** High

Form — RPR
33 **1** **Relkida**[27] 2328 2-9-0 TedDurcan 4 — 73
(M R Channon) *pressed ldr after 2f: rdn to ld wl over 1f out: drvn and kpt on fnl f* **6/4**[1]
2 *1 1/4* **Fanlight Fanny (USA)** 2-9-0 JimCrowley 11 — 69
(P Winkworth) *in tch in midfield: shkn up 2f out: styd on to take 2nd ins fnl f: no imp on wnr nr fin* **9/1**
40 **3** *1* **Cuppacocoa**[41] 1922 2-8-11 AdamKirby[(3)] 8 — 65
(C G Cox) *restless stalls: led for 1f: styd prom: swtchd lft and rdn 2f out: nt qckn over 1f out: kpt on* **6/1**[3]
4 *1* **Ishi Adiva** 2-9-0 SteveDrowne 6 — 61
(Tom Dascombe) *chsd ldrs: rdn 2f out: hanging lft over 1f out: fdd fnl f* **25/1**
5420 **5** *1 3/4* **Splendidio**[14] 2709 2-8-7 JamesMillman[(7)] 5 — 55
(D K Ivory) *led after 1f to wl over 1f out: wknd fnl f* **40/1**
6 *5* **Miss Jenny (IRE)** 2-9-0 RyanMoore 1 — 37
(B J Meehan) *completely missed break: detached in last tl sme prog 2f out: pushed along and no ch* **3/1**[2]
6 **7** *hd* **Damhsoir (IRE)**[14] 2703 2-8-9 EmmettStack[(5)] 10 — 36
(H S Howe) *fly-jmpd leaving stalls: bhd: swtchd to wd outside and hrd rdn fnl 2f: no ch* **66/1**
8 *nk* **Morning Song (IRE)** 2-9-0 MickyFenton 7 — 35
(N P Littmoden) *chsd ldrs: rdn and outpcd over 2f out: steadily wknd* **20/1**
004 **9** *1/2* **Queensgate**[14] 2710 2-9-0 FergusSweeney 2 — 33
(M Blanshard) *hld up bhd ldrs: wknd rapidly over 1f out* **16/1**
10 *1 1/4* **Ken's Girl** 2-9-0 AlanMunro 9 — 29
(W S Kittow) *struggling in rr after 2f: sn no ch* **18/1**
11 *3* **Tafis Beach** 2-9-0 SebSanders 3 — 18
(J R Jenkins) *outpcd after 2f: struggling after* **40/1**

60.64 secs (-0.46) **Going Correction** -0.175s/f (Firm) 11 Ran SP% **115.4**
Speed ratings (Par 91):96,94,92,90,88 80,79,79,78,76 71
CSF £14.83 TOTE £2.60: £1.10, £2.50, £2.10; EX 19.30.
Owner M J Watson **Bred** M J Watson **Trained** West Ilsley, Berks
■ Stewards' Enquiry : Emmett Stack one-day ban: used whip when out of contention (July 15)

FOCUS
Just an ordinary fillies' maiden, particularly by Windsor's standards. The fifth holds down the form.

NOTEBOOK
Relkida had shown plenty of ability when third round here on both her previous starts and confirmed the promise of those two efforts to get off the mark with a straightforward success. This was by no means a particularly strong race, but she is clearly going the right way and looks a nice type for nurseries. (op 11-10 tchd 13-8)
Fanlight Fanny(USA), a 22,000gns first foal of an unraced half-sister to multiple US sprint winner Rahy Cat, was supported in the market and made a very pleasing introduction. Her stable is becoming noted for its juveniles these days, and this one looks capable of making her mark. (op 12-1 tchd 14-1)
Cuppacocoa, who shaped promisingly on her debut at Nottingham only to blow her chance at the start next time, again got restless at the start, but seemed to have every chance in the race itself. (op 8-1)
Ishi Adiva, a 10,000gns half-sister to Lindus Atenor, a dual six-furlong winner at two, out of a successful sprinter, made an encouraging racecourse debut. This was not a great race, but she should improve and find her level. (op 33-1)
Splendidio had been beaten in sellers on her last three starts and her proximity suggests the form is pretty limited. (tchd 50-1)
Miss Jenny(IRE), a half-sister to smart sprinter Autumnal, and to multiple winning sprinters Lord Pacal, Storyteller and Mazepa, lost her chance with a very slow start. She is bred to make a nice sprinter and can surely do better. Official explanation: jockey said filly missed break (op 11-4)
Morning Song(IRE) Official explanation: jockey said filly hung left

3149 TOTE TEXT BETTING 60021 CLAIMING STKS — 1m 67y
7:10 (7:10) (Class 5) 3-Y-O+ — £3,886 (£1,156; £577; £288) Stalls High

Form — RPR

-045 **1** **Right Ted (IRE)**[7] 2932 3-8-8 76 .... RyanMoore 6 — 70
(R Hannon) *chsd clr ldr: clsd to ld jst over 2f out: sn pressed: rdn clr fr over 1f out* **10/11**[1]

2020 **2** 2 ½ **Desert Dreamer (IRE)**[19] 2555 5-9-10 79 .... AlanMunro 5 — 73
(P R Chamings) *hld up: wnt 3rd 1/2-way: clsd to chal wnr 2f out: sn rdn and fnd nil* **3/1**[2]

2203 **3** 5 **Holiday Cocktail**[142] 375 4-9-4 66 .... SaleemGolam(3) 7 — 58
(S C Williams) *chsd clr ldng pair to 1/2-way: drvn over 2f out: outpcd and btn over 1f out* **10/3**[3]

0-00 **4** 1 ½ **Gran Clicquot**[6] 2952 11-8-10 37 .... RobynBrisland(5) 3 — 49?
(G P Enright) *restless stalls: dwlt: off the pce in last pair: lost tch 1/2-way: brief effrt over 2f out: sn btn* **50/1**

0000 **5** 1 **Kilmeena Magic**[20] 2531 4-8-12 40 .... PatDobbs 2 — 44
(J C Fox) *off the pce in last pair: lost tch 1/2-way: brief effrt over 2f out: sn wknd* **80/1**

-000 **6** 2 ½ **European (ARG)**[20] 2531 6-9-1 63 ....(b[1]) NelsonDeSouza(3) 1 — 44
(R M Beckett) *led: tk ferocious hold and sn clr: wknd and hdd jst over 2f out* **11/1**

1m 41.99s (-3.61) **Going Correction** -0.425s/f (Firm)
WFA 3 from 4yo+ 9lb — 6 Ran SP% **112.0**
Speed ratings (Par 103):101,98,93,92,91 88
CSF £3.92 TOTE £1.80: £1.30, £2.00; EX 4.10.Right Ted was claimed by T. Wall for £16,000.
Owner Fergus Jones **Bred** Rathasker Stud **Trained** East Everleigh, Wilts

FOCUS
Not a very competitive claimer and the proximity of the 37-rated Gran Clicquot in fourth does little for the form, with the front three way below their best. European set a strong pace, but weakened out of contention quite quickly
European(ARG) Official explanation: jockey said gelding ran too free

3150 TOTESPORT 0800 221 221 H'CAP — 6f
7:40 (7:43) (Class 4) (0-85,85) 3-Y-O — £6,477 (£1,927; £963; £481) Stalls High

Form — RPR

31 **1** **Home Sweet Home (IRE)**[12] 2763 3-8-10 74 .... TedDurcan 4 — 85+
(P D Evans) *trckd ldr gng wl: effrt to ld over 1f out: rdn and wl in command fnl f* **3/1**[2]

41-0 **2** 2 ½ **Lipizza (IRE)**[9] 2864 3-8-12 76 .... SteveDrowne 6 — 79+
(N A Callaghan) *trckd ldrs: rdn and nt qckn 2f out: effrt and hit by rival's whip over 1f out: chsd wnr ins fnl f: no imp* **5/2**[1]

0010 **3** 1 ¾ **Catspraddle (USA)**[16] 2652 3-8-8 72 .... RyanMoore 3 — 70
(R Hannon) *led: crossed to nr side rail after 2f: drvn and hdd over 1f out: sn outpcd: kpt on nr fin* **15/2**

441- **4** ½ **Bertie Southstreet**[366] 3121 3-9-7 85 .... GeorgeBaker 5 — 82
(J R Best) *trckd ldrs: rdn wl over 1f out: no imp ent fnl f: fdd* **11/1**

0-00 **5** hd **Pearly Poll**[17] 2609 3-8-9 73 ow1 .... SebSanders 2 — 69
(R M Beckett) *in tch in last pair: rdn 1/2-way: struggling 2f out: kpt on last 100yds* **25/1**

0640 **6** ¾ **Makabul**[7] 2931 3-9-2 80 .... AlanMunro 1 — 74
(B R Millman) *racd on outer: trckd ldrs: effrt over 1f out: sn nt qckn and no imp* **11/2**

0001 **7** 5 **Savernake Blue**[2] 3087 3-8-12 83 6ex .... ThomasO'Brien(7) 7 — 62
(M R Channon) *fly-jmpd s: pushed along to rcvr after 2f: rdn and struggling 2f out: wknd* **4/1**[3]

1m 12.52s (-1.15) **Going Correction** -0.175s/f (Firm) — 7 Ran SP% **112.9**
Speed ratings (Par 102):100,96,94,93,93 92,85
CSF £10.65 TOTE £3.80: £2.20, £2.20; EX 9.10.
Owner John P Jones **Bred** Western Bloodstock **Trained** Pandy, Abergavenny

FOCUS
Just an ordinary sprint handicap for the grade, but decent efforts from Home Sweet Home, who is progressing into a useful filly, and Lipizza. The fourth sets the standard.
Savernake Blue Official explanation: jockey said gelding reared on leaving stalls

3151 TOTESPORTCASINO.COM H'CAP — 1m 2f 7y
8:10 (8:11) (Class 4) (0-80,84) 3-Y-O+ — £5,829 (£1,734; £866; £432) Stalls Low

Form — RPR

4-23 **1** **Cusoon**[21] 2510 4-9-8 72 .... RyanMoore 8 — 81
(G L Moore) *hld up in 5th: prog to chal wl over 2f out: sn drvn: disp ld fr 2f out tl forced into narrow advantage fnl f* **5/2**[1]

23-5 **2** nk **Great Orator (USA)**[17] 2615 4-9-10 74 .... DaneO'Neill 6 — 82
(H Candy) *t.k.h: trckd ldng trio: effrt to chal over 2f out: disp ld fr 2f out tl nt qckn ins fnl f* **5/2**[1]

3031 **3** 1 **Active Asset (IRE)**[2] 3081 4-9-13 84 6ex .... ThomasO'Brien(7) 1 — 90
(M R Channon) *hld up in 6th: effrt over 2f out: pressed ldng pair over 1f out: urged along and nt qckn last 150yds* **7/1**

-506 **4** 2 ½ **Zilcash**[24] 2404 3-9-0 75 .... SteveDrowne 3 — 76
(A King) *pressed ldr: chal wl over 2f out: sn rdn and outpcd: one pce after* **14/1**

0-06 **5** 1 ½ **Bentley Brook (IRE)**[92] 843 4-9-11 75 .... MickyFenton 4 — 74
(P A Blockley) *hld up in last: pushed along over 3f out: prog 2f out to chse ldng trio 1f out: wknd* **50/1**

-240 **6** ¾ **Firesong**[45] 1830 4-9-9 73 .... RichardHughes 5 — 70
(Pat Eddery) *led: rdn and hdd 2f out: steadily wknd* **9/2**[2]

0000 **7** ½ **Northside Lodge (IRE)**[33] 2149 8-8-8 61 ....(p) SaleemGolam(3) 7 — 57
(W R Swinburn) *trckd ldng pair: effrt to chal on wd outside 3f out: sn nt qckn and lost pl: n.d after* **16/1**

0242 **8** 1 ½ **Alekhine (IRE)**[24] 2401 5-9-10 74 ....(p) AlanMunro 2 — 67
(J R Boyle) *hld up in 7th: drvn over 2f out: sn struggling and btn* **13/2**[3]

2m 4.45s (-3.85) **Going Correction** -0.425s/f (Firm)
WFA 3 from 4yo+ 11lb — 8 Ran SP% **115.7**
Speed ratings (Par 105):98,97,96,94,93 93,92,91
CSF £8.68 CT £37.33 TOTE £2.90: £1.40, £1.60, £1.40; EX 8.90.
Owner The Winning Hand **Bred** Mrs Dare Wigan And Dominic Wigan **Trained** Woodingdean, E Sussex

FOCUS
An ordinary handicap for the grade and a moderate winning time. Sound-enough form from the first two.

3152 ARENA LEISURE PLC FILLIES' H'CAP — 1m 3f 135y
8:40 (8:41) (Class 5) (0-70,69) 3-Y-O+ — £3,238 (£963; £481; £240) Stalls Low

Form — RPR

0412 **1** **Madhavi**[6] 2953 4-9-9 60 .... RichardHughes 11 — 71
(R Hannon) *mde all: shkn up and drew 2 l clr over 2f out: jnd ins fnl f: hld on wl* **6/1**[2]

0001 **2** shd **Celtique**[18] 2577 4-9-9 60 .... NickyMackay 12 — 71
(M Wigham) *hld up towards rr: prog over 2f out: nt clr run briefly sn after: chsd wnr over 1f out: upsides fnl f: jst pipped* **6/1**[2]

-000 **3** 3 **Sand And Stars (IRE)**[17] 2628 5-10-0 65 .... GeorgeBaker 3 — 71
(M H Tompkins) *hld up in last pair: hrd rdn and last wl over 2f out: prog wl over 1f out: styd on fnl f: nrst fin* **9/1**

-362 **4** ¾ **Italic**[23] 2434 3-9-5 69 ....(b) RyanMoore 13 — 74
(Mrs A J Perrett) *trckd ldrs: gng strly 3f out: rdn and no rspnse 2f out: one pce after* **3/1**[1]

414- **5** nk **Ellina**[238] 6285 5-10-0 65 .... JimmyQuinn 10 — 70
(J Pearce) *in tch: outpcd and dropped to last trio over 2f out: kpt on again fr over 1f out* **12/1**

505 **6** ¾ **Fondness**[40] 1940 3-9-5 69 .... SteveDrowne 8 — 72
(R Charlton) *trckd wnr for 4f: styd in tch: rdn and effrt towards outer over 2f out: fdd over 1f out* **17/2**

3265 **7** nk **Nina Fontenail (FR)**[8] 2902 5-9-9 60 .... RobertHavlin 7 — 63
(B R Millman) *in tch in rr: effrt on outer wl over 2f out: no imp over 1f out: fdd* **6/1**[2]

0310 **8** ½ **Gambling Spirit**[28] 2305 4-9-12 63 .... DaneO'Neill 9 — 65
(H Candy) *dwlt: rcvrd to trck wnr after 4f: rdn over 2f out: wknd over 1f out* **8/1**[3]

300- **9** 4 **Avicia**[235] 6307 4-9-9 60 .... FergusSweeney 4 — 56
(C A Horgan) *hld up in last pair: taken to wd outside and effrt 3f out: wknd 2f out* **40/1**

0-30 **10** 6 **Grateful**[31] 2188 3-8-10 60 .... SebSanders 5 — 46
(R M Beckett) *hld up: prog and prom after 5f: rdn 3f out: wknd rapidly 2f out* **12/1**

0-05 **11** 7 **Always Turn Left (IRE)**[15] 2673 3-8-0 55 .... EmmettStack(5) 2 — 30
(H S Howe) *in tch: effrt on wd outside 3f out: sn wknd* **33/1**

2m 25.43s (-4.67) **Going Correction** -0.425s/f (Firm)
WFA 3 from 4yo+ 13lb — 11 Ran SP% **120.3**
Speed ratings (Par 100):98,97,95,95,95 94,94,94,91,87 82
CSF £42.96 CT £328.76 TOTE £4.80: £2.10, £2.70, £3.20; EX 29.60.
Owner White Beech Farm **Bred** Elsdon Farms **Trained** East Everleigh, Wilts

FOCUS
A modest fillies' handicap, but solid form. The first two both slightly improved on recent wins and were both rated higher last year.
Grateful Official explanation: jockey said filly hung right

3153 ANN HOKE BIRTHDAY CELEBRATION H'CAP — 1m 67y
9:10 (9:10) (Class 5) (0-70,70) 3-Y-O+ — £3,238 (£963; £481; £240) Stalls High

Form — RPR

0054 **1** **Deeper In Debt**[5] 2969 8-10-0 65 .... SebSanders 2 — 73
(J Akehurst) *drvn to ld: mde all: looked in command over 1f out: hld on u.p nr fin* **4/1**[2]

4-60 **2** ¾ **Woodcote Place**[16] 2642 3-9-10 70 .... AlanMunro 10 — 74+
(P R Chamings) *stdd s: hld up in last: plenty to do over 3f out: rapid prog on outer 2f out: clsd w rdr waving whip to take 2nd nr fin* **12/1**

0-63 **3** shd **Mythical Charm**[9] 2860 7-9-7 58 ....(t) RyanMoore 4 — 64
(J J Bridger) *t.k.h: trckd wnr: rdn over 2f out: no imp over 1f out: kpt on* **15/2**

0256 **4** 1 ¼ **Jools**[14] 2708 8-9-6 64 .... JamesMillman(7) 3 — 67
(D K Ivory) *trckd ldng pair: rdn wl over 2f out: no imp: one pce fr over 1f out* **7/2**[1]

2342 **5** 1 ¾ **Taranaki**[7] 2936 8-9-9 60 .... DaneO'Neill 1 — 59
(P D Cundell) *dwlt: sn in midfield: rdn wl over 2f out: one pce and no imp* **5/1**[3]

0000 **6** hd **Lady Duxyana**[2] 3099 3-8-2 51 ow3 .... NelsonDeSouza(3) 6 — 48
(M D I Usher) *trckd ldrs: rdn over 2f out: grad fdd over 1f out* **33/1**

2030 **7** ½ **Rowan Warning**[16] 2645 4-9-8 59 .... NickyMackay 9 — 57
(J R Boyle) *settled midfield: rdn 3f out: no prog and btn wl over 1f out* **7/1**

0005 **8** nk **Celtic Spa (IRE)**[34] 2113 4-9-10 61 .... SteveDrowne 7 — 58
(P D Evans) *hld up in rr: nt clr run wl over 1f out and swtchd lft: shuffled along whn nt clr run ins fnl f: nvr nr ldrs* **9/1**

2000 **9** 2 ½ **Silver Court**[17] 2601 4-8-10 47 oh1 ow1 .... RichardHughes 8 — 38
(A W Carroll) *dwlt: t.k.h and hld up in last pair: rdn and no rspnse over 2f out* **10/1**

1450 **10** 4 **Boogie Magic**[21] 2510 6-8-11 51 .... AdamKirby(3) 11 — 33
(T Keddy) *settled in midfield: rdn 3f out: wknd 2f out* **12/1**

1m 42.5s (-3.10) **Going Correction** -0.425s/f (Firm)
WFA 3 from 4yo+ 9lb — 10 Ran SP% **120.6**
Speed ratings (Par 103):98,97,97,95,94 93,93,93,90,86
CSF £53.20 CT £360.76 TOTE £4.10: £1.60, £4.50, £2.10; EX 76.60 Place 6 £26.30, Place 5 £18.14..
Owner Tipp-Ex Rapid Racing II **Bred** P And Mrs Venner **Trained** Epsom, Surrey

FOCUS
A modest handicap and the time was ordinary, the winner making all.
Celtic Spa(IRE) Official explanation: jockey said filly was denied clear run
Silver Court Official explanation: jockey said gelding was unsuited by good to firm, firm in places ground
T/Plt: £25.20 to a £1 stake. Pool: £72,337.75. 2,090.20 winning tickets. T/Qpdt: £18.20 to a £1 stake. Pool: £4,030.40. 163.10 winning tickets. JN

3096 WOLVERHAMPTON (A.W) (L-H)
Monday, July 3

OFFICIAL GOING: Standard
Wind: Light; against Weather: Hot

3154 WBX.COM WORLD BET EXCHANGE H'CAP — 5f 216y(P)
2:30 (2:30) (Class 6) (0-65,65) 3-Y-O — £2,730 (£806; £403) Stalls Low

Form — RPR

655 **1** **Xpres Maite**[19] 2542 3-8-13 60 .... AmirQuinn(3) 10 — 73
(S R Bowring) *chsd ldrs: rdn over 2f out: led wl ins fnl f: r.o* **20/1**

-202 **2** 1 **Hoh Wotanite**[19] 2553 3-9-3 61 .... LPKeniry 4 — 71
(A M Balding) *hld up in mid-div: rdn over 2f out: hdwy over 1f out: r.o wl ins fnl f: nt rch wnr* **6/1**[2]

-051 **3** 1 **Steel City Boy (IRE)**[7] 2939 3-9-4 65 7ex .... DanielTudhope(3) 13 — 72
(D Carroll) *w ldrs: led over 2f out: rdn wl over 1f out: edgd rt and hdd wl ins fnl f: no ex* **11/8**[1]

0063 **4** 1 ½ **Crusader's Gold (FR)**[7] 2939 3-8-9 53 ow1 .... ShaneKelly 7 — 56
(T D Easterby) *bhd: rdn and hdwy over 2f out: one pce fnl f* **16/1**

0524 **5** 5 **Mystic Queen (IRE)**[18] 2576 3-8-8 52 .... FrankieMcDonald 11 — 40
(A P Jarvis) *mid-div: hung rt over 2f out: no hdwy* **33/1**

2630 **6** 1 ¾ **Glenargo (USA)**[7] [2937] 3-8-10 **54**..........................(p) AdrianMcCarthy 6 36
(R A Harris) *led: rdn and hdd over 2f out: wknd over 1f out* **33/1**

042 **7** ¾ **Artie's Son (IRE)**[7] [2939] 3-9-2 **60**.................................. TedDurcan 1 40
(T D Easterby) *sn chsng ldrs: rdn over 3f out: wknd over 2f out* **6/1**[2]

5310 **8** 2 ½ **Miss Lopez (IRE)**[9] [2856] 3-9-6 **64**.................................. SebSanders 9 37
(K R Burke) *s.i.s: nvr nr ldrs* **20/1**

04-3 **9** ¾ **Butterfly Bud (IRE)**[24] [2399] 3-9-2 **65**............................ GregFairley(5) 5 35
(J O'Reilly) *sn chsng ldrs: rdn over 3f out: sn wknd* **9/1**

0-53 **10** 3 ½ **Shunkawakhan (IRE)**[10] [2833] 3-9-3 **61**.......................... OscarUrbina 3 21
(G C H Chung) *sn outpcd* **8/1**[3]

0352 **11** 5 **Fikri**[10] [2833] 3-9-0 **65**...(vt[1]) JamesO'Reilly(7) 12 10
(T J Pitt) *sn outpcd* **16/1**

-500 **12** 2 **She's Our Beauty (IRE)**[14] [2701] 3-9-2 **60**................(v[1]) SamHitchcott 8 —
(D Nicholls) *w ldr tl rdn 3f out: sn wknd* **66/1**

0000 **13** 11 **Grafton (IRE)**[34] [2109] 3-9-5 **63**.. AlanMunro 2 —
(J D Bethell) *outpcd* **12/1**

1m 14.56s (-1.25) **Going Correction** -0.075s/f (Stan) 13 Ran SP% **128.1**
Speed ratings (Par 98):105,103,102,100,93 91,90,87,86,81 74,72,57
CSF £139.11 CT £292.81 TOTE £29.70: £5.90, £2.30, £1.30; EX 194.60 TRIFECTA Not won..
Owner Charterhouse Holdings Plc **Bred** S R Bowring **Trained** Edwinstowe, Notts

FOCUS
A strong pace led to a smart winning time for a race like this. Quite ordinary form, but the winner is unexposed.

Xpres Maite ♦ Official explanation: trainer said, regarding the improved form shown, the gelding had benefited from today's drop in trip

Mystic Queen(IRE) Official explanation: jockey said filly hung badly right

3155 JOHN SMITH'S EXTRA SMOOTH (S) STKS 5f 20y(P)

3:00 (3:01) (Class 6) 3-Y-O+ **£2,388** (£705; £352) **Stalls** Low

Form RPR

0004 **1** **Sovereignty (JPN)**[12] [2748] 4-9-4 60.................................. TomEaves 8 64
(I Semple) *mid-div: rdn 3f out: hdwy over 1f out: str run to ld cl home* **6/1**[3]

5360 **2** 1 ¾ **Aswan (IRE)**[11] [2793] 8-9-1 52..................................(t) AmirQuinn(3) 4 58
(S R Bowring) *hld up in tch: rdn over 1f out: r.o ins fnl f* **15/2**

0-50 **3** nk **Sir Loin**[6] [2949] 5-9-4 48...(v) AlanMunro 6 57
(N Tinkler) *led 1f: chsd ldr: led over 1f out: rdn fnl f: hdd cl home* **12/1**

-405 **4** 2 **Rudi's Pet (IRE)**[12] [2748] 12-8-11 65..........................(v) VictoriaBehan(7) 3 50
(D Nicholls) *chsd ldrs: one pce fnl 2f* **7/2**[1]

2016 **5** ½ **Mirasol Princess**[16] [2632] 5-8-11 50.......................... JamesMillman(7) 11 48
(D K Ivory) *outpcd: hdwy over 1f out: n.m.r briefly on ins wl ins fnl f: nt rch ldrs* **10/1**

5414 **6** 1 **Edged In Gold**[23] [2444] 4-9-4 50..................................(e) SebSanders 10 44
(P J Makin) *hld up: hdwy on ins over 2f out: rdn over 1f out: wknd ins fnl f* **5/1**[2]

0305 **7** ¾ **Detonate**[6] [2949] 4-9-4 54.. NCallan 1 42
(Mrs C A Dunnett) *led after 1f: rdn and hdd over 1f out: wknd wl ins fnl f* **13/2**

2000 **8** 1 ¼ **He's A Rocket (IRE)**[16] [2632] 5-8-13 48..................(b) AndrewElliott(5) 12 37
(K R Burke) *prom tl wknd over 1f out* **14/1**

1640 **9** 3 **Twinned (IRE)**[31] [2187] 3-9-4 62..(b[1]) LPKeniry 7 30
(J S Moore) *prom tl rdn and wknd over 1f out* **14/1**

0000 **10** nk **Mind That Fox**[55] [1571] 4-9-4 45.. JimmyQuinn 5 25
(T Wall) *s.i.s: a bhd* **50/1**

04- **11** hd **Binty**[291] [5256] 4-8-6 49.. MarkCoumbe(7) 2 20
(A J Chamberlain) *s.v.s: a in rr* **33/1**

003 **12** 1 ¼ **Lucky Lucioni (IRE)**[18] [2573] 3-8-10 65.......................... AdamKirby(3) 9 19
(G A Butler) *swtchd lft sn after s: sn outpcd* **10/1**

62.32 secs (-0.50) **Going Correction** -0.075s/f (Stan)
WFA 3 from 4yo+ 5lb 12 Ran SP% **122.4**
Speed ratings (Par 101):101,98,97,94,93 92,90,88,84,83 83,81
CSF £52.38 TOTE £8.70: £2.70, £2.60, £3.50; EX 69.90 TRIFECTA Not won..The winner was sold to D Ivory for 6,500gns.
Owner R Hyndman **Bred** Darley Stud Management, L L C **Trained** Carluke, S Lanarks

FOCUS
A weakish seller, in which not many showed their form. The front two are better than this at their best.

Binty Official explanation: jockey said filly missed break

Lucky Lucioni(IRE) Official explanation: jockey said gelding was outpaced

3156 WORLD BET EXCHANGE WBX.COM H'CAP 1m 4f 50y(P)

3:30 (3:30) (Class 5) (0-75,72) 3-Y-O **£3,238** (£963; £481; £240) **Stalls** Low

Form RPR

0-31 **1** **Bedouin Blue (IRE)**[77] [1044] 3-9-0 **65**.............................. LeeEnstone 5 73+
(P C Haslam) *hld up in tch: rdn wl over 1f out: led and inched lft wl ins fnl f: rdn out* **15/2**

-356 **2** ¾ **Rajaall**[17] [2607] 3-9-7 **72**.. SamHitchcott 7 79
(M R Channon) *chsd ldr: led over 4f out: rdn over 2f out: edgd lft and hdd wl ins fnl f: nt qckn* **9/1**

600 **3** shd **Russian Dream (IRE)**[14] [2712] 3-9-3 **68**.......................... OscarUrbina 8 75
(W R Swinburn) *hld up: hdwy over 4f out: rdn and ev ch fr over 1f out: edgd lft ins fnl f: nt qckn* **40/1**

-422 **4** 10 **Phone In**[11] [2795] 3-9-6 **71**.. SebSanders 2 62+
(Sir Mark Prescott) *prom: lost pl 4f out: sn nt clr run: styd on fnl f: n.d* **6/4**[1]

100 **5** ½ **Marmota (IRE)**[31] [2209] 3-9-0 **65**.................................... DeanMcKeown 9 55
(M Johnston) *hld up: hdwy 5f out: sn rdn: wknd wl over 1f out* **16/1**

5536 **6** 5 **Archimboldo (USA)**[16] [2633] 3-9-0 **65**............................ ShaneKelly 4 47
(T Wall) *nvr nr ldrs* **25/1**

-033 **7** 3 **Million All Day (IRE)**[4] [3016] 3-8-2 **53**.......................... RichardMullen 1 30
(W R Muir) *hld up: rdn over 4f out: sn bhd* **7/1**[3]

0-00 **8** 1 ¼ **Pay On (IRE)**[17] [2622] 3-8-11 **62**.......................................(v[1]) AlanMunro 6 37
(W Jarvis) *s.i.s: hdwy on outside over 3f out: wknd over 2f out* **33/1**

-343 **9** 9 **Greenwich Village**[23] [2434] 3-9-3 **68**................................ PaulDoe 10 29
(W J Knight) *hld up in tch: rdn and wknd over 3f out* **10/3**[2]

1530 **10** 134 **Petrichan (IRE)**[33] [2128] 3-9-1 **66**.......................................(p) NCallan 3 —
(K A Ryan) *led: hdd over 4f out: sn wknd: t.o* **33/1**

2m 41.6s (-0.82) **Going Correction** -0.075s/f (Stan) 10 Ran SP% **115.4**
Speed ratings (Par 100):99,98,98,91,91 88,86,85,79,—
CSF £68.80 CT £2510.31 TOTE £9.30: £2.40, £2.50, £7.70; EX 64.90 Trifecta £272.90 Part won. Pool £384.38 - 0.35 winning units..
Owner Blue Lion Racing VI **Bred** John Weld **Trained** Middleham Moor, N Yorks

FOCUS
Not a bad handicap, but with only four still in contention at the three-furlong pole, this was not that competitive. The winner probably did not match his turf form.

Phone In Official explanation: jockey said gelding suffered interference in running

3157 DIXONS ESTATE AGENTS EBF MAIDEN STKS 7f 32y(P)

4:00 (4:00) (Class 5) 2-Y-O **£3,886** (£1,156; £577; £288) **Stalls** High

Form RPR

43 **1** **Capannina**[16] [2638] 2-8-12 .... TPQueally 2 66+
(J Noseda) *mde all: hung rt fr over 2f out: flashed tail whn hit w whip ins fnl f: r.o* **4/7**[1]

0 **2** 1 ¼ **Our Herbie**[21] [2506] 2-9-3 .... FrankieMcDonald 1 68
(J W Hills) *s.i.s: hdwy on ins over 2f out: rdn over 1f out: edgd rt ins fnl f: kpt on* **20/1**

0 **3** shd **Zelos (IRE)**[17] [2619] 2-9-3 .... ShaneKelly 4 68
(J A Osborne) *a.p: rdn over 2f out: swtchd lft ins fnl f: kpt on* **4/1**[2]

52 **4** 3 ½ **Kaladar (IRE)**[35] [2072] 2-9-3 .... NCallan 11 59
(K A Ryan) *a.p: rdn and ev ch over 2f out: wknd wl ins fnl f* **8/1**[3]

5 1 ½ **Arabellas Homer** 2-8-12 .... TomEaves 7 51+
(Miss J A Camacho) *s.i.s: towards rr: rdn and hdwy on ins over 1f out: nvr trbld ldrs* **25/1**

6 shd **Purple Sands (IRE)** 2-9-3 .... SebSanders 12 55
(B J Meehan) *s.i.s: sn mid-div: hdwy 3f out: sn rdn: wknd ins fnl f* **12/1**

7 3 ½ **Gold Response** 2-9-0 .... PatrickMathers(3) 6 47
(D Shaw) *nvr bttr than mid-div* **50/1**

4 **8** 1 ¼ **Fleetwood Image**[9] [2854] 2-9-3 .... JimmyQuinn 5 43
(J R Weymes) *w ldr tl over 3f out: sn rdn: wknd over 2f out* **33/1**

9 6 **Mujart** 2-8-5 .... RussellKennemore(7) 9 23
(J A Pickering) *s.i.s: short-lived effrt on outside over 2f out* **33/1**

10 2 **Field Sport (FR)** 2-9-3 .... TedDurcan 8 23
(C E Brittain) *prom tl wknd over 2f out* **25/1**

11 18 **Mr Chocolate Drop (IRE)** 2-9-0 .... DominicFox(3) 10 —
(M J Attwater) *s.i.s: bhd: rdn 4f out: sn struggling* **40/1**

12 3 **Blue Mak** 2-9-3 .... HayleyTurner 3 —
(D Shaw) *s.v.s: a in rr* **50/1**

1m 31.62s (1.22) **Going Correction** -0.075s/f (Stan) 12 Ran SP% **127.2**
Speed ratings (Par 94):90,88,88,84,82 82,78,77,70,68 47,44
CSF £21.96 TOTE £1.70: £1.10, £5.90, £1.50; EX 25.70 Trifecta £123.70 Pool £439.29 - 2.52 winning units..
Owner Peter R Pritchard **Bred** Tarworth Bloodstock Investments Ltd **Trained** Newmarket, Suffolk

FOCUS
The winner, third and fourth probably did not need to improve and only time will show the value of this form.

NOTEBOOK

Capannina, a well-backed favourite, seemed suited by the extra furlong on this switch to sand. She did not prove to be an easy ride and also showed signs of temperament. (op 8-11 tchd 4-5 in places)

Our Herbie ♦, a half-brother to several winners, showed tremendous improvement on his debut effort over this longer trip. He is certainly going the right way.

Zelos(IRE) ♦, a half-brother to course-and-distance winner Keel, is another who is progressing along the right lines. (tchd 9-2)

Kaladar(IRE) may be better suited to six furlongs for the time being. (op 9-1)

Arabellas Homer, a half-sister to Lincolneurocruiser, was apparently unfancied and should be better for the experience.

Purple Sands(IRE), a half-brother to Richmond Stakes winner Carrizo Creek, is another who should come on for the outing. (op 14-1)

3158 JOHN SMITH'S NO NONSENSE DAY APPRENTICE CLAIMING STKS 7f 32y(P)

4:30 (4:30) (Class 6) 4-Y-O+ **£2,730** (£806; £403) **Stalls** High

Form RPR

-450 **1** **Le Chiffre (IRE)**[6] [2947] 4-8-8 68..................................(p) TolleyDean(3) 9 62
(R A Harris) *hld up: hdwy 5f out: led 3f out: hrd rdn and edgd rt ins fnl f: r.o* **11/1**

5310 **2** nk **Wings Of Morning (IRE)**[31] [2208] 5-8-2 47...........(v) KellyHarrison(3) 10 55
(D Carroll) *a.p: rdn to chse ldr over 2f out: edgd rt ins fnl f: kpt on* **22/1**

2044 **3** 1 ¼ **Noorain**[13] [2728] 4-7-13 47 ow4..................................(t) MarkCoumbe(5) 7 51
(Stef Liddiard) *hld up in mid-div: hdwy over 2f out: sn rdn: kpt on ins fnl f* **25/1**

0001 **4** 5 **Mister Elegant**[11] [2793] 4-8-13 55.................................... MarcHalford 12 47
(J L Spearing) *chsd ldrs: rdn over 3f out: wknd over 1f out* **6/1**

5641 **5** 1 **Sawwaah (IRE)**[9] [2874] 9-9-0 70................................(p) VictoriaBehan(5) 3 50+
(D Nicholls) *hld up: rdn over 4f out: swtchd rt over 1f out: nvr nrr* **11/2**[3]

1160 **6** 3 **Bollin Edward**[6] [2947] 7-9-0 67.. NSLawes(5) 6 42
(K A Ryan) *chsd ldrs tl wknd over 2f out* **9/2**[2]

0000 **7** 1 ½ **Local Poet**[12] [2749] 5-9-2 78..(bt) LiamJones(3) 8 38
(I Semple) *s.i.s: hdwy on outside over 3f out: sn rdn: wknd over 2f out* **2/1**[1]

0-03 **8** 1 ½ **Lucky Lil**[32] [2160] 4-7-9 48.. LauraReynolds(5) 5 16
(R M Whitaker) *nvr nr ldrs* **40/1**

9 ½ **Littleton Aldor (IRE)**[31] 6-8-5 .... AndrewElliott 2 19
(W G M Turner) *prom: lost pl whn n.m.r on ins and hit rails over 3f out: sn bhd* **33/1**

0625 **10** hd **Gem Bien (USA)**[24] [2413] 8-8-6 50 ow2...................(b) RonanKeogh(3) 4 23
(D W Chapman) *s.i.s: hld up and bhd: short-lived effrt over 2f out* **14/1**

/0-0 **11** shd **Jeune Loup**[11] [97] 4-8-9 60.. GregFairley 11 22
(P C Haslam) *s.i.s: hdwy 5f out: rdn over 3f out: sn wknd* **50/1**

0006 **12** 2 **Fraternity**[24] [2413] 9-8-4 50.................................. RussellKennemore(3) 1 15
(J A Pickering) *led: hdd 3f out: sn wknd* **20/1**

1m 29.22s (-1.18) **Going Correction** -0.075s/f (Stan) 12 Ran SP% **116.5**
Speed ratings (Par 101):103,102,101,95,94 90,89,87,86,86 86,84
CSF £231.77 TOTE £15.60: £2.80, £4.70, £4.10; EX 213.60 TRIFECTA Not won..
Owner www.gardenshedracing.com **Bred** Agricola Del Parco **Trained** Earlswood, Monmouths
■ Stewards' Enquiry : Tolley Dean three-day ban: used whip with excessive frequency and hit gelding in the incorrect place (Jul 15-17)

FOCUS
A modest claimer. The winner ran to this year's limited form, but was capable of a stone better last year.

Sawwaah(IRE) Official explanation: jockey said gelding was never travelling

Littleton Aldor(IRE) Official explanation: jockey said gelding resented kickback

3159 TAKE CONTROL WITH WBX.COM H'CAP 1m 141y(P)

5:00 (5:00) (Class 6) (0-65,64) 3-Y-O+ **£2,730** (£806; £403) **Stalls** Low

Form RPR

0004 **1** **Inside Story (IRE)**[9] [2874] 4-9-5 **55**..................................(b) TomEaves 11 69
(M W Easterby) *hld up and bhd: hdwy over 4f out: rdn over 2f out: led and hung rt jst over 1f out: all out* **14/1**

0-05 **2** nk **Woolly Back (IRE)**[10] [2808] 5-9-4 **54**................................ RobertHavlin 7 67
(A C Whillans) *hld up in rr: rdn and hdwy over 3f out: r.o ins fnl f* **10/1**

3140 **3** *5* **Bridgewater Boys**[17] 2627 5-10-0 **64**......(b) NCallan 9 67+
(K A Ryan) *s.i.s: outpcd and sn wl bhd: hdwy on outside 2f out: r.o ins fnl f: nrst fin* **10/3**[2]
2040 **4** *nk* **Primeshade Promise**[24] 2414 5-9-2 **52**...... RichardThomas 10 54
(D Burchell) *hld up and bhd: rdn and hdwy over 2f out: hung lft ins fnl f: one pce* **12/1**
-506 **5** *1 ½* **Patavium (IRE)**[18] 2592 3-9-3 **63**...... RichardMullen 13 62
(E J O'Neill) *sn chsng ldrs: led over 3f out: rdn over 2f out: hdd jst over 1f out: wknd ins fnl f* **20/1**
0046 **6** *5* **Danzare**[5] 2969 4-9-3 **53**...... JimmyQuinn 6 42
(Mrs A J Hamilton-Fairley) *hld up towards rr: n.m.r and squeezed through wl over 1f out: nvr nr ldrs* **9/1**
5600 **7** *2* **Carpet Ride**[14] 2702 4-9-3 **53**...... HayleyTurner 1 37
(B G Powell) *led 1f: prom: rdn 4f out: wknd wl over 1f out* **33/1**
1455 **8** *6* **Chater Knight (IRE)**[11] 2790 5-9-3 **53**......(b[1]) AdrianMcCarthy 2 25
(R A Harris) *pushed along to ld after 1f: t.k.h: hdd over 3f out: sn rdn: wknd over 2f out* **6/1**[3]
1600 **9** *3* **The Bonus King**[27] 2317 6-9-6 **61**...... GregFairley(5) 3 26
(J Jay) *chsd ldrs: pushed along over 4f out: sn lost pl* **9/1**
10-0 **10** *11* **Filey Buoy**[67] 1258 4-9-2 **52**...... VHalliday 4 —
(R M Whitaker) *hld up in mid-div: rdn 4f out: sn bhd* **33/1**
45-0 **11** *3 ½* **Knock Bridge (IRE)**[174] 77 4-9-5 **58**...... DanielTudhope(3) 5 —
(D Carroll) *hld up in mid-div: rdn 4f out: wknd 3f out* **10/1**
-022 **P** **La Viola**[11] 2794 4-9-1 **56**......(b) AndrewElliott(5) 8 —
(K R Burke) *hdwy 6f out: rdn and wknd wl over 2f out: p.u lame ins fnl f* **3/1**[1]

1m 51.08s (-0.68) **Going Correction** -0.075s/f (Stan)
WFA 3 from 4yo+ 10lb **12** Ran SP% **125.5**
Speed ratings (Par 101):100,99,95,95,93 89,87,82,79,69 66,—
CSF £152.31 CT £587.77 TOTE £16.40: £3.50, £6.00, £2.30; EX 113.90 TRIFECTA Not won. Place 6 £1,820.12, Place 5 £1,078.96..
Owner K Wreglesworth **Bred** Arthur S Phelan **Trained** Sheriff Hutton, N Yorks

FOCUS
A modest handicap run at a strong pace which suited those coming from behind. The first two were well in on old form and finished clear.
Danzare Official explanation: jockey said filly was unlucky in running
La Viola Official explanation: jockey said filly lost her action
T/Plt: £2,669.60 to a £1 stake. Pool: £49,736.40. 13.60 winning tickets. T/Qpdt: £322.40 to a £1 stake. Pool: £4,052.40. 9.30 winning tickets. KH

2950 BRIGHTON (L-H)
Tuesday, July 4

OFFICIAL GOING: Firm
There was a huge bias towards the outside of the track. Four of the six winners were in front racing next to the stands' rail with three furlongs left to run.
Wind: Slight, half-against

3160 RESIDENTIAL APPROVED INSPECTORS CLAIMING STKS 5f 213y
2:30 (2:31) (Class 6) 2-Y-O £2,590 (£770; £385; £192) Stalls Low

Form RPR
0014 **1** **Just Dust**[18] 2598 2-8-6 ......(p) MarcHalford(5) 1 65
(W G M Turner) *mde all: rdn appr fnl f: edgd lft ins but r.o* **11/2**
3021 **2** *1* **Peggys Flower**[15] 2709 2-8-9 ...... RyanMoore 3 60
(N A Callaghan) *t.k.h in 3rd pl: swtchd lft and hdwy 2f out: 2nd and ev ch 1f out: rdn and no imp ins fnl f* **11/8**[1]
032 **3** *1 ¾* **Hester Brook (IRE)**[10] 2878 2-8-5 ...... DominicFox(3) 4 53
(J G M O'Shea) *trckd ldr tl appr fnl f: one pce ins* **9/4**[2]
0661 **4** *7* **Fair 'n Square (IRE)**[14] 2726 2-8-5 ...... JamieMackay 5 28
(J L Spearing) *racd wd towards rr: lost tch over 1f out* **5/1**[3]
U06 **5** *8* **Kaptain Kate**[8] 2916 2-8-5 ...... EdwardCreighton(3) 2 5
(R Brotherton) *s.i.s: outpcd thrght* **40/1**

1m 10.9s (0.80) **Going Correction** -0.10s/f (Good) **5** Ran SP% **107.4**
Speed ratings (Par 92):90,88,86,77,66
CSF £12.94 TOTE £8.50: £3.20, £1.20; EX 17.70.
Owner T.O.C.S. Ltd **Bred** T O C S Ltd And W G M Turner **Trained** Sigwells, Somerset

FOCUS
A modest claimer, but at least the principals had some fair previous form and the form is rated around the runner-up and fourth. With the track dolled quite a fair way out from the inside rail, the field were inclined to race down the middle.

NOTEBOOK
Just Dust goes well in the cheekpieces, and fast ground suits him, though his rider felt this was firmer than ideal. His tendency to edge left up the hill was just typical of many runners here, and he should stay seven furlongs. (op 9-2 tchd 6-1)
Peggys Flower, who was retained for 9,400 guineas after winning a seller last time, ran well enough and should be placed to recoup the auction costs. (op 6-4 tchd 13-8 in a place)
Hester Brook(IRE) was trying an extra furlong and seemed to stay it alright, though lack of acceleration was a problem up the hill. She has been running well and deserves to find a little race. (op 2-1 tchd 5-2)
Fair 'n Square(IRE) has looked more effective over five furlongs. (op 6-1)
Kaptain Kate continues to show little. (op 50-1)

3161 TRENTON FIRE (S) STKS 7f 214y
3:00 (3:02) (Class 6) 3-4-Y-O £2,266 (£674; £337; £168) Stalls Low

Form RPR
0000 **1** **Silver Visage (IRE)**[4] 3033 4-9-3 49......(p) BrianReilly 9 55
(Miss J Feilden) *mde all: c over to stands' side 3f out: rdn out fnl f* **8/1**[3]
6210 **2** *1 ¾* **Beau Marche**[19] 2567 4-9-8 45......(b) RyanMoore 6 56
(G G Margarson) *in tch: swtchd lft over 2f out: rdn and wnt 2nd over 1f out: no imp ins fnl f* **9/2**[1]
0-00 **3** *4* **Macs Ransom (USA)**[11] 2823 3-8-3 55...... ChrisCatlin 1 35
(N A Callaghan) *a in tch: chsd wnr over 2f out tl over 1f out: one pce after* **9/2**[1]
0034 **4** *4* **Khyber Knight (IRE)**[6] 2968 3-8-3 42...... AdrianMcCarthy 3 26
(Jane Southcombe) *mid-div: rdn and sme hdwy 3f out: one pce after* **9/2**[1]
0006 **5** *5* **Chookie Windsor**[6] 2968 3-8-13 53......(p) JohnEgan 4 24
(M S Saunders) *trckd ldrs tl rdn and wknd over 1f out* **5/1**[2]
0040 **6** *2* **Rosiella**[5] 3024 4-8-7 41......(t) MarcHalford(5) 5 12
(M Appleby) *trckd wnr: rdn over 3f out: wknd over 2f out* **8/1**[3]
-000 **7** *3 ½* **Canvas (IRE)**[8] 2937 3-8-1 48 ow5...... JemmaMarshall(7) 10 6
(Miss Z C Davison) *t.k.h: a bhd* **50/1**
-000 **8** *3* **Ferrara Flame (IRE)**[50] 1723 4-8-12 50...... ShaneKelly 11 —
(R Brotherton) *slowly away: a bhd* **12/1**

0000 **9** *3 ½* **Keresforth**[4] 3033 4-9-0 36......(p) EdwardCreighton(3) 2 —
(Mrs L C Jewell) *a bhd* **20/1**

1m 33.63s (-1.41) **Going Correction** -0.10s/f (Good)
WFA 3 from 4yo 9lb **9** Ran SP% **107.8**
Speed ratings (Par 101):103,101,97,93,88 86,82,79,76
CSF £37.28 TOTE £10.60: £3.40, £1.60, £1.80; EX 60.10 Trifecta £156.30 Pool: £286.29 - 1.30 winning tickets..There was no bid for the winner.
Owner Hoofbeats Racing Club **Bred** Trickledown Stud D Magnier And P J Hernon **Trained** Exning, Suffolk

FOCUS
Jockey Brian Reilly had won the last race at the last meeting by bringing his mount Multahab over to the stands' rail and the tactic worked a treat here aboard a horse that had become hard to win with. However, because of this the form is suspect and the runner-up is the best guide. This tactic rather set the trend for the following races.

3162 BUTLER & YOUNG MAIDEN STKS 1m 1f 209y
3:30 (3:31) (Class 5) 3-Y-O+ £3,238 (£963; £481; £240) Stalls High

Form RPR
-342 **1** **Areyoutalkingtome**[52] 1670 3-9-1 97...... EddieAhern 4 61+
(C A Cyzer) *trckd ldr: led over 3f out: clr 2f out: eased ins fnl f* **2/7**[1]
0550 **2** *2* **Guadiana (GER)**[17] 2636 4-9-7 37......(v) ShaneKelly 5 45
(A W Carroll) *t.k.h: hld up: rdn over 1f out: styd on to go 2nd ins fnl f: no ch w wnr* **50/1**[3]
660 **3** *1* **Ten Commandments (IRE)**[10] 2861 3-8-5 39...... EmmettStack(5) 3 43
(K J Burke) *t.k.h: led tl hdd over 3f out: wknd appr fnl f and lost 2nd ins fnl f* **66/1**
052 **4** *9* **Art Man**[22] 2498 3-9-1 77...... RyanMoore 2 31+
(Mrs A J Perrett) *racd 3rd: wnt 2nd over 3f out: hung lft fr 2f out and wknd over 1f out: eased: lame* **10/3**[2]

2m 5.56s (2.96) **Going Correction** -0.10s/f (Good)
WFA 3 from 4yo 11lb **4** Ran SP% **104.3**
Speed ratings (Par 103):84,82,81,74
CSF £13.35 TOTE £1.30; EX 12.90.
Owner Mrs Charles Cyzer **Bred** C A Cyzer **Trained** Maplehurst, W Sussex

FOCUS
A non-event with the second favourite finishing lame, making this a one-horse race with the winner having plenty in hand. The winning time was pedestrian and therefore the form adds up to very little.
Art Man Official explanation: trainer's representative said gelding finished lame

3163 BUTLER & YOUNG TRAINING H'CAP 1m 3f 196y
4:00 (4:01) (Class 5) (0-70,70) 3-Y-O+ £3,886 (£1,156; £577; £288) Stalls High

Form RPR
1003 **1** **Lucky Lark**[10] 2882 3-9-7 **70**...... JohnEgan 5 84+
(M Johnston) *trckd ldr: led over 3f out on favoured stands rail: clr over 1f out: easily* **5/1**
-042 **2** *7* **Girardii**[25] 2391 3-9-1 **64**......(b) RichardHughes 2 67
(R Charlton) *racd 3rd: chsd wnr over 1f out: but no imp* **6/4**[1]
0230 **3** *3* **Iberian Light (USA)**[5] 3017 3-8-9 **58**......(v[1]) ChrisCatlin 3 56
(N A Callaghan) *hld up in last: rdn 2f out: plugged on to go 3rd fnl f* **4/1**[3]
3012 **4** *8* **Icannshift (IRE)**[4] 3035 6-9-0 **50**...... FergusSweeney 1 43+
(T M Jones) *led: rdn 4f out: hdd over 3f out: wknd over 1f out* **9/4**[2]

2m 29.78s (-2.42) **Going Correction** -0.10s/f (Good)
WFA 3 from 6yo+ 13lb **4** Ran SP% **107.4**
Speed ratings (Par 103):104,99,97,92
CSF £12.75 TOTE £5.40; EX 7.60.
Owner Gainsborough Stud **Bred** Gainsborough Stud Management Ltd **Trained** Middleham Moor, N Yorks

FOCUS
They finished pretty strung out in this modest handicap, a race in which the advantage of racing under the stands' rail was again clear to see. The form is not strong.

3164 BYL GROUP H'CAP 6f 209y
4:30 (4:30) (Class 5) (0-70,70) 3-Y-O £3,238 (£963; £481; £240) Stalls Low

Form RPR
-353 **1** **Cindertrack**[10] 2881 3-9-7 **70**...... ShaneKelly 3 84
(J A Osborne) *mde all: grabbed favoured stands rail 3f out: rdn clr fnl f* **7/1**[3]
0-64 **2** *5* **High Class Problem (IRE)**[25] 2403 3-9-2 **65**...... EddieAhern 7 66
(P F I Cole) *hld up: hdwy over 2f out: chsd clr wnr fr over 1f out* **11/10**[1]
-054 **3** *½* **Sunset Ridge (IRE)**[29] 2285 3-8-4 **53**...... ChrisCatlin 8 53
(Rae Guest) *trckd wnr tl rdn wl over 1f out: kpt on one pl fnl f* **16/1**
6334 **4** *nk* **Danish Blues (IRE)**[19] 2583 3-8-13 **62**......(p) RyanMoore 6 61
(N P Littmoden) *t.k.h: hld up: rdn 2f out: kpt on u.p fnl f* **6/1**[2]
3061 **5** *1 ¼* **Elusive Warrior (USA)**[14] 2727 3-9-0 **63**......(p) JimCrowley 9 59+
(Mrs A J Perrett) *hld up in rr: nt clr run over 2f out: one pce fr over 1f out* **15/2**
000- **6** *4* **Wonderful Desert**[288] 5355 3-8-12 **61**...... NickyMackay 5 46
(L M Cumani) *s.i.s: nvr got into r* **7/1**[3]
3506 **7** *½* **Mid Valley**[23] 2479 3-8-5 **54** ow2......(p) JohnEgan 4 38
(J R Jenkins) *mid-div: hmpd over 2f out: wknd over 1f out* **10/1**
-030 **8** *hd* **Royal Agreement**[10] 2877 3-8-5 **57** ow3...... AdamKirby(3) 2 41
(B G Powell) *chsd ldrs: rdn 3f out: wknd wl over 1f out* **20/1**

1m 21.45s (-1.25) **Going Correction** -0.10s/f (Good) **8** Ran SP% **118.4**
Speed ratings (Par 100):103,97,96,96,94 90,89,89
CSF £15.73 CT £126.61 TOTE £9.50: £3.10, £1.10, £3.30; EX 20.00 Trifecta £235.60 Pool: £458.04 - 1.38 winning tickets..
Owner Mrs W W Fleming **Bred** Wyck Hall Stud Ltd **Trained** Upper Lambourn, Berks

FOCUS
A modest handicap in which the winner made all with the advantage of the faster strip of ground under the stands' rail. The form should be treated with caution although the proximity of the third and fourth does represent an element of soundness.

3165 BYL CONSTRUCTION CONSULTANTS H'CAP 5f 59y
5:00 (5:00) (Class 4) (0-80,80) 3-Y-O+ £6,309 (£1,888; £944; £472; £235) Stalls Low

Form RPR
0-30 **1** **One Way Ticket**[18] 2624 6-10-0 **80**......(p) RyanMoore 3 90
(J M Bradley) *mde all: grabbed favoured stands' rail 3f out: rdn clr fnl f* **9/2**[3]
0051 **2** *3 ½* **Misaro (GER)**[10] 2858 5-9-7 **73**......(b) AdrianMcCarthy 5 70
(R A Harris) *towards rr: hdwy in centre over 2f out: rdn to go 2nd ins fnl f* **3/1**[1]
0425 **3** *½* **Willhewiz**[5] 3027 6-9-9 **75**...... JohnEgan 1 71
(M S Saunders) *chsd wnr tl hrd rdn and lost 2nd ins fnl f* **4/1**[2]
1422 **4** *1 ½* **Malapropism**[5] 3027 6-9-12 **78**...... IanMongan 7 68
(M R Channon) *chsd ldrs: rdn and fdd appr fnl f* **9/2**[3]

4-01 **5** 1 1/4 **Multahab**[7] 2955 7-8-9 **61** 6ex oh8 ......(t) BrianReilly 6 47
(Miss D A McHale) *trckd ldrs tl rdn and wknd appr fnl f* **5/1**
-006 **6** 8 **Hornpipe**[16] 2674 4-10-0 **80** ...... JimCrowley 4 37
(M S Saunders) *hld up: a bhd: lost tch over 1f out* **9/1**
61.20 secs (-1.10) **Going Correction** -0.10s/f (Good) **6** Ran SP% **108.0**
Speed ratings (Par 105):104,98,97,95,93 80
CSF £16.86 CT £49.28 TOTE £5.00: £2.30, £2.40; EX 20.50 Trifecta £175.60 Pool: £529.56 - 2.14 winning tickets. Place 6 £61.65, Place 5 £34.02.
Owner Saracen Racing **Bred** Woodsway Stud And Chao Racing And Bloodstock Ltd **Trained** Sedbury, Gloucs
FOCUS
A competitive handicap on paper but another race ruined by the huge bias towards those racing next to the stands'-side rail. The form cannot be taken at face value.
Misaro(GER) Official explanation: jockey said saddle slipped
T/Plt: £93.10 to a £1 stake. Pool: £57,512.50. 450.70 winning tickets. T/Qpdt: £28.20 to a £1 stake. Pool: £3,573.10. 93.60 winning tickets. JS

2998 HAMILTON (R-H)
Tuesday, July 4

OFFICIAL GOING: Good
Wind: Almost nil

3166 RECTANGLE GROUP CLAIMING STKS 6f 5y
2:15 (2:15) (Class 6) 3-5-Y-0 **£2,730** (£806; £403) **Stalls** Centre

Form RPR
0050 **1** **Limonia (GER)**[19] 2574 4-8-3 45 ...... JamesDoyle(5) 7 57
(N P Littmoden) *trckd ldrs: led over 1f out: hld on wl* **11/1**[3]
2-53 **2** nk **Howards Princess**[13] 2749 4-9-5 68 ...... TomEaves 6 67
(I Semple) *keen: trckd ldrs: wnt 2nd over 1f out: effrt and ev ch ins fnl f: kpt on: jst hld* **1/2**[1]
0003 **3** 5 **Special Gold**[12] 2785 4-9-3 54 ......(b) DavidAllan 5 50
(T D Easterby) *led to over 1f out: sn outpcd* **7/2**[2]
0500 **4** hd **Shatin Leader**[8] 2928 4-8-7 41 ......(p) RoystonFfrench 2 39
(Miss L A Perratt) *in tch: rdn over 2f out: edgd rt and sn no imp* **33/1**
466 **5** 9 **Forestelle (IRE)**[34] 2129 3-8-6 52 ...... BenSwarbrick(3) 4 18
(M Dods) *trckd ldrs: rdn over 2f out: sn outpcd* **20/1**
2000 **6** 1 1/4 **Ariesanne (IRE)**[11] 2811 5-8-8 40 ......(p) PaulHanagan 3 9
(A C Whillans) *in tch: rdn 1/2-way: sn btn* **28/1**
1m 12.18s (-0.92) **Going Correction** -0.25s/f (Firm)
WFA 3 from 4yo+ 6lb **6** Ran SP% **108.4**
Speed ratings (Par 101):96,95,88,88,76 75
CSF £16.32 TOTE £8.80: £3.10, £1.10; EX 22.60.
Owner M Murphy **Bred** D Furstin Zu Oettingen-Wallerstein **Trained** Newmarket, Suffolk
FOCUS
An uncompetitive race in which the field raced stands' side. The pace was fair but the favourite was below her best and the form is not solid with the fourth the best guide.

3167 RACING UK H'CAP 1m 65y
2:45 (2:45) (Class 5) (0-70,68) 3-Y-0 **£3,238** (£963; £481; £240) **Stalls** High

Form RPR
6531 **1** **Touch Of Ivory (IRE)**[21] 2529 3-8-8 **55** ......(p) PaulHanagan 11 68
(R A Fahey) *prom: led over 2f out: rdn and kpt on wl fnl f* **5/2**[1]
642 **2** 1/2 **Wind Star**[14] 2734 3-9-7 **68** ...... DeanMcKeown 3 80+
(G A Swinbank) *hld up: hdwy whn nt clr run over 3f to appr 2f out: effrt and chsd wnr 1f out: kpt on wl fnl f* **4/1**[2]
0000 **3** 5 **Cape Of Storms**[9] 2896 3-9-5 **66** ...... TonyCulhane 9 66
(M R Channon) *cl up: ev ch over 2f out: no ex over 1f out* **16/1**
2203 **4** 1/2 **Wednesdays Boy (IRE)**[13] 2746 3-8-6 **53** ...... DaleGibson 2 52
(P D Niven) *keen: hld up: effrt outside over 2f out: no imp over 1f out* **7/1**
3240 **5** shd **Airbound (USA)**[11] 2809 3-9-5 **66** ...... JoeFanning 6 65
(M Johnston) *hld up towards rr: shkn up and hdwy 4f out: no ex fr over 1f out* **13/2**[3]
50-5 **6** 1 **Princess Of Aeneas (IRE)**[24] 2448 3-9-1 **62** ...... TomEaves 7 58
(I Semple) *s.i.s: bhd tl hdwy over 1f out: n.d* **20/1**
-500 **7** 1 1/2 **Inchdhuaig (IRE)**[13] 2746 3-8-9 **56** ...... LeeEnstone 8 49
(P C Haslam) *in tch: drvn 3f out: no imp* **10/1**
0056 **8** 3/4 **Sunbolt (IRE)**[12] 2795 3-9-0 **61** ......(b[1]) PhillipMakin 1 52
(T D Barron) *bhd: effrt outside over 2f out: n.d* **12/1**
00-0 **9** 6 **Knickerless (IRE)**[29] 2284 3-8-0 **52** ow2 ...... JamesDoyle(5) 12 29
(N P Littmoden) *led to over 2f out: sn btn* **12/1**
2000 **10** 15 **Trumpita**[55] 1593 3-8-5 **52** ...... DavidAllan 5 —
(T D Easterby) *chsd ldrs tl wknd over 2f out* **25/1**
5-00 **11** 3 1/2 **Kasarami (IRE)**[13] 2746 3-8-3 **50** oh1 ow1 ...... AdrianTNicholls 10 —
(J S Goldie) *midfield: rdn over 3f out: sn outpcd* **33/1**
0-00 **12** 2 1/2 **Considerthelilies (IRE)**[10] 2856 3-8-7 **54** ...... RoystonFfrench 4 —
(Miss L A Perratt) *in tch tl rdn and wknd fr over 2f out* **100/1**
1m 46.68s (-2.62) **Going Correction** -0.15s/f (Firm) **12** Ran SP% **117.3**
Speed ratings (Par 100):107,106,101,101,100 99,98,97,91,76 73,70
CSF £11.24 CT £133.43 TOTE £3.80: £1.70, £1.60, £4.30; EX 16.50.
Owner Colin Jarvis **Bred** John Hutchinson **Trained** Musley Bank, N Yorks
FOCUS
An ordinary handicap in which the pace was fair and the winning time was good for the grade. The runner-up looks better than the bare form and those just outside the places give the form credibility.

3168 DM HALL H'CAP (QUALIFIER FOR THE HAMILTON PARK SERIES FINAL) 1m 1f 36y
3:15 (3:15) (Class 5) (0-75,73) 3-Y-0+ **£3,886** (£1,156; £577; £288) **Stalls** High

Form RPR
-054 **1** **Chief Scout**[11] 2810 4-10-0 **73** ...... TomEaves 1 83
(I Semple) *prom: effrt and led 2f out: kpt on wl fnl f* **13/2**[3]
0060 **2** 1 1/4 **Qualitair Wings**[39] 1996 7-8-13 **58** ...... DerekMcGaffin 4 65
(J Hetherton) *hld up: hdwy 1/2-way: effrt and edgd rt fr 2f out: chsd wnr ins fnl f: r.o* **9/1**
0652 **3** hd **Burnley Al (IRE)**[1] 3139 4-8-12 **57** ......(b) TonyHamilton 10 64
(R A Fahey) *led to 2f out: kpt on same pce ins fnl f* **7/1**
0-45 **4** 1 3/4 **Shy Glance (USA)**[29] 2298 4-9-4 **63** ...... AdrianTNicholls 5 67
(G A Swinbank) *prom: effrt over 2f out: kpt on same pce fnl f* **7/2**[1]
022 **5** 1/2 **Middlemarch (IRE)**[10] 2853 6-9-11 **70** ......(p) DaleGibson 3 73
(J S Goldie) *in tch: rdn and outpcd 2f out: n.d after* **9/2**[2]
4116 **6** nk **Ulysees (IRE)**[10] 2853 7-9-10 **69** ...... PaulHanagan 8 71
(I Semple) *hld up: checked on ins 1/2-way: effrt 2f out: no imp fnl f* **8/1**
0000 **7** nk **Pianoforte (USA)**[29] 2286 4-8-10 **55** ...... DavidAllan 2 56
(E J Alston) *hld up: n.m.r over 2f out: edgd rt and sn no imp* **25/1**
1603 **8** 1 3/4 **Dispol Veleta**[13] 2747 5-9-6 **68** ...... BenSwarbrick(3) 6 66
(T D Barron) *hld up: rdn over 3f out: n.d* **15/2**
43-5 **9** 10 **Michaels Pride (IRE)**[62] 1419 4-9-10 **69** ...... JoeFanning 9 47
(M Johnston) *chsd ldrs tl over 2f out: wkng whn hmpd over 1f out* **9/1**
1m 58.3s (-1.36) **Going Correction** -0.15s/f (Firm) **9** Ran SP% **113.0**
Speed ratings (Par 103):100,98,98,97,96 96,96,94,85
CSF £61.75 CT £419.19 TOTE £8.50: £2.40, £2.70, £2.60; EX 78.50.
Owner Black & White Communication (Scotland) L **Bred** J R And Mrs P Good **Trained** Carluke, S Lanarks
FOCUS
Another ordinary event but the steady gallop suited those racing prominently. The form could work out but it is hard to be confident.
Shy Glance(USA) Official explanation: jockey said gelding had a breathing problem
Dispol Veleta Official explanation: jockey said mare hung right-handed throughout

3169 ALWAYS TRYING H'CAP 1m 4f 17y
3:45 (3:50) (Class 5) (0-70,68) 3-Y-0 **£3,238** (£963; £481; £240) **Stalls** High

Form RPR
-042 **1** **Baltic Princess (FR)**[12] 2786 3-9-6 **67** ...... JoeFanning 6 78+
(M Johnston) *cl up: led 1/2-way: jnd over 2f out: kpt on strly fnl f* **4/5**[1]
-660 **2** 5 **Virginia Rose (IRE)**[24] 2466 3-8-8 **55** ...... PaulHanagan 5 58
(J G Given) *hld up: rdn 3f out: hdwy over 1f out: chsd wnr ins last: no imp* **12/1**
0-22 **3** 1 1/2 **Minthare (IRE)**[13] 2750 3-9-4 **65** ...... TonyHamilton 1 66+
(C Grant) *trckd ldrs: effrt and chal over 2f out: hung rt over 1f out: sn no ex* **4/1**[2]
0-00 **4** 1 1/2 **Orange Stravinsky**[40] 1948 3-9-4 **65** ...... DeanMcKeown 2 64
(P C Haslam) *prom: effrt 3f out: no imp over 1f out* **14/1**
1-00 **5** 6 **Entranced**[34] 2124 3-9-7 **68** ...... TomEaves 7 57
(Miss J A Camacho) *trckd ldrs: rdn 3f out: btn over 1f out* **13/2**[3]
0-00 **6** 15 **Katsumoto (IRE)**[34] 2124 3-8-5 **57** ...... JamesDoyle(5) 4 22
(N P Littmoden) *led to 1/2-way: hung rt and wknd fr over 2f out* **10/1**
2m 38.21s (-0.97) **Going Correction** -0.15s/f (Firm) **6** Ran SP% **112.3**
Speed ratings (Par 100):97,93,92,91,87 77
CSF £11.86 TOTE £1.70: £1.10, £4.60; EX 12.80.
Owner J Conroy & J Regan **Bred** 6 C Stallions Limited **Trained** Middleham Moor, N Yorks
FOCUS
An uncompetitive event in which the pace was only fair and the form is rated around those in the frame behind the winner.

3170 PHOTOFUN UK H'CAP 5f 4y
4:15 (4:17) (Class 5) (0-75,73) 3-Y-0+ **£5,181** (£1,541; £770; £384) **Stalls** Centre

Form RPR
0136 **1** **Dizzy In The Head**[11] 2830 7-9-11 **70** ......(b) TomEaves 4 81
(I Semple) *racd stands side: mde all: rdn and r.o wl fr 2f out* **5/1**[3]
4502 **2** 1 **Aegean Dancer**[12] 2784 4-9-7 **66** ...... DerekMcGaffin 5 73
(B Smart) *cl up stands side: effrt over 2f out: kpt on ins fnl f* **5/1**[3]
6421 **3** 3/4 **Kings College Boy**[12] 2780 6-9-6 **65** ......(b) PaulHanagan 1 69+
(R A Fahey) *in tch stands side: effrt 2f out: kpt on fnl f: no imp* **3/1**[1]
2341 **4** 3 **Blackheath (IRE)**[17] 2661 10-9-11 **73** ...... SilvestreDeSousa(3) 7 67+
(D Nicholls) *led duo to r on far side: no imp w stands side fr over 1f out* **7/2**[2]
0000 **5** 1 3/4 **Jadan (IRE)**[21] 2521 5-8-10 **55** ...... DavidAllan 9 42+
(E J Alston) *keen: chsd far side ldr: rdn and no imp fr 2f out* **6/1**
5-30 **6** 1 1/4 **Shrink**[12] 2784 5-9-10 **69** ...... PhillipMakin 3 52
(M Dods) *prom stands side tl rdn and no imp fr over 1f out* **16/1**
0150 **7** 1/2 **Brut**[4] 3041 4-9-4 **68** ...... MarkLawson(5) 2 49
(D W Barker) *in tch stands side: effrt over 2f out: wknd over 1f out* **9/1**
59.66 secs (-1.54) **Going Correction** -0.25s/f (Firm) **7** Ran SP% **110.7**
Speed ratings (Par 103):102,100,99,94,91 89,88
CSF £27.90 CT £92.59 TOTE £4.80: £2.80, £3.20; EX 29.40.
Owner Gordon McDowall **Bred** Bearstone Stud And T Herbert Jackson **Trained** Carluke, S Lanarks
FOCUS
An ordinary event in which the two that raced on the far side could never get competitive. The form is not that strong but looks sound enough.

3171 FAIR FRIDAY NEXT WEEK H'CAP 6f 5y
4:45 (4:45) (Class 6) (0-60,60) 3-Y-0+ **£2,730** (£806; £403)

Form RPR
5265 **1** **Blue Maeve**[7] 2949 6-9-4 **53** ...... SilvestreDeSousa(3) 8 64
(A D Brown) *mde all: edgd lft 2f out: kpt on wl fnl f* **6/1**[2]
4600 **2** 2 **Obe One**[15] 2700 6-9-6 **52** ...... AdrianTNicholls 10 57+
(D Nicholls) *bhd: rdn 1/2-way: nt clr run and swtchd rt over 1f out: chsd wnr ins fnl f: r.o: no imp* **7/1**[3]
1510 **3** nk **Union Jack Jackson (IRE)**[49] 1764 4-9-9 **55** ...... DaleGibson 11 59
(J G Given) *bhd and outpcd: hdwy whn nt clr run over 1f out: kpt on fnl f: no imp* **10/1**
0006 **4** 2 **Elkhorn**[13] 2749 4-9-12 **58** ......(p) TomEaves 3 60+
(Miss J A Camacho) *s.i.s: wl bhd: gd hdwy whn no room over 1f out: kpt on fnl f: no imp* **14/1**
2150 **5** hd **Piccolo Prince**[57] 1528 5-9-7 **58** ...... JamesDoyle(5) 5 63+
(E J Alston) *in tch: effrt whn nt clr run over 2f to over 1f out: kpt on same pce ins fnl f* **16/1**
0602 **6** 1 3/4 **Rancho Cucamonga (IRE)**[10] 2856 4-9-7 **53** ......(b) J-PGuillambert 14 45
(T D Barron) *racd wd: in tch: effrt and chsd wnr over 1f out to ins last: sn btn* **11/2**[1]
0-44 **7** hd **Grey Cossack**[26] 2380 9-9-9 **55** ...... RoystonFfrench 13 47
(Mrs L Stubbs) *in tch on outside: rdn and edgd rt 2f out: sn outpcd* **7/1**[3]
6206 **8** 4 **Compton Classic**[20] 2550 4-8-13 **48** ......(p) DanielTudhope(3) 6 28
(J S Goldie) *keen: prom: rdn 2f out: no ex whn chkd ins fnl f* **8/1**
-040 **9** 1/2 **Mozakhraf (USA)**[18] 2611 4-10-0 **60** ...... DO'Donohoe 4 38
(K A Ryan) *prom tl rdn and wknd over 1f out* **7/1**[3]
00-3 **10** 1 1/2 **Bond Becks (IRE)**[8] 2928 6-9-7 **53** ...... DerekMcGaffin 7 27
(B Smart) *bhd: hdwy over 2f out: wknd over 1f out* **14/1**
10-0 **11** 4 **My Rascal (IRE)**[62] 1414 4-9-8 **54** ......(p) TonyCulhane 2 16
(J Balding) *cl up tl rdn and wknd over 1f out* **18/1**
20-0 **12** 5 **Sholto**[7] 2949 8-9-2 **48** ......(b) PaulHanagan 1 —
(J O'Reilly) *cl up tl wknd fr 2f out* **20/1**
1m 12.2s (-0.90) **Going Correction** -0.25s/f (Firm) **12** Ran SP% **116.6**
Speed ratings (Par 101):96,93,92,90,90 87,87,82,81,79 74,67
CSF £46.87 CT £415.68 TOTE £8.50: £3.10, £2.80, £3.80; EX 39.80 Place 6 £84.50, Place 5 £63.12.
Owner R G Fell **Bred** P J And Mrs Nolan **Trained** Pickering, York
■ Stewards' Enquiry : Tom Eaves one-day ban: careless riding (Jul 15)
FOCUS
A modest handicap featuring several unreliable sorts and one that was started using a flip start. The field raced centre to stands' side and the placed horses set the level for the form.

Grey Cossack Official explanation: jockey said gelding hung right-handed from 2f out
Sholto Official explanation: jockey said gelding bled from the nose
T/Jkpt: Not won. T/Plt: £157.70 to a £1 stake. Pool: £49,396.00. 228.60 winning tickets. T/Qpdt: £53.30 to a £1 stake. Pool: £3,482.80. 48.30 winning tickets. RY

2731 THIRSK (L-H)
Tuesday, July 4

OFFICIAL GOING: Straight course - good to firm; round course - firm
Wind: Virtually nil.

3172 RACE FOR LIFE 9TH JULY APPRENTICE STKS (FILLIES' H'CAP) 5f
6:30 (6:30) (Class 5) (0-70,67) 3-Y-O+ £3,886 (£1,156; £577; £288) Stalls High

Form				RPR
00-3	1		**Aahgowangowan (IRE)**[10] 2856 7-9-4 **60**....(t) LiamJones(3) 7 (M Dods) *mde all: rdn wl over 1f out: kpt on strly* 11/4[1]	73
4510	2	1 ½	**Ashes (IRE)**[17] 2661 4-10-0 **67**.... AndrewElliott 3 (K R Burke) *cl up: rdn and ev ch wl over 1f out: drvn and one pce ent last* 9/2[2]	75
3600	3	½	**Safranine (IRE)**[9] 2897 9-8-8 **50**.... MichaelJStainton(3) 8 (Miss A Stokell) *towards rr: hdwy over 2f out: swtchd lft and rdn over 1f out: styd on ins last: nrst fin* 14/1	56
500-	4	2 ½	**Elisha (IRE)**[15] 2715 4-9-3 **56**.... GregFairley 9 (Anthony Mullins, Ire) *prom: rdn along and edgd lft 2f out: sn drvn and wknd appr last* 5/1[3]	53
1204	5	1 ¼	**Mystery Pips**[8] 2925 6-9-5 **63**....(v) DanielleMcCreery(5) 6 (N Tinkler) *bmpd s and in rr tl styd on fnl 2f* 7/1	56
-402	6	2	**Yorke's Folly (USA)**[7] 2949 5-8-6 **48** oh3....(b) KellyHarrison(3) 5 (C W Fairhurst) *chsd ldrs: rdn along 1/2-way: wkng whn sltly hmpd wl over 1f out* 7/1	33
1000	7	¾	**Missperon (IRE)**[17] 2637 4-8-12 **56**....(p) HelenGarner(5) 4 (K A Ryan) *chsd ldrs to 1/2-way: sn wknd* 25/1	39
3-00	8	12	**Elvina**[22] 2494 5-8-10 **52**.... JamesMillman(3) 2 (A G Newcombe) *a towards rr* 11/2	—
0000	9	1 ¼	**Madam Moschata**[25] 2399 3-8-2 **51** oh5 ow3.... VictoriaBehan(5) 1 (D W Barker) *wnt lft s: a rr* 66/1	—

58.34 secs (-1.56) **Going Correction** -0.125s/f (Firm)
WFA 3 from 4yo+ 5lb 9 Ran SP% **113.9**
Speed ratings (Par 100):107,104,103,99,97 94,93,74,72
CSF £14.78 CT £144.27 TOTE £3.40: £1.10, £2.70, £3.10; EX 11.80.
Owner Les Waugh **Bred** Seamus Phelan **Trained** Denton, Co Durham

FOCUS
A decent winning time for a race like this and the form looks fair rated through the runner-up.

3173 EUROPEAN BREEDERS FUND MAIDEN STKS 6f
7:00 (7:00) (Class 4) 2-Y-O £6,477 (£1,927; £963; £481) Stalls High

Form				RPR
	1		**He's A Humbug (IRE)** 2-9-3.... NCallan 4 (K A Ryan) *trckd ldrs: hdwy to ld over 2f out: sn clr: easily* 11/2[3]	88+
4	2	3 ½	**Fourfoot Bay (IRE)**[16] 2680 2-9-3.... GrahamGibbons 6 (J D Bethell) *dwlt and bhd: pushed along and hdwy 1/2-way: rdn along 2f out: styd on to take 2nd ins last: no ch w wnr* 5/2[2]	72
2	3	¾	**Weekend Fling (USA)**[9] 2890 2-8-12.... JoeFanning 3 (M Johnston) *cl up: led over 3f out: rdn along and hdd over 2f out: kpt on same pce* 1/1[1]	64
0	4	3	**Tarraburn (USA)**[24] 2439 2-9-3.... DarryllHolland 1 (J Howard Johnson) *racd wd: prom: rdn along and edgd lft 2f out: sn one pce* 16/1	60
4405	5	nk	**Onenightinlisbon (IRE)**[9] 2890 2-8-12.... LeeEnstone 2 (P T Midgley) *prom: rdn along and hung lft over 2f out: sn wknd* 14/1	54
0565	6	½	**First Valentini**[16] 2680 2-8-5.... SuzzanneFrance(7) 8 (N Bycroft) *bhd: hdwy 1/2-way: rdn to chse ldrs over 2f out: sn drvn and wknd* 33/1	53
00	7	6	**Eldon Endeavour**[6] 2972 2-9-3.... DeanMcKeown 5 (B Storey) *led: rdn along and hdd over 3f out: sn wknd* 200/1	40

1m 12.66s (0.16) **Going Correction** -0.125s/f (Firm) 7 Ran SP% **109.9**
Speed ratings (Par 96):93,88,87,83,82 82,74
CSF £18.10 TOTE £4.60: £2.00, £2.30; EX 20.00.
Owner David Fravigar, Kathy Dixon **Bred** Denis McDonnell **Trained** Hambleton, N Yorks

FOCUS
A fair juvenile maiden, run at a sound enough pace, and the impressive debutant winner is value for further.

NOTEBOOK
He's A Humbug(IRE) ◆, brother to a dual winner in Spain and who cost 32,000gns, proved very easy to back on-course ahead of this racecourse debut. However, he was quickly into his stride from the gates and ultimately ran out a facile winner, being value for plenty further than the winning margin. He has plenty of scope, is entitled to improve for the outing, and is most likely to have his next outing in the Gimcrack at York next month, which indicates he is very well-regarded by his shrewd trainer. (op 7-2)
Fourfoot Bay(IRE), fourth on debut at York 16 days previously, struggled to go the early pace yet eventually picked up for pressure and was doing his best work towards the finish. He is flattered by his proximity to the easy winner, however, and still looked in need of this experience. (op 11-4 tchd 3-1)
Weekend Fling(USA), runner-up against her own sex at Pontefract on debut nine days previously, was made to look one paced when the winner asserted nearing the two-furlong marker and was ultimately well held. She still left the impression she can be found an opening before too long, however. (op 6-5 tchd 5-4)
Tarraburn(USA) improved a touch on the form of his debut at Haydock 24 days previously and got home well enough over the extra furlong. He looks more of a nursery type. (op 20-1 tchd 14-1)
Onenightinlisbon(IRE) Official explanation: jockey said filly hung left-handed

3174 MACDONALD BLACK SWAN HELMSLEY (S) STKS 7f
7:30 (7:31) (Class 5) 2-Y-O £3,238 (£963; £481; £240) Stalls Low

Form				RPR
	1		**Slavonic Lake** 2-8-11.... NCallan 4 (I A Wood) *cl up: pushed along 3f out: rdn wl over 1f out: styd on ins last to ld last 50 yds* 13/2	58
4	2	¾	**Dispol Splendid (IRE)**[15] 2695 2-8-6.... PhilipRobinson 7 (T D Barron) *led: rdn along 2f out: hdd and no ex last 50 yds* 9/2[3]	51
004	3	1 ¼	**Providence Farm**[18] 2626 2-8-11.... PaulMulrennan 3 (M W Easterby) *trckd ldrs: sltly hmpd over 3f out: hdwy 2f out: rdn to chal ent last: sn wandered and one pce* 11/4[1]	52+
642	4	4	**Dispol Truly (IRE)**[14] 2731 2-8-6.... GrahamGibbons 2 (A G Newcombe) *trckd ldrs effrt on inner whn nt clr run and hmpd over 3f out: rdn 2f out and sn btn* 3/1[2]	37+
3	5	¾	**Bridget's Team**[52] 1682 2-8-6.... JoeFanning 5 (P C Haslam) *hld up: swtchd wd and hdwy over 2f out: rdn to chse ldrs over 1f out: sn wknd* 11/4[1]	35
0	6	1 ¾	**Ellies Faith**[35] 2106 2-7-13.... SuzzanneFrance(7) 8 (N Bycroft) *cl up: rdn along wl over 2f out and sn wknd* 25/1	31

1m 27.41s (0.31) **Going Correction** -0.125s/f (Firm) 6 Ran SP% **113.7**
Speed ratings (Par 94):93,92,90,86,85 83
CSF £35.60 TOTE £6.90: £2.00, £2.30; EX 47.10.The winner was bought in for 12,500gns.
Owner Neardown Stables **Bred** Vidin Gate Stud **Trained** Upper Lambourn, Berks

FOCUS
A weak juvenile event, run at just a modest pace, and the first three came clear.

NOTEBOOK
Slavonic Lake, the first foal of an unraced sister to Direct Play, a triple six-furlong winner at two, was making his debut at a lowly level and was well backed to get off the mark. He ran green when push came to shove, but was given a strong ride by Callan, and eventually had a deal in hand at the finish. The quick surface proved to his liking, he looked to need all of this trip, and is entitled to improve for the experience. (op 10-1)
Dispol Splendid(IRE), fourth on her debut over five furlongs at Carlisle 15 days previously, was given a positive ride on this step up in trip and only gave way to the winner inside the final furlong. She left the definite impression she ought to be going one better at this level before too long, although she may benefit for the drop to six furlongs. (op 7-2)
Providence Farm ran his race over this extra furlong and helps to set the level of this form. He may just need holding onto for longer over this trip at present. (op 3-1 tchd 7-2)
Dispol Truly(IRE) was ridden more prominently on this first attempt at a seventh furlong and failed to get home. (tchd 10-3)
Bridget's Team, third on debut in a claimer at this track 52 days previously, did little to convince that she wants this longer trip and may do better when reverting to a sharper test in due course. Official explanation: jockey said filly hung right-handed (op 3-1 tchd 5-2 and 4-1 in a place)

3175 BUCK INN MAUNBY MAIDEN AUCTION STKS 7f
8:00 (8:00) (Class 5) 2-Y-O £3,562 (£1,059; £529; £264) Stalls Low

Form				RPR
645	1		**Rosbay (IRE)**[27] 2361 2-8-11.... DavidAllan 9 (T D Easterby) *mde all: rdn clr 2f out: kpt on* 6/4[1]	78+
	2	2	**Babieca (USA)** 2-8-11.... PhillipMakin 6 (T D Barron) *in tch on outer: reminders 1/2-way: hdwy over 2f out: sn rdn and styd on ins last* 6/1[3]	73
6644	3	5	**Generist**[9] 2899 2-8-1.... DominicFox(3) 2 (M J Attwater) *in tch: hdwy over 2f out: sn rdn and kpt on same pce* 12/1	53
	4	2 ½	**Ingleby Flame (IRE)** 2-8-6.... BenSwarbrick(3) 3 (T D Barron) *hld up in tch: effrt and sme hdwy over 2f out: sn rdn and no imp* 12/1	51
03	5	½	**Autour Du Monde**[6] 2972 2-8-8.... DarryllHolland 1 (P C Haslam) *chsd wnr: rdn along over 2f out: grad wknd* 8/1	49
	6	nk	**Olgarena (IRE)** 2-8-8.... MickyFenton 4 (T D Easterby) *dwlt: a rr* 22/1	48
5	7	1 ½	**Keep Your Distance**[20] 2545 2-8-11.... PatCosgrave 5 (K R Burke) *prom: rdn along over 2f out: sn drvn and wknd* 14/1	47
	U		**Always Best** 2-8-9.... JoeFanning 7 (M Johnston) *wnt bdly rt and uns rdr s* 4/1[2]	—

1m 27.17s (0.07) **Going Correction** -0.125s/f (Firm) 8 Ran SP% **111.8**
Speed ratings (Par 94):94,91,86,83,82 82,80,—
CSF £10.24 TOTE £2.50: £1.50, £1.40, £3.60; EX 13.90.
Owner Croft, Taylor, Stone & Hebdon **Bred** Alan Dargan **Trained** Great Habton, N Yorks

FOCUS
Just a fair contest in which the winner dominated and the field finished fairly strung out.

NOTEBOOK
Rosbay(IRE), who had shown fairly solid form, relished this step up to seven furlongs and, putting his experience to good use, made all for a decisive victory. He looks the type of horse who can improve further and he promises to make his presence felt in nursery company. (op 7-4 tchd 15-8 in places)
Babieca(USA), out of a half-sister to high-class performer Mukaddamah, is a well-grown individual who was noisy and a bit coltish in the preliminaries. He ran well in second and, sure to improve with time and experience, he should win a race. (op 8-1)
Generist, who has been beaten in selling company, was comfortably held in third, having raced rather keenly through the early parts. (op 14-1)
Ingleby Flame(IRE), whose dam was a winning sprinter, was a stablemate of the runner-up and showed a hint of promise on his debut. (op 11-1)
Autour Du Monde failed to improve for this step up in trip but is now eligible for nurseries. (op 7-1 tchd 6-1)

3176 CARLETON FURNITURE H'CAP 1m
8:30 (8:30) (Class 3) (0-90,89) 3-Y-O £9,067 (£2,697; £1,348; £673) Stalls Low

Form				RPR
231	1		**Minister Of State**[18] 2615 3-9-3 **85**.... PhilipRobinson 3 (M A Jarvis) *led: rdn along 2f out: hdd and drvn over 1f out: rallied ins last to ld nr fin* 11/8[1]	92+
-002	2	½	**North Walk (IRE)**[45] 1855 3-8-11 **79**.... NCallan 1 (K A Ryan) *trckd ldrs: hdwy over 2f out: rdn to ld over 1f out: edgd lft ins last: hdd and no ex nr fin* 16/1	85
5436	3	1 ¼	**Damelza (IRE)**[14] 2735 3-8-6 **74**....(t) DavidAllan 2 (T D Easterby) *dwlt and hld up in rr: hdwy on inner over 2f out: rdn to chse ldrs over 1f out: kpt on same pce ins last* 18/1	77
250-	4	2 ½	**Always Baileys (IRE)**[260] 5949 3-8-11 **79**.... JoeFanning 4 (M Johnston) *hld up in tch: hdwy over 2f out: sn rdn and no imp appr last* 16/1	76
3146	5	3	**Neardown Beauty (IRE)**[10] 2880 3-8-7 **75**.... DarryllHolland 6 (I A Wood) *hld up in rr: hdwy over 2f out: sn rdn and btn* 10/1	65
2-21	6	18	**Northern Boy (USA)**[24] 2448 3-9-0 **82**.... PhillipMakin 5 (T D Barron) *sn trcking ldrs: effrt 3f out: sn rdn along and wknd: eased over 1f out* 11/4[2]	31
311-	7	3	**Natural Force (IRE)**[231] 6352 3-9-7 **89**.... KerrinMcEvoy 7 (Saeed Bin Suroor) *trckd ldrs: pushed along 3f out: rdn and btn 2f out: eased* 5/1[3]	31

1m 36.61s (-3.09) **Going Correction** -0.125s/f (Firm) 7 Ran SP% **111.6**
Speed ratings (Par 104):110,109,108,105,102 84,81
CSF £24.16 TOTE £2.50: £1.70, £3.20; EX 26.60.
Owner Cheveley Park Stud **Bred** Cheveley Park Stud Ltd **Trained** Newmarket, Suffolk

FOCUS
A fairly competitive line-up and a decent winning time for a contest of its type. Solid form, rated around the third and fourth, with the first two showing improvement.

NOTEBOOK
Minister Of State ◆ is clearly going the right way and, given a canny ride from the front, rallied in tremendous style to get the better of the runner-up after staring defeat firmly in the face inside the final furlong. He can improve further. (op 6-4 tchd 13-8 in a place)

North Walk(IRE) ◆, returning from a short break, ran a blinder on ground arguably a bit quick for him. It was only close home that he was finally outpointed and there are races to be won with him. (tchd 18-1)
Damelza(IRE), reverting to hold-up tactics, ran a fair race and may have benefited from the fitting of a tongue-tie. (op 16-1)
Always Baileys(IRE) made a satisfactory return to action and there should be improvement to come on easier ground. (op 14-1)
Neardown Beauty(IRE), back over a mile, found little when the pressure was on. (op 8-1)
Northern Boy(USA) was ultimately well beaten on his handicap debut. Official explanation: jockey said colt lost its action (op 7-2 tchd 5-2)
Natural Force(IRE), on his first run since November, came off the bridle before the straight and was soon in trouble. (op 9-2)

3177 LADIES DAY H'CAP — 2m
9:00 (9:00) (Class 4) (0-85,81) 3-Y-0+ **£6,477** (£1,927; £963; £481) **Stalls** Low

Form				RPR
0002	**1**		**Whispering Death**[16] 2684 4-8-12 **65**.....(v) TonyCulhane 5 (W J Haggas) *hld up in tch: hdwy on bit over 2f out: led over 1f out: rdn clr ins last* **5/2**[1]	79+
1030	**2**	*5*	**Trance (IRE)**[14] 2723 6-10-0 **81**.....(p) NCallan 3 (T D Barron) *hld up: hdwy on outer over 2f out: rdn to chse wnr and edgd lft ent last: sn one pce* **7/2**[3]	88+
3503	**3**	*5*	**Kristensen**[10] 2879 7-9-2 **69**.....(v) PaulHanagan 1 (Karen McLintock) *trckd ldr: rdn along 3f out: wknd fnl 2f* **6/1**	69
0451	**4**	*¾*	**Let It Be**[10] 2871 5-8-9 **62**..... DavidAllan 4 (K G Reveley) *trckd ldrs: effrt 3f out: sn rdn and wknd wl over 1f out* **6/1**	61
0520	**5**	*¾*	**Incursion**[14] 2723 5-9-3 **70**..... AdrianTNicholls 6 (D Nicholls) *trckd ldr: effrt 3f out: sn rdn and wknd fnl 2f* **10/1**	68
503	**6**	*1*	**Calcutta Cup (UAE)**[52] 1691 3-8-3 **75**..... JoeFanning 2 (M Johnston) *set stdy pce: rn wd bnd into bk st and j. path: rdn along 3f out: drvn and hdd over 1f out: wknd qckly and eased* **11/4**[2]	72+

3m 29.13s (-2.07) **Going Correction** -0.125s/f (Firm)
WFA 3 from 4yo+ 19lb — **6** Ran SP% **115.1**
Speed ratings (Par 105):100,97,95,94,94 93
CSF £12.02 TOTE £3.80: £1.80, £2.30; EX 15.00 Place 6 £137.96, Place 5 £72.38..
Owner G Roberts/F M Green **Bred** Milton Park Stud **Trained** Newmarket, Suffolk

FOCUS
Just an ordinary staying handicap. There was no pace on and this is not strong form.
Calcutta Cup(UAE) Official explanation: jockey said colt hung right-handed throughout
T/Plt: £132.30 to a £1 stake. Pool: £44,159.10. 243.60 winning tickets. T/Qpdt: £38.40 to a £1 stake. Pool: £2,514.20. 48.40 winning tickets. JR

2394 CATTERICK (L-H)
Wednesday, July 5

OFFICIAL GOING: Firm (good to firm in places)
The watered ground was described as 'just on the fast side of good with a very good cover of grass'.
Wind: Light; half behind Weather: Fine, sunny and very warm

3187 EUROPEAN BREEDERS FUND ZETLAND MEDIAN AUCTION MAIDEN STKS — 7f
2:30 (2:30) (Class 5) 2-Y-0 **£3,886** (£1,156; £577; £288) **Stalls** Low

Form				RPR
2	**1**		**Kirklees (IRE)**[15] 2733 2-9-3..... JoeFanning 1 (M Johnston) *mde all: shkn up over 1f out: sn drew clr readily* **4/9**[1]	85+
234	**2**	*5*	**Pires**[11] 2844 2-9-3..... TonyCulhane 2 (M R Channon) *stdd s: sn drvn along and hung rt: hmpd bnd over 4f out: wnt 2nd over 1f out: no ch w wnr* **2/1**[2]	72+
5	**3**	*4*	**Centenary (IRE)**[15] 2733 2-9-3..... DarryllHolland 3 (J Howard Johnson) *w wnr: rdn over 2f out: one pce* **16/1**[3]	62
0	**4**	*8*	**Bollin Freddie**[26] 2409 2-9-3..... MickyFenton 4 (T D Easterby) *s.i.s: sn chsng ldrs: outpcd 3f out: lost pl over 1f out* **100/1**	41

1m 25.37s (-1.99) **Going Correction** -0.45s/f (Firm) — **4** Ran SP% **109.5**
Speed ratings (Par 94):93,87,82,73
CSF £1.62 TOTE £1.50; EX 1.70.
Owner Jumeirah Racing **Bred** Darley **Trained** Middleham Moor, N Yorks

FOCUS
An interesting little juvenile maiden, won by a colt who can rate higher, and the field came home strung out.

NOTEBOOK
Kirklees(IRE) ◆, a narrow runner-up on his debut at Thirsk, was all the rage in the betting to go one better and duly rewarded his followers with a comfortable success. He was edgy in the preliminaries, and just before the start, but when the gates opened he was very professional and ultimately full value for his winning margin. Considering the runner-up had finished fourth in the Chesham Stakes at Royal Ascot previously, this has to rate a decent effort, and it will be very interesting to see where this progressive colt is pitched in next. (op 8-13 after early 8-11 in a place)
Pires, fourth in the Listed Chesham Stakes last time and whose trainer had been successful with his only two previous runners in this event, never looked particularly at ease on this undulating track and his fate was already sealed before he was hampered on the turn for home. He did finish clear in second, and time may tell there was little disgrace in this defeat, so he should be given one more chance when reverting to a more galloping track and slightly easier ground. (op 13-8)
Centenary(IRE), behind the winner on his debut at Thirsk, finished further behind that rival this time and was another who may not have enjoyed this track. He looks in need of further experience and may fare better when eligible for nurseries. (op 14-1 tchd 12-1)
Bollin Freddie, as on his Haydock debut over six furlongs last time, was always playing catch-up after a sluggish start and never figured. (op 66-1)

3188 EUROPEAN BREEDERS FUND MAIDEN FILLIES' STKS — 5f
3:00 (3:00) (Class 5) 2-Y-0 **£3,886** (£1,156; £577; £288) **Stalls** Low

Form				RPR
04	**1**		**Valley Of The Moon (IRE)**[19] 2623 2-9-0..... PaulHanagan 8 (R A Fahey) *chsd ldrs: styd on to ld towards fin* **9/2**[2]	74
5	**2**	*nk*	**Durova (IRE)**[12] 2827 2-9-0..... MickyFenton 5 (T D Easterby) *led: hung lft over 1f out: hdd and no ex wl ins last* **11/2**[3]	73
34	**3**	*1 ¼*	**Malaaq**[10] 2890 2-9-0..... RHills 4 (M A Jarvis) *w ldr: chal over 1f out: kpt on same pce ins last* **4/5**[1]	68
	4	*2*	**Frontline In Focus (IRE)** 2-9-0..... PatCosgrave 9 (K R Burke) *s.s: hdwy over 1f out: styd on wl ins last* **20/1**	61+
0	**5**	*3 ½*	**Nanny State (IRE)**[7] 2973 2-9-0..... JoeFanning 3 (P C Haslam) *chsd ldrs: wknd 1f out: eased towards fin* **33/1**	49
	6	*1 ¼*	**Golden Topaz (IRE)** 2-9-0..... DarryllHolland 7 (J Howard Johnson) *mid-div: effrt over 2f out: hung lft and wknd fnl f* **9/1**	44
	7	*5*	**Flying Valentino** 2-9-0..... DeanMcKeown 1 (G A Swinbank) *hmpd sn after s: t.k.h in rr: sme hewady 2f out: hung lft over 1f out: sn wknd* **20/1**	26
0	**8**	*7*	**Laurels Lady**[16] 2703 2-9-0..... RoystonFfrench 6 (I W McInnes) *s.i.s: in rr and hung rt 2f out: swvd bdly lft over 1f out* **100/1**	—
0	**9**	*5*	**Kyoto City**[13] 2791 2-9-0..... PaulQuinn 2 (D W Chapman) *in tch: outpcd over 2f out: sn wknd* **100/1**	—

58.68 secs (-1.92) **Going Correction** -0.45s/f (Firm) — **9** Ran SP% **113.6**
Speed ratings (Par 91):97,96,94,91,85 83,75,64,56
CSF £26.79 TOTE £6.20: £1.80, £1.10, £1.10; EX 24.30.
Owner T Elsey,S A Elsey,R Mustill,J Tunstall **Bred** Mrs P Grubb **Trained** Musley Bank, N Yorks

FOCUS
A modest juvenile fillies' maiden, run at a solid pace, and the first two came clear giving the form a sound appearance.

NOTEBOOK
Valley Of The Moon(IRE) just did enough to get on top of the runner-up close home and break her duck at the third time of asking. She had shown promise on both her previous outings, and she put that experience to good use this time, acting well on the quick surface. Her future lies with the Handicapper and she ought to relish the return to a sixth furlong in due course. (tchd 4-1 and 5-1)
Durova(IRE), who missed the break when fifth on her debut at Redcar on similar ground, showed decent early speed this time and was only reeled in by the winner late on. She is going the right way, finished a clear second best, and can be placed to get off the mark before too long. (tchd 5-1)
Malaaq, dropping back in trip, is bred to relish this sort of surface and has to rate disappointing. She displayed the required pace for this distance, but while she may be more at home when reverting to a more conventional track, at this stage she does not look like living up to her pedigree. (op 10-11 tchd evens in a place)
Frontline In Focus(IRE), a precocious type on breeding, shaped with ability and was keeping on well enough in the latter stages after a slow start. She can be expected to benefit from this debut experience and go closer next time. (op 16-1)

3189 WE RACE AGAIN NEXT WEDNESDAY MEDIAN AUCTION MAIDEN STKS — 5f 212y
3:30 (3:30) (Class 6) 3-4-Y-0 **£2,730** (£806; £403) **Stalls** Low

Form				RPR
4550	**1**		**Lord Mayfair (USA)**[5] 3034 4-9-2 44.....(b) AnnStokell(7) 3 (Miss A Stokell) *mde all: rdn clr over 1f out: styd on* **40/1**	61
-000	**2**	*4*	**Graceful Flight**[14] 2758 4-9-4 35..... LeeEnstone 1 (P T Midgley) *chsd ldrs: wnt 2nd over 2f out: no imp* **100/1**	44
4-03	**3**	*½*	**Bijli (IRE)**[11] 2859 3-9-3 69..... TPQueally 5 (J Noseda) *trckd ldrs: effrt over 2f out: kpt on same pce* **7/4**[1]	47
-060	**4**	*nk*	**Strong Approach (IRE)**[12] 2809 3-9-3 67.....(b[1]) PhillipMakin 7 (T D Barron) *s.i.s: hdwy on outside 2f out: kpt on: nt rch ldrs* **5/2**[2]	46+
-330	**5**	*nk*	**Takanewa (IRE)**[16] 2699 3-8-12 68..... DarryllHolland 6 (J Howard Johnson) *hld up in rr: hdwy over 3f out: kpt on same pce fnl 2f* **3/1**[3]	40
54	**6**	*1 ½*	**Just Lille (IRE)**[8] 2948 3-8-12..... RoystonFfrench 2 (Mrs A Duffield) *in rr: stmbld bnd over 3f out: kpt on fnl 2f: nvr nr ldrs* **10/1**	35+
-046	**7**	*½*	**Laphonic (USA)**[30] 2285 3-9-0 50..... SaleemGolam(3) 8 (T J Etherington) *chsd ldrs: rdn and hung lft over 2f out: one pce* **14/1**	39
0050	**8**	*½*	**Madame Guillotine**[119] 618 4-9-4 37.....(p) MickyFenton 9 (P T Midgley) *chsd ldrs: lost pl over 2f out: sme hdwy 2f out: nvr a threat* **100/1**	33
00-4	**9**	*2 ½*	**The Keep**[27] 2377 4-9-4 40.....(b) TomEaves 4 (R E Barr) *prom: wknd over 1f out* **40/1**	26

1m 12.22s (-1.78) **Going Correction** -0.45s/f (Firm)
WFA 3 from 4yo 6lb — **9** Ran SP% **112.6**
Speed ratings (Par 101):93,87,87,86,86 84,83,82,79
CSF £1726.50 TOTE £18.00: £4.90, £12.00, £1.10; EX 400.20.
Owner Ms Caron Stokell **Bred** C A Hansen And Daniel D Hansen **Trained** Brompton-on-Swale, N Yorks

FOCUS
A very moderate winning time allowing for the conditions and the form is most dubious with the first two home officially rated just 44 and 35 respectively.

3190 PROJECT MANAGEMENT SCOTLAND H'CAP — 5f
4:00 (4:01) (Class 5) (0-70,67) 3-Y-0+ **£5,181** (£1,541; £770; £384) **Stalls** Low

Form				RPR
0600	**1**		**Ryedane (IRE)**[23] 2504 4-9-9 **62**..... J-PGuillambert 11 (T D Easterby) *chsd ldrs: styd on to ld nr fin* **10/1**	74
4213	**2**	*nk*	**Kings College Boy**[1] 3170 6-9-5 **65**.....(b) JamesReveley(7) 8 (R A Fahey) *chsd ldrs: led jst ins last: hdd and no ex nr fin* **7/2**[1]	76
-026	**3**	*1*	**Strensall**[13] 2784 9-9-13 **66**..... PaulHanagan 13 (R E Barr) *chsd ldrs: kpt on same pce ins last* **11/2**[3]	73
5401	**4**	*¾*	**Sharp Hat**[9] 2928 12-8-9 **48** 6ex..... TonyCulhane 3 (D W Chapman) *led tl hdd jst ins last: wknd towards fin* **11/2**[3]	52
-000	**5**	*1*	**Betsen (IRE)**[25] 2449 4-10-0 **67**..... AdrianTNicholls 5 (D Nicholls) *s.i.s: hdwy on inner over 2f out: hrd rdn over 1f out: kpt on same pce* **8/1**	68+
3006	**6**	*¾*	**Champagne Cracker**[9] 2925 5-9-10 **63**..... TonyHamilton 14 (I Semple) *s.i.s: hdwy on outer over 2f out: kpt on: nvr rchd ldrs* **14/1**	61+
0640	**7**	*nk*	**Borzoi Maestro**[20] 2571 5-9-1 **54**.....(p) DarryllHolland 7 (M Wellings) *w ldr: one pce appr fnl f* **17/2**	51
-001	**8**	*¾*	**Dark Champion**[12] 2833 6-8-13 **59**.....(b) MarkCoumbe(7) 15 (R E Barr) *hld up on wd outside: effrt 2f out: nvr trbld ldrs* **18/1**	53
0000	**9**	*¾*	**Percy Douglas**[9] 2928 6-8-6 **52**.....(bt) AnnStokell(7) 10 (Miss A Stokell) *sn outpcd and in rr: nvr a factor* **14/1**	44
6251	**10**	*3 ½*	**Never Without Me**[13] 2784 6-9-13 **66**..... MickyFenton 12 (J F Coupland) *sn outpcd in rr on outer: bhd fnl 2f* **5/1**[2]	45

58.20 secs (-2.40) **Going Correction** -0.45s/f (Firm)
WFA 3 from 4yo+ 5lb — **10** Ran SP% **119.0**
Speed ratings (Par 103):101,100,98,97,96 94,94,93,92,86
CSF £45.96 CT £218.79 TOTE £12.50: £3.70, £1.70, £2.60; EX 78.60.
Owner Ryedale Partners No 5 **Bred** Tally-Ho Stud **Trained** Great Habton, N Yorks

FOCUS
An ordinary sprint handicap and not as competitive as it might have been with the five non-runners. The form looks solid enough rated through the third.

3191 CATTERICKBRIDGE.CO.UK H'CAP — 7f
4:30 (4:30) (Class 3) (0-90,90) 3-Y-0+ **£9,715** (£2,890; £1,444; £721) **Stalls** Low

Form				RPR
2503	**1**		**Hartshead**[6] 3020 7-10-0 **90**..... DeanMcKeown 6 (G A Swinbank) *trckd ldrs: styd on to ld towards fin* **5/2**[1]	98
1260	**2**	*hd*	**Byron Bay**[41] 1949 4-9-6 **82**..... TomEaves 1 (I Semple) *led after 1f: kpt on fnl f: hdd nr fin* **17/2**	89

6610 **3** *1* **Tough Love**[7] [2974] 7-8-11 **73**..(p) MickyFenton 5 77
(T D Easterby) *hld up in rr: hdwy and swtchd rt over 1f out: styd on* **13/2**

-446 **4** *nk* **Heureux (USA)**[12] [2809] 3-8-7 **77**...............................(b[1]) DarryllHolland 2 77
(J Howard Johnson) *trckd ldrs: drvn over 2f out: nt clr run ins last: kpt on same pce* **14/1**

5542 **5** *2* **Serieux**[15] [2737] 7-8-12 **74**...(v) AdrianTNicholls 4 72
(D Nicholls) *t.k.h: effrt over 2f out: kpt on: nvr rchd ldrs* **5/1**[3]

3140 **6** *½* **Fiefdom (IRE)**[13] [2776] 4-9-8 **87**....................................... LeeVickers(3) 3 83
(I W McInnes) *chsd ldrs: outpcd and n.m.r 2f out: no threat after* **15/2**

6430 **7** *1 ½* **H Harrison (IRE)**[8] [2946] 6-8-10 **72**............................. RoystonFfrench 7 64
(I W McInnes) *led 1f: chsd ldrs: fdd fnl f* **10/1**

5232 **8** *1 ½* **Madaares (USA)**[8] [2948] 3-8-8 **78**.. RHills 8 63
(M Johnston) *s.i.s: sn drvn along on outer: nvr a threat* **9/2**[2]

1m 24.09s (-3.27) **Going Correction** -0.45s/f (Firm)
WFA 3 from 4yo+ 8lb **8** Ran SP% **114.8**
Speed ratings (Par 107):100,99,98,98,96 95,93,92
CSF £24.77 CT £124.41 TOTE £3.20: £1.30, £3.10, £3.40; EX 35.40.

Owner B Valentine **Bred** Gainsborough Stud Management Ltd **Trained** Melsonby, N Yorks

■ Stewards' Enquiry : Dean McKeown caution: used whip with excessive frequency

FOCUS
A decent handicap though the time was modest for the grade give the fast conditions. The form appears sound enough rated around the placed horses.

NOTEBOOK
Hartshead, only declared for this when the race was reopened, put up a career-best effort to win this being off a mark 4lb higher than for his last success. He also needed every yard of this trip to get up near the line and despite this win is probably better suited by a mile these days. (tchd 11-4)

Byron Bay, a springer in the market, was obviously expected by someone to run a big race and duly did so. Soon bustled into the lead from the inside stall, he refused to be overtaken but the winners' last-gasp effort proved one challenge too many. This ground would have been plenty fast enough for him, so this was a decent effort in defeat. (op 12-1)

Tough Love, who has managed just one victory in the past three years, had a lot to do turning for home and probably did well to finish where he did. His victory at Thirsk two outings ago was over this trip, but that was in a strongly-run race and this was not quite run the same way. (op 11-2)

Heureux(USA) ◆, dropping in trip, did by far the better of the two three-year-olds and may have been a bit closer had he seen more daylight in the home straight. He is gradually dropping in the weights and looks to have a race in him before too long. (tchd 16-1)

Serieux finished further behind Tough Love than he had at Thirsk last time despite meeting him on 2lb better terms for a half-length beating. He has proved very hard to win with in recent seasons and does not look the easiest of rides. (op 6-1)

Fiefdom(IRE) could never really get involved and looks held off his current mark. His victory at Lingfield three starts ago may have been down to him enjoying the advantage of a faster strip of ground. (op 8-1)

Madaares(USA), still a maiden, missed the break and then appeared to have a real problem negotiating the home bend which was the last thing he needed over this shorter trip. He needs a stiffer test and is better than this. (op 4-1)

3192 STOCKTON H'CAP — 1m 3f 214y
5:00 (5:00) (Class 6) (0-65,59) 4-Y-0+ **£3,412** (£1,007; £504) **Stalls** Low

Form RPR

6050 **1** **Abstract Folly (IRE)**[16] [2697] 4-9-2 **54**........................... DarryllHolland 3 60+
(J D Bethell) *hld up in rr: hmpd over 2f out: styd on wl to ld nr fin* **7/1**

0055 **2** *nk* **Melvino**[9] [2927] 4-9-6 **58**... PhillipMakin 4 64
(T D Barron) *s.i.s: hld up: hdwy 4f out: styd on to ld ins last: hdd and no ex towards fin* **6/1**[3]

-520 **3** *1 ¼* **Colway Ritz**[11] [2871] 12-8-2 **43**.............................. SilvestreDeSousa(3) 1 47+
(W Storey) *trckd ldrs: outpcd whn n.m.r 2f out: swtchd rt and styd on: kpt on wl ins last* **8/1**

1325 **4** *½* **Acuzio**[13] [2788] 5-8-13 **51**.. PaulMulrennan 9 54
(W M Brisbourne) *trckd ldrs: led over 2f out: hdd and no ex ins last* **9/2**[2]

5130 **5** *1 ¾* **Nicozetto (FR)**[2] [3141] 6-8-10 **51**.. DNolan(3) 5 51
(N Wilson) *hld up towards rr: effrt over 2f out: styd on same pce fnl f* **16/1**

0-30 **6** *1* **Zeydnaa (IRE)**[17] [2684] 6-8-12 **50**.. TonyHamilton 8 48
(C R Wilson) *led 1f: chsd ldrs: one pce whn n.m.r on inner 1f out* **7/1**

7 *½* **Starofthemorning (IRE)**[174] [5561] 5-7-11 **40** oh4.. DuranFentiman(5) 11 38
(A W Carroll) *s.i.s: drvn 7f out: hdwy on wd outside over 2f out: kpt on same pce appr fnl f* **25/1**

4606 **8** *1 ½* **Platinum Charmer (IRE)**[13] [2788] 6-9-6 **58**..................(p) PatCosgrave 6 53
(K R Burke) *in tch: sn pushed along: fdd fnl f* **10/1**

6011 **9** *1 ¼* **Hezaam (USA)**[14] [2762] 5-9-7 **59**.. DO'Donohoe 2 52
(Mrs A Duffield) *trckd ldrs: drvn on inner 4f out: keeping on same pce whn n.m.r appr fnl f: eased ins last* **9/4**[1]

35-0 **10** *12* **Rockpiler**[12] [2829] 4-8-2 **47**... MarkCoumbe(7) 7 21
(D W Thompson) *t.k.h: led after 1f: hdd over 6f out: hmpd over 2f out: lost pl over 1f out: eased* **100/1**

0546 **11** *6* **Viscount Rossini**[61] [1462] 4-8-2 **40**................................. PaulHanagan 10 4
(A W Carroll) *w ldrs: led over 6f out: faltered and hdd over 2f out: eased and sn lost pl* **33/1**

2m 33.86s (-5.14) **Going Correction** -0.45s/f (Firm) **11** Ran SP% **122.1**
Speed ratings (Par 101):99,98,97,97,96 95,95,94,93,85 81
CSF £50.06 CT £352.63 TOTE £10.60: £2.30, £2.30, £2.40; EX 78.50 Place 6 £39.68, Place 5 £26.05.

Owner Clarendon Thoroughbred Racing **Bred** John Neary **Trained** Middleham Moor, N Yorks

FOCUS
A competitive if modest handicap, but trouble for a few after Viscount Rossini took a bad step soon after turning for home and, as he faltered, it caused a ripple effect back through the field. The form is best rated through the third.

Hezaam(USA) Official explanation: jockey said gelding suffered interference and was denied a clear run

Viscount Rossini Official explanation: jockey said gelding lost its action

T/Plt: £41.20 to a £1 stake. Pool: £38,780.25 - 687.05 winning units T/Qpdt: £38.30 to a £1 stake. Pool: £2,502.90 - 48.35 winning units WG

2916 CHEPSTOW (L-H)
Wednesday, July 5

OFFICIAL GOING: Good to firm changing to good after race 1 (6.40)
The meeting was delayed due to an inspection of the track after the first race. The last race was abandoned due to bad light.
Wind: Nil

3193 32RED MAIDEN STKS — 6f 16y
6:40 (6:41) (Class 5) 2-Y-O **£3,562** (£1,059; £529; £264) **Stalls** High

Form RPR

0 **1** **Kyshanty**[30] [2287] 2-9-0 .... RichardSmith(3) 12 77
(R Hannon) *trckd ldrs: chal over 2f out tl led over 1f out: drvn out* **50/1**

0 **2** *1 ¼* **Auction Oasis**[58] [1542] 2-8-12 .... FrancisFerris 13 68
(B Palling) *slt ld on stands side: rdn over 2f out: hdd over 1f out: styd on but nt pce of wnr ins last* **33/1**

20 **3** *1 ¼* **Goodbye Cash (IRE)**[12] [2800] 2-8-12 .... FrancisNorton 1 65
(P D Evans) *s.i.s: sn in tch: drvn to chal over 1f out: kpt on same pce ins last* **6/1**[3]

66 **4** *1 ½* **Marine Parade**[39] [2029] 2-9-3 .... PatDobbs 10 65
(R Hannon) *chsd ldrs: challenged fr half way and stl ev ch over 1f out: wknd ins last* **5/2**[1]

5 *2* **Shantina's Dream (USA)** 2-8-12 .... SteveDrowne 14 57+
(H Morrison) *rr but in tch: stmbld ins fnl 3f: kpt on fr over 1f out but nvr gng pce to rch ldrs* **4/1**[2]

6 *¾* **Reebal** 2-9-3 .... TPQueally 11 57
(B J Meehan) *chsd ldrs: rdn 3f out: wknd over 1f out* **11/1**

0 **7** *½* **Up In Arms (IRE)**[34] [2172] 2-9-3 .... JimCrowley 2 55
(P Winkworth) *s.i.s: rr but in tch: hdwy 1/2-way: rdn 2f out: wknd fnl f* **50/1**

8 *½* **Only Hope** 2-8-5 .... ThomasO'Brien(7) 15 49
(M R Channon) *bhd: stl plenty to do 2f out: r.o appr fnl f: kpt on cl home but nvr in contention* **16/1**

55 **9** *shd* **Road To Recovery**[19] [2617] 2-9-3 .... FergusSweeney 6 53
(A M Balding) *chsd ldrs: rdn over 2f out: wknd over 1f out* **6/1**[3]

5 **10** *1 ¼* **Dansilver**[19] [2598] 2-9-3 .... VinceSlattery 8 50
(D J Wintle) *chsd ldrs: rdn 1/2-way: wknd ins fnl 2f* **50/1**

0 **11** *1 ¾* **Movethegoalposts**[13] [2783] 2-9-3 .... KDarley 3 44
(M Johnston) *w ldr 4f: wknd over 1f out* **12/1**

12 *5* **Soffooh (USA)** 2-9-0 .... EdwardCreighton(3) 4 29
(M R Channon) *outpcd most of way* **12/1**

13 *2 ½* **Majestas (IRE)** 2-9-3 .... RobertHavlin 5 22
(J G M O'Shea) *a outpcd in rr* **33/1**

14 *1* **Our Archie** 2-9-3 .... AdrianMcCarthy 7 19
(M J Attwater) *s.i.s: in tch 1/2-way: wkng whn sltly hmpd over 2f out* **20/1**

1m 12.78s (0.38) **Going Correction** -0.075s/f (Good) **14** Ran SP% **123.3**
Speed ratings (Par 94):94,92,90,88,86 85,84,83,83,81 79,72,69,68
CSF £1192.82 TOTE £60.50: £12.10, £6.30, £1.60; EX 775.80.
Owner D J Walker, Dr M M Smith & R C Smith **Bred** Lady Whent **Trained** East Everleigh, Wilts
■ Aquilegia was withdrawn at the start (6/1, deduct 10p in the £ under Rule 4).

FOCUS
The rain had got into the ground and it was closer to good than anything else. This juvenile event saw a shock result but the form looks fair, rated through the third and fourth.

NOTEBOOK
Kyshanty, who is out of a half-sister to Bold Edge, a high-class sprinter for the Hannon yard, went off a big price but seemed to win on merit. This represented a huge improvement on his debut effort, where he never got competitive, and he is obviously going the right way. He holds entries in the Weatherbys Super Sprint and the Doncaster St Leger Sales race, but he will need to come on again for this to figure in those two events. (old market op 66-1 new market op 40-1)
Auction Oasis beat just one home on her Windsor debut but this was much better, although she had the benefit of racing near the stands' rail. There may well be a nursery in her after another outing. (old market op 40-1)
Goodbye Cash(IRE), who took her chance in the Albany Stakes at Royal Ascot last time, is now eligible for nurseries and that is where her future lies. (old market op 9-1 new market op 7-1)
Marine Parade, a stablemate of the big-priced winner, had every chance. He has a race or two in him, possibly over another furlong in nurseries. (old market op 11-4 new market tchd 9-4)
Shantina's Dream(USA), who comes from a decent American family, was a shade unlucky on this debut as she was about to come with an effort when she stumbled over two furlongs out and is a bit better than her finishing position suggests. It would be no surprise if she reversed this form with most of those that finished in front of her if they met again. Official explanation: jockey said filly stumbled 2 1/2f out (old market op 5-1 tchd 11-2)
Reebal, whose dam won the Cherry Hinton Stakes, is a half-brother to winners in France and the USA. He was not given a hard time when held and should come on for this. (old market op 16-1 new market tchd 12-1)

3194 32RED.COM CLAIMING STKS — 1m 14y
7:10 (7:52) (Class 6) 3-Y-O+ **£2,590** (£770; £385; £192) **Stalls** High

Form RPR

0004 **1** **Nashaab (USA)**[4] [3068] 9-9-5 75.................................(v) SteveDrowne 10 55
(P D Evans) *rrd s and v.s.a: stl plenty to do over 2f out:swtchd rt ins fnl 2f: rapid hdwy fnl f: led last strides* **7/2**[2]

4350 **2** *½* **Emperor Cat (IRE)**[16] [1395] 5-9-0 40.. FrancisFerris 11 49
(Mrs N S Evans) *chsd ldrs: chal over 1f out tl led jst ins last: ct last strides* **66/1**

0000 **3** *1* **Comeintothespace (IRE)**[13] [2794] 4-8-12 50................. AdamKirby(3) 5 48
(Miss Victoria Roberts) *chsd ldrs: led appr fnl 2f: sn rdn: hdd jst ins last: styd on same pce nr fin* **50/1**

0003 **4** *1 ¼* **Zafarshah (IRE)**[20] [2566] 7-9-2 45.............................(b) AdrianMcCarthy 3 46
(R A Harris) *chsd ldrs: rdn 2f out. styd on same pce ins fnl f* **11/1**

0606 **5** *nk* **What-A-Dancer (IRE)**[29] [2319] 9-8-10 63.................(b[1]) TolleyDean(7) 8 46
(R A Harris) *s.i.s: hdwy 1/2-way: rdn 3f out: one pce fnl 2f* **5/1**[3]

0001 **6** *1 ½* **Wild Lass**[22] [2531] 5-8-9 49...(b) LPKeniry 9 35
(J C Fox) *chsd ldrs: outpcd 3f out: pushed along and kpt on again ins last* **16/1**

0466 **7** *¾* **Priorina (IRE)**[32] [2245] 4-8-11 49...................................(v) RobertHavlin 1 35
(D Haydn Jones) *led after 2f: hdd appr fnl 2f: wknd fnl f* **20/1**

00-0 **8** *6* **A One (IRE)**[19] [2599] 7-8-12 57.. EmmettStack(5) 13 27
(H J Manners) *chsd ldrs: rdn 3f out: wknd 2f out* **40/1**

5244 **9** *1* **Spy Gun (USA)**[46] [1573] 6-8-10 45.................................. SladeO'Hara(7) 6 25
(T Wall) *chsd ldrs: rdn 3f out: sn btn* **25/1**

6-00 **10** *3* **Dara Mac**[145] [363] 7-9-1 52.. VinceSlattery 14 16
(L P Grassick) *nvr bttr than mid-div: no ch fnl 3f* **66/1**

06-0 **11** *2 ½* **Mabella (IRE)**[7] [2966] 4-8-9 42......................................(tp) DavidKinsella 2 —
(B J Llewellyn) *s.i.s: a bhd* **100/1**

0136 **12** *13* **Lord Chamberlain**[7] [2978] 13-9-5 59..............................(b) TPQueally 15 —
(J M Bradley) *s.i.s: hdwy tyo chse ldrs 1/2-way: wknd 3f out* **11/2**
-000 **13** *3½* **Factual Lad**[28] [2351] 8-9-7 65.............................. GeorgeBaker 7 —
(B R Millman) *led 2f: wknd over 2f out* **11/1**
00- **14** *11* **Huw The News**[23] [265] 7-8-7 .... DonnaCaldwell(7) 12 —
(S C Burrough) *a in rr* **100/1**
0165 **15** *7* **Makai**[8] [2947] 3-8-10 66.. KDarley 16 —
(M Johnston) *nvr travelling and sn bhd* **3/1**[1]

1m 37.37s (1.37) **Going Correction** +0.10s/f (Good)
WFA 3 from 4yo+ 9lb **15** Ran SP% **119.8**
Speed ratings (Par 101):97,96,95,94,93 92,91,85,84,81 79,66,62,51,44
CSF £239.22 TOTE £5.10: £2.50, £12.60, £9.20; EX 192.80.
Owner M W Lawrence **Bred** Shadwell Farm Inc **Trained** Pandy, Abergavenny

FOCUS
This claimer was delayed by over 40 minutes as the course was formally inspected by the stewards after Steven Drowne, whose mount stumbled in the opener, reported that the ground was inconsistent. The form of this race has to be treated with the utmost caution as many of the horses are likely to have boiled over due to the wait, and the form is weak in any case. They all wanted to be away from the stands' rail.
Factual Lad Official explanation: jockey said gelding was unsuited by the good ground
Makai Official explanation: vet said gelding had tied up

3195 32RED ONLINE CASINO (S) STKS — 7f 16y
7:40 (8:15) (Class 6) 3-Y-O — **£2,266** (£674; £337; £168) **Stalls** High

Form — RPR
4546 **1** **Mocha Java**[36] [2101] 3-9-0 60.............................. JosedeSouza 13 55+
(P F I Cole) *racd alone stands side and a in tch w main gp: drvn to ld wl over 1f out: readily* **4/1**[1]
6000 **2** *2½* **Baytown Valentina**[18] [2632] 3-8-9 37..............................(p) LPKeniry 15 43
(R Brotherton) *racd towards stands side and a in tch: rdn and styd on to chse wnr ins fnl f but a readily hld* **66/1**
4436 **3** *nk* **Three Feathers**[6] [3006] 3-8-7 46.............................. JamesMillman(7) 16 47
(M Salaman) *bhd: hdwy over 2f out: r.o wl fnl f: gng on cl home but nt rch ldrs* **15/2**
0660 **4** *1½* **Reality Time (IRE)**[16] [2704] 3-8-9 50.............................. PaulDoe 3 38
(W J Knight) *in tch: hdwy 3f out: drvn to chal over 1f out: outpcd ins last* **14/1**
-000 **5** *7* **Baytown Lulu**[17] [2678] 3-8-4 48.............................. EmmettStack(5) 11 20
(H S Howe) *mid-div: hdwy 2f out: kpt on same pce fnl f* **33/1**
2433 **6** *2½* **The Jailer**[7] [2968] 3-8-9 42..............................(v[1]) DavidKinsella 9 14+
(J G M O'Shea) *led: 5l clr 3f out: sn rdn: wknd and hdd wl over 1f out* **6/1**[2]
000 **7** *hd* **Silvabella (IRE)**[7] [2968] 3-8-9 45..............................(p) RobertHavlin 5 13
(D Haydn Jones) *in tch: rdn and effrt over 2f out: nvr gng pce to rch ldrs and wknd over 1f out* **50/1**
10-0 **8** *1* **Fun Time**[20] [2589] 3-8-6 60.............................. EdwardCreighton(3) 14 11
(M R Channon) *mid-div: rdn and effrt 3f out: nt rch ldrs: wknd over 1f out* **13/2**[3]
4002 **9** *½* **Crush On You**[11] [2877] 3-8-7 52.............................. RussellKennemore(7) 4 14
(R Hollinshead) *nvr gng pce to rch ldrs* **6/1**[2]
6206 **10** *5* **Cecchetti (IRE)**[26] [2415] 3-8-4 45.............................. RichardKingscote(5) 1 —
(Mrs H Sweeting) *chsd ldrs: rdn 3f out: sn btn* **12/1**
0046 **11** *1¾* **Legal Call**[11] [2877] 3-9-0 41..............................(v) JimCrowley 8 —
(M Appleby) *sn outpcd* **25/1**
00-0 **12** *6* **Wizard Prince**[83] [1003] 3-9-0 45..............................(p) FergusSweeney 6 —
(J G M O'Shea) *chsd ldrs: rdn 3f out: sn btn* **33/1**
-000 **13** *15* **Misterbianco (IRE)**[6] [3030] 3-9-0 60..............................(b[1]) TPQueally 12 —
(B J Meehan) *chsd ldrs: rdn 3f out: wknd qckly over 2f out* **11/1**
60-0 **14** *¾* **Young Flavio**[15] [2730] 3-9-0 62..............................(p) SteveDrowne 10 —
(J M Bradley) *chsd ldrs over 4f* **11/1**
0266 **15** *16* **Fallal Parc**[32] [2249] 3-9-0 41.............................. FrancisNorton 2 —
(M F Harris) *sn bhd* **20/1**

1m 25.18s (1.88) **Going Correction** +0.10s/f (Good) **15** Ran SP% **122.6**
Speed ratings (Par 98):93,90,89,88,80 77,77,75,75,69 67,60,43,42,24
CSF £329.39 TOTE £4.10: £2.80, £15.80, £2.50; EX 234.50.The winner was bought in for 8,000gns.
Owner P F I Cole Ltd **Bred** A H And C E Robinson Partnership **Trained** Whatcombe, Oxon
■ The first winner in Britain for experienced Brazilian rider Jose de Souza, older brother of Nelson de Souza.

FOCUS
A modest time, even for a seller. A weak race, the form compromised by a bias towards those racing near the stands' side.

3196 32REDPOKER.COM H'CAP — 1m 4f 23y
8:10 (8:41) (Class 6) (0-55,58) 4-Y-0+ — **£2,914** (£867; £433; £216) **Stalls** Low

Form — RPR
4000 **1** **Padre Nostro (IRE)**[37] [2075] 7-8-11 51.............................. ChrisGlenister(7) 1 60+
(J R Holt) *in tch: chsd ldrs over 3f out: nt clr run over 1f out: swtchd rt and styd on strly ins last to ld fnl 50yds: readily* **20/1**
4126 **2** *¾* **Plain Champagne (IRE)**[12] [2822] 4-9-5 52.............................. RichardThomas 9 58
(Dr J R J Naylor) *sn led: rdn over 2f out: kpt narrow advantage fr 2f out tl hdd and outpcd fnl 50yds* **7/1**
0534 **3** *1* **Harare**[7] [2966] 5-8-11 49.............................. JamesDoyle(5) 12 53
(R J Price) *bhd: rdn over 3f out: hdwy 2f out: chsd ldrs fnl f: no ex nr fin* **9/2**[2]
05/2 **4** *1½* **Dareneur (IRE)**[19] [2601] 6-9-4 51.............................. DavidKinsella 13 53
(J G M O'Shea) *bhd: rdn and hdwy fr 2f out: styd on fnl f but nvr gng pce to rch ldrs* **6/1**[3]
0026 **5** *hd* **Olivino (GER)**[7] [1729] 5-9-3 50.............................. SteveDrowne 8 51
(B J Llewellyn) *bhd: hdwy on outside over 2f out: chsd ldrs 1f out: wknd ins last* **4/1**[1]
-000 **6** *½* **Bubbling Fun**[3] [3115] 5-8-12 52.............................. SladeO'Hara(7) 10 52
(T Wall) *chsd ldrs: rdn 3f out: ev ch appr fnl f: wknd ins last* **16/1**
-550 **7** *4* **Financial Future**[32] [2221] 6-9-2 52..............................(b) NeilChalmers(3) 4 46
(C Roberts) *in tch: drvn to chse ldr 3f out: no imp fr 2f out: wknd fnl f* **12/1**
0000 **8** *2* **Lawood (IRE)**[3] [3115] 6-9-8 55..............................(v) VinceSlattery 15 46
(L P Grassick) *bhd: rdn over 3f out: sme hdwy fnl 2f: n.d* **25/1**
00-0 **9** *¾* **Laurollie**[10] [2902] 4-9-3 53.............................. AdamKirby(3) 2 43
(Dr J R J Naylor) *chsd ldrs: rdn 3f out: wknd 2f out* **14/1**
/055 **10** *18* **Lets Try Again (IRE)**[8] [2483] 9-9-2 49..............................(v[1]) RobertHavlin 5 10
(R A Farrant) *bhd: effrt 4f out: nvr bttr then mid-div* **12/1**
4012 **11** *29* **Scamperdale**[26] [2414] 4-9-8 55.............................. KDarley 3 —
(B P J Baugh) *chsd ldrs: rn wd bnd 5f out: n.d after and no ch fnl 3f* **8/1**
0-00 **12** *1¾* **Xacobeo (IRE)**[58] [1548] 4-9-0 50.............................. StephaneBreux(3) 11 —
(R Hannon) *chsd ldrs tl sddle slipped bnd 5f out: nt rcvr and rdr lost irons: t.o* **14/1**

2050 **R** **Screen Test**[16] [2483] 4-9-6 53..............................(b[1]) GeorgeBaker 6 —
(B G Powell) *ref to r* **7/1**

2m 42.31s (3.59) **Going Correction** +0.275s/f (Good) **13** Ran SP% **131.8**
Speed ratings (Par 101):99,98,97,96,96 96,93,92,91,79 60,59,—
CSF £169.53 CT £771.08 TOTE £27.90: £8.50, £2.30, £3.40; EX 209.60.
Owner Mrs E Glenister **Bred** Mrs G P Gaffney **Trained** Peckleton, Leics
■ The first winner as an apprentice for Chris Glenister, following one winner as an amateur.

FOCUS
Very little to get carried away about in this modest handicap as far as the future is concerned, and probably weak form with the third the best guide. Delta Force was withdrawn (7/1, got loose and galloped to Chepstow town centre). R4 applies, deduct 10p in the £.
Padre Nostro(IRE) Official explanation: trainer said, regarding the improved form shown, yard was out of form at the time of the previous run
Lets Try Again(IRE) Official explanation: jockey said gelding had slipped on the bend
Scamperdale Official explanation: jockey said gelding had slipped on the bend
Xacobeo(IRE) Official explanation: jockey said colt had slipped on the bend

3197 WEATHERBYS BANK H'CAP — 1m 14y
8:40 (9:10) (Class 5) (0-75,78) 3-Y-0+ — **£4,533** (£1,348; £674; £336) **Stalls** High

Form — RPR
0600 **1** **Fabrian**[16] [2708] 8-9-9 65.............................. JamesDoyle(5) 2 83
(R J Price) *led afer 1f: rdn 2f out: hld on wl u.p fnl f* **11/4**[1]
-042 **2** *2* **Carloman**[18] [2648] 3-8-10 59..............................(b) NelsonDeSouza(3) 4 70
(R M Beckett) *chsd ldrs: wnt 2nd and rdn 2f out: kpt on ins last but nt pce of wnr* **5/1**[3]
0503 **3** *5* **The Gaikwar (IRE)**[7] [2969] 7-9-11 65..............................(b) AmirQuinn(3) 8 67
(R A Harris) *s.i.s: sn rcvrd to chse ldrs: rdn 2f out: wknd and edgd lft appr fnl f* **4/1**[2]
5431 **4** *5* **Trevian**[13] [2789] 5-9-3 54.............................. TPQueally 5 44
(J M Bradley) *bhd: pushed along and sme hdwy fr over 1f out but nvr in contention* **4/1**[2]
0100 **5** *3* **Tuscarora (IRE)**[137] [451] 7-9-4 62.............................. JackDean(7) 1 46
(A W Carroll) *unruly stalls: in tch: effrt over 2f out: sn wknd* **25/1**
0404 **6** *6* **Primeshade Promise**[2] [3159] 5-9-1 52..............................(p) RichardThomas 10 22
(D Burchell) *rdn 4f out: a in rr* **13/2**
600- **7** *6* **Air Of Supremacy (IRE)**[333] [4168] 5-9-4 55.............................. FrancisNorton 6 11
(J L Spearing) *early spd: bhd fr 1/2-way* **28/1**
44U1 **8** *1½* **Wizby**[9] [2921] 3-8-6 59 6ex.............................. DonnaCaldwell(7) 3 9
(P D Evans) *a in rr* **10/1**
26-6 **9** *nk* **Pelham Crescent (IRE)**[172] [118] 3-10-0 74.............................. FrancisFerris 7 24
(B Palling) *t.k.h: chsd ldrs 5f* **16/1**

1m 35.55s (-0.45) **Going Correction** +0.10s/f (Good)
WFA 3 from 5yo+ 9lb **9** Ran SP% **118.9**
Speed ratings (Par 103):106,104,99,94,91 85,79,77,77
CSF £17.34 CT £55.78 TOTE £4.30: £1.60, £2.00, £2.20; EX 43.70 Place 6 £272.64, Place 5 £45.86.
Owner Glyn Byard **Bred** Juddmonte Farms **Trained** Ullingswick, H'fords

FOCUS
Once again, it appeared that the stands' side rail was the place to be on an evening when jockeys did not seem to know where to go. They finished well strung out. An ordinary race, but fair efforts from the front two.
Wizby Official explanation: jockey said saddle slipped

3198 32RED ONLINE POKER ROOM H'CAP — 6f 16y
() (Class 6) (0-65,) 3-Y-0+ — £

T/Plt: £1,197.10 to a £1 stake. Pool: £58,382.50 - 35.60 winning units T/Qpdt: £32.30 to a £1 stake. Pool: £4,550.20 - 104 winning units ST

[2978]KEMPTON (A.W) (R-H)
Wednesday, July 5

OFFICIAL GOING: Standard
Wind: Slight; half behind

3199 SURREY HERALD & NEWS H'CAP — 5f (P)
7:00 (7:00) (Class 5) (0-75,72) 3-Y-0+ — **£3,238** (£963; £481; £240) **Stalls** High

Form — RPR
0531 **1** **Heavens Walk**[4] [3071] 5-8-12 56 6ex..............................(t) SebSanders 3 68+
(P J Makin) *lw: a.p: led ent fnl f: rdn out* **5/2**[1]
2636 **2** *1¼* **After The Show**[28] [2340] 5-10-0 72.............................. MartinDwyer 2 79
(Rae Guest) *bhd: hdwy and swtchd lft over 1f out: r.o to go 2nd ins fnl f* **9/2**[2]
1313 **3** *1¼* **Forest Dane**[12] [2813] 6-9-2 60.............................. OscarUrbina 5 63+
(Mrs N Smith) *lw: in tch: n.m.r ovr 1f out: r.o ins fnl f* **9/2**[2]
321 **4** *hd* **Spirit Of Coniston**[28] [2340] 3-8-12 61.............................. RichardHughes 7 61
(Peter Grayson) *a.p: ev ch over 1f out: wknd ins fnl f* **9/2**[2]
000- **5** *1¼* **Fern House (IRE)**[346] [3785] 4-8-9 53 oh23.............................. RichardMullen 8 50
(Peter Grayson) *slowly away: hdwy whn nt clr run over 1f out: nvr on terms* **33/1**
12-0 **6** *¾* **Nistaki (USA)**[7] [2981] 5-9-11 72.............................. PatrickMathers(3) 1 67
(D Shaw) *settled in rr: nvr on terms* **20/1**
4035 **7** *nk* **Pride Of Joy**[9] [2939] 3-9-4 67.............................. DaneO'Neill 4 59
(D K Ivory) *chsd ldrs: rdn 2f out: sn wknd* **12/1**
0060 **8** *2* **Campeon (IRE)**[35] [2136] 4-8-13 57.............................. TedDurcan 10 43
(J M Bradley) *led for 2f: wknd sn after* **7/1**[3]

60.35 secs (-0.05) **Going Correction** +0.125s/f (Slow)
WFA 3 from 4yo+ 5lb **8** Ran SP% **111.0**
Speed ratings (Par 103):105,103,101,100,98 97,97,93
CSF £12.90 CT £44.31 TOTE £2.00: £1.02, £4.10, £2.30; EX 14.40.
Owner Mrs P J Makin **Bred** Mrs P J Makin **Trained** Ogbourne Maisey, Wilts
■ Stewards' Enquiry : Oscar Urbina caution: careless riding

FOCUS
A modest sprint, run at a decent clip, and the form looks solid for the class.

3200 SURREY HERALD & NEWS MAIDEN FILLIES' STKS — 1m 2f (P)
7:28 (7:31) (Class 5) 3-Y-0+ — **£3,238** (£963; £481; £240) **Stalls** High

Form — RPR
44 **1** **Millistar**[30] [2304] 3-8-12 .... PhilipRobinson 1 71+
(M A Jarvis) *trckd ldr: rdn to ld 1f out: edgd rt nr fin but r.o* **3/1**[1]
3- **2** *1½* **Very Agreeable**[222] [6424] 3-8-12 .... SebSanders 10 68
(W R Swinburn) *unf: scope: trckd ldrs: rdn over 1f out: kpt on u.p to go 2nd cl home* **11/1**
03 **3** *hd* **Kinvara Lass (IRE)**[29] [2325] 3-8-12 .... NickyMackay 12 68
(L M Cumani) *leggy: led tl rdn and hdd 1f out: kpt on but lost 2nd cl home* **5/1**[3]

5 **4** 1¾ **Aegean Pearl (USA)**[14] 2753 3-8-12 .... JimmyFortune 9 64
(J H M Gosden) *unf: trckd ldrs: rdn over 1f out: kpt on one pce fnl f* **7/2**[2]
0 **5** 1 **Juicy Fruits**[44] 1901 3-8-12 .... EddieAhern 7 62
(E A L Dunlop) *leggy: slowly away: sn in tch: rdn over 2f out: kpt on but nvr nr to chal* **33/1**
6 2½ **Kalandara (IRE)** 3-8-12 .... KerrinMcEvoy 4 58+
(Sir Michael Stoute) *w'like: leggy: s.i.s: in rr tl hdwy and styd on fr over 1f out* **6/1**
7 ¾ **Ninetails (IRE)** 3-8-12 .... RichardMullen 14 56
(E J O'Neill) *w'like: cl cpld: bit bkwd: slowly away: sn mid-div: no hdwy fnl 2f* **25/1**
5 **8** 1 **Selkirk Lady**[44] 1901 3-8-12 .... OscarUrbina 3 54
(W R Swinburn) *leggy: lw: in rear: effrt over 3f out: nvr on terms* **10/1**
9 2½ **Broughtons Revival** 4-9-9 .... TedDurcan 2 50
(W J Musson) *unf: bit bkwd: slowly away: a towards rr* **25/1**
6- **10** 2½ **Lovingly**[319] 4559 3-8-12 .... MartinDwyer 5 45
(W Jarvis) *unf: scope: bit bkwd: mid-div: rdn over 3f out: sn btn* **16/1**
11 1 **Sunley Song** 3-8-12 .... DaneO'Neill 6 43
(B G Powell) *unf: angular: a towards rr* **33/1**
12 3½ **Love Or Money** 3-8-12 .... MichaelHills 13 36
(W J Haggas) *w'like: a bhd* **16/1**
0- **13** 8 **The Lady Mandarin**[232] 6351 3-8-12 .... NCallan 11 21
(G Wragg) *in tch tl wknd 3f out* **50/1**
14 13 **Miss Marlene** 3-8-12 .... HayleyTurner 8 —
(B G Powell) *unf: mid-div tl rdn and wknd wl over 2f out* **33/1**

2m 10.94s (1.94) **Going Correction** +0.125s/f (Slow)
WFA 3 from 4yo 11lb **14** Ran SP% **125.8**
Speed ratings (Par 100):97,95,95,94,93 91,90,90,88,86 85,82,76,65
CSF £36.41 TOTE £5.40: £1.90, £3.30, £2.40; EX 60.40.
Owner Helena Springfield Ltd **Bred** Meon Valley Stud **Trained** Newmarket, Suffolk

FOCUS
A modest fillies' maiden, run at a steady early pace, and the form is worth treating with a degree of caution and has not been rated too positively.
Kalandara(IRE) Official explanation: jockey said filly missed the break

3201 EUROPEAN BREEDERS FUND MAIDEN FILLIES' STKS 7f (P)
7:56 (8:00) (Class 5) 2-Y-O **£3,886** (£1,156; £577; £288) **Stalls** High

Form RPR
1 **Sesmen** 2-9-0 .... OscarUrbina 1 80
(M Botti) *leggy: w'like: trckd ldrs. rdn appr fnl f: r.o: led post* **20/1**
3 **2** shd **Laureldean Express**[7] 2980 2-9-0 .... RichardMullen 6 80
(E J O'Neill) *w'like: mde most tl rdn and hdd last stride* **4/1**[1]
0 **3** 2½ **Sweet Lilly**[25] 2456 2-9-0 .... TedDurcan 7 74
(M R Channon) *lw: s.i.s: hdwy 2f out: r.o fnl f: nvr nrr* **16/1**
5 **4** ½ **Guacamole**[11] 2867 2-9-0 .... MichaelHills 12 72
(B W Hills) *s.i.s: gd hdwy over 2f out: ev ch ent fnl f: no ex ins* **5/1**[2]
40 **5** 2½ **Sweet Candy**[37] 2076 2-9-0 .... NCallan 8 66
(K A Ryan) *leggy: t.k.h: in tch: effrt over 2f out: one pce after* **14/1**
6 hd **Darrfonah (IRE)** 2-9-0 .... SebSanders 10 65+
(C E Brittain) *unf: slowly away: wl in rr tl styd on wl ins fnl 2f: nt rch ldrs* **10/1**[3]
46 **7** 3½ **Rosie Cross (IRE)**[25] 2456 2-9-0 .... StephenCarson 2 56
(R F Johnson Houghton) *w ldr tl rdn and wknd over 1f out* **14/1**
00 **8** ½ **Susanna's Prospect (IRE)**[9] 2930 2-9-0 .... JimmyFortune 3 55
(B J Meehan) *w'like: s.i.s: hdwy 2f out: one pce appr fnl f* **5/1**[2]
5 **9** nk **Splendored Love (USA)**[8] 2957 2-9-0 .... RichardHughes 1 54
(R Hannon) *nvr bttr than mid-div* **5/1**[2]
10 2½ **Zoorina** 2-9-0 .... (t) MartinDwyer 5 48
(M P Tregoning) *w'like: a towards rr* **11/1**
04 **11** nk **Bertrada (IRE)**[6] 3010 2-9-0 .... EddieAhern 9 47
(H Morrison) *a bhd* **25/1**
12 ½ **Killer Heels** 2-9-0 .... JohnEgan 14 45
(S Kirk) *w'like: cl cpld: bit bkwd: slowly away: nvr on terms* **25/1**
0 **13** 1¼ **High Bullen**[71] 1203 2-9-0 .... DaneO'Neill 4 42
(M Meade) *w'like: in tch on outside: wknd over 2f out* **50/1**
0 **14** 2½ **Tranquility**[18] 2638 2-9-0 .... JimmyQuinn 13 36
(J Pearce) *w'like: bit bkwd: in tch tl rdn over 3f out: wknd qckly* **33/1**

1m 27.83s (1.03) **Going Correction** +0.125s/f (Slow) **14** Ran SP% **124.0**
Speed ratings (Par 91):99,98,96,95,92 92,88,87,87,84 84,83,82,79
CSF £96.85 TOTE £36.20: £11.00, £2.40, £3.60; EX 378.50.
Owner Scuderia Rencati Srl **Bred** Peter Ebdon Racing **Trained** Newmarket, Suffolk
■ Stewards' Enquiry : Stephen Carson three-day ban: careless riding (Jul 16-18)

FOCUS
A decent winning time for a race like this and the form looks sound with the first two coming clear.

NOTEBOOK
Sesmen, a 27,000gns purchase closely related to winners at up to 11 furlongs, got her career off to a perfect start with a very narrow success. There was plenty to like about her attitude inside the final furlong, she deserves extra credit considering that she was drawn widest of all, and clearly has a future. (tchd 16-1)
Laureldean Express ◆ was ridden more aggressively than was the case on her recent course and distance debut and ultimately was only denied by the smallest of margins. She progressed as expected for the step up to this longer trip, proved game in defeat, and can be considered a winner without a penalty ahead of her next assignment. (op 7-2)
Sweet Lilly, as on her Newbury debut 25 days previously, was slow to break and always playing catch up thereafter. However, this was certainly a step in the right direction, and she looked to need of all of this longer trip.
Guacamole, fifth on debut at Newmarket last time, had no more to offer after entering the final furlong and was eventually well held. She will be suited by a mile before the season's end and appeals as the type to fare better when switching to nurseries.
Susanna's Prospect(IRE) Official explanation: jockey said filly clipped heels on final bend
Splendored Love(USA) was supported in the betting ring on this step up to seven furlongs, but never seriously figured through the race, and ran below the form of her Newbury debut eight days previously. (op 7-1)
Tranquility Official explanation: trainer said filly had a breathing problem

3202 MARTIN COLLINS ENTERPRISE H'CAP (LONDON MILE QUALIFIER) 1m (P)
8:24 (8:28) (Class 4) (0-80,80) 3-Y-O+ **£5,505** (£1,637; £818; £408) **Stalls** High

Form RPR
3245 **1** **Cross The Line (IRE)**[22] 2536 4-9-8 71 .... EddieAhern 5 80
(A P Jarvis) *a.p: led 2f out: rdn: jst hld on* **11/4**[1]
26-0 **2** nk **Brave Fight**[30] 2290 3-9-2 74 .... DaneO'Neill 1 80
(A King) *in rr tl hdwy on outside over 2f out: fin wl: to go 2nd ins fnl f and clsng on wnr fin* **16/1**
4520 **3** 1¼ **Mujood**[19] 2620 3-9-6 78 .... StephenCarson 3 81
(R F Johnson Houghton) *in tch on outside: rdn 3f out: ev ch ins fnl f: no ex fnl 100yds* **12/1**
000- **4** 1¾ **Leoballero**[197] 6629 6-10-0 77 .... (t) JohnEgan 4 78
(D J Daly) *lw: bhd tl hdwy ins fnl 2f: nvr nrr* **16/1**
6-00 **5** 2 **Dr Thong**[16] 2708 5-10-0 77 .... JimmyFortune 6 73
(P F I Cole) *bhd: outpcd 2f out: styd on fnl f* **7/1**
0-00 **6** 2 **Overlord Way (GR)**[7] 2983 4-9-12 75 .... IanMongan 9 67
(P R Chamings) *led after 1f: rdn and hdd 2f out: sn btn* **10/1**
1550 **7** nk **Scot Love (IRE)**[14] 2757 3-9-8 80 .... (v[1]) ShaneKelly 8 69
(J Noseda) *slowly away: hld up: n.m.r 2f out: nvr on terms* **9/2**[2]
3166 **8** ½ **Parkview Love (USA)**[14] 2752 5-9-4 70 .... (v) PatrickMathers(3) 7 60
(D Shaw) *prom: disp ld over 2f out: wknd fnl f* **10/1**
4642 **9** 1¼ **Luck In Running (USA)**[4] 3101 3-8-11 69 .... JoeFanning 2 54
(M Johnston) *lw: prom on outside tl wknd over 1f out* **5/1**[3]
060 **10** 26 **Doctor David**[65] 1336 3-8-9 67 .... RichardHughes 10 —
(Ernst Oertel) *led for 1f: rdn 3f out: eased over 1f out* **20/1**

1m 40.76s (-0.04) **Going Correction** +0.125s/f (Slow)
WFA 3 from 4yo+ 9lb **10** Ran SP% **116.4**
Speed ratings (Par 105):105,104,103,101,99 97,97,96,95,69
CSF £50.22 CT £459.47 TOTE £4.40: £1.80, £4.10, £3.40; EX 60.80.
Owner Eurostrait Ltd **Bred** Genesis Green Stud Ltd **Trained** Twyford, Bucks

FOCUS
A decent little handicap and the winning time was about as you would expect for the class. The form looks sound rated around the winner and third.
Leoballero Official explanation: jockey said gelding hung right

3203 KEMPTON FOR WEDDINGS H'CAP 2m (P)
8:52 (8:54) (Class 3) (0-90,90) 4-Y-O+
£7,790 (£2,332; £1,166; £583; £291; £146) **Stalls** High

Form RPR
3/10 **1** **Prins Willem (IRE)**[15] 2723 7-9-4 87 .... (vt) OscarUrbina 10 95
(J R Fanshawe) *lw: hld up: hdwy on outside over 2f out: strly rdn to ld last strides* **9/2**[1]
-106 **2** hd **Velvet Heights (IRE)**[34] 2176 4-8-11 80 .... TedDurcan 2 88
(J L Dunlop) *hld up: rdn and str hdwy in ins wl over 1f out: r.o to go 2nd nr fin* **5/1**[2]
440 **3** ½ **Follow On**[16] 2712 4-8-4 73 .... MartinDwyer 8 80
(A P Jarvis) *in tch: led over 2f out: rdn: no ex ins fnl f: hdd and lost 2nd nr fin* **20/1**
2-65 **4** 2 **Theatre (USA)**[32] 2219 7-8-4 73 oh1 ow2 .... JohnEgan 1 78
(Jamie Poulton) *lw: in rr tl styd on ins fnl 2f: nvr nrr* **8/1**
3510 **5** ¾ **Salute (IRE)**[12] 2817 7-8-2 71 .... NickyMackay 7 75
(P G Murphy) *trckd ldr to over 2f out: one pce after* **11/2**[3]
1-02 **6** 2½ **Colloquial**[25] 2437 5-9-7 90 .... (v) DaneO'Neill 5 91
(H Candy) *led tl rdn and hdd over 2f out: wknd over 1f out* **9/2**[1]
0314 **7** 5 **Madiba**[32] 2219 7-8-2 71 oh11 .... FrankieMcDonald 3 66
(P Howling) *bhd: nvr on terms* **33/1**
-240 **8** ½ **Archduke Ferdinand (FR)**[15] 2723 8-8-9 78 .... EddieAhern 6 73
(A King) *hld up: nvr got into r* **13/2**
-006 **9** 4 **Fortune Island (IRE)**[12] 2817 7-9-2 85 .... (vt) JimmyFortune 9 75
(D E Pipe) *mid-div: rdn over 3f out: sn btn* **16/1**
04-5 **10** 27 **Darasim (IRE)**[19] 2625 8-9-5 88 .... (v) JoeFanning 4 45
(M Johnston) *trckd ldrs: rdn over 3f out: wknd qckly* **25/1**
0-60 **11** ½ **Stolen Song**[9] 2935 6-7-11 71 oh18 .... (b) MarcHalford(5) 11 28
(J Ryan) *prom tl wknd over 3f out* **100/1**
300- **12** 15 **Hunting Lodge (IRE)**[15] 4389 5-8-7 83 .... (b) JosephWalsh(7) 12 22
(H J Manners) *in rdn and lost tch 5f out* **33/1**

3m 30.11s (-1.29) **Going Correction** +0.125s/f (Slow) **12** Ran SP% **114.2**
Speed ratings (Par 107):108,107,107,106,106 105,102,102,100,86 86,79
CSF £24.16 CT £404.30 TOTE £5.10: £1.70, £2.50, £8.40; EX 37.10.
Owner Chris Van Hoorn **Bred** Mrs A Hughes **Trained** Newmarket, Suffolk

FOCUS
A very decent staying handicap run at a good pace thanks to Colloquial. The form looks solid and should prove reliable.

NOTEBOOK
Prins Willem(IRE), winner of his only previous outing on sand at Lingfield earlier in the year, obviously likes this surface and maintained his unbeaten record following a patient ride, though only narrowly and until the last couple of strides it did not appear that he would get up. There is a £50,000 handicap over this trip coming up back on the Lingfield Polytrack and that could be a tempting target for him. (op 4-1 tchd 7-2)
Velvet Heights(IRE), like the winner successful in his only previous try on sand, in his case over course and distance back in April, only just failed to maintain his unbeaten record off a 3lb higher mark having been given a similarly patient ride to his rival. The forthcoming Lingfield race could be an ideal target for him too. (op 9-2)
Follow On ◆, stepping up in trip and making his handicap and sand debuts after three outings in turf maidens, hardly deserved to be beaten. Quickening to the front soon after turning for home, he looked to have the race won but his two much more streetwise rivals swamped him on either side in the shadow of the post. Considering his lack of experience, this was a cracking effort and he is entitled to build on this.
Theatre(USA) has only been seen once on sand in about three and a half years, but is proven on the surface and did not perform at all badly in this warm contest. He still has the ability to win an ordinary staying handicap on Polytrack. (op 10-1)
Salute(IRE) had the leader in his sights the whole way and had every chance turning in, but lacked the pace to go with the principals thereafter. He is not the most consistent. (op 6-1 tchd 5-1)
Colloquial, not seen on sand since finishing unplaced on his racecourse debut and racing off a career-high mark, set a decent pace but failed to get home and did not transfer his recent turf form back onto Polytrack. (op 10-3)

3204 WEATHERBYS MESSAGING SERVICE APPRENTICE H'CAP (ROUND 5) 6f (P)
9:20 (9:26) (Class 5) (0-75,74) 3-Y-O+ **£3,238** (£963; £481; £240) **Stalls** High

Form RPR
0006 **1** **Norcroft**[7] 2981 4-9-10 70 .... (p) KirstyMilczarek 7 76
(Mrs C A Dunnett) *mde all: strly rdn ent fnl f: jst hld on* **9/1**
2324 **2** shd **Nautical**[7] 2981 8-9-10 70 .... LiamJones 9 76
(A W Carroll) *t.k.h in mid-div: gd hdwy over 1f out: r.o strly: jst failed* **11/4**[1]
4250 **3** 3½ **A Teen**[43] 1909 8-8-4 57 oh12 ow2 .... JPFeatherstone(7) 2 52
(P Howling) *chsd ldrs: rdn over 1f out: kpt on one pce* **33/1**
4536 **4** hd **Arctic Desert**[19] 2603 6-9-9 74 .... JamesRogers(5) 4 69
(A M Balding) *v.s.a: in rr tl hdwy and n.m.r on ins over 1f out: nvr nr to chal* **11/2**[2]
0046 **5** hd **Mountain Pass (USA)**[5] 3052 4-8-10 56 .... (v) DerekNolan 10 50
(M J Wallace) *mid-div: effrt over 1f out: nvr on terms* **13/2**
4-01 **6** nk **Finsbury**[21] 2553 3-8-13 72 .... JonjoMilczarek(7) 5 65
(C F Wall) *s.i.s: swtchd rt and effrt 2f out: no ex appr fnl f* **11/2**[2]

0-62 **7** 3/4 **Stormy Monday**[21] [2554] 3-9-0 **71**.................................... PatrickHills(5) 1 62
(J W Hills) *lw: hld up: effrt on outside 2f out but nvr on terms* **6/1**[3]
-600 **8** *nk* **Siraj**[141] [408] 7-8-4 **55** oh4...(p) BRoper(5) 6 45
(J Ryan) *chsd wnr tl rdn and wknd 2f out* **33/1**
0-30 **9** *5* **Bellanora**[19] [2602] 3-8-8 **60**... ThomasO'Brien 8 35
(R F Johnson Houghton) *chsd ldrs: rdn 1/2-way: sn bhd* **16/1**
1m 15.19s (1.49) **Going Correction** +0.125s/f (Slow)
WFA 3 from 4yo+ 6lb **9** Ran SP% **106.8**
Speed ratings (Par 103):95,94,90,89,89 89,88,87,81
CSF £29.60 CT £660.61 TOTE £13.40: £4.60, £1.10, £4.50; EX 49.60 Place 6 £58.94, Place 5 £45.85.
Owner Mrs Christine Dunnett **Bred** Norcroft Park Stud **Trained** Hingham, Norfolk
FOCUS
A rather messy contest and surprisingly there was no pace on for this sprint. As a result the winning time was moderate for a race of its class and the form looks dubious. That rather played into the hands of the winner, and both the front pair pulled well clear of the rest.
T/Plt: £78.60 to a £1 stake. Pool: £47,230.55. 438.20 winning tickets. T/Qpdt: £22.80 to a £1 stake. Pool: £2,974.20. 96.30 winning tickets. JS

3205 - 3208a (Foreign Racing) - See Raceform Interactive

[2224]EPSOM (L-H)
Thursday, July 6
OFFICIAL GOING: Good (good to firm in places)
Wind: Almost nil Weather: Fine

3209 BETFREDPOKER.COM H'CAP 1m 4f 10y
6:15 (6:21) (Class 5) (0-75,73) 4-Y-0+ **£4,533** (£1,348; £674; £336) **Stalls** Centre

Form RPR
0111 **1** **Mostarsil (USA)**[9] [2953] 8-9-3 **69** 5ex.................................(p) RyanMoore 5 76
(G L Moore) *mde all: dictated modest pce to 1/2-way: steadily increased tempo: 4l clr over 1f out: drvn to hold on fnl f* **3/1**[1]
2-33 **2** *nk* **Hawridge King**[10] [2918] 4-9-1 **67**.. MickyFenton 6 74
(W S Kittow) *chsd ldrs: wnt 2nd over 2f out: clsd on wnr fnl f: jst hld* **5/1**[3]
-350 **3** 2 1/2 **Double Spectre (IRE)**[9] [2956] 4-8-13 **65**.......................... VinceSlattery 9 68+
(Jean-Rene Auvray) *stdd s: t.k.h and bhd: rdn and hdwy 2f out: edgd lft and wnt 3rd 1f out: nt rch ldng pair* **10/1**
-004 **4** 3 **Estrelle (GER)**[15] [2762] 4-9-4 **70**................................... TedDurcan 2 68
(H R A Cecil) *prom: wnt 2nd 1/2-way tl over 2f out: one pce* **7/1**
4000 **5** 2 1/2 **The Violin Player (USA)**[26] [2447] 5-9-7 **73**.................... JoeFanning 10 68
(H J Collingridge) *hld up and bhd: pushed along 4f out: nvr rchd ldrs* **8/1**
0404 **6** *nk* **Blackmail (USA)**[9] [2953] 8-8-9 **61** ow2...........................(b) SebSanders 1 55
(Miss B Sanders) *hld up towards rr: hdwy 4f out: effrt in centre 3f out: no ex over 1f out* **9/2**[2]
0006 **7** 1 1/4 **Play Up Pompey**[9] [2956] 4-7-11 **54** oh2.......................... MarcHalford(5) 3 46
(J J Bridger) *chsd wnr to 1/2-way: prom tl wknd 2f out* **14/1**
0/6- **8** *11* **Space Cowboy (IRE)**[32] [4219] 6-9-1 **72**.................... RobynBrisland(5) 7 48
(G L Moore) *chsd ldrs tl wknd ent st* **33/1**
-550 **9** *hd* **Montage (IRE)**[21] [2577] 4-8-2 **54** oh2.............................. JimmyQuinn 8 29
(J Akehurst) *s.i.s: sn in midfield: wknd over 3f out* **9/1**
00/0 **10** 1 1/2 **Danakil**[44] [1926] 11-8-6 **65**... ThomasBubb(7) 4 38
(S Dow) *t.k.h: chsd ldrs tl wknd 4f out* **66/1**
2m 38.69s (-0.04) **Going Correction** +0.025s/f (Good) **10** Ran SP% **113.7**
Speed ratings (Par 103):101,100,99,97,95 95,94,87,86,85
CSF £17.22 CT £130.38 TOTE £2.90: £1.30, £2.10, £3.20; EX 14.80.
Owner G A Jackman **Bred** Shadwell Farm Inc **Trained** Woodingdean, E Sussex
FOCUS
Not a strong handicap rated through the winner.

3210 FLEMING RUSSELL STENT E B F MEDIAN AUCTION MAIDEN STKS 7f
6:45 (6:49) (Class 4) 2-Y-0 **£4,533** (£1,348; £674; £336) **Stalls** Low

Form RPR
43 **1** **The Old Fella**[16] [2724] 2-9-3 .... RyanMoore 7 78
(R Hannon) *chsd ldr: hung lft and led wl over 1f out: hrd rdn fnl f: jst hld on* **4/7**[1]
030 **2** *shd* **Tudor Prince (IRE)**[16] [2719] 2-9-3 .... DarryllHolland 3 78
(B J Meehan) *t.k.h: chsd ldrs: n.m.r on rail ent st: sn outpcd: rallied to press wnr ins fnl f: jst failed* **5/1**[2]
56 **3** 2 1/2 **Atheneum (IRE)**[30] [2321] 2-9-3 .... JoeFanning 5 72
(M Johnston) *led: rdn and hdd over 1f out: one pce* **14/1**
2636 **4** 2 1/2 **Silca Soprano**[11] [2890] 2-8-12 .... TedDurcan 4 64+
(M R Channon) *hld up towards rr: hmpd and slipped bnd 4f out: effrt on rail 3f out: styd on steadily: nt pce to rch ldrs* **12/1**
506 **5** 1/2 **It's No Problem (IRE)**[8] [2967] 2-8-12 .... RobertHavlin 8 59
(Jean-Rene Auvray) *chsd ldrs: hung lft over 2f out: one pce* **50/1**
0 **6** 3/4 **Bobbish**[20] [2619] 2-9-3 .... OscarUrbina 1 62+
(N A Callaghan) *sn bhd: styd on fr over 1f out: nvr rchd chalng position* **40/1**
6 **7** 1/2 **Pagan Rules (IRE)**[20] [2604] 2-9-3 .... SebSanders 9 61+
(Mrs A J Perrett) *wnt rt s and s.i.s: sn in midfield: rdn and no hdwy fnl 3f* **11/1**[3]
0 **8** *nk* **Revisionist (IRE)**[40] [2009] 2-9-3 .... PatDobbs 6 60
(R Hannon) *in tch: outpcd over 3f out: n.d after* **33/1**
9 *7* **Mayireneyrbel** 2-8-12 .... MickyFenton 2 38
(R Ingram) *s.v.s: a outpcd and wl bhd* **66/1**
1m 24.54s (0.59) **Going Correction** +0.025s/f (Good) **9** Ran SP% **111.8**
Speed ratings (Par 96):97,96,94,91,90 89,89,88,80
CSF £3.29 TOTE £1.50: £1.10, £1.60, £3.10; EX 5.00.
Owner M Sines **Bred** T E Pocock **Trained** East Everleigh, Wilts
FOCUS
An uncompetitive event dominated by the form horses with the runner-up setting the level.
NOTEBOOK
The Old Fella, whose strong-finishing third in the Windsor Castle represented easily the best form on offer, looked sure to be suited by further than that, but seven furlongs was a big step up for him, and on a very different track. In the end the combination almost proved too much for him, as he was inclined to edge left, looking ill at ease on the track, and was unable to pull away as one might have expected. This was nothing like his Ascot form, but Richard Hannon junior reckons he did not stay, and the plan now is to drop him back to six furlongs for a novice at Newmarket's July meeting, then aim for the valuable sales race at Doncaster. (op 4-9 tchd 8-13 in places)
Tudor Prince(IRE) ◆ was also dropped in class, having finished in rear in the Coventry. His problem here was that he did not handle the downhill turn into the straight at all well, as a result of which he was left with too much to do. Still a good five lengths down two out, he was gaining rapidly at the finish and was unlucky not to win. (op 6-1 tchd 13-2 in places)
Atheneum(IRE) made a bold bid from the front but was put firmly in his place. He has the nursery option now. (op 20-1)
Silca Soprano lost her back legs going into the bend so ran a bit better than the bare facts suggest.
It's No Problem(IRE) had her chance although she did not look totally happy on the track, but looks limited.
Bobbish is worth keeping in mind for a small race in due course, as he made steady late headway from a hopeless position having struggled early on. Official explanation: jockey said gelding lost its action

3211 NIKON H'CAP 6f
7:20 (7:21) (Class 3) (0-95,93) 3-Y-0+ **£8,096** (£2,408; £1,203; £601) **Stalls** High

Form RPR
5064 **1** **Steel Blue**[19] [2661] 6-8-10 **76**.. HayleyTurner 6 87
(R M Whitaker) *mde virtually all: hrd rdn over 1f out: hld on wl* **6/1**[3]
4240 **2** 3/4 **Idle Power (IRE)**[5] [3092] 8-9-7 **90**.................................... AmirQuinn(3) 8 99
(J R Boyle) *trckd ldng pair gng wl: rdn to press wnr fnl f: a hld* **11/2**[2]
6050 **3** 1 1/2 **Fantasy Believer**[5] [3077] 8-9-2 **82**.................................. DarryllHolland 4 87
(J J Quinn) *hld up towards rr: hdwy and edgd lft fr over 2f out: styd on to take 3rd fnl f* **11/2**[2]
3010 **4** *1* **Beaver Patrol (IRE)**[12] [2847] 4-9-13 **93**.............................. ShaneKelly 1 95
(R F Johnson Houghton) *hld up towards rr: sme hdwy whn hmpd jst ins fnl f: swtchd rt: nrst fin* **11/4**[1]
5501 **5** *shd* **Purus (IRE)**[15] [2757] 4-9-3 **83**.. JoeFanning 7 84
(P Mitchell) *pressed wnr: rdn over 2f out: no ex fnl f* **12/1**
-604 **6** 1 3/4 **Fast Heart**[61] [1475] 5-9-3 **83**...(t) LPKeniry 2 79
(D Nicholls) *chsd ldrs: rdn over 2f out: no ex fnl f* **8/1**
0056 **7** 3/4 **Pic Up Sticks**[8] [2983] 7-9-3 **83**... RyanMoore 3 77
(B G Powell) *hld up towards rr: mod effrt over 2f out: nvr able to chal* **10/1**
5600 **8** 1/2 **Jayanjay**[26] [2429] 7-9-4 **87**.. NelsonDeSouza(3) 5 79
(Miss B Sanders) *mid-div: outpcd over 2f out: n.d after* **12/1**
3100 **9** *14* **Bird Over**[26] [2438] 4-9-4 **84**.. SebSanders 9 34
(R M Beckett) *stdd s and swtchd lft to ins: a bhd: no ch fnl 2f* **12/1**
68.77 secs (-1.86) **Going Correction** -0.125s/f (Firm) **9** Ran SP% **115.0**
Speed ratings (Par 107):107,106,104,102,102 100,99,98,79
CSF £38.74 CT £193.16 TOTE £8.90: £2.40, £2.10, £2.00; EX 61.40.
Owner Country Lane Partnership **Bred** R T And Mrs Watson **Trained** Scarcroft, W Yorks
FOCUS
A decent handicap in which it proved hard to come from behind and the form looks sound with the placed horses to recent form.
NOTEBOOK
Steel Blue won over seven furlongs here in soft ground last year, but he was highly effective off much higher marks at this trip in his prime and still has enough toe if he has plenty of use made of him. He made all the running and was always holding on the runner-up.
Idle Power(IRE), who got no sort of run at Windsor last weekend, did not have that excuse this time. He travelled really well, but when he was asked to go after the winner he did not really pick up. He may well return to his favourite track Goodwood for the Stewards' Cup, but he needs plenty to come out in order to get a run. (op 5-1)
Fantasy Believer, last year's winner, is well treated these days, and this is his time of year, so it was no surprise to see him step up on previous efforts this season and finish a respectable third. However, he was inclined to hang left in the straight, where he was wide of the rest, and he never looked like repeating last year's victory. Official explanation: jockey said gelding hung left (tchd 5-1)
Beaver Patrol(IRE), a course and distance winner last month, looks high enough in the handicap now, although in fairness it was hard coming from off he pace. (op 3-1 tchd 10-3 in a place)
Purus(IRE) acts on good ground but would ideally have liked some rain. The four-year-old pressed the leader but could not pull out any extra when it was needed. (op 14-1)
Fast Heart ◆ is probably the interesting one for the future, as this was his first run for David Nicholls and is the type with which he excels, for he was once rated 101 and is now down to 83, a mark which could well drop another pound or two after this. He had not run for two months, and he was a bit short of room on the rail near the finish, otherwise he would have been a shade closer. (tchd 9-1)
Bird Over Official explanation: jockey said filly was never travelling

3212 CHISHOLM & WINCH H'CAP 7f
7:50 (7:53) (Class 4) (0-85,85) 3-Y-0+ **£6,477** (£1,927; £963; £481) **Stalls** Low

Form RPR
1532 **1** **Phluke**[9] [2954] 5-9-5 **77**.. NelsonDeSouza(3) 12 88
(R F Johnson Houghton) *pressed ldrs: rdn to ld ins fnl f: hld on wl* **12/1**
4100 **2** 1/2 **Quantum Leap**[22] [2555] 9-9-0 **69**..(v) JimmyQuinn 16 78+
(S Dow) *s.s: outpcd and wl bhd: gd hdwy and eased outside 1f out: fin wl* **20/1**
0135 **3** *hd* **Marmooq**[13] [2831] 3-8-10 **73**... JoeFanning 11 79
(M Johnston) *mid-div on outside: hdwy in centre 2f out: hung lft: r.o to chse wnr 50 yds out: kpt on: lost 2nd on line* **12/1**
-054 **4** *nk* **Scarlet Flyer (USA)**[19] [2650] 3-8-12 **75**............................. RyanMoore 5 80
(G L Moore) *mid-div: hdwy and hung lft fnl 2f: nrst fin* **9/2**[1]
06-4 **5** 1 1/4 **Inch By Inch**[19] [2635] 7-9-0 **72**..(b) AmirQuinn(3) 6 77
(P J Makin) *chsd ldrs: led over 2f out tl ins fnl f: no ex* **16/1**
5566 **6** 1/2 **Katiypour (IRE)**[15] [2757] 9-9-11 **80**.................................. SebSanders 3 86+
(Miss B Sanders) *chsd ldrs: hrd rdn 2f out: nt qckn appr fnl f* **8/1**[3]
5263 **7** 1 3/4 **Call My Number (IRE)**[15] [2760] 3-9-3 **80**.......................... TedDurcan 2 76
(M R Channon) *in tch: hrd rdn and no imp fnl 2f* **9/1**
-643 **8** 3 1/2 **Yo Pedro (IRE)**[11] [2900] 4-9-9 **78**...................................... OscarUrbina 15 69
(J R Fanshawe) *in tch: effrt over 2f out: wknd over 1f out* **13/2**[2]
-040 **9** 1/2 **Toffee Vodka (IRE)**[26] [2459] 4-9-3 **72**.......................... FrankieMcDonald 4 66+
(J W Hills) *hld up towards rr: promising hdwy on rail whn hmpd over 2f out: nt rcvr* **10/1**
0000 **10** 3/4 **Sky Crusader**[14] [2776] 4-9-13 **82**....................................(v1) RobertHavlin 14 69
(R Ingram) *s.s: sn in midfield: rdn and no hdwy fnl 2f* **9/1**
4410 **11** 1/2 **Ocean Pride (IRE)**[19] [2650] 3-9-8 **85**..................................(b) PatDobbs 9 68
(R Hannon) *prom 5f* **14/1**
000 **12** 1/2 **Pachello (IRE)**[20] [2624] 4-9-6 **75**................................... DarryllHolland 17 60
(J M Bradley) *sn led and c across fr wd draw: hdd over 2f out: sn wknd* **50/1**
4-05 **13** 3/4 **Blu Manruna**[20] [2620] 3-8-1 **64** oh1.................................(b) DavidKinsella 10 44
(J Akehurst) *s.s: a bhd* **20/1**
2000 **14** *hd* **Kabeer**[13] [2820] 8-8-9 **64**...(t) MickyFenton 13 47
(P S McEntee) *a bhd* **33/1**
33-0 **15** *16* **Goodwood Spirit**[26] [2443] 4-9-11 **80**.................................. ShaneKelly 7 23
(J M Bradley) *a towards rr: rdn and no ch fnl 2f* **33/1**
00-0 **16** *35* **Neon Blue**[18] [2681] 5-9-2 **71**..(v) HayleyTurner 8 —
(R M Whitaker) *s.s: sn t.o* **25/1**
1m 23.23s (-0.72) **Going Correction** +0.025s/f (Good)
WFA 3 from 4yo+ 8lb **16** Ran SP% **120.9**
Speed ratings (Par 105):105,104,104,103,102 101,99,95,95,94 93,93,92,92,73 33
CSF £241.50 CT £2936.62 TOTE £15.70: £3.30, £4.10, £4.90, £1.10; EX 390.40.

Owner Mrs R F Johnson Houghton **Bred** Mrs R F Johnson Houghton **Trained** Blewbury, Oxon

FOCUS
A big field for this competitive handicap, but there was less trouble in running than one might have expected. There was a good blend of prominent racers and hold-up horses in the first six, suggesting there was no great pace bias, but the form is nothing special.
Toffee Vodka(IRE) Official explanation: jockey said saddle slipped
Kabeer Official explanation: jockey said gelding was unsuited by the track
Goodwood Spirit Official explanation: jockey said gelding hung right
Neon Blue Official explanation: jockey said gelding was unsuited by the track

3213 DRIVERS JONAS CLAIMING STKS — 1m 114y
8:25 (8:27) (Class 5) 3-Y-0+ — £3,238 (£963; £481; £240) Stalls Low

Form — RPR
-004 **1** **Envision**[6] 3045 3-9-3 85 ... RyanMoore 1 — 75
(R Hannon) *hld up towards rr: rdn and hdwy 2f out: led 1f out: slt ld fnl f: hld on wl* 11/4[1]
4222 **2** nk **Border Artist**[8] 2969 7-9-1 50 ... OscarUrbina 5 — 62
(B G Powell) *stdd s: hld up towards rr: rdn and hdwy 2f out: jnd wnr 1f out: r.o: jst hld* 6/1
0451 **3** 4 **Fortune Point (IRE)**[9] 2952 8-9-5 50 ... (v) ShaneKelly 4 — 57
(A W Carroll) *rdn and sn led: hdd and no ex 1f out* 12/1
1220 **4** 2 **Molem**[19] 2647 4-9-13 70 ... (vt[1]) SebSanders 7 — 61
(Lady Herries) *trckd ldrs: chal on bit 3f out: shkn up 2f out: fnd little* 7/1
310- **5** nk **Nanton (USA)**[278] 5599 4-9-10 85 ... NelsonDeSouza(3) 3 — 60
(P F I Cole) *in tch: outpcd 3f out: hung lft whn btn* 3/1[2]
0650 **6** hd **Alchemist Master**[8] 2974 7-9-3 75 ... HayleyTurner 2 — 50
(R M Whitaker) *chsd ldrs tl wknd over 1f out* 9/2[3]
0150 **7** 6 **Zinging**[21] 2585 7-8-8 47 ... MarcHalford(5) 6 — 33
(J J Bridger) *w ldr: rdn 3f out: sn wknd* 33/1
0503 **8** nk **Postmaster**[20] 2599 4-9-1 52 ... MickyFenton 8 — 34
(R Ingram) *a bhd: no ch fnl 2f* 16/1

1m 45.03s (-0.71) **Going Correction** +0.025s/f (Good)
WFA 3 from 4yo+ 10lb — 8 Ran SP% **113.2**
Speed ratings (Par 103):104,103,100,98,98 97,92,92
CSF £19.24 TOTE £3.80: £1.50, £1.50, £2.80; EX 19.40.Alchemist Master was claimed by C. R. Dore for £10,000.
Owner Mrs J Wood **Bred** Cheveley Park Stud Ltd **Trained** East Everleigh, Wilts
■ A treble on the night for championship-leading jockey Ryan Moore.
■ Stewards' Enquiry : Oscar Urbina caution: used whip with excessive frequency

FOCUS
An ordinary claimer in which few had a realistic chance based on official ratings and the runner-up governs the level of the form.

3214 LEWIS SILKIN H'CAP — 1m 2f 18y
8:55 (8:58) (Class 4) (0-85,83) 3-Y-0+ — £5,505 (£1,637; £818; £408) Stalls Low

Form — RPR
0006 **1** **Magic Sting**[19] 2640 5-9-5 74 ... HayleyTurner 4 — 85+
(M L W Bell) *trckd ldng pair: led 3f out: qcknd clr 2f out: easily* 16/1
4402 **2** 3 **Fire Two**[14] 2779 3-8-10 76 ... TedDurcan 2 — 82
(M R Channon) *trckd ldrs: rdn to chse wnr over 2f out: no imp* 8/1
0462 **3** ¾ **Prime Contender**[23] 2519 4-9-1 70 ... SebSanders 9 — 74
(B W Hills) *in tch: effrt over 2f out: one pce* 5/1[2]
45-1 **4** nk **Inchloch**[35] 2169 4-9-13 82 ... ShaneKelly 8 — 86
(B G Powell) *s.i.s: hld up in 6th: effrt whn hmpd over 3f out: drvn to chse ldrs fnl 2f: one pce* 7/1
1014 **5** nk **Secretary General (IRE)**[19] 2640 5-9-11 80 ... RyanMoore 5 — 83
(P F I Cole) *hld up towards rr: rdn and hung lft fnl 3f: nvr nrr* 11/2[3]
-006 **6** 1 ½ **Diktatorial**[13] 2819 4-10-0 83 ... (t) DarryllHolland 7 — 83
(G A Butler) *hld up detached last: shkn up and sme hdwy over 1f out: nvr in chalng position* 12/1
2411 **7** 4 **Dove Cottage (IRE)**[20] 2601 4-9-3 72 ... MickyFenton 1 — 65
(W S Kittow) *disp ld: led 4f out tl 3f out: wknd over 2f out* 8/1
0501 **8** ¾ **Burgundy**[15] 2752 9-9-1 70 ... (b) OscarUrbina 6 — 62
(P Mitchell) *s.i.s: hld up and bhd: rdn over 2f out: nvr a factor* 6/1
3101 **9** 55 **Sir Arthur (IRE)**[14] 2781 3-8-13 79 ... JoeFanning 3 — —
(M Johnston) *disp ld tl 4f out: lost pl qckly ent st: virtually p.u* 4/1[1]

2m 8.37s (-0.67) **Going Correction** +0.025s/f (Good)
WFA 3 from 4yo+ 11lb — 9 Ran SP% **114.6**
Speed ratings (Par 105):103,100,100,99,99 98,95,94,50
CSF £136.02 CT £739.57 TOTE £22.70: £6.10, £3.50, £1.90; EX 215.10 Place 6 £83.02, Place 5 £44.28.
Owner Mrs P T Fenwick **Bred** Michael Watt And Exors Of The Late Miss Jemima Joh **Trained** Newmarket, Suffolk
■ A double on the night for 2005 joint-champion apprentice Hayley Turner.

FOCUS
A fair handicap run at just an ordinary early pace and the form looks sound.
Secretary General(IRE) Official explanation: jockey said gelding hung left
Sir Arthur(IRE) Official explanation: trainer's representative had no explanation for the poor form shown
T/Plt: £41.50 to a £1 stake. Pool: £55,262.95. 970.60 winning tickets. T/Qpdt: £29.10 to a £1 stake. Pool: £3,911.10. 99.45 winning tickets. LM

2436 HAYDOCK (L-H)
Thursday, July 6
OFFICIAL GOING: Good to firm (good in places)
Wind: Almost nil Weather: Hot and sunny

3215 HAYDOCK PARK BADGEHOLDERS CLUB FILLIES' H'CAP — 1m 3f 200y
2:20 (2:21) (Class 5) (0-75,74) 3-Y-0+ — £4,533 (£1,348; £674; £336) Stalls High

Form — RPR
-043 **1** **Generosia**[10] 2929 3-8-4 62 ... (t) FrancisNorton 3 — 70
(A M Balding) *hld up: hdwy over 3f out: led 2f out: sn edgd lft: abt 3l clr over 1f out: tail flashed u.p: all out towards fin* 4/1[2]
506- **2** hd **Patxaran (IRE)**[88] 5220 4-9-9 73 ... (t) GregFairley(5) 2 — 80
(P C Haslam) *chsd ldrs: rdn and ev ch over 2f out: nt qckn over 1f out: r.o ins fnl f: clsd qckly towards fin* 9/1
-611 **3** 3 ½ **Spring Dream (IRE)**[34] 2209 3-9-2 74 ... TonyCulhane 8 — 75
(M R Channon) *chsd ldrs: rdn over 2f out: styd on same pce fnl f* 5/1[3]
0061 **4** ½ **Topflight Wildbird**[15] 2747 3-8-5 63 ... DeanMcKeown 4 — 63
(Mrs G S Rees) *chsd ldr: led 9f out: rdn and hdd 2f out: wknd ins fnl f* 9/1
003 **5** nk **Gaze**[19] 2655 3-8-12 70 ... MartinDwyer 5 — 70
(W Jarvis) *in rr div: niggled along at times: rdn and hung lft over 2f out: kpt on ins fnl f: nvr trbld ldrs* 4/1[2]
4-35 **6** 6 **Bouquet**[13] 2822 4-9-8 67 ... NCallan 1 — 57
(J R Fanshawe) *led: hdd 9f out: chsd ldr to 3f out: sn rdn: wknd over 1f out* 9/4[1]
-000 **7** 1 ½ **Farne Isle**[25] 1144 7-9-1 60 ... (tp) TomEaves 6 — 48
(G A Harker) *s.i.s: rdn 4f out: a bhd* 33/1

2m 33.22s (-1.77) **Going Correction** -0.20s/f (Firm)
WFA 3 from 4yo+ 13lb — 7 Ran SP% **110.4**
Speed ratings (Par 100):97,96,94,94,94 90,89
CSF £35.73 CT £171.12 TOTE £5.20: £2.40, £4.00; EX 41.80.
Owner Winterbeck Manor Stud **Bred** Addison Racing Ltd Inc **Trained** Kingsclere, Hants

FOCUS
An ordinary fillies' handicap but pretty solid form rated through the runner-up and third.

3216 EBF MARKETAVENUERACINGCLUB.CO.UK NOVICE FILLIES' STKS — 6f
2:50 (2:50) (Class 5) 2-Y-0 — £4,533 (£1,348; £674; £336) Stalls Centre

Form — RPR
51 **1** **Precocious Star (IRE)**[11] 2890 2-9-5 ... PatCosgrave 6 — 90+
(K R Burke) *hld up bhd ldrs: hdwy to ld over 1f out: r.o wl and edgd lft ins fnl f: wl in command* 6/1[3]
1 **2** 2 **Ela Aleka Mou**[18] 2680 2-9-5 ... PhilipRobinson 2 — 81
(M A Jarvis) *led: hdd over 1f out: sn rdn: hung lft ins fnl f: nt pce of wnr* 6/4[1]
1 **3** 1 ¼ **Tender Moments**[40] 2026 2-9-5 ... NCallan 5 — 77
(K A Ryan) *trckd ldrs: rdn and outpcd 2f out: edgd lft and styd on ins fnl f* 6/1[3]
2 **4** ¾ **Abby Road (IRE)**[17] 2703 2-8-12 ... SteveDrowne 3 — 68
(B J Meehan) *racd keenly: cl up: ev ch under 2f out: sn rdn and hung lft: no ex ins fnl f* 9/4[2]
104 **5** 3 ½ **Ask Don't Tell (IRE)**[48] 1824 2-8-12 ... JohnEgan 1 — 58
(Tom Dascombe) *w ldr: rdn and ev ch whn hung lft 2f out: wknd over 1f out* 25/1
6 1 **Park's Girl** 2-8-8 ... KDarley 4 — 51
(P C Haslam) *in rr: hdwy to r in tch 4f out: ev ch under 2f out: sn rdn and edgd lft: wknd 1f out* 16/1

1m 15.41s (0.51) **Going Correction** -0.10s/f (Good) — 6 Ran SP% **109.1**
Speed ratings (Par 91):92,89,87,86,82 80
CSF £14.63 TOTE £7.60: £2.50, £1.50; EX 15.50.
Owner Market Avenue Racing Club Ltd **Bred** Tom Twomey **Trained** Middleham Moor, N Yorks

FOCUS
An interesting race featuring two or three promising fillies who could well go on to contest races in Pattern company.

NOTEBOOK
Precocious Star(IRE) picked up well from off the pace and ran out a clear winner, despite edging left in the closing stages. That sign of inexperience made no difference as she had the race in the bag at the time, and she deserves a crack at a black-type event now. She holds an entry in the Group 2 Debutante Stakes at Leopardstown but connections may opt to aim a little lower to begin with. (op 13-2)
Ela Aleka Mou travelled best for much of the way next to the stands' rail but could not match the winner's turn of foot. This was still a good effort, though, and her breeding suggests she should appreciate stepping up to seven furlongs. (tchd 13-8)
Tender Moments, who won in heavy ground on her debut, had very different conditions to deal with this time. She got outpaced when the leaders stepped up the tempo and took a while to get into her stride, but she saw her race out well and slower ground is likely to see her in a better light in future. (op 7-1)
Abby Road(IRE), who was a well-backed favourite when beaten on her debut, again attracted support in the market. She holds a Moyglare Stud Stakes entry and is clearly well regarded, but she carried her head to one side and never really looked happy here, and connections will be scratching their heads now. (tchd 5-2 in places)
Ask Don't Tell(IRE), the most experienced filly in the line-up, might be better over five furlongs but she was taking on useful opposition here anyway and was found wanting. (op 28-1 tchd 33-1)
Park's Girl, whose dam was a useful multiple winner at two over sprint distances, was the only newcomer in the race and had a tough task on her debut. She will come on for the run and success in maiden company at a lesser track would not come as a surprise.

3217 EASIBED H'CAP — 6f
3:20 (3:21) (Class 4) (0-80,80) 3-Y-0+ — £6,477 (£1,927; £963; £481) Stalls Centre

Form — RPR
0211 **1** **Blue Tomato**[6] 3041 5-9-9 80 6ex ... LiamTreadwell(5) 8 — 96+
(J M Bradley) *hld up: hdwy 2f out: swtchd lft over 1f out: sn led: r.o wl* 9/2[1]
-433 **2** 2 ½ **Knot In Wood (IRE)**[19] 2661 4-9-8 74 ... PaulHanagan 4 — 83
(R A Fahey) *led: rdn and hdd over 1f out: edgd lft ent fnl f: nt pce of wnr after* 9/2[1]
-545 **3** ½ **No Grouse**[19] 2661 6-8-10 62 ... DavidAllan 9 — 69
(E J Alston) *hld up: rdn and hdwy over 1f out: r.o ins fnl f: nrst fin* 7/1[2]
1600 **4** nk **High Ridge**[8] 2981 7-9-9 75 ... (p) NCallan 7 — 81
(J M Bradley) *trckd ldrs: rdn over 2f out: styd on same pce fnl f* 16/1[3]
0200 **5** ½ **Countdown**[31] 2302 4-9-9 75 ... (b) TomEaves 5 — 80
(Miss J A Camacho) *midfield: rdn over 2f out: styd on ins fnl f: nt pce to chal* 20/1
0-10 **6** 1 ¾ **Rosein**[27] 2417 4-9-1 67 ... J-PGuillambert 1 — 66
(Mrs G S Rees) *racd keenly: w ldrs: rdn and ev ch wl over 1f out: wknd ins fnl f* 50/1
600- **7** nk **Orphan (IRE)**[257] 6022 4-10-0 80 ... PatCosgrave 12 — 78
(K R Burke) *hld up: rdn 2f out: kpt on ins fnl f: nvr able to chal* 16/1[3]
5351 **8** ¾ **Guildenstern (IRE)**[23] 2536 4-9-11 77 ... (t) SteveDrowne 11 — 76+
(H Morrison) *dwlt: sn in tch: rdn 2f out: sn lost pl: swtchd lft and kpt on ent fnl f: eased whn no imp towards fin* 9/2[1]
2126 **9** shd **Dvinsky (USA)**[12] 2864 5-9-0 73 ... KellyHarrison(7) 2 — 69
(D Carroll) *s.i.s: sn in tch: rdn over 2f out: wknd ins fnl f* 16/1[3]
6001 **10** shd **Pomfret Lad**[14] 2785 8-9-7 76 ... DerekNolan(3) 6 — 72
(J J Quinn) *w ldr: rdn and ev ch over 1f out: sn wknd* 20/1
00-0 **11** nk **Bold Haze**[19] 2661 4-8-13 65 ... TonyHamilton 3 — 60
(Miss S E Hall) *in tch: rdn over 2f out: wknd over 1f out* 25/1
-631 **12** 5 **Rosapenna (IRE)**[21] 2590 4-9-8 74 ... KDarley 10 — 66+
(C F Wall) *a bhd* 7/1[2]

1m 13.31s (-1.59) **Going Correction** -0.10s/f (Good) — 12 Ran SP% **112.5**
Speed ratings (Par 105):106,102,102,101,100 98,98,97,97,96 96,89
CSF £20.82 CT £139.14 TOTE £5.00: £2.00, £1.60, £2.60; EX 22.00.
Owner Dab Hand Racing **Bred** Bearstone Stud **Trained** Sedbury, Gloucs

FOCUS
A competitive sprint handicap on paper but the well-handicapped winner did it easily in the end. The form looks solid based on the performances of the placed horses.
Rosapenna(IRE) Official explanation: jockey said filly was never travelling

3218 DALKIA H'CAP — 1m 30y
3:50 (3:52) (Class 3) (0-95,90) 3-Y-0+ £9,715 (£2,890; £1,444; £721) Stalls Low

Form RPR

1-20 **1** **Banknote**[38] 2086 4-9-5 **87** .... FrancisNorton 4 99
(A M Balding) *chsd ldrs: led over 1f out: sn edgd lft: r.o ins fnl f* **11/2**[2]

0-45 **2** 1 ½ **Mutawaffer**[23] 2520 5-9-4 **86** .... PaulHanagan 3 96+
(R A Fahey) *led early: chsd ldrs after: rdn to take 2nd over 1f out: cl up whn n.m.r ins fnl f: hld by wnr after* **9/2**[1]

4-00 **3** nk **Very Wise**[19] 2657 4-9-0 **82** .... TonyCulhane 9 90
(W J Haggas) *hld up: hdwy whn nt clr run and swtchd rt over 1f out: styd on ins fnl f* **9/2**[1]

6451 **4** nk **Sew'N'So Character (IRE)**[8] 2988 5-9-5 **87** 6ex .... KDarley 6 94
(M Blanshard) *in tch: rdn over 2f out: styd on ins fnl f* **11/2**[2]

0331 **5** 4 **Diamonds And Dust**[14] 2787 4-9-3 **85** ....(b) NCallan 5 83
(M H Tompkins) *sn chsd ldr tl rdn over 2f out: n.m.r and lost grnd over 1f out: no imp after* **8/1**[3]

0024 **6** 1 ¼ **Calcutta**[8] 2988 10-9-8 **90** .... MartinDwyer 8 85
(B W Hills) *towards rr: rdn over 4f out: sme hdwy over 1f out: no imp fnl f* **8/1**[3]

0100 **7** shd **Baylaw Star**[23] 2527 5-9-6 **88** .... CatherineGannon 7 83
(K A Ryan) *sn led: rdn over 2f out: hdd over 1f out: wknd fnl f* **50/1**

-000 **8** 1 **Stagbury Hill (USA)**[14] 2776 4-9-3 **85** .... JohnEgan 10 78
(J W Hills) *hld up in rr: pushed along over 3f out: nvr trbld ldrs* **20/1**

6440 **9** nk **Stoic Leader (IRE)**[5] 3079 6-8-12 **80** .... SteveDrowne 2 72
(R F Fisher) *midfield: rdn over 2f out: outpcd over 1f out: wknd fnl f* **12/1**

6600 **10** nk **Boo**[82] 1017 4-9-8 **90** ....(v) PatCosgrave 1 81
(K R Burke) *a rdn along in midfield: swtchd lft and outpcd over 1f out: wknd fnl f* **10/1**

1m 41.62s (-3.89) **Going Correction** -0.20s/f (Firm) 10 Ran SP% **112.9**
Speed ratings (Par 107):111,109,109,108,104 103,103,102,102,101
CSF £29.40 CT £122.24 TOTE £4.30: £1.90, £2.20, £2.10; EX 23.00.
Owner The Queen **Bred** Exors Of The Late Queen Elizabeth **Trained** Kingsclere, Hants
■ Stewards' Enquiry : Francis Norton one-day ban: careless riding (Jul 17)
Tony Culhane one-day ban: careless riding (Jul 17)

FOCUS
Not a bad handicap and it was run at a good clip thanks to the trailblazing Baylaw Star, but there was a fair amount of trouble in running, too. The form is rated quite positively through the winner.

NOTEBOOK
Banknote, who won this race last year off a 9lb lower mark, had the ground in his favour and the strong early pace ensured that he did not throw his race away by racing too keenly. A winner of five of his 12 career starts, he has developed into a very useful performer and apparently the plan is now to step him into Pattern company. (tchd 6-1)
Mutawaffer, hampered by the winner inside the final furlong, is the sort of horse who always seems to find bad luck. Winless since September 2003, few would argue he is on a mark he has the ability to win off, but whether he will is another matter. (op 5-1 tchd 6-1)
Very Wise, who was backed into joint-favouritism, enjoyed a luckless run as he was attempting to make up ground from the back of the field. He has the ability to win off this sort of mark. (op 5-1)
Sew'N'So Character(IRE) has a poor strike-rate and, although a winner on his previous start, he was always more than likely going to find one or two too strong here, especially as the ground was quicker than ideal. (op 5-1 tchd 6-1)
Diamonds And Dust paid the price for chasing the strong early gallop set by Baylaw Star.
Calcutta was disappointing as he had the ground in his favour and the race was run to suit. (op 6-1)
Baylaw Star set an unsustainably fast early gallop. (op 33-1)

3219 BINGLEY MAIDEN STKS — 1m 30y
4:20 (4:21) (Class 5) 3-Y-0+ £3,238 (£963; £481; £240) Stalls Low

Form RPR

3 **1** **Abwaab**[39] 2048 3-9-0 ....(t) MartinDwyer 5 79+
(W J Haggas) *a.p: rdn over 2f out: led ins fnl f: r.o* **9/4**[3]

02- **2** 1 ½ **Dynamic Rhythm (USA)**[328] 4346 3-9-0 .... ShaneKelly 7 76
(J Noseda) *a.p: rdn and nt qckn over 1f out: styd on ins fnl f: wnt 2nd towards fin* **2/1**[2]

3422 **3** ½ **Pirouetting**[12] 2881 3-8-9 78 .... TonyCulhane 3 69
(B W Hills) *led: rdn over 1f out: hdd ins fnl f: no ex towards fin* **15/8**[1]

-06 **4** 7 **Weet For Ever (USA)**[12] 2881 3-9-0 .... RobbieFitzpatrick 6 58+
(P A Blockley) *s.i.s: racd keenly: in rr: rdn over 1f out and sn wnt 4th: jinked rt towards fin: no imp* **33/1**

0 **5** 4 **Norakit**[8] 2985 3-8-9 .... JohnEgan 2 44+
(M R Channon) *racd keenly: hld up: hdwy 3f out: rdn whn chsd ldrs over 2f out: wknd over 1f out* **25/1**

66-3 **6** 3 ½ **Distant Vision (IRE)**[6] 3039 3-8-9 ....(t) FrancisNorton 4 36+
(A Berry) *hld up: effrt 3f out: sn edgd lft and no imp: bhd over 1f out* **66/1**

1m 46.29s (0.78) **Going Correction** -0.20s/f (Firm)
WFA 3 from 5yo 9lb 6 Ran SP% **107.2**
Speed ratings (Par 103):88,86,86,79,75 71
CSF £6.42 TOTE £2.80: £1.50, £1.80; EX 6.20.
Owner Hamdan Al Maktoum **Bred** R T And Mrs Watson **Trained** Newmarket, Suffolk

FOCUS
An average maiden run at a steady early gallop and the time was 4.67 seconds slower than the preceding handicap, but the first two home should soon be winning in handicap company.

3220 GOOSE GREEN H'CAP — 1m 6f
4:50 (4:50) (Class 4) (0-85,79) 4-Y-0+ £6,477 (£1,927; £963; £481) Stalls Low

Form RPR

3-33 **1** **Nobelix (IRE)**[26] 2447 4-9-4 **76** .... MartinDwyer 7 89+
(J R Fanshawe) *mde all at stdy pce: qcknd tempo over 2f out: clr over 1f out: styd on wl* **9/2**[2]

-611 **2** 7 **Ti Adora (IRE)**[19] 2653 4-9-7 **79** .... FrancisNorton 4 83
(P W D'Arcy) *racd keenly: prom: rdn over 3f out: wnt 2nd over 1f out: no ch w wnr: pressed for 2nd cl home* **5/1**[3]

346- **3** shd **Bucks**[58] 6482 9-8-12 **70** .... KDarley 1 74
(Ian Williams) *in tch: rdn over 3f out: sn outpcd: kpt on ins fnl f: chalng for 2nd cl home* **9/1**

0000 **4** 1 ¾ **Dancer's Serenade (IRE)**[15] 2761 4-9-0 **72** .... JohnEgan 6 73
(T P Tate) *hld up: hdwy 5f out: rdn and hung lft fr 3f out: kpt on same pce fnl 2f* **16/1**

5-14 **5** nk **Crathorne (IRE)**[14] 2242 6-8-6 **64** .... PaulHanagan 5 65
(M Todhunter) *hld up: rdn 3f out: kpt on ins fnl f: nvr able to chal* **3/1**[1]

45-5 **6** hd **Foursquare Flyer (IRE)**[7] 3009 4-9-0 **72** .... DaleGibson 2 73
(J Mackie) *hld up: rdn over 4f out: kpt on ins fnl f: nvr able to chal* **20/1**

0-03 **7** ¾ **Border Tale**[76] 597 6-8-0 **63** ow3 .... AndrewMullen(5) 9 63
(James Moffatt) *prom: rdn and ev ch 3f out: wknd over 1f out* **20/1**

4161 **8** 5 **Haatmey**[12] 2869 4-9-3 **75** ....(v) TonyCulhane 3 68
(M R Channon) *in tch: rdn 3f out: wknd wl over 1f out* **5/1**[3]

000/ **9** 24 **Glimmer Of Light (IRE)**[61] 5258 6-8-7 **65** .... AdrianTNicholls 8 27
(S A Brookshaw) *hld up in rr: rdn over 4f out: nvr on terms* **11/1**

3m 9.82s (3.53) **Going Correction** -0.20s/f (Firm) 9 Ran SP% **110.3**
Speed ratings (Par 105):81,77,76,75,75 75,75,72,58
CSF £25.25 CT £179.69 TOTE £5.60: £2.10, £1.50, £2.60; EX 22.60 Place 6 £65.49, Place 5 £18.70.
Owner Rupert Hambro **Bred** Horst Rapp And Dieter Burkle **Trained** Newmarket, Suffolk

FOCUS
There was an unsatisfactorily steady early pace dictated by the eventual winner in this staying handicap and the time was pedestrian, but he was still impressive.
T/Plt: £129.80 to a £1 stake. Pool: £48,217.40. 271.00 winning tickets. T/Qpdt: £10.60 to a £1 stake. Pool: £3,334.30. 232.25 winning tickets. DO

2956 NEWBURY (L-H)
Thursday, July 6

OFFICIAL GOING: Good
Wind: Almost nil

3221 STANJAMESUK.COM APPRENTICE H'CAP — 1m 3f 5y
6:00 (6:01) (Class 5) (0-70,69) 3-Y-0+ £3,238 (£963; £481; £240) Stalls Centre

Form RPR

0532 **1** **Ollie George (IRE)**[8] 2990 3-8-12 **65** .... StephenDonohoe 11 76
(A M Balding) *mid-div: hrd drvn 3f out: slt ld appr fnl 2f: drvn out ins last* **9/2**[1]

064U **2** 4 **Hatch A Plan (IRE)**[8] 2966 5-9-7 **62** .... TravisBlock 6 66
(Mrs A J Hamilton-Fairley) *bhd: hdwy 3f out: styd on u.p to chse wnr fnl f but a wl hld* **14/1**

/600 **3** 1 **Bukit Fraser (IRE)**[47] 1847 5-9-2 **60** ....(t) DerekNolan(3) 12 62
(P F I Cole) *bhd: hrd drvn fr 3f out: styd on u.p to go 3rd fnl f but nvr gng pce to rch ldrs* **16/1**

6040 **4** 3 **Mixing**[19] 2647 4-9-1 **61** .... BRoper(5) 8 58
(W Jarvis) *chsd ldrs: drvn to chal fr 3f out: stl ev ch ins fnl 2f: wknd fnl f* **25/1**

30-5 **5** nk **Bienheureux**[12] 2862 5-9-1 **56** ....(v) JerryO'Dwyer 2 52
(Miss Gay Kelleway) *bhd: rdn and hdwy over 2f out: kpt on ins last but nvr gng pce to rch ldrs* **12/1**

0432 **6** nk **Danger Zone**[7] 3024 4-9-11 **69** ....(p) LiamJones(3) 10 65
(Mrs A J Perrett) *in tch: hdwy 3f out: chsd ldrs 2f out: wknd over 1f out* **5/1**[2]

0033 **7** 1 ½ **Serramanna**[9] 2956 5-8-7 **51** oh2 .... SladeO'Hara(3) 4 44
(Dr J R J Naylor) *chsd ldrs: slt ld fr over 3f out tl narrowly hdd over 2f out: wknd over 1f out* **5/1**[2]

330 **8** 1 ½ **Follow The Colours (IRE)**[23] 2518 3-8-9 **67** .... PatrickHills(5) 1 58
(J W Hills) *chsd ldrs: slt advantage 4f oit tl hdd appr fnl 3f: stl ev ch 2f out: sn btn* **5/1**[2]

4125 **9** 1 **Gallego**[10] 2918 4-9-6 **61** .... JamesDoyle 7 50
(R J Price) *s.i.s: bhd: sme hdwy 3f out: wknd 2f out* **6/1**[3]

-100 **10** nk **John Charles (IRE)**[84] 1002 4-9-11 **66** .... RichardKingscote 3 54
(B De Haan) *chsd ldrs: rdn over 3f out: wknd 2f out* **22/1**

0004 **11** 26 **Under Fire (IRE)**[12] 2877 3-7-9 **53** oh3 ow2 .... JamesRogers(5) 5 —
(A W Carroll) *plld hrd: in tch a m* **50/1**

0-00 **12** 13 **Shortbread**[21] 2585 4-8-8 **54** .... JosephWalsh(5) 9 —
(M Salaman) *led tl hdd 4f out: sn wknd* **100/1**

2m 21.53s (-0.74) **Going Correction** -0.025s/f (Good)
WFA 3 from 4yo+ 12lb 12 Ran SP% **113.9**
Speed ratings (Par 103):101,98,97,95,94 94,93,92,91,91 72,63
CSF £63.00 CT £917.80 TOTE £3.70: £1.90, £3.30, £6.10; EX 68.00.
Owner Peter R Grubb **Bred** Lawrence Walsh **Trained** Kingsclere, Hants

FOCUS
This probably did not take too much winning although the form looks fair enough.
Shortbread Official explanation: jockey said gelding hung right-handed

3222 STAN JAMES EUROPEAN BREEDERS FUND MAIDEN STKS — 6f 8y
6:30 (6:35) (Class 4) 2-Y-0 £6,477 (£1,927; £963; £481) Stalls High

Form RPR

1 **Traffic Guard (USA)** 2-9-3 .... JohnEgan 4 85+
(J S Moore) *trckd ldrs: chal 2f out: led over 1f out: shkn up: green but sn clr ins last: comf* **33/1**

2 1 **Prime Defender** 2-9-3 .... MichaelHills 3 82+
(B W Hills) *chsd ldrs: rdn and styd on to chse wnr ins last but a hld* **11/1**[3]

3 1 ½ **Chataway** 2-9-3 .... SteveDrowne 14 78+
(B J Meehan) *chsd ldrs: rdn over 2f out: styd on ins last but nvr gng pce to chal* **20/1**

4 nk **Magic Mountain (IRE)** 2-9-3 .... DaneO'Neill 9 77
(R Hannon) *chsd ldrs: rdn over 2f out: kpt on same pce ins last* **12/1**

6 **5** 2 ½ **Tracer**[17] 2710 2-9-3 .... RichardHughes 12 69+
(R Hannon) *led: rdn 2f out: hdd over 1f out: wknd ins last* **7/2**[2]

6 ½ **Buckie Massa** 2-9-3 .... JimmyFortune 8 68
(S Kirk) *s.i.s: hdwy to chse ldrs 1/2-way: outpcd fnl f* **12/1**

3 **7** ½ **Kilburn**[27] 2402 2-9-0 .... AdamKirby(3) 6 66
(C G Cox) *chsd ldrs: pushed along 2f out: wknd ins fnl f* **3/1**[1]

8 3 ½ **Lordswood (IRE)** 2-9-3 .... MartinDwyer 5 56
(A M Balding) *in tch: sltly hmpd over 4f out: shkn up and no prog fnl 2f* **20/1**

9 ½ **Last Dog Standing (IRE)** 2-8-12 .... JamesDoyle(5) 11 54
(B G Powell) *bhd: rdn 3f out: styd on fnl 2f but nvr gng pce to rch ldrs* **33/1**

10 1 ¼ **Shake On It** 2-9-3 .... StephenCarson 2 50
(R F Johnson Houghton) *bhd: hdwy to trck ldrs 2f out: wknd fnl f* **12/1**

11 11 **Fereeji** 2-9-3 .... TonyCulhane 16 17
(M R Channon) *s.i.s: outpcd most of way* **11/1**[3]

12 1 **Avoid The Cat** 2-9-3 .... JimCrowley 10 14
(Mrs A J Perrett) *s.i.s: outpcd most of way* **25/1**

13 ¾ **Moddlij (IRE)** 2-9-0 .... EdwardCreighton(3) 13 12
(M R Channon) *slowly away: a outpcd* **33/1**

14 ½ **Master Golfer (USA)** 2-9-3 .... KDarley 7 11
(B W Hills) *a outpcd* **12/1**

P **Xaaretta (IRE)** 2-8-9 .... RichardSmith(3) 1 —
(R Hannon) *slowly away: rr whn broke leg over 1f out: destroyed* **33/1**

1m 14.78s (0.46) **Going Correction** +0.05s/f (Good) 15 Ran SP% **119.8**
Speed ratings (Par 96):98,96,94,94,90 90,89,84,84,82 67,66,65,64,—
CSF £337.13 TOTE £43.80: £9.70, £3.10, £7.50; EX 521.00.

The Form Book, Raceform Ltd, Compton, RG20 6NL

Owner Uplands Acquisitions Limited **Bred** F Penn And John R Penn **Trained** Upper Lambourn, Berks

FOCUS
Plenty of the big yards were represented in this juvenile maiden and it could throw up a few future winners.

NOTEBOOK
Traffic Guard(USA), sold for 42,000gns at the breeze-ups earlier this year, was always up there on his debut and in the end he ran on well to win. He looked a shade green when hitting the front so there could well be plenty more improvement in him. He will not mind further and he can go on from here. (op 25-1)
Prime Defender, whose dam was a winning sprinter, did little wrong on his debut and he will improve plenty for the experience. He is another who will be suited by another furlong and should have little difficulty getting his head in front.
Chataway, who is already a gelding, is out of a maiden half-sister to high-class sprinter Averti. He hails from a yard whose youngsters come on for the run and he can be found an opportunity in the not too distant future.
Magic Mountain(IRE) is related to winners over further, including smart handicapper Gryffindor, out of a half-sister to smart middle-distance performer/hurdler Midnight Legend. There was nothing wrong with this debut effort as he was clear of the others and will need another furlong or so to be seen to better effect.
Tracer, upped in trip, did best of those with a run under their belt. He showed pace but once again did not find a lot and nurseries after another run could be the way forward with him in the longer term. (op 9-2 tchd 5-1)
Buckie Massa, a half-brother to seven-furlong winner Zafantage, made a satisfactory start to his career. (tchd 10-1)
Kilburn showed promise on his debut at Goodwood in what looked a decent race and this was disappointing. (op 9-4)

3223 STANSPOKER.CO.UK H'CAP — 7f (S)
7:05 (7:08) (Class 3) (0-95,93) 3-Y-0+ **£9,067** (£2,697; £1,348; £673) **Stalls** High

Form | | | | RPR
-050 **1** **Paper Talk (USA)**[14] 2776 4-9-13 **92** .... MichaelHills 9 — 102
(B W Hills) *hld up: hdwy on outside over 1f out: hung rt u.p ins last: led last half f: drvn out* **13/2**[3]
6642 **2** ½ **Grizedale (IRE)**[12] 2860 7-8-9 **74** .... (t) PaulDoe 12 — 83
(J Akehurst) *hld up in rr: swtchd lft to outside wl over 1f out: hdwy, carried rt and ev ch ins last: no ex cl home* **16/1**
2303 **3** 1 **Binanti**[14] 2776 6-9-7 **86** .... FrancisNorton 3 — 92
(P R Chamings) *trckd ldrs: n.m.r fr 2f out tl led gng wl jst ins fnl f: hdd and one pce last half f* **8/1**
1033 **4** ¾ **King's Caprice**[5] 3092 5-9-11 **90** .... (t) RichardThomas 5 — 94
(J A Geake) *led: hdd jst ins fnl f: sn one pce* **11/2**[1]
0014 **5** nk **Blue Trojan (IRE)**[7] 3020 6-8-13 **78** .... JimmyFortune 8 — 81
(S Kirk) *in tch: drvn to chse ldrs fr 2f out: one pce ins last* **6/1**[2]
-034 **6** 5 **Red Romeo**[13] 2830 5-9-4 **83** .... DeanMcKeown 13 — 73
(G A Swinbank) *s.i.s: bhd: hdwy into mid-div 1/2-way: n.m.r fr over 2f out: one pce whn hmpd last half f* **13/2**[3]
5-00 **7** 1¾ **Emilio**[5] 3092 5-9-11 **90** .... (t) FJohansson 7 — 76
(R A Kvisla) *chsd ldrs: rdn over 2f out: wkng whn sltly hmpd last half f* **100/1**
1406 **8** 8 **Loyal Royal (IRE)**[18] 2675 3-9-6 **93** .... JohnEgan 1 — 55
(D R C Elsworth) *chsd ldrs: rdn over 2f out: wknd and no ch whn hmpd last half f* **16/1**
6364 **9** 12 **Isphahan**[21] 2581 3-7-10 **76** .... (v) JamesRogers(7) 2 — 7
(A M Balding) *in tch: rdn 3f out: wknd fr 2f out: no ch whn hmpd last half f* **10/1**
4-00 **10** 13 **Cape Presto (IRE)**[60] 1505 3-9-0 **87** .... RichardHughes 10 — —
(R Hannon) *chsd ldr early: wknd 2f out* **16/1**
0000 **11** 3 **Millennium Force**[14] 2776 8-9-6 **85** .... TonyCulhane 6 — 86
(M R Channon) *bhd: hdwy over 2f out: wkng whn bdly hmpd last half f* **14/1**
0230 **B** **Surwaki (USA)**[20] 2606 4-8-9 **77** .... AdamKirby(3) 4 — 79
(C G Cox) *trckd ldrs: chal fr 3f out: one pce and hld whn hmpd and b.d last half f* **16/1**
-000 **B** **Postgraduate (IRE)**[29] 2364 4-9-8 **87** .... (v) SteveDrowne 11 — —
(W J Knight) *bhd: swtchd to outside and sme hdwy over 1f out: no ch w ldrs whn bdly hmpd and b.d last half f* **12/1**

1m 27.46s (0.46) **Going Correction** +0.05s/f (Good)
WFA 3 from 4yo+ 8lb — **13** Ran SP% **115.4**
Speed ratings (Par 107):99,98,97,96,96 90,88,79,65,50 47,—,—
CSF £102.41 CT £869.32 TOTE £7.90: £2.80, £3.00, £2.30; EX 260.30.
Owner Gainsborough Stud **Bred** Gainsborough Farm Llc **Trained** Lambourn, Berks
■ Stewards' Enquiry : Michael Hills two-day ban: careless riding (Jul 17-18)

FOCUS
A wide-open handicap and the form looks sound.

NOTEBOOK
Paper Talk(USA), well beaten after making the running at Royal Ascot, reverted to hold-up tactics and ran on down the outside of the pack to show ahead inside the last. He did well under his big weight but may struggle after he has been reassessed. (op 6-1)
Grizedale(IRE) was raised 3lb for his Lingfield second. He made his challenge with the winner down the outside but, losing momentum when slightly hampered in the melee, was just held. He is proving hard to win with. (op 20-1)
Binanti ran another solid race but, after showing ahead going best, he was run out of it. He holds no secrets from the Handicapper.
King's Caprice, back over seven, adopted his usual tactics but had been under pressure for a time before being collared entering the final furlong. He is running well but may need to be dropped a couple of pounds before he is winning again. (op 5-1 tchd 6-1)
Blue Trojan(IRE), back down in trip, was not disgraced but is always going to be up against it in this grade. Official explanation: jockey said gelding moved poorly (op 8-1)
Red Romeo was returning to seven furlongs but did not get the breaks. (op 5-1)
Surwaki(USA) sweated up beforehand. He raced prominently, but was feeling the pinch when squeezed up and coming down inside the last. (tchd 14-1)

3224 PUMP TECHNOLOGY & JUNG PUMPEN PARTNERSHIP CELEBRATION H'CAP — 1m (S)
7:35 (7:44) (Class 4) (0-85,85) 3-Y-0 **£6,153** (£1,830; £914; £456) **Stalls** High

Form | | | | RPR
1335 **1** **Illustrious Blue**[15] 2754 3-9-2 **80** .... PaulDoe 2 — 96
(W J Knight) *trckd ldrs: led appr fnl 2f: hrd rdn and styd on wl fnl f* **20/1**
-240 **2** 1¼ **Acheekyone (IRE)**[47] 1841 3-9-6 **84** .... JimmyFortune 8 — 97
(B J Meehan) *hld up in rr: stdy hdwy fr 3f out to trck wnr 1f out: hrd rdn and r.o fnl f but a hld* **4/1**[1]
-002 **3** 3½ **Shogun Prince (IRE)**[10] 2932 3-9-2 **80** .... DaneO'Neill 4 — 85
(A King) *rrd stalls: hdwy 1/2-way: rdn to chse ldrs and edgd lft ins fnl 2f: one pce fnl f* **16/1**
4465 **4** 2 **Star Of The Desert (IRE)**[27] 2404 3-8-7 **74** .... AdamKirby(3) 3 — 75
(C G Cox) *chsd ldr: chal fr 5f out tl rdn 2f out: wknd fnl f* **20/1**
32-4 **5** nk **Ebert**[54] 1681 3-8-9 **73** .... FergusSweeney 14 — 73
(P J Makin) *s.i.s: sn in tch: rdn and hdwy on stands side over 2f out: kpt on same pce fnl f* **16/1**
0604 **6** 1 **Cool Sting (IRE)**[12] 2863 3-8-5 **72** .... NeilChalmers(3) 5 — 70
(A M Balding) *chsd ldrs: rdn over 2f out: wknd fnl f* **25/1**
-421 **7** 1 **Jihaaz (IRE)**[10] 2919 3-9-7 **85** 6ex .... RHills 6 — 81
(B W Hills) *chsdf ldrs: pushed along 3f out: wknd over 1f out* **9/2**[2]
0-03 **8** 3 **Princess Lavinia**[55] 1630 3-8-8 **72** .... SteveDrowne 10 — 61
(G Wragg) *bhd: sme prog fr over 1f out: nvr in contention* **33/1**
21-1 **9** shd **Music Note (IRE)**[40] 2033 3-9-7 **85** .... TonyCulhane 7 — 74
(M R Channon) *slt ld tl hdd appr fnl 2f: wknd over 1f out* **7/1**
136 **10** 5 **Odessa Star (USA)**[10] 2921 3-7-12 **67** oh1 ow1 .... JamesDoyle(5) 11 — 45
(J G Portman) *bhd: sme hdwy fr 3f out: nvr rchd ldrs and sn btn* **40/1**
-012 **11** 5 **Ingratitude (IRE)**[48] 1828 3-9-7 **85** .... JohnEgan 12 — 52
(R M Beckett) *nvr bttr than mid-div* **13/2**[3]
12 3½ **Dream Catcher (SWE)**[217] 3-9-5 **83** .... (t) FJohansson 1 — 42
(R A Kvisla) *chsd ldrs over 5f* **50/1**
1-3 **13** 1½ **Just Intersky (USA)**[13] 2809 3-9-1 **79** .... DeanMcKeown 15 — 35
(G A Swinbank) *racd towards stands side: chsd ldrs over 5f* **7/1**
2052 **14** 15 **Carmenero (GER)**[12] 2863 3-9-4 **82** .... MartinDwyer 13 — —
(W R Muir) *racd stands side: chsd ldrs over 5f: lost tch fnl 2f* **11/1**

1m 40.17s (-0.45) **Going Correction** +0.05s/f (Good) — **14** Ran SP% **117.3**
Speed ratings (Par 102):104,102,99,97,96 95,94,91,91,86 81,78,76,61
CSF £90.50 CT £1384.02 TOTE £20.70: £6.00, £1.60, £5.40; EX 115.30.
Owner Mr & Mrs I H Bendelow **Bred** B J And Mrs Crangle **Trained** Patching, W Sussex

FOCUS
A competitive-looking affair and the form of those behind the first two looks reasonable.
Carmenero(GER) Official explanation: jockey said gelding pulled hard and was unsteerable in the early stages

3225 GARDNER MECHANICAL SERVICES MAIDEN STKS — 1m 4f 5y
8:10 (8:11) (Class 5) 3-Y-0+ **£5,181** (£1,541; £770; £384) **Stalls** Centre

Form | | | | RPR
2223 **1** **Ermine Sea**[13] 2804 3-9-0 93 .... JimmyFortune 9 — 86
(J H M Gosden) *trckd ldrs 1m out: slt ld 3f out: rdn and narrowly hdd 2f out: rallied u.p to ld again ins last: drvn out* **5/4**[1]
-523 **2** 1¾ **Altenburg (FR)**[37] 2118 4-9-8 80 .... JamesDoyle(5) 5 — 83
(Mrs N Smith) *bhd: hdwy on outside fr 3f out: chal 1f out: hung lft and no ex ins last* **16/1**
2 **3** shd **Hyperalert (USA)**[13] 2829 3-9-0 .... KDarley 2 — 83
(M Johnston) *chsd ldr 4f: styd prom: slt ld 2f out: hdd ins last: styd on samme pce* **5/2**[2]
-033 **4** 3 **Reinstated (IRE)**[8] 2970 3-8-9 82 .... MichaelHills 6 — 73
(B W Hills) *in tch: trckd ldrs and pushed along 2f out: wknd ins fnl f* **14/1**
3 **5** hd **Well Hidden**[27] 2412 3-8-9 .... RHills 3 — 73
(Sir Michael Stoute) *in tch: rdn and effrt 2f out: nvr quite gng pce to press ldrs: wknd ins last* **5/1**[3]
6 5 **Crossbow Creek**[114] 8-9-13 .... JimCrowley 7 — 70
(M G Rimell) *s.i.s: sn in tch: rdn and kpt on fr 3f out but nvr gng pce to rch ldrs: wknd fnl 2f* **20/1**
00 **7** 2½ **Brief History**[31] 2304 3-9-0 .... DaneO'Neill 4 — 66
(H Candy) *sn led: narrowly hdd 3f out: wknd 2f out* **40/1**
4 **8** 8 **Valuta (USA)**[13] 2815 3-9-0 .... (t) FJohansson 1 — 53
(R A Kvisla) *bhd most of way* **33/1**
00-0 **9** dist **Come To Daddy (IRE)**[27] 2411 4-9-13 40 .... PaulFitzsimons 8 — —
(F Jordan) *lost tch fnl 5f: t.o* **100/1**

2m 34.28s (-1.71) **Going Correction** -0.025s/f (Good)
WFA 3 from 4yo+ 13lb — **9** Ran SP% **113.4**
Speed ratings (Par 103):104,102,102,100,100 97,95,90,—
CSF £22.59 TOTE £2.10: £1.10, £3.20, £1.50; EX 29.50.
Owner Lady Bamford **Bred** Lady Bamford **Trained** Newmarket, Suffolk

FOCUS
A decent maiden and the form looks solid enough.

3226 STANJAMESUK.COM STKS (H'CAP) — 6f 8y
8:45 (8:47) (Class 4) (0-80,80) 3-Y-0 **£5,505** (£1,637; £818; £408) **Stalls** High

Form | | | | RPR
0004 **1** **Sleeping Storm (IRE)**[10] 2932 3-8-7 **71** .... KMay(7) 3 — 79+
(B J Meehan) *in tch: hdwy fr 2f out to ld 1f out: drvn and styd on wl fnl f* **33/1**
0366 **2** ½ **Brandywell Boy (IRE)**[6] 3049 3-9-1 **77** .... JamesDoyle(5) 8 — 84
(D J S Ffrench Davis) *slt ld: rdn over 2f out: hdd 1f out: kpt on ins fnl f but a hld by wnr* **33/1**
1401 **3** ½ **Roman Quest**[20] 2609 3-8-12 **74** .... TravisBlock(5) 14 — 85+
(H Morrison) *hld up in rr: hdwy whn nt clr run fr over 1f out and ins last: rapid hdwy fnl half f: fin fast: unlucky* **7/1**[3]
251 **4** nk **River Kirov (IRE)**[38] 2080 3-9-4 **75** .... AdrianMcCarthy 1 — 79
(P W Chapple-Hyam) *chsd ldrs: rdn to dispute ld 1f out: kpt on same pce u.p ins last* **9/2**[2]
5154 **5** ½ **Starlight Gazer**[20] 2609 3-9-5 **76** .... RichardThomas 7 — 79
(J A Geake) *chsd ldrs: rdn 2f out: kpt on ins last but nvr gng pce to chal* **14/1**
-213 **6** ½ **Cheney Hill**[24] 2509 3-8-12 **69** .... DaneO'Neill 5 — 70
(H Candy) *chsd ldrs: t.k.h early: rdn over 1f out: one pce whn n.m.r ins last* **7/1**[3]
311 **7** nk **Home Sweet Home (IRE)**[3] 3150 3-9-4 **80** 6ex... StephenDonohoe(5) 6 — 80
(P D Evans) *pressed ldrs early: styd prom: rdn and kpt on fr over 1f out but nt pce to chal ins last* **3/1**[1]
000 **8** 1¼ **Littledodayno (IRE)**[12] 2863 3-8-8 **65** .... JamieMackay 9 — 61
(M Wigham) *in tch: pushed along over 1f out: kpt on ins last: gng on cl home* **40/1**
0645 **9** ¾ **Spearit (IRE)**[10] 2931 3-9-2 **73** .... JohnEgan 13 — 67
(D R C Elsworth) *in tch: rdn and hdwy 2f out: chsd ldrs u.p 1f out: sn no imp* **12/1**
0402 **10** 1 **Valentino Swing (IRE)**[10] 2931 3-8-13 **70** .... (p) FrancisNorton 2 — 61
(J L Spearing) *w ldr over 3f: one pce whn hmpd 1f out: sn btn* **14/1**
0-06 **11** hd **River Kintyre**[15] 2760 3-9-7 **78** .... MichaelHills 15 — 69
(B W Hills) *bhd: swtchd rt and sme hdwy fnl f: nvr in contention* **40/1**
10-0 **12** 1 **Eversden (USA)**[20] 2609 3-9-2 **76** .... AdamKirby(3) 10 — 64
(C G Cox) *chsd ldrs: rdn over 2f out: wknd over 1f out* **50/1**
5305 **13** nk **Blue Aura (IRE)**[20] 2609 3-9-4 **75** .... SteveDrowne 4 — 62
(R Charlton) *in tch: hdwy and n.m.r over 1f out: n.d after* **12/1**
052 **14** nk **Disco Ball**[26] 2458 3-9-1 **72** .... KDarley 11 — 58
(G Wragg) *chsd ldrs: rdn 2f: wknd over 1f out* **7/1**[3]

1406 **15** *1* **African Concerto (IRE)**[67] 1312 3-8-5 **62**.................... MartinDwyer 12 45
(S Kirk) *a outpcd* **50/1**

1m 14.77s (0.45) **Going Correction** +0.05s/f (Good) **15** Ran SP% **124.1**
Speed ratings (Par 102):99,98,97,97,96 95,95,93,92,91 91,89,89,89,87
CSF £858.55 CT £8388.46 TOTE £39.30: £6.50, £5.70, £3.00; EX 857.40 Place 6 £2,871.04, Place 5 £761.67.
Owner Miss J Semple **Bred** Michael O'Mahony **Trained** Manton, Wilts

FOCUS
A fair three-year-old handicap with quite a few potential improvers in the line up. The runner-up sets the standard.
Roman Quest ◆ Official explanation: jockey said gelding was denied a clear run
Cheney Hill Official explanation: jockey said gelding hung badly right-handed
T/Plt: £3,183.50 to a £1 stake. Pool: £54,512.30. 12.50 winning tickets. T/Qpdt: £102.30 to a £1 stake. Pool: £5,588.50. 40.40 winning tickets. ST

2586 YARMOUTH (L-H)

Thursday, July 6

OFFICIAL GOING: Firm
Wind: Light, across Weather: Hot and sunny

3227 EUROPEAN BREEDERS FUND MAIDEN FILLIES' STKS 7f 3y
2:30 (2:31) (Class 5) 2-Y-O **£3,886** (£1,156; £577; £288) **Stalls** Low

Form RPR

33 **1** **Majounes Song**[19] 2660 2-9-0 .... RoystonFfrench 2 77+
(M Johnston) *mde all: rdn 2f out: wl in command fnl f* **6/4**[1]

0 **2** *3 ½* **Millestan (IRE)**[19] 2638 2-9-0 .... EddieAhern 3 68+
(H R A Cecil) *cl up: rdn 2f out: wnt 2nd 1f out: kpt on but no ch w wnr* **12/1**

3 *2 ½* **Mizzle (USA)** 2-9-0 .... KerrinMcEvoy 5 61+
(Saeed Bin Suroor) *keen: sn pressing wnr: rdn 2f out: rn green and lost 2nd 1f out: wknd* **9/4**[2]

4 *2* **Zefooha (FR)** 2-9-0 .... TedDurcan 1 56
(M R Channon) *dwlt: drvn wl over 2f out: sn struggling* **10/1**

3 **5** *6* **Dancing Granny**[9] 2943 2-9-0 .... JamieSpencer 4 41
(M L W Bell) *keen early: chsd ldrs tl rdn and wknd over 2f out* **5/1**[3]

6 *16* **Group Force (IRE)** 2-9-0 .... TPQueally 6 —
(M H Tompkins) *dwlt: last pair and struggling: no ch fr 1/2-way: eased and t.o fnl f* **20/1**

1m 27.3s (0.70) **Going Correction** -0.05s/f (Good) **6** Ran SP% **109.0**
Speed ratings (Par 91):94,90,87,84,78 59
CSF £18.70 TOTE £2.40: £1.40, £3.00; EX 16.20.
Owner Mrs R J Jacobs **Bred** Newsells Park Stud Limited **Trained** Middleham Moor, N Yorks

FOCUS
An interesting little juvenile fillies' maiden, run at a solid pace, and the field came home strung out. The runner-up sets the standard.

NOTEBOOK
Majounes Song was always in control at the head of affairs and eventually came right away from her rivals to score at the third attempt. She clearly enjoyed racing over the extra furlong, was full value for her winning margin, and should be high on confidence after this. (op 15-8)
Millestan(IRE), up in trip, travelled sweetly for most of the race and posted a much-improved effort in defeat. She is a big, scopey filly and looks sure to find an opening before too long. (op 11-1)
Mizzle(USA), whose dam was a top-class mile winner as a juvenile and was then placed in the French Oaks at three, was the first juvenile runner of the current campaign from her leading connections. She was well away, but ultimately lost out through her lack of experience and was well held at the finish. She ought to improve plenty for this. (tchd 2-1)
Zefooha(FR), half-sister to a six-furlong juvenile debut winner and whose dam was successful over ten furlongs at three, took too long to find her stride following a sluggish start and never figured. She is entitled to come on for the experience. (op 17-2 tchd 8-1)
Dancing Granny, dropping in trip, failed to improve on her Beverley debut nine days previously and eventually paid for running too freely through the early parts. (tchd 11-2)

3228 BET365 (S) STKS 6f 3y
3:00 (3:00) (Class 6) 2-Y-O **£2,266** (£674; £337; £168) **Stalls** High

Form RPR

301 **1** **Feisty**[6] 3054 2-8-11 .... FrancisFerris 6 60
(Rae Guest) *keen pressing ldrs: rdn to ld over 1f out and edgd rt briefly: drvn and a jst holding chalr* **7/1**

0632 **2** *nk* **House Arrest**[6] 3054 2-8-6 ....(p) DarryllHolland 7 54
(I A Wood) *cl up: drvn and ev ch through fnl f: tail gng and nt keen to overtake* **3/1**[2]

603 **3** *3* **Denton Hawk**[10] 2922 2-8-11 .... PhillipMakin 5 50
(M Dods) *drvn early: a struggling to go pce: sme prog over 1f out: nvr able to chal* **9/4**[1]

5 **4** *3* **Ladas Lad**[10] 2916 2-8-11 .... RobertMiles 4 40
(W G M Turner) *bhd: rdn and outpcd 1/2-way: n.d* **12/1**

5 *½* **Eastern Playboy (IRE)** 2-8-11 .... TPQueally 1 39
(J Jay) *prom: led over 2f out tl rdn and hdd over 1f out: sn fdd* **17/2**

06 **6** *14* **Lady Davali**[9] 2943 2-8-6 ....(b[1]) RoystonFfrench 3 —
(S Parr) *sn drvn and nvr looked keen: wl bhd after 2f: t.o* **40/1**

4665 **7** *4* **All Talk**[17] 2709 2-8-7 ow1 .... JamieSpencer 2 —
(Mrs C A Dunnett) *led: drvn and hdd over 2f out: lost pl qckly: eased and t.o* **7/2**[3]

1m 14.54s (0.84) **Going Correction** -0.05s/f (Good) **7** Ran SP% **111.1**
Speed ratings (Par 92):92,91,87,83,82 64,58
CSF £26.64 TOTE £9.20: £2.80, £1.80; EX 17.00.There was no bid for the winner.
Owner Rae Guest **Bred** Miss Rachel E Flynn **Trained** Newmarket, Suffolk

FOCUS
A weak juvenile event, run at a sound pace, and the first two came clear, suggesting the form is solid enough.

NOTEBOOK
Feisty, off the mark in this grade at Wolverhampton last time, proved most game inside the final furlong and followed up on this drop back in trip. She confirmed her All-Weather form with the runner-up on 5lb worse terms, handled the quick surface without fuss, and is a progressive filly for this sort of level. (op 11-2)
House Arrest held every chance, but could not get past the game winner, and failed to reverse Wolverhampton form with that rival despite racing on 5lb better terms. Her attitude will be scrutinised after this, but she certainly has a race of this nature well within her compass. (op 5-2 tchd 11-4)
Denton Hawk, well backed, took too long to hit full stride and was never a serious threat to the first pair. He may need an easier surface. (op 10-3)
Ladas Lad shaped as though he needs further, an opinion which is strongly backed up by his pedigree. (op 14-1)
Lady Davali Official explanation: jockey said filly was unsuited by the firm ground
All Talk, making her debut for a new yard, dropped out tamely when headed and is going the wrong way. Official explanation: jockey said filly was eased in the closing stages after losing her action (tchd 4-1)

3229 PKF (UK) LLP H'CAP 7f 3y
3:30 (3:31) (Class 5) (0-75,75) 3-Y-0+ **£3,562** (£1,059; £529; £264) **Stalls** High

Form RPR

0-00 **1** **Scrummage**[23] 2532 3-8-3 **59**..................................(v[1]) RoystonFfrench 2 67+
(Sir Michael Stoute) *mde all: rdn and styd on strly fnl f* **12/1**

0002 **2** *1 ¼* **Dr Synn**[20] 2606 5-9-3 **65**.. KerrinMcEvoy 4 73
(J Akehurst) *pushed along and outpcd in rr: hdwy 2f out: wnt 2nd ins fnl f: drvn and a hld* **5/1**[3]

1554 **3** *3* **Charlie Bear**[19] 2645 5-8-10 **58**.. AdrianMcCarthy 3 58
(Miss Z C Davison) *sn chsng wnr: rdn over 1f out: lost 2nd and wknd fnl 100 yds* **7/1**

0004 **4** *½* **Life's A Whirl**[5] 3089 4-8-8 **56** oh2......................................(p) TPQueally 1 55
(Mrs C A Dunnett) *unwilling to go bhd stalls: chsd ldrs: rdn over 2f out: btn over 1f out* **10/1**

-055 **5** *5* **Curtain Bluff**[12] 2860 4-9-9 **71**... JamieSpencer 7 57
(M R Channon) *dwlt: drvn after 3f: struggling to get on terms over 2f out* **7/2**[2]

0506 **6** *1* **Panshir (FR)**[14] 2789 5-8-5 **56** oh11............................ SaleemGolam[(3)] 6 39
(Mrs C A Dunnett) *pressed ldrs: drvn over 2f out: sn racing awkwardly and btn* **12/1**

5252 **7** *¾* **Favouring (IRE)**[9] 2947 4-8-5 **56** oh6........................(v) JohnMcAuley[(3)] 8 37
(M C Chapman) *racd alone stands rail w rest in centre: wknd 2f out* **8/1**

00-4 **8** *3* **Keyaki (IRE)**[63] 1432 5-9-13 **75**.. GeorgeBaker 9 49
(C F Wall) *stdd s: bhd: nvr gng wl fr 1/2-way* **11/4**[1]

0460 **9** *14* **Goodbye Girl (IRE)**[21] 2589 3-8-0 **56** oh13..................(v) FrancisFerris 5 —
(Mrs C A Dunnett) *rdn and struggling over 3f out: poor last over 2f out: t.o* **66/1**

1m 25.17s (-1.43) **Going Correction** -0.05s/f (Good)
WFA 3 from 4yo+ 8lb **9** Ran SP% **115.1**
Speed ratings (Par 103):106,104,101,100,94 93,92,89,73
CSF £70.67 CT £458.29 TOTE £10.30: £3.30, £2.00, £2.20; EX 82.80 Trifecta £246.10 Pool: £603.36 - 1.74 winning tickets..
Owner J Wigan & G Strawbridge **Bred** G Strawbridge And London Thoroughbred Services Lt **Trained** Newmarket, Suffolk

FOCUS
A moderate handicap, run at a fair pace, and the winner is value for slightly further with the runner-up to recent form.
Scrummage Official explanation: trainer's rep said, regarding the improved form shown, the colt had benefited from today's fitting of a visor
Keyaki(IRE) Official explanation: jockey said mare was never travelling from halfway

3230 HI-SPAN H'CAP 1m 2f 21y
4:00 (4:01) (Class 5) (0-70,69) 3-Y-0+ **£3,562** (£1,059; £529; £264) **Stalls** Low

Form RPR

63-6 **1** **Swains Bridge (USA)**[36] 2143 4-10-0 **69**........................ NickyMackay 5 83+
(L M Cumani) *cl up: led gng wl 3f out: clr 1f out: eased: comf* **2/1**[1]

3230 **2** *1 ½* **Ten-Cents**[13] 2822 4-9-3 **58**.. GeorgeBaker 6 61
(C F Wall) *hld up last pair: stl last on rails over 1f out: swtchd outside and drvn hrd: fin fast to snatch 2nd but given far too much* **7/1**[3]

-000 **3** *1 ¼* **Penmara**[10] 2929 3-8-5 **57**... JamieMackay 11 57
(M H Tompkins) *t.k.h: led after 3f out: hdd 3f out: rdn and no ch w wnr 1f out: lost 2nd cl home* **25/1**

040 **4** *1* **Musical Magic**[17] 2712 3-8-13 **65**... TPQueally 4 63
(J Noseda) *chsng ldrs whn stmbld ent st and lost pl briefly: rdn over 2f out: no imp fnl f* **17/2**

/024 **5** *hd* **Inch Lodge**[19] 2647 4-9-6 **68**................................... ChrisCavanagh[(7)] 1 66
(Miss D Mountain) *chsd ldrs: rdn over 2f out: one pce and no imp after* **9/2**[2]

0506 **6** *nk* **Capitalise (IRE)**[13] 2814 3-8-0 **52**................................... FrancisFerris 10 49
(V Smith) *hld up towards rr: rdn over 2f out: weaved through and sme prog fnl f but n.d* **20/1**

202- **7** *1 ¼* **Lennel**[352] 3611 8-8-4 **52**... JamieHamblett[(7)] 7 47
(A Bailey) *midfield: pushed along 3f out: one pce and no imp after* **14/1**

00-0 **8** *nk* **Perfectionist**[9] 2944 4-8-9 **50** oh5................................. RoystonFfrench 2 44
(Mrs C A Dunnett) *led 3f: prom: ev ch 3f out: fdd over 1f out* **50/1**

0600 **9** *shd* **Nassar (IRE)**[10] 2932 3-8-10 **69**................................. KirstyMilczarek[(7)] 8 63
(G Prodromou) *plld hrd in midfield: shkn up 2f out: sn btn* **33/1**

0001 **10** *nk* **Orpen Wide (IRE)**[6] 2947 4-9-8 **66** 6ex......................(b) LeeVickers[(3)] 3 60
(M C Chapman) *midfield: rdn wl over 2f out: nt stride out and btn wl over 1f out* **8/1**

300 **11** *1 ½* **Dubai Sunday (JPN)**[12] 2849 5-9-0 **55**......................(bt) BrianReilly 9 46
(P S McEntee) *stdd s: hld up in rr: shortlived effrt over 3f out: drvn and btn over 2f out* **16/1**

2m 12.01s (3.91) **Going Correction** -0.05s/f (Good)
WFA 3 from 4yo+ 11lb **11** Ran SP% **111.7**
Speed ratings (Par 103):82,80,79,79,78 78,77,77,77,77 75
CSF £14.23 CT £255.99 TOTE £2.40: £1.50, £2.00, £6.00; EX 20.00 Trifecta £295.90 Part won. Pool: £416.78 - 0.70 winning tickets..
Owner Christopher Wright **Bred** Stratford Place Stud **Trained** Newmarket, Suffolk

FOCUS
A moderate handicap, run at a fair early pace though the final time was very slow. The progressive winner is value for further and the form looks sound on paper.

3231 GREAT YARMOUTH TOURISM INDUSTRY MEDIAN AUCTION MAIDEN STKS 1m 3f 101y
4:30 (4:31) (Class 5) 3-4-Y-O **£3,238** (£963; £481; £240) **Stalls** Low

Form RPR

2-23 **1** **Billich**[26] 2465 3-9-0 **77**.. RichardMullen 6 81
(E J O'Neill) *settled rr: pushed along 4f out: impr to 2nd 2f out: rdn to ld over 1f out: easily outbattled rival and sn clr* **11/2**[3]

-542 **2** *3* **Alasoun (IRE)**[32] 2261 3-9-0 **80**................................(v[1]) KerrinMcEvoy 5 76
(Sir Michael Stoute) *sn led: rdn 2f out: hdd over 1f out: fnd nil* **6/5**[1]

6462 **3** *2 ½* **Soulard (USA)**[23] 2526 3-9-0 **74**...................................(v[1]) TPQueally 3 71
(J Noseda) *chsd ldrs: rdn wl over 2f out: one pce: no ch w ldrs over 1f out* **4/1**[2]

2334 **4** *5* **Sweet Medicine**[72] 1213 4-9-7 **72**.................................... NickyMackay 4 58
(P Howling) *trckd ldrs: wnt 2nd 4f out tl drvn 2f out: sn fdd* **8/1**

5 *7* **Always Stylish (IRE)** 3-9-0 .... RoystonFfrench 8 51
(M Johnston) *chsd ldr tl rdn 4f out: lost tch over 2f out* **12/1**

-504 **6** *14* **Finnegans Rainbow**[22] 2398 4-9-9 **35**................................. LeeVickers[(3)] 1 28
(M C Chapman) *last pair: struggling 4f out: t.o fnl 2f* **50/1**

0-40 **7** *9* **Alf Tupper**[33] [2243] 3-9-0 62 EddieAhern 7 13
(M H Tompkins) *struggling in rr over 4f out: t.o fnl 2f* **10/1**
2m 23.84s (-3.66) **Going Correction** -0.05s/f (Good)
WFA 3 from 4yo 12lb **7** Ran SP% **110.7**
Speed ratings (Par 103):111,108,107,103,98 88,81
CSF £11.72 TOTE £7.90: £2.80, £1.40; EX 12.70 Trifecta £57.70 Pool: £428.77 - 5.27 winning tickets..
Owner Mrs Julie Mitchell **Bred** Mrs S J Hearn **Trained** Averham Park, Notts
FOCUS
A modest maiden which saw the field trail home behind the comfortable winner who is the best guide to the form. The winning time was smart however, almost four seconds faster than the following apprentice handicap.
Alasoun(IRE) Official explanation: trainer's representative said colt lost a front shoe

3232 TELETEXT RACING "HANDS AND HEELS" APPRENTICE H'CAP 1m 3f 101y
5:00 (5:00) (Class 6) (0-60,60) 3-Y-0+ **£2,590** (£770; £385; £192) **Stalls** Low

Form RPR
25-2 **1** **Looks The Business (IRE)**[9] [2956] 5-10-0 **60** PJBenson 8 67
(W G M Turner) *hld up: 9th st: stdy run up far rails fnl 3f: led 100 yds out: rdn out* **5/1**[2]
3220 **2** *½* **Coffin Dodger**[5] [3075] 3-8-2 **46** KirstyMilczarek 3 52
(C N Allen) *dwlt: bhd: 15th st: gd prog in 7th ent fnl f: styd on wl to snatch 2nd: nt quite rch wnr* **8/1**[3]
3662 **3** *nk* **Granary Girl**[10] [2935] 4-8-9 **46** StevenCorrigan(5) 14 52
(J Pearce) *hld up: prog 4f out: jnd ldr 2f out: ev ch tl nt qckn fnl 100 yds* **12/1**
0143 **4** *hd* **Darghan (IRE)**[11] [2902] 6-9-10 **59** AlanRutter(3) 15 64
(W J Musson) *keen: settled trcking ldrs: effrt to take narrow advantage fr 3f out: rdn over 1f out: hdd and one pce fnl 100 yds* **4/1**[1]
6013 **5** *½* **String Serenade (IRE)**[9] [2952] 5-8-12 **47** LukeMorris(3) 11 51
(V Smith) *chsd ldrs: rdn 3f out: styd on steadily at one pce after: no ex fnl 100 yds* **12/1**
-004 **6** *shd* **Spaceman**[21] [2569] 3-8-9 **53** AshleyHamblett 6 57
(L M Cumani) *hld up towards rr: stl 8th but gd prog ent fnl f: kpt on wl* **8/1**[3]
0054 **7** *½* **Agilete**[6] [3035] 4-8-11 **43** JamesMillman 5 46
(J R Boyle) *s.i.s: stdy prog fnl 3f: kpt on cl home* **10/1**
0516 **8** *1* **Tata Naka**[5] [3095] 6-9-11 **57** RonanKeogh 12 59
(Mrs C A Dunnett) *hld up midfield: effrt 4f out: ev ch 2f out: no ex fnl f* **12/1**
6000 **9** *6* **Jadeeron**[12] [2869] 7-8-8 **45** (p) JPFeatherstone(5) 2 37
(Miss D A McHale) *dwlt: hdwy on outside after 3f: led over 4f out tl 3f out: fdd wl over 1f out* **16/1**
0100 **10** *5* **Shaika**[21] [2591] 3-8-5 **49** StacyRenwick 4 32
(G Prodromou) *keen: hmpd early and again after 2f where rdr shot up in sddle: nvr bttr than midfield: btn 2f out* **28/1**
0650 **11** *1* **Pitsi Kahtoh**[9] [2952] 4-8-7 **42** oh6 ChrisHough(3) 13 24
(P W Hiatt) *hld up towards rr: n.d* **33/1**
-631 **12** *½* **True (IRE)**[13] [2832] 5-8-11 **43** TolleyDean 16 24
(Mrs S Lamyman) *s.s: keen and racing awkwardly: a bhd: btn over 2f out* **12/1**
-000 **13** *¾* **Tiptoeing**[21] [2573] 3-8-5 **52** MarkWaite(3) 10 32
(M H Tompkins) *chsd ldrs: chal ent st: wknd over 2f out* **40/1**
000 **14** *shd* **Alan The Aussie**[31] [2291] 3-7-9 **42** oh22 SophieDoyle(3) 9 21
(G Prodromou) *led tl over 4f out: sn lost pl* **100/1**
0-01 **15** *¾* **Three Ships**[149] [328] 5-9-7 **53** RobbieMills 7 31
(Miss J Feilden) *cl up: lost pl 4f out: n.d after* **14/1**
-000 **16** *28* **King Of Chav's (IRE)**[42] [1950] 3-7-12 **45** JamieHamblett(3) 1 —
(A Bailey) *keen in rr: last st: rdr lost irons 4f out and continued t.o* **25/1**
2m 27.8s (0.30) **Going Correction** -0.05s/f (Good)
WFA 3 from 4yo+ 12lb **16** Ran SP% **125.0**
Speed ratings (Par 101):96,95,95,95,94 94,94,93,89,85 85,84,84,84,83 63
CSF £44.01 CT £472.14 TOTE £5.80: £2.30, £1.80, £2.30, £2.10; EX 41.00 Trifecta £223.00 Pool: £408.32 - 1.30 winning tickets. Place 6 £73.58, Place 5 £40.80.
Owner M J B Racing **Bred** Mrs M O'Callaghan **Trained** Sigwells, Somerset
FOCUS
A moderate event of its type, run at no more than a fair pace and the winning time was nearly four seconds slower than the preceding maiden. The first seven were closely covered at the finish so the form should be treated with caution.
Shaika Official explanation: jockey said saddle slipped
True(IRE) Official explanation: trainer said mare was found to have pulled a muscle in her near hind quarter
King Of Chav's(IRE) Official explanation: jockey said he lost his stirrup irons
T/Plt: £44.40 to a £1 stake. Pool: £44,060.85. 724.30 winning tickets. T/Qpdt: £14.60 to a £1 stake. Pool: £3,018.60. 152.30 winning tickets. IM

3233 - 3238a (Foreign Racing) - See Raceform Interactive

2943 BEVERLEY (R-H)
Friday, July 7
OFFICIAL GOING: Firm (good to firm in places)
Wind: Virtually nil

3239 EUROPEAN BREEDERS FUND NOVICE STKS 5f
6:40 (6:40) (Class 4) 2-Y-O **£5,311** (£1,580; £789; £394) **Stalls** High

Form RPR
62 **1** **Siren's Gift**[9] [2984] 2-8-7 FergusSweeney 1 85+
(A M Balding) *mde all: rdn over 1f out: styd on wl* **5/4**[1]
1260 **2** *2* **Avertuoso**[17] [2724] 2-9-2 DerekMcGaffin 2 87
(B Smart) *cl up: rdn and ev ch over 1f out: kpt on same pce ins ins last* **15/2**
15 **3** *hd* **Opal Noir**[37] [2127] 2-9-0 PaulHanagan 3 84+
(J Howard Johnson) *sn outpcd and pushed along in rr: hdwy 2f out: swtchd lft and rdn over 1f out: sn one pce* **6/4**[2]
055 **4** *5* **Baileys Hilight (IRE)**[58] [1587] 2-8-12 JoeFanning 4 64
(M Johnston) *chsd ldng pair: rdn along 2f out: sn wknd* **7/1**[3]
63.20 secs (-0.80) **Going Correction** -0.325s/f (Firm) **4** Ran SP% **108.7**
Speed ratings (Par 96):93,89,89,81
CSF £9.87 TOTE £1.80; EX 8.10.
Owner J C Smith **Bred** Littleton Stud **Trained** Kingsclere, Hants
FOCUS
An ordinary maiden but sound enough with the runner-up to his mark.
NOTEBOOK
Siren's Gift fulfilled previous promise by coming good, showing plenty of speed throughout and sticking to her guns in pleasing style. She is not that big but is very pacey and it looks only now that she is starting to get the hang of what racing is about. (op 6-5 tchd 11-10)
Avertuoso, whose previous win was on similar ground, ran a fair race under top-weight and sets the standard. (op 6-1 tchd 9-1)
Opal Noir appeared to find this ground too lively and was soon taken off his legs. He picked up willingly under pressure inside the final quarter mile but flattened out towards the finish. (op 13-8)
Baileys Hilight(IRE) chased the leaders but her measure had been taken approaching the final furlong and, on ground that may have been catching her out, was eased when her chance had gone. (op 10-1)

3240 WESTWOOD (S) H'CAP 7f 100y
7:10 (7:11) (Class 6) (0-60,59) 3-Y-O+ **£3,238** (£963; £481; £240) **Stalls** High

Form RPR
5-00 **1** **Legal Dram**[164] [183] 5-9-6 **45** PaulMulrennan 14 55
(M Dods) *a.p: effrt over 2f out: rdn over 1f out: styd on to ld ins last: drvn out* **9/1**
20-0 **2** *nk* **Baby Barry**[28] [2414] 9-9-11 **50** PaulHanagan 7 59
(R A Fahey) *towards rr: rdn along 3f out: hdwy 2f out: drvn and styd on ent last: jst hld* **5/1**[1]
0005 **3** *¾* **Mill By The Stream**[15] [2785] 4-8-12 **42** RoryMoore(5) 15 49
(P T Midgley) *hld up towards rr: hdwy on inner over 3f out: swtchd lft 2f out: rdn over 1f out: ev ch ins last: no ex towards fin* **6/1**[2]
6050 **4** *nk* **Motu (IRE)**[20] [2641] 5-9-10 **49** (v) JoeFanning 11 55
(I W McInnes) *hld up in rr: hdwy 3f out: swtchd ins and effrt over 1f out: sn rdn and ev ch ins last tl no ex towards fin* **8/1**
0-00 **5** *1* **Filey Buoy**[4] [3159] 4-8-7 **39** MichaelJStainton(7) 16 43
(R M Whitaker) *chsd ldr: led 3f out: rdn wl over 1f out: drvn and hdd ins last: one pce* **13/2**[3]
-003 **6** *nk* **Parchment (IRE)**[14] [2832] 4-9-5 **49** MarkLawson(5) 5 52
(A J Lockwood) *towards rr on inner: swtchd lft and hdwy over 2f out: rdn over 1f out: styd on strly ins last: nrst fin* **13/2**[3]
-050 **7** *2* **Frimley's Mattery**[4] [3137] 6-8-13 **45** AdeleRothery(7) 10 43
(R E Barr) *in tch: hdwy 3f out: sn rdn and n.m.r wl over 1f out: sn no imp* **8/1**
4500 **8** *½* **Kalani Star (IRE)**[15] [2789] 6-9-6 **45** (v) DavidAllan 4 42
(I W McInnes) *towards rr tl styd on fnl 2f: nt rch ldrs* **14/1**
6000 **9** *1 ½* **Eliminator**[15] [2782] 3-8-7 **45** NataliaGemelova(5) 6 38
(I W McInnes) *bhd tl sme late hdwy* **28/1**
0-40 **10** *nk* **Shamwari Fire (IRE)**[15] [2789] 6-8-13 **41** SaleemGolam(3) 9 33
(I W McInnes) *chsd ldrs: rdn along over 2f out: sn wknd* **14/1**
0000 **11** *1 ½* **Faithisflying**[52] [1765] 4-9-1 **40** (p) TonyCulhane 8 29
(D W Chapman) *dwlt: sn in tch: rdn along 3f out: sn wknd* **12/1**
0050 **12** *2* **Aqua**[18] [2697] 4-9-8 **47** (b[1]) MickyFenton 1 31
(P T Midgley) *wnt lft s: sn led and set str pce tl hdd & wknd 3f out* **28/1**
000- **13** *hd* **Wizardmicktee (IRE)**[214] [6512] 4-9-1 **40** FergusSweeney 3 23
(A Bailey) *a rr* **25/1**
00-0 **14** *3* **Drury Lane (IRE)**[18] [2700] 6-9-2 **44** (p) DanielTudhope(3) 12 20
(D W Chapman) *towards rr: hdwy on inner 3f out: in tch whn n.m.r wl over 1f out and sn wknd* **20/1**
1m 32.12s (-2.19) **Going Correction** -0.325s/f (Firm)
WFA 3 from 4yo+ 8lb **14** Ran SP% **126.4**
Speed ratings (Par 101):99,98,97,97,96 95,93,93,91,91 89,87,86,83
CSF £53.80 CT £309.54 TOTE £14.20: £4.30, £1.40, £2.00; EX 83.20.There was no bid for the winner.
Owner Les Waugh **Bred** L Waugh **Trained** Denton, Co Durham
■ Stewards' Enquiry : Adele Rothery three-day ban; careless riding (Jul 18-19 + 1)
FOCUS
A poor seller but sound enough, with the first three near their respective marks.
Legal Dram Official explanation: trainer said, regarding the improved form shown, the gelding was having its first run on turf and its first run in a seller
Mill By The Stream Official explanation: jockey said gelding ran too free early
Drury Lane(IRE) Official explanation: jockey said gelding was denied a clear run

3241 AUNT BESSIE'S YORKSHIRE PUDDING H'CAP 1m 100y
7:40 (7:40) (Class 4) (0-85,83) 4-Y-O+ **£6,477** (£1,927; £963; £481) **Stalls** High

Form RPR
0502 **1** **Claret And Amber**[7] [3040] 4-9-0 **74** PaulHanagan 5 86
(R A Fahey) *hld up in tch: hdwy over 2f out: effrt: nt clr run and swtchd lft over 1f out: rdn ins last and styd on to ld nr fin* **11/4**[1]
0112 **2** *nk* **Riley Boys (IRE)**[9] [2974] 5-9-9 **83** 6ex TonyCulhane 1 94
(J G Given) *hld up and bhd: hdwy over 2f out: effrt and nt clr run over 1f out: swtchd lft and rdn to ld ins last: hdd nr line* **11/4**[1]
3144 **3** *2* **Jubilee Street (IRE)**[15] [2787] 7-9-4 **81** SaleemGolam(3) 6 88
(Mrs A Duffield) *led: rdn along 2f out: drvn over 1f out: hdd and one pce ins last* **9/2**[2]
0510 **4** *1* **Nevada Desert (IRE)**[21] [2627] 6-8-3 **70** MichaelJStainton(7) 7 75
(R M Whitaker) *trckd ldrs: hdwy over 2f out: rdn to chal over 1f out and ev ch tl drvn and nt qckn ins last* **8/1**
3535 **5** *¾* **Wing Commander**[4] [3147] 7-8-8 **68** (p) DavidAllan 8 71
(I W McInnes) *trckd ldrs: hdwy on inner over 2f out: sn rdn and kpt on same pce appr last* **11/2**[3]
6-55 **6** *½* **Thistle**[16] [2761] 5-8-8 **68** PaulMulrennan 4 70
(J Howard Johnson) *cl up: rdn along 2f out: drvn and edgd lft over 1f out: sn wknd* **25/1**
6635 **7** *5* **Baillieborough (IRE)**[7] [3040] 7-9-5 **79** (v) NCallan 9 70
(Robert Gray) *dwlt: in tch: rdn along to chse ldrs over 2f out: drvn and wknd over 1f out* **8/1**
1m 43.73s (-3.67) **Going Correction** -0.325s/f (Firm) **7** Ran SP% **113.0**
Speed ratings (Par 105):105,104,102,101,100 100,95
CSF £9.99 CT £31.19 TOTE £3.90: £1.80, £1.90; EX 10.00.
Owner The Matthewman Partnership **Bred** D R Tucker **Trained** Musley Bank, N Yorks
FOCUS
A decent prize for this handicap, which resulted in a nail-biting finish and the form looks sound.

3242 COME RACING AT BEVERLEY TOMORROW MAIDEN STKS 5f
8:10 (8:11) (Class 4) 2-Y-O **£4,533** (£1,348; £674; £336) **Stalls** High

Form RPR
6 **1** **Evens And Odds (IRE)**[36] [2159] 2-9-3 NCallan 1 81+
(K A Ryan) *trckd ldrs: hdwy 2f out: rdn to ld ins last: styd on* **3/1**[3]
2 *2* **Makshoof (IRE)** 2-9-3 RHills 2 74
(M A Jarvis) *chsd ldrs: hdwy on outer 2f out: rdn and ev ch 1f out: kpt on same pce* **4/1**
5432 **3** *hd* **Perlachy**[24] [2523] 2-9-3 DavidAllan 4 73
(T D Easterby) *led: rdn along 2f out: drvn and edgd lft 1f out: hdd & wknd ins last* **11/4**[2]
4 *2 ½* **Fujisan** 2-9-3 JoeFanning 6 64
(M Johnston) *cl up: rdn 2f out: wknd over 1f out* **9/4**[1]

00 **5** *1 ½* **King Charles**[11] 2930 2-9-3 .... DO'Donohoe 7 59
(E A L Dunlop) *dwlt: sn rdn along in rr: n.d* **9/1**
6 *17* **Nihil Petere (IRE)** 2-8-12 .... MickyFenton 3 —
(P T Midgley) *dwlt: sn outpcd and wl bhd fr 1/2-way* **40/1**
62.84 secs (-1.16) **Going Correction** -0.325s/f (Firm) **6** Ran SP% **114.9**
Speed ratings (Par 96):96,92,92,88,86 58
CSF £15.78 TOTE £3.30: £2.00, £1.40; EX 10.20.
Owner Mrs Catherine O'Flynn **Bred** Old Carhue Stud **Trained** Hambleton, N Yorks

FOCUS
A reasonable little race with the third to form.

NOTEBOOK
Evens And Odds(IRE), who flopped at odds-on on his debut at Ayr, set the record straight with a sound display. Having raced freely with the leaders first time and then fallen in a heap, he was dropped in and proved a different proposition, quickening to win in pleasing style. Connections felt this ground was too firm for him but rate him highly and a Group 2 race at Maisons-Laffitte was mentioned as an option. (op 5-2 tchd 7-2)
Makshoof(IRE) ◆, a 100,000gns purchase from the family of Aragon, made a pleasing debut and should not be long in winning. (tchd 7-2)
Perlachy, who is pretty well exposed, probably ran his best race yet in finishing a close-up third, comfortably clear of the rest. (op 4-1)
Fujisan showed promise but faded in the closing stages; he can probably do better. (op 5-2 tchd 11-4 in places)

3243 FERGUSON FAWSITT ARMS H'CAP — 1m 4f 16y
8:40 (8:40) (Class 5) (0-70,76) 3-Y-0+ **£4,857** (£1,445; £722; £360) **Stalls** High

Form RPR
0222 **1** **Intavac Boy**[16] 2762 5-9-6 **57** .... NCallan 8 63
(C W Thornton) *trckd ldrs: swtchd lft and hdwy over 2f out: rdn to ld over 1f out: drvn and edgd rt ins last: hld on gamely* **11/4**[2]
0315 **2** *hd* **Shekan Star**[8] 2998 4-9-1 **52** .... TonyCulhane 5 57
(K G Reveley) *hld up in tch: pushed along and hdwy 2f out: rdn over 1f out: drvn to chal ins last and ev ch: jst hld* **11/2**
0031 **3** *2 ½* **Lucky Lark**[3] 3163 3-9-12 **76** 6ex .... JoeFanning 1 77
(M Johnston) *trckd ldr: effrt 3f out: rdn along 2f out: drvn and one pce appr last* **11/8**[1]
-400 **4** *nk* **Red River Rebel**[15] 2788 8-8-11 **48** oh2 .... PaulMulrennan 3 49
(J R Norton) *led: rdn along 3f out: hdd over 1f out: n.m.r and wknd ins last* **11/1**
-452 **5** *nk* **Tedsdale Mac**[10] 2945 7-9-3 **61** .... SuzzanneFrance(7) 2 62
(N Bycroft) *hld up: hdwy 3f out: rdn along wl over 1f out and sn btn* **4/1**[3]
2m 37.59s (-2.62) **Going Correction** -0.325s/f (Firm)
WFA 3 from 4yo+ 13lb **5** Ran SP% **112.5**
Speed ratings (Par 103):95,94,93,93,92
CSF £17.59 TOTE £3.90: £2.00, £2.50; EX 16.60.
Owner B J Kellett **Bred** C And Mrs Wilson **Trained** Middleham Moor, N Yorks
■ Stewards' Enquiry : N Callan caution: careless riding

FOCUS
A moderate handicap and a modest winning time for the grade. The form is weak but sound enough rated around the principals.

3244 WILLIAM JACKSON BAKERY STKS (FILLIES' H'CAP) — 1m 1f 207y
9:10 (9:11) (Class 5) (0-70,61) 3-Y-0 **£3,886** (£1,156; £577; £288) **Stalls** High

Form RPR
00-4 **1** **Trick Or Treat**[34] 2246 3-9-3 **56** .... TonyCulhane 3 66+
(J G Given) *hld up and bhd: gd hdwy on outer over 2f out: rdn over 1f out: styd on ins last to ld last 100 yds* **14/1**
4604 **2** *1 ¾* **Dream Of Paradise (USA)**[11] 2923 3-9-1 **59** .... GregFairley(5) 2 66
(Mrs L Williamson) *led: rdn clr 2f out: drvn ent last: hdd and no ex last 100 yds* **14/1**
2200 **3** *2* **Tangarita**[26] 2480 3-9-5 **58** .... FergusSweeney 1 61
(A M Balding) *trckd ldrs: hdwy to chse ldr 4f out: rdn along over 2f out: drvn and kpt on same pce appr last* **7/1**
5311 **4** *1 ½* **Touch Of Ivory (IRE)**[3] 3167 3-9-1 **61** 6ex .... (p) JamesReveley(7) 5 61
(R A Fahey) *hld up in tch: hdwy over 2f out: rdn over 1f out: kpt on same pce* **5/4**[1]
0-00 **5** *nk* **Quintin**[28] 2412 3-8-6 **45** .... PaulHanagan 6 45
(T D Easterby) *in tch: hdwy on inner 3f out: rdn pover 2f out: kpt on same pce* **16/1**
1204 **6** *2* **Keisha Kayleigh (IRE)**[12] 2891 3-9-7 **60** .... TomEaves 8 56
(B Ellison) *hld up: n.m.r after 1f: a rr* **5/1**[3]
0021 **7** *½* **Bella Fiorella (IRE)**[14] 2814 3-8-9 **51** .... DominicFox(3) 7 46
(Miss V Haigh) *chsd ldr: rdn along 3f out: wknd 2f out* **7/2**[2]
3-00 **8** *22* **Graze On Too (IRE)**[37] 2129 3-9-2 **55** .... JoeFanning 4 8
(J J Quinn) *keen: chsd ldrs: riudden along wl over 2f out and sn wknd* **25/1**
2m 4.79s (-2.51) **Going Correction** -0.325s/f (Firm) **8** Ran SP% **118.9**
Speed ratings (Par 97):97,95,94,92,92 90,90,72
CSF £192.90 CT £1498.02 TOTE £23.10: £2.40, £4.50, £2.00; EX 135.30 Place 6 £330.01, Place 5 £159.68.
Owner Peter Onslow **Bred** P Onslow **Trained** Willoughton, Lincs

FOCUS
A moderate fillies' handicap rated through the second.
T/Plt: £435.20 to a £1 stake. Pool: £50,436.50. 84.60 winning tickets T/Qpdt: £66.60 to a £1 stake. Pool: £3,352.90. 37.20 winning tickets JR

3215 HAYDOCK (L-H)
Friday, July 7

OFFICIAL GOING: Good to firm (good in places)
Wind: Light, half-against Weather: Sunny

3245 JOHN CARROLL APPRENTICE H'CAP (SPONSORED BY JOSEPH HELER ESQ.) — 6f
6:50 (6:51) (Class 5) (0-70,70) 3-Y-0+ **£3,886** (£1,156; £577; £288) **Stalls** Centre

Form RPR
0062 **1** **Celtic Thunder**[15] 2780 5-8-11 **56** .... (b) JamesMillman(3) 14 65
(T J Etherington) *bhd: rdn and hdwy over 1f out: sn edgd rt: r.o ins fnl f to ld fnl strides* **5/1**[1]
-000 **2** *nk* **Gavioli (IRE)**[6] 3094 4-8-3 **52** .... BarrySavage(7) 10 60
(J M Bradley) *chsd ldrs: rdn over 1f out: led ins fnl f: hdd fnl strides* **25/1**
0-50 **3** *1 ½* **Convince (USA)**[12] 2897 5-9-8 **67** .... AshleyHamblett(3) 6 71
(J M Bradley) *in tch: rdn over 1f out: nt qckn ins fnl f* **7/1**[3]
0302 **4** *nk* **Blessed Place**[9] 2971 6-9-6 **62** .... JamesDoyle 13 65
(D J S Ffrench Davis) *led: rdn over 1f out: hdd ins fnl f: no ex cl home* **5/1**[1]
0-60 **5** *hd* **Disguise**[28] 2396 4-9-6 **62** .... AndrewMullen 8 64
(J J Quinn) *in tch: rdn 2f out: styd on cl home: nt pce to chal* **11/2**[2]
4010 **6** *2* **Full Spate**[6] 3094 11-9-9 **65** .... JerryO'Dwyer 4 61
(J M Bradley) *hld up: rdn and hdwy over 2f out: one pce ins fnl f* **10/1**
5003 **7** *hd* **Val De Maal (IRE)**[7] 3052 6-9-0 **56** .... (b) GregFairley 1 52
(Miss J A Camacho) *prom: rdn over 2f out: fdd fnl f* **11/2**[2]
0000 **8** *1 ½* **Mis Chicaf (IRE)**[25] 2505 5-8-5 **52** .... (t) BRoper(5) 3 43
(Robert Gray) *bhd: hdwy over 1f out: no imp fnl f* **14/1**
0-00 **9** *2 ½* **Cate Washington**[23] 2554 3-8-0 **51** oh4 .... KellyHarrison(3) 9 35
(Mrs L Williamson) *midfield: rdn 2f out: sn wknd* **50/1**
0-00 **10** *hd* **Rectangle (IRE)**[15] 2780 6-8-8 **53** .... (t) ThomasO'Brien(3) 5 36
(Micky Hammond) *towards rr: rdn 2f out: nvr on terms* **16/1**
4240 **11** *shd* **Alexia Rose (IRE)**[94] 864 4-9-1 **60** .... KevinGhunowa(3) 2 43
(A Berry) *prom: pushed along 1/2-way: wknd 2f out* **16/1**
0000 **12** *2* **Torrent**[66] 1396 11-8-2 **51** oh10 .... (b) KevinMachent(7) 7 28
(J M Saville) *midfield tl rdn and wknd 2f out* **33/1**
1m 15.17s (0.27) **Going Correction** -0.10s/f (Good)
WFA 3 from 4yo+ 6lb **12** Ran SP% **112.9**
Speed ratings (Par 103):94,93,91,91,90 88,88,86,82,82 82,79
CSF £126.99 CT £879.60 TOTE £4.00: £1.70, £10.60, £2.80; EX 241.80.
Owner Ian Smith **Bred** K Benson **Trained** Norton, N Yorks

FOCUS
A very moderate winning time, about half a second slower than the two-year-old maiden. Sound, if modest form.

3246 M.E.N. - NUMBER 1 ARENA IN THE WORLD (S) STKS — 6f
7:20 (7:21) (Class 4) 2-Y-0 **£4,533** (£1,348; £674; £336) **Stalls** Centre

Form RPR
20 **1** **Merry Moon (IRE)**[14] 2807 2-8-6 .... DaleGibson 10 52
(M Dods) *in tch: hdwy over 1f out: r.o to ld wl ins fnl f: rdn out cl home* **12/1**
5143 **2** *¾* **Yerevan**[22] 2586 2-8-11 .... SamHitchcott 15 55
(M R Channon) *led: edgd lft over 1f out: hdd wl ins fnl f: nt qckn cl home* **6/5**[1]
030 **3** *½* **Ensign's Trick**[17] 2731 2-8-1 .... LiamJones(5) 5 48
(W M Brisbourne) *towards rr: hdwy whn carried rt sltly over 1f out: r.o ins fnl f: clsng nr fin* **100/1**
0 **4** *nk* **Disco Queen (IRE)**[78] 1096 2-8-6 .... KDarley 14 47
(P C Haslam) *chsd ldrs: rdn and edgd lft over 1f out: edgd rt ins fnl f: styd on* **16/1**
0353 **5** *hd* **Flamestone**[17] 2731 2-8-11 .... DarryllHolland 3 52
(J D Bethell) *midfield: pushed along 1/2-way: hdwy over 2f out: one pce nr fin* **12/1**
00 **6** *¾* **Take My Turn**[23] 2552 2-8-11 .... OscarUrbina 1 50
(M Blanshard) *bhd: hdwy over 1f out: edgd lft ins fnl f: kpt on: nvr nr to chal* **66/1**
052 **7** *½* **Put It On The Card**[21] 2626 2-8-11 .... (v) GrahamGibbons 13 48
(P D Evans) *prom: rdn 2f out: edgd rt over 1f out: outpcd fater* **13/2**[2]
014 **8** *shd* **Cheshire Prince**[22] 2586 2-9-2 .... ShaneKelly 4 53
(W M Brisbourne) *chsd ldrs: rdn 1/2-way: sn hung lft: no ex fnl f* **9/1**[3]
00 **9** *1 ¼* **Rose Court**[24] 2523 2-8-6 .... TonyHamilton 8 39+
(K G Reveley) *towards rr: hdwy into midfield 1/2-way: nvr trbld ldrs* **40/1**
32 **10** *5* **La Esperanza**[11] 2922 2-8-6 .... PaulFessey 2 24
(T D Barron) *racd keenly: handy for 1f: sn towards rr* **10/1**
505 **11** *½* **Daruma (IRE)**[11] 2922 2-8-11 .... (b) RobbieFitzpatrick 6 27
(Peter Grayson) *racd keenly: midfield: rdn over 2f out: wknd over 1f out* **33/1**
12 *2 ½* **Spin Dancer** 2-8-8 ow2 .... PatCosgrave 11 17
(W M Brisbourne) *s.s: a bhd* **40/1**
05 **13** *3* **Totally Free**[9] 2967 2-8-8 .... RichardSmith(3) 7 11
(M D I Usher) *prom: rdn over 2f out: sn wknd: eased whn btn ins fnl f* **40/1**
1m 15.71s (0.81) **Going Correction** -0.10s/f (Good) **13** Ran SP% **111.9**
Speed ratings (Par 96):90,89,88,87,87 86,86,85,84,77 76,73,69
CSF £24.20 TOTE £15.20: £4.20, £1.10, £19.90; EX 44.70.The winner was bought in for 10,500gns. Yerevan was claimed by Richard Phillips for £14,000
Owner Moneyleague Ltd **Bred** David Fenlon **Trained** Denton, Co Durham

FOCUS
Fair selling form, the winner back to the level of her debut effort.

NOTEBOOK
Merry Moon(IRE) was five lengths behind Yerevan when making her debut at Nottingham, but was 3lb better off here and knew a lot more. Staying on, she got on top of her old rival close home. (op 11-1)
Yerevan, dropped in grade, showed plenty of pace to get most most of her rivals off the bridle but, after wandering in front, she was cut down in the last 50 yards. She is not progressing. (op 11-10 tchd 5-4 and 11-8 in places)
Ensign's Trick, one of three from the Brisbourne yard, is learning with experience and this was her best run to date. Out of a prolific winner at up to ten furlongs, she should stay a bit further.
Disco Queen(IRE) showed more than she had on her debut in a soft-ground maiden. Official explanation: jockey said filly hung left throughout
Flamestoneran his race but is starting to look exposed. (op 11-1 tchd 10-1)
Take My Turn kept on in encouraging fashion and is not without hope.

3247 MTB GROUP MAIDEN AUCTION STKS — 6f
7:50 (7:52) (Class 5) 2-Y-0 **£3,238** (£963; £481; £240) **Stalls** Centre

Form RPR
0 **1** **El Bosque (IRE)**[21] 2617 2-8-11 .... GrahamGibbons 11 82
(B R Millman) *mde all: rdn ins fnl f: kpt on* **14/1**
2 *½* **Celtic Sultan (IRE)** 2-9-2 .... DarryllHolland 2 85
(T P Tate) *towards rr: rdn and hdwy over 1f out: edgd lft and chsd wnr ins fnl f: r.o: clsng nr fin* **11/2**[3]
4 **3** *2 ½* **Transpique (IRE)**[11] 2930 2-8-11 .... PhilipRobinson 9 73
(C G Cox) *a.p: rdn over 1f out and carried hd awkwardly: nt pce of ldng pair ins fnl f* **9/4**[1]
4 *1 ½* **Valdan (IRE)** 2-8-9 .... SteveDrowne 1 66
(P D Evans) *s.s: bhd: rdn and hdwy over 1f out: kpt on ins fnl f: nt trble ldrs* **20/1**
5 *nk* **Captain Nemo (USA)** 2-8-9 .... PaulFessey 3 65
(T D Barron) *hld up: hdwy 2f out: sn rdn: kpt on ins fnl f: nt trble ldrs* **14/1**
5 **6** *½* **Pavlovia**[9] 2973 2-8-6 .... TPQueally 12 61
(T D Easterby) *cl up: rdn over 1f out: no ex ins fnl f* **7/2**[2]

7 2 1/2 **My Secrets** 2-8-13 .... KDarley 10 60
(M Johnston) *towards rr: sme hdwy over 3f out: rdn and wknd over 1f out* **8/1**

8 1 **Terry Molloy (IRE)** 2-8-9 .... PatCosgrave 4 53
(K R Burke) *racd keenly and green: hld up: kpt on fnl f: will improve* **20/1**

0 9 3 1/2 **Better Off Red (USA)**[23] 2552 2-8-7 ow1 .... ShaneKelly 7 41
(B J Meehan) *midfield: rdn over 2f out: edgd lft and wknd over 1f out* **20/1**

0 10 shd **Perfect Style (IRE)**[20] 2638 2-8-6 .... OscarUrbina 8 39
(M Blanshard) *midfield: rdn whn carried lft over 1f out: sn wknd* **25/1**

0 11 2 1/2 **Silly Gilly (IRE)**[64] 1442 2-8-4 .... JimmyQuinn 5 30
(A Berry) *in tch: rdn 2f out: wknd over 1f out* **50/1**

12 9 **Whats Your Game (IRE)** 2-8-9 .... TonyHamilton 6 —
(A Berry) *prom tl rdn and wknd over 1f out: eased whn btn ins fnl f* **66/1**

1m 14.68s (-0.22) **Going Correction** -0.10s/f (Good) 12 Ran SP% **114.4**
Speed ratings (Par 94):97,96,93,91,90 89,86,85,80,80 77,65
CSF £78.26 TOTE £17.60: £4.50, £2.10, £1.30; EX 77.90.
Owner Wessex Racing **Bred** Mrs M Campbell-Andenaes **Trained** Kentisbeare, Devon

FOCUS
Not an easy race to rate with little previous form to go on. The first two came clear.

NOTEBOOK
El Bosque(IRE) was too green to do himself justice on his debut at Sandown but knew a lot more here and made all the running down the centre of the track. He should be able to improve again. (op 16-1)
Celtic Sultan(IRE) ◆, whose dam was a winning sprinter, is a half-brother to a couple of winners at seven furlongs and a mile. Still last with two furlongs to run, he was a bit short of room when first trying to improve before running on well inside the last to cut the gap to the winner. He ought to be able to go one better, perhaps over seven furlongs. (op 7-1)
Transpique(IRE) was a little unlucky on his debut but, while running respectably, he did not build on that. He looked less than straightforward, carrying his head to one side when under pressure to pick up. (op 2-1)
Valdan(IRE), second foal of an unraced dam, did well to reach his final position after a slow start and should benefit from the outing. (op 16-1)
Captain Nemo(USA), from a decent North American family, was keeping on late and should improve for the experience.
Pavlovia had seemed likely to appreciate this step up in trip but after showing pace she faded inside the last. (tchd 9-2)
Terry Molloy(IRE) gave the impression that he should be capable of better with this experience behind him. (op 28-1)
Whats Your Game(IRE) Official explanation: jockey said gelding lost its action

3248 TONY AND KIERAN MEMORIAL H'CAP — 1m 3f 200y
8:20 (8:20) (Class 4) (0-80,80) 3-Y-0+ **£6,477** (£1,927; £963; £481) **Stalls** High

Form RPR

4001 1 **Gringo**[14] 2822 4-9-10 **76** .... OscarUrbina 8 85+
(B W Hills) *hld up: hdwy over 2f out: led over 1f out: r.o wl and pushed out ins fnl f* **3/1**[1]

0-02 2 2 1/2 **Lucky Leo**[12] 2902 6-9-2 **68** .... DarryllHolland 2 73
(Ian Williams) *midfield: rdn over 3f out: hdwy whn nt clr run and swtchd rt over 1f out: r.o ins fnl f: wnt 2nd towards fin: no ch w wnr* **10/3**[2]

0016 3 nk **The Composer**[9] 2989 4-9-6 **72** .... SteveDrowne 9 77
(M Blanshard) *in tch: rdn over 2f out: nt qckn ins fnl f* **8/1**

0210 4 shd **Sualda (IRE)**[9] 2975 7-10-0 **80** .... TonyHamilton 6 84
(R A Fahey) *trckd ldrs: rdn to ld over 2f out: hdd over 1f out: styd on same pce ins fnl f: lost 2nd towards fin* **7/1**

0-16 5 3/4 **Count Kristo**[30] 2351 4-9-9 **75** .... PhilipRobinson 4 78
(C G Cox) *hld up: rdn and hung lft over 1f out: styd on ins fnl f: nvr able to chal* **6/1**[3]

1340 6 1 1/4 **Soho Square**[38] 2117 3-8-9 **74** .... KDarley 7 75
(M Johnston) *prom: niggled along over 5f out: rdn over 2f out: wknd wl ins fnl f* **8/1**

0250 7 shd **Khanjar (USA)**[8] 3022 6-9-9 **75** .... PatCosgrave 1 76
(K R Burke) *led: rdn over 3f out: hdd over 2f out: wknd wl ins fnl f* **12/1**

200- 8 1 1/4 **Neutrino**[120] 5053 4-9-7 **73** .... LeeEnstone 5 74+
(P C Haslam) *hld up: rdn over 3f out: hdwy 2f out: nt clr run whn effrt over 1f out: eased whn no real prog wl ins fnl f* **40/1**

2m 34.01s (-0.98) **Going Correction** -0.20s/f (Firm)
WFA 3 from 4yo+ 13lb 8 Ran SP% **107.2**
Speed ratings (Par 105):95,93,93,93,92 91,91,90
CSF £11.36 CT £57.88 TOTE £3.20: £1.10, £1.30, £1.90; EX 6.10.
Owner Guy Reed **Bred** Guy Reed **Trained** Lambourn, Berks

FOCUS
The pace was pretty sedate, resulting in something of a sprint up the straight and a very moderate time for a race of its class. Not a strong race, but the winner did it well.
Lucky Leo Official explanation: jockey said gelding was denied a clear run
Count Kristo Official explanation: jockey said gelding hung left in straight

3249 MIKE PENNINGTON 50TH BIRTHDAY H'CAP — 1m 6f
8:50 (8:50) (Class 5) (0-70,70) 3-Y-0 **£3,238** (£963; £481; £240) **Stalls** Low

Form RPR

331 1 **Cape Secret (IRE)**[21] 2607 3-9-1 **67** .... NelsonDeSouza(3) 7 83
(R M Beckett) *mde all: qckned pce 3f out: rdn over 1f out: a holding on towards fin* **4/1**[2]

-601 2 3/4 **Shore Thing (IRE)**[22] 2592 3-9-3 **66** .... TPQueally 4 81
(M H Tompkins) *hld up: hdwy over 3f out: chsd wnr over 2f out: sn edgd lft: styd on ins fnl f: hld towards fin* **7/1**[3]

-302 3 7 **Karlani (IRE)**[22] 2584 3-9-6 **69** .... J-PGuillambert 3 75
(Sir Michael Stoute) *handy: lost pl 5f out: rallied to chse ldrs 3f out: wknd fnl f* **4/1**[2]

6053 4 6 **Plemont Bay**[8] 3017 3-8-8 **57** .... DarryllHolland 9 55
(M L W Bell) *prom: rdn over 4f out: wknd over 1f out* **7/1**[3]

0231 5 1 3/4 **Collette's Choice**[4] 3145 3-8-10 **59** 6ex .... TonyHamilton 5 55
(R A Fahey) *hld up: hdwy over 3f out: rdn over 2f out: wknd over 1f out* **3/1**[1]

-050 6 14 **Loch Awe**[22] 2591 3-8-4 **53** .... JimmyQuinn 2 31
(J G Given) *hld up: hdwy 6f out: wknd over 4f out* **66/1**

5004 7 3/4 **Myrtle Bay (IRE)**[23] 2548 3-9-5 **68** .... PatCosgrave 10 45
(K R Burke) *in tch: tk clsr order 6f out: rdn and wknd over 2f out* **25/1**

0010 8 6 **Arsad (IRE)**[22] 2592 3-8-10 **59** .... ShaneKelly 11 28
(C E Brittain) *hld up: rdn over 3f out: nvr on terms* **33/1**

-000 9 18 **Zingbat (IRE)**[23] 2539 3-8-2 **51** oh1 .... PaulFessey 1 —
(J G Given) *in tch: lost pl 1/2-way: bhd after* **40/1**

3-15 10 6 **Spanish Lace**[39] 2081 3-9-7 **70** .... KDarley 6 8
(Miss J A Camacho) *hld up: hdwy over 6f out: wknd qckly over 3f out: eased whn btn over 1f out* **10/1**

3m 0.63s (-5.66) **Going Correction** -0.20s/f (Firm) 10 Ran SP% **109.8**
Speed ratings (Par 100):108,107,103,100,99 91,90,87,77,73
CSF £28.85 CT £108.50 TOTE £5.20: £2.10, £2.40, £1.90; EX 27.80.
Owner Larkin, Legge And Milner **Bred** Declan And Catherine Macpartlin **Trained** Whitsbury, Hants

FOCUS
A decent winning time for a race like this. Strong form, with the first two, both progressive, pulling clear of the remainder.
Zingbat(IRE) Official explanation: jockey said gelding hung left throughout
Spanish Lace Official explanation: jockey said filly lost its action

3250 GLADYS & GORDON GOLDEN ANNIVERSARY FILLIES' H'CAP — 1m 30y
9:20 (9:21) (Class 5) (0-75,75) 3-Y-0 **£3,238** (£963; £481; £240) **Stalls** Low

Form RPR

21 1 **Robema**[23] 2542 3-9-7 **75** .... GrahamGibbons 8 81
(J J Quinn) *hld up: hdwy 3f out: rdn over 1f out: edgd lft and led ins fnl f: pushed out cl home* **5/2**[1]

551 2 1/2 **Gelder**[19] 2673 3-9-4 **72** .... SteveDrowne 11 77
(H Morrison) *a.p and tail flashed several times: led 2f out: hdd ins fnl f: nt qckn cl home* **7/1**

-653 3 1/2 **Myths And Verses**[4] 3138 3-8-0 **59** .... JamesDoyle(5) 3 63
(K A Ryan) *hld up: gd hdwy 3f out: rdn to chse ldrs over 1f out: styd on wl towards fin* **11/1**

-000 4 2 **Tiber Tilly**[21] 2609 3-8-12 **66** .... DarryllHolland 5 65
(N P Littmoden) *led: rdn and hdd 2f out: styd on same pce fnl f* **14/1**

64-2 5 1 **Antigoni (IRE)**[22] 2583 3-9-2 **70** .... FrancisNorton 7 67
(A M Balding) *hld up: pushed along over 3f out: rdn over 2f out: hdwy and edgd lft over 1f out: kpt on ins fnl f: nt rch ldrs* **9/2**[2]

446 6 3/4 **Dallma (IRE)**[29] 2383 3-9-1 **69** .... KDarley 1 64
(C E Brittain) *bhd: rdn over 1f out: styd on u.p fnl f: nt trble ldrs* **10/1**

4211 7 nk **Whistleupthewind**[6] 3072 3-8-6 **60** 6ex .... (b) ShaneKelly 6 54
(J M P Eustace) *midfield: effrt over 2f out: one pce ins fnl f* **13/2**[3]

0435 8 2 1/2 **Dancing Flame**[16] 2750 3-8-2 **56** oh3 .... JimmyQuinn 2 45
(E J Alston) *midfield: rdn and hdwy 3f out: nt clr run over 2f out: sn rdn: wknd over 1f out* **14/1**

32-4 9 12 **Munaa (IRE)**[21] 2613 3-9-1 **69** .... PatCosgrave 10 30
(K R Burke) *racd keenly: sn dropped to midfield: rdn over 2f out: wknd over 1f out* **16/1**

0600 10 2 **Bellsbank (IRE)**[6] 3067 3-9-4 **72** .... SamHitchcott 4 28
(A Bailey) *racd keenly: prom tl rdn and wknd over 2f out* **66/1**

0-6 11 12 **Westering Home (IRE)**[8] 3007 3-9-5 **73** .... (b) DaleGibson 9 2
(J Mackie) *t.k.h: wnt cl up after 2f: wknd over 2f out* **66/1**

1m 43.84s (-1.67) **Going Correction** -0.20s/f (Firm) 11 Ran SP% **112.2**
Speed ratings (Par 97):100,99,99,97,96 95,94,92,80,78 66
CSF £18.88 CT £161.58 TOTE £3.50: £1.50, £3.50, £4.50; EX 22.60 Place 6 £29.22, Place 5 £9.20.
Owner Mrs J O'Connor **Bred** Newsells Park Stud Limited **Trained** Settrington, N Yorks

FOCUS
The first two are unexposed and progressive and this form looks solid enough.
Whistleupthewind Official explanation: jockey said filly had no more to give
Dancing Flame Official explanation: jockey said filly was denied a clear run
Westering Home(IRE) Official explanation: jockey said filly lost its action
T/Plt: £35.80 to a £1 stake. Pool: £63,159.20. 1,284.65 winning tickets. T/Qpdt: £6.50 to a £1 stake. Pool: £3,857.70. 436.75 winning tickets. DO

2649 SANDOWN (R-H)
Friday, July 7

OFFICIAL GOING: Good to firm (good in places on round course)
Wind: Virtually nil Weather: Overcast, beconing fine. Humid.

3251 BIG NIGHT DOWN UNDER ON 26 JULY H'CAP — 5f 6y
2:05 (2:08) (Class 3) (0-95,93) 3-Y-0+ **£8,096** (£2,408; £1,203; £601) **Stalls** High

Form RPR

0560 1 **Pic Up Sticks**[1] 3211 7-9-2 **83** .... RyanMoore 12 93
(B G Powell) *hld up midfield: prog 2f out: got through 1f out: drvn to ld last 75yds* **11/1**

5510 2 nk **Royal Challenge**[20] 2661 5-8-13 **80** .... MichaelHills 8 89
(M H Tompkins) *hld up in last trio: effrt on outer 2f out: rdn and r.o wl fnl f to take 2nd nr fin: nt rch wnr* **7/1**[2]

525 3 shd **Quality Street**[13] 2858 4-8-7 **74** .... KerrinMcEvoy 3 83
(P Butler) *prom: rdn to chse ldr over 1f out: led last 150yds: hdd and no ex fnl 75yds* **20/1**

3021 4 1 **Devon Flame**[20] 2635 7-8-13 **80** .... JimCrowley 11 85
(R J Hodges) *lw: chsd ldrs on inner: rdn 2f out: styd on u.p to chal ins fnl f: one pce last 100yds* **15/2**[3]

0011 5 shd **Intriguing Glimpse**[19] 2674 5-9-10 **91** .... SebSanders 9 96
(Miss B Sanders) *lw: hld up towards rr: nt clr run over 1f out and swtchd lft: clsng on ldrs whn nt clr run ins fnl f: r.o: no ch* **6/1**[1]

1000 6 1/2 **The Jobber (IRE)**[6] 3092 5-9-5 **86** .... TedDurcan 5 89
(M Blanshard) *lw: b: wl in tch: prog to press ldrs over 1f out: one pce ins fnl f* **25/1**

0436 7 3/4 **Cape Royal**[7] 3038 6-9-7 **93** .... (b) LiamTreadwell(5) 6 93
(J M Bradley) *led after 1f: gng wl 2f out: hdd and fdd last 150yds* **8/1**

-153 8 hd **Auwitesweetheart**[36] 2173 4-9-1 **82** .... AlanMunro 10 81
(B R Millman) *lw: lost pl over 3f out and in rr: rdn 1/2-way: plugged on fnl f: n.d* **8/1**

12 9 1/2 **Golden Dixie (USA)**[10] 2946 7-9-6 **90** .... AmirQuinn(3) 1 88
(R A Harris) *hld up towards rr and racd on outer: outpcd 1/2-way: sn rdn: styd on fnl f: no ch* **8/1**

1104 10 nk **Cashel Mead**[30] 2340 6-8-9 **81** .... TravisBlock(5) 4 78
(J L Spearing) *dwlt: rdn in last pair after 2f: kpt on fnl f: nvr nrr* **12/1**

0-00 11 3 **Hoh Hoh Hoh**[34] 2227 4-9-5 **86** .... MartinDwyer 2 72
(A M Balding) *lw: free to post: prom: rdn 1/2-way: wknd over 1f out* **12/1**

0601 12 3 **Graze On**[6] 3069 4-9-8 **89** 3ex .... (b) AdrianMcCarthy 7 64
(R A Harris) *lw: led for 1f: chsd ldr to over 1f out: wkng whn n.m.r and hit rail ent fnl f* **10/1**

1-00 13 5 **Kenmore**[31] 2323 4-9-10 **91** .... JohnEgan 13 48
(D Nicholls) *sn rdn in last: nvr gng wl: eased over 1f out* **25/1**

61.31 secs (-0.90) **Going Correction** 0.0s/f (Good) 13 Ran SP% **117.1**
Speed ratings (Par 107):107,106,106,104,104 103,102,102,101,101 96,91,83
CSF £82.08 CT £1565.59 TOTE £12.60: £3.70, £2.60, £4.40; EX 124.50.
Owner The Vintage Group **Bred** J P Coggan **Trained** Morestead, Hants

FOCUS
A solid-looking handicap run at a sound pace.

NOTEBOOK
Pic Up Sticks, who ran moderately the night before off a slower pace, came home strongly to land the spoils close the line. He is not an easy horse to predict and is far from certain to run the same race again, but he had to negotiate some traffic problems when making his effort, and is value for slightly further than the winning distance. He is capable, if in the mood, of going close next time even when reassessed. (tchd 12-1)
Royal Challenge, dropping down in trip, flew home on the outside of the pack after having every chance. He seemed to run up to his best at a course he had run well at before, but remains a bit high in the weights on the balance of his winning form. (op 13-2)
Quality Street, who has a habit of running well at Sandown, was produced with her effort with a furlong to go, but was swamped by the finishers inside the final half furlong. It was a decent effort from a modest draw and she should add to her only success to date, which was in claiming company on her racecourse debut, fairly soon.
Devon Flame continues to run well, which does not get him any respite from the Handicapper. He is a fair sort to rate the race around. (tchd 7-1)
Intriguing Glimpse looked the unlucky horse in the race, as she suffered plenty of traffic problems just behind the leaders on the far-side rail. She can be rated a bit better than her final position suggests. (op 13-2 tchd 7-1)
The Jobber(IRE) had every chance but finished like a horse that is in the grip of the Handicapper. Official explanation: jockey said filly lost a front shoe
Cape Royal, with the blinkers back on, went off like a scalded cat in front and it was not surprising to see him not last out up the hill. He needs to come down the weights a bit to have an obvious chance of winning. (op 15-2)
Auwitesweetheart Official explanation: jockey said filly hung left and lost her action
Golden Dixie(USA) did not have the best of draws but kept on well enough to suggest he is still performing close to his recent best. (op 7-1)

3252 SMITH & WILLIAMSON DRAGON STKS (LISTED RACE) 5f 6y
2:40 (2:42) (Class 1) 2-Y-O

£13,343 (£5,057; £2,530; £1,261; £632; £317) **Stalls** High

Form				RPR
116	**1**		**Bahama Mama (IRE)**[14] 2800 2-8-11 ShaneKelly 9	98
			(J Noseda) *lw: cl up: nt clr run 2f out to 1f out: pushed along and r.o strly to ld last 75yds: won gng away* **7/2**[2]	
2126	**2**	1 1/4	**Mood Music**[15] 2771 2-9-2 MartinDwyer 1	99
			(E J O'Neill) *trckd ldrs: effrt 2f out: rdn to ld jst over 1f out: hdd and outpcd last 75yds* **12/1**	
2100	**3**	1 3/4	**Scented Present**[15] 2771 2-9-2 AlanMunro 4	92
			(B J Meehan) *taken down early: hld up: last 2f out: rdn and styd on fnl f to take 3rd nr fin* **25/1**	
1264	**4**	nk	**La Neige**[10] 2960 2-9-2 TedDurcan 2	91
			(M R Channon) *lw: hld up in last trio: rdn over 1f out: styd on fnl f: nvr rchd ldrs* **6/1**[3]	
21	**5**	shd	**Southandwest (IRE)**[20] 2631 2-9-2 JohnEgan 3	91
			(J S Moore) *lw: sn trckd ldr: rdn to ld wl over 1f out to jst over 1f out: wknd last 100yds* **15/2**	
3520	**6**	nk	**Fairfield Princess**[6] 3084 2-8-11 KerrinMcEvoy 5	85
			(N A Callaghan) *hld up in last trio: shkn up over 1f out: styd on ins fnl f: no ch* **20/1**	
61	**7**	1/2	**Resignation (IRE)**[20] 2630 2-9-2 PatDobbs 7	88
			(R Hannon) *lw: t.k.h: hld up in tch and gng wl: rdn whn nt clr run and bmpd jst over 1f out: sn btn* **7/2**[2]	
1223	**8**	1 3/4	**Cav Okay (IRE)**[15] 2771 2-9-2 RyanMoore 6	82
			(R Hannon) *mde most to wl over 1f out: wknd rapidly ins fnl f* **3/1**[1]	

61.94 secs (-0.27) **Going Correction** 0.0s/f (Good) **8** Ran SP% **111.8**
Speed ratings (Par 102):102,100,97,96,96 96,95,92
CSF £41.95 TOTE £4.20: £1.30, £3.00, £6.60; EX 68.00.
Owner Lucayan Stud **Bred** C J Foy **Trained** Newmarket, Suffolk
FOCUS
A Listed race that looked up to standard and is best rated through the fourth. The winner was impressive enough, after looking blocked in at one stage, and upholds the Albany Stakes form.
NOTEBOOK
Bahama Mama(IRE), who ran well despite being unplaced in the Albany Stakes at Royal Ascot last time, came home a convincing winner despite meeting some trouble in running. The drop in trip clearly did not inconvenience her and she is a smart sprinting juvenile. Connections have made plenty of entries for her, including a Group 2 event over seven furlongs in Ireland at the end of July. However, the Princess Margaret would still seem the logical next race for her. (op 11-4)
Mood Music, who was giving the winner weight due to her sex allowance, easily reversed Norfolk Stakes form with Cav Okay, and got back on track with a pleasing performance. He looks a real sprinter and should give a good account of himself wherever connections take him next. (tchd 14-1)
Scented Present stayed on strongly from the rear of the pack after the first two had gone beyond recall. Another furlong may well be within his scope and it was a sound effort behind decent-looking sprinters. He has entries in some of the big sales races later in the year, and looks to be the type to run well in one of those.
La Neige, who was fitted with a Monty Robert's rug for stalls entry, has been kept on the go recently and did not appear to be fully suited by the drop down in trip, even though it was on a stiff track. His Coventry form looks rock-solid and, if anything, a step up to seven furlongs is most likely to suit him in the future. (op 13-2 tchd 7-1)
Southandwest(IRE) ran a fair race and was not disgraced in face of a stiff task. He is a half-brother to the decent filly La Mottie, so more improvement can be expected. (op 8-1 tchd 10-1)
Resignation(IRE) got unbalanced when the winner moved out into the middle of the track from off the rail, and failed to get home thereafter. He is probably not up to Listed class quite yet, but has the physical scope to make improvement. (tchd 10-3)
Cav Okay(IRE), who did not appear to move to post very fluently, again gave the impression that five furlongs tests his stamina, especially on a stiff track. He emerged from the race with a genuine excuse, but a sharper track would suit him much better and it is also possible we may not see the best of him until he strengthens up. Official explanation: vet said colt finished lame on its left foreleg (op 11-4 tchd 7-2)

3253 JOHN O'NEILL & PARTNERS EBF MAIDEN STKS 7f 16y
3:15 (3:19) (Class 4) 2-Y-O **£5,181** (£1,541; £770; £384) **Stalls** High

Form				RPR
0	**1**		**Nur Tau (IRE)**[28] 2402 2-9-3 MartinDwyer 9	78
			(M P Tregoning) *lw: chsd ldng trio: rdn 2f out: no imp tl picked up ent fnl f: r.o to ld last 50yds* **12/1**	
3	**2**	1/2	**Hurlingham**[12] 2899 2-9-3 RoystonFfrench 11	76
			(M Johnston) *lw: led: hrd rdn fr over 2f out: kpt on u.p: hdd last 50yds* **3/1**[2]	
36	**3**	1/2	**Golden Balls (IRE)**[10] 2960 2-9-3 RyanMoore 7	75
			(R Hannon) *lw: pressed ldr: rdn to chal over 2f out: nt qckn and hld fr over 1f out: lost 2nd last 100yds* **9/4**[1]	
	4	1	**Laish Ya Hajar (IRE)** 2-9-3 TedDurcan 10	73
			(M R Channon) *str: scope: bit bkwd: dwlt: rcvrd into midfield after 3f: nt on terms w ldrs fr 3f out: styd on fnl f: nrst fin* **14/1**	
	5	nk	**Karoo Blue (IRE)** 2-9-3 SebSanders 4	72
			(C E Brittain) *w'like: pressed ldng pair: rdn over 2f out: a jst hld fr over 1f out : wknd last 100yds* **20/1**	
	6	2 1/2	**Deccan Express (IRE)** 2-9-3 JohnEgan 3	66+
			(R Hannon) *w'like: scope: hld up wl in rr: shkn up 2f out: kpt on steadily but nvr on terms* **14/1**	
	7	3	**Greek God** 2-9-3 AlanMunro 8	58
			(W Jarvis) *scope: bit bkwd: nvr beyond midfield: brief effrt 2f out but nt on terms: wknd 1f out* **9/1**[3]	
	8	3	**Perfect Reward** 2-9-3 JimCrowley 2	51
			(Mrs A J Perrett) *neat: scope: bit bkwd: in tch to 1/2-way: wl in rr and struggling wl over 2f out* **20/1**	
	9	1 3/4	**Hoh Me Hoh You (IRE)** 2-9-3 PatDobbs 6	46
			(S Kirk) *cmpt: bit bkwd: dwlt: hld up in rr: sme prog to midfield 3f out but nt on terms: wknd 2f out* **40/1**	
	10	52	**Almondillo (IRE)** 2-9-3 KerrinMcEvoy 1	—
			(C F Wall) *str: bit bkwd: s.v.s: a last: wknd 3f out: wl bhd whn virtually p.u ins fnl f* **16/1**	

1m 32.83s (1.74) **Going Correction** +0.15s/f (Good) **10** Ran SP% **104.6**
Speed ratings (Par 96):96,95,94,93,93 90,87,83,81,22
CSF £46.08 TOTE £13.30: £3.20, £1.30, £1.30; EX 51.80.
Owner Millrace Partners **Bred** C H Wacker Iii **Trained** Lambourn, Berks
■ Palamoun was withdrawn (8/1, refused to enter stalls). R4 applies, deduct 10p in the £.
■ Stewards' Enquiry : Royston Ffrench one-day ban: used whip with excessive frequency (Jul 18)
Ryan Moore one-day ban: used whip with excessive frequency (Jul 18)
FOCUS
A reasonable-looking maiden on paper containing a few horses that look sure to come on for the experience and not a race to be totally certain about at this stage.
NOTEBOOK
Nur Tau(IRE), who showed very little on his debut over six furlongs, came with a late flourish to steal the prize late on. He clearly relished the seventh furlong, so can be expected to stay at least a mile as a juvenile. The dam's side of his pedigree has plenty of class, and it would be no surprise to see him make up into a decent sort, despite the winning time being ordinary. (op 11-1)
Hurlingham looked all set to collect before being passed in the closing stages. Much like his debut, he showed greenness in the latter stages and can be expected to progress again for the run, as he has plenty of scope for improvement. (op 4-1)
Golden Balls(IRE) had every chance but did not appear to see the race out as well as some of the others. A less-demanding track might suit him better at the trip, and he could be the sort for a nice nursery. (op 7-4 tchd 13-8)
Laish Ya Hajar(IRE), from the family of Zafeen, was surprisingly weak in the market for a trainer/owner that often produces a nice juvenile. Clearly not as sharp as many of the two-year-olds that come from the yard, he kept on really nicely just behind the leading bunch and can be expected to come on for the experience. The fact that he holds no fancy entries suggests he has been slow to come to hand. (op 12-1)
Karoo Blue(IRE) ◆ held every chance two from home but failed to get home on his racecourse debut. He has plenty of class in his pedigree and should win his share of races if making normal progress from the race.
Deccan Express(IRE) never threatened to get strike a blow, but was noted staying on in his own time from off the pace. He can progress with experience. (tchd 16-1)
Greek God had every chance up the straight but failed to trouble the leaders. He was not unfancied in the market prior to the race and must be though capable of better. His pedigree suggests he may need middle distances next season to be at his best. (op 14-1)
Perfect Reward, an attractive sort, faded out of the picture after being close up early. (op 20-1)
Hoh Me Hoh You(IRE) looked to be the weakest of the horses in the paddock and will improve with time. (op 33-1)
Almondillo(IRE), who did not look as straight as a few of the others in the race, came out of the race with an excuse for his poor showing. Official explanation: jockey said colt lost its action

3254 SEYMOUR PIERCE GALA STKS (LISTED RACE) 1m 2f 7y
3:50 (3:51) (Class 1) 3-Y-O+

£15,898 (£6,025; £3,015; £1,503; £753; £378) **Stalls** High

Form				RPR
1156	**1**		**Kandidate**[17] 2722 4-9-8 108 (t) SebSanders 6	117
			(C E Brittain) *lw: restrained bhd ldng pair: effrt on inner over 1f out: rdn to ld jst ins fnl f: styd on wl and sn clr* **9/1**	
1/3-	**2**	2 1/2	**Windsor Knot (IRE)**[293] 5290 4-9-5 107 KerrinMcEvoy 4	109
			(Saeed Bin Suroor) *bit bkwd: t.k.h: trckd ldr: led 2f out: rdn over 1f out: hdd jst ins fnl f: fnd nil* **8/1**	
121	**3**	1 1/4	**Alfie Flits**[12] 2893 4-9-8 107 DeanMcKeown 3	110
			(G A Swinbank) *swtg: trckd ldrs: rdn over 2f out: plugged on same pce and nvr able to chal* **5/2**[2]	
3403	**4**	nk	**Crosspeace (IRE)**[14] 2803 4-9-8 108 RoystonFfrench 1	109
			(M Johnston) *lw: trckd ldrs: rdn over 3f out: chal u.p 2f out: fdd fnl f* **4/1**[3]	
6104	**5**	3	**Mulaqat**[15] 2775 3-8-11 111 MartinDwyer 2	104
			(M P Tregoning) *lw: plld hrd early: hld up in last: shkn up over 2f out: struggling whn nt clr run briefly over 1f out: nt qckn* **7/4**[1]	
5615	**6**	2 1/2	**Weightless**[22] 2597 6-9-5 105 JimCrowley 5	96
			(Mrs A J Perrett) *lw: racd freely: led to 2f out: wknd over 1f out* **20/1**	

2m 8.28s (-1.96) **Going Correction** +0.15s/f (Good)
WFA 3 from 4yo+ 11lb **6** Ran SP% **110.8**
Speed ratings (Par 111):113,111,110,109,107 105
CSF £71.43 TOTE £10.20: £3.50, £2.80; EX 65.50.
Owner A J Richards **Bred** Proton Partnership **Trained** Newmarket, Suffolk
FOCUS
A decent contest with a solid winning time for a Listed race and best rated through the winner.
NOTEBOOK
Kandidate, taking a considerable drop in class after contesting two Group 1 races in a row, stretched away from his field in the final stages, after being held up just behind the leaders, to record a clear-cut success. He obviously has plenty of talent and should be a force when kept to a realistic level. (op 14-1)
Windsor Knot(IRE), who holds a Group 1 Juddmonte International entry, does not see the racecourse too often but is a decent sort when he does. A winner of the Solario Stakes at the course at two, he kept on when put under pressure after pulling quite hard early, and is sure to progress from his first run since September last year. (op 9-1)
Alfie Flits was very weak in the market prior to the off, presumably because he got very warm before the race. Always close to the pace, he could not quicken when asked to by his jockey, and could be feeling the effects on a busy year now - which includes his impressive efforts in bumpers. It was still a fair effort, however, and he is sure to hold his own in similar company wherever his connections decide to take him next. (op 7-4)
Crosspeace(IRE) is a useful yardstick to the form and was not beaten that far in a race not run to suit him. He always gives his all and deserves to win another decent race before too long. (tchd 9-2)
Mulaqat, the only three-year-old in the line-up, ran a lifeless race after travelling very keenly early, slightly detached from the main body of the field. There did not seem to be an obvious reason as to why he ran so moderately. (op 5-2)
Weightless was easily swallowed up at the two-furlong marker by the chasing pack when they closed in. (op 14-1)

3255 GVA GRIMLEY H'CAP 1m 2f 7y

4:25 (4:28) (Class 2) (0-100,98) 3-Y-0+

£11,217 (£3,358; £1,679; £840; £419; £210) Stalls High

Form RPR

0010 1 **Dansili Dancer**16 [2742] 4-9-3 90 AdamKirby(3) 8 101
(C G Cox) *lw: hld up bhd ldrs: shkn up and effrt over 2f out: disp ld wl over 1f out: def advantage ins fnl f: kpt on wl* 10/1

1-4 2 ¾ **Book Of Music (IRE)**41 [2030] 3-9-1 96 KerrinMcEvoy 6 105
(Sir Michael Stoute) *hld up in last trio: prog over 2f out: chsd ldrs over 1f out: nt qckn: kpt on fnl f to take 2nd last 50yds* 4/1²

0004 3 hd **Coup D'Etat**21 [2621] 4-8-12 82 RyanMoore 2 91
(J L Dunlop) *lw: hld up in last pair: effrt on inner whn nt clr run 2f out: drvn and r.o fnl f: fin best of all* 11/2

1-62 4 ½ **In Full Cry**6 [3081] 3-8-2 83 RoystonFfrench 9 91
(M Johnston) *sn trckd ldng pair: rdn over 2f out: effrt to dispute ld wl over 1f out to ins fnl f: one pce* 10/3¹

1201 5 nk **Goodbye Mr Bond**20 [2657] 6-9-5 89 FrancisNorton 4 96
(E J Alston) *lw: t.k.h: hld up in midfield: rdn and prog on outer 2f out: chsd ldrs ent fnl f: one pce last 150yds* 9/2³

251- 6 1¼ **Foxhaven**345 [3838] 4-10-0 98 SebSanders 7 103
(P R Chamings) *lw: settled in midfield: effrt on inner over 2f out: chsd ldrs over 1f out: fdd ins fnl f* 12/1

6002 7 1¼ **Yakimov (USA)**19 [2672] 7-8-8 81 EdwardCreighton(3) 10 84
(D J Wintle) *snatched up after 1f and dropped to last: shuffled along over 2f out: stl last wl over 1f out: styd on: nvr nr ldrs* 25/1

30-0 8 1½ **Cavallini (USA)**9 [2989] 4-9-0 84 JimCrowley 5 84
(G L Moore) *b: b.hind: mde most to wl over 1f out: wknd rapidly fnl f* 40/1

-153 9 3 **Miss Provvidence (IRE)**12 [2892] 4-9-6 90 AlanMunro 3 84
(W R Swinburn) *lw: t.k.h: trckd ldrs: lost pl and btn over 2f out: eased whn no ch f inal f* 8/1

6-01 10 13 **Tashkandi (IRE)**11 [2918] 6-8-11 81 6ex VinceSlattery 1 50
(P Bowen) *pressed ldr: led briefly over 2f out: sn wknd rapidly* 33/1

2m 11.45s (1.21) **Going Correction** +0.15s/f (Good)
WFA 3 from 4yo+ 11lb 10 Ran SP% 113.8
Speed ratings (Par 109):101,100,100,99,99 98,97,96,94,83
CSF £47.78 CT £244.61 TOTE £11.10: £3.40, £1.60, £2.10; EX 66.40.
Owner The Troupers **Bred** The Magic Slipper Partnership **Trained** Lambourn, Berks

FOCUS
A good handicap but a very moderate winning time for a race of this class and 3.17 seconds slower than the Listed contest. However, the form looks sound on paper.

NOTEBOOK
Dansili Dancer, with cheekpieces removed after running down the field in the Royal Hunt Cup, resumed winning ways over a trip he was far from proven at. Always close to the pace, he was ideally positioned when the tempo increased and won by a comfortable margin. Considering the early gallop was far from strong, it still remains to be seen whether he truly stays ten furlongs. (op 12-1)
Book Of Music(IRE) ◆ belied his inexperience with a decent performance against solid handicappers. The form of his seasonal debut back in May has worked out pretty nicely and it would be a surprise if his shrewd trainer did not have a race in mind for his charge, off what could be a lenient handicap mark. (tchd 9-2)
Coup D'Etat was finishing the fastest of all as the winner past the line. He found his path blocked a couple of times, after switching from the middle of the track to the inside, and then back again, and can be considered a bit unlucky. He is a talented-enough handicapper when he puts his mind to it but is just not very easy to predict. (op 15-2)
In Full Cry, one of only two three-year-olds in the race taking on older rivals, tried his very best to go with Dansili Dancer when that rival went for home, but was unable to match his finishing kick. There was still plenty to like about the performance and he looks sure to win more races. (op 11-4)
Goodbye Mr Bond had every chance up the home straight but may have found the stiff ten furlongs just stretching his stamina. He has been in a rich vein of form this season but is suffering in the weights for it. (op 4-1)
Foxhaven, not seen for almost a year, made a satisfactory return to the racecourse and can be expected to come on for the run. He has run well at Goodwood in the past and one suspects he is being lined up for a race at their Glorious meeting at the start of August.
Yakimov(USA) ◆ caught the eye in behind, keeping on for pressure after being held up towards the rear. While he was no doubt unsuited by the lack of early pace, it was noticeable that the jockey never went for his stick in the final stages, preferring to use hands and heels instead - although it is worth noting that he has run similar races in the past from off the pace. He arguably should have been ridden much closer to the pace for a horse guaranteed to stay, much like when he won at Warwick earlier in the season, and is better than his final position suggests.
Miss Provvidence(IRE) pulled very hard in the early stages and failed to get home. (tchd 9-1)
Tashkandi(IRE), a winner last time, dropped out tamely after making the early gallop. One suspects he was running well above his proper grade.

3256 UCL HOSPITALS/NATIONAL HOSPITAL H'CAP 1m 6f

5:00 (5:01) (Class 4) (0-85,85) 3-Y-0+ £6,477 (£1,927; £963; £481) Stalls Centre

Form RPR

6013 1 **Mudawin (IRE)**14 [2817] 5-10-0 85 JohnEgan 4 92
(Jane Chapple-Hyam) *lw: hld up towards rr: prog over 3f out to chal over 2f out: looked hld ent fnl f: styd on again to ld last stride* 5/1³

0-45 2 shd **Rio De Janeiro (IRE)**19 [847] 5-8-11 68 AlanMunro 3 75
(Miss E C Lavelle) *trckd ldng pair: effrt to ld wl over 2f out: sn pressed: rdn and looked wnr ins fnl f: collared on line* 9/1

3416 3 1¾ **Mister Right (IRE)**17 [2723] 5-9-5 76 RyanMoore 1 81
(D J S Ffrench Davis) *hld up in last: prog on outer to chal 2f out: sn rdn and nt qckn: one pce and hld after* 7/2¹

556 4 2 **Riff Raff**32 [2292] 3-8-2 74 ow1 MartinDwyer 8 76
(W Jarvis) *led: jinked lft bnd after 2f and hdd: effrt to chal and upsides 3f out: nt qckn over 2f out: hld after* 8/1

65-1 5 ½ **Captain General**57 [1614] 4-8-10 67 KerrinMcEvoy 6 68
(J A R Toller) *t.k.h: hld up in midfield: rdn over 2f out: one pce and no imp on ldrs after* 4/1²

2052 6 1½ **Dubai Ace (USA)**13 [2869] 5-8-6 66 NeilChalmers(3) 9 65
(Miss Sheena West) *hld up in midfield: rdn and outpcd over 2f out: n.d after* 6/1

0060 7 nk **Love Angel (USA)**24 [2534] 4-8-4 66 oh6 MarcHalford(5) 7 65
(J J Bridger) *hld up towards rr: n.m.r bnd 4f out: sn outpcd: plugged on one pce fnl 2f* 40/1

5-30 8 16 **Smart Gal (IRE)**38 [2117] 3-7-13 71 JamieMackay 2 49
(J L Dunlop) *hld up in last pair: wl outpcd and btn over 2f out* 15/2

0/0- 9 5 **Tycoon Hall (IRE)**314 [3812] 6-9-4 75 VinceSlattery 5 47
(P Bowen) *bit bkwd: t.k.h: led after 2f to wl over 2f out: wknd rapidly* 20/1

3m 8.20s (3.69) **Going Correction** +0.15s/f (Good)
WFA 3 from 4yo+ 15lb 9 Ran SP% 113.3
Speed ratings (Par 105):95,94,93,92,92 91,91,82,79
CSF £48.08 CT £175.95 TOTE £6.40: £1.90, £2.60, £1.60; EX 54.60 Place 6 £1,180.24, Place 5 £ 261.88.
Owner Franconson Partners **Bred** Shadwell Estate Company Limited **Trained** Newmarket, Suffolk

FOCUS
A very moderate winning time for the grade and not that strong a contest, rated through the winner..
T/Jkpt: Not won. T/Plt: £1,355.70 to a £1 stake. Pool: £66,954.20. 36.05 winning tickets. T/Qpdt: £77.00 to a £1 stake. Pool: £5,162.30. 49.60 winning tickets. JN

2244 SOUTHWELL (L-H)

Friday, July 7

OFFICIAL GOING: Standard
Wind: Light, half-behind

3257 WBX.COM WORLD BET EXCHANGE H'CAP 5f (F)

2:00 (2:00) (Class 6) (0-55,55) 3-Y-0 £2,730 (£806; £403) Stalls High

Form RPR

-063 1 **Miss Mujahid Times**37 [2138] 3-8-6 42 (b) SilvestreDeSousa(3) 2 52
(A D Brown) *disp ld tl led 2f out: sn rdn and hdd: rallied to ld and hung lft ins fnl f: r.o* 8/1

5245 2 hd **Mystic Queen (IRE)**4 [3154] 3-9-5 52 JimmyFortune 4 61
(A P Jarvis) *chsd ldrs: rdn to ld and edgd lft over 1f out: hdd ins fnl f: r.o* 11/2²

0-04 3 4 **Vicky Pollard**7 [3034] 3-9-2 52 DeanCorby(3) 6 47
(P Howling) *chsd ldrs: rdn over 1f out: styd on same pce* 18/1

002 4 1¾ **Sarah's Prince (IRE)**11 [2937] 3-9-3 50 NCallan 8 38
(D K Ivory) *sn outpcd: styd on ins fnl f: nrst fin* 4/1¹

601 5 hd **Money Mate (IRE)**13 [2876] 3-9-3 55 StephenDonohoe(5) 5 43
(J O'Reilly) *dwlt: outpcd: styd on ins fnl f: nvr nrr* 4/1¹

-233 6 1½ **Stoneacre Fred (IRE)**150 [335] 3-9-6 53 RobbieFitzpatrick 14 35
(Peter Grayson) *s.s: outpcd: hrd rdn and hung lft over 1f out: n.d* 6/1³

60-0 7 1 **Martharum**23 [2543] 3-8-10 43 TomEaves 3 22
(J J Quinn) *disp ld 3f: sn rdn and wknd* 33/1

000- 8 nk **Hotchpotch (USA)**295 [5245] 3-9-3 50 MickyFenton 9 28
(J R Best) *s.i.s: outpcd* 12/1

0000 9 ¾ **Teddy Monty (IRE)**51 [1771] 3-8-7 47 (b) ChrisCavanagh(7) 10 22
(M Quinn) *dwlt: outpcd* 33/1

1644 10 1¼ **Axis Shield (IRE)**10 [2949] 3-9-0 52 EmmettStack(5) 13 22
(M C Chapman) *mid-div: rdn 1/2-way: sn wknd* 8/1

005- 11 1½ **Globe**358 [3477] 3-8-8 41 StephenCarson 11 —
(M S Saunders) *s.i.s: sn chsng ldrs: rdn and wknd 1/2-way* 20/1

5-20 12 5 **Tatstheticket**91 [910] 3-9-1 48 (b) BrianReilly 12 —
(J Balding) *mid-div: rdn and wknd 1/2-way* 25/1

62.23 secs (1.93) **Going Correction** +0.35s/f (Slow) 12 Ran SP% 119.3
Speed ratings (Par 98):98,97,91,88,88 85,84,83,82,80 78,70
CSF £49.70 CT £773.99 TOTE £9.20: £4.20, £2.30, £4.90; EX 67.40 TRIFECTA Not won..
Owner John Wills **Bred** John Wills And Gordon Kendrick **Trained** Pickering, York

FOCUS
A very poor handicap and, as is normally the case over the straight five here, those drawn low, and therefore raced down the centre of the track, enjoyed a distinct advantage and could be a few pounds out either way.

3258 BIG RACING WEEKEND MAIDEN STKS (DIV I) 1m 3f (F)

2:30 (2:31) (Class 5) 3-Y-0+ £2,590 (£770; £385; £192) Stalls Low

Form RPR

5223 1 **New Guinea**19 [2682] 3-9-0 86 PhilipRobinson 1 93+
(M A Jarvis) *mde all: clr over 2f out: eased fnl f* 1/3¹

3 2 17 **Ha'Penny Beacon**47 [1866] 3-8-6 DanielTudhope(3) 8 61+
(D Carroll) *hld up: hdwy over 4f out: wknd over 2f out: wnt remote 2nd over 1f out* 7/1²

03 3 7 **Fairlight Express (IRE)**11 [2917] 6-9-12 MickyFenton 2 55
(Stef Liddiard) *prom: rdn to chse wnr over 3f out: wknd over 2f out* 16/1

00-0 4 3 **Sara Mana Mou**77 [1118] 3-8-9 45 TPQueally 5 45
(J G Portman) *hld up: rdn and wknd over 3f out* 80/1

404 5 9 **Tirol Livit (IRE)**60 [1533] 3-8-11 49 DNolan(3) 9 35
(N Wilson) *chsd wnr tl rdn over 3f out: sn wknd* 25/1

0-0 6 6 **Lihusn Al Haz (USA)**22 [2578] 3-8-9 HayleyTurner 4 21
(C E Brittain) *chsd ldrs: rdn 1/2-way: sn wknd* 50/1

0 7 4 **Suzuki (IRE)**30 [2350] 3-8-9 RobertHavlin 6 14
(H Morrison) *prom 7f* 16/1

0- 8 shd **Celtic Empire (IRE)**286 [5455] 3-9-0 DaleGibson 10 19
(Jedd O'Keeffe) *s.i.s: hld up: wknd over 4f out* 50/1

9 20 **Lourdes (IRE)** 3-8-9 NCallan 11 —
(J R Fanshawe) *s.i.s: sn chsng ldrs: rdn and wknd over 3f out* 8/1³

60-0 10 16 **Earthling**185 [27] 5-9-12 40 PaulQuinn 3 —
(D W Chapman) *prom to 1/2-way* 80/1

30-0 11 1 **Montrachet Belle**7 [3039] 4-9-2 45 (t) DeclanMcGann(5) 7 —
(R Johnson) *sn outpcd and bhd* 80/1

2m 27.67s (-1.23) **Going Correction** +0.225s/f (Slow)
WFA 3 from 4yo+ 12lb 11 Ran SP% 121.9
Speed ratings (Par 103):113,100,95,93,86 82,79,79,64,53 52
CSF £3.39 TOTE £1.20: £1.02, £1.40, £2.90; EX 3.50 Trifecta £23.10 Pool £445.85, 13.70 winning units..
Owner Jumeirah Racing **Bred** Milton Park Stud Partnership **Trained** Newmarket, Suffolk

FOCUS
Very few ever got into this and a non-event, with the winner proving several classes above his rivals and little to focus on otherwise. A very smart winning time indeed for a race like this, 1.82 seconds faster than the second division.

3259 DOSCO 50TH ANNIVERSARY MEDIAN AUCTION MAIDEN STKS 6f (F)

3:05 (3:05) (Class 6) 2-Y-0 £2,730 (£806; £403) Stalls Low

Form RPR

52 1 **Naayla (IRE)**10 [2957] 2-8-12 JimmyFortune 8 83+
(B J Meehan) *trckd ldrs: led on bit wl over 1f out: shkn up and r.o wl: eased nr fin* 11/8¹

442 2 1¾ **Persian Peril**14 [2807] 2-9-3 TomEaves 4 80
(G A Swinbank) *led: hdd 5f out: rdn and ev ch over 1f out: sn outpcd* 8/1

3 3 7 **Follow The Flag (IRE)**21 [2604] 2-9-3 NCallan 7 59
(N P Littmoden) *chsd ldrs: rdn over 2f out: wknd over 1f out* 11/2³

4 3 **Fen Dream** 2-9-3 TPQueally 2 50
(E F Vaughan) *chsd ldrs over 3f* 40/1

044 5 1½ **Sparkling Eyes**16 [2743] 2-8-12 PhilipRobinson 3 41
(C E Brittain) *s.i.s: rcvrd to ld 5f out: rdn and hdd wl over 1f out: sn wknd* 7/4²

6 33 **Only A Splash** 2-9-3 .... PaulQuinn 5 —
(D W Chapman) *s.i.s: sn pushed along in rr: wknd over 3f out* **50/1**

1m 19.37s (2.47) **Going Correction** +0.225s/f (Slow) **6** Ran SP% **109.4**
Speed ratings (Par 92):92,89,80,76,74 30
CSF £12.30 TOTE £2.10: £1.30, £2.10; EX 9.40 Trifecta £16.30 Pool £428.02, 18.55 winning units..

Owner Saleh Al Homaizi & Imad Al Sagar **Bred** J Hanly **Trained** Manton, Wilts

FOCUS
A fair little contest of its type with a few of these already having shown some form. The field all came down the middle once in line for home.

NOTEBOOK
Naayla(IRE) confirmed the promise of her Newbury effort and the race was hers as soon as she took it up on the bridle a quarter of a mile from home. She won this with a bit in hand and can now look for something a bit better. (op 11-10)
Persian Peril was always up with the pace and kept going, but had no answer to the winner. He seemed to handle the surface well enough and pulled clear of the rest, but may be better off in nurseries. (op 9-1)
Follow The Flag(IRE) did not progress from his Goodwood debut performance and did not appear to see out the trip on this slower surface. (tchd 5-1)
Fen Dream, a 15,000gns colt, never looked like getting involved but should come on for the experience and there is plenty of stamina in his pedigree, so he may improve for further in time.
Sparkling Eyes, fourth in the Queen Mary, showed up with the pace for a while but eventually capitulated very tamely. The different surface gives her a viable excuse, but equally the Queen Mary form continues to take a battering. Official explanation: jockey said filly was unsuited by the fibresand surface (op 2-1)
Only A Splash, a half-brother to three winners including Soaked, looked as green as grass on this debut. (op 40-1)

3260 POCHIN @ LONG EATON PLUMBERS CLUB CLAIMING STKS — 1m 4f (F)
3:40 (3:41) (Class 6) 3-Y-0+ **£2,730** (£806; £403) **Stalls** Low

Form RPR

6203 **1** **Starcross Maid**[15] 2777 4-9-1 50 .... MickyFenton 9 53
(J F Coupland) *chsd ldrs: led over 1f out: styd on u.p* **8/1**

4435 **2** ½ **Romil Star (GER)**[24] 2528 9-8-12 52 .... (v) PatrickDonaghy(7) 12 56
(K R Burke) *chsd ldrs: led over 8f out: hdd over 4f out: rdn over 1f out: styd on* **4/1**[1]

3032 **3** 1 **Iamback**[8] 3013 6-8-8 38 .... (t) RoryMoore(5) 10 49
(Miss D A McHale) *chsd ldrs: led over 4f out: rdn and hdd over 1f out: no ex nr fin* **7/1**[2]

0065 **4** 8 **Chookie Windsor**[3] 3161 3-8-0 53 .... EmmettStack(5) 4 42
(M S Saunders) *hld up: hdwy over 3f out: rdn and hung lft over 2f out: styd on same pce* **14/1**

0005 **5** 5 **Gravardlax**[8] 3013 5-9-3 30 .... BrianReilly 6 33
(Miss D A McHale) *s.i.s: hdwy over 4f out: rdn over 2f out: sn wknd* **40/1**

0434 **6** 7 **Citelle (IRE)**[20] 2633 3-8-2 54 .... (t) FrankieMcDonald 11 21
(Mrs P N Dutfield) *s.i.s: hdwy 8f out: wknd over 3f out* **4/1**[1]

4036 **7** 10 **Molly's Secret**[66] 1385 8-8-6 40 ow1 .... (p) RonanKeogh(7) 5 4
(Miss S J Wilton) *hld up: rdn 1/2-way: sn wknd* **14/1**

4002 **8** 6 **Tennessee Belle (IRE)**[7] 3051 4-8-5 32 .... KirstyMilczarek(7) 8 —
(C N Allen) *hld up: a bhd* **14/1**

9 1½ **Dechiper (IRE)**[619] 6431 4-9-1 .... DeclanMcGann(5) 7 —
(R Johnson) *chsd ldrs over 8f* **40/1**

060 **10** 17 **Muscari**[18] 2712 4-9-3 69 .... JimmyFortune 1 —
(A P Jarvis) *led: hdd over 8f out: rdn and wknd over 3f out* **4/1**[1]

4605 **11** 8 **Gawrosz (POL)**[34] 2245 7-9-4 41 .... DavidKinsella 3 —
(G J Smith) *prom: lost pl over 7f out: wknd over 5f out* **40/1**

0-06 **R** **Collect**[7] 3036 4-8-12 59 .... (b) TPQueally 2 —
(M H Tompkins) *ref to r* **15/2**[3]

2m 45.07s (2.98) **Going Correction** +0.225s/f (Slow)
WFA 3 from 4yo+ 13lb **12** Ran SP% **122.7**
Speed ratings (Par 101):99,98,98,92,89 84,78,74,73,61 56,—
CSF £41.07 TOTE £10.20: £3.10, £1.60, £1.40; EX 35.20 Trifecta £76.70 Pool £361.17, 3.34 winning units..Romil Star was claimed by M. Attwater for £7,000.

Owner J F Coupland **Bred** D M Beresford **Trained** Grimsby, Lincs

FOCUS
A moderate claimer in which nothing was able to make up ground from off the pace and the principals came centre to stands' side on reaching the home straight. The first three pulled well clear, but with those most favoured by the weights running so poorly the form looks very modest.
Muscari Official explanation: jockey said filly had no more to give; vet said filly suffered from heat stress
Gawrosz(POL) Official explanation: jockey said gelding lost its action

3261 BIG RACING WEEKEND MAIDEN STKS (DIV II) — 1m 3f (F)
4:15 (4:17) (Class 5) 3-Y-0+ **£2,590** (£770; £385; £192) **Stalls** Low

Form RPR

23 **1** **Hernando Royal**[20] 2646 3-9-0 .... MickyFenton 7 88+
(H Morrison) *chsd ldr 9f out: led over 2f out: styd on u.p* **5/2**[2]

3-6 **2** 6 **Born Wild (GER)**[22] 2580 3-8-9 .... NCallan 9 73
(Sir Michael Stoute) *led 10f out: rdn and hdd over 2f out: styd on same pce appr fnl f* **10/3**[3]

44 **3** 1½ **Kentucky Warbler (IRE)**[21] 2600 3-8-9 .... RobertHavlin 3 71
(H Morrison) *led 1f: chsd ldrs: rdn over 1f out: styd on same pce* **7/1**

4 8 **Burnt Oak (UAE)**[114] 4-9-12 .... TomEaves 8 63
(C W Fairhurst) *s.i.s: hdwy 7f out: rdn over 3f out: wknd over 2f out* **2/1**[1]

60 **5** 6 **Hill Billy Rock (IRE)**[23] 2542 3-9-0 .... PaulQuinn 10 54
(G A Swinbank) *hld up: a in rr* **16/1**

00P0 **6** 7 **Prophet Preacher (IRE)**[29] 2379 3-8-6 48 .... (v[1]) BenSwarbrick(3) 5 37
(M J Attwater) *prom 7f* **66/1**

0 **7** hd **Stockholder**[27] 2465 3-9-0 .... HayleyTurner 4 42
(C A Cyzer) *mid-div: rdn and wknd over 4f out* **28/1**

8 1½ **Gallileo Figaro (USA)** 3-8-6 ow2 .... StephenDonohoe(5) 1 37
(W M Brisbourne) *sn pushed along in rr: bhd fr 1/2-way* **20/1**

05 **9** 30 **Cortina**[24] 2526 3-8-9 .... TPQueally 6 —
(J Jay) *chsd ldrs to 1/2-way* **100/1**

0- **10** ½ **Royalties**[334] 4191 4-9-4 .... DeanCorby(3) 11 —
(M A Allen) *s.s: a in rr* **100/1**

11 17 **Westcourt Phoenix** 3-8-9 .... PaulMulrennan 2 —
(M W Easterby) *chsd ldrs 4f* **50/1**

2m 29.49s (0.59) **Going Correction** +0.225s/f (Slow)
WFA 3 from 4yo 12lb **11** Ran SP% **117.0**
Speed ratings (Par 103):106,101,100,94,90 85,85,84,62,61 49
CSF £10.72 TOTE £3.50: £1.10, £1.60, £1.80; EX 11.60 Trifecta £22.20 Pool £595.18, 19.01 winning units..

Owner A N Solomons **Bred** The White's Farmers **Trained** East Ilsley, Berks

FOCUS
Once again those that raced up with the pace were favoured and the race only concerned the front three over the last half-mile. Although the winning time was 1.82 seconds slower than the first division, it was still creditable for the type of race and the form looks sound.

3262 TAKE CONTROL WITH WBX.COM H'CAP — 7f (F)
4:50 (4:50) (Class 5) (0-70,70) 3-Y-0+ **£3,238** (£963; £481; £240) **Stalls** Low

Form RPR

2060 **1** **Shifty**[18] 2702 7-9-4 63 .... DanielTudhope(3) 7 74
(D Carroll) *s.i.s: hld up: hdwy over 2f out: led and edgd lft over 1f out: r.o* **7/1**[3]

5441 **2** ½ **Lincolneurocruiser**[6] 3089 4-9-0 63 .... RussellKennemore(7) 2 73
(Mrs N Macauley) *s.s: hld up: hdwy 1/2-way: led over 1f out: sn rdn and hdd: styd on* **9/2**[2]

1062 **3** 2 **Chickado (IRE)**[34] 2248 5-8-9 51 oh1 .... (p) RobertHavlin 4 56
(D Haydn Jones) *in rr: hdwy and hung lft over 1f out: nt rch ldrs* **9/1**

0500 **4** 2½ **Elrafa Mujahid**[11] 2936 4-9-4 60 .... (b) NCallan 12 59
(Ernst Oertel) *chsd ldrs: led over 2f out: rdn and hdd over 1f out: no ex* **8/1**

000 **5** 5 **Nan Jan**[42] 1993 4-9-6 62 .... (t) StephenCarson 5 48
(R Ingram) *sn outpcd: styd on ins fnl f: nrst fin* **16/1**

0540 **6** ½ **Apex**[29] 2384 5-9-11 67 .... KimTinkler 10 52
(N Tinkler) *sn pushed along and prom: rdn and wknd wl over 1f out* **10/1**

2213 **7** 4 **Sir Bond (IRE)**[71] 1257 5-9-7 63 .... TomEaves 9 38
(B Smart) *dwlt: hdwy over 5f out: wknd over 2f out* **10/3**[1]

0140 **8** 3 **Golden Square**[38] 2098 4-9-3 59 .... JimmyFortune 6 27
(A W Carroll) *chsd ldrs: rdn over 4f out: hung lft and wknd 2f out* **7/1**[3]

1201 **9** 4 **Exit Smiling**[42] 1996 4-10-0 70 .... MickyFenton 11 28
(P T Midgley) *chsd ldr: led over 4f out: rdn and hdd over 2f out: wknd over 1f out* **7/1**[3]

0000 **10** 5 **Warden Warren**[6] 3089 8-9-2 58 .... (p) BrianReilly 8 3
(Mrs C A Dunnett) *prom: lost pl whn swtchd wd 5f out: sn bhd* **20/1**

2-03 **11** 2½ **Our Mary (IRE)**[13] 2873 3-8-8 61 .... BenSwarbrick(3) 1 —
(Robert Gray) *led: hdd over 4f out: wknd 2f out* **25/1**

1m 32.17s (1.37) **Going Correction** +0.225s/f (Slow)
WFA 3 from 4yo+ 8lb **11** Ran SP% **123.5**
Speed ratings (Par 103):101,100,98,95,89 89,84,81,76,70 67
CSF £40.60 CT £296.80 TOTE £7.20: £3.30, £1.70, £2.10; EX 63.40 TRIFECTA Not won..

Owner W R B Racing 39 (wrbracing.com) **Bred** Biddestone Stud And Partner **Trained** Warthill, N Yorks

■ Stewards' Enquiry : Russell Kennemore two-day ban: using whip with excessive frequency (Jul 18-19)

FOCUS
A modest handicap, though competitive in its own right, and once again the field came down the middle. Unlike in the other races on the day, the front three all came from well off the pace which suggests the leaders went off too quick. The form looks sound rated through the placed horses.

3263 BOOK TICKETS ON-LINE H'CAP — 1m (F)
5:25 (5:26) (Class 6) (0-60,58) 3-Y-0+ **£2,730** (£806; £403) **Stalls** Low

Form RPR

3-56 **1** **California Laws**[15] 2792 4-9-1 52 .... BenSwarbrick(3) 13 72+
(T D Barron) *trckd ldrs: led 2f out: sn rdn clr* **4/1**[1]

6250 **2** 5 **Gem Bien (USA)**[4] 3158 8-9-2 50 .... (b) PaulQuinn 7 55
(D W Chapman) *chsd ldrs: outpcd 2f out: swtchd rt over 1f out: styd on: no ch w wnr* **22/1**

1306 **3** 5 **Tacid**[34] 2248 4-9-0 48 .... RobertHavlin 5 42
(Dr J D Scargill) *broke wl: sn lost pl and swtchd wd: hdwy over 2f out: wknd 2f out* **9/1**

-003 **4** shd **Teide Lady**[27] 2466 3-9-0 57 .... FrancisFerris 14 51
(Rae Guest) *hld up in tch: rdn over 2f out: edgd lft and wknd over 1f out* **15/2**[3]

0501 **5** nk **Dispol Peto**[37] 2137 6-9-1 54 .... (p) DeclanMcGann(5) 10 47
(R Johnson) *chsd ldrs: ev ch 3f out: rdn and wknd over 1f out* **5/1**[2]

1003 **6** 1¼ **Monte Mayor Junior**[71] 1259 3-9-1 58 .... (v) FrankieMcDonald 1 48
(D Haydn Jones) *hld up in tch: rdn over 2f out: wknd over 1f out* **20/1**

1524 **7** 1½ **Legal Lover (IRE)**[34] 2245 4-8-9 50 .... RussellKennemore(7) 8 37
(R Hollinshead) *led: rdn and hdd 2f out: sn wknd* **15/2**[3]

6050 **8** 1 **Simply St Lucia**[39] 443 4-9-6 54 .... JimmyFortune 9 39
(J R Weymes) *chsd ldrs over 5f* **8/1**

4500 **9** 1 **Boogie Magic**[4] 3153 6-8-12 46 .... (p) BrianReilly 12 29
(T Keddy) *sn outpcd* **20/1**

-600 **10** 5 **Inchloss (IRE)**[37] 2137 5-9-4 52 .... PaulEddery 11 24
(C N Kellett) *sn pushed along in rr: n.d* **50/1**

60-2 **11** 4 **Broughton Buzzer**[39] 2070 5-8-10 49 .... StephenDonohoe(5) 6 12
(A G Newcombe) *chsd ldrs: rdn and lost pl over 4f out: wknd wl over 2f out* **9/1**

0443 **12** 6 **Noorain**[4] 3158 4-8-9 48 ow1 .... (t) DerekNolan(5) 2 —
(Stef Liddiard) *w ldr: ev ch 3f out: sn rdn and wknd* **8/1**

-200 **13** 12 **Hand Of Destiny (USA)**[8] 3030 3-9-1 58 .... (bt) StephenCarson 4 —
(N P Littmoden) *a in rr* **33/1**

0350 **14** 20 **Zando**[7] 3056 4-9-7 55 .... HayleyTurner 3 —
(E G Bevan) *sn outpcd* **20/1**

1m 46.26s (1.66) **Going Correction** +0.225s/f (Slow)
WFA 3 from 4yo+ 9lb **14** Ran SP% **126.0**
Speed ratings (Par 101):100,95,90,89,89 88,86,85,84,79 75,69,57,37
CSF £103.90 CT £796.88 TOTE £5.10: £2.00, £6.10, £4.00; EX 63.50 TRIFECTA Not won. Place 6 £79.51, Place 5 £23.02..

Owner Rupert Bear Racing **Bred** P Balding **Trained** Maunby, N Yorks

FOCUS
A decent pace early with several battling for the early lead, but a one-horse race in the end. The form looks sound through those behind the winner, who can win again.
Zando Official explanation: jockey said gelding did not face the kickback

T/Plt: £34.10 to a £1 stake. Pool: £42,441.75. 907.75 winning tickets. T/Qpdt: £4.70 to a £1 stake. Pool: £3,516.60. 548.00 winning tickets. CR

3110 WARWICK (L-H)

Friday, July 7

OFFICIAL GOING: Good (good to soft in places)

Wind: Moderrate behind Weather: Fine

3264 TITAN 02 MOBILITY (S) STKS — 1m 2f 188y

2:20 (2:22) (Class 6) 3-Y-O £2,388 (£705; £352) Stalls Low

Form RPR

-455 1 **Joy In The Guild (IRE)**[9] [2968] 3-8-8 43 FergusSweeney 8 51
(W S Kittow) *hld up and bhd: rdn and hdwy over 2f out: edgd lft and led 1f out: edgd lft fnl f: r.o* 11/2[3]

0050 2 2 **Simplified**[9] [2968] 3-8-8 48 JimmyQuinn 2 47
(J Pearce) *hld up towards rr: rdn and hdwy 2f out: r.o ins fnl f: wnt 2nd nr fin* 10/1

0004 3 ¾ **Flashing Floozie**[5] [3115] 3-8-8 44 RichardThomas 9 46
(M F Harris) *chsd ldr: rdn 3f out: led over 1f out: sn hdd: nt qckn* 5/1[2]

0-50 4 2½ **Beauchamp United**[67] [1350] 3-8-13 67 NickyMackay 10 46
(G A Butler) *hld up in mid-div: rdn 3f out: hdwy fnl f: nt rch ldrs* 6/1

54 5 nk **Anasena**[12] [2895] 3-8-8 EddieAhern 11 41
(G G Margarson) *a.p: outpcd over 5f out: rdn whn edgd rt 2f out: no real prog* 5/2[1]

U05 6 shd **Lucy Babe**[25] [2498] 3-8-3 LiamJones(5) 1 41
(G Prodromou) *swvd lft sn after s: in rr: rdn over 2f out: swtchd lft ins fnl f: styd on: nrst fin* 9/1

006 7 1 **Fentastic**[6] [3074] 3-8-8 FrancisFerris 4 39
(Rae Guest) *hld up towards rr: rdn and hdwy 3f out: nt clr run 2f out: edgd lft and rdr dropped whip over 1f out: no imp* 33/1

-003 8 2½ **Kirkstall Lane**[22] [2568] 3-8-13 44 (b) DaneO'Neill 5 39
(R Hannon) *prom: led over 3f out: rdn whn edgd lft and hdd over 1f out: sn wknd* 9/1

6040 9 11 **Sahara Style**[27] [2463] 3-8-13 37 (b) LPKeniry 3 20
(R Hollinshead) *led: hdd over 3f out: rdn over 2f out: wknd wl over 1f out* 16/1

00-0 10 45 **Katejackiera (IRE)**[38] [2107] 3-8-8 36 DavidAllan 6 —
(W M Brisbourne) *hld up in mid-div: rdn over 7f out: sn struggling: t.o fnl 3f* 80/1

0-05 11 15 **Tay Bridge (IRE)**[38] [2101] 3-8-13 45 DarryllHolland 7 —
(G F Bridgwater) *prom tl wknd over 5f out: t.o* 33/1

2m 21.89s (2.49) **Going Correction** +0.175s/f (Good) 11 Ran SP% **117.0**
Speed ratings (Par 98):97,95,95,93,92 92,92,90,82,49 38
CSF £58.34 TOTE £6.40: £2.00, £3.40, £1.70; EX 100.80.There was no bid for the winner.
Owner The Racing Guild **Bred** Trickledown Stud D Magnier And P J Hernon **Trained** Blackborough, Devon

FOCUS
A modest seller full of horses down in class and poor form.
Anasena Official explanation: jockey said filly did not handle the loose ground
Tay Bridge(IRE) Official explanation: jockey said gelding hung left and had a breathing problem

3265 BOTT LTD NOVICE AUCTION STKS — 7f 26y

2:55 (2:56) (Class 5) 2-Y-O £3,238 (£963; £481; £240) Stalls Low

Form RPR

521 1 **Sans Reward (IRE)**[24] [2530] 2-8-10 EddieAhern 2 77+
(B J Meehan) *led 1f: a.p: rdn to ld over 1f out: edgd lft ins fnl f: eased cl home* 8/13[1]

01 2 1½ **Jane Of Arc (FR)**[17] [2733] 2-8-10 DavidAllan 6 70
(T D Easterby) *led after 1f: rdn whn edgd lft and hdd over 1f out: nt qckn ins fnl f* 3/1[2]

6 3 nk **Down The Brick (IRE)**[77] [1107] 2-8-9 DaneO'Neill 3 69
(B R Millman) *hld up in tch: rdn and outpcd wl over 1f out: kpt on towards fin* 25/1

5331 4 hd **Ten Dollars More (IRE)**[37] [2139] 2-8-11 DarryllHolland 5 70
(J A Osborne) *s.i.s: sn chsng ldr: rdn 2f out: kpt on same pce fnl f* 6/1[3]

03 5 8 **Tres Hombres**[8] [3005] 2-8-9 SteveDrowne 1 48
(Tom Dascombe) *hld up in rr: outpcd fnl 2f* 25/1

5 6 3½ **Lucknam (IRE)**[46] [1876] 2-8-6 ow2 LPKeniry 4 36
(M Meade) *hld up in tch: wknd and edgd lft over 1f out* 66/1

1m 27.48s (2.48) **Going Correction** +0.175s/f (Good) 6 Ran SP% **110.4**
Speed ratings (Par 94):92,90,89,89,80 76
CSF £2.55 TOTE £1.70: £1.10, £1.90; EX 3.20.
Owner Sandy Briddon & Edward Butler **Bred** Rathbarry Stud **Trained** Manton, Wilts

FOCUS
Sans Reward had the form in the book and readily justified being an odds-on favourite and sets the standard.

NOTEBOOK
Sans Reward(IRE) continues to progress and duly appreciated the extra furlong. Scoring with a fair bit in hand, she is now likely to step up in class. (op 4-5)
Jane Of Arc(FR) had more to do this time but underlined the fact that she gets this trip well and was by no means disgraced against an improving sort. (op 2-1 tchd 4-1)
Down The Brick(IRE) ◆ had obviously learnt a lot when running over an inadequate five furlongs at Kempton in April. Bred for this sort of trip, there are races to be won with him. (op 28-1 tchd 33-1)
Ten Dollars More(IRE), not inconvenienced by the extra furlong, had more on his plate than when winning on the Fibresand at Southwell. (op 9-1 tchd 5-1)

3266 SYSTIMAX SOLUTIONS MAIDEN STKS — 7f 26y

3:30 (3:31) (Class 5) 3-4-Y-O £3,238 (£963; £481; £240) Stalls Low

Form RPR

0335 1 **Southport Star (IRE)**[14] [2823] 3-9-3 74 OscarUrbina 10 78+
(J R Fanshawe) *hld up and bhd: hdwy on outside and hung lft over 1f out: rdn to ld ins fnl f: r.o* 9/4[1]

420- 2 ¾ **Grand Entrance (IRE)**[259] [6010] 3-9-3 76 SteveDrowne 2 76
(C R Egerton) *a.p: rdn over 1f out: ev ch ins fnl f: nt qckn* 5/1[3]

3656 3 nk **Pab Special (IRE)**[36] [2160] 3-9-3 68 PatCosgrave 11 75
(K R Burke) *stdd s: hld up and bhd: rdn and hdwy over 1f out: nt qckn ins fnl f* 25/1

032- 4 nk **Call Me Waki (USA)**[306] [4974] 3-8-12 76 DarryllHolland 9 70
(A M Balding) *led 3f: chsd ldr: rdn to ld over 1f out: hdd and no ex ins fnl f* 4/1[2]

04 5 1½ **Dance Spirit (IRE)**[21] [2605] 3-9-3 MichaelTebbutt 6 71
(B J Meehan) *hld up in mid-div: rdn and hdwy over 1f out: one pce fnl f* 7/1

60 6 5 **Princess Danah (IRE)**[28] [2406] 3-8-12 EddieAhern 8 53
(W R Swinburn) *s.i.s: hld up in rr: rdn 2f out: late hdwy: nvr nrr* 18/1

6 7 1¾ **Tropical Climate (USA)**[79] [1088] 3-8-12 TonyCulhane 4 58+
(B W Hills) *prom: led 4f out: rdn and hdd over 1f out: eased whn btn ins fnl f: sddle slipped: b.b.v* 5/1[3]

8 shd **Kims Rose (IRE)** 3-8-5 TolleyDean(7) 3 49
(R A Harris) *s.i.s: hld up and bhd: stdy hdwy on ins 3f out: sn rdn: wknd over 1f out* 25/1

-0P5 9 6 **Look Here's May**[13] [2881] 4-9-6 40 LPKeniry 7 34
(R Hollinshead) *hld up in tch: rdn 2f out: wknd qckly* 100/1

0 10 5 **Cosmic Girl**[9] [2985] 3-8-12 DaneO'Neill 1 21
(H Candy) *prom: rdn 2f out: wknd qckly* 22/1

0-00 11 1¼ **Lady Luisa (IRE)**[7] [3032] 4-8-13 38 (t) AnnStokell(7) 5 18
(Miss A Stokell) *s.i.s: hld up: bhd fnl 3f* 100/1

1m 24.73s (-0.27) **Going Correction** +0.175s/f (Good)
WFA 3 from 4yo 8lb 11 Ran SP% **115.9**
Speed ratings (Par 103):108,107,106,106,104 99,97,96,90,84 82
CSF £12.67 TOTE £3.70: £1.50, £2.30, £5.40; EX 19.80.
Owner The Southport Star Partnership **Bred** Swordlestown Stud **Trained** Newmarket, Suffolk

FOCUS
A moderate maiden that has been rated slightly negatively with the third limiting the form.
Tropical Climate(USA) Official explanation: jockey said saddle slipped and filly bled from the nose
Look Here's May Official explanation: jockey said filly lost its action

3267 SYSTIMAX GIGASPEED XL FILLIES' H'CAP — 5f 110y

4:05 (4:06) (Class 5) (0-70,64) 3-Y-O+ £3,238 (£963; £481; £240) Stalls Low

Form RPR

6003 1 **Safranine (IRE)**[3] [3172] 9-8-5 50 AnnStokell(7) 11 61
(Miss A Stokell) *hld up in mid-div: hdwy over 1f out: rdn to ld wl ins fnl f: r.o wl* 16/1

0031 2 1½ **Ruby's Dream**[8] [3004] 4-9-3 55 5ex (p) SteveDrowne 4 61
(J M Bradley) *hld up in mid-div: rdn over 2f out: hdwy whn swtchd rt jst over 1f out: r.o to take 2nd nr fin* 11/2[2]

2530 3 nk **My Girl Pearl (IRE)**[6] [3094] 6-8-11 49 NickyMackay 10 54
(M S Saunders) *s.i.s: hld up and bhd: rdn over 1f out: gd hdwy on outside fnl f: fin wl* 14/1

0-31 4 shd **Aahgowangowan (IRE)**[3] [3172] 7-9-8 60 (t) PhillipMakin 6 65
(M Dods) *led: rdn and edgd lft jst over 1f out: hdd and no ex wl ins fnl f* 9/4[1]

0014 5 hd **Blakeshall Quest**[38] [2096] 6-9-0 52 (b) DaneO'Neill 12 56
(R Brotherton) *a.p: rdn over 2f out: no ex towards fin* 22/1

-000 6 ½ **Zimbali**[10] [2949] 4-8-9 47 JosedeSouza 1 49
(J M Bradley) *chsd ldrs on ins: rdn 2f out: one pce fnl f* 28/1

0220 7 shd **Cerulean Rose**[10] [2962] 7-9-10 62 DarryllHolland 5 64
(A W Carroll) *hld up and bhd: rdn 3f out: hdwy over 1f out: kpt on towards fin* 15/2[3]

0000 8 nk **Extremely Rare (IRE)**[27] [2462] 5-9-10 62 TonyCulhane 13 63
(M S Saunders) *mid-div: effrt on outside over 1f out: one pce fnl f* 12/1

-603 9 ¾ **The Lady Caster**[18] [2704] 3-8-5 52 (v) NelsonDeSouza(3) 16 51
(R M Beckett) *wnt rt s: sn prom: rdn 2f out: edgd lft 1f out: wknd ins fnl f* 16/1

0204 10 ½ **Sahara Silk (IRE)**[27] [2462] 5-9-9 64 (v) PatrickMathers(3) 2 61
(D Shaw) *bhd: rdn and hdwy on ins over 1f out: no further prog fnl f* 12/1

0534 11 hd **Divine White**[18] [2704] 3-8-9 53 EddieAhern 9 49
(Mrs A J Perrett) *chsd ldrs: rdn over 2f out: wknd over 1f out* 17/2

00/0 12 ½ **Royal Supremacy (IRE)**[25] [2494] 5-8-7 45 oh6 RichardThomas 3 40
(J M Bradley) *chsd ldrs: rdn over 1f out: sn edgd lft: wknd ins fnl f* 50/1

/00- 13 1 **Speed Of Sound**[392] [2451] 4-9-12 64 LPKeniry 8 55
(A M Balding) *hld up in mid-div: wknd over 1f out* 40/1

1-60 14 ½ **Largs**[169] [146] 6-8-5 46 (p) JasonEdmunds(3) 15 36
(J Balding) *wnt rt s: a bhd* 25/1

5560 15 1½ **Attitude Annie**[91] [902] 3-8-10 54 JimmyQuinn 14 39
(S Dow) *a bhd* 33/1

0/00 16 shd **Kool Acclaim**[13] [2864] 5-9-10 62 J-PGuillambert 7 46
(S C Williams) *s.i.s: a bhd* 16/1

65.89 secs (1.58) **Going Correction** +0.10s/f (Good)
WFA 3 from 4yo+ 5lb 16 Ran SP% **127.1**
Speed ratings (Par 100):101,99,98,98,98 97,97,97,96,95 95,94,93,92,90 90
CSF £99.29 CT £1355.15 TOTE £15.20: £3.10, £1.80, £2.70, £1.30; EX 112.30.
Owner Ms Caron Stokell **Bred** Mrs A Whitehead **Trained** Brompton-on-Swale, N Yorks

FOCUS
a moderate contest and although the pack were closing in the final furlong not many really looked like winning. The form is solid but modest.
Attitude Annie Official explanation: trainer said filly was found to be in season

3268 SYSTIMAX IPATCH H'CAP — 5f

4:40 (4:40) (Class 4) (0-80,76) 3-Y-O £6,477 (£1,927; £963; £481) Stalls Low

Form RPR

3431 1 **Toy Top (USA)**[7] [3042] 3-9-4 73 6ex (b) PhillipMakin 4 80
(M Dods) *mde all: rdn over 1f out: r.o wl* 7/2[3]

1415 2 1¼ **Jakeini (IRE)**[7] [3042] 3-9-2 71 DaneO'Neill 1 73
(E S McMahon) *chsd wnr: rdn over 1f out: nt qckn ins fnl f* 9/4[1]

11-3 3 1¾ **Queen Cobra (IRE)**[46] [1900] 3-9-7 76 SteveDrowne 8 72
(H Morrison) *a.p: rdn over 1f out: one pce fnl f* 4/1

0040 4 1 **Supercast (IRE)**[31] [2329] 3-9-6 75 (b[1]) EddieAhern 5 67
(J S Moore) *hld up in tch: rdn over 1f out: edgd lft ent fnl f: one pce* 12/1

1353 5 3 **Lucayos**[11] [2931] 3-9-6 75 (b) GeorgeBaker 3 56
(Mrs H Sweeting) *s.i.s: hung lft thrght: a bhd* 3/1[2]

-000 6 ¾ **Smart Cassie**[14] [2826] 3-8-12 70 PatrickMathers(3) 6 49
(D Shaw) *s.i.s: rdn 2f out: a bhd* 28/1

59.36 secs (-0.84) **Going Correction** +0.10s/f (Good) 6 Ran SP% **109.1**
Speed ratings (Par 102):104,102,99,97,92 91
CSF £11.11 CT £27.71 TOTE £3.80: £2.00, £1.50; EX 8.90.
Owner D Vic Roper **Bred** L Kengye **Trained** Denton, Co Durham

FOCUS
A tightly-knit little handicap that could have been rated a little higher.

3269 SYSTIMAX GIGASPEED X10D H'CAP — 2m 39y

5:15 (5:15) (Class 5) (0-75,79) 3-Y-O+ £4,533 (£1,348; £674; £336) Stalls Low

Form RPR

6441 1 **Raslan**[5] [3114] 3-9-9 79 6ex J-PGuillambert 1 91+
(M Johnston) *led 1f: a.p: led 3f out: rdn and wandered over 1f out: sn clr: eased towards fin* 5/4[1]

-004 2 2½ **Trials 'n Tribs**[22] [2577] 4-8-9 46 oh4 TonyCulhane 9 51
(C A Cyzer) *hld up and bhd: rdn and hdwy over 2f out: styd on to take 2nd ins fnl f: no ch w wnr* 14/1

3603 **3** ½ **Ritsi**[21] 2607 3-9-0 **70**....................(t) EddieAhern 6 74
(Mrs A J Perrett) *hld up: hdwy over 6f out: ev ch 2f out: sn rdn: one pce* **11/4**[2]

53/0 **4** 1¾ **Schooner (GER)**[41] 2035 6-9-12 **63**.................... GeorgeBaker 3 65
(Lady Herries) *hld up: hdwy 4f out: sn rdn: edgd lft 1f out: one pce* **11/1**

3044 **5** ½ **Openide**[12] 2894 5-10-0 **65**.................... JimmyQuinn 7 67
(B W Duke) *led after 1f: hdd over 6f out: rdn over 5f out: lost pl over 3f out: styd on fnl f* **10/1**[3]

-460 **6** 4 **Bobsleigh**[34] 2219 7-9-5 **56**.................... DaneO'Neill 5 53
(H S Howe) *hld up and bhd: rdn 3f out: no rspnse* **12/1**

6000 **7** 2½ **Shingle Street (IRE)**[34] 2219 4-9-6 **57**....................(b) NickyMackay 8 51
(I A Wood) *prom: led over 6f out: rdn and hdd 3f out: wknd over 1f out* **16/1**

0-50 **8** 12 **Kaluana Court**[86] 975 10-8-11 **48**.................... RichardThomas 2 28
(A W Carroll) *hld up in tch: rdn over 3f out: sn wknd* **20/1**

3m 35.94s (3.24) **Going Correction** +0.175s/f (Good)
WFA 3 from 4yo+ 19lb **8** Ran SP% **113.5**
Speed ratings (Par 103):98,96,96,95,95 93,92,86
CSF £20.86 CT £42.35 TOTE £2.10: £1.50, £2.20, £1.30; EX 16.10.
Owner Jumeirah Racing **Bred** Darley **Trained** Middleham Moor, N Yorks

FOCUS
A modest winning time for a race like this but the winner is value for more than the winning margin.

3270 SYSTIMAX CUSTOMER DAY AT WARWICK APPRENTICE H'CAP 1m 4f 134y
5:45 (5:45) (Class 6) (0-60,60) 3-Y-0+ **£2,730** (£806; £403) **Stalls** Low

Form RPR

3254 **1** **Acuzio**[2] 3192 5-9-5 **51**....................(p) PJBenson 6 60
(W M Brisbourne) *hld up towards rr: hdwy on ins 3f out: rdn and hung lft over 1f out: r.o to ld nr fin* **4/1**[1]

1430 **2** nk **Figaro's Quest (IRE)**[13] 2869 4-9-10 **56**....................(b) RobbieMills 11 65
(P F I Cole) *chsd ldr: led over 5f out: clr over 1f out: rdn and ct nr fin* **11/2**[2]

044- **3** 1¼ **Kernel Dowery (IRE)**[305] 5008 6-8-13 **48**.................... JamieHamblett(3) 12 55
(W R Swinburn) *hld up in mid-div: hdwy 2f out: sn rdn: kpt on ins fnl f* **7/1**

0640 **4** 2½ **Eamon An Chnoic (IRE)**[22] 2577 5-8-13 **50**.................... SophieDoyle(5) 7 53
(B W Duke) *chsd ldrs: one pce fnl 2f* **20/1**

0026 **5** ½ **Ganymede**[12] 2902 5-9-8 **59**....................(p) WilliamCarson(5) 10 61
(J G M O'Shea) *hld up towards rr: hdwy on ins 2f out: sn rdn: one pce fnl f* **10/1**

/000 **6** ¾ **Garston Star**[13] 2871 5-8-9 **49**.................... JosephWalsh(8) 9 50
(J S Moore) *led: hdd over 5f out: chsd ldr: rdn over 2f out: wknd fnl f* **16/1**

015 **7** 1¾ **Boulevin (IRE)**[30] 2360 6-8-12 **49**.................... JamesRogers(5) 2 48
(R J Price) *s.s: hld up and bhd: hdwy on ins 2f out: rdn over 1f out: nvr trbld ldrs* **13/2**[3]

0004 **8** hd **Summer Bounty**[21] 2601 10-9-11 **60**.................... LukeMorris(3) 3 58
(F Jordan) *hld up: rdn and hdwy 3f out: edgd lft ins fnl f: no imp* **13/2**[3]

51-0 **9** 3 **Picot De Say**[17] 379 4-9-3 **56**.................... PaulPickard(7) 5 50
(C Roberts) *s.i.s: hld up and bhd: sme hdwy on outside over 6f out: wknd over 2f out* **14/1**

0000 **10** 1¾ **Mustakhlas (USA)**[15] 2788 5-8-4 **44** oh2.................... SoniaEaton(8) 4 36
(B P J Baugh) *a bhd* **14/1**

6500 **11** ½ **Pitsi Kahtoh**[1] 3232 4-8-7 **44** oh8.................... ChrisHough(5) 1 35
(P W Hiatt) *chsd ldrs: rdn over 2f out: wknd wl over 1f out* **28/1**

-020 **12** 2½ **Rafelite**[16] 2751 4-9-6 **57**.................... DeanHeslop(5) 8 44
(Lady Herries) *bhd fnl 3f* **12/1**

2m 44.69s (1.09) **Going Correction** +0.175s/f (Good) **12** Ran SP% **118.8**
Speed ratings (Par 101):103,102,102,100,100 99,98,98,96,95 95,93
CSF £25.04 CT £151.71 TOTE £4.50: £1.80, £1.90, £2.70; EX 25.60 Place 6 £13.84, Place 5 £4.07.
Owner Derek Hartland and Peter Gradwell **Bred** D W Hartland **Trained** Great Ness, Shropshire

FOCUS
A weak handicap but the form looks reliable with the runner-up to form.
T/Plt: £23.00 to a £1 stake. Pool: £37,296.70. 1,179.20 winning tickets. T/Qpdt: £4.80 to a £1 stake. Pool: £2,790.70. 430.00 winning tickets. KH

3271 - 3278a (Foreign Racing) - See Raceform Interactive

3239 BEVERLEY (R-H)
Saturday, July 8

OFFICIAL GOING: Firm
7mm water was put on the final four furlongs since the previous night. The ground was described as 'very firm'.
Wind: Light, half-against Weather: Fine but overcast

3279 AWARD WINNING COACHMAN CARAVANS (S) STKS 7f 100y
2:15 (2:16) (Class 5) 2-Y-O **£3,562** (£1,059; £529; £264) **Stalls** High

Form RPR

4 **1** **The Slider**[8] 3054 2-8-1 ow2.................... KevinGhunowa(7) 4 54
(P A Blockley) *led 1f: t.k.h: led over 5f out: hld on towards fin* **5/1**[3]

3202 **2** ½ **Lansdown**[14] 2870 2-8-3 .... BenSwarbrick(3) 3 51
(Robert Gray) *chsd ldrs: effrt over 2f out: kpt on ins last: no ex cl home* **3/1**[1]

025 **3** nk **Tumble Jill (IRE)**[14] 2870 2-8-3 .... EdwardCreighton(3) 6 50
(J S Moore) *chsd ldrs: effrt over 2f out: wnt rt 1f out: kpt on same pce* **7/2**[2]

0063 **4** 2½ **Moist**[8] 3054 2-8-6 .... DO'Donohoe 5 44
(N A Callaghan) *chsd ldrs: hung lft and lost pl bnd over 5f out: hdwy over 2f out: wknd fnl f* **3/1**[1]

04 **5** 1¼ **Wakeys Wizzard**[16] 2778 2-8-6 .... TomEaves 7 41
(M E Sowersby) *restless in stalls: sn trcking ldrs: hung lft over 1f out: sn wknd* **11/1**

056 **6** 1¾ **Compton Verney**[14] 2870 2-8-11 ....(b[1]) PaulMulrennan 2 42
(M W Easterby) *crossed over and led after 1f: hdd over 5f out: wandered and wknd over 1f out* **8/1**

0 **7** 15 **Alevic (IRE)**[29] 2416 2-8-6 .... DuranFentiman(5) 1 7
(J R Norton) *chsd ldrs: lost pl over 3f out: sn bhd* **33/1**

1m 36.9s (2.59) **Going Correction** -0.075s/f (Good) **7** Ran SP% **111.3**
Speed ratings (Par 94):82,81,81,78,76 74,57
CSF £19.22 TOTE £4.30: £2.00, £1.90; EX 15.80.There was no bid for the winner.
Owner Market Avenue Racing Club Ltd **Bred** Stanley J Sharp **Trained** Lambourn, Berks

FOCUS
No one wanted to make the running resulting in a moderate time, even for a low-grade juvenile seller and the form is just average for the grade.

NOTEBOOK
The Slider, noisy in the paddock, regained the advantage leaving the back stretch and in the end did just enough. (op 4-1)
Lansdown, lightly-made, made hard work of it but was closing the gap all the way to the line. (op 5-2 tchd 10-3)
Tumble Jill(IRE) put a poor effort at Redcar last time behind her and in the end was only just found lacking. (op 4-1)
Moist failed to handle the bend leaving the back stretch. Back on the heels of the first three coming to the final furlong, she did not see it out anywhere near as well as the first three. (op 7-2 tchd 11-4)
Wakeys Wizzard played up in the stalls. She was going nowhere when coming off a straight line coming to the final furlong. (op 16-1)
Compton Verney, on his toes in the paddock, wore blinkers for the first time. He overcame his outside draw but never looked happy in the headgear and wanted to do nothing but hang left.
Official explanation: jockey said colt would not face the blinkers and hung left round bottom bend (op 11-1)

3280 GO RACING AT RIPON ON MONDAY NOVICE STKS 7f 100y
2:45 (2:45) (Class 4) 2-Y-O **£5,181** (£1,541; £770; £384) **Stalls** High

Form RPR

1 **1** **Champery (USA)**[7] 3080 2-9-5 .... RoystonFfrench 3 88+
(M Johnston) *mde all: shkn up 3f out: styd on strly* **2/9**[1]

6 **2** 3 **Billy Dane (IRE)**[12] 2930 2-8-12 .... TPQueally 4 74+
(B J Meehan) *hld up last but in tch: effrt 3f out: swtchd outside over 1f out: r.o to take 2nd ins last: no ch w wnr* **10/1**[3]

3 2½ **Pennyrock (IRE)** 2-8-8 .... DO'Donohoe 2 64
(K A Ryan) *sn trcking ldr: shkn up over 4f out: drvn 3f out: wknd ins last* **8/1**[2]

10 **4** 3½ **Love In May (IRE)**[81] 1066 2-9-0 .... TonyCulhane 1 62
(J S Moore) *trckd ldrs on outer: t.k.h: effrt over 3f out: wknd fnl f: eased* **16/1**

1m 34.02s (-0.29) **Going Correction** -0.075s/f (Good) **4** Ran SP% **107.9**
Speed ratings (Par 96):98,94,91,87
CSF £3.14 TOTE £1.30; EX 3.00.
Owner Jumeirah Racing **Bred** Darley **Trained** Middleham Moor, N Yorks

FOCUS
The winner was given his own way in front and was never threatened at any stage and can be expected to rate higher.

NOTEBOOK
Champery(USA) ◆ ambled round in front and strode up the final hill with real purpose. A grand type, he can only get better. (op 1-4 tchd 2-7 tchd 1-3 in a place)
Billy Dane(IRE), a keen type, was dropped out in last. His rider seemed to take an age to ask him for a real effort but when switched outside he really picked up to finish clear second best. He may well be being prepared for a nursery campaign with one more day trip to come. (op 7-1)
Pennyrock(IRE), an April foal, is up in the air and narrow. He tended to be on and off the bridle before becoming leg-weary and losing second spot inside the last. This will have taught him a fair bit. (op 12-1 tchd 13-2)
Love In May(IRE), absent for 11 weeks, again tended to hang left and in the end the extended seven proved way beyond her. (op 14-1)

3281 COACHMAN CARAVANS QUALITY H'CAP 5f
3:20 (3:20) (Class 3) (0-90,85) 3-Y-O+ **£11,658** (£3,468; £1,733; £865) **Stalls** High

Form RPR

6320 **1** **Oranmore Castle (IRE)**[14] 2864 4-9-4 **75**....................(t) RoystonFfrench 7 86
(B W Hills) *chsd ldrs: styd on to ld ins last: hld on wl* **11/2**[3]

6025 **2** ½ **Pawan (IRE)**[11] 2946 6-8-7 **71**....................(b) AnnStokell(7) 9 80
(Miss A Stokell) *s.i.s: hdwy over 2f out: styd on wl ins last: jst hld* **14/1**

0603 **3** ¾ **Caribbean Coral**[15] 2830 7-9-6 **80**....................(p) DNolan(3) 8 86
(J J Quinn) *chsd ldrs on inner: n.m.r 2f out: swtchd ins 1f out: kpt on same pce last 100yds* **7/1**

4021 **4** nk **Bo McGinty (IRE)**[11] 2946 5-10-0 **85**....................(b) TonyHamilton 10 90
(R A Fahey) *chsd ldrs: hrd rdn and hung rt over 1f out: kpt on same pce* **11/4**[1]

2061 **5** nk **Harry Up**[7] 3097 5-9-4 **82**.................... NSLawes(7) 12 86
(K A Ryan) *led tl hdd and no ex ins last* **5/1**[2]

0-22 **6** 1½ **Lake Garda**[18] 2732 5-9-5 **76**.................... DO'Donohoe 3 75+
(K A Ryan) *chsd ldrs: styd on same pce appr fnl f* **8/1**

3500 **7** ½ **Trojan Flight**[8] 3041 5-9-2 **73**.................... TonyCulhane 2 70+
(D W Chapman) *sn outpcd and bhd: hdwy on inner and n.m.r 2f out: nvr rchd ldrs* **16/1**

0532 **8** 1¾ **Canadian Danehill (IRE)**[9] 3004 4-8-7 **69**.................... GregFairley(5) 5 60
(R M H Cowell) *s.i.s: kpt on fnl 2f: nvr a threat* **10/1**

3560 **9** nk **Brigadore**[10] 2981 7-8-12 **69**.................... TPQueally 4 59
(J G Given) *slowly away: bhd tl kpt on fnl 2f: nvr on terms* **16/1**

0342 **10** ¾ **Ptarmigan Ridge**[14] 2852 10-8-11 **73**.................... MarkLawson(5) 1 60
(Miss L A Perratt) *a in rr* **20/1**

1050 **11** 4 **Wicked Uncle**[11] 2946 7-9-6 **77**....................(v) PaulMulrennan 11 49
(S Gollings) *chsd ldrs: lost pl appr fnl f: sn bhd* **25/1**

62.53 secs (-1.47) **Going Correction** -0.075s/f (Good) **11** Ran SP% **118.5**
Speed ratings (Par 107):108,107,106,105,105 102,101,99,98,97 90
CSF £80.48 CT £551.08 TOTE £7.10: £2.50, £2.60, £2.30; EX 104.00.
Owner Sangster Family, Cavendish Inv, P Savill **Bred** Gigginstown House Stud **Trained** Lambourn, Berks

FOCUS
High numbers as usual held sway. The form looks solid, rated through the first two.

NOTEBOOK
Oranmore Castle(IRE), dropping back to five, was hunted along. He really stretched out when asked a question and in the end did just enough to record career victory number two. (op 7-1 tchd 5-1)
Pawan(IRE) threw away his high draw with a sluggish start. Making ground on the outer at halfway, he really found his stride inside the last and in the end was just held at bay. His stable has struck a purple patch. (op 12-1)
Caribbean Coral, 16lb below his last success two years ago, had the cheekpieces back on. He had little luck and his long losing run must surely end sooner rather than later. (op 6-1 tchd 11-2)
Bo McGinty(IRE), 6lb higher, had the leader in his sights but he persisted in hanging right and this was not one his better days. Official explanation: jockey said gelding hung right throughout (op 10-3 tchd 7-2)
Harry Up, without a win on turf for three years, had the plum draw and looked in charge until suddenly being overwhelmed inside the last. (op 9-2)
Lake Garda was always struggling to overcome his outside draw. (op 11-1)
Trojan Flight, drawn one from the outside, made his effort against the far rail and deserves credit for this. (op 20-1)

3282 BRANTINGHAM H'CAP 1m 100y
3:55 (3:55) (Class 4) (0-80,78) 3-Y-O **£7,124** (£2,119; £1,059; £529) **Stalls** High

Form RPR

6023 **1** **Nelsons Column (IRE)**[9] 3007 3-9-0 **71**.................... PaulMulrennan 6 79
(G M Moore) *led: shkn up 3f out: hrd rdn and hung rt over 1f out: edgd lft and regained ld last 75yds* **5/1**[3]

The Form Book, Raceform Ltd, Compton, RG20 6NL

3001 **2** *1* **Paraguay (USA)**[8] 3045 3-9-3 **77**........................... EdwardCreighton[(3)] 3 83
(Miss V Haigh) *t.k.h: trckd ldr: slt ld jst ins last: hdd and no ex last 75yds* **10/1**

6245 **3** *1 ½* **Royal Composer (IRE)**[28] 2441 3-8-10 **67**...................... DO'Donohoe 4 70
(T D Easterby) *hld up: t.k.h: outpcd over 3f out: hdwy 2f out: styd on ins last* **11/4**[1]

4-1 **4** *hd* **It's Unbelievable (USA)**[32] 2325 3-9-2 **73**........................ TPQueally 2 75
(B J Meehan) *t.k.h: trckd ldrs: kpt on same pce fnl f* **3/1**[2]

6130 **5** *nk* **Abbey Cat (IRE)**[33] 2297 3-9-6 **77**.. NeilPollard 7 79
(G A Swinbank) *sn trcking ldrs: effrt on inner over 3f out: nt clr run 2f out: hit on hd by rival rdr's whip: nt qckn fnl f* **5/1**[3]

-520 **6** *5* **Superior Star**[9] 3023 3-8-3 **60**....................................(b) RoystonFfrench 1 51
(R A Fahey) *hld up: outpcd 4f out: no threat after* **5/1**[3]

1m 46.14s (-1.26) **Going Correction** -0.075s/f (Good) 6 Ran SP% **110.8**
Speed ratings (Par 102):103,102,100,100,100 95
CSF £48.13 TOTE £7.50: £2.80, £3.30; EX 50.50.
Owner Ean Muller Associates **Bred** E A C Muller **Trained** Middleham Moor, N Yorks
■ Stewards' Enquiry : Paul Mulrennan three-day ban: used whip with excessive frequency, down the shoulder in the forehand position and without giving gelding time to respond (Jul 19-21); caution: careless riding
FOCUS
A modest handicap but a messy one with the first four getting in each others' way.

3283 ELTHERINGTON H'CAP 1m 1f 207y
4:30 (4:30) (Class 5) (0-75,72) 3-Y-0+ **£5,181** (£1,541; £770; £384) **Stalls High**

Form RPR

0-05 **1** **Our Teddy (IRE)**[21] 2640 6-9-12 **70**................................ TonyCulhane 5 81
(P A Blockley) *hld up: hdwy over 3f out: hrd rdn to ld over 1f out: all out* **9/2**[2]

5641 **2** *½* **Mount Usher**[8] 3037 4-9-4 **67**... GregFairley[(5)] 7 81+
(G A Swinbank) *tk fierce hold: hdwy on ins and nt clr run fr over 2f out: swtchd ins 1f out: r.o wl: nt quite rch wnr* **4/6**[1]

-660 **3** *3* **Boquilobo**[22] 2622 3-8-12 **67**....................................... RoystonFfrench 1 71
(M Johnston) *led 1f: chsd ldr: one pce fnl f* **10/1**[3]

0-00 **4** *hd* **Apsara**[17] 2761 5-9-1 **59**.. PaulMulrennan 3 63
(G M Moore) *led after 1f: quite keen: edgd lft and hdd over 1f out: one pce* **16/1**

-000 **5** *hd* **Peters Delite**[11] 2947 4-8-9 **53**.. TonyHamilton 6 57
(R A Fahey) *stl had hood on whn stalls opened: s.i.s: kpt on on inner fnl 2f: nvr a threat* **12/1**

0-06 **6** *1* **Edas**[11] 2945 4-9-11 **72**.. DNolan[(3)] 2 74
(J J Quinn) *chsd ldrs: one pce appr fnl f* **28/1**

0404 **7** *1 ¼* **Fairy Monarch (IRE)**[5] 3147 7-8-6 **53** oh3.............(v[1]) BenSwarbrick[(3)] 4 52
(P T Midgley) *hld up: hdwy on outside 3f out: one pce and nvr a threat* **10/1**[3]

2m 5.13s (-2.17) **Going Correction** -0.075s/f (Good)
WFA 3 from 4yo+ 11lb 7 Ran SP% **113.4**
Speed ratings (Par 103):105,104,102,102,101 101,100
CSF £7.73 TOTE £4.70: £2.00, £1.10; EX 9.90.
Owner The Beare Family **Bred** Vizcaya Ag **Trained** Lambourn, Berks
FOCUS
A modest handicap in which the winner stole first run, the runner-up must be accounted an unlucky loser and is rated the winner with Our Teddy to form.

3284 THINK BEVERLEY RACECOURSE FOR CONFERENCES AND WEDDINGS STKS (H'CAP) 2m 35y
5:00 (5:00) (Class 5) (0-70,67) 3-Y-0+ **£5,181** (£1,541; £770; £384) **Stalls High**

Form RPR

2141 **1** **Rose Bien**[8] 3035 4-9-2 **56**....................................(p) EdwardCreighton[(3)] 7 65
(P J McBride) *hld up: hdwy on outer over 4f out: styd on wl to ld 1f out: kpt on wl* **4/1**[2]

6124 **2** *1 ½* **Call Me George**[20] 2677 3-8-11 **67**.............................. RoystonFfrench 5 74
(M Johnston) *chsd ldrs: chal 7f out: styd on same pce fnl f* **2/1**[1]

6-00 **3** *1 ¾* **Thewhirlingdervish (IRE)**[15] 2828 8-9-9 **65**........... DuranFentiman[(5)] 3 70
(T D Easterby) *chsd ldrs on outer: styd on to ld over 1f out: sn hdd and nt qckn* **12/1**

6406 **4** *nk* **The Grey Man**[31] 2357 5-9-9 **63**.. DNolan[(3)] 8 68
(E S McMahon) *led: hdd over 1f out: kpt on same pce* **11/1**

-030 **5** *¾* **Paradise Flight (IRE)**[13] 2894 5-9-13 **64**.....................(b) DO'Donohoe 9 68
(K A Ryan) *hld up in tch: pushed along 4f out: hung rt and one pce appr fnl f* **10/1**

16 **6** *1 ¾* **Mulligan's Pride (IRE)**[9] 3019 5-9-3 **59**.................... GregFairley[(5)] 10 61
(G A Swinbank) *trckd ldrs: effrt on inner and n.m.r over 3f out: edgd lft and one pce fnl 2f* **8/1**[3]

-236 **7** *2 ½* **Overstrand (IRE)**[13] 2894 7-9-7 **63**.......................... TomGreenway[(5)] 6 62
(Robert Gray) *hld up in tch: effrt on wd outside over 3f out: one pce* **9/1**

6-60 **8** *1* **Best Port (IRE)**[20] 2684 10-9-6 **57**................................ TonyCulhane 1 54
(J Parkes) *swtchd rt s: hld up in last: hdwy on inner over 2f out: nvr a threat* **20/1**

-306 **9** *1 ¾* **Zeydnaa (IRE)**[3] 3192 6-8-13 **50**.................................... TonyHamilton 2 45
(C R Wilson) *chsd ldrs: lost pl over 1f out* **9/1**

-004 **10** *9* **Sahem (IRE)**[25] 2528 9-9-9 **60**.. TPQueally 4 44
(Robert Gray) *chsd ldrs: chal 7f out: wknd 2f out* **40/1**

3m 37.9s (-1.60) **Going Correction** -0.075s/f (Good)
WFA 3 from 4yo+ 19lb 10 Ran SP% **116.8**
Speed ratings (Par 103):101,100,99,99,98 97,96,96,95,90
CSF £12.39 CT £87.76 TOTE £5.20: £2.00, £1.40, £2.90; EX 9.50.
Owner P J Pateman **Bred** Mrs J F Budgett **Trained** Newmarket, Suffolk
FOCUS
Just a steady pace to past halfway in this low-grade handicap and the winner did well making her run up the outer. The form is modest.

3285 YORKSHIRE CANCER RESEARCH MAIDEN STKS 5f
5:35 (5:37) (Class 5) 3-Y-0+ **£3,562** (£1,059; £529; £264) **Stalls High**

Form RPR

3-00 **1** **Hotham**[8] 3042 3-9-0 67.. DNolan[(3)] 15 73
(N Wilson) *mde all: hld on towards fin* **10/1**

655 **2** *hd* **Cordelia**[18] 2734 3-8-12 63.. TonyCulhane 6 67
(B W Hills) *mid-div: hdwy on ins 2f out: styd on to chal ins last: no ex nr fin* **6/1**

0234 **3** *2 ½* **Chanteuse Noire (USA)**[35] 2235 3-8-12 61..................(v) TPQueally 12 58
(J Noseda) *chsd ldrs: effrt over 1f out: kpt on same pce* **3/1**[2]

0 **4** *2* **Rigat**[18] 2734 3-9-0 .... BenSwarbrick[(3)] 7 56+
(T D Barron) *s.i.s: bhd hdwy 2f out: styd on wl ins last* **33/1**

30 **5** *nk* **Conrad**[21] 2658 3-9-3 75... TonyHamilton 5 55
(R A Fahey) *mid-div: outpcd after 2f: kpt on fnl 2f* **7/2**[3]

0-54 **6** *nk* **Indian Ballet**[8] 3053 3-8-12 62... MatthewHenry 11 49
(M A Jarvis) *chsd ldrs: one pce appr fnl f* **5/2**[1]

7 *1 ¾* **Bond Free Spirit (IRE)** 3-8-7 .... DuranFentiman[(5)] 13 43
(G R Oldroyd) *s.s: sme hdwy on outside over 1f out: nvr on terms* **40/1**

0- **8** *nk* **Star Of Siam (IRE)**[414] 1857 3-8-7 .... GregFairley[(5)] 14 42
(J D Bethell) *sn outpcd and pushed along: sme hdwy on inner 2f out: nvr on terms* **25/1**

05- **9** *¾* **That's Blue Chip**[250] 6196 3-9-3 .... RoystonFfrench 1 44
(P W D'Arcy) *chsd ldrs on outer: wknd over 1f out* **25/1**

004 **10** *shd* **Waggledance (IRE)**[16] 2780 4-9-1 46............................... KellyHarrison[(7)] 4 43
(D Carroll) *chsd ldrs: lost pl over 1f out* **16/1**

36-0 **11** *1 ½* **Quote Unquote**[187] 10 3-8-9 67... NeilChalmers[(3)] 10 33
(J Parkes) *chsd ldrs: wkng whn n.m.r over 1f out* **20/1**

12 *5* **Longy The Lash** 3-9-3 .... DO'Donohoe 8 20
(K G Reveley) *s.s: a last: detached 2f out* **25/1**

63.51 secs (-0.49) **Going Correction** -0.075s/f (Good)
WFA 3 from 4yo 5lb 12 Ran SP% **126.7**
Speed ratings (Par 103):100,99,95,92,92 91,88,88,87,86 84,76
CSF £67.57 TOTE £13.90: £3.30, £2.00, £2.10; EX 71.60 Place 6 £87.81, Place 5 £41.53.
Owner Paul & Linda Dixon **Bred** Capt J H Wilson **Trained** Upper Helmsley, N Yorks
■ Stewards' Enquiry : Tony Culhane one-day ban: used whip with excessive frequency (Jul 22)
FOCUS
A modest sprint maiden, the first two clear. The winner had the best of the draw but the form looks sound.
T/Plt: £196.70 to a £1 stake. Pool: £39,426.65. 146.25 winning tickets. T/Qpdt: £48.70 to a £1 stake. Pool: £1,758.70. 26.70 winning tickets. WG

[2972]CARLISLE (R-H)
Saturday, July 8

OFFICIAL GOING: Good to firm (firm in places)
Wind: Breezy, half-against

3286 STORY WORKFORCE MAIDEN AUCTION STKS 5f
7:00 (7:01) (Class 5) 2-Y-O **£3,238** (£963; £481; £240) **Stalls High**

Form RPR

34 **1** **Argentine (IRE)**[56] 1664 2-8-13 .... KDarley 1 85+
(M Johnston) *mde all: rdn 2f out: kpt on strly fnl f* **15/8**[1]

0 **2** *½* **Ice Mountain**[10] 2973 2-8-11 .... DerekMcGaffin 11 81
(B Smart) *sn pushed along bhd ldrs: effrt and chsd wnr over 1f out: kpt on fnl f: hld towards fin* **11/2**[3]

3 *5* **Wicked Wilma (IRE)** 2-8-4 .... PaulQuinn 4 56
(A Berry) *dwlt: m green in rr: hdwy over 1f out: kpt on: no ch w first two* **80/1**

02 **4** *½* **Okikoki**[12] 2930 2-8-13 .... RobertHavlin 2 63
(W R Muir) *w ldrs tl rdn and no ex over 1f out* **5/2**[2]

5 **5** *½* **Lemon Silk (IRE)**[16] 2783 2-9-2 .... PaulHanagan 5 64
(T P Tate) *towards rr: outpcd 1/2-way: hdwy over 1f out: n.d* **9/1**

6 *1* **Kyrenia Girl (IRE)** 2-8-6 .... DavidAllan 7 51
(T D Easterby) *s.i.s: sme late hdwy: nvr rchd ldrs* **25/1**

7 *2 ½* **Triple Shadow** 2-8-11 .... PhillipMakin 8 47
(T D Barron) *cl up tl edgd rt and wknd wl over 1f out* **11/2**[3]

006 **8** *2 ½* **Focus Star**[25] 2523 2-8-9 .... TomEaves 9 36
(J M Jefferson) *towards rr: outpcd 1/2-way: n.d after* **40/1**

0 **9** *1 ½* **Piccolini**[16] 2791 2-8-6 .... CatherineGannon 6 27
(Mrs G S Rees) *in tch tl wknd over 2f out* **66/1**

000 **10** *nk* **Devilfishpoker Com**[15] 2806 2-8-13 .... NeilPollard 3 33
(R C Guest) *in tch: hung rt 1/2-way: sn wknd* **150/1**

62.15 secs (0.65) **Going Correction** +0.15s/f (Good) 10 Ran SP% **113.8**
Speed ratings (Par 94):100,99,91,90,89 88,84,80,77,77
CSF £12.09 TOTE £2.90: £1.20, £1.90, £5.30.
Owner Mrs S J Brookhouse **Bred** Tony Hirschfeld And L K Piggott **Trained** Middleham Moor, N Yorks
■ Stewards' Enquiry : Robert Havlin two-day ban: careless riding (Jul 19-20)
FOCUS
An ordinary event in which the first two pulled clear in the closing stages. The pace was sound, resulting in a good time, and, although not easy to assess, this bare form should prove reliable.
NOTEBOOK
Argentine(IRE) took the eye in the paddock and left his latest below-par run behind him on this first start on fast ground. Although his main market rival disappointed he showed a good attitude, should stay six furlongs and may be capable of a bit better. (op 5-2 tchd 11-4)
Ice Mountain ◆ duly improved a fair bit for his debut run and did well to pull clear of the remainder. He left the impression that the step up to six furlongs plus would be in his favour and he looks sure to win a small event in due course. (op 8-1)
Wicked Wilma(IRE), the first foal of a half-sister to a six furlong winner and a mile and six winner, shaped with a bit of promise, despite her greenness on this racecourse debut. She is entitled to improve for this experience. (op 50-1)
Okikoki looked in good shape in the paddock but had his limitations exposed back in trip and on this much quicker ground. He should be suited by the return to further and more give in the ground and is one to keep an eye on in nursery company when getting those conditions. (tchd 9-4 and 11-4)
Lemon Silk(IRE), who hinted at ability over six furlongs on his debut, did not look suited by the drop to this trip but should be seen to better effect over six furlongs and beyond in modest nursery company. (op 11-1 tchd 8-1)
Kyrenia Girl(IRE), the first foal of a half-sister to a couple of winners up to middle distances, only hinted at ability on this racecourse debut. She should do better with time and experience.

3287 MARTIN ARMSTRONG MEMORIAL H'CAP 5f 193y
7:30 (7:31) (Class 5) (0-75,73) 3-Y-0+ **£3,238** (£963; £481; £240) **Stalls High**

Form RPR

2111 **1** **Our Sheila**[14] 2873 3-9-3 **73**.. MarkLawson[(5)] 3 81
(B Smart) *cl up: edgd rt and led over 1f out: hld on wl fnl f* **4/1**[1]

1-00 **2** *nk* **Kool Ovation**[8] 3041 4-9-6 **65**.. DavidAllan 7 73
(A Dickman) *dwlt: outpcd: hdwy over 1f out: kpt on wl fnl f* **20/1**

0056 **3** *½* **Cree**[13] 2898 4-8-9 **54**... RobertHavlin 4 61
(W R Muir) *chsd ldrs: effrt over 2f out: kpt on fnl f: hld towards fin* **9/1**

0400 **4** *nk* **Mozakhraf (USA)**[4] 3171 4-9-1 **60**......................(p) CatherineGannon 10 66
(K A Ryan) *led: drvn fr over 2f out: hdd over 1f out: no ex wl ins fnl f* **16/1**

3040 **5** *1 ½* **Defi (IRE)**[8] 3040 4-9-4 **63**.......................................(b) TomEaves 2 64
(I Semple) *racd wd: hld up in tch: effrt and hung lft 2f out: no imp fnl f* **6/1**[2]

2000 **6** *hd* **Distant Times**[21] 2661 5-9-3 **62**..............................(b) GrahamGibbons 1 62
(T D Easterby) *prom: rdn over 2f out: no ex over 1f out* **6/1**[2]

-061 **7** *¾* **Snow Bunting**[15] 2811 8-8-13 **58**...................................... PaulHanagan 11 56
(Jedd O'Keeffe) *prom: effrt over 2f out: no ex appr fnl f* **6/1**[2]

3210 **8** *2* **Bel Cantor**[13] 2896 3-9-3 **73**.... RichardKingscote(5) 5 64
(W J H Ratcliffe) *cl up tl rdn and outpcd wl over 1f out* **8/1**[3]
0026 **9** *2 ½* **Dispol Katie**[10] 2977 5-10-0 **73**.... PhillipMakin 6 57
(T D Barron) *bhd: rdn 1/2-way: n.d* **6/1**[2]
/000 **10** *3 ½* **Shank On Fourteen (IRE)**[16] 2785 5-9-6 **65**.... NeilPollard 8 39
(K R Burke) *prom tl rdn and wknd fr 2f out* **33/1**
-000 **11** *21* **Geordie Dancer (IRE)**[12] 2926 4-8-9 **54** oh1....(b) JoeFanning 9 —
(A Berry) *sn w ldrs: wknd fr 1/2-way: t.o* **50/1**
1m 14.12s (0.51) **Going Correction** +0.15s/f (Good)
WFA 3 from 4yo+ 6lb **11** Ran SP% **113.8**
Speed ratings (Par 103):102,101,100,100,98 98,97,94,91,86 58
CSF £86.46 CT £675.34 TOTE £3.10: £2.10, £6.00, £3.00; EX 147.70.
Owner Anthony D Gee **Bred** Mrs C R Philipson **Trained** Hambleton, N Yorks

FOCUS
An ordinary handicap in which the pace was sound and the form is just fair. The field stayed centre to far side in the straight.

3288 VENTURE IFA (S) STKS — 7f 200y
8:00 (8:09) (Class 6) 3-Y-O — **£2,730** (£806; £403) **Stalls** High

Form RPR
0-50 **1** **River Logic (IRE)**[36] 2195 3-8-12 49.... TomEaves 1 57
(J Howard Johnson) *hld up: hdwy to ld 1f out: r.o strly* **8/1**
56 **2** *2 ½* **Roman History (IRE)**[19] 2696 3-8-12 46.... GylesParkin 7 51
(Miss Tracy Waggott) *prom: effrt and ev ch over 1f out: kpt on fnl f: nt rch wnr* **14/1**
-050 **3** *¾* **Coronation Flight**[18] 2734 3-8-7 41.... DeanMcKeown 2 45
(F P Murtagh) *s.i.s: bhd tl c stands side and hdwy over 2f out: kpt on fnl f: nrst fin* **33/1**
0-20 **4** *nk* **Elite Land**[25] 2529 3-8-5 50....(b) SuzzanneFrance(7) 6 49
(N Bycroft) *midfield: hmpd and swtchd 3f out: wd and led briefly over 1f out: one pce fnl f* **8/1**
0052 **5** *2 ½* **Pontefract Glory**[9] 3006 3-8-12 39....(p) PhillipMakin 17 43
(M Dods) *keen in midfield: effrt over 2f out: no imp over 1f out* **4/1**[1]
-000 **6** *1 ¾* **The Flying Peach**[39] 2101 3-8-7 41.... PaulQuinn 9 34
(W M Brisbourne) *towards rr: hdwy far side 2f out: no imp fnl f* **40/1**
0540 **7** *nk* **Wensleydale Star**[30] 2379 3-8-5 40.... DeanHeslop(7) 16 38
(T D Barron) *cl up tl rdn and outpcd fr 2f out* **14/1**
-065 **8** *shd* **Eurana**[19] 2699 3-8-7 47.... PaulHanagan 10 33
(Jedd O'Keeffe) *keen in tch: effrt over 2f out: no ex over 1f out* **11/2**[3]
9 *1 ¼* **Madame Diktatit** 3-8-4 ow2.... RichardKingscote(5) 8 32
(Ms Deborah J Evans) *in tch: drvn over 3f out: no imp over 1f out* **25/1**
0300 **10** *2 ½* **Distinctly Jim (IRE)**[12] 2923 3-8-12 55....(b[1]) DerekMcGaffin 15 30
(B Smart) *keen: chsd ldrs to 2f out: sn btn* **5/1**[2]
0005 **11** *2 ½* **Salisbury World (IRE)**[16] 2782 3-8-12 47.... DaleGibson 14 24
(J F Coupland) *s.i.s: n.d* **12/1**
-500 **12** *3 ½* **Boumsong (IRE)**[12] 2923 3-8-12 40.... NeilPollard 12 16
(R C Guest) *dwlt: rdn in rr over 2f out: n.d* **66/1**
0-04 **13** *3 ½* **Mandarin Grand (IRE)**[36] 2192 3-8-7 36....(p) JoeFanning 13 —
(Miss L A Perratt) *led to over 1f out: sn btn* **16/1**
-000 **14** *10* **Our Serendipity**[14] 2874 3-8-7 40.... DavidAllan 3 —
(K G Reveley) *prom tl rdn and wknd over 2f out* **25/1**
50-0 **15** *3* **Happy Harry (IRE)**[24] 2546 3-8-12 44.... RobertHavlin 4 —
(B Storey) *racd wd in midfield: rdn 3f out: sn btn* **50/1**
0-0 **16** *½* **Flick N Flack**[48] 1866 3-8-9 ow2.... MarkLawson(5) 5 —
(D W Thompson) *uns rdr and loose bef s: nvr on terms* **80/1**
0 **17** *21* **Talbot Street**[33] 2298 3-8-12 ....(t) CatherineGannon 11 —
(Robert Gray) *cl up tl wknd fr 3f out* **100/1**
1m 41.61s (1.52) **Going Correction** +0.15s/f (Good) **17** Ran SP% **119.9**
Speed ratings (Par 98):98,95,94,94,91 90,89,89,88,86 83,80,76,66,63 63,42
CSF £105.83 TOTE £12.10: £4.00, £5.70, £5.40; EX 191.40.The winner was sold to R. G. Fell for 8,000gns.
Owner Transcend Bloodstock LLP **Bred** J K Beckitt And Son **Trained** Billy Row, Co Durham

FOCUS
A weak event but one in which the pace was sound throughout. The field fanned across the course in the straight.
Mandarin Grand(IRE) Official explanation: jockey said filly lost its action

3289 COORS FINE LIGHT H'CAP — 7f 200y
8:30 (8:36) (Class 4) (0-80,80) 3-Y-O+ — **£6,477** (£1,927; £963; £481) **Stalls** High

Form RPR
-120 **1** **Whitethorne**[14] 2851 4-9-4 **73**.... PaulHanagan 2 83
(R A Fahey) *prom: led over 2f out: hld on wl fnl f* **9/2**[3]
5031 **2** *½* **Regent's Secret (USA)**[10] 2974 6-9-7 **79**.... DanielTudhope(3) 7 88
(J S Goldie) *hld up: rdn 3f out: gd hdwy wl over 1f out: chsd wnr wl ins fnl f: r.o* **11/4**[1]
-104 **3** *1 ¼* **Vicious Warrior**[10] 2974 7-9-11 **80**.... DeanMcKeown 4 86
(R M Whitaker) *cl up: ev ch over 2f out: one pce fnl f* **9/2**[3]
1153 **4** *2* **Hula Ballew**[10] 2974 6-9-6 **75**.... PhillipMakin 3 76
(M Dods) *trckd ldrs: effrt and ev ch over 2f out: one pce over 1f out* **10/3**[2]
020- **5** *1 ¾* **Mayadeen (IRE)**[24] 2622 4-9-11 **80**.... TomEaves 8 77
(J G M O'Shea) *bhd: rdn over 3f out: kpt on fnl f: n.d* **20/1**
3553 **6** *3* **Efidium**[15] 2831 8-8-7 **69**.... SuzzanneFrance(7) 1 59
(N Bycroft) *dwlt: hld up: effrt over 2f out: edgd rt and sn outpcd* **8/1**
-500 **7** *1 ½* **Kirkby's Treasure**[47] 1885 8-9-1 **70**.... JoeFanning 6 57
(A Berry) *hld up: short-lived effrt 2f out: sn btn* **20/1**
0600 **8** *10* **Redwood Rocks (IRE)**[19] 2697 5-8-12 **67**....(b[1]) DerekMcGaffin 5 31
(B Smart) *keen: set str pce to over 2f out: wknd over 1f out* **16/1**
1m 40.69s (0.60) **Going Correction** +0.15s/f (Good) **8** Ran SP% **112.6**
Speed ratings (Par 105):103,102,101,99,97 94,93,83
CSF £16.74 CT £57.35 TOTE £4.80: £1.70, £1.60, £1.90; EX 32.40.
Owner Mrs Doreen M Swinburn **Bred** Genesis Green Stud Ltd **Trained** Musley Bank, N Yorks
■ Stewards' Enquiry : Paul Hanagan one-day ban: using whip with excessive frequency (Jul 19)

FOCUS
No progressive sorts for this fair prize but the pace was sound throughout and the form is solid enough.
Redwood Rocks(IRE) Official explanation: jockey said gelding ran too free having been fitted with blinkers first time

3290 AZURE SUPPORT SERVICES H'CAP — 6f 192y
9:00 (9:02) (Class 5) (0-70,66) 3-Y-O — **£3,238** (£963; £481; £240) **Stalls** High

Form RPR
0210 **1** **Jellytot (USA)**[25] 2525 3-9-0 **59**.... CatherineGannon 3 70
(K A Ryan) *hld up: hdwy to ld 1f out: hld on wl fnl f* **10/1**
4030 **2** *hd* **Kasumi**[27] 2479 3-9-1 **60**.... TomEaves 1 70
(H Morrison) *in tch: outpcd 1/2-way: rallied and hung rt 2f out: chal 1f out: kpt on: hld cl home* **5/1**[3]
4412 **3** *3* **Esoterica (IRE)**[5] 3138 3-9-7 **66**....(b) PaulFessey 7 69
(T D Barron) *prom: effrt over 1f out: edgd rt: one pce fnl f* **3/1**[1]
5043 **4** *½* **Carr Hall (IRE)**[16] 2782 3-8-9 **54**.... DavidAllan 5 55
(T D Easterby) *chsd ldrs: outpcd 2f out: rallied fnl f: no imp* **8/1**
3006 **5** *nk* **Josarty**[13] 2896 3-8-9 **54**.... GrahamGibbons 4 55
(J J Quinn) *in tch: effrt over 2f out: no imp fnl f* **20/1**
0003 **6** *shd* **Cape Of Storms**[4] 3167 3-9-4 **63**.... TonyCulhane 9 63
(M R Channon) *led to 1f out: one pce whn n.m.r ins fnl f* **13/2**
5-05 **7** *2* **Pitbull**[13] 2896 3-8-12 **60**.... BenSwarbrick(3) 8 55
(Mrs G S Rees) *cl up: rdn over 2f out: sn btn* **7/1**
-542 **8** *5* **Jaassey**[16] 2782 3-9-0 **59**.... KDarley 6 41
(T D Walford) *hld up: rdn over 2f out: no imp over 1f out* **4/1**[2]
3100 **9** *2 ½* **Miss Lopez (IRE)**[5] 3154 3-9-5 **64**.... PaulHanagan 10 40
(K R Burke) *dwlt: sn trcking ldrs: rdn and wknd over 1f out* **25/1**
0-00 **10** *27* **True Valentine**[51] 1791 3-8-2 **47** oh3.... JoeFanning 2 —
(A Berry) *bhd: lost tch fr 1/2-way* **100/1**
1m 27.73s (0.63) **Going Correction** +0.15s/f (Good) **10** Ran SP% **117.3**
Speed ratings (Par 100):102,101,98,97,97 97,95,89,86,55
CSF £58.71 CT £194.67 TOTE £8.50: £2.00, £2.10, £1.50; EX 111.20.
Owner David Fravigar, Kathy Dixon **Bred** Gallagher's Stud **Trained** Hambleton, N Yorks
■ The first winner in Britain for former Irish apprentice champion Cathy Gannon.

FOCUS
An ordinary handicap in which the riders reported that the evening's rain had started to get into the ground and the form is limited. The field came centre to stands' side in the straight but the principals edged towards the far side in the closing stages.
True Valentine Official explanation: jockey said bit slipped through filly's mouth

3291 BARBOURS OF DUMFRIES MAIDEN H'CAP — 2m 1f 52y
9:30 (9:32) (Class 6) (0-60,59) 4-Y-O+ — **£2,730** (£806; £403) **Stalls** High

Form RPR
20-4 **1** **Lodgician (IRE)**[14] 2871 4-9-1 **53**.... GrahamGibbons 9 65+
(J J Quinn) *trckd ldrs gng wl: led over 3f out: rdn and r.o strly fr 2f out* **5/1**[3]
4553 **2** *3 ½* **Arch Folly**[35] 2219 4-9-7 **59**.... TomEaves 1 65
(J G Portman) *hld up in tch: effrt on outside and chsd wnr over 2f out: no imp fnl f* **9/2**[2]
005- **3** *2 ½* **Kanpai (IRE)**[10] 5973 4-9-0 **52**....(v) PaulFessey 3 55
(J G M O'Shea) *prom: effrt 3f out: no ex over 1f out* **9/2**[2]
-505 **4** *8* **Hugs Destiny (IRE)**[10] 1562 5-8-12 **50**....(t) DeanMcKeown 2 43
(M A Barnes) *chsd ldrs: effrt and ev ch over 2f out: wknd over 1f out* **8/1**
-544 **5** *½* **Totally Scottish**[16] 1184 10-8-5 **50**.... JamesReveley(7) 4 43
(K G Reveley) *in tch: outpcd over 4f out: no imp fr 2f out* **4/1**[1]
06/0 **6** *3* **Scratch The Dove**[35] 2219 9-8-2 **40** oh1.... DaleGibson 7 29
(A E Price) *s.s: hld up: rdn and short-lived effrt over 3f out: sn btn* **25/1**
60-0 **7** *shd* **Grandma's Girl**[21] 2242 4-8-11 **49**....(p) CatherineGannon 8 38
(Robert Gray) *s.i.s: hld up: rdn over 3f out: sn btn* **33/1**
5/02 **8** *29* **Tipu Sultan**[29] 2395 6-8-10 **48**.... PaulHanagan 5 —
(Micky Hammond) *in tch: effrt over 3f out: wknd over 2f out* **10/1**
0600 **9** *15* **Longing For Cindy (USA)**[27] 1724 4-8-3 **41**....(p) PaulQuinn 10 —
(W M Brisbourne) *led to over 3f out: wknd 2f out* **50/1**
0345 **10** **College Rebel**[26] 2501 5-8-3 **48**.... KevinGhunowa(7) 6 —
(J F Coupland) *keen: w ldr tl wknd 3f out* **13/2**
3m 54.96s (5.06) **Going Correction** +0.15s/f (Good) **10** Ran SP% **115.3**
Speed ratings (Par 101):94,92,91,87,87 85,85,72,65,65
CSF £26.99 CT £108.31 TOTE £6.60: £2.50, £3.00, £2.50; EX 39.30 Place 6 £212.19, Place 5 £116.16.
Owner J Henderson (co Durham) **Bred** Sir Eric Parker **Trained** Settrington, N Yorks

FOCUS
A modest event and an ordinary gallop but an improved effort from the winner on his first try over this trip with the winner setting the standard.
T/Plt: £326.90 to a £1 stake. Pool: £48,972.25. 109.35 winning tickets. T/Qpdt: £57.30 to a £1 stake. Pool: £2,869.60. 37.00 winning tickets. RY

3245 HAYDOCK (L-H)
Saturday, July 8

OFFICIAL GOING: Good to firm
Wind: Almost nil Weather: Overcast; some light drizzle

3292 H2O JULY TROPHY H'CAP — 1m 3f 200y
2:20 (2:23) (Class 2) (0-105,92) 3-Y-O — **£19,431** (£5,781; £2,889; £1,443) **Stalls** High

Form RPR
3-12 **1** **Futun**[50] 1813 3-9-7 **92**.... NickyMackay 5 101+
(L M Cumani) *t.k.h: hld up: hdwy 2f out: nt clr run and swtchd rt over 1f out: r.o ins fnl f to ld towards fin* **7/1**
-301 **2** *½* **Prowess (IRE)**[20] 2682 3-9-4 **89**.... RyanMoore 1 97
(B W Hills) *led: rdn over 2f out and hrd pressed: hdd towards fin* **5/1**[1]
4140 **3** *¾* **Numeric (GER)**[15] 2805 3-8-11 **82**....(b[1]) JimmyFortune 4 89
(J H M Gosden) *t.k.h: midfield: hdwy to go prom after 4f: rdn and ev ch fr 2f out: nt qckn wl ins fnl f* **5/1**[1]
-611 **4** *½* **Cresta Gold**[10] 2975 3-9-7 **92**.... DavidAllan 8 98
(A Bailey) *hld up: pushed along in rr over 4f out: hdwy over 1f out: r.o ins fnl f: nt rch ldrs* **11/2**[2]
6466 **5** *½* **Doctor Scott**[15] 2805 3-8-10 **81**.... JoeFanning 7 86
(M Johnston) *cl up: rdn over 2f out: lugged lft fr over 1f out: styd on ins fnl f: one pce towards fin* **6/1**[3]
2200 **6** *½* **Salute The General**[15] 2805 3-8-10 **81**.... RichardMullen 2 86
(W R Muir) *trckd ldrs: outpcd wl over 2f out: sn n.m.r: styd on ins fnl f: no imp towards fin* **8/1**
-120 **7** *2 ½* **Idarah (USA)**[15] 2805 3-9-5 **90**.... MartinDwyer 3 91
(W J Haggas) *prom: rdn over 2f out: wknd over 1f out* **10/1**
-122 **8** *2* **Solva**[11] 2961 3-8-9 **80**.... JimmyQuinn 6 78
(B J Meehan) *hld up: nt clr run over 2f out: n.m.r and hmpd wl over 1f out: sn no imp* **20/1**
1150 **9** *2 ½* **Peppertree Lane (IRE)**[16] 2774 3-9-5 **90**.... KDarley 9 84
(M Johnston) *t.k.h: in tch: rdn over 2f out: sn hung lft: wknd over 1f out* **17/2**
2m 30.96s (-4.03) **Going Correction** -0.25s/f (Firm) **9** Ran SP% **111.0**
Speed ratings (Par 106):103,102,102,101,101 101,99,98,96
CSF £39.42 CT £183.27 TOTE £5.90: £2.10, £2.10, £2.10; EX 24.40 Trifecta £90.00 Pool: £507.24 - 4 winning units.
Owner Scuderia Rencati Srl **Bred** Azienda Agricola Francesca **Trained** Newmarket, Suffolk

FOCUS
A good three-year-old handicap run at an average gallop. The form looks solid, rated around the runner-up and fourth, and should work out.

NOTEBOOK
Futun, not seen since the middle of May and giving weight away to all his rivals, displaying a nice turn of foot in the final furlong to grab victory close to the line, confirming the good impression he made much earlier in the season. Sure to keep on improving as the season unfolds, his astute trainer will surely find another opening for him. (op 5-1)
Prowess(IRE) set an average gallop from the off and kept on bravely when challenged for the lead in the final stages. She has some useful form to her name, which should make her a valuable mare in the paddocks, and it is conceivable that she may get a bit further given her pedigree - she is by a French Derby/Arc winner out of mare by another Arc winner (amongst other top-class middle-distance races.) (tchd 11-2)
Numeric(GER), in first-time blinkers, made a rush for the line up the inside rail but did not get home as well as the first two - possibly because he pulled quite hard early in the race. He did, however, reverse form with the two horses that finished in front of him at Royal Ascot, but does not completely convince that he is an easy ride.
Cresta Gold was held up towards the rear and had all of her rivals to pass up the home straight. The jockey persevered with her all the way up the way to the winning post, and she responded extremely well for pressure. One suspects that she will get further than a mile and a half in time. (op 13-2)
Doctor Scott was never that far away from the lead and had every chance. It might be that he needs further but, even so, it was a bit disappointing that he did not get involved at the business end of the race after such a fine effort at Royal Ascot. (op 11-2)
Salute The General would have finished a bit closer had he not met some traffic problems about two furlongs from home. Although he has performed well on a quick surface and handles it, it might be that he really comes into his own when there is some ease in the ground, as his only win came on the Fibresand and he was a very commendable second at Newbury earlier in the season on soft ground. (op 9-1)
Idarah(USA) was unable to dominate again and was beaten halfway up the home straight. Ten furlongs could easily end up being his ideal trip, although he has the size and scope to make his mark at the winter game if he went through the Sales ring. (op 14-1)
Peppertree Lane(IRE), stepping up half a mile in trip, ran like a horse that did not see out the trip. (op 12-1)

3293 BET365 LANCASHIRE OAKS (GROUP 2) (F&M) 1m 3f 200y
2:50 (2:54) (Class 1) 3-Y-O+

£51,102 (£19,368; £9,693; £4,833; £2,421; £1,215) **Stalls** High

Form				RPR
5-61	**1**		**Allegretto (IRE)**[22] 2600 3-8-6 84 ... RyanMoore 6 (Sir Michael Stoute) *a cl up: rdn over 2f out: led over 1f out: r.o ins fnl f: wl in command towards fin* **13/2**[3]	108
-331	**2**	*3*	**Local Spirit (USA)**[7] 3073 3-8-6 69 ... JoeFanning 9 (C E Brittain) *hld up in rr: gd hdwy 3f out: led over 2f out: hdd over 1f out: flashed tail u.p: no ex ins fnl f* **66/1**	103
2-11	**3**	*3*	**Princess Nada**[23] 2582 3-8-6 101 ... NickyMackay 5 (L M Cumani) *racd keenly: hld up: hdwy 3f out: chsd ldrs 2f out: one pce fnl f* **6/4**[1]	99
01-3	**4**	*4*	**Play Me**[19] 2706 4-9-5 90 ... AdrianMcCarthy 1 (P W Chapple-Hyam) *racd keenly: prom: rdn over 2f out: wknd over 1f out* **25/1**	93
21-5	**5**	*shd*	**Innocent Air**[50] 1819 3-8-6 103 ... RobertHavlin 7 (J H M Gosden) *sn led: rdn and hdd over 2f out: sn checked whn losing pl: wknd over 1f out* **13/2**[3]	92
1-25	**6**	*1 ¼*	**Guilia**[36] 2203 3-8-6 100 ... KDarley 8 (Rae Guest) *midfield: pushed along 4f out: wl btn over 1f out* **3/1**[2]	90
1-10	**7**	*nk*	**Alessandria**[16] 2772 3-8-6 98 ... MartinDwyer 4 (E A L Dunlop) *hld up: rdn over 2f out: no imp* **8/1**	90
3503	**8**	*40*	**Marachi Band (USA)**[25] 2537 3-8-6 85 ... (b) RichardMullen 2 (E J O'Neill) *cl up: pushed along 4f out: wknd qckly 3f out: t.o* **50/1**	28

2m 28.44s (-6.55) **Going Correction** -0.25s/f (Firm)
WFA 3 from 4yo 13lb **8** Ran SP% **110.1**
Speed ratings (Par 115):111,109,107,104,104 103,103,76
CSF £311.31 TOTE £7.40: £1.70, £4.70, £1.40; EX 171.80 Trifecta £408.20 Part won. Pool: £575.07 - 0.20 winning tickets..
Owner Cheveley Park Stud **Bred** Miss K Rausing And Airlie Stud **Trained** Newmarket, Suffolk

FOCUS
The winner apart, the form should be treated with caution due to the official mark of the runner-up, but the winning time was virtually par for a race of its stature.

NOTEBOOK
Allegretto(IRE) is getting better with racing and ran right away from her rivals in the closing stages. Her pedigree is all class, being by a Derby winner out of a highly progressive racemare, and she, much like her dam, is improving with time. There was plenty to like about the effort and she is sure to hold her own in stronger company, although the race did not appear to be the strongest Group 2 ever run. Connections did not have any solid plans for her after the race, although they have plenty of options, but the St Leger might come into their minds depending how the season unfolds with the colts. (op 8-1)
Local Spirit(USA), from a stable in decent form, almost pulled off a massive shock when surging to the front over two furlongs from home despite, one again, flashing her tail under pressure - which looks more of a trait than any sign of being ungenuine. A full-sister to the top-class mare Crimplene, this was far and above anything she had achieved in the past and it remains to be seen whether the run was a fluke. Nothing really suggested that it was sheer luck that got her placed, and she can probably operate from ten furlongs to a mile and a half.
Princess Nada moved with ominous ease throughout the race but found her stamina giving out in the final two furlongs, much like her illustrious half-brother's did in the Derby. A lesser grade may see her win over a mile and a half, but it is likely that ten furlongs will be her most suitable trip. (tchd 13-8)
Play Me, who was close to the early gallop, looked very one paced in the last quarter of a mile and a combination of the trip and the grade was too much for her.
Innocent Air made the early pace but folded tamely when joined two from home. She does not seem to have progressed over the winter after being a half-decent juvenile. (tchd 7-1)
Guilia had plenty of form lines that gave her an obvious chance of going close. However, she was never really going with any fluency wide of her rivals, and the effort must go down as a really disappointing one, considering the official rating of the runner-up. It will be back to the drawing board for connections with her. (op 5-2)
Alessandria once again proved a bitter disappointment. She has not progressed as anticipated since being raised in class after such an impressive display on the All-Weather back in May. Official explanation: jockey said filly lost its action (tchd 17-2)
Marachi Band(USA) Official explanation: vet said filly finished lame

3294 BET365 OLD NEWTON CUP (HERITAGE H'CAP) 1m 3f 200y
3:30 (3:34) (Class 2) 4-Y-O+

£52,972 (£15,861; £7,930; £3,969; £1,980; £994) **Stalls** High

Form				RPR
-030	**1**		**Consular**[14] 2848 4-8-8 90 ... NCallan 14 (M A Jarvis) *a.p: led over 3f out: rdn and edgd rt over 1f out: r.o ins fnl f* **16/1**	102
-222	**2**	*1*	**Ouninpohja (IRE)**[7] 3085 5-9-10 106 ... DeanMcKeown 1 (G A Swinbank) *trckd ldrs: chsd wnr over 2f out: carried hd high and hung lft over 1f out: r.o ins fnl f: a hld* **7/1**[2]	116
-135	**3**	*3*	**Star Of Light**[15] 2803 5-8-11 100 ... MichaelJStainton(7) 4 (B J Meehan) *midfield: nt clr run and hmpd over 3f out: sn swtchd rt: hdwy and edgd lft over 2f out: styd on ins fnl f: nt* **7/1**[2]	105+
12-1	**4**	*1 ½*	**Signatory (USA)**[43] 1991 4-9-1 97 ... JimmyFortune 3 (J H M Gosden) *in tch: rdn 3f out: styd on same pce fnl f* **9/2**[1]	100
/100	**5**	*1 ¾*	**Vengeance**[14] 2848 6-8-12 94 ... PatDobbs 7 (S Dow) *hld up: rdn and hdwy over 1f out: styd on ins fnl f: nvr nrr* **66/1**	94+
461	**6**	*½*	**Young Mick**[14] 2848 4-8-11 93 ... (v) JimmyQuinn 15 (G G Margarson) *in tch: outpcd over 3f out: rdn and kpt on fr 2f out: one pce ins fnl f* **11/1**[3]	93
-001	**7**	*nk*	**Nordwind (IRE)**[33] 2296 5-8-3 85 ... FrancisNorton 10 (W R Swinburn) *hld up: rdn and hdwy over 2f out: one pce ins fnl f* **25/1**	84
232-	**8**	*1 ½*	**Royal Jet**[277] 5690 4-8-3 85 ... RichardMullen 11 (M R Channon) *hld up: rdn over 2f out: hdwy over 1f out: one pce ins fnl f* **40/1**	82
0004	**9**	*shd*	**Polygonal (FR)**[14] 2848 6-8-4 91 ... JamesDoyle(5) 9 (Ernst Oertel) *hld up: rdn over 2f out: sme hdwy over 1f out: no imp on ldrs* **25/1**	88
00-5	**10**	*¾*	**Red Lancer**[36] 2201 5-8-11 93 ... PaulHanagan 12 (R A Fahey) *midfield: hdwy 6f out: rdn and wknd over 2f out* **7/1**[2]	88
5232	**11**	*3*	**Lets Roll**[14] 2850 5-8-5 90 ... DanielTudhope(3) 5 (C W Thornton) *hld up: effrt on rail whn nt clr run over 2f out: no imp after* **14/1**	81+
3-35	**12**	*shd*	**Thunder Rock (IRE)**[14] 2848 4-8-8 90 ... RyanMoore 16 (Sir Michael Stoute) *in tch: rdn over 2f out: carried hd to one side: wknd and eased fnl f* **9/2**[1]	81+
0000	**13**	*hd*	**Crow Wood**[14] 2848 7-8-8 90 ... GrahamGibbons 17 (J J Quinn) *prom: rdn 3f out: wknd over 2f out* **40/1**	80
0125	**14**	*10*	**Gavroche (IRE)**[15] 2840 5-9-4 100 ... MartinDwyer 13 (J R Boyle) *s.i.s: midfield: lost pl over 2f out: n.d after* **25/1**	75
-203	**15**	*5*	**Dunaskin (IRE)**[21] 2656 6-8-11 93 ... KDarley 8 (Karen McLintock) *t.k.h: hld up: midfield after 3f: losing pl whn n.m.r over 2f out: sn eased* **66/1**	60+
0-46	**16**	*2*	**Brahminy Kite (USA)**[50] 1815 4-9-4 100 ... (v) JoeFanning 6 (M Johnston) *led: hdd over 3f out: wknd over 2f out* **25/1**	64

2m 28.83s (-6.16) **Going Correction** -0.25s/f (Firm) **16** Ran SP% **118.0**
Speed ratings (Par 109):110,109,107,106,105 104,104,103,103,103 101,101,100,94,90 89
CSF £110.71 CT £866.83 TOTE £20.40: £3.90, £2.10, £2.40, £1.80; EX 167.70 Trifecta £887.90 Pool: £2,001 - 1.60 winning units..
Owner Mrs P Good **Bred** Mrs P Good **Trained** Newmarket, Suffolk
■ Stewards' Enquiry : Francis Norton two-day ban: careless riding (Jul 19-20)
Jimmy Quinn two-day ban: used whip with whip arm above shoulder height (Jul 19,20)

FOCUS
A strong handicap, run slightly slower time than the Lancashire Oaks, but still around par for the class. It seemed an advantage to race up with the pace but the form looks solid enough and should work out.

NOTEBOOK
Consular, whose best efforts have all now come at Haydock, was always well placed to make a winning bid up the home straight. Although possibly flattered by being so close to the pace, he took up the running going well and won with a bit more in hand than the winning distance suggests. The Handicapper is bound to take a dim view of the win, because of the official marks of the next five home, and he will find things more difficult for him now. (op 14-1)
Ouninpohja(IRE)put his head in the air the instant Dean McKeown asked for him to quicken. Only slightly hampered by the winner as that horse edged into the middle of the course, he is not one to trust at the moment to go through with his effort after finishing second for the fourth time in a row. Considering he won five races last season, it would never be a surprise to see him land a nice prize again at some stage, and it would be interesting to see if some ease in the ground improved his attitude under pressure. (op 15-2)
Star Of Light was possibly given a bit too much to do, like a few in the race, and was not helped by being forced to switch a couple of times to get a run. That said, he ran a sound race and is the best marker to the form.
Signatory(USA)had every chance but was just not good enough on the day. It is not easy to ascertain whether the rise in the weights or the quicker ground contributed to the seemingly modest effort - he was due to be pulled out if the ground was not suitable - but a step up in trip may bring about some improvement. (op 4-1)
Vengeance had a mountain to climb entering the home straight and was gaining on the leaders all too late. He should not be harshly treated by the Handicapper and remains capable of winning again.
Young Mick appeared to have every chance but failed to land a blow under stiff pressure. He has had a fine season, which includes a success at Royal Ascot, and can be excused a modest effort. (op 16-1 tchd 10-1)
Royal Jet, having his first race of the season, shaped a bit better than his final position suggested, although he did not look to be putting his head down when asked to pass rivals. A set of headgear may be required again.
Red Lancer never featured with any chance and ran a very modest race. Without a win since landing the Chester Vase in 2004, he is obviously very hard to win with.
Thunder Rock(IRE) alway seems to be well-fancied for big handicaps, despite a lack of winning form at the grade. He had finished in front of the winner at Royal Ascot when down the field in the Duke Of Edinburgh Stakes, Consular was 3lb better off with him on that run, so it must go down as a below-par effort. It was noticeable that the jockey did not give him a hard time throughout the final stages, suggesting all may not have been right with him. Official explanation: jockey said colt lost its action (op 5-1 tchd 11-2 in places)
Dunaskin(IRE) Official explanation: trainer said gelding suffered interference in running

3295 CASINO 36 STOCKPORT CLASSIC CONDITIONS STKS 6f
4:05 (4:08) (Class 2) 3-Y-O+

£12,464 (£3,732; £1,866; £934; £466; £234) **Stalls** Centre

Form				RPR
5-35	**1**		**Somnus**[30] 2386 6-8-11 109 ... NCallan 7 (T D Easterby) *trckd ldrs: rdn to ld and edgd sltly rt over 1f out: drvn out whn pressed towards fin* **11/4**[2]	106
-640	**2**	*shd*	**Excusez Moi (USA)**[16] 2776 4-8-11 97 ... (tp) RyanMoore 9 (C E Brittain) *s.i.s: hld up: hdwy over 2f out: chsd wnr over 1f out: lugged lft and ev ch ins fnl f: r.o* **13/2**[3]	106
2160	**3**	*2 ½*	**Kodiac**[121] 621 5-8-11 104 ... (b) KDarley 6 (J L Dunlop) *w ldr: led 1/2-way: rdn and hdd over 1f out: edgd rt ins fnl f: nt pce of ldng pair after* **8/1**	99
0000	**4**	*2*	**Just James**[7] 3079 7-8-11 96 ... JoeFanning 10 (D Nicholls) *in rr: rdn and hdwy over 1f out: kpt on ins fnl f: nt pce to chal* **16/1**	93
6433	**5**	*2*	**Bahamian Pirate (USA)**[14] 2847 11-8-11 99 ... FrancisNorton 4 (D Nicholls) *in rr: rdn and sme hdwy over 1f out: no imp on ldrs* **10/1**	87

0561 **6** *4* **Indian Trail**[7] 3077 6-8-11 94........................ AdrianTNicholls 3 87+
(D Nicholls) *in tch: rdn over 2f out: wknd 1f out: eased whn btn ins fnl f* **5/2**[1]

0002 **7** *3/4* **Beckermet (IRE)**[7] 3076 4-9-2 102........................ MartinDwyer 1 77
(R F Fisher) *led: hdd 1/2-way: rdn over 2f out: wknd over 1f out* **13/2**[3]

3000 **8** *5* **Jonny Ebeneezer**[15] 2824 7-8-11 82........................ MickyFenton 8 57
(M Wellings) *in tch: rdn over 2f out: sn wknd* **50/1**

1m 11.99s (-2.91) **Going Correction** -0.25s/f (Firm) **8** Ran SP% **109.9**
Speed ratings (Par 109):109,108,105,102,100 94,93,87
CSF £19.24 TOTE £3.90: £1.30, £2.10, £2.30; EX 29.50.
Owner Legard Sidebottom & Sykes **Bred** Lady Legard **Trained** Great Habton, N Yorks

FOCUS
A solid-looking conditions race, that included a couple of Group 1 winners of the distant past but not a race to go over board about.

NOTEBOOK
Somnus, who had not won since landing a Group 1 at Longchamp in late 2004, looked a bit fortunate to gain success after the runner-up appeared to do his very best to throw it away. However, one could not fault the way he kept on all the way to the line, on a track he goes well at, and he could easily return for the William Hill Sprint Cup later in the season. (op 5-2 tchd 3-1 in places)
Excusez Moi(USA), who had plenty to do with the winner on official figures, appeared to throw away certain victory by hanging in towards Somnus throughout the final furlong. It certainly looked like he could have won had he steered a straight course, and is one to treat with caution until he proves he is a straightforward ride. (op 10-1)
Kodiac, running his first race for his old yard after being trained in Dubai for a spell, showed plenty of enthusiasm on his first run since March, despite edging right under a left-hand drive inside the final furlong. He should come on for the run and is entitled to plenty of respect next time. (op 9-1)
Just James always seems to run virtually the same race every time he makes the track. He is making his way down the handicap very slowly and will never be a horse that can be easily predicted. (op 14-1)
Bahamian Pirate(USA) is a grand old campaigner who had been running well of late. However, he did not run up to his recent best and might be better suited by larger fields now. (op 9-1 tchd 8-1)
Indian Trail tracked the leaders with the eventual winner, but found nothing when asked to quicken. There did not seem to be an obvious excuse for the poor effort, apart from racing quite keenly in the first part of the race, so it might be that a busy recent period has had an effect on him. He has won in small fields before so it is difficult to give that as a reason for failure, although his style of racing might be better suited by a race with many more runners. Official explanation: trainer said gelding hung right-handed closing stages (op 9-4)
Beckermet(IRE) showed a lot of early pace but could not sustain it at the business end of the race. (op 6-1)
Jonny Ebeneezer was predictably outclassed. (tchd 40-1)

3296 DUKE OF LANCASTER'S OWN YEOMANRY H'CAP 6f
4:35 (4:41) (Class 3) (0-90,90) 3-Y-0 **£11,334** (£3,372; £1,685; £841) **Stalls** Centre

Form RPR

5002 **1** **King Orchisios (IRE)**[14] 2866 3-9-7 **90**........................(p) NCallan 17 103
(K A Ryan) *mde all: rdn over 1f out: pressed ins fnl f: jst hld on* **9/1**

2231 **2** *shd* **Burning Incense (IRE)**[12] 2931 3-8-13 **82**........................ RyanMoore 16 95
(R Charlton) *hld up: hdwy over 2f out: rdn to chse wnr over 1f out: ev ch ins fnl f: r.o u.p: jst failed* **13/8**[1]

1 **3** *1 1/2* **Nusoor (IRE)**[56] 1687 3-8-6 **75**........................ MartinDwyer 12 83
(W J Haggas) *s.i.s: hld up: hdwy 2f out: rdn over 1f out: edgd lft ins fnl f: r.o: nt pce of ldng pair* **7/1**[2]

0126 **4** *3* **Garstang**[24] 2553 3-8-4 **73** oh3 ow2........................(b) RobbieFitzpatrick 7 72
(Peter Grayson) *bhd: rdn over 2f out: hdwy over 1f out: styd on ins fnl f: nt rch ldrs* **20/1**

6522 **5** *3/4* **Creative Mind (IRE)**[21] 2642 3-8-10 **79**........................ RichardMullen 15 76
(E J O'Neill) *prom: rdn over 2f out: fdd ins fnl f* **12/1**

-014 **6** *nk* **Charlie Delta**[17] 2760 3-8-11 **83**........................ DanielTudhope(3) 11 79
(D Carroll) *s.s: hld up: rdn 2f out: hdwy over 1f out: styd on: nt pce of ldrs* **25/1**

4103 **7** *1/2* **Rochdale**[14] 2866 3-9-1 **84**........................ JimmyFortune 2 79
(M A Jarvis) *midfield: rdn over 1f out: no imp fnl f* **8/1**[3]

6200 **8** *1/2* **Grazeon Gold Blend**[21] 2639 3-9-1 **84**........................ GrahamGibbons 8 77
(J J Quinn) *chsd ldrs: rdn over 2f out: hung lft over 1f out: wknd fnl f* **40/1**

4160 **9** *shd* **Rainbow Bay**[31] 2363 3-8-7 **76**........................ PaulHanagan 14 69
(R A Fahey) *in tch: rdn over 1f out: one pce fnl f* **33/1**

-100 **10** *1 1/2* **Greek Secret**[17] 2760 3-8-4 **73**........................ JimmyQuinn 9 61
(T D Easterby) *midfield: rdn over 2f out: wknd over 1f out* **33/1**

3340 **11** *nk* **Ryedale Ovation (IRE)**[30] 2385 3-8-10 **79**........................(p) DavidAllan 6 66
(T D Easterby) *towards rr: rdn and hdwy 2f out: no imp* **20/1**

5116 **12** *5* **Gavarnie Beau (IRE)**[17] 2756 3-9-4 **87**........................ FrancisNorton 3 59
(M Blanshard) *midfield: n.m.r 2f out: sn bhd* **33/1**

4025 **13** *4* **The History Man (IRE)**[10] 2976 3-8-7 **76**........................(b) DaleGibson 4 36
(M W Easterby) *prom tl rdn and wknd over 2f out* **50/1**

-000 **14** *3/4* **Crosby Hall**[10] 2976 3-8-2 **71** oh1........................(t) KimTinkler 1 29
(N Tinkler) *sn pushed along: a bhd* **50/1**

1-46 **15** *nk* **Bajan Parkes**[21] 2639 3-9-0 **83**........................ FergusSweeney 5 40
(H Candy) *in tch: rdn over 3f out: wknd over 2f out* **9/1**

1m 12.51s (-2.39) **Going Correction** -0.25s/f (Firm) **15** Ran SP% **118.0**
Speed ratings (Par 104):105,104,102,98,97 97,96,96,96,94 93,86,81,80,80
CSF £20.63 CT £112.29 TOTE £12.10: £3.30, £1.30, £2.50; EX 33.50.
Owner Mr & Mrs Julian And Rosie Richer **Bred** Rathbarry Stud **Trained** Hambleton, N Yorks

FOCUS
A competitive three-year-old handicap, in which the winner held a decent advantage over his rivals for much of the race. The draw appeared to play its part in the result as wellm but the race has been rated positively.

NOTEBOOK
King Orchisios(IRE), fitted with first-time cheekpieces, set off in front and stretched his rivals from the start. He looked all set to be swallowed up inside the final furlong before sticking his head out, denying the well-backed favourite all the way to the line. Always well regarded by his stable, the headgear may have helped to concentrate and, if they work for a second time, he ought to go close next time. (op 17-2 tchd 8-1)
Burning Incense(IRE) looked all set to collect approaching the final furlong before the winner pulled out more for pressure. Arguably putting up his best performance to date, he may not have finished improving yet, although it is a slight worry that he did not pass the winner when it looked like he could have at any stage inside the distance. He can be given the benefit of doubt at this stage. (op 2-1)
Nusoor(IRE) ◆ came into the race very inexperienced but put up a good effort, travelling well just off the lead before not quite getting home, still appearing a little green under pressure. Looking to have plenty of physical scope for improvement, he is one to take out of the race. (op 15-2)
Garstang, running from out of the handicap, is a credit to everyone connected to him, and he ran right up to his very best form, staying on well after being held up. He is going to find his handicap mark rising a bit for the run, so more improvement will be needed for him to have an obvious chance next time.
Creative Mind(IRE), steadily dropping down in trip, was always to the fore of the chasing pack before only staying on at the one pace throughout the final two furlongs, drifting to the 'wrong' side in the process. The step up in grade was probably just too much for her. (op 14-1 tchd 11-1)
Charlie Delta is a consistent sort who appeared to run right up to his best. However, the Handicapper probably has his measure for the time being, after raising him 10lb for his win in Class 5 company last month.
Rochdale, only just behind the winner last time at Newmarket and trying six furlongs for the first time, was never able to get on terms from a draw that was not advantageous on the day. (op 15-2)
Grazeon Gold Blend did not run without promise but was hanging to his left throughout the final stages. (op 33-1)
Crosby Hall Official explanation: vet said colt finished distressed
Bajan Parkes was beaten by the halfway point and ran a lacklustre race. Official explanation: jockey said gelding had no more to give (op 8-1)

3297 PAUL SALISBURY H'CAP 5f
5:10 (5:11) (Class 5) (0-70,70) 3-Y-0+ **£3,238** (£963; £481; £240) **Stalls** Centre

Form RPR

-323 **1** **Endless Summer**[22] 2618 9-9-1 **62**........................ JamesDoyle(5) 12 73
(A W Carroll) *hld up in rr: rdn and hdwy over 1f out: edgd lft ins fnl f: r.o to ld nr fin* **11/2**[1]

3065 **2** *1/2* **Henry Hall (IRE)**[16] 2784 10-9-11 **67**........................ KimTinkler 8 76
(N Tinkler) *sn chsng ldrs: rdn to ld ins fnl f: hdd nr fin* **14/1**

0003 **3** *1 1/2* **Harrison's Flyer (IRE)**[11] 2962 5-10-0 **70**........................(p) RyanMoore 4 74
(J M Bradley) *hld up towards rr: rdn and hdwy over 1f out: hung lft ins fnl f: r.o* **15/2**

1143 **4** *shd* **Soba Jones**[67] 1388 9-9-5 **64**........................ JasonEdmunds(3) 16 67
(J Balding) *a.p: rdn over 1f out: kpt on ins fnl f* **12/1**

3621 **5** *nk* **Drumming Party (USA)**[11] 2962 4-9-9 **65**........................(t) FergusSweeney 17 67
(A M Balding) *s.i.s: hld up: hdwy over 2f out: rdn over 1f out: kpt on towards fin* **6/1**[2]

0605 **6** *hd* **Town House**[9] 3004 4-8-2 **51** oh6........................ SoniaEaton(7) 15 52
(B P J Baugh) *led: rdr and hdd ins fnl f: no ex* **66/1**

1060 **7** *nk* **Jahia (NZ)**[16] 2780 7-8-9 **51** oh3........................ MickyFenton 2 51
(P T Midgley) *w ldr: rdn and ev ch over 1f out: nt qckn ins fnl f* **66/1**

2503 **8** *hd* **Highland Song (IRE)**[14] 2855 3-9-6 **67**........................ NCallan 11 67
(R F Fisher) *w ldrs: rdn over 2f out: edgd lft jst ins fnl f: one pce* **14/1**

06 **9** *shd* **Diamond Katie (IRE)**[14] 2856 4-9-0 **56**........................ DaleGibson 6 55
(N Tinkler) *chsd ldrs: lost pl after 2f: rdn over 1f out: sme late prog* **20/1**

0062 **10** *hd* **Whitbarrow (IRE)**[7] 3071 7-9-1 **64**........................ JamesMillman(7) 9 63
(B R Millman) *chsd ldrs: lost pl after 2f: rdn over 1f out: sme late prog* **7/1**[3]

4006 **11** *1/2* **Whistler**[22] 2618 9-9-6 **62**........................(p) PaulFitzsimons 3 59
(Miss J R Tooth) *s.i.s: rdn over 1f out: effrt whn carried lft jst ins fnl f: n.d* **16/1**

0-00 **12** *nk* **Flaran**[16] 2784 6-8-9 **51**........................ JimmyQuinn 7 47
(J A R Toller) *bhd fnl 2f* **20/1**

0-00 **13** *3/4* **Flur Na H Alba**[16] 2784 7-9-10 **66**........................(v) GrahamGibbons 1 59
(J J Quinn) *chsd ldrs: rdn 2f out: carried lft jst ins fnl f: sn swtchd rt: n.d after* **22/1**

0-00 **14** *hd* **Beyond The Clouds (IRE)**[16] 2780 10-9-5 **61**........................ AdrianMcCarthy 5 53
(J S Wainwright) *s.i.s: a bhd* **50/1**

0005 **15** *5* **Jadan (IRE)**[4] 3170 5-8-13 **55**........................ FrancisNorton 13 29
(E J Alston) *mid-div: rdn 2f out: sn bhd* **8/1**

6400 **16** *5* **Borzoi Maestro**[3] 3190 5-8-12 **54**........................(p) JoeFanning 14 10
(M Wellings) *prom: hung lft and losing pl whn n.m.r jst over 1f out: eased fnl f* **16/1**

60.03 secs (-2.04) **Going Correction** -0.25s/f (Firm)
WFA 3 from 4yo+ 5lb **16** Ran SP% **116.7**
Speed ratings (Par 103):106,105,102,102,102 101,101,101,100,100 99,99,98,97,89 81
CSF £71.65 CT £602.50 TOTE £6.40: £1.60, £3.20, £2.30, £3.00; EX 125.40.
Owner Seasons Holidays **Bred** Juddmonte Farms **Trained** Cropthorne, Worcs
■ Stewards' Enquiry : N Callan one-day ban: careless riding (Jul 19)

FOCUS
A modest sprint, in which the first 14 home were covered by less than five lengths and the form looks strong enough for the grade, backed up by the time.
Diamond Katie(IRE) Official explanation: jockey said filly hung right-handed
Whitbarrow(IRE) Official explanation: jockey said gelding hung right-handed
Borzoi Maestro Official explanation: jockey said gelding lost its action

3298 MR & MRS STEVEN CHADWICK WEDDING DAY H'CAP 1m 30y
5:45 (5:46) (Class 5) (0-70,71) 3-Y-0+ **£3,238** (£963; £481; £240) **Stalls** Low

Form RPR

0-02 **1** **She's Our Lass (IRE)**[22] 2627 5-9-5 **64**........................ DanielTudhope(3) 2 74+
(D Carroll) *hld up and bhd: rdn and hdwy on ins over 2f out: led over 1f out: r.o wl* **7/2**[2]

-005 **2** *3/4* **Missed A Beat**[14] 2865 4-9-9 **65**........................ FrancisNorton 3 73
(M Blanshard) *a.p: rdn and ev ch over 1f out: kpt on ins fnl f* **7/1**

-011 **3** *1/2* **Prince Evelith (GER)**[7] 3082 3-9-6 **71**........................ DeanMcKeown 4 78+
(G A Swinbank) *hld up towards rr: rdn and hung lft fr over 2f out: hdwy over 1f out: styd on towards fin* **5/2**[1]

2054 **4** *1/2* **Champain Sands (IRE)**[19] 2697 7-8-9 **56**........................ TravisBlock(5) 10 62
(E J Alston) *hld up and bhd: hdwy over 3f out: rdn and ev ch over 1f out: sn hung lft: nt qckn* **14/1**

/030 **5** *2 1/2* **Tamatave (IRE)**[48] 1864 4-9-10 **66**........................ NCallan 5 66
(K A Ryan) *a.p: rdn and ev ch wl over 1f out: one pce whn n.m.r jst ins fnl f* **16/1**

3103 **6** *2 1/2* **Takes Tutu (USA)**[5] 3147 7-10-0 **70**........................ RobbieFitzpatrick 7 64
(C R Dore) *hld up in rr: rdn over 2f out: sme hdwy on ins 1f out: eased whn no imp towards fin* **6/1**[3]

3000 **7** *3/4* **Uhuru Peak**[24] 2541 5-8-11 **53**........................(t) DaleGibson 8 46
(M W Easterby) *t.k.h: prom: rdn over 2f out: sn wknd* **40/1**

2402 **8** *1/2* **Bond Diamond**[15] 2831 9-9-5 **61**........................ MickyFenton 9 52
(P T Midgley) *plld hrd: led early: chsd ldr: led over 3f out: rdn and hdd over 1f out: wknd ins fnl f* **14/1**

5000 **9** *3* **Anduril**[24] 2551 5-9-12 **68**........................(b) JimmyQuinn 12 53
(Miss M E Rowland) *plld hrd in mid-div: hdwy 3f out: rdn 2f out: wknd jst over 1f out* **33/1**

4314 **10** *1/2* **Trevian**[3] 3197 5-8-12 **54**........................ AdrianTNicholls 1 37
(J M Bradley) *hld up in mid-div: rdn 3f out: wknd 2f out* **9/1**

220/ **11** *1 3/4* **Explode**[24] 6548 9-8-8 **53** oh3 ow2........................ JasonEdmunds(3) 11 32
(Miss L C Siddall) *s.i.s: a bhd* **50/1**

1000 **12** *30* **Mystic Man (FR)**[61] 1531 8-9-11 **70**.......................... PatrickMathers(3) 6 —
(I W McInnes) *sn led: rdn and hdd over 3f out: wknd qckly wl over 2f out: t.o* **33/1**

1m 44.12s (-1.39) **Going Correction** -0.25s/f (Firm)
WFA 3 from 4yo+ 9lb **12** Ran SP% **117.1**
Speed ratings (Par 103):96,95,94,94,91 89,88,88,85,84 82,52
CSF £27.14 CT £71.79 TOTE £4.80: £1.80, £2.40, £1.50; EX 24.40 Place 6 £24.93, Place 5 £14.18.
Owner We-Know Partnership **Bred** Illuminatus Investments **Trained** Warthill, N Yorks

FOCUS
A modest handicap run at a slow early tempo and the time was modest. The fourth sets the level for the form.
Trevian Official explanation: jockey said gelding hung right-handed
T/Plt: £43.30 to a £1 stake. Pool: £101,095.20. 1,702.35 winning tickets. T/Qpdt: £15.20 to a £1 stake. Pool: £4,275.80. 208.10 winning tickets. DO

3004 LEICESTER (R-H)

Saturday, July 8

OFFICIAL GOING: Good (good to firm in places)
Wind: Light, behind

3299 LADBROKESCASINO.COM FILLIES' H'CAP — 5f 218y
2:25 (2:25) (Class 5) (0-70,70) 3-Y-O **£5,181** (£1,541; £770; £384) **Stalls** Low

Form RPR

01 **1** **Bakhoor (IRE)**[19] 2704 3-8-8 **57**.. LPKeniry 12 72+
(W Jarvis) *chsd ldrs: led over 1f out: r.o wl* **5/2**[1]

31 **2** *2* **China Cherub**[14] 2859 3-9-5 **68**.. DaneO'Neill 9 74
(H Candy) *s.i.s: hdwy 1/2-way: chsd wnr over 1f out: styd on same pce* **4/1**[2]

0233 **3** *nk* **Making Music**[8] 3042 3-9-4 **67**....................................(p) J-PGuillambert 4 72
(T D Easterby) *prom: outpcd 1/2-way: hdwy over 1f out: styd on* **14/1**

0-06 **4** *nk* **Night Rainbow (IRE)**[21] 2648 3-8-4 **56** ow1................. AdamKirby(3) 13 60
(C Tinkler) *chsd ldrs: rdn 1/2-way: edgd lft ins fnl f: styd on same pce* **50/1**

-415 **5** *1 1/4* **Orange Dancer (IRE)**[26] 2511 3-9-2 **70**........................ TravisBlock(5) 3 72+
(H Morrison) *chsd ldrs: rdn, nt clr run and lost pl over 1f out: n.d after* **13/2**[3]

2340 **6** *shd* **Red Vixen (IRE)**[10] 2987 3-7-13 **55**.......................... KirstyMilczarek(7) 2 55
(C N Allen) *hld up: swtchd rt and hdwy over 1f out: nt trble ldrs* **16/1**

-000 **7** *3/4* **Forces Sweetheart**[32] 2316 3-7-13 **55**.......................... LukeMorris(7) 8 53
(M L W Bell) *hld up: hdwy 1/2-way: rdn over 1f out: no ex* **33/1**

1601 **8** *hd* **Just Down The Road (IRE)**[10] 2987 3-8-13 **65**... NelsonDeSouza(3) 10 62
(R A Harris) *led over 4f: wknd ins fnl f* **8/1**

2214 **9** *hd* **Piccostar**[10] 2987 3-9-7 **70**.. SamHitchcott 5 67
(A B Haynes) *a in rr* **14/1**

3364 **10** *nk* **Spectacular Show (IRE)**[8] 3047 3-9-7 **70**...................... PatCosgrave 6 66
(M Quinn) *in rr: swtchd rt and sme hdwy over 1f out: wknd ins fnl f* **9/1**

003 **11** *2* **Cabriole**[17] 2763 3-9-0 **63**.. HayleyTurner 1 53
(H R A Cecil) *chsd ldrs over 4f* **8/1**

0431 **12** *3/4* **Sapphire Storm (IRE)**[21] 2644 3-8-0 **54** oh1 ow3........ RoryMoore(5) 11 42
(P T Midgley) *hld up: hdwy 1/2-way: wknd wl over 1f out* **28/1**

1m 11.07s (-2.13) **Going Correction** -0.30s/f (Firm) **12** Ran SP% **121.7**
Speed ratings (Par 97):102,99,98,98,96 96,95,95,95,94 92,91
CSF £12.08 CT £122.23 TOTE £4.00: £2.00, £1.70, £5.20; EX 14.00 TRIFECTA Not won..
Owner Ziad A Galadari **Bred** Galadari Sons Stud Company Limited **Trained** Newmarket, Suffolk

FOCUS
This looks a strong handicap for the grade. An improved effort from the winner, with the runner-up to form.
Red Vixen(IRE) Official explanation: jockey said filly lost a front shoe

3300 LADBROKES.COM (S) STKS — 5f 2y
3:00 (3:01) (Class 6) 2-Y-O **£2,590** (£770; £385; £192) **Stalls** Low

Form RPR

0430 **1** **Pat Will (IRE)**[6] 3117 2-8-7 ow1.......................... J-PGuillambert 7 60+
(P D Evans) *chsd ldrs: hung rt 1/2-way: rdn to ld over 1f out: hdd ins fnl f: rallied to ld nr fin* **8/11**[1]

5004 **2** *nk* **Caj (IRE)**[30] 2382 2-8-6.. PatCosgrave 3 58
(M Quinn) *chsd ldrs: edgd lft 2f out: rdn to ld ins fnl f: hdd nr fin* **7/1**[3]

5006 **3** *2 1/2* **Loch Clutha (IRE)**[12] 2922 2-8-3 ....(p) NelsonDeSouza(3) 5 49
(K R Burke) *s.i.s: outpcd: styd on ins fnl f: nrst fin* **17/2**

5403 **4** *hd* **Alittleriskie (IRE)**[12] 2916 2-8-11 ....(b) LPKeniry 4 53
(J S Moore) *led over 3f: no ex ins fnl f* **9/1**

055 **5** *1 1/2* **Mr Mini Scule**[37] 2179 2-8-11 ....(b[1]) DaneO'Neill 1 48
(A B Haynes) *chsd ldrs: rdn 1/2-way: wknd fnl f* **16/1**

6003 **6** *nk* **Cyprus Rose**[26] 2495 2-8-4 ow1................................ AdamKirby(3) 2 43
(V Smith) *chsd ldrs: rdn whn bmpd wl over 1f out: wknd fnl f* **11/2**[2]

4040 **7** *13* **Lenard Frank (IRE)**[6] 3117 2-8-11 .... HayleyTurner 6 —
(M D I Usher) *sn outpcd* **33/1**

60.67 secs (-0.23) **Going Correction** -0.30s/f (Firm) **7** Ran SP% **115.1**
Speed ratings (Par 92):89,88,84,84,81 81,60
CSF £6.69 TOTE £1.50: £1.10, £3.70; EX 5.70.The winner was bought in for 5,000gns. Caj was the subject of a friendly claim.
Owner D Healy **Bred** Tally-Ho Stud **Trained** Pandy, Abergavenny
■ Stewards' Enquiry : Pat Cosgrave two-day ban: careless riding (Jul 18-19)

FOCUS
Typical form for the grade. The winner can improve on this.

NOTEBOOK
Pat Will(IRE) had the best form in the book and obliged at short odds, despite being made to work hard in the final furlong. She appreciated the drop back to the minimum trip in selling company, but she is clearly only modest, and she showed a definite tendency to lug to her right in the early stages. She will find life tougher in nurseries. (op 4-5 tchd 10-11)
Caj(IRE) shaped better than in recent starts, seeing out the trip much better than she had been doing and only being denied close home. (op 9-1 tchd 10-1)
Loch Clutha(IRE) became outpaced in the early stages and was some six lengths adrift at halfway. She stayed on past beaten rivals late in the day, shaping as though she would appreciate another furlong or two. (op 10-1 tchd 8-1)
Alittleriskie(IRE), beaten in sellers on her last three starts, cut out the early running but was swallowed up passing the furlong pole. (op 10-1 tchd 15-2)

3301 LADBROKES.COM H'CAP — 1m 60y
3:35 (3:35) (Class 4) (0-80,78) 3-Y-O
£7,478 (£2,239; £1,119; £560; £279; £70) **Stalls** High

Form RPR

5553 **1** **Rationale (IRE)**[22] 2616 3-8-7 **64**.................................... HayleyTurner 4 72
(S C Williams) *chsd ldrs: rdn over 1f out: styd on to ld wl ins fnl f* **10/1**

2121 **2** *1/2* **Angaric (IRE)**[38] 2126 3-9-0 **74**.............................. NelsonDeSouza(3) 9 81
(B Smart) *led: rdn over 1f out: hdd wl ins fnl f* **13/2**

-020 **3** *1* **Fregate Island (IRE)**[16] 2781 3-9-2 **78**......................... LiamJones(5) 10 83
(W J Haggas) *chsd ldrs: rdn over 2f out: styd on* **11/1**

3034 **4** *1/2* **Blacktoft (USA)**[15] 2823 3-8-9 **66**.................................... PatCosgrave 1 69
(E A L Dunlop) *hld up in tch: rdn over 2f out: styd on* **16/1**

5-32 **5** *1/2* **Danski**[43] 1978 3-9-4 **78**.. AmirQuinn(3) 8 80
(P J Makin) *hld up: swtchd lft over 2f out: hung rt over 1f out: r.o ins fnl f: nt rch ldrs* **6/1**[3]

U416 **6** *1/2* **Ahlawy (IRE)**[16] 2781 3-9-0 **78**.............................. AshleyHamblett(7) 6 79+
(L M Cumani) *s.i.s: hld up: outpcd over 2f out: r.o ins fnl f: nrst fin* **14/1**

1141 **6** *dht* **Punjabi**[15] 2809 3-9-4 **75**.. J-PGuillambert 7 76
(Mrs G S Rees) *hld up: hdwy over 2f out: rdn over 1f out: styd on same pce* **4/1**[2]

3-24 **8** *nk* **Villa Sonata**[22] 2615 3-9-1 **72**.. OscarUrbina 11 72
(J R Fanshawe) *hld up in tch: rdn over 2f out: no ex fnl f* **11/4**[1]

-015 **9** *3* **Zamala**[31] 2359 3-9-6 **77**.. DaneO'Neill 3 71
(J L Dunlop) *hld up: hdwy over 2f out: sn rdn: wknd fnl f* **14/1**

1006 **10** *3 1/2* **Fangorn Forest (IRE)**[7] 3067 3-9-1 **72**..............................(p) LPKeniry 2 57
(R A Harris) *hld up: a in rr* **50/1**

0146 **11** *3 1/2* **Stanley Goodspeed**[21] 2650 3-9-1 **75**.......................... AdamKirby(3) 5 52
(J W Hills) *hld up in tch: rdn over 3f out: sn lost pl* **16/1**

1m 44.12s (-1.18) **Going Correction** -0.05s/f (Good) **11** Ran SP% **118.8**
Speed ratings (Par 102):103,102,101,101,100 100,100,99,96,93 89
CSF £74.40 CT £751.85 TOTE £8.60: £2.00, £2.30, £4.80; EX 61.50 TRIFECTA Not won..
Owner Alasdair Simpson **Bred** Middle Park Stud Ltd **Trained** Newmarket, Suffolk

FOCUS
A wide-open handicap with several unexposed performers on show, but there was only around four lengths covering the first eight home and few got into this despite the overall gallop appearing brisk enough. The winner did not quite run to his Nottingham form, but the overall level of the race seems sound rated around the third and fourth.
Danski Official explanation: jockey said colt stumbled early on
Punjabi Official explanation: jockey said gelding ran flat
Stanley Goodspeed Official explanation: jockey said gelding hung right

3302 EUROPEAN BREEDERS FUND FILLIES' H'CAP — 1m 3f 183y
4:10 (4:10) (Class 4) (0-85,80) 3-Y-O-**£7,478** (£2,239; £1,119; £560; £279) **Stalls** High

Form RPR

6013 **1** **Wannabe Posh (IRE)**[23] 2584 3-8-13 **70**.......................... EddieAhern 1 86+
(J L Dunlop) *chsd ldr: rdn and hung rt fr over 2f out: led over 1f out: styd on strly* **6/4**[1]

1223 **2** *5* **Winds Of Change**[8] 3046 3-8-12 **69**.............................. J-PGuillambert 2 76+
(M Johnston) *led: rdn and hdd whn hmpd over 1f out: wknd ins fnl f* **11/4**[2]

0-22 **3** *1 1/4* **Kerriemuir Lass (IRE)**[35] 2220 3-9-2 **73**.......................... DaneO'Neill 5 77
(M A Jarvis) *trckd ldrs: racd keenly: n.m.r over 3f out: sn rdn: styd on same pce appr fnl f* **7/2**[3]

-213 **4** *4* **Tasjeel (USA)**[20] 2679 3-9-9 **80**.................................. OscarUrbina 4 80+
(W J Haggas) *hld up: rdn over 2f out: wknd over 1f out* **5/1**

/36- **5** *1* **Swindon (USA)**[229] 6405 4-9-9 **70**.......................... NelsonDeSouza(3) 3 67
(P F I Cole) *hld up: racd keenly: wknd over 2f out* **22/1**

2m 33.38s (-1.12) **Going Correction** -0.05s/f (Good)
WFA 3 from 4yo 13lb **5** Ran SP% **109.9**
Speed ratings (Par 102):101,97,96,94,93
CSF £5.86 TOTE £1.90: £1.50, £1.40; EX 2.70.
Owner Nicholas Cooper **Bred** Vizcaya Ag **Trained** Arundel, W Sussex

FOCUS
They went a modest gallop. The level of the form looks sound, rated through the second, third and fourth.

3303 LADBROKES.COM CLAIMING STKS — 1m 1f 218y
4:40 (4:40) (Class 5) 3-Y-O **£4,533** (£1,348; £505; £505) **Stalls** High

Form RPR

3003 **1** **Participation**[8] 3045 3-9-2 75.................................(p) DerekNolan(5) 9 73
(M J Wallace) *s.i.s: hld up: hdwy 7f out: rdn to ld ins fnl f: r.o* **11/4**[1]

0 **2** *1* **Dik Dik**[42] 2028 3-8-13 ....(v[1]) OscarUrbina 1 63
(J R Fanshawe) *s.i.s: hld up: hdwy over 2f out: rdn and edgd rt over 1f out: ev ch ins fnl f: no ex nr fin* **9/1**

00 **3** *1 1/2* **Fluted Crystal**[17] 2753 3-8-8 .... LPKeniry 3 55
(H Candy) *chsd ldrs: led 2f out: rdn and hdd ins fnl f: no ex* **40/1**

55 **3** *dht* **Matinee Idol**[10] 2970 3-8-8 .... DaneO'Neill 8 55
(H Candy) *s.i.s: hld up: r.o ins fnl f: nrst fin* **7/1**

5404 **5** *2* **Mister Maq**[19] 2698 3-9-1 57.....................................(p) J-PGuillambert 7 58
(M Dods) *hld up in tch: rdn and n.m.r over 1f out: no ex ins fnl f* **5/1**[3]

-000 **6** *3/4* **Sea Grain (IRE)**[24] 2539 3-8-11 52.............................. HayleyTurner 10 53
(Robert Gray) *chsd ldr: rdn over 2f out: styd on same pce appr fnl f* **25/1**

0-65 **7** *3* **Mighty Observer (IRE)**[23] 2591 3-8-9 48............................ EddieAhern 6 46+
(M H Tompkins) *sn led: rdn and hdd 2f out: wknd fnl f* **8/1**

4405 **8** *shd* **Tora Petcha (IRE)**[9] 3008 3-8-6 69.................... RussellKennemore(7) 11 49
(R Hollinshead) *s.s: rdn 3f out: wknd over 1f out* **7/2**[2]

0030 **9** *3 1/2* **Carpeting**[8] 3045 3-8-6 57...(v) AdamKirby(3) 5 38
(D Morris) *hld up: rdn over 4f out: a in rr* **16/1**

0105 **10** *25* **Tallyhobye**[15] 2832 3-8-7 49.. PatCosgrave 4 —
(M E Sowersby) *hld up: plld hrd: rdn and wknd 4f out* **20/1**

00-0 **11** *48* **Fairytale Of York (IRE)**[24] 2539 3-8-2 37...................(v[1]) FrancisFerris 2 —
(D Carroll) *hld up: rdn and wknd 1/2-way* **50/1**

2m 7.71s (-0.59) **Going Correction** -0.05s/f (Good) **11** Ran SP% **118.1**
Speed ratings (Par 100):100,99,98,98,96 95,93,93,90,70 32
PL: Fluted Crystal 3.80, Matinee Idol £1.30; TC: Participation/Dik Dik/FC £26.80; Participation/Dik Dik/MI £26.80 CSF £27.38 TOTE £2.20: £1.90, £2.30; EX 31.30.Dik Dik was claimed by Conrad Allen for £10,000. The winner was the subject of a friendly claim.
Owner B Walsh & Mrs R G Hillen **Bred** Juddmonte Farms Ltd **Trained** Newmarket, Suffolk

FOCUS
Little strength in depth in this claimer but the form looks solid enough rated around the winhner, fifth and sixth.
Carpeting Official explanation: jockey said gelding slipped on the bend

3304 LADBROKES.COM CLASSIFIED STKS 7f 9y
5:15 (5:18) (Class 5) 3-Y-0+ £5,047 (£1,510; £755; £377; £188) Stalls Low

Form RPR

2-00 1 **Certain Justice (USA)**[177] 100 8-9-3 70 HayleyTurner 8 76
(Stef Liddiard) *a.p: racd keenly: trckd ldr 4f out: led 2f out: edgd rt and hdd over 1f out: rallied to ld nr fin* **20/1**

-463 2 *shd* **Imperial Gain (USA)**[13] 2896 3-8-6 70 (p) AdamKirby(3) 3 76
(W R Swinburn) *hld up: swtchd rt over 2f out: hdwy to ld: hung rt and lft over 1f out: sn rdn: hdd nr fin* **11/4**[2]

0111 3 *nk* **Electric Warrior (IRE)**[9] 3023 3-9-5 80 PatCosgrave 7 85+
(K R Burke) *hld up: hdwy and nt clr run over 1f out: sn rdn: r.o* **6/4**[1]

1-00 4 1 ½ **Sweet Emily**[7] 3099 4-9-0 67 OscarUrbina 2 69
(J R Fanshawe) *chsd ldrs: rdn: hung rt and ev ch over 1f out: no ex ins fnl f* **7/2**[3]

200 5 5 **Poker Player (IRE)**[7] 3089 4-9-3 66 (b) FrancisFerris 1 59
(G C Bravery) *led 5f: hung rt over 1f out: sn wknd* **14/1**

30-0 6 5 **El Capitan (FR)**[14] 2868 3-8-9 70 DaneO'Neill 6 47
(Miss Gay Kelleway) *chsd ldrs 5f* **25/1**

1m 24.5s (-1.60) **Going Correction** -0.30s/f (Firm)
WFA 3 from 4yo+ 8lb 6 Ran SP% **104.2**
Speed ratings (Par 103):97,96,96,94,89 83
CSF £62.29 TOTE £19.60: £5.40, £1.50; EX 141.40 TRIFECTA Not won. Place 6 £73.65, Place 5 £47.77.
Owner Foursure Partners **Bred** Knoll Enterprises Inc **Trained** Great Shefford, Berks
■ Stewards' Enquiry : Oscar Urbina one-day ban: careless riding (Jul 19)

FOCUS
A tight classified stakes and fair form for the level. They went without Premier Fantasy and Drawback after the former lashed out in the stalls, injuring Drawback.
T/Plt: £101.30 to a £1 stake. Pool: £38,910.45. 280.15 winning tickets. T/Qpdt: £18.80 to a £1 stake. Pool: £1,951.30. 76.80 winning tickets. CR

2610 NOTTINGHAM (L-H)
Saturday, July 8

OFFICIAL GOING: Firm (good to firm in places)
Wind: Virtually nil Weather: Overcast

3305 AMATEUR JOCKEYS ASSOCIATION INVESTING IN RACING LADY RIDERS' H'CAP 1m 1f 213y
6:10 (6:10) (Class 6) (0-60,60) 4-Y-0+ £2,637 (£811; £405) Stalls Low

Form RPR

1044 1 **Gala Sunday (USA)**[19] 2702 6-9-7 **46** (b) MissSBrotherton 9 67+
(M W Easterby) *chsd ldr: led after 1f: mde rest: drew clr over 3f out: unchal after* **9/1**

6245 2 8 **Ermine Grey**[19] 2708 5-10-7 **60** MrsSBosley 10 66
(A W Carroll) *hld up wl bhd: pushed along and effrt over 3f out: n.m.r 1f out: styd on to go 2nd on line: no ch w wnr* **7/1**

0201 3 *shd* **Orpen Quest (IRE)**[6] 3112 4-9-12 **51** 6ex (v) MissLEllison 12 57
(M J Attwater) *t.k.h: hld up in midfield: c wd st: rdn 3f out: chsd wnr over 1f out: hung lft fnl f: lost 2nd on line* **8/1**

0223 4 1 **Friends Hope**[21] 2636 5-9-13 **55** MissFayeBramley(3) 4 59
(P A Blockley) *settled in midfield: effrt and rdn over 3f out: kpt on: nvr nr wnr* **4/1**[2]

3023 5 ¾ **Fiore Di Bosco (IRE)**[15] 2808 5-9-13 **52** MrsCBartley 8 55
(T D Barron) *s.s: wl bhd: rdn and styd on fr 3f out: nvr on terms* **11/2**[3]

6642 6 *hd* **Wood Fern (UAE)**[10] 2966 6-9-0 **44** MissMSowerby(5) 3 46
(W M Brisbourne) *hld up wl bhd: rdn 3f out: styd on fnl f: nvr nrr* **3/1**[1]

0005 7 ¾ **Hillhall (IRE)**[7] 3068 4-9-9 **48** MissEJJones 14 49
(W M Brisbourne) *t.k.h: chsd ldrs: rdn and outpcd 3f out: wknd fnl f* **25/1**

-000 8 2 ½ **Emperor's Well**[8] 3056 7-10-0 **60** ow2 (b) MissJCoward(7) 13 56
(M W Easterby) *led for 1f: chsd wnr: rdn and outpcd over 3f out: wkng whn sltly hmpd 1f out* **33/1**

0132 9 ½ **Miss Monica (IRE)**[11] 2952 5-9-1 **45** MrsMarieKing(5) 5 40
(P W Hiatt) *t.k.h: hld up in midfield: pushed along 3f out: no prog* **7/1**

0030 10 9 **Full Of Zest**[14] 2862 4-9-11 **57** (b) MissLauraGray(7) 2 35
(Mrs L J Mongan) *chsd ldrs tl rdn and wknd 3f out: sn wl bhd* **33/1**

0/00 11 4 **Didifon**[10] 2966 11-9-7 **53** ow5 (p) MissJBuck(7) 11 23
(Mrs L J Young) *bhd and pushed along 1/2-way: t.o* **66/1**

2m 6.24s (-3.46) **Going Correction** -0.35s/f (Firm) 11 Ran SP% **117.7**
Speed ratings (Par 101):99,92,92,91,91 90,90,88,87,80 77
CSF £68.47 CT £531.72 TOTE £9.40: £3.00, £2.50, £2.90; EX 65.60.
Owner M W Easterby **Bred** Juddmonte Farms Inc **Trained** Sheriff Hutton, N Yorks
■ Blue Hedges was withdrawn (14/1, vet's advice). R4 applies, deduct 5p in the £, new market formed.

FOCUS
A moderate handicap run at a good early gallop. It has been rated negatively through the third.
Orpen Quest(IRE) Official explanation: jockey said gelding hung left throughout
Fiore Di Bosco(IRE) Official explanation: jockey said mare missed the break

3306 KONICA MINOLTA EAST (S) H'CAP 6f 15y
6:40 (6:42) (Class 6) (0-65,60) 3-4-Y-0 £2,730 (£806; £403) Stalls High

Form RPR

6140 1 **Namir (IRE)**[9] 3004 4-9-10 59 (vt) AmirQuinn(3) 6 68
(S R Bowring) *swtchd to stands' side sn after s: hld up: prog over 2f out: rdn to chal 1f out: led last 100yds: styd on* **11/2**[2]

0033 2 ¾ **Special Gold**[4] 3166 4-9-8 54 (b) J-PGuillambert 16 61
(T D Easterby) *chsd ldrs stands' side: wnt 2nd 3f out: rdn to ld 1f out: hdd and no ex last 100yds* **4/1**[1]

0540 3 1 **Smokincanon**[16] 2785 4-8-11 48 MarcHalford(5) 5 52+
(W G M Turner) *chsd ldrs on far side: led 3f out: clr of that gp over 1f out: ev ch fnl f: nt qckn last 100yds* **11/1**

0250 4 *hd* **Suhezy (IRE)**[16] 2782 3-8-11 49 PatCosgrave 17 52
(J S Wainwright) *led on stands' side: rdn 3f out: hdd 1f out: kpt on one pce* **7/1**[3]

-000 5 ¾ **Princely Vale (IRE)**[11] 2955 4-9-1 52 (b[1]) LiamJones(5) 12 53
(W G M Turner) *dwlt: sn rcvrd and prom on stands' side: rdn and ev ch 2f out: wknd fnl f* **8/1**

2204 6 1 ¼ **Bahhmirage (IRE)**[11] 2951 3-9-8 60 (v) EddieAhern 14 57
(Stef Liddiard) *dwlt: bhd on stands' side: rdn over 3f out: kptn on fnl f: nt rch ldrs* **7/1**[3]

0000 7 2 **Centreofattention**[14] 2874 3-8-3 44 SaleemGolam(3) 8 35+
(Mrs A Duffield) *bhd on far side: effrt u.p over 2f out: chsd ldr far side over 1f out: nt trble ldrs* **33/1**

00-0 8 ¾ **Sham Ruby**[23] 2575 4-8-12 44 (t) LPKeniry 11 33
(M R Bosley) *chsd ldrs on stands' side: hung lft and wknd wl over 2f out* **33/1**

04-0 9 *shd* **Binty**[5] 3155 4-8-10 49 MarkCoumbe(7) 10 38
(A J Chamberlain) *in tch on stands' side: rdn 3f out: wl btn over 1f out* **33/1**

-660 10 ¾ **First Among Equals**[36] 2187 3-8-9 47 SamHitchcott 15 33
(Miss J R Tooth) *chsd ldrs on stands' side tl rdn and wknd over 2f out* **33/1**

2000 11 *shd* **Von Wessex**[8] 3033 4-8-13 45 RobertMiles 4 31+
(W G M Turner) *in tch on far side: rdn 3f out: nvr on terms* **14/1**

00-0 12 3 **Carrietau**[22] 2616 3-9-6 58 (b[1]) JamieMackay 9 35
(J G Given) *sn bhd on stands' side: no ch 3f out* **33/1**

5360 13 *shd* **Coalite (IRE)**[16] 2782 3-8-13 54 (b) SilvestreDeSousa(3) 3 31+
(A D Brown) *led far side gp tl 3f out: sn rdn: wknd 2f out* **11/1**

0000 14 *nk* **Reviving (IRE)**[11] 2955 3-9-3 55 StephenCarson 2 31+
(R F Johnson Houghton) *prom on far side: rdn 3f out: wknd wl over 1f out* **20/1**

0000 15 ¾ **Maylea Gold (IRE)**[8] 3045 3-8-9 50 DeanCorby(3) 1 24+
(Miss J Feilden) *chsd ldrs on far side: rdn 3f out: sn no ch* **66/1**

4000 16 3 ½ **Dream Factor (IRE)**[9] 3006 3-8-7 45 PaulEddery 7 8+
(J O'Reilly) *racd far side: a wl bhd* **40/1**

0500 17 6 **Charming Princess**[14] 2876 3-8-2 45 EmmettStack(5) 13 —
(J S Wainwright) *chsd ldrs on stands' side tl hung lft and wknd qckly 3f out* **33/1**

1m 14.94s (-0.06) **Going Correction** -0.25s/f (Firm)
WFA 3 from 4yo 6lb 17 Ran SP% **121.2**
Speed ratings (Par 101):90,89,87,87,86 84,82,81,80,79 79,75,75,75,74 69,61
CSF £24.38 CT £247.56 TOTE £8.30: £2.20, £1.10, £3.10, £1.40; EX 27.30.There was no bid for the winner.
Owner ownaracehorse.co.uk (S A Mapletoft) **Bred** B Kennedy **Trained** Edwinstowe, Notts
■ Stewards' Enquiry : Amir Quinn two-day ban: using whip without allowing mount time to respond (Jul 19-20)

FOCUS
An ordinary selling handicap run in a poor time even for seller, 0.16 seconds slower than the two-year-old fillies' maiden. Nevertheless the form looks sound although very moderate.
Sham Ruby Official explanation: jockey said filly hung left
Von Wessex Official explanation: jockey said gelding ran flat

3307 HARRY RICHMOND & PARTNER LTD MAIDEN AUCTION FILLIES' STKS 6f 15y
7:15 (7:17) (Class 5) 2-Y-0 £3,238 (£963; £481; £240) Stalls High

Form RPR

542 1 **Harvest Joy (IRE)**[28] 2456 2-8-4 AlanMunro 4 72+
(B R Millman) *slipped as stalls opened and slowly away: bhd tl swtchd lft and hdwy 3f out: led over 1f out: sn clr: pushed out* **10/11**[1]

2 2 2 ½ **Beautiful Madness (IRE)**[9] 3005 2-8-1 DominicFox(3) 8 65
(M G Quinlan) *t.k.h: trckd ldrs tl pushed along and outpcd 3f out: rallied over 1f out: r.o to go 2nd nr fin: no ch w wnr* **9/2**[2]

6 3 *shd* **Bert's Memory**[16] 2791 2-8-8 EddieAhern 10 68
(K A Ryan) *chsd ldrs: rdn over 2f out: kpt on to chse wnr ins fnl f: lost 2nd nr fin* **12/1**

50 4 2 **Violet's Pride**[6] 3110 2-8-4 JosedeSouza 11 58
(S Parr) *led: qcknd clr 3f out: hdd over 1f out: wknd ins fnl f* **28/1**

0 5 6 **Grand Lucre**[56] 1675 2-8-8 RichardMullen 12 44
(E J O'Neill) *trckd ldrs: hung lft and rn green wl over 1f out: sn no ch* **13/2**[3]

5 6 3 **Namarian (IRE)**[26] 2500 2-8-8 J-PGuillambert 7 35
(T D Easterby) *prom: rdn 3f out: sn struggling and wl bhd* **8/1**

06 7 2 **Shes Millie**[56] 1688 2-7-13 EmmettStack(5) 1 25
(J G M O'Shea) *wnt lft s: sn rcvrd and prom: rdn 3f out: wknd 2f out* **20/1**

6 8 13 **Foxies Firstglance**[12] 2938 2-8-6 ow2 PaulMulrennan 2 —
(R D E Woodhouse) *chsd ldr tl lost pl qckly over 3f out: sn wl bhd: t.o* **66/1**

1m 14.78s (-0.22) **Going Correction** -0.25s/f (Firm) 8 Ran SP% **112.4**
Speed ratings (Par 91):91,87,87,84,76 72,70,52
CSF £4.88 TOTE £1.80: £1.02, £2.00, £2.10; EX 7.30.
Owner R S Jeffery **Bred** John Hutchinson **Trained** Kentisbeare, Devon

FOCUS
Just a fair maiden and the winner did not have to be at her best to score.

NOTEBOOK
Harvest Joy(IRE), runner-up at Newbury last time, had less to do in this company, but she lost her footing as the stalls opened and had to do it the hard way, coming from last to first. In the end she was easily the best, though, and there could be further success to come in nurseries. (op 11-10 after 5-4 in places)
Beautiful Madness(IRE), runner-up on her debut at Leicester, raced a bit too keen for her own good and could not live with the winner. She may struggle to win a maiden and nurseries look likely to give her a better chance of success in time. (tchd 5-1)
Bert's Memory, whose dam won over ten furlongs at three, is by a sire who is an influence for speed. Improving on her debut effort at Wolverhampton, she appreciated the extra furlong, but is another who will hold stronger claims in handicap company in due course. (tchd 10-1)
Violet's Pride bagged the stands'-side rail and once again showed good speed. The sixth furlong found her out, though, and a drop back to the minimum distance should suit. (op 25-1 tchd 33-1)
Grand Lucre, whose dam won over seven furlongs at three, still looked green on this second career start. She probably needs more time. (op 11-2 tchd 7-1)
Namarian(IRE), being by Namid, may well do a lot better when she can get her toe in. (tchd 15-2 and 9-1)

3308 STAPLEFORD PARK MEDIAN AUCTION MAIDEN STKS 5f 13y
7:45 (7:46) (Class 6) 2-Y-0 £3,412 (£1,007; £504) Stalls High

Form RPR

252 1 **Conquest (IRE)**[18] 2724 2-9-3 (b) JimmyFortune 2 93+
(W J Haggas) *mde all: clr 3f out: unchal after: eased nr fin* **2/13**[1]

3 2 5 **Castano**[87] 987 2-9-3 AlanMunro 4 75
(B R Millman) *a chsng wnr: rdn over 1f out: sn no ch w wnr* **6/1**[2]

3 15 **Lady Saffron (IRE)** 2-8-12 JosedeSouza 3 14
(J Balding) *sn outpcd in 3rd: t.o fr 1/2-way* **66/1**

4 12 **Express Willy** 2-9-3 PaulMulrennan 1 —
(J R Weymes) *taken steadily to post: dwlt: sn totally outpcd and t.o* **40/1**[3]

59.89 secs (-1.91) **Going Correction** -0.25s/f (Firm) 4 Ran SP% **104.9**
Speed ratings (Par 92):105,97,73,53
CSF £1.28 TOTE £1.10; EX 1.40.
Owner Highclere Thoroughbred Racing XXXVIII **Bred** Gerrardstown House Stud **Trained** Newmarket, Suffolk

FOCUS
An uncompetitive maiden but the winner clocked a very smart time for the type of contest and the form is rated at face value.

NOTEBOOK

Conquest(IRE) was in a different class to the rest and had no trouble getting off the mark at the fourth attempt. Runner-up in the Windsor Castle Stakes last time out, he deserved to win a race and, although he had little to beat, he recorded a fast time in victory. He will now return to Pattern company, with the choice being between the Molcomb Stakes at Goodwood and the Prix Robert Papin at Maisons-Laffitte. (tchd 1-6)

Castano, well backed when third on his debut over the course and distance in soft ground back in April, had different conditions to deal with this time. He had no chance with the very useful winner, but he tried his best to hang onto his coattails and was not disgraced. He will find his niche in nurseries in time. (op 7-1)

Lady Saffron(IRE), a half-sister to five winners, including useful Waterside, a smart multiple winner over six and seven furlongs, and multiple winning sprinter Seven No Trumps, struggled to go the pace from an early stage and was never seen with a chance. She should do better in time. (op 50-1)

3309 MATTHEWS AND TANNERT H'CAP — 1m 1f 213y

8:15 (8:15) (Class 4) (0-80,80) 3-Y-0+ — **£6,477** (£1,927; £963; £481) **Stalls** Low

Form				RPR
1250	**1**		**Gallego**[2] 3221 4-8-4 **61** oh1 ... LiamJones(5) 4 (R J Price) *s.s: hld up bhd: hdwy on outside 2f out: rdn to ld 1f out: r.o* **6/1**[3]	68
4106	**2**	¾	**Bright Sun (IRE)**[17] 2761 5-9-4 **70** ... (t) AlanMunro 2 (N Tinkler) *led: rdn 2f out: hdd 1f out: one pce* **6/1**[3]	76
3131	**3**	1 ½	**Dragon Slayer (IRE)**[8] 3048 4-10-0 **80** ... EddieAhern 3 (M J Attwater) *hld up in tch: rdn over 2f out: nt clr run and swtchd 1f out: r.o: wnt 3rd on line* **13/8**[1]	83
2500	**4**	shd	**Voice Mail**[10] 2969 7-9-4 **70** ... (b) LPKeniry 6 (A M Balding) *in tch: rdn over 2f out: fnd little and one pce fnl f: lost 3rd on line* **7/1**	73
1-20	**5**	3	**Press Express (IRE)**[37] 2162 4-9-11 **77** ... HayleyTurner 1 (M L W Bell) *t.k.h: chsd ldrs: nt clr run 2f out: rdn and wknd over 1f out* **3/1**[2]	74
-000	**6**	1	**Evolution Ex (USA)**[22] 2621 4-9-7 **73** ... PatCosgrave 5 (K R Burke) *chsd ldr: rdn over 2f out: wknd over 1f out* **12/1**	68

2m 6.09s **Going Correction** -0.35s/f (Firm) — 6 Ran SP% **111.9**

Speed ratings (Par 105):100,99,98,98,95 94

CSF £39.73 TOTE £8.00: £2.60, £4.20; EX 40.00.

Owner My Left Foot Racing Syndicate **Bred** Mrs C C Regalado-Gonzalez **Trained** Ullingswick, H'fords

FOCUS

An ordinary handicap and average form for the grade, rated around the first two. The winner benefited from being held up off the decent early pace.

3310 CITY LIFE AND COUNTRY LIVING MAGAZINE H'CAP — 1m 1f 213y

8:45 (8:45) (Class 5) (0-75,74) 3-Y-0 — **£3,238** (£963; £481; £240) **Stalls** Low

Form				RPR
3404	**1**		**Keel (IRE)**[38] 2142 3-9-7 **74** ... ShaneKelly 6 (J A Osborne) *led: sn clr: pushed 8l clr over 4f out: drvn 2f out: unchal* **15/2**	81+
4533	**2**	3 ½	**Markington**[16] 2786 3-9-3 **70** ... AlanMunro 3 (J D Bethell) *chsd ldr: rdn over 4f out: 3rd over 3f out: wnt 2nd again over 1f out: kpt on: nt rch wnr* **9/4**[1]	70
2234	**3**	1 ½	**Apt To Run (USA)**[10] 2990 3-9-5 **72** ... (b) RichardMullen 7 (E A L Dunlop) *hld up in last: rdn and effrt over 2f out: kpt on but nvr nr wnr* **7/2**[3]	70
0135	**4**	2 ½	**Secret Liaison**[38] 2142 3-9-6 **73** ... JamieMackay 5 (Sir Mark Prescott) *hld up: rdn and hdwy 4f out: wnt 2nd and hung lft over 3f out: wknd over 1f out* **11/4**[2]	66
6540	**5**	2	**Vodkatini**[22] 2620 3-9-0 **67** ... (v) FergusSweeney 4 (P J Makin) *t.k.h: chsd ldrs: rdn and outpcd 4f out: no ch after* **5/1**	56

2m 7.66s **Going Correction** -0.35s/f (Firm) — 5 Ran SP% **108.1**

Speed ratings (Par 100):94,91,90,88,86

CSF £23.64 TOTE £6.70: £2.60, £2.30; EX 30.60.

Owner Mountgrange Stud **Bred** Oak Lodge Bloodstock **Trained** Upper Lambourn, Berks

FOCUS

A fair handicap stolen by the winner under a good tactical ride. The race could have been rated higher but the winning time was moderate for the type of contest.

3311 PLANET FASHIONS H'CAP — 1m 54y

9:15 (9:15) (Class 5) (0-75,70) 3-Y-0+ — **£3,886** (£1,156; £577; £288) **Stalls** Low

Form				RPR
5023	**1**		**Barons Spy (IRE)**[7] 3089 5-9-3 **58** ... JamesDoyle(5) 3 (R J Price) *t.k.h: chsd ldr for 2f: settled in midfield: smooth hdwy to ld over 1f out: rdn clr: eased nr fin* **85/40**[1]	69+
0541	**2**	1 ¾	**Deeper In Debt**[5] 3153 8-10-1 **70** 6ex ... RoryMoore(5) 2 (J Akehurst) *sn led: rdn 2f out: hdd over 1f out: one pce* **5/2**[2]	77
0430	**3**	½	**Libre**[23] 2585 6-10-0 **64** ... JimmyFortune 6 (F Jordan) *hld up: rdn and effrt over 3f out: kpt on u.p fnl f* **4/1**[3]	70
-000	**4**	3 ½	**El Rey Royale**[15] 2808 4-8-13 **49** ... JimmyQuinn 4 (Micky Hammond) *t.k.h: chsd ldr after 2f: rdn 3f out: wknd fnl f* **6/1**	47
646	**5**	¾	**Mexican Bob**[12] 2919 3-9-10 **69** ... LPKeniry 1 (Heather Dalton) *t.k.h: chsd ldrs: rdn over 2f out: wknd 1f out* **20/1**	63
0410	**6**	3	**Adobe**[10] 2969 11-9-4 **59** ... LiamJones(5) 7 (W M Brisbourne) *s.s: hld up: rdn and effrt 3f out: no ch wl over 1f out* **9/1**	48
0030	**7**	42	**Donya One**[102] 783 4-8-9 **45** oh8 ... AlanMunro 5 (John A Harris) *bhd: in tch tl over 4f out: t.o* **50/1**	—

1m 43.44s (-2.96) **Going Correction** -0.35s/f (Firm)

WFA 3 from 4yo+ 9lb — 7 Ran SP% **111.6**

Speed ratings (Par 103):100,98,97,94,93 90,48

CSF £7.27 TOTE £4.10: £2.10, £1.30; EX 12.70 Place 6 £93.31, Place 5 £12.61.

Owner Barry Veasey **Bred** Tally-Ho Stud **Trained** Ullingswick, H'fords

FOCUS

A modest handicap that has been rated through the runner-up to the form of his Windsor win.

T/Plt: £64.00 to a £1 stake. Pool: £40,647.55. 463.25 winning tickets. T/Qpdt: £12.50 to a £1 stake. Pool: £2,749.10. 162.30 winning tickets. SP

3251 SANDOWN (R-H)

Saturday, July 8

OFFICIAL GOING: Good to firm (good in places on round course)

Wind: Light, across Weather: Fine and warm

3312 LAURENT-PERRIER CHAMPAGNE SPRINT STKS (GROUP 3) — 5f 6y

2:05 (2:07) (Class 1) 3-Y-0+

£28,390 (£10,760; £5,385; £2,685; £1,345; £675) **Stalls** High

Form				RPR
0630	**1**		**Pivotal Point**[14] 2846 6-9-3 110 ... SebSanders 11 (P J Makin) *sn trckd ldrs and racd against far side rail: effrt over 1f out: drvn and r.o fnl f to ld last 50yds* **5/1**[2]	117
-222	**2**	½	**Benbaun (IRE)**[6] 3124 5-9-7 111 ... (v) JamieSpencer 12 (M J Wallace) *racd against far side rail: pressed ldrs: led 1/2-way: rdn and tail swishing fnl f: hdd and nt qckn last 50yds* **5/2**[1]	119
-020	**3**	1	**The Trader (IRE)**[18] 2720 8-9-3 110 ... (b) TedDurcan 4 (M Blanshard) *s.i.s: hld up and sn wl bhd: gd prog against far side rail 2f out: nt clr run over 1f out: r.o fnl f* **16/1**	112
1212	**4**	hd	**Tawaassol (USA)**[21] 2658 3-8-12 93 ... (t) RHills 9 (Sir Michael Stoute) *trckd ldrs: nt clr run briefly wl over 1f out: sn rdn and nt qckn: styd on fnl f: nvr able to chal* **9/1**	111
1410	**5**	nk	**Reverence**[18] 2720 5-9-9 111 ... EddieAhern 6 (E J Alston) *settled in last trio: rdn on outer 2f out: r.o ins fnl f: nrst fin* **8/1**	116
4006	**6**	hd	**The Tatling (IRE)**[14] 2846 9-9-7 110 ... DarryllHolland 3 (J M Bradley) *towards rr: rdn 2f out: prog u.p 1f out: kpt on same pce* **9/1**	113
4253	**7**	hd	**Pivotal Flame**[20] 2675 4-9-3 105 ... (p) MJKinane 8 (E S McMahon) *prom: rdn to press ldr over 1f out tl wknd jst ins fnl f* **7/1**[3]	108
/12-	**8**	1 ¾	**Musadif (USA)**[300] 5163 8-9-3 106 ... (t) FJohansson 7 (R A Kvisla) *towards rr: rdn 2f out: hanging but kpt on fnl f: n.d* **100/1**	102
1300	**9**	1 ½	**Corridor Creeper (FR)**[18] 2720 9-9-3 107 ... (p) ShaneKelly 10 (J M Bradley) *led to 1/2-way: wknd over 1f out* **20/1**	97
1-00	**10**	13	**Boogie Street**[18] 2720 5-9-3 108 ... RichardHughes 5 (R Hannon) *pressed ldr for 2f: wknd rapidly 2f out: eased fnl f: t.o* **20/1**	50
6110	**11**	2	**One Putra (IRE)**[14] 2847 4-9-3 106 ... (t) PhilipRobinson 1 (M A Jarvis) *dwlt: racd wd: a struggling in rr: t.o* **11/1**	43
3-0F	**12**	9	**Tabaret**[18] 2720 3-8-12 103 ... AlanMunro 2 (R M Whitaker) *in tch in rr to 1/2-way: sn wknd: t.o* **40/1**	10+

60.83 secs (-1.38) **Going Correction** 0.0s/f (Good)

WFA 3 from 4yo+ 5lb — **12** Ran SP% **116.0**

Speed ratings (Par 113):111,110,108,108,107 107,107,104,101,81 77,63

CSF £16.70 TOTE £6.10: £2.10, £1.40, £5.70; EX 14.70 Trifecta £178.00 Pool: £1,304.26 - 5.20 winning units..

Owner R A Bernard **Bred** T R Lock **Trained** Ogbourne Maisey, Wilts

FOCUS

A typically tight Group 3 sprint with not much covering the front seven at the line, but a race in which the usual track bias played its part with the front pair, who set the standard, starting from the two highest stalls and the third following them up the far rail.

NOTEBOOK

Pivotal Point showed that his effort to finish third in last month's King's Stand was no fluke but, as was the case then, the draw was very much in his favour here, as was this stiff five. Getting a lovely tow from the leaders against the far rail, once he was pulled out for his effort he found more than enough to go and win his race. He may turn out again for the July Cup, but although he did not run so well in the Golden Jubilee just four days after the King's Stand, he has won when turned out again quickly before now so there should not be any worries on that score. (tchd 11-2)

Benbaun(IRE), who finished just in front of Pivotal Point in the King's Stand, was rightly given a positive ride from the plum draw and looked to be in control approaching the distance, but he looked rather ungainly in the last furlong and was eventually worried out of it. He has plenty of ability but is a bit of a lad, hence the headgear, and after four consecutive second places at a high level in a relatively short space of time, he is now likely to be given a well-earned rest. (tchd 11-4 and 9-4 in places)

The Trader(IRE), who had no chance from his draw in the King's Stand, returned to the sort of form that saw him chase home Reverence in the Temple Stakes here in May. Taken over from his low draw to race against the far rail, he had the whole field in front of him at halfway but managed to sneak through to reach a challenging position a furlong from home, but he then found the winner blocking his path and therefore halting his momentum. By the time daylight presented itself, he had run out of time. As talented as he is and as well as he retains his ability, he has always just missed out in domestic Group company.

Tawaassol(USA), dropped to the minimum trip for the first time, faced a stiff task for a three-year-old stepping out of handicap company and was also by far the worst horse in the race based on official ratings. However, he showed that not to be the case and was coming home as well as anything over a trip that was probably on the sharp side. He still has the scope to improve and looks up to winning in Listed company at least, which is probably just as well as he has almost certainly blown his handicap mark apart. (op 10-1)

Reverence, not as well drawn as he was when winning the Temple Stakes here in May and carrying a penalty for that success, rather found himself trapped on the outside of the field throughout and did not look entirely happy on the ground, so it is a sign of his ability that he kept plugging away to finish as close as he did. He has had a tough season already, so it may be worth giving him a break now and bring him back for an autumn campaign when the ground is likely to be more in his favour. (op 13-2 tchd 17-2)

The Tatling(IRE) never really threatened down the middle of the track, but although he was not helped by the draw he is still a bit below his very best. (op 8-1)

Pivotal Flame was not disgraced, but that has been the story with him at this level for a while now and he is still without a win since he was a two-year-old. (op 8-1 tchd 17-2)

One Putra(IRE) missed the break from the outside stall and that made an already difficult task impossible. Official explanation: jockey said colt missed the break (op 12-1)

Tabaret Official explanation: jockey said colt moved poorly throughout; vet said colt returned stiff behind

3313 TOTESCOOP6 STKS (HERITAGE H'CAP) — 1m 14y

2:35 (2:39) (Class 2) 3-Y-0+

£62,320 (£18,660; £9,330; £4,670; £2,330; £1,170) **Stalls** High

Form				RPR
0-14	**1**		**Hinterland (IRE)**[17] 2742 4-9-3 **99** ... PhilipRobinson 11 (M A Jarvis) *t.k.h: prom: prog to ld over 1f out: drvn and wl in command last 150yds: r.o wl* **7/2**[1]	110
0020	**2**	1 ¼	**Ace Of Hearts**[17] 2742 7-9-5 **101** ... GeorgeBaker 4 (C F Wall) *fast away: racd wd: cl up: effrt 2f out: drvn to press wnr 1f out: readily hld ins fnl.f* **12/1**	109
0240	**3**	½	**Momtic (IRE)**[15] 2803 5-9-10 **106** ... AlanMunro 13 (W Jarvis) *prom: rdn and nt qckn 2f out: styd on wl fnl f: nvr able to chal* **14/1**	113

3000 **4** ¾ **Capable Guest (IRE)**[17] 2742 4-8-11 **93**.................... JamieSpencer 15 98
(M R Channon) *hld up in midfield: effrt on inner over 2f out: nt clr run over 1f out: r.o ins fnl f: nrst fin* **10/1**[3]

2502 **5** ½ **Granston (IRE)**[21] 2657 5-8-5 **87**.................................... KerrinMcEvoy 7 91
(J D Bethell) *pressed ldr: upsides 2f out to over 1f out: one pce after* **12/1**

11-0 **6** *shd* **Stagelight (IRE)**[17] 2742 4-9-8 **104**.................................. ShaneKelly 10 108
(J Noseda) *hld up towards rr: plenty to do over 2f out: nt clr run 2f out and briefly over 1f out: r.o fnl f: no ch* **25/1**

0340 **7** 1¼ **Kings Quay**[15] 2803 4-9-0 **96**.. DarryllHolland 9 99+
(J J Quinn) *t.k.h: cl up: rdn 2f out: hld ent fnl f: eased last 100yds* **16/1**

-001 **8** *hd* **Humble Opinion**[28] 2440 4-8-5 **87**...................................... EddieAhern 8 88
(B J Meehan) *hld up bhd ldrs: prog on outer 2f out: nt qckn over 1f out: fdd ins fnl f* **13/2**[2]

4341 **9** *nk* **Flipando (IRE)**[9] 3020 5-8-9 **91**... PaulFessey 3 91
(T D Barron) *hld up towards rr: prog wl over 1f out: one pce u.p sn after* **10/1**[3]

56/0 **10** 1¼ **Seulement (USA)**[36] 2200 4-9-1 **97**.................................... CSoumillon 1 94
(L M Cumani) *settled towards rr: no real imp on ldrs fnl 2f* **14/1**

1005 **11** *nk* **Pentecost**[17] 2742 7-9-7 **103**....................................... RichardHughes 14 99
(A M Balding) *t.k.h: cl up tl wknd over 1f out* **12/1**

0353 **12** *hd* **My Paris**[31] 2358 5-9-0 **101**.. AndrewMullen(5) 16 97
(K A Ryan) *mde most to over 1f out: wknd fnl f* **16/1**

0-20 **13** 2½ **Desert Realm (IRE)**[16] 2774 3-8-7 **98**................................... JohnEgan 2 88
(M Johnston) *hld up wl in rr: effrt on outer over 2f out: no prog over 1f out: wknd* **33/1**

0300 **14** 3 **Chrysander**[35] 2226 4-9-4 **100**... TedDurcan 5 83
(M R Channon) *dwlt: hld up wl in rr: no real prog fnl 3f* **33/1**

0066 **15** ¾ **Bahar Shumaal (IRE)**[28] 2435 4-9-0 **96**.................................... RHills 6 77
(C E Brittain) *hld up wl in rr: rdn 3f out: no prog* **50/1**

-305 **16** *hd* **Langford**[9] 3020 6-8-11 **96**... SaleemGolam(3) 17 77+
(M H Tompkins) *rrd in stalls and lft at least 15l: ct up at bk of field after 3f: rdn and struggling 3f out* **16/1**

604/ **17** 7 **Beauchamp Pilot**[742] 3323 8-9-6 **102**................................ MJKinane 12 67
(G A Butler) *hld up: a wl in rr: nt moving wl and struggling over 2f out: t.o* **40/1**

1m 41.92s (-2.03) **Going Correction** 0.0s/f (Good)
WFA 3 from 4yo+ 9lb **17** Ran SP% **121.9**
Speed ratings (Par 109):110,108,108,107,107 106,105,105,105,103 103,103,100,97,97 96,89
CSF £42.78 CT £559.67 TOTE £3.50: £1.50, £3.00, £2.90, £2.60; EX 59.70 Trifecta £858.80 Pool: £37,376.06 - 30.90 winning units..
Owner Sheikh Mohammed **Bred** Gerald W Leigh **Trained** Newmarket, Suffolk

FOCUS

A red-hot and competitive handicap as it should be for the money and the form looks strong, but the early pace was more modest than might have been expected though the final time was perfectly acceptable, 0.32 seconds faster than the later Listed race for three-year-old fillies. Because of the way the race was run, it was a big advantage to race handily and four of the first five home were in the leading group throughout. However, despite the ordinary early gallop there was not as much trouble late on as might have been the case, with only two possible hard-luck stories.

NOTEBOOK

Hinterland(IRE) ◆, who ran such a big race in the Royal Hunt Cup, was ridden with a little more patience this time but was still handy enough in a contest not run at a strong gallop. When asked to go and win his race, he found plenty and was well on top at the line. It is less than a year since he made his racecourse debut, so there is every chance he is still improving and he may stick at this trip for the Totesport Mile at Glorious Goodwood. In the longer term, it would be no surprise to see him tackling Pattern company. (tchd 10-3 and 4-1 in places)

Ace Of Hearts, winner of this race last year off a 9lb lower mark, was always up with the pace after bursting the gates and kept battling all the way to the line, finishing much closer to Hinterland than he had in the Royal Hunt Cup despite meeting him on the same terms. However, like the winner he was favoured by racing handily in a race run at an ordinary pace and this effort will not get him any help from the Handicapper.

Momtic(IRE), just beaten by Ace Of Hearts in this race last year, was weighted to dead-heat with his old rival on that piece of form and very nearly did so, but he was yet another to benefit from racing close to the pace. This was still a fine effort under top weight, but he may now be something of a twilight horse - too high in the handicap but not quite up to winning in Pattern company, domestically at least. (op 12-1)

Capable Guest(IRE), who ran such a good race from an awful draw in the Hunt Cup, did much the best of those that tried to come off the pace, though in reality he did not have luck on his side here either. Trying for a run up the inside, he found himself caught in a pocket at a vital stage and by the time he managed to get through it was too late. Fortune has not been smiling on him this year, but on the other hand a record of just two wins from 27 starts is poor for a horse of his ability. Official explanation: jockey said gelding suffered interference in running (tchd 11-1)

Granston(IRE) was always up with the pace and that was a major contributory factor in him finishing as close as he did. This is his trip, but he was put up 2lb for getting beaten last time so will need to improve to win off this sort of mark. (op 14-1)

Stagelight(IRE) ◆, all the better for his run in the Hunt Cup when returning from a very long layoff, can be considered unlucky not to have done even better this time. Trying to come from well off the pace in a contest favouring those that raced prominently, he did not enjoy the clearest of passages in the home straight, but was finishing to some purpose. It would have been understandable had he 'bounced' from Ascot, but that did not appear to be the case and he shapes as though he would get a bit further. Perhaps the Cambridgeshire would be his sort of race. (tchd 33-1)

Kings Quay was never far away on this drop back in trip but he could never make any impact on the leaders and was not knocked about when his chance had gone. He has not won for nearly two years and the Handicapper still appears to have hold of him. Official explanation: jockey said colt hung left-handed

Humble Opinion, raised 4lb for his Haydock victory, managed to get himself into a challenging position entering the last couple of furlongs before finding the demands too much. (op 7-1 tchd 15-2)

Flipando(IRE), just 2lb higher than for his Newcastle victory, could never land a serious blow and this race would not have suited his style of running. (op 9-1)

My Paris had the run of the race out in front yet still capitulated tamely. He has won on fast ground, but does look better with ease.

Langford lost all chance at the start and this effort can be safely ignored. Official explanation: jockey said gelding reared and sat down in stalls missing break

3314 CORAL-ECLIPSE STKS (GROUP 1) 1m 2f 7y

3:15 (3:16) (Class 1) 3-Y-O+

£260,620 (£98,776; £49,434; £24,648; £12,347; £6,196) **Stalls** High

Form RPR

1-14 **1** **David Junior (USA)**[17] 2741 4-9-7 123................................ JamieSpencer 2 122
(B J Meehan) *hld up in last pair: prog on outer over 2f out: drvn to ld 1f out: r.o strly* **9/4**[2]

-115 **2** 1½ **Notnowcato**[17] 2741 4-9-7 113... MJKinane 6 119+
(Sir Michael Stoute) *trckd ldr for 2f: styd prom: effrt on inner and nt clr run over 1f out: swtchd lft: r.o fnl f to take 2nd nr fin* **9/1**

2114 **3** *nk* **Blue Monday**[15] 2803 5-9-7 .... SteveDrowne 8 118
(R Charlton) *hld up in midfield: tried for run up inner and nowhere to go 2f out: swtchd to outer over 1f out: r.o to take 3rd last stri* **8/1**

-410 **4** *shd* **Aussie Rules (USA)**[34] 2278 3-8-10 .... AlanMunro 3 116
(A P O'Brien, Ire) *hld up in midfield: prog on outer over 2f out: drvn to chal and upsides jst over 1f out: hanging rt after: lost 2 pls nr fi* **11/2**[3]

4321 **5** 2 **Ouija Board**[17] 2741 5-9-4 117.. CSoumillon 7 115+
(E A L Dunlop) *hld up: lost pl and in last pair 3f out: prog over 2f out: rn into trble repeatedly fr over 1f out: nt rcvr* **2/1**[1]

1301 **6** 1 **Snoqualmie Boy**[16] 2775 3-8-10 .... JohnEgan 5 111
(D R C Elsworth) *prom: chal over 2f out: drvn to ld over 1f out: hdd & wknd 1f out* **22/1**

1233 **7** 1¾ **Royal Alchemist**[17] 2740 4-9-4 102.................................. MichaelTebbutt 9 106
(B J Meehan) *led: stepped up pce after 3f: hdd & wknd over 1f out* **100/1**

0434 **8** ¾ **Hattan (IRE)**[20] 2693 4-9-7 108... KerrinMcEvoy 1 108
(C E Brittain) *hld up in last pair: effrt on wd outside 3f out: no prog 2f out: wknd* **66/1**

3-25 **9** 7 **Notable Guest (USA)**[36] 2202 5-9-7 112..................... RichardHughes 4 94
(Sir Michael Stoute) *trckd ldr after 2f tl over 2f out: n.m.r wl over 1f out: sn wknd: eased fnl f* **16/1**

2m 7.31s (-2.93) **Going Correction** 0.0s/f (Good)
WFA 3 from 4yo+ 11lb **9** Ran SP% **113.3**
Speed ratings (Par 117):111,109,109,109,107 107,105,105,99
CSF £22.05 TOTE £3.20: £1.30, £3.00, £3.40; EX 25.40 Trifecta £118.50 Pool: £3,023.46 - 18.10 winning units..
Owner Roldvale Limited **Bred** A I Appleton **Trained** Manton, Wilts

FOCUS

A famous race and billed as a match between David Junior and Ouija Board, but whilst one received a copybook ride and made full use of it, the other endured a nightmare. Despite the presence of a pacemaker, the early pace did not look that strong and the presence of a couple of Group 3 performers in the frame could be said to drag the form down a little. Also the winning time was moderate for a race of its stature, 3/100ths of a second slower than the later 70-85 three-year-old handicap over the same trip. Having said that, the winner could hardly have done much more.

NOTEBOOK

David Junior(USA), a bit disappointing behind Ouija Board at Royal Ascot when it was thought the slow pace went against him, had the help of a pacemaker this time, but even so this was by no means a strongly-run race in which he was held up last for much of the way. Once in line for home, he was switched wide of the field to make his effort and that was to prove crucial, as whilst he was able to maintain a trouble-free run down the outside while his main rival was getting caught in an equine spider's web. He had to be ridden right out to beat a couple of Group 3 winners and the winning time was not great, but he could not really have done much more than win like this. The big ten-furlong races such as the Juddmonte International and the Irish Champion are obviously on the agenda for him now, whilst in the longer term his trainer has made no secret of his ambition to aim the colt at the Breeders' Cup Classic. (op 11-4 tchd 3-1 and 100-30 in a place)

Notnowcato, only just behind David Junior in the Prince Of Wales Stakes at Royal Ascot, was never far off the pace. He had to be switched about a furlong out to avoid the pacemaker before running on well, but it made no difference to the result. He lost nothing in defeat especially as he returned with a puncture wound on his near-fore joint, but it remains to be seen how he would cope in a truly-run Group 1. (tchd 10-1)

Blue Monday, a supplementary entry, fully justified his inclusion and stayed on really well to make the frame after having to be switched when his route up the inside was blocked. He has a decent turn of foot when things pan out for him and he is well up to winning again in slightly lesser Group company. (op 10-1 tchd 11-1 in a place)

Aussie Rules(USA), on whom Munro was a late replacement following the removal of Kieren Fallon's licence and the injury to his proposed replacement Johnny Murtagh, came to win his race approaching the last furlong but he then appeared to empty and first impressions were that he might not have stayed. (op 5-1 tchd 4-1 and 6-1 in a place)

Ouija Board, bidding to become only the third filly to win this race, was switched off early and only had David Junior behind her turning for home. However, whilst her old rival made his bid down the outside, Soumillon tried to steer a route through the middle of the field and her problems were only beginning when the gap she was attempting to go through between Aussie Rules and Snoqualmie Boy closed. From then on things only got worse, and when she did finally see daylight she crossed the line full of running. This was X-rated stuff, but we all know how good she is and the decider between her and David Junior should be well worth travelling to see. (op 7-4 tchd 85-40 in places)

Snoqualmie Boy, another supplementary entry, had his chance a furlong out and was not disgraced, but the return to the top level was too much for him at this stage of his career. (op 20-1)

Royal Alchemist, recently purchased to fulfil pacemaker duties in this, did not go mad and set just a reasonable gallop before gradually winding things up. She hung on for longer than might have been expected, but she is a decent filly and is well up to winning a Group race in her own right. (op 66-1)

Hattan(IRE), without a win since last year's Chester Vase, tried to get into the race down the outside once in line for home but could never get involved. He continues to find this level beyond him. (op 50-1)

Notable Guest(USA), who beat David Junior in last season's Rose Of Lancaster Stakes, has not improved at anything like the same rate as his old rival since and this was another moderate effort. (tchd 20-1)

3315 ADDLESHAW GODDARD STKS (REGISTERED AS THE ESHER STAKES) (LISTED RACE) 2m 78y

3:45 (3:47) (Class 1) 4-Y-O+ **£15,898** (£6,025; £3,015; £1,503; £753) **Stalls** Centre

Form RPR

1555 **1** **Land 'n Stars**[28] 2453 6-9-3 103... PaulDoe 4 109
(Jamie Poulton) *hld up in 3rd tl chsd ldr 6f out: rdn 5f out: clsd grad fr 2f out: led last 100yds: hld on wl* **16/1**

-425 **2** *nk* **Sergeant Cecil**[16] 2773 7-9-0 111....................................... AlanMunro 3 106
(B R Millman) *hld up in 4th: effrt over 3f out: rdn to dispute 2nd fr 2f out and clsd grad: chal last 100yds: jst hld* **5/6**[1]

5020 **3** 1½ **Winged D'Argent (IRE)**[16] 2773 5-9-0 108.......................... JohnEgan 2 104
(M Johnston) *led: drvn and qcknd 5f out: kpt on wl tl collared last 100yds* **13/2**

0-30 **4** 1¾ **Barolo**[16] 2773 7-9-0 108... TedDurcan 5 102
(W R Swinburn) *trckd ldr to 6f out: outpcd 4f out: tried to cl fr 2f out: no imp fr over 1f out* **9/2**[2]

-253 **5** 42 **Vinando**[14] 2849 5-9-0 103...(bt) JamieSpencer 1 51
(C R Egerton) *s.s: a last: rdn and lost tch 5f out: nvr looked happy after: virtually p.u fnl f* **5/1**[3]

3m 39.72s (1.49) **Going Correction** 0.0s/f (Good) **5** Ran SP% **108.6**
Speed ratings (Par 111):96,95,95,94,73
CSF £29.86 TOTE £18.00: £3.10, £1.20; EX 35.10.
Owner Paul Blows **Bred** C A Cyzer **Trained** Telscombe, E Sussex

FOCUS

They went no gallop in this staying event and the pace did not pick up until approaching the end of the back straight. The winning time was therefore very slow for a Listed race and the form, best rated through the winner, has to be treated with some caution as a consequence.

The Form Book, Raceform Ltd, Compton, RG20 6NL

NOTEBOOK

Land 'n Stars was worst in on adjusted official ratings, just as he was when winning a Listed race at Newmarket last autumn which landed him his 3lb penalty for this. He looked very unlikely to win soon after turning in as he was under pressure and apparently going nowhere, but his stamina then kicked in and with the leader hanging away from the inside rail a furlong out, he took full advantage and just outbattled the favourite. He is likely to try and confirm the form with the runner-up in the Goodwood Cup, whilst the Melbourne Cup has also been mentioned as a possibility. (op 14-1)

Sergeant Cecil was the best horse in the race on official ratings, but a moderately-run race in a small field is not really his cup of tea and he was inclined to take a keen grip behind the leaders. Caught a little flat-footed soon after straightening up for home, he managed to get himself into a position where he had a chance of winning and collared the pacemaker, but just lost out in the battle to the line. He will bid for compensation in the Goodwood Cup, where he will hopefully get a stronger pace and a bigger field. (tchd 10-11 and evens in places)

Winged D'Argent(IRE) was allowed to dominate at his own pace, which is a dangerous thing to allow a Johnston-trained horse to do. Quickening from the front exiting the back straight, he seemed to have his rivals in trouble but the distress signals were going out coming to the last furlong. Hanging away from the rail as he tired, he was eventually swamped on both sides by the front pair and he had nothing more to give. He tries his best, but has not won a race for 15 months. (op 6-1 tchd 7-1 in a place)

Barolo was rather inclined to race in snatches and lacked a turn of foot at a vital stage. He has not really built on his promising return in the Henry II Stakes here in May, though he ran almost to the pound with Winged D'Argent on that form. (tchd 5-1)

Vinando dropped off the back of the field exiting the back straight and something must have been amiss. Official explanation: jockey said horse never travelled (op 11-2 tchd 6-1 in a place)

3316 WEATHERBYS VAT SERVICES STKS (REGISTERED AS THE DISTAFF STAKES) (LISTED RACE) (FILLIES) 1m 14y

4:20 (4:21) (Class 1) 3-Y-O

£15,898 (£6,025; £3,015; £1,503; £753; £378) **Stalls** High

Form	Pos	Dist	Horse / comment	RPR
1-24	1		**Star Cluster**[23] 2582 3-8-12 94 .... RichardHughes 8 (H R A Cecil) *trckd ldng pair: rdn to ld over 1f out: hrd pressed ins fnl f: hld on gamely* **5/1**[2]	101
10	2	*shd*	**Silver Touch (IRE)**[55] 1719 3-8-12 .... TedDurcan 2 (M R Channon) *hld up in last: gd prog on outer fr over 2f out: drvn to chal ins fnl f: nt qckn nr fin* **13/2**[3]	100
10-0	3	*hd*	**Expensive**[17] 2744 3-8-12 105 .... AlanMunro 6 (C F Wall) *trckd ldng trio: rdn and nt qckn 2f out: swtchd lft 1f out: r.o fnl f: gaining nr fin* **9/1**	100
0-12	4	*nk*	**La Mottie**[17] 2744 3-8-12 102 .... DarryllHolland 3 (J Noseda) *hld up in 8th: dropped to last over 2f out and plenty to do: rapid prog over 1f out: fin strly: hopeless task* **10/11**[1]	99+
4004	5	4	**Tara Too (IRE)**[14] 2880 3-8-12 80 .... PhilipRobinson 9 (D W P Arbuthnot) *led: rdn and jnd 2f out: hdd over 1f out: wknd* **50/1**	90?
-156	6	1 ¾	**Illuminise (IRE)**[17] 2744 3-8-12 88 .... CSoumillon 7 (E A L Dunlop) *trckd ldr: chal over 2f out: upsides over 1f out: sn wknd* **16/1**	86
0-20	7	2 ½	**Arm Candy (IRE)**[50] 1819 3-8-12 91 .... JohnEgan 1 (J A R Toller) *trckd ldng trio tl rdn and wknd 2f out* **20/1**	80
1004	8	3	**My Amalie (IRE)**[43] 1990 3-8-12 92 .... KerrinMcEvoy 10 (C E Brittain) *dwlt: hld up in last pair: no real prog 2f out: wknd over 1f out* **25/1**	73
1-66	9	½	**Dictatrix**[50] 1834 3-8-12 94 .... ShaneKelly 5 (J M P Eustace) *dwlt: sn in tch in 7th: rdn and struggling over 2f out: wknd* **66/1**	72
4-50	10	22	**Stage Flight**[17] 2744 3-8-12 98 .... JamieSpencer 4 (B J Meehan) *racd in 6th tl wknd over 2f out: hanging bdly over 1f out and eased: t.o* **25/1**	22

1m 42.24s (-1.71) **Going Correction** 0.0s/f (Good) **10** Ran SP% **114.2**
Speed ratings (Par 105):108,107,107,107,103 101,99,96,95,73
CSF £33.94 TOTE £5.40: £1.80, £2.20, £2.30; EX 30.30.

Owner K Abdulla **Bred** Juddmonte Farms Ltd **Trained** Newmarket, Suffolk

FOCUS

Despite little covering the front four at the line, there was a good pace on early resulting in a creditable winning time for a race like this, although the form is limited by the proximity of the fifth and sixth.

NOTEBOOK

Star Cluster ◆, stepping down from ten furlongs, clearly appreciated it and was always in a good position to strike. She had to knuckle down to some serious work after taking up the running, but her resolution could not be faulted and she ground out a game victory. This was only her fourth outing, so she is entitled to improve a bit more yet. (op 6-1)

Silver Touch(IRE) ◆, who ran so poorly when faced with such a severe test in the French Guineas on only her second start, was much more at home in this. Held up early, her rider took no chances of being stopped in her run by pulling her out widest of all in order to make her effort. She got there in plenty of time, but whether it was having to do so much running in order to get to the front or the winner's toughness, she was just unable to get on top. This ground looked much more suitable for her and she still has plenty of scope. (op 9-2 tchd 7-1 in a place)

Expensive ◆, all the better for her promising effort on her belated return at Royal Ascot, was close enough starting up the home straight, but took an age to respond to pressure and looked most unlikely to make the frame coming to the last furlong. However, she then found her second wind and finished to such a degree that she was right alongside the front pair at the line. She may come on again for this and should soon be winning if she does, whilst she shapes as through she would get a bit further. (op 10-1)

La Mottie, who had three of today's rivals behind her when runner-up to Red Evie in the Sandringham at Royal Ascot, was given a lot to do though to be fair her starting position was no worse than the eventual runner-up. She tried to make her effort through the field rather than around it, but although she had to weave her way through she was never stopped in her run and this looked a case of getting the timing wrong rather than taking the wrong route. (tchd evens in place and 5-6 in places)

Tara Too(IRE) tried to make all the running, but she faced an impossible task on official ratings and was readily brushed aside. (op 40-1)

Illuminise(IRE) had no apparent excuses this time and was just not good enough.

Arm Candy(IRE) Official explanation: jockey said filly moved poorly throughout; vet said filly returned sore

My Amalie(IRE) Official explanation: jockey said filly missed the break

Dictatrix Official explanation: trainer said filly had a breathing problem

Stage Flight Official explanation: jockey said filly lost its action; vet said filly returned sore

3317 INKERMAN H'CAP 7f 16y

4:50 (4:56) (Class 3) (0-95,90) 3-Y-O

£8,724 (£2,612; £1,306; £653; £326; £163) **Stalls** High

Form	Pos	Dist	Horse / comment	RPR
6336	1		**The Snatcher (IRE)**[42] 2014 3-9-7 90 .... RichardHughes 8 (R Hannon) *settled in midfield: shkn up and prog 2f out: led over 1f out: in command fnl f: drvn out* **8/1**	97
0053	2	¾	**Ans Bach**[15] 2824 3-9-3 86 .... (p) PhilipRobinson 6 (M A Jarvis) *hld up towards rr: gng wl 2f out: prog whn nt clr run over 1f out: r.o to take 2nd last 50yds: nt rch wnr* **9/2**[3]	92+
-233	3	½	**Escape Clause (USA)**[22] 2615 3-9-0 83 .... KerrinMcEvoy 2 (Sir Michael Stoute) *t.k.h: trckd ldng trio: rdn and hanging 2f out: nt qckn over 1f out: styd on ins fnl f* **7/2**[1]	87
63-0	4	*nk*	**Jamieson Gold (IRE)**[63] 1490 3-9-5 88 .... DarryllHolland 7 (B W Hills) *chsd ldr to over 1f out: chsd wnr sn after: no imp ins fnl f: lost 2 pls nr fin* **25/1**	91
4000	5	1	**Guest Connections**[16] 2774 3-9-7 90 .... JohnEgan 3 (M R Channon) *hld up towards rr: effrt on outer and rdn over 2f out: styd on fnl f: nvr able to chal* **16/1**	90
0526	6	½	**Mister Benedictine**[21] 2642 3-8-9 78 .... SteveDrowne 10 (W R Muir) *t.k.h: prom: rdn over 2f out: grad fdd fr over 1f out* **12/1**	77
322	7	3	**Mumaathel (IRE)**[31] 2343 3-8-11 80 .... RHills 4 (M P Tregoning) *restless stalls: plld hrd early: trckd ldrs: rdn and nt qckn 2f out: no ch whn squeezed out 1f out* **9/2**[3]	71
1522	8	¾	**Damika (IRE)**[17] 2760 3-8-13 82 .... JamieSpencer 5 (R M Whitaker) *hld up in last pair: effrt on outer over 2f out: no prog over 1f out: wknd* **4/1**[2]	71
633-	9	½	**Crocodile Bay (IRE)**[274] 5716 3-9-6 89 .... ShaneKelly 9 (Carl Llewellyn) *led to over 1f out: wknd rapidly* **20/1**	77
210-	10	2	**Playtotheaudience**[325] 4477 3-9-7 90 .... JimCrowley 1 (R A Fahey) *hld up in last pair: rdn over 2f out: no prog* **20/1**	73

1m 29.46s (-1.63) **Going Correction** 0.0s/f (Good) **10** Ran SP% **116.6**
Speed ratings (Par 104):109,108,107,107,106 105,102,101,100,98
CSF £42.63 CT £155.00 TOTE £10.50: £2.90, £1.70, £1.70; EX 50.50.

Owner Mrs R Ablett **Bred** Miss Eileen Grealish **Trained** East Everleigh, Wilts

FOCUS

A good pace set by Crocodile Bay resulted in a fair time for a race like this and the form looks sound rated around the first two.

NOTEBOOK

The Snatcher(IRE), given a short break since his last appearance, looked exposed coming into this and did not look particularly well handicapped having already been beaten three times off this mark. However, there was no denying his determination when asked to go and win his race and he made full use of getting first run on the runner-up. He is a tough colt, but this was his fourth win in his 16th outing, so he hardly possesses much in the way of scope. (op 7-1)

Ans Bach was just behind the eventual winner for most of the way and followed him through when he made his move, but he had more of a problem getting through and by the time he got into gear, his rival had gone beyond recall. He looks capable of winning off this sort of mark, but does not look the easiest of rides. (op 4-1 tchd 5-1)

Escape Clause(USA), not for the first time, was inclined to race rather keenly on the outside of the field and when asked for his effort he was made to look one paced. The drop in trip probably did not help him. (op 4-1)

Jamieson Gold(IRE) raced handily and hung in there until well inside the last furlong. This was a much better effort than on his reappearance (tchd 28-1)

Guest Connections ran better than of late under joint top weight, but will still need a bit more help from the Handicapper. (tchd 20-1)

Mister Benedictine semed to have every chance this time, though he may have done a bit too much early.

Mumaathel(IRE), making his handicap debut, pulled far too hard early to give himself any chance of getting home. Official explanation: jockey said colt pulled hard early (tchd 5-1)

Damika(IRE), given a patient ride, was brought with his effort widest of all in the home straight but after looking a likely threat his effort soon petered out. He has won over this trip, but perhaps he is better over shorter. (tchd 9-2)

3318 THE SUGABABES AT SANDOWN ON 16 AUGUST H'CAP 1m 2f 7y

5:25 (5:30) (Class 4) (0-85,85) 3-Y-O **£7,772** (£2,312; £1,155; £577) **Stalls** High

Form	Pos	Dist	Horse / comment	RPR
-620	1		**Road To Love (IRE)**[15] 2805 3-9-6 84 .... JohnEgan 7 (M Johnston) *mde all: drew clr over 4f out: 6l clr over 1f out: rdn fnl f: unchal* **9/1**	103
314-	2	3	**Noble Gent (IRE)**[284] 5524 3-9-7 85 .... KerrinMcEvoy 1 (Saeed Bin Suroor) *hld up bhd ldrs: prog over 2f out: chsd clr wnr over 1f out: clsd grad but nvr any ch* **4/1**[1]	99
6031	3	3	**Kahlua Kiss**[11] 2961 3-8-12 76 .... ShaneKelly 3 (W R Muir) *s.i.s and rousted along early in last pair: prog on outer over 2f out: tk modest 3rd 1f out: kpt on* **16/1**	84
-304	4	¾	**Merveilles**[16] 2786 3-9-6 84 .... (b[1]) SteveDrowne 9 (J H M Gosden) *s.v.s: last tl stdy prog on outer 2f out: nt clr run over 1f out: plld out and shkn up sn after: kpt on* **20/1**	91
221	5	4	**Incidentally (IRE)**[22] 2605 3-9-7 85 .... RichardHughes 4 (R Hannon) *hld up wl in rr: drvn and prog over 2f out: no imp on clr ldrs over 1f out: wknd* **9/1**	84
-232	6	1 ½	**Midnight Traveller**[22] 2608 3-9-1 79 .... DarryllHolland 5 (L M Cumani) *mostly chsd wnr: clr of rest 4f out: no imp over 2f out: wknd wl over 1f out* **5/1**[3]	75+
1-00	7	*shd*	**Altilhar (USA)**[8] 3046 3-8-6 70 .... JimCrowley 11 (G L Moore) *chsd ldrs: u.p and wkng over 2f out* **33/1**	66
0213	8	*nk*	**Mystic Storm**[29] 2404 3-8-10 74 .... JamieSpencer 6 (Lady Herries) *prom in chsng gp: effrt wl over 2f out: no imp sn after: wknd over 1f out* **9/2**[2]	69
1000	9	1 ¼	**Gracechurch (IRE)**[15] 2805 3-8-9 80 .... ThomasO'Brien[(7)] 2 (M R Channon) *nvr beyond midfield: no prog 3f out: wknd 2f out* **12/1**	73
2144	10	1	**Bin Rahy (IRE)**[21] 2659 3-9-4 82 .... TedDurcan 10 (M R Channon) *prom in chsng gp: wkng whn n.m.r on inner over 2f out* **13/2**	73
1-03	11	5	**Dansa Queen**[14] 2865 3-8-7 76 .... AndrewMullen[(5)] 13 (W R Swinburn) *reluctant to go to post: chsd ldrs: lost pl after 2f: struggling and btn over 2f out* **16/1**	58

2m 7.28s (-2.96) **Going Correction** 0.0s/f (Good) **11** Ran SP% **115.3**
Speed ratings (Par 102):111,108,106,105,102 101,101,100,99,99 95
CSF £43.99 CT £573.08 TOTE £11.20: £2.90, £1.90, £3.60; EX 52.80 Place 6 £56.12, Place 5 £34.20.

Owner Grant Mercer **Bred** South House Stud **Trained** Middleham Moor, N Yorks

FOCUS

A strongly-run race in which the field were soon strung out and finished like that. A very decent winning time for the type of contest, fractionally faster even than the Eclipse, suggesting the form is strong and the race has been rated positively as a consequence.

Merveilles ◆ Official explanation: jockey said gelding missed the break
Mystic Storm Official explanation: jockey said gelding never travelled
Dansa Queen Official explanation: jockey said filly lost her action
T/Jkpt: Not won. T/Plt: £73.20 to a £1 stake. Pool: £127,125.05. 1,267.10 winning tickets.
T/Qpdt: £18.40 to a £1 stake. Pool: £4,235.40. 170.30 winning tickets. JN

3319 - 3321a (Foreign Racing) - See Raceform Interactive

2764 LEOPARDSTOWN (L-H)
Saturday, July 8

OFFICIAL GOING: Good

3322a IRISH STALLION FARMS EUROPEAN BREEDERS FUND BROWNSTOWN STKS (GROUP 3) (F&M) — 7f
7:20 (7:20) 3-Y-0+ **£40,344** (£11,793; £5,586; £1,862)

RPR
1 **Spinning Queen**[14] 2880 3-8-12 MichaelHills 6 109
(B W Hills) *in rr: hdwy on outer 2f out: rdn to chal in 2nd fr over 1f out: styd on wl fnl f to ld last strides* **7/2**[2]
2 *hd* **Wake Up Maggie (IRE)**[15] 2802 3-8-12 FMBerry 3 109
(C F Wall) *trckd ldrs: impr to ld fr 2f out: strly pressed ins fnl f: hdd last strides* **2/1**[1]
3 *4 ½* **Modeeroch (IRE)**[31] 2369 3-8-12 105 KJManning 2 98
(J S Bolger, Ire) *chsd ldrs: mainly 6th: nt clr run and dropped to rr under 2f out: rdn and kpt on wout threatening fr over 1f out* **11/2**[3]
4 *hd* **Beauty Bright (IRE)**[41] 2054 3-8-12 100 KFallon 7 97
(A P O'Brien, Ire) *towards rr: hdwy into 3rd fr under 2f out: no imp u.p and kpt on same pce fr over 1f out* **10/1**
5 *1* **Ugo Fire (IRE)**[41] 2054 3-9-1 106 DPMcDonogh 4 98
(Kevin Prendergast, Ire) *trckd ldrs: 5th 2f out: sn no imp u.p: kpt on same pce* **12/1**
6 *1* **Shersha (IRE)**[16] 2776 7-9-6 98 WSupple 1 92
(Kevin F O'Donnell, Ire) *led early: sn hdd: remained prom: 4th 2f out: sn no imp u.p* **25/1**
7 *2* **Utterly Heaven (IRE)**[84] 1026 4-9-6 105 (b) PJSmullen 8 87
(D K Weld, Ire) *sn led: strly pressed and hdd 2f out: sn no ex* **14/1**
8 *1 ½* **Violette**[69] 1328 3-9-1 SebSanders 5 86
(Sir Mark Prescott) *sn trckd ldrs: no ex u.p in 2nd fr 2f out* **7/2**[2]

1m 26.5s **Going Correction** -0.60s/f (Hard)
WFA 3 from 4yo+ 8lb — 8 Ran SP% **120.5**
Speed ratings: 108,107,102,102,101 100,97,96
CSF £11.63 TOTE £5.10: £1.70, £1.50, £1.70; DF 10.20.
Owner Marston Stud & Cavendish Investing Ltd **Bred** R A Bonnycastle And Marston Stud **Trained** Lambourn, Berks

NOTEBOOK
Spinning Queen seems to have had her confidence boosted by her easy Warwick victory and was produced with precision timing to follow up on this return to Group company. She was reversing 1,000 Guineas form with the runner-up and looks to be a filly on the up. (op 7/2 tchd 4/1)
Wake Up Maggie(IRE) made her bid for glory soon after turning for home, but although she put daylight between herself and the rest she proved vulnerable to the winner's turn of foot. She has not had much luck in five starts since winning a valuable sales race at The Curragh last autumn, losing out in photos in three of them. (op 9/4 tchd 5/2)
Violette was easily left behind and it remains to be seen whether she has trained on.

3323 - 3325a (Foreign Racing) - See Raceform Interactive

1659 JAGERSRO (R-H)
Friday, July 7

OFFICIAL GOING: Standard

3326a SVENSKT OAKS (FILLIES) (DIRT) — 1m 4f
7:35 (12:00) 3-Y-0
£18,485 (£8,503; £3,697; £2,588; £1,848; £1,109)

RPR
1 **Red Dress On (SWE)**[24] 2564 3-9-2 DDelgado 2 —
(T Gustafsson, Sweden)
2 *3* **Negra Del Oro (GER)**[24] 2564 3-9-2 LHammer-Hansen 10 —
(A Lund, Norway)
3 *½* **Mrs Moneybags (IRE)** 3-9-2 (b) FDiaz 8 —
(L Kelp, Sweden)
4 *3* **Aura (SWE)** 3-9-2 NCordrey 1 —
(T Gustafsson, Sweden)
5 *hd* **Auchroisk (SWE)**[24] 2564 3-9-2 (b) MSvanberg 5 —
(Bruno Nilsson, Sweden)
6 *3* **Will Be (IRE)**[24] 2564 3-9-2 FJohansson 12 —
(R A Kvisla) *midfield, progress and 4th after 3f, soon niggled along, u.p 5f out and lost place, stayed on again in straight SP 21-10F* **21/10**[1]
7 *1 ½* **Casata (IRE)**[24] 2564 3-9-2 MMartinez 6 —
(F Reuterskiold, Sweden)
8 *nk* **Xaara (SWE)**[24] 2564 3-9-2 YvonneDurant 3 —
(M Kahn, Sweden)
9 *hd* **Fredrika** 3-9-2 GSolis 11 —
(F Reuterskiold, Sweden)
10 *1* **La Parrilla (IRE)** 3-9-2 (b) DinaDanekilde 9 —
(H I Larsen)
11 *3* **Safariknight (IRE)** 3-9-2 SaraSlot 7 —
(Kerstin Helander, Sweden)
12 *12* **Mrs Miskovsky (SWE)** 3-9-2 CathrineWeilby 4 —
(Ewa Breitholtz)

2m 38.4s — 12 Ran SP% **32.3**
(Including 1SKr stake): WIN 8.10; PL 1.20, 6.60, 3.60; DF 43.00.
Owner Stall Rio **Bred** Stall Magnum **Trained** Sweden

NOTEBOOK
Will Be(IRE), surprisingly sent off favourite, was in trouble down the back straight, and though she stayed on past some beaten horses in the final stages, never looked dangerous

2850 AYR (L-H)
Sunday, July 9

OFFICIAL GOING: Good
Wind: Virtually nil.

3328 IRVINE HERALD MEDIAN AUCTION MAIDEN STKS — 7f 50y
2:10 (2:11) (Class 5) 2-Y-0 **£3,368** (£1,002; £500; £250) **Stalls** Low

Form — RPR
4 1 **Frosty Night (IRE)**[23] 2619 2-9-3 JoeFanning 8 90+
(M Johnston) *mde all: pushed clr 2f out: easily* **11/10**[1]
2 *2 ½* **Steam Cuisine** 2-8-12 TPQueally 5 74
(M G Quinlan) *hld up towards rr: hdwy on outer over 2f out: rdn over 1f out: styd on to chse wnr ins last* **12/1**
3 3 *2* **Karma Llama (IRE)**[13] 2924 2-8-12 PaulEddery 6 69
(B Smart) *trckd ldrs: hdwy to chse wnr over 2f out: sn rdn and kpt on same pce* **10/1**[3]
4 4 *1 ¾* **Musical Land (IRE)**[13] 2924 2-9-3 PaulHanagan 4 69
(J R Weymes) *chsd ldrs: rdn along over 2f out: sn one pce* **11/1**
0 5 *2 ½* **Heywood**[11] 2979 2-9-3 TonyCulhane 1 68+
(M R Channon) *keen: in tch: pushed along over 2f out: sn no imp* **20/1**
0 6 *2* **Salto Chico**[15] 2854 2-9-3 DavidAllan 7 58
(W M Brisbourne) *sn outpcd and bhd tl sme late hdwy* **100/1**
7 *2* **Chookie Hamilton** 2-9-3 TomEaves 3 53
(I Semple) *dwlt: a rr* **40/1**
0 8 *3* **Meridian Grey (USA)**[19] 2733 2-9-3 NCallan 2 46
(K A Ryan) *chsd wnr: rdn along over 2f out: sn edgd rt and btn* **5/2**[2]

1m 34.67s (1.95) **Going Correction** -0.05s/f (Good) — 8 Ran SP% **109.5**
Speed ratings (Par 94):86,83,80,78,76 73,71,68
CSF £14.38 TOTE £2.10: £1.50, £4.20, £2.60; EX 19.40.
Owner A D Spence **Bred** Annalee Bloodstock And Rockhart Trading Ltd **Trained** Middleham Moor, N Yorks

FOCUS
An uncompetitive event in which the pace was only fair and the winning time modest. The winner dictated but appeals as the type to improve again for this yard and the third and fourth help back up the form.

NOTEBOOK
Frosty Night(IRE) ◆ had the rub of this uncompetitive race but fully confirmed debut promise and won in the manner of one that can hold his own in slightly better company. He should stay a mile and is sure to win another race. (op 6-5 tchd 5-4 in places)
Steam Cuisine ◆, from a stable that can get one ready first time, was easy to back but showed definite promise on this racecourse debut. This first foal of a triple seven-furlong winner looks capable of winning a similar event. (op 10-1)
Karma Llama(IRE), who shaped well on her debut at Musselburgh on firm ground, ran to a similar level on this easier surface. Although vulnerable to the better types in this grade, she appeals as the sort to win a minor event. (op 7-1)
Musical Land(IRE), who showed ability at a modest level on his debut, finished a similar distance behind Karma Llama as he had done at Musselburgh. He looks the sort to do better over a bit further once qualified for a handicap mark. (op 10-1 tchd 12-1)
Heywood, edgy and coltish in the paddock, failed to settle on this turf debut and, although not totally disgraced, will have to become more amenable to restraint if he is to progress in this sphere. (op 16-1)
Salto Chico again achieved little and is likely to continue to look vulnerable in this type of event. (op 50-1)
Meridian Grey(USA) was well supported but failed by a long chalk to confirm the bit of promise shown on his reappearance. However he is in very good hands and would not be one to write off just yet. Official explanation: jockey said colt hung right-handed throughout (op 3-1)

3329 AYRSHIRE POST H'CAP — 1m
2:45 (2:45) (Class 6) (0-60,59) 3-Y-0 **£3,238** (£963; £481; £240) **Stalls** Low

Form — RPR
0400 1 **Noble Nova**[17] 2782 3-8-12 51 JoeFanning 6 63
(M R Channon) *trckd ldrs:hdwy to ld wl over 1f out: sn rdn and styd on gamely ins last* **16/1**
306- 2 *nk* **Signal Hill**[250] 6212 3-9-5 58 TonyCulhane 12 69
(W J Haggas) *hld up and bhd: swtchd wd and gd hdwy over 2f out: rdn and ev ch over 1f out: sn drvn and kpt on* **6/1**[3]
-504 3 *1 ¾* **Three Strings (USA)**[26] 2529 3-8-13 52 (p) PaulHanagan 3 59
(P D Niven) *a.p: hdwy over 2f out: sn rdn and ev ch tl drvn and one pce ins last* **8/1**
-004 4 *1 ½* **Farne Island**[17] 2782 3-9-5 58 GrahamGibbons 4 62
(J J Quinn) *hld up in tch: hdwy 3f out: rdn to chal wl over 1f out and ev ch tl drvn and one pce ent last* **9/2**[2]
-100 5 *3 ½* **Queen Jean**[18] 2746 3-9-6 59 (p) TPQueally 1 55
(J G Given) *towards rr: hdwy 3f out: n.m.r and swtchd rt wl over 1f out: sn rdn and kpt on: nrst fin* **12/1**
6-60 6 *5* **Prince Duval (IRE)**[26] 2525 3-8-10 52 DanielTudhope(3) 10 37
(D Carroll) *cl up: effrt and ev ch over 2f out: sn rdn: edgd rt and wknd* **9/1**
00-6 7 *shd* **Ruby Rubble**[20] 2699 3-8-13 52 PatCosgrave 2 37
(K R Burke) *in tch: rdn along 3f out: sn wknd* **25/1**
-500 8 *1 ¼* **English Archer**[14] 2896 3-9-2 55 PhillipMakin 9 38
(J R Weymes) *s.i.s: a towards rr* **66/1**
-600 9 *1 ¾* **Dzhani**[29] 2466 3-9-1 54 PaulMulrennan 13 33
(Jedd O'Keeffe) *cl up: led wl over 2f out: sn rdn and edgd lft: hdd wl over 1f out and grad wknd* **33/1**
0353 10 *1 ½* **Hogan's Heroes**[16] 2823 3-9-6 59 TomEaves 5 34
(G A Butler) *hld up and bhd: swtchd wd and sme hdwy wl over 2f out: sn rdn and btn* **4/1**[1]
0-60 11 *2 ½* **Colton**[24] 2583 3-9-5 58 NCallan 14 28
(J M P Eustace) *trckd ldrs: hdwy 3f out: cl up and rdn over 2f out: sn wknd* **8/1**
50-6 12 *1 ½* **Silver Mont (IRE)**[31] 2379 3-9-3 56 PaulFessey 7 23
(Mrs A Duffield) *midfield: hdwy 3f out: sn rdn along and n.m.r wl over 1f out: sn wknd* **20/1**
-005 13 *24* **Bold Tiger (IRE)**[6] 3138 3-9-0 53 GylesParkin 8 —
(Miss Tracy Waggott) *led: rdn along over 3f out: sn hdd & wknd* **66/1**
-000 14 *3* **Considerthelilies (IRE)**[5] 3167 3-9-1 54 RoystonFfrench 11 —
(Miss L A Perratt) *a towards rr* **100/1**

1m 42.6s (-0.89) **Going Correction** -0.05s/f (Good) — 14 Ran SP% **113.8**
Speed ratings (Par 98):102,101,99,98,94 89,89,88,86,85 82,81,57,54
CSF £97.98 CT £851.27 TOTE £18.10: £4.30, £2.70, £2.10; EX 174.30.
Owner M Channon **Bred** Bloodhorse International Limited **Trained** West Ilsley, Berks
■ Stewards' Enquiry : Tony Culhane one-day ban: careless riding (Jul 20); caution: used whip with excessive frequency

FOCUS
An ordinary handicap, but the pace was fair and the form looks reasonable and should stand up at a similar level.
Noble Nova Official explanation: trainer's rep said, regarding the improved form shown, filly was better suited by today's good ground
Colton Official explanation: jockey said gelding had no more to give

3330 WEST SOUND H'CAP 6f
3:20 (3:20) (Class 5) (0-70,70) 3-Y-O+ **£4,210** (£1,252; £625; £312) **Stalls** Low

Form RPR
2112 **1** **Yorkshire Blue**[9] [3041] 7-9-11 **70**................................ DanielTudhope(3) 3 81+
(J S Goldie) *towards rr: hdwy and swtchd outside over 2f out: rdn to ld over 1f out: sn clr* **9/4**[1]
-003 **2** 1 ½ **Prospect Court**[6] [3137] 4-8-4 **51** oh4........................ AndrewMullen(5) 12 57
(A C Whillans) *trckd ldrs: hdwy 1/2-way: rdn to ld over 2f out: hdd wl over 1f out and kpt on same pce* **9/1**[3]
4502 **3** 1 **Newsround**[16] [2811] 4-8-9 **51** oh2.................................(b) TonyCulhane 6 54
(D W Chapman) *hmpd s and bhd: hdway on outer over 2f out: sn rdn and kpt on appr last: nrst fin* **10/1**
5403 **4** ½ **Haulage Man**[20] [2700] 8-8-9 **51** oh5...................................(p) DavidAllan 4 53
(Karen McLintock) *towards rr: hdwy over 2f out: sn rdn and kpt on ins last: nrst fin* **9/1**[3]
053 **5** ½ **Pride Of Kinloch**[16] [2811] 6-8-10 **52**.............................(p) TonyHamilton 9 52
(N Wilson) *led: rdn along and hdd over 2f out: grad wknd* **10/1**
1060 **6** 2 **George The Best (IRE)**[10] [3003] 5-9-4 **60**...................... PaulHanagan 8 54
(Micky Hammond) *hmpd s: sn chsng ldrs: rdn along over 2f out and grad wknd* **9/1**[3]
030 **7** ½ **Dunn Deal (IRE)**[13] [2920] 6-9-13 **69**.................................... PaulQuinn 10 62
(W M Brisbourne) *hld up: hdwy 1/2-way: rdn alontg 2f out and sn no imp* **10/1**
5000 **8** 1 ¾ **Salviati (USA)**[10] [3004] 9-9-9 **65**.. NCallan 1 52
(J M Bradley) *in tch: effrt over 2f out: sn rdn and no hdwy* **8/1**[2]
-000 **9** nk **Roonah (FR)**[10] [3023] 3-8-4 **52**.. PaulFessey 5 38
(Karen McLintock) *wnt rt s: sn chsng ldrs: rdn along over 2f out and sn wknd* **100/1**
0154 **10** 2 **Boanerges (IRE)**[12] [2955] 9-9-3 **59**.................................... JoeFanning 11 39
(J M Bradley) *trckd ldrs: effrt over 2f out: sn rdn and wknd over 1f out* **8/1**[2]
1100 **11** 5 **Obe Bold (IRE)**[10] [3004] 5-9-0 **56**.................................... FrancisNorton 2 21
(A Berry) *chsd ldrs: rdn along 1/2-way: sn wknd* **25/1**
0-00 **12** 9 **Cd Flyer (IRE)**[54] [1760] 9-9-8 **64**..................................... PaulMulrennan 7 2
(R C Guest) *cl up: rdn along 1/2-way: sn wknd* **33/1**
1m 14.23s (0.56) **Going Correction** +0.075s/f (Good)
WFA 3 from 4yo+ 6lb **12** Ran SP% **118.0**
Speed ratings (Par 103):99,97,95,95,94 91,91,88,88,85 78,66
CSF £22.43 CT £174.81 TOTE £2.80: £1.30, £4.20, £2.10; EX 29.60.
Owner Thoroughbred Leisure Racing Club 2 **Bred** R T And Mrs Watson **Trained** Uplawmoor, E Renfrews

FOCUS
An ordinary handicap in which the field raced centre to far side. The pace seemed sound and the form looks solid.

3331 LADIES NIGHT ON SATURDAY 12 AUGUST H'CAP 1m
3:55 (3:55) (Class 4) (0-80,80) 3-Y-O+ **£6,477** (£1,927; £963; £481) **Stalls** Low

Form RPR
-040 **1** **Primo Way**[29] [2454] 5-10-0 **78**.. TomEaves 8 87
(I Semple) *hld up in tch: hdwy over 2f out: rdn to chse wnr over 1f out: styd on to ld last 100 yds* **9/1**
6000 **2** 1 ¼ **Major Magpie (IRE)**[6] [3147] 4-9-5 **69**................................ PaulFessey 6 76
(M Dods) *hld up in rr: hdwy over 2f out: sn rdn and styd on wl fnl f* **6/1**[3]
3302 **3** nk **Jaad**[7] [3113] 3-9-7 **80**... RoystonFfrench 3 86
(M Johnston) *cl up: led after 1f: pushed clr 2f out: rdn over 1f out: drvn ins last: hdd and no ex last 100 yds* **11/4**[1]
1100 **4** 1 **Commitment Lecture**[15] [2853] 6-9-4 **68**.........................(t) PhillipMakin 2 72
(M Dods) *in tch: hdwy to chse ldrs 3f out: rdn 2f out and kpt on same pce* **8/1**
0304 **5** 2 ½ **Fair Shake (IRE)**[9] [3040] 6-9-4 **68**.................................(v) TonyHamilton 1 66
(Karen McLintock) *hld up in rr: swtchd wd and gd hdwy over 2f out: rdn wl over 1f out and sn one pce* **6/1**[3]
5612 **6** nk **Hawkit (USA)**[8] [3068] 5-9-8 **72**.. NCallan 9 70
(A Bailey) *hld up towards rr: swtchd wd and hdwy over 2f out: sn rdn and no imp fr wl over 1f out* **11/2**[2]
0000 **7** 2 ½ **Bolton Hall (IRE)**[12] [2947] 4-8-12 **62**.............................. PaulHanagan 4 54
(R A Fahey) *led 1f: cl up tl rdn along wl over 2f out and sn wknd* **9/1**
-046 **8** 2 ½ **Ignition**[22] [2634] 4-8-12 **62**...(p) JoeFanning 7 49
(W M Brisbourne) *chsd ldng pair: rdn along wl over 2f out and sn wknd* **10/1**
1m 42.19s (-1.30) **Going Correction** -0.05s/f (Good)
WFA 3 from 4yo+ 9lb **8** Ran SP% **110.8**
Speed ratings (Par 105):104,102,102,101,98 98,96,93
CSF £57.79 CT £181.87 TOTE £10.20: £3.70, £3.00, £1.10; EX 76.40.
Owner Gordon McDowall **Bred** Mrs P A Reditt And M J Reditt **Trained** Carluke, S Lanarks

FOCUS
An ordinary event, but the pace was sound and the form could prove a little better than initially rated.

3332 EBF LAND O'BURNS FILLIES' STKS (LISTED RACE) 5f
4:30 (4:31) (Class 1) 3-Y-O+
£15,898 (£6,025; £3,015; £1,503; £753; £378) **Stalls** Low

Form RPR
0- **1** **Free Roses (IRE)**[11] [2993] 3-8-12 .... FMBerry 4 97
(Edward Lynam, Ire) *trckd ldrs: gd hdwy over 1f out: sn rdn and kpt on wl to ld last 100 ydss* **7/2**[2]
-343 **2** 1 **Clear Impression (IRE)**[29] [2438] 4-9-3 97.................... J-PGuillambert 1 93
(S C Williams) *cl up on outer: effrt 2f out: rdn to ld ent last: sn edgd rt and drvn: hdd and nt qckn last 100 yds* **2/1**[1]
0-05 **3** 1 **Bowness**[38] [2173] 4-9-3 76.. TonyCulhane 7 89?
(J G Given) *chsd ldrs: rdn wl over 1f out: drvn and kpt on ins last* **18/1**
-055 **4** shd **Clare Hills (IRE)**[22] [2651] 3-8-12 93..............................(p) PatCosgrave 8 89
(K R Burke) *cl up: led after 1f: rdn 2f out: drvn and hdd ent last: kpt on same pce* **10/1**
4-02 **5** ¾ **Dixie Belle**[22] [2651] 3-8-12 95...(t) TPQueally 3 86
(M G Quinlan) *cl up: rdn along 2f out: drvn and hld whn n.m.r ent last* **11/2**[3]
1410 **6** nk **Glenviews Youngone (IRE)**[22] [2651] 3-8-12 83...... RobbieFitzpatrick 9 85
(Peter Grayson) *in tch: hdwy 2f out: sn rdn and no imp ins last* **9/1**
3600 **7** 2 **Enchantment**[9] [3038] 5-9-3 87...(p) JoeFanning 5 78
(J M Bradley) *led 1f: cl up tl rdn 2f out and grad wknd appr last* **10/1**
2511 **8** 1 ½ **Pippa's Dancer (IRE)**[14] [2898] 4-9-3 73.......................... FrancisNorton 2 73
(W R Muir) *chsd ldrs: rdn along 2f out: sn wknd* **12/1**
00-4 **9** 3 ½ **Vondova**[10] [3002] 4-9-3 77.. TomEaves 6 60
(D A Nolan) *a rr* **300/1**
60.18 secs (-0.26) **Going Correction** +0.075s/f (Good)
WFA 3 from 4yo+ 5lb **9** Ran SP% **112.4**
Speed ratings (Par 108):105,103,101,101,100 99,96,94,88
CSF £10.49 TOTE £4.50: £1.90, £1.40, £5.70; EX 10.60.
Owner Lady O'Reilly **Bred** David Fenlon **Trained** Dunshaughlin, Co Meath

FOCUS
Not a strong race for the money or the grade, and the 76-rated third holds the form down, although the pace was sound. The stalls were on the far side, but the field ended up against the stands' rail.

NOTEBOOK
Free Roses(IRE) ◆ is a filly on the upgrade and she had no problems with the drop in distance or the step up in class. A return to six furlongs will not inconvenience and, although this bare form looks shaky, she is the type to progress again. (tchd 4-1 and 9-2 in a place)
Clear Impression(IRE) looked to have solid claims at the weights and looked the winner for much of the way. Although failing to pick up as well as the winner late on, she ran creditably and is sure to be placed to advantage in non-handicap company. (op 7-4 tchd 9-4)
Bowness's proximity as an inconsistent 76-rated handicapper holds this form down to a large degree. She will be suited by the return to six furlongs but she may be flattered, as the leaders went off plenty quick enough, so her short term future lies with the assessor. (op 16-1 tchd 20-1)
Clare Hills(IRE) fared the best of those that helped to force the generous pace and she was not disgraced. She will be of more interest in this company when allowed an uncontested lead. (op 12-1)
Dixie Belle jumped off much better than at Sandown and helped to force the generous gallop. Not surprisingly she could not sustain her effort in the closing stages and she would not be one to write off just yet. (op 7-1)
Glenviews Youngone(IRE) had something to find at the weights and was not disgraced, but she left the impression that she would be worth another try over six furlongs. (op 8-1)

3333 KILMARNOCK STANDARD H'CAP 1m 2f
5:00 (5:00) (Class 6) (0-65,65) 4-Y-O+ **£3,238** (£963; £481; £240) **Stalls** Low

Form RPR
4362 **1** **Donna's Double**[10] [3022] 11-8-6 **50**..............................(p) TonyHamilton 9 57
(Karen McLintock) *hld up: hdwy over 2f out: rdn over 1f out: squeezed through to ld ins last: drvn out* **10/1**
5403 **2** ¾ **Royal Flynn**[9] [3037] 4-8-13 **57**.. PaulFessey 10 63
(M Dods) *trckd ldrs: hdwy over 2f out: rdn and ev ch ent tl drvn and nt qckn towards fin* **6/1**[3]
6135 **3** shd **Inch High**[16] [2811] 8-8-7 **51**.. PaulHanagan 2 56
(J S Goldie) *in tch: hdwy over 2f out: rdn over 1f out: ev ch ins last: nt qckn last 50 yds* **8/1**
0602 **4** shd **Ruby Legend**[16] [2832] 8-8-7 **51**..(b) JoeFanning 13 56
(K G Reveley) *hld up in midfield: hdwy on outer wl over 2f out: rdn over 1f out: satyed on wl fnl f: nrst fin* **14/1**
016- **5** hd **Neil's Legacy (IRE)**[253] [6141] 4-8-1 **50**.................... AndrewMullen(5) 12 55
(Miss L A Perratt) *chsd ldrs: hdwy over 2f out: rdn to chse ldrs over 1f out: kpt on u.p ins last* **33/1**
651 **6** 1 **Brief Statement (IRE)**[16] [2808] 4-8-10 **59**........................ LiamJones(5) 3 62
(W M Brisbourne) *towards rr: rdn along 4f out: gd hdwy 2f out: chsd ldrs and nt clr run ins last: kpt on* **9/2**[1]
1652 **7** nk **Balwearie (IRE)**[16] [2812] 5-9-2 **60**..............................(p) RoystonFfrench 6 63
(Miss L A Perratt) *led: rdn along and hdd over 2f out: led again over 1f out: drvn: edgd lft and hdd inside last: wknd* **5/1**[2]
00-4 **8** 2 **Fair Spin**[43] [1187] 6-8-6 **50**.. FrancisNorton 8 49
(Micky Hammond) *hld up in rr: swtchd outside and hdwy over 2f out: sn rdn and kpt on appr last: nt rch ldrs* **25/1**
3664 **9** ½ **Jordans Elect**[15] [2853] 6-9-7 **65**.................................. PaulMulrennan 11 63
(P Monteith) *cl up: rdn to ld over 2f out: drvn and hdd over 1f out: sn wknd* **11/1**
600/ **10** ¾ **Culcabock (IRE)**[51] [5479] 6-8-2 **46** oh3...................... CatherineGannon 5 43
(Miss Lucinda V Russell) *chsd ldrs on inner: rdn along over 2f out: sn wknd* **12/1**
0060 **11** 3 ½ **Frogs' Gift (IRE)**[17] [2789] 4-8-2 **46** oh3................................ PaulQuinn 7 36
(G M Moore) *a rr* **66/1**
5052 **12** 7 **Insubordinate**[16] [2808] 5-8-10 **57**.............................. DanielTudhope(3) 1 35
(J S Goldie) *s.i.s: a rr* **5/1**[2]
2m 10.81s (-0.91) **Going Correction** -0.05s/f (Good) **12** Ran SP% **117.0**
Speed ratings (Par 101):101,100,100,100,100 99,99,97,97,96 93,88
CSF £67.05 CT £510.34 TOTE £13.10: £3.60, £2.30, £2.60; EX 94.90.
Owner J R Adams (Newcastle) Limited **Bred** Aston Park Stud **Trained** Ingoe, Northumberland

FOCUS
An ordinary handicap, but a decent gallop from the outset and the form appears solid enough for the level.

3334 ANTHEA MORSHEAD "GOOD LUCK" FROM AYR RACECOURSE AMATEUR RIDERS' H'CAP 5f
5:30 (5:30) (Class 6) (0-55,55) 4-Y-O+ **£2,966** (£912; £456) **Stalls** Low

Form RPR
2060 **1** **Compton Classic**[5] [3171] 4-10-9 **48**.................(p) MissMMullineaux(5) 11 57
(J S Goldie) *outpcd and towards rr: hdwy on outer over 1f out: str run ins last to ld nr fin* **15/2**
-000 **2** ½ **Viewforth**[18] [2748] 8-10-12 **53**......................................(b) MrCMcGaffin(7) 7 60
(I Semple) *midfield: swtchd lft and hdwy over 1f out: rdn to ld ins last hdd nr fin* **14/1**
2260 **3** 2 **Rowanberry**[23] [2611] 4-10-13 **47**.. MrSDobson 4 47
(R M H Cowell) *chsd ldrs: hdwy over 1f out: rdn to ld ent last: sn hdd and one pce* **5/1**[2]
5004 **4** hd **Shatin Leader**[5] [3166] 4-9-13 **38**....................................(p) MissARyan(5) 5 37
(Miss L A Perratt) *in tch: hdwy 2f out: rdn and ev ch ent last: kpt on same pce* **16/1**
0-00 **5** ½ **Instinct**[20] [2700] 5-10-0 **37**...................................... MissFayeBramley(3) 13 34
(Micky Hammond) *midfield: hdwy over 1f out: styd on ins last: nrst fin* **33/1**
0630 **6** nk **Rosie's Result**[13] [2928] 6-10-4 **43**.. CJCallow(5) 9 39
(M Todhunter) *in tch: hdwy over 1f out: sn rdn and kpt on same pce ins last* **8/1**
0000 **7** nk **On The Trail**[47] [1909] 9-10-7 **41**..................................(p) MissSBrotherton 6 36
(D W Chapman) *cl up: led 1/2-way: rdn and hdd over 1f out: sn wknd* **16/1**

0063 **8** 3/4 **Seven No Trumps**[12] 2949 9-11-0 **55**........................ MissSBradley(7) 14 48
(J M Bradley) *chsd ldrs: rdn wl over 1f out: wknd ent last* **5/2**[1]
000- **9** *nk* **Choreographic (IRE)**[243] 6293 4-9-12 **37**........................ MrBMcHugh(5) 8 29
(R A Fahey) *towards rr: sme hdwy over 1f out: styng on whn n.m.r ins last* **16/1**
000- **10** *shd* **Hebenus**[314] 4824 7-9-12 **37**........................ MissHCuthbert(5) 10 28
(T A K Cuthbert) *prom: effrt to chal over 1f out: rdn to ld ent last: sn edged lft: hdd & wknd* **50/1**
00-5 **11** 2 1/2 **Telepathic (IRE)**[59] 1611 6-11-2 **50**........................ MrsCBartley 2 32
(A Berry) *led to 1/2-way: sn rdn and wknd wl over 1f out* **16/1**
00-0 **12** 3/4 **Alfie Lee (IRE)**[13] 2928 9-9-11 **38**........................(tp) MissEJTuck(7) 12 17
(D A Nolan) *a rr* **66/1**
0360 **13** 1 3/4 **Sundried Tomato**[20] 2700 7-10-9 **43**........................(p) MissLEllison 3 16
(D W Chapman) *chsd ldrs: rdn along 2f out: sn wknd* **12/1**
1404 **14** 6 **Bahrain Gold (IRE)**[9] 3052 6-11-1 **54**........................(b) MrMJJSmith(5) 1 6
(N P McCormack) *chsd ldrs: rdn along over 2f out: sn wknd* **6/1**[3]

61.28 secs (0.84) **Going Correction** +0.075s/f (Good) **14** Ran SP% **126.7**
Speed ratings (Par 101):96,95,92,91,90 90,89,88,88,88 84,82,80,70
CSF £113.21 CT £604.93 TOTE £10.00: £3.40, £4.70, £1.50; EX 133.80 Place 6 £97.14, Place 5 £61.19.
Owner J S Goldie **Bred** James Thom And Sons And Peter Orr **Trained** Uplawmoor, E Renfrews
■ Stewards' Enquiry : Mrs C Bartley one-day ban: failed to keep straight from stalls (Jul 28)

FOCUS
A low-grade handicap, but the pace was solid throughout and the form looks sound but limited. The field fanned across most of the track and the winner came towards the stands' side.
T/Jkpt: Not won. T/Plt: £90.80 to a £1 stake. Pool: £59,715.55. 480.00 winning tickets. T/Qpdt: £28.80 to a £1 stake. Pool: £3,289.80. 84.40 winning tickets. JR

3160 BRIGHTON (L-H)
Sunday, July 9

OFFICIAL GOING: Firm
As at the last meeting, there appeared to be an advantage in heading for the stands' rail, with Desert Dreamer the only winner not to come across.
Wind: Fresh, against Weather: Cloudy start, fine later

3335 EBF SKYBET.COM WIMBLEDON FINAL NEXT GAME WINNER MEDIAN AUCTION MAIDEN STKS 6f 209y
2:30 (2:31) (Class 6) 2-Y-O £2,590 (£770; £385; £192) **Stalls** Low

Form RPR
422 **1** **Tencendur (IRE)**[55] 1730 2-9-3 .... KDarley 2 76
(M Johnston) *led after 1f: c to stands' rail: edgd lft over 1f out: drvn to hold on fnl f* **2/1**[1]
025 **2** 1/2 **Dee Jay Wells**[26] 2530 2-9-3 .... RyanMoore 6 75
(R Hannon) *led 1f: cl 2nd after: hrd rdn and ev ch fnl f: edgd lft: nt qckn fnl 50 yds* **4/1**[3]
05 **3** 2 1/2 **Sunley Sovereign**[20] 2710 2-9-3 .... SamHitchcott 7 68
(M R Channon) *t.k.h in 4th: effrt and rdr dropped whip over 1f out: one pce fnl f* **8/1**
0 **4** 9 **Rubilini**[12] 2957 2-8-12 .... AlanMunro 5 40
(M R Channon) *s.i.s: sn bhd: rdn over 2f out: nvr trbld ldrs* **10/1**
02 **5** *shd* **Law Of The Land (IRE)**[9] 3031 2-9-3 .... MartinDwyer 4 45
(W R Muir) *t.k.h: chsd ldng pair: hrd rdn and wknd 2f out* **9/4**[2]
0 **6** 3 1/2 **Sepia Print (IRE)**[23] 2604 2-8-12 .... PaulDoe 3 31
(W J Knight) *sn bhd: pushed along and n.d final 3f* **33/1**

1m 25.13s (2.43) **Going Correction** +0.20s/f (Good) **6** Ran SP% **107.2**
Speed ratings (Par 92):94,93,90,80,80 76
CSF £9.33 TOTE £2.60: £1.20, £2.70; EX 9.30.
Owner Joy And Valentine Feerick **Bred** Michael O'Mahony **Trained** Middleham Moor, N Yorks

FOCUS
An ordinary maiden, run at a modest pace for the first three furlongs and rated around the first three.

NOTEBOOK
Tencendur(IRE) was able to bag the stands' rail, which had been hugely favourable at the last meeting, but - if there was an advantage this time - he gave it away again by hanging left down the camber. That said, he was well at home over this longer trip and battled bravely to hold off a strong challenge from the runner-up. (tchd 15-8)
Dee Jay Wells came to have a real chance, but edged left down the camber and changed his legs on the final hill, which is forgiveable around here on the prevailing firm ground. Until then, he had handled the track pretty well. (op 5-1)
Sunley Sovereign, presented with a perfect opening when the winner edged left and gave him the plum position on the stands' rail, was not knocked about after his rider lost his whip on the run to the final furlong. He is now qualified for nurseries, and will be interesting next time. (op 9-1 tchd 10-1)
Rubilini will be qualified for nurseries after one more run, and that looks to be her sphere. (op 7-1)
Law Of The Land(IRE) did not run his race, and may not have been at his best on this unconventional track. (tchd 5-2)
Sepia Print(IRE) needs another run to qualify for nurseries, and should be more at home in that company, though improvement is required. (tchd 40-1)

3336 ITALY V FRANCE IN-PLAY BETTING WITH SKYBET.COM MAIDEN STKS 7f 214y
3:05 (3:05) (Class 5) 3-Y-O £3,886 (£1,156; £577; £288) **Stalls** Low

Form RPR
2-34 **1** **Heather Moor (USA)**[39] 2129 3-8-12 75........................ RyanMoore 5 71
(Sir Michael Stoute) *mde all: c to stands' rail st: hrd rdn over 1f out: hld on wl* **6/4**[1]
42 **2** 1/2 **Quintrell**[45] 1956 3-8-12 .... DaneO'Neill 4 70
(H Candy) *sn prom: wnt 2nd over 4f out: str chal fnl f: r.o* **9/4**[2]
50 **3** 3 **True West (USA)**[43] 2028 3-8-12 .... ShaneKelly 3 63
(J Noseda) *chsd ldrs: rdn and lost pl 3f out: styd on to take 3rd ins fnl f* **18/1**
02-6 **4** 1 1/4 **With Style**[32] 2350 3-8-12 83........................ EddieAhern 6 60
(E A L Dunlop) *chsd ldrs: hrd rdn over 2f out: one pce* **6/1**[3]
5033 **5** *nk* **Shinko (IRE)**[12] 2951 3-8-9 56........................(p) DeanCorby(3) 2 59?
(Miss J Feilden) *in tch: rdn to chse ldng pair over 2f out: no ex* **33/1**
4 **6** 4 **Casual Affair**[7] 3112 3-9-3 .... RichardMullen 1 55
(E J O'Neill) *chsd ldrs: hrd rdn over 2f out: sn wknd* **15/2**
-00 **7** 6 **Eastlands (IRE)**[13] 2934 3-9-3 .... PaulDoe 7 41
(Jamie Poulton) *s.s: outpcd and bhd: short-lived effrt in centre over 2f out: eased whn no ch fnl f* **50/1**
2050 **8** 7 **Picture Show (USA)**[10] 3011 3-8-12 63........................ SebSanders 8 19
(C E Brittain) *prom 5f: wkng whn hung lft fnl 2f* **16/1**

1m 36.91s (1.87) **Going Correction** +0.20s/f (Good) **8** Ran SP% **112.9**
Speed ratings (Par 100):98,97,94,93,92 88,82,75
CSF £4.81 TOTE £2.00: £1.70, £1.20, £1.60; EX 4.70 Trifecta £56.60 Pool: £502.23 - 6.29 winning units.
Owner K Abdulla **Bred** Juddmonte Farms Inc **Trained** Newmarket, Suffolk
■ Stewards' Enquiry : Dane O'Neill two-day ban: used whip with excessive frequency (Jul 20-21)

FOCUS
A routine maiden, but one with several big stables involved. The first two were close to form but the race has not been rated positively.

3337 SKYBET.COM ITALY V FRANCE CORRECT SCORE BETTING IN-PLAY H'CAP 6f 209y
3:40 (3:40) (Class 4) (0-80,79) 3-Y-O+ £6,232 (£1,866; £933; £467; £233; £117) **Stalls** Low

Form RPR
0202 **1** **Desert Dreamer (IRE)**[6] 3149 5-10-0 **79**........................ AlanMunro 9 88
(P R Chamings) *stdd s: t.k.h in rr: eased lft and hdwy 2f out: qcknd to ld in centre fnl 50 yds* **15/2**
0555 **2** 3/4 **Curtain Bluff**[3] 3229 4-9-6 **71**........................(v[1]) MartinDwyer 10 78
(M R Channon) *hld up in tch: nt clr run 3f out: styd on u.p to take 2nd on line* **14/1**
6161 **3** *shd* **Ivory Lace**[12] 2954 5-9-5 **75**........................ JamesDoyle(5) 4 82
(S Woodman) *chsd ldrs: swtchd lft and led 2f out: hrd rdn fnl f: hdd and nt qckn fnl 50 yds* **9/2**[2]
0060 **4** 1 3/4 **Border Edge**[33] 2327 8-8-9 **60**........................(v) HayleyTurner 3 62
(J J Bridger) *prom: led 3f out to 2f out: one pce fnl f* **16/1**
0656 **5** *hd* **Landucci**[10] 3012 5-10-0 **79**........................ MichaelHills 5 80
(J W Hills) *in tch: drvn to press ldrs 2f out: one pce fnl f* **11/4**[1]
1-00 **6** 1 3/4 **Pillars Of Wisdom**[36] 2232 4-9-11 **76**........................(t) PaulDoe 6 73
(J L Dunlop) *dwlt: hdwy to press ldrs 2f out: no ex fnl f* **10/1**
-223 **7** 3/4 **Keep Bacckinhit (IRE)**[12] 2954 4-8-9 **60**........................ RyanMoore 8 55
(G L Moore) *mid-div: effrt over 2f out: no imp* **5/1**[3]
-002 **8** *nk* **Kings Heir (IRE)**[33] 2318 3-9-6 **79**........................ SebSanders 7 73
(R M Beckett) *prom over 4f* **5/1**[3]
0006 **9** 4 **Acomb**[12] 2954 6-9-5 **70**........................ RichardThomas 2 53
(Mrs L Richards) *led: c to stands' rail st: hdd 3f out: sn wknd and hung lft* **25/1**
0354 **10** 4 **Hurricane Coast**[16] 2831 7-9-3 **68**........................(bt) ShaneKelly 1 40
(C R Dore) *a bhd* **14/1**

1m 22.81s (0.11) **Going Correction** +0.20s/f (Good)
WFA 3 from 4yo+ 8lb **10** Ran SP% **122.1**
Speed ratings (Par 105):107,106,106,104,103 101,100,100,96,91
CSF £111.61 CT £550.13 TOTE £9.00: £2.90, £4.10, £2.40; EX 125.50 Trifecta £703.60 Part won. Pool: £991.08 - 0.50 winning units..
Owner Patrick Chamings Sprint Club **Bred** Gainsborough Stud Management Ltd **Trained** Baughurst, Hants

FOCUS
A typical Brighton handicap, run at a decent pace and rated through the winner, but not the strongest contest.

3338 ITALY V FRANCE SKYBET 1ST PLAYER CARDED H'CAP 1m 1f 209y
4:15 (4:16) (Class 5) (0-70,70) 3-Y-O £3,886 (£1,156; £577; £288) **Stalls** High

Form RPR
0-15 **1** **Prince Picasso**[55] 1736 3-9-5 **68**........................ SebSanders 6 79+
(Sir Mark Prescott) *mde all: rdn and hung lft fnl 3f: c to stands' rail: drew clr fnl f* **1/1**[1]
0206 **2** 2 1/2 **Cantabilly (IRE)**[13] 2932 3-9-5 **68**........................ MartinDwyer 3 72
(M R Channon) *dwlt: towards rr: rdn 3f out: styd on fnl 2f: tk 2nd fnl 100 yds* **8/1**
-365 **3** 1 1/4 **Salvestro**[28] 2480 3-8-13 **62**........................(b[1]) RyanMoore 7 64
(Mrs A J Perrett) *prom: jnd wnr 4f out: one pce fnl f* **6/1**[2]
2010 **4** 2 1/2 **Nikki Bea (IRE)**[13] 2929 3-8-10 **59**........................ PaulDoe 4 56
(Jamie Poulton) *in tch: rdn 3f out: one pce* **9/1**
0302 **5** 1 1/4 **Penang Cinta**[11] 2968 3-8-11 **60**........................ NickyMackay 2 55
(G A Butler) *in rr: outpcd and lost tch 4f out: mod effrt in centre whn hung lft 2f out: edgd rt 1f out: no imp* **7/1**[3]
0300 **6** 1 3/4 **Kavachi (IRE)**[13] 2933 3-9-3 **66**........................ EddieAhern 1 58
(E A L Dunlop) *prom: hrd rdn 3f out: wknd over 1f out* **6/1**[2]
0450 **7** 16 **Devon Ruby**[28] 2484 3-7-11 **51** oh6........................ EmmettStack(5) 8 12
(C L Popham) *dwlt: sn in tch: wknd 3f out: sn bhd* **66/1**

2m 5.11s (2.51) **Going Correction** +0.20s/f (Good) **7** Ran SP% **113.7**
Speed ratings (Par 100):97,95,94,92,91 89,76
CSF £9.82 CT £32.63 TOTE £1.80: £1.30, £2.50; EX 12.00 Trifecta £35.00 Pool: £859.05 - 17.39 winning units.
Owner Syndicate 2004 **Bred** Cheveley Park Stud Ltd **Trained** Newmarket, Suffolk

FOCUS
A modest race, run at a moderate pace until the last half-mile, but the form is relatively solid and the winner can progress.

3339 BARKING BRICKWORK H'CAP 7f 214y
4:50 (4:50) (Class 6) (0-60,60) 3-Y-O+ £2,590 (£770; £385; £192) **Stalls** Low

Form RPR
5000 **1** **Out For A Stroll**[22] 2645 7-9-6 **55**........................ SaleemGolam(3) 14 70+
(S C Williams) *hld up in midfield: hdwy and nt clr run on stands' rail over 1f out: fnd gap ins fnl f: str run to ld fnl stride* **6/1**[3]
2222 **2** *hd* **Border Artist**[3] 3213 7-9-3 **52**........................ EdwardCreighton(3) 4 62
(B G Powell) *dwlt: towards rr: hdwy and nt clr run fr 2f out: led ins fnl f: kpt on: ct fnl stride* **9/2**[1]
3526 **3** *nk* **Fantasy Defender (IRE)**[16] 2820 4-9-0 **46**........................(v) LPKeniry 7 55
(Ernst Oertel) *t.k.h in midfield: hdwy to chal over 1f out: kpt on* **17/2**
0240 **4** 1 3/4 **Hadath (IRE)**[39] 2135 9-9-5 **51**........................(b) GeorgeBaker 12 56
(B G Powell) *hld up towards rr: hdwy whn nt clr run and swtchd lft over 1f out: styd on* **14/1**
1500 **5** 1/2 **Zinging**[3] 3213 7-9-1 **47**........................(v) RyanMoore 11 51
(J J Bridger) *chsd ldrs: led 2f out: edgd off stands' rail and hdd ins fnl f: no ex* **20/1**
0423 **6** *shd* **Blue Empire (IRE)**[12] 2947 5-9-12 **58**........................ HayleyTurner 10 62
(C R Dore) *chsd ldrs: n.m.r over 1f out: one pce* **5/1**[2]
1330 **7** 3 **Welsh Dragon**[42] 2050 3-9-4 **59**........................ MartinDwyer 6 56
(A M Balding) *w ldrs: led briefly over 2f out: wknd 1f out* **8/1**
0003 **8** *nk* **Didoe**[11] 2966 7-8-12 **44**........................ PaulDoe 5 40
(P W Hiatt) *mid-div: lost pl after 3f: rdn and styd on fnl 2f* **16/1**

-204 **9** 2 1/2 **Whatatodo**[22] [2634] 4-9-0 **53** .... LukeMorris[(7)] 8 44
(M L W Bell) *chsd ldrs tl hrd rdn and wknd over 1f out* **11/1**
205 **10** *shd* **Tuning Fork**[11] [2969] 6-9-8 **54** .... AlanMunro 9 44
(T M Jones) *led tl over 2f out: sn btn* **7/1**
0026 **11** 1 3/4 **Love's Design (IRE)**[12] [2952] 9-8-10 **45** ....(v) DeanCorby[(3)] 13 31
(Miss J Feilden) *mid-div: effrt over 2f out: wknd over 1f out* **33/1**
00-0 **12** 1 1/4 **Royal Sailor (IRE)**[13] [2935] 4-9-0 **53** ....(b) DonnaCaldwell[(7)] 15 36
(J Ryan) *s.s: wl bhd most of way* **100/1**
0400 **13** 1 1/2 **Eclipse Park**[41] [2065] 3-9-5 **60** ....(p) ShaneKelly 3 40
(M J McGrath) *a bhd* **50/1**
3106 **14** 20 **Tamora**[8] [3099] 4-9-3 **49** ....(v) FrankieMcDonald 1 —
(A P Jarvis) *mid-div: n.m.r on ins rail and lost pl 5f out: sn wl bhd* **20/1**
00-0 **15** 29 **Ridgeway Cross (IRE)**[186] [31] 3-9-0 **55** .... SebSanders 2 —
(Ernst Oertel) *prom 5f* **40/1**

1m 36.4s (1.36) **Going Correction** +0.20s/f (Good)
WFA 3 from 4yo+ 9lb **15** Ran SP% **122.0**
Speed ratings (Par 101):101,100,100,98,98 98,95,94,92,92 90,89,87,67,38
CSF £31.09 CT £242.42 TOTE £7.30: £2.60, £2.20, £2.00; EX 32.40 Trifecta £213.60 Pool: £436.38 - 1.45 winning units.
Owner The Nomads **Bred** Exors Of The Late Mrs F G Allen **Trained** Newmarket, Suffolk

FOCUS
A low-grade race, but very competitive, and run at a good clip, with three horses vying for the early lead, and the field soon stretched out. The form looks reliable enough.
Hadath(IRE) Official explanation: jockey said gelding was denied a clear run
Zinging Official explanation: jockey said gelding ran too free
Ridgeway Cross(IRE) Official explanation: jockey said filly ran too free

3340 SKYBET.COM FOR ALL YOUR WORLD CUP BETTING H'CAP 5f 59y
5:20 (5:21) (Class 6) (0-60,55) 3-Y-0 **£2,590** (£770; £385; £192) **Stalls** Low

Form RPR
-562 **1** **Mullady Penelope**[15] [2876] 3-9-7 **55** .... SebSanders 4 62+
(Mrs A Duffield) *hld up in tch: nt clr run and swtchd to stands' rail ins fnl 2f: led ins fnl f: rdn out* **6/5**[1]
400 **2** 1 1/2 **Neardown Queen**[15] [2859] 3-8-11 **50** .... JamesDoyle[(5)] 8 52
(I A Wood) *outpcd and bhd: gd hdwy towards ins to ld over 1f out: hdd and one pce ins fnl f* **10/1**
0565 **3** 1/2 **Thoughtsofstardom**[16] [2826] 3-9-6 **54** ....(p) BrianReilly 1 54
(P S McEntee) *prom: rdn 4f out: chal over 1f out: one pce fnl f* **11/2**[3]
-000 **4** 2 **Song Huntress**[37] [2208] 3-8-11 **45** .... RichardThomas 6 38
(A G Newcombe) *towards rr: effrt over 2f out: hung lft: styd on same pce* **16/1**
3040 **5** 1 1/4 **Danny The Dip**[7] [3118] 3-9-7 **55** .... RyanMoore 3 44
(J J Bridger) *prom: hrd rdn and edging lft wn bmpd over 1f out: no ex* **4/1**[2]
-060 **6** 2 1/2 **Wotavadun (IRE)**[167] [177] 3-8-8 **42** ....(b) HayleyTurner 2 22
(C R Dore) *led: c to stands' rail st: hung bdly lft 2f out: edgd rt and hdd over 1f out: wknd* **14/1**
0-00 **7** *nk* **Pink Pyjamas**[19] [2730] 3-8-7 **41** ....(v) AlanMunro 7 19
(J A R Toller) *towards rr: effrt over 2f out: sn btn* **10/1**
-604 **8** 8 **Watch Out Jess**[19] [2730] 3-9-1 **49** .... LPKeniry 5 —
(M Madgwick) *prom to 1/2-way* **6/1**

64.33 secs (2.03) **Going Correction** +0.20s/f (Good) **8** Ran SP% **121.5**
Speed ratings (Par 98):91,88,87,84,82 78,78,65
CSF £16.32 CT £54.94 TOTE £2.00: £1.10, £2.70, £1.80; EX 19.70 Trifecta £88.50 Pool: £224.60 - 1.80 winning units. Place 6 £26.06, Place 5 £14.85.
Owner Middleham Park Racing XXXIX **Bred** Llety Stud **Trained** Constable Burton, N Yorks

FOCUS
A moderate race, but run at a good sprint tempo. However, yet again it was won by a horse on the stands' rail and it may not be form to get carried away with.
Danny The Dip Official explanation: jockey said gelding hung left
Wotavadun(IRE) Official explanation: jockey said gelding hung both ways
T/Plt: £17.20 to a £1 stake. Pool: £66,788 - 2,822.95 winning units T/Qpdt: £9.00 to a £1 stake. Pool: £4,193 - 342.60 winning units LM

2799 CHANTILLY (R-H)
Sunday, July 9

OFFICIAL GOING: Good to soft

3342a PRIX JEAN PRAT (GROUP 1) (C&F) 1m
3:15 (3:22) 3-Y-O **£157,628** (£63,062; £31,531; £15,752; £7,890)

RPR
1 **Stormy River (FR)**[19] [2721] 3-9-2 .... TThulliez 6 118+
(N Clement, France) *held up, last straight, angled out over 2f out, strong run final f to lead last strides* **7/4**[1]
2 1/2 **Kentucky Dynamite (USA)**[28] [2489] 3-9-2 .... C-PLemaire 2 117
(A De Royer-Dupre, France) *always close up, went 2nd entering straight, driven to lead 150yds out, caught last strides* **16/1**
3 1 1/2 **Dilek (FR)**[13] [2942] 3-9-2 .... CSoumillon 12 114
(A De Royer-Dupre, France) *always close up, 4th straight, 3rd and under pressure 2f out, kept on same pace under driving* **2/1**[2]
4 1/2 **Kendargent (FR)**[28] [2489] 3-9-2 .... RMarchelli 1 113
(Y Fouin, France) *soon led, set good pace, hard ridden and headed 150 yds out, kept on* **33/1**
5 1/2 **Garnica (FR)**[56] [1718] 3-9-2 .... IMendizabal 7 111
(J-C Rouget, France) *mid division, 6th straight, 4th 2f out, stayed on one pace* **16/1**
6 1/2 **Impressionnante**[35] [2275] 3-8-13 .... OPeslier 10 107
(C Laffon-Parias, France) *held up, 8th straight, headway on outsdie 2f out, never near to challenge* **13/2**
7 *nk* **Boris De Deauville (IRE)**[60] [1600] 3-9-2 .... YBarberot 3 110
(S Wattel, France) *held up, 9th straight, headway on rails over 2f out, kept on at one pace final 1 1/2f* **33/1**
8 1 1/2 **Ivan Denisovich (IRE)**[19] [2721] 3-9-2 .... KFallon 8 106
(A P O'Brien, Ire) *held up, 10th straight, effort on outside from over 2f out, ridden and found nothing 1 1/2f out* **4/1**[3]
9 1 1/2 **Royal Power (IRE)**[19] [2721] 3-9-2 .... TedDurcan 5 103
(M R Channon) *7th straight on inside, disputed 4th over 2f out, hard ridden well over 1f out, no extra final f* **28/1**
10 5 **Arabian Prince (USA)**[7] [3129] 3-9-2 .... JAHeffernan 9 92
(A P O'Brien, Ire) *raced in 4th, 5th straight, soon weakened* **66/1**
11 **Marchand D'Argent (FR)**[42] 3-9-2 .... J-MBreux 4 92
(N Clement, France) *driven to try and lead, tracked leader til 3rd straight, eased over 2f out, tailed off* **150/1**

1m 37.8s **Going Correction** +0.05s/f (Good) **11** Ran SP% **126.3**
Speed ratings: 114,113,112,111,111 110,110,108,107,102 102
PARI-MUTUEL: WIN 3.40 (coupled with Marchand D'Argent); PL 1.30, 2.10, 1.40; DF 18.30.
Owner Ecurie Mister Ess A S **Bred** J & Mlle Marie-Laure Collet **Trained** Chantilly, France

NOTEBOOK
Stormy River(FR), held up in last position, he was still at the back of the field rounding the home turn. Just before the two-furlong marker he was switched to the outside and showed an incredible turn of foot to sweep past the field to win by half a length. He is likely to be aimed at the Prix Jacques le Marois at Deauville.
Kentucky Dynamite(USA), up with the pace early on, he was moving easily in third position mid-race. Entering the straight he moved up to second and 150 yards from the post hit the front. He responded well and led up the straight only to be caught close home by the fast finishing Stormy River. There are more Group races in him.
Dilek(FR), supplemented for this event, was quickly into a good position despite his outside draw. Going round the bend he got a little unbalanced and was short of room, from which point he was always being pushed along. He battled bravely up the straight but was only staying on one paced.
Kendargent(FR), quickly out of the stalls, he took advantage of his good draw to lead the field along at a good pace. Running up the inside rail, he only relinquished his lead when headed 150 yards out by the eventual second.

2693 SAN SIRO (R-H)
Sunday, July 9

OFFICIAL GOING: Good

3343a PREMIO LUCIANO MANTOVANI (LISTED RACE) (FILLIES) 7f 110y
4:30 (4:40) 2-Y-O **£21,724** (£9,559; £5,214; £2,607)

RPR
1 **Sweet Wind Music** 2-9-0 .... PSirigu 9 98
(B Grizzetti, Italy)
2 1 1/4 **Biz Bar** 2-9-0 .... MEsposito 2 95
(M Guarnieri, Italy)
3 *snk* **Trans Gold (IRE)**[42] [2062] 2-9-0 .... MDemuro 5 95
(A Renzoni, Italy)
4 2 1/2 **Sopran Slam (IRE)** 2-9-0 .... DVargiu 8 89
(B Grizzetti, Italy)
5 *snk* **Baldovina**[22] [2638] 2-9-0 .... URispoli 13 88?
(M Botti) *rcd on outside, last but one st, gd prog fr 3f out, no ex appr fnl f (5.78/1)* **58/10**[1]
6 1/2 **Iuturna (USA)**[42] [2062] 2-9-0 .... LManiezzi 6 87
(R Menichetti, Italy)
7 *shd* **Pussy Galore (ITY)** 2-9-0 .... SUrru 12 87
(M Innocenti, Italy)
8 *snk* **Almusa (IRE)** 2-9-0 .... EBotti 1 87
(A & G Botti, Italy)
9 2 **Vola Vola (IRE)**[25] [2565] 2-9-0 .... MTellini 4 82
(R Feligioni, Italy)
10 *hd* **Gegyp (IRE)** 2-9-0 .... FBranca 7 82
(L Riccardi, Italy)
11 1 1/4 **Edelfa (IRE)** 2-9-0 .... ADiNapoli 10 79
(C Marinelli, Italy)
12 **Lady Enza (IRE)** 2-9-0 .... SGuerrieri 3 79
(S Lanteri, Italy)
13 **Kilkenny (ITY)**[29] [2475] 2-9-0 .... PConvertino 11 79
(A Marcialis, Italy)

1m 33.9s **13** Ran SP% **14.7**
(including 1 euro stake): WIN 7.85; PL 2.81, 3.27, 1.92; SF 139.32..
Owner Scuderia Razza Rossonera **Bred** Azienda Agricola Colareti Antonio **Trained** Italy

NOTEBOOK
Baldovina handled the step up in distance without a problem, and was not beaten too far. However, on this evidence she does not look up to Listed company just yet.

2966 BATH (L-H)
Monday, July 10

OFFICIAL GOING: Good
The jockeys came middle to stands' side in the home straight in the 3.45 onwards which normally only happens when the ground is soft.
Wind: Moderate against Weather: Intermittent light rain

3344 E.B.F./VERTESE OMEGA 369 MAIDEN STKS 5f 11y
2:15 (2:31) (Class 5) 2-Y-O **£3,562** (£1,059; £529; £264) **Stalls** Low

Form RPR
62 **1** **Abunai**[21] [2710] 2-8-12 .... SteveDrowne 7 72+
(R Charlton) *a.p: led wl over 1f out: rdn fnl f: r.o wl* **3/1**[1]
04 **2** 2 1/2 **Piccolena Boy**[12] [2967] 2-9-3 .... JimCrowley 11 68
(P Winkworth) *a.p: rdn wl over 1f out: nt qckn ins fnl f* **28/1**
04 **3** 1/2 **Star Strider**[23] [2631] 2-9-3 .... MartinDwyer 9 66
(A M Balding) *dwlt: sn hld up in mid-div: rdn and hdwy on outside 2f out: r.o one pce fnl f* **10/1**
04 **4** *nk* **Indian Song (IRE)**[12] [2984] 2-8-12 .... StephenCarson 6 60
(R F Johnson Houghton) *chsd ldrs on ins: rdn wl over 1f out: one pce fnl f* **7/2**[2]
05 **5** 1/2 **Dancing Daisy (IRE)**[23] [2631] 2-8-7 .... JamesDoyle[(5)] 10 58
(Mrs P N Dutfield) *rrd and s.s: outpcd and bhd: rdn 2f out: swtchd rt jst over 1f out: r.o wl towards fin* **66/1**
6 1/2 **Equuleus Pictor** 2-9-3 .... FrancisNorton 13 62
(J L Spearing) *dwlt: rdn 2f out: hdwy whn nt clr run jst ins fnl f: bttr for r* **12/1**
7 1 1/4 **Kyllachy Storm** 2-9-3 .... AlanMunro 4 57+
(R J Hodges) *bhd: rdn 2f out: late hdwy: nrst fin* **20/1**
63 **8** 1 3/4 **Colchium (IRE)**[33] [2354] 2-8-12 .... RyanMoore 2 46
(H Morrison) *w ldr: led jst over 2f out: hdd wl over 1f out: sn rdn: wknd ins fnl f* **7/1**[3]
9 1/2 **Bathwick Leti (IRE)** 2-8-9 .... NeilChalmers[(3)] 12 44
(A M Balding) *s.i.s: nvr nr ldrs* **40/1**
5 **10** 1 1/2 **Auction Boy**[54] [1770] 2-9-3 .... FrancisFerris 8 44
(B Palling) *hld up in mid-div: rdn 3f out: eased whn btn wl ins fnl f* **10/1**

63 **11** 1 ½ **Land Ahoy**[27] 2530 2-9-3 .... FrankieMcDonald 1 38
(D W P Arbuthnot) *led: rdn and hdd jst over 2f out: sn wknd: stmbld ins fnl f* **7/2**[2]

06 **12** 5 **Linkslade Lad**[10] 3031 2-9-3 ....(b) RichardMullen 3 20
(W R Muir) *s.s: outpcd* **100/1**

62.98 secs (0.48) **Going Correction** +0.025s/f (Good) **12** Ran SP% **121.0**
Speed ratings (Par 94):97,93,92,91,90 90,88,85,84,82 79,71
CSF £98.89 TOTE £3.80: £1.30, £7.50, £3.10; EX 108.80 Trifecta £236.70 Part won. Pool: £333.44 - 0.35 winning units..
Owner A E Oppenheimer **Bred** Hascombe And Valiant Studs **Trained** Beckhampton, Wilts

FOCUS
An interesting if modest maiden featuring a few who have already become course regulars. Weakish form as it stands.

NOTEBOOK
Abunai, who did not get the run of the race on her first two starts, came home a clear-cut winner. Connections are toying with trying to get her some black type but that would mean a big step up from this. (op 10-3 tchd 4-1)
Piccolena Boy, whose two previous outings were over slightly further here, ran his best race so far and the trip may have helped. (op 33-1)
Star Strider was having his third run over course and distance and again had to recover from an indifferent start. Like the runner-up, he does seem to be on an upward curve. (op 14-1)
Indian Song(IRE) had run a similar race at Salisbury on her previous outing but this time there were no excuses.
Dancing Daisy(IRE) ◆ finished with a flourish after getting the start all wrong. She looks capable of improvement especially over a longer trip. Official explanation: jockey said filly had reared as gates opened
Equuleus Pictor ◆ is a half-brother to Grand Rapide who won over a mile here. A springer in the market, he was shaping promisingly when encountering traffic problems. With the benefit of this experience losses can be recouped. (op 20-1 tchd 25-1)
Kyllachy Storm ◆ was nibbled at in the market but it took a long time for the penny to drop. Finishing as well as any, he is one to keep an eye on especially when tackling further. (op 28-1)
Land Ahoy Official explanation: jockey said colt failed to handle the loose ground

3345 WESTERN DAILY PRESS RACE CLUB (S) STKS 5f 11y
2:45 (2:57) (Class 6) 2-Y-O **£2,266** (£674; £337; £168) **Stalls** Low

Form RPR

000 **1** **River Rosie (IRE)**[11] 3010 2-8-9 .... EddieAhern 10 51
(J G Portman) *a.p: chal gng wl over 1f out: rdn fnl f: led cl home* **8/1**

2550 **2** nk **Fly Time**[11] 3010 2-8-9 .... ChrisCatlin 5 50
(M R Channon) *led: hrd rdn fnl f: hdd cl home* **5/1**[2]

3 ¾ **Cookies Quiff (IRE)** 2-9-0 .... JohnEgan 11 52
(J S Moore) *s.i.s: hdwy 3f out: rdn over 1f out: hung lft ent fnl f: kpt on* **14/1**

20 **4** ½ **Meru Camp (IRE)**[24] 2617 2-9-0 .... JimCrowley 7 50
(P Winkworth) *a.p: rdn over 2f out: kpt on ins fnl f* **9/2**[1]

00 **5** ½ **Stunningjo**[77] 1181 2-8-9 ....(b[1]) FrancisNorton 2 44
(J L Spearing) *bhd: rdn over 2f out: gd late hdwy: nrst fin* **11/1**

5530 **6** nk **Diminuto**[8] 3117 2-8-9 .... HayleyTurner 1 43
(M D I Usher) *chsd ldrs on ins: outpcd over 2f out: rdn and kpt on fnl f: nt rch ldrs* **5/1**[2]

005 **7** 1 **Tagula Music (IRE)**[41] 2094 2-8-9 .... FrancisFerris 3 39
(B Palling) *dwlt: bhd: rdn over 2f out: sme hdwy 1f out: n.d* **33/1**

0020 **8** nk **Emergency Services**[7] 3136 2-9-0 .... RyanMoore 4 43
(Tom Dascombe) *bhd: rdn over 2f out: n.d* **8/1**

0061 **9** 1 ½ **Suzieblue (IRE)**[14] 2916 2-9-0 ....(p) LPKeniry 6 37
(J S Moore) *hld up in tch: rdn over 2f out: wknd fnl f* **6/1**[3]

020 **10** 1 **Bathwick Style**[41] 2094 2-8-9 .... DaneO'Neill 8 29
(B R Millman) *mid-div: rdn over 2f out: wknd over 1f out* **12/1**

11 ¾ **Temple Air (IRE)** 2-9-0 .... RobertMiles 9 31
(W G M Turner) *prom over 2f* **33/1**

63.77 secs (1.27) **Going Correction** +0.025s/f (Good) **11** Ran SP% **116.6**
Speed ratings (Par 92):90,89,88,87,86 86,84,84,81,80 78
CSF £47.33 TOTE £11.90: £3.20, £1.50, £7.80; EX 51.00 TRIFECTA Not won..There was no bid for the winner. Fly Time was claimed by H J Manners for £6,000.
Owner Christopher Shankland **Bred** Patrick O'Neill **Trained** Compton, Berks

FOCUS
An ordinary seller in which they finished in a heap.

NOTEBOOK
River Rosie(IRE) took advantage of a return to the minimum distance and a drop into selling company. (op 9-1)
Fly Time had finished half a length in front of River Rosie over seven on the Polytrack at Lingfield last time. She showed the right attitude under strong pressure but eventually got worn down. (op 4-1)
Cookies Quiff(IRE) ◆ did not help his chances by hanging but this was still an encouraging start to his career, albeit at a low level. Normal improvement should see him take a similar contest. (op 12-1)
Meru Camp(IRE) had been highly tried on his previous outing after his second to a multiple winner in a claimer on his debut. He seems ready for a step up to six. (op 6-1)
Stunningjo, tried in blinkers on this drop in grade, was supported in the market. She is crying out for further on this evidence. (op 16-1)
Diminuto, back in the right sort of company, requires a return to six. (tchd 9-2)
Temple Air(IRE) Official explanation: jockey said gelding hung left

3346 SUMMERSOUNDSPECTACULAR.COM MAIDEN STKS 1m 2f 46y
3:15 (3:20) (Class 5) 3-Y-O+ **£3,238** (£963; £481; £240) **Stalls** Low

Form RPR

6-23 **1** **Fleeting Memory**[33] 2350 3-8-12 81...................................(t) RyanMoore 1 81
(Sir Michael Stoute) *hld up in tch: hdwy 3f out: rdn to ld over 1f out: r.o wl* **1/1**[1]

435 **2** 2 ½ **Star Crowned (USA)**[35] 2304 3-9-3 87......................(bt) JimmyFortune 4 82+
(B J Meehan) *chsd ldr: rdn over 3f out: led jst over 2f out tl over 1f out: no ex ins fnl f* **7/4**[2]

035 **3** 1 ¼ **Grave Matters (USA)**[8] 3122 3-8-12 .... GregFairley(5) 5 79
(M Johnston) *led: rdn and hdd jst over 2f out: wknd over 1f out* **6/1**[3]

0 **4** 13 **Chifney Rush (IRE)**[19] 2753 3-8-12 .... MichaelHills 2 49
(B W Hills) *bhd: rdn over 3f out: styd on to take modest 4th ins fnl f* **40/1**

0 **5** 3 ½ **Indian Girl**[21] 2712 3-8-12 .... TedDurcan 9 43
(M R Channon) *hld up: sme hdwy over 4f out: rdn over 3f out: sn struggling* **40/1**

04 **6** shd **Indian Pride**[28] 2498 4-9-9 .... TPQueally 3 42
(D J Coakley) *a bhd: fin lame* **40/1**

0 **7** 6 **Winning Connection (IRE)**[8] 3112 3-9-3 .... ChrisCatlin 8 36
(P A Blockley) *a bhd* **100/1**

05 **8** 5 **Monsignor Fred**[17] 2815 4-10-0 .... DaneO'Neill 7 27
(H Candy) *prom: lost pl over 4f out: rdn over 3f out: sn bhd* **28/1**

2m 10.21s (-0.79) **Going Correction** +0.025s/f (Good)
WFA 3 from 4yo 11lb **8** Ran SP% **112.4**
Speed ratings (Par 103):104,102,101,90,87 87,82,78
CSF £2.76 TOTE £1.80: £1.10, £1.60, £1.40; EX 3.40 Trifecta £9.30 Pool: £741.23 - 56.33 winning units..
Owner The Queen **Bred** The Queen **Trained** Newmarket, Suffolk

FOCUS
The cream had come to the top a long way out in this weak maiden. The winner and third were roughly to form.
Indian Pride Official explanation: vet said filly finished with a high heart rate and was lame

3347 SUMMER SOUNDS SPECTACULAR AT BATH RACECOURSE MAIDEN H'CAP 1m 3f 144y
3:45 (3:49) (Class 5) (0-75,75) 3-Y-O **£3,562** (£1,059; £529; £264) **Stalls** Low

Form RPR

6352 **1** **Mull Of Dubai**[17] 2814 3-8-6 60... JohnEgan 4 69
(J S Moore) *hld up in mid-div: hdwy 3f out: rdn to ld wl over 1f out: sn hung rt: r.o* **8/1**

-002 **2** ¾ **Storm Of Arabia (IRE)**[14] 2933 3-8-9 63........................... TedDurcan 6 71
(W R Swinburn) *hld up in mid-div: hdwy over 4f out: rdn over 2f out: carried rt over 1f out: styd on ins fnl f* **9/1**

05-0 **3** ½ **Malakiya (IRE)**[85] 1032 3-8-8 65....................................... AdamKirby(3) 8 72
(G A Butler) *s.i.s: bhd: rdn 4f out: hdwy 2f out: swtchd lft over 1f out: styd on ins fnl f* **20/1**

543 **4** 3 **Regent's Park**[19] 2753 3-9-6 74.. SteveDrowne 2 76
(R Charlton) *a.p: led briefly 2f out: sn carried rt and rdn: wknd wl ins fnl f* **7/1**[3]

0-50 **5** 1 ½ **Roya**[30] 2434 3-8-13 67... DaneO'Neill 7 67
(R Hannon) *hld up in mid-div: rdn over 1f out: hdwy fnl f: nt rch ldrs* **22/1**

26-3 **6** nk **Mortarboard**[37] 2220 3-9-7 75... RichardMullen 5 75
(E J O'Neill) *hld up in tch: rdn over 2f out: sn btn* **7/1**[3]

4004 **7** 3 **Floodlight Fantasy**[14] 2933 3-8-9 63.................................. RyanMoore 3 58
(E S McMahon) *led: rdn and hdd 2f out: wkng whn carried rt over 1f out* **6/1**[2]

6006 **8** 1 ¼ **Kapellmeister (IRE)**[12] 2990 3-9-3 71......................(p) JimmyFortune 14 64
(C R Egerton) *prom: rdn over 3f out: wkng whn n.m.r on stands' rail over 1f out* **14/1**

3060 **9** 1 ¼ **Synonymy**[9] 3075 3-8-6 60... FrancisNorton 9 51
(M Blanshard) *bhd: rdn over 3f out: sme hdwy over 1f out: eased whn btn ins fnl f* **28/1**

-030 **10** ¾ **Rebelling (IRE)**[42] 2082 3-8-10 64............................... StephenCarson 16 54
(R F Johnson Houghton) *s.s: n.d* **20/1**

5355 **11** nk **Coda Agency**[16] 2882 3-8-6 60.. EddieAhern 13 49
(D W P Arbuthnot) *hld up in tch: rdn 3f out: wknd 2f out* **16/1**

3432 **12** ½ **Conservation (FR)**[56] 1738 3-9-6 74................................... AlanMunro 10 62
(P W Chapple-Hyam) *prom: rdn and ev ch over 2f out: wknd over 1f out* **9/2**[1]

500 **13** hd **Dream Witness (FR)**[23] 2646 3-8-6 60.......................... NickyMackay 11 48
(W R Muir) *hld up in mid-div: rdn 4f out: wknd 3f out* **66/1**

0404 **14** nk **On Air (USA)**[11] 3008 3-8-6 65.. GregFairley(5) 12 52
(M Johnston) *prom: rdn over 3f out: wknd over 2f out* **18/1**

006 **15** 10 **Seal Of Hope**[17] 2815 3-8-11 65... MartinDwyer 1 36
(M P Tregoning) *s.i.s: a bhd* **25/1**

6-00 **16** 10 **Kick And Prance**[47] 1941 3-8-3 57.................................(t) ChrisCatlin 15 12
(J A Geake) *a bhd* **66/1**

2m 31.02s (0.72) **Going Correction** +0.025s/f (Good) **16** Ran SP% **120.5**
Speed ratings (Par 100):98,97,97,95,94 93,91,91,90,89 89,89,89,88,82 75
CSF £70.60 CT £1400.53 TOTE £11.30: £2.20, £2.40, £3.00, £2.00; EX 83.80 TRIFECTA Not won..
Owner Mrs Fitri Hay **Bred** B Walters **Trained** Upper Lambourn, Berks

FOCUS
They came middle to stands' side in the home straight. This was a decent race of its type, with some unexposed runners in the frame, and the form should be sound.
Kapellmeister(IRE) Official explanation: jockey said gelding hung right

3348 BATH CHRONICLE H'CAP 5f 11y
4:15 (4:20) (Class 6) (0-65,65) 3-Y-O+ **£2,461** (£732; £365; £182) **Stalls** Low

Form RPR

2104 **1** **King Egbert (FR)**[9] 3071 5-8-5 49.................................... TolleyDean(7) 5 59
(A W Carroll) *towards rr: hdwy over 2f out: sn rdn: edgd rt and led wl ins fnl f: r.o* **9/1**

004 **2** nk **Kitchen Sink (IRE)**[9] 3094 4-8-13 50..............................(e) RyanMoore 11 59
(P J Makin) *chsd ldrs: rdn over 1f out: carried sltly rt ins fnl f: r.o* **7/2**[1]

2-45 **3** 1 ¼ **Tomthevic**[9] 3071 8-8-6 46 oh4..............................(p) NelsonDeSouza(3) 16 51
(J M Bradley) *led: rdn over 1f out: hdd and no ex wl ins fnl f* **16/1**

5363 **4** 1 ¼ **Cosmic Destiny (IRE)**[9] 3071 4-9-4 55 .... DaneO'Neill 4 55
(E F Vaughan) *hld up in mid-div: rdn over 1f out: hdwy fnl f: nvr able to chal* **15/2**[3]

0060 **5** shd **Whistler**[2] 3297 9-9-11 62...(p) PaulFitzsimons 8 62
(Miss J R Tooth) *s.i.s and sltly hmpd: bhd: rdn and hdwy over 1f out: nt rch ldrs* **11/1**

0045 **6** ½ **Pro Tempore**[23] 2637 4-8-9 46 .... FergusSweeney 9 44
(David Pinder) *wnt sltly lft s: a.p: rdn wl over 1f out: one pce fnl f* **11/1**

0620 **7** ¾ **Whitbarrow (IRE)**[2] 3297 7-9-6 64............................ JamesMillman(7) 12 59
(B R Millman) *mid-div: rdn over 2f out: no real prog fnl f* **6/1**[2]

0105 **8** ½ **Jucebabe**[8] 3118 3-8-13 55 .... FrancisNorton 15 46+
(J L Spearing) *hld up in mid-div: rdn over 1f out: sme hdwy whn nt clr run ins fnl f: nt rcvr* **10/1**

0/00 **9** 1 ¼ **Royal Supremacy (IRE)**[3] 3267 5-8-9 46 oh7.................... ChrisCatlin 6 35
(J M Bradley) *chsd ldr: rdn over 1f out: wkng whn carried sltly rt ins fnl f* **28/1**

3500 **10** ½ **Ceredig**[23] 2652 3-9-4 60 .... EddieAhern 2 45
(W R Muir) *hld up in tch: rdn 2f out: wkng whn n.m.r over 1f out* **14/1**

00-0 **11** 1 ¼ **Exmoor Dancer (IRE)**[27] 2531 3-7-13 46 oh6............. EmmettStack(5) 7 27
(H S Howe) *s.i.s: outpcd* **66/1**

4030 **12** 1 ¼ **Xaar Breeze**[10] 3033 3-8-4 46 oh3................................... FrancisFerris 10 23
(Mrs P Townsley) *prom: rdn over 2f out: wkng whn hmpd on stands' rail ins fnl f* **33/1**

0016 **13** hd **Parkside Pursuit**[9] 3071 8-9-9 65.......................... LiamTreadwell(5) 14 42+
(J M Bradley) *bhd: effrt on stands' rail whn n.m.r 2f out: sme hdwy whn nt clr run ins fnl f: nt rcvr* **9/1**

00-2 **14** nk **Epineuse**[10] 3034 3-8-8 50 .... LPKeniry 3 24
(J R Best) *a bhd* **20/1**

6060 **15** ½ **Jinksonthehouse**[11] 3004 5-8-9 46 oh1 .... HayleyTurner 1 20
(M D I Usher) *chsd ldrs tl rdn and wknd over 2f out* **33/1**

000- **16** 7 **Rileys Dream**[29] 5897 7-8-9 46 oh6 .... FrankieMcDonald 13 —
(C J Price) *outpcd* **66/1**

62.46 secs (-0.04) **Going Correction** +0.025s/f (Good)
WFA 3 from 4yo+ 5lb **16** Ran SP% **123.7**
Speed ratings (Par 101):101,100,98,96,96 95,94,93,91,90 88,86,86,85,85 73
CSF £38.55 CT £534.55 TOTE £13.40: £3.90, £1.50, £3.60, £2.10; EX 67.30 Trifecta £285.30 Part won. Pool: £401.94 - 0.20 winning units..
Owner Bob Dean **Bred** Eric Puerari **Trained** Cropthorne, Worcs
■ Stewards' Enquiry : Tolley Dean one-day ban: used whip in an incorrect place (Jul 21); one-day ban: careless riding (Sep 14)

FOCUS
They again tacked over towards the stands' side in this modest handicap. The form looks solid for the grade.

3349 BET365.COM H'CAP 5f 161y
4:45 (4:48) (Class 5) (0-75,72) 3-Y-0 **£3,886** (£1,156; £577; £288) **Stalls** Low

Form RPR

322 **1** **Libor (IRE)**[19] 2763 3-9-4 69 .... NickyMackay 4 81+
(L M Cumani) *s.i.s: hld up and bhd: hdwy over 2f out: rdn to ld ins fnl f: drvn out* **11/4**[1]

5050 **2** 1 ¾ **Boldinor**[10] 3055 3-8-12 63 .... AlanDaly 3 69
(N E Berry) *bhd: rdn over 2f out: hdwy over 1f out: r.o ins fnl f* **50/1**

06-1 **3** hd **Safari Mischief**[10] 3034 3-9-2 67 .... JimCrowley 1 72
(P Winkworth) *led: rdn and hung rt over 1f out: hdd ins fnl f: nt qckn* **33/1**

1401 **4** 1 **Musical Romance (IRE)**[8] 3118 3-9-0 72 6ex .... (b) KMay(7) 5 74
(B J Meehan) *s.i.s: rdn over 2f out: hdwy over 1f out: kpt on ins fnl f* **14/1**

0-44 **5** 1 **Gift Aid**[27] 2535 3-8-2 53 oh2 .... ChrisCatlin 9 52
(P J Makin) *chsd ldrs: rdn and sltly outpcd over 2f out: kpt on one pce fnl f* **10/1**

-441 **6** ½ **Namu**[8] 3111 3-9-4 69 6ex .... MichaelHills 11 66
(B W Hills) *a.p: rdn and one pce fnl 2f* **11/2**[2]

-240 **7** 1 ½ **Royal Citadel (IRE)**[25] 2583 3-9-1 69 .... (p) AdamKirby(3) 7 61
(C G Cox) *bhd: rdn 4f out: hdwy over 1f out: one pce fnl f* **8/1**

0066 **8** nk **Matterofact (IRE)**[12] 2987 3-8-11 67 .... TravisBlock(5) 15 58
(Mrs P N Dutfield) *prom: rdn 2f out: wknd ins fnl f* **12/1**

0022 **9** 2 **Balian**[8] 3118 3-8-13 64 .... (b[1]) RyanMoore 6 48
(G L Moore) *hld up in mid-div: rdn over 2f out: no hdwy* **6/1**[3]

-200 **10** hd **Indian Lady (IRE)**[11] 3004 3-8-11 62 .... (p) HayleyTurner 12 45
(Mrs A L M King) *s.i.s: hld up: sn mid-div: hdwy over 3f out: rdn and wknd over 1f out* **25/1**

-005 **11** ½ **Pearly Poll**[7] 3150 3-9-4 72 .... NelsonDeSouza(3) 8 54
(R M Beckett) *a bhd* **33/1**

3344 **12** 2 ½ **Guilded Warrior**[28] 2496 3-9-3 68 .... (v) FergusSweeney 2 41
(W S Kittow) *s.i.s: sn chsng ldrs: rdn over 2f out: sn wknd* **8/1**

4442 **13** 5 **Succeed (IRE)**[137] 487 3-8-6 62 .... RichardKingscote(5) 13 18
(Mrs H Sweeting) *w ldr: rdn over 2f out: wknd over 1f out* **40/1**

-000 **14** 5 **Catabound (USA)**[17] 2814 3-8-2 53 oh1 .... FrancisFerris 10 —
(B R Millman) *s.i.s: outpcd* **50/1**

0-00 **15** 2 ½ **Be My Charm**[28] 2511 3-8-4 55 .... FrancisNorton 14 —
(M Blanshard) *s.i.s: hdwy 4f out: rdn and wknd 2f out: sddle sn slipped and eased* **50/1**

1m 11.16s (-0.04) **Going Correction** +0.025s/f (Good) **15** Ran SP% **120.1**
Speed ratings (Par 100):101,98,98,97,95 95,93,92,90,89 89,85,79,72,69
CSF £182.47 CT £2659.01 TOTE £2.80: £1.50, £11.80, £7.60; EX 156.50 TRIFECTA Not won. Place 6 £143.54, Place 5 £47.86.
Owner Mrs Angie Silver **Bred** James Cosgrove **Trained** Newmarket, Suffolk

FOCUS
The tactic of coming over towards the stands' side was now set in stone. The form is not totally convincing but a positive view has been taken of it, with the winner progressing on his handicap debut.
Be My Charm Official explanation: jockey said saddle slipped
T/Plt: £55.30 to a £1 stake. Pool: £70,644.45 - 931.50 winning units T/Qpdt: £9.50 to a £1 stake. Pool: £4,365.00 - 336.90 winning units KH

3135 MUSSELBURGH (R-H)
Monday, July 10
OFFICIAL GOING: Good (good to firm in places)
Wind: Slight against

3350 WATCH LIVE ON RUK CHANNEL 432 H'CAP 2m
2:30 (2:30) (Class 6) (0-55,58) 4-Y-0+ **£2,730** (£806; £403) **Stalls** Low

Form RPR

0-51 **1** **Ostfanni (IRE)**[7] 3135 6-9-11 58 6ex .... PatCosgrave 7 66
(M Todhunter) *trckd ldrs: hdwy over 3f out: chsd clr ldr over 2f out and sn rdn: drvn over 1f out: styd on ins fnl f to ld last 50 yds* **10/11**[1]

4214 **2** hd **Senor Set (GER)**[16] 2869 5-9-8 55 .... DeanMcKeown 10 63
(J Pearce) *in tch: hdwy over 3f out: rdn 2f out: drvn and styd on to ld briefly wl ins last: hdd and no ex last 50 yds* **7/2**[2]

-030 **3** 1 ¾ **Rouge Et Noir**[7] 3135 8-9-3 50 .... PaulMulrennan 5 56
(P Monteith) *led after 2f: pushed clr 3f out: rdn wl over 1f out: drvn and hdd wl ins last* **25/1**

02-0 **4** 4 **Lennel**[4] 3230 8-9-5 52 .... (v) DavidAllan 1 53
(A Bailey) *hld up: hdwy on inner 3f out: rdn to chse ldrs 2f out: sn drvn and no imp appr last* **12/1**

4063 **5** 1 ¾ **Transit**[7] 3135 7-9-5 52 .... TomEaves 2 51
(B Ellison) *hld up in midfield: hdwy 3f out: rdn to chse ldrs 2f out: sn drvn and no imp* **10/1**[3]

0-16 **6** 6 **King's Envoy (USA)**[22] 938 7-8-5 43 .... AndrewMullen(5) 11 35
(Mrs J C McGregor) *chsd ldrs: rdn along 3f out: sn wknd* **25/1**

0052 **7** 4 **Bolshoi Ballet**[7] 3135 8-8-9 42 .... (b) PaulHanagan 6 29
(R A Fahey) *hld up: hdwy to chse ldrs over 5f out: rdn along over 3f out: sn btn* **14/1**

5-60 **8** 11 **Acca Larentia (IRE)**[7] 3135 5-7-9 35 oh5 .... (p) KellyHarrison(7) 4 9
(Mrs H O Graham) *prom: riddne along 4f out: sn wknd* **100/1**

000/ **9** 3 ½ **North Landing (IRE)**[33] 4449 6-8-5 38 ow3 .... NeilPollard 3 8
(R C Guest) *led 2f: prom tl rdn along 4f out and sn wknd* **66/1**

0/0- **10** 31 **Taili**[356] 3611 5-8-2 35 oh15 .... CatherineGannon 8 —
(D A Nolan) *a rr* **200/1**

6-00 **11** 4 **Paint The Lily (IRE)**[11] 2998 5-8-3 36 ow1 .... AdrianTNicholls 9 —
(F Watson) *midfield: rdn along after 5f:sn lost pl and bhd* **100/1**

3m 33.09s (-0.81) **Going Correction** -0.05s/f (Good) **11** Ran SP% **109.7**
Speed ratings (Par 101):100,99,99,97,96 93,91,85,83,68 66
CSF £3.35 CT £35.11 TOTE £1.60: £1.10, £1.60, £8.20; EX 4.30.
Owner Ian Hall Racing **Bred** Mrs Brigitte Schlueter **Trained** Orton, Cumbria

FOCUS
Weak form, rated through the third. The winner did not need to run to her previous best.
North Landing(IRE) Official explanation: jockey said gelding had no more to give

3351 EUROPEAN BREEDERS FUND MEDIAN AUCTION MAIDEN STKS 5f
3:00 (3:03) (Class 5) 2-Y-0 **£4,210** (£1,252; £625; £312) **Stalls** Low

Form RPR

02 **1** **Rainbow Fox**[12] 2973 2-9-3 .... PaulHanagan 3 78
(R A Fahey) *chsd ldrs: pushed along 1/2-way: hdwy wl over 1f out: sn rdn and styd on to ld ins last: kpt on* **7/4**[1]

25 **2** ½ **Grange Lili (IRE)**[19] 2755 2-8-12 .... RobbieFitzpatrick 1 71
(Peter Grayson) *s.i.s: swtchd rt and gd hdwy wl over 1f out: rdn and styd on strly ent last* **8/1**

0 **3** ½ **Crow's Nest Lad**[31] 2409 2-9-3 .... DavidAllan 4 78+
(T D Easterby) *wnt rt s and sn pushed along in rr: hdwy wl over 1f out: swtchd rt and rdn ent last: styd on strly* **16/1**

02 **4** ½ **Ronnie Howe**[19] 2759 2-9-3 .... PhillipMakin 8 73
(M Dods) *dwlt: sn prom: effrt 1/2-way: rdn to ld wl over 1f out: hdd ins last: kpt on same pce* **5/1**[2]

34 **5** 1 **Davaye**[30] 2439 2-8-12 .... PatCosgrave 10 64
(K R Burke) *cl up: led after 2f: rdn along and hdd wl over 1f out: sn drvn and one pce* **5/1**[2]

03 **6** 3 **Mamora Reef**[12] 2973 2-8-12 .... PaulMulrennan 2 53
(J R Weymes) *cl up: rdn along 2f out: sn wknd* **7/1**[3]

50 **7** 1 ¼ **Animated**[24] 2623 2-9-3 .... AdrianTNicholls 7 54
(D Nicholls) *led 2f: sn rdn along and wknd 2f out* **12/1**

3002 **8** 5 **Our Toy Soldier**[11] 2999 2-9-3 .... PaulEddery 5 36
(B Smart) *chsd ldrs: rdn along 2f out: sn wknd* **25/1**

50 **9** 3 **Sophie's Dream**[35] 2281 2-9-3 .... JoeFanning 6 25+
(J G Given) *chsd ldrs: rdn along 2f out: sn wknd* **20/1**

60.99 secs (0.49) **Going Correction** -0.05s/f (Good) **9** Ran SP% **115.5**
Speed ratings (Par 94):94,93,92,91,90 85,83,75,70
CSF £16.60 TOTE £2.40: £1.10, £2.80, £4.70; EX 20.10.
Owner Kevin Lee & David Barlow **Bred** Ms R A Myatt **Trained** Musley Bank, N Yorks

FOCUS
An average juvenile maiden, with the form not looking that strong, but it should produce the odd winner. It has been rated through the winner and fourth.

NOTEBOOK
Rainbow Fox, who looked slightly unfortunate not to collect at Carlisle late last month, stayed on strongly inside the final furlong to win going away. Evidently a progressive colt, six furlongs is going to bring about further improvement and he looks one to keep on side, with a venture into nurseries now likely. (op 2-1 tchd 9-4)
Grange Lili(IRE), who seemed to find seven furlongs stretching her at Kempton last time, was reverting to the minimum here and handled it well enough, but just lacked the winner's finishing kick. She is another now qualified for nurseries and a return to six furlongs should see her in an even better light. (op 11-1)
Crow's Nest Lad, slowly away and never involved on his debut at Haydock, did not shape that day as though a drop to five furlongs was the answer and it was no surprise to see him readily outpaced early on. To his credit though he finished strongly and either a maiden or a nursery should soon be coming his way, with a return to further undoubtedly set to suit.
Ronnie Howe has seemed more at home over this trip the past twice, but it is unlikely he will be winning until contesting handicaps off a lowly mark. (op 6-1)
Davaye has shown ability on each start to date and she looks another likely nursery sort. (op 4-1)

3352 WATCH LIVE ON THEBETTINGSITE.CO.UK H'CAP 1m 4f
3:30 (3:30) (Class 6) (0-55,55) 3-Y-0+ **£2,730** (£806; £403) **Stalls** High

Form RPR

0-62 **1** **Alambic**[7] 3140 3-8-6 46 .... SebSanders 4 66+
(Sir Mark Prescott) *sn trcking ldr: led over 3f out: rdn clr 2f out: drvn over 1f out and styd on strly* **11/8**[1]

3021 **2** 8 **Sudden Impulse**[7] 3140 5-9-4 48 6ex .... SilvestreDeSousa(3) 2 55
(A D Brown) *prom: lost pl and pushed along 1/2-way: rdn and hdwy on inner over 2f out: drvn to chse wnr over 1f out: no imp* **3/1**[2]

34-0 **3** 3 **Onyergo (IRE)**[61] 1590 4-9-11 52 .... PhillipMakin 6 54
(J R Weymes) *a.p: rdn along 3f out: drvn fnl 2f and plugged on same pce* **25/1**

6-06 **4** hd **Kristiansand**[7] 3140 6-9-13 54 .... PaulHanagan 1 56
(P Monteith) *in tch: hdwy to chse ldrs 5f out: rdn along 3f out: sn drvn and no imp* **12/1**

-030 **5** 3 ½ **Danzatrice**[22] 2684 4-9-10 51 .... DeanMcKeown 10 47
(C W Thornton) *hld up in midfield: hdwy on outer 3f out: rdn over 2f out and sn btn* **16/1**

0313 **6** ½ **Kyle Of Lochalsh**[7] 3140 6-9-13 54 .... TonyCulhane 7 49
(J S Goldie) *hld up: hdwy over 2f out and sn no hdwy* **9/2**[3]

6204 **7** 9 **Fiddlers Creek (IRE)**[11] 2998 7-10-0 55 .... (t) TomEaves 11 36
(R Allan) *in tch: hdwy 5f out: rdn along 3f out and sn wknd* **10/1**

-000 **8** 5 **Safe Shot**[7] 3140 7-8-11 38 oh3 .... (b[1]) CatherineGannon 12 11
(Mrs J C McGregor) *a towards rr* **66/1**

605/ **9** 7 **Blushing Prince (IRE)**[537] 1037 8-8-13 40 .... NeilPollard 8 2
(R C Guest) *a towards rr* **100/1**

-005 **10** 7 **Drawn Out (IRE)**[153] 329 3-8-7 50 .... (v) DanielTudhope(3) 13 1
(P C Haslam) *a rr* **33/1**

460 **11** dist **Claudia May**[26] 2548 5-9-2 43 .... PaulMulrennan 3 —
(Miss Lucinda V Russell) *led: rdn along 5f out: hdd wl over 3f out: sn wknd: lost action and virtually p.u fnl 2f* **200/1**

2m 36.04s (-0.86) **Going Correction** -0.05s/f (Good)
WFA 3 from 4yo+ 13lb **11** Ran SP% **117.7**
Speed ratings (Par 101):100,94,92,92,90 89,83,80,75,71 —
CSF £5.29 CT £68.20 TOTE £2.50: £1.10, £1.50, £4.90; EX 6.50.
Owner Lady O'Reilly **Bred** Miss K Rausing And Mrs S M Rogers **Trained** Newmarket, Suffolk

FOCUS
The race won at the course last week by Sudden Impulse was key to this with the front three all re-opposing. This was a modest handicap, but the form is sound for the grade with the winner progressing to the tune of 9lb.

3353 EDINBURGH TRADES (S) STKS 1m
4:00 (4:00) (Class 6) 3-Y-0+ **£2,730** (£806; £403) **Stalls** Low

Form RPR

6415 **1** **Sawwaah (IRE)**[7] 3158 9-9-7 70 .... (p) AdrianTNicholls 11 67
(D Nicholls) *trckd ldrs: hdwy over 2f out: rdn to chal ent last: kpt on to ld last 50 yds* **4/1**[2]

6523 **2** nk **Burnley Al (IRE)**[6] 3168 4-9-7 57 .... (b) PaulHanagan 13 66
(R A Fahey) *prom: effrt 3f out: rdn to ld over 1f out: drvn ins last: hdd and no ex last 50 yds* **7/2**[1]

5020 **3** *1* **Desert Lightning (IRE)**[26] [2546] 4-9-2 55..................... PaulMulrennan 8 59
(K R Burke) *trckd ldrs gng wl: effrt 2f out and sn shkn up: rdn ent last and kpt on same pce* **14/1**

4443 **4** *2* **Ballyhurry (USA)**[7] [3139] 9-9-2 67................................... TonyCulhane 1 54
(J S Goldie) *towards rr: hdwy on outer 3f out: rdn to chse ldrs and edgd rt over 1fd out: sn drvn and no imp* **7/2**[1]

-036 **5** *shd* **Son Of Thunder (IRE)**[21] [2697] 5-9-2 54............................ PhillipMakin 7 54
(M Dods) *in tch: hdwy to chse ldrs over 2f out: sn rdn: n.m.r and one pce ent last* **4/1**[2]

2500 **6** *nk* **Linden's Lady**[7] [3137] 6-8-11 54.......................................(v) SebSanders 2 48
(J R Weymes) *in tch: hdwy on inner over 2f out: rdn along and n.m.r over 1f out: no imp* **13/2**[3]

-040 **7** *nk* **Mandarin Grand (IRE)**[2] [3288] 3-7-11 36............(p) DuranFentiman(5) 10 45?
(Miss L A Perratt) *led: rdn along over 2f out: drvn and hdd over 1f out: wknd* **50/1**

0600 **8** *7* **Annals**[62] [1575] 4-8-11 38.. NeilPollard 6 31
(R C Guest) *hld up: effrt and sme hdwy 3f out: sn rdn and btn 2f out* **100/1**

0-05 **9** *2* **Keyalzao (IRE)**[10] [3051] 4-8-8 30.............................. DanielTudhope(3) 9 27
(A Crook) *prom: rdn along 3f out: sn wknd* **100/1**

0-00 **10** *5* **Wood Dalling (USA)**[7] [3137] 8-9-2 41....................... CatherineGannon 3 20
(Mrs J C McGregor) *a rr* **100/1**

0-00 **11** *3* **Kristalchen**[11] [3001] 4-8-11 45.. GylesParkin 4 8
(D W Thompson) *a rr* **100/1**

12 *2* **My Best Secret**[40] 7-9-2 .... TomEaves 5 9
(L Lungo) *s.i.s: a rr* **25/1**

1m 41.34s (-1.16) **Going Correction** -0.05s/f (Good)
WFA 3 from 4yo+ 9lb **12** Ran SP% **114.2**
Speed ratings (Par 101):103,102,101,99,99 99,99,92,90,85 82,80
CSF £17.33 TOTE £4.30: £1.80, £1.70, £3.20; EX 11.00.There was no bid for the winner.
Owner Fayzad Thoroughbred Limited **Bred** Shadwell Estate Company Limited **Trained** Sessay, N Yorks

FOCUS
A typically competitive seller. It has been rated through the second and third, with the seventh limiting the form.

3354 LE GARCON D'OR H'CAP 5f
4:30 (4:30) (Class 4) (0-80,78) 3-Y-0+ **£6,477** (£1,927; £963; £481) **Stalls** Low

Form RPR

4054 **1** **Rudi's Pet (IRE)**[7] [3155] 12-8-5 65..........................(v) VictoriaBehan(7) 1 74
(D Nicholls) *mde all: rdn over 1f out: edgd rt ins last: kpt on strly* **20/1**

0121 **2** *1 ½* **Glencairn Star**[16] [2852] 5-9-8 75.................................. TonyCulhane 4 79
(J S Goldie) *chsd ldrs: hdwy 2f out: rdn over 1f out: drvn and edgd rt ins last: styd on* **4/1**[1]

3651 **3** *hd* **Lady Bahia (IRE)**[14] [2925] 5-8-12 65..................(b) RobbieFitzpatrick 9 68+
(Peter Grayson) *dwlt and towards rr: gd hdwy on outer 2f out: rdn over 1f out: edgd lft and ev ch ins last: no ex towards fin* **12/1**

0040 **4** *hd* **Colonel Cotton (IRE)**[10] [3041] 7-9-4 71.......................(b) PaulHanagan 8 73
(R A Fahey) *chsd ldrs: hdwy wl over 1f out: swtchd rt and ch whn bmpd ins last: kpt on* **4/1**[1]

-503 **5** *shd* **Conjecture**[11] [3004] 4-9-3 70.. SebSanders 6 72
(R Bastiman) *cl up: effrt and ev ch over 1f out: sn rdn and nt qckn ins last* **11/2**[3]

0263 **6** *2 ½* **Strensall**[5] [3190] 9-8-13 66.. JoeFanning 5 59
(R E Barr) *cl up: ev ch wl over 1f out: sn rdn and hld whn n.m.r and wknd ins last* **10/1**

4502 **7** *1* **Plateau**[9] [3069] 7-9-11 78... AdrianTNicholls 3 67
(D Nicholls) *hld up: a towards rr* **5/1**[2]

-532 **8** *hd* **Howards Princess**[6] [3166] 4-9-1 68.................................(p) TomEaves 2 57
(I Semple) *s.i.s: a towards rr* **10/1**

5102 **9** *4* **Ashes (IRE)**[6] [3172] 4-9-0 67.. PaulMulrennan 10 41
(K R Burke) *chsd ldrs: rdn along wl over 1f out: wknd ent last* **10/1**

59.27 secs (-1.23) **Going Correction** -0.05s/f (Good) **9** Ran SP% **111.8**
Speed ratings (Par 105):107,104,104,103,103 99,98,97,91
CSF £94.33 CT £1014.46 TOTE £23.90: £5.10, £1.70, £2.80; EX 110.40.
Owner D Nicholls **Bred** Declan Macpartlin **Trained** Sessay, N Yorks
■ Stewards' Enquiry : Adrian T Nicholls caution: used whip when out of contention

FOCUS
A typically competitive sprint handicap. Ordinary form, but sound enough.

3355 SCOTTISH RACING "YOUR BEST BET" H'CAP 1m 1f
5:00 (5:01) (Class 6) (0-65,60) 3-Y-0 **£3,412** (£1,007; £504) **Stalls** Low

Form RPR

5043 **1** **Three Strings (USA)**[1] [3329] 3-8-13 52..............................(p) TomEaves 2 60
(P D Niven) *trckd ldrs: hdwy 3f out: rdn to ld over 1f out: sn drvn and edgd rt: kpt on wl* **11/2**[3]

0044 **2** *½* **Farne Island**[1] [3329] 3-9-2 58... DNolan(3) 7 65
(J J Quinn) *in tch: smooth hdwy on inner 3f out: rdn to chal over 1f out and ev ch tl drvn ins last and no ex towards fin* **11/2**[3]

0310 **3** *2* **Apache Nation (IRE)**[14] [2923] 3-9-7 60............................. PhillipMakin 11 63
(M Dods) *trckd ldrs: hdwy 3f out: rdn along and n.m.r over 1f out: swtchd lft and styd on u.p ins last* **4/1**[1]

0051 **4** *1* **Gigs Magic (USA)**[19] [2746] 3-8-11 50................................... JoeFanning 1 54+
(M Johnston) *trckd ldng pair: hdwy 3f out: rdn 2f out: drvn and ev ch whn hmpd over 1f out: swtchd lft and kpt on same pce* **9/2**[2]

-000 **5** *1* **Lambency (IRE)**[25] [2589] 3-8-8 47.. PaulHanagan 10 46
(J G Given) *led: rdn along over 2f out: drvn and edgd lft over 1f out: sn hdd & wknd* **16/1**

0-64 **6** *¾* **Dubai Around (IRE)**[32] [2379] 3-9-1 54............................ DeanMcKeown 6 52
(Micky Hammond) *hld up in midfield: hdwy 3f out: rdn to chse ldrs 2f out: sn drvn and kpt on same pce* **10/1**

00-0 **7** *nk* **Allouette**[11] [3001] 3-8-7 49 ow3.................................. DanielTudhope(3) 8 46
(W J H Ratcliffe) *hld up towards rr: hdwy over 2f out: swtchd rt to inner and drvn over 1f out: no imp* **33/1**

1005 **8** *2 ½* **Queen Jean**[1] [3329] 3-9-6 59...(p) SebSanders 4 51
(J G Given) *chsd ldrs: rdn along over 2f out: grad wknd* **9/1**

2666 **9** *8* **Mandarin Rocket (IRE)**[7] [3138] 3-9-0 58.................. DuranFentiman(5) 3 34
(Miss L A Perratt) *a rr* **16/1**

0-60 **10** *2* **Silver Mont (IRE)**[1] [3329] 3-9-3 56.. TonyCulhane 5 28
(Mrs A Duffield) *a bhd* **16/1**

0-63 **11** *33* **Pappas Ruby (USA)**[46] [1950] 3-8-6 45.......................... AdrianTNicholls 9 —
(J S Goldie) *midfield: rdn along over 4f out: sn wknd* **12/1**

1m 56.57s (0.57) **Going Correction** -0.05s/f (Good) **11** Ran SP% **116.3**
Speed ratings (Par 98):95,94,92,91,91 90,90,87,80,78 49
CSF £35.43 CT £137.08 TOTE £6.00: £2.10, £2.50, £1.60; EX 43.70.
Owner The Wednesday Club **Bred** Gaucho Ltd **Trained** Barton-le-Street, N Yorks

FOCUS
A modest handicap run in a poor time. The first two more or less ran relative to their efforts at Ayr the day before.

3356 LINKS H'CAP 5f
5:30 (5:31) (Class 6) (0-60,60) 3-Y-0+ **£3,071** (£906; £453) **Stalls** Low

Form RPR

-005 **1** **Strawberry Patch (IRE)**[14] [2928] 7-8-13 48..........(p) DanielTudhope(3) 6 58
(J S Goldie) *cl up: rdn to ld over 1f out: drvna nd kpt on wl fnl f* **7/1**[3]

0000 **2** *1* **Percy Douglas**[5] [3190] 6-8-11 50.................................(bt) AnnStokell(7) 5 56
(Miss A Stokell) *a.p: rdn and ev ch over 1f out: kpt on ins last* **14/1**

0622 **3** *1 ¼* **Montillia (IRE)**[14] [2928] 4-9-4 50... SebSanders 3 52
(C F Wall) *led: rdn along and hdd over 1f out:drvn and kpt on same pce ins last* **11/4**[1]

450 **4** *1* **Angelofthenorth**[28] [2505] 4-9-7 60............................. JohnCavanagh(7) 9 58
(C J Teague) *towards rr: hdwy 2f out: rdn and styd on wl fnl f: nrst fin* **16/1**

00-5 **5** *hd* **Fern House (IRE)**[5] [3199] 4-8-9 41 oh11.................. RobbieFitzpatrick 13 38+
(Peter Grayson) *in tch on outer: hdwy and nt clr run wl over 1f out: swtchd rt and rdn: styd on ins last* **15/2**

0044 **6** *shd* **Shatin Leader**[1] [3334] 4-8-4 41 oh3.......................(p) DuranFentiman(5) 15 38
(Miss L A Perratt) *a.p: rdn wl over 1f out: kpt on same pce ent last* **20/1**

4606 **7** *1 ¾* **Lady Hopeful (IRE)**[48] [1913] 4-8-13 45...........................(b) DeanMcKeown 1 36
(Peter Grayson) *dwlt and towards rr: effrt and n.m.r in inner wl over 1f out: styd on ins last: nt rch ldrs* **12/1**

3000 **8** *hd* **New Options**[14] [2928] 9-8-10 42..(b) GylesParkin 4 32
(Peter Grayson) *chsd ldrs: rdn wl over 1f out: sn one pce* **25/1**

6263 **9** *shd* **Jun Fan (USA)**[31] [2396] 4-10-0 60... TomEaves 8 49
(B Ellison) *chsd ldrs: rdn along 1/2-way: sn drvn and kpt on same pce* **5/1**[2]

0000 **10** *½* **On The Trail**[1] [3334] 9-8-9 41..(p) TonyCulhane 11 29
(D W Chapman) *chsd ldrs: rdn along 2f out: sn wknd* **12/1**

0000 **11** *nk* **He's A Rocket (IRE)**[7] [3155] 5-8-9 48...................(p) PatrickDonaghy(7) 10 35
(K R Burke) *cl up: rdn along 2f out: grad wknd* **16/1**

0-00 **12** *½* **Drury Lane (IRE)**[3] [3240] 6-8-12 44...(p) PaulQuinn 7 29
(D W Chapman) *n.d* **33/1**

4-00 **13** *shd* **Binty**[2] [3306] 4-8-10 49... MarkCoumbe(7) 12 33
(A J Chamberlain) *s.i.s: a towards rr* **50/1**

0000 **14** *2 ½* **Mister Marmaduke**[11] [3003] 5-8-9 41 oh2............(p) CatherineGannon 14 16
(D A Nolan) *chsd ldrs: rdn along over 2f out: sn wknd* **66/1**

0-00 **15** *½* **Mutayam**[14] [2928] 6-8-12 44...(tp) PaulHanagan 2 18
(D A Nolan) *in tch: rdn along 2f out: sn wknd* **20/1**

60.41 secs (-0.09) **Going Correction** -0.05s/f (Good) **15** Ran SP% **121.2**
Speed ratings (Par 101):98,96,94,92,92 92,89,89,89,88 87,86,86,82,82
CSF £92.78 CT £339.31 TOTE £8.00: £2.50, £4.30, £1.40; EX 80.30 Place 6 £18.72, Place 5 £15.18.
Owner Mrs Lucille Bone **Bred** Mrs G Doyle **Trained** Uplawmoor, E Renfrews

FOCUS
A modest event, the form not up to much.
Lady Hopeful(IRE) Official explanation: jockey said filly hung right-handed throughout
Mister Marmaduke Official explanation: gelding lost a sheepskin cheekpiece in first furlong
T/Plt: £15.60 to a £1 stake. Pool: £51,061.55. 2,381.30 winning tickets. T/Qpdt: £6.30 to a £1 stake. Pool: £2,569.00. 299.30 winning tickets. JR

2783 RIPON (R-H)
Monday, July 10

OFFICIAL GOING: Good to firm
3mm water had been put on the track every night since the previous meeting. The ground was described as 'just on the quick side with an excellent cover'.
Wind: Light; half behind Weather: Heavy shower race one, then fine

3357 MARKET PLACE (S) STKS 1m 1f 170y
6:50 (6:54) (Class 6) 3-Y-0 **£2,730** (£806; £403) **Stalls** High

Form RPR

0005 **1** **Moonlight Fantasy (IRE)**[11] [3006] 3-8-12 40........................ KimTinkler 4 52
(N Tinkler) *trckd ldr: led over 3f out: styd on* **11/1**

0-00 **2** *2 ½* **Carrietau**[2] [3306] 3-8-12 58... J-PGuillambert 1 47
(J G Given) *swvd rt s: sn chsng ldrs: hung rt and wnt 2nd 2f out: kpt on: no real imp* **9/1**

5400 **3** *1* **Wensleydale Star**[2] [3288] 3-8-5 40.................................. DeanHeslop(7) 2 45
(T D Barron) *bmpd s: sn mid-div: hdwy over 3f out: kpt on same pce fnl 2f* **9/1**

0 **4** *2 ½* **Sweet Lavinia**[34] [2325] 3-8-8 ow1............................ GrahamGibbons 11 36
(J D Bethell) *mid-div: hdwy u.p over 4f out: n.m.r on inner 2f out and over 1f out: kpt on* **20/1**

-204 **5** *nk* **Elite Land**[2] [3288] 3-8-5 50...................................(b) SuzzanneFrance(7) 5 40
(N Bycroft) *mid-div: hdwy on outer over 2f out: nvr nr ldrs* **4/1**[1]

0003 **6** *2* **Ebony Lady**[41] [2107] 3-8-1 37 ow1.......................(v) MichaelJStainton(7) 7 32
(R M Whitaker) *chsd ldrs: one pce fnl 3f* **6/1**[2]

0-00 **7** *1* **Elli Lewtia**[40] [2143] 3-8-2 40.. LiamJones(5) 6 29
(J Jay) *prom: rdn over 3f out: one pce* **25/1**

0-40 **8** *3 ½* **Ayala Cove (USA)**[153] [333] 3-8-0 40......................(t) KellyHarrison(7) 12 22
(P C Haslam) *rrd s: bhd tl sme hdwy 3f out: nvr on terms* **50/1**

4430 **9** *1* **Augustus Livius (IRE)**[14] [2923] 3-8-12 45...................(p) PaulFessey 10 26
(W Storey) *led tl over 3f out: lost pl 2f out* **8/1**[3]

6000 **10** *1 ½* **For No One (IRE)**[17] [2832] 3-8-12 60.......................... RoystonFfrench 14 23
(M Johnston) *chsd ldrs: drvn over 3f out: lost pl over 1f out* **6/1**[2]

-400 **11** *3 ½* **Thornton Princess**[7] [3138] 3-8-2 49........................ AndrewMullen(5) 15 11
(B S Rothwell) *rrd s: haewady over 3f out: wknd and eased 1f out* **8/1**[3]

00-0 **12** *9* **Prince Richard**[56] [1736] 3-8-7 45.. MarkLawson(5) 3 —
(B Smart) *trckd ldrs: t.k.h: reminders after 2f: sn lost pl* **20/1**

0 **13** *11* **Bamalam**[21] [2696] 3-8-7 .... TonyHamilton 9 —
(C R Wilson) *restless in stalls: a in rr: bhd fnl 3f* **100/1**

2m 5.92s (0.92) **Going Correction** -0.025s/f (Good) **13** Ran SP% **115.4**
Speed ratings (Par 98):95,93,92,90,89 88,87,84,83,82 79,72,63
CSF £96.55 TOTE £9.90: £3.10, £3.50, £4.00; EX 105.50.There was no bid for the winner.
Owner Mount Pleasant Farm Racing Partnership **Bred** Rockhart Trading Ltd **Trained** Langton, N Yorks
■ Anasena (5/1, vet's advice) & Moraadi (100/1, unruly & uns rdr gng to s) were withdrawn. R4 applies, new market formed.

FOCUS
A poor race even by selling standards. The time was poor and for the time being it has been rated through the winner.
Sweet Lavinia Official explanation: jockey said filly was denied a clear run

Augustus Livius(IRE) Official explanation: jockey said gelding hung left-handed throughout

3358 CERTAINTY INTERIORS MAIDEN AUCTION FILLIES' STKS 5f

7:20 (7:20) (Class 5) 2-Y-O **£3,886** (£1,156; £577; £288) **Stalls** Low

Form RPR

4 **1** **Frontline In Focus (IRE)**[5] 3188 2-8-7 .... PatCosgrave 12 80
(K R Burke) *in tch: hdwy 2f out: swtchd lft 1f out: styd on to ld post* **9/2**[1]

4 **2** *shd* **Ishi Adiva**[7] 3148 2-8-7 .... JimmyQuinn 4 80
(Tom Dascombe) *chsd ldr: led over 1f out: hdd post* **11/2**[3]

0 **3** *4* **Sister Etienne (IRE)**[18] 2791 2-8-4 .... PaulFessey 6 62
(T D Barron) *led tl over 1f out: kpt on same pce* **20/1**

4 *½* **Catlivius (IRE)** 2-8-7 .... NCallan 7 63
(K A Ryan) *chsd ldrs: hung rt over 1f out: kpt on same pce* **11/2**[3]

64 **5** *1* **Mickleberry (IRE)**[28] 2500 2-8-7 .... TonyHamilton 2 60
(J D Bethell) *w ldrs: one pce fnl 2f* **13/2**

0 **6** *1 ¾* **Nomoreblondes**[19] 2759 2-8-0 ow1 .... RoryMoore(5) 8 52
(P T Midgley) *mid-div: kpt on fnl 2f: nvr rchd ldrs* **100/1**

5656 **7** *3 ½* **First Valentini**[6] 3173 2-8-7 ....(b¹) RoystonFfrench 9 41
(N Bycroft) *chsd ldrs over 2f: wknd over 1f out* **16/1**

025 **8** *1 ¾* **The Italian Job**[31] 2394 2-8-10 .... DavidAllan 11 38
(T D Easterby) *a in rr* **5/1**[2]

5 **9** *1 ½* **Fine Leg**[18] 2791 2-8-1 .... EdwardCreighton(3) 3 26
(P J McBride) *a towards rr* **16/1**

0 **10** *hd* **Rue Soleil**[12] 2973 2-8-0 ow1 .... AndrewMullen(5) 13 27
(J R Weymes) *swvd rt s: a bhd* **33/1**

11 *¾* **Amaretto Venture** 2-8-7 .... GrahamGibbons 5 26
(J J Quinn) *s.i.s: a in rr* **12/1**

03 **12** *18* **Bonny Scotland (IRE)**[16] 2878 2-8-2 .... LiamJones(5) 1 —
(Miss V Haigh) *s.v.s: a detached in last* **16/1**

59.64 secs (-0.56) **Going Correction** -0.175s/f (Firm) 12 Ran SP% **113.0**
Speed ratings (Par 91):97,96,90,89,88 85,79,76,74,74 72,44
CSF £26.82 TOTE £6.50: £2.10, £2.40, £2.80; EX 18.00.
Owner Frontline Bathrooms **Bred** Christan Syndicate **Trained** Middleham Moor, N Yorks

FOCUS
Modest form, but sound for the grade. The first two finished clear and the winner, who overcame an outside draw, deserves credit.

NOTEBOOK
Frontline In Focus(IRE), making a quick return, did well to overcome her outside draw. She had to switch inside the leader and showed real spirit to put her head in front on the line. She deserves a short break now and will relish a step up to six. (op 6-1)
Ishi Adiva, a close-coupled filly, took charge but was nailed on the line. She deserves to go one better. (op 6-1)
Sister Etienne(IRE), already entered in a seller, took them along but in the end the first two ran right away from her.
Catlivius(IRE), on the leg, tended to race away from the running rail and, on this tricky track for a newcomer, was always tending to hang out. The experience will not be lost on her. (tchd 5-1)
Mickleberry(IRE), very fit, showed bags of toe but even over this shorter trip she did not get home. (op 6-1)
The Italian Job never went a yard and did not seem to take to this undulating track. Official explanation: jockey said filly was not suited by the track (op 9-2)
Rue Soleil Official explanation: jockey said filly was not suited by the track
Bonny Scotland(IRE) Official explanation: jockey said filly missed the break

3359 RIPON LAND ROVER H'CAP 1m 4f 10y

7:50 (7:50) (Class 4) (0-80,80) 3-Y-O **£6,477** (£1,927; £963; £481) **Stalls** High

Form RPR

4210 **1** **Scotland Yard (UAE)**[12] 2975 3-9-6 **79** .... RoystonFfrench 3 92+
(M Johnston) *trckd ldr: led over 3f out: edgd rt 2f out: styd on strly fnl f* **4/1**[2]

4312 **2** *4* **Princess Cocoa (IRE)**[18] 2781 3-8-6 **65** .... TonyHamilton 6 69
(R A Fahey) *s.i.s: stdy hdwy on ins 4f out: swtchd lft 2f out: hung rt and no imp* **7/2**[1]

6-04 **3** *¾* **Hunting Haze**[18] 2781 3-8-3 **62** .... JimmyQuinn 2 64
(Miss S E Hall) *t.k.h in rr: effrt 3f out: sn chsng 1st 2: styd on same pce* **13/2**

0522 **4** *5* **Is It Me (USA)**[12] 2970 3-8-9 **68** .... NCallan 4 62
(P A Blockley) *led tl over 3f out: lost pl over 1f out* **9/2**[3]

3344 **5** *1* **Blushing Hilary (IRE)**[11] 3001 3-8-11 **70** .... DavidAllan 5 63
(Miss J A Camacho) *sn trcking ldrs: effrt over 3f out: edgd rt and lost pl over 1f out* **14/1**

361- **6** *2 ½* **Fenners (USA)**[269] 5878 3-9-5 **78** ....(t) J-PGuillambert 7 67
(M Johnston) *in rr: sn pushed along: hdwy u.p 3f out: lost pl over 1f out* **14/1**

2m 35.25s (-1.75) **Going Correction** -0.025s/f (Good) 6 Ran SP% **87.1**
Speed ratings (Par 102):104,101,100,97,96 95
CSF £10.70 TOTE £3.50: £1.70, £1.60.
Owner Jumeirah Racing **Bred** Darley **Trained** Middleham Moor, N Yorks
■ Jidaar (7/2) was withdrawn on vet's advice. R4 applies, deduct 20p in the £.

FOCUS
Quite a tactical affair but a clear-cut and improving winner. The form is not that strong but seems sound.

3360 COMMERCIAL FIRST MORTGAGES H'CAP 6f

8:20 (8:20) (Class 3) (0-90,89) 3-Y-O **£9,715** (£2,890; £1,444; £721) **Stalls** Low

Form RPR

2000 **1** **Grazeon Gold Blend**[2] 3296 3-9-2 **84** .... GrahamGibbons 6 91
(J J Quinn) *chsd ldrs: styd on to ld last 100yds* **8/1**

6-40 **2** *¾* **Come Out Fighting**[67] 1438 3-9-7 **89** .... PatCosgrave 1 94
(P A Blockley) *w ldr: led over 3f out: hdd and no ex ins last* **7/2**[2]

3200 **3** *1* **Soto**[10] 3041 3-8-2 **70** .... DaleGibson 4 72
(M W Easterby) *led over 2f: kpt on same pce fnl f* **13/2**

1600 **4** *½* **Rainbow Bay**[2] 3296 3-8-8 **76** ....(p) TonyHamilton 7 76
(R A Fahey) *in tch: hdwy on outer to chse ldrs over 2f out: kpt on same pce* **14/1**

4210 **5** *3* **Westport**[32] 2385 3-8-10 **78** .... NCallan 3 72+
(K A Ryan) *chsd ldrs: rdn 3 out: nvr a real threat: wknd and eased jst ins last* **15/8**[1]

1262 **6** *hd* **Welcome Approach**[12] 2976 3-8-4 **72** .... DavidAllan 2 63
(J R Weymes) *trckd ldrs: effrt over 2f out: lost pl over 1f out* **4/1**[3]

1006 **7** *3 ½* **Rondo**[12] 2976 3-8-6 **74** .... PaulFessey 5 54
(T D Barron) *dwlt: a outpcd in last* **25/1**

1m 11.76s (-1.24) **Going Correction** -0.175s/f (Firm) 7 Ran SP% **112.0**
Speed ratings (Par 104):101,100,98,98,94 93,89
CSF £34.45 TOTE £9.40: £4.10, £2.90; EX 54.20.
Owner J R Rowbottom **Bred** Mrs E McKee **Trained** Settrington, N Yorks

FOCUS
A fair handicap and sound form, although lacking progressive types overall.

NOTEBOOK
Grazeon Gold Blend, making a quick return, has an awkward head carriage, hence the sheepskin noseband. He seemed to relish the sixth furlong and in the end was right on top.
Come Out Fighting, absent for over two months, travelled strongly but in the end found the winner just too good. He might be marginally better over the minimum trip. (op 9-2)
Soto, on a losing run stretching back sixteen races now and racing from a career-low mark, went down fighting. (op 5-1)
Rainbow Bay, who along with the winner ran at Haydock two days earlier, had the cheepieces on this time but was always struggling to get in a blow from his outside draw. (op 9-1)
Westport, 8lb higher than Redcar, was back after a month on the sidelines but he never really went at any stage and in the end his rider called it a day. (op 11-4 tchd 3-1 in a place)
Welcome Approach, 3lb higher, was keen to get on with it in the early stages. He dropped away in disappointing fashion and five furlongs seems to suit him better.

3361 ABACUS H'CAP 1m

8:50 (8:50) (Class 5) (0-70,75) 3-Y-O+ **£3,886** (£1,156; £577; £288) **Stalls** High

Form RPR

0000 **1** **Pianoforte (USA)**[6] 3168 4-9-0 **55** .... JimmyQuinn 10 68+
(E J Alston) *hld up in rr: hdwy on inner and nt clr run over 2f out: styd on strly to ld ins last: readily* **20/1**

5203 **2** *1 ¾* **Sedge (USA)**[18] 2789 6-8-9 **55** ....(p) RoryMoore(5) 11 61
(P T Midgley) *sn trcking ldrs: led over 1f out: hdd and no ex ins last* **7/1**[3]

-004 **3** *nk* **Apsara**[2] 3283 5-9-4 **59** .... PaulMulrennan 1 64+
(G M Moore) *sltly hmpd s: sn chsng ldrs: chal over 3f out: styd on ins last* **16/1**

1603 **4** *2* **Attacca**[14] 2926 5-9-0 **55** .... DavidAllan 8 56
(J R Weymes) *in rr: hdwy 3f out: styd on fnl f* **16/1**

-000 **5** *¾* **Kabis Amigos**[45] 1996 4-9-0 **55** .... PaulFessey 3 54
(D Nicholls) *t.k.h: trckd ldr: led over 6f out tl over 1f out: hung rt and sn wknd* **9/1**

5U63 **6** *nk* **Grande Terre (IRE)**[7] 3142 5-9-1 **56** ....(p) TonyHamilton 12 54
(R A Fahey) *mid-div: effrt over 3f out: kpt on: n.d* **9/2**[2]

2000 **7** *2* **Flaxby**[18] 2789 4-8-9 **50** ....(b) GrahamGibbons 4 44
(J D Bethell) *trckd ldrs: edgd rt and wknd appr fnl f* **11/1**

0530 **8** *2* **Ali D**[5] 3113 8-9-7 **62** .... NCallan 7 51
(G Woodward) *chsd ldrs: wknd over 1f out* **9/1**

4011 **9** *1 ½* **Kaymich Perfecto**[7] 3147 6-9-13 **75** 6ex .... MichaelJStainton(7) 9 61
(R M Whitaker) *in rr: sme hdwy on outer over 3f out: nvr on terms* **4/1**[1]

4265 **10** *3* **Spanish Law**[14] 2926 4-8-11 **52** ....(b) PhillipMakin 2 31
(M Dods) *wnt lft s: a in rr* **8/1**

1006 **11** *2 ½* **Pauline's Prince**[44] 2025 4-9-8 **63** .... RoystonFfrench 6 36
(R Hollinshead) *mid-div: drvn 3f out: sn wknd* **25/1**

30-0 **12** *19* **Ocean Sunrise (IRE)**[39] 2160 3-9-1 **65** .... JoeFanning 5 —
(M Johnston) *swtchd rt after s: led tl over 6f out: lost pl 3f out: sn bhd and eased* **33/1**

1m 39.47s (-1.63) **Going Correction** -0.025s/f (Good)
WFA 3 from 4yo+ 9lb 12 Ran SP% **113.4**
Speed ratings (Par 103):107,105,104,102,102 101,99,97,96,93 90,71
CSF £144.90 CT £2322.40 TOTE £27.00: £5.30, £2.50, £4.90; EX 140.40.
Owner Honest Traders **Bred** Cashmark Farm **Trained** Longton, Lancs

FOCUS
A modest handicap, but solid form for the grade. The winner has slipped to a nice mark.
Kaymich Perfecto Official explanation: jockey said gelding was not suited by the track

3362 KIRKGATE MAIDEN STKS 1m

9:20 (9:20) (Class 5) 3-Y-O+ **£3,886** (£1,156; £577; £288) **Stalls** High

Form RPR

3-04 **1** **Tawaafud**[22] 2673 3-8-12 75 .... RHills 3 72
(B W Hills) *led: shkn up 4f out: styd on fnl 2f: unchal* **5/4**[1]

2-20 **2** *2* **Tafiya**[114] 668 3-8-12 75 .... NickyMackay 9 68
(G A Butler) *wnt lft s: hld up: hdwy and swtchd outside over 2f out: wnt 2nd 1f out: no imp* **3/1**[3]

34 **3** *1 ½* **My Arch**[33] 2366 4-9-12 .... NCallan 6 71+
(K A Ryan) *trckd ldrs: keeping on same pce whn sltly hmpd over 1f out* **5/2**[2]

05 **4** *shd* **Hassaad**[40] 2146 3-9-3 ....(b¹) TonyCulhane 7 69
(W J Haggas) *sltly hmpd s: settled in last: hdwy and drvn along 3f out: kpt on: nvr a threat* **10/1**

03 **5** *3* **Final Award (IRE)**[13] 2948 3-8-12 .... TomEaves 1 57
(G M Moore) *t.k.h: trckd wnr: edgd rt over 1f out: sn wknd* **33/1**

6 *10* **Spittal Point** 4-9-7 .... GrahamGibbons 2 36
(J J Quinn) *chsd ldrs: lost pl over 1f out: sn bhd* **50/1**

1m 41.7s (0.60) **Going Correction** -0.025s/f (Good)
WFA 3 from 4yo 9lb 6 Ran SP% **112.0**
Speed ratings (Par 103):96,94,92,92,89 79
CSF £5.32 TOTE £2.30: £1.40, £2.00; EX 6.30 Place 6 £486.51, Place 5 £78.33.
Owner Hamdan Al Maktoum **Bred** Shadwell Estate Company Limited **Trained** Lambourn, Berks

FOCUS
A tactical affair run in a moderate time with the winner always in pole position.
T/Plt: £1,265.10 to a £1 stake. Pool: £64,558.80. 37.25 winning tickets. T/Qpdt: £105.30 to a £1 stake. Pool: £4,967.10. 34.90 winning tickets. WG

3148 WINDSOR (R-H)

Monday, July 10

OFFICIAL GOING: Good to firm (good in places)
Wind: Nil Weather: Overcast

3363 CLAUDIA SWINBURN EBF MAIDEN STKS 6f

6:35 (6:35) (Class 5) 2-Y-O **£4,533** (£1,348; £674; £336) **Stalls** High

Form RPR

25 **1** **Jo'Burg (USA)**[20] 2719 2-9-3 .... MJKinane 1 79+
(Mrs A J Perrett) *t.k.h: racd on outer and trckd ldrs: hanging fr 1/2-way: rdn to ld last 150yds: kpt on wl* **2/5**[1]

03 **2** *1 ¼* **Cheap Street**[12] 2967 2-9-3 .... TPQueally 4 75
(J G Portman) *led after 2f and sn racd against nr side rail: rdn and hdd last 150yds: one pce* **25/1**

3 *nk* **Sakhee's Secret** 2-9-3 .... SteveDrowne 14 74
(H Morrison) *hld up in midfield: nt clr run on inner 2f out: prog over 1f out: swtchd lft and r.o ins fnl f: nrst fin* **10/1**[3]

0 **4** *½* **Masai Moon**[27] 2530 2-9-3 .... AlanMunro 3 73
(B R Millman) *towards rr: prog on outer over 2f out: shkn up and kpt on fr over 1f out: nvr able to chal* **50/1**

5 5 1/2 **Sri Pekan Two**[31] 2402 2-9-3 .... JamieSpencer 13 73+
(P F I Cole) *trckd ldng pair: lost pl over 2f out: renewed effrt over 1f out: kpt on ins fnl f* **7/1**[2]

0 6 *shd* **Eager Igor (USA)**[28] 2506 2-9-3 .... StephenCarson 7 71
(R F Johnson Houghton) *sn prom: chsd ldr briefly over 1f out: one pce whn carried lft ins fnl f* **50/1**

7 1 1/4 **L'Oiseau De Feu (USA)** 2-9-3 .... DO'Donohoe 11 70+
(E A L Dunlop) *s.i.s: wl in rr: prog on outer 2f out: keeping on but no ch whn squeezed out nr fin* **20/1**

0 8 *shd* **Blackwater Stream (IRE)**[27] 2530 2-9-3 .... RobertHavlin 8 67
(Mrs P N Dutfield) *prom: shkn up and outpcd wl over 1f out: swtchd lft ins fnl f: one pce* **100/1**

9 2 1/2 **Buccellati** 2-9-3 .... MartinDwyer 16 60
(A M Balding) *s.s: rn green and detached in last pair: hanging but kpt on fr 1/2-way: n.d* **33/1**

10 2 **Wilmington** 2-9-3 .... RichardHughes 2 54+
(R Hannon) *trckd ldng gp: shkn up 2f out: grad wknd* **40/1**

0 11 *shd* **Spinning Crystal (IRE)**[33] 2354 2-8-12 .... EddieAhern 6 48+
(B W Hills) *nvr beyond midfield: rn green and fdd wl over 1f out* **50/1**

0 12 1 1/2 **Bertie Swift**[98] 849 2-9-3 .... GeorgeBaker 9 49
(J Gallagher) *led for 2f: prom tl wknd 2f out* **100/1**

13 8 **Bertoliver** 2-9-3 .... DarryllHolland 12 25
(D K Ivory) *hld up in rr: wknd and eased 2f out* **100/1**

14 17 **Vietnam** 2-9-3 .... JimmyFortune 10 —
(S Kirk) *s.s: a bhd: t.o* **50/1**

1m 12.01s (-1.66) **Going Correction** -0.35s/f (Firm) **14** Ran SP% **117.8**
Speed ratings (Par 94):97,95,94,94,93 93,91,91,88,85 85,83,72,50
CSF £18.85 TOTE £1.40: £1.10, £3.20, £3.10; EX 11.90.

Owner A D Spence **Bred** T Cooper **Trained** Pulborough, W Sussex

FOCUS
There were showers prior to racing that eased the ground a little but it remained generally good to firm. This was a decent contest judged on paddock inspection and the previous form on offer. The field stayed stands' side. The winner was well below his Ascot form and this race does not looks as strong as it might have been.

NOTEBOOK
Jo'Burg(USA) , an honourable fifth in the Coventry at Ascot, had to overcome another bad draw. He had gone to post with his head on one side and did likewise coming out of the stalls (he was loaded with a Monty Roberts blanket) with the result that the bit slipped through his mouth. He had to work a bit but won well in the end, straightening up as he had to be driven out through the last furlong. He now heads for the Group 2 Vintage Stakes at Goodwood, won last year by Sir Percy, with connections hoping for a sound surface.

Cheap Street probably got the best ground under the rails and momentarily looked like winning when kicking a couple of lengths clear past halfway. There is not a lot of him but he is progressing apace and should win his maiden.

Sakhee's Secret has plenty to live up to coming from a prolific winning family, being a half-brother to six winners including Palace Affair, Duke Of Modena and King's Caprice. He got no run through against the stands' rail at a vital time but was finishing to effect and should soon make amends. Official explanation: jockey said colt was denied a clear run (op 11-1 tchd 12-1)

Masai Moon was unfavoured by the draw and he kept on well after staying midtrack. This well-grown early foal looks progressive.

Sri Pekan Two ran a fair race, although he ended up midtrack despite his high draw. Slightly hampered in the final furlong as others edged out to get runs, he was keeping on and is going the right way.

Eager Igor(USA) travelled well through the race to build on his debut effort at this track. He could possibly do with a shade further as he was outpaced into the final two furlongs before rallying. (tchd 66-1)

L'Oiseau De Feu(USA), from the family of the top-class Hatoof, took the eye in the paddock. He ran better than the bare form as he laid down a strong challenge mid-track going inside the final two furlongs before starting to flatten out and being hampered and eased in the final strides.

Blackwater Stream(IRE) was one of the first ridden along but he kept finding and looks to be going the right way. (op 66-1)

Bertoliver Official explanation: jockey said colt hung right throughout

3364 TOTESPORT.COM H'CAP 1m 67y
7:05 (7:06) (Class 5) (0-70,70) 3-Y-O **£3,238** (£963; £481; £240) **Stalls** High

Form RPR

-036 1 **Night Cru**[31] 2391 3-9-3 **66** .... EddieAhern 14 73
(C F Wall) *trckd ldrs: effrt against nr side rail 2f out: clr passage and r.o wl fnl f to ld last stride* **5/1**[1]

-602 2 *hd* **Woodcote Place**[7] 3153 3-9-7 **70** .... AlanMunro 2 76
(P R Chamings) *t.k.h: hld up last: prog on outer 3f out: rdn ent fnl f: led last 75yds: hdd fnl stride* **6/1**[2]

6302 3 *hd* **Sgt Schultz (IRE)**[24] 2616 3-9-2 **65** .... JohnEgan 3 71
(J S Moore) *sn trckd ldrs: effrt over 2f out: rdn to ld over 1f out: hdd and jst outpcd last 75yds* **5/1**[1]

0226 4 1 3/4 **Mucho Loco (IRE)**[25] 2583 3-8-13 **62** ....(b) TPQueally 10 64
(J G Portman) *hld up in rr: last 2f out: swtchd to outer and r.o fnl f: no ch* **9/1**

5400 5 *nk* **Chia (IRE)**[14] 2921 3-8-8 **57** .... TedDurcan 13 58
(D Haydn Jones) *sn restrained bhd ldng pair: rdn to chal 2f out: one pce fnl f* **16/1**

2106 6 *shd* **Titus Lumpus (IRE)**[11] 3011 3-8-12 **61** .... DarryllHolland 12 62
(R M Flower) *led: hrd pressed over 2f out: hdd and no ex over 1f out* **14/1**

054 7 3/4 **Dab Hand (IRE)**[14] 2940 3-9-4 **67** .... RyanMoore 7 66
(D M Simcock) *trckd ldrs: effrt but hanging fr 3f out: chal 2f out: nt qckn and btn 1f out* **8/1**[3]

100- 8 *nk* **Sakabula (USA)**[298] 5252 3-9-5 **68** .... MartinDwyer 1 67
(G C Bravery) *sn trckd ldr: chal over 2f out: hld whn squeezed out jst over 1f out: no ch after* **50/1**

0011 9 *nk* **Emotive**[16] 2877 3-9-1 **64** .... ChrisCatlin 9 62+
(I A Wood) *plld hrd early: hld up midfield: pushed along 3f out: nt clr run over 1f out: swtchd lft ins fnl f: kpt on* **6/1**[2]

0003 10 *shd* **Possessed**[25] 2589 3-9-0 **63** .... RobertHavlin 8 61
(T D McCarthy) *hld up in rr: rdn and no prog over 2f out* **14/1**

0210 11 3/4 **Fratt'n Park (IRE)**[9] 3072 3-9-5 **68** .... SteveDrowne 5 67+
(J J Bridger) *hld up in midfield: rdn wl over 2f out: no real prog: btn whn nowhere to go last 100yds and eased* **14/1**

0500 12 *hd* **Orphina (IRE)**[11] 3011 3-8-11 **60** .... ShaneKelly 6 55
(Pat Eddery) *trckd ldrs: rdn over 2f out: fdd wl over 1f out* **14/1**

1m 44.36s (-1.24) **Going Correction** -0.175s/f (Firm) **12** Ran SP% **117.5**
Speed ratings (Par 100):99,98,98,96,96 96,95,95,95,95 94,94
CSF £33.79 CT £161.39 TOTE £6.70: £2.20, £2.50, £2.10; EX 43.20.

Owner John Bridge & The Late Geoffrey Bovill **Bred** Jeremy Green And Sons **Trained** Newmarket, Suffolk

FOCUS
A muddling race with a strong pace considerably eased, as often happens around the bend, before the sprint home in which there was considerable scrimmaging. As a result the form cannot be viewed positively overall.

Mucho Loco(IRE) Official explanation: jockey said gelding hung right final furlong
Titus Lumpus(IRE) Official explanation: jockey said gelding hung left into the straight
Emotive Official explanation: jockey said gelding was denied a clear run
Fratt'n Park(IRE) Official explanation: jockey said filly was denied a clear run

3365 SUNLEY EBF H'CAP 1m 3f 135y
7:35 (7:37) (Class 4) (0-80,78) 3-Y-O+ **£6,477** (£1,927; £963; £481) **Stalls** Low

Form RPR

5-04 1 **Alessano**[45] 1991 4-9-9 **75** ....(b) RyanMoore 8 84
(G L Moore) *prom: urged along over 2f out: drvn to chal 1f out: led last 75yds: kpt on wl* **11/2**[2]

-203 2 *nk* **Ocean Avenue (IRE)**[27] 2534 7-9-9 **75** .... DarryllHolland 4 83
(C A Horgan) *trckd ldr: led over 4f out and increased pce: hrd rdn 2f out: hdd last 75yds* **8/1**

0065 3 *nk* **Spinning Coin**[16] 2869 4-9-8 **74** .... TPQueally 11 82
(J G Portman) *hld up: n.m.r bnd 6f out: rdn 4f out: prog on outer fr 3f out: drvn to chal ins fnl f: nt qckn* **16/1**

0401 4 1 3/4 **Eldorado**[11] 3024 5-9-3 **69** .... JimmyFortune 9 74
(S Kirk) *hld up in midfield: gng wl enough 4f out: lost pl over 2f out: drvn over 1f out: r.o fnl f: no ch* **11/1**

411 5 *shd* **Olimpo (FR)**[35] 2305 5-9-11 **77** .... AlanMunro 1 82
(B R Millman) *plld hrd: cl up: rdn to chse ldr over 2f out tl wknd 1f out* **5/1**[1]

0-00 6 1 3/4 **Mutamaasek (USA)**[35] 2305 4-8-13 **65** .... TedDurcan 7 67+
(Lady Herries) *hld up towards rr: shkn up over 4f out: prog u.p 2f out : nt rch ldrs: fdd fnl f* **33/1**

0610 7 *shd* **Winners Delight**[10] 3048 5-9-12 **78** .... RichardHughes 12 80
(C F Wall) *hld up in rr: hrd rdn over 2f out: one pce and no imp* **11/1**

-051 8 5 **Love Always**[22] 2672 4-9-7 **73** .... PatDobbs 5 67
(S Dow) *hld up in last pair: pushed along over 4f out: effrt u.p over 2f out: no ch: wknd fnl f* **12/1**

0425 9 1/2 **Risk Runner (IRE)**[25] 2584 3-8-12 **77** ....(v) JDSmith 2 70+
(A King) *hld up: prog into midfield 1/2-way: rdn on outer 3f out: steadily wknd: eased fnl f* **8/1**

-504 10 1 3/4 **Hawridge Star (IRE)**[41] 2097 4-9-4 **70** ....(v) ChrisCatlin 6 60
(W S Kittow) *hld up in last pair: rdn over 4f out: sn struggling: no ch fnl 2f* **16/1**

3104 11 5 **Smooth Jazz**[10] 3048 4-9-9 **75** .... JamieSpencer 3 57
(R M Beckett) *t.k.h: hld up in midfield: rdn and no rspnse over 2f out: heavily eased over 1f out* **6/1**[3]

3233 12 1 1/4 **Velvet Waters**[11] 3009 5-9-0 **66** .... StephenCarson 10 46
(R F Johnson Houghton) *sweating: led to over 4f out: sn rdn: wknd fr 3f out* **9/1**

2m 26.15s (-3.95) **Going Correction** -0.175s/f (Firm)
WFA 3 from 4yo+ 13lb **12** Ran SP% **117.6**
Speed ratings (Par 105):106,105,105,104,104 103,103,99,99,98 94,94
CSF £48.75 CT £667.80 TOTE £7.30: £2.20, £3.30, £4.10; EX 69.30.

Owner D J Deer **Bred** D J And Mrs Deer **Trained** Woodingdean, E Sussex

FOCUS
Another muddling contest with a lack of pace until into the home straight, which saw another bunched field. Just ordinary form, but pretty solid, the third and fourth running to their latest marks.

Smooth Jazz Official explanation: jockey said gelding had no more to give

3366 JOBS@PERTEMPS H'CAP 1m 2f 7y
8:05 (8:06) (Class 4) (0-85,85) 3-Y-O+ **£6,477** (£1,927; £963; £481) **Stalls** Low

Form RPR

-520 1 **Brief Goodbye**[10] 3048 6-9-6 75 .... MickyFenton 2 84
(John Berry) *dwlt: hld up in last pair: taken to wd outside and prog over 2f out : sustained effrt fr over 1f out to ld wl ins fnl f* **11/1**

0015 2 3/4 **Forthright**[10] 3044 5-9-0 74 .... JamesDoyle(5) 4 82
(A W Carroll) *trckd ldrs: effrt 3f out: rdn to ld over 1f out: hdd and one pce wl ins fnl f* **9/1**

6031 3 2 **Urban Tiger (GER)**[24] 2622 3-8-11 77 .... TedDurcan 11 81
(A King) *hld up in last trio: prog to midfield 4f out: rdn over 3f out: kpt on u.p: nvr able to chal* **5/1**[2]

2221 4 1/2 **Folio (IRE)**[19] 2761 6-9-9 83 .... StephenDonohoe(5) 6 86
(W J Musson) *hld up: last trio 4f out: stdy prog to chse ldrs wl over 1f out: one pce u.p after* **6/1**[3]

-006 5 *nk* **Night Spot**[14] 2918 5-9-5 74 .... GeorgeBaker 10 77
(B R Millman) *prom: trckd ldr 4f out: rdn to ld 2f out to over 1f out: one pce and sn btn* **14/1**

0006 6 *nk* **Rawdon (IRE)**[10] 3048 5-9-11 80 ....(v) HayleyTurner 3 82
(M L W Bell) *led: rdn and hdd 2f out: hmpd sn after: eased whn btn fnl f but lost no more grnd* **10/1**

0323 7 6 **South O'The Border**[24] 2621 4-9-1 77 .... JamesMillman(7) 5 68
(T G Mills) *chsd ldrs: drvn and wknd 2f out* **5/1**[2]

-006 8 1/2 **Bridegroom**[10] 3056 4-8-4 64 oh16 ....(v[1]) RichardKingscote(5) 1 54
(Lady Herries) *t.k.h: pressed ldr to 4f out: wknd rapidly wl over 1f out* **66/1**

6001 9 1 1/4 **Della Salute**[9] 3095 4-9-6 75 .... AlanMunro 9 62
(Miss E C Lavelle) *hld up in last pair: rdn and no prog whn bdly hmpd over 2f out* **12/1**

23-1 10 45 **Conkering (USA)**[81] 1100 3-9-5 85 .... JamieSpencer 7 —+
(J R Fanshawe) *trckd ldrs: rdn over 3f out: effrt on inner whn hmpd jst over 2f out: virtually p.u after* **11/4**[1]

2m 6.06s (-2.24) **Going Correction** -0.175s/f (Firm)
WFA 3 from 4yo+ 11lb **10** Ran SP% **117.6**
Speed ratings (Par 105):101,100,98,98,98 97,93,92,91,55
CSF £106.68 CT £563.33 TOTE £13.80: £3.60, £3.40, £1.60; EX 150.60.

Owner J McCarthy **Bred** Chippenham Lodge Stud Ltd **Trained** Newmarket, Suffolk

■ Stewards' Enquiry : George Baker caution: careless riding
Hayley Turner two-day ban: careless riding (Jul 21-22)

FOCUS
A steadily-run contest. Ordinary form, the winner back to his 2005 best.

3367 COOLMORE FOOTSTEPSINTHESAND MAIDEN FILLIES' STKS 1m 67y
8:35 (8:36) (Class 5) 3-4-Y-O **£3,886** (£1,156; £577; £288) **Stalls** High

Form RPR

-42 1 **Sabah**[21] 2712 3-9-0 .... NeilChalmers(3) 3 77
(A M Balding) *trckd ldr: rdn to chal over 1f out: led ins fnl f: hld on wl* **12/1**

The Form Book, Raceform Ltd, Compton, RG20 6NL

0-2 **2** *nk* **Early Evening**[31] 2406 3-9-3 DaneO'Neill 9 76
(H Candy) *led: rdn and pressed over 1f out: hdd ins fnl f: kpt on but a hld* **7/2**[2]

4- **3** *hd* **Regal Velvet**[279] 5692 3-9-3 RobertHavlin 14 76
(J H M Gosden) *hld up in midfield: prog to trck ldrs 2f out: plld out over 1f out: shkn up to chal ins fnl f: nt qckn nr fin* **11/1**

4 *1 1/2* **Aryaamm (IRE)** 3-9-3 PhilipRobinson 10 72+
(M A Jarvis) *trckd ldng pair: shkn up 2f out: hanging lft and nt qckn over 1f out: one pce* **3/1**[1]

5 **5** *1* **Spirit Of The Fen (IRE)**[31] 2406 3-9-3 JimmyFortune 5 70
(J H M Gosden) *settled midfield: shkn up and effrt on outer 3f out: chsd ldrs over 1f out: one pce after* **7/2**[2]

62 **6** *hd* **Mcnairobi**[25] 2575 3-9-3 LPKeniry 8 69
(P D Cundell) *t.k.h: trckd ldng trio: hanging lft and nt qckn fr 2f out* **33/1**

0 **7** *nk* **Moon Empress (FR)**[19] 2753 3-9-3 MartinDwyer 6 69+
(W R Muir) *hld up midfield: shkn up and outpcd over 2f out: kpt on again fnl f* **66/1**

8 *3* **Lady Songbird (IRE)** 3-9-3 TedDurcan 11 62
(W R Swinburn) *settled in midfield: pushed along 3f out: outpcd and btn 2f out* **33/1**

0 **9** *1* **Dream Dance**[14] 2934 3-9-3 SteveDrowne 2 59+
(H Morrison) *mulish to post: trckd ldrs: rdn over 2f out: wknd over 1f out* **50/1**

0 **10** *1/2* **Warden Rose**[12] 2985 3-9-3 JohnEgan 4 58
(D R C Elsworth) *hld up wl in rr: pushed along over 2f out: no prog* **33/1**

0- **11** *1/2* **Excellent**[279] 5688 3-9-3 RyanMoore 12 57
(Sir Michael Stoute) *settled in last pair: pushed along and no prog 3f out* **6/1**[3]

05 **12** *hd* **Norakit**[4] 3219 3-9-3 ChrisCatlin 1 57?
(M R Channon) *hld up wl in rr: pushed along over 2f out: no prog* **66/1**

6-0 **13** *4* **Hazelnut**[14] 2934 3-9-3 JamieSpencer 7 47
(J R Fanshawe) *s.i.s: sn pushed along: a struggling in last* **14/1**

1m 43.88s (-1.72) **Going Correction** -0.175s/f (Firm) **13** Ran SP% **120.2**
Speed ratings (Par 100):101,100,100,99,98 97,97,94,93,93 92,92,88
CSF £52.29 TOTE £12.90: £2.40, £1.60, £4.90; EX 46.20.

Owner Sir Roger Buckley **Bred** C H Bothway **Trained** Kingsclere, Hants

FOCUS
This was probably only a fair maiden with the form unlikely to prove that strong, although it makes sense at face value.

3368 LADBROKES.COM H'CAP 6f
9:05 (9:06) (Class 5) (0-70,70) 3-Y-0+ **£3,238** (£963; £481; £240) **Stalls** High

Form RPR

5420 **1** **Bold Argument (IRE)**[23] 2650 3-9-8 **70** RobertHavlin 10 78
(Mrs P N Dutfield) *chsd ldrs: rdn 1/2-way: prog u.p over 1f out: styd on to ld last 50yds* **50/1**

0-33 **2** *nk* **Inka Dancer (IRE)**[24] 2603 4-9-0 **56** FrancisFerris 16 64
(B Palling) *led and racd against nr side rail: rdn over 1f out: hdd and no ex last 50yds* **12/1**

2431 **3** *hd* **Hammer Of The Gods (IRE)**[11] 3012 6-9-2 **58**.....(bt) JamieSpencer 15 65
(P S McEntee) *trckd ldr: rdn to chal 1f out: nt qckn and hld last 75yds* **11/4**[1]

6606 **4** *nk* **Who's Winning (IRE)**[23] 2635 5-9-13 **69** GeorgeBaker 4 76+
(B G Powell) *hld up wl in rr: prog over 2f out: styd on fr over 1f out: nt quite pce to chal* **25/1**

0054 **5** *1* **Born To Be Bold**[21] 2711 4-9-10 **66** RichardHughes 11 70
(R Hannon) *trckd ldrs: effrt over 2f out: tried to cl over 1f out: kpt on same pce* **7/1**[3]

5001 **6** *1 1/4* **Linda Green**[9] 3094 5-9-10 **66** ChrisCatlin 5 66+
(M R Channon) *hld up wl in rr: effrt 2f out: kpt on fr over 1f out: nvr able to rch ldrs* **11/2**[2]

2200 **7** *1* **Cerulean Rose**[3] 3267 7-9-5 **61** JimmyFortune 8 58
(A W Carroll) *chsd ldrs: rdn over 2f out: no imp over 1f out: wknd ins fnl f* **9/1**

0000 **8** *3/4* **Sweetest Revenge (IRE)**[9] 3094 5-9-3 **59** HayleyTurner 3 54
(M D I Usher) *hld up wl in rr: effrt on outer 2f out: kpt on: n.d* **33/1**

-666 **9** *hd* **Lady Edge (IRE)**[21] 2702 4-8-13 **55** ShaneKelly 6 49
(A W Carroll) *dwlt: wl in rr: effrt towards outer 2f out: plugged on same pce* **50/1**

0135 **10** *hd* **Bens Georgie (IRE)**[9] 3094 4-9-11 **67** DaneO'Neill 9 60
(D K Ivory) *in tch: effrt on outer to chse ldrs 2f out: wknd over 1f out* **10/1**

0501 **11** *hd* **Limonia (GER)**[6] 3166 4-8-4 **51** 6ex JamesDoyle(5) 12 44
(N P Littmoden) *restless stalls: dwlt: hld up wl in rr: sme prog over 2f out: wknd over 1f out* **16/1**

5505 **12** *3/4* **Cayman Breeze**[15] 2898 6-8-11 **53** RyanMoore 1 43
(J M Bradley) *swtchd fr wdst draw to r on inner after 2f: nvr any ch* **16/1**

6005 **13** *1 1/2* **Currency**[10] 3041 9-9-9 **70** LiamTreadwell(5) 2 56
(J M Bradley) *racd on wd outside: nvr on terms: no prog u.p 2f out: wknd over 1f out* **20/1**

40-6 **14** *1/2* **Stokesies Wish**[14] 2920 6-8-12 **57** AdamKirby(3) 13 41
(J L Spearing) *prom nr side tl wknd 2f out* **25/1**

1002 **15** *hd* **Caustic Wit (IRE)**[9] 3094 8-9-7 **70**.....(p) TolleyDean(7) 7 54
(M S Saunders) *racd on outer: nvr on terms: wknd over 1f out* **10/1**

0000 **16** *1 1/4* **Royal Orissa**[32] 2384 4-9-13 **69** SteveDrowne 14 49
(D Haydn Jones) *chsd ldng pair to 1/2-way: lost pl rapidly* **25/1**

1m 11.7s (-1.97) **Going Correction** -0.35s/f (Firm)
WFA 3 from 4yo+ 6lb **16** Ran SP% **125.4**
Speed ratings (Par 103):99,98,98,97,96 94,93,92,92,92 91,90,88,88,87 86
CSF £558.10 CT £2233.40 TOTE £62.60: £9.80, £2.80, £1.80, £6.60; EX 908.10 Place 6 £187.75, Place 5 £157.56.

Owner Simon Dutfield **Bred** K S Lee **Trained** Axmouth, Devon

FOCUS
No coincidence that those drawn high dominated. Ordinary form, but sound.

Limonia(GER) Official explanation: jockey said filly slipped on leaving stalls

T/Plt: £250.30 to a £1 stake. Pool: £79,154.40. 230.80 winning tickets. T/Qpdt: £82.70 to a £1 stake. Pool: £4,180.30. 37.40 winning tickets. JN

3369 - 3371a (Foreign Racing) - See Raceform Interactive

3141 PONTEFRACT (L-H)
Tuesday, July 11

OFFICIAL GOING: Good to firm
Wind: Moderate behind

3372 DIANNE NURSERY 6f
2:45 (2:46) (Class 4) 2-Y-0 **£6,477** (£1,927; £963; £481) **Stalls** Low

Form RPR

541 **1** **Bodes Galaxy (IRE)**[13] 2967 2-9-5 **81** MickyFenton 2 99
(N P Littmoden) *qckly away: mde all: rdn wl over 1f out and styd on strly* **9/2**[2]

01 **2** *7* **Dhanyata (IRE)**[31] 2456 2-9-7 **83** JamieSpencer 9 98
(B J Meehan) *sn chsng wnr: effrt over 2f out: rdn wl over 1f out: drvn and kpt on ins last: nt rch wnr* **5/6**[1]

351 **3** *6* **Monkey Glas (IRE)**[28] 2523 2-8-11 **73** PatCosgrave 4 70
(K R Burke) *trckd ldrs: hdwy to chse ldng pair 2f out: sn rdn and one pce* **15/2**[3]

3505 **4** *3 1/2* **Everyman**[32] 2416 2-8-0 **62** ow2.....(v) FrancisNorton 5 49
(P D Evans) *dwlt and bhd: rdn along 1/2-way: styd on u.p fnl 2f: nrst fin* **25/1**

0250 **5** *3* **Nota Liberata**[25] 2623 2-8-3 **68** NelsonDeSouza(3) 3 46
(G M Moore) *in tch: hdwy to chse ldrs over 2f out: sn rdn and weeakened* **20/1**

4213 **6** *9* **The Mighty Ogmore**[8] 3136 2-8-3 **65** JoeFanning 7 16
(R C Guest) *a towards rr* **12/1**

2504 **7** *4* **Suhayl Star (IRE)**[21] 2733 2-9-1 **77** TonyCulhane 1 16
(M R Channon) *chsd ldrs: rdn along 1/2-way: sn wknd* **14/1**

0156 **8** *1 1/4* **Spinning Game**[25] 2626 2-7-12 **60** oh5 PaulQuinn 8 —
(D W Chapman) *a rr* **50/1**

3115 **9** *3/4* **Emma Told Lies**[8] 3136 2-7-12 **60** oh1 DaleGibson 6 —
(M W Easterby) *racd wd: chsd ldrs to 1/2-way: sn rdn along and wknd* **20/1**

1m 16.22s (-1.18) **Going Correction** -0.175s/f (Firm) **9** Ran SP% **114.2**
Speed ratings (Par 96):100,98,90,86,82 70,64,63,62
CSF £8.09 CT £26.27 TOTE £5.50: £1.50, £1.10, £2.00; EX 11.00.

Owner Mark Harniman **Bred** T Stewart **Trained** Newmarket, Suffolk

FOCUS
The official ratings shown next to each horse are estimated and for information purposes only. This looked a decent nursery and the pace was noticeably strong. Very few ever got into it and the front three were in those positions throughout, whilst the first two eventually pulled well clear.

NOTEBOOK
Bodes Galaxy(IRE) ◆ pinged the gates from his low draw and adopted the same tactics that proved so effective at Bath. Relishing this stiff six, he only had the favourite to worry about from halfway and found more than enough to keep her at bay. He should get further and ought to continue to progress. (op 6-1 tchd 13-2)
Dhanyata(IRE), whose Newbury victory has worked out well, was unable to apply the same front-running tactics this time thanks to the winner stealing her thunder. She could never quite pick him up, but this was still a fair effort by a filly under top weight. (op 10-11 tchd evens)
Monkey Glas(IRE) was always in about the same place, but could do nothing to stop the front two forging clear of him. He still kept the others at bay comfortably enough and should find an ordinary nursery at some point under similar conditions. (op 7-1 tchd 13-2)
Everyman deserves a bit of credit for finishing fourth as he was last to break from the stalls. Considering how far he was beaten it would be wrong to get too carried away, but he will surely improve when he is faced with a greater test of stamina.
Nota Liberata never looked like getting involved and does not seem to be progressing. (op 18-1)
Emma Told Lies, whether by accident or design, raced very wide of her rivals until the home bend but it did her no favours. (op 18-1)

3373 RACING WELFARE MAIDEN STKS 1m 2f 6y
3:15 (3:16) (Class 5) 3-Y-0+ **£4,533** (£1,348; £674; £336) **Stalls** Low

Form RPR

- **1** **Virtuosity** 3-8-10 RyanMoore 4 80
(Sir Michael Stoute) *dwlt: hld up in rr: hdwy 4f out: swtchd wd and effrt 3f out: rdn to ld wl over 1f out and sn qcknd clr* **11/4**[2]

2 *5* **Longhill Tiger** 3-9-1 NCallan 6 76
(G G Margarson) *hld up in rr: gd hdwy on inner whn bmpd 2f out: sn rdn and kpt on: no ch w wnr* **33/1**

432 **3** *3 1/2* **Greek Easter (IRE)**[20] 2753 3-8-10 **80** JamieSpencer 1 67+
(B J Meehan) *set stdy pce: edgd lft over 2f out: sn shkn up: rdn and hdd wl over 1f out: sn btn* **4/6**[1]

3 **4** *3* **Hayden Grace**[12] 3001 3-8-10 KDarley 5 58
(M Johnston) *hld up in tch: effrt and sme hdwy 4f out: sn rdn and btn wl over 2f out* **11/2**[3]

0 **5** *15* **Golden Groom**[14] 2948 3-9-1 LeeEnstone 3 35
(C W Fairhurst) *keen: chsd ldrs: rdn along 4f out: sn wknd* **125/1**

05 **6** *2 1/2* **Oasis Flower**[14] 2948 3-8-10 .....(v[1]) EddieAhern 2 25
(J R Fanshawe) *chsd ldrs: rdn along 4f out: sn wknd* **33/1**

7 *29* **Sagemacca (IRE)** 4-9-7 GrahamGibbons 7 —
(J J Quinn) *chsd ldr on outer: rdn along 1/2-way: sn wknd* **66/1**

2m 11.4s (-2.68) **Going Correction** -0.175s/f (Firm)
WFA 3 from 4yo 11lb **7** Ran SP% **110.2**
Speed ratings (Par 103):103,99,96,93,81 79,56
CSF £62.00 TOTE £4.20: £1.40, £6.70; EX 68.80.

Owner Cheveley Park Stud **Bred** Cheveley Park Stud Ltd **Trained** Newmarket, Suffolk

■ Stewards' Enquiry : Jamie Spencer one-day ban: careless riding (Jul 22)

FOCUS
Just a fair pace for this maiden, but unlike in the the first race the first two home came from the back of the field. The runners were inclined to race down the middle of the track in the home straight. Not an easy race to rate for now, particularly with the favourite disappointing.

3374 KING RICHARD III H'CAP 6f
3:45 (3:45) (Class 3) (0-90,90) 3-Y-0+
£11,217 (£3,358; £1,679; £840; £419; £210) **Stalls** Low

Form RPR

0503 **1** **Fantasy Believer**[5] 3211 8-9-4 **80** DarryllHolland 7 91
(J J Quinn) *trckd ldrs: hdwy 2f out: rdn to ld ins last: styd on wl* **6/1**[3]

25-4 **2** *1/2* **Wyatt Earp (IRE)**[14] 2946 5-9-8 **84** TonyHamilton 2 94
(R A Fahey) *cl up: led over 2f out: rdn over 1f out: hdd and nt qckn ins last* **4/1**[2]

1260 **3** *1 3/4* **Dvinsky (USA)**[5] 3217 5-8-11 **73** RyanMoore 8 78
(D Carroll) *hld up: hdwy 2f out: rdn over 1f out: styd on ins last* **12/1**

5661 **4** *hd* **Waterline Twenty (IRE)**[10] 3067 3-8-13 **81**................ FrancisNorton 11 84
(P D Evans) *chsd ldrs: rdn wl over 1f out: drvn and kpt on same pce ins last* **28/1**

4253 **5** *nk* **Ice Planet**[10] 3077 5-10-0 **90**.. JoeFanning 3 93
(D Nicholls) *chsd ldrs: rdn along wl over 1f out: drvn and one pce ins last* **7/2**[1]

5435 **6** *½* **Titinius (IRE)**[20] 2749 6-8-9 **71** oh2................................ DeanMcKeown 6 73
(Micky Hammond) *hld up towards rr: gd hdwy on inner over 2f out: rdn and ch over 1f out: drvn and wknd ins last* **25/1**

5000 **7** *¾* **Trojan Flight**[3] 3281 5-8-11 **73**.................................(p) TonyCulhane 9 72
(D W Chapman) *bhd: rdn along over 2f out: styd on ins last: nvr nr ldrs* **12/1**

2023 **8** *2* **Circuit Dancer (IRE)**[21] 2732 6-8-11 **73**...................... AdrianTNicholls 5 66
(D Nicholls) *keen: hld up towards rr: sme hdwy over 2f out: rdn and edgd rt wl over 1f out: sn no imp* **7/1**

5320 **9** *½* **Canadian Danehill (IRE)**[3] 3281 4-8-9 **71** oh2............... EddieAhern 10 63
(R M H Cowell) *cl up: rdn along over 2f out: wknd wl over 1f out* **12/1**

-000 **10** *1 ¼* **Thunderwing (IRE)**[13] 2974 4-8-13 **75**............................ PatCosgrave 1 63
(K R Burke) *led: rdn along and hdd over 2f out: sn wknd* **66/1**

0046 **11** *2 ½* **Banjo Patterson**[21] 2732 4-9-8 **84**..................................(b[1]) DO'Donohoe 4 65
(G A Huffer) *chsd ldrs: rdn along 2f out: wkng whn hmpd wl over 1f out* **6/1**[3]

1m 15.06s (-2.34) **Going Correction** -0.175s/f (Firm)
WFA 3 from 4yo+ 6lb **11** Ran SP% **115.2**
Speed ratings (Par 107):108,107,105,104,104 103,102,100,99,97 94
CSF £29.05 CT £284.50 TOTE £6.30: £2.20, £1.60, £4.30; EX 20.30.
Owner The Fantasy Fellowship B **Bred** John Khan **Trained** Settrington, N Yorks

FOCUS
A decent sprint handicap run at a true pace, and solid form which should prove reliable. The whole field decided to move to the centre of the track early, despite the stalls being placed next to the inside rail, and it did appear that the middle of the track was riding quicker.

NOTEBOOK
Fantasy Believer ◆, who always seems to hit form at around this time of year, had hinted at a return to form last time and took full advantage of a mark 8lb lower than for his last win just over a year ago. He battled on really well to score and will still be well handicapped under a penalty, so now that he has regained winning form a quick follow up would not be a surprise. (tchd 11-2)
Wyatt Earp(IRE), appreciating the extra furlong and stiff track, put in a brave effort in defeat having been up with the pace throughout. He has returned from his lengthy layoff in good heart and should be able to go one better before long. (op 11-2)
Dvinsky(USA), 7lb higher than when scoring over course and distance last month, stayed on nicely from the home turn to snatch third and continues to perform well, but he does not have the greatest win record. (op 14-1)
Waterline Twenty(IRE), raised 5lb for her Chester victory, had every chance from the outside stall but failed to quicken and may prefer the extra furlong now. (op 25-1)
Ice Planet ran another creditable race off this sort of mark having raced much more prominently early than in recent starts. Still 10lb higher than when winning last season's Great St Wilfrid, he is still one to watch out for if contesting one of the big sprint handicaps in the next couple of months. (op 10-3 tchd 3-1)
Titinius(IRE) was not disgraced considering he made his effort closer to the inside rail than his rivals and that he is probably better over a bit further. His losing run, stretching back more than three years, is a bit misleading as he was absent for two of those, and he does look capable of winning off this sort of mark. (op 20-1)
Banjo Patterson, sporting first-time blinkers, already looked beaten when getting badly hampered soon after turning for home. He continues to perform below his best. (op 11-2)

3375 CATTERICK ARE RACING TOMORROW H'CAP — 1m 2f 6y
4:15 (4:15) (Class 5) (0-75,74) 3-Y-O — £4,533 (£1,348; £674; £336) Stalls Low

Form RPR

-023 **1** **Nesno (USA)**[29] 2502 3-9-7 **74**..................................(b[1]) DarryllHolland 3 83
(J D Bethell) *cl up: led after 2f: rdn 2f out: hdd over 1f out: carried rt and bmpd twice ins last and rdr dropped whip: r.o. fin 2nd, nk: awrdd r* **5/2**[1]

6404 **2** *nk* **Truly Fruitful (IRE)**[29] 2502 3-9-2 **69**............................. PatCosgrave 1 78
(K R Burke) *trckd ldrs: hdwy on inner 3f out: rdn to chal 2f out: led over 1f out: hung bdly rt ins last: jst hld on: fin 1st, nk: pl 2nd* **5/1**[3]

6030 **3** *8* **Suits Me**[19] 2781 3-9-5 **72**.. GrahamGibbons 2 66
(J J Quinn) *hld up in rr: smooth hdwy 3f out: rdn to chse ldng pair wl over 1f out: sn drvn and one pce* **15/2**

-506 **4** *1 ¼* **Regal Connection (USA)**[23] 2679 3-9-3 **70**......................... KDarley 8 61
(M Johnston) *led 2f: cl up tl rdn along 3f out and sn wknd* **9/2**[2]

6146 **5** *½* **King's Revenge**[26] 2584 3-9-7 **74**..................................(b) TedDurcan 6 64
(T D Easterby) *chsd ldrs: rdn along over 3f out: sn wknd* **17/2**

0-33 **6** *nk* **Luna Landing**[19] 2779 3-9-7 **74**...................................... DaleGibson 4 64
(Jedd O'Keeffe) *hld up towards rr: effrt and sme hdwy 3f out: sn rdn and btn* **10/1**

4053 **7** *34* **Bolckow**[19] 2795 3-8-10 **63**... NCallan 7 —
(K A Ryan) *trckd ldrs on outer: rdn along 4f out: sn wknd* **6/1**

2m 11.53s (-2.55) **Going Correction** -0.175s/f (Firm) **7** Ran SP% **109.1**
Speed ratings (Par 100):102,103,96,95,94 94,67
CSF £13.58 CT £71.24 TOTE £2.80: £1.50, £2.90; EX 16.10.
Owner Elliott Brothers **Bred** Mrs Elisabeth Fabre **Trained** Middleham Moor, N Yorks
■ Stewards' Enquiry : Pat Cosgrave four-day ban: careless riding (Jul 22-25); two-day ban: used whip down the shoulder in the forehand position (Jul 26-27)

FOCUS
A modest little handicap in which the runners decided to stay more towards the inside of the track on reaching the home straight, at least until the front pair went on their travels, and they proved different class to the others. The Stewards decided to reverse the placings of the first two and in view of the interference that took place it looked the right decision. Ordinary form, but the first two showed improved form in finishing clear.

3376 BRADLEY MAIDEN STKS — 1m 4f 8y
4:45 (4:45) (Class 5) 3-Y-O+ — £4,533 (£1,348; £674; £336) Stalls Low

Form RPR

43 **1** **Belanak (IRE)**[71] 1343 3-8-13 .... RyanMoore 3 79+
(Sir Michael Stoute) *mde virtually all: rdn wl over 1f out: drvn and edgd rt ins last: kpt on* **8/15**[1]

4-4 **2** *nk* **Gordonsville**[13] 2970 3-8-13 .... JamieSpencer 1 79+
(A M Balding) *trckd ldrs: hdwy over 2f out: rdn to chse wnr over 1f out: drvn to chal and ev ch wl ins last: no ex nr fin* **13/2**[2]

52 **3** *7* **Beldon Hill (USA)**[10] 3100 3-8-8 .... TedDurcan 6 62
(C E Brittain) *trckd ldng pair: rdn along on outer 3f out: drvn 2f out and plugged on same pce* **10/1**[3]

2 **4** *1 ¼* **Particle (IRE)**[16] 2901 3-8-13 .... JoeFanning 5 65
(M Johnston) *cl up: rdn along 3f out: wknd 2f out* **13/2**[2]

30 **5** *hd* **Don And Gerry (IRE)**[27] 566 5-9-7 .... FrancisNorton 4 60
(P D Evans) *hld up: effrt 4f out: sn rdn alonga nd nvr a factor* **40/1**

3 **6** *7* **Primitive Academy**[16] 2901 4-9-12 .... EddieAhern 7 54+
(H R A Cecil) *chsd ldng pair on outer: rdn along 4f out: sn wknd* **20/1**

0/6 **7** *11* **Tanmeya**[16] 2901 5-9-7 .... NeilPollard 2 31
(R C Guest) *hld up towards rr: sme hdwy on inner over 4f out: sn rdn along and wknd over 3f out* **150/1**

2m 39.48s (-0.82) **Going Correction** -0.175s/f (Firm)
WFA 3 from 4yo+ 13lb **7** Ran SP% **108.9**
Speed ratings (Par 103):95,94,90,89,89 84,77
CSF £3.85 TOTE £1.50: £1.40, £2.40; EX 5.00.
Owner H H Aga Khan **Bred** His Highness The Aga Khan's Studs S C **Trained** Newmarket, Suffolk

FOCUS
An uncompetitive maiden and no pace on at all for the first mile, resulting in a modest winning time. Again the runners came centre-field on reaching the straight and the first two continually edged right, eventually finishing right under the stands' rail. The first two finished clear and may rate higher.

3377 BETFAIR.COM APPRENTICE SERIES (ROUND 3) H'CAP — 1m 2f 6y
5:15 (5:15) (Class 5) (0-70,74) 4-Y-O+ — £3,886 (£1,156; £577; £288) Stalls Low

Form RPR

0200 **1** **Splodger Mac (IRE)**[27] 2541 7-8-5 **50**........................ SuzzanneFrance 2 55
(N Bycroft) *mde all: clr 1/2-way: rdn 2f out: drvn and kpt on ins last: hld on wl* **50/1**

0 **2** *hd* **Otranto (USA)**[15] 2918 4-8-10 **60**................................(t) WilliamCarson(5) 8 65
(M Johnston) *hld up in rr: hdwy over 2f out: rdn over 1f out: styd on strly ins last: jst hld* **16/1**[3]

-024 **3** *nk* **Finished Article (IRE)**[38] 2221 9-9-3 **65**........................ AlanRutter(3) 1 69
(W J Musson) *hld up in rr: hdwy 3f out: rdn 2f out: styd on strly ins last* **9/1**[2]

12-6 **4** *1 ¾* **Hilltime (IRE)**[11] 1748 6-8-2 **52**....................................... NSLawes(5) 7 53
(J S Wainwright) *in tch: hdwy to chse ldr over 3f out: rdn 2f out: drvn and kpt on same pce appr last* **9/1**[2]

3-61 **5** *1 ¼* **Swains Bridge (USA)**[5] 3230 4-10-1 **74** 5ex.............. AshleyHamblett 6 72
(L M Cumani) *keen: trckd ldng pair: pushed along and outpcd 3f out: rdn wl over 1f out: kpt on ins last* **4/11**[1]

-004 **6** *9* **Rudaki**[18] 2832 4-8-5 **50**.. ThomasO'Brien 5 31
(M E Sowersby) *trckd ldr: effrt 3f out: sn rdn and wknd fnl 2f* **28/1**

0500 **7** *5* **Mccormack (IRE)**[22] 2707 4-8-5 **50** oh3......................... TolleyDean 3 22
(Micky Hammond) *chsd ldrs: rdn along 3f out: sn wknd* **33/1**

0104 **8** *24* **Zarova (IRE)**[15] 2927 4-8-8 **58**..................................(b[1]) AdeleRothery(5) 4 —
(M W Easterby) *plld hrd: racd wd: a rr* **16/1**[3]

2m 12.95s (-1.13) **Going Correction** -0.175s/f (Firm) **8** Ran SP% **113.4**
Speed ratings (Par 103):97,96,96,95,94 87,83,63
CSF £654.47 CT £7641.41 TOTE £20.20: £4.90, £3.60, £1.80; EX 314.20 Place 6 £121.93, Place 5 £107.33.
Owner Mrs J Dickinson **Bred** John Brady **Trained** Brandsby, N Yorks
■ Stewards' Enquiry : Thomas O'Brien caution: careless riding; one-day ban: careless riding

FOCUS
A modest winning time thanks to a very ordinary early gallop and the shock 50-1 winner was gifted the race to a certain degree. The form does not look reliable because of that.
Swains Bridge(USA) Official explanation: trainer's rep had no explanation for the poor form shown
T/Plt: £495.20 to a £1 stake. Pool: £63,874.55. 94.15 winning tickets. T/Qpdt: £83.40 to a £1 stake. Pool: £3,942.50. 34.95 winning tickets. JR

3257 SOUTHWELL (L-H)
Tuesday, July 11

OFFICIAL GOING: Standard
Wind: Light; half behind Weather: Fine

3378 WBX.COM WORLD BET EXCHANGE CLAIMING STKS — 1m (F)
2:30 (2:31) (Class 5) 3-Y-O — £3,238 (£963; £481; £240) Stalls Low

Form RPR

6445 **1** **Opera Writer (IRE)**[11] 3055 3-9-3 64................................(e) DavidAllan 7 67
(T D Easterby) *sn in rr and drvn along: hdwy over 3f out: wnt 2nd over 1f out: styd on to ld jst ins last: drew clr* **7/2**[2]

0050 **2** *3* **Welcome Releaf**[10] 3087 3-8-13 55.................................(v) ShaneKelly 2 57
(G C H Chung) *led: clr over 2f out: edgd rt: hdd and no ex ins last* **16/1**

1-23 **3** *½* **Ruffie (IRE)**[32] 2415 3-8-13 66....................................... AdamKirby(3) 9 59
(Miss Gay Kelleway) *trckd ldrs on outer: lost pl after 2f: sn bhd and drvn along: hdwy on outside 2f out: styd on wl fnl f* **5/2**[1]

6000 **4** *2 ½* **Apres Ski (IRE)**[13] 2968 3-8-8 52.................................. DeanCorby(3) 14 49
(J W Hills) *s.i.s: sn chsng ldrs on outer: one pce fnl 2f* **33/1**

-000 **5** *5* **Paddy Moon**[47] 1950 3-8-7 50 ow3........................ StephenDonohoe(5) 4 40
(J G Given) *in rr: kpt on fnl 2f: nvr nr ldrs* **25/1**

3300 **6** *¾* **Franky'N'Jonny**[53] 1829 3-7-8 52................................ KirstyMilczarek(7) 6 28
(Mrs C A Dunnett) *trckd ldrs: swtchd ins bnd over 4f out: one pce fnl 2f* **15/2**[3]

0560 **7** *nk* **Sunbolt (IRE)**[7] 3167 3-9-7 61......................................(b) PaulFessey 13 47
(T D Barron) *racd wd: lost pl over 4f out: kpt on fnl 2f* **9/1**

0-60 **8** *¾* **Marvin Gardens**[43] 2070 3-8-9 40...................................... BrianReilly 3 33
(P S McEntee) *chsd ldrs: wknd over 1f out* **80/1**

0600 **9** *1* **Meohmy**[8] 3145 3-8-8 50..(v) ChrisCatlin 5 30
(M R Channon) *s.i.s: bhd tl sme hdwy fnl 2f* **16/1**

4665 **10** *14* **Forestelle (IRE)**[7] 3166 3-8-9 52.............................. BenSwarbrick(3) 10 6
(M Dods) *mid-div: rdn 4f out: wknd and eased over 1f out* **20/1**

0000 **11** *3* **Grafton (IRE)**[8] 3154 3-8-10 63 ow1.................................. SebSanders 8 —
(J D Bethell) *chsd ldrs: rdn over 2f out: sn btn: eased ins last* **15/2**[3]

5000 **12** *15* **Xpres Boy (IRE)**[17] 2877 3-9-0 59.................................. AmirQuinn(3) 1 —
(S R Bowring) *chsd ldrs: wknd over 2f out: bhd whn heavily eased ins last* **18/1**

0000 **P** **Bond Cruz**[28] 2529 3-8-7 42...(p) GylesParkin 11 —
(G R Oldroyd) *lost pl after 1f: sn bhd: t.o over 3f out: p.u over 1f out* **66/1**

1m 46.24s (1.64) **Going Correction** +0.225s/f (Slow) **13** Ran SP% **115.6**
Speed ratings (Par 100):100,97,96,94,89 88,87,87,86,72 69,54,—
CSF £52.92 TOTE £4.50: £1.60, £5.70, £1.30; EX 62.60 Trifecta £215.40 Part won. Pool: £303.52 - 0.69 winning units..The winner was claimed by Mustafa Khan for £10,000.
Owner Norman Jackson **Bred** J Davison **Trained** Great Habton, N Yorks

FOCUS
A moderate claimer, but at least the pace seemed decent.
Ruffie(IRE) Official explanation: jockey said filly did not face the kickback
Sunbolt(IRE) Official explanation: jockey said gelding did not face the kickback
Forestelle(IRE) Official explanation: jockey said filly finished lame
Xpres Boy(IRE) Official explanation: jockey said gelding moved poorly throughout
Bond Cruz Official explanation: jockey said gelding moved poorly throughout

3379 TAKE CONTROL WITH WBX.COM MAIDEN FILLIES' H'CAP 1m (F)
3:00 (3:00) (Class 6) (0-55,55) 3-Y-0+ **£2,730** (£806; £403) **Stalls** Low

Form RPR

-000 **1** **Aberdeen Park**[64] 1537 4-8-9 **45**........................(b) RichardKingscote(5) 5 57
(Mrs H Sweeting) *s.s: gd hdwy over 2f out: swtchd lft appr fnl f: led jst ins last: hung lft: styd on* **10/1**

5300 **2** 2 **Tabulate**[10] 3099 3-8-13 **53**.. ChrisCatlin 8 61
(P L Gilligan) *hld up in rr: hdwy on outer over 3f out: led over 2f out: wandered over 1f out: hdd and no ex jst ins last* **13/2**[1]

23-0 **3** 10 **Food For Thought**[39] 2195 3-8-12 **55**............................(v[1]) DNolan(3) 12 43
(J J Quinn) *s.i.s: hdwy on outer over 3f out: hung lft and kpt on fnl f* **13/2**[1]

0050 **4** shd **Whisper Inthe Wind (IRE)**[10] 3072 3-8-12 **55**............. DominicFox(3) 6 43
(Miss J Feilden) *chsd ldrs on inner: one pce fnl 2f* **20/1**

0006 **5** 1 ½ **Opera Belle**[37] 2261 4-8-11 **45**..(t) AdamKirby(3) 9 30
(Miss Gay Kelleway) *w ldrs: led 3f out: sn hdd: fdd appr fnl f* **9/1**[3]

0-30 **6** 2 **Sister Gee (IRE)**[36] 2288 4-8-5 **43**...................... RussellKennemore(7) 1 24
(R Hollinshead) *hld up towards rr: hdwy 3f out: wknd over 1f out* **25/1**

000- **7** hd **Madge**[43] 3185 4-9-0 **45**...(v) PaulFessey 7 25
(W Storey) *bhd: styd on fnl 2f: nvr on terms* **14/1**

0035 **8** ½ **Kissi Kissi**[17] 2877 3-8-11 **54**....................................... BenSwarbrick(3) 3 33
(M J Attwater) *hld up towards rr: smooth hdwy 4f out: rdn and wknd over 1f out* **8/1**[2]

0000 **9** nk **Algorithm**[8] 3142 4-8-8 **44**.. DuranFentiman(5) 2 23
(T D Easterby) *drvn and to chse ldrs: one pce fnl 2f* **20/1**

0-00 **10** 13 **Westlake Bond (IRE)**[57] 1728 4-8-13 **44**........................ GylesParkin 11 —
(G R Oldroyd) *sn chsng ldrs on outer: lost pl over 2f out: bhd whn eased ins last* **50/1**

455 **11** ½ **Eternal Legacy (IRE)**[41] 2129 4-9-8 **53**............................ DavidAllan 14 5
(J Parkes) *trckd ldrs on outer: hung lft and lost pl over 2f out: bhd whn eased ins last* **8/1**[2]

00 **12** 7 **Bellabelini (IRE)**[17] 2877 3-9-1 **55**...................................(b) ShaneKelly 13 —
(S Kirk) *mde most: hdd 3f out: sn wknd: bhd whn eased* **12/1**

0500 **13** 2 **Muckle**[12] 3017 3-8-12 **52**.. SebSanders 4 —
(S C Williams) *chsd ldrs: drvn 4f out: lost pl over 2f out: eased whn bhd* **13/2**[1]

005 **14** 2 **Azerley (IRE)**[43] 2080 3-8-13 **53**.. SteveDrowne 10 —
(J D Bethell) *chsd ldrs: lost pl over 2f out: bhd whn eased* **10/1**

1m 46.34s (1.74) **Going Correction** +0.225s/f (Slow)
WFA 3 from 4yo 9lb **14** Ran SP% **120.1**
Speed ratings (Par 98):100,98,88,87,86 84,84,83,83,70 69,62,60,58
CSF £70.04 CT £476.07 TOTE £13.50: £4.50, £3.40, £2.10; EX 109.40 TRIFECTA Not won..
Owner The Kennet Connection **Bred** Miss K Whitehouse **Trained** Lockeridge, Wilts

FOCUS
A very moderate a race, which is hardly surprising given it was restricted to maiden fillies rated 55 or below. They seemed to go off too fast and the first two both came from well off the pace.
Azerley(IRE) Official explanation: jockey said filly had no more to give

3380 WBX.COM WORLD BET EXCHANGE (S) STKS 5f (F)
3:30 (3:31) (Class 6) 2-Y-0 **£2,388** (£705; £352) **Stalls** High

Form RPR

6230 **1** **Minimum Fuss (IRE)**[25] 2626 2-8-6 ....(b) PaulMulrennan 1 55
(M W Easterby) *racd wd: mde all: edgd lft over 1f out: all out* **7/1**[3]

0000 **2** ¾ **Gibsons**[22] 2709 2-8-11 .... RobertHavlin 4 57
(Mrs P N Dutfield) *sn outpcd and drvn along: hdwy 2f out: edgd lft and styd on wl fnl f: jst hld* **50/1**

4205 **3** nk **Splendidio**[8] 3148 2-8-6 .... RoystonFfrench 2 51
(D K Ivory) *sn chsng wnr: kpt on fnl f: no ex wl ins last* **9/4**[1]

0356 **4** 3 **Lovers Kiss**[18] 2806 2-8-7 ow1.. ShaneKelly 8 41
(N Wilson) *chsd ldrs: rdn 2f out: one pce* **14/1**

4036 **5** 3 ½ **Elizabeth Garrett**[27] 2538 2-8-4 ow1..........................(p) AdamKirby(3) 3 29
(R M H Cowell) *trckd ldrs: rdn and outpcd over 2f out: no threat after* **9/4**[1]

2143 **6** 3 ½ **Baytown Paikea**[27] 2538 2-8-11 .... BrianReilly 9 20
(P S McEntee) *chsd ldrs: hrd rdn 2f out: sn wknd* **7/2**[2]

7 4 **Nice One** 2-8-7 ow1.. TomEaves 6 —
(J R Turner) *dwlt: a last* **14/1**

61.59 secs (1.29) **Going Correction** +0.075s/f (Slow) **7** Ran SP% **111.6**
Speed ratings (Par 92):92,90,90,85,79 74,67
CSF £214.86 TOTE £7.70: £4.20, £8.30; EX 140.10 Trifecta £356.90 Part won. Pool: £502.78 - 0.69 winning units..The winner was bought in for 4,800gns.
Owner Winton Bloodstock Ltd **Bred** M Day **Trained** Sheriff Hutton, N Yorks
■ Stewards' Enquiry : Paul Mulrennan three-day ban: used whip with excessive frequency and without giving filly time to respond (Jul 22-24)

FOCUS
As is to be expected in selling company, particularly in the juvenile division, the form looks pretty poor.

NOTEBOOK
Minimum Fuss(IRE), racing wide of the main body of the field, made every yard. She hung across to the far side and there was nothing at all to spare at the line. (op 8-1)
Gibsons, an excitable type, was soon being run off his feet. Despite edging left he was reeling them in throughout the final furlong and would have made it in a few more strides. He really needs six. (op 40-1)
Splendidio, edgy beforehand, was having just her second start for this handler and in the end was just found lacking. (tchd 5-2)
Lovers Kiss looked really well but lacked the basic speed to be effective over this trip. (op 16-1)
Elizabeth Garrett, a handful to load, sported first-time cheekpieces and is looking fully exposed. (op 5-2)
Baytown Paikea, having her second try on this surface, again did not shine on it. (op 3-1)

3381 TAKE CONTROL WITH WBX.COM H'CAP 6f (F)
4:00 (4:00) (Class 5) (0-70,67) 3-Y-0 **£3,886** (£1,156; £577; £288) **Stalls** Low

Form RPR

6551 **1** **Xpres Maite**[8] 3154 3-9-3 **66** 6ex.. AmirQuinn(3) 5 80+
(S R Bowring) *w ldrs: led over 1f out: r.o wl* **5/1**[2]

-500 **2** 2 ½ **Tilly's Dream**[27] 2554 3-9-6 **66**.. ShaneKelly 12 72
(G C H Chung) *sltly hmpd s: racd wd: sn chsng ldrs: led over 4f out tl over 1f out: kpt on same pce* **7/1**

6600 **3** nk **Immaculate Red**[16] 2896 3-8-7 **53**.............................(b[1]) RoystonFfrench 2 58
(R Bastiman) *mid-div: hdwy over 2f out: styd on wl ins last* **25/1**

063 **4** 2 **Nightstrike (IRE)**[11] 3053 3-9-2 **62**... DaneO'Neill 3 61
(H Candy) *led tl over 4f out: chsd ldrs: one pce fnl f* **9/2**[1]

-306 **5** hd **The City Kid (IRE)**[43] 2068 3-9-2 **67**...................(b) StephenDonohoe(5) 8 66
(P D Evans) *in rr: hdwy on ins over 2f out: styd on fnl f* **12/1**

60-0 **6** 6 **Bitter Chill**[18] 2823 3-9-3 **63**... SteveDrowne 13 44
(H Morrison) *racd wd: in rr: hdwy over 2f out: kpt on* **11/1**

0420 **7** 4 **The London Gang**[35] 2318 3-8-13 **59**.................................... TomEaves 1 28
(P D Evans) *bhd and drvn along: sme hdwy over 2f out: nvr on terms* **6/1**

3021 **8** 1 ¾ **Elegant Times (IRE)**[11] 3050 3-9-6 **66**............................ SebSanders 10 29
(T D Easterby) *wnt rt s: bhd and drvn along: sme hdwy on wd outside over 2f out: nvr on terms* **11/2**[3]

0140 **9** ¾ **Mister Becks (IRE)**[17] 2876 3-8-0 **49**......................... JohnMcAuley(3) 6 10
(M C Chapman) *mid-div: rdn over 3f out: sn btn* **25/1**

4003 **10** 3 **Crafty Fox**[10] 3087 3-9-0 **60**.. FrankieMcDonald 7 12
(A P Jarvis) *rr-div: hrd drvn over 3f out: sn lost pl* **9/1**

-030 **11** 5 **Our Mary (IRE)**[4] 3262 3-8-10 **61**................................ AndrewMullen(5) 4 —
(Robert Gray) *mid-div: outpcd and lost pl over 4f out: sn bhd* **20/1**

6000 **12** 32 **Beverley Polo (IRE)**[54] 1792 3-8-5 **51** ow1.............(b) PaulMulrennan 11 —
(M W Easterby) *sltly hmpd s: racd wd: sn chsng ldrs: lost pl over 3f out: bhd whn hmpd over 2f out: wl t.o:* **50/1**

1m 18.47s (1.57) **Going Correction** +0.225s/f (Slow) **12** Ran SP% **117.5**
Speed ratings (Par 100):98,94,94,91,91 83,78,75,74,70 64,21
CSF £37.65 CT £813.14 TOTE £5.50: £2.10, £2.60, £7.00; EX 84.90 TRIFECTA Not won..
Owner Charterhouse Holdings Plc **Bred** S R Bowring **Trained** Edwinstowe, Notts

FOCUS
They went a strong pace from the start and few got involved in what was a modest sprint handicap. The winner is progressive and this has been rated through the runner-up.
Nightstrike(IRE) Official explanation: vet said filly lost a front shoe

3382 WBX.COM WORLD BET EXCHANGE H'CAP 1m 6f (F)
4:30 (4:30) (Class 6) (0-55,55) 4-Y-0+ **£2,730** (£806; £403) **Stalls** Low

Form RPR

-000 **1** **Optimum (IRE)**[17] 2862 4-9-4 **54**.. MickyFenton 1 67
(J T Stimpson) *mde all: styd on fnl 2f: all out* **50/1**

3603 **2** hd **Ego Trip**[18] 2812 5-9-4 **54**..(b) PaulMulrennan 2 67
(M W Easterby) *trckd ldrs: wnt 2nd over 3f out: rdn to chal 2f out: no ex nr fin* **13/2**

4352 **3** 5 **Romil Star (GER)**[4] 3260 9-8-9 **52**........................(v) KevinGhunowa(7) 14 58
(M J Attwater) *chsd ldrs: hdwy on ins over 3f out: wknd fnl f* **5/1**[3]

/20- **4** 8 **Lillebror (GER)**[418] 1822 8-9-0 **50**... TPQueally 9 45
(B J Curley) *hld up in mid-div: effrt over 4f out: one pce fnl 2f* **9/2**[2]

6551 **5** 9 **Bold Trump**[23] 1572 5-8-13 **49**... J-PGuillambert 4 31
(Mrs N S Evans) *in tch: drvn 6f out: outpcd fnl 4f* **12/1**

-600 **6** 2 ½ **Stolen Song**[6] 3203 6-8-10 **51**....................................(e) MarcHalford(5) 11 29
(J Ryan) *in rr and drvn 6f out: nvr a factor* **20/1**

3000 **7** 3 ½ **Dubai Sunday (JPN)**[5] 3230 5-9-5 **55**..............................(t) BrianReilly 5 29
(P S McEntee) *chsd ldrs: rdn over 4f out: lost pl 3f out* **18/1**

0101 **8** 5 **Galantos (GER)**[49] 1540 5-9-5 **55**...................................... GeorgeBaker 7 22
(G L Moore) *hld up in rr: reminders and sme hdwy 6f out: rdn over 4f out: nvr a factor* **7/2**[1]

00/0 **9** 3 ½ **Kaparolo (USA)**[11] 1138 7-9-2 **55**.............................. BenSwarbrick(3) 12 17
(John A Harris) *s.i.s: hdwy on outside after 4f: lost pl over 3f out* **50/1**

61-0 **10** 3 ½ **Mungo Jerry (GER)**[20] 318 5-9-0 **55**..................(t) TomMessenger(5) 8 12
(B N Pollock) *in rr: hdwy after 5f: lost pl over 5f out: sn bhd* **14/1**

00-3 **11** 21 **Ashstanza**[15] 2935 5-8-12 **48**... TomEaves 3 —
(R D E Woodhouse) *chsd ldrs: lost pl over 5f out: sn bhd: t.o* **40/1**

020/ **12** 12 **Littlestar (FR)**[43] 5320 5-8-7 **50**......................... RussellKennemore(7) 13 —
(B D Leavy) *in rr: sn rdn along: t.o 4f out* **66/1**

6050 **13** 25 **Bullseye**[11] 3035 4-9-2 **52**... SebSanders 6 —
(J R Boyle) *chsd ldrs: lost pl 6f out: sn wl t.o* **7/1**

100- **14** 64 **Woolstone Boy (USA)**[49] 6540 5-9-5 **55**...............(t) MichaelTebbutt 10 —
(K C Bailey) *sn drvn along in rr: detached 6f out: sn t.o: virtually p.u: btn 50 l* **14/1**

3m 10.2s (0.60) **Going Correction** +0.225s/f (Slow) **14** Ran SP% **121.8**
Speed ratings (Par 101):107,106,104,99,94 92,90,88,86,84 72,65,50,14
CSF £348.82 CT £1957.17 TOTE £51.10: £8.60, £2.30, £1.50; EX 207.40 TRIFECTA Not won..
Owner J T Stimpson **Bred** Mrs Brid Cosgrove **Trained** Newcastle-Under-Lyme, Staffs

FOCUS
A modest handicap but the form seems reasonable for the grade. As is usually the case in a staying races round here, they finished well strung out. They went a sound pace and that resulted in a decent winning time for a race like this.
Galantos(GER) Official explanation: jockey said gelding never travelled

3383 WBX.COM WORLD BET EXCHANGE MAIDEN STKS (DIV I) 6f (F)
5:00 (5:01) (Class 5) 3-4-Y-0 **£2,590** (£770; £385; £192) **Stalls** Low

Form RPR

2U **1** **Advancement**[26] 2575 3-9-3 .... SebSanders 2 73
(R A Fahey) *chsd ldrs: styd on to ld ins last: r.o* **7/4**[1]

-033 **2** 1 ½ **Bijli (IRE)**[6] 3189 3-9-3 69... TPQueally 8 68
(J Noseda) *chsd ldrs: led 2f out: hdd and no ex ins last* **10/3**[3]

0604 **3** nk **Strong Approach (IRE)**[6] 3189 3-9-3 67......................... PaulFessey 11 67
(T D Barron) *chsd ldrs: outpcd over 3f out: hdwy 2f out: styd on fnl f* **11/4**[2]

-05 **4** 3 **Hot Agnes**[11] 3053 3-8-12 .... MichaelTebbutt 10 53
(H J Collingridge) *hld up towards rr: hdwy over 2f out: kpt on: nvr trbld ldrs* **8/1**

0-0 **5** 12 **Wolf Pack**[10] 3090 4-9-6 .... EdwardCreighton(3) 4 23
(R W Price) *s.i.s: sn bhd and drvn along: sme hdwy 2f out: nvr a factor* **50/1**

0/0- **6** 1 ¼ **Mill End Chateau**[267] 5952 4-9-9 45................................... ShaneKelly 6 19
(D K Ivory) *w ldr: led 3f out: hdd 2f out: sn wknd* **66/1**

0060 **7** 2 **Millbrook Star (IRE)**[39] 2192 3-9-0 35.......................... AdamKirby(3) 3 12
(M C Chapman) *mid-div: outpcd over 4f out: no ch after* **80/1**

0000 **8** 4 **Eathie**[9] 3112 4-9-9 47..(v) FrancisFerris 9 —
(M J Attwater) *reminders after s: sn bhd* **25/1**

00-0 **9** 2 ½ **Beautiful South**[41] 2129 3-8-10 47 ow1................................(b) DNolan(3) 1 —
(N Wilson) *s.i.s: outpcd over 4f out: sn bhd* **25/1**

0-00 **10** 2 **Dancing Moonlight (IRE)**[134] 533 4-8-11 27................ AnnStokell(7) 5 —
(Mrs N Macauley) *dwlt: a in rr* **80/1**

0- **11** 3 **Miacarla**[291] 5428 3-8-12 .... MickyFenton 7 —
(A Berry) *led tl 3f out: wkng whn heavily eased over 1f out: virtually p.u* **33/1**

1m 18.29s (1.39) **Going Correction** +0.225s/f (Slow)
WFA 3 from 4yo 6lb **11** Ran SP% **113.8**
Speed ratings (Par 103):99,97,96,92,76 74,72,66,63,60 56
CSF £7.01 TOTE £2.60: £1.10, £1.30, £1.40; EX 6.60 Trifecta £12.70 Pool: £434.43 - 24.24 winning units.
Owner R Cowie **Bred** Raymond Cowie **Trained** Musley Bank, N Yorks

FOCUS
A modest maiden and the slower of the two divisions; the first four well clear of deadwood and the form is not solid.
Miacarla Official explanation: jockey said filly filly lost its action

3384 WBX.COM WORLD BET EXCHANGE MAIDEN STKS (DIV II) 6f (F)
5:30 (5:31) (Class 5) 3-4-Y-0 £2,590 (£770; £385; £192) Stalls Low

Form RPR
00 **1** **Indian Sabre (IRE)**[17] [2859] 3-9-3 .... ShaneKelly 8 81+
(J Noseda) *sn chsng ldrs: led over 1f out: kpt on wl* **8/1**[3]
64 **2** 1¼ **Benandonner (USA)**[17] [2859] 3-9-3 .... SteveDrowne 6 77
(E A L Dunlop) *chsd ldrs: chal over 1f out: no ex ins last* **2/1**[2]
3524 **3** 6 **Spinning**[46] [2001] 3-9-3 72 .... PaulFessey 2 59
(T D Barron) *outpcd and in rr over 4f out: hdwy 2f out: kpt on to take modest 3rd ins last: nvr nr 1st 2* **5/6**[1]
0-00 **4** 4 **Active Audience (IRE)**[61] [1609] 3-8-12 55 ....(b[1]) TPQueally 9 42
(A Berry) *chsd ldrs: rdn and edgd rt 2f out: one pce* **20/1**
033 **5** 1¼ **All Clued Up (IRE)**[11] [3034] 3-8-12 55 .... ChrisCatlin 10 38
(Rae Guest) *led tl over 1f out: sn wknd* **12/1**
6 1¾ **Tetrode (USA)** 4-9-9 .... MickyFenton 5 39
(R M H Cowell) *chsd ldrs: edgd rt and wknd 2f out* **18/1**
00 **7** nk **Pronto Vende (IRE)**[11] [3050] 3-9-0 .... AdamKirby(3) 4 37
(G A Butler) *hld up in rr: bhd after 2f: sme hdwy 2f out: nvr a factor* **25/1**
0000 **8** 5 **Wilmas Gal**[12] [3006] 3-8-7 31 ....(t) AndrewMullen(5) 3 17
(R Bastiman) *sn outpcd: bhd after 2f* **66/1**
9 nk **Vibrato (USA)** 4-9-9 .... FrancisFerris 7 22
(C J Teague) *s.i.s: sn chsng ldrs: wknd over 2f out* **33/1**
00/6 **10** 24 **Villa Chigi (IRE)**[17] [2875] 4-9-9 46 .... GylesParkin 1 —
(G R Oldroyd) *sn bhd: virtually p.u fnl f* **66/1**

1m 17.67s (0.77) **Going Correction** +0.225s/f (Slow)
WFA 3 from 4yo 6lb **10** Ran SP% **126.5**
Speed ratings (Par 103):103,101,93,88,86 84,83,76,76,44
CSF £25.74 TOTE £11.70: £2.10, £1.10, £1.10; EX 39.70 Trifecta £44.60 Pool: £528.55 - 8.41 winning units. Place 6 £526.87, Place 5 £312.89..
Owner Sheikh Khaled Duaij Al Sabah **Bred** Irish National Stud **Trained** Newmarket, Suffolk

FOCUS
Like the first division, not many of these could be seriously considered, but a positive view has been taken of the form with the front pair clear. The winning time was over half a second faster than the previous race.
T/Jkpt: Not won. T/Plt: £575.30 to a £1 stake. Pool: £59,700.40. 75.75 winning tickets. T/Qpdt: £213.70 to a £1 stake. Pool: £2,975.10. 10.30 winning tickets. WG

3154 WOLVERHAMPTON (A.W) (L-H)
Tuesday, July 11

OFFICIAL GOING: Standard
Wind: Light; across

3385 WILLIAMHILLPOKER.COM MAIDEN AUCTION STKS 7f 32y(P)
6:50 (6:50) (Class 5) 2-Y-0 £3,238 (£963; £481; £240) Stalls High

Form RPR
1 **Supa Sal** 2-8-6 .... RyanMoore 7 71
(P F I Cole) *w ldr: led over 5f out: shkn up over 1f out: pushed out* **7/1**[3]
2 3 **Brenin Gwalia** 2-8-9 .... FergusSweeney 1 67
(D M Simcock) *led early: a.p: chsd wnr 2f out: sn rdn: no imp fnl f* **25/1**
2 **3** nk **Cape Schanck**[13] [2979] 2-8-11 .... JohnEgan 11 68
(Jane Chapple-Hyam) *s.i.s: sn in tch: rdn wl over 1f out: edgd lft ins fnl f: nt qckn* **11/10**[1]
4 3 **Arch Of Titus (IRE)** 2-8-12 .... JamieSpencer 5 61
(M L W Bell) *s.i.s: bhd tl rdn and hdwy on wd outside 2f out: kpt on ins fnl f: nt trble ldrs* **11/2**[2]
05 **5** ½ **Having A Ball**[15] [2938] 2-8-11 .... DaneO'Neill 3 59
(P D Cundell) *broke wl: sn stdd: hld up in mid-div: rdn and no hdwy fnl 2f* **33/1**
5 **6** 3 **Noverfancy (IRE)**[31] [2475] 2-8-2 .... NelsonDeSouza(3) 10 46
(M Botti) *prom tl wknd wl over 1f out* **12/1**
03 **7** 2½ **Mr Wall Street**[12] [2999] 2-8-13 .... TomEaves 9 47
(Mrs L Williamson) *s.i.s: bhd: rdn 3f out: nvr nr ldrs* **40/1**
8 ½ **Inflagrantedelicto (USA)** 2-8-12 .... RoystonFfrench 6 45
(M Johnston) *prom: rdn 3f out: sn wknd* **10/1**
046 **9** 7 **Spanish Air**[20] [2755] 2-8-0 .... JamesDoyle(5) 4 21
(J W Hills) *sn led: hdd over 5f out: rdn over 2f out: wknd wl over 1f out* **14/1**
10 7 **Swan Of Raunds** 2-8-8 .... DanielTudhope(3) 2 9
(J R Norton) *outpcd* **50/1**
000 **11** 41 **Marryl**[62] [1595] 2-8-10 ....(b[1]) PaulMulrennan 8 —
(M W Easterby) *s.i.s: a in rr: t.o fnl 4f* **100/1**

1m 29.93s (-0.47) **Going Correction** -0.25s/f (Stan) **11** Ran SP% **111.1**
Speed ratings (Par 94):92,88,88,84,84 80,77,77,69,61 14
CSF £164.85 TOTE £6.70: £1.60, £6.20, £1.10; EX 226.60.
Owner Ben & Sir Martyn Arbib **Bred** Arbib Bloodstock Partnership **Trained** Whatcombe, Oxon

FOCUS
With the favourite well below form this was probably not a strong race.

NOTEBOOK
Supa Sal ◆ is a half-sister to this season's mile winner Supaseus and ten- and twelve-furlong winner Swellmova. She probably could have done with a lead for longer but did her job well and can go on to better things. (op 13-2 tchd 15-2)
Brenin Gwalia only cost 3,500 gns and connections are entitled to be delighted with this debut against an above-average sort for the grade. (op 20-1)
Cape Schanck was sent off a hot favourite on the strength of his second in a similar event at Kempton last month. He could not overhaul the second let alone bother the winner. (op 4-5)
Arch Of Titus(IRE) is a half-brother to a dual winner in Norway. He had to come the scenic route but shaped promisingly enough in the closing stages. (op 7-1)
Having A Ball did run better over this longer distance but the improvement was hardly dramatic.

3386 WOLVERHAMPTON-RACECOURSE.CO.UK (S) H'CAP 1m 141y(P)
7:20 (7:20) (Class 6) (0-55,53) 3-Y-0+ £2,388 (£705; £352) Stalls Low

Form RPR
2502 **1** **Gem Bien (USA)**[4] [3263] 8-9-2 50 ....(b) TonyCulhane 7 61
(D W Chapman) *hld up in tch: led 2f out: rdn over 1f out: r.o* **6/1**[3]
-533 **2** 1¾ **Naval Attache**[12] [3014] 4-9-1 49 .... RyanMoore 4 56
(B R Johnson) *hld up in tch: rdn 2f out: kpt on ins fnl f: nt trble wnr* **9/2**[1]
6-50 **3** 1¾ **Able Mind**[13] [2966] 6-8-13 47 .... JohnEgan 2 50
(D W Thompson) *hld up in mid-div: hdwy over 2f out: chsd wnr wl over 1f out tl rdn and no ex ins fnl f* **15/2**
0000 **4** 1¼ **Samson Quest**[11] [3056] 4-9-0 53 ....(v) RoryMoore(5) 13 54
(G F Bridgwater) *hld up and bhd: rdn and hdwy on outside wl over 1f out: one pce fnl f* **16/1**
5323 **5** ¾ **Frank's Quest (IRE)**[32] [2413] 6-9-2 50 .... DaneO'Neill 11 49
(A B Haynes) *hld up in mid-div: rdn over 3f out: hdwy over 2f out: one pce fnl f* **8/1**
0532 **6** 2½ **Paso Doble**[32] [2413] 8-8-12 53 ....(v) JamesMillman(7) 5 47
(B R Millman) *bhd: rdn over 2f out: sme hdwy on ins over 1f out: nvr trbld ldrs* **9/1**
0004 **7** 1½ **Riska King**[77] [1217] 6-9-1 49 .... RoystonFfrench 9 40
(P A Blockley) *hld up towards rr: rdn over 2f out: sme hdwy over 1f out: n.d* **11/2**[2]
5100 **8** 1 **Welsh Whisper**[22] [2702] 7-8-9 46 .... NeilChalmers(3) 3 35
(S A Brookshaw) *s.i.s: a bhd* **16/1**
3120 **9** 4 **Bob Baileys**[57] [1723] 4-9-1 49 ....(b) SebSanders 1 29
(P R Chamings) *led: rdn and hdd 2f out: wknd over 1f out* **15/2**
000 **10** 2 **Maya's Prince**[10] [3073] 4-8-13 47 .... HayleyTurner 10 23
(M D I Usher) *prom: chsd ldr over 6f out: rdn and ev ch over 2f out: wknd wl over 1f out* **66/1**
2066 **11** 1½ **Eijaaz (IRE)**[8] [3139] 5-8-11 52 .... KristinStubbs(7) 12 25
(Mrs L Stubbs) *s.i.s: rdn over 3f out: a bhd* **14/1**
0-03 **12** 17 **Shaaban (IRE)**[11] [3051] 5-8-11 50 ....(p) LiamJones(5) 6 —
(R J Price) *nvr gng wl: sn bhd: t.o* **40/1**
0000 **13** 9 **Pyramid**[11] [3053] 4-9-0 48 .... BrianReilly 8 —
(P L Gilligan) *chsd ldr 2f: pushed along over 5f out: rdn over 3f out: wknd over 2f out: eased wl over 1f out: t.o* **33/1**

1m 49.69s (-2.07) **Going Correction** -0.25s/f (Stan) **13** Ran SP% **117.8**
Speed ratings (Par 101):99,97,95,94,94 91,90,86,84 83,67,59
CSF £32.26 CT £208.14 TOTE £3.30: £1.40, £1.80, £4.60; EX 20.40.There was no bid for the winner. Naval Attache was claimed by Paul Blockley for £6,000.
Owner J M Chapman **Bred** George Pruette **Trained** Stillington, N Yorks

FOCUS
An open-looking selling handicap. The form looks sound for the grade.
Pyramid Official explanation: jockey said gelding had been hanging badly left

3387 PUNCH TAVERNS RETAILERS MEDIAN AUCTION MAIDEN STKS 1m 141y(P)
7:50 (7:51) (Class 6) 3-4-Y-0 £2,730 (£806; £403) Stalls Low

Form RPR
2- **1** **Dash To The Front**[295] [5361] 3-8-12 .... JamieSpencer 13 73+
(J R Fanshawe) *hld up in mid-div: hdwy over 2f out: led 1f out: rdn out* **4/9**[1]
000 **2** 2 **Esteem**[26] [2587] 3-9-3 71 .... SebSanders 11 74
(W Jarvis) *a.p: led jst over 2f out: rdn whn edgd lft and hdd 1f out: sn hung rt: nt qckn* **11/1**
3 ¾ **Our Faye** 3-8-12 .... JohnEgan 6 67
(S Kirk) *hld up and bhd: hdwy on outside over 1f out: kpt on ins fnl f* **50/1**
00 **4** 1¼ **Evening**[25] [2615] 3-8-12 .... RyanMoore 10 65
(B W Hills) *hld up and bhd: hdwy on outside over 1f out: r.o one pce fnl f* **16/1**
50 **5** 3 **Stumped**[35] [2325] 3-9-3 ....(t) TonyCulhane 4 64
(W J Haggas) *hld up in mid-div: hdwy wl over 1f out: no further prog f fnl f* **9/1**[2]
6 shd **Pothos Way (GR)** 3-9-3 .... JimCrowley 7 63
(P R Chamings) *hld up in mid-div: rdn 3f out: hdwy 2f out: no further prog* **100/1**
3 **7** 2½ **Can Can Star**[27] [2542] 3-9-3 .... GrahamGibbons 8 58
(J G Given) *led: hdd over 6f out: rdn and ev ch 2f out: wknd over 1f out* **10/1**[3]
3564 **8** 1 **Pop Music (IRE)**[75] [1254] 3-9-0 72 .... DeanCorby(3) 9 56
(Miss J Feilden) *prom: led 3f out tl jst over 2f out: wknd fnl f* **14/1**
9 4 **Mill End (IRE)** 4-9-13 .... RichardMullen 2 48
(R M H Cowell) *hld up in tch: rdn over 2f out: wknd wl over 1f out* **66/1**
0 **10** ½ **Pickwick Miss (USA)**[26] [2575] 3-8-12 .... FergusSweeney 5 41
(D M Simcock) *s.i.s: rdn over 4f out: a bhd* **150/1**
0 **11** hd **Cankara (IRE)**[10] [3100] 3-8-9 .... DanielTudhope(3) 1 41
(D Carroll) *a bhd* **50/1**
60 **12** 5 **Midnight Diamond (IRE)**[34] [2366] 3-9-3 .... TomEaves 12 36
(Mrs L Williamson) *w ldr: led over 6f out to 3f out: sn wknd* **100/1**
00 **13** 3 **Miss Ruby**[26] [2587] 4-9-8 .... DaneO'Neill 3 24
(Rae Guest) *a bhd* **150/1**

1m 49.77s (-1.99) **Going Correction** -0.25s/f (Stan)
WFA 3 from 4yo 10lb **13** Ran SP% **117.9**
Speed ratings (Par 101):98,96,95,94,91 91,89,88,85,84 84,79,77
CSF £6.27 TOTE £1.40: £1.10, £1.90, £15.60; EX 10.60.
Owner Helena Springfield Ltd **Bred** Meon Valley Stud **Trained** Newmarket, Suffolk

FOCUS
A weakish maiden and not strong form.

3388 WILLIAMHILLCASINO.COM H'CAP 1m 4f 50y(P)
8:20 (8:20) (Class 5) (0-75,72) 3-Y-0+ £3,238 (£963; £481; £240) Stalls Low

Form RPR
0-12 **1** **Warsaw Pact (IRE)**[39] [2209] 3-8-11 68 .... SebSanders 5 88+
(Sir Mark Prescott) *mde all: hung rt ent back str over 5f out: pushed clr wl over 1f out: eased cl home* **8/15**[1]
6004 **2** 3 **Bowled Out (GER)**[12] [3009] 4-9-5 63 .... RichardMullen 8 67
(P J McBride) *hld up: hdwy 3f out: sn rdn to chse wnr: no imp* **16/1**
0-60 **3** nk **Plenty Cried Wolf**[41] [2150] 4-9-1 59 .... RoystonFfrench 4 63
(R A Fahey) *hld up in tch: rdn 4f out: styd on one pce fnl 2f* **50/1**
2023 **4** 5 **Digger Boy**[10] [3100] 3-8-11 68 .... PhilipRobinson 7 64
(M A Jarvis) *w wnr: rdn 3f out: wknd 2f out* **8/1**[3]
1202 **5** 5 **Caraman (IRE)**[10] [3098] 8-9-11 69 .... GrahamGibbons 3 57
(J J Quinn) *prom: rdn 3f out: wknd 2f out* **9/2**[2]
5000 **6** 16 **Monte Mayor Boy**[30] [2482] 4-8-11 55 ....(p) FrankieMcDonald 6 17
(D Haydn Jones) *bhd: pushed along 8f out: short-lived effrt over 3f out* **50/1**
0-00 **7** 5 **Archivist (IRE)**[19] [2795] 3-7-5 55 .... LauraReynolds(7) 2 9
(M Blanshard) *stmbld bdly and s.v.s: a in rr: t.o fnl 3f* **33/1**
1600 **8** 21 **Desperation (IRE)**[10] [3098] 4-10-0 72 .... JamieSpencer 1 —
(B D Leavy) *hld up: pushed along 8f out: rdn over 5f out: struggling whn eased 3f out: t.o* **22/1**

2m 38.68s (-3.74) **Going Correction** -0.25s/f (Stan)
WFA 3 from 4yo+ 13lb **8** Ran SP% **111.6**
Speed ratings (Par 103):102,100,99,96,93 82,79,65
CSF £9.97 CT £198.33 TOTE £1.50: £1.02, £2.90, £4.40; EX 9.30.
Owner J Fishpool - Osborne House **Bred** Saad Bin Mishrif **Trained** Newmarket, Suffolk

FOCUS
An uncompetitive handicap. The progressive winner was value for a wider-margin of victory, but the placed form is not strong.
Desperation(IRE) Official explanation: jockey said gelding had never been travelling

3389 WILLIAMHILL.CO.UK H'CAP 5f 216y(P)
8:50 (8:50) (Class 6) (0-60,60) 3-Y-0+ £2,730 (£806; £403) Stalls Low

Form RPR
3024 1 **Blessed Place**[4] [3245] 6-9-0 **53**....................................(t) JamieSpencer 6 64
(D J S Ffrench Davis) *sn led: edgd rt over 1f out: rdn out* **4/1**[1]
6005 2 1 ½ **Mind Alert**[11] [3052] 5-8-13 **52**....................................(v) JohnEgan 10 59
(S R Bowring) *hld up in mid-div: hdwy over 2f out: rdn over 1f out: kpt on ins fnl f: nt trble wnr* **15/2**
2201 3 ½ **Bodden Bay**[22] [2700] 4-8-13 **55**.................................... DanielTudhope(3) 8 60
(D Carroll) *a.p: rdn over 2f out: nt qckn ins fnl f* **8/1**
334/ 4 ½ **Athboy Nights (IRE)**[375] [3102] 4-8-13 **57**.................... DerekNolan(5) 12 61
(M J Wallace) *led early: hld up and sn lost pl: hdwy over 2f out: rdn wl over 1f out: kpt on ins fnl f* **20/1**
0000 5 1 **Sentiero Rosso (USA)**[11] [3041] 4-9-7 **60**..........................(t) TomEaves 5 61
(B Ellison) *chsd ldrs: rdn over 2f out: one pce fnl f* **9/1**
0042 6 hd **Peruvian Style (IRE)**[19] [2785] 5-8-11 **53**.................. NelsonDeSouza(3) 3 53
(J M Bradley) *a.p: rdn over 1f out: no ex ins fnl f* **6/1**[2]
0006 7 2 **El Potro**[12] [3004] 4-9-0 **53**.. RichardMullen 9 47
(J R Holt) *sn bhd: rdn over 2f out: sme hdwy over 1f out: n.d* **14/1**
2300 8 1 ¼ **Orchestration (IRE)**[19] [2792] 5-9-0 **53**..........................(v) FrancisFerris 13 43
(M J Attwater) *nvr nr ldrs* **16/1**
0360 9 ½ **Cherokee Nation**[12] [3004] 5-8-11 **53**..........................(v[1]) AdamKirby(3) 2 42
(P W D'Arcy) *hld up in tch: rdn and wknd over 2f out* **7/1**[3]
-000 10 ¾ **White Ledger (IRE)**[11] [3052] 7-8-13 **52**..........................(v) SebSanders 11 38
(R E Peacock) *sn bhd* **33/1**
0040 11 2 **Willofcourse**[15] [2920] 5-9-2 **55**..(v[1]) DaneO'Neill 4 35
(H Candy) *s.i.s: a bhd* **9/1**
0000 12 3 ½ **Bold Cheverak**[26] [2590] 4-8-12 **51**.. BrianReilly 1 21
(Mrs C A Dunnett) *mid-div: n.m.r on ins 4f out: sn bhd* **16/1**
-000 13 2 **Canary Island (IRE)**[14] [2955] 4-9-0 **58**.......................... JamesDoyle(5) 7 22
(J M Bradley) *chsd wnr: rdn 3f out: sn wknd* **50/1**

1m 14.33s (-1.48) **Going Correction** -0.25s/f (Stan) **13 Ran SP% 117.8**
Speed ratings (Par 101):99,97,96,95,94 94,91,89,89,88 85,80,78
CSF £31.99 CT £231.68 TOTE £5.50: £1.50, £2.20, £2.90; EX 29.20.
Owner S J Edwards **Bred** Mrs W H Gibson Fleming **Trained** Lambourn, Berks
■ Stewards' Enquiry : Derek Nolan one-day ban: failed to keep straight from stalls (Jul 22)

FOCUS
A tightly-knit low grade handicap. Modest, but sound form.

3390 WILLIAM HILL 0800 44 40 40 H'CAP 7f 32y(P)
9:20 (9:21) (Class 6) (0-60,60) 3-Y-0+ £2,730 (£806; £403) Stalls High

Form RPR
6004 1 **Captain Darling (IRE)**[126] [612] 6-8-10 **54**.......... EdwardCreighton(3) 10 67
(R W Price) *led after 1f: clr whn rdn over 1f out: r.o wl* **33/1**
3425 2 2 ½ **Taranaki**[8] [3153] 8-9-5 **60**.. SebSanders 8 67
(P D Cundell) *hld up in mid-div: hdwy on outside over 2f out: rdn to chse wnr over 1f out: no imp* **6/1**[3]
0664 3 nk **Spark Up**[10] [3099] 6-8-7 **53**....................................(b) StephenDonohoe(5) 4 59
(J W Unett) *s.i.s: bhd tl hdwy over 1f out: r.o ins fnl f* **9/1**
0465 4 hd **Mountain Pass (USA)**[6] [3204] 4-8-10 **56**....................(p) DerekNolan(5) 12 61
(M J Wallace) *hld up and bhd: hdwy 2f out: rdn and hung lft fr over 1f out: nt qckn* **20/1**
-561 5 shd **California Laws**[4] [3263] 4-9-0 **58** 6ex.......................... BenSwarbrick(3) 2 63
(T D Barron) *prom: lost pl on ins over 2f out: rallied wl over 1f out: one pce fnl f* **6/4**[1]
0000 6 ½ **Ronsard (IRE)**[91] [965] 4-9-5 **60**.. JohnEgan 9 64
(T J Pitt) *s.i.s: hdwy on outside fnl f: nvr nrr* **12/1**
0150 7 4 **Downland (IRE)**[17] [2874] 10-9-0 **55**.. KimTinkler 5 48
(N Tinkler) *prom: chsd wnr over 3f out: rdn over 2f out: lost 2nd over 1f out: wknd fnl f* **25/1**
4062 8 4 **Arian's Lad**[25] [2602] 5-8-5 **53**.. TolleyDean(7) 3 36
(B Palling) *led 1f: chsd wnr tl rdn over 3f out: wknd wl over 1f out* **14/1**
3000 9 ¾ **Tribute (IRE)**[19] [2780] 5-8-13 **54**............................(be[1]) GrahamGibbons 1 35
(P A Blockley) *prom: sn nt clr run on ins and lost pl: hdwy over 4f out: rdn over 2f out: sn wknd* **20/1**
6-00 10 shd **Mel's Moment (USA)**[9] [3116] 4-8-9 **55**.............................. LiamJones(5) 6 36
(R J Price) *hld up in tch: lost pl over 5f out: n.d after* **66/1**
4012 11 nk **Resplendent Prince**[19] [2793] 4-8-11 **57**....................(v) JamesDoyle(5) 7 37
(P Howling) *prom: rdn over 2f out: sn wknd* **10/1**
0660 12 29 **Tipsy Lad**[60] [1644] 4-8-13 **54**..(t) JamieSpencer 11 —
(D J S Ffrench Davis) *bhd: rdn over 3f out: no rspnse: eased whn no ch wl over 1f out* **5/1**[2]

1m 28.75s (-1.65) **Going Correction** -0.25s/f (Stan) **12 Ran SP% 122.2**
Speed ratings (Par 101):99,96,95,95,95 94,90,85,84,84 84,51
CSF £216.83 CT £1998.63 TOTE £40.60: £10.30, £1.30, £2.90; EX 459.50 Place 6 £28.92 Place 5 £19.90..
Owner Phil Pearce **Bred** Knocktoran Stud **Trained** Newmarket, Suffolk

FOCUS
A strong pace led to the fastest time of the meeting compared with standard. A modest handicap, but the form should prove reliable.
T/Plt: £30.10 to a £1 stake. Pool: £58,772.50. 1,423.95 winning tickets. T/Qpdt: £16.60 to a £1 stake. Pool: £3,151.30. 140.20 winning tickets. KH

3391 - 3393a (Foreign Racing) - See Raceform Interactive

3187 CATTERICK (L-H)
Wednesday, July 12

OFFICIAL GOING: Good to firm (firm in places)
The well watered ground was described as 'fast side of good with a very good cover of grass'.
Wind: Moderate; half against Weather: Overcast and cool

3394 MALTON SUITE (S) STKS 5f
2:10 (2:11) (Class 6) 2-Y-0 £2,730 (£806; £403) Stalls Low

Form RPR
0624 1 **Bowl Em Over**[16] [2922] 2-8-6 ....(p) RoystonFfrench 3 52
(M E Sowersby) *mde virtually all: kpt on wl ins last* **6/1**[3]
624 2 ¾ **Me And Mine (USA)**[19] [2806] 2-8-11 .... PhillipMakin 1 54
(T D Barron) *drvn along to chse ldrs: outpcd over 2f out: hrd rdn and kpt on to chal jst ins last: no ex* **4/5**[1]
65 3 1 **Lord Blue Boy**[81] [1142] 2-8-11 .... TonyCulhane 5 51
(W G M Turner) *t.k.h: w wnr: chal over 1f out: fdd wl ins last* **5/2**[2]
3400 4 1 ¾ **Minnie Magician**[37] [2294] 2-8-7 ow1................................ PatCosgrave 6 40
(C Grant) *chsd ldrs: kpt on same pce appr fnl f* **16/1**
0 5 1 **The Brat**[21] [2759] 2-8-3 .... PatrickMathers(3) 4 36
(James Moffatt) *chsd ldrs: rdn and wl outpcd over 2f out: kpt on fnl f* **12/1**

61.29 secs (0.69) **Going Correction** -0.05s/f (Good) **5 Ran SP% 112.0**
Speed ratings (Par 92):92,90,89,86,84
CSF £11.68 TOTE £7.50: £2.20, £1.10; EX 9.60.There was no bid for the winner.
Owner Keith Brown Properties (hull) Ltd **Bred** J A And Mrs M A Knox **Trained** Goodmanham, E Yorks

FOCUS
A poor race by selling race standards, run at just a steady pace and weak form.

NOTEBOOK
Bowl Em Over, with the cheekpieces back on, was given a canny ride from the front and in the end did enough. Races don't come much worse than this. (op 11-2 tchd 13-2)
Me And Mine(USA) looked to have been found a golden opportunity but, drawn one, his lack of early pace proved a handicap. Working hard to get upsides, he could never force his head in front. (op 8-11 tchd 10-11 and evens in places)
Lord Blue Boy, absent since April, went down best. He sat upsides on the bridle but tired noticeably in the final 75 yards. He might just have needed this. (op 4-1)
Minnie Magician, out of sorts on her two most recent starts, was dropping back to five. Highest drawn, she was always playing catch-up on the outer. (tchd 18-1)
The Brat, having just her second start, was soon struggling, but the fact that she finished as close as she did at the line emphasises the low quality of this seller.

3395 PADDOCK SUITE H'CAP 7f
2:45 (2:45) (Class 5) (0-75,76) 3-Y-0 £3,886 (£1,156; £577; £288) Stalls Low

Form RPR
3531 1 **Cindertrack**[8] [3164] 3-9-9 **76** 6ex.. ShaneKelly 4 84
(J A Osborne) *led over 1f: led over 3f out: qcknd over 2f out: hld on wl* **5/1**[2]
0554 2 ¾ **Final Tune (IRE)**[9] [3137] 3-8-10 **63**.............................. AdrianTNicholls 5 69
(D Nicholls) *chsd ldrs: sn drvn along: rallied 2f out: no ex ins last* **8/1**
6352 3 1 ½ **Viva Volta**[13] [3023] 3-9-5 **72**.. DavidAllan 1 74
(T D Easterby) *chsd ldrs: styd on same pce fnl f* **3/1**[1]
5554 4 ½ **Sir Orpen (IRE)**[11] [3087] 3-9-7 **74**.. PhillipMakin 2 75
(T D Barron) *trckd ldrs: outpcd over 2f out: swtchd rt 1f out: styd on* **3/1**[1]
2530 5 ½ **Il Castagno (IRE)**[11] [3067] 3-9-2 **74**.............................. MarkLawson(5) 7 73
(B Smart) *t.k.h: led over 5f out tl over 3f out: wknd ins last* **11/2**[3]
-331 6 1 ¾ **First Approval**[37] [2298] 3-9-7 **74**.. TonyCulhane 6 69
(B W Hills) *s.i.s: effrt over 2f out: nvr trbld ldrs* **6/1**
-560 7 1 ½ **Flylowflylong (IRE)**[14] [2977] 3-9-0 **67**............................ PaulMulrennan 3 58
(I Semple) *t.k.h: trckd ldrs: outpcd over 2f out: btn whn sltly hmpd 1f out* **12/1**
0000 8 ½ **The Thrifty Bear**[12] [3042] 3-8-9 **62**...................................... LeeEnstone 8 51
(C W Fairhurst) *t.k.h in rr: drvn 3f out: nvr a threat* **33/1**

1m 24.4s (-2.96) **Going Correction** -0.30s/f (Firm) **8 Ran SP% 118.1**
Speed ratings (Par 100):104,103,101,100,100 98,96,96
CSF £45.63 CT £142.71 TOTE £5.10: £1.70, £2.70, £1.40; EX 39.60.
Owner Mrs W W Fleming **Bred** Wyck Hall Stud Ltd **Trained** Upper Lambourn, Berks
■ Stewards' Enquiry : Phillip Makin one-day ban: careless riding (Jul 23)

FOCUS
An ordinary handicap but the form looks very sound.
First Approval Official explanation: jockey said filly was hampered on leaving stalls

3396 "TURMERIC" H'CAP 1m 7f 177y
3:20 (3:20) (Class 4) (0-85,80) 3-Y-0+ £6,477 (£1,927; £963; £481) Stalls Low

Form RPR
1-12 1 **Key Time (IRE)**[10] [3114] 4-8-13 **65**.. SebSanders 4 84+
(Sir Mark Prescott) *trckd ldrs: shkn up to ld 3f out: 12l clr 1f out: heavily eased* **2/5**[1]
5-51 2 5 **Industrial Star (IRE)**[40] [2196] 5-9-2 **68**.............................. TonyCulhane 3 72
(Micky Hammond) *sn detached in last and drvn along: laboured hdwy 4f out: kpt on u.str.p to go 2nd 1f out: no ch w wnr* **7/1**[2]
0040 3 3 ½ **Ten Carat**[11] [3078] 6-10-0 **80**..(b[1]) PatCosgrave 1 80
(M Todhunter) *drvn to take clr ld after 1f: jnd over 6f out: hdd 3f out: wknd 1f out* **18/1**
3030 4 8 **Double Obsession**[22] [2723] 6-9-12 **78**....................(b) AdrianTNicholls 2 68
(D Nicholls) *led 1f: chsd ldrs: rdn over 5f out: btn over 3f out* **9/1**[3]
06-2 5 10 **Patxaran (IRE)**[6] [3215] 4-9-2 **73**..(t) GregFairley(5) 6 51
(P C Haslam) *chsd ldrs: reminders 6f out: lost pl over 3f out: sn bhd* **9/1**[3]

3m 42.59s (11.19) **Going Correction** -0.30s/f (Firm) **5 Ran SP% 109.2**
Speed ratings (Par 105):60,57,55,51,46
CSF £3.66 TOTE £1.40: £1.10, £2.10; EX 2.90.
Owner G Moore - Osborne House **Bred** Airlie Stud **Trained** Newmarket, Suffolk

FOCUS
A totally one-sided contest with the facile winner still on the up and value for 13 lengths.
Double Obsession Official explanation: jockey said gelding hung left-handed throughout

3397 LUNCHEON SUITE H'CAP 5f 212y
3:55 (3:55) (Class 5) (0-70,70) 3-Y-0 £3,886 (£1,156; £577; £288) Stalls Low

Form RPR
-053 1 **Desert Hunter (IRE)**[23] [2701] 3-8-2 **51** oh1........................ JimmyQuinn 5 55
(Micky Hammond) *prom: hrd rdn: hung lft and hdwy 2f out: styd on to ld last strides* **9/2**[3]
0354 2 nk **Mulligan's Gold (IRE)**[14] [2976] 3-9-7 **70**............................ SebSanders 1 73
(T D Easterby) *sn chsng ldrs: led over 1f out: jst ct* **11/4**[1]
5653 3 shd **Thoughtsofstardom**[3] [3340] 3-8-0 **54**....................(p) DuranFentiman(5) 3 57
(P S McEntee) *prom: effrt over 2f out: styd on: no ex wl ins last* **13/2**
0010 4 ¾ **Seesawmilu (IRE)**[55] [1792] 3-8-3 **52**.......................... AdrianTNicholls 9 53+
(E J Alston) *hld up in tch: hdwy on ins over 2f out: nt clr run and swtchd rt ins last: r.o towards fin* **16/1**
0050 5 1 ¾ **Bold Tiger (IRE)**[3] [3329] 3-8-6 **55** ow2............................(b) GylesParkin 8 50
(Miss Tracy Waggott) *sn led: hdd over 1f out: wknd towards fin* **50/1**
-066 6 2 ½ **Musette (IRE)**[18] [2876] 3-8-2 **58** oh9 ow7................ MichaelJStainton(7) 7 46
(R E Barr) *sn outpcd and bhd: hdwy 2f out: kpt on ins last* **50/1**
5020 7 2 **Soviet Legend (IRE)**[62] [1612] 3-8-2 **51** oh1..............(v) RoystonFfrench 2 33
(T J Etherington) *chsd ldrs: wknd appr fnl f* **11/1**
2224 8 ½ **Northern Chorus (IRE)**[12] [3042] 3-9-4 **67**......................(v) DavidAllan 10 47+
(A Dickman) *led early: tk fierce hold: m v wd bnd and lost pl over 3f out: hdwy and edgd lft 2f out: sn fdd* **7/2**[2]
-332 9 1 ¾ **Discotheque (USA)**[32] [2445] 3-9-1 **64**................................ TonyCulhane 11 39
(P Howling) *sn outpcd and bhd: sme hdwy 2f out: nvr on terms* **8/1**
00-0 10 nk **Cole (IRE)**[41] [2163] 3-8-6 **55**.. PatCosgrave 6 29
(J Howard Johnson) *s.i.s: bhd tl sme late hdwy: nvr a factor* **33/1**
0-00 11 19 **Maayafushi**[70] [1413] 3-8-2 **51** oh6.. DaleGibson 4 —
(Micky Hammond) *s.i.s: a detached in last: t.o 2f out* **40/1**

1m 12.41s (-1.59) **Going Correction** -0.30s/f (Firm) **11 Ran SP% 115.0**
Speed ratings (Par 100):98,97,97,96,94 90,88,87,85,84 59
CSF £16.47 CT £78.31 TOTE £4.90: £1.80, £1.60, £2.30; EX 18.10.

Owner A Walker & Belarus Partnership **Bred** Meridian Stud **Trained** Middleham Moor, N Yorks
FOCUS
A modest handicap rated through the first two and the form does not look strong, limited by the fifth and sixth.
Discotheque(USA) Official explanation: jockey said filly was unsuited by the track

3398 MIDDLEHAM SUITE H'CAP 7f
4:30 (4:30) (Class 6) (0-65,65) 3-Y-0+ £2,730 (£806; £403) Stalls Low

Form RPR
0-21 **1** **Pay Time**[9] 3137 7-8-8 **52** 6ex.................................. MichaelJStainton(7) 1 64
(R E Barr) *chsd ldrs: led over 1f out: styd on wl: readily* **8/1**
6002 **2** *1 ¼* **Obe One**[8] 3171 6-9-1 **52**.................................. AdrianTNicholls 14 61
(D Nicholls) *s.i.s: hdwy and edgd rt over 1f out: styd on to take 2nd nr line* **8/1**
6042 **3** *hd* **Second Reef**[9] 3137 4-9-2 **53**.................................. ShaneKelly 12 61
(E J Alston) *hld up in mid-field: hdwy 2f out: tk 2nd ins last: no ex* **13/2**[2]
0331 **4** *1 ¼* **Joshua's Gold (IRE)**[16] 2936 5-9-4 **62**....................(v) KellyHarrison(7) 8 67
(D Carroll) *chsd ldrs: styd on same pce fnl f* **6/1**[1]
/035 **5** *2 ½* **Quicks The Word**[28] 2544 6-8-5 **47**.................................. GregFairley(5) 5 45
(T A K Cuthbert) *rr-div: hdwy over 2f out: kpt on same pce fnl f* **20/1**
0-02 **6** *hd* **Sir Don (IRE)**[26] 2611 7-9-2 **53**.................................. SebSanders 7 50
(E S McMahon) *mid-div: drvn 4f out: kpt on same pce fnl 2f* **7/1**[3]
0540 **7** *1* **Diamond Heritage**[10] 3112 4-8-6 **50**....................(b) MarkCoumbe(7) 17 45
(S Parr) *s.i.s: in rr tl kpt on fnl 2f: nvr nr ldrs* **66/1**
26-0 **8** *shd* **Sincerely**[11] 3099 4-9-9 **60**.................................. TonyCulhane 11 54
(B W Hills) *t.k.h in mid-field: kpt on fnl 2f: nvr a threat* **16/1**
2-00 **9** *1 ½* **Borodinsky**[60] 1683 5-8-8 **50**.................................. DuranFentiman(5) 15 40
(R E Barr) *bhd and drvn along: kpt on fnl 2f: nvr on terms* **20/1**
5501 **10** *nk* **Lord Mayfair (USA)**[7] 3189 4-8-6 **50** 6ex....................(b) AnnStokell(7) 3 40
(Miss A Stokell) *sn chsng ldrs: hung lft and wknd over 1f out* **12/1**
6260 **11** *hd* **Witchelle**[9] 3142 5-9-4 **58**.................................. DNolan(3) 10 47
(R Craggs) *sn led: hdd over 2f out: wknd fnl f* **20/1**
-516 **12** *1 ¼* **Outrageous Flirt (IRE)**[16] 2926 4-9-2 **53**.................................. DavidAllan 6 39+
(A Dickman) *bhd and drvn along: hdwy on ins and nt clr run 2f out: n.d after* **8/1**
13 *1* **Barry The Brave**[164] 4-10-0 **65**.................................. DeanMcKeown 9 48
(Micky Hammond) *s.i.s: a in rr* **33/1**
0500 **14** *nk* **Montana**[19] 2833 6-8-9 **46** oh1.................................. LeeEnstone 4 28
(C W Fairhurst) *led eraly: chsd ldr: led over 2f out tl over 1f out: wkng whn hmpd and heavily eased ins last* **33/1**
-000 **15** *2 ½* **Navigation (IRE)**[25] 2661 4-9-8 **59**.................................. RoystonFfrench 2 34
(T J Etherington) *mid-div: effrt over 2f out: sn wknd* **16/1**
0-23 **16** *5* **Riverhill (IRE)**[21] 2750 3-9-1 **60**.................................. PatCosgrave 13 19
(J Howard Johnson) *chsd ldrs on outer: lost pl 2f out: eased* **16/1**

1m 24.66s (-2.70) **Going Correction** -0.30s/f (Firm)
WFA 3 from 4yo+ 8lb 16 Ran SP% **120.5**
Speed ratings (Par 101):103,101,101,99,97 96,95,95,93,93 93,91,90,90,87 81
CSF £63.31 CT £466.95 TOTE £9.40: £2.10, £2.30, £1.90, £1.40; EX 92.60.
Owner Mrs R E Barr **Bred** M Paver And M D M Racing Thoroughbreds Ltd **Trained** Seamer, N Yorks
FOCUS
A searching gallop and a ready, bang-in-form winner. The form is only modest but has a solid look about it.
Lord Mayfair(USA) Official explanation: jockey said gelding was denied a clear run
Outrageous Flirt(IRE) Official explanation: jockey said filly was denied a clear run

3399 RICHMOND SUITE MEDIAN AUCTION MAIDEN STKS 1m 5f 175y
5:05 (5:05) (Class 5) 3-4-Y-0 £3,886 (£1,156; £577; £288) Stalls Low

Form RPR
4623 **1** **Soulard (USA)**[6] 3231 3-8-12 74....................(v) ShaneKelly 6 65
(J Noseda) *mde all: shkn up and qcknd over 3f out: edgd rt 2f out: styd on* **5/6**[1]
0044 **2** *1* **Estrelle (GER)**[6] 3209 4-9-8 70.................................. JimmyQuinn 4 59
(H R A Cecil) *trckd ldr: chal over 3f out: kpt on same pce fnl f* **7/4**[2]
-400 **3** *4* **Kalantera (IRE)**[26] 2607 3-8-12 58....................(v) SebSanders 2 58
(A M Balding) *trckd ldrs: chal 3f out: hrd rdn 2f out: hung lft and wknd appr fnl f* **8/1**[3]
0-06 **4** *8* **Gettysburg (IRE)**[29] 2529 3-8-12 49.................................. PatCosgrave 3 47
(J Howard Johnson) *hld up in tch: drvn and outpcd over 4f out: nvr a threat* **16/1**
0 **5** *37* **Salawat**[76] 1254 3-8-7 .... DeanMcKeown 1 —
(T T Clement) *in tch: lost pl over 7f out: t.o 4f out: btn 37l* **100/1**
-000 **6** *19* **Lady Luisa (IRE)**[5] 3266 4-9-1 32....................(t) AnnStokell(7) 5 —
(Miss A Stokell) *hld up in tch: lost pl over 6f out: t.o 5f out* **66/1**

2m 59.25s (-5.25) **Going Correction** -0.30s/f (Firm)
WFA 3 from 4yo 15lb 6 Ran SP% **110.4**
Speed ratings (Par 103):103,102,100,95,68 57
CSF £2.39 TOTE £1.90: £1.30, £1.10; EX 2.40 Place 6 £5.59, Place 5 £3.82.
Owner Budget Stable **Bred** Lazy Lane Stables Inc **Trained** Newmarket, Suffolk
FOCUS
A very weak maiden with the winner able to dictate things.
Salawat Official explanation: jockey said filly was unsuited by the good to firm (firm in places) ground
T/Plt: £6.20 to a £1 stake. Pool: £36,001.85 - 4,206.35 winning units. T/Qpdt: £2.50 to a £1 stake. Pool: £1,887.50 - 541.10 winning units. WG

3199 KEMPTON (A.W) (R-H)
Wednesday, July 12

OFFICIAL GOING: Standard
Wind: Virtually nil Weather: Fine

3400 REDACTIVE MEDIA GROUP FILLIES' H'CAP 1m 2f (P)
7:00 (7:02) (Class 5) (0-75,74) 3-Y-0 £3,238 (£963; £481; £240) Stalls High

Form RPR
1360 **1** **Odessa Star (USA)**[6] 3224 3-8-12 **65**.................................. OscarUrbina 3 74
(J G Portman) *s.i.s: hld up in rr: stdy hdwy on outside over 3f out: str run to ld ins fnl f: comf* **16/1**
2532 **2** *2 ½* **Shamila**[12] 3036 3-9-5 **72**.................................. JohnEgan 6 76+
(G A Butler) *s.i.s: sn in tch: hdwy 2f out: styd on to chse wnr ins fnl f but a readily hld* **8/1**[3]
2142 **3** *1 ¼* **Lucky Token (IRE)**[18] 2865 3-9-7 **74**.................................. GeorgeBaker 11 76
(E A L Dunlop) *disp ld tl def advantage after 3f: rdn 2f out: hdd ins fnl f: sn wknd and lost 2nd* **4/1**[2]
-664 **4** *1 ¾* **Snake Skin**[16] 2929 3-8-2 **55** oh3.................................. DavidKinsella 1 53
(J Gallagher) *s.i.s: sn rcvrd to chse ldrs: pushed along 2f out: wknd ins fnl f* **16/1**
6-63 **5** *½* **Theatre Royal**[16] 2932 3-8-9 **62**.................................. MartinDwyer 5 59
(A M Balding) *chsd ldrs: pushed along over 2f out: wknd fnl f* **9/4**[1]
-533 **6** *nk* **Veronica's Girl**[164] 234 3-9-5 **72**.................................. RichardHughes 2 69
(W J Knight) *bhd: shkn up and sme hdwy on ins 2f out: nvr rchd ldrs* **14/1**
6003 **7** *½* **Haiti Dancer**[19] 2814 3-8-3 **56**....................(v[1]) ChrisCatlin 7 52
(C G Cox) *disp ld 3f: styd chsng ldr tl wknd qckly 1f out* **8/1**[3]
0201 **8** *3 ½* **October Ben**[14] 2978 3-8-12 **65**.................................. FergusSweeney 10 54
(M D I Usher) *s.i.s: bhd: rapid hdwy on outside 4f out: chsd ldrs 3f out: wknd ins fnl 2f* **4/1**[2]
5-60 **9** *6* **Baileys Polka**[58] 1732 3-9-0 **67**.................................. JamieMackay 4 45
(J G Given) *in tch: rdn 3f out: sn btn* **50/1**
0 **10** *2 ½* **Rosalie**[32] 2434 3-8-12 **65**.................................. TPQueally 8 38
(C F Wall) *s.i.s: a in rr* **33/1**
3-60 **11** *1 ½* **Sophie'Jo**[14] 2990 3-9-1 **68**....................(v[1]) StephenCarson 9 38
(H R A Cecil) *chsd ldrs: rdn over 4f out: wknd rapidly 3f out* **16/1**

2m 8.59s (-0.41) **Going Correction** +0.10s/f (Slow) 11 Ran SP% **122.2**
Speed ratings (Par 97):105,103,102,100,100 99,99,96,91,89 88
CSF £143.62 CT £625.25 TOTE £22.50: £5.50, £2.40, £1.80; EX 225.10.
Owner Pump Technology Limited **Bred** Sugar Maple Farm **Trained** Compton, Berks
FOCUS
Only a modest handicap for fillies but the form is sound rated through the placed horses. The winner goes well on an All-Weather surface, while the runner-up seems to like being runner-up.
Haiti Dancer Official explanation: jockey said filly hung right

3401 LEONARD CURTIS H'CAP 1m 2f (P)
7:28 (7:31) (Class 3) (0-90,88) 3-Y-0+
£7,790 (£2,332; £1,166; £583; £291; £146) Stalls High

Form RPR
1541 **1** **Acrobatic (USA)**[21] 2754 3-8-10 **81**.................................. RichardHughes 4 96+
(R Charlton) *led 2f: styd trcking ldr tl led appr fnl 2f: drvn 5l clr over 1f out: kpt that advantage and r.o strly* **2/1**[1]
1530 **2** *5* **Obrigado (USA)**[18] 2848 6-10-0 **88**.................................. DarryllHolland 5 94+
(W J Haggas) *stdd s: hld up in rr:stl plenty to do 2f out:swtchd to rail and rapid hdwy fnl f and sn 2nd: but no ch w wnr* **5/1**[3]
5-60 **3** *1* **Punta Galera (IRE)**[39] 2224 3-9-2 **87**.................................. DaneO'Neill 10 91
(R Hannon) *prom: chsd wnr over 1f out but nvr any ch: outpcd and lost 2nd ins last* **20/1**
04-6 **4** *1 ¼* **Buster Hyvonen (IRE)**[26] 2621 4-8-12 **72**.................................. OscarUrbina 1 74
(J R Fanshawe) *rr but in tch: hday 3f out: styd on fr 2f out but nvr gng pce to rch ldr: sn one pce* **7/2**[2]
6-52 **5** *3 ½* **Jack Of Trumps (IRE)**[61] 1631 6-9-11 **85**.................................. SteveDrowne 8 80
(G Wragg) *chsd ldrs: rdn over 2f out: wknd qckly fnl f* **15/2**
-215 **6** *1 ¼* **Custodian (IRE)**[147] 421 4-8-9 **69** oh1.................................. EddieAhern 6 62
(H R A Cecil) *chsd ldrs: rdn 3f out: wknd 2f out* **14/1**
0402 **7** *¾* **Dower House**[32] 2447 11-9-8 **82**....................(t) ChrisCatlin 3 73
(Andrew Turnell) *bhd: rdn over 3f out and styd on same pce: nvr nrr* **16/1**
2-20 **8** *4* **Master Of The Race**[25] 2657 4-9-8 **82**.................................. MartinDwyer 2 66
(Sir Michael Stoute) *plld hrd: led after 2f: hdd appr fnl 2f and wknd rapidly* **7/1**
4015 **9** *shd* **Charlie Kennet**[21] 2752 8-8-5 **70**.................................. RichardKingscote(5) 11 53
(Mrs H Sweeting) *chsd ldrs: rdn 3f out: sn wknd* **22/1**
0100 **10** *2 ½* **Cool Hunter**[34] 2387 5-9-9 **83**....................(v[1]) TedDurcan 9 62
(W R Swinburn) *in tch: rdn 3f out and sn wknd* **20/1**
1-00 **11** *7* **Highest Regard**[11] 3101 4-9-1 **75**.................................. BrianReilly 7 40
(P L Gilligan) *plld hrd in rr: a bhd* **50/1**

2m 7.23s (-1.77) **Going Correction** +0.10s/f (Slow)
WFA 3 from 4yo+ 11lb 11 Ran SP% **124.9**
Speed ratings (Par 107):111,107,106,105,102 101,100,97,97,95 89
CSF £12.38 CT £166.04 TOTE £3.20: £1.40, £2.60, £7.20; EX 18.00.
Owner K Abdulla **Bred** Juddmonte Farms Inc **Trained** Beckhampton, Wilts
FOCUS
A solid-looking handicap won by a horse given a positive ride and rated around the fourth.
NOTEBOOK
Acrobatic(USA), whose last success at the course worked out really well, enjoyed the run of the race and was most impressive in victory. A horse with winning form on turf and an All-Weather surface, he can win another handicap at least before connections consider anything in better company. (op 5-2 and 3-1 in places and 11-4 in places)
Obrigado(USA), who is still 8lb higher in the weights than his last victory, needs riding a certain way - held up off a strong pace - and got his optimum race conditions throughout the race. However, punters on this occasion could afford to feel a little aggrieved that they did not get more of a run for their money, as he had plenty to do turning down the side of the course. A longer run-in, even though he has won over the trip at Kempton before, would suit him. (op 9-2)
Punta Galera(IRE), dropping in grade, failed to live with the winner as he quickened away, but kept on well enough to hold the chasing bunch at bay. He is probably not the easiest horse to place at the moment off his current handicap mark, but connections are sure to find the right opportunities for him. (op 25-1)
Buster Hyvonen(IRE) once again gave the impression that he would have been ideally suited by racing over further than this trip. He is capable of winning more races but is now starting to look a bit exposed. (op 5-1 tchd 11-2)
Jack Of Trumps(IRE) is still racing off a mark above his last winning one, and will not really be of any serious interest until dropped a few more pounds. (op 6-1 tchd 8-1)
Dower House had quite a lot to do off the pace and was never nearer. (op 14-1)
Master Of The Race, again fitted with a sheepskin noseband, led the field early before dropping out under pressure. He is probably better suited by coming off the pace, but, even then, can never be expected to put his best forward. (tchd 15-2 and 8-1 in a place)
Charlie Kennet Official explanation: jockey said gelding ran flat

3402 EUROPEAN BREEDERS FUND MEDIAN AUCTION MAIDEN FILLIES' STKS 6f (P)
7:56 (7:59) (Class 4) 2-Y-0 £4,533 (£1,348; £674; £336) Stalls High

Form RPR
1 **Pinkabout (IRE)** 2-9-0 .... JimmyFortune 3 76+
(J H M Gosden) *in tch: rapid hdwy on outside 2f out:led wl over 1f out:sn hung rt to far rail: qcknd clr: pushed out* **9/2**[2]
0 **2** *2 ½* **Bright Moon**[15] 2957 2-9-0 .... DaneO'Neill 1 69
(R Hannon) *sn chsng ldr: rdn: hmpd and outpcd over 1f out: styd on again fnl f to take 2nd last strides: no ch w wnr* **25/1**
320 **3** *nk* **Baltic Belle (IRE)**[19] 2800 2-9-0 .... RichardHughes 10 68
(R Hannon) *sn led: rdn and over 2f out: hdd wl over 1f out: no ch w wnr fnl f: lost 2nd last strides* **4/9**[1]
0 **4** *¾* **Astroangel**[25] 2638 2-9-0 .... NCallan 8 65
(M H Tompkins) *chsd ldrs: wnt 2nd 2f out: styd on one pce fnl f* **50/1**

45 **5** *1 1/4* **Miss Ippolita**[47] 1989 2-9-0 .... EddieAhern 11 62
(J R Jenkins) *chsd ldrs: rdn 2f out: outpcd appr fnl f* **10/1**[3]
6 *3 1/2* **Eastern Princess** 2-9-0 .... RichardThomas 9 51
(J A Geake) *s.i.s: sn in tch: rdn 3f out: wknd ins fnl 2f* **33/1**
7 *1 1/4* **Artistic Liason** 2-9-0 .... ChrisCatlin 6 47
(G C H Chung) *slowly away: bhd: sme hdwy over 2f out but nvr in contention* **22/1**
8 *3* **Inimical** 2-9-0 .... FergusSweeney 5 38
(W S Kittow) *bhd: brief effrt 3f out but nvr in contention* **25/1**
00 **9** *17* **Pineapple Poll**[12] 3043 2-9-0 .... BrianReilly 4 —
(P L Gilligan) *a outpcd* **66/1**

1m 16.29s (2.59) **Going Correction** +0.10s/f (Slow) **9** Ran SP% **115.0**
Speed ratings (Par 93):86,82,82,81,79 74,73,69,46
CSF £97.91 TOTE £4.20: £1.20, £4.10, £1.02; EX 38.30.
Owner H R H Princess Haya Of Jordan **Bred** Swordlestown Stud **Trained** Newmarket, Suffolk
■ Stewards' Enquiry : Jimmy Fortune one-day ban: careless riding (Jul 23)

FOCUS
A fair maiden run at only a modest early gallop. The winner looks smart but the form is anything but solid.

NOTEBOOK
Pinkabout(IRE), a half-sister to Carry On Katie, a very good juvenile in 2003, showed a tremendous turn of foot when asked to quicken and, despite hanging over to the inside rail from the middle of the track, won very impressively. She looks certain to hold her own in much better company. (op 11-4)
Bright Moon, a stablemate of the odds-on favourite, was outdone by the winner's burst of speed and never had an answer to that move. She did, however, keep on well for pressure and looks sure to win any ordinary maiden. (op 33-1)
Baltic Belle(IRE), who ran respectably in the Albany Stakes at Royal Ascot, set the race up from the front but was left behind when Pinkabout flew past. There can be little doubt she bumped into a potentially smart sort, but a seventh furlong at least still looks required. (op 8-11 tchd 4-5 in a place)
Astroangel shaped much more encouragingly after a modest debut effort, and can progress again for a step up in trip.
Miss Ippolita, who finished just behind Sander Camillo last time, has now had three races and one would believe that nurseries are the objective with her. (op 11-1 tchd 12-1)
Artistic Liason was well beaten by the principals but did not shape without some promise. If making normal progress, she should be more competitive next time kept to ordinary company. (op 16-1)
Pineapple Poll Official explanation: jockey said filly stumbled on leaving stalls

3403 AMIGO H'CAP 6f (P)
8:24 (8:26) (Class 4) (0-85,80) 3-Y-O **£5,505** (£1,637; £818; £408) **Stalls** High

Form RPR
-330 **1** **Sant Elena**[18] 2865 3-9-0 **73** .... SteveDrowne 5 85
(G Wragg) *trckd ldrs: drvn to take slt ld over 1f out: drvn and kpt on wl cl home* **12/1**
0-61 **2** *1 1/4* **Greek Renaissance (IRE)**[12] 3053 3-9-7 **80** .... MartinDwyer 9 91+
(M P Tregoning) *hld up in tch: hdwy on rails over 2f out: nt clr run 1f out and ins last: swtchd lft and qckng cl home to take 2nd* **11/8**[1]
4203 **3** *hd* **Woodnook**[21] 2756 3-9-1 **74** .... JimmyFortune 6 82
(J A R Toller) *in tch: hdwy over 1f out: qckng and r.o wl fnl f but nvr gng pce of wnr: ct for 2nd cl home* **7/1**
-032 **4** *nk* **Matuza (IRE)**[30] 2509 3-9-7 **80** .... JohnEgan 7 87
(W R Muir) *chsd ldrs: t.k.h: drvn and qcknd to chal over 1f out: nt qckn last half f* **3/1**[2]
50-0 **5** *2 1/2* **Violet Ballerina (IRE)**[53] 1843 3-9-2 **75** .... IanMongan 8 75
(B J Meehan) *s.i.s: bhd: pushed along over 2f out: kpt on fr over 1f out but nvr gng pce to rch ldrs* **25/1**
-155 **6** *2* **Spiritual Peace (IRE)**[28] 2553 3-9-5 **78** .... NCallan 4 72
(K A Ryan) *led tl hdd over 1f out: wknd ins last* **9/1**
0462 **7** *hd* **Rapsgate (IRE)**[11] 3087 3-8-13 **72** .... (b) RichardHughes 3 65
(R Hannon) *bhd: sme hdwy on ins over 2f out: nvr rchd ldrs and sn one pce* **16/1**
6056 **8** *1 1/4* **Brunelleschi**[11] 3087 3-8-11 **70** .... (v) ChrisCatlin 10 59
(P L Gilligan) *sn wl off the pce in rr: kpt on fr over 1f out but nvr in contention* **25/1**
1052 **9** *1/2* **Blushing Thief (USA)**[14] 2981 3-9-7 **80** .... (b) EddieAhern 2 68
(W Jarvis) *chsd ldrs: rdn 2f out: wknd ins fnl 2f* **13/2**[3]

1m 13.76s (0.06) **Going Correction** +0.10s/f (Slow) **9** Ran SP% **124.2**
Speed ratings (Par 102):103,101,101,100,97 94,94,92,92
CSF £31.23 CT £136.25 TOTE £14.20: £3.60, £1.10, £2.60; EX 35.90.
Owner The Eclipse Partnership **Bred** Car Colston Hall Stud **Trained** Newmarket, Suffolk

FOCUS
A decent sprint handicap tghat appears sound enough with those immediately behind the first two close to form and a race likely to produce winners.

3404 MARTIN COLLINS ENTERPRISES H'CAP (LONDON MILE QUALIFIER) 1m (P)
8:52 (8:54) (Class 4) (0-80,80) 3-Y-O+ **£5,505** (£1,637; £818; £408) **Stalls** High

Form RPR
3052 **1** **Tumbleweed Glory (IRE)**[13] 3008 3-9-5 **78** .... TedDurcan 9 87
(B J Meehan) *hld up in rr: stdy hdwy fr 3f out: drvn and qcknd to ld jst ins fnl f: hld on all out* **10/1**
31 **2** *hd* **Our Putra**[16] 2934 3-9-4 **77** .... (t) PhilipRobinson 2 85
(M A Jarvis) *hld up in tch: stdy hdwy on outside 3f out: qcknd to chal appr fnl: str burst cl home: jst failed* **4/1**[2]
0000 **3** *1 3/4* **Logsdail**[12] 3044 6-9-2 **66** .... (p) IanMongan 8 72
(G L Moore) *behind: hdwy fr 3f out: drvn to chal ins last: outpcd cl home* **9/2**[3]
0001 **4** *nk* **Out For A Stroll**[3] 3339 7-8-8 **61** 6ex .... SaleemGolam(3) 5 67
(S C Williams) *chsd ldrs: led ins fnl 2f: hdd jst ins last: kpt on same pce* **3/1**[1]
5203 **5** *nk* **Mujood**[7] 3202 3-9-5 **78** .... (p) StephenCarson 1 81
(R F Johnson Houghton) *bhd: hdwy 3f out: chsd ldrs over 1f out: outpcd ins last* **16/1**
-065 **6** *3 1/2* **Kingsholm**[48] 1957 4-9-9 **73** .... MartinDwyer 3 70
(A M Balding) *bhd: hdwy on ins 3f out: chsd ldrs ins fnl 2f: wknd fnl f* **10/1**
4400 **7** *8* **Feu D'Artifice (USA)**[14] 2990 3-9-0 **73** .... (b) RichardHughes 14 50
(R Hannon) *disp ld tl slt advantage 3f out: hdd ins fnl 2f: wknd fnl f* **16/1**
5-34 **8** *2* **Rowan Lodge (IRE)**[14] 2983 4-9-11 **75** .... (b) TPQueally 4 49
(M H Tompkins) *sn trcking ldrs: pushed along 3f out: wknd over 2f out* **12/1**
4-60 **9** *8* **Mr Rooney (IRE)**[21] 2760 3-9-7 **80** .... KDarley 7 34
(M Johnston) *chsd ldrs: rdn 3f out: wknd over 2f out* **20/1**
2330 **10** *18* **White Bear (FR)**[32] 2464 4-9-2 **66** .... (b) HayleyTurner 13 —
(C R Dore) *sn rdn in rr: a bhd* **20/1**
00-0 **11** *shd* **Jay Gee's Choice**[14] 2983 6-9-11 **75** .... GeorgeBaker 12 —
(B G Powell) *in tch 5f* **50/1**
1166 **12** *3/4* **Indian Edge**[28] 2551 5-9-6 **70** .... FrancisFerris 11 —
(B Palling) *sn slt ld: hdd 3f out: wknd sn after* **16/1**
-400 **13** *nk* **Reaching Out (IRE)**[12] 3048 4-9-4 **68** .... DarryllHolland 10 —
(N P Littmoden) *a in rr* **16/1**
0-00 **14** *nk* **Wrighty Almighty (IRE)**[28] 2555 4-10-0 **78** .... EddieAhern 6 —
(P R Chamings) *chsd ldrs tl wknd ins fnl 3f* **20/1**

1m 39.88s (-0.92) **Going Correction** +0.10s/f (Slow)
WFA 3 from 4yo+ 9lb **14** Ran SP% **128.8**
Speed ratings (Par 105):108,107,106,105,105 101,93,91,83,65 65,65,64,64
CSF £50.88 CT £222.70 TOTE £11.50: £2.30, £1.70, £3.10; EX 50.30.
Owner The Tumbleweed Partnership **Bred** Kilcarn Stud **Trained** Manton, Wilts

FOCUS
A competitive handicap and the time was good, suggesting the form is solid and reliable.
White Bear(FR) Official explanation: jockey said gelding bled from the nose
Reaching Out(IRE) Official explanation: jockey said gelding lost its action
Wrighty Almighty(IRE) Official explanation: jockey said gelding had no more to give

3405 WEATHERBYS VAT SERVICES APPRENTICE H'CAP (ROUND 6) 7f (P)
9:20 (9:26) (Class 5) (0-70,67) 3-Y-O+ **£3,238** (£963; £481; £240) **Stalls** High

Form RPR
0014 **1** **Mister Elegant**[9] 3158 4-8-11 **55** .... JamieHamblett(5) 2 64
(J L Spearing) *trckd ldrs: hung lft to centre crse over 2f out: edgd rt and hdwy over 1f out: styd on to ld fnl 50yds* **7/2**[2]
6000 **2** *3/4* **Seneschal**[14] 2971 5-9-11 **64** .... ThomasO'Brien 9 71
(A B Haynes) *chsd ldrs: led over 1f out: hdd and no ex fnl 50yds* **10/3**[1]
-014 **3** *1 1/4* **Vibe**[16] 2920 5-8-11 **50** .... JamieJones 3 54
(A W Carroll) *rr but in tch: rdn and hdwy over 1f out: styd on ins last but nvr gng pce to chal ldrs* **5/1**[3]
30-0 **4** *1* **My Michelle**[64] 1568 5-8-5 **49** .... WilliamCarson(5) 10 50
(B Palling) *chsd ldrs: rdn over 2f out: kpt on same pce fnl f* **7/1**
000 **5** *2 1/2* **Helen Wood**[21] 2753 3-7-10 **48** oh3 .... FrankiePickard(5) 5 40
(M D I Usher) *sn led: hdd over 1f out and sn btn* **14/1**
000- **6** *14* **Arkholme**[86] 4005 5-9-9 **67** .... (b) JosephWalsh(5) 1 26
(A M Hales) *slowly away: sn in tch: wknd over 3f out* **20/1**

1m 29.13s (2.33) **Going Correction** +0.10s/f (Slow)
WFA 3 from 4yo+ 8lb **6** Ran SP% **85.9**
Speed ratings (Par 103):90,89,87,86,83 67
CSF £8.45 CT £15.98 TOTE £3.60: £2.10, £1.50; EX 10.60 Place 6 £34.24, Place 5 £7.34.
Owner M Lawrence & W Cooper **Bred** J Spearing And Kate Ive **Trained** Kinnersley, Worcs
■ Arian's Lad (11/4F, ref ent stalls), Tom Forest (7/1, bolted bef s), & Tipsy Lad (7/1, reared over in stalls) all WD. R4, deduct 45p.

FOCUS
A plethora of non-runners and withdrawals for one reason or another, but Mister Elegant put up a fair performance and won with a bit to spare. The form does not looks that solid and is best rated around the winner and third.
Arkholme Official explanation: jockey said gelding hung right
T/Plt: £24.60 to a £1 stake. Pool: £59,494.80. 1,760.55 winning tickets. T/Qpdt: £3.70 to a £1 stake. Pool: £3,373.00. 663.70 winning tickets. ST

3070 LINGFIELD (L-H)
Wednesday, July 12

OFFICIAL GOING: Turf course - good to firm; all-weather - standard
Wind: Almost nil

3406 LINGFIELDPARK.CO.UK MEDIAN AUCTION MAIDEN STKS 6f (P)
1:45 (1:46) (Class 5) 3-4-Y-O **£3,238** (£963; £481; £240) **Stalls** Low

Form RPR
6 **1** **Al Qasi (IRE)**[18] 2868 3-9-3 .... AdrianMcCarthy 10 85+
(P W Chapple-Hyam) *chsd ldng gp: effrt on wd outside bnd 2f out: led ins fnl f: sn clr* **7/4**[1]
0300 **2** *4* **Even Bolder**[12] 3055 3-9-0 67 .... StephaneBreux(3) 11 70
(S Kirk) *pressed ldr: rdn to chal 2f out: upsides ent fnl f: sn outpcd by wnr* **10/1**
2020 **3** *1 1/4* **Bobby Rose**[13] 3011 3-9-3 64 .... TPQueally 6 66
(D K Ivory) *trckd ldrs: rdn and effrt wl over 1f out: kpt on one pce* **7/2**[2]
2265 **4** *hd* **Best Double**[13] 3000 3-8-12 66 .... FJohansson 9 61
(G A Butler) *dwlt: hld up in last pair: gng wl enough but stl in last pair wl over 1f out: rdn and r.o wl fnl f: hopeless task* **11/2**[3]
0200 **5** *1/2* **Lady Zanzara (USA)**[73] 1312 3-8-12 57 .... WandersonD'Avila 8 59
(J W Hills) *dwlt: towards rr: effrt and hmpd wl over 1f out: pushed along and kpt on: n.d* **33/1**
6 *nk* **Fastrac Boy** 3-9-3 .... LPKeniry 7 63
(J R Best) *led: rdn 2f out: hdd & wknd rapidly ins fnl f* **40/1**
000 **7** *1 1/4* **Cativo Cavallino**[11] 3094 3-9-3 62 .... PaulDoe 5 60
(Jamie Poulton) *chsd ldrs: drvn wl over 1f out: no rspnse: fdd fnl f* **14/1**
4- **8** *1/2* **Fen Guest**[358] 3614 3-8-5 .... RobbieMills(7) 3 53
(Rae Guest) *towards rr: outpcd over 2f out: urged along and no ch after: kpt on last 100yds* **11/1**
60 **9** *4* **Tajjree**[10] 3112 3-8-12 .... (p) StephenCarson 4 41
(Miss K B Boutflower) *prom: drvn on inner 2f out: wknd rapidly over 1f out* **20/1**
305 **10** *1* **King Of Charm (IRE)**[12] 3034 3-9-3 62 .... (b1) JimCrowley 12 43
(G L Moore) *prom tl wknd v rapidly wl over 1f out* **20/1**
11 *1 1/2* **Granakey (IRE)** 3-8-9 .... DominicFox(3) 2 34
(M G Quinlan) *s.s: a in last pair: lost tch 1/2-way* **40/1**

1m 12.11s (-0.70) **Going Correction** +0.10s/f (Slow) **11** Ran SP% **115.4**
Speed ratings (Par 103):104,98,97,96,96 95,94,93,88,86 84
CSF £18.57 TOTE £2.80: £1.40, £4.10, £1.40; EX 33.10 Trifecta £140.10 Pool: £205.30 - 1.04 winning units.
Owner Ziad A Galadari **Bred** T C Butler **Trained** Newmarket, Suffolk

FOCUS
A typically weak older-horse sprint maiden for the time of year, but a potentially useful winner in Al Qasi and the form has been rated positively.

3407 LINGFIELD PARK GOLF COURSE MAIDEN AUCTION STKS (DIV I) 6f (P)
2:20 (2:22) (Class 5) 2-Y-O **£2,590** (£770; £385; £192) **Stalls** Low

Form RPR
4 **1** **Lakshmi (IRE)**[15] 2957 2-8-7 .... ChrisCatlin 1 71+
(M R Channon) *chsd ldr: urged along and led over 1f out: rdn clr fnl f* **6/5**[1]

3 **2** *3 ½* **Smokey Oakey (IRE)**[16] [2930] 2-8-12 .... TPQueally 4 65
(M H Tompkins) *chsd ldng pair: rdn and effrt over 1f out: kpt on same pce to take 2nd ins fnl f* **9/4**[2]

605 **3** *2 ½* **Bookiesindex Boy**[18] [2878] 2-8-12 ....(b[1]) RobertHavlin 9 58
(J R Jenkins) *led: rdn and hdd over 1f out: sn btn* **40/1**

4 *5* **Madam Gaffer** 2-8-3 .... KMay(7) 6 41
(B J Meehan) *s.s: rn green in rr and nvr on terms: wnt remote 4th on inner over 1f out* **33/1**

6 **5** *1* **Ambrosiano**[27] [2579] 2-9-1 .... GeorgeBaker 10 43
(Miss E C Lavelle) *rn green but sn chsd ldrs: qckly outpcd 2f out: no ch after* **11/2**[3]

00 **6** *1* **Fongalong**[13] [3026] 2-8-1 .... EdwardCreighton(3) 5 29+
(Tom Dascombe) *outpcd and a wl in rr: no ch whn nt clr run wl over 1f out* **14/1**

0 **7** *1 ¼* **Iced Tango**[29] [2530] 2-8-9 .... PaulFitzsimons 3 30
(F Jordan) *chsd ldrs but nvr on terms: struggling fr 1/2-way* **100/1**

8 *3 ½* **Hucking Heat (IRE)** 2-9-1 .... LPKeniry 2 25
(J R Best) *chsd ldrs but nvr on terms: struggling bef 1/2-way: wknd fnl f* **25/1**

0005 **9** *18* **Piccolo Prezzo**[15] [2950] 2-8-4 .... FrancisFerris 7 —
(I A Wood) *v fractious in stalls: removed and reloaded: nvr happy: t.o after 2f* **33/1**

1m 13.91s (1.10) **Going Correction** +0.10s/f (Slow) **9** Ran SP% **111.4**
Speed ratings (Par 94):96,91,88,81,80 78,77,72,48
CSF £3.57 TOTE £2.10: £1.10, £1.40, £11.20; EX 4.40 Trifecta £38.00 Pool: £331.32 - 6.18 winning units.
Owner Box 41 **Bred** The Lavington Stud **Trained** West Ilsley, Berks

FOCUS
A weak maiden, but quite a nice performance from Lakshmi. The winning time was slightly faster than the second division.

NOTEBOOK
Lakshmi(IRE) ♦, an encouraging fourth on her debut at Newbury, would have found the race less competitive but still appeared to show improved form and was a most decisive winner. Considering she has not beaten a great deal, the Handicapper should not be too harsh and she may get into nurseries off a fair mark. (op Evens tchd 5-4 in places)
Smokey Oakey(IRE), beaten only a head and a neck in an ordinary maiden at Windsor on his debut, seemed to run his race but was no match whatsoever for the winner. (tchd 2-1)
Bookiesindex Boy has looked very quirky on his last two runs, swerving left both times, but he had shown ability in a good maiden at Newmarket on his debut and, fitted with blinkers for the first time, he confirmed that initial promise, behaving better this time. He is not one to give up on just because of his wayward tendencies and, with speed to burn, he could do even better over five furlongs.
Madam Gaffer, a 16,500gns half-sister to five winners, including high-class sprinter Pivotal Point, out of a fair triple five- to seven-furlong winner, made a pleasing introduction under a 7lb claimer and should improve quite a bit for the experience.
Ambrosiano still seemed in need of the experience and failed to confirm the promise he showed on his debut at Newbury. (op 7-1)

3408 LINGFIELD PARK GOLF COURSE MAIDEN AUCTION STKS (DIV II) 6f (P)
2:55 (2:56) (Class 5) 2-Y-O **£2,590** (£770; £385; £192) **Stalls** Low

Form RPR
0 **1** **Ede's Dot Com (IRE)**[16] [2930] 2-8-12 .... PaulDoe 9 74+
(W J Knight) *trckd ldr after 2f: rdn to ld wl over 1f out: clr fnl f: eased nr fin* **4/1**[2]

42 **2** *1 ¾* **Early Promise (IRE)**[15] [2950] 2-8-6 ow2.............................. BrianReilly 4 63
(P L Gilligan) *trckd ldrs: rn qckn and outpcd 2f out: hanging but styd on to chse wnr ins fnl f: clsd but no ch* **7/2**[1]

020 **3** *4* **La Marmotte (IRE)**[31] [2478] 2-8-7 .... FrankieMcDonald 1 52
(J W Hills) *trckd ldr for 2f: outpcd over 2f out: kpt on fnl f to take 3rd nr fin* **6/1**[3]

40 **4** *nk* **Billy Red**[23] [2710] 2-9-1 .... RobertHavlin 5 59
(J R Jenkins) *led: drvn and hdd wl over 1f out: wknd rapidly ins fnl f* **4/1**[2]

00 **5** *½* **Gifted Heir (IRE)**[29] [2530] 2-8-9 .... DavidKinsella 10 51
(I A Wood) *dwlt: trckd ldrs: bdly outpcd over 2f out: kpt on again fnl f* **33/1**

6 *1 ½* **Prince Of Charm (USA)** 2-9-1 .... PatDobbs 3 53
(P Mitchell) *s.s: t.o after 1f: prog to midfield 1/2-way but nt on terms: shkn up over 1f out: kpt on* **10/1**

7 *½* **Falcon Flyer** 2-8-10 .... TPQueally 7 46
(J R Best) *sn wl outpcd and pushed along: nvr on terms: plugged on fr over 1f out* **7/1**

0 **8** *18* **Cavendish**[16] [2930] 2-8-12 .... ChrisCatlin 8 —
(J M P Eustace) *sn wl outpcd: t.o fr 1/2-way* **20/1**

9 *¾* **Rubber Duck (IRE)** 2-8-5 ow1.............................. RobbieFitzpatrick 6 —
(Peter Grayson) *sn wl outpcd: t.o fr 1/2-way* **14/1**

10 *shd* **Port Luanda (IRE)** 2-8-9 .... AdrianMcCarthy 2 —
(R M Flower) *s.s: a t.o* **16/1**

1m 14.15s (1.34) **Going Correction** +0.10s/f (Slow) **10** Ran SP% **118.4**
Speed ratings (Par 94):95,92,87,86,86 84,83,59,58,58
CSF £18.75 TOTE £5.10: £2.60, £2.00, £1.90; EX 18.10 Trifecta £24.60 Pool: £199.66 - 5.74 winning units.
Owner Tony Smith **Bred** Maurice Burns **Trained** Patching, W Sussex

FOCUS
Another modest juvenile maiden, the winner doing well but beating little. The winning time was slightly slower than the first division.

NOTEBOOK
Ede's Dot Com(IRE), not beaten that far in a bunch finish in what looked a pretty ordinary maiden by Windsor's standards on his debut, showed improved form to get off the mark at the second attempt. He never looked in danger from the moment he was asked to pick up and, with more improvement possible, he could do well in nurseries. (tchd 9-2)
Early Promise(IRE) seems to be progressing nicely at a modest level, but she was basically no match for the winner. She could find her level in nursery company. (tchd 4-1 and 9-2 in places)
La Marmotte(IRE), up in trip and switched to Polytrack, was well held by the front two and does not seem to be progressing. She may benefit from a drop in grade. (op 11-2)
Billy Red weakened rather disappointingly in the straight and has not gone on from an encouraging debut effort. (op 11-2)
Gifted Heir(IRE) ran quite a nice race and can probably do better over slightly further when able to run in nurseries.
Falcon Flyer, a 21,000gns half-sister to five winners abroad, out of a winner at up to ten furlongs, was solid enough in the market beforehand but ran very green. She could be capable of quite a bit better in time. (tchd 15-2)

3409 WAYMENT FLOORING NURSERY 5f (P)
3:30 (3:31) (Class 5) 2-Y-O **£3,886** (£1,156; £577; £288) **Stalls** High

Form RPR
0510 **1** **Il Palio (IRE)**[37] [2300] 2-9-0 **76**.................................... JamesMillman(7) 6 85
(B R Millman) *pressed ldng pair for 2f: trckd them after: effrt to chse ldr over 1f out: drvn and r.o to ld last 50yds* **5/1**[2]

042 **2** *¾* **Inflight (IRE)**[22] [2726] 2-8-7 **62**...................................... FergusSweeney 3 68
(R M Beckett) *led: kicked at least 2l clr over 1f out: tired and hdd last 50yds* **9/1**

632 **3** *2 ½* **Shreddy Shrimpster**[16] [2916] 2-8-1 **59**.................... StephaneBreux(3) 8 56
(A B Haynes) *off the pce in midfield: effrt 2f out: styd on fnl f to take 3rd nr fin* **18/1**

320 **4** *½* **Whiskey Junction**[37] [2281] 2-9-4 **76**............................ NeilChalmers(3) 7 72
(A M Balding) *trckd ldng trio: outpcd 2f out: drvn and kpt on to chse clr ldng pair ins fnl f: lost 3rd nr fin* **5/1**[2]

4534 **5** *5* **Nicada (IRE)**[15] [2950] 2-8-9 **64**.. ChrisCatlin 10 42
(Miss Gay Kelleway) *sn wl off the pce in last trio: nvr a factor: passed wkng rivals fnl f* **25/1**

6616 **6** *½* **Autumn Storm**[10] [3120] 2-8-7 **62**.................................... StephenCarson 1 38
(R Ingram) *s.s: wl bhd in last trio: hrd rdn and no ch fnl 2f* **16/1**

654 **7** *shd* **La Quinta (IRE)**[11] [3070] 2-8-8 **70**... KMay(7) 4 45
(B J Meehan) *pressed ldr to 2f out: lost 2nd over 1f out and wknd rapidly* **7/1**[3]

4311 **8** *1* **Top Tier**[9] [3136] 2-8-5 **60** 6ex.. RobbieFitzpatrick 2 32
(Peter Grayson) *chsd ldrs but no on terms: reminder over 3f out: hmpd on inner 1/2-way: no ch after* **5/2**[1]

0212 **9** *1 ¼* **Peggys Flower**[8] [3160] 2-8-10 **65**...................................... DO'Donohoe 9 32
(N A Callaghan) *v s.i.s: a wl off the pce: pushed along and no prog 2f out* **8/1**

3405 **10** *5* **She Wont Wait**[11] [3070] 2-8-2 **57**.. HayleyTurner 5 6
(T M Jones) *rdn in midfield and nt on terms: wknd 2f out* **33/1**

60.52 secs (0.74) **Going Correction** +0.10s/f (Slow) **10** Ran SP% **113.4**
Speed ratings (Par 94):98,96,92,92,84 83,83,81,79,71
CSF £47.97 CT £758.24 TOTE £6.20: £2.10, £2.40, £4.50; EX 81.20 TRIFECTA Not won..
Owner Mrs L S Millman **Bred** Blue Bloodstock Limited **Trained** Kentisbeare, Devon

FOCUS
The two top weights were racing off estimated handicap marks of 82, but this still looked just an ordinary nursery and the form appears sound.

NOTEBOOK
Il Palio(IRE) had little chance in a very hot race at Windsor on his previous start, but the switch to nursery company suited well and he benefited from cool ride from his 7lb claimer - Millman did not panic despite Inflight kicking into a clear lead early in the straight - to gain his third success of the season. He is clearly useful, but could get harder to place as the season goes on. (op 13-2)
Inflight(IRE) looked all over the winner when kicking well clear early in the straight, but she was not the first horse and will not be the last to end up treading water through what seems a particularly challenging final furlong. She looks well up to finding a similar race. (op 15-2)
Shreddy Shrimpster, beaten at odds-on in a seller at Chepstow when with Mark Wallace on her previous start, ran well switched to nursery company and her new connections looks to have found themselves a nice, fun horse. (op 16-1 tchd 20-1)
Whiskey Junction seemed to boil over when a disappointing beaten favourite at Carlisle on his previous start, but this was better and he again showed his liking for Polytrack. Official explanation: jockey said gelding resented the kickback (op 13-2)
Nicada(IRE), without the cheekpieces this time, was given plenty to do by the Handicapper. (op 16-1)
Top Tier, chasing the hat-trick after landing a seller and a nursery at Musselburgh, lost her chance when hampered at about halfway. Official explanation: jockey said filly hung right throughout (tchd 9-4 and 11-4 in places)

3410 FURLONGS & FAIRWAYS H'CAP 7f (P)
4:05 (4:06) (Class 6) (0-65,65) 3-Y-O **£2,388** (£705; £352) **Stalls** Low

Form RPR
2022 **1** **Hoh Wotanite**[9] [3154] 3-9-3 **61**.. LPKeniry 1 74
(A M Balding) *dwlt: sn chsd ldrs: cl 4th and clr of rest 2f out: n.m.r over 1f out: got through to ld last 150yds: drvn clr* **4/1**[1]

0-34 **2** *2 ½* **Young Bertie**[36] [2316] 3-8-11 **60**..............................(p) TravisBlock(5) 3 67
(H Morrison) *led: clr w 3 chalrs 2f out: hdd and outpcd last 150yds* **9/2**[2]

4000 **3** *1 ¾* **Air Biscuit (IRE)**[28] [2554] 3-9-2 **60**..................................(t) GeorgeBaker 8 62+
(C F Wall) *hld up towards rr: stmbld bdly over 5f out: gng wl enough 3f out: nt clr run over 2f out: r.o to take 3rd nr fin: no ch* **12/1**

4-05 **4** *½* **Musical Echo**[13] [3011] 3-9-7 **65**.. ChrisCatlin 11 66
(G C H Chung) *settled midfield: rdn wl over 2f out: no prog tl styd on fr over 1f out: nrst fin* **11/1**

0623 **5** *½* **Some Diva**[14] [2987] 3-9-1 **59**... StephenCarson 9 58
(W R Swinburn) *pressed ldr: rdn to chal 2f out: hanging and wknd fnl f* **11/1**

2545 **6** *½* **Simpsons Ross (IRE)**[14] [2978] 3-9-2 **60**................................ PaulDoe 2 58
(R M Flower) *prom: drvn to chal 2f out: nrly upsides jst over 1f out: hung lft and wknd* **12/1**

0242 **7** *nk* **Panic Stations**[11] [3099] 3-8-8 **59**.................................. LukeMorris(7) 10 56
(M L W Bell) *racd towards outer and in rr: rdn 3f out: no prog tl styd on fnl f: n.d* **7/1**

053 **8** *5* **Blushing Light (USA)**[12] [3050] 3-9-7 **65**......................... FJohansson 13 49
(M A Magnusson) *chsd ldrs early: rdn in midfield wl over 2f out: wknd over 1f out* **25/1**

-040 **9** *hd* **Sorrel Point**[69] [1430] 3-9-2 **60**.................................... MichaelTebbutt 7 44+
(H J Collingridge) *hld up and sn last: gng wl enough but stl last 2f out: shuffled along fnl f: nvr nr ldrs* **66/1**

0501 **10** *shd* **Tuscany Queen (IRE)**[27] [2573] 3-8-11 **55**............................. PatDobbs 5 39
(R Hannon) *nvr beyond midfield: rdn and no prog over 2f out: wknd over 1f out* **10/1**

-502 **11** *shd* **Sanctity**[33] [2418] 3-9-0 **58**.. MickyFenton 6 41
(J R Fanshawe) *dwlt: a towards rr: rdn and struggling over 2f out* **5/1**[3]

0000 **12** *nk* **Mujelle**[24] [2678] 3-9-2 **60**..(p) TPQueally 14 43
(D K Ivory) *racd wd: in tch: rdn and struggling over 2f out: wknd* **50/1**

6-00 **13** *8* **Bee Seventeen (USA)**[14] [2987] 3-9-6 **64**.................(bt[1]) JosedeSouza 4 26
(P F I Cole) *dwlt and early reminders to rch midfield: wknd over 2f out* **40/1**

1m 25.94s (0.05) **Going Correction** +0.10s/f (Slow) **13** Ran SP% **118.2**
Speed ratings (Par 98):103,100,98,97,97 96,96,90,90,90 89,89,80
CSF £20.73 CT £207.31 TOTE £4.60: £1.70, £2.10, £4.00; EX 25.10 TRIFECTA Not won..
Owner D F Allport **Bred** Dunchurch Lodge Stud Co **Trained** Kingsclere, Hants

FOCUS
A modest handicap, which appeared to be run at a fair tempo. The form is ordinary but sound, rated through the fourth.
Air Biscuit(IRE) Official explanation: trainer said filly had clipped heels and lost both front shoes
Some Diva Official explanation: jockey said filly had been hanging right

Simpsons Ross(IRE) Official explanation: jockey said gelding had been hanging left

3411 GOLF & GAMBLE (S) STKS — 1m 2f
4:40 (4:40) (Class 6) 3-Y-O+ **£2,388** (£705; £352) **Stalls** Low

Form | RPR

4000 **1** **Bishops Finger**[18] 2862 6-9-12 50.....(b) RobertHavlin 6 63
(Jamie Poulton) *trckd ldng trio: effrt on inner over 2f out: rdn to ld wl over 1f out: in command fnl f* **11/2**[3]

6503 **2** *2 ½* **Milk And Sultana**[10] 3115 6-9-7 48..... TPQueally 7 53
(G A Ham) *trckd ldr: effrt to chal and upsides 2f out: outpcd by wnr fr jst over 1f out* **7/2**[2]

-355 **3** *2* **Beauchamp Unique**[61] 1634 3-8-4 62..... ChrisCatlin 4 43
(G A Butler) *dwlt: hld up in rr: sme prog on outer over 3f out: plugged on fnl 2f: no ch w ldng pair* **5/2**[1]

0654 **4** *nk* **Chookie Windsor**[5] 3260 3-9-1 51..... JimCrowley 8 53
(M S Saunders) *chsd ldrs: rdn and outpcd over 2f out: kpt on one pce after* **8/1**

0146 **5** *2 ½* **Danish Monarch**[22] 2725 5-9-5 52..... ChrisCavanagh(7) 10 49
(David Pinder) *led to wl over 1f out: wknd* **8/1**

0060 **6** *½* **Fentastic**[5] 3264 3-8-4 40..... FrancisFerris 1 37+
(Rae Guest) *hld up: rn into trble downhill and detached last 3f out: hrd rdn and kpt on: no ch* **20/1**

0060 **7** *2 ½* **Duxford**[14] 2978 5-8-13 39.....(be) RussellKennemore(7) 5 37
(D K Ivory) *hld up in tch: hrd rdn and outpcd 3f out: sn btn* **20/1**

0000 **8** *3 ½* **Jazrawy**[14] 2978 4-9-6 52..... MickyFenton 9 30
(Miss Gay Kelleway) *trckd ldr to 3f out: wknd rapidly* **11/1**

00-0 **9** *10* **Bold Brownie**[27] 2573 4-9-1 32..... AdrianMcCarthy 2 6
(Miss Z C Davison) *in tch in rr: hrd rdn over 3f out: sn wknd* **100/1**

0050 **10** *7* **Glenviews Oldport (USA)**[21] 2752 4-9-1 42.....(b) RobbieFitzpatrick 11 —
(Peter Grayson) *s.s: a in rr: rdn and wl bhd over 2f out* **25/1**

2m 8.50s (-1.22) **Going Correction** -0.075s/f (Good)
WFA 3 from 4yo+ 11lb **10** Ran SP% **111.1**
Speed ratings (Par 101):101,99,97,97,95 94,92,89,81,76
CSF £22.63 TOTE £9.00: £2.90, £1.10, £1.10; EX 30.10 Trifecta £50.70 Pool: £191.75 - 2.68 winning units.There was no bid for the winner. Beauchamp Unique was claimed by D J Moffatt for £6,000.
Owner Jamie Poulton **Bred** Cheveley Park Stud Ltd And Mrs J Druce **Trained** Telscombe, E Sussex

FOCUS
A bad race that is unlikely to have any bearing on future events, despite the time being reasonable and the runner-up to recent form.

3412 RYDON FILLIES' H'CAP — 1m 3f 106y
5:15 (5:15) (Class 5) (0-70,70) 3-Y-O+ **£3,238** (£963; £481; £240) **Stalls** High

Form | RPR

-026 **1** **Aimee Vibert**[40] 2186 4-9-9 65..... StephenCarson 2 72
(W R Swinburn) *prom in chsng gp: wnt 3rd 4f out: clsd u.p fr 3f out: led over 1f out: drvn out* **17/2**

3060 **2** *½* **Boot 'n Toot**[13] 3028 5-10-0 70..... J-PGuillambert 5 76
(C A Cyzer) *hld up towards rr: rdn over 3f out: clsd grad fr 2f out: r.o to take 2nd last 75yds: nt rch wnr* **7/1**[3]

0003 **3** *1* **Sand And Stars (IRE)**[9] 3152 5-9-9 65..... GeorgeBaker 1 69
(M H Tompkins) *hld up in midfield: rdn over 3f out: clsd grad fr 2f out: kpt on fnl f: nvr able to chal* **9/2**[1]

6111 **4** *hd* **Another Con (IRE)**[10] 3115 5-8-12 **54** 6ex..... RobbieFitzpatrick 7 58
(P A Blockley) *hld up in last pair: drvn over 3f out: styd on wd outside and kpt on fnl 2f: nvr quite rchd ldrs* **9/2**[1]

0050 **5** *shd* **Cantrip**[19] 2822 6-8-10 **52**..... RobertHavlin 8 56
(Miss B Sanders) *led for 1f: chsd clr ldr: rdn to cl fr 5f out: led wl over 2f out: collared over 1f out: no ex* **9/2**[1]

2234 **6** *¾* **Lady Taverner**[51] 1879 5-8-13 **60**..... NataliaGemelova(5) 3 64+
(J E Long) *hld up: last 5f out: prog on inner 3f out: clsng whn nt clr run wl over 1f out: one pce and no imp fnl f* **7/1**[3]

0453 **7** *3* **Missie Baileys**[12] 3035 4-8-13 **58**..... AmirQuinn(3) 4 56
(Mrs L J Mongan) *in tch in midfield: rdn over 3f out: tried to cl fr 2f out: no hdwy over 1f out* **6/1**[2]

000 **8** *6* **Light Dreams**[16] 2917 3-8-8 **62**.....(v[1]) PaulDoe 10 50
(W J Knight) *s.i.s: drvn to ld after 1f and sn clr: hdd wl over 2f out: wkng whn n.m.r over 1f out: eased* **14/1**

0-00 **9** *19* **Al Dhahab (USA)**[13] 3017 3-8-5 **59**..... HayleyTurner 6 17
(C E Brittain) *chsd clr ldng pair to 4f out: wknd rapidly: t.o* **25/1**

2m 28.32s (-1.60) **Going Correction** -0.075s/f (Good)
WFA 3 from 4yo+ 12lb **9** Ran SP% **114.9**
Speed ratings (Par 100):102,101,100,100,100 100,97,93,79
CSF £66.10 CT £303.24 TOTE £11.00: £3.80, £2.50, £1.50; EX 103.40 Trifecta £175.40 Part won. Pool: £247.13 - 0.35 winning units. Place 6 £16.94, Place 5 £12.50.
Owner Mrs P W Harris **Bred** Pendley Farm **Trained** Aldbury, Herts

FOCUS
A modest fillies' handicap run at an average pace and weakish form.
Light Dreams Official explanation: jockey said filly had been hanging left
T/Plt: £22.60 to a £1 stake. Pool: £37,424.35. 1,206.55 winning tickets. T/Qpdt: £11.10 to a £1 stake. Pool: £2,095.00. 138.70 winning tickets. JN

3083
NEWMARKET (JULY) (R-H)
Wednesday, July 12

OFFICIAL GOING: Good to firm
Meeting now held from Wednesday to Friday and rebranded the July Festival.
Wind: Light, across Weather: Hot and sunny

3413 RACING POST BLOODSTOCK H'CAP — 1m
1:30 (1:31) (Class 3) (0-90,90) 3-Y-O+ **£11,658** (£3,468; £1,733; £865) **Stalls** Low

Form | RPR

-214 **1** **Smart Enough**[20] 2774 3-9-8 **89**..... KerrinMcEvoy 18 101+
(M A Magnusson) *lw: racd stands' side: mde all: rdn out* **9/2**[1]

2210 **2** *1 ¾* **Plum Pudding (IRE)**[20] 2774 3-9-9 **90**..... RyanMoore 3 98+
(R Hannon) *racd far side: chsd ldrs: led that gp over 1f out: sn rdn: r.o: 1st of 11 in gp* **8/1**[2]

-402 **3** *hd* **Dry Ice (IRE)**[19] 2819 4-9-7 **79**..... DaneO'Neill 11 88
(H Candy) *racd stands' side: hld up: hdwy and edgd lft over 2f out: rdn to chse wnr over 1f out: r.o: 2nd of 8 in gp* **28/1**

0621 **4** *½* **Optimus (USA)**[12] 3044 4-9-2 **77**..... AdamKirby(3) 1 85
(G A Butler) *b. nr hind: racd far side: hld up in tch: chsd ldr of that gp over 1f out: styd on: 2nd of 11 that side* **11/1**

-050 **5** *½* **Norton (IRE)**[14] 2988 9-10-0 **86**..... IanMongan 19 93
(T G Mills) *racd stands' side: chsd ldrs: rdn over 1f out: styd on: 3rd of 8 in gp* **25/1**

4514 **6** *½* **Sew'N'So Character (IRE)**[6] 3218 5-9-13 **85**..... TedDurcan 13 91
(M Blanshard) *racd stands' side: hld up: swtchd lft and hdwy over 1f out: nt rch ldrs: 4th of 8 in gp* **16/1**

-201 **7** *2* **Along The Nile**[12] 3040 4-9-8 **80**.....(t) JamieSpencer 7 81+
(K G Reveley) *racd far side: hld up: hdwy and nt clr run over 1f out: nt rch ldrs: 3rd of 11 in gp* **10/1**[3]

66-2 **8** *½* **Bolodenka (IRE)**[13] 3020 4-9-9 **81**..... PaulHanagan 2 81
(R A Fahey) *racd far side: prom: rdn over 1f out: no ex: 4th of 11 in gp* **8/1**[2]

2004 **9** *¾* **Namroc (IRE)**[19] 2824 5-9-8 **80**..... JimmyFortune 8 78
(N A Callaghan) *racd far side: hld up: rdn over 1f out: nt trble ldrs: 5th of 11 in gp* **10/1**[3]

0003 **10** *shd* **Krugerrand (USA)**[25] 2657 7-9-9 **86**..... StephenDonohoe(5) 6 84
(W J Musson) *lw: racd far side: hld up: hdwy u.p over 1f out: nvr trbld ldrs: 6th of 11 in gp* **16/1**

6263 **11** *½* **Everest (IRE)**[12] 3040 9-9-8 **80**..... EddieAhern 16 77
(B Ellison) *racd stands' side: hld up: nvr trbld ldrs: 5th of 8 in gp* **14/1**

1024 **12** *2* **Tyzack (IRE)**[17] 2900 5-9-11 **83**..... MickyFenton 17 75
(Stef Liddiard) *racd stands' side: chsd ldrs: hung lft over 1f out: sn wknd: 6th of 8 in gp* **20/1**

301- **13** *1* **Ninth House (USA)**[205] 6623 4-9-11 **83**.....(t) RichardHughes 15 73
(D J Daly) *lw: swtchd to r far side: hld up: n.d: 7th of 11 in gp* **66/1**

33-6 **14** *3 ½* **Kingdom Of Dreams (IRE)**[32] 2440 4-9-9 **81**..... LDettori 9 63
(J Noseda) *racd far side: chsd ldrs: led that gp over 5f out: rdn and hdd over 1f out: sn wknd: 8th of 11 in gp* **12/1**

6-23 **15** *½* **Toshi (USA)**[18] 2872 4-9-9 **81**..... TomEaves 14 62
(I Semple) *racd stands' side: chsd ldrs 6f: 7th of 8 in gp* **33/1**

1100 **16** *4* **Rain Stops Play (IRE)**[19] 2810 4-9-10 **82**..... NCallan 12 54
(M Quinn) *racd stands' side: chsd ldrs: rdn over 2f out: sn wknd: last of 8 in gp* **50/1**

0245 **17** *3* **Inch Lodge**[6] 3230 4-8-10 **68**..... RobertMiles 4 33
(Miss D Mountain) *b: racd far side: led that side: hdd over 5f out: wknd 2f out: 9th of 11 in gp* **66/1**

5415 **18** *1* **Boundless Prospect (USA)**[19] 2819 7-9-11 **83**..... JohnEgan 10 45
(Miss Gay Kelleway) *racd far side: hld up: rdn over 2f out: a in rr: 10th of 11 in gp* **20/1**

0063 **19** *8* **Capricho (IRE)**[19] 2819 9-8-12 **70**..... DarryllHolland 5 14
(J Akehurst) *racd far side: chsd ldrs over 5f: last of 11 in gp* **25/1**

1m 37.61s (-2.82) **Going Correction** -0.125s/f (Firm)
WFA 3 from 4yo+ 9lb **19** Ran SP% **121.6**
Speed ratings (Par 107):109,107,107,106,106 105,103,103,102,102 101,99,98,95,94 90,87,86,78
CSF £32.12 CT £938.05 TOTE £5.20: £1.80, £2.50, £4.60, £3.00; EX 44.40 Trifecta £486.10 Part won. Pool: £684.70 - 0.50 winning units..
Owner East Wind Racing Ltd **Bred** Whitsbury Manor Stud And Mrs M E Slade **Trained** Upper Lambourn, Berks

FOCUS
A good, competitive handicap run at a sound gallop. It was run in a time 3.28sec faster than the slowly-run Group 1 later in the afternoon and the form looks solid. The field split into two groups but there did not appear to be a significant advantage.

NOTEBOOK
Smart Enough ◆, who ran such a good race from the front in the Britannia Handicap at Royal Ascot, justified favouritism in good style. He was quite keen in the early stages and taken on for the lead by Inch Lodge, but his rider was able to keep something in reserve and he picked up well to resist the challenge of the runner-up on the other flank. He looks to have room for further improvement and, despite the inevitable rise in the weights, looks set to be a major player in the big mile handicaps leading up to the Cambridgeshire.
Plum Pudding(IRE) ◆, who finished well behind the winner in the Britannia, ran much better on this occasion and was the only one from the far-side group to pose a significant threat in the last couple of furlongs. He could not trouble the winner up the hill but was clear of the rest and looks sure to pick up a decent handicap on this evidence.
Dry Ice(IRE), a relatively lightly-raced gelding who showed what he was capable of at Goodwood on his previous outing, gave the winner a race until fading up the hill. He hung on for the minor placing and looks capable of adding to his juvenile maiden success off what looks a competitive mark. (op 33-1)
Optimus(USA) ◆, a course-and-distance winner last month, handled the better-class contest and higher mark and was doing his best work late on. He can make his mark at a slightly lower, and is open to further improvement. (op 10-1)
Norton(IRE), a reliable old handicapper, was settled close to the pace and ran his race, and is a fair guide to the level of the form.
Sew'N'So Character(IRE), another capable sort in this grade, is holding his form well and should continue to run with credit, although he may struggle to add to his score off his current mark.
Along The Nile is a progressive sort but was well held in this grade.
Bolodenka(IRE), a previous course-and-distance winner, ran a fair race on the far side before fading in the closing stages.
Kingdom Of Dreams(IRE) showed up on the far side until fading in the last quarter mile.

3414 TOTESPORT.COM STKS (HERITAGE H'CAP) — 6f
2:00 (2:02) (Class 2) (0-105,100) 3-Y-O
£52,972 (£15,861; £7,930; £3,969; £1,980; £994) **Stalls** Low

Form | RPR

0422 **1** **Dark Missile**[21] 2756 3-8-6 **85**..... MartinDwyer 1 96
(A M Balding) *racd far side: chsd ldrs: rdn over 1f out: r.o to ld nr fin: 1st of 11 in gp* **16/1**

-001 **2** *hd* **Mutamarres**[21] 2760 3-8-8 **87**.....(v) RHills 6 97
(Sir Michael Stoute) *racd far side: led and overall ldr: rdn and hdd nr fin: 2nd of 11 in gp* **12/1**

2411 **3** *shd* **Prince Tamino**[25] 2658 3-9-7 **100**..... SteveDrowne 3 110
(H Morrison) *lw: racd far side: mid-div: hdwy over 1f out: r.o: 3rd of 11 in gp* **4/1**[1]

1156 **4** *shd* **Ripples Maid**[25] 2658 3-8-10 **89**..... RichardThomas 2 99
(J A Geake) *racd far side: a.p: rdn over 1f out: r.o: 4th of 11 in gp* **14/1**

12-0 **5** *1 ¼* **Grantley Adams**[88] 1020 3-9-0 **93**..... TedDurcan 4 99
(M R Channon) *racd far side: hld up: hdwy over 1f out: styd on: 5th of 11 in gp* **50/1**

-204 **6** *2* **Orpsie Boy (IRE)**[25] 2658 3-8-1 **85**.....(b[1]) JamesDoyle(5) 16 85+
(N P Littmoden) *racd stands' side: hld up: hdwy over 1f out: r.o to ld that gp nr fin: no ch w far side: 1st of 9 in gp* **12/1**

-023 **7** *shd* **High Curragh**[25] 2658 3-8-8 **87**..... NCallan 8 87
(K A Ryan) *racd far side: chsd ldrs: rdn over 1f out: styd on same pce: 6th of 11 in gp* **10/1**[3]

1105 **8** *hd* **Ingleby Arch (USA)**[11] 3077 3-9-4 **97**.............................. PaulFessey 13 96+
(T D Barron) *racd stands' side: mid-div: hdwy 2f out: sn rdn: styd on: 2nd of 9 in gp* **16/1**

1501 **9** *3/4* **Angus Newz**[25] 2651 3-9-7 **100**.............................. DarryllHolland 12 97+
(M Quinn) *racd stands' side: led that gp tl hdd over 3f out: styd on sam pce appr fnl f: 3rd of 9 in gp* **20/1**

1544 **10** *shd* **Total Impact**[18] 2866 3-8-9 **88**.............................. EddieAhern 17 85+
(C A Cyzer) *lw: racd stands' side: chsd ldr tl led that gp over 3f out: rdn over 1f out: wknd fnl f: 4th of 9 in gp* **25/1**

-403 **11** *1/2* **Johannes (IRE)**[15] 2959 3-9-2 **95**.............................. RichardHughes 5 90
(D Nicholls) *racd far side: chsd ldrs: rdn over 1f out: sn wknd: 7th of 11 in gp* **14/1**

0-00 **12** *1/2* **Godfrey Street**[22] 2720 3-9-7 **100**.............................. RyanMoore 7 94
(R Hannon) *racd far side: hld up: nvr trbld ldrs: 8th of 11 in gp* **33/1**

41-4 **13** *1/2* **Bertie Southstreet**[9] 3150 3-8-6 **85**.............................. KerrinMcEvoy 20 77+
(J R Best) *racd stands's ide: chsd ldrs: rdn over 1f out: sn wknd: 5th of 9 in gp* **33/1**

-315 **14** *1/2* **Trafalgar Bay (IRE)**[25] 2658 3-9-3 **96**.............................. LDettori 9 87
(S Kirk) *lw: racd far side: hld up: n.d: 9th of 11 in gp* **6/1**[2]

6210 **15** *hd* **Phantom Whisper**[25] 2639 3-8-10 **89**.............................. GrahamGibbons 15 79+
(B R Millman) *racd stands' side: prom: rdn over 2f out: wknd over 1f out: 6th of 9 in gp* **33/1**

1360 **16** *shd* **Green Park (IRE)**[12] 3038 3-9-1 **94**.............................. PaulHanagan 10 84
(R A Fahey) *racd far side: n.d: 10th of 11 in gp* **33/1**

1220 **17** *nk* **Pearly Wey**[25] 2658 3-8-13 **95**.............................. AdamKirby(3) 14 84+
(C G Cox) *racd stands' side: plld hrd and prom: wknd over 1f out: 7th of 9 in gp* **14/1**

1610 **18** *1 1/4* **Mr Sandicliffe**[25] 2658 3-8-10 **89**..............................(p) JamieSpencer 19 74+
(B W Hills) *racd stands' side: s.i.s: hld up: nt clr run fr over 2f out: n.d: 8th of 9 in gp* **25/1**

0033 **19** *3/4* **Charles Darwin (IRE)**[18] 2863 3-8-6 **85**.............................. FrancisNorton 18 68+
(M Blanshard) *lw: racd stands's ide: prom: hmpd over 2f out: wknd over 1f out: last of 9 in gp* **33/1**

-010 **20** *5* **Red Cape (FR)**[14] 2988 3-8-11 **90**.............................. JohnEgan 11 58
(N A Callaghan) *lw: racd far side: dwlt: hld up: a in rr: last of 11 in gp* **25/1**

1m 10.88s (-2.47) **Going Correction** -0.125s/f (Firm) **20** Ran SP% **123.5**
Speed ratings (Par 106):111,110,110,110,108 106,106,105,104,104 103,103,102,101,101 101,101,99,98,91
CSF £172.33 CT £671.48 TOTE £22.00: £4.20, £2.50, £1.80, £4.50; EX 172.20 Trifecta £730.70 Part won. Pool: £1,029.20 - 0.10 winning units..
Owner J C Smith **Bred** Littleton Stud **Trained** Kingsclere, Hants

FOCUS
A highly-competitive sprint handicap in which four progressive sorts fought out the finish. The form has been rated positively, but those who raced on the far side seemed to be at a distinct advantage.

NOTEBOOK
Dark Missile ◆, who appreciated the return to this distance when an unlucky second at Kempton last month, settled nicely just in behind the leaders and got a nice tow through from her rails pitch. Appearing to appreciate the good pace in a big field, she came through to challenge over a furlong out and held on doggedly once edging ahead. A scopey filly who has the speed for five furlongs, she is to be given a break now, but it is entirely possible she will return in even better shape and she is most definitely one to keep on the right side of.
Mutamarres got his act together in the first-time visor at Ripon last month where the combination of front-running tactics over six furlongs appeared to work well. Despite racing off a 7lb higher mark, he really served it up to his rivals and it was only late on he gave way to the winner. The headgear has clearly made a huge difference to him and he should continue to go well under similarly forcing tactics. (op 9-1)
Prince Tamino, a most progressive sprint handicapper who took the valuable William Hill Trophy at York last time off a mark of 92, was rightly at the head of the market, but he was being niggled along from an early stage and never looked to be going particularly well. He did however find plenty under pressure and still looked as though he may get there as they raced towards the line, but the substantial weight difference told in the end. (tchd 9-2)
Ripples Maid, who lost all chance when slipping badly at the start against Prince Tamino on their York meeting, was 8lb better off here and this improved showing came as no surprise. Never far away, she kept on right to the line and, although 9lb higher than when last winning, she remains generally progressive. (tchd 12-1 in a place)
Grantley Adams made a pleasing reappearance at Kempton and this generally consistent gelding did best of those to come from behind. He was never in with a chance of challenging the principals, but did enough to suggest he is capable of scoring off this sort of mark.
Orpsie Boy(IRE), significantly better off with Prince Tamino on York form, again ran well, 'winning' his race on the stands' side, but he was never quite on terms and ran as well as could have been expected. The first-time blinkers did not appear to have a negative effect and he remains capable of better still.
High Curragh was unable to build on his good third at York and lacked a finishing kick.
Ingleby Arch(USA) left a couple of disappointing efforts behind, but he continues to give the impression he is worth a try back at seven furlongs. (op 20-1)
Trafalgar Bay(IRE), a progressive sprinter who looked to hold obvious claims on his York fifth, never got into it having been held up and appeared to have no obvious excuse. Official explanation: jockey said colt was unsuited by the good to firm ground (op 7-1 tchd 15-2 in a place)
Pearly Wey Official explanation: jockey said gelding hung right
Mr Sandicliffe failed to get the gaps when he wanted them and never had a chance to shine.
Charles Darwin(IRE) quickly lost his place having been hampered and should have the run ignored.

3415 CHIPPENHAM LODGE STUD CHERRY HINTON STKS (GROUP 2) (FILLIES) 6f

2:35 (2:35) (Class 1) 2-Y-O

£39,746 (£15,064; £7,539; £3,759; £1,883; £945) **Stalls** Low

Form RPR

41 **1** **Sander Camillo (USA)**[19] 2800 2-8-12 .... LDettori 4 116
(J Noseda) *chsd ldr: led over 2f out: rdn clr over 1f out: edgd rt: r.o* **11/8**[1]

31 **2** *5* **Alzerra (UAE)**[33] 2409 2-8-12 .... TedDurcan 8 101
(M R Channon) *plld hrd and prom: rdn to chse wnr over 1f out: styd on same pce* **12/1**

1111 **3** *nk* **Gilded (IRE)**[21] 2743 2-9-1 .... RichardHughes 10 103
(R Hannon) *lw: hld up: hdwy over 2f out: rdn over 1f out: styd on same pce* **11/1**

11 **4** *1 1/2* **Hope'N'Charity (USA)**[11] 3084 2-8-12 .... AdamKirby 9 96
(C G Cox) *chsd ldrs: outpcd over 2f out: n.d after* **12/1**

1 **5** *shd* **Alderney (USA)**[25] 2660 2-8-12 .... PhilipRobinson 1 95
(M A Jarvis) *plld hrd and prom: rdn over 1f out: wknd ins fnl f* **10/3**[2]

12 **6** *hd* **Silk Blossom (IRE)**[19] 2800 2-8-12 .... MichaelHills 3 95
(B W Hills) *b.hind: hld up: effrt and nt clr run over 1f out: nvr trbld ldrs* **5/1**[3]

1 **7** *2 1/2* **Divine Right**[26] 2604 2-8-12 .... JimmyFortune 6 87
(B J Meehan) *lw: hld up: rdn over 2f out: n.d* **28/1**

4153 **8** *nk* **Slipasearcher (IRE)**[10] 3120 2-8-12 .... SteveDrowne 5 86
(P D Evans) *lw: sn pushed along in rr: n.d* **66/1**

613 **9** *3/4* **Nina Blini**[21] 2743 2-8-12 .... JamieSpencer 2 84
(B J Meehan) *hld up: rdn over 2f out: n.d* **25/1**

0314 **10** *6* **Three Decades (IRE)**[11] 3084 2-8-12 .... EddieAhern 7 66
(C A Cyzer) *sn led: hdd over 2f out: sn rdn and wknd* **100/1**

1m 12.12s (-1.23) **Going Correction** -0.125s/f (Firm) **10** Ran SP% **115.3**
Speed ratings (Par 103):103,96,95,93,93 93,90,89,88,80
CSF £19.48 TOTE £2.60: £1.30, £3.80, £2.10; EX 28.60 Trifecta £233.70 Pool: £1,115.90 - 3.39 winning units.
Owner Sir Robert Ogden **Bred** P Robertson And Brenda Robertson **Trained** Newmarket, Suffolk

FOCUS
A good renewal with both the Queen Mary and Albany winners in action and it was the hot favourite that ran out an impressive winner, cementing her position at the head of the 1000 Guineas market.

NOTEBOOK
Sander Camillo(USA) showed her debut running in soft ground to be all wrong when trouncing her rivals in the Albany Stakes at Royal Ascot, a performance that led to her being promoted to the head of the 2007 1000 Guineas betting, and her lofty reputation led to her being made a short-priced favourite for this tougher assignment. Prominent throughout, she strode on effortlessly with a quarter of a mile to run and quickly put the result beyond doubt, just having to be ridden out inside the final furlong. Cut to as short as 7/1 for next year's opening fillies' Classic, she is going to stay further and now has the Moyglare Stud Stakes as a likely target, but it would be unwise to get carried away despite Dettori's comment that she's "as good a two-year-old filly as I've ridden" as the key juvenile 1000 Guineas trials, the Rockfel, Fillies' Mile and Cheveley Park, have yet to take place. (tchd 13-8)
Alzerra(UAE), one place ahead of Sander Camillo on her debut at Newmarket, went on to win her maiden in good style at Haydock and she looked one of the likelier dangers to the favourite with her trainer rating her as "the best I've got". Unfortunately for her though, she failed to settle and was left trailing by the winner's burst. This was a cracking effort nonetheless to beat the Queen Mary winner a neck, and she remains capable of better once learning to settle better.
Gilded(IRE), a prolific two-year-old bidding for her sixth consecutive success, took an average renewal of the Queen Mary in typically workmanlike style and she again gave her all against better rivals here, but the winner simply possessed a superior kick and she was found wanting under her penalty. She may struggle to score again at this level, but her masterful juvenile trainer no doubt has the Super Sprint at the forefront of his mind for the filly, who is likely to spearhead a typically strong Hannon attack on the Newbury race.
Hope'N'Charity(USA), a workmanlike winner of a Listed race here last time, stepped up on that with a sound effort, but she did not give the impression she is up to winning at this level and it may be that any Group success she enjoys comes at a lower level. (op 14-1)
Alderney(USA), a mightily impressive winner on her debut at York, spoiled her chance by pulling hard and her rider reported she hung right. She is obviously believed to be a lot better than this and deserves another chance to show what she can do. Official explanation: jockey said filly hung right (op 3-1 tchd 7-2 in a place)
Silk Blossom(IRE), given plenty to do when a staying-on second in the Albany, was still in with a chance of reaching the frame when denied a clear run just over a furlong out and she was unable to make any impression afterwards. She rates a little better than her finishing position suggests. (op 7-1)

3416 UAE EQUESTRIAN AND RACING FEDERATION FALMOUTH STKS (GROUP 1) (F&M) 1m

3:10 (3:12) (Class 1) 3-Y-O+

£113,560 (£43,040; £21,540; £10,740; £5,380; £2,700) **Stalls** Low

Form RPR

0505 **1** **Rajeem**[19] 2802 3-8-10 96.............................. KerrinMcEvoy 4 114
(C E Brittain) *mde virtually all: edgd lft ins fnl f: rdn out* **50/1**

1-01 **2** *3/4* **Nannina**[19] 2802 3-8-10 113.............................. JimmyFortune 2 113
(J H M Gosden) *lw: chsd ldrs: rdn and ev ch fr over 1f out tl unable qckn nr fin* **2/1**[2]

3-02 **3** *3/4* **Musicanna**[40] 2199 5-9-5 102..............................(t) OscarUrbina 7 113
(J R Fanshawe) *lw: trckd ldrs: outpcd over 1f out: r.o ins fnl f* **33/1**

4-14 **4** *nk* **Peeress**[22] 2722 5-9-5 118.............................. MJKinane 5 112
(Sir Michael Stoute) *lw: b.hind: hld up: hdwy over 1f out: sn rdn: styd on same pce towards fin* **9/2**[3]

1303 **5** *1/2* **Nasheej (USA)**[19] 2802 3-8-10 107.............................. RyanMoore 1 109
(R Hannon) *with wnr: rdn and ev ch over 1f out: styng on same pce whn n.m.r ins fnl f* **16/1**

2-41 **6** *1 3/4* **Soviet Song (IRE)**[21] 2740 6-9-5 119.............................. JamieSpencer 3 107
(J R Fanshawe) *swtg: hld up and bhd: hdwy over 1f out: no ex ins fnl f* **6/5**[1]

-033 **7** *1* **Cape Columbine**[34] 2386 4-9-5 100.............................. JohnEgan 6 105
(D R C Elsworth) *h.d.w: hld up: plld hrd: wknd over 1f out* **50/1**

1m 40.89s (0.46) **Going Correction** -0.125s/f (Firm)
WFA 3 from 4yo+ 9lb **7** Ran SP% **109.7**
Speed ratings (Par 117):92,91,90,90,89 87,86
CSF £137.78 TOTE £23.70: £4.40, £2.20; EX 112.90.
Owner Saeed Manana **Bred** Usk Valley Stud **Trained** Newmarket, Suffolk

FOCUS
A top-class contest for fillies and mares bringing together the leaders of three generations. However, the pace was very modest, resulting in a time 3.28sec slower than the opening three-year-old handicap, and it produced a shock outcome, suggesting the form should be treated with caution.

NOTEBOOK
Rajeem, who ran her best race of the season when an unlucky-in-running fifth to Nannina in the Coronation Stakes at Royal Ascot, was able to reverse placings under totally different tactics. Instead of being held up, this time she settled at the head of affairs, along with Nasheej. When challenged by the runner-up a furlong and a half from home, she responded really well and came away for a decisive success. She is clearly going the right way and is likely to go for the Nassau Stakes next, but it remains to be seen if she will be able to repeat this given she had the run of the race.
Nannina, who beat today's winner decisively in the Coronation Stakes, was always well placed on the heels of the leaders and when asked to make her challenge looked as if she would win. However, Rajeem responded and was always holding her on the run to the line. She beat the rest well enough and connections blamed the slow gallop for her defeat, but although she can win again at this level, with the Prix d'Astarte at Deauville the most likely target, she does not look the outstanding filly she promised to be at Ascot. (tchd 9-4)
Musicanna is a useful mare but has yet to prove any better than Group 3 class. Her proximity along with the winner backs up the impression that the slow early gallop led to a suspect result, but connections will be delighted with her Group 1 placing.
Peeress held up at the back off a steady gallop, failed to pick up as well as would have been hoped but the ground would not have been totally in her favour and this generally consistent mare can be give a chance to atone. (tchd 5-1)

Nasheej(USA), along with the winner, set a very steady pace but when asked to pick up she could not respond. Although placed at this level more than once, she has not won above Group 2 class and may have to drop to that level to score again, or alternatively seek easier pickings abroad. (op 20-1)
Soviet Song(IRE), who won so well at Royal Ascot, was a well-backed favourite to win this for a third successive time. However, she was held up at the back off a slow pace and as she made her move the leaders were quickening and she could never get into contention. She is clearly better than this but needs a sounder gallop and the Sussex Stakes, which she won in 2004 and was runner-up in last season, will be next on the agenda. Official explanation: trainer had no explanation for the poor form shown (op 11-10 tchd 5-4)
Cape Columbine, who has been well held in three attempts at this level, did not help her chances by failing to settle off the slow pace.

3417 STRUTT & PARKER EBF MAIDEN STKS 7f
3:45 (3:45) (Class 3) 2-Y-O **£7,772** (£2,312; £1,155; £577) **Stalls** Low

Form				RPR
54	**1**		**Kalgoorlie (USA)**[22] 2719 2-9-3 .... LDettori 2 (J Noseda) *lw: mde virtually all: drvn out* **8/11**[1]	87
	2	*shd*	**Safe Investment (USA)** 2-9-3 .... PhilipRobinson 12 (J H M Gosden) *gd sort: hld up: hdwy over 1f out: sn rdn and edgd lft: r.o* **14/1**	87
	3	*nk*	**Many Volumes (USA)** 2-9-3 .... RichardHughes 1 (H R A Cecil) *gd sort: trckd ldrs: rdn and ev ch fr over 1f out: r.o* **11/2**[2]	86
	4	*1 ¼*	**Old Romney** 2-9-3 .... JoeFanning 16 (M Johnston) *w'like: scope: lw: w wnr tl rdn over 2f out: no ex ins fnl f* **16/1**	83
	5	*shd*	**Maslak (IRE)** 2-9-3 .... MartinDwyer 10 (E A L Dunlop) *gd sort: bkwd: chsd ldrs: edgd lft and outpcd over 1f out: r.o ins fnl f* **16/1**	82
	6	*4*	**Priory Bay (USA)** 2-9-3 .... RichardMullen 5 (E A L Dunlop) *w'like: scope: hld up: hdwy over 2f out: rdn and edgd lft over 1f out: sn wknd* **50/1**	72
550	**7**	*1 ¼*	**Mint State**[11] 3083 2-9-3 .... JohnEgan 4 (D R C Elsworth) *swtg: dwlt: hld up: nvr trbld ldrs* **33/1**	69
	8	*2*	**My Learned Friend (IRE)** 2-9-3 .... SteveDrowne 8 (A M Balding) *w'like: scope: lw: prom: rdn 1/2-way: wknd over 1f out* **50/1**	64
	9	*½*	**Perfect Courtesy (IRE)** 2-9-3 .... JimmyFortune 11 (P W Chapple-Hyam) *neat: s.i.s: hld up: nvr nrr* **20/1**	62
	10	*3*	**Zaahid (IRE)** 2-9-3 .... RHills 15 (B W Hills) *leggy: scope: s.i.s: hld up: hdwy 1/2-way: edgd lft and wknd over 1f out* **12/1**[3]	55
0	**11**	*2*	**Mulvany (IRE)**[27] 2579 2-9-3 .... NCallan 13 (B J Meehan) *lw: prom swtchd lft over 2f out: sn wknd* **66/1**	49
	12	*1 ¾*	**Italian Stallion (IRE)** 2-9-3 .... RyanMoore 7 (R Hannon) *cmpt: bkwd: s.i.s: outpcd* **20/1**	45
0	**13**	*7*	**Master Golfer (USA)**[6] 3222 2-9-3 .... MichaelHills 6 (B W Hills) *str: cmpt: chsd ldrs to 1/2-way* **66/1**	27
	14	*¾*	**Jafaru** 2-9-3 .... JamieSpencer 14 (G A Butler) *w'like: scope: chsd ldrs: hung lft and wknd over 2f out* **28/1**	25
	15	*2 ½*	**Say Great (IRE)** 2-9-0 .... RossStudholme(3) 9 (V Smith) *wl grwn: s.i.s: sn outpcd* **100/1**	18
0	**16**	*2 ½*	**Wickedish**[12] 3043 2-8-12 .... TedDurcan 3 (P Howling) *bkwd: chsd ldrs: lost pl over 5f out: wknd 2f out* **100/1**	7

1m 26.69s (-0.09) **Going Correction** -0.125s/f (Firm) **16** Ran SP% **124.2**
Speed ratings (Par 98):95,94,94,93,93 88,87,84,84,80 78,76,68,67,64 61
CSF £11.61 TOTE £1.80: £1.30, £3.60, £1.90; EX 21.60.
Owner Sheikh Marwan Al Maktoum **Bred** R J O'Neill **Trained** Newmarket, Suffolk

FOCUS
A good maiden with Coventry fourth Kalgoorlie just edging out a couple of highly promising newcomers. The race has been rated positively and should produce plenty of winners.

NOTEBOOK
Kalgoorlie(USA), well beaten in soft ground on his debut at Newmarket, showed what he is truly capable of when thrown in at the deep end in the Coventry Stakes, flashing home to claim a never-nearer fourth having been outpaced in rear, and this represented a significantly easier target. He made mighty hard work of it though, being unable to quicken, but he was just able to hold on. (op 4-5)
Safe Investment(USA) ◆, whose stable are beginning to bring out some of their better two-year-olds, is a good-looking sort, but found himself dismissed in the betting with his owner's retained jockey choosing to ride Many Volumes. That did not stop him running a big race though, keeping on well inside the final furlong and just missing out. He is entitled to come on a deal for the outing and looks one to keep on side, with a normal maiden almost certain to come his way.
Many Volumes(USA) ◆, who has apparently been putting in some decent work at home, made good headway to hold every chance inside the final furlong, but like the runner-up he was never quite getting there. He too is a nice-looking colt who should have little trouble finding an ordinary maiden before going on to better things. (op 6-1)
Old Romney ◆, like so many of his stable's juveniles, is a fine, scopey sort and anything he achieved here was always going to be improved upon in future. He was soon helping to force the pace, but lacked a change of gear and could only keep on inside the final furlong. He should come on appreciably for the outing and winning a maiden should prove a formality for the son of Halling, who is going to stay further in time.
Maslak(IRE) ◆, sporting Sheikh Hamdan's second colours, upstaged the first string and overcame greenness to make a highly pleasing debut, running on nicely inside the final furlong having been outpaced to just miss out on fourth. He should be one of many of these to strike in a similar race in the coming months. (op 14-1)
Priory Bay(USA), bred to be effective at this trip, shaped very much indeed as though the experience was needed, but he made a brief move with a quarter of a mile to run and is clearly not without ability. Most of his stable's juveniles tend to improve a good deal for their debut outing and he looks sure to improve.
Mint State continues to find a few too good in decent maidens, but he is one to watch out for once tackling nurseries. (tchd 40-1 in a place)
My Learned Friend(IRE) comes from a stable whose juveniles tend to need their initial outing and that theory was borne out, but he showed up well for a long way and is certain to find easier opportunities.
Zaahid(IRE), although bred to appreciate further in time, should be effective at this distance at this stage of his career, but he never really recovered from a slow start and was not given a hard time. It is reasonable to expect significant improvement on this. (op 14-1)
Jafaru Official explanation: jockey said bit slipped through colt's mouth

3418 EBF RACING POST FILLIES' H'CAP 7f
4:20 (4:20) (Class 2) (0-100,94) 3-Y-O
£15,580 (£4,665; £2,332; £1,167; £582; £292) **Stalls** Low

Form				RPR
-156	**1**		**Heaven Sent**[18] 2851 3-8-8 **81** .... RyanMoore 3 (Sir Michael Stoute) *lw: s.i.s: hld up: hmpd over 2f out: hdwy and swtchd rt over 1f out: rdn to ld ins fnl f: r.o* **6/1**[3]	92+
-660	**2**	*1 ¼*	**Jeanmaire (IRE)**[21] 2744 3-9-1 **88** .... SteveDrowne 1 (H Morrison) *hld up: swtchd rt and hdwy over 2f out: swtchd lft over 1f out: sn rdn and ev ch: unable qckn wl ins fnl f* **12/1**	96
2-03	**3**	*nk*	**Blades Girl**[11] 3067 3-8-9 **82** .... (p) NCallan 2 (K A Ryan) *chsd ldrs: rdn to ld over 1f out: edgd lft and hdd ins fnl f: unable qckn* **16/1**	89
15-0	**4**	*3 ½*	**Oceans Apart**[18] 2880 3-9-0 **90** .... NelsonDeSouza(3) 6 (P F I Cole) *hld up in tch: rdn and edgd lft over 2f out: styd on same pce appr fnl f* **16/1**	88
-010	**5**	*nk*	**Silver Dip**[25] 2650 3-8-11 **84** .... MichaelHills 11 (B W Hills) *lw: chsd ldrs: led over 2f out: rdn and hdd over 1f out: wknd ins fnl f* **7/1**	81
1403	**6**	*2*	**Polliwilline (IRE)**[19] 2818 3-8-8 **81** .... RichardHughes 5 (R Hannon) *hld up: hdwy and hmpd over 1f out: wknd ins fnl f* **20/1**	72
0-01	**7**	*½*	**Lady Livius (IRE)**[15] 2959 3-9-7 **94** .... DaneO'Neill 9 (R Hannon) *b. off hind: hld up: hdwy over 2f out: rdn and edgd lft over 1f out: sn wknd* **14/1**	84
-115	**8**	*1 ¾*	**Harvest Queen (IRE)**[21] 2744 3-9-6 **93** .... EddieAhern 7 (P J Makin) *chsd ldr tl led 1/2-way: hdd over 2f out: wknd fnl f* **9/4**[1]	78
16-3	**9**	*7*	**Melaaya (USA)**[43] 2103 3-9-3 **90** .... RHills 8 (M Johnston) *chsd ldrs: rdn 1/2-way: wknd wl over 2f out* **12/1**	56
24-1	**10**	*2 ½*	**Amy Louise (IRE)**[12] 3039 3-8-5 **78** .... KDarley 4 (T D Barron) *led to 1/2-way: wknd 2f out* **5/1**[2]	38
0-30	**11**	*3*	**Queen Of Fire**[27] 2582 3-9-6 **93** .... (v[1]) TedDurcan 10 (M R Channon) *reminders sn after s: hld up: wknd over 2f out* **25/1**	45

1m 24.26s (-2.52) **Going Correction** -0.125s/f (Firm) **11** Ran SP% **116.6**
Speed ratings (Par 103):109,107,107,103,102 100,100,98,90,87 83
CSF £75.19 CT £772.21 TOTE £7.40: £2.60, £5.00, £3.70; EX 101.70.
Owner Cheveley Park Stud **Bred** Cheveley Park Stud Ltd **Trained** Newmarket, Suffolk
■ Stewards' Enquiry : Steve Drowne one-day ban: careless riding (Jul 23)

FOCUS
A good competitive fillies' handicap run at a decent pace, the time being 2.43sec faster than the preceding juvenile maiden and those that made the running faded in the closing stages. However, the form is not obviously strong.

NOTEBOOK
Heaven Sent had disappointed a couple of times since winning her maiden, but things worked out better for her this time. The good gallop seemed to suit her and she picked up really well up the hill having started slowly and been held up. It remains to be seen whether she can progress enough to earn some black type. (op 5-1)
Jeanmaire(IRE), has generally been struggling this season, but a slight drop in class and some help from the handicapper brought about a return to form. She could not match the winner up the hill but this was a decent effort and she may have more to offer. (op 14-1)
Blades Girl, stepping up in grade, ran another good race in the cheekpieces and briefly looked as if she might win. She is relatively inexperienced and her shrewd connections may be able to find a race for her over this trip on a slightly easier track.
Oceans Apart, a filly who has been highly tried, was left behind by the front three up the hill. She looks high enough in the weights at present, but is one to bear in mind for when she races on a flatter track with the blinkers re-applied.
Silver Dip travelled well and looked the likely winner when going to the front, but the pace had been strong early on and she had nothing in reserve when the challenges came from off the pace.
Polliwilline(IRE) seems well suited by a flat track and easier ground than she encountered her, and in the circumstances ran well as she did not get the best of passages.
Lady Livius(IRE), trying a longer trip and raised 7lb for her last success, appeared not to last home.
Harvest Queen(IRE) was the big disappointment of the race, but raced close to the early pace that in hindsight was probably too strong and dropped out in the last quarter-mile. She has something to prove now, but the Handicapper may have over-reacted to her Nottingham win and may need to drop her a few pounds. Official explanation: jockey said filly was unsuited by the good to firm ground (tchd 5-2)
Amy Louise(IRE) , who made all to win her maiden last time, set off at a good gallop, but like the favourite paid the penalty at the business end. (op 15-2)

3419 KLEINWORT BENSON MAIDEN STKS 1m 2f
4:55 (4:55) (Class 4) 3-Y-O **£7,772** (£2,312; £1,155; £577) **Stalls** Centre

Form				RPR
2-04	**1**		**Zaif (IRE)**[46] 2034 3-9-0 82 .... AntonyProcter(3) 9 (D R C Elsworth) *hld up: hdwy over 2f out: rdn to ld and edgd rt ins fnl f: r.o* **14/1**	88
322	**2**	*1 ¼*	**Garafena**[27] 2578 3-8-12 81 .... JamieSpencer 7 (Pat Eddery) *hld up: swtchd rt and hdwy over 1f out: sn rdn: r.o* **6/1**	80
342	**3**	*2 ½*	**Jewaar (USA)**[18] 2868 3-8-12 81 .... RHills 3 (M A Jarvis) *lw: chsd ldrs: led over 1f out: hdd and no ex ins fnl f* **11/2**[3]	75
4-06	**4**	*¾*	**Wassfa**[28] 2556 3-8-12 75 .... KerrinMcEvoy 6 (C E Brittain) *chsd ldrs: nt clr run and lost pl over 2f out: hmpd over 1f out: styd on ins fnl f* **16/1**	76+
6	**5**	*3*	**Rainbow Zest**[33] 2412 3-9-3 .... JimmyFortune 2 (P W Chapple-Hyam) *lw: hld up: hdwy over 3f out: rdn and hung lft over 2f out: wknd over 1f out* **33/1**	73
3	**6**	*¾*	**Road Home**[19] 2825 3-9-3 .... NCallan 4 (G Wragg) *dwlt: sn chsng ldrs: rdn and ev ch over 1f out: sn wknd* **7/2**[2]	72
333	**7**	*8*	**Montpellier (IRE)**[37] 2304 3-9-3 84 .... SteveDrowne 1 (E A L Dunlop) *chsd ldrs: led over 3f out: rdn and hdd over 1f out: wknd qckly* **11/4**[1]	57
0-4	**8**	*½*	**Gnillah**[110] 710 3-8-12 .... LDettori 10 (B W Hills) *hld up: rdn over 2f out: sn wknd* **16/1**	51
4-	**9**	*1 ¾*	**Battalion (IRE)**[252] 6227 3-9-3 .... RyanMoore 11 (Sir Michael Stoute) *hld up: lost tch fnl 4f* **11/2**[3]	52
3046	**10**	*3*	**Hunting Party (IRE)**[19] 2825 3-9-3 75 .... (t) MichaelHills 5 (B W Hills) *lw: led over 6f: wknd 2f out* **20/1**	47

2m 5.09s (-1.35) **Going Correction** -0.125s/f (Firm) **10** Ran SP% **120.1**
Speed ratings (Par 102):100,99,97,96,94 93,87,86,85,82
CSF £98.49 TOTE £20.80: £4.80, £2.10, £2.00; EX 137.70 Place 6 £128.10, Place 5 £47.06.
Owner Miss R Wakeford **Bred** Bobby Donworth And Miss Honora Corridan **Trained** Newmarket, Suffolk
■ Stewards' Enquiry : Jamie Spencer 16-day ban (takes into account previous offences; three days deferred): careless riding (Jul 28-Aug 9)

FOCUS
Just a fair maiden but sound enough rated through the runner-up and fourth.
Rainbow Zest Official explanation: jockey said colt hung left
Montpellier(IRE) Official explanation: jockey said colt ran too free
Battalion(IRE) Official explanation: jockey said colt never travelled
T/Jkpt: Not won. T/Plt: £137.80 to a £1 stake. Pool: £128,507.75. 680.40 winning tickets. T/Qpdt: £63.50 to a £1 stake. Pool: £6,247.30. 72.80 winning tickets. CR

3420 - 3426a (Foreign Racing) - See Raceform Interactive

3343 SAN SIRO (R-H)

Wednesday, July 12

OFFICIAL GOING: Good

3427a PREMIO CALDE (CLAIMER) 6f
4:35 (4:37) 2-Y-O **£4,311** (£1,899; £1,035; £517)

RPR
1 **Joybee** 2-8-11 .... DVargiu 9 —
(B Grizzetti, Italy)
2 3 1/2 **Black Joke (IRE)** 2-8-2 .... SMulas 4 —
(P Paciello, Italy)
3 1/2 **Sopran Nyda (ITY)** 2-8-2 .... SUrru 10 —
(V Ficara, Italy)
4 3 1/2 **Soviet Kiri (IRE)** 2-8-6 .... PConvertino 3 —
(S Ibido, Italy)
5 6 **Cincia (ITY)** 2-8-2 .... MEsposito 1 —
(G Livraghi, Italy)
6 10 **Rosada (ITY)** 2-8-6 .... LManiezzi 7 —
(M Innocenti, Italy)
7 6 **Nicofonte (ITY)** 2-8-9 .... ACarboni 8 —
(P Caravati, Italy)
8 dist **Mac Zanna (ITY)** 2-8-9 .... APolli 6 —
(M G Quinlan) *never in contention*

8 Ran

(Including 1 Euro stake): WIN 1.50; PL 1.11, 2.23, 1.47; DF 13.04.
Owner B Grizzetti **Bred** B Grizzetti **Trained** Italy

NOTEBOOK
Mac Zanna(ITY) never threatened to land a blow, though her jockey was not hard on her once it became clear she had no chance.

3428a PREMIO ANGERA FIA (MAIDEN) (FILLIES) 7f 110y
5:35 (5:52) 2-Y-O **£6,897** (£3,034; £1,655; £828)

RPR
1 **Muccia (IRE)** 2-9-0 .... MEsposito 1 —
(G Miliani, Italy)
2 7 **Douby Douby (IRE)**[28] [2565] 2-9-0 .... MDemuro 11 —
(P Paciello, Italy)
3 nk **Clodia (IRE)** 2-9-0 .... DVargiu 7 —
(B Grizzetti, Italy)
4 1 **Zarina Caterina** 2-9-0 .... SMulas 2 —
(B Grizzetti, Italy)
5 1 1/4 **Curitiba** 2-8-10 .... APolli 3 —
(M G Quinlan) *mid-division, 5th half-way, pushed along straight, stayed on til no extra from 1f out*
6 1 1/2 **Thathshan (ITY)**[32] [2475] 2-9-0 .... GArena 10 —
(S Billeri, France)
7 2 **Narratrice (IRE)** 2-8-10 .... NMurru 6 —
(M Gasparini, Italy)
8 7 **Filara** 2-9-0 .... LManiezzi 4 —
(R Menichetti, Italy)
9 1 **White Visor (IRE)** 2-9-0 .... PConvertino 8 —
(A Angelelli, Italy)
10 9 **Simpatica (ITY)** 2-9-0 .... DDettori 12 —
(G Avvisati, Italy)

10 Ran

WIN 5.29; PL 1.74, 1.85, 1.55; DF 15.47.
Owner Scuderia Razza Rossonera **Bred** Allevamento Gialloblu Srl **Trained** Italy

NOTEBOOK
Curitiba produced a pleasing performance on her debut, running well for a long way, but she just got a little tired in the final furlong.

3209 EPSOM (L-H)

Thursday, July 13

OFFICIAL GOING: Good (good to firm in places)
Wind: Nil Weather: Overcast becoming fine

3429 TATTENHAM CORNER APPRENTICE H'CAP 1m 2f 18y
6:20 (6:23) (Class 5) (0-75,80) 4-Y-O+ **£3,886** (£1,156; £577; £288) **Stalls** Low

Form RPR
4046 1 **Blackmail (USA)**[7] [3209] 8-8-8 **59** ....(b) AdamKirby 10 66
(Miss B Sanders) *racd wd: trckd ldng trio: c alone to nr side st: sn wl on terms: r.o wl fnl f: jst prevailed* **10/1**
0061 2 nk **Magic Sting**[7] [3214] 5-9-8 **80** 6ex .... LukeMorris(7) 2 86
(M L W Bell) *trckd ldng pair: led main gp on far side over 2f out: drvn and hld on nr fin: jst pipped by lone runner nr side* **2/1**[1]
5300 3 nk **Transvestite (IRE)**[17] [2918] 4-9-3 **75** .... PatrickHills(7) 8 80
(J W Hills) *hld up: 8th st: prog on outer over 2f out: styd on fnl f to take 2nd of main gp nr fin* **10/1**
0020 4 3/4 **Lysandra (IRE)**[13] [3037] 4-9-0 **72** .... DanielleMcCreery(7) 7 76
(N Tinkler) *t.k.h: hld up: 6th st: prog to chse main gp ldr over 1f out: hld ins fnl f* **25/1**
0602 5 1 1/4 **Qualitair Wings**[9] [3168] 7-8-4 **58** .... LiamJones(3) 9 60
(J Hetherton) *trckd ldrs: 5th st: cl up 2f out: fdd fnl f* **5/1**[2]
5010 6 3/4 **Burgundy**[7] [3214] 9-9-5 **70** ....(b) AmirQuinn 4 70
(P Mitchell) *s.i.s: hld up: 9th and c alone down centre st: no imp on ldrs fr 2f out: kpt on* **12/1**
-013 7 1 **Catskill**[31] [2499] 4-9-5 **70** .... SaleemGolam 6 68
(E F Vaughan) *trckd ldr: chal 3f out: chsd new ldr over 2f out to over 1f out: wknd* **8/1**
64U2 8 7 **Hatch A Plan (IRE)**[7] [3221] 5-8-9 **62** .... TravisBlock(3) 1 47
(Mrs A J Hamilton-Fairley) *hld up in tch: 7th st: no prog and struggling over 2f out* **13/2**[3]
0060 9 3 **Play Up Pompey**[7] [3209] 4-8-0 **56** oh6 .... TolleyDean(5) 5 35
(J J Bridger) *racd freely: led to over 2f out: sn wknd* **20/1**
0/00 10 1/2 **Danakil**[7] [3209] 11-8-7 **65** .... ThomasBubb(7) 3 43
(S Dow) *sn last: detached st: nvr a factor* **100/1**

2m 10.43s (1.39) **Going Correction** +0.225s/f (Good) **10** Ran SP% **109.9**
Speed ratings (Par 103):103,102,102,101,100 100,99,93,91,91
CSF £27.98 CT £193.15 TOTE £13.10: £4.30, £1.10, £2.30; EX 41.90.
Owner Peter Crate **Bred** Skymarc Farm Inc **Trained** Headley, Surrey
■ Stewards' Enquiry : Adam Kirby one-day ban: used whip with excessive frequency (Jul 24)

FOCUS
Just a fair pace for this apprentice handicap and a difference of opinion coming into the home straight. Originally three horses looked as though they were going to come across to the stands' side, but two of them decided to return to the far side, leaving the eventual winner to enjoy a solo against the stands' rail. As a result the form may be unreliable.

3430 CHALK LANE MAIDEN AUCTION STKS 6f
6:50 (6:52) (Class 5) 2-Y-O **£3,886** (£1,156; £577; £288) **Stalls** High

Form RPR
0 1 **Addictive**[26] [2638] 2-8-2 ow1 .... SaleemGolam(3) 4 70+
(S C Williams) *dwlt: detached in last: abt 8 l bhd ldr whn c alone to nr side st: overall ldr over 1f out: sn wl clr* **11/2**[3]
6 2 5 **Pango's Legacy**[31] [2506] 2-8-11 .... TravisBlock(5) 2 66
(H Morrison) *chsd clr ldng pair: styd far side st: rdn to chse ldr over 1f out: plugged on to ld trio nr fin: no ch* **8/1**
623 3 3/4 **Cosmopolitan Lady**[14] [3026] 2-8-8 .... KDarley 1 56
(D M Simcock) *led: styd far side st: rdn over 1f out: no ch w wnr fnl f and hdd nr fin on his side* **4/6**[1]
663 4 12 **Bahamian Love**[31] [2500] 2-8-5 ow1 .... EddieAhern 3 17
(B W Hills) *pressed ldr: styd far side st: wknd rapidly over 1f out: eased* **4/1**[2]

1m 10.48s (-0.15) **Going Correction** -0.175s/f (Firm) **4** Ran SP% **106.5**
Speed ratings (Par 94):94,87,86,70
CSF £35.33 TOTE £5.60; EX 17.30.
Owner Paul W Stevens **Bred** Whitsbury Manor Stud **Trained** Newmarket, Suffolk

FOCUS
Arguments could be made for each of the quartet on what they had shown in their limited racecourse starts to date, in what looked a fairly decent little race. Once again though, the faster strip of ground on the stands' side proved to be the place to be. The form is rated at face value for the present.

NOTEBOOK
Addictive left the form of her Leicester debut well behind to come home well clear of her rivals, but as in the first race she undoubtedly benefited from racing alone against the stands' rail. The form looks dubious as a result. (op 11-1)
Pango's Legacy, ridden at a sensible pace early on, was severely handicapped by staying on the far side in the home straight though he eventually came out best of the trio that raced on that side. He is going the right way and should win one soon. (op 5-1)
Cosmopolitan Lady jinked left at the start and did not look the easiest of rides. Staying on the far side did not help, but this was still well below recent efforts. (tchd 8-11)
Bahamian Love dropped away tamely after going off too quickly early on. Official explanation: jockey said filly lost its action (op 7-2)

3431 SODEXHO PRESTIGE JUMP JOCKEYS DERBY H'CAP (TO BE RIDDEN BY NATIONAL HUNT JOCKEYS) 1m 4f 10y
7:25 (7:30) (Class 4) (0-80,77) 4-Y-O+ **£6,477** (£1,927; £963; £481) **Stalls** Centre

Form RPR
3114 1 **Great View (IRE)**[10] [3141] 7-11-2 **69** ....(p) TomScudamore 10 83
(Mrs A L M King) *hld up and sn last: 10th and making str prog st: led 2f out : pushed out and a holding on fnl f* **10/1**
0552 2 3/4 **Melvino**[8] [3192] 4-10-5 **58** oh1 .... PJBrennan 1 71
(T D Barron) *s.s: hld up: prog and cl 7th st: led 3f out to 2f out: hanging lft but rallied fnl f: a hld* **8/1**
5/65 3 9 **King Kasyapa (IRE)**[17] [2917] 4-11-6 **73** .... JasonMaguire 3 72
(P Bowen) *trckd ldrs: cl 6th st: effrt against nr side rail over 2f out: sn outpcd by ldng pair: plugged on* **33/1**
043- 4 hd **Fair Along (GER)**[98] [634] 4-11-0 **67** .... RichardJohnson 2 65
(P J Hobbs) *sn pressed ldr: led ent st: hdd 3f out: outpcd fr over 2f out* **11/2**[3]
1262 5 2 1/2 **Cormorant Wharf (IRE)**[10] [3141] 6-11-0 **67** .... JamieMoore 9 61
(G L Moore) *dwlt: in tch in midfield: u.p in 9th and struggling st: no ch after: plugged on* **9/2**[2]
0/40 6 nk **Kristoffersen**[36] [2357] 6-10-5 **58** oh1 .... WayneHutchinson 6 52
(Ian Williams) *settled midfield: 8th and u.p st: sn n.d* **25/1**
2500 7 2 **Cherished Number**[25] [1400] 7-10-8 **61** ....(b) ChristianWilliams 12 52
(A M Hales) *s.i.s: a towards rr: 11th and struggling st: nt on terms 3f out: n.d after* **33/1**
-030 8 shd **Border Tale**[7] [3220] 6-10-7 **60** .... EddieAhern 7 50
(James Moffatt) *prom: pressed ldr ent st: sn rdn and wknd* **16/1**
-040 9 1/2 **Stolen Hours (USA)**[30] [2534] 6-11-6 **73** .... LeightonAspell 5 63
(J Akehurst) *prom: cl 4th st: outpcd fr 3f out: wknd* **11/1**
0/60 10 8 **Sir Laughalot**[14] [3014] 6-10-5 **58** oh2 .... BarryFenton 4 35
(Miss E C Lavelle) *mde most tl hdd & wknd ent st: eased over 1f out* **25/1**
15-6 11 11 **Annibale Caro**[50] [1943] 4-11-10 **77** .... JimCrowley 8 36
(Sir Mark Prescott) *pressed ldng pair tl 5th and rdn st: sn wknd rapidly* **7/2**[1]
6636 12 11 **Papeete (GER)**[15] [2982] 5-10-10 **63** .... AndrewTinkler 13 5
(Miss B Sanders) *chsd ldrs for 5f: sn lost pl: last and wkng st* **17/2**
0-10 13 53 **Explosive Fox (IRE)**[25] [1748] 5-10-5 **58** ....(p) TimmyMurphy 11 —
(S Curran) *taken v steadily to post: in tch to 1/2-way: 12th and wkng st: virtually p.u 2f out* **16/1**

2m 40.08s (1.35) **Going Correction** +0.225s/f (Good) **13** Ran SP% **120.2**
Speed ratings (Par 105):104,103,97,97,95 95,94,94,93,88 81,73,38
CSF £84.84 CT £2539.31 TOTE £10.10: £2.50, £2.10, £9.30; EX 67.10.
Owner All The Kings Horses **Bred** Terry McGrath **Trained** Wilmcote, Warwicks

FOCUS
A mixed bag ability-wise for the second running of the Jump Jockeys Derby. Seven of the 13 jockeys were having their first ride at the track, but unlike their Flat counterparts in the previous race, all the riders looked to have paid attention to what had happened earlier, electing to come up the favoured stands' side rail in the home straight. The form is rated positively around the principals.
Cormorant Wharf(IRE) Official explanation: jockey said gelding hung right
Annibale Caro Official explanation: trainer's rep had no explanation for the poor form shown
Papeete(GER) Official explanation: jockey said mare hung right
Explosive Fox(IRE) Official explanation: jockey said gelding lost its action

3432 FRIENDS OF JONATHAN COOPER CONDITIONS STKS 1m 2f 18y
7:55 (7:59) (Class 3) 3-Y-O+ **£9,348** (£2,799; £1,399; £700) **Stalls** Low

Form RPR
0005 1 **Impeller (IRE)**[15] [2989] 7-9-0 91 .... EddieAhern 3 101
(W R Muir) *trckd ldng pair: cruising 2f out: led jst over 1f out: pushed out: cleverly* **14/1**
115- 2 1/2 **True Cause (USA)**[291] [5494] 3-8-3 105 ....(v[1]) KerrinMcEvoy 2 100
(Saeed Bin Suroor) *disp ld mostly: hanging lft and rdn over 2f out: looked uneasy on crse: hdd jst over 1f out: rallied fnl f: a hld* **4/1**[3]

2226 **3** 1 1/4 **Boule D'Or (IRE)**[20] [2803] 5-9-0 107 .... MichaelHills 4 98
(J Akehurst) *awkward and stdd s: hld up in last: cl up 2f out: effrt over 1f out: sn rdn and nt qckn* **2/1**[2]

4034 **4** *shd* **Crosspeace (IRE)**[6] [3254] 4-9-0 108 .... RoystonFfrench 1 97
(M Johnston) *disp ld: rdn over 2f out: hdd jst over 1f out: one pce* **1/1**[1]

2m 10.73s (1.69) **Going Correction** +0.225s/f (Good)
WFA 3 from 4yo+ 11lb 4 Ran SP% **110.0**
Speed ratings (Par 107):102,101,100,100
CSF £60.12 TOTE £9.90; EX 29.30.
Owner D G Clarke & C L A Edginton **Bred** P E Banahan **Trained** Lambourn, Berks

FOCUS
Another small but intriguing race where arguments could be made for each of the quartet. The form is rated through the winner to this year's best.

NOTEBOOK
Impeller(IRE) was travelling very strongly when hitting the front just over a furlong from home and was good value for his winning margin. He is a tough sort with bags of form in big-field handicaps. (op 11-1)
True Cause(USA) posted a respectable effort on his first start since finishing fifth in last season's Royal Lodge. He looked more straightforward than on that occasion and put his head down late when headed. On this evidence, he will not be taking up his Sussex Stakes engagement, but he does have another race in him. (op 9-4 tchd 9-2 in places)
Boule D'Or(IRE) is well below the sort of form he has posted regularly over the past two years and, having gone 21 runs without a win, he is starting to get frustrating. (op 3-1)
Crosspeace(IRE) may be starting to pay the price for his recent exertions. (op 11-8 tchd 6-4)

3433 EPSOM & EWELL H'CAP — 1m 114y
8:25 (8:30) (Class 4) (0-85,82) 3-Y-0+ **£6,477** (£1,927; £963; £481) **Stalls** Low

Form RPR
0012 **1** **Paraguay (USA)**[5] [3282] 3-8-10 **77** .... EdwardCreighton(3) 2 85
(Miss V Haigh) *stdd s: hld up in detached last: stdy prog fr 2f out: shkn up and r.o to ld last 75yds: readily* **11/2**[3]

5666 **2** 1 **Katiypour (IRE)**[7] [3212] 9-9-12 **80** .... KerrinMcEvoy 7 87
(Miss B Sanders) *hld up bhd ldrs: cl 5th st: shkn up and nt qckn 2f out: r.o ins fnl f: snatched 2nd last stride* **7/2**[2]

6606 **3** *shd* **My Princess (IRE)**[19] [2865] 4-9-2 **70** .... JimmyFortune 1 77
(N A Callaghan) *pressed ldrs: 3rd st: chal 2f out: nt qckn over 1f out: renewed effrt and upsides ins fnl f: nt qckn again* **13/2**

5412 **4** *nk* **Deeper In Debt**[5] [3311] 8-9-2 **70** 6ex .... DarryllHolland 4 76
(J Akehurst) *led: hrd pressed 2f out: hanging lft fr over 1f out: hdd & wknd last 75yds* **3/1**[1]

-000 **5** 1 **Joseph Henry**[25] [2683] 4-10-0 **82** .... KDarley 5 86
(M Johnston) *pressed ldrs: cl 4th st: rdn to chal 2f out: stl upsides ent fnl f: wknd last 100yds* **7/1**

-606 **6** 3 **Cape Maya**[26] [2655] 3-8-5 **69** .... EddieAhern 3 66
(B J Meehan) *wl in tch: cl 6th st: effrt on outer 2f out: hanging lft and wknd over 1f out* **12/1**

0006 **7** 3 1/2 **Sekula Pata (NZ)**[15] [2988] 7-9-8 **79** .... (b) SaleemGolam(3) 6 69
(Christian Wroe, UAE) *t.k.h: trckd ldr to over 3f out: sn wknd* **6/1**

1m 46.03s (0.29) **Going Correction** +0.225s/f (Good)
WFA 3 from 4yo+ 10lb 7 Ran SP% **110.4**
Speed ratings (Par 105):107,106,106,105,104 102,99
CSF £23.21 TOTE £6.50: £3.50, £1.60; EX 26.50.
Owner R J Budge **Bred** Nutbush Farm **Trained** Wiseton, Notts

FOCUS
Very little recent winning form but plenty of these were handicapped to win. The form is rated around the fourth backed up by the runner-up.
Deeper In Debt Official explanation: jockey said gelding hung left

3434 WALTON DOWNS H'CAP — 6f
8:55 (8:57) (Class 4) (0-80,75) 3-Y-0+ **£5,505** (£1,637; £818; £408) **Stalls** High

Form RPR
0020 **1** **Caustic Wit (IRE)**[3] [3368] 8-9-2 **70** .... (p) TolleyDean(7) 9 81
(M S Saunders) *trckd ldng pair: nt clr run over 1f out and hanging: got through ent fnl f to ld last 150yds: r.o wl* **8/1**

3331 **2** 1 1/4 **Louphole**[15] [2971] 4-9-4 **65** .... FergusSweeney 4 72
(P J Makin) *rrd s: wl in rr: 9th st: prog wl over 1f out: hanging lft after: bmpd 1f out: styd on to take 2nd nr fin* **7/2**[1]

0054 **3** *hd* **Buy On The Red**[14] [3012] 5-9-12 **73** .... (b) KerrinMcEvoy 1 79
(W R Muir) *chsd ldr: rdn 2f out: nt qckn 1f out: kpt on same pce after* **4/1**[2]

0000 **4** *hd* **Pachello (IRE)**[7] [3212] 4-10-0 **75** .... KDarley 2 81
(J M Bradley) *blazed off in front: rdn over 1f out: hdd and fdd last 150yds* **25/1**

3034 **5** 1 **Summer Recluse (USA)**[15] [2971] 7-9-6 **67** .... (t) DarryllHolland 7 70
(J M Bradley) *chsd clr ldrs: 6th st: rdn 2f out: no imp over 1f out: kpt on ins fnl f* **15/2**

0-05 **6** 3/4 **Vegas Boys**[31] [2496] 3-9-8 **75** .... JimmyFortune 10 75
(N A Callaghan) *chsd ldng trio: rdn over 2f out: cl up ent fnl f: wknd sn after* **11/2**[3]

4332 **7** 1 **Sweet Pickle**[13] [3033] 5-9-1 **65** .... (e) AmirQuinn(3) 8 63
(J R Boyle) *dwlt: towards rr: 7th st: effrt on outer 2f out: cl up jst over 1f out: bmpd rival sn after and wknd* **7/1**

0-60 **8** 1 1/2 **Stokesies Wish**[3] [3368] 6-8-7 **57** .... AdamKirby(3) 6 50
(J L Spearing) *chsd clr ldrs: 5th st: rdn wl over 2f out: wkng whn n.m.r jst over 1f out* **20/1**

0/0- **9** 6 **Khalidia (USA)**[506] [451] 5-9-9 **70** .... EddieAhern 5 45
(M A Magnusson) *a wl in rr: 8th st: wknd over 2f out* **12/1**

0000 **10** 5 **Middleton Grey**[79] [1220] 8-9-11 **72** .... (p) LPKeniry 3 32
(A G Newcombe) *s.i.s: outpcd and a wl bhd in last* **16/1**

68.98 secs (-1.65) **Going Correction** +0.225s/f (Good)
WFA 3 from 4yo+ 6lb 10 Ran SP% **115.2**
Speed ratings (Par 105):104,102,102,101,100 99,98,96,88,81
CSF £35.68 CT £132.47 TOTE £9.20: £2.80, £1.30, £2.00; EX 39.30 Place 6 £5,848.43, Place 5 £3,026.17.
Owner Mrs Sandra Jones **Bred** Gainsborough Stud Management Ltd **Trained** Green Ore, Somerset

FOCUS
There was a suspicion beforehand that this could turn in to a messy affair, with the likes of Sweet Pickle, Louphole and Stokesies Wish tending to come from off the pace, and although there were no real hard luck stories, a few of them got into a bit of a mess late on. Nevertheless, the form looks solid enough on paper.
Caustic Wit(IRE) Official explanation: trainer's representative said, regarding the improved form shown, gelding was poorly drawn and forced wide last time out
T/Plt: £1,592.70 to a £1 stake. Pool: £57,164.65. 26.20 winning tickets. T/Qpdt: £160.40 to a £1 stake. Pool: £4,402.60. 20.30 winning tickets. JN

3031 **FOLKESTONE** (R-H)
Thursday, July 13

OFFICIAL GOING: Good to firm (firm in places)
Wind: Virtually nil Weather: Sunny and warm

3435 EBF MEDIAN AUCTION MAIDEN FILLIES' STKS — 7f (S)
2:20 (2:20) (Class 5) 2-Y-0 **£3,238** (£963; £481; £240) **Stalls** Low

Form RPR
5 **1** **Dora Explora**[20] [2816] 2-9-0 .... JimmyFortune 7 66
(P W Chapple-Hyam) *pressed ldr tl led over 2f out: rdn over 1f out: styd on strly to go clr ins fnl f* **11/8**[1]

35 **2** 2 1/2 **Little Miss Wizzy**[14] [3010] 2-9-0 .... HayleyTurner 9 60
(M L W Bell) *trckd ldrs on outer: rdn and chsd wnr 2f out tl 1f out: outpcd by wnr fnl f: wnt 2nd again last 100 yds* **13/2**

0 **3** *nk* **Doubly Guest**[52] [1896] 2-9-0 .... OscarUrbina 5 59
(G G Margarson) *dwlt: sn rcvrd and hld up in tch: rdn and hdwy over 2f out: kpt on one pced fnl f* **25/1**

500 **4** 1/2 **Whipchord (IRE)**[26] [2631] 2-9-0 .... RichardSmith 10 57
(R Hannon) *hld up in tch: rdn wl over 2f out: chsd wnr 1f out: flashed tail and wknd last 100 yds* **4/1**[2]

5 2 1/2 **Poyle Kiera** 2-9-0 .... FergusSweeney 1 51
(M Blanshard) *bhd: kpt on steadily fr over 1f out: nt rch ldrs* **40/1**

6 1/2 **Minnow** 2-8-11 .... SaleemGolam(3) 6 50
(S C Williams) *dwlt: hld up bhd: rdn and hdwy wl over 2f out: sn chsng ldrs: wknd 1f out* **25/1**

05 **7** 1/2 **Saxenberg**[34] [2388] 2-8-9 .... JerryO'Dwyer(5) 8 48
(Miss J R Gibney) *trckd ldrs: rdn wl over 2f out: wkng whn sltly hmpd over 1f out* **50/1**

8 1 3/4 **Avina Laugh** 2-9-0 .... RobertHavlin 2 44
(P W Chapple-Hyam) *cl up: rdn 3f out: sn struggling and wl bhd* **20/1**

06 **9** 1 **Gorgeous Girl**[14] [3010] 2-8-11 .... AdamKirby(3) 3 41
(P W D'Arcy) *slt ld tl wl over 2f out: sn rdn: wknd over 1f out* **20/1**

03 **10** 3 **Abounding**[14] [3010] 2-9-0 .... SebSanders 4 33
(R M Beckett) *trckd ldrs: rdn wl over 2f out: sn wknd: no ch whn sltly hmpd over 1f out* **9/2**[3]

1m 26.8s (-1.10) **Going Correction** -0.30s/f (Firm) 10 Ran SP% **115.2**
Speed ratings (Par 91):94,91,90,90,87 86,86,84,83,79
CSF £9.43 TOTE £2.10: £1.10, £2.30, £5.70; EX 9.50 Trifecta £115.40 Part won. Pool £162.62 - 0.10 winning units..
Owner Sills Racing **Bred** Catridge Farm Stud And Mrs J Hall **Trained** Newmarket, Suffolk

FOCUS
This didn't look the strongest of juvenile fillies' maidens and so the time, within a second of standard, can be attributed to the very fast ground. The runner-up and the time are the best guides to the level.

NOTEBOOK
Dora Explora had shown enough promise at Goodwood on her debut to suggest she would be a different proposition upped in trip and with the experience under her belt. Connections believe she will not be seen at her best until next year, but given the way she stayed on strongly in the final furlong of this contest, she can make an impact in nurseries later this summer. (tchd 5-4)
Little Miss Wizzy reversed recent Lingfield form with Abounding, and this was better after a lacklustre effort on the All-Weather last time. Given her breeding and running style, she may be the type to appreciate an easier surface, and she should begin nursery life off a pretty modest mark. (op 7-1 tchd 6-1)
Doubly Guest was never going the pace over five furlongs at Windsor on her debut, but this was a much improved effort over this longer trip. She was always travelling nicely off the pace before making good headway passing the two-pole and kept on nicely in the closing stages. She can build on this, especially over further.
Whipchord(IRE), the most experienced filly in field, could not maintain her effort approaching the furlong marker and she now has something to prove.
Poyle Kiera was not given a hard time on this debut but was noted making late headway from the rear and she looked as though the run would bring her on significantly.
Minnow, bred to be speedy, was another to show promise before flattening out in the closing stages and may be of more interest dropped back to six furlongs.
Avina Laugh Official explanation: jockey said filly was unsuited by the good to firm (firm in places) ground

3436 FOLKESTONE-RACECOURSE.CO.UK MAIDEN STKS — 7f (S)
2:55 (2:55) (Class 5) 3-Y-0 **£3,562** (£1,059; £529; £264) **Stalls** Low

Form RPR
4- **1** **Macedon**[356] [3680] 3-9-3 .... LPKeniry 2 70+
(J S Moore) *trckd ldrs on stands rail: plld out over 1f out: shkn up and qcknd to ld last 100 yds: readily* **3/1**[2]

-002 **2** 1 3/4 **High Octave (IRE)**[14] [3011] 3-9-0 66 .... AdamKirby(3) 3 66
(B G Powell) *hld up bhd: hdwy over 2f out: rdn to ld over 1f out: hdd last 100 yds: no ch w wnr* **11/2**[3]

5650 **3** 1 **Alwariah**[29] [2554] 3-8-12 49 .... HayleyTurner 7 58
(C E Brittain) *t.k.h: chsd ldr tl led wl over 2f out: rdn and hdd over 1f out: no ex ins fnl f* **12/1**

3-52 **4** 4 **Secret Assassin (IRE)**[11] [3112] 3-9-3 74 .... SebSanders 5 52
(W R Muir) *hld up in midfield: effrt u.p 2f out: sn no prog* **1/1**[1]

0 **5** 13 **Boysie Brigador (USA)**[12] [3090] 3-9-3 .... (t) FJohansson 4 17
(R A Kvisla) *hld up in last pair: swtchd rt and rdn 2f out: sn struggling: t.o* **66/1**

0 **6** 2 **Kims Rose (IRE)**[6] [3266] 3-8-5 .... TolleyDean(7) 8 7
(R A Harris) *wnt rt s: t.k.h and sn prom: rdn over 2f out: sn wknd* **14/1**

7 1 1/2 **Mocairde (USA)**[424] [1728] 3-8-12 .... JimmyFortune 1 —
(J R Best) *t.k.h: hld up: rdn over 2f out: sn struggling: t.o* **8/1**

0-0 **8** 6 **Patitiri (USA)**[19] [2859] 3-8-7 .... JerryO'Dwyer(5) 6 —
(M G Quinlan) *led tl rdn and hdd wl over 2f out: sn wknd: t.o* **33/1**

1m 25.9s (-2.00) **Going Correction** -0.30s/f (Firm) 8 Ran SP% **120.3**
Speed ratings (Par 100):99,97,95,91,76 74,72,65
CSF £21.17 TOTE £4.20: £1.30, £1.70, £3.10; EX 24.20 Trifecta £136.40 Pool: £219.13 - 1.14 winning units..
Owner Mrs Fitri Hay **Bred** Cheveley Park Stud Ltd **Trained** Upper Lambourn, Berks

FOCUS
A modest maiden but the winner looks capable of going on to better things. The third is the best guide to the form.

3437 CURZON PLACE RECRUITMENT H'CAP — 2m 93y
3:30 (3:30) (Class 6) (0-55,54) 4-Y-0+ **£2,730** (£806; £403) **Stalls** Low

Form — RPR

0205 **1** **Mustang Ali (IRE)**[146] 443 5-9-2 **48** .... AlanDaly 7 — 60
(Dr J R J Naylor) *hld up midfield: wl in tch: hdwy 6f out: wnt 2nd 3f out: led and edgd rt 2f out: sn rdn clr: easily* **12/1**

4060 **2** *5* **Lysander's Quest (IRE)**[13] 3035 8-8-8 **40** .... OscarUrbina 9 — 46
(R Ingram) *trckd ldrs: hdwy to trck ldng pair 5f out: rdn over 2f out: sn outpcd by wnr: kpt on to go 2nd nr fin* **11/2**[2]

6-00 **3** *hd* **Irish Ballad**[13] 3035 4-9-5 **54** .... (t) AdamKirby[(3)] 10 — 60
(W R Swinburn) *led: rdn over 2f out: hdd 2f out: no ch w wnr after: lost 2nd nr fin* **7/1**

260/ **4** *1* **Dear Sir (IRE)**[72] 3851 6-8-13 **45** .... RobertHavlin 13 — 50
(Mrs P N Dutfield) *t.k.h: hld up midfield: drvn and outpcd 5f out: styd on over 1f out: nt trble ldrs* **40/1**

2-66 **5** *¾* **Equilibria (USA)**[36] 2345 4-9-2 **48** .... JimmyFortune 4 — 52
(G L Moore) *towards rr: effrt u.p over 3f out: kpt on fnl f: nt trble ldrs* **8/1**

0-20 **6** *1* **Redspin (IRE)**[19] 2871 6-8-7 **39** .... LPKeniry 2 — 41
(J S Moore) *towards rr: rdn 6f out: styd on fnl f: n.d* **6/1**[3]

-006 **7** *nk* **Harlestone Linn**[32] 2483 4-9-2 **48** .... JamieMackay 8 — 50
(J L Dunlop) *chsd ldrs: wnt 2nd 1/2-way tl 3f out: sn rdn: wknd over 1f out* **12/1**

6404 **8** *hd* **Eamon An Chnoic (IRE)**[6] 3270 5-8-11 **50** .... SophieDoyle[(7)] 11 — 52
(B W Duke) *t.k.h: trckd ldrs: rdn 3f out: wknd wl over 1f out* **14/1**

6036 **9** *2* **Lenwade**[13] 3035 5-8-10 **42** .... SebSanders 14 — 41
(G G Margarson) *chsd ldrs: rdn over 3f out: keeping on one pced whn hmpd and hit rail over 2f out: no ch after* **6/1**[3]

0035 **10** *½* **Barnbrook Empire (IRE)**[16] 2944 4-8-2 **41** .... TolleyDean[(7)] 1 — 40
(R A Harris) *hld up in tch: rdn over 3f out: nvr on terms* **14/1**

6050 **11** *5* **Bhutan (IRE)**[17] 2935 11-8-1 **38** .... RobynBrisland[(5)] 6 — 31
(Jim Best) *hld up in last pair: sme prog 3f out: n.d* **50/1**

03-0 **12** *7* **Frontlinefinancier**[61] 1690 6-9-1 **54** .... MarkCoumbe[(7)] 12 — 38
(N I M Rossiter) *chsd ldr tl 1 1/2-way: rdn and lost pl qckly 4f out* **5/1**[1]

00-5 **13** *44* **Just Beware**[46] 1879 4-8-8 **43** .... (p) SaleemGolam[(3)] 5 — —
(Miss Z C Davison) *a last pair: t.o 3f out: eased over 1f out* **66/1**

3m 37.2s (-3.50) **Going Correction** -0.30s/f (Firm) **13** Ran SP% **118.8**
Speed ratings (Par 101):96,93,93,92,92 92,91,91,90,90 88,84,62
CSF £75.83 CT £508.40 TOTE £10.80: £3.40, £2.10, £3.10; EX 44.90 Trifecta £141.30 Part won. Pool: £199.15 - 0.50 winning units..
Owner Ascot Brew Racing **Bred** Pat Dowling **Trained** Shrewton, Wilts
■ Stewards' Enquiry : Sophie Doyle two-day ban: careless riding (Jul 24-25)

FOCUS
A extremely weak handicap rated through the third.
Frontlinefinancier Official explanation: vet said gelding finished lame

3438 LADBROKES TOTAL BETTING SERVICE, REGISTER TODAY H'CAP — 5f
4:05 (4:05) (Class 5) (0-70,68) 3-Y-0+ **£3,886** (£1,156; £577; £288) **Stalls** Low

Form — RPR

0463 **1** **Witchry**[15] 2971 4-10-0 **68** .... FergusSweeney 1 — 78
(A G Newcombe) *trckd ldrs on stands rail: rdn over 1f out: styd on to ld last 100 yds: sn in command* **4/1**[2]

0160 **2** *1¼* **Parkside Pursuit**[3] 3348 8-9-11 **65** .... SebSanders 2 — 70
(J M Bradley) *bhd: rdn and outpcd over 2f out: rallied and nt clr run over 1f out: swtchd lft and r.o last 100 yds: wnt 2nd nr fin* **6/1**

/152 **3** *hd* **Millfields Dreams**[17] 2920 7-8-7 **52** .... JerryO'Dwyer[(5)] 4 — 56
(M G Quinlan) *led: rdn and hung rt 2f out: hdd last 100 yds: outpcd by wnr* **11/4**[1]

0320 **4** *hd* **Mostanad**[27] 2602 4-8-7 **50** .... AdamKirby[(3)] 5 — 54
(J M Bradley) *chsd ldr: rdn and ev ch 2f out: no ex wl ins fnl f* **18/1**

0456 **5** *nk* **Pro Tempore**[3] 3348 4-8-6 **49** oh3 .... NeilChalmers[(3)] 7 — 51
(David Pinder) *prom: ev ch and rdn 2f out: one pced ins fnl f* **12/1**

0300 **6** *¾* **Trace Clip**[16] 2962 8-8-2 **49** oh1 .... (e[1]) MarkCoumbe[(7)] 6 — 49
(N I M Rossiter) *slowly away: rcvrd and in tch after 2f: effrt whn pushed rt 1f out: nt rch ldrs* **20/1**

3036 **7** *nk* **Enjoy The Buzz**[31] 2494 7-9-1 **55** .... JimmyFortune 3 — 54
(J M Bradley) *hld up midfield: rdn and n.m.r 2f out: swtchd rt and bmpd rival twice over 1f out: no prog after* **5/1**[3]

6215 **8** *1¼* **Drumming Party (USA)**[5] 3297 4-9-11 **65** .... (t) LPKeniry 8 — 59
(A M Balding) *t.k.h: hld up: effrt whn bmpd twice over 1f out: no prog after* **4/1**[2]

400- **9** *4* **Spinetail Rufous (IRE)**[348] 3947 8-8-6 **49** oh3 .... (b) SaleemGolam[(3)] 9 — 29
(Miss Z C Davison) *in tch: rdn 2f out: sn no prog* **28/1**

59.44 secs (-1.36) **Going Correction** -0.30s/f (Firm) **9** Ran SP% **118.8**
Speed ratings (Par 103):98,96,95,95,94 93,93,91,84
CSF £29.19 CT £77.63 TOTE £5.70: £2.20, £2.90, £1.10; EX 44.10 Trifecta £156.30 Pool: £273.14 - 1.24 winning units..
Owner M K F Seymour **Bred** Darley **Trained** Yarnscombe, Devon

FOCUS
A modest handicap but solid rated through the next four behind the winner, and one that can produce future winners at a similar level.
Enjoy The Buzz Official explanation: jockey said horse hung right under pressure

3439 LADBROKES NUMBER 1 FOR LOTTO H'CAP — 1m 4f
4:40 (4:40) (Class 5) (0-70,65) 3-Y-0 **£3,886** (£1,156; £577; £288) **Stalls** Low

Form — RPR

-621 **1** **Alambic**[3] 3352 3-8-8 **52** 6ex .... SebSanders 7 — 65+
(Sir Mark Prescott) *mde all: rdn and veered bdly lft over 1f out: rcvrd and styd on to assert nr fin* **4/9**[1]

5321 **2** *hd* **Ollie George (IRE)**[7] 3221 3-9-7 **65** .... (v) LPKeniry 8 — 78
(A M Balding) *a chsng wnr: rdn over 2f out: lft w ev ch and bmpd ins fnl f: nt qckn nr fin* **7/2**[2]

4003 **3** *6* **Zizou (IRE)**[12] 3075 3-8-2 **46** oh4 .... HayleyTurner 5 — 49
(J J Bridger) *w.w midfield: effrt and rdn 3f out: sn outpcd: kpt on and wnt 3rd over 1f out: nt trble ldrs* **28/1**

1411 **4** *7* **Bob's Your Uncle**[17] 2933 3-9-7 **65** .... JimmyFortune 1 — 57
(J G Portman) *hld up: prog to chse ldng pair 5f out: rdn 3f out: sn outpcd* **7/1**[3]

0-05 **5** *1¾* **The Spread**[14] 3017 3-8-11 **55** .... FergusSweeney 6 — 44
(M Blanshard) *hld up in last: gd hdwy to chse ldrs 4f out: rdn and wknd wl over 2f out* **66/1**

6-02 **6** *3½* **Alwaysforsale (IRE)**[19] 2861 3-8-2 **46** .... FrancisFerris 3 — 29
(J S Moore) *chsd ldrs: drvn 5f out: wknd 3f out* **50/1**

-004 **7** *2* **Delorain (IRE)**[28] 2591 3-8-3 **54** .... (v) RonanKeogh[(7)] 2 — 34
(J A R Toller) *dwlt: hld up in rr: effrt u.p over 3f out: no ch 2f out* **40/1**

0020 **8** *28* **It's Basil**[14] 3016 3-8-8 **52** .... (b) JamieMackay 4 — —
(R M Flower) *chsd ldrs tl lost pl after 3f: last and rdn 3f out: no prog: eased fnl f: t.o* **80/1**

2m 34.93s (-5.57) **Going Correction** -0.30s/f (Firm) **8** Ran SP% **114.5**
Speed ratings (Par 100):106,105,101,97,96 93,92,73
CSF £2.20 CT £15.02 TOTE £1.40: £1.10, £1.20, £4.60; EX 2.30 Trifecta £42.30 Pool: £406.99 - 6.82 winning units..
Owner Lady O'Reilly **Bred** Miss K Rausing And Mrs S M Rogers **Trained** Newmarket, Suffolk

FOCUS
A moderate and uncompetitive race that produced a close finish between two progressive types who could rate higher.
Delorain(IRE) Official explanation: jockey said colt clipped heels in back straight

3440 LADBROKES "ANY 2 WILL DO" FILLIES' H'CAP — 1m 1f 149y
5:15 (5:16) (Class 5) (0-70,70) 3-Y-0+ **£3,886** (£1,156; £577; £288) **Stalls** Low

Form — RPR

3100 **1** **Gambling Spirit**[10] 3152 4-9-10 **63** .... FergusSweeney 3 — 70
(H Candy) *chsd ldrs: wnt 2nd 3f out: led 1f out: hld on gamely: all out* **8/1**

0466 **2** *nk* **Danzare**[10] 3159 4-8-10 **52** .... NeilChalmers[(3)] 9 — 58
(Mrs A J Hamilton-Fairley) *chsd ldrs tl lost pl over 4f out: gd hdwy on inner 2f out: wnt 2nd last 100 yds: jst hld* **9/1**

04-4 **3** *¾* **Quantum (IRE)**[28] 2587 3-9-6 **70** .... JimmyFortune 2 — 80+
(J H M Gosden) *s.s: wl bhd: rdn and hung lft bnd over 2f out: r.o strly fnl f: nrst fin* **7/4**[1]

00-1 **4** *1* **Thornfield Clo (IRE)**[15] 2968 3-8-1 **54** .... StephaneBreux[(3)] 7 — 57
(R Hannon) *t.k.h: chsd ldr after 1f: led 7f out: rdn and hdd 1f out: lost 2nd and wknd last 100 yds* **6/1**[2]

0304 **5** *1¼* **Depressed**[12] 3095 4-9-6 **64** .... (p) RichardKingscote[(5)] 10 — 64
(Ernst Oertel) *chsd ldrs: rdn and outpcd over 2f out: kpt on again fnl f* **7/1**[3]

-004 **6** *nk* **Greenmeadow**[13] 3036 4-9-4 **57** .... LPKeniry 1 — 57
(S Kirk) *chsd ldrs: 3rd and rdn over 2f out: wknd over 1f out* **12/1**

606 **7** *hd* **Jabbara (IRE)**[28] 2587 3-9-4 **68** .... OscarUrbina 5 — 67
(C E Brittain) *hld up bhd: last pair over 3f out: kpt on over 1f out: nvr on terms* **9/1**

300- **8** *¾* **Proud Scholar (USA)**[256] 6183 4-9-7 **60** .... (t) FJohansson 12 — 58
(R A Kvisla) *midfield tl lost pl 5f out: last pair 3f out: styd on over 1f out: n.d* **50/1**

0 **9** *2½* **Wilderness Bay (IRE)**[27] 2601 4-10-0 **67** .... GeorgeBaker 11 — 60
(M R Bosley) *midfield in tch: rdn over 3f out: sn struggling* **20/1**

-000 **10** *¾* **Vinska (USA)**[14] 3016 3-8-2 **52** .... DavidKinsella 8 — 44
(J W Hills) *t.k.h: sn led: hdd 7f out: rdn and wknd wl over 2f out* **66/1**

-060 **11** *½* **Adage**[28] 2584 3-9-1 **65** .... HayleyTurner 4 — 56
(David Pinder) *chsd ldrs: lost pl over 3f out: n.d after* **20/1**

0003 **12** *7* **Penmara**[7] 3230 3-8-5 **55** .... JamieMackay 6 — 33
(M H Tompkins) *sn bhd and pushed along: gd hdwy to chse ldrs 4f out: wknd wl over 2f out* **14/1**

2m 1.74s (-3.49) **Going Correction** -0.30s/f (Firm)
WFA 3 from 4yo 11lb **12** Ran SP% **121.6**
Speed ratings (Par 100):101,100,100,99,98 98,97,97,95,94 94,88
CSF £77.06 CT £185.73 TOTE £10.70: £2.80, £2.70, £1.30; EX 122.90 TRIFECTA Not won. Place 6 £39.14, Place 5 £21.30.
Owner Simon Broke And Partners **Bred** Beech Park Bloodstock Ltd **Trained** Kingston Warren, Oxon

FOCUS
A modest fillies' handicap run at a steady early pace and the form is ordinary.
T/Plt: £64.40 to a £1 stake. Pool: £43,054.80. 487.45 winning tickets. T/Qpdt: £11.80 to a £1 stake. Pool: £3,004.70. 188.30 winning tickets. SP

3413 NEWMARKET (JULY) (R-H)
Thursday, July 13

OFFICIAL GOING: Good to firm
Wind: Light, half-behind Weather: Overcast becoming cloudy with sunny spells after race 2

3441 BAHRAIN TROPHY (LISTED RACE) — 1m 5f
1:30 (1:30) (Class 1) 3-Y-O **£15,898** (£6,025; £3,015; £1,503; £753) **Stalls** Centre

Form — RPR

-130 **1** **Youmzain (IRE)**[20] 2801 3-9-0 106 .... TonyCulhane 1 — 113+
(M R Channon) *hld up: swtchd lft and hdwy over 1f out: led ins fnl f: rdn out* **3/1**[2]

21-5 **2** *1* **Jadalee (IRE)**[75] 1300 3-9-0 97 .... MartinDwyer 3 — 112+
(M P Tregoning) *chsd ldrs: nt clr run and lost pl over 2f out: swtchd lft over 1f out: r.o* **6/1**[3]

2124 **3** *5* **Degas Art (IRE)**[20] 2801 3-9-0 107 .... JohnEgan 2 — 104
(D R C Elsworth) *lw: trckd ldrs: racd keenly: rdn to ld over 1f out: hdd and no ex ins fnl f* **11/8**[1]

4-40 **4** *4* **Private Business (USA)**[20] 2804 3-9-0 102 .... (p) RichardHughes 6 — 98
(B W Hills) *lw: led: rdn over 5f out: hdd over 1f out: sn wknd* **13/2**

-636 **5** *14* **Morghim (IRE)**[20] 2801 3-9-0 97 .... RHills 4 — 77
(J L Dunlop) *chsd ldr: rdn over 2f out: wknd over 1f out* **8/1**

2m 43.85s (-8.15) **5** Ran SP% **105.8**
CSF £18.24 TOTE £3.50: £1.50, £2.50; EX 14.60.
Owner Jaber Abdullah **Bred** Frank Dunne **Trained** West Ilsley, Berks
■ Stewards' Enquiry : John Egan caution: careless riding

FOCUS
A new distance for this race, previously run over just short of 1m 7f. This was a decent race for the grade. There is more to come from the winner, while the second showed big improvement.

NOTEBOOK
Youmzain(IRE), one of two St Leger entries in the line-up, travelled well under a patient ride and won in style. He lost his footing on the bend and was always in rear in the King Edward VII, but he returned to nearer his good Leopardstown form here. Having been held up in last, he moved up easily on the outside, but Culhane held on to him still until the furlong marker, no doubt with one eye on keeping Dwyer and Jadalee hemmed in and forcing them to challenge wide. When asked to go the response was immediate - admittedly against slowish rivals - and he stretched more than two lengths clear without resort to the whip before being eased close home. He is 20-1 from 40-1 for the St Leger with sponsors Ladbrokes, and his trainer can choose between the Voltigeur, the Gordon and the March Stakes in the interim. (op 5-2)
Jadalee(IRE), patiently ridden, improved for the step up in trip on this first start since April. He came clear of the rest and might have given the winner a bit more to do if he had been able to get out sooner. (op 8-1)
Degas Art(IRE) had finished a long way ahead of Youmzain in the King Edward VII but, after taking a narrow lead, was made to look rather one paced in the latter stages. (op 5-4)

Private Business(USA), a disappointment over two miles when quietly fancied for the Queen's Vase, wore cheekpieces for the first time. He had plenty of use made of him over this shorter trip but was getting reminders with six furlongs to run and eventually dropped out to finish well beaten. (op 8-1)
Morghim(IRE), who had kept on for a remote sixth in the King Edward VII, three places ahead of Youmzain, pressed the leader for a long way but was beaten with more than two furlongs to go and eased down in the end. He has become disappointing. (op 10-1)

3442 TNT JULY STKS (GROUP 2) (C&G) 6f
2:00 (2:00) (Class 1) 2-Y-O

£39,746 (£15,064; £7,539; £3,759; £1,883; £945) **Stalls** Low

Form RPR
15 **1** **Strategic Prince**[21] 2771 2-8-12 .... EddieAhern 4 106+
(P F I Cole) *chsd ldrs: n.m.r and lost pl over 2f out: hdwy over 1f out: r.o to ld wl ins fnl f* **16/1**
22 **2** *1 3/4* **Armigerent (IRE)**[10] 3143 2-8-12 .... KDarley 5 101
(M Johnston) *mid-div: lost pl 4f out: r.o ins fnl f* **50/1**
6411 **3** *1 1/4* **Dubai's Touch**[10] 3143 2-8-12 .... JoeFanning 8 97
(M Johnston) *hld up in tch: racd keenly: rdn and ev ch fr over 1f out tl no ex wl ins fnl f* **33/1**
3151 **4** *1/2* **Dazed And Amazed**[16] 2960 2-8-12 .... RichardHughes 3 96
(R Hannon) *b.hind: led: hdd 4f out: led over 1f out: sn rdn: hdd wl ins fnl f: wknd towards fin* **10/1**[3]
1 **5** *hd* **Danebury Hill**[43] 2144 2-8-12 .... AlanMunro 9 95
(B J Meehan) *lw: s.i.s: hld up: hdwy over 2f out: rdn and ev ch fr over 1f out: tl wknd wl ins fnl f* **12/1**
1 **6** *1 1/4* **Narrjoo (USA)**[29] 2545 2-8-12 .... TonyCulhane 2 91
(M R Channon) *w ldr: racd keenly: led 4f out: rdn and hdd over 1f out: wknd fnl f* **6/1**[2]
2112 **7** *nk* **Hoh Mike (IRE)**[21] 2771 2-8-12 .... JamieSpencer 1 90
(M L W Bell) *dwlt: hdwy over 4f out: nt clr run over 1f out: sn rdn: wknd ins fnl f* **4/6**[1]
1140 **8** *4* **Mubaashir (IRE)**[23] 2719 2-8-12 .... LDettori 7 78
(E A L Dunlop) *lw: hld up: rdn over 2f out: wknd over 1f out* **12/1**
301 **9** *2 1/2* **Dubai Magic (USA)**[14] 3025 2-8-12 ....(t) RyanMoore 6 71
(C E Brittain) *prom: rdn 1/2-way: wknd over 1f out* **50/1**

1m 12.15s (-1.20) **Going Correction** +0.05s/f (Good) **9** Ran SP% **111.5**
Speed ratings (Par 106):110,107,106,105,105 103,103,97,94
CSF £572.26 TOTE £18.60: £3.10, £11.40, £6.20; EX 428.50 Trifecta £545.70 Part won. Pool: £768.66 - 0.10 winning units..
Owner H R H Sultan Ahmad Shah **Bred** The Ausherra Partnership **Trained** Whatcombe, Oxon

FOCUS
A very creditable winning time, even for a race like this. A muddling sort of contest, but no doubting the authority of the winner and the form could prove reasonable.

NOTEBOOK
Strategic Prince ◆, fifth in the Norfolk at Ascot, comprehensively reversed the placings with Hoh Mike. As befits his breeding - he is out of a half-sister to Oaks winner Ramruma - he proved well served by the step up to six furlongs and, if anything, can be seen in an even better light when put over farther. He looked to be going nowhere when coming under pressure two furlongs out but the picture changed dramatically in the final furlong when he quickened up to lead on the outside and soon pulled clear. He could go for the Richmond or Champagne Stakes at Goodwood next and can win more races at this level.
Armigerent(IRE) had finished runner-up in his first two starts and again had to settle for that berth but put in an encouraging effort. He was behind and was being pushed along over half a mile from home but stuck to his task well and kept on well in the final furlong. The loss of his maiden tag should be a formality before he steps back up in grade, perhaps over further.
Dubai's Touch was 6lb better off with the runner-up for a short-head success at Pontefract last time but the placings were easily reversed on these revised terms. He came through to throw down his challenge in the final furlong but could only keep on at the same pace. He had looked progressive beforehand but may have to be slightly dropped in class to add to his score.
Dazed And Amazed has progressed nicely with experience and was soon bowling along at a steady gallop. He could only keep on at the same pace when headed but probably ran to his mark and can win again in Listed class.
Danebury Hill stayed on in the closing stages on his first start since his debut success in May. He should come for the experience and should soon be making his mark once more.
Narrjoo(USA), stepping up markedly in grade, was soon in the thick of the action but faded in the closing stages, having raced keenly. He found this company just a little too hot but should also find further opportunities. (op 11-2 tchd 5-1)
Hoh Mike(IRE) was a major disappointment after his luckless run in the Norfolk Stakes. After missing the break he soon recovered to race in touch. Short of room with over a furlong to run, he was unable to quicken up when in the clear. This was not his running and he is better than he showed on this occasion. The longer trip might have been partly to blame. (op 8-11)
Mubaashir(IRE) Official explanation: jockey said colt ran flat

3443 BLANDFORD BLOODSTOCK JOSS COLLINS STKS (HERITAGE H'CAP) 1m 2f
2:35 (2:38) (Class 2) (0-105,97) 3-Y-O

£31,160 (£9,330; £4,665; £2,335; £1,165; £585) **Stalls** Centre

Form RPR
-211 **1** **Formal Decree (GER)**[31] 2502 3-8-13 **89**...................... JamieSpencer 6 101+
(G A Swinbank) *hld up: hdwy and hung lft over 1f out: rdn to ld and hung rt over 1f out: hung lft ins fnl f: drvn out* **3/1**[1]
1200 **2** *1 1/4* **Porters (USA)**[21] 2774 3-8-11 **87**.................................. RichardHughes 7 96
(R Hannon) *s.i.s: hld up: hdwy u.p and swtchd rt over 1f out: edgd lft ins fnl f: styd on* **50/1**
231 **3** *1* **Alcyon (IRE)**[36] 2366 3-8-9 **85**.. LDettori 2 92
(E A L Dunlop) *lw: chsd clr ldr: rdn over 2f out: ev ch whn hmpd over 1f out: styd on* **25/1**
-143 **4** *1 1/4* **King's Head (IRE)**[26] 2659 3-9-7 **97**.............................. PhilipRobinson 4 102
(M A Jarvis) *mid-div: outpcd 3f out: hdwy and swtchd lft over 1f out: styd on u.p* **8/1**[3]
-020 **5** *hd* **Military Cross**[21] 2774 3-9-5 **95**.................................... DarryllHolland 10 100
(W J Haggas) *hld up: hdwy over 2f out: hung lft over 1f out: no ex ins fnl f* **9/1**
2134 **6** *nk* **Lake Poet (IRE)**[20] 2805 3-9-0 **90**.................................. KerrinMcEvoy 3 94
(C E Brittain) *mid-div: outpcd 3f out: styd on ins fnl f: nt trble ldrs* **8/1**[3]
6012 **7** *shd* **Salute Him (IRE)**[11] 3119 3-8-11 **87**.................................. TedDurcan 13 91
(M R Channon) *chsd ldrs: rdn and ev ch over 1f out: wknd ins fnl f* **25/1**
2130 **8** *nk* **Kalankari (IRE)**[21] 2774 3-9-3 **93**.................................. MartinDwyer 5 96
(A M Balding) *lw: mid-div: hdwy u.p over 3f out: wknd ins fnl f* **12/1**
-340 **9** *nk* **Ahmedy (IRE)**[28] 2584 3-7-13 **75**.................................. AdrianMcCarthy 8 78
(M R Channon) *mid-div: hdwy over 2f out: rdn and nt clr run over 1f out: wknd ins fnl f* **100/1**
4600 **10** *5* **Silver Blue (IRE)**[15] 2988 3-9-5 **95**.................................. RyanMoore 14 88
(R Hannon) *lw: hld up: rdn over 3f out: n.d* **50/1**
1320 **11** *1 1/4* **Crime Scene (IRE)**[21] 2774 3-9-3 **93**.................................. KDarley 12 84
(M Johnston) *prom: rdn over 3f out: wknd fnl f* **12/1**
6201 **12** *5* **Road To Love (IRE)**[5] 3318 3-9-0 **90** 6ex.............................. JohnEgan 9 71
(M Johnston) *b. off fore: led and sn clr: rdn: edgd rt: hdd and hmpd over 1f out: sn wknd* **9/2**[2]
2-36 **13** *18* **Jumbajukiba**[21] 2774 3-8-13 **89**.. EddieAhern 1 36
(Mrs A J Perrett) *hld up: wknd over 2f out* **9/1**
-550 **14** *6* **Beau Nash (USA)**[20] 2805 3-8-11 **87**.................................. AlanMunro 11 23
(P W Chapple-Hyam) *chsd ldrs over 7f* **25/1**

2m 4.59s (-1.85) **Going Correction** +0.05s/f (Good) **14** Ran SP% **117.2**
Speed ratings (Par 106):109,108,107,106,106 105,105,105,105,101 100,96,81,77
CSF £189.22 CT £3169.33 TOTE £4.10: £1.60, £10.10, £3.70; EX 279.80 Trifecta £1305.90 Part won. Pool: £1,839.41 - 0.60 winning units..
Owner Mrs Karen S Pratt **Bred** Gestut Olympia **Trained** Melsonby, N Yorks

FOCUS
This is invariably an informative event, and there should once again be winners emerging from it before long. The form looks pretty solid. The winner improved again by 5lb, and can do better still. They went a very strong pace, set by the eventual twelfth.

NOTEBOOK
Formal Decree(GER) is lazy and does not look the most straightforward of rides, but he is going from strength to strength and completed his hat-trick with a most authoritative win, off a mark 17lb higher than for his first victory. He was being driven along with plenty to do half a mile out, and when he made his ground on the far side of the field he carried his head to the right and then hung in that direction. He took it up readily enough with more than a furlong to run, however, and was firmly in charge up the hill. A step up to a mile and a half will suit him. (op 7-2)
Porters(USA) belied his odds with a good effort, proving well suited by the step up from a mile and coming from a fair way back on the near side of the pack to be nearest at the finish. This was a good effort and the trip was presumably important to him. He will go to Goodwood next.
Alcyon(IRE) made a highly creditable handicap debut and fared much the best of those that raced prominently. He is clearly going to hold his own in this sort of company, and on this evidence he will not have any trouble getting further.
King's Head(IRE) looked vulnerable under top weight and ran at least as well as he was entitled to, staying on up the far side of the pack after getting outpaced. He looks worth a try over further. (op 9-1 tchd 10-1 in places)
Military Cross, back up to ten furlongs after a troubled run in the Britannia, was held up in rear through the early stages. After improving to chase the leaders, he edged left and weakened inside the final furlong. (op 15-2)
Lake Poet(IRE) ◆, a tough sort, got warm and was on his toes in the paddock, but he ran well nevertheless, staying on quite takingly as if he needs a return to further. (tchd 17-2 and 9-1 in places)
Salute Him(IRE) ran a respectable race in this warm company.
Kalankari(IRE) (tchd 11-1 tchd 14-1 in places)
Silver Blue(IRE) continues to struggle and needs dropping a few pounds.
Road To Love(IRE), under a 6lb penalty but officially 3lb well in, was soon clear and led them all up the middle of the straight, deliberately shunning the stands' rail, before the effort started to tell on him approaching the two pole and he was eventually swamped. (op 4-1)
Jumbajukiba was particularly disappointing, as he was in trouble a long time before stamina became an issue, having been dropped in on the rail from his outside draw. He had not impressed on his way to post and may do better when he gets the chance to race on easier ground again. Official explanation: jockey said colt ran flat (tchd 10-1 in places)

3444 PRINCESS OF WALES'S WBX.COM STKS (GROUP 2) 1m 4f
3:10 (3:11) (Class 1) 3-Y-O+ **£51,102** (£19,368; £9,693; £4,833) **Stalls** Centre

Form RPR
1211 **1** **Soapy Danger**[20] 2804 3-8-3 96.. KDarley 1 121
(M Johnston) *lw: led: rdn and hdd 2f out: rallied to ld and edgd rt over 1f out: styd on u.p* **5/1**[3]
-122 **2** *3/4* **Mountain High (IRE)**[19] 2845 4-9-2 110.............................. RyanMoore 2 120
(Sir Michael Stoute) *lw: trckd wnr: rdn and ev ch over 1f out: styd on* **4/7**[1]
4533 **3** *3/4* **Enforcer**[19] 2845 4-9-2 116.. MartinDwyer 3 119
(W R Muir) *s.i.s: sn trcking ldrs: led 2f out: sn rdn: hung rt and hdd: styd on same pce ins fnl f* **9/2**[2]
-360 **4** *2* **Bandari (IRE)**[19] 2845 7-9-2 115.. RHills 4 116
(M Johnston) *hld up: rdn over 1f out: nvr able to chal* **10/1**

2m 32.82s (-0.09) **Going Correction** +0.05s/f (Good)
WFA 3 from 4yo+ 13lb **4** Ran SP% **107.6**
Speed ratings (Par 115):102,101,101,99
CSF £8.51 TOTE £4.30; EX 7.50.
Owner Mrs R J Jacobs **Bred** Newsells Park Stud Limited **Trained** Middleham Moor, N Yorks

FOCUS
The smallest field since 1992, and not a particularly distinguished bunch by Group 2 standards. Not strong form for the grade although the second and third ran close to their Ascot running.

NOTEBOOK
Soapy Danger , on paper, had a lot to find, as his official rating had remained on 96 after his win in the two-mile Queen's Vase, where he had needed plenty of rousting along, and the shorter trip was hardly likely to be to his advantage. However, he was given a really positive ride, and having been challenged on either side and headed, his stamina came into play in the closing stages and he came back strongly. Only the third three-year-old to win this in the last 20 years - Fruits of Love, from the same stable, was the last in 1998 - he has come a very long way in a short time, having started his career with a defeat on the Polytrack at Wolverhampton only in February. There is no doubt more to come, but he hardly looks the type for the King George, for which he holds an entry, and a return to further for the St Leger looks much more his thing. (op 9-2)
Mountain High(IRE) looked hard to beat on his Hardwicke second to Maraahel, but having had every chance and come to win the race he was beaten fair and square by the winner. He ran pretty much to his Ascot form, but bumped into an improver. (op 8-11)
Enforcer, who had previously run well in the Coronation Cup, which helps give the form some credibility, made his effort at the same time as Mountain High, but on the opposite side of the winner, and he too had every chance. He may still run in the King George, but if not there are alternative options abroad in Cologne and Deauville. (op 4-1)
Bandari(IRE) had disappointed in the Hardwicke, and also on his previous start, but this race seems to bring out the best in him and he won it in 2004 as well as finishing second to Millenary in 2003. A switch to more patient tactics was tried here - not surprisingly with stablemate Soapy Danger making the running - and although he is not the force he was he ran his best race in a while.

3445 CAPANNELLE RACECOURSE EBF NOVICE STKS 6f
3:45 (3:45) (Class 2) 2-Y-O **£9,715** (£2,890; £1,444; £721) **Stalls** Low

Form RPR
1 **Hamoody (USA)** 2-8-8 .... AlanMunro 7 85+
(P W Chapple-Hyam) *gd sort: scope: lw: s.i.s: plld hrd and sn prom: led ins fnl f: r.o wl* **2/1**[1]
2 *2* **Romanov Dynasty (IRE)** 2-8-8 .... MartinDwyer 8 79
(R Hannon) *w'like: scope: lw: s.s: hld up: hung lft over 1f out: r.o ins fnl f: no ch w wnr* **25/1**

1 **3** 3/4 **Chin Wag (IRE)**[14] 3005 2-9-2 RichardMullen 6 85
(E S McMahon) *w ldr: plld hrd: led 1/2-way: rdn and hdd over 1f out: styd on same pce ins fnl f* **4/1**[3]

41 **4** *hd* **Top Bid**[45] 2072 2-9-2 DavidAllan 9 84
(T D Easterby) *lw: chsd ldrs: rdn to ld over 1f out: hdd and no ex ins fnl f* **8/1**

431 **5** *shd* **The Old Fella**[7] 3210 2-9-5 RyanMoore 3 87
(R Hannon) *trckd ldrs: plld hrd: rdn over 2f out: ev ch ins fnl f: no ex* **7/2**[2]

6 **6** 2 1/2 **Reebal**[8] 3193 2-8-12 LDettori 2 72
(B J Meehan) *led to 1/2-way: rdn and ev ch over 1f out: wknd ins fnl f* **14/1**

7 3/4 **Habalwatan (IRE)** 2-8-8 KerrinMcEvoy 4 66
(C E Brittain) *w'like: cmpt: s.i.s: hld up: effrt over 2f out: wknd over 1f out* **33/1**

8 1 3/4 **Rule Of Life** 2-8-8 RichardHughes 1 61
(B W Hills) *wl grwn: str: bkwd: hld up: wknd over 1f out* **7/1**

1m 13.21s (-0.14) **Going Correction** +0.05s/f (Good) **8** Ran SP% **112.6**
Speed ratings (Par 100):102,99,98,98,97 94,93,91
CSF £53.90 TOTE £2.90: £1.40, £4.70, £1.70; EX 65.40.

Owner Saleh Al Homaizi & Imad Al Sagar **Bred** Ragged Mountain Farm **Trained** Newmarket, Suffolk

FOCUS

This was probably quite a decent event rated around the third and fourth.

NOTEBOOK

Hamoody(USA), a $210,000 buy at the breeze-ups, ran out a convincing winner despite pulling hard. He looked an athletic type in the paddock and took the preliminaries pretty well, but once the stalls opened he was pretty keen and did not really settle that well through the race. However, when pulled out to lead a furlong from home he still had plenty to offer and quickened up in the style of a good horse. This experience should prove of major benefit for his next start now the freshness is out of him and his trainer will step him up to seven furlongs next time. He looks a useful prospect and more should certainly be heard from him. (op 15-8 tchd 9-4 in places)

Romanov Dynasty(IRE) ◆ , who fetched 58,000gns this year, shaped with considerable promise. Slowly away, he was settled in last place until asked for his effort over two furlongs out and finished well to take second spot. Rather green here, he should derive considerable benefit from this run and is one to be with next time.

Chin Wag(IRE) , giving 8lb to the front two for a debut success at Leicester, was keen in the early stages. He came through to lead over two furlongs out and kept on quite well without proving quite good enough. Time may well tell that he had an impossible task at the weights and he can win more races in a similar grade. (op 11-2 tchd 6-1 in places)

Top Bid, who had hacked up by eight lengths on his last outing at Leicester, acquitted himself well. He was soon close up and had every chance in the final two furlongs until the winner swooped. He is another who can find further opportunities at this sort of level. (op 9-1)

The Old Fella, a winner at Epsom a week earlier, was conceding 11lb to the winner and put in a sound effort. He tried to make progress towards the far side in the final two furlongs and kept on at the same pace, but is another for whom there will be further visits to the winner's enclosure. (op 10-3 tchd 3-1 in places)

Reebal, who made the early running, is certainly capable of making his mark in lesser company. (tchd 16-1 in places)

Habalwatan(IRE), who had two handlers in the paddock, chased the leaders until two out and should improve.

Rule Of Life, whose dam won the Cheveley Park Stakes, looked a big, raw colt who can improve for the experience, but may do better in his second season. (op 13-2)

3446 GIST H'CAP — 2m 24y

4:20 (4:20) (Class 3) (0-90,84) 4-Y-O+ **£9,715** (£2,890; £1,444; £721) **Stalls** Centre

Form				RPR
1-33	**1**		**Mersey Sound (IRE)**[11] 3114 8-7-11 **65** oh1 MarcHalford(5) 6 (D R C Elsworth) *chsd ldrs: led ins fnl f: edgd rt: rdn out* **11/2**[3]	76
-012	**2**	1 1/2	**Our Monogram**[18] 2894 10-8-9 **72** RichardHughes 8 (R M Beckett) *led and sn clr: rdn 5f out: hdd ins fnl f: styd on same pce* **6/1**	81
6112	**3**	2 1/2	**Ti Adora (IRE)**[7] 3220 4-9-1 **78** JohnEgan 7 (P W D'Arcy) *lw: hld up: hdwy over 2f out: rdn over 1f out: no ex ins fnl f* **6/1**	84
4300	**4**	2	**Establishment**[19] 2849 9-8-13 **76** EddieAhern 5 (C A Cyzer) *chsd clr ldr: rdn over 3f out: styd on same pce appr fnl f* **9/1**	80
6126	**5**	*nk*	**Wise Owl**[12] 3098 4-9-7 **84** DarryllHolland 9 (J Pearce) *hld up: hdwy over 2f out: sn rdn: styd on same pce appr fnl f* **14/1**	87
5202	**6**	5	**Dovedon Hero**[11] 3116 6-8-7 **70** (b) RichardMullen 1 (P J McBride) *hld up: hdwy over 2f out: rdn and wknd over 1f out* **7/1**	67
6603	**7**	3	**John Forbes**[18] 2894 4-8-5 **68** PaulFessey 2 (B Ellison) *hld up: rdn over 2f out: n.d* **14/1**	62
0302	**8**	2 1/2	**Trance (IRE)**[9] 3177 6-9-4 **81** (p) RyanMoore 4 (T D Barron) *hld up: effrt over 2f out: sn wknd* **5/1**[2]	72
4403	**9**	10	**Follow On**[8] 3203 4-8-10 **73** AlanMunro 3 (A P Jarvis) *lw: chsd ldrs: rdn over 3f out: wknd over 2f out* **9/2**[1]	52

3m 28.46s (1.47) **Going Correction** +0.05s/f (Good) **9** Ran SP% **114.6**
Speed ratings (Par 107):98,97,96,95,94 92,90,89,84
CSF £38.09 CT £204.24 TOTE £7.20: £2.00, £2.40, £2.10; EX 45.00.

Owner A Heaney **Bred** Airlie Stud **Trained** Newmarket, Suffolk

FOCUS

A moderate winning time for the grade. An ordinary staying handicap, the winner running up to his best form of the last two years and sound enough form.

NOTEBOOK

Mersey Sound(IRE) is pretty much a reformed character these days, and he came here on a good mark on his favoured fast ground, and with a capable apprentice taking off 5lb. His recent Warwick third had been boosted by the subsequent good wins of the pair that beat him, and he franked that form once again by travelling well throughout under a patient ride and picking up the leader readily enough up the final hill.

Our Monogram soon established a long lead and, sticking on gallantly, was collared only inside the final furlong. (op 15-2)

Ti Adora(IRE) made her effort on the outside and looked a danger a furlong out, but this was her first try at two miles and she did not get home as well as the winner.

Establishment is a regular in these races and ran creditably enough, but remains high enough in the weights. (op 8-1)

Wise Owl, back on turf for the first time this year, ran about as well as could be expected under his big weight.

Dovedon Hero, a market mover, had to be ridden to get into contention after being held up in rear and ideally needs to get there on the bridle if he is ever to win these days. (op 10-1)

Follow On looked interesting following his improved effort over two miles on sand last time, but failed to run much of a race and remains a maiden. (op 4-1)

3447 CLASSIC FM H'CAP — 5f

4:55 (4:55) (Class 4) (0-85,85) 3-Y-O+ **£8,096** (£2,408; £1,203; £601) **Stalls** Low

Form				RPR
1000	**1**		**Matsunosuke**[27] 2618 4-9-2 **73** DarryllHolland 7 (A B Coogan) *hld up: racd keenly: hdwy over 1f out: rdn to ld ins fnl f: r.o* **16/1**	85+
4124	**2**	1 1/2	**Handsome Cross (IRE)**[12] 3069 5-9-11 **85** SilvestreDeSousa(3) 9 (D Nicholls) *lw: chsd ldrs: led over 1f out: hdd and unable qck ins fnl f* **7/1**	92
6046	**3**	*hd*	**Fast Heart**[7] 3211 5-9-12 **83** (t) AdrianTNicholls 8 (D Nicholls) *s.i.s: hld up: hdwy over 1f out: r.o: nrst fin* **5/1**[2]	89
2132	**4**	*nk*	**Kings College Boy**[8] 3190 6-8-9 **66** oh1 (b) PaulFessey 13 (R A Fahey) *mid-div: hmpd and nt clr run over 1f out: r.o ins fnl f: nt trble ldrs* **13/2**[3]	76+
4224	**5**	1 1/2	**Malapropism**[9] 3165 6-9-7 **78** JohnEgan 12 (M R Channon) *lw: chsd ldrs: rdn over 1f out: edgd rt: no ex fnl f* **10/1**	78
1-02	**6**	*hd*	**Lipizza (IRE)**[10] 3150 3-9-0 **76** LDettori 5 (N A Callaghan) *s.i.s: hld up: swtchd lft and hdwy over 1f out: nt trble ldrs* **9/2**[1]	73
3050	**7**	1/2	**Detonate**[10] 3155 4-8-2 **66** oh14 (p) KirstyMilczarek(7) 15 (Mrs C A Dunnett) *hld up in tch: rdn over 1f out: no ex fnl f* **100/1**	63
0005	**8**	*nk*	**Betsen (IRE)**[8] 3190 4-8-10 **67** JoeFanning 3 (D Nicholls) *chsd ldrs: rdn and ev ch over 1f out: wknd ins fnl f* **20/1**	63
3000	**9**	*nk*	**Figaro Flyer (IRE)**[19] 2866 3-9-9 **85** RichardMullen 11 (P Howling) *mid-div: outpcd 3f out: r.o ins fnl f* **33/1**	78
224	**10**	3/4	**Millinsky (USA)**[19] 2858 5-8-9 **73** RobbieMills(7) 6 (Rae Guest) *s.i.s: nvr nrr* **14/1**	65
3241	**11**	*nk*	**Hello Roberto**[14] 3027 5-9-3 **74** (p) AdrianMcCarthy 10 (R A Harris) *lw: led over 3f: wknd ins fnl f* **11/1**	65
01-5	**12**	1 1/4	**Bold Minstrel (IRE)**[27] 2624 4-9-9 **80** JamieSpencer 4 (M Quinn) *swtg: chsd ldrs: rdn and ev ch over 1f out: wknd fnl f* **7/1**	67
5520	**13**	4	**Financial Times (USA)**[15] 2981 4-9-3 **74** MickyFenton 1 (Stef Liddiard) *chsd ldrs: rdn over 1f out: wknd fnl f* **16/1**	46
6300	**14**	5	**Polar Force**[19] 2864 6-8-11 **68** RichardHughes 2 (Mrs C A Dunnett) *mid-div: wknd over 1f out* **20/1**	22

58.66 secs (-0.90) **Going Correction** +0.05s/f (Good)
WFA 3 from 4yo+ 5lb **14** Ran SP% **122.5**
Speed ratings (Par 105):109,106,106,105,103 103,102,101,101,100 99,97,91,83
CSF £121.75 CT £658.34 TOTE £22.20: £6.60, £3.00, £2.70; EX 254.00 Place 6 £6,444.78, Place 5 £2,568.96.

Owner A B Coogan **Bred** R Coogan **Trained** Soham, Cambs

FOCUS

A typical run-of-the mill sprint but sound form, with the second running to his best.

Kings College Boy Official explanation: jockey said gelding was denied a clear run

Financial Times(USA) Official explanation: jockey said gelding lost its action

Polar Force Official explanation: jockey said gelding didn't feel right

T/Jkpt: £120,031.10 to a £1 stake. Pool: £169,058.00. 1.00 winning ticket. T/Plt: £3,515.50 to a £1 stake. Pool: £115,096.60. 23.90 winning tickets. T/Qpdt: £73.40 to a £1 stake. Pool: £9,555.60. 96.25 winning tickets. CR

3264 WARWICK (L-H)

Thursday, July 13

OFFICIAL GOING: Good to firm

Wind: Virtually nil

3448 HALL BROS MAIDEN AUCTION STKS — 7f 26y

2:10 (2:12) (Class 5) 2-Y-O **£3,238** (£963; £481; £240) **Stalls** Low

Form				RPR
6	**1**		**Iron Fist (IRE)**[12] 3083 2-9-1 RichardMullen 9 (E J O'Neill) *sn chsng ldr: drvn along 2f out: styd on to ld fnl 50yds* **13/8**[1]	78
0	**2**	*nk*	**Anthea**[16] 2958 2-8-6 NickyMackay 1 (B R Millman) *trckd ldrs: drvn and hung rt 1f out: styd on to take 2nd cl home and gaining on wnr: nt quite get up* **4/1**[2]	68
4	**3**	1	**Lusolly**[33] 2474 2-8-11 TPQueally 11 (M G Quinlan) *led: rdn 2f out: hdd and outpcd fnl 50yds* **7/1**[3]	71
0	**4**	1 3/4	**Bathwick Breeze**[14] 3025 2-8-11 GrahamGibbons 4 (B R Millman) *s.i.s: sn rcvrd to chse ldrs: rdn 2f out: wknd ins last* **40/1**	66
00	**5**	2 1/2	**High Bullen**[8] 3201 2-8-9 ow1 DaneO'Neill 6 (M Meade) *chsd ldrs: drvn along over 2f out: wknd fnl f* **66/1**	58
6004	**6**	3/4	**Fasuby (IRE)**[24] 2709 2-8-6 FrancisNorton 7 (P D Evans) *chsd ldr early: styd front rnk: rdn over 3f out: wknd over 1f out* **12/1**	53
0	**7**	1 1/2	**Love Brothers**[14] 3025 2-8-12 EdwardCreighton(3) 10 (M R Channon) *in tch: rdn and effrt over 3f out: nvr in contention but styd on fnl f* **8/1**	58
U	**8**	1/2	**Always Best**[9] 3175 2-8-9 RoystonFfrench 2 (M Johnston) *sn bdly outpcd in rr and rdn along: styd on fr over 1f out but nvr in contention* **15/2**	51
6	**9**	3/4	**Nihil Petere (IRE)**[6] 3242 2-8-0 ow1 RoryMoore(5) 8 (P T Midgley) *s.i.s and wl bhd: rdn after 2f: styd on fr over 1f out but nvr in contention* **66/1**	45
04	**10**	2	**Pas De Trois**[14] 3005 2-8-11 StephenCarson 3 (R F Johnson Houghton) *in tch early: rdn 1/2-way and sn no ch* **9/1**	46
0	**11**	2	**Mr Chocolate Drop (IRE)**[10] 3157 2-8-9 RobbieFitzpatrick 5 (M J Attwater) *a in rr* **66/1**	39

1m 24.49s (-0.51) **Going Correction** -0.125s/f (Firm) **11** Ran SP% **118.1**
Speed ratings (Par 94):97,96,95,93,90 89,88,87,86,84 82
CSF £7.81 TOTE £2.40: £1.10, £1.60, £1.80; EX 12.00.

Owner J C Fretwell **Bred** Pier House Stud **Trained** Averham Park, Notts

FOCUS

This did not look a great maiden on paper and and very few ever got into it. The second and sixth are the best guides.

NOTEBOOK

Iron Fist(IRE) showed the right sort of resolution to get on top having raced close to the pace throughout. Described as still a big baby by his trainer, he had shown ability in a much better race at Newmarket on his debut and should continue to progress. (op 5-2 tchd 11-4 in a place)

Anthea had also run in a much better race at Newbury on her debut and improved on that, but was inclined to hang inside the last furlong either through greenness or because she was feeling the ground. There is certainly a race in her. (op 7-2 tchd 9-2)

Lusolly, whose debut effort at San Siro was difficult to fathom, ran well from the front here and battled on well when challenged. (op 13-2)

Bathwick Breeze, a stablemate of the runner-up, performed much better than when last of 11 at Salisbury on his debut and reversed form with Love Brothers, who had finished in front of him then. (op 50-1)

High Bullen put up her best performance to date in terms of finishing position, but she probably achieved little in terms of form.
Love Brothers Official explanation: jockey said colt hung throughout
Always Best was completely taken off his feet, even over this trip. A much stiffer test of stamina and more time are needed. (op 9-1 tchd 7-1)

3449 CHURCHILL OFFICE SOLUTIONS LTD H'CAP 5f 110y
2:45 (2:46) (Class 4) (0-85,86) 3-Y-O+
£5,297 (£1,586; £793; £396; £198; £99) Stalls Centre

Form				RPR
6033	1		**Caribbean Coral**[5] 3281 7-10-0 80 (p) GrahamGibbons 10 (J J Quinn) *stdd s: hld up and taken towards ins: stdy hdwy over 1f out: led under hand driving fnl 50yds: readily* 4/1[1]	91
4154	2	nk	**Bluebok**[14] 3027 5-9-12 78 TomEaves 8 (J M Bradley) *chsd ldrs: led over 1f out: hdd and no ex fnl 50yds* 9/2[2]	88
0030	3	1 ½	**Desperate Dan**[14] 3027 5-9-7 80 (b) FrankiePickard(7) 7 (J A Osborne) *trckd ldrs: pushed along and edgd lft over 1f out: fnd no ex ins fnl f* 25/1	85
0252	4	shd	**Pawan (IRE)**[5] 3281 6-8-12 71 (b) AnnStokell(7) 3 (Miss A Stokell) *s.i.s: hdwy on ins 2f out: qcknd to chal 1f out: one pce ins last* 4/1[1]	76
4054	5	1 ¾	**Peter Island (FR)**[22] 2756 3-9-2 74 NCallan 2 (J Gallagher) *slt ld tl hdd over 1f out: wknd ins last* 12/1	72
1-00	6	¾	**Niteowl Lad (IRE)**[27] 2624 4-9-6 75 (t) JasonEdmunds(3) 4 (J Balding) *s.i.s: styng on whn checked over 1f out: one pce after* 8/1	71
2036	7	nk	**Fizzlephut (IRE)**[14] 3027 4-9-10 76 RichardThomas 9 (Miss J R Tooth) *in tch: rdn 1/2-way: kpt on fnl f but nvr gng pce to rch ldrs* 10/1	71
0105	8	½	**Devine Dancer**[19] 2866 3-9-5 77 DaneO'Neill 5 (H Candy) *chsd ldrs: drvn to chal over 1f out: wknd ins last* 12/1	69
-301	9	1 ¼	**One Way Ticket**[9] 3165 6-10-1 86 6ex (p) LiamTreadwell(5) 6 (J M Bradley) *w ldr over 3f: wknd over 1f out* 7/1[3]	75
0605	10	1 ¼	**Whistler**[3] 3348 9-8-10 62 (p) PaulFitzsimons 1 (Miss J R Tooth) *a outpcd* 12/1	47

65.38 secs (-0.12) **Going Correction** +0.125s/f (Good)
WFA 3 from 4yo+ 5lb 10 Ran SP% 117.8
Speed ratings (Par 105):105,104,102,102,100 99,98,98,96,94
CSF £22.12 CT £335.81 TOTE £6.10: £1.70, £2.00, £7.40; EX 28.50.
Owner Dawson, Green, Quinn, Roberts **Bred** P And C Scott **Trained** Settrington, N Yorks

FOCUS
A fair sprint handicap despite the smallish field and no shortage of early pace thanks to One Way Ticket and Peter Island duelling for the early lead. The form is solid backed up by a decent time.
Pawan(IRE) Official explanation: trainer said gelding received a cut to its stifle on leaving the stalls
Fizzlephut(IRE) Official explanation: jockey said saddle slipped

3450 EUROPEAN BREEDERS FUND FILLIES' H'CAP 7f 26y
3:20 (3:20) (Class 4) (0-80,79) 3-Y-O+ £7,772 (£2,312; £1,155; £577) Stalls Low

Form				RPR
3116	1		**Meditation**[19] 2860 4-9-2 72 JamesDoyle(5) 5 (I A Wood) *mde virtually all: rdn over 1f out: styd on strly ins last* 7/2[1]	83
6026	2	1	**Saxon Lil (IRE)**[16] 2947 4-9-2 67 FrancisNorton 9 (J L Spearing) *chsd ldr thrght: swtchd lft appr fnl f and kpt on but a hld* 6/1	75
0050	3	1 ¼	**Celtic Spa (IRE)**[10] 3153 4-8-3 61 JamieJones(7) 3 (P D Evans) *chsd ldrs: drvn along fr 3f out: outpcd ins last* 7/1	66
0400	4	hd	**Toffee Vodka (IRE)**[7] 3212 4-9-7 72 MichaelHills 8 (J W Hills) *t.k.h early: chsd ldrs: rdn and one pce over 1f out: styd on again u.p cl home* 9/2[3]	76
10-0	5	1 ¼	**Nephetriti Way (IRE)**[72] 1382 5-9-7 72 NCallan 1 (P R Chamings) *s.i.s: bhd: rdn and sme hdwy 2f oit: kpt on fnl f but nvr gng pce to chal* 14/1	73
-013	6	1	**Miss Meggy**[19] 2851 4-10-0 79 (b) TomEaves 4 (Miss J A Camacho) *chsd ldrs: rdn 3f out: wknd fnl f* 4/1[2]	78
2001	7	nk	**Peace Lily**[25] 2676 4-8-10 61 StephenCarson 7 (R F Johnson Houghton) *in tch: rdn 3f out: wknd ins fnl 2f* 9/2[3]	59
0-06	8	1 ½	**Lady Cree (IRE)**[20] 2818 3-8-11 70 DaneO'Neill 2 (W R Muir) *s.i.s: rdn 1/2-way and nvr gng pce to trble ldrs* 20/1	61
0300	9	4	**Catherines Cafe (IRE)**[31] 2511 3-8-4 63 NickyMackay 6 (Mrs P N Dutfield) *a outpcd in rr* 20/1	44

1m 24.15s (-0.85) **Going Correction** -0.125s/f (Firm)
WFA 3 from 4yo+ 8lb 9 Ran SP% 121.6
Speed ratings (Par 102):99,97,96,96,94 93,93,91,87
CSF £26.40 CT £141.07 TOTE £4.50: £1.60, £1.20, £2.90; EX 35.00.
Owner Paddy Barrett **Bred** P E Barrett **Trained** Upper Lambourn, Berks

FOCUS
A fair fillies' handicap, though few managed to get into it. The winning time was 0.34 seconds faster than the juveniles in the opener but the form looks pretty sound.

3451 DLA PIPER MAIDEN STKS 1m 2f 188y
3:55 (3:56) (Class 5) 3-Y-O+ £3,238 (£963; £481; £240) Stalls Low

Form				RPR
5-3	1		**Zero (IRE)**[63] 1605 3-9-0 NCallan 5 (M A Jarvis) *trckd ldrs: shkn up and qcknd to ld over 1f out: sn in command: comf* 11/4[2]	84+
3	2	1 ¾	**Kibara**[36] 2366 3-8-9 NickyMackay 1 (L M Cumani) *hld up in tch: hdwy on ins to chal wl over 1f out: kpt on but sn no ch w wnr* 3/1[3]	76
3-30	3	1 ½	**Materialize (USA)**[61] 1669 3-8-9 70 FrancisNorton 4 (H R A Cecil) *chsd ldrs: led 2f out:sn rdn: hdd over 1f out and sn outpcd* 9/1	73
0	4	2	**Florimund**[87] 1055 3-9-0 StephenDavies 3 (Sir Michael Stoute) *s.i.s: hld up: hdwy into mid-div over 3f out: shkn up and kpt on fnl f but nvr gng pce to rch ldrs* 16/1	74
2-2	5	nk	**Piety (IRE)**[10] 3146 3-8-9 RoystonFfrench 9 (M Johnston) *chsd ldrs: hung rt bnd 3f out: continued to hang and sn btn* 13/8[1]	69
04	6	¾	**Dream Shared**[22] 2753 3-8-9 DO'Donohoe 10 (E A L Dunlop) *chsd ldrs: rdn over 2f out: wknd fnl f* 20/1	68
	7	8	**The Iron Giant (IRE)**[24] 2578 4-9-12 StephenCarson 6 (B G Powell) *led tl hdd 2f out: sn btn* 80/1	58?
0	8	5	**Sunley Song**[8] 3200 3-8-9 DaneO'Neill 7 (B G Powell) *a in rr* 100/1	44
00-5	9	2	**Annies Valentine**[16] 2951 3-8-9 40 TPQueally 11 (J Gallagher) *a in rr* 100/1	41
05	10	13	**Indian Girl**[3] 3346 3-8-6 EdwardCreighton(3) 8 (M R Channon) *plld hrd: chsd ldrs: wknd 3f out* 50/1	17

2m 16.78s (-2.62) **Going Correction** -0.125s/f (Firm)
WFA 3 from 4yo 12lb 10 Ran SP% 115.6
Speed ratings (Par 103):104,102,101,100,99 99,93,89,88,79
CSF £11.09 TOTE £3.50: £1.40, £1.50, £2.20; EX 14.70.
Owner Mohammed Al Nabouda **Bred** Darley **Trained** Newmarket, Suffolk

FOCUS
Only half of this field seemed to have a realistic chance in this maiden and the form is pretty ordinary, rated through the third.
Piety(IRE) Official explanation: jockey said filly hung right throughout

3452 COLLIERS CRE RATING SERVICES H'CAP (PART OF THE WARWICK STAYERS SERIES) 1m 6f 213y
4:30 (4:30) (Class 4) (0-80,78) 3-Y-O+ £6,477 (£1,927; £963; £481) Stalls Low

Form				RPR
0052	1		**Takafu (USA)**[14] 3028 4-9-6 70 FrankieMcDonald 4 (W S Kittow) *trckd ldr: chal over 4f out tl led ins fnl 3f: hrd drvn and r.o wl whn strly chal thrght fnl f* 9/2[3]	83
0021	2	shd	**Whispering Death**[9] 3177 4-9-7 71 6ex (v) TonyCulhane 6 (W J Haggas) *rr but in tch:pushed along 7f out and 4f out: hdwy to trck ldrs 2f out:chal gng wl 1f out: upsides ins last: no ex cl home* 6/4[1]	84
0421	3	9	**Baltic Princess (FR)**[9] 3169 3-8-6 73 6ex J-PGuillambert 1 (M Johnston) *led: hdd ins fnl 3f: wknd qckly fnl f* 13/8[2]	74
0-00	4	6	**Karlu (GER)**[15] 2975 4-10-0 78 PaulEddery 3 (Pat Eddery) *s.i.s: rr: rdn 7f out: no rspnse* 14/1	71
4004	5	hd	**Akritas**[14] 3013 5-9-8 72 (bt[1]) DaneO'Neill 7 (P F I Cole) *s.i.s: sn in tch: rdn and hdwy to chse ldrs 5f out: wknd qckly 2f out* 22/1	65
0004	6	24	**Eastborough (IRE)**[19] 2879 7-9-5 69 NCallan 5 (B G Powell) *chsd ldrs: rdn and wknd qckly over 3f out* 14/1	31

3m 14.14s (-1.76) **Going Correction** -0.125s/f (Firm)
WFA 3 from 4yo+ 17lb 6 Ran SP% 114.0
Speed ratings (Par 105):99,98,94,90,90 78
CSF £12.02 TOTE £6.20: £2.20, £1.30; EX 18.40.
Owner Midd Shire Racing **Bred** G W Humphrey Jr **Trained** Blackborough, Devon

FOCUS
There was always the danger of a lack of early pace in this staying event due to the small field, but after not going very quick in the early stages Baltic Princess soon stepped up the gallop and this probably became a fair test of stamina. The form might be reasonable with the first two well clear.
Whispering Death Official explanation: jockey said, regarding the apparent tender ride, his orders were to get gelding to rail, cover it up early on and make his challenge as late as possible, adding that gelding travelled well early on but came off the bridle mid-race, and he expected gelding to pick up readily when asked for an effort, delaying a challenge until final furlong, in accordance with successful tactics employed in previous races, but was disappointed with the failure to quicken
Eastborough(IRE) Official explanation: jockey said gelding had no more to give

3453 SEE MORE ON RACING UK H'CAP 7f 26y
5:05 (5:06) (Class 5) (0-75,76) 3-Y-O £3,238 (£963; £481; £240) Stalls Low

Form				RPR
13-0	1		**Balik Pearls**[19] 2864 3-9-7 75 (b) NCallan 5 (N A Callaghan) *chsd ldrs: rdn over 2f out: led 1f out: drvn out* 4/1[2]	83
5502	2	1	**Royal Tavira Girl (IRE)**[12] 3072 3-8-0 57 DominicFox(3) 3 (M G Quinlan) *hld up rr: hdwy on ins over 2f out: chal appr fnl f and kpt on u.p ins last but a hld* 9/2[3]	62
5311	3	1 ¾	**Cindertrack**[1] 3395 3-9-8 76 6ex ShaneKelly 8 (J A Osborne) *led: rdn and hdd 1f out: sn btn* 8/11[1]	76
3-05	4	4	**Kineta (USA)**[17] 2921 3-8-11 65 DaneO'Neill 7 (W R Muir) *chsd ldr over 5f out tl rdn 2f out: sn btn* 12/1	55
0-00	5	6	**Missdevina (IRE)**[29] 2554 3-8-10 64 TPQueally 6 (M G Quinlan) *chsd ldr until over 5f out: styd front rnk: rdn 3f out: wknd fr 2f out* 25/1	38
5-00	6	1	**Lyrical Blues (IRE)**[36] 2353 3-8-11 65 GrahamGibbons 4 (B R Millman) *s.i.s: a in rr* 16/1	37
000-	7	nk	**Double Oh Seven (IRE)**[199] 6663 3-8-4 63 JamesDoyle(5) 2 (J W Unett) *in tch: rdn and wknd 3f out* 12/1	34

1m 23.41s (-1.59) **Going Correction** -0.125s/f (Firm) 7 Ran SP% 121.2
Speed ratings (Par 100):104,102,100,96,89 88,87
CSF £24.02 CT £27.16 TOTE £5.90: £2.20, £2.20; EX 24.00 Place 6 £57.07, Place 5 £44.47.
Owner Alan Brazil Racing Club Ltd **Bred** T K And Mrs P A Knox **Trained** Newmarket, Suffolk

FOCUS
Just a fair handicap to end the card, but the fastest of the three races run over the trip at the meeting with the runner-up the best guide.
T/Plt: £58.40 to a £1 stake. Pool: £36,652.85. 458.00 winning tickets. T/Qpdt: £28.70 to a £1 stake. Pool: £2,037.80. 52.50 winning tickets. ST

3385 WOLVERHAMPTON (A.W) (L-H)
Thursday, July 13

OFFICIAL GOING: Standard
Wind: Light, across Weather: Sunny

3454 WBX.COM WORLD BET EXCHANGE APPRENTICE H'CAP 2m 119y(P)
6:40 (6:40) (Class 5) (0-70,65) 3-Y-O+ £3,238 (£963; £481; £240) Stalls Low

Form				RPR
3140	1		**Madiba**[8] 3203 7-9-2 60 JPFeatherstone(7) 2 (P Howling) *s.i.s: sn mid-div: hdwy over 5f out: styd on to ld wl ins fnl f* 7/1	68
0311	2	½	**Eforetta (GER)**[43] 2140 4-9-4 60 FrankiePickard(5) 3 (D J Wintle) *hld up and bhd: hdwy over 3f out: styd on towards fin* 5/2[1]	67
5366	3	1	**Archimboldo (USA)**[10] 3156 3-8-9 65 SladeO'Hara 6 (T Wall) *s.i.s: hld up: hdwy over 5f out: led 3f out: sn rdn: hdd wl ins fnl f: no ex* 14/1	71
0320	4	5	**Jolizero**[56] 1808 5-9-6 57 MichaelJStainton 7 (John Berry) *keen early: prom: outpcd over 6f out: rallied over 3f out: styd on same pce fnl 2f* 9/2[2]	57
6005	5	5	**Halland**[20] 2812 8-9-11 65 NeilBrown(3) 4 (T J Fitzgerald) *hld up and bhd: hdwy over 5f out: wknd over 2f out* 12/1	59
5200	6	½	**Blue Hills**[11] 2140 5-9-5 59 (p) PJBenson(3) 9 (P W Hiatt) *hld up in tch: wknd over 4f out* 8/1	52
60-0	7	½	**Mcqueen (IRE)**[35] 955 6-9-9 RussellKennemore 1 (B D Leavy) *prom: n.m.r on ins and lost pl after 2f: rdn over 9f out: bhd fnl 7f* 33/1	53
0000	8	9	**Boss Mak (IRE)**[28] 2591 3-8-1 57 ThomasO'Brien 10 (V Smith) *sn chsng ldr: led over 5f out to 3f out: sn wknd* 25/1	39

5415 **9** *2* **Rare Coincidence**[10] 3140 5-9-3 **54**....(p) JamesO'Reilly 5 33
(R F Fisher) *led: pushed along and hdd over 5f out: wknd 3f out* **11/2**

3510 **10** *11* **Mister Completely (IRE)**[37] 1754 5-8-13 **55**.... JosephWalsh(5) 8 21
(Miss Sheena West) *hld up in tch: rdn and wknd over 4f out* **5/1**[3]

3m 41.86s (-1.27) **Going Correction** -0.125s/f (Stan)
WFA 3 from 4yo+ 19lb **10** Ran SP% **123.6**
Speed ratings (Par 103):97,96,96,93,91 91,91,86,85,80
CSF £26.43 CT £251.79 TOTE £6.10: £1.90, £1.40, £3.00; EX 41.10.
Owner Eastwell Manor Racing Ltd **Bred** M L Roberts **Trained** Newmarket, Suffolk
■ The first winner for Johnny Featherstone, son of trainer Lucinda Featherstone.
■ Stewards' Enquiry : Michael J Stainton caution: careless riding

FOCUS
A moderate handicap with the runner-up to form.
Mister Completely(IRE) Official explanation: jockey said gelding had no more to give

3455 SPONSOR A RACE CALL 0870 220 2442 NOVICE MEDIAN AUCTION STKS 7f 32y(P)

7:10 (7:10) (Class 5) 2-Y-0 **£3,886** (£1,156; £577; £288) **Stalls** High

Form RPR

4 **1** **Princeton (IRE)**[14] 3025 2-8-12 .... TedDurcan 1 76
(M R Channon) *a.p: rdn and wnt 2nd 2f out: led 1f out: sn edgd rt: rdn out* **4/1**[3]

3314 **2** *1 ½* **Ten Dollars More (IRE)**[6] 3265 2-9-2 .... ShaneKelly 5 76
(J A Osborne) *led: rdn 2f out: hdd 1f out: sn edgd lft: nt qckn* **9/2**

4012 **3** *1 ¼* **Hart Of Gold**[17] 2924 2-9-6 .... JamieSpencer 6 77
(M J Wallace) *hld up: rdn and hdwy on ins wl over 1f out: one pce fnl f* **2/1**[1]

4 *shd* **Beech Games** 2-8-12 .... RichardMullen 7 69
(E J O'Neill) *s.i.s: sn prom: rdn and ev ch over 2f out: one pce fnl f* **10/1**

31 **5** *5* **Apollo Five**[41] 2185 2-9-6 .... TPQueally 2 64
(D J Coakley) *prom: ev ch over 2f out: sn rdn: wknd 1f out* **11/4**[2]

0 **6** *11* **Gold Response**[10] 3157 2-8-9 .... PatrickMathers(3) 3 29
(D Shaw) *hld up: rdn over 3f out: sn struggling* **40/1**

1m 30.5s (0.10) **Going Correction** -0.125s/f (Stan) **6** Ran SP% **109.7**
Speed ratings (Par 94):94,92,90,90,85 72
CSF £20.85 TOTE £6.10: £3.10, £2.80; EX 18.70.
Owner Jumeirah Racing **Bred** Darley **Trained** West Ilsley, Berks

FOCUS
This was well-contested despite the small field although the level is hard to be sure about.

NOTEBOOK
Princeton(IRE) built on the promise of his Salisbury debut and scored in workmanlike fashion. (tchd 7-2)
Ten Dollars More(IRE) did not do a lot wrong but the task of conceding 4lb to the winner proved too much. (op 7-2 tchd 5-1)
Hart Of Gold could not sustain a promising-looking run but was giving weight away to the first two. (op 3-1)
Beech Games ◆, a 56,000 gns half-brother to dual six-furlong juvenile winner Viking Spirit, had already been gelded. He turned in a sound effort on his debut and a suitable opportunity can be found. (op 8-1)
Apollo Five got away on level terms for the first time but appeared to get found out by the longer distance. (op 2-1)

3456 RINGSIDE SUITE 700 THEATRE STYLE CONFERENCE CLAIMING STKS 1m 4f 50y(P)

7:45 (7:45) (Class 5) 3-5-Y-0 **£3,886** (£1,156; £577; £288) **Stalls** Low

Form RPR

1432 **1** **La Via Ferrata (IRE)**[12] 3075 3-8-10 60.... JamieSpencer 3 73
(P F I Cole) *stmbld s: hld up: hdwy to ld over 4f out: rdn over 3f out: c wd and edgd rt over 1f out: flashed tail: r.o* **7/2**[2]

4224 **2** *2* **Phone In**[10] 3156 3-8-12 71.... SebSanders 4 72
(Sir Mark Prescott) *led: hung rt bnd 7f out: hdd over 4f out: sn rdn: styd on same pce fnl 2f* **4/7**[1]

0P06 **3** *9* **Prophet Preacher (IRE)**[6] 3261 3-8-2 48....(v) DaleGibson 5 47
(M J Attwater) *hld up in tch: rdn over 4f out: wknd over 3f out* **50/1**

4353 **4** *5* **Macho Dancer (IRE)**[12] 3066 3-7-12 53.... EmmettStack(5) 7 40
(K J Burke) *prom tl wknd over 3f out* **20/1**

0005 **5** *2 ½* **Mystified (IRE)**[21] 2795 3-8-7 62....(b) FrancisNorton 1 40
(R F Fisher) *prom tl wknd over 3f out* **20/1**

3020 **6** *17* **Keshya**[19] 2869 5-9-4 62.... RyanMoore 2 11+
(N P Littmoden) *s.v.s: a wl bhd: t.o* **7/1**[3]

0020 **7** *25* **Tennessee Belle (IRE)**[6] 3260 4-8-5 40.... KirstyMilczarek(7) 6 —
(C N Allen) *hld up: struggling over 5f out: t.o fnl 4f* **33/1**

2m 40.62s (-1.80) **Going Correction** -0.125s/f (Stan)
WFA 3 from 4yo+ 13lb **7** Ran SP% **112.8**
Speed ratings (Par 103):101,99,93,90,88 77,60
CSF £5.69 TOTE £4.00: £1.20, £1.10; EX 7.20.The winner was claimed by M. K. F. Seymour for £20,000. Phone In was claimed by Roy Brotherton for £25,000.
Owner P F I Cole Ltd **Bred** Roland H Alder **Trained** Whatcombe, Oxon

FOCUS
An uncompetitive claimer but the winner looks improved.
Keshya Official explanation: jockey said mare missed the break
Tennessee Belle(IRE) Official explanation: jockey said filly was never travelling

3457 THE RED DEVILS DISPLAY AT WOLVERHAMPTON JULY 17TH MAIDEN STKS 5f 216y(P)

8:15 (8:15) (Class 4) 2-Y-0 **£5,181** (£1,541; £770; £384) **Stalls** Low

Form RPR

0 **1** **Al Khaleej (IRE)**[54] 1838 2-9-3 .... JamieSpencer 1 79
(E A L Dunlop) *s.i.s: rdn and hdwy on ins over 2f out: led 1f out: r.o wl* **2/5**[1]

2 *1 ½* **Si Foo (USA)** 2-9-3 .... RyanMoore 6 75
(A M Balding) *hld up in mid-div: rdn and hdwy on ins wl over 1f out: swtchd rt ins fnl f: kpt on* **10/1**[3]

3 *½* **Dream Eile (IRE)**[12] 3103 2-9-3 .... RichardMullen 8 73
(P D Deegan, Ire) *bhd: hdwy on outside wl over 1f out: r.o wl ins fnl f: nrst fin* **50/1**

52 **4** *1 ¼* **Ghost Dancer**[21] 2783 2-9-3 .... NickyMackay 11 69
(L M Cumani) *prom: led over 4f out: rdn 2f out: hdd 1f out: sn edgd lft: one pce* **13/2**[2]

60 **5** *1 ¾* **Candyland (IRE)**[28] 2572 2-8-12 .... TedDurcan 2 59
(M R Channon) *hld up in mid-div: hdwy to chse ldr over 2f out: rdn wl over 1f out: wknd ins fnl f* **11/1**

6 *1 ¼* **Sundae** 2-9-3 .... AlanMunro 13 60
(C F Wall) *prom: hung rt bnd over 2f out: wknd over 1f out* **25/1**

04 **7** *2 ½* **Spence's Choice (IRE)**[21] 2783 2-9-3 .... DaleGibson 10 53
(M W Easterby) *mid-div: rdn 3f out: no hdwy fnl 2f* **40/1**

04 **8** *3* **Disco Queen (IRE)**[6] 3246 2-8-12 .... DeanMcKeown 5 39
(P C Haslam) *outpcd* **33/1**

0 **9** *1 ¾* **Pertemps Networks**[38] 2287 2-8-10 .... AdeleRothery(7) 12 39
(M W Easterby) *s.i.s: outpcd* **50/1**

03 **10** *7* **Storm Mission (USA)**[14] 3018 2-9-0 .... DominicFox(3) 9 18
(Miss V Haigh) *chsd ldrs: hung rt bnd over 2f out: sn wknd* **33/1**

6 **11** *9* **Tu Sei Romantica (IRE)**[29] 2565 2-8-12 .... NCallan 4 —
(K A Ryan) *prom tl rdn and wknd 2f out* **20/1**

0 **12** *2 ½* **Blue Mak**[10] 3157 2-9-0 .... PatrickMathers(3) 3 —
(D Shaw) *s.s: a in rr* **66/1**

0 **13** *7* **Our Archie**[8] 3193 2-9-3 .... RobbieFitzpatrick 7 —
(M J Attwater) *led over 1f: rdn 3f out: sn wknd* **50/1**

1m 14.85s (-0.96) **Going Correction** -0.125s/f (Stan) **13** Ran SP% **126.5**
Speed ratings (Par 96):101,99,98,96,94 92,89,85,83,73 61,58,49
CSF £5.15 TOTE £1.40: £1.10, £3.50, £11.80; EX 9.30.
Owner Mayoof Sultan **Bred** A Stroud And J Hanly **Trained** Newmarket, Suffolk

FOCUS
An ordinary maiden in which there were plenty available at fancy prices and only time will show the value of the form. However, the race time was reasonable.

NOTEBOOK
Al Khaleej(IRE), who had shaped well enough on his debut on soft ground at Newbury in May, found this a lot easier and justified the tag of being a well-backed favourite. (op 8-13)
Si Foo(USA) ◆ gave a good account of himself on his debut and should not be hard to place given normal improvement. (tchd 12-1)
Dream Eile(IRE), who had failed to beat another horse in two outings in Ireland, was without the blinkers he had sported on his previous start. Taking to the surface, he finished in a style of one who would appreciate further.
Ghost Dancer, switching to sand, had plenty of use made of him from a wide draw. (op 6-1)
Candyland(IRE) again shaped as though she may benefit from a return to five. (tchd 12-1)
Sundae is a 50,000gns brother to this season's Abernant and Cecil Frail winner Paradise Isle and dual six-furlong juvenile scorer Murfreesboro. Very colty in the paddock, he did not handle the bend well and should have learnt something from this. (op 28-1)

3458 ENJOY RACING FROM THE ZONGALERO RESTAURANT MAIDEN STKS 1m 141y(P)

8:45 (8:46) (Class 5) 3-Y-0+ **£4,533** (£1,348; £674; £336) **Stalls** Low

Form RPR

5-6 **1** **Strawberry Lolly**[75] 1306 3-8-12 .... RyanMoore 6 80+
(Sir Michael Stoute) *hld up in mid-div: hdwy 2f out: sn rdn: led jst ins fnl f: r.o wl* **9/4**[1]

0 **2** *3 ½* **Border News**[83] 1120 3-9-3 .... TedDurcan 10 72
(H R A Cecil) *chsd ldr: rdn over 2f out: ev ch 1f out: one pce* **11/2**[3]

0 **3** *2* **William's Way**[11] 3122 4-9-13 .... NCallan 1 68
(I A Wood) *led: rdn over 2f out: hdd 1f out: wknd ins fnl f* **16/1**

0 **4** *3* **Tiz Timely (USA)**[56] 1798 3-8-12 .... FrancisNorton 4 57+
(A M Balding) *hld up: lost pl 6f out: rdn 3f out: no real prog fnl 2f* **12/1**

5 *1 ¾* **Brigydon (IRE)** 3-9-3 .... JamieSpencer 2 58
(J R Fanshawe) *prom: rdn over 2f out: wkng whn edgd rt 1f out* **10/3**[2]

0 **6** *1 ¾* **Sasetti (IRE)**[19] 2868 3-8-12 ....(t) MickyFenton 3 50
(J R Fanshawe) *s.i.s: bhd: rdn 3f out: nvr nr ldrs* **14/1**

6-50 **7** *¾* **Spanish Story**[38] 2293 3-8-12 48....(p) ShaneKelly 9 48
(A M Balding) *s.i.s: sn prom: rdn over 2f out: wknd wl over 1f out* **20/1**

0 **8** *1 ¼* **Sprinkle**[15] 2985 3-8-12 .... SebSanders 5 45
(R M Beckett) *a bhd* **20/1**

9 *3 ½* **Osiris Way** 4-9-13 .... AlanMunro 12 43
(P R Chamings) *s.i.s: short-lived effrt on outside over 4f out* **14/1**

10 *5* **Thunder S (USA)** 3-8-12 .... NickyMackay 7 28
(L M Cumani) *sn bhd: rdn over 3f out: no rspnse* **8/1**

1m 50.25s (-1.51) **Going Correction** -0.125s/f (Stan)
WFA 3 from 4yo 10lb **10** Ran SP% **116.8**
Speed ratings (Par 103):101,97,96,93,91 90,89,88,85,81
CSF £14.79 TOTE £3.10: £1.10, £1.10, £6.50; EX 19.90.
Owner Mrs R J Jacobs **Bred** Newsells Park Stud Limited **Trained** Newmarket, Suffolk

FOCUS
An interesting if ordinary maiden rated around the third.

3459 WORLD BET EXCHANGE WBX.COM H'CAP 7f 32y(P)

9:15 (9:15) (Class 5) (0-75,75) 3-Y-0+ **£3,886** (£1,156; £577; £288) **Stalls** High

Form RPR

5552 **1** **Curtain Bluff**[4] 3337 4-9-8 **71**....(v) TedDurcan 3 82
(M R Channon) *hld up in tch: rdn to ld jst over 1f out: r.o wl* **9/2**[3]

-106 **2** *3* **Rosein**[7] 3217 4-9-4 **67**.... SebSanders 4 70
(Mrs G S Rees) *led: rdn and hdd jst over 1f out: one pce* **7/1**

0001 **3** *shd* **Joyeaux**[13] 3052 4-9-1 **64**....(v) DerekMcGaffin 2 67
(J Hetherton) *s.i.s: hld up: rdn over 2f out: hdwy 1f out: r.o* **8/1**

0430 **4** *nk* **Treasure House (IRE)**[12] 3101 5-9-4 **67**.... FrancisNorton 5 69
(M Blanshard) *hld up in tch: rdn over 2f out: kpt on ins fnl f* **3/1**[1]

1104 **5** *½* **Full Victory (IRE)**[12] 3101 4-9-7 **75**.... JamesDoyle(5) 8 76
(R A Farrant) *hld up and bhd: rdn over 2f out: hdwy on outside over 1f out: sn hung lft: kpt on ins fnl f* **4/1**[2]

0000 **6** *1* **Happy As Larry (USA)**[29] 2547 4-9-3 **73**....(bt[1]) JamesO'Reilly(7) 9 71
(T J Pitt) *s.i.s: t.k.h: sn prom: ev ch 2f out: sn rdn: wkng whn edgd rt wl ins fnl f* **16/1**

0032 **7** *2* **Bond Playboy**[13] 3052 6-8-13 **62**....(p) GylesParkin 7 55
(G R Oldroyd) *hld up in tch: rdn over 2f out: btn whn nt clr run wl ins fnl f* **8/1**

1660 **8** *1* **Parkview Love (USA)**[8] 3202 5-9-4 **70**....(v) PatrickMathers(3) 1 60
(D Shaw) *prom: rdn over 2f out: sn wknd* **3/1**[1]

020- **9** *¾* **Turn Around**[402] 2334 6-9-2 **65**.... DeanMcKeown 6 53
(J Pearce) *s.i.s: a bhd* **16/1**

1m 28.37s (-2.03) **Going Correction** -0.125s/f (Stan) **9** Ran SP% **134.7**
Speed ratings (Par 103):106,102,102,102,101 100,98,96,96
CSF £42.59 CT £264.17 TOTE £7.00: £2.00, £1.90, £5.80; EX 20.20 Place 6 £69.57, Place 5 £33.73.
Owner Mrs M Findlay **Bred** Mike Channon Bloodstock Ltd **Trained** West Ilsley, Berks

FOCUS
This modest handicap was won in a fast time and the form looks sound.
Full Victory(IRE) Official explanation: jockey said gelding hung left
T/Plt: £80.00 to a £1 stake. Pool: £51,875.50. 473.30 winning tickets. T/Qpdt: £6.80 to a £1 stake. Pool: £4,275.00. 463.10 winning tickets. KH

3460 - 3466a (Foreign Racing) - See Raceform Interactive

3193 CHEPSTOW (L-H)

Friday, July 14

OFFICIAL GOING: Good to firm

Wind: Brisk, across

3467 BETFAIR APPRENTICE TRAINING SERIES H'CAP 1m 4f 23y

6:40 (6:41) (Class 5) (0-70,70) 3-Y-O+ £3,368 (£1,002; £500; £250) Stalls Low

Form RPR

2200 1 **Robbie Can Can**[46] 2075 7-8-5 54 JackDean(7) 12 60
(A W Carroll) *hld up in rr: rdn and hdwy over 2f out: slt ld 1f out: hld on wl whn strly chal thrght fnl f* 4/1[3]

6-06 2 shd **Siakira**[18] 2929 3-8-3 65 ow3 JPFeatherstone(7) 9 70
(I A Wood) *t.k.h: hld up in rr: hdwy over 2f out: drvn to chal thrght fnl f: no ex last strides* 12/1

0330 3 1 1/4 **Serramanna**[8] 3221 5-8-11 53 oh4 SladeO'Hara 1 56
(Dr J R J Naylor) *t.k.h: chsd ldrs: rdn over 2f out: pressed ldrs appr fnl f: kpt on same pce* 7/2[2]

0000 4 1 1/2 **Dayoff (IRE)**[14] 3035 5-8-11 53 oh6 (v) JamieJones 8 54
(P D Evans) *in tch: rdn 3f out: hdwy 2f out: chsd ldrs 1f out: sn one pce* 20/1

5/24 5 hd **Dareneur (IRE)**[9] 3196 6-8-11 53 oh2 TolleyDean 4 54
(J G M O'Shea) *chsd ldrs: chal 4f out: led 3f out: hdd 1f out: wknd ins last* 9/2

6003 6 1/2 **Bukit Fraser (IRE)**[8] 3221 5-9-4 60 (t) JamesMillman 2 60
(P F I Cole) *led tl hdd 3f out: styd pressing ldr tl ins fnl 2f: wknd ins fnl f* 11/4[1]

60-4 7 shd **Proprioception (IRE)**[18] 2918 4-8-7 54 LukeMorris(5) 6 54
(W K Goldsworthy) *chsd ldrs tl dropped rr 5f out: rdn 3f out: kpt on fr over 1f out but nvr gng pce to rch ldrs* 10/1

00/0 8 16 **Heriot**[28] 2601 5-9-1 57 ThomasO'Brien 11 31
(S C Burrough) *chsd ldrs tl wknd over 3f out* 50/1

2m 42.24s (3.52) **Going Correction** -0.225s/f (Firm)
WFA 3 from 4yo+ 13lb 8 Ran SP% **110.6**
Speed ratings (Par 103):79,78,78,77,76 76,76,65
CSF £46.53 CT £172.74 TOTE £4.60: £1.50, £4.00, £1.70; EX 45.60.
Owner K F Coleman **Bred** I Robinson & A W Robinson **Trained** Cropthorne, Worcs
■ A first winner for Jack Dean, whose older brother Tolley also took part in this race.

FOCUS
They went no gallop, resulting in a very pedestrian winning time and the form is weak.

3468 EUROPEAN BREEDERS FUND/S.E.T. OFFICE SUPPLIES NOVICE STKS 5f 16y

7:10 (7:11) (Class 4) 2-Y-O £5,678 (£1,699; £849; £424; £211) Stalls High

Form RPR

1003 1 **Scented Present**[7] 3252 2-9-0 RobertHavlin 1 88+
(B J Meehan) *trckd ldrs: led over 1f out: qcknd ins last: easily* 1/1[1]

331 2 2 **Relkida**[11] 3148 2-8-11 ChrisCatlin 5 70
(M R Channon) *trckd ldrs: nt clr run over 1f out and ins last: swtchd lft between horses and qcknd to take 2nd cl hime: no ch w wnr* 5/2[2]

231 3 hd **Racing Stripes (IRE)**[25] 2710 2-9-5 PatDobbs 4 77
(A B Haynes) *led: rdn 2f out: hdd over 1f out: styd on one pce and lost 2nd cl home* 5/1[3]

1203 4 1 1/4 **No Worries Yet (IRE)**[46] 2076 2-8-9 SteveDrowne 3 63
(J L Spearing) *pressed ldr early: styd in 2nd and rdn over 2f out: wknd ins last* 10/1

00 5 1/2 **Red**[31] 2530 2-8-4 NelsonDeSouza(3) 2 59
(R M Beckett) *sn pushed along in rr: kpt on fnl f and r.o cl home but nvr gng pce to be competitive* 33/1

59.52 secs (-0.08) **Going Correction** -0.30s/f (Firm) 5 Ran SP% **107.3**
Speed ratings (Par 96):88,84,84,82,81
CSF £3.47 TOTE £2.00: £1.10, £1.40; EX 3.70.
Owner The Calvera Partnership **Bred** Mrs M Holdcroft And Mrs M Forsyth **Trained** Manton, Wilts

FOCUS
An ordinary maiden with the winner in a different leagyue and the fourth and fifth set the level.

NOTEBOOK
Scented Present took full advantage of the drop in grade and won easing down. He would have had more on his plate had the runner-up obtained a clear run, but scored with enough in hand to suggest he would have won in any case. (op 10-11 tchd 11-10 and 6-5 in a place)
Relkida, reverting to five furlongs, found herself trapped in a pocket at a crucial stage. She quickened up well when free to secure second spot, but the favourite was long gone by that stage. (tchd 9-4)
Racing Stripes(IRE) was attempting to concede upwards of 5lb to his rivals and this was a decent effort. He was pulled out of a race over six furlongs the next day but on this evidence might prove happiest over five. (op 11-2 tchd 9-2)
No Worries Yet(IRE) has proved herself better than a plater but nurseries are likely to be her level now.
Red, last all the way, should be seen in a better light when stepped up in trip.

3469 CROWN AT WHITEBROOK H'CAP 1m 14y

7:40 (7:40) (Class 5) (0-75,79) 3-Y-O+ £5,181 (£1,541; £770; £384) Stalls High

Form RPR

5033 1 **The Gaikwar (IRE)**[9] 3197 7-9-5 66 (b) RichardKingscote(5) 6 76
(R A Harris) *hld up rr but in tch: hdwy over 2f out: slt ld 1f out: drvn out* 8/1

0001 2 1 1/2 **Personify**[16] 2969 4-9-10 69 (p) AdamKirby(3) 4 75
(C G Cox) *front rnk: rdn and kpt on to chse wnr ins last but nvr gng pce to chal* 11/2[3]

6001 3 nk **Fabrian**[9] 3197 8-9-9 70 5ex JamesDoyle(5) 8 76
(R J Price) *chsd ldrs: slt ld ins fnl 3f: hdd ins fnl 2f: styd front rnk but kpt on same pce ins last* 5/2[1]

0505 4 1 3/4 **Linda's Colin (IRE)**[32] 2499 4-9-6 62 SteveDrowne 11 64
(R A Harris) *chsd ldrs: led ins fnl 2f: hdd 1f out: sn outpcd* 25/1

0451 5 nk **Right Ted (IRE)**[11] 3149 3-9-7 79 5ex SladeO'Hara(7) 7 78?
(T Wall) *chsd ldrs: pushed along fr 3f out: kpt on same pce fnl 2f* 14/1

6500 6 5 **Crimson Flame (IRE)**[15] 3030 3-9-0 65 ChrisCatlin 5 53
(M R Channon) *bhd: sn drvn along: mod prog fr over 1f out* 12/1

00P0 7 hd **Halcyon Magic**[14] 3044 8-8-6 51 oh1 (b) DominicFox(3) 3 40
(M Wigham) *bhd: stl plenty to do 2f out: drvn and r.o ins fnl f but nvr in contention* 40/1

4040 8 shd **Red Contact (USA)**[16] 2983 5-8-12 57 NelsonDeSouza(3) 10 46
(J R Best) *awkward stalls: sn led: hdd ins fnl 3f: wknd over 1f out* 9/1

5232 9 1 1/2 **Foolish Groom**[14] 3044 5-9-3 59 (v) FergusSweeney 2 44
(R Hollinshead) *s.i.s: bhd: hdwy to get in tch 3f out: nvr rchd ldrs and wknd ins fnl 2f* 7/2[2]

5502 10 1 1/2 **Quel Ange (FR)**[18] 2918 4-10-0 70 JimCrowley 9 52
(R J Hodges) *chsd ldrs: rdn 3f out: wknd ins fnl 2f* 16/1

1m 33.3s (-2.70) **Going Correction** -0.30s/f (Firm)
WFA 3 from 4yo+ 9lb 10 Ran SP% **113.8**
Speed ratings (Par 103):101,99,99,97,97 92,91,91,90,88
CSF £50.30 CT £141.69 TOTE £8.80: £2.50, £2.10, £1.60; EX 59.60.
Owner Leeway Group Limited **Bred** Burton Agnes Stud Co Ltd **Trained** Earlswood, Monmouths

FOCUS
A fair handicap in which the winner and second ran to form.
Linda's Colin(IRE) Official explanation: jockey said gelding hung left
Foolish Groom Official explanation: jockey said gelding was unsuited by the good to firm ground

3470 SCOTTISH EQUITABLE/JOCKEYS' ASSOCIATION H'CAP 7f 16y

8:10 (8:10) (Class 3) (0-95,95) 3-Y-O £9,463 (£2,832; £1,416; £708; £352) Stalls High

Form RPR

3310 1 **Irony (IRE)**[22] 2776 7-9-11 85 (p) SteveDrowne 5 91
(A M Balding) *trckd ldrs: pushed along 2f out: swtchd lft ins last: qcknd to ld fnl 50yds: comf* 3/1[2]

-250 2 1/2 **Material Witness (IRE)**[22] 2776 9-9-13 87 SebSanders 3 92
(W R Muir) *led: rdn along fr 3f out: kpt on wl tl hdd and outpcd fnl 50yds* 11/2

0545 3 2 1/2 **Pure Imagination (IRE)**[13] 3101 5-8-9 72 AdamKirby(3) 4 70
(J M Bradley) *rr but in tch: hdwy over 2f out to chse ldr over 1f out: no imp and outpcd ins last* 11/4[1]

5030 4 2 **Puya**[16] 2983 4-9-5 79 FergusSweeney 1 74+
(H Candy) *chsd ldrs: rdn to take 2nd over 3f out: wkng whn hmpd ins fnl f* 10/3[3]

0004 5 1 1/4 **Lizarazu (GER)**[12] 3113 7-8-10 77 (p) TolleyDean(7) 2 66
(R A Harris) *chsd ldrs: rdn 3f out: wknd fr 2f out* 11/2

1m 20.5s (-2.80) **Going Correction** -0.30s/f (Firm)
WFA 3 from 4yo+ 8lb 5 Ran SP% **105.5**
Speed ratings (Par 107):104,103,100,98,96
CSF £17.03 TOTE £2.60: £1.70, £1.90; EX 5.70.
Owner John Nicholls Ltd/mobley Homes **Bred** Mrs G Doyle **Trained** Kingsclere, Hants
■ Stewards' Enquiry : Steve Drowne one-day ban: careless riding (Jul 25)

FOCUS
Despite the small field they went a fair pace and the form looks pretty solid.

NOTEBOOK
Irony(IRE), who had the cheekpieces back on, found this much less competitive than the Buckingham Palace Handicap at Ascot in which he finished down the field. He had to be switched off the rail to get a run before despatching the leader a shade readily. (op 11-4 tchd 10-3 in places)
Material Witness(IRE), winner of the Bunbury Cup two years ago this week, finished one place behind Irony on his latest start at Ascot. Getting across to the rail and trying to make all, he fought well but was run out of it close home. (op 4-1)
Pure Imagination(IRE), who tried his luck over an extended mile on sand last time, was racing off his last winning mark and appeared to have no excuses. (op 5-2 tchd 3-1)
Puya, back down in trip and reverting to turf, had her chance but was held when running out of room inside the last. (op 4-1 tchd 3-1)
Lizarazu(GER) has been found wanting off this sort of mark since his win at Warwick in May and was the first of these to crack. (tchd 13-2)

3471 AVONBRIDGE AT WHITSBURY MANOR STUD SPRINT (H'CAP) 6f 16y

8:40 (8:42) (Class 2) (0-100,100) 3-Y-O+

£15,580 (£4,665; £2,332; £1,167; £582; £292) Stalls High

Form RPR

0334 1 **King's Caprice**[8] 3223 5-9-6 92 (t) RichardThomas 12 101
(J A Geake) *chsd wnr: rdn 2f out: styd on strly u.p to ld last strides* 12/1

0362 2 shd **Woodcote (IRE)**[13] 3077 4-9-4 93 (p) AdamKirby(3) 15 102
(C G Cox) *led: rdn over 2f out: kpt on wl fnl f: ct last strides* 5/1[1]

4040 3 1/2 **Mine Behind**[13] 3092 6-8-7 86 KylieManser(7) 11 94
(J R Best) *in tch: pushed along and hdwy over 1f out: kpt on wl fnl f: gng on cl home but nt rch ldrs* 16/1

0331 4 1/2 **Caribbean Coral**[1] 3449 7-9-0 86 6ex (p) SebSanders 6 92
(J J Quinn) *bhd: rdn over 2f out: kpt on wl to chse ldrs ins last but nt qckn fnl 75yds* 13/2[3]

6-60 5 shd **Tony The Tap**[13] 3092 5-8-7 86 TolleyDean(7) 9 92
(B Palling) *chsd ldrs: rdn 1/2-way: kpt on same pce fnl f* 10/1

2200 6 2 **Rising Shadow (IRE)**[12] 3125 5-9-3 89 PatDobbs 16 89
(T D Barron) *bhd: pushed along and hdwy over 1f out: kpt on ins last but nvr gng pce to rch ldrs* 15/2

120 7 nk **Golden Dixie (USA)**[7] 3251 7-9-5 91 HayleyTurner 1 90
(R A Harris) *bhd: pushed along over 2f out: kpt on wl fnl f but nvr in contention* 20/1

-510 8 1/2 **Don Pele (IRE)**[14] 3038 4-9-3 89 NCallan 7 86
(K A Ryan) *chsd ldrs: rdn 1/2-way: wknd ins fnl f* 11/2[2]

0504 9 nk **Obe Gold**[13] 3092 4-10-0 100 ChrisCatlin 8 96
(M R Channon) *sn pushed along in rr: styd on fr 2f out but nvr gng pce to rch ldrs* 14/1

0240 10 1 **Kingscross**[31] 2520 8-8-9 81 FergusSweeney 2 74
(M Blanshard) *bhd: sn pushed along styd on fr over 1f out but nvr in contention* 25/1

3-00 11 hd **Goodwood Spirit**[8] 3212 4-8-6 81 oh1 NelsonDeSouza(3) 5 74
(J M Bradley) *pressed ldrs: rdn 1/2-way: wknd fnl f* 40/1

0-11 12 3/4 **Balakiref**[46] 2074 7-8-4 81 oh4 JamesDoyle(5) 4 72
(M Dods) *chsd ldrs: rdn along fr over 3f out: wknd fnl f* 12/1

0-20 13 1 3/4 **Fisberry**[74] 1359 4-8-10 82 RobertHavlin 10 67
(M S Saunders) *s.i.s: sn rcvrd into mid-div: rdn 1/2-way: wknd fr 2f out* 25/1

60-0 14 1/2 **Cyclical**[13] 3092 4-9-1 87 SteveDrowne 14 71
(G A Butler) *s.i.s and bmpd s: a outpcd* 18/1

0214 15 1 **Devon Flame**[7] 3251 7-8-9 81 oh1 JimCrowley 3 62
(R J Hodges) *nvr gng pce to rch ldrs: bhd fnl 2f* 9/1

69.05 secs (-3.35) **Going Correction** -0.30s/f (Firm) 15 Ran SP% **124.3**
Speed ratings (Par 109):110,109,109,108,108 105,105,104,104,102 102,101,99,98,97
CSF £69.68 CT £699.29 TOTE £18.70: £5.00, £2.20, £5.90; EX 113.10.
Owner Miss B Swire **Bred** Miss B Swire **Trained** Kimpton, Hants
■ Stewards' Enquiry : Adam Kirby one-day ban: used whip with excessive frequency (Jul 25)

FOCUS
A valuable and competitive handicap. A high draw proved an advantage. A decent handicap, and soild enough form.

NOTEBOOK
King's Caprice was due to be dropped a pound after four defeats from this mark. Unable to lead as he normally does but racing in second spot, he forced his head in front near the line. A strongly-run six furlongs seems ideal. (tchd 14-1)

Woodcote(IRE), who was raised 2lb in defeat last time, tried valiantly to make all against the rail but was claimed near the line. He is in good heart at present. (op 13-2 tchd 7-1)
Mine Behind was keeping on well against the rail in the latter stages but could not land a telling blow at the two leaders, who dominated throughout. (op 12-1)
Caribbean Coral ran a good race under the penalty he collected for his win at Warwick the previous afternoon. (op 7-1 tchd 6-1)
Tony The Tap ran another respectable race but remains in the Handicapper's grip, 6lb above his last winning mark. (op 20-1)
Rising Shadow(IRE) , a victim of his own consistency, remains 7lb above his last winning mark despite a 16-race losing streak. (op 8-1)
Balakiref Official explanation: jockey said gelding was unsuited by the good to firm ground
Cyclical Official explanation: jockey said gelding was unsuited by the track

3472 GG RACING SYNDICATE FILLIES' H'CAP — 1m 14y
9:10 (9:14) (Class 5) (0-70,75) 3-Y-O — **£5,181** (£1,541; £770; £384) **Stalls** High

Form — RPR
0-60 **1** **Dancing Storm**[74] 1348 3-8-8 **56**.................................. FergusSweeney 6 — 61
(W S Kittow) *mde all: hrd rdn and hld on all out fnl f* — **18/1**
4413 **2** *nk* **My Lovely Lady (IRE)**[13] 3088 3-9-7 **69**........................ HayleyTurner 12 — 73
(M L W Bell) *chsd ldrs: drvn to chal ins fnl f: kpt on but no ex last strides* — **3/1**[1]
0344 **3** *½* **Khyber Knight (IRE)**[10] 3161 3-8-1 **54** oh8 ow4........... JamesDoyle(5) 3 — 57
(Jane Southcombe) *chsd ldrs: over 2f out: ev ch ins last: no ex cl home* — **40/1**
-302 **4** *nk* **Starboard Light**[27] 2634 3-8-7 **55**....................................... SebSanders 1 — 57+
(R M Beckett) *racd alone far side and a up w ldrs: ev ch wl ins last: no ex cl home* — **7/1**
0004 **5** *hd* **Zafantage**[18] 2921 3-9-0 **62**... FrankieMcDonald 10 — 64
(S Kirk) *bhd: rdn 3f out: hdwy in centre crse 2f out: styd on u.p ins last: no ex cl home* — **12/1**
0201 **6** *shd* **Dream Rose (IRE)**[11] 3142 3-9-13 **75** 6ex........................... ChrisCatlin 9 — 77+
(M R Channon) *bhd: rdn and hdwy over 2f out: styd on to chse ldrs ins last: one pce cl home* — **9/2**[2]
4U10 **7** *5* **Wizby**[9] 3197 3-8-7 **55** ow1.. SteveDrowne 13 — 45
(P D Evans) *slowly away: bhd: hrd rdn over 3f out: sme prog fr over 1f out but n.d* — **8/1**
000 **8** *shd* **Flying Visitor**[28] 2615 3-7-13 **50** oh5....................(b[1]) NelsonDeSouza(3) 7 — 40
(J M P Eustace) *chsd ldrs: rdn 1/2-way: wknd 2f out* — **50/1**
5000 **9** *shd* **Orphina (IRE)**[4] 3364 3-8-12 **60**... PatDobbs 2 — 50
(Pat Eddery) *chsd ldrs: rdn over 3f out: wknd ins fnl 2f* — **10/1**
0000 **10** *13* **Jessica Wigmo**[20] 2877 3-8-2 **50** oh4........................ RichardThomas 11 — 10
(A W Carroll) *chsd ldrs over 5f* — **100/1**
0424 **11** *6* **Imperial Lucky (IRE)**[14] 3055 3-8-12 **60**................................ NCallan 14 — 6
(M J Wallace) *in tch: rdn and hdwy 1/2-way: wknd over 2f out* — **11/2**[3]
350 **12** *3* **Diamond Winnie**[46] 2077 3-7-11 **52** ow2.................... JosephWalsh(7) 8 — —
(Mrs N S Evans) *slowly away: a bhd* — **33/1**
-360 **13** *1 ¼* **Just Devine (IRE)**[56] 1823 3-9-4 **69**................................ AdamKirby(3) 5 — 5
(B Palling) *chsd ldrs 5f* — **10/1**

1m 33.36s (-2.64) **Going Correction** -0.30s/f (Firm) **13** Ran SP% **121.6**
Speed ratings (Par 97):101,100,100,99,99 99,94,94,94,81 75,72,71
CSF £72.02 CT £2283.54 TOTE £21.60: £4.60, £1.70, £11.50; EX 110.10 Place 6 £85.77, Place 5 £31.99.
Owner The Quintet Partnership **Bred** D R Tucker **Trained** Blackborough, Devon

FOCUS
A modest handicap lacking progressive types, but the form seems sound enough for the grade. One filly raced alone down the far side, and the field fanned out across the track in the latter stages.
My Lovely Lady(IRE) Official explanation: jockey said filly hung left
Imperial Lucky(IRE) Official explanation: jockey said filly ran flat
Just Devine(IRE) Official explanation: jockey said filly hung left
T/Plt: £152.20 to a £1 stake. Pool: £53,310.85. 255.55 winning tickets. T/Qpdt: £37.70 to a £1 stake. Pool: £3,021.30. 59.30 winning tickets. ST

3064 CHESTER (L-H)
Friday, July 14

OFFICIAL GOING: Good to firm (firm in places)
Wind: Light, across Weather: Hot and sunny

3473 ETHEL AUSTIN PROPERTIES H'CAP — 7f 122y
6:30 (6:32) (Class 4) (0-80,80) 3-Y-O — **£5,829** (£1,734; £866; £432) **Stalls** Low

Form — RPR
-026 **1** **Glenmuir (IRE)**[51] 1934 3-9-6 **79**.. AlanMunro 4 — 86
(B R Millman) *hld up: hdwy 2f out: led ins fnl f: r.o* — **6/1**
-050 **2** *1* **Pitbull**[6] 3290 3-8-2 **61** oh1.. JimmyQuinn 1 — 65
(Mrs G S Rees) *hld up: hdwy whn nt clr run over 2f out: nt clr run again over 1f out: ev ch whn hung lft ins fnl f: nt qckn* — **16/1**
4635 **3** *1* **Stainley (IRE)**[43] 2171 3-8-5 **64**....................................... FrancisNorton 3 — 66
(J D Bethell) *trckd ldrs: rdn over 3f out: styd on same pce ins fnl f* — **5/1**[3]
0022 **4** *nk* **North Walk (IRE)**[10] 3176 3-9-6 **79**.................................. DO'Donohoe 7 — 80
(K A Ryan) *in tch: pushed along briefly after 1f: hdwy 3f out: rdn over 2f out: kpt on same pce ins fnl f* — **9/2**[2]
234 **5** *1 ¾* **Feelin Irie (IRE)**[13] 3082 3-8-4 **63**..................................... KimTinkler 2 — 59
(N Tinkler) *led: rdn over 1f out: hdd ins fnl f: sn btn* — **8/1**
1100 **6** *1 ½* **Trans Sonic**[84] 1115 3-9-2 **80**... GregFairley(5) 8 — 73
(A P Jarvis) *racd keenly: prom: rdn over 2f out: wknd ins fnl f* — **15/2**
-000 **7** *6* **Observatory Star (IRE)**[17] 2947 3-8-8 **67**............................ DavidAllan 6 — 45
(T D Easterby) *s.s: bhd: nvr on terms* — **28/1**
-331 **8** *10* **Mahrajaan (USA)**[20] 2881 3-9-6 **79**.. RHills 5 — 32
(J H M Gosden) *prom tl rdn and wknd over 2f out* — **11/4**[1]

1m 32.36s (-2.39) **Going Correction** -0.30s/f (Firm) **8** Ran SP% **108.0**
Speed ratings (Par 102):99,98,97,96,94 93,87,77
CSF £82.95 CT £451.16 TOTE £7.70: £2.50, £3.60, £2.10; EX 231.10.
Owner Glenmuir Partnership **Bred** Frank Dunne **Trained** Kentisbeare, Devon

FOCUS
This looked a very ordinary race for the grade but the form looks sound enough rated through the runner-up.
Glenmuir(IRE) Official explanation: trainer's representative said gelding had improved following a break from running
Mahrajaan(USA) Official explanation: jockey said colt hung left-handed throughout

3474 HIGHSTREETVOUCHERS.COM CONDITIONS STKS — 5f 16y
7:00 (7:01) (Class 2) 2-Y-O — **£10,094** (£3,020; £1,510; £755; £376) **Stalls** Low

Form — RPR
021 **1** **Not For Me (IRE)**[18] 2938 2-8-9 .... GregFairley(5) 1 — 97
(T J Pitt) *mde all: rdn over 1f out: kpt on wl* — **11/2**[3]
3415 **2** *1* **Bridge It Jo**[13] 3084 2-8-9 .... AlanMunro 2 — 88
(Miss J Feilden) *chsd ldrs: rdn and swtchd rt over 1f out: wnt 2nd ins fnl f: r.o: nt rch wnr* — **11/2**[3]
145 **3** *2* **Kerry's Dream**[44] 2125 2-8-9 .... DavidAllan 4 — 81
(T D Easterby) *prom: rdn and ev ch 2f out: no ex ins fnl f* — **9/2**[2]
2211 **4** *3* **Invincible Force (IRE)**[13] 3064 2-9-0 .... FrancisNorton 5 — 75+
(Ms Deborah J Evans) *hmpd s: bhd: effrt over 1f out: no imp* — **7/2**[1]
120 **5** *1* **Just Joey**[21] 2800 2-8-9 .... PhillipMakin 3 — 67
(J R Weymes) *chsd ldrs: rdn over 2f out: sn wknd* — **11/2**[3]
241 **6** *12* **Minaash (USA)**[13] 3070 2-9-0 .... ShaneKelly 6 — 29
(J Noseda) *racd keenly: chsd ldrs tl rdn and wknd over 2f out* — **7/2**[1]

60.06 secs (-1.99) **Going Correction** -0.30s/f (Firm) 2y crse rec **6** Ran SP% **108.8**
Speed ratings (Par 100):103,101,98,93,91 72
CSF £32.36 TOTE £5.80: £2.00, £2.70; EX 27.90.
Owner Ms K O'Hare **Bred** Floral Partnership **Trained** Bawtry, S Yorks

FOCUS
Previous winners of this race include Majestic Missile (03) and Beckermet (04), and Amadeus Wolf was second last year. While it remains to be seen if there was anything of that sort of class in this year's renewal, it looked a reasonable contest, backed up by the time.

NOTEBOOK
Not For Me(IRE) showed just fair form when off the mark over six furlongs at Wolverhampton on his previous start, but the drop back in trip suited well and he took advantage of the best draw of all to follow up. He clearly has bundles of pace and looks a useful type. (op 7-1 tchd 15-2)
Bridge It Jo, the winner of a maiden at Nottingham before running fifth in an ordinary six-furlong Listed event at Newmarket, ran a creditable race dropped in both grade and trip. She was clear of the rest and should continue to go well in similar events. (op 5-1)
Kerry's Dream ran well from a bad draw in the Hilary Needler at Beverley on her previous start, but she could not quite match that form this time. (op 3-1)
Invincible Force(IRE), chasing the hat-trick after landing his maiden at Warwick and a novice event over course and distance, did not have the best of the draws and could never get involved after getting hampered at the start. Official explanation: jockey said geling suffered interference at the start (op 9-2)
Just Joey, who was second in the Hilary Needler but beat only two home in the Albany Stakes, proved disappointing dropped in class. (op 6-1)
Minaash(USA) had the worst of the draw, met with a little trouble at the start, and raced keenly, so this run is probably best forgotten. Official explanation: jockey said colt was unsuited by the track (op 3-1)

3475 KATHLEEN B. CORBETT MEMORIAL H'CAP — 5f 16y
7:30 (7:31) (Class 3) (0-95,94) 3-Y-O£10,094 (£3,020; £1,510; £755; £376) **Stalls** Low

Form — RPR
6033 **1** **Azygous**[14] 3049 3-8-5 **78**.. AlanMunro 5 — 86
(J Akehurst) *mde all: pushed out and kpt on ins fnl f* — **7/1**
2422 **2** *½* **Blazing Heights**[20] 2855 3-8-0 **78**.................................... LiamJones(5) 7 — 84+
(J S Goldie) *s.s: in rr: clsd to r bhd main gp over 3f out and t.k.h: rdn and hdwy over 1f out: r.o ins fnl f* — **9/2**[1]
3346 **3** *nk* **Scooby Dude (IRE)**[43] 2168 3-8-5 **78**............................ FrancisNorton 8 — 83
(Ms Deborah J Evans) *a.p: rdn and ev ch over 1f out: nt qckn ins fnl f* **7/1**
-400 **4** *1 ½* **Gallery Girl (IRE)**[27] 2658 3-9-2 **89**...................................... DavidAllan 1 — 89
(T D Easterby) *chsd ldrs: rdn over 1f out: styd on same pce ins fnl f* **9/2**[1]
1441 **5** *1 ½* **Moorhouse Lad**[20] 2866 3-8-11 **84**.................................... JimmyQuinn 6 — 78
(G Woodward) *cl up on outside over 3f out: rdn over 1f out: no ex ins fnl f* — **11/2**[3]
0-50 **6** *¾* **Titus Alone (IRE)**[14] 3038 3-9-7 **94**.................................... PaulEddery 3 — 86
(B Smart) *racd keenly: in tch: rdn over 2f out: nvr able to chal: eased whn btn wl ins fnl f* — **14/1**
4151 **7** *5* **Glasshoughton**[16] 2976 3-8-8 **81**... PhillipMakin 4 — 55
(M Dods) *in tch: rdn whn n.m.r and hmpd 2f out: lost pl qckly and bhd after* — **5/1**[2]
0201 **8** *9* **Stoneacre Lad (IRE)**[27] 2639 3-9-3 **90**..................(b) RobbieFitzpatrick 2 — 31
(Peter Grayson) *in tch: outpcd after 1f: bhd after* — **7/1**

60.10 secs (-1.95) **Going Correction** -0.30s/f (Firm) **8** Ran SP% **112.6**
Speed ratings (Par 104):103,102,101,99,96 95,87,73
CSF £37.19 CT £227.46 TOTE £8.80: £2.30, £1.90, £1.60; EX 48.50.
Owner The Grass Is Greener Partnership V **Bred** Mrs R D Peacock **Trained** Epsom, Surrey

FOCUS
This looked like just an ordinary sprint handicap for the grade but it has been rated at face value with the third setting the standard.

NOTEBOOK
Azygous, racing off a career-low mark, got the run of the race out in front and ended a losing run stretching back to April 2005. He will go up in the weights for this and things will not always fall so kindly.
Blazing Heights, an unlucky loser at Ayr on his previous start, again looked as though he may well have won had things fallen right. Slowly away, he raced very keenly in behind and just got going too late when switched widest of all with his run. He may not be that straightforward, but is in good enough form to get his head back in front when granted more luck. (op 7-2 tchd 5-1)
Scooby Dude(IRE), returning from a 43-day break, seemed to have every chance and ran well. (tchd 15-2)
Gallery Girl(IRE) has been given a chance by the Handicapper and this was a little better than of late. (op 5-1)
Moorhouse Lad did not have the best of draws and could not defy a 4lb higher mark than when winning at Newmarket on his previous start.
Glasshoughton, 6lb higher than when winning at Carlisle on his previous start, lost his chance when hampered around two furlongs out and can be forgiven this. (op 6-1)
Stoneacre Lad(IRE) Official explanation: trainer said colt was unsuited by the track

3476 ASTBURY WREN NURSERY — 5f 16y
8:00 (8:00) (Class 4) 2-Y-O — **£5,440** (£1,618; £808; £404) **Stalls** Low

Form — RPR
21 **1** **Vale Of Belvoir (IRE)**[35] 2394 2-8-6 **74**.......................... FrancisNorton 6 — 81+
(K R Burke) *trckd ldrs: qcknd to ld 1f out: r.o wl* — **9/2**[3]
2241 **2** *1 ¼* **Frisky Talk (IRE)**[25] 2703 2-8-5 **73** ow1.................................... RHills 1 — 76
(B W Hills) *led: rdn and hdd 1f out: nt pce of wnr after* — **9/4**[1]
422 **3** *1 ½* **Riotous (IRE)**[25] 2695 2-8-2 **70**... JimmyQuinn 2 — 67
(A Dickman) *racd keenly: hld up: rdn over 1f out: hdwy whn forced rt ins fnl f: styd on towards finsih* — **5/1**
2330 **4** *hd* **Spoof Master (IRE)**[15] 3026 2-9-0 **89**.............................. PJBenson(7) 4 — 85
(W G M Turner) *trckd ldrs: rdn over 1f out: edgd rt ins fnl f: styd on same pce* — **9/2**[3]

521 **5** 2 ½ **Bollin Franny**[23] [2759] 2-8-10 **78**.. DavidAllan 5 65
(T D Easterby) *w ldr: rdn and ev ch 2f out: hld whn carried rt ins fnl f* **4/1**[2]

0045 **6** 1 ½ **Almora Guru**[31] [2517] 2-7-8 **67** oh4 ow1........................... LiamJones(5) 3 49
(W M Brisbourne) *hld up: rdn 2f out: no real imp whn carried rt and hmpd ins fnl f* **20/1**

60.69 secs (-1.36) **Going Correction** -0.30s/f (Firm) **6** Ran SP% **108.6**
Speed ratings (Par 96):98,96,93,93,89 86
CSF £14.02 TOTE £5.30: £2.90, £1.30; EX 14.90.
Owner S Marley & Tweenhills Racing IX **Bred** Denis And Mrs Teresa Bergin **Trained** Middleham Moor, N Yorks

FOCUS
The official ratings shown next to each horse are estimated and for information purposes only. This looked like a reasonable enough nursery with the runner-up the best guide to the level.

NOTEBOOK
Vale Of Belvoir(IRE) ◆, off the mark at the second attempt in a Catterick maiden on her previous start, overcame her wide draw and followed up in this better company. She never looked in any danger and is progressing very nicely indeed. (op 13-2)
Frisky Talk(IRE), who finally managed to get her head in front in a maiden at Warwick last time, had the best draw and seemed to have every chance, but she was no match for the winner. This would appear to be as good as she is. (op 7-4)
Riotous(IRE), who showed ability in three runs in maiden company, got behind early on and was never seen with a serious chance. He is a little bit better than the bare form. (op 13-2 tchd 7-1)
Spoof Master(IRE), dropped a furlong in trip, looked on a stiff enough mark for his nursery debut but did not run badly. (tchd 5-1)
Bollin Franny could not build on the form he showed when winning his maiden at Ripon last time. (op 7-2)

3477 SHELL UK H'CAP 1m 2f 75y
8:30 (8:30) (Class 4) (0-85,83) 3-Y-O **£5,829** (£1,734; £866; £432) **Stalls** High

Form RPR
0651 **1** **Stotsfold**[15] [3015] 3-9-2 **78**.. AlanMunro 4 84+
(W R Swinburn) *hld up in tch: hdwy on outside 2f out: r.o to ld ins fnl f: pushed out cl home* **7/4**[1]

3-60 **2** 1 **Shaydreambeliever**[39] [2290] 3-8-7 **69**.............................. GylesParkin 3 73
(R A Fahey) *prom: led over 4f out: rdn over 2f out: hdd and edgd lft ins fnl f: hld cl home* **16/1**

5053 **3** hd **Hill Of Almhuim (IRE)**[28] [2622] 3-8-6 **68**....................(v) FrancisNorton 2 72
(K R Burke) *t.k.h: led: hdd over 4f out: rallied and ev ch ins fnl f: nt qckn cl home* **4/1**[2]

2414 **4** ¾ **Flying Clarets (IRE)**[19] [2892] 3-9-2 **78**.......................... TonyHamilton 5 80
(R A Fahey) *t.k.h: trckd ldrs: rdn over 2f out: ev ch ins fnl f: one pce cl home* **9/2**[3]

-200 **5** hd **Nihal (IRE)**[41] [2224] 3-9-7 **83**.. JoeFanning 1 89+
(M Johnston) *trckd ldrs: effrt whn nt clr run and swtchd lft over 1f out: nt clr run again and swtchd rt ins fnl f: nt rcvr* **5/1**

4466 **6** 3 **Dallma (IRE)**[7] [3250] 3-8-7 **69**.. RHills 7 65
(C E Brittain) *hld up: rdn and outpcd over 3f out: nvr able to chal* **9/1**

0-54 **7** 25 **Gamesters Lady**[13] [3065] 3-8-9 **76**.............................. LiamJones(5) 6 25
(W M Brisbourne) *s.i.s: a bhd: lost tch 3f out* **20/1**

2m 11.59s (-1.55) **Going Correction** -0.30s/f (Firm) **7** Ran SP% **111.9**
Speed ratings (Par 102):94,93,93,92,92 89,69
CSF £30.57 TOTE £2.80: £1.70, £3.60; EX 43.70.
Owner Mrs P W Harris **Bred** Pendley Farm **Trained** Aldbury, Herts
■ A treble for jockey Alan Munro following earlier wins on Glenmuir and Azygous.

FOCUS
A fair handicap which looks sound enough rated through the placed horses.

3478 CHESHIRE YEOMANRY FILLIES' H'CAP 6f 18y
9:00 (9:00) (Class 5) (0-75,72) 3-Y-O+ **£3,432** (£1,021; £510; £254) **Stalls** Low

Form RPR
-314 **1** **Aahgowangowan (IRE)**[7] [3267] 7-8-11 **60**..................(t) LiamJones(5) 4 70
(M Dods) *mde all: rdn ins fnl f: hld on gamely towards fin* **9/4**[1]

0031 **2** nk **Safranine (IRE)**[7] [3267] 9-8-3 **54** 6ex.............................. AnnStokell(7) 1 63
(Miss A Stokell) *trckd ldrs: rdn to chse wnr over 1f out: sn edgd rt: r.o towards fin* **6/1**

0016 **3** 1 **Linda Green**[4] [3368] 5-9-5 **66**.............................. EdwardCreighton(3) 6 72+
(M R Channon) *hld up: plld wd whn rdn and hdwy over 1f out: r.o ins fnl f: nt rch front pair* **4/1**[2]

0656 **4** 3 **Highland Cascade**[14] [3041] 4-9-13 **71**.............................. ShaneKelly 2 68
(J M P Eustace) *trckd ldrs: rdn over 1f out: one pce ins fnl f* **5/1**[3]

4033 **5** hd **Dorn Dancer (IRE)**[14] [3041] 4-9-6 **64**.............................. JimmyQuinn 5 67+
(D W Barker) *hld up: effrt whn n.m.r and hmpd over 1f out: n.d after* **4/1**[2]

-000 **6** 1 **Cate Washington**[7] [3245] 3-7-12 **55** oh6 ow2.................. KellyHarrison(7) 8 47
(Mrs L Williamson) *in rr: rdn over 1f out: nvr on terms* **33/1**

6246 **7** 2 ½ **Miskina**[77] [1273] 5-8-4 **53** oh8.............................. GregFairley(5) 3 39
(W M Brisbourne) *prom: rdn over 2f out: wknd ins fnl f* **10/1**

1m 13.67s (-1.98) **Going Correction** -0.30s/f (Firm)
WFA 3 from 4yo+ 6lb **7** Ran SP% **113.8**
Speed ratings (Par 100):101,100,99,95,95 93,90
CSF £16.14 CT £50.11 TOTE £3.20: £1.90, £2.80; EX 8.20 Place 6 £287.51, Place 5 £66.46.
Owner Les Waugh **Bred** Seamus Phelan **Trained** Denton, Co Durham

FOCUS
Both Aahgowangowan and Safranine, two in-form mares, were racing off lower marks than in future and this looked a good sprint for the grade with the form sound.
T/Plt: £569.50 to a £1 stake. Pool: £58,666.45. 75.20 winning tickets. T/Qpdt: £26.40 to a £1 stake. Pool: £3,572.10. 100.00 winning tickets. DO

3166 HAMILTON (R-H)
Friday, July 14

OFFICIAL GOING: Good to firm (firm in places on the loop)
Wind: Almost nil

3479 JOHN SMITH'S EXTRA COLD H'CAP 5f 4y
6:50 (6:50) (Class 5) (0-70,70) 3-Y-O **£3,238** (£963; £481; £240) **Stalls** Centre

Form RPR
21 **1** **Urbe Condita (IRE)**[37] [2356] 3-9-7 **70**.............................. KDarley 3 92+
(T J Etherington) *keen: prom: led gng wl over 1f out: sn clr: easily* **1/1**[1]

3053 **2** 5 **Rothesay Dancer**[15] [3000] 3-8-13 **65**..........................(p) DNolan(3) 4 69
(J S Goldie) *chsd ldrs: effrt and ev ch over 1f out: kpt on fnl f: no ch w wnr* **7/2**[3]

0306 **3** 2 ½ **Egyptian Lord**[18] [2939] 3-8-6 **58**..........................(b) PatrickMathers(3) 2 53
(Peter Grayson) *mde most to over 1f out: sn outpcd* **10/1**

-654 **4** 2 ½ **Howards Prince**[20] [2855] 3-9-0 **63**..........................(p) PatCosgrave 5 49
(I Semple) *w ldrs: rdn 1/2-way: ev ch over 1f out: sn btn* **3/1**[2]

60-0 **5** 1 ½ **Compton Lad**[64] [1612] 3-8-2 **51** oh3..........................(p) RoystonFfrench 1 32
(D A Nolan) *w ldrs tl wknd over 1f out* **100/1**

58.65 secs (-2.55) **Going Correction** -0.35s/f (Firm) **5** Ran SP% **107.3**
Speed ratings (Par 100):106,98,94,90,87
CSF £4.53 TOTE £1.70: £1.10, £2.00; EX 3.60.
Owner Miss Z C Willis **Bred** Bryan Ryan **Trained** Norton, N Yorks

FOCUS
An uncompetitive race in which the pace was sound and the runner-up is the best guide to the level.

3480 NO NONSENSE (S) STKS 1m 65y
7:20 (7:21) (Class 5) 3-Y-O+ **£3,238** (£963; £481; £240) **Stalls** High

Form RPR
0-02 **1** **Baby Barry**[7] [3240] 9-9-4 **50**.. DaleGibson 5 60
(R A Fahey) *trckd ldrs: rdn to ld over 1f out: hld on wl fnl f* **11/4**[1]

022P **2** ½ **La Viola**[11] [3159] 4-8-13 **57**..........................(v) PatCosgrave 7 54
(K R Burke) *hld up in tch: effrt over 2f out: chsd wnr over 1f out: kpt on fnl f: hld towards fin* **7/2**[2]

16-5 **3** ½ **Neil's Legacy (IRE)**[5] [3333] 4-8-8 **50**.............................. AndrewMullen(5) 6 53
(Miss L A Perratt) *hld up ins: outpcd 3f out: rallied over 1f out: kpt on wl fnl f* **11/2**

2335 **4** nk **Alisdanza**[23] [2747] 4-8-13 **49**.. PaulQuinn 1 52
(G A Swinbank) *hld up in tch: hdwy and ev ch over 1f out: no ex ins fnl f* **5/1**[3]

-060 **5** 3 **Jordans Spark**[30] [2546] 5-9-4 **45**.............................. RoystonFfrench 10 50
(P Monteith) *keen: trckd ldrs tl rdn and no ex over 1f out* **14/1**

0004 **6** 5 **El Rey Royale**[6] [3311] 4-9-4 **49**..........................(v[1]) KDarley 3 39
(Micky Hammond) *keen: led to over 2f out: wknd over 1f out* **6/1**

4000 **7** 1 **Zantero**[20] [2881] 4-9-1 **42**.. DNolan(3) 4 36
(W M Brisbourne) *s.i.s: hld up: short-lived effrt over 2f out: sn btn* **40/1**

560- **8** 1 **Lowicz**[371] [3312] 4-8-10 **34**.............................. DanielTudhope(3) 2 29
(D Carroll) *pressed ldr: led over 2f out to over 1f out: sn btn* **14/1**

9 44 **Deer Park Countess**[74] 5-8-10.............................. PatrickMathers(3) 9 —
(D A Nolan) *hld up: pushed along 4f out: sn btn: t.o* **66/1**

1m 47.61s (-1.69) **Going Correction** -0.225s/f (Firm) **9** Ran SP% **112.5**
Speed ratings (Par 103):99,98,98,97,94 89,88,87,43
CSF £11.93 TOTE £2.40: £1.10, £1.90, £1.80; EX 8.40.There was no bid for the winner.
Owner Mrs Annette C Barlow **Bred** Capt J H Wilson **Trained** Musley Bank, N Yorks
■ Stewards' Enquiry : Pat Cosgrave caution: careless riding

FOCUS
A moderate race in which the pace was steady and this bare form does not look reliable.

3481 JOHN SMITH'S EXTRA SMOOTH NURSERY (A QUALIFIER FOR THE HAMILTON PARK 2-Y-O SERIES FINAL) 6f 5y
7:50 (7:50) (Class 3) 2-Y-O **£7,772** (£2,312; £1,155; £577) **Stalls** Centre

Form RPR
21 **1** **Adaptation**[15] [2999] 2-9-4 **79**.. KDarley 5 85+
(M Johnston) *cl up: led over 2f out: kpt on strly fnl f* **4/5**[1]

0042 **2** 1 ½ **Dolly Coughdrop (IRE)**[12] [3117] 2-8-6 **67**.............................. PatCosgrave 3 66
(K R Burke) *prom: effrt 2f out: sn chsng wnr: r.o fnl f* **9/2**[2]

5221 **3** 1 ½ **My Valerina (IRE)**[25] [2695] 2-8-10 **71**.............................. RoystonFfrench 4 65
(Mrs A Duffield) *cl up: rdn over 2f out: edgd rt appr fnl f: kpt on same pce* **9/2**[2]

2136 **4** shd **The Mighty Ogmore**[3] [3372] 2-8-1 **67**.............................. AndrewMullen(5) 2 61
(R C Guest) *in tch: rdn over 2f out: kpt on fnl f: no imp* **25/1**

01 **5** 1 ¼ **Moonwalking**[21] [2807] 2-9-7 **82**.. DaleGibson 6 72
(Jedd O'Keeffe) *plld hrd: led to over 2f out: wknd over 1f out* **14/1**

0140 **6** nk **Cheshire Prince**[7] [3246] 2-8-4 **65**.. PaulQuinn 1 54
(W M Brisbourne) *keen: trckd ldrs tl wknd fr 2f out* **10/1**[3]

1m 13.24s (0.14) **Going Correction** -0.225s/f (Firm) **6** Ran SP% **111.5**
Speed ratings (Par 98):90,88,86,85,84 83
CSF £4.68 TOTE £1.50: £1.10, £1.90; EX 4.00.
Owner J Shack **Bred** Newsells Park Stud Limited **Trained** Middleham Moor, N Yorks

FOCUS
An ordinary event and a fair pace but another step in the right direction for Adaptation with the form of those behind looking solid. The official ratings shown next to each horse are estimated and for information purposes only.

NOTEBOOK
Adaptation ◆, who did not have to improve to win over course and distance in uncompetitive company last time, turned in her best effort to win with a bit more in hand than the margin suggests. She again shaped as though the step up to seven furlongs would suit and remains capable of better. (op Evens tchd 11-10 in places)
Dolly Coughdrop(IRE) is a consistent sort who jumped off better than at Windsor last time and seemed to give it her best shot. She looks a good guide to the worth of this form and should continue to give a good account. (op 7-2)
My Valerina(IRE) is not very big but had the run of the race and was not disgraced. The return to five furlongs may suit but she may not be the easiest to place in this type of event from her current mark in the mid-70s. (tchd 5-1)
The Mighty Ogmore, mainly a consistent sort, has only raced over sprint distances to date but left the impression that she would be worth a try over seven furlongs. (op 16-1)
Moonwalking took the eye in the preliminaries but failed to settle and may not have been suited by making his own running. The step up to seven furlongs on a more conventional track should suit when more patient tactics are adopted. (tchd 16-1)
Cheshire Prince has not really improved since his Yarmouth selling win and had his limitations exposed on this nursery debut after failing to settle. He will have to improve a fair bit to win from this mark in this company.

3482 JOHN SMITH'S SCOTTISH STEWARDS CUP H'CAP 6f 5y
8:20 (8:21) (Class 2) (0-105,103) 3-Y-O+
£21,812 (£6,531; £3,265; £1,634; £815; £409) **Stalls** Centre

Form RPR
1104 **1** **Bayeux (USA)**[22] [2776] 5-9-11 **94**.. NickyMackay 1 107
(G A Butler) *in tch: effrt and swtchd rt 2f out: led ins fnl f: kpt on fnl f* **5/2**[1]

-500 **2** ¾ **Machinist (IRE)**[41] [2230] 6-9-2 **88**.............................. SilvestreDeSousa(3) 3 99
(D Nicholls) *prom: led over 1f out: edgd lft: hdd ins fnl f: kpt on* **8/1**[3]

1121 **3** ¾ **Yorkshire Blue**[5] [3330] 7-8-9 **78** 6ex oh2.............................. RoystonFfrench 8 87
(J S Goldie) *midfield: outpcd after 2f: hdwy over 1f out: kpt on fnl f: nrst fin* **7/1**[2]

5031 **4** ½ **Fantasy Believer**[3] [3374] 8-9-0 **86** 6ex.............................. DNolan(3) 13 93
(J J Quinn) *hld up on outside: gd hdwy over 2f out: ch ins fnl f: edgd lft and no ex last 75yds* **7/1**[2]

5210 **5** nk **Dhaular Dhar (IRE)**[13] [3077] 4-8-12 **84**.............................. DanielTudhope(3) 9 90
(J S Goldie) *hld up: hdwy centre 2f out: kpt on tl no imp wl ins fnl f* **25/1**

0124 **6** hd **My Gacho (IRE)**[13] [3077] 4-8-12 **84**..........................(v) BenSwarbrick(3) 4 90
(T D Barron) *w ldrs: rdn over 2f out: kpt on same pce fnl f* **8/1**[3]

0100 **7** *3* **Zomerlust**[20] [2847] 4-9-11 **94** .... GrahamGibbons 7 91
(J J Quinn) *hld up: rdn over 2f out: kpt on fnl f: n.d* **10/1**

6034 **8** *1 1/4* **Continent**[14] [3038] 9-9-1 **91** .... VictoriaBehan(7) 6 84
(D Nicholls) *led to over 1f out: sn outpcd* **10/1**

1361 **9** *nk* **Dizzy In The Head**[10] [3170] 7-8-4 **78** 6ex oh2........(b) DuranFentiman(5) 2 70
(I Semple) *w ldrs tl wknd over 1f out* **25/1**

2411 **10** *1 3/4* **Folga**[11] [3144] 4-9-10 **93** 6ex........ KDarley 5 80
(J G Given) *awkward s: bhd and sn rdn along: nvr on terms* **14/1**

43-0 **11** *1/2* **Curtail (IRE)**[27] [2651] 3-10-0 **103** .... PatCosgrave 11 88
(I Semple) *prom tl rdn and wknd fr 2f out* **25/1**

0004 **12** *2 1/2* **Just James**[6] [3295] 7-9-11 **94** .... PaulQuinn 12 72
(D Nicholls) *sn wl bhd: nvr on terms* **12/1**

0000 **13** *9* **Northern Svengali (IRE)**[15] [3003] 10-8-6 **78** oh41(t) PatrickMathers(3) 10 29
(D A Nolan) *in tch: rdn over 2f out: sn btn* **200/1**

1m 10.65s (-2.45) **Going Correction** -0.225s/f (Firm)
WFA 3 from 4yo+ 6lb **13** Ran SP% **120.4**
Speed ratings (Par 109):107,106,105,104,103 103,99,98,97,95 94,91,79
CSF £21.68 CT £132.95 TOTE £3.80: £2.00, £3.80, £1.40; EX 45.40.
Owner Michael Tabor **Bred** Darley **Trained** Blewbury, Oxon

FOCUS
A competitive event in which the field converged in the centre but the best of the pace was more towards the stands' side. The form looks solid and has been rated positively.

NOTEBOOK
Bayeux(USA), dropped in both trip and grade, had the race run to suit and ran as well as he ever had done. A good pace suits him ideally and he appeals as the type to win again over sprint distances. (op 7-2 tchd 4-1 in places)
Machinist(IRE) ◆ ran his best race on turf of the year and may be a bit better than the bare form as he was up with the strong pace throughout. This was a clear sign that a return to winning ways is imminent and he is one to keep an eye on. (op 9-1 tchd 10-1)
Yorkshire Blue, up in the weights and in grade, was anything but disgraced from just out of the handicap. His run style means he needs things to fall right but he has been at the top of his game of late and should continue to give a good account. (tchd 13-2 and 8-1)
Fantasy Believer, who returned to winning ways at Pontefract, was another to shape as though better than the bare form as he was isolated away from the best of the pace on the wide outside. He did well to get into a challenging position where he did and remains capable of winning again this summer. (op 4-1)
Dhaular Dhar(IRE) is not the most consistent but ran creditably having raced on the outside of the main field. The return to seven furlongs will be more to his liking but he is not really one to place maximum faith in. (tchd 33-1)
My Gacho(IRE) has been running creditably and did so again, especially as he was right up with the strong pace throughout. He has edged up in the weights this year but should continue to give a good account around this trip. (op 7-1)
Zomerlust has little margin for error from his current mark but left the impression that he would be worth another try over seven furlongs. (op 9-1)
Folga Official explanation: jockey said filly became upset in the stalls and didn't make the break well

3483 JOHN SMITH'S STAYERS H'CAP 1m 5f 9y
8:50 (8:51) (Class 4) (0-85,81) 3-Y-0+ **£7,772** (£2,312; £1,155; £577) **Stalls** High

Form RPR

2325 **1** **Bronze Dancer (IRE)**[21] [2828] 4-9-2 **62** .... PaulQuinn 3 75
(G A Swinbank) *hld up: effrt over 2f out: qcknd to ld ins fnl f: r.o wl* **8/1**[3]

4665 **2** *2* **Doctor Scott**[6] [3292] 3-9-7 **81** .... RoystonFfrench 6 91
(M Johnston) *chsd ldrs: pushed along 4f out: led over 1f out to ins fnl f: r.o same pce* **5/4**[1]

-125 **3** *3* **Reluctant Suitor**[57] [1809] 4-9-5 **68** .... DanielTudhope(3) 4 74
(J S Goldie) *in tch: effrt whn nt clr run over 2f out: one pce appr fnl f* **3/1**[2]

6520 **4** *1 1/4* **Balwearie (IRE)**[5] [3333] 5-8-9 **60** .... AndrewMullen(5) 1 64
(Miss L A Perratt) *hld up in tch: hdwy and ev ch over 1f out: no ex ins fnl f* **9/1**

1343 **5** *2 1/2* **Oldenway**[15] [3022] 7-9-6 **66** .... DaleGibson 2 66
(R A Fahey) *keen: led to over 1f out: sn outpcd* **8/1**[3]

6102 **6** *5* **Norman Beckett**[13] [3065] 3-8-12 **72** ....(p) PatCosgrave 5 64
(I Semple) *keen: in tch: effrt over 2f out: wknd over 1f out* **10/1**

6060 **7** *4* **Motafarred (IRE)**[22] [2773] 4-9-13 **73** .... KDarley 7 59
(Micky Hammond) *cl up tl rdn and wknd fr 2f out* **14/1**

2m 47.94s (-5.46) **Going Correction** -0.225s/f (Firm)
WFA 3 from 4yo+ 14lb **7** Ran SP% **117.4**
Speed ratings (Par 105):107,105,103,103,101 98,96
CSF £19.33 TOTE £9.60: £3.30, £1.30; EX 23.00.
Owner Mrs I Gibson **Bred** Lisieux Stud **Trained** Melsonby, N Yorks

FOCUS
An ordinary event but the winner did well to come from off an ordinary early gallop and record a decent time and may be a bit better than the bare form.

3484 JOHN SMITH'S H'CAP (A QUALIFIER FOR THE HAMILTON PARK HANDICAP SERIES) 1m 1f 36y
9:20 (9:20) (Class 5) (0-70,69) 3-Y-0+ **£3,886** (£1,156; £577; £288) **Stalls** High

Form RPR

0520 **1** **Insubordinate**[5] [3333] 5-8-13 **57** .... DanielTudhope(3) 7 66+
(J S Goldie) *hld up ins: hdwy whn nt clr run over 2f to over 1f out: rdn and led ins fnl f: r.o strly* **6/1**

2211 **2** *1* **Cottingham (IRE)**[35] [2414] 5-9-3 **61** .... BenSwarbrick(3) 4 67
(T D Barron) *upset in stalls: missed break: sn in tch: effrt and ev ch over 1f out: kpt on ins last: nt rch wnr* **2/1**[1]

0000 **3** *1* **Anthemion (IRE)**[25] [2697] 9-8-5 **51** .... AndrewMullen(5) 8 55
(Mrs J C McGregor) *led and clr to over 2f out: hdd ins fnl f: kpt on same pce* **11/2**[3]

1166 **4** *shd* **Ulysees (IRE)**[10] [3168] 7-10-0 **69** .... RoystonFfrench 3 73
(I Semple) *prom: outpcd 3f out: rallied fnl f: kpt on: nrst fin* **4/1**[2]

3000 **5** *2* **Royal Pardon**[19] [2891] 4-8-9 **50** ....(p) PaulQuinn 5 50
(R C Guest) *bhd tl styd on fr 2f out: nvr rchd ldrs* **25/1**

0654 **6** *2* **Campbells Lad**[11] [3139] 5-8-6 **50** oh10........ PatrickMathers(3) 2 46
(Mrs G S Rees) *chsd clr ldr: ev ch over 2f out: wknd over 1f out* **25/1**

4002 **7** *1/2* **Hansomelle (IRE)**[23] [2747] 4-9-2 **57** .... DaleGibson 9 52
(B Mactaggart) *chsd ldrs: outpcd 3f out: n.d after* **7/1**

6010 **8** *1 1/4* **Royal Indulgence**[22] [2789] 6-9-0 **55** .... PatCosgrave 1 47
(W M Brisbourne) *hld up: rdn over 3f out: sn btn* **9/1**

5000 **9** *23* **Mccormack (IRE)**[3] [3377] 4-8-9 **50** oh3........(v1) KDarley 6 —
(Micky Hammond) *hld up in tch: rdn over 3f out: sn btn* **16/1**

1m 56.75s (-2.91) **Going Correction** -0.225s/f (Firm) **9** Ran SP% **119.1**
Speed ratings (Par 103):103,102,101,101,99 97,97,96,75
CSF £19.02 CT £70.15 TOTE £7.00: £2.10, £1.80, £2.40; EX 33.20 Place 6 £5.43, Place 5 £3.82.
Owner Mrs D I Goldie **Bred** Charlock Farm Stud **Trained** Uplawmoor, E Renfrews

FOCUS
An ordinary handicap in which the pace was sound throughout and this bare form should stand up at a similar level.
T/Plt: £7.50 to a £1 stake. Pool: £45,281.50. 4,374.90 winning tickets. T/Qpdt: £7.10 to a £1 stake. Pool: £2,396.00. 249.30 winning tickets. RY

3406 LINGFIELD (L-H)
Friday, July 14

OFFICIAL GOING: Turf course - good to firm; all-weather - standard
Wind: Light, half-against Weather: Sunny and warm

3485 JACK SHEPPARD 90TH BIRTHDAY EBF MAIDEN STKS 6f
2:25 (2:25) (Class 5) 2-Y-0 **£4,533** (£1,348; £674; £336) **Stalls** High

Form RPR

22 **1** **Simply Perfect**[23] [2743] 2-8-12 .... ShaneKelly 2 77+
(J Noseda) *dwlt: hld up bhd ldrs: effrt to ld jst over 1f out: shuffled along and in n.d fnl f* **2/13**[1]

33 **2** *1 1/4* **Follow The Flag (IRE)**[7] [3259] 2-9-3 .... GeorgeBaker 3 66
(N P Littmoden) *reminder sn after s: chsd ldr to 2f out: sn rdn: chsd wnr ins fnl f: no imp* **16/1**[3]

60 **3** *1 1/4* **Ron In Ernest**[15] [3025] 2-9-3 .... StephenCarson 5 62
(J A Geake) *led: rdn and hdd jst over 1f out: fdd ins fnl f* **40/1**

4 *3/4* **Jawaab (IRE)** 2-9-3 .... DaneO'Neill 1 60
(E A L Dunlop) *s.s: rn green in last but in tch: outpcd and rdn 2f out: kpt on again last 100yds* **14/1**[2]

5 *nk* **Fares (IRE)** 2-9-3 .... J-PGuillambert 4 59
(C E Brittain) *dwlt: in tch: rdn and outpcd 2f out: plugged on ins fnl f* **28/1**

1m 11.61s (-0.06) **Going Correction** -0.275s/f (Firm) **5** Ran SP% **105.1**
Speed ratings (Par 94):89,87,85,84,84
CSF £3.01 TOTE £1.10: £1.02, £3.50; EX 3.00.
Owner D Smith, M Tabor & Mrs J Magnier **Bred** Trehedyn Stud And Quarry Bloodstock **Trained** Newmarket, Suffolk

FOCUS
A muddling contest with the field being covered by around three lengths at the line, but no doubting the class of cosy winner Simply Perfect, and the placed horses set the level for the form.

NOTEBOOK
Simply Perfect was the clear choice on the form of her placed efforts behind Dutch Art at Windsor and her second at the Royal meeting behind the prolific Gilded in the Queen Mary. Although taking on the colts, she proved far too classy, merely having to be pushed out once getting to the front, and she looks ready for a return to Group company. Seven furlongs will be within range this season and she has the Moyglare Stud stakes next month as a possible target. (op 1-7 tchd 1-6 in places and 2-11 in a place)
Follow The Flag(IRE) had to be woken up early on with a reminder and he stuck on well enough into second, but was never a threat to the winner. He is in need of a seventh furlong and should make his mark in nurseries. (op 20-1)
Ron In Ernest stepped up on previous efforts and was ridden aggressively by Carson, but he was readily brushed aside inside the final furlong and is another likely handicap type. (op 33-1)
Jawaab(IRE) was quite costly at 130,000gns, but his stable's juveniles usually benefit from a run and, considering he is bred to stay a good bit further, he was always likely to find himself tapped for speed. That proved to be the case as his lack of experience told, but he was going on at the end and better can be expected next time. (op 12-1)
Fares(IRE) is bred to be effective at this distance, but his trainer rarely has his juveniles ready first time up and he looked in need of the experience. (op 25-1)

3486 FORMOST FABRICATIONS H'CAP 6f
2:55 (2:55) (Class 3) (0-90,90) 3-Y-0+ **£9,067** (£2,697; £1,348; £673) **Stalls** High

Form RPR

2015 **1** **Adantino**[16] [2981] 7-8-7 **76** ....(b) JamesMillman(7) 5 86
(B R Millman) *hld up in last trio: prog against nr side rail over 2f out: gap opened and effrt to ld jst over 1f out: pushed out* **7/1**[3]

2111 **2** *2* **Blue Tomato**[8] [3217] 5-9-6 **87** 5ex........ LiamTreadwell(5) 3 91
(J M Bradley) *hld up in last trio: prog 2f out: squeezed through and hanging lft 1f out: chsd wnr fnl f: no imp* **7/4**[1]

0460 **3** *1/2* **Banjo Patterson**[3] [3374] 4-9-8 **84** ....(v1) IanMongan 9 87
(G A Huffer) *trckd ldrs: gng wl whn nt clr run 2f out: swtchd lft jst over 1f out: styd on fnl f: nvr able to chal* **8/1**

1302 **4** *1* **Romany Nights (IRE)**[21] [2824] 6-9-9 **85** ....(b) GeorgeBaker 2 85
(Miss Gay Kelleway) *racd on outer: trckd ldrs: effrt 2f out: cl up jst over 1f out: one pce after* **9/1**

2402 **5** *1 1/4* **Idle Power (IRE)**[8] [3211] 8-9-11 **90** .... AmirQuinn(3) 7 86
(J R Boyle) *pressed ldr: led 2f out to jst over 1f out: wknd fnl f* **9/2**[2]

50-0 **6** *1* **Safari Sunset (IRE)**[34] [2429] 4-9-4 **80** .... JimCrowley 1 73
(P Winkworth) *in tch in rr: hrd rdn over 2f out: struggling wl over 1f out* **20/1**

4253 **7** *3/4* **Willhewiz**[10] [3165] 6-8-6 **75** .... TolleyDean(7) 8 66
(M S Saunders) *led to 2f out: sn wknd* **12/1**

6302 **8** *nk* **Roman Quintet (IRE)**[15] [3012] 6-8-10 **72** .... DaneO'Neill 6 62
(D W P Arbuthnot) *pressed ldrs: rdn and losing pl whn n.m.r jst over 1f out: wknd* **8/1**

-020 **9** *2* **Goodenough Mover**[22] [2776] 10-9-8 **84** .... LPKeniry 4 68
(Andrew Turnell) *racd on outer: pressed ldrs: rdn 1/2-way: wknd wl over 1f out* **25/1**

69.50 secs (-2.17) **Going Correction** -0.275s/f (Firm) **9** Ran SP% **115.6**
Speed ratings (Par 107):103,100,99,98,96 95,94,93,91
CSF £19.65 CT £102.33 TOTE £9.90: £2.20, £1.10, £2.50; EX 15.80.
Owner Tarka Two Racing **Bred** S D Bevan **Trained** Kentisbeare, Devon

FOCUS
A decent handicap in which they went a decent gallop and the form looks sound rated around the runner-up and fourth.

NOTEBOOK
Adantino, a slight disappointment off this mark at Kempton last time, bounced back to his best under a confident ride to win off a career-high mark. He got the splits when required and seems to be progressing at the age of seven, but whether he can defy a further rise is doubtful. (op 15-2 tchd 8-1)
Blue Tomato, bidding for a four-timer, was well-suited by the decent gallop and he performed well under his 7lb penalty, but that did not stop him going close. He was no match for the winner though and things are only going to get harder from now on. (tchd 13-8 and 2-1)
Banjo Patterson, who failed to fire in first-time blinkers latest, had the visor on instead and he ran much better, not getting the clearest of runs and looking unfortunate not to get second. He is most inconsistent however and there is no guarantee the headgear will have the same effect in future. (op 7-1)
Romany Nights(IRE) was forced to race away from the favoured rail and he ran well considering, just being able to keep on at the one pace. He may not be up to winning off this mark, but should continue to pay his way. (op 15-2)

Idle Power(IRE) went on with two to run, but he was left trailing as the principals burst through inside the final furlong and he really needs a little help from the Handicapper. (tchd 5-1)
Safari Sunset(IRE) has yet to offer a great deal this season and is another who needs some help from the Handicapper. (op 16-1)

3487 LADIES EVENING JULY 22ND H'CAP 7f
3:30 (3:30) (Class 3) (0-90,82) 3-Y-0 £9,067 (£2,697; £1,348; £673) Stalls High

Form RPR
5225 1 **Creative Mind (IRE)**[6] 3296 3-9-4 79 DaneO'Neill 5 87
(E J O'Neill) *mde virtually all: rdn over 2f out: hrd pressed fnl f: jst hld on* 4/1[2]
0544 2 *shd* **Scarlet Flyer (USA)**[8] 3212 3-9-0 75 GeorgeBaker 2 83
(G L Moore) *reminder sn after s: hld up in last pair: prog over 2f out: chsd wnr over 1f out: hrd rdn and r.o: jst failed* 4/1[2]
6614 3 *2 ½* **Waterline Twenty (IRE)**[3] 3374 3-9-6 81 J-PGuillambert 6 82
(P D Evans) *racd against nr side rail: pressed wnr to over 2f out: sn drvn and outpcd: kpt on again ins fnl f* 7/1[3]
4013 4 *nk* **Roman Quest**[8] 3226 3-8-8 74 TravisBlock(5) 7 74
(H Morrison) *t.k.h: hld up bhd ldrs: trckd wnr over 2f out to over 1f out: rdn and no rspnse: fdd* 5/4[1]
2300 5 *1 ½* **His Master's Voice (IRE)**[105] 822 3-8-11 72 FrankieMcDonald 1 68
(D W P Arbuthnot) *racd on outer and wl in tch: rdn over 2f out: grad wknd fr over 1f out* 25/1
0520 6 *1* **Carmenero (GER)**[8] 3224 3-9-7 82 IanMongan 3 75
(W R Muir) *hld up in last pair: effrt over 2f out: cl up over 1f out: wknd* 16/1
13 7 *12* **Ask No More**[14] 3055 3-8-8 69 BrianReilly 4 30
(P L Gilligan) *t.k.h: hld up bhd ldrs: rdn 1/2-way: sn wknd: t.o* 14/1

1m 22.62s (-1.59) **Going Correction** -0.275s/f (Firm) 7 Ran SP% 113.3
Speed ratings (Par 104):98,97,95,94,92 91,78
CSF £19.91 TOTE £4.70: £1.90, £2.70; EX 20.60.
Owner Adrian & Rachael Archer **Bred** Farmers Hill Stud **Trained** Averham Park, Notts
■ Stewards' Enquiry : George Baker two-day ban: used whip with excessive force (Jul 25-26)

FOCUS
The front two pulled clear in what was an ordinary handicap and the form could rate fractionally higher.

NOTEBOOK
Creative Mind(IRE) comes from a stable that is in decent form now and this consistent sort gained a deserved first success in over a year. She rarely runs a bad race and, although she will go up for this, it should not be too much and there may be a little progression in her. (op 11-2)
Scarlet Flyer(USA) has been running as though a win is near and he very nearly got up under Baker, having been behind early on. Clear of the third, he can soon gain compensation for his astute trainer. (tchd 5-1)
Waterline Twenty(IRE) is definitely in need of this trip these days, and judging by the way she kept on again inside the final, may even be worth a try at a mile. (op 11-2 tchd 8-1)
Roman Quest took quite a grip early on and that counted against him in the finish as he found little. He is a fair bit better than this and deserves another chance to show it. (op 11-8 tchd 11-10 and 6-4 in places)
His Master's Voice(IRE) has shown enough to suggest he has a small race in him and, given this was his first start on turf, it is reasonable to think he may have some improvement in him. (tchd 28-1)
Carmenero(GER) is finding winning tough off this sort of mark and on this evidence he is going to continue to struggle until the Handicapper relents. Official explanation: trainer said gelding bled from the nose

3488 TOM EARLE MEMORIAL AND M&E CIVIL ENGINEERING LTD CLAIMING STKS 1m (P)
4:05 (4:05) (Class 5) 3-Y-0 £3,886 (£1,156; £577; £288) Stalls High

Form RPR
1146 1 **Piano Player (IRE)**[28] 2608 3-9-2 73 RichardKingscote(5) 2 81
(J A Osborne) *hld up in tch: effrt over 2f out: chsd ldr over 1f out: rdn to ld ins fnl f: sn clr* 11/8[1]
0060 2 *1 ¾* **Surely Truly (IRE)**[23] 2760 3-8-2 68 ow2 (v[1]) SaleemGolam(3) 5 61
(K R Burke) *trckd ldrs: effrt to ld over 2f out: hdd and outpcd ins fnl f* 11/2[3]
0031 3 *6* **Participation**[6] 3303 3-8-11 75 (p) IanMongan 1 53
(M J Wallace) *hld up bhd ldrs: drvn over 3f out: outpcd and btn over 2f out : plugged on one pce* 2/1[2]
125 4 *nk* **Mon Petite Amour**[39] 2293 3-7-13 47 ow1 (p) FrankieMcDonald 6 41
(D W P Arbuthnot) *led after 2f and maintained stdy pce: rdn and hdd over 2f out: wknd rapidly fnl f* 10/1
5 *1* **Dixieland Boy (IRE)** 3-8-11 AmirQuinn(3) 3 53
(P J Makin) *ses slowly and lost 6l: sn in tch: outpcd over 2f out: shkn up and one pce after* 12/1
0050 6 *9* **Musical Chimes**[15] 3016 3-8-6 48 J-PGuillambert 4 25
(C A Cyzer) *led at stdy pce for 2f: prom after: rdn 3f out: wknd over 2f out* 33/1

1m 41.37s (1.94) **Going Correction** +0.025s/f (Slow) 6 Ran SP% 110.5
Speed ratings (Par 100):91,89,83,82,81 72
CSF £9.18 TOTE £2.00: £1.50, £2.30; EX 7.90.Participation was claimed by Mr John Spence for £15,000. Surely Truly was claimed by Mr N. F. Glynn for £12,000.
Owner Mountgrange Stud **Bred** B W Hills And Mrs H Theodorou **Trained** Upper Lambourn, Berks

FOCUS
An uncompetitive claimer in which favourite ran out a ready winner and the form is rated through the runner-up.

3489 J B RINEY & CO FILLIES' H'CAP 1m 2f (P)
4:40 (4:40) (Class 3) (0-90,87) 3-Y-0+ £9,067 (£2,697; £1,348; £673) Stalls Low

Form RPR
-162 1 **Grain Of Truth**[26] 2679 3-8-9 84 JamieHamblett(7) 3 98+
(Sir Michael Stoute) *hld up in cl tch: trckd ldr over 2f out: led over 1f out: shkn up and sn clr: comf* 11/4[2]
2324 2 *2 ½* **Nice Tune**[37] 2341 4-10-0 85 J-PGuillambert 2 94
(C E Brittain) *trckd ldr: led over 3f out: drvn and hdd over 1f out: no ch w wnr after* 9/4[1]
2-21 3 *5* **Fyvie**[19] 2895 3-8-9 77 DaneO'Neill 5 77
(E A L Dunlop) *hld up in cl tch: rdn over 2f out: sn wl outpcd and btn* 4/1
21-0 4 *3 ½* **In Dubai (USA)**[43] 2174 3-9-5 87 JosedeSouza 1 80
(M P Tregoning) *led to over 3f out: rdn over 2f out: sn wknd* 9/1
-320 5 *7* **Moi Aussi (USA)**[139] 522 3-9-5 87 (b) SebSanders 4 67
(Sir Mark Prescott) *hld up in cl tch: rdn over 2f out: wknd rapidly wl over 1f out* 7/2[3]
-16 6 *10* **Divine River**[17] 2961 3-9-0 82 FrankieMcDonald 6 43
(A P Jarvis) *t.k.h: pressed ldng pair tl wknd over 3f out: t.o over 2f out* 33/1

2m 6.27s (-1.52) **Going Correction** +0.025s/f (Slow)
WFA 3 from 4yo 11lb 6 Ran SP% 112.6
Speed ratings (Par 104):107,105,101,98,92 84
CSF £9.44 TOTE £2.90: £1.10, £2.60; EX 13.80.
Owner Gainsborough Stud **Bred** W And R Barnett Ltd **Trained** Newmarket, Suffolk

FOCUS
A fair handicap in which the field finished well strung out and the form looks sound with the runner-up the best guide.

NOTEBOOK
Grain Of Truth, who bounced back from a poor effort when second at York last month, looked to hold every chance on this All-Weather debut with her rider's allowance coming in handy. Held up early, she moved into an ominous position turning into the straight and quickly put the result beyond doubt. This was a nice performance and, with further likely to suit in time, she is most definitely one to keep on-side. (op 3-1 tchd 10-3 in places)
Nice Tune, although setting a fair standard, was always likely to be vulnerable under her big weight and she was quickly left trailing by the winner. Consistency is her game and she will no doubt continue to run well, but winning will probably continue to be difficult. (op 5-2 tchd 11-4 and 3-1 in a place)
Fyvie, who looked more than happy over a 12 furlongs when breaking her duck at Pontefract, quite simply found the drop back in trip against her and could only keep on at the one pace. She remains capable of better back up in distance. (op 7-2)
In Dubai(USA), for the second time this season, failed to see her race out and, whilst it may be she is not staying the ten-furlong trip, there is also the possibility she has not trained on. Her breeding suggested she would be most effective on the surface and she has something to prove. (op 8-1 tchd 10-1)
Moi Aussi(USA), down the field in a French Listed contest latest, should have fared much better and the way she stopped suggested the trip may have been beyond her. She's got quite a bit to prove at present. (op 4-1)

3490 LINGFIELD PARK GOLF CLUB H'CAP 1m 4f (P)
5:15 (5:15) (Class 4) (0-85,83) 3-Y-0+ £6,477 (£1,927; £963; £481) Stalls Low

Form RPR
-121 1 **Warsaw Pact (IRE)**[3] 3388 3-8-6 74 5ex ow1 SebSanders 7 87+
(Sir Mark Prescott) *trckd ldr: led 4f out: kicked clr 3f out: 4 l ahd 1f out: drvn and hld on to dwindling advantage nr fin* 1/1[1]
10-0 2 *½* **Rayhani (USA)**[85] 1095 3-8-12 80 JosedeSouza 1 92
(M P Tregoning) *hld up in tch: outpcd 3f out: prog on inner over 2f out: drvn to chse wnr 1f out and flashed tail: clsng wl at fin* 14/1
1-6 3 *5* **I Have Dreamed (IRE)**[104] 834 4-9-11 80 IanMongan 9 84
(T G Mills) *trckd ldrs: rdn over 4f out: prog to chse wnr over 3f out: no imp: lost 2nd 1f out: wknd* 7/1[3]
3455 4 *shd* **Wingman (IRE)**[21] 2817 4-10-0 83 FrankieMcDonald 3 87
(J W Hills) *hld up in rr: effrt on outer over 3f out: drvn and outpcd over 2f out: styd on again ins fnl f* 14/1
-525 5 *2* **Desert Cristal (IRE)**[49] 1992 5-9-11 83 AmirQuinn(3) 8 85+
(J R Boyle) *t.k.h early: prom: rdn to dispute 2nd 3f out: n.m.r over 2f out: btn whn squeezed out wl over 1f out* 14/1
-231 6 *1 ¾* **Billich**[8] 3231 3-9-0 82 5ex DaneO'Neill 2 80
(E J O'Neill) *t.k.h early: cl up: rdn to dispute 2nd 3f out: struggling over 2f out: wknd over 1f out* 9/2[2]
0325 7 *7* **Santando**[27] 2647 6-8-12 67 (b) J-PGuillambert 6 54
(C E Brittain) *led to 4f out: wknd 3f out* 12/1
2005 8 *11* **Eloquent Knight (USA)**[16] 2982 4-9-4 73 (t) LPKeniry 4 42
(W R Muir) *pressed ldrs tl wknd rapidly jst over 3f out: t.o* 25/1
62-4 9 *dist* **True Companion**[184] 88 7-9-8 77 GeorgeBaker 5 —
(N P Littmoden) *s.s: hld up in detached last: pushed along and no prog 4f out: eased 3f out: t.o* 16/1

2m 32.92s (-1.47) **Going Correction** +0.025s/f (Slow)
WFA 3 from 4yo+ 13lb 9 Ran SP% 118.1
Speed ratings (Par 105):105,104,101,101,99 98,94,86,—
CSF £18.19 CT £71.98 TOTE £1.60: £1.20, £2.40, £2.40; EX 14.90 Place 6 £8.99, Place 5 £8.35.
Owner J Fishpool - Osborne House **Bred** Saad Bin Mishrif **Trained** Newmarket, Suffolk
■ Stewards' Enquiry : Jose de Souza two-day ban: careless riding (Jul 25-26)

FOCUS
Two progressive sorts pulled right away in what was a good handicap. The time was decent and the form should work out.
True Companion Official explanation: jockey said gelding was slowly away, resented the kickback and was never travelling
T/Plt: £24.10 to a £1 stake. Pool: £32,988.50. 996.60 winning tickets. T/Qpdt: £12.10 to a £1 stake. Pool: £1,919.80. 117.20 winning tickets. JN

3441 NEWMARKET (JULY) (R-H)
Friday, July 14

OFFICIAL GOING: Good to firm
They tended to race down the middle in races run on the straight course, but those drawn high and closest to the near-side rail still had a big advantage.
Wind: Fresh, against Weather: Fine and sunny

3491 CURTIS MEDICAL CENTRES H'CAP 1m
1:30 (1:31) (Class 2) (0-100,98) 3-Y-0
£18,696 (£5,598; £2,799; £1,401; £699; £351) Stalls Low

Form RPR
230 1 **Dark Islander (IRE)**[22] 2774 3-9-1 92 EddieAhern 15 104
(J W Hills) *hld up: hdwy over 2f out: led over 1f out: edgd lft: rdn out* 12/1
-310 2 *1 ¾* **Dunelight (IRE)**[22] 2774 3-9-3 94 (v[1]) PhilipRobinson 9 102+
(C G Cox) *disp ld tl led over 2f out: rdn and hdd over 1f out: no ex nr fin* 15/2[3]
210- 3 *hd* **Charlie Cool**[292] 5494 3-9-2 93 AlanMunro 14 101
(W J Haggas) *hld up: hdwy 2f out: sn rdn: styd on* 33/1
1050 4 *nk* **South Cape**[16] 2988 3-8-13 90 TonyCulhane 5 97
(M R Channon) *hld up: hdwy over 1f out: r.o* 33/1
-350 5 *3* **Zato (IRE)**[22] 2774 3-9-7 98 NCallan 12 98
(M R Channon) *hld up: hdwy over 2f out: rdn over 1f out: styd on same pce* 50/1
4601 6 *1 ¾* **Louie Louie (IRE)**[27] 2650 3-8-8 85 KerrinMcEvoy 6 81+
(N A Callaghan) *lw: chsd ldrs: rdn and ev ch over 1f out: wknd ins fnl f* 8/1
416 7 *1 ¼* **Adventuress**[56] 1819 3-8-12 89 JimmyFortune 13 82
(B J Meehan) *lw: hld up in tch: rdn over 2f out: wknd fnl f* 33/1

2-10 **8** ½ **Supaseus**[22] 2774 3-8-10 **87** .... SteveDrowne 8 79+
(H Morrison) *chsd ldrs: rdn over 2f out: wknd over 1f out* **11/2**[2]

140 **9** 3 **Leningrad (IRE)**[22] 2775 3-9-2 **93** .... JamieSpencer 3 78
(M L W Bell) *disp ld over 5f: wknd over 1f out* **16/1**

3322 **10** 1 ¾ **Multakka (IRE)**[28] 2605 3-8-7 **84** .... MartinDwyer 2 65
(M P Tregoning) *prom: rdn over 2f out: wknd over 1f out* **10/1**

0205 **11** 3 **Regal Royale**[22] 2774 3-9-3 **94** .... MJKinane 7 68
(Sir Michael Stoute) *lw: hld up. effrt over 2f out: sn wknd* **4/1**[1]

-133 **12** 7 **King Of The Moors (USA)**[42] 2205 3-8-7 **84** .... PaulFessey 11 42
(T D Barron) *hld up: rdn over 3f out: wknd over 2f out* **16/1**

0055 **13** 3 **Renderoc (USA)**[15] 3007 3-8-4 **81** .... JohnEgan 4 32
(J S Moore) *s.i.s: hld up: rdn 1/2-way: wknd over 2f out* **66/1**

1-30 **14** 5 **Giganticus (USA)**[22] 2774 3-9-3 **94** .... MichaelHills 1 34
(B W Hills) *hld up: hdwy over 2f out: sn rdn and wknd* **11/2**[2]

1m 38.06s (-2.37) **Going Correction** +0.05s/f (Good) **14** Ran SP% **114.5**
Speed ratings (Par 106):113,111,111,110,107 106,104,104,101,99 96,89,86,81
CSF £90.95 CT £2870.41 TOTE £15.00: £4.50, £2.80, £5.20; EX 149.20 Trifecta £710.40 Part won. Pool: £1,000.60 - 0.20 winning units..
Owner Donald M Kerr **Bred** Addison Racing Ltd Inc **Trained** Upper Lambourn, Berks

FOCUS
A good three-year-old handicap run at what appeared a reasonable enough pace. They all raced towards the middle of the track, but those drawn high still seemed to be at an advtantage. Solid form.

NOTEBOOK
Dark Islander(IRE), a creditable tenth in the Britannia Stakes at Royal Ascot on his previous start, would have found this a little less competitive but showed improved form in any case and won nicely. His effort is all the more creditable considering he raced keenly early on. His trainer is of the opinion he could get ten furlongs if learning to settle and thinks he could be very good over that distance.
Dunelight(IRE), with a visor fitted for the first time, looked to return to the sort of form he showed when winning on Newmarket's Rowley Mile course two starts previously, but could not reverse Britannia Stakes placings with Dark Islander. He seemed to rally a touch in the final furlong, suggesting he could just have been keeping something back for himself in the first place, and it would be no surprise to see visor swapped for blinkers next time. He has a serious amount of ability, but is just not quite progressing as one might have hoped for one reason or another. (op 7-1 tchd 8-1)
Charlie Cool ◆, seventh of eight in an ordinary renewal of the Royal Lodge when last seen 292 days previously, ran a fine race on his belated reappearance. A Great Voltigeur entry, his connections clearly expect him to stay further and there should be plenty more to come. He looks capable of exploiting his current handicap mark and must be kept on the right side of. (op 25-1)
South Cape has been given a bit of a chance by the Handicapper and ran a very creditable race in fourth, keeping on after having to be switched towards the near side of the pack for his run. One gets the impression, though, that he will remain vulnerable in this sort of company.
Zato(IRE) could not reverse Britannia form with Dark Islander and Dunelight, but still posted a very respectable effort off top weight. He looks one of those horses who might not be up to pattern level this season, and is plenty high enough in the weights for handicaps.
Louie Louie(IRE) seemed to have every chance but could not defy a 3lb higher mark than when winning a lesser race over seven furlongs at Sandown on his previous start. However, he raced more towards the far side of the track than many of these and may have been on slightly slower ground. He may also be better over shorter. (op 9-1)
Supaseus was disappointing considering he had Dark Islander, Dunelight and Zato behind him when eighth of 30 in the Britannia Stakes at Royal Ascot. (tchd 6-1 in places)
Regal Royale found little when asked to pick up and was a major disappointment considering he had beaten a few of these in the Britannia Stakes, not least Dark Islander and Dunelight. (op 7-2)
Giganticus(USA) is surely better than he showed this time. (op 6-1 tchd 13-2 in places)

3492 WEATHERBYS SUPERLATIVE STKS (GROUP 2) 7f
2:00 (2:00) (Class 1) 2-Y-O
£39,746 (£15,064; £7,539; £3,759; £1,883; £945) **Stalls** Low

Form RPR

1 **1** **Halicarnassus (IRE)**[20] 2867 2-9-0 .... TonyCulhane 5 109
(M R Channon) *lw: prom: outpcd 1/2-way: r.o wl ins fnl f to ld nr fin* **33/1**

1 **2** ½ **He's A Decoy (IRE)**[26] 2686 2-9-0 .... MJKinane 6 108
(David Wachman, Ire) *gd sort: neat: hld up: hdwy over 2f out: rdn to ld and edgd lft ins fnl f: hdd nr fin* **5/1**[3]

3 1 ½ **Admiralofthefleet (USA)**[19] 2906 2-9-0 .... JMurtagh 7 104
(A P O'Brien, Ire) *gd sort: lw: sn chsng ldr: led over 1f out: rdn: edgd lft and hdd ins fnl f: styd on same pce* **6/1**

1 **4** 1 **Rallying Cry (USA)**[13] 3083 2-9-0 .... JimmyFortune 4 102
(J H M Gosden) *trckd ldrs: rdn and nt clr run over 1f out: kpt on* **9/2**[2]

21 **5** 1 ¼ **Charlie Farnsbarns (IRE)**[21] 2821 2-9-0 .... LDettori 2 99
(B J Meehan) *chsd ldrs: rdn over 1f out: wknd ins fnl f* **15/2**

1 **6** ½ **Hinton Admiral**[23] 2745 2-9-0 .... JoeFanning 3 97
(M Johnston) *lw: led over 5f: wknd ins fnl f* **12/1**

31 **7** 2 **Champlain**[20] 2844 2-9-0 .... PhilipRobinson 1 92
(M A Jarvis) *lw: hld up: effrt over 2f out: wknd over 1f out* **13/8**[1]

1m 26.02s (-0.76) **Going Correction** +0.05s/f (Good) **7** Ran SP% **109.6**
Speed ratings (Par 106):106,105,103,102,101 100,98
CSF £172.44 TOTE £27.90: £5.90, £2.30; EX 139.20.
Owner Box 41 **Bred** Yeomanstown Lodge Stud **Trained** West Ilsley, Berks

FOCUS
The last two winners of the Superlative Stakes, Horatio Nelson and Dubawi, went on to prove themselves high-class Group 1 horses, resulting in this race being upgraded to a Group 2 for the first time. However, this looked a less distinguished renewal and did not really do justice to his new status. The early gallop did not seem that fast, but plenty of pace was injected from at least half way, perhaps too early a stage as all bar the eventual winner, who dropped back when the tempo was stepped up, appeared to struggle to sustain their efforts. As a result, it remains to be seen just how this form will work out. They all raced towards the middle of the track.

NOTEBOOK
Halicarnassus(IRE) showed just fair form when dead-heating over course and distance on his debut, so this represented quite significant improvement. Handy enough early, he was caught out badly when the pace increased at about halfway, and looked set to finish last at one stage, but he responded well to strong pressure and managed to get up near the line. While it is hard to knock an unbeaten Group 2 winner, it may well be that his six rivals were all asked for maximum effort too far out and, in getting outpaced, he was able to keep something back for the business end, when he may only have been passing horses who were slowing down having already given their maximum. Only time will show if that theory is right or not.
He's A Decoy(IRE), off the mark on his debut over this trip before dropping back to six furlongs to take a Cork Listed race, was always travelling with plenty of enthusiasm and may just have committed for home a little too soon, as he had little left when challenged late on. A more evenly-run seven furlongs is likely to suit better. (tchd 11-2)
Admiralofthefleet(USA), a six-length winner of a Gowran Park maiden, seemed to have every chance but was just found out in this much higher grade. He is, though, open to more improvement. (tchd 13-2)
Rallying Cry(USA), a course and distance maiden winner on his debut, ran respectably, stepped up significantly in class, especially as he was a little short of room when trying to stay on.
Charlie Farnsbarns(IRE), a three-length winner of a fair six-furlong maiden here on his previous start, ran creditably, upped significantly in class. He may even be a little bit better than the bare form, as he raced more towards the unfavoured far side than some of these. (op 8-1)
Hinton Admiral would have found this significantly tougher than the Hamilton maiden he won on his debut, but probably quickened the pace too soon in any case. (op 11-1)
Champlain showed himself a smart prospect when winning the Chesham Stakes at Royal Ascot on his previous start, but that form is not working out that well and he proved very disappointing here on this step up to Group company. Official explanation: trainer had no explanation for the poor form shown (tchd 6-4 tchd 15-8 and 2-1 in places)

3493 LADBROKES BUNBURY CUP (HERITAGE H'CAP) 7f
2:35 (2:35) (Class 2) (0-105,102) 3-Y-O **£45,339** (£13,489; £6,741; £3,367) **Stalls** Low

Form RPR

0000 **1** **Mine (IRE)**[23] 2742 8-9-10 **102** ....(v) MJKinane 14 116
(J D Bethell) *lw: hld up: hdwy over 1f out: led ins fnl f: r.o wl* **10/1**

0-60 **2** 2 **Intrepid Jack**[20] 2847 4-9-4 **96** .... EddieAhern 17 104
(H Morrison) *hld up: hdwy 2f out: rdn and ev ch over 1f out: styd on same pce* **12/1**

-520 **3** ½ **Marching Song**[22] 2776 4-9-2 **94** .... RyanMoore 18 101
(R Hannon) *hld up: hdwy 2f out: rdn to ld over 1f out: hdd and unable qck ins fnl f* **14/1**

1006 **4** hd **Swinbrook (USA)**[13] 3092 5-8-10 **88** ....(v) AlanMunro 15 94
(J A R Toller) *hld up: nt clr run over 1f out: swtchd lft: r.o u.p* **16/1**

1422 **5** 2 **Easy Air**[22] 2774 3-8-8 **94** .... LDettori 3 92+
(E A L Dunlop) *chsd ldrs: rdn over 2f out: styd on same pce fnl f* **7/1**[2]

-210 **6** ¾ **Kostar**[20] 2847 5-8-13 **94** .... AdamKirby(3) 19 93
(C G Cox) *chsd ldrs: rdn over 1f out: wknd ins fnl f* **14/1**

0211 **7** nk **Imperial Echo (USA)**[13] 3079 5-8-6 **84** .... PaulFessey 12 82+
(T D Barron) *s.i.s: hld up: hdwy over 1f out: nt clr run ins fnl f: nt rch ldrs* **20/1**

3202 **8** nk **Appalachian Trail (IRE)**[22] 2776 5-9-7 **99** ....(b) TomEaves 7 96
(I Semple) *prom: rdn over 1f out: no ex* **16/1**

0-40 **9** ¾ **Another Bottle (IRE)**[23] 2742 5-9-6 **98** .... SteveDrowne 13 99+
(R Charlton) *lw: hld up: hdwy and nt clr run over 1f out: nt trble ldrs* **8/1**[3]

0002 **10** 1 ¼ **Compton's Eleven**[13] 3079 5-9-5 **97** .... TonyCulhane 9 89
(M R Channon) *hld up: nt clr run over 2f out and over 1f out: n.d* **33/1**

3033 **11** 1 **Binanti**[8] 3223 6-8-8 **86** .... MartinDwyer 1 75
(P R Chamings) *hld up: hdwy over 2f out: wknd fnl f* **33/1**

2030 **12** ¾ **Bahiano (IRE)**[20] 2847 5-9-8 **100** .... KerrinMcEvoy 10 87
(C E Brittain) *chsd ldrs: hmpd and wknd over 1f out* **25/1**

2121 **13** 1 ½ **Zidane**[20] 2864 4-8-12 **90** .... JamieSpencer 11 73+
(J R Fanshawe) *lw: hld up: hdwy and nt clr run over 1f out: sn rdn and wknd* **11/2**[1]

0230 **14** 2 ½ **Prince Of Thebes (IRE)**[23] 2742 5-9-2 **94** .... PaulDoe 8 70
(J Akehurst) *w ldrs over 4f: n.m.r and wknd over 1f out* **25/1**

2161 **15** 1 **Wavertree Warrior (IRE)**[27] 2649 4-8-11 **89** .... JimmyFortune 6 63
(N P Littmoden) *w ldrs over 4f: wknd fnl f* **20/1**

1453 **16** 2 **Akona Matata (USA)**[23] 2742 4-9-2 **94** .... SebSanders 2 62
(C E Brittain) *hld up: hdwy over 2f out: wknd over 1f out* **8/1**[3]

2103 **17** 1 ¼ **Malcheek (IRE)**[13] 3079 4-8-8 **86** .... DavidAllan 20 51
(T D Easterby) *w ldrs tl led 3f out: hdd & wknd over 1f out* **50/1**

0000 **18** 3 **Traytonic**[13] 3079 5-8-7 **85** ....(v[1]) AdrianTNicholls 4 42
(D Nicholls) *w ldrs tl rdn 1/2-way: wknd 2f out* **33/1**

2012 **19** ½ **Pintle**[12] 3121 6-8-6 **84** .... JohnEgan 16 40
(J L Spearing) *mde most 4f: wkng whn hmpd over 1f out* **20/1**

1m 24.26s (-2.52) **Going Correction** +0.05s/f (Good)
WFA 3 from 4yo+ 8lb **19** Ran SP% **124.8**
Speed ratings (Par 109):116,113,113,112,110 109,109,109,108,106 105,104,103,100,99 96,95,91,91
CSF £108.41 CT £1706.27 TOTE £10.40: £2.30, £3.50, £3.90, £5.90; EX 140.60 TRIFECTA Not won..
Owner M J Dawson **Bred** David John Brown **Trained** Middleham Moor, N Yorks
■ Mine became the first horse to win three Bunbury Cups, adding to his successes of 2002 and 2005. He was also second in 2003.

FOCUS
A good renewal of the Bunbury Cup, run at what appeared at even pace, and the winning time was decent. They all raced down the middle of the track, but a high draw was a big advantage still and the first four raced nearest the stands' rail. Fifth-placed Easy Air was the only one in the first seven from a single-figure stall

NOTEBOOK
Mine(IRE), the winner of this race in 2002 (off 87), second in 2003 (93), and successful again last year (104), gained an unprecedented third Bunbury Cup, and it was by far his easiest success out of the three to boot. Always going well, he made his move closer to the near-side rail than many of these and never looked in any danger. He had often shown a tendency to idle in front, but kept finding to pull well clear this time, suggesting he is maturing with age. He may now be aimed at the International Stakes, although he was only tenth in that race last year (when staged at Newbury) having won this race. (tchd 11-1)
Intrepid Jack, tenth of 28 in the Wokingham on his previous start, got this extra furlong well enough to beat all bar the Bunbury Cup specialist. Connections will have more options now, and he clearly has the ability to land a decent handicap.
Marching Song, eighth of 27 in the Buckingham Palace at Royal Ascot on his previous start, appeared to have every chance and ran a good race in third. (op 16-1)
Swinbrook(USA), given another chance over seven furlongs, kept on well after having to be switched with his challenge and emerges with plenty of credit. He has never won beyond six furlongs, but this trip appeared to suit.
Easy Air ◆ could not quite reproduce the form he showed to finish second in the Britannia Stakes on his previous start, but raced more towards the far side of the track than those in front of him and is better than he showed. He fared best of those drawn in single figures.
Kostar ran well but could not see out this stiff seven furlongs.
Imperial Echo(USA) ◆, chasing the hat-trick, needs things to fall just right for him, which they did not this time. Still, he showed enough to warrant keeping on the right side of off his current sort of mark. (op 22-1)
Appalachian Trail(IRE) was below the form he showed to finish second in the Buckingham Palace at Royal Ascot on his previous start, but did not have a great draw.
Another Bottle(IRE) appeared unsuited by the drop back to seven furlongs. (op 9-1)
Bahiano(IRE) ◆ was not given a hard time after getting hampered and is quite a bit better than the bare form suggests. Official explanation: jockey said gelding was denied a clear run
Zidane, 10lb higher than when winning over six furlongs here on his previous start, met with some trouble in-running but did not pick up when in the clear and looked to be racing on the unfavoured part of the track, towards the far side. (op 6-1)
Akona Matata(USA), third in the Royal Hunt Cup on his previous start, can be forgiven this as he raced closest of all to the far rail and that was certainly not the place to be. (op 15-2)
Malcheek(IRE) Official explanation: jockey said colt ran too free
Traytonic Official explanation: jockey said gelding lost its action
Pintle Official explanation: trainer said mare bled from the nose

3494 DARLEY JULY CUP (GROUP 1) 6f
3:10 (3:22) (Class 1) 3-Y-0+

£204,408 (£77,472; £38,772; £19,332; £9,684; £4,860) **Stalls** Low

Form				RPR
2001	**1**		**Les Arcs (USA)**[20] 2846 6-9-5 110 .... JohnEgan 15 (T J Pitt) *lw: b: hld up in tch: rdn to ld ins fnl f: r.o* **10/1**	122
10-0	**2**	*hd*	**Iffraaj**[20] 2846 5-9-5 114 .... LDettori 12 (Saeed Bin Suroor) *trckd ldrs: outpcd over 1f out: r.o wl ins fnl f* **11/2**[2]	124+
-004	**3**	*3/4*	**Ashdown Express (IRE)**[20] 2846 7-9-5 111 .... AlanMunro 16 (C F Wall) *hld up: hdwy over 1f out: r.o* **20/1**	119
1-05	**4**	*shd*	**Amadeus Wolf**[20] 2846 3-8-13 120 .... NCallan 13 (K A Ryan) *chsd ldrs: rdn to ld over 1f out: sn hdd: styd on* **10/1**	118
0110	**5**	*3/4*	**Moss Vale (IRE)**[24] 2720 5-9-5 114 .... AdrianTNicholls 9 (D Nicholls) *chsd ldrs: rdn and ev ch over 1f out: styd on* **14/1**	117+
3210	**6**	*shd*	**Quito (IRE)**[20] 2846 9-9-5 111 ....(b) TonyCulhane 17 (D W Chapman) *b: hld up: r.o ins fnl f: nt rch ldrs* **25/1**	116
13	**7**	*shd*	**Takeover Target (AUS)**[20] 2846 7-9-5 .... JayFord 1 (J Janiak, Australia) *w ldr: led 1f out: edgd lft: hdd and no ex ins fnl f* **9/2**[1]	116+
6301	**8**	*1 1/4*	**Pivotal Point**[6] 3312 6-9-5 105 .... SebSanders 6 (P J Makin) *plld hrd and prom: stdd and dropped rr 5f out: r.o ins fnl f: nt trble ldrs* **16/1**	112+
0-50	**9**	*1 1/4*	**Gift Horse**[20] 2846 6-9-5 106 .... EddieAhern 8 (D Nicholls) *s.i.s: hld up: nvr trbld ldrs* **16/1**	109
4501	**10**	*1/2*	**Fayr Jag (IRE)**[13] 3076 7-9-5 109 .... DavidAllan 14 (T D Easterby) *lw: chsd ldrs: rdn over 1f out: wknd ins fnl f* **33/1**	107
12-0	**11**	*nk*	**La Cucaracha**[24] 2720 5-9-2 112 .... MichaelHills 7 (B W Hills) *lw: hld up: hdwy over 1f out: wknd ins fnl f* **9/1**	103+
-106	**12**	*3 1/2*	**Red Clubs (IRE)**[23] 2739 3-8-13 117 .... RyanMoore 2 (B W Hills) *lw: hld up: hdwy over 1f out: wknd fnl f* **10/1**	95+
4	**13**	*1 1/2*	**Falkirk (NZ)**[24] 2720 6-9-5 ....(bt) JMurtagh 10 (Lee Freedman, Australia) *lw: trckd ldrs: plld hrd: rdn and ev ch over 1f out: sn wknd* **13/2**[3]	91
-224	**14**	*shd*	**Marcus Andronicus (USA)**[24] 2721 3-8-13 .... MJKinane 4 (A P O'Brien, Ire) *chsd ldrs: rdn over 2f out: sn wknd* **20/1**	90
1-02	**15**	*2 1/2*	**Murfreesboro**[17] 2959 3-8-13 98 .... JimmyFortune 11 (J H M Gosden) *led over 4f: sn hmpd and wknd* **66/1**	82

1m 11.16s (-2.19) **Going Correction** +0.05s/f (Good)
WFA 3 from 4yo+ 6lb **15** Ran SP% **120.4**
Speed ratings (Par 117):116,115,114,114,113 113,113,111,110,109 108,104,102,102,98
CSF £59.60 TOTE £11.30: £3.30, £2.10, £8.90; EX 51.40 Trifecta £518.20 Pool: £4,525.73 - 6.20 winning units..
Owner Willie McKay **Bred** Elk Manor Farm **Trained** Bawtry, S Yorks
■ Les Arcs, in following up his Royal Ascot win, became the first horse older than five to win the July Cup since 1938.

FOCUS
There were no stand-out performer on show and this was just an average renewal of the July Cup. Unfortunately for a Group 1 there was a draw bias, with those in high stalls significantly favoured. They all raced down the middle of the track, but again, those closest to the near-side rail had a distinct advantage. The pace, although not frantic early on, appeared reasonable.

NOTEBOOK
Les Arcs(USA) has been a revelation since dropped back to sprinting and followed up his success in the Golden Jubilee Stakes at Royal Ascot to gain back-to-back Group 1 wins. He could be considered a slightly fortunate winner with eventual runner-up Iffraaj forced to sit and wait for a gap at a crucial stage, but he is clearly one of the best sprinters this country has to offer at the moment and should continue to go well in the top sprints both here and abroad for the remainder of the season. One could hardly have predicted this in August 2004, when he was eighth of 12 in a maiden hurdle at Cartmel.
Iffraaj ◆, seventh behind Les Arcs in the Golden Jubilee Stakes at Royal Ascot when his yard were still not firing, put up an improved effort and should have reversed form with Les Arcs. As that one was beginning his move, Dettori was forced to sit and wait for a gap to appear, and got in the clear just too late. He has plenty of options from six furlong to a mile, and provided he gets the fast ground he needs he will be very hard to beat if connections opt for Goodwood's Lennox Stakes in preference to the Sussex or the Maurice De Gheest. (op 6-1 tchd 5-1)
Ashdown Express(IRE), runner-up in this race two years previously, and sixth last year, had a good draw and ran to a similar level of form as when fourth in the Golden Jubilee Stakes last time.
Amadeus Wolf ◆, fifth in the Golden Jubilee Stakes on his previous start, ran another cracker and was easily the best of the three-year-olds. A likeable type, he looks capable of improving with the benefit of further racing. He may now be aimed at the Haydock Sprint Cup and must go there with a big chance.
Moss Vale(IRE) ◆, eighth of 28 when a slow-starting favourite for the King's Stand at Royal Ascot on his previous start, fared best of the single-figure stalls and looks better than the bare form as he racing closer to the unfavoured far side than those in front of him. He ought to give a good account in the Nunthorpe at York. (tchd 16-1 in a place)
Quito(IRE) had a good draw and ran as we have come to expect, giving his all late on and finishing strongly.
Takeover Target(AUS), an Australian raider who won the King's Stand at Royal Ascot and was then third in the Golden Jubilee, had the worst of the draw and, after tacking across to race down the centre of the track, could not sustain his effort. He has won over seven furlongs in his homeland, but from what we have seen over here, the minimum trip looks to suit best. (op 11-2 tchd 6-1)
Pivotal Point did not help his chance by racing keenly, but still posted a good effort.
Gift Horse ran better than he did in the Golden Jubilee and is going the right way. (op 14-1)
Fayr Jag(IRE) had every chance but is maybe not quite up to this level anymore. (op 28-1)
La Cucaracha was well below form and pretty disappointing. She will have to bounce back considerably to defend her Nunthorpe crown. Official explanation: jockey said mare ran flat (op 10-1)
Red Clubs(IRE) raced on the unfavoured part of the track, but was never going in anycase. (op 12-1)
Falkirk(NZ), another Australian raider, was well below the form he showed when fourth of 28 in the King's Stand at Royal Ascot. (op 7-1 tchd 15-2 and 8-1 in places)
Marcus Andronicus(USA) did not appear suited by the switch to top-class sprinting, although he did race on the unfavoured part of the track. (op 16-1)
Murfreesboro, rated just 98, was seemingly out of his depth. (op 100-1)

3495 HEATHAVON STUD EBF MAIDEN FILLIES' STKS 6f
3:45 (3:50) (Class 3) 2-Y-0 **£7,772** (£2,312; £1,155; £577) **Stalls** Low

Form				RPR
24	**1**		**Medley**[21] 2800 2-9-0 .... RyanMoore 6 (R Hannon) *w ldr tl led over 2f out: pushed out* **8/15**[1]	82+
	2	*2*	**Cartimandua** 2-9-0 .... JimmyFortune 3 (E S McMahon) *w'like: scope: chsd ldrs: rdn over 1f out: styd on same pce ins fnl f* **10/1**[3]	76
3	**3**	*nk*	**Silkie Smooth (IRE)**[57] 1807 2-9-0 .... JamieSpencer 5 (B W Hills) *chsd ldrs: effrt over 1f out: styd on same* **9/2**[2]	75
	4	*1 1/4*	**Freedom At Last (IRE)** 2-9-0 .... AlanMunro 4 (W Jarvis) *w'like: chsd ldrs: rdn over 1f out: styd on same pce* **28/1**	71
6	**5**	*shd*	**Darrfonah (IRE)**[9] 3201 2-9-0 .... PhilipRobinson 2 (C E Brittain) *s.i.s: hld up: hdwy over 2f out: ev ch over 1f out: wknd ins fnl f* **14/1**	71
00	**6**	*7*	**Silver Flame**[27] 2638 2-9-0 .... EddieAhern 7 (B J Meehan) *led over 3f: wknd over 1f out* **33/1**	50
	7	*6*	**Featherlight** 2-9-0 .... JohnEgan 1 (N A Callaghan) *neat: bhd fr 1/2-way* **25/1**	32

1m 15.23s (1.88) **Going Correction** +0.05s/f (Good) **7** Ran SP% **109.4**
Speed ratings (Par 95):89,86,85,84,84 74,66
CSF £5.90 TOTE £1.50: £1.10, £3.40; EX 8.30.
Owner The Queen **Bred** The Queen **Trained** East Everleigh, Wilts

FOCUS
They raced middle to near side, and the pace was very steady early on. As a result, a few of these could be flattered by their proximity to Medley, who probably didn't need to run anywhere near her Royal Ascot level.

NOTEBOOK
Medley ◆, runner-up on her debut at Windsor before showing improved form when fourth in a decent renewal of the Albany Stakes at Royal Ascot, found this a straightforward opportunity and didn't need to be at her best. She is probably value for a little more than the margin suggests, as she helped force only a steady early pace and was not out to record any spectacular figures. She should not be underestimated when stepped back up in grade. (op 4-6)
Cartimandua, a half-sister to Terentia, triple five-furlong winner at two to three, out of a useful dual seven-furlong juvenile winner who was later fairly useful over six furlongs, made a pleasing debut. With the early pace very steady, she looks a little flattered to get so close to the winner, but clearly possesses a fair amount of ability and is open to improvement.
Silkie Smooth(IRE), well beaten into third behind two nice types on her debut at York, ran a respectable race but lacked any kind of finishing kick. A return to easier ground may suit and she could also benefit from a step up in trip. (op 4-1)
Freedom At Last(IRE), a 60,000gns half-sister to Aldo L'Argentin, who was placed over seven furlongs at two, was seemingly unfancied but made a respectable debut.
Darrfonah(IRE) did not really build on the form she showed on her debut at Kempton.

3496 COMMUNITY UNION FOR SAFER BETTING SHOPS NURSERY 7f
4:20 (4:20) (Class 2) 2-Y-0 **£12,954** (£3,854; £1,926; £962) **Stalls** Low

Form				RPR
051	**1**		**Eddie Jock (IRE)**[35] 2388 2-9-4 **83** .... JamieSpencer 4 (M L W Bell) *hld up: hdwy over 2f out: rdn to ld ins fnl f: r.o* **6/1**[1]	90
024	**2**	*1*	**Ebn Reem**[35] 2416 2-9-1 **80** .... PhilipRobinson 6 (M A Jarvis) *led: rdn and hdd ins fnl f: unable qck* **7/1**[3]	84
026	**3**	*nk*	**Miss Saafend Plaza (IRE)**[17] 2958 2-8-12 **77** .... RyanMoore 7 (R Hannon) *hld up: nt clr run over 2f out: swtchd rt and hdwy over 1f out: sn hit over hd w rivals whip: r.o: nt rch ldrs* **10/1**	81
11	**4**	*1 1/2*	**Ingleby Princess**[18] 2924 2-8-9 **74** .... PaulFessey 11 (T D Barron) *hld up: hdwy 4f out: rdn and ev ch over 1f out: styd on same pce fnl f* **13/2**[2]	74
3100	**5**	*1*	**Zafonical Storm (USA)**[12] 3126 2-8-9 **74** .... JohnEgan 8 (B W Duke) *chsd ldrs: rdn over 1f out: edgd lft and no ex fnl f* **9/1**	71
003	**6**	*5*	**Regal Ovation**[17] 2950 2-8-3 **68** ow2 .... MartinDwyer 3 (W R Muir) *chsd ldrs over 5f* **25/1**	52
61	**7**	*nk*	**Charlie Tipple**[15] 3018 2-9-1 **80** .... MickyFenton 10 (T D Easterby) *lw: trckd ldrs: edgd lft over 1f out: sn wknd* **15/2**	63
2201	**8**	*1*	**See In The Dark (IRE)**[12] 3117 2-9-6 **85** 6ex .... JimmyFortune 1 (B J Meehan) *in rr: rdn 1/2-way: n.d* **8/1**	66
01	**9**	*3/4*	**Easy Lover**[23] 2755 2-8-13 **78** .... EddieAhern 9 (J A Osborne) *prom: rdn and edgd rt over 1f out: sn wknd* **13/2**[2]	57
1054	**10**	*4*	**Stir Crazy (IRE)**[11] 3136 2-8-8 **73** .... TonyCulhane 12 (M R Channon) *hld up: hdwy 2f out: sn rdn: wknd over 1f out* **10/1**	41
0216	**11**	*9*	**Cavort (IRE)**[15] 3026 2-9-2 **86** .... EmmettStack(5) 5 (Pat Eddery) *s.i.s: hdwy 1/2-way: wkng whn hmpd over 1f out* **25/1**	31
1544	**12**	*19*	**Urban Warrior**[46] 2084 2-8-12 **77** .... AlanMunro 2 (J R Best) *s.i.s: bhd fr 1/2-way* **25/1**	—

1m 27.12s (0.34) **Going Correction** +0.05s/f (Good) **12** Ran SP% **116.0**
Speed ratings (Par 100):100,98,98,96,95 89,89,88,87,83 72,51
CSF £44.93 CT £408.26 TOTE £6.20: £2.40, £2.70, £3.90; EX 55.20.
Owner C A Gershinson **Bred** J Egan, J Corcoran And J Judd **Trained** Newmarket, Suffolk
■ Stewards' Enquiry : Eddie Ahern two-day ban: careless riding (Jul 25-26)

FOCUS
This looked a decent nursery and it should work out well. They raced down the middle of the track early on, but became more spread out in the closing stages, right the way across to the near-side rail in the end. The early pace looked just ordinary, but they finished well-strung out. The official ratings shown next to each horse are estimated and for information purposes only.

NOTEBOOK
Eddie Jock(IRE) would have found this quite a bit tougher than the six-furlong Brighton maiden he won on his previous start but, upped in trip, he found the necessary improvement to follow up. There could be more to come, but things can only get tougher for the time being. (op 5-1)
Ebn Reem, turned over at odds on in a six-furlong Wolverhampton maiden on his previous start, ran much better upped in trip and switched to nursery company. He was a touch keen early and his best is probably yet to come. (tchd 8-1)
Miss Saafend Plaza(IRE) ◆, making her nursery debut, took a bump after having to be switched with her run and just got going too late. She also appeared to be hit over the head by another rider's whip, so all things considered this was a good effort, and she ought to be placed to effect.
Ingleby Princess, the winner of two minor races up North, tried her luck tight against the near-side rail and ran well faced with undoubtedly her trickiest task to date. (op 7-1)
Zafonical Storm(USA) was surely flattered by his proximity in the Railway Stakes at Curragh on his previous start and, switched to nursery company, he ran a respectable race to confirm this is more his sort of level. (op 8-1)
See In The Dark(IRE), carrying a 6lb penalty for his success in a six-furlong nursery at Windsor on his previous start, raced on the unfavoured side of the track from the worst draw of all and can be forgiven this.
Easy Lover could not build on the form she showed when winning a seven-furlong nursery at Kempton on her previous start. Official explanation: jockey said filly was unsuited by the good to firm ground (op 7-1)

3497 EGERTON HOUSE STABLES H'CAP 1m 4f
4:55 (4:55) (Class 3) (0-90,86) 3-Y-0+ **£9,715** (£2,890; £1,444; £721) **Stalls** Centre

Form				RPR
-050	**1**		**Best Prospect (IRE)**[16] 2989 4-9-9 **81** .... JamieSpencer 9 (M Dods) *hld up: hdwy over 1f out: led ins fnl f: r.o* **10/1**	87
1004	**2**	*1*	**Top Seed (IRE)**[13] 3093 5-10-0 **86** .... TonyCulhane 7 (M R Channon) *lw: hld up: hdwy over 1f out: nt clr run ins fnl f: nvr able to chal* **15/2**	92+
-621	**3**	*shd*	**Green Room (FR)**[19] 2901 3-8-11 **82** .... EddieAhern 1 (J L Dunlop) *lw: a.p: chsd ldr 3f out: rdn and edgd lft over 1f out: styd on same pce ins fnl f* **7/1**[3]	86

02-0 **4** *shd* **Kinrande (IRE)**[41] 2229 4-9-13 **85**.................................... MartinDwyer 5 89
(P J Makin) *led: rdn and edgd lft over 1f out: hdd and edgd rt ins fnl f: unable qck* **8/1**

2301 **5** *1 3/4* **Snowed Under**[27] 2640 5-9-9 **81**.................................... PhilipRobinson 8 82
(J D Bethell) *lw: chsd ldrs: rdn over 1f out: styd on same pce fnl f* **11/2**[2]

0-63 **6** *nk* **Sweet Indulgence (IRE)**[14] 3048 5-9-2 **79**.......... StephenDonohoe(5) 6 80
(W J Musson) *hld up: hdwy over 1f out: one pce ins fnl f* **4/1**[1]

2042 **7** *2* **Cripsey Brook**[14] 3037 8-8-12 **77**............................(t) JamesReveley(7) 4 74
(K G Reveley) *hld up: nt clr run over 2f out: nvr trbld ldrs* **10/1**

-031 **8** *12* **Mexican Pete**[12] 3116 6-9-4 **76** 6ex.................................... RyanMoore 3 54
(A W Carroll) *hld up in tch: rdn over 2f out: wknd over 1f out* **11/2**[2]

-625 **9** *1/2* **Wellington Hall (GER)**[14] 3048 8-9-7 **79**...................... JimmyFortune 2 56
(P W Chapple-Hyam) *chsd ldr 9f: rdn and wknd over 1f out* **8/1**

2m 36.51s (3.60) **Going Correction** +0.05s/f (Good)
WFA 3 from 4yo+ 13lb **9** Ran SP% **115.4**
Speed ratings (Par 107):90,89,89,89,88 87,86,78,78
CSF £82.34 CT £563.29 TOTE £11.60: £3.60, £2.80, £1.80; EX 88.90 Place 6 £1,570.39, Place 5 £235.36.
Owner Mrs Karen S Pratt **Bred** Farmers Hill Stud **Trained** Denton, Co Durham

FOCUS
The top weight, Top Seed, was rated 4lb below the ceiling of 90 and this looked like an ordinary handicap for the grade. They did not appear to go any great pace early on.

NOTEBOOK
Best Prospect(IRE) had never previously been tried over a trip this far, but he got it well enough to gain his first success since landing his maiden back in May 2005. Things fell just right for him this time, with his rider getting a gap when going for a daring run up the rail, and things will not always fall so kindly, but he will have more options now he has proven his stamina. (op 9-1)
Top Seed(IRE) would not have been suited by the steady early pace and picked up just too late. He tried to follow the eventual winner through a gap tight against the near rail, and did not get the clearest of runs, but he had basically left his challenge too late. (op 13-2)
Green Room(FR), upped in trip and switched to handicaps, found this tougher than the Warwick maiden she won on her previous start but was a big improver. (op 8-1)
Kinrande(IRE) ran much better than on his reappearance at Epsom and seems to be going the right way again now. (op 10-1)
Snowed Under, given another chance over a mile and a half, was below the form he showed to win at Leicester on his previous start off an 8lb higher mark. (tchd 6-1)
Sweet Indulgence(IRE) promised to be suited by the return to this distance, but he was disappointing. (op 5-1 tchd 11-2 in places)
Mexican Pete, carrying a 6lb penalty, ran nowhere near the form he showed when winning at Warwick on his previous start. (op 13-2)
T/Jkpt: Not won. T/Plt: £1,762.30 to a £1 stake. Pool: £130,730.50. 54.15 winning tickets. T/Qpdt: £77.60 to a £1 stake. Pool: £9,312.35. 88.75 winning tickets. CR

[2679] YORK (L-H)
Friday, July 14

OFFICIAL GOING: Good to firm
The ground had been watered and was described as 'good to firm, not firm at all and with the best cover of grass at this track so far this year'.
Wind: Light 1/2 against Weather: Fine, sunny and hot

3498 HOVIS MAIDEN STKS — 7f
2:15 (2:15) (Class 4) 2-Y-O **£6,541** (£1,946; £972; £485) **Stalls** Low

Form RPR

1 **Medicine Path** 2-9-3 .... RichardMullen 4 88+
(E J O'Neill) *trckd ldrs: effrt over 1f out: rdn and qcknd to ld ins last: r.o* **7/2**[3]

26 **2** *1 1/4* **Cumin (USA)**[20] 2844 2-8-12 .... RHills 3 80
(B W Hills) *cl up: led over 2f out: rdn wl over 1f out: hdd and one pce ins last* **7/4**[1]

35 **3** *1 1/4* **Gweebarra**[20] 2844 2-9-3 .... DO'Donohoe 8 82
(K A Ryan) *trckd ldrs on outer: effrt 2f out: rdn and ev ch over 1f out: kpt on same pce* **3/1**[2]

4 *3* **Stark Contrast (USA)** 2-9-3 .... DarryllHolland 9 74
(G A Butler) *well-made: hld up in tch: hdwy 3f out: styd on ins last: bttr for r* **16/1**

5 *1 1/4* **Obe Royal** 2-9-3 .... TedDurcan 7 70
(M R Channon) *tall: dwlt and bhd: hdwy on outer over 2f out: rdn to chse ldrs wl over 1f out: sn edgd lft and wknd* **20/1**

0 **6** *2 1/2* **Bed Fellow (IRE)**[16] 2979 2-9-3 .... DeanMcKeown 1 64
(A P Jarvis) *prom: effrt 3f out and ev ch tl rdn and hung lft 2f out: sn wknd* **40/1**

6 **7** *1 3/4* **Darfour**[26] 2680 2-9-3 .... RoystonFfrench 2 59
(M Johnston) *hld up: hdwy 3f out: rdn to chse ldrs over 2f out: sn wknd* **16/1**

0 **8** *5* **Go Red**[24] 2733 2-9-3 .... PaulMulrennan 5 46
(M W Easterby) *led: rdn along 3f out: sn hdd & wknd* **66/1**

6 **9** *1 3/4* **Deccan Express (IRE)**[7] 3253 2-9-3 .... RichardHughes 6 42
(R Hannon) *hld up: hdwy and in tch over 2f out: sn rdn and btn* **10/1**

1m 23.44s (-1.96) **Going Correction** -0.175s/f (Firm) **9** Ran SP% **113.1**
Speed ratings (Par 96):104,102,101,97,96 93,91,85,83
CSF £9.61 TOTE £4.80: £1.70, £1.20, £1.40; EX 12.50.
Owner J C Fretwell **Bred** Jenny Hall Bloodstock Ltd **Trained** Averham Park, Notts

FOCUS
A very quick time and the winner looks a very useful prospect. It should prove a well above average maiden.

NOTEBOOK
Medicine Path ◆, whose stable took this a year ago with subsequent Doncaster Champagne Stakes winner Silent Times, is a tall individual with quite a round action. After being temporarily outpaced he won going away and looks a fine prospect. (op 10-3)
Cumin(USA), who looked very fit indeed, travelled best much of the way but ran into a classy looking winner. She ran close to her Royal Ascot level again and should win a similar race before long. (op 13-8 tchd 15-8 in places)
Gweebarra, a neck in front of the runner-up at Royal Ascot, went down fighting and is sure to make his mark at this level. (tchd 10-3, 7-2 in a place)
Stark Contrast(USA) ◆ stayed on nicely from off the pace without being in anyway knocked about. He will learn from this sympathetic introduction. (tchd 14-1)
Obe Royal gave a rodeo display on the way down. After a very tardy start he did well to get involved before dropping away in the closing stages. The experience should have done him a power of good. (op 16-1)
Bed Fellow(IRE), who has plenty of size and scope, has a very round action. He showed ability but looked to be feeling the ground before dropping away.
Darfour showed a moderate action going down and probably did not appreciate the quick ground. (op 14-1)
Deccan Express(IRE) Official explanation: jockey said colt was unsuited by the good to firm ground

3499 CUISINE DE FRANCE SUMMER STKS (GROUP 3) (F&M) — 6f
2:45 (2:46) (Class 1) 3-Y-O+
£28,390 (£10,760; £5,385; £2,685; £1,345; £675) **Stalls** Centre

Form RPR

2-00 **1** **La Chunga (USA)**[24] 2720 3-8-10 **109**............................ DarryllHolland 5 107
(J Noseda) *in tch and pshd along 1/2-way: hdwy over 2f out: rdn over 1f out: styd on to ld ins last* **11/4**[1]

1-00 **2** *1 1/4* **Donna Blini**[21] 2802 3-8-10 **109**.................................... MichaelTebbutt 4 103
(B J Meehan) *led: rdn 2f out: hdd over 1f out: drvn and rallied ins last: kpt on* **7/1**

-101 **3** *shd* **Paradise Isle**[34] 2438 5-9-2 **105**.................................... KDarley 11 104
(C F Wall) *cl up: rdn 2f out: drvn to ld jst over 1f out: hdd ins last and kpt on same pce* **3/1**[2]

2615 **4** *hd* **Yomalo (IRE)**[20] 2847 6-9-4 **102**.................................... NickyMackay 3 105
(Rae Guest) *dwlt: sn pushed along and outpcd in rr: swtchd rt and hdwy wl over 1f out: styd on strly ins last* **8/1**

0101 **5** *1* **Tagula Sunrise (IRE)**[20] 2851 4-9-2 **92**.......................... PaulHanagan 2 100
(R A Fahey) *towards rr: hdwy over 2f out: sn rdn and kpt on ins last: nrst fin* **20/1**

0115 **6** *nk* **Intriguing Glimpse**[7] 3251 5-9-2 **91**.............................. JimmyQuinn 8 99
(Miss B Sanders) *hld up towards rr: hdwy 2f out: rdn to chse ldrs over 1f out: kpt on same pce ins last* **25/1**

1-63 **7** *3/4* **Gimasha**[14] 3047 4-9-2 **92**.. TedDurcan 1 97
(W Jarvis) *hld up in rr: hdwy on outer over 2f out: rdn to chse ldrs wl over 1f out: sn drvn and wknd appr last* **20/1**

15-2 **8** *1 1/4* **Nidhaal (IRE)**[34] 2438 3-8-10 **104**.. RHills 9 92
(E A L Dunlop) *chsd ldrs: rdn along over 2f out: grad wknd* **11/2**[3]

-214 **9** *5* **Leopoldine**[27] 2651 3-8-10 **88**.................................... FrancisNorton 6 77
(H Morrison) *hld up: hdwy to chse ldrs 2f out: sn rdn and wknd* **28/1**

-100 **10** *2 1/2* **Nantyglo**[21] 2802 3-8-10 **101**.................................... HayleyTurner 7 70
(M L W Bell) *chsd ldrs: rdn along wl over 2f out and sn wknd* **33/1**

3-01 **11** *3 1/2* **Jewel In The Sand (IRE)**[14] 3047 4-9-2 **101**............ RichardHughes 10 60
(R Hannon) *in tch: pushed along to chse ldrs 1/2-way: sn rdn and wknd fnl 2f* **14/1**

1m 10.14s (-2.42) **Going Correction** -0.175s/f (Firm)
WFA 3 from 4yo+ 6lb **11** Ran SP% **117.1**
Speed ratings (Par 113):109,107,107,106,105 105,104,102,95,92 87
CSF £20.33 TOTE £3.90: £1.90, £2.40, £1.30; EX 22.70 Trifecta £33.40 Pool: £167.00 - 15.80 winning units..
Owner Sir Robert Ogden **Bred** Brilliant Stables Inc Et Al **Trained** Newmarket, Suffolk

FOCUS
A decent renewal of this fillies' Group 3, run at an end-to-end gallop. Sound form.

NOTEBOOK
La Chunga(USA), a winner over this course and distance at the Royal meeting last year, needed every yard of the six. Soon pushed along, she really put her head down and battled and was right on top at the line. She should continue to give a good account of herself at this level. (op 3-1)
Donna Blini, back over a more suitable trip, flew the traps and took them along at a fierce pace. She went down fighting and the Cheveley Park winner should continue to give a good account of herself in high-class sprints. (op 13-2)
Paradise Isle, winner of eight races, had a few pounds to find with the first two and this admirable mare ran right up to her very best. (tchd 7-2 and 10-3 in places)
Yomalo(IRE), under a 2lb penalty, had a bit to find and after a tardy start and then being forced to switch, she was staying on in fine style at the end.
Tagula Sunrise(IRE), dropping back in trip and on ground plenty quick enough for her, had a mountain to climb on official ratings and deserves plenty of credit for this. However her handicap mark might well suffer.
Intriguing Glimpse, who had the least chance on official figures, seemed to run out of her skin, especially considering all her six wins have been over the minimum trip. She too could pay heavily when her new rating clicks in. (op 20-1)
Gimasha, another with plenty to find, was walked to post. She showed she is right back to her very best. (op 16-1)
Nidhaal(IRE), who suffered a stress fracture in the Cheveley Park, was reportedly jarred up after finishing runner-up behind Paradise Isle on her return at Haydock. She was well below her best and may not have appreciated the quick ground. (tchd 6-1)
Jewel In The Sand(IRE) looked at her very best beforehand but turned in a disappointing effort on the back of her Newmarket success. (op 16-1)

3500 HEARTHSTEAD HOMES STKS (H'CAP) — 7f
3:20 (3:20) (Class 4) (0-85,83) 3-Y-O+ **£6,800** (£2,023; £1,011; £505) **Stalls** Low

Form RPR

0005 **1** **Gallantry**[13] 3079 4-9-13 **82**.. JimmyQuinn 1 91
(D W Barker) *hld up in tch: hdwy over 2f out: rdn to ld ins last: styd on* **8/1**

4020 **2** *1 1/4* **Bond Diamond**[6] 3298 9-8-4 **64** oh3.............................. RoryMoore(5) 2 70
(P T Midgley) *hedl up towards rr: gd hdwy on outer over 2f out: rdn to chal over 1f out and ev ch tl nt qckn ins last* **33/1**

1016 **3** *1* **Royal Dignitary (USA)**[13] 3079 6-9-11 **83**.......(v) SilvestreDeSousa(3) 11 86+
(D Nicholls) *cl up: wd st: led wl over 2f out: rdn over 1f out: hdd and no ex ins last* **7/1**[3]

160- **4** *3/4* **Sam's Secret**[273] 5880 4-9-1 **70**.................................... DeanMcKeown 3 71
(S Parr) *hld up towards rr: hdwy 2f out: sn rdn and styd on ins last: nrst fin* **25/1**

2603 **5** *shd* **Dvinsky (USA)**[3] 3374 5-9-1 **73**.................................. DanielTudhope(3) 4 74
(D Carroll) *trckd ldrs: hdwy 3f out: rdn to chal wl over 1f out and ev ch tl drvn and wknd ins last* **5/1**[2]

0-00 **6** *nk* **Lago D'Orta (IRE)**[16] 2974 6-9-2 **78**.......................... VictoriaBehan(7) 9 78
(D Nicholls) *towards rr: hdwy over 2f out: styd on appr last: nrst fin* **10/1**

6103 **7** *3/4* **Tough Love**[9] 3191 7-9-4 **73**....................................(p) GrahamGibbons 10 71
(T D Easterby) *chsd ldrs: rdn aloong over 2f out: drvn and wandered over 1f out: sn wknd* **7/1**[3]

3004 **8** *1 1/2* **Breaking Shadow (IRE)**[13] 3079 4-9-9 **78**.......................... PhillipMakin 6 72
(T D Barron) *midfield: effrt and sme hdwy 2f out: sn rdn: switched lft and no imp fr over 1f out* **4/1**[1]

4525 **9** *3/4* **Tedsdale Mac**[7] 3243 7-8-2 **64**.............................. SuzzanneFrance(7) 12 56
(N Bycroft) *a towards rr* **16/1**

20-0 **10** *1 3/4* **Vanadium**[14] 3040 4-9-9 **78**.. DarryllHolland 8 65
(J G Given) *led: rdn along 3f out: sn hdd: grad wknd fnl 2f* **12/1**

0103 **11** *1 1/2* **Li Shih Chen**[73] 1384 3-8-11 **74**.. TPQueally 5 57
(A P Jarvis) *chsd ldng pair: rdn along over 2f out: sn wknd* **14/1**

4000 **12** *1* **Harvest Warrior**[28] 2627 4-9-5 **74**..(b) TedDurcan 7 55
(T D Easterby) *in tch: rdn along over 2f out: sn wknd* **10/1**

1m 22.97s (-2.43) **Going Correction** -0.175s/f (Firm)
WFA 3 from 4yo+ 8lb **12** Ran SP% **118.0**
Speed ratings (Par 105):106,104,103,102,102 102,101,99,98,96 94,93
CSF £239.58 CT £1963.85 TOTE £12.50: £3.40, £8.00, £2.70; EX 516.30.

Owner The Circle Bloodstock I Limited **Bred** Cheveley Park Stud Ltd **Trained** Scorton, N Yorks

FOCUS

Not a strong handicap by York standards, and the proximity of the runner-up is a bit of a worry.

Tough Love Official explanation: jockey said gelding was unsuited by the good to firm ground

Vanadium Official explanation: jockey said gelding was unsuited by the good to firm ground

3501 JOHN WEST TUNA STKS (H'CAP) 1m 4f

3:55 (3:55) (Class 2) (0-100,99) 3-Y-O+ **£11,658** (£3,468; £1,733; £865) **Stalls** Centre

Form RPR

-541 **1** **Luberon**[13] 3093 3-9-0 **98** ... KDarley 3 108+
(M Johnston) *set stdy pce qcknd 3f out: sn clr: rdn and styd on strly fr over 1f out* **9/2**[2]

0011 **2** *2* **Gringo**[7] 3248 4-8-11 **79** 3ex ... OscarUrbina 4 91+
(B W Hills) *hld up in rr: effrt and hdwy 2f out: nt clr run and swtchd rt over 1f out: rdn and styd on ins last* **7/2**[1]

4002 **3** *hd* **Pevensey (IRE)**[13] 3093 4-8-11 **82** ... PaulHanagan 6 86
(M A Buckley) *hld up towards rr: hdwy on outer over 2f out: rdn to chse wnr ins last: lost 2nd towards fin* **17/2**

/5-6 **4** *nk* **Premier Dane (IRE)**[27] 2657 4-9-4 **89** ... PatCosgrave 7 93
(N G Richards) *trckd ldrs: hdwy over 3f out: rdn 2f out and kpt on same pce appr last* **8/1**

32-0 **5** *1 ½* **Royal Jet**[6] 3294 4-9-0 **85** ... TedDurcan 1 86+
(M R Channon) *hld up: hdwy over 2f out: rdn and nt much over 1f out: sn no imp* **7/1**[3]

2446 **6** *1* **Rehearsal**[20] 2848 5-9-7 **92** ... RichardHughes 2 92
(L Lungo) *trckd ldng pair: hdwy 3f out: rdn wl over 1f out: wknd appr last* **7/2**[1]

0560 **7** *3* **Most Definitely (IRE)**[13] 3078 6-8-12 **83** ... GrahamGibbons 5 78
(T D Easterby) *keen: trckd ldrs: hdwy to chse wnr over 3f out: rdn along over 2f out: sn drvn and wknd over 1f out* **16/1**

14-0 **8** *3* **Kerashan (IRE)**[140] 512 4-10-0 **99** ... RichardMullen 8 89
(Saeed Bin Suroor) *chsd ldrs: rdn along on outer over 3f out: wkng whn hmpd over 1f out* **9/1**

2m 32.24s (-0.16) **Going Correction** +0.025s/f (Good)
WFA 3 from 4yo+ 13lb 8 Ran SP% **112.6**

Speed ratings (Par 109):101,99,99,99,98 97,95,93

CSF £19.98 CT £126.40 TOTE £4.10: £1.40, £1.60, £2.90; EX 8.90.

Owner Brian Yeardley Continental Ltd **Bred** Card Bloodstock **Trained** Middleham Moor, N Yorks

FOCUS

A fine tactical ride by Kevin Darley, dictating his own pace until winding it up in the home straight, and not surprisingly the winning time was moderate. They never really looked like being overhauled. The race has been rated through the third.

NOTEBOOK

Luberon, 9lb higher, was allowed his own way in front and, stepping up the gallop in the final half-mile, he never looked in any danger. He is progressing nicely and it would be dangerous to assume he was flattered. (op 4-1 tchd 5-1 in a place)

Gringo ◆, under his 3lb penalty, was keen to get on with it. He met all sorts of traffic problems before staying on strongly to snatch second spot near the line. He must be kept on the right side, with a trip to Redcar significant. (tchd 4-1)

Pevensey(IRE), meeting the winner on 8lb better terms, gave him plenty of rope. He worked hard to take second place inside the last only to be pipped for that place near the line. (op 9-1)

Premier Dane(IRE) could do no more than plug on at the same pace and would have appreciated a much stronger gallop. (op 9-1)

Royal Jetdidn't really improve on his reappearance effort. (op 8-1)

Rehearsal looks rated to the hilt now. (op 4-1)

Kerashan(IRE) looked very fit but was the first to come under real pressure and the cloud over the stable hasn't lifted yet. (op 7-1)

3502 MR KIPLING EXCEEDINGLY GOOD STKS (H'CAP) 1m 5f 197y

4:30 (4:30) (Class 3) (0-90,82) 3-Y-O **£9,715** (£2,890; £1,444; £721) **Stalls** Low

Form RPR

0121 **1** **Bauer (IRE)**[29] 2584 3-8-11 **72** ... NickyMackay 5 89+
(L M Cumani) *trckd ldng pair: hdwy 3f out: led over 2f out: rdn over 1f out: styd on wl fnl f* **2/1**[1]

1212 **2** *1* **Liberate**[26] 2677 3-8-11 **72** ... JamieMackay 2 85
(Sir Mark Prescott) *hld up in rr: hdwy over 2f out: swtchd outside and rdn wl over 1f out: drvn to chse wnr ins last: kpt on* **13/2**

6012 **3** *2 ½* **Shore Thing (IRE)**[7] 3249 3-8-5 **66** ... TPQueally 4 75
(M H Tompkins) *trckd ldrs: hdwy over 3f out: rdn to chal 2f out and ev ch tl edgd lft and one pce appr last* **3/1**[3]

4241 **4** *hd* **Som Tala**[26] 2677 3-9-3 **78** ... TedDurcan 3 87
(M R Channon) *trfacked ldr: hdwy to ld over 3f out: rdn and hdd over 2f out: drvn and wknd over 1f out* **9/1**

51-5 **5** *2* **Sin City**[16] 2986 3-8-12 **73** ... PaulHanagan 1 79
(R A Fahey) *led: rdn and qcknd over 4f out: hdd over 3f out: drvn 2f out and sn wknd* **11/4**[2]

3m 0.92s (2.48) **Going Correction** +0.025s/f (Good) 5 Ran SP% **108.3**

Speed ratings (Par 104):93,92,91,90,89

CSF £14.29 TOTE £2.50: £1.50, £2.60; EX 13.10.

Owner Aston House Stud **Bred** Aston House Stud **Trained** Newmarket, Suffolk

FOCUS

The top-weight was 12lb below the race ceiling, so this was not the strongest of races for the grade. The gallop was anything but strong too, resulting in a very moderate winning time for a race like this. Nevertheless, there were some progressive sorts in the field. The form has been rated through the fourth, with the first two both showing improved form.

NOTEBOOK

Bauer(IRE), a finely-made individual, is a good walker. Racing from a 7lb higher than when winning at Newbury, he travelled best and took this in tidy fashion. He should continue on the up. (op 13-8)

Liberate, a big horse, eventually made his way to the outside. He stayed on in most determined fashion but was never going to finish anywhere but second best. The stiffer test the better with him. (op 6-1)

Shore Thing(IRE), due to go up 7lb after finishing clear second best at Haydock, had no excuse and will struggle unless his rating is revised. (op 10-3 tchd 7-2 in places)

Som Tala, meeting Liberate on 2lb worse terms, didn't shine. (op 12-1)

Sin City, a lightly-made individual, had his own way in front, but after setting sail for home he was swallowed up. (op 3-1)

3503 FIT AS A BUTCHER'S DOG STKS (H'CAP) 5f

5:05 (5:05) (Class 3) (0-90,83) 3-Y-O+ **£8,096** (£2,408; £1,203; £601) **Stalls** Centre

Form RPR

2245 **1** **Malapropism**[1] 3447 6-9-10 **78** ... TedDurcan 3 88
(M R Channon) *cl up: rdn wl over 1f out: led wl ins last: kpt on* **11/4**[1]

1325 **2** *¾* **Coconut Moon**[13] 3069 4-8-12 **69** ... EdwardCreighton(3) 1 77
(E J Alston) *chsd ldng pair: hdwy to ld 1/2-way: rdn over 1f out: hdd and nt qckn wl ins last* **11/4**[1]

0404 **3** *¾* **Colonel Cotton (IRE)**[4] 3354 7-9-3 **71** ...(b) TonyHamilton 5 76
(R A Fahey) *s.i.s: hdwy 1/2-way: rdn to chse ldng pair over 1f out: sn drvn and no imp* **3/1**[2]

-000 **4** *3* **Flur Na H Alba**[6] 3297 7-8-12 **66** ...(v) TPQueally 6 60
(J J Quinn) *a rr* **9/1**

1-00 **5** *2* **Triskaidekaphobia**[43] 2168 3-9-10 **83** ... PaulFitzsimons 8 68
(Miss J R Tooth) *led: rdn along and hdd 1/2-way: sn wknd* **8/1**

0320 **6** *¾* **Catch The Cat (IRE)**[41] 2237 7-8-12 **66** ...(p) CatherineGannon 2 50
(Robert Gray) *dwlt: sn chsng ldrs: rdn along over 2f out and sn btn: fin lame* **6/1**[3]

58.00 secs (-1.32) **Going Correction** -0.175s/f (Firm)
WFA 3 from 4yo+ 5lb 6 Ran SP% **113.7**

Speed ratings (Par 107):103,101,100,95,92 91

CSF £10.86 CT £22.87 TOTE £3.90: £2.20, £1.80; EX 10.30 Place 6 £25.99, Place 5 £22.59.

Owner Michael A Foy **Bred** Michael A Foy **Trained** West Ilsley, Berks

■ Blackheath was withdrawn (7/2, rdr inj in paddock.) R4 applies, deduct 20p in the £. New market formed.

FOCUS

The highest rated horse was 7lb below the race ceiling. Straightforward to rate, though, with the second and third to form and the winner stepping up slightly on his recent best.

NOTEBOOK

Malapropism, having his second outing in two days, simply would not be denied and deserves full credit for this. (old market op 7-2 new market op 3-1)

Coconut Moon, still on the up, pushed the winner hard and deserves to find another opening. (old market tchd 9-2 in a place new market op 3-1 tchd 5-2, 10-3 in a place)

Colonel Cotton(IRE), in blinkers again, gave away more ground in the early stages than he was eventually beaten by, but the fact remains he has not visted the winner's enclosure for over two years now. (new market op 4-1)

Flur Na H Alba, due to drop another 3lb in the rtaings, hasn't shone at all in four starts this time. (new market op 12-1 tchd 8-1)

Triskaidekaphobia, with the blinkers left off, showed all his old speed but was well beaten off in the end. (new market op 14-1)

Catch The Cat(IRE) Official explanation: jockey said gelding finished lame

T/Plt: £23.90 to a £1 stake. Pool: £71,500.15. 2,181.90 winning tickets. T/Qpdt: £14.50 to a £1 stake. Pool: £2,870.20. 146.40 winning tickets. JR

3504 - 3514a (Foreign Racing) - See Raceform Interactive

2941 LONGCHAMP (R-H)

Friday, July 14

OFFICIAL GOING: Good

3515a PRIX DE THIBERVILLE (LISTED RACE) (FILLIES) 1m 4f

6:15 (6:18) 3-Y-O **£17,241** (£6,897; £5,172; £3,448; £1,724)

RPR

1 **Village Fete**[24] 3-8-9 ... DBoeuf 3 102
(D Smaga, France) **14/1**

2 *nk* **Penne (FR)**[41] 2257 3-8-9 ... IMendizabal 2 102
(J-C Rouget, France) **9/1**[3]

3 *¾* **Going Day (USA)**[61] 1720 3-8-9 ... TGillet 10 101
(J E Pease, France) **12/1**

4 *1* **Souvenance**[26] 2694 3-9-0 ... J-BEyquem 6 104
(Sir Mark Prescott) *tracked leader to straight, ridden 2f out, every chance over 1f out, ran on same pace (11/2)* **5/1**[2]

5 *nse* **Ioannina** 3-8-9 ... ASuborics 5 99
(P Schiergen, Germany) **9/1**[3]

6 *¾* **Mary Louhana**[24] 3-8-9 ... SMaillot 7 98
(M Delzangles, France) **10/1**

7 *nk* **Ivory Gala (FR)**[39] 2292 3-8-9 ... KerrinMcEvoy 1 98
(B J Meehan) *always in touch, 5th straight, ridden & disputing 3rd when hampered by winner over 1f out, not recover (40/1)* **20/1**

8 *1 ½* **Ponte Tresa (FR)**[41] 2257 3-9-0 ... CSoumillon 13 100
(Y De Nicolay, France)

9 *nse* **Pearl Sky (FR)**[33] 2491 3-8-9 ... DBonilla 11 95
(Y De Nicolay, France)

10 *shd* **Perstrovka (IRE)**[75] 3-8-9 ...(b) OPeslier 9 95
(E Lellouche, France)

11 **Seracina**[16] 3-8-9 ... TThulliez 8 —
(P Bary, France)

12 **Sweet Shop**[19] 3-8-9 ... KFallon 12 —
(A Fabre, France)

13 **Flow Chart (UAE)**[31] 2537 3-8-9 ... LDettori 4 —
(H-A Pantall, France) **7/2**[1]

2m 30.0s 13 Ran SP% **87.1**

PARI-MUTUEL: WIN 11.10; PL 3.70, 3.40, 4.30; DF 70.30.

Owner K Abdulla **Bred** Juddmonte Farms Ltd **Trained** Lamorlaye, France

NOTEBOOK

Souvenance, having her fifth successive race abroad since winning a maiden at Ayr last season, did not really build on her Italian Oaks third in this lesser grade.

Ivory Gala(FR), winner of a Leicester maiden on her previous outing, ran with credit and would have finished closer but for being hampered by the winner in th straight.

3516a PRIX MAURICE DE NIEUIL (GROUP 2) 1m 6f

6:45 (6:48) 4-Y-O+ **£51,103** (£19,724; £9,414; £6,276; £3,138)

RPR

1 **Bellamy Cay**[40] 2277 4-8-12 ... KFallon 1 115
(A Fabre, France) *raced in 3rd to straight, switched left 2f out, led inside final f, ran on well* **7/2**[2]

2 *1 ½* **Montare (IRE)**[54] 1875 4-8-13 ... TGillet 6 114
(J E Pease, France) *held up, 6th straight, headway towards inside from over 2f out, ran on to take 2nd last strides* **7/2**[2]

3 *hd* **Ostankino (FR)**[54] 1875 5-9-2 ... OPeslier 7 117
(E Lellouche, France) *held up, 7th straight, closing on outside when carried left 2f out, ran on under pressure to take 3rd last strides* **13/2**[3]

4 *nk* **Shamdala (IRE)**[26] 2693 4-9-1 ... CSoumillon 2 115
(A De Royer-Dupre, France) *held up, 8th straight, beginning move on outside when hampered 2f out, ran on to take 4th last strides* **6/4**[1]

5 *shd* **Bussoni (GER)**[55] 1860 5-8-12 ... ADeVries 5 112
(H Blume, Germany) *tracked leader til led well over 1f out, soon hard ridden, headed inside final f, no extra & lost 2nd close home* **12/1**

6 *4* **The Whistling Teal**[63] 1628 10-8-12 .... TThulliez 4 107
(G Wragg) *always close up, 4th straight, disputing 4th when carried left 2f out, kept on one pace* **9/1**

7 *1 ½* **El Biba D'Or (IRE)**[40] 7-8-12 .... SLandi 3 105
(P Giannotti, Italy) *first to show, settled in 5th, 4th on rails when switched left 2f out, soon beaten* **50/1**

8 *5* **Lord Sunshine (FR)**[61] 4-8-12 .... FSpanu 9 99?
(A Spanu, France) *last to straight, never a factor* **60/1**

9 *1 ½* **Belle Suisse (FR)**[24] 4-8-8 .... DBonilla 8 93
(Y De Nicolay, France) *soon led, headed well over 1f out, weakened from distance* **34/1**

3m 1.90s **9** Ran SP% **121.9**

PARI-MUTUEL: WIN 5.50; PL 2.50, 2.20, 3.20; DF 11.30.

Owner K Abdulla **Bred** Juddmonte Farms **Trained** Chantilly, France

NOTEBOOK

Bellamy Cay raced in third on the inside and made his move halfway up the straight. Switched left two furlongs out, he led inside the final furlong and won with authority. His next race is likely to be the Darley Prix Kergorlay at Deauville next month.

Montare(IRE) broke slowly, was held up at the back and was sixth entering the straight. She progressed up the inside rail from over two furlongs out and then produced a strong finish to take second in the last strides.

Ostankino(FR) was held up and was seventh turning into the straight. He was closing on the outside when carried left by the eventual sixth, but ran on under pressure to take third in the last strides.

Shamdala(IRE), a supplementary entry, was held up out the back alongside the eventual second. She was beginning her move on the outside when hampered two furlongs out, being pushed left and losing momentum, but ran on again and took fourth in the last strides.

The Whistling Teal ran his race under a positive ride, and was beginning to struggle when hampered a quarter mile out.

3517a JUDDMONTE GRAND PRIX DE PARIS (GROUP 1) (ENTIRE COLTS & FILLIES) 1m 4f

7:20 (7:25) 3-Y-O **£197,034** (£78,828; £39,414; £19,960; £9,862)

RPR

1 **Rail Link**[24] 2738 3-9-2 .... CSoumillon 3 121+
(A Fabre, France) *always close up, 4th straight on outside, headway from 2f out, led 150yds out, ran on well* **2/1**[1]

2 *2* **Red Rocks (IRE)**[21] 2801 3-9-2 .... LDettori 10 117
(B J Meehan) *led after 1f, headed 150yds out, ran on* **5/1**[3]

3 *hd* **Sudan (IRE)**[24] 2738 3-9-2 .... TThulliez 2 117
(E Lellouche, France) *raced in 5th to straight, ran on last 2f to take 3rd well inside final f* **20/1**

4 *snk* **Grand Couturier**[48] 3-9-2 .... TJarnet 9 116
(J-C Rouget, France) *raced in 6th to straight, kept on final 2f, never nearer* **14/1**

5 *1* **Art Deco (IRE)**[40] 2278 3-9-2 .... OPeslier 8 115
(C R Egerton) *a prom, trckd ldr after 2f, 2nd str, rdn & ev ch wl over 1f out, no ex fnl f, lost 3rd closing stages* **15/2**

6 *1 ½* **Gravitas**[27] 3-9-2 .... KerrinMcEvoy 1 113
(A Fabre, France) *held up, 7th straight, effort on inside from over 2f out, switched left over 1f out, one pace* **14/1**

7 *hd* **Mountain (IRE)**[12] 3127 3-9-2 .... KFallon 5 112
(A P O'Brien, Ire) *led 1f, settled in 3rd, 3rd straight, 4th 1f out, gradually weakened* **6/1**

8 *2 ½* **Numide (FR)**[40] 2278 3-9-2 .... IMendizabal 4 109
(J-C Rouget, France) *slowly into stride, raced in rear, last most of the way* **29/10**[2]

9 *¾* **Puerto Rico (IRE)**[12] 3127 3-9-2 .... CO'Donoghue 6 108
(A P O'Brien, Ire) *always in rear, 8th straight, hard ridden 2f out, no headway* **14/1**

2m 26.4s **9** Ran SP% **126.5**

PARI-MUTUEL: WIN 2.00; PL 1.10, 1.50, 2.10; DF 4.60.

Owner K Abdulla **Bred** Juddmonte Farms Ltd **Trained** Chantilly, France

NOTEBOOK

Rail Link, always up with the pace, came to join the leaders at the furlong marker and 150 yards out he hit the front and ran on well to win by two lengths with authority.

Red Rocks(IRE), quickly into the lead, set a good, sound pace, and although headed 150 yards out by the winner stayed on to hold second place. He lost his off-fore plate during the race and the trainer reported that he will now have a break.

Sudan(IRE) sat in fifth position to the straight and ran on from the two-furlong pole producing a strong finish to take third well inside the final furlong.

Grand Couturier was raced in sixth to the straight and at the two-furlong marker he was asked to quicken on the outside and stayed on to take fourth position.

Art Deco(IRE), a close fourth in the Prix du Jockey-Club following his Dee Stakes victory, had every chance but may have found this longer trip beyond him.

Mountain(IRE), beaten for the third successive time at this level, looks to need a drop in grade.

3473 CHESTER (L-H)

Saturday, July 15

OFFICIAL GOING: Good to firm (firm in places; watered)

Wind: Light behind Weather: Hot and sunny

3518 TOTESCOOP6 CHESTER CONDITIONS STKS 7f 2y

2:25 (2:25) (Class 2) 3-Y-O+ **£13,248** (£3,964; £1,982; £991; £493) **Stalls** Low

Form RPR

15-2 **1** **Prince Of Light (IRE)**[14] 3091 3-8-8 109 .... J-PGuillambert 1 107+
(M Johnston) *mde all at stdy pce: rdn to qckn over 1f out: r.o* **11/8**[1]

4-15 **2** *1 ¼* **Vanderlin**[69] 1527 7-9-10 112 .... FrancisNorton 4 112
(A M Balding) *chsd ldrs: rdn over 1f out: edgd lft and wnt 2nd ins fnl f: styd on: nt trble wnr* **7/2**[3]

-232 **3** *hd* **Mac Love**[14] 3086 5-8-13 107 .... TonyCulhane 5 100
(R Charlton) *stdd s: racd keenly: hld up: rdn over 1f out: hdwy whn nt clr run and swtchd lft ins fnl f: r.o: nrst fin* **2/1**[2]

0020 **4** *shd* **Beckermet (IRE)**[7] 3295 4-9-2 106 .... RHills 2 103
(R F Fisher) *stdd s: hld up bhd ldrs: rdn to chse wnr over 1f out: lost 2nd and nt qckn ins fnl f* **8/1**

1506 **5** *1 ¼* **Will He Wish**[13] 3121 10-8-13 90 .... DO'Donohoe 3 97
(S Gollings) *sn w wnr: rdn and ev ch 2f out: no ex ins fnl f* **33/1**

1m 26.48s (-1.99) **Going Correction** -0.075s/f (Good)

WFA 3 from 4yo+ 8lb **5** Ran SP% **111.7**

Speed ratings (Par 109):108,106,106,106,104

CSF £6.72 TOTE £2.30: £1.40, £1.80; EX 6.30.

Owner Claire Riordan And Kieran Coughlan **Bred** High Bramley Grange Stud Ltd **Trained** Middleham Moor, N Yorks

FOCUS

A steadily-run race in which Prince Of Light dominated throughout, although the form is limited by the fifth.

NOTEBOOK

Prince Of Light(IRE) ◆, a three-time winning juvenile, including at Group level, did more than enough to suggest he had trained on when running hot favourite Librettist close at Windsor earlier in the month, and the drop back to seven furlongs proved to be no problem. Soon in the lead from stall one, he was able to dominate at his own tempo and quickened well as they turned for home before staying on strongly. Evidently a progressive type, the return to a mile is likely to bring about further improvement and races such as the Totesport Mile and Group 2 Celebration Mile, both at Goodwood in August, may prove suitable targets. He should stay ten furlongs in time and is certainly one to keep on-side. (op 6-4 tchd 13-8)

Vanderlin, last seen finishing a close-up fifth behind top-class miler Bullish Luck in the Champions Mile at Sha Tin in May, looked a major threat to the favourite despite being badly in at the weights, but he lacked the winner's change of gear and could only keep on at the one pace under pressure. This was a fair effort in a race he has a fine record in and the return to a mile is going to help. (op 9-2)

Mac Love, who did not get the best of runs, has now performed creditably in defeat on each of his four starts this season, but he keeps finding himself done for a change of pace and it is surely time he was returned to a mile. (op 15-8 tchd 9-4)

Beckermet(IRE) is usually a trail-blazer at shorter, but he was ridden with restraint on this first try at seven furlongs, and having come through to chase the winner, he emptied out inside the final furlong and was run out of second. He is a very capable sprinter on his day and has a decent race in him. (op 15-2)

Will He Wish was always likely to struggle and he only ran as well as he did due to racing prominently in a moderately-run race. (op 25-1)

3519 TOTECOURSE TO COURSE H'CAP 1m 2f 75y

3:00 (3:00) (Class 4) (0-80,77) 4-Y-O+ **£5,829** (£1,734; £866; £432) **Stalls** High

Form RPR

0340 **1** **Instructor**[14] 3081 5-9-7 77 .... J-PGuillambert 4 86
(R A Fahey) *led: rdn and hdd over 1f out: rallied to regain ld ins fnl f: styd on gamely and in command cl home* **6/1**[3]

0512 **2** *1* **Billy One Punch**[28] 2640 4-8-8 64 .... TonyCulhane 2 71
(G G Margarson) *racd keenly: trckd ldr: rdn to ld over 1f out: hdd ins fnl f: no ex cl home* **3/1**[2]

0213 **3** *1* **Go Solo**[17] 2975 5-9-7 77 .... DeanMcKeown 3 82
(G A Swinbank) *trckd ldrs: rdn over 2f out: sn outpcd by ldng pair: styd on ins fnl f* **9/4**[1]

-350 **4** *¾* **Barbirolli**[28] 2640 4-8-1 62 .... LiamJones(5) 1 66
(W M Brisbourne) *hld up in midfield: rdn over 2f out: styd on ins fnl f: nvr able to chal* **6/1**[3]

0041 **5** *3* **Nashaab (USA)**[10] 3194 9-8-13 69 .... (v) FrancisNorton 7 67
(P D Evans) *t.k.h: hld up: rdn over 3f out: no imp: eased whn btn wl ins fnl f* **6/1**[3]

0-06 **6** *2* **Paparaazi (IRE)**[168] 223 4-9-2 72 .... GylesParkin 5 66
(R A Fahey) *racd keenly: hld up: rdn over 3f out: nvr on terms* **12/1**

5410 **7** *5* **Scotty's Future (IRE)**[23] 2788 8-8-5 61 .... DO'Donohoe 6 46
(A Berry) *hld up in midfield: hdwy over 6f out: rdn over 3f out: wknd over 2f out: eased whn btn ins fnl f* **16/1**

2m 13.08s (-0.06) **Going Correction** -0.075s/f (Good) **7** Ran SP% **112.2**

Speed ratings (Par 105):97,96,95,94,92 90,86

CSF £23.37 TOTE £7.40: £3.70, £1.90; EX 35.10.

Owner Yorkshire Racing Club Owners Group 1990 **Bred** Cheveley Park Stud Ltd **Trained** Musley Bank, N Yorks

FOCUS

A tricky handicap on paper, but Instructor and Billy One Punch dominated throughout and were allowed to fight the race out between them. The form looks reasonable if not rock solid and has been rated at face value.

Instructor Official explanation: trainer's representative had no explanation for the improved form shown

3520 TOTESPORT.COM CHESTER CITY WALL STKS (LISTED RACE) 5f 16y

3:35 (3:35) (Class 1) 3-Y-O+

£15,898 (£6,025; £3,015; £1,503; £753; £378) **Stalls** Low

Form RPR

0-05 **1** **Tournedos (IRE)**[13] 3124 4-9-0 103 .... TonyCulhane 1 103
(R Charlton) *chsd ldrs: rdn to take 2nd over 1f out: r.o to ld towards fin* **5/2**[1]

1051 **2** *½* **Desert Lord**[42] 2227 6-9-0 100 .... (b) DO'Donohoe 3 101
(K A Ryan) *led: rdn over 1f out: hdd towards fin* **5/1**[3]

3036 **3** *nk* **Ooh Aah Camara (IRE)**[12] 3144 3-8-4 84 .... RobbieFitzpatrick 2 93
(T J Pitt) *sn rdn and outpcd: hdwy over 1f out: swtchd rt ins fnl f: r.o: nrst fin* **14/1**

0330 **4** *1 ¼* **Strike Up The Band**[21] 2847 3-8-9 106 .... AdrianTNicholls 4 101+
(D Nicholls) *dwlt: hld up: hdwy over 1f out: ev ch on rail whn n.m.r and hmpd ins fnl f: nt rcvr* **4/1**[2]

-200 **5** *¾* **Bond City (IRE)**[25] 2720 4-9-0 100 .... MickyFenton 7 93
(B Smart) *midfield: rdn over 2f out: kpt on ins fnl f: nt pce to chal* **20/1**

0-24 **6** *nk* **Dhekraa (IRE)**[35] 2438 3-8-4 97 .... RHills 9 85
(M A Jarvis) *in rr: rdn over 1f out: kpt on ins fnl f: nvr trbld ldrs* **11/1**

4402 **7** *nk* **Talbot Avenue**[29] 2624 8-9-0 96 .... DeanMcKeown 6 91
(M Mullineaux) *prom: rdn over 1f out: one pce ins fnl f* **12/1**

302 **8** *nk* **Treasure Cay**[23] 2799 5-9-0 102 .... (v[1]) FrancisNorton 5 89
(P W D'Arcy) *prom: rdn 2f out: wknd wl ins fnl f* **11/1**

4243 **9** *2* **Sierra Vista**[15] 3038 6-8-9 101 .... J-PGuillambert 8 77
(D W Barker) *in tch on outside: rdn over 1f out: sn wknd* **7/1**

60.61 secs (-1.44) **Going Correction** -0.075s/f (Good)

WFA 3 from 4yo+ 5lb **9** Ran SP% **113.5**

Speed ratings (Par 111):108,107,106,104,103 103,102,102,98

CSF £14.64 TOTE £3.40: £1.40, £1.90, £2.00; EX 15.40.

Owner Vimal Khosla **Bred** Pat Grogan **Trained** Beckhampton, Wilts

■ Stewards' Enquiry : D O'Donohoe one-day ban: careless riding (Jul 26); caution: used whip without giving mount time to respond

FOCUS

A decent Listed contest won for the second successive year by Tournedos but the form is ordinary for the grade with the draw a factor.

NOTEBOOK

Tournedos(IRE), shock winner of this contest last year for John Akehurst, had the benefit of stall one and he enjoyed a nice tow round before going in pursuit of Desert Lord and quickening past him close home. His keeping-on fifth behind the high-class Dandy Man at the Curragh recently suggested he was ready to return to winning ways and he is now likely to be aimed at some of the season's remaining top sprints. (op 3-1 tchd 7-2 and 10-3 in places)

Desert Lord is perhaps one of the quickest around, hence his victory in the Vodafone Dash, and he was soon blazing the trail. He led them into the final furlong, but hung to his left under pressure and the winner proved too strong in the closing stages. (tchd 9-2)

Ooh Aah Camara(IRE) had a bit to find with the principals, but she is twice a course winner and her knowledge of the place was an obvious advantage. Struggling early, she began to hit top stride as they raced into the straight and was coming home strongly, but the line came too soon. Most of her best form has come at this distance.

Strike Up The Band, narrowly touched off by Ooh Aah Camara on his only previous visit to the course, found himself behind early, but he picked up strongly in the straight and came with his challenge over a furlong out, but soon found himself squeezed for room and was then hampered by the runner-up. This ended his chance, but the drop to five furlongs for the first time in a while clearly suited.

Bond City(IRE) found himself outclassed in the King's Stand, but this was more realistic and he ran much better. He has a decent race in him if able to repeat his Vodafone Dash Form. (op 14-1)

Dhekraa(IRE) was entitled to run well and she did just that, getting going late on having been behind early. She has shown enough this season to suggest she is capable of winning at this level. (op 12-1 tchd 10-1)

Talbot Avenue had a fair bit to find and was always likely to struggle. (op 14-1)

Treasure Cay fell away rather quickly having shown up well early, but he ran well enough to suggest the visor can become a permanent fixture. (op 9-1 tchd 12-1 in a place)

Sierra Vista was beaten by her outside draw and should have the run ignored. (op 6-1)

3521 TOTEPOOL TEXT BETTING 60021 MAIDEN AUCTION STKS 5f 16y

4:10 (4:10) (Class 5) 2-Y-0 **£3,400** (£1,011; £505; £252) **Stalls** Low

Form RPR

64 **1** **Gold Spirit (IRE)**[25] 2726 2-8-7 .... FrancisNorton 1 80+
(E J O'Neill) *mde all: shkn up and qcknd clr over 1f out: r.o wl: eased towards fin* **3/1**[2]

52 **2** *1* **Durova (IRE)**[10] 3188 2-7-13 .... DuranFentiman(5) 2 73+
(T D Easterby) *trckd ldrs: lft 2nd 1/2-way: sn rdn: outpcd by wnr over 1f out: kpt on ins fnl f: flattered* **1/1**[1]

3 **3** *7* **Wicked Wilma (IRE)**[7] 3286 2-8-3 ow1 .... AdrianTNicholls 3 47
(A Berry) *racd keenly: w wnr tl hung rt and rdn 1/2-way: sn wknd* **6/1**[3]

5050 **4** *4* **Daruma (IRE)**[8] 3246 2-8-7 ....(b) RobbieFitzpatrick 5 37
(Peter Grayson) *in tch: sn hung rt and rdn: wknd 1/2-way* **33/1**

06 **5** *½* **Imprimis Tagula (IRE)**[32] 2517 2-8-9 .... LiamJones(5) 4 42
(A Bailey) *rdn 1/2-way: a bhd* **14/1**

6 *4* **Miss Capricorn** 2-8-6 .... DO'Donohoe 6 19
(K A Ryan) *s.s: a bhd* **7/1**

61.73 secs (-0.32) **Going Correction** -0.075s/f (Good) **6** Ran SP% **111.4**

Speed ratings (Par 94):99,97,86,79,79 72

CSF £6.29 TOTE £4.10: £1.80, £1.40; EX 5.20.

Owner Roadmate Racing **Bred** Norelands Bloodstock **Trained** Averham Park, Notts

FOCUS

An ordinary maiden dominated by those at the head of the market and rated through the runner-up, but could be higher.

NOTEBOOK

Gold Spirit(IRE) failed to get home when seemingly unable to handle the track at Brighton last time, but he had the best stall here and Norton made full use, leading throughout and showing a tidy change of pace to go clear a furlong out. Value for probably five lengths, he looks a good nursery prospect and this speedy sort may yet have more to offer. (op 11-4 tchd 10-3)

Durova(IRE) held a decent position throughout and had every chance, but the winner was far too speedy and she could only keep on at the one pace. She is now qualified for nurseries though, and the fact she was clear of the third is encouraging. (op 6-5 tchd 6-4)

Wicked Wilma(IRE), who halved in price in the betting, did far too much in the first half of the race and did not look comfortable on the course. She is clearly thought capable of better, but may not show it until contesting nurseries. (op 12-1)

Daruma(IRE) has been running in sellers and it will be a surprise if he scores outside of that grade. (tchd 25-1)

Imprimis Tagula(IRE) has shown enough to suggest he can find a small race in nurseries. (op 12-1)

Miss Capricorn, the only debutant in the line-up, missed the break and was struggling all the way. This is a tough course to debut at and she should be capable of better in time. Official explanation: jockey said filly was never travelling (op 7-2)

3522 TOTEEXACTA H'CAP 1m 7f 195y

4:40 (4:40) (Class 4) (0-80,74) 3-Y-0+ **£5,829** (£1,734; £866; £432) **Stalls** Low

Form RPR

5360 **1** **Merrymaker**[21] 2850 6-9-9 **72** .... PatrickMathers(3) 7 79
(W M Brisbourne) *hld up: rdn and hdwy over 3f out: edgd lft and led wl ins fnl f: r.o* **9/1**

3 **2** *¾* **Behlaya (IRE)**[16] 3019 5-10-0 **74** .... J-PGuillambert 2 80
(T D Easterby) *midfield: hdwy 3f out: rdn to ld over 1f out: hdd and edgd rt wl ins fnl f: hld after* **4/1**[1]

00/5 **3** *nk* **Almah (SAF)**[58] 1800 8-9-12 **72** ....(b) FrancisNorton 1 78
(Miss Venetia Williams) *rn in snatches: chsd ldrs: sltly outpcd over 1f out: nt clr run and swtchd rt wl ins fnl f: styd on* **7/1**

0505 **4** *1 ½* **Turner**[13] 3114 5-8-4 **55** .... LiamJones(5) 3 59
(W M Brisbourne) *hld up: rdn and hdwy over 1f out: one pce ins fnl f* **4/1**[1]

6131 **5** *½* **Lake Wakatipu**[16] 2998 4-9-0 **60** .... DeanMcKeown 6 64
(M Mullineaux) *chsd ldrs: wnt 2nd over 4f out: rdn over 2f out: ev ch 1f out: no ex wl ins fnl f* **9/2**[2]

0445 **6** *nk* **Openide**[8] 3269 5-9-0 **60** .... RobbieFitzpatrick 4 63
(B W Duke) *led: hdd after 2f: remained prom: pushed along 5f out: outpcd 3f out: kpt on ins fnl f: eased whn hld towards fin* **5/1**[3]

-105 **7** *2* **Red Sun**[143] 270 9-9-2 **62** ....(t) MickyFenton 8 63
(J Mackie) *led after 2f: rdn and hung rt over 2f out: hdd over 1f out: wknd ins fnl f* **8/1**

00/0 **8** *55* **Glimmer Of Light (IRE)**[9] 3220 6-9-0 **60** .... AdrianTNicholls 5 —
(S A Brookshaw) *midfield: rdn over 3f out: wkng whn n.m.r 2f out: eased fnl f: t.o* **16/1**

3m 28.97s (-4.63) **Going Correction** -0.075s/f (Good) **8** Ran SP% **114.3**

Speed ratings (Par 105):108,107,107,106,106 106,105,77

CSF £44.83 CT £268.99 TOTE £12.20: £3.10, £1.70, £2.80; EX 53.80.

Owner The Blacktoffee Partnership **Bred** Hascombe And Valiant Studs **Trained** Great Ness, Shropshire

FOCUS

An ordinary contest and not much of a pace on with the result that anyone of five had a chance with a furlong to run. The third sets the level, backed up by the winner and fifth.

3523 TOTESPORT 0800 221 221 APPRENTICE H'CAP 7f 122y

5:15 (5:16) (Class 5) (0-70,70) 3-Y-0+ **£3,562** (£1,059; £529; £264) **Stalls** Low

Form RPR

014 **1** **Out For A Stroll**[3] 3404 7-9-5 **61** 6ex .... LiamTreadwell 10 70+
(S C Williams) *hld up: rdn and hdwy over 1f out: sn swtchd lft: r.o strly ins fnl f to ld fnl strides* **7/2**[1]

-410 **2** *nk* **Chicken Soup**[141] 504 4-9-9 **70** .... JamesO'Reilly(5) 7 78
(T J Pitt) *in tch: rdn to ld over 1f out: hdd fnl strides* **11/2**

4146 **3** *½* **Iced Diamond (IRE)**[19] 2936 7-8-11 **56** .... LiamJones(3) 5 63
(W M Brisbourne) *midfield: hdwy over 2f out: rdn over 1f out: styd on ins fnl f* **4/1**[2]

4236 **4** *nk* **Blue Empire (IRE)**[6] 3339 5-9-2 **58** .... AndrewMullen 9 64
(C R Dore) *prom: rdn to ld over 2f out: hdd over 1f out: kpt on u.p: one pce fnl strides* **9/2**[3]

0000 **5** *1* **Hypnotic**[12] 3147 4-9-3 **64** ....(t) PJBenson(5) 1 68
(D Nicholls) *in tch: rdn 2f out: kpt on same pce fnl f* **7/1**

-406 **6** *2* **Kirstys Lad**[15] 3050 4-8-2 **51** oh13 ....(b) SophieDoyle(7) 8 50
(M Mullineaux) *hld up: niggled along over 3f out: styd on ins fnl f: nt rch ldrs* **50/1**

6000 **7** *1 ½* **Queens Rhapsody**[68] 1528 6-9-1 **57** ....(p) PatrickMathers 4 52
(A Bailey) *in tch: rdn 3f out: one pce over 1f out* **14/1**

1400 **8** *2 ½* **Golden Square**[6] 3262 4-8-11 **53** ....(p) MarcHalford 3 42
(A W Carroll) *prom: rdn over 3f out: wknd 2f out: btn whn n.m.r and hmpd over 1f out* **12/1**

-503 **9** *3 ½* **Sir Loin**[12] 3155 5-8-2 **51** oh3 ....(v) DanielleMcCreery(7) 2 31
(N Tinkler) *racd keenly: sn led: hung rt and hdd over 2f out: wknd over 1f out* **14/1**

0045 **10** *1 ½* **Khetaab (IRE)**[21] 2875 4-8-4 **53** ....(b) JamesRogers(7) 11 29
(E J Alston) *sn wl bhd* **25/1**

1m 33.39s (-1.36) **Going Correction** -0.075s/f (Good) **10** Ran SP% **115.1**

Speed ratings (Par 103):103,102,102,101,100 98,97,94,91,89

CSF £22.55 CT £79.45 TOTE £4.30: £1.90, £1.70, £1.60; EX 26.00 Place 6 £23.98, Place 5 £14.13.

Owner The Nomads **Bred** Exors Of The Late Mrs F G Allen **Trained** Newmarket, Suffolk

FOCUS

A competitive handicap and a tight finish with the third and fourth setting the standard.

T/Plt: £46.30 to a £1 stake. Pool: £85,566.25. 1,348.50 winning tickets. T/Qpdt: £10.10 to a £1 stake. Pool: £3,470.60. 252.00 winning tickets. DO

3479 HAMILTON (R-H)

Saturday, July 15

OFFICIAL GOING: Good to firm (firm in places on the loop)

Wind: Light, across.

3524 SUNDAY MAIL APPRENTICE RIDERS' H'CAP (ROUND 2) 6f 5y

6:50 (6:50) (Class 6) (0-60,53) 3-Y-0+ **£2,730** (£806; £403) **Stalls** Low

Form RPR

6026 **1** **Rancho Cucamonga (IRE)**[11] 3171 4-9-13 **52** ....(b) PJMcDonald 14 62
(T D Barron) *missed break: bhd: hdwy centre to ld over 1f out: kpt on strly* **8/1**

-615 **2** *nk* **Paddywack (IRE)**[12] 3137 9-9-9 **48** ....(b) JamesMillman 16 57
(D W Chapman) *hld up centre: hdwy: hung rt and chal over 1f out: kpt on fnl f* **7/1**[3]

0002 **3** *1 ½* **Viewforth**[6] 3334 8-9-11 **53** ....(b) NeilBrown(3) 15 58
(I Semple) *prom on outside: led over 2f to over 1f out: edgd lft: one pce ins fnl f* **5/1**[2]

-000 **4** *shd* **Drury Lane (IRE)**[5] 3356 6-9-0 **39** ....(p) LeanneKershaw 9 43
(D W Chapman) *s.i.s: bhd tl kpt on fnl 2f: nrst fin* **20/1**

3600 **5** *nk* **Sundried Tomato**[6] 3334 7-8-13 **43** ....(p) BRoper(5) 4 46
(D W Chapman) *chsd ldrs: rdn over 2f out: one pce over 1f out* **25/1**

0-40 **6** *hd* **The Keep**[10] 3189 4-8-10 **40** ....(b) MarkCoumbe(5) 7 43
(R E Barr) *bhd and sn outpcd: hdwy over 2f out: no imp fnl f* **100/1**

0-64 **7** *1 ¾* **Cut Ridge (IRE)**[31] 2543 7-9-5 **44** .... KellyHarrison 5 41
(J S Wainwright) *chsd ldrs: effrt and edgd rt 2f out: sn outpcd* **14/1**

0022 **8** *hd* **Obe One**[3] 3398 6-9-10 **52** .... VictoriaBehan(3) 10 49
(D Nicholls) *midfield: drvn 1/2-way: no imp fr 2f out* **3/1**[1]

5-60 **9** *1 ¾* **Tartan Special**[46] 2112 4-9-1 **45** ....(p) PatrickDonaghy(5) 8 37
(K R Burke) *led to over 2f out: wknd over 1f out* **22/1**

-000 **10** *¾* **Stormingmichaelori**[23] 2782 3-9-1 **46** .... SladeO'Hara 3 35
(N Wilson) *w ldr tl wknd over 1f out* **66/1**

6414 **11** *shd* **Beverley Beau**[19] 2928 4-9-8 **47** .... KristinStubbs 1 36
(Mrs L Stubbs) *w ldrs tl wknd over 1f out* **11/1**

0305 **12** *1* **Underthemistletoe (IRE)**[15] 3039 4-9-1 **40** .... MichaelJStainton 2 26
(R E Barr) *dwlt: nvr on terms* **33/1**

0-00 **13** *1 ¼* **Beautiful South**[4] 3383 3-8-13 **47** .... RobbieMills(3) 13 29
(N Wilson) *cl up to 2f out: sn rdn and wknd* **100/1**

0662 **14** *½* **Smirfys Party**[16] 3003 8-9-1 **45** ....(v) WilliamCarson(5) 12 26
(W M Brisbourne) *chsd ldrs tl wknd fr 2f out* **7/1**[3]

0320 **15** *2* **Weakest Link**[31] 2544 5-9-10 **49** ....(p) StephanieHollinshead 11 24
(E J Alston) *prom: rdn over 2f out: sn wknd* **12/1**

1m 12.04s (-1.06) **Going Correction** -0.325s/f (Firm)

WFA 3 from 4yo+ 6lb **15** Ran SP% **119.8**

Speed ratings (Par 101):94,93,91,91,91 90,88,88,85,84 84,83,81,81,78

CSF £58.62 CT £251.61 TOTE £7.80: £1.90, £2.60, £2.60; EX 86.30.

Owner P D Savill **Bred** P D Savill **Trained** Maunby, N Yorks

■ The first winner on the Flat in Britain for Patrick McDonald, who is better known as a jumps rider.

FOCUS

An ordinary event in which the field raced centre to stands' side. The pace was sound and this form should stand up at a similar level.

Weakest Link Official explanation: trainer said gelding had lost a front shoe

3525 JOHN BANKS H'CAP 5f 4y

7:20 (7:21) (Class 5) (0-70,68) 3-Y-0+ **£3,886** (£1,156; £577; £288) **Stalls** Low

Form RPR

1324 **1** **Kings College Boy**[2] 3447 6-9-7 **68** ....(b) JamesReveley(7) 6 77+
(R A Fahey) *keen: cl up: led over 1f out: edgd lft ins fnl f: r.o* **10/11**[1]

0051 **2** *1 ¼* **Strawberry Patch (IRE)**[5] 3356 7-8-11 **54** 6ex ....(p) DanielTudhope(3) 3 58
(J S Goldie) *chsd ldrs: drvn 1/2-way: kpt on fnl f: tk 2nd cl home* **3/1**[2]

0356 **3** *shd* **Raccoon (IRE)**[24] 2748 6-9-7 **66** ....(v) PJMcDonald(5) 1 72+
(D W Chapman) *chsd ldrs: effrt 2f out: ch whn hung rt ins fnl f: no ex and lost 2nd cl home* **9/2**[3]

-000 4 5 **Beyond The Clouds (IRE)**[7] 3297 10-8-10 57..... MichaelJStainton(7) 4 43
(J S Wainwright) *in tch: effrt and edgd rt 2f out: sn outpcd* 12/1
060- 5 3/4 **Black Oval**[208] 6613 5-8-2 49 oh12.............. MarkCoumbe(7) 5 32
(S Parr) *led to over 1f out: sn btn* 25/1
0000 6 3 1/2 **Geordie Dancer (IRE)**[7] 3287 4-8-7 52 ow2.....(b) StephenDonohoe(5) 2 22
(A Berry) *chsd ldrs tl wknd over 2f out* 33/1
59.92 secs (-1.28) **Going Correction** -0.325s/f (Firm) 6 Ran SP% 110.0
Speed ratings (Par 103):97,95,94,86,85 80
CSF £3.64 TOTE £1.90: £1.10, £1.70; EX 3.90.
Owner The Cosmic Cases **Bred** Lady Jennifer Green **Trained** Musley Bank, N Yorks
■ The first winner on the Flat for James Reveley.
■ Stewards' Enquiry : James Reveley two-day ban: careless riding (Jul 26-27)
FOCUS
An uncompetitive event but one in which the pace was sound and the race is rated around the runner-up to latest form.

3526 SUNDAY MAIL MEDIAN AUCTION MAIDEN STKS 5f 4y
7:50 (7:50) (Class 5) 3-Y-O **£3,238** (£963; £481; £240) **Stalls** Low

Form RPR
0460 1 **Laphonic (USA)**[10] 3189 3-9-3 48.............(t) KDarley 6 51
(T J Etherington) *pressed ldr: drvn over 1f out: led ins fnl f: r.o wl* 7/1[3]
6050 2 1/2 **Signor Whippee**[19] 2939 3-9-3 44..............(b) TonyHamilton 7 49
(A Berry) *led to ins fnl f: kpt on: hld towards fin* 50/1
0-46 3 1 3/4 **The Salwick Flyer (IRE)**[78] 1272 3-8-12 52......... StephenDonohoe(5) 8 43
(A Berry) *outpcd tl hdwy over 1f out: nrst fin* 20/1
0666 4 1/2 **Musette (IRE)**[3] 3397 3-8-5 42.............. MichaelJStainton(7) 3 36
(R E Barr) *sn outpcd: hdwy and edgd rt 2f out: kpt on fnl f: no imp* 14/1
2530 5 hd **Newkeylets**[21] 2856 3-8-12 53..............(p) PaulFessey 2 35
(I Semple) *squeezed out s: outpcd tl gd hdwy fnl f: r.o wl* 11/4[2]
0-24 6 nk **Slipperfoot**[26] 2701 3-8-12 58.............. GrahamGibbons 1 34
(J J Quinn) *hung rt thrght: chsd ldrs tl outpcd over 1f out* 4/5[1]
0-00 7 3/4 **Nautico**[37] 2377 3-8-9 45.............. DanielTudhope(3) 4 31
(Miss L A Perratt) *in tch: outpcd 1/2-way: no imp fr 2f out* 50/1
0-05 8 4 **Compton Lad**[1] 3479 3-9-3 48..............(p) PatCosgrave 5 22
(D A Nolan) *keen: chsd ldrs tl wknd over 1f out* 50/1
60.06 secs (-1.14) **Going Correction** -0.325s/f (Firm) 8 Ran SP% 112.0
Speed ratings (Par 100):96,95,92,91,91 90,89,83
CSF £266.34 TOTE £7.20: £2.00, £6.40, £4.30; EX 245.00.
Owner Ownaracehorse Ltd (ownaracehorse.co.uk) **Bred** Florel Farm And Jackie McClure **Trained** Norton, N Yorks
FOCUS
A low-grade event in which the two market leaders disappointed and consequently this race took very little winning. The runner-up sets the level.

3527 SCOTTISH RACING CLAIMING STKS 1m 3f 16y
8:20 (8:20) (Class 6) 3-5-Y-O **£2,730** (£806; £403) **Stalls** High

Form RPR
051 1 **Awaken**[26] 2696 5-9-6 50.............. PhillipMakin 3 61
(Miss Tracy Waggott) *chsd ldrs: smooth hdwy over 3f out: led 2f out: rdn out* 2/1[1]
0265 2 3 **Ganymede**[8] 3270 5-9-4 57..............(p) StephenDonohoe(5) 4 59
(J G M O'Shea) *hld up in tch: hdwy 3f out: chsd wnr over 1f out: kpt on ins fnl f* 3/1[2]
0040 3 2 1/2 **Myrtle Bay (IRE)**[8] 3249 3-8-13 65..............(v[1]) PatCosgrave 2 57
(K R Burke) *cl up: led briefly over 2f out: no ex over 1f out* 2/1[1]
400- 4 1 3/4 **United Spirit (IRE)**[32] 5206 5-9-3 52.............. PaulMulrennan 1 46
(Jedd O'Keeffe) *led to over 2f out: wknd over 1f out* 4/1[3]
2m 22.01s (-4.25) **Going Correction** -0.325s/f (Firm)
WFA 3 from 4yo+ 12lb 4 Ran SP% 111.7
Speed ratings (Par 101):102,99,98,96
CSF £8.36 TOTE £2.20; EX 4.70.
Owner Miss T Waggott **Bred** Juddmonte Farms **Trained** Spennymoor, Co Durham
FOCUS
An uncompetitive race in which the pace was only fair and the form does not look solid.

3528 SUNDAY MAIL H'CAP 1m 65y
8:50 (8:52) (Class 4) (0-80,78) 3-Y-O+ **£5,505** (£1,637; £818; £408) **Stalls** High

Form RPR
-101 1 **Mistress Twister**[20] 2892 5-9-5 73.............. PaulFessey 2 81
(T D Barron) *in tch: rdn and outpcd over 3f out: rallied over 1f out: styd on wl to ld nr fin* 6/4[1]
0155 2 hd **Dark Charm (FR)**[21] 2853 7-9-2 70..............(p) TonyHamilton 4 77
(R A Fahey) *chsd ldrs: effrt over 2f out: kpt on u.p towards fin* 10/3[2]
1500 3 shd **Wahoo Sam (USA)**[17] 2974 6-9-5 73.............. CatherineGannon 5 80
(K A Ryan) *led and clr to 1/2-way: rdn 2f out: kpt on: hdd towards fin* 7/2[3]
0-00 4 5 **Coalpark (IRE)**[42] 2239 3-8-12 75.............. KDarley 1 69
(M Johnston) *chsd ldr: effrt over 2f out: sn outpcd* 8/1
20-5 5 3 1/2 **Mayadeen (IRE)**[7] 3289 4-9-5 78.............. StephenDonohoe(5) 3 65
(J G M O'Shea) *bhd: outpcd 1/2-way: nvr on terms* 11/2
1m 45.06s (-4.24) **Going Correction** -0.325s/f (Firm)
WFA 3 from 4yo+ 9lb 5 Ran SP% 111.8
Speed ratings (Par 105):108,107,107,102,99
CSF £6.89 TOTE £2.30: £1.60, £2.40; EX 5.60.
Owner Dave Scott **Bred** Mrs F A Veasey **Trained** Maunby, N Yorks
■ Stewards' Enquiry : Catherine Gannon caution: used whip in the incorrect place
FOCUS
An ordinary event but a decent gallop and the form is rated at face value, despite slight doubts over the placed horses.

3529 HAMILTON PARK SUPER SIX H'CAP 1m 65y
9:20 (9:20) (Class 6) (0-60,58) 3-Y-O **£2,730** (£806; £403) **Stalls** High

Form RPR
4001 1 **Noble Nova**[6] 3329 3-9-6 57 6ex.............. KDarley 1 62+
(M R Channon) *prom: hdwy to ld over 2f out: edgd rt: drvn out* 6/4[2]
0006 2 3 **The Flying Peach**[7] 3288 3-8-2 39 oh5.............. CatherineGannon 6 37
(W M Brisbourne) *hld up in tch: effrt and chsd wnr over 1f out: edgd rt: no imp fnl f* 16/1
0-01 3 3 **Walnut Grove**[23] 2782 3-9-1 55.............. BenSwarbrick(3) 3 46
(T D Barron) *trckd ldrs: effrt 3f out: edgd rt and outpcd fr 2f out* 11/8[1]
4000 4 1 1/2 **Thornton Princess**[5] 3357 3-8-9 46..............(p) PaulMulrennan 5 34
(B S Rothwell) *set decent gallop to over 2f out: sn no ex* 12/1
5044 5 7 **Joking John**[12] 3138 3-7-13 41.............. LeanneKershaw(5) 4 13
(C W Fairhurst) *bolted to post: keen: pressed ldr tl wknd fr 3f out* 7/1[3]
00-0 6 5 **Isharram (IRE)**[64] 1633 3-8-2 39 oh3.............. PaulFessey 7 —
(A Berry) *bhd: struggling 1/2-way: nvr on terms* 20/1
1m 47.04s (-2.26) **Going Correction** -0.325s/f (Firm) 6 Ran SP% 112.9
Speed ratings (Par 98):98,95,92,90,83 78
CSF £24.15 CT £38.70 TOTE £2.10: £1.90, £3.70; EX 39.20 Place 6 £140.69, Place 5 £53.51.
Owner M Channon **Bred** Bloodhorse International Limited **Trained** West Ilsley, Berks
FOCUS
Another ordinary handicap with a number of non-runners in which the market leader proved a bit of a disappointment and the winner is rated to his juvenile form.
T/Plt: £334.00 to a £1 stake. Pool: £59,754.10. 130.60 winning tickets. T/Qpdt: £66.60 to a £1 stake. Pool: £3,010.30. 33.40 winning tickets. RY

3485 LINGFIELD (L-H)
Saturday, July 15

OFFICIAL GOING: Standard
Transferred from Ascot
Wind: Virtually nil. Weather: Sunny.

3530 PLAY BACKGAMMON AT LADBROKES.COM NURSERY 6f (P)
2:00 (2:00) (Class 4) 2-Y-O **£4,857** (£1,445; £722; £360) **Stalls** Low

Form RPR
621 1 **Market Day**[14] 3096 2-9-4 84.............. NickyMackay 4 98+
(L M Cumani) *trckd ldrs: rdn and hdwy 2f out: led 1f out: sn clr: pushed out: comf* 11/10[1]
0364 2 3 **High Style**[13] 3117 2-8-8 74.............. RyanMoore 8 76
(R Hannon) *wnt rt and lost grnd s: sn in tch: rdn 2f out: styd on wl fnl f: wnt 2nd nr fin: no ch w wnr* 6/1[2]
0403 3 1 **Tom Paris**[13] 3117 2-8-1 67..............(b) FrancisFerris 1 66
(W R Muir) *led: hrd rdn 2f out: hdd 1f out: sn outpcd: lost 2nd nr fin* 12/1[3]
4310 4 1/2 **Hythe Bay**[24] 2743 2-9-1 81.............. LDettori 7 79
(R T Phillips) *hld up in rr: rdn and effrt 2f out: no imp tl kpt on last 100 yds* 6/1[2]
3140 5 1 **Three Decades (IRE)**[3] 3415 2-9-5 90.............. DerekNolan(5) 3 85
(C A Cyzer) *chsd ldr 4f out tl 1f out: wknd u.p fnl f* 14/1
1460 6 1 3/4 **Hucking Hill (IRE)**[45] 2127 2-8-11 77.............. JimmyFortune 2 66
(J R Best) *chsd ldrs: rdn over 2f out: kpt on onepced* 14/1
1045 7 1 1/2 **Ask Don't Tell (IRE)**[9] 3216 2-7-12 64 oh1.............. DavidKinsella 6 49
(Tom Dascombe) *hung rt thrght: chsd ldrs tl rdn and wknd 2f out* 20/1
6130 8 16 **Beckenham's Secret**[13] 3117 2-8-12 78.............. JamieSpencer 5 15
(B R Millman) *chsd ldr tl 4f out: wknd wl over 2f out: eased fnl f: t.o* 6/1[2]
1m 14.12s (1.31) **Going Correction** -0.025s/f (Stan) 8 Ran SP% 116.3
Speed ratings (Par 96):90,86,84,84,82 80,78,57
CSF £8.31 CT £53.49 TOTE £1.70: £1.10, £1.80, £2.60; EX 7.60 Trifecta £61.70 Pool: £121.79 - 1.40 winning units..
Owner Allevamento Gialloblu **Bred** Biddestone Stud **Trained** Newmarket, Suffolk
FOCUS
Market Day looked different class here and can hold her own in Listed races and possibly better. The second and third ran close to their Windsor form and give the form a solid feel. The official ratings shown next to each horse are estimated and for information purposes only.
NOTEBOOK
Market Day ◆, off the mark at the third attempt over six furlongs on Wolverhampton's Polytrack on her previous start, was different class to this lot on her handicap debut and followed up in good style. She looks Listed class at least and must be kept on the right side of. (tchd 5-4)
High Style lost his chance with a very slow start and probably did well to get up for second near the line, but he is highly unlikely to have beaten the winner had he got away on terms, such was that one's superiority. (op 7-1)
Tom Paris ran a good race off his light weight under a positive ride, but just failed to confirm recent Windsor placings with slow-starting High Style.
Hythe Bay, returned to a more sensible grade and stepped back up in trip, stayed on widest of all without ever looking like winning. (tchd 11-2)
Three Decades(IRE) had it all to do off top weight, and would most likely have found this coming too soon in any case, having run down the field in the Cherry Hinton just three days earlier.
Ask Don't Tell(IRE) Official explanation: jockey said filly hung right-handed throughout

3531 BET IN PLAY AT LADBROKES.COM NOVICE STKS 7f (P)
2:35 (2:36) (Class 4) 2-Y-O **£4,857** (£1,445; £722; £360) **Stalls** Low

Form RPR
01 1 **Norisan**[21] 2867 2-9-5 .... RichardHughes 4 92
(R Hannon) *chsd ldr tl over 1f out: rdn to ld ins fnl f: drvn out* 7/4[1]
010 2 3/4 **Johannesburg Jack (IRE)**[25] 2719 2-9-5 .... RyanMoore 6 90
(H Morrison) *settled in tch: rdn and effrt over 2f out: led over 1f out: hdd ins fnl f: onepced* 11/4[2]
4105 3 5 **Deadshot Keen (IRE)**[18] 2960 2-9-0 .... LDettori 2 72
(B J Meehan) *led tl rdn and hdd over 1f out: wknd fnl f* 11/4[2]
06 4 2 **Bobbish**[9] 3210 2-8-12 .... JimmyFortune 1 65
(N A Callaghan) *s.s: racd in last pair: lost tch over 2f out: wnt 4th nr fin* 25/1
5 1/2 **Orange Pekoe (USA)** 2-8-8 .... NickyMackay 5 60
(P Mitchell) *s.s: racd in last pair: pushed along 4f out: lost tch over 2f out* 25/1
1 6 shd **Fuji (IRE)**[15] 3031 2-9-2 .... JamieSpencer 3 67
(M L W Bell) *t.k.h: trckd ldrs: rdn 3f out: wknd 2f out: lost 2 pls nr fin* 5/1[3]
1m 26.57s (0.68) **Going Correction** -0.025s/f (Stan) 6 Ran SP% 114.1
Speed ratings (Par 96):95,94,88,86,85 85
CSF £7.06 TOTE £2.80: £1.60, £1.80; EX 9.60.
Owner The Waney Racing Group Inc **Bred** The National Stud Owner Breeders Club Ltd **Trained** East Everleigh, Wilts
FOCUS
A reasonable enough novice event, featuring a couple of horses who ran at Royal Ascot, as well as some form that tied in very closely with the Group 2 Superlative Stakes from the July Meeting. Only four of the six runners could be seriously considered beforehand, but a solid little race nevertheless.
NOTEBOOK
Norisan, who dead-heated with subsequent Superlative Stakes winner Halicarnassus in a seven-furlong maiden on the July course on his previous start, had an obvious chance on that form and proved good enough to follow up, despite not looking comfortable on the turning track. He came a little wide on the bend and just took a few strides to really get going, but he was well on top in the end. Given both this success, and how his maiden has worked out, his connections are more than entitled to step him up in grade next time. (op 15-8 tchd 2-1)
Johannesburg Jack(IRE), off the mark at Brighton before running 13th of 21 in the Coventry Stakes at Royal Ascot, seemed to have every chance and was just held. He finished clear of the remainder and is clearly a useful sort, so he should continue to go well in races like this one and nurseries. (op 10-3)

Deadshot Keen(IRE), fifth of nine in a Listed race at Newbury on his previous start having finished behind Johannesburg Jack in the Coventry Stakes at Royal Ascot, was left behind by the front two and did not improve for the step up to seven furlongs. (op 3-1 tchd 10-3)
Bobbish never posed a threat, but he is now eligible for nurseries and could do better. (op 20-1)
Orange Pekoe(USA) ◆, a 50,000gns half-brother to eight winners, including prolific US sprint winner First Watch, out of a top-class prolific six to ten-furlong winner in the US, needed this experience and was not given a hard time. He should develop into a nice sort in time; he is certainly bred to.
Fuji(IRE) would have found this a lot tougher than the Folkestone maiden he won on his debut, but did not fire in any case. (op 4-1)

3532 180+ CASINO GAMES AT LADBROKESCASINO.COM H'CAP 1m (P)
3:10 (3:11) (Class 4) (0-85,85) 3-Y-0+ **£6,477** (£1,927; £963; £481) **Stalls** High

Form				RPR
01	**1**		**Royal Oath (USA)**[36] 2411 3-8-12 **85**..........................(t) JimmyFortune 6 (J H M Gosden) *slowly away: sn rcvrd and settled midfield: hdwy over 2f out: rdn to ld 1f out: sn clr: rdn out* **2/1**[1]	102+
0304	**2**	*3*	**Mina A Salem**[35] 2443 4-9-5 **83**.. RyanMoore 2 (C E Brittain) *slowly away: sn chsng ldrs: rdn and outpcd over 1f out: kpt on fnl f: wnt 2nd on line: no ch w wnr* **12/1**	93
0-11	**3**	*shd*	**Bee Stinger**[13] 3121 4-8-12 **76**...................................... JamieSpencer 11 (I A Wood) *chsd ldrs early: stdd and rr of main gp 4f out: rdn and hdwy over 2f out: styd on: wnt 3rd on line: no ch w wnr* **7/2**[2]	86
5321	**4**	*shd*	**Phluke**[9] 3212 5-9-2 **80**.. StephenCarson 3 (R F Johnson Houghton) *chsd ldr tl rdn to ld 2f out: hdd 1f out: sn outpcd: lost 2 pls on line* **20/1**	90
1011	**5**	*2 ½*	**Samuel Charles**[29] 2614 8-9-2 **80**... LDettori 9 (C R Dore) *hld up on outer: bhd and rdn 3f out: kpt on fnl f: n.d* **6/1**[3]	84
0001	**6**	*hd*	**Hits Only Heaven (IRE)**[17] 2983 4-9-3 **84**......(e) SilvestreDeSousa(3) 12 (D Nicholls) *prom on outside: rdn 2f out: sn outpcd* **15/2**	88
5642	**7**	*1 ¾*	**Glencalvie (IRE)**[17] 2983 5-9-1 **79**..............................(v) KerrinMcEvoy 4 (J Akehurst) *chsd ldrs on outer: rdn 3f out: wknd wl over 1f out* **15/2**	79
3220	**8**	*½*	**Merrymadcap (IRE)**[33] 2510 4-9-0 **78**............................ NickyMackay 8 (M Blanshard) *hld up bhd: bdly hmpd and stmbld over 2f out: keeping on onepced whn nt clr run 1f out: n.d* **16/1**	77+
2021	**9**	*1*	**Desert Dreamer (IRE)**[6] 3337 5-9-5 **83** 5ex..................... SebSanders 5 (P R Chamings) *steaded s: hld up midfield on inner: hmpd over 2f out: n.d after* **20/1**	79+
2006	**10**	*5*	**Trifti**[73] 1410 5-8-13 **82**... DerekNolan(5) 10 (C A Cyzer) *hld up in rr: hmpd over 2f out: no ch after* **33/1**	67+
5015	**11**	*1 ¼*	**Purus (IRE)**[9] 3211 4-9-4 **82**.. RichardHughes 1 (P Mitchell) *led tl rdn and hdd 2f out: sn wknd: eased ins fnl f* **16/1**	64
	12	*18*	**Black Chief (SWE)**[362] 5-8-13 **77**...............................(vt[1]) FJohansson 7 (R A Kvisla) *s.s: detached last after 2f: t.o and eased fnl f* **66/1**	18

1m 37.55s (-1.88) **Going Correction** -0.025s/f (Stan)
WFA 3 from 4yo+ 9lb **12** Ran SP% **127.9**
Speed ratings (Par 105):108,105,104,104,102 102,100,99,98,93 92,74
CSF £30.99 CT £89.28 TOTE £3.70: £1.60, £3.60, £1.90; EX 49.80 Trifecta £59.70 Pool: £269.24 - 3.20 winning units..
Owner W S Farish & William S Farish Jnr **Bred** Farish And Farish Llc **Trained** Newmarket, Suffolk
■ Stewards' Enquiry : Jimmy Fortune two-day ban: careless riding (Jul 26-27)

FOCUS
A very competitive race for the grade, for the 12 runners had won 17 races between them already this season, and half the field scored last time. Strong form.
Glencalvie(IRE) Official explanation: jockey said gelding was never travelling
Merrymadcap(IRE) Official explanation: jockey said gelding clipped heels approaching bend
Purus(IRE) Official explanation: jockey said gelding hung left

3533 24 HOUR LADBROKES BETTING ON 0800 777 888 STKS (HERITAGE H'CAP) 2m (P)
3:45 (3:46) (Class 2) (0-105,104) 3-Y-0+
£31,160 (£9,330; £4,665; £2,335; £1,165; £585) **Stalls** Low

Form				RPR
4110	**1**		**Finalmente**[14] 3078 4-8-13 **93**.. LDettori 6 (N A Callaghan) *settled in tch: prog to chse ldng trio over 3f out: sn rdn: styd on strly ins fnl f to ld nr fin* **8/1**	104
-020	**2**	*nk*	**Elusive Dream**[25] 2723 5-8-11 **91**.................................... SebSanders 11 (Sir Mark Prescott) *pushed up to ld after 1f: hrd pressed and rdn wl over 2f out: battled on gamely tl hdd and no ex nr fin* **9/2**[1]	102
5610	**3**	*2*	**Bulwark (IRE)**[14] 3078 4-9-2 **96**.............................(be) KerrinMcEvoy 4 (Mrs A J Perrett) *hld up in midfield: smooth hdwy over 4f out: sn chsng ldng pair: rdn 2f out: hung lft and fnd little 1f out: wnt 3rd nr fin* **5/1**[2]	105
0-30	**4**	*nk*	**Odiham**[14] 3078 5-9-0 **94**..(v) NickyMackay 10 (H Morrison) *w.w in midfield: hdwy to chse ldr over 3f out: rdn to chal 2f out: wknd ins fnl f* **10/1**	102
/101	**5**	*8*	**Prins Willem (IRE)**[10] 3203 7-8-11 **91**.....................(vt) JamieSpencer 13 (J R Fanshawe) *hld up in rr: hdwy 5f out: plld outside and hrd rdn 3f out: sn wl outpcd* **13/2**[3]	90
0/64	**6**	*½*	**Dorothy's Friend**[14] 3078 6-8-10 **90**............................... JimmyFortune 2 (R Charlton) *led for 1f: prom: pushed up to press ldr 10f out: rdn over 3f out: sn wknd* **9/2**[1]	88
5102	**7**	*¾*	**Solent (IRE)**[22] 2817 4-9-3 **97**.. RichardHughes 8 (R Hannon) *settled in midfield: effrt u.p over 4f out: outpcd over 2f out* **12/1**	94
1425	**8**	*14*	**Mceldowney**[25] 2723 4-8-3 **86**............................... SilvestreDeSousa(3) 1 (M Johnston) *settled in midfield: lost pl 6f out: no ch after: t.o* **12/1**	66
5310	**9**	*shd*	**Alfie Noakes**[21] 2848 4-8-8 **88**.. JimCrowley 14 (Mrs A J Perrett) *hld up bhd: hdwy 6f out: rdn over 4f out: sn struggling: t.o* **16/1**	68
0021	**10**	*¾*	**Ski Jump (USA)**[29] 2625 6-8-2 **82**..........................(v) AdrianMcCarthy 3 (R A Fahey) *chsd ldrs tl rdn and wknd over 4f out: t.o* **16/1**	61
0	**11**	*4*	**Freddy (ARG)**[14] 3093 7-8-2 **82**.....................................(t) FrancisFerris 5 (Ernst Oertel) *hld up: wl bhd: rdn 6f out: sn no ch: t.o* **66/1**	57
03-0	**12**	*7*	**Inchnadamph**[88] 1071 6-8-5 **85**..............................(t) FergusSweeney 7 (T J Fitzgerald) *a bhd: rdn and lost tch 6f out: t.o* **25/1**	51
0/0-	**13**	*1*	**Unleash (USA)**[17] 1465 7-9-1 **95**....................................... VinceSlattery 9 (P J Hobbs) *midfield tl rdn and lost pl 7f out: t.o last 3f* **50/1**	60
-246	**14**	*2*	**Dancing Bay**[21] 2849 9-9-10 **104**.. RyanMoore 12 (N J Henderson) *t.k.h: chsd ldr after 3f tl 10f out: sn rdn and lost pl: t.o and eased last 3f* **16/1**	67

3m 22.39s (-6.40) **Going Correction** -0.025s/f (Stan) **14** Ran SP% **126.9**
Speed ratings (Par 109):115,114,113,113,109 109,109,102,102,101 99,96,95,94
CSF £45.85 CT £208.26 TOTE £10.80: £3.20, £2.20, £2.80; EX 85.50 Trifecta £461.30 Part won. Pool: £649.74 - 0.70 winning units..
Owner Edward M Kirtland **Bred** Helshaw Grange Stud Ltd **Trained** Newmarket, Suffolk

FOCUS
As good a staying handicap as we've seen on the all weather, and run at a strong pace pretty much throughout. The winning time was smart for the grade, a Polytrack course record for the trip. It paid to stay reasonably handy, for of those held up early, only Bulwark managed to get involved.

NOTEBOOK
Finalmente ◆ did not enjoy a clear run when only mid-division in the Northumberland Plate on his last outing, but he had previously looked progressive and got back on track with a narrow victory. He still had a bit to do in the last half mile, and did not seem at all happy negotiating the final bend, but he came into his own in the straight and got up virtually on the line. This was a very good effort considering he did not appear totally at home on the track and he promises to do even better returned to a more galloping course. He could be interesting if turning up in something like the Ebor, and later in the season the Cesarewitch appeals as a suitable target. (tchd 17-2 in a place)
Elusive Dream, seventh in the Ascot Stakes on his previous start, made this a good test under a really positive ride and was only just denied. He deserves to get his head back in front, but things will not get any easier if the Handicapper raises his turf mark off the back of this effort. (op 11-2)
Bulwark(IRE), perhaps a little unlucky when two places in front of Finalmente in the Northumberland Plate on his previous start, seemed to be produced with every chance this time but hung a little under pressure and could not confirm form with that rival. Although some may question whether he went through with his effort, he still fared the best of those held up early by some way and, in making his move into a challenging position, he may have been forced to use up too much energy. He obviously has his quirks, but still gives the impression there is a decent prize to be won with him when everything falls right. (tchd 11-2)
Odiham, 15th of 20 in the Northumberland Plate on his previous start, swapped the blinkers for a visor and looked the most likely winner when ranging upsides Elusive Dream on the turn into the straight, but he did not appear to go through with his effort and his jockey had to stop riding late on due to a slipped saddle. But for that he would probably have finished third. On this evidence, even allowing for the mishap with the tack, he looks one to have reservations about. Official explanation: jockey said saddle slipped (op 8-1)
Prins Willem(IRE), the winner of his last two outings on Polytrack, was not at his best off a 4lb higher mark than when winning at Kempton on his previous start, but he was held up early and only Bulwark got into the contest having raced in a similar position early. (op 6-1)
Dorothy's Friend tried to ensure Elusive Dream did not get an easy time of things up front, but may have compromised his own chance in doing so and was a long way below the form he showed when fourth in the Northumberland Plate on his previous start. Connections reckon he needs a more galloping track. (op 4-1 tchd 5-1)
Solent(IRE) Official explanation: jockey said colt hung left throughout
Dancing Bay Official explanation: jockey said gelding was never travelling

3534 LADBROKES SUMMER MILE STKS (GROUP 3) 1m (P)
4:15 (4:17) (Class 1) 4-Y-0+
£56,780 (£21,520; £10,770; £5,370; £2,690; £1,350) **Stalls** High

Form				RPR
110-	**1**		**Echo Of Light**[273] 5902 4-9-1 110...................................... KerrinMcEvoy 5 (Saeed Bin Suroor) *sn led: mde rest: styd on strly over 1f out: in command fnl f* **7/1**	121+
/0-1	**2**	*2 ½*	**Satchem (IRE)**[35] 2431 4-9-1 112...(t) LDettori 12 (Saeed Bin Suroor) *chsd ldrs on outside: chsd wnr wl over 3f out: rdn 2f out: outpcd by wnr* **3/1**[2]	114
0-60	**3**	*1 ¼*	**Notability (IRE)**[23] 2776 4-9-1 99................................... PhilipRobinson 8 (M A Jarvis) *chsd ldr tl over 3f out: riden over 2f out: onepced whn edgd lft ins fnl f* **11/1**	111
1022	**4**	*½*	**Stronghold**[24] 2742 4-9-1 115.. RichardHughes 3 (J H M Gosden) *chsd ldrs on inner: rdn over 2f out: keeping on onepced whn swtchd ins fnl f: kpt on* **7/4**[1]	110+
4-12	**5**	*hd*	**Spectait**[47] 2086 4-9-1 98.. SebSanders 11 (Sir Mark Prescott) *sn bustled along: rr in tch: styd on u.p fnl f: n.d* **8/1**	109
2461	**6**	*1*	**Suggestive**[14] 3086 8-9-1 111......................................(b) NickyMackay 7 (W J Haggas) *rr: rdn 4f out: effrt on outer 3f out: wknd fnl f* **12/1**	107
2330	**7**	*1 ½*	**Royal Alchemist**[7] 3314 4-8-12 103.............................. MichaelTebbutt 9 (B J Meehan) *chsd ldrs: rdn 2f out: wknd 1f out* **20/1**	101
2263	**8**	*1*	**Boule D'Or (IRE)**[2] 3432 5-9-1 105...................................... DeanCorby 2 (J Akehurst) *stated slowly: bhd: rdn 3f out: nvr on terms* **20/1**	101
6220	**9**	*1 ¾*	**Babodana**[24] 2742 6-9-1 105.. JimmyFortune 4 (M H Tompkins) *midfield wl in tch: rdn over 2f out: sn outpcd* **16/1**	97
3-01	**10**	*1*	**Cesare**[24] 2742 5-9-1 102.. JamieSpencer 10 (J R Fanshawe) *w.w in midfield on outer: hdwy 3f out: hrd rdn 2f out: wknd over 1f out: eased ins fnl f* **5/1**[3]	95+
0-00	**11**	*23*	**Gig Harbor**[29] 2621 7-9-1 97... DavidKinsella 6 (Miss E C Lavelle) *s.s: rdn and lost tch 4f out: t.o* **66/1**	42

1m 36.23s (-3.20) **Going Correction** -0.025s/f (Stan) course record **11** Ran SP% **134.6**
Speed ratings (Par 113):115,112,111,110,110 109,108,107,105,104 81
CSF £32.09 TOTE £9.60: £3.00, £2.00, £2.60; EX 44.40 Trifecta £325.80 Pool: £504.80 - 1.10 winning units..
Owner Godolphin **Bred** Kilcarn Stud **Trained** Newmarket, Suffolk
■ This was run last year as the Ladbrokes Silver Trophy.

FOCUS
The second running of this race on the all-weather, and unfortunately the last, as it reverts to Ascot next year. It attracted a classy field, but Echo Of Light led from start to finish at a good pace and came nicely clear, looking a natural for this surface. The strong handicap form of the third to the fifth give the form credibility, and the winning time was very solid for a Group 3.

NOTEBOOK
Echo Of Light ◆, the winner of a maiden and a conditions race before going off far too fast when seemingly making the pace for a stablemate in the Champion Stakes on his final start last term, led at a good, but more sensible gallop this time and was able to sustain his effort right the way to the line, ultimately winning in good style. The drop back to a mile did not bother him in the slightest and this was a cracking performance considering he was reappearing off the back of a 273-day break for a stable whose horses may only just be hitting top form. He is entered in both the Celebration Mile and International Stakes but, while those sorts of races are quite a step up from this level, he certainly deserves his chance in a higher grade, especially with improvement likely. He will probably be best, though, with a bit of cut in the ground. (tchd 15-2)
Satchem(IRE), a very narrow winner of a Goodwood Listed race on his reappearance, ran well stepped up in class but was no match for his impressive stablemate. This was a good effort, but he is obviously going to have to find improvement to make the grade at a higher level. (after 4-1 in places tchd 7-2 in places)
Notability(IRE) ◆, a major disappointment in the Buckingham Palace Stakes at Royal Ascot when the ground was probably too fast for his liking, appreciated the switch to this much kinder surface and showed what he is capable of. He has always looked pattern-class in the making and this effort confirms he is well worth his place in these sorts of races/Listed company. However, he is entered in a valuable mile handicap at Goodwood and, with the weights already decided for that contest, he could find himself on an attractive mark, although a bit of cut in the ground is seemingly an absolute must. (op 10-1)
Stronghold, just denied in the Royal Hunt Cup on his previous start, ran respectably stepped up to Group company for the first time, but could not reverse Goodwood placings with Satchem from two starts back. He was a little short of room when beginning to stay on, but was by no means unlucky. (op 5-2 tchd 11-4 and 3-1 in a place)

Spectait ◆ was beaten at odds on at Sandown when last seen 47-days previously, but is much better than he showed there and confirmed that with a fine effort stepped up to Group company. He finished well having not had the greatest of runs through when trying to pick and there could be even better to come yet. He is entered in both the International Stakes Handicap at Ascot and a valuable mile handicap at Goodwood and, with the weights already set, he could look on a very attractive mark if turning up for either/both of those, although he needs easy ground. (op 7-1)
Suggestive, an impressive winner at Wolverhampton on his only previous try on Polytrack, could not repeat the form he showed to win the Criterion Stakes at Newmarket on his previous start. (op 14-1)
Royal Alchemist was turned out very quickly after making the pace for David Junior in the Eclipse. (op 25-1)
Cesare, a winner over course and distance on his only previous try on Polytrack, was below the form he showed when beating Stronghold a neck in the Royal Hunt Cup on his previous start, but then he was 14lb worse off with that rival. (tchd 11-2)

3535 PLAY POKER AT LADBROKES.COM H'CAP — 5f (P)

4:50 (4:51) (Class 2) (0-105,100) 3-Y-0+

£12,464 (£3,732; £1,866; £934; £466; £234) **Stalls** High

Form				RPR
3256	**1**		**Green Manalishi**[13] 3124 5-9-10 **99** .... LDettori 10 (D W P Arbuthnot) *w.w in tch: hdwy over 2f out: rdn to ld ins fnl f: r.o wl* **7/2**[2]	108
0000	**2**	¾	**Texas Gold**[21] 2847 8-9-9 **98** .... KerrinMcEvoy 8 (W R Muir) *hld up in tch: rdn 2f out: carried hd awkwardly and fnd little tl styd on strly last 100 yds: nt rch wnr* **5/1**[3]	105
2010	**3**	*nk*	**Trinculo (IRE)**[52] 1936 9-8-12 **90** .... SilvestreDeSousa(3) 5 (D Nicholls) *led for 1f: chsd ldr: ev ch 1f out: unable qck u.p* **8/1**	96
6400	**4**	*hd*	**Saabiq (USA)**[24] 2744 3-8-12 **92** .... JamieSpencer 3 (C E Brittain) *s.s: hld up bhd: rdn and styd on wl fnl f: nvr nrr* **6/1**	95+
4360	**5**	*nk*	**Cape Royal**[8] 3251 6-9-4 **93** ....(b) RyanMoore 7 (J M Bradley) *led after 1f: edgd rt u.p 1f out: hdd ins fnl f: one pce* **8/1**	97
6010	**6**	*hd*	**Graze On**[8] 3251 4-9-3 **92** ....(b) AdrianMcCarthy 6 (R A Harris) *chsd ldrs: rdn 2f out: styng on one pce whn squeezed out ins fnl f* **14/1**	95+
30-0	**7**	½	**Classic Encounter (IRE)**[70] 1485 3-9-6 **100** .... RichardHughes 9 (D M Simcock) *t.k.h: hld up in rr: rdn 2f out: kpt on ins fnl f: nt rch ldrs* **20/1**	99
2300	**8**	*hd*	**Judd Street**[14] 3092 4-9-5 **94** ....(t) StephenCarson 1 (R F Johnson Houghton) *in tch on inner: rdn and effrt 2f out: kpt on one pce fnl f* **10/3**[1]	94
	9	2	**Maxim's (ARG)**[247] 5-9-8 **97** ....(t) FJohansson 4 (R A Kvisla) *chsd ldrs rdn 2f out: wknd wl ins fnl f* **40/1**	90
060-	**10**	9	**Dance Night (IRE)**[301] 5288 4-9-6 **95** .... JimmyFortune 2 (R Charlton) *hung rt thrght: wl bhd after 2f: t.o and eased st* **16/1**	56

59.90 secs (0.12) **Going Correction** -0.025s/f (Stan)
WFA 3 from 4yo+ 5lb **10** Ran SP% **118.2**
Speed ratings (Par 109):98,96,96,96,95 95,94,94,90,76
CSF £21.82 CT £135.02 TOTE £3.40: £2.00, £1.60, £3.60; EX 15.50 Trifecta £196.50 Pool: £304.53 - 1.10 winning units..
Owner Derrick C Broomfield **Bred** E Aldridge **Trained** Upper Lambourn, Berks

FOCUS
A very competitive sprint handicap, but they finished in a bunch behind Green Manalishi, who won in good style, and the winning time was moderate for a race of this class.

NOTEBOOK
Green Manalishi, sixth of eight in a good Listed sprint at the Curragh on his previous start, appreciated the return to handicap company and, always well placed by the former champion jockey, picked up well to win pretty nicely - a good bit of riding from stall ten of ten. He should continue to go well and could give a good account of himself in something like the Hong Kong Jockey Club Sprint Stakes at Ascot. (op 3-1 tchd 11-4 and 4-1 in a place)
Texas Gold, second in this race last year off a 2lb lower mark, ran his best race of the season so far without ever really looking like winning. There should be plenty more to come and the Stewards' Cup is his main aim. (op 6-1)
Trinculo(IRE), returning from a 52-day break, ran an honest race under a positive ride and is entitled to be even sharper next time. (op 7-1)
Saabiq(USA) ◆, without the cheekpieces and dropped back from a mile to try five furlongs for the first time, found herself well back after missing the break, but she had the necessary speed to stay in touch and would have been even closer had she got a gap when initially staying on in the straight. Now she has proven her effectiveness as a sprinter, her connections should have plenty more options. Official explanation: jockey said filly jumped awkwardly out of stalls (op 8-1)
Cape Royal helped force the pace with Trinculo and can have few excuses. (op 9-1)
Graze On did not appear to have any major excuses.
Classic Encounter(IRE) ◆, making both his handicap and Polytrack debut off the back of a 70-day break, did well to finish so close given how keenly he raced. He could be pretty decent if learning to settle.
Judd Street, the winner of his last three starts on Lingfield's Polytrack, failed to fire with a tongue-tie fitted for the first time. (op 11-4)
Dance Night(IRE) Official explanation: jockey said colt hung right throughout

3536 PLAY BINGO AT LADBROKES.COM H'CAP — 6f (P)

5:20 (5:20) (Class 5) (0-70,72) 3-Y-0+ **£3,238** (£963; £481; £240) **Stalls** Low

Form				RPR
5210	**1**		**Russian Rocket (IRE)**[14] 3094 4-9-7 **64** .... KerrinMcEvoy 7 (Mrs C A Dunnett) *trckd ldrs: rdn to ld 1f out: hld on wl nr fin* **5/1**[2]	74
1130	**2**	½	**Up Tempo (IRE)**[16] 3012 8-9-6 **68** ....(b) TravisBlock(5) 4 (C R Dore) *bhd: rdn 3f out: styd on strly ins fnl f: nrst fin* **8/1**	76
4640	**3**	1	**Vindication**[14] 3089 6-9-4 **61** ....(v) JamieSpencer 3 (R M H Cowell) *stdd s: hld up: hdwy to trck ldrs 3f out: ev ch 1f out: fnd little u.p fnl f* **11/2**[3]	66
0002	**4**	*nk*	**Seneschal**[3] 3405 5-9-7 **64** .... LDettori 10 (A B Haynes) *w.w in tch: rdn and effrt 2f out: kpt on onepced ins fnl f* **5/2**[1]	68
2503	**5**	1 ¼	**A Teen**[10] 3204 8-8-7 **53** oh1 ow2 .... DeanCorby(3) 6 (P Howling) *bhd: rdn over 2f out: kpt on last 100 yds: n.d* **25/1**	53
5600	**6**	*shd*	**Attitude Annie**[8] 3267 3-8-5 **54** .... PaulDoe 12 (S Dow) *drvn to go prom: lft in ld after 1f: rdn 3f out: hdd 1f out: wknd last 100 yds* **33/1**	53
4630	**7**	2	**Humility**[16] 3014 5-9-3 **60** .... RyanMoore 5 (C A Cyzer) *rr: rdn over 2f out: nvr trbld ldrs* **9/1**	54
0061	**8**	½	**Norcroft**[10] 3204 4-9-8 **72** ....(p) KirstyMilczarek(7) 9 (Mrs C A Dunnett) *hld up in rr: rdn 2f out: nvr on terms* **9/1**	65
2502	**9**	1	**Desert Opal**[43] 2208 6-9-5 **62** .... RichardThomas 8 (C R Dore) *a rr: rdn over 2f out: no imp* **8/1**	52
2-06	**10**	1 ½	**Nistaki (USA)**[10] 3199 5-9-12 **69** .... JimmyFortune 2 (D Shaw) *prom: lft 2nd after 1f tl over 1f out: sn wknd* **8/1**	54
5000	**11**	12	**Great Belief (IRE)**[14] 3071 4-8-9 **52** .... DavidKinsella 1 (T D McCarthy) *led tl hung bdly rt and hdd after 1f: chsd ldrs on wd outside: btn and eased bnd 2f out: t.o* **50/1**	1

1m 14.17s (1.36) **Going Correction** -0.025s/f (Stan)
WFA 3 from 4yo+ 6lb **11** Ran SP% **122.7**
Speed ratings (Par 103):89,88,87,86,84 84,82,81,80,78 62
CSF £46.15 CT £234.44 TOTE £7.30: £2.00, £2.80, £2.50; EX 86.40 Trifecta £96.50 Part won. Pool: £136.02 - 0.10 winning units. Place 6 £37.93, Place 5 £25.03..
Owner Mrs Christine Dunnett **Bred** Tally-Ho Stud **Trained** Hingham, Norfolk

FOCUS
A modest handicap and, like the previous sprint, a very moderate winning time, slower even than the earlier nursery.
Great Belief(IRE) Official explanation: jockey said gelding hung badly left throughout
T/Plt: £66.40 to a £1 stake. Pool: £66,960.35. 736.00 winning tickets. T/Qpdt: £35.70 to a £1 stake. Pool: £3,382.70. 70.10 winning tickets. SP

3305 NOTTINGHAM (L-H)

Saturday, July 15

OFFICIAL GOING: Good to firm (firm in places)
Wind: Light, behind Weather: Fine and sunny

3537 EUROPEAN BREEDERS FUND MAIDEN FILLIES' STKS — 6f 15y

2:15 (2:15) (Class 5) 2-Y-0 **£4,533** (£1,348; £674; £336) **Stalls** High

Form				RPR
	1		**Boreal Applause** 2-9-0 .... OscarUrbina 11 (E A L Dunlop) *dwlt: hdwy over 2f out: led ins fnl f: edgd lft: r.o* **9/2**[2]	74
0	**2**	*nk*	**Zonta Zitkala**[15] 3043 2-8-11 .... AmirQuinn(3) 3 (R M Beckett) *hung lft thrght: chsd ldrs: rdn over 2f out: r.o* **7/2**[1]	73
0	**3**	1 ½	**Proud**[38] 2354 2-9-0 .... HayleyTurner 10 (M L W Bell) *chsd ldrs: rdn over 1f out: edgd lft ins fnl f: styd on same pce* **17/2**	69
36	**4**	*nk*	**Diamond Light (USA)**[18] 2957 2-9-0 .... TPQueally 5 (J L Dunlop) *led: rdn and hdd ins fnl f: no ex* **13/2**[3]	68
	5	5	**Sahara Crystal** 2-9-0 .... DaneO'Neill 7 (H Candy) *chsd ldr: rdn over 2f out: wknd fnl f* **10/1**	53
	6	*nk*	**Tiger Tango (USA)** 2-9-0 .... GeorgeBaker 8 (W J Haggas) *s.s: hung lft fr over 2f out: nt trble ldrs* **8/1**	52
	7	7	**What A Treasure (IRE)** 2-9-0 .... JamieMackay 6 (L M Cumani) *sn hung lft and outpcd* **16/1**	31
0	**8**	1	**Poor Nelly**[28] 2638 2-9-0 .... PaulEddery 9 (J L Dunlop) *prom: rdn and hung lft over 3f out: sn lost pl* **40/1**	28
	9	½	**Koffiefontein (USA)** 2-9-0 .... RoystonFfrench 4 (L M Cumani) *sn outpcd* **20/1**	26
	10	3	**Show Trial (IRE)** 2-9-0 .... TedDurcan 2 (M R Channon) *prom: rdn and hung lft over 2f out: sn wknd and eased* **8/1**	17
	11	1 ¼	**Cushat Law (IRE)** 2-8-9 .... GregFairley(5) 1 (W Jarvis) *s.s: outpcd* **28/1**	14

1m 13.16s (-1.84) **Going Correction** -0.45s/f (Firm) **11** Ran SP% **112.1**
Speed ratings (Par 91):94,93,91,91,84 84,74,73,72,68 67
CSF £19.03 TOTE £6.60: £2.90, £1.90, £1.80; EX 38.50.
Owner Mrs G A Rupert **Bred** Summerhill Stud **Trained** Newmarket, Suffolk

FOCUS
Just an average juvenile maiden, but one that should still produce winners in nursery company.

NOTEBOOK
Boreal Applause, a Redcar Two-Year-Old Trophy entrant, is bred to be fully effective at this trip and she overcame a tardy start to make a winning debut. This was not a great race, but her stable's juveniles often come on for the outing and she may be the type to improve, especially over further. (op 4-1 tchd 5-1)
Zonta Zitkala, a keeping-on seventh on her debut at Newmarket, was tackling lesser opposition and would probably have won had she not continually lugged to her left throughout the race. She is going to stay further in time and can win her maiden. (op 4-1)
Proud, always struggling after a slow start on her debut, knew more this time and was soon in a good position, but she was unable to quicken under pressure and got left behind in the final furlong. This was a much better effort and she is very much a type for nurseries. (op 10-1)
Diamond Light(USA) has shown enough in three starts to suggest she can pick up a race once contesting nurseries, especially over further. (op 7-1)
Sahara Crystal, a first juvenile runner of the season for Candy and very much bred to appreciate a mile plus in time, appeared to know her job and was up there early on, but she became readily outpaced inside the final quarter mile and faded late on. There were enough positives to be taken from this though and she is going to improve for further. (op 9-1 tchd 17-2)
Tiger Tango(USA), a son of Johannesburg, was slowly away and hung under pressure, but she was at least going on towards the end of her race and can be expected to improve on the outing. (op 9-1)
Poor Nelly Official explanation: jockey said filly stumbled 4f out
Show Trial(IRE), whose trainer has an excellent record with juveniles, dropped away tamely having been up there early on and was most disappointing. She is surely capable of better. (op 7-1)

3538 LES STONE MEMORIAL H'CAP — 6f 15y

2:50 (2:59) (Class 6) (0-65,65) 3-Y-0 **£3,238** (£963; £481; £240)

Form				RPR
006	**1**		**Wheelavit (IRE)**[19] 2934 3-9-7 **65** .... GeorgeBaker 11 (B G Powell) *chsd ldrs: rdn and hung lft over 2f out: styd on u.p to ld post* **6/1**[2]	72
4-30	**2**	*shd*	**Butterfly Bud (IRE)**[12] 3154 3-9-5 **63** .... PaulEddery 15 (J O'Reilly) *hung lft thrght: mde most: rdn over 1f out: hdd post* **13/2**[3]	69
-064	**3**	*shd*	**Night Rainbow (IRE)**[7] 3299 3-8-8 **55** .... EdwardCreighton(3) 7 (C Tinkler) *w ldr: rdn over 2f out: sn edgd lft: r.o* **9/1**	61
3320	**4**	1 ½	**Discotheque (USA)**[3] 3397 3-9-6 **64** .... TedDurcan 9 (P Howling) *chsd ldrs: rdn over 1f out: styd on same pce ins fnl f* **10/1**	66
5000	**5**	*nk*	**Inchdhuaig (IRE)**[11] 3167 3-8-4 **53** .... GregFairley(5) 8 (P C Haslam) *chsd ldrs: outpcd 1/2-way: r.o ins fnl f* **6/1**[2]	54
5621	**6**	*nk*	**Mullady Penelope**[6] 3340 3-9-3 **61** 6ex .... RoystonFfrench 4 (Mrs A Duffield) *chsd ldrs: rdn and ev ch 1f out: styd on same pce* **7/1**	61
500	**7**	1 ½	**Decider (USA)**[14] 3090 3-8-2 **49** oh1 ow3 .... StephaneBreux(3) 14 (J M Bradley) *hld up: hdwy over 2f out: hmpd over 1f out: nt trble ldrs* **50/1**	47+
0000	**8**	¾	**Trumpita**[11] 3167 3-8-2 **46** .... JamieMackay 3 (T D Easterby) *hld up: hdwy over 2f out: rdn and ev ch over 1f out: wknd ins fnl f* **20/1**	39
0040	**9**	1 ½	**Under Fire (IRE)**[9] 3221 3-8-6 **50** ow2 .... RobertMiles 13 (A W Carroll) *chsd ldrs: rdn 1/2-way: sn lost pl* **16/1**	38
6600	**10**	1	**Dispol Valentine**[24] 2758 3-8-0 **49** oh8 ow3 ....(p) RoryMoore(5) 10 (P T Midgley) *n.d* **50/1**	34

The Form Book, Raceform Ltd, Compton, RG20 6NL

3600 **11** ½ **Bermuda Beauty (IRE)**[26] 2704 3-8-3 **47** oh1 ow1..... PaulFitzsimons 5 31
(J M Bradley) *hld up: effrt over 2f out: sn wknd* **22/1**
500- **12** 4 **Magical World**[381] 3016 3-7-13 **46** oh11.................... DominicFox(3) 16 18
(J M Bradley) *s.s: hdwy over 2f out: wknd over 1f out* **66/1**
6062 **13** 3 **Good Companion (IRE)**[14] 3090 3-9-5 **63**..................... DaneO'Neill 6 26
(J L Dunlop) *prom: rdn and lost pl over 3f out: sn bhd* **9/2**[1]
-200 **14** 10 **Tatstheticket**[8] 3257 3-8-3 **47**...............................(v[1]) HayleyTurner 2 —
(J Balding) *chsd ldrs over 3f* **66/1**
1400 **15** 2 **Mister Becks (IRE)**[4] 3381 3-8-2 **49**..................(b[1]) JohnMcAuley(3) 12 —
(M C Chapman) *s.s: a wl bhd* **33/1**
0-00 **16** 1 **Young Flavio**[10] 3195 3-8-11 **55**...................................(p) TPQueally 1 —
(J M Bradley) *s.s: a wl bhd* **40/1**

1m 13.2s (-1.80) **Going Correction** -0.45s/f (Firm) **16** Ran SP% **119.0**
Speed ratings (Par 98):94,93,93,91,91 90,88,87,85,84 83,78,74,61,58 57
CSF £40.26 CT £366.63 TOTE £6.20: £1.30, £2.00, £2.80, £2.40; EX 31.30.
Owner Nameless & Shameless **Bred** John Bourke **Trained** Morestead, Hants

FOCUS
Flip start. A modest handicap and a moderate winning time, fractionally slower than the preceding two-year-old fillies' maiden. However, the form looks sound enough rated through the placed horses.
Wheelavit(IRE) Official explanation: trainer said, regarding the improved form shown, the gelding had benefited from today's drop in trip to 6f
Tatstheticket Official explanation: jockey said gelding lost its action
Young Flavio Official explanation: jockey said gelding ducked right-handed at start

3539 XLI LTD H'CAP 1m 6f 15y
3:25 (3:25) (Class 4) (0-85,81) 3-Y-0 **£6,477** (£1,927; £963; £481) **Stalls** Low

Form RPR
4241 **1** **Strategic Mount**[17] 2970 3-9-2 **76**.................................... TPQueally 4 90
(P F I Cole) *mde all: rdn clr over 3f out: eased ins fnl f* **5/2**[2]
41-6 **2** 5 **Los Cabos (IRE)**[24] 2754 3-9-6 **80**............................... RobertHavlin 1 87
(J H M Gosden) *hld up: hdwy to chse wnr over 2f out: sn rdn and no imp* **14/1**
2123 **3** 6 **Meadow Mischief (FR)**[27] 2677 3-9-4 **78**..................(b) OscarUrbina 5 81+
(E A L Dunlop) *hld up: hdwy 9f out: rdn and hung lft over 2f out: sn wknd* **9/1**
3121 **4** 6 **Dream Champion**[14] 3065 3-9-7 **81**............................... TedDurcan 6 72
(M R Channon) *chsd ldr: rdn over 4f out: wknd over 2f out* **7/2**[3]
342 **5** 3½ **Sybella**[13] 3122 3-9-5 **79**.. DaneO'Neill 2 65
(J L Dunlop) *hld up: rdn and wknd 4f out* **9/1**
0-13 **6** 7 **El Alamein (IRE)**[28] 2633 3-8-3 **63**............................. JamieMackay 3 39
(Sir Mark Prescott) *trckd ldrs: racd keenly: shkn up over 6f out: rdn and hung lft 4f out: sn wknd* **7/4**[1]

3m 0.40s (-6.70) **Going Correction** -0.45s/f (Firm) **6** Ran SP% **113.8**
Speed ratings (Par 102):101,98,94,91,89 85
CSF £34.36 TOTE £3.50: £2.50, £4.50; EX 55.60.
Owner Ben & Sir Martyn Arbib **Bred** Arbib Bloodstock Partnership **Trained** Whatcombe, Oxon

FOCUS
A fair staying handicap in which runners finished well strung out with the third close to previous form.
El Alamein(IRE) Official explanation: trainer had no explanation for the poor form shown

3540 EVENING POST FAMILY DAY H'CAP 1m 1f 213y
4:00 (4:01) (Class 5) (0-70,74) 3-Y-0 **£3,886** (£1,156; £577; £288) **Stalls** Low

Form RPR
-040 **1** **Benbrook**[22] 2814 3-8-12 **60**.. DaneO'Neill 2 67
(J L Dunlop) *mde virtually all: rdn over 2f out: r.o wl: eased nr fin* **12/1**[3]
-155 **2** 2½ **High Seasons**[19] 2933 3-9-5 **67**.................................. GeorgeBaker 3 69
(B R Millman) *a.p: rdn and hung lft fr over 3f out: chsd wnr over 1f out: no imp* **10/3**[1]
0404 **3** 2½ **Musical Magic**[9] 3230 3-9-2 **64**....................................... TPQueally 9 61
(J Noseda) *sn chsng wnr: rdn over 2f out: wknd fnl f* **10/1**[2]
6000 **4** ½ **Nassar (IRE)**[9] 3230 3-9-1 **66**...................................... AmirQuinn(3) 4 62
(G Prodromou) *hld up: rdn over 3f out: nvr trbld ldrs* **20/1**

2m 9.00s (-0.70) **Going Correction** -0.45s/f (Firm) **4** Ran SP% **44.6**
Speed ratings (Par 100):84,82,80,79
CSF £8.26 TOTE £6.00; EX 23.00.
Owner Mrs J M Khan **Bred** P D And Mrs Player **Trained** Arundel, W Sussex
■ Prince Picasso (8/15F) was withdrawn on vet's advice. R4 applies, deduct 65p in the £.

FOCUS
A weak handicap run in a pedestrian winning time in what was a depleted field and the form is far from solid.

3541 HELP A HORSE WITH THE BROOKE CHARITY (S) STKS 1m 54y
4:30 (4:30) (Class 6) 3-4-Y-0 **£2,730** (£806; £403) **Stalls** Low

Form RPR
5420 **1** **Al Rayanah**[19] 2929 3-8-10 63.. AmirQuinn(3) 3 55
(G Prodromou) *hld up in tch: chsd ldr 5f out: rdn to ld over 2f out: hdd over 1f out: styd on u.p to ld ins fnl f* **7/2**[1]
4660 **2** ½ **Priorina (IRE)**[10] 3194 4-9-8 44...................................(v) RobertHavlin 8 56
(D Haydn Jones) *hld up: hdwy 5f out: rdn to ld over 1f out: hdd ins fnl f: styd on* **8/1**
0400 **3** ½ **Spring Time Girl**[17] 2966 4-8-11 43.........................(b[1]) GregFairley(5) 6 49
(B Ellison) *hld up: rdn 1/2-way: hdwy over 2f out: r.o* **6/1**[3]
0203 **4** shd **Desert Lightning (IRE)**[5] 3353 4-9-7 55............................ GeorgeBaker 14 54
(K R Burke) *broke wl: sn stdd: hdwy u.p over 2f out: styd on* **4/1**[2]
0003 **5** nk **Comeintothespace (IRE)**[10] 3194 4-9-4 45............ NeilChalmers(3) 15 53
(Miss Victoria Roberts) *hld up: swtchd leat and hdwy over 1f out: styd on* **12/1**
5660 **6** 3 **Ming Vase**[45] 2137 4-9-7 42... LeeEnstone 11 46
(P T Midgley) *plld hrd and prom: rdn over 3f out: styd on same pce fnl f* **22/1**
0-60 **7** 5 **Soviet Promise (IRE)**[16] 3006 3-8-7 40.........................(b[1]) TedDurcan 5 28
(G G Margarson) *s.s: nvr nrr* **33/1**
6003 **8** 1½ **Bertie Bear**[16] 3006 3-8-12 39...(v) TPQueally 1 29
(G G Margarson) *hld up: hdwy u.p over 3f out: wknd over 1f out* **16/1**
0001 **9** 4 **Silver Visage (IRE)**[11] 3161 4-9-13 45...........................(p) BrianReilly 2 28
(Miss J Feilden) *sn led: rdn and hdd over 2f out: wknd over 1f out* **9/1**
00-0 **10** hd **Ello Lucky (IRE)**[15] 3032 4-9-2 36.................................. PaulFitzsimons 9 16
(J M Bradley) *prom over 5f* **66/1**
0600 **11** 1½ **Millbrook Star (IRE)**[4] 3383 3-8-5 35.................... JamieHamblett(3) 12 16
(M C Chapman) *sn outpcd* **50/1**
2046 **12** 12 **Bahhmirage (IRE)**[7] 3306 3-8-7 58.............................(b) HayleyTurner 10 —
(Stef Liddiard) *sn pushed along in rr: rdn over 3f out: no rspnse* **13/2**
0002 **13** 2½ **Baytown Valentina**[10] 3195 3-8-7 40..........................(p) JamieMackay 4 —
(R Brotherton) *chsd ldrs 5f* **33/1**

-600 **14** 1¾ **Tantien**[14] 3089 4-9-2 37.. RoystonFfrench 7 —
(John A Harris) *chsd ldrs over 4f* **66/1**

1m 42.37s (-4.03) **Going Correction** -0.45s/f (Firm)
WFA 3 from 4yo 9lb **14** Ran SP% **119.7**
Speed ratings (Par 101):102,101,101,100,100 97,92,91,87,86 85,73,70,69
CSF £29.87 TOTE £6.00: £2.30, £2.80, £2.80; EX 69.40.The winner was bought in for 7,200gns
Owner Faisal Al-Nassar **Bred** R P Kernohan **Trained** East Harling, Norfolk
■ Stewards' Enquiry : Robert Havlin caution: used whip with excessive frequency
Amir Quinn three-day ban: used whip with excessive frequency and without giving time to respond (Jul 26-28)

FOCUS
A moderate race for the grade, although the time was reasonable, in which the runner-up sets the standard.
Tantien Official explanation: trainer's representative said filly was unsuited by the good to firm, firm in places ground

3542 RACING UK ON CHANNEL 432 H'CAP 1m 54y
5:05 (5:05) (Class 5) (0-75,77) 3-Y-0+ **£3,238** (£963; £481; £240) **Stalls** Low

Form RPR
0052 **1** **Missed A Beat**[7] 3298 4-9-6 **66**...................................... OscarUrbina 1 73
(M Blanshard) *chsd ldrs: rdn over 3f out: styd on to ld ins fnl f* **3/1**[1]
2520 **2** 1¾ **Favouring (IRE)**[9] 3229 4-8-6 **55** oh3.....................(v) JohnMcAuley(3) 2 58
(M C Chapman) *led and sn clr: rdn over 1f out: hdd and unable to qckn ins fnl f* **14/1**
0231 **3** ¾ **Barons Spy (IRE)**[7] 3311 5-9-3 **63**................................ RobertMiles 8 64
(R J Price) *chsd ldrs: rdn over 3f out: styd on same pce ins fnl f* **4/1**[3]
-102 **4** 1¼ **Malech (IRE)**[63] 1681 3-9-3 **72**..................................... HayleyTurner 4 68
(M L W Bell) *chsd clr ldr tl rdn 3f out: styd on same pce appr fnl f* **5/1**
5521 **5** 1 **Curtain Bluff**[2] 3459 4-10-3 **77** 6ex...............................(v) TedDurcan 6 73
(M R Channon) *hld up: rdn over 2f out: nvr trbld ldrs* **10/3**[2]
6021 **6** ½ **Murrumbidgee (IRE)**[16] 3030 3-8-2 **64**........................ PatrickHills(7) 5 57
(J W Hills) *hld up: rdn over 3f out: n.d* **7/1**
0-50 **7** 2 **Malinsa Blue (IRE)**[17] 2977 4-10-0 **74**....................... RoystonFfrench 7 64
(S Parr) *hld up: plld hrd: n.d* **33/1**
3000 **8** nk **Will The Till**[29] 2601 4-8-5 **56**................................... GregFairley(5) 3 46
(J M Bradley) *hld up: rdn 1/2-way: n.d* **14/1**

1m 41.93s (-4.47) **Going Correction** -0.45s/f (Firm)
WFA 3 from 4yo+ 9lb **8** Ran SP% **113.5**
Speed ratings (Par 103):104,102,101,100,99 98,96,96
CSF £44.27 CT £169.88 TOTE £5.60: £1.50, £3.80, £2.10; EX 69.10 Place 6 £196.60, Place 5 £113.75.
Owner The First Timers **Bred** Whitsbury Manor Stud **Trained** Upper Lambourn, Berks
■ Stewards' Enquiry : Oscar Urbina caution: used whip with excessive frequency

FOCUS
A competitive handicap in which Favouring tried to slip the field and the form looks slightly dubious.
Will The Till Official explanation: vet said gelding was found to have a fibrilating heart after the race
T/Plt: £2,129.60 to a £1 stake. Pool: £38,800.25. 13.30 winning tickets. T/Qpdt: £930.70 to a £1 stake. Pool: £1,886.60. 1.50 winning tickets. CR

3024 SALISBURY (R-H)
Saturday, July 15

OFFICIAL GOING: Good to firm
The far side rail was still out several metres to save ground for later in the season.
Wind: Virtually nil.

3543 BATHWICK TYRES LADY RIDERS' SERIES H'CAP 6f
6:35 (6:35) (Class 5) (0-75,74) 3-Y-0+ **£3,435** (£1,065; £532; £266) **Stalls** High

Form RPR
6430 **1** **Stagnite**[38] 2347 6-9-4 **55** oh9...........................(p) MissFayeBramley(3) 11 61
(P A Blockley) *mde v all: rdn 2f out: edgd rt u.p wl ins last: hld on all out* **33/1**
-060 **2** ½ **Miss Porcia**[148] 446 5-9-7 **55** oh10......................... MissCHannaford 3 60
(P A Blockley) *in tch: hdwy on rails over 1f out: styng on to chse wnr but hld whn hmpd last strides* **33/1**
5364 **3** nk **Arctic Desert**[10] 3204 6-10-4 **71**............................. MissMSowerby(5) 2 75
(A M Balding) *slowly away: bhd: hdwy and swtchd to far rail 3f out:swtchd lft 2f out: styd on: hung bdly rt and chal ins last: fnd little* **6/1**[1]
1030 **4** 2½ **Greenwood**[21] 2864 8-10-10 **72**...................................... MissEJJones 9 68
(P G Murphy) *in tch: rdn 3f out: styd on fnl f: nvr gng pce to rch ldrs* **6/1**[1]
3244 **5** nk **Patavium Prince (IRE)**[16] 3004 3-9-8 **69**.................... MissKFerguson(7) 1 63+
(J R Best) *racd wd: bhd: hdwy fr 2f out: kpt on fnl f but nvr gng pce to chal* **6/1**[1]
0000 **6** nk **Salviati (USA)**[6] 3330 9-9-10 **65**.........................(p) MissSBradley(7) 12 59
(J M Bradley) *s.i.s: sn mid-div: hdwy 2f out: one pce ins last* **14/1**
0-00 **7** nk **The Crooked Ring**[14] 3069 4-10-9 **74**........................ MissEFolkes(3) 8 67
(P D Evans) *chsd ldrs: rdn 3f out: wknd ins fnl f* **14/1**
0005 **8** nk **Sentiero Rosso (USA)**[4] 3389 4-9-12 **60**........................(t) MissLEllison 5 53
(B Ellison) *racd wd and in rr: sme hdwy fnl 2f* **17/2**
0001 **9** ½ **Scuba (IRE)**[23] 2792 4-9-10 **63**.............................(b) MissVCartmel(5) 7 54
(H Morrison) *racd wd: outpcd: kpt on fnl 2f: nvr rchd ldrs* **6/1**[1]
4004 **10** ½ **Mozakhraf (USA)**[7] 3287 4-9-6 **59**.............................. MissARyan(5) 4 49
(K A Ryan) *chsd ldrs: rdn over 2f out: wknd fnl f* **7/1**[3]
5303 **11** 1¼ **My Girl Pearl (IRE)**[8] 3267 6-9-7 **55** oh6................... MrsSBosley 13 41
(M S Saunders) *chsd ldrs: rdn over 2f out: wknd fnl f* **13/2**[2]
0546 **12** 3 **Indian Gem**[25] 2729 5-9-2 **55** oh18.......................... MissMMullineaux(5) 6 32
(A J Chamberlain) *slowly away: a in rr* **50/1**
0-00 **13** 8 **Yorkies Boy**[30] 2573 11-9-2 **55** oh20.........................(p) MissAWallace(5) 10 8
(N E Berry) *sn bhd* **66/1**

1m 14.47s (-0.51) **Going Correction** -0.025s/f (Good)
WFA 3 from 4yo+ 6lb **13** Ran SP% **116.2**
Speed ratings (Par 103):102,101,100,97,97 96,96,96,95,94 93,89,78
CSF £817.78 CT £7454.71 TOTE £36.50: £9.10, £9.30, £2.10; EX 651.20.
Owner Mrs Joanna Hughes **Bred** D A And Mrs Hicks **Trained** Lambourn, Berks
■ Stewards' Enquiry : Miss Faye Bramley caution: careless riding

FOCUS
A moderate line-up, but better than some for a race of this type and the time was reasonable.
My Girl Pearl(IRE) Official explanation: jockey said mare lost its action

3544 UPTON MCGOUGAN CONSULTING ENGINEERS 25TH ANNIVERSARY NOVICE AUCTION STKS 6f

7:05 (7:05) (Class 4) 2-Y-O £4,533 (£1,348; £674; £336) **Stalls** High

Form RPR

01 **1** **Kyshanty**[10] 3193 2-9-5 .... RichardHughes 8 77
(R Hannon) *mde all: hrd rdn fnl f: kpt on wl* **9/4**[1]

2 ¾ **Rambo Honours (IRE)** 2-8-11 .... SebSanders 7 67
(R M Beckett) *trckd ldrs: swtchd lft and effrt ins fnl 2f: rn green over 1f out: kpt on ins last: gng on cl home but a hld* **9/1**

006 **3** 1 **Cesc**[61] 1737 2-8-11 .... FergusSweeney 5 64
(P J Makin) *in tch: rdn and hdwy over 1f out: styd on to chse wnr ins last: no imp: ct for 2nd cl home* **13/2**

0 **4** hd **Avoid The Cat**[9] 3222 2-8-9 .... JimCrowley 3 61
(Mrs A J Perrett) *chsd ldr tl over 3f out: rdn and one pce 2f out: kpt on again ins last but nvr gng pce to rch wnr* **25/1**

05 **5** 2½ **Red Hot Jazz (IRE)**[35] 2456 2-8-4 .... MartinDwyer 2 49
(Mrs P N Dutfield) *plld hrd: chsd wnr over 3f out: wknd fnl f* **5/1**[3]

6 shd **Cantique (IRE)** 2-8-6 .... NickyMackay 4 50
(R M Beckett) *s.i.s: rr but in tch: rdn over 2f out: kpt on same pce ins last* **8/1**

1 **7** 1¼ **Hephaestus**[114] 701 2-9-1 .... EdwardCreighton(3) 1 59
(M R Channon) *rr: rdn along fr 3f out: nvr gng pce to get competitive and a struggling* **11/4**[2]

1m 15.93s (0.95) **Going Correction** -0.025s/f (Good) **7** Ran SP% **112.4**
Speed ratings (Par 96):92,91,89,89,86 85,84
CSF £22.17 TOTE £2.70: £1.60, £4.10; EX 21.60.
Owner D J Walker, Dr M M Smith & R C Smith **Bred** Lady Whent **Trained** East Everleigh, Wilts

FOCUS
Probably an ordinary maiden, though they were all either lightly-raced or making their debuts, so can improve a bit.

NOTEBOOK
Kyshanty grabbed the far side rail and was able to dictate his own tempo under a well-judged ride. Having had the run of the race, he battled well to hold the others at bay and was always just in control. (op 2-1 tchd 15-8)
Rambo Honours(IRE), a 12,000 euro Dilshaan newcomer, made a promising debut and should all the better for the experience, with longer trips likely to suit. (op 16-1)
Cesc did better over the longer trip, and looks a likely sort for six-furlong nurseries. (op 8-1)
Avoid The Cat seemed to have benefited from his debut run, and looks capable of landing a little race. He will be ready for nurseries after one more outing, with sprint trips likely to suit this season. (op 20-1)
Red Hot Jazz(IRE) is now qualified for nurseries, and is capable of a good show, but she must learn to settle much better than she did here. (op 4-1)
Cantique(IRE), a cheap filly by Danetime, is bred to be speedy, and this was a satisfactory debut upon which she can improve. (op 10-1)
Hephaestus, a winner on his debut on Polytrack, did not show nearly as much here. (tchd 3-1, 10-3 in a place)

3545 HERITAGE AUDI QUATTRO CELEBRATION E B F MAIDEN STKS 6f 212y

7:35 (7:36) (Class 4) 2-Y-O £4,857 (£1,445; £722; £360) **Stalls** Centre

Form RPR

363 **1** **Golden Balls (IRE)**[8] 3253 2-9-3 .... RichardHughes 10 85
(R Hannon) *trckd ldrs: n.m.r ins fnl 3f: slt ld 2f out: sn narrowly hdd: led again ins last: hrd rdn: all out* **7/2**[3]

2 shd **Snake's Head** 2-8-12 .... SebSanders 5 80+
(J L Dunlop) *bhd: gd hdwy to chse ldrs and bmpd 3f out and again over 2f out: led ins fnl 2f: hdd ins last: rallied gamely: jst failed* **14/1**

2 **3** 2½ **Spanish Hidalgo (IRE)**[20] 2899 2-9-3 .... JamieSpencer 11 78
(J L Dunlop) *chsd ldrs: edgd lft 3f out: wnt lft again over 2f out: sn chalng: rdn over 1f out: wknd last half f* **3/1**[2]

4 6 **Messiah Garvey** 2-9-0 .... EdwardCreighton(3) 6 63
(M R Channon) *bhd: pushed along 1/2-way: kpt on fr over 1f out and styd on ins last but nvr in contention* **25/1**

5 hd **Streets Ahead** 2-9-3 .... FergusSweeney 8 62
(A M Balding) *s.i.s: bhd: rdn and sme hdwy over 2f out: nvr in contention and sn one pce* **33/1**

3 **6** 8 **Raffaas**[16] 3025 2-9-3 .... MartinDwyer 3 41
(M P Tregoning) *s.i.s: sn chsng ldrs: j. shadow 3f out: led wl over 2f out: hdd 2f out: wknd rapidly over 1f out* **5/4**[1]

0 **7** 4 **Boogie Dancer**[35] 2456 2-8-12 .... MichaelTebbutt 4 26
(H S Howe) *in tch on outside: shkn up and green 3f out: wknd and hung rt over 2f out* **80/1**

30 **8** 1¾ **Clewer**[17] 2980 2-8-12 .... VinceSlattery 7 21
(P A Blockley) *t.k.h: in tch 4f* **33/1**

0 **9** 1 **Last Dog Standing (IRE)**[9] 3222 2-9-3 .... StephenCarson 9 24
(B G Powell) *a in rr: no ch whn hung rt into far rail over 2f out* **40/1**

0 **10** ½ **Brave Amber**[39] 2328 2-8-12 .... NickyMackay 13 17
(M Blanshard) *keen hold: led tl hdd wl over 2f out: sn btn* **66/1**

0 **11** 1½ **Fun In The Sun**[17] 2967 2-9-3 .... AdrianMcCarthy 1 19
(Jane Southcombe) *chsd ldrs: bmpd 3f out: wknd and bmpd again 2f out* **125/1**

0 **12** 13 **Color Man**[17] 2979 2-9-3 .... JimCrowley 12 —
(Mrs A J Perrett) *extremely slowly away and lost 18l: nt rcvr and a in rr* **50/1**

1m 28.0s (-1.06) **Going Correction** -0.025s/f (Good) **12** Ran SP% **116.0**
Speed ratings (Par 96):105,104,102,95,94 85,81,79,78,77 75,60
CSF £45.17 TOTE £4.30: £1.60, £3.80, £1.70; EX 49.80.
Owner M Sines **Bred** Mrs Noelle Walsh **Trained** East Everleigh, Wilts

FOCUS
Likely to prove a decent maiden, and a very smart winning time for a race like this suggests the form will prove sound.

NOTEBOOK
Golden Balls(IRE) confirmed that that this trip does suit him, though he had to dig deep to hold the persistent challenge of the runner-up. His future now lies in the hands of the Handicapper. (op 3-1 tchd 4-1)
Snake's Head ◆, a half-sister to several winners including the dual juvenile winner Zabaglione, made a fine debut despite being knocked about during the race and looking very green. She looks sure to improve greatly on this, and is one to note. (op 16-1)
Spanish Hidalgo(IRE) again showed enough to suggest he can win a similar race. He should improve with racing, like many in his family. (op 10-3 tchd 7-2)
Messiah Garvey, a well-bred 40,000 guineas Lear Fan filly, took a while to get going but was getting the hang of things late on. She can step up on this encouraging debut. (op 28-1)
Streets Ahead, a 20,000 guineas son of Beat Hollow, shaped reasonably well on this debut run, and can do better with the experience under his belt.
Raffaas came to win the race, only to fold up tamely. He needs to redeem himself following this weak effort. (op 11-8 tchd 6-5)

3546 COLD SERVICE LIMITED H'CAP 1m

8:05 (8:05) (Class 4) (0-85,84) 3-Y-O £7,124 (£2,119; £1,059; £529) **Stalls** High

Form RPR

2-45 **1** **Ebert**[9] 3224 3-8-10 73 .... SebSanders 8 79
(P J Makin) *patiently rdn and hld up in tch: swtchd lft and qcknd over 1f out: led jst ins last: drvn out* **9/2**[2]

-213 **2** 1 **Storm On The Run (IRE)**[35] 2443 3-9-5 82 .... RichardHughes 3 86
(R Hannon) *hld up in rr: nt clr run and switched lft to outside over 1f out: drvn and qcknd to chal ins last: nt pce of wnr* **9/2**[2]

-162 **3** nk **Sharplaw Autumn (USA)**[16] 3007 3-9-1 78 .... JamieSpencer 9 81
(W J Haggas) *led 1f: trckd ldrs: n.m.r on ins 2f out: sn rdn: kpt on to chse ldrs ins last but nvr gng pce to chal* **4/1**[1]

0-43 **4** ¾ **Imperial Harry**[19] 2919 3-8-4 70 .... EdwardCreighton(3) 1 71
(M R Channon) *plld hrd and pressed ldr after 1f: slt ld over 2f out: hdd over 1f out: styd on on same pce ins last* **11/1**

1261 **5** 1½ **Tempsford Flyer (IRE)**[30] 2581 3-9-7 84 .... RyanMoore 7 82
(J W Hills) *chsd ldrs: rdn 3f out: slt ld over 1f out: hdd jst ins last: sn btn* **4/1**[1]

6046 **6** 1¼ **Cool Sting (IRE)**[9] 3224 3-8-7 70 .... FergusSweeney 6 65
(A M Balding) *in tch: hdwy on outside over 2f out to chse press ldrs wl over 1f out: wknd ins last* **14/1**

1 **7** 1¾ **Baleegh (USA)**[15] 3032 3-9-0 77 .... MartinDwyer 2 68
(M P Tregoning) *bmpd s: plld hrd and led after 1f: hdd over 1f out: wknd over 1f out: eased whn no ch* **11/2**[3]

03-5 **8** 1¼ **Trimlestown (IRE)**[21] 2868 3-9-1 78 .... DaneO'Neill 4 66
(H Candy) *chsd ldrs: rdn to chal ins fnl 2f: wknd qckly fnl f* **16/1**

1m 41.95s (-1.14) **Going Correction** -0.025s/f (Good) **8** Ran SP% **112.6**
Speed ratings (Par 102):104,103,102,101,100 99,97,96
CSF £24.22 CT £86.23 TOTE £5.40: £2.20, £1.10, £2.30; EX 31.80.
Owner R A Henley and Mrs N E Lyon **Bred** Grasshopper 2000 Ltd **Trained** Ogbourne Maisey, Wilts

FOCUS
A decent handicap for the track, largely contested by unexposed types. Baleegh and Imperial Harry ended up setting the pace, with both running too freely and being heavily restrained in front.
Tempsford Flyer(IRE) Official explanation: jockey said colt hung left

3547 EDMUND NUTTALL H'CAP 1m 4f

8:35 (8:35) (Class 5) (0-75,76) 3-Y-O+ £3,562 (£1,059; £529; £264) **Stalls** High

Form RPR

051 **1** **Our Teddy (IRE)**[7] 3283 6-10-1 76 .... JamieSpencer 5 84
(P A Blockley) *hld up rr but in tch: swtchd lft 2f out: qcknd to ld 1f out and styd on under hand driving thrght fnl f* **6/1**[3]

0222 **2** hd **Soufah (IRE)**[22] 2822 4-9-5 66 .... SebSanders 8 74
(J L Dunlop) *chsd ldrs: drvn to chal 1f out and styd pressing wnr ins last but a jst hld* **11/4**[1]

6521 **3** nk **Fort Churchill (IRE)**[16] 3022 5-9-9 70 .... (bt) RyanMoore 2 78
(B Ellison) *chsd ldr after 3f: rdn to ld ins fnl 4f: hrd drvn fr 3f out: hdd 1f out: no ex cl home* **4/1**[2]

-035 **4** 4 **Snark (IRE)**[15] 3046 3-9-1 75 .... FergusSweeney 7 76
(P J Makin) *chsd ldr 3f: styd front rnk rdn and outpcd over 2f out: styd on same pce fnl f* **15/2**

5414 **5** ½ **Stellenbosch (USA)**[15] 3046 3-8-10 70 .... RichardHughes 4 70
(J W Hills) *led: hdd ins fnl 4f: styd pressing ldrs and ev ch u.p over 1f out: wknd ins last* **6/1**[3]

0-25 **6** 2½ **Darling Deanie (IRE)**[16] 3028 4-9-10 71 .... JohnEgan 3 67
(D R C Elsworth) *hld up rr but in tch: hdwy to chse ldrs 3f out: sn drvn: wknd ins fnl 2f* **4/1**[2]

0 **7** 2 **Montevideo**[14] 3093 6-10-0 75 .... JimCrowley 1 68
(Jonjo O'Neill) *bhd: sme hdwy 5f out: wknd over 2f out* **22/1**

000/ **8** 1 **Sharmy (IRE)**[583] 6172 10-10-0 75 .... DaneO'Neill 6 67
(Ian Williams) *hld up in rr: pushed along 4f out: nvr in contention* **40/1**

9 10 **Brave Hiawatha (FR)**[33] 4-9-10 70 .... VinceSlattery 9 46
(J A B Old) *rr and rdn 5f out: sn no ch* **50/1**

2m 38.03s (1.67) **Going Correction** +0.225s/f (Good)
WFA 3 from 4yo+ 13lb **9** Ran SP% **115.8**
Speed ratings (Par 103):103,102,102,100,99 98,96,96,89
CSF £22.61 CT £74.33 TOTE £5.80: £2.20, £1.30, £1.80; EX 19.90.
Owner The Beare Family **Bred** Vizcaya Ag **Trained** Lambourn, Berks

FOCUS
Just a fair handicap, run at a modest pace until the final half-mile but a reasonable time.

3548 E B F LADIES EVENING FILLIES' H'CAP 1m

9:05 (9:07) (Class 3) (0-95,87) 3-Y-O
£11,217 (£3,358; £1,679; £840; £419; £210) **Stalls** High

Form RPR

-211 **1** **Caressed**[21] 2865 3-9-2 82 .... JamieSpencer 2 95+
(J R Fanshawe) *hld up in rr: rdn and qcknd fr 2f out: chsd ldrs and hung bdly rt last half f: swtchd lft and rapid hdwy to ld last stride* **4/7**[1]

-231 **2** hd **Usk Poppy**[17] 2985 3-8-11 77 .... JohnEgan 1 82
(D R C Elsworth) *trckd ldrs: rdn to ld ins fnl 2f: styd on gamely whn strly chal thrght fnl f: ct last stride* **4/1**[2]

4405 **3** shd **Dame Hester (IRE)**[21] 2880 3-8-13 79 .... (b) MartinDwyer 5 84
(E J O'Neill) *t.k.h: trckd ldrs: drvn to chal over 1f out: stl upsides u.p thrght fnl f no ex last strides* **11/1**

45 **4** 2 **Penfection (IRE)**[16] 3021 3-9-7 87 .... NickyMackay 4 87
(M Botti) *s.i.s: hld up rr but in tch: pushed along: hdwy and hung rt over 1f out: kpt on ins last: nvr gng pce to rch ldrs* **33/1**

4-25 **5** 1 **Antigoni (IRE)**[8] 3250 3-8-8 74 ow5 .... RichardHughes 6 72
(A M Balding) *sn ld: hdd ins fnl 2f: wknd fnl f* **20/1**

4132 **6** ½ **My Lovely Lady (IRE)**[1] 3472 3-7-10 69 .... LukeMorris(7) 3 66
(M L W Bell) *chsd ldr to 2f out: wknd fnl f* **8/1**[3]

1m 42.4s (-0.69) **Going Correction** -0.025s/f (Good) **6** Ran SP% **110.8**
Speed ratings (Par 101):102,101,101,99,98 98
CSF £3.04 TOTE £1.70: £1.10, £1.70; EX 3.30 Place 6 £42.15, Place 5 £7.86.
Owner Cheveley Park Stud **Bred** Cheveley Park Stud Ltd **Trained** Newmarket, Suffolk

FOCUS
Decent prizemoney for this handicap, and a good line-up, though lacking in numbers, and run at a modest pace to halfway.

NOTEBOOK
Caressed was not seen at her best here, having been restrained in the rear off a weak early pace. However, the fact that she got there in the end, albeit narrowly - and with something of a scare when she hung badly away from the whip - suggests that she can do much better with a proper gallop. (op 4-6 tchd 8-11)
Usk Poppy got the extra furlong well, and gave the odds-on favourite a real scare. She looks a tough sort who will continue to give punters a run from their money if the Handicapper does not over-burden her for this. Official explanation: jockey said filly hung left (op 5-1 tchd 7-2)

Dame Hester(IRE) ran her best race to date, though she sat closer to the modest pace than the winner, so is probably flattered a bit by the bare result. That said, she battled well and deserves credit. (op 12-1 tchd 14-1)
Penfection(IRE) had a tough task trying to concede weight to these useful fillies, and attempting to come from behind off a very ordinary early gallop sealed her fate. (op 22-1 tchd 20-1)
Antigoni(IRE) had the run of the race, setting a moderate tempo, but was ultimately brushed aside. She has the ability to win but needs to drop a few pounds. (op 11-1)
My Lovely Lady(IRE) has been in good form of late, and was not beaten far here, but there were several improvers in this field, and she was more exposed. Official explanation: jockey said filly hung left (op 15-2 tchd 7-1)
T/Plt: £36.30 to a £1 stake. Pool: £57,396.25. 1,153.00 winning tickets. T/Qpdt: £3.40 to a £1 stake. Pool: £4,184.40. 889.60 winning tickets. ST

3498 YORK (L-H)

Saturday, July 15

OFFICIAL GOING: Good to firm (firm in places)

5mm water was put on the track since the previous day. The ground was described as 'good, fast ground, not firm with an excellent cover'.
Wind: Light, half-behind. Weather: Hot and sunny

3549 JOHN SMITH'S CASK H'CAP 1m

2:10 (2:10) (Class 3) (0-90,87) 3-Y-O+ £9,715 (£2,890; £1,444; £721) Stalls Low

Form				RPR
0/01	1		**Fremen (USA)**12 3139 6-9-7 **82** JoeFanning 3 (D Nicholls) *trckd ldrs gng wl: nt clr run and swtchd outside over 2f out: r.o to ld ins last* 5/1[3]	91+
2110	2	1 1/4	**Grey Boy (GER)**23 2776 5-9-7 **82** PaulHanagan 6 (R A Fahey) *trckd ldrs: led 2f out: hdd and no ex ins last* 11/4[1]	88
1030	3	nk	**Tough Love**1 3500 7-8-12 **73** (p) DavidAllan 4 (T D Easterby) *hld up in last: effrt over 3f out: kpt on wl fnl f* 7/1	78
1443	4	1/2	**Jubilee Street (IRE)**8 3241 7-9-6 **81** PaulFessey 7 (Mrs A Duffield) *hld up in rr: effrt over 3f out: styd on same pce fnl 2f* 13/2	85
-452	5	1 1/2	**Mutawaffer**9 3218 5-9-12 **87** TonyHamilton 8 (R A Fahey) *hld up: effrt over 3f out: kpt on same pce fnl 2f* 7/2[2]	87
1210	6	1 1/4	**Sake (IRE)**17 2974 4-8-12 **73** KimTinkler 5 (N Tinkler) *w ldr: led over 3f ou: hdd 2f out: wknd fnl f* 10/1	71
-040	7	1 3/4	**Top Dirham**17 2974 8-9-2 **77** DaleGibson 2 (M W Easterby) *trckd ldrs: hrd drvn over 3f out: one pce* 12/1	71
012/	8	2	**Atlantic Story (USA)**62 6176 4-9-7 **82** (t) PaulMulrennan 1 (M W Easterby) *set mod pce: hdd over 3f out: lost pl over 1f out* 22/1	71

1m 37.77s (-1.73) **Going Correction** -0.025s/f (Good) 8 Ran SP% **112.5**
Speed ratings (Par 107):107,105,105,104,103 102,100,98
CSF £18.52 CT £94.26 TOTE £5.20: £1.90, £1.30, £1.80; EX 12.90 Trifecta £85.60 Pool: £699.69 - 5.80 winning units..
Owner Miss C King Mrs A Seed Ms Finola Devaney **Bred** Flaxman Holdings Ltd **Trained** Sessay, N Yorks

FOCUS
A fair handicap run at just a steady gallop until the final three furlongs but in the end a respectable time. The form has a solid look.

NOTEBOOK
Fremen(USA), once rated 11lb higher, had his confidence boosted by his claiming-race success. He travelled smoothly but had to switch for a run and was right on top at the line. He should continue to give a good account of himself at this level. (op 4-1)
Grey Boy(GER) went down fighting and should continue in good form for his new yard. (tchd 3-1 in places)
Tough Love was having his second outing here in two days and is better over a mile than shorter. He did well improving from last in a race that was a tactical affair. (op 8-1)
Jubilee Street(IRE), weighted to the limit, deserves credit staying on from off what was not a strong early pace. (op 7-1)
Mutawaffer, without a win for over two years, is proving frustrating and the ground here was plenty fast enough for him. (tchd 4-1)
Sake(IRE), 5lb higher than his last win, found this too tough. (op 12-1)

3550 JOHN SMITH'S EXTRA COLD H'CAP 6f

2:45 (2:45) (Class 3) (0-95,93) 3-Y-O+ £9,715 (£2,890; £1,444; £721) Stalls Centre

Form				RPR
5-42	1		**Wyatt Earp (IRE)**4 3374 5-9-4 **84** PaulHanagan 1 (R A Fahey) *w ldrs: led over 2f out: hld on towards fin* 13/8[1]	93
0104	2	nk	**Beaver Patrol (IRE)**9 3211 4-9-13 **93** AlanMunro 7 (R F Johnson Houghton) *mde most: hdd over 2f out: rallied fnl f: no ex towards fin* 5/2[2]	101
0500	3	1	**Connect**14 3077 9-9-13 **93** (b) NCallan 3 (M H Tompkins) *in rr: sn pushed along: hdwy over 2f out: styd on fnl f* 11/2[3]	98
25	4	shd	**First Order**14 3092 5-9-7 **87** JohnEgan 5 (Ernst Oertel) *trckd ldrs: n.m.r over 1f out: styd on wl* 7/1	92
3000	5	1/2	**High Reach**21 2847 6-9-10 **90** RichardMullen 8 (W R Muir) *w ldrs: chal over 3f out: kpt on same pce fnl f* 16/1	93
5440	6	nk	**Roman Maze**49 2017 6-9-6 **86** DavidAllan 4 (W M Brisbourne) *chsd ldrs: effrt and hung lft over 2f out: kpt on* 12/1	88
0250	7	12	**The History Man (IRE)**7 3296 3-7-9 **74** (b) AdeleRothery(7) 6 (M W Easterby) *rrd s: hdwy on outside to chse ldrs after 2f: hung lft and lost pl over 1f out* 25/1	40

1m 11.2s (-1.36) **Going Correction** -0.225s/f (Firm)
WFA 3 from 4yo+ 6lb 7 Ran SP% **112.0**
Speed ratings (Par 107):100,99,98,98,97 97,81
CSF £5.54 CT £15.93 TOTE £2.30: £1.60, £1.70; EX 5.20 Trifecta £17.90 Pool: £643.62 - 25.50 winning units..
Owner Los Bandidos Racing **Bred** J W Parker And Keith Wills **Trained** Musley Bank, N Yorks

FOCUS
A moderate winning time for the class but it looks sound form with the winner and the fourth duplicating their most recent mark

NOTEBOOK
Wyatt Earp(IRE), in top form, was making a quick return and with the leader covered in what was not a strong gallop, he was always doing just enough. He should continue to give a good account of himself. (op 7-4 tchd 2-1 and 15-8 in a place)
Beaver Patrol(IRE), allowed to set his own pace, was coming back for more at the line and deserves full marks. (op 11-4)
Connect, still 3lb higher than his last win, showed he is fully effective over six but he would have preferred an end-to-end gallop. (op 5-1)
First Order, best described as 'a bit of a monkey', has done all his winning over the minimum trip but that was over two years ago. He was messed about at a crucial stage and deserves credit for this especially as he would have prefered a stronger gallop. (op 6-1)
High Reach, down 3lb, likes flat tracks and ran a lot better than of late.
Roman Maze, back after a seven-week break, is slipping to a favourable mark and the outing will not be lost on him.
The History Man(IRE) Official explanation: jockey said gelding missed the break

3551 JOHN SMITH'S EXTRA SMOOTH SILVER CUP H'CAP (LISTED RACE) 1m 5f 197y

3:20 (3:22) (Class 1) (0-110,105) 3-Y-O+
£19,873 (£7,532; £3,769; £1,879; £941; £472) Stalls Low

Form				RPR
-211	1		**Linas Selection**22 2805 3-8-10 **103** KDarley 1 (M Johnston) *trckd ldr: shkn up over 4f out: led over 3f out: styd on strly: eased towards fin* 8/11[1]	112+
4210	2	1	**Balkan Knight**21 2848 6-9-13 **105** JohnEgan 2 (D R C Elsworth) *hld up: smooth hdwy to chal over 2f out: nt qckn ins last* 6/1[2]	113
30-3	3	1 1/2	**Lost Soldier Three (IRE)**20 2893 5-9-13 **105** EddieAhern 4 (L M Cumani) *trckd ldrs: effrt 4f out: styd on same pce fnl 2f* 7/1[3]	111
2203	4	2	**Palomar (USA)**21 2848 4-9-10 **102** ShaneKelly 8 (R Charlton) *t.k.h in rr: hdwy 3f out: kpt on same pce: nvr rchd ldrs* 8/1	105
-016	5	1	**Kiswahili**27 2689 4-9-3 **95** NCallan 5 (Sir Mark Prescott) *t.k.h in rr: effrt over 3f out: n.m.r over 1f out: nvr rchd ldrs* 20/1	97
2535	6	4	**Vinando**7 3315 5-9-10 **102** (bt) PaulHanagan 6 (C R Egerton) *s.i.s: sn drvn along: hdwy to chse ldrs after 3f: outpcd over 3f out: kpt on fnl f* 25/1	98
2-13	7	21	**Hearthstead Wings**73 1409 4-9-11 **103** (v) JoeFanning 3 (M Johnston) *led tl over 3f out: lost pl over 1f out: eased and sn bhd* 12/1	70

2m 57.57s (-0.87) **Going Correction** -0.025s/f (Good)
WFA 3 from 4yo+ 15lb 7 Ran SP% **112.1**
Speed ratings (Par 111):101,100,99,98,97 95,83
CSF £5.27 CT £16.65 TOTE £1.70: £1.20, £3.00; EX 6.40 Trifecta £18.60 Pool: £832.14 - 31.74 winning units..
Owner Mrs R J Jacobs **Bred** Newsells Park Stud Limited **Trained** Middleham Moor, N Yorks

FOCUS
Hearthstead Wings dropped anchor in front resulting a a very moderate winning time for a race of its stature. However, the form looks strong rated through the two placed horses.

NOTEBOOK
Linas Selection, 13lb higher, worked hard to get his head in front. He really battled and was able to take things easily near the line. He is a highly progressive young stayer and the St Leger must be in his sights now. sdf sdf sdf, 13lb higher, worked hard to get his head in front. He really battled and was able to take things easily near the line. He is a highly progressive young stayer and the St Leger must be in his sights now. (op 4-5 tchd 5-6 and 4-6 in places)

Balkan Knight moved upsides travelling the better but in the end he was very much second best. He should continue to give a good account of himself in these highly competitive handicaps.
Lost Soldier Three(IRE), who took this a year ago from a 1lb lower mark, appreciated the step up in trip but, on ground plenty lively enough for him, he never really threatened to get in a blow.
Palomar(USA), again fitted with earplugs, was keen to get on with it. He tended to edge left under pressure and never really got competitive. (op 7-1)
Kiswahili, who looked her best, was as usual loaded with the help of a blanket. The race was definitely not run to suit her, she is basically just a stayer. (tchd 25-1)
Vinando, who showed a moderate action going to post, ran a stale sort of race. (tchd 28-1)
Hearthstead Wings, who moved poorly to post, dropped anchor in front. In the end he dropped right out and was reported to have finished lame behind.

3552 47TH JOHN SMITH'S CUP (HERITAGE H'CAP) 1m 2f 88y

3:55 (3:56) (Class 2) 3-Y-O+
£93,480 (£27,990; £13,995; £7,005; £3,495; £1,755) Stalls Low

Form				RPR
0012	1		**Fairmile**17 2989 4-8-12 **91** AdamKirby(3) 9 (W R Swinburn) *hld up towards rr: hdwy and swtchd outside over 2f out: r.o wl to ld last 100yds* 6/1[1]	101+
4060	2	3/4	**Bravo Maestro (USA)**21 2848 5-8-9 **90** JamesDoyle(5) 3 (N P Littmoden) *lw: hld up in mid-div: hdwy and nt clr run 2f out: r.o wl fnl f: no ex wl ins last* 12/1	99+
6000	3	1/2	**Boo**9 3218 4-9-0 **90** PatCosgrave 2 (K R Burke) *wl in tch: hdwy over 3f out: led over 1f out: hdd and no ex ins last* 50/1	98
-410	4	shd	**Forgery (IRE)**24 2742 4-9-3 **93** JohnEgan 16 (G A Butler) *in rr: hdwy on ins over 3f out: styd on wl fnl 2f* 8/1[3]	101+
2100	5	nk	**Chantaco (USA)**21 2848 4-9-4 **94** LPKeniry 5 (A M Balding) *hld up in mid-div: hdwy over 3f out: swtchd outside over 2f out: kpt on same pce ins last* 8/1[3]	101
0020	6	1	**Bustan (IRE)**24 2742 7-9-8 **98** PhillipMakin 1 (G C Bravery) *trckd ldr: led over 2f out: hdd appr fnl f: wknd towards fin* 50/1	103
1353	7	shd	**Star Of Light**7 3294 5-9-10 **100** AlanMunro 4 (B J Meehan) *chsd ldrs: styng on same pce whn n.m.r ins last* 6/1[1]	105
-500	8	1 1/2	**Courageous Duke (USA)**22 2803 7-9-10 **100** ShaneKelly 18 (J Noseda) *hld up in rr: hdwy on outside over 2f out: styd on: nt rch ldrs* 25/1	102+
0440	9	1	**El Coto**24 2742 6-9-2 **92** CatherineGannon 20 (K A Ryan) *in rr: hdwy u.p on ins over 3f out: nvr nr ldrs* 40/1	92+
6001	10	2	**Go Tech**21 2872 6-8-11 **87** 5ex DavidAllan 7 (T D Easterby) *hld up in rr: hdwy on outer over 2f out: nvr nr ldrs* 25/1	83
0310	11	1 1/2	**Divine Gift**24 2742 5-9-7 **97** NCallan 6 (K A Ryan) *chsd ldrs: chal over 2f out: sn wknd* 33/1	91
03-3	12	1 1/4	**Motive (FR)**77 1298 5-9-4 **94** TonyHamilton 17 (J Howard Johnson) *trckd ldrs: wknd over 1f out* 25/1	85
-651	13	1	**Great Plains**17 2989 4-9-4 **94** 5ex EddieAhern 14 (Mrs A J Perrett) *rr-div: effrt on outer whn bmpd over 2f out: n.d after* 14/1	83
0310	14	1	**Blue Spinnaker (IRE)**22 2803 7-9-9 **99** PaulMulrennan 19 (M W Easterby) *in rr: sme hdwy on outer 3f out: nvr on terms* 25/1	86
0051	15	1 3/4	**Impeller (IRE)**2 3432 7-9-3 **98** RichardMullen 15 (W R Muir) *mid-div: hrd drvn over 3f out: nvr on terms* 20/1	77
06-3	16	hd	**James Caird (IRE)**35 2435 6-8-9 **88** SaleemGolam(3) 10 (M H Tompkins) *hld up in rr: nvr a factor* 16/1	72
0330	17	9	**Focus Group (USA)**42 2229 5-8-13 **89** GrahamGibbons 12 (J J Quinn) *a in rr* 20/1	56

-551 **18** 1 ½ **I'm So Lucky**22 2803 4-9-11 101 5ex JoeFanning 13 65
(M Johnston) *led tl over 2f out: sn lost pl* 7/1[2]

2030 **19** 9 **Dunaskin (IRE)**7 3294 6-9-3 93 PaulFessey 8 40
(Karen McLintock) *chsd ldrs: lost pl over 3f out: bhd whn eased over 1f out* 66/1

1-10 **20** 1 ½ **Public Forum**22 2803 4-9-6 96 KDarley 11 40
(Sir Michael Stoute) *mid-div: drvn over 3f out: sn lost pl: bhd whn eased over 1f out* 10/1

2m 7.66s (-2.82) **Going Correction** -0.025s/f (Good) **20** Ran SP% **128.3**
Speed ratings (Par 109):110,109,109,108,108 107,107,106,105,104 103,102,101,100,99 98,91,90,83,82
CSF £68.50 CT £3358.10 TOTE £8.20: £1.90, £4.30, £6.10, £3.00; EX 116.20 Trifecta £5496.30 Pool: £40,828.95 - 5.30 winning units..
Owner Mrs P W Harris **Bred** Pendley Farm **Trained** Aldbury, Herts

FOCUS
A traditionally strong handicap but with no three-year-olds in the line-up this time, and those drawn in double figures again struggled to make an impact. The gallop was sound throughout and four out of the first five came from off the pace. The form looks both strong and solid.

NOTEBOOK
Fairmile, due to race from a 6lb higher mark in future, travelled strongly towards the rear. Pulled outside, he moved forward with real determination and was firmly in command at the line. The boy was very cool. (op 7-1 tchd 15-2 in a place)
Bravo Maestro(USA), leniently treated compared with his All-Weather mark, looked at his very best. Denied a run at a crucial stage, he would have given the winner more to do but on the day looked only second best.
Boo showed the benfit of his Haydock outing and went down with all guns blazing.
Forgery(IRE) ◆, 4lb higher than Newbury, had an outside draw to overcome. Last of all turning in, he enjoyed a dream run up the inner and was catching the three ahead of him at the line. He seemed to appreciate the step back up in trip and deserves to find another good prize.
Chantaco(USA), full of beans in the parade, likes the hurly burly of these big handicaps. Pulled outside, he was only found lacking in the closing stages.
Bustan(IRE) rolled back the clock but he saw the front plenty soon enough and he had no more to offer near the line.
Star Of Light, back over his best trip and reunited with his favourite rider, was only keeping on in his own time when left short of racing room inside the last. (tchd 13-2)
Courageous Duke(USA), having his second outing after a break, had an outside draw to overcome. He made steady ground down the wide outside but was never going to get close enough to take a real hand.
El Coto had the worst of the draw.
I'm So Lucky, under his 5lb penalty, had to be rousted along to lead. Given no peace in front, in the end he dropped right away. (op 8-1)
Dunaskin(IRE) Official explanation: jockey said gelding lost its action

3553 JOHN SMITH'S MEDIAN AUCTION MAIDEN STKS 6f
4:25 (4:27) (Class 4) 2-Y-O **£6,800** (£2,023; £1,011; £505) **Stalls** Centre

Form RPR

1 **Codeword (IRE)** 2-9-3 JoeFanning 5 92+
(M Johnston) *rangy: scope: led over 1f: w ldr: styd on to ld last 100yds: r.o wl* 13/2[3]

22 **2** 1 **Vauquelin (IRE)**18 2960 2-9-3 RichardMullen 1 89
(E S McMahon) *sn trcking ldrs: led over 4f out: hdd and no ex ins last* 1/2[1]

3 1 ¼ **All You Need (IRE)** 2-9-3 LPKeniry 4 85
(R Hollinshead) *lengthy: trckd ldrs: kpt on wl fnl f* 33/1

0 **4** 2 **World's Heroine (IRE)**22 2816 2-8-9 AdamKirby(3) 6 74
(G A Butler) *sn outpcd and in rr: hdwy over 1f out: styd on ins last* 16/1

5 4 **Inspirina (IRE)** 2-9-3 EddieAhern 7 67
(T R George) *gd sort: chsd ldrs: drvn over 2f out: lost pl over 1f out* 4/1[2]

0 **6** 10 **Bowman's Boy (IRE)**66 1588 2-9-3 PaulMulrennan 3 37
(M W Easterby) *chsd ldrs: lost pl over 2f out: sn bhd* 66/1

00 **7** 4 **Ruthles Philly**16 3018 2-8-12 PaulHanagan 2 20
(D W Barker) *keen: in tch: outpcd after 2f: lost pl 2f out* 66/1

1m 11.42s (-1.14) **Going Correction** -0.225s/f (Firm) **7** Ran SP% **111.8**
Speed ratings (Par 96):98,96,95,92,87 73,68
CSF £9.81 TOTE £5.20: £2.40, £1.20; EX 9.40.
Owner Jumeirah Racing **Bred** Mrs Lisa Kelly **Trained** Middleham Moor, N Yorks

FOCUS
A decent juvenile event run in a decent fast time and the winner looks Group class already.

NOTEBOOK
Codeword(IRE) ◆, who has plenty of size and scope, looked to be carrying a fair amount of condition. He knew his job and buckled down well to get right on top at the line. It was a quick time and he looks a very good prospect. (op 7-1)
Vauquelin(IRE) soon showed ahead but in the end he simply met on too good. His turn is surely only delayed. (op 4-7 tchd 4-6 and 8-13 in places)
All You Need(IRE), sold for 10,000gns at the breeze-up sales, seemed to run very well on his debut.
World's Heroine(IRE) stayed on in her won time after struggling to go the pace and a seventh furlong will aid her cause. (op 14-1)
Inspirina(IRE), who changed trainer's the previous day, looks the part and changed hands for 58,000gns at the breeze-up sales. Deep-bodied, he might not appreciate the ground as quick as this and is surely better than he showed on this day. (op 7-2)

3554 JOHN SMITH'S "NO NONSENSE RACING" MAIDEN FILLIES' STKS 7f
5:00 (5:01) (Class 4) 3-4-Y-O **£6,800** (£2,023; £1,011; £505) **Stalls** Low

Form RPR

0 **1** **Josie Marcus (USA)**30 2587 3-9-0 ShaneKelly 9 83
(J Noseda) *trckd ldrs: led over 1f out: r.o strly* 12/1

3-44 **2** 2 ½ **Pearl's Girl**36 2406 3-9-0 77 PaulHanagan 7 76+
(W J Haggas) *swvd rt s: hdwy over 2f out: nt clr run 1f out: styd on to take 2nd nr fin* 4/1[3]

6 **3** nk **Mail Express (IRE)**21 2859 3-9-0 NCallan 8 76
(L M Cumani) *lw: hmpd and carried rt s: hld up: hdwy over 3f out: n.m.r 2f out: styd on ins last* 7/2[2]

32-4 **4** hd **Call Me Waki (USA)**8 3266 3-9-0 70 LPKeniry 2 75
(A M Balding) *led tl over 1f out: kpt on same pce* 5/1

-320 **5** 1 ¼ **Another Genepi (USA)**29 2620 3-9-0 72 AlanMunro 4 72
(J W Hills) *chsd ldrs: kpt on same pce appr fnl f* 11/2

50 **6** 9 **Footstepsinthesnow (IRE)**14 3090 3-9-0 DavidAllan 6 47
(M A Buckley) *hdwy on ins to chse ldrs over 4f out: lost pl over 1f out* 40/1

4 **7** nk **Tilbury**17 2985 3-9-0 EddieAhern 5 47
(H R A Cecil) *in tch: drvn over 3f out: sn lost pl* 10/3[1]

0- **8** 5 **Whoopee (USA)**391 2735 3-9-0 JoeFanning 1 33
(M Johnston) *chsd ldrs: lost pl over 1f out* 14/1

000- **9** ¾ **Ochil Hills Dancer (IRE)**299 5360 4-9-5 40 DNolan(3) 10 31
(A Crook) *chsd ldrs on outer: lost pl over 2f* 100/1

1m 23.1s (-2.30) **Going Correction** -0.225s/f (Firm)
WFA 3 from 4yo 8lb **9** Ran SP% **115.1**
Speed ratings (Par 102):104,101,100,100,99 88,88,82,81
CSF £59.39 TOTE £14.00: £3.30, £1.80, £1.80; EX 51.20.
Owner Edward J Kelly Jr & Michael M Kelly **Bred** Indian Springs Farm Inc **Trained** Newmarket, Suffolk

FOCUS
An ordinary fillies' maiden race but the winner was a big improver on her debut effort when well supported. The fourth is officially rated just 70 and with the runner-up sets the standard with the time reasonable.

3555 JOHN SMITH'S "PREMIER CLUB" STKS (NURSERY) 5f
5:30 (5:31) (Class 3) 2-Y-O **£7,772** (£2,312; £1,155; £577) **Stalls** Centre

Form RPR

2602 **1** **Avertuoso**8 3239 2-9-2 88 MarkLawson(5) 5 93
(B Smart) *trckd ldr: edgd rt and led over 1f out: r.o wl* 13/2

645 **2** 1 ¼ **Danum Dancer**29 2623 2-8-5 72 AlanMunro 2 73
(N Bycroft) *chsd ldrs: hung rt 1f out: no ex ins last* 8/1

01 **3** ¾ **Compton Fields**13 3110 2-8-5 77 RichardKingscote(5) 7 75
(R Charlton) *hld up: hdwy over 2f out: n.m.r over 1f out: styd on same pce* 7/2[1]

041 **4** ¾ **Valley Of The Moon (IRE)**10 3188 2-8-7 74 PaulHanagan 3 69
(R A Fahey) *sn pushed along in rr: hdwy 2f out: styd on same pce appr fnl f* 4/1[2]

6130 **5** nk **Mr Klick (IRE)**49 2009 2-8-13 83 DNolan(3) 1 77
(N Wilson) *in rr: drvn and hdwy over 2f out: kpt on same pce appr f* 16/1

4653 **6** 1 **The Nifty Fox**29 2623 2-8-7 74 DavidAllan 8 64
(T D Easterby) *chsd ldrs on inner: wknd fnl f* 9/2[3]

026 **7** 2 ½ **La Vecchia Scuola (IRE)**17 2973 2-8-4 71 PaulQuinn 4 52
(D Nicholls) *chsd ldrs: wknd fnl f* 12/1

053 **8** 2 ½ **Hawaii Prince**14 3080 2-8-9 76 JoeFanning 6 48
(D Nicholls) *led: hdd and hmpd over 1f out: sn wknd* 9/2[3]

58.66 secs (-0.66) **Going Correction** -0.225s/f (Firm) **8** Ran SP% **116.6**
Speed ratings (Par 98):96,94,92,91,91 89,85,81
CSF £57.88 CT £213.58 TOTE £9.30: £2.30, £3.00, £1.60; EX 93.50 Place 6 £12.57, Place 5 £7.38.
Owner Pinnacle Averti Partnership **Bred** P A Mason **Trained** Hambleton, N Yorks
■ Stewards' Enquiry : Mark Lawson caution: careless riding

FOCUS
Fair nursery form and the winner must be worth another try in Listed company now. The official ratings shown next to each horse are estimated and for information purposes only.

NOTEBOOK
Avertuoso looked at his very best and defied topweight in game fashion. He is well worth another try in Listed company. (tchd 7-1)
Danum Dancer went down fighting but looked ill at ease on the quick ground.
Compton Fields, who lacks a bit of size and scope, was put to sleep at the back. He was tightened up when trying to improve and looked second best on the day. (op 3-1 tchd 4-1 in places)
Valley Of The Moon(IRE) struggled to go the pace but stuck on in willing fashion and looks ready for a step up to six furlongs. (op 3-1)
Mr Klick(IRE), edgy beforehand, has started life in nursery company on a stiffish mark. (op 14-1)
The Nifty Fox, in the thick of things, dropped out in disappointing fashion. (op 8-1)
Hawaii Prince, dropping back to the minimum trip, took them along but his chance had slipped when he was forced to take evasive action. Official explanation: jockey said colt suffered interference in running (op 5-1 tchd 11-2)
T/Jkpt: Not won. T/Plt: £16.70 to a £1 stake. Pool: £160,017.30. 6,983.20 winning tickets. T/Qpdt: £9.20 to a £1 stake. Pool: £5,595.70. 447.55 winning tickets. WG

3556 - 3558a (Foreign Racing) - See Raceform Interactive

3123 CURRAGH (R-H)
Saturday, July 15

OFFICIAL GOING: Good to firm

3559a LADBROKES.COM INTERNATIONAL STKS (GROUP 3) 1m
4:00 (4:04) 3-Y-O+ **£33,620** (£9,827; £4,655; £1,551)

RPR

1 **Mustameet (USA)**13 3129 5-9-7 115 DPMcDonogh 3 115
(Kevin Prendergast, Ire) *trckd ldrs: mainly 4th: 3rd under 2f out: rdn to chal and ld over 1f out: styd on wl fnl f: all out* 9/4[2]

2 hd **Ace (IRE)**24 2741 5-9-7 116 KFallon 7 115
(A P O'Brien, Ire) *racd mainly 5th: clsr in 4th over 1f out: sn rdn in 2nd: styd on wl: nt rch wnr: jst failed* 5/4[1]

3 2 **Modeeroch (IRE)**7 3322 3-8-9 103 KJManning 6 106
(J S Bolger, Ire) *towards rr in 6th: clsr in 4th fr 2f out: rdn to chal in 2nd 1f out: sn dropped to 3rd and kpt on same pce* 14/1

4 shd **Killybegs (IRE)**70 1486 3-9-1 MJKinane 4 111+
(B W Hills) *trckd ldrs in 3rd: 5th and no imp u.p fr over 1f out: kpt on ins fnl f* 5/1[3]

5 ½ **Hurricane Cat (USA)**41 2278 3-9-1 105 JAHeffernan 2 110
(A P O'Brien, Ire) *trckd ldr in 2nd: rdn fr 3f out: no imp u.p and kpt on same pce fr over 1f out* 12/1

6 nk **Latino Magic (IRE)**135 564 6-9-7 RMBurke 1 109
(R J Osborne, Ire) *s.i.s: in rr: no imp u.p and kpt on same pce fr over 1f out* 25/1

7 4 **Kings Point (IRE)**42 2226 5-9-7 (p) PJSmullen 5 101
(R A Fahey) *led: strly pressed and hdd over 1f out where checked: sn no ex* 14/1

1m 39.3s
WFA 3 from 5yo+ 9lb **7** Ran SP% **116.8**
CSF £5.65 TOTE £2.50: £1.80, £1.80; DF 7.10.
Owner Hamdan Al Maktoum **Bred** Shadwell Farm LLC **Trained** Friarstown, Co Kildare
■ Stewards' Enquiry : D P McDonogh caution: careless riding

NOTEBOOK
Mustameet(USA) is enjoying a terrific campaign, and made it four wins from six starts this season with a game performance under a well-judged ride. Declan McDonogh stole a couple of vital lengths on his main rival when going for home over one furlong out, and it provided sufficient cushion to secure a second Group 3 success of an increasingly worthy career. Five of his six wins have come over a mile, and he has all the attributes that one would look for in a miler at this level. (op 7/4)

Ace(IRE) performed with great credit on the international stage last year, but it is becoming difficult not to make repeated reference to the cold statistic that he has failed to win a race since August 2004. It would be churlish to criticise him for his failure to win during last season's top-level campaign, but there is no doubt that he came here with something to prove, on the temperamental front at least, after flops at Epsom and Royal Ascot. Although he failed to rectify an important omission in terms of obtaining a confidence-boosting win, this was by no means an unsatisfactory performance, since he seemed much more relaxed through the race, and stayed on all the way to the line once his challenge developed momentum. From an overall perspective, he deserves to win a big pot. (op 6/4 tchd 7/4)
Modeeroch(IRE), a smart juvenile who is still seeking her first win as a three-year-old, did nothing wrong in a race in which the two market principals stood out at the weights. She has the ability to win a good prize before too long. (op 10/1)
Killybegs(IRE) ran a sound race on his first run since finishing down the field in the 2000 Guineas. He may not be quite in the front rank of his generation in the way one might expect of a Craven winner, but there is no reason why he should fail to participate effectively at Group 3 level in the second half of the season. (op 5/1 tchd 6/1)
Kings Point(IRE), whose rating of 103 left him well short of the standard required here, led for a long way before dropping out of contention a furlong out. (op 12/1)

3561a LADBROKES ROCKINGHAM H'CAP (PREMIER HANDICAP) 5f
5:00 (5:00) 3-Y-O+
£41,448 (£13,172; £6,275; £2,137; £1,448; £758)

RPR

1 **Osterhase (IRE)**[13] 3124 7-10-3 110 (b) FMBerry 1 118
(J E Mulhern, Ire) *led: strly pressed and narrowly hdd 1f out: rallied to regain ld cl home* **6/4**[1]

2 *hd* **Leitra (IRE)**[27] 2688 3-9-2 100 JMurtagh 9 107
(M Halford, Ire) *sn trckd ldr in 2nd: rdn to chal and ld 1f out: kpt on wl u.p: hdd cl home* **7/1**[3]

3 *3/4* **Bo McGinty (IRE)**[7] 3281 5-8-6 85 (b) WSupple 13 90
(R A Fahey) *mid-div: 8th under 2f out: rdn to go mod 3rd under 1f out: styd on wl without rching ldrs* **9/1**

4 *3 1/2* **Coseadrom (IRE)**[15] 3059 4-8-1 83 CDHayes(3) 10 75
(Peter Henley, Ire) *mid-div: 6th 2f out: rdn and kpt on wout threatening into 4th fnl f* **20/1**

5 *shd* **Vintage Year (IRE)**[15] 3059 4-7-11 83 MACleere(7) 2 75
(T J O'Mara, Ire) *chsd ldrs: 4th 2f out: sn no imp u.p: kpt on same pce* **16/1**

6 *1/2* **Waterways (IRE)**[27] 2688 3-9-2 100 NGMcCullagh 3 90
(P J Prendergast, Ire) *prom: no imp u.p and kpt on same pce fr over 1f out* **10/1**

7 *3/4* **Benwilt Breeze (IRE)**[13] 3125 4-8-13 92 (t) DPMcDonogh 12 79
(G M Lyons, Ire) *prom: rdn and no imp fr over 1f out: kpt on same pce* **16/1**

8 *1/2* **Point Calimere (IRE)**[13] 3125 5-7-13 83 (t) DJMoran(5) 6 68
(Liam McAteer, Ire) *cl up: rdn bef 1/2-way: no imp fr under 2f out* **20/1**

9 *nk* **Libras Child (IRE)**[3] 3422 7-7-13 83 SMGorey(5) 5 67
(P Delaney, Ire) *towards rr for most: nvr a factor* **40/1**

10 *3* **Free Roses (IRE)**[6] 3332 3-9-2 100 KFallon 4 73
(Edward Lynam, Ire) *chsd ldrs early: towards rr and no imp u.p fr over 1 1/2f out* **5/1**[2]

11 *1/2* **Belleinga (IRE)**[41] 2269 5-8-11 90 PJSmullen 11 62
(T F Lacy, Ire) *sn chsd ldrs: 8th 2f out: sn no imp u.p* **16/1**

12 *1* **Tigim (IRE)**[15] 3059 7-8-4 83 (b) MCHussey 7 51
(Peter Henley, Ire) *dwlt: towards rr for most: nvr a factor* **25/1**

13 *1 3/4* **Namaya (IRE)**[40] 2311 3-9-2 100 KJManning 8 62
(J S Bolger, Ire) *mid-div: 7th 1/2-way: no imp u.p fr under 2f out* **33/1**

58.90 secs
WFA 3 from 4yo+ 5lb **13** Ran SP% **124.7**
CSF £11.61 CT £80.64 TOTE £2.40: £1.60, £1.90, £2.90; DF 17.50.
Owner Michael Rosenfeld **Bred** E Kopica & M Rosenfeld **Trained** the Curragh, Co Kildare

NOTEBOOK
Bo McGinty(IRE) has been in good form in British sprint handicaps and ran right up to his best, producing a strong late surge that saw him draw well clear of the remainder (op 7/1)

3560 - 3562a (Foreign Racing) - See Raceform Interactive

HAMBURG (R-H)
Saturday, July 15

OFFICIAL GOING: Good

3563a JAXX-POKAL (HAMBURGER MEILE) (GROUP 3) 1m
4:40 (4:46) 3-Y-O+ **£22,069** (£6,897; £3,448; £2,069)

RPR

1 **Lateral**[40] 2314 3-8-9 WMongil 10 110
(P Schiergen, Germany) *always close up, 5th straight, led 2f out, soon clear, ran on well* **6/4**[1]

2 *4* **Willingly (GER)**[27] 2692 7-9-6 ADeVries 9 104
(M Trybuhl, Germany) *mid-division, stayed on final 2f to take 2nd last strides* **61/10**[2]

3 *hd* **Azarole (IRE)**[77] 1299 5-9-6 PatDobbs 1 104
(J S Moore) *tracked leaders, 3rd straight, soon ridden & outpaced, ran on to take 2nd inside final f, no extra & lost 2nd last strides* **76/10**

4 *1 1/4* **Binary File (USA)**[20] 8-9-6 THellier 11 101
(L Kelp, Sweden) *dwelt start, behind to straight, headway on outside from 2f out, one pace final f* **124/10**

5 *hd* **Jubilation**[27] 7-9-6 ABoschert 7 101
(F Reuterskiold, Sweden) *mid-division, 6th straight, switched left over 1f out, not clear run inside final f, never nearer* **82/10**

6 *2* **Lord Areion (GER)**[265] 6049 4-9-2 TMundry 8 93
(H J Groschel, Germany) *never near to challenge* **103/10**

7 *1 1/2* **Lucidor (GER)**[40] 2314 3-8-9 AStarke 6 92
(Frau E Mader, Germany) *always towards rear* **15/2**[3]

8 *hd* **Rushing Dasher (GER)** 4-9-2 EPedroza 5 89
(A Wohler, Germany) *led to 2f out* **101/10**

9 *3* **Silex (GER)**[34] 3-8-9 FilipMinarik 3 85
(P Schiergen, Germany) *mid-division, slipped through on inside to dispute 3rd straight, beaten well over 1f out* **14/1**

10 *2* **Proudance (GER)**[43] 2217 4-9-6 AHelfenbein 4 83
(R Suerland, Germany) *prominent, went 2nd half-way, 2nhd straight, soon weakened* **79/10**

1m 35.75s
WFA 3 from 4yo+ 9lb **10** Ran SP% **131.6**
(including ten euro stakes): WIN 25; PL 13, 16, 21; SF 140.

Owner Stiftung Gestut Fahrhof **Bred** Stiftung Gestut Fahrhof **Trained** Germany

NOTEBOOK
Azarole(IRE), having raced prominently, got outpaced at the top of the home straight. Finding his second wind, he went second soon after the furlong pole, only to lose that position right on the line. This was a good effort after an 11-week break, although he did have a hard race which might leave its mark.

3132 MAISONS-LAFFITTE (R-H)
Saturday, July 15

OFFICIAL GOING: Good to soft

3564a PRIX DE RIS-ORANGIS (GROUP 3) 6f (S)
3:20 (3:21) 3-Y-O+ **£27,586** (£11,034; £8,276; £5,517; £2,759)

RPR

1 **Presto Shinko (IRE)**[27] 2675 5-9-0 TThulliez 1 111
(R Hannon) *always close up on rails, headway & switched right well over 1f out, quickened to lead 150yds out, driven out* **108/10**

2 *nk* **Satri (IRE)**[40] 2313 4-9-4 OPeslier 2 113
(J-M Beguigne, France) *always in touch, staying on when hmpd by 3rd well over 1f out, rallied inside final f, finished 4th, nk shd 3/4l, placed 2nd* **46/10**[2]

3 *shd* **Tycoon's Hill (IRE)**[23] 2799 7-9-0 JAuge 6 108
(Robert Collet, France) *pressed leader, every chance final f, ridden & unable to quicken closing stages, finished 2nd, nk, disq and placed 3rd* **47/10**[3]

4 *3/4* **Biniou (IRE)**[19] 2941 3-8-8 CSoumillon 4 108
(Robert Collet, France) *trckd ldrs, rdn & hung left well over 1f out, ev ch fnl f, unable to quicken cl hme, fin 3rd, nk shd, disq & plcd 4th* **47/10**[3]

5 *nse* **Karlo Guitar (BRZ)**[23] 2799 6-9-0 FSpanu 8 107?
(M Delzangles, France) *prominent on outside, every chance 1f out, kept on same pace* **33/1**

6 *3/4* **Marchand D'Or (FR)**[19] 2941 3-8-13 DBonilla 3 110
(F Head, France) *led on rails, headed 150yds out, one pace* **1/1**[1]

7 *1* **Abundance (USA)**[42] 4-8-10 RonanThomas 7 98
(Mme C Head-Maarek, France) *prominent on outside til no extra final f* **6/1**

8 *3* **Chantilly Beauty (FR)**[24] 2740 4-8-10 (b) TJarnet 5 89
(R Pritchard-Gordon, France) *always towards rear* **15/1**

9 *2 1/2* **Kuaicoss (IRE)**[55] 1871 4-9-1 MTellini 9 87
(A Renzoni, Italy) *in touch to over 1f out* **18/1**

1m 11.7s
WFA 3 from 4yo+ 6lb **9** Ran SP% **140.2**
PARI-MUTUEL: WIN 11.80; PL 3.10, 2.10, 4.10; DF 24.80.
Owner Major A M Everett **Bred** Mrs S O'Riordan **Trained** East Everleigh, Wilts

NOTEBOOK
Presto Shinko(IRE) gained his first Group win at the first attempt having previously been placed in Listed company. He was always close up just behind the leaders on the rails, made his move over a furlong out when switched right and quickened to lead 150 yards out to score in a blanket finish.
Satri(IRE), always up with the pace, he looked in a winning position before being bumped and interfered with a furlong out. He finished fourth but was promoted to second after the second and third were demoted.
Tycoon's Hill(IRE) tracked the leaders until making his move at the furlong marker. He hit the front inside the final furlong before being unable to resist the late surge of the winner. He finished second but was later demoted by the Stewards to third.
Biniou(IRE) tracked his stablemate for much of the race before trying to go up the inside and pass between the eventual third and sixth and then bumped the second. He produced a good finish but was demoted to fourth after a Stewards' enquiry

3292 HAYDOCK (L-H)
Sunday, July 16

OFFICIAL GOING: Good to firm
'Football Furlong' day, with riders representing Premiership clubs in a points competition and wearing club colours instead of owners' silks.
Wind: Light, across Weather: Hot and sunny

3565 32RED ONLINE CASINO H'CAP 7f 30y
2:20 (2:21) (Class 5) (0-70,70) 4-Y-O+ **£5,505** (£1,637; £818; £408) **Stalls** Low

Form RPR

4501 1 **Le Chiffre (IRE)**[13] 3158 4-8-9 **65** (p) MichaelJStainton(7) 2 75
(R A Harris) *a.p: rdn to ld over 2f out: a holding on cl home* **10/1**

3314 2 *nk* **Joshua's Gold (IRE)**[4] 3398 5-8-10 **62** (v) DanielTudhope(3) 7 71
(D Carroll) *midfield: hdwy 3f out: rdn to chse wnr over 2f out: sn edgd lft: r.o cl home* **5/1**[1]

4412 3 *1 1/4* **Lincolneurocruiser**[9] 3262 4-8-12 **68** RussellKennemore(7) 5 74
(Mrs N Macauley) *in tch: rdn over 2f out: kpt on ins fnl f: nt trble front pair* **5/1**[1]

1246 4 *1/2* **Franksalot (IRE)**[15] 3094 6-9-4 **67** RoystonFfrench 10 71
(I W McInnes) *midfield: rdn over 2f out: hdwy over 1f out: styd on ins fnl f: nt rch ldrs* **10/1**

1036 5 *1 1/2* **Takes Tutu (USA)**[8] 3298 7-9-7 **70** (p) PhilipRobinson 3 71
(C R Dore) *hld up: rdn over 2f out: styd on fnl f: nvr nrr* **15/2**[2]

5536 6 *3/4* **Efidium**[8] 3289 8-9-4 **67** ChrisCatlin 8 66
(N Bycroft) *hld up: hdwy ove r4f out: rdn over 2f out: one pce fnl f* **10/1**

3402 7 *shd* **Mistral Sky**[36] 2464 7-9-2 **65** (v) FrancisNorton 1 63
(Stef Liddiard) *midfield: rdn over 2f out: no imp* **8/1**[3]

-503 8 *2 1/2* **Convince (USA)**[9] 3245 5-8-13 **65** AdamKirby(3) 4 57
(J M Bradley) *racd keenly: led: rdn and hdd over 2f out: wknd over 1f out* **10/1**

0305 9 *hd* **Tamatave (IRE)**[8] 3298 4-9-1 **64** DO'Donohoe 6 55
(K A Ryan) *trckd ldrs: rdn over 2f out: wknd 1f out* **14/1**

0341 10 *1* **Stamford Blue**[20] 2920 5-8-13 **62** (b) AdrianMcCarthy 9 51
(R A Harris) *s.s: a bhd: eased whn n.d ins fnl f* **8/1**[3]

1m 29.66s (-2.40) **Going Correction** -0.325s/f (Firm) **10** Ran SP% **110.4**
Speed ratings (Par 103):100,99,98,97,95 95,94,92,91,90
CSF £55.50 CT £272.74 TOTE £12.40: £4.80, £1.90, £2.30; EX 110.60.
Owner www.gardenshedracing.com **Bred** Agricola Del Parco **Trained** Earlswood, Monmouths

FOCUS
A competitive race in which they went 5-1 the field, but it is modest handicap form.
Stamford Blue Official explanation: jockey said saddle slipped

3566 32RED POKER H'CAP — 1m 2f 120y

2:50 (2:50) (Class 5) (0-70,70) 3-Y-0+ £5,505 (£1,637; £818; £408) Stalls High

Form RPR

6024 **1** **Ruby Legend**[7] [3333] 8-8-9 **51**.......................................(b) DavidAllan 10 60
(K G Reveley) *trckd ldrs: wnt 2nd 4f out: led over 2f out: sn rdn and edgd lft: drvn out towards fin* **9/1**

-040 **2** *1* **Daring Affair**[29] [2656] 5-10-0 **70**....................................... PatCosgrave 8 77
(K R Burke) *trckd ldr to 4f out: rdn over 2f out: wnt 2nd again over 1f out: r.o towards fin* **18/1**

0332 **3** *1 ½* **Oddsmaker (IRE)**[17] [3019] 5-9-7 **63**.............................(t) FrancisNorton 6 67
(M A Barnes) *plld hrd: hld up: rdn and hdwy over 1f out: styd on ins fnl f* **7/2**[1]

0-00 **4** *1* **Lobengula (IRE)**[177] [163] 4-9-6 **62**........................... RoystonFfrench 5 65
(I W McInnes) *led: rdn and hdd over 2f out: one pce fnl f* **66/1**

2501 **5** *hd* **Gallego**[8] [3309] 4-9-3 **64**.. LiamJones(5) 9 66
(R J Price) *stdd s: racd keenly: hld up: rdn over 2f out: lugged lft over 1f out: styd on fnl f: nt rch ldrs* **7/2**[1]

2213 **6** *nk* **Trouble Mountain (USA)**[15] [3081] 9-10-0 **70**.................(t) DaleGibson 7 72
(M W Easterby) *midfield: hdwy over 4f out: rdn over 3f out: outpcd 2f out: kpt on ins fnl f* **9/2**[2]

5004 **7** *2* **Voice Mail**[8] [3309] 7-10-0 **70**..(b) LPKeniry 2 68
(A M Balding) *plld hrd: prom: rdn over 2f out: sn edgd lft: wknd over 1f out* **7/1**[3]

5350 **8** *nk* **Western Roots**[113] [723] 5-9-2 **58**....................................... ChrisCatlin 3 55
(M Appleby) *hld up: hdwy over 3f out: rdn over 2f out: wknd 1f out* **14/1**

0005 **9** *5* **Peters Delite**[8] [3283] 4-8-11 **53**....................................... PaulHanagan 4 41
(R A Fahey) *midfield tl pushed along and wknd over 3f out* **7/1**[3]

2m 15.35s (-2.38) **Going Correction** -0.325s/f (Firm) **9** Ran SP% **111.0**
Speed ratings (Par 103):95,94,93,92,92 92,90,90,86
CSF £146.01 CT £652.55 TOTE £10.40: £2.10, £4.00, £1.80; EX 101.10.
Owner Mrs J M Grimston **Bred** Huttons Ambo Stud **Trained** Lingdale, Redcar & Cleveland

FOCUS
A modest handicap run at a steady early pace.

3567 32RED.COM H'CAP — 6f

3:20 (3:23) (Class 4) (0-85,84) 4-Y-0+ £8,096 (£2,408; £1,203; £601) Stalls Centre

Form RPR

4332 **1** **Knot In Wood (IRE)**[10] [3217] 4-8-11 **74**.......................... PaulHanagan 5 87
(R A Fahey) *a.p: rdn to ld over 1f out: r.o wl* **2/1**[1]

0050 **2** *3* **Currency**[6] [3368] 9-8-7 **70**.. RoystonFfrench 7 74
(J M Bradley) *in tch: rdn and outpcd over 2f out: r.o to take 2nd post: no ch w wnr* **16/1**

02-5 **3** *shd* **Sir Nod**[90] [1042] 4-9-1 **78**.. TomEaves 9 82
(Miss J A Camacho) *sn prom: rdn 2f out: r.o same pce ins fnl f* **6/1**[2]

0130 **4** *hd* **Bond Boy**[36] [2450] 9-9-7 **84**.......................................(b) PhilipRobinson 3 87
(B Smart) *led: rdn and hdd over 1f out: no ex fnl strides* **8/1**[3]

0030 **5** *hd* **Looks Could Kill (USA)**[15] [3077] 4-9-5 **82**......................... EddieAhern 6 85
(E J Alston) *towards rr: rdn 1/2-way: r.o fnl f: nrst fin* **8/1**[3]

102 **6** *3* **Pick A Nice Name**[22] [2864] 4-8-1 **71** ow1............ MichaelJStainton(7) 10 65
(R M Whitaker) *s.i.s: in rr: effrt over 2f out: wknd 1f out* **8/1**[3]

0000 **7** *2 ½* **Prince Tum Tum (USA)**[28] [2681] 6-9-3 **80**......................(v[1]) JohnEgan 4 66+
(D W Barker) *in tch: rdn over 1f out: sn wknd: eased whn btn ins fnl f* **8/1**[3]

6004 **8** *5* **High Ridge**[10] [3217] 7-8-8 **74**..(p) AdamKirby(3) 1 45
(J M Bradley) *in tch: rdn over 2f out: sn wknd: eased whn btn ins fnl f* **10/1**

00-0 **9** *¾* **Orphan (IRE)**[10] [3217] 4-9-2 **79**.. PatCosgrave 2 48+
(K R Burke) *in tch: n.m.r after 1f and lost pl: keeping on but no imp on ldrs whn lost action and eased ins fnl f* **16/1**

1m 12.43s (-2.47) **Going Correction** -0.45s/f (Firm) **9** Ran SP% **112.9**
Speed ratings (Par 105):98,94,93,93,93 89,86,79,78
CSF £36.56 CT £164.15 TOTE £2.70: £1.10, £5.00, £3.20; EX 40.80.
Owner Rhodes, Kenyon & Gill **Bred** Rathbarry Stud **Trained** Musley Bank, N Yorks

Prince Tum Tum(USA) Official explanation: jockey said gelding had no more to give
High Ridge Official explanation: trainer said jockey was unable to get gelding covered up
Orphan(IRE) Official explanation: trainer said gelding was unsuited by the good to firm ground

3568 32RED CASINO H'CAP — 5f

3:50 (3:51) (Class 4) (0-80,80) 3-Y-0 £8,096 (£2,408; £1,203; £601) Stalls Centre

Form RPR

2202 **1** **Shes Minnie**[17] [3000] 3-9-1 **74**... TonyCulhane 7 83
(J G M O'Shea) *in tch: rdn over 1f out: sn wandered: r.o ins fnl f to ld towards fin* **9/2**[2]

4311 **2** *½* **Toy Top (USA)**[9] [3268] 3-9-7 **80**....................................(b) PhillipMakin 8 87
(M Dods) *a.p: led over 1f out: sn rdn: edgd lft ins fnl f: hdd towards fin* **4/1**[1]

5-00 **3** *1* **Rag Tag (IRE)**[17] [3027] 3-9-6 **79**...(t) LPKeniry 6 83
(A M Balding) *led: rdn and hdd over 1f out: stl ev ch ins fnl f: no ex fnl strides* **9/1**

6555 **4** *¾* **Choysia**[25] [2760] 3-9-4 **77**.. JohnEgan 10 78
(D W Barker) *s.i.s: in rr: rdn 1/2-way: edgd lft and hdwy over 1f out: styd on ins fnl f: nt pce of ldrs* **9/2**[2]

0545 **5** *½* **Peter Island (FR)**[3] [3449] 3-9-1 **74**..............................(v[1]) ChrisCatlin 3 73
(J Gallagher) *chsd ldrs: rdn and ev ch 2f out: styd on same pce fnl f* **11/2**[3]

101 **6** *10* **Mormeatmic**[22] [2855] 3-9-5 **78**.. PaulMulrennan 5 41
(M W Easterby) *in tch tl rdn and wknd 2f out* **8/1**

-060 **7** *1 ¾* **Christa Bee**[17] [3000] 3-9-1 **74**... FrancisNorton 4 31
(A Berry) *s.s: a bhd* **33/1**

3535 **8** *6* **Lucayos**[9] [3268] 3-8-10 **74**..............................(b) RichardKingscote(5) 2 9
(Mrs H Sweeting) *s.s: a wl bhd* **7/1**

58.75 secs (-3.32) **Going Correction** -0.45s/f (Firm) **10** Ran SP% **108.3**
Speed ratings (Par 102):108,107,105,104,103 87,84,75
CSF £20.32 CT £133.90 TOTE £5.00: £1.10, £2.20, £2.40; EX 11.30 Trifecta £382.00 Pool £538.05 - one winning unit..
Owner Alan Purvis **Bred** S Martin And Alan Purvis **Trained** Elton, Gloucs

FOCUS
A fair handicap run at a good pace throughout.
Lucayos Official explanation: jockey said colt was reluctant to leave the stalls

3569 32RED PROUDLY SPONSORS ASTON VILLA F.C. H'CAP — 1m 30y

4:25 (4:25) (Class 5) (0-70,71) 3-Y-0 £5,505 (£1,637; £818; £408) Stalls Low

Form RPR

0354 **1** **Cool Ebony**[17] [3030] 3-9-6 **69**.. PhillipMakin 2 76
(M Dods) *mde virtually all: rdn over 2f out: r.o ins fnl f whn pressed* **8/1**

3023 **2** *nk* **Sgt Schultz (IRE)**[6] [3364] 3-9-2 **65**... JohnEgan 8 71
(J S Moore) *hld up: hdwy over 2f out: ev ch wl ins fnl f: r.o* **4/1**[2]

0622 **3** *hd* **Daaweitza**[15] [3082] 3-9-6 **69**... TomEaves 5 75
(B Ellison) *midfield: swtchd lft whn rdn and hdwy over 2f out: ev ch fnl f over 1f out: nt qckn fnl strides* **5/1**[3]

6563 **4** *1* **Pab Special (IRE)**[9] [3266] 3-9-8 **71**................................... PatCosgrave 1 75
(K R Burke) *trckd ldrs: rdn over 1f out: ev ch ins fnl f: nt qckn* **16/1**

5-00 **5** *1 ¾* **Gates Of Eden (USA)**[20] [2929] 3-9-2 **65**.......................... HayleyTurner 6 65
(M L W Bell) *prom: rdn over 2f out: ev ch over 1f out: no ex ins fnl f* **12/1**

000 **6** *2* **Littledodayno (IRE)**[10] [3226] 3-8-13 **62**........................ FrancisNorton 10 57
(M Wigham) *stdd s: hld up: rdn and hdwy over 1f out: one pce ins fnl f* **22/1**

-642 **7** *nk* **High Class Problem (IRE)**[12] [3164] 3-9-2 **65**...............(b[1]) EddieAhern 4 59
(P F I Cole) *s.i.s: sn trckd ldrs: rdn and lost pl over 2f out: no imp after* **3/1**[1]

-545 **8** *½* **Moonstreaker**[22] [2873] 3-8-8 **64**........................... MichaelJStainton(7) 9 57
(R M Whitaker) *s.i.s: bhd: rdn and hdwy over 2f out: wknd fnl f* **14/1**

0323 **9** *2 ½* **Great Chieftain (IRE)**[27] [2698] 3-9-7 **70**.......................... PaulHanagan 7 57
(R A Fahey) *midfield tl rdn and wknd 2f out* **6/1**

00-0 **10** *2 ½* **Ditton Dancer**[33] [2518] 3-9-3 **66**.................................. GrahamGibbons 3 48
(J J Quinn) *racd keenly: w wnr tl rdn and wknd over 2f out* **25/1**

1m 42.77s (-2.74) **Going Correction** -0.325s/f (Firm) **10** Ran SP% **115.5**
Speed ratings (Par 100):100,99,99,98,96 94,94,93,91,88
CSF £39.65 CT £182.33 TOTE £9.30: £2.90, £1.60, £1.90; EX 59.50.
Owner Wedgewood Estates **Bred** Wedgewood Estates **Trained** Denton, Co Durham

FOCUS
An ordinary handicap featuring a number of performers who have struggled to get their heads in front.

3570 32RED POKER FOOTBALL FURLONG FREEROLL H'CAP — 1m 30y

5:00 (5:00) (Class 6) (0-65,68) 4-Y-0+ £3,238 (£963; £481; £240) Stalls Low

Form RPR

0041 **1** **Inside Story (IRE)**[13] [3159] 4-9-2 **60**...........................(b) PaulMulrennan 9 71
(M W Easterby) *hld up: hdwy 3f out: rdn over 1f out: r.o ins fnl f to ld fnl strides* **14/1**

0001 **2** *hd* **Pianoforte (USA)**[6] [3361] 4-9-0 **58** 6ex............................ FrancisNorton 5 69
(E J Alston) *midfield: hdwy over 2f out: rdn over 1f out: led ins fnl f: hdd fnl strides* **10/3**[3]

141 **3** *1 ¼* **Out For A Stroll**[1] [3523] 7-9-0 **61** 6ex.......................... SaleemGolam(3) 1 73+
(S C Williams) *racd keenly: midfield: nt clr run over 2f out: sn swtchd lft: hdwy over 1f out: ran on whn swtchd rt ins fnl f: nt rch frnt* **5/2**[1]

-021 **4** *nk* **She's Our Lass (IRE)**[8] [3298] 5-9-7 **68**.......................... DanielTudhope(3) 8 75
(D Carroll) *hld up: hdwy over 2f out: rdn to ld over 1f out: sn edgd lft: hdd ins fnl f: no ex towards fin* **3/1**[2]

6065 **5** *1 ½* **What-A-Dancer (IRE)**[11] [3194] 9-9-4 **62**.................(p) AdrianMcCarthy 2 66
(R A Harris) *racd keenly: hld up: rdn over 2f out: hdwy over 1f out: styd on ins fnl f: eased towards fin* **20/1**

0450 **6** *1* **Khetaab (IRE)**[1] [3523] 4-8-9 **53**..(b) DavidAllan 7 55
(E J Alston) *led: rdn over 3f out: hdd over 1f out: kpt on same pce* **66/1**

0060 **7** *nk* **Pauline's Prince**[6] [3361] 4-8-12 **63**.......................... RussellKennemore(7) 6 64
(R Hollinshead) *prom: rdn and ev ch 2f out: no ex ins fnl f* **33/1**

0365 **8** *½* **Son Of Thunder (IRE)**[6] [3353] 5-8-10 **54**.......................... PhillipMakin 10 54
(M Dods) *hld up: rdn over 2f out: hdwy over 1f out: one pce wl ins fnl f* **12/1**

4106 **9** *1 ¼* **Adobe**[8] [3311] 11-8-9 **58**... LiamJones(5) 3 55
(W M Brisbourne) *trckd ldrs: rdn over 3f out: wknd over 1f out* **14/1**

-000 **10** *3 ½* **Hawridge Sensation**[18] [2969] 4-8-11 **55**............................ ChrisCatlin 4 44
(W S Kittow) *prom tl rdn and wknd 2f out* **14/1**

1m 43.05s (-2.46) **Going Correction** -0.325s/f (Firm) **10** Ran SP% **113.5**
Speed ratings (Par 101):99,98,97,97,95 94,94,93,92,89
CSF £57.94 CT £162.04 TOTE £14.90: £3.40, £1.30, £1.50; EX 55.40 Place 6 £44.18, Place 5 £21.95..
Owner K Wreglesworth **Bred** Arthur S Phelan **Trained** Sheriff Hutton, N Yorks
■ Stewards' Enquiry : Paul Mulrennan caution: used whip without regard to gelding's stride pattern

FOCUS
Not a bad handicap for the grade and it was dominated by the four last-time-out winners in the field.
T/Jkpt: Not won. T/Plt: £80.60 to a £1 stake. Pool: £73,499.70. 665.60 winning tickets. T/Qpdt: £7.60 to a £1 stake. Pool: £3,971.75. 384.00 winning tickets. DO

3571 - (Foreign Racing) - See Raceform Interactive

3556 CURRAGH (R-H)

Sunday, July 16

OFFICIAL GOING: Good to firm (firm in places; firm on the stands' side)

3572a EMIRATES AIRLINE MINSTREL STKS (GROUP 3) — 7f

2:35 (2:36) 4-Y-0+ £38,068 (£10,482; £4,965)

RPR

1 **Jedburgh**[24] [2776] 5-9-1 ....(b) SebSanders 1 107
(J L Dunlop) *trckd ldr in 2nd: rdn to ld ins fnl f: kpt on wl: all out* **10/11**[1]

2 *nk* **Noelani (IRE)**[22] [2846] 4-9-1 105................................. MJKinane 2 106
(John M Oxx, Ire) *led: rdn and hdd ins fnl f: kpt on wl cl home* **15/8**[2]

3 *18* **Tiger Dance (USA)**[32] [2559] 4-9-1 101..............................(t) KFallon 3 58
(A P O'Brien, Ire) *a last: outpcd 1/2-way: rdn and bhd fr 2f out* **4/1**[3]

1m 28.6s **Going Correction** -0.25s/f (Firm) **3** Ran SP% **107.2**
Speed ratings: 83,82,62
CSF £2.86 TOTE £1.80; DF 2.90.
Owner The Earl Cadogan **Bred** The Earl Cadogan **Trained** Arundel, W Sussex

FOCUS
A poor turnout for this Group Three event and, not surprisingly, it turned into a tactical affair.

NOTEBOOK
Jedburgh, a smart handicapper who finished sixth under a big weight in the Buckingham Palace Stakes at Royal Ascot, always had the leader in his sights in a race in which the early pace was pedestrian, and he quickened up to take the initiative inside the final furlong, holding enough in reserve to see off a rally by the runner-up. As serious Group Three form this has to be treated with extreme caution, since Jedburgh had never contested a Group race in 25 previous outings and had never managed better than fourth in four attempts in Listed races. That said, he is a smart type at the trip (at which he has recorded his seven victories), and his trainer will no doubt be prepared to travel with him in search of further opportunities. (op 11/10)
Noelani(IRE), who won a six-furlong Group Three event at the venue last season, was stepping up to seven furlongs for the first time and the slow early pace should have played to her strengths. However, she never looked particularly happy after being asked to raise the tempo and was picked off fairly readily before trying to claw her way back in the closing stages. She is probably best with some ease in the ground. (op 11/8)
Tiger Dance(USA) Official explanation: vet said colt was blowing hard post race

3574a DUBAI DUTY FREE ANGLESEY STKS (GROUP 3) 6f 63y
3:35 (3:35) 2-Y-O £33,672 (£9,879; £4,706; £1,603)

RPR

1 **Regional Counsel**[23] [2837] 2-9-1 92 DPMcDonogh 6 103
(Kevin Prendergast, Ire) *trckd ldrs: 4th 1/2-way: rdn in cl 3rd 1 1/2f out: styd on wl fnl f: ld cl home* **12/1**

2 *nk* **Sadeek**[26] [2719] 2-9-1 NCallan 8 102
(K A Ryan) *chsd ldr in 2nd: disp ld briefly 1/2-way: rdn fr 2f out: disp ld again ins fnl f: hdd cl home* **4/1**[2]

3 *nk* **Chivalrous (IRE)**[15] [3103] 2-9-1 JAHeffernan 7 101
(A P O'Brien, Ire) *led: jnd briefly 1/2-way: rdn fr 2f out: kpt on wl fnl f: hdd cl home* **10/1**

4 *1/2* **Gaudeamus (USA)**[16] [3060] 2-8-12 KJManning 1 97
(J S Bolger, Ire) *hld up: 6th 1/2-way: rdn fr 2f out: kpt on wout threatening fnl f* **13/2**[3]

5 *shd* **Finicius (USA)**[15] [3103] 2-9-1 JMurtagh 3 99
(Eoin Griffin, Ire) *hld up on stands rail: pushed along fr 3f out: 5th 2f out: kpt on same pce fnl f* **5/2**[1]

6 *2 1/2* **King Of Swords (IRE)**[29] [2665] 2-9-1 PShanahan 4 92
(C Collins, Ire) *a in rr: no imp fr 2 1/2f out* **16/1**

7 *nk* **Abide With Me (USA)** 2-9-1 KFallon 5 91
(A P O'Brien, Ire) *dwlt sltly: sn trckd ldrs: 3rd 1/2-way: rdn and no imp fr 2f out* **4/1**[2]

1m 16.8s **Going Correction** 0.0s/f (Good) 8 Ran SP% **104.6**
Speed ratings: 104,103,103,102,102 99,98
CSF £49.35 TOTE £15.30: £4.50, £1.90; DF 85.20.
Owner Colm McEvoy **Bred** Cheveley Park Stud Ltd **Trained** Friarstown, Co Kildare

NOTEBOOK
Regional Counsel produced a fine effort to follow up his maiden win at Limerick over this shorter trip. He was being ridden along in behind the front pair with over a furlong to go, but he ran on bravely to challenge between those horses and get up in the final strides. He could head for the National Stakes where the return to seven furlongs will suit. (op 10/1)

Sadeek, who won the Woodcote Stakes at Epsom, and was eighth in the Coventry Stakes at Royal Ascot prior to this, helped to force the pace and looked to have the race won before the winner's late surge. He should be able to score at this level. (op 9/2 tchd 5/1)

Chivalrous(IRE) finished fourth to today's beaten favourite Finicius on his debut here two weeks earlier and improved on that effort. He set out to make all and it was only late on that he was run out of it. A maiden looks a formality. (op 10/1 tchd 12/1)

Gaudeamus(USA) , who won a Listed race over seven here just over two weeks ago, ran well and was keeping on over the final furlong. She looks as though she will do better when returning to further. (op 6/1)

Finicius(USA), who created a good impression on his debut, was trapped on the inside rail for much of the race. By the time the gap came for him it was too late, but he was still only beaten only just over a length. He can improve and may also be seen to better effect over further. (op 2/1)

Abide With Me(USA), making his debut, raced prominently but started to weaken in the closing stages. He should improve a fair amount for the outing. (op 5/2)

3575a DARLEY IRISH OAKS (GROUP 1) (FILLIES) 1m 4f
4:10 (4:10) 3-Y-O
£165,862 (£52,758; £25,172; £8,620; £5,862; £3,103)

RPR

1 **Alexandrova (IRE)**[44] [2203] 3-9-0 117 KFallon 2 121+
(A P O'Brien, Ire) *hld up in rr: last ent st: smooth prog fr 2 1/2f out: swtchd to far rail 2f out: led over 1f out: kpt on wl: easily* **8/15**[1]

2 *4* **Scottish Stage (IRE)**[24] [2772] 3-9-0 MJKinane 4 112
(Sir Michael Stoute) *trckd ldr in mod 2nd: rdn to ld 3f out: hdd over 1f out: kpt on one pced fnl f* **13/2**[3]

3 *1* **Rising Cross**[28] [2694] 3-9-0 MartinDwyer 1 110
(J R Best) *trckd ldrs in mod 3rd: rdn along fr in 2nd 2 1/2f out: dropped to 3rd again 1 1/2f out: no ex fnl f* **20/1**

4 *hd* **Mont Etoile (IRE)**[24] [2772] 3-9-0 MichaelHills 3 110
(W J Haggas) *trckd ldrs in mod 4th: rdn along 3f out: kpt on same pce wout threatening fnl f* **11/1**

5 *2 1/2* **Confidential Lady**[35] [2491] 3-9-0 SebSanders 6 106
(Sir Mark Prescott) *hld up in 5th: rdn along fr 3f out: no imp fr 2f out* **5/1**[2]

6 *10* **Flyingit (USA)**[8] [3323] 3-9-0 79 JMurtagh 5 90?
(Thomas Mullins, Ire) *led and clr: reduced advantage and rdn along fr 4f out: hdd 3f out: sn wknd and dropped towards rr* **200/1**

2m 29.6s **Going Correction** -0.50s/f (Hard) 6 Ran SP% **108.8**
Speed ratings: 111,108,107,107,105 99
CSF £4.21 TOTE £1.50: £1.10, £3.30; DF 4.20.
Owner Mrs John Magnier **Bred** Quay Bloodstock **Trained** Ballydoyle, Co Tipperary
■ Alexandrova, Aidan O'Brien's first Irish Oaks winner, was the 11th filly to complete the Epsom-Curragh Oaks double.

FOCUS
Alexandrova stamped herself in a league of her own in this division but the proximity of the sixth limits the level of the form somewhat.

NOTEBOOK
Alexandrova(IRE) confirmed the impression left by her Epsom triumph that she is quite simply in a league of her own among the three-year-old fillies at a mile and a half. After the outsider set a good pace , she came through on the inside and stretched away in commanding fashion to gain a second Classic triumph. She could take on the colts in the King George or Juddmonte International, but the Yorkshire Oaks will provide easier pickings. (op 4/7 tchd 1/2)

Scottish Stage(IRE), the Ribblesdale runner-up, won the battle for second with an honest performance. She led the pursuit of the pacesetter and had a spell at the head of affairs before the winner surged past. Never worse than second in five starts, she is a high-class filly who can continue to progress.

Rising Cross, the Epsom runner-up, continues to prove a credit to connections. A supplementary entry here, she put her disappointing Oaks d'Italia showing behind her and that race probably came a bit soon after her Epsom exertions.

Mont Etoile(IRE) failed to confirm Royal Ascot form with Scottish Stage but, considering that she was a 25-1 chance for the Ribblesdale, that was no real surprise. There is a suspicion that this year's Ribblesdale was not the strongest of renewals, but this Montjeu filly has not done much wrong this term. (op 10/1)

Confidential Lady was patently below her best, which was a shame, as a good run would have put the winner's performance in context. She was being driven along three furlongs out and was in trouble too soon to claim that lack of stamina was the main issue. This was her second disappointing run at the Curragh, though on very different going to her heavy-ground Irish 1000 Guineas flop.

3576 - 3578a (Foreign Racing) - See Raceform Interactive

3563 HAMBURG (R-H)
Sunday, July 16

OFFICIAL GOING: Good

3579a IDEE HANSA-PREIS (GROUP 2) 1m 3f
4:15 (4:30) 3-Y-O+ £41,379 (£14,483; £7,586; £3,793; £1,724)

RPR

1 **Egerton (GER)**[37] 5-9-2 THellier 6 112
(P Rau, Germany) *raced in 5th on outside, 3rd straight, led 1f out, ridden out* **49/10**

2 *1* **Song Writer (GER)**[266] [6050] 6-9-2 ABoschert 5 110
(Carmen Bocskai, Switzerland) *held up in rear, 7th straight, stayed on down outside to go 2nd 150 yards out, ran on* **29/1**

3 *2 1/2* **Nordtanzerin (GER)**[42] [2279] 3-7-12 FilipMinarik 7 99
(P Schiergen, Germany) *not settled pressing leader, led 1 1/2f out to 1f out, one pace* **11/10**[1]

4 *1 1/4* **Simonas (IRE)**[21] [2910] 7-9-2 EPedroza 2 104
(A Wohler, Germany) *held up in 6th on inside, stayed on at one pace final 2f* **33/10**[2]

5 *1/2* **Expensive Dream (GER)**[49] [2061] 7-9-2 ASuborics 9 103
(P Vovcenko, Germany) *held up in last, headway well over 2f out, ridden and one pace final 1 1/2f* **124/10**

6 *6* **Donaldson (GER)**[21] [2910] 4-9-6 TMundry 1 98
(P Rau, Germany) *led to 1 1/2f out, weakened* **36/10**[3]

7 *9* **Day Walker**[17] 4-9-2 (b) AStarke 8 79
(Rune Haugen, Norway) *raced in 3rd, 4th straight, soon weakened* **135/10**

8 *1/2* **All Spirit (GER)**[21] [2910] 4-9-4 ADeVries 3 80
(N Sauer, Germany) *close up in 4th til lost place over 3f out* **20/1**

2m 16.82s
WFA 3 from 4yo+ 11lb 8 Ran SP% **132.0**
PARI-MUTUEL (including 10 euro stake): WIN 59; PL 15, 32, 12; SF 1464.
Owner Stall Reckendorf **Bred** Gestut Rottgen **Trained** Germany

LE TOUQUET (L-H)
Friday, July 14

OFFICIAL GOING: Good

3580a GRAND PRIX DU TOUQUET 1m 3f
3:00 (3:00) 4-Y-O+ £4,828 (£1,931; £1,448; £966; £483)

RPR

1 **Londra (IRE)**[244] 5-8-8 (b) TCastanheira 51
(S Smrczek, Germany)

2 *shd* **Alqaayid**[100] [888] 5-8-8 DBreux(3) 54
(P W Hiatt)

3 *6* **Dream Machine (IRE)**[10] 5-9-3 (b) CHanotel 50
(Ron Caget, France)

4 *1* **Special Reggae (IRE)**[223] 4-9-4 DDehens 50
(L Lannoo, France)

5 *1* **Esta Bella (FR)**[294] 4-8-7 XChalaron 37
(H Hosselet, France)

6 *2* **Orlano (FR)** 4-8-11 SPolleux 38
(D Baillif, France)

7 *2 1/2* **Cosmoledo (FR)**[10] 6-8-10 JCrocquevieille 33
(Mlle A-C Trouve, France)

7 Ran

No PMUs available.
Owner Frau H Focke **Bred** Mrs Hildegard Focke **Trained** Germany

NOTEBOOK
Alqaayid, an All-Weather performer who had several runs in France in the second half of last year, did better on this return visit only just losing out ina close finish, the first two clear.

3328 AYR (L-H)
Monday, July 17

OFFICIAL GOING: Firm (good to firm in places)
Wind: Breezy, against

3581 EBF GILES PREMIER MAIDEN STKS 6f
2:00 (2:00) (Class 4) 2-Y-O £4,533 (£1,348; £674; £336) **Stalls** Centre

Form RPR

1 **Big Timer (USA)** 2-9-3 TomEaves 5 80
(I Semple) *s.i.s: keen in tch: smooth hdwy 1/2-way: led over 1f out: drifted lft: kpt on strly* **14/1**[3]

2 2 *2* **Gazboolou**[31] [2610] 2-9-3 PatCosgrave 2 74
(K R Burke) *chsd ldrs: outpcd over 2f out: kpt on fnl f: wnt 2nd cl home: no ch w wnr* **4/6**[1]

3 *1/2* **Palo Verde** 2-9-3 JoeFanning 3 73
(M Johnston) *led at stdy gallop: rdn over 2f out: hdd over 1f out: one pce ins last: lost 2nd cl home* **2/1**[2]

4 *shd* **Coconut Queen (IRE)** 2-8-12 PaulFessey 1 67
(Mrs A Duffield) *keen: prom: rdn and outpcd over 2f out: kpt on fnl f* **25/1**

5 *1* **Emirate Isle** 2-9-3 PaulMulrennan 6 69
(J Wade) *in tch: outpcd over 2f out: kpt on fnl f: no imp* **50/1**

06 6 *15* **Seriously Lucky (IRE)**[30] [2660] 2-9-3 AdrianTNicholls 4 24
(D Nicholls) *cl up: rdn 1/2-way: sn wknd: eased whn no ch* **20/1**

1m 13.75s (0.08) **Going Correction** -0.30s/f (Firm) 6 Ran SP% **110.6**
Speed ratings (Par 96):87,84,83,83,82 62
CSF £23.87 TOTE £11.80: £4.60, £1.10; EX 33.60.
Owner David McKenzie **Bred** Mt Brilliant Farm Llc **Trained** Carluke, S Lanarks

FOCUS
An ordinary event but a fair performance from Big Timer, who looks the sort to improve with experience. The gallop was only modest in the first half.

NOTEBOOK
Big Timer(USA) ◆, who is related to a host of winners up to a mile, was green in the paddock and looked as though the race would do him good but created a favourable impression on this racecourse debut. He should stay seven furlongs and appeals as the type to win more races.

Gazboolou, who shaped well on his debut at Nottingham, ran to a similar level but left the impression that a much stiffer overall test of stamina would have been in his favour. He looks sure to pick up a small event. (tchd 8-13 and 8-11 in places)

Palo Verde, who has several winners in his pedigree, had the run of the race and showed ability on this racecourse debut. He is not the most robust of individuals and should improve for the experience. (op 9-4 tchd 5-2)

Coconut Queen(IRE), green in the preliminaries, is related to a couple of six-furlong winners. She showed ability at a modest level and should improve for the experience, especially granted a stiffer test of stamina.

Emirate Isle, from a stable that does not have many runners in this sphere, shaped as though a much stiffer test of stamina will suit in due course but is going to remain vulnerable in this type of event.

Seriously Lucky(IRE) was again soundly beaten and will have to show a good deal more before he is worth a bet. Official explanation: jockey said colt was unsuited by the firm (good to firm in places) ground (tchd 25-1)

3582 GILES CHARITIES H'CAP — 7f 50y

2:30 (2:31) (Class 5) (0-70,65) 3-Y-O **£4,533** (£1,348; £674; £336) **Stalls** Low

Form RPR

546 **1** **Just Lille (IRE)**[12] [3189] 3-9-0 **58** .... RoystonFfrench 3 — 73
(Mrs A Duffield) *trckd ldrs: rdn 1/2-way: rallied and led over 1f out: styd on wl* **8/1**

2504 **2** *5* **Suhezy (IRE)**[9] [3306] 3-8-4 **48** .... PaulHanagan 7 — 50
(J S Wainwright) *set stdy pce: rdn and hdd over 1f out: kpt on same pce* **5/1**[3]

-026 **3** *3/4* **Ours (IRE)**[18] [3023] 3-9-3 **61** .... (p) SebSanders 4 — 61
(J D Bethell) *s.i.s: hld up: hdwy to chse clr ldrs 3f out: sn rdn and hung lft: kpt on fnl f: no imp* **9/4**[1]

0554 **4** *nk* **Electron Pulse**[23] [2856] 3-8-12 **59** .... DanielTudhope(3) 2 — 58
(J S Goldie) *keen: hld up: rdn over 2f out: kpt on fnl f: nvr rchd ldrs* **3/1**[2]

60-0 **5** *4* **Heads Turn (IRE)**[42] [2284] 3-8-3 **47** .... JimmyQuinn 1 — 36
(E J Alston) *keen: trckd ldrs tl wknd fr 3f out* **10/1**

-035 **6** *3* **Silk Merchant (IRE)**[46] [2160] 3-9-3 **61** .... TomEaves 6 — 42
(J Howard Johnson) *cl up: rdn 3f out: sn wknd* **7/1**

6000 **7** *3/4* **Bellsbank (IRE)**[10] [3250] 3-9-2 **65** .... GregFairley(5) 5 — 44
(A Bailey) *hled up in tch: effrt over 3f out: sn wknd* **16/1**

1m 30.13s (-2.59) **Going Correction** -0.30s/f (Firm) **7** Ran SP% **111.0**
Speed ratings (Par 100):102,96,95,95,90 87,86
CSF £44.29 CT £115.30 TOTE £10.10: £4.40, £2.60; EX 43.10.
Owner Granville J Harper **Bred** Sweetmans Bloodstock **Trained** Constable Burton, N Yorks

FOCUS
An uncompetitive race in which the steady pace suited those racing closest to the pace. This bare form is not up to much and does not look entirely reliable.

Bellsbank(IRE) Official explanation: jockey said filly swallowed its tongue

3583 AXA INSURANCE H'CAP — 1m 2f

3:05 (3:06) (Class 5) (0-70,68) 4-Y-O+ **£4,533** (£1,348; £674; £336) **Stalls** Low

Form RPR

02 **1** **Otranto (USA)**[6] [3377] 4-8-13 **60** .... (t) RoystonFfrench 4 — 69
(M Johnston) *prom: rdn to ld 2f out: edgd rt ins fnl f: r.o wl* **5/2**[1]

0002 **2** *1 1/4* **Major Magpie (IRE)**[8] [3331] 4-9-6 **67** .... TomEaves 9 — 73
(M Dods) *missed break: keen early: hld up: hdwy 2f out: chsd wnr ins fnl f: r.o* **4/1**[2]

1353 **3** *shd* **Inch High**[8] [3333] 8-8-4 **51** .... PaulHanagan 1 — 57
(J S Goldie) *chsd ldr: effrt and ev ch over 2f out: edgd lft over 1f out: kpt on ins fnl f* **4/1**[2]

5204 **4** *3/4* **Balwearie (IRE)**[3] [3483] 5-8-8 **60** .... (p) AndrewMullen(5) 5 — 65
(Miss L A Perratt) *chsd ldrs: led briefly over 2f out: one pce fnl f* **9/2**[3]

5-00 **5** *6* **Knock Bridge (IRE)**[14] [3159] 4-9-4 **68** .... DanielTudhope(3) 6 — 61
(D Carroll) *hld up in tch: rdn 3f out: sn btn* **20/1**

/56- **6** *1* **Winslow Boy (USA)**[315] [4998] 5-8-8 **55** .... PaulMulrennan 7 — 46
(P Monteith) *keen: hld up: rdn 3f out: sn btn* **33/1**

100- **7** *10* **Constable Burton**[276] [5884] 5-8-12 **59** .... PaulFessey 3 — 31
(Mrs A Duffield) *led to over 2f out: sn wknd* **6/1**

2m 7.01s (-4.71) **Going Correction** -0.30s/f (Firm) **7** Ran SP% **108.7**
Speed ratings (Par 103):106,105,104,104,99 98,90
CSF £11.32 CT £32.67 TOTE £3.20: £1.60, £2.30; EX 10.10.
Owner Al Saharaa Holding Syndicate **Bred** Gainsborough Farm Llc **Trained** Middleham Moor, N Yorks

FOCUS
An ordinary handicap but one in which the gallop was fair and this bare form, rated through the third, should prove reliable.

3584 GILES CORPORATE H'CAP — 6f

3:35 (3:35) (Class 4) (0-80,76) 3-Y-O+ **£6,477** (£1,927; £963; £481) **Stalls** Centre

Form RPR

0446 **1** **Ellens Academy (IRE)**[16] [3077] 11-9-0 **68** .... JimmyQuinn 2 — 79
(E J Alston) *hld up centre: rdn 1/2-way: hdwy 2f out: led ins fnl f: r.o wl* **11/2**[3]

1222 **2** *1* **Geojimali**[16] [3097] 4-8-12 **69** .... DanielTudhope(3) 4 — 77+
(J S Goldie) *trckd centre ldrs: rdn to ld over 1f out: hdd ins fnl f: kpt on* **15/8**[1]

3563 **3** *2* **Raccoon (IRE)**[2] [3525] 6-8-12 **66** .... (v) SebSanders 7 — 68
(D W Chapman) *racd alone stands side: a cl up: rdn 2f out: r.o fnl f* **9/2**[2]

00-0 **4** *shd* **High Voltage**[91] [1042] 5-9-2 **70** .... (t) PatCosgrave 5 — 72
(K R Burke) *disp ld centre to over 1f out: one pce fnl f* **12/1**

0250 **5** *5* **Whinhill House**[31] [2624] 6-8-11 **70** .... (p) MarkLawson(5) 6 — 57
(D W Barker) *slt ld centre to over 1f out: sn btn* **9/1**

0-05 **6** *nk* **Millfield (IRE)**[27] [2732] 3-9-2 **75** .... PaulHanagan 1 — 61
(J Howard Johnson) *dwlt: sn in tch: outpcd over 2f out: n.d after* **7/1**

3610 **7** *5* **Dizzy In The Head**[3] [3482] 7-9-8 **76** .... (b) TomEaves 3 — 47
(I Semple) *racd alone towards far side: cl up tl rdn and wknd wl over 1f out* **7/1**

1m 11.45s (-2.22) **Going Correction** -0.30s/f (Firm)
WFA 3 from 4yo+ 5lb **7** Ran SP% **111.0**
Speed ratings (Par 105):102,100,98,97,91 90,84
CSF £15.30 TOTE £7.60: £3.70, £1.40; EX 18.00.
Owner K Lee And I Davies **Bred** Mrs Chris Harrington **Trained** Longton, Lancs

FOCUS
A muddling race with runners all over the course but a strong gallop teed things up for a finisher. The runner-up is the best guide to the level.

3585 GILES INSURANCE BROKERS STKS (HERITAGE H'CAP) — 5f

4:10 (4:11) (Class 2) 3-Y-O+ **£32,385** (£9,635; £4,815; £2,405) **Stalls** Centre

Form RPR

1211 **1** **Fantasy Explorer**[17] [3049] 3-8-0 **83** .... JimmyQuinn 1 — 94+
(J J Quinn) *prom: effrt 2f out: led ins fnl f: drvn out* **5/1**[1]

0615 **2** *1* **Harry Up**[9] [3281] 5-7-12 **82** .... AndrewMullen(5) 2 — 90
(K A Ryan) *led to ins fnl f: kpt on u.p* **12/1**

424B **3** *shd* **Orientor**[27] [2720] 8-9-7 **103** .... DanielTudhope(3) 4 — 111+
(J S Goldie) *bhd tl hdwy over 1f out: kpt on fnl f: nrst fin* **20/1**

0201 **4** *1/2* **Peace Offering (IRE)**[17] [3038] 6-9-7 **100** .... AdrianTNicholls 3 — 106
(D Nicholls) *hld up in tch: effrt over 2f out: kpt on ins fnl f: no imp* **10/1**

2100 **5** *nk* **Highland Warrior**[17] [3038] 7-8-6 **85** .... PaulHanagan 5 — 90+
(J S Goldie) *s.i.s: bhd tl hdwy over 1f out: nvr rchd ldrs* **12/1**

1242 **6** *1* **Handsome Cross (IRE)**[4] [3447] 5-8-3 **85** .... SilvestreDeSousa(3) 10 — 86
(D Nicholls) *prom: rdn over 2f out: no ex over 1f out* **5/1**[1]

-402 **7** *1* **Come Out Fighting**[7] [3360] 3-8-7 **90** ow1 .... GrahamGibbons 8 — 87
(P A Blockley) *chsd ldrs tl rdn and no ex over 1f out* **8/1**[3]

1212 **8** *shd* **Glencairn Star**[7] [3354] 5-7-12 **77** oh2 .... DaleGibson 6 — 74
(J S Goldie) *bhd and rdn 1/2-way: kpt on fnl f: nvr rchd ldrs* **10/1**

02-5 **9** *1/2* **Masta Plasta (IRE)**[16] [3076] 3-9-5 **107** .... MarkLawson(5) 7 — 101
(J Howard Johnson) *chsd ldrs tl rdn and no ex over 1f out* **20/1**

1200 **10** *hd* **Fyodor (IRE)**[17] [3038] 5-9-7 **100** .... GeorgeBaker 11 — 95
(W J Haggas) *hld up: rdn 2f out: n.d* **17/2**

3420 **11** *1 1/2* **Ptarmigan Ridge**[9] [3281] 10-7-12 **77** oh5 .... PaulFessey 9 — 66
(Miss L A Perratt) *chsd ldrs tl rdn and wknd over 1f out* **25/1**

3002 **12** *3/4* **Grigorovitch (IRE)**[17] [3038] 4-8-6 **85** .... TomEaves 13 — 72
(I Semple) *plld hrd: hld up: rdn over 2f out: nvr a factor* **6/1**[2]

4106 **13** *1* **Glenviews Youngone (IRE)**[8] [3332] 3-8-2 **85** ow2 RobbieFitzpatrick 12 — 67
(Peter Grayson) *in tch: drvn 1/2-way: sn btn* **16/1**

58.15 secs (-2.29) **Going Correction** -0.30s/f (Firm)
WFA 3 from 4yo+ 4lb **13** Ran SP% **122.1**
Speed ratings (Par 109):106,104,104,103,102 101,99,99,98,98 96,94,93
CSF £65.08 CT £792.36 TOTE £7.30: £2.20, £5.20, £6.00; EX 103.30 TRIFECTA Not won..
Owner The Fantasy Fellowship E **Bred** Sexton Enterprises **Trained** Settrington, N Yorks
■ Stewards' Enquiry : Andrew Mullen one-day ban: failed to keep straight from stalls (Jul 28)

FOCUS
A fair field for this valuable handicap and a race where the field came up the centre of the course. Although the pace was sound and the form looks solid, very few got into the race.

NOTEBOOK

Fantasy Explorer ◆, a most progressive sort, looked in good condition and turned in his best effort yet from this 9lb higher mark. He goes really well on fast ground and, although he will be up in the weights again, should continue to give a good account. (op 10-1)

Harry Up is a tough and consistent sort who was allowed to dominate and he ran right up to his best. He will be up in the weights again for this but should continue to run well away from progressive sorts on turf or Polytrack. (op 14-1)

Orientor, who has not won for over two years, ran a typical race and fared the best of those to come from off the pace to show himself none-the-worse for his Ascot mishap. However, his style of racing is always dependent on pace and getting the gaps and he is not one for shortish odds next time.

Peace Offering(IRE), who broke a long losing run in a valuable Newcastle handicap last time, ran creditably from this 5lb higher mark having been ridden with a touch more patience this time. He should continue to go well in this type of event.

Highland Warrior got closer to Peace Offering than in the Gosforth Park Cup last time and ran creditably considering this race suited those racing close to the pace. However, he is another that needs things to fall perfectly. (op 10-1)

Handsome Cross(IRE) back up in grade, had the run of the race and ran creditably. However, he again showed that he is vulnerable from his current mark in this type of event. (op 6-1)

Come Out Fighting, returned to five furlongs, was not disgraced on this first run on very quick ground. He has not had much racing and is not one to be writing off just yet, though. (op 7-1)

Grigorovitch(IRE) is the type that needs things to fall right but failed by a long chalk to reproduce his Gosforth Park Cup second placing after getting no cover and failing to settle. He is not one to dismiss just yet, though.

3586 AXA INSURANCE FOR YOUR BUSINESS H'CAP — 1m

4:40 (4:40) (Class 6) (0-60,58) 3-Y-O **£3,238** (£963; £481; £240) **Stalls** Low

Form RPR

0011 **1** **Noble Nova**[2] [3529] 3-9-6 **57** 6ex .... JoeFanning 8 — 67
(M R Channon) *trckd ldrs: effrt 2f out: led 1f out: kpt on wl* **11/4**[2]

0-05 **2** *1* **Taranis**[16] [3075] 3-8-11 **48** .... SebSanders 10 — 56
(Sir Mark Prescott) *keen early: sn led: rdn over 2f out: edgd rt and hdd 1f out: kpt on u.p* **6/1**[3]

0-00 **3** *2* **Silver Sail**[14] [3138] 3-8-4 **41** .... PaulHanagan 4 — 44
(J S Wainwright) *chsd ldrs: outpcd over 2f out: rallied fnl f: nt rch first two* **50/1**

06-2 **4** *1* **Signal Hill**[8] [3329] 3-9-7 **58** .... GeorgeBaker 5 — 59
(W J Haggas) *hld up: effrt over 2f out: kpt on fnl f: no imp* **8/11**[1]

0060 **5** *nk* **Beginners Luck (IRE)**[21] [2923] 3-8-2 **39** .... PaulFessey 7 — 39
(D Carroll) *dwlt: bhd tl kpt on fnl f: n.d* **25/1**

-040 **6** *hd* **Honor Me (IRE)**[28] [2704] 3-9-3 **54** .... GrahamGibbons 9 — 54
(J J Quinn) *chsd ldrs: rdn over 2f out: no ex over 1f out* **28/1**

0400 **7** *3/4* **Mandarin Grand (IRE)**[7] [3353] 3-7-11 **39** oh3 .... (p) DuranFentiman(5) 3 — 37
(Miss L A Perratt) *hld up: rdn 3f out: n.d* **100/1**

-630 **8** *2* **Pappas Ruby (USA)**[7] [3355] 3-8-5 **45** .... DanielTudhope(3) 1 — 38
(J S Goldie) *hld up in tch: rdn over 3f out: sn btn* **50/1**

0000 **9** *nk* **Megalo Maniac**[34] [2529] 3-8-9 **46** .... TomEaves 2 — 39
(K G Reveley) *in tch: outpcd over 2f out: sn btn* **33/1**

1m 40.02s (-3.47) **Going Correction** -0.30s/f (Firm) **9** Ran SP% **114.0**
Speed ratings (Par 98):105,104,102,101,100 100,99,97,97
CSF £17.24 CT £661.80 TOTE £3.90: £1.10, £1.50, £7.90; EX 16.30.
Owner M Channon **Bred** Bloodhorse International Limited **Trained** West Ilsley, Berks

FOCUS
An ordinary handicap but a steady pace in the first half of the contest meant those held up were at a disadvantage. The form looks sound enough but is limited by the proximity of the third.

3587 AXA INSURANCE - EASY TO DO BUSINESS WITH H'CAP — 5f

5:10 (5:10) (Class 6) (0-65,65) 3-Y-O
£2,866 (£858; £429; £214; £107; £53) **Stalls** Centre

Form RPR

0532 **1** **Rothesay Dancer**[3] [3479] 3-9-4 **65** .... (p) DanielTudhope(3) 3 — 71
(J S Goldie) *chsd ldrs: led wl over 1f out: hld on wl fnl f* **5/2**[2]

0-26 **2** *nk* **Dulce Sueno**[23] [2855] 3-8-12 **56** .... TomEaves 5 — 61
(I Semple) *s.i.s: hld up in tch: rdn over 2f out: no imp tl kpt on wl fnl f* **5/1**[3]

14 **3** *nk* **Spirit Of Coniston**[12] [3199] 3-9-2 **60** .... (b) RobbieFitzpatrick 7 — 64
(Peter Grayson) *disp ld: rdn and hung lft over 1f out: rallied: no ex wl ins fnl f* **9/4**[1]

-400 **4** *2 ½* **Alugat (IRE)**[28] 2701 3-8-11 **55**..(p) PaulFessey 4 50
(Mrs A Duffield) *keen: chsd ldrs: effrt over 2f out: no ex over 1f out* **11/2**

-000 **5** *¾* **Nautico**[2] 3526 3-8-2 **46** oh1.. RoystonFfrench 1 38
(Miss L A Perratt) *in tch: hung lft and outpcd 1/2-way: kpt on fnl f: nrst fin* **20/1**

0004 **6** *6* **Mytton's Pride**[21] 2939 3-8-13 **57**...................................... JimmyQuinn 6 28
(A Bailey) *led to wl over 1f out: sn btn* **7/1**

59.60 secs (-0.84) **Going Correction** -0.30s/f (Firm) **6** Ran SP% **108.7**
Speed ratings (Par 98):94,93,93,89,87 78
CSF £14.12 TOTE £3.20: £2.00, £1.80; EX 14.80 Place 6 £171.25, Place 5 £110.23.
Owner Frank Brady **Bred** Frank Brady **Trained** Uplawmoor, E Renfrews

FOCUS
An ordinary race and one in which the pace was sound and the form is solid. The field raced in the centre of the track.
T/Jkpt: Not won. T/Plt: £269.20 to a £1 stake. Pool: £62,939.05. 170.65 winning tickets. T/Qpdt: £21.00 to a £1 stake. Pool: £4,267.00. 150.30 winning tickets. RY

3363 WINDSOR (R-H)
Monday, July 17

OFFICIAL GOING: Good to firm
Wind: Nil

3588 LADBROKES.COM EBF MEDIAN AUCTION MAIDEN STKS 5f 10y
6:25 (6:28) (Class 5) 2-Y-O **£3,886** (£1,156; £577; £288) **Stalls** High

Form RPR

1 **Fabuleux Millie (IRE)** 2-8-9 .... NelsonDeSouza(3) 15 71
(R M Beckett) *racd on stands rail and pressed ldrs: chal 1/2-way tl slt ld jst ins fnl f: hld on all out* **16/1**

00 **2** *nk* **Stargazy**[27] 2724 2-8-12 .... RichardKingscote(5) 12 75
(R Charlton) *w ldrs tl slt advantage 2f out: sn rdn: hdd jst ins last: styd on strly: no ex last strides* **9/2**[2]

3 *1* **Averticus** 2-9-3 .... RHills 6 71
(B W Hills) *in tch: n.m.r and outpcd 2f out: drvn and styd on again ins last: fin wl* **20/1**

4 *nk* **Black Moma (IRE)** 2-8-12 .... RichardSmith 13 65
(R Hannon) *chsd ldrs: rdn 1/2-way: kpt on wl fnl f but nvr quite gng pce to chal ins last* **33/1**

5 *hd* **Sacre Coeur** 2-8-12 .... EddieAhern 2 65
(J L Dunlop) *chsd ldrs: rdn 1/2-way: styd on fnl f but nvr quite gng pce to chal* **12/1**

30 **6** *1 ½* **Mogok Ruby**[46] 2172 2-9-3 .... MickyFenton 14 64
(L Montague Hall) *led tl narrowly hdd 2f out: styd w ldrs tl wknd ins last* **33/1**

7 *1 ¼* **Popolo (IRE)** 2-8-12 .... JamieSpencer 8 55
(M L W Bell) *s.i.s: effrt and n.m.r over 2f out: kpt on ins last: gng on cl home* **15/2**

640 **8** *¾* **Mac Gille Eoin**[19] 2967 2-9-3 .... TedDurcan 7 57
(J Gallagher) *chsd ldrs: rdn ½-way: wknd fnl f* **66/1**

9 *¾* **Pretty Miss** 2-8-12 .... DaneO'Neill 11 49
(H Candy) *s.i.s: sn rcvrd into mid-div: pushed along 2f out: kpt on fnl f but nvr in contention* **11/4**[1]

10 *nk* **Nepos** 2-9-3 .... ShaneKelly 1 53
(J A Osborne) *sn bhd: nvr in contention* **33/1**

06 **11** *1* **Chingford (IRE)**[19] 2984 2-8-12 .... PhilipRobinson 3 45
(D W P Arbuthnot) *chsd ldrs: rdn 2f out: wknd over 1f out* **50/1**

5 **12** *2 ½* **The Jay Factor (IRE)**[46] 2172 2-9-3 .... JimmyFortune 5 41
(Pat Eddery) *mid-div: rdn and one pce whn carried lft ins fnl 2f: n.d after* **11/2**[3]

56 **13** *½* **Lucknam (IRE)**[10] 3265 2-8-12 .... SteveDrowne 4 34
(M Meade) *mid-div: rdn 1/2-way: sn wknd* **66/1**

4 **14** *1* **Equal And Approved**[23] 2878 2-9-3 .... RichardHughes 9 35
(R Hannon) *towards rr: carried lft ins fnl 2f and nvr in contention* **13/2**

0 **15** *4* **Respect My Wishes**[21] 2930 2-8-12 .... RobertHavlin 10 16
(R Ingram) *s.i.s: bhd: rdn and hung bdly lft 2f out: nvr in contention* **100/1**

60.00 secs (-1.10) **Going Correction** -0.325s/f (Firm) **15** Ran SP% **118.4**
Speed ratings (Par 94):95,94,92,92,92 89,87,86,85,84 83,79,78,76,70
CSF £80.19 TOTE £17.30: £3.50, £2.40, £5.00; EX 118.80.
Owner Mrs Ralph Beckett **Bred** Ashley Guest And Mrs John Guest **Trained** Whitsbury, Hants

FOCUS
The bare form looks just ordinary but, like most Windsor maidens, it should still produce winners.

NOTEBOOK
Fabuleux Millie(IRE), the first foal of Flying Millie, who won as a two-year-old for Richard Hannon and was later a useful sprinter for Ralph Beckett, winning the Shergar Cup Distaff, is certainly bred to be pretty precocious and proved good enough to make a winning debut. This was not that strong a maiden, but she created a good impression and is worth her place in better company with improvement likely.
Stargazy ◆, who had shown ability on his debut at Goodwood but finished last in the Windsor Castle on his previous start, appreciated the return to maiden company and was just held. He has bags of pace and is clearly well up to winning a sprint maiden. He is also now eligible to run in nurseries. (op 4-1 tchd 7-2)
Averticus, out of a half-sister to quite useful miler Blaise Castle, stayed on nicely having been short of room when beginning his challenge. He should improve for the experience. (tchd 22-1)
Black Moma(IRE), a 10,500gns purchase, out of a mare from the family of the smart Irish performer Friendly Persuasion, was seemingly unfancied but showed plenty of ability.
Sacre Coeur ◆, a 57,000gns half-sister to four winners, including Lonely Heart, a quite useful dual ten-furlong winner, and Indian Trail, a successful winning sprinter, out of a multiple winner over seven to ten furlongs, looked a serious threat when throwing down her challenge towards the outside, but was ultimately just held. This should sharpen her up no end and she could be one to be with in similar company next time. (op 14-1)
Popolo(IRE), a 50,000euros half-sister to Zelo, a prolific winner in Italy at up to ten furlongs, and to Yaky Romani, a multiple mile scorer in the same country, kept on quite nicely in the latter stages having missed the break and been a little short of room about two furlongs out. She should step up considerably on this form next time. (op 13-2)
Pretty Miss, a half-sister to several winners, including top-class sprinter Kyllachy out of a five-furlong juvenile winner, ran below market expectations on her debut. She probably just needed this first racecourse experience and should be capable of a lot better. (op 9-4 tchd 3-1)
The Jay Factor(IRE) failed to build on the form he showed when fifth on his debut at Sandown and was disappointing. The ground was much faster this time and may not have been ideal. (op 13-2 tchd 7-1)
Equal And Approved showed just a moderate level of form when fourth in a weak maiden at Warwick on his debut and failed to build on that. Official explanation: jockey said colt missed the break (op 7-1)

3589 RBS H'CAP 1m 3f 135y
6:55 (6:56) (Class 4) (0-85,84) 3-Y-O **£6,309** (£1,888; £944; £472; £235) **Stalls** Low

Form RPR

1122 **1** **Cool Customer (USA)**[52] 1975 3-9-5 **82**........................ JamieSpencer 5 90+
(E A L Dunlop) *hld up in rr: hdwy over 2f our: carried rt 1f out: swtchd lft and qckmd ins last: drvn to ld fnl 50yds: readily* **7/1**

2234 **2** *¾* **Robustian**[15] 3119 3-9-3 **80**.. RyanMoore 6 87
(R F Johnson Houghton) *hld up rr but in tch: drvn and hdwy on outside over 2f out: led and hung rt 1f out: hdd and outpcd fnl 50yds* **4/1**[2]

3521 **3** *4* **Mull Of Dubai**[7] 3347 3-8-3 **66** 6ex.. JohnEgan 7 66
(J S Moore) *hld up rr: hdwy on outside over 3f out: led over 2f out: hdd and carried lft 1f out: sn btn* **7/1**

0013 **4** *1 ½* **Bon Viveur**[31] 2608 3-8-7 **70**..(p) RichardHughes 1 68
(R Hannon) *led 1f: styd chsng ldrs: hrd drvn ins fnl 4f: styd front rnk tl wknd and hung lft over 1f out* **14/1**

1-42 **5** *shd* **Faith And Reason (USA)**[18] 3015 3-9-7 **84**........................(v[1]) LDettori 2 82
(Saeed Bin Suroor) *led after 1f: rdn 3f out: hdd over 2f out: hung rt ins fnl 2f: no ch w ldrs whn n.m.r 1f out: styd on cl home* **9/4**[1]

0-01 **6** *1* **Fear To Tread (USA)**[23] 2882 3-8-13 **76**............................ EddieAhern 8 72
(J L Dunlop) *chsd ldrs: rdn and hld whn n.m.r on rail ins fnl 2f: btn whn bdly hmpd jst ins fnl f* **8/1**

015 **7** *1 ½* **Masterofthecourt (USA)**[46] 2174 3-9-4 **81**..................... SteveDrowne 3 75
(H Morrison) *chsd ldrs: drvn to chal 3f out: wknd ins fnl 2f* **5/1**[3]

-000 **8** *1 ¼* **Altilhar (USA)**[9] 3318 3-8-4 **67**.. RichardMullen 4 58
(G L Moore) *rdn over 3f out: a towards rr and nvr in contention* **33/1**

2m 25.53s (-4.57) **Going Correction** -0.325s/f (Firm) **8** Ran SP% **113.2**
Speed ratings (Par 102):102,101,98,97,97 97,96,95
CSF £34.32 CT £202.75 TOTE £6.40: £2.00, £1.80, £2.70; EX 46.20.
Owner Gainsborough Stud **Bred** Dell Ridge Farm **Trained** Newmarket, Suffolk

FOCUS
This looked a reasonable enough handicap and the form appears sound, but the pace was just ordinary for much of the way.

3590 TOTESPORT.COM FILLIES' H'CAP 1m 67y
7:25 (7:25) (Class 4) (0-85,82) 3-Y-O+ **£4,098** (£4,098; £944; £472; £235) **Stalls** High

Form RPR

0-25 **1** **Zaafran**[66] 1650 3-9-2 **74**.. PhilipRobinson 4 80
(M A Jarvis) *led tl hdd over 5f out:styd in tch:rdn 2f out:swtchd lft 1f out: drvn to ld wl ins last: ct last stride* **12/1**

21-1 **1** *dht* **Starship (IRE)**[24] 2823 3-9-7 **79**...................................... JamieSpencer 3 85+
(W J Haggas) *bhd: pushed along over 3f out: styd on u.p and qckmd 1f out: chal last half f: forced dead-heat last stride* **9/4**[1]

3445 **3** *1* **Rakata (USA)**[37] 2457 4-9-4 **68**...(t) LDettori 6 74
(P F I Cole) *led over 5f out: 4l clr over 3f out: sn rdn: kpt slt advantage tl hdd and outpcd wl ins lst* **8/1**

-053 **4** *2 ½* **All Quiet**[15] 3121 5-10-0 **78**.. RichardHughes 7 85+
(R Hannon) *t.k.h: hld up rr but in tch: hday and rdn 2f out: swtchd lft over 1f: styng on one pce whn hmpd ins last* **11/4**[2]

0503 **5** *1 ¾* **Celtic Spa (IRE)**[4] 3450 4-8-2 **59**.................................... JamieJones(7) 1 55
(P D Evans) *in tch: rdn over 3f out: chsd ldrs 2f out: wknd fnl f* **11/1**

1 **6** *¾* **Sama Dubai (AUS)**[34] 2532 3-9-10 **82**................................... RyanMoore 8 74
(Sir Michael Stoute) *t.k.h early: chsd ldrs: rdn over 2f out: wknd appr fnl f* **9/2**[3]

3112 **7** *¾* **Smart Ass (IRE)**[135] 583 3-8-10 **68**...................................... JohnEgan 2 59
(J S Moore) *t.k.h: chsd ldrs: rdn over 2f out: wknd over 1f out* **10/1**

-633 **8** *2* **Mythical Charm**[14] 3153 7-8-9 **59** oh1.............................(t) SteveDrowne 5 47
(J J Bridger) *hld up in tch: rdn and effrt fr 3f out: nvr gng pce to rch ldrs: sn wknd* **20/1**

1m 42.8s (-2.80) **Going Correction** -0.325s/f (Firm)
WFA 3 from 4yo+ 8lb **8** Ran SP% **116.6**
Speed ratings (Par 102):101,101,100,97,95 95,94,92
WIN: Starship £1.60, Zaafran £8.00. PL: S £1.60, Z £3.90. EX: S/Z £28.90, Z/S £19.80. CSF: S/Z £15.54, Z/S £20.10. TRIC: S/Z/Rakata £93.73, Z/S/R £118.91..
Owner Sheikh Ahmed Al Maktoum **Bred** Darley **Trained** Newmarket, Suffolk
Owner Mrs Magnier/Scott/Hirschfeld & Piggott **Bred** L K Piggott And A Hirschfeld **Trained** Newmarket, Suffolk

FOCUS
A reasonable fillies' handicap run at a decent early pace and the form should prove reasonable with the front two progressive.

3591 SUNLEY MAIDEN STKS 6f
7:55 (7:58) (Class 5) 2-Y-O **£3,886** (£1,156; £577; £288) **Stalls** High

Form RPR

03 **1** **Lord Theo**[21] 2938 2-8-10 .... JamesMillman(7) 13 76
(D K Ivory) *trckd ldrs untl slt ld ins fnl 3f: hrd drvn fnl 2f: hld on wl fnl f* **15/2**[3]

2 *1* **Herb Paris (FR)** 2-8-12 .... MartinDwyer 14 68
(M P Tregoning) *in tch: rdn and hdwy over 2f out: chsd wnr ins last: kpt on but a hld* **14/1**

3 *nk* **Maker's Mark (IRE)** 2-9-3 .... DaneO'Neill 4 72
(H Candy) *bhd: hdwy on outside fr 2f out: shkn up and styd on wl fnl f: gng on cl home but nvr gng pce to chal* **14/1**

0 **4** *1 ¼* **Bertoliver**[7] 3363 2-9-3 .... JohnEgan 15 68
(D K Ivory) *chsd ldrs: rdn over 2f out: one pce ins last* **66/1**

0 **5** *hd* **Jost Van Dyke**[65] 1688 2-9-3 .... RobertHavlin 10 68
(B R Millman) *chsd ldrs: drvn to chal over 1f out: wknd ins last* **50/1**

6 *¾* **Nobilissima (IRE)** 2-8-12 .... EddieAhern 5 61
(J L Spearing) *chsd ldrs: drvn to chal over 2f out: stl ev ch over 1f out: wknd ins last* **66/1**

4 **7** *2 ½* **Magic Mountain (IRE)**[11] 3222 2-9-3 .... RyanMoore 8 58
(R Hannon) *chsd ldrs: chal 3f out: rdn over 2f out: wknd ins fnl f* **11/8**[1]

8 *1* **Mister Lucky (FR)** 2-9-3 .... JimmyFortune 6 55
(Sir Michael Stoute) *chsd ldrs: rdn 3f out: wknd fnl f* **8/1**

9 *½* **Bateleur** 2-9-3 .... ChrisCatlin 9 54
(M R Channon) *mid-div: pushed along over 2f out: kpt on fnl f but nvr in contention* **16/1**

10 *nk* **Tiburon** 2-9-3 .... SteveDrowne 1 53
(H Morrison) *in tch: rdn 1/2-way: sn outpcd* **33/1**

11 *nk* **Distant Sunset (IRE)** 2-9-3 .... RHills 11 52
(B W Hills) *t.k.h: sn rr and n.m.r on rails: sme prog fnl f* **20/1**

0 **12** *1 ½* **King Of Tricks**[31] 2617 2-9-3 .... RichardSmith 3 47
(M D I Usher) *nvr bttr than mid-div* **100/1**

13 *1* **Alfresco** 2-9-3 .... ShaneKelly 7 44
(Pat Eddery) *slowly away: sn pushed along: sme prog fnl f* **20/1**

14 nk **Polly Jones (USA)** 2-8-12 .... TedDurcan 2 38
(B G Powell) *slowly away: a outpcd* **50/1**
6 **15** nk **Purple Sands (IRE)**[14] 3157 2-9-3 .... PatDobbs 16 42
(B J Meehan) *led tl hdd ins fnl 3f: sn wknd* **12/1**
16 11 **Mighty Missouri (IRE)** 2-9-3 .... LDettori 12 9
(W R Swinburn) *s.i.s: nvr travelling and a wl bhd* **5/1**[2]

1m 13.17s (-0.50) **Going Correction** -0.325s/f (Firm) **16** Ran SP% **128.9**
Speed ratings (Par 94):90,88,88,86,86 85,82,80,80,79 79,77,75,75,75 60
CSF £107.30 TOTE £10.10: £2.40, £5.30, £4.60; EX 180.70.
Owner R D Hartshorn **Bred** M J Perkins **Trained** Radlett, Herts

FOCUS
This looked an alright maiden beforehand but, as it turned out, the bare form does not look anything special.

NOTEBOOK
Lord Theo, eight lengths clear of the remainder when third to subsequent conditions-race winner Not For Me in a Wolverhampton maiden on his previous start, continued his progression with a decisive success, keeping on well to get off the mark at the third attempt having always been well placed by his improving 7lb claimer. He looks a nice type for nurseries. (op 8-1)
Herb Paris(FR), the first foal of a quite useful ten-furlong winner in France at three, was not that fancied in the market but made a pleasing debut. She should improve and it will be disappointing if she does not find a similar race. (op 12-1 tchd 11-1)
Maker's Mark(IRE) ♦, a 19,000gns half-brother to Impressive Flight, a dual six-furlong winner at three, later a winner in the US, ran a cracker on his debut considering he had to come widest of all with his run in the straight. He should go very close in similar company next time.
Bertoliver, a stablemate of the winner, was always struggling to get one continuous run through, but he was not unlucky. This represents a big improvement on his debut effort and he is clearly going the right way.
Jost Van Dyke improved on the form he showed on his debut at Warwick and is another going the right way.
Nobilissima(IRE), a 5,000euros half-sister to Watchmyeyes, a dual nine-furlong winner at two and Perugino's Shadow, a winner over hurdles, showed plenty of speed and this was an encouraging introduction.
Magic Mountain(IRE) ran nowhere near the form he showed when fourth on his debut at Newbury and was a major disappointment. He might just have been feeling the fast ground a touch late on. Official explanation: jockey said colt had no more to give (op 13-8 tchd 7-4 in a place)
Mister Lucky(FR), a 100,000gns half-brother to the high-class Ruwi, a multiple mile to ten-furlong winner in France, out of a dual winner over ten to 12 furlongs, was given plenty of encouragement from the saddle from quite an early stage, but did not respond. He could well benefit from a bit of give in the ground, but there was little encouragement in this effort. (op 9-1 tchd 10-1 in places)
Mighty Missouri(IRE), a 90,000gns first foal of a seven-furlong winner at two, who was later Listed placed over nine furlongs at three, was solid in the market but ran no sort of race. He was never going a yard after starting slowly, but is surely better than this. Official explanation: jockey said colt never travelled (op 15-2)

3592 RITZ CLUB (S) STKS — 1m 3f 135y
8:25 (8:27) (Class 5) 3-4-Y-O — **£3,238** (£963; £481; £240) **Stalls** Low

Form / RPR
0060 **1** **Kapellmeister (IRE)**[7] 3347 3-8-9 71 ....(p) JohnEgan 2 67
(C R Egerton) *mde all: drvn clr over 2f out: unchal* **1/1**[1]
-043 **2** 9 **Tip Toes (IRE)**[16] 3074 4-8-13 36 .... DeanCorby(3) 3 48
(P Howling) *prom: chsd wnr fr over 6f out: no ch fr over 2f out: hld on all out for wl btn 2nd* **40/1**
-000 **3** nk **Glory Be (ITY)**[40] 2360 4-9-2 40 .... EddieAhern 11 47
(J L Spearing) *chsd ldrs: rdn fr over 3f out: styd on to chal for modest 2nd cl home* **16/1**
5502 **4** 1 ¼ **Guadiana (GER)**[13] 3162 4-9-2 37 ....(v) ShaneKelly 10 45
(A W Carroll) *bhd: rdn over 3f out: styd on fnl 2f out: kpt on cl home to take modest 4th* **12/1**
6040 **5** 1 ¼ **Shaheer (IRE)**[22] 2902 4-9-12 47 ....(b[1]) JimCrowley 13 53
(J Gallagher) *in tch: chsd ldrs 5f out: sn rdn: nvr gng pce to rch wnr: wknd over 1f out* **16/1**
0030 **6** 2 ½ **Kirkstall Lane**[10] 3264 3-8-9 44 ....(b) DaneO'Neill 4 44
(R Hannon) *rr: hdwy into mid-div 5f out: sn rdn: wknd 2f out* **16/1**
0033 **7** 1 ¼ **Zizou (IRE)**[4] 3439 3-8-9 42 .... HayleyTurner 12 42
(J J Bridger) *chsd ldrs: rdn 4f out: wknd over 2f out* **6/1**[2]
0406 **8** 2 ½ **Rosiella**[13] 3161 4-9-2 40 ....(t) MickyFenton 9 33
(M Appleby) *s.i.s: bhd: rdn and mod hdwy fnl 2f* **66/1**
-026 **9** ½ **Alwaysforsale (IRE)**[4] 3439 3-8-9 46 .... PatDobbs 7 37
(J S Moore) *bhd: sme hdwy fnl 3f* **12/1**
6000 **10** 2 ½ **Carpet Ride**[6] 3159 4-9-7 50 .... RyanMoore 5 33
(B G Powell) *chsd ldrs: rdn 4f out: wknd 3f out* **8/1**[3]
6000 **11** 6 **Meohmy**[6] 3378 3-8-4 45 .... ChrisCatlin 6 18
(M R Channon) *prom early: bhd fr 1/2-way* **16/1**
0-50 **12** nk **Victor Buckwell**[70] 1540 4-9-7 39 ....(b) SteveDrowne 1 22
(G L Moore) *chsd ldrs 1m* **20/1**
-060 **13** 15 **Trackattack**[91] 636 4-9-0 45 .... JPFeatherstone(7) 8 —
(P Howling) *a in rr* **66/1**

2m 26.11s (-3.99) **Going Correction** -0.325s/f (Firm)
WFA 3 from 4yo 12lb **13** Ran SP% **124.5**
Speed ratings (Par 103):100,94,93,92,92 90,89,87,87,85 81,81,71
CSF £69.80 TOTE £1.90: £1.10, £4.30, £5.50; EX 54.00.The winner was sold to M. S. Saunders for 10,000gns.
Owner Mrs Evelyn Hankinson **Bred** Churchtown House Stud **Trained** Chaddleworth, Berks
■ Stewards' Enquiry : J P Featherstone two-day ban: used whip with excessive force and with whip arm from above shoulder height (Jul 28, 30)

FOCUS
An awful race - unusual for Windsor - and certainly not worth dwelling on despite the placed form being sound enough.

3593 FINSPREADS H'CAP — 5f 10y
8:55 (8:56) (Class 5) (0-75,73) 3-Y-0+ — **£3,238** (£963; £481; £240) **Stalls** High

Form / RPR
-020 **1** **Bahamian Ballet**[17] 3041 4-9-6 **68** .... RichardMullen 6 81
(E S McMahon) *chsd ldrs: drvn to chal 1f out: led ins last: drvn out* **12/1**
3231 **2** 1 **Endless Summer**[9] 3297 9-8-12 **65** .... JamesDoyle(5) 7 74+
(A W Carroll) *bhd: rdn over 1f out: swtchd lft and qcknd u.p ins last: tk 2nd last strides: nt rch wnr* **15/8**[1]
0241 **3** shd **Blessed Place**[6] 3389 6-8-10 **65** 6ex........(t) AshleyHamblett(7) 8 74
(D J S Ffrench Davis) *led: rdn over 2f out: hdd ins last and hung lft cl home* **6/1**[3]
5054 **4** nk **Gwilym (GER)**[15] 3118 3-8-11 **63** .... RobertHavlin 2 70
(D Haydn Jones) *carried lft s: bhd: hdwy on outside 2f out: ev ch 1f out: one pce ins last* **14/1**
0000 **5** ½ **Extremely Rare (IRE)**[10] 3267 5-8-13 **61** .... MickyFenton 4 67
(M S Saunders) *wnt lft s: rr but in tch: hdwy 2f out: drvn to chal 1f out: no ex ins last* **6/1**[3]

0203 **6** ¾ **Chinalea (IRE)**[18] 3027 4-9-11 **73** .... PhilipRobinson 1 76
(C G Cox) *chsd ldrs: drvn to chal over 1f out: wknd fnl half f* **3/1**[2]
0006 **7** 1 ¾ **Silver Prelude**[37] 2444 5-9-3 **65** .... DaneO'Neill 3 62
(D K Ivory) *carried lft s: bhd: haedway 2f out: chsd ldrs 1f out: wknd ins last* **16/1**
0500 **8** 1 **Dancing Mystery**[23] 2858 12-9-0 **62** ....(b) EddieAhern 5 56
(E A Wheeler) *chsd ldr 3f: wknd over 1f out* **12/1**

59.71 secs (-1.39) **Going Correction** -0.325s/f (Firm)
WFA 3 from 4yo+ 4lb **8** Ran SP% **116.3**
Speed ratings (Par 103):98,96,96,95,94 93,90,89
CSF £35.61 CT £150.69 TOTE £14.40: £3.80, £1.10, £2.00; EX 54.60 Place 6 £280.24, Place 5 £70.13.
Owner B N Toye **Bred** B N And Mrs Toye **Trained** Hopwas, Staffs

FOCUS
A modest sprint handicap, but the form does not look too bad for the grade.
T/Plt: £468.40 to a £1 stake. Pool: £81,626.05. 127.20 winning tickets. T/Qpdt: £31.90 to a £1 stake. Pool: £5,393.60. 125.10 winning tickets. ST

3454 WOLVERHAMPTON (A.W) (L-H)
Monday, July 17

OFFICIAL GOING: Standard
Wind: Light, half-against

3594 SUPPORT THE BROOKE HOSPITAL FOR ANIMALS CLASSIFIED CLAIMING STKS — 1m 4f 50y(P)
6:40 (6:40) (Class 6) 3-Y-0+ — **£2,730** (£806; £403) **Stalls** Low

Form / RPR
0243 **1** **Finished Article (IRE)**[6] 3377 9-9-6 57 .... StephenDonohoe(5) 8 64+
(W J Musson) *hld up towards rr: hdwy on outside: led appr fnl f: styd on wl: sn clr* **9/4**[2]
0360 **2** 4 **Molly's Secret**[10] 3260 8-8-11 40 ....(p) RonanKeogh(7) 1 51
(Miss S J Wilton) *hld up in tch: rdn 2f out: ev ch 1f out: styd on but nt pce of wnr* **16/1**
4-00 **3** 3 **Park Lane Princess (IRE)**[21] 2929 3-8-6 57 .... KirstyMilczarek(7) 6 53
(D M Simcock) *hld up in rr: hdwy over 1f out: styd on but nvr nr to chal* **9/1**[3]
0111 **4** ¾ **Zalkani (IRE)**[17] 3051 6-10-0 60 .... DeanMcKeown 7 55
(J Pearce) *hld up in tch: hdwy 1/2-way: ev ch over 1f out: fdd ins fnl f* **1/1**[1]
0-00 **5** ¾ **Perfectionist**[11] 3230 4-9-4 45 .... AdamKirby(3) 3 47
(Mrs C A Dunnett) *prom tl lost pl on inside over 2f out: swtchd rt over 1f out: one pce* **20/1**
1000 **6** ½ **Welsh Whisper**[6] 3386 7-9-2 46 .... NeilChalmers(3) 4 44
(S A Brookshaw) *slowly away: in rr and nvr on terms* **33/1**
04-6 **7** hd **Nutley Queen (IRE)**[33] 59 7-8-13 35 ....(t) RoryMoore(5) 5 42
(M Appleby) *trckd ldr: led 3f out: rdn and hdd appr fnl f: wknd ins* **66/1**
01-4 **8** 2 ½ **Tanning**[12] 63 4-9-0 43 ....(v) LiamJones(5) 2 39
(M Appleby) *led tl hdd 3f out: sn wknd* **20/1**

2m 43.62s (1.20) **Going Correction** 0.0s/f (Stan)
WFA 3 from 4yo+ 12lb **8** Ran SP% **110.6**
Speed ratings (Par 101):96,93,91,90,90 90,89,88
CSF £31.23 TOTE £2.90: £1.30, £2.20, £2.30; EX 25.40.The winner was claimed by P. A. Blockley for £7,000.
Owner W J Musson **Bred** Dr D Davis **Trained** Newmarket, Suffolk

FOCUS
This moderate contest was run at a very steady pace.

3595 MEET THE MEN IN RED (S) STKS — 5f 20y(P)
7:10 (7:10) (Class 6) 3-4-Y-O — **£2,388** (£705; £352) **Stalls** Low

Form / RPR
6306 **1** **Glenargo (USA)**[14] 3154 3-9-0 50 ....(p) AdrianMcCarthy 6 58
(R A Harris) *led to over 3f out: styd prom: rdn to ld ins fnl f: hld on wl* **16/1**
6206 **2** nk **Lady Algarhoud (FR)**[20] 2962 4-9-4 61 .... IanMongan 8 58
(D K Ivory) *chsd ldrs: ev ch ins fnl f: no imp cl home* **9/4**[1]
0004 **3** 2 **Dysonic (USA)**[24] 2833 4-9-1 37 ....(v[1]) JasonEdmunds(3) 10 51
(J Balding) *led over 3f out: edgd rt u.p and hdd ins fnl f: no ex* **25/1**
6400 **4** 1 ¼ **Twinned (IRE)**[14] 3155 3-8-12 59 ....(p) StevenGibson(7) 12 51
(J S Moore) *a in tch on outside: rdn 1f out: kpt on one pce fnl f* **25/1**
0440 **5** nk **Flying Dancer**[154] 402 4-8-10 40 .... SaleemGolam(3) 7 40
(R A Harris) *towards rr: hdwy over 1f out: nvr nr to chal* **25/1**
000 **6** ½ **Maya's Prince**[6] 3386 4-9-4 47 .... J-PGuillambert 4 44
(M D I Usher) *towards rr: mde sme late hdwy* **33/1**
0400 **7** hd **Roko**[26] 2758 4-8-11 37 ....(bt) MSemple(7) 2 43
(S R Bowring) *mid-div: wknd appr fnl f* **33/1**
4002 **8** shd **Neardown Queen**[8] 3340 3-8-9 55 .... NCallan 13 37
(I A Wood) *a towards rr on outside* **7/1**[2]
-106 **9** 3 ½ **Charley's Aunt (IRE)**[21] 2937 3-8-11 60 .... AdamKirby(3) 3 28
(Mrs C A Dunnett) *in tch: rdn 2f out: wknd over 1f out* **9/1**[3]
0606 **10** 4 **Wotavadun (IRE)**[8] 3340 3-9-0 42 .... TonyHamilton 5 15
(C R Dore) *mid-div: rdn 1/2-way: sn bhd* **33/1**
6000 **11** 3 **Bermuda Beauty (IRE)**[2] 3538 3-8-9 45 .... PaulFitzsimons 1 —
(J M Bradley) *mid-div: rdn 1/2-way: sn bhd* **14/1**
0400 **12** 46 **Stoneacre Boy (IRE)**[16] 3097 3-8-12 78 ....(b) RonanKeogh(7) 9 —
(Peter Grayson) *v.s.a and lost all ch at s: t.o* **9/4**[1]

62.86 secs (0.04) **Going Correction** 0.0s/f (Stan)
WFA 3 from 4yo 4lb **12** Ran SP% **116.9**
Speed ratings (Par 101):99,98,95,93,92 92,91,91,85,79 74,1
CSF £47.80 TOTE £24.70: £5.80, £1.20, £7.20; EX 60.90.The winner was bought in for 5,500gns. Lady Algarhoud was claimed by Michael Appleby for £6,000.
Owner Leeway Group Limited **Bred** Ocala Stud Farms & Karl D Koontz Revocable Trust **Trained** Earlswood, Monmouths

FOCUS
A poor contest but only a few ever got into this.
Charley's Aunt(IRE) Official explanation: jockey said filly hung right-handed
Wotavadun(IRE) Official explanation: jockey said gelding bled from the nose
Stoneacre Boy(IRE) Official explanation: jockey said gelding was very reluctant to race

3596 THE RED DEVILS DROP IN TONIGHT MAIDEN AUCTION STKS — 5f 216y(P)
7:40 (7:43) (Class 5) 2-Y-O — **£3,238** (£963; £481; £240) **Stalls** Low

Form / RPR
1 **Crumbs Of Comfort (USA)** 2-8-10 .... NickyMackay 11 75+
(L M Cumani) *outpcd in mid-div: rdn 2f out: hdwy and styd on to ld ins fnl f: kpt on wl* **7/2**[2]
2 1 ½ **Tipsy Prince** 2-8-6 .... JasonEdmunds(3) 10 70
(Mrs G S Rees) *a.p: led 2f out: rdn and hdd ins fnl f: nt pce of wnr* **25/1**

6 **3** 5 **Park's Girl**[11] 3216 2-8-8 ...... J-PGuillambert 2 54
(P C Haslam) *a.p: led 1/2-way: hdd 2f out: wknd ins fnl f* **4/1**[3]
0 **4** 3 **Bellapais Boy**[68] 1595 2-8-13 ...... NCallan 6 50
(T D Easterby) *sn outpcd: hdwy over 1f out: nvr nr to chal* **8/1**
0 **5** 1 **Dories Dream**[87] 1113 2-8-4 ...... AdrianMcCarthy 7 38
(Jane Southcombe) *towards rr: mde sme late hdwy* **33/1**
0 **6** 3/4 **Billy Ruffian**[65] 1664 2-8-13 ...... PaulQuinn 3 44
(T D Easterby) *mid-div whnn clipped heels over 4f out: outpcd over 2f out and sn btn* **16/1**
0 **7** 1 **Wool Mart**[21] 2930 2-8-9 ...... FergusSweeney 13 37
(M Blanshard) *outpcd and a bhd* **33/1**
0 **8** 5 **Misaine (IRE)**[19] 2973 2-8-6 ...... SaleemGolam(3) 12 22
(T J Etherington) *slowly away: bhd whn c wd into st* **33/1**
0 **9** 1/2 **Julatten (IRE)**[35] 2500 2-8-6 ...... DeanMcKeown 1 18
(G A Swinbank) *led to 1/2-way: wknd wl over 1f out* **11/4**[1]
0 **10** 5 **Mujart**[14] 3157 2-8-4 ...... FrancisFerris 4 1
(J A Pickering) *prom tl bdly hmpd 2f out: nt persevered w after and wknd fnl f* **33/1**
11 5 **Imperial Style (IRE)** 2-8-6 ...... PatrickMathers(3) 9 —
(D Shaw) *slowly away: a bhd* **25/1**

1m 15.4s (-0.41) **Going Correction** 0.0s/f (Stan) 11 Ran SP% **105.3**
Speed ratings (Par 94):102,100,93,89,88 87,85,79,78,71 65
CSF £77.11 TOTE £3.60: £1.70, £8.10, £1.10; EX 56.20.
Owner Christopher Wright **Bred** Brookdale **Trained** Newmarket, Suffolk
■ Multitude (6/1) was withdrawn on vet's advice. R4 applies, deduct 10p in the £.

FOCUS
That went a decent pace and the field was soon strung out.

NOTEBOOK
Crumbs Of Comfort(USA), a $60,000 yearling, is a half-sister to seven-furlong winner Becky Moss by a high-class dirt performer. She was outpaced through the early stages but began to pick up once the penny dropped and ran on well to cut down the leader inside the last. (op 11-4)
Tipsy Prince ◆, already a gelding, is bred for speed, being a half-sister to winning sprinters Castelletto, Piccolo Cattivo and Baby Barry. Always up with the pace, he travelled strongly prior to leading off the home turn but ran a little green in front and was gathered in by the winner. This was a promising debut and he can land a similar race. (op 16-1)
Park's Girl showed promise on her debut despite finishing last and confirmed that she has ability, although she was readily outpaced by the first two once into the straight. (tchd 9-2)
Bellapais Boy, whose dam was a high-class miler in Germany, cut little ice on his debut in May. He made late progress and is one to keep an eye out for when eligible for nurseries after another run. (op 12-1)
Dories Dream, down in grade for this second run after three months' absence, was never a factor. (tchd 40-1)
Billy Ruffian, returning after two months off, was not disgraced considering he stumbled quite badly after about two furlongs. Official explanation: jockey said colt clipped heels and stumbled approaching 4f marker (op 20-1)
Misaine(IRE) Official explanation: jockey said gelding hung right
Julatten(IRE) set the pace to halfway and dropped away tamely once into the straight. This was disappointing but she probably needs further. (op 10-3)
Mujart, who showed little on her debut here over an extra furlong, ran a lot better than her finishing position indicates as she was in third place when having to be snatched up with two to run and her rider did not persevere afterwards. (tchd 40-1)

3597 CELEBRATE AT DUNSTALL PARK H'CAP 1m 5f 194y(P)
8:10 (8:11) (Class 6) (0-55,55) 4-Y-0+ **£2,730** (£806; £403) **Stalls** Low

Form RPR
5500 **1** **Montage (IRE)**[11] 3209 4-9-2 **49** ...... TPQueally 6 62
(J Akehurst) *hld up in tch: hdwy 4f out: led over 2f out: edgd rt over 1f out: styd on wl ins fnl f* **6/1**[2]
5205 **2** 3 **Star Rising**[29] 2684 4-8-10 **48** ...... StephenDonohoe(5) 1 57
(W J Musson) *mid-div: rdn and hdwy to go 2nd 2f out: swtchd lft ent fnl f: kpt on but no imp* **10/3**[1]
-060 **3** 3 1/2 **So Elegant (IRE)**[36] 2483 4-9-4 **51** ...... DerekMcGaffin 3 55
(J Jay) *towards rr: styd on ins fnl 2f but nvr nr to chal* **12/1**
-605 **4** nk **Ocean Rock**[32] 2577 5-9-3 **50** ...... OscarUrbina 5 54
(C A Horgan) *slowly away: in rr tl hdwy on outside over 3f out: no ex fnl f and lost 3rd cl home* **10/3**[1]
-060 **5** 2 **Ashwell Rose**[83] 1219 4-8-12 **45** ...... J-PGuillambert 11 46
(R T Phillips) *hld up in rr: hdwy over 2f out: one pce fnl f* **33/1**
0006 **6** 5 **Bubbling Fun**[12] 3196 5-8-9 **49** ...... SladeO'Hara(7) 2 43
(T Wall) *mid-div: effrt over 2f out but nvr on terms* **12/1**
0550 **7** 4 **Lets Try Again (IRE)**[12] 3196 9-9-2 **49** ...... FergusSweeney 12 37
(R A Farrant) *led tl hdd over 2f out: wknd over 1f out* **16/1**
0000 **8** nk **Shingle Street (IRE)**[10] 3269 4-9-8 **55** ......(b) NCallan 9 43
(I A Wood) *mid-div: rdn over 3f out: wknd over 2f out* **8/1**
/012 **9** 1 1/2 **Major Blade (GER)**[17] 1724 8-9-0 **47** ...... LPKeniry 8 33
(Heather Dalton) *prom to 1/2-way: rdn 4f out: sn wknd* **13/2**[3]
1-00 **10** 1/2 **Komreyev Star**[51] 2025 4-8-12 **45** ...... IanMongan 13 30
(M Mullineaux) *trckd ldrs: wnt 2nd 1/2-way: rdn and wknd over 2f out* **12/1**

3m 7.59s (0.22) **Going Correction** 0.0s/f (Stan) 10 Ran SP% **116.8**
Speed ratings (Par 101):99,97,95,95,93 91,88,88,87,87
CSF £26.35 CT £235.17 TOTE £8.70: £2.00, £1.60, £4.40; EX 40.40.
Owner A D Spence **Bred** The Thoroughbred Corporation **Trained** Epsom, Surrey

FOCUS
This banded-class handicap was run at only a steady pace.
Montage(IRE) Official explanation: trainer's rep had no explanation for the improved form shown
Major Blade(GER) Official explanation: jockey said gelding lost its action

3598 BETFAIR.COM H'CAP 7f 32y(P)
8:40 (8:40) (Class 5) (0-75,75) 3-Y-0+ **£3,886** (£1,156; £577; £288) **Stalls** High

Form RPR
-002 **1** **Corrib (IRE)**[17] 3055 3-8-12 **70** ...... FrancisFerris 8 75
(B Palling) *slowly away: hdwy after 3f: rdn to ld over 1f out: drvn out* **10/1**
0030 **2** 1/2 **Golden Alchemist**[24] 2823 3-9-0 **72** ...... IanMongan 12 76
(M D I Usher) *a.p: ev ch appr fnl f: kpt on ins* **16/1**
1010 **3** 1 1/4 **African Gift**[17] 3041 4-9-1 **71** ...... StephenDonohoe(5) 6 75
(J G Given) *a.p: rdn to press wnr ins fnl f* **9/1**
0010 **4** 3/4 **Scuba (IRE)**[2] 3543 4-8-7 **63** ......(b) TravisBlock(5) 2 65
(H Morrison) *trckd ldr: led 1/2-way: hdd over 1f out: nt qckn ins fnl f* **5/1**[2]
5041 **5** 1 3/4 **Passion Fruit**[19] 2977 5-9-10 **75** ...... DeanMcKeown 5 72
(C W Fairhurst) *outpcd in rr: hdwy on outside over 1f out: nvr nr to chal* **6/1**[3]
600 **6** 3 **Middle Eastern**[16] 3089 4-8-13 **64** ...... FergusSweeney 9 53
(P A Blockley) *nvr bttr than mid-div: rdn 2f out: no further hdwy* **20/1**
3020 **7** 1 **Hits Only Cash**[19] 2981 4-9-5 **70** ...... J-PGuillambert 11 57
(J Pearce) *a towards rr* **12/1**
1160 **8** hd **Prettilini**[95] 1004 3-8-12 **70** ...... NickyMackay 1 53
(Stef Liddiard) *in tch to 1/2-way* **20/1**
0241 **9** 2 1/2 **Vienna's Boy (IRE)**[37] 2464 5-9-6 **71** ...... TPQueally 10 51
(W J Musson) *v.s.a and nvr got into r* **7/2**[1]
0500 **10** 6 **Loaderfun (IRE)**[17] 3041 4-9-2 **70** ...... DNolan(3) 3 34
(N Wilson) *led to 1/2-way: wknd 2f out* **33/1**
0320 **11** 3 **Poppys Footprint (IRE)**[122] 660 5-9-4 **69** ...... NCallan 4 25
(K A Ryan) *prom tl wknd over 2f out* **8/1**
6506 **F** **Alchemist Master**[11] 3213 7-9-7 **72** ...... TonyHamilton 7 —
(C R Dore) *in rr whn broke down and fell 1/2-way: dead* **14/1**

1m 29.74s (-0.66) **Going Correction** 0.0s/f (Stan)
WFA 3 from 4yo+ 7lb 12 Ran SP% **116.1**
Speed ratings (Par 103):103,102,101,100,98 94,93,93,90,83 80,—
CSF £151.34 CT £1512.05 TOTE £8.70: £2.20, £3.20, £3.50; EX 88.70.
Owner Derek And Jean Clee **Bred** Dr John Waldron **Trained** Tredodridge, Vale Of Glamorgan

FOCUS
This fair handicap was run at a decent pace and the form appears sound enough.
Hits Only Cash Official explanation: jockey said gelding would not face the kickback
Vienna's Boy(IRE) Official explanation: jockey said gelding missed the break and was slowly away from the stalls

3599 BOOK YOUR CHRISTMAS PARTY NOW H'CAP 1m 141y(P)
9:10 (9:10) (Class 6) (0-55,60) 3-Y-0+ **£2,730** (£806; £403) **Stalls** Low

Form RPR
2013 **1** **Orpen Quest (IRE)**[9] 3305 4-8-7 **55** ......(v) KevinGhunowa(7) 8 64
(M J Attwater) *sn trckd ldr: led over 2f out: drvn out fnl f* **10/1**
6643 **2** 1/2 **Spark Up**[6] 3390 6-8-7 **53** ......(b) StephenDonohoe(5) 13 61
(J W Unett) *s.i.s: bhd tl hdwy 2f out: rdn and pressed wnr ins fnl f* **8/1**
0120 **3** 3/4 **Scamperdale**[12] 3196 4-9-0 **55** ...... NCallan 7 61
(B P J Baugh) *stdd s: hld up: hdwy 3f out: wnt 2nd over 1f out but nt qckn ins fnl f* **8/1**
6602 **4** 2 1/2 **Band**[17] 3056 6-8-7 **55** ...... RussellKennemore(7) 5 56+
(E S McMahon) *sn in tch: short of room over 1f out and could nt qckn fnl f* **3/1**[1]
0041 **5** 1 1/2 **Captain Darling (IRE)**[6] 3390 6-9-2 **60** 6ex...... EdwardCreighton(3) 6 58
(R W Price) *led tl hdd over 2f out: wknd over 1f out* **9/1**
2564 **6** 1/2 **Jools**[14] 3153 8-8-12 **53** ...... OscarUrbina 2 50
(D K Ivory) *towards rr: effrt over 2f out: nvr on terms* **7/2**[2]
5021 **7** nk **Gem Bien (USA)**[6] 3386 8-9-1 **56** 6ex......(b) PaulQuinn 12 52+
(D W Chapman) *prom tl sltly hmpd 4f out: nvr on terms after* **7/1**[3]
1500 **8** 3 **Downland (IRE)**[6] 3390 10-9-0 **55** ...... KimTinkler 4 45
(N Tinkler) *nvr bttr than mid-div* **25/1**
3005 **9** hd **Shannon Arms (USA)**[17] 3056 5-9-0 **55** ...... LPKeniry 10 45
(R Brotherton) *in tch tl wknd wl over 1f out* **16/1**
0032 **10** 10 **Danielle's Lad**[31] 2599 10-8-12 **53** ...... FrancisFerris 3 22
(B Palling) *trckd ldrs: rdn and wknd over 2f out* **8/1**

1m 50.5s (-1.26) **Going Correction** 0.0s/f (Stan) 10 Ran SP% **121.9**
Speed ratings (Par 101):105,104,103,101,100 99,99,96,96,87
CSF £91.39 CT £685.73 TOTE £15.00: £5.40, £4.80, £2.70; EX 150.90 Place 6 £589.97, Place 5 £266.25.
Owner Mrs J Osbaldeston **Bred** Pursuit Of Truth Syndicate **Trained** Wysall, Notts

FOCUS
A low-grade handicap but run at a decent gallop and reasonably sound form.
T/Plt: £1,585.10 to a £1 stake. Pool: £56,674.45. 26.10 winning tickets. T/Qpdt: £237.80 to a £1 stake. Pool: £4,402.90. 13.70 winning tickets. JS

3600 - 3603a (Foreign Racing) - See Raceform Interactive

3279 BEVERLEY (R-H)
Tuesday, July 18

OFFICIAL GOING: Good to firm (firm in places)
Wind: Light, behind. Weather: Hot & sunny.

3604 RACING UK ON SKY 432 CLAIMING STKS 7f 100y
2:15 (2:15) (Class 5) 3-Y-0 **£3,400** (£1,011; £505; £252) **Stalls** High

Form RPR
3114 **1** **Touch Of Ivory (IRE)**[11] 3244 3-8-6 61 ......(p) PaulHanagan 6 65
(R A Fahey) *hld up: hdwy over 2f out: rdn to chse ldr ins last: styd on wl to ld last 50 yds* **7/4**[1]
4123 **2** 3/4 **Esoterica (IRE)**[10] 3290 3-9-1 68 ......(b) PaulFessey 5 72
(T D Barron) *hld up in tch: hdwy on outer 3f out: led 2f out: rdn and hung rt ent last: drvn: hdd and no ex last 50 yds* **9/4**[2]
4310 **3** 5 **Sapphire Storm (IRE)**[10] 3299 3-8-0 50 ow1...... RoryMoore(5) 2 50
(P T Midgley) *prom: effrt 3f out: rdn over 2f out and ev ch tl drvn and one pce appr last* **16/1**
3000 **4** shd **Distinctly Jim (IRE)**[10] 3288 3-8-5 50 ...... DavidAllan 8 49
(B Smart) *hld up in tch: swtchd outside and hdwy over 2f out: sn rdn and kpt on same pce appr last* **12/1**
1000 **5** 2 **Greek Secret**[10] 3296 3-8-13 71 ...... GrahamGibbons 4 52
(T D Easterby) *prom: rdn along over 2f out: wknd wl over 1f out* **9/2**[3]
0000 **6** 1 **Kings Cavalier (USA)**[26] 2782 3-8-8 47 ow3......(v) TomEaves 9 45
(I W McInnes) *hld up: a towards rr* **50/1**
3600 **7** nk **Coalite (IRE)**[10] 3306 3-8-7 52 ...... CatherineGannon 3 43
(A D Brown) *keen: chsd eladers: led after 1f: rdn along 3f out: hdd 2f out and sn wknd* **33/1**
0-00 **8** 1/2 **Knickerless (IRE)**[14] 3167 3-8-2 46 ...... RichardThomas 1 37
(N P Littmoden) *hld up: a rr* **33/1**
3305 **9** 1 1/4 **Takanewa (IRE)**[13] 3189 3-9-2 64 ...... PaulMulrennan 7 48
(J Howard Johnson) *keen: led 1f: cl up tl rdn along wl over 2f out and sn wknd* **14/1**

1m 32.44s (-1.87) **Going Correction** -0.35s/f (Firm) 9 Ran SP% **113.4**
Speed ratings (Par 100):96,95,89,89,87 85,85,84,83
CSF £5.55 TOTE £2.90: £1.10, £1.30, £4.20; EX 5.50.Touch of Ivory (IRE) was claimed by Mr E. Nisbet for £10,000.
Owner Colin Jarvis **Bred** John Hutchinson **Trained** Musley Bank, N Yorks

FOCUS
An ordinary claimer run at a decent pace. Sound enough form.

3605 MEDIEVAL NIGHT HERE NEXT MONDAY MAIDEN AUCTION STKS 5f
2:45 (2:45) (Class 4) 2-Y-0 **£4,533** (£1,348; £674; £336) **Stalls** High

Form RPR
02 **1** **Ice Mountain**[10] 3286 2-8-7 ...... PhilipRobinson 6 90
(B Smart) *mde all: shkn up wl over 1f out and sn qcknd clr: easily* **10/11**[1]
4323 **2** 5 **Perlachy**[11] 3242 2-8-10 ...... DavidAllan 5 75
(T D Easterby) *trckd ldrs: swtchd lft and hdwy 2f out: rdn to chse wnr over 1f out: no imp ins last* **11/4**[2]

005 **3** 3½ **Emefdream**[53] 1982 2-8-10 .... NCallan 2 62
(K A Ryan) *cl up: rdn along 2f out: drvn over 1f out and kpt on same pce* **20/1**

402 **4** ½ **Dotty's Daughter**[66] 1682 2-8-2 .... PaulFessey 7 53
(Mrs A Duffield) *cl up: rdn along 1/2-way: drvn wl over 1f out and sn wknd* **10/1**

334 **5** 1 **Josr's Magic (IRE)**[70] 1559 2-8-7 .... DO'Donohoe 4 54
(Mrs A Duffield) *trckd ldrs: effrt 2f out: sn rdn and btn* **11/2**[3]

0 **6** ½ **Blissfully**[35] 2523 2-8-5 .... DeanMcKeown 1 50
(S Parr) *s.i.s: a rr* **50/1**

030 **7** 5 **Bonny Scotland (IRE)**[8] 3358 2-7-13 .... DominicFox(3) 3 29
(Miss V Haigh) *dwlt: a rr* **50/1**

61.62 secs (-2.38) **Going Correction** -0.525s/f (Hard) **7** Ran SP% **112.2**
Speed ratings (Par 96):98,90,84,83,82 81,73
CSF £3.37 TOTE £2.00: £1.40, £1.70; EX 3.90.
Owner Pinnacle Kyllachy Partnership **Bred** Miss K Rausing **Trained** Hambleton, N Yorks

FOCUS
A fairly uncompetitive maiden but a nice performance from the winner, who is progressing. The race has been rated through the consistent runner-up.

NOTEBOOK
Ice Mountain looked the one to beat on his Carlisle second, and he proved much too good for this lot. His sire and dam won over the minimum trip as juveniles and so it is no surprise that he has inherited plenty of speed. He deserves to step up in grade now. (op 5-4 tchd 11-8 in a place)
Perlachy could not get near Ice Mountain, who won easily, but he is a consistent performer - he has been awarded an RPR of 73 on each of his last four starts - and his performance is a good guide to the winner's merit. (op 7-2)
Emefdream running on the quickest ground he has encountered on turf to date, ran his best race so far, but he needs dropping in grade. (op 12-1)
Dotty's Daughter, who would have won a claimer last time out but for jockey error, will be happier back in that sort of company. (op 7-1)
Josr's Magic(IRE), gelded since his last run in May, was disappointing on his return to the track. (op 4-1)

3606 JOIN RACING UK CLUB H'CAP 7f 100y
3:15 (3:15) (Class 4) (0-85,82) 3-Y-O **£7,772** (£2,312; £1,155; £577) **Stalls** High

Form RPR

-163 **1** **Stonehaugh (IRE)**[28] 2737 3-9-0 **75** ....(t) TomEaves 7 81+
(J Howard Johnson) *led 2f: trckd ldrs: swtchd lft and effrt over 1f out: sn rdn and squeezed through to ld last 50 yds* **10/1**

1212 **2** nk **Angaric (IRE)**[10] 3301 3-9-1 **76** .... PhilipRobinson 4 79
(B Smart) *trckd ldrs gng wl: hdwy over 2f out: rdn to ld ent last: hdd and nt qckn last 50 yds* **5/2**[1]

-624 **3** nk **Zennerman (IRE)**[17] 3067 3-9-6 **81** .... DavidAllan 8 83
(W M Brisbourne) *hld up in rr: hdwy on inner 2f out: rdn ent last and ev ch tl drvn and no ex last 100 yds* **8/1**

0225 **4** ½ **Jimmy The Guesser**[17] 3067 3-9-5 **80** .... RichardThomas 3 81
(N P Littmoden) *trckd ldrs: hdwy wl over 2f out: rdn over 1f out: drvn and kpt on ins last* **10/1**

5511 **5** nk **Xpres Maite**[7] 3381 3-8-12 **73** 6ex........ PhillipMakin 9 73
(S R Bowring) *hld up towards rr: hdwy on outer wl over 2f out: sn rdn and kpt on ins last: nrst fin* **11/1**

0550 **6** ½ **Renderoc (USA)**[4] 3491 3-9-6 **81** ....(p) NCallan 2 80
(J S Moore) *prom: effrt over 2f out: rdn to ld briefly over 1f out: sn hdd & wknd ins last* **20/1**

-440 **7** 2 **Aspen Falls (IRE)**[32] 2620 3-9-1 **76** .... SebSanders 1 70+
(Sir Mark Prescott) *stdd s: hld up in rr: hdwy wl over 2f out: rdn to chse ldrs whn n.m.r over 1f out: sn wknd* **7/1**

-216 **8** ½ **Northern Boy (USA)**[14] 3176 3-9-7 **82** .... PaulFessey 6 75
(T D Barron) *s.i.s: rapid hdwy to ld after 2f: rdn along 2f out: drvn and hdd over 1f out: sn wknd* **5/1**[2]

2453 **9** 1¼ **Royal Composer (IRE)**[10] 3282 3-8-6 **67** .... DO'Donohoe 5 56
(T D Easterby) *a towards rr* **13/2**[3]

1m 31.41s (-2.90) **Going Correction** -0.35s/f (Firm) **9** Ran SP% **113.5**
Speed ratings (Par 102):102,101,101,100,100 99,97,96,95
CSF £34.65 CT £214.66 TOTE £11.50: £3.50, £1.50, £2.80; EX 49.00.
Owner Transcend Bloodstock LLP **Bred** Yakup Demir Tokdemir **Trained** Billy Row, Co Durham

FOCUS
A competitive handicap that resulted in a bunch finish. The form does not look all that strong.
Northern Boy(USA) Official explanation: jockey said colt had no more to give

3607 121ST YEAR OF THE WATT MEMORIAL H'CAP 2m 35y
3:45 (3:45) (Class 4) (0-85,74) 3-Y-O+ **£7,124** (£2,119; £1,059; £529) **Stalls** High

Form RPR

-121 **1** **Key Time (IRE)**[6] 3396 4-9-12 **74** 6ex........ SebSanders 3 91+
(Sir Mark Prescott) *trckd ldr: hdwy to ld 3f out: rdn clr wl over 1f out: styd on* **2/5**[1]

0331 **2** 3½ **Mister Arjay (USA)**[19] 3019 6-8-12 **60** .... TomEaves 1 71
(B Ellison) *led 11/2f: trckd ldng pair: hdwy to chse wnr over 2f out and sn rdn: drvn over 1f out and sn no imp* **9/2**[2]

1610 **3** 9 **Haatmey**[12] 3220 4-9-12 **74** ....(v) TonyCulhane 2 77
(M R Channon) *dwlt: hdwy to ld after 11/2f: rdn along over 3f out: sn hdd and kpt on same pce* **9/1**[3]

31-0 **4** 8 **You Too**[50] 2078 4-9-10 **72** .... JoeFanning 4 68+
(M Johnston) *hld up: effrt and hdwy 4f out: rdn along 3f out and sn btn* **12/1**

3m 32.37s (-7.13) **Going Correction** -0.35s/f (Firm) **4** Ran SP% **107.3**
Speed ratings (Par 105):103,101,96,92
CSF £2.48 TOTE £1.60; EX 2.10.
Owner G Moore - Osborne House **Bred** Airlie Stud **Trained** Newmarket, Suffolk

FOCUS
A weakish handicap, but solid enough form based on the performance of the runner-up.
You Too Official explanation: vet said filly returned lame left fore

3608 GO RACING AT PONTEFRACT ON FRIDAY NIGHT H'CAP 5f
4:15 (4:16) (Class 6) (0-55,61) 3-Y-O+ **£3,238** (£963; £481; £240) **Stalls** High

Form RPR

6152 **1** **Paddywack (IRE)**[3] 3524 9-9-0 **48** ....(b) TonyCulhane 13 59
(D W Chapman) *towards rr: gd hdwy 2f out: rdn to ld ins last: sn drvn: edgd rt and jst hld on* **4/1**[1]

4140 **2** shd **Beverley Beau**[3] 3524 4-8-6 **47** .... KristinStubbs(7) 20 57
(Mrs L Stubbs) *chsd ldrs: hdwy 2f out: sn rdn and ev ch ent last: kpt on wl: jst hld* **11/1**

-300 **3** 3 **Flying Tackle**[21] 2949 8-9-2 **50** ....(v) PaulHanagan 11 49
(I W McInnes) *outpcd and in rr: hdwy 2f out: sn rdn and styd on strly ins last: nrst fin* **11/1**

0-30 **4** 1 **Bond Becks (IRE)**[14] 3171 6-8-13 **52** .... MarkLawson(5) 19 48
(B Smart) *cl up: led 2f out and sn rdn: hdd ins last and sn wknd* **8/1**[3]

1410 **5** ½ **Misty Princess**[71] 1539 4-9-1 **49** .... RobbieFitzpatrick 10 43
(M J Attwater) *midfield: hdwy whn swtchd rt wl over 1f out: sn rdn and kpt on: nrst fin* **20/1**

0630 **6** 1¼ **Seven No Trumps**[9] 3334 9-9-0 **55** .... BarrySavage(7) 15 51+
(J M Bradley) *towards rr: gd hdwy whn hmpd wl over 1f out: swtchd lft and kpt on wl fnl f* **7/1**[2]

0002 **7** 2 **Percy Douglas**[8] 3356 6-8-8 **49** ....(bt) AnnStokell(7) 12 31
(Miss A Stokell) *chsd ldrs: rdn along wl oiver 1f out: n.m.r ent last kpt on same pce* **16/1**

0600 **8** hd **Campeon (IRE)**[13] 3199 4-9-6 **54** ....(p) NCallan 14 35
(J M Bradley) *led: rdn along and hdd 2f out: grad wknd* **12/1**

4-11 **9** nk **Bahamian Bay**[105] 873 4-8-13 **47** .... PhilipRobinson 6 27
(M Brittain) *cl up: rdn along 2f out: wknd wl over 1f out* **12/1**

6216 **10** 1¼ **Mullady Penelope**[3] 3538 3-9-4 **61** 6ex........ GregFairley(5) 7 37
(Mrs A Duffield) *a midfield* **16/1**

0000 **11** 1 **Fairgame Man**[21] 2949 8-8-12 **46** ....(p) GylesParkin 16 18
(J S Wainwright) *in rr: hdwy whn hmpd wl over 1f out: n.d* **10/1**

-000 **12** 1¼ **Valiant Romeo**[70] 1571 6-9-2 **50** ....(p) PaulMulrennan 9 18
(R Bastiman) *chsd ldrs: rdn along 2f out: sn wknd* **50/1**

015 **13** nk **Money Mate (IRE)**[11] 3257 3-8-9 **54** .... JamesO'Reilly(7) 18 21+
(J O'Reilly) *in tch on inner whn hmpd wl over 1f out: nt rcvr* **10/1**

5000 **14** hd **Kingsmaite**[34] 2541 5-8-10 **51** ....(b) MSemple(7) 8 17
(S R Bowring) *sn rdn along: a rr* **25/1**

0000 **15** ½ **Mis Chicaf (IRE)**[11] 3245 5-9-0 **48** ....(t) TomEaves 4 12
(Robert Gray) *nvr a factor* **33/1**

0-00 **16** ½ **My Rascal (IRE)**[14] 3171 4-9-4 **52** ....(p) DavidAllan 5 14
(J Balding) *chsd ldrs on outer to 1/2-way: sn wknd* **33/1**

5000 **17** 36 **She's Our Beauty (IRE)**[15] 3154 3-9-2 **54** ....(v) PaulQuinn 17 —+
(D Nicholls) *midfield on inner whn bdly hmpd wl over 1f out: no ch after* **50/1**

61.43 secs (-2.57) **Going Correction** -0.525s/f (Hard)
WFA 3 from 4yo+ 4lb **17** Ran SP% **124.0**
Speed ratings (Par 101):99,98,94,92,91 89,86,86,85,83 82,80,79,79,78 77,20
CSF £44.67 CT £477.14 TOTE £4.10: £1.50, £3.20, £1.80, £2.50; EX 56.60.
Owner David W Chapman **Bred** Colm McEvoy **Trained** Stillington, N Yorks
■ Stewards' Enquiry : Robbie Fitzpatrick four-day ban: careless riding (Jul 30-31, Aug 1,3)

FOCUS
A typical Beverley sprint, run at a decent pace, and pretty solid form. Those drawn in double figures dominated. The three non-runners, who no doubt coincidentally were drawn in the lowest three stalls, all had sick notes from their respective vets.
My Rascal(IRE) Official explanation: jockey said saddle slipped
She's Our Beauty(IRE) Official explanation: jockey said filly suffered interference

3609 STARS OF THE FUTURE APPRENTICE H'CAP 1m 100y
4:45 (4:46) (Class 6) (0-65,63) 3-Y-O **£3,238** (£963; £481; £240) **Stalls** High

Form RPR

0442 **1** **Farne Island**[8] 3355 3-9-2 **58** .... DNolan 1 65
(J J Quinn) *hld up towards rr: hdwy 3f out: swtchd lft and rdn over 1f out: drvn and edgd rt ins last: styd on to ld nr fin* **7/4**[1]

2205 **2** nk **Mambo Sun**[31] 2633 3-9-2 **63** .... SophieDoyle(5) 7 69
(P A Blockley) *led and sn clr: rdn over 2f out: drvn ent last: hdd and no ex nr fin* **4/1**[2]

-120 **3** 2 **Markestino**[27] 2746 3-8-3 **48** .... DuranFentiman(3) 3 50
(T D Easterby) *chsd ldr: rdn along over 2f out: drvn over 1f out: kpt on ins last* **6/1**[3]

5000 **4** 1¼ **Twilight Avenger (IRE)**[46] 2198 3-8-8 **50** .... SilvestreDeSousa 4 50
(W M Brisbourne) *chsd ldrs: rdn along over 2f out: kpt on same pce* **12/1**

2045 **5** 1 **Elite Land**[8] 3357 3-8-3 **50** ....(b) SuzzanneFrance(5) 6 47
(N Bycroft) *chsd ldrs: rdn along over 2f out: sn one pce* **8/1**

0350 **6** 1½ **Kissi Kissi**[7] 3379 3-8-8 **50** .... DominicFox 8 44
(M J Attwater) *hld up in rr: hdwy on outer wl over 2f out: sn rdn and wknd appr last* **8/1**

006 **7** 9 **Bold Medicean**[25] 2829 3-8-9 **54** .... GregFairley(3) 5 29
(T P Tate) *a towards rr* **7/1**

060- **8** 1¼ **Decent (IRE)**[267] 6077 3-8-8 **50** .... BenSwarbrick 2 23
(W J H Ratcliffe) *a rr* **33/1**

1m 46.47s (-0.93) **Going Correction** -0.35s/f (Firm) **8** Ran SP% **116.0**
Speed ratings (Par 98):90,89,87,86,85 83,74,73
CSF £8.89 CT £34.15 TOTE £2.10: £1.10, £1.60, £2.10; EX 6.60.
Owner G Shiel **Bred** G G Shiel **Trained** Settrington, N Yorks

FOCUS
A moderate handicap featuring only two previous winners (both on Fibresand). The winner did not need to improve and the front three all ran to form.

3610 MARIE TINKLER LADY RIDERS H'CAP (FOR LADY AMATEUR RIDERS) 1m 1f 207y
5:15 (5:15) (Class 6) (0-55,55) 3-Y-O+ **£3,123** (£968; £484; £242) **Stalls** High

Form RPR

0441 **1** **Gala Sunday (USA)**[10] 3305 6-10-10 **55** ....(b) MissSBrotherton 13 68
(M W Easterby) *trckd ldrs: gd hdwy over 2f out: rdn to chal ent last: styd on to ld nr line* **11/4**[1]

0036 **2** shd **Parchment (IRE)**[11] 3240 4-9-10 **48** .... MissWGibson(7) 2 61
(A J Lockwood) *midfield: hdwy wl over 2f out: rdn to ld wl over 1f out: jnd ent last: hdd no ex nr line* **12/1**

-501 **3** 3 **River Logic (IRE)**[10] 3288 3-9-5 **51** .... MissMSowerby(5) 8 58
(A D Brown) *hld up: hdwy on outer over 2f out: edgd lft to stands rails and rdn over 1f out: kpt on ins last* **10/1**

2234 **4** nk **Friends Hope**[10] 3305 5-10-6 **54** .... MissFayeBramley(3) 4 60
(P A Blockley) *stdd s: hld up in rr: hdwy wl over 2f out: rdn over 1f out: kpt on ins last: nrst fin* **6/1**[2]

0-00 **5** 1¾ **Eddies Jewel**[24] 2874 6-9-3 **39** .... MissJRiding(5) 15 42
(I W McInnes) *led: rdn along wl over 2f out: hdd wl over 1f out and grad wknd* **25/1**

6426 **6** ¾ **Wood Fern (UAE)**[10] 3305 6-9-12 **43** .... MissEJJones 6 45
(W M Brisbourne) *trckd ldrs on inner: hdwy over 2f out: sn rdn and no imp appr last* **7/1**

0-00 **7** 2 **Expression Echo (IRE)**[36] 2497 4-9-11 **42** ....(p) MissCHannaford 11 40
(A G Newcombe) *bhd tl sme late hdwy* **18/1**

2001 **8** 1¾ **Splodger Mac (IRE)**[7] 3377 7-10-5 **50** .... MissLEllison 9 45
(N Bycroft) *prom: effrt to chse ldr 4f out: rdn along over 2f out and grad wknd* **7/1**

0000 **9** hd **Futoo (IRE)**[32] 2612 5-10-0 **50** ....(p) MissNJefferson(5) 14 44
(D W Chapman) *prom: rdn along over 3f out: sn wknd* **20/1**

0235 **10** 1/2 **Fiore Di Bosco (IRE)**[10] 3305 5-10-7 52 .... MrsCBartley 3 45
(T D Barron) *hld up: a rr* **13/2**[3]

006/ **11** 1 1/2 **Only Words (USA)**[16] 3508 9-8-13 35 oh1 .... MissARyan(5) 7 25
(A J Lockwood) *hld up towards rr: swtchd wd and sme hdwy wl over 2f out: sn rdn and wknd* **25/1**

0000 **12** 5 **Emperor's Well**[10] 3305 7-10-3 55 .... (b) MissJCoward(7) 1 36
(M W Easterby) *chsd ldrs: sddle slipped after 3f: b ehind fr over 4f out* **16/1**

540/ **13** 12 **Power And Demand**[34] 1573 9-8-11 35 oh5 .... MrsDWilkinson(7) 10 —
(C W Thornton) *a bhd* **50/1**

0600 **14** 8 **Frogs' Gift (IRE)**[9] 3333 4-9-5 43 .... MissEJTuck(7) 5 —
(G M Moore) *prom on outer: rdn along over 3f out and sn wknd* **33/1**

2m 5.59s (-1.71) **Going Correction** -0.35s/f (Firm)
WFA 3 from 4yo+ 10lb **14** Ran SP% **124.6**
Speed ratings (Par 101):92,91,89,89,87 87,85,84,84,83 82,78,68,62
CSF £37.16 CT £304.83 TOTE £3.30: £1.90, £3.60, £2.90; EX 54.80 Place 6 £6.22, Place 5 £4.59..
Owner M W Easterby **Bred** Juddmonte Farms Inc **Trained** Sheriff Hutton, N Yorks

FOCUS
A very ordinary handicap featuring a number of banded-class performers. Modest form, but it should prove reliable.
Emperor's Well Official explanation: jockey said saddle slipped
T/Plt: £4.90 to a £1 stake. Pool: £58,325.25. 8,671.45 winning tickets. T/Qpdt: £3.30 to a £1 stake. Pool: £2,552.40. 563.70 winning tickets. JR

3335 BRIGHTON (L-H)

Tuesday, July 18

OFFICIAL GOING: Firm
Wind: Light, against. Weather: Hot & sunny.

3611 MATTHEW CLARK MEDIAN AUCTION MAIDEN STKS 5f 213y
2:30 (2:30) (Class 6) 3-4-Y-0 **£2,590** (£770; £385; £192) **Stalls** Low

Form RPR

5204 **1** **Kahlua Bear**[25] 2813 4-9-5 41 .... (v[1]) AdamKirby(3) 4 59
(Miss K B Boutflower) *led tl hdd 2f out: rallied u.p to ld again wl ins fnl f: all out* **12/1**[3]

0220 **2** shd **Balian**[8] 3349 3-9-3 66 .... (p) IanMongan 1 59
(G L Moore) *chsd wnr: led 2f out: rdn and hdd wl ins fnl f: jst denied* **2/1**[1]

0565 **3** shd **Danawi (IRE)**[17] 3090 3-9-3 62 .... DaneO'Neill 2 58
(R Hannon) *racd 4th: picked up wl ins fnl f and fin strly: only narrowly btn* **2/1**[1]

33-0 **4** 2 **Turn Me On (IRE)**[33] 2575 3-9-3 70 .... (t) HayleyTurner 3 52
(M L W Bell) *racd 3rd: hung lft over 1f out: one pce fnl f* **9/4**[2]

-000 **5** 7 **Astronova**[18] 3032 3-8-5 45 .... PatrickHills(7) 5 26
(M H Tompkins) *brought to ins rail fr ins draw s: a bhd and lost tch over 1f out* **33/1**

69.00 secs (-1.10) **Going Correction** -0.30s/f (Firm)
WFA 3 from 4yo 5lb **5** Ran SP% **108.1**
Speed ratings (Par 101):95,94,94,92,82
CSF £34.89 TOTE £9.30: £2.20, £1.70; EX 22.50.
Owner P Uniacke **Bred** J E Jones **Trained** Blewbury, Oxon
■ Stewards' Enquiry : Dane O'Neill one-day ban: used whip with excessive frequency (Jul 30)

FOCUS
A weak race. The winner has been rated to the best view of his banded form.

3612 BETFRED SPRINT SERIES H'CAP STKS (QUALIFIER) 5f 213y
3:00 (3:00) (Class 5) (0-75,75) 3-Y-0+ **£3,886** (£1,156; £577; £288) **Stalls** Low

Form RPR

6064 **1** **Who's Winning (IRE)**[8] 3368 5-9-6 69 .... GeorgeBaker 9 75
(B G Powell) *hmpd after 1f: outpcd 3f out: hdwy 2f out: hung lft sn after: rdn to ld post* **5/1**[2]

0-30 **2** shd **Make My Dream**[19] 3011 3-8-5 59 .... JimCrowley 11 64
(J Gallagher) *c over to stands' side sn after s and sn led: hrd rdn and hdd post* **33/1**

1613 **3** hd **Ivory Lace**[9] 3337 5-9-7 75 .... JamesDoyle(5) 2 80
(S Woodman) *in tch: swtchd rt 2f out: r.o to press first 2 cl home* **11/2**[3]

6-45 **4** nk **Inch By Inch**[12] 3212 7-9-5 71 .... (b) AmirQuinn(3) 8 75
(P J Makin) *in tch on stands' side: rdn over 2f out: rallied and r.o fnl f* **4/1**[1]

5050 **5** 1/2 **Cayman Breeze**[8] 3368 6-8-4 56 oh3 .... NelsonDeSouza(3) 4 59
(J M Bradley) *bdly hmpd after 1f: hdwy over 2f out: rdn and nt qckn ins fnl f* **14/1**

-056 **6** 3/4 **Vegas Boys**[5] 3434 3-9-7 75 .... ChrisCatlin 5 74
(N A Callaghan) *carried lft sn after s: rdn to chse ldrs over 2f out: one pce fnl f* **8/1**

2-35 **7** 1 **Dance To The Blues (IRE)**[21] 2962 5-9-3 69 .... (p) AdamKirby(3) 10 66
(B De Haan) *carried lft after s but prom: rdn 1/2-way: one pce appr fnl f* **8/1**

0041 **8** 2 1/2 **Sovereignty (JPN)**[15] 3155 4-8-4 60 .... JamieJones(7) 6 50
(D K Ivory) *hmpd after 1f: bhd effrt over 2f out: no hdwy fr over 1f out* **12/1**

0345 **9** 4 **Regal Dream (IRE)**[21] 2954 4-9-2 72 .... PatrickHills(7) 1 50+
(J W Hills) *slowly away: bhd whn hmpd after 1f: nvr on terms* **8/1**

1202 **10** 8 **Sarah's Art (IRE)**[18] 3049 3-9-0 68 .... (b) BrianReilly 7 21+
(Miss D A McHale) *hmpd after 1f: a bhd* **13/2**

5330 **11** 9 **Berties Brother**[70] 1576 3-8-1 62 oh12 ow6 .... JemmaMarshall(7) 3 —
(D G Bridgwater) *in tch whn bdly hmpd after 1f: bhd sn after* **66/1**

68.29 secs (-1.81) **Going Correction** -0.30s/f (Firm)
WFA 3 from 4yo+ 5lb **11** Ran SP% **117.5**
Speed ratings (Par 103):100,99,99,99,98 97,96,92,87,76 64
CSF £153.64 CT £960.71 TOTE £7.10: £1.90, £9.90, £2.50; EX 246.00 TRIFECTA Not won..
Owner Tony Head and Caroline Andrus **Bred** Colin Kennedy **Trained** Morestead, Hants
■ Stewards' Enquiry : Jim Crowley eight-day ban: careless riding (Jul 29-Aug 5)

FOCUS
A rough race, in which there was a nasty incident after a furlong or so which saw several horses effectively put out of the race. The field fanned across the course in the latter stages and not many got into it. Very ordinary form.

3613 GAYMERS CIDER (S) STKS 6f 209y
3:30 (3:31) (Class 6) 2-Y-0 **£2,266** (£674; £337; £168) **Stalls** Low

Form RPR

004 **1** **Sunstroke (IRE)**[31] 2643 2-8-6 .... TPQueally 6 55
(M G Quinlan) *hld up: led 2f out: led 1f out: r.o wl* **8/1**

6322 **2** 2 **House Arrest**[12] 3228 2-8-6 .... PaulDoe 8 50
(I A Wood) *chsd ldr: ev ch 1f out: rdn and jst hld on for 2nd* **4/1**[2]

0555 **3** shd **Mr Mini Scule**[10] 3300 2-8-11 .... DaneO'Neill 2 55
(A B Haynes) *led tl hrd rdn and hdd 1f out: kpt on one pce fnl f* **12/1**

41 **4** 1 3/4 **The Slider**[10] 3279 2-8-4 .... KevinGhunowa(7) 5 50
(P A Blockley) *chsd ldrs: rdn 1/2-way: one pce ins fnl 2f* **5/1**[3]

0253 **5** hd **Tumble Jill (IRE)**[10] 3279 2-8-6 .... LPKeniry 7 44
(J S Moore) *hld up: rdn 1/2-way: sn outpcd* **7/1**

0200 **6** 2 **Emergency Services**[8] 3345 2-8-11 .... JimCrowley 4 44
(Tom Dascombe) *mid-div: outpcd in rr fr 1/2-way 6* **14/1**

0634 **7** 1 3/4 **Moist**[10] 3279 2-8-6 .... ChrisCatlin 1 35
(N A Callaghan) *s.i.s: sn outpcd* **11/2**

0513 **R** **Sad Times (IRE)**[24] 2870 2-8-6 .... (p) LiamJones(5) 3 —
(W G M Turner) *ref to r* **7/2**[1]

1m 22.41s (-0.29) **Going Correction** -0.30s/f (Firm) **8** Ran SP% **112.2**
Speed ratings (Par 92):89,86,86,84,84 82,80,—
CSF £38.46 TOTE £8.70: £2.50, £1.50, £5.80; EX 43.40 Trifecta £255.30 Pool £496.23. - 1.38 winning units..There was no bid for the winner.
Owner The Afternoon Syndicate **Bred** Peter Savill **Trained** Newmarket, Suffolk

FOCUS
A fair race of its type, with an improved effort from the winner. Sound form.

NOTEBOOK
Sunstroke(IRE) ran out an appropriate winner on one of the hottest days of the year. Down in grade, she belied her sprinting pedigree over this longer trip and, if anything, will stay a bit further too.
House Arrest, with the cheekpieces left off, had her chance but the winner pulled away in the final furlong. She has finished runner-up in three of these now. (op 3-1)
Mr Mini Scule ran a fair race on this first outing on fast ground, coupled with a rise in trip and the loss of the blinkers. (op 14-1)
The Slider won over an extended seven at Beverley and, shoved along from halfway, seemed to find this slightly shorter trip too sharp. (op 7-2)
Sad Times(IRE) had a decent chance on form, but was first reluctant to go round behind the stalls and then refused point blank to race. Official explanation: jockey said filly refused to race (tchd 10-3 and 4-1)

3614 PIPER HEIDSIECK CHAMPAGNE H'CAP 7f 214y
4:00 (4:02) (Class 6) (0-60,54) 3-Y-0+ **£3,238** (£963; £481; £240) **Stalls** Low

Form RPR

-330 **1** **Start Of Authority**[20] 2969 5-9-4 43 .... JimCrowley 13 55
(J Gallagher) *prom: led over 2f out: rdn and hld on cl home* **9/1**

2221 **2** nk **Prince Valentine**[28] 2728 5-9-8 47 .... (p) IanMongan 10 58
(G L Moore) *mid-div: swtchd rt: hdwy 2f out: pressed wnr thrght fnl f* **6/1**[2]

-003 **3** 2 1/2 **Macs Ransom (USA)**[14] 3161 3-9-3 50 .... ChrisCatlin 5 53
(N A Callaghan) *a.p: kpt on one pce ins fnl 2f* **10/1**

2404 **4** 2 1/2 **Hadath (IRE)**[9] 3339 9-9-12 51 .... (b) GeorgeBaker 3 51+
(B G Powell) *in rr: rdn and hdwy on outside over 2f out: r.o fnl f: nvr nrr* **7/1**[3]

5263 **5** 1 **Fantasy Defender (IRE)**[9] 3339 4-9-7 46 .... (v) LPKeniry 8 43
(Ernst Oertel) *s.i.s: sn mid-div: rdn over 3f out: one pce appr fnl f* **9/2**[1]

4363 **6** 1 1/4 **Three Feathers**[13] 3195 3-8-8 44 .... SaleemGolam(3) 4 36
(M Salaman) *t.k.h in mid-div: rdn 1/2-way: fdd appr fnl f* **14/1**

-400 **7** nk **Shamwari Fire (IRE)**[11] 3240 6-8-10 38 .... (b[1]) PatrickMathers(3) 1 32
(I W McInnes) *mid-div: effrt on ins over 2f out: sn one pce* **33/1**

-000 **8** 1/2 **Arthurs Dream (IRE)**[46] 2186 4-9-4 48 .... JamesDoyle(5) 12 40
(A W Carroll) *bhd: rdn 3f out and sn mde effrt: n.d* **9/1**

055- **9** 1 **Zafarilla (IRE)**[384] 3013 3-8-12 50 .... EmmettStack(5) 14 47+
(Pat Eddery) *in rr: rdn over 3f out: nt clr run over 1f out and no ch after* **9/1**

00-0 **10** 1/2 **Pragmatica**[37] 42 5-8-13 41 .... (p) AdamKirby(3) 11 30
(R M H Cowell) *led for over 1f: rdn 1/2-way: wknd wl over 1f out* **16/1**

5005 **11** 3/4 **Zinging**[9] 3339 7-9-8 47 .... (v) HayleyTurner 9 34
(J J Bridger) *prom: led over 6f out: hdd over 2f out: sn wknd* **12/1**

0-00 **12** hd **Savernake Brave (IRE)**[71] 1538 5-8-11 36 .... (v[1]) FergusSweeney 7 23
(Mrs H Sweeting) *a towards rr* **25/1**

0-00 **13** 5 **Royal Sailor (IRE)**[9] 3339 4-10-0 53 .... (b) MichaelTebbutt 6 28
(J Ryan) *in tch tl rdn 3f out: sn btn* **66/1**

0000 **14** 1 **Tally (IRE)**[44] 2260 6-8-7 39 .... JemmaMarshall(7) 2 12
(D G Bridgwater) *a in rr* **50/1**

0400 **15** 6 **Squadron Leader (IRE)**[35] 2531 3-9-7 54 .... DaneO'Neill 15 11
(R Hannon) *a bhd* **16/1**

1m 32.42s (-2.62) **Going Correction** -0.30s/f (Firm)
WFA 3 from 4yo+ 8lb **15** Ran SP% **120.4**
Speed ratings (Par 101):101,100,98,95,94 93,93,92,91,91 90,90,85,84,78
CSF £60.18 CT £574.52 TOTE £14.60: £4.50, £2.30, £4.20; EX 80.90 Trifecta £275.40 Part won. Pool £387.97. - 0.35 winning units.
Owner Adweb Ltd **Bred** Gunther Knoerzer **Trained** Chastleton, Oxon

FOCUS
A very modest event, with the topweight running off just 53. It was run at a sound pace and the form should prove sound.

3615 BLACKSTONE WINERY H'CAP 1m 1f 209y
4:30 (4:32) (Class 6) (0-60,60) 3-Y-0+ **£2,590** (£770; £385; £192) **Stalls** High

Form RPR

0000 **1** **Factual Lad**[13] 3194 8-9-12 58 .... GeorgeBaker 2 66
(B R Millman) *a in tch: rdn over 2f out: str run fnl f to ld post* **7/1**

0514 **2** shd **Gigs Magic (USA)**[8] 3355 3-8-5 50 .... SaleemGolam(3) 6 58
(M Johnston) *nvr far away: rdn to ld over 1f out: hdd post* **7/2**[1]

1520 **3** 2 **Fantasy Crusader**[19] 3014 7-9-5 54 .... AdamKirby(3) 5 58+
(R M H Cowell) *hld up in rr: hdwy on outside 3f out: str run fnl f: fin fast to go 3rd nr fin* **13/2**[3]

0030 **4** shd **Didoe**[9] 3339 7-8-12 44 .... PaulDoe 10 48
(P W Hiatt) *s.i.s but sn trckd ldr: lost 2nd over 2f out: one pce and lost 3rd cl home* **12/1**

1114 **5** 3/4 **Another Con (IRE)**[6] 3412 5-8-10 49 .... KevinGhunowa(7) 9 51+
(P A Blockley) *trckd ldrs: rdn 2f out: one pce fnl f* **9/2**[2]

4513 **6** 3/4 **Fortune Point (IRE)**[12] 3213 8-9-8 59 .... (v) JamesDoyle(5) 3 60
(A W Carroll) *led tl hdd over 1f out: sn wknd* **7/1**

240- **7** hd **Take A Mile (IRE)**[83] 6008 4-9-7 60 .... JPFeatherstone(7) 7 61
(B G Powell) *bhd: effrt 3f out: nvr on terms* **7/1**

0500 **8** 1 1/4 **Sweet Boulangere**[41] 2352 3-9-1 57 .... DaneO'Neill 8 55
(R Hannon) *racd wd: nvr on terms* **25/1**

5000 **9** shd **Kalani Star (IRE)**[11] 3240 6-8-8 43 .... (v) PatrickMathers(3) 1 41
(I W McInnes) *trckd ldrs: wnt 2nd over 2f out: rdn and wknd over 1f out* **16/1**

0-00 **10** *7* **Laurollie**[13] 3196 4-9-3 **49**.. AlanDaly 4 34
(Dr J R J Naylor) *a in rr* **20/1**
1m 59.53s (-3.07) **Going Correction** -0.30s/f (Firm)
WFA 3 from 4yo+ 10lb **10** Ran SP% **113.4**
Speed ratings (Par 101):100,99,98,98,97 97,96,95,95,90
CSF £30.79 CT £166.60 TOTE £8.50: £3.30, £1.40, £2.10; EX 25.60 Trifecta £356.30 Part won. Pool £501.89. - 0.69 winning units.
Owner Tarka Racing **Bred** Wheelersland Stud **Trained** Kentisbeare, Devon
FOCUS
The field made for the centre of the track once in line for home. Pretty ordinary form.

3616 CATERING SERVICES INTERNATIONAL APPRENTICE H'CAP 1m 3f 196y
5:00 (5:03) (Class 6) (0-65,63) 4-Y-0+ **£2,730** (£806; £403) **Stalls** High

Form RPR
0636 **1** **Monash Lad (IRE)**[19] 3022 4-8-13 **62**.............................. PatrickHills(7) 8 70
(M H Tompkins) *in rr: swtchd lft over 3f out: rdn and kpt on to ld wl ins fnl f* **25/1**
6462 **2** *nk* **Meelup (IRE)**[16] 3115 6-9-1 **57**..(p) AmirQuinn 6 65
(P G Murphy) *trckd ldr: led on ins over 2f out: rdn and hdd wl ins fnl f* **7/1**[3]
0135 **3** *7* **String Serenade (IRE)**[12] 3232 5-8-5 **47**...................... SaleemGolam 2 44
(V Smith) *in tch tl outpcd appr fnl f* **12/1**
-665 **4** *hd* **Equilibria (USA)**[5] 3437 4-8-1 **48**.................................. JamieJones(5) 9 44
(G L Moore) *t.k.h in mid-div: chsd ldrs over 2f out: outpcd appr fnl f* **15/2**
0124 **5** *hd* **Icannshift (IRE)**[14] 3163 6-8-10 **52**................................. NeilChalmers 5 48
(T M Jones) *led tl c into centre and hdd over 2f out: wknd over 1f out* **9/1**
44-3 **6** *hd* **Kernel Dowery (IRE)**[11] 3270 6-8-8 **50**........................... AdamKirby 10 46
(W R Swinburn) *in tch: rdn over 2f out: sn one pce* **9/2**[1]
3004 **7** *1 ¼* **Ulshaw**[37] 2481 9-8-0 **45** oh8 ow1.................................. JamesDoyle(3) 4 39
(J M Bradley) *hld up: a in rr* **25/1**
2513 **8** *shd* **Seattle Robber**[15] 3141 4-9-2 **63**.........................(p) KevinGhunowa(5) 1 57
(P A Blockley) *in rr: effrt 4f out but nvr on terms* **5/1**[2]
3310 **9** *1* **Twentytwosilver (IRE)**[7] 2577 6-8-4 **49**.................. LiamJones(3) 7 41
(D B Feek) *slowly away: effrt 3f out: sn btn* **7/1**[3]
1262 **10** *12* **Plain Champagne (IRE)**[13] 3196 4-8-7 **54**............ AshleyHamblett(5) 3 27
(Dr J R J Naylor) *trckd ldrs: rdn 3f out: sn wknd* **9/2**[1]
2m 27.73s (-4.47) **Going Correction** -0.30s/f (Firm) **10** Ran SP% **115.2**
Speed ratings (Par 101):102,101,97,97,96 96,95,95,95,87
CSF £188.34 CT £2208.39 TOTE £19.70: £5.00, £2.80, £3.20; EX 147.10 TRIFECTA Not won. Place 6 £722.63, Place 5 £286.85..
Owner Miss Clare Hollest **Bred** Eoin And Stephanie Hanly **Trained** Newmarket, Suffolk
FOCUS
This was run at a steady pace and turned into something of a sprint. The three to stay on the far rail filled the first three places, with the front two, who have been rated to last year's best, finishing well clear.
Icannshift(IRE) Official explanation: jockey said gelding lost the bridle over one ear
Plain Champagne(IRE) Official explanation: jockey said filly was unsuited by the firm ground
T/Jkpt: Not won. T/Plt: £962.60 to a £1 stake. Pool £68,574.80. 52 winning tickets. T/Qpdt: £55.30 to a £1 stake. Pool £5,325.70. 71.20 winning tickets. JS

3076 NEWCASTLE (L-H)
Tuesday, July 18
OFFICIAL GOING: Good to firm (firm in places)
Wind: Breezy, behind

3617 TRANSCEND BLOODSTOCK APPRENTICE H'CAP 6f
6:40 (6:40) (Class 6) (0-60,60) 3-Y-0+ **£2,590** (£770; £385; £192) **Stalls** Centre

Form RPR
0032 **1** **Prospect Court**[9] 3330 4-9-1 **49**.................................... AndrewMullen 2 60
(A C Whillans) *chsd far side ldrs: rdn 1/2-way: led and overall ldr ins fnl f: r.o wl* **8/1**
0006 **2** *½* **Tuscan Flyer**[26] 2785 8-8-3 **42** ow1...........................(b) RobbieMills(5) 1 51
(R Bastiman) *led far side to ins fnl f: 2nd of 9 in gp* **25/1**
4014 **3** *hd* **Sharp Hat**[13] 3190 12-9-2 **50**.. MarcHalford 9 58
(D W Chapman) *cl up stands side: led that gp 2f out: hung into centre and hdd by far side ins fnl f: r.o: 1st of 8 in gp* **16/1**
0 **4** *¾* **Dechiper (IRE)**[11] 3260 4-8-10 **47** ow4.................. DeclanMcGann(3) 16 53
(R Johnson) *bhd stands side: rdn 1/2-way: r.o wl fnl f: nrst fin: 2nd of 8 in gp* **66/1**
4026 **5** *1 ¼* **Yorke's Folly (USA)**[14] 3172 5-8-5 **45**...............(b) LeanneKershaw(3) 14 47
(C W Fairhurst) *chsd stands side ldrs: effrt and edgd into centre over 1f out: one pce fnl f: 3rd of 8 in gp* **12/1**
0010 **6** *¾* **Dark Champion**[13] 3190 6-9-5 **58**...........................(b) MarkCoumbe(5) 3 58
(R E Barr) *cl up far side tl rdn and no ex appr fnl f: 3rd of 9 in gp* **20/1**
4040 **7** *1* **Bahrain Gold (IRE)**[9] 3334 6-9-1 **54**...................... JamieHamblett(5) 13 51
(N P McCormack) *chsd stands side ldrs tl rdn and nt qckn over 1f out: 4th of 8 in gp* **20/1**
2000 **8** *½* **Quantica (IRE)**[26] 2785 7-8-9 **48**.........................(t) DanielleMcCreery(5) 7 44
(N Tinkler) *swtchd to stands side and hld up sn after s: effrt over 2f out: no imp tl styd on fnl f: 5th of 8 in gp* **22/1**
0140 **9** *1 ¼* **Haroldini (IRE)**[26] 2793 4-8-9 **43**.........................(p) StephenDonohoe 5 35
(J Balding) *s.i.s: bhd far side tl kpt on last 2f: n.d: 4th of 9 in gp* **14/1**
0053 **10** *¾* **Mill By The Stream**[11] 3240 4-8-8 **42**........................ RoryMoore 11 32
(P T Midgley) *hld up stands side: rdn over 2f out: nvr rchd ldrs: 6th of 8 in gp* **9/1**
2606 **11** *½* **Whittinghamvillage**[15] 3137 5-9-2 **55**...........................(p) NeilBrown(5) 6 43
(D W Whillans) *hld up far side: rdn over 2f out: btn over 1f out: 5th of 9 in gp* **16/1**
0006 **12** *hd* **Born For Diamonds (IRE)**[25] 2831 4-8-5 **42**....... MichaelJStainton(3) 10 30
(R E Barr) *swtchd to far side sn after s: prom tl rdn and outpcd fr 2f out: 6th of 9 in gp* **66/1**
5020 **13** *½* **Hamaasy**[21] 2949 5-8-12 **49**.. HMuya(3) 17 35
(D Nicholls) *led stands side to 2f out: hung lft and sn outpcd: 7th of 8 in gp* **15/2**[3]
5160 **14** *hd* **Outrageous Flirt (IRE)**[6] 3398 4-9-2 **53**.................. KellyHarrison(3) 15 38
(A Dickman) *in tch stands side: rdn over 2f out: btn over 1f out: last of 8 in gp* **10/1**
6600 **15** *1 ¾* **Wolfman**[21] 2949 4-8-9 **43**..(p) DerekNolan 8 23
(D W Barker) *chsd far side ldrs tl wknd over 2f out: 7th of 9 in gp* **50/1**
-605 **16** *3 ½* **Disguise**[11] 3245 4-9-7 **60**.. PJBenson(5) 12 30
(J J Quinn) *swtchd to far side sn after s: chsd ldrs tl wknd over 2f out: 8th of 9 in gp* **9/2**[1]
0621 **17** *1 ¼* **Celtic Thunder**[11] 3245 5-9-7 **58**...............................(b) JamesMillman(3) 4 24
(T J Etherington) *s.i.s: sn wl bhd far side: nvr on terms: last of 9 in gp* **7/1**[2]
1m 13.48s (-1.61) **Going Correction** -0.45s/f (Firm) **17** Ran SP% **121.4**
Speed ratings (Par 101):92,91,91,90,88 87,86,85,83,82 82,81,81,80,78 73,72
CSF £201.15 CT £3203.65 TOTE £10.40: £2.60, £4.90, £3.50, £19.60; EX 213.70.
Owner Mrs L M Whillans **Bred** Mrs G Slater **Trained** Newmill-On-Slitrig, Borders
■ Stewards' Enquiry : Robbie Mills one-day ban: careless riding (Sep 14); one-day ban: used whip with excessive frequency (Jul 30)
FOCUS
An ordinary event in which the field split evenly. The far side edged it this time but, in truth, there was little between the sides. Average for the grade.
Disguise Official explanation: vet said gelding bled from the nose
Celtic Thunder Official explanation: trainer said gelding was unsuited by the good to firm (firm in places) ground

3618 SIMPSON & GREGG LTD NOVICE AUCTION STKS 6f
7:10 (7:11) (Class 6) 2-Y-0 **£2,914** (£867; £433; £216) **Stalls** Centre

Form RPR
10 **1** **Holdin Foldin (IRE)**[26] 2771 2-9-3 .... PatCosgrave 1 90+
(K R Burke) *mde all: clr 1/2-way: v easily* **1/12**[1]
2 *17* **Desert Maze (IRE)** 2-8-9 .... TonyHamilton 4 31
(J Wade) *chsd wnr thrght: rdn 1/2-way: sn outpcd* **40/1**
3 *2 ½* **Chastity (IRE)** 2-8-9 .... KimTinkler 3 24
(N Tinkler) *prom: outpcd after 2f: no ch after* **16/1**[2]
4 *16* **Miss Puffle** 2-8-5 ow1.. DeanMcKeown 2 —
(S Parr) *sn wl bhd: t.o* **28/1**[3]
1m 13.45s (-1.64) **Going Correction** -0.45s/f (Firm) **4** Ran SP% **104.1**
Speed ratings (Par 92):92,69,66,44
CSF £4.68 TOTE £1.10; EX 3.90.
Owner Tweenhills Racing & P Timmins J Rhodes **Bred** Paul Starr **Trained** Middleham Moor, N Yorks
■ Stewards' Enquiry : Pat Cosgrave one-day ban: failed to ride to draw (Jul 30)
FOCUS
A non-event with the very short-priced favourite coasting to a very easy win over vastly inferior rivals. He could rate much better.
NOTEBOOK
Holdin Foldin(IRE), far from disgraced in the Norfolk at Royal Ascot on his previous start, did not have to turn a hair to beat vastly inferior rivals in this very one-sided event over this longer trip. This told us nothing new about him but he remains worth a try back in stronger company. (tchd 1-10 in as place)
Desert Maze(IRE) was absolutely no match for the useful winner on this racecourse debut but did hint at ability and may do better in modest nursery company over further in due course.
Chastity(IRE) has winners in her pedigree but achieved little on this racecourse debut. (tchd 20-1)
Miss Puffle offered no immediate promise on this racecourse debut. (op 33-1)

3619 HOLYSTONE DEMOLITION LTD CLAIMING STKS 7f
7:40 (7:40) (Class 6) 2-Y-0 **£2,266** (£674; £337; £168) **Stalls** Centre

Form RPR
0141 **1** **Just Dust**[14] 3160 2-8-12 ....(p) MarcHalford(5) 4 65
(W G M Turner) *keen: mde all: hld on wl fnl f* **5/1**[2]
53 **2** *½* **Centenary (IRE)**[13] 3187 2-9-7 .... TomEaves 3 68
(J Howard Johnson) *cl up: effrt over 2f out: kpt on fnl f* **9/2**[1]
1 **3** *½* **Beau Sancy**[35] 2524 2-9-5 .... JimmyQuinn 2 64
(J Pearce) *chsd ldrs: effrt whn hung lft and carried hd high over 1f out: kpt on fnl f* **13/2**
2022 **4** *1 ¼* **Lansdown**[10] 3279 2-7-13 ....(p) AndrewMullen(5) 6 46
(B Ellison) *sn pushed along towards rr: hdwy outside over 1f out: kpt on fnl f: nrst fin* **9/2**[1]
000 **5** *½* **Up The Pole**[28] 2733 2-8-8 .... PaulMulrennan 9 49
(M W Easterby) *hld up in tch: effrt over 2f out: no imp fnl f* **25/1**
0043 **6** *shd* **Providence Farm**[14] 3174 2-8-13 .... DaleGibson 5 54
(M W Easterby) *in tch: outpcd after 3f: hung lft and rallied over 1f out: no imp fnl f* **7/1**
05 **7** *1 ½* **The Dandy Fox**[42] 2321 2-9-2 .... PaulHanagan 1 53
(D Nicholls) *in tch: drvn over 2f out: no ex over 1f out* **10/1**
3535 **8** *5* **Flamestone**[11] 3246 2-9-1 .... GrahamGibbons 7 39
(J D Bethell) *in tch: drvn over 2f out: btn fnl f* **11/2**[3]
000 **9** *17* **Rose Court**[11] 3246 2-8-9 .... JamesReveley(7) 8 —
(K G Reveley) *hld up: rdn over 2f out: sn btn* **18/1**
1m 26.97s (-1.03) **Going Correction** -0.45s/f (Firm) **9** Ran SP% **112.4**
Speed ratings (Par 92):88,87,86,85,84 83,77,57
CSF £26.83 TOTE £4.10: £1.40, £2.20, £2.00; EX 29.70.The winner was claimed by D. R. C. Elsworth for £10,000. Beau Sancy was claimed by R. A. Harris £11,000. Centenary (IRE) was claimed by J. S. Wainwright for £12,000
Owner T.O.C.S. Ltd **Bred** T O C S Ltd And W G M Turner **Trained** Sigwells, Somerset
■ Stewards' Enquiry : Paul Mulrennan one-day ban: failed to ride to draw (Jul 30)
FOCUS
A low-grade event in which the pace was only fair and those racing close to the gallop held the edge. The time looks good but the form is not that strong.
NOTEBOOK
Just Dust failed to settle on his first run over this longer distance but he saw the trip out well after enjoying the run of the race to notch his third win in his last four starts. He is a versatile sort who goes well on fast ground and has now joined David Elsworth. (op 4-1)
Centenary(IRE), dropped in grade, ran creditably and again left the impression that the step up to a mile would suit. He was claimed by John Wainwright and appeals as the type to win a small race granted a stiffer test. (op 7-1)
Beau Sancy, who won an uncompetitive race on his debut, was not disgraced on this first run for new connections but did not impress with the way he hung or carried his head under pressure. He was claimed by Ron Harris and it will be interesting to see how he progresses. (op 6-1 tchd 7-1)
Lansdown, tried in the cheekpieces, shaped as though a bit better than the bare form as she finished the best of those held up. However, she looks the type that needs things to drop just right and may be one to watch until getting her head in front where it matters. (tchd 4-1)
Up The Pole, dropped in grade, had something to find on these terms but left the impression that a stiffer overall test of stamina would have suited. She is likely to remain vulnerable in this type of race, though. (op 22-1)
Providence Farm also shaped as though a stiffer test of stamina would have suited but he did not look entirely straightforward under pressure on this very quick ground. (op 8-1)

3620 TRANSCEND BLOODSTOCK MAIDEN STKS 1m 2f 32y
8:10 (8:10) (Class 5) 3-4-Y-0 **£3,562** (£1,059; £529; £264) **Stalls** Centre

Form RPR
02- **1** **Act Friendly (IRE)**[270] 6007 3-8-11 .... KerrinMcEvoy 5 57+
(Saeed Bin Suroor) *pressed ldr: led over 2f out: shkn up and wnt clr fnl f* **1/9**[1]
0-00 **2** *6* **Fadansil**[15] 3138 3-9-2 **47**... TonyHamilton 4 51
(J Wade) *led to over 2f out: kpt on: no ch w wnr* **33/1**[3]

3-0 **3** *1 ¼* **Knight Valiant**[41] [2366] 3-9-2 .... TomEaves 2 49
(J Howard Johnson) *keen: chsd ldrs: effrt over 2f out: sn one pce* **12/1**[2]
0 **4** *hd* **Carabinieri (IRE)**[19] [3001] 3-9-2 .... PaulHanagan 6 48
(J Barclay) *s.i.s: hld up in tch: effrt and edgd lft over 2f out: sn outpcd* **66/1**
-050 **5** *8* **Keyalzao (IRE)**[8] [3353] 4-9-4 30.......... DNolan(3) 3 28
(A Crook) *in tch tl rdn and wknd over 2f out* **100/1**
56 **6** *7* **Musical Giant (USA)**[19] [3001] 3-9-2 .... PaulMulrennan 1 20
(J Howard Johnson) *hld up: rdn 3f out: sn btn* **33/1**[3]
2m 11.73s (-0.07) **Going Correction** -0.05s/f (Good)
WFA 3 from 4yo 10lb **6 Ran SP% 106.1**
Speed ratings (Par 103):98,93,92,92,85 80
CSF £6.98 TOTE £1.10: £1.02, £5.80; EX 5.00.
Owner Godolphin **Bred** Gainsborough Stud Management Ltd **Trained** Newmarket, Suffolk
FOCUS
The second very one-sided contest on this modest card and Act Friendly did not have to better her previous run to beat a 47-rated rival with a good deal more in hand than the margin suggested. The time was poor.

3621 CLOSE HOUSE COUNTRY CLUB H'CAP 1m 2f 32y
8:40 (8:40) (Class 5) (0-75,71) 3-Y-O+ **£3,886** (£1,156; £577; £288) **Stalls** Centre

Form RPR
2112 **1** **Cottingham (IRE)**[4] [3484] 5-9-1 **61**.......... BenSwarbrick(3) 2 70
(T D Barron) *trckd ldr: led 2f out: kpt on wl fnl f* **15/8**[1]
-614 **2** *1 ¼* **Fossgate**[18] [3037] 5-9-7 **64**.......... JimmyQuinn 1 71
(J D Bethell) *prom: effrt 2f out: chsd wnr ins fnl f: kpt on* **11/2**[3]
-003 **3** *1* **Leslingtaylor (IRE)**[27] [2762] 4-9-8 **65**.......... GrahamGibbons 6 70
(J J Quinn) *in tch: effrt over 2f out: kpt on fnl f: no imp* **11/2**[3]
1062 **4** *¾* **Bright Sun (IRE)**[10] [3309] 5-10-0 **71**..........(t) KimTinkler 7 75
(N Tinkler) *led to 2f out: kpt on same pce fnl f* **13/2**
2405 **5** *1* **Airbound (USA)**[14] [3167] 3-8-10 **63**.......... KDarley 5 65
(M Johnston) *prom: drvn 3f out: no imp fr over 1f out* **4/1**[2]
-005 **6** *1 ½* **Red Chairman**[17] [3081] 4-9-5 **62**.......... TomEaves 4 61
(R Johnson) *plld hrd: hld up: rdn over 2f out: n.d* **20/1**
1006 **7** *nk* **George's Flyer (IRE)**[19] [3008] 3-8-9 **62**..........(b) PaulHanagan 8 60
(R A Fahey) *hld up: rdn 3f out: sn btn* **12/1**
2m 10.61s (-1.19) **Going Correction** -0.05s/f (Good)
WFA 3 from 4yo+ 10lb **7 Ran SP% 111.3**
Speed ratings (Par 103):102,101,100,99,98 97,97
CSF £11.82 CT £45.08 TOTE £2.50: £2.30, £3.20; EX 10.90.
Owner Twinacre Nurseries Ltd **Bred** B Kennedy **Trained** Maunby, N Yorks
FOCUS
An ordinary event in which the gallop was on the steady side. The winner is continuing his recent progress back to his best, while the second and third ran to this year's form.

3622 SENDRIG CONSTRUCTION 25TH ANNIVERSARY H'CAP 5f
9:10 (9:10) (Class 4) (0-80,75) 3-Y-O+ **£5,505** (£1,637; £818; £408) **Stalls** Centre

Form RPR
6001 **1** **Ryedane (IRE)**[13] [3190] 4-9-3 **67**.......... DavidAllan 9 77
(T D Easterby) *keen early: mde all: clr over 1f out: rdn out* **7/1**
0040 **2** *1 ¾* **True Magic**[17] [3097] 5-9-3 **67**.......... GrahamGibbons 2 71
(J D Bethell) *cl up: drvn over 2f out: kpt on fnl f: no ch w wnr* **16/1**
1500 **3** *shd* **Brut**[14] [3170] 4-8-11 **66**.......... MarkLawson(5) 7 70
(D W Barker) *towards rr: drvn 1/2-way: hdwy over 1f out: kpt on: nrst fin* **16/1**
4043 **4** *shd* **Colonel Cotton (IRE)**[4] [3503] 7-9-7 **71**..........(v) PaulHanagan 6 74+
(R A Fahey) *s.i.s: bhd tl hdwy over 1f out: r.o fnl f: nrst fin* **4/1**[2]
2636 **5** *hd* **Strensall**[8] [3354] 9-8-9 **66**.......... MichaelJStainton(7) 3 69
(R E Barr) *prom: rdn over 2f out: one pce over 1f out* **7/1**
-006 **6** *1 ½* **Niteowl Lad (IRE)**[5] [3449] 4-9-8 **75**..........(t) JasonEdmunds(3) 5 72
(J Balding) *prom: effrt over 2f out: no ex over 1f out* **8/1**
0000 **7** *¾* **Shank On Fourteen (IRE)**[10] [3287] 5-8-8 **58**.......... PatCosgrave 1 52
(K R Burke) *in tch tl rdn and wknd wl over 1f out* **16/1**
0652 **8** *hd* **Henry Hall (IRE)**[10] [3297] 10-9-4 **68**.......... KimTinkler 4 62
(N Tinkler) *plld hrd in tch: rdn over 2f out: btn fnl f* **5/1**[3]
1430 **9** *nk* **Divine Spirit**[18] [3041] 5-9-4 **68**.......... DO'Donohoe 8 61
(M Dods) *hld up: rdn over 2f out: n.d* **3/1**[1]
59.25 secs (-2.25) **Going Correction** -0.45s/f (Firm) **9 Ran SP% 115.4**
Speed ratings (Par 105):100,97,97,96,96 94,92,92,92
CSF £110.09 CT £1731.89 TOTE £9.10: £2.40, £3.70, £6.30; EX 157.40 Place 6 £148.22, Place 5 £18.31.
Owner Ryedale Partners No 5 **Bred** Tally-Ho Stud **Trained** Great Habton, N Yorks
FOCUS
An ordinary but competitive sprint in which the whole field raced on the far side. Nothing ever got in a blow at the winner, who got an easy lead, but was well in old form and did not seem flattered.
Divine Spirit Official explanation: jockey said due to not being able to get covered up gelding hung right-handed
T/Plt: £106.90 to a £1 stake. Pool: £54,106.40. 369.25 winning tickets. T/Qpdt: £23.50 to a £1 stake. Pool: £3,828.30. 120.10 winning tickets. RY

3227 YARMOUTH (L-H)
Tuesday, July 18

OFFICIAL GOING: Firm
Wind: Nil Weather: Hot

3623 AEROPAK E B F MAIDEN STKS 7f 3y
6:20 (6:20) (Class 4) 2-Y-O **£4,857** (£1,445; £722; £360) **Stalls** High

Form RPR
0 **1** **Tobosa**[25] [2821] 2-9-3 .... LDettori 8 81
(W Jarvis) *chsd ldr: rdn 2f out: led 1f out: styd on* **17/2**
2 *1* **Sahrati** 2-9-3 .... SebSanders 5 78
(C E Brittain) *trckd ldrs: rdn and outpcd 4f out: rallied 2f out: kpt on to go 2nd: nr fin: nt rch wnr* **16/1**
05 **3** *nk* **Heywood**[9] [3328] 2-9-3 .... TedDurcan 1 78
(M R Channon) *led: rdn over 2f out: hdd 1f out: unable qck ins fnl f* **22/1**
4 *hd* **King's Causeway (USA)** 2-9-3 .... ShaneKelly 3 77
(W J Haggas) *midfield: in tch: rdn 3f out: kpt on steadily fnl f: nrst fin* **13/2**[3]
5 *4* **Passage Of Time** 2-8-12 .... EddieAhern 6 62
(H R A Cecil) *midfield: in tch: rdn wl over 2f out: kpt on one pce* **15/8**[1]
563 **6** *2 ½* **Atheneum (IRE)**[12] [3210] 2-9-3 .... J-PGuillambert 7 60
(M Johnston) *slowly away: sn rcvrd: pressed ldrs 5f out tl rdn wl over 2f out: wknd 1f out* **4/1**[2]
7 *3* **Diggs Lane (IRE)** 2-9-3 .... SteveDrowne 4 52
(N A Callaghan) *slowly away: bhd whn stmbld after 1f: lost tch 1/2-way* **12/1**
8 *nk* **Furmigadelagiusta** 2-9-3 .... NickyMackay 2 52
(L M Cumani) *a bhd: rdn and lost tch 1/2-way* **13/2**[3]
1m 23.86s (-2.74) **Going Correction** -0.45s/f (Firm) **8 Ran SP% 109.9**
Speed ratings (Par 96):97,95,95,95,90 87,84,84
CSF £119.63 TOTE £11.50: £3.40, £3.40, £3.60; EX 81.10.
Owner Collins, Randall, Rich & Turnbull **Bred** G S Shropshire **Trained** Newmarket, Suffolk
FOCUS
Just an average maiden but a couple of promising debuts suggest there will be future winners come from the race.
NOTEBOOK
Tobosa, the pick of the paddock, improved on his debut at Newmarket last month and scored well having been close to the pace throughout. He can improve further and should get a mile. (op 10-1)
Sahrati ◆, a half-brother to Hazeymm making his debut for an in-form yard, raced close up towards the far side on his debut and showed plenty of promise. He should improve for the run and will be better on better ground, but looks capable of winning a similar event. (op 14-1)
Heywoodby the same sire as the winner, ran his best race to date and, qualified for nurseries now, could well have more to offer. (op 20-1)
King's Causeway(USA) ◆ looked fit for his debut and was the eyecatcher of the race, running green but keeping on nicely in the closing stages. He should come on considerably for the experience and on this evidence will be winning before long. (op 8-1)
Passage Of Time, a half-sister to the useful Sandglass, ran below market expectations on this debut, being unable to find extra when asked. She should improve with this behind her. (op 9-4 tchd 5-2)
Atheneum(IRE), the most experienced runner in the field, missed the break but was soon in contention. It may be that he did too much too soon, but has something to prove and may be better off in nurseries. (op 3-1)

3624 DIOMED DEVELOPMENTS (S) NURSERY 5f 43y
6:50 (6:50) (Class 6) 2-Y-O **£2,266** (£674; £337; £168) **Stalls** High

Form RPR
063 **1** **Danger Alley**[16] [3110] 2-9-4 **67**..........(b) RichardMullen 1 63
(E J O'Neill) *chsd ldr tl led after 1f: mde rest: rdn wl over 1f out: styd on wl* **2/1**[1]
2120 **2** *1 ½* **Peggys Flower**[6] [3409] 2-9-7 **70**.......... LDettori 3 61
(N A Callaghan) *t.k.h: chsd wnr over 3f out: rdn 2f out: outpcd by wnr ins fnl f* **11/4**[2]
2053 **3** *1 ¾* **Splendidio**[7] [3380] 2-8-7 **56**.......... JohnEgan 5 40
(D K Ivory) *chsd ldrs: rdn 2f out: wnt 3rd ins fnl f: no imp* **6/1**
1436 **4** *1 ¼* **Baytown Paikea**[7] [3380] 2-8-3 **52**.......... FrancisFerris 4 32
(P S McEntee) *led for 1f: chsd ldrs: rdn over 2f out: wknd ins fnl f* **11/2**[3]
0036 **5** *½* **Cyprus Rose**[10] [3300] 2-7-9 **51**.......... LukeMorris(7) 2 29
(V Smith) *a bhd: rdn 3f out: kpt on one pce: n.d* **9/1**
0610 **6** *½* **Suzieblue (IRE)**[8] [3345] 2-7-12 **54**..........(b[1]) JosephWalsh(7) 6 30
(J S Moore) *chsd ldrs on rail: hmpd after 1f: rdn 2f out: no prog: btn whn nt clr run last 100 yds* **14/1**
62.08 secs (-0.72) **Going Correction** -0.45s/f (Firm) **6 Ran SP% 106.3**
Speed ratings (Par 92):87,84,81,79,79 78
CSF £6.76 TOTE £3.30: £1.80, £1.70; EX 5.40.The winner was bought-in for 8,200gns
Owner Scholes,Kirkham & Fretwell **Bred** J S Middleton And Miss K S Buckley **Trained** Averham Park, Notts
FOCUS
A modest selling nursery. The official ratings shown next to each horse are estimated and for information purposes only.
NOTEBOOK
Danger Alley, dropping in class, was well backed and made no mistake under a positive ride. He had shown what he was capable of in the first-time blinkers on his previous outing, and with the headgear retained ran out a comfortable winner. He was bought-in at the auction, so connections must feel he has more to offer. (op 11-4 tchd 15-8)
Peggys Flower had lost her chance at the start at Lingfield last week but it was different this time and she was soon tracking the winner. She was quite keen early but performed with credit and could find a similar event. (tchd 10-3)
Splendidio, having her eighth race, had been behind the runner-up at Windsor earlier in the season but finished much closer and continues to perform with credit, despite being exposed. There could be a similar race for her back on the All-Weather. (op 5-1 tchd 13-2)
Baytown Paikea, who had a busy time in the first half of last month, has not been in the same form since returning from a short break, but this is her level. (op 5-1 tchd 9-2)
Cyprus Rose is clearly very moderate and never really figured. (op 7-1 tchd 10-1)
Suzieblue(IRE) found herself short of room in the closing stages when trying to mount a challenge towards the stands' rail. (op 10-1)

3625 4HEAD H'CAP 5f 43y
7:20 (7:20) (Class 4) (0-85,85) 3-Y-O+
£6,232 (£1,866; £933; £467; £233; £117) **Stalls** High

Form RPR
1542 **1** **Bluebok**[5] [3449] 5-9-7 **78**.......... JamieSpencer 1 91
(J M Bradley) *prom: rdn to ld over 1f out: styd on strly and drew clr ins fnl f* **2/1**[1]
2451 **2** *1 ¾* **Malapropism**[4] [3503] 6-9-12 **83** 6ex.......... TedDurcan 3 90
(M R Channon) *led: sn hdd: pressed ldr: ev ch and rdn 2f out: outpcd by wnr ins fnl f* **11/2**[3]
5311 **3** *nk* **Heavens Walk**[13] [3199] 5-8-7 **64**..........(t) SebSanders 4 70
(P J Makin) *hld up bhd: effrt 2f out: hrd rdn over 1f out: no imp ins fnl f* **9/4**[2]
3606 **4** *nk* **Silver Dane (IRE)**[29] [2711] 4-9-0 **71**..........(v) JohnEgan 2 76
(Mrs C A Dunnett) *in tch: rdn 2f out: kpt on one pce ins fnl f* **11/1**
0000 **5** *1 ½* **Figaro Flyer (IRE)**[5] [3447] 3-9-10 **85**.......... RichardMullen 5 84
(P Howling) *chsd ldrs: rdn and outpcd wl over 2f out: kpt on ins fnl f* **20/1**
0200 **6** *5* **Spanish Ace**[30] [2674] 5-9-11 **82**.......... LDettori 6 63
(J M Bradley) *sn led: rdn 2f out: hdd over 1f out: sn wknd: eased last 100 yds* **6/1**
60.01 secs (-2.79) **Going Correction** -0.45s/f (Firm)
WFA 3 from 4yo+ 4lb **6 Ran SP% 106.9**
Speed ratings (Par 105):104,101,100,100,97 89
CSF £11.91 TOTE £2.80: £1.90, £2.70; EX 11.40.
Owner E A Hayward **Bred** E Duggan And D Churchman **Trained** Sedbury, Gloucs
FOCUS
Just a fair handicap but the first two are in form. Solid form despite the small field, the winner and second running to this year's best.
Spanish Ace Official explanation: jockey said gelding hung left and moved poorly

3626 ADIOS CLAIMING STKS — 1m 2f 21y
7:50 (7:50) (Class 6) 3-Y-O+ £2,331 (£693; £346; £173) Stalls Low

Form				RPR
U35	1		**Luis Melendez (USA)**^{15} [3139] 4-9-8 67 (t) SteveDrowne 1 (Tom Dascombe) *mde all: rdn wl over 1f out: kpt on wl: in command last 100 yds* **5/2**^{2}	60
5143	2	1 ¼	**Ionian Spring (IRE)**^{17} [3068] 11-9-8 79 DanielTudhope$^{(3)}$ 8 (D Carroll) *hld up in last pair: hdwy on bit over 3f out: chsd wnr 2f out: rdn over 1f out: one pce* **5/4**^{1}	61
-000	3	¾	**Is**^{20} [2968] 3-7-7 45 LukeMorris$^{(7)}$ 2 (Rae Guest) *chsd ldrs: rdn over 3f out: chsd wnr 3f out tl 2f out: kpt on one pce* **33/1**	44
-000	4	1 ½	**Pay On (IRE)**^{15} [3156] 3-8-8 58 (v) LDettori 7 (W Jarvis) *t.k.h: hld up in last: rdn and effrt on inner 3f out: swtchd rt over 1f out: no imp* **3/1**^{3}	49
0010	5	nk	**Wodhill Gold**^{48} [2148] 5-9-1 43 (v) DerekMcGaffin 4 (D Morris) *settled in midfield: rdn wl over 3f out: one pce* **16/1**	46
00	6	40	**Genevieve**^{33} [2587] 4-9-1 OscarUrbina 3 (Mrs C A Dunnett) *t.k.h: chsd ldr tl 3f out: sn wl bhd: eased 1f out: t.o* **50/1**	—

2m 8.61s (0.51) **Going Correction** -0.275s/f (Firm)
WFA 3 from 4yo+ 10lb **6** Ran SP% **108.8**
Speed ratings (Par 101):86,85,84,83,82 50
CSF £5.60 TOTE £3.00: £1.90, £1.30.
Owner Oneway **Bred** Bloomsbury Stud **Trained** Lambourn, Berks

FOCUS
An uncompetitive claimer in which only half the field had a serious chance on official ratings and the winner was below par. Suspect form given the proximity of the third and fifth.

3627 FREEDERM VIRGINIA STKS (F&M) (LISTED RACE) — 1m 2f 21y
8:20 (8:20) (Class 1) 3-Y-O+
£15,705 (£5,978; £2,993; £1,495; £747; £375) Stalls Low

Form				RPR
1-15	1		**Reunite (IRE)**^{26} [2772] 3-8-8 101 LDettori 5 (Saeed Bin Suroor) *led at stdy pce tl 6f out: led again 2f out: pushed clr fnl f: eased nr fin* **10/11**^{1}	106+
3312	2	2 ½	**Local Spirit (USA)**^{10} [3293] 3-8-8 102 SebSanders 2 (C E Brittain) *chsd ldr tl led 6f out: hdd 2f out: sn rdn and tail swishing: kpt on but no ch w wnr fnl f* **11/2**^{3}	95+
450-	3	2	**Ruby Wine**^{329} [4663] 4-9-4 100 TedDurcan 6 (J M P Eustace) *hld up bhd: hdwy 5f out: rdn 3f out: wnt 3rd ins fnl f: kpt on: no ch w wnr* **22/1**	91
-014	4	2	**Pine Cone (IRE)**^{29} [2706] 4-9-4 89 SteveDrowne 9 (A King) *chsd ldrs tl lost pl 5f out: rdn over 3f out: styd on fnl f: wnt 4th nr fin* **40/1**	87
0-03	5	½	**Expensive**^{10} [3316] 3-8-8 101 EddieAhern 7 (C F Wall) *chsd ldrs: 3rd and rdn over 2f out: sn outpcd: lost 2 pls ins fnl f* **5/1**^{2}	86
1/62	6	1 ½	**Mamela (GER)**^{36} [2503] 5-9-4 98 NickyMackay 3 (L M Cumani) *trckd ldrs: rdn 3f out: sn outpcd* **16/1**	84
5160	7	5	**Tata Naka**^{12} [3232] 6-9-4 55 JohnEgan 4 (Mrs C A Dunnett) *hld up bhd: rdn over 3f out: sn wl outpcd* **150/1**	74?
1-1	8	6	**Postage Stampe**^{38} [2446] 3-8-8 90 JamieSpencer 8 (D M Simcock) *hld up: rdn 4f out: sn struggling: no ch after: t.o* **11/2**^{3}	63
0050	9	7	**Virginia Plain**^{16} [3115] 3-8-8 45 ShaneKelly 1 (Miss Diana Weeden) *a bhd: lost tch 3f out: t.o* **300/1**	49?

2m 2.83s (-5.27) **Going Correction** -0.275s/f (Firm) course record
WFA 3 from 4yo+ 10lb **9** Ran SP% **113.5**
Speed ratings (Par 111):110,108,106,104,104 103,99,94,88
CSF £6.07 TOTE £2.00: £1.10, £1.60, £3.00; EX 8.40.
Owner Godolphin **Bred** Darley **Trained** Newmarket, Suffolk

FOCUS
An ordinary Listed event, and not all that strong for the grade. The first two were aways prominent and are progressive, with the winner looking capable of winning in Group company.

NOTEBOOK
Reunite(IRE) took this in impressive fashion. A close fifth in the Ribblesdale on her previous outing, she appreciated the drop back in trip and made the early running. Going on again a quarter-mile out, she gained her first Pattern success with something in hand. She looks progressive and there should be more to come. (op Evens tchd 11-10)
Local Spirit(USA), whose debut on turf last time resulted in her finishing runner-up in the Lancashire Oaks, took over after half a mile but had no answer to the winner's pace and may be better over further at this level. (op 9-2)
Ruby Wine ran an encouraging race on her first start since finishing well beaten in this race last season. She should improve for the outing and looks capable of winning more races at this level. (op 25-1)
Pine Cone(IRE) ran as well as could be expected as she had a difficult task judged on official ratings. Fourth twice now at Listed level, she deserves to earn black type before long. (op 33-1)
Expensive, stepped up in trip, did not appear to stay and a return to shorter will help. (op 7-1)
Mamela(GER), another whose form has been at shorter, failed to pick up in the straight. (op 14-1 tchd 20-1)
Postage Stampe Official explanation: jockey said filly never travelled

3628 BAZUKA H'CAP — 1m 6f 17y
8:50 (8:50) (Class 5) (0-70,69) 3-Y-O+ £3,562 (£1,059; £529; £264) Stalls High

Form				RPR
6211	1		**Alambic**^{5} [3439] 3-7-12 53 6ex JamieMackay 4 (Sir Mark Prescott) *chsd ldr: rdn 3f out: led 2f out: edgd lft: clr 1f out: comf* **4/6**^{1}	59+
6060	2	1 ¾	**Platinum Charmer (IRE)**^{13} [3192] 6-8-9 55 (p) AndrewElliott$^{(5)}$ 6 (K R Burke) *midfield: rdn 5f out: outpcd over 3f out: styd on over 1f out: wnt 2nd nr fin: nt rch wnr* **16/1**	56
0005	3	nk	**Phoebe Woodstock (IRE)**^{17} [3095] 4-10-0 69 JamieSpencer 3 (W R Swinburn) *settled midfield: outpcd over 3f out: rdn over 2f out: styd on fnl f: nt rch wnr* **10/1**^{3}	70
5304	4	¾	**Ariodante**^{25} [2822] 4-9-8 63 ShaneKelly 1 (J M P Eustace) *led at stdy pce: qcknd over 4f out: hdd 2f out: one pced u.p: lost 2 pls last 100 yds* **11/1**	63
5066	5	hd	**Capitalise (IRE)**^{12} [3230] 3-7-5 53 oh2 LukeMorris$^{(7)}$ 8 (V Smith) *t.k.h: hld up bhd: rdn 3f out: styd on fnl f: nvr nrr* **25/1**	53
-206	6	2	**Redspin (IRE)**^{5} [3437] 6-8-12 53 oh14 JohnEgan 2 (J S Moore) *settled midfield: rdn over 5f out: outpcd 4f out: n.d after* **16/1**	50?
0161	7	½	**Lefonic**^{19} [3013] 4-9-2 57 OscarUrbina 7 (G C H Chung) *trckd ldng pair: rdn 4f out: no ch w ldrs after: wknd fnl f* **8/1**^{2}	53
2202	8	1 ¼	**Coffin Dodger**^{12} [3232] 3-7-7 55 oh7 ow2 KirstyMilczarek$^{(7)}$ 5 (C N Allen) *slowly away: hld up in last: effrt u.p 3f out: nvr on terms* **12/1**	49

3m 2.73s (-2.57) **Going Correction** -0.275s/f (Firm)
WFA 3 from 4yo+ 14lb **8** Ran SP% **111.8**
Speed ratings (Par 103):96,95,94,94,94 93,92,92
CSF £12.67 CT £59.10 TOTE £1.50: £1.10, £3.10, £1.90; EX 15.70 Place 6 £35.16, Place 5 £2.75.
Owner Lady O'Reilly **Bred** Miss K Rausing And Mrs S M Rogers **Trained** Newmarket, Suffolk

FOCUS
A modest staying handicap in which the well-handicapped winner completed a quick hat-trick. The pace was only steady and the form looks far from solid.
T/Plt: £90.00 to a £1 stake. Pool: £55,164.05. 446.95 winning tickets. T/Qpdt: £2.30 to a £1 stake. Pool: £4,900.90. 1,541.20 winning tickets. SP

3629 - 3632a (Foreign Racing) - See Raceform Interactive

3394 CATTERICK (L-H)
Wednesday, July 19

OFFICIAL GOING: Firm (good to firm in places)
Wind: Vitually nil

3633 JOHN SMITH'S EXTRA SMOOTH NOVICE AUCTION STKS — 7f
2:30 (2:30) (Class 5) 2-Y-O £3,886 (£1,156; £577; £288) Stalls Low

Form				RPR
2	1		**Dollar Chick (IRE)**^{22} [2943] 2-8-8 KDarley 3 (M Johnston) *cl up: rdn to ld over 1f out: kpt on ins last* **4/9**^{1}	66
6451	2	2 ½	**Rosbay (IRE)**^{15} [3175] 2-9-3 DavidAllan 2 (T D Easterby) *led: rdn along over 2f out: drvn and hdd over 1f out: kpt on same pce ins last* **5/2**^{2}	69
4	3	hd	**Ingleby Flame (IRE)**^{15} [3175] 2-8-9 PaulFessey 4 (T D Barron) *chsd ldng pair: rdn along 1/2-way: styd on u.p appr last: nrst fin* **16/1**^{3}	60
	4	11	**Admiral Savannah (IRE)** 2-8-9 PaulQuinn 1 (T D Easterby) *s.i.s: sn outpcd and bhd* **50/1**	31

1m 25.75s (-1.61) **Going Correction** -0.50s/f (Hard) **4** Ran SP% **105.7**
Speed ratings (Par 94):89,86,85,73
CSF £1.67 TOTE £1.40; EX 1.40.
Owner Ascot In Mind **Bred** Airlie Stud And Sir Thomas Pilkington **Trained** Middleham Moor, N Yorks

FOCUS
A modest contest, and the form is far from solid, but Dollar Chick looks a good nursery prospect.

NOTEBOOK
Dollar Chick(IRE), a highly promising second on her debut at Beverley last month, was a hot favourite to build on that and, although not winning easily, she had a fair amount in hand at the line. As with most of her trainer's juveniles, she looks progressive and, with the step up to a mile expected to bring about further improvement, she is most definitely one to keep on side. There may be a decent nursery in her. (op 4-11)
Rosbay(IRE), a well-experienced colt, faced a stiff task giving 9lb to the winner and he ran as well as could have been expected, just hanging on for second. He will remain difficult to place however and may be more of a nursery type. (op 7-2)
Ingleby Flame(IRE), who did not shape too badly on his debut at Thirsk, found himself struggling for speed with three furlongs to run, but he came home strongly and would have finished second in a few more strides. He is clearly heading the right way and is going to appreciate a mile in time. (op 12-1)
Admiral Savannah(IRE), bred to appreciate a bit further in time, his sire Dilshaan having been a strong stayer at two, was always struggling after a slow start and may benefit from a combination of more time and slower ground.

3634 EAT, SLEEP AT THE NAGS HEAD, PICKHILL H'CAP — 1m 3f 214y
3:00 (3:01) (Class 5) (0-70,68) 3-Y-O £5,181 (£1,541; £770; £384) Stalls Low

Form				RPR
5224	1		**Is It Me (USA)**^{9} [3359] 3-9-7 68 PhillipMakin 6 (P A Blockley) *sn led: rdn over 2f out: drvn over 1f out: styd on gamely ins last* **9/2**^{3}	74
0024	2	nk	**Osolomio (IRE)**^{26} [2814] 3-8-9 56 MickyFenton 8 (J G Given) *trckd ldrs: hdwy to chse wnr 3f out: rdn 2f out: edgd lft over 1f out: drvn and kpt on ins last* **4/1**^{2}	62
00-0	3	1	**Lolla's Spirit (IRE)**^{26} [2814] 3-8-10 57 KDarley 4 (M L W Bell) *hld up towards rr: hdwy over 4f out: rdn to chse ldrs 2f out: drvn and kpt on ins last* **8/1**	61
3626	4	nk	**Azurine (IRE)**^{16} [3142] 3-9-2 63 JoeFanning 1 (M Johnston) *trckd ldrs: rdn along and outpcd over 4f out: swtchd rt and drvn 2f out: styd on ins last* **13/2**	67
0002	5	½	**Vice Admiral**^{16} [3145] 3-8-5 52 DaleGibson 2 (M W Easterby) *prom: rdn along over 3f out: drvn 2f out: kpt on appr last* **13/2**	55
2315	6	7	**Collette's Choice**^{12} [3249] 3-9-0 61 TonyHamilton 9 (R A Fahey) *hld up: swtchd rt and hdwy over 3f out: rdn to chse ldrs on outer 2f out: sn drvn and btn* **11/4**^{1}	53
5160	7	28	**Zabeel Tower**^{39} [2441] 3-8-4 58 GemmaAnderson$^{(7)}$ 3 (James Moffatt) *in tch: rdn along over 3f out: sn wknd* **40/1**	5
400-	8	6	**Herninski**^{232} [6467] 3-8-9 63 JamieHamblett$^{(7)}$ 5 (M C Chapman) *dwlt: a rr* **28/1**	1
4-50	9	6	**Find It Out (USA)**^{23} [2933] 3-9-0 61 PaulFessey 7 (T D Barron) *in tch: hdwy to chse ldrs 1/2-way: rdn along over 4f out and sn wknd* **16/1**	—

2m 33.26s (-5.74) **Going Correction** -0.50s/f (Hard) **9** Ran SP% **114.4**
Speed ratings (Par 100):99,98,98,97,97 92,74,70,66
CSF £22.63 CT £138.62 TOTE £4.20: £1.70, £1.60, £3.00; EX 18.30.
Owner J T Billson **Bred** Audley Farm Inc **Trained** Lambourn, Berks

FOCUS
A competitive handicap in which it was an advantage to be ridden prominently.
Find It Out(USA) Official explanation: jockey said gelding lost its action

3635 ROOPAL PARMAR CATTERICK EXPERIENCE (S) STKS — 5f 212y
3:30 (3:32) (Class 6) 3-Y-O+ £2,730 (£806; £403) Stalls Low

Form				RPR
0-43	1		**The Old Soldier**^{25} [2874] 8-9-0 51 DavidAllan 14 (A Dickman) *midfield: hdwy over 2f out: rdn to ld over 1f out: clr ins last* **7/2**^{2}	59
5403	2	2 ½	**Smokincanon**^{11} [3306] 4-8-9 47 MarcHalford$^{(5)}$ 11 (W G M Turner) *cl up: led 2f out: rdn and hdd over 1f out: kpt on same pce ins last* **6/1**^{3}	51
0000	3	1 ¼	**Algorithm**^{8} [3379] 4-8-9 41 (b^{1}) KDarley 4 (T D Easterby) *dwlt and towards rr: hdwy 1/2-way: rdn to chse ldrs over 1f out: styd on ins last: nrst fin* **12/1**	42

The Form Book, Raceform Ltd, Compton, RG20 6NL

3050 **4** *shd* **Underthemistletoe (IRE)**[4] 3524 4-8-2 40........(v) MichaelJStainton(7) 8 42
(R E Barr) *chsd ldrs: rdn along 2f out: edgd lft and one pce appr last* **40/1**

0000 **5** *nk* **Fox Covert (IRE)**[20] 3003 5-8-9 40................................ MarkLawson(5) 2 46
(D W Barker) *cl up on inner: effrt and ev ch 2f out: sn rdn and one pce appr last* **10/1**

4301 **6** *nk* **Stagnite**[4] 3543 6-9-6 46..(p) MickyFenton 6 51
(P A Blockley) *cl up: rdn along over 2f out: sn drvn and wknd* **3/1**[1]

4006 **7** *1* **Attila The Hun**[20] 3003 7-9-0 43.. PaulFessey 1 44+
(F Watson) *led: rdn along over 2f out: sn hdd & wknd appr last* **10/1**

000 **8** *2* **Binty**[9] 3356 4-8-2 47... MarkCoumbe(7) 10 31
(A J Chamberlain) *s.i.s and bhd tl styd on fnl 2f* **40/1**

3044 **9** *1 ¼* **King Forever**[153] 427 4-9-0 50.. DaleGibson 9 32
(D E Cantillon) *bhd tl sme late hdwy* **16/1**

036- **10** *5* **Swallow Senora (IRE)**[274] 5957 4-8-2 45..........(b[1]) JamieHamblett(7) 12 12
(M C Chapman) *s.i.s: a rr* **33/1**

0000 **11** *1 ¾* **Torrent**[12] 3245 11-8-7 41..(b) KevinMachent(7) 13 12
(J M Saville) *a towards rr* **66/1**

00-0 **12** *1* **King Henrik (USA)**[70] 1594 4-8-7 40............................ SladeO'Hara(7) 3 9
(A Crook) *a towards rr* **100/1**

0500 **13** *3* **Aqua**[12] 3240 4-8-9 42...(b) JoeFanning 7 —
(P T Midgley) *in tch whn hmpd after 2f: sn bhd* **50/1**

0250 **P** **St Ivian**[18] 3089 6-8-11 44.. DNolan(3) 5 —
(Mrs N Macauley) *midfield whn stmbld after 2f: lost action and sn p.u* **8/1**

1m 11.75s (-2.25) **Going Correction** -0.50s/f (Hard) **14** Ran SP% **116.6**
Speed ratings (Par 101):95,91,90,89,89 89,87,85,83,76 74,73,69,—
CSF £23.06 TOTE £3.80: £1.60, £1.90, £2.50; EX 31.50.There was no bid for the winner.
Owner The Maroon Stud **Bred** Snowdrop Stud Co Ltd **Trained** Sandhutton, N Yorks

FOCUS
A pretty uncompetitive seller in which only a handful could be given a chance.
Aqua Official explanation: jockey said filly was hampered into bend leaving back straight

3636 JOHN SMITH'S NO NONSENSE H'CAP 5f
4:00 (4:01) (Class 4) (0-85,80) 3-Y-O **£7,772** (£2,312; £1,155; £577) **Stalls** Low

Form RPR

2-1 **1** **Buachaill Dona (IRE)**[89] 1126 3-9-6 **79**........................ AdrianTNicholls 1 89+
(D Nicholls) *dwlt: trckd ldrs: hdwy 2f out: rdn to ld ins last: comf* **4/1**[3]

5321 **2** *1 ½* **Rothesay Dancer**[2] 3587 3-8-9 **71** 6ex..............................(p) DNolan(3) 5 76
(J S Goldie) *tracked ldr: hdwy 2f out: rdn to ld over 1f out: drvn and hdd ins last* **5/1**

1222 **3** *1* **Hypnosis**[19] 3042 3-8-6 **65**.. RoystonFfrench 4 66
(D W Barker) *led: rdn along 2f out: sn drvn and hdd over 1f out: kpt on same pce* **9/4**[2]

3112 **4** *nk* **Toy Top (USA)**[3] 3568 3-9-2 **80**....................................(b) LiamJones(5) 2 80
(M Dods) *trckd ldrs: effrt and hung bdly rt over 1f out: kpt on ins last* **13/8**[1]

0600 **5** *13* **Christa Bee**[3] 3568 3-9-1 **74**..(b[1]) JoeFanning 3 28
(A Berry) *dwlt: a rr* **50/1**

57.46 secs (-3.14) **Going Correction** -0.575s/f (Hard) **5** Ran SP% **107.5**
Speed ratings (Par 102):102,99,98,97,76
CSF £21.71 TOTE £5.40: £2.70, £2.50; EX 25.60.
Owner Mike Browne **Bred** John O Browne **Trained** Sessay, N Yorks

FOCUS
Just the five runners, but the first four home had finished either first or second last time and the form looks reliable.

3637 SEE MORE ON RACING UK CLAIMING STKS 1m 3f 214y
4:30 (4:31) (Class 5) 3-Y-O+ **£3,412** (£1,007; £504) **Stalls** Low

Form RPR

-000 **1** **Kristalchen**[9] 3353 4-8-11 45.. GylesParkin 4 41
(D W Thompson) *trckd ldrs: hdwy 3f out: rdn 2f out: led 1f out: drvn ins last and hld on wl* **50/1**

1655 **2** *hd* **Regency Red (IRE)**[125] 647 8-9-5 51............................. LiamJones(5) 6 54
(W M Brisbourne) *hld up in tch: hdwy over 4f out: effrt to chse ldrs 2f out: rdn to chal over 1f out and ev ch: jst hld* **4/1**[1]

61-6 **3** *½* **Fenners (USA)**[9] 3359 3-9-2 78...(t) DaleGibson 2 57+
(G P Kelly) *trckd ldrs tl lost pl and bhd 5f out: hdwy 3f out: rdn 2f out: styd on strly ins last* **9/2**[2]

3200 **4** *3* **King Of Meze (IRE)**[26] 2811 5-9-10 46........................(p) TonyHamilton 5 48
(J S Wainwright) *led: rdn along over 2f out: drvn and hdd 1f out: wknd ins last* **7/1**[3]

0-00 **5** *9* **Sovereign State (IRE)**[10] 1560 9-9-5 49......................(p) RoryMoore(5) 7 34
(D W Thompson) *keen: chsd ldrs: rdn along over 3f out and sn wknd* **8/1**

0-00 **6** *1 ½* **Tojoneski**[23] 2927 7-9-8 44...(p) RoystonFfrench 8 30
(I W McInnes) *hld up in rr: sme hdwy 1/2-way: rdn along over 3f out and nvr a factgor* **9/1**

0505 **7** *1 ¼* **Keyalzao (IRE)**[1] 3620 4-8-10 30.. DNolan(3) 3 19
(A Crook) *a rr* **66/1**

3553 **8** *nk* **Beauchamp Unique**[7] 3411 3-8-9 62.................................. MickyFenton 9 26
(James Moffatt) *in tch: headway to chse ldr after 4f: rdn along over 3f out and sn wknd* **9/2**[2]

/020 **9** *43* **Tipu Sultan**[11] 3291 6-9-8 46.. DeanMcKeown 1 —
(Micky Hammond) *in tch: lost pl and in rr after 5f: hdwy on outer to chse ldrs 5f out: sn rdn and wknd over 3f out* **9/2**[2]

2m 34.93s (-4.07) **Going Correction** -0.50s/f (Hard)
WFA 3 from 4yo+ 12lb **9** Ran SP% **111.6**
Speed ratings (Par 103):93,92,92,90,84 83,82,82,53
CSF £231.07 TOTE £75.40: £10.20, £1.90, £1.60; EX 449.00.
Owner D Paterson **Bred** The Wheet Partnership **Trained** Bolam, Co Durham

FOCUS
A very moderate claimer, but the pace seemed decent enough.
Tojoneski Official explanation: jockey said gelding hung right throughout
Tipu Sultan Official explanation: jockey said gelding was unsuited by the firm ground

3638 RACING UK LIVE ON 432 MEDIAN AUCTION MAIDEN STKS 7f
5:00 (5:03) (Class 6) 3-Y-O **£2,730** (£806; £403) **Stalls** Low

Form RPR

-524 **1** **Secret Assassin (IRE)**[6] 3436 3-9-3 73.............................. PhillipMakin 1 74
(W R Muir) *mde all: rdn 2f out: drvn and kpt on ins last* **3/1**[2]

3223 **2** *1 ½* **Lucksin (IRE)**[17] 3112 3-9-3 73... JoeFanning 6 70
(N Tinkler) *in tch: hdwy to trck ldrs 1/2-way: effrt to chse wnr wl over 1f out: sn rdn and hung lft ent last: drvn and one pce* **5/2**[1]

30 **3** *3 ½* **Can Can Star**[8] 3387 3-9-3.. KDarley 4 61
(J G Given) *chsd wnr: rdn along 2f out: drvn over 1f out and sn wknd* **3/1**[2]

6043 **4** *1 ¼* **Strong Approach (IRE)**[8] 3383 3-9-3 65........................(b) PaulFessey 2 57
(T D Barron) *chsd ldng pair: effrt over 2f out and sn ridde: drvn wl over 1f out and sn wknd* **4/1**[3]

0-00 **5** *13* **Mighty Duel**[33] 2615 3-9-3 42.. MickyFenton 3 22
(J R Norton) *sn outpcd and a bhd* **50/1**

0 **6** *3* **It's Gone**[41] 2383 3-9-3.. DeanMcKeown 5 14
(J G Given) *outpcd and bhd fr 1/2-way* **33/1**

0-0 **7** *16* **Star Of Siam (IRE)**[11] 3285 3-8-12.............................. GrahamGibbons 7 —
(J D Bethell) *chsd ldrs 3f: sn outpcd and bhd* **18/1**

1m 24.24s (-3.12) **Going Correction** -0.50s/f (Hard) **7** Ran SP% **108.7**
Speed ratings (Par 98):97,95,91,89,75 71,53
CSF £9.79 TOTE £4.10: £1.80, £1.50; EX 12.00 Place 6 £109.51, Place 5 74.24.
Owner David Kerwood **Bred** Gerry Flannery **Trained** Lambourn, Berks

FOCUS
Only four of the seven runners could be seriously considered beforehand and this was a weak maiden.
Star Of Siam(IRE) Official explanation: jockey said saddle slipped
T/Plt: £41.90. Pool £41,353.75, 719.25 winning tickets T/Qpdt: £15.70. Pool £1,844.90, 86.80 winning tickets JR

3400 KEMPTON (A.W) (R-H)
Wednesday, July 19

OFFICIAL GOING: Standard
Wind: Light, behind Weather: Fine, hot

3639 WEATHERBYS PRINTING APPRENTICE H'CAP (ROUND 7) 1m 2f (P)
7:00 (7:00) (Class 4) (0-80,78) 3-Y-O+ **£5,505** (£1,637; £818; £408) **Stalls** High

Form RPR

300 **1** **Follow The Colours (IRE)**[13] 3221 3-8-0 **65**................ PatrickHills(5) 4 76
(J W Hills) *lw: trckd ldr: clr of rest over 2f out: led wl over 1f out: pushed out and in n.d after* **4/1**[2]

2 *2 ½* **Call My Bluff (FR)**[51] 3-8-3 **66**... RobbieMills(3) 2 72
(Rae Guest) *plld hrd: hld up in 5th: prog to chse clr ldng pair 2f out: styd on to take 2nd ins fnl f: no ch* **25/1**

0106 **3** *1* **Burgundy**[6] 3429 9-9-6 **70**..(b) AshleyHamblett 5 74
(P Mitchell) *hld up in last: bdly outpcd over 2f out and rdn: kpt on fr over 1f out: no ch* **3/1**[1]

-003 **4** *shd* **King's Thought**[28] 2752 7-10-0 **78**.................................. JamesMillman 1 82
(S Gollings) *led at stdy pce: tried to kick on over 2f out: hdd wl over 1f out: fdd fnl f* **9/2**[3]

-463 **5** *2* **Dumaran (IRE)**[31] 2088 8-9-8 **75**.................................... PJBenson(3) 8 75
(W J Musson) *trckd ldng pair: outpcd over 2f out: wknd fnl f* **9/2**[3]

-065 **6** *1 ¼* **Bentley Brook (IRE)**[16] 3151 4-9-4 **68**.......................... KevinGhunowa 7 66
(P A Blockley) *hld up in last pair: bdly outpcd and rdn over 2f out: no ch after* **5/1**

0 **7** *5* **Best Of The Lot (USA)**[18] 3081 4-9-8 **75**........................ NeilBrown(3) 6 63
(T J Fitzgerald) *trckd ldng pair tl wknd rapidly 2f out* **12/1**

2m 10.36s (1.36) **Going Correction** +0.175s/f (Slow)
WFA 3 from 4yo+ 10lb **7** Ran SP% **109.6**
Speed ratings (Par 105):101,99,98,98,96 95,91
CSF £78.88 CT £311.08 TOTE £4.50: £2.10, £4.40; EX 41.30.
Owner M Wauchope,Sir Simon Dunning,R Cottam **Bred** Cathal Ryan **Trained** Upper Lambourn, Berks

FOCUS
A steadily-run race and Follow The Colours was ideally positioned throughout. The form is not strong with the fourth the best guide.

3640 EUROPEAN BREEDERS FUND MAIDEN FILLIES' STKS 7f (P)
7:28 (7:30) (Class 4) 2-Y-O **£5,181** (£1,541; £770; £384) **Stalls** High

Form RPR

54 **1** **Guacamole**[14] 3201 2-9-0 .... MichaelHills 5 79
(B W Hills) *racd wd and trckd ldrs: prog 3f out: carried lft fr 2f out: led jst ins fnl f: styd on wl* **5/1**[3]

30 **2** *¾* **Elizabeth Street (USA)**[26] 2800 2-9-0 .... EddieAhern 8 77
(P F I Cole) *w ldr: led over 2f out: rdn and hung lft after: hdd jst ins fnl f: styd on but a hld* **5/1**[3]

3 *3 ½* **Farley Star** 2-9-0 .... SteveDrowne 9 68
(R Charlton) *unf: bit bkwd: hld up in rr: hmpd over 4f out and dropped rr: prog over 2f out: pushed along and styd on to take 3rd fnl f* **14/1**

4 *1* **Flying Encore (IRE)** 2-9-0 .... SebSanders 6 65
(W R Swinburn) *unf: hld up wl in rr: plenty to do whn hmpd over 2f out: styd on wl after: nrst fin* **33/1**

4 **5** *½* **Madam Gaffer**[7] 3407 2-9-0 .... RyanMoore 3 64
(B J Meehan) *str: mde most to over 2f out: one pce u.p* **33/1**

3 **6** *1 ¼* **Mizzle (USA)**[13] 3227 2-9-0 .... LDettori 11 61
(Saeed Bin Suroor) *leggy: tall: w ldrs gng wl: rdn 2f out: fnd nil and sn btn* **4/1**[2]

22 **7** *1 ¼* **Spritza (IRE)**[37] 2506 2-9-0 .... JamieSpencer 2 58
(M L W Bell) *trckd ldrs: hrd rdn 2f out: one pce and sn btn* **7/4**[1]

8 *3 ½* **Bright Dance** 2-9-0 .... NickyMackay 12 48
(L M Cumani) *w'like: bit bkwd: nvr beyond midfield: rdn and struggling over 2f out: fdd* **16/1**

9 *3* **Vodka Luge** 2-8-11 .... DeanCorby(3) 14 41
(J W Hills) *w'like: bit bkwd: hld up on inner: shkn up over 2f out: no prog: wknd over 1f out* **50/1**

0 **10** *6* **Roxy Singer**[33] 2626 2-8-9 .... StephenDonohoe(5) 4 25
(W J Musson) *dwlt: hld up in last: pushed along and no real prog over 2f out* **66/1**

11 *¾* **Byanita (IRE)** 2-9-0 .... FrancisFerris 10 23
(B Palling) *w'like: unf: chsd ldrs: hrd rdn 3f out: sn wknd* **66/1**

0 **12** *4* **Miss Silver Spurs**[24] 2899 2-9-0 .... HayleyTurner 7 13
(M D I Usher) *w'like: t.k.h: hld up in tch: wknd over 2f out* **100/1**

13 *1* **Sweet Soul Diva** 2-8-11 .... DominicFox(3) 13 —
(Miss V Haigh) *leggy: t.k.h: hld up in midfield: stmbld bdly over 4f out: nt rcvr* **66/1**

14 *nk* **Best Warning** 2-9-0 .... JohnEgan 1 —
(J Ryan) *w'like: bit bkwd: wnt lft s: wl in rr tl rdn and effrt into midfield 3f out: sn wknd* **50/1**

1m 28.59s (1.79) **Going Correction** +0.175s/f (Slow) **14** Ran SP% **117.5**
Speed ratings (Par 93):96,95,91,90,89 88,86,82,79,72 71,66,65,65
CSF £28.33 TOTE £6.10: £1.60, £1.90, £3.50; EX 39.10.
Owner Jeremy Gompertz & Patrick Milmo **Bred** Jeremy Gompertz **Trained** Lambourn, Berks
■ Stewards' Enquiry : Eddie Ahern caution: careless riding

FOCUS
A fair maiden rated around the first two and likely to produce winners.

NOTEBOOK

Guacamole, who ran well in a course and distance maiden here last time, seemingly took another step forward and got on top inside the final furlong. The front pair were clear of the third and the daughter of Inchinor may yet do better still in nurseries. (op 9-2)

Elizabeth Street(USA), highly tried behind Sander Camillo at Royal Ascot, had previously shown plenty of ability when third to Queen Mary winner Gilded and she appreciated the step up to seven furlongs, keeping on well despite edging left under pressure. She should win her maiden before going on to nurseries. (op 6-1 tchd 13-2 and 9-2)

Farley Star, a sister to the stable's smart juvenile Luvah Girl, lost her position after being quite badly impeded, but she made great strides down the stretch to claim a never-nearer third and is most definitely one to take from the race. Official explanation: jockey said filly was hampered on bend (op 12-1)

Flying Encore(IRE), whose in-form trainer's juveniles often benefit from a run, found herself struggling in rear early on, but she made some good headway down the straight, despite being interfered with, and was closing well as they crossed the line. She was another to shape with immense promise and winning a maiden should prove a formality before going on to nurseries. (op 25-1)

Madam Gaffer stepped up on her debut effort and will be qualified for nurseries after one more run.

Mizzle(USA), Godolphin's first juvenile runner of the season who finished third at Yarmouth, failed to build on that, dropping away tamely having travelled well into the straight. She is clearly a horse of limited ability. (tchd 7-2)

Spritza(IRE) set the standard on the evidence of her Haydock and Windsor seconds, but the step up in trip did not suit as well as expected and she dropped away at the business end. (op 15-8 tchd 2-1 and 9-4 in a place)

Sweet Soul Diva Official explanation: jockey said filly clipped heels on bend

3641 TFM NETWORKS NURSERY 7f (P)

7:56 (7:58) (Class 5) 2-Y-O £3,238 (£963; £481; £240) Stalls High

Form				RPR
042	1		**Stagehand (IRE)**[25] 2857 2-8-1 **66** ... AdrianMcCarthy 13 (B R Millman) *mde all: rdn and hrd pressed wl over 1f out: styd on wl and pushed out fnl f* **14/1**	75
0302	2	1	**Tudor Prince (IRE)**[13] 3210 2-9-3 **82** ... LDettori 12 (B J Meehan) *cl up: trckd wnr gng easily over 2f out: rdn over 1f out: nt qckn and hld after* **11/8**[1]	89
012	3	3	**Blue Madeira**[34] 2586 2-8-13 **78** ... TomEaves 10 (Mrs L Stubbs) *dwlt: hld up towards rr: prog over 2f out: rdn to chse ldng pair over 1f out: no imp* **15/2**[2]	77
303	4	shd	**Goose Green (IRE)**[99] 968 2-7-12 **66** ... EdwardCreighton(3) 3 (M R Channon) *lw: hld up: last 1/2-way: pushed along and stdy prog on inner fr over 2f out: nvr nrr* **25/1**	65
3142	5	½	**Ten Dollars More (IRE)**[6] 3455 2-8-11 **77** ... ShaneKelly 8 (J A Osborne) *towards rr: rdn and effrt over 2f out: kpt on but nvr pce to rch ldrs* **15/2**[2]	73
455	6	2 ½	**Vadinka**[29] 2726 2-8-5 **70** ow2 ... (p) JohnEgan 7 (P Winkworth) *mostly chsd wnr to over 2f out: fdd* **20/1**	61
0263	7	3	**Straight Face (IRE)**[21] 2979 2-8-12 **77** ... PaulDoe 4 (W J Knight) *prom towards outside: rdn 3f out: fdd fr over 2f out* **14/1**	60
10	8	½	**Carson's Spirit (USA)**[29] 2719 2-9-7 **86** ... ChrisCatlin 9 (W S Kittow) *hld up in last pair: rdn on outer over 2f out: no real prog* **10/1**[3]	68
651	9	4	**Babylon Sister (IRE)**[20] 3010 2-8-7 **72** ... RyanMoore 11 (R Hannon) *chsd ldrs: rdn 3f out: no prog whn swtchd lft over 1f out: wknd* **15/2**[2]	43
1512	10	2 ½	**Mrs Crossy (IRE)**[30] 2709 2-7-5 **63** oh3 ... LukeMorris(7) 2 (A W Carroll) *mostly in midfield: urged along 3f out: no imp over 2f out: wknd* **20/1**	28
0046	11	6	**Princely Royal**[50] 2094 2-8-0 **65** ... HayleyTurner 5 (J J Bridger) *w ldrs tl wknd 3f out* **66/1**	14
0206	12	hd	**Colditz (IRE)**[24] 2899 2-8-8 **73** ... TedDurcan 6 (M R Channon) *lw: nvr beyond midfield: struggling u.p 3f out: wknd* **20/1**	22
640	13	½	**Fort Worth (IRE)**[40] 2402 2-8-1 **66** ... FrancisFerris 1 (B Gubby) *swtg: prog on wd outside and prom 1/2-way: sn rdn and wknd* **33/1**	14

1m 27.97s (1.17) **Going Correction** +0.175s/f (Slow) 13 Ran SP% **122.4**
Speed ratings (Par 94):100,98,95,95,94 91,88,87,83,80 73,73,72
CSF £31.59 CT £172.13 TOTE £17.20: £3.40, £1.10, £2.90; EX 53.00.
Owner Always Hopeful Partnership **Bred** Crone Stud Farms Ltd **Trained** Kentisbeare, Devon

FOCUS

Not a bad nursery and the form looks sound with the first two clear and the race should produce winners. The official ratings shown next to each horse are estimated and for information purposes only.

NOTEBOOK

Stagehand(IRE), who did not look a winner waiting to happen when hammered by Simba Sun at Lingfield last time, showed improved form for the switch to nurseries and led throughout under a fine ride from McCarthy, finding plenty under pressure when hard pressed. Evidently on the up, he should stay a mile and looks to have more to offer. (op 12-1)

Tudor Prince(IRE), touched off by a decent sort at Epsom earlier in the month, was a hot favourite to make a successful handicap debut and it looked a question of how far as they raced into the straight, but there was little response and he was ultimately outbattled. He has a bit to prove now. (op 9-4 tchd 5-2 in a place)

Blue Madeira, runner-up to a useful sort at Yarmouth, was a bit adrift of the second and shaped as though a return to sprinting would help, albeit he ran well. (op 7-1)

Goose Green(IRE), stepping up two furlongs in trip for this nursery debut, was going on nicely at the end without being given too hard a time and he should have little trouble finding a similar race for his top juvenile trainer. (op 20-1)

Ten Dollars More(IRE) has been running well, but he has become rather exposed and is likely to remain vulnerable to an improver off this sort of mark. (op 7-1)

Straight Face(IRE) showed up well for a long way towards the outside and has a race in him off this sort of mark.

Babylon Sister(IRE) Official explanation: jockey said filly had no more to give

3642 MARTIN COLLINS ENTERPRISES H'CAP (LONDON MILE QUALIFIER) 1m (P)

8:24 (8:25) (Class 5) (0-70,70) 3-Y-O+ £3,238 (£963; £481; £240) Stalls High

Form				RPR
0003	1		**Logsdail**[7] 3404 6-9-10 **66** ... (p) RyanMoore 3 (G L Moore) *b: hld up wl in rr: prog over 2f out: swtchd lft over 1f out: drvn and r.o wl to ld last 75yds* **9/4**[1]	74+
0365	2	nk	**Takes Tutu (USA)**[3] 3565 7-9-8 **64** ... (p) EddieAhern 12 (C R Dore) *settled in midfield: rdn and effrt over 2f out: r.o to chal ins fnl f: no ex nr fin* **7/1**	71
003-	3	hd	**Primo Gold**[246] 6360 3-8-8 **58** ... SebSanders 14 (W R Swinburn) *settled in midfield on inner: prog over 2f out: drvn to chal ins fnl f: nt qckn last 50yds* **14/1**	63
0-0	4	shd	**Mohawk Star (IRE)**[17] 3121 5-9-7 **68** ... JamesDoyle(5) 9 (I A Wood) *trckd ldr to over 5f out: styd prom: rdn to ld 2f out: worn down last 75yds* **25/1**	75
0330	5	5	**Barathea Dreams (IRE)**[18] 3101 5-10-0 **70** ... LPKeniry 10 (J S Moore) *lw: trckd ldrs: effrt over 2f out: rdn and cl enough over 1f out: sn wl outpcd* **11/2**[2]	65
2406	6	½	**Firesong**[16] 3151 4-9-9 **70** ... EmmettStack(5) 4 (Pat Eddery) *hld up in rr: effrt on outer over 2f out: sn no real prog and struggling* **7/1**	64
0050	7	hd	**Height Of Spirits**[25] 2862 4-8-8 **57** ... TolleyDean(7) 8 (T D McCarthy) *b: s.i.s and rousted along early: rn in snatches after: a in rr: struggling 3f out* **14/1**	51
00-0	8	½	**Oh Danny Boy**[19] 3044 5-9-11 **67** ... JohnEgan 7 (Jane Chapple-Hyam) *chsd ldrs: rdn over 2f out: wkng whn sltly impeded over 1f out* **20/1**	60
005	9	nk	**Nan Jan**[12] 3262 4-9-1 **57** ... (t) DaneO'Neill 13 (R Ingram) *chsd ldrs: rdn 3f out: no prog: wknd over 1f out* **16/1**	49
000/	10	½	**Cashel Bay (USA)**[1538] 1210 8-8-6 **51** oh1 ... EdwardCreighton(3) 5 (Luke Comer, Ire) *racd wd in rr: effrt over 3f out: sn no prog and btn* **25/1**	42
0105	11	2 ½	**Polish Index**[39] 2443 4-9-2 **58** ... (p) LDettori 2 (J R Jenkins) *swtg: trckd ldr over 5f out: rdn to ld briefly over 2f out: pressed ldr to over 1f out: wknd rapidly fnl f* **13/2**[3]	43
004	12	1 ¾	**Wodhill Schnaps**[19] 3032 5-9-6 **62** ... DerekMcGaffin 11 (D Morris) *prom: rdn on inner 3f out: sn lost pl: wknd rapidly fnl f* **66/1**	43
00-0	13	1 ½	**Lifted Way**[21] 2969 7-9-11 **67** ... GeorgeBaker 6 (P R Chamings) *led to over 2f out: wknd rapidly wl over 1f out* **66/1**	44

1m 42.02s (1.22) **Going Correction** +0.175s/f (Slow)
WFA 3 from 4yo+ 8lb 13 Ran SP% **119.1**
Speed ratings (Par 103):100,99,99,99,94 93,93,92,92 89,88,86
CSF £16.62 CT £187.11 TOTE £3.10: £1.70, £2.10, £2.80; EX 20.70.
Owner D T L Limited **Bred** Stetchworth Park Stud Ltd **Trained** Woodingdean, E Sussex

FOCUS

Just a modest handicap, but they appeared to go a reasonable gallop and the first three home came from off the pace. The first four finished in a bunch, but were clear of the rest and the form looks reliable enough.

3643 BOOK NOW FOR IRISH NIGHT FILLIES' H'CAP 1m (P)

8:52 (8:53) (Class 4) (0-85,84) 3-Y-O £5,505 (£1,637; £818; £408) Stalls High

Form				RPR
0013	1		**Dancing Guest (IRE)**[24] 2891 3-8-8 **71** ... EddieAhern 3 (G G Margarson) *hld up in 4th: prog to trck ldr over 2f out: sn upsides: forced ahd 1f out: styd on* **4/1**[3]	79
2010	2	¾	**October Ben**[7] 3400 3-7-9 **65** ... FrankiePickard(7) 7 (M D I Usher) *s.s: hld up in last pair: outpcd over 2f out: prog on outer over 1f out: urged along and styd on to take 2nd nr fin* **10/1**	71
-262	3	½	**Lunar Express (USA)**[18] 3067 3-9-6 **83** ... RyanMoore 1 (W J Haggas) *b.hind: led at stdy pce: kicked on 3f out: jnd 2f out: hdd and one pce 1f out* **13/8**[1]	88
10-1	4	1 ¾	**Best Guess (USA)**[51] 2087 3-8-13 **76** ... AdrianMcCarthy 5 (P W Chapple-Hyam) *swtg: hld up in last pair: rdn wl over 2f out: no prog tl kpt on over 1f out: n.d* **7/1**	77
-320	5	½	**Famcred**[18] 3088 3-9-7 **84** ... NickyMackay 6 (L M Cumani) *lw: t.k.h: trckd ldr tl over 2f out: nt qckn wl over 1f out: fdd fnl f* **3/1**[2]	84
55-0	6	5	**Pommes Frites**[43] 2330 3-9-2 **79** ... RichardMullen 4 (W R Muir) *t.k.h early: trckd ldng pair to 3f out: hrd rdn over 2f out: wknd over 1f out* **16/1**	68

1m 43.33s (2.53) **Going Correction** +0.175s/f (Slow) 6 Ran SP% **110.6**
Speed ratings (Par 99):94,93,92,91,90 85
CSF £38.89 TOTE £5.00: £1.80, £4.40; EX 43.10.
Owner John Guest **Bred** Kevin Foley **Trained** Newmarket, Suffolk

FOCUS

Not a bad fillies' handicap but it was run at a steady early pace and the form rated around the winner and third, may not be totally reliable.

3644 TFM NETWORKS H'CAP 7f (P)

9:20 (9:20) (Class 5) (0-75,75) 3-Y-O £3,238 (£963; £481; £240) Stalls High

Form				RPR
-016	1		**Finsbury**[14] 3204 3-9-4 **72** ... GeorgeBaker 7 (C F Wall) *hld up wl in rr: stdy prog and weaved through fr over 2f out: rdn to ld last 50yds: readily* **12/1**	86+
06-1	2	½	**Mataram (USA)**[20] 3011 3-8-13 **67** ... LDettori 11 (W Jarvis) *swtg: hld up towards rr: prog over 2f out: rdn to ld ins fnl f: hdd and outpcd last 50yds* **5/2**[1]	80
1465	3	1	**Neardown Beauty (IRE)**[15] 3176 3-9-2 **75** ... JamesDoyle(5) 9 (I A Wood) *trckd ldrs: smooth prog to ld over 1f out: hdd and nt qckn ins fnl f* **13/2**[3]	85
0530	4	¾	**Press The Button (GER)**[23] 2932 3-9-2 **70** ... NickyMackay 12 (J R Boyle) *led for 1f: styd prom: effrt to chal 2f out: kpt on same pce fnl f* **16/1**	78
4632	5	2 ½	**Imperial Gain (USA)**[11] 3304 3-8-13 **70** ... AdamKirby(3) 10 (W R Swinburn) *chsd ldrs: rdn and nt qckn over 2f out: no imp after: kpt on fnl f* **4/1**[2]	71
00-0	6	½	**Sun Catcher (IRE)**[33] 2620 3-9-7 **75** ... PatDobbs 8 (R Hannon) *led after 1f: drvn and hdd over 1f out: wknd ins fnl f* **33/1**	75
-540	7	¾	**You Call That Art (USA)**[39] 2458 3-9-7 **75** ... (b[1]) RyanMoore 3 (R Hannon) *hld up wl in rr: rdn on outer over 2f out: no imp on ldrs* **20/1**	73
00-4	8	1	**King's Ransom**[36] 2532 3-9-7 **75** ... FergusSweeney 13 (A M Balding) *swtg: dwlt: hld up in last pair: prog on inner over 2f out: rchd midfield over 1f out: no hdwy after* **9/1**	70
-356	9	3 ½	**Broken Spur (FR)**[79] 1349 3-9-5 **73** ... (t) MichaelHills 1 (B W Hills) *wl in rr: struggling in last trio over 2f out: no ch after* **10/1**	59
0060	10	nk	**Mount Sinai**[20] 3030 3-9-3 **71** ... PaulDoe 2 (W J Knight) *w ldrs: chal and upsides wl over 1f out: wknd and eased fnl f* **33/1**	56
34-0	11	½	**Bouzouki (USA)**[107] 851 3-9-4 **72** ... EddieAhern 4 (W R Swinburn) *chsd ldrs: rdn over 2f out: wknd jst over 1f out* **20/1**	56
0-06	12	6	**El Capitan (FR)**[11] 3304 3-8-13 **67** ... (v[1]) DaneO'Neill 5 (Miss Gay Kelleway) *b: w ldr after 2f to over 2f out: wknd rapidly* **33/1**	34
-500	13	hd	**Satin Doll**[18] 3073 3-8-11 **65** ... (b[1]) TedDurcan 6 (M P Tregoning) *s.s: nvr gng wl and a in last pair* **25/1**	32

-310 **14** *6* **Proud Killer**[28] [2739] 3-9-5 **73** JohnEgan 14 24
(J R Jenkins) *lw: chsd ldrs: rdn 1/2-way: sn struggling: eased whn no ch over 1f out* **11/1**

1m 26.75s (-0.05) **Going Correction** +0.175s/f (Slow) **14** Ran SP% **125.1**
Speed ratings (Par 100):107,106,105,104,101 101,100,99,95,94 94,87,87,80
CSF £40.19 CT £221.95 TOTE £20.10: £6.50, £1.60, £2.20; EX 81.70 Place 6 £332.35, Place 5 £85.20..
Owner O Pointing **Bred** O Pointing **Trained** Newmarket, Suffolk

FOCUS
A fair handicap run at a decent enough pace, and the form, rated through the third and fourth, looks reasonable enough for the grade.
T/Plt: £574.60 to a £1 stake. Pool: £56,559.55. 71.85 winning tickets. T/Qpdt: £18.20 to a £1 stake. Pool: £3,792.40. 154.10 winning tickets. JN

3530 LINGFIELD (L-H)

Wednesday, July 19

OFFICIAL GOING: Standard

3645 EUROPEAN BREEDERS FUND MAIDEN FILLIES' STKS 6f (P)

2:20 (2:21) (Class 5) 2-Y-O **£3,886** (£1,156; £577; £288) **Stalls** Low

Form RPR
3 **1** **Chervil**[30] [2703] 2-9-0 RyanMoore 12 76
(Mrs A J Perrett) *chsd ldrs: wnt 2nd over 2f out: rdn to ld over 1f out: edgd lft: styd on wl* **11/4**[1]

2 *1 1/4* **Empress Olga (USA)** 2-9-0 RichardMullen 4 72
(E A L Dunlop) *trckd ldrs: chsd ldr briefly over 2f out: sn rdn: chsd wnr ins fnl f: kpt on* **5/1**[3]

3 *1 1/4* **Baylini** 2-8-9 JamesDoyle(5) 1 69
(Ms J S Doyle) *racd in midfield: rdn over 2f out: sn chsng ldng trio: kpt on wl fnl f: nt rch ldrs* **25/1**

4 *3* **Veenwouden** 2-9-0 JamieSpencer 10 60
(J R Fanshawe) *slowly away: wl bhd: styd on fr over 1f out: nvr nrr* **11/2**

4 **5** *1* **Ama De Casa (USA)**[39] [2442] 2-9-0 LDettori 5 57
(J Noseda) *pressed ldr tl led over 3f out: rdn and hdd over 1f out: wknd qckly last 100 yds* **7/2**[2]

0 **6** *1 1/2* **My Tiger Lilly**[26] [2816] 2-9-0 PaulDoe 2 52
(W J Knight) *bhd: nt clr run over 2f out: sme prog over 1f out: n.d* **9/1**

0 **7** *3* **Hemispear**[32] [2638] 2-9-0 PaulFitzsimons 11 43
(Miss J R Tooth) *hld in midfield: rdn over 2f out: sn struggling* **50/1**

8 *2 1/2* **Cape Runaway (IRE)** 2-9-0 NickyMackay 6 36
(L M Cumani) *a bhd: pushed along 3f out: nvr on terms* **12/1**

50 **9** *1 1/2* **Fine Leg**[9] [3358] 2-9-0 (t) TonyCulhane 9 31
(P J McBride) *midfield in tch: rdn 2f out: sn wknd* **25/1**

0 **10** *8* **Countyourblessings**[21] [2984] 2-9-0 TPQueally 7 7
(J G Portman) *a rr: rdn over 2f out: sn lost tch: eased last 100 yds: t.o* **33/1**

0 **11** *11* **Rubber Duck (IRE)**[7] [3408] 2-9-0 RobbieFitzpatrick 3 —
(Peter Grayson) *led tl over 3f out: sn wknd: eased ins fnl f: t.o* **66/1**

1m 14.2s (1.39) **Going Correction** +0.125s/f (Slow) **11** Ran SP% **112.7**
Speed ratings (Par 91):95,93,91,87,86 84,80,77,75,64 49
CSF £14.93 TOTE £3.20: £1.50, £1.90, £4.40; EX 15.10 Trifecta £220.00 Part won. Pool £309.94, 0.84 winning units..
Owner K Abdulla **Bred** Juddmonte Farms Ltd **Trained** Pulborough, W Sussex

FOCUS
Likely to prove above average for a race of its type on this track and surface.

NOTEBOOK
Chervil, well suited by the extra furlong, had to overcome a wide draw, but was given an excellent ride to get into a handy position. She is progressing nicely, and can improve again. (tchd 5-2)
Empress Olga(USA) ◆ a 1.5 million dollar sister to the top-class Russian Rhythm, has a lot to live up to but made an encouraging debut, and finding a maiden should be a formality. She should be be judged on her own merits, rather than those of her illustrious sister, but the early signs are positive. (op 6-1)
Baylini a bargain-basement Bertolini filly, is bred to be quick and made a smart debut behind two promising sorts. A routine maiden, at least, is within her range. (op 33-1)
Veenwouden ◆, a half-sister by Desert Prince to the smart middle-distance performer Delsarte, caught the eye after missing the break. She will be sharper next time, and is capable of winning a similar event before going on to better things. (op 7-2)
Ama De Casa(USA) has performed with some credit, without setting the world alight, on both her runs to date - the first of them on turf. A run-of-the-mill maiden is within reach, but she will come into her own when handicapped after one more run. (tchd 4-1)
My Tiger Lilly again ran quite well, and will be interesting when ready for nurseries following her next race. (op 10-1)

3646 BELLWAY H'CAP 6f (P)

2:50 (2:50) (Class 5) (0-75,75) 3-Y-O **£3,238** (£963; £481; £240) **Stalls** Low

Form RPR
1264 **1** **Garstang**[11] [3296] 3-9-7 **75** (b) RobbieFitzpatrick 2 82
(Peter Grayson) *sn chsng ldr: rdn to ld over 2f out: hld on wl cl home: all out* **6/1**[3]

0021 **2** *hd* **Xaluna Bay (IRE)**[28] [2756] 3-9-4 **72** RichardMullen 3 78
(W R Muir) *chsd ldrs:rdn and chsd wnr 2f out: kpt on u.p last 100 yds: jst hld* **7/2**[1]

0146 **3** *1/2* **Charlie Delta**[11] [3296] 3-9-4 **75** DanielTudhope(3) 5 82+
(D Carroll) *midfield: rdn over 2f out: hmpd bnd 2f out: r.o strly ins fnl f: nrst fin* **8/1**

0-05 **4** *1 1/2* **Violet Ballerina (IRE)**[7] [3403] 3-9-7 **75** LDettori 6 75
(B J Meehan) *in tch: rdn to press ldrs 2f out: kpt on onepced ins fnl f* **9/1**

-620 **5** *hd* **Stormy Monday**[14] [3204] 3-9-2 **70** EddieAhern 12 69
(J W Hills) *midfield: in tch: rdn over 2f out: kpt on fnl f: nt rch ldrs* **16/1**

0050 **6** *shd* **Ockums Razor (IRE)**[19] [3055] 3-8-12 **66** JohnEgan 7 65
(C A Dwyer) *bhd: rdn 3f out: weaved through over 1f out: r.o wl: nt rch ldrs* **28/1**

-430 **7** *2* **Music By Mozart**[41] [2383] 3-9-7 **75** JimmyFortune 10 68
(P W Chapple-Hyam) *rr: rdn and effrt on outside over 2f out: kpt on onepced fnl f* **8/1**

2140 **8** *hd* **Piccostar**[11] [3299] 3-9-1 **69** RyanMoore 4 62
(A B Haynes) *hld up rr: rdn over 2f out: nvr trbld ldrs* **12/1**

-046 **9** *3/4* **What Do You Know**[32] [2652] 3-9-4 **75** AdamKirby(3) 8 65
(G A Butler) *a rr: rdn 2f out: n.d* **18/1**

4060 **10** *5* **African Concerto (IRE)**[13] [3226] 3-8-5 **59** FrankieMcDonald 1 34
(S Kirk) *sn led: rdn and hdd 2f out: wknd qckly* **33/1**

-432 **11** *9* **And I**[19] [3050] 3-9-4 **72** DaneO'Neill 11 20
(M P Tregoning) *rr on outer: rdn over 3f out: sn wl bhd: eased fnl f: t.o* **15/2**

441 **12** *3/4* **Falmassim**[18] [3090] 3-9-2 **70** NickyMackay 9 16
(L M Cumani) *a bhd: plld to outer and rdn over 3f out: sn no ch: eased fnl f: t.o* **5/1**[2]

1m 13.9s (1.09) **Going Correction** +0.125s/f (Slow) **12** Ran SP% **122.4**
Speed ratings (Par 100):97,96,96,94,93 93,91,90,89,83 71,70
CSF £28.18 CT £175.60 TOTE £7.50: £2.10, £2.00, £3.20; EX 41.50 Trifecta £144.50 Pool £380.61, 1.87 winning units..
Owner The Foulrice Twenty **Bred** Mrs S E Barclay **Trained** Formby, Lancs

FOCUS
A fair handicap producing a close finish.
Xaluna Bay(IRE) Official explanation: jockey said filly lost a near-fore shoe
Falmassim Official explanation: jockey said colt never travelled

3647 LADIES EVENING THIS SATURDAY MEDIAN AUCTION MAIDEN STKS 1m (P)

3:20 (3:22) (Class 6) 3-4-Y-O **£2,730** (£806; £403) **Stalls** High

Form RPR
626 **1** **Mcnairobi**[9] [3367] 3-8-12 SebSanders 7 75
(P D Cundell) *hld up in midfield: pushed along and nt clr run 2f out: r.o over 1f out: led last 50 yds* **7/4**[1]

3 **2** *hd* **Magic Rush**[108] [844] 4-9-11 SteveDrowne 3 82
(Mrs Norma Pook) *trckd ldrs on inner: rdn to ld jst ins fnl f: hdd last 50 yds: kpt on* **13/2**[3]

3 *3/4* **Mr Chad** 3-9-3 RichardMullen 10 78
(E J O'Neill) *w.w in tch: hdwy on outer 3f out: rdn and ch over 1f out: kpt on last 100 yds* **10/1**

3 **4** *1* **Our Faye**[8] [3387] 3-8-12 JohnEgan 11 71
(S Kirk) *chsd ldrs: rdn and ev ch 2f out: unable qckn ins fnl f* **11/2**[2]

03 **5** *5* **William's Way**[6] [3458] 4-9-11 RyanMoore 5 66
(I A Wood) *led after 1f: rdn over 2f out: hdd jst ins fnl f: wknd qckly* **8/1**

04 **6** *1/2* **Piper's Song (IRE)**[23] [2919] 3-9-3 DaneO'Neill 2 63
(H Candy) *midfield in tch: rdn over 2f out: kpt on onepced* **8/1**

7 *2* **Star Berry** 3-8-5 KMay(7) 8 53
(B J Meehan) *s.s: rr of main gp: rdn whn hmpd 2f out: kpt on: n.d* **20/1**

0 **8** *3/4* **Rowe Park**[17] [3122] 3-9-0 AdamKirby(3) 9 57
(Mrs L C Jewell) *led for 1f: chsd ldr: rdn 2f out: wknd qckly 1f out* **50/1**

9 *1* **Nahlass** 3-8-7 JamesDoyle(5) 12 49
(Ms J S Doyle) *rr of main gp: rdn over 4f out: nvr on terms* **33/1**

0-0 **10** *nk* **Compton Express**[175] [191] 3-8-12 PaulDoe 6 49
(Jamie Poulton) *chsd ldrs: rdn over 2f out: wknd wl over 1f out* **33/1**

11 *11* **Forementor** 3-8-12 ChrisCatlin 4 23
(D K Ivory) *s.s: sn bhd: lost tch 5f out: t.o* **33/1**

0 **12** *shd* **Birbalini**[130] [630] 3-8-12 TonyCulhane 1 23
(P J McBride) *s.s: sn wl bhd in last pair: t.o* **50/1**

1m 40.4s (0.97) **Going Correction** +0.125s/f (Slow)
WFA 3 from 4yo 8lb **12** Ran SP% **113.9**
Speed ratings (Par 101):100,99,99,98,93 92,90,89,88,88 77,77
CSF £11.32 TOTE £2.20: £1.10, £1.80, £3.00; EX 15.20 Trifecta £51.80 Pool £266.72, 3.65 winning units..
Owner Ian M Brown **Bred** Roden House Stud **Trained** Compton, Berks

FOCUS
A maiden contested by late-developing types, many of them not without ability.

3648 EBF PAUL KELLEWAY MEMORIAL CLASSIFIED STKS 1m (P)

3:50 (3:50) (Class 3) 3-Y-O+ **£10,594** (£3,172; £1,586; £793; £396; £198) **Stalls** High

Form RPR
1- **1** **Lightning Flash**[424] [1896] 4-9-3 88 JamieSpencer 1 105+
(J R Fanshawe) *slowly away: hld up: plld wd 2f out: jnd ldrs on bit 1f out: shkn up to assert last 100 yds* **7/2**[2]

4150 **2** *1 1/4* **Indian Steppes (FR)**[27] [2776] 7-9-0 89 LDettori 4 95
(P S McEntee) *chsd ldr tl led after 1f tl 5f out: rdn and ev ch 2f out: nt pce of wnr last 100 yds* **5/2**[1]

0504 **3** *1/2* **South Cape**[5] [3491] 3-8-9 90 TonyCulhane 2 95
(M R Channon) *led for 1f: trckd ldrs: rdn over 2f out: kpt on onepced fnl f* **5/2**[1]

1- **4** *3/4* **Demon Docker (IRE)**[229] [6477] 3-8-9 82 EddieAhern 3 93
(P W Chapple-Hyam) *t.k.h: pressed ldrs tl led 5f out: rdn 2f out: hdd last 100 yds:wknd nr fin* **6/1**[3]

3205 **5** *1 3/4* **Moi Aussi (USA)**[5] [3489] 3-8-6 87 (b) SebSanders 6 86
(Sir Mark Prescott) *chsd ldrs on outer: rdn and ev ch 2f out: wknd over 1f out* **14/1**

0600 **6** *25* **Lygeton Lad**[26] [2820] 8-9-3 88 (t) SteveDrowne 5 34+
(Miss Gay Kelleway) *stdd s: hld up in last pair: rdn over 2f out: sn lost tch: eased fnl f: t.o* **9/1**

1m 40.25s (0.82) **Going Correction** +0.125s/f (Slow)
WFA 3 from 4yo+ 8lb **6** Ran SP% **110.3**
Speed ratings (Par 107):100,98,98,97,95 70
CSF £12.20 TOTE £2.70: £1.60, £1.80; EX 8.70.
Owner Mrs Nicolas Kairis **Bred** Matthews Breeding And Racing Ltd **Trained** Newmarket, Suffolk

FOCUS
Quite a useful field, with an unexposed winner who has now won twice from just two outings, both on Polytrack.

NOTEBOOK
Lightning Flash ◆ made it two from two in his first race since making a winning debut 14 months ago. In doing so, he created a favourable impression and he is one to keep on the right side, though it is interesting that both his runs to date have been on Polytrack. (op 15-8 tchd 4-1 in a place)
Indian Steppes(FR) came back to form after one below-par effort, followed by a tough assignment at Royal Ascot, and was beaten only by a progressive sort. This trip suits her well nowadays. (op 7-2)
South Cape made a good All-Weather debut, giving his connections a new range of options for the future. He is running well at present, and capable of winning either on this surface, or on turf. (op 10-3 tchd 7-2)
Demon Docker(IRE) was running in better company than when he made a winning debut at Wolverhampton last December. Nonetheless, he acquitted himself well, and looks capable of finding a race. (op 15-2 tchd 8-1)
Moi Aussi(USA) is more effective at a mile than ten furlongs, but she was not quite up to this stiff challenge. (op 12-1)
Lygeton Lad had a difficult task at the weights, but - even so - is better than he looked here. Official explanation: jockey said gelding had no more to give (op 8-1)

3649 **HASTINGS PRINTING COMPANY H'CAP** **2m (P)**
4:20 (4:21) (Class 5) (0-75,74) 3-Y-0+ **£3,238** (£963; £481; £240) **Stalls** Low

Form RPR
2122 **1** **Liberate**[5] [3502] 3-8-10 **72** SebSanders 6 88+
(Sir Mark Prescott) *led after 1f: mde rest: drew clr 3f out: in n.d after: v easily* **8/13**[1]
0144 **2** *9* **Dark Parade (ARG)**[18] [3098] 5-8-13 **65** JamieJones(7) 4 67
(G L Moore) *trckd ldrs: wnt 2nd over 4f out tl 3f out: sn no ch w wnr: regained 2nd 2f out: no imp* **17/2**
-654 **3** *nk* **Theatre (USA)**[14] [3203] 7-10-0 **73** JohnEgan 7 75
(Jamie Poulton) *hld up bhd: rdn over 4f out: sn wl outpcd: styd on over 1f out: wnt 3rd nr fin* **8/1**[3]
0000 **4** *½* **Grey Paint (USA)**[23] [2933] 3-8-12 **74** (t) RyanMoore 1 75
(R Hannon) *w.w in midfield: effrt u.p to ch wnr 3f out: sn btn: lost 2nd 2f out: plugged on* **20/1**
2150 **5** *1* **Linden Lime**[37] [2501] 4-9-0 **59** PaulDoe 8 59
(Jamie Poulton) *hld up in last: effrt over 4f out: sn rdn and struggling: no ch last 3f* **14/1**
6005 **6** *8* **Global Challenge (IRE)**[32] [2653] 7-9-6 **65** SteveDrowne 2 55
(P G Murphy) *sn nudged along: racd in midfield tl lost tch 4f out: sn no ch* **50/1**
0600 **7** *1 ½* **Love Angel (USA)**[12] [3256] 4-8-12 **57** J-PGuillambert 3 45
(J J Bridger) *hld up bhd: brief effrt over 4f out: sn wl bhd* **33/1**
6033 **8** *1* **Ritsi**[12] [3269] 3-8-7 **69** (t) EddieAhern 9 56
(Mrs A J Perrett) *chsd ldr after 2f tl over 4f out: wknd u.p 3f out: eased* **15/2**[2]
0066 **P** **Fiddlers Ford (IRE)**[46] [2219] 5-9-1 **60** (p) ChrisCatlin 5 —
(T Keddy) *led for 1f chsd ldrs tl rdn and lost pl 5f out: lost action 3f out: tailed after: p.u and dismntd over 1f out* **14/1**

3m 28.17s (-0.62) **Going Correction** +0.125s/f (Slow)
WFA 3 from 4yo+ 17lb 9 Ran SP% **118.3**
Speed ratings (Par 103):106,101,101,101,100 96,95,95,—
CSF £6.78 CT £25.53 TOTE £1.50: £1.10, £2.10, £2.00; EX 8.00 Trifecta £30.20 Pool £428.47, 10.05 winning units..
Owner Eclipse Thoroughbreds-Osborne House III **Bred** Miss K Rausing **Trained** Newmarket, Suffolk

FOCUS
A fair stayers' race, won easily by a progressive sort who looked a class above the rest.
Ritsi Official explanation: jockey said gelding had no more to give

3650 **LINGFIELDPARK.CO.UK H'CAP** **1m 2f (P)**
4:50 (4:50) (Class 6) (0-65,64) 3-Y-0 **£2,388** (£705; £352) **Stalls** Low

Form RPR
1613 **1** **Maidford (IRE)**[23] [2921] 3-8-12 **55** FergusSweeney 5 63
(M Meade) *trckd ldrs: rdn to chal 2f out: led wl ins fnl f: jst hld on* **6/1**[2]
0034 **2** *shd* **Teide Lady**[12] [3263] 3-8-12 **55** JamieSpencer 4 63
(Rae Guest) *hld up in midfield: hdwy wl over 2f out: plld out and rdn wl over 1f out: str run ins fnl f: jst failed* **4/1**[1]
0040 **3** *shd* **Floodlight Fantasy**[9] [3347] 3-9-6 **63** (p) RichardMullen 2 71
(E S McMahon) *chsd ldrs: wnt 2nd 3f out: led over 2f out: sn hrd pressed: rdn over 1f out: hdd wl ins fnl f: no ex* **6/1**[2]
-060 **4** *3* **Henchman**[19] [3055] 3-9-5 **62** (b[1]) JimmyFortune 10 64
(Lady Herries) *chsd ldrs: rdn and wnt 2nd briefly over 2f out: kpt on onepced fnl f* **25/1**
0056 **5** *2* **Pactolos Way**[20] [3016] 3-8-11 **54** JimCrowley 12 53
(P R Chamings) *bhd: hdwy on inner whn hmpd 2f out: swtchd over 1f out: kpt on* **25/1**
0110 **6** *2* **Emotive**[9] [3364] 3-9-7 **64** SebSanders 8 59
(I A Wood) *hld up bhd: hdwy on outer 3f out: kpt on: nvr able to chal* **8/1**
0554 **7** *1 ¼* **Peak Seasons (IRE)**[24] [2901] 3-8-10 **53** AdrianMcCarthy 3 45
(W De Best-Turner) *led: rdn and hdd over 2f out: wknd wl over 1f out* **33/1**
4000 **8** *1* **Super Frank (IRE)**[20] [3011] 3-9-2 **62** AdamKirby(3) 1 52
(G A Butler) *chsd ldrs on inner: rdn and effrt over 2f out: wknd wl over 1f out* **8/1**
3010 **9** *hd* **Mae Cigan (FR)**[36] [2518] 3-9-7 **64** TedDurcan 14 54
(M Blanshard) *hld up in last: prog on inner 3f out: rdn and no hdwy over 2f out* **14/1**
000 **10** *4* **Atwirl**[44] [2304] 3-8-9 **52** (b[1]) ShaneKelly 13 34
(D J Daly) *hld up in tch on outer: rdn 2f out: wknd over 1f out* **33/1**
606 **11** *1 ½* **Princess Danah (IRE)**[12] [3266] 3-9-3 **60** EddieAhern 9 40
(W R Swinburn) *hld up in rr: rdn 3f out: nvr on terms* **7/1**[3]
3653 **12** *3 ½* **Salvestro**[10] [3338] 3-9-5 **62** (b) RyanMoore 11 35
(Mrs A J Perrett) *t.k.h: hld up in rr: rdn over 2f out: no prog* **7/1**[3]
0005 **13** *6* **Blue Army (IRE)**[23] [2940] 3-8-7 **50** (p) ChrisCatlin 7 12
(Jane Southcombe) *chsd ldr: rdn over 3f out: sn wknd: t.o* **50/1**
-450 **14** *24* **Henry Holmes**[102] [918] 3-9-5 **62** (e[1]) RichardThomas 6 —
(Mrs L Richards) *t.k.h and chsd ldrs early: lost pl 4f out: t.o last 2f* **40/1**

2m 8.76s (0.97) **Going Correction** +0.125s/f (Slow) 14 Ran SP% **120.4**
Speed ratings (Par 98):101,100,100,98,96 95,94,93,93,90 88,86,81,62
CSF £28.15 CT £154.38 TOTE £5.60: £2.10, £1.90, £3.70; EX 22.40 Trifecta £153.70 Part won. Pool £216.51, 0.94 winning units. Place 6 £9.33, Place 5 £4.96.
Owner Ladyswood Stud **Bred** T Wada **Trained** Sherston,Wilts

FOCUS
A modest race, but competitive enough, with two short heads covering the first three home.
Princess Danah(IRE) Official explanation: jockey said filly was struck into
Salvestro Official explanation: jockey said colt ran too free
T/Jkpt: £2,281.10. Pool £96,385, 3563.75 winning tickets T/Plt: £12.40. Pool £60,858.60, 3,563.75 winnnig tickets T/Qpdt: £4.30. Pool £2,668.20, 457.20 winning tickets SP

3651 - 3657a (Foreign Racing) - See Raceform Interactive

[3319]LEOPARDSTOWN (L-H)
Wednesday, July 19

OFFICIAL GOING: Good

3658a **SILVER FLASH STKS (LISTED RACE) (FILLIES)** **6f**
8:00 (8:01) 2-Y-0 **£22,448** (£6,586; £3,137; £1,068)

RPR
1 **Chanting (USA)**[28] [2764] 2-8-12 KFallon 3 102
(David Wachman, Ire) *racd in 4th: rdn in 3rd bef st: chal fr 1 1/2f out: 2nd under 1f out: led ins fnl f: styd on wl* **11/10**[1]
2 *1 ¼* **Miss Beatrix (IRE)**[19] [3060] 2-8-12 DPMcDonogh 1 98
(Kevin Prendergast, Ire) *attempted to make all: strly pressed 1 1/2f out: hdd and kpt on same pce ins fnl f* **5/1**[3]
3 *1* **Gee Kel (IRE)**[21] [2992] 2-8-12 WSupple 2 95
(Francis Ennis, Ire) *trckd ldr in 2nd: rdn to chal 1 1/2f out: 3rd and kpt on same pce fr under 1f out* **9/4**[2]
4 *4* **Musthav (IRE)**[3] [3577] 2-8-12 WMLordan 6 83
(T Stack, Ire) *mainly in rr: rdn to go mod 4th 1 1/2f out: kpt on same pce* **16/1**
5 *3 ½* **Unlock (IRE)**[63] [1782] 2-8-12 PJSmullen 5 73
(D K Weld, Ire) *racd mainly in 5th: rdn to go 4th into st: sn no imp u.p: eased ins fnl f* **14/1**
6 *12* **Simonetta (IRE)**[19] [3060] 2-8-12 (p) KJManning 4 37
(J S Bolger, Ire) *trckd ldrs in 3rd: rdn bef 1/2-way: sn lost pl and no imp: last and eased ins fnl f* **7/1**

1m 14.6s **Going Correction** +0.20s/f (Good) 6 Ran SP% **120.1**
Speed ratings: 100,98,97,91,87 71
CSF £8.08 TOTE £2.00: £1.50, £2.80; DF 11.60.
Owner Michael Tabor **Bred** Tower Bloodstock **Trained** Goolds Cross, Co Tipperary

NOTEBOOK
Chanting(USA), a cosy winner on her most recent start at the course, held strong claims on this rise in class and, having been restrained early on, she came through to chase the runner-up and got well on top inside the final furlong. She is clearly progressing well and there may well be more to come from her upped to seven furlongs. (op 6/4)
Miss Beatrix(IRE), a disappointment in this grade at the Curragh last time, showed that running to be all wrong on this drop back in trip and she made a bold bid to make all. The winner proved too classy in the end, but she probably has a Listed contest in her if continuing to progress. (op 4/1)
Gee Kel(IRE), runner-up in a Naas Group 2 last month, went on to lose her maiden tag back there last time and this return to Pattern company brought about another sound effort. She looks worth a try at seven furlongs. (op 9/4 tchd 5/2)

3660a **CHALLENGE STKS (LISTED RACE)** **1m 6f**
9:00 (9:00) 3-Y-0+ **£22,448** (£6,586; £2,103; £2,103)

RPR
1 **Foreign Affairs**[26] [2840] 8-9-12 DPMcDonogh 3 110
(Sir Mark Prescott) *sn led and disp: led sn after 2f: sn clr: niggled along fr 6f out: sltly reduced ld bef st: styd on wl u.p* **4/1**[3]
2 *3* **Mkuzi**[18] [3107] 7-9-9 110 MJKinane 5 103+
(John M Oxx, Ire) *chsd ldrs: mainly mod 4th: clsr in 2nd fr early st: no imp u.p and kpt on same pce fnl f* **15/8**[2]
3 *6* **Simple Exchange (IRE)**[42] [2371] 5-9-9 105 PJSmullen 2 96
(D K Weld, Ire) *towards rr: poor 7th over 5f out: rdn to go mod 5th bef st: kpt on without threatening fr 2f out* **8/1**
3 *dht* **Virginia Woolf**[18] [3107] 4-9-6 98 FMBerry 1 93
(John M Oxx, Ire) *chsd ldrs: mainly mod 3rd: wnt 2nd 6f out: clsd appr st: sn dropped to 3rd and no imp: kpt on same pce* **14/1**
5 *3* **Ice Princess (IRE)**[26] [2840] 3-8-7 91 WSupple 6 91
(David Wachman, Ire) *mid-div: poor 6th over 5f out: no imp u.p and kpt on same pce fr bef st* **16/1**
6 *2 ½* **Sable D'Olonne (IRE)**[26] [2840] 3-8-7 90 WMLordan 7 88
(T Stack, Ire) *towards rr: poor last and rdn 6f out: mod 7th and kpt on same pce fr bef st* **25/1**
7 *2 ½* **Road To Mandalay (IRE)**[26] [2804] 3-8-10 KFallon 4 88
(A P O'Brien, Ire) *chsd ldrs: mainly mod 5th: clsd bef st: sn 4th: swished tail and no ex u.p fr 2f out* **7/4**[1]
8 *dist* **Rocksham (IRE)**[12] [3278] 6-9-6 49 JAHeffernan 8 —
(J J Lennon, Ire) *sn led and disp: hdd sn after 2f: chsd ldr after: dropped to 3rd 6f out: lost pl and wknd fr 4f out: virtually p.u st: t.o* **66/1**

2m 57.6s **Going Correction** -0.25s/f (Firm)
WFA 3 from 4yo+ 14lb 8 Ran SP% **120.1**
Speed ratings: 113,111,106,106,105 103,102,—
Tote Place: Simple Exchange 1.40, Virginia Woolf 1.60. CSF £12.64 TOTE £4.60: £1.60, £1.60; DF 14.40.
Owner Charles C Walker - Osborne House **Bred** Miss K Rausing **Trained** Newmarket, Suffolk

NOTEBOOK
Foreign Affairs, who was winning for the 12th time in a 36-race career, had never won beyond a mile and a half. He established a clear advantage after a couple of furlongs, and responded well to pressure to record his seventh Listed win and his third in Ireland. (op 7/2)
Mkuzi, a former dual winner of the Curragh Cup over this trip, chased the winner early in the straight. He drew a long way clear of the remainder, but was making no impression on the winner in the final furlong. (op 7/4 tchd 2/1)
Simple Exchange(IRE), held up in an effort to get the trip, stuck to his task well enough but was too far back when making his effort to get into contention. He would have been closer but for meeting interference, and ended up sharing third place with Virginia Woolf, who is a handicapper. (op 12/1)
Road To Mandalay(IRE) Official explanation: jockey said colt lost its action turning into the home straight; vet said colt was blowing hard post race
T/Jkpt: @72.10. Pool of @10,000.00 - 104 winning units. T/Plt: @10.00. Pool of @1,387.50 - 104 winning units. II

3659 - 3660a (Foreign Racing) - See Raceform Interactive

[3579]HAMBURG (R-H)
Wednesday, July 19

OFFICIAL GOING: Good

3661a **ALICE-CUP (EX FAHRHOFER STUTENPREIS) (GROUP 3) (F&M)** **1m**
6:40 (6:41) 3-Y-0+ **£22,069** (£6,897; £3,448; £2,069)

RPR
1 **Molly Art (GER)**[24] [2912] 4-9-6 (b) ASuborics 5 110
(U Ostmann, Germany) *in touch, 5th straight, ran on to lead 1f out, pushed out* **66/10**
2 *1 ¼* **Sexy Lady (GER)**[17] [3133] 3-8-10 TMundry 11 105
(P Rau, Germany) *mid-division, effort 1 1/2f out, went 2nd 150 yards out, not reach winner* **14/10**[1]
3 *2* **Squaw Dance**[20] [3002] 4-9-4 AStarke 6 101
(W J Haggas) *led to 1f out, just held on for 3rd* **28/10**[2]
4 *½* **Amateis (GER)**[53] [2059] 3-8-10 JBojko 7 100
(P Rau, Germany) *held up in mid-division, stayed on well final stages, just missed 3rd* **136/10**
5 *1 ¼* **Madura (GER)**[53] [2059] 3-8-10 J-PCarvalho 12 98
(Mario Hofer, Germany) *mid-division, stayed on at one pace final furlong* **262/10**
6 *nse* **Jalta (GER)**[284] [5750] 3-8-10 AHelfenbein 10 97
(H Steinmetz, Germany) *prominent til one pace final 1 1/2f* **151/10**

The Form Book, Raceform Ltd, Compton, RG20 6NL

7 *hd* **Deauville (GER)**[24] 2912 3-8-10 ....(b) ADeVries 2 97
(Frau E Mader, Germany) *held up, effort on outside early straight, some headway til one pace inside last* **18/1**

8 *1 1/4* **Funny Legend (NOR)**[50] 2123 5-9-6 .... FJohansson 4 97
(Wido Neuroth, Norway) *mid-division, never a factor* **61/10**[3]

9 *1 1/2* **Norwegian Pride (FR)**[24] 2912 4-9-6 .... WMongil 3 94
(P Schiergen, Germany) *held up, never a danger* **132/10**

10 *1 1/2* **Birthday Art (GER)** 4-9-4 .... WPanov 9 89
(P Vovcenko, Germany) *in touch til weakened from over 1f out* **491/10**

11 *17* **Zackmunde (GER)**[305] 3-8-10 .... JPalik 8 55
(Frau A Glodde, Germany) *held up in rear on inside, never a factor* **38/1**

12 *7* **Annatira (GER)**[1020] 5353 5-9-4 .... JVictoire 1 41
(E Kurdu, Germany) *in touch, pushed along straight, weakened quickly from over 1f out* **298/10**

1m 36.17s
WFA 3 from 4yo+ 8lb **12** Ran SP% **132.1**
(Including 10 Euro stake): WIN 76; PL 15, 12, 14; SF 235.
Owner Gestut Auenquelle **Bred** Gestut Auenquelle **Trained** Germany

NOTEBOOK
Molly Art(GER) came from off the pace well and was a deserving winner. She appears to be a four-year-old on the upgrade.
Sexy Lady(GER), a four-time winner, including in a French Group 3 prior to this, was beaten fair and square but gives the form a solid look.
Squaw Dance ran to form and connections were pleased with her effort. She is in foal to Dubawi, and may have one more run before being retired to the paddocks.

VICHY

Wednesday, July 19

OFFICIAL GOING: Good to soft

3662a GRAND PRIX DE VICHY (GROUP 3) 1m 2f
8:45 (9:02) 3-Y-0+ **£27,586** (£11,034; £8,276; £5,517; £2,759)

RPR

1 **Touch Of Land (FR)**[116] 742 6-9-9 .... OPeslier 1 120
(H-A Pantall, France) *raced in 3rd, close 4th straight, headway 2f out, led 1 1/2f out, ran on strongly, ridden out* **29/10**[3]

2 *1 1/2* **Ruwi**[53] 4-9-2 .... IMendizabal 6 111
(J-C Rouget, France) *racd in 5th, 3rd str, sn pushed along and ran on, rdn to chal fnl f, ran on but not rch wnr* **14/10**[1]

3 *1 1/2* **Mohandas (FR)**[21] 5-9-2 .... DBoeuf 3 108
(W Hefter, Germany) *raced in 2nd, ridden 1 1/2f out, dropped to 4th over 1f out, rallied under pressure and took 3rd close home* **25/1**

4 *shd* **Special Envoy (FR)**[21] 4-9-2 .... TThulliez 2 108
(N Clement, France) *led to 1 1/2f out, kept on under pressure, narrowly lost 3rd close home* **10/1**

5 *2* **Advice**[21] 5-9-2 .... TJarnet 4 104
(A Fabre, France) *raced in 4th, disputing last straight, driven over 1 1/2f out, not quicken* **59/10**

6 *shd* **Archange D'Or (IRE)**[34] 2597 4-9-2 .... CSoumillon 5 104
(A Fabre, France) *held up in last, disputing last straight, shaken up 1 1/2f out, no response* **27/10**[2]

2m 10.19s **6** Ran SP% **121.8**
PARI-MUTUEL (Including 1 Euro stake): WIN 3.90; PL 1.90, 1.30;SF 11.30.
Owner Gary A Tanaka **Bred** Chevotel De La Hauquerie **Trained** France

NOTEBOOK
Touch Of Land(FR), held up in third place early on when the pace was of a moderate nature, quickened well on the rail to lead a furlong and a half out and outclassed the other five runners who were all in receipt of 7lb. He appears to have kept his form well with age and will now have a second attempt to win the Arlington Million.
Ruwi raced in last place and was caught for speed when things quickened up rapidly in the straight. He ran on during the final furlong but never had a chance with the winner.
Mohandas(FR) settled in second place early on was another one to be caught for speed when things quickened up. He stayed on gamely to take third place inside the final furlong.
Special Envoy(FR) tried to go from pillar to post at a moderate pace. He was under pressure from a furlong and a half out and lost third place close home.

3429 EPSOM (L-H)

Thursday, July 20

OFFICIAL GOING: Good to firm (firm in places)
Wind: Light, against Weather: Sunny and warm

3663 EUROPEAN BREEDERS FUND MEDIAN AUCTION MAIDEN STKS 7f
6:15 (6:16) (Class 5) 2-Y-0 **£4,533** (£1,348; £674; £336) **Stalls** Low

Form RPR

1 **Five A Side** 2-9-3 .... J-PGuillambert 6 84
(M Johnston) *w'like: cl cpld: bit bkwd: w ldr: rdn 2f out: pressed new ldr 1f out but looked hld: rallied to ld nr fin* **10/1**

62 2 *nk* **Billy Dane (IRE)**[12] 3280 2-9-0 .... NelsonDeSouza(3) 5 83
(B J Meehan) *b.hind: trckd ldng pair: effrt to ld over 1f out: hanging lft after: nt qckn and hdd nr fin* **2/1**[1]

03 3 *2 1/2* **Sweet Lilly**[15] 3201 2-8-12 .... TedDurcan 1 72
(M R Channon) *dwlt: sn prom: cl 4th st: wandering and nt qckn wl over 1f out: kpt on to take 3rd nr fin* **7/2**[2]

0252 4 *nk* **Dee Jay Wells**[11] 3335 2-9-3 .... RyanMoore 4 76
(R Hannon) *swtg: mde most: hdd over 1f out: fdd fnl f* **4/1**[3]

02 5 *3* **Our Herbie**[17] 3157 2-9-3 .... EddieAhern 3 68
(J W Hills) *s.s: outpcd: 7th st: sme prog to 5th 2f out: no imp ldrs* **9/1**

00 6 *1* **Revisionist (IRE)**[14] 3210 2-9-3 .... PatDobbs 7 66
(R Hannon) *lw: sn outpcd: 6th and wl off the pce st: no prog* **50/1**

60 7 *shd* **Pagan Rules (IRE)**[14] 3210 2-9-3 .... KerrinMcEvoy 8 65
(Mrs A J Perrett) *dwlt: nvr gng wl and off the pce: 5th and nt on terms st: sn btn* **14/1**

00 8 *6* **Numerical (IRE)**[21] 3025 2-9-3 .... IanMongan 2 50
(J L Dunlop) *sn outpcd: last and struggling st: bhd fnl 3f* **20/1**

1m 23.07s (-0.88) **Going Correction** -0.15s/f (Firm) **8** Ran SP% **108.0**
Speed ratings (Par 94):99,98,95,95,92 90,90,83
CSF £27.08 TOTE £7.40: £2.10, £1.40, £1.50; EX 22.10.
Owner Jumeirah Racing **Bred** Michael Ng **Trained** Middleham Moor, N Yorks
■ Zelos (12/1) was withdrawn. R4 applies, deduct 5p in the £.

FOCUS
Just an ordinary maiden and the first four home were in the first four throughout. Despite that the form looks pretty solid and should prove reliable.
NOTEBOOK
Five A Side, a 28,000gns half-brother to Goodbye Mr Bond, a multiple mile to ten-furlong winner, and to Anfield Dream, a multiple five to six-furlong scorer, showed good early speed to race bang up with the pace from the start, but ran green when asked for his effort in the straight. However, he had the rail to run against and, with the eventual runner-up not going on as expected when hitting the front, he was able to get back on top near the line. There was a lot to like about this performance, not least his attitude, and he gives the impression he will improve quite a bit for the experience, although it should probably be noted he was not exactly given an easy time of things by his jockey. (op 15-2 tchd 7-1)
Billy Dane(IRE), on his toes beforehand, confirmed the ability he showed on his two previous runs, but appeared to throw away a good winning opportunity. With Five A Side running green, he looked all over the winner when hitting the front inside the last couple of furlongs, but he hung to his left and failed to really go through with his effort, handing the initiative to the eventual winner. It may be that he simply failed to handle the camber, but there has to be a slight question mark about his attitude after this effort. (op 11-4)
Sweet Lilly, who looked very fit indeed beforehand, did not seem to handle the track that well, struggling to cope with both the downhill run and the camber, so is likely to prove better than she was able to show. (op 3-1 tchd 11-4)
Dee Jay Wells did not offer much under pressure and was not at his best. He may be better suited by a bit of give in the ground. (op 5-1)
Our Herbie was never seen with a chance, but he will probably show improved form when sent handicapping. (tchd 10-1)
Numerical(IRE), despite having his third run, was still carrying condition. (op 16-1)

3664 MALL ASHLEY CLAIMING STKS 7f
6:45 (6:47) (Class 5) 3-Y-0+ **£3,886** (£1,156; £577; £288) **Stalls** Low

Form RPR

0041 1 **Envision**[14] 3213 3-9-1 78 .... RyanMoore 7 75
(R Hannon) *off the pce in midfield: 6th st: rdn 3f out: sustained prog to ld jst over 1f out: drvn out* **7/4**[1]

4505 2 *3/4* **Bessemer (JPN)**[19] 3097 5-9-9 75 ....(p) DanielTuhope(3) 5 80
(D Carroll) *trckd clr ldrs: 4th st: hanging but prog to ld briefly over 1f out: nt qckn and hld ins fnl f* **11/1**

2222 3 *1 3/4* **Border Artist**[11] 3339 7-9-0 55 .... OscarUrbina 9 63
(B G Powell) *lw: hld up wl in rr: 9th st: prog over 2f out: rdn and kpt on fr over 1f out: no imp ldng pair last 150yds* **4/1**[2]

0106 4 *5* **Renegade (IRE)**[20] 3033 5-9-0 46 ....(b) IanMongan 10 50
(Mrs L J Mongan) *led at fast pce: clr over 2f out: hdd & wknd over 1f out* **33/1**

00-0 5 *1 3/4* **Parisi Princess**[26] 2860 5-8-5 40 ow1 .... NeilChalmers(3) 4 39
(D L Williams) *chsd ldr to over 4f out: 3rd st: rdn and no prog over 2f out: wknd wl over 1f out* **66/1**

5425 6 *2* **Serieux**[15] 3191 7-9-12 73 ....(v) AdrianTNicholls 3 51
(D Nicholls) *t.k.h: trckd ldr over 4f out to 2f out: wknd rapidly* **5/1**[3]

-056 7 *1* **Underscore (USA)**[25] 2900 4-9-4 73 .... AdrianMcCarthy 2 41
(R A Harris) *off the pce towards rr: 8th st: rdn and no prog over 2f out* **15/2**

005 8 *2 1/2* **Mandarin Spirit (IRE)**[40] 2464 6-9-8 68 ....(p) J-PGuillambert 8 38
(G C H Chung) *s.s: last and wl off the pce: nvr a factor* **9/1**

025 9 *9* **For Life (IRE)**[19] 3089 4-9-4 53 ....(p) EddieAhern 6 10
(A P Jarvis) *stdd s: hld up towards rr: 7th st: sn rdn and btn: hanging bdly and wknd fnl 2f* **20/1**

0526 10 *shd* **Princess Kai (IRE)**[23] 2955 5-8-2 41 .... JosephLoveridge(7) 1 —
(R Ingram) *t.k.h and restrained bhd ldrs: awkward downhill: 5th and losing pl st: sn wknd and bhd* **40/1**

1m 21.83s (-2.12) **Going Correction** -0.15s/f (Firm)
WFA 3 from 4yo+ 7lb **10** Ran SP% **114.8**
Speed ratings (Par 103):106,105,103,97,95 93,92,89,78,78
CSF £21.71 TOTE £2.70: £2.10, £2.80, £1.50; EX 27.90.Border Artist was claimed by Jeff Pearce for £8,000.
Owner Mrs J Wood **Bred** Cheveley Park Stud Ltd **Trained** East Everleigh, Wilts

FOCUS
Just an ordinary claimer, but they went a good pace and the winning time was slightly quicker than the three-year-old handicap later on in the card. The form looks pretty sound with the first and third close to recent course form.
Serieux Official explanation: jockey said gelding lost its action
Underscore(USA) Official explanation: jockey said colt was unsuited by the track
Mandarin Spirit(IRE) Official explanation: jockey said gelding missed the break

3665 THE SPORTSMAN NEWSPAPER H'CAP 1m 2f 18y
7:15 (7:17) (Class 4) (0-80,79) 3-Y-0 **£7,772** (£2,312; £1,155; £577) **Stalls** Low

Form RPR

2062 1 **Cantabilly (IRE)**[11] 3338 3-8-10 **68** .... TedDurcan 2 73
(M R Channon) *lw: settled in 4th: swtchd rt over 2f out: effrt to chal fnl f: drvn to ld narrowly last 75yds* **10/3**[3]

05-6 2 *nk* **Ned Ludd (IRE)**[31] 2712 3-9-7 **79** .... RyanMoore 1 83
(R Hannon) *settled in 3rd tl trckd ldr 3f out: led wl over 1f out: sn drvn: hdd last 75yds: jst hld* **5/1**

6410 3 *2* **Nefski Alexander (USA)**[21] 3008 3-9-2 **74** .... EddieAhern 5 74
(P F I Cole) *swtg: hld up in last: cl up st and gng wl: poised to chal over 1f out: hrd rdn and fnd nil fnl f* **11/1**

50-4 4 *3* **Always Baileys (IRE)**[16] 3176 3-9-5 **77** .... J-PGuillambert 4 72
(M Johnston) *chsd ldr to 3f out: sn rdn and struggling: fdd* **11/4**[2]

0121 5 *1* **Pagan Crest**[21] 3008 3-8-11 **69** ....(b[1]) KerrinMcEvoy 3 62
(Mrs A J Perrett) *lw: t.k.h: led: rdn and hdd wl over 1f out: wknd tamely* **15/8**[1]

2m 8.35s (-0.69) **Going Correction** -0.15s/f (Firm) **5** Ran SP% **109.5**
Speed ratings (Par 102):96,95,94,91,90
CSF £19.00 TOTE £4.30: £2.10, £2.60; EX 21.20.
Owner A R Parrish **Bred** W P Iceton **Trained** West Ilsley, Berks

FOCUS
Just the five runners, but an interesting little contest and the form does not look too bad. Having said that, it is worth keeping in mind that the pace was pretty steady early on and the favourite was well below his best, suggesting the form is not the most solid.
Pagan Crest Official explanation: jockey said gelding ran too free

3666 COMPTON HELLYER 60TH BIRTHDAY H'CAP 1m 4f 10y
7:50 (7:51) (Class 5) (0-75,74) 3-Y-0+ **£5,505** (£1,637; £818; £408) **Stalls** Centre

Form RPR

3144 1 **Croon**[21] 3028 4-10-0 **74** .... EddieAhern 6 83+
(H Morrison) *lw: hld up in 5th: gng easily in st: stdy prog 2f out: shkn up to ld ent fnl f: sn in command* **3/1**[1]

4121 **2** *1 1/2* **Madhavi**[17] 3152 4-9-5 **65**.. RichardHughes 3 72
(R Hannon) *pressed ldr: reminders over 6f out: rdn to ld 2f out: hdd and outpcd ent fnl f* **4/1**[2]

4-35 **3** *1 1/4* **Tavalu (USA)**[20] 3035 4-9-0 **60**.. RyanMoore 4 65
(G L Moore) *led: rdn and hdd 2f out: stl nrly upsides 1f out: one pce after* **3/1**[1]

0461 **4** *3 1/2* **Blackmail (USA)**[7] 3429 8-8-12 **58**..............................(b) KerrinMcEvoy 5 57
(Miss B Sanders) *trckd ldrs: 4th and c wd st: sn rdn and no imp: n.d fnl 2f* **5/1**[3]

4246 **5** *hd* **Desert Island Disc**[32] 2672 9-9-5 **72**........................... SladeO'Hara[(7)] 1 71
(Dr J R J Naylor) *hld up in cl last: outpcd and rdn st: nvr on terms after* **9/1**

6113 **6** *1 1/4* **Spring Dream (IRE)**[14] 3215 3-9-2 **74**............................... TedDurcan 2 71
(M R Channon) *trckd ldng pair: rdn st: outpcd 2f out: wknd fnl f* **6/1**

2m 37.58s (-1.15) **Going Correction** -0.15s/f (Firm)
WFA 3 from 4yo+ 12lb **6** Ran SP% **111.0**
Speed ratings (Par 103):97,96,95,92,92 91
CSF £14.77 TOTE £4.20: £2.00, £2.40; EX 17.90.
Owner de La Warr Racing **Bred** D J And Mrs Deer **Trained** East Ilsley, Berks

FOCUS
Only six runners, and they went a steady pace for much of the way, but the form looks reasonable enough for the level and pretty sound rated around the placed horses.
Blackmail(USA) Official explanation: trainer said gelding finished lame

3667 LONDON FOCUS H'CAP 7f
8:20 (8:26) (Class 4) (0-80,79) 3-Y-O **£7,772** (£2,312; £1,155; £577) **Stalls** Low

Form RPR

-001 **1** **Scrummage**[14] 3229 3-8-6 **64**.......................................(v) KerrinMcEvoy 7 79+
(Sir Michael Stoute) *mde all: clr fnl 2f: shkn up briefly over 1f out: unchal* **5/2**[1]

4653 **2** *3* **Neardown Beauty (IRE)**[1] 3644 3-8-12 **73**............ NelsonDeSouza[(3)] 1 80+
(I A Wood) *lw: hld up in tch: 6th st: nt clr run over 2f out to over 1f out: r.o to take 2nd last 50yds: no ch w wnr* **7/2**[2]

5266 **3** *nk* **Mister Benedictine**[12] 3317 3-9-5 **77**.............................. SteveDrowne 2 83
(W R Muir) *lw: prom: 4th st: rdn to chse wnr over 2f out: no imp: lost 2nd last 50yds* **5/1**

4604 **4** *1 1/2* **Critic (IRE)**[21] 3007 3-9-7 **79**...(v[1]) EddieAhern 6 81
(M L W Bell) *lw: prom: 3rd st: disp 2nd over 2f out: rdn and one pce fr over 1f out* **8/1**

-050 **5** *1/2* **Blu Manruna**[14] 3212 3-8-4 **62** ow1.......................................(p) PaulDoe 9 63
(J Akehurst) *wl in rr: detached in 7th st and rdn: styd on fnl 2f: n.d* **10/1**

4461 **6** *6 1/2* **Arzaag**[24] 2937 3-8-5 **66** ow1.......................................(b) AdamKirby[(3)] 10 50
(D M Simcock) *hld up: detached in last st and rdn: no ch after* **14/1**

0000 **7** *1* **Bollywood (IRE)**[34] 2609 3-7-11 **60** oh5....................... MarcHalford[(5)] 8 41
(J J Bridger) *racd freely: chsd wnr tl over 2f out: sn wknd* **50/1**

-21 **D** **Miss McGuire**[23] 2951 3-9-6 **78**.. RyanMoore 4 66
(G L Moore) *chsd ldrs: bmpd 5f out: 5th st: no prog over 2f out: wknd and eased over 1f out: fin 6th, 5l: disq* **4/1**[3]

1m 22.08s (-1.87) **Going Correction** -0.15s/f (Firm) **8** Ran SP% **116.3**
Speed ratings (Par 102):104,100,100,98,97 90,89,92
CSF £11.60 CT £40.52 TOTE £3.20: £1.60, £2.10, £1.90; EX 17.70.
Owner J Wigan & G Strawbridge **Bred** G Strawbridge And London Thoroughbred Services Lt **Trained** Newmarket, Suffolk

FOCUS
A fair handicap but an easy success for Scrummage, who enjoyed the run of the race, leading at no more than an ordinary pace. The winning time was slightly slower than the earlier claimer, which just goes to show how easy a time the winner had up front. The third sets the standard for the form. Miss McGuire disq: (prohibited substance in sample). oore fined £1,300.
Arzaag Official explanation: jockey said colt was unsuited by the track
Miss McGuire Official explanation: jockey said filly suffered interference in running

3668 PIONEER MAIDEN H'CAP 1m 114y
8:50 (8:57) (Class 5) (0-70,65) 3-Y-O **£3,238** (£963; £481; £240) **Stalls** Low

Form RPR

0422 **1** **Carloman**[15] 3197 3-9-2 **60**..(b) RyanMoore 9 70
(R M Beckett) *mde all: drvn clr over 1f out: wandered u.str.p fnl f: unchal* **5/2**[1]

5022 **2** *1 3/4* **Royal Tavira Girl (IRE)**[7] 3453 3-8-10 **57**................... DominicFox[(3)] 12 63
(M G Quinlan) *swtchd to inner fr wd draw sn after s: hld up: 10th st: prog to chse wnr over 1f out: kpt on but unable to chal* **7/1**[3]

-000 **3** *3* **Giverny Spring**[17] 3142 3-9-4 **62**.. EddieAhern 6 62
(J W Hills) *towards rr: 11th st: rdn on outer wl over 2f out: styd on fr over 1f out to take 3rd ins fnl f* **20/1**

-000 **4** *1/2* **Cunegonde**[24] 2929 3-8-4 **48**... PaulDoe 13 47
(G L Moore) *wl in rr: last st: rdn on outer over 2f out: styd on fr over 1f out: nrst fin* **33/1**

00-2 **5** *1 1/2* **Snow Symphony (IRE)**[23] 2951 3-9-4 **65**...................... AdamKirby[(3)] 1 61
(D M Simcock) *chsd wnr: no imp over 2f out: wknd and lost 2nd over 1f out* **12/1**

0504 **6** *1 1/2* **Whisper Inthe Wind (IRE)**[9] 3379 3-8-8 **55**............. SaleemGolam[(3)] 8 48
(Miss J Feilden) *swtg: settled midfield: 7th st: rdn and no prog over 2f out: fdd* **33/1**

0400 **7** *3/4* **Tilsworth Charlie**[35] 2589 3-8-0 **47** oh1 ow1.......... NelsonDeSouza[(3)] 3 38
(J R Jenkins) *nvr bttr than midfield: 8th st: no prog over 2f out* **33/1**

0335 **8** *hd* **Shinko (IRE)**[11] 3336 3-8-9 **56**...................................(p) DeanCorby[(3)] 4 47
(Miss J Feilden) *hld up towards rr: 9th st and gng wl enough: drvn and no prog over 2f out* **16/1**

5542 **9** *nk* **Final Tune (IRE)**[8] 3395 3-9-6 **64**................................. AdrianTNicholls 2 54
(D Nicholls) *trckd ldrs: 6th and cl enough on inner st: wknd 2f out* **10/3**[2]

-044 **10** *nk* **Captain Bolsh**[48] 2210 3-8-11 **55**....................................(v) DO'Donohoe 7 44
(J Pearce) *prom: 3rd st: rdn and wknd over 2f out* **14/1**

4060 **11** *3* **Perfect Order (USA)**[21] 3016 3-8-6 **50**...............................(p) TPQueally 5 33
(N A Callaghan) *hld up: n.m.r 6f out: 12th st: no prog* **11/1**

3443 **12** *5* **Khyber Knight (IRE)**[6] 3472 3-8-2 **46** oh5............... AdrianMcCarthy 10 19
(Jane Southcombe) *chsd ldrs: 4th st: wknd over 2f out* **8/1**

0006 **13** *nk* **Lady Duxyana**[17] 3153 3-8-2 **46** oh2................................. HayleyTurner 11 18
(M D I Usher) *lw: b: prom: 5th and losing pl st: sn wknd* **33/1**

1m 44.6s (-1.14) **Going Correction** -0.15s/f (Firm) **13** Ran SP% **120.4**
Speed ratings (Par 100):99,97,94,94,93 91,91,90,90,90 87,83,82
CSF £19.08 CT £284.78 TOTE £3.70: £1.60, £2.70, £5.10; EX 26.50 Place 6 £26.82, Place 5 £18.73.
Owner R S G Jones,J M Blyth Currie & A R Adams **Bred** Dr Karen Monica Sanderson **Trained** Whitsbury, Hants

FOCUS
As is to be expected in a maiden handicap, just modest form but solid enough rated around the fourth and fifth.
Whisper Inthe Wind(IRE) Official explanation: jockey said filly slipped on the bend
Khyber Knight(IRE) Official explanation: jockey said filly never travelled
T/Plt: £52.60 to a £1 stake. Pool: £61,670.70. 855.55 winning tickets. T/Qpdt: £24.00 to a £1 stake. Pool: £2,861.20. 88.20 winning tickets. JN

3524 HAMILTON (R-H)
Thursday, July 20

OFFICIAL GOING: Good to firm (firm in places)
Wind: Almost nil

3669 WEATHERBYS BANK MAIDEN AUCTION STKS (A QUALIFIER FOR THE HAMILTON PARK 2-Y-O SERIES FINAL) 6f 5y
2:20 (2:20) (Class 5) 2-Y-O **£3,238** (£963; £481; £240) **Stalls** Centre

Form RPR

00 **1** **Movethegoalposts**[15] 3193 2-8-12 .... RoystonFfrench 5 68
(M Johnston) *w ldrs: drvn over 2f out: led ins fnl f: hld on wl* **9/1**

2 **2** *nk* **Brenin Gwalia**[9] 3385 2-8-7 .... MartinDwyer 2 62
(D M Simcock) *led: rdn and edgd rt over 1f out: hdd ins fnl f: kpt on* **11/10**[1]

55 **3** *3/4* **Lemon Silk (IRE)**[12] 3286 2-8-12 .... MickyFenton 4 65
(T P Tate) *hung rt thrght: prom: outpcd over 2f out: kpt on wl fnl f* **9/2**[2]

6 **4** *1* **Stay Active (USA)**[27] 2807 2-8-9 .... TomEaves 1 59
(I Semple) *s.i.s: sn prom: outpcd over 2f out: kpt on steadily fnl f* **6/1**[3]

30 **5** *3* **Tobago Reef**[22] 2973 2-8-7 .... TonyHamilton 6 48
(Mrs L Stubbs) *chsd ldrs: rdn and hung rt over 2f out: sn one pce* **6/1**[3]

00 **6** *17* **Piccolini**[12] 3286 2-8-3 .... CatherineGannon 3 —
(Mrs G S Rees) *w ldrs: rdn over 3f out: sn wknd* **40/1**

1m 12.2s (-0.90) **Going Correction** -0.20s/f (Firm) **6** Ran SP% **106.8**
Speed ratings (Par 94):98,97,96,95,91 68
CSF £17.69 TOTE £7.50: £3.30, £1.10; EX 19.70.
Owner Favourites Racing XXI **Bred** Barry Taylor **Trained** Middleham Moor, N Yorks

FOCUS
An ordinary event in which the pace was sound with the third probably the best guide to the form.

NOTEBOOK
Movethegoalposts, easy to back, turned in a seemingly much improved effort on this third start. He is a chunky type with scope for further progress, should stay seven furlongs and may be the sort to win a race in nursery company. Official explanation: trainer had no explanation for the apparent improvement in form (op 10-1)
Brenin Gwalia, who shaped well on his debut over seven furlongs; failed to build on that dropped in distance for this turf debut. The return to seven will suit and, although this bare form is ordinary, he looks capable of winning a small event. (op 6-5 tchd 5-4 in places)
Lemon Silk(IRE) did not look very happy at this unconventional course but ran his best race yet. He has improved with every outing, should appreciate the step up to seven furlongs and is the type to win a small event in due course. (op 4-1 tchd 5-1)
Stay Active(USA) bettered the form of his debut and left the impression that he would be capable of a bit better over seven furlongs and in ordinary nursery company in due course. (op 13-2 tchd 11-2)
Tobago Reef has not really built on a fair debut effort but is another from this race that may be capable of a bit better in modest nursery company granted a stiffer test of stamina on a flatter track. (op 5-1)
Piccolini, upped to six furlongs, was again soundly beaten and is of no immediate interest. (op 33-1)

3670 DOROTHY AND ARTHUR BALDING STKS (H'CAP) 6f 5y
2:50 (2:50) (Class 5) (0-70,66) 3-Y-O+ **£3,886** (£1,156; £577; £288) **Stalls** Centre

Form RPR

0023 **1** **Viewforth**[5] 3524 8-9-1 **53**..(b) TomEaves 3 63
(I Semple) *prom: effrt over 2f out: styd on wl fnl f to ld cl home* **10/3**[2]

0261 **2** *nk* **Rancho Cucamonga (IRE)**[5] 3524 4-9-0 **52**...............(b) MartinDwyer 5 61
(T D Barron) *dwlt: sn in tch: hdwy over 2f out: led appr fnl f: edgd rt and hdd towards fin* **6/4**[1]

0325 **3** *shd* **Chairman Bobby**[21] 3003 8-8-4 **47**.........................(p) AndrewMullen[(5)] 2 56
(D W Barker) *led to appr fnl f: rallied: hld towards fin* **9/2**[3]

0-00 **4** *3* **Bold Haze**[14] 3217 4-9-10 **62**... MickyFenton 1 62
(Miss S E Hall) *outpcd: effrt and drifted to stands rail over 2f out: kpt on fnl f: no imp* **10/1**

100- **5** *nk* **Minimum Bid**[317] 5033 5-9-9 **66**..................................... MarkLawson[(5)] 4 65
(B Smart) *chsd ldrs: drvn 1/2-way: wknd over 1f out: eased ins last* **13/2**

0-50 **6** *5* **Telepathic (IRE)**[11] 3334 6-8-12 **50**............................ GrahamGibbons 6 34
(A Berry) *cl up tl rdn and wknd over 2f out* **33/1**

1m 11.75s (-1.35) **Going Correction** -0.20s/f (Firm) **6** Ran SP% **106.6**
Speed ratings (Par 103):101,100,100,96,96 89
CSF £7.83 TOTE £4.00: £1.40, £1.60; EX 5.90.
Owner Gordon McDowall **Bred** Britton House Stud And R J Gorringe **Trained** Carluke, S Lanarks

FOCUS
Not the most competitive of handicaps but a sound pace and this form should prove reliable with the placed horses to recent form.

3671 WEATHERBYS BANK CONDITIONS STKS 1m 65y
3:20 (3:21) (Class 3) 3-Y-O **£9,971** (£2,985; £1,492) **Stalls** High

Form RPR

-225 **1** **Metropolitan Man**[30] 2721 3-8-12 108............................. MartinDwyer 1 104+
(D M Simcock) *set slow pce: pushed along over 2f out: comf* **1/4**[1]

-200 **2** *2 1/2* **Desert Realm (IRE)**[12] 3313 3-8-12 95............................. JoeFanning 3 98
(M Johnston) *chsd wnr: effrt 3f out: edgd rt and no ex over 1f out* **3/1**[2]

0 **3** *70* **Onlybayinvillage (IRE)**[69] 1633 3-8-5 .... ChristopherEly[(7)] 2 —
(A Berry) *wnt lft s: chsd ldrs 3f: sn lost tch* **100/1**[3]

1m 49.78s (0.48) **Going Correction** -0.20s/f (Firm) **3** Ran SP% **106.0**
Speed ratings (Par 104):89,86,16
CSF £1.27 TOTE £1.30; EX 1.10.
Owner The Metropolitans **Bred** Mrs G Slater **Trained** Newmarket, Suffolk

FOCUS
An uncompetitive event for the money and one in which the winner, the clear pick on BHB ratings, was allowed to do his own thing in front.

NOTEBOOK
Metropolitan Man, the clear pick on ratings and on form, faced a straightforward task and was also allowed the run of the race. This told us nothing new about him but he is likely to remain vulnerable back in Group company. (op 4-11 tchd 2-5 in a place)
Desert Realm(IRE) had 13lb to find with the winner on official ratings but, although not disgraced, is almost certainly flattered by his proximity in this muddling event. He is likely to remain vulnerable back in handicaps from his current mark. (op 9-4)
Onlybayinvillage(IRE) faced an impossible task on only this second racecourse start but picked up nearly £1,500 for ambling round. (op 66-1)

3672 BILL MCHARG H'CAP — 1m 65y

3:55 (3:56) (Class 6) (0-65,63) 3-Y-O+ — £3,238 (£963; £481; £240) Stalls High

Form — RPR

0405 1 **Defi (IRE)**[12] 3287 4-10-0 **61**................(b) TomEaves 6 — 76
(I Semple) *hld up: smooth hdwy to ld 2f out: pushed clr* **9/2**[2]

3404 2 4 **Thornaby Green**[28] 2789 5-8-4 **44**................ DeanHeslop(7) 1 — 50
(T D Barron) *in tch: effrt over 2f out: rallied to chse wnr ins fnl f: kpt on* **11/2**[3]

0111 3 1 1/2 **Noble Nova**[3] 3586 3-9-2 **57** 6ex................ JoeFanning 7 — 58
(M R Channon) *chsd ldrs: hdwy to ld briefly over 2f out: one pce over 1f out* **6/4**[1]

0003 4 1 **Anthemion (IRE)**[6] 3484 9-8-13 **51**................ AndrewMullen(5) 5 — 51
(Mrs J C McGregor) *led to over 3f out: outpcd fr 2f out* **11/2**[3]

5201 5 3 **Insubordinate**[6] 3484 5-9-13 **63** 6ex................ DNolan(3) 3 — 56
(J S Goldie) *hld up: rdn 3f out: edgd rt and no imp fr 2f out* **6/1**

6546 6 5 **Campbells Lad**[6] 3484 5-8-7 **43**................ PatrickMathers(3) 4 — 25
(Mrs G S Rees) *w ldr: led over 3f to over 2f out: sn wknd* **20/1**

1m 45.68s (-3.62) **Going Correction** -0.20s/f (Firm)
WFA 3 from 4yo+ 8lb — 6 Ran SP% **108.0**
Speed ratings (Par 101):110,106,104,103,100 95
CSF £26.27 TOTE £4.40: £1.90, £2.30; EX 32.60.
Owner Gordon McDowall **Bred** Skymarc Farm Inc And Dr A J O'Reilly **Trained** Carluke, S Lanarks

FOCUS
An ordinary handicap but a decent gallop teed things for something coming from just off the pace. The form is rated around the first two but may not be totally solid.

3673 AMANDA FORSYTH "FORTY FABULOUS YEARS" CLAIMING STKS — 6f 5y

4:30 (4:31) (Class 5) 3-Y-O+ — £3,238 (£963; £481; £240) Stalls Centre

Form — RPR

5010 1 **Limonia (GER)**[10] 3368 4-8-10 52................ MickyFenton 8 — 53
(N P Littmoden) *keen: mde all: rdn over 2f out: hld on wl fnl f* **7/1**[3]

5320 2 hd **Howards Princess**[10] 3354 4-9-3 66................(p) TomEaves 3 — 59
(I Semple) *keen: trckd ldrs: effrt and edgd rt over 1f out: ev ch ins fnl f: hld towards fin* **3/1**[2]

0005 3 1 **Fox Covert (IRE)**[1] 3635 5-8-7 40................ MarkLawson(5) 2 — 51
(D W Barker) *chsd ldrs: rdn and outpcd 2f out: kpt on wl fnl f* **33/1**

0010 4 1 1/4 **Pomfret Lad**[14] 3217 8-9-8 74................ GrahamGibbons 5 — 57
(J J Quinn) *trckd ldrs: effrt and ev ch 2f out: one pce fnl f* **1/1**[1]

0446 5 3 **Shatin Leader**[10] 3356 4-8-7 38................(p) RoystonFfrench 1 — 33
(Miss L A Perratt) *prom: drvn and outpcd over 2f out: no imp fnl f* **20/1**

5/0 6 1 3/4 **Night Prayers (IRE)**[118] 719 4-9-5 80................ GylesParkin 4 — 40
(B Smart) *bhd: outpcd 1/2-way: hung rt and sn no imp* **11/1**

1000 7 5 **Obe Bold (IRE)**[11] 3330 5-8-12 56................ JoeFanning 7 — 18
(A Berry) *chsd ldrs tl rdn and wknd over 2f out* **20/1**

/00- 8 17 **Second Wind**[297] 5508 11-8-9 33................(t) PatrickMathers(3) 6 — —
(D A Nolan) *s.i.s: hung rt thrght: lost tch fr 1/2-way* **200/1**

1m 11.8s (-1.30) **Going Correction** -0.20s/f (Firm) — 8 Ran SP% **108.8**
Speed ratings (Par 103):100,99,98,96,92 90,83,61
CSF £25.21 TOTE £9.80: £2.00, £1.10, £5.50; EX 18.00.
Owner M Murphy **Bred** D Furstin Zu Oettingen-Wallerstein **Trained** Newmarket, Suffolk
■ Stewards' Enquiry : Tom Eaves three-day ban: used whip with excessive frequency (Jul 31, Aug 1,3)

FOCUS
A modest event but one that took less winning than seemed likely beforehand with the market leader disappointing. The pace was sound but the third anchors the form.

3674 DAILY RECORD H'CAP — 1m 5f 9y

5:00 (5:00) (Class 5) (0-70,68) 3-Y-O+ — £4,533 (£1,348; £674; £336) Stalls High

Form — RPR

2111 1 **Alambic**[2] 3628 3-7-13 **52** 6ex................ JamieMackay 8 — 60+
(Sir Mark Prescott) *set stdy pce: mde all: pushed along and edgd lft over 1f out: kpt on strly* **4/11**[1]

4500 2 2 1/2 **King's Fable (USA)**[17] 3145 3-8-0 **53**................ RoystonFfrench 4 — 57
(M Johnston) *sn trcking wnr: effrt over 2f out: edgd rt over 1f out: kpt on ins fnl f* **50/1**

3251 3 2 **Bronze Dancer (IRE)**[6] 3483 4-9-7 **68** 6ex................ AshleyHamblett(7) 7 — 69
(G A Swinbank) *stdd in tch: effrt 3f out: no imp fr 2f out* **9/2**[2]

-344 4 3/4 **Easibet Dot Net**[14] 2549 6-10-0 **68**................(p) TomEaves 5 — 68
(I Semple) *keen: hld up in tch: outpcd 3f out: kpt on fnl f: nrst fin* **20/1**

0501 5 2 1/2 **Abstract Folly (IRE)**[15] 3192 4-9-6 **60**................ GrahamGibbons 2 — 56
(J D Bethell) *prom tl rdn and outpcd over 2f out* **16/1**[3]

-030 6 8 **Millennium Hall**[21] 2998 7-9-4 **58**................ JoeFanning 6 — 42
(Miss Lucinda V Russell) *dwlt: hdwy and in tch 1/2-way: hung rt and wknd fr 3f out* **100/1**

-006 7 nk **Rajam**[34] 2628 8-9-6 **60**................ TonyHamilton 1 — 44
(G A Harker) *hld up: rdn 4f out: sn btn* **66/1**

2m 51.9s (-1.50) **Going Correction** -0.20s/f (Firm)
WFA 3 from 4yo+ 13lb — 7 Ran SP% **106.6**
Speed ratings (Par 103):96,94,93,92,91 86,86
CSF £28.47 CT £30.23 TOTE £1.30: £1.20, £6.40; EX 20.10.
Owner Lady O'Reilly **Bred** Miss K Rausing And Mrs S M Rogers **Trained** Newmarket, Suffolk

FOCUS
An ordinary event in which the one progressive sort was allowed to do her own thing in front and the race is rated through the runner-up. The pace was only fair.

3675 BETFAIR APPRENTICE SERIES H'CAP (ROUND 3) (PART OF THE "APPRENTICE TRAINING RACE" SERIES) — 1m 3f 16y

5:35 (5:35) (Class 6) (0-55,55) 3-Y-O+ — £2,730 (£806; £403) Stalls High

Form — RPR

6-16 1 **The Pen**[17] 3141 4-10-0 **55**................ DeanWilliams 6 — 63
(C W Fairhurst) *hld up in tch: effrt 3f out: rallied to ld ins fnl f: kpt on wl* **5/1**[3]

3136 2 1 **Kyle Of Lochalsh**[10] 3352 6-9-12 **53**................ KevinGhunowa 7 — 59
(J S Goldie) *trckd ldrs: led over 3f out: rdn and edgd lft over 2f out: hdd ins fnl f: kpt on same pce* **5/2**[1]

0634 3 3 **Nakwa (IRE)**[17] 3140 8-9-4 **45**................ MichaelJStainton 2 — 46
(E J Alston) *prom: effrt 3f out: kpt on same pce fnl f* **11/4**[2]

6252 4 3 **Grande Roche (IRE)**[36] 2548 4-9-13 **54**................ AshleyHamblett 4 — 50
(G A Swinbank) *stdd in tch: effrt and hung lft over 2f out: outpcd over 1f out* **5/2**[1]

/0-0 5 13 **Taili**[10] 3350 5-8-4 **36** oh16................ NBazeley(5) 5 — 9
(D A Nolan) *slowly away: bhd: outpcd 4f out: no ch after* **200/1**

-600 6 1 1/4 **Acca Larentia (IRE)**[10] 3350 5-8-9 **36** oh6................(p) KellyHarrison 1 — 7
(Mrs H O Graham) *w ldr: ev ch over 3f out: wknd over 2f out* **33/1**

606/ 7 50 **Phoenix Nights (IRE)**[669] 5673 6-9-1 **47**................ ChristopherEly(5) 3 — —
(A Berry) *led to over 3f out: sn wknd: t.o* **50/1**

2m 22.27s (-3.99) **Going Correction** -0.20s/f (Firm) — 7 Ran SP% **105.9**
Speed ratings (Par 101):106,105,103,100,91 90,54
CSF £15.19 TOTE £5.90: £2.70, £1.80; EX 16.90 Place 6 £50.30, Place 5 £16.80.
Owner William Hill **Bred** Mrs R D Peacock **Trained** Middleham Moor, N Yorks

FOCUS
A modest event in which the pace was sound and this bare form should prove reliable through the runner-up.
T/Plt: £50.30 to a £1 stake. Pool: £39,029.40. 565.35 winning tickets. T/Qpdt: £16.80 to a £1 stake. Pool: £1,471.40. 64.50 winning tickets. RY

3299 LEICESTER (R-H)

Thursday, July 20

OFFICIAL GOING: Firm (good to firm in places)
Wind: Light, behind Weather: Overcast, but hot and humid

3676 MOUNTSORREL MEDIAN AUCTION MAIDEN STKS — 1m 1f 218y

2:10 (2:10) (Class 5) 3-4-Y-O — £3,238 (£963; £481; £240) Stalls High

Form — RPR

02 1 **Diamond Shower (USA)**[21] 3029 3-9-0................ JimmyFortune 2 — 84
(E A L Dunlop) *mde all: rdn over 2f out: styd on* **11/10**[1]

44- 2 1 1/4 **Raucous (GER)**[290] 5658 3-9-0................ JohnEgan 4 — 82
(T P Tate) *trckd wnr: racd keenly: rdn over 2f out: styd on same pce fnl f* **9/4**[2]

55 3 2 1/2 **Amazing Charlie (IRE)**[20] 3032 3-8-9................ JimCrowley 5 — 72
(Mrs A J Perrett) *trckd ldrs: racd keenly: rdn over 2f out: no ex fnl f* **12/1**

4 3/4 **Shumookh (IRE)** 3-9-0................ RHills 8 — 76
(M A Jarvis) *s.s: hdwy 7f out: rdn over 2f out: sn hung lft: styd on same pce appr fnl f* **7/2**[3]

00 5 44 **Stockholder**[13] 3261 3-9-0................ HayleyTurner 3 — —
(C A Cyzer) *hld up: rdn 1/2-way: wknd over 3f out:sddle slipped* **33/1**

2m 6.56s (-1.74) **Going Correction** -0.20s/f (Firm)
WFA 3 from 4yo 10lb — 5 Ran SP% **111.2**
Speed ratings (Par 103):98,97,95,94,59
CSF £3.90 TOTE £1.70: £1.10, £1.90; EX 3.90 Trifecta £6.60 Pool: £186.86 - 19.97 winning tickets..
Owner Gainsborough Stud **Bred** Gainsborough Farm Llc **Trained** Newmarket, Suffolk

FOCUS
A fair maiden but the winner set just a steady pace before winding things up. The second is the best guide to the form.
Shumookh(IRE) Official explanation: jockey said gelding hung left
Stockholder Official explanation: jockey said saddle slipped

3677 RACEDAY HOSPITALITY (S) STKS — 5f 2y

2:40 (2:40) (Class 6) 2-Y-O — £2,590 (£770; £385; £192) Stalls Low

Form — RPR

060 1 **Shes Millie**[12] 3307 2-8-6................ FrankieMcDonald 1 — 55
(J G M O'Shea) *chsd ldrs: outpcd 1/2-way: rallied over 1f out: led and hung rt ins fnl f: r.o* **11/1**

050 2 1 **Totally Free**[13] 3246 2-8-11................(v[1]) HayleyTurner 2 — 56
(M D I Usher) *hld up in tch: plld hrd: rdn and ev ch ins fnl f : unable qckn* **16/1**

4364 3 hd **Baytown Paikea**[2] 3624 2-8-6................ JamesDoyle(5) 4 — 55
(P S McEntee) *disp ld: rdn and hung rt over 1f out: hdd and unable qckn ins fnl f* **15/2**

6241 4 2 1/2 **Bowl Em Over**[8] 3394 2-8-11................(p) PaulHanagan 7 — 46
(M E Sowersby) *disp ld: rdn over 1f out: wknd ins fnl f* **11/2**

50 5 1 1/4 **Dansilver**[15] 3193 2-8-11................ VinceSlattery 5 — 42
(D J Wintle) *chsd ldrs: rdn 1/2-way: outpcd and hung lft over 1f out: styd on ins fnl f* **5/1**[3]

0001 6 1 3/4 **River Rosie (IRE)**[10] 3345 2-8-11................ SebSanders 9 — 35
(J G Portman) *chsd ldrs: edgd rt 2f out: wknd over 1f out* **10/3**[2]

0 7 1 1/4 **Bronco's Filly (IRE)**[24] 2916 2-8-7 ow1................ FergusSweeney 3 — 27
(J G M O'Shea) *hld up: rdn 1/2-way: sn wknd* **33/1**

8 2 1/2 **Tora Warning** 2-8-11................ DeanMcKeown 6 — 22
(John A Harris) *s.s: outpcd* **20/1**

653 9 9 **Lord Blue Boy**[8] 3394 2-8-6................ MarcHalford(5) 8 — —
(W G M Turner) *chsd ldrs: rdn 1/2-way: sn wknd* **3/1**[1]

61.36 secs (0.46) **Going Correction** -0.35s/f (Firm) — 9 Ran SP% **113.8**
Speed ratings (Par 92):82,80,80,76,74 71,69,65,50
CSF £166.83 TOTE £17.60: £4.40, £4.20, £2.00; EX 234.30 Trifecta £150.40 Part won. Pool: £211.95 - 0.10 winning tickets..There was no bid for the winner.
Owner Alan Purvis **Bred** S Martin And Alan Purvis **Trained** Elton, Gloucs

FOCUS
A truly-run race but modest form rated around the placed horses.

NOTEBOOK
Shes Millie, out of the money in three maidens, got off the mark on this drop in grade. The strongly-run five furlongs on fast ground suited her. (op 12-1)
Totally Free, well beaten over a furlong further in this grade last time, raced keenly in the first-time visor but put in an improved effort. It remains to be seen whether the headgear works so well again.
Baytown Paikea set the pace against the rail, but jinked approaching the final furlong and was collared inside the last. Her limitations are there for all to see. Official explanation: jockey said filly jinked right (op 7-1)
Bowl Em Over, winner of a particularly poor race at Catterick, disputed the lead with the eventual third, racing freely, before dropping away inside the last. She gave the impression that she did not like this ground. (op 5-1)
Dansilver, down in grade after showing little in a couple of six-furlong races at Chepstow, gave the impression he needs to step back up in trip.
Lord Blue Boy was in trouble by halfway. Official explanation: jockey said colt was unsuited by the firm ground (op 7-2)

3678 RACECOURSE VIDEO SERVICES NURSERY — 5f 218y

3:10 (3:13) (Class 4) 2-Y-O

£6,232 (£1,866; £933; £467; £233; £117) Stalls Low

Form — RPR

232 1 **Lipocco**[33] 2631 2-9-7 **83**................ SebSanders 9 — 88
(R M Beckett) *prom: jnd ldr over 4f out: rdn to ld ins fnl f: r.o* **9/2**[2]

341 2 nk **Argentine (IRE)**[12] 3286 2-9-4 **80**................ KDarley 4 — 84
(M Johnston) *led: rdn over 1f out: hdd ins fnl f: nt qckn nr fin* **8/13**[1]

0540 3 1 **Stir Crazy (IRE)**[6] 3496 2-8-7 **69**................ ChrisCatlin 5 — 70
(M R Channon) *chsd ldrs: rdn over 2f out: no ex ins fnl f* **10/1**

104 4 6 **Love In May (IRE)**[12] 3280 2-8-10 **72** JohnEgan 2 55
(J S Moore) *chsd ldrs: rdn 1/2-way: wknd over 1f out* **16/1**
6323 5 3 ½ **Shreddy Shrimpster**[8] 3409 2-7-13 **61** oh1 ow1 HayleyTurner 7 34
(A B Haynes) *s.i.s: hld up: rdn 1/2-way: n.d: sddle slipped* **20/1**
040 6 ½ **Spirit Rising**[33] 2631 2-7-12 **60** oh9 PaulHanagan 8 31
(J M Bradley) *s.i.s and wnt lft s: sme hdwy 1/2-way: sn wknd* **66/1**
0031 7 ½ **Party Palace**[34] 2626 2-7-13 **61** ow1 FrankieMcDonald 6 31
(J A Osborne) *prom to 1/2-way* **9/1[3]**
5054 8 3 ½ **Everyman**[9] 3372 2-7-7 **60** (b[1]) DuranFentiman(5) 3 19
(P D Evans) *s.i.s: outpcd* **20/1**
0333 9 ½ **Aggbag**[43] 2346 2-7-6 **61** oh8 ow1 SoniaEaton(7) 1 19
(B P J Baugh) *sn outpcd* **33/1**

1m 11.39s (-1.81) **Going Correction** -0.35s/f (Firm) **9** Ran SP% **119.0**
Speed ratings (Par 96):98,97,96,88,83 82,82,77,76
CSF £7.59 CT £27.38 TOTE £6.40: £1.60, £1.10, £2.70; EX 9.40 Trifecta £33.00 Pool: £513.24 - 11.01 winning tickets..
Owner The Anagram Partnership **Bred** C Scott And T Leigh **Trained** Whitsbury, Hants

FOCUS
Official ratings are estimated. Few got into this, but with the first three coming home well clear the form looks solid.

NOTEBOOK
Lipocco, whose three previous runs were all at Bath, was tackling six furlongs for the first time. One of three battling it out in the final furlong, he stuck his neck out well to secure victory. A tough sort who is well at home on top of the ground, he will stay a bit further. (op 4-1)
Argentine(IRE), stepped up to six furlongs for the first time, was sent off a pretty short price for this nursery bow. Always to the fore but harried for the lead, he had to admit defeat near the line but did not do much wrong. (op 4-6 after early 8-11)
Stir Crazy(IRE), back down in trip, was one of three vying for the lead with a furlong or so to run but was the first of them to crack. He finished well ahead of the rest and this was a creditable effort. (tchd 9-1)
Love In May(IRE), who failed to stay an extended seven furlongs last time, was in fourth place and making no inroads on the three in front of her by the halfway stage. (op 18-1)
Shreddy Shrimpster, tackling six furlongs for the first time, was merely best of the rest. Official explanation: jockey said saddle slipped (op 16-1)

3679 FREE TIPS @ GG.COM H'CAP 7f 9y
3:45 (3:47) (Class 4) (0-80,79) 3-Y-0+

£6,232 (£1,866; £933; £467; £233; £117) **Stalls** Low

Form RPR
0145 1 **Blue Trojan (IRE)**[14] 3223 6-9-10 77 GeorgeBaker 9 93
(S Kirk) *racd centre: outpcd: hdwy u.p over 1f out: r.o to ld wl ins fnl f* **3/1[2]**
-006 2 1 ½ **Pillars Of Wisdom**[11] 3337 4-9-9 76 (t) SebSanders 10 88
(J L Dunlop) *racd centre: chsd ldr tl overall ldr over 4f out: clr over 1f out: rdn and hdd wl ins fnl f* **9/1**
0044 3 5 **Life's A Whirl**[14] 3229 4-8-7 60 oh6 (p) JohnEgan 8 58
(Mrs C A Dunnett) *racd centre: led: hdd over 4f out: rdn over 2f out: sn outpcd* **16/1**
3010 4 ¾ **Torquemada (IRE)**[19] 3089 5-8-9 62 PaulDoe 3 58
(W Jarvis) *s.i.s: racd centre: hdwy over 2f out: no imp fr over 1f out* **13/2**
5042 5 ½ **Rezzago (USA)**[36] 2555 6-9-12 79 JimmyFortune 2 74
(W R Swinburn) *racd centre: prom: rdn over 2f out: styd on same pce* **11/4[1]**
-000 6 nk **Goodwood Spirit**[6] 3471 4-9-10 77 (p) NCallan 5 71
(J M Bradley) *racd centre: prom: rdn over 2f out: wknd over 1f out* **20/1**
4100 7 10 **Sands Of Barra (IRE)**[26] 2863 3-9-2 76 ChrisCatlin 7 43
(N A Callaghan) *racd centre: chsd ldrs over 4f* **16/1**
0262 8 1 **Saxon Lil (IRE)**[7] 3450 4-9-0 67 SteveDrowne 4 32
(J L Spearing) *racd centre: chsd ldrs 5f* **5/1[3]**
0-00 9 1 **Palatinate (FR)**[18] 3121 4-9-3 73 (v[1]) AdamKirby(3) 1 35
(C G Cox) *racd alone stands' side: w ldrs 3f: sn rdn and hung rt: wknd 2f out* **25/1**
0-00 10 6 **Red Lantern**[28] 2789 5-8-7 60 oh24 RobbieFitzpatrick 6 6
(M J Attwater) *racd centre: sn pushed along in rr: bhd fnl 3f* **100/1**

1m 23.03s (-3.07) **Going Correction** -0.35s/f (Firm)
WFA 3 from 4yo+ 7lb **10** Ran SP% **113.0**
Speed ratings (Par 105):103,101,95,94,94 93,82,81,80,73
CSF £28.47 CT £302.30 TOTE £4.00: £1.50, £2.10, £4.10; EX 34.80 Trifecta £296.30 Part won. Pool: £417.38 - 0.60 winning tickets..
Owner The Ex Katy Boys **Bred** Patrick Cassidy **Trained** Upper Lambourn, Berks

FOCUS
This fair handicap was run at a strong pace and the first two finished clear so the race is rated positively.
Saxon Lil(IRE) Official explanation: jockey said filly had no more to give

3680 GG.COM CLAIMING STKS 1m 3f 183y
4:20 (4:20) (Class 5) 4-Y-0+ **£3,886** (£1,156; £577; £288) **Stalls** High

Form RPR
-300 1 **Tedstale (USA)**[22] 2975 8-9-7 78 (b) NCallan 8 71
(K A Ryan) *hld up: hdwy over 3f out: rdn to ld and hung rt over 1f out: styd on* **3/1[2]**
0000 2 1 ½ **Jazrawy**[8] 3411 4-8-7 52 ChrisCatlin 3 55
(Miss Gay Kelleway) *racd keenly: w wnr tl rdn, hung lft and outpcd over 1f out: styd on ins fnl f* **25/1**
2500 3 1 ¾ **Khanjar (USA)**[13] 3248 6-9-7 72 PatCosgrave 4 66
(K R Burke) *mde most over 10f: no ex ins fnl f* **4/1[3]**
3435 4 2 ½ **Oldenway**[6] 3483 7-8-9 66 PaulHanagan 6 50
(R A Fahey) *chsd ldrs: rdn over 3f out: styd on same pce fnl 2f* **10/11[1]**
0504 5 5 **Three Boars**[28] 2788 4-9-7 50 (b) JohnEgan 7 54
(S Gollings) *hld up: rdn over 3f out: n.d* **11/1**
5000 6 2 ½ **Pitsi Kahtoh**[13] 3270 4-7-7 35 (p) LukeMorris(7) 5 29
(P W Hiatt) *chsd ldrs over 9f* **66/1**
00-0 7 14 **Raul Sahara**[22] 41 4-8-10 47 AdamKirby(3) 2 20
(J W Unett) *chsd ldrs over 9f* **33/1**

2m 32.04s (-2.46) **Going Correction** -0.20s/f (Firm) **7** Ran SP% **114.0**
Speed ratings (Par 103):100,99,97,96,92 91,81
CSF £63.47 TOTE £3.80: £1.60, £7.50; EX 61.30 TRIFECTA Not won..Jazrawy was claimed by P. W. Hiatt for £5,000. Oldenway was claimed by John A. Harris for £6,000.
Owner Yorkshire Racing Club & Derek Blackhurst **Bred** Gainesway Thoroughbreds Limited **Trained** Hambleton, N Yorks

FOCUS
A modest claimer but not strong form with the fifth to his recent mark.
Three Boars Official explanation: jockey said gelding was unsuited by the firm ground

3681 MELTON MOWBRAY CONDITIONS STKS 1m 1f 218y
4:50 (4:51) (Class 3) 3-Y-0

£7,790 (£2,332; £1,166; £583; £291; £146) **Stalls** High

Form RPR
14- 1 **Ashaawes (USA)**[338] 4455 3-9-3 102 LDettori 3 101
(Saeed Bin Suroor) *s.i.s: sn rcvrd to ld: rdn and hung rt over 1f out: styd on: eased nr fin* **7/2[2]**
6-03 2 1 ½ **Humungous (IRE)**[19] 3091 3-9-3 100 SteveDrowne 4 98
(C R Egerton) *prom: chsd wnr over 2f out: outpcd over 1f out: styd on ins fnl f* **11/1[3]**
-160 3 shd **Gandor (IRE)**[28] 2774 3-9-3 87 DavidKinsella 2 98
(J H M Gosden) *chsd wnr tl rdn over 2f out: sn outpcd: styd on ins fnl f* **33/1**
-260 4 1 ¾ **Tell**[28] 2775 3-9-3 102 SebSanders 6 94
(J L Dunlop) *hld up: hdwy to chse wnr 2f out: sn rdn and ev ch: no ex ins fnl f* **14/1**
511 5 18 **Imperial Star (IRE)**[18] 3119 3-9-3 102 JimmyFortune 1 86+
(J H M Gosden) *trckd ldrs: rdn over 2f out: wknd over 1f out: eased* **4/11[1]**
0 6 34 **Dark Emotion**[62] 1822 3-9-3 JohnEgan 5 —
(W De Best-Turner) *s.i.s: hld up: bhd fnl 4f* **200/1**

2m 4.14s (-4.16) **Going Correction** -0.20s/f (Firm) **6** Ran SP% **114.0**
Speed ratings (Par 104):108,106,106,105,90 63
CSF £38.93 TOTE £3.70: £1.60, £2.50; EX 32.40.
Owner Godolphin **Bred** Jayeff 'B' Stables **Trained** Newmarket, Suffolk

FOCUS
A decent conditions event in which the field came down the centre in the home straight. The time was decent but the form is rated positively.

NOTEBOOK
Ashaawes(USA), off the track since the Ebor meeting 11 months ago, was soon in front and stayed on strongly in the latter stages to draw clear. Described by Dettori as 'very lazy', there is improvement to come from him over 12 furlongs. (tchd 4-1)
Humungous(IRE), upped in trip, could not go with the winner in the run to the final furlong but did stay on to get the better of a tussle for second. He is not going to be easy to place. (op 12-1 tchd 14-1)
Gandor(IRE), like the runner-up, was staying on at the end after being outpaced by the eventual winner and fourth. This was a decent effort at the weights.
Tell challenged the eventual winner on the run to the final furlong, but did not get home and was relegated two places inside the last. He needs to return to a mile. (op 12-1)
Imperial Star(IRE), a half-brother to last year's Derby winner Motivator, proved disappointing but picked up a muscle injury and this was not his running. Official explanation: jockey said colt lost its action (op 4-9)

3682 GREAT GLEN H'CAP 5f 218y
5:25 (5:26) (Class 5) (0-70,70) 3-Y-0+ **£5,181** (£1,541; £770; £384) **Stalls** Low

Form RPR
3312 1 **Louphole**[7] 3434 4-9-7 **65** SebSanders 5 76
(P J Makin) *s.i.s: hld up: swtchd rt and hdwy over 1f out: r.o to ld wl ins fnl f* **10/3[1]**
0563 2 ¾ **Cree**[12] 3287 4-8-10 **54** RichardMullen 12 62
(W R Muir) *chsd ldrs: rdn over 2f out: led 1f out: hdd wl ins fnl f* **8/1**
0312 3 ¾ **Safranine (IRE)**[6] 3478 9-8-5 **56** AnnStokell(7) 11 62
(Miss A Stokell) *chsd ldrs: led wl over 1f out: rdn and hdd 1f out: styd on same pce* **18/1**
0004 4 ¾ **Pink Bay**[32] 2676 4-8-9 **53** (b[1]) FergusSweeney 3 57
(W S Kittow) *hld up: rdn 1/2-way: r.o ins fnl f: nrst fin* **14/1**
-026 5 1 ¾ **Sir Don (IRE)**[8] 3398 7-8-9 **53** NCallan 2 52
(E S McMahon) *chsd ldrs: rdn over 2f out: styd on same pce appr fnl f* **17/2**
5605 6 ½ **Danehill Stroller (IRE)**[22] 2971 6-9-6 **64** (p) JimmyFortune 10 61
(R M Beckett) *s.i.s: rdn over 2f out: nvr nrr* **6/1[3]**
2013 7 2 ½ **Bodden Bay**[9] 3389 4-8-11 **55** RobbieFitzpatrick 9 45
(D Carroll) *chsd ldrs: rdn over 2f out: wknd fnl f* **12/1**
0502 8 hd **Boldinor**[10] 3349 3-9-0 **63** AlanDaly 4 52
(N E Berry) *chsd ldrs 4f* **16/1**
3030 9 1 ¼ **My Girl Pearl (IRE)**[5] 3543 6-8-7 **51** oh2 JohnEgan 1 36
(M S Saunders) *chsd ldrs: hung rt 1/2-way: sn rdn and wknd* **20/1**
0004 10 2 **Pachello (IRE)**[7] 3434 4-9-12 **70** KDarley 8 49
(J M Bradley) *led: hdd wl over 1f out: sn wknd* **5/1[2]**
10-3 P **Smirfys Night**[36] 2544 7-8-8 **52** DavidKinsella 6 —
(E S McMahon) *s.s: outpcd: p.u and dismntd 2f out* **7/1**

1m 10.84s (-2.36) **Going Correction** -0.35s/f (Firm)
WFA 3 from 4yo+ 5lb **11** Ran SP% **118.4**
Speed ratings (Par 103):101,100,99,98,95 95,91,91,89,87 —
CSF £30.44 CT £432.90 TOTE £3.20: £1.60, £2.70, £3.30; EX 42.10 Trifecta £171.50 Part won. Pool: £241.67 - 0.98 winning tickets. Place 6 £280.17, Place 5 £237.63.
Owner Ten Of Hearts **Bred** Mrs P Harford **Trained** Ogbourne Maisey, Wilts

FOCUS
A moderate handicap in which the field raced down the centre, with the first two home ending up on the far side of the bunch. The form is straightforward and sound rated through the third.
T/Plt: £722.50 to a £1 stake. Pool: £55,430.95. 56.00 winning tickets. T/Qpdt: £30.90 to a £1 stake. Pool: £3,460.40. 82.70 winning tickets. CR

3594 WOLVERHAMPTON (A.W) (L-H)
Thursday, July 20

OFFICIAL GOING: Standard
Wind: Moderate, behind

3683 WOLVERHAMPTON-RACECOURSE.CO.UK APPRENTICE H'CAP 5f 20y(P)
6:35 (6:35) (Class 6) (0-60,60) 3-Y-0+ **£3,071** (£906; £453) **Stalls** Low

Form RPR
5030 1 **Sir Loin**[5] 3523 5-8-7 **48** (v) DanielleMcCreery(6) 2 59
(N Tinkler) *broke wl: t.k.h: mde all: rdn and edgd rt ins fnl f: r.o* **5/1[2]**
1523 2 ¾ **Millfields Dreams**[7] 3438 7-9-0 **52** BRoper(3) 12 60
(M G Quinlan) *hld up towards rr: hdwy on ins wl over 1f out: kpt on ins fnl f: nt trble wnr* **13/2[3]**
0145 3 1 ¾ **Blakeshall Quest**[13] 3267 6-9-0 **52** (b) JamesRogers(3) 11 54
(R Brotherton) *chsd ldrs: rdn over 1f out: kpt on same pce fnl f* **16/1**
122- 4 ¾ **Dellagio (IRE)**[205] 6668 5-8-13 **51** MarkCoumbe(3) 1 50
(R W Price) *chsd ldrs: wnt 2nd over 1f out: no ex towards fin* **4/1[1]**
3620 5 hd **Global Achiever**[48] 2208 5-8-3 **46** (b) MarvinCheung(8) 3 45
(G C H Chung) *chsd wnr tl wl over 1f out: one pce* **9/1**
3000 6 ¾ **Byo (IRE)**[59] 1899 8-8-9 **50** JPFeatherstone(6) 6 46
(P Howling) *hld up in tch: lost pl after 1f: kpt on fnl f: n.d* **14/1**

504 **7** 1 ¾ **Angelofthenorth**[10] 3356 4-9-5 **60**.......... JohnCavanagh(6) 8 — 50
(C J Teague) *hmpd s: nvr nr ldrs* **16/1**

-346 **8** 1 **Talcen Gwyn (IRE)**[151] 455 4-9-8 **60**.......... JosephWalsh(3) 7 — 46
(M F Harris) *bmpd s: prom: rdn over 2f out: wknd over 1f out* **9/1**

0500 **9** 1 ¼ **Imtalkinggibberish**[44] 2317 5-8-11 **49**.......... WilliamCarson(3) 4 — 30
(V Smith) *s.i.s: bhd whn carried lft over 1f out: n.d* **7/1**

0335 **10** 1 **All Clued Up (IRE)**[9] 3384 3-9-2 **55**.......... LukeMorris 5 — 33
(Rae Guest) *t.k.h: chsd ldrs: rdn over 2f out: sn wknd: hung lft over 1f out* **11/1**

4610 **11** 10 **Secret Vision (USA)**[34] 2611 5-8-8 **46**.......... PatrickDonaghy(3) 9 — —
(R M H Cowell) *wnt lft and bmpd s: sn wl bhd* **11/1**

62.72 secs (-0.10) **Going Correction** -0.10s/f (Stan)
WFA 3 from 4yo+ 4lb — **11** Ran SP% **117.6**
Speed ratings (Par 101):96,94,92,90,90 89,86,84,82,81 65
CSF £37.58 CT £495.74 TOTE £5.10: £1.60, £2.00, £8.10; EX 46.80.
Owner W F Burton **Bred** Britton House Stud And C Gregson **Trained** Langton, N Yorks
■ Stewards' Enquiry : Luke Morris two-day ban: careless riding (Jul 31, Aug 1)

FOCUS
A poor handicap rated around the first two.
Secret Vision(USA) Official explanation: vet said mare was wrong behind

3684 EUROPEAN BREEDERS FUND NOVICE FILLIES' STKS — 5f 20y(P)
7:05 (7:05) (Class 4) 2-Y-O — **£4,533** (£1,348; £674; £336) **Stalls** Low

Form — RPR

1 **1** **Enticing (IRE)**[22] 2984 2-9-3 .... MichaelHills 4 — 95+
(W J Haggas) *wnt rt s: sn led: drew clr fnl f: easily* **2/11**[1]

05 **2** 7 **Seaflower Reef (IRE)**[18] 3120 2-8-10 .... LPKeniry 2 — 63
(A M Balding) *led early: chsd wnr to 3f out: sn rdn: outpcd wl over 1f out: kpt on to take 2nd wl ins fnl f: no ch w wnr* **20/1**[3]

4100 **3** 1 ½ **Christmas Tart (IRE)**[19] 3084 2-9-3 .... ChrisCatlin 1 — 64
(V Smith) *hld up: hdwy to chse wnr 2f out: sn rdn: hung lft over 1f out: sn btn* **7/1**[2]

0 **4** 3 **Blakeshall Rose**[43] 2355 2-8-10 .... DeanMcKeown 5 — 47
(A J Chamberlain) *carried rt s: chsd wnr 3f out to 2f out: wknd over 1f out* **150/1**

62.09 secs (-0.73) **Going Correction** -0.10s/f (Stan) — **4** Ran SP% **102.5**
Speed ratings (Par 93):101,89,87,82
CSF £3.98 TOTE £1.10; EX 3.60.
Owner Lael Stable **Bred** Lael Stables **Trained** Newmarket, Suffolk

FOCUS
This turned out to be the expected cakewalk for Enticing who could be Pattern class.

NOTEBOOK
Enticing(IRE) outclassed her three rivals in the style of a long odds-on shot. She is now likely to be stepped up to Listed class in the St Hugh's Stakes at Newbury next month. (op 2-9 tchd 1-6)
Seaflower Reef(IRE) did nothing more than finish best of the rest but is bred to need further and it showed. (op 14-1)
Christmas Tart(IRE), trying her luck on sand, proved no match for the winner and lugged over to the inside rail. (op 11-2 tchd 15-2)
Blakeshall Rose ran better than on her debut but that is not saying a lot. (op 80-1)

3685 FAMILY FUN DAYS AT WOLVERHAMPTON RACECOURSE NOVICE STKS — 5f 216y(P)
7:35 (7:35) (Class 4) 2-Y-O — **£4,533** (£1,348; £674; £336) **Stalls** Low

Form — RPR

21 **1** **Ponty Rossa (IRE)**[22] 2973 2-8-10 .... DavidAllan 4 — 78
(T D Easterby) *hld up: hdwy wl over 1f out: hrd rdn to ld cl home* **11/4**[1]

2225 **2** nk **Dowlleh**[19] 3080 2-8-11 .... ChrisCatlin 3 — 78
(M R Channon) *led after 1f: rdn clr over 1f out: ct cl home* **11/4**[1]

3 5 **Quiddity (IRE)** 2-8-3 .... RichardMullen 6 — 55
(E J O'Neill) *hld up in tch: wnt 2nd 2f out: sn rdn and edgd lft: wknd ins fnl f* **6/1**[3]

021 **4** nk **Rainbow Fox**[10] 3351 2-9-1 .... PaulHanagan 7 — 67
(R A Fahey) *plld hrd: in tch on outside: rdn 2f out: wknd ins fnl f* **3/1**[2]

0 **5** 3 ½ **Stevie Gee (IRE)**[19] 3080 2-8-11 .... DeanMcKeown 1 — 52
(G A Swinbank) *hld up: nt clr run on ins and lost pl over 4f out: n.d after* **33/1**

6 5 **Daddy Cool** 2-8-3 .... LiamJones(5) 2 — 34
(W G M Turner) *led 1f: prom tl rdn and wknd wl over 1f out* **22/1**

516 **7** nk **Juan Bol (IRE)**[62] 1824 2-8-11 .... MichaelTebbutt 5 — 36
(V Smith) *prom: chsd ldr over 3f out: rdn over 2f out: wknd wl over 1f out* **8/1**

1m 16.16s (0.35) **Going Correction** -0.10s/f (Stan) — **7** Ran SP% **111.0**
Speed ratings (Par 96):93,92,85,85,80 74,73
CSF £9.93 TOTE £3.80: £1.50, £2.20; EX 16.90.
Owner The Lapin Blanc Racing Partnership **Bred** Jim McDonald **Trained** Great Habton, N Yorks

FOCUS
There were three previous winners in this quite interesting novice contest and the form looks reasonable rated through the winner.

NOTEBOOK
Ponty Rossa(IRE), back up to six, had quite a hard race in eventually wearing down the runner-up. Well regarded by connections, they will know where they stand with her after she has run in the Princess Margaret at Ascot on Diamond Day. (tchd 10-3)
Dowlleh tried to steal it once in line for home and the tactics very nearly paid off. He deserves a change of fortune. (op 3-1 tchd 5-2)
Quiddity(IRE) ran well for a long way and should come on for the experience. (op 4-1 tchd 7-1)
Rainbow Fox ran too freely on this step up to six. (op 9-2 tchd 5-2)
Daddy Cool Official explanation: vet said colt was struck into on its right hind leg

3686 SUPPORT THE BROOKE HOSPITAL FOR ANIMALS H'CAP — 1m 4f 50y(P)
8:05 (8:05) (Class 4) (0-80,80) 3-Y-O+ — **£6,477** (£1,927; £963; £481) **Stalls** Low

Form — RPR

1211 **1** **Warsaw Pact (IRE)**[6] 3490 3-8-9 **73** 6ex.......... SebSanders 8 — 93+
(Sir Mark Prescott) *sn led: rdn clr 2f out: eased towards fin* **2/7**[1]

1550 **2** 5 **Shaunas Vision (IRE)**[19] 3098 7-9-3 **76**.......... JamesMillman(7) 9 — 83
(D K Ivory) *hld up towards rr: hdwy over 4f out: sn rdn: tk 2nd ins fnl f: no ch w wnr* **50/1**

0042 **3** 1 ½ **Bowled Out (GER)**[9] 3388 4-8-11 **63**.......... RichardMullen 11 — 68
(P J McBride) *hld up in tch: hdwy over 5f out: chsd wnr over 3f out: no imp fnl 2f* **20/1**

0206 **4** 3 ½ **Keshya**[7] 3456 5-8-5 **62**.......... JamesDoyle(5) 1 — 61
(N P Littmoden) *bhd: hdwy on outside over 1f out: nvr trbld ldrs* **50/1**

6102 **5** 2 **Birthday Star (IRE)**[43] 2345 4-8-10 **62** oh1.......... JDSmith 5 — 58
(W J Musson) *hld up towards rr: swtchd rt wl over 1f out: nvr nrr* **20/1**

0145 **6** 3 **Secretary General (IRE)**[14] 3214 5-10-0 **80**.......... JimmyFortune 7 — 71
(P F I Cole) *prom: chsd wnr after 2f tl rdn over 3f out: wknd over 1f out* **9/1**[2]

060- **7** 1 ¼ **Astronomical (IRE)**[122] 5525 4-9-12 **78**.......... ChrisCatlin 4 — 67
(Miss S J Wilton) *led early: prom tl rdn and wknd over 4f out* **50/1**

6404 **8** 3 **Heathyards Pride**[110] 832 6-9-6 **79**.......... RussellKennemore(7) 10 — 63
(R Hollinshead) *a bhd* **20/1**

-603 **9** hd **Plenty Cried Wolf**[9] 3388 4-8-10 **62** oh3.......... PaulHanagan 2 — 46
(R A Fahey) *mid-div: rdn over 4f out: sn struggling* **25/1**

2230 **10** 3 **Rocket Force (USA)**[26] 2850 6-9-1 **70**.......... DNolan(3) 3 — 49
(N Wilson) *prom: rdn over 3f out: sn wknd* **16/1**[3]

6003 **11** 3 ½ **Russian Dream (IRE)**[17] 3156 3-8-6 **70**.......... StephenCarson 6 — 43
(W R Swinburn) *t.k.h in tch: rdn over 3f out: sn wknd* **20/1**

2m 39.09s (-3.33) **Going Correction** -0.10s/f (Stan)
WFA 3 from 4yo+ 12lb — **11** Ran SP% **122.4**
Speed ratings (Par 105):107,103,102,100,99 97,96,94,94,92 89
CSF £35.66 CT £154.82 TOTE £1.30: £1.10, £11.90, £2.20; EX 21.50.
Owner J Fishpool - Osborne House **Bred** Saad Bin Mishrif **Trained** Newmarket, Suffolk

FOCUS
A fair handicap and no surprises here with the long odds-on winner 8lb well-in. The form is not that strong and is rated around the placed horses.

3687 STAY AT THE HOLIDAY INN WOLVERHAMPTON FILLIES' H'CAP — 7f 32y(P)
8:35 (8:35) (Class 3) (0-95,93) 3-Y-O+ — **£9,715** (£2,890; £1,444; £721) **Stalls** High

Form — RPR

2600 **1** **Kindlelight Debut**[90] 1111 6-9-7 **84**.......... JamesDoyle(5) 3 — 94
(N P Littmoden) *hld up in tch: rdn 2f out: led ins fnl f: r.o wl* **8/1**

4004 **2** 2 ½ **Toffee Vodka (IRE)**[7] 3450 4-9-8 **80**.......... MichaelHills 9 — 84
(J W Hills) *a.p: rdn to ld jst over 1f out: hdd ins fnl f: nt qckn* **7/1**

5/0 **3** 1 ½ **Nebraska Lady (IRE)**[26] 2851 4-9-5 **77**.......... RichardMullen 8 — 77
(E J O'Neill) *s.i.s: hld up and bhd: rdn over 2f out: hdwy wl over 1f out: kpt on one pce fnl f* **11/1**

-110 **4** ½ **Song Of Passion (IRE)**[29] 2744 3-10-0 **93**.......... JimmyFortune 5 — 88
(R Hannon) *chsd ldr: rdn to ld 2f out: hdd jst over 1f out: one pce* **15/8**[1]

00-0 **5** ¾ **Ginger Spice (IRE)**[105] 898 4-8-11 **74**.......... LiamJones(5) 1 — 70
(W J Haggas) *led: hung rt and hdd 2f out: wknd ins fnl f* **16/1**

4363 **6** shd **Damelza (IRE)**[16] 3176 3-8-9 **74**..........(t) DavidAllan 4 — 67
(T D Easterby) *hld up and bhd: rdn 2f out: hdwy over 1f out: nvr trbld ldrs* **11/2**[2]

6-00 **7** 2 ½ **Siena Gold**[26] 2851 4-9-11 **83**.......... DeanMcKeown 6 — 73
(J G Given) *hld up in tch: rdn and wknd over 2f out* **50/1**

-053 **8** 1 **Bowness**[11] 3332 4-9-4 **76**.......... SebSanders 7 — 63
(J G Given) *hld up and bhd: hdwy on outside over 3f out: rdn over 2f out: wknd over 1f out* **13/2**[3]

0136 **9** hd **Miss Meggy**[7] 3450 4-9-3 **75**..........(b) PaulHanagan 2 — 61
(Miss J A Camacho) *hld up in tch: rdn over 2f out: wknd 1f out* **7/1**

1m 29.09s (-1.31) **Going Correction** -0.10s/f (Stan)
WFA 3 from 4yo+ 7lb — **9** Ran SP% **115.8**
Speed ratings (Par 104):103,100,98,97,97 96,94,92,92
CSF £62.84 CT £624.93 TOTE £8.80: £2.10, £1.50, £3.70; EX 25.90.
Owner Kindlelight Ltd **Bred** Cheveley Park Stud Ltd **Trained** Newmarket, Suffolk

FOCUS
A fair fillies' handicap and the form is pretty straightforward with the runner-up the best guide.

NOTEBOOK
Kindlelight Debut returned refreshed after a three-month break and defied a career-high mark to register her sixth course win in decisive fashion. (op 7-1)
Toffee Vodka(IRE) was 5lb higher than when winning over a mile on the Polytrack at Lingfield last August. She has a tremendous record on limited appearances on this surface and is yet to finish out of the first two.
Nebraska Lady(IRE), a six-furlong juvenile winner at Ballinrobe, was making her sand debut having probably needed her first outing for her new connections at Ayr last month. (tchd 12-1)
Song Of Passion(IRE) was well backed against these older horses but her welter burden proved too much. (op 2-1 tchd 5-2)
Ginger Spice(IRE) lost the lead after hanging away from the rail on the home turn and perhaps lack of a recent run took its toll in the closing stages.
Damelza(IRE), again in a tongue strap, came in for support but did not seem to be suited to the drop back from a mile. (op 10-1)

3688 COME TO FAMILY FUN DAY ON 28TH JULY H'CAP — 1m 141y(P)
9:05 (9:05) (Class 4) (0-85,85) 3-Y-O+ — **£6,477** (£1,927; £963; £481) **Stalls** Low

Form — RPR

6200 **1** **Given A Choice (IRE)**[26] 2850 4-10-0 **85**.......... SebSanders 9 — 92
(J G Given) *sn chsng ldr: rdn over 2f out: led wl ins fnl f: r.o* **12/1**

0115 **2** ½ **Samuel Charles**[5] 3532 8-9-9 **80**.......... RobbieFitzpatrick 6 — 86
(C R Dore) *hld up in mid-div: rdn over 3f out: hdwy over 2f out: r.o wl towards fin* **7/1**

060- **3** shd **United Nations**[311] 5176 5-8-9 **69**.......... DNolan(3) 3 — 75
(N Wilson) *hld up in mid-div: rdn over 2f out: r.o wl towards fin* **66/1**

0656 **4** nk **Kingsholm**[8] 3404 4-9-2 **73**.......... LPKeniry 8 — 78
(A M Balding) *hld up in tch: rdn over 3f out: kpt on ins fnl f* **13/2**[3]

1354 **5** shd **Secret Liaison**[12] 3310 3-8-4 **70**.......... JamieMackay 1 — 74
(Sir Mark Prescott) *led: rdn over 1f out: hdd wl ins fnl f* **11/4**[1]

5021 **6** shd **Claret And Amber**[13] 3241 4-9-7 **78**.......... PaulHanagan 7 — 83
(R A Fahey) *hld up towards rr: rdn over 3f out: hdwy over 2f out: kpt on ins fnl f* **11/4**[1]

10-5 **7** 1 ¼ **Nanton (USA)**[14] 3213 4-9-12 **83**.......... JimmyFortune 4 — 85
(P F I Cole) *prom: rdn over 2f out: one pce fnl f* **14/1**

3411 **8** ½ **Bijou Dan**[19] 3101 5-8-9 **71**..........(b) DuranFentiman(5) 10 — 72
(W G Harrison) *a bhd* **5/1**[2]

6065 **9** 2 **Flighty Fellow (IRE)**[22] 2974 6-9-1 **72**..........(v) DavidAllan 2 — 69
(Miss J A Camacho) *hld up in mid-div: rdn over 3f out: wknd over 1f out* **12/1**

1m 49.23s (-2.53) **Going Correction** -0.10s/f (Stan)
WFA 3 from 4yo+ 9lb — **9** Ran SP% **119.4**
Speed ratings (Par 105):107,106,106,106,106 106,104,104,102
CSF £96.03 CT £5309.91 TOTE £17.90: £4.70, £2.80, £14.30; EX 205.10 Place 6 £242.91, Place 5 £96.66 .
Owner The G-Guck Group **Bred** Rathasker Stud **Trained** Willoughton, Lincs
■ Stewards' Enquiry : Paul Hanagan one-day ban: used whip with excessive frequency (Jul 31)

FOCUS
The first six home were covered by around a length in this very competitive little handicap. The pace was decent and the form looks solid enough rated around the first two.
T/Plt: £72.00 to a £1 stake. Pool: £51,704.10. 523.90 winning tickets. T/Qpdt: £15.20 to a £1 stake. Pool: £3,501.00. 169.70 winning tickets. KH

3662 VICHY

Thursday, July 20

OFFICIAL GOING: Good to soft

3692a PRIX MUNET (GENTLEMEN-RIDERS) 5f

7:23 (7:21) 3-Y-0+ **£6,897** (£2,759; £2,069; £1,379; £690)

			RPR
1		**Protector (SAF)**[140] 563 5-10-12 ... MrEMonfort 5 (Diego Lowther, France)	95
2	½	**Kourka (FR)**[28] 4-10-2 ... MrFGuy 4 (J-M Beguigne, France)	84
3	2	**Prinsycios (FR)**[547] 11-10-9 ... MrJFonzo 3 (J Fonzo, France)	84
4	hd	**Lord Mayor**[43] 2341 5-10-5 ... MrDHDunsdon 7 (R M H Cowell) *held up, ridden & outpaced 2f out, headway on outside from distance, nearest at finish (7/1 cpld)* 7/1[1]	79
5	1	**Canadian Danehill (IRE)**[9] 3374 4-10-5 ... MrESelter 12 (R M H Cowell) *broke well on ouside, close up til outpaced half-way, ridden 2f out, kept on steadily (7/1cpld)* 7/1[1]	76
6	nk	**American Gatto (USA)**[195] 4-10-12 ...(b) MrCRossi 2 (J Rossi, France)	81
7	shd	**Spyros (FR)**[315] 8-10-5 ... MrVGelhay 8 (H Gelhay, France)	74
8	nk	**Forever Bond (BRZ)**[28] 5-10-5 ...(b) MrHNaggar 11 (Robert Collet, France)	73
9	2 ½	**Lothaire (FR)**[410] 5-10-5 ... MrTBeaurain 10 (D Allard, France)	64
10	1	**Frescatie (FR)**[84] 4-10-2 ... MrYMergirie 6 (R Kleparski, France)	58
11		**First Hostess (IRE)**[18] 3-9-12 ...(b) MrBVaubernier 9 (J-J Boutin, France)	58
12		**Blazing Fact (IRE)**[28] 8-10-5 ...(b) MrJ-PBoisgontier 1 (Alex Vanderhaeghen, Belgium)	61

56.00 secs
WFA 3 from 4yo+ 4lb 12 Ran SP% **25.0**
PARI-MUTUEL (including one euro stakes): WIN 4.70; PL 1.70, 1.30,1.50; DF 8.20.
Owner James L Atkinson **Bred** Dr M Thomson (ambiance Stud) **Trained** France

NOTEBOOK
Lord Mayor ran quite well considering the big drop in trip, but he looks sure to do better when returning to a more suitable distance.
Canadian Danehill(IRE) is more suited to this trip than his stablemate, but he is rated a stone lower on official ratings and came out second-best.

3286 CARLISLE (R-H)

Friday, July 21

OFFICIAL GOING: Firm (good to firm in places)

Wind: Breezy, across

3693 ARCHITECTS PLUS MAIDEN AUCTION STKS 5f

2:10 (2:10) (Class 5) 2-Y-O **£3,238** (£963; £481; £240) **Stalls High**

Form				RPR
330	1		**Startolini**[52] 2106 2-8-7 ... PaulEddery 4 (B Smart) *mde all: rdn over 1f out: r.o strly* 13/2[2]	67
232	2	1 ½	**Princess Ileana (IRE)**[19] 3120 2-8-7 ... FrancisNorton 5 (K R Burke) *keen: trckd ldrs: effrt and chsd wnr over 1f out: edgd lft: kpt on same pce ins fnl f* 1/4[1]	61
65	3	2	**Wanchai Night**[23] 2972 2-8-12 ... DavidAllan 3 (T D Easterby) *keen: prom: rdn 1/2-way: kpt on same pce fnl f* 11/1[3]	59
060	4	1 ¾	**Alavana (IRE)**[26] 2890 2-8-7 ... PaulHanagan 2 (D W Barker) *cl up tl rdn and no ex over 1f out* 25/1	48
	5	50	**Neveronamonday (IRE)** 2-8-4 ... PaulQuinn 1 (A Berry) *s.v.s: a wl bhd* 40/1	—

61.78 secs (0.28) **Going Correction** -0.125s/f (Firm) 5 Ran SP% **108.0**
Speed ratings (Par 94):92,89,86,83,3
CSF £8.42 TOTE £6.50: £2.40, £1.02; EX 11.30.
Owner Gerry Slater & Allen Evans **Bred** Lt-Col And Mrs R Bromley Gardner **Trained** Hambleton, N Yorks

FOCUS
An uncompetitive race in which the gallop was only fair and the form does not look solid.

NOTEBOOK
Startolini, disappointing and beaten before stamina became an issue upped to six furlongs at Redcar last time, showed that to be all wrong with this workmanlike success. She should prove effective over that longer trip but her short-term future depends on how the Handicapper views this win. (op 6-1 tchd 7-1)
Princess Ileana(IRE) looked the one to beat on previous evidence but proved a disappointment after taking a fair grip early on and edging off a true line when asked for an effort. However, she may prove better suited to softer ground and is capable of winning a similar event. (op 1-3)
Wanchai Night took the eye in the paddock and ran his best race yet. Although he is likely to remain vulnerable in this type of event, he will be of more interest over six furlongs in ordinary nursery company. (op 9-1)
Alavana(IRE), who turned in an improved effort at Pontefract last time, failed to build on that back in distance and she is going to continue to look vulnerable in this type of event. (op 16-1)
Neveronamonday(IRE) looked in need of the outing on this racecourse debut and showed nothing after a very sluggish start. (op 33-1)

3694 DONLEYS CLAIMING STKS 1m 3f 107y

2:45 (2:45) (Class 6) 3-Y-O+ **£2,730** (£806; £403) **Stalls Low**

Form				RPR
2104	1		**Sualda (IRE)**[14] 3248 7-9-13 79 ... PaulHanagan 1 (R A Fahey) *chsd ldr: led 2f out: sn pushed clr: eased ins fnl f* 4/11[1]	78+
6552	2	5	**Regency Red (IRE)**[2] 3637 8-9-0 51 ... LiamJones(5) 4 (W M Brisbourne) *dwlt: hld up: effrt 3f out: kpt on to go 2nd wl ins fnl f: no ch w wnr* 6/1[2]	57
0006	3	nk	**Evolution Ex (USA)**[13] 3309 4-9-13 70 ... PatCosgrave 3 (K R Burke) *led to 2f out: sn one pce* 7/1[3]	65
-000	4	3 ½	**Buddy Brown**[50] 2162 4-9-13 72 ... TomEaves 2 (J Howard Johnson) *chsd ldrs: drvn over 2f out: sn btn* 14/1	59

2m 23.02s (-4.98) **Going Correction** 0.0s/f (Good) 4 Ran SP% **106.8**
Speed ratings (Par 101):99,95,95,92
CSF £2.86 TOTE £1.40; EX 2.10.The winner was claimed by Diamond Racing Ltd for £15,000.
Owner J H Tattersall **Bred** St Simon Foundation **Trained** Musley Bank, N Yorks

FOCUS
A most uncompetitive event in which the market leader did not have to improve to win with plenty in hand. The runner-up sets the standard.

3695 CUBBY CONSTRUCTION H'CAP 1m 1f 61y

3:15 (3:15) (Class 5) (0-70,74) 3-Y-O **£3,238** (£963; £481; £240) **Stalls High**

Form				RPR
-151	1		**Prince Picasso**[12] 3338 3-9-13 74 6ex ... SebSanders 2 (Sir Mark Prescott) *pressed ldr: led 2f out: drvn out* 6/4[1]	85+
2052	2	1 ¾	**Mambo Sun**[3] 3609 3-9-2 63 ... PaulHanagan 3 (P A Blockley) *led to 2f out: kpt on u.p fnl f* 7/1[3]	70
1244	3	1 ¼	**English City (IRE)**[29] 2795 3-8-9 56 ... PaulEddery 1 (B Smart) *hld up: effrt over 2f out: kpt on fnl f: nt rch first two* 12/1	61
4421	4	3	**Farne Island**[3] 3609 3-8-11 58 ... GrahamGibbons 8 (J J Quinn) *keen: chsd ldrs: effrt over 2f out: no ex over 1f out* 11/4[2]	57
5006	5	1 ½	**Crimson Flame (IRE)**[7] 3469 3-9-4 65 ...(v) TonyCulhane 10 (M R Channon) *hld up ins: effrt over 2f out: no imp* 16/1	61
-516	6	1	**Decree Nisi**[20] 3082 3-9-4 65 ... RoystonFfrench 4 (Mrs A Duffield) *prom tl rdn and outpcd fr 2f out* 20/1	59
0012	7	¾	**Jill Dawson (IRE)**[22] 3030 3-8-11 58 ... FrancisNorton 7 (John Berry) *hld up midfield: effrt outside 3f out: hung lft and sn no imp* 7/1[3]	50
4350	8	¾	**Dancing Flame**[14] 3250 3-8-6 53 ... DavidAllan 6 (E J Alston) *hld up: drvn over 3f out: nvr on terms* 16/1	44
5600	9	2	**Sunbolt (IRE)**[10] 3378 3-8-11 58 ... PhillipMakin 9 (T D Barron) *hld up: rdn over 3f out: sn btn* 33/1	45

1m 55.65s (-1.91) **Going Correction** 0.0s/f (Good) 9 Ran SP% **118.8**
Speed ratings (Par 100):108,106,105,102,101 100,99,99,97
CSF £13.38 CT £96.25 TOTE £2.20: £1.40, £2.10, £3.00; EX 13.80.
Owner Syndicate 2004 **Bred** Cheveley Park Stud Ltd **Trained** Newmarket, Suffolk

FOCUS
A run-of-the-mill event but one in which it paid to race up with the ordinary pace and Prince Picasso continued on his upward curve. The placed horses set the level for the form.
Jill Dawson(IRE) Official explanation: trainer said filly was found to have pulled muscles in her hindquarters

3696 WEATHERBYS INSURANCE BURGH BARONY PLATE (H'CAP) 2m 1f 52y

3:50 (3:50) (Class 4) (0-80,74) 4-Y-O+ **£6,477** (£1,927; £963; £481) **Stalls High**

Form				RPR
1211	1		**Key Time (IRE)**[3] 3607 4-9-13 74 6ex ... SebSanders 5 (Sir Mark Prescott) *chsd ldrs: pushed along 5f out: rallied and ev ch fr 3f out: led ins fnl f: styd on wl* 1/3[1]	84+
0-41	2	1 ¼	**Lodgician (IRE)**[13] 3291 4-8-13 60 ... GrahamGibbons 1 (J J Quinn) *keen: trckd ldrs: led 1/2-way: rdn over 2f out: hdd ins fnl f: r.o: no ex towards fin* 15/2[2]	68
3312	3	2	**Mister Arjay (USA)**[3] 3607 6-8-13 60 ... TomEaves 4 (B Ellison) *led to 1/2-way: chsd ldrs: drvn and outpcd over 3f out: rallied over 1f out: no ch w first two* 8/1[3]	66
166	4	3 ½	**Mulligan's Pride (IRE)**[13] 3284 5-8-5 57 ... AndrewElliott(5) 2 (G A Swinbank) *hld up in tch: effrt outside over 3f out: outpcd and hung rt over 2f out: n.d after* 20/1	59
0505	5	½	**Rule For Ever**[22] 3019 4-8-8 60 ...(t) GregFairley(5) 3 (M Johnston) *cl up tl rdn and wknd fr 2f out* 20/1	61

3m 48.2s (-1.70) **Going Correction** 0.0s/f (Good) 5 Ran SP% **107.4**
Speed ratings (Par 105):104,103,102,100,100
CSF £3.12 TOTE £1.30: £1.10, £2.50; EX 3.50.
Owner G Moore - Osborne House **Bred** Airlie Stud **Trained** Newmarket, Suffolk
■ Stewards' Enquiry : Seb Sanders one-day ban: used whip with excessive frequency (Aug 1)

FOCUS
A modest race in which the progressive types filled the first two places but only run at an ordinary gallop for much of the way. The form is relatively weak with the fourth the best guide.

3697 ASD METAL SERVICES CARLISLE H'CAP 6f 192y

4:25 (4:26) (Class 5) (0-70,62) 3-Y-O+ **£3,238** (£963; £481; £240) **Stalls High**

Form				RPR
0544	1		**Champain Sands (IRE)**[13] 3298 7-8-12 55 ... StephenDonohoe(5) 7 (E J Alston) *hld up: smooth hdwy 2f out: rdn to ld wl ins fnl f: comf* 9/2[2]	66
-211	2	1	**Pay Time**[9] 3398 7-8-13 56 6ex ... MichaelJStainton(5) 5 (R E Barr) *keen: trckd ldrs: led 2f out to wl ins fnl f: no ex* 6/1[3]	64
25-1	3	1 ¼	**Carnivore**[25] 2926 4-9-9 61 ... PaulFessey 2 (T D Barron) *prom: effrt and swtchd to r along stands side over 2f out: rdn and hung rt over 1f out: no ex ins fnl f* 6/4[1]	66+
0000	4	shd	**Uhuru Peak**[13] 3298 5-8-13 51 ...(t) DaleGibson 8 (M W Easterby) *prom: effrt 2f out: kpt on same pce ins fnl f* 16/1	55
2000	5	1	**Out Of India**[66] 1760 4-9-5 62 ... MarkLawson(5) 6 (B Smart) *hld up in tch: effrt over 2f out: no imp over 1f out* 12/1	64
-000	6	nk	**Borodinsky**[9] 3398 5-8-12 50 ... TomEaves 1 (R E Barr) *led to 2f out: wknd appr fnl f* 25/1	51
0000	7	½	**Flaxby**[11] 3361 4-8-12 50 ...(b) FrancisNorton 3 (J D Bethell) *hld up: rdn over 2f out: nvr rchd ldrs* 10/1	50
6034	8	½	**Attacca**[11] 3361 5-9-3 55 ... SebSanders 4 (J R Weymes) *chsd ldr: effrt over 2f out: wknd ins fnl f* 13/2	54

1m 26.02s (-1.08) **Going Correction** 0.0s/f (Good) 8 Ran SP% **112.3**
Speed ratings (Par 103):106,104,103,103,102 101,101,100
CSF £30.29 CT £57.78 TOTE £4.60: £1.40, £1.80, £1.10; EX 33.40.
Owner Geoff & Astrid Long **Bred** Gerrardstown House Stud **Trained** Longton, Lancs

FOCUS
An ordinary handicap run at a fair pace and one in which the market leader was the only one to switch to the stands' side early in the straight. The form is sound enough rated around the first two.

3698 BAINES WILSON MAIDEN STKS 6f 192y

4:55 (4:58) (Class 5) 3-Y-O+ **£3,238** (£963; £481; £240) **Stalls High**

Form				RPR
5-33	1		**Grand Opera (IRE)**[66] 1759 3-9-3 77 ... TomEaves 5 (J Howard Johnson) *missed break: hdwy 1/2-way: drvn to ld ent fnl f: styd on wl* 5/4[1]	59
5243	2	nk	**Spinning**[10] 3384 3-9-3 72 ... PaulFessey 6 (T D Barron) *dwlt: bhd: effrt ins over 2f out: ev ch 1f out: kpt on fnl f: jst hld* 9/4[2]	58
5332	3	1	**Naval Attache**[10] 3386 4-9-10 49 ... PhillipMakin 7 (P A Blockley) *led: hrd pressed fr over 2f out: hdd 1f out: kpt on same pce towards fin* 9/2[3]	58
0000	4	6	**Zantero**[7] 3480 4-9-7 42 ... DNolan(3) 1 (W M Brisbourne) *keen: chsd ldrs: chal over 2f out tl wknd over 1f out* 33/1	42

-050 **5** *shd* **Inchmarlow (IRE)**[39] 2504 3-8-12 50...................... DuranFentiman(5) 10 39
(T H Caldwell) *s.i.s: bhd tl sme hdwy on ins over 1f out: n.d* **12/1**
004 **6** *1 3/4* **Active Audience (IRE)**[10] 3384 3-8-12 55...............(b) FrancisNorton 11 29
(A Berry) *chsd ldrs tl wknd fr 2f out* **25/1**
4-00 **7** *10* **Bottomless Wallet**[35] 2615 5-9-5 42..........................(p) TonyHamilton 9 5
(F Watson) *in tch tl rdn and wknd fr 2f out* **66/1**
0000 **8** *8* **Warren Place**[21] 3050 6-9-7 36.............................. SilvestreDeSousa(3) 8 —
(A D Brown) *bhd: drvn 1/2-way: nvr on terms* **66/1**
00-0 **9** *1 1/2* **Beacon Rambler**[22] 3001 4-9-5 44............................... MarkLawson(5) 2 —
(F Watson) *chsd ldrs: rdn 3f out: sn btn* **100/1**
00 **10** *19* **Wee Ziggy**[86] 1230 3-9-3.. PaulQuinn 3 —
(D Nicholls) *unruly bef s: racd wd in rr: struggling fr 1/2-way* **40/1**
0- **11** *4* **Newcastles Owen (IRE)**[262] 6212 3-8-12 .... DeclanMcGann(5) 4 —
(R Johnson) *s.i.s: sn midfield on outside: effrt over 3f out: wknd over 2f out* **50/1**

1m 26.86s (-0.24) **Going Correction** 0.0s/f (Good)
WFA 3 from 4yo+ 7lb **11** Ran SP% **116.3**
Speed ratings (Par 103):100,99,98,91,91 89,78,68,67,45 40
CSF £3.86 TOTE £2.40: £1.10, £1.30, £1.50; EX 5.40.
Owner Transcend Bloodstock LLP **Bred** Ballyhane Stud **Trained** Billy Row, Co Durham
■ Stewards' Enquiry : Paul Fessey one-day ban: used whip with excessive frequency (Aug 1)
Tom Eaves one-day ban: used whip with excessive frequency (Aug 4)

FOCUS
A race lacking any strength and the proximity of the 49-rated third confirms this form is modest at best.

3699 ROSS LLOYD LTD H'CAP 5f
5:25 (5:26) (Class 5) (0-70,68) 3-Y-0+ **£3,238** (£963; £481; £240) **Stalls** High

Form RPR
5022 **1** **Aegean Dancer**[17] 3170 4-9-6 **68**................................ MarkLawson(5) 4 77
(B Smart) *chsd ldrs: disp ld 2f out: sn rdn: kpt on wl fnl f to ld cl home* **7/2**[2]
0402 **2** *hd* **True Magic**[3] 3622 5-9-10 **67**... SebSanders 1 75
(J D Bethell) *cl up: led over 1f out: edgd rt u.p ins fnl f: hdd cl home* **9/2**[3]
0541 **3** *1 1/4* **Rudi's Pet (IRE)**[11] 3354 12-9-2 **66** 6ex....................(v) VictoriaBehan(7) 9 70
(D Nicholls) *chsd ldrs: effrt 2f out: edgd rt: kpt on fnl f* **5/1**
1602 **4** *1 1/2* **Parkside Pursuit**[8] 3438 8-9-8 **65**................................ PhillipMakin 10 63
(J M Bradley) *hld up in tch: effrt 2f out: no imp fnl f* **13/2**
-453 **5** *3/4* **Tomthevic**[11] 3348 8-8-6 **49** oh7.......................................(p) PaulFessey 7 44
(J M Bradley) *led to over 1f out: sn outpcd* **10/1**
024 **6** *2* **Trick Cyclist**[27] 2852 5-9-5 **62**.......................................(p) DaleGibson 8 50
(M W Easterby) *s.i.s: rdn in rr 1/2-way: no imp over 1f out* **11/4**[1]
0004 **7** *2* **Beyond The Clouds (IRE)**[6] 3525 10-9-0 **57**.................. GylesParkin 3 38
(J S Wainwright) *hld up outside: rdn over 2f out: sn btn* **33/1**
0000 **8** *1/2* **Fairgame Man**[3] 3608 8-8-1 **49** oh3.......................(v) DuranFentiman(5) 6 28
(J S Wainwright) *in tch to 1/2-way: sn rdn and btn* **16/1**

60.32 secs (-1.18) **Going Correction** -0.125s/f (Firm) **8** Ran SP% **115.0**
Speed ratings (Par 103):104,103,101,99,98 94,91,90
CSF £19.79 CT £78.02 TOTE £3.90: £1.50, £2.00, £1.90; EX 26.30 Place 6 £1.80, Place 5 £1.73.
Owner Pinnacle Piccolo Partnership **Bred** Theobalds Stud **Trained** Hambleton, N Yorks

FOCUS
An ordinary event run at a decent gallop but favouring those racing close to the pace. The runner-up is the best guide to the form.
Trick Cyclist Official explanation: jockey said gelding slipped on leaving stalls
T/Plt: £2.80 to a £1 stake. Pool: £32,271.60. 8,267.95 winning tickets. T/Qpdt: £1.90 to a £1 stake. Pool: £1,994.90. 767.40 winning tickets. RY

[3221]NEWBURY (L-H)
Friday, July 21

OFFICIAL GOING: Good to firm (firm in places in back straight)
Wind: Very slight, across

3700 HILLWOOD STUD E B F MAIDEN FILLIES' STKS 6f 8y
2:00 (2:02) (Class 4) 2-Y-0 **£6,477** (£1,927; £963; £481) **Stalls** Centre

Form RPR
4264 **1** **Vital Statistics**[21] 3043 2-9-0 .... JohnEgan 3 77
(D R C Elsworth) *trckd ldrs: led ins final 2f: pushed along ins last: rdn to hold narrow advantage cl home* **4/1**[2]
36 **2** *hd* **Party (IRE)**[21] 3043 2-9-0 .... RichardHughes 12 76
(R Hannon) *in tch: drvn and qcknd to chse wnr 1f out: str run cl home: nt quite get up* **13/2**[3]
3 *2 1/2* **Small Fortune** 2-9-0 .... SteveDrowne 5 69
(R Charlton) *unf: scope: mid-div: drvn and one pce 2f out: styd on wl fnl f: gng on cl home* **14/1**
4 *nk* **Russian Rosie (IRE)** 2-9-0 .... TPQueally 1 68
(J G Portman) *leggy: slowly away: sn rcvrd to get into mid-div: trckd ldrs 2f out: kpt on same pce ins last* **40/1**
5 *1/2* **Alecia (IRE)** 2-8-11 .... AdamKirby(3) 13 67
(C G Cox) *w'like: strong: b.bkwd: slt ld tl hdd ins fnl 2f: styd front rnk tl wknd ins last* **20/1**
6 *1* **Regal Quest (IRE)** 2-9-0 .... JimmyFortune 6 64
(S Kirk) *unf: scope: b.bkwd: bhd: rdn over 2f out: kpt on ins last: styng on cl home* **14/1**
7 *1/2* **Roshanak (IRE)** 2-9-0 .... JamieSpencer 8 62
(B J Meehan) *w'like: b.bkwd: s.i.s: bhd: drvn over 2f out: edgd rt ins last: kpt on wl cl home* **16/1**
50 **8** *shd* **Splendored Love (USA)**[16] 3201 2-9-0 .... RyanMoore 7 62
(R Hannon) *w ldrs: rdn 2f out: wknd ins fnl f* **16/1**
9 *shd* **Nadawat (USA)** 2-9-0 .... RHills 15 61
(J L Dunlop) *w'like: scope: sn in tch: pushed along over 2f out: one pce fnl f* **7/2**[1]
0 **10** *shd* **Blue Mistral (IRE)**[24] 2957 2-9-0 .... PaulDoe 4 61
(W J Knight) *w ldrs: rdn over 2f out: wknd fnl f* **50/1**
0 **11** *1 1/2* **Apache Dream (IRE)**[24] 2957 2-9-0 .... LDettori 2 57+
(B J Meehan) *chsd ldrs: shkn up over 1f out: eased whn btn ins last* **13/2**[3]
12 *3/4* **Cow Girl (IRE)** 2-9-0 .... MartinDwyer 14 54
(A M Balding) *unf: b.bkwd: bhd sme hdwy into mid-div 1/2-way: nvr in contention* **33/1**
13 *3/4* **Queen Of Fools (IRE)** 2-9-0 .... PatDobbs 11 52
(R Hannon) *b.bkwd: s.i.s: a outpcd* **33/1**
14 *3 1/2* **Lake Pontchartrain (IRE)** 2-9-0 .... GeorgeBaker 10 42
(S Kirk) *w'like: w ldrs over 3f* **33/1**
15 *1/2* **Queen's Fortune (IRE)** 2-9-0 .... TedDurcan 9 40
(M R Channon) *unf: b.bkwd: slowly away and sn bdly outpcd: nvr in contention but did stay on fnl f* **16/1**

1m 13.25s (-1.07) **Going Correction** -0.275s/f (Firm) **15** Ran SP% **117.9**
Speed ratings (Par 93):96,95,92,92,91 90,89,89,89,88 86,85,84,80,79
CSF £27.01 TOTE £4.70: £1.60, £2.50, £5.00; EX 20.10.
Owner Setsquare Recruitment **Bred** M P B Bloodstock Ltd **Trained** Newmarket, Suffolk

FOCUS
A race that has produced several subsequent two-year-old Group 1 winners in the past, although with the betting market going 14/1 bar four and the race dominated by two of the most experienced it will be surprising if this year's renewal lives up to previous seasons'. However, the winner seemed to run right up to her Royal Ascot form.

NOTEBOOK
Vital Statistics, who finished sixth in the Queen Mary before getting beaten in a Newmarket maiden, finally came good and confirmed Headquarters running with today's runner-up. The pair had the race to themselves in the final furlong and set the standard for the form. (op 7-2)
Party(IRE) who was hampered late on when finishing two lengths behind today's winner at Newmarket, followed that rival through and had every chance inside the final furlong, but was always just being held. She should be not too long in getting off the mark. (op 11-2)
Small Fortune ◆ made an encouraging debut, staying on really well in the closing stages without troubling the first two, having been held up at the back. She should come on for this and has races in her.
Russian Rosie(IRE) ◆, a half-sister to the useful Russian Ruby, caught the eye making late progress, having been slowly into her stride. She was doing her best work at the finish and shapes as though another furlong will suit her.
Alecia(IRE) ◆, the first British representative of her sire, who won the Lockinge here in his racing days, made a promising debut, showing up throughout and only fading in the last furlong or so. She looks sure to come on for the run and a maiden is within her compass. (tchd 22-1)
Regal Quest(IRE), who is bred to get middle-distances, was noted keeping on at the end despite running green and should do better when getting a stiffer test of stamina.
Roshanak(IRE) was supported in the market but never really figured on this debut.
Nadawat(USA), the first foal of the useful Tashawak, looked fit enough but got upset in the stalls and, after showing up early, was well beaten. Her dam was a steady improver and it will be a surprise if she cannot do better with this behind her. (op 5-1 tchd 11-2 in a place)
Apache Dream(IRE) ran better than on her debut under a positive ride, but dropped away when the principals kicked on. (op 11-2)

3701 HIGHCLERE THOROUGHBRED RACING MAIDEN STKS 7f (S)
2:30 (2:38) (Class 4) 2-Y-0 **£6,477** (£1,927; £963; £481) **Stalls** Centre

Form RPR
1 **Aqmaar** 2-9-3 .... RHills 6 86
(J L Dunlop) *w'like: scope: lengthy: chsd ldrs: led wl over 1f out: sn drvn: kpt on strly cl home* **9/1**
2 *1 1/4* **Putra Square** 2-9-3 .... EddieAhern 7 83
(P F I Cole) *w'like: scope: sn led: rdn and hdd wl over 1f out: styd chsng wnr but a readily hld* **16/1**
3 *nk* **Monzante (USA)** 2-9-3 .... SteveDrowne 15 82
(R Charlton) *leggy: bhd: pushed along 1/2-way: hdwy fr 2f out: styd on wl fnl f: gng on cl home* **20/1**
4 *nk* **Regal Flush** 2-9-3 .... JimmyFortune 4 81
(Sir Michael Stoute) *scope: lw: in tch: rdn over 2f out: kpt on fr over 1f out but nvr gng pce to chal* **3/1**[2]
5 *2* **Sowdrey** 2-9-3 .... TedDurcan 18 76
(M R Channon) *unf: chsd ldrs: rdn over 2f out: outpcd ins last* **33/1**
4 **6** *1/2* **Eager Lover (USA)**[101] 961 2-9-3 .... JamieSpencer 16 75
(B W Hills) *missed break and plld hrd: sn racing alone towards stands' side and chsng wnr: rdn 2f out: wknd ins last* **7/1**[3]
22 **7** *1* **Folio (USA)**[33] 2680 2-9-3 .... RichardHughes 1 72
(B W Hills) *lw: in tch: rdn over 2f out: nvr gng pce to rch ldrs and one pce* **11/4**[1]
8 *2 1/2* **Irish Dancer** 2-8-12 .... TPQueally 3 61
(J L Dunlop) *leggy: mid-div: pushed along 1/2-way: sme prog fnl f* **66/1**
9 *1 3/4* **Bold Abbott (USA)** 2-9-3 .... JimCrowley 17 61
(Mrs A J Perrett) *unf: b.bkwd: hld up in rr: pushed along and green 3f out: kpt on ins last but nvr in contention* **40/1**
10 *hd* **Leonide** 2-9-3 .... MichaelTebbutt 11 60
(B J Meehan) *w'like: strong: mid-div: pushed along 1/2-way: nvr in contention* **100/1**
0 **11** *1 1/4* **Alnwick**[36] 2572 2-9-3 .... FergusSweeney 5 57
(P D Cundell) *nvr bttr than mid-div* **66/1**
12 *3/4* **Cry Presto (USA)** 2-9-3 .... RyanMoore 9 55
(R Hannon) *strong: b.bkwd: s.i.s: sn rdn: outpcd most of way* **10/1**
13 *1/2* **Toggle** 2-9-3 .... PatDobbs 13 54
(R Hannon) *b.bkwd: chsd ldrs: rdn over 2f out: wknd wl over 1f out* **66/1**
0 **14** *nk* **Grimes Glory**[23] 2979 2-9-3 .... RichardSmith 12 53
(R Hannon) *pressed ldrs: rdn over 2f out: wknd over 1f out* **100/1**
15 *3/4* **Moheebb (IRE)** 2-9-3 .... MartinDwyer 8 51
(M P Tregoning) *w'like: scope: wnt lft s: a in rr* **9/1**
16 *2 1/2* **Dan Tucker** 2-9-3 .... LDettori 2 45
(B J Meehan) *w'like: scope: nvr bttr than mid-div: no ch fnl 2f* **16/1**
17 *11* **Straw Boy** 2-9-3 .... ChrisCatlin 10 16
(M R Channon) *unf: scope: b.bkwd: s.i.s: a outpcd* **50/1**

1m 26.57s (-0.43) **Going Correction** -0.275s/f (Firm) **17** Ran SP% **123.6**
Speed ratings (Par 96):91,89,89,88,86 86,84,82,80,79 78,77,76,76,75 72,60
CSF £137.88 TOTE £11.00: £2.90, £5.50, £6.40; EX 270.60.
Owner Hamdan Al Maktoum **Bred** Shadwell Estate Company Limited **Trained** Arundel, W Sussex

FOCUS
A decent maiden featuring a number of well-bred sorts. However, it was run at a steady gallop - the time was the slowest of the three over the trip on the day - and few came from off the pace.

NOTEBOOK
Aqmaar ◆, a half-brother to the same owner's Estiqraar, was not easy to load on this debut but travelled well in the race, just behind the leaders, and having picked up to lead over a furlong out, ran on well to repel several challengers. He looked as if the outing will bring him on and he could well make up into a decent colt. (op 12-1)
Putra Square ◆, a speedily-bred newcomer from an in-form yard, knew his job and made the running until headed by the winner. However, he did not drop away and was running on again at the line. He has a fair amount of scope and should be winning before too long. (op 14-1)
Monzante(USA) ◆, a debutant related to a number of winners, did well to finish where he did, having been held up off a steady gallop. He was doing his best work in the final furlong and can be expected to improve a good deal for the run. (tchd 16-1)
Regal Flush ◆, a half-brother to the Cheveley Park winner Regal Rose, drifted out from favourite and was restive in the stalls. However, he performed well despite running green and, like several of those around him, will be better for the outing. (op 5-2)
Sowdrey, by In The Wings out of a decent racemare, ran a fine race over a trip that will be on the short side for him in time. After racing prominently, he just got outpaced when the leaders quickened but picked up again inside the last furlong. He may need a little more time, but is one to keep an eye on.

Eager Lover(USA), who had been absent for over 14 weeks since his debut, clearly benefited from being given time to develop. He showed promise, having raced keenly up with the leaders, but isolated towards the stands' side, for a long way. (op 9-1 tchd 10-1)
Folio(USA) backed down to favourite and with two decent efforts at six furlongs under his belt, was held up and never got into a challenging position in a race run at a steady gallop. However, he was upsides the eventual fourth inside the quarter-mile pole so this has to be viewed as a disappointing effort. (op 4-1)
Irish Dancer never got involved but did not run too badly and will appreciate longer trips. (op 50-1)
Leonide stoutly-bred on the dam's side, was another who shaped quite promisingly but looks as if he will need more time. (op 80-1)

3702 LILLIAN SUMMERS MEMORIAL CONDITIONS STKS — 7f (S)
3:05 (3:06) (Class 3) 3-Y-0+ **£8,101** (£2,425; £1,212; £607) **Stalls** Centre

Form | | | | RPR
112- **1** **Caradak (IRE)**[293] 5638 5-9-0 114 ... LDettori 2 — 105+
(Saeed Bin Suroor) *lw: led 1f: styd trcking ldr: chal appr fnl f: led ins: drvn to assert fnl 100yds* **2/7**[1]
0-10 **2** ½ **Saville Road**[30] 2739 3-8-7 97 ... ShaneKelly 4 — 101
(D J Daly) *led after 1f: rdn 2f out: narrowly hdd ins last: outpcd fnl 100yds* **7/1**[2]
0-23 **3** 6 **Grimes Faith**[92] 1091 3-8-1 83 ... StephaneBreux(3) 3 — 82
(R Hannon) *chsd ldrs in 3rd: rdn and no imp over 2f out: no ch fr over 1f out* **28/1**
21- **4** 9 **Rosinka (IRE)**[359] 3840 3-7-13 ... NickyMackay 1 — 54+
(J L Dunlop) *a last: rdn 1/2-way: lost tch fnl 2f* **8/1**[3]

1m 23.01s (-3.99) **Going Correction** -0.275s/f (Firm)
WFA 3 from 4yo+ 7lb — 4 Ran SP% **104.8**
Speed ratings (Par 107):111,110,103,93
CSF £2.45 TOTE £1.20; EX 2.20.
Owner Godolphin **Bred** His Highness The Aga Khan's Studs S C **Trained** Newmarket, Suffolk

FOCUS
An uncompetitive conditions' event which went much as the betting suggested, with Caradak different class. The time was decent, being much faster than the two other races over the trip on the day.

NOTEBOOK
Caradak(IRE) had not been seen since finishing runner-up in the Group 1 Prix de La Foret when owned by the Aga Khan but had 17lb and more in hand of his rivals on official ratings. In the end he scored more cosily than the official margin suggests, but this was nowhere near his best form. It will do his confidence good though, and he can be expected to be contesting Group races again from now . (tchd 1-4)
Saville Road, with 17lb to find with the winner on official ratings, was given a positive ride and briefly over a furlong out looked like he might hold on. However, he could not resist that rival's challenge and is slightly flattered by the official margin. It is hoped that the Handicapper does not take the form too literally. (op 13-2 tchd 8-1)
Grimes Faith, a decent handicapper returning after a 13-week break, had two stone to find with the winner on official ratings and ran as well as could be expected. (op 20-1)
Rosinka(IRE), relatively unexposed but returning from just short of a year off, did not give much cause for optimism and was well beaten. (op 6-1)

3703 TURFSURF EQUINE SURFACING FILLIES' H'CAP — 1m 2f 6y
3:35 (3:35) (Class 4) (0-80,77) 3-Y-0+ **£5,505** (£1,637; £818; £408) **Stalls** Centre

Form | | | | RPR
0313 **1** **Kahlua Kiss**[13] 3318 3-9-3 76 ... MartinDwyer 5 — 86
(W R Muir) *lw: t.k.h: trckd ldrs: led over 2f out: hrd drvn and hld on wl fnl f* **7/2**[1]
-625 **2** 1½ **Noora (IRE)**[26] 2892 5-9-11 77 ... (v) AdamKirby(3) 3 — 85
(C G Cox) *lw: hld up in rr: swtchd to outside and gd hdwy fr 2f out to chse wnr fnl f: sn hrd drvn and a hld* **6/1**
16-3 **3** 2½ **Bracklinn**[20] 3095 4-9-3 66 ... JamieSpencer 1 — 69
(J R Fanshawe) *chsd ldr 7f out tl led ins fnl 4f: hdd and rdn over 2f out: wknd ins last* **9/2**[2]
0010 **4** ½ **Della Salute**[11] 3366 4-9-12 75 ... LPKeniry 8 — 77
(Miss E C Lavelle) *hld up in rr: hdwy 3f out: drvn to chse ldrs over 2f out: nvr gng pce to chal: wknd fnl f* **20/1**
-001 **5** 2½ **Golden Applause (FR)**[21] 3036 4-9-10 73 ... EddieAhern 2 — 70
(Mrs A L M King) *chsd ldrs: rdn 3f out: wknd over 1f out* **15/2**
033 **6** 1 **Kinvara Lass (IRE)**[16] 3200 3-8-11 70 ... NickyMackay 7 — 65
(L M Cumani) *t.k.h: in tch: hdwy 3f out: wknd 2f out* **5/1**[3]
0431 **7** 1¼ **Generosia**[15] 3215 3-8-8 67 ... (t) RichardHughes 6 — 60
(A M Balding) *s.i.s: bhd: rdn over 2f out: nvr in contention* **9/2**[2]
0506 **8** 7 **Uig**[53] 2067 5-9-5 68 ... JimmyFortune 4 — 48
(H S Howe) *led tl hdd ins fnl 4f: wknd ins fnl 3f* **16/1**
0600 **9** 9 **Muscari**[14] 3260 4-9-6 69 ... FrankieMcDonald 9 — 32
(A P Jarvis) *t.k.h: chsd ldr 3f: wknd ins fnl 3f* **50/1**

2m 4.81s (-3.90) **Going Correction** -0.275s/f (Firm)
WFA 3 from 4yo+ 10lb — 9 Ran SP% **113.9**
Speed ratings (Par 102):104,102,100,100,98 97,96,91,83
CSF £24.37 CT £94.73 TOTE £4.70: £1.50, £2.00, £2.00; EX 30.40 Trifecta £316.00 Pool: £623.24 - 1.40 winning tickets..
Owner M J Caddy **Bred** Whitsbury Manor Stud **Trained** Lambourn, Berks

FOCUS
A fair fillies' handicap run at a sound gallop. It has been rated fairly positively around the third and fourth, with the winner progressing and the runner-up still going the right way.
Generosia Official explanation: jockey said filly was unsuited by the good to firm (firm in places) ground

3704 SPORTING INDEX H'CAP — 1m 3f 5y
4:10 (4:10) (Class 5) (0-75,75) 3-Y-0+ **£4,857** (£1,445; £722; £360) **Stalls** Centre

Form | | | | RPR
1434 **1** **Darghan (IRE)**[15] 3232 6-8-12 59 ... TPQueally 7 — 69
(W J Musson) *swtg: hld up rr: hdwy on outside over 2f out: led over 1f out: drvn out fnl f* **6/1**[3]
4U20 **2** nk **Hatch A Plan (IRE)**[8] 3429 5-8-10 62 ... TravisBlock(5) 1 — 74+
(Mrs A J Hamilton-Fairley) *s.i.s: hdwy on ins 3f out: nt clr run over 2f out: effrt and nt clr run 1f out:sn chsng wnr but a jst hld* **18/1**
4014 **3** 1½ **Eldorado**[11] 3365 5-9-8 69 ... JimmyFortune 4 — 76
(S Kirk) *in tch: chsd ldrs 7f out: led ins fnl 3f: sn hrd drvn: hdd over 1f out: styd on same pce ins last* **9/2**[2]
36-5 **4** ½ **Swindon (USA)**[13] 3302 4-9-4 65 ... RyanMoore 10 — 71
(P F I Cole) *in tch: drvn and hdwy to chse ldrs 2f out: no ex appr fnl f* **14/1**
-022 **5** 1¾ **Lucky Leo**[14] 3248 6-9-12 73 ... JamieSpencer 5 — 76
(Ian Williams) *lw: hld up in rr: hdwy on outside over 2f out: sn rdn: no ex 1f out: wknd ins last* **2/1**[1]
3562 **6** 4 **Rajaall**[18] 3156 3-9-3 75 ... TedDurcan 6 — 71
(M R Channon) *swtg: led 1f: styd chsng ldr tl led ins fnl 4f: hdd ins fnl 3f: wknd appr fnl f* **7/1**
0011 **7** 1 **Star Of Canterbury (IRE)**[41] 2434 3-9-1 73 ... LDettori 9 — 67
(A P Jarvis) *t.k.h: led after 1f: hdd ins fnl 4f: wknd over 1f out* **9/2**[2]
0060 **8** 2½ **Hayyani (IRE)**[21] 3048 4-10-0 75 ... RichardHughes 8 — 65
(K McAuliffe) *chsd ldrs: rdn over 3f out: wknd qckly 2f out* **20/1**

2m 19.24s (-3.03) **Going Correction** -0.275s/f (Firm)
WFA 3 from 4yo+ 11lb — 8 Ran SP% **113.2**
Speed ratings (Par 103):100,99,98,98,97 94,93,91
CSF £100.12 CT £527.71 TOTE £7.60: £2.30, £3.90, £1.80; EX 154.70.
Owner S Rudolf **Bred** His Highness The Aga Khan's Studs S C **Trained** Newmarket, Suffolk

FOCUS
An ordinary handicap by Newbury standards, and the gallop was nothing special. Sound enough though, with the winner, third and fourth all to their recent form and the second rated unlucky not to win.
Lucky Leo Official explanation: jockey said gelding finished lame
Star Of Canterbury(IRE) Official explanation: jockey said gelding ducked away from horses in front approaching 3f marker

3705 SPORTING INDEX APPRENTICE H'CAP — 7f (S)
4:45 (4:46) (Class 5) (0-75,72) 3-Y-0+ **£3,238** (£963; £481; £240) **Stalls** Centre

Form | | | | RPR
5054 **1** **Linda's Colin (IRE)**[7] 3469 4-8-13 62 ... WilliamCarson(5) 4 — 73
(R A Harris) *swtg: trckd ldrs: rdn over 1f out: styd on wl to ld fnl 50yds* **9/1**
0/5- **2** 1¼ **Villarosi (IRE)**[545] 180 4-9-10 68 ... KylieManser 1 — 76
(J R Best) *chsd ldrs: pushed along 3f out: led last half f: hdd and no ex fnl 50yds* **40/1**
-342 **3** ¾ **Young Bertie**[9] 3410 3-8-4 60 ... (p) NBazeley(5) 6 — 63
(H Morrison) *lw: disp ld tl def advantage ins fnl 4f: rdn over 2f out: kpt slt advantage tl hdd and outpcd last half f* **4/1**[1]
5011 **4** ¾ **Le Chiffre (IRE)**[5] 3565 4-9-8 71 6ex ... (p) BRoper(5) 8 — 75
(R A Harris) *hld up in rr: rdn and hdwy over 2f out: chsd ldrs fr over 1f out: no ex cl home* **6/1**[3]
4252 **5** ½ **Taranaki**[10] 3390 8-9-1 59 ... JamieHamblett 7 — 61
(P D Cundell) *swtg: chsd ldrs: rdn 2f out: one pce ins last* **6/1**[3]
-000 **6** nk **Kareeb (FR)**[20] 3089 9-9-1 62 ... AlanRutter(3) 3 — 63
(W J Musson) *lw: hld up in rr: hdwy 2f out: chsd ldrs 1f out: sn one pce* **13/2**
0022 **7** shd **Dr Synn**[15] 3229 5-9-3 66 ... MarkCoumbe(5) 11 — 67
(J Akehurst) *lw: in tch: rdn over 3f out: hdwy to press ldrs over 1f out: wknd ins last* **9/2**[2]
5453 **8** nk **Pure Imagination (IRE)**[7] 3470 5-10-0 72 ... PJBenson 5 — 72
(J M Bradley) *hld up in rr: hdwy over 2f out: chsd ldrs 1f out: sn one pce* **7/1**
5456 **9** 1½ **Simpsons Ross (IRE)**[9] 3410 3-8-9 60 ... KMay 10 — 53
(R M Flower) *pressed ldrs: rdn over 2f out: wknd ins last* **25/1**
0640 **10** 3½ **Megalala (IRE)**[24] 2956 5-8-4 53 oh6 ... JosephWalsh(5) 2 — 40
(J J Bridger) *disp ld tl ins fnl 4f: styd chsng ldr: rdn over 2f out: wknd appr fnl f* **66/1**
0604 **11** 4 **Border Edge**[12] 3337 8-9-2 60 ... (v) RobbieMills 9 — 36
(J J Bridger) *outpcd most of way* **16/1**

1m 25.27s (-1.73) **Going Correction** -0.275s/f (Firm)
WFA 3 from 4yo+ 7lb — 11 Ran SP% **116.2**
Speed ratings (Par 103):98,96,95,94,94 93,93,93,91,87 83
CSF £318.89 CT £1696.40 TOTE £11.10: £3.20, £7.50, £2.10; EX 535.70 Place 6 £442.92, Place 5 £172.18.
Owner C Waters **Bred** Saud Bin Saad **Trained** Earlswood, Monmouths

FOCUS
A modest contest for the track, run 2.26sec slower than the earlier conditions race but faster than the juvenile maiden. The winner ran to this year's all-weather best, and the lightly raced runner-up improved significantly on her juvenile form.
T/Jkpt: Not won. T/Plt: £526.30 to a £1 stake. Pool: £66,193.55. 91.80 winning tickets. T/Qpdt: £38.70 to a £1 stake. Pool: £3,981.40. 75.95 winning tickets. ST

3491 NEWMARKET (JULY) (R-H)
Friday, July 21

OFFICIAL GOING: Good to firm
Wind: Light, across Weather: Overcast, but humid

3706 HOME OF HORSE RACING H'CAP — 1m 2f
5:45 (5:47) (Class 5) (0-70,70) 3-Y-0+ **£3,886** (£1,156; £577; £288) **Stalls** Centre

Form | | | | RPR
0012 **1** **Celtique**[18] 3152 4-9-8 64 ... DO'Donohoe 3 — 73
(M Wigham) *hld up: hdwy over 2f out: rdn to ld wl ins fnl f: r.o* **11/2**[2]
0001 **2** 1¼ **Padre Nostro (IRE)**[16] 3196 7-8-7 56 ... ChrisGlenister(7) 8 — 63
(J R Holt) *chsd ldrs: lost pl over 5f out: hdwy over 1f out: r.o* **25/1**
2022 **3** shd **Glendale**[27] 2862 5-8-10 52 ... JohnEgan 11 — 58
(D K Ivory) *a.p: chsd ldr over 3f out: rdn to ld ins fnl f: sn hdd and unable qckn* **11/2**[2]
6025 **4** ½ **Qualitair Wings**[8] 3429 7-9-3 59 ... DerekMcGaffin 5 — 64
(J Hetherton) *s.i.s: hdwy over 6f out: rdn over 1f out: styd on* **10/1**
5242 **5** hd **Top Spec (IRE)**[22] 3009 5-10-0 70 ... JimmyQuinn 4 — 75
(J Pearce) *dwlt: hld up: hdwy over 1f out: nt rch ldrs* **5/1**[1]
2204 **6** 1¼ **Molem**[15] 3213 4-9-12 68 ... (vt) KerrinMcEvoy 1 — 71
(Lady Herries) *led: rdn over 1f out: hdd and no ex ins fnl f* **10/1**
0000 **7** ¾ **Dubai Sunday (JPN)**[10] 3382 5-8-10 52 ... BrianReilly 9 — 53
(P S McEntee) *chsd ldr over 2f: remained handy: rdn over 2f out: styd on same pce appr fnl f* **33/1**
-213 **8** ½ **Dinner Date**[23] 2982 4-9-6 62 ... ShaneKelly 12 — 62
(T Keddy) *s.i.s: hld up: effrt and swtchd lft over 1f out: nvr nrr* **11/2**[2]
4000 **9** nk **Lenoir (GER)**[40] 2480 3-8-8 60 ... (v) ChrisCatlin 10 — 60
(V Smith) *s.i.s: hld up: nt trble ldrs* **28/1**
0-1 **10** 12 **Paradise Expected**[174] 219 3-9-4 70 ... AlanMunro 6 — 47
(P W Chapple-Hyam) *prom: rdn over 2f out: sn wknd* **8/1**[3]
30-0 **11** 6 **River Mist Image (USA)**[147] 503 4-9-10 66 ... JamieSpencer 7 — 32
(J R Fanshawe) *chsd ldrs: rdn over 1f out: sn wknd and eased* **10/1**
0305 **12** 6 **Busy Man (IRE)**[22] 3014 7-8-10 52 ... PaulDoe 2 — 6
(J R Jenkins) *s.i.s: plld hrd and sn prom: trckd ldr over 7f out tl rdn over 3f out: wkng whn nt clr run over 2f out* **25/1**

2m 4.78s (-1.66) **Going Correction** -0.05s/f (Good)
WFA 3 from 4yo+ 10lb — 12 Ran SP% **115.3**
Speed ratings (Par 103):104,103,102,102,102 101,100,100,100,90 85,80
CSF £139.07 CT £790.59 TOTE £6.30: £1.80, £6.60, £2.00; EX 95.90.

Owner D T L Limited **Bred** Wretham Stud **Trained** Newmarket, Suffolk

FOCUS

A modest handicap run at a steady early pace although the overall time was reasonable. The first two set the standard.

Busy Man(IRE) Official explanation: jockey said gelding ran too free

3707 SEE MORE ON RACING UK MAIDEN FILLIES' STKS — 7f

6:15 (6:17) (Class 4) 2-Y-O — **£4,533** (£1,348; £674; £336) **Stalls** High

Form — RPR

1 **Princess Taise (USA)** 2-9-0 .... JoeFanning 12 — 85
(M Johnston) *w ldr tl led 1/2-way: hung lft fr over 2f out: rdn over 1f out: r.o* **12/1**

2 **2** ½ **Cast In Gold (USA)**[24] [2958] 2-9-0 .... LDettori 1 — 84
(B J Meehan) *hld up: hdwy over 2f out: ev ch whn carried lft ins fnl f: unable qckn nr fin* **13/8**[1]

2 **3** 2 **Light Shift (USA)**[21] [3043] 2-9-0 .... TedDurcan 7 — 79
(H R A Cecil) *chsd ldrs: rdn and ev ch whn hung lft over 1f out: styng on same pce whn nt clr run ins fnl f* **7/4**[2]

4 1 **Free Offer** 2-9-0 .... EddieAhern 6 — 76
(J L Dunlop) *hld up: hdwy over 1f out: nt trble ldrs* **40/1**

5 **5** 1 **Nicomedia (IRE)**[24] [2958] 2-9-0 .... RyanMoore 4 — 73
(R Hannon) *led to 1/2-way: rdn over 1f out: no ex* **8/1**[3]

0 **6** 3 **Look Who's Dancing**[24] [2957] 2-9-0 .... KerrinMcEvoy 10 — 66
(J L Dunlop) *chsd ldrs: rdn over 2f out: wknd over 1f out* **25/1**

0 **7** hd **Split Briefs (IRE)**[41] [2456] 2-9-0 .... ShaneKelly 3 — 65
(D J Daly) *chsd ldrs: bmpd wl over 1f out: sn wknd* **100/1**

0 **8** nk **Security Tiger (IRE)**[24] [2958] 2-8-11 .... EdwardCreighton(3) 11 — 64
(M R Channon) *s.i.s: sn prom: hung lft and wknd over 1f out* **100/1**

9 1 ¼ **On The Go** 2-9-0 .... PhilipRobinson 2 — 61
(M A Jarvis) *s.i.s: hld up: hung lft thrght: rdn over 2f out: sn wknd* **14/1**

10 ½ **Shanawa (IRE)** 2-9-0 .... ChrisCatlin 5 — 60
(M R Channon) *s.s: a in rr* **66/1**

0 **11** 3 **Featherlight**[7] [3495] 2-9-0 .... OscarUrbina 9 — 52
(N A Callaghan) *hld up: wknd 2f out* **100/1**

12 2 **Summer Of Love (IRE)** 2-8-11 .... NelsonDeSouza(3) 8 — 47
(P F I Cole) *hld up: rdn over 2f out: sn wknd* **20/1**

1m 26.33s (-0.45) **Going Correction** -0.05s/f (Good) — **12** Ran SP% **115.4**

Speed ratings (Par 93):100,99,97,96,94 91,91,90,89,88 85,83

CSF £30.12 TOTE £16.40: £3.30, £1.30, £1.40; EX 51.00.

Owner Gainsborough Stud **Bred** Gainsborough Farm Llc **Trained** Middleham Moor, N Yorks

FOCUS

This looked a decent maiden but they did not go that fast early on and the form could be a little high. It should produce winners, however.

NOTEBOOK

Princess Taise(USA), a half-sister to Graphic Design, a dual middle-distance winner at three in France, grabbed the favoured stands'-side rail and was in pole position throughout. Despite hanging left, she bravely fought off the attentions of the favourite, who had the benefit of a previous run under her belt, and looks a useful filly in the making. She will easily get a mile this season and should make a nice middle-distance filly at three. (op 10-1)

Cast In Gold(USA) ran with plenty of promise on her debut and looked one of the two main contenders here. She was handed the worst draw, though, and had to challenge widest of all, and in the end the Johnston filly outbattled her. This was a good maiden, she came clear of the rest, and will surely make it third time lucky. (op 6-4 tchd 7-4 in places)

Light Shift(USA), another who offered plenty of hope on her debut, could not go with the first two but finished a clear third. She remains a useful prospect and will not always run into a such smart opposition. (op 2-1)

Free Offer, whose dam won over a mile at two and is a half-sister to Chelsea Barracks, a 12-furlong winner, and Guard Duty, a winner over two miles, is by Generous and bred to get quite a bit further than this in time. She was unfancied on this debut but put in some good late work, and some improvement for this outing might well see her off the mark, especially if she is stepped up to a mile later in the season. (op 33-1 tchd 50-1)

Nicomedia(IRE) ran well at Newbury first time up and was well positioned throughout, but she ended up being beaten further by Cast In Gold this time than she was on her debut. She could be one for nurseries over a mile later in the season. (tchd 9-1)

Look Who's Dancing, a half-sister to Spotlight, a useful juvenile over seven furlongs and a mile who later became a high-class nine-furlong winner in the US, looked likely to appreciate the extra furlong and duly improved for her debut effort, but she still finished adrift of the first five. (op 33-1)

On The Go Official explanation: jockey said filly hung left throughout

3708 HALVERTON REIM H'CAP — 7f

6:45 (6:46) (Class 4) (0-85,85) 3-Y-O — **£5,505** (£1,637; £818; £408) **Stalls** High

Form — RPR

1 **1** **Bustin Justin (USA)**[41] [2458] 3-9-0 **78** .... LDettori 5 — 85+
(J Noseda) *mde all: shkn up and hung lft fr over 1f out: r.o* **8/11**[1]

-010 **2** ½ **Lyrical Sound (IRE)**[20] [3067] 3-9-0 **78** .... MichaelHills 8 — 84
(B W Hills) *hld up: rdn over 1f out: r.o wl ins fnl f: nt rch wnr* **14/1**

6016 **3** nk **Louie Louie (IRE)**[7] [3491] 3-9-7 **85** .... KerrinMcEvoy 4 — 90
(N A Callaghan) *chsd wnr: rdn and ev ch whn hung lft over 1f out: unable qckn ins fnl f* **11/4**[2]

2445 **4** ½ **Patavium Prince (IRE)**[6] [3543] 3-8-6 **70** ow1 .... EddieAhern 3 — 74
(J R Best) *trckd ldrs: racd keenly: rdn and hung lft over 1f out: styd on same pce ins fnl f* **10/1**[3]

0466 **5** 1 ¼ **Cool Sting (IRE)**[6] [3546] 3-8-6 **70** .... (p) RichardMullen 6 — 70
(A M Balding) *s.i.s: sn chsng ldrs: rdn and hung lft over 1f out: no ex* **16/1**

0060 **6** 9 **Fangorn Forest (IRE)**[13] [3301] 3-8-6 **70** .... (p) AdrianMcCarthy 7 — 46
(R A Harris) *hld up: rdn 1/2-way: wknd 2f out* **33/1**

0506 **7** 1 ¾ **Ockums Razor (IRE)**[2] [3646] 3-8-4 **68** ow2 .... JohnEgan 1 — 39
(C A Dwyer) *hld up: plld hrd: rdn over 2f out: sn wknd* **28/1**

-000 **P** **Ocean Of Dreams (FR)**[30] [2756] 3-9-1 **79** .... JamieSpencer 2 — —
(J D Bethell) *hld up: p.u over 4f out* **20/1**

1m 25.59s (-1.19) **Going Correction** -0.05s/f (Good) — **8** Ran SP% **117.4**

Speed ratings (Par 102):104,103,103,102,101 90,88,—

CSF £13.58 CT £22.56 TOTE £1.80: £1.10, £2.30, £1.10; EX 8.20.

Owner Zayat Stables Ltd **Bred** A U Jones & Marie D Jones **Trained** Newmarket, Suffolk

FOCUS

A fair handicap in which Bustin Justin looked to have got in quite lightly on his handicap debut against a bunch of mainly exposed types. He was allowed the run of the race, but the form looks pretty solid.

Fangorn Forest(IRE) Official explanation: jockey said filly was unsuited by the good to firm ground

Ockums Razor(IRE) Official explanation: jockey said colt was unsuited by the good to firm ground

Ocean Of Dreams(FR) Official explanation: jockey said colt moved poorly

3709 DAVIS GROUP CONDITIONS STKS — 5f

7:20 (7:20) (Class 3) 3-Y-0+ — **£8,724** (£2,612; £1,306; £653; £326; £163) **Stalls** High

Form — RPR

-002 **1** **Donna Blini**[7] [3499] 3-8-11 109 .... LDettori 9 — 95
(B J Meehan) *disp ld tl led over 1f out: rdn out* **11/4**[2]

0-00 **2** ¾ **Majestic Missile (IRE)**[31] [2720] 5-9-0 110 .... (t) JamieSpencer 5 — 91
(W J Haggas) *s.s: hld up: plld hrd: nt clr run over 1f out: r.o wl ins fnl f: nt rch wnr* **5/2**[1]

0203 **3** nk **The Trader (IRE)**[13] [3312] 8-9-1 109 .... (b) TedDurcan 2 — 91
(M Blanshard) *hld up: swtchd lft and hdwy over 1f out: sn ev ch and rdr dropped reins: edgd lft: unable qckn towards fin* **3/1**[3]

0403 **4** ¾ **Celtic Mill**[20] [3076] 8-9-1 105 .... (p) KerrinMcEvoy 1 — 89
(D W Barker) *chsd ldrs: rdn and ev ch over 1f out: styd on same pce* **7/1**

2101 **5** 1 ¼ **Russian Rocket (IRE)**[6] [3536] 4-8-9 64 .... JohnEgan 8 — 78
(Mrs C A Dunnett) *chsd ldrs: rdn over 1f out: styd on same pce* **66/1**

00-0 **6** 1 ½ **Dizzy Dreamer (IRE)**[94] [1068] 3-8-0 94 .... AdrianMcCarthy 4 — 68
(P W Chapple-Hyam) *sn pushed along and prom: rdn over 1f out: no ex* **33/1**

0610 **7** 1 **Norcroft**[6] [3536] 4-8-9 65 .... (p) ChrisCatlin 6 — 69
(Mrs C A Dunnett) *w wnr over 3f: wknd ins fnl f* **100/1**

0330 **8** 6 **Gone'N'Dunnett (IRE)**[20] [3094] 7-8-9 62 .... (v) J-PGuillambert 3 — 47
(Mrs C A Dunnett) *mid-div: sn drvn along: wknd over 1f out* **100/1**

-000 **9** 6 **Boogie Street**[13] [3312] 5-9-0 105 .... RichardHughes 7 — 31
(R Hannon) *chsd ldrs: wknd qckly over 1f out* **7/1**

58.69 secs (-0.87) **Going Correction** -0.05s/f (Good)

WFA 3 from 4yo+ 4lb — **9** Ran SP% **111.7**

Speed ratings (Par 107):104,102,102,101,99 96,95,85,75

CSF £9.50 TOTE £3.10: £1.30, £1.30, £1.60; EX 10.00.

Owner Mrs T S M Cunningham **Bred** James Thom And Sons **Trained** Manton, Wilts

FOCUS

An ordinary conditions race run at a fairly steady early pace. The proximity of the 64-rated fifth, who was only beaten three lengths, anchors the form and makes it look less than solid.

NOTEBOOK

Donna Blini ran well in defeat in a Group Three race last time and the drop back to the minimum trip looked unlikely to present her with any problems as she possesses plenty of speed. She enjoyed the run of the race next to the stands'-side rail but had a bit in hand at the finish and deserves another crack at a Pattern contest now. (tchd 5-2 and 3-1 in places)

Majestic Missile(IRE) was best in at the weights but was awkward leaving the stalls, did not settle for his rider at the back of the field and had his work cut out to make up ground from the rear in the closing stages. He finished well but it was all too late and, not for the first time, his supporters were left disappointed. A real layers' favourite, he has now been beaten eight times at 5-1 or shorter since his successful juvenile campaign, winning only once since that time, at 13-8. (tchd 11-4)

The Trader(IRE) came with his challenge down the outside, which was not the place to be, and, while his rider dropped his reins briefly, he would still not have won. His style of running demands a race to be run at a stronger pace than this. (tchd 10-3 and 7-2 in a place)

Celtic Mill would have probably been seen to better effect had his rider allowed him to bowl along in front. His best performances have come when he has made every yard, setting a good pace from the start. On paper it looked as though the lead was going to be well-contested, as there were five potential front-runners in the line-up, but as it transpired Donna Blini was gifted a fairly uncontested lead. (op 6-1)

Russian Rocket(IRE) has been in good form recently but he had a mountain to climb in this company. Rated 31lb lower on adjusted official ratings than the winner, his good performance holds down the value of the form and is owed to the fact that the early pace was far from frantic.

Dizzy Dreamer(IRE), having only her second start of the campaign, has clearly had her problems and was once again well held.

Boogie Street came in for market support but he once again disappointed. Out of sorts this season, it looks as though he may have a problem. (op 10-1)

3710 RACING UK ON SKY 432 H'CAP — 1m 2f

7:50 (7:51) (Class 3) (0-95,92) 3-Y-O — **£7,790** (£2,332; £1,166; £583; £291; £146) **Stalls** High

Form — RPR

-140 **1** **Steppe Dancer (IRE)**[28] [2801] 3-9-0 **87** .... EddieAhern 6 — 97
(D J Coakley) *chsd ldrs: rdn to ld ins fnl f: edgd lft: r.o* **14/1**

14-2 **2** hd **Noble Gent (IRE)**[13] [3318] 3-9-1 **88** .... LDettori 2 — 98
(Saeed Bin Suroor) *chsd ldr: rdn to ld over 1f out: hung lft and hdd ins fnl f: r.o* **10/11**[1]

-624 **3** 2 **In Full Cry**[14] [3255] 3-8-12 **85** .... JoeFanning 4 — 91
(M Johnston) *led: rdn and hdd over 1f out: styd on same pce* **7/1**

-130 **4** 2 ½ **High Command**[57] [1951] 3-9-3 **90** .... (t) JamieSpencer 3 — 91
(E A L Dunlop) *trckd ldrs: rdn 2f out: wknd fnl f* **5/1**[3]

2002 **5** ½ **Porters (USA)**[8] [3443] 3-9-0 **87** .... RichardHughes 1 — 88
(R Hannon) *hld up: rdn over 2f out: hung lft and wknd fnl f* **4/1**[2]

5300 **6** 5 **Wovoka (IRE)**[54] [2046] 3-9-2 **92** .... EdwardCreighton(3) 5 — 83
(M R Channon) *hld up: rdn and wknd over 1f out* **25/1**

2m 5.04s (-1.40) **Going Correction** -0.05s/f (Good) — **6** Ran SP% **112.1**

Speed ratings (Par 104):103,102,101,99,98 94

CSF £27.58 TOTE £14.20: £4.00, £1.10; EX 31.80.

Owner Chris Van Hoorn **Bred** Maggiorelli Ice Guarnieri **Trained** West Ilsley, Berks

FOCUS

A decent handicap run at a fair pace and the form looks sound.

NOTEBOOK

Steppe Dancer(IRE), who did not settle when faced with a stiff task in the King Edward VII Stakes last time, was much less keen on this drop back into handicap company. The good early pace suited him and he came through having travelled well to nail the hot favourite inside the final furlong. Clearly well regarded, there should be more to come from him.

Noble Gent(IRE), runner-up at Sandown on his reappearance, did little wrong in filling the same position again. The winner is well regarded and ran in a Group Two race last time, so there was little disgrace in conceding 1lb to him and getting beaten a head, regardless of what the betting market would suggest. (op 5-6 tchd Evens)

In Full Cry, a beaten favourite on his last two starts, set a decent pace in front and kept going after being headed. He is an honest type but needs to dig out some improvement from somewhere if he is to defy his current mark. (tchd 15-2)

High Command, tongue tied for the first time, may need a bit of cut in the ground to be seen at his best, but he too needs to find some improvement to win off a mark 7lb higher than for his last success. (op 6-1 tchd 9-2)

Porters(USA), who put up an improved display on his first go at this trip over the course and distance last time, failed to repeat that performance eight days later. Perhaps the race came too soon. (op 5-1, tchd 5-1 in a place)

3711 NGK SPARK PLUGS MAIDEN STKS — 1m
8:20 (8:21) (Class 5) 3-Y-O — £5,181 (£1,541; £770; £384) Stalls High

Form				RPR
02	1		**Border News**[8] 3458 3-9-3 .... RichardHughes 1 (H R A Cecil) *chsd ldr: rdn over 2f out: looked hld whn hmpd and lft in ld wl ins fnl f* **3/1**[2]	73
0	2	shd	**Somersault**[22] 3029 3-8-12 .... RyanMoore 3 (Sir Michael Stoute) *hld up in tch: rdn over 1f out: lft 2nd wl ins fnl f: styd on* **4/1**[3]	68
0	3	3 1/2	**Manipulate**[28] 2825 3-9-3 .... NickyMackay 6 (L M Cumani) *hld up: rdn over 3f out: n.d: fin 4th, shd, 1l and 2 1/2l: plcd 3rd* **7/1**	65
	4	hd	**Cool Tiger** 3-9-0 .... DeanCorby(3) 7 (P Howling) *plld hrd and prom: rdn over 1f out: wknd fnl f: fin 5th, hd: plcd 4th* **20/1**	65
0	5	26	**Mocairde (USA)**[8] 3436 3-8-6 ow1 .... KylieManser(7) 2 (J R Best) *s.s: hdwy over 4f out: wknd over 2f out: fin 6th, 26l: plcd 5th* **40/1**	—
3040	D		**Alhaitham (USA)**[28] 2815 3-9-3 85 .... (t) RHills 5 (J L Dunlop) *led: rdn and looked in command whn sddle slipped and lost weight cloth wl ins fnl f: sn hdd: fin 3rd, shd and 1l: disq* **6/5**[1]	75+

1m 41.35s (0.92) **Going Correction** -0.05s/f (Good) 6 Ran SP% **110.2**
Speed ratings (Par 100):93,92,89,89,63 91
CSF £14.63 TOTE £3.70: £2.20, £2.00; EX 7.40.
Owner K Abdulla **Bred** Juddmonte Farms Ltd **Trained** Newmarket, Suffolk

FOCUS
A fair maiden but a very fortunate winner who sets the level, with the disqualified third rated a length winner. Alhaitham disq: weighed in light.

3712 NEWMARKET NIGHTS H'CAP — 1m
8:50 (8:50) (Class 5) (0-75,77) 4-Y-0+ — £3,886 (£1,156; £577; £288) Stalls High

Form				RPR
2343	1		**Fasylitator (IRE)**[20] 3101 4-8-13 67 .... JohnEgan 12 (D K Ivory) *hld up in tch: rdn to ld wl ins fnl f* **9/2**[2]	76
6063	2	nk	**My Princess (IRE)**[8] 3433 4-9-2 70 .... LDettori 8 (N A Callaghan) *led 1f: chsd ldrs: rdn and ev ch ins fnl f: r.o* **5/2**[1]	78
6-06	3	shd	**Sonny Parkin**[21] 3044 4-8-13 70 .... (v) AdamKirby(3) 5 (G A Huffer) *hld up: hdwy over 2f out: rdn and ev ch whn hung rt ins fnl f: kpt on* **15/2**	78
5300	4	shd	**Ali D**[11] 3361 8-8-7 61 .... JimmyQuinn 4 (G Woodward) *chsd ldrs: led 2f out: sn rdn: hdd wl ins fnl f* **12/1**	69
0521	5	1 1/4	**Missed A Beat**[6] 3542 4-9-4 72 6ex .... OscarUrbina 9 (M Blanshard) *chsd ldrs: rdn and ev ch over 1f out: styd on same pce ins fnl f* **13/2**[3]	77
0331	6	2	**The Gaikwar (IRE)**[7] 3469 7-8-13 72 6ex .... (b) RichardKingscote(5) 10 (R A Harris) *hld up: rdn over 1f out: r.o: nt rch ldrs* **8/1**	73
0116	7	shd	**Bold Diktator**[19] 3113 4-9-7 75 .... (b) EddieAhern 11 (W R Muir) *hld up: hdwy over 3f out: rdn and nt clr run over 1f out: styd on same pce* **12/1**	75
5215	8	hd	**Curtain Bluff**[6] 3542 4-9-9 77 6ex .... (v) TedDurcan 7 (M R Channon) *hld up: rdn over 1f out: nvr trbld ldrs* **10/1**	77
4420	9	shd	**Tiber Tiger (IRE)**[21] 3044 6-8-4 65 .... (b) JemmaMarshall(7) 6 (N P Littmoden) *hld up in tch: racd keenly: rdn over 1f out: no ex* **9/1**	65
0P00	10	nk	**Halcyon Magic**[7] 3469 8-7-13 56 oh6 .... (b) DominicFox(3) 3 (M Wigham) *s.i.s: hld up: n.d* **66/1**	55
500-	11	12	**King Of Diamonds**[321] 4951 5-8-9 70 .... KylieManser(7) 2 (J R Best) *plld hrd: led 7f out: sn clr: hdd & wknd 2f out* **33/1**	41

1m 39.18s (-1.25) **Going Correction** -0.05s/f (Good) 11 Ran SP% **121.9**
Speed ratings (Par 103):104,103,103,103,102 100,100,99,99,99 87
CSF £16.77 CT £87.49 TOTE £7.00: £2.10, £1.40, £3.10; EX 23.50 Place 6 £15.59, Place 5 £3.90.
Owner Mrs A Shone **Bred** Gerard Callanan **Trained** Radlett, Herts

FOCUS
A competitive handicap run at a steady early pace which resulted in something of a sprint and a tight finish. The form seems sound enough with the first five close to their marks.
T/Plt: £14.50 to a £1 stake. Pool: £62,661.25. 3,148.90 winning tickets. T/Qpdt: £5.60 to a £1 stake. Pool: £3,996.35. 526.65 winning tickets. CR

3372 PONTEFRACT (L-H)
Friday, July 21

OFFICIAL GOING: Firm (good to firm in places)
Wind: Slight, across

3713 CORAL - BOOKMAKER OF THE YEAR MAIDEN AUCTION STKS — 6f
6:30 (6:32) (Class 4) 2-Y-O — £4,533 (£1,348; £674; £336) Stalls Low

Form				RPR
00	1		**Mundo's Magic**[72] 1588 2-8-9 .... AdrianTNicholls 2 (D W Barker) *mde all: rdn clr wl over 1f out: drvn ins last and kpt on wl* **16/1**	77
43	2	1 1/4	**Cassie's Choice (IRE)**[28] 2807 2-8-4 .... RoystonFfrench 8 (B Smart) *chsd ldrs: hdwy on outer over 2f out: sn rdn and edgd lft wl over 1f out: kpt on u.p ins last: nt rch wnr* **7/2**[2]	68
0	3	4	**My Secrets**[14] 3247 2-8-13 .... KDarley 6 (M Johnston) *chsd ldrs: pushed along 1/2-way: rdn over 2f out: styd on same pce* **10/3**[1]	65
	4	1 1/4	**Fadeyev (IRE)** 2-8-11 .... PatCosgrave 5 (K A Ryan) *clsd up: rdn along over 2f out: edgd lft wl over 1f out and sn wknd* **10/3**[1]	59
0	5	1/2	**Only Hope**[16] 3193 2-8-6 .... DavidAllan 9 (M R Channon) *unruly in parade ring: sn pushed along in rr: hdwy on outer over 1f out: kpt on ins last: nrst fin* **9/2**[3]	53
	6	2	**The Graig** 2-8-9 .... RobbieFitzpatrick 1 (C Drew) *dwlt and sn pushed along in rr: styd on fnl 2f: nrst fin* **40/1**	50
55	7	1 1/4	**Ocean Of Champagne**[30] 2745 2-8-4 .... PaulHanagan 3 (A Dickman) *chsd ldrs on inner: rdn along and wkng whn hmpd wl over 1f out* **8/1**	41
0	8	1	**Lost Inheritance**[73] 1559 2-8-0 ow1 .... RoryMoore(5) 10 (P T Midgley) *in tch on outer: pushed along and lost pl 1/2-way: sn bhd* **100/1**	39
06	9	nk	**Gold Response**[8] 3455 2-8-8 .... PatrickMathers(3) 4 (D Shaw) *a towards rr* **66/1**	44
00	10	1 1/2	**Fire Alarm**[22] 3018 2-8-4 .... LeanneKershaw(5) 7 (J J Quinn) *a rr* **25/1**	38

1m 17.49s (0.09) **Going Correction** -0.375s/f (Firm) 10 Ran SP% **112.3**
Speed ratings (Par 96):84,82,77,75,74 72,70,69,68,66
CSF £67.84 TOTE £23.90: £3.90, £1.10, £1.80; EX 99.20.
Owner Fishing 4 Fun **Bred** Bearstone Stud **Trained** Scorton, N Yorks

FOCUS
A modest maiden in which the front two pulled clear and the runner-up sets the standard.

NOTEBOOK
Mundo's Magic, nibbled at in the market beforehand, was smartly into his stride and bagged the rail from stall two before quickening into a clear lead and winning with a bit in hand. This was a big step up on his two previous efforts and he has clearly benefited from a break, so there may be more to come in nurseries. (op 22-1 tchd 25-1)
Cassie's Choice(IRE) continues to head the right way and, although proving no match for the winner, she came right away from the third and it should be just a matter of time before she gets off the mark. She is another likely nursery prospect. (op 3-1)
My Secrets, outpaced throughout on his debut at Haydock, was expected to be much wiser on this occasion and was rightly towards the head of the market with his stable's juveniles in cracking form. He came out well, but was soon outpaced and could only keep on at the same pace. Seven furlongs plus is going to suit in time and he has yet to fulfil his promise. (op 4-1)
Fadeyev(IRE), bred to appreciate trips upward of seven furlongs in time, comes from a stable who have had multiple juvenile winners this season and he appeared to know his job, but just lacked the speed of the front two. He should improve with experience and may be able to pick up a small race. (op 3-1)
Only Hope, as was the case on her debut, got going once the race was all over and she still looks inexperienced. The step up to seven furlongs is going to help and we have not seen the best of her yet. (op 7-2)

3714 TOTESPORT.COM FILLIES' H'CAP — 1m 4f 8y
7:05 (7:07) (Class 5) (0-75,74) 3-Y-O+ — £5,181 (£1,541; £770; £384) Stalls Low

Form				RPR
0-41	1		**Trick Or Treat**[14] 3244 3-8-3 61 .... JamieMackay 5 (J G Given) *hld up in rr: swtchd outside and hdwy wl over 2f out: rdn to chse clr ldr over 1f out: styd on wl to ld last 75 yds* **7/2**[3]	72+
0-56	2	1/2	**Bollin Dolly**[72] 1598 3-8-7 65 .... DavidAllan 2 (T D Easterby) *led: pushed along 3f out: rdn clr 2f out: drvn ins last: hdd and no ex last 75 yds* **10/1**	76
0010	3	11	**Richtee (IRE)**[22] 3009 5-9-8 68 .... PaulHanagan 4 (R A Fahey) *trckd ldr: effrt 3f out: sn rdn along: drvn and wknd wl over 1f out* **11/4**[2]	61
0653	4	10	**Spinning Coin**[11] 3365 4-10-0 74 .... PatCosgrave 6 (J G Portman) *chsd ldng pair: effrt and hdwy 3f out: rdn over 2f out and sn btn* **15/8**[1]	51
0040	5	2 1/2	**Kiama**[45] 2326 4-8-11 57 .... KDarley 1 (M Johnston) *trckd ldrs: hdwy over 4f out: rdn along 3f out and sn btn* **4/1**	30

2m 37.74s (-2.56) **Going Correction** -0.275s/f (Firm)
WFA 3 from 4yo+ 12lb 5 Ran SP% **112.8**
Speed ratings (Par 100):97,96,89,82,81
CSF £33.30 TOTE £3.10: £1.80, £2.70; EX 42.80.
Owner Peter Onslow **Bred** P Onslow **Trained** Willoughton, Lincs

FOCUS
A tricky heat on paper, but the front two ended up 11 lengths clear of the third. However, the form may not be that strong.

3715 ANTONIA DEUTERS H'CAP — 5f
7:35 (7:35) (Class 3) (0-90,84) 3-Y-O+
£11,217 (£3,358; £1,679; £630; £630; £210) Stalls Low

Form				RPR
0100	1		**Mr Wolf**[28] 2830 5-9-11 84 .... (p) NCallan 10 (D W Barker) *qckly away and sn clr: rdn over 1f out: styd on strly* **10/1**	100
3314	2	2	**Caribbean Coral**[7] 3471 7-9-11 84 3ex .... (p) GrahamGibbons 1 (J J Quinn) *dwlt and towards rr: hdwy whn n.m.r over 2f out: rdn over 1f out: drvn on inner and kpt on wl fnl f* **5/1**[1]	93
0001	3	nk	**Matsunosuke**[8] 3447 4-8-10 76 3ex .... LukeMorris(7) 9 (A B Coogan) *towards rr: hdwy 2f out: sn rdn: sswtchd rt and styd on ins last: drvn: edgd lft last 100yds* **13/2**[2]	84+
3241	4	1/2	**Kings College Boy**[6] 3525 6-8-12 71 3ex .... (b) PaulHanagan 3 (R A Fahey) *midfield: effrt when n.m.r over 2f out: swtchd rt and rdn over 1f out: drvn and styd on ins last* **8/1**	77+
4512	4	dht	**Malapropism**[3] 3625 6-9-7 80 3ex .... TonyCulhane 11 (M R Channon) *chsd wnr: rdn 2f out: drvn whn hmpd ins last: no ex* **8/1**	86
253	6	hd	**Quality Street**[14] 3251 4-9-3 76 .... RobbieFitzpatrick 5 (P Butler) *chsd wnr: rdn wl over 1f out: drvn ins last: edgd rt and no ex last 100 yds* **16/1**	81
0151	7	1 1/2	**Adantino**[7] 3486 7-8-13 79 3ex .... (b) JamesMillman(7) 4 (B R Millman) *dwlt and towards rr tl styd on fnl f* **7/1**[3]	79
0011	8	3/4	**Ryedane (IRE)**[3] 3622 4-8-11 70 3ex .... DavidAllan 2 (T D Easterby) *in tch on inner: rdn along whn n.m.r over 2f out: sn drvn and btn over 1f out* **5/1**[1]	67
-113	9	11	**Our Little Secret (IRE)**[25] 2925 4-8-3 69 .... KevinGhunowa(7) 7 (A Berry) *chsd ldrs: rdn along 2f out: sn wknd* **18/1**	27
5600	10	nk	**Brigadore**[13] 3281 7-8-8 67 .... KDarley 8 (J G Given) *dwlt and towards rr: hdwy on outer 1/2-way: rdn and in tch wl over 1f out: sn drvn and wknd* **9/1**	24
0000	P		**Wanchai Lad**[35] 2624 5-9-5 78 .... AdrianTNicholls 6 (D Nicholls) *dwlt and towards rr: hdwy whn bdly hmpd over 2f out: sn lost action: p.u and dismntd 1f out* **20/1**	—

61.37 secs (-2.43) **Going Correction** -0.375s/f (Firm) 11 Ran SP% **116.4**
Speed ratings (Par 107):104,100,100,99,99 99,96,95,78,77 —
CSF £58.78 CT £359.76 TOTE £10.60: £3.10, £2.70, £2.50; EX 50.10.
Owner P Asquith **Bred** P Asquith **Trained** Scorton, N Yorks
■ Stewards' Enquiry : Luke Morris two-day ban: careless riding (Aug 1,3)

FOCUS
A competitive sprint handicap full of in-form sprinters and the form is solid rated around the first three.

NOTEBOOK
Mr Wolf, a useful sprinter on his day who goes well on turning tracks, has done most of his winning at six furlongs, but he is fully effective at five and, having burst into an early lead, he powered clear to win with plenty in hand. Consistency is not his strong point and he is more likely to bomb out next time than win, but he is one to always bear in mind when the emphasis is on speed. (op 12-1)
Caribbean Coral has come back to form in recent weeks and he has performed creditably in defeat the last twice now. He would have given the winner more to think about had he been able to obtain a better early position and received a clear run through, but it was not to be. He can probably find a race off this sort of mark. (op 11-2)

Matsunosuke, as was the case with the runner-up, found himself in an uncompromising early position and the winner poached first run on him. He finished well and, although the race was beyond him, he should remain competitive off this sort of mark. (op 5-1)
Kings College Boy did not get the clearest of runs through and should have been challenging for second, but he is on good form at the present and there will be other days for him. (tchd 9-1)
Malapropism was never too far off the gallop and, although hampered late on, he was already held. This was another good effort, but he will remain vulnerable off this sort of mark. (tchd 9-1)
Quality Street ran well for a long way, but was run out of the places inside the final furlong. She has not won since her debut, but this was a decent effort nonetheless.
Adantino has been in decent form, winning two of his last three starts, but he soon found himself behind and the late headway he made was not enough to see him involved. (op 13-2)
Ryedane(IRE), on a hat-trick following wins at Catterick and Newcastle, did not get a clear run, but he failed to pick up as expected anyhow and may struggle off this new mark, albeit he deserves a chance to show this running to be wrong.
Wanchai Lad Official explanation: jockey said gelding had lost a shoe and returned sore

3716 DANETHORPE RACING PURPLE AND PINK H'CAP 1m 4y
8:05 (8:05) (Class 5) (0-70,70) 3-Y-0+ **£4,533** (£1,348; £674; £336) **Stalls** Low

Form RPR
0043 **1** **Apsara**[11] [3361] 5-9-3 **59** TomEaves 4 70
(G M Moore) *chsd clr ldr: hdwy over 2f out: rdn to ld 1/2f out: drvn ins last and styd on wl* **7/1[3]**
4102 **2** *¾* **Chicken Soup**[6] [3523] 4-9-7 **70** JamesO'Reilly[(7)] 7 79+
(T J Pitt) *hld up in rr: stdy hdwy 3f out: effrt over 1f out: ev ch and swtchd lft ins last: sn rdn and nt qckn towards fin* **7/2[2]**
5013 **3** *shd* **River Logic (IRE)**[3] [3610] 3-7-12 **51** SilvestreDeSousa[(3)] 10 58
(A D Brown) *chsd ldng pair: hdwy over 2f out: rdn over 1f out: kpt on ins last* **8/1**
0100 **4** *1 ¾* **Royal Indulgence**[7] [3484] 6-8-8 **55** LiamJones[(5)] 6 60
(W M Brisbourne) *s.i.s and bhd: hdwy on inner wl over 1f out: rdn and styd on strly ins last: nrst fin* **33/1**
0010 **5** *hd* **Splodger Mac (IRE)**[3] [3610] 7-8-2 **51** oh1 (b) SuzzanneFrance[(7)] 12 55
(N Bycroft) *led and sn clr: rdn along over 2f out: hdd 11/2f out and grad wknd* **20/1**
0504 **6** *3* **Motu (IRE)**[14] [3240] 5-8-6 **51** oh2 (v) PatrickMathers[(3)] 1 48
(I W McInnes) *in tch: hdwy to chse ldrs 3f out: rdn 2f out and kpt on same pce* **20/1**
0012 **7** *¾* **Pianoforte (USA)**[5] [3570] 4-9-2 **58** 6ex FrancisNorton 3 54
(E J Alston) *hld up in midfield: smooth hdwy over 3f out: rdn along wl over 1f out and sn no imp* **9/4[1]**
4040 **8** *nk* **Fairy Monarch (IRE)**[13] [3283] 7-8-4 **51** oh2 (b) RoryMoore[(5)] 5 46
(P T Midgley) *bhd tl sme late hdwy* **25/1**
0431 **9** *3* **Three Strings (USA)**[11] [3355] 3-8-8 **58** 6ex (p) NCallan 9 44
(P D Niven) *in tch: rdn along 3f out: drvn over 2f out and sn wknd* **9/1**
00-0 **10** *1 ¾* **Passionately Royal**[33] [2681] 4-9-8 **64** PaulHanagan 11 48
(R A Fahey) *midfield: rdn along 3f out and sn wknd* **25/1**
5355 **11** *5* **Wing Commander**[14] [3241] 7-9-10 **66** (b) RoystonFfrench 13 39
(I W McInnes) *chsd ldrs: rdn along wl over 2f out and sn wknd* **11/1**
56-0 **12** *13* **Danceinthevalley (IRE)**[52] [2108] 4-9-12 **68** DeanMcKeown 8 11
(G A Swinbank) *a rr* **16/1**
0-00 **13** *10* **Kalush**[145] [526] 5-8-2 **51** oh19 (t) PaulPickard[(7)] 2 —
(J Hetherton) *s.i.s: a rr* **100/1**

1m 43.23s (-2.47) **Going Correction** -0.275s/f (Firm)
WFA 3 from 4yo+ 8lb **13** Ran SP% **122.0**
Speed ratings (Par 103):101,100,100,98,98 95,94,94,91,89 84,71,61
CSF £29.71 CT £214.51 TOTE £8.80: £2.80, £1.40, £2.90; EX 35.20.
Owner Mrs Mary And Miss Susan Hatfield **Bred** St Clare Hall Stud **Trained** Middleham Moor, N Yorks

FOCUS
A modest but competitive handicap and the form looks solid with the first five close to their marks.
Pianoforte(USA) Official explanation: jockey said gelding had no more to give
Fairy Monarch(IRE) Official explanation: jockey said gelding bled from the nose
Three Strings(USA) Official explanation: jockey said gelding hung right from 2f out

3717 WEATHERBYS STALLION BOOK MAIDEN STKS 1m 2f 6y
8:35 (8:35) (Class 4) 3-4-Y-0 **£5,829** (£1,734; £866; £432) **Stalls** Low

Form RPR
3 **1** **Dawera (IRE)**[44] [2349] 3-8-12 TomEaves 4 79+
(Sir Michael Stoute) *mde virtually all: clr 3f out: easily* **1/8[1]**
6 **2** *6* **Pochard**[18] [3146] 3-8-7 StephenDonohoe[(5)] 5 56
(J M P Eustace) *hld up: hdwy over 2f out: rdn over 1f out: styd on to take 2nd pl ins last: no ch w wnr* **9/1[2]**
0 **3** *¾* **Princess Toto**[72] [1598] 3-8-7 LeanneKershaw[(5)] 3 55
(P C Haslam) *chsd wnr: rdn along 3f out: sn drvn and one pce* **16/1[3]**
0 **4** *hd* **Maseem**[20] [3073] 3-9-3 NCallan 2 59
(Rae Guest) *chsd wnr: rdn over 2f out: drvn wl over 1f out and plugged on same pce* **16/1[3]**

2m 11.22s (-2.86) **Going Correction** -0.275s/f (Firm) **4** Ran SP% **110.7**
Speed ratings (Par 105):100,95,94,94
CSF £2.16 TOTE £1.10; EX 2.70.
Owner H H Aga Khan **Bred** His Highness The Aga Khan's Studs S C **Trained** Newmarket, Suffolk

FOCUS
An uncompetitive maiden and an easy success for hot favourite Dawera who is value for much more than the official margin.

3718 COUNTRYWIDE FREIGHT H'CAP 6f
9:05 (9:05) (Class 5) (0-75,73) 3-Y-0+ **£4,533** (£1,348; £674; £336) **Stalls** Low

Form RPR
2651 **1** **Blue Maeve**[17] [3171] 6-8-9 **59** SilvestreDeSousa[(3)] 2 75
(A D Brown) *qckly away: mde all: rdn wl over 1f out: drvn ins last and kpt on gamely* **7/2[1]**
-002 **2** *½* **Kool Ovation**[13] [3287] 4-9-6 **67** DavidAllan 6 81
(A Dickman) *in tch: hdwy on inner 2f out: swtchd rt and rdn to chse wnr ins last: sn drvn and kpt on* **5/1[2]**
-303 **3** *4* **The Terrier**[22] [3023] 3-9-5 **71** NCallan 1 72
(G A Swinbank) *trckd ldrs: hdwy to chse wnr 2f out and sn rdn: drvn ins last and sn one pce* **6/1[3]**
0163 **4** *½* **Linda Green**[7] [3478] 5-9-5 **66** TonyCulhane 8 67
(M R Channon) *towards rr: hdwy 2f out: sn rdn: kpt on ins last: nrst fin* **7/2[1]**
5160 **5** *1 ¼* **True Night**[81] [1341] 9-9-9 **70** AdrianTNicholls 11 67
(D Nicholls) *outpcd and bhd tl styd on fr over 1f out: nrst fin* **14/1**
0000 **6** *4* **Throw The Dice**[21] [3041] 4-9-3 **69** MarkLawson[(5)] 3 54
(D W Barker) *chsd ldng pair: rdn along 2f out: sn wknd* **12/1**
2100 **7** *3 ½* **Bel Cantor**[13] [3287] 3-8-13 **72** JamesMillman[(7)] 7 45
(W J H Ratcliffe) *cl up: rdn along over 2f out: sn drvn and wknd* **16/1**
6035 **8** *½* **Dvinsky (USA)**[7] [3500] 5-9-11 **72** RobbieFitzpatrick 4 45
(S R Bowring) *towards rr: rdn along over 2f out and nvr a factor* **7/2[1]**

1m 15.11s (-2.29) **Going Correction** -0.375s/f (Firm)
WFA 3 from 4yo+ 5lb **8** Ran SP% **117.9**
Speed ratings (Par 103):100,99,94,93,91 86,81,81
CSF £22.00 CT £103.63 TOTE £5.10: £2.00, £2.40, £1.60 Place 6 £117.16, Place 5 £62.42.
Owner R G Fell **Bred** P J And Mrs Nolan **Trained** Pickering, York

FOCUS
Modest form but solid enough rated around the first two.
True Night Official explanation: jockey said gelding was hanging badly early on
T/Plt: £85.60 to a £1 stake. Pool: £59,297.80. 505.30 winning tickets. T/Qpdt: £15.40 to a £1 stake. Pool: £3,724.20. 178.70 winning tickets. JR

3661 HAMBURG (R-H)
Friday, July 21

OFFICIAL GOING: Good

3719a FAHRHOFER STUTENPREIS (GROUP 3) (F&M) 1m 3f
6:00 (6:08) 3-Y-0+ **£22,069** (£6,897; £3,448; £2,069)

RPR
1 **Wurfscheibe (GER)**[47] [2280] 4-9-6 TMundry 2 104
(P Rau, Germany) *held up, 5th straight on outside, ridden to track leader 2f out, driven to lead well inside final f, ran on* **23/10[2]**
2 *½* **Cliffrose (GER)**[55] 4-9-6 AStarke 4 103
(Frau E Mader, Germany) *tracked leader to straight, led on outside 2f out, ridden over 1f out, headed well inside final f* **23/10[2]**
3 *1 ¾* **Litalia (IRE)**[26] [2913] 3-8-7 FilipMinarik 1 98
(P Schiergen, Germany) *disputed 3rd, 4th straight, kept on one pace final 2f* **26/10[3]**
4 *½* **Koffibini (IRE)**[299] [5498] 4-9-4 WMongil 5 97
(H J Groschel, Germany) *disputed 3rd, 3rd straight, effort on outside final 2f, never able to challenge* **142/10**
5 *1 ¼* **Aramina (GER)**[47] [2279] 3-8-7 ASuborics 3 95
(P Schiergen, Germany) *held up, always in touch, last straight, headway on inside well over 1f out, soon one pace* **19/10[1]**
6 *nk* **Daytona (GER)**[55] 5-9-6 ABest 6 97
(P Rau, Germany) *led to 2f out, one pace* **94/10**

2m 21.05s
WFA 3 from 4yo+ 11lb **6** Ran SP% **139.1**
(including ten euro stakes): WIN 33; PL 21, 20; SF 160.
Owner Gestut Ravensberg **Bred** Gestut Ravensberg **Trained** Germany

3565 HAYDOCK (L-H)
Saturday, July 22

OFFICIAL GOING: Good to firm
Wind: Almost nil Weather: Cloudy but very warm

3720 HAYDOCK PARK PONY CLUB NURSERY 5f
6:40 (6:41) (Class 5) 2-Y-0 **£3,238** (£963; £481; £240) **Stalls** Centre

Form RPR
2213 **1** **My Valerina (IRE)**[8] [3481] 2-8-2 **70** SaleemGolam[(3)] 6 73
(Mrs A Duffield) *sn outpcd: swtchd rt 2f out: hdwy whn hung lft 1f out: r.o strly ins fnl f to ld cl home* **3/1[1]**
4003 **2** *nk* **Stolt (IRE)**[21] [3064] 2-9-4 **86** DNolan[(3)] 2 88
(N Wilson) *led: rdn over 1f out: sn edgd rt: hdd cl home* **4/1[2]**
1300 **3** *1* **Bazroy (IRE)**[32] [2724] 2-8-10 **80** (b[1]) StephenDonohoe[(5)] 4 78
(P D Evans) *chsd ldrs: rdn and sltly outpcd over 2f out: rallied and hung lft over 1f out: r.o ins fnl f* **12/1**
1432 **4** *shd* **Yerevan**[15] [3246] 2-8-4 **69** NickyMackay 3 67
(R T Phillips) *a cl up: rdn and edgd rt over 1f out: nt qckn cl home* **4/1[2]**
0422 **5** *1 ½* **Inflight (IRE)**[10] [3409] 2-8-1 **69** NelsonDeSouza[(3)] 7 62
(R M Beckett) *prom: rdn and ev ch over 1f out: no ex wl ins fnl f* **4/1[2]**
0250 **6** *5* **The Italian Job**[12] [3358] 2-7-11 **67** DuranFentiman[(5)] 1 42
(T D Easterby) *in tch: rdn over 2f out: wknd 1f out* **25/1**
0554 **7** *1 ¼* **Baileys Hilight (IRE)**[15] [3239] 2-8-8 **73** KDarley 5 43+
(M Johnston) *dwlt: towards rr: effrt over 2f out: wknd over 1f out: eased whn btn ins fnl f* **7/1[3]**
054 **8** *2 ½* **Amelie Brown (IRE)**[46] [2321] 2-7-12 **63** oh7 KimTinkler 8 24
(N Tinkler) *hung lft thrght: a bhd* **33/1**

60.60 secs (-1.47) **Going Correction** -0.35s/f (Firm) **8** Ran SP% **112.0**
Speed ratings (Par 94):97,96,94,94,92 84,82,78
CSF £14.43 CT £121.42 TOTE £3.70: £1.50, £1.40, £3.70; EX 11.60.
Owner V Hubbard D Clinton S Gale & M Milns **Bred** C H Wacker Iii **Trained** Constable Burton, N Yorks
■ Stewards' Enquiry : D Nolan one-day ban: careless riding (Aug 3)

FOCUS
A fair nursery run at a strong pace from the beginning. The form does not look that great, though, as the fourth was beaten in a seller last time. The official ratings shown next to each horse are estimated and for information purposes only.

NOTEBOOK
My Valerina(IRE) struggled to go the early pace but the leaders went off too fast and the race fell into her lap late on. She appeared to see the trip out strongly, suggesting a return to six might suit, but it was probably a case of those in front stopping. (tchd 7-2)
Stolt(IRE) went fast from the start, perhaps too fast, as he helped set up the race for the fast-finishing favourite. This was a good performance under top-weight, and he probably put up a personal best in defeat. (op 9-2)
Bazroy(IRE), set stiff tasks since winning on his debut in a Polytrack maiden, was wearing blinkers for the first time and appreciated the drop in class. He benefited from racing off the pace and challenging late off what was a strong gallop. (op 14-1)
Yerevan had shown plenty of speed on her previous starts over six furlongs and she was not inconvenienced by the drop back to the minimum trip. She was beaten in a seller last time though, and her performance does not do a lot for the value of the form. (op 9-2)
Inflight(IRE) could not secure the outright lead this time but helped force a strong pace which eventually put paid to her chance. (op 7-2 tchd 9-2)
The Italian Job has now thrown in three disappointing efforts since her fair effort at Catterick on her second start. (tchd 20-1)
Amelie Brown(IRE) Official explanation: jockey said filly hung left-handed throughout

3721 RACINGUK.TV E B F MAIDEN STKS — 6f

7:10 (7:11) (Class 5) 2-Y-O — £3,886 (£1,156; £577; £288) Stalls Centre

Form — RPR

2 **1** **Celtic Sultan (IRE)**[15] 3247 2-9-3 .... KDarley 5 — 85+
(T P Tate) *s.i.s: sn rcvrd to ld: rdn out and in command ins fnl f* **4/11**[1]

2 *1 1/4* **Fishforcompliments** 2-9-3 .... PaulHanagan 1 — 78
(R A Fahey) *s.i.s: sn chsd ldrs & rdn along: outpcd over 2f out: rallied & hung lft 1f out: tk 2nd ins fnl f: rdr dropped whip: a hld* **9/1**[3]

3 *3 1/2* **Naughty Thoughts (IRE)** 2-8-12 .... NCallan 2 — 63
(K A Ryan) *dwlt: prom: rdn over 2f out: ev ch over 1f out: wknd ins fnl f* **16/1**

4 *7* **Mick Is Back** 2-8-12 .... StephenDonohoe(5) 4 — 47
(P D Evans) *s.i.s: rn green and towards rr: tk mod 4th ins fnl f: nt trble ldrs* **33/1**

05 **5** *2* **The Brat**[10] 3394 2-8-9 .... PatrickMathers(3) 7 — 36
(James Moffatt) *chsd ldrs: rdn over 2f out: wknd over 1f out* **100/1**

6 *2 1/2* **Sherjawy (IRE)** 2-9-3 .... NickyMackay 6 — 33
(L M Cumani) *broke wl to ld briefly: sn bhd and outpcd* **10/1**

7 *7* **Aquilegia (IRE)** 2-8-12 .... FergusSweeney 3 — 7
(E S McMahon) *s.i.s: bhd: hung lft 1/2-way: effrt over 2f out: no imp on ldrs: wknd over 1f out* **8/1**[2]

1m 12.41s (-2.49) **Going Correction** -0.35s/f (Firm) — 7 Ran SP% **113.3**
Speed ratings (Par 94):102,100,95,86,83 80,71
CSF £4.52 TOTE £1.40: £1.10, £2.40; EX 3.70.
Owner Mrs Sylvia Clegg **Bred** Miss C Lyons **Trained** Tadcaster, N Yorks

FOCUS
The market did not speak in favour of the newcomers and this maiden turned out to be pretty uncompetitive. The winner is the best guide to the level at this stage.

NOTEBOOK
Celtic Sultan(IRE), who was backed and ran with plenty of promise when finishing runner-up to El Bosque over this course and distance on his debut, saw that form given a boost when the winner ran fourth in the Weatherbys Super Sprint earlier in the day. Backed as though defeat was out of the question, he is clearly well regarded and only had to pushed out to score. He can now take a deserved step up in class. (op 4-6 tchd 1-3, 8-11 in places)
Fishforcompliments, a brother to Playtotheaudience, a winner over this trip at two, overcame greenness to run on for second place. It did not help that his rider dropped his whip and he should improve for the run. (op 7-1 tchd 10-1)
Naughty Thoughts(IRE), a half-sister to Blue Bajan, a multiple winner between nine and 12 furlongs, is bred to need middle distances next season. This was a fair debut over what would appear to be an inadequate trip, even at two, and she can do better in time over further. (op 10-1)
Mick Is Back, a half-brother to Princess Celo, a six-furlong winner at two, showed distinct signs of inexperience on his debut and can do better with this run under his belt.
The Brat, last in a seller on her previous start, is of very moderate ability.
Sherjawy(IRE), a half-brother to Sohgol, a winner over a mile at three, hails from a stable that rarely strikes with its juveniles first time out. (op 14-1)

3722 BROWNS MITSUBISHI H'CAP — 6f

7:40 (7:42) (Class 4) (0-85,84) 3-Y-O — £6,232 (£1,866; £933; £467; £233; £117) Stalls Centre

Form — RPR

1030 **1** **Rochdale**[14] 3296 3-9-7 **84** .... PhilipRobinson 5 — 97+
(M A Jarvis) *a.p: led over 1f out: rdn ins fnl f: r.o wl* **4/1**[2]

0330 **2** *1 1/2* **Charles Darwin (IRE)**[10] 3414 3-9-7 **84** .... FrancisNorton 10 — 92
(M Blanshard) *racd keenly: chsd ldrs: nt clr run over 1f out: r.o to take 2nd ins fnl f: nt rch wnr* **10/1**

2003 **3** *1 3/4* **Soto**[12] 3360 3-8-6 **69** .... DaleGibson 1 — 72
(M W Easterby) *led: rdn and hdd over 1f out: no ex ins fnl f* **20/1**

6004 **4** *3/4* **Rainbow Bay**[12] 3360 3-8-11 **74** .... (p) PaulHanagan 11 — 77+
(R A Fahey) *towards rr: reminder early: rdn and hdwy over 1f out: nt clr run ins fnl f: styd on: nt trble ldrs* **20/1**

3221 **5** *1 1/2* **Libor (IRE)**[12] 3349 3-8-13 **76** .... NickyMackay 3 — 72
(L M Cumani) *hld up: hdwy over 2f out: rdn over 1f out: one pce ins fnl f* **6/4**[1]

2333 **6** *3/4* **Making Music**[14] 3299 3-8-5 **68** ow1 .... (p) DavidAllan 9 — 62
(T D Easterby) *chsd ldrs: rdn 2f out: edgd lft over 1f out: wknd ins fnl f* **14/1**

0010 **7** *1 3/4* **Savernake Blue**[19] 3150 3-9-5 **82** .... KDarley 2 — 71
(M R Channon) *in tch: rdn over 1f out: sn wknd* **20/1**

310 **8** *3/4* **Rydal Mount (IRE)**[31] 2739 3-9-5 **82** .... FergusSweeney 6 — 68
(W S Kittow) *prom: rdn 2f out: edgd lft over 1f out: sn wknd* **9/1**[3]

5554 **9** *1/2* **Choysia**[6] 3568 3-9-0 **77** .... NCallan 8 — 62
(D W Barker) *hld up: rdn and sme hdwy over 1f out: wknd ins fnl f* **12/1**

0060 **10** *1 1/4* **Rondo**[12] 3360 3-8-8 **71** .... PhillipMakin 4 — 52
(T D Barron) *s.i.s: a bhd* **50/1**

-306 **11** *10* **Mint**[22] 3042 3-8-8 **71** .... TomEaves 7 — 22
(D W Barker) *hld up in midfield: pushed along over 2f out: sn wknd* **22/1**

1m 12.45s (-2.45) **Going Correction** -0.35s/f (Firm) — 11 Ran SP% **114.0**
Speed ratings (Par 102):102,100,97,96,94 93,91,90,89,88 74
CSF £37.75 CT £720.66 TOTE £4.80: £1.50, £3.30, £4.30; EX 41.70.
Owner Jumeirah Racing **Bred** R F And S D Knipe **Trained** Newmarket, Suffolk

FOCUS
There was just a modest early pace to this sprint handicap and that favoured those who raced prominently.n The runner-up is the best guide to the level.
Rydal Mount(IRE) Official explanation: jockey said filly was unsuited by the good to firm ground
Choysia Official explanation: jockey said filly had no more to give
Rondo Official explanation: jockey ssid gelding missed the break

3723 SECURITY GUARD COMPANY UK LTD H'CAP — 1m 6f

8:10 (8:11) (Class 4) (0-80,80) 4-Y-O+ — £6,477 (£1,927; £963; £481) Stalls Low

Form — RPR

3323 **1** **Oddsmaker (IRE)**[6] 3566 5-8-5 **64** .... (t) DeanMcKeown 7 — 73
(M A Barnes) *rrd s: plld hrd: hld up: hdwy 9f out: led 8f out: rdn 2f out: r.o ins fnl f* **5/1**

-003 **2** *3 1/2* **Thewhirlingdervish (IRE)**[14] 3284 8-8-1 **65** .... DuranFentiman(5) 5 — 69
(T D Easterby) *led to 8f out: remained prom: rdn to take 2nd over 3f out: kpt on same pce fnl f and n.d to wnr* **9/1**

0004 **3** *1* **Dancer's Serenade (IRE)**[16] 3220 4-8-11 **70** .... KDarley 3 — 73
(T P Tate) *restless in stalls: hld up: rdn and hdwy to chse ldrs over 3f out: one pce ins fnl f* **10/1**

2124 **4** *nk* **Compton Eclaire (IRE)**[20] 3114 6-8-2 **61** oh3 .... (v) PaulHanagan 8 — 62
(B Ellison) *hld up: pushed along and outpcd over 4f out: styd on towards fin: nvr able to chal: fin 5th, 3 1/2l, 1l, 1l and nk: plcd 4th* **7/2**[2]

4514 **5** *shd* **Let It Be**[18] 3177 5-8-2 **61** .... FrancisNorton 4 — 62
(K G Reveley) *prom: lost pl over 6f out: renewed effrt 3f out: eased whn no ex wl ins fnl f: fin 6th, shd: plcd 5th* **9/2**[3]

4606 **6** *1/2* **Bobsleigh**[15] 3269 7-7-11 **61** oh7 .... (p) EmmettStack(5) 6 — 61
(H S Howe) *prom: lost pl over 6f out: rdn and outpcd over 4f out: styd on towards fin: fin 7th, 1/2l, plcd 6th* **25/1**

0-25 **D** *1* **Mandatum**[42] 2447 5-9-7 **80** .... NickyMackay 1 — 82+
(L M Cumani) *cl up: sddle slipped 8f out: disp 4th whn lost weight cloth over 1f out: eased whn no ex wl ins fnl f: fin 4th: disq & plcd last* **2/1**[1]

3m 7.05s (0.76) **Going Correction** -0.10s/f (Good) — 7 Ran SP% **113.3**
Speed ratings (Par 105):93,91,90,89,89 89,89
CSF £46.67 CT £429.78 TOTE £6.20: £2.30, £2.20; EX 20.00.
Owner D Maloney **Bred** Margaret Conlon **Trained** Farlam, Cumbria
■ Stewards' Enquiry : Francis Norton caution: allowed mare to coast home without assistance

FOCUS
There was little early pace to this staying handicap and Dean McKeown took the initiative to take on front-running duties a mile out, which proved a race-winning move. The form does not look strong or reliable with the winner the best guide. Mandatum disq: weighed in light.

3724 ABACUS SECURITIES H'CAP — 1m 2f 120y

8:40 (8:40) (Class 5) (0-75,73) 3-Y-O+ — £3,238 (£963; £481; £240) Stalls High

Form — RPR

0402 **1** **Daring Affair**[6] 3566 5-9-11 **70** .... NCallan 4 — 79
(K R Burke) *trckd ldrs: n.m.r over 5f out: led over 2f out: edgd lft over 1f out: edgd rt wl ins fnl f: r.o* **7/2**[3]

0204 **2** *2 1/2* **Lysandra (IRE)**[9] 3429 4-9-13 **72** .... KimTinkler 8 — 76
(N Tinkler) *towards rr: hdwy over 2f out: styd on to take 2nd over 1f out: nt trble wnr* **20/1**

455 **3** *1 1/2* **Gobi King**[21] 3100 4-9-8 **67** .... NickyMackay 1 — 68
(L M Cumani) *in tch: rdn over 3f out: kpt on same pce fnl f* **11/4**[1]

4331 **4** *1* **Silverhay**[19] 3141 5-10-0 **73** .... (p) PhillipMakin 6 — 73
(T D Barron) *led: rdn and hdd over 2f out: one pce fnl f* **9/2**

0041 **5** *5* **Mr Aitch (IRE)**[23] 3009 4-9-8 **72** .... JamesDoyle(5) 7 — 63
(R T Phillips) *prom: rdn and ev ch over 2f out: wknd over 1f out* **3/1**[2]

-004 **6** *5* **Coalpark (IRE)**[7] 3528 3-9-1 **71** .... KDarley 3 — 53
(M Johnston) *bhd: pushed along over 4f out: eased whn n.d fnl f* **9/1**

00-2 **7** *shd* **Wizard Of Us**[56] 2025 6-8-4 **56** .... SophieDoyle(7) 2 — 37
(M Mullineaux) *prom tl pushed along and wknd over 3f out* **14/1**

2m 15.56s (-2.17) **Going Correction** -0.10s/f (Good)
WFA 3 from 4yo+ 11lb — 7 Ran SP% **113.5**
Speed ratings (Par 103):103,101,100,99,95 92,92
CSF £63.14 CT £217.09 TOTE £4.30: £2.20, £4.40; EX 83.90.
Owner Nigel Shields **Bred** N R Shields And K R Burke **Trained** Middleham Moor, N Yorks

FOCUS
An ordinary handicap and modest form rated around the runner-up.

3725 BINGLEY H'CAP — 1m 30y

9:10 (9:10) (Class 5) (0-70,67) 3-Y-O — £3,238 (£963; £481; £240) Stalls Low

Form — RPR

5461 **1** **Just Lille (IRE)**[5] 3582 3-9-4 **64** 6ex .... RoystonFfrench 7 — 77
(Mrs A Duffield) *trckd ldrs: rdn over 3f out: wandered over 2f out: led over 1f out: r.o wl and wl in command fnl f* **9/4**[1]

5206 **2** *3* **Superior Star**[14] 3282 3-8-12 **58** .... (v[1]) PaulHanagan 8 — 64
(R A Fahey) *trckd ldrs: rdn over 3f out: outpcd over 2f out: hung lft and styd on to take 2nd ins fnl f: no ch w wnr* **8/1**

6533 **3** *2 1/2* **Myths And Verses**[15] 3250 3-8-9 **60** .... JamesDoyle(5) 4 — 60+
(K A Ryan) *hld up: rdn over 3f out: hdwy over 2f out: kpt on ins fnl f* **6/1**[3]

2345 **4** *3/4* **Feelin Irie (IRE)**[8] 3473 3-8-11 **57** .... KimTinkler 10 — 59
(N Tinkler) *led: rdn and hdd over 1f out: wknd ins fnl f* **11/1**

0036 **5** *1/2* **Cape Of Storms**[14] 3290 3-9-2 **62** .... TomEaves 9 — 59+
(R Brotherton) *midfield: rdn over 3f out: kpt on ins fnl f: nvr able to chal* **16/1**

0065 **6** *shd* **Crimson Flame (IRE)**[1] 3695 3-9-2 **62** .... (v) NCallan 11 — 59
(M R Channon) *prom: rdn over 2f out: wknd ins fnl f* **8/1**

0-60 **7** *1 1/4* **Sunny Parkes**[21] 3100 3-7-11 **50** .... SophieDoyle(7) 3 — 44
(M Mullineaux) *dwlt: hld up: rdn and wnt lft 2f out: edgd rt over 1f out: kpt on: nvr rchd ldrs* **50/1**

0502 **8** *4* **Pitbull**[8] 3473 3-8-11 **62** .... AndrewElliott(5) 2 — 47
(Mrs G S Rees) *s.i.s: hld up: rdn 3f out: no imp* **5/1**[2]

0460 **9** *5* **Tranos (USA)**[24] 2990 3-9-7 **67** .... NickyMackay 5 — 40
(L M Cumani) *s.i.s: hld up: rdn over 3f out: nvr on terms* **10/1**

50-4 **10** *2* **Stanley Bay (IRE)**[28] 2873 3-8-9 **55** .... DavidAllan 1 — 24
(T D Easterby) *rdn 5f out: a bhd* **20/1**

00-0 **11** *7* **Gypsy's Kiss**[42] 2465 3-8-7 **53** .... FergusSweeney 6 — 6
(B P J Baugh) *racd keenly: midfield: rdn 3f out: wknd 2f out* **66/1**

1m 44.37s (-1.14) **Going Correction** -0.10s/f (Good) — 11 Ran SP% **115.5**
Speed ratings (Par 100):101,98,95,94,94 94,92,88,83,81 74
CSF £19.95 CT £95.69 TOTE £2.70: £1.50, £2.60, £1.50; EX 24.90 Place 6 £328.73, Place 5 £163.95.
Owner Granville J Harper **Bred** Sweetmans Bloodstock **Trained** Constable Burton, N Yorks
■ Stewards' Enquiry : Andrew Elliott two-day ban: used whip when out of contention (Aug 3,4)

FOCUS
A modest three-year-old handicap run at a steady early pace and in which very few got competitive; as such the form is not rated positively.
Pitbull Official explanation: jockey said gelding hung left
T/Plt: £228.40 to a £1 stake. Pool: £59,220.70. 189.20 winning tickets. T/Qpdt: £108.40 to a £1 stake. Pool: £3,034.90. 20.70 winning tickets. DO

3645 LINGFIELD (L-H)

Saturday, July 22

OFFICIAL GOING: Turf course - good to firm (firm in places); all-weather - standard
Wind: Almost nil

3726 JOHN GODFREY ASSOCIATES EBF MAIDEN STKS — 7f

6:20 (6:21) (Class 5) 2-Y-O — £3,886 (£1,156; £577; £288) Stalls High

Form — RPR

60 **1** **Darfour**[8] 3498 2-9-3 .... J-PGuillambert 2 — 76
(M Johnston) *trckd ldr: rdn to ld over 1f out: drvn out* **7/2**[2]

00 **2** *1/2* **Up In Arms (IRE)**[17] 3193 2-9-3 .... StephenCarson 7 — 75
(P Winkworth) *led tl rdn and hdd appr fnl f: kpt on u.p* **40/1**

3 *1 1/4* **Serene Highness (IRE)** 2-8-12 .... TPQueally 3 — 66
(J L Dunlop) *hld up in rr: hdwy 2f out: styd on wl fnl f* **14/1**

0000 **4** *5* **Venir Rouge**[21] 3083 2-9-3 .... AlanDaly 5 — 58
(M Salaman) *t.k.h: in tch whn short of room and swtchd lft over 1f out: sn btn* **9/1**[3]

00 **5** 2 ½ **Color Man**[7] 3545 2-9-3 .... JimCrowley 6 52
(Mrs A J Perrett) *s.i.s: rdn over 3f out: wknd over 1f out* **40/1**

6 **6** 2 **Priory Bay (USA)**[10] 3417 2-9-3 .... RichardMullen 4 47
(E A L Dunlop) *in tch: edgd rt and wknd over 1f out* **4/7**[1]

7 18 **Extractor** 2-9-3 .... PaulDoe 1 —
(J L Dunlop) *s.i.s: sn in tch: edgd rt and wknd wl over 1f out: eased* **20/1**

1m 23.95s (-0.26) **Going Correction** -0.325s/f (Firm) 7 Ran SP% **112.2**
Speed ratings (Par 94):88,87,86,80,77 75,54
CSF £114.31 TOTE £5.60: £1.90, £5.00; EX 68.30.
Owner A M A Al Shorafa **Bred** Hascombe And Valiant Studs **Trained** Middleham Moor, N Yorks

FOCUS
A modest juvenile maiden, run at an average pace. The first three came clear.

NOTEBOOK
Darfour, who had proved distinctly green on his previous two outings, was able to race handily for the first time and showed a game attitude to break his duck at the third attempt. He is clearly going the right way, promises to do better as he steps up in trip, and should make his mark in nuseries. (op 4-1)
Up In Arms(IRE), slow to break on his previous two outings, was given a very positive ride on this step up in distance and posted by far his best effort to date. Now he has seemingly learnt to break on terms he should have more to offer, so he ought to have little trouble in going one better before too long. (op 33-1)
Serene Highness(IRE), bred to make her mark over a longer trip, was doing her best work towards the finish and posted a pleasing debut effort. She is entitled to improve for the experience and looks to have a future. (op 12-1 tchd 11-1)
Venir Rouge ran below his recent level and spoilt his chances by running too freely. (op 12-1)
Priory Bay(USA), sixth on debut in a much hotter contest at Newmarket ten days previously, failed to run his race and proved bitterly disappointing. Something may have been amiss, but he has it all to prove now. Official explanation: jockey said colt never travelled (tchd 8-13)
Extractor Official explanation: jockey said gelding had no more to give

3727 WYPALL WIPERS CHALLENGE NURSERY 6f
6:50 (6:50) (Class 5) 2-Y-O **£3,886** (£1,156; £577; £288) **Stalls** High

Form RPR
5403 **1** **Stir Crazy (IRE)**[2] 3678 2-7-12 **69** .... EdwardCreighton(3) 1 67
(M R Channon) *mde all: rdn out fnl f* **2/1**[2]

4153 **2** 1 **King's Bastion (IRE)**[35] 2630 2-9-7 **89** .... EddieAhern 5 84
(M L W Bell) *chsd wnr thrght: rdn and no imp fnl f* **13/8**[1]

4606 **3** 5 **Hucking Hill (IRE)**[7] 3530 2-8-5 **73** .... LPKeniry 2 53
(J R Best) *chsd ldrs: rdn over 2f out: one pce fnl f* **6/1**

5440 **4** 2 ½ **Urban Warrior**[8] 3496 2-8-4 **72** .... StephenCarson 4 45
(J R Best) *trckd ldrs: rdn 1/2-way: wknd over 1f out* **11/2**[3]

0460 **5** 3 ½ **Princely Royal**[3] 3641 2-7-13 **72** ow5 .... RoryMoore(5) 3 34
(J J Bridger) *stdd s: a towards rr* **25/1**

040 **6** ½ **Bertrada (IRE)**[17] 3201 2-7-12 **66** oh11 .... DavidKinsella 6 27
(H Morrison) *chsd ldrs tl rdn and outpcd 1/2-way* **16/1**

1m 10.78s (-0.89) **Going Correction** -0.325s/f (Firm) 6 Ran SP% **110.8**
Speed ratings (Par 94):92,90,84,80,76 75
CSF £5.48 TOTE £2.40: £1.20, £1.60; EX 6.00.
Owner Miss F V Cove & Mrs V Beech **Bred** Paddy Kennedy **Trained** West Ilsley, Berks

FOCUS
This looks fair form for the grade, with the first two coming clear, although they did get the run of the race. The official ratings shown next to each horse are estimated and for information purposes only.

NOTEBOOK
Stir Crazy(IRE), third at Leicester three days previously, pinged out of the gates and never saw another rival en route to a ready success. He had very much the run of the race though, and a future weight rise will make life harder. (op 15-8)
King's Bastion(IRE) finished well clear of the remainder on this return to a sixth furlong, but simply found the burden of top weight beyond him. He needs some respite from the Handicapper on this evidence, but remains in good form all the same. (tchd 6-4, 7-4 in places)
Hucking Hill(IRE) was found wanting nearing the two-furlong pole and left the impression he needs to revert to the minimum trip in order to get closer in this sphere. (op 11-2)
Urban Warrior, dropping back from seven furlongs, lacks size and is in real danger of regressing. (op 10-1)
Princely Royal Official explanation: jockey said gelding never travelled

3728 LADBROKES.COM SUPPORTING SPINAL INJURIES ASSOCIATION H'CAP 6f
7:20 (7:20) (Class 6) (0-60,59) 3-Y-O+ **£2,388** (£705; £352) **Stalls** High

Form RPR
0405 **1** **Banjo Bay (IRE)**[61] 1899 8-9-8 **58** .... AdamKirby(3) 5 68
(Miss Gay Kelleway) *mid-div: rdn and hdwy over 2f out: led ins fnl f: drvn out* **14/1**

2102 **2** nk **Beau Marche**[18] 3161 4-8-12 **45** ....(b) SebSanders 8 54
(G G Margarson) *chsd ldrs: nt clr run over 2f out: rdn and r.o wl fnl f* **10/1**[3]

5114 **3** 1 ½ **Diamond Josh**[22] 3033 4-9-2 **56** .... JamieHamblett(7) 1 61
(P D Evans) *racd far side: overall ldr tl rdn: edgd lft and hdd ins fnl f* **10/1**[3]

6000 **4** hd **Siraj**[17] 3204 7-9-2 **49** ....(p) J-PGuillambert 18 53
(J Ryan) *hld up on stands' side: r.o fnl f: nvr nrr* **25/1**

0006 **5** hd **Zimbali**[15] 3267 4-8-13 **46** .... JosedeSouza 7 49
(J M Bradley) *trckd ldrs: swtchd rt 2f out: kpt on fnl f* **33/1**

0165 **6** shd **Mirasol Princess**[19] 3155 5-8-9 **49** .... JamesMillman(7) 13 52
(D K Ivory) *mid-division: rdn 2f out: r.o one pce fnl f* **11/1**

4313 **7** 3 **Hammer Of The Gods (IRE)**[12] 3368 6-9-12 **59** ....(bt) AlanMunro 15 53
(P S McEntee) *prom on stands' side: rdn over 2f out: sn btn* **10/3**[1]

0643 **8** nk **Night Rainbow (IRE)**[7] 3538 3-9-3 **58** .... EdwardCreighton(3) 4 51
(C Tinkler) *prom: rdn over 2f out: wknd appr fnl f* **16/1**

0410 **9** shd **Jennverse**[37] 2574 4-9-0 **47** .... JimmyQuinn 11 40
(D K Ivory) *nvr bttr than mid-div* **14/1**

0650 **10** nk **Miss Madame (IRE)**[22] 3044 5-9-5 **52** .... IanMongan 12 44
(T G Mills) *chsd ldrs in centre of crse: rdn over 2f out: wknd over 1f out* **11/1**

0312 **11** nk **Ruby's Dream**[15] 3267 4-9-9 **56** ....(p) RyanMoore 17 47
(J M Bradley) *prom tl rdn and bhd fr 1/2-way* **4/1**[2]

0403 **12** hd **Riolo (IRE)**[20] 3111 4-9-3 **57** ....(p) KevinGhunowa(7) 10 47
(K F Clutterbuck) *mid-div: rdn 1/2-way: swtchd rt over 1f out: sn wknd* **14/1**

540- **13** 2 **Pinafore**[271] 6070 4-9-5 **52** .... JimCrowley 16 36
(P Winkworth) *in tch: rdn 1/2-way: sn btn* **50/1**

0/00 **14** ½ **Galloway Boy (IRE)**[159] 401 9-9-0 **47** ....(t) RobertMiles 3 30
(J F Panvert) *mid-div: rdn and wknd wl over 1f out* **100/1**

3006 **15** ¾ **Trace Clip**[9] 3438 8-8-8 **48** ....(e) MarkCoumbe(7) 9 29
(N I M Rossiter) *v.s.a: a bhd* **25/1**

0000 **16** nk **Canary Island (IRE)**[11] 3389 4-9-6 **53** .... GeorgeBaker 6 33
(J M Bradley) *a in rr* **33/1**

0002 **17** 1 ¼ **Gavioli (IRE)**[15] 3245 4-8-13 **53** .... BarrySavage(7) 14 29
(J M Bradley) *in tch to 1/2-way* **11/1**

1m 10.6s (-1.07) **Going Correction** -0.325s/f (Firm)
WFA 3 from 4yo+ 5lb 17 Ran SP% **128.7**
Speed ratings (Par 101):94,93,91,91,91 90,86,86,86,86 85,85,82,82,81 80,78
CSF £146.64 CT £1498.45 TOTE £19.50: £2.90, £2.20, £2.30, £11.90; EX 164.30.
Owner Miss Zora Fakirmohamed **Bred** Yeomanstown Stud **Trained** Exning, Suffolk

FOCUS
A moderate sprint, but there was no real draw advantage and the form looks sound.
Trace Clip Official explanation: trainer said gelding lost a front shoe

3729 KIMBERLY-CLARK PROFESSIONAL CLAIMING STKS 1m (P)
7:50 (7:50) (Class 6) 3-5-Y-O **£2,388** (£705; £352) **Stalls** High

Form RPR
4451 **1** **Opera Writer (IRE)**[11] 3378 3-8-11 65 ....(e) EddieAhern 1 74
(J R Boyle) *in tch: wnt 2nd 3f out: rdn to ld over 1f out: sn clr* **9/4**[2]

041 **2** 5 **Writ (IRE)**[23] 3014 4-8-13 61 .... SebSanders 4 59
(Ernst Oertel) *led tl rdn and hdd over 1f out: one pce after* **10/11**[1]

0500 **3** 5 **Angel River**[29] 2820 4-8-6 42 ....(e) JimmyQuinn 2 40
(J Ryan) *mid-div: chsd ldrs over 2f out: fdd over 1f out* **25/1**

5340 **4** nk **Musiotal**[38] 2546 5-8-6 45 .... ManavNem(7) 7 46
(P A Blockley) *plld hrd on outside: btn over 2f out* **12/1**

140/ **5** 1 **Bathwick Finesse (IRE)**[638] 6334 4-8-10 75 .... JamesMillman(7) 3 48
(B R Millman) *mid-div: wknd 2f out* **10/1**[3]

0160 **6** ¾ **Inescapable (USA)**[60] 1914 5-8-10 42 .... JackDean(7) 5 46
(A W Carroll) *slowly away: a in rr* **20/1**

000 **7** 5 **Bare Rambler**[27] 2573 3-8-3 39 ....(v[1]) JamieMackay 6 27
(Stef Liddiard) *s.i.s: t.k.h: sn in tch: wknd over 2f out* **80/1**

0 **8** 20 **Miss Marlene**[17] 3200 3-7-12 .... FrancisFerris 8 —
(B G Powell) *trckd ldr to 3f out: sn wknd* **50/1**

1m 39.0s (-0.43) **Going Correction** 0.0s/f (Stan)
WFA 3 from 4yo+ 8lb 8 Ran SP% **111.7**
Speed ratings (Par 101):102,97,92,91,90 89,84,64
CSF £4.33 TOTE £3.40: £1.30, £1.10, £2.50; EX 4.90.Writ and Opera Writer were both the subject of a friendly claim.
Owner M Khan X2 **Bred** J Davison **Trained** Epsom, Surrey

FOCUS
A weak claimer, and although the winner is up 5lb on his previous all-weather pick, the overall form is far from solid

3730 RON HUGGINS (S) STKS 1m 2f (P)
8:20 (8:21) (Class 6) 3-Y-O+ **£2,388** (£705; £352) **Stalls** Low

Form RPR
05 **1** **Medfae (KSA)**[26] 2934 3-8-9 .... AlanMunro 4 67
(C F Wall) *trckd ldr: rdn to ld appr fnl f: readily* **6/1**[3]

5-00 **2** 2 **Gateland**[68] 1738 3-8-9 64 .... EddieAhern 2 63
(W R Swinburn) *trckd ldrs: styd on to go 2nd ins fnl f* **12/1**

5000 **3** 1 ¼ **At The Helm (IRE)**[21] 3095 4-9-0 49 .... PaulDoe 1 56
(W J Knight) *led tl rdn and hdd appr fnl f: one pce* **18/1**

0031 **4** 1 ¼ **Good Article (IRE)**[21] 3074 5-9-11 55 .... RyanMoore 10 65
(D K Ivory) *racd wd: hdwy on outside 3f out: one pce appr fnl f* **7/2**[1]

0600 **5** 3 ½ **Linning Wine (IRE)**[100] 1001 10-9-11 65 ....(p) GeorgeBaker 14 58+
(P A Blockley) *hld up in rr: hdwy over 1f out: nvr nr to chal: lame* **9/1**

0004 **6** ½ **Samson Quest**[11] 3386 4-9-6 52 ....(v) RoryMoore(5) 8 57+
(G F Bridgwater) *in rr: styd on ins fnl 2f nvr nr to chal* **20/1**

0065 **7** 1 ¼ **Salinger (USA)**[21] 3074 4-9-5 45 ....(b) IanMongan 12 49
(Mrs L J Mongan) *t.k.h: in tch: rdn 3f out: nvr nr to chal* **33/1**

5032 **8** 1 **Milk And Sultana**[10] 3411 6-9-6 50 .... JimmyQuinn 5 48
(G A Ham) *in tch tl rdn and wknd over 1f out* **8/1**

0001 **9** nk **Bishops Finger**[10] 3411 6-9-11 57 ....(b) RobertHavlin 11 52
(Jamie Poulton) *a in rr* **4/1**[2]

5326 **10** 2 **Paso Doble**[11] 3386 8-8-12 51 .... JamesMillman(7) 13 42
(B R Millman) *racd wd: a bhd* **14/1**

00P0 **11** 3 ½ **Barton Sands (IRE)**[37] 2577 9-9-11 50 ....(t) J-PGuillambert 3 42
(Ernst Oertel) *mid-div: rdn 3f out: sn btn* **20/1**

0-00 **12** nk **Miracle Baby**[24] 2971 4-8-9 36 .... MarcHalford(5) 7 30
(A J Chamberlain) *trckd ldrs tl rdn and wknd over 2f out* **100/1**

00-6 **13** 4 **Arkholme**[10] 3405 5-9-5 60 .... LPKeniry 9 28
(A M Hales) *hld up: a bhd* **50/1**

3025 **14** 6 **Penang Cinta**[13] 3338 3-8-12 58 .... AdamKirby(3) 6 22
(G A Butler) *mid-div til rdn and wknd 3f out* **12/1**

2m 7.41s (-0.38) **Going Correction** 0.0s/f (Stan)
WFA 3 from 4yo+ 10lb 14 Ran SP% **120.3**
Speed ratings (Par 101):101,99,98,97,94 94,93,92,92,90 87,87,84,79
CSF £71.81 TOTE £8.10: £2.70, £3.20, £5.60; EX 65.10.The winner was bought in for 17,200gns. Gateland was claimed by Jason Parfitt for £6,000.
Owner S Fustok **Bred** Salah M Fustok **Trained** Newmarket, Suffolk
■ Medfae is the first Saudi Arabian-bred winner in Britain.

FOCUS
An above-average seller and the winning time was over half a second faster than the following fillies' handicap. Sound form, rated around the third.
Linning Wine(IRE) Official explanation: vet said gelding returned lame
Penang Cinta Official explanation: jockey said gelding ran too free

3731 9TH YEAR OF THE DAVID WOODHOUSE BIRTHDAY FILLIES' H'CAP 1m 2f (P)
8:50 (8:51) (Class 5) (0-75,75) 3-Y-O+ **£3,238** (£963; £481; £240) **Stalls** Low

Form RPR
1032 **1** **Let Slip**[31] 2752 4-10-0 **75** .... AlanMunro 10 85+
(W Jarvis) *mid-div: hdwy 4f out: rdn over 1f out: led ins fnl f: readily* **4/1**[1]

55-5 **2** 1 ½ **Lunar River (FR)**[26] 2929 3-8-7 **64** ....(t) RichardMullen 13 71
(E A L Dunlop) *trckd ldrs: led briefly 1f out: rdn and nt pce of wnr* **20/1**

2650 **3** nk **Nina Fontenail (FR)**[19] 3152 5-8-10 **57** .... RobertHavlin 11 63
(B R Millman) *hld up in tch: hdwy 2f out: r.o fnl f: nvr nrr* **8/1**

0363 **4** ¾ **Kalatime (IRE)**[26] 2933 3-8-11 **68** .... LPKeniry 12 73
(A M Balding) *led tl hdd 1f out: rdn and fdd ins fnl f* **12/1**

5322 **5** 2 ½ **Shamila**[10] 3400 3-9-0 **74** .... AdamKirby(3) 7 74
(G A Butler) *in tch: rdn 3f out: one pce ins fnl 2f* **5/1**[2]

443 **6** 1 **Kentucky Warbler (IRE)**[15] 3261 3-8-8 **65** .... SteveDrowne 4 63
(H Morrison) *trckd ldrs: rdn 3f out: one pce after* **11/2**[3]

-430 **7** 1 ½ **Reflecting (IRE)**[26] 2929 3-9-3 **74** .... EddieAhern 8 70
(J W Hills) *mid-div: chsd ldrs over 3f out: sn btn* **33/1**

00 **8** hd **Wilderness Bay (IRE)**[9] 3440 4-9-1 **62** .... GeorgeBaker 1 57
(M R Bosley) *in tch: rdn over 3f out: sn bhd* **50/1**

5-33 **9** ½ **Silken Act (CAN)**[23] 3029 3-9-4 **75** .... RyanMoore 6 69
(Mrs A J Perrett) *a bhd* **5/1**[2]

5004 **10** *1 3/4* **Elrafa Mujahid**[15] 3262 4-8-10 **57** AlanDaly 9 48
(Ernst Oertel) *bhd whn c wd into st: nvr on terms* **20/1**
5-00 **11** *hd* **Saucy**[52] 2148 5-8-9 **56** oh10 JimmyQuinn 5 46
(A W Carroll) *plld hrd: a bhd* **25/1**
0003 **12** *1* **Bride To Be (USA)**[23] 3030 3-8-13 **70** SebSanders 2 59
(C E Brittain) *slowly away: a bhd* **14/1**
0104 **P** **Nikki Bea (IRE)**[13] 3338 3-8-4 **61** ow2 PaulDoe 3 —
(Jamie Poulton) *bhd whn sddle slipped: p.u over 3f out* **12/1**
2m 8.12s (0.33) **Going Correction** 0.0s/f (Stan)
WFA 3 from 4yo+ 10lb **13** Ran SP% **120.2**
Speed ratings (Par 100):98,96,96,95,93 93,91,91,90 89,89,—
CSF £91.62 CT £623.72 TOTE £4.50: £1.90, £5.70, £2.80; EX 153.00 Place 6 £266.96, Place 5 £63.20.
Owner The Let Slip Partnership **Bred** John And Susan Davis **Trained** Newmarket, Suffolk
FOCUS
A fair fillies' handicap, but the winning time was over half a second slower than the earlier seller. It may have been an advantage to race up with the pace.
Saucy Official explanation: jockey said mare ran too free
Nikki Bea(IRE) Official explanation: jockey said saddle slipped
T/Plt: £827.40 to a £1 stake. Pool: £50,780.65. 44.80 winning tickets. T/Qpdt: £148.70 to a £1 stake. Pool: £4,260.70. 21.20 winning tickets. JS

3700 NEWBURY (L-H)
Saturday, July 22

OFFICIAL GOING: Good (good to soft in places on straight course after race 2 (3.00)
Half an inch of rain fell on the track in the hour before racing, chainging the ground from good to firm, firm in places, to the easy side of good.
Wind: Virtually nil

3732 STAN JAMES HACKWOOD STKS (GROUP 3) 6f 8y
2:25 (2:27) (Class 1) 3-Y-O+
£28,390 (£10,760; £5,385; £2,685; £1,345; £675) **Stalls** Centre

Form RPR
5010 **1** **Fayr Jag (IRE)**[8] 3494 7-9-7 108 DavidAllan 8 116
(T D Easterby) *trckd ldr 1/2-way: drvn to ld over 1f out: hld on wl u.p fnl f* **16/1**
1603 **2** *nk* **Kodiac**[14] 3295 5-9-3 102 (b) SebSanders 7 111
(J L Dunlop) *lw: trckd ldrs: n.m.r over 1f out: swtchd rt ins last: stayed on wl to take 2nd last strides: nt rch wnr* **25/1**
2124 **3** *shd* **Tawaassol (USA)**[14] 3312 3-8-12 108 (t) RHills 2 110
(Sir Michael Stoute) *chsd ldrs: drvn to chal appr fnl f: stl ev ch ins last: no ex last strides* **5/1**
-042 **4** *shd* **Balthazaar's Gift (IRE)**[28] 2846 3-8-12 115 KerrinMcEvoy 1 110+
(T R George) *hld up rr but in tch: pushed along over 2f out: one pce over 1f out tl styd on wl cl home* **11/4**[2]
0361 **5** *nk* **Baltic King**[28] 2847 6-9-3 114 (t) JimmyFortune 3 110
(H Morrison) *lw: chsd ldrs: ev ch appr fnl f and ins last: no ex cl home* **5/2**[1]
0043 **6** *3/4* **Ashdown Express (IRE)**[8] 3494 7-9-3 111 AlanMunro 10 107
(C F Wall) *lw: t.k.h: hld up rr but in tch: rdn and hdwy appr fnl f: kpt on cl home but nvr quite gng pce to chal* **10/3**[3]
2-00 **7** *1 3/4* **Ajigolo**[28] 2846 3-8-12 106 TedDurcan 4 102
(M R Channon) *led tl hdd over 1f out: wknd ins last* **40/1**
1m 12.41s (-1.91) **Going Correction** -0.075s/f (Good)
WFA 3 from 5yo+ 5lb **7** Ran SP% **107.2**
Speed ratings (Par 113):109,108,108,108,107 106,104
CSF £273.96 TOTE £16.90: £4.40, £5.70; EX 87.80.
Owner Jonathan Gill **Bred** Canice M Farrell Jnr **Trained** Great Habton, N Yorks
FOCUS
Upgraded from Listed level for the first time, but by no means the classiest of Group 3 sprints. Only about half a length covered the first five home and it would be impossible to rate the form highly.
NOTEBOOK
Fayr Jag(IRE), who picked up a weak Group 3 at Newcastle earlier in the month, shaded a five-way photo in what was a competitive sprint. He did not have a lot going for him on paper as he was having to give weight to higher rated rivals and the rain had turned the ground softer than he would like, but he raced prominently throughout and held on well as his rivals closed in near the line. He will apparently take in the Nunthorpe next, a race in which he was sixth last year. (op 14-1)
Kodiac ran well on his return from a break at Haydock last time and followed up that effort with a positive display here. The weights gave him plenty to find with the market principals and the ground turned out to be slower than he would ideally want, but he still only narrowly failed to notch his first success at Pattern level. As we know, there is currently very little between the top sprint handicappers and the Pattern-class sprinters, so it should not have been a total surprise to see him run so well. (op 16-1)
Tawaassol(USA), who has a progressive profile and was expected to appreciate the return to six furlongs, did best of the three-year-olds. He once again got the better of higher rated rivals and a similar race at this level can be won with him in the coming months. (op 4-1 tchd 11-2)
Balthazaar's Gift(IRE), the best of these according to official ratings, has plenty of form on ground with cut in it so the deluge of rain which fell on the track prior to racing ought not to have inconvenienced him. Racing for a new stable, he took a while to pick up from off the pace and was never quite going to get there. He is better than this. (op 3-1)
Baltic King, the Wokingham winner, has still to win in Group company despite numerous tries. He is a consistent type but always worth taking on at a short price - he has only won twice from 11 starts when sent off favourite. (op 11-4 tchd 9-4)
Ashdown Express(IRE) has difficulty winning at the best of times but his record of 122 in this race ensured that he was sent off a pretty short price. The going had turned against him, however, and he struggled to make up ground from the back of the field. (op 3-1)
Ajigolo, who led the field in the Golden Jubilee last time, again adopted front-running tactics. He was well held in the end, though, and does not appear to have retained the ability he showed at two. (op 33-1)

3733 LADBROKES.COM STKS (HERITAGE H'CAP) 1m (S)
3:00 (3:00) (Class 2) 3-Y-O+
£28,044 (£8,397; £4,198; £2,101; £1,048; £526) **Stalls** Centre

Form RPR
03-0 **1** **Salinja (USA)**[24] 2988 4-9-1 **93** RyanMoore 13 102
(Mrs A J Perrett) *hld up in rr: shkn up and hdwy over 2f out: led ins last: edgd rt u.p cl home: all out* **18/1**
0033 **2** *nk* **Audience**[24] 2988 6-8-10 **88** (p) PaulDoe 12 96
(J Akehurst) *in tch: hdwy on stands rail 2f out: str chal ins last: nt qckn cl home* **13/2**
0004 **3** *shd* **Capable Guest (IRE)**[14] 3313 4-9-1 **93** TedDurcan 3 101
(M R Channon) *lw: rr but in tch: hdwy over 2f out: r.o strly ins last to press ldrs wl ins last: no ex cl home* **4/1**[1]
0005 **4** *1* **Joseph Henry**[9] 3433 4-8-2 **80** JoeFanning 5 87+
(M Johnston) *rr but in tch: rdn and hdwy over 2f out: styd on ins last: one pce whn hmpd cl home* **16/1**
2421 **5** *nk* **Kelucia (IRE)**[21] 3088 5-8-12 **90** SebSanders 9 95
(R M Beckett) *bhd: hdwy over 2f out: styd on u.p ins last: gng on cl home but nt pce to rch ldrs* **11/2**[3]
0202 **6** *hd* **Ace Of Hearts**[14] 3313 7-9-10 **102** GeorgeBaker 4 106
(C F Wall) *lw: chsd ldrs: led 2f out: sn rdn: hdd ins last and sn one pce* **5/1**[2]
6/00 **7** *3/4* **Seulement (USA)**[14] 3313 4-9-3 **95** KerrinMcEvoy 6 98
(L M Cumani) *chsd ldrs: chal ins fnl 2f: one pce ins last* **15/2**
-235 **8** *shd* **Spirit Of France (IRE)**[148] 507 4-9-2 **94** RoystonFfrench 1 96
(Christian Wroe, UAE) *pitched leaving stalls: sn rcvrd to chhase ldrs: ev ch 1f out: outpcd ins last* **33/1**
10-1 **9** *3/4* **Namroud (USA)**[29] 2810 7-8-7 **85** PaulHanagan 11 86
(R A Fahey) *t.k.h: led ins fnl 2f: hdd 2f out: styd pressing ldrs tl wknd ins last* **9/1**
0246 **10** *nk* **Calcutta**[16] 3218 10-8-11 **89** MichaelHills 2 89
(B W Hills) *lw: bhd: hdwy over 2f out: chsd ldrs over 1f out: sn one pce* **14/1**
0066 **11** *shd* **Diktatorial**[16] 3214 4-8-4 **82** AlanMunro 10 82
(G A Butler) *chsd ldrs tl outpcd 2f out: kpt on again wl ins last* **20/1**
04/0 **12** *49* **Beauchamp Pilot**[14] 3313 8-9-2 **97** AdamKirby(3) 7 —
(G A Butler) *led tl hdd ins fnl 4f: wknd rapidly: t.o* **33/1**
1m 39.59s (-1.03) **Going Correction** -0.075s/f (Good) **12** Ran SP% **115.6**
Speed ratings (Par 109):102,101,101,100,100 100,99,99,98,98 98,49
CSF £125.02 CT £573.55 TOTE £21.20: £5.20, £2.90, £1.90; EX 182.10 Trifecta £997.40 Part won. Pool £1,404.80, 0.50 winning units..
Owner Mrs Priscilla Graham **Bred** C Beam **Trained** Pulborough, W Sussex
FOCUS
Most of these are pretty exposed, and a fairly steady early pace resulted in something of a sprint to the line and a bunch finish. Not strong form for the grade.
NOTEBOOK
Salinja(USA) travelled well towards the rear of the bunched field and picked up in good style when the sprint for home began. He likes a bit of cut in the ground so the heavy rain which changed the ground description would have been in his favour. He also stays further than this, and is likely to be seen out next at Goodwood over an extra two furlongs. (tchd 16-1)
Audience, a generally consistent type, is another who does not mind getting his toe in. He is rated to win at present, as he is on a mark 5lb lower than when last successful, but he is hardly prolific. (op 7-1)
Capable Guest(IRE), beaten by the draw at Ascot and unlucky in running last time out, had no such excuses this time. He was sent off favourite for this competitive heat, but whether that was merited judging by his modest strike-rate is open to question. He should continue to go well off this sort of mark but is generally worth opposing. (op 9-2)
Joseph Henry would have finished a touch closer had he not been hampered close home but he would not have gained another place. He is now on a mark he really ought to be able to capitalise on.
Kelucia(IRE), 5lb higher than when successful at Newmarket last time out, finished well next to the stands'-side rail, but it was all too late. She needs a stronger pace than she got here. (op 6-1)
Ace Of Hearts, runner-up a couple of times this year so far off a mark of 101, was back on his highest ever mark of 102 here. The rain would not have been in his favour but he still was not beaten that far. (op 9-2 tchd 11-2)
Seulement(USA) was going well enough entering the final two furlongs but he did not find as much as looked likely under pressure. He might need to drop a bit more in the weights before he regains the winning thread. (tchd 8-1)
Spirit Of France(IRE), having his first run back in this country since changing stables, is going to need to drop a few pounds from his current high mark before he starts winning again. Official explanation: jockey said gelding stumbled after leaving stalls
Namroud(USA) should not have been inconvenienced by the easing underfoot conditions, but he disappointed. (op 8-1)
Beauchamp Pilot Official explanation: jockey said gelding's stride shortened from 4f out

3734 WEATHERBYS SUPER SPRINT 5f 34y
3:30 (3:33) (Class 2) 2-Y-O
£76,725 (£28,685; £13,975; £6,100; £2,800; £1,445) **Stalls** Centre

Form RPR
161 **1** **Elhamri**[32] 2724 2-9-4 DPMcDonogh 12 106
(S Kirk) *racd in centre course: mde all: hrd rdn fr over 1f out: r.o gamely* **9/1**[3]
42 **2** *1* **Ishi Adiva**[12] 3358 2-8-1 ow1 RichardThomas 15 85
(Tom Dascombe) *racd in centre crse: in tch: hrd drvn 1/2-way: styd on strly fnl f to take 2nd cl home but nt rch wnr* **100/1**
216 **3** *hd* **We'll Confer**[32] 2724 2-8-13 NCallan 13 97
(K A Ryan) *pressed wnr in centre crse: chal over 1f out: sn hrd rdn: no ex ins last and lost 2nd cl home* **20/1**
01 **4** *1 1/4* **El Bosque (IRE)**[15] 3247 2-8-11 AlanMunro 11 90
(B R Millman) *lw: racd in centre crse: bhd and sn rdn: kpt on wl ins fnl f: nt rch ldrs* **33/1**
1 **5** *1 1/4* **Ingleby Image**[113] 814 2-8-0 PaulFessey 9 75
(T D Barron) *w'like: racd far side: s.i.s: sn in tch: rdn 1/2-way: kpt on wl fnl f but nvr gng pce to chal* **12/1**
1113 **6** *shd* **Gilded (IRE)**[10] 3415 2-8-10 RichardHughes 14 84+
(R Hannon) *racd stands side: s.i.s: sn in tch: styd on wl to ld that gp jst ins last and sn clr that bunch: no ch w centre* **11/4**[1]
410 **7** *1/2* **Riverside Dancer (USA)**[29] 2800 2-8-6 CatherineGannon 1 79
(K A Ryan) *racd far side: chse ldrs: rdn and one pce fnl 2f* **28/1**
641 **8** *1* **Gold Spirit (IRE)**[7] 3521 2-8-5 RichardMullen 10 74
(E J O'Neill) *racd far side: chsd ldrs: hrd drvn fr 1/2-way: kpt on same pce fnl f* **25/1**
3152 **9** *nk* **Satulagi (USA)**[21] 3084 2-7-13 JimmyQuinn 6 67
(J S Moore) *racd far side: sn pushed along in rr: hdwy fnl f: kpt on wl cl home* **10/1**
1210 **10** *1* **Everymanforhimself (IRE)**[32] 2719 2-8-6 JoeFanning 2 70
(J G Given) *lw: racd far side: bhd: hdwy over 1f out: kpt on ins last: nt rch ldrs* **16/1**
610 **11** *1 1/4* **Resignation (IRE)**[15] 3252 2-8-9 JimmyFortune 19 69+
(R Hannon) *racd stand side: s.i.s: bhd: rdn 1/2-way: styd on fnl f to go 2nd that gp but nvr gng pce to get competitive* **12/1**
2412 **12** *1 1/2* **Frisky Talk (IRE)**[8] 3476 2-8-6 MichaelHills 17 60+
(B W Hills) *racd stands side: in tch: rdn and one pce fnl 2f* **66/1**
0031 **13** *1 1/2* **Scented Present**[8] 3468 2-8-12 SteveDrowne 8 61
(B J Meehan) *racd far side: bhd: sn pushed along: kpt on fr over 1f out: nt rch ldrs* **25/1**

6053 **14** *nk* **Bookiesindex Boy**[10] 3407 2-8-7 ....(b) AdamKirby 3 55
(J R Jenkins) *racd far side: chsd ldrs: sn rdn: wknd fnl f* **150/1**

021 **15** *1 ½* **Ice Mountain**[4] 3605 2-8-5 .... PhilipRobinson 18 47+
(B Smart) *racd stand side: led that gp tl jst ins last: sn wknd* **8/1**[2]

0314 **16** *¾* **Proper (IRE)**[35] 2630 2-8-3 .... AdrianMcCarthy 7 43
(M R Channon) *swtg: racd far side: chsd ldrs over 3f* **100/1**

10 **17** *2 ½* **Hephaestus**[7] 3544 2-8-8 .... DaneO'Neill 16 39+
(M R Channon) *racd stands side: in tch over 3f* **100/1**

2230 **18** *¾* **Cav Okay (IRE)**[15] 3252 2-8-12 .... RyanMoore 21 40+
(R Hannon) *lw: racd stands side: chsd ldrs tl wknd appr fnl f* **14/1**

044 **19** *2 ½* **Indian Song (IRE)**[12] 3344 2-7-13 .... JamieMackay 4 18
(R F Johnson Houghton) *racd far side: outpcd most of way* **100/1**

2644 **20** *2* **La Neige**[15] 3252 2-9-1 .... TedDurcan 22 27+
(M R Channon) *lw: rced stands side: outpcd most of way* **20/1**

6130 **21** *¾* **Nina Blini**[10] 3415 2-8-5 .... KerrinMcEvoy 23 14+
(B J Meehan) *racd stands side: a outpcd* **10/1**

6021 **22** *5* **Avertuoso**[7] 3555 2-9-0 .... RoystonFfrench 5 5
(B Smart) *racd far side: chsd ldrs over 3f* **33/1**

404 **23** *13* **Billy Red**[10] 3408 2-8-10 ....(v[1]) SebSanders 20 —
(J R Jenkins) *racd stands side: bhd fr 1/2-way* **100/1**

61.32 secs (-1.24) **Going Correction** -0.075s/f (Good) **23** Ran SP% **127.5**
Speed ratings (Par 100):106,104,104,102,100 99,99,97,97,95 93,91,88,88,85 84,80,79,75,72 70,62,42
CSF £751.56 TOTE £11.70: £2.60, £33.30, £6.90; EX 2404.90 Trifecta £8519.30 Part won. Pool £11,999.05, 0.10 winning units..
Owner Norman Ormiston **Bred** Highfield Stud Ltd **Trained** Upper Lambourn, Berks

FOCUS
A fair renewal on paper but, in contrast to previous years, those drawn in the middle and who raced up the centre of the track were strongly favoured. The group racing close to the stands' rail were that Gilded headed were at a massive disadvantage (perhaps as much as 14lb to 20lb), and that clearly undermines the overall strength of the form. There's no knocking Elhamri, however, and he is well worth his place in a Group race.

NOTEBOOK
Elhamri, a game winner of the Windsor Castle Stakes last time out, showed that bravery again in fighting off the attentions of the eventual third when strongly challenged inside the final two furlongs. He made every yard, gave weight and a beating to the rest and shrugged off concerns that the rain had put paid to his chances. He is clearly a smart performer and deserves a crack at a Group contest now - connections are pondering the Prix Morny. (tchd 10-1)
Ishi Adiva, narrowly beaten at Ripon last time out, improved on that form on her third outing. She benefited from racing in the group which came up the centre of the track but was perhaps suited by the easier ground, and an auction maiden should come her way on this evidence.
We'll Confer was over three lengths behind Elhamri at Ascot but the turnaround in the weights (5lb pull) gave him some hope of reversing the form. He threw down a determined challenge inside the final quarter mile but lost the battle and that probably cost him the runner-up spot, too. He should pay his way in good nursery company. (op 25-1)
El Bosque(IRE), a winner over six furlongs last time out, benefited, like the first three, from racing on the faster ground up the middle of the track. He found this an inadequate test, though, and will be happier when he gets to race over an extra furlong again.
Ingleby Image, a heavy-ground maiden winner, came out best of the group which raced on the far side. She was the least experienced in the line-up, but looked particularly fit so there may not be much more to come. (tchd 14-1 in a place)
Gilded(IRE) had to overcome a slow start but still won the race on the stands' side by four lengths. Considering that, she can be regarded as unlucky to have only placed sixth overall. She is a speedy filly and the Molecomb looks the ideal target for her. (op 10-3 tchd 4-1)
Riverside Dancer(USA), seventh in the Albany Stakes last time out, came home second from the far-side group. She ran with plenty of credit considering her disadvantageous draw and can do better. (op 25-1 tchd 33-1)
Gold Spirit(IRE) did not run up the form of his Chester maiden win a week earlier and might have found the race coming a bit too soon.
Satulagi(USA) needs six furlongs nowadays. (op 15-2)
Resignation(IRE) ran better than the bare form suggests as he was second home from those who raced on the slower ground up the stands' side, and he wasn't well away. (tchd 11-1)
Frisky Talk(IRE) showed speed on the disadvantaged stands' side but may have found the ground slower than ideal.
Ice Mountain showed up well among those who were at a big disadvantage near the stands' rail. He ran much better than the bare facts suggest. (op 15-2)
Cav Okay(IRE) Official explanation: jockey said colt lost its action

3735 TRAILFINDERS CONDITIONS STKS 7f (S)
4:00 (4:03) (Class 3) 2-Y-O
£7,478 (£2,239; £1,119; £560; £279; £140) **Stalls** Centre

Form RPR

1 **1** **Thousand Words**[37] 2579 2-8-13 .... RichardHughes 6 98+
(B W Hills) *w'like: lw: hld up in rr: hdwy over 2f out: trckd ldr appr fnl f: drvn and qcknd to ld nr fin: readily* **15/8**[2]

1 **2** *nk* **Drumfire (IRE)**[30] 2778 2-8-13 .... JoeFanning 1 97+
(M Johnston) *w'like: scope: led: drvn and qcknd over 2f out: edgd lft u.p ins last: hdd and no ex cl home* **5/4**[1]

3 *2* **Striving Storm (USA)** 2-8-7 .... AlanMunro 5 86
(P W Chapple-Hyam) *w'like: t.k.h: hld up in tch: hdwy over 2f out: wnt 3rd appr fnl f: nt pce of ldrs ins last but styd on wl* **12/1**[3]

41 **4** *3 ½* **Princeton (IRE)**[9] 3455 2-8-10 .... TedDurcan 7 81
(M R Channon) *lw: bhd: rdn over 2f out: hdwy over 1f out: sn hanging lft but styd on ins last: nvr in contention* **14/1**

0 **5** *1* **Little Miss Tara (IRE)**[53] 2106 2-8-5 .... JimmyQuinn 2 73
(A B Haynes) *unf: bhd: rdn and effrt over 2f out: nt rch ldrs: wknd over 1f out* **33/1**

1 **6** *1 ¾* **Monachello (USA)**[27] 2899 2-8-13 .... RyanMoore 3 77
(Mrs A J Perrett) *chsd ldrs: rdn over 2f out: wknd over 1f out* **12/1**[3]

513 **7** *1 ¾* **As One Does**[19] 3143 2-8-13 .... NCallan 4 72
(K A Ryan) *t.k.h: chsd ldr to 2f out: sn btn* **16/1**

1m 25.73s (-1.27) **Going Correction** -0.075s/f (Good) **7** Ran SP% **110.1**
Speed ratings (Par 98):104,103,101,97,96 94,92
CSF £4.17 TOTE £2.70: £1.50, £1.40; EX 4.90.
Owner K Abdulla **Bred** Juddmonte Farms Ltd **Trained** Lambourn, Berks

FOCUS
A decent conditions event featuring four last-time-out winners. Strong form, and the first two, who finished clear, are destined for better things.

NOTEBOOK
Thousand Words ◆ once again showed that he is in posession of a smart turn of foot and, having travelled strongly off the pace, mowed down the favourite in impressive style in the closing stages. A return to faster ground is likely to see him in an even better light and he looks a smart prospect, well up to winning at Pattern level. The Acomb and Champagne Stakes are the likely targets, and he is available at 40-1 for next year's 2000 Guineas. (op 7-4 tchd 2-1)
Drumfire(IRE) ◆, well supported throughout the day, set out to make every yard and did little wrong in defeat, only succumbing to a well-timed challenge from a smart rival. He too can make his mark at a higher level, and he might be a Vintage Stakes candidate for a trainer who has a cracking record in that contest over recent seasons, saddling two winners, a runner-up and two thirds from six runners over the past five years. (op 13-8 tchd 6-5)
Striving Storm(USA) ◆, an athletic sort who is a half-brother to a juvenile sprint winner in the US, is out of a mare who was a triple sprint winner in America. He ran a blinder considering he was making his racecourse debut against smart opposition, and this well-regarded colt looks nailed on to win his maiden on the way to better things. (op 13-2 tchd 6-1)
Princeton(IRE), workmanlike in winning on the Polytrack last time, had a lot more to do against this opposition and tended to hang left while struggling to get into contention. (op 25-1)
Little Miss Tara(IRE), well held on her debut, looked out of her depth in this company and did quite well to beat a couple home. As a daughter of Namid she was no doubt helped by the easing of the ground. (op 100-1)
Monachello(USA) failed to build on the promise of his debut win at Warwick and the judgement has to be that he was unsuited by the easier ground. (tchd 14-1)
As One Does was the most experienced of these but he raced a touch keenly and disappointed. (op 12-1)

3736 DAVID WILSON HOMES STEVENTON STKS (LISTED RACE) 1m 2f 6y
4:35 (4:35) (Class 1) 3-Y-0+ **£15,898** (£6,025; £3,015; £1,503) **Stalls** Centre

Form RPR

115 **1** **Tam Lin**[29] 2801 3-8-10 105.................... RyanMoore 2 114+
(Sir Michael Stoute) *lw: racd in 3rd: hdwy 2f out: wnt 2nd 1f out: flashed tail u.p: hung rt ins last: styd on to ld last strides* **5/2**[2]

/3-2 **2** *hd* **Windsor Knot (IRE)**[15] 3254 4-9-3 107.................... KerrinMcEvoy 3 111
(Saeed Bin Suroor) *trckd ldr: drvn to chal 2f out: led appr fnl f: ct last strides* **7/4**[1]

121- **3** *1 ¼* **Khyber Kim**[273] 6025 4-9-3 103.................... DaneO'Neill 4 109
(H Candy) *led: rdn over 2f out: hdd over 1f out and sn one pce* **5/2**[2]

1045 **4** *27* **Mulaqat**[15] 3254 3-8-10 111.................... RichardHughes 5 60+
(M P Tregoning) *lw: a last: reminder 4f out: rdn 3f out: wknd rapidly over 2f out* **7/1**[3]

2m 4.46s (-4.25) **Going Correction** -0.075s/f (Good)
WFA 3 from 4yo 10lb **4** Ran SP% **106.0**
Speed ratings (Par 111):114,113,112,91
CSF £6.96 TOTE £3.60; EX 5.60.
Owner Gainsborough Stud **Bred** Gainsborough Stud Management Ltd **Trained** Newmarket, Suffolk

FOCUS
A competitive conditions event despite the small field, and solid form for the grade. None of the first three was fully exposed and it is worth taking a positive view of the form.

NOTEBOOK
Tam Lin did not look the most enthusiastic as his tail flashed under pressure, but his rider still managed to get him to put his head in front near the line. He is a talented animal and has now won three of his four starts, but whether he will always put it in, especially in tougher company, is open to question. (op 2-1 tchd 11-4)
Windsor Knot(IRE), who got a little warm beforehand, looked to have been found a good opportunity to finally get back to winning ways, and he looked the likeliest winner when taking the measure of Khyber Kim, but he was eventually collared near the line. He has the ability to win at this level but is short of his two-year-old best. (tchd 13-8)
Khyber Kim, a lightly-raced four-year-old, has gone well fresh in the past so it was no great concern that he was making his seasonal reappearance, especially as he looked fit beforehand. He also likes a bit of give in the ground so it was no surprise to see some money for him in the market. He set a good pace in front, kept fighting after being headed and, while he needs to progress to win at this level, he is sufficiently unexposed to be open to further improvement. (op 10-3 tchd 7-2)
Mulaqat would not have been suited by the easing of the ground at all and trailed in well beaten. Official explanation: jockey said colt never travelled (op 11-2)

3737 SPORTING INDEX H'CAP 1m 2f 6y
5:10 (5:11) (Class 3) (0-95,92) 3-Y-0+
£7,790 (£2,332; £1,166; £583; £291; £146) **Stalls** Centre

Form RPR

5-14 **1** **Inchloch**[16] 3214 4-9-9 82.................... RichardHughes 10 91
(B G Powell) *hld up rr but in tch: hdwy on outside over 2f out: hrd drvn to ld 1f out: kpt on strly cl home* **5/1**[3]

6 **2** *1 ½* **Starnevees (FR)**[30] 2787 5-10-0 87.................... KerrinMcEvoy 2 93
(L M Cumani) *swtg: chsd ldrs: wnt 2nd 2f out: chal 1f out: nt qckn ins last: jst hld on for 2nd* **12/1**

0010 **3** *shd* **Humble Opinion**[14] 3313 4-10-0 87.................... JimmyFortune 4 93
(B J Meehan) *in tch: rdn and hdwy over 2f out: styd on u.p to press for 2nd cl home but no imp on wnr* **7/2**[2]

600- **4** *2 ½* **She's My Outsider**[249] 6350 4-9-3 76.................... JimmyQuinn 9 77
(I A Wood) *chsd ldr: led over 3f out: hdd 1f out: sn wknd* **11/1**

0000 **5** *¾* **Gracechurch (IRE)**[14] 3318 3-8-10 79.................... TedDurcan 3 79
(M R Channon) *rr but in tch: rdn and hdwy 3f out: nvr gng pce to rch ldrs: wknd fnl f* **6/1**

3-52 **6** *nk* **Great Orator (USA)**[19] 3151 4-9-3 76.................... DaneO'Neill 7 75
(H Candy) *swtg: chsd ldrs: rdn 3f out: wknd appr fnl f* **5/2**[1]

6000 **7** *3* **Silver Blue (IRE)**[9] 3443 3-9-9 92.................... PatDobbs 6 86
(R Hannon) *bhd: rdn 3f out: nvr in contention* **14/1**

1010 **8** *3 ½* **Sir Arthur (IRE)**[16] 3214 3-8-10 79.................... JoeFanning 8 66
(M Johnston) *led tl hdd over 3f out: wknd 2f out* **11/2**

2m 8.18s (-0.53) **Going Correction** -0.075s/f (Good)
WFA 3 from 4yo+ 10lb **8** Ran SP% **119.8**
Speed ratings (Par 107):99,97,97,95,95 94,92,89
CSF £64.76 CT £240.54 TOTE £5.70: £1.80, £2.80, £1.80; EX 38.10 Place 6 £4,765.14, Place 5 £154.09..
Owner Jimmy & Rita Wenman **Bred** Lord Vestey **Trained** Morestead, Hants
■ Stewards' Enquiry : Jimmy Fortune one-day ban: careless riding (Aug 3)

FOCUS
An ordinary handicap for the grade and the early pace was steady. The form, assessed through the third, has not been rated positively.

NOTEBOOK
Inchloch, held up off a steady pace, was brought with a withering run down the outside, where the ground had been proven to be quickest earlier on the card, and ran out a ready winner. A relatively lightly-raced four-year-old, he is improving for his current trainer, for whom he has now won twice from three starts. (op 6-1)
Starnevees(FR), having only his second start for Cumani, improved for his seasonal return, the easier ground and the step up to ten furlongs. Together with the third, he pulled clear of the rest, and if he can build on this he could soon end his two-year losing streak. (op 7-1)
Humble Opinion usually runs his race and today was no exception, despite not having ground conditions to suit him ideally. He finished well clear of the third, but he is hardly well handicapped on a career-high mark of 87. (tchd 4-1 and 9-2 in a place)
She's My Outsider, who came in for some each-way support at big prices, was not disgraced on her seasonal reappearance. Her stamina for this trip was unproven and she struggled to see it out. (op 25-1)

Gracechurch(IRE), who is back on the mark he last won off, should not have been inconvenienced by the easing ground conditions, but he proved disappointing. (op 8-1)
Great Orator(USA), a beaten favourite three times now, is becoming expensive to follow. He ran well on easy ground in a course and distance maiden last autumn, so that is no excuse. (op 3-1 tchd 7-2)
Silver Blue(IRE) could not take advantage of a drop in grade and looks handicapped up to the hilt. (op 12-1)
Sir Arthur(IRE) was granted an uncontested lead and was able to set just a steady pace, but he was totally unable to capitalise. He does not look straightforward and may require headgear. (op 5-1 tchd 6-1)
T/Jkpt: Not won. T/Plt: £24,121.30 to a £1 stake. Pool: £142,084.50. 4.30 winning tickets. T/Qpdt: £245.70 to a £1 stake. Pool: £7,340.60. 22.10 winning tickets. ST

3706 NEWMARKET (JULY) (R-H)

Saturday, July 22

OFFICIAL GOING: Good to firm

Wind: Light, half-behind until race 3 then turning fresh Weather: Overcast and humid until after race 3 then turning showery

3738 LETTERGOLD PLASTICS MAIDEN STKS — 6f

2:10 (2:10) (Class 4) 2-Y-O — **£4,533** (£1,348; £674; £336) **Stalls** High

Form				RPR
	1		**Cockney Rebel (IRE)** 2-9-3 .... DO'Donohoe 1 (G A Huffer) *trckd ldrs: led over 1f out: sn rdn and hung lft: r.o* **10/1**	83
	2	1 ¼	**Cavalry Guard (USA)** 2-9-3 .... EddieAhern 5 (H R A Cecil) *hmpd s: hld up: hdwy over 2f out: rdn and ev ch 1f out: sn edgd lft: no ex towards fin* **5/1**[3]	80+
2	**3**	3 ½	**Gentleman Pirate**[36] [2617] 2-9-3 .... TPQueally 7 (M H Tompkins) *hmpd s: sn chsng ldr: rdn and ev ch over 1f out: sn edgd lft: wknd ins fnl f* **11/8**[1]	69
	4	nk	**College Scholar (GER)** 2-9-3 .... ChrisCatlin 6 (M R Channon) *dwlt and hmpd s: hdwy over 4f out: rdn over 1f out: edgd lft and wknd* **7/1**	68
66	**5**	4	**Reebal**[9] [3445] 2-9-3 ....(b[1]) LDettori 8 (B J Meehan) *swvd lft s: led: rdn and hdd over 1f out: sn wknd* **9/2**[2]	56
	6	5	**Lawyer To World** 2-9-3 .... ShaneKelly 4 (N A Callaghan) *hmpd s: outpcd* **8/1**	41
	7	5	**Nou Camp** 2-9-3 .... JohnEgan 3 (N A Callaghan) *hmpd s: hld up: rdn and wknd over 2f out* **25/1**	26

1m 13.81s (0.46) **Going Correction** 0.0s/f (Good) **7** Ran SP% **113.5**
Speed ratings (Par 96):96,94,89,89,83 77,70
CSF £57.55 TOTE £8.40: £2.50, £3.10; EX 82.20.
Owner Phil Cunningham **Bred** Oak Lodge Bloodstock **Trained** Newmarket, Suffolk

FOCUS
This maiden featured mainly unraced or inexperienced colts and there was little strength in depth, so the value of the form is hard to pin down. Sound efforts by the first two, though. They raced down the centre of the track.

NOTEBOOK
Cockney Rebel(IRE) ◆, a half-brother to four winners who holds a Derby entry, was said to be a doubtful runner unless the rains came but took his chance and seemed to handle the ground. Always travelling well just behind the leaders, he showed signs of greenness when hitting the front - which was the reason for him hanging - but did it nicely in the end. He looks capable of going on to better things. (op 12-1)
Cavalry Guard(USA) ◆, a $200,000 American-bred colt with a Gimcrack entry, ran a nice race on this debut. After being slightly hampered by the wayward Reebal at the start, he settled off the pace before coming through looking likely to score. However, the winner proved too strong up the hill. He lost nothing in defeat and was clear of the rest, so should be winning before too long. (op 7-2)
Gentleman Pirate, narrowly beaten in what looks an ordinary Sandown maiden on his debut, was expected to appreciate this extra furlong. He was well backed and appeared to have every chance, but was brushed aside by the two newcomers. His future is likely to lie in nurseries. (op 13-8 and tchd 7-4 in a place)
College Scholar(GER), another newcomer and one who is bred to appreciate at least a mile, ran well despite showing his inexperience. He is likely to be better for the outing. (tchd 8-1)
Reebal, who had run reasonably in a couple of fair maidens previously, had the blinkers on for the first time. He swerved badly left leaving the stalls, slightly hampering several of his rivals, then made the running until the principals swept by coming out of the dip. He will be better off in nurseries, but needs to get in the frame to qualify. (op 6-1 tchd 13-2)
Lawyer To World, a 125,000gns brother to Stormont, appeared clueless on this debut and was always at the back. (tchd 9-1)
Nou Camp, related to several winners at around a mile, like his stable companion showed very little on this debut. (op 22-1)

3739 VC BET APHRODITE STKS (LISTED RACE) (F&M) — 1m 4f

2:40 (2:43) (Class 1) 3-Y-O+ — **£15,898** (£6,025; £3,015; £1,503; £753; £378) **Stalls** Centre

Form				RPR
216	**1**		**Quenched**[30] [2772] 3-8-4 100 .... RobertHavlin 8 (J H M Gosden) *led 1f: chsd ldr to 6f out: rdn over 2f out: swtchd lft over 1f out: r.o to ld wl ins fnl f* **4/1**[2]	105+
6114	**2**	½	**Cresta Gold**[14] [3292] 3-8-4 93 .... MartinDwyer 3 (A Bailey) *led 11f out: rdn over 1f out: hdd wl ins fnl f* **14/1**	104
22-1	**3**	nk	**Pictavia (IRE)**[23] [3021] 4-9-5 107 .... LDettori 7 (Saeed Bin Suroor) *a.p: swtchd lft over 6f out: sn chsng ldr: rdn and ev ch fnl f: styd on* **1/1**[1]	107
1111	**4**	1	**Gower Song**[22] [3046] 3-8-4 84 .... JohnEgan 1 (D R C Elsworth) *hld up: hdwy over 4f out: rdn and ev ch 1f out: styd on same pce* **8/1**	102
4-10	**5**	nk	**Sindirana (IRE)**[30] [2772] 3-8-7 92 .... J-PGuillambert 2 (Sir Michael Stoute) *hld up: hdwy over 1f out: sn rdn: styd on* **10/1**	104
53-1	**6**	hd	**Power Girl (GER)**[33] [2706] 4-9-5 94 .... ShaneKelly 4 (P F I Cole) *hld up: effrt and nt clr run over 1f out: nvr able to chal* **16/1**	104
1112	**7**	3 ½	**Reem Three**[23] [3021] 3-8-4 97 .... NickyMackay 6 (L M Cumani) *plld hrd and prom: bmpd over 6f out: rdn over 1f out: wknd fnl f* **15/2**[3]	96
033-	**8**	5	**Desert Move (IRE)**[338] [4515] 4-9-2 97 .... ChrisCatlin 5 (M R Channon) *s.i.s: hld up: rdn over 2f out: wknd over 1f out* **50/1**	88

2m 33.32s (0.41) **Going Correction** 0.0s/f (Good)
WFA 3 from 4yo 12lb **8** Ran SP% **116.5**
Speed ratings (Par 111):98,97,97,96,96 96,94,90
CSF £57.92 TOTE £5.20: £1.60, £3.60, £1.10; EX 86.80.
Owner K Abdulla **Bred** Juddmonte Farms Ltd **Trained** Newmarket, Suffolk

FOCUS
A decent-looking Listed contest in which they came up the stands' rail in the straight, but it was run at a steady pace and those behind early never really figured. The second and fourth showed improved form, particularly the latter.

NOTEBOOK
Quenched, who ran well in what is proving to be a good renewal of the Ribblesdale last time, settled in behind the leader on the rail but had to wait for a run. When the gap opened she picked up well and scored nicely, securing her paddock value at the same time. She is in the Yorkshire Oaks but would come up against the likes of Alexandrova there, and may be better off tackling the Galtres Stakes at the same meeting. (tchd 9-2)
Cresta Gold, a handicapper who has gone up 23lb in the ratings since the beginning of June, is likely to be going up again after this effort, but having earned black type connections will no doubt view this as mission accomplished. She was given a clever ride, waiting in front and then battling on bravely to hold off all bar the winner. She should continue to give a good account.
Pictavia(IRE) was always in the right place in a steadily-run race, but failed to pick up as well as could have been expected and just seemed to lack an extra gear. It may be she did not stay this longer trip, although she seemed to get it in last year's Oaks, but it would be no surprise if the headgear she sometimes wore when with Jim Bolger was re-applied. (tchd 11-10)
Gower Song, another handicapper who was bidding for a five-timer, had gone up 20lb in the ratings since her run began but was still rated just 84. She went close to earning black type despite not being suited by the way the race was run, which suggests she may not have finished winning yet. (op 10-1)
Sindirana(IRE) finished a lot closer to the winner than she had in the Ribblesdale, but was another who was probably unsuited by the way the race was run.
Power Girl(GER) ◆, a winner in similar grade last time, looked unlucky in this stronger race as she could get no sort of run in the closing stages. Her stable is in good form at present and she may be capable of finding compensation, with the Chalice Stakes at Newbury early next month a possible target.
Reem Three was meeting today's third on 3lb better terms for a length and a quarter defeat at Newcastle, but faded in the closing stages and may not have stayed this longer trip. (op 8-1)

3740 CHRIS BLACKWELL MEMORIAL H'CAP — 1m

3:15 (3:16) (Class 2) (0-100,95) 3-Y-O — **£12,464** (£3,732; £1,866; £934; £466; £234) **Stalls** High

Form				RPR
1	**1**		**Multidimensional (IRE)**[28] [2868] 3-9-7 **95** .... EddieAhern 5 (H R A Cecil) *trckd ldr: led 2f out: hung lft ins fnl f: rdn out* **5/4**[1]	104+
0121	**2**	nk	**Paraguay (USA)**[9] [3433] 3-8-4 **81** .... EdwardCreighton(3) 3 (Miss V Haigh) *s.i.s: hld up: hdwy over 1f out: chsd wnr fnl f: r.o* **6/1**[3]	89
2046	**3**	4	**Orpsie Boy (IRE)**[10] [3414] 3-8-6 **85** ....(b) JamesDoyle(5) 7 (N P Littmoden) *chsd ldrs: rdn over 1f out: no ex fnl f* **3/1**[2]	84
31-0	**4**	1 ¼	**Annabelle Ja (FR)**[64] [1819] 3-8-11 **85** .... JohnEgan 2 (D R C Elsworth) *led 6f: wknd fnl f* **14/1**	81
6325	**5**	1 ¼	**Rubenstar (IRE)**[29] [2809] 3-8-7 **81** .... TPQueally 4 (M H Tompkins) *hld up: hdwy 2f out: sn rdn: wknd fnl f* **9/1**	74
0005	**6**	2 ½	**Guest Connections**[14] [3317] 3-9-0 **88** .... ChrisCatlin 1 (M R Channon) *chsd ldrs: rdn over 2f out: wknd over 1f out* **12/1**	75

1m 40.51s (0.08) **Going Correction** 0.0s/f (Good) **6** Ran SP% **108.1**
Speed ratings (Par 106):99,98,94,93,92 89
CSF £8.44 TOTE £2.10: £1.60, £2.10; EX 6.00.
Owner Niarchos Family **Bred** The Niarchos Family **Trained** Newmarket, Suffolk

FOCUS
A decent handicap despite the small turnout. The pace was steady until the last three furlongs but the first two came clear and the form has been taken at face value. The field raced up the centre of the track.

NOTEBOOK
Multidimensional(IRE) ◆, winner of a course and distance maiden on his debut four weeks previously, did not look especially well treated but was well supported and travelled well throughout. He ran green once in front but did enough to hold off the progressive runner-up and, with more improvement almost certain, he looks likely to be racing in Pattern company before too long. (op 11-8)
Paraguay(USA) ◆, who has progressed really well for current connections since winning a claimer over course and distance last month, gave the winner a real race and came clear of the rest. He looks well worth the £18,000 his trainer gave for him and can gain compensation for this defeat before long. (tchd 11-2)
Orpsie Boy(IRE), stepping up in trip having run well in decent handicaps over six furlongs, had the blinkers on again and appeared to run his race, but possibly did not last home up the hill. A drop back to seven may prove to be the answer. (tchd 10-3 tchd 7-2 in places)
Annabelle Ja(FR), back after a break and dropped in trip, set the pace but was brushed aside by the principals. She may be better off racing against her own sex. (op 11-1)
Rubenstar(IRE) may not have been suited by the steady pace but never really landed a blow. Some of his better efforts have been on right-handed, turning tracks. (op 15-2)
Guest Connections, who had shown signs of a revival last time, had every chance the way the race was run but dropped away and is struggling to make an impression despite dropping 9lb in the handicap since the start of the season. (tchd 14-1)

3741 INVESCO PERPETUAL E B F FILLIES' H'CAP — 6f

3:50 (3:51) (Class 3) (0-95,92) 3-Y-O+ — **£8,724** (£2,612; £1,306; £653; £326; £163) **Stalls** High

Form				RPR
4110	**1**		**Folga**[8] [3482] 4-9-12 **92** .... LDettori 2 (J G Given) *trckd ldr: shkn up 2f out: r.o to ld post* **3/1**[1]	99
1041	**2**	nk	**Daniella**[29] [2818] 4-8-9 **75** ....(p) FrancisFerris 4 (Rae Guest) *led: pushed clr over 1f out: rdn and hung lft ins fnl f: hdd post* **5/1**[3]	81
4352	**3**	2	**Secret Night**[28] [2880] 3-8-13 **84** .... JohnEgan 1 (J A R Toller) *trckd ldrs: rdn over 1f out: styng on same pce whn hung rt ins fnl f* **4/1**[2]	83
0041	**4**	¾	**Sleeping Storm (IRE)**[16] [3226] 3-7-11 **75** .... KMay(7) 3 (B J Meehan) *hld up: effrt over 1f out: nt trble ldrs* **6/1**	72
3640	**5**	½	**Spectacular Show (IRE)**[14] [3299] 3-8-2 **73** oh5 .... ChrisCatlin 6 (M Quinn) *chsd ldrs: rdn over 1f out: no ex* **20/1**	68
-004	**6**	½	**Qusoor (IRE)**[19] [3144] 3-8-12 **83** .... MartinDwyer 7 (J L Dunlop) *hld up: effrt over 1f out: nvr trbld ldrs* **10/1**	77

1m 11.95s (-1.40) **Going Correction** 0.0s/f (Good)
WFA 3 from 4yo 5lb **6** Ran SP% **89.8**
Speed ratings (Par 104):109,108,105,104,104 103
CSF £11.08 TOTE £2.90: £1.60, £2.30; EX 14.30.
Owner The Thrill Seekers **Bred** P Onslow **Trained** Willoughton, Lincs
■ Lipizza (7/2) was withdrawn; failed to enter the stalls. Rule 4 deduct 20p in £.

FOCUS
A fair sprint handicap run at a decent gallop and producing a close finish, with the four-year-olds dominating. The field raced up the centre of the track.

NOTEBOOK

Folga, a tough and genuine mare, has been in fine form this season and gained her third win with a late thrust. She is climbing the handicap but connections may now be thinking in terms of getting her some black type. (tchd 10-3)

Daniella, 8lb better off for a length and a quarter defeat by the winner earlier in the season, set the pace and quickened clear going into the dip. She looked to have the race in safe keeping inside the last, but then seemed to tire and got caught on the line. Her wins have been on flatter or easier tracks, and so she may be able to gain compensation before long.

Secret Night, placed in Listed company last time, was dropping back in trip but was always in the right place to strike. However, she was in trouble as soon as the runner-up quickened and it looks on this evidence as if she will have to race over further from now on. (op 10-3)

Sleeping Storm(IRE), who recaptured something of her juvenile form last time when dropped back to this distance, was 4lb higher but failed to build on that effort. She is another who may prefer racing on a flatter track. (op 7-1)

Spectacular Show(IRE), racing from 5lb out of the handicap, never landed a blow.

Qusoor(IRE), 7lb better off with the winner for a near five-length beating at Pontefract, finished a little closer but never really got into contention.

3742 DODSON AND HORRELL MAIDEN STKS — 7f

4:25 (4:26) (Class 5) 3-Y-O — £5,181 (£1,541; £770; £384) Stalls High

Form				RPR
20-2	1		**Grand Entrance (IRE)**[15] [3266] 3-9-3 75 ... LDettori 10	74
			(C R Egerton) *chsd ldr: rdn to ld ins fnl f: r.o* **13/8**[2]	
6	2	*nk*	**Silent Applause**[38] [2542] 3-9-3 ... RobertHavlin 9	74
			(Dr J D Scargill) *hld up in tch: shkn up over 1f out: r.o* **25/1**	
3-50	3	*1*	**Trimlestown (IRE)**[7] [3546] 3-9-3 75 ... MartinDwyer 7	71
			(H Candy) *led: rdn over 1f out: hdd and unable qck ins fnl f* **10/1**[3]	
0-0	4	*1*	**Goodwood March**[94] [1085] 3-8-12 ... IanMongan 6	63
			(J L Dunlop) *hld up: hdwy 2f out: styd on* **25/1**	
4-	5	*3/4*	**Pertemps Green**[357] [3957] 3-8-12 ... JamesDoyle(5) 2	66
			(Stef Liddiard) *s.i.s: hld up: plld hrd: hdwy over 1f out: styd on* **16/1**	
04	6	*1*	**Mambonow (USA)**[35] [2662] 3-9-3 ... ShaneKelly 4	64
			(J Noseda) *chsd ldrs: rdn over 1f out: no ex* **6/4**[1]	
	7	*2*	**Another Gladiator (USA)** 3-9-3 ... DO'Donohoe 12	59
			(K A Ryan) *mid-div: hdwy 3f out: sn rdn: wknd over 1f out* **12/1**	
00	8	*1*	**Warden Rose**[12] [3367] 3-8-12 ... JohnEgan 3	51
			(D R C Elsworth) *hld up: nvr nr to chal* **20/1**	
0-0	9	*hd*	**Gold Express**[28] [2868] 3-9-3 ... OscarUrbina 11	56
			(W A O'Gorman) *s.i.s: hld up: swtchd lft over 1f out: nvr nr to chal* **33/1**	
	10	*7*	**Kindallachan** 3-8-12 ... EddieAhern 5	32
			(G C Bravery) *s.i.s: hld up: hdwy u.p over 2f out: wknd over 1f out* **33/1**	
	11	*1*	**Lady Suffragette (IRE)** 3-8-5 ... FrankiePickard(7) 8	30
			(John Berry) *sn outpcd* **66/1**	
0-00	12	*6*	**Prima Markova**[21] [3073] 3-8-12 45 ... ChrisCatlin 1	14
			(D J Daly) *chsd ldrs over 4f* **66/1**	

1m 24.79s (-1.99) **Going Correction** 0.0s/f (Good) 12 Ran SP% **122.1**

Speed ratings (Par 100):111,110,109,108,107 106,104,102,102,94 93,86

CSF £50.57 TOTE £2.70: £1.30, £5.50, £2.70; EX 51.50.

Owner Mrs Evelyn Hankinson **Bred** Joseph Rogers **Trained** Chaddleworth, Berks

FOCUS

Little strength in depth - they went 10/1 bar two - but the form, rated around the third, has been treated reasonably positively. They raced centre to stands' side.

3743 JOIN THE RACING UK CLUB H'CAP — 1m 6f 175y

4:55 (4:56) (Class 4) (0-85,82) 4-Y-O+ — £5,505 (£1,637; £818; £408) Stalls Centre

Form				RPR
-331	1		**Mersey Sound (IRE)**[9] [3446] 8-8-5 71 ... MarcHalford(5) 1	83
			(D R C Elsworth) *hld up: hdwy over 3f out: hung rt and led over 2f out: styd on wl* **5/2**[1]	
2443	2	*5*	**Maystock**[23] [3028] 6-8-8 69 ... JohnEgan 4	74
			(B G Powell) *led: rdn and hdd over 2f out: styd on same pce appr fnl f* **5/1**[3]	
/4-0	3	*5*	**Tiyoun (IRE)**[21] [3078] 8-9-7 82 ... ShaneKelly 5	81
			(Jedd O'Keeffe) *chsd ldrs: rdn over 4f out: wknd fnl f* **20/1**	
6103	4	*3*	**Haatmey**[4] [3607] 4-8-13 74 ... (v) ChrisCatlin 3	69
			(M R Channon) *rn in snatches in rr: rdn 1/2-way: nvr nrr* **8/1**	
0121	5	*5*	**Taxman (IRE)**[21] [3098] 4-8-11 72 ... (p) MartinDwyer 7	60
			(C E Brittain) *prom: rdn to chse ldr over 4f out: wknd over 1f out* **3/1**[2]	
340	6	*22*	**River City (IRE)**[21] [3100] 9-8-9 70 ... VinceSlattery 2	30
			(Noel T Chance) *chsd ldr tl rdn over 4f out: wknd over 3f out* **15/2**	
0006	P		**Spanish Ridge (IRE)**[28] [2869] 4-8-10 71 ow1 ... IanMongan 6	—
			(J L Dunlop) *hld up: hdwy over 5f out: rdn and wknd over 2f out: p.u and dismntd over 1f out* **7/1**	

3m 6.50s (-5.97) **Going Correction** 0.0s/f (Good) 7 Ran SP% **110.4**

Speed ratings (Par 105):112,109,106,105,102 90,—

CSF £14.17 TOTE £3.10: £2.00, £2.50; EX 13.00.

Owner A Heaney **Bred** Airlie Stud **Trained** Newmarket, Suffolk

FOCUS

Not a strong staying handicap, but it was run at a sound gallop and turned into a procession by the in-form winner.

Taxman(IRE) Official explanation: jockey said gelding had no more to give

Spanish Ridge(IRE) Official explanation: trainer said gelding had a breathing problem

3744 PLANTATION STUD H'CAP — 5f

5:30 (5:30) (Class 3) (0-95,93) 3-Y-O+ — £8,096 (£2,408; £1,203; £601) Stalls High

Form				RPR
5601	1		**Pic Up Sticks**[15] [3251] 7-9-2 87 ... RichardKingscote(5) 8	93
			(B G Powell) *trckd ldrs: shkn up over 1f out: r.o to ld post* **4/1**[1]	
2033	2	*hd*	**Woodnook**[10] [3403] 3-8-4 74 ... JohnEgan 3	78
			(J A R Toller) *hld up: hdwy over 1f out: rdn to ld ins fnl f: hdd post* **9/2**[2]	
0005	3	*1/2*	**High Reach**[7] [3550] 6-9-9 89 ... MartinDwyer 2	92
			(W R Muir) *chsd ldrs: rdn and ev ch ins fnl f: styd on* **6/1**	
0331	4	*shd*	**Azygous**[8] [3475] 3-8-9 84 ... JamesDoyle(5) 9	86
			(J Akehurst) *led: rdn and hdd ins fnl f: kpt on: edgd lft nr fin* **9/1**	
-605	5	*nk*	**Tony The Tap**[8] [3471] 5-8-13 86 ... TolleyDean(7) 1	88
			(B Palling) *chsd ldrs: rdn 1/2-way: styd on u.p* **5/1**[3]	
0006	6	*1*	**The Jobber (IRE)**[15] [3251] 5-9-4 84 ... LDettori 4	82
			(M Blanshard) *chsd ldr: rdn and ev ch 1f out: styng on same pce whn n.m.r towards fin* **13/2**	
3605	7	*nk*	**Cape Royal**[7] [3535] 6-9-13 93 ... OscarUrbina 6	90
			(J M Bradley) *hld up in tch: rdn over 1f out: styd on same pce* **13/2**	
-005	8	*2 1/2*	**Triskaidekaphobia**[8] [3503] 3-8-9 79 ... PaulFitzsimons 7	66
			(Miss J R Tooth) *chsd ldrs: rdn over 1f out: wknd fnl f* **22/1**	
1-50	9	*3 1/2*	**Bold Minstrel (IRE)**[9] [3447] 4-8-12 78 ... ShaneKelly 5	53
			(M Quinn) *hld up: wknd over 1f out* **14/1**	

59.03 secs (-0.53) **Going Correction** 0.0s/f (Good)

WFA 3 from 4yo+ 4lb 9 Ran SP% **116.8**

Speed ratings (Par 107):104,103,102,102,102 100,100,96,90

CSF £22.28 CT £107.89 TOTE £3.50: £1.70, £1.80, £2.60; EX 22.50 Place 6 £63.66, Place 5 £8.71..

Owner The Vintage Group **Bred** J P Coggan **Trained** Morestead, Hants

FOCUS

A decent, competitive sprint handicap in which the majority of the field had a chance over a furlong out. The winner came up the stands' side. The form is probably sound enough on balance.

NOTEBOOK

Pic Up Sticks is not the most regular winner, but is in good form at present and followed up his recent Sandown victory off a 4lb higher mark. He travelled well and responded best to prevail in a tight finish. He has won off marks in the 90s in the past, so may have more to offer. (op 9-2 tchd 13-2 in places)

Woodnook, a relatively inexperienced three-year-old filly, has been performing consistently this season without winning. She did nothing wrong on this occasion and deserves to win a race before long. (op 5-1)

High Reach has not won since April last year but his yard is in good form at present and he ran his race. The Handicapper has only reluctantly eased him in the weights, but he has shown in the past that he is capable of scoring off this sort of mark. (tchd 13-2)

Azygous, raised 6lb after his Chester win last time, again tried to make all but did not get any peace in front and did well to hold on for so long. His previous form suggests a sharper track is more in his favour. (op 8-1 tchd 10-1)

Tony The Tap has not won for the best part of two years, but he likes this track, having finished third in this race last season. He had every chance and was only just run out of the placings. His consistency means he is still 6lb above his last winning mark. (op 9-2)

The Jobber(IRE), despite being 6lb better off, finished slightly further behind the winner than he had at Sandown. He is one to bear in mind for when there is a little more cut in the ground. (op 7-1)

Cape Royal, another on a long losing run, is still 6lb higher than his last winning mark. His best chance of ending the sequence may come back at Epsom, where he goes so well. (tchd 7-1)

T/Plt: £61.90 to a £1 stake. Pool: £78,129.80. 920.85 winning tickets. T/Qpdt: £8.50 to a £1 stake. Pool: £3,228.40. 279.70 winning tickets. CR

3357 RIPON (R-H)

Saturday, July 22

OFFICIAL GOING: Good to firm changing to good after race 3 (3.20pm)

Wind: Virtually nil.

3745 EBF DOBSONS GASKETS MAIDEN FILLIES' STKS — 5f

2:20 (2:21) (Class 4) 2-Y-O — £4,533 (£1,348; £674; £336) Stalls Low

Form				RPR
24	1		**Abby Road (IRE)**[16] [3216] 2-9-0 ... KDarley 3	89+
			(B J Meehan) *mde virtually all: rdn clr ent last: styd on strly* **5/2**[2]	
522	2	*5*	**Durova (IRE)**[7] [3521] 2-8-9 ... DuranFentiman(5) 4	71
			(T D Easterby) *cl up: ev ch 2f out: sn rdn and kpt on same pce fnl f* **7/2**[3]	
30	3	*1 1/2*	**Princess Georgina**[21] [3084] 2-9-0 ... RobbieFitzpatrick 7	66
			(S C Williams) *trckd ldng pair: effrt and ev ch 2f out: sn rdn and wknd appr last* **6/4**[1]	
03	4	*shd*	**Sister Etienne (IRE)**[12] [3358] 2-9-0 ... PhillipMakin 2	65
			(T D Barron) *chsd ldrs: hdwy 2f out: sn rdn and kpt on ins last* **10/1**	
6	5	*1/2*	**Mazin Lady**[24] [2972] 2-9-0 ... TomEaves 1	63
			(Miss J A Camacho) *trckd ldrs: effrt 2f out: sn rdn and no imp appr last* **16/1**	
	6	*11*	**My Two Girls (IRE)** 2-9-0 ... LeeEnstone 6	24
			(P T Midgley) *wnt rt s: a outpcd in rr* **33/1**	
0	7	*1 1/2*	**Mystic**[70] [1664] 2-8-9 ... MarkLawson(5) 5	18
			(D W Barker) *sn outpcd and bhd fr 1/2-way* **33/1**	
	8	*7*	**Wilde Jasmine (IRE)** 2-8-9 ... AndrewMullen(5) 8	—
			(J R Weymes) *s.s: a bhd* **50/1**	

60.03 secs (-0.17) **Going Correction** 0.0s/f (Good) 8 Ran SP% **113.6**

Speed ratings (Par 93):101,93,90,90,89 72,69,58

CSF £11.47 TOTE £3.10: £1.30, £1.40, £1.20; EX 7.20 Trifecta £6.10 Pool £86.43 - 10.02 winning units..

Owner Andrew Rosen **Bred** Western Bloodstock **Trained** Manton, Wilts

FOCUS

Not a bad maiden and Abby Road ran out a most impressive winner and the race could rate higher.

NOTEBOOK

Abby Road(IRE), who failed to see out six furlongs at Haydock last time, was able to confirm the promise of her initial effort and evidently prospered from the drop back to the minimum trip. Soon on the rail, she coasted clear in impressive fashion and looks a real speedball, suggesting she can more than hold her own up in grade. (tchd 11-4)

Durova(IRE) has developed into a consistent sort, but she continues to find at least one too good and may find life easier in nurseries. She will stay six furlongs in time and has a race in her. (op 11-4)

Princess Georgina, who received no luck in running when ninth in a modest Listed contest at Newmarket last time, did not look sure to be suited by this return to five furlongs and, having been up there early, she found herself readily outpaced and outclassed by the winner. This was disappointing, but she is now qualified for nurseries and it will be interesting to see what sort of mark she gets. (op 2-1)

Sister Etienne(IRE) ran well in a lesser race at the course last time and this was another fair effort, but it is unlikely she will be winning until contesting nurseries and stepping up to six furlongs. (op 12-1)

Mazin Lady, as on her debut, ran better than her finishing position suggested and she should have little trouble finding a race, whether it be a maiden or a nursery.

Wilde Jasmine(IRE) Official explanation: jockey said filly missed the break

3746 MARY KAY SHAW BIRTHDAY CELEBRATION (S) STKS — 6f

2:50 (2:50) (Class 6) 2-Y-O — £2,590 (£770; £385; £192) Stalls Low

Form				RPR
0303	1		**Ensign's Trick**[15] [3246] 2-8-1 ... LiamJones(5) 2	68+
			(W M Brisbourne) *led 1f: trckd ldrs: swtchd rt and hdwy to ld 11/2f out: sn rdn clr* **4/1**[2]	
0063	2	*9*	**Loch Clutha (IRE)**[14] [3300] 2-8-6 ... (p) FrancisNorton 3	41
			(K R Burke) *cl up: led after 1f: hdd 4f out: swtchd rt and rdn 2f out: kpt on to take remote 2nd ins last* **4/1**[2]	
4024	3	*3*	**Dotty's Daughter**[4] [3605] 2-8-3 ... SaleemGolam(3) 4	32
			(Mrs A Duffield) *outpcd and pushed along in rr after 2f: hdxway on outer 2f out: sn rdn and kpt on ins last* **9/4**[1]	
050	4	*3*	**Poniard (IRE)**[70] [1682] 2-8-6 ... MarkLawson(5) 7	28
			(D W Barker) *towards rr and pushed along after 2f: rdn and hdwy 2f out: kpt on ins last* **9/2**[3]	

000 **5** *1 1/4* **Vodkat**[24] [2973] 2-8-6 .... KimTinkler 1 19
(N Tinkler) *s.i.s: hdwy 1/2-way: rdn 2f out: sn no imp* **7/1**

00 **5** *dht* **Dockside Dancer (IRE)**[53] [2106] 2-8-6 .... RobbieFitzpatrick 5 19
(P T Midgley) *chsd ldrs: led after 2f: rdn along and hdd 1 1/2f out: sn wknd* **66/1**

0 **7** *1* **Nice One**[11] [3380] 2-8-8 ow2........................ TomEaves 9 18
(J R Turner) *cl up: rdn 2f out: sn wknd* **50/1**

4 **8** *21* **Express Willy**[14] [3308] 2-8-11 .... PhillipMakin 8 —
(J R Weymes) *bolted bef s: s.i.s: a bhd* **16/1**

5 **9** *5* **Eastern Playboy (IRE)**[16] [3228] 2-8-11 .... DerekMcGaffin 6 —
(J Jay) *chsd ldrs: rdn along 1/2-way: sn wknd* **16/1**

1m 14.1s (1.10) **Going Correction** 0.0s/f (Good) **9** Ran SP% **116.7**
Speed ratings (Par 92):92,80,76,72,70 70,69,41,34
CSF £20.66 TOTE £5.70: £1.90, £1.80, £1.70; EX 22.80 Trifecta £90.00 Pool £164.82 - 1.30 winning units..The winner was bought in for 20,000gns.
Owner Mrs Mary Brisbourne **Bred** W M Brisbourne **Trained** Great Ness, Shropshire

FOCUS
A modest seller and the runners finished well strung out behind the winner, who put up a cracking performance for the level.

NOTEBOOK
Ensign's Trick, who was always prominent, galloped them into the ground inside the final furlong and ran out a most easy winner. She has been beaten at this level before, but seemed to show improved form so could go on to success at a higher level. (op 7-2)
Loch Clutha(IRE) has been running well in similar races and this was another sound effort on her first try at six furlongs. She was clear of the third and should find a race eventually.
Dotty's Daughter, who ran well for a long way against much better opposition at Beverley earlier in the week, was unable to capitalise on this drop in grade and was struggling to lay up from a very early stage. Her lack of pace was disappointing, especially as she has been racing over five furlongs, but she can find a race at this level. (op 3-1)
Poniard(IRE) has now disappointed the last twice, his best effort to date coming in a fair maiden, and although making a brief move towards the outside, he never threatened to get involved.
Vodkat failed to improve for the drop in grade/rise in distance and she is another likely to continue to struggle. (op 50-1)
Dockside Dancer(IRE) is a horse of limited ability and she is going to struggle to find races. Official explanation: jockey said filly finished lame (op 50-1)
Nice One Official explanation: jockey said filly did not handle the track
Eastern Playboy(IRE) Official explanation: jockey said colt became unbalanced on the undulations

3747 BISHOPTON H'CAP 1m 1f 170y
3:20 (3:20) (Class 4) (0-85,84) 3-Y-O **£7,886** (£2,360; £1,180; £590; £293) **Stalls** High

Form RPR

0231 **1** **Nelsons Column (IRE)**[14] [3282] 3-8-9 **75**........................ TomEaves 8 85
(G M Moore) *trckd ldr: hdwy to ld wl over 3f out: rdn wl over 1f out: styd on strly ins last* **6/1**

1043 **2** *3* **Vicious Warrior**[14] [3289] 7-9-5 **80**........................ MichaelJStainton(5) 6 84
(R M Whitaker) *trckd ldng pair: hdwy 3f out: rdn to chal 2f out and ev ch tl drvn: edgd lft and one pce ent last* **8/1**

0313 **3** *1/2* **Active Asset (IRE)**[19] [3151] 4-10-0 **84**........................ KDarley 4 87
(M R Channon) *keen: hld up in rr: hdwy 3f out: rdn over 1f out: kpt on ins last: nrst fin* **9/2**[2]

3250 **4** *1* **Augustine**[24] [2989] 5-9-5 **75**........................ PhillipMakin 3 76
(P W Hiatt) *hld up in rr: hdwy 3f out: rdn over 1f out: edgd lft and kpt on ins last* **7/1**

6412 **5** *1 1/2* **Mount Usher**[14] [3283] 4-9-2 **72**........................ DeanMcKeown 7 70
(G A Swinbank) *trckd ldrs: hdwy 3f out: rdn wl over 1f out and sn btn* **15/8**[1]

5250 **6** *4* **Tedsdale Mac**[8] [3500] 7-8-2 **65** oh3........................ SuzzanneFrance(7) 2 56
(N Bycroft) *keen: hld up towards rr: effrt 3f out: rdn 2f out and sn no imp* **33/1**

1313 **7** *1 1/2* **Dragon Slayer (IRE)**[14] [3309] 4-9-10 **80**........................ RobbieFitzpatrick 5 68
(M J Attwater) *keen: chsd ldrs: rdn along on outer over 2f out: sn drvn and wknd* **11/2**[3]

12/0 **8** *8* **Atlantic Story (USA)**[7] [3549] 4-9-9 **79**........................ DaleGibson 1 52
(M W Easterby) *led: rdn along over 4f out: hdd wl over 3f out: drvn and wknd over 2f out* **40/1**

2m 5.89s (0.89) **Going Correction** +0.35s/f (Good)
WFA 3 from 4yo+ 10lb **8** Ran SP% **111.6**
Speed ratings (Par 105):110,107,107,106,105 102,100,94
CSF £49.96 CT £230.90 TOTE £6.50: £1.90, £2.00, £1.60; EX 50.20 Trifecta £95.20 Part won. Pool £134.20 - 0.10 winning units..
Owner Ean Muller Associates **Bred** E A C Muller **Trained** Middleham Moor, N Yorks

FOCUS
An ordinary handicap in which they went a just a fair gallop and the form does not appear strong.

3748 RIPON BELL-RINGER H'CAP 1m 4f 10y
3:55 (3:56) (Class 3) (0-90,87) 3-Y-O+
£11,217 (£3,358; £1,679; £840; £419; £210) **Stalls** High

Form RPR

0152 **1** **Forthright**[12] [3366] 5-9-4 **77**........................ FrancisNorton 1 84+
(A W Carroll) *trckd ldrs: smooth hdwy over 2f out: cl up over 1f out: rdn to ld jst ins last: styd on* **12/1**

0405 **2** *1* **Nero's Return (IRE)**[42] [2435] 5-9-6 **79**........................ KDarley 9 85
(M Johnston) *trckd ldr: hdwy to ld over 3f out: jnd and rdn 2f out hdd jst ins last: drvn and no ex* **5/1**[2]

6012 **3** *1/2* **Lucayan Dancer**[24] [2975] 6-9-8 **81**........................ AdrianTNicholls 11 86
(D Nicholls) *trckd ldng pair: hdwy over 2f out: swtchd lft and rdn wl over 1f out: styd on ins last* **12/1**

4213 **4** *nk* **Baltic Princess (FR)**[9] [3452] 3-7-11 **73**........................ DuranFentiman(5) 12 78
(M Johnston) *led: pushed along over 4f out: rdn and hdd over 3f out: drvn and kpt on same pce appr last* **13/2**[3]

-106 **5** *1/2* **Stretton (IRE)**[47] [2296] 8-9-3 **81**........................ AndrewElliott(5) 6 85+
(J D Bethell) *hld up towards rr: gd hdwy on outer over 2f out: rdn to chse ldrs over 1f out: drvn and kpt on same pce ent last* **25/1**

0511 **6** *shd* **Our Teddy (IRE)**[7] [3547] 6-9-7 **80**........................ PhillipMakin 5 84
(P A Blockley) *hld up in tch: hdwy 3f out: rdn 2f out: drvn and styd on same pce appr last* **13/2**[3]

0042 **7** *1 1/4* **Top Seed (IRE)**[8] [3497] 5-10-0 **87**........................ TomEaves 10 89
(M R Channon) *hld up in midfield: hdwy 3f out: rdn along 2f out and sn no imp* **4/1**[1]

5600 **8** *3/4* **Most Definitely (IRE)**[8] [3501] 6-9-8 **81**........................ TonyHamilton 4 81
(T D Easterby) *hld up in rr: hdwy over 3f out: rdn over 2f out and sn btn* **10/1**

2026 **9** *2* **Dovedon Hero**[9] [3446] 6-8-10 **69**........................(b) DerekMcGaffin 2 66
(P J McBride) *hld up: a rr* **16/1**

2316 **10** *3 1/2* **Billich**[8] [3490] 3-8-12 **83**........................ RobbieFitzpatrick 3 75
(E J O'Neill) *trckd ldrs: hdwy 4f out: rdn along wl over 2f out and sn wknd* **8/1**

0040 **11** *shd* **Sharp Reply (USA)**[24] [2975] 4-8-12 **76**........................ MichaelJStainton(5) 7 67
(R M Whitaker) *hld up: sme hdwy on outer3f out: sn rdn along and nvr a factor* **12/1**

-000 **12** *32* **Ringsider (IRE)**[82] [1357] 5-9-6 **84**........................ AndrewMullen(5) 8 24
(G A Butler) *a rr* **25/1**

2m 40.53s (3.53) **Going Correction** +0.35s/f (Good)
WFA 3 from 4yo+ 12lb **12** Ran SP% **120.2**
Speed ratings (Par 107):102,101,101,100,100 100,99,99,97,95 95,74
CSF £72.00 CT £746.33 TOTE £18.90: £4.30, £2.30, £3.10; EX 125.60 Trifecta £186.50 Part won. Pool £262.80 - 0.10 winning units..
Owner Mrs B Quinn **Bred** Wyck Hall Stud Ltd **Trained** Cropthorne, Worcs

FOCUS
A highly-competitive handicap in which they went only a fair gallop. The third, fourth and fifth are the best guides to the form.

NOTEBOOK
Forthright, trying this trip for the first time, has really come back to form in recent weeks and, having travelled nicely into contention, he edged ahead of Nero's Return and kept on right the way to the line, winning with a little bit to spare considering he does not do a lot in front. He is progressing nicely and looks open to further improvement at this distance. (op 11-1)
Nero's Return(IRE), another trying this trip for the first time, went on just under half a mile out, but the winner always looked to have him covered and he could only keep on at the one pace under pressure. This was an improved effort and he is back on a decent mark now, so expect him to be winning soon for his in-form stable. (op 6-1)
Lucayan Dancer has performed well off higher marks since winning at Chester last month and he kept on well into third, but was never getting to the front pair. (op 11-1)
Baltic Princess(FR), a progressive filly who failed to see out 15 furlongs at Warwick last time, was much more at home over this distance and she took them along until her stable companion went on three out. She kept plugging away under pressure and did enough to suggest she is capable of winning off this mark, possibly at 14 furlongs. (op 7-1)
Stretton(IRE) was quite the eye-catcher, making good late headway having been in rear early and going on well close home. He has clearly benefited from a short break, but remains 4lb higher than when last winning. (op 18-1 tchd 16-1)
Our Teddy(IRE), up 4lb for his narrow Salisbury win, never really got into it, but he was given enough to do and may have benefited from a more positive ride. (op 7-1 tchd 6-1)
Top Seed(IRE) has been in decent form, but he faced a tough task under top weight. He ran reasonably well, but is likely to continue to be vulnerable off this sort of mark. (op 9-2)
Billich Official explanation: jockey said colt was unsuited by the good ground

3749 KEVIN KAI LOWERY MEMORIAL MAIDEN H'CAP 6f
4:30 (4:31) (Class 5) (0-70,66) 3-Y-O+ **£3,886** (£1,156; £577; £288) **Stalls** Low

Form RPR

4000 **1** **Tadlil**[36] [2602] 4-9-4 **53**........................ PhillipMakin 15 66
(J M Bradley) *hld up in tch far side: hdwy over 2f out: rdn to ld that gp wl over 1f out: overall ldr ent last: styd on wl* **14/1**

-604 **2** *1 3/4* **Fortress**[33] [2699] 3-9-1 **55**........................(b) AdrianTNicholls 5 61
(E J Alston) *overall ldr stands side: rdn 2f out: drvn and hdd ent last kpt on same pce* **8/1**

0064 **3** *3/4* **Elkhorn**[18] [3171] 4-9-7 **56**........................(p) TomEaves 4 61
(Miss J A Camacho) *hld up and bhd stands side: swtchd rt and hdwy 2f out: sn rdn and styd on ins last: nrst fin* **6/1**[2]

654 **4** *3/4* **Best Double**[10] [3406] 3-9-7 **66**........................ AndrewMullen(5) 16 68
(G A Butler) *chsd ldrs far side: rdn over 2f out: kpt on same pce appr last* **15/2**[3]

020- **5** *1 1/4* **Lottie**[418] [2131] 5-8-2 **42** oh6........................ LiamJones(5) 2 41
(G Woodward) *cl up stands side: rdn along 2f out: drvn and one pce appr last* **33/1**

0-03 **6** *hd* **Dazzler Mac**[53] [2112] 5-9-0 **52**........................ SilvestreDeSousa(3) 17 50
(N Bycroft) *swtchd lft s and in tch on outer of far side gp: effrt over 2f out: sn rdn: edgd rt and styd on same pce ins last* **5/1**[1]

6660 **7** *shd* **Lady Edge (IRE)**[12] [3368] 4-9-3 **52**........................(v[1]) FrancisNorton 9 50
(A W Carroll) *hld up in rr stands side: hdwy 2f out: sn rdn and styd on ins last: nrst fin* **20/1**

6003 **8** *1* **Immaculate Red**[11] [3381] 3-8-10 **53**........................(b) SaleemGolam(3) 12 47
(R Bastiman) *chsd ldrs far side: rdn along 2f out: drvn and one pce over 1f out* **14/1**

0606 **9** *1* **Harrington Bates**[22] [3053] 5-8-1 **43**........................ LukeMorris(7) 8 35
(R M Whitaker) *in tch stands side: rdn along over 2f out: sn wknd* **20/1**

5034 **10** *nk* **Kashtanka (IRE)**[116] [783] 4-8-4 **42** oh5........................(p) JasonEdmunds(3) 20 33
(J Balding) *cl up far side: rdn along over 2f out and sn wknd* **33/1**

0-03 **11** *1/2* **Malelane (IRE)**[28] [2876] 3-7-13 **44**........................ AndrewElliott(5) 3 33
(A Dickman) *prom stands side: effrt and cl up 2f out: sn rdn and wknd ent last* **12/1**

3204 **12** *nk* **Mostanad**[9] [3438] 4-8-12 **50**........................ DanielTudhope(3) 10 39
(J M Bradley) *in tch stands side: rdn along over 2f out: sn wknd* **11/1**

0500 **13** *hd* **Madame Guillotine**[17] [3189] 4-8-7 **42** oh5........................ DeanMcKeown 7 30
(P T Midgley) *chsd ldrs stands side: rdn along over 2f out: sn wknd* **100/1**

-406 **14** *3/4* **The Keep**[7] [3524] 4-8-7 **42** oh3........................(b) DerekMcGaffin 18 28
(R E Barr) *led far side gp: rdn along and hdd wl over 2f out: edgd lft and wknd wl over 1f out* **33/1**

0065 **15** *1 3/4* **Josarty**[14] [3290] 3-8-8 **53**........................ MarkLawson(5) 14 33
(J J Quinn) *cl up far side: rdn along over 2f out: grad wknd* **12/1**

03-0 **16** *1* **Lake Suprima (IRE)**[191] [99] 3-8-5 **50**........................ MichaelJStainton(5) 1 27
(R M Whitaker) *chsd ldr stands side: rdn along 1/2-way: sn wknd* **66/1**

5000 **17** *1 1/4* **Aqua**[3] [3635] 4-8-7 **42**........................(b) RobbieFitzpatrick 19 16
(P T Midgley) *a rr far side* **66/1**

0003 **18** *1 1/2* **Algorithm**[3] [3635] 4-8-7 **42** oh1........................(b) TonyHamilton 6 11
(T D Easterby) *in tch stands side: rdn along over 2f out: sn wknd* **12/1**

0000 **19** *10* **Qaasi (USA)**[25] [2947] 4-9-5 **59**........................(b[1]) GregFairley(5) 13 —
(Mrs K Walton) *prom far side: rdn along 1/2-way: sn wknd* **14/1**

40/0 **20** *dist* **Miss Sudbrook (IRE)**[49] [2223] 4-9-1 **50**........................ DaleGibson 11 —
(A W Carroll) *a rr far side: bhd 1/2-way: t.o fnl 2f* **100/1**

1m 13.7s (0.70) **Going Correction** 0.0s/f (Good)
WFA 3 from 4yo+ 5lb **20** Ran SP% **128.6**
Speed ratings (Par 103):95,92,91,90,89 88,88,87,85,85 84,84,84,83,80 79,77,75,62,—
CSF £116.34 CT £781.59 TOTE £16.00: £3.50, £2.70, £1.80, £2.80; EX 285.60 TRIFECTA Not won..
Owner E A Hayward **Bred** Wheelersland Stud **Trained** Sedbury, Gloucs

FOCUS
A moderate but highly-competitive sprint handicap and the form looks straightforward and solid, with the third, fourth and fifth to form.
Harrington Bates Official explanation: jockey said gelding hung right
Malelane(IRE) Official explanation: jockey said filly was hanging from 2f out

The Form Book, Raceform Ltd, Compton, RG20 6NL

3750 BIRCHALL CATERING SUPPLIES MEDIAN AUCTION MAIDEN STKS 1m
5:05 (5:05) (Class 5) 3-4-Y-O £4,533 (£1,348; £674; £336) Stalls High

Form RPR
0-64 1 **Dado Mush**[68] [1736] 3-9-3 52 PhillipMakin 2 59
(T T Clement) *hld up in rr: hdwy over 2f out: swtchd rt and nt clr run wl over 1f out: swtchd lft and rdn ent last: led last 100 yds* 7/1[3]
0003 2 3/4 **Giverny Spring**[2] [3668] 3-8-5 62 PatrickHills(7) 4 52
(J W Hills) *keen: trckd ldng pair: hdwy 3f out: cl up 2f out: rdn to ld ent last: hdd and one pce last 100 yds* 1/1[1]
06 3 hd **Silk Topper (IRE)**[25] [2948] 3-9-3 TonyHamilton 6 57
(R A Fahey) *led 2f: cl up tl eld again over 3f out: rdn 2f out: drvn and hdd ent last: kpt on same pce* 7/1[3]
6 4 6 **Lady's Law**[22] [3032] 3-8-12 TomEaves 5 38
(G G Margarson) *keen: trckd ldrs on inner: effrt over 2f out: sn rdn and wknd wl over 1f out* 14/1
5 5 2 1/2 **Chrisjen**[29] [2829] 4-9-6 DaleGibson 1 32
(M W Easterby) *keen: rapid hdwy on outer to ld after 2f: rdn along and hdd over 3f out: wknd over 2f out* 10/3[2]
00-0 6 14 **Fancy You (IRE)**[63] [1859] 3-8-12 49 FrancisNorton 3 —
(A W Carroll) *keen: chsd ldrs: hdwy over 3f out: rdn over 2f out and sn wknd* 16/1

1m 43.26s (2.16) **Going Correction** +0.35s/f (Good)
WFA 3 from 4yo 8lb 6 Ran SP% 110.6
Speed ratings (Par 103):103,102,102,96,93 79
CSF £14.16 TOTE £10.20: £3.40, £1.20; EX 22.20 Place 6 £54.90, Place 5 £38.50..
Owner Dr M Edres **Bred** Bellow Hill Stud **Trained** Newmarket, Suffolk

FOCUS
Weak maiden form rated around the winner and runner-up.
T/Plt: £94.90 to a £1 stake. Pool £64,882.05. 862.60 winning tickets. T/Qpdt: £38.50 to a £1 stake. Pool £2,021.00. 38.80 winning tickets. JR

3751 - 3754a (Foreign Racing) - See Raceform Interactive

3719 HAMBURG (R-H)
Saturday, July 22

OFFICIAL GOING: Good

3755a LOTTO-TROPHY (GROUP 3) 6f
4:25 (4:28) 3-Y-O+ £27,586 (£12,414; £6,207; £3,448; £2,069)

RPR
1 **Electric Beat**[62] 3-8-9 AHelfenbein 2 110
(Andreas Lowe, Germany) *outpaced early, last straight, brought to outside and soon hard ridden, ran on well to lead inside final f, driven out* 5/2[2]
2 1 1/2 **Matrix (GER)**[30] [2799] 5-9-2 JVictoire 1 108
(W Baltromei, Germany) *led to inside final f, ran on same pace* 86/10
3 2 1/2 **Lucky Strike**[26] [2941] 8-9-4 ADeVries 8 102
(A Trybuhl, Germany) *always close up, 2nd straight, ridden & one pace from over 1f out* 7/10[1]
4 hd **Diable**[58] [1973] 7-9-2 TMundry 9 99
(H Hesse, Germany) *5th straight, disputed 3rd over 1f out, one pace* 137/10
5 1 3/4 **Stormiano (GER)**[30] [2799] 4-9-0 ASuborics 6 92
(Dr A Bolte, Germany) *3rd straight on inside, soon ridden & one pace* 78/10
6 1 1/2 **Omasheriff (IRE)**[30] [2799] 4-9-0 THellier 7 88
(Bruce Hellier, Germany) *6th straight, no headway* 71/10[3]
7 3/4 **Austrian (GER)**[62] [1869] 5-9-0 AStarke 3 85
(M Sowa, Germany) *tracked leader to half-way, 4th straight, soon beaten* 21/1

1m 10.54s
WFA 3 from 4yo+ 5lb 7 Ran SP% 132.9
(including ten euro stakes): WIN 35; PL 11, 15, 11; SF 448.
Owner Rennstall Directa **Bred** T E Pocock **Trained** Germany

2476 BELMONT PARK (L-H)
Saturday, July 22

OFFICIAL GOING: Muddy

3757a COACHING CLUB AMERICAN OAKS (GRADE 1) (FILLIES) (DIRT) 1m 2f (D)
9:45 (9:45) 3-Y-O
£104,651 (£34,884; £17,442; £8,721; £5,233; £872)

RPR
1 **Wonder Lady Anne L (USA)**[78] 3-8-9 EPrado 4 115
(R Dutrow Jr, U.S.A) 93/10
2 3/4 **Pine Island (USA)**[21] 3-8-9 JCastellano 7 114
(C McGaughey III, U.S.A) 5/4[1]
3 1 3/4 **Miss Shop (USA)**[125] 3-8-9 RMigliore 3 111
(H A Jerkens, U.S.A) 145/10
4 6 1/2 **Lemons Forever (USA)**[21] 3-8-9 MGuidry 2 99
(D Stewart, U.S.A) 57/10[3]
5 nk **Teammate (USA)**[21] 3-8-9 CVelasquez 1 99
(H A Jerkens, U.S.A) 166/10
6 13 3/4 **Unbridled Belle (USA)** 3-8-9 (b) MLuzzi 9 74
(T Pletcher, U.S.A) 183/10
7 3/4 **Sugar Shake (USA)** 3-8-9 (b) JRVelazquez 5 73
(R J Frankel, U.S.A) 51/10[2]
8 11 3/4 **Baghdaria (USA)**[22] 3-8-9 FJara 6 51
(T Amoss, U.S.A) 184/10
9 18 **Vague (USA)**[29] [2802] 3-8-9 KDesormeaux 8 19
(J Noseda) *raced in 4th til lost place after 4f, soon dropped to last and beaten* 83/10

2m 4.63s 9 Ran SP% 118.7
PARI-MUTUEL (Including $2 stake): WIN 20.60; PL (1-2) 6.60, 2.80;SHOW (1-2-3) 4.30, 2.50, 5.70; SF 56.00.
Owner IEAH Stables, Jachen Farms & H Sanford **Bred** Dan White & Highland Farm **Trained** USA

NOTEBOOK
Vague(USA) turned in an appalling effort and was last and beaten before halfway. She was encountering a longer trip and a muddy dirt track for the first time here, but even so was very disappointing.

2870 REDCAR (L-H)
Sunday, July 23

OFFICIAL GOING: Good to firm (firm in places)
After 16mm rain the previous day the ground was described as 'lovely, fast summer ground with a very good cover'.
Wind: Light, half behind Weather: Fine and sunny

3758 EBF BROOKE EQUINE CHARITY MAIDEN STKS 7f
2:20 (2:21) (Class 5) 2-Y-O £3,886 (£1,156; £577; £288) Stalls Centre

Form RPR
2342 1 **Pires**[18] [3187] 2-9-3 TonyCulhane 7 89
(M R Channon) *mde virtually all: qcknd over 3f out: drvn clr fnl f* 4/9[1]
4 2 2 1/2 **White Deer (USA)**[25] [2972] 2-9-3 KDarley 5 82
(M Johnston) *w wnr: drvn 3f out: kpt on same pce fnl f* 5/1[2]
33 3 4 **Karma Llama (IRE)**[14] [3328] 2-8-12 PaulEddery 9 67
(B Smart) *trckd ldrs: chal over 2f out: wknd fnl f* 8/1[3]
4 5 **Firestorm (IRE)** 2-9-3 LeeEnstone 2 59
(C W Fairhurst) *lengthy: dwlt: sn pushed along and in tch: hung rt and lost pl over 1f out* 25/1
5 2 **Sendali (FR)** 2-9-3 JamieSpencer 6 54
(J D Bethell) *rangy: scope: stdd s: sn trcking ldrs: lost pl over 1f out* 10/1
6 3 1/2 **Bollin Felix** 2-9-3 DavidAllan 8 45
(T D Easterby) *leggy: unf: scope: s.s: sn in tch: outpcd over 3f out: sn lost pl* 20/1
00 7 9 **Rue Soleil**[13] [3358] 2-8-12 JoeFanning 4 16
(J R Weymes) *chsd ldrs: lost pl 3f out: sn bhd* 33/1
0 8 21 **Wrynoes Pass (IRE)**[27] [2922] 2-9-3 GylesParkin 1 —
(R F Fisher) *restless in stalls: chsd ldrs: lost pl 3f out: bhd whn eased over 1f out* 66/1

1m 23.15s (-1.75) **Going Correction** -0.30s/f (Firm) 8 Ran SP% 119.2
Speed ratings (Par 94):98,95,90,84,82 78,68,44
CSF £3.14 TOTE £1.40: £1.02, £1.80, £2.00; EX 4.20.
Owner Mrs K Duggan & Mrs H Grove **Bred** J Duggan **Trained** West Ilsley, Berks

FOCUS
No strength in depth and the pace was just modest to the halfway mark. Pires was hardly winning out of turn and the success will have done his confidence good.

NOTEBOOK
Pires, quite a big individual, looked very fit indeed. Happier on this much flatter, more galloping track, he dictated it and, winding up the gallop from halfway, in the end he ran out a most decisive winner. The more time he is given from now on, the better. (op 8-13 tchd 4-6 in places)
White Deer(USA), long in the back, seemed happier on much quicker ground. He stepped up on his debut effort over this extra furlong and should find a race. (op 4-1)
Karma Llama(IRE) looked likely to give the winner a race when moving upsides, but in the end she did not see it out. At least this opens up the nursery route for her.
Firestorm(IRE), a March foal, is a son of Celtic Swing. A lazy walker, he hung as he tired and may not have appreciated the quick ground. (op 40-1)
Sendali(FR), a March foal, is a keen type. He fell in a heap late on and hopefully will improve for the experience. (op 9-1)
Bollin Felix, an April foal, is up in the air and narrow and will probably not come into his own until he tackles middle-distances at three.

3759 ELECTROLUX H'CAP 5f
2:50 (2:50) (Class 5) (0-70,69) 3-Y-O £3,238 (£963; £481; £240) Stalls Centre

Form RPR
2240 1 **Northern Chorus (IRE)**[11] [3397] 3-9-2 67 (v) DanielTudhope(3) 2 76
(A Dickman) *mde virtually all: hung bdly rt fnl f: kpt on wl* 7/2[1]
-450 2 1 **Lyndalee (IRE)**[34] [2701] 3-9-4 66 DavidAllan 12 71
(T D Easterby) *chsd ldrs: kpt on to take 2nd ins last: no real imp* 8/1
6305 3 3/4 **Trombone Tom**[27] [2937] 3-8-8 56 PaulHanagan 5 58
(J R Norton) *chsd ldrs: checked jst ins last: kpt on same pce* 6/1
-001 4 1/2 **Hotham**[15] [3285] 3-9-4 69 DNolan(3) 10 70
(N Wilson) *chsd ldrs: styd on same pce appr fnl f* 11/2[3]
-600 5 1/2 **Networker**[29] [2876] 3-8-2 50 oh10 PaulQuinn 4 49
(K G Reveley) *prom: outpcd over 2f out: kpt on same pce appr fnl f* 33/1
-302 6 1 **Butterfly Bud (IRE)**[8] [3538] 3-8-12 67 JamesO'Reilly(7) 9 62
(J O'Reilly) *rr-div: sn drvn along: kpt on fnl 2f: nvr nr to chal* 5/1[2]
5030 7 3 **Highland Song (IRE)**[15] [3297] 3-9-4 66 (p) TonyCulhane 1 50
(R F Fisher) *trckd ldrs: rdn 2f out: wknd fnl f* 5/1[2]
0505 8 1 1/4 **Bold Tiger (IRE)**[11] [3397] 3-7-11 50 (b) MarcHalford(5) 8 30
(Miss Tracy Waggott) *swvd rt s: chsd ldrs: wknd over 1f out* 14/1
0-00 9 1 **Martharum**[16] [3257] 3-7-11 50 oh10 LiamJones(5) 3 26
(J J Quinn) *w ldrs: wknd over 1f out* 25/1
10 1/2 **Megavegas**[81] 3-8-2 50 oh14 PaulFessey 11 24
(P T Midgley) *sn outpcd and in rr* 40/1
20-0 11 1 **Midnight Pearl (USA)**[80] [1437] 3-9-1 63 TomEaves 6 34
(J Howard Johnson) *sn outpcd: nvr on terms* 14/1
6-00 12 nk **Quote Unquote**[15] [3285] 3-8-12 60 ChrisCatlin 7 30
(J Parkes) *sn outpcd and in rr* 25/1

57.77 secs (-0.93) **Going Correction** -0.30s/f (Firm) 12 Ran SP% 122.7
Speed ratings (Par 100):95,93,92,91,90 89,84,82,80,79 78,77
CSF £32.15 CT £170.96 TOTE £4.10: £1.40, £3.00, £2.20; EX 50.30.
Owner The Future Generation **Bred** Mark Commins **Trained** Sandhutton, N Yorks
■ Stewards' Enquiry : Daniel Tudhope caution: careless riding

FOCUS
A low-grade three-year-old sprint handicap with few going into the race in good form and although the front two ran to their marks it is not guaranteed to prove reliable form.
Megavegas Official explanation: jockey said filly moved poorly throughout

3760 GAFFNEY INDUSTRIAL & WELDING SUPPLIES H'CAP 1m 3f
3:20 (3:20) (Class 4) (0-80,76) 3-Y-O £5,505 (£1,637; £818; £408) Stalls Low

Form RPR
5332 1 **Markington**[15] [3310] 3-9-1 70 JamieSpencer 2 78
(J D Bethell) *hld up wl in tch in last: hdwy on outer over 4f out: rdn to ld over 1f out: edgd lft ins last: styd on* 6/4[1]
4022 2 1 1/4 **Fire Two**[17] [3214] 3-9-7 76 TedDurcan 3 82
(M R Channon) *trckd ldr: wnt 2nd over 5f out: led over 2f out: hdd over 1f out: unable qckn* 7/4[2]

-602 **3** *1¾* **Shaydreambeliever**[9] 3477 3-9-0 **69** .... PaulHanagan 4 72
(R A Fahey) *set modest pce: shkn up over 4f out: hdd over 2f out: rallied: kpt on same pce appr fnl f* **9/2**[3]

3103 **4** *7* **Apache Nation (IRE)**[13] 3355 3-8-5 **60** .... DaleGibson 1 51
(M Dods) *trckd ldr: crowded bnd 6f out: drvn over 3f out: no imp: eased fnl f* **13/2**

2m 21.51s (0.51) **Going Correction** +0.075s/f (Good) **4** Ran SP% **107.9**
Speed ratings (Par 102):101,100,98,93
CSF £4.41 TOTE £2.30; EX 3.30.
Owner Clarendon Thoroughbred Racing **Bred** Minster Enterprises Ltd **Trained** Middleham Moor, N Yorks

FOCUS
A very steady gallop and the first two were longstanding maidens going into this handicap. However, it appears sound enough with the placed horses to recent form.

3761 WEATHERBYS INSURANCE SUMMER SPRINT (HERITAGE H'CAP) 6f
3:50 (3:52) (Class 2) (0-105,96) 3-Y-O **£32,385** (£9,635; £4,815; £2,405) **Stalls** Centre

Form RPR

-210 **1** **Bentong (IRE)**[65] 1836 3-9-4 **96** .... NelsonDeSouza(3) 12 108
(P F I Cole) *trckd ldrs stands' side: effrt and edgd lft over 1f out: led ins last: edgd lft: r.o* **4/1**[2]

4004 **2** *½* **Gallery Girl (IRE)**[9] 3475 3-8-12 **87** .... DavidAllan 4 97
(T D Easterby) *led: hdd ins last: no ex* **25/1**

5220 **3** *nk* **Damika (IRE)**[15] 3317 3-8-7 **82** .... DeanMcKeown 6 91
(R M Whitaker) *sn chsng ldrs: n.m.r over 1f out: crowded and carried lft wl ins last: no ex* **20/1**

4030 **4** *4* **Johannes (IRE)**[11] 3414 3-9-4 **93** .... AdrianTNicholls 10 94+
(D Nicholls) *chsd ldrs: rdn whn hmpd over 1f out: kpt on same pce* **16/1**

0001 **5** *½* **Grazeon Gold Blend**[13] 3360 3-8-13 **88** .... GrahamGibbons 3 84
(J J Quinn) *chsd ldrs on outer: kpt on same pce fnl 2f* **25/1**

4222 **6** *½* **Blazing Heights**[9] 3475 3-8-6 **81** .... TomEaves 14 75+
(J S Goldie) *s.i.s: hld up stands' side: nt clr run over 2f out: hdwy and edgd rt over 1f out: nvr nr ldrs* **7/1**[3]

0-00 **7** *¾* **Colorus (IRE)**[45] 2385 3-8-8 **83** .... PaulHanagan 8 75
(R A Fahey) *mid-div: effrt over 2f out: keeping on same pce whn hmpd over 1f out* **50/1**

5-31 **8** *nk* **Charles Parnell (IRE)**[29] 2875 3-8-0 **75** .... ChrisCatlin 13 66
(M Dods) *in rr stands' side: kpt on fnl 2f: nvr nr ldrs* **16/1**

0012 **8** *dht* **Mutamarres**[11] 3414 3-9-1 **90** .... (v) MartinDwyer 9 81+
(Sir Michael Stoute) *w ldr: wkng whn bdly hmpd over 1f out* **5/2**[1]

1220 **10** *nk* **Imperial Sword**[36] 2658 3-8-11 **86** .... PaulFessey 2 76
(T D Barron) *sn outpcd in rr far side: kpt on fnl 2f: nvr nrr* **8/1**

4004 **11** *¾* **Saabiq (USA)**[8] 3535 3-9-4 **93** .... JamieSpencer 1 81
(C E Brittain) *sn outpcd in rr on far side: nvr a factor* **7/1**[3]

1-40 **12** *¾* **Bertie Southstreet**[11] 3414 3-8-7 **82** .... JoeFanning 7 68+
(J R Best) *mi-div: keeping on same pce whn hmpd over 1f out* **20/1**

3600 **13** *¾* **Green Park (IRE)**[11] 3414 3-9-4 **93** .... TonyHamilton 11 76
(R A Fahey) *s.i.s: nvr a factor* **33/1**

-506 **14** *1* **Titus Alone (IRE)**[9] 3475 3-9-1 **90** .... PaulEddery 5 70
(B Smart) *stdd s: hld up: sme hdwy whn hmpd over 1f out* **50/1**

69.06 secs (-2.64) **Going Correction** -0.30s/f (Firm) **14** Ran SP% **120.5**
Speed ratings (Par 106):105,104,103,98,97 97,96,95,95,95 94,93,92,91
CSF £107.15 CT £1846.26 TOTE £5.20: £1.90, £8.40, £5.30; EX 112.40 TRIFECTA Not won..
Owner H R H Sultan Ahmad Shah **Bred** J Egan, J Corcoran And J Judd **Trained** Whatcombe, Oxon
■ The first running of this £50,000 Heritage Handicap.
■ Stewards' Enquiry : Nelson De Souza one-day ban: careless riding (Aug 3)

FOCUS
A decent, competitive handicap although the top-weight was 9lb below the race ceiling. The winner went badly left before striking the front causing mayhem but the first three finished clear in the end and the form looks solid, rated around the placed horses.

NOTEBOOK
Bentong(IRE), 10lb higher than Salisbury, has been absent since York after being cast in his box. A grand type, turned out in tip-top condition, he travelled strongly but edged left before taking charge, causing a domino effect. He went even more left in front leaving the third very short of room. He is due to carry a 3lb penalty in the Stewards Cup and should give a good account of himself. (op 7-2)
Gallery Girl(IRE), slipping to a lenient mark, ran a lot better even though she only looked third best on the day. Her sole success came in August at two.
Damika(IRE), 17lb higher than Newcastle and 11lb higher than his Lingfield success, was sticking on in gallant fashion when left very short of room between the first two near the line. He looked second best and has 12 days to turn out before his increased new rating kicks in.
Johannes(IRE), down 11lb this time, continues to struggle to make any real impact.
Grazeon Gold Blend, 4lb higher, found this a much tougher contest. (op 20-1)
Blazing Heights, a headstrong type, likes to come from the back and as a result needs plenty of luck in running, which is reflected by his career strike-rate - just one success from 11 starts now. (op 8-1 tchd 10-1)
Colorus(IRE), down 7lb after two outings this time, was going nowhere when caught up in the melee.
Mutamarres, 10lb higher than Ripon, was starting to struggle when knocked completely out of his stride by the winner. (op 9-4)
Saabiq(USA) Official explanation: jockey said filly never travelled

3762 COURT HOMEMAKERS H'CAP 1m 1f
4:20 (4:23) (Class 6) (0-65,63) 3-Y-O+ **£3,238** (£963; £481; £240) **Stalls** Low

Form RPR

6435 **1** **Apache Point (IRE)**[37] 2612 9-9-5 **54** .... KimTinkler 8 64
(N Tinkler) *trckd ldrs: chal 1f out: bmpd ins last: led last stride* **8/1**

0362 **2** *shd* **Parchment (IRE)**[5] 3610 4-8-8 **48** .... MarkLawson(5) 10 58
(A J Lockwood) *hld up in mid-field: hdwy over 3f out: led on ins 1f out: edgd rt: jst ct* **9/2**[2]

4042 **3** *1* **Thornaby Green**[3] 3672 5-8-2 **44** .... DeanHeslop(7) 3 52
(T D Barron) *led after 1f: qcknd over 6f out: hdd 1f out: no ex* **5/1**[3]

0511 **4** *nk* **Awaken**[8] 3527 5-9-8 **57** .... MichaelTebbutt 13 64
(Miss Tracy Waggott) *uns rrn and rn loose bef s: hld up: hdwy over 3f out: sn chsng ldrs: styd on fnl f* **12/1**

40-0 **5** *1¼* **Authenticate**[24] 3009 4-9-11 **60** .... ChrisCatlin 5 65
(E J O'Neill) *hld up in tch: effrt over 3f out: styd on same pce appr fnl f* **12/1**

3354 **6** *¾* **Alisdanza**[9] 3480 4-9-0 **49** .... RobbieFitzpatrick 7 52
(G A Swinbank) *hld up in rr: hdwy on outer over 2f out: styd on ins last* **11/1**

5420 **7** *1½* **Jaassey**[15] 3290 3-9-0 **58** .... KDarley 2 58
(T D Walford) *chsd ldrs: fdd fnl f* **15/2**

0152 **8** *¾* **Leighton Buzzard**[31] 2789 4-9-11 **63** .... DanielTudhope(3) 14 62
(Mrs A Duffield) *hld up in rr: hdwy on outside 3f out: hung rt: kpt on: nvr nr ldrs* **4/1**[1]

5400 **9** *nk* **Diamond Heritage**[11] 3398 4-8-6 **48** .... (b) MarkCoumbe(7) 9 46
(S Parr) *hld up in rr: hdwy on outer 3f out: nvr nr ldrs* **40/1**

0046 **10** *1¼* **Rudaki**[12] 3377 4-9-0 **49** .... (p) TomEaves 12 45
(M E Sowersby) *led 1f: chsd ldrs: wknd fnl 2f* **25/1**

0000 **11** *2½* **Typhoon Ginger (IRE)**[21] 3115 11-9-2 **56** .... AndrewElliott(5) 4 47
(G Woodward) *s.i.s: a in rr* **12/1**

562 **12** *1½* **Roman History (IRE)**[15] 3288 3-8-2 **46** .... PaulFessey 11 34
(Miss Tracy Waggott) *trckd ldrs: effrt 4f out: wknd over 2f out* **20/1**

-600 **13** *3* **Ronnies Lad**[24] 3022 4-8-4 **44** oh4 .... (v) DuranFentiman(5) 1 26
(J R Norton) *t.k.h: trckd ldrs on inner: lost pl 3f out* **66/1**

-005 **14** *21* **Mighty Duel**[4] 3638 3-8-0 **44** oh2 .... PaulHanagan 6 —
(J R Norton) *in rr: bhd, hung right and eased over 1f out* **50/1**

1m 52.76s (-0.64) **Going Correction** +0.075s/f (Good)
WFA 3 from 4yo+ 9lb **14** Ran SP% **123.6**
Speed ratings (Par 101):105,104,104,103,102 101,100,99,99,98 96,95,92,73
CSF £43.13 CT £210.70 TOTE £9.00: £3.00, £1.70, £2.10; EX 45.70.
Owner Bull Boys Syndicate I **Bred** Newgate Stud Co **Trained** Langton, N Yorks

FOCUS
A low-grade handicap with the first four covered by a large horse blanket at the line and close to their marks, so the form appears sound enough.
Mighty Duel Official explanation: jockey said gelding hung right-handed throughout

3763 HOT CHOCOLATE PLAYS REDCAR - 24TH AUGUST - APPRENTICE H'CAP 1m 6f 19y
4:50 (4:50) (Class 5) (0-70,61) 4-Y-O+ **£3,238** (£963; £481; £240) **Stalls** Low

Form RPR

1411 **1** **Rose Bien**[15] 3284 4-9-7 **61** .... (p) EdwardCreighton 5 69
(P J McBride) *trckd ldrs: effrt over 2f out: led over 1f out: drvn out* **4/1**[2]

-600 **2** *2* **Best Port (IRE)**[15] 3284 10-8-10 **53** .... MarkLawson(3) 3 58
(J Parkes) *hld up in rr: hdwy over 3f out: styd on to take 2nd ins last: no ch w wnr* **10/1**

0602 **3** *1¾* **Platinum Charmer (IRE)**[5] 3628 6-8-12 **55** .... (p) AndrewElliott(3) 4 58
(K R Burke) *trckd ldrs: led over 2f out: hdd over 1f out: kpt on same pce* **9/2**[3]

0230 **4** *3* **Toss The Caber (IRE)**[27] 2927 4-9-0 **59** .... (t) JamesReveley(5) 7 58
(K G Reveley) *led 1f: trckd ldr: led 4f out: hdd over 2f out: fdd fnl f* **12/1**

5512 **5** *hd* **Mr Majestic**[30] 2828 4-9-2 **61** .... (p) MichaelJStainton(5) 1 60
(R M Whitaker) *trckd ldrs: chal over 3f out: hung rt: wknd 1f out* **2/1**[1]

2541 **6** *7* **Acuzio**[16] 3270 5-8-11 **56** ow1 .... (p) PJBenson(5) 6 45
(W M Brisbourne) *uns rdr gng to s: rrd s: hld up in rr: hdwy over 3f out: hung lft and lost pl over 1f out: eased ins last* **11/2**

2-04 **7** *7* **Lennel**[13] 3350 8-8-10 **50** .... (b) DominicFox 2 29
(A Bailey) *s.s: hdwy on outside after 4f: drvn over 5f out: sn lost pl* **12/1**

4640 **8** *hd* **Esquillon**[51] 2196 4-7-13 **46** ow1 .... MarkCoumbe(7) 8 25
(S Parr) *led after 1f: hdd 4f out: sn lost pl* **40/1**

3m 4.74s (-0.28) **Going Correction** +0.075s/f (Good) **8** Ran SP% **113.8**
Speed ratings (Par 103):103,101,100,99,99 95,91,90
CSF £42.44 CT £185.50 TOTE £4.20: £2.00, £1.60, £1.70; EX 40.40 Place 6 £93.83, Place 5 £86.20..
Owner P J Pateman **Bred** Mrs J F Budgett **Trained** Newmarket, Suffolk

FOCUS
A moderate handicap, no better than a seller and a very steady pace, so the form is rated as average for the grade.
T/Jkpt: £9,494.10 to a £1 stake. Pool £26,744.00. 2 winning tickets. T/Plt: £123.10 to a £1 stake. Pool £53,295.10. 315.85 winning tickets. T/Qpdt: £55.20 to a £1 stake. Pool £2,173.40. 29.10 winning tickets. WG

3764 - 3766a (Foreign Racing) - See Raceform Interactive

3507 FAIRYHOUSE (R-H)
Sunday, July 23

OFFICIAL GOING: Good to firm

3767a BULMERS BELGRAVE STKS (LISTED RACE) 6f
3:55 (3:55) 3-Y-O+ **£24,693** (£7,244; £3,451; £1,175)

RPR

1 **Osterhase (IRE)**[8] 3561 7-9-11 114 .... (b) FMBerry 3 112
(J E Mulhern, Ire) *led: rdn and strly pressed ent st: hdd 1 1/2f out: rallied ins fnl f: regained ld under 100 yds out: styd on wl* **7/4**[2]

2 *hd* **Borderlescott**[29] 2847 4-9-6 .... RoystonFfrench 1 107
(R Bastiman) *chsd ldrs in 3rd: impr to chal on outer ent st: led 1 1/2f out: hdd under 100 yds out: kpt on* **6/4**[1]

3 *1¼* **That's Hot (IRE)**[21] 3125 3-8-12 93 .... MJKinane 2 99
(G M Lyons, Ire) *hld up in rr: prog early st: 3rd and kpt on fnl f* **20/1**

4 *½* **Sweet Afton (IRE)**[9] 3508 3-8-12 92 .... MCHussey 4 98
(Eamon Tyrrell, Ire) *chsd ldrs in 4th: last early st: kpt on same pce fr over 1f out* **14/1**

5 *1¾* **An Tadh (IRE)**[21] 3129 3-9-6 107 .... JMurtagh 5 100
(G M Lyons, Ire) *trckd ldr in 2nd: cl up and chal early st: no ex fnl f: eased cl home* **7/2**[3]

1m 12.0s **Going Correction** +0.025s/f (Good)
WFA 3 from 4yo+ 5lb **5** Ran SP% **110.0**
Speed ratings: 104,103,102,101,99
CSF £4.75 TOTE £2.00: £1.30, £1.60; DF 4.10.
Owner Michael Rosenfeld **Bred** E Kopica & M Rosenfeld **Trained** the Curragh, Co Kildare

FOCUS
A cracking race fought out by two tough and progressive sprinters.

NOTEBOOK
Osterhase(IRE) is as tough as they come and, although replaced by Borderlescott at the head of the market, he still looked the one to beat. Just as effective at six furlongs, he battled back doggedly having looked beaten and nobody could begrudge him the win. It now looks likely he will head to York for the Nunthorpe and, given front runners often go well there, it is not hard to see him playing a leading role. (op 11/10)
Borderlescott, a tough and progressive sprinter who ran a cracker in the Wokingham last time, went on over a furlong out and looked set to score, but Osterhase is a tough customer and he was run out of it in the dying strides. This was another fine effort from the gelding and he fully deserves to take his chance at Group level. He may well develop into a leading sprinter next season if contuinuing to progress. (op 2/1)
An Tadh(IRE) has shown most of his best form over further, so it was somewhat disappointing he found so little under pressure. (op 4/1)

3768 - 3774a (Foreign Racing) - See Raceform Interactive

3755 HAMBURG (R-H)

Sunday, July 23

OFFICIAL GOING: Good

3775a AIR BERLIN-CUP (LISTED RACE) — 2m

1:50 (1:53) 4-Y-0+ **£9,655** (£3,793; £2,069; £1,034; £690)

RPR

1 **Elusive Dream**[8] 3533 5-9-2 ... THellier 1 — 106
(Sir Mark Prescott) *pushed along to lead, narrowly headed after 5f, led again 5f out, ridden 2f out, ran on gamely to line* **7/5**[1]

2 3/4 **El Tango (GER)**[28] 2910 4-9-4 ... WMongil 3 — 107
(P Schiergen, Germany) **17/10**[2]

3 5 **Soterio (GER)**[37] 2629 6-9-0 ... JVictoire 4 — 98
(W Baltromei, Germany) **23/10**[3]

4 9 **Palais Tiff (GER)**[64] 1860 7-8-9 ... J-PCarvalho 5 — 84
(Frau M Fechner, Germany) **37/2**

5 1 1/2 **Evinado (GER)**[302] 5482 7-8-9 ... FilipMinarik 6 — 83
(P Vovcenko, Germany) **12/1**

6 nk **Peruginos Flyer (IRE)**[721] 4380 7-8-9 ... EPedroza 2 — 82
(F Reuterskiold, Sweden) **97/10**

3m 23.57s — 6 Ran SP% **131.2**

(including ten euro stakes); WIN 24; PL 15, 16; SF 54.

Owner Cheveley Park Stud **Bred** Cheveley Park Stud Ltd **Trained** Newmarket, Suffolk

NOTEBOOK

Elusive Dream may have conceded the lead, but he kept his place on the rail and never allowed the new leader an advantage of more than one length. He had to be driven right out but was always holding the runner-up. It was his first win since September 2004 and well deserved. He is now most likely to take his chance in the Ebor.

3776a BMW DEUTSCHES DERBY (GROUP 1) (C&F) — 1m 4f

4:20 (4:23) 3-Y-0 **£165,517** (£55,172; £33,103; £16,552; £5,517)

RPR

1 **Schiaparelli (GER)**[28] 2910 3-9-2 ... AStarke 12 — 115
(P Schiergen, Germany) *always in touch, 4th straight, led well over 1f out, driven out* **11/4**[1]

2 3/4 **Dickens (GER)**[22] 3-9-2 ... MDemuro 1 — 114
(H Blume, Germany) *held up in rear, last until good headway from 4f out, 5th straight, chased winner final f, kept on under pressure* **25/1**

3 1 3/4 **Oriental Tiger (GER)**[21] 3131 3-9-2 ... ABoschert 11 — 111
(U Ostmann, Germany) *held up in rear early, mid-division at half-way, 8th straight, stayed on final 2f to take 3rd last strides* **16/1**

4 nk **Saddex**[14] 3-9-2 ... TMundry 2 — 111
(P Rau, Germany) *a prom, 3rd straight, every chance well over 1f out, disputed 2nd approaching final f, one pace & lost 3rd last strides* **4/1**[2]

5 1 1/4 **Dark Dancer (GER)**[48] 2314 3-9-2 ... ABest 8 — 109
(W Kelkel, Germany) *mid-division, 9th straight, staying on when hampered by weakening horse over 1f out, switched left 1f out, fin wl* **20/1**

6 hd **Aspectus (IRE)**[21] 3131 3-9-2 ... ADeVries 14 — 108
(H Blume, Germany) *always in touch, 6th straight, ridden 2f out, kept on one pace* **9/2**[3]

7 3 **Lauro (GER)**[21] 3131 3-9-2 ... WMongil 15 — 104
(P Schiergen, Germany) *tracked leaders, 2nd straight, weakened well over 1f out* **4/1**[2]

8 shd **Quelle Amore (GER)**[49] 2279 3-8-12 ... EPedroza 13 — 100
(A Wohler, Germany) *never nearer than mid-division* **14/1**

9 3 **Prince Flori (GER)**[33] 2738 3-9-2 ... HGrewe 5 — 99
(S Smrczek, Germany) *prominent, led half-way to well over 1f out, soon weakened* **33/1**

10 5 **Elcanos (GER)**[22] 3-9-2 ... J-PCarvalho 7 — 92
(Mario Hofer, Germany) *mid-division, 7th straight on inside, beaten well over 1f out* **40/1**

11 5 **Katalog (GER)**[14] 3-9-2 ... JBojko 10 — 84
(Tim Gibson, Germany) *always towards rear* **100/1**

12 hd **Sadler's Star (GER)**[22] 3-9-2 ... FilipMinarik 9 — 84
(H J Groschel, Germany) *14th half-way, always towards rear* **66/1**

13 1 3/4 **Imonso (GER)**[21] 3131 3-9-2 ... ASuborics 4 — 81
(P Schiergen, Germany) *always towards rear (reported to have spread a plate on first turn)* **14/1**

14 4 1/2 **Nobileo**[38] 3-9-2 ... THellier 6 — 75
(Wido Neuroth, Norway) *13th half-way, always in rear* **20/1**

15 43 **Diarius (GER)**[36] 2671 3-9-2 ... JVictoire 3 — 10
(H Blume, Germany) *driven to lead after 1f, headed half-way, tailed off* **150/1**

2m 30.94s — 15 Ran SP% **126.0**

WIN 37; PL 20, 50, 36; SF 896.

Owner Stall Blankenese **Bred** Gestut Karlshof **Trained** Germany

NOTEBOOK

Schiaparelli(GER), a full-brother to 2000 German Derby winner Samum and 2002 German Oaks winner Salve Regina, showed his true colours under a well-judged ride and ran out a ready winner. He is clearly an improving colt, may well next line-up in the Grosser Preis von Baden, and is expected to do even better as a four-year-old.

Dickens(GER), markedly upped in class, emerged from off the pace to throw down a decent late challenge to the winner and ran the race of his life in defeat. This looked about as far as he wants to go and he is capable of finding a race at this level in due course.

3564 MAISONS-LAFFITTE (R-H)

Sunday, July 23

OFFICIAL GOING: Good

3777a PRIX ROBERT PAPIN (GROUP 2) (C&F) — 5f 110y

2:50 (2:52) 2-Y-0 **£51,103** (£19,724; £9,414; £6,276; £3,138)

RPR

1 **Boccassini (GER)**[21] 3132 2-8-13 ... DBonilla 5 — 108
(M Rulec, Germany) *prominent, 4th 1/2-way, ridden over 1 1/2f out and ran on, quickened well to lead 100 yards out, ridden out* **14/1**

2 hd **Golden Titus (IRE)**[36] 2670 2-9-2 ... SLandi 1 — 110
(A Renzoni, Italy) *in touch, close 2nd half-way, ridden to lead 2f out, headed 100 yards out, ran on* **11/2**[3]

3 shd **Magic America (USA)**[21] 3132 2-8-13 ... (b) DBoeuf 3 — 107
(Mme C Head-Maarek, France) *held up, last 1/2-way, headway 1 1/2f out, ridden to chal fnl f, every chance close home, just missed 2nd on line* **9/1**

4 2 **Beauty Is Truth**[17] 2-8-13 ... OPeslier 7 — 100
(Robert Collet, France) *in touch on outside, disputing 5th half-way, ran on 1 1/2f out til no extra final 100 yards* **7/2**[2]

5 1 **Not For Me (IRE)**[9] 3474 2-9-2 ... JohnEgan 2 — 100
(T J Pitt) *prominent on rail, ridden to lead half-way, headed 2f out, no extra* **14/1**

6 4 **Grand Vista**[19] 2-9-2 ... CSoumillon 8 — 87
(A Fabre, France) *very free to post, held up, 7th half-way, never a threat* **6/5**[1]

7 1 1/2 **Adelphos (FR)**[31] 2-9-2 ... RonanThomas 4 — 82
(Mme N Rossio, France) *led in centre to half-way, weakened 1 1/2f out* **16/1**

8 shd **Evens And Odds (IRE)**[16] 3242 2-9-2 ... NCallan 6 — 82
(K A Ryan) *reluctant to load, disputed 5th half-way, outpaced 2f out, soon beaten* **14/1**

64.50 secs — 8 Ran SP% **118.9**

PARI-MUTUEL: WIN 7.40; PL 2.10, 2.00, 2.70; DF 16.20.

Owner Stall Nik **Bred** Stall Westerberg **Trained** Germany

NOTEBOOK

Boccassini(GER) is a game little filly. Held up early on, she came under pressure one and a half out and fought all the way to the line. Connections of this bargain filly will now target the Cheveley Park Stakes at Newmarket, and she may tackle the Prix Morny at Deauville beforehand.

Golden Titus(IRE) always well to the fore from his number one draw, looked the winner passing the furlong marker, but was ultimately headed in the closing stages. He will now have a rest and tackle top-class company again in the autumn.

Magic America(USA), blinkered as usual, put up a pretty good performance on this occasion. Racing behind the leaders, she started her challenge one and a half out, but did not quite go through with her effort. The Prix Morny is now on the cards.

Beauty Is Truth was given a waiting ride and was putting in her best work at the finish up the centre of the track. She is only a small individual and looks out of her depth at this level.

Not For Me(IRE) was outpaced before the final furlong and then just stayed on near the stands' rail.

Grand Vista probably spoilt his chances on the way to the start and failed to run his race.

Evens And Odds(IRE) held up in sixth position, he never looked like finishing in the frame.

3778a PRIX EUGENE ADAM (GROUP 2) (STRAIGHT COURSE) — 1m 2f (S)

3:20 (3:21) 3-Y-0 **£78,621** (£30,345; £14,483; £9,655; £4,828)

RPR

1 **Flashing Numbers (USA)**[14] 3341 3-8-11 ... IMendizabal 4 — 117
(Mario Hofer, Germany) *raced in 4th, shaken up 2 1/2f out, ran on to lead 1 1/2f out on outside, went clear final furlong, pushed out* **16/1**

2 2 **Dragon Dancer**[21] 3127 3-8-11 ... AlanMunro 1 — 113
(G Wragg) *raced in 2nd, pressing leader 3f out, led 2 1/2f out to 1 1/2f out, held 2nd comfortably, not pace of winner* **13/8**[1]

3 3 **Linda's Lad**[50] 2228 3-8-11 ... CSoumillon 5 — 108
(A Fabre, France) *last, under pressure over 3f out, driven and stayed on at one pace to take 3rd final stages but never in contention* **2/1**[2]

4 3/4 **Markovitch**[57] 2030 3-8-11 ... OPeslier 2 — 107
(P W Chapple-Hyam) *led to 2 1/2f out, stayed on under pressure til no extra from over 1f out* **16/1**

5 2 1/2 **Multiplex**[19] 3186 3-8-11 ... LDettori 3 — 102
(A Fabre, France) *raced in 3rd, pushed along to take closer order 3f out, driven over 2f out soon one pace* **5/2**[3]

2m 0.80s — 5 Ran SP% **111.8**

PARI-MUTUEL: WIN 11.30; PL 2.70, 1.60; SF 39.80.

Owner Turf Syndikat 2006 **Bred** Little Man Farm **Trained** Germany

NOTEBOOK

Flashing Numbers(USA) bided his time until the field passed the stands one and a half out. He then quickened impressively and was not under significant pressure as he passed the post. He has no fancy engagements, but he could turn out for the Prix Guillaume d'Ornano at Deauville.

Dragon Dancer was given every possible chance. He settled in second place before taking a narrow advantage at the one and a half furlong marker and, although he battled on well, had nothing in reserve when challenged by the winner. He will now be rested until the autumn, when he will return to a mile and a half.

Linda's Lad ran a strange sort of race. Dropped back to last, he looked in trouble at the two-furlong marker before making some late progress without ever getting competitive. It was a disappointing effort and he is another who will return to 12 furlongs after a rest.

Markovitch tried to make every yard of the running and he surrendered his lead to the runner-up passing the stands. He was then one paced to the line, but still picked up 14,000euros.

Multiplex, who came into this unbeaten in his previous three outings, was found wanting when push came to shove and was another of his trainer's runners to perform well below expectations on the day.

3779a PRIX MESSIDOR (GROUP 3) (STRAIGHT COURSE) — 1m (S)

3:55 (3:55) 3-Y-0+ **£27,586** (£11,034; £8,276; £5,517; £2,759)

RPR

1 **Librettist (USA)**[22] 3091 4-9-1 ... LDettori 1 — 116
(Saeed Bin Suroor) *made all, ridden 1 1/2f out, driven out & ran on well* **7/4**[2]

2 1 **Helios Quercus (FR)**[27] 2941 4-9-1 ... IMendizabal 4 — 113
(C Diard, France) *raced in 4th, headway on outside 2f out, chased winner final 1 1/2f, kept on same pace under pressure* **16/1**

3 1 1/2 **Manduro (GER)**[32] 2741 4-9-8 ... CSoumillon 7 — 116
(A Fabre, France) *broke well on outside, restrained to dispute 6th, went 5th over 4f out, ran on under pressure to take 3rd close home* **6/4**[1]

4 hd **Racinger (FR)**[42] 2489 3-8-8 ... DBonilla 3 — 108
(F Head, France) *disputed 2nd, ridden 1 1/2f out, kept on one pace* **25/1**

5 1/2 **Ryono (USA)**[51] 2217 7-9-1 ... TCastanheira 8 — 108
(S Smrczek, Germany) *held up in rear, headway 2f out, never able to challenge* **40/1**

6 snk **Together (FR)**[27] 2941 6-8-12 ... (b) SMaillot 2 — 104
(Mme C Vergne, France) *disputed 2nd, ridden & no extra from over 1f out* **28/1**

7 snk **Special Kaldoun (IRE)**[63] 1873 7-9-1 ... DBoeuf 5 — 107
(D Smaga, France) *raced in 5th on rails, ridden well over 1f out, kept on but never a factor* **20/1**

8 8 **Apsis**[42] 2490 5-9-6 .... OPeslier 6 94
(A Fabre, France) *disputed 6th for over 3f, 7th half-way, beaten 2f out* **7/2**[3]

1m 36.0s
WFA 3 from 4yo+ 8lb 8 Ran SP% **119.0**
PARI-MUTUEL: WIN 3.90; PL 1.80, 2.00, 1.20; DF 31.00.
Owner Godolphin **Bred** Calumet Farm **Trained** Newmarket, Suffolk

NOTEBOOK
Librettist(USA) looked in great condition in the paddock and won this Group 3 event with something in reserve. His jockey set a sensible pace until things were quickened up before the two-furlong marker, and shortly after defeat was out of the question. Connections feel he will come on even further and he may even tackle the Sussex Stakes, but the Prix Jacques Le Marois is definitely on the cards.
Helios Quercus(FR) ran up to his very best form without excuses on this occasion. He tracked the leaders and started his challenge 400m from the post. He then stayed on well but never looked like catching the winner. It is most likely he will next be seen in the Jacques Le Marois.
Manduro(GER) dropped out early on, he had a lot of ground to make up from two furlongs out. He was putting in his best work at the finish, but was never a danger to the winner and runner-up. He was giving three kilos to the winner, and the runner-up, and still could go for the Jacques le Marois although a return to ten furlongs is also a likelihood.
Racinger(FR) well up from the start, he kept up the good work to the end and only lost third place in the final strides.
Apsis, the winner of Listed event and a Group 3 on his previous two outings, dropped out tamely a fair way out and proved bitterly disappointing.

3581 AYR (L-H)
Monday, July 24

OFFICIAL GOING: Good to firm (firm in places)
Wind: Breezy, half against

3780 LADIES NIGHT ON SATURDAY 12 AUGUST MEDIAN AUCTION MAIDEN STKS 6f
2:15 (2:15) (Class 5) 2-Y-O **£3,368** (£1,002; £500; £250) **Stalls** Low

Form RPR
226 1 **Voodoo Moon**[60] 1945 2-8-12 .... JoeFanning 3 76+
(M Johnston) *mde all: rdn over 1f out: r.o strly to go clr fnl f* **11/10**[1]
2 6 **Carillon (IRE)** 2-8-12 .... KDarley 7 61+
(M Johnston) *sn chsng wnr: rdn 2f out: no ex whn edgd lft ins fnl f: eased towards fin* **5/4**[2]
3 8 **The Grey Berry** 2-9-3 .... TonyHamilton 4 39
(C Grant) *prom: outpcd 1/2-way: kpt on fnl f: no ch w first two* **16/1**
0000 4 shd **Devilfishpoker Com**[16] 3286 2-8-10 .... (e[1]) JamesO'Reilly(7) 2 39
(R C Guest) *chsd ldrs: outpcd 1/2-way: n.d after* **100/1**
6 5 nk **Only A Splash**[17] 3259 2-9-3 .... PaulQuinn 1 38
(D W Chapman) *in tch: outpcd over 3f out: no imp fr 2f out* **100/1**
6 2 **Hansomis (IRE)** 2-8-12 .... DaleGibson 5 27
(B Mactaggart) *prom tl rdn and outpcd over 2f out* **10/1**[3]
04 7 40 **Perfect Reflection**[25] 2999 2-8-12 .... TomEaves 6 —
(A Berry) *sn outpcd: lost tch after 2f* **100/1**

1m 12.63s (-1.04) **Going Correction** -0.275s/f (Firm) 7 Ran SP% **110.0**
Speed ratings (Par 94):95,87,76,76,75 73,19
CSF £2.47 TOTE £1.90: £1.40, £1.20; EX 3.40.
Owner Mrs R Dick **Bred** Angmering Park Stud **Trained** Middleham Moor, N Yorks

FOCUS
An uncompetitive race in which the winner had the run of the race against the inside rail. The winner sets the level for the form.

NOTEBOOK
Voodoo Moon, who disappointed after getting worked up in the preliminaries on her first run on soft ground last time, was much more relaxed and turned in her best effort back on a sound surface. She had the run of the race though, and will find life tougher in competitive nursery company. (op 6-4 tchd 13-8 in a place)
Carillon(IRE) ◆, a half-sister to a couple of winners up to middle distances, took the eye in the paddock and, although easy to back near the off, showed ability on this racecourse debut. The step up to seven furlongs will suit and she looks the sort to win a similar event. (op 10-11 tchd 6-4, 4-5 in a place)
The Grey Berry, a half-brother to a dual six-furlong winner, showed a modicum of ability on this debut but, although the step up to seven furlongs may help, he is likely to continue to look vulnerable in this type of event. (tchd 20-1)
Devilfishpoker Com had finished last in each of his previous outings but fared a little better in the first time eyeshield. He is going to have to have his sights lowering considerably if he is to win a race, though. (op 66-1)
Only A Splash, tailed off on his debut on Fibresand earlier in the month, fared better on this turf debut but is going to continue to look vulnerable in this type of event. (op 66-1)
Hansomis(IRE), a sister to juvenile winners The History Man and Hansomelle, did not show enough on this racecourse debut to suggest she is of much short-term interest in this type of event. (op 12-1)
Perfect Reflection Official explanation: jockey said filly hung right throughout

3781 BOOK NOW FOR THE TOTESPORT GOLD CUP H'CAP 5f
2:45 (2:46) (Class 6) (0-60,59) 3-Y-O+ **£3,238** (£963; £481; £240) **Stalls** Low

Form RPR
-304 1 **Bond Becks (IRE)**[6] 3608 6-9-2 **52** .... PJBenson(7) 12 64
(B Smart) *led centre gp: effrt 2f out: overall ldr ins fnl f: kpt on strly* **13/2**[2]
6306 2 1 **Rosie's Result**[15] 3334 6-8-8 **42** .... AndrewMullen(5) 3 50
(M Todhunter) *led far side gp: hdd by centre wnr ins fnl f: edgd rt: kpt on: 1st of 9 in gp* **17/2**
0231 3 hd **Viewforth**[4] 3670 8-10-2 **59** 6ex .... (b) TomEaves 1 67
(I Semple) *chsd far side ldrs: effrt 2f out: kpt on ins fnl f: 2nd of 9 in gp* **7/1**[3]
3003 4 1 **Flying Tackle**[6] 3608 8-9-7 **50** .... (v) RoystonFfrench 7 54+
(I W McInnes) *bhd far side: hdwy over 1f out: kpt on fnl f: nrst fin: 3rd of 9 in gp* **8/1**
0143 5 nk **Sharp Hat**[6] 3617 12-9-7 **50** .... PaulQuinn 14 53
(D W Chapman) *cl up centre: drvn and outpcd 2f out: r.o ins fnl f: 2nd of 6 in gp* **7/1**[3]
040 6 1 1/4 **Waggledance (IRE)**[16] 3285 4-8-10 **46** .... KellyHarrison(7) 2 45
(D Carroll) *trckd far side ldrs: rdn over 2f out: no ex whn edgd rt over 1f out: 4th of 9 in gp* **33/1**
6013 7 1 1/4 **Muara**[25] 3003 4-9-7 **55** .... MarkLawson(5) 15 49
(D W Barker) *prom centre: rdn over 2f out: no ex over 1f out: 3rd of 6 in gp* **6/1**[1]
0650 8 nk **Zap Attack**[32] 2785 6-8-9 **38** ow1 .... PhillipMakin 6 31
(J Parkes) *hld up in tch far side: effrt over 2f out: no imp over 1f out: 5th of 9 in gp* **16/1**
0512 9 hd **Strawberry Patch (IRE)**[9] 3525 7-9-10 **56** .... (p) DNolan(3) 4 48
(J S Goldie) *trckd far side ldrs tl edgd rt and outpcd over 1f out: 6th of 9 in gp* **6/1**[1]
6000 10 1 **Wolfman**[6] 3617 4-9-0 **43** .... (p) AdrianTNicholls 16 32
(D W Barker) *in tch centre: outpcd 1/2-way: n.d after: 4th of 6 in gp* **33/1**
30-0 11 3/4 **Four Kings**[181] 181 5-8-3 **37** .... GregFairley(5) 8 23
(R Allan) *prom far side tl wknd fr 2f out: 7th of 9 in gp* **100/1**
0000 12 hd **Fairgame Man**[3] 3699 8-8-10 **46** .... (p) DanielleMcCreery(7) 9 31
(J S Wainwright) *bhd far side: rdn 1/2-way: nvr on terms: 8th of 9 in gp* **20/1**
-000 13 1/2 **Mutayam**[14] 3356 6-8-12 **41** .... (t) CatherineGannon 13 24
(D A Nolan) *prom centre tl rdn and wknd fr 2f out: 5th of 6 in gp* **100/1**
-005 14 nk **Instinct**[15] 3334 5-8-8 **37** .... DeanMcKeown 11 19
(Micky Hammond) *in tch centre: outpcd over 2f out: sn btn: last of 6 in gp* **18/1**
0-00 15 8 **Alfie Lee (IRE)**[15] 3334 9-8-8 **37** oh1 .... (t) KimTinkler 10 —
(D A Nolan) *in tch far side tl wknd fr 2f out: last of 9 in gp* **100/1**

58.98 secs (-1.46) **Going Correction** -0.275s/f (Firm) 15 Ran SP% **113.3**
Speed ratings (Par 101):100,98,98,96,96 94,92,91,91,89 88,88,87,86,74
CSF £53.89 CT £402.12 TOTE £8.20: £3.10, £2.80, £3.00; EX 70.90.
Owner R C Bond **Bred** Dr Paschal Carmody **Trained** Hambleton, N Yorks

FOCUS
A moderate handicap in which the field split into two groups but, although the best of the pace was on the far side, the winner came clear of those to race in the centre and may be a bit better than the bare form, which looks sound enough.
Muara Official explanation: trainer's representative said filly was found to be lame on returning to the stables

3782 HORSERACINGBREAKS.COM H'CAP 1m
3:20 (3:20) (Class 5) (0-75,73) 3-Y-O **£3,886** (£1,156; £577; £288) **Stalls** Low

Form RPR
6422 1 **Wind Star**[20] 3167 3-9-7 **73** .... DeanMcKeown 5 80+
(G A Swinbank) *chsd ldrs: effrt outside 2f out: qcknd to ld ent fnl f: comf* **1/1**[1]
-540 2 2 **Crosby Vision**[59] 1999 3-9-7 **73** .... PhillipMakin 6 75
(J R Weymes) *led to 2f out: rallied: kpt on fnl f: nt rch wnr* **6/1**
2101 3 hd **Jellytot (USA)**[16] 3290 3-8-7 **64** .... AndrewMullen(5) 1 65
(K A Ryan) *in tch on ins: hdwy to ld 2f out: hdd ent fnl f: one pce* **3/1**[2]
1113 4 1 1/2 **Noble Nova**[4] 3672 3-9-3 **69** 6ex .... JoeFanning 7 67
(M R Channon) *pressed ldr: ev ch 2f out: one pce fnl f* **11/2**[3]
1-0 5 5 **Roscommon**[51] 2239 3-9-3 **69** .... TomEaves 3 56
(I Semple) *in tch tl rdn over 2f out: sn outpcd* **20/1**

1m 42.47s (-1.02) **Going Correction** -0.275s/f (Firm) 5 Ran SP% **109.4**
Speed ratings (Par 100):94,92,91,90,85
CSF £7.41 TOTE £1.90: £1.10, £3.80; EX 7.50.
Owner D G Williams **Bred** Mrs N F M Sampson **Trained** Melsonby, N Yorks

FOCUS
An uncompetitive event in which the pace was on the steady side and the form is far from solid.

3783 WEATHERBYS BANK FILLIES' H'CAP 6f
3:50 (3:54) (Class 4) (0-85,76) 3-Y-O+ **£7,478** (£2,239; £1,119; £560; £279; £140) **Stalls** Low

Form RPR
3141 1 **Aahgowangowan (IRE)**[10] 3478 7-9-2 **65** .... (t) LiamJones(5) 3 82
(M Dods) *mde all: clr over 1f out: pushed out* **10/3**[2]
0000 2 5 **Obe Bold (IRE)**[4] 3673 5-8-4 **53** .... NataliaGemelova(5) 4 55
(A Berry) *sn pushed along in rr: hdwy over 1f out: kpt on wl fnl f to take 2nd nr fin* **33/1**
0242 3 shd **Riquewihr**[21] 3144 6-10-0 **72** .... (p) TonyHamilton 2 74
(J S Wainwright) *chsd wnr: rdn over 2f out: one pce over 1f out: lost 2nd cl home* **10/3**[2]
1634 4 nk **Linda Green**[3] 3718 5-9-5 **66** .... EdwardCreighton(3) 6 67
(M R Channon) *bhd: rdn over 2f out: kpt on fnl f: no imp* **11/4**[1]
3123 5 3 1/2 **Safranine (IRE)**[4] 3682 9-8-6 **57** .... AnnStokell(7) 5 47
(Miss A Stokell) *prom: lost pl over 2f out: n.d after* **8/1**
0-40 6 1 **Vondova**[15] 3332 4-9-10 **68** .... TomEaves 1 55
(D A Nolan) *chsd ldrs tl wknd fr 2f out* **100/1**
1111 7 4 **Our Sheila**[16] 3287 3-9-8 **76** .... MarkLawson(5) 7 51
(B Smart) *v unruly gng to post: stmbld bdly s: sn prom: rdn and hung lft over 2f out: wknd wl over 1f out* **4/1**[3]

1m 11.3s (-2.37) **Going Correction** -0.275s/f (Firm)
WFA 3 from 4yo+ 5lb 7 Ran SP% **107.9**
Speed ratings (Par 102):104,97,97,96,92 90,85
CSF £79.54 TOTE £4.20: £1.80, £7.60; EX 68.10.
Owner Les Waugh **Bred** Seamus Phelan **Trained** Denton, Co Durham

FOCUS
An ordinary handicap but, although the gallop was sound, nothing ever looked like posing a serious threat to the winner, who is better than ever in her current state.
Our Sheila Official explanation: trainer said filly was suffering the effects of a busy season

3784 RACINGUK.TV H'CAP 1m 2f
4:25 (4:25) (Class 5) (0-70,67) 3-Y-O+ **£5,181** (£1,541; £770; £384) **Stalls** Low

Form RPR
6640 1 **Jordans Elect**[15] 3333 6-9-6 **63** .... (v[1]) MarkLawson(5) 3 71
(P Monteith) *mde all: rdn and edgd rt 2f out: hld on wl fnl f* **7/1**
3540 2 1 1/2 **Rotuma (IRE)**[31] 2808 7-9-0 **52** .... (b) TomEaves 1 57
(M Dods) *hld up in tch: effrt over 2f out: hdwy to chse wnr ins fnl f: no imp* **8/1**
1121 3 3/4 **Cottingham (IRE)**[6] 3621 5-9-12 **67** 6ex .... BenSwarbrick(3) 2 71
(T D Barron) *trckd ldrs: effrt over 2f out: one pce ins fnl f* **5/4**[1]
5064 4 1 3/4 **Regal Connection (USA)**[13] 3375 3-9-0 **67** .... (b[1]) GregFairley(5) 7 68
(M Johnston) *pressed wnr: rdn and ev ch over 2f out: no ex ins fnl f* **7/1**
3533 5 1 1/2 **Inch High**[7] 3583 8-8-10 **51** .... DNolan(3) 4 49
(J S Goldie) *prom: effrt over 2f out: no ex over 1f out* **11/2**[3]
2044 6 5 **Balwearie (IRE)**[7] 3583 5-9-7 **59** .... (p) RoystonFfrench 6 47
(Miss L A Perratt) *prom: outpcd over 2f out: btn over 1f out* **5/1**[2]
000- 7 26 **No Commission (IRE)**[64] 5149 4-8-7 **50** .... AndrewMullen(5) 5 —
(R F Fisher) *s.i.s: bhd: eased whn no ch fr 3f out* **100/1**

2m 8.41s (-3.31) **Going Correction** -0.275s/f (Firm)
WFA 3 from 4yo+ 10lb 7 Ran SP% **113.6**
Speed ratings (Par 103):102,100,100,98,97 93,72
CSF £58.90 TOTE £12.10: £4.60, £3.50; EX 94.90.
Owner B A Jordan **Bred** James Thom And Sons **Trained** Rosewell, Midlothian

FOCUS
Another run-of-the-mill handicap and one in which the gallop was only fair. This bare form may not be reliable, rated around the winner and fourth.

No Commission(IRE) Official explanation: jockey said gelding was unsuited by the good to firm (firm in places) ground

3785 JIM MCKERRELL RETIRAL H'CAP 1m 2f
4:55 (4:56) (Class 6) (0-55,55) 3-Y-0 **£2,914** (£867; £433; £216) **Stalls** Low

Form RPR
0133 **1** **River Logic (IRE)**[3] [3716] 3-9-1 **51** SilvestreDeSousa(3) 2 57+
(A D Brown) *prom: effrt and led over 1f out: hung lft: rdn and r.o wl* **5/2**[1]
-646 **2** 1 1/4 **Dubai Around (IRE)**[14] [3355] 3-9-5 **52** DeanMcKeown 14 56
(Micky Hammond) *towards rr: hdwy over 2f out: kpt on to go 2nd wl ins fnl f: nt rch wnr* **16/1**
0051 **3** 3/4 **Moonlight Fantasy (IRE)**[14] [3357] 3-9-0 **47** KimTinkler 12 49
(N Tinkler) *keen: led to over 1f out: lost 2nd wl ins fnl f* **7/1**[3]
4003 **4** shd **Wensleydale Star**[14] [3357] 3-8-0 **40** DeanHeslop(7) 1 42
(T D Barron) *dwlt: sn midfield on ins: effrt over 2f out: kpt on fnl f* **10/1**
0503 **5** 3/4 **Coronation Flight**[16] [3288] 3-8-8 **41** RoystonFfrench 11 42
(F P Murtagh) *hld up: hdwy over 2f out: kpt on fnl f: no imp* **20/1**
3355 **6** 1/2 **Linton Dancer (IRE)**[28] [2923] 3-9-4 **51** PhillipMakin 3 51
(J R Weymes) *chsd ldrs: effrt over 2f out: one pce over 1f out* **5/1**[2]
-000 **7** 12 **Mycenean Prince (USA)**[81] [1441] 3-8-7 **47** JamesO'Reilly(7) 4 24
(R C Guest) *in tch tl rdn and wknd over 2f out* **40/1**
050 **8** 1/2 **Indian Girl**[11] [3451] 3-9-5 **55** EdwardCreighton(3) 10 31
(M R Channon) *s.i.s: nvr rchd ldrs* **33/1**
4-00 **9** nk **Andorran (GER)**[46] [2379] 3-9-2 **54** GregFairley(5) 7 29
(A Dickman) *bhd: drvn over 3f out: nvr on terms* **20/1**
0000 **10** 3/4 **Eliminator**[17] [3240] 3-8-5 **43** NataliaGemelova(5) 6 17
(I W McInnes) *bhd: rdn over 3f out: nvr on terms* **33/1**
1203 **11** 1/2 **Markestino**[6] [3609] 3-9-1 **48** (t) TonyHamilton 9 21
(T D Easterby) *keen: cl up tl wknd over 2f out* **5/1**[2]
0000 **12** 5 **King Of Chav's (IRE)**[18] [3232] 3-8-5 **43** LiamJones(5) 8 6
(A Bailey) *keen: in tch on outside tl wknd fr over 3f out* **40/1**
6300 **13** 1 3/4 **Pappas Ruby (USA)**[7] [3586] 3-8-10 **43** (p) TomEaves 13 3
(J S Goldie) *chsd ldrs tl wknd over 2f out* **20/1**

2m 10.1s (-1.62) **Going Correction** -0.275s/f (Firm) 13 Ran SP% **114.4**
Speed ratings (Par 98):95,94,93,93,92 92,82,82,82,81 81,77,75
CSF £39.83 CT £245.30 TOTE £3.60: £1.50, £4.30, £2.40; EX 54.20.
Owner R G Fell **Bred** J K Beckitt And Son **Trained** Pickering, York

FOCUS
A modest handicap and one in which the pace was sound and the form looks solid enough.

3786 DAWN HOMES H'CAP 7f 50y
5:25 (5:27) (Class 6) (0-55,55) 3-Y-0+ **£3,071** (£906; £453) **Stalls** Low

Form RPR
5046 **1** **Motu (IRE)**[3] [3716] 5-9-1 **49** (v) RoystonFfrench 7 59
(I W McInnes) *prom: rdn over 2f out: led over 1f out: rdn out* **11/1**
0355 **2** 2 1/2 **Quicks The Word**[12] [3398] 6-8-5 **46** KellyHarrison(7) 1 50
(T A K Cuthbert) *midfield on ins: hdwy and ev ch over 1f out: kpt on same pce ins fnl f* **12/1**
0000 **3** 3/4 **Quantica (IRE)**[6] [3617] 7-9-0 **48** (t) KimTinkler 8 50
(N Tinkler) *bhd tl hdwy over 2f out: kpt on wl fnl f* **11/1**
1600 **4** hd **Outrageous Flirt (IRE)**[6] [3617] 4-8-13 **52** GregFairley(5) 2 53
(A Dickman) *w ldr: led over 2f out to over 1f out: no ex ins last* **16/1**
00-0 **5** shd **Nevinstown (IRE)**[188] [134] 6-9-2 **50** TonyHamilton 4 51
(C Grant) *prom: effrt and hrd rdn fr 2f out: one pce fnl f* **11/2**[1]
0340 **6** 1 1/4 **Attacca**[3] [3697] 5-9-2 **55** MarkLawson(5) 6 53
(J R Weymes) *hld up: hdwy over 2f out: no imp fnl f* **11/1**
0423 **7** 3/4 **Second Reef**[12] [3398] 4-9-2 **55** TravisBlock(5) 9 51
(E J Alston) *hld up: effrt over 2f out: no imp over 1f out* **6/1**[2]
0030 **8** hd **Margaret's Dream (IRE)**[31] [2811] 5-9-0 **48** PaulQuinn 3 43
(D Carroll) *bhd: rdn over 2f out: sme late hdwy: n.d* **25/1**
0005 **9** 1 1/2 **Royal Pardon**[10] [3484] 4-8-6 **47** (p) JamesO'Reilly(7) 12 38
(R C Guest) *bhd: drvn over 3f out: nvr rchd ldrs* **25/1**
0535 **10** 1 1/2 **Pride Of Kinloch**[15] [3330] 6-9-1 **52** (p) DNolan(3) 10 39
(N Wilson) *chsd ldrs: effrt over 2f out: wknd over 1f out* **12/1**
-001 **11** 1 1/4 **Legal Dram**[17] [3240] 5-9-0 **48** PhillipMakin 13 32
(M Dods) *prom tl rdn and wknd over 2f out* **7/1**[3]
-013 **12** 1/2 **Walnut Grove**[9] [3529] 3-8-11 **55** BenSwarbrick(3) 11 35
(T D Barron) *prom: rdn over 2f out: sn wknd* **12/1**
5006 **13** 1 **Linden's Lady**[14] [3353] 6-9-1 **49** (b) CatherineGannon 5 29
(J R Weymes) *keen in rr: rdn 3f out: n.d* **20/1**
00-2 **14** 4 **Bandos**[28] [2926] 6-9-7 **55** (t) TomEaves 14 25
(I Semple) *keen: led to over 2f out: sn wknd* **8/1**

1m 30.75s (-1.97) **Going Correction** -0.275s/f (Firm)
WFA 3 from 4yo+ 7lb 14 Ran SP% **119.7**
Speed ratings (Par 101):100,97,96,96,95 94,93,93,91,90 88,88,86,82
CSF £132.34 CT £1526.43 TOTE £16.70: £5.30, £4.00, £4.00; EX 173.00 Place 6 £258.54, Place 5 £240.87.
Owner G Parkinson **Bred** J Hanly **Trained** Catwick, E Yorks

FOCUS
A modest handicap but a sound pace throughout and this bare form, rated through the winner, should prove reliable.
Bandos Official explanation: jockey said gelding sulked when headed
T/Jkpt: Part won. £7,100.00 to a £1 stake. Pool: £10,000.00. 0.50 winning tickets. T/Plt: £352.80 to a £1 stake. Pool: £60,535.75. 125.25 winning tickets. T/Qpdt: £168.80 to a £1 stake. Pool: £3,241.00. 14.20 winning tickets. RY

3604 BEVERLEY (R-H)
Monday, July 24

OFFICIAL GOING: Good to firm
Heavy rain two days earlier on watered ground resulted in the going being described as 'just on the quick side of good with an excellent cover'.
Wind: Light, half-behind Weather: Fine and sunny

3787 MEDIEVAL NIGHT CLAIMING STKS 5f
6:30 (6:30) (Class 5) 2-Y-0 **£3,412** (£1,007; £504) **Stalls** High

Form RPR
4055 **1** **Onenightinlisbon (IRE)**[20] [3173] 2-9-0 LeeEnstone 1 78
(P T Midgley) *sn chsng ldrs: led 1f out: drvn clr* **20/1**
1112 **2** 4 **Granny Peel (IRE)**[21] [3136] 2-8-11 DO'Donohoe 6 61
(K A Ryan) *chsd ldrs: drvn over 2f out: hung lft ins last: styd on to take 2nd nr line* **5/4**[1]
3643 **3** hd **Ishibee (IRE)**[23] [3096] 2-8-9 (p) PaulFessey 3 58
(Mrs A Duffield) *unruly in paddock: led tl 1f out: wknd towards fin* **13/2**[3]
242 **4** nk **Fractured Foxy**[81] [1442] 2-8-11 GrahamGibbons 2 59
(J J Quinn) *swvd lft s: sn chsng ldrs: kpt on same pce fnl f* **3/1**[2]
6033 **5** 1 1/2 **Denton Hawk**[18] [3228] 2-8-13 (p) DavidAllan 5 56
(M Dods) *chsd ldrs: outpcd over 2f out: kpt on fnl f* **20/1**
6 2 **Birdie Birdie** 2-8-7 PaulHanagan 8 42
(R A Fahey) *s.i.s: reminders after s: in rr tl sme hdwy fnl 2f* **13/2**[3]
0 **7** 5 **West Warning**[26] [2973] 2-9-0 (b) MickyFenton 7 31
(M W Easterby) *dwlt: a bhd and sn drvn along* **100/1**
0 **8** 1 1/4 **Imperial Style (IRE)**[7] [3596] 2-8-9 PatrickMathers(3) 9 25
(D Shaw) *chsd ldrs: drvn over 2f out: lost pl over 1f out* **66/1**
00 **9** 8 **Laurels Lady**[19] [3188] 2-7-13 (b[1]) AndrewElliott(5) 4 —
(I W McInnes) *swvd lft s: hung rt on outer: sme hdwy 3f out: wandered and sn lost pl* **150/1**

63.86 secs (-0.14) **Going Correction** -0.175s/f (Firm) 9 Ran SP% **108.8**
Speed ratings (Par 94):94,87,87,86,84 81,73,71,58
CSF £41.86 TOTE £20.20: £4.10, £1.10, £2.20; EX 42.00.The winner was claimed by Nigel Shields for £15,000
Owner M E Elsworthy **Bred** Stephen Moloney **Trained** Westow, N Yorks

FOCUS
A fair seller with a clear-cut winner. The form looks reasonable for the grade.

NOTEBOOK
Onenightinlisbon(IRE) overcame the worst draw and in the end won going away. She now joins Karl Burke and will be interesting in nursery company. (op 16-1 tchd 22-1)
Granny Peel(IRE), in trouble at halfway, came off a straight line inside the last but in the end did just enough to secure second spot. (op 10-11)
Ishibee(IRE), a handful in the paddock, showed them a clean pair of heels but she faded noticeably near the line. (op 7-1)
Fractured Foxy, dropped to claiming company, went sideways out of the traps. This looks as good as she is. (op 4-1)
Denton Hawk, in first-time cheekpieces, will be suited by a step up to six. (op 16-1)
Birdie Birdie, very green to post, was clueless coming back and this should have at least opened her eyes. (op 7-1)

3788 EUROPEAN BREEDERS FUND NOVICE STKS 7f 100y
7:00 (7:00) (Class 4) 2-Y-0 **£5,181** (£1,541; £770; £384) **Stalls** High

Form RPR
1 **1** **Silent Waves (USA)**[30] [2854] 2-9-5 JoeFanning 4 95+
(M Johnston) *mde all: qcknd over 2f out: drvn wl clr: edgd lft ins last: heavily eased towards fin* **1/7**[1]
2 9 **Lady Best (IRE)** 2-8-3 PaulHanagan 1 53
(J R Weymes) *chsd ldrs: wnt 2nd 2f out: no ch w wnr* **40/1**
4 **3** 2 **Coconut Queen (IRE)**[7] [3581] 2-8-7 PaulFessey 2 52
(Mrs A Duffield) *trckd ldrs: effrt on outer over 2f out: kpt on same pce* **14/1**[3]
4 7 **Petrosian** 2-8-8 KDarley 3 37
(M Johnston) *dwlt: sn trcking ldrs taking t.k.h: wnt 2nd over 5f out: hung bdly lft over 2f out: wknd and eased 1f out* **8/1**[2]

1m 33.37s (-0.94) **Going Correction** -0.05s/f (Good) 4 Ran SP% **107.7**
Speed ratings (Par 96):103,92,90,82
CSF £8.44 TOTE £1.10; EX 8.50.
Owner Salem Suhail **Bred** M375 Thoroughbreds, R Murphy & Dr S Price-Murphy **Trained** Middleham Moor, N Yorks

FOCUS
An uncompetitive race but the winner scored eased down in a fair time.

NOTEBOOK
Silent Waves(USA), a lazy walker, dominated and came clear but he edged left and ended up towards the stands'-side rail. He still looks to have something to learn but this powerful galloper may not appreciate really fast ground. (op 2-11 tchd 1-5)
Lady Best(IRE), who stands over a fair amount of ground, still looks weak. What she actually achieved on her debut is open to doubt. (op 20-1)
Coconut Queen(IRE), making a quick return and stepping up in trip, is unlikely to have improved on her debut effort. (op 16-1)
Petrosian, a tall, narrow individual was very noisy in the paddock. He hung badly left almost throughout and came to a standstill in the end. (tchd 13-2)

3789 MKM BUILDING SUPPLIES H'CAP 7f 100y
7:30 (7:30) (Class 4) (0-80,80) 3-Y-0+ **£6,477** (£1,927; £963; £481) **Stalls** High

Form RPR
3214 **1** **Phluke**[9] [3532] 5-10-0 **80** StephenCarson 7 91
(R F Johnson Houghton) *trckd ldrs: kpt on to ld jst ins last: r.o* **9/4**[1]
2U1 **2** 1 **Advancement**[13] [3383] 3-8-12 **71** PaulHanagan 8 78
(R A Fahey) *trckd ldrs: t.k.h: drvn 3f out: styd on ins last: no real imp* **9/2**[3]
0000 **3** 1 **Trojan Flight**[13] [3374] 5-9-4 **70** TonyCulhane 6 76
(D W Chapman) *t.k.h in rr: hdwy on ins and nt clr run over 2f out: styd on same pce fnl f* **5/1**
0202 **4** 1 1/2 **Bond Diamond**[10] [3500] 9-8-7 **64** RoryMoore(5) 1 66+
(P T Midgley) *stl had hood on whn stalls opened: s.s: t.k.h in last: hdwy on inner and nt clr run over 1f out: swtchd and kpt on* **15/2**
-500 **5** 1/2 **Malinsa Blue (IRE)**[9] [3542] 4-9-6 **72** (b) J-PGuillambert 4 73
(S Parr) *t.k.h in front: hdd jst ins fnl f: wknd* **33/1**
2464 **6** 1 1/2 **Franksalot (IRE)**[8] [3565] 6-8-12 **67** PatrickMathers(3) 3 64
(I W McInnes) *chsd ldrs: kpt on same pce fnl 2f* **12/1**
0303 **7** 1 3/4 **Tough Love**[9] [3549] 7-9-7 **73** (p) DavidAllan 5 66
(T D Easterby) *hld up in rr: effrt over 2f out: swtchd rt 1f out: nvr a threat* **10/3**[2]
3200 **8** 3/4 **Poppys Footprint (IRE)**[7] [3598] 5-9-2 **68** (b) DO'Donohoe 2 59
(K A Ryan) *hld up towards rr: effrt on outer over 2f out: hung rt: wknd fnl f* **14/1**

1m 33.5s (-0.81) **Going Correction** -0.05s/f (Good)
WFA 3 from 4yo+ 7lb 8 Ran SP% **117.8**
Speed ratings (Par 105):102,100,99,98,97 95,93,92
CSF £13.16 CT £46.29 TOTE £3.70: £1.30, £2.20, £2.60; EX 13.30.
Owner Mrs R F Johnson Houghton **Bred** Mrs R F Johnson Houghton **Trained** Blewbury, Oxon

FOCUS
A fair handicap and not a flat-out gallop but the form looks very sound and the winner continues to progress.

3790 NATWEST AGRICULTURAL TEAM H'CAP 1m 1f 207y
8:00 (8:00) (Class 5) (0-75,69) 3-Y-0 **£4,533** (£1,348; £674; £336) **Stalls** High

Form RPR
3122 **1** **Princess Cocoa (IRE)**[14] [3359] 3-9-3 **65** PaulHanagan 2 78+
(R A Fahey) *led early: trckd ldr: effrt over 2f out: led over 1f out: rdn clr* **5/4**[1]
4310 **2** 5 **Three Strings (USA)**[3] [3716] 3-8-9 **57** (p) DavidAllan 1 61
(P D Niven) *trckd ldrs: t.k.h: effrt over 3f out: tk 2nd 1f out: no ch w wnr* **7/1**

2443 **3** *nk* **English City (IRE)**^{3} [3695] 3-8-8 **56** DerekMcGaffin 4 59
(B Smart) *trckd ldrs: t.k.h: effrt over 3f out: kpt on same pce fnl f* **5/2**^{2}
-043 **4** *5* **Hunting Haze**^{14} [3359] 3-8-13 **61** MickyFenton 3 55
(Miss S E Hall) *sn led: set mod pce: qcknd over 5f out: sltly hmpd and hdd over 1f out: sn wknd* **9/2**^{3}
0530 **5** *9* **Bolckow**^{13} [3375] 3-8-12 **60** DO'Donohoe 6 36
(K A Ryan) *t.k.h in last: in tch: effrt on outer 3f out: wknd over 1f out: eased whn wl btn* **11/1**

2m 5.56s (-1.74) **Going Correction** -0.05s/f (Good) **5** Ran SP% **112.0**
Speed ratings (Par 100):104,100,99,95,88
CSF £10.68 TOTE £2.00: £1.10, £3.30; EX 8.40.
Owner P Ashton **Bred** Corduff Stud **Trained** Musley Bank, N Yorks

FOCUS
A modest handicap but the form rated through the second and third looks solid and an improved effort from the progressive winner.

3791 FAMILY DAY HERE NEXT TUESDAY MAIDEN H'CAP 2m 35y
8:30 (8:31) (Class 6) (0-55,55) 3-Y-O **£3,238** (£963; £481; £240) **Stalls** High

Form RPR
0046 **1** **Leo McGarry (IRE)**^{21} [3145] 3-8-12 **48** SaleemGolam$^{(3)}$ 4 56+
(S C Williams) *hld up toward rr: hdwy on outer over 4f out: hung lft and led over 1f out: sn drvn clr* **9/2**^{1}
0025 **2** *2 1/2* **Vice Admiral**^{5} [3634] 3-9-5 **52** JoeFanning 14 57
(M W Easterby) *led 2f: chsd ldrs: led over 2f out: hdd over 1f out: kpt on same pce* **5/1**^{2}
0403 **3** *2 1/2* **Myrtle Bay (IRE)**^{9} [3527] 3-9-3 **55** AndrewElliott$^{(5)}$ 6 57
(K R Burke) *led after 2f: hdd over 2f out: kpt on one pce* **9/1**
00-0 **4** *1 1/4* **Monashee Grey (IRE)**^{21} [3140] 3-8-5 **38** PaulHanagan 8 39
(R A Fahey) *in rr: reminders after 5f: styd on fnl 3f: nvr trbld ldrs* **14/1**
3206 **5** *shd* **Wise Choice**^{23} [3075] 3-9-6 **53** MickyFenton 11 53
(N P Littmoden) *mid-div: hdwy 5f out: kpt on same pce fnl 2f* **5/1**^{2}
06-0 **6** *nk* **Tiltili (IRE)**^{64} [1866] 3-9-3 **50** TonyCulhane 13 50
(P C Haslam) *mid-div: kpt on fnl 3f: nvr nr ldrs* **12/1**
-600 **7** *shd* **Silver Mont (IRE)**^{14} [3355] 3-9-5 **52** (v^{1}) PaulFessey 15 52
(Mrs A Duffield) *chsd ldrs: one pce fnl 2f* **20/1**
6602 **8** *4* **Virginia Rose (IRE)**^{20} [3169] 3-9-7 **54** J-PGuillambert 10 49
(J G Given) *hld up in rr: stdy hdwy over 3f out: rdn 2f out: wknd over 1f out* **7/1**^{3}
5000 **9** *1 1/2* **Dream Witness (FR)**^{14} [3347] 3-9-8 **55** FrancisNorton 2 48
(W R Muir) *mid-div: hdwy to chse ldrs over 4f out: wknd over 1f out* **20/1**
P063 **10** *1/2* **Prophet Preacher (IRE)**^{11} [3456] 3-8-6 **46** (v) KevinGhunowa$^{(7)}$ 12 39
(M J Attwater) *mid-div: effrt and prom over 3f out: lost pl over 1f out* **25/1**
0026 **11** *17* **Travolta**^{25} [3017] 3-9-7 **54** (p) KDarley 3 26+
(C G Cox) *chsd ldrs: chal 6f out: lost pl 2f out* **5/1**^{2}
0-00 **12** *3 1/2* **Navajo Warrior (IRE)**^{21} [3145] 3-8-7 **40** DavidAllan 9 8
(T D Easterby) *in rr: drvn 6f out: bhd fnl 3f* **33/1**
000 **13** *3* **Whiston Lad (IRE)**^{38} [2615] 3-8-8 **48** MSemple$^{(7)}$ 5 13
(S R Bowring) *s.i.s: in rr: wl bhd fnl 5f* **40/1**
0600 **14** *21* **Every Inch (IRE)**^{21} [3145] 3-8-3 **36** DO'Donohoe 1 —
(T D Easterby) *w ldrs: sn drvn along: lost pl over 3f out: sn bhd: virtually p.u: t.o* **50/1**

3m 39.81s (0.31) **Going Correction** -0.05s/f (Good) **14** Ran SP% **125.8**
Speed ratings (Par 98):97,95,94,93,93 93,93,91,90,90 82,80,78,68
CSF £25.65 CT £203.89 TOTE £5.80: £1.90, £1.90, £3.10; EX 39.00.
Owner E Murphy Racing **Bred** Sugar Puss Corporation **Trained** Newmarket, Suffolk

FOCUS
A low-grade stayers' handicap but the pace was sound and the form looks reliable. The improvement shown by the winner over this extended trip was mirrored by the market confidence.

3792 SIR LUPIN OF PIPWITHERS RIDES AGAIN H'CAP 1m 1f 207y
9:00 (9:01) (Class 5) (0-75,75) 4-Y-O+ **£3,562** (£1,059; £529; £264) **Stalls** High

Form RPR
0000 **1** **Terminate (GER)**^{44} [2455] 4-8-5 **59** (b^{1}) JoeFanning 3 67
(N P Littmoden) *trckd ldrs: tk fierce hold: hdwy to ld 2f out: hung rt: kpt on wl* **7/1**^{3}
1552 **2** *1 1/4* **Dark Charm (FR)**^{9} [3528] 7-9-2 **70** (p) PaulHanagan 2 77+
(R A Fahey) *set modest pce: qcknd over 3f out: hdd 2f out: hmpd and swtchd lft over 1f out: styd on: no real imp* **5/2**^{2}
2504 **3** *2 1/2* **Augustine**^{2} [3747] 5-9-7 **75** TonyCulhane 5 76
(P W Hiatt) *t.k.h in last: effrt over 3f out: kpt on: nvr nr to chal* **5/2**^{2}
4032 **4** *3* **Royal Flynn**^{15} [3333] 4-8-3 **57** (p) PaulFessey 4 53
(M Dods) *dwlt: hdwy to go 2nd over 6f out: chal over 2f out: sn rdn: hung rt and wknd jst ins last: eased* **9/4**^{1}

2m 10.31s (3.01) **Going Correction** -0.05s/f (Good) **4** Ran SP% **100.4**
Speed ratings (Par 103):85,84,82,79
CSF £20.30 TOTE £10.70; EX 26.70 Place 6 £60.44, Place 5 £41.01.
Owner Bill Hinge **Bred** Gestut Hofgut Mappen **Trained** Newmarket, Suffolk
■ Suivez Moi (12/1) was withdrawn on vet's advice. R4 applies, deduct 5p in the £.

FOCUS
A weak handicap, slowly-run and only the first two were seriously involved.
T/Plt: £935.80 to a £1 stake. Pool £53,910. 42.05 winning tickets T/Qpdt: £664.10 to a £1 stake. Pool £3,141. 3.50 winning tickets WG

3588 WINDSOR (R-H)
Monday, July 24

OFFICIAL GOING: Good to firm
Wind: Nil Weather: Sunny and hot

3793 ATKINS FOR LONDON FILLIES' H'CAP 1m 67y
6:20 (6:20) (Class 5) (0-75,75) 3-Y-O **£3,238** (£963; £481; £240) **Stalls** High

Form RPR
130 **1** **Wagtail**^{47} [2344] 3-9-5 **73** (t) JimmyFortune 8 83+
(E A L Dunlop) *t.k.h: trckd ldr: hanging lft and wnt alone to far side fr 3f out: overall ldr over 2f out: drvn and in command 1f out* **11/1**
0116 **2** *1 1/4* **Diamond De Triano (USA)**^{31} [2823] 3-9-4 **75** DanielTudhope$^{(3)}$ 7 82
(P W Chapple-Hyam) *trckd ldrs: rdn over 2f out: hanging lft and ended nr far side fnl f: chsd wnr: styd on* **8/1**^{3}
2016 **3** *2* **Dream Rose (IRE)**^{10} [3472] 3-9-7 **75** IanMongan 10 78
(M R Channon) *chsd ldrs: hrd rdn and no imp over 2f out: styd on fr over 1f out and led main gp ins fnl f* **12/1**
-601 **4** *nk* **Dancing Storm**^{10} [3472] 3-8-4 **58** FrankieMcDonald 6 60
(W S Kittow) *t.k.h: prom: rdn and nt qckn over 2f out: styd on fnl f* **10/1**
-060 **5** *1 1/4* **Lady Cree (IRE)**^{11} [3450] 3-8-11 **65** (b^{1}) MartinDwyer 11 64
(W R Muir) *dwlt: hld up wl in rr: lots of whip flourishing fr over 2f out: r.o fnl f: nvr nr ldrs* **33/1**
5512 **6** *shd* **Gelder**^{17} [3250] 3-9-6 **74** SteveDrowne 12 73
(H Morrison) *prom: pressed nr side ldr 3f out: led gp over 1f out: usual tail swishing after: wknd ins fnl f* **4/1**^{1}
600- **7** *1/2* **Suesam**^{276} [6004] 3-9-2 **70** AlanMunro 1 68
(B R Millman) *stdd fr wide draw and hld up in rr: rdn over 2f out: plugged on one pce* **50/1**
032 **8** *1* **Lilac Star**^{26} [2985] 3-9-4 **72** PaulEddery 9 67
(Pat Eddery) *kicked bef s: hld up towards rr: rdn over 2f out: one pce and no imp* **6/1**^{2}
6060 **9** *3/4* **Jabbara (IRE)**^{11} [3440] 3-8-12 **66** KerrinMcEvoy 13 60
(C E Brittain) *hld up towards rr: rdn over 2f out: no prog* **10/1**
-454 **10** *hd* **Aristofilia**^{34} [2727] 3-8-6 **63** NelsonDeSouza$^{(3)}$ 4 56
(P F I Cole) *dwlt: hld up in last pair: taken to outer and shkn up over 2f out: one pce after* **14/1**
0-14 **11** *hd* **Thornfield Clo (IRE)**^{11} [3440] 3-7-13 **56** oh3 StephaneBreux$^{(3)}$ 3 49
(R Hannon) *v free to post: t.k.h: trckd ldrs: wknd 2f out* **16/1**
2400 **12** *1 1/2* **Royal Citadel (IRE)**^{14} [3349] 3-8-13 **67** (v) PhilipRobinson 2 56
(C G Cox) *led and urged along early: hdd over 2f out: lost ld on nr side over 1f out: wknd* **14/1**
0045 **13** *2 1/2* **Zafantage**^{10} [3472] 3-8-8 **62** RyanMoore 5 46
(S Kirk) *chsd ldrs: rdn 1/2-way: struggling over 2f out* **10/1**
050 **14** *4* **Consuelita**^{21} [3146] 3-8-8 **62** RichardHughes 14 36
(B J Meehan) *hld up wl in rr: rdn over 2f out: no rspnse: eased fnl f* **20/1**

1m 44.13s (-1.47) **Going Correction** -0.05s/f (Good) **14** Ran SP% **117.6**
Speed ratings (Par 97):105,103,101,101,100 100,99,98,97,97 97,95,93,89
CSF £92.34 CT £1083.42 TOTE £11.10: £3.40, £2.90, £3.30; EX 149.10.
Owner Hesmonds Stud **Bred** Jeremy Gompertz **Trained** Newmarket, Suffolk

FOCUS
A modest three-year-old fillies' handicap, run at a fair pace, and the first two home drifted to the far side in the home straight. The third and fourth give the form some substance.
Lilac Star Official explanation: jockey said filly was kicked at start; vet said filly was sound post-race
Aristofilia Official explanation: jockey said filly stumbled shortly after start
Consuelita Official explanation: jockey said filly had no more to give

3794 PSP ASSOCIATION MAIDEN STKS 1m 2f 7y
6:50 (6:52) (Class 5) 3-4-Y-O **£3,238** (£963; £481; £240) **Stalls** Low

Form RPR
0- **1** **Farringdon**^{388} [3084] 3-9-3 MartinDwyer 6 79+
(M P Tregoning) *settled midfield: shkn up and prog 2f out: drvn and r.o wl fnl f to ld last strides* **14/1**
63 **2** *nk* **Miss Trinidad (USA)**^{38} [2600] 3-8-12 SteveDrowne 12 73
(B J Meehan) *chsd ldrs: pushed along 4f out: rdn and effrt over 2f out: r.o to chal nr fin: jst outpcd by wnr* **10/1**
063- **3** *hd* **Best Lady (IRE)**^{300} [5534] 3-8-12 70 MichaelHills 18 73
(B W Hills) *trckd ldng pair: effrt to ld 2f out: drvn and looked wnr 1f out: worn down last strides* **14/1**
4 *2* **Phebe** 3-8-5 HeatherMcGee$^{(7)}$ 13 69+
(L M Cumani) *hld up towards rr: stdy prog on bit fr over 3f out: styd on fnl f: nvr nrr: promising debut* **33/1**
2300 **5** *1/2* **Beckett Hall (IRE)**^{26} [2986] 3-9-3 76 RichardHughes 1 73
(R Hannon) *pressed ldr to over 2f out: sn one pce u.p* **13/2**^{3}
00 **6** *3/4* **Naini Tal**^{25} [3029] 3-8-12 JohnEgan 9 67
(D R C Elsworth) *hld up in rr: sme prog 3f out: reminder over 2f out: shuffled along and kpt on steadily fr over 1f out: do bttr* **25/1**
2-32 **7** *1/2* **Montjeu Man**^{44} [2465] 3-9-3 80 JimmyFortune 8 71
(E A L Dunlop) *restless in stalls: mde most to 2f out: sn btn* **15/8**^{1}
05 **8** *2 1/2* **Juicy Fruits**^{19} [3200] 3-8-12 RichardMullen 2 61
(E A L Dunlop) *chsd ldrs: rdn wl over 2f out: wknd fnl f* **33/1**
00- **9** *nk* **Cetshwayo**^{126} [5990] 4-9-8 StephenDonohoe$^{(5)}$ 15 66
(J M P Eustace) *mostly towards rr: rdn and no imp on ldrs fnl 2f* **100/1**
6 **10** *1/2* **Strong Survivor (USA)**^{37} [2662] 3-9-3 NickyMackay 17 65
(L M Cumani) *wl in tch: rdn over 2f out: grad fdd* **33/1**
04 **11** *nk* **Florimund**^{11} [3451] 3-9-3 StephenDavies 3 64+
(Sir Michael Stoute) *hld up in last pair: stdy prog into midfield over 2f out and gng wl: shuffled along and no ch after: should improve* **10/1**
12 *1 3/4* **You Live And Learn** 3-8-12 RobertHavlin 14 56
(H Morrison) *nvr beyond midfield: rdn and struggling over 2f out* **50/1**
13 *1/2* **Squiffy** 3-9-3 FergusSweeney 4 60
(P D Cundell) *dwlt: settled in last pair: nvr a factor* **66/1**
14 *3/4* **Persian Warrior (IRE)** 3-9-3 SebSanders 16 58
(W R Swinburn) *dwlt: a wl in rr: pushed along and no prog over 4f out* **14/1**
00 **15** *1 1/2* **Silk Purse**^{33} [2753] 3-8-9 NeilChalmers$^{(3)}$ 19 50
(M Madgwick) *dwlt: sn in midfield: gng wl enough over 4f out: shkn up and wknd 2f out* **100/1**
4-4 **16** *1/2* **Zalzaar (IRE)**^{30} [2881] 4-9-13 PhilipRobinson 7 55
(C G Cox) *chsd ldng pair tl wknd 3f out* **16/1**
17 *8* **Arabian Tiger** 3-9-3 AlanMunro 11 39
(P W Chapple-Hyam) *s.s: a wl in rr: t.o* **20/1**
18 *3 1/2* **Save The Secret (AUS)** 3-9-3 RyanMoore 5 33
(Sir Michael Stoute) *sn rdn and struggling: rn v green: bhd fnl 3f: t.o* **6/1**^{2}
0 **19** *9* **Hensting House**^{37} [2655] 3-9-3 AlanDaly 10 16
(Dr J R J Naylor) *prom tl wknd rapidly over 3f out: t.o* **100/1**

2m 8.65s (0.35) **Going Correction** -0.05s/f (Good)
WFA 3 from 4yo 10lb **19** Ran SP% **130.3**
Speed ratings (Par 103):96,95,95,94,93 93,92,90,90,89 89,88,87,87,86 85,79,76,69
CSF £145.57 TOTE £16.80: £4.30, £3.70, £3.90; EX 213.80.
Owner A E Oppenheimer **Bred** Hascombe And Valiant Studs **Trained** Lambourn, Berks
■ Stewards' Enquiry : Stephen DaviesH 32-day ban: in breach of Rule 157 (Aug 4-Sep 4)

FOCUS
A fair maiden likely to produce a number of winners and rated around the third and fifth.
Phebe ◆ Official explanation: jockey said, regarding the apparent tender ride, her orders were to jump out well, settle mid-division and make an effort after the intersection, adding that filly had become unbalanced around the bend and had been ridden to her best ability, taking into account her inexperience in the closing stages
Florimund Official explanation: 40-day ban: (Aug 8-Sep 16)

3795 MARKETFORM H'CAP — 6f
7:20 (7:21) (Class 4) (0-85,85) 3-Y-O **£6,477** (£1,927; £963; £481) **Stalls** High

Form				RPR
1-	**1**		**Fast Bowler**[330] 4790 3-8-10 **79** ... StephenDonohoe(5) 8 (J M P Eustace) *hld up in last pair: prog over 1f out: hrd rdn and r.o fnl f to ld last strides* **12/1**	86+
3110	**2**	*hd*	**Home Sweet Home (IRE)**[18] 3226 3-9-4 **82** ... JimmyFortune 2 (P D Evans) *settled in tch: effrt on outer 2f out: hrd rdn to ld ins fnl f: hdd last strides* **5/1**[3]	88
0324	**3**	*3/4*	**Matuza (IRE)**[12] 3403 3-9-2 **80** ... MartinDwyer 4 (W R Muir) *pressed ldr: upsides fr wl over 1f out: hd high and nt looking keen fnl f: nt qckn* **3/1**[1]	84
0101	**4**	*shd*	**Didn't We (IRE)**[42] 2496 3-9-7 **85** ... (v) IanMongan 7 (T G Mills) *mde most: hanging lft fr over 2f out: jnd wl over 1f out: hdd and nt qckn ins fnl f* **9/2**[2]	88
4020	**5**	*nk*	**Valentino Swing (IRE)**[18] 3226 3-8-6 **70** ... (p) KerrinMcEvoy 5 (J L Spearing) *w ldng pair to 1/2-way: cl up after: rdn and nt qckn wl over 1f out: kpt on ins fnl f* **15/2**	73
4201	**6**	*hd*	**Bold Argument (IRE)**[14] 3368 3-8-9 **73** ... RobertHavlin 6 (Mrs P N Dutfield) *in tch: hrd rdn on nr side over 1f out: kpt on same pce* **15/2**	75
3662	**7**	*1 3/4*	**Brandywell Boy (IRE)**[18] 3226 3-8-10 **79** ... JamesDoyle(5) 1 (D J S Ffrench Davis) *hld up in last pair: prog on wd outside 2f out: chal 1f out: wknd* **16/1**	76
-233	**8**	*8*	**Grimes Faith**[3] 3702 3-9-5 **83** ... RichardHughes 3 (R Hannon) *chsd ldrs tl wknd rapidly and eased jst over 1f out* **5/1**[3]	56+

1m 12.43s (-1.24) **Going Correction** -0.05s/f (Good) 8 Ran SP% **113.6**
Speed ratings (Par 102):106,105,104,104,104 103,101,90
CSF £69.66 CT £230.47 TOTE £13.30: £3.00, £1.90, £1.50; EX 114.40.
Owner J C Smith **Bred** Littleton Stud **Trained** Newmarket, Suffolk

FOCUS
A fair three-year-old handicap, run at a decent enough pace, and the first six were very closely covered at the finish. The form looks sound.
Grimes Faith Official explanation: trainer said colt appeared sore on leaving course but was subsequently found to be sound

3796 SEI EBF MAIDEN FILLIES' STKS — 6f
7:50 (7:52) (Class 4) 2-Y-O **£5,181** (£1,541; £770; £384) **Stalls** High

Form				RPR
1		**English Ballet (IRE)** 2-9-0 ... MichaelHills 3 (B W Hills) *dwlt: sn trckd ldrs and racd towards far side: chsd ldr over 1f out: sustained chal and r.o wl to ld last strides* **11/1**	78
3	**2**	*shd*	**Mason Ette**[31] 2816 2-9-0 ... PhilipRobinson 5 (C G Cox) *mde most and racd towards far side: wandered over 1f out: jnd ins fnl f: r.o but hdd last strides* **4/1**[3]	78
403	**3**	*5*	**Ripping**[26] 2984 2-9-0 ... RyanMoore 9 (R Hannon) *w ldrs: readily outpcd and fdd fnl f* **11/4**[2]	63
6	**4**	*1*	**Eastern Princess**[12] 3402 2-9-0 ... RichardThomas 8 (J A Geake) *wl in tch: chsd ldr briefly wl over 1f out: sn outpcd* **50/1**	60
0	**5**	*hd*	**Oh So Saucy**[28] 2930 2-9-0 ... AlanMunro 2 (C F Wall) *racd towards far side: cl up: shkn up and wknd over 1f out* **25/1**	59
2	**6**	*shd*	**Centreboard (USA)**[37] 2643 2-9-0 ... RichardHughes 15 (R Charlton) *racd towards nr side: w ldrs to over 1f out: wknd* **9/4**[1]	59
7	*1 3/4*	**Breezeway (IRE)** 2-9-0 ... SteveDrowne 10 (B J Meehan) *nvr on terms w ldrs: n.d fr over 1f out* **25/1**	54
8	*nk*	**Dubai Shadow (IRE)** 2-9-0 ... KerrinMcEvoy 7 (C E Brittain) *racd towards far side: cl up 4f: wknd and eased* **16/1**	53
9	*3/4*	**Baarrij** 2-9-0 ... IanMongan 13 (M R Channon) *dwlt: a wl in rr: shkn up and no real prog over 1f out* **20/1**	50
10	*hd*	**Pret A Porter (UAE)** 2-9-0 ... MartinDwyer 1 (M R Channon) *s.s: a wl in rr: shkn up and one pce fnl f* **33/1**	50
11	*1*	**Its Moon (IRE)** 2-9-0 ... JohnEgan 12 (M R Channon) *s.s: rn green and a wl in rr* **16/1**	47
12	*1/2*	**Career Girl (USA)** 2-9-0 ... RichardMullen 6 (E A L Dunlop) *blindfold only jst removed in time and s.s: a in rr: shkn up and no prog over 1f out* **28/1**	45
13	*11*	**Peggy's Pearl** 2-9-0 ... FergusSweeney 14 (J S Moore) *w ldrs to 1/2-way: wknd rapidly* **66/1**	12

1m 13.49s (-0.18) **Going Correction** -0.05s/f (Good) 13 Ran SP% **119.8**
Speed ratings (Par 93):99,98,92,90,90 90,88,87,86,86 85,84,69
CSF £51.10 TOTE £11.70: £2.40, £2.10, £1.80; EX 46.70.
Owner David Reid Scott & Sangster Family **Bred** Swettenham Stud **Trained** Lambourn, Berks

FOCUS
A fair juvenile fillies' maiden in which the front two pulled clear. The form looks sound and the race should produce its share of winners.

NOTEBOOK
English Ballet(IRE), a 70,00euros purchase related to several speedy juveniles, was steady in the market and she knew her job, soon tracking the leaders. The race looked beyond her when the runner-up went into a lead, but she picked up well to get on terms and just shaded it. She has the potential to leave this form behind and should stay seven furlongs in time. (op 12-1 tchd 10-1)
Mason Ette, who would have gone close but for hanging on her debut at Goodwood, raced into the lead and looked the likeliest winner, but English Ballet covered the move and she was run out of it in the dying strides. Winning a similar contest should prove a formality and, although bred to be a middle-distance performer in time, she shows enough speed to suggest she could win back at five furlongs. (op 9-2 tchd 5-1 in a place)
Ripping ran another sound race, but was well held back in third and is likely to remain vulnerable to those less-exposed. Nurseries may be her best option, depending on what mark she gets. (op 10-3 tchd 7-2)
Eastern Princess stepped up on her debut effort and will benefit from the combination of a rise in distance/move into handicap company in time.
Oh So Saucy, a Redcar Two-Year-Old Trophy entrant, looks to be going the right way and she showed up well to a point, but looks another nursery type.
Centreboard(USA), turned over at odds on his debut at Lingfield, was expected to be suited by this extra furlong, but he took a fierce hold in the early stages and that told late on as he tried to make his move. He clearly has ability, but looks a tricky customer. (op 7-4 tchd 5-2 in a place)
Breezeway(IRE) ◆, a 340,000euros purchase related to several useful performers, kept on nicely without being given an overly hard time and she looks sure to benefit from the outing. Further is going to suit in time and she looks a fair prospect.
Dubai Shadow(IRE) comes from a stable whose juveniles often need a run and he looks set to benefit from a bit more time.
Baarrij, a half-sister to Remaadd, is bred to be better at further and she was never going after a slowish start. The experience should do her good and she should show herself to be better than this in time. (op 16-1)
Pret A Porter(UAE) never recovered from a slow start and lacked the experience to get involved. She is another who should leave this behind in time.
Its Moon(IRE), the third and final Channon newcomer, shaped similarly to the others in that she raced green and lacked the pace to get involved. She is likely to benefit from the outing. Official explanation: jockey said filly hung left (op 25-1)
Career Girl(USA) ◆, a well-bred filly bred to appreciate trips upwards of seven furlongs, blew the start after her blindfold was removed very late, but she still travelled strongly into contention. She was unsure what was required of her when asked to challenge though and ultimately fell away. There were many positives to take from this and she should not be underestimated next time. (op 25-1)

3797 SOUTHERN ELECTRIC CUSTOMER PRICE PROMISE (S) STKS — 1m 3f 135y
8:20 (8:22) (Class 5) 3-Y-O+ **£3,238** (£963; £481; £240) **Stalls** Low

Form				RPR
6361	**1**		**Monash Lad (IRE)**[6] 3616 4-9-0 62 ... PatrickHills(7) 9 (M H Tompkins) *hld up wl in rr: stdy prog fr 3f out: led wl over 1f out: pushed clr* **5/2**[1]	60
060	**2**	*3 1/2*	**Yenaled**[30] 2862 9-9-7 54 ... SteveDrowne 4 (J M Bradley) *prom in chsng gp: clsd fr 3f out: chal 2f out: sn outpcd by wnr* **12/1**	54
-004	**3**	*nk*	**Gran Clicquot**[21] 3149 11-8-11 43 ... RobynBrisland(5) 5 (G P Enright) *wl in rr: styd on fr over 2f out: chal for 2nd fnl f: no ch w wnr* **50/1**	49
00-6	**4**	*3/4*	**Tetragon (IRE)**[23] 3068 6-9-4 64 ... DanielTudhope(3) 10 (D Carroll) *hld up: prog and prom in chsng gp 5f out: tried to cl fr 3f out: one pce fnl 2f* **10/1**	53
-404	**5**	*3/4*	**Arabian Moon (IRE)**[27] 2952 10-9-7 45 ... GeorgeBaker 8 (R Brotherton) *hld up wl in rr: prog 3f out: clsng whn nt clr run and swtchd rt 2f out: one pce after* **10/1**	54+
2652	**6**	*4*	**Ganymede**[9] 3527 5-9-2 55 ... (v) StephenDonohoe(5) 3 (J G M O'Shea) *dwlt: hld up wl in rr: effrt 3f out: nvr rchd ldrs* **9/2**[3]	45
4-00	**7**	*shd*	**Lucefer (IRE)**[54] 2132 8-9-7 44 ... (b) OscarUrbina 2 (G C H Chung) *chsd ldr: clr of rest 1/2-way: led over 2f out to 2f out: wknd* **25/1**	45
600-	**8**	*3/4*	**Dream Alive**[26] 3751 5-9-2 48 ... JamesDoyle(5) 6 (S Curran) *wl in rr: rdn and struggling 4f out: sn n.d* **33/1**	44
2050	**9**	*nk*	**Skin Sure Thing**[70] 1726 3-7-12 41 ow1 ... (p) MarkCoumbe(7) 12 (D G Bridgwater) *chsd clr ldng trio to over 3f out: stl chsng over 1f out: wknd* **80/1**	39
0025	**10**	*hd*	**Chocolate Boy (IRE)**[70] 1729 7-9-7 42 ... (b) RyanMoore 14 (G L Moore) *in tch in chsng gp: chsd clr ldng pair over 3f out: cl up but looked hld whn squeezed out wl over 1f out* **4/1**[2]	46+
4504	**11**	*9*	**Ambersong**[23] 3074 8-9-7 36 ... RichardThomas 1 (A W Carroll) *a wl in rr: lost tch over 3f out* **16/1**	29
5655	**12**	*11*	**Sky At Night (IRE)**[25] 3016 3-8-9 50 ... (b) JimmyQuinn 7 (P Mitchell) *dwlt: rchd midfield 1/2-way: wknd over 3f out: t.o* **14/1**	11
0200	**13**	*3*	**It's Basil**[11] 3439 3-8-9 50 ... (b) SebSanders 11 (R M Flower) *led: clr w one rival 1/2-way: hdd & wknd rapidly over 2f out* **25/1**	6
-000	**14**	*45*	**Shortbread**[18] 3221 4-9-7 48 ... AlanDaly 15 (M Salaman) *plld hrd: prom to 5f out: wknd rapidly: sn t.o* **66/1**	—

2m 28.63s (-1.47) **Going Correction** -0.05s/f (Good)
WFA 3 from 4yo+ 12lb 14 Ran SP% **120.5**
Speed ratings (Par 103):102,99,99,98,98 95,95,95,95,94 88,81,79,49
CSF £32.89 TOTE £3.60: £1.80, £3.20, £6.20; EX 47.50.The winner was sold for 11,500gns to Nick Shutts. Ganymede was claimed by Mrs L. J. Mongan for £6,000
Owner Miss Clare Hollest **Bred** Eoin And Stephanie Hanly **Trained** Newmarket, Suffolk
■ Stewards' Enquiry : Patrick Hills one-day ban: careless riding (Aug 4)

FOCUS
A very weak event which saw the winner score as he was entitled to on official figures.

3798 VC CASINO.COM H'CAP — 1m 2f 7y
8:50 (8:51) (Class 5) (0-70,70) 3-Y-O+ **£3,238** (£963; £481; £240) **Stalls** Low

Form				RPR
0134	**1**		**Bon Viveur**[7] 3589 3-9-8 **70** ... (p) RichardHughes 6 (R Hannon) *mde virtually all: styd against nr side rail in st: hrd pressed fnl f: hld on wl* **2/1**[1]	75
0000	**2**	*nk*	**Silver Court**[21] 3153 4-8-4 47 oh5 ... JamesDoyle(5) 4 (A W Carroll) *hld up: wnt towards far side in st and trckd ldrs: swtchd to nr side and chsd wnr over 1f out: str chal: jst hld* **16/1**	51
0046	**3**	*2*	**Eastborough (IRE)**[11] 3452 7-9-13 **65** ... RyanMoore 3 (B G Powell) *dwlt: hld up in tch: wnt towards far side in st and prom: one pce over 1f out* **9/2**[2]	65
000-	**4**	*1/2*	**Qik Dip (IRE)**[294] 5665 3-8-10 **61** ... DanielTudhope(3) 2 (P D Evans) *t.k.h: hld up: trckd ldrs towards far side in st: kpt on but nvr able to chal* **33/1**	60
0000	**5**	*1*	**Northside Lodge (IRE)**[21] 3151 8-9-7 **59** ... (p) SebSanders 7 (W R Swinburn) *pressed wnr: upsides over 5f out tl wnt to far side rail over 3f out: nt on terms over 1f out* **7/1**	56
0000	**6**	*3/4*	**Native American**[24] 3035 4-9-5 **57** ... RobertHavlin 1 (T D McCarthy) *cl up: wnt towards far side in st and prom: one pce fnl 2f* **16/1**	53
0000	**7**	*1*	**Scottish River (USA)**[35] 2708 7-10-0 **66** ... RichardSmith 8 (M D I Usher) *dwlt: hld up in last: styd towards nr side in st: effrt over 2f out: nvr rchd ldrs* **15/2**	60
4662	**8**	*2 1/2*	**Danzare**[11] 3440 4-9-2 **54** ... JimmyQuinn 10 (Mrs A J Hamilton-Fairley) *wl in tch: styd against nr side rail in st and chsd wnr to 2f out: wknd* **11/2**[3]	43
1000	**9**	*nk*	**John Charles (IRE)**[18] 3221 4-9-11 **63** ... MartinDwyer 5 (B De Haan) *t.k.h: trckd ldrs: styd towards nr side in st: wknd 2f out* **10/1**	52
0600	**10**	*5*	**Romanova (IRE)**[44] 2460 4-8-9 **54** ow1 ... (b[1]) SladeO'Hara(7) 9 (Dr J R J Naylor) *dwlt: in tch tl wknd over 2f out* **50/1**	33

2m 8.69s (0.39) **Going Correction** -0.05s/f (Good)
WFA 3 from 4yo+ 10lb 10 Ran SP% **116.9**
Speed ratings (Par 103):96,95,94,93,92 92,91,89,89,85
CSF £38.83 CT £133.22 TOTE £2.80: £1.40, £6.00, £1.80; EX 63.80 Place 6 £279.31, Place 5 £63.68.
Owner Mrs J Wood **Bred** Khorshed And Ian Deane **Trained** East Everleigh, Wilts

FOCUS
Modest handicap form and far from solid form with the time modest.
Romanova(IRE) Official explanation: jockey said filly was hampered on the bend
T/Plt: £551.60 to a £1 stake. Pool: £82,068.65. 108.60 winning tickets. T/Qpdt: £20.40 to a £1 stake. Pool: £6,599.50. 238.90 winning tickets. JN

3623 YARMOUTH (L-H)

Monday, July 24

OFFICIAL GOING: Firm

Wind: Light, behind Weather: Sunny

3799 EBF / FABERSCAFFOLDING.CO.UK MEDIAN AUCTION MAIDEN STKS — 5f 43y

2:30 (2:30) (Class 6) 2-Y-O — £2,590 (£770; £385; £192) Stalls High

Form	Pos	Dist	Horse	Jockey	RPR
0540	1		**Loves Bidding**[32] [2771] 2-9-3 ... DaneO'Neill 2 (R Ingram) *mde all: rdn over 2f out: styd on wl* **15/8**[2]		75
04	2	1 ¼	**Astroangel**[12] [3402] 2-8-12 ... TPQueally 1 (M H Tompkins) *slowly away: chsd ldrs: rdn over 2f out: swished tail u.p: wnt 2nd ins fnl f: no imp* **9/2**[3]		65
042	3	shd	**Piccolena Boy**[14] [3344] 2-9-3 ... JimCrowley 5 (P Winkworth) *chsd ldr: rdn over 2f out: kpt on one pce fnl f* **6/4**[1]		70
3	4	8	**Cookies Quiff (IRE)**[14] [3345] 2-9-3 ... LPKeniry 3 (J S Moore) *chsd ldrs: rdn and edgd lft wl over 2f out: sn struggling* **9/1**		41
	5	nk	**Julilla** 2-8-12 ... EddieAhern 4 (G G Margarson) *slowly away: sn wl outpcd* **16/1**		35

61.80 secs (-1.00) **Going Correction** -0.40s/f (Firm) 5 Ran SP% **108.8**

Speed ratings (Par 92):92,90,89,77,76

CSF £10.18 TOTE £2.80: £1.30, £2.40; EX 11.80.

Owner Ellangowan Racing Partners **Bred** R Ingram, Llety Farms And A Wright **Trained** Epsom, Surrey

FOCUS

An ordinary maiden in which the form looks sound but modest.

NOTEBOOK

Loves Bidding appreciated the drop in class after being outclassed in the Norfolk Stakes at Ascot. Getting over to the rail to lead, he made all the running and was always in command. He will now be aimed at a nursery over a stiff five furlongs or an easy six. (op 3-1)

Astroangel had not shaped as if a drop back to the the minimum trip was required and the way she was keeping on, albeit flashing her tail, suggests she will appreciate the return to six furlongs. She is now qualified for nurseries. (op 11-2)

Piccolena Boy, whose three previous runs were all at Bath, was always chasing the leader, but he could not muster the pace to get any closer and was pipped for second. (op 5-4)

Cookies Quiff(IRE) had made an encouraging debut in a seller but his limitations were exposed in this better grade. (op 13-2 tchd 10-1)

Julilla, whose dam was a dual winner over six furlongs, was always at the back of the field after a slow start. (op 10-1)

3800 WBX.COM WORLD BET EXCHANGE NURSERY — 7f 3y

3:00 (3:00) (Class 5) 2-Y-O — £3,238 (£963; £481; £240) Stalls High

Form	Pos	Dist	Horse	Jockey	RPR
352	1		**Little Miss Wizzy**[11] [3435] 2-8-1 **62** ... HayleyTurner 4 (M L W Bell) *s.s: hld up in tch: hdwy 2f out: rdn over 1f out: styd on gamely to ld nr fin* **7/2**[3]		67
3010	2	nk	**Dubai Magic (USA)**[11] [3442] 2-9-6 **81** ... JamieSpencer 1 (C E Brittain) *settled in midfield: rdn and chsd ldr over 2f out: led jst over 1f out: hdd and no ex nr fin* **5/2**[1]		85
064	3	¾	**Bobbish**[9] [3531] 2-8-9 **70** ... ChrisCatlin 7 (N A Callaghan) *chsd ldr tl pushed along and outpcd 3f out: rallied and ev ch 1f out: unable qckn u.p* **10/3**[2]		72
5345	4	¾	**Nicada (IRE)**[12] [3409] 2-8-4 **65** ... AdrianMcCarthy 6 (Miss Gay Kelleway) *hld up in midfield: effrt and rdn wl over 1f out: kpt on same pce ins fnl f* **14/1**		65
0123	5	½	**Hart Of Gold**[11] [3455] 2-9-2 **82** ... StephenDonohoe(3) 3 (M J Wallace) *taken down early: sn led: rdn wl over 1f out: hdd and faltered jst over 1f out: wknd last 100 yds* **11/2**		81
5040	6	15	**Suhayl Star (IRE)**[13] [3372] 2-9-0 **75** ...(v1) TedDurcan 2 (M R Channon) *wnt lft s: hld up bhd: effrt and shortlived effrt over 2f out: no ch last 2f: t.o* **10/1**		35
030	7	shd	**Storm Mission (USA)**[11] [3457] 2-8-8 **72** ... DominicFox(3) 5 (Miss V Haigh) *trckd ldrs tl rdn and lost pl qckly 3f out: no ch last 2f: t.o* **18/1**		32

1m 24.4s (-2.20) **Going Correction** -0.40s/f (Firm) 7 Ran SP% **110.3**

Speed ratings (Par 94):96,95,94,93,93 76,76

CSF £11.73 TOTE £4.30: £2.20, £1.80; EX 15.90.

Owner Caine, Miller, Myers & Phillips **Bred** Witney And Warren Enterprises Ltd **Trained** Newmarket, Suffolk

FOCUS

A fair nursery that was run at a decent pace and rated through the fourth. The field raced some way from the stands' rail. The official ratings shown next to each horse are estimated and for information purposes only.

NOTEBOOK

Little Miss Wizzy, on her nursery debut, soon recovered from a slow start. Making headway on the near side of the bunch, she snatched the race in the last strides. (tchd 10-3)

Dubai Magic(USA), well beaten in the July Stakes at Newmarket when wearing a tongue tie, was back up in trip against this more suitable opposition. After getting to the front, he edged first left and then right, and was just run out of it. (op 11-4)

Bobbish broke better this time and is getting the hang of things. Just held in the latter stages, he may need a mile now. (op 4-1 tchd 3-1)

Nicada(IRE) was keeping on at the end and looks well worth another try at this trip. (op 16-1 tchd 20-1)

Hart Of Gold set a decent pace, but could not pull out any extra once headed. The impression he gave was that he was not at home on such fast ground. (op 10-3)

3801 LETHEBY & CHRISTOPHER (S) STKS — 6f 3y

3:35 (3:35) (Class 6) 2-Y-O — £2,266 (£674; £337; £168) Stalls High

Form	Pos	Dist	Horse	Jockey	RPR
05	1		**Jost Van Dyke**[7] [3591] 2-8-12 ... DaneO'Neill 9 (B R Millman) *slowly away: bhd: hdwy 4f out: rdn over 2f out: led jst ins fnl f: drvn out* **5/4**[1]		61+
204	2	1 ¼	**Meru Camp (IRE)**[14] [3345] 2-8-12 ... JimCrowley 5 (P Winkworth) *chsd ldrs: rdn over 2f out: led over 1f out: hdd jst ins fnl f: kpt on one pce* **13/2**[3]		57
5306	3	1	**Diminuto**[14] [3345] 2-8-7 ... HayleyTurner 7 (M D I Usher) *hld up in midfield: effrt whn nt clr run and swtchd lft over 1f out: kpt on same pce ins fnl f* **13/2**[3]		49
0041	4	1	**Sunstroke (IRE)**[6] [3613] 2-8-13 ...(b1) TPQueally 1 (M G Quinlan) *chsd ldr: rdn and hung rt over 1f out: wknd ins fnl f* **4/1**[2]		52
0365	5	5	**Elizabeth Garrett**[13] [3380] 2-8-7 ...(p) EddieAhern 8 (R M H Cowell) *chsd ldrs for 2f: sn outpcd: kpt on ins fnl f: nt trble ldrs* **11/1**		31
0365	6	1 ¾	**Cyprus Rose**[6] [3624] 2-8-7 ... ChrisCatlin 2 (V Smith) *a bhd: rdn over 2f out: kpt on ins fnl f: n.d* **20/1**		26
3643	7	nk	**Baytown Paikea**[4] [3677] 2-8-8 ... DuranFentiman(5) 4 (P S McEntee) *led: sn crossed to stands rail: rdn 2f out: hdd over 1f out: sn wknd* **20/1**		31
0300	8	½	**Bonny Scotland (IRE)**[6] [3605] 2-8-4 ... DominicFox(3) 3 (Miss V Haigh) *v.s.a: a bhd* **33/1**		24
060	9	shd	**Champagne Perry**[39] [2588] 2-8-11 ow2 ... RossStudholme(3) 6 (V Smith) *sn rdn and hanging rt: wl bhd fr 3f out* **66/1**		30

1m 13.14s (-0.56) **Going Correction** -0.40s/f (Firm) 9 Ran SP% **113.4**

Speed ratings (Par 92):87,85,84,82,76 73,73,72,72

CSF £9.07 TOTE £2.20: £1.30, £1.70, £1.60; EX 10.30 Trifecta £116.50 Pool £579.28, 3.53 winning units.The winner was bought in for 7,400gns

Owner Bigwigs Bloodstock XII **Bred** T E Pocock **Trained** Kentisbeare, Devon

FOCUS

A slightly better than average juvenile seller despite the moderate time.

NOTEBOOK

Jost Van Dyke, dropped in grade, was a little slow to break. Switched to the outer of the bunch, he needed a bit of driving to find full stride but was well on top at the end. (op 11-10)

Meru Camp(IRE), suited by this longer trip, came through to lead but found the favourite too strong in the latter stages. (op 6-1 tchd 7-1)

Diminuto, better for this return to six furlongs, had to switch for a clear run but that can not be used as an excuse. Official explanation: jockey said filly suffered interference in running (op 9-1)

Sunstroke(IRE), a little keen in the first-time blinkers, was unsuited by the drop in trip and will appreciate the return to seven furlongs plus. (op 9-2 tchd 5-1)

Elizabeth Garrett, returning to turf, seemed to stay this longer trip but is a very modest performer. (op 12-1 tchd 10-1)

Baytown Paikea, having her fifth run in a fortnight, showed pace but did not see out this longer trip. (op 16-1)

3802 WBX.COM WORLD BET EXCHANGE H'CAP — 5f 43y

4:05 (4:06) (Class 4) (0-80,79) 3-Y-O+ — £5,505 (£1,637; £818; £408) Stalls High

Form	Pos	Dist	Horse	Jockey	RPR
6064	1		**Silver Dane (IRE)**[6] [3625] 4-9-5 **71** ...(v) ChrisCatlin 6 (Mrs C A Dunnett) *bhd: hdwy over 2f out: rdn to chal over 1f out: r.o wl to ld cl home* **5/1**[3]		81
5035	2	nk	**Conjecture**[14] [3354] 4-9-4 **70** ... RobbieFitzpatrick 4 (R Bastiman) *led: rdn wl over 1f out: kpt on gamely tl hdd cl home* **7/2**[2]		79
2135	3	2 ½	**Mannikko (IRE)**[48] [2329] 3-9-7 **77** ... TedDurcan 7 (G Wragg) *sn outpcd in last: styd on over 1f out: wnt 3rd wl ins fnl f: nt rch ldrs* **5/2**[1]		77
6403	4	¾	**Vindication**[9] [3536] 6-8-12 **64** ...(v) EddieAhern 2 (R M H Cowell) *chsd ldrs: wnt 2nd wl over 1f out: sn rdn: fnd little and fdd fnl f* **8/1**		61
2020	5	nk	**Fisola (IRE)**[24] [3049] 3-9-6 **76** ... DaneO'Neill 5 (C G Cox) *chsd ldrs: rdn wl over 2f out: kpt on same pce* **9/1**		72
-050	6	2	**Polish Emperor (USA)**[36] [2674] 6-9-13 **79** ...(p) ShaneKelly 1 (W R Swinburn) *sn drvn along on outer: chsd ldrs tl wknd over 1f out* **15/2**		68
-003	7	3 ½	**Rag Tag (IRE)**[8] [3568] 3-9-9 **79** ...(t) LPKeniry 3 (A M Balding) *chsd ldr tl 2f out: sn rdn and wknd* **15/2**		55

60.45 secs (-2.35) **Going Correction** -0.40s/f (Firm)

WFA 3 from 4yo+ 4lb 7 Ran SP% **112.1**

Speed ratings (Par 105):102,101,97,96,95 92,87

CSF £21.84 TOTE £6.30: £2.80, £2.70; EX 21.80.

Owner The Smart Syndicate **Bred** Tally-Ho Stud **Trained** Hingham, Norfolk

FOCUS

The field raced away from the stands' rail. The form looks straightforward and sound, rated through the runner-up.

3803 WEATHERBYS BANK FILLIES' H'CAP — 1m 3f 101y

4:40 (4:40) (Class 6) (0-65,60) 3-Y-O+ — £2,590 (£770; £385; £192) Stalls Low

Form	Pos	Dist	Horse	Jockey	RPR
0000	1		**Baboosh (IRE)**[154] [462] 5-9-11 **55** ... MichaelTebbutt 5 (M Wigham) *hld up in midfield: plld out and smooth prog to chse ldr over 2f out: led 1f out: rdn out* **4/1**[1]		62+
-620	2	½	**Fonic Rock (IRE)**[21] [3145] 3-9-1 **56** ... JamieSpencer 7 (M L W Bell) *hld up in rr: rdn wl over 3f out: gd hdwy to ld wl over 2f out: hdd 1f out: kpt on u.p* **9/2**[2]		62
4004	3	nk	**Lady Georgette (IRE)**[23] [3072] 3-9-2 **57** ... ChrisCatlin 11 (E J O'Neill) *hld up wl bhd: hdwy over 3f out: rdn over 2f out: wnt 3rd over 1f out: styd on wl last 100 yds: nvr nrr* **14/1**		63
0360	4	3 ½	**Lenwade**[11] [3437] 5-8-12 **42** ... JimmyQuinn 10 (G G Margarson) *slowly away: hld up wl bhd: hdwy 3f out: rdn over 2f out: kpt on: nt pce to trble ldrs* **6/1**[3]		42
4000	5	2	**Ruling Reef**[37] [2636] 4-9-2 **46** ... HayleyTurner 3 (M D I Usher) *rn in snatches: effrt u.p on inner over 2f out: kpt on same pce fr over 1f out* **25/1**		43
1300	6	3	**Miss Glory Be**[54] [2132] 8-8-10 **47** ...(p) AshleyHamblett(7) 4 (Ernst Oertel) *chsd ldrs: wnt 2nd 4f out tl wl over 2f out: wknd: b.b.v* **25/1**		39
5-00	7	3	**Shamsalmaidan (IRE)**[45] [2391] 3-9-5 **60** ... TedDurcan 6 (C E Brittain) *hld up in midfield: effrt u.p wl over 2f out: wknd over 1f out* **16/1**		48
00-0	8	1	**Liameliss**[42] [2497] 4-8-12 **45** ... DeanCorby(3) 9 (M A Allen) *chsd ldr tl 5f out: rdn over 4f out: sn wknd* **100/1**		31
1353	9	shd	**String Serenade (IRE)**[6] [3616] 5-8-10 **47** ... LukeMorris(7) 1 (V Smith) *prom: chsd ldr 5f out tl 4f out: sn rdn: wknd wl over 2f out* **8/1**		33
3103	10	1	**Red Sail**[24] [3036] 5-9-11 **55** ...(b) ShaneKelly 2 (Dr J D Scargill) *racd in midfield: hdwy to chse ldrs over 3f out: rdn over 2f out : sn wknd* **9/2**[2]		39
0323	11	¾	**Iamback**[17] [3260] 6-9-1 **45** ...(t) JamieMackay 8 (Miss D A McHale) *led tl wl over 2f out: sn lost pl and no ch* **9/1**		28

2m 24.1s (-3.40) **Going Correction** -0.40s/f (Firm)

WFA 3 from 4yo+ 11lb 11 Ran SP% **113.0**

Speed ratings (Par 98):96,95,95,92,91 89,87,86,86,85 84

CSF £20.42 CT £224.60 TOTE £4.00: £1.80, £2.00, £4.30; EX 18.90 Trifecta £149.40 Pool £349.33, 1.66, w/u.

Owner D Hassan **Bred** Lord Halifax **Trained** Newmarket, Suffolk

FOCUS

The pace was steady and the runners fanned out across the course in the straight. This did not look strong beforehand but might turn out to be reasonable for the grade, the first three finishing clear. The winner was very well in on old form and is value for a bit extra, while the second and third are slight improvers.

Miss Glory Be Official explanation: trainer said mare bled from the nose

3804 **MINT CASINO GREAT YARMOUTH H'CAP** **1m 2f 21y**
5:10 (5:10) (Class 6) (0-60,60) 3-Y-O **£2,590** (£770; £385; £192) **Stalls** Low

Form RPR
-066 **1** **Gizmondo**[25] 3030 3-8-13 **52** JamieSpencer 7 66+
(M L W Bell) *stdd s: hld up bhd: plld out and rdn over 3f out: hdwy to ld over 2f out: clr 1f out: comf* **11/2**[2]
2003 **2** *5* **Tangarita**[17] 3244 3-9-4 **57** LPKeniry 1 62
(A M Balding) *trckd ldrs on inner: squeezed through to chse wnr over 2f out: no imp u.p after* **11/2**[2]
0030 **3** *1* **Penmara**[11] 3440 3-9-2 **55** TPQueally 3 58
(M H Tompkins) *t.k.h early: hld up in midfield: hdwy to trck ldrs 4f out: rdn over 2f out: kpt on same pce* **8/1**
0030 **4** *1 ½* **Mighty Dancer (IRE)**[32] 2795 3-9-6 **59** ShaneKelly 5 59
(S Kirk) *hld up bhd: hdwy on inner over 3f out: swtchd rt over 2f out: sn drvn and outpcd: kpt on ins fnl f* **9/2**[1]
0000 **5** *½* **Mamichor**[25] 3016 3-8-11 **50** EddieAhern 6 49
(J R Boyle) *hld up in rr: plld wd and effrt over 2f out: hung lft fnl f: kpt on: nt pce to trble ldrs* **10/1**
6042 **6** *½* **Dream Of Paradise (USA)**[17] 3244 3-9-7 **60** JamieMackay 11 58
(Mrs L Williamson) *t.k.h: chsd ldr: ev ch 3f out: rdn and wknd wl over 1f out* **15/2**
0004 **7** *4* **Nassar (IRE)**[9] 3540 3-9-4 **60** (v) AmirQuinn(3) 9 51
(G Prodromou) *t.k.h: trckd ldrs: rdn 2f out: sn btn* **9/1**
003 **8** *9* **Fluted Crystal**[16] 3303 3-9-0 **53** DaneO'Neill 8 27
(H Candy) *hld up in midfield: lost pl 4f out: rallied u.p 3f out: sn btn: t.o* **7/1**[3]
2600 **9** *3* **Saxon Star (IRE)**[26] 2968 3-8-2 **41** oh1 HayleyTurner 10 9
(M D I Usher) *racd wd: chsd ldrs: rdn 4f out: wknd wl over 2f out: t.o* **50/1**
0500 **10** *¾* **Picture Show (USA)**[15] 3336 3-9-7 **60** TedDurcan 2 26
(C E Brittain) *hld up in rr: swtchd rt and nt clr run wl over 2f out: no ch after: t.o* **16/1**
-000 **11** *10* **Woolfall King (IRE)**[39] 2591 3-8-3 **42** JimmyQuinn 4 —
(G G Margarson) *led: rdn 3f out: hdd over 2f out: sn wknd: t.o* **25/1**

2m 5.58s (-2.52) **Going Correction** -0.40s/f (Firm) **11** Ran SP% **115.1**
Speed ratings (Par 98):94,90,89,88,87 87,84,76,74,73 65
CSF £35.01 CT £241.16 TOTE £6.00: £2.50, £2.50, £2.40; EX 32.80 Trifecta £226.40 Part won. Pool: £318.94 - 0.54 winning units. Place 6 £44.45, Place 5 £20.05.
Owner K J Mercer **Bred** Usk Valley Stud **Trained** Newmarket, Suffolk

FOCUS
A modest handicap. The winner was much improved and should rate higher and the form looks fairly sound.
Gizmondo ◆ Official explanation: trainer said, regarding the improved form shown, the horse had taken time to recover from being gelded and had benefited from today's step up in trip
Mamichor Official explanation: jockey said gelding hung left
Nassar(IRE) Official explanation: jockey said colt was unsuited by today's firm ground
T/Plt: Div £107.50 Tkts 378.50 Pool £55,753.25 T/Qpdt: Div £29.20 Tkts 98.80 Pool £3,899.50 SP

3805 - 3808a (Foreign Racing) - See Raceform Interactive

3780 AYR (L-H)
Tuesday, July 25

OFFICIAL GOING: Firm (good to firm in places)
Wind: Light, half-against

3809 **EUROPEAN BREEDERS FUND MAIDEN STKS** **7f 50y**
2:15 (2:15) (Class 4) 2-Y-O **£4,533** (£1,348; £674; £336) **Stalls** Low

Form RPR
62 **1** **Valbenny (IRE)**[32] 2806 2-8-12 DeanMcKeown 4 67
(G A Swinbank) *stdd in tch: hdwy over 1f out: led ins fnl f: styd on wl* **9/1**
65 **2** *¾* **Al Raahi**[24] 3083 2-9-3 TonyCulhane 3 70
(M R Channon) *set modest gallop: shkn up 2f out: hdd ins fnl f: kpt on u.p* **9/4**[2]
3 *1 ¼* **Tartan Tie** 2-9-3 JoeFanning 1 67
(M Johnston) *cl up: ev ch over 2f out: no ex ins fnl f* **11/2**[3]
0 **4** *2 ½* **Chookie Hamilton**[16] 3328 2-9-3 TomEaves 2 60
(I Semple) *in tch: rdn over 2f out: sn outpcd: kpt on ins fnl f: no imp* **50/1**
4 **5** *½* **Snowflight**[24] 3080 2-9-3 PaulHanagan 5 59
(R A Fahey) *keen: trckd ldrs: ev ch wl over 1f out: sn rdn and outpcd* **1/1**[1]

1m 33.44s (0.72) **Going Correction** -0.20s/f (Firm) **5** Ran SP% **108.1**
Speed ratings (Par 96):87,86,84,81,81
CSF £28.28 TOTE £9.50: £2.80, £1.40; EX 27.30.
Owner A Butler **Bred** Ken Lynch **Trained** Melsonby, N Yorks

FOCUS
An uncompetitive race in which the market leader disappointed. The runner-up was allowed to dictate an ordinary gallop.

NOTEBOOK
Valbenny(IRE) has improved markedly with every outing and turned in her best effort to get off the mark. The step up to this trip proved ideal and, with the prospect of a stronger gallop likely to suit in future, she may well be capable of better still. (op 10-1)
Al Raahi, who attracted market support, took the eye in the paddock and was allowed to do his own thing in front. He ran up to his best and, although vulnerable to the more progressive sorts in this grade, looks sure to win an ordinary event. (op 10-3 tchd 7-2)
Tartan Tie has several winners in his pedigree and, although he had the run of the race, showed enough on this racecourse debut for his in-form stable to suggest he is capable of winning a similar event with this experience behind him. (op 3-1)
Chookie Hamilton bettered the form of his course-and-distance run earlier in the month and, although likely to remain vulnerable in this type of event, will be of more interest granted a stiffer test of stamina once handicapped.
Snowflight, who shaped well behind a subsequent winner on his debut, failed to settle and proved a disappointment over a trip that should have suited. He is not one to write off yet but will have to settle better if he is to progress. (tchd 10-11 and 11-10)

3810 **BOOK FOR THE TOTESPORT AYR GOLD CUP H'CAP** **1m 7f**
2:45 (2:45) (Class 6) (0-55,55) 4-Y-O+ **£3,238** (£963; £481; £240) **Stalls** Low

Form RPR
0004 **1** **Dayoff (IRE)**[11] 3467 5-8-10 **48** (v) StephenDonohoe(5) 4 59+
(P D Evans) *hld up: gd hdwy to ld over 1f out: edgd lft: styd on strly* **11/2**[2]
6343 **2** *4* **Nakwa (IRE)**[5] 3675 8-8-12 **45** DavidAllan 6 51
(E J Alston) *in tch: hdwy to ld over 2f out: edgd lft: hdd over 1f out: kpt on same pce fnl f* **6/1**[3]
2340 **3** *shd* **Caymans Gift**[26] 2998 6-9-3 **55** AndrewMullen(5) 2 61
(A C Whillans) *hld up: hdwy and ev ch over 1f out: sn one pce* **6/1**[3]
-040 **4** *1* **Lennel**[2] 3763 8-9-3 **50** (b) FrancisNorton 7 55
(A Bailey) *hld up: rdn 3f out: kpt on fnl f: nvr rchd ldrs* **7/1**
-064 **5** *½* **Kristiansand**[15] 3352 6-9-2 **49** PaulHanagan 3 53
(P Monteith) *keen: in tch: rdn over 2f out: kpt on fnl f: no imp* **11/2**[2]
00/0 **6** *1 ½* **Culcabock (IRE)**[16] 3333 6-8-10 **43** JoeFanning 5 45
(Miss Lucinda V Russell) *chsd ldrs tl rdn and wknd 2f out* **10/1**
0300 **7** *3 ½* **Border Tale**[12] 3431 6-9-3 **55** MarkLawson(5) 9 53
(James Moffatt) *chsd ldrs to 3f out: sn rdn and wknd* **8/1**
/06- **8** *1* **Spartan Odyssey**[515] 489 5-8-2 **35** PaulQuinn 1 31
(A Bailey) *keen: led 4f: cl up tl wknd fr 3f out* **50/1**
0303 **9** *nk* **Rouge Et Noir**[9] 3350 8-9-4 **51** PaulMulrennan 6 47
(P Monteith) *led after 4f to over 2f out: wknd qckly* **5/1**[1]

3m 17.73s (-4.74) **Going Correction** -0.20s/f (Firm) **9** Ran SP% **110.7**
Speed ratings (Par 101):104,101,101,101,101 100,98,97,97
CSF £35.89 CT £193.52 TOTE £6.60: £2.10, £2.10, £3.00; EX 45.70.
Owner John P Jones **Bred** John Flynn And Mrs Eimear Mulhern **Trained** Pandy, Abergavenny

FOCUS
A modest handicap but one in which the gallop was soon fair. The form looks sound, the second running to his recent best with the winner value for a bit extra.
Border Tale Official explanation: jockey said gelding was unsuited by the firm (good to firm in places) ground

3811 **SERENDIPITY INTERACTIVE H'CAP** **6f**
3:20 (3:20) (Class 5) (0-75,72) 3-Y-O+ **£5,181** (£1,541; £770; £384) **Stalls** Low

Form RPR
2222 **1** **Geojimali**[8] 3584 4-9-8 **69** DNolan(3) 4 78+
(J S Goldie) *stdd in tch: gd hdwy on outside to ld ins fnl f: r.o wl* **2/1**[1]
0034 **2** *1 ½* **Flying Edge (IRE)**[30] 2898 6-9-2 **65** TravisBlock(5) 5 70
(E J Alston) *keen: cl up: led over 1f out to ins fnl f: edgd lft: kpt on* **5/1**[3]
0000 **3** *1 ¼* **Fairgame Man**[1] 3781 8-8-2 **53** oh7 DanielleMcCreery(7) 2 54
(J S Wainwright) *keen: chsd ldrs: effrt over 1f out: r.o ins fnl f* **33/1**
2423 **4** *¾* **Riquewihr**[1] 3783 6-10-0 **72** (p) TonyHamilton 1 71
(J S Wainwright) *led to over 1f out: kpt on same pce* **8/1**
0321 **5** *1 ¼* **Prospect Court**[7] 3617 4-8-4 **53** oh1 AndrewMullen(5) 6 48
(A C Whillans) *chsd ldrs tl rdn and no ex over 1f out* **5/2**[2]
-000 **6** *nk* **Big Bradford**[28] 2952 5-9-2 **60** (v) PaulHanagan 3 54
(R A Fahey) *prom: outpcd 1/2-way: kpt on u.p fnl f: n.d* **5/1**[3]

1m 11.82s (-1.85) **Going Correction** -0.20s/f (Firm) **6** Ran SP% **109.3**
Speed ratings (Par 103):104,102,100,99,97 97
CSF £11.65 TOTE £2.60: £1.70, £2.40; EX 15.20.
Owner Fyffees 2 **Bred** Jim Goldie **Trained** Uplawmoor, E Renfrews

FOCUS
An ordinary handicap in which the gallop to halfway was only fair. The winner and second ran pretty much to form but the overall level is not solid.

3812 **DAWN CONSTRUCTION H'CAP** **1m**
3:50 (3:50) (Class 4) (0-85,82) 4-Y-O+ **£7,772** (£2,312; £1,155; £577) **Stalls** Low

Form RPR
0054 **1** **Joseph Henry**[3] 3733 4-9-5 **80** JoeFanning 7 91
(M Johnston) *hld up ins: hdwy 3f out: led over 1f out: pushed out* **3/1**[1]
0525 **2** *1 ½* **Little Jimbob**[28] 2945 5-9-2 **77** PaulHanagan 4 84
(R A Fahey) *led: rdn over 2f out: hdd over 1f out: kpt on same pce* **3/1**[1]
1534 **3** *shd* **Hula Ballew**[17] 3289 6-9-0 **75** PhillipMakin 6 82
(M Dods) *pressed ldr: effrt over 2f out: ev ch over 1f out: kpt on same pce ins fnl f* **8/1**
4434 **4** *1 ¼* **Jubilee Street (IRE)**[10] 3549 7-9-5 **80** PaulFessey 5 84
(Mrs A Duffield) *keen: sn prom: outpcd over 2f out: kpt on fnl f* **13/2**[3]
0415 **5** *1* **Nashaab (USA)**[10] 3519 9-8-6 **67** (v) FrancisNorton 8 69
(P D Evans) *missed break: bhd: rdn 3f out: no imp tl styd on wl fnl f* **16/1**
4400 **6** *shd* **Stoic Leader (IRE)**[19] 3218 6-9-3 **78** PaulMulrennan 1 80
(R F Fisher) *in tch: effrt over 2f out: no imp over 1f out* **20/1**
0110 **7** *shd* **Kaymich Perfecto**[15] 3361 6-8-11 **77** MichaelJStainton(5) 3 78
(R M Whitaker) *chsd ldrs: outpcd over 2f out: n.d after* **10/1**
0401 **8** *hd* **Primo Way**[16] 3331 5-9-7 **82** TomEaves 9 83
(I Semple) *hld up: effrt over 2f out: sn btn* **9/2**[2]

1m 40.57s (-2.92) **Going Correction** -0.20s/f (Firm) **8** Ran SP% **112.4**
Speed ratings (Par 105):106,104,104,103,102 102,101,101
CSF £11.34 CT £62.13 TOTE £3.60: £1.50, £1.40, £2.30; EX 12.90.
Owner John Brown & Megan Dennis **Bred** John Brown & Megan Dennis **Trained** Middleham Moor, N Yorks

FOCUS
A fair handicap but as the modest gallop suited those racing up with the pace, the winner may be a bit better than the bare form. The third holds down the form slightly.

3813 **CONFERENCE CENTRE AT AYR RACECOURSE H'CAP** **7f 50y**
4:25 (4:25) (Class 4) (0-85,85) 3-Y-O+ **£6,477** (£1,927; £963; £481) **Stalls** Low

Form RPR
0124 **1** **Confide (IRE)**[35] 2737 4-8-11 **66** DeanMcKeown 8 74+
(G A Swinbank) *hld up in tch: effrt over 1f out: led ins fnl f: rdn and r.o wl* **7/4**[1]
0-00 **2** *½* **Neon Blue**[19] 3212 5-8-9 **69** (p) MichaelJStainton(5) 2 76
(R M Whitaker) *mde most tl hdd ins fnl f: kpt on* **16/1**
4013 **3** *½* **Queen's Composer (IRE)**[23] 3113 3-8-9 **76** MarkLawson(5) 6 79
(B Smart) *prom: effrt and ev ch over 1f out: no ex wl ins fnl f* **11/4**[2]
0305 **4** *¾* **Alfonso**[54] 2164 5-9-3 **72** TomEaves 4 76
(I Semple) *prom: rdn to chal 2f out: kpt on same pce fnl f* **7/1**
5-U0 **5** *7* **Flying Bantam (IRE)**[110] 898 5-9-4 **73** TonyHamilton 3 59
(R A Fahey) *keen: w ldr: rdn over 2f out: wknd over 1f out* **8/1**
0260 **P** **Lord Of The East**[37] 2681 7-10-0 **83** PaulHanagan 9 —
(I W McInnes) *uns rdr to post: bucked repeatedly, swished tail and v rel to r sn after s: p.u* **5/1**[3]

1m 31.08s (-1.64) **Going Correction** -0.20s/f (Firm)
WFA 3 from 4yo+ 7lb **6** Ran SP% **109.2**
Speed ratings (Par 105):101,100,99,99,91 —
CSF £27.45 CT £66.42 TOTE £2.10: £1.30, £5.00; EX 31.60.
Owner Elsa Crankshaw & G Allan Ii **Bred** Kevin Foley **Trained** Melsonby, N Yorks
■ Stewards' Enquiry : Dean McKeown caution: used whip with excessive frequency and without giving mount time to respond

FOCUS
An ordinary event in which the pace was just fair.

3814 **LADIES NIGHT ON SATURDAY 12 AUGUST H'CAP** **6f**
4:55 (4:57) (Class 6) (0-60,60) 3-Y-O **£3,238** (£963; £481; £240) **Stalls** Low

Form RPR
4200 **1** **The London Gang**[14] 3381 3-9-2 **60** (v) StephenDonohoe(5) 6 67
(P D Evans) *hld up: effrt centre over 1f out: led ins fnl f: kpt on wl* **5/1**[1]
5305 **2** *½* **Newkeylets**[10] 3526 3-8-13 **52** (b[1]) TomEaves 13 58
(I Semple) *racd alone centre: overall ldr: hdd ins fnl f: no ex* **10/1**

0050 **3** *3* **Azerley (IRE)**[14] [3379] 3-8-11 **50**.................................... FrancisNorton 11 47
(J D Bethell) *in tch: effrt over 2f out: no imp fnl f* **16/1**
0104 **4** *3/4* **Seesawmilu (IRE)**[13] [3397] 3-8-13 **52**........................... AdrianTNicholls 5 46
(E J Alston) *keen: chsd ldrs: effrt over 2f out: no ex fnl f* **7/1**[3]
0-60 **5** *hd* **Gifted Glori**[61] [1950] 3-8-6 **45**.. DavidAllan 1 39
(J J Quinn) *dwlt: sn prom: effrt over 2f out: one pce over 1f out* **8/1**
4000 **6** *nk* **Mandarin Grand (IRE)**[8] [3586] 3-7-11 **41** oh1.......(p) DuranFentiman(5) 7 34
(Miss L A Perratt) *midfield: drvn 1/2-way: rallied over 1f out: no imp* **50/1**
0531 **7** *hd* **Desert Hunter (IRE)**[13] [3397] 3-9-0 **53**......................... DeanMcKeown 8 45
(Micky Hammond) *in tch: drvn over 2f out: no imp over 1f out* **5/1**[1]
0525 **8** *2 1/2* **Pontefract Glory**[17] [3288] 3-8-2 **41** oh2...........................(p) PaulFessey 12 26
(M Dods) *bhd: rdn and hung rt over 2f out: sn btn* **11/2**[2]
0605 **9** *3 1/2* **Beginners Luck (IRE)**[8] [3586] 3-8-2 **41** oh2......................... PaulQuinn 2 15
(D Carroll) *bhd and sn rdn along: nvr on terms* **25/1**
0005 **10** *1 1/2* **Nautico**[8] [3587] 3-8-3 **42**...(b[1]) PaulHanagan 9 12
(Miss L A Perratt) *cl up tl hung lft and wknd over 2f out* **16/1**
-463 **11** *7* **The Salwick Flyer (IRE)**[10] [3526] 3-8-11 **50**................. TonyCulhane 10 —+
(A Berry) *led main gp tl faltered bdly over 2f out: nt rcvr* **25/1**
0000 **P** **Madam Moschata**[21] [3172] 3-8-0 **44** ow1.................. AndrewMullen(5) 3 —
(D W Barker) *chsd ldrs tl lost pl over 2f out: p.u over 1f out: lame* **100/1**

1m 13.06s (-0.61) **Going Correction** -0.20s/f (Firm) 12 Ran SP% **103.8**
Speed ratings (Par 98):96,95,91,90,90 89,89,86,81,79 70,—
CSF £41.55 CT £542.57 TOTE £7.40: £2.00, £4.00, £5.70; EX 70.80.
Owner D Healy **Bred** Lostford Manor Stud **Trained** Pandy, Abergavenny
■ Rosita Mia was withdrawn (9/1, unruly in stalls). rule 4 applies, deduct 10p in the pound.

FOCUS
A modest event in which the majority raced towards the far side but the runner-up showed that the centre of the course was no slower. The form does not look rock solid.
Pontefract Glory Official explanation: jockey said gelding hung right throughout
The Salwick Flyer(IRE) Official explanation: jockey said gelding lost its action
Madam Moschata Official explanation: jockey said filly felt lame but returned sound

3815 JOIN THE RACING UK CLUB H'CAP 1m
5:25 (5:28) (Class 6) (0-60,55) 3-Y-0+ **£3,238** (£963; £481; £240) **Stalls** Low

Form RPR
0605 **1** **Jordans Spark**[11] [3480] 5-8-13 **45**................................. MarkLawson(5) 8 56
(P Monteith) *hld up: hdwy on ins to ld over 1f out: kpt on wl fnl f* **10/1**
-503 **2** *2* **Able Mind**[14] [3386] 6-9-2 **46**.. DNolan(3) 13 52
(D W Thompson) *hld up midfield: effrt on outside over 2f out: hung lft over 1f out: kpt on fnl f: nt rch wnr* **11/2**[1]
0034 **3** *nk* **Anthemion (IRE)**[5] [3672] 9-9-4 **50**........................... AndrewMullen(5) 11 56
(Mrs J C McGregor) *trckd ldr: led over 3f out to over 1f out: no ex ins fnl f* **6/1**[2]
0-00 **4** *1* **Never Say Deya**[42] [2529] 3-9-2 **51**..................................... TonyCulhane 2 52
(M R Channon) *in tch: effrt over 2f out: one pce ins fnl f* **17/2**
4000 **5** *3/4* **Shamwari Fire (IRE)**[7] [3614] 6-8-11 **38**.............................(b) DavidAllan 4 40
(I W McInnes) *dwlt: sn midfield: effrt over 2f out: hung lft over 1f out: no imp* **10/1**
6060 **6** *1 1/4* **Whittinghamvillage**[7] [3617] 5-9-9 **55**.............................. GregFairley(5) 5 54
(D W Whillans) *in tch: effrt over 2f out: no ex over 1f out* **8/1**[3]
3650 **7** *1/2* **Son Of Thunder (IRE)**[9] [3570] 5-9-13 **54**...................(v[1]) PhillipMakin 14 52
(M Dods) *hld up: rdn 3f out: kpt on fnl f: no imp* **6/1**[2]
0046 **8** *1* **El Rey Royale**[11] [3480] 4-9-6 **47**.................................... DeanMcKeown 6 42
(Micky Hammond) *trckd ldrs: effrt over 2f out: wknd over 1f out* **9/1**
006- **9** *1/2* **Charlie George**[44] [5924] 5-8-11 **38**....................................... PaulFessey 7 32
(P Monteith) *hld up: rdn 3f out: no imp fr 2f out* **40/1**
5-00 **10** *2 1/2* **Royal Glen (IRE)**[9] [1436] 8-9-1 **42**.. TomEaves 1 30
(W S Coltherd) *bhd and sn outpcd: kpt on fnl f: nvr on terms* **14/1**
-005 **11** *6* **Eddies Jewel**[7] [3610] 6-8-12 **39**.......................................(v) TonyHamilton 10 14
(I W McInnes) *led to over 3f out: wknd over 1f out* **10/1**
0000 **12** *15* **Sparkbridge (IRE)**[47] [2379] 3-9-6 **55**........................... PaulMulrennan 12 —
(R F Fisher) *bhd and sn drvn along: nvr on terms* **33/1**
4600 **13** *1* **Claudia May**[15] [3352] 5-8-13 **40**.. JoeFanning 3 —
(Miss Lucinda V Russell) *prom to 3f out: sn wknd* **50/1**

1m 40.13s (-3.36) **Going Correction** -0.20s/f (Firm)
WFA 3 from 4yo+ 8lb 13 Ran SP% **116.9**
Speed ratings (Par 101):108,106,105,104,103 102,102,101,100,98 92,77,76
CSF £62.01 CT £364.39 TOTE £12.80: £3.00, £2.00, £2.20; EX 37.60 Place 6 £92.22, Place 5 £25.77.
Owner B A Jordan **Bred** Egerton Stud Farms **Trained** Rosewell, Midlothian

FOCUS
An ordinary event but the strong pace teed things up for a finisher. The form looks sound, the winner running his best race since 2004.
T/Jkpt: Not won. T/Plt: £147.30 to a £1 stake. Pool: £58,615.35. 290.40 winning tickets. T/Qpdt: £15.80 to a £1 stake. Pool: £4,165.60. 194.70 winning tickets. RY

3676 LEICESTER (R-H)
Tuesday, July 25

OFFICIAL GOING: Good to firm (firm in places)
Wind: Nil Weather: Hot and sunny

3816 SAMWORTH BROTHERS H'CAP 1m 1f 218y
6:20 (6:20) (Class 5) (0-70,70) 3-Y-0 **£5,362** (£1,604; £802; £401; £199) **Stalls** High

Form RPR
0401 **1** **Benbrook**[10] [3540] 3-9-2 **65**.. DaneO'Neill 5 73+
(J L Dunlop) *mde all: rdn over 1f out: styd on: eased nr fin* **8/11**[1]
6310 **2** *1* **Lester Leaps In (USA)**[36] [2713] 3-9-7 **70**............................ PatDobbs 1 73
(R Hannon) *trckd wnr: rdn over 2f out: styd on* **6/4**[2]
0-60 **3** *3/4* **Westering Home (IRE)**[18] [3250] 3-9-2 **65**....................... MickyFenton 6 67
(J Mackie) *hld up: hung rt fr 1/2-way: rdn 4f out: hdwy over 2f out: nt rch ldrs* **20/1**
00-0 **4** *10* **Aeronaut**[39] [2602] 3-8-0 **52** oh13 ow1......................(t) NelsonDeSouza(3) 4 35
(J M Bradley) *plld hrd and prom: rdn over 3f out: wknd over 1f out* **66/1**
00-0 **5** *3* **Double Oh Seven (IRE)**[12] [3453] 3-8-9 **58**................. FergusSweeney 3 35
(J W Unett) *hld up: rdn over 4f out: wknd over 3f out* **14/1**[3]

2m 6.85s (-1.45) **Going Correction** -0.30s/f (Firm) 5 Ran SP% **110.8**
Speed ratings (Par 100):93,92,91,83,81
CSF £2.07 TOTE £1.90: £1.10, £1.20; EX 2.00.
Owner Mrs J M Khan **Bred** P D And Mrs Player **Trained** Arundel, W Sussex

FOCUS
A modest race that will probably be unreliable formwise. The winner was value for a bit extra and the race has been rated through the runner-up.

3817 WARNING ZONE H'CAP 7f 9y
6:50 (6:52) (Class 6) (0-60,58) 4-Y-0+ **£3,238** (£963; £481; £240) **Stalls** Low

Form RPR
04-5 **1** **The Cayterers**[64] [1877] 4-8-10 **50**............................... NelsonDeSouza(3) 1 66
(J M Bradley) *plld hrd and prom: led and hung rt over 2f out: r.o* **33/1**
2032 **2** *1* **Sedge (USA)**[15] [3361] 6-8-13 **55**......................................(p) RoryMoore(5) 2 68
(P T Midgley) *chsd ldrs: rdn and ev ch fr over 1f out: unable qck nr fin* **9/2**[1]
0034 **3** *3 1/2* **Zafarshah (IRE)**[20] [3194] 7-8-8 **45**............................(b) AdrianMcCarthy 7 49
(R A Harris) *hld up: hdwy over 1f out: nt rch ldrs* **12/1**
0610 **4** *1 1/4* **Snow Bunting**[17] [3287] 8-9-6 **57**.. SebSanders 14 58
(Jedd O'Keeffe) *hld up: swtchd rt and hdwy over 1f out: nt trble ldrs* **5/1**[2]
140- **5** *2 1/2* **Rem Time (IRE)**[295] [5663] 6-8-12 **49**...................................... MickyFenton 13 43
(John Berry) *mid-div: hdwy and hung rt over 2f out: rdn over 1f out: wknd over 1f out* **22/1**
0605 **6** *nk* **Grezie**[40] [2574] 4-8-6 **48**.. LiamJones(5) 4 41
(T D McCarthy) *s.i.s: plld hrd and sn prom: rdn over 2f out: wknd over 1f out* **11/1**
1463 **7** *1 1/4* **Iced Diamond (IRE)**[10] [3523] 7-9-5 **56**.......................... FergusSweeney 17 46
(W M Brisbourne) *s.i.s: hld up: styd on ins fnl f: nrst fin* **9/1**[3]
5260 **8** *1/2* **Green Pirate**[25] [3052] 4-9-1 **52**...(p) DaneO'Neill 5 41
(M Wellings) *s.s: hdwy over 2f out: hung rt and wknd over 1f out* **14/1**
0016 **9** *1/2* **Wild Lass**[20] [3194] 5-8-12 **49**..(b) LPKeniry 9 37
(J C Fox) *wnt rt s: outpcd: nvr nrr* **25/1**
1360 **10** *shd* **Lord Chamberlain**[20] [3194] 13-8-13 **57**...................(b) BarrySavage(7) 11 44
(J M Bradley) *s.i.s and hmpd s: outpcd: nrst fin* **25/1**
0060 **11** *shd* **Yorkie**[32] [2811] 7-9-2 **53**.. JimmyQuinn 8 40
(J Pearce) *hld up: effrt over 2f out: wknd over 1f out* **10/1**
6602 **12** *shd* **Priorina (IRE)**[10] [3541] 4-8-10 **47**..................................(v) RobertHavlin 15 34
(D Haydn Jones) *chsd ldrs over 5f* **9/1**[3]
0004 **13** *shd* **Blue Knight (IRE)**[26] [3003] 7-9-4 **58**.....................(vt) DanielTudhope(3) 12 45
(D Carroll) *chsd ldrs: led over 2f out: sn hdd: rdn: hung lft and wknd over 1f out* **11/1**
5030 **14** *5* **Postmaster**[19] [3213] 4-8-13 **50**... RichardSmith 10 24
(R Ingram) *chsd ldrs over 4f* **25/1**
5066 **15** *hd* **Panshir (FR)**[19] [3229] 5-8-8 **45**... PatDobbs 18 18
(Mrs C A Dunnett) *chsd ldrs 5f* **20/1**
0050 **16** *nk* **Shannon Arms (USA)**[8] [3599] 5-9-4 **55**................. RobbieFitzpatrick 6 27
(R Brotherton) *led: hdd & wknd over 2f out* **25/1**
0060 **17** *18* **El Potro**[14] [3389] 4-8-13 **50**... RichardMullen 16 —
(J R Holt) *hld up: bhd fr 1/2-way* **33/1**
-000 **18** *10* **Mel's Moment (USA)**[14] [3390] 4-8-8 **50**.......................... JamesDoyle(5) 3 —
(R J Price) *mid-div: wknd 1/2-way* **66/1**

1m 23.64s (-2.46) **Going Correction** -0.30s/f (Firm) 18 Ran SP% **126.8**
Speed ratings (Par 101):102,100,96,95,92 92,90,90,89,89 89,89,89,83,83 82,62,50
CSF £163.95 CT £1960.14 TOTE £34.40: £6.70, £1.50, £2.90, £1.30; EX 142.50.
Owner R D Willis and M C Watts **Bred** Acrum Lodge Stud **Trained** Sedbury, Gloucs

FOCUS
A very moderate race indeed, but solid form. The winner was impressive enough and can go in again. The race can be rated around the second, who is a solid sort at the level.
Shannon Arms(USA) Official explanation: jockey said gelding hung right-handed
Mel's Moment(USA) Official explanation: jockey said gelding hit its head on the stalls

3818 HIGH SHERIFFS' MAIDEN AUCTION STKS 5f 2y
7:20 (7:21) (Class 6) 2-Y-0 **£3,238** (£963; £481; £240) **Stalls** Low

Form RPR
4 **1** **Black Moma (IRE)**[8] [3588] 2-8-6 .... RichardSmith 2 61+
(R Hannon) *trckd ldrs: pushed along 2f out: edgd rt over 1f out: rdn to ld ins fnl f: r.o* **8/11**[1]
504 **2** *nk* **Violet's Pride**[17] [3307] 2-7-11 .... CharlotteKerton(7) 1 58
(S Parr) *led: hung rt thrght: rdn and hdd ins fnl f: r.o* **8/1**[3]
2 **3** *5* **Tipsy Prince**[8] [3596] 2-8-7 .... JasonEdmunds(3) 3 46
(Mrs G S Rees) *w ldr 3f: rdn and nt clr run over 1f out: wknd fnl f* **7/4**[2]
060 **4** *3 1/2* **Jojesse**[85] [1342] 2-8-7 .... DanielTudhope(3) 4 33
(S Parr) *chsd ldrs over 3f* **25/1**

59.80 secs (-1.10) **Going Correction** -0.30s/f (Firm) 4 Ran SP% **109.2**
Speed ratings (Par 92):96,95,87,81
CSF £6.97 TOTE £1.80; EX 5.50.
Owner B Bull **Bred** Poulton Farm Stud **Trained** East Everleigh, Wilts

FOCUS
A modest race run in a reasonable time considering the small field - it was quicker than the three-year-old handicap that ended the card. However, the form is probably not worth a great deal.

NOTEBOOK
Black Moma(IRE) made hard work of winning but is probably a bit better than the bare result suggests. She shapes as though a sixth furlong would not be a problem. (op 11-8)
Violet's Pride had shown glimpses of ability before and ran up to her best. She is capable of landing a modest race judged on this run, and stronger handling may also bring out a little extra improvement. (op 5-1)
Tipsy Prince, dropping down in trip by a furlong, failed to build on his first run, which came on an All-Weather surface. He will be much easier to assess properly after his next run. (op 6-4 tchd 5-4 and 2-1)
Jojesse, returning after a break, again showed very little and needs to find some improvement from somewhere to get involved in a finish in the foreseeable future. (op 22-1)

3819 NEXT H'CAP 1m 3f 183y
7:50 (7:50) (Class 3) (0-90,87) 3-Y-0 **£11,217** (£3,358; £1,679; £840) **Stalls** High

Form RPR
0601 **1** **Kapellmeister (IRE)**[8] [3592] 3-8-9 **75** 6ex.....................(p) MickyFenton 3 83
(M S Saunders) *mde all: rdn clr over 1f out: styd on wl* **8/1**
2242 **2** *5* **Phone In**[12] [3456] 3-8-4 **70**.. RoystonFfrench 4 70
(R Brotherton) *a.p: chsd wnr over 5f out: rdn over 2f out: styd on same pce appr fnl f* **15/2**[3]
3160 **3** *1 1/2* **Billich**[3] [3748] 3-9-3 **83**.. RichardMullen 2 81
(E J O'Neill) *hld up: hdwy and nt clr run over 2f out: sn rdn: styd on same pce appr fnl f* **10/3**[2]
1 **4** *26* **Eta Draconis (IRE)**[32] [2829] 3-9-7 **87**.. LDettori 1 65+
(Saeed Bin Suroor) *chsd wnr tl rdn over 5f out: wknd over 2f out* **4/6**[1]

2m 28.87s (-5.63) **Going Correction** -0.30s/f (Firm) 4 Ran SP% **105.9**
Speed ratings (Par 104):106,102,101,84
CSF £47.94 TOTE £7.70; EX 38.30.
Owner M S Saunders **Bred** Churchtown House Stud **Trained** Green Ore, Somerset

FOCUS
This form is not rock solid, especially with the favourite well below par, but a positive view has been taken of it with the time comparing favourably to the other round-course races.

NOTEBOOK

Kapellmeister(IRE) set off in front and maintained the gallop all the way to the line. Having won only a seller last time, albeit fairly easily from a horse rated only 36, he will need to continue improvement to maintain his winning form. (op 7-1 tchd 13-2)

Phone In kept on strongly to the line but was never getting to the winner. He is a consistent sort but needs to come down the weights to have an obvious chance. (op 10-1)

Billich tried to come off the pace but never bridged the gap to the eventual winner. The evidence of the Form Book suggests that he is too high in the weights after his success earlier in the month. (op 7-2 tchd 5-2)

Eta Draconis(IRE) failed to run up to the promise he showed when winning on his debut, but was later reported to have a problem. This run can be easily ignored. Official explanation: jockey said colt had a breathing problem (op 8-13 tchd 8-11)

3820 PICK EVERARD H'CAP — 1m 60y

8:20 (8:20) (Class 6) (0-65,63) 3-Y-0+ — **£3,238** (£963; £481; £240) — **Stalls** High

Form — RPR

0004 **1** — **Cantarna (IRE)**[25] 3056 5-9-2 **55** .... MickyFenton 5 — 65
(J Mackie) *chsd ldrs: rdn to ld ins fnl f: r.o* — **12/1**

2313 **2** ½ **Barons Spy (IRE)**[10] 3542 5-9-5 **63** .... JamesDoyle(5) 3 — 72
(R J Price) *hld up: hdwy over 2f out: rdn and hung rt over 1f out: r.o* — **5/1**[3]

2364 **3** *nk* **Blue Empire (IRE)**[10] 3523 5-9-4 **57** .... JimmyQuinn 1 — 65
(C R Dore) *led: rdn over 1f out: hdd and unable qck ins fnl f* — **7/1**

2413 **4** ½ **Magic Warrior**[31] 2862 6-9-4 **57** .... PatDobbs 13 — 65+
(J C Fox) *chsd ldrs: rdn over 2f out: nt clr run over 1f out: swtchd lft ins fnl f: r.o* — **4/1**[1]

000- **5** 1½ **Veiled Applause**[314] 5219 3-9-1 **62** .... SebSanders 2 — 63
(R M Beckett) *hld up: hdwy over 2f out: edgd rt fr over 1f out: styd on* — **14/1**

0655 **6** ½ **What-A-Dancer (IRE)**[9] 3570 9-9-2 **62** .... (p) TolleyDean(7) 6 — 64
(R A Harris) *chsd ldr: rdn over 1f out: no ex ins fnl f* — **16/1**

0400 **7** *shd* **Wind Chime (IRE)**[27] 2969 9-9-1 **54** .... FergusSweeney 9 — 56
(A G Newcombe) *hld up: hmpd over 6f out: hdwy over 2f out: nt clr run over 1f out: nt rch ldrs* — **20/1**

3140 **8** 1½ **Trevian**[17] 3298 5-9-0 **53** .... RoystonFfrench 12 — 52
(J M Bradley) *hld up: hdwy over 4f out: rdn over 2f out: styd on same pce appr fnl f* — **9/1**

2264 **9** ½ **Dudley Docker (IRE)**[28] 2947 4-9-7 **63** .... DanielTudhope(3) 10 — 60
(D Carroll) *s.i.s and stmbld s: hld up: hdwy over 2f out: wknd over 1f out* — **9/2**[2]

1060 **10** 5 **Adobe**[9] 3570 11-8-12 **58** .... PJBenson(7) 8 — 44
(W M Brisbourne) *chsd ldrs: rdn 3f out: wknd over 1f out* — **40/1**

013- **11** ¾ **King After**[236] 5366 4-9-1 **61** .... KylieManser(7) 11 — 45
(J R Best) *s.i.s and wnt lft s: hmpd over 6f out: n.d* — **33/1**

0606 **12** *hd* **Simplify**[26] 3014 4-8-7 **51** .... (b) RoryMoore(5) 4 — 35
(T M Jones) *plld and prom: rdn over 2f out: sn wknd* — **8/1**

3500 **13** ½ **Western Roots**[9] 3566 5-5-9 **58** .... DaneO'Neill 7 — 41
(M Appleby) *s.i.s: hld up: a in rr* — **25/1**

1m 43.77s (-1.53) **Going Correction** -0.30s/f (Firm)
WFA 3 from 4yo+ 8lb — **13** Ran SP% **122.7**

Speed ratings (Par 101):95,94,94,93,92 91,91,90,89,84 83,83,83

CSF £70.20 CT £363.89 TOTE £15.70: £4.40, £2.50, £2.30; EX 242.60.

Owner Milltown House & Co **Bred** Newberry Stud Farm Ltd **Trained** Church Broughton , Derbys

FOCUS

A moderate affair in which the early gallop was not strong. Those who raced close to the pace had the edge and quite a few finished well from off the pace. The form looks sound, with the winner, third and fifth to form.

Trevian Official explanation: jockey said gelding suffered interference in running

Simplify Official explanation: jockey said gelding had steering problems

3821 HARVEY INGRAM H'CAP — 5f 2y

8:50 (8:50) (Class 6) (0-65,65) 3-Y-0 — **£3,238** (£963; £481; £240) — **Stalls** Low

Form — RPR

000 **1** — **Two Acres (IRE)**[74] 1646 3-8-6 **50** .... FergusSweeney 10 — 58+
(A G Newcombe) *hmpd s: outpcd: hdwy 1/2-way: led 1f out: r.o* — **9/1**

3061 **2** 1¼ **Glenargo (USA)**[8] 3595 3-9-5 **63** 5ex .... (p) AdrianMcCarthy 12 — 66
(R A Harris) *w ldr tl led over 1f out: sn hdd: styd on* — **15/2**

0150 **3** *nk* **Money Mate (IRE)**[7] 3608 3-8-4 **55** ow1 .... JamesO'Reilly(7) 14 — 57
(J O'Reilly) *prom: rdn over 1f out: styd on* — **6/1**[2]

-000 **4** 1 **Jackie Francis (IRE)**[53] 2187 3-8-2 **46** oh2 .... RoystonFfrench 4 — 44
(R Brotherton) *mde most over 3f: styd on same pce* — **40/1**

4040 **5** 1½ **Master Malarkey**[38] 2644 3-7-13 **46** .... (b) NelsonDeSouza(3) 7 — 39
(Mrs C A Dunnett) *chsd ldrs: rdn and n.m.r over 1f out: styd on same pce* — **9/1**

6503 **6** *shd* **Alwariah**[12] 3436 3-9-1 **59** .... SebSanders 11 — 51
(C E Brittain) *mid-div: sn pushed along: hdwy over 1f out: nt trble ldrs* — **9/2**[1]

1500 **7** *shd* **Phinerine**[23] 3118 3-8-11 **62** .... (b) TolleyDean(7) 5 — 54
(R A Harris) *dwlt: hdwy 1/2-way: rdn over 1f out: no ex* — **13/2**[3]

0000 **8** *hd* **Nilsatisoptimum (USA)**[78] 1549 3-8-0 **49** .... LiamJones(5) 3 — 40
(M Mullineaux) *chsd ldrs: hung rt fr 1/2-way: wknd fnl f* — **10/1**

0006 **9** 1 **Smart Cassie**[18] 3268 3-9-4 **65** .... PatrickMathers(3) 8 — 53
(D Shaw) *hld up: effrt and hung rt over 1f out: n.d* — **8/1**

3300 **10** 1¾ **Berties Brother**[7] 3612 3-7-13 **50** oh2 ow4 .... MarkCoumbe(7) 2 — 31
(D G Bridgwater) *sn outpcd* — **20/1**

0200 **11** *shd* **Soviet Legend (IRE)**[13] 3397 3-8-0 **49** .... (b) AndrewElliott(5) 6 — 30
(T J Etherington) *chsd ldrs: rdn whn stmbld 1/2-way: wknd over 1f out* — **6/1**[2]

0000 **12** 2 **Teddy Monty (IRE)**[18] 3257 3-8-2 **46** oh2 .... (b) JimmyQuinn 1 — 20
(M Quinn) *s.i.s: outpcd* — **33/1**

-000 **13** 3½ **Young Flavio**[10] 3538 3-8-2 **53** ow6 .... (p) BarrySavage(7) 9 — 14
(J M Bradley) *rrd s: sn prom: lost pl 3f out: sn bhd* — **40/1**

60.16 secs (-0.74) **Going Correction** -0.30s/f (Firm) — **13** Ran SP% **124.6**

Speed ratings (Par 98):93,91,90,88,86 86,86,85,84,81 81,78,72

CSF £75.75 CT £345.10 TOTE £12.00: £3.10, £4.20, £2.40; EX 124.00 Place 6 £373.91, Place 5 £355.94.

Owner Samuel Jefford **Bred** Noel Finegan **Trained** Yarnscombe, Devon

FOCUS

A moderate sprint handicap won by a horse who appeared after the race to have pounds in hand on his first run in handicap company. Not strong form overall.

Nilsatisoptimum(USA) Official explanation: jockey said saddle slipped

T/Plt: £213.20 to a £1 stake. Pool: £62,584.15. 214.20 winning tickets. T/Qpdt: £193.80 to a £1 stake. Pool: £3,196.00. 12.20 winning tickets. CR

3799 YARMOUTH (L-H)

Tuesday, July 25

OFFICIAL GOING: Firm

Wind: Light, across Weather: Hot and sunny

3822 EUROPEAN BREEDERS FUND / CARLSBERG UK MAIDEN STKS — 5f 43y

2:00 (2:00) (Class 5) 2-Y-0 — **£4,210** (£1,252; £625; £312) — **Stalls** High

Form — RPR

303 **1** — **Princess Georgina**[3] 3745 2-8-12 .... J-PGuillambert 3 — 65
(S C Williams) *t.k.h early: mde all in slt ld: shkn up 1f out: styd on wl* — **11/4**[2]

002 **2** *shd* **Stargazy**[8] 3588 2-9-3 .... JamieSpencer 4 — 70
(R Charlton) *pressed ldr thrght: rdn 2f out: unable qck u.p nr fin* — **4/11**[1]

55 **3** ¾ **Retaliate**[32] 2806 2-8-12 .... SebSanders 5 — 62
(M Quinn) *cl up: rdn 2f out: kpt on onepced ins fnl f* — **33/1**[3]

00 **4** 1¼ **Bertie Swift**[15] 3363 2-9-3 .... JimCrowley 1 — 62
(J Gallagher) *chsd ldrs: outpcd after 1f: rdn wl over 2f out: styd fnl f: nt rch ldrs* — **66/1**

5 *nk* **Distant Flash** 2-8-12 .... TedDurcan 2 — 56
(M J Wallace) *dwlt: sn outpcd and detached: rdn over 2f out: kpt on wl fnl f: nrst fin* — **40/1**

62.04 secs (-0.76) **Going Correction** -0.35s/f (Firm) — **5** Ran SP% **106.9**

Speed ratings (Par 94):92,91,90,88,88

CSF £3.96 TOTE £3.70: £1.20, £1.10; EX 5.30.

Owner J W Parry **Bred** Old Mill Stud And S C Williams **Trained** Newmarket, Suffolk

■ Stewards' Enquiry : J-P Guillambert one-day ban: failed to ride to draw (Aug 6)
Jamie Spencer one-day ban: failed to ride to draw (Aug 10)

FOCUS

A modest juvenile maiden, run at a sound pace, and the first three came clear. The form looks straightforward enough.

NOTEBOOK

Princess Georgina pulled her way to the front early on and ultimately dug deep to repel the runner-up and gain her first success by the smallest of margins. She had disappointed at Ripon three days previously on slightly easier ground, but there was no faulting her attitude this time, and she ought to hold her own when switching to nurseries. (op 9-4)

Stargazy, all the rage in the betting ring, held every chance under maximum pressure late on but could not get past the winner try as he might. He only just lost out and, while he is starting to look exposed, he does deserve to get off the mark. (op 4-9 tchd 1-2 in places)

Retaliate had her chance and posted a personal-best effort. She appreciated the faster ground, looks to be going the right way, and should fare better when switched to nurseries. (op 25-1)

Bertie Swift, dropping back in distance, was keeping on after being outpaced around halfway and, on this evidence, really looks in need of a stiffer test. An easier surface is also likely to be to his benefit. (op 40-1)

Distant Flash, a cheap purchase, proved very easy to back ahead of this debut experience and looked much in need of the run. She ought to be sharper next time. (op 33-1)

3823 SOUTH PIER LEISURE COMPLEX (LOWESTOFT) H'CAP — 1m 3f 101y

2:30 (2:31) (Class 6) (0-55,55) 3-Y-0 — **£2,590** (£770; £385; £192) — **Stalls** Low

Form — RPR

0046 **1** — **Spaceman**[19] 3232 3-9-6 **53** .... (v) NickyMackay 7 — 66
(L M Cumani) *hld up in midfield: prog to join ldr 3f out: led 2f out: rdn clr ins fnl f* — **13/2**[3]

5142 **2** 2½ **Gigs Magic (USA)**[7] 3615 3-9-3 **50** .... RoystonFfrench 1 — 59
(M Johnston) *prom: wnt 2nd 4f out: sn led and rdn: hdd 2f out: outpcd ins fnl f* — **11/4**[1]

0050 **3** 5 **Hurry Up Helen (IRE)**[39] 2607 3-9-5 **52** .... ShaneKelly 6 — 52
(Mrs L Stubbs) *led: rdn and hdd wl over 3f out: kpt on but no ch w first 2 after* — **14/1**

0004 **4** 2½ **Polish Welcome**[26] 3016 3-9-7 **54** .... SebSanders 3 — 50
(S C Williams) *trckd ldrs: rdn over 4f out: outpcd over 2f out: no ch after* — **7/1**

0-00 **5** *hd* **Cut Glass**[22] 3137 3-9-8 **55** .... KerrinMcEvoy 13 — 51
(C E Brittain) *hld up in midfield: rdn 4f sn struggling: kpt on again ins fnl f* — **28/1**

2020 **6** 1 **Coffin Dodger**[7] 3628 3-8-6 **46** .... KirstyMilczarek(7) 8 — 40
(C N Allen) *slowly away: hld up in rr: rdn wl over 3f out: nvr on terms* — **7/1**

0665 **7** 1¼ **Capitalise (IRE)**[7] 3628 3-9-1 **51** .... RossStudholme(3) 9 — 43
(V Smith) *chsd ldrs: rdn over 3f out: wknd wl over 2f out* — **16/1**

0000 **8** 1½ **Tiptoeing**[19] 3232 3-8-11 **47** .... SaleemGolam(3) 4 — 36
(M H Tompkins) *hld up bhd: rdn and effrt into midfield 3f out: no hdwy last 2f* — **50/1**

000- **9** *hd* **Mighty Splash**[279] 5970 3-9-8 **55** .... JamieSpencer 10 — 44
(R Charlton) *hld up bhd: rdn and effrt 3f out: no real prog* — **4/1**[2]

U056 **10** 1 **Lucy Babe**[18] 3264 3-8-3 **41** .... LiamJones(5) 2 — 28
(G Prodromou) *slowly away: hld up bhd: rdn 3f out: no prog* — **33/1**

0005 **11** 7 **Lambency (IRE)**[15] 3355 3-8-13 **46** .... JamieMackay 11 — 22
(J G Given) *sn chsng ldr: rdn over 4f out: wknd 3f out: sn no ch: t.o* — **33/1**

0500 **12** 5 **Virginia Plain**[7] 3627 3-8-7 **45** .... EmmettStack(5) 5 — 12
(Miss Diana Weeden) *chsd ldrs: effrt to press ldrs 4f out: wknd 3f out: t.o* — **66/1**

0005 **13** 23 **Go Amwell**[32] 2814 3-8-11 **44** .... AlanMunro 12 — —
(J R Jenkins) *t.k.h: hld up in rr: rdn over 3f out: no prog: eased: t.o* — **25/1**

2m 24.71s (-2.79) **Going Correction** -0.35s/f (Firm) — **13** Ran SP% **114.2**

Speed ratings (Par 98):96,94,90,88,88 87,86,85,85,84 79,76,59

CSF £22.01 CT £241.88 TOTE £7.60: £2.50, £1.20, £4.80; EX 26.40 Trifecta £266.00 Part won. Pool: £374.72 - 0.94 winning tickets..

Owner Fittocks Stud **Bred** Fittocks Stud **Trained** Newmarket, Suffolk

FOCUS

A modest three-year-old handicap, run at a sound pace, and the form looks sound enough. The first two finished clear and the third and fourth ran to their handicap form.

Coffin Dodger Official explanation: jockey said filly ran flat

Mighty Splash Official explanation: jockey said filly ran green

Go Amwell Official explanation: jockey said gelding was kicked at the start, hung right and lost its action

3824 PETTITTS ANIMAL ADVENTURE PARK AT REEDHAM (S) STKS — 1m 2f 21y

3:05 (3:05) (Class 6) 3-Y-0 — **£2,266** (£674; £337; £168) — **Stalls** Low

Form — RPR

5540 **1** — **Peak Seasons (IRE)**[6] 3650 3-8-12 53 .... (b[1]) AdrianMcCarthy 5 — 58
(W De Best-Turner) *t.k.h: chsd ldr tl led 7f out: mde rest: drew clr 2f out: easily* — **6/1**[3]

0050 **2** *6* **Cool Isle**[31] 2861 3-8-7 42 ow3......(b) DeanCorby(3) 4 45
(P Howling) *prom: chsd ldr 6f out: rdn wl over 2f out: sn no ch w wnr: kpt on* **8/1**

0502 **3** *¾* **Simplified**[18] 3264 3-8-7 45...... JimmyQuinn 6 40
(J Pearce) *hld up in midfield: hdwy over 3f out: rdn over 2f out: kpt on onepced* **7/2[2]**

1000 **4** *2½* **Shaika**[19] 3232 3-8-8 48...... LiamJones(5) 8 41
(G Prodromou) *hld up in rr: rdn and hdwy on outer over 2f out: kpt on but nvr nr ldrs* **13/2**

-600 **5** *3* **Soviet Promise (IRE)**[10] 3541 3-8-7 40...... BrianReilly 7 30
(G G Margarson) *hld up in rr: rdn and effrt over 3f out: nvr on terms* **40/1**

0003 **6** *¾* **Is**[7] 3626 3-8-7 45...... FrancisFerris 3 28
(Rae Guest) *chsd ldrs: rdn over 4f out: fdd wl over 2f out* **7/1**

4600 **7** *10* **Goodbye Girl (IRE)**[19] 3229 3-8-7 43......(p) JohnEgan 1 9
(Mrs C A Dunnett) *a bhd: rdn over 3f out: no prog: t.o* **12/1**

0033 **8** *10* **Madam Mac (IRE)**[31] 2877 3-8-7 44...... AlanMunro 2 —
(B J Meehan) *trckd ldrs: pushed along and effrt over 3f out: btn over 2f out: eased: t.o* **11/4[1]**

2m 5.02s (-3.08) **Going Correction** -0.35s/f (Firm) **8** Ran SP% **110.3**
Speed ratings (Par 98):98,93,92,90,88 87,79,71
CSF £48.70 TOTE £7.40: £2.10, £2.80, £1.80; EX 66.60 Trifecta £434.90 Pool: £624.91 - 1.02 winning tickets..The winner was sold to Michael Chapman for 6,400gns.
Owner De Best racing **Bred** Peter Gleeson **Trained** West Overton, Wilts
■ William de Best-Turner's first winner for more than two years.

FOCUS
A weak seller, run at an average pace. The form is not solid but the winner, the only gelding in a line-up otherwise comprising fillies, is value for further.
Madam Mac(IRE) Official explanation: jockey said filly was unsuited by today's firm ground

3825 BRITANNIA PIER THEATRE SUMMER SEASON H'CAP 5f 43y
3:35 (3:35) (Class 6) (0-60,60) 4-Y-O+ **£2,388** (£705; £352) **Stalls** High

Form RPR

6046 **1** **Davids Mark**[63] 1914 6-8-2 41...... NickyMackay 4 52+
(J R Jenkins) *hld up bhd: hdwy over 1f out: chsd ldr over 1f out: led last 100 yds: sn clr* **20/1**

0-24 **2** *2* **Smiddy Hill**[50] 2295 4-9-7 60...... RoystonFfrench 5 64
(R Bastiman) *chsd ldrs: rdn over 2f out: hung rt over 1f out: kpt on fnl f: wnt 2nd nr fin* **9/2[1]**

0-00 **3** *shd* **Knead The Dough**[27] 2971 5-7-11 41 oh2...... NataliaGemelova(5) 9 45
(A E Price) *chsd ldrs: rdn 2f out: hung rt over 1f out: kpt on ins fnl f* **80/1**

4654 **4** *nk* **Mountain Pass (USA)**[14] 3390 4-9-2 55......(p) JamieSpencer 6 58
(M J Wallace) *hld up in midfield: rdn 2f out: styd on wl ins fnl f: nrst fin* **10/1**

0500 **5** *¾* **Detonate**[12] 3447 4-8-11 50......(v) JohnEgan 8 50
(Mrs C A Dunnett) *led: clr over 1f out: hdd last 100 yds: wknd and lost 3 pls nr fin* **10/1**

1402 **6** *nk* **Beverley Beau**[7] 3608 4-8-0 46...... KristinStubbs(7) 1 45
(Mrs L Stubbs) *wnt rt sn after s: chsd ldrs: rdn 3f out: kpt on same pce fnl f* **8/1[3]**

-015 **7** *nk* **Multahab**[21] 3165 7-9-0 53......(t) BrianReilly 14 51
(Miss D A McHale) *chsd ldrs: rdn over 2f out: kpt on same pce* **10/1**

/000 **8** *½* **Kool Acclaim**[18] 3267 5-9-2 58...... SaleemGolam(3) 11 54+
(S C Williams) *outpcd and wl bhd: styd on wl fnl f: nrst fin* **14/1**

-404 **9** *1* **Salon Prive**[104] 986 6-9-3 56...... ShaneKelly 7 48
(C A Cyzer) *chsd ldrs: rdn over 2f out: wknd ins fnl f* **16/1**

1000 **10** *½* **Amanda's Lad (IRE)**[113] 858 6-8-6 50...... EmmettStack(5) 15 41
(M C Chapman) *chsd ldrs: rdn 3f out: sn struggling* **33/1**

-600 **11** *½* **Largs**[18] 3267 6-8-1 45......(b) MarcHalford(5) 13 34
(J Balding) *wnt rt s: bhd: rdn 3f out: nvr trbld ldrs* **40/1**

3634 **12** *shd* **Cosmic Destiny (IRE)**[15] 3348 4-9-1 54...... JimCrowley 12 42
(E F Vaughan) *prom: rdn 2f out: wknd 1f out* **8/1[3]**

0600 **13** *1* **Stephanie's Mind**[41] 2543 4-7-13 41 oh3...... EdwardCreighton(3) 10 26
(M Quinn) *racd in midfield: rdn over 2f out: nvr trbld ldrs* **40/1**

2603 **14** *nk* **Rowanberry**[16] 3334 4-8-7 46...... KerrinMcEvoy 3 30
(R M H Cowell) *s.s: a wl bhd: no ch* **5/1[2]**

-000 **15** *2* **Flaran**[17] 3297 6-8-9 48...... JimmyQuinn 16 24
(J A R Toller) *in tch: rdn over 2f out: sn lost pl: eased ins fnl f* **14/1**

61.27 secs (-1.53) **Going Correction** -0.35s/f (Firm) **15** Ran SP% **117.4**
Speed ratings (Par 101):98,94,94,94,92 92,92,91,89,88 88,87,86,85,82
CSF £101.41 CT £6986.29 TOTE £22.30: £5.60, £3.10, £16.40; EX 167.90 TRIFECTA Not won..
Owner Mrs Wendy Jenkins **Bred** D Lowe **Trained** Royston, Herts

FOCUS
A modest handicap but the form looks pretty sound although there is a slight doubt about the proximity of the third.
Salon Prive Official explanation: jockey said gelding was unsuited by today's firm ground
Largs Official explanation: jockey said mare hung right-handed throughout
Rowanberry Official explanation: jockey said filly missed the break

3826 WELLINGTON PIER AND WINTER GARDENS YARMOUTH MAIDEN STKS 7f 3y
4:10 (4:11) (Class 5) 3-4-Y-O **£3,238** (£963; £481; £240) **Stalls** High

Form RPR

5252 **1** **Chalentina**[25] 3032 3-8-12 66...... TedDurcan 4 70
(H R A Cecil) *mde all: rdn wl over 1f out: outbattled runner up last 50 yds* **7/2[3]**

0223 **2** *hd* **Madame Medusa (IRE)**[22] 3144 3-8-12 72......(v) AlanMunro 5 69
(J A R Toller) *a pressing ldr: upsides over 1f out: rdn ins fnl f: nt go past and outbattled last 50 yds* **2/1[1]**

62 **3** *2* **Silent Applause**[3] 3742 3-9-3...... ShaneKelly 9 69
(Dr J D Scargill) *bhd: hdwy over 2f out: rdn to chse ldng pair and hung lft over 1f out: hung rt ins fnl f: kpt on same pce* **3/1[2]**

-434 **4** *1¼* **Imperial Harry**[10] 3546 3-9-0 70...... EdwardCreighton(3) 3 66
(M R Channon) *t.k.h: chsd ldrs: drvn 2f out: kpt on onepced ins fnl f* **4/1**

0-0 **5** *9* **Whoopee (USA)**[10] 3554 3-8-12...... RoystonFfrench 1 38
(M Johnston) *chsd ldrs: rdn over 3f out: sn struggling and no ch after* **20/1**

50 **6** *shd* **Sajaaya (AUS)**[37] 2673 3-8-5......(t) JamieHamblett(7) 7 37
(Sir Michael Stoute) *rrd and s.s: sn in tch: rdn 4f out: no ch fr 3f out* **14/1**

7 *7* **Always A Story** 4-9-10...... PaulEddery 2 24
(Miss D Mountain) *in tch for 2f: sn outpcd: t.o* **50/1**

0 **8** *17* **Haughton Hope**[99] 1049 3-8-12...... MarcHalford(5) 6 —
(J Balding) *wnt rt s: a bhd: t.o over 3f out* **100/1**

1m 24.1s (-2.50) **Going Correction** -0.35s/f (Firm)
WFA 3 from 4yo 7lb **8** Ran SP% **114.9**
Speed ratings (Par 103):100,99,97,96,85 85,77,58
CSF £10.88 TOTE £4.10: £1.60, £1.20, £1.40; EX 12.00 Trifecta £18.90 Pool: £686.85 - 25.79 winning tickets..
Owner Chalentina Partnership **Bred** Bearstone Stud **Trained** Newmarket, Suffolk

FOCUS
A modest maiden, run at a sound pace, and the first two came clear. It has been rated through the winner, who got the run of the race.
Haughton Hope Official explanation: jockey said gelding hung right

3827 STANLEY M THREADWELL MEMORIAL H'CAP 7f 3y
4:40 (4:40) (Class 5) (0-70,70) 3-Y-O+ **£3,238** (£963; £481; £240) **Stalls** High

Form RPR

3166 **1** **Lii Najma**[25] 3055 3-9-2 65...... KerrinMcEvoy 2 72
(C E Brittain) *chsd ldrs tl stdd into midfield after 1f: hdwy over 2f out: rdn over 1f out: r.o to ld nr fin* **7/2[1]**

0030 **2** *½* **Silent Storm**[34] 2757 6-9-10 66...... J-PGuillambert 5 75
(C A Cyzer) *w.w in tch: rdn and hdwy 2f out: led jst ins fnl f:hdd and no ex nr fin* **7/1**

6564 **3** *3* **Highland Cascade**[11] 3478 4-10-0 70...... ShaneKelly 7 71
(J M P Eustace) *chsd ldrs: rdn to chse ldr over 2f out: led 1f out: sn hdd: wknd last 100 yds* **7/1**

4020 **4** *2* **Mistral Sky**[9] 3565 7-9-9 65......(v) JamieSpencer 3 61
(Stef Liddiard) *hld up bhd: hdwy 2f out: hrd rdn over 1f out: no imp fnl f* **7/2[1]**

5202 **5** *1* **Favouring (IRE)**[10] 3542 4-8-8 55......(v) EmmettStack(5) 8 48
(M C Chapman) *sn led: rdn over 2f out: hdd 1f out: fdd* **9/2[2]**

000 **6** *6* **Deserted Prince (IRE)**[25] 3045 3-8-6 55......(p) JohnEgan 1 29
(M J Wallace) *hld up bhd: effrt u.p over 2f out: nt pce to trble ldrs* **25/1**

2040 **7** *2* **Whatatodo**[16] 3339 4-8-9 51 oh1...... HayleyTurner 6 22
(M L W Bell) *chsd ldr tl over 2f out: sn rdn: wknd wl over 1f out* **11/2[3]**

0000 **8** *5* **Warden Warren**[18] 3262 8-8-4 51 oh1......(b) MarcHalford(5) 4 9
(Mrs C A Dunnett) *swtchd lft after1f: nvr bttr than midfield: rdn over 3f out: no ch last 2f: t.o* **14/1**

1m 23.76s (-2.84) **Going Correction** -0.35s/f (Firm)
WFA 3 from 4yo+ 7lb **8** Ran SP% **113.5**
Speed ratings (Par 103):102,101,98,95,94 87,85,79
CSF £27.97 CT £161.58 TOTE £4.40: £1.60, £2.70, £1.60; EX 33.50 Trifecta £165.80 Pool: £483.40 - 2.07 winning tickets..
Owner Saeed Manana **Bred** Zubieta Ltd **Trained** Newmarket, Suffolk

FOCUS
A moderate handicap, which saw the first two come clear, and the form makes sense.
Deserted Prince(IRE) Official explanation: jockey said gelding lost its action

3828 WALTON PIER WALTON ON THE NAZE FILLIES' H'CAP 1m 3y
5:10 (5:12) (Class 5) (0-70,70) 3-Y-O+ **£3,562** (£1,059; £529; £264) **Stalls** High

Form RPR

0443 **1** **Life's A Whirl**[5] 3679 4-8-12 54......(p) JohnEgan 2 62
(Mrs C A Dunnett) *chsd ldrs: wnt 2nd over 2f out: rdn to ld over 1f out: sn hdd: rallied to ld ins fnl f: styd on* **6/1[3]**

2014 **2** *1* **Bavarica**[109] 905 4-8-11 60...... SladeO'Hara(7) 1 66
(Miss J Feilden) *t.k.h: hld up in midfield: hdwy over 2f out: led jst over 1f out: hdd ins fnl f: kpt on onepced* **25/1**

4201 **3** *1½* **Al Rayanah**[10] 3541 3-8-10 63...... SaleemGolam(3) 5 63+
(G Prodromou) *squeezed s: hld up bhd: rdn and hdwy over 2f out: r.o ins fnl f: nt rch ldrs* **12/1**

0632 **4** *hd* **My Princess (IRE)**[4] 3712 4-10-0 70...... KerrinMcEvoy 7 72
(N A Callaghan) *bhd: niggled along after 2f: drvn and sme hdwy over 2f out: kpt on ins fnl f: nt rch ldrs* **7/4[1]**

2110 **5** *1½* **Whistleupthewind**[18] 3250 3-8-11 61......(b) ShaneKelly 4 58
(J M P Eustace) *led: clr over 3f out: rdn 2f out: hdd over 1f out: wknd fnl f* **9/1**

-600 **6** *1¾* **Baileys Polka**[13] 3400 3-8-12 62...... JamieMackay 6 55
(J G Given) *settled midfield: rdn 3f out: kpt on onepced and no imp over 1f out* **66/1**

6644 **7** *11* **Snake Skin**[13] 3400 3-8-3 53...... DavidKinsella 9 20
(J Gallagher) *chsd ldr rdn 4f out: wknd wl over 2f out: t.o* **8/1**

200 **8** *22* **Catherine Medici**[52] 2244 3-8-5 55......(v[1]) NickyMackay 8 —
(R M H Cowell) *w.w in tch: rdn over 3f out: sn lost pl: t.o* **50/1**

1326 **9** *10* **My Lovely Lady (IRE)**[10] 3548 3-9-6 70...... JamieSpencer 3 —
(M L W Bell) *hld up in tch: shkn up wl over 3f out: sn btn and eased: t.o* **3/1[2]**

1m 37.26s (-2.64) **Going Correction** -0.35s/f (Firm)
WFA 3 from 4yo 8lb **9** Ran SP% **111.8**
Speed ratings (Par 100):99,98,96,96,94 93,82,60,50
CSF £131.53 CT £1711.04 TOTE £7.90: £1.80, £6.00, £2.80; EX 171.90 Trifecta £535.40 Part won. Pool: £754.13 - 0.44 winning tickets. Place 6 £27.05, Place 5 £27.00.
Owner Life's a Whirl Partnership **Bred** The Queen **Trained** Hingham, Norfolk

FOCUS
A modest fillies' handicap, run at a fair pace. The form looks sound but limited.
My Princess(IRE) Official explanation: jockey said filly got bumped at the start
Catherine Medici Official explanation: jockey said saddle slipped
My Lovely Lady(IRE) Official explanation: trainer said filly was in season
T/Plt: £70.40 to a £1 stake. Pool: £59,721.45. 618.70 winning tickets. T/Qpdt: £38.40 to a £1 stake. Pool: £3,730.30. 71.70 winning tickets. SP

3829 - (Foreign Racing) - See Raceform Interactive

3633

CATTERICK (L-H)
Wednesday, July 26

OFFICIAL GOING: Firm (good to firm in places)
After 10mm rain and 10mm water over the previous week the ground was described as 'very firm'.
Wind: Light, half-against Weather: Fine and sunny

3830 LOUISBURG MAIDEN STKS 5f 212y
2:20 (2:20) (Class 5) 2-Y-O **£3,886** (£1,156; £577; £288) **Stalls** Low

Form RPR

532 **1** **Algol**[25] 3080 2-9-3...... TomEaves 7 67+
(J Howard Johnson) *mde all: clr over 1f out: unchal* **8/11[1]**

0 **2** *5* **Soffooh (USA)**[21] 3193 2-9-3...... TonyCulhane 8 52
(M R Channon) *a chsng wnr: kpt on same pce fnl 2f* **9/1[3]**

0 **3** *1¼* **Mandurah (IRE)**[77] 1587 2-9-3...... AdrianTNicholls 4 48
(D Nicholls) *chsd ldrs: one pce fnl 2f* **11/1**

00 **4** *½* **Micky Mac (IRE)**[51] 2281 2-9-3......(b[1]) RoystonFfrench 1 46
(I W McInnes) *s.i.s: sn chsng ldrs: edgd rt and lft fnl 2f: one pce* **100/1**

4 **5** *¾* **Alberts Story (USA)**[69] 1807 2-9-3...... PaulHanagan 6 44
(R A Fahey) *chsd ldrs: outpcd over 3f out: no imp after* **11/4[2]**

The Form Book, Raceform Ltd, Compton, RG20 6NL

6 *hd* **Monet's Lady (IRE)** 2-8-12 .... TonyHamilton 5 38
(R A Fahey) *s.i.s: outpcd and bhd: kpt on fnl 2f* **16/1**

0 7 *4* **Darcy's Pride (IRE)**[27] 3018 2-8-7 .... MarkLawson(5) 2 26
(D W Barker) *s.i.s: a in rr: edgd rt fnl 2f* **100/1**

00 8 *6* **Pertemps Networks**[13] 3457 2-8-10 .... AdeleRothery(7) 3 12
(M W Easterby) *stdd s: t.k.h and taken wd after 1f: lost pl over 2f out: eased ins last* **40/1**

1m 13.14s (-0.86) **Going Correction** -0.25s/f (Firm) **8** Ran SP% **113.2**
Speed ratings (Par 94):95,88,86,86,85 84,79,71
CSF £8.44 TOTE £1.50: £1.10, £1.90, £2.90; EX 8.60.
Owner Transcend Bloodstock LLP **Bred** W L Caley **Trained** Billy Row, Co Durham

FOCUS
A one-sided contest, the winner was never in any danger. Those behind look very modest.

NOTEBOOK
Algol, very fit indeed, was the most experienced in the line-up and had by far the best credentials. He never looked in any danger but may now be forced down the nursery route. (op 10-11 tchd 11-10)
Soffooh(USA), a close-coupled colt, is not the best of movers. He improved on his debut effort but the winner was different class. He will appreciate less-firm ground. (op 10-1 tchd 8-1)
Mandurah(IRE), absent for 11 weeks, showed a fair bit more than he had done on his debut when worst drawn. (op 10-1 tchd 12-1)
Micky Mac(IRE), last on his first two starts when he hung right and then suffered a slipped saddle, ducked and dived in first-time blinkers and looks anything but straightfoward.
Alberts Story(USA), a nice type, was racing on totally different ground but in truth showed very little. Hopefully he is better than he showed here. (op 9-4 tchd 2-1)
Monet's Lady(IRE), up in the air and narrow, was noisy in the paddock. She stayed on nicely late in the day after a tardy start and can do a fair bit better in time. (op 20-1)
Pertemps Networks Official explanation: jockey said gelding ran too free; trainer said gelding was found to be jarred up the following day

3831 SPHINX & HONDEGHEM (S) STKS 7f
2:50 (2:52) (Class 6) 2-Y-O **£2,730** (£806; £403) **Stalls** Low

Form RPR

2060 1 **Colditz (IRE)**[7] 3641 2-8-11 .... TonyCulhane 9 60
(M R Channon) *chsd ldrs: led over 2f out: drvn out* **3/1**[1]

060 2 *2* **Only A Grand**[38] 2680 2-8-6 .... (b[1]) RoystonFfrench 7 50
(R Bastiman) *chsd ldrs: wnt 2nd over 1f out: kpt on: no imp* **25/1**

050 3 *7* **The Dandy Fox**[8] 3619 2-8-6 .... AdrianTNicholls 3 32
(D Nicholls) *chsd ldrs: sn drvn along: tk modest 3rd ins last* **7/2**[2]

0436 4 *2* **Providence Farm**[8] 3619 2-8-11 .... (b[1]) PaulMulrennan 8 31
(M W Easterby) *sn chsng ldrs on outer: led over 4f out: hung lft and hdd over 2f out: nt keen: wknd ins last* **6/1**

045 5 *3 ½* **Wakeys Wizzard**[18] 3279 2-8-7 ow1 .... TomEaves 5 18
(M E Sowersby) *led over 2f: wknd fnl 2f* **5/1**

00 6 *shd* **Little Tiny Tom**[30] 2938 2-8-4 .... (b[1]) PaulPickard(7) 6 22
(C N Kellett) *s.s: sn bhd: sme hdwy 2f out: nvr on terms* **66/1**

000 7 *nk* **Dispol Moonlight (IRE)**[32] 2870 2-8-11 .... PaulFessey 4 21
(T D Barron) *sn outpcd and bhd: sme hdwy 2f out: nvr on terms* **12/1**

54 8 *38* **Ladas Lad**[20] 3228 2-8-11 .... (p) PhillipMakin 2 —
(W G M Turner) *chsd ldrs: drvn and lost pl over 3f out: eased over 1f out: t.o* **9/2**[3]

0000 9 *½* **Marryl**[15] 3385 2-8-11 .... DaleGibson 1 —
(M W Easterby) *s.i.s: sn drvn along: bhd after 2f: eased ins last: t.o* **50/1**

1m 26.66s (-0.70) **Going Correction** -0.25s/f (Firm) **9** Ran SP% **111.3**
Speed ratings (Par 92):94,91,83,81,77 77,76,33,32
CSF £74.00 TOTE £3.20: £1.60, £6.00, £2.40; EX 89.20.The winner was sold to D. W. Barker for 12,500gns.
Owner Jumeirah Racing **Bred** Darley **Trained** West Ilsley, Berks

FOCUS
A modest event even by selling race standards.

NOTEBOOK
Colditz(IRE), who continually swished his tail in the paddock, had his mind made up for him. He changed hands at at the auction. (op 5-2)
Only A Grand, who showed little on her first three starts, had the blinkers on and seemed to appreciate the step up in trip. (op 28-1 tchd 40-1)
The Dandy Fox, taken very quietly to post, was down to selling company for the first time. She looks fairly paceless. (op 3-1)
Providence Farm, in first-time blinkers, moved up on the outer to show ahead but he looked anything but keen infront and is one to have severe reservations about. Official explanation: trainer said colt was found to be jarred up the following day (op 11-2)
Ladas Lad Official explanation: jockey said gelding had no more to give
Marryl Official explanation: trainer said gelding was found to be jarred up the following day

3832 5TH REGIMENT ROYAL ARTILLERY H'CAP 5f
3:20 (3:22) (Class 4) (0-85,88) 3-Y-O+ **£6,477** (£1,927; £963; £481) **Stalls** Low

Form RPR

6365 1 **Strensall**[8] 3622 9-8-8 **66** oh1 .... PaulHanagan 8 76
(R E Barr) *chsd ldrs: styd on to ld towards fin* **9/1**

2223 2 *nk* **Hypnosis**[7] 3636 3-8-4 **66** oh1 .... RoystonFfrench 2 74
(D W Barker) *chsd ldrs: led over 1f out: hdd and no ex towards fin* **10/1**

0110 3 *1 ½* **Ryedane (IRE)**[5] 3715 4-9-1 **73** 6ex .... DavidAllan 7 77
(T D Easterby) *chsd ldrs: hung lft 1f out: styd on same pce* **6/1**

-353 4 *1* **Atlantic Viking (IRE)**[35] 2748 11-8-8 **66** .... JoeFanning 5 66
(D Nicholls) *in tch: edgd rt 2f out: nvr trbld ldrs* **11/2**

5003 5 *nk* **Brut**[8] 3622 4-8-5 **68** ow2 .... MarkLawson(5) 1 67
(D W Barker) *mid-div: hdwy 2f out: kpt on: nvr rchd ldrs* **4/1**[2]

3010 6 *1 ¾* **One Way Ticket**[13] 3449 6-9-13 **85** .... (p) TomEaves 4 78
(J M Bradley) *led tl hdd over 1f out: sn fdd* **5/1**[3]

0463 7 *13* **Fast Heart**[13] 3447 5-9-13 **85** .... AdrianTNicholls 6 31
(D Nicholls) *s.i.s: nvr wnt pce and a detached in last: rdn and put hd in air over 1f out: no rspnse: eased* **11/4**[1]

58.46 secs (-2.14) **Going Correction** -0.25s/f (Firm)
WFA 3 from 4yo+ 4lb **7** Ran SP% **112.1**
Speed ratings (Par 105):107,106,104,102,102 99,78
CSF £87.14 CT £580.54 TOTE £11.20: £4.10, £2.70; EX 53.50.
Owner R E Barr **Bred** M Paver And M D M Racing Thoroughbreds Ltd **Trained** Seamer, N Yorks

FOCUS
A modest handicap but run at a sound pace and reasonable enough form.
Fast Heart Official explanation: trainer had no explanation for the poor form shown

3833 DRAGON CLAIMING STKS 5f
3:50 (3:50) (Class 6) 3-Y-O+ **£2,730** (£806; £403) **Stalls** Low

Form RPR

3253 1 **Chairman Bobby**[6] 3670 8-8-7 47 .... (p) MarkLawson(5) 1 59
(D W Barker) *w ldrs: led 1f out: edgd lft: hld on towards fin* **7/2**[2]

4004 2 *nk* **Alugat (IRE)**[9] 3587 3-8-8 55 .... (p) RoystonFfrench 3 57+
(Mrs A Duffield) *chsd ldrs: outpcd over 2f out: rallied and hung lft 1f out: hrd rdn and styd on: jst hld* **6/1**[3]

5413 3 *½* **Rudi's Pet (IRE)**[5] 3699 12-9-7 70 .... (v) AdrianTNicholls 2 65
(D Nicholls) *led tl 1f out: bmpd and carried rt: no ex* **5/4**[1]

6000 4 *1 ½* **Campeon (IRE)**[8] 3608 4-8-11 54 .... (b[1]) TomEaves 7 50
(J M Bradley) *w ldrs: kpt on same pce fnl f* **15/2**

0000 5 *4* **On The Trail**[16] 3356 9-8-9 40 .... (p) TonyCulhane 5 33
(D W Chapman) *chsd ldrs: wknd appr fnl f* **16/1**

0043 6 *½* **Dysonic (USA)**[9] 3595 4-8-10 37 .... (v) JasonEdmunds(3) 10 35
(J Balding) *w ldrs: wknd over 1f out* **14/1**

0502 7 *¾* **Signor Whippee**[11] 3526 3-8-9 52 .... (b) TonyHamilton 9 32
(A Berry) *s.i.s: sme hdwy on outside over 2f out: nvr nr ldrs* **25/1**

0060 8 *nk* **Revien (IRE)**[42] 2544 4-8-13 43 .... PaulFitzsimons 4 32
(Miss J R Tooth) *in tch: effrt over 2f out: lost pl over 1f out* **50/1**

0000 9 *¾* **Torrent**[7] 3635 11-8-2 41 .... (b) KevinMachent(7) 6 25
(J M Saville) *in rr: swtchd lft after 1f: nvr on terms* **66/1**

6/0 10 *3* **Panfield Belle (IRE)**[23] 3139 5-8-7 .... CatherineGannon 8 12
(R Allan) *in tch: outpcd over 2f out: sn bhd* **100/1**

59.42 secs (-1.18) **Going Correction** -0.25s/f (Firm)
WFA 3 from 4yo+ 4lb **10** Ran SP% **113.6**
Speed ratings (Par 101):99,98,97,95,88 88,86,86,85,80
CSF £23.58 TOTE £3.70: £1.10, £1.50, £1.20; EX 18.10.
Owner J Johnson **Bred** J Johnson **Trained** Scorton, N Yorks
■ Stewards' Enquiry : Mark Lawson one-day ban: careless riding (Aug 6)

FOCUS
A poor claimer in which the favourite ran well below his official rating.

3834 Q BATTERY SANNA'S POST NURSERY 7f
4:20 (4:22) (Class 5) 2-Y-O **£3,886** (£867; £867; £288) **Stalls** Low

Form RPR

3011 1 **Feisty**[20] 3228 2-8-6 **62** .... FrancisFerris 2 60
(Rae Guest) *hld up in tch: effrt over 2f out: styd on wl fnl f: led nr fin* **7/1**

3345 2 *¾* **Josr's Magic (IRE)**[8] 3605 2-9-3 **73** .... (b[1]) RoystonFfrench 1 69
(Mrs A Duffield) *led after 1f: rdn over 2f out: hdd nr fin* **6/1**[3]

4221 2 *dht* **Tencendur (IRE)**[17] 3335 2-9-6 **76** .... AdrianTNicholls 6 72
(D Nicholls) *chsd ldrs: drvn over 4f out: wnt 2nd over 2f out: styd on towards fin* **9/4**[2]

431 4 *2 ½* **Capannina**[23] 3157 2-9-7 **77** .... ShaneKelly 4 67
(J Noseda) *trckd ldrs: rdn over 2f out: kpt on same pce* **13/8**[1]

040 5 *2 ½* **Spence's Choice (IRE)**[13] 3457 2-8-5 **61** .... PaulMulrennan 3 44
(M W Easterby) *sn detached in last: kpt on fnl 2f: nvr nr ldrs* **14/1**

0406 6 *2 ½* **Suhayl Star (IRE)**[2] 3800 2-9-5 **75** .... TonyCulhane 5 52
(M R Channon) *led 1f: chsd ldrs: rdn 3 out: wknd over 1f out* **9/1**

1m 26.87s (-0.49) **Going Correction** -0.25s/f (Firm) **6** Ran SP% **112.3**
Speed ratings (Par 94):92,91,91,88,85 82
WIN: Feisty £5.80. PL: £2.70, Tencendur £0.80, Josr's Magic £0.70. EX: F/T £11.00, F/JM £23.00. CSF: F/T £11.58, F/JM £23.23..
Owner Rae Guest **Bred** Miss Rachel E Flynn **Trained** Newmarket, Suffolk

FOCUS
An improved effort from the winner and solid enough form with the placed horses to their pre-race marks. The official ratings shown next to each horse are estimated and for information purposes only.

NOTEBOOK
Feisty, who is only small, has a big heart and battled away to put her head in front near the line. On this evidence a mile will suit her even better.
Josr's Magic(IRE), having his second outing after being gelded, had the blinkers on for the first time. He soon took them along but seemed to rather hang fire and was edged out near the line. He is anything but straightforward. (tchd 5-2)
Tencendur(IRE), who has changed hands for 12,000gns, would have finished clear second but for being eased near the line. He seemed to be struck by Ffrench's whip on his inner and the winner went slightly across him anticipating the bend soon after the line. (tchd 5-2)
Capannina, back on turf on her nursery debut, was flat out turning in and never really looked like taking a hand. (op 7-4 tchd 6-4, 15-8 in a place)
Spence's Choice(IRE), soon remote in last, stayed on when it was all over. Official explanation: trainer said gelding was found to be jarred up the following day (op 10-1)
Suhayl Star(IRE), with the headgear left off, kept tabs on the leader, but his response to pressure was very limited to say the very least. (op 8-1 tchd 10-1)

3835 5TH REGIMENT ROYAL ARTILLERY WORKSHOPS H'CAP 5f 212y
4:50 (4:50) (Class 6) (0-65,65) 3-Y-O+ **£3,238** (£963; £481; £240) **Stalls** Low

Form RPR

0004 1 **Drury Lane (IRE)**[11] 3524 6-8-9 **46** oh7 .... (p) TonyCulhane 1 52
(D W Chapman) *chsd ldrs: wnt 2nd 2f out: carried rt and led ins last: hld on* **11/1**

5632 2 *1* **Cree**[6] 3682 4-9-3 **54** .... PhillipMakin 2 57
(W R Muir) *chsd ldrs: hung lft over 1f out: styd on wl ins last* **5/2**[1]

0050 3 *shd* **Betsen (IRE)**[13] 3447 4-10-0 **65** .... AdrianTNicholls 4 68
(D Nicholls) *drvn to ld: edgd rt and hdd ins last: no ex* **5/1**[3]

0004 4 *hd* **Siraj**[4] 3728 7-8-12 **49** .... (p) MichaelTebbutt 8 51+
(J Ryan) *hld up in rr: hdwy on outside 2f out: kpt on wl ins last* **12/1**

0505 5 *shd* **Cayman Breeze**[8] 3612 6-8-13 **50** .... TomEaves 12 52+
(J M Bradley) *hld up towards rr: gd hdwy 2f out: swtchd lft ins last: no ex* **11/2**

2612 6 *¾* **Rancho Cucamonga (IRE)**[6] 3670 4-9-4 **55** ....(b) RoystonFfrench 5 55+
(T D Barron) *in rr: hdwy over 2f out: styd on fnl f: nt rch ldrs* **4/1**[2]

60-5 7 *3 ½* **Black Oval**[11] 3525 5-8-2 **46** oh7 .... MarkCoumbe(7) 10 35
(S Parr) *chsd ldrs: wknd fnl f* **50/1**

4105 8 *hd* **Misty Princess**[8] 3608 4-8-5 **49** .... KevinGhunowa(7) 13 37
(M J Attwater) *sn chsng ldrs on outer: edgd rt over 1f out: sn wknd* **16/1**

0053 9 *1 ½* **Fox Covert (IRE)**[6] 3673 5-8-5 **47** oh6 ow1 .... MarkLawson(5) 7 31
(D W Barker) *prom: lost pl over 3f out: no threat after* **14/1**

0504 10 *hd* **Underthemistletoe (IRE)**[7] 3635 4-8-4 **46** oh8.(v) MichaelJStainton(5) 9 29
(R E Barr) *in tch on outer: outpcd over 2f out: n.d after* **66/1**

0006 11 *3* **Geordie Dancer (IRE)**[11] 3525 4-8-10 **47** .... (p) TonyHamilton 3 21
(A Berry) *in tch: effrt over 2f out: wknd over 1f out* **66/1**

0-00 12 *1* **Chilsdown**[49] 2366 3-9-6 **62** .... DeanMcKeown 11 33
(Ronald Thompson) *s.i.s: a in rr* **100/1**

50-0 13 *9* **Sam The Sorcerer**[171] 300 5-8-9 **46** oh14 .... PaulMulrennan 6 —
(J R Norton) *chsd ldrs: lost pl over 2f out: bhd whn eased ins last* **100/1**

1m 12.86s (-1.14) **Going Correction** -0.25s/f (Firm)
WFA 3 from 4yo+ 5lb **13** Ran SP% **116.1**
Speed ratings (Par 101):97,95,95,95,95 94,89,89,87,86 82,81,69
CSF £37.45 CT £148.96 TOTE £11.60: £3.60, £1.70, £1.90; EX 44.40.

Owner David W Chapman **Bred** Tipperary Bloodstock And Eclipse Bloodstock **Trained** Stillington, N Yorks
FOCUS
A low-grade handicap and little separating the first six at the line.

3836 WILLIE CARSON - PINKER'S POND APPRENTICE H'CAP — 1m 3f 214y
5:20 (5:20) (Class 6) (0-55,51) 3-Y-O+ — **£2,730** (£806; £403) **Stalls** Low

Form — RPR
5054 **1** — **Hugs Destiny (IRE)**[6] 3291 5-9-11 **48** .... MCGeran 6 — 56+
(M A Barnes) *trckd ldrs: led over 2f out: shkn up ins last: r.o* — **3/1**[2]
6623 **2** 1 1/4 **Granary Girl**[20] 3232 4-9-9 **46** .... StevenCorrigan 4 — 51
(J Pearce) *hld up and bhd: hdwy over 4f out: wnt 2nd over 1f out: no ex ins last* — **2/1**[1]
000- **3** 2 1/2 **Comical Errors (USA)**[49] 6289 4-9-10 **47** ....(t) JosephLoveridge 7 — 48
(P C Haslam) *mid-div: sn pushed along: hdwy on outer 3f out: nvr on terms* — **10/1**
0603 **4** 11 **So Elegant (IRE)**[9] 3597 4-10-0 **51** .... JonjoMilczarek 2 — 34
(J Jay) *hld up in rr: drvn over 4f out: hung rt: nvr on terms* — **11/2**
0001 **5** 1/2 **Kristalchen**[7] 3637 4-9-7 **44** 6ex........ PaulPickard 1 — 27
(D W Thompson) *s.s: hld up in last: drvn over 3f out: nvr on terms* — **9/2**[3]
050 **6** 3 **Cortina**[19] 3261 3-8-1 **36** ow1........(bt[1]) BarrySavage 5 — 14
(J Jay) *set str pce: hdd over 2f out: wandered and sn wknd* — **28/1**
-004 **7** 3/4 **Loaded Gun**[27] 3022 6-9-6 **43** .... KirbyHarris 3 — 20
(W Storey) *chsd ldr: lost pl over 1f out* — **9/1**

2m 37.74s (-1.26) **Going Correction** -0.25s/f (Firm)
WFA 3 from 4yo+ 12lb — **7** Ran SP% **114.4**
Speed ratings (Par 101):94,93,91,84,83 81,81
CSF £9.46 TOTE £3.70: £2.00, £1.40; EX 12.40 Place 6 £36.30, Place 5 £21.90.
Owner J G White **Bred** Matt Gleeson **Trained** Farlam, Cumbria
■ A first success on his third ride for 17-year-old Michael Geran.
■ Stewards' Enquiry : Jonjo Milczarek seven-day ban: used whip with excessive force, frequency and down the shoulder in the forehand position (Aug 6-12)
FOCUS
A low-grade handicap confined to apprentices who had not ridden a winner.
T/Plt: £36.30 to a £1 stake. Pool: £38,763.90. 777.65 winning tickets. T/Qpdt: £21.90 to a £1 stake. Pool: £2,216.80. 74.85 winning tickets. WG

3816 LEICESTER (R-H)
Wednesday, July 26

OFFICIAL GOING: Good to firm (firm in places)
Wind: Almost nil Weather: Hot and humid

3837 BBC RADIO LEICESTER 104.9 FM NURSERY — 5f 218y
6:15 (6:15) (Class 4) 2-Y-O — **£4,533** (£1,348; £674; £336) **Stalls** Low

Form — RPR
4033 **1** — **Tom Paris**[11] 3530 2-8-1 **67** ....(b) MartinDwyer 5 — 69
(W R Muir) *prom: rdn over 2f out: styd on u.p to ld wl ins fnl f* — **7/2**[3]
3102 **2** 1 **Dimboola**[25] 3064 2-9-7 **87** .... RHills 3 — 86
(B W Hills) *chsd ldrs: led and edgd lft over 1f out: rdn and hdd wl ins fnl f* — **2/1**[1]
2261 **3** 2 **Voodoo Moon**[2] 3780 2-9-0 **80** 6ex........ JoeFanning 1 — 73
(M Johnston) *led to 1/2-way: sn rdn: no ex fnl f* — **5/2**[2]
0422 **4** 3/4 **Dolly Coughdrop (IRE)**[12] 3481 2-7-13 **70** .... AndrewElliott(5) 2 — 61
(K R Burke) *w ldr tl led 1/2-way: rdn and hdd over 1f out: no ex ins fnl f* — **9/2**
5120 **5** 6 **Mrs Crossy (IRE)**[7] 3641 2-7-5 **64** oh2........ LukeMorris(7) 4 — 37
(A W Carroll) *outpcd* — **14/1**

1m 11.27s (-1.93) **Going Correction** -0.225s/f (Firm) — **5** Ran SP% **109.0**
Speed ratings (Par 96):103,101,99,98,90
CSF £10.68 TOTE £4.60: £3.60, £1.20; EX 8.30.
Owner M J Caddy **Bred** Lostford Manor Stud **Trained** Lambourn, Berks
FOCUS
Just the five runners and this looked an ordinary nursery. The form should prove reliable, though. The official ratings shown next to each horse are estimated and for information purposes only.
NOTEBOOK
Tom Paris confirmed earlier promise to get off the mark at the sixth attempt. Although he wears blinkers and has already been gelded, he seems genuine enough and should continue to go well. (op 11-2)
Dimboola seemed to get this extra furlong well enough but found the concession of 20lb to Tom Paris just too much. He is likely to remain vulnerable. (op 9-4)
Voodoo Moon only really had one horse to beat when winning her maiden at Ayr two days previously and would have found this more competitive. The race may also have come too soon. (tchd 11-4 in places)
Dolly Coughdrop(IRE) was below the form she showed when second on her two previous starts in nursery company and proved disappointing. (op 10-3)
Mrs Crossy(IRE) was never seen with a chance. Official explanation: trainer said filly never travelled (op 12-1)

3838 GG.COM MAIDEN AUCTION STKS — 7f 9y
6:45 (6:45) (Class 4) 2-Y-O — **£4,533** (£1,348; £674; £336) **Stalls** Low

Form — RPR
U0 **1** — **Always Best**[13] 3448 2-8-9 .... JoeFanning 4 — 65
(M Johnston) *chsd ldrs: led wl over 1f out: r.o: eased nr fin* — **7/2**[2]
005 **2** 1 3/4 **Gifted Heir (IRE)**[14] 3408 2-8-8 .... TPQueally 1 — 59
(I A Wood) *led: rdn and hdd wl over 1f out: styd on same pce fnl f* — **6/1**[3]
3 1 1/2 **Belvedere Vixen** 2-8-6 .... MartinDwyer 6 — 54
(J A Osborne) *dwlt: hdwy over 2f out: shkn up over 1f out: styd on same pce: should improve* — **5/2**[1]
0 **4** 5 **Oedipuss (IRE)**[53] 2218 2-8-4 .... EmmettStack(5) 3 — 44
(K J Burke) *chsd ldr tl rdn over 2f out: hung rt and wknd over 1f out* — **22/1**
5 **5** 1 **Poyle Kiera**[13] 3435 2-8-3 .... DaleGibson 7 — 35
(M Blanshard) *sn outpcd* — **5/2**[1]
00 **6** nk **Elle's Angel (IRE)**[27] 3005 2-8-2 ow1........ SaleemGolam(3) 5 — 36
(B R Millman) *sn pushed along in rr: rdn 1/2-way: wknd 2f out* — **7/1**

1m 25.34s (-0.76) **Going Correction** -0.225s/f (Firm) — **6** Ran SP% **110.5**
Speed ratings (Par 96):95,93,91,85,84 84
CSF £23.16 TOTE £4.50: £2.00, £2.00; EX 25.80.
Owner Always Trying Partnership III **Bred** Mrs R D Peacock **Trained** Middleham Moor, N Yorks
FOCUS
A weak maiden. The runners ignored the stands' rail and finished spread across the track.
NOTEBOOK
Always Best, who unseated at the start on his racecourse debut and ran very green next time at Warwick, knew his job much better and found this a good opportunity to get off the mark at the third attempt. He should not be given too harsh a handicap mark and, open to more improvement, he could add to this. (op 2-1)
Gifted Heir(IRE), upped to seven furlongs, ran well under a positive ride, despite edging right, and seems to be going the right way. He is now eligible for nurseries and could find his level. (op 9-1 tchd 10-1)
Belvedere Vixen, a 20,000gns sister to very smart triple five- to six-furlong winning juvenile B A Foxtrot, made a respectable introduction and should know more next time. (op 4-1)
Oedipuss(IRE) ran better than on his debut at Chepstow but was still well held. Official explanation: jockey said colt hung right-handed throughout (op 14-1)
Poyle Kiera never looked happy and failed to build on the form she showed in a modest maiden at Folkestone on her debut. Official explanation: jockey said filly never travelled (op 9-4 tchd 15-8)

3839 NEWTON HARCOURT (S) STKS — 1m 60y
7:15 (7:15) (Class 6) 3-Y-O — **£2,590** (£770; £385; £192) **Stalls** High

Form — RPR
5420 **1** — **Final Tune (IRE)**[6] 3668 3-8-11 66........ JoeFanning 4 — 55
(D Nicholls) *hld up: plld hrd: hdwy to ld over 2f out: styd on* — **7/4**[1]
0020 **2** 1 **Crush On You**[21] 3195 3-8-5 50........ RussellKennemore(7) 7 — 54
(R Hollinshead) *hld up: hdwy over 3f out: rdn and hung rt over 1f out: styd on* — **14/1**
0033 **3** 1 1/4 **Macs Ransom (USA)**[8] 3614 3-8-3 50........ SaleemGolam(3) 8 — 45+
(N A Callaghan) *hld up: nt clr run over 3f out: hdwy whn rdr dropped whip over 2f out: styd on* — **3/1**[2]
0400 **4** 2 1/2 **Under Fire (IRE)**[11] 3538 3-8-11 47........ ShaneKelly 5 — 44
(A W Carroll) *chsd ldr tl led over 3f out: rdn and hdd over 2f out: styd on same pce appr fnl f* — **20/1**
0-00 **5** shd **Tuscany Rose**[32] 2877 3-8-6 50........ MartinDwyer 2 — 39
(W R Muir) *prom: rdn over 2f out: styd on same pce appr fnl f* — **10/1**
3220 **6** shd **Psycho Cat**[106] 969 3-8-11 60........(p) PaulHanagan 1 — 44
(P A Blockley) *hld up: plld hrd: styd on fnl f: nrst fin* — **13/2**[3]
0220 **7** 6 **Lucys Lady**[27] 3006 3-8-1 47........ AndrewElliott(5) 6 — 25
(K R Burke) *s.i.s: hld up: a in rr* — **7/1**
0 **8** 3 **Madame Diktatit**[18] 3288 3-8-6 .... DaleGibson 10 — 18
(Ms Deborah J Evans) *chsd ldrs: rdn over 3f out: wknd over 2f out* — **33/1**
0005 **9** 3/4 **Baytown Lulu**[21] 3195 3-8-1 40........ EmmettStack(5) 3 — 16
(H S Howe) *chsd ldrs 6f* — **50/1**
0000 **10** 5 **Mytass**[27] 3006 3-8-8 35........(b) AdamKirby(3) 11 — 10
(J A Pickering) *sn led: hdd over 3f out: sn rdn: wknd 2f out* — **66/1**

1m 43.48s (-1.82) **Going Correction** -0.225s/f (Firm) — **10** Ran SP% **114.1**
Speed ratings (Par 98):100,99,97,95,95 95,89,86,85,80
CSF £26.99 TOTE £2.50: £1.10, £3.30, £1.70; EX 27.00.The winner was sold to Malcolm Shirley for 9,000gns. Macs Ransom was claimed by Paul Howling for £6,000.
Owner Fayzad Thoroughbred Limited **Bred** Shortgrove Manor Stud **Trained** Sessay, N Yorks
FOCUS
Just an ordinary seller. The form looks sound.
Lucys Lady Official explanation: jockey said filly hung left-handed throughout

3840 AXMINSTER CARPETS PALAIS H'CAP — 1m 3f 183y
7:45 (7:45) (Class 4) (0-85,83) 4-Y-O+ **£5,362** (£1,604; £802; £401; £199) **Stalls** High

Form — RPR
0023 **1** — **Pevensey (IRE)**[12] 3501 4-9-7 **83** .... MartinDwyer 3 — 92
(M A Buckley) *hld up: hdwy over 2f out: led ins fnl f: pushed out* — **5/2**[1]
4052 **2** 1 1/4 **Nero's Return (IRE)**[4] 3748 5-9-3 **79** .... JoeFanning 1 — 86
(M Johnston) *a.p: led 2f out: sn rdn: hdd and unable qck ins fnl f* — **5/2**[1]
3401 **3** 2 **Instructor**[11] 3519 5-9-5 **81** .... PaulHanagan 6 — 85
(R A Fahey) *stmbld s: sn led: hdd 8f out: chsd ldr tl led 3f out: rdn and hdd 2f out: no ex fnl f* — **7/1**
0400 **4** nk **Stolen Hours (USA)**[13] 3431 6-8-7 **69** .... TPQueally 8 — 72
(J Akehurst) *chsd ldr 2f: remained handy: rdn over 2f out: styd on same pce fnl f* — **16/1**
-054 **5** 2 **Sky Quest (IRE)**[29] 2945 8-8-11 **76** ....(tp) SaleemGolam(3) 5 — 76
(W R Swinburn) *hld up: hdwy and nt clr run over 2f out: rdn over 1f out: sn wknd* — **13/2**[3]
5340 **6** 1 1/2 **Wester Lodge (IRE)**[26] 3037 4-8-8 **70** .... ShaneKelly 2 — 68
(J M P Eustace) *hld up: hdwy 5f out: rdn and wknd 2f out* — **10/1**
-165 **7** 1 **Count Kristo**[19] 3248 4-8-9 **74** ....(p) AdamKirby(3) 4 — 70
(C G Cox) *chsd ldr 10f out: led 8f out: hdd 3f out: sn rdn: wknd over 1f out* — **6/1**[2]

2m 31.18s (-3.32) **Going Correction** -0.225s/f (Firm) — **7** Ran SP% **112.2**
Speed ratings (Par 105):102,101,99,99,98 97,96
CSF £8.09 CT £35.86 TOTE £3.70: £2.40, £1.40; EX 9.80.
Owner C C Buckley **Bred** Barronstown Stud And Orpendale **Trained** Castle Bytham, Lincs
■ Mark Buckley's first winner of the year.
FOCUS
A fair handicap, not strongly-run. It has been rated though the second and third.
Count Kristo Official explanation: jockey said gelding ran too freely

3841 EUROPEAN BREEDERS FUND WATERLOO FILLIES' H'CAP — 7f 9y
8:20 (8:20) (Class 4) (0-80,80) 3-Y-O
£7,478 (£2,239; £1,119; £560; £279; £140) **Stalls** Low

Form — RPR
1055 **1** — **Deira (USA)**[25] 3072 3-8-9 **68** .... TPQueally 4 — 77
(C E Brittain) *racd centre: a.p: rdn and hung lft over 1f out: r.o to ld post* — **12/1**
4115 **2** hd **Inaminute (IRE)**[25] 3099 3-8-5 **69** .... AndrewElliott(5) 2 — 77
(K R Burke) *racd centre: led: hdd over 4f out: rdn to ld ins fnl f: hdd post* — **7/1**
0212 **3** 1 1/2 **Xaluna Bay (IRE)**[7] 3646 3-8-13 **72** .... MartinDwyer 6 — 76
(W R Muir) *racd centre: plld hrd and prom: led over 1f out: rdn: hung lft and hdd ins fnl f: styd on same pce* — **5/1**[3]
312 **4** 1 **China Cherub**[18] 3299 3-8-10 **69** .... DaneO'Neill 10 — 71
(H Candy) *wnt rt s: racd centre: hld up: hdwy over 2f out: rdn and ev ch over 1f out: styd on same pce fnl f* — **9/4**[1]
4400 **5** nk **Aspen Falls (IRE)**[8] 3606 3-9-3 **76** .... SebSanders 8 — 77
(Sir Mark Prescott) *s.i.s: racd centre: hld up: hdwy u.p over 1f out: no imp ins fnl f* — **7/1**
3316 **6** 1/2 **First Approval**[14] 3395 3-9-0 **73** .... RHills 5 — 72
(B W Hills) *racd centre: chsd ldrs: rdn and ev ch over 1f out: no ex ins fnl f* — **16/1**
1443 **7** 1 1/4 **Hypocrisy**[40] 2609 3-9-4 **77** .... J-PGuillambert 3 — 73
(S C Williams) *hld up: plld hrd: hdwy and swtchd to r alone stands' side over 5f out: w ldrs: rdn and hung rt over 1f out: no ex* — **7/2**[2]
3-01 **8** 1 1/2 **Balik Pearls**[13] 3453 3-9-7 **80** .... PaulHanagan 1 — 72
(N A Callaghan) *racd centre: hld up: rdn 1/2-way: nvr trbld ldrs* — **12/1**
0356 **9** 1/2 **Amygdala**[92] 1210 3-7-10 **62** ....(p) NicolPolli(7) 9 — 53
(M Botti) *racd centre: mid-div: rdn over 2f out: sn wknd* — **66/1**

-000 **10** *7* **Titian Saga (IRE)**[25] 3087 3-8-11 **70**.................................. JoeFanning 7 43
(C N Allen) *racd centre: plld hrd and prom: led over 4f out: rdn and hdd over 1f out: wknd qckly: eased fnl f* **40/1**

1m 26.17s (0.07) **Going Correction** -0.225s/f (Firm) **10** Ran SP% **119.9**

Speed ratings (Par 99):90,89,88,86,86 86,84,82,82,74

CSF £95.98 CT £484.60 TOTE £15.30: £3.30, £2.50, £3.00; EX 164.90.

Owner Ali Saeed **Bred** Darley **Trained** Newmarket, Suffolk

FOCUS

A fair fillies' handicap, but they went a noticeably steady pace early on. All bar Hypocrisy, who raced stands' side, came up the middle of the track. Not strong form, rated though the second and fifth.

3842 EUROPEAN BREEDERS FUND MEDIAN AUCTION MAIDEN STKS 5f 2y

8:50 (8:50) (Class 5) 3-Y-0 **£3,238** (£963; £481; £240) **Stalls** Low

Form RPR

2232 **1** **Lucksin (IRE)**[7] 3638 3-9-3 73.. JoeFanning 3 71
(N Tinkler) *trckd ldrs: led over 1f out: hung rt ins fnl f: r.o* **5/6**[1]

5000 **2** *1 ½* **Ceredig**[16] 3348 3-9-3 57.. MartinDwyer 1 66
(W R Muir) *a.p: chsd wnr over 1f out: sn rdn: nt qckn ins fnl f* **9/1**[3]

-043 **3** *5* **Vicky Pollard**[19] 3257 3-8-12 50.. TonyCulhane 2 43
(P Howling) *led over 3f: wknd fnl f* **12/1**

544 **4** *¾* **Best Double**[4] 3749 3-8-7 66.. AndrewMullen(5) 5 40
(G A Butler) *chsd ldrs: rdn over 3f out: wknd over 1f out* **9/4**[2]

-350 **5** *4* **Optical Seclusion (IRE)**[32] 2873 3-9-0 54............(b[1]) SaleemGolam(3) 4 31
(T J Etherington) *sn outpcd* **14/1**

0-00 **6** *6* **Exmoor Dancer (IRE)**[16] 3348 3-8-7 40...................... EmmettStack(5) 6 4
(H S Howe) *chsd wnr tl rdn and wknd 2f out* **66/1**

59.46 secs (-1.44) **Going Correction** -0.225s/f (Firm) **6** Ran SP% **111.2**

Speed ratings (Par 100):102,99,91,90,84 74

CSF £9.34 TOTE £1.60: £1.40, £2.50; EX 5.90 Place 6 £58.12, Place 5 £31.97 .

Owner P Burton,M Gosse,A Mornin,T Stanley **Bred** M Duffy **Trained** Langton, N Yorks

FOCUS

A weak maiden, with the winner taking advantage of her market rival's poor run. The runner-up sets the standard.

T/Plt: £148.90 to a £1 stake. Pool: £51,472.60. 252.25 winning tickets. T/Qpdt: £21.10 to a £1 stake. Pool: £4,275.10. 149.90 winning tickets. CR

3726 LINGFIELD (L-H)

Wednesday, July 26

OFFICIAL GOING: All-weather - standard; turf course - good to firm

Wind: Virtually nil Weather: Sunny and hot

3843 GO RACING AT FOLKESTONE TOMORROW EVENING E B F MEDIAN AUCTION MAIDEN STKS (DIV I) 7f (P)

2:00 (2:02) (Class 5) 2-Y-0 **£2,590** (£770; £385; £192) **Stalls** Low

Form RPR

053 **1** **Heywood**[8] 3623 2-9-3 .... TedDurcan 9 78
(M R Channon) *pressed ldr: led after 3f: mde rest: drvn and kpt on steadily fr over 1f out* **5/1**[3]

2 *1* **Abbotts Ann** 2-8-12 .... MichaelHills 11 70
(B W Hills) *plld hrd: a ldng trio: pressed wnr after 3f: drvn and no imp over 1f out: kpt on* **11/2**

3 *½* **Fever** 2-9-3 .... RyanMoore 4 74
(R Hannon) *chsd ldrs: pushed along 1/2-way: drvn and styd on fr over 1f out : nvr able to chal* **8/1**

4 **4** *½* **Beech Games**[13] 3455 2-9-3 .... RichardMullen 6 73
(E J O'Neill) *chsd ldrs: rdn over 2f out: nt qckn over 1f out: one pce after* **3/1**[2]

5 *1 ¼* **Beverly Hill Billy** 2-9-3 .... DaneO'Neill 10 70
(A King) *settled towards rr: pushed along 3f out: no real prog tl rdn and r.o fnl f: nrst fin* **50/1**

6 *1* **Satyricon** 2-9-3 .... OscarUrbina 1 67
(M Botti) *dwlt: settled in rr: shkn up over 2f out: kpt on same pce: n.d* **20/1**

00 **7** *1* **Spiderback (IRE)**[30] 2930 2-9-3 .... PatDobbs 2 64
(R Hannon) *chsd ldrs on inner: cl enough over 2f out: sn rdn and no prog* **25/1**

8 *shd* **Wind Flow** 2-9-3 .... JamieSpencer 5 64
(E A L Dunlop) *dwlt: nvr gng pce and a struggling towards rr: effrt on outer over 2f out: no prog* **11/4**[1]

04 **9** *½* **Bathwick Breeze**[13] 3448 2-8-10 .... JamesMillman(7) 8 63
(B R Millman) *led for 3f: lost pl and rdn 3f out: grad wknd* **40/1**

10 *½* **The Bronx** 2-9-3 .... JohnEgan 14 61
(M J Wallace) *towards rr: sme prog over 2f out: no imp over 1f out: fdd* **25/1**

0 **11** *10* **Dawson Creek (IRE)**[41] 2572 2-9-3 .... RichardThomas 12 35
(B Gubby) *chsd ldrs: drvn 1/2-way: sn struggling: bhd over 1f out* **66/1**

0 **12** *5* **Port Luanda (IRE)**[14] 3408 2-9-3 .... PaulDoe 3 22
(R M Flower) *dwlt: a struggling in rr: bhd fnl 2f* **100/1**

04 **13** *53* **Private Peachey (IRE)**[85] 1372 2-9-3 .... AlanMunro 13 —
(B R Millman) *s.i.s: sn last: wd bnd over 4f out and wknd: t.o* **25/1**

1m 26.8s (0.91) **Going Correction** +0.075s/f (Slow) **13** Ran SP% **118.0**

Speed ratings (Par 94):97,95,95,94,93 92,91,90,90,89 78,72,12

CSF £29.37 TOTE £5.50: £1.90, £2.10, £3.40; EX 33.90 Trifecta £56.10 Pool: £448.59 - 5.87 winning tickets..

Owner Jumeirah Racing **Bred** R F And S D Knipe **Trained** West Ilsley, Berks

FOCUS

The first division of this maiden looked basically ordinary on paper, although there were a couple of expensive purchases making their debuts. They went 20/1 bar five and, the favourite excepted, the other four dominated the race.

NOTEBOOK

Heywood, who had been gradually progressive in three previous outings, appreciated this easier surface having raced on very fast ground at Yarmouth, and after going on off the turn always had matters under control. A half-brother to Ratio, he can make his mark in handicaps. (op 9-2)

Abbotts Ann ♦, the only filly in the line-up and out of an unraced half-sister to Annus Mirabilis, showed plenty of promise considering how freely she ran from her wide draw. However, she knuckled down to her work in the straight and should not be long in winning. (op 9-2)

Fever, a 75,000gns brother to High Curragh, was being pushed along to hold his place after a couple of furlongs but kept going well and should improve with this experience under his belt. (op 7-1)

Beech Games built on his Wolverhampton debut but appeared to have every chance and could not quicken in the straight. (op 9-2)

Beverly Hill Billy stayed on nicely from the back and is bred to be a juvenile winner.

Satyricon was another to show promise and should benefit from the experience.

Wind Flow was backed in to favourite, but ended up racing wide and never got involved. The support suggests he has more ability than he was able to show on this debut. (op 5-2)

Port Luanda(IRE) Official explanation: vet said colt finished distressed

Private Peachey(IRE) Official explanation: jockey said colt never travelled

3844 GO RACING AT FOLKESTONE TOMORROW EVENING E B F MEDIAN AUCTION MAIDEN STKS (DIV II) 7f (P)

2:30 (2:30) (Class 5) 2-Y-0 **£2,590** (£770; £385; £192) **Stalls** Low

Form RPR

1 **Valiance (USA)** 2-9-3 .... RobertHavlin 11 80
(J H M Gosden) *dwlt: in tch on wd outside: effrt over 2f out: rdn and r.o wl fr over 1f out to ld last stride* **5/1**[3]

0 **2** *hd* **Nightinshining (IRE)**[27] 3025 2-9-3 .... DaneO'Neill 7 79
(A King) *pressed ldr: led over 2f out: drvn and kpt on wl fnl f: hdd last stride* **33/1**

3 **3** *½* **Astronomic View**[41] 2572 2-9-3 .... JamieSpencer 9 78
(E A L Dunlop) *trckd ldrs: prog 2f out to press ldr wl over 1f out: str chal fnl f: nt qckn and hld nr fin* **13/8**[1]

4 *½* **Kid Mambo (USA)** 2-9-3 .... IanMongan 10 77
(T G Mills) *rn green towards outer: in tch: squeezed through and prog wl over 1f out: chsd ldng trio fnl f: kpt on* **10/3**[2]

5 **5** *5* **Fares (IRE)**[12] 3485 2-9-3 .... SebSanders 14 64
(C E Brittain) *sn wl in rr: struggling 3f out: kpt on u.p fnl 2f: n.d* **20/1**

30 **6** *½* **Tension Point**[32] 2844 2-9-3 .... SteveDrowne 4 63
(J A Osborne) *trckd ldrs: pushed along over 2f out: no prog and hld whn n.m.r jst over 1f out: fdd* **14/1**

04 **7** *¾* **Kerswell**[33] 2816 2-8-6 ow1... JamesMillman(7) 12 57
(B R Millman) *w ldrs and racd wd: outpcd fr 2f out* **20/1**

8 *shd* **Magena Gold** 2-8-12 .... RichardKingscote(5) 5 60
(R Charlton) *dwlt: settled towards rr: shkn up wl over 1f out: no real prog* **33/1**

63 **9** *¾* **Down The Brick (IRE)**[19] 3265 2-9-3 .... AlanMunro 13 58
(B R Millman) *a in rr: n.d fr over 2f out* **12/1**

0 **10** *nk* **Wilmington**[16] 3363 2-9-3 .... RyanMoore 2 58
(R Hannon) *chsd ldrs: cl enough on inner over 2f out: wkng whn n.m.r jst over 1f out* **14/1**

0 **11** *1 ¼* **Distant Sunset (IRE)**[9] 3591 2-9-3 .... MichaelHills 3 54
(B W Hills) *dwlt: a wl in rr* **33/1**

00 **12** *shd* **Rowan Venture**[28] 2979 2-9-3 ....(b[1]) NCallan 1 54
(M H Tompkins) *mde most to over 2f out: wknd rapidly jst over 1f out* **100/1**

050 **13** *hd* **Saxenberg**[13] 3435 2-8-12 .... JohnEgan 6 49
(Miss J R Gibney) *w ldrs: drvn 3f out: wknd 2f out* **100/1**

14 *1 ½* **Palmiro** 2-9-3 .... NickyMackay 8 50
(W J Haggas) *settled in last pair: no prog 2f out* **20/1**

1m 27.14s (1.25) **Going Correction** +0.075s/f (Slow) **14** Ran SP% **124.0**

Speed ratings (Par 94):95,94,94,93,87 87,86,86,85,85 83,83,83,81

CSF £170.62 TOTE £6.70: £2.20, £8.80, £1.20; EX 219.00 Trifecta £145.90 Part won. Pool: £205.57 - 0.10 winning tickets..

Owner H R H Princess Haya Of Jordan **Bred** Hascombe Stud And Valiant Stud **Trained** Newmarket, Suffolk

FOCUS

The second division of this maiden contained mainly inexperienced juveniles and they went 12/1 bar three, all of whom finished in the frame.

NOTEBOOK

Valiance(USA) ♦, a 130,000gns Derby entry from the family of Prize Giving and Pridwell, made a pleasing debut. He had to race wide throughout but, under a fine, sympathetic ride, gradually reeled in the runner-up to lead near the line. He looks sure to come on a fair amount for this. (op 9-2)

Nightinshining(IRE) improved considerably for his Salisbury debut and went very close to causing a surprise. He showed a good attitude and should be able to find compensation before long.

Astronomic View had every chance but was unable to pick up in the closing stages and may have found the extra furlong beyond him at this stage. (op 7-4 tchd 6-4 in a place)

Kid Mambo(USA), who cost 115,000gns earlier this year, is from the family of Selkirk and showed plenty of promise in finishing on the heels of the placed horses and clear of the rest, despite running green. (op 3-1 tchd 7-2 in places)

Fares(IRE) was best of the remainder, running a similar race to his debut in that he stayed on at the end, and he will do better once qualified for handicaps.

Kerswell Official explanation: jockey said filly hung right

3845 GOLF AND GAMBLE H'CAP 7f (P)

3:00 (3:00) (Class 5) (0-70,70) 3-Y-0+ **£3,238** (£963; £481; £240) **Stalls** Low

Form RPR

3005 **1** **His Master's Voice (IRE)**[12] 3487 3-9-2 **70**.......................... AlanMunro 13 78
(D W P Arbuthnot) *a ldng trio: pressed ldr over 2f out and gng wl: led over 1f out: rdn and styd on stoutly* **9/1**

1302 **2** *1 ¼* **Up Tempo (IRE)**[11] 3536 8-9-9 **70**..............................(b) RyanMoore 3 78
(C R Dore) *trckd ldrs: effrt 2f out: hrd rdn to chse wnr fnl f: no imp* **10/3**[1]

4030 **3** *nk* **Hollow Jo**[50] 2331 6-9-3 **64**... MickyFenton 6 71
(J R Jenkins) *hld up in rr: prog wl over 1f out: nt qckn ent fnl f: kpt on same pce* **10/1**

0410 **4** *1* **Sovereignty (JPN)**[8] 3612 4-8-13 **60**.. NCallan 4 65
(D K Ivory) *wnt lft s: sn in tch in midfield: drvn and nt qckn over 1f out: styd on ins fnl f* **10/1**

0013 **5** *hd* **Joyeaux**[13] 3459 4-9-3 **64**..(v) DerekMcGaffin 2 68
(J Hetherton) *pressed ldrs: effrt 2f out: nt qckn over 1f out: one pce after* **11/1**

6205 **6** *½* **Stormy Monday**[7] 3646 3-9-2 **70**.. MichaelHills 8 73
(J W Hills) *settled towards rr: prog 2f out: chsd ldrs 1f out: one pce after* **6/1**[2]

0010 **7** *3 ½* **Moon Bird**[25] 3099 4-9-0 **61**.. TedDurcan 7 55
(C A Cyzer) *dwlt: t.k.h: hld up in rr: gng wl enough whn nt clr run briefly 2f out: shkn up and no prog over 1f out* **14/1**

03P0 **8** *¾* **Storm Centre**[28] 2969 4-8-10 **62**...................................... JamesDoyle(5) 9 54
(Miss J S Davis) *pressed ldr: led over 2f out to over 1f out: wknd* **50/1**

2-00 **9** *1* **Morgan Lewis (IRE)**[65] 1882 5-9-1 **62**......................(p) SteveDrowne 11 51
(J A Geake) *racd towards outer: in tch: effrt 3f out: drvn and struggling over 2f out* **8/1**

0000 **10** *5* **Jonny Ebeneezer**[18] 3295 7-9-3 **64**..............................(v[1]) DaneO'Neill 1 40
(M Wellings) *s.v.s: hld up in last pair and sn jst in tch: rdn and no prog 2f out: eased fnl f* **12/1**

0010 **11** *1* **Peace Lily**[13] 3450 4-9-0 **61**.. StephenCarson 12 35
(R F Johnson Houghton) *racd v wd: in tch: effrt over 2f out: sn wknd* **13/2**[3]

0060 **12** *1 ¾* **Acomb**[17] 3337 6-9-4 **65**.. RichardThomas 5 34
(Mrs L Richards) *led to over 2f out: wknd rapidly* **33/1**

00-P **13** 3 1/2 **Empty Gesture**[50] 2317 4-8-12 **59** .... JohnEgan 14 19
(J R Best) *s.v.s: a last and nvr rcvrd* **66/1**
1m 26.46s (0.57) **Going Correction** +0.075s/f (Slow)
WFA 3 from 4yo+ 7lb **13** Ran SP% **119.1**
Speed ratings (Par 103):99,97,97,96,95 95,91,90,89,83 82,80,76
CSF £38.53 CT £325.24 TOTE £11.80: £3.10, £1.50, £3.00; EX 54.40 Trifecta £163.20 Part won. Pool: £229.86 - 0.30 winning tickets..
Owner The Moving Partnership **Bred** Yeomanstown Stud **Trained** Upper Lambourn, Berks
FOCUS
Just a modest handicap, run slightly faster than both divisions of the maiden earlier in the day.
Empty Gesture Official explanation: jockey said gelding missed the break

3846 FURLONGS & FAIRWAYS H'CAP 6f (P)
3:30 (3:30) (Class 5) (0-70,70) 3-Y-0+ **£3,238** (£963; £481; £240) **Stalls** Low

Form RPR
2-03 **1** **Portmeirion**[25] 3097 5-9-7 **63** .... SebSanders 11 73
(S C Williams) *dwlt: wl off the pce tl clsd fr 2f out: drvn and styd on to ld last 75yds* **7/2**[1]
2413 **2** 1/2 **Blessed Place**[9] 3593 6-9-4 **60** ....(t) NCallan 4 68
(D J S Ffrench Davis) *led and sn clr at fast pce: tired over 1f out: hdd last 75yds: kpt on* **5/1**[2]
3300 **3** nk **Gone'N'Dunnett (IRE)**[5] 3709 7-9-6 **62** ....(v) JohnEgan 7 69
(Mrs C A Dunnett) *chsd clr ldrs: no imp fr 1/2-way tl styd on fnl f: jst unable to chal* **14/1**
4155 **4** hd **Orange Dancer (IRE)**[18] 3299 3-9-9 **70** .... SteveDrowne 2 76
(H Morrison) *mostly chsd clr ldr to 1f out: one pce u.p* **8/1**
0050 **5** nk **Mandarin Spirit (IRE)**[6] 3664 6-9-12 **68** ....(b) OscarUrbina 1 74
(G C H Chung) *dwlt: sn rcvrd to chse ldng pair: disp 2nd 1f out: one pce ins fnl f* **11/1**
2212 **6** 1/2 **Million Percent**[49] 2347 7-9-1 **62** .... RoryMoore(5) 3 66
(C R Dore) *dwlt: outpcd in midfield: urged along and kpt on fr 2f out: nt rch ldrs* **13/2**[3]
5020 **7** 1 1/4 **Desert Opal**[11] 3536 6-9-2 **61** .... AdamKirby(3) 12 61
(C R Dore) *bdly outpcd in last: styd on fr over 1f out: no ch* **25/1**
/0-0 **8** shd **Khalidia (USA)**[13] 3434 5-9-3 **64** .... RichardKingscote(5) 6 64
(M A Magnusson) *dwlt: outpcd and nvr on terms: kpt on fnl f* **50/1**
0024 **9** nk **Seneschal**[11] 3536 5-9-9 **65** .... RyanMoore 10 64
(A B Haynes) *outpcd in rr: shkn up 2f out: no real prog over 1f out* **7/1**
-060 **10** 2 1/2 **Nistaki (USA)**[11] 3536 5-9-7 **66** .... PatrickMathers(3) 5 58
(D Shaw) *dwlt: sn in midfield and off the pce: effrt on inner whn bdly hmpd over 2f out: no ch after* **33/1**
34/4 **11** 1 1/2 **Athboy Nights (IRE)**[15] 3389 4-9-1 **57** .... JamieSpencer 9 44
(M J Wallace) *outpcd in midfield: no imp wl over 1f out: eased* **5/1**[2]
2000 **12** shd **Indian Lady (IRE)**[16] 3349 3-8-5 **59** ....(v[1]) RussellKennemore(7) 8 45
(Mrs A L M King) *rrd bdly s: outpcd in midfield: struggling whn hmpd on inner over 2f out: no ch* **40/1**
1m 13.31s (0.50) **Going Correction** +0.075s/f (Slow)
WFA 3 from 4yo+ 5lb **12** Ran SP% **118.7**
Speed ratings (Par 103):99,98,97,97,97 96,94,94,94,91 89,88
CSF £19.86 CT £223.19 TOTE £4.40: £1.90, £1.80, £3.30; EX 26.20 Trifecta £289.40 Part won. Pool: £407.68 - 0.54 winning tickets..
Owner Usk Valley Stud **Bred** Usk Valley Stud **Trained** Newmarket, Suffolk
FOCUS
An ordinary sprint run at a scorching early pace.
Athboy Nights(IRE) Official explanation: jockey said filly moved badly
Indian Lady(IRE) Official explanation: jockey said filly missed the break and was denied a clear run

3847 SIMON TAYLOR 18TH BIRTHDAY FILLIES' H'CAP 5f (P)
4:00 (4:00) (Class 6) (0-55,54) 3-Y-0+ **£2,388** (£529; £529) **Stalls** High

Form RPR
6340 **1** **Cosmic Destiny (IRE)**[1] 3825 4-9-5 **54** .... DaneO'Neill 9 67
(E F Vaughan) *dwlt: t.k.h: hld up in last pair: sweeping run on outer to ld last 150yds: sn clr* **11/2**[2]
1453 **2** 3 **Blakeshall Quest**[6] 3683 6-9-3 **52** ....(b) RyanMoore 8 54
(R Brotherton) *racd on outer towards rr: rdn wl over 1f out: r.o ins fnl f: no ch w wnr* **5/1**[1]
6006 **2** dht **Attitude Annie**[11] 3536 3-8-12 **51** .... PaulDoe 2 52
(S Dow) *chsd ldng pair: rdn to chal and upsides 1f out: sn outpcd by wnr: jnd for 2nd on line* **20/1**
1656 **4** shd **Mirasol Princess**[4] 3728 5-8-7 **49** .... JamesMillman(7) 7 51+
(D K Ivory) *in tch: rdn whn nt clr run 1f out: r.o nr fin* **5/1**[1]
4100 **5** shd **Jennverse**[4] 3728 4-8-12 **47** .... JohnEgan 1 48
(D K Ivory) *dwlt: sn chsd ldrs: effrt and nt clr run briefly on inner 1f out: kpt on same pce* **6/1**[3]
6223 **6** nk **Montillia (IRE)**[16] 3356 4-8-11 **49** .... AdamKirby(3) 5 49
(J W Unett) *pressed ldr: led over 3f out: hdd and fnd nil last 150yds* **5/1**[1]
-000 **7** hd **Elvina**[22] 3172 5-9-1 **50** .... FergusSweeney 3 49
(A G Newcombe) *chsd ldrs: effrt over 1f out: nt qckn fnl f* **11/1**
4146 **8** 1 1/4 **Edged In Gold**[23] 3155 4-9-0 **49** ....(e) SebSanders 10 44+
(P J Makin) *hld up in tch: effrt whn nowhere to go over 1f out to ins fnl f: nt rcvr* **7/1**
4420 **9** 1/2 **Succeed (IRE)**[16] 3349 3-8-10 **54** .... RichardKingscote(5) 4 46
(Mrs H Sweeting) *led to over 3f out: pressed ldr after: upsides 1f out: wknd rapidly* **16/1**
-610 **10** 1 **Limited Magician**[42] 2543 5-8-12 **47** ....(v) RobbieFitzpatrick 6 37
(C Smith) *outpcd and a struggling in rr* **33/1**
59.87 secs (0.09) **Going Correction** +0.075s/f (Slow)
WFA 3 from 4yo+ 4lb **10** Ran SP% **114.1**
Speed ratings (Par 98): **102,97,97,97,96 96,96,94,93,91**WIN: Cosmic Destiny £7.80. PL: £3.00, Blakeshall Quest £2.00, Attitude Annie £4.20. EX: CD/BQ £21.90. CD/AA £63.50. CSF: CD/BQ £16.19, CD/AA £52.70. TRIC: CD/BQ/AA £259.87. CD/AA/BQ £297.50. TRIF: £80.70. Pool: £227.40 - 0.50 w/u. £113.70 c/f to Saturday.27 CSF £Owner CT £A M Pickering TOTE £Bred: £The Cruelle People, £Trained, £Newmarket, Suffolk.
FOCUS
A very moderate fillies' handicap, but competitive nonetheless, with only 7lb separating the whole field on official ratings.
Edged In Gold Official explanation: jockey said filly was denied a clear run

3848 WHIPS AND TEES H'CAP 1m 3f 106y
4:30 (4:30) (Class 5) (0-75,81) 3-Y-0 **£3,238** (£963; £481; £240) **Stalls** High

Form RPR
1221 **1** **Liberate**[7] 3649 3-10-0 **81** 7ex .... SebSanders 4 94+
(Sir Mark Prescott) *mde all: clr 3f out: drvn over 1f out: styd on wl: unchal* **1/3**[1]
6506 **2** 3 1/2 **Jebel Ali (IRE)**[27] 3015 3-9-2 **74** .... JamesDoyle(5) 7 79
(B Gubby) *hld up in midfield: prog 4f out: chsd wnr over 2f out: tried to cl over 1f out: hanging and no imp after* **20/1**
5064 **3** 6 **Zilcash**[23] 3151 3-9-7 **74** .... DaneO'Neill 3 69
(A King) *trckd ldng pair: outpcd and lost pl bdly over 3f out: plugged on again fnl 2f to snatch 3rd nr fin* **8/1**[2]
2353 **4** 1/2 **Moonlight Music (IRE)**[25] 3073 3-9-7 **74** .... RichardMullen 6 69
(E J O'Neill) *chsd wnr to over 2f out: wknd over 1f out* **12/1**
-062 **5** 2 1/2 **Siakira**[12] 3467 3-8-11 **64** .... NCallan 8 55
(I A Wood) *dwlt: sn chsd ldrs: effrt over 3f out: sn outpcd and btn* **10/1**[3]
46 **6** 6 **Will Be (IRE)**[19] 3326 3-9-6 **73** ....(t) SteveDrowne 5 54
(R A Kvisla) *a in rr: last and wl bhd over 4f out: no ch after* **25/1**
-000 **7** 2 1/2 **El Faro (FR)**[58] 2082 3-8-9 **62** .... ChrisCatlin 2 39
(M R Channon) *a in rr: struggling to stay in tch over 4f out: no ch after* **14/1**
5336 **8** 1 1/4 **Veronica's Girl**[14] 3400 3-9-4 **71** .... PaulDoe 1 46
(W J Knight) *hld up in last: prog over 4f out: effrt on outer 3f out: wknd rapidly 2f out* **16/1**
2m 28.54s (-1.38) **Going Correction** 0.0s/f (Good) **8** Ran SP% **124.1**
Speed ratings (Par 100):105,102,98,97,95 91,89,88
CSF £12.40 CT £35.57 TOTE £1.30: £1.10, £4.50, £1.90; EX 19.00 Trifecta £66.90 Pool: £280.94 - 2.98 winning tickets..
Owner Eclipse Thoroughbreds-Osborne House III **Bred** Miss K Rausing **Trained** Newmarket, Suffolk
FOCUS
A fair turf handicap but uncompetitive in nature.

3849 COME RACING HERE ON SATURDAY EVENING MAIDEN STKS 1m 3f 106y
5:00 (5:01) (Class 5) 3-Y-0+ **£3,238** (£963; £481; £240) **Stalls** High

Form RPR
32 **1** **Kibara**[13] 3451 3-8-11 .... NickyMackay 9 75+
(L M Cumani) *led 9f out: mde rest: drew clr fr 3f out: easily* **4/6**[1]
40 **2** 5 **Valuta (USA)**[20] 3225 3-9-2 ....(t) SteveDrowne 3 67
(R A Kvisla) *chsd wnr 7f out: shkn up 3f out: no imp and wl hld fnl 2f* **28/1**
5 **3** nk **Valart**[27] 3029 3-8-11 .... AlanDaly 5 61
(C Tinkler) *in tch: effrt over 3f out: disp 2nd fnl 2f: nt qckn and no ch w wnr* **14/1**
-505 **4** 2 **Roya**[16] 3347 3-9-2 65 .... RyanMoore 2 63
(R Hannon) *hld up in tch: outpcd over 3f out: kpt on fnl 2f: n.d* **6/1**[3]
0 **5** 3 1/2 **Noddies Way**[53] 2228 3-9-2 .... RobertMiles 6 57
(J F Panvert) *hld up: nowhere to go and snatched up after 1f: last tl effrt on wd outside 3f out: plugged on: nvr a factor* **14/1**
2 **6** 5 **Longhill Tiger**[15] 3373 3-9-2 .... NCallan 7 49
(G G Margarson) *t.k.h: hld up: outpcd 3f out: grad wknd* **4/1**[2]
0 **7** 2 1/2 **Janaah**[41] 2580 3-8-11 .... OscarUrbina 4 40
(C E Brittain) *hld up in tch: rdn and wknd 3f out* **33/1**
06- **8** 1 1/4 **Mayden Dawn**[256] 6319 3-8-11 .... MickyFenton 1 38
(Miss E C Lavelle) *led to 9f out: prom tl wknd u.p 3f out* **50/1**
005 **9** 10 **Stockholder**[6] 3676 3-9-2 .... HayleyTurner 8 27
(C A Cyzer) *a in rr: wknd over 3f out* **50/1**
2m 30.51s (0.59) **Going Correction** 0.0s/f (Good) **9** Ran SP% **117.9**
Speed ratings (Par 103):97,93,93,91,89 85,83,82,75
CSF £31.28 TOTE £1.70: £1.10, £3.70, £3.00; EX 31.00 Trifecta £217.80 Pool: £306.86 - 1.00 winning ticket. Place 6 £41.85, Place 5 £11.47.
Owner Fittocks Stud **Bred** Fittocks Stud **Trained** Newmarket, Suffolk
FOCUS
An uncompetitive turf maiden with the well-supported odds-on favourite making the majority of the running and coming home at her leisure.
Noddies Way Official explanation: jockey said colt suffered interference on first bend
Longhill Tiger Official explanation: jockey said colt hung right
T/Jkpt: Not won. T/Plt: £15.20 to a £1 stake. Pool: £50,780.85. 2,436.65 winning tickets. T/Qpdt: £7.20 to a £1 stake. Pool: £2,744.10. 281.00 winning tickets. JN

3312 SANDOWN (R-H)
Wednesday, July 26

OFFICIAL GOING: Good to firm (good in places on round course; firm in places on sprint course)
Wind: Nil

3850 PANMURE GORDON INSTITUTIONAL EQUITIES APPRENTICE H'CAP 1m 2f 7y
6:05 (6:06) (Class 5) (0-75,75) 3-Y-0+ **£3,238** (£963; £481; £240) **Stalls** High

Form RPR
3003 **1** **Transvestite (IRE)**[13] 3429 4-9-7 **75** .... PatrickHills(7) 3 87
(J W Hills) *stdd s: hld up rr but in tch: hdwy over 2f out: led appr fnl f: clr ins last: comf* **3/1**[1]
-500 **2** 3 1/2 **Resonate (IRE)**[28] 2974 8-9-9 **75** .... JamesMillman(5) 7 80
(A G Newcombe) *hld up rr but in tch: hdwy and rdn 2f out: styd on ins last to take 2nd nr fin but no ch w wnr* **11/2**[3]
2600 **3** nk **Christmas Truce (IRE)**[39] 2647 7-8-12 **62** ....(v) JamesDoyle(3) 8 67
(Ms J S Doyle) *trckd ldrs: slt ld over 5f out: def advantage 3f out: hdd appr fnl f: sn one pce: ct for 2nd cl home* **10/1**
0040 **4** 1 1/4 **Voice Mail**[10] 3566 7-9-6 **70** ....(b) StephenDonohoe(3) 6 72
(A M Balding) *swtg: chsd ldrs 4f out: outpcd over 2f out: styd on again fnl f but n.d* **15/2**
0060 **5** 1 1/2 **Trifti**[11] 3532 5-8-8 **60** .... AshleyHamblett(5) 9 60
(C A Cyzer) *lw: chsd ldrs: rdn 3f out: one pce fnl 2f* **15/2**
50-6 **6** 2 **Acknowledgement**[24] 3122 4-9-3 **69** .... StephanieHollinshead(5) 5 65
(D R C Elsworth) *disp 2nd tl chal 5f out to 3f out: wknd over 1f out* **12/1**
030- **7** 5 **James Street (IRE)**[278] 6010 3-8-4 **66** .... KylieManser(5) 4 52
(J R Best) *sn led: hdd over 5f out: styd chsng ldrs tl wknd 2f out* **11/1**
0012 **8** 3 **Padre Nostro (IRE)**[5] 3706 7-8-2 **56** .... ChrisGlenister(7) 2 37+
(J R Holt) *sddle slipped sn after s: plld hrd: in tch tl wknd fr 3f out* **10/3**[2]
2m 9.15s (-1.09) **Going Correction** -0.20s/f (Firm)
WFA 3 from 4yo+ 10lb **8** Ran SP% **112.1**
Speed ratings (Par 103):96,93,92,91,90 89,85,82
CSF £18.93 CT £142.11 TOTE £3.40: £1.40, £2.00, £2.40; EX 21.70.
Owner Nigel Howlett Partnership **Bred** Rathasker Stud **Trained** Upper Lambourn, Berks
FOCUS
A modest handicap run at a steady early pace. The form is not strong.
Acknowledgement Official explanation: jockey said gelding was unsuited by the good to firm (good in places) ground
Padre Nostro(IRE) Official explanation: jockey said saddle slipped on leaving stalls

The Form Book, Raceform Ltd, Compton, RG20 6NL

3851 PANMURE GORDON INVESTMENT TRUST E B F MAIDEN STKS 7f 16y
6:35 (6:37) (Class 5) 2-Y-O £4,533 (£1,348; £674; £336) Stalls High

Form RPR
4 1 **Old Romney**14 3417 2-9-3 .... KDarley 8 83+
(M Johnston) *mde all: pushed along over 2f out: shkn up to go clr appr fnl f: readily* **2/5**1
2 2 **Colonel Flay** 2-9-3 .... RobertHavlin 5 78
(Mrs P N Dutfield) *w'like: attractive: lw: in tch: hdwy 2f ot: styd on fnl f to take 2nd cl home but no ch w wnr* **66/1**
0 3 ¾ **Perfect Courtesy (IRE)**14 3417 2-9-3 .... AlanMunro 4 76
(P W Chapple-Hyam) *lw: chsd ldrs: rdn to go 2nd 2f out: nvr gng pce to trble wnr: outpcd and lost 2nd nr fin* **4/1**2
60 4 3½ **Deccan Express (IRE)**12 3498 2-9-3 .... RichardHughes 7 67
(R Hannon) *chsd wnr: rdn 3f out: lost 2nd 2f out: wknd fnl f* **14/1**3
0 5 ½ **Mayireneyrbel**20 3210 2-8-12 .... MickyFenton 3 60
(R Ingram) *leggy: s.i.s: rr: pushed along over 2f out: kpt on ins last and gng on cl home but nvr in contention* **66/1**
6 nk **So Sweet (IRE)** 2-8-12 .... TedDurcan 2 60
(M R Channon) *leggy: v.s.a and bhd: hdwy but plenty to do fr 2f out: styng on whn hmpd ins last: kpt on again cl home* **14/1**3
0 7 ¾ **Converti**44 2506 2-9-0 .... NelsonDeSouza(3) 10 63
(P F I Cole) *leggy: chsd ldrs: rdn 3f out: wknd ins fnl 2f* **25/1**
0 8 1¼ **Hoh Me Hoh You (IRE)**19 3253 2-9-3 .... PatDobbs 6 59
(S Kirk) *chsd ldrs: rdn 3f ouut: wknd over 1f out* **40/1**
6 9 4 **Prince Of Charm (USA)**14 3408 2-9-3 .... ChrisCatlin 9 49
(P Mitchell) *w'like: s.i.s: bhd: pushed along over 3f out: rdn and hung rt over 1f out: nvr in contention* **50/1**
10 1¾ **Garrya** 2-9-3 .... RyanMoore 1 45
(R Hannon) *w'like: bit bkwd: bhd most of way* **20/1**

1m 29.74s (-1.35) **Going Correction** -0.20s/f (Firm) **10 Ran SP% 120.8**
Speed ratings (Par 94):99,96,95,91,91 90,90,88,84,82
CSF £69.23 TOTE £1.40: £1.10, £9.10, £1.40; EX 55.50.
Owner Gainsborough Stud **Bred** Gainsborough Stud Management Ltd **Trained** Middleham Moor, N Yorks

FOCUS
A pretty uncompetitive maiden by Sandown standards, in which the winner did not have to run up to the form of his debut effort to get off the mark.

NOTEBOOK
Old Romney, who did not look quite as well in his coat as he had done on his debut at Newmarket, had much less to beat here and duly landed the odds in workmanlike fashion. He will get a mile this year and, while the bare form does not amount to much, he has plenty of potential. (op 4-9 tchd 1-2 in places)
Colonel Flay, pretty green beforehand, just edged the battle for second spot. An attractive half-brother to In Deep, a winner over 14 furlongs at four, he really is not bred to excel at two, but this was a fair effort and he should improve for the run. (op 50-1)
Perfect Courtesy(IRE), whose dam is a half-sister to high-class jumper Song Of The Sword and to juvenile winner Mrs Pankhurst, was a well-backed second favourite as punters looked for the proverbial each-way good thing. He had the best part of eight lengths to make up on the favourite on their Newmarket form and did step up on that debut effort, but he looks to need a mile already and could be a nursery type after one more run. (tchd 9-2)
Deccan Express(IRE) has not progressed from his debut outing but connections now have the option of going the nursery route, and that could well see him in a better light. (op 12-1)
Mayireneyrbel, who looked lean and very fit, is a half-sister to Presidum Travel, a multiple winner in Italy between seven and 13 furlongs. She again lost ground at the start and struggled to get into contention afterwards. (op 50-1)
So Sweet(IRE), who was making her racecourse debut, looked fit beforehand. A sister to the smart, multiple-winner Crosspeace, she ran better than her finishing position suggests as she missed the break badly and had a lot of ground to make up turning into the straight. She will come on for the experience and leave this form behind in time. Official explanation: jockey said filly missed the break
Garrya is quite a chunky type.

3852 LORD MCGOWAN H'CAP 7f 16y
7:05 (7:08) (Class 3) (0-90,88) 3-Y-O £8,096 (£2,408; £1,203; £601) Stalls High

Form RPR
0532 1 **Ans Bach**18 3317 3-9-7 88 .... (p) PhilipRobinson 2 97
(M A Jarvis) *hld up in rr: hdwy on outside over 2f out: qcknd to chse ldr ins last: styd on u.p to ld last strides* **5/1**3
0011 2 shd **Scrummage**6 3667 3-8-3 70 6ex .... (v) KerrinMcEvoy 6 79
(Sir Michael Stoute) *lw: sn trcking ldr: led appr fnl 2f: drvn fnl f: ct last strides* **2/1**1
1-3 3 2½ **Alfie Tupper (IRE)**41 2581 3-9-3 84 .... RichardHughes 7 86
(S Kirk) *b.hind: trckd ldrs: rdn 2f out: chsd ldr jst ins last but no imp: outpcd fnl 100yds* **10/3**2
1510 4 shd **Orchard Supreme**50 2330 3-9-4 85 .... RyanMoore 3 87
(R Hannon) *bhd: stl plenty to do over 2f out: hdwy on outside over 1f out: kpt on wl fnl f: gng on cl home but nt rch ldrs* **25/1**
5-04 5 nk **Oceans Apart**14 3418 3-9-4 88 .... NelsonDeSouza(3) 8 89
(P F I Cole) *t.k.h: chsd ldrs: rdn over 2f out: styd on u.p ins last: nt pce to chal fnl 100yds* **14/1**
1113 6 nk **Electric Warrior (IRE)**18 3304 3-8-13 80 .... NCallan 11 80
(K R Burke) *chsd ldrs: wnt 2nd ins fnl 2f: wknd ins last* **8/1**
6022 7 1 **Woodcote Place**16 3364 3-8-5 72 .... AlanMunro 4 69+
(P R Chamings) *lw: stdd s: rr: hdwy and n.m.r 2f out and 1f out: nvr gng pce to rch ldrs after* **16/1**
0105 8 ½ **Silver Dip**14 3418 3-9-2 83 .... MichaelHills 1 79
(B W Hills) *chsd ldrs: rdn 2f out: wknd ins fnl f* **14/1**
0045 9 7 **Tara Too (IRE)**18 3316 3-9-3 84 .... TedDurcan 9 61
(D W P Arbuthnot) *bhd: rdn 3f out: nvr a danger* **12/1**
2100 10 2½ **Fratt'n Park (IRE)**16 3364 3-7-11 69 oh2 .... MarcHalford(5) 5 39
(J J Bridger) *plld hrd early: a bhd: rdn and hung lft 3f out* **50/1**
33-0 11 ½ **Crocodile Bay (IRE)**18 3317 3-9-6 87 .... ChrisCatlin 10 56
(Carl Llewellyn) *set str pce tl hdd appr fnl 2f: sn wknd* **50/1**

1m 27.48s (-3.61) **Going Correction** -0.20s/f (Firm) **11 Ran SP% 118.9**
Speed ratings (Par 104):112,111,109,108,108 108,107,106,98,95 95
CSF £15.34 CT £39.15 TOTE £5.90: £1.90, £1.40, £1.90; EX 18.70.
Owner Sheikh Ahmed Al Maktoum **Bred** Darley **Trained** Newmarket, Suffolk

FOCUS
Not a bad handicap and it was notable for being run at a strong gallop, which suited those who were held up off the pace. Solid form, rated through the second and fifth.

NOTEBOOK
Ans Bach has looked ready to strike of late and he was very much suited by the way this race was run. Held up towards the rear in a fast-run affair, he was able to put in a strong finish and just get up near the line. He and the runner-up finished well clear of the rest and can expect to go up a fair bit in the handicap now. (op 6-1)
Scrummage was denied the clear lead he enjoyed when winning on his last two starts but still raced up with the strong pace. He did remarkably well in the circumstances to be only narrowly denied, and he remains an improving colt. (op 7-4 tchd 9-4)
Alfie Tupper(IRE), the least exposed of the field, settled better off this strong pace and just shaded the bunch finish for third place. Given the way the race was run, he could possibly have done with being held up further back. (tchd 11-4)
Orchard Supreme wants softer ground than this, but the way the race was run suited him and he stayed on well from well off the pace. He would not be guaranteed to repeat this effort next time. (op 33-1)
Oceans Apart, taking another drop in class, raced keenly despite the decent gallop, and she remains on a mark which makes her difficult to place.
Electric Warrior(IRE) enjoyed a successful spell last month but now appears to be in the grip of the Handicapper. (op 17-2)
Woodcote Place ◆ had the race run to suit but the gaps never opened up for him. He would have been placed at least with a clear run, finished full of running, and this performance can be ignored. He remains a winner waiting to happen. Official explanation: jockey said colt was denied a clear run (tchd 20-1)
Fratt'n Park(IRE), who was on his toes beforehand, failed to settle. (op 66-1)

3853 PANMURE GORDON CORPORATE FINANCE H'CAP 1m 6f
7:35 (7:42) (Class 4) (0-80,80) 4-Y-O+ £6,477 (£1,927; £963; £481) Stalls Centre

Form RPR
-041 1 **Alessano**16 3365 4-9-5 78 .... (b) RyanMoore 7 86
(G L Moore) *led 1f: styd trcking ldr: led over 2f out: hrd drvn fr over 1f out: hld on all out* **7/2**1
6-05 2 ¾ **Boxhall (IRE)**46 2460 4-8-10 69 .... (t) AlanMunro 1 76
(W R Swinburn) *led after 1f: rdn over 3f out: hdd over 2f out: styd chsng wnr and kpt on wl fnl f but a hld* **5/1**3
4163 3 hd **Mister Right (IRE)**19 3256 5-9-3 76 .... RichardHughes 6 83+
(D J S Ffrench Davis) *in tch: chsd ldrs 5f out: rdn and effrt over 2f out: kpt on wl u.p fnl f but nvr gng pce to chal* **4/1**2
0521 4 nk **Takafu (USA)**13 3452 4-9-3 76 .... FrankieMcDonald 3 82
(W S Kittow) *lw: t.k.h: chsd ldrs: rdn 3f out: styd on wl fnl 2f but nvr gng pce to chal* **6/1**
5232 5 1½ **Altenburg (FR)**20 3225 4-9-7 80 .... KerrinMcEvoy 10 84
(Mrs N Smith) *t.k.h: chsd ldrs: rdn over 2f out: styd on same pce* **11/2**
2465 6 ½ **Desert Island Disc**6 3666 9-8-6 72 .... SladeO'Hara(7) 5 76
(Dr J R J Naylor) *bhd: rdn over 3f out: hdwy on outside over 1f out: kpt on ins last but nvr rchd ldrs* **14/1**
0602 7 ½ **Boot 'n Toot**14 3412 5-8-12 71 .... MichaelHills 2 74
(C A Cyzer) *stdd s: hld up in rr: hdwy on ins 2f out: sn rdn: kpt on fnl f but nvr a danger* **12/1**
0510 8 nk **Love Always**16 3365 4-8-13 72 .... PatDobbs 9 74
(S Dow) *hdwy into mid-div 1/2-way: rdn and effrt 2f out: kpt on fnl f but nvr gng pce to trble ldrs* **16/1**
6360 9 nk **Papeete (GER)**13 3431 5-8-3 62 .... JimmyQuinn 4 64
(Miss B Sanders) *ready: hdwy 5f out: rdn 3f out: kpt on under presure fr over 1f out but nvr in contention* **20/1**
6000 10 ¾ **Love Angel (USA)**7 3649 4-7-11 61 oh1 .... MarcHalford(5) 8 62
(J J Bridger) *a towards rr but styd on fnl 2f: nvr in contention* **33/1**

3m 4.53s (0.02) **Going Correction** -0.20s/f (Firm) **10 Ran SP% 116.5**
Speed ratings (Par 105):91,90,90,90,89 89,88,88,88,88
CSF £21.03 CT £72.77 TOTE £3.40: £1.70, £1.60, £1.90; EX 20.40.
Owner D J Deer **Bred** D J And Mrs Deer **Trained** Woodingdean, E Sussex

FOCUS
They went no great pace and the principals were always to the fore. The field was separated by only around five lengths and the race cannot be rated too positively.
Altenburg(FR) Official explanation: jockey said gelding ran too free

3854 PANMURE GORDON H'CAP 1m 14y
8:10 (8:11) (Class 4) (0-80,80) 3-Y-O+ £6,477 (£1,927; £963; £481) Stalls High

Form RPR
1251 1 **Habshan (USA)**24 3113 6-10-0 80 .... AlanMunro 1 89
(C F Wall) *in tch: hdwy on outside 2f out: drvn to ld appr fnl f: hld on wl cl home* **7/2**1
0013 2 nk **Fabrian**12 3469 8-9-0 71 .... JamesDoyle(5) 7 80
(R J Price) *sn led: rdn 2f out: hdd appr fnl f: styd on ins last but a jst hld cl home* **4/1**2
3316 3 2 **The Gaikwar (IRE)**5 3712 7-9-1 72 .... (b) RichardKingscote(5) 9 76
(R A Harris) *b: t.k.h: chsd ldrs: rdn and effrt 2f out: nt pce to chal: wknd fnl 100yds* **9/1**
2200 4 hd **Merrymadcap (IRE)**11 3532 4-9-8 74 .... FrancisNorton 6 78
(M Blanshard) *mid-div: hdwy and rdn over 2f out: chsd ldrs over 1f out: styd on same pce fnl f* **6/1**
0065 5 2½ **Night Spot**16 3366 5-9-0 73 .... JamesMillman(7) 2 71
(B R Millman) *hld up in rr: pushed along and hdwy over 2f out: nvr gng pce to rch ldrs but kpt on ins last* **11/2**3
2043 6 2 **Undeterred**55 2180 10-9-4 70 .... NCallan 4 63
(K J Burke) *bhd: rdn and hdwy on outside 3f out: nvr in contention: wknd u.p fnl f* **9/1**
1002 7 ½ **Quantum Leap**20 3212 9-9-4 70 .... (v) JimmyQuinn 5 62
(S Dow) *in tch: rdn 3f out: wknd over 1f out* **6/1**
6330 8 shd **Mythical Charm**9 3590 7-8-9 61 oh3 .... (t) RyanMoore 8 53
(J J Bridger) *swtg: b.hind: t.k.h: chsd ldrs: rdn 3f out: wknd ins fnl 2f* **16/1**
0004 9 ½ **Dream Forest (IRE)**27 3011 3-8-5 65 .... RobertHavlin 3 56
(Mrs P N Dutfield) *chsd ldrs: rdn 3f out: wknd ins fnl 2f* **33/1**

1m 42.47s (-1.48) **Going Correction** -0.20s/f (Firm)
WFA 3 from 4yo+ 8lb **9 Ran SP% 115.0**
Speed ratings (Par 105):99,98,96,96,94 92,91,91,90
CSF £17.41 CT £115.51 TOTE £4.70: £1.80, £1.80, £3.20; EX 13.80.
Owner Alan & Jill Smith **Bred** Darley Stud Management, L L C **Trained** Newmarket, Suffolk

FOCUS
The pace was only steady and it turned into a a bit of a sprint up the straight. Probably sound form, the winner maintaining his gradual improvement.

3855 PANMURE CAPITAL H'CAP 5f 6y
8:40 (8:43) (Class 5) (0-75,75) 4-Y-O+ £4,533 (£1,348; £674; £336) Stalls High

Form RPR
000- 1 **Little Edward**364 3841 8-9-6 72 .... JimCrowley 6 84
(R J Hodges) *trckd ldrs: led over 1f out: hld on wl cl home* **25/1**
2036 2 1 **Chinalea (IRE)**9 3593 4-9-7 73 .... (p) PhilipRobinson 7 81
(C G Cox) *led tl hdd over 1f out: styd on but a hld ins last* **7/2**2
0641 3 ½ **Who's Winning (IRE)**8 3612 5-9-4 75 6ex......... RichardKingscote(5) 10 81
(B G Powell) *chsd ldrs: rdn 2f out: one pce ins last* **9/2**3

0512 **4** 3/4 **Misaro (GER)**[22] [3165] 5-9-7 **73**................................(b) AdrianMcCarthy 9 77
(R A Harris) *rr but in tch: rdn 1/2-way: kpt on fnl f to take 4th last strides but nvr gng pce to be competitive* **5/2**[1]

2006 **5** *shd* **Kallista's Pride**[110] [902] 6-8-8 **67**.................................. KylieManser(7) 2 70
(J R Best) *lw: s.i.s: bhd: hdwy 2f out: styd on to take 4th ins last: nvr gng pce to rch ldrs: ct for 4th last stride* **20/1**

060 **6** 1 1/4 **Diamond Katie (IRE)**[18] [3297] 4-8-2 **54**........................... JimmyQuinn 3 53
(N Tinkler) *lw: bhd: rdn 1/2-way: kpt on fnl f and gng on cl home but nvr gng pce to be competitive* **7/1**

-000 **7** *shd* **Meikle Barfil**[38] [2674] 4-8-11 **63**.. RyanMoore 8 61
(J M Bradley) *chsd ldrs: rdn 2f out: btn over 1f out* **14/1**

2530 **8** 3/4 **Willhewiz**[12] [3486] 6-9-6 **72**..(v) JohnEgan 5 68
(M S Saunders) *chsd ldr tl wl over 1f out: wknd ins last* **6/1**

0006 **9** 3/4 **Salviati (USA)**[11] [3543] 9-8-10 **62**..(p) NCallan 4 55
(J M Bradley) *b: slowly away: swtchd to far rail after 1f: effrt 1/2-way: nvr in contention* **10/1**

60.80 secs (-1.41) **Going Correction** -0.20s/f (Firm) **9** Ran SP% **120.1**
Speed ratings (Par 103):103,101,100,99,99 97,97,95,94
CSF £115.30 CT £489.47 TOTE £29.60: £4.50, £1.90, £1.90; EX 218.10 Place 6 £9.73, Place 5 £5.06.
Owner J W Mursell **Bred** J W Mursell **Trained** Charlton Adam, Somerset
■ Stewards' Enquiry : Kylie Manser four-day ban: dropped hands and lost 4th place (Aug 6-9)

FOCUS
An ordinary handicap, run in a decent time, and this is solid form, rated through the runner-up.
Who's Winning(IRE) Official explanation: jockey said gelding was denied a clear run
Misaro(GER) Official explanation: jockey said gelding missed the break
T/Plt: £15.60 to a £1 stake. Pool: £64,663.50. 3,021.00 winning tickets. T/Qpdt: £7.30 to a £1 stake. Pool: £4,169.80. 421.10 winning tickets. ST

[3344] BATH (L-H)
Thursday, July 27

OFFICIAL GOING: Firm
Wind: Light, against Weather: Sunny and warm

3860 PLATINUM TROWBRIDGE MEDIAN AUCTION MAIDEN STKS 5f 161y
2:20 (2:20) (Class 6) 2-Y-O **£2,590** (£770; £385; £192) **Stalls** Low

Form RPR

0 **1** **Bateleur**[10] [3591] 2-9-3 .... ChrisCatlin 7 67
(M R Channon) *led over 4f out: rdn over 1f out: r.o wl* **9/4**[1]

0 **2** 2 **Nepos**[10] [3588] 2-9-3 .... ShaneKelly 2 60
(J A Osborne) *a.p: rdn over 2f out: chsd wnr over 1f out: kpt on same pce* **4/1**[3]

5502 **3** 5 **Fly Time**[17] [3345] 2-8-7 .... StephenDonohoe(5) 3 39
(H J Manners) *a.p: rdn to chse wnr over 2f out tl over 1f out: wknd fnl f* **5/1**

0 **4** 1 3/4 **Straw Boy**[6] [3701] 2-8-10 .... ThomasO'Brien(7) 1 38
(M R Channon) *chsd ldrs: rdn 3f out: wknd over 1f out* **14/1**

055 **5** 8 **Dancing Daisy (IRE)**[17] [3344] 2-8-12 .... RobertHavlin 6 6
(Mrs P N Dutfield) *chsd ldrs: rdn 3f out: wknd wl over 1f out* **7/2**[2]

50 **6** 10 **Auction Boy**[17] [3344] 2-9-3 .... FrancisFerris 4 —
(B Palling) *led tl over 4f out: rdn over 3f out: wknd over 2f out* **8/1**

7 5 **The Power Of Phil** 2-9-0 .... EdwardCreighton(3) 8 —
(R Brotherton) *s.v.s: a in rr: eased whn no ch over 1f out* **50/1**

060 **8** 26 **Linkslade Lad**[17] [3344] 2-9-3 .... MartinDwyer 5 —
(W R Muir) *rel to r: a t.o* **33/1**

1m 11.9s (0.70) **Going Correction** -0.075s/f (Good) **8** Ran SP% **112.3**
Speed ratings (Par 92):92,89,82,80,69 56,49,15
CSF £10.98 TOTE £3.00: £1.10, £2.00, £1.60; EX 18.00 Trifecta £166.60 Pool: £445.84 - 1.90 winning tickets..
Owner Dave and Gill Hedley **Bred** G Hedley And Mike Channon Bloodstock Limited **Trained** West Ilsley, Berks

FOCUS
A weak juvenile maiden little better than a seller.

NOTEBOOK
Bateleur, never a danger on his debut in an ordinary maiden at Windsor, stepped up on that effort to get off the mark at the second attempt. He is clearly progressing, but is likely to find things tougher from now on. (op 3-1)
Nepos, like Bateleur, was well held on his racecourse debut in a Windsor maiden, but this was easier and he ran creditably in second. (op 5-1)
Fly Time, claimed out of Mick Channon's yard after her neck-second in a course seller last time, was well held by the front two and does not look up to winning a maiden. (op 4-1)
Straw Boy, last of 17 on his debut at Newbury, would have found this much less competitive and ran better. (op 8-1)
Dancing Daisy(IRE) had appeared to be going the right way, but she was well beaten this time and proved pretty disappointing. (op 5-1)

3861 BRIDGES MOTOR GROUP/E.B.F. NOVICE STKS 5f 11y
2:55 (2:55) (Class 5) 2-Y-O **£3,562** (£1,059; £529; £264) **Stalls** Low

Form RPR

215 **1** **Southandwest (IRE)**[20] [3252] 2-9-0 .... JohnEgan 5 86+
(J S Moore) *chsd ldr: led over 1f out: sn rdn: r.o wl* **4/9**[1]

3312 **2** 1 3/4 **Relkida**[13] [3468] 2-8-11 .... ChrisCatlin 1 74
(M R Channon) *a.p: rdn 2f out: chsd wnr fnl f: no imp* **3/1**[2]

3 2 1/2 **Mr Loire** 2-8-3 .... RichardKingscote(5) 4 61
(R Charlton) *hld up: hdwy 2f out: rdn over 1f out: edgd lft ins fnl f: one pce* **12/1**[3]

6166 **4** 2 1/2 **Autumn Storm**[15] [3409] 2-8-9 .... StephenCarson 2 53
(R Ingram) *led: hdd over 1f out: sn rdn: wknd ins fnl f* **50/1**

100 **5** 2 1/2 **Hephaestus**[5] [3734] 2-8-9 .... ThomasO'Brien(7) 3 51
(M R Channon) *sn outpcd* **16/1**

62.15 secs (-0.35) **Going Correction** -0.075s/f (Good) **5** Ran SP% **109.8**
Speed ratings (Par 94):99,96,92,88,84
CSF £2.03 TOTE £1.40: £1.10, £1.20; EX 2.00.
Owner B McNicholas & M Feehan **Bred** Paul Hardy **Trained** Upper Lambourn, Berks

FOCUS
A pretty ordinary novice event with the winner not needing to be at his best to score.

NOTEBOOK
Southandwest(IRE), the winner of a course and distance maiden before running fifth in a Sandown Listed race, found this a straightforward enough opportunity dropped in class. He is probably worth stepping back up in grade. (op 4-7 tchd 4-6)
Relkida is a consistent sort and ran an honest race in second, she was just no match for Southandwest when it mattered. (tchd 5-2)
Mr Loire, a 22,000gns half-brother to Miss L'Augeval, a seven-furlong juvenile winner at two, out of a seven-furlong two-year-old winner, ran as though this experience would do him good and he should improve. (op 10-1)
Autumn Storm has struggled since winning her maiden and was well held. (op 40-1)
Hephaestus, 17th of 23 in the Super Sprint on his previous start, could not take advantage of this drop in grade and does not seem to be progressing. (op 12-1)

3862 PLATINUM BATH (S) STKS 1m 2f 46y
3:25 (3:25) (Class 6) 4-Y-O+ **£2,266** (£674; £337; £168) **Stalls** Low

Form RPR

5130 **1** **Seattle Robber**[9] [3616] 4-8-10 63.................................(p) ManavNem(7) 3 52
(P A Blockley) *hld up in rr: hdwy on outside over 2f out: rdn fnl f: r.o to ld cl home* **11/8**[1]

0405 **2** 3/4 **Shaheer (IRE)**[10] [3592] 4-9-8 47.......................................(b) JimCrowley 5 56
(J Gallagher) *hld up in tch: rdn over 2f out: led 1f out: hdd cl home* **8/1**

1465 **3** 1 1/4 **Danish Monarch**[15] [3411] 5-9-1 49........................... ChrisCavanagh(7) 8 54
(David Pinder) *led: rdn and hdd 2f out: ev ch 1f out: nt qckn* **12/1**

0304 **4** 1 3/4 **Didoe**[9] [3615] 7-8-12 42... FrancisFerris 6 40
(P W Hiatt) *a.p: rdn over 4f out: one pce fnl 2f* **7/2**[2]

0320 **5** *shd* **Milk And Sultana**[5] [3730] 6-9-3 48.. AlanDaly 7 45
(G A Ham) *hld up in mid-div: hdwy over 3f out: led 2f out: sn rdn: hdd 1f out: one pce* **5/1**[3]

0500 **6** 2 1/2 **Bullseye**[16] [3382] 4-9-3 43..(b[1]) GeorgeBaker 2 40
(J R Boyle) *chsd ldr tl rdn 3f out: eased whn btn wl ins fnl f* **8/1**

4-60 **7** 16 **Nutley Queen (IRE)**[8] [3594] 7-8-12 35..........................(t) RobertHavlin 9 5
(M Appleby) *rdn 4f out: a bhd* **50/1**

6-00 **8** 1 1/4 **Mabella (IRE)**[22] [3194] 4-8-12 40...................................... DavidKinsella 1 3
(B J Llewellyn) *hld up towards rr: struggling 4f out* **66/1**

000/ **9** 9 **Boom Or Bust (IRE)**[10] [3637] 7-9-3 42...........................(p) VinceSlattery 4 —
(Karen George) *rdn over 3f out: a bhd* **50/1**

2m 9.35s (-1.65) **Going Correction** -0.075s/f (Good) **9** Ran SP% **116.3**
Speed ratings (Par 101):103,102,101,100,99 97,85,84,76
CSF £13.69 TOTE £2.30: £1.10, £2.90, £3.40; EX 17.40 Trifecta £73.10 Pool: £514.26 - 4.99 winning tickets..The winner was bought in for 8,500gns.
Owner J T Billson **Bred** Littleton Stud **Trained** Lambourn, Berks
■ A first career success for Mauritius-born apprentice Manav Nem.

FOCUS
A moderate seller and Seattle Robber did not have to be at his best to justify favouritism with the runner-up running his best race for a while.

3863 A.K.S. YEOVIL CLAIMING STKS 5f 11y
4:00 (4:01) (Class 6) 3-Y-O+ **£2,331** (£693; £346; £173) **Stalls** Low

Form RPR

0500 **1** **Carcinetto (IRE)**[44] [2531] 4-8-12 41...............................(p) FrancisFerris 8 53
(B Palling) *w ldr: rdn over 2f out: led over 1f out: r.o* **10/1**

0000 **2** *nk* **Ballybunion (IRE)**[30] [2949] 7-9-2 52..................... RichardKingscote(5) 1 61
(R A Harris) *a.p: rdn over 2f out: ev ch ins fnl f: kpt on* **11/2**[3]

6306 **3** 1 1/4 **Seven No Trumps**[9] [3608] 9-9-0 54................................ BarrySavage(7) 6 56
(J M Bradley) *hld up and bhd: swtchd rt and hdwy over 1f out: sn swtchd lft: r.o ins fnl f* **11/2**[3]

4535 **4** 1 1/2 **Tomthevic**[6] [3699] 8-9-3 44..(b) ShaneKelly 7 47
(J M Bradley) *led: rdn and hdd over 1f out: one pce fnl f* **5/1**[2]

4004 **5** 4 **Twinned (IRE)**[10] [3595] 3-8-6 59...............................(p) StevenGibson(7) 9 33
(J S Moore) *prom: rdn over 2f out: wknd fnl f* **6/1**

0600 **6** 1 **Jinksonthehouse**[17] [3348] 5-7-13 43........................ FrankiePickard(7) 10 18
(M D I Usher) *nvr trbld ldrs* **16/1**

5010 **7** 1 **Ardkeel Lass (IRE)**[76] [1645] 5-8-5 45............................... TolleyDean(7) 5 20
(R A Harris) *sn pushed along and carried hd high: nvr nr ldrs* **15/2**

0000 **8** *shd* **Shank On Fourteen (IRE)**[9] [3622] 5-9-13 58................. MartinDwyer 11 35
(K R Burke) *s.i.s: a bhd* **4/1**[1]

045- **9** 1 1/2 **Indian Bazaar (IRE)**[239] [6471] 10-8-10 43................ JasonLetherby(7) 4 20
(R A Harris) *chsd ldrs tl wknd over 2f out* **33/1**

-000 **10** 5 **Ms Polly Garter**[36] [2758] 4-8-3 35..............................(p) SaleemGolam(3) 2 —
(J M Bradley) *sn outpcd* **66/1**

62.50 secs **Going Correction** -0.075s/f (Good)
WFA 3 from 4yo+ 4lb **10** Ran SP% **112.9**
Speed ratings (Par 101):97,96,94,92,85 84,82,82,79,71
CSF £62.05 TOTE £15.80: £3.80, £1.50, £2.50; EX 123.80 Trifecta £463.60 Part won. Pool: £653.03 - 0.34 winning tickets..
Owner Bryn Palling **Bred** M A Doyle **Trained** Tredodridge, Vale Of Glamorgan

FOCUS
A moderate claimer rated around the principals and could be a little higher.

3864 CITY MOTORS & S.J. COOK & SONS H'CAP 5f 11y
4:35 (4:35) (Class 5) (0-70,67) 3-Y-O **£3,886** (£1,156; £577; £288) **Stalls** Low

Form RPR

0003 **1** **Montzando**[25] [3118] 3-8-5 **54**.......................................(v) SaleemGolam(3) 7 58
(B R Millman) *sn prom: rdn to ld over 1f out: drvn out* **4/1**[2]

1050 **2** *nk* **Jucebabe**[17] [3348] 3-8-7 **53**.. JimCrowley 3 56
(J L Spearing) *a.p: rdn over 1f out: r.o to take 2nd nr fin* **8/1**

0660 **3** *nk* **Matterofact (IRE)**[17] [3349] 3-9-5 **65**................................. RobertHavlin 1 67
(Mrs P N Dutfield) *led: rdn and hdd over 1f out: kpt on ins fnl f* **13/2**

6552 **4** *hd* **Cordelia**[19] [3285] 3-9-3 **63**.. JohnEgan 2 64
(B W Hills) *bhd: rdn over 2f out: hdwy on ins 1f out: no ex cl home* **11/4**[1]

0-00 **5** 2 1/2 **Me**[33] [2864] 3-9-7 **67**...(t) MartinDwyer 6 59
(P W Chapple-Hyam) *bhd: rdn and sme hdwy on outside over 1f out: one pce fnl f* **7/1**

143 **6** 1/2 **Spirit Of Coniston**[10] [3587] 3-9-0 **60**.......................(b) RobbieFitzpatrick 5 50
(Peter Grayson) *chsd ldrs: rdn over 2f out: eased whn btn wl ins fnl f* **9/2**[3]

6010 **7** 3 **Just Down The Road (IRE)**[19] [3299] 3-9-4 **64**............... FrancisFerris 8 44
(R A Harris) *w ldr: rdn over 2f out: wkng whn n.m.r 1f out* **6/1**

62.46 secs (-0.04) **Going Correction** -0.075s/f (Good) **7** Ran SP% **116.1**
Speed ratings (Par 100):97,96,96,95,91 90,86
CSF £36.03 CT £204.33 TOTE £6.40: £2.80, £3.30; EX 35.60 Trifecta £205.40 Pool: £494.78 - 1.71 winning tickets..
Owner The Links Partnership **Bred** Peter Baldwin **Trained** Kentisbeare, Devon
■ Stewards' Enquiry : Jim Crowley caution: careless riding

FOCUS
A modest sprint handicap but sound enough rated through the third and fourth.

3865 RENAULT VANS FILLIES' H'CAP 1m 2f 46y
5:10 (5:11) (Class 5) (0-70,70) 3-Y-O **£3,886** (£1,156; £577; £288) **Stalls** Low

Form RPR

062 **1** **Hanella (IRE)**[31] [2919] 3-9-6 **69**.. GeorgeBaker 7 73
(R M Beckett) *hld up: sn in rr: rdn over 2f out: hdwy over 1f out: r.o to ld last strides* **5/2**[2]

-635 **2** *hd* **Theatre Royal**[15] [3400] 3-8-12 **61**.. MartinDwyer 5 65
(A M Balding) *a.p: swtchd rt over 1f out: led ins fnl f: hrd rdn and hdd last strides* **9/4**[1]

-202 **3** 3/4 **Tafiya**[17] [3362] 3-9-7 **70** .... AliAlSaffar 1 73
(G A Butler) *t.k.h in tch: stdd and lost pl over 6f out: swtchd rt and hdwy wl over 1f out: ev ch ins fnl f: hld whn n.m.r last strides* **11/2**

2P20 **4** 3 1/2 **Dimelight**[29] [2990] 3-9-6 **69** .... JohnEgan 3 65
(D R C Elsworth) *hld up: hdwy over 3f out: rdn to ld over 1f out: hdd ins fnl f: wknd* **5/1**[3]

0-02 **5** 1 1/4 **Golden Sprite**[46] [2480] 3-8-12 **61** .... RobertHavlin 4 55
(B R Millman) *led 1f: chsd ldr: rdn to ld briefly wl over 1f out: wknd wl ins fnl f* **6/1**

3620 **6** 8 **Aurora Jane (FR)**[27] [3036] 3-9-1 **64** .... PaulEddery 2 42
(B W Hills) *led after 1f: rdn and hdd wl over 1f out: sn wknd* **10/1**

4000 **7** 1 1/2 **Tilsworth Charlie**[7] [3668] 3-8-2 **51** oh6 .... FrankieMcDonald 6 27
(J R Jenkins) *hld up: hdwy over 3f out: sn rdn: wkng whn edgd lft over 1f out* **40/1**

2m 10.09s (-0.91) **Going Correction** -0.075s/f (Good) 7 Ran SP% **117.2**
Speed ratings (Par 97):100,99,99,96,95 89,87
CSF £8.97 TOTE £4.20: £2.20, £1.70; EX 10.60 Place 6 £33.10, Place 5 £21.76.
Owner Frank Brady **Bred** Cathal Ryan **Trained** Whitsbury, Hants

FOCUS
Just a modest fillies' handicap, but not bad form for the grade and rated fairly positively.
Theatre Royal Official explanation: jockey said filly lost its action just before line
T/Plt: £108.50 to a £1 stake. Pool: £46,263.45. 311.05 winning tickets. T/Qpdt: £102.30 to a £1 stake. Pool: £2,571.70. 18.60 winning tickets. KH

3435 FOLKESTONE (R-H)

Thursday, July 27

OFFICIAL GOING: Good to firm (firm in places)
Wind: Nil Weather: Fine but cloudy

3866 LADBROKES TOTAL BETTING SERVICE, REGISTER TODAY APPRENTICE H'CAP 6f
5:50 (5:55) (Class 5) (0-70,69) 3-Y-O **£3,886** (£1,156; £577; £288) **Stalls** Low

Form RPR

4416 **1** **Namu**[17] [3349] 3-9-5 **69** .... SladeO'Hara(5) 4 76
(B W Hills) *racd against nr side rail: trckd ldrs: chal fr 1/2-way: led jst ins fnl f: pushed out* **7/2**[2]

4454 **2** nk **Patavium Prince (IRE)**[6] [3708] 3-9-4 **68** .... KylieManser(5) 7 78+
(J R Best) *dwlt: hld up wl in rr: stl plenty to do over 1f out: effrt ent fnl f: r.o wl and gaining at fin* **10/3**[1]

3003 **3** 1/2 **Musical Script (USA)**[26] [3094] 3-8-10 **58** .... TravisBlock(3) 5 63
(Mrs A J Hamilton-Fairley) *w ldr: led wl over 2f out: rdn and hdd jst ins fnl f: kpt on* **9/2**[3]

0-00 **4** 1 **Fun Time**[22] [3195] 3-8-2 **50** .... MarcHalford(3) 1 52
(M R Channon) *chsd ldrs: rdn over 2f out: styd on same pce ins fnl f: nvr able to chal* **20/1**

-000 **5** 1 3/4 **Be My Charm**[17] [3349] 3-7-12 **50** .... LauraReynolds(7) 8 46
(M Blanshard) *chsd ldrs: rdn and one pce fnl 2f* **50/1**

4434 **6** hd **Overwing (IRE)**[27] [3049] 3-9-7 **66** .... AdamKirby 3 65+
(R M H Cowell) *dwlt: wl in rr: rdn and effrt whn nt clr run 1f out: swtchd out wd and kpt on: no ch* **15/2**

0000 **7** 1/2 **Forces Sweetheart**[19] [3299] 3-8-0 **52** .... LukeMorris(7) 9 46
(M L W Bell) *trckd ldrs: effrt on outer to chal 2f out: wknd ins fnl f* **20/1**

-530 **8** shd **Shunkawakhan (IRE)**[24] [3154] 3-8-10 **60** .... DeanWilliams(5) 13 54
(G C H Chung) *trckd rival on far side: led over 2f out: clr over 1f out but nvr on terms w main gp* **16/1**

6030 **9** 1 **The Lady Caster**[20] [3267] 3-8-7 **52** ....(v) NelsonDeSouza 6 43
(R M Beckett) *led to wl over 2f out: nt look keen after: wknd fnl f* **11/1**

6533 **10** 2 1/2 **Thoughtsofstardom**[15] [3397] 3-8-7 **55** ....(p) DuranFentiman(3) 12 38
(P S McEntee) *led the pair on far side to over 2f out: no ch* **16/1**

3344 **11** 2 1/2 **Danish Blues (IRE)**[23] [3164] 3-8-13 **61** ....(p) JamesDoyle(3) 10 37
(N P Littmoden) *trckd ldrs tl wknd rapidly over 1f out* **10/1**

05-0 **12** 8 **Globe**[20] [3257] 3-8-2 **50** oh9 .... LiamJones(3) 2 2
(M S Saunders) *a detached in last and rdr frequently looking down: eased fnl f* **66/1**

1m 11.11s (-2.49) **Going Correction** -0.425s/f (Firm) 12 Ran SP% **117.4**
Speed ratings (Par 100):99,98,97,96,94 94,93,93,91,88 85,74
CSF £14.75 CT £53.40 TOTE £5.20: £2.20, £1.30, £2.00; EX 22.10.
Owner Philip G Harvey **Bred** Philip Graham Harvey **Trained** Lambourn, Berks

FOCUS
A moderate three-year-old sprint, run at a sound pace, and a low draw proved an advantage. The form looks dubious and is best rated through winner and third.
Overwing(IRE) Official explanation: jockey said filly suffered interference in running
Danish Blues(IRE) Official explanation: jockey said gelding hung right
Globe Official explanation: jockey said filly lost its action

3867 LADBROKES NUMBER 1 FOR LOTTO (S) STKS 6f
6:20 (6:21) (Class 6) 3-Y-O+ **£2,730** (£806; £403) **Stalls** Low

Form RPR

-060 **1** **Piddies Pride (IRE)**[41] [2611] 4-8-4 58 ....(v) JamesDoyle(5) 7 53+
(Miss Gay Kelleway) *squeezed out s: wl in rr: rdn and prog on outer fr 2f out: sustained effrt to ld last 100yds* **11/1**

0005 **2** nk **Princely Vale (IRE)**[19] [3306] 4-9-0 50 ....(b) RobertMiles 2 57
(W G M Turner) *racd against nr side rail: led: rdn over 1f out: edgd rt and hdd last 100yds: nt qckn* **25/1**

3-04 **3** nk **Turn Me On (IRE)**[9] [3611] 3-8-9 70 ....(t) HayleyTurner 9 56
(M L W Bell) *pressed ldrs: outpcd over 2f out: renewed effrt over 1f out: chal ent fnl f: nt qckn last 100yds* **7/1**

0055 **4** 1/2 **Snow Wolf**[27] [3033] 5-8-11 52 .... AdamKirby(3) 1 55
(J M Bradley) *hld up in last pair: effrt against nr side rail whn nt clr run over 1f out and ins fnl f: r.o nr fin* **6/1**[3]

0106 **5** 1 **Full Spate**[20] [3245] 11-9-6 63 .... RyanMoore 3 58
(J M Bradley) *sn trckd ldrs: rdn and lost pl over 2f out: tried to rally over 1f out: one pce* **11/4**[1]

0300 **6** 1/2 **My Girl Pearl (IRE)**[7] [3682] 6-8-9 49 .... FergusSweeney 6 45
(M S Saunders) *pressed ldr to 1f out: wknd* **7/1**

4032 **7** 1/2 **Smokincanon**[8] [3635] 4-8-9 47 .... MarcHalford(5) 8 49
(W G M Turner) *a towards rr: rdn and no real prog fnl 2f* **11/2**[2]

6604 **8** nk **Reality Time (IRE)**[22] [3195] 3-8-4 47 .... PaulDoe 11 43
(W J Knight) *dwlt: wl in rr: effrt on outer 2f out: fdd fnl f* **25/1**

3016 **9** hd **Stagnite**[8] [3635] 6-8-13 57 ....(p) KevinGhunowa(7) 4 53
(P A Blockley) *chsd ldrs: rdn and nt qckn over 2f out: lost pl: n.d fnl f* **7/1**

0300 **10** 7 **Xaar Breeze**[17] [3348] 3-7-13 43 .... LiamJones(5) 10 21
(Mrs P Townsley) *racd on outer: in tch: wknd rapidly over 1f out* **25/1**

1m 11.48s (-2.12) **Going Correction** -0.425s/f (Firm)
WFA 3 from 4yo+ 5lb 10 Ran SP% **113.7**
Speed ratings (Par 101):97,96,96,95,94 93,92,92,92,82
CSF £249.50 TOTE £8.60: £3.00, £4.70, £1.90; EX 229.50.The winner was bought in for 6,000gns.
Owner Countrywide Classics Limited **Bred** B Kennedy **Trained** Exning, Suffolk

FOCUS
A weak affair, run at a solid pace, and the form looks fair for the class rated through the second.
Xaar Breeze Official explanation: jockey said filly was never travelling

3868 EUROPEAN BREEDERS FUND MAIDEN FILLIES' STKS 7f (S)
6:50 (6:51) (Class 5) 2-Y-O **£4,533** (£1,348; £674; £336) **Stalls** Low

Form RPR

4 **1** **Zefooha (FR)**[21] [3227] 2-9-0 .... RichardHughes 5 73
(M R Channon) *dwlt: sn trckd ldrs: effrt to press ldr over 1f out and rn green: rdn to ld nr fin* **9/2**[3]

6 **2** hd **Ronaldsay**[29] [2980] 2-9-0 .... RyanMoore 6 72
(R Hannon) *pressed ldr: led wl over 1f out: idled and wandered in front: drvn fnl f: hdd nr fin* **7/2**[2]

00 **3** 2 **Bay Of Light**[30] [2958] 2-9-0 .... JimmyQuinn 4 67
(P W Chapple-Hyam) *led: rdn and hdd wl over 1f out: nt qckn* **5/4**[1]

4 3/4 **Power Ballad** 2-9-0 .... PaulDoe 3 65
(W J Knight) *plld hrd: hld up in last pair: prog on outer over 2f out: nt qckn and hld 1f out* **40/1**

5065 **5** 2 1/2 **It's No Problem (IRE)**[21] [3210] 2-9-0 .... FergusSweeney 8 58
(Jean-Rene Auvray) *t.k.h: hld up in last pair: effrt over 2f out: wknd fnl f* **16/1**

0 **6** 1 **Killer Heels**[22] [3201] 2-9-0 .... LPKeniry 1 56
(S Kirk) *trckd ldrs: pushed along 3f out: wknd 2f out* **20/1**

03 **7** 3/4 **Doubly Guest**[14] [3435] 2-9-0 .... OscarUrbina 2 54
(G G Margarson) *t.k.h early: trckd ldrs tl wknd 2f out* **8/1**

1m 26.61s (-1.29) **Going Correction** -0.425s/f (Firm) 7 Ran SP% **109.0**
Speed ratings (Par 91):90,89,87,86,83 82,81
CSF £18.59 TOTE £5.40: £2.20, £1.90; EX 18.10.
Owner Sheikh Ahmed Al Maktoum **Bred** Darley Stud Management Co Ltd **Trained** West Ilsley, Berks

FOCUS
A fair juvenile fillies' maiden which saw the first two come clear but the form is not that solid.

NOTEBOOK
Zefooha(FR), popular in the betting ring, showed the benefit of her debut experience at Yarmouth and just did enough to get off the mark at the second attempt. She is clearly going the right way, is evidently well thought of by connections as she holds a Group 1 entry in Ireland, and another furlong is also likely to suit in due course. (op 13-2)
Ronaldsay ◆ broke much better than had been the case on her Kempton debut last time and only lost out through greeness in the final furlong. She was nicely clear of the remainder and ought to be placed to get off the mark in the coming weeks. (op 9-4)
Bay Of Light had her chance from the front, but proved disappointingly one paced when pressed approaching the final furlong. She has a bit to prove now, but may be the type to fare better now she is eligible for a nursery mark. (op 6-4)
Power Ballad, a half-sister to High Dancer, a mile winner at three and also successful over timber at that age, proved very free through the early stages and looked in need of the experience. She still showed ability, however, and ought to know more next time out. (op 25-1 tchd 50-1)

3869 JIM WALL'S 80TH BIRTHDAY H'CAP 7f (S)
7:20 (7:24) (Class 6) (0-60,60) 3-Y-O **£2,730** (£806; £403) **Stalls** Low

Form RPR

-100 **1** **Takitwo**[28] [3011] 3-9-6 **60** .... SebSanders 12 71
(P D Cundell) *racd wd: in tch in rr: prog and drvn over 2f out: styd on u.p to ld ins fnl f: hld on* **12/1**

5461 **2** nk **Mocha Java**[22] [3195] 3-9-6 **60** .... JosedeSouza 2 70
(P F I Cole) *w ldr: led over 2f out: sn rdn: hdd and nt qckn ins fnl f: kpt on nr fin* **6/1**[2]

3406 **3** 3 1/2 **Red Vixen (IRE)**[19] [3299] 3-8-6 **53** .... KirstyMilczarek(7) 10 54
(C N Allen) *wl in rr: swtchd sharply rt 2f out and shkn up: styd on after to take 3rd nr fin* **16/1**

3003 **4** 1/2 **Fateful Attraction**[44] [2535] 3-8-10 **55** .... JamesDoyle(5) 13 55
(I A Wood) *reluctant to go bhd stalls: w ldrs: stl nrly upsides wl over 1f out: nt qckn after* **15/2**

0222 **5** 2 **Royal Tavira Girl (IRE)**[7] [3668] 3-9-2 **59** .... DominicFox(3) 5 53
(M G Quinlan) *chsd ldrs: rdn over 2f out: grad outpcd after* **7/1**[3]

1066 **6** hd **Titus Lumpus (IRE)**[17] [3364] 3-9-6 **60** .... PaulDoe 9 54
(R M Flower) *mde most to over 2f out: wknd jst over 1f out* **16/1**

5065 **7** 2 **Patavium (IRE)**[24] [3159] 3-9-6 **60** .... ChrisCatlin 6 49
(E J O'Neill) *w ldrs: outpcd jst over 2f out: shkn up over 1f out: no prog after* **8/1**

0050 **8** 1 1/4 **Precautionary**[111] [902] 3-9-0 **57** .... AdamKirby(3) 3 42
(Miss J Feilden) *nvr on terms w ldrs: struggling and outpcd fr over 2f out* **25/1**

0000 **9** 3 1/2 **Orphina (IRE)**[13] [3472] 3-9-3 **57** ....(b[1]) PatDobbs 4 33
(Pat Eddery) *chsd ldrs: rdn 3f out: wknd 2f out* **16/1**

6500 **10** 1 **Cheveley Flyer**[77] [1616] 3-8-12 **52** ....(v[1]) JimmyQuinn 8 26+
(J Pearce) *dwlt: wl in rr: lost tch w ldrs sn after 1/2-way: no ch after* **16/1**

4560 **11** shd **Simpsons Ross (IRE)**[6] [3705] 3-9-5 **59** .... EddieAhern 11 32+
(R M Flower) *chsd ldrs over 4f out: wknd and eased wl over 1f out* **17/2**

0-00 **12** 4 **Sprouston (FR)**[70] [1801] 3-9-1 **55** ....(b[1]) LPKeniry 14 18
(J S Moore) *dwlt: racd alone far side: nvr on terms: bhd whn c across to join main gp over 2f out* **11/1**

5506 **13** 5 **Dora's Green**[86] [1378] 3-9-1 **55** .... FergusSweeney 7 5
(M Blanshard) *chsd ldrs tl wknd rapidly fr over 2f out* **66/1**

-140 **14** 16 **Thornfield Clo (IRE)**[3] [3793] 3-8-13 **53** .... RichardHughes 1 —
(R Hannon) *cl up: rdn after 3f: sn struggling: bhd whn virtually p.u fnl f* **11/2**[1]

1m 26.15s (-1.75) **Going Correction** -0.425s/f (Firm) 14 Ran SP% **120.5**
Speed ratings (Par 98):93,92,88,88,85 85,83,81,77,76 76,72,66,48
CSF £82.36 CT £1204.80 TOTE £19.10: £5.50, £2.90, £2.50; EX 119.20.
Owner Miss M C Fraser **Bred** Roden House Stud **Trained** Compton, Berks

FOCUS
A moderate three-year-old handicap and the form looks sound enough with the first two coming clear and the runner-up setting the standard.
Red Vixen(IRE) Official explanation: jockey said filly was denied a clear run
Simpsons Ross(IRE) Official explanation: jockey said gelding hung left
Sprouston(FR) Official explanation: jockey said gelding hung left throughout
Thornfield Clo(IRE) Official explanation: jockey said filly ran too free to post

3870 EASTWELL MANOR H'CAP — 1m 4f
7:50 (7:50) (Class 6) (0-60,60) 3-Y-O — **£2,730** (£806; £403) **Stalls** Low

Form — RPR

4551 **1** **Joy In The Guild (IRE)**[20] 3264 3-8-10 **49** .... FergusSweeney 1 — 57
(W S Kittow) *hld up in last pair and off the pce: prog over 2f out: rdn to ld jst over 1f out: sn clr* **10/1**

00-5 **2** *2 ½* **Irish Whispers (IRE)**[47] 2434 3-9-7 **60** .... RyanMoore 8 — 64+
(B G Powell) *trckd ldrs: rdn to ld 2f out: sn hdd and outpcd: kpt on ins fnl f* **6/1**

0440 **3** *¾* **Captain Bolsh**[7] 3668 3-9-2 **55** .... JimmyQuinn 3 — 58
(J Pearce) *hld up in tch: prog on inner over 2f out: led wl over 1f out: hdd jst over 1f out: wknd ins fnl f* **14/1**

-036 **4** *1 ¼* **Peas 'n Beans (IRE)**[25] 3115 3-8-13 **59** .... LukeMorris(7) 2 — 60
(M L W Bell) *t.k.h: trckd ldrs: rdn and nt qckn over 2f out: styd on again fnl f* **11/2**[3]

0000 **5** *1 ¼* **Sa Nau**[31] 2933 3-8-9 **48** .... J-PGuillambert 5 — 47
(T Keddy) *hld up in tch: rdn and effrt on wd outside 3f out: outpcd 2f out : plugged on* **33/1**

0044 **6** *4* **Polish Welcome**[2] 3823 3-9-1 **54** .... SebSanders 7 — 47
(S C Williams) *pushed up to ld and set decent pce: hdd & wknd 2f out* **5/1**[2]

5002 **7** *¾* **King's Fable (USA)**[7] 3674 3-8-9 **53** .... GregFairley(5) 6 — 44
(M Johnston) *pressed ldr: rdn over 3f out: wknd 2f out* **11/8**[1]

6400 **8** *6* **Lewis Lloyd (IRE)**[29] 2968 3-8-5 **44** .... PaulDoe 4 — 26
(I A Wood) *pressed ldrs tl wknd wl over 2f out* **25/1**

000 **9** *29* **Rockatorri**[50] 2349 3-8-2 **41** oh3.......................................(p) ChrisCatlin 9 — —
(G G Margarson) *a struggling in last: lost tch 7f out: t.o 4f out* **50/1**

2m 36.96s (-3.54) **Going Correction** -0.425s/f (Firm) **9** Ran SP% **112.9**
Speed ratings (Par 98):94,92,91,91,90 87,87,83,63
CSF £65.79 CT £839.30 TOTE £9.50: £2.30, £1.80, £4.60; EX 36.50.
Owner The Racing Guild **Bred** Trickledown Stud D Magnier And P J Hernon **Trained** Blackborough, Devon

FOCUS
A poor three-year-old handicap, run at a generous early pace, and those coming from behind were at an advantage. The third sets the standard.
Peas 'n Beans(IRE) Official explanation: trainer said gelding was unsuited by the track
Polish Welcome Official explanation: jockey said filly hung left

3871 LADBROKES "ANY 2 WILL DO" H'CAP — 1m 1f 149y
8:20 (8:20) (Class 4) (0-85,82) 3-Y-O
£7,790 (£2,332; £1,166; £583; £291; £146) **Stalls** Low

Form — RPR

4053 **1** **Dame Hester (IRE)**[12] 3548 3-9-7 **79** .... ChrisCatlin 1 — 88
(E J O'Neill) *trckd ldng trio: plld out and effrt ins fnl 2f: led jst over 1f out: pushed clr* **10/1**

1142 **2** *2* **Black Beauty**[41] 2622 3-9-7 **79** .... RyanMoore 3 — 84
(M G Quinlan) *hld up in 6th: rdn over 2f out: hanging but styd on fnl f to take 2nd nr fin* **5/2**[2]

1511 **3** *hd* **Prince Picasso**[6] 3695 3-9-10 **82** 6ex.............................. SebSanders 2 — 87
(Sir Mark Prescott) *trckd ldr: rdn to dispute ld 2f out: hdd and outpcd jst over 1f out* **5/4**[1]

3400 **4** *½* **Ahmedy (IRE)**[14] 3443 3-8-12 **73** .... EdwardCreighton(3) 7 — 77+
(M R Channon) *t.k.h early: hld up in last: rdn and outpcd over 2f out: kpt on fnl f: no ch* **8/1**

-341 **5** *shd* **Heather Moor (USA)**[18] 3336 3-9-3 **75** .... RichardHughes 6 — 79
(Sir Michael Stoute) *trckd ldng pair: effrt on inner to dispute ld 2f out: hdd jst over 1f out: one pce* **7/1**[3]

4201 **6** *2 ½* **Empire Dancer (IRE)**[31] 2940 3-8-9 **74** .... KirstyMilczarek(7) 5 — 73
(C N Allen) *led at fair pce: hdd 2f out: wknd fnl f* **25/1**

650- **7** *1 ¾* **Al Hazim (IRE)**[300] 5582 3-8-5 **70** .... AshleyHamblett(7) 4 — 66
(L M Cumani) *hld up in 5th: rdn and floundering 2f out: sn wknd* **20/1**

2m 0.29s (-4.94) **Going Correction** -0.425s/f (Firm) **7** Ran SP% **114.3**
Speed ratings (Par 102):102,100,100,99,99 97,96
CSF £35.27 TOTE £14.20: £4.40, £1.80; EX 38.80 Place 6 £1,463.56, Place 5 £1,028.74.
Owner Miss A H Marshall **Bred** Miss Honora Corridan **Trained** Averham Park, Notts

FOCUS
A fair three-year-old handicap and the form looks sound enough for the class.
T/Plt: £2,034.00 to a £1 stake. Pool: £53,637.15. 19.25 winning tickets. T/Qpdt: £80.30 to a £1 stake. Pool: £4,621.20. 42.55 winning tickets. JN

3850 SANDOWN (R-H)
Thursday, July 27
OFFICIAL GOING: Good to firm (firm in places)
Wind: Nil Weather: Hot and humid

3872 "CHOSEN ONES" QUALIFY ON-LINE MAIDEN AUCTION STKS — 5f 6y
2:10 (2:12) (Class 5) 2-Y-O — **£3,886** (£1,156; £577; £288) **Stalls** High

Form — RPR

2 **1** **Prime Defender**[21] 3222 2-8-11 .... MichaelHills 4 — 91+
(B W Hills) *a travelling wl bhd ldrs: jnd ldrs on bit over 2f out: led jst over 1f out: sn qcknd clr: readily* **11/10**[1]

43 **2** *3* **Transpique (IRE)**[20] 3247 2-8-13 .... PhilipRobinson 3 — 79
(C G Cox) *lw: prom: led over 2f out tl over 1f out: kpt on but nt pce of wnr* **11/2**[3]

00 **3** *3* **Blackwater Stream (IRE)**[17] 3363 2-8-4 .... JamesDoyle(5) 1 — 64
(Mrs P N Dutfield) *s.i.s: sn pushed along in last trio: styd on but edgd rt fr over 1f out: wnt 3rd ins fnl f* **20/1**

032 **4** *¾* **Cheap Street**[17] 3363 2-8-11 .... RyanMoore 2 — 64
(J G Portman) *led after 1f tl over 2f out: sn rdn: hung rt and one pce fnl f* **9/4**[2]

5 *¾* **Honest Danger** 2-8-9 .... LDettori 6 — 59
(J R Best) *w'like: leggy: s.i.s: bhd: drvn along 3f out: styd on fnl f: nvr on terms* **20/1**

00 **6** *2* **Perfect Style (IRE)**[20] 3247 2-8-8 .... TedDurcan 8 — 51
(M Blanshard) *broke wl: led for 1f: chsd ldrs: rdn over 2f out: sn btn* **66/1**

7 *2* **Another True Story** 2-8-13 .... RichardHughes 7 — 48
(R Hannon) *w'like: str: bit bkwd: s.i.s and a in last trio* **14/1**

0 **8** *2* **Hucking Heat (IRE)**[15] 3407 2-8-11 .... LPKeniry 5 — 39
(J R Best) *chsd ldrs: rdn 2f out: sn wknd* **66/1**

61.05 secs (-1.16) **Going Correction** -0.25s/f (Firm) **8** Ran SP% **112.9**
Speed ratings (Par 94):99,94,89,88,87 83,80,77
CSF £7.29 TOTE £2.00: £1.10, £1.80, £3.10; EX 8.80.
Owner S Falle, M Franklin, J Sumsion **Bred** Christopher J Mason **Trained** Lambourn, Berks

FOCUS
They came home well strung out in this fair juvenile maiden and the form should stand up.

NOTEBOOK
Prime Defender, runner-up at Newbury on his debut, had learnt from that and proved much too good for this opposition. He handled the drop back to the minimum trip well, showing good speed throughout, and came home an easy winner. The Doncaster Sales race, this year run at York, is being targeted by connections. (op Evens tchd 6-5)
Transpique(IRE) did not build on his promising debut when a beaten favourite at Haydock last time but he did little wrong. The winner was in a different class but it was a perfectly sound performance in second. (op 9-2)
Blackwater Stream(IRE) struggled to go the early pace on the drop back to the minimum trip but he kept on well and appears to be improving with racing. Nurseries are now open to him, and a return to six should suit. Official explanation: jockey said colt missed the break
Cheap Street proved a bit disappointing as it was expected that the drop back to five furlongs would suit him. A return to a sharper track might help. (op 3-1 tchd 100-30 in places)
Honest Danger, who is bred to need further than this, struggled with the pace over this minimum trip and should do better when stepping up in distance. (op 16-1)
Perfect Style(IRE)

3873 £500,000 WILLIAM HILL GRAND PRIX II H'CAP — 5f 6y
2:45 (2:46) (Class 5) (0-75,74) 3-Y-O — **£3,886** (£1,156; £577; £288) **Stalls** High

Form — RPR

0544 **1** **Gwilym (GER)**[10] 3593 3-8-10 **63** .... TedDurcan 11 — 68
(D Haydn Jones) *chsd ldrs: rdn over 2f out: swtchd lft over 1f out: r.o to ld ins fnl f: jst hld on* **4/1**[2]

0405 **2** *hd* **Danny The Dip**[18] 3340 3-7-11 **55** oh2...................... MarcHalford(5) 10 — 59
(J J Bridger) *sn restrained towards rr: drifted lft and hdwy fr over 2f out: str run ins fnl f: jst failed* **33/1**

2202 **3** *¾* **Balian**[9] 3611 3-8-12 **65**...(p) RyanMoore 1 — 66
(G L Moore) *lw: hld up: rdn and hdwy fr 2f out: styd on to go 3rd ins fnl f: nrst fin* **8/1**

3002 **4** *½* **Even Bolder**[15] 3406 3-9-0 **67** .... PatDobbs 3 — 67
(S Kirk) *trckd ldr: rdn and effrt over 1f out: kpt on same pce* **14/1**

4152 **5** *nk* **Jakeini (IRE)**[20] 3268 3-9-6 **73**.......................................(p) DaneO'Neill 6 — 71
(E S McMahon) *swtg: sn led: rdn over 1f out: hdd ins fnl f: no ex* **5/1**[3]

4014 **6** *½* **Musical Romance (IRE)**[17] 3349 3-9-4 **71**.......................(b) LDettori 12 — 68
(B J Meehan) *hld up mid-div: rdn over 2f out: kpt on same pce* **7/2**[1]

0-00 **7** *½* **Eversden (USA)**[21] 3226 3-9-6 **73** .... PhilipRobinson 9 — 68
(C G Cox) *sn outpcd in rr: styd on fnl f: n.d* **15/2**

5544 **8** *shd* **City For Conquest (IRE)**[28] 3000 3-9-4 **71**......................(v) LPKeniry 4 — 65
(K R Burke) *in tch: rdn over 2f out: swtchd lft over 1f out: sltly hmpd ins fnl f whn hld* **14/1**

2315 **9** *nk* **Pititana (IRE)**[75] 1672 3-9-7 **74** .... RichardHughes 7 — 67
(R Hannon) *chsd ldrs: rdn over 2f out: one pce fnl f* **13/2**

0000 **10** *½* **Bollywood (IRE)**[7] 3667 3-8-0 **58** ow3.......................... JamesDoyle(5) 8 — 50
(J J Bridger) *chsd ldrs for 3f* **33/1**

61.35 secs (-0.86) **Going Correction** -0.25s/f (Firm) **10** Ran SP% **114.3**
Speed ratings (Par 100):96,95,94,93,93 92,91,91,90,90
CSF £120.18 CT £1016.30 TOTE £5.20: £2.00, £6.00, £2.50; EX 101.20.
Owner S Kon, D Llewelyn and J Runeckles **Bred** B Krutmann **Trained** Efail Isaf, Rhondda C Taff

FOCUS
A modest sprint handicap in which they finished in something of a heap but the form looks sound rated around the winner and third.
City For Conquest(IRE) Official explanation: jockey said saddle slipped
Bollywood(IRE) Official explanation: jockey said gelding hung right

3874 WILLIAM HILL GODS OF POKER STKS (REGISTERED AS THE STAR STAKES) (LISTED RACE) (FILLIES) — 7f 16y
3:15 (3:16) (Class 1) 2-Y-O
£13,343 (£5,057; £2,530; £1,261; £632; £317) **Stalls** High

Form — RPR

1 **1** **Sudoor**[30] 2958 2-8-11 .... RHills 1 — 95+
(J L Dunlop) *lw: hld up but in tch: smooth hdwy to join ldrs 3f out: w.w: shkn up to ld over 1f out: hung rt: rdn out* **11/8**[1]

511 **2** *1* **Precocious Star (IRE)**[21] 3216 2-8-11 .... SebSanders 5 — 92
(K R Burke) *trckd ldrs: rdn to chal over 2f out: ev ch whn bmpd jst over 1f out: kpt on but no ex ins fnl f* **5/1**[3]

5421 **3** *¾* **Harvest Joy (IRE)**[19] 3307 2-8-11 .... AlanMunro 7 — 90
(B R Millman) *lw: sn niggled along in rr: rdn 3f out: no impession tl styd on ins fnl f: wnt 3rd cl home: nrst fin* **16/1**

5 **4** *nk* **Onida (IRE)**[27] 3043 2-8-11 .... PhilipRobinson 8 — 90
(C G Cox) *swtg: led: rdn and hrd pressed fr 3f out: hdd and bmpd jst over 1f out: 3rd and hld whn n.m.r on rails ins fnl f* **11/1**

51 **5** *hd* **Dora Explora**[14] 3435 2-8-11 .... RyanMoore 6 — 89
(P W Chapple-Hyam) *lw: trckd ldrs: rdn to chal over 3f out: ev ch 2f out: cl up but hld whn bmpd jst over 1f out* **10/1**

331 **6** *1 ¾* **Majounes Song**[21] 3227 2-8-11 .... RoystonFfrench 2 — 85
(M Johnston) *chsd ldrs: rdn 3f out: kpt on same pce fnl 2f* **10/3**[2]

1530 **7** *3* **Slipasearcher (IRE)**[15] 3415 2-8-11 .... SteveDrowne 3 — 77
(P D Evans) *hld up but in tch: effrt and nt clr run on rails 3f out: sn swtchd lft: no imp after* **16/1**

1m 28.12s (-2.97) **Going Correction** -0.25s/f (Firm) **7** Ran SP% **111.0**
Speed ratings (Par 99):106,104,104,103,103 101,98
CSF £8.01 TOTE £2.00: £1.40, £2.50; EX 7.00.
Owner Hamdan Al Maktoum **Bred** Shadwell Estate Company Limited **Trained** Arundel, W Sussex
■ Stewards' Enquiry : R Hills one-day ban: careless riding (Aug 7)

FOCUS
A decent Listed contest in which five of the seven runners were last-time-out scorers but they finished in something of a heap and the form may not be that strong despite the good time.

NOTEBOOK
Sudoor hails from a stable whose juveniles invariably improve for their debut runs, so the fact that she was able to win on her first outing marked her out as potentially useful. She duly stepped up on that form on her second start, running out an authoritative winner of this Listed contest, and it was no surprise to hear that connections are considering the Fillies' Mile for her later in the season. She will not have any trouble getting the extra furlong, looks a bright prospect and has already been given quotes of around 40-1 for next year's 1000 Guineas. (op 13-8 tchd 7-4)
Precocious Star(IRE), who has improved with every run and was chasing a hat-trick, looked a possibility two furlongs out having travelled well to that point but the winner proved just too good for her. She seemed to get the longer trip well enough. (op 9-2)
Harvest Joy(IRE), who won her maiden at Nottingham last time out, was struggling to go the pace for much of the way but her rider's persistence paid off and she finished well to claim valuable black type. The dam's side of her pedigree has plenty of stamina in it and she should have no trouble getting a mile. (op 14-1)
Onida(IRE), who ran a promising race on her debut behind another John Dunlop-trained filly, was far from disgraced on this step up in class. She should not be troubled to win a maiden. (op 12-1)

Dora Explora found this tougher than the Folkestone maiden she won last time out, but was far from disgraced and should be capable of winning more races at a lower level. (op 8-1)
Majounes Song did not make the running as she had at Yarmouth and lacked the speed required over this trip at this level. She is bred to need at least middle distances next year though, and so the best is surely yet to come. (op 7-2)
Slipasearcher(IRE), the most experienced of these, arguably had the best form on offer, but the step up in trip hardly looked likely to suit this speedily-bred filly, and being denied a clear run three furlongs out made no difference to the result. (op 20-1)

3875 WILLIAMHILLCASINO.COM MINIMUM £1 MAIDEN STKS 1m 14y
3:50 (3:51) (Class 5) 3-4-Y-O **£3,886** (£1,156; £577; £288) **Stalls** High

Form					RPR
	1		**Desert Authority (USA)** 3-9-2 ... LDettori 6 (Saeed Bin Suroor) *w/like: scope: athletic: lw: trckd ldrs in 3rd: smooth prog to ld over 2f out: sn in command: v comf* **6/5**[1]		95+
0-	2	1 ½	**Mulaazem**[293] 5708 3-9-2 ... RHills 1 (M P Tregoning) *w/like: str: bit bkwd: trckd ldrs in 4th: chsd wnr in vain fr 2f out but drew wl clr of remainder* **7/1**[2]		85
00	3	31	**Little Miss Verity**[44] 2532 3-8-11 ... RichardThomas 4 (J A Geake) *led: rdn and hdd over 2f out: sn wknd* **100/1**		8
2333	4	2	**Escape Clause (USA)**[19] 3317 3-9-2 84 ... RyanMoore 3 (Sir Michael Stoute) *w ldr: rdn over 3f out: sn wandered u.p and wknd* **6/5**[1]		9
	5	5	**Hello Deauville (FR)** 3-8-11 ... DaneO'Neill 2 (J Akehurst) *slowly away: nvr on terms w ldng quartet: wknd 3f out* **40/1**[3]		—

1m 41.24s (-2.71) **Going Correction** -0.25s/f (Firm) 5 Ran SP% **106.8**
Speed ratings (Par 103):103,101,70,68,63
CSF £9.94 TOTE £2.10: £1.10, £2.10; EX 5.40.
Owner Godolphin **Bred** Stoneside Stable **Trained** Newmarket, Suffolk

FOCUS
Not a strong maiden but the first two, who are both well bred, came home well clear of the rest and the form has been rated positively.
Escape Clause(USA) Official explanation: vet said colt was found to have an irregular heartbeat post-race

3876 WILLIAM HILL GALWAY PLATE NEXT WEDNESDAY H'CAP 1m 2f 7y
4:25 (4:25) (Class 3) (0-90,87) 3-Y-0+ **£8,096** (£2,408; £1,203; £601) **Stalls** High

Form				RPR
1-63	1		**I Have Dreamed (IRE)**[13] 3490 4-9-1 79 ... IanMongan 4 (T G Mills) *trckd ldr: led over 3f out: rdn over 2f out: wandered ins fnl f but a in command* **3/1**[2]	94+
5302	2	3	**Obrigado (USA)**[15] 3401 6-9-9 87 ... TonyCulhane 3 (W J Haggas) *lw: hld up in 3rd: rdn to chse wnr over 2f out: no further imp* **11/4**[1]	93
5201	3	3	**Brief Goodbye**[17] 3366 6-9-2 80 ... MickyFenton 5 (John Berry) *hld up in 5th: rdn 3f out: wnt 3rd over 1f out: no further imp* **9/2**	80
1122	4	3 ½	**Riley Boys (IRE)**[20] 3241 5-9-8 86 ... EddieAhern 1 (J G Given) *restrained in 4th: rdn 3f out: sn one pce* **4/1**[3]	80
4115	5	5	**Olimpo (FR)**[17] 3365 5-8-13 77 ... AlanMunro 6 (B R Millman) *led at decent pce: hdd ovr 3f out: sn rdn: btn fnl 2f: eased cl home* **4/1**[3]	61

2m 6.80s (-3.44) **Going Correction** -0.25s/f (Firm) 5 Ran SP% **109.8**
Speed ratings (Par 107):103,100,98,95,91
CSF £11.48 TOTE £4.40: £2.40, £1.30; EX 13.40.
Owner T G Mills **Bred** Dr T A Ryan **Trained** Headley, Surrey

FOCUS
Olimpo set a decent pace in this handicap and they finished well strung out. The form should hold up.

NOTEBOOK
I Have Dreamed(IRE), who had disappointed connections on the Polytrack on his last two starts, getting beaten off a mark of 80 both times, came in for good market support and clearly appreciated the switch back to racing on grass. He is now two from two on turf and, open to plenty more improvement, should be kept on side even after reassessment. (op 7-2 tchd 4-1)
Obrigado(USA) had the race run to suit but the unexposed and well-handicapped winner proved too good for him. In hindsight he was probably trying the impossible in giving him 8lb, so there was no disgrace in finishing a clear second. A fairly consistent type, his performance is probably a good guide to the level of the form. (op 3-1 tchd 5-2)
Brief Goodbye found this race run in a different way to the one that he won at Windsor last time, and the stronger pace caught him out. (op 5-1)
Riley Boys(IRE), who is now on a career-high mark, has only once been out of the first two in ten outings at Beverley, but he tends not to fare so well elsewhere. Despite having the race run to suit, he could not get close enough to throw down a challenge. (op 7-2 tchd 9-2 in places)
Olimpo(FR), whose wins earlier in the season came when he was held up, made the running this time, at a pace which proved unsustainable as it turned out. (op 7-2)

3877 WILLIAMHILLGAMES.COM MINIMUM 10P H'CAP 1m 6f
5:00 (5:00) (Class 3) (0-95,84) 3-Y-0 **£8,096** (£2,408; £1,203; £601) **Stalls** Centre

Form				RPR
6652	1		**Doctor Scott**[13] 3483 3-9-7 84 ... RoystonFfrench 2 (M Johnston) *cl up: hrd rdn wl over 2f out: edgd rt over 1f out: styd on wl to ld ins fnl: drvn out* **4/1**[2]	92
-400	2	1 ¾	**Twill (IRE)**[42] 2584 3-9-0 77 ... SteveDrowne 4 (H Morrison) *trck ldrs: led 2f out: sn rdn and veered bdly lft: hdd jst over 1f out: drifted rt but r.o to regain 2nd cl home* **40/1**	83+
2211	3	nk	**Liberate**[1] 3848 3-9-2 79 5ex ... SebSanders 1 (Sir Mark Prescott) *led: rdn and hdd 2f out: regained ld jst over 1f out: no ex whn hdd again ins fnl f* **11/10**[1]	84
2414	4	nk	**Som Tala**[13] 3502 3-9-1 78 ... TedDurcan 9 (M R Channon) *swtg: cl up: rdn 3f out: no imp tl styd on ins fnl f* **15/2**	83
-510	5	¾	**Brigadore (USA)**[27] 3046 3-8-13 76 ... IanMongan 6 (W R Muir) *hld up in last pair: outpcd 3f out: styd on fnl f* **33/1**	80
1-62	6	3 ½	**Los Cabos (IRE)**[12] 3539 3-9-3 80 ... LDettori 7 (J H M Gosden) *trckd ldr: rdn 3f out: wknd 1f out* **9/2**[3]	79
6213	7	1 ¼	**Green Room (FR)**[13] 3497 3-9-5 82 ... EddieAhern 8 (J L Dunlop) *hld up in last pair: rdn 3f out: wknd 1f out* **10/1**	79

3m 2.36s (-2.15) **Going Correction** -0.25s/f (Firm) 7 Ran SP% **112.0**
Speed ratings (Par 104):96,95,94,94,94 92,91
CSF £114.66 CT £282.65 TOTE £5.30: £2.20, £7.10; EX 78.60 Place 6 £74.83, Place 5 £47.56.
Owner Irene White And Helen Bogie **Bred** The Kingwood Partnership **Trained** Middleham Moor, N Yorks

FOCUS
A fair staying handicap featuring some interesting types who were unexposed at the trip. The form looks sound enough, rated around the principals.

NOTEBOOK
Doctor Scott, back against his own age-group, got quite warm but battled on strongly to defy top-weight and confirmed himself a useful stayer in the making. Two miles should be well within his compass and staying events look set to open up new opportunities for him. Goodwood next week is likely to be on the agenda, where he will bid to repeat his half-brother Scott's View's success. (tchd 9-2)
Twill(IRE) had been disappointing so far this season but he returned to form on this step up in trip, and may well have won had he not thrown away his chance by hanging left in the closing stages. He hung left at Newbury last time, too, so is clearly not the most straightforward.
Liberate did not have the easiest of races when landing short odds the previous day at Lingfield, but he did get to compete off a 2lb lower this time. He once again set out to make all and rallied well after being headed, but the impression left was that the race came too soon after the previous day's exertions. He will have to find further improvement to defy his new mark in the high 80s. (op Evens tchd 6-5 in places)
Som Tala, who came in for some support, was 7lb better off at the weights with Liberate compared with when they met at York 13 days earlier, and he managed to reduce the deficit from just over two and a half lengths to a neck. (op 10-1)
Brigadore(USA) stayed on from off the pace and was closest at the finish, but he still looks fairly harshly treated based on what he has achieved. (op 25-1)
Los Cabos(IRE) did not see out the trip as well as the principals and may well be more at home over a mile and a half. (op 5-1)
Green Room(FR) won a weak maiden last month and her handicap mark looks stiff for what she has achieved to date. Official explanation: jockey said filly was unsuited by the good to firm (firm in places) ground (op 9-1 tchd 11-1)
T/Jkpt: £7,708.20 to a £1 stake. Pool: £21,713.50. 2.00 winning tickets. T/Plt: £183.00 to a £1 stake. Pool: £64,180.85. 255.90 winning tickets. T/Qpdt: £36.90 to a £1 stake. Pool: £3,052.20. 61.20 winning tickets. TM

3549 YORK (L-H)
Thursday, July 27

OFFICIAL GOING: Good to firm
Transferred from Doncaster, this was York's first evening meeting since 1971.
Wind: Almost nil Weather: Fine, hot and sunny

3878 FOUR HIGH PETERGATE HOTEL AND SAWFISH SOFTWARE FILLIES' MAIDEN AUCTION STKS 7f
6:00 (6:01) (Class 4) 2-Y-O **£6,541** (£1,946; £972; £485) **Stalls** Low

Form				RPR
04	1		**World's Heroine (IRE)**[12] 3553 2-8-11 ... NickyMackay 9 (G A Butler) *hld up in rr: hdwy over 3f out: led 1f out: pushed out* **11/4**[1]	82
35	2	2 ½	**Dancing Granny**[21] 3227 2-8-9 ... JamieSpencer 15 (M L W Bell) *led tl 1f out: no ex* **9/2**[3]	73
0	3	2 ½	**Falimar**[47] 2461 2-8-9 ... TomEaves 2 (Miss J A Camacho) *chsd ldrs: kpt on same pce fnl 2f* **33/1**	67
3	4	shd	**Cape Dancer (IRE)**[33] 2854 2-8-9 ... PaulMulrennan 12 (J S Wainwright) *trckd ldrs: effrt over 2f out: one pce* **22/1**	66
	5	1 ½	**Onatopp (IRE)** 2-8-9 ... DavidAllan 10 (T D Easterby) *s.i.s: hdwy on outer over 3f out: kpt on fnl f* **25/1**	62
	6	3 ½	**Annual Event (IRE)** 2-8-7 ... RichardMullen 4 (E J O'Neill) *chsd ldrs: outpcd over 2f out: no threat after* **3/1**[2]	51
	7	nk	**By The Edge (IRE)** 2-8-4 ... DaleGibson 11 (T D Barron) *chsd ldrs: wknd 2f out* **33/1**	47
	8	¾	**Juvenescent (USA)** 2-8-4 ... AndrewElliott[(5)] 5 (R D E Woodhouse) *mid-div: rn green and outpcd over 4f out: kpt on fnl 2f* **12/1**	51
42	9	3 ½	**Dispol Splendid (IRE)**[23] 3174 2-8-4 ... PaulFessey 1 (T D Barron) *chsd ldrs: wknd over 2f out* **12/1**	36
	10	shd	**Double Precedent** 2-8-5 ... JoeFanning 7 (M Johnston) *s.i.s: a outpcd* **6/1**	37
60	11	14	**Nihil Petere (IRE)**[14] 3448 2-8-0 ... RoryMoore[(5)] 3 (P T Midgley) *s.i.s: a in rr: bhd and eased fnl 2f* **66/1**	1

1m 25.24s (-0.16) **Going Correction** -0.125s/f (Firm) 11 Ran SP% **115.1**
Speed ratings (Par 93):95,92,89,89,87 83,83,82,78,78 62
CSF £14.04 TOTE £4.10: £1.60, £1.20, £7.50; EX 16.20.
Owner The Distaff Partnership **Bred** Quay Bloodstock **Trained** Blewbury, Oxon

FOCUS
After 2" of water and 1/2" of rain over the previous 11 days the ground was reckoned to be 'fast but no jar and with a very good cover of grass'. There was little strength in depth behind the winner in what was probably a very ordinary maiden. The runner-up is the best guide to the level.

NOTEBOOK
World's Heroine(IRE), awash with sweat and with two handlers in the paddock, came from off the pace to score in most decisive fashion in the end. She will be even better suited by a mile but it remains to be seen how much she can progress. (op 5-2 tchd 3-1, 10-3 in a place)
Dancing Granny, worst drawn, put her below-par Yarmouth effort behind her but in the end she was very much second best. (op 4-1)
Falimar, who made her debut on the All-Weather, shaped much better and should improve again. (op 40-1)
Cape Dancer(IRE), quite keen, seemed to step up on her debut effort a month ago. (op 25-1)
Onatopp(IRE), who has quite a pronounced knee action, had a stable attendant to make sure she gave no problems in the stalls. She made ground from the rear down the outside after a tardy start and can only improve.
Annual Event(IRE), quite a plain filly, was clearly expected to give a good account of herself on her debut but she was tapped for toe when the pace increased and could never get back into the mix. (op 7-2)
Double Precedent, a rangy newcomer, has a round action and after missing the break slightly she never figured. (tchd 13-2)

3879 FIRST TRANSPENNINE EXPRESS H'CAP 6f
6:30 (6:31) (Class 4) (0-80,79) 3-Y-O **£6,477** (£1,927; £963; £481) **Stalls** Centre

Form				RPR
61	1		**Al Qasi (IRE)**[15] 3406 3-9-5 77 ... AdrianMcCarthy 4 (P W Chapple-Hyam) *chsd ldrs: rdn over 2f out: styd on to ld last 100yds* **10/11**[1]	87+
2500	2	¾	**The History Man (IRE)**[12] 3550 3-8-5 70 ... (b) AdeleRothery[(7)] 6 (M W Easterby) *led: t.k.h: hdd and no ex ins last* **40/1**	77
0630	3	shd	**Night In (IRE)**[27] 3042 3-8-11 69 ... (t) KimTinkler 7 (N Tinkler) *chsd ldrs: kpt on wl fnl f* **33/1**	76
5544	4	1	**Sir Orpen (IRE)**[15] 3395 3-9-1 73 ... JamieSpencer 5 (T D Barron) *sn outpcd: reminders after 2: edgd rt and styd on fnl 2f* **11/2**[2]	77+
4113	5	nk	**Bahamian Duke**[29] 2976 3-8-6 64 ... FrancisNorton 12 (K R Burke) *mid-div: hdwy over 2f out: kpt on fnl f* **8/1**[3]	67

3542 **6** 2 **Mulligan's Gold (IRE)**[15] 3397 3-8-13 **71** KDarley 9 68
(T D Easterby) *hld up: hdwy over 2f out: one pce fnl f* **11/1**
0615 **7** 1 **Elusive Warrior (USA)**[23] 3164 3-8-4 **62** PaulHanagan 2 56
(R A Fahey) *s.i.s: hdwy over 2f out: nvr nr ldrs* **25/1**
-216 **8** nk **Sea Salt**[68] 1857 3-9-6 **78** PhillipMakin 3 71
(T D Barron) *chsd ldrs: wknd fnl f* **10/1**
1220 **9** 3 ½ **Maison Dieu**[29] 2976 3-8-1 **64** AndrewElliott(5) 1 47
(E J Alston) *chsd ldrs: lost pl over 1f out* **16/1**
000P **10** 2 ½ **Ocean Of Dreams (FR)**[6] 3708 3-9-7 **79** GrahamGibbons 11 54
(J D Bethell) *a outpcd and in rr* **33/1**

1m 11.25s (-1.31) **Going Correction** -0.125s/f (Firm) **10** Ran SP% **114.4**
Speed ratings (Par 102):103,102,101,100,100 97,96,95,91,87
CSF £57.46 CT £749.22 TOTE £1.90: £1.10, £6.30, £5.00; EX 39.00.
Owner Ziad A Galadari **Bred** T C Butler **Trained** Newmarket, Suffolk

FOCUS
The first five finished in a heap but the form looks very reliable rated through the placed horses.

3880 SKYBET.COM PORTLAND TRIAL H'CAP 5f 89y
7:00 (7:00) (Class 3) (0-90,85) 3-Y-0+ **£8,096** (£2,408; £1,203; £601) Stalls Centre

Form RPR
5102 **1** **Royal Challenge**[20] 3251 5-9-9 **82** TPQueally 8 88
(M H Tompkins) *hld up: hdwy 2f out: r.o to ld post* **11/4**[1]
2414 **2** shd **Kings College Boy**[6] 3715 6-9-1 **74** (v) PaulHanagan 6 80
(R A Fahey) *trckd ldrs: led over 1f out: jst ct* **9/2**[3]
0020 **3** shd **Grigorovitch (IRE)**[10] 3585 4-9-12 **85** TomEaves 7 91
(I Semple) *rrd s: t.k.h: sn in tch: swtchd outside over 1f out: styd on wl: jst failed* **10/1**
-300 **4** 1 ¼ **Mimi Mouse**[41] 2624 4-9-9 **82** DavidAllan 1 83
(T D Easterby) *w ldr: kpt on same pce fnl f* **15/2**
2524 **5** hd **Pawan (IRE)**[14] 3449 6-8-7 **73** (b) AnnStokell(7) 3 73
(Miss A Stokell) *s.i.s: sn chsng ldrs: edgd lft and kpt on same pce fnl f* **12/1**
0013 **6** shd **Matsunosuke**[6] 3715 4-9-7 **80** JamieSpencer 2 80
(A B Coogan) *trckd ldrs: effrt over 1f out: kpt on same pce* **7/2**[2]
0006 **7** nk **Happy As Larry (USA)**[14] 3459 4-8-12 **71** (bt) FrancisNorton 5 70
(T J Pitt) *led tl over 1f out: fdd* **11/2**

63.04 secs (-1.96) **7** Ran SP% **111.0**
CSF £14.37 CT £99.98 TOTE £3.40: £2.30, £1.90; EX 10.80.
Owner Killarney Glen **Bred** Capt A L Smith-Maxwell **Trained** Newmarket, Suffolk
■ A new distance in readiness for the Portland itself at the St Leger meeting which will be run here in September.

FOCUS
Ordinary form and the whole field finished in a bunch.

NOTEBOOK
Royal Challenge, in fine form at present, came from off the pace to get up right on the line. (op 7-2)
Kings College Boy continues in top form and after hitting the front plenty soon enough, in the end he just missed out. (op 6-1)
Grigorovitch(IRE), something of a character, was on his back legs when the stalls opened. Taking a keen grip, when pulled wide he really picked up and would have made it in one more stride. He has plenty of ability but is not easy to predict. (op 8-1)
Mimi Mouse, down 3lb this time, was having her first outing for six weeks after bleeding from the nose. This was a much more encouraging effort. (op 7-1)
Pawan(IRE), an habitual slow starter, has not won for a year and a half now. This was a good effort over a trip short of his best.
Matsunosuke, who looked at his very best, for some reason or other did not really fire and never looked like picking up sufficiently to prove a real threat. (tchd 10-3 and 4-1)
Happy As Larry(USA), with the blinkers back on, was a major mover on the morning line. He took them along but in truth put up little fight when tackled. (op 9-2)

3881 SMITH BROTHERS CONDITIONS STKS 1m
7:30 (7:30) (Class 3) 4-Y-0+ **£10,363** (£3,083; £1,540; £769) Stalls Low

Form RPR
2403 **1** **Momtic (IRE)**[19] 3313 5-8-9 106 AlanMunro 4 108
(W Jarvis) *trckd ldrs: effrt over 4f out: chal over 2f out: led over 1f out: hld on wl* **10/11**[1]
3660 **2** 1 **Kings Point (IRE)**[12] 3559 5-8-12 102 PaulHanagan 5 109
(R A Fahey) *hld up: hdwy over 3f out: plld outside over 1f out: nt qckn ins last* **12/1**
-640 **3** 1 ½ **Rocamadour**[68] 1840 4-8-9 110 TonyCulhane 2 103
(M R Channon) *led early: chsd ldr: led over 2f out: sn rdn: hdd over 1f out: unable qckn* **5/2**[2]
2602 **4** 7 **Byron Bay**[22] 3191 4-8-9 84 TomEaves 1 86
(I Semple) *sn led: clr over 6f out: hdd over 2f out: wknd over 1f out* **28/1**
-256 **5** 22 **Vortex**[25] 3134 7-9-2 109 (t) JamieSpencer 3 43+
(Miss Gay Kelleway) *hld up: effrt over 3f out: nt clr run and swtchd outside over 2f out: nvr a threat: lost pl over 1f out: heavily eased towards fin* **5/1**[3]

1m 36.95s (-2.55) **Going Correction** -0.05s/f (Good) **5** Ran SP% **108.8**
Speed ratings (Par 107):110,109,107,100,78
CSF £12.22 TOTE £1.90: £1.20, £4.20; EX 9.20.
Owner Heath, Keenan & Verrier **Bred** Janic Thoroughbreds **Trained** Newmarket, Suffolk

FOCUS
A breakneck gallop and the winner thoroughly deserved this first success this year. The runner-up sets the standard.

NOTEBOOK
Momtic(IRE), clear best on official figures, made the most of a golden opportunity but his trainer may struggle to find other openings for him unless he looks abroad. (tchd Evens in places)
Kings Point(IRE), who had 7lb to find with the winner, could not dominate this time but he stuck to his task and deserves credit. He is another rated over 100 who will struggle for winning opportunities. (op 10-1 tchd 16-1)
Rocamadour, rated 4lb ahead of the winner, was having his first outing for over two months. After hitting the front, he was firmly put in his place over a trip that is his minimum now. (tchd 9-4)
Byron Bay, who had an impossible task, set a breakneck gallop and it was just a question of time before he ran out of petrol. (op 25-1)
Vortex ran very flat after his abortive trip to America and in the end his rider was content to let him complete in his own time. Official explanation: jockey said gelding ran flat (op 6-1)

3882 GARROWBY H'CAP 1m 4f
8:00 (8:00) (Class 2) (0-100,99) 3-Y-0 **£12,954** (£3,854; £1,926; £962) Stalls Centre

Form RPR
2005 **1** **Nihal (IRE)**[13] 3477 3-8-5 **83** JoeFanning 2 93+
(M Johnston) *trckd ldrs: c centre over 4f out: led over 2f out: edgd lft ins fnl f: hld on wl* **9/1**[3]
-121 **2** ½ **Futun**[19] 3292 3-9-5 **97** NickyMackay 3 107+
(L M Cumani) *t.k.h: led after 1f: styd far side over 4f out: hung rt over 3f out: hdd over 2f out: carried lft and no ex ins last* **4/5**[1]
2101 **3** 1 **Scotland Yard (UAE)**[17] 3359 3-8-7 **85** KDarley 4 93
(D E Pipe) *led 1f: trckd ldrs: c wd over 4f out: swtchd lft over 2f out: styd on same pce fnl f* **7/4**[2]
-030 **4** 17 **Auction Room (USA)**[39] 2679 3-8-3 **81** PaulHanagan 1 76+
(B W Hills) *trckd ldrs: drvn along over 6f out: styd far side over 4f out: nvr a real threat: lost pl and eased over 1f out* **16/1**

2m 32.01s (-0.39) **Going Correction** -0.05s/f (Good) **4** Ran SP% **107.8**
Speed ratings (Par 106):99,98,98,86
CSF £17.09 TOTE £7.80; EX 12.90.
Owner Jaber Abdullah **Bred** Mrs C L Weld **Trained** Middleham Moor, N Yorks

FOCUS
The runner-up would not settle in front and they ended up all over the shop in the home straight. The gallop was not strong and the third looks the key to the overall value of the form.

NOTEBOOK
Nihal(IRE), who looked to have come to herself beforehand, proved suited by the step up in trip and in the end simply would not be denied. She will not be resting on her laurels. (op 7-1 tchd 10-1)
Futun, lit up, gave his rider a torrid time. He hung out to join the other two racing wide and carried left by the winner inside the last, to his credit he fought back all the way to the line. He may need to be treated with kid gloves after this. (op 5-6 tchd Evens and 10-11 in places)
Scotland Yard(UAE), who has changed stables, was done no favours when Futun cut across his bows to take charge. Brought wide in the home straight, he had his ground taken and had to switch inside the first two. He stayed on all the way to the line and no doubt will be seen over hurdles soon rather than later. All his best efforts have come in small fields. (op 2-1)
Auction Room(USA), again up in trip, was in trouble before the home turn. She elected to remain alone on the far side and was left further and further behind. After this she has an awful lot to prove. (op 14-1 tchd 12-1)

3883 SGT PEPPER'S H'CAP 1m 208y
8:30 (8:30) (Class 5) (0-75,72) 3-Y-0+ **£5,505** (£1,637; £818; £408) Stalls Low

Form RPR
5122 **1** **Billy One Punch**[12] 3519 4-9-8 **66** TonyCulhane 1 75+
(G G Margarson) *trckd ldrs: led 3f out: hrd rdn and hld on towards fin* **7/2**[1]
-066 **2** ½ **Paparaazi (IRE)**[12] 3519 4-9-12 **70** PaulHanagan 4 78
(R A Fahey) *chsd ldrs: kpt on wl fnl f: no ex towards fin* **12/1**
0214 **3** nk **She's Our Lass (IRE)**[11] 3570 5-9-7 **68** DanielTudhope(3) 6 75
(D Carroll) *in tch: hdwy over 2f out: styd on wl: nt qckn ins last* **4/1**[2]
0624 **4** 1 **Bright Sun (IRE)**[9] 3621 5-9-13 **71** (t) KimTinkler 2 76
(N Tinkler) *led tl 3f out: kpt on same pce fnl f* **10/1**
0303 **5** nk **Suits Me**[16] 3375 3-9-3 **70** GrahamGibbons 7 73
(J J Quinn) *chsd ldrs: styd on same pce appr fnl f* **12/1**
0650 **6** 3 **Flighty Fellow (IRE)**[7] 3688 6-10-0 **72** (p) TomEaves 13 70
(Miss J A Camacho) *hld up in mid-div: effrt over 2f out: nvr nr to chal* **14/1**
2506 **7** nk **Tedsdale Mac**[5] 3747 7-8-11 **62** SuzzanneFrance(7) 3 60
(N Bycroft) *mid-div: effrt over 2f out: nvr a threat* **16/1**
0411 **8** 1 ¼ **Inside Story (IRE)**[11] 3570 4-9-8 **66** 6ex (b) PaulMulrennan 9 61
(M W Easterby) *hld up in last pl: effrt on inner over 2f out: nvr nr ldrs* **7/1**[3]
0000 **9** nk **Typhoon Ginger (IRE)**[4] 3762 11-8-7 **56** AndrewElliott(5) 5 51
(G Woodward) *hld up in rr: effrt on wd outside 3f out: nvr nr ldrs* **12/1**
60-4 **10** nk **Sam's Secret**[13] 3500 4-9-12 **70** DeanMcKeown 8 64
(S Parr) *stdd and swtchd lft s: nvr a factor* **12/1**
6420 **11** 1 ¾ **Luck In Running (USA)**[22] 3202 3-9-2 **69** JoeFanning 12 59
(M Johnston) *chsd ldrs: lost pl over 1f out* **8/1**

1m 52.72s (1.73) **Going Correction** -0.05s/f (Good)
WFA 3 from 4yo+ 9lb **11** Ran SP% **118.2**
Speed ratings (Par 103):90,89,89,88,88 85,85,84,83,83 82
CSF £46.63 CT £180.50 TOTE £4.40: £1.80, £4.90, £2.10; EX 84.30 Place 6 £110.37, Place 5 £56.45.
Owner Norcroft Park Stud **Bred** Norcroft Park Stud, And A J Hollis **Trained** Newmarket, Suffolk

FOCUS
An ordinary handicap and a tactical affair in which the winner was always in the right place and had first run. Despite that the form looks reliable rated around the runner-up, fourth and fifth.
Inside Story(IRE) Official explanation: trainer had no explanation for the poor form shown
Sam's Secret Official explanation: jockey said filly lost a near-fore shoe
T/Plt: £116.20 to a £1 stake. Pool: £64,264.00. 403.60 winning tickets. T/Qpdt: £60.30 to a £1 stake. Pool: £3,990.40. 48.90 winning tickets. WG

3884 - 3887a (Foreign Racing) - See Raceform Interactive

2844 ASCOT (R-H)
Friday, July 28

OFFICIAL GOING: Good
Wind: Nil Weather: Sunny, very warm

3888 JOHN GUEST BROWN JACK STKS (H'CAP) 2m
2:05 (2:06) (Class 2) (0-100,90) 3-Y-0+ **£16,192** (£4,817; £2,407; £1,202) Stalls High

Form RPR
1245 **1** **Lightning Strike (GER)**[35] 2804 3-8-9 **88** JoeFanning 6 98
(T G Mills) *led for 1f: trckd ldr: led over 2f out: in command over 1f out: drvn out* **9/4**[1]
0010 **2** 1 ¼ **Nordwind (IRE)**[20] 3294 5-9-9 **85** AlanMunro 9 94
(W R Swinburn) *t.k.h: trckd ldng pair: rdn to chse wnr 2f out: no imp fnl f* **12/1**
-540 **3** 1 ½ **Mirjan (IRE)**[27] 3078 10-10-0 **90** (b) JimCrowley 8 97
(L Lungo) *settled in midfield: outpcd and rdn over 3f out: styd on fnl 2f to take 3rd nr last strides* **12/1**
1265 **4** nk **Wise Owl**[15] 3446 4-9-7 **83** JimmyQuinn 3 90
(J Pearce) *hld up in last in steadily run r: prog 4f out: rdn to chse ldng pair over 1f out: no ex fnl f: too much to do* **28/1**
4250 **5** 3 **Mceldowney**[13] 3533 4-9-5 **86** GregFairley(5) 2 89
(M Johnston) *settled in midfield: rdn 7f out: lost tch w ldrs 4f out: kpt on u.p fr over 2f out: no ch* **8/1**
-100 **6** 1 **Mikao (IRE)**[27] 3078 5-9-10 **86** GeorgeBaker 4 88
(M H Tompkins) *trckd ldng pair: rdn over 2f out: nt qckn: wknd fnl f* **7/1**[3]
0613 **7** 15 **Kames Park (IRE)**[34] 2850 4-9-11 **87** TomEaves 5 71
(I Semple) *s.s: hld up in last pair: rdn over 4f out: sn lost tch: t.o* **12/1**
-306 **8** ½ **Escayola (IRE)**[27] 3078 6-9-8 **84** (b) TonyCulhane 1 67
(W J Haggas) *led after 1f and set stdy pce: increased tempo fr over 4f out: hdd & wknd rapidly over 2f out* **9/2**[2]

The Form Book, Raceform Ltd, Compton, RG20 6NL

0131 **9** *29* **Mudawin (IRE)**[21] 3256 5-9-12 **88**........................ JohnEgan 7 36
(Jane Chapple-Hyam) *hld up in rr: rdn 5f out: lost tch over 3f out: no ch after: eased over 1f out: t.o: lame* **8/1**

3m 32.32s (-4.18) **Going Correction** -0.025s/f (Good)
WFA 3 from 4yo+ 17lb **9** Ran SP% **110.2**
Speed ratings (Par 109):109,108,107,107,105 105,97,97,83
CSF £28.61 CT £245.29 TOTE £2.80: £1.50, £4.30, £3.10; EX 48.30 Trifecta £370.60 Pool £1,137.92 - 2.18 winning units..

Owner T G Mills **Bred** Dr Chr Berglar **Trained** Headley, Surrey

FOCUS
Not the strongest race for the class, run at a modest early pace, but the form looks sound enough and the winner remains open to further improvement over this sort of distance.

NOTEBOOK
Lightning Strike(GER), fifth in the Queen's Vase last time and the sole three-year-old in the line-up, justified strong support in the betting ring with a ready success. He lacks a real turn of foot, but he clearly stays very well, and should be high on confidence again after this. His connections have plenty of options now they know he stays, which reportedly may include a shot at the Melbourne Cup, and it will be very interesting to see where he is pitched in next. (op 5-2 tchd 2-1)

Nordwind(IRE) did well to finish as close as he did on this step up in trip, as he pulled hard through the early stages. He is somewhat inconsistent these days, but on this evidence is well worth another chance over this distance. (op 11-1)

Mirjan(IRE), eighth in the Northumberland Plate last time, was doing his best towards the finish and really would have appreciated a stronger early pace. He retains all of his ability, and can be rated a little better than the bare form, but is never one for win-only purposes. (op 10-1)

Wise Owl ◆ made up his ground quickly when asked to improve approaching the turn for home, and looked a threat when switching wide for his challenge in the home straight, but ultimately had no more to give inside the final furlong. This was a good effort considering he was held up off just an average early gallop and he looks weighted to win at present when things go more his way. (op 25-1)

Mceldowney was being ridden a fair way out and merely kept on at his own pace in the home straight. He may well be in need of a break now.

Mikao(IRE), down in class, again ran below expectations and has not really gone on as could have been expected after winning on his seasonal bow in April. (op 8-1)

Escayola(IRE) failed to improve for the switch to front-running tactics and continues to frustrate. Official explanation: jockey said gelding had no more to give (tchd 4-1)

Mudawin(IRE) Official explanation: vet said gelding returned lame

3889 LONDON CLUBS INTERNATIONAL STKS (HERITAGE H'CAP) 1m (S)

2:40 (2:42) (Class 2) 3-Y-O

£46,740 (£13,995; £6,997; £3,502; £1,747; £877) **Stalls** Low

Form RPR

3102 **1** **Dunelight (IRE)**[14] 3491 3-9-2 **95**........................(v) PhilipRobinson 15 111
(C G Cox) *racd towards far side: mde all: clr of two rivals over 2f out: in n.d after: unchal: 1st of 3 in gp* **7/1**[3]

4225 **2** *5* **Easy Air**[14] 3493 3-9-1 **94**........................ LDettori 13 100+
(E A L Dunlop) *racd towards far side: chsd wnr: lft bhd fr over 2f out but stl clr of nr side gp: 2nd of 3 in gp* **4/1**[2]

0205 **3** *2 1/2* **Military Cross**[15] 3443 3-9-2 **95**........................ TonyCulhane 8 93
(W J Haggas) *hld up nr side: trckd ldrs gng easily over 2f out: led gp wl over 1f out: r.o wl: no ch w far side but 1st of 13 in gp* **9/1**

3-04 **4** *1* **Jamieson Gold (IRE)**[20] 3317 3-8-9 **88**........................ MichaelHills 2 84
(B W Hills) *trckd nr side ldrs: effrt 2f out: chsd ldr 1f out: r.o but no ch: 2nd of 13 in gp* **25/1**

011 **5** *3/4* **Royal Oath (USA)**[13] 3532 3-9-0 **93**........................(t) JimmyFortune 10 87
(J H M Gosden) *hld up in rr nr side: drvn over 2f out: styd on u.p fr over 1f out: nrst fin and no ch: 3rd of 13 in gp* **3/1**[1]

0521 **6** *nk* **Tumbleweed Glory (IRE)**[16] 3404 3-7-10 **82**........................ KMay(7) 11 76
(B J Meehan) *hld up on outer of nr side: prog 3f out: pressed ldrs over 1f out : fdd ins fnl f: 4th of 13 in gp* **16/1**

3255 **7** *3/4* **Rubenstar (IRE)**[6] 3740 3-8-2 **81**........................ JimmyQuinn 14 73+
(M H Tompkins) *swtchd fr wd draw to r against nr side rail: last pair tl 2f out: gd prog over 1f out: nvr nrr: no ch: 5th of 13 in gp* **66/1**

2623 **8** *3/4* **Lunar Express (USA)**[9] 3643 3-8-4 **83**........................ NickyMackay 3 76+
(W J Haggas) *wl in tch nr side: effrt and cl up over 1f out: wkng whn n.m.r ins fnl f: 6th of 13 in gp* **16/1**

1460 **9** *1 1/2* **Yarqus**[38] 2721 3-9-7 **100**........................ SebSanders 16 87
(C E Brittain) *racd towards far side: a last of trio: wknd 2f out but stl beat 7 rivals on nr side* **33/1**

221- **10** *nk* **Ordnance Row**[265] 6249 3-8-11 **90**........................ RyanMoore 4 76
(R Hannon) *pressed nr side ldr: led gp over 2f out to wl over 1f out: wknd fnl f: 7th of 13 in gp* **10/1**

3505 **11** *3* **Zato (IRE)**[14] 3491 3-9-3 **96**........................ TedDurcan 1 75
(M R Channon) *dwlt: hld up towards rr nr side: effrt over 2f out: wknd over 1f out: no ch* **20/1**

00-0 **12** *1* **Doctor Dash**[91] 1268 3-9-0 **93**........................ LPKeniry 12 70
(D R C Elsworth) *racd on outer of nr side gp: in tch: hanging and wknd over 2f out* **50/1**

10-0 **13** *3* **Playtotheaudience**[20] 3317 3-8-9 **88**........................ PaulHanagan 9 58
(R A Fahey) *racd nr side: a wl in rr: wknd 2f out* **100/1**

215 **14** *2 1/2* **Incidentally (IRE)**[20] 3318 3-8-5 **84**........................ EddieAhern 7 48
(R Hannon) *w nr side ldrs: rdn 1/2-way: wknd over 2f out* **25/1**

130 **15** *3/4* **Against The Grain**[27] 3079 3-8-6 **85**........................ JoeFanning 6 47
(M Johnston) *mde most nr side to over 2f out: wknd rapidly* **11/1**

5506 **16** *3 1/2* **Renderoc (USA)**[10] 3606 3-7-12 **77** oh1........................(p) FrancisFerris 5 31
(J S Moore) *trckd nr side ldrs: rdn over 3f out: sn wknd* **50/1**

1m 39.83s (-1.97) **Going Correction** +0.025s/f (Good) **16** Ran SP% **118.5**
Speed ratings (Par 106):110,105,102,101,100 100,99,98,97,97 94,93,90,87,86 83
CSF £31.35 CT £270.35 TOTE £8.60: £2.00, £1.20, £2.60, £4.20; EX 36.00 Trifecta £234.40 Pool £1,875.76 - 5.68 winning units..

Owner Mr and Mrs P Hargreaves **Bred** D And Ms B Egan **Trained** Lambourn, Berks

■ Stewards' Enquiry : K May caution: careless riding

FOCUS
A strong three-year-old handicap, which totally contradicted the apparent draw bias of the recent Royal Meeting, with the three racing down the middle of the track at a real advantage. There's a chance the stands' side group rather ignored the trio racing wide, and they could be significantly beter than the bare form, but the winner could hardly have been more impressive.

NOTEBOOK
Dunelight(IRE) ◆ comfortably made all, racing down the middle of the track, and confirmed that he is a fast-improving young handicapper. Obviously his canny rider's decision to keep to his draw paid dividends, but the manner of this success suggests he would have most likely still have prevailed even if racing on the stands' side. He is in the Totesport Mile at Goodwood, in which he would carry only a 3lb penalty, but his trainer was reluctant to commit him to that event, as that is on a very different track and may well come too soon. (op 9-1)

Easy Air, fifth against his elders from an unfavourable draw in the Bunbury Cup last time, was at an advantage this time in keeping to the middle of the track and posted another solid effort in defeat on ground that probably turned against him. He never really looked like getting to the winner back over this extra furlong, however, and the jury is still out as to his optimum trip. (op 7-2 tchd 10-3)

Military Cross emerged the best of those to race on the stands' side and ran another sound race on this drop back to a mile. He just looks to be in the Handicapper's grip at present, but should continue to pay his way, and does deserve a change of fortune.

Jamieson Gold(IRE) posted another improved effort in defeat and is clearly now coming back to form. He can build on this while his yard remains in decent form

Royal Oath(USA) ◆, bidding for the hat-trick from an 8lb higher mark, was doing all of his best work towards the finish in this much better race and deserves credit considering his inexperience. He looked to need every yard of this trip and, with further improvement still likely, it would be a surprise if we had seen the best of him just yet. (tchd 7-2)

Tumbleweed Glory(IRE), raised 6lb for winning on the All-Weather last time, posted a sound effort yet failed to see out the race all that well.

Rubenstar(IRE) ◆ was dropped across the back of the field and held up on the rail, when in hindsight he would have been much better off keeping to his high draw and racing with the small group down the centre of the track. He did well to finish as close in the circumstances and can be rated better than the bare form.

Yarqus, whose last two outings have been at the top level, was never really on terms racing with the first two down the middle of the track and was well held under top weight.

Ordnance Row ◆, who had some fair form as a juvenile last term and was making his seasonal bow after a 265-day break, shaped as though the race would be of real benefit and is probably capable of better. (op 11-1)

Against The Grain was given an aggressive ride over this longer trip and has to rate a non-stayer. (op 10-1)

3890 NATIONAL BANK OF DUBAI CUP (HERITAGE H'CAP) 1m 4f

3:15 (3:15) (Class 2) (0-105,98) 3-Y-0+

£46,740 (£13,995; £6,997; £3,502; £1,747; £877) **Stalls** High

Form RPR

616 **1** **Young Mick**[20] 3294 4-9-5 **93**........................(v) RobertWinston 10 102
(G G Margarson) *trckd ldng trio tl wnt 2nd over 2f out: rdn to ld over 1f: edgd rt ins fnl f: styd on wl* **10/1**

2-05 **2** *1 1/4* **Royal Jet**[14] 3501 4-8-11 **85**........................ JohnEgan 7 92
(M R Channon) *plld hrd early: hld up in 8th: rdn and prog over 2f out: styd on fnl f to take 2nd last strides* **16/1**

5-62 **3** *hd* **Glistening**[34] 2848 4-9-10 **98**........................ LDettori 8 105
(L M Cumani) *settled in 6th: rdn fr over 4f out: effrt u.p 2f out: styd on to take 3rd last strides* **2/1**[1]

0301 **4** *shd* **Consular**[20] 3294 4-9-8 **96**........................ PhilipRobinson 1 103
(M A Jarvis) *led: drvn and hdd by wnr over 1f out but clr of rest: one pce and lost 2 pls last strides* **4/1**[2]

1441 **5** *1 1/2* **Croon**[8] 3666 4-8-6 **80** 6ex........................ SteveDrowne 9 85
(H Morrison) *hld up in 5th: gng wl enough 3f out: shkn up and nt qckn 2f out: no imp after* **9/1**

0112 **6** *1/2* **Gringo**[14] 3501 4-8-10 **84**........................ KDarley 4 88
(B W Hills) *hld up in 9th: rdn 3f out: kpt on fnl 2f: nvr rchd ldrs* **11/2**[3]

4554 **7** *2* **Wingman (IRE)**[14] 3490 4-8-11 **85**........................ EddieAhern 3 86
(J W Hills) *hld up in 10th: rdn over 3f out: struggling after: plugged on over 1f out* **16/1**

4013 **8** *1 1/2* **Instructor**[2] 3840 5-8-7 **81**........................ PaulHanagan 6 79
(R A Fahey) *hld up in 7th: rdn and no imp wl over 2f out: n.d after* **25/1**

3200 **9** *1/2* **Crime Scene (IRE)**[15] 3443 3-8-6 **92**........................ JoeFanning 2 89
(M Johnston) *pressed ldr to over 2f out: wkng whn hmpd jst over 1f out* **9/1**

50-0 **10** *7* **Hawridge Prince**[101] 1071 6-9-5 **93**........................ AlanMunro 5 79
(B R Millman) *hld up in last: detached and struggling over 3f out: bhd after* **40/1**

0660 **11** *8* **Bahar Shumaal (IRE)**[20] 3313 4-9-4 **92**........................ SebSanders 11 65
(C E Brittain) *trckd ldng pair to over 2f out: wknd rapidly* **50/1**

2m 32.8s (-0.20) **Going Correction** -0.025s/f (Good)
WFA 3 from 4yo+ 12lb **11** Ran SP% **117.8**
Speed ratings (Par 109):99,98,98,97,96 96,95,94,93,89 83
CSF £155.39 CT £451.21 TOTE £8.60: £2.10, £4.00, £1.40; EX 216.50 Trifecta £494.10 Pool £2,157.74 - 3.10 winning units..

Owner M F Kentish **Bred** M F Kentish **Trained** Newmarket, Suffolk

■ Stewards' Enquiry : L Dettori two-day ban: careless riding (Aug 8-9)

FOCUS
A decent handicap for the class, but run at just a moderate early pace, and those coming from off the pace were at a disadvantage. The highly-progressive winner continues on an upwards curve.

NOTEBOOK
Young Mick proved at an advantage in racing handily, but still showed a neat turn of foot to settle the issue after passing the two-furlong marker, and readily confirmed his recent course and distance form with Glistening despite racing on 4lb worse terms. He really has been an incredibly progressive horse this season, indeed he is currently rated 39lb higher than when getting off the mark in an All-Weather claimer at the start of the year, and is evidently still improving. While he now picks up a only a 4lb penalty for the Ebor at York next month, his stamina for that longer trip must still be taken on trust. His trainer stated that the Cox Plate and Melbourne Cup were possible future targets and it would be fascinating to see him travel for either of those events. (op 9-1)

Royal Jet ◆ was keeping on stoutly towards the finish and did really well considering he raced too freely under restraint through the early parts. A stronger pace would have been much more to his liking and, on this evidence, his season may just be about to kick off.

Glistening ◆, up 3lb for his narrow defeat over course and distance to Young Mick at the Royal Meeting 34 days previously, was being hard ridden by Dettori before the turn for home and was unsuited by the modest early pace. He kept on in the manner of a horse who needs a stiffer test, and it was no surprise that he remains the ante-post favourite for the Ebor next month, as he really does appeal as the ideal type for that event. However, it must be noted that he has only a maiden success to his name thus far. (op 7-4 tchd 9-4 in places)

Consular, raised 6lb for winning the Old Newton Cup at Haydock last time, got very much the run of the race out in front and can have no excuses. He remains in good form. (op 5-1)

Croon looked a brief threat at the top of the straight, but he failed to quicken when it really mattered and was found out by his penalty for winning a much lesser race at Epsom eight days previously. (op 8-1)

Gringo ◆ has to rate better than the bare form as he was unsuited by being held up off the modest early pace and kept on all too late in the day. (op 6-1 tchd 13-2)

Wingman(IRE) was another who was at a disadvantage in racing off the early pace and is capable of a little better.

3891 INDEPENDENT NEWSPAPER EBF VALIANT STKS (LISTED RACE) (F&M) 1m (R)

3:50 (3:51) (Class 1) 3-Y-O+

£22,712 (£8,608; £4,308; £2,148; £1,076; £540) **Stalls** High

Form RPR

3-01 **1** **Wasseema (USA)**[49] [2406] 3-8-7 93 .... RHills 3 114+
(Sir Michael Stoute) *mde all: clr 3f out: rdn over 1f out: galloped on strly: impressive* **11/2**

4- **2** *7* **Highway To Glory (IRE)**[117] 3-8-7 94 .... OscarUrbina 9 98
(M Botti) *chsd ldrs: rdn wl over 2f out: effrt to go 2nd over 1f out: no imp on wnr* **25/1**

-413 **3** *½* **Squaw Dance**[9] [3661] 4-9-1 100 .... KerrinMcEvoy 10 99
(W J Haggas) *chsd wnr after 2f: no imp over 2f out: lost 2nd over 1f out: kpt on* **4/1**[3]

-035 **4** *1 ½* **Expensive**[10] [3627] 3-8-7 101 .... EddieAhern 4 93
(C F Wall) *hld up in midfield: prog over 3f out: drvn over 2f out: no hdwy over 1f out: one pce* **10/3**[2]

-241 **5** *3* **Star Cluster**[20] [3316] 3-8-11 102 .... RichardHughes 6 90
(H R A Cecil) *pushed along in midfield over 5f out: drvn over 2f out: no prog and sn btn* **9/4**[1]

2621 **6** *1* **Distinctive Look (IRE)**[35] [2815] 3-8-7 83 ....(t) RyanMoore 5 84
(B J Meehan) *off the pce in rr: last over 3f out: no ch after* **14/1**

0040 **7** *1 ¼* **My Amalie (IRE)**[20] [3316] 3-8-7 90 .... SebSanders 7 81
(C E Brittain) *sn drvn and outpcd in rr: a struggling to stay in tch: no ch fnl 2f* **33/1**

-442 **8** *22* **Little Miss Gracie**[29] [3002] 4-9-1 98 ....(b[1]) DaneO'Neill 8 33
(A B Haynes) *chsd wnr for 2f: prom tl wknd rapidly over 3f out: t.o* **11/1**

1201 **P** **Whitethorne**[20] [3289] 4-9-1 78 .... PaulHanagan 1 —
(R A Fahey) *reluctant to r: sn t.o: p.u after 3f: lame* **33/1**

1m 39.4s (-2.70) **Going Correction** -0.025s/f (Good)
WFA 3 from 4yo 8lb **9** Ran **SP% 114.0**
Speed ratings (Par 111):112,105,104,103,100 99,97,75,—
CSF £128.17 TOTE £5.60: £1.70, £6.40, £1.80; EX 170.40 Trifecta £777.00 Pool £2,101.44 - 1.92 winning units..
Owner Hamdan Al Maktoum **Bred** Swettenham Stud And Ben Sangster **Trained** Newmarket, Suffolk

FOCUS
A fair line-up for the class, and although the sixth limits the form overall the winner could not have been much more impressive in making all. She is well worth her place in a Group race.

NOTEBOOK
Wasseema(USA) ◆, who refused to go into the stalls on her intended start at the Royal Meeting, had the aid of earplugs this time and gave no trouble. She made all to score most impressively and looked to have plenty up her sleeve on passing the line. She had been somewhat disappointing to date, having been well-touted during the off-season, but is clearly now finding her feet and her trainer has few peers at improving fillies. Another rise in class is now well deserved and she can hold her own in Group company, as she looked full value for the winning margin. (op 7-2)
Highway To Glory(IRE), making her British debut after a 117-day break, was no match for the winner yet turned in a very respectable effort in defeat. She is clearly at home in this class, looked to enjoy the ground, and is entitled to improve for the run. (op 20-1)
Squaw Dance, down in class, ran her race in defeat and has developed into a consistent filly. She is in-foal to Dubawi and will no doubt be off the paddocks before too long. (op 5-1)
Expensive failed to improve for this drop back to a more suitable trip. She is proving a little frustrating to follow now. (op 7-2)
Star Cluster, under a penalty for her Listed success last time, was never really travelling all that well and failed to confirm her recent Sandown form with Expensive. She has a little to prove now. (op 5-2 tchd 11-4)
Whitethorne, currently in-foal, was later found to have finished lame. Official explanation: vet said filly pulled up lame

3892 JOHN GUEST EBF MAIDEN STKS 7f

4:25 (4:26) (Class 4) 2-Y-O **£6,477** (£1,927; £963; £481) **Stalls** Low

Form RPR

1 **One To Follow** 2-9-3 .... PhilipRobinson 7 80
(C G Cox) *pressed ldng pair: shuffled along fr 1/2-way: looked in trble 2f out: rallied over 1f out: led jst ins fnl f: styd on wl* **12/1**

2 *nk* **Big Robert** 2-9-3 .... KerrinMcEvoy 6 80
(W R Muir) *s.s: in tch: stdy prog on outer fr 3f out: rdn to chal 1f out: nt qckn but kpt on nr fin* **20/1**

0 **3** *shd* **King Joshua (IRE)**[35] [2821] 2-9-3 .... LDettori 8 79
(G A Butler) *hld up in rr: prog 2f out: effrt to chal 1f out: pressed wnr after: hld last 100yds and lost 2nd nr fin* **7/1**[2]

4 *2* **Record Breaker (IRE)** 2-9-3 .... JoeFanning 5 74
(M Johnston) *pressed ldr: led over 2f out to over 1f out: cose up ins fnl f: wknd last 100yds* **9/4**[1]

5 *1 ¼* **Minos (IRE)** 2-9-3 .... RichardHughes 9 71
(R Hannon) *racd on outer: in tch: stdy prog gng wl to ld over 1f out: hdd jst ins fnl f: wknd rapidly* **15/2**[3]

4 **6** *1 ¼* **Mesbaah (IRE)**[27] [3083] 2-9-3 .... RHills 3 68
(M A Jarvis) *hld up in rr: nt clr run 2f out: no ch after: styd on last 150yds* **9/4**[1]

7 *5* **Daylami Dreams** 2-9-3 .... JohnEgan 4 56+
(J S Moore) *dwlt: in tch: wl outpcd 2f out: eased whn no ch fnl f* **25/1**

8 *1 ½* **Majuro (IRE)** 2-9-3 .... TedDurcan 1 52
(M R Channon) *s.i.s: urged along in last pair early: lost tch over 2f out: no ch after* **20/1**

65 **9** *13* **Ambrosiano**[16] [3407] 2-9-3 .... MickyFenton 10 19
(Miss E C Lavelle) *fast away: led to over 2f out: wknd rapidly: t.o* **16/1**

10 *1 ¼* **Six Of Trumps (IRE)** 2-9-3 .... ShaneKelly 2 16
(J A Osborne) *a in last trio: wknd over 2f out: t.o* **33/1**

1m 29.98s (0.98) **Going Correction** +0.025s/f (Good) **10** Ran **SP% 115.7**
Speed ratings (Par 96):90,89,89,87,85 84,78,76,62,60
CSF £224.77 TOTE £18.90: £3.70, £3.40, £2.10; EX 264.80 TRIFECTA Not won.
Owner Pat and Brian Makepeace & Stephen Barrow **Bred** D R Wellicome **Trained** Lambourn, Berks

FOCUS
Probably just a modest maiden for the track, featuring mainly juveniles bred to appreciate longer distances in time. The first three came clear.

NOTEBOOK
One To Follow, the first foal of an unraced half-sister to numerous winners over longer trips, dug deep when getting outpaced nearing two out and ultimately did just enough to make a winning debut. He should improve plenty for this experience and is bred to been seen to better effect over a stiffer test. Whatever the form is worth, he has a future. (op 14-1 tchd 11-1)
Big Robert, the first foal of a ten-furlong winner, was doing his best work towards the finish and can be rated a little better than the bare form as he made a sluggish start. He will be suited by longer trips in due course and really ought to be placed to get off the mark on one of the smaller tracks before too long.
King Joshua(IRE), eighth at Newmarket on debut 35 days previously, came through to hold every chance inside the final furlong and posted a much-improved effort in defeat. He still looked green this time and a maiden should really be his for the taking in the coming weeks. (op 5-1)
Record Breaker(IRE), who cost 110,000gns as a two-year-old and is half-brother to Irish Oaks heroine Vintage Tipple amongst others, failed to see out the race as well as the principals having been subject to a positive ride. A step up in trip will be much to his advantage in due course and he is entitled to improve for this debut experience. (op 5-2 tchd 11-4 in a place)
Minos(IRE), a half-brother to winners at this trip and beyond, got no cover racing on the outside of the pack and was found wanting inside the final furlong. A future Group 2 engagement suggests he is thought capable of much better. (op 10-1 tchd 7-1 in places)
Mesbaah(IRE) failed to improve on the level of his Newmarket debut and proved disappointing. He probably needs more experience. Official explanation: jockey said colt ran very green (op 2-1 tchd 3-1)

3893 BETEX OCTOBER CLUB MAIDEN FILLIES' STKS 6f

5:00 (5:00) (Class 4) 2-Y-O **£6,477** (£1,927; £963; £481) **Stalls** Low

Form RPR

1 **Italian Girl** 2-9-0 .... AlanMunro 4 85
(A P Jarvis) *wl in tch: stdy prog on outer fr over 2f out: led 1f out: shkn up and a holding on* **7/1**

65 **2** *¾* **Darrfonah (IRE)**[14] [3495] 2-9-0 .... KerrinMcEvoy 5 83
(C E Brittain) *w ldrs: rdn to chal and upsides 1f out: kpt on but a hld by wnr* **8/1**

3 *1* **Silca Chiave** 2-9-0 .... TedDurcan 6 80
(M R Channon) *in tch: chsd ldrs 2f out: pushed along and styd on wl to take 3rd nr fin* **11/4**[1]

4 *nk* **Elusive Flash (USA)** 2-8-11 .... NelsonDeSouza(3) 3 79
(P F I Cole) *w ldrs: led over 1f out to 1f out: one pce* **13/2**

5 *3* **Passing Hour (USA)** 2-9-0 .... LDettori 8 70
(G A Butler) *dwlt and wnt rt s: last tl sme prog fr 2f out: kpt on fnl f but no ch w ldrs* **11/2**[3]

6 *2 ½* **Selinka** 2-9-0 .... RichardHughes 2 63
(R Hannon) *a towards rr: shkn up and struggling over 2f out: plugged on fnl f* **10/1**

53 **7** *7* **Tee Off (IRE)**[31] [2957] 2-9-0 .... MichaelHills 1 42
(B W Hills) *mde most to over 1f out: wknd rapidly* **7/2**[2]

0 **8** *3* **Polly Jones (USA)**[11] [3591] 2-9-0 .... OscarUrbina 7 33
(B G Powell) *dwlt: prog fr rr on outer 1/2-way: wknd rapidly 2f out* **66/1**

1m 15.6s (-0.40) **Going Correction** +0.025s/f (Good) **8** Ran **SP% 111.8**
Speed ratings (Par 93):96,95,93,93,89 85,76,72
CSF £58.18 TOTE £8.70: £1.80, £2.90, £1.50; EX 65.00 Trifecta £1223.50 Part won. Pool £1,723.37 - 0.78 winning units. Place 6 £262.42, Place 5 £126.13..
Owner Eurostrait Ltd **Bred** Barton Stud **Trained** Twyford, Bucks

FOCUS
This was run at a sound pace and could prove to be a fair fillies' maiden. The debut winner is value for slightly further.

NOTEBOOK
Italian Girl ◆, a half-sister to a dual ten furlong winner in France, was very well backed to make a winning bow and duly rewarded her supporters with a ready display. She is value for a little further than the winning margin and it will not come as a surprise to see her upped markedly in class before too long. (op 16-1)
Darrfonah(IRE) posted her best effort to date and finished nicely clear of the remainder. She is going the right way, helps to set the standard for this form, and would enjoy the step back up to a seventh furlong on this evidence. (tchd 15-2)
Silca Chiave ◆, a half-sister to the high-class Silca's Sister, who landed this maiden in 2005 before winning the Group 1 Prix Morny, ran green when push came to shove and was doing most of her best work towards the finish. She holds three Group 1 entries and looks sure to improve for this debut experience. (tchd 3-1, 5-2 in places)
Elusive Flash(USA), a $300,000 purchase and half-sister to five winners, showed up nicely for a long way and should improve for the experience. (op 9-2)
Passing Hour(USA), a half-sister to most notably Queen Mary winner Shining Hour, was popular in the betting ring ahead of this debut yet ultimately lost her chance at the start. Her stable's juveniles appear to be starting to find their feet now and she ought to be sharper for this experience. (op 8-1)
Tee Off(IRE), very easy to back, dropped out tamely once headed and shaped as though something may have been amiss. (op 9-4)
T/Jkpt: Not won. T/Plt: £536.90 to a £1 stake. Pool: £128,580.40. 174.80 winning tickets. T/Qpdt: £147.80 to a £1 stake. Pool: £6,913.40. 34.60 winning tickets. JN

[3467] CHEPSTOW (L-H)

Friday, July 28

OFFICIAL GOING: Good to firm
Wind: Light, across Weather: fine and warm

3894 32RED POKER AMATEUR RIDERS' H'CAP 1m 4f 23y

6:20 (6:21) (Class 6) (0-55,55) 3-Y-O+ **£2,248** (£697; £348; £174) **Stalls** Low

Form RPR

0262 **1** **Cemgraft**[66] [1415] 5-10-5 46 ....(tp) MissZoeLilly(7) 12 56
(A J Lidderdale) *hld up in rr: hdwy over 2f out: styd on fnl f to ld nr fin* **9/1**

6654 **2** *nk* **Equilibria (USA)**[10] [3616] 4-10-7 46 .... MissHayleyMoore(5) 11 55
(G L Moore) *trckd ldrs: led 4f out: rdn over 2f out: hdd nr fin* **9/1**

1406 **3** *2* **Montosari**[23] [3013] 7-10-12 51 .... JackMitchell(5) 3 57
(P Mitchell) *in tch: ev ch 1f out: no ex fnl 50yds* **33/1**

0006 **4** *2* **Garston Star**[21] [3270] 5-10-13 47 .... MrsSMoore 13 50
(J S Moore) *mid-div: hdwy over 4f out to chse ldrs: one pce fnl f* **20/1**

2001 **5** *1 ½* **Robbie Can Can**[14] [3467] 7-11-1 54 .... MrMWall(5) 16 54
(A W Carroll) *stdd s: bhd: hdwy over 3f out: one pce ins fnl 2f* **9/2**[2]

5500 **6** *3 ½* **Lets Try Again (IRE)**[11] [3597] 9-10-12 49 .... MrDEdwards(3) 9 44
(R A Farrant) *trckd ldrs: rdn over 2f out: wknd fnl f* **28/1**

602 **7** *1* **Yenaled**[4] [3797] 9-10-13 54 .... MissHDavies(7) 8 47
(J M Bradley) *bhd: rdn and hdwy over 2f out: nvr nrr* **11/1**

000/ **8** *½* **New Diamond**[30] [2787] 7-10-9 50 .... MrKFord(7) 2 42
(Mrs P Ford) *trckd ldr: ev ch 4f out: wknd appr fnl f* **66/1**

5343 **9** *1 ¼* **Harare**[23] [3196] 5-10-8 49 .... MrMPrice(7) 14 39
(R J Price) *hld up in rr: effrt over 2f out: nvr on terms* **9/1**

0041 **10** *2* **Dayoff (IRE)**[3] [3810] 5-11-2 53 5ex ....(v) MissEFolkes(3) 10 40
(P D Evans) *bhd whn hung lft over 3f out: nvr on terms* **7/2**[1]

4040 **11** *½* **Eamon An Chnoic (IRE)**[15] [3437] 5-10-13 47 .... GerardTumelty 6 33
(B W Duke) *sn in tch: rdn over 3f out: wknd wl over 1f out* **14/1**

3502 **12** *¾* **Emperor Cat (IRE)**[23] [3194] 5-10-6 45 .... MissABevan(5) 4 30
(Mrs N S Evans) *mid-div: rdn over 3f out: sn bhd* **33/1**

/245 **13** *6* **Dareneur (IRE)**[14] [3467] 6-11-1 49 .... MissSBrotherton 5 25
(J G M O'Shea) *trckd ldrs: rdn over 2f out: wknd over 1f out* **6/1**[3]

6636 **14** *3 ½* **Smoothie (IRE)**[58] [2150] 8-10-7 48 ....(p) MrJRavenall(7) 15 18
(Ian Williams) *a bhd* **10/1**

The Form Book, Raceform Ltd, Compton, RG20 6NL

/00- **15** *shd* **Mrs Philip**[274] 4994 7-11-0 55 MissKHobbs(7) 1 25
(P J Hobbs) *led tl hdd 4f out: sn wknd* **33/1**
30/0 **16** *7* **Davoski**[26] 3116 12-10-11 45 MissEJJones 7 4
(Dr P Pritchard) *s.i.s: sn mid-div: rdn and wknd over 3f out* **66/1**
2m 36.9s (-1.82) **Going Correction** -0.10s/f (Good) **16** Ran SP% **128.8**
Speed ratings (Par 101):102,101,100,99,98 95,95,94,93,92 92,91,87,85,85 80
CSF £87.52 CT £2604.85 TOTE £13.20: £3.60, £3.20, £6.30, £5.30; EX 125.50.
Owner Entertainments Committee **Bred** Hamilton Nash Inc **Trained** Eastbury, Berks
FOCUS
A typically low-grade line-up for a race of this type, but run at a good gallop and the form is probably sound.

3895 32RED ONLINE CASINO MAIDEN AUCTION STKS 6f 16y
6:50 (6:51) (Class 5) 2-Y-O **£3,562** (£1,059; £529; £264) **Stalls** High

Form RPR
024 **1** **Okikoki**[20] 3286 2-8-11 RobertHavlin 8 80
(W R Muir) *hld up in tch: effrt and nt clr rn over 1f out: styd on to ld nr fin* **8/1**
24 **2** *½* **Gremlin**[53] 2287 2-8-4 RichardKingscote(5) 4 77
(A King) *a.p: rdn to ld over 1f out: hdd nr fin* **5/2**[1]
0 **3** *1* **Dubai Builder**[57] 2172 2-8-11 LPKeniry 3 76
(J S Moore) *in tch: rdn over 2f out: swtchd lft over 1f out: rn green: styd on* **7/2**[2]
4 *2* **Fish Called Johnny** 2-8-13 SteveDrowne 9 72
(B J Meehan) *s.i.s: rdn and hdwy over 2f out: kpt on fnl f* **14/1**
62 **5** *hd* **Pango's Legacy**[15] 3430 2-8-6 TravisBlock(5) 2 69
(H Morrison) *prom: rdn 2f out: wknd ins fnl f* **4/1**[3]
02 **6** *5* **Auction Oasis**[23] 3193 2-8-4 FrancisFerris 6 47
(B Palling) *led tl hdd over 1f out: wknd ins fnl f* **5/1**
7 *hd* **Oldjoesaid** 2-8-13 DaneO'Neill 1 55
(H Candy) *outpcd on outside fr 1/2-way* **7/1**
00 **8** *8* **Fun In The Sun**[13] 3545 2-8-9 RichardSmith 5 27
(Jane Southcombe) *chsd ldrs: rdn 1/2-way: wknd over 1f out* **100/1**
1m 10.0s (-2.40) **Going Correction** -0.275s/f (Firm) **8** Ran SP% **118.7**
Speed ratings (Par 94):94,93,92,89,89 82,82,71
CSF £29.55 TOTE £11.40: £2.30, £2.00, £1.80; EX 45.80.
Owner M J Caddy **Bred** Redmyre Bloodstock And Stuart McPhee **Trained** Lambourn, Berks
FOCUS
Probably a maiden of reasonable standard, with some likely improvers, and run at a good sprint gallop, suggesting the form is sound.
NOTEBOOK
Okikoki is more effective at six furlongs than five, and was later reported to have found the minimum trip on fast ground too sharp last time out. Tracking the leaders this time, rather than helping to set the pace, he produced a decisive late burst to clinch it despite meeting trouble in running, and looks useful at a sensible level. (op 9-1)
Gremlin ran well enough to continue to suggest than he is good enough to win a routine maiden, but he is now also qualified for nurseries. (tchd 7-2)
Dubai Builder ◆ is still filling into his good-sized frame, but he is said to be one of his stable's best two-year-olds, and he was fitter than on his debut. Seeming to get a bit unbalanced on the undulations, he nonetheless put in an improved effort, and looks the type to improve as the season progresses. (op 8-1)
Fish Called Johnny, a 31,000 guinea son of the speedy Kyllachy, comes from a good winning family. Despite missing the break, thus losing his position against the rail, he came home well and looks capable of winning races. (op 12-1)
Pango's Legacy has shown enough in his three maidens to suggest he can make an impact in nurseries now he is qualified. (op 5-1 tchd 11-2)
Auction Oasis showed good early pace, but merely set the race up for the others. She is now qualified for nurseries, and can hold her own in that sphere if conserving more for the finish. (op 11-4)
Oldjoesaid, the most expensive in the field at 40,000 guineas, is by the top-class sprinter Royal Applause, and from a good family with winning form from six to ten furlongs. Though looking distinctly uncomfortable on the fast ground, he could be capable of better when there is more cut. (op 15-2 tchd 11-2)
Fun In The Sun ran well for four furlongs, but was ultimately outclassed. (tchd 66-1)

3896 DASHCASINO.COM CLAIMING STKS 2m 49y
7:20 (7:20) (Class 6) 3-Y-O+ **£2,331** (£693; £346; £173) **Stalls** Low

Form RPR
5532 **1** **Arch Folly**[20] 3291 4-9-11 60 NeilChalmers(3) 7 56+
(J G Portman) *hld up in rr: hdwy 5f out: rdn 2f out: nt clr rn over 1f out: styd on to ld wl ins fnl f* **4/5**[1]
0432 **2** *nk* **Tip Toes (IRE)**[11] 3592 4-9-2 36 DeanCorby(3) 4 47
(P Howling) *slowly away: in rr tl hdwy 6f out: led 4f out: hdd over 2f out: kpt on and ev ch ins fnl f: outlasted cl home* **7/1**
0350 **3** *¾* **Barnbrook Empire (IRE)**[15] 3437 4-9-5 40 SteveDrowne 3 46
(B J Llewellyn) *led for 1f: led again over 2f out: hdd wl ins fnl f and no ex fnl 50yds* **10/1**
4045 **4** *1 ¼* **Arabian Moon (IRE)**[4] 3797 10-9-11 45 GeorgeBaker 2 51
(R Brotherton) *hld up: hdwy 4f out: chsd ldrs 2f out: hung lft appr fnl f: one pce ins* **6/1**[3]
60/4 **5** *11* **Dear Sir (IRE)**[15] 3437 6-9-7 45 JamesMillman(7) 9 40
(Mrs P N Dutfield) *trckd ldrs: led 6f out tl hdd 4f out: wknd wl over 1f out* **14/1**
4060 **6** *¾* **Rosiella**[5] 3592 4-9-2 40 (t) DaneO'Neill 12 27
(M Appleby) *t.k.h: hld up in rr: nvr on terms* **33/1**
-600 **7** *1* **Skelligs Rock (IRE)**[39] 2707 6-9-7 48 JamesDoyle(5) 1 36
(A W Carroll) *hld up: hdwy over 5f out: rdn and wknd 3f out* **50/1**
8 *17* **Scarface**[43] 9-9-11 60 ChrisCatlin 11 15
(J L Spearing) *led after 1f: hdd after 3f: wknd 4f out* **11/2**[2]
0/00 **9** *17* **Heriot**[14] 3467 5-10-0 55 (b) VinceSlattery 8 —
(S C Burrough) *led after 3f tl after 4f: wknd over 4f out* **100/1**
10 *11* **Kossies Mate**[85] 7-9-2 MickyFenton 5 —
(P W Hiatt) *v.s.a: plld hrd and led after 4f: rdn 6f out: sn hdd & wknd* **66/1**
000/ **11** *46* **Fuero Real (FR)**[433] 1367 11-9-10 35 (v[1]) LPKeniry 6 —
(R Brotherton) *in tch tl wknd 7f out: t.o* **100/1**
3m 37.79s (-1.61) **Going Correction** -0.10s/f (Good) **11** Ran SP% **121.9**
Speed ratings (Par 101):100,99,99,98,93 92,92,83,75,69 46
CSF £7.46 TOTE £1.80: £1.10, £1.30, £3.20; EX 9.00.Arch Folly was claimed by Bill Gavan for £10,000. Barnbrook Empire was claimed by Luke Dace for £6,000. Tip Toes was the subject of a friendly claim (£6,000).
Owner Simon Skinner **Bred** Mrs R Pease **Trained** Compton, Berks
FOCUS
A modest race, but a respectable performance from the winner at the weights. The early pace was only fair, and the form looks weak.
Barnbrook Empire(IRE) Official explanation: jockey said filly hung left-handed
Arabian Moon(IRE) Official explanation: trainer said gelding lost a shoe
Dear Sir(IRE) Official explanation: jockey said gelding had no more to give
Scarface Official explanation: jockey said gelding was unsuited by the good to firm ground

3897 EBF/TRANSBAND DRIVER RECRUITMENT CALL 0800 587 7550 FILLIES' H'CAP 7f 16y
7:50 (7:56) (Class 5) (0-70,70) 3-Y-O+ **£4,210** (£1,252; £625; £312) **Stalls** High

Form RPR
5035 **1** **Celtic Spa (IRE)**[11] 3590 4-9-6 60 StephenDonohoe(5) 5 71
(P D Evans) *trckd ldrs. led appr fnl f: rdn out* **7/2**[1]
5340 **2** *1 ¼* **Divine White**[21] 3267 3-8-10 52 ShaneKelly 8 57
(Mrs A J Perrett) *led: rdn over 2f out: hdd appr fnl f: nt pce of wnr* **7/1**
0044 **3** *1 ¼* **Pink Bay**[8] 3682 4-9-4 53 (b) FergusSweeney 2 58
(W S Kittow) *hdwy on outside 1/2-way: ev ch appr fnl f: kpt on one pce ins* **5/1**[2]
1005 **4** *shd* **Tuscarora (IRE)**[23] 3197 7-9-6 60 JamesDoyle(5) 7 64
(A W Carroll) *in tch: rdn and n.m.r 2f out: kpt on fnl f* **7/1**
-000 **5** *shd* **Waiting For Mary (IRE)**[45] 2535 3-8-8 50 RobertHavlin 9 51
(J G M O'Shea) *hld up: hdwy whn n.m.r over 1f out: one pce after* **14/1**
0602 **6** *2* **Miss Porcia**[13] 3543 5-8-13 55 KevinGhunowa(7) 1 54
(P A Blockley) *in tch on outside: rdn over 2f out: wknd over 1f out* **11/2**[3]
1600 **7** *1 ¼* **Prettilini**[11] 3598 3-9-10 66 ChrisCatlin 11 58
(Stef Liddiard) *prom to 1/2-way* **14/1**
000- **8** *3 ½* **Madam Patti**[282] 5969 3-8-13 55 FrancisFerris 6 38
(B Palling) *chsd ldr: rdn 2f out: wknd over 1f out* **20/1**
3120 **9** *shd* **Ruby's Dream**[6] 3728 4-9-7 56 (p) SteveDrowne 4 42
(J M Bradley) *hld up: rdn over 2f out: wknd over 1f out* **6/1**
0460 **10** *24* **Bahhmirage (IRE)**[13] 3541 3-8-11 53 (b) MickyFenton 3 —
(Stef Liddiard) *sn outpcd and a bhd* **16/1**
1m 21.7s (-1.60) **Going Correction** -0.275s/f (Firm)
WFA 3 from 4yo+ 7lb **10** Ran SP% **117.5**
Speed ratings (Par 100):98,96,95,95,94 92,91,87,87,59
CSF £28.42 CT £126.26 TOTE £4.30: £1.80, £2.80, £2.20; EX 45.90.
Owner Derek Buckley **Bred** Miss A R Byrne **Trained** Pandy, Abergavenny
FOCUS
A modest race, but a competitive one containing low-grade sprinters capable of winning in their turn. The form is sound rated around the placed horses.
Tuscarora(IRE) Official explanation: jockey said mare was denied a clear run

3898 WEATHERBYS BANK H'CAP 7f 16y
8:20 (8:21) (Class 5) (0-75,75) 3-Y-O+ **£5,181** (£1,541; £770; £384) **Stalls** High

Form RPR
6556 **1** **What-A-Dancer (IRE)**[3] 3820 9-9-1 62 (b) AdrianMcCarthy 5 65
(R A Harris) *in tch: rdn to ld over 1f out: all out* **5/1**
4000 **2** *shd* **Golden Square**[13] 3523 4-8-9 56 oh4 ShaneKelly 3 59
(A W Carroll) *led tl hdd over 1f out: rdn and pressed wnr to line* **14/1**
0201 **3** *½* **Caustic Wit (IRE)**[15] 3434 8-9-13 74 FergusSweeney 7 81+
(M S Saunders) *t.k.h: hld up: dropped to rr and not clr run 2f out: r.o wl fnl f: unlucky* **11/4**[1]
-000 **4** *1* **Wrighty Almighty (IRE)**[16] 3404 4-10-0 75 (p) GeorgeBaker 6 74
(P R Chamings) *t.k.h: hld up: rdn over 1f out: kpt on ins fnl f* **10/1**
0335 **5** *nk* **Ten Shun**[29] 3030 3-8-7 61 (v[1]) SteveDrowne 9 56
(P D Evans) *trckd ldrs: rdn over 1f out: wknd fnl f* **4/1**[3]
0114 **6** *½* **Le Chiffre (IRE)**[7] 3705 4-9-3 71 6ex (p) TolleyDean(7) 4 68
(R A Harris) *trckd ldrs: rdn over 2f out: one pce fnl f* **10/3**[2]
0000 **7** *3* **Arthurs Dream (IRE)**[10] 3614 4-8-4 56 oh8 JamesDoyle(5) 8 45
(A W Carroll) *hld up: hdwy over 2f out: wknd fnl f* **10/1**
5200 **P** **Chief Exec**[93] 1246 4-9-7 68 J-PGuillambert 1 —
(C A Cyzer) *prom tl rdn over 2f out: wknd rapidly: p.u 1f out: b.b.v* **8/1**
1m 21.8s (-1.50) **Going Correction** -0.275s/f (Firm)
WFA 3 from 4yo+ 7lb **8** Ran SP% **122.4**
Speed ratings (Par 103):97,96,96,95,94 94,90,—
CSF £75.10 CT £236.93 TOTE £6.00: £1.60, £4.80, £1.40.
Owner Sheedy Scrap Metals (1976) Ltd **Bred** Miss V Charlton **Trained** Earlswood, Monmouths
FOCUS
A fair handicap, with little more than two lengths covering the first six and the form is not solid.
Caustic Wit(IRE) ◆ Official explanation: jockey said gelding was denied a clear run
Chief Exec Official explanation: vet said gelding returned distressed

3899 32RED.COM H'CAP 5f 16y
8:50 (8:51) (Class 5) (0-70,69) 3-Y-O+ **£4,210** (£1,252; £625; £312) **Stalls** High

Form RPR
0002 **1** **Ballybunion (IRE)**[1] 3863 7-8-5 52 RichardKingscote(5) 4 60
(R A Harris) *a.p: led 2f out: strly rdn: jst hld on* **9/2**[1]
6200 **2** *nk* **Whitbarrow (IRE)**[18] 3348 7-8-13 62 (v[1]) JamesMillman(7) 8 69
(B R Millman) *hld up in tch: swtchd rt 2f out: r.o fnl f to snatch 2nd cl home* **10/1**
5030 **3** *shd* **Convince (USA)**[12] 3565 5-9-9 65 ShaneKelly 6 72
(J M Bradley) *trckd ldr: rdn and ev ch 1f out: kpt on but lost 2nd cl home* **12/1**
041 **4** *nk* **King Egbert (FR)**[18] 3348 5-8-4 53 TolleyDean(7) 3 59
(A W Carroll) *mid-div: hmpd after 1f: hdwy over 2f out: r.o fnl f: nvr nrr* **5/1**[2]
2000 **5** *nk* **Cerulean Rose**[18] 3368 7-8-11 58 JamesDoyle(5) 5 63
(A W Carroll) *s.i.s: in rr tl hdwy on outside 1/2-way: nt qckn fnl f* **5/1**[2]
0033 **6** *½* **Harrison's Flyer (IRE)**[20] 3297 5-9-13 69 (p) SteveDrowne 7 72
(J M Bradley) *hld up: rdn over 2f out: kpt on fnl f: nvr able chal* **5/1**[2]
6024 **7** *1 ¼* **Parkside Pursuit**[7] 3699 8-9-8 67 AdamKirby(3) 1 66
(J M Bradley) *mid-div: hdwy 2f out: fdd ins fnl f* **7/1**[3]
4565 **8** *¾* **Pro Tempore**[15] 3438 4-8-8 50 oh1 FergusSweeney 2 46
(David Pinder) *led tl hdd 2f out: wknd appr fnl f* **16/1**
2062 **9** *1 ½* **Lady Algarhoud (FR)**[11] 3595 4-9-1 57 ChrisCatlin 9 47
(M Appleby) *mid-div: rdn over 2f out: sn btn* **11/1**
0300 **10** *4* **Hit's Only Money (IRE)**[74] 1746 6-9-7 63 AdrianMcCarthy 10 39
(R A Harris) *a bhd* **12/1**
58.10 secs (-1.50) **Going Correction** -0.275s/f (Firm) **10** Ran SP% **119.4**
Speed ratings (Par 103):101,100,100,99,99 98,96,95,93,86
CSF £51.05 CT £513.27 TOTE £6.80: £2.60, £3.50, £5.00; EX 61.10 Place 6 £93.81, Place 5 £16.45..
Owner The Over The Bridge Partnership **Bred** La Pescaia S A S Di Miuta Pontello **Trained** Earlswood, Monmouths
FOCUS
A modest handicap, but run at a good gallop, and producing a blanket finish. The third and fourth were close to this year's form.
T/Plt: £243.40 to a £1 stake. Pool £61,635.60. 184.85 winning tickets. T/Qpdt: £16.00 to a £1 stake. Pool £5,882.10. 271.50 winning tickets. JS

[3738] NEWMARKET (R-H)

Friday, July 28

OFFICIAL GOING: Good to soft (good in places)

Wind: Nil Weather: Fine and sunny, but humid

3900 BOLLINGER CHAMPAGNE CHALLENGE SERIES H'CAP (FOR GENTLEMAN AMATEUR RIDERS) 1m 2f

5:45 (5:46) (Class 5) (0-70,70) 3-Y-O+ £3,747 (£1,162; £580; £290) Stalls Centre

Form RPR

0-00 **1** **Mighty Moon**[42] 2607 3-10-4 **60**..........(bt[1]) MrSWalker 4 71
(Lady Herries) *a.p: rdn to ld ins fnl f: r.o* **20/1**

0254 **2** *1 ½* **Qualitair Wings**[7] 3706 7-10-5 **58**.......... MrCMcGaffin(7) 6 66
(J Hetherton) *s.i.s: hld up: hdwy over 3f out: led over 1f out: sn rdn: hung lft and hdd ins fnl f: no ex* **13/2**[3]

0121 **3** *2 ½* **Celtique**[7] 3706 4-11-4 **69** 5ex.......... MrDHutchison(5) 11 72
(M Wigham) *hld up: hdwy over 2f out: styd on same pce fnl f* **2/1**[1]

5522 **4** *nk* **Dark Charm (FR)**[4] 3792 7-11-5 **70**.......... MrBMcHugh(5) 14 73
(R A Fahey) *trckd ldrs: rdn and hung lft over 2f out: styd on same pce fnl f* **9/2**[2]

0000 **5** *3* **Oakley Absolute**[29] 3024 4-10-6 **59**..........(p) MrHSkelton(7) 9 56
(R Hannon) *chsd ldr: rdn over 2f out: wknd fnl f* **33/1**

0130 **6** *shd* **Catskill**[15] 3429 4-11-6 **69**.......... MrJOwen(3) 8 66
(E F Vaughan) *prom: racd keenly: led over 2f out: rdn and hdd over 1f out: wknd ins fnl f* **10/1**

1150 **7** *shd* **Brave Dane (IRE)**[32] 2918 8-10-11 **62**.......... MrMJJSmith(5) 1 59
(A W Carroll) *hld up: hrd rdn over 1f out: nt trble ldrs* **10/1**

0000 **8** *1 ½* **Dubai Sunday (JPN)**[7] 3706 5-10-0 **51** oh1.......... MrPCollington(5) 12 45
(P S McEntee) *hld up: effrt over 1f out: n.d* **18/1**

4/1- **9** *1 ¼* **Dark Society**[103] 248 8-10-6 **55**.......... MrDEngland(3) 2 47
(A W Carroll) *s.i.s: hld up: n.d* **40/1**

2134 **10** *2 ½* **Ramsgill (USA)**[26] 3116 4-11-1 **66**.......... MrSPearce(5) 3 53
(J Pearce) *hld up: rdn over 3f out: wknd over 1f out* **10/1**

0543 **11** *3 ½* **Love You Always (USA)**[26] 3116 6-10-2 **55**..........(t) MrRBirkett(7) 13 35
(Miss J Feilden) *mid-div: rdn over 2f out: sn wknd* **10/1**

4000 **12** *11* **Reaching Out (IRE)**[16] 3404 4-11-1 **64**.......... MrNMoore(3) 10 23
(N P Littmoden) *led over 7f: sn wknd* **16/1**

04-4 **13** *nk* **Power Glory**[50] 243 4-10-0 **51** oh3.......... MrSFMagee(5) 5 10
(M J Gingell) *chsd ldrs 7f* **100/1**

2m 8.71s (2.27) **Going Correction** +0.05s/f (Good)
WFA 3 from 4yo+ 10lb **13** Ran SP% **123.5**
Speed ratings (Par 103):92,90,88,88,86 86,86,84,83,81 79,70,69
CSF £146.74 CT £387.17 TOTE £24.30: £4.20, £2.50, £1.70; EX 155.50.
Owner Lady Herries **Bred** Angmering Park Stud **Trained** Patching, W Sussex
■ Stewards' Enquiry : Mr M J J Smith two-day ban: used whip with excessive force (Aug 9,15)

FOCUS
Not strong form, but it looks sound with the second and third close to the previous week's form.

3901 CORPORATE FX FOREIGN CURRENCY MAIDEN STKS 1m 4f

6:10 (6:17) (Class 5) 3-Y-O £5,181 (£1,541; £770; £384) Stalls Centre

Form RPR

3-2 **1** **Very Agreeable**[23] 3200 3-8-12.......... SebSanders 8 86+
(W R Swinburn) *prom: t.k.h: lost pl 9f out: nt clr run over 2f out: hdwy over 1f out: rdn to ld ins fnl f: styd on* **9/1**

5 **2** *½* **Topjeu (IRE)**[70] 1823 3-9-3.......... NickyMackay 7 89
(L M Cumani) *hld up: racd keenly: hdwy u.p over 2f out: edgd rt over 1f out: styd on* **11/4**[1]

-242 **3** *1* **Spell Casting (USA)**[40] 2682 3-9-3 87.......... NCallan 9 87
(M H Tompkins) *trckd ldrs: led over 1f out: rdn and hdd ins fnl f: no ex towards fin* **10/3**[2]

54 **4** *5* **Aegean Pearl (USA)**[23] 3200 3-8-12.......... JimmyFortune 5 74
(J H M Gosden) *led: rdn and hdd over 1f out: wknd fnl f* **12/1**

0 **5** *1 ½* **Ninetails (IRE)**[23] 3200 3-8-12.......... RichardMullen 6 72
(E J O'Neill) *unruly in stalls: s.i.s: sn prom: rdn over 4f out: wknd over 1f out* **40/1**

453- **6** *nk* **Art Investor**[310] 5401 3-9-3 78.......... JohnEgan 3 76
(D R C Elsworth) *hld up: hdwy u.p over 1f out: wknd fnl f* **9/1**

-443 **7** *1 ¾* **Thumpers Dream**[25] 3146 3-8-12 83.......... EddieAhern 1 68
(H R A Cecil) *chsd ldr tl rdn over 2f out: wknd over 1f out* **6/1**

64 **8** *¾* **Zirkel (IRE)**[41] 2655 3-9-3.......... RobertWinston 4 72
(Mrs A L M King) *s.i.s: hld up: effrt over 2f out: wknd over 1f out* **28/1**

6 **9** *19* **Kalandara (IRE)**[23] 3200 3-8-12.......... RyanMoore 2 37
(Sir Michael Stoute) *prom: rdn over 3f out: wknd 2f out* **5/1**[3]

2m 33.17s (0.26) **Going Correction** +0.05s/f (Good) **9** Ran SP% **114.3**
Speed ratings (Par 100):101,100,100,96,95 95,94,93,81
CSF £33.65 TOTE £8.60: £2.00, £1.70, £1.60; EX 32.80.
Owner J M Greetham **Bred** J M Greetham **Trained** Aldbury, Herts

FOCUS
A fair maiden on paper, but the time was modest and the form might not stand up. The first two showed improvement.
Kalandara(IRE) Official explanation: trainer's rep had no explanation for the poor form shown

3902 SEE MORE ON RACING UK NURSERY 7f

6:40 (6:42) (Class 5) 2-Y-O £3,886 (£1,156; £577; £288) Stalls High

Form RPR

0643 **1** **Bobbish**[4] 3800 2-8-11 **70**.......... NCallan 6 72
(N A Callaghan) *racd alone stands' side: disp ld tl overall ldr 2f out: rdn out* **11/2**[3]

364 **2** *¾* **Diamond Light (USA)**[13] 3537 2-8-8 **67**.......... JimmyQuinn 3 67
(J L Dunlop) *racd centre: disp ld 5f: sn rdn: edgd rt: kpt on* **5/2**[1]

061 **3** *1 ½* **Disco Dan**[31] 2950 2-9-4 **77**.......... JimmyFortune 4 73
(D M Simcock) *racd centre: hld up in tch: rdn over 1f out: styd on same pce ins fnl f* **5/1**[2]

0263 **4** *1 ½* **Miss Saafend Plaza (IRE)**[14] 3496 2-9-7 **80**.......... RyanMoore 5 73
(R Hannon) *racd centre: chsd ldrs: rdn over 2f out: no ex fnl f* **5/2**[1]

035 **5** *1 ¾* **Tres Hombres**[21] 3265 2-8-1 **60**.......... RichardThomas 1 48
(Tom Dascombe) *racd centre: in tch: outpcd 1/2-way: n.d after* **20/1**

3034 **6** *5* **Goose Green (IRE)**[9] 3641 2-8-9 **68**.......... TonyCulhane 2 44
(M R Channon) *racd centre: chsd ldr tl rdn over 2f out: wknd over 1f out* **11/2**[3]

1m 27.54s (0.76) **Going Correction** +0.05s/f (Good) **6** Ran SP% **109.3**
Speed ratings (Par 94):97,96,94,92,90 85
CSF £18.56 TOTE £6.60: £3.00, £1.90; EX 19.30.
Owner J G Davis & Star Pointe Ltd **Bred** J G Davis And Star Pointe Ltd **Trained** Newmarket, Suffolk

FOCUS
The winner raced alone up the stands' rail, the other five coming down the centre of the track. A sound race, the second and fourth fitting in well. The official ratings shown next to each horse are estimated and for information purposes only.

NOTEBOOK
Bobbish, making a quick reappearance, raced in isolation against the stands' rail. Taking an overall lead with two furlongs to run, he kept up the gallop to see off the persistent runner-up. The give in the ground suited him. (op 7-1)
Diamond Light(USA), upped in trip for her nursery bow, led the quintet who raced down the centre throughout but had to give best to a rival racing on his own near the stands' rail. She lost little in defeat and should continue to acquit herself well. (tchd 11-4)
Disco Dan, tackling easy ground for the first time, lacked the pace to get to the principals late on but did stay the seven furlongs. (op 4-1)
Miss Saafend Plaza(IRE), raised 6lb after finishing third in a similar race over course and distance, ran her race but may appreciate the return to a quicker surface. (op 2-1 tchd 9-4)
Tres Hombres looked to be well beaten when dropping to rear at halfway but did plug on again.
Goose Green(IRE) was disappointing after his promising return to action at Kempton, and might appreciate a return to sand. (op 7-1)

3903 CORPORATE FX EBF CONDITIONS STKS 6f

7:10 (7:11) (Class 3) 2-Y-O £7,124 (£2,119; £1,059; £529) Stalls High

Form RPR

13 **1** **Chin Wag (IRE)**[15] 3445 2-9-3.......... RichardMullen 5 86
(E S McMahon) *mde all: rdn and hung lft fr over 1f out: r.o* **5/4**[1]

5140 **2** *½* **Dickie Le Davoir**[31] 2960 2-9-3.......... RobertWinston 7 85
(K R Burke) *hld up: pushed along 1/2-way: hdwy over 2f out: rdn and ev ch fr over 1f out: unable qckn nr fin* **15/2**

51 **3** *5* **Part Timer (IRE)**[48] 2439 2-9-5.......... TedDurcan 1 72
(M R Channon) *chsd wnr: rdn and ev ch over 1f out: wknd ins fnl f* **5/2**[2]

4 *3* **Brainy Benny (IRE)** 2-8-10.......... LDettori 2 54
(N A Callaghan) *chsd ldrs over 4f* **3/1**[3]

460 **5** *2 ½* **Breckland Boy**[32] 2938 2-8-13..........(p) JohnEgan 6 49
(Mrs C A Dunnett) *chsd ldrs over 4f* **40/1**

1m 14.04s (0.69) **Going Correction** +0.05s/f (Good) **5** Ran SP% **112.2**
Speed ratings (Par 98):97,96,89,85,82
CSF £11.45 TOTE £2.40: £1.20, £4.30; EX 11.70.
Owner J C Fretwell **Bred** R N Auld **Trained** Hopwas, Staffs

FOCUS
A decent little conditions race in which the first two finished clear.

NOTEBOOK
Chin Wag(IRE) returned to winning ways after a good run in defeat in a warm novice race at the July festival here. Making all, he hung to his left under pressure but held on well when strongly challenged. He is a useful juvenile, if not wholly straightforward. (op 6-4)
Dickie Le Davoir emerged as the main threat to the favourite, but despite battling on he was just held by his larger rival. He got the six furlongs well, having failed to run his race on his first try at this trip. (op 7-1 tchd 8-1)
Part Timer(IRE), returning to six furlongs, was attempting to give weight all round. He had his chance, but was squeezed up a little on the approach to the final furlong and could produce no extra from then on. (op 9-4)
Brainy Benny(IRE), a 58,000gns yearling, showed his inexperience on this debut and there should be improvement in him, particularly over further given he is out of a mare who won over 14 furlongs. (op 4-1)
Breckland Boy faced a stiff task in this company and was well beaten in the first-time cheekpieces. He is not progressing. (op 33-1)

3904 PORTLAND PLACE PROPERTIES H'CAP 6f

7:40 (7:41) (Class 3) (0-90,88) 3-Y-O+ £8,096 (£2,408; £1,203; £601) Stalls High

Form RPR

0505 **1** **Fullandby (IRE)**[28] 3038 4-9-7 **83**.......... NickyMackay 5 94
(T J Etherington) *hld up: hdwy and nt clr run over 1f out: swtchd lft: rdn to ld wl ins fnl f: jst hld on* **5/1**[1]

0230 **2** *shd* **Circuit Dancer (IRE)**[17] 3374 6-8-10 **72**.......... AdrianTNicholls 14 83
(D Nicholls) *led 1f: led again 2f out: rdn and hdd wl ins fnl f: r.o* **14/1**

2400 **3** *nk* **Kingscross**[14] 3471 8-9-3 **79**.......... TedDurcan 7 89
(M Blanshard) *s.i.s: hld up: r.o wl ins fnl f* **12/1**

/563 **4** *½* **Seamus Shindig**[29] 3012 4-9-5 **81**.......... JimmyFortune 4 89
(H Candy) *trckd ldrs: rdn and ev ch fr over 1f out: kpt on* **10/1**

-000 **5** *½* **Kenmore**[21] 3251 4-9-10 **86**.......... TomEaves 12 93+
(D Nicholls) *s.i.s: hld up: r.o wl ins fnl f: nt rch ldrs* **20/1**

6450 **6** *¾* **Spearit (IRE)**[22] 3226 3-8-5 **72**.......... JohnEgan 9 76
(D R C Elsworth) *hld up: rdn over 2f out: r.o ins fnl f: nrst fin* **20/1**

0015 **7** *hd* **Prince Cyrano**[34] 2864 7-8-11 **73**.......... TPQueally 8 77
(W J Musson) *chsd ldrs: rdn over 1f out: styd on same pce* **14/1**

3024 **8** *3 ½* **Romany Nights (IRE)**[14] 3486 6-9-8 **84**..........(b) KerrinMcEvoy 3 77
(Miss Gay Kelleway) *led 5f out: hdd 2f out: sn rdn: wknd fnl f* **7/1**[3]

0-00 **9** *½* **Russian Symphony (USA)**[27] 3092 5-9-8 **84**..........(p) LDettori 15 76
(C R Egerton) *hld up: rdn over 2f out: n.d* **9/1**

-026 **10** *½* **Lipizza (IRE)**[15] 3447 3-8-9 **76**.......... DO'Donohoe 6 65
(N A Callaghan) *s.i.s: sn plld in mid-div: hdwy and nt clr run over 1f out: wknd ins fnl f* **8/1**

0-06 **11** *2 ½* **Safari Sunset (IRE)**[14] 3486 4-9-1 **77**.......... JimCrowley 10 60
(P Winkworth) *mid-div: rdn and n.m.r 1/2-way: sn lost pl* **16/1**

1000 **12** *1 ¼* **Bird Over**[22] 3211 4-9-7 **83**.......... SebSanders 2 62
(R M Beckett) *hmpd s: hdwy 4f out: rdn over 2f out: hung lft and wknd over 1f out* **25/1**

5100 **13** *6* **Don Pele (IRE)**[14] 3471 4-9-12 **88**.......... NCallan 1 49+
(K A Ryan) *wnt rt s: chsd ldrs: rdn over 2f out: wknd and eased over 1f out* **9/1**

4603 **14** *8* **Banjo Patterson**[14] 3486 4-9-8 **84**..........(v) RyanMoore 13 21
(G A Huffer) *prom: rdn 2f out: sn wknd* **13/2**[2]

1m 12.55s (-0.80) **Going Correction** +0.05s/f (Good)
WFA 3 from 4yo+ 5lb **14** Ran SP% **123.0**
Speed ratings (Par 107):107,106,106,105,105 104,103,99,98,97 94,92,84,74
CSF £75.63 CT £835.96 TOTE £6.30: £2.40, £4.90, £4.40; EX 101.70.
Owner Miss M Greenwood **Bred** Mrs A Haskell Ellis **Trained** Norton, N Yorks

FOCUS
A solid handicap, the winner and third running to form. The field raced in the centre of the track before fanning out.

NOTEBOOK
Fullandby(IRE) was runner-up in this event a year ago off an 8lb lower mark. Suited by the step back up in trip and easier ground, he ran on well to notch his first win of the season. (op 9-2 tchd 11-2)
Circuit Dancer(IRE) was always up in the van and just missed out. This was his best effort so far this year and he can find a race from this sort of mark.
Kingscross was favoured by the ease in the ground and was putting in some good late work. This was a solid effort.

Seamus Shindig ran his best race of the season and, as he is relatively lightly raced, there could be more to come from him.
Kenmore ♦, a stablemate of the runner-up, finished in good style after switching to the near side for a clear run. He has dropped to an attractive mark, a pound lower than when scoring for Barry Hills at Newmarket last autumn. (op 16-1)
Spearit(IRE), who is creeping down the weights, is another who was doing his best work at the end.
Romany Nights(IRE) Official explanation: jockey said gelding ran too free
Banjo Patterson Official explanation: trainer had no explanation for the poor form shown

3905 CORPORATE FX OVERSEAS PROPERTY CONDITIONS STKS 1m 4f
8:10 (8:10) (Class 3) 3-Y-O+ **£8,724** (£2,612; £1,306; £653; £326) **Stalls** Centre

Form RPR
23-6 **1** **Guadalajara (GER)**[36] [2773] 5-8-10 108 .... LDettori 4 101+
(Saeed Bin Suroor) *mde all: shkn up over 1f out: comf* **1/1**[1]
2222 **2** *2 ½* **Ouninpohja (IRE)**[20] [3294] 5-9-1 110 .... DeanMcKeown 2 100+
(G A Swinbank) *a.p: chsd wnr over 3f out: rdn and hung lft over 1f out: nt run on* **6/4**[2]
36-6 **3** *7* **Something Exciting**[56] [2202] 4-8-10 109 .... JohnEgan 5 83+
(D R C Elsworth) *prom: rdn over 2f out: wknd over 1f out* **6/1**[3]
6303 **4** *14* **Amwell Brave**[27] [3085] 5-9-1 55 .... RyanMoore 1 66?
(J R Jenkins) *hld up: rdn over 2f out: sn wknd* **50/1**
-000 **5** *61* **Three Counties (IRE)**[26] [3114] 5-9-1 60 .... EddieAhern 3 —
(N I M Rossiter) *chsd wnr tl hung lft and wknd over 3f out* **66/1**
2m 31.5s (-1.41) **Going Correction** +0.05s/f (Good) **5** Ran SP% **107.7**
Speed ratings (Par 107):106,104,99,90,49
CSF £2.60 TOTE £2.00: £1.20, £1.40; EX 3.00.
Owner Godolphin **Bred** G Baron Von Ullmann **Trained** Newmarket, Suffolk

FOCUS
This decent conditions race was run in a modest time and the fourth anchors the form, which is hard to pin down.
NOTEBOOK
Guadalajara(GER), who became warm in the preliminaries, made all the running and did not have to exert herself too much to score. Likely to stay at this sort of trip, having failed to see out the extra mile of the Gold Cup, what she actually achieved here is hard to assess but it was an encouraging performance nonetheless. (op 8-13)
Ouninpohja(IRE), winner of his final five starts last year, has now finished second on his first five runs of this season. Never able to get to the mare, he is a smart performer but notoriously unenthusiastic. (op 2-1)
Something Exciting, runner-up to Eswarah in last year's Oaks, has plenty of questions to answer now having been well held this term in the Coronation Cup and in this lesser company. (op 8-1)
Amwell Brave, who ran well above himself in a Listed race here last time, again faced a thankless task but picked up another slice of prizemoney for his enterprising connections.

3906 RACING UK ON SKY 432 H'CAP 1m
8:40 (8:41) (Class 5) (0-75,75) 3-Y-O **£3,886** (£1,156; £577; £288) **Stalls** High

Form RPR
0361 **1** **Night Cru**[18] [3364] 3-9-1 **69** .... EddieAhern 9 75
(C F Wall) *hld up: hdwy over 2f out: led over 1f out: rdn out* **7/2**[1]
3034 **2** *nk* **Titian Dancer**[37] [2757] 3-9-5 **73** .... (t) TedDurcan 7 78
(W R Swinburn) *s.i.s: hld up: swtchd rt and hdwy over 1f out: r.o* **11/2**
642 **3** *shd* **Benandonner (USA)**[17] [3384] 3-9-4 **72** .... LDettori 1 77
(E A L Dunlop) *led: hdd over 1f out: r.o* **4/1**[2]
2035 **4** *shd* **Mujood**[16] [3404] 3-9-7 **75** .... StephenCarson 8 80
(R F Johnson Houghton) *chsd ldr: rdn and ev ch fr over 1f out: no ex nr fin* **13/2**
0216 **5** *½* **Murrumbidgee (IRE)**[13] [3542] 3-8-3 **64** .... PatrickHills(7) 4 68
(J W Hills) *hld up: hdwy over 2f out: shkn up over 1f out: styd on* **9/1**
0422 **6** *2 ½* **Musicmaestroplease (IRE)**[27] [3089] 3-8-10 **64** .... DeanMcKeown 5 62
(S Parr) *trckd ldrs: plld hrd: rdn over 1f out: no ex* **5/1**[3]
1120 **7** *1* **Smart Ass (IRE)**[11] [3590] 3-9-0 **68** .... JohnEgan 2 67+
(J S Moore) *trckd ldrs: plld hrd: rdn over 1f out: wknd ins fnl f* **13/2**
4-00 **8** *6* **Madame Constanze (IRE)**[121] [797] 3-8-2 **56** oh3 .... JimmyQuinn 6 38
(Miss Gay Kelleway) *hld up: hdwy 2f out: sn rdn and wknd* **25/1**
055- **9** *26* **Huggle**[268] [6228] 3-8-9 **63** .... NCallan 3 —
(P S McEntee) *mid-div: rdn and wknd over 2f out* **16/1**
1m 41.06s (0.63) **Going Correction** +0.05s/f (Good) **9** Ran SP% **120.7**
Speed ratings (Par 100):98,97,97,97,97 94,93,87,61
CSF £24.21 CT £82.44 TOTE £4.90: £1.70, £2.60, £1.70; EX 29.30 Place 6 £28.00, Place 5 £10.20..
Owner John Bridge & The Late Geoffrey Bovill **Bred** Jeremy Green And Sons **Trained** Newmarket, Suffolk
■ Stewards' Enquiry : L Dettori one-day ban: used whip with excessive frequency and without giving gelding time to respond (Aug 10)

FOCUS
A fair handicap in which the runners raced in a bunch towards the far side. The first five finished in a heap but the form looks reasonable with the third and fourth to recent marks.
Smart Ass(IRE) Official explanation: jockey said filly ran too free
T/Plt: £28.00 to a £1 stake. Pool: £53,539.35. 1,395.75 winning tickets. T/Qpdt: £10.20 to a £1 stake. Pool: £3,790.40. 274.40 winning tickets. CR

3172 THIRSK (L-H)
Friday, July 28

OFFICIAL GOING: Round course - firm; straight course - good to firm (firm in places)
Wind: Nil

3907 THIRSK FAMILY DAY - 4TH AUGUST MEDIAN AUCTION MAIDEN STKS 5f
2:00 (2:00) (Class 4) 2-Y-O **£5,181** (£1,541; £770; £384) **Stalls** High

Form RPR
03 **1** **Crow's Nest Lad**[18] [3351] 2-9-3 .... DavidAllan 1 74
(T D Easterby) *a.p: effrt 2f out: rdn to ld ent last: kpt on* **11/10**[1]
06 **2** *½* **Eager Igor (USA)**[18] [3363] 2-9-3 .... StephenCarson 4 72
(R F Johnson Houghton) *dwlt and slt hmpd s: sn pushed along in rr: rdn over 2f out: swtchd outside and drvn over 1f out: styd on wl fnl f* **7/2**[3]
2540 **3** *hd* **Pernomente (IRE)**[52] [2315] 2-9-3 .... (t) MartinDwyer 5 71
(J S Moore) *led: rdn along wl over 1f out: hdd ent last: nt qckn towards fin* **12/1**
024 **4** *¾* **Ronnie Howe**[18] [3351] 2-9-3 .... PhillipMakin 2 69
(M Dods) *trckd ldrs: hdwy 2f out: rdn over 1f out: kpt on same pce ins last* **10/3**[2]
6 **5** *½* **My Two Girls (IRE)**[6] [3745] 2-8-12 .... LeeEnstone 7 62
(P T Midgley) *dwlt: sn in tch: rdn 2f out: kpt on ins last* **100/1**
0243 **6** *2 ½* **Dotty's Daughter**[6] [3746] 2-8-12 .... (b[1]) PaulFessey 3 53
(Mrs A Duffield) *prom: rdn along 2f out: wknd appr last* **18/1**
7 *20* **Lafontaine Bleu** 2-8-12 .... TonyHamilton 6 —
(R A Fahey) *rdn along and outpcd fr 1/2-way: eased wl over 1f out* **22/1**
58.82 secs (-1.08) **Going Correction** -0.30s/f (Firm) **7** Ran SP% **111.2**
Speed ratings (Par 96):96,95,94,93,92 88,56
CSF £4.84 TOTE £2.10: £1.50, £2.30; EX 6.30.
Owner Ron George **Bred** Capt J H Wilson **Trained** Great Habton, N Yorks

FOCUS
An ordinary sprint maiden rated through the third and sixth and limited.
NOTEBOOK
Crow's Nest Lad confirmed the promise he showed when a much-improved third at Musselburgh on his previous start with a workmanlike display. Progressing nicely, he should find his level in nurseries. (op 11-8)
Eager Igor(USA), dropped back in trip, had a bit to do after getting slightly hampered at the start and there was plenty to like about the way he stayed on the closing stages. A return to six furlongs should suit, and he looks up to winning a maiden, but connections will now also have the option of going handicapping. (op 4-1)
Pernomente(IRE) kept on really well when strongly challenged and this has to rate as one of his best efforts to date. He has had a few chances, but certainly seems to have the right attitude. (op 9-1)
Ronnie Howe was not beaten far and posted a respectable effort. He could do even better in nurseries. (tchd 7-2)
My Two Girls(IRE) improved on the form she showed on her debut at Ripon and is going the right way. Official explanation: jockey said filly was unsuited by the good to firm (firm in places) ground (op 66-1)
Lafontaine Bleu Official explanation: jockey said filly lost its action

3908 EBF "MICHAEL J. WOOD CHANTRY CHEMICALS" MAIDEN FILLIES' STKS 7f
2:30 (2:30) (Class 4) 2-Y-O **£6,477** (£1,927; £963; £481) **Stalls** Low

Form RPR
1 **Carwell (IRE)** 2-9-0 .... RoystonFfrench 5 67
(M Johnston) *cl up: led over 2f out: rdn over 1f out: styd on wl* **7/2**[2]
0 **2** *1 ½* **Avina Laugh**[15] [3435] 2-9-0 .... AdrianMcCarthy 4 63
(P W Chapple-Hyam) *led: rdn along and hdd over 2f out: drvn over 1f out: kpt on u.p ins last* **11/2**
6 **3** *nk* **Golden Topaz (IRE)**[23] [3188] 2-9-0 .... PaulMulrennan 1 62
(J Howard Johnson) *chsd ldrs: swtchd rt and hdwy 2f out: sn rdn and kpt on ins last* **5/1**[3]
4 *1 ¾* **Porcelain (IRE)** 2-8-11 .... DanielTudhope(3) 3 58
(A Dickman) *dwlt and towards rr: hdwy 1/2-way: styd on appr last: nrst fin* **13/2**
5 *2 ½* **Livalex** 2-9-0 .... PhillipMakin 6 51
(M Dods) *chsd ldrs: rdn along 2f out: sn one pce* **17/2**
6 *3* **Decent Proposal** 2-9-0 .... DavidAllan 7 43
(T D Easterby) *sn outpcd and pushed along in rr tl sme hdwy fnl 2f* **3/1**[1]
0 **7** *7* **Grazie Mille**[35] [2827] 2-8-9 .... DuranFentiman(5) 2 25
(T D Easterby) *outpcd and bhd fr 1/2-way* **33/1**
8 *1 ¾* **Semahs Holly** 2-8-7 .... JamesO'Reilly(7) 8 21
(J O'Reilly) *a rr* **33/1**
9 *3 ½* **Star Of Night** 2-9-0 .... TonyHamilton 10 12
(C Grant) *a rr* **33/1**
10 *8* **Loose Canon** 2-9-0 .... HayleyTurner 9 —
(Mrs C A Dunnett) *keen: chsd ldrs tl rn v wd home turn: sn bhd* **16/1**
1m 26.32s (-0.78) **Going Correction** -0.125s/f (Firm) **10** Ran SP% **117.8**
Speed ratings (Par 93):99,97,96,94,92 88,80,78,74,65
CSF £23.06 TOTE £3.70: £1.30, £2.60, £1.90; EX 16.50.
Owner Ali Saeed **Bred** Darley **Trained** Middleham Moor, N Yorks

FOCUS
A very ordinary fillies' maiden and it is difficult to be confident about the level..
NOTEBOOK
Carwell(IRE), out of an unraced half-sister to smart Japanese performer Sugino Top Gun, was easy to back but proved good enough to make a winning debut. Always well placed, she stayed on strongly for pressure in the straight and never really looked like being reeled in. She is not that big, but there should be better to come in the short term at least. (op 9-4 tchd 4-1 in a place)
Avina Laugh did not show much on her debut at Folkestone, but this was a lot better. A moderate maiden could come her way, but her long-term future is very much lies in handicaps. (op 9-2)
Golden Topaz(IRE) improved on the form she showed on her debut over five furlongs at Catterick and clearly benefited from this longer trip. (op 7-1)
Porcelain(IRE), a half-sister to Propellor, a six-furlong juvenile winner, and Poker, a mile scorer at three, out of a multiple sprint winner, stayed on nicely after missing the break and this has to rate as a very pleasing introduction. (op 9-1)
Livalex, a 5,000gns half-sister to Arran Scout, a dual eight/nine-furlong winner at three, made a satisfactory introduction and is open to improvement. (op 11-1)
Decent Proposal ♦, out of a mare placed over six furlongs at two, was clearly fancied to make a winning debut but she basically ran far too green early on. She will know a lot more next time. (op 6-1 tchd 11-4)
Loose Canon Official explanation: jockey said filly hung violently right

3909 NATTRASS CONSTRUCTION MAIDEN STKS 7f
3:05 (3:07) (Class 5) 3-Y-O+ **£5,181** (£1,541; £770; £384) **Stalls** Low

Form RPR
04 **1** **Rigat**[20] [3285] 3-9-3 .... PhillipMakin 11 54+
(T D Barron) *trckd ldrs: hdwy 2f out: swtchd rt and rdn to chse ldng pair whn hung rt ins last: drvn and styd on to ld nr line* **9/1**[3]
220- **2** *nk* **Turkish Sultan (IRE)**[307] [5455] 3-9-3 77 .... DavidAllan 3 53
(T D Easterby) *cl up: led 2f out and sn rdn: drvn ins last: hdd nr line* **15/2**[2]
4-3 **3** *½* **Mashaair (IRE)**[69] [1845] 3-9-3 .... MartinDwyer 2 52
(B W Hills) *sn led: rdn and hdd 2f out: drvn: rallied and ev ch ins last: no ex towards fin* **30/100**[1]
0000 **4** *3* **Stormingmichaelori**[13] [3524] 3-9-3 43 .... (p) VHalliday 13 44
(N Wilson) *in tch: hdwy to chse ldrs 2f out: sn rdn and no imp* **150/1**
00-0 **5** *hd* **Compton Bay**[122] [783] 6-9-7 36 .... DanielTudhope(3) 8 46
(M Brittain) *midfield: hdwy on outer 3f out: rdn along 2f out: sn no imp* **125/1**
0 **6** *½* **Bond Free Spirit (IRE)**[20] [3285] 3-8-12 .... GylesParkin 7 37
(G R Oldroyd) *chsd ldrs: rdn along over 2f out: sn no imp* **40/1**
66- **7** *1 ¼* **Danzar**[412] [2498] 4-9-10 .... RoystonFfrench 9 42
(M Brittain) *midfield: hdwy 3f out: sn rdn along and no imp fr over 1f out* **80/1**
0-00 **8** *¾* **Gypsy Royal (IRE)**[49] [2418] 4-9-5 38 .... PaulFessey 4 35
(G Woodward) *midfield: hdwy 3f out: sn rdn along and no imp appr last* **200/1**
05 **9** *1 ¾* **Golden Groom**[17] [3373] 3-9-3 .... DeanMcKeown 1 32
(C W Fairhurst) *bhd tl sme late hdwy* **50/1**

0060 **10** *nk* **Born For Diamonds (IRE)**[10] 3617 4-9-0 42........ MichaelJStainton(5) 6 29
(R E Barr) *chsd ldrs: rdn along 3f out: grad wknd* **100/1**

04 **11** *1 1/4* **Beautiful Summer (IRE)**[25] 3146 3-8-12 .... TonyHamilton 10 23
(R A Fahey) *s.i.s: a towards rr* **20/1**

0-00 **12** *1 3/4* **Champagne Rossini (IRE)**[24] 2195 4-9-3 40............... PJBenson(7) 12 26
(M C Chapman) *a rr* **150/1**

0006 **13** *3* **Lady Luisa (IRE)**[16] 3399 4-8-12 28...........................(bt) AnnStokell(7) 5 13
(Miss A Stokell) *s.i.s: a rr* **100/1**

1m 25.18s (-1.92) **Going Correction** -0.125s/f (Firm)
WFA 3 from 4yo+ 7lb **13** Ran SP% **113.7**
Speed ratings (Par 103):105,104,104,100,100 99,98,97,95,95 93,91,88
CSF £68.26 TOTE £12.70: £1.90, £1.40, £1.10; EX 61.60.
Owner Mrs Janis Macpherson **Bred** Mrs M Chaworth-Musters **Trained** Maunby, N Yorks

FOCUS
A fair time but the proximity of the 43-rated Stormingmichaelori and the 36-rated Compton Bay suggest this was a very weak maiden indeed.
Mashaair(IRE) Official explanation: trainer's rep had no explanation for the poor form shown
Golden Groom Official explanation: jockey said gelding suffered interference in running

3910 HUMBER (S) H'CAP 1m
3:40 (3:41) (Class 6) (0-60,59) 3-Y-O **£3,238** (£963; £481; £240) **Stalls** Low

Form RPR

4045 **1** **Mister Maq**[20] 3303 3-9-5 57..(b) PaulFessey 6 64
(M Dods) *midfield: effrt and rdn along over 2f out: swtchd outside and hdwy over 1f out: styd on ins last: led nr line* **5/1**[2]

0602 **2** *nk* **Jenny Soba**[25] 3142 3-8-12 50.................................. DeanMcKeown 3 56
(R M Whitaker) *in tch: hdwy over 2f out: rdn over 1f out: drvn and led wl ins last: hdd nr line* **5/1**[2]

6000 **3** *1/2* **Millbrook Star (IRE)**[13] 3541 3-7-9 40 oh5..............(b[1]) SophieDoyle(7) 2 45
(M C Chapman) *in tch: hdwy on inner and n.m.r 2f out: squeezed through and rdn over 1f out: led ins last: hdd and no ex last 100 yds* **100/1**

0455 **4** *2* **Elite Land**[10] 3609 3-8-2 47.................................. SuzzanneFrance(7) 10 47
(N Bycroft) *midfield: rdn along wl over 2f out: styd on ins last: nrst fin* **9/1**

-000 **5** *nk* **Canary Girl**[32] 2940 3-7-12 41 oh2 ow1...................... AndrewElliott(5) 12 41
(Mrs C A Dunnett) *prom: effrt over 2f out: rdn to ld wl over 1f out: drvn and hdd jst ins last: one pce* **50/1**

0-40 **6** *1 1/2* **Stanley Bay (IRE)**[6] 3725 3-9-3 55....................................... DavidAllan 9 51
(T D Easterby) *bhd: rdn along 3f out: swtchd ins and hdwy 2f out: kpt on u.p ins last: nrst fin* **20/1**

3530 **7** *3/4* **Hogan's Heroes**[19] 3329 3-9-6 58.................................... MartinDwyer 1 52
(G A Butler) *led: rdn along and edgd rt 2f out: sn hdd: drvn and wknd over 1f out* **7/2**[1]

3006 **8** *shd* **Franky'N'Jonny**[17] 3378 3-8-12 50................................(p) HayleyTurner 16 44
(Mrs C A Dunnett) *in tch: hdwy 3f out: effrt and rdn 2f out: sn ev ch tl drvn and one pce ent last* **14/1**

0006 **9** *nk* **Kings Cavalier (USA)**[10] 3604 3-8-6 47.............(v) PatrickMathers(3) 15 40
(I W McInnes) *towards rr tl styd on fnl 2f* **40/1**

040- **10** *1 1/2* **Caribbean Nights (IRE)**[245] 6420 3-9-2 59........... DuranFentiman(5) 17 49
(T D Easterby) *towards rr: hdwy 3f out: rdn to chse ldrs on outer over 1f out: sn drvn: edgd lft and wknd* **25/1**

0050 **11** *1 3/4* **Salisbury World (IRE)**[20] 3288 3-8-6 44.................... TonyHamilton 13 30
(J F Coupland) *slowly away: a rr* **33/1**

0062 **12** *1* **The Flying Peach**[13] 3529 3-7-11 40 oh1........................ LiamJones(5) 5 24
(W M Brisbourne) *s.i.s: a rr* **7/1**[3]

0-60 **13** *4* **Ruby Rubble**[19] 3329 3-8-12 50....................................... PhillipMakin 14 24
(K R Burke) *chsd ldrs: rdn along over 2f out: grad wknd* **12/1**

0000 **14** *2 1/2* **Centreofattention**[20] 3306 3-8-4 42...........................(p) StephenCarson 7 11
(Mrs A Duffield) *cl up: rdn wl over 2f out: sn drvn and wknd* **20/1**

0000 **15** *3* **Wilmas Gal**[17] 3384 3-8-2 40 oh9...............................(t) RoystonFfrench 4 2
(R Bastiman) *chsd ldrs: rdn along wl over 2f out: sn wknd* **100/1**

0-00 **16** *7* **Cole (IRE)**[16] 3397 3-8-12 50.................................... PaulMulrennan 11 —
(J Howard Johnson) *a rr* **25/1**

1m 39.45s (-0.25) **Going Correction** -0.125s/f (Firm) **16** Ran SP% **119.0**
Speed ratings (Par 98):96,95,95,93,92 91,90,90,90,88 87,86,82,79,76 69
CSF £25.01 CT £1462.36 TOTE £6.70: £2.30, £1.40, £14.80, £2.10; EX 35.40.There was no bid for the winner.
Owner Harrison, Kirkupp, Smith & Allan **Bred** Hedgeholme Stud **Trained** Denton, Co Durham
■ Eurana withdrawn (14/1, broke out of stalls). R4 applies, deduct 5p in the £.
■ Stewards' Enquiry : Martin Dwyer caution: careless riding

FOCUS
A competitive selling handicap run at a good pace from the start, but the form is not solid and the runner-up is the best guide.
Salisbury World(IRE) Official explanation: jockey said gelding missed the break

3911 WARWICK DRYERS H'CAP 1m 4f
4:15 (4:15) (Class 4) (0-80,80) 3-Y-O **£6,477** (£1,927; £963; £481) **Stalls** Low

Form RPR

6264 **1** **Azurine (IRE)**[9] 3634 3-8-4 63.................................... RoystonFfrench 5 70
(M Johnston) *mde all: qcknd 3f out: rdn and edgd rt 2f out: drvn and styd on wl fnl f* **5/1**[3]

2342 **2** *2 1/2* **Robustian**[11] 3589 3-9-7 80.. StephenCarson 2 83
(R F Johnson Houghton) *hld up: hdwy over 3f out: rdn to chal wl over 1f out: drvn and edgd lft ent last: kpt on same pce* **5/6**[1]

0035 **3** *hd* **Gaze**[22] 3215 3-8-10 69..(v[1]) MartinDwyer 1 72
(W Jarvis) *trckd wnr: hdwy whn n.m.r and swtchd lft wl over 1f out: sn rdn and no imp* **10/1**

532 **4** *nk* **Avelian (IRE)**[27] 3066 3-8-5 69....................................... LiamJones(5) 4 72
(W J Haggas) *trckd ldng pair: hdwy and nt clr run wl over 1f out: swtchd rt: rdn and hung lft ent last: styd on towards fin* **5/2**[2]

2m 38.89s (3.69) **Going Correction** -0.125s/f (Firm) **4** Ran SP% **108.9**
Speed ratings (Par 102):82,80,80,80
CSF £9.89 TOTE £5.00; EX 12.20.
Owner F Towey **Bred** Gerrardstown House Stud **Trained** Middleham Moor, N Yorks

FOCUS
A disappointing turnout, especially considering there was £10,000 up for grabs, and Azurine made every yard having been allowed to dictate on her own terms. The form is not solid and limited by the proximity of the third.
Gaze Official explanation: jockey said filly hung left

3912 DEEPDALE SOLUTIONS NSPCC FILLIES' H'CAP 6f
4:45 (4:45) (Class 5) (0-70,71) 3-Y-O+ **£5,181** (£1,541; £770; £384) **Stalls** High

Form RPR

1411 **1** **Aahgowangowan (IRE)**[4] 3783 7-9-13 71 6ex..........(t) LiamJones(5) 14 85
(M Dods) *mde all: rdn clr wl over 1f out: styd on* **6/4**[1]

0265 **2** *2 1/2* **Yorke's Folly (USA)**[10] 3617 5-8-4 48 oh3.........(b) LeanneKershaw(5) 17 54
(C W Fairhurst) *trckd ldrs stands rail: hdwy to chse wnr over 1f out: sn rdn and kpt on same pce ins last* **12/1**[3]

0-50 **3** *hd* **Black Oval**[2] 3835 5-8-2 48 oh9.................................... MarkCoumbe(7) 15 53
(S Parr) *in tch stands side: hdwy 2f out: sn rdn and kpt on ins last: nrst fin* **100/1**

-640 **4** *2 1/2* **Cut Ridge (IRE)**[13] 3524 7-8-9 48 oh6.......................... TonyHamilton 16 46
(J S Wainwright) *hld up: hdwy 2f out: rdne and kpt on ins last: nrst fin* **25/1**

-000 **5** *3/4* **Westlake Bond (IRE)**[17] 3379 4-8-4 48 oh10.....(p) DuranFentiman(5) 11 44
(G R Oldroyd) *midfield: hdwy 2f out: sn rdn and no imp appr last* **100/1**

3336 **6** *1 1/4* **Making Music**[6] 3722 3-9-9 67...(p) DavidAllan 10 59
(T D Easterby) *chsd wnr: rdn along 2f out: drvn and wknd over 1f out* **14/1**

1652 **7** *3/4* **Petite Mac**[30] 2977 6-9-0 60...................................... SuzzanneFrance(7) 1 50+
(N Bycroft) *racd wd: midfield: rdn along and hdwy 2f out: kpt on u.p ins last* **8/1**[2]

4022 **8** *1 1/4* **True Magic**[7] 3699 5-9-11 67.. DanielTudhope(3) 5 53
(J D Bethell) *dwlt and hmpd s: bhd tl styd on fnl 2f: nvr a factor* **8/1**[2]

2112 **9** *1/2* **Pay Time**[7] 3697 7-9-0 58... MichaelJStainton(5) 6 42+
(R E Barr) *hmpd s: bhd tl sme hdwy on outer wl over 1f out: nvr a factor* **8/1**[2]

1235 **10** *4* **Safranine (IRE)**[4] 3783 9-8-11 57.. AnnStokell(7) 3 29
(Miss A Stokell) *nvr nr ldrs* **16/1**

00-4 **11** *hd* **Elisha (IRE)**[24] 3172 4-8-9 55... NSLawes(7) 12 27
(K A Ryan) *chsd ldrs: rdn 2f out: sn wknd* **14/1**

0002 **12** *shd* **Graceful Flight**[23] 3189 4-8-9 48 oh13.............................. LeeEnstone 13 20
(P T Midgley) *a towards rr* **100/1**

00-5 **13** *3* **Minimum Bid**[8] 3670 5-9-6 66.. PJBenson(7) 8 29
(B Smart) *chsd ldrs: rdn along 1/2-way: sn wknd* **16/1**

0000 **14** *2* **Mis Chicaf (IRE)**[10] 3608 5-8-9 48.................................(t) PaulMulrennan 9 5
(Robert Gray) *chsd ldrs: rdn along 1/2-way: sn wknd* **66/1**

0300 **15** *2 1/2* **Our Mary (IRE)**[17] 3381 3-8-10 54................................ RoystonFfrench 7 3
(Robert Gray) *a rr* **50/1**

0/0- **16** *3/4* **First Eclipse (IRE)**[556] 143 5-8-4 48 oh8..................... AndrewElliott(5) 2 —
(G Woodward) *racd wd: a rr* **100/1**

4004 **U** **Sounds Simla (IRE)**[37] 2758 3-9-2 60.................................. PaulFessey 4 —
(J F Coupland) *bmpd s: a rr: stmbld and uns rdr 2f out* **50/1**

1m 10.71s (-1.79) **Going Correction** -0.30s/f (Firm)
WFA 3 from 4yo+ 5lb **17** Ran SP% **119.3**
Speed ratings (Par 100):99,95,95,92,91 89,88,86,86,80 80,80,76,73,70 69,—
CSF £19.25 CT £1116.94 TOTE £2.30: £1.50, £3.20, £8.50, £3.30; EX 29.50.
Owner Les Waugh **Bred** Seamus Phelan **Trained** Denton, Co Durham

FOCUS
She only beat a bunch of modest sprinters, but Aahgowangowan was impressive in gaining her fourth win from her last five starts and the form has been rated positively. The first six home were drawn in double-figure stalls.
Graceful Flight Official explanation: jockey said filly lost its action
Our Mary(IRE) Official explanation: jockey said filly was unsuited by the good to firm (firm in places) ground

3913 TELETEXT "HANDS AND HEELS" APPRENTICE H'CAP 5f
5:20 (5:20) (Class 5) (0-75,72) 3-Y-O+ **£5,181** (£1,541; £770; £384) **Stalls** High

Form RPR

0000 **1** **Shank On Fourteen (IRE)**[1] 3863 5-8-10 58.............. LukeMorris(3) 10 67
(K R Burke) *wnt lft s: in tch: hdwy 2f out: rdn over 1f out: led ins last: styd on* **7/1**

1521 **2** *1* **Paddywack (IRE)**[10] 3608 9-8-8 56 6ex............(b) DanielleMcCreery(3) 8 61
(D W Chapman) *dwlt and hmpd s: bhd: rdn and hdwy wl over 1f out: styd on wl towards fin* **4/1**[2]

2240 **3** *nk* **Millinsky (USA)**[15] 3447 5-9-12 71..................................... RobbieMills 5 75
(Rae Guest) *cl up: led wl over 1f out: sn rdn:hdd ins last and kpt on same pce* **10/3**[1]

2510 **4** *shd* **Never Without Me**[23] 3190 6-9-6 65.................................... PJBenson 1 69+
(J F Coupland) *cl up on outer: effrt and ev ch wl over 1f out tl nt qckn ins last* **14/1**

-036 **5** *1/2* **Dazzler Mac**[6] 3749 5-8-8 53 oh1................................ SuzzanneFrance 6 58+
(N Bycroft) *in tch: hdwy whn hmpd over 1f out:s witched lft and styd on wl towards fin* **8/1**

0106 **6** *shd* **Dark Champion**[10] 3617 6-8-10 58............................(b) MarkCoumbe(3) 9 59
(R E Barr) *hmpd s and bhd: hdwy and swtchd sharply lft over 1f out: kpt on ins last: nrst fin* **9/1**

0260 **7** *nk* **Dispol Katie**[20] 3287 5-9-10 72.. DeanHeslop(3) 11 72
(T D Barron) *chsd ldrs: pushed along wl over 1f out: one pce appr last* **11/2**[3]

0000 **8** *2* **Amanda's Lad (IRE)**[3] 3825 6-8-8 53 oh3.................... JamieHamblett 4 46
(M C Chapman) *cl up: ev ch 2f out: wkng whn hmpd over 1f out* **25/1**

3206 **9** *2* **Catch The Cat (IRE)**[14] 3503 7-9-5 64............................(v) RonanKeogh 7 50
(Robert Gray) *cl up: pushed along 2f out: sn wknd* **12/1**

0020 **10** *3/4* **Percy Douglas**[10] 3608 6-8-5 53 oh1........................(bt) SophieDoyle(3) 2 36
(Miss A Stokell) *in tch tl wknd fnl 2f* **25/1**

6440 **11** *3* **Axis Shield (IRE)**[21] 3257 3-7-13 53 oh3........................ PaulPickard(5) 3 26
(M C Chapman) *led: pushed along over 2f out: hdd wl over 1f out and sn wknd* **50/1**

58.94 secs (-0.96) **Going Correction** -0.30s/f (Firm)
WFA 3 from 5yo+ 4lb **11** Ran SP% **116.1**
Speed ratings (Par 103):95,93,92,92,91 91,91,88,84,83 78
CSF £34.00 CT £113.54 TOTE £8.10: £2.60, £1.70, £1.80; EX 47.30 Place 6 £77.18, Place 5 £52.78..
Owner Lee Westwood **Bred** Martyn J McEnery **Trained** Middleham Moor, N Yorks
■ Stewards' Enquiry : Mark Coumbe six-day ban: careless riding (Aug 8-13)
Sophie Doyle 10-day ban: use of whip in a hands and heels race (Aug 9-10,14-15,17-18,23-25,31)

FOCUS
A moderate sprint handicap run in a time slightly slower than the earlier two-year-old maiden and rated negatively through the runner-up.
Shank On Fourteen(IRE) Official explanation: trainer's representative had no explanation for the apparent improvement in form
Amanda's Lad(IRE) Official explanation: jockey said saddle slipped
Catch The Cat(IRE) Official explanation: jockey said gelding pulled up lame but returned sound
T/Plt: £47.00 to a £1 stake. Pool: £39,054.75. 605.40 winning tickets. T/Qpdt: £35.10 to a £1 stake. Pool: £2,009.30. 42.30 winning tickets. JR

3683 WOLVERHAMPTON (A.W) (L-H)

Friday, July 28

OFFICIAL GOING: Standard

Wind: Almost nil Weather: Sunny, hot

3914 STAY AT THE WOLVERHAMPTON HOLIDAY INN CLAIMING STKS 1m 141y(P)

2:20 (2:21) (Class 6) 3-Y-O+ **£2,730** (£806; £403) **Stalls** Low

Form				RPR
U351	**1**		**Luis Melendez (USA)**[10] [3626] 4-9-11 67.............(t) EdwardCreighton(3) 13 *(Tom Dascombe) mde all: rdn over 1f out: drvn out* **15/2**	80
00-0	**2**	*nk*	**Formidable Will (FR)**[199] [77] 4-9-10 60.......................(tp) DaleGibson 6 *(M W Easterby) a.p: rdn over 2f out: chsd wnr wl over 1f out: r.o ins fnl f* **14/1**	75
0560	**3**	*nk*	**Underscore (USA)**[8] [3664] 4-9-9 73......................... LiamTreadwell(5) 10 *(R A Harris) s.i.s: hld up: hdwy on ins over 3f out: sn rdn: hung lft ins fnl f: r.o towards fin* **8/1**	78
0210	**4**	*3 ½*	**Gem Bien (USA)**[11] [3599] 8-9-4 55..................................(p) PaulQuinn 11 *(D W Chapman) hld up in mid-div: rdn and hdwy over 3f out: one pce fnl 2f* **14/1**	61
0-00	**5**	*hd*	**Oh Danny Boy**[9] [3642] 5-9-10 67.. RobertHavlin 9 *(Jane Chapple-Hyam) hld up in mid-div: hdwy wl over 1f out: sn hung lft: no imp fnl f* **14/1**	67
1650	**6**	*1 ¼*	**Makai**[23] [3194] 3-9-5 68.. J-PGuillambert 5 *(M Johnston) chsd wnr: rdn and ev ch over 2f out: lost 2nd wl over 1f out: wknd fnl f* **11/1**	68
22P2	**7**	*2 ½*	**La Viola**[14] [3480] 4-8-11 56...(v) PatCosgrave 12 *(K R Burke) hld up in tch: lost pl and n.m.r over 3f out: sn rdn: n.d after* **10/1**	46
5354	**8**	*hd*	**Go Garuda**[32] [2936] 5-9-1 59.................................. StephenDonohoe(5) 4 *(Miss Gay Kelleway) mid-div: rdn over 5f out: no hdwy fnl 2f* **9/2**[2]	54
	9	*6*	**City Minx** 4-9-1 .... DerekMcGaffin 8 *(D Morris) s.i.s and hmpd s: a bhd* **80/1**	37
2-31	**10**	*1 ¾*	**Grecian Gold (IRE)**[53] [2291] 4-9-8 73......................... FergusSweeney 1 *(J R Boyle) prom: rdn wl over 3f out: wknd 2f out* **11/4**[1]	40
2033	**11**	*2*	**Holiday Cocktail**[25] [3149] 4-9-11 66........................... SaleemGolam(3) 3 *(S C Williams) hld up and bhd: rdn over 2f out: no rspnse* **11/2**[3]	42
0	**12**	*3 ½*	**Granakey (IRE)**[16] [3406] 3-8-5 .... DominicFox(3) 7 *(M G Quinlan) wnt rt s: a bhd* **80/1**	23
5/06	**13**	*2 ½*	**Night Prayers (IRE)**[8] [3673] 4-9-9 80.................. MarkLawson(5) 2 *(B Smart) plld hrd in tch: rdn and wknd over 3f out* **40/1**	29

1m 50.9s (-0.86) **Going Correction** +0.075s/f (Slow)

WFA 3 from 4yo+ 9lb **13** Ran SP% **125.4**

Speed ratings (Par 101):106,105,105,102,102 101,98,98,93,91 90,86,84

CSF £113.08 TOTE £11.60: £3.40, £1.40, £10.80; EX 227.30.Luis Melendez was the subject of a friendly claim of £12,000.

Owner Oneway **Bred** Bloomsbury Stud **Trained** Lambourn, Berks

FOCUS

A competitive claimer in which the front three were separated by two necks. The race has been rated positively with the third and fourth to last year's form, and should produce winners.

Grecian Gold(IRE) Official explanation: jockey said gelding finished lame

Night Prayers(IRE) Official explanation: jockey said gelding ran too free and hung right-handed

3915 TO SPONSOR A RACE CALL 0870 220 2442 FILLIES' (S) STKS 7f 32y(P)

2:55 (2:57) (Class 6) 2-Y-O **£2,388** (£705; £352) **Stalls** High

Form				RPR
513R	**1**		**Sad Times (IRE)**[10] [3613] 2-8-13 ....(p) MarcHalford(5) 8 *(W G M Turner) s.i.s: sn chsng ldrs: rdn over 2f out: c wd st: led over 1f out: r.o* **5/1**[3]	61
414	**2**	*1 ¼*	**The Slider**[10] [3613] 2-8-11 .... KevinGhunowa(7) 5 *(P A Blockley) mid-div: rdn and hdwy over 2f out: kpt on ins fnl f* **3/1**[1]	58
0	**3**	*½*	**Marist Madame**[58] [2145] 2-8-6 ow1......................... JamesMillman(7) 10 *(D K Ivory) led: rdn over 2f out: hdd over 1f out: nt qckn ins fnl f* **16/1**	52
00	**4**	*5*	**Bathwick Princess**[108] [962] 2-8-12 .... GrahamGibbons 6 *(P D Evans) chsd ldrs: rdn over 3f out: outpcd over 2f out: styd on ins fnl f* **16/1**	38
	5	*hd*	**Porjenski** 2-8-12 .... FergusSweeney 4 *(A B Haynes) s.i.s: sn chsng ldrs: rdn and ev ch 2f out: wknd ins fnl f* **12/1**	38
00	**6**	*1 ¾*	**Taran Tregarth**[32] [2938] 2-8-9 .... EdwardCreighton(3) 3 *(A Bailey) s.i.s: bhd tl hdwy over 1f out: n.d* **40/1**	33
00	**7**	*1 ¼*	**Roxy Singer**[9] [3640] 2-8-7 .... StephenDonohoe(5) 2 *(W J Musson) hld up towards rr: rdn over 3f out: no rspnse* **10/3**[2]	30
00	**8**	*2 ½*	**Countyourblessings**[9] [3645] 2-8-9 .... AdamKirby(3) 9 *(J G Portman) prom: rdn over 2f out: wknd wl over 1f out* **14/1**	24
0	**9**	*6*	**Spin Dancer**[21] [3246] 2-8-12 .... RobbieFitzpatrick 12 *(W M Brisbourne) w ldr: rdn over 3f out: wknd over 2f out* **40/1**	9
	10	*9*	**Bell Amica** 2-8-5 .... StacyRenwick(7) 7 *(M J Attwater) s.s: outpcd* **16/1**	—
	11	*1*	**Wingsinmotion (IRE)** 2-8-12 .... PatCosgrave 1 *(K R Burke) s.s: outpcd* **11/2**	—
	12	*1*	**Rathnait** 2-8-9 .... DominicFox(3) 11 *(M J Attwater) s.s: outpcd* **25/1**	—

1m 33.44s (3.04) **Going Correction** +0.075s/f (Slow) **12** Ran SP% **120.9**

Speed ratings (Par 89):85,83,83,77,77 75,73,70,63,53 52,51

CSF £20.44 TOTE £6.10: £2.50, £1.20, £6.30; EX 21.40.There was no bid for the winner.

Owner Nutty Partners **Bred** John J Cosgrave **Trained** Sigwells, Somerset

FOCUS

A bad seller in which the front three drew clear and rated around the first two.

NOTEBOOK

Sad Times(IRE), who refused to take part at Brighton last time, was on a going day and she stayed on strongly for a workmanlike win. Her trainer does not have the best of records with his juveniles here, but she is a tough sort likely to continue to pay her way at a similar level. (op 11-2)

The Slider, whose sole previous victory came in a bad race at Beverley earlier in the month, was held at Brighton last time, but this was a much better effort and she shaped as though worth a try at a mile. She is clearly moderate, but has another race in her. (op 5-2 tchd 9-4)

Marist Madame, never involved on her debut at Yarmouth, left that form behind and kept on well once headed. She is another for whom a mile may suit and it will be both disappointing and surprising if she cannot find a race at this level. (op 14-1)

Bathwick Princess was a bit adrift of the front three, but this was her best effort to date and the step up to seven furlongs from five clearly made the difference. (op 20-1)

Porjenski, who cost just £600, recovered from a sluggish start to move into a challenging position, but she faded late on and clearly needed the experience. (op 9-1)

Roxy Singer was the disappointment of the race, failing to make an impact on this drop back down in grade. She looks regressive already. (op 6-1)

Countyourblessings tired off the home bend and could be the type for selling nurseries back at six furlongs. (op 10-1)

Bell Amica Official explanation: jockey said filly never travelled

Wingsinmotion(IRE) was one of the more interesting runners on show, but she was struggling from a very early stage and needs to improve massively if she is to be winning races. (op 7-1)

3916 PRIORY PARK AMATEUR BOXING MEDIAN AUCTION MAIDEN STKS 5f 216y(P)

3:30 (3:33) (Class 6) 3-4-Y-O **£3,071** (£906; £453) **Stalls** Low

Form				RPR
4-0	**1**		**Fen Guest**[16] [3406] 3-8-12 .... JamieMackay 8 *(Rae Guest) broke wl: sn stdd: hdwy over 2f out: rdn to ld wl over 1f out: r.o wl* **7/1**[3]	58+
0	**2**	*1 ¾*	**Whistle Away**[28] [3050] 3-9-0 .... SaleemGolam(3) 6 *(W R Swinburn) led early: a.p: rdn and ev ch over 2f out: nt qckn ins fnl f* **15/2**	58
0634	**3**	*½*	**Crusader's Gold (FR)**[25] [3154] 3-9-3 50.................(v[1]) J-PGuillambert 10 *(T D Easterby) a.p: led 2f out: sn rdn and hdd: one pce fnl f* **9/4**[1]	56
	4	*hd*	**How's She Cuttin' (IRE)** 3-8-9 .... BenSwarbrick(3) 3 *(T D Barron) s.i.s: sn wl bhd: hdwy over 1f out: swtchd lft ins fnl f: kpt on* **7/1**[3]	50+
00	**5**	*3*	**One More Than Ten**[28] [3053] 3-9-3 .... GrahamGibbons 9 *(T D Easterby) s.i.s: bhd: rdn over 3f out: hdwy over 1f out: hung lft ent fnl f: no imp* **16/1**	46
2000	**6**	*nk*	**Tatstheticket**[13] [3538] 3-9-0 43...............................(v) JasonEdmunds(3) 7 *(J Balding) chsd ldrs: n.m.r over 1f out: sn wknd* **33/1**	46
	7	*1*	**Arabian Breeze** 3-8-12 .... TPQueally 12 *(M Mullineaux) n.d* **33/1**	38
	8	*2 ½*	**Orchard House (FR)** 3-9-3 .... DerekMcGaffin 5 *(J Jay) s.i.s: a bhd* **20/1**	35
336	**9**	*¾*	**Stoneacre Fred (IRE)**[21] [3257] 3-9-3 52.................... RobbieFitzpatrick 1 *(Peter Grayson) chsd ldrs: rdn over 2f out: nt clr run on ins ent st sn wknd* **11/4**[2]	43+
00	**10**	*¾*	**Cankara (IRE)**[17] [3387] 3-8-5 .... KellyHarrison(7) 4 *(D Carroll) s.s: outpcd* **14/1**	26
/0-6	**11**	*7*	**Mill End Chateau**[17] [3383] 4-9-1 45.......................... JamesMillman(7) 2 *(D K Ivory) sn led: rdn and hdd 2f out: sn wknd: eased whn btn ins fnl f* **40/1**	10
0	**U**		**Miss Imperious**[28] [3053] 3-8-7 .... MarkLawson(5) 11 *(B Smart) sn outpcd: last whn clipped heels and uns rdr over 1f out* **33/1**	—

1m 16.39s (0.58) **Going Correction** +0.075s/f (Slow)

WFA 3 from 4yo 5lb **12** Ran SP% **122.8**

Speed ratings (Par 101):99,96,96,95,91 91,90,86,85,84 75,—

CSF £57.42 TOTE £7.10: £1.70, £2.30, £1.60; EX 51.50.

Owner C J Murfitt **Bred** Stowell Hill Ltd **Trained** Newmarket, Suffolk

FOCUS

Moderate maiden form limited by the sixth.

How's She Cuttin'(IRE) Official explanation: jockey said filly would not face the kick-back

Cankara(IRE) Official explanation: jockey said, regarding running and riding, her orders were to sit mid-division and see how the race developed, adding that the filly missed the break, which she had done in the past, and then plugged on in the home straight; trainer's rep said that the filly would probably be stepped back up in trip; vet said that filly was slightly lame behind

Mill End Chateau Official explanation: jockey said gelding lost its action

3917 WOLVERHAMPTON-RACECOURSE.CO.UK NURSERY 5f 216y(P)

4:00 (4:00) (Class 5) 2-Y-O **£3,886** (£1,156; £577; £288) **Stalls** Low

Form				RPR
405	**1**		**Sweet Candy**[23] [3201] 2-8-7 **68**.. DO'Donohoe 7 *(K A Ryan) a.p: rdn over 3f out: led ins fnl f: r.o wl* **11/2**[3]	76+
252	**2**	*3*	**Drifting Gold**[36] [2791] 2-8-6 **70**... AdamKirby(3) 4 *(C G Cox) chsd ldrs: nt clr run and lost pl over 4f out: sn bhd: rn wd ent st: gd late hdwy to take 2nd nr post* **4/1**[2]	69
01	**3**	*hd*	**Ede's Dot Com (IRE)**[16] [3408] 2-9-2 **82**................ StephenDonohoe(5) 5 *(W J Knight) chsd ldrs: rdn over 3f out: sltly outpcd out 2f out: rallying whn hung lft 1f out: kpt on* **7/2**[1]	80
0155	**4**	*½*	**Down The Well (IRE)**[51] [2342] 2-8-7 **73**............... RichardKingscote(5) 6 *(J A Osborne) w ldr: led over 2f out: sn rdn: hdd and no ex ins fnl f* **8/1**	70
4031	**5**	*3*	**Stir Crazy (IRE)**[6] [3727] 2-8-11 **75** 6ex.................. EdwardCreighton(3) 10 *(M R Channon) led early: prom: ev ch over 2f out: sn rdn: wknd fnl f* **11/2**[3]	63
201	**6**	*¾*	**Merry Moon (IRE)**[21] [3246] 2-8-3 **64**.................................. DaleGibson 8 *(M Dods) hld up: rdn over 3f out: nvr nr ldrs* **7/1**	50
3204	**7**	*¾*	**Whiskey Junction**[16] [3409] 2-9-1 **76**................................ FrancisNorton 3 *(A M Balding) sn led: hdd over 2f out: sn rdn: wkng whn hmpd on ins 1f out* **8/1**	59
1560	**8**	*1 ¼*	**Spinning Game**[17] [3372] 2-7-12 **59** oh5................................ PaulQuinn 2 *(D W Chapman) chsd ldrs: nt clr run and stmbld after 1f: sn bhd: carried wd ent st* **33/1**	39
4500	**9**	*3*	**Smirfy's Silver**[35] [2807] 2-8-7 **68**............................... RobbieFitzpatrick 9 *(W M Brisbourne) outpcd* **33/1**	39
030	**10**	*1 ½*	**Abdu**[52] [2321] 2-7-12 **59** oh3.. FrankieMcDonald 1 *(M W Easterby) prom tl rdn and wknd over 3f out* **66/1**	25

1m 16.62s (0.81) **Going Correction** +0.075s/f (Slow) **10** Ran SP% **115.1**

Speed ratings (Par 94):97,93,92,92,88 87,86,84,80,78

CSF £27.08 CT £87.72 TOTE £5.00: £2.90, £2.30, £2.10; EX 50.80.

Owner Pedro Rosas **Bred** David John Brown **Trained** Hambleton, N Yorks

FOCUS

A fair nursery and sound form with the winner value for a little more. The official ratings shown next to each horse are estimated and for information purposes only.

NOTEBOOK

Sweet Candy, dropping back to six furlongs for this nursery debut, took time to hit top stride, but she drew right away inside the final furlong and made it yet another juvenile winner for the Ryan yard. She gives the impression she will stay seven furlongs and there may yet be more to come from the daughter of Cadeaux Genereux. (op 7-1 tchd 8-1)

Drifting Gold has developed into a consistent sort, having now finished second in three of her last four starts, and although not enjoying the best of runs through here, she would never have beaten the winner. She deserves to find a race, but her tasks are going to continue to get harder. (tchd 7-2)

Ede's Dot Com(IRE), an easy winner at Lingfield earlier in the month, was starting out nursery life on a stiff enough mark of 88 and he did not look good enough. A step up to seven furlongs may enable him to improve, but winning handicaps is not going to be easy. (tchd 10-3 and 4-1)

Down The Well(IRE) shaped a little better on this drop in grade and may well be worth dropping back down to the minimum, as she again showed a lot of speed. (op 13-2)

Stir Crazy(IRE), penalised for his Lingfield win, was up there from an early stage and held every chance, but he dropped away from a furlong out and seemed to find this a step too far. (op 9-2 after 4-1)

3918 MATTHEW CHANEY'S 13TH BIRTHDAY H'CAP 1m 141y(P)

4:35 (4:37) (Class 5) (0-75,75) 3-Y-O+ **£3,238** (£963; £481; £240) **Stalls** Low

Form RPR

6223 **1** **Daaweitza**[12] [3569] 3-8-8 **74** StephenDonohoe(5) 8 82
(B Ellison) *a.p: rdn 2f out: led ins fnl f: r.o* **7/1**[3]

210 **2** *1* **Don Pietro**[32] [2932] 3-8-9 **73** EdwardCreighton(3) 10 79
(D J Coakley) *chsd ldr: rdn 2f out: ev ch ins fnl f: r.o* **8/1**

0000 **3** *½* **Crail**[65] [1943] 6-9-8 **74** IanMongan 1 79+
(C F Wall) *a.p: rdn over 2f out: n.m.r 1f out: r.o* **5/1**[1]

1460 **4** *nk* **Stanley Goodspeed**[20] [3301] 3-8-10 **74** (t) AdamKirby(3) 5 78
(J W Hills) *hld up mid-div: rdn over 2f out: kpt on fnl f* **25/1**

60-3 **5** *nk* **United Nations**[8] [3688] 5-9-0 **69** DNolan(3) 2 73+
(N Wilson) *hld up in tch: rdn whn nt clr run on ins fr over 1f out tl ins fnl f: nt rch ldrs* **9/1**

0000 **6** *hd* **Thunderwing (IRE)**[17] [3374] 4-9-4 **70** PatCosgrave 13 73
(K R Burke) *a.p: rdn over 3f out: c wd and lost pl bnd over 2f out: styng on whn hung lft ins fnl f* **16/1**

1000 **7** *hd* **Lord Of Dreams (IRE)**[36] [2794] 4-8-13 **65** FrankieMcDonald 9 68
(D W P Arbuthnot) *led: rdn 2f out: hdd ins fnl f: no ex* **12/1**

0000 **8** *hd* **Anduril**[20] [3298] 5-8-12 **64** (b) J-PGuillambert 7 66
(Miss M E Rowland) *rrd and s.s: hdwy on wd outside over 2f out: nvr nrr* **20/1**

5000 **9** *1* **Western Roots**[3] [3820] 5-9-0 **66** AlanDaly 12 66
(M Appleby) *hld up and bhd: rdn over 2f out: n.d* **33/1**

00-0 **10** *1¼* **Constable Burton**[11] [3583] 5-9-1 **67** TPQueally 3 64
(Mrs A Duffield) *hmpd sn after s: a towards rr* **16/1**

162/ **11** *½* **Cadeaux Des Mages**[1036] [5194] 6-9-9 **75** JamieMackay 4 71
(J G Given) *plld hrd: sn bhd* **25/1**

2123 **12** *¾* **New England**[147] [571] 4-8-12 **64** RobbieFitzpatrick 11 59
(W M Brisbourne) *awkward leaving stalls and s.s: a bhd* **6/1**[2]

1m 52.19s (0.43) **Going Correction** +0.075s/f (Slow)
WFA 3 from 4yo+ 9lb **12** Ran SP% **99.4**
Speed ratings (Par 103):101,100,99,99,99 98,98,98,97,96 96,95
CSF £39.50 CT £165.00 TOTE £8.40: £2.20, £3.00, £1.50; EX 58.00.
Owner Mrs Andrea M Mallinson **Bred** C Mallinson **Trained** Norton, N Yorks
■ Treasure House (7/2F) was withdrawn on vet's advice. R4 applies, deduct 20p in the £.

FOCUS
A competitive handicap in which they went just a steady gallop and the form is rated at face value around the fourth.
New England Official explanation: jockey said gelding reared as stalls opened

3919 DINE AT DUNSTALL PARK APPRENTICE H'CAP 2m 119y(P)

5:10 (5:12) (Class 6) (0-55,55) 4-Y-O+ **£2,730** (£806; £403) **Stalls** Low

Form RPR

4544 **1** **Ice And Fire**[36] [2790] 7-8-10 **45** (b) AshleyHamblett(5) 13 57
(J T Stimpson) *hld up and bhd: hdwy on outside over 5f out: led 3f out: hung rt fr over 1f out: hrd rdn ins fnl f: styd on* **12/1**

5001 **2** *2* **Montage (IRE)**[11] [3597] 4-9-11 **55** 6ex AdamKirby 12 65
(J Akehurst) *hld up in tch: led over 8f out to 3f out: sn rdn: hung rt and rn wd ent st: edgd lft ins fnl f: styd on* **2/1**[1]

5012 **3** *9* **High Frequency (IRE)**[45] [2528] 5-8-12 **47** SladeO'Hara(5) 10 46
(A Crook) *hld up in tch: rdn over 3f out: one pce* **10/1**

0635 **4** *1¾* **Transit**[18] [3350] 7-8-11 **44** (p) StephenDonohoe(3) 7 41
(B Ellison) *hld up and bhd: hdwy 3f out: edgd lft wl over 1f out: no further prog* **11/2**[2]

-500 **5** *2½* **Kaluana Court**[21] [3269] 10-8-10 **45** FrankiePickard(5) 1 39
(A W Carroll) *hld up towards rr: styd on fnl 2f: nvr nr ldrs* **12/1**

0055 **6** *5* **Gravardlax**[21] [3260] 5-8-0 **35** (t) KirstyMilczarek(5) 4 23
(Miss D A McHale) *hld up in mid-div: struggling over 3f out* **28/1**

006 **7** *4* **Ballymena**[32] [2917] 5-8-10 **45** TolleyDean(5) 9 28
(R A Harris) *hld up in mid-div: hdwy over 8f out: wknd over 3f out* **25/1**

5000 **8** *6* **Indian Chase**[74] [1745] 9-9-7 **51** EdwardCreighton 3 27
(Dr J R J Naylor) *a bhd* **33/1**

-263 **9** *7* **Tharua (IRE)**[178] [256] 4-9-3 **47** (v) SaleemGolam 5 14
(Ernst Oertel) *hld up in mid-div: hdwy 5f out: wknd over 3f out* **16/1**

3450 **10** *1½* **College Rebel**[20] [3291] 5-8-11 **46** KevinGhunowa(5) 6 12
(J F Coupland) *hld up in tch: wknd over 5f out* **20/1**

4005 **11** *30* **Aristi (IRE)**[73] [1766] 5-9-4 **48** (p) DNolan 2 —
(M Quinn) *led 2f: prom tl rdn 4f out: sn wknd: sddle slipped: t.o* **6/1**[3]

4-35 **12** *5* **Encrypt (IRE)**[51] [2357] 4-9-3 **52** JosephWalsh(5) 11 —
(O Brennan) *prom tl wknd 4f out: t.o* **8/1**

000- **13** *37* **Meikle Beoch**[258] [6331] 4-8-2 **32** oh5 DominicFox 8 —
(Mrs H Sweeting) *prom: led after 2f tl over 8f out: wknd over 6f out: t.o fnl 5f* **50/1**

3m 44.16s (1.03) **Going Correction** +0.075s/f (Slow) **13** Ran SP% **121.4**
Speed ratings (Par 101):100,99,94,94,92 90,88,85,82,81 67,65,47
CSF £34.81 CT £265.81 TOTE £18.50: £5.80, £1.10, £2.10; EX 58.50 Place 6 £60.66, Place 5 £9.68..
Owner J T Stimpson & B Trubshaw **Bred** Abdullah Saeed Bul Hab **Trained** Newcastle-Under-Lyme, Staffs

FOCUS
Modest handicap form. The front two drew clear.
Aristi(IRE) Official explanation: jockey said saddle slipped
Encrypt(IRE) Official explanation: jockey said filly had no more to give
T/Plt: £81.10 to a £1 stake. Pool: £42,676.55. 383.90 winning tickets. T/Qpdt: £6.80 to a £1 stake. Pool: £3,208.10. 345.40 winning tickets. KH

3920 - 3922a (Foreign Racing) - See Raceform Interactive

3888 ASCOT (R-H)

Saturday, July 29

OFFICIAL GOING: Good to firm (good in places)

3923 EUROPEAN BREEDERS FUND CROCKER BULTEEL MAIDEN STKS (C&G) 6f

2:00 (2:01) (Class 4) UNRACED 2-Y-O **£6,477** (£1,927; £963; £481) Stalls Low

Form RPR

1 **To The Max (IRE)** 2-9-0 JimmyFortune 4 94
(R Hannon) *unf: scope: lw: dwlt: in tch in rr: prog 2f out: rdn and styd on wl fr over 1f out to ld last 75yds* **15/2**

2 *¾* **Dijeerr (USA)** 2-9-0 PhilipRobinson 6 92
(M A Jarvis) *cmpt: str: lw: cl up: trckd ldr over 2f out: shkn up to ld 1f out: hdd and outpcd last 75yds* **11/4**[1]

3 *1½* **Winged Flight (USA)** 2-9-0 JoeFanning 2 87
(M Johnston) *rangy: mde most: rdn and hdd 1f out: one pce* **7/2**[2]

4 *½* **Dodge City (USA)** 2-9-0 LDettori 3 86
(J Noseda) *str: scope: trckd ldrs: shkn up wl over 1f out: rn green and nt qckn* **4/1**[3]

5 *4* **Paceman (USA)** 2-9-0 RichardHughes 1 74
(R Hannon) *str: lw: dwlt: in tch tl wknd over 1f out* **9/2**

6 *10* **Mo (USA)** 2-9-0 (t) FJohansson 7 44
(R A Kvisla) *wl grwn: lw: wnt rt s: rcvrd to join ldr: wkng rapidly whn veered rt jst over 2f out: t.o* **33/1**

7 *9* **Bad Habit** 2-9-0 TedDurcan 5 17
(M R Channon) *lengthy: sn outpcd and reminders: t.o fr 1/2-way* **10/1**

1m 14.41s (-1.59) **Going Correction** 0.0s/f (Good) **7** Ran SP% **110.9**
Speed ratings (Par 96):103,102,100,99,94 80,68
CSF £26.67 TOTE £10.00: £3.30, £2.20; EX 41.10.
Owner The Max Partnership **Bred** Timothy J Rooney **Trained** East Everleigh, Wilts

FOCUS
This was confined to newcomers, so it is very hard to know how good a maiden it was. There were, though, some decent stables represented and all eight runners had attractive enough pedigrees, so it should be considered a pretty good race until proven otherwise. The winning time only 0.25 seconds slower than the Group 3 Princess Margaret Stakes later on in the card. They all raced towards the stands'-side rail.

NOTEBOOK
To The Max(IRE), a 42,000euros half-brother to useful dual seven/eight-furlong winner Bon Nuit, and six-furlong two-year-old scorer In A Silent Way, was seemingly the less fancied of the Hannon pair, but still attracted some support and proved good enough to make a winning debut. Having tracked the leaders early on, he found plenty when switched out with his run, displaying a particularly willing attitude. This cannot exactly be considered an easy introduction, but he looks the type who will take his racing with little bother. With no previous form to go on, only time will tell how good a maiden this was, but it looked pretty decent and he deserves to step up in class. It would be no surprise to see him turn up in something like the Solario Stakes at Sandown. (op 12-1 tchd 7-1)
Dijeerr(USA) ◆, a $500,000 half-brother to Sharp Writer, a quite useful miler, was made favourite for his racecourse debut, but having looked the most likely winner when hitting the front about a furlong out he was just unable to resist To The Max's challenge. He is likely to benefit from this outing and should be good enough next time. (op 3-1 tchd 7-2)
Winged Flight(USA), a $95,000 purchase, out of a quite useful nine-furlong winner, had every chance against the stands'-side rail, but just lacked a change of pace in the closing stages. He ought to come on for this and it will be disappointing if he does not win his maiden next time. (tchd 10-3 and 4-1)
Dodge City(USA), not sold at $275,000, is the first foal of a dual winner at around a mile in the US. Easy to back on course, he looked in need of the experience at the business end and was not given a hard time. There should be much better to come. (op 5-2)
Paceman(USA), not sold at $60,000, is a half-brother to Melanosporum, a mile winner at three. Sent off a shorter price than his successful stablemate and seemingly the yard's number one on jockey bookings, he found little under pressure and ran below expectations. He is surely better than this. (op 4-1tchd 5-1 in places)
Mo(USA), a 46,000gns purchase, out of a half-sister to high-class Fairy Garden, a multiple mile to a 12-furlong winner in France and the US, showed speed early but was weakening when possibly bumped slightly over two furlongs out. (tchd 25-1)
Bad Habit, a 32,000gns half-brother to Diction, a triple six to eight-furlong winner, never went a yard. (op 16-1)

3924 INDORE PEARS DIAMOND WINKFIELD STKS (LISTED RACE) 7f

2:35 (2:37) (Class 1) 2-Y-O

£14,195 (£5,380; £2,692; £1,342; £672; £337) **Stalls** Low

Form RPR

1520 **1** **Satulagi (USA)**[7] [3734] 2-8-11 JohnEgan 7 96
(J S Moore) *dwlt: hld up in last pair: plld to outer and rdn 2f out: prog to ld jst over 1f out: edgd lft: styd on wl* **10/1**

3421 **2** *1½* **Pires**[6] [3758] 2-9-2 TedDurcan 3 97
(M R Channon) *sn trckd ldr: chal 2f out: upsides over 1f out: hanging and nt qckn fnl f* **13/2**

011 **3** *shd* **Norisan**[14] [3531] 2-9-2 RichardHughes 2 97
(R Hannon) *lw: mde most: rdn 2f out: hdd jst over 1f out: one pce* **7/2**[2]

222 **4** *1¾* **Armigerent (IRE)**[16] [3442] 2-9-2 KDarley 1 92
(M Johnston) *lw: chsd ldrs: rdn and nt clr run jst over 2f out: one pce fr over 1f out* **6/4**[1]

3120 **5** *7* **Captain Marvelous (IRE)**[39] [2719] 2-9-2 MichaelHills 4 74
(B W Hills) *rrd s: hld up in last pair: pushed along over 3f out: lost tch over 2f out* **7/1**

513 **6** *3½* **Prince Of Elegance**[32] [2960] 2-9-2 MJKinane 6 65
(Mrs A J Perrett) *lw: pressed ldrs tl wknd rapidly wl over 1f out* **11/2**[3]

1m 28.46s (-0.54) **Going Correction** 0.0s/f (Good) **6** Ran SP% **112.5**
Speed ratings (Par 102):97,95,95,93,85 81
CSF £69.81 TOTE £14.20: £5.00, £2.50; EX 93.20.
Owner Mrs Fitri Hay **Bred** Lantern Hill Farm Llc **Trained** Upper Lambourn, Berks

FOCUS
This looked a pretty ordinary race for the grade, but they seemed to go a decent pace throughout and the form should be reliable. They all raced towards the stands'-side rail.

NOTEBOOK
Satulagi(USA) has been on the go since making her debut in only the second juvenile race of the season, but she has tended to progress with racing and had shown very useful form on more than one occasion, including when fifth to Sander Camillo in the Albany Stakes. Stepped up to seven furlongs for the first time following her ninth of 23 in the Super Sprint, she was held up behind the leaders, who seemed to be going plenty quick enough, and picked up best of all when switched out with her run, seeing the trip out very well. A fine effort considering she was the only filly in the line up. She may now be aimed the Lowther Stakes at York, but that Group 2 will be much tougher and the drop back in distance is unlikely to suit. (tchd 12-1)
Pires, fourth in the Chesham Stakes over course and distance at the Royal meeting, had since taken two more runs to break his maiden, justifying odds of 4/9 on his latest outing. Returned to Listed company, he seemed to run his race and can have few excuses. (op 9-1 tchd 11-2)
Norisan, who dead-heated with subsequent Superlative Stakes winner Halicarnassus in a seven-furlong maiden on the July course before following up in a novice event on Lingfield's Polytrack, ran respectably stepped up in grade, but just finished a touch weakly and may have gone too fast. He may be better ridden with slightly more patience. (tchd 4-1)
Armigerent(IRE), returned to seven furlongs, never looked happy chasing what was a decent enough pace and kept on without ever looking likely to pose a threat. This was some way off the form he showed when second in the July Stakes on his previous start and was disappointing. (op 6-5 tchd 7-4 and 15-8 in a place)
Captain Marvelous(IRE), 11th of 21 in the Coventry Stakes on his previous start, reared coming out of the stalls and was below form stepped up in trip and dropped in grade. (op 9-1)
Prince Of Elegance, off the mark in a maiden at Goodwood before running third in a six-furlong Newbury Listed event, got little cover on this step up in trip and weakened very tamely. (op 13-2 tchd 7-1 in a place)

3925 PRINCESS MARGARET STKS (GROUP 3) (FILLIES) 6f
3:10 (3:11) (Class 1) 2-Y-O

£25,551 (£9,684; £4,846; £2,416; £1,210; £607) **Stalls** Low

Form	Pos	Dist	Horse	RPR
013	**1**		**Scarlet Runner**[36] 2800 2-8-12 ...... KerrinMcEvoy 7 (J L Dunlop) *lw: trckd ldr towards centre: led wl over 1f out: hrd pressed fnl f: styd on wl* **5/1**[2]	106
2641	**2**	½	**Vital Statistics**[8] 3700 2-8-12 ...... JohnEgan 10 (D R C Elsworth) *hld up in rr of gp towards centre: prog on outer 2f out: pressed wnr fnl f: styd on but a hld* **20/1**	105
221	**3**	nk	**Simply Perfect**[15] 3485 2-8-12 ...... CSoumillon 1 (J Noseda) *trckd nr side ldr tl jnd main gp after 3f: rdn and outpcd over 1f out: styd on again fnl f* **11/2**[3]	104
01	**4**	hd	**Indian Ink (IRE)**[32] 2957 2-8-12 ...... RichardHughes 5 (R Hannon) *trckd ldrs towards centre: hrd rdn and prog over 1f out: one pce ins fnl f* **4/1**[1]	103
312	**5**	1 ½	**Alzerra (UAE)**[17] 3415 2-8-12 ...... TedDurcan 2 (M R Channon) *led nr side trio and wl on terms: one pce fr over 1f out* **6/1**	99
3	**6**	nk	**Love On Sight**[49] 2456 2-8-12 ...... NCallan 8 (A P Jarvis) *lw: in tch towards centre: outpcd over 1f out: kpt on again ins fnl f* **14/1**	98
114	**7**	¾	**Hope'N'Charity (USA)**[17] 3415 2-8-12 ...... PhilipRobinson 6 (C G Cox) *led gp towards centre to wl over 1f out: one pce after* **9/1**	95
521	**8**	6	**Naayla (IRE)**[22] 3259 2-8-12 ...... LDettori 9 (B J Meehan) *in tch towards centre: rdn and hanging bdly fr 2f out: wknd* **14/1**	77
1	**9**	6	**Pinkabout (IRE)**[17] 3402 2-8-12 ...... JimmyFortune 3 (J H M Gosden) *last of nr side trio: struggling to stay in tch over 2f out: wknd* **15/2**	59
1	**10**	56	**Pelican Key (IRE)**[27] 3120 2-8-12 ...... MJKinane 4 (D M Simcock) *lw: a towards rr: wknd over 2f out: virtually p.u fnl f* **10/1**	—

1m 14.16s (-1.84) **Going Correction** 0.0s/f (Good) **10** Ran SP% **115.3**
Speed ratings (Par 101):104,103,102,102,100 100,99,91,83,8
CSF £97.40 TOTE £6.40: £2.40, £4.10, £1.80; EX 151.70 Trifecta £1627.70 Pool: £2,521.88 - 1.10 winning units..
Owner Nicholas Jones **Bred** Coln Valley Stud **Trained** Arundel, W Sussex
■ Stewards' Enquiry : John Egan two-day ban: careless riding (Aug 9-10); caution: careless riding

FOCUS
Nine of the ten runners were previous winners, and the sole maiden came from the stable which had taken two of the last three runnings of this race, so this was certainly a competitive renewal of the Princess Margaret. However, there did not look to be any stand-out performer on show, and the winning time was only 0.25 seconds quicker than the earlier maiden for unraced colts and geldings. The field split into two groups early on, with Alzerra, Simply Perfect and Pinkabout racing towards the stands'-side, and the remainder just a little way off the rail, but they all came together in the closing stages.

NOTEBOOK
Scarlet Runner, the winner of a Windsor maiden before running third to Sander Camillo in the Albany Stakes at Royal Ascot, was always well positioned by the excellent McEvoy and sustained her challenge right the way to the line. She has the option of going for the Lowther Stakes next time, but if that comes too soon she could be aimed at the Cheveley Park. While she is a likeable filly and certainly going the right way, those races would require improvement on the bare form of this success. (op 4-1)
Vital Statistics, the Queen Mary sixth who was getting off the mark at the fifth attempt when winning a maiden at Newbury on her previous start, had to be switched widest of all to get a clear run and finished strongly. This was a cracking effort and she is clearly still improving. Official explanation: vet said filly returned with cuts to hind legs, caused in stalls (op 33-1)
Simply Perfect, off the mark at odds of 2/13 in maiden company at Lingfield (turf) on her previous start, ran well back up in grade but could not confirm Queen Mary form with Vital Statistics. (op 4-1)
Indian Ink(IRE), the comfortable winner of a six-furlong maiden at Newbury on her previous start, ran with credit, stepped up significantly in class, and was clear of the remainder in fourth. She is open to more improvement. (op 7-2)
Alzerra(UAE), a five-length second to Sander Camillo in the Cherry Hinton on her previous start, raced on arguably slightly slower ground against the stands'-side rail and was ultimately well held in fifth.
Love On Sight ◆, well clear of the remainder when third on her debut in a six-furlong maiden at Newbury, represented the yard who had won two of the last three runnings of this race. She ran with real credit and gave the impression she is open to more improvement. She can win her maiden before stepping back up in class. (tchd 16-1)
Hope'N'Charity(USA), the winner of a maiden and Listed race before running fourth to Sander Camillo in the Cherry Hinton at Newmarket, raced a little keenly early on and could not reverse form with Alzerra. (op 11-1)
Naayla(IRE) would have found this a lot tougher than the Southwell (Fibresand) maiden she won last time and, hanging in the last third, finished up well held. (op 20-1)
Pinkabout(IRE), an impressive winner of a six-furlong Kempton maiden on her debut but, upped in class, was well beaten. Official explanation: jockey said filly lost its action (op 9-1)
Pelican Key(IRE) looked a cracking prospect when winning a Windsor conditions race on her debut, but something was presumably amiss this time. Official explanation: vet said filly finished distressed (op 12-1)

3926 TOTESPORT INTERNATIONAL STKS (HERITAGE H'CAP) 7f
3:45 (3:47) (Class 2) 3-Y-O+

£93,480 (£27,990; £13,995; £7,005; £3,495; £1,755) **Stalls** Low

Form	Pos	Dist	Horse	RPR
1130	**1**		**Dabbers Ridge (IRE)**[38] 2742 4-8-9 **97** ...... MichaelHills 12 (B W Hills) *trckd ldrs nr side: prog to ld 2f out: clr over 1f out: drvn and hld on wl nr fin* **12/1**	109
5001	**2**	nk	**Uhoomagoo**[37] 2776 8-8-7 **95** ......(b) NCallan 14 (K A Ryan) *hld up wl in rr nr side: drvn and gd prog on outer fr 2f out: clsd on wnr ins fnl f: jst hld* **16/1**	106
5203	**3**	1 ½	**Marching Song**[15] 3493 4-8-6 **94** ...... RichardHughes 7 (R Hannon) *hld up midfield nr side: prog to chse ldrs 2f out: drvn and styd on fnl f: unable to chal* **11/1**	101
2020	**4**	shd	**Appalachian Trail (IRE)**[15] 3493 5-8-11 **99** ......(b) TomEaves 10 (I Semple) *lw: wl in rr nr side: gd prog u.p wl over 1f out: styd on ins fnl f* **16/1**	106
1041	**5**	nk	**Bayeux (USA)**[15] 3482 5-8-9 **97** 3ex ...... JohnEgan 1 (G A Butler) *towards rr nr side and sn pushed along: effrt u.p over 2f out: styd on: nrst fin* **10/1**	103
3-14	**6**	¾	**Polar Magic**[54] 2289 5-8-11 **99** ...... LDettori 5 (J R Fanshawe) *dwlt: hld up in last trio nr side: rdn and prog fr wl over 1f out: styd on: unable to chal* **11/1**	103
0051	**7**	nk	**Gallantry**[15] 3500 4-7-12 **86** oh4 ...... JimmyQuinn 4 (D W Barker) *pressed nr side ldrs: rdn to chal 2f out: btn over 1f out: fdd ins fnl f* **25/1**	89
1042	**8**	1 ¾	**Beaver Patrol (IRE)**[14] 3550 4-8-5 **93** ...... KerrinMcEvoy 16 (R F Johnson Houghton) *lw: racd on outer of nr side gp: rdn over 2f out: one pce and no imp ldrs* **20/1**	91
-141	**9**	shd	**Hinterland (IRE)**[21] 3313 4-9-0 **102** 3ex ...... PhilipRobinson 20 (M A Jarvis) *racd towards far side: pressed ldr but nvr on terms w main gp: led his gp of 4 over 2f out: kpt on but no ch with pack* **7/2**[1]	100+
0001	**10**	¾	**Mine (IRE)**[15] 3493 8-9-3 **105** 3ex ......(v) MJKinane 17 (J D Bethell) *hld up last of gp towards far side: effrt over 2f out: pressed ldr nr fin: 2nd of 4 in gp* **11/2**[2]	101+
6100	**11**	hd	**Mr Sandicliffe**[17] 3414 3-7-12 **93** oh4 ......(b[1]) FrancisFerris 3 (C N Allen) *dwlt: wl in rr nr side: struggling over 2f out: hung rt wl over 1f out: plugged on* **100/1**	86
5023	**12**	1 ½	**New Seeker**[28] 3086 6-9-4 **109** ......(b) AdamKirby[(3)] 9 (C G Cox) *led nr side gp after 2f to over 2f out: wknd over 1f out* **8/1**[3]	100
2105	**13**	shd	**Dhaular Dhar (IRE)**[15] 3482 4-7-7 **86** oh2 ...... DuranFentiman[(5)] 19 (J S Goldie) *chsd ldng pair towards far side: rdn 1/2-way: struggling fnl 2f: 3rd of 4 in gp* **50/1**	77+
0300	**14**	nk	**Bahiano (IRE)**[15] 3493 5-8-12 **100** ...... CSoumillon 6 (C E Brittain) *racd nr side: nvr beyond midfield: no prog and btn wl over 1f out* **16/1**	90
0040	**15**	1	**Just James**[15] 3482 7-8-6 **94** ...... JoeFanning 8 (D Nicholls) *a towards rr nr side: rdn and one pce fnl 2f: no prog* **33/1**	82
3341	**16**	hd	**King's Caprice**[15] 3471 5-8-7 **95** 3ex ......(t) RichardThomas 11 (J A Geake) *overall ldr nr side for 2f: pressed ldr: led again over 2f out to 2f out: wknd* **50/1**	82
0330	**17**	3 ½	**Binanti**[15] 3493 6-7-12 **86** ...... FrankieMcDonald 18 (P R Chamings) *led far side gp to over 2f out: nvr on terms w nr side: wknd: last of 4 in gp* **40/1**	64+
-620	**18**	¾	**Marshman (IRE)**[28] 3079 7-8-0 **95** ow7 ...... PatrickHills[(7)] 2 (M H Tompkins) *nvr beyond midfield on nr side: wknd 2f out* **40/1**	71
0033	**19**	20	**King Marju (IRE)**[133] 667 4-8-4 **92** ...... MartinDwyer 13 (K R Burke) *lw: v fractious preliminaries: a towards rr nr side: t.o* **25/1**	14
5616	**20**	3 ½	**Indian Trail**[21] 3295 6-9-0 **102** ...... AdrianTNicholls 15 (D Nicholls) *lw: t.k.h: trckd nr side ldrs tl wknd rapidly jst over 2f out: t.o* **25/1**	14

1m 25.89s (-3.11) **Going Correction** -0.10s/f (Good)
WFA 3 from 4yo+ 7lb **20** Ran SP% **128.8**
Speed ratings (Par 109):112,111,109,109,109 108,108,106,106,105 105,103,103,102,101 101,97,96,73,69
CSF £179.80 CT £2245.43 TOTE £17.80: £4.10, £2.40, £3.00, £6.00; EX 396.90 Trifecta £7267.60 Pool: £60,393.02 - 50.90 winning units..
Owner Maurice Mogg **Bred** Franco Castelfranci **Trained** Lambourn, Berks

FOCUS
Maybe not quite as big a field as many might have expected, but this looked a decent enough renewal of this valuable handicap. Hinterland, Mine, Dhaular Dhar and Binanti tried their luck towards the far side of the track, but the much larger group who raced on the near side but off the rail were at a significant advantage. Needless to say, though, they were all well spread out in the closing stages. The first four home were all drawn towards the middle.

NOTEBOOK
Dabbers Ridge(IRE) did not appear to see out a mile when only 12th in the Royal Hunt Cup on his previous start, but the drop back in trip suited and he just proved good enough. He had previously shown a preference for a bit of give in the ground, but this surface did not pose a problem for him. A seven-furlong specialist, he is probably worth taking on over any other trip. (op 14-1)
Uhoomagoo, having his 99th career start, ran a terrific race off a mark 5lb higher than when winning the Buckingham Palace Stakes at the Royal meeting. He won at the Galway Festival last year and could head back there for this year's meeting.
Marching Song, third to Mine in the Bunbury Cup on his previous outing, ran another fine race in defeat and can have few excuses. (op 10-1 tchd 12-1)
Appalachian Trail(IRE), second to Uhoomagoo in the Buckingham Palace Stakes before running eighth in the Bunbury Cup, looks a little bit better than the bare form as he had to be switched closer to the stands'-side rail than many of these with his run and got going too late. (op 14-1)
Bayeux(USA), 2lb well-in under the penalty he picked up for winning over six furlongs at Hamilton on his previous start, is another who looks a little bit better than the bare form as he had to be switched with his run. (op 12-1)
Polar Magic found himself further back than was ideal after starting slowly and was never a serious danger. He can do better.
Gallantry ran well from 4lb out of the handicap, but would have found this tougher than the York handicap he won last time.
Beaver Patrol(IRE) was 2lb lower than in future, but it might be that six furlongs suits best. (op 25-1)
Hinterland(IRE), the Royal Hunt Cup fourth, was 3lb well-in under the penalty he picked up for winning at Sandown on his previous start, but was unfavoured by racing with only three other horses towards the far side of the track. He is clearly better than he was able to show. (tchd 4-1 in places)
Mine(IRE), 3lb well-in under the penalty he picked up for winning his third Bunbury Cup, would have been totally unsuited by racing with just three other horses towards the far side of the track and is better than he was able to show. (tchd 6-1)
Mr Sandicliffe ◆, with blinkers replacing cheekpieces, and upped to seven furlongs for the first time, ran a blinder on his debut for new connections considering he was 4lb out of the handicap and hung badly right when trying to stay on. He looks as though he will stay this trip and that will create more opportunities for him. (op 66-1)
New Seeker, successful in this race in both 2003 and last year, faded in the latter stages and struggled to concede weight all round. He was reported to have hit his head on the stalls, so can be excused. Official explanation: jockey said gelding hit its head in stalls (tchd 9-1)
Indian Trail Official explanation: jockey said gelding had no more to give

3927 KING GEORGE VI AND QUEEN ELIZABETH DIAMOND STKS (GROUP 1) 1m 4f
4:20 (4:22) (Class 1) 3-Y-O+

£425,850 (£161,400; £80,775; £40,275; £20,175; £10,125) **Stalls** High

Form	Pos	Dist	Horse	RPR
1-12	**1**		**Hurricane Run (IRE)**[34] 2914 4-9-7 ...... CSoumillon 4 (A Fabre, France) *lw: trckd ldr to 4f out: 4th and rdn wl over 2f out: rallied over 1f out: r.o to ld last 100yds* **5/6**[1]	126+
-112	**2**	½	**Electrocutionist (USA)**[38] 2741 5-9-7 124 ...... LDettori 1 (Saeed Bin Suroor) *lw: b: hld up: prog to trck ldr 4f out: rdn to chal wl over 1f out: hanging rt but upsides fnl f: nt qckn last 100yds* **4/1**[3]	125
/2-1	**3**	½	**Heart's Cry (JPN)**[126] 741 5-9-7 ...... C-PLemaire 3 (K Hashiguchi, Japan) *w'like: lw: trckd ldng pair for 5f: 5th over 4f out: prog 3f out: led wl over 1f out: hdd and nt qckn last 100yds* **3/1**[2]	124
5333	**4**	1 ¾	**Enforcer**[16] 3444 4-9-7 116 ...... MartinDwyer 2 (W R Muir) *lw: hld up in last: effrt over 2f out: chsd ldng trio 1f out: no imp* **50/1**	121

0311 **5** 1 ½ **Maraahel (IRE)**35 2845 5-9-7 120.....(v) RHills 6 119
(Sir Michael Stoute) *hld up in last pair: shkn up and no prog over 2f out: kpt on to grab 5th nr fin* **14/1**

0-06 **6** ½ **Cherry Mix (FR)**71 1833 5-9-7 114.....(t) KerrinMcEvoy 5 118
(Saeed Bin Suroor) *b: led to wl over 1f out: wknd* **50/1**

2m 30.29s (-2.71) **Going Correction** -0.10s/f (Good) **6** Ran SP% **110.1**
Speed ratings (Par 117):105,104,104,103,102 101
CSF £4.36 TOTE £1.80: £1.10, £2.40; EX 5.10.
Owner Michael Tabor **Bred** Gestut Ammerland **Trained** Chantilly, France
■ Hurricane Run emulated his sire Montjeu, the 2000 winner. They are the only French-trained winners since Pawneese in 1976.
■ Stewards' Enquiry : C Soumillon six-day ban: used whip with excessive frequency (Aug 9-14)
L Dettori caution: used whip with excessive frequency

FOCUS
The smallest field since 1970 and no three-year-olds, but a cracking renewal nevertheless, with three of the best middle-distance horses in the world on show in Hurricane Run, Electrocutionist and Heart's Cry, and three more who are very smart performers in their own right. It lived up to expectations and more, with the 'big three' virtually in a line inside the final furlong in a most memorable finish. The others were a little too close for comfort, so it's difficult to rate the form highly by King George standards - the winner's provisional mark of 126 is the lowest of any winner in the last 10 years - but the way the race was run contributed to that, for Cherry Mix had only increased the tempo after about four and a half furlongs.

NOTEBOOK
Hurricane Run(IRE) ◆ had been turned over in his prep for this race in the Grand Prix de Saint-Cloud, but memories of that slight blip were banished with a fantastic performance. Having always been well placed, he suddenly came off the bridle as the field rounded the final bend, and looked a pretty unlikely winner for a second or two, but Soumillon, reunited with him due to Fallon's enforced absence, quickly got after him. The response was by no means immediate, but he was racing on the fastest ground he had encountered since landing last year's Irish Derby, and also became short of room as Heart's Cry loomed up on his outside. As he finally began to hit full stride a gap opened up for him towards the inside rail and he showed a fine change of pace to quicken past Electrocutionist. To many he may not have been as visually impressive as he was in the Arc, and this effort might not have matched the performance figures he recorded that day, but marked him down as arguably the best middle-distance turf horse in the world. His season will now be geared towards defending his Arc crown, and if he turns up at Longchamp at his best, stablemate Shirocco and the Japanese-trained Deep Impact will have to be very special indeed to stop him. (op 10-11 tchd Evens and 4-5)
Electrocutionist(USA), the winner of this year's Dubai World Cup before running second to Ouija Board in the Prince Of Wales's Stakes at the Royal meeting off the back of an interrupted preparation, was the subject of late scare, having pulled out stiff in the morning after probably getting cast in his box overnight. This was another fantastic performance from a particularly game sort, but one cannot but help think he might have been feeling something in the closing stages, for having been produced with every chance, he began carrying his head slightly awkwardly and was inclined to hang to his left when under maximum pressure. There is cause for suggesting he would have benefited from his rider pulling his whip through to his left hand, but he has had some hard races this season and it will be interesting to see what he is capable of next time. (op 7-2 tchd 9-2)
Heart's Cry(JPN), who upset the much-heralded and otherwise unbeaten Deep Impact in Japan on Christmas day before winning the Sheema Classic in Dubai, ran a terrific race on his British debut. Having loomed up on the outside with every chance, he came out worst in a terrific three-way battle and his rider thought he could even have blown up, having been off the track for four months. He will now head back to Japan and has done his homeland proud. (op 11-4)
Enforcer has been running fantastically well in the face of some stiff tasks this season and he again did his connections proud. His proximity will be used by many to hold the form of this race down, but he has already been placed in the Coronation Cup this season and the way he tends to be ridden means he can stay on late and try and pick off horses who have already given their best effort.
Maraahel(IRE) had a bit to find with the principals, but could not even confirm Hardwicke form with Enforcer and was not at his best. (op 16-1tchd 18-1 in a place)
Cherry Mix(FR) set the pace for his stablemate. The fact he was not beaten very far adds weight to theory he did not go very fast in the first part of the contest. (op 66-1)

3928 IDOL'S EYE DIAMOND H'CAP (LADIES RACE) 7f
4:55 (4:56) (Class 3) (0-90,90) 3-Y-O+ **£8,744** (£2,711; £1,355; £677) **Stalls** Low

Form RPR

4123 **1** **Lincolneurocruiser**13 3565 4-9-5 71 oh3..... MrsMMorris 10 80
(Mrs N Macauley) *wl in tch: effrt 2f out: led 1f out: hld on nr fin* **20/1**

0304 **2** ½ **Greenwood**14 3543 8-9-5 71..... MrsSMoore 11 79
(P G Murphy) *trckd ldrs: prog to ld wl over 1f out: hdd 1f out: kpt on wl nr fin* **20/1**

4406 **3** *shd* **Roman Maze**14 3550 6-10-5 85..... MissNCarberry 7 93+
(W M Brisbourne) *hld up: smooth prog 2f out: rdn to chal fnl f: nt qckn last 75yds* **11/2**1

230B **4** ¾ **Surwaki (USA)**23 3223 4-9-4 75..... MissJFerguson(5) 2 81
(C G Cox) *mde most to over 2f out: outpcd: r.o again ins fnl f* **25/1**

6422 **5** ¾ **Grizedale (IRE)**23 3223 7-9-9 75.....(t) MissEJJones 18 79
(J Akehurst) *racd in centre gp early: prog whn jnd main gp: pressed wnr jst ins fnl f: one pce* **12/1**

-000 **6** ½ **Emilio**23 3223 5-10-5 85.....(t) MrsCGraberg 8 87
(R A Kvisla) *dwlt: wl in rr: taken towards centre and r.o fnl f: nt rch ldrs* **100/1**

0305 **7** ½ **Looks Could Kill (USA)**13 3567 4-9-10 81. MissMichelleSaunders(5) 4 82
(E J Alston) *trckd ldrs: lost pl over 2f out: swtchd lft over 1f out: kpt on fnl f: no ch* **20/1**

0163 **8** ½ **Royal Dignitary (USA)**15 3500 6-10-3 83..... MsKWalsh 6 83
(D Nicholls) *w ldrs: led over 2f out to wl over 1f out: fdd fnl f* **9/1**3

6662 **9** 3 **Katiypour (IRE)**16 3433 9-10-0 80..... MrsCBartley 14 72
(Miss B Sanders) *w ldrs tl wknd over 1f out* **10/1**

1212 **10** ½ **Paraguay (USA)**7 3740 3-9-12 85..... MissSBrotherton 15 72
(Miss V Haigh) *hld up: prog to chse ldrs over 1f out: wknd fnl f* **7/1**2

3643 **11** 1 **Arctic Desert**14 3543 6-9-0 71 oh1..... MissMSowerby(5) 20 58
(A M Balding) *s.s: racd in centre: nvr on terms: kpt on* **20/1**

4150 **12** *hd* **Boundless Prospect (USA)**17 3413 7-10-2 82..... MrsACooke 9 69
(Miss Gay Kelleway) *sn wl bhd: kpt on fr over 1f out: no ch* **20/1**

2141 **13** *shd* **Blue Java**43 2606 5-9-5 76..... MissFCumani(5) 13 63
(H Morrison) *w ldrs: upsides over 2f out to wl over 1f out: wknd* **11/2**1

2630 **14** 1 ½ **Everest (IRE)**17 3413 9-10-0 80..... MissLEllison 23 63
(B Ellison) *racd centre: nvr on terms: bhd over 1f out* **20/1**

6001 **15** ½ **Kindlelight Debut**9 3687 6-10-10 90..... MrsEmmaLittmoden 3 71
(N P Littmoden) *chsd ldrs: u.p over 2f out: sn wknd* **20/1**

6040 **16** 1 **Border Edge**8 3705 8-9-0 71 oh13.....(v) MissJRiding(5) 16 50
(J J Bridger) *led gp in centre but nt on terms: wknd 2f out* **66/1**

0240 **17** 2 **Tyzack (IRE)**17 3413 5-9-11 82..... MrsSLiddiard(5) 1 55
(Stef Liddiard) *prom for 4f: sn wknd* **14/1**

4302 **18** 2 **Treetops Hotel (IRE)**40 2707 7-9-0 71 oh18..... MissAWallace(5) 22 39
(B R Johnson) *racd towards far side: nvr on terms: bhd fnl 2f* **40/1**

-166 **19** 10 **Divine River**15 3489 3-9-1 79..... MissKellyBurke(5) 17 17
(A P Jarvis) *racd centre gp: chsd ldrs to 1/2-way: wknd rapidly* **50/1**

0403 **20** 21 **Mine Behind**15 3471 6-10-7 87..... MrsSBosley 19 —
(J R Best) *chsd ldr in centre to 1/2-way: wknd rapidly: t.o* **12/1**

1m 28.63s (-0.37) **Going Correction** -0.10s/f (Good)
WFA 3 from 4yo+ 7lb **20** Ran SP% **128.5**
Speed ratings (Par 107):96,95,95,94,93 93,92,91,88,87 86,86,86,84,84 82,80,78,66,42
CSF £359.04 CT £2522.25 TOTE £28.80: £4.70, £6.90, £2.00, £7.40; EX 459.90 Trifecta £2151.30 Part won. Pool: £3,030.14 - 0.30 winning units..
Owner Peter Smith P C Coaches Limited **Bred** David Brown, Slatch Farm Stud And G B Turnbull L **Trained** Sproxton, Leics

FOCUS
A very competitive renewal of this lady riders' handicap and, as is so often the case in these types of races, it proved a minefield for punters. The field tended to race middle to stands' side and it was those who had raced in the larger near-side group from the start who appeared at a distinct advantage. The first three home came from middle stalls.

NOTEBOOK
Lincolneurocruiser ◆ seems to be improving and proved good enough to win from 3lb out of the handicap. Having picked up well to lead, he appeared particularly game when strongly challenged to hold on for his third success of the year. Although the form from these types of races does not always work out, he looks one to keep on the right side of.
Greenwood goes well in these types of races and ran a cracker in second. He is just hard to win with.
Roman Maze, partnered by arguably the pick of the jockeys, stayed on for pressure without perhaps finding as much as one might have expected. (op 5-1)
Surwaki(USA) raced closer to the stands' rail than many of these and kept on to the line.
Grizedale(IRE) has not won for nearly a year, but is in good form and this was another decent effort from a far from ideal draw. (op 11-1)
Emilio ◆, a multiple winner in Scandinavia, had not shown much in this country so far this season, but this was a very eye-catching performance. Well off the pace for much of the way, he was forced to switch wide with his run and just got going too late. It will be interesting to see if he can confirm this next time.
Looks Could Kill(USA) ◆ is another better than the bare form as, after losing his place, he had to be switched inside with his run and got going too late.
Paraguay(USA) has been in fine form lately, but was not at his best this time. (tchd 15-2 in a place)
Blue Java, 4lb higher than when winning at Goodwood on his previous start, did not find much under pressure and proved disappointing. (op 6-1)
Mine Behind Official explanation: jockey said gelding lost its action

3929 DIAMOND RESEARCH ANNIVERSARY CLASSIFIED STKS 1m 2f
5:30 (5:31) (Class 2) 3-Y-O+
£12,464 (£3,732; £1,866; £934; £466; £234) **Stalls** High

Form RPR

4310 **1** **Senor Dali (IRE)**37 2775 3-8-10 95..... KerrinMcEvoy 6 103
(J L Dunlop) *racd freely: trckd ldr: rdn to ld 2f out: in command fr over 1f out: readily* **6/1**3

2002 **2** 1 ¼ **Desert Realm (IRE)**9 3671 3-8-10 95..... JoeFanning 4 101
(M Johnston) *hit stalls s: hld up in 5th: effrt on inner over 2f out: chsd wnr over 1f out: hung lft and no imp* **8/1**

1-1 **3** ½ **Portal**50 2404 3-8-7 92..... OscarUrbina 2 97
(J R Fanshawe) *hld up in last: effrt on outer over 2f out: nt qckn wl over 1f out: styd on ins fnl f* **6/4**1

0510 **4** 1 ¾ **Impeller (IRE)**14 3552 7-9-6 94..... MartinDwyer 7 97
(W R Muir) *t.k.h: trckd ldng pair: rdn and nt qckn 2f out: n.m.r over 1f out: one pce* **6/1**3

0003 **5** ½ **Boo**14 3552 4-9-6 92..... PatCosgrave 5 96
(K R Burke) *t.k.h: hld up in 4th: rdn and struggling over 2f out: wl btn whn hmpd jst ins fnl f* **5/1**2

3100 **6** 3 **Divine Gift**14 3552 5-9-6 95..... NCallan 3 90
(K A Ryan) *led to 2f out: wknd fnl f* **13/2**

2m 11.57s (3.57) **Going Correction** -0.10s/f (Good)
WFA 3 from 4yo+ 10lb **6** Ran SP% **109.7**
Speed ratings (Par 109):81,80,79,78,77 75
CSF £47.47 TOTE £8.50: £3.50, £3.10; EX 53.10 Place 6 £1,292.76, Place 5 £489.27.
Owner Mrs M E Slade **Bred** Frank Dunne **Trained** Arundel, W Sussex

FOCUS
This looked quite an interesting classified event, with just 3lb separating the entire field at the weights on BHB figures, but they went a steady pace early and it developed into something of a sprint in the straight.

NOTEBOOK
Senor Dali(IRE), the Predominate Stakes third, was always well placed given the way the race was run and picked up nicely in the straight to win well. He might find things tougher when reassessed, but is clearly smart when things fall right for him. (op 7-1 tchd 8-1)
Desert Realm(IRE), upped in trip, was not as well placed as the winner when the pace increased but kept on in the closing stages. (op 13-2)
Portal ◆, the winner of a Folkestone maiden last year and successful off a mark of 82 in a handicap over this sort of trip at Goodwood on her reappearance, appeared to be given too much to do considering how steady they went early. She could not make up the required ground in the straight but can do better. (tchd 11-8 and 13-8 in places)
Impeller(IRE) did not run badly but seems more suited by switch-back tracks like Epsom. (tchd 11-2 and 7-1 in places)
Boo did not help his chance by racing keenly early and probably would have preferred a stronger gallop. (tchd 9-2 and 11-2 in a place)
T/Jkpt: Not won. T/Plt: £1,860.00 to a £1 stake. Pool: £193,267.59. 75.85 winning tickets. T/Qpdt: £83.80 to a £1 stake. Pool: £12,850.10. 113.40 winning tickets. JN

3843 LINGFIELD (L-H)
Saturday, July 29

OFFICIAL GOING: Turf course - good to firm; all-weather - standard
Wind: Fresh, behind Weather: Cloudy

3930 LINGFIELDPARK.CO.UK MAIDEN AUCTION STKS 5f
6:00 (6:00) (Class 5) 2-Y-O **£3,238** (£963; £481; £240) **Stalls** High

Form RPR

6 **1** **Nobilissima (IRE)**12 3591 2-8-4..... AdrianTNicholls 7 65
(J L Spearing) *racd on stands' rail: mde most: edgd lft off rail ins fnl 2f: rdn out* **9/1**

3 **2** 1 ¼ **Averticus**12 3588 2-8-12..... MichaelHills 3 68
(B W Hills) *hld up: rdn and hdwy 2f out: swtchd rt to stands' rail over 1f out: r.o to take 2nd ins fnl f* **4/7**1

306 **3** 1 ½ **Mogok Ruby**12 3588 2-8-13..... MickyFenton 5 64
(L Montague Hall) *w wnr tl nt qckn appr fnl f* **16/1**

0440 **4** 3/4 **Indian Song (IRE)**[7] 3734 2-8-5 .... JohnEgan 1 53
(R F Johnson Houghton) *hld up: drvn to chse ldng pair 2f out: one pce* **11/2**[2]

60 **5** 2 1/2 **City Bhoy**[29] 3031 2-8-10 .... SteveDrowne 4 49
(Tom Dascombe) *hld up towards rr: effrt and sltly hmpd ins fnl 2f: nvr able to chal* **40/1**

6 *shd* **Convivial Spirit** 2-8-10 .... TedDurcan 6 49
(E F Vaughan) *dwlt: sn in tch in rr: effrt and rn green 2f out: hmpd on rail over 1f out: n.d after* **33/1**

333 **7** 1 1/4 **Bush Breakfast**[28] 3070 2-8-13 .... IanMongan 2 47
(P Winkworth) *hld up towards rr: rdn and n.d fnl 2f* **7/1**[3]

57.77 secs (-1.17) **Going Correction** -0.275s/f (Firm) 7 Ran SP% **112.8**
Speed ratings (Par 94):98,96,93,92,88 88,86
CSF £14.27 TOTE £16.80: £3.50, £1.20; EX 22.30.
Owner Nine Traders Syndicate **Bred** Sea Syndicate **Trained** Kinnersley, Worcs

FOCUS
An ordinary maiden, with a beaten odds-on favourite who gave the winner too much start and not form to be confident about.

NOTEBOOK
Nobilissima(IRE) made good use of the stands' rail draw, though she edged left and let the favourite take over against the fence in the final quarter-mile. However, she still had more than enough in the tank to hold on over a trip which seemed to suit her better than the six furlongs which she encountered on her debut. (op 8-1)
Averticus eventually got over to the stands' rail, but by then the winner was almost home. Though a shade disappointing here, he can win over an extra furlong. (tchd 4-9 tchd 8-13 in a place)
Mogok Ruby did well to match the winner for a long way, and looks likely to switch to nurseries soon. (op 20-1 tchd 33-1)
Indian Song(IRE) was running at a more realistic level this time, but still fell short. Nurseries look to be the obvious route from now on. (op 5-1 tchd 6-1)
City Bhoy is now qualified for nurseries, and that looks his level. (op 33-1)
Convivial Spirit, a cheap purchase from a speedy family, had already been gelded for this debut. Despite running green, he ran quite well until running out of room on the stands' rail nearing the final furlong, and should improve for the experience. (op 25-1)
Bush Breakfast ran below the level of previous efforts, and can do better in nurseries. (op 8-1 tchd 11-1)

3931 TRACKSIDE CARVERY MEDIAN AUCTION MAIDEN STKS 7f
6:30 (6:31) (Class 5) 3-5-Y-0 **£3,238** (£963; £481; £240) **Stalls** High

Form RPR

-503 **1** **Trimlestown (IRE)**[7] 3742 3-9-3 73.......... FergusSweeney 5 71
(H Candy) *pressed ldr: led over 2f out: rdn out* **7/4**[1]

0540 **2** 2 1/2 **Dab Hand (IRE)**[19] 3364 3-9-0 65.......... AdamKirby(3) 6 64
(D M Simcock) *sn led: hdd over 2f out: hrd rdn over 1f out: nt qckn* **9/1**

32 **3** 3/4 **Magic Rush**[10] 3647 4-9-10 .... SteveDrowne 3 65
(Mrs Norma Pook) *hld up in tch: effrt and edgd lft over 2f out: styd on same pce* **10/3**[2]

0-3 **4** 1/2 **Distant Drums (IRE)**[44] 2575 3-8-12 .... MichaelHills 4 56
(B W Hills) *t.k.h: trckd ldng pair: rdn over 2f out: one pce* **4/1**[3]

50 **5** 1/4 **Divo Noro (IRE)**[44] 2587 3-8-10 .... AshleyHamblett(7) 1 59+
(L M Cumani) *chsd ldrs: rdn over 2f out: one pce* **25/1**

5-60 **6** 2 **Athena's Dream**[47] 2511 3-8-12 65.......... JohnEgan 7 51+
(C F Wall) *hld up towards rr: promising hdwy over 2f out: sn rdn and no imp* **13/2**

4000 **7** 1 1/4 **Diamond Heritage**[6] 3762 4-9-10 48..........(b) MickyFenton 9 53
(S Parr) *a towards rr: rdn and n.d fr 1/2-way* **50/1**

0040 **8** 2 1/2 **Wodhill Schnaps**[10] 3642 5-9-10 62.......... DerekMcGaffin 10 46
(D Morris) *sn pushed along in rr: nvr a factor* **33/1**

00 **9** 4 **Cosmic Girl**[22] 3266 3-8-12 .... FrancisFerris 2 27
(H Candy) *stdd s: t.k.h in midfield: rdn over 2f out: sn lost tch* **66/1**

1m 22.27s (-1.94) **Going Correction** -0.275s/f (Firm)
WFA 3 from 4yo+ 7lb 9 Ran SP% **113.0**
Speed ratings (Par 103):100,97,96,95,94 92,91,88,83
CSF £17.78 TOTE £2.80: £1.30, £2.90, £1.50; EX 14.50.
Owner Thurloe Thoroughbreds XVI **Bred** Liam Brennan **Trained** Kingston Warren, Oxon

FOCUS
A fair older-horse maiden, with an improving winner but the form limited by the seventh.
Diamond Heritage Official explanation: jockey said gelding kept changing its legs

3932 DEREK BURRIDGE RACING & GOLF TROPHIES H'CAP 7f
7:00 (7:00) (Class 5) (0-70,70) 3-Y-0 **£3,238** (£963; £481; £240) **Stalls** High

Form RPR

6325 **1** **Imperial Gain (USA)**[10] 3644 3-9-4 70..........(v[1]) AdamKirby(3) 5 76
(W R Swinburn) *chsd ldrs: led 2f out: hrd drvn and r.o* **7/2**[2]

5003 **2** 2 **Endless Night**[30] 3011 3-8-13 62..........(p) SteveDrowne 9 63
(H Morrison) *dwlt: towards rr: rdn and hdwy over 2f out: styd on to take 2nd on stands' rail ins fnl f* **10/3**[1]

5060 **3** 1 1/2 **Mid Valley**[25] 3164 3-8-2 51..........(v[1]) FrankieMcDonald 10 50+
(J R Jenkins) *sn bhd: effrt and nt clr run ins fnl 2f: hrd rdn and r.o fnl f: nvr nrr* **12/1**

0000 **4** 1/2 **Bollywood (IRE)**[2] 3873 3-8-1 55.......... MarcHalford(5) 7 51
(J J Bridger) *chsd ldrs: drvn along fnl 3f: n.m.r over 1f out: styd on same pce* **20/1**

0646 **5** *hd* **Smile For Us**[28] 3089 3-8-13 67..........(b) JerryO'Dwyer(5) 6 62
(C Drew) *led tl 2f out: btn whn edgd lft over 1f out* **13/2**[3]

0022 **6** *nk* **High Octave (IRE)**[16] 3436 3-9-3 66.......... TedDurcan 3 60
(B G Powell) *bhd: effrt in centre over 2f out: no imp over 1f out* **7/2**[2]

0030 **7** 6 **Possessed**[19] 3364 3-8-13 62.......... JohnEgan 8 40
(T D McCarthy) *dwlt: sn rdn along in midfield: outpcd fnl 2f* **9/1**

000 **8** *nk* **Cativo Cavallino**[17] 3406 3-8-11 60.......... PaulDoe 4 37
(Jamie Poulton) *in tch: rdn 1/2-way: wknd over 1f out* **14/1**

-000 **9** 1 1/4 **Ameliore (IRE)**[27] 3118 3-8-2 51 oh8.......... FrancisFerris 1 25
(S Woodman) *w ldr tl wknd qckly over 1f out* **50/1**

0005 **10** 24 **Helen Wood**[17] 3405 3-8-3 52 oh8 ow1.......... AdrianTNicholls 2 —
(M D I Usher) *dwlt: sn wl bhd: eased whn no ch fnl 2f* **33/1**

1m 22.27s (-1.94) **Going Correction** -0.275s/f (Firm) 10 Ran SP% **114.9**
Speed ratings (Par 100):100,97,96,95,95 94,88,87,86,58
CSF £15.03 CT £127.16 TOTE £4.80: £1.80, £1.90, £3.90; EX 13.60.
Owner Mrs P W Harris **Bred** Lantern Hill Farm Llc **Trained** Aldbury, Herts

FOCUS
A modest race, but the pace looked good enough and the form appears sound through the second and fourth.
Helen Wood Official explanation: jockey said filly was unsuited by the good to firm ground

3933 LADIES EVENING AUGUST 12TH H'CAP 7f 140y
7:30 (7:33) (Class 6) (0-55,55) 3-Y-0+ **£2,388** (£705; £352) **Stalls** Centre

Form RPR

2635 **1** **Fantasy Defender (IRE)**[11] 3614 4-8-10 **47**..........(v) AdamKirby(3) 6 55
(Ernst Oertel) *bhd: rdn and hdwy 3f out: led ins fnl f: all out* **7/1**[2]

0000 **2** *nk* **Balerno**[30] 3014 7-9-5 **53**.......... AlanDaly 11 60
(Mrs L J Mongan) *bhd: gd hdwy 2f out: r.o wl u.p fnl f* **33/1**

0150 **3** *shd* **Diamond Dan (IRE)**[31] 2966 4-8-11 **52**.......... JamieHamblett(7) 1 59
(P D Evans) *in tch: effrt over 2f out: styd on wl fnl f* **12/1**

46-0 **4** *nk* **Pearl Farm**[44] 2574 5-9-1 **49**.......... SteveDrowne 13 55
(C A Horgan) *trckd ldrs gng wl: led 2f out: hdd and no ex ins fnl f* **14/1**

0300 **5** *shd* **Postmaster**[4] 3817 4-9-2 **50**.......... IanMongan 12 56
(R Ingram) *outpcd and bhd: drvn along 1/2-way: rapid hdwy fr over 1f out: fin fast* **16/1**

5140 **6** 1 1/4 **Dexileos (IRE)**[31] 2978 7-8-9 **46**..........(t) NeilChalmers(3) 3 49
(David Pinder) *a.p: one pce appr fnl f* **20/1**

0440 **7** 1/2 **Blue Line**[28] 3095 4-9-5 **53**..........(v) AdrianTNicholls 4 54
(M Madgwick) *dwlt and bmpd s: towards rr tl hdwy 2f out: no imp fnl f* **14/1**

4044 **8** 1 1/2 **Hadath (IRE)**[11] 3614 9-9-2 **50**..........(b) GeorgeBaker 2 48
(B G Powell) *mid-div: drvn to chse ldrs 2f out: one pce appr fnl f* **7/1**[2]

6050 **9** 1/2 **Free Silver (IRE)**[31] 2987 3-8-13 **55**.......... JohnEgan 8 51
(Miss K B Boutflower) *towards rr: rdn and edgd rt towards stands' rail fr 2f out: nvr rchd ldrs* **20/1**

6400 **10** 4 **Megalala (IRE)**[8] 3705 5-8-8 **47**.......... MarcHalford(5) 18 39+
(J J Bridger) *rdn along to chse ldrs: outpcd over 2f out: btn in midfield whn hmpd over 1f out* **33/1**

1022 **11** *nk* **Beau Marche**[7] 3728 4-8-12 **46**..........(b) MartinDwyer 14 32+
(G G Margarson) *mid-div: shkn up and no prog 2f out: eased whn btn 1f out* **7/2**[1]

3350 **12** 1/2 **Ballare (IRE)**[28] 3089 7-8-12 **46**..........(v) FergusSweeney 5 30
(P J Makin) *dwlt: wnt lft and bmpd s: nvr nr ldrs* **16/1**

0000 **13** 1 3/4 **Hawridge Sensation**[13] 3570 4-9-5 **53**..........(t) MickyFenton 9 33
(W S Kittow) *held up towards rr: nt clr rn ins fnl 2f: n.d* **20/1**

0205 **14** 1 **Penny Glitters**[26] 3142 3-8-6 **55**..........(b[1]) AshleyHamblett(7) 7 33
(S Parr) *stmbld s: prom over 5f: wkng whn bmpd over 1f out* **16/1**

553- **15** 1 1/2 **Constructor**[224] 6596 5-9-7 **55**.......... NCallan 15 29
(C A Cyzer) *plld hrd: prom 5f* **12/1**

0250 **16** 1 3/4 **For Life (IRE)**[9] 3664 4-9-3 **51**..........(p) FrankieMcDonald 17 20
(A P Jarvis) *s.i.s: sn in midfield on stands' rail: wknd over 2f out* **12/1**

2050 **17** 3 1/2 **Tuning Fork**[20] 3339 6-9-5 **53**.......... PaulDoe 10 14
(T M Jones) *led tl wknd 2f out* **10/1**[3]

-000 **18** 4 **Royal Sailor (IRE)**[11] 3614 4-9-0 **48**..........(b) MichaelTebbutt 16 —
(J Ryan) *a bhd* **50/1**

1m 30.79s (-0.67) **Going Correction** -0.275s/f (Firm)
WFA 3 from 4yo+ 8lb 18 Ran SP% **132.5**
Speed ratings (Par 101):92,91,91,91,91 89,89,87,87,83 83,82,80,79,78 76,73,69
CSF £244.03 CT £2853.62 TOTE £9.30: £2.40, £4.20, £2.40, £4.50; EX 1753.40.
Owner The Fantasy Fellowship D **Bred** Patrick Brady **Trained** Newmarket, Suffolk

FOCUS
A low-grade handicap containing mostly exposed types, run at a strong gallop, and producing a blanket finish. The form looks solid enough.
Ballare(IRE) Official explanation: jockey said gelding suffered interference soon after start
Hawridge Sensation Official explanation: jockey said gelding was denied a clear run
Penny Glitters Official explanation: jockey said filly stumbled badly on leaving stalls
Constructor Official explanation: jockey said gelding ran too free
Tuning Fork Official explanation: jockey said gelding stopped quickly 2f out
Royal Sailor(IRE) Official explanation: jockey said gelding hung right throughout

3934 BOB COOMBER MEMORIAL H'CAP 1m 2f (P)
8:00 (8:01) (Class 6) (0-65,65) 3-Y-0+ **£2,388** (£705; £352) **Stalls** Low

Form RPR

0223 **1** **Glendale**[8] 3706 5-9-8 **60**.......... MartinDwyer 4 68
(D K Ivory) *led after 1f and dictated mod tempo: qcknd 3f out: hrd rdn and hung bdly rt fnl f: hld on gamely whn chal* **7/2**[1]

004 **2** *hd* **Evening**[18] 3387 3-9-3 **65**.......... MichaelHills 7 73+
(B W Hills) *stdd s: hld up in rr: gd hdwy on outside over 2f out: str chal fnl f: r.o: jst hld* **10/1**

0412 **3** 2 **Writ (IRE)**[7] 3729 4-9-9 **61**.......... MickyFenton 5 65
(Ernst Oertel) *prom: rdn 3f out: hung lft over 1f out: one pce* **7/1**[3]

-112 **4** 1 3/4 **Revolve**[67] 1910 6-8-12 **50**..........(p) IanMongan 1 50
(Mrs L J Mongan) *led 1f: remained prom: rdn 3f out: one pce fnl 2f* **8/1**

2500 **5** 1/2 **Blue Hedges**[58] 2181 4-9-6 **58**.......... TedDurcan 8 58
(H J Collingridge) *mid-div on rail: effrt 3f out: styd on same pce* **20/1**

3050 **6** *nk* **Busy Man (IRE)**[8] 3706 7-8-12 **50**.......... SteveDrowne 9 49
(J R Jenkins) *s.s: towards rr tl hrd rdn and styd on fnl 2f* **33/1**

-000 **7** *nk* **Eastlands (IRE)**[20] 3336 3-8-13 **61**.......... JohnEgan 3 59
(Jamie Poulton) *s.i.s: sn chsng ldrs: rdn 3f out: one pce fnl 2f* **7/1**[3]

5203 **8** 1 **Fantasy Crusader**[11] 3615 7-8-13 **54**.......... AdamKirby(3) 12 51
(R M H Cowell) *wd: towards rr: rdn 3f out: nvr rchd ldrs* **12/1**

0150 **9** 1/2 **Charlie Kennet**[17] 3401 8-9-13 **65**.......... GeorgeBaker 10 61
(Mrs H Sweeting) *towards rr: rdn 3f out: n.d* **10/1**

2130 **10** 2 **Dinner Date**[8] 3706 4-9-9 **61**.......... FrankieMcDonald 6 53
(T Keddy) *in tch: rdn 3f out: sn outpcd* **13/2**[2]

3344 **11** 4 **General Flumpa**[32] 2956 5-9-3 **55**.......... NCallan 2 39
(C F Wall) *chsd ldrs: outpcd 3f out: btn whn n.m.r bnd into st* **8/1**

0060 **12** 1 **African Sahara (USA)**[31] 2982 7-9-12 **64**..........(t) PaulEddery 13 46
(Miss D Mountain) *towards rr: rdn and n.d fnl 3f* **20/1**

2m 7.72s (-0.07) **Going Correction** -0.125s/f (Stan)
WFA 3 from 4yo+ 10lb 12 Ran SP% **121.1**
Speed ratings (Par 101):95,94,93,91,91 91,90,90,89,88 84,84
CSF £39.29 CT £239.53 TOTE £4.90: £1.40, £3.70, £3.40; EX 22.50.
Owner Mrs J A Cornwell **Bred** Mrs J A Cornwell **Trained** Radlett, Herts

FOCUS
A moderate contest run at a tactical pace, with the winner getting the run of the race from the front and setting the standard, and the runner-up doing well to come from so far back.
African Sahara(USA) Official explanation: vet said horse returned lame

3935 GOLF & RACING AT LINGFIELD PARK H'CAP 2m (P)
8:30 (8:31) (Class 5) (0-70,70) 3-Y-0+ **£3,238** (£963; £481; £240) **Stalls** Low

Form RPR

0012 **1** **Desert Sea (IRE)**[30] 3017 3-8-8 **67**.......... FergusSweeney 9 85
(C Tinkler) *t.k.h in midfield: hdwy 4f out: led over 1f out: rdn clr: readily* **8/1**

-136 **2** *7* **El Alamein (IRE)**[14] 3539 3-8-6 **65** ow2 SebSanders 14 75
(Sir Mark Prescott) *trckd ldr: led 7f out tl over 1f out: nt pce of wnr* **9/2**[1]

3-02 **3** *½* **Primondo (IRE)**[50] 2408 4-9-3 **59** NCallan 12 68
(J R Fanshawe) *mid-div: hdwy 5f out: styd on same pce fnl 3f* **5/1**[2]

1505 **4** *2 ½* **Linden Lime**[10] 3649 4-9-1 **57** PaulDoe 6 63
(Jamie Poulton) *stdd s: hld up towards rr: gd hdwy 6f out: one pce fnl 3f* **16/1**

2504 **5** *6* **Nawow**[49] 2460 6-9-13 **69** MartinDwyer 8 68
(P D Cundell) *bhd: mod effrt 3f out: nt rch ldrs* **7/1**

3400 **6** *shd* **Moon Emperor**[95] 1213 9-9-13 **69** (be) GeorgeBaker 13 68
(J R Jenkins) *stdd s: wl bhd tl mod late hdwy* **25/1**

060- **7** *shd* **Heart Springs**[290] 5837 6-9-0 **56** AlanDaly 5 55
(Dr J R J Naylor) *mid-div: hrd rdn 3f out: no imp* **40/1**

6023 **8** *3 ½* **High Hope (FR)**[30] 3013 8-8-12 **59** (b) RobynBrisland[(5)] 4 53
(G L Moore) *hld up in midfield: no hdwy fnl 3f* **20/1**

2142 **9** *1 ¼* **Senor Set (GER)**[19] 3350 5-9-2 **58** TedDurcan 1 51
(J Pearce) *mid-div: rdn and btn 3f out* **6/1**[3]

1120 **10** *10* **Tycheros**[116] 866 4-9-2 **61** SaleemGolam[(3)] 11 42
(S C Williams) *chsd ldrs tl wknd 3f out* **6/1**[3]

400 **11** *2 ½* **Soubriquet (IRE)**[30] 3029 3-8-11 **70** IanMongan 7 48
(T G Mills) *chsd ldrs: rdn along 1/2-way: wknd 3f out* **12/1**

4530 **12** *hd* **Missie Baileys**[17] 3412 4-9-0 **56** AdrianTNicholls 2 34
(Mrs L J Mongan) *in tch: lost pl rapidly bnd 5f out: sn bhd* **40/1**

00-0 **13** *12* **Avicia**[26] 3152 4-9-3 **59** SteveDrowne 3 22
(C A Horgan) *prom tl wknd 4f out* **50/1**

0053 **14** *34* **Phoebe Woodstock (IRE)**[11] 3628 4-9-11 **70** AdamKirby[(3)] 10 —
(W R Swinburn) *led tl 7f out: wknd qckly 5f out: bhd and eased fnl 2f* **12/1**

3m 23.57s (-5.22) **Going Correction** -0.125s/f (Stan)
WFA 3 from 4yo+ 17lb **14** Ran SP% **123.7**
Speed ratings (Par 103):108,104,104,103,100 99,99,98,97,92 91,91,85,68
CSF £42.94 CT £206.17 TOTE £11.30: £3.50, £2.50, £2.90; EX 51.70 Place 6 £43.86, Place 5 £32.96.
Owner Bonusprint **Bred** Peter McGlynn **Trained** Compton, Berks

FOCUS
A fair stayers' race, run at a solid gallop, and won by a improving type. The fourth sets the standard.
Avicia Official explanation: jockey said filly had no more to give
Phoebe Woodstock(IRE) Official explanation: jockey said filly stopped quickly
T/Plt: £56.30 to a £1 stake. Pool: £51,652.45. 668.75 winning tickets. T/Qpdt: £23.90 to a £1 stake. Pool: £3,966.80. 122.80 winning tickets. LM

3617 NEWCASTLE (L-H)
Saturday, July 29

OFFICIAL GOING: Straight course - good to firm (firm in places); round course - firm
Wind: Breezy, behind

3936 BETFRED POKER SPRINT SERIES FINAL H'CAP 6f
2:25 (2:25) (Class 2) 3-Y-O+
£12,464 (£3,732; £1,866; £934; £466; £234) **Stalls** High

Form RPR
0033 **1** **Soto**[7] 3722 3-8-9 **68** PaulMulrennan 4 78
(M W Easterby) *mde virtually all: rdn 2f out: edgd lft and hld on wl fnl f* **14/1**

5232 **2** *1* **Millfields Dreams**[9] 3683 7-7-11 **54** DominicFox[(3)] 2 63+
(M G Quinlan) *chsd ldrs: effrt over 1f out: chekced ins fnl f: r.o to go 2nd cl home* **9/1**

0022 **3** *nk* **Kool Ovation**[8] 3718 4-9-2 **70** TonyHamilton 5 77
(A Dickman) *trckd ldrs: effrt and ch ent fnl f: no ex and lost 2nd cl home* **6/1**[3]

4461 **4** *nk* **Ellens Academy (IRE)**[12] 3584 11-8-13 **72** MichaelJStainton[(5)] 7 78+
(E J Alston) *hld up: hdwy 2f out: kpt on fnl f* **4/1**[2]

1213 **5** *3* **Yorkshire Blue**[15] 3482 7-9-7 **78** DanielTudhope[(3)] 10 75
(J S Goldie) *bhd and outpcd: hdwy over 1f out: nvr rchd ldrs* **5/2**[1]

6000 **6** *nk* **Brigadore**[8] 3715 7-8-10 **64** TonyCulhane 9 60
(J G Given) *hld up: effrt over 2f out: no imp over 1f out* **12/1**

-302 **7** *shd* **Make My Dream**[11] 3612 3-7-11 **61** ow1 AndrewElliott[(5)] 3 56
(J Gallagher) *w wnr tl rdn and no ex over 1f out* **14/1**

0335 **8** *5* **Dorn Dancer (IRE)**[15] 3478 4-8-5 **64** MarkLawson[(5)] 6 45
(D W Barker) *towards rr: outpcd and hung lft 1/2-way: n.d* **6/1**[3]

-350 **9** *1 ¾* **Dance To The Blues (IRE)**[11] 3612 5-9-0 **68** (b[1]) J-PGuillambert 1 44
(B De Haan) *wnt lft s: sn outpcd: nvr on terms* **16/1**

300 **10** *6* **Dunn Deal (IRE)**[20] 3330 6-8-12 **66** PaulQuinn 8 24
(W M Brisbourne) *towards rr: rdn and outpcd fr 1/2-way* **16/1**

1m 10.71s (-4.38) **Going Correction** -0.65s/f (Hard)
WFA 3 from 4yo+ 5lb **10** Ran SP% **119.9**
Speed ratings (Par 109):103,101,101,100,96 96,96,89,87,79
CSF £137.31 CT £850.60 TOTE £18.50: £3.60, £3.50, £1.90; EX 150.60 Trifecta £335.20 Part won. Pool: £472.17 - 0.20 winning units..
Owner Woodford Group Plc **Bred** D Sugars And B Parker **Trained** Sheriff Hutton, N Yorks
■ Stewards' Enquiry : Paul Mulrennan two-day ban: careless riding (Aug 9-10)

FOCUS
An ordinary event in which the field raced in the centre and, although the pace seemed sound, those held up were at a disadvantage. Solid form amongst the principals.

NOTEBOOK
Soto gained due reward for a string of consistent efforts to notch his first win on grass. He did have the run of the race in a handicap that favoured racing close to the pace, though, and he will find things tougher after reassessment. (op 12-1)
Millfields Dreams has been a model of consistency this year and ran to his best, despite getting checked for room in the closing stages. The interference made little difference to the result but he should continue to give a good account. (op 10-1)
Kool Ovation had the run of the race and extended his run of creditable efforts but, not for the first time, seemed to be saving a little bit for himself and, although capable of winning a similar event, may not be one for maximum faith.
Ellens Academy(IRE), who broke a losing run at Ayr on his previous start, fared the best of those that attempted to come from off the pace. However, he remains the type that needs things to fall right and so would not be one for maximum faith. (tchd 9-2)
Yorkshire Blue was not totally disgraced in a race that suited those racing prominently but he is now high enough in the weights and his style of racing means things will have to drop perfectly if he is to win from this mark. Official explanation: jockey said gelding never travelled (op 11-4)
Brigadore, returned to six furlongs, was not totally disgraced in a race where it paid to race prominently and, as his style of racing means he needs things to drop just right, he remains one to tread very carefully with.
Dorn Dancer(IRE) Official explanation: jockey said filly was unsuited by the good to firm (firm in places) ground
Dance To The Blues(IRE) Official explanation: jockey said mare did not face the first time blinkers

3937 WOODFORDGROUP.COM BEESWING H'CAP 7f
2:55 (2:56) (Class 3) (0-95,93) 3-Y-O+
£11,217 (£3,358; £1,679; £840; £419; £210) **Stalls** High

Form RPR
5031 **1** **Hartshead**[24] 3191 7-9-9 **93** AndrewElliott[(5)] 9 103
(G A Swinbank) *hld up midfield: hdwy 2f out: led ins fnl f: pushed out* **6/1**[3]

0060 **2** *¾* **Mezuzah**[29] 3040 6-8-9 **74** oh1 PaulMulrennan 10 82
(M W Easterby) *mde most tl hdd ins fnl f: kpt on* **25/1**

4530 **3** *1 ¼* **Pure Imagination (IRE)**[8] 3705 5-8-4 **74** oh4 (b[1]) GregFairley[(5)] 8 79
(J M Bradley) *s.i.s: bhd tl hdwy over 1f out: nrst fin* **16/1**

4006 **4** *¾* **Stoic Leader (IRE)**[4] 3812 6-8-13 **78** GylesParkin 13 81
(R F Fisher) *prom: effrt over 2f out: one pce fnl f* **20/1**

0040 **5** *1* **Breaking Shadow (IRE)**[15] 3500 4-8-11 **76** (p) FrancisNorton 11 76
(T D Barron) *hld up: effrt and hdwy over 1f out: kpt on fnl f: nrst fin* **7/1**

2110 **6** *nk* **Imperial Echo (USA)**[15] 3493 5-9-5 **84** PhillipMakin 12 83
(T D Barron) *hld up: effrt over 2f out: no imp fnl f* **4/1**[1]

2122 **7** *shd* **Angaric (IRE)**[11] 3606 3-8-6 **78** J-PGuillambert 4 74
(B Smart) *prom: effrt over 2f out: edgd lft and no ex over 1f out* **11/2**[2]

0000 **8** *1* **Millennium Force**[23] 3223 8-9-3 **82** TonyCulhane 1 78
(M R Channon) *bhd: rdn 1/2-way: hdwy over 1f out: n.d* **14/1**

-060 **9** *½* **Laith (IRE)**[38] 2756 3-7-13 **74** DominicFox[(3)] 14 66
(Miss V Haigh) *hld up: effrt over 2f out: nvr rchd ldrs* **50/1**

1406 **10** *½* **Fiefdom (IRE)**[24] 3191 4-9-2 **86** NataliaGemelova[(5)] 3 79
(I W McInnes) *cl up tl edgd lft and outpcd fr 2f out* **20/1**

2010 **11** *1* **Along The Nile**[17] 3413 4-8-12 **80** (t) DanielTudhope[(3)] 6 71
(K G Reveley) *hld up midfield: rdn over 2f out: no imp whn n.m.r appr fnl f* **11/2**[2]

5245 **12** *3* **Pawan (IRE)**[2] 3880 6-8-2 **74** oh1 (b) AnnStokell[(7)] 7 57
(Miss A Stokell) *dwlt: sn midfield: edgd lft over 2f out: sn outpcd* **25/1**

-650 **13** *1 ¼* **Silidan**[28] 3079 3-8-5 **82** MichaelJStainton[(5)] 2 58
(T P Tate) *keen: cl up tl wknd fr 2f out* **25/1**

1030 **14** *hd* **Malcheek (IRE)**[15] 3493 4-9-6 **85** TonyHamilton 5 64
(T D Easterby) *keen: trckd ldrs: rdn over 2f out: wknd wl over 1f out* **11/1**

1m 23.55s (-4.45) **Going Correction** -0.65s/f (Hard)
WFA 3 from 4yo+ 7lb **14** Ran SP% **121.5**
Speed ratings (Par 107):99,98,96,95,94 94,94,93,92,91 90,87,85,85
CSF £157.87 CT £2296.55 TOTE £6.90: £2.50, £8.00, £3.80; EX 228.60.
Owner B Valentine **Bred** Gainsborough Stud Management Ltd **Trained** Melsonby, N Yorks

FOCUS
A decent event in which the gallop was sound but once again those held up were at a disadvantage. Fair form for the grade, and sound.

NOTEBOOK
Hartshead is an improved performer this year and turned in his best effort yet. On this evidence he will be equally effective over a mile and he should continue to give a good account away from progressive sorts. (op 11-2)
Mezuzah had the run of the race but ran really well on ground that is considered plenty quick enough. A much softer surface will suit and he will be one to keep in mind when he encounters suitable conditions.
Pure Imagination(IRE), tried in first time blinkers, ran his best race of the year and fared the best of those to come from off the ordinary gallop. He looks a bit better than the bare form and looks capable of winning an ordinary event.
Stoic Leader(IRE), who has not won on turf since May of last year, raced closer to the pace than has been the case of late and ran creditably. He is a consistent sort who should continue to give a good account but is vulnerable from this mark.
Breaking Shadow(IRE), with the cheekpieces refitted, ran a typical race in that he was set a fair amount to do and failed to make up the deficit in the closing stages. Horses of this ilk remain ones to tread very carefully with. (op 13-2 tchd 6-1 in a place)
Imperial Echo(USA), dropped in grade after a fair run in the Bunbury Cup, was not disgraced given he found himself in a race where the leaders did not come back. He has done well this year and is not one to write off just yet.
Angaric(IRE), up in the weights and in grade, had his limitations exposed back in this lesser grade and he may continue to look vulnerable to progressive or well-handicapped sorts from his current mark. (op 7-1)
Pawan(IRE) Official explanation: jockey said gelding was unsuited by the good to firm (firm in places) ground

3938 PIMMS SUMMER CLASSIC H'CAP 5f
3:30 (3:30) (Class 4) (0-85,84) 3-Y-O+
£6,232 (£1,866; £933; £467; £233; £117) **Stalls** High

Form RPR
0203 **1** **Grigorovitch (IRE)**[2] 3880 4-9-10 **84** DanielTudhope[(3)] 6 94+
(I Semple) *covered up in tch: n.m.r over 1f out: rdn and styd on strly to ld post* **3/1**[1]

5124 **2** *shd* **Malapropism**[8] 3715 6-9-12 **83** TonyCulhane 1 90
(M R Channon) *led: rdn over 1f out: kpt on wl: ct post* **6/1**

4142 **3** *1 ¼* **Kings College Boy**[2] 3880 6-9-2 **73** (v) TonyHamilton 2 76
(R A Fahey) *trckd ldrs: effrt 2f out: kpt on same pce ins fnl f* **5/1**[3]

0221 **4** *1* **Aegean Dancer**[8] 3699 4-8-10 **74** ow2 PJBenson[(7)] 8 73
(B Smart) *hld up in tch: effrt and chsd ldrs over 1f out: one pce fnl f* **5/1**[3]

5421 **5** *shd* **Bluebok**[11] 3625 5-9-13 **84** FrancisNorton 3 83
(J M Bradley) *trckd ldrs tl rdn and nt qckn appr fnl f* **4/1**[2]

3651 **6** *2* **Strensall**[3] 3832 9-8-10 **72** 7ex MichaelJStainton[(5)] 5 63
(R E Barr) *keen: chsd ldrs tl no ex over 1f out* **8/1**

5633 **7** *10* **Raccoon (IRE)**[12] 3584 6-8-10 **67** (v) J-PGuillambert 7 22+
(D W Chapman) *chsd ldrs tl rdn and wknd over 1f out* **10/1**

58.26 secs (-3.24) **Going Correction** -0.65s/f (Hard) **7** Ran SP% **112.8**
Speed ratings (Par 105):99,98,96,95,95 91,75
CSF £20.63 CT £85.22 TOTE £3.90: £2.40, £2.70; EX 23.80.
Owner newkeylets **Bred** Middle Park Stud Ltd **Trained** Carluke, S Lanarks

FOCUS
A tightly knit handicap, a decent pace and no advantage in any style of racing. Sound form, rated through the runner-up, with the winner a little bit bette than the bare form.

3939 WOODFORDGROUP.COM H'CAP 1m 2f 32y
4:00 (4:01) (Class 4) (0-80,80) 3-Y-O+
£5,297 (£1,586; £793; £396; £198; £99) **Stalls** Centre

Form RPR
-000 **1** **Highest Regard**[17] 3401 4-8-12 **64** J-PGuillambert 5 69
(N P McCormack) *keen: set stdy pce: qcknd 3f out: hld on wl fnl f* **14/1**

0420 **2** *nk* **Cripsey Brook**[15] 3497 8-9-4 **77**..............................(t) JamesReveley(7) 7 81
(K G Reveley) *hld up: hdwy over 1f out: chsd wnr wl ins fnl f: kpt on* **4/1**[3]

0300 **3** *1 1/4* **Ransom Strip (USA)**[28] 3081 3-8-0 **67**........................ AndrewElliott(5) 3 69
(M Johnston) *prom: effrt over 2f out: rallied over 1f out: kpt on fnl f: no ex towards fin* **7/1**

006- **4** *1 1/4* **Planters Punch (IRE)**[72] 6236 5-8-9 **61**............................ PhillipMakin 2 61
(G M Moore) *hld up: hdwy on ins over 1f out: no ex ins fnl f* **8/1**

0432 **5** *2* **Vicious Warrior**[7] 3747 7-9-9 **80**........................... MichaelJStainton(5) 4 76
(R M Whitaker) *keen: chsd ldrs: effrt over 2f out: no ex fnl f* **5/2**[1]

066 **6** *hd* **Edas**[21] 3283 4-9-1 **70**... DanielTudhope(3) 1 66
(J J Quinn) *prom: rdn over 2f out: no ex over 1f out* **8/1**

4411 **7** *3 1/2* **Gala Sunday (USA)**[11] 3610 6-8-9 **61** oh1................(b) PaulMulrennan 8 50
(M W Easterby) *cl up: rdn over 2f out: sn wknd* **3/1**[2]

2m 8.57s (-3.23) **Going Correction** -0.25s/f (Firm)
WFA 3 from 4yo+ 10lb **7** Ran SP% **115.0**
Speed ratings (Par 105):102,101,100,99,98 98,95
CSF £69.32 CT £433.39 TOTE £25.30: £5.60, £2.20; EX 73.40.
Owner Mrs D McCormack **Bred** Kingwood Stud **Trained** Medomsley, Co Durham

FOCUS
A modest event, and a steady pace means this may not be a reliable form guide.

3940 ASPERS CASINO MAIDEN AUCTION STKS 7f
4:35 (4:35) (Class 5) 2-Y-O **£3,238** (£963; £481; £240) **Stalls** High

Form RPR

2 **1** **Babieca (USA)**[25] 3175 2-8-11 .... PhillipMakin 1 74+
(T D Barron) *chsd ldr: rdn to ld over 1f out: styd on strly* **10/11**[1]

435 **2** *1 1/2* **Fongs Gazelle**[36] 2807 2-8-7 .... J-PGuillambert 3 66
(M Johnston) *led to over 1f out: kpt on same pce fnl f* **7/2**[2]

0 **3** *3/4* **Smugglers Bay (IRE)**[39] 2733 2-8-12 .... PaulMulrennan 6 69
(T D Easterby) *sn niggled in tch: hdwy 1/2-way: rdn 2f out: kpt on ins fnl f: nt rch first two* **6/1**

244 **4** *1* **Intersky Sports (USA)**[30] 3018 2-8-10 .... CatherineGannon 5 65
(K A Ryan) *in tch: hdwy 1/2-way: effrt and hung lft over 1f out: sn no ex* **9/2**[3]

56 **5** *10* **Ishetoo**[30] 3018 2-8-6 .... DanielTudhope(3) 2 38
(A Dickman) *chsd ldrs tl wknd fr 2f out* **10/1**

2 **6** *12* **Desert Maze (IRE)**[11] 3618 2-8-8 .... TonyHamilton 4 5
(J Wade) *keen: cl up tl wknd over 2f out* **16/1**

1m 26.48s (-1.52) **Going Correction** -0.65s/f (Hard) **6** Ran SP% **122.0**
Speed ratings (Par 94):82,80,79,78,66 53
CSF £5.10 TOTE £2.00: £1.60, £2.40; EX 4.00.
Owner R G Toes and Patrick Toes **Bred** Overbrook Farm **Trained** Maunby, N Yorks
■ Stewards' Enquiry : Phillip Makin caution: used whip down the shoulder in the forehand position

FOCUS
An ordinary event in which the pace was sound and the field again raced in the centre. An ice effort from the winner, but the fourth holds down the form a little.

NOTEBOOK
Babieca(USA) ◆ fully confirmed debut promise to win an ordinary event with more in hand than the bare margin suggests. He is a colt with scope for further improvement and, although this bare form is ordinary, should continue to give a good account (op 11-8 tchd 7-4 and 15-8 in places)
Fongs Gazelle, upped to this more suitable trip, had the run of the race and ran creditably. She seems effective on most ground and looks capable of picking up a small event. (op 11-4)
Smugglers Bay(IRE) bettered his debut effort and left the impression that an even stiffer test of stamina would have been in his favour. He will stay a mile and, although vulnerable to progressive sorts in this grade, looks capable of winning a small event. (op 7-1 tchd 11-2)
Intersky Sports(USA) failed to improve for the step up to this trip and did not look the most straightforward under pressure. He is capable of winning a small event but remains one to have reservations about. (op 7-2 tchd 5-1)
Ishetoo attracted support but again failed to improve on this first run over a trip that should have suited. He looks capable of winning a small event but is not really one to place much faith in. Official explanation: jockey said gelding lost its action (op 12-1 tchd 8-1)
Desert Maze(IRE) failed to build on a moderate debut effort and is likely to continue to look vulnerable in this type of event. Official explanation: jockey said gelding hung right throughout (op 25-1 tchd 14-1)

3941 SALTWELL SIGNS APPRENTICE H'CAP 1m 2f 32y
5:05 (5:06) (Class 6) (0-55,57) 3-Y-O+ **£2,388** (£705; £352) **Stalls** Centre

Form RPR

0423 **1** **Thornaby Green**[6] 3762 5-8-12 **44**.................................. DeanHeslop(5) 5 52
(T D Barron) *keen: mde all: rdn over 1f out: hld on wl fnl f* **3/1**[2]

02-6 **2** *1/2* **Master Nimbus**[13] 2707 6-9-3 **44**.. RobbieMills 7 51
(J J Quinn) *keen: cl up: effrt and ev ch over 1f out: r.o fnl f: hld towards fin* **9/2**[3]

0005 **3** *1 1/4* **Shamwari Fire (IRE)**[4] 3815 6-8-9 **36**..................(b) NeilBrown 6 41
(I W McInnes) *prom: effrt 2f out: rdn and one pce fnl f* **8/1**

0002 **4** *4* **House Martin**[58] 2181 4-9-6 **52**................................(p) JamesRogers(5) 4 49
(C R Dore) *keen: prom: effrt over 2f out: outpcd over 1f out* **11/2**

0241 **5** *nk* **Ruby Legend**[13] 3566 8-10-2 **57**..............................(b) JamesReveley 9 54
(K G Reveley) *trckd ldrs: effrt and ev ch 2f out: wknd ent fnl f* **2/1**[1]

0-00 **6** *2 1/2* **Ello Lucky (IRE)**[14] 3541 4-8-2 **36**................................ BarrySavage(7) 1 28
(J M Bradley) *stdd in rr: effrt 3f out: nvr rchd ldrs* **20/1**

000- **7** *10* **Belton**[76] 5697 4-9-2 **48**.. MarkWaite(5) 8 21
(Ronald Thompson) *missed break and wl bhd: nvr on terms* **40/1**

0000 **8** *2 1/2* **Futoo (IRE)**[11] 3610 5-9-1 **45**..................(p) DanielleMcCreery(3) 10 13
(D W Chapman) *midfield: outpcd over 4f out: sn btn* **10/1**

5050 **9** *1 1/4* **Keyalzao (IRE)**[10] 3637 4-8-8 **35** oh5.......................... CharlotteKerton 2 1
(A Crook) *in tch: effrt ovr 2f out: sn btn* **66/1**

0-00 **10** *1 3/4* **Allouette**[19] 3355 3-8-4 **46**...................................... AdeleRothery(5) 3 8
(W J H Ratcliffe) *hld up: rdn over 4f out: sn btn* **25/1**

2m 10.61s (-1.19) **Going Correction** -0.25s/f (Firm)
WFA 3 from 4yo+ 10lb **10** Ran SP% **124.6**
Speed ratings (Par 101):94,93,92,89,89 87,79,77,76,74
CSF £17.76 CT £103.41 TOTE £5.10: £1.70, £2.00, £3.00; EX 37.50 Place 6 £766.44, Place 5 £183.86.
Owner K J Alderson **Bred** Mrs S Broadhurst **Trained** Maunby, N Yorks

FOCUS
A weak handicap in which the steady pace suited those ridden close to the gallop. The first thre basically ran to form but the bare form may not prove reliable.
T/Plt: £979.50 to a £1 stake. Pool: £79,436, 59.20 winning tickets T/Qpdt: £27.10 to a £1 stake. Pool: £4,644.20. 126.40 winning tickets RY

3537 NOTTINGHAM (L-H)
Saturday, July 29

OFFICIAL GOING: Good to firm
After 7mm rain and 20mm watering over the previous four days the ground was described as 'definitely firm'. The home turn had been moved out 3yds.
Wind: Light, half-against Weather: Fine and sunny

3942 EUROPEAN BREEDERS FUND MAIDEN FILLIES' STKS 6f 15y
2:30 (2:30) (Class 5) 2-Y-O **£3,886** (£1,156; £577; £288) **Stalls** High

Form RPR

1 **Danetime Music (IRE)** 2-9-0 .... DO'Donohoe 1 71
(M J Wallace) *mde all: hld on towards fin* **25/1**

0 **2** *nk* **Keidas (FR)**[29] 3043 2-9-0 .... EddieAhern 8 70+
(C F Wall) *chsd ldrs: outpcd over 2f out: styd on wl fnl f: jst hld* **11/2**

03 **3** *nk* **Proud**[14] 3537 2-9-0 .... SebSanders 4 69
(M L W Bell) *trckd ldrs: chal over 1f out: no ex ins last* **5/2**[2]

0 **4** *6* **Sahara Dawn (IRE)**[58] 2166 2-9-0 ....(b[1]) DaneO'Neill 9 51
(C G Cox) *s.i.s: sn rdn along: kpt on fnl 2f: nvr on terms* **12/1**

30 **5** *4* **Su Doku (USA)**[38] 2743 2-8-9 .... JamesDoyle(5) 6 39
(N P Littmoden) *dwlt: drvn along and hdwy 3f out: lost pl over 1f out* **9/4**[1]

5 **6** *3* **River Tarrant**[36] 2821 2-9-0 .... AlanMunro 2 30
(P W Chapple-Hyam) *sn trcking ldrs: hung lft thrght: lost pl over 1f out* **10/3**[3]

7 *shd* **Clappers (IRE)** 2-9-0 .... PatDobbs 7 30
(T D Easterby) *swvd lft s: hung lft: nvr on terms* **50/1**

8 *13* **Delaporte** 2-9-0 .... RobbieFitzpatrick 5 —
(M A Buckley) *chsd ldrs: lost pl over 2f out: sn bhd* **66/1**

9 *6* **Frill A Minute** 2-8-7 .... DawnRankin(7) 3 —
(Miss L C Siddall) *hung bdly lft thrght: sn detached in last* **100/1**

1m 15.5s (0.50) **Going Correction** -0.10s/f (Good) **9** Ran SP% **113.8**
Speed ratings (Par 91):92,91,91,83,77 73,73,56,48
CSF £152.26 TOTE £15.90: £3.40, £2.80, £1.30; EX 138.40.
Owner Mrs T P Hyde **Bred** Patrick J Connolly **Trained** Newmarket, Suffolk
■ Stewards' Enquiry : D O'Donohoe caution: careless riding

FOCUS
Nothing much to look at in the paddock and probably a weak maiden fillies' event, rated for now through the third.

NOTEBOOK
Danetime Music(IRE), a tall newcomer, was allowed to dictate. She edged right at the two-furlong marker, tightening up the runner-up, and in the end she did only just enough. (op 22-1 tchd 20-1)
Keidas(FR), racing hard against the rail, was left short of room and lost a couple of lengths two furlongs from home. She came back strongly inside the last and must be accounted a shade unlucky. (op 8-1 tchd 9-1)
Proud, who showed a moderate action going down, threw down the gauntlet but in the end was just found lacking. (tchd 9-4)
Sahara Dawn(IRE), whose saddle slipped on her debut, had blinkers on this time but she never went a yard. (op 11-1)
Su Doku(USA), who missed a beat at the start, never looked happy on this very quick ground. Official explanation: jockey said filly had been unsuited by the good to firm ground (op 10-3)
River Tarrant, nothing at all to look at, was on one rein throughout and does not appreciate the ground this quick. Official explanation: jockey said filly had been unsuited by the good to firm ground (op 9-4)

3943 CHRISTOPHER MCANDREW'S THE BIG 40 H'CAP 6f 15y
3:00 (3:00) (Class 5) (0-75,75) 3-Y-O **£3,238** (£963; £481; £240) **Stalls** High

Form RPR

2514 **1** **River Kirov (IRE)**[23] 3226 3-9-7 **75**...............................(t) AlanMunro 3 84+
(P W Chapple-Hyam) *trckd ldrs: effrt over 1f out: rdn to ld jst ins last: jst hld on* **11/8**[1]

5455 **2** *shd* **Peter Island (FR)**[13] 3568 3-8-11 **72**....................(v) AshleyHamblett(7) 4 81
(J Gallagher) *hld up: effrt and swtchd outside 2f out: edgd lft: hrd rdn and r.o fnl f: jst hld* **10/1**

4161 **3** *1 1/2* **Namu**[2] 3866 3-8-8 **69**.. SladeO'Hara(7) 2 74
(B W Hills) *w ldrs: led 3f out tl jst ins last: no ex* **7/2**[2]

5115 **4** *3 1/2* **Xpres Maite**[11] 3606 3-9-1 **72**.. AmirQuinn(3) 5 66
(S R Bowring) *led 3f: edgd lft and wknd fnl f* **6/1**[3]

0005 **5** *1 3/4* **Greek Secret**[11] 3604 3-9-0 **68**..(p) SebSanders 8 57
(T D Easterby) *w ldrs on stands' side: wknd appr fnl f* **12/1**

300 **6** *hd* **Fayr Sky (IRE)**[29] 3042 3-8-11 **65**................................ DO'Donohoe 7 53
(J J Quinn) *chsd ldrs: hung lft and lost pl over 1f out* **18/1**

0600 **7** *2* **Rondo**[7] 3722 3-8-10 **67**.. BenSwarbrick(3) 6 49
(T D Barron) *hld up: hdwy to join ldrs after 2f: rdn and lost pl over 2f out* **40/1**

0205 **8** *1/2* **Valentino Swing (IRE)**[5] 3795 3-9-2 **70**..........................(p) EddieAhern 1 51
(J L Spearing) *chsd ldrs: rdn over 3f out: lost pl over 1f out* **8/1**

1m 14.64s (-0.36) **Going Correction** -0.10s/f (Good) **8** Ran SP% **114.2**
Speed ratings (Par 100):98,97,95,91,88 88,85,85
CSF £16.68 CT £40.95 TOTE £1.80: £1.20, £2.50, £1.10; EX 14.00.
Owner R J Arculli and B Vuchot **Bred** Kildaragh Stud **Trained** Newmarket, Suffolk

FOCUS
Just ordinary form, rated through the runner-up with an unpenalised previous winner a good third.
Xpres Maite Official explanation: jockey said gelding had been unsuited by the good to firm ground

3944 BET WITH THE BOOKIES (S) H'CAP 1m 1f 213y
3:35 (3:36) (Class 6) (0-60,58) 4-Y-O+ **£2,730** (£806; £403) **Stalls** Low

Form RPR

6606 **1** **Ming Vase**[14] 3541 4-8-5 **42**.. RobbieFitzpatrick 7 50+
(P T Midgley) *trckd ldrs: wnt 2nd 3f out: led over 1f out: hung violently rt ins last: hld on* **10/1**

5024 **2** *1/2* **Guadiana (GER)**[12] 3592 4-8-0 **42** oh2 ow3.................. JamesDoyle(5) 8 48
(A W Carroll) *bhd: hdwy over 2f out: styd on ins last: jst hld* **11/2**[2]

0460 **3** *1 1/4* **Rudaki**[6] 3762 4-8-9 **49**.. JasonEdmunds(3) 9 53
(M E Sowersby) *bhd: hdwy over 2f out: styd on wl fnl f* **10/1**

0005 **4** *1 1/4* **Ruling Reef**[5] 3803 4-8-9 **46**.. RichardSmith 2 47
(M D I Usher) *hld up in rr: hdwy 2f out: styd on strly fnl f* **13/2**[3]

0000 **5** *1* **Kalani Star (IRE)**[11] 3615 6-8-2 **42** ow1..................... SaleemGolam(3) 12 41
(I W McInnes) *hld up in mid-div: effrt over 2f out: kpt on same pce fnl f* **12/1**

0-00 **6** *1 1/4* **Rock Haven (IRE)**[76] 405 4-9-3 **54**.. PatDobbs 3 51
(J Mackie) *s.i.s: bhd: hdwy over 2f out: kpt on: nvr rchd ldrs* **33/1**

6310 **7** 1/2 **True (IRE)**[23] [3232] 5-8-5 **42** ow1 EddieAhern 1 38
(Mrs S Lamyman) *in tch: effrt over 3f out: one pce fnl 2f* **9/2**[1]
2004 **8** 3/4 **King Of Meze (IRE)**[10] [3637] 5-8-3 **45** (p) AndrewMullen(5) 5 40
(J S Wainwright) *anticipated s: first away: led: clr over 4f out: hdd over 1f out: sn wknd* **13/2**[3]
0050 **9** 4 **Hillhall (IRE)**[21] [3305] 4-8-9 **46** ShaneKelly 13 33
(W M Brisbourne) *chsd ldrs: wknd over 2f out* **9/1**
2440 **10** 1 1/2 **Spy Gun (USA)**[24] [3194] 6-8-3 **47** ow6 SladeO'Hara(7) 6 31
(T Wall) *s.i.s: nvr on terms* **16/1**
000- **11** 2 **Keon (IRE)**[242] [6468] 4-9-0 **58** RussellKennemore(7) 4 38
(R Hollinshead) *sn chsng ldrs: effrt on outer over 2f out: sn lost pl* **28/1**
5460 **12** 5 **Viscount Rossini**[24] [3192] 4-7-12 **40** EmmettStack(5) 10 11
(A W Carroll) *t.k.h in rr: hdwy u.p 4f out: hung rt and lost pl over 2f out* **33/1**
-400 **13** 1/2 **King Nicholas (USA)**[60] [2108] 7-8-4 **41** (bt) JamieMackay 15 11
(J Parkes) *chsd ldr: lost pl over 2f out* **25/1**
000 **14** 16 **Lets Be Lucky (IRE)**[50] [2413] 4-8-7 **44** AlanMunro 14 —
(F Jordan) *t.k.h: sn prom: lost pl 4f out: t.o 2f out* **28/1**
00-6 **15** 12 **Ivana Illyich (IRE)**[37] [2777] 4-8-2 **39** oh2 (p) DO'Donohoe 11 —
(J S Wainwright) *in rr: reminders 7f out: sn bhd: t.o 3f out* **28/1**

2m 9.43s (-0.27) **Going Correction** -0.10s/f (Good) **15** Ran SP% **122.1**
Speed ratings (Par 101):97,96,95,94,93 92,92,91,88,87 85,81,81,68,59
CSF £59.69 CT £575.79 TOTE £14.00: £4.70, £2.30, £3.40; EX 85.30.There was no bid for the winner.
Owner Michael Ng **Bred** Cheveley Park Stud Ltd **Trained** Westow, N Yorks
FOCUS
King Of Meze seemed to charge the gates and came out a length or so ahead of the others. It was a poor race even by selling race standards, rated around the first two.

3945 KONICA MINOLTA EAST H'CAP 1m 54y
4:10 (4:12) (Class 4) (0-85,85) 3-Y-O
£6,232 (£1,866; £933; £467; £233; £117) **Stalls** Centre

Form RPR
6453 **1** **Airbuss (IRE)**[28] [3082] 3-8-13 **77** RobertHavlin 1 86
(M R Channon) *s.i.s: drvn along to r promly: effrt over 2f out: wnt 2nd 1f out: edgd lft: led towards fin* **5/1**[3]
-221 **2** hd **Safqa**[42] [2662] 3-9-1 **79** EddieAhern 4 88
(B W Hills) *led after 1f: rdn 1f out: hdd nr fin* **7/2**[1]
0224 **3** 2 1/2 **North Walk (IRE)**[15] [3473] 3-8-12 **81** AndrewMullen(5) 2 84
(K A Ryan) *led 1f: chsd ldrs: wnt 2nd over 1f out: kpt on same pce* **7/2**[1]
3155 **4** 1 **Methusaleh (IRE)**[47] [2502] 3-8-13 **77** AlanMunro 7 78
(T D Easterby) *s.i.s: in rr: hdwy over 1f out: styd on wl towards fin* **12/1**
3230 **5** 1/2 **Great Chieftain (IRE)**[13] [3569] 3-8-4 **68** DO'Donohoe 5 68
(R A Fahey) *w ldrs: one pce fnl 2f* **16/1**
0130 **6** 1 1/4 **Kaveri (USA)**[28] [3088] 3-9-7 **85** SebSanders 9 82
(C E Brittain) *sn trcking ldrs: chal over 3f out: fdd appr fnl f* **16/1**
6243 **7** hd **Zennerman (IRE)**[11] [3606] 3-9-4 **82** ShaneKelly 8 78
(W M Brisbourne) *trckd ldrs: rdn over 2f out: sn outpcd* **14/1**
2132 **8** hd **Storm On The Run (IRE)**[14] [3546] 3-9-5 **83** DaneO'Neill 6 79
(R Hannon) *mid-div: effrt 3f out: sn chsng ldrs: fdd appr fnl f* **9/2**[2]
113- **9** 1 **Startori**[285] [5942] 3-9-7 **85** PaulEddery 3 78
(B Smart) *s.i.s: a in rr* **14/1**
4515 **10** 2 1/2 **Right Ted (IRE)**[15] [3469] 3-8-4 **75** SladeO'Hara(7) 10 63
(T Wall) *in rr: effrt on outer over 3f out: nvr on terms* **16/1**

1m 43.31s (-3.09) **Going Correction** -0.10s/f (Good) **10** Ran SP% **118.0**
Speed ratings (Par 102):111,110,108,107,106 105,105,105,104,101
CSF £23.16 CT £69.92 TOTE £8.00: £2.10, £2.40, £1.30; EX 30.70.
Owner Sheikh Ahmed Al Maktoum **Bred** Roger Charlton And Floors Farming **Trained** West Ilsley, Berks
■ Stewards' Enquiry : Robert Havlin two-day ban: used whip with excessive frequency (Aug 9-10)
FOCUS
Solid form, improved efforts from the winner and more especially the second, rated through the third and fourth.

3946 SANDICLIFFE NEW TRANSIT FEEL THE DIFFERENCE MAIDEN FILLIES' STKS 1m 1f 213y
4:45 (4:46) (Class 5) 3-Y-O **£3,238** (£963; £481; £240) **Stalls** Low

Form RPR
0-22 **1** **Early Evening**[19] [3367] 3-9-0 77 DaneO'Neill 4 72
(H Candy) *led: shkn up over 3f out: rdn over 1f out: hld on wl* **11/10**[1]
23 **2** 1 **Majestic Halo**[41] [2673] 3-9-0 EddieAhern 6 70
(E A L Dunlop) *trckd ldrs: chal 3f out: no ex ins last* **7/2**[2]
04 **3** hd **Izadore (IRE)**[33] [2917] 3-9-0 DO'Donohoe 2 70
(E A L Dunlop) *dwlt: sn trcking ldrs: swished tail and kpt on same pce fnl f* **22/1**
4 1/2 **Shahmina (IRE)** 3-9-0 RobertHavlin 11 69
(J H M Gosden) *in rr: hdwy over 4f out: kpt on wl fnl f* **7/1**[3]
5 3/4 **Tidal Chorus** 3-9-0 JamieMackay 9 67
(J G Given) *chsd ldrs: drvn over 5f out: hung lft and kpt on same pce fnl 2f* **20/1**
0 **6** shd **Lady Songbird (IRE)**[19] [3367] 3-9-0 SebSanders 1 67
(W R Swinburn) *stdd s: hld up in mid-div: kpt on fnl 2f: nvr trbld ldrs* **25/1**
55 **7** 1/2 **Spirit Of The Fen (IRE)**[19] [3367] 3-9-0 DavidKinsella 7 66
(J H M Gosden) *mid-div: effrt on outside 4f out: kpt on steadily fnl 2f* **8/1**
6 **8** hd **Aphorism**[28] [3100] 3-8-9 RoryMoore(5) 8 66
(J R Fanshawe) *hld up in rr: kpt on fnl 2f: nvr a factor* **28/1**
06 **9** 3 1/2 **Sasetti (IRE)**[16] [3458] 3-8-11 SaleemGolam(3) 10 59
(J R Fanshawe) *hld up: a in rr* **66/1**
50 **10** 11 **Selkirk Lady**[24] [3200] 3-9-0 AlanMunro 3 38+
(W R Swinburn) *restless in stalls: s.i.s: effrt 4f out: wknd over 2f out: sn bhd* **16/1**
0-0 **11** 5 **The Lady Mandarin**[24] [3200] 3-9-0 PatDobbs 5 29
(G Wragg) *chsd ldrs: drvn 4f out: sn lost pl and bhd* **80/1**

2m 11.06s (1.36) **Going Correction** -0.10s/f (Good) **11** Ran SP% **118.5**
Speed ratings (Par 97):90,89,89,88,88 87,87,87,84,75 71
CSF £4.37 TOTE £2.00: £1.10, £2.10, £4.80; EX 6.00.
Owner Sarah Lakin & Tony Solomons **Bred** Lakin Bloodstock, Hillard Bloodstock And Trading L **Trained** Kingston Warren, Oxon
FOCUS
A tactical affair with the winner given her own way infront. Early Evening has an official rating of 77 and sets the standard.

3947 NOTTINGHAMSHIRE LIFEBOATS H'CAP 1m 54y
5:15 (5:15) (Class 6) (0-60,60) 3-Y-O+ **£2,730** (£806; £403) **Stalls** Centre

Form RPR
3643 **1** **Blue Empire (IRE)**[4] [3820] 5-9-10 **57** EddieAhern 10 68
(C R Dore) *mde all: hrd rdn and styd on fnl 2f: unchal* **7/2**[1]
2420 **2** 2 **Panic Stations**[17] [3410] 3-9-4 **59** HayleyTurner 7 63
(M L W Bell) *chsd ldrs: wnt 2nd 4f out: kpt on same pce fnl 2f: no real imp* **10/1**
1004 **3** 1/2 **Royal Indulgence**[8] [3716] 6-9-2 **54** LiamJones(5) 6 59
(W M Brisbourne) *sn in tch: effrt over 2f out: kpt on same pce fnl f* **11/1**
0600 **4** 1/2 **Pauline's Prince**[13] [3570] 4-9-4 **58** RussellKennemore(7) 4 62
(R Hollinshead) *hld up in mid-div: hdwy to chse ldrs over 3f out: kpt on same pce appr fnl f* **33/1**
-400 **5** 3 **Balearic Star (IRE)**[31] [2978] 5-9-6 **53** (b[1]) AlanMunro 5 50
(B R Millman) *in rr: hdwy over 2f out: kpt on: nvr rchd ldrs* **7/1**[3]
0050 **6** 1/2 **Peters Delite**[13] [3566] 4-9-4 **51** DO'Donohoe 12 47
(R A Fahey) *t.k.h in rr: hdwy on wd outside 3f out: edgd lft: nvr nr ldrs* **16/1**
0006 **7** 3/4 **Ronsard (IRE)**[18] [3390] 4-9-6 **60** JamesO'Reilly(7) 1 54
(T J Pitt) *unruly and reluctant to go to s: bhd: sme hdwy over 2f out: nvr nr ldrs* **14/1**
6000 **8** 4 **The Bonus King**[10] [3159] 6-9-10 **57** DaneO'Neill 8 42
(J Jay) *in tch: effrt 3f out: wknd over 1f out* **20/1**
6041 **9** 1 1/2 **Burton Ash**[34] [2891] 4-9-9 **56** (p) JamieMackay 15 37
(J G Given) *chsd ldrs: wknd over 1f out* **7/1**[3]
006 **10** 4 **Louise Dupin (IRE)**[27] [3112] 3-9-5 **60** SebSanders 17 30
(R M Beckett) *hld up towards rr on outer: effrt over 2f out: sn wknd* **9/1**
-004 **11** 1 1/2 **Heartcrusher (IRE)**[36] [2808] 4-9-8 **55** RobbieFitzpatrick 3 24
(G A Swinbank) *s.i.s: nvr a factor* **8/1**
0131 **12** 6 **Orpen Quest (IRE)**[12] [3599] 4-9-4 **58** (v) KevinGhunowa(7) 13 13
(M J Attwater) *in rr: effrt on outer over 2f out: sn lost pl* **13/2**[2]
5-10 **13** 1 1/4 **Sonderborg**[186] [183] 5-8-12 **50** (p) AndrewMullen(5) 16 2
(J Mackie) *in tch: lost pl over 3f out* **28/1**
05-3 **14** 9 **Sion Hill (IRE)**[207] [26] 5-8-12 **45** PatDobbs 11 —
(Mrs N Macauley) *trckd ldrs: lost pl over 3f out: sn bhd* **66/1**
0000 **15** hd **Ellens Princess (IRE)**[26] [3142] 4-9-3 **50** (b) LeeEnstone 9 —
(J S Wainwright) *sn chsng ldrs: lost pl 3f out: sn bhd* **50/1**

1m 44.27s (-2.13) **Going Correction** -0.10s/f (Good)
WFA 3 from 4yo+ 8lb **15** Ran SP% **126.2**
Speed ratings (Par 101):106,104,103,103,100 99,98,94,93,89 87,81,80,71,71
CSF £39.05 CT £367.46 TOTE £4.20: £2.10, £2.40, £3.50; EX 63.60 Place 6 £57.16, Place 5 £15.75.
Owner Mrs Jennifer Marsh **Bred** Yeomanstown Stud **Trained** West Pinchbeck, Lincs
FOCUS
The winner went hard infront and never looked in any real danger. The form looks rock solid rathed though the placed horses.
Ellens Princess(IRE) Official explanation: jockey said filly would not face the blinkers
T/Plt: £43.30 to a £1 stake. Pool: £45,711.15. 770.20 winning tickets T/Qpdt: £17.30 to a £1 stake. Pool: £2,432.10. 103.90 winning tickets. WG

3543 SALISBURY (R-H)
Saturday, July 29

OFFICIAL GOING: Good to firm
Wind: Moderate, half against

3948 CORAL.CO.UK CARNARVON AMATEUR RIDERS' H'CAP 1m
6:10 (6:12) (Class 5) (0-75,70) 3-Y-O+ **£3,747** (£1,162; £580; £290) **Stalls** High

Form RPR
5543 **1** **Charlie Bear**[23] [3229] 5-10-3 **57** MissGDGracey-Davison(5) 2 66
(Miss Z C Davison) *a.p: led over 1f out: rdn out* **6/1**[2]
0436 **2** hd **Undeterred**[3] [3854] 10-11-7 **70** GerardTumelty 4 81+
(K J Burke) *mid-div: swtchd lft and r.o* *n.m.r ent fnl f: swtchd lft and r.o* **7/1**[3]
0000 **3** 1/2 **Will The Till**[14] [3542] 4-9-11 **53** MissHDavies(7) 12 60
(J M Bradley) *hld up in rr: hdwy 2f out: r.o fnl f: nvr nrr* **9/1**
-406 **4** hd **Prince Of The May**[48] [2482] 4-9-12 **52** MissVCartmel(5) 8 59
(H Morrison) *trckd ldr: led over 2f out: hdd over 1f out: one pce fnl f* **15/2**
200/ **5** 3 1/2 **Johannian**[626] [6612] 8-10-13 **67** MrNPearce(5) 6 66
(J M Bradley) *hld up: swtchd rt and hdwy over 2f out: wknd ins fnl f* **40/1**
3260 **6** 1 1/2 **Paso Doble**[7] [3730] 8-9-9 **51** oh6 MissDO'Brien(7) 3 46
(B R Millman) *nvr bttr than mid-div* **20/1**
1001 **7** hd **Sol Rojo**[29] [3056] 4-10-3 **57** MrSPearce(5) 9 52
(J Pearce) *mid-div: rdn 2f out: wknd fnl f* **10/3**[1]
0160 **8** shd **Stagnite**[2] [3867] 6-10-1 **57** (p) MissFGuillambert(7) 7 52
(P A Blockley) *led tl hdd over 2f out: wknd ent fnl f* **12/1**
60-6 **9** shd **Piano Man**[51] [1926] 4-10-4 **58** MissSarah-JaneDurman(5) 5 53
(J C Fox) *in rr and nvr on terms* **22/1**
3600 **10** 3 **Lord Chamberlain**[4] [3817] 13-10-1 **57** (b) MissSBradley(7) 11 45
(J M Bradley) *in tch tl wknd wl over 1f out* **12/1**
0023 **11** 1 1/4 **Consonant (IRE)**[30] [3024] 9-10-10 **66** MrBAdams(7) 1 51
(D G Bridgwater) *in tch tl wknd wl over 1f out* **6/1**[2]
305- **12** 1 3/4 **Suivez Moi (IRE)**[90] [5990] 4-10-9 **65** MissIsabelTompsett(7) 10 46
(M F Harris) *mid-div: bhd fr over 2f out* **20/1**
60-0 **13** 17 **Rocket (IRE)**[85] [1460] 5-9-9 **51** oh6 MissKWhitbread(7) 13 —
(H J Manners) *mid-div to 1/2-way: sn wl bhd* **80/1**

1m 44.87s (1.78) **Going Correction** +0.25s/f (Good) **13** Ran SP% **118.8**
Speed ratings (Par 103):101,100,100,100,96 95,94,94,94,91 90,88,71
CSF £44.21 CT £392.58 TOTE £8.30: £3.00, £2.40, £4.20; EX 55.30.
Owner Mervyn Merwood **Bred** Old Road Securities Plc **Trained** Hammerwood, E Sussex
FOCUS
A fairly moderate race that will probably not work out with the runner-up the best guide.

3949 HIGHLAND PARK SINGLE MALT SCOTCH WHISKY MAIDEN STKS 6f
6:40 (6:40) (Class 4) 2-Y-O **£4,857** (£1,445; £722; £360) **Stalls** High

Form RPR
40 **1** **Magic Mountain (IRE)**[12] [3591] 2-9-3 (t) RyanMoore 2 83
(R Hannon) *trckd ldr: shkn up 2f out: led over 1f out: r.o wl* **7/4**[1]
2 2 **St Philip (USA)** 2-9-0 NelsonDeSouza(3) 6 77
(R M Beckett) *outpcd: rdn and styd on fnl 2f to chse wnr ins fnl f* **9/4**[2]
3 2 **Cool Box (USA)** 2-9-3 RichardHughes 5 71
(Mrs A J Perrett) *prom: rdn over 1f out: no ex ins fnl f* **9/2**[3]
00 **4** 3 1/2 **Mulvany (IRE)**[17] [3417] 2-8-10 (b[1]) KMay(7) 1 61
(B J Meehan) *trckd ldr: led over 2f out: hdd over 1f out: wknd ins fnl f* **25/1**

5 ½ **Sharpazmax (IRE)** 2-9-3 ... JimmyQuinn 8 59
(P J Makin) *slowly away: a bhd* **7/1**

0 6 ½ **Mighty Missouri (IRE)**[12] 3591 2-9-3 ... StephenCarson 4 58
(W R Swinburn) *in tch tl rdn 1/2-way: sn btn* **12/1**

0 7 1 **The Grey Bam Bam**[31] 2984 2-8-12 ... LPKeniry 7 50
(R J Hodges) *led tl hdd over 2f out: sn wknd* **50/1**

1m 15.82s (0.84) **Going Correction** +0.25s/f (Good) 7 Ran SP% **111.3**
Speed ratings (Par 96):104,101,98,94,93 92,91
CSF £5.53 TOTE £2.80: £1.40, £2.00; EX 6.40.
Owner Lord Carnarvon **Bred** Lodge Park Stud **Trained** East Everleigh, Wilts

FOCUS
A modest race won by the form horse with the fourth close to form.

NOTEBOOK
Magic Mountain(IRE), who was slightly disappointing last time at Windsor, made no mistake this time in the tongue tie and won going away. His future will probably be in handicaps now. (op 5-4 tchd 6-5)
St Philip(USA), who holds a Gimcrack entry, finished to good effect and will have derived plenty for the run. Clearly expected to go close considering his market position, he should be capable of going close in any ordinary maiden next time. (op 11-4 tchd 3-1)
Cool Box(USA) momentarily looked dangerous approaching the final furlong, but found his effort flatten out under full pressure, coming home steadily throughout the final furlong. He may need further than six furlongs next time. (op 4-1 tchd 5-1)
Mulvany(IRE)probably ran his best race to date, with the blinkers applied for the first time, but rarely looked like winning. Low-grade handicaps will be his best option in the near future.
Sharpazmax(IRE), a half-brother to four winners, did not shape as badly as his final position suggested, as he was hampered leaving the stalls and looked green under pressure. If making normal improvement, he would be of some interest next time if kept to a sensible level. Official explanation: jockey said colt missed the break (op 11-1 tchd 13-2)
Mighty Missouri(IRE) failed to show a great deal again, looking green from some way out. It would, however, be surprising if this son of Danehill did not prove to be much better in time. (op 20-1)

3950 GLENSIDE MANOR HEALTHCARE SERVICES LTD MAIDEN STKS 6f
7:10 (7:10) (Class 4) 3-Y-O+ **£5,505** (£1,637; £818; £408) **Stalls** High

Form RPR

0322 1 **Kansas Gold**[27] 3111 3-9-3 69 ... RyanMoore 11 72
(W R Muir) *mde all: shkn up over 2f out: drvn out fnl f* **9/4**[2]

-023 2 ½ **Rogue**[28] 3090 4-9-3 63 ... AdrianMcCarthy 6 65
(Jane Southcombe) *a.p: rdn over 1f out: r.o to go 2nd ins fnl f* **9/2**[3]

00 3 ½ **Sprinkle**[16] 3458 3-8-12 ... JosedeSouza 1 64+
(R M Beckett) *slowly away: hdwy whn short of room and swtchd lft over 1f out: r.o ins fnl f: nvr nrr* **40/1**

2-44 4 hd **Call Me Waki (USA)**[14] 3554 3-8-12 70 ... RichardHughes 2 63
(A M Balding) *trckd wnr tl rdn and no ex ins fnl f* **7/4**[1]

5205 5 1 **Arculinge**[31] 2987 3-8-12 55 ... RichardMullen 7 61+
(M Blanshard) *trckd ldrs: rdn and one pce ins fnl f* **14/1**

0634 6 shd **Nightstrike (IRE)**[18] 3381 3-8-12 61 ... LPKeniry 10 60
(H Candy) *in tch: rdn and nt qckn ins fnl f* **7/1**

00 7 5 **Parthenope**[31] 2985 3-8-12 ... StephenCarson 3 45
(J A Geake) *hld up: bhd fnl 2f* **66/1**

5-4 8 6 **John Bratby (USA)**[65] 1960 4-9-8 ... JimmyQuinn 8 32
(P J Makin) *prom tl rdn and wknd over 1f out* **16/1**

50 9 6 **Question (USA)**[28] 3090 3-8-9 ... EdwardCreighton(3) 5 9
(J M Bradley) *a bhd* **50/1**

1m 15.81s (0.83) **Going Correction** +0.25s/f (Good)
WFA 3 from 4yo 5lb 9 Ran SP% **116.3**
Speed ratings (Par 105):104,103,102,102,101 100,94,86,78
CSF £12.94 TOTE £3.60: £1.30, £1.50, £6.00; EX 16.80.
Owner C L A Edginton **Bred** Coln Valley Stud **Trained** Lambourn, Berks
■ Stewards' Enquiry : Adrian McCarthy two-day ban: careless riding (Aug 9-10)

FOCUS
Only a modest maiden, in which the first six home were involved in a bunch finish with the fifth and sixth limiting the form.

3951 TURFSURF EQUINE SURFACING CLAIMING STKS 1m
7:40 (7:40) (Class 5) 3-4-Y-O **£3,562** (£1,059; £529; £264) **Stalls** High

Form RPR

0411 1 **Envision**[9] 3664 3-8-12 76 ... RyanMoore 5 77+
(R Hannon) *trckd ldr: rdn to ld 2f out: sn clr: easily* **10/11**[1]

1461 2 6 **Piano Player (IRE)**[15] 3488 3-9-1 71 ... ShaneKelly 6 66
(J A Osborne) *hld up in tch: rdn to go 2nd over 1f out: no ch w wnr* **4/1**[3]

0206 3 1 **Scutch Mill (IRE)**[30] 3024 4-9-3 62 ... RichardHughes 2 60
(Karen George) *slowly away: rdn and effrt 2f out: kpt on to go 3rd fnl f* **8/1**

0-50 4 1¼ **Nanton (USA)**[9] 3688 4-9-6 81 ... NelsonDeSouza(3) 3 63
(P F I Cole) *hld up: hdwy after 3f: rdn over 1f out: one pce fnl f* **3/1**[2]

6020 5 ½ **Croft (IRE)**[36] 2814 3-8-3 57 ... (v) JamesDoyle(5) 4 53
(R M Stronge) *led: qckn pce 3f out: rdn and hdd 2f out: wknd ins fnl f* **25/1**

1m 45.19s (2.10) **Going Correction** +0.25s/f (Good)
WFA 3 from 4yo 8lb 5 Ran SP% **112.3**
Speed ratings (Par 103):99,93,92,90,90
CSF £5.11 TOTE £1.80: £1.10, £1.60; EX 4.50.Envision was the subject of a friendly claim of £20,000.
Owner Mrs J Wood **Bred** Cheveley Park Stud Ltd **Trained** East Everleigh, Wilts

FOCUS
The winner was in a different league to his rivals and won with plenty in hand. Piano Player is a better horse on the All-Weather and can be given another chance, but the rest are disappointing.

3952 WESTOVER GROUP H'CAP 1m 6f 15y
8:10 (8:11) (Class 5) (0-70,69) 3-Y-O+ **£3,886** (£1,156; £577; £288)

Form RPR

-450 1 **Rehearsed (IRE)**[43] 2607 3-8-4 62 ... EdwardCreighton(3) 3 68
(H Morrison) *prom early: sn settled in mid-div: rdn 4f out: led u.p 1f out: hld on* **9/1**

0143 2 ½ **Eldorado**[8] 3704 5-10-0 69 ... RichardHughes 4 74
(S Kirk) *hld up: hdwy to ld 2f out: rdn and hdd 1f out: kpt on one pce* **9/2**[2]

-400 3 ¾ **Ocean Of Storms (IRE)**[63] 2013 11-9-3 65 ... MarkCoumbe(7) 8 69
(N I M Rossiter) *wl bhd: rdn over 4f out: styd on u.p ins fnl 2f: nvr nrr* **33/1**

0004 4 1 **Grey Paint (USA)**[10] 3649 3-8-12 67 ... (t) RyanMoore 11 70
(R Hannon) *mid-div: rdn and styd on one pce ins fnl 2f* **4/1**[1]

6060 5 ½ **Bobsleigh**[7] 3723 7-9-0 55 ... VinceSlattery 7 57
(H S Howe) *led after 4f: sn clr: rdn and hdd 2f out: no ex fnl f* **10/1**

0 6 1¾ **The Iron Giant (IRE)**[16] 3451 4-8-13 59 ... RichardKingscote(5) 13 58+
(B G Powell) *towards rr: hdwy to chse ldrs 3f out: wknd 1f out* **33/1**

-533 7 1½ **Red Forest (IRE)**[35] 2871 7-9-1 56 ... (t) RichardMullen 9 53
(J Mackie) *sn bhd and nvr on terms after* **6/1**[3]

-300 8 nk **Grateful**[26] 3152 3-7-13 57 ... (b[1]) NelsonDeSouza(3) 14 54
(R M Beckett) *t.k.h: trckd ldrs: chsd ldr over 3f out but hung bdly rt and hit rail: sn btn* **33/1**

556- 9 3½ **Jayer Gilles**[266] 6267 6-9-3 58 ... LPKeniry 1 50
(Dr J R J Naylor) *mid-div: rdn 4f out: sn btn* **17/2**

-003 10 6 **Irish Ballad**[16] 3437 4-8-13 54 ... (t) StephenCarson 6 38
(W R Swinburn) *led for 4f: wknd over 3f out* **13/2**

040- 11 14 **Beaufort**[341] 4640 4-9-12 67 ... ShaneKelly 2 31
(D K Ivory) *prom early: lost pl 6f out: sn wl bhd* **40/1**

6-54 12 1 **Swindon (USA)**[8] 3704 4-9-9 64 ... JosedeSouza 10 27
(P F I Cole) *t.k.h: mid-div tl wknd over 3f out* **9/1**

3m 7.50s (1.27) **Going Correction** +0.25s/f (Good)
WFA 3 from 4yo+ 14lb 12 Ran SP% **116.7**
Speed ratings (Par 103):106,105,105,104,104 103,102,102,100,96 88,88
CSF £47.05 CT £1289.63 TOTE £9.60: £3.80, £2.60, £4.50; EX 66.70.
Owner Mrs G C Maxwell & J D N Tillyard **Bred** J C Condon **Trained** East Ilsley, Berks
■ Stewards' Enquiry : Mark Coumbe one-day ban: used whip with excessive frequency (Aug 14)

FOCUS
A flip start was used. Race hand-timed. A modest staying handicap and limited form best rated through the fourth.

3953 UNITED TAXIS FILLIES' H'CAP 6f 212y
8:40 (8:41) (Class 4) (0-85,80) 3-Y-O+ **£8,096** (£2,408; £1,203; £601) **Stalls** Centre

Form RPR

1161 1 **Meditation**[16] 3450 4-9-7 76 ... JamesDoyle(5) 1 84
(I A Wood) *mde virtually all: drvn out fnl f* **7/2**[2]

4220 2 ¾ **Gaelic Princess**[30] 3020 6-9-7 78 ... JamesMillman(7) 3 84+
(A G Newcombe) *hld up: rdn and swtchd lft to stands' side over 2f out: r.o strly fnl f to snatch 2nd cl home* **10/1**

0534 3 ½ **All Quiet**[12] 3590 5-10-0 78 ... RichardHughes 5 83
(R Hannon) *prom: disp ld 1/2-way: rdn and lost 2nd cl home* **7/2**[2]

0025 4 2½ **Way To The Stars**[39] 2735 3-9-1 72 ... RyanMoore 2 68
(A M Balding) *trckd wnr to 1/2-way: one pce ins fnl 2f* **7/1**[3]

0-05 5 2½ **Nephetriti Way (IRE)**[16] 3450 5-9-4 71 ... NelsonDeSouza(3) 9 63
(P R Chamings) *trckd ldrs tl wknd over 1f out* **14/1**

01 6 ½ **Josie Marcus (USA)**[14] 3554 3-9-9 80 ... ShaneKelly 8 68
(J Noseda) *hld up: rdn 2f out: nt qckn* **9/4**[1]

0100 7 2½ **Peace Lily**[3] 3845 4-8-11 61 ... StephenCarson 6 45
(R F Johnson Houghton) *hld up in tch: rdn over 2f out: sn btn* **16/1**

5/03 8 1½ **Nebraska Lady (IRE)**[9] 3687 4-9-11 75 ... RichardMullen 7 55
(E J O'Neill) *hld up in tch: rdn 3f out: no hdwy after* **10/1**

1m 30.23s (1.17) **Going Correction** +0.25s/f (Good)
WFA 3 from 4yo+ 7lb 8 Ran SP% **118.4**
Speed ratings (Par 102):103,102,101,98,95 95,92,90
CSF £39.32 CT £133.06 TOTE £4.30: £1.50, £2.70, £1.30; EX 28.10 Place 6 £66.82, Place 5 £24.59.
Owner Paddy Barrett **Bred** P E Barrett **Trained** Upper Lambourn, Berks

FOCUS
A reasonable handicap for fillies won by a very in-form sort. The race has not been rated positively.
T/Plt: £64.30 to a £1 stake. Pool: £42,911.55. 486.55 winning tickets. T/Qpdt: £12.00 to a £1 stake. Pool: £3,567.00. 218.95 winning tickets. JS

[3878]YORK (L-H)
Saturday, July 29

OFFICIAL GOING: Good to firm
Wind: Slight, behind

3954 SKYBET.COM EBF FILLIES' STKS (H'CAP) 1m 2f 88y
2:10 (2:10) (Class 3) (0-90,89) 3-Y-O+ **£9,715** (£2,890; £1,444; £721) **Stalls** Low

Form RPR

3131 1 **Kahlua Kiss**[8] 3703 3-9-6 81 ... RobertWinston 1 95+
(W R Muir) *trckd ldrs: smooth hdwy over 3f out: led on bit over 2f out: sn pushed clr: easily* **11/4**[1]

1011 2 5 **Mistress Twister**[14] 3528 5-9-9 74 ... PaulFessey 4 78
(T D Barron) *hld up in rr: hdwy 3f out: rdn wl over 1f out: styd on to chse wnr ins last: no imp* **5/1**[3]

4144 3 ½ **Flying Clarets (IRE)**[15] 3477 3-9-3 78 ... PaulHanagan 2 81
(R A Fahey) *dwlt: sn led: rdn along over 3f out: hdd over 2f out: sn drvn and one pce* **10/1**

2042 4 2½ **Lysandra (IRE)**[7] 3724 4-9-7 72 ... KimTinkler 7 70
(N Tinkler) *hld up: pushed along and hdwy over 2f out: sn rdn and no imp* **16/1**

1-11 5 ½ **Starship (IRE)**[12] 3590 3-9-2 82 ... LiamJones(5) 6 79+
(W J Haggas) *cl up: pushed along 3f out: rdn over 2f out: sn drvn and wknd* **7/2**[2]

-1 6 ¾ **Virtuosity**[18] 3373 3-10-0 89 ... RyanMoore 5 85
(Sir Michael Stoute) *prom: pushed along over 3f out: rdn wl over 2f out: sn drvn and wknd* **11/4**[1]

2m 10.36s (-0.12) **Going Correction** +0.025s/f (Good)
WFA 3 from 4yo+ 10lb 6 Ran SP% **107.2**
Speed ratings (Par 104):101,97,96,94,94 93
CSF £15.08 TOTE £3.80: £1.90, £2.10; EX 14.90.
Owner M J Caddy **Bred** Whitsbury Manor Stud **Trained** Lambourn, Berks

FOCUS
A fair fillies' handicap, run at a fair pace, and the impressive winner is value for plenty further. The form is sound enough.

NOTEBOOK
Kahlua Kiss, 5lb higher than when scoring at Newbury eight days previously, was always travelling supremely well and ultimately followed up by coming home to score as she pleased. She is value for plenty further, this was her third success from her last four outings, and she is clearly most progressive. Now may well be the time to try and gain some valuable black type. (op 10-3)
Mistress Twister, runner-up in this event last year from a 5lb lower mark, kept on towards the finish without threatening the winner to fill the same position this time around. She has been in grand form in the main since resuming life this term and may not be weighted out of winning in this sphere just yet. (op 11-2 tchd 6-1)
Flying Clarets(IRE) was made to look very one paced when the winner asserted yet was not disgraced. She just looks in the Handicapper's grip at present. (tchd 9-1)
Starship(IRE), raised 3lb for dead-heating at Windsor last time, failed to see out the longer trip as was expected and proved somewhat disappointing.
Virtuosity, off the mark on debut at Pontefract last time, proved very one paced when push came to shove on this handicap bow under her big weight. She is not one to write off just yet. Official explanation: trainer had no explanation for the poor form shown (op 9-4)

3955 SKYBET PRESS RED TO BET ON C4 STKS (H'CAP) 2m 2f
2:40 (2:40) (Class 4) (0-80,76) 3-Y-O+ **£8,096** (£2,408; £1,203; £601) **Stalls** Low

Form RPR
0212 **1** **Whispering Death**[16] [3452] 4-9-9 **76**.........................(v) LiamJones(5) 11 86
(W J Haggas) *hld up in rr: smooth hdwy 4f out: led 2f out: rdn over 1f out and styd on wl* **7/1**[3]
-412 **2** *3 1/2* **Lodgician (IRE)**[8] [3696] 4-9-1 **63**................................ GrahamGibbons 7 70
(J J Quinn) *midfield: hdwy over 4f out: rdn along 3f out: chsd wnr and drvn over 1f out: kpt on same pce* **9/1**
3112 **3** *4* **Eforetta (GER)**[16] [3454] 4-8-13 **61**.. ChrisCatlin 8 63
(D J Wintle) *midfield: hdwy over 4f out: rdn to chse ldrs 3f out: sn drvn and kpt on same pce* **25/1**
3123 **4** *shd* **Mister Arjay (USA)**[8] [3696] 6-8-8 **61**...................... StephenDonohoe(5) 3 63
(B Ellison) *led 2f: cl up tl led again 1/2-way: rdn along over 4f out: hdd 3f out: sn drvn and grad wknd fnl 2f* **12/1**
4111 **5** *1/2* **Rose Bien**[6] [3763] 4-8-10 **61**.................................(p) EdwardCreighton(3) 9 62
(P J McBride) *hld up in rr: hdwy over 3f out: sn rdn and kpt on same pce fnl 2f* **7/2**[1]
-511 **6** *3 1/2* **Ostfanni (IRE)**[19] [3350] 6-9-0 **62**.................................... RobertWinston 4 60
(M Todhunter) *midfield: hdwy over 4f out: sn pushed along: rdn wl over 2f out and nvr rch ldrs* **5/1**[2]
0032 **7** *4* **Thewhirlingdervish (IRE)**[7] [3723] 8-9-3 **65**....................... DavidAllan 6 58
(T D Easterby) *trckd ldrs: hdwy 5f out: rdn to ld 3f out: drvn and hdd 2f out: sn wknd* **10/1**
-512 **8** *shd* **Industrial Star (IRE)**[17] [3396] 5-9-6 **68**............................ PaulHanagan 2 61
(Micky Hammond) *trckd ldrs: hdwy over 4f out: pushed along to chse ldrs 3f out: rdn and edgd lft over 2f out: sn drvn and btn wl over 1f out* **11/1**
4456 **9** *2* **Openide**[7] [3522] 5-8-11 **59**.. RyanMoore 10 50
(B W Duke) *cl up: led after 2f: rdn along 10f out: hdd 1/2-way: drvn along 4f out: sn wknd* **7/1**[3]
5125 **10** *7* **Mr Majestic**[6] [3763] 4-8-13 **61**.. DeanMcKeown 5 44
(R M Whitaker) *in tch: hdwy over 4f out: chsd ldrs 3f out: sn rdn and wkng whn n.m.r 2f out* **14/1**
3601 **11** *hd* **Merrymaker**[14] [3522] 6-9-10 **75**................................ PatrickMathers(3) 1 58
(W M Brisbourne) *hld up: a rr* **20/1**

3m 54.65s (6.65) **11** Ran SP% **114.3**
CSF £66.53 CT £1478.09 TOTE £7.40: £2.20, £3.60, £6.30; EX 83.40.
Owner G Roberts/F M Green **Bred** Milton Park Stud **Trained** Newmarket, Suffolk

FOCUS
A modest marathon handicap, run at a solid pace, and the winner defied top weight in good style. The race has been rated through the third and fourth.
Rose Bien Official explanation: jockey said filly ran flat
Ostfanni(IRE) Official explanation: trainer had no explanation for the poor form shown
Thewhirlingdervish(IRE) Official explanation: jockey said gelding lost its action

3956 SKYBET DASH (HERITAGE H'CAP) 6f
3:15 (3:16) (Class 2) (0-105,103) 3-Y-O+
£31,160 (£9,330; £4,665; £2,335; £1,165; £585) **Stalls** Centre

Form RPR
-421 **1** **Wyatt Earp (IRE)**[14] [3550] 5-8-8 **87**.............................. RoystonFfrench 6 98
(R A Fahey) *in tch: rdn along and sltly outpcd 1/2-way: hdwy 2f out: sn rdn and styd on to ld ins last: drvn out* **6/1**[2]
2535 **2** *3/4* **Ice Planet**[18] [3374] 5-8-10 **89**... RobertWinston 5 98
(D Nicholls) *chsd ldrs: rdn and hdwy wl over 1f out: drvn and ev ch ins last: kpt on same pce towards fin* **6/1**[2]
1112 **3** *shd* **Blue Tomato**[15] [3486] 5-8-4 **88**... LiamJones(5) 14 97
(J M Bradley) *towards rr: gd hdwy on outer 2f out: rdn to chal ins last and ev ch tl no ex towards fin* **7/1**[3]
3321 **4** *hd* **Knot In Wood (IRE)**[13] [3567] 4-8-2 **81**............................. PaulHanagan 3 89
(R A Fahey) *chsd ldrs: hdwy 2f out: rdn to ld briefly over 1f out: drvn and hdd ins last: no ex towards fin* **9/2**[1]
1246 **5** *nk* **My Gacho (IRE)**[15] [3482] 4-8-4 **83**.................................(b) DaleGibson 11 90
(T D Barron) *cl up: rdn along 2f out: ev ch over 1f out: sn drvn and nt qckn ins last* **16/1**
6154 **6** *2* **Yomalo (IRE)**[15] [3499] 6-9-9 **102**...................................... NickyMackay 13 103
(Rae Guest) *sn outpcd and bhd: hdwy over 1f out: styd on strly ins last: nrst fin* **15/2**
5040 **7** *hd* **Obe Gold**[15] [3471] 4-9-5 **98**..(v) ChrisCatlin 9 99
(M R Channon) *towards rr: rdn along over 2f out: styd on appr last: nrst fin* **16/1**
0314 **8** *hd* **Fantasy Believer**[15] [3482] 8-8-6 **85**.................................. RyanMoore 12 85
(J J Quinn) *prom: rdn along wl over 1f out: wknd ent last* **8/1**
641 **9** *1 3/4* **Steel Blue**[23] [3211] 6-8-0 **79**.. HayleyTurner 4 74
(R M Whitaker) *prom: rdn along 2f out: wknd over 1f out* **10/1**
1005 **10** *3/4* **Highland Warrior**[12] [3585] 7-8-6 **85**............................. DeanMcKeown 2 78
(J S Goldie) *dwlt: hdwy and in tch 2f out: sn rdn and btn* **25/1**
0303 **11** *2* **Desperate Dan**[16] [3449] 5-7-8 **80**..........................(b) FrankiePickard(7) 10 67
(J A Osborne) *keen: sn led: rdn along 2f out: hdd & wknd over 1f out* **40/1**
0-16 **12** *8* **Dazzling Bay**[53] [2323] 6-8-12 **91**.. DavidAllan 1 54
(T D Easterby) *a rr* **16/1**

68.78 secs (-3.78) **Going Correction** -0.40s/f (Firm) course record **12** Ran SP% **115.2**
Speed ratings (Par 109):109,108,107,107,107 104,104,104,101,100 98,87
CSF £40.59 CT £261.46 TOTE £5.00: £2.00, £2.40, £1.80; EX 40.00 Trifecta £133.50 Pool: £1,204.20 - 6.40 winning units..
Owner Los Bandidos Racing **Bred** J W Parker And Keith Wills **Trained** Musley Bank, N Yorks

FOCUS
A strong sprint handicap, which produced a tight finish, and the form looks rock solid, with the winner up 5lb and the second and third to form.

NOTEBOOK
Wyatt Earp(IRE), raised 3lb for his narrow success over course and distance a fortnight previously, advertised his current rude health and followed up in ready fashion. He is clearly still improving, is in the right hands, and his connections are very keen to aim him at the Ayr Gold Cup in September.
Ice Planet turned in an improved effort in defeat and, while he has proving hard to actually win with to date this term, this display certainly leaves the impression his turn is not far off. (op 7-1)
Blue Tomato came with his customary late challenge and posted another solid effort. He continues to hold his form very well and is a decent benchmark for this form. (op 8-1)
Knot In Wood(IRE), up 7lb for winning at Haydock 13 days previously, may have hit the front a touch too soon this time yet still lost very little in defeat off this higher mark. Like his winning stablemate, he remains capable of further improvement, and probably needs slightly easier ground. (op 5-1)
My Gacho(IRE) ran his race in defeat and, while he remains in fair form, just left the impression he is weighted to his best at present.
Yomalo(IRE), reverting to handicap company, struggled to go the early pace and was doing her best work towards the finish. This was a respectable effort under her big weight. (op 8-1)
Steel Blue Official explanation: jockey said gelding was unsuited by the good to firm ground

3957 SKYBET YORK STKS (GROUP 2) 1m 2f 88y
3:50 (3:50) (Class 1) 3-Y-O+ **£56,780** (£21,520; £10,770; £5,370; £2,690) **Stalls** Low

Form RPR
-263 **1** **Best Alibi (IRE)**[27] [3127] 3-8-6 116.................................... RyanMoore 3 119+
(Sir Michael Stoute) *led after 1f: shkn up 2f out: rdn ent last and kpt on: comf* **2/5**[1]
4340 **2** *2* **Hattan (IRE)**[21] [3314] 4-9-2 106.. TPQueally 2 113
(C E Brittain) *hld up: gd hdwy 3f out: chal 2f out: sn rdn and edgd lft over 1f out: sn one pce* **14/1**
211/ **3** *1 3/4* **Crocodile Dundee (IRE)**[727] [4380] 5-9-2 .... NickyMackay 4 110
(L M Cumani) *led 1f: chsd wnr tl rdn along over 2f out and sn one pce* **7/1**[2]
1046 **4** *3* **Yasoodd**[39] [2721] 3-8-6 108.. ChrisCatlin 1 104
(M R Channon) *hld up: effrt and sme hdwy 3f out: sn rdn and no imp* **9/1**[3]
-034 **5** *18* **Zayn Zen**[38] [2740] 4-8-13 103... RobertWinston 5 67+
(M A Jarvis) *trckd ldng apir: hdwy 4f out: rdn along over 2f out and sn wknd* **9/1**[3]

2m 7.93s (-2.55) **Going Correction** +0.025s/f (Good)
WFA 3 from 4yo+ 10lb **5** Ran SP% **110.6**
Speed ratings (Par 115):111,109,108,105,91
CSF £7.35 TOTE £1.40: £1.10, £4.90; EX 7.50.
Owner Gainsborough Stud **Bred** Robert Scarborough **Trained** Newmarket, Suffolk

FOCUS
The inaugural running of this Group 2 event, and not the strongest event for the prize, but the winner is a high-class performer at least and value for further than his winning margin. The form is not rock solid although the second ran to his best.

NOTEBOOK
Best Alibi(IRE), down in class after a fine effort to finish third in the Irish Derby last time, gained a nice confidence boosting success and must be rated value for further. This is his ground, he was rightly given a positive ride by Moore, and this success was well deserved. He is entered in the Group 1 Juddmonte International at this venue next month, but the drop back in trip may be a concern in that, as 12 furlongs really does look to be his optimum trip. (op 4-9 tchd 1-2 in places)
Hattan(IRE), who beat only one home in the Eclipse last time, turned in an improved effort on this drop in grade yet was eventually put in his place by the winner over the longer trip. He has been highly-tried, and deserves a change of fortune, so may be worth dropping again to Group 3 company. (op 12-1)
Crocodile Dundee(IRE), returning from a 727-day layoff, showed up well enough from the front until understandably tiring from two out. He ought to come on a bundle for the run and, considering his trainer excels with this type of horse, he is one to keep a close eye on. (tchd 8-1)
Yasoodd failed to really improve a great deal for this drop in grade and did not really convince over this longer trip. (op 7-1 tchd 10-1)
Zayn Zen Official explanation: jockey said filly lost its action

3958 SKYBET MAIDEN AUCTION STKS 6f
4:25 (4:26) (Class 4) 2-Y-O **£6,541** (£1,946; £972; £485) **Stalls** Centre

Form RPR
4 **1** **Valdan (IRE)**[22] [3247] 2-8-6 ow2.......................... StephenDonohoe(5) 6 83
(P D Evans) *stdd s: trckd ldrs: swtchd rt and hdwy over 1f out: rdn ins last: led nr fin* **7/2**[2]
3 **2** *3/4* **All You Need (IRE)**[14] [3553] 2-8-10 .... RobertWinston 5 80
(R Hollinshead) *a.p: chal 2f out: rdn ent last: drvn to ld last 75 yds: hdd and no ex nr fin* **5/4**[1]
63 **3** *hd* **Park's Girl**[12] [3596] 2-8-7 .... RoystonFfrench 4 76
(P C Haslam) *a.p: rdn to ld jst inside last: sn drvn: hdd and no ex last 75 yds* **22/1**
3232 **4** *2 1/2* **Perlachy**[11] [3605] 2-8-13 .... DavidAllan 8 75
(T D Easterby) *sn led: rdn 2f out: drvn and hdd jst ins last: one pce* **5/1**[3]
0 **5** *4* **Mandy's Maestro (USA)**[30] [3018] 2-8-12 .... DeanMcKeown 7 62
(R M Whitaker) *prom: pushed along 1/2-way: rdn over 2f out and sn wknd* **16/1**
6 *1* **Sunnyside Tom (IRE)** 2-8-9 .... PaulHanagan 3 56
(R A Fahey) *dwlt: in tch: rdn along wl over 2f out and sn wknd* **11/1**
7 *3* **Homecroft Boy** 2-8-11 .... TPQueally 2 49
(J A Osborne) *s.i.s: a rr* **10/1**
3 **8** *1/2* **Lady Saffron (IRE)**[21] [3308] 2-8-6 .... DaleGibson 9 42
(J Balding) *in tch: rdn along over 2f out: sn wknd* **50/1**

1m 10.65s (-1.91) **Going Correction** -0.40s/f (Firm) **8** Ran SP% **112.9**
Speed ratings (Par 96):96,95,94,91,86 84,80,80
CSF £8.01 TOTE £4.80: £1.60, £1.10, £4.30; EX 8.20.
Owner D Maloney **Bred** Herbertstown Stud Ltd **Trained** Pandy, Abergavenny

FOCUS
A modest juvenile maiden, but the pace was sound, and the form looks quite strong for the grade with the first three coming clear.

NOTEBOOK
Valdan(IRE), fourth at Haydock on his debut in a race that is working out well, showed the benefit of that experience and came with a decisive late challenge to get off the mark at the second attempt, despite his rider carrying 2lb overweight. He is value for a little further and clearly has a future. (op 5-1 tchd 10-3)
All You Need(IRE), whose stable won this last year, probably ran very close to the level of his recent debut over course and distance and was simply denied by a superior rival on the day. He got very warm beforehand and is certainly capable of winning a similar event in the coming weeks. (op 10-11 tchd 4-5 in a place and 11-8 in places)
Park's Girl had every chance and only gave way late on. She has a fair bit of scope, and it would come as no surprise were she to fare better when switching to nurseries, for which she now becomes eligible. (op 25-1 tchd 20-1)
Perlachy was again soon to the fore, but ultimately the burden of top weight told, and he again found a few too good. He does help set the level for this form. (op 11-2)

3959 SKYBET.COM CLAIMING STKS 7f
5:00 (5:00) (Class 4) 3-Y-O+ **£6,477** (£1,927; £963; £481) **Stalls** Low

Form RPR
002 **1** **Neon Blue**[4] [3813] 5-9-3 69...(p) DeanMcKeown 8 79
(R M Whitaker) *trckd ldr: effrt 2f out: rdn over 1f out: led ins last: kpt on wl* **8/1**
6350 **2** *nk* **Bailieborough (IRE)**[22] [3241] 7-8-9 77.................. StephenDonohoe(5) 6 75
(B Ellison) *trckd ldng pair: hdwy to ld 2f out: rdn over 1f out: hdd ins last: drvn and kpt on wl* **9/2**[3]
2460 **3** *2* **Calcutta**[7] [3733] 10-9-8 87.. RobertWinston 1 78
(B W Hills) *hld up in tch: hdwy 3f out: effrt wl over 1f out: sn rdn and no imp ins last* **15/8**[1]
0-00 **4** *1 1/2* **Cyclical**[15] [3471] 4-9-3 84.. NickyMackay 7 69
(G A Butler) *rr tl styd on fnl 2f: n.d* **8/1**
3113 **5** *2 1/2* **Cindertrack**[16] [3453] 3-9-1 82... TPQueally 3 61
(J A Osborne) *led: rdn along 3f out: hdd 2f out and sn wknd* **7/2**[2]

2001 **6** *5* **The London Gang**[4] 3814 3-8-5 60 ....(v) PaulHanagan 4 37+
(P D Evans) *hld up in tch: effrt over 2f out: sn rdn and wknd wl over 1f out* **7/1**

1m 22.53s (-2.87) **Going Correction** -0.40s/f (Firm)
WFA 3 from 4yo+ 7lb **6** Ran SP% **109.9**
Speed ratings (Par 105):100,99,97,95,92 87
CSF £40.92 TOTE £7.90: £2.90, £3.10; EX 48.00.
Owner Country Lane Partnership **Bred** R And Mrs Watson And Mrs A J Ralli **Trained** Scarcroft, W Yorks

■ Stewards' Enquiry : Stephen Donohoe three-day ban: used whip with excessive frequency, without giving gelding time to respond and down the shoulder in the forehand position (Aug 9-11)

FOCUS
A fair event of its type which was run at a sound enough pace. The time does not back up the improved run from the winner, for whom this was personal-best form.
The London Gang Official explanation: jockey said colt lost ist action

3960 FULFORD GOLF CLUB CENTENARY STKS (H'CAP) 1m 4f
5:35 (5:35) (Class 4) (0-80,77) 4-Y-0+ **£8,096** (£2,408; £1,203; £601) **Stalls** Centre

Form RPR

5213 **1** **Fort Churchill (IRE)**[14] 3547 5-8-12 **73** ....(bt) StephenDonohoe(5) 9 87
(B Ellison) *a.p: hdwy over 3f out: led wl over 2f out: rdn over 1f out and styd on strly* **9/1**

1253 **2** *3 ½* **Reluctant Suitor**[15] 3483 4-8-10 **69** ow1 .... DNolan(3) 2 77
(J S Goldie) *hld up towards rr: hdwy over 3f out: rdn to chse wnr over 1f out: kpt on* **6/1**[3]

021 **3** *nk* **Otranto (USA)**[12] 3583 4-8-8 **64** ....(t) RoystonFfrench 4 72
(M Johnston) *hld up towards rr: hdwy over 3f out: swtchd lft and rdn wl over 1f out: kpt on* **11/4**[1]

0560 **4** *nk* **Sporting Gesture**[31] 2975 9-9-3 **73** .... DaleGibson 3 80
(M W Easterby) *chsd ldrs: hdwy 3f out: rdn over 2f out: kpt on same pce appr last* **6/1**[3]

1141 **5** *6* **Great View (IRE)**[16] 3431 7-9-7 **77** ....(p) RobertWinston 6 75
(Mrs A L M King) *hld up in rr: stdy hdwy on inner 4f out: rdn and ch 2f out: sn drvn and wknd over 1f out: eased* **13/2**

0600 **6** *6* **Motafarred (IRE)**[15] 3483 4-9-0 **70** .... DeanMcKeown 1 58
(Micky Hammond) *led: rdn along over 3f out: hdd wl over 2f out and sn wknd* **28/1**

0033 **7** *2 ½* **Leslingtaylor (IRE)**[11] 3621 4-8-9 **65** .... GrahamGibbons 8 49
(J J Quinn) *chaed ldrs: effrt 3f out: rdn over 2f out and sn wknd* **12/1**

0103 **8** *6* **Richtee (IRE)**[8] 3714 5-8-10 **66** ....(p) PaulHanagan 5 41
(R A Fahey) *hld up: effrt and sme haedway over 3f out: rdn and btn wl over 2f out* **5/1**[2]

5041 **9** *6* **Maneki Neko (IRE)**[39] 2736 4-8-13 **74** .... MarkLawson(5) 7 39
(E W Tuer) *in tch: hdwaay to chse ldr 7f out: rdn along 4f out and sn wknd* **12/1**

2m 29.86s (-2.54) **Going Correction** +0.025s/f (Good) **9** Ran SP% **114.1**
Speed ratings (Par 105):109,106,106,106,102 98,96,92,88
CSF £61.16 CT £188.39 TOTE £10.10: £3.20, £2.60, £1.50; EX 134.20 Place 6 £206.03, Place 5 £97.44.
Owner L D Gamble and Mr & Mrs J H Mathias **Bred** P H Betts **Trained** Norton, N Yorks

FOCUS
A modest handicap, run at an average pace, and the winner did the job with plenty in hand. The runner-up ran to form and the overall level looks sound.
T/Plt: £177.80 to a £1 stake. Pool: £108,313.35. 444.65 winning tickets. T/Qpdt: £11.20 to a £1 stake. Pool: £5,224.20. 342.70 winning tickets. JR

3961 - (Foreign Racing) - See Raceform Interactive

3654 LEOPARDSTOWN (L-H)
Saturday, July 29
OFFICIAL GOING: Good (good to yielding in places)

3962a KOREAN RACING ASSOCIATION TYROS STKS (LISTED RACE) 7f
6:20 (6:21) 2-Y-0 **£22,448** (£6,586; £3,137; £1,068)

RPR

1 **Teofilo (IRE)**[13] 3573 2-9-1 .... KJManning 1 102
(J S Bolger, Ire) *hld up in tch: 8th into st: 4th and hdwy over 1f out: led ins fnl f: r.o wl: comf* **7/2**[1]

2 *1 ¾* **Middleham (IRE)**[35] 2844 2-9-1 .... WSupple 10 98
(M Johnston) *settled 2nd: chal and led early st: hdd ins fnl f: nt pce of wnr* **11/2**[3]

3 *1* **Whatsthescript (IRE)**[19] 3369 2-9-1 .... WMLordan 5 96
(David Wachman, Ire) *trckd ldrs: 5th 1/2-way: 4th and chal on outer early st: kpt on ins fnl f* **6/1**

4 *1 ¼* **Blackberry Boy (IRE)**[83] 1518 2-9-1 .... PJSmullen 6 92
(D K Weld, Ire) *hld up: 9th into st: 5th under 1f out: kpt on* **8/1**

5 *shd* **Hammers Boy (IRE)**[39] 2719 2-9-1 .... JAHeffernan 4 92
(T Stack, Ire) *settled 3rd: cl up and chal early st: ev ch 1f out: sn no ex* **14/1**

6 *¾* **Country Song (USA)**[35] 2844 2-9-1 ....(b[1]) KFallon 9 90
(David Wachman, Ire) *chsd ldrs: 7th into st: rdn and no fr 1 1/2f out* **4/1**[2]

7 *3 ½* **The Real Thing (IRE)**[29] 3060 2-8-12 .... PShanahan 3 79
(C Collins, Ire) *chsd ldrs: 6th and rdn ent st: no ex fr 1 1/2f out* **10/1**

8 *¾* **Jopau**[41] 2685 2-9-1 .... JMurtagh 11 80
(G M Lyons, Ire) *sn led: hdd under 2f out: sn wknd* **10/1**

9 *2 ½* **Streetofchampions (USA)**[31] 2994 2-9-1 .... DPMcDonogh 2 73
(T J O'Mara, Ire) *chsd ldrs in 4th: wknd early st* **10/1**

10 *3* **Bold Apache (IRE)** 2-9-1 .... CO'Donoghue 7 66
(A P O'Brien, Ire) *bhd thrght* **20/1**

11 *5 ½* **Friarscourt (USA)**[28] 3103 2-9-1 .... RMBurke 8 52
(R J Osborne, Ire) *a bhd: trailing st* **100/1**

1m 30.0s **11** Ran SP% **122.7**
CSF £23.96 TOTE £4.40: £1.30, £2.50, £2.00; DF 34.30.
Owner Mrs J S Bolger **Bred** J S Bolger **Trained** Coolcullen, Co Carlow

FOCUS
A strong Listed race featuring several interesting maiden winners as well as the second and third from the Chesham Stakes at Royal Ascot.

NOTEBOOK
Teofilo(IRE) produced a cracking effort to score and stamp himself a high-class colt. Successful in a decent looking Curragh maiden two weeks ago, he took the step up in class in his stride. He only had a couple of rivals behind him heading into the final quarter of a mile but he picked up well as the field fanned out and got to the front inside the final furlong before pulling clear for a decisive success. Trainer Jim Bolger pointed the way towards the National Stakes, adding that his juvenile could run in the Futurity Stakes in the meantime. (op 4/1)

Middleham(IRE) ran well and reversed Chesham form with Country Song. The former had no answer to the winner's charge, but he kept on well for second and this represented an improvement on his Royal Ascot run. He should be able to win at this level. (op 9/2)

Whatsthescript(IRE), who was stepping up in class having won a Roscommon maiden earlier this month, was never that far away and took closer order heading towards the final furlong. He probably was not helped when appearing to be flicked by a rival rider's whip, but then stayed on again. Having improved with each run, further progress looks quite likely.

Blackberry Boy(IRE) acquitted himself well as he was having his first run since May and was taking a marked step up in class from the Gowran maiden he won on his debut. There should be more to come from him. (op 7/1)

Hammers Boy(IRE) posted a sound effort on his first run since finishing unplaced in the Coventry. He held every chance heading towards the final furlong but was not able to contain the challenges of several of his rivals

Country Song(USA) did not match the form of his run in the Chesham. Wearing first-time blinkers, he made his challenge on the outside entering the straight but could never quite pick up the leaders. (op 5/2)

The Real Thing(IRE) ran respectably but found this tougher than the Listed race in which she finished second to Gaudeamus at the Curragh last month. (op 8/1)

3963a ROBERT H. GRIFFIN DEBUTANTE STKS (GROUP 2) (FILLIES) 7f
6:50 (6:51) 2-Y-0 **£56,034** (£16,379; £7,758; £2,586)

RPR

1 **Gaudeamus (USA)**[13] 3574 2-8-12 .... KJManning 1 100
(J S Bolger, Ire) *settled 2nd: 3rd 1/2-way: rdn to chal early st: kpt on wl u.p ins fnl f to ld cl home* **9/4**[2]

2 *hd* **Dimenticata (IRE)**[10] 3656 2-8-12 .... DPMcDonogh 2 100
(Kevin Prendergast, Ire) *led: strly pressed ent st: narrowly hdd 1 1/2f out: regained ld briefly ins fnl f: hdd cl home* **5/2**[3]

3 *shd* **Alexander Tango (IRE)**[14] 3556 2-8-12 .... WMLordan 4 99
(T Stack, Ire) *trckd ldrs in 3rd: 2nd 1/2-way: chal on outer ent st: narrow advantage 1 1/2f out: hdd ins fnl f: kpt on u.p* **7/4**[1]

4 *shd* **Aleagueoftheirown (IRE)** 2-8-12 .... KFallon 5 99
(David Wachman, Ire) *hld up in tch: 5th and rdn st: 4th and kpt on wl ins fnl f* **9/1**

5 *1 ½* **Petite Cherie (IRE)**[25] 3178 2-8-12 .... JMurtagh 3 95+
(G M Lyons, Ire) *hld up in tch: 5th 1/2-way: rdn st: styng on whn nt clr run wl ins fnl f* **16/1**

1m 31.9s **5** Ran SP% **111.6**
CSF £8.40 TOTE £3.00: £2.00, £1.40; DF 6.90.
Owner Mrs J S Bolger **Bred** Manganard LLC **Trained** Coolcullen, Co Carlow

FOCUS
A small field for this average renewal, and it was run in a slow time. There was little between them at the finish.

NOTEBOOK
Gaudeamus(USA) produced a brave effort to record her second Stakes race success. Successful in a Listed event at the Curragh last month, she looked as though she would appreciate stepping back up to this trip having run fourth to Regional Counsel in the Anglesey Stakes a fortnight ago. She was being ridden along but responded well and was challenging for the lead heading towards the final furlong, and she pulled out that little bit more to get to the front close home. Her trainer felt that her previous experience stood her in good stead and indicated that the Moyglare is a likely target. A smart filly, she will stay further. (op 2/1 tchd 5/2)

Dimenticata(IRE) was a stylish winner of a mile maiden here ten days ago and seemed to improve on that effort. She set out to make all, cutting out a steady pace, and found plenty under pressure when strongly pressed by both the winner and Alexander Tango. She was only just touched off close home and appeals as the type that can score at Stakes level. (op 7/2)

Alexander Tango(IRE) looked a nice prospect when making a winning debut in a Curragh maiden earlier this month. She loomed up, travelling well, to challenge for the lead early in the straight, but just was not able to contain the renewed efforts of the first two. There should be more to come from her after only two starts. (op 6/4)

Aleagueoftheirown(IRE) made a bright start to her career, staying on quite nicely in the closing stages. She should not have any trouble making her mark if dropping back to maiden company for her next start. (op 7/1)

Petite Cherie(IRE) looked to be facing much stronger opposition than that which she encountered when winning a Gowran maiden last time and was unlucky not to finish closer as she found herself tight for room inside the final furlong. (op 14/1)

3964a MELD STKS (GROUP 3) 1m 2f
7:20 (7:20) 3-Y-0+ **£31,379** (£9,172; £4,344; £1,448)

RPR

1 **Heliostatic (IRE)**[27] 3127 3-8-11 114 .... KJManning 1 112+
(J S Bolger, Ire) *mde all: rdn and strly pressed under 2f out: styd on wl fnl f* **11/10**[1]

2 *2* **Lord Admiral (USA)**[45] 2559 5-9-7 111 .... KFallon 5 108
(Charles O'Brien, Ire) *settled 4th: prog 3f out: 2nd and rdn to chal ent st: ev ch under 2f out: nt run on: one pce* **5/2**[2]

3 *¾* **Kendor Dine (FR)**[69] 1873 4-9-10 110 .... JMurtagh 4 110
(Eoin Griffin, Ire) *prom: 3rd 1/2-way: 4th appr st: 3rd and kpt on fr 2f out* **10/1**

4 *4 ½* **Latino Magic (IRE)**[14] 3559 6-9-7 108 .... RMBurke 3 99
(R J Osborne, Ire) *hld up towards rr: last and in tch 4f out: rdn and one pce st* **9/1**

5 *1* **Valentina Guest (IRE)**[10] 3657 5-9-4 93 .... FMBerry 6 94
(Peter Casey, Ire) *hld up towards rr: 5th and in tch 4f out: no imp st* **16/1**

6 *3* **Simple Exchange (IRE)**[10] 3660 5-9-7 104 ....(b[1]) PJSmullen 2 91
(D K Weld, Ire) *cl 2nd: rdn over 3f out: wknd early st* **8/1**[3]

2m 6.50s
WFA 3 from 4yo+ 10lb **6** Ran SP% **112.3**
CSF £4.01 TOTE £2.20: £1.20, £1.80; DF 3.40.
Owner Mrs J S Bolger **Bred** J S Bolger **Trained** Coolcullen, Co Carlow

FOCUS
Just an ordinary Group 3.

NOTEBOOK
Heliostatic(IRE) ◆, a Listed winner before running seven of 13th in the Irish Derby, proved himself well to group-class with a ready success. On the evidence of this performance, he could be up to fulfilling to potential he showed earlier in his career. (op 5/4 tchd 11/8)

Lord Admiral(USA), returned to ten furlongs, ran a creditable enough race in defeat and just bumped into a nice horse. He is not the easiest to win with.

Kendor Dine(FR) was making his debut for new connections have formerly been trained in France and ran well in defeat. (op 8/1)

Latino Magic(IRE) is vulnerable in this sort of company. (op 8/1)

3967a IRISH STALLION FARMS EUROPEAN BREEDERS FUND SWEET MIMOSA STKS (LISTED RACE) (F&M) 6f

8:50 (8:50) 3-Y-0+ **£31,427** (£9,220; £4,393; £1,496)

RPR

1 **Indian Maiden (IRE)**[49] 2438 6-9-6 FMBerry 6 104
(M S Saunders) *hld up towards rr: hdwy on outer over 1f out: styd on wl to ld nr fin: edgd lft last strides* **4/1**[3]

2 *shd* **Beauty Bright (IRE)**[21] 3322 3-8-12 98 JAHeffernan 7 101
(A P O'Brien, Ire) *prom: 3rd 1/2-way: chal st: led briefly ins fnl f: narrowly hdd cl home: sltly hmpd last strides* **12/1**

3 *½* **That's Hot (IRE)**[6] 3767 3-8-12 96 JMurtagh 2 100
(G M Lyons, Ire) *hld up in tch: swtchd to inner early st: r.o wl ins fnl f: 3rd cl home* **12/1**

4 *nk* **Absolutelyfabulous (IRE)**[17] 3422 3-8-12 101 KFallon 4 99
(David Wachman, Ire) *trckd ldrs in 5th: rdn and no imp early st: kpt on wl ins fnl f* **7/4**[1]

5 *hd* **Ripples Maid**[17] 3414 3-8-12 RichardThomas 1 98
(J A Geake) *trckd ldrs on inner: 4th 3f out: rdn st: kpt on fnl f* **9/1**

6 *½* **Sweet Afton (IRE)**[6] 3767 3-8-12 95 MCHussey 3 97
(Eamon Tyrrell, Ire) *led: strly pressed st: hdd ins fnl f: kpt on u.p* **16/1**

7 *shd* **Modeeroch (IRE)**[14] 3559 3-9-1 104 KJManning 5 99
(J S Bolger, Ire) *trckd ldr in 2nd: rdn to chal early st: ev ch over 1f out: sn no ex* **11/4**[2]

1m 15.8s
WFA 3 from 6yo 5lb **7** Ran SP% **114.3**
CSF £48.42 TOTE £4.90: £2.70, £3.30; DF 77.00.
Owner Chris Scott & Peter Hall **Bred** Shadwell Estate Co Ltd **Trained** Green Ore, Somerset
■ Stewards' Enquiry : F M Berry one-day ban: careless riding (Aug 7)

FOCUS
Just an ordinary Listed race.

NOTEBOOK
Indian Maiden(IRE) really is a terrific mare and gained the sixth Listed success of her fantastic career. She should continue to go well in this sort of company, especially when there is more give in the ground.
Beauty Bright(IRE), dropped in trip and grade, ran a fine race and was just denied. She is clearly up to winning in similar company. (op 10/1)
That's Hot(IRE), third in a similar event at Fairyhouse the previous week, again ran well. (op 10/1)
Absolutelyfabulous(IRE), chasing the hat-trick following two wins in handicap company, the latest one by six lengths off a mark of 80, ran well but looked to be found out by the step up in class. (op 6/4)
Ripples Maid had a bit to find at the weights but was not beaten that far. (op 8/1 tchd 10/1)
T/Jkpt: @164.60. Pool @13,170.50. 60 winning units T/Plt: @74.00. Pool @1,382.00. 14 winning units II

3923 ASCOT (R-H)

Sunday, July 30

OFFICIAL GOING: Good to firm
Wind: Moderate, across

3970 WOODCOTE STUD H'CAP 6f

1:40 (1:40) (Class 2) (0-100,99) 3-Y-0 **£16,192** (£4,817; £2,407; £1,202) **Stalls** Low

Form RPR

3302 **1** **Charles Darwin (IRE)**[8] 3722 3-8-8 86 NCallan 3 95
(M Blanshard) *w ldrs: led 2f out: hrd pressed fnl f: hld on wl nr fin* **8/1**

215 **2** *nk* **Third Set (IRE)**[39] 2757 3-8-6 84 (t) SteveDrowne 6 92
(R Charlton) *dwlt: hld up: prog 2f out: pressed wnr jst over 1f out: str chal fnl f: no ex last 50yds* **11/2**[3]

2-05 **3** *shd* **Grantley Adams**[18] 3414 3-9-1 93 TedDurcan 7 101
(M R Channon) *hld up: prog 2f out: hrd rdn to chal fnl f: kpt on same pce* **5/1**[2]

2254 **4** *2½* **Jimmy The Guesser**[12] 3606 3-8-2 80 JoeFanning 1 80
(N P Littmoden) *trckd ldrs: chsd wnr briefly over 1f out: outpcd fnl f* **10/1**

0463 **5** *¾* **Orpsie Boy (IRE)**[8] 3740 3-8-1 84 (b) JamesDoyle(5) 4 82
(N P Littmoden) *dwlt: hld up: outpcd over 1f out: one pce and nvr able to chal* **4/1**[1]

6620 **6** *4* **Brandywell Boy (IRE)**[6] 3795 3-8-2 80 oh1 FrankieMcDonald 8 66
(D J S Ffrench Davis) *racd on outer: mde most to 2f out: wknd rapidly fnl f* **33/1**

-000 **7** *2½* **Godfrey Street**[18] 3414 3-9-5 97 RyanMoore 10 75
(R Hannon) *racd on outer: trckd ldrs: wknd rapidly over 1f out* **9/1**

-246 **8** *½* **Dhekraa (IRE)**[15] 3520 3-9-4 96 RHills 2 73
(M A Jarvis) *hld up: outpcd and struggling 2f out: no ch after* **6/1**

1020 **9** *1¼* **Guto**[43] 2651 3-9-2 99 AndrewMullen(5) 5 72
(K A Ryan) *racd towards outer: w ldr to 2f out: wknd rapidly* **11/1**

3-00 **10** *shd* **Curtail (IRE)**[16] 3482 3-9-6 98 TomEaves 9 71
(I Semple) *racd towards outer: trckd ldrs gng wl: wknd rapidly over 1f out* **20/1**

1m 14.14s (-1.86) **Going Correction** +0.025s/f (Good) **10** Ran SP% **112.6**
Speed ratings (Par 106):106,105,105,102,101 95,92,91,90,90
CSF £49.72 CT £241.70 TOTE £8.30: £2.20, £2.40, £2.00; EX 70.30 Trifecta £660.90 Part won. Pool £930.98 - 0.20 winning units..
Owner J M Beever **Bred** M And P Associates **Trained** Upper Lambourn, Berks

FOCUS
Just an ordinary three-year-old sprint for the grade. The raced towards the near side, but a little way off the rail. The first three finished clear and the form should prove sound.

NOTEBOOK
Charles Darwin(IRE) gained his first success of the year off an 8lb higher mark than when winning the second of his two nurseries last season, and did so in particularly game fashion. A rise in the weights will make things tougher.
Third Set(IRE) ◆ was slightly disappointing on his handicap debut over seven furlongs at Kempton on his previous start but, dropped in trip and returned to turf, with a tongue-tie fitted for the first time, he was just held. This was arguably a career-best effort and there could be better to come again. (op 5-1)
Grantley Adams, having just his third start of the season, ran a cracker in third and was just held. He is another who could have more to offer. (op 11-2)
Jimmy The Guesser probably just found six furlongs on fast ground on the sharp side and ran well considering. (op 8-1)
Orpsie Boy(IRE), dropped back in trip, kept on without ever looking like winning and is proving hard to win with. (tchd 9-2 in places)
Dhekraa(IRE), down in grade from Listed company, was well beaten and has to be considered disappointing. (op 5-1)

3971 BRUNSWICK H'CAP 1m 2f

2:10 (2:11) (Class 2) (0-105,102) 3-Y-0+
£18,696 (£5,598; £2,799; £1,401; £699; £351) **Stalls** High

Form RPR

2010 **1** **Road To Love (IRE)**[17] 3443 3-8-9 93 RHills 9 113
(M Johnston) *mde all and set str pce: rdn and drew rt away fr 2f out: impressive* **3/1**[1]

2405 **2** *7* **London Express (IRE)**[37] 2805 3-8-6 90 JoeFanning 6 97
(M Johnston) *chsd wnr: rdn 3f out: lft bhd fnl 2f: jst hld on for 2nd* **3/1**[1]

0600 **3** *hd* **Kamanda Laugh**[64] 2012 5-9-4 92 NCallan 8 99
(K A Ryan) *racd in 4th tl chsd ldng pair over 3f out: sn rdn: kpt on to press runner-up fnl f but no ch w wnr* **16/1**

3022 **4** *¾* **Obrigado (USA)**[3] 3876 6-8-13 87 PaulHanagan 4 92+
(W J Haggas) *dwlt: hld up in last and wl off the pce: stl last 3f out: effrt and nt clr run over 2f out: styd on: no ch* **6/1**[3]

5000 **5** *nk* **Courageous Duke (USA)**[15] 3552 7-9-10 98 ShaneKelly 5 103
(J Noseda) *hld up in midfield: effrt over 3f out: kpt on but no ch w wnr* **5/1**[2]

0312 **6** *½* **Regent's Secret (USA)**[22] 3289 6-8-6 83 oh1 DanielTudhope(3) 1 87
(J S Goldie) *hld up in last pair and wl off the pce: effrt over 3f out: plugged on fnl 2f: n.d* **12/1**

0206 **7** *4* **Bustan (IRE)**[15] 3552 7-9-9 97 RyanMoore 7 93
(G C Bravery) *chsd ldrs: 4th and struggling wl over 2f out: sn wknd* **9/1**

000- **8** *8* **Invasian (IRE)**[302] 5607 5-8-13 90 JohnMcAuley(3) 11 71
(B J McMath) *plld hrd early: hld up in midfield and off the pce: no prog and btn over 2f out* **50/1**

0040 **9** *shd* **Compton Bolter (IRE)**[37] 2803 9-10-0 102 (t) NickyMackay 2 83
(G A Butler) *hld up in last trio and wl off the pce: nvr a factor: wknd 2f out* **33/1**

-640 **10** *nk* **Cruise Director**[36] 2848 6-8-10 84 EddieAhern 10 64
(Ian Williams) *chsd ldng pair to over 3f out: wknd rapidly* **20/1**

2m 4.71s (-3.29) **Going Correction** -0.075s/f (Good)
WFA 3 from 5yo+ 10lb **10** Ran SP% **114.2**
Speed ratings (Par 109):110,104,104,103,103 103,99,93,93,93
CSF £10.92 CT £119.38 TOTE £4.10: £1.60, £1.60, £5.50; EX 8.40 Trifecta £148.00 Pool £1,188.89 - 5.70 winning units..
Owner Grant Mercer **Bred** South House Stud **Trained** Middleham Moor, N Yorks

FOCUS
With the older horses looking pretty exposed the door was open for one of the Mark Johnston-trained three-year-olds to win what was probably just a fair handicap. It has ben rated around the third and the sixth.

NOTEBOOK
Road To Love(IRE) went too fast in front at Newmarket last time, and may well have found the race coming too soon after his all-the-way win at Sandown, but he returned to form here. Once again setting out to make all, his rider, who excels on this type of horse, gave him a breather before the straight and then kicked clear once in line for home. He ran out an impressive winner and looks well up to competing at Pattern level on this evidence, but he could well turn out at Goodwood over this trip under a penalty before stepping up in class. (op 7-2)
London Express(IRE), who ran well in the King George V Handicap on his previous start, was back on a mark only 5lb higher than when beating older horses at Pontefract in the spring. He just held on for second, finding his well-handicapped stable-companion much too strong, but could well still be capable of winning off this sort of mark, especially back over further. (op 11-4)
Kamanda Laugh has not had the best of seasons so far but he has dropped back to his last winning mark now and, trying a new trip following a two-month break, offered some hope. He got the extra distance well and this should open up new opportunities for him.
Obrigado(USA) again found himself up against a well-handicapped rival he could not compete with, but he continues to run solid races in defeat. The contest was perhaps not run ideally to suit but he is running consistently at the moment, leaving the Handicapper unable to drop him at all. (tchd 13-2, 7-1 in places)
Courageous Duke(USA), who ran well from a wide draw in the John Smith's Cup last time, has only come home first in one of his last 22 starts and remains 3lb above his last winning mark. This was a fair effort but he remains difficult to win with. (op 9-2 tchd 11-2)
Regent's Secret(USA), who raced from 1lb out of the handicap, struggled to get into it from off the pace and has a bit of a task on his hands now off a mark in the low 80s.
Bustan(IRE) was flattered by his favourable draw at York last time. (tchd 10-1)

3972 HONG KONG JOCKEY CLUB SPRINT STKS (HERITAGE H'CAP) 5f

2:40 (2:44) (Class 2) 3-Y-0+
£43,624 (£13,062; £6,531; £3,269; £1,631; £819) **Stalls** Low

Form RPR

5002 **1** **Machinist (IRE)**[16] 3482 6-8-4 88 JoeFanning 23 97
(D Nicholls) *settled bhd ldrs: prog to ld wl over 1f out: hrd pressed fnl f: jst hld on* **10/1**[3]

0001 **2** *shd* **One More Round (USA)**[29] 3092 8-8-8 97 (b) JamesDoyle(5) 8 106+
(N P Littmoden) *hld up wl in rr: rapid prog jst over 1f out: str run fnl f: needed one more stride* **14/1**

200 **3** *nk* **Golden Dixie (USA)**[16] 3471 7-8-7 91 TedDurcan 20 99
(R A Harris) *hld up towards rr: prog over 1f out: chal ins fnl f: jst hld nr fin* **14/1**

2000 **4** *¾* **Fyodor (IRE)**[13] 3585 5-9-2 100 ShaneKelly 19 105
(W J Haggas) *wl in tch: effrt over 1f out: styd on fnl f: nt quite pce to chal* **33/1**

5020 **5** *¾* **Plateau**[20] 3354 7-7-12 82 oh4 NickyMackay 4 85+
(D Nicholls) *nt on terms towards nr side: prog over 1f out: styd on wl fnl f: unable to chal* **33/1**

2014 **6** *hd* **Peace Offering (IRE)**[13] 3585 6-8-9 100 VictoriaBehan(7) 15 102
(D Nicholls) *led for 1f: w ldr: led again briefly 2f out: fdd fnl f* **14/1**

2143 **7** *hd* **Bo McGinty (IRE)**[15] 3561 5-8-1 85 (b) PaulHanagan 1 86+
(R A Fahey) *taken down early: off the pce towards nr side: gd prog jst over if out: r.o fnl f: nrst fin* **7/1**[2]

2120 **8** *shd* **Glencairn Star**[13] 3585 5-7-7 82 oh7 DuranFentiman(5) 2 83+
(J S Goldie) *wl off the pce towards nr side: swtchd lft ent fnl f: r.o strly nr fin: no ch* **33/1**

2426 **9** *shd* **Handsome Cross (IRE)**[13] 3585 5-8-1 85 DavidKinsella 10 85
(D Nicholls) *pressed ldrs tl one pce fnl f* **20/1**

5003 **10** *¾* **Connect**[15] 3550 9-8-9 93 (b) RHills 11 91
(M H Tompkins) *hld up in midfield: nt qckn over 1f out: one pce after* **12/1**

0606 **11** *shd* **Kay Two (IRE)**[29] 3069 4-8-5 89 ow1 JohnEgan 22 86
(R J Price) *w ldrs: upsides jst over 1f out: wknd ins fnl f* **16/1**

0106 **12** *nk* **Graze On**[15] 3535 4-8-9 93 (b) AdrianMcCarthy 14 89
(R A Harris) *chsd ldrs: one pce and no imp over 1f out* **33/1**

0002 **13** *nk* **Texas Gold**[15] 3535 8-9-0 98 SteveDrowne 17 93
(W R Muir) *chsd ldrs: n.m.r over 2f out: one pce and btn fnl f* **12/1**

24B3 **14** *nk* **Orientor**[13] 3585 8-9-2 **103**.......... DanielTudhope(3) 5 — 97
(J S Goldie) *hld up in rr: effrt but no real ch whn hmpd 1f out* **11/1**

245- **15** *3/4* **Maltese Falcon**[304] 5573 6-9-10 **108**.......... (t) MichaelHills 24 — 99
(P F I Cole) *hld up in rr: prog on wd outside and cl up over 1f out: wknd* **33/1**

4034 **16** *shd* **Celtic Mill**[9] 3709 8-9-7 **105**.......... (p) NCallan 12 — 96
(D W Barker) *led after 1f to 2f out: wknd over 1f out* **16/1**

3252 **17** *3/4* **Coconut Moon**[16] 3503 4-7-12 **82** oh13.......... JimmyQuinn 13 — 70
(E J Alston) *nvr beyond midfield: no prog over 1f out* **40/1**

0300 **18** *shd* **If Paradise**[29] 3092 5-8-10 **94**.......... PatDobbs 7 — 82+
(R Hannon) *off the pce towards nr side: no ch over 1f out* **33/1**

0360 **19** *2 1/2* **Fizzlephut (IRE)**[17] 3449 4-7-13 **83** oh6 ow1.......... FrankieMcDonald 21 — 62
(Miss J R Tooth) *w ldrs over 3f: wknd* **66/1**

2-44 **20** *3* **Lafi (IRE)**[78] 1663 7-9-6 **104**.......... EddieAhern 9 — 72
(D Nicholls) *dwlt: nvr on terms: bhd fr over 1f out* **11/2**[1]

0103 **21** *1/2* **Trinculo (IRE)**[15] 3535 9-8-9 **93**.......... AdrianTNicholls 16 — 59
(D Nicholls) *taken down early and walked to post: prom 1f: lost pl and n.m.r: sn struggling* **25/1**

000P **22** *3/4* **Wanchai Lad**[9] 3715 5-7-12 **82** oh4.......... PaulQuinn 18 — 46
(D Nicholls) *nvr beyond midfield: wknd wl over 1f out* **66/1**

0136 **U** **Matsunosuke**[3] 3880 4-7-5 **81** 8ex.......... LukeMorris(7) 6 — —
(A B Coogan) *hld up wl in rr: stmbld and uns rdr 1/2-way* **16/1**

60.59 secs (-0.81) **Going Correction** +0.025s/f (Good) 23 Ran SP% **130.0**
Speed ratings (Par 109):107,106,106,105,103 103,103,103,103,101 101,101,100,100,99 98,97,97,93,88 87,86,—
CSF £130.71 CT £2021.41 TOTE £11.10: £2.70, £4.20, £3.00, £12.00; EX 268.00 Trifecta £2164.00 Part won. Pool £3,048.00 - 0.20 winning units..
Owner Berry & Gould Partnership **Bred** Ballymacoll Stud Farm Ltd **Trained** Sessay, N Yorks

FOCUS
A typically competitive renewal in which the action developed up the middle of the track and those to race more stands' side seemed disadvantaged. The form makes sense.

NOTEBOOK
Machinist(IRE) had signalled a return to form at Hamilton last time when runner-up in the Scottish Stewards Cup, and he built on that to run out a narrow winner of this valuable handicap on his first attempt at the minimum trip. He is clearly just as effective over five as he is over six, and the Stewards' Cup would have been the ideal target, but he was apparently left out of that race by mistake and will now likely contest the seven-furlong handicap at Goodwood instead. While a winner over that trip as a two-year-old, this success shows that he is more effective over shorter these days. (op 9-1)
One More Round(USA) had things drop right at Windsor last time and, unbelievably, almost followed up. His impressive rider timed the tricky gelding's challenge almost perfectly but the line came just a stride too soon. While he remains in this form he must be considered in similar company (he is in the Stewards' Cup) but he remains one to back each-way rather than win only, as the margins are so fine with him. (op 12-1)
Golden Dixie(USA), poorly drawn on his last two starts, showed what he is capable of under his optimum conditions, finishing strongly from off the pace for third place. He is likely to take in the Stewards' Cup next. (op 12-1)
Fyodor(IRE) ran a blinder off what had looked a mark he was struggling to justify, at least on turf, and hopefully this is a sign that he is returning to form. A strongly-run race over the minimum trip suits him.
Plateau, a winner of only one of his last 33 starts, came out best of those who raced towards the stands' side. This was a good effort from 4lb out of the handicap but his record suggests he remains opposable.
Peace Offering(IRE), in good form of late, was prominent throughout and, given that the finish was dominated by hold-up performers, he ran a very creditable race. He seems to go well for this rider and is another with the option of running in the Stewards' Cup, although his winning form is over the minimum trip. (op 16-1)
Bo McGinty(IRE), third in Ireland on his previous start, remains in good heart. He finished well on the stands' side, coming home second best, and he can remain competitive off this sort of mark. He is not in the Stewards' Cup. (tchd 8-1)
Glencairn Star had plenty to do a furlong out but finished to some purpose. Considering he was racing from 7lb out of the handicap it was a good effort, and he confirmed himself an improving type. A strongly-run five furlongs on good ground or faster suits him well.
Handsome Cross(IRE) is more effective on a sharper track. Dominating a field this size proved too difficult.
Kay Two(IRE), who has dropped 7lb in the handicap since joining his current stable, showed good speed for a long way but, along with the other pace-setters, found the pack swamping him inside the final furlong.
Texas Gold, 6lb lower than at the beginning of the season, did not run badly on his final prep for the Stewards' Cup. He has a good record at Goodwood and it would not be a surprise to see him run well there granted a favourable draw.
Lafi(IRE), the 2004 Wokingham winner, lost a shoe and returned lame so this run can be forgiven. Official explanation: trainer said gelding lost a right-fore shoe and returned lame (tchd 6-1)

3973 CATHAY PACIFIC 60TH ANNIVERSARY H'CAP — 1m (S)
3:15 (3:18) (Class 3) (0-90,88) 3-Y-0+ **£9,067** (£2,697; £1,348; £673) **Stalls** Low

Form — RPR

-550 **1** **Champions Gallery**[38] 2774 3-9-6 **88**.......... JohnEgan 17 — 103+
(D R C Elsworth) *hld up in rr: smooth prog 3f out: led 2f out: rdn and edgd lft fr over 1f out: r.o wl* **7/1**

212- **2** *1 3/4* **Cross My Mind**[337] 4753 4-9-8 **82**.......... SteveDrowne 7 — 94
(T Keddy) *hld up towards rr: prog over 2f out: rdn to chse wnr over 1f out: styd on but no imp* **20/1**

1451 **3** *nk* **Blue Trojan (IRE)**[10] 3679 6-9-9 **83**.......... GeorgeBaker 15 — 94
(S Kirk) *hld up in detached last: swtiched to outer and rapid prog 2f out: chsd ldng pair fnl f: kpt on* **13/2**[3]

0132 **4** *3* **Fabrian**[4] 3854 8-8-6 **71**.......... JamesDoyle(5) 6 — 75
(R J Price) *in tch in midfield: outpcd and struggling over 2f out: styd on wl again ins fnl f* **9/1**

-113 **5** *shd* **Bee Stinger**[15] 3532 4-9-2 **76**.......... NCallan 8 — 80
(I A Wood) *w ldrs: upsides over 2f out: sn rdn and outpcd* **6/1**[2]

1152 **6** *hd* **Samuel Charles**[10] 3688 8-9-4 **78**.......... JimmyQuinn 10 — 81
(C R Dore) *hld up wl in rr: prog on outer over 2f out: drvn and no imp over 1f out: fdd* **20/1**

6214 **7** *1 3/4* **Optimus (USA)**[18] 3413 4-9-1 **78**.......... AdamKirby(3) 9 — 77
(G A Butler) *dwlt: wl in rr: prog on outer over 2f out: fdd over 1f out* **5/1**[1]

5146 **8** *shd* **Sew'N'So Character (IRE)**[18] 3413 5-9-12 **86**.......... TedDurcan 4 — 85
(M Blanshard) *hld up wl in rr: outpcd over 2f out: plugged on fr over 1f out: n.d* **11/1**

1-00 **9** *5* **I'm In Love (USA)**[53] 2359 3-9-0 **82**.......... NickyMackay 12 — 68
(M A Magnusson) *w ldrs: led briefly over 2f out: sn wknd* **66/1**

31 **10** *5* **Abwaab**[24] 3219 3-9-2 **84**.......... (t) EddieAhern 3 — 58
(R F Johnson Houghton) *trckd ldrs gng wl: rdn and wknd rapidly 2f out* **16/1**

0505 **11** *12* **Norton (IRE)**[18] 3413 9-9-12 **86**.......... IanMongan 14 — 35
(T G Mills) *mde most to over 2f out: wknd rapidly: t.o* **8/1**

3315 **12** *1 1/4* **Diamonds And Dust**[24] 3218 4-9-4 **85**.......... (b) PatrickHills(7) 5 — 31
(M H Tompkins) *w ldr to 3f out: wknd rapidly: t.o* **16/1**

1010 **13** *1/2* **Royal Amnesty**[39] 2754 3-8-6 **74**.......... OscarUrbina 2 — 17
(G C H Chung) *nvr on terms: pushed along and struggling 1/2-way: sn wknd: t.o* **25/1**

4-30 **14** *5* **Killena Boy (IRE)**[32] 2983 4-9-7 **81**.......... PaulHanagan 16 — 14
(W Jarvis) *chsd ldrs tl wknd 3f out: t.o* **20/1**

0060 **15** *11* **Sekula Pata (NZ)**[17] 3433 7-9-0 **77**.......... (b) SaleemGolam(3) 11 — —
(Christian Wroe, UAE) *prom to 1/2-way: wknd rapidly: t.o* **66/1**

1m 40.09s (-1.71) **Going Correction** +0.025s/f (Good)
WFA 3 from 4yo+ 8lb 15 Ran SP% **119.1**
Speed ratings (Par 107):109,107,106,103,103 103,101,101,96,91 79,78,78,73,62
CSF £147.20 CT £977.27 TOTE £9.00: £2.90, £7.30, £2.60; EX 238.80 Trifecta £483.30 Pool £1,279.96 - 1.88 winning units..
Owner Champions Gallery **Bred** Middle Park Stud Ltd **Trained** Newmarket, Suffolk

FOCUS
A competitive handicap, and solid form. The first two are unexposed. They went a strong pace and it suited those held up in the early stages. Again they raced towards the near side but off the rail.

NOTEBOOK
Champions Gallery ◆, unsuited by easy ground on his first two starts of the season and then poorly drawn in the Britannia Stakes at the Royal meeting, looked to have conditions to suit this time and, strongly supported in the market, ran out a ready winner. A fine-looking individual, he appeals as one to keep on your side. (op 13-2 tchd 15-2)
Cross My Mind ◆, who showed a useful level of form in maiden and handicap company at up to seven furlongs last year, ran a fine race behind the clearly well-handicapped winner on his belated reappearance, seeing the mile out well. Considering this was his first run in 337 days, he is open to improvement and should go very close next time.
Blue Trojan(IRE), 6lb higher than when winning over seven furlongs at Leicester on his previous start, stayed on in the closing stages having been detached in the early stages, but his run appeared to flatten out a touch near the line. (op 9-2)
Fabrian nearly always seems to hit a flat spot when first coming under pressure and looks as though he will be capable of better back over further these days. (op 10-1)
Bee Stinger, having travelled as well as anything for much of the way, found himself in front too soon and did not really see out his race. On this evidence he could prove effective over a strongly-run seven furlongs. (tchd 7-1)
Optimus(USA) had conditions to suit but was well held off a career-high mark. (op 11-2 tchd 6-1)
Abwaab Official explanation: jockey said gelding hung right

3974 CANISBAY BLOODSTOCK H'CAP — 1m 4f
3:50 (3:51) (Class 4) (0-85,85) 3-Y-0 **£6,477** (£1,927; £963; £481) **Stalls** High

Form — RPR

0-02 **1** **Rayhani (USA)**[16] 3490 3-9-7 **85**.......... JosedeSouza 11 — 99+
(M P Tregoning) *hld up in last trio: prog on outer over 2f out: sustained effrt to ld last 75yds* **4/1**[2]

3212 **2** *hd* **Ollie George (IRE)**[17] 3439 3-8-7 **71**.......... (v) LPKeniry 7 — 82
(A M Balding) *settled in midfield: pushed along over 4f out: prog over 2f out: led wl over 1f out: battled on but hdd last 75yds: jst hld* **4/1**[2]

61 **3** *1/2* **Peppertree**[28] 3122 3-9-4 **82**.......... OscarUrbina 8 — 92
(J R Fanshawe) *hld up in last trio: prog on outer over 2f out: pressed ldr over 1f out: upsides ins fnl f: nt qckn* **7/1**[3]

0621 **4** *5* **Cantabilly (IRE)**[10] 3665 3-8-6 **70**.......... TedDurcan 12 — 72
(M R Channon) *hld up in midfield: effrt and squeezed through 2f out: sn outpcd* **10/1**

0042 **5** *3/4* **Counting House (IRE)**[30] 3046 3-9-0 **78**.......... SteveDrowne 13 — 82+
(R Charlton) *trckd ldrs: nt clr run over 2f out: sn outpcd: kpt on but n ch* **3/1**[1]

1403 **6** *1/2* **Herring (IRE)**[31] 3015 3-8-12 **76**.......... EddieAhern 1 — 76
(D J Coakley) *hld up in last trio: rdn over 3f out: sn outpcd: plugged on fnl 2f* **14/1**

-064 **7** *7* **Wassfa**[18] 3419 3-8-11 **75**.......... RyanMoore 10 — 64
(C E Brittain) *led to wl over 1f out: wknd rapidly* **14/1**

0311 **8** *3 1/2* **Unique Moment**[33] 2944 3-8-6 **70**.......... JoeFanning 5 — 53
(D J S Ffrench Davis) *prom: chsd ldr over 4f out: wknd rapidly 2f out* **11/1**

5564 **9** *3* **Riff Raff**[23] 3256 3-8-8 **72**.......... PaulHanagan 6 — 50
(W Jarvis) *chsd ldr to over 4f out: sn rdn: wknd 2f out* **20/1**

2m 31.85s (-1.15) **Going Correction** -0.075s/f (Good) 9 Ran SP% **113.0**
Speed ratings (Par 102):100,99,99,96,95 95,90,88,86
CSF £19.91 CT £106.32 TOTE £5.30: £1.80, £1.50, £2.10; EX 23.40 Trifecta £79.20 Pool £1,383.35 - 12.40 winning units..
Owner Sheikh Ahmed Al Maktoum **Bred** Darley **Trained** Lambourn, Berks

FOCUS
This did not look that strong a handicap for the grade. The form is fair and looks sound, the first three finishing clear and the fourth setting the standard.

3975 OWEN BROWN MAIDEN FILLIES' STKS — 1m (R)
4:25 (4:27) (Class 4) 3-Y-O **£6,477** (£1,927; £963; £481) **Stalls** High

Form — RPR

-442 **1** **Pearl's Girl**[15] 3554 3-9-0 75.......... PaulHanagan 7 — 80
(W J Haggas) *trckd ldrs: swtchd lft and effrt over 1f out: rdn to ld last 150yds: hld on wl* **9/2**[3]

3423 **2** *nk* **Jewaar (USA)**[18] 3419 3-9-0 80.......... RHills 4 — 79
(M A Jarvis) *led: rdn and pressed 2f out: edgd lft and hdd last 150yds: nt qckn* **7/2**[2]

3 *hd* **Moon Valley** 3-9-0.......... EddieAhern 9 — 79+
(M P Tregoning) *settled in rr: pushed along over 3f out: prog 2f out: clsd on ldrs fnl f: jst unable to chal* **7/1**

4 *2* **Sularina (IRE)** 3-9-0.......... NickyMackay 8 — 74+
(L M Cumani) *rn green in last: stdy prog fr 2f out: gng on wl at fin* **14/1**

422 **5** *hd* **Quintrell**[21] 3336 3-9-0 74.......... FergusSweeney 12 — 73
(H Candy) *trckd ldr for 2f: styd prom: tried to chal over 1f out: one pce* **9/1**

4-3 **6** *6* **Regal Velvet**[20] 3367 3-9-0.......... RyanMoore 5 — 67+
(J H M Gosden) *trckd ldr after 2f: chal over 2f out: edgd lft and wknd rapidly wl over 1f out* **6/4**[1]

-000 **7** *12* **Smoking Star**[32] 2968 3-8-9 50.......... JamesDoyle(5) 10 — 32
(N I M Rossiter) *a in rr: lost tch over 2f out* **100/1**

00 **8** *nk* **Useful**[32] 2985 3-8-7.......... WilliamCarson(7) 6 — 31
(A W Carroll) *hld up in rr: hung lft bnd 3f out: carried hd high and nt run on* **66/1**

06 **9** *61* **Kims Rose (IRE)**[17] 3436 3-9-0.......... TedDurcan 3 — —
(R A Harris) *t.k.h: trckd ldrs: wknd rapidly 3f out: eased: t.o* **66/1**

1m 41.25s (-0.85) **Going Correction** -0.075s/f (Good) 9 Ran SP% **113.5**
Speed ratings (Par 99):101,100,100,98,98 92,80,80,19
CSF £20.25 TOTE £5.70: £1.40, £1.40, £2.50; EX 15.60 Trifecta £63.20 Pool £1,076.64 - 12.08 winning units. Place 6 £148.58, Place 5 £75.04..

Owner Winterbeck Manor Stud **Bred** Goldford Stud And P E Clinton **Trained** Newmarket, Suffolk
FOCUS
No more than a fair maiden, but it featured a couple of interesting newcomers. An improved effort from the winner, with the runner-up and fifth to form.
Kims Rose(IRE) Official explanation: jockey said filly lost its action
T/Jkpt: Not won. T/Plt: £192.50 to a £1 stake. Pool: £141,150.05. 535.10 winning tickets. T/Qpdt: £50.40 to a £1 stake. Pool: £8,874.40. 130.25 winning tickets. JN

3900 **NEWMARKET (JULY)** (R-H)
Sunday, July 30
OFFICIAL GOING: Good to firm
Wind: Light, half-behind Weather: Cloudy with sunny periods

3976 NSPCC EBF MAIDEN STKS — 7f
2:20 (2:23) (Class 4) 2-Y-O — **£4,533** (£1,348; £674; £336) **Stalls** Low

Form — RPR
2 **1** **Safe Investment (USA)**[18] [3417] 2-9-3 .... RichardHughes 5 — 85
(J H M Gosden) *chsd ldrs: led over 1f out: rdn out* **4/9**[1]
5 **2** *1 1/2* **Eglevski (IRE)**[31] [3025] 2-9-3 .... JimmyFortune 14 — 81
(J L Dunlop) *w ldr: rdn and ev ch over 1f out: styd on same pce ins fnl f* **12/1**
3 *1/2* **Loch Tay** 2-9-3 .... LDettori 15 — 80
(M L W Bell) *s.i.s: sn prom: rdn over 1f out: styd on* **11/1**[3]
4 *3/4* **Hadahoo (USA)** 2-9-3 .... PhilipRobinson 12 — 78
(M A Jarvis) *led 6f out: rdn and hdd over 1f out: no ex ins fnl f* **9/1**[2]
5 *1 1/2* **Overturn (IRE)** 2-9-3 .... HayleyTurner 13 — 74+
(W R Swinburn) *chsd ldrs: rdn over 1f out: styd on same pce* **33/1**
00 **6** *nk* **Love Brothers**[17] [3448] 2-9-0 .... EdwardCreighton(3) 1 — 73
(M R Channon) *hld up: styd on fnl f: nvr trbld ldrs* **50/1**
7 *1/2* **Balnagore** 2-9-3 .... SebSanders 9 — 72
(J L Dunlop) *s.i.s: hld up: rdn 1/2-way: styd on ins fnl f: nrst fin* **33/1**
8 *nk* **Morning Farewell** 2-9-3 .... RobertHavlin 11 — 71
(P W Chapple-Hyam) *s.i.s: sn prom: rdn over 1f out: sn wknd* **33/1**
9 *2* **Tumby Lawn (USA)** 2-9-3 .... RichardMullen 4 — 66
(E A L Dunlop) *mid-div: rdn over 2f out: n.d* **33/1**
4 **10** *2 1/2* **Fen Dream**[23] [3259] 2-9-0 .... NelsonDeSouza(3) 7 — 59
(E F Vaughan) *led 1f: chsd ldrs tl wknd over 1f out* **33/1**
0 **11** *3* **Diggs Lane (IRE)**[12] [3623] 2-8-12 .... GregFairley(5) 6 — 52
(N A Callaghan) *hld up in tch: rdn 3f out: soon wknd* **33/1**
12 *hd* **Massive (IRE)** 2-9-3 .... ChrisCatlin 2 — 51
(M R Channon) *s.i.s: hld up: a in rr* **33/1**
13 *1 3/4* **Bold Adventure** 2-8-12 .... StephenDonohoe(5) 16 — 47
(W J Musson) *s.i.s: outpcd* **50/1**
14 *3 1/2* **Kingsmead (USA)** 2-9-3 .... MickyFenton 8 — 37
(Miss J Feilden) *sn outpcd* **66/1**
15 *nk* **Ski For Luck (IRE)** 2-9-3 .... JamieMackay 3 — 37
(J L Dunlop) *s.i.s: outpcd* **50/1**
16 *24* **King's Regiment (IRE)** 2-9-3 .... MatthewHenry 10 — —
(M A Jarvis) *chsd ldrs over 4f* **50/1**

1m 25.9s (-0.88) **Going Correction** -0.15s/f (Firm) **16** Ran SP% **125.2**
Speed ratings (Par 96):99,97,96,95,94 93,93,92,90,87 84,84,82,78,77 50
CSF £5.65 TOTE £1.50: £1.10, £2.70, £2.60; EX 8.60.
Owner K Abdulla **Bred** Juddmonte Farms Inc **Trained** Newmarket, Suffolk
FOCUS
This could prove to be an above-average juvenile maiden and should produce its share of future winners. The winner was slightly off his debut form.
NOTEBOOK
Safe Investment(USA) confirmed the promise of his recent debut effort over course and distance and got off the mark at the second attempt with a bit up his sleeve. He clearly acts well on fast ground, shapes as though he will have no trouble in getting a mile, and it will be very interesting to see where he is pitched in next. (op 8-13 tchd 4-6 in places)
Eglevski(IRE), fifth on his debut at Salisbury a month ago, showed much-improved form but could not match the winner's speed when it really mattered. He will stay plenty further as a three-year-old, but is clearly up to breaking his duck over this sort of trip before too long. (op 14-1)
Loch Tay ◆, who cost 45,000gns and is related to winners at up to two miles, stayed on takingly inside the final furlong and deserves extra credit considering he missed the break. He ought to be plenty sharper with this debut experience under his belt. (op 12-1)
Hadahoo(USA), a $150,000 purchase who boasts a smart American pedigree, showed up well from the front until being done for speed inside the final furlong. He already looks in need of a mile and should not be too long in finding a maiden.
Overturn(IRE), related to numerous winners and out of a half-sister to high-class juveniles Primo Valentino and Dora Carrington, shaped with a deal of promise and did more than enough to suggest he has a future. His stable has yet to start firing with their two-year-olds and this colt could well be the first of them to strike this term in the coming weeks.
Love Brothers was doing his best work towards the finish and left the clear impression he will fare better when switching to nurseries. (op 40-1)
Balnagore, a 10,000gns purchase bred to make his mark over this sort of trip, looked badly in need of the experience yet still hinted at ability. (op 28-1)

3977 JULY COURSE FAMILY DAY H'CAP — 1m 2f
2:50 (2:58) (Class 5) (0-75,73) 3-Y-O — **£3,886** (£1,156; £577; £288) **Stalls** Centre

Form — RPR
4-43 **1** **Quantum (IRE)**[17] [3440] 3-9-5 **71** .... JimmyFortune 7 — 88+
(J H M Gosden) *a.p: jnd ldr over 3f out: rdn to ld 1f out: edgd lft: r.o* **11/4**[1]
-223 **2** *3* **Kerriemuir Lass (IRE)**[22] [3302] 3-9-7 **73** .... PhilipRobinson 9 — 84
(M A Jarvis) *led: rdn and hdd 1f out: sn outpcd* **7/2**[2]
4004 **3** *1 3/4* **Ahmedy (IRE)**[3] [3871] 3-9-4 **73** .... EdwardCreighton(3) 5 — 81
(M R Channon) *slowly into stride: hld up: hdwy over 2f out: rdn over 1f out: styd on same pce* **9/2**[3]
5100 **4** *7* **Leamington Lad (IRE)**[44] [2616] 3-8-11 **63** .... RichardHughes 1 — 58
(J A Geake) *hld up: effrt and hmpd over 2f out: n.m.r and wknd over 1f out* **8/1**
1024 **5** *6* **Malech (IRE)**[15] [3542] 3-9-6 **72** .... LDettori 6 — 55
(M L W Bell) *hld up: hdwy over 4f out: hung rt and wknd over 1f out* **5/1**
3550 **6** *3/4* **Coda Agency**[20] [3347] 3-8-5 **57** .... ChrisCatlin 4 — 39
(D W P Arbuthnot) *chsd ldr over 6f: wkng whn hmpd over 1f out* **20/1**
5-00 **7** *1* **Lord Laing (USA)**[51] [2403] 3-8-7 **62** .... NelsonDeSouza(3) 11 — 42
(H J Collingridge) *hld up: rdn over 2f out: sn wknd* **50/1**
00-0 **8** *shd* **Sakabula (USA)**[20] [3364] 3-9-1 **67** .... SebSanders 3 — 47
(G C Bravery) *prom: riden over 3f out: hung rt and wknd over 1f out* **33/1**
-010 **9** *12* **Swayze (IRE)**[58] [2209] 3-9-1 **67** .... RichardMullen 10 — 24
(N P Littmoden) *chsd ldrs 8f* **11/1**

2m 4.25s (-2.19) **Going Correction** -0.15s/f (Firm) **9** Ran SP% **112.8**
Speed ratings (Par 100):102,99,98,92,87 87,86,86,76
CSF £11.81 CT £40.17 TOTE £3.00: £1.30, £1.60, £1.50; EX 11.70.
Owner H R H Princess Haya Of Jordan **Bred** Norelands Bloodstock **Trained** Newmarket, Suffolk
■ Campanile (14/1) was withdrawn (got loose before s). R4 applies, deduct 5p in the £, new market formed. Levin (33/1) also w/d.
FOCUS
A fair handicap, won by a progressive filly, and the form looks sound with the first three finishing clear. The first two are progressive.
Malech(IRE) Official explanation: trainer said gelding hung right

3978 NSPCC FAMILY DAY H'CAP — 1m
3:25 (3:29) (Class 3) (0-90,90) 3-Y-O
£7,790 (£2,332; £1,166; £583; £291; £146) **Stalls** Low

Form — RPR
12 **1** **Bosset (USA)**[29] [3088] 3-9-5 **88** .... LDettori 1 — 99+
(J Noseda) *hld up in tch: led over 1f out: rdn out* **11/4**[2]
1400 **2** *1 1/2* **Leningrad (IRE)**[16] [3491] 3-9-7 **90** .... RichardHughes 2 — 97
(M L W Bell) *hld up: hdwy to chse wnr fnl f: sn rdn: no imp wl ins fnl f* **12/1**
5043 **3** *5* **South Cape**[11] [3648] 3-9-7 **90** .... ChrisCatlin 5 — 85
(M R Channon) *chsd ldrs: rdn over 2f out: wknd fnl f* **5/1**[3]
2311 **4** *2 1/2* **Minister Of State**[26] [3176] 3-9-6 **89** .... PhilipRobinson 4 — 78
(M A Jarvis) *led: rdn and hdd over 1f out: wknd fnl f* **15/8**[1]
1-4 **5** *nk* **Demon Docker (IRE)**[11] [3648] 3-9-4 **87** .... JimmyFortune 3 — 76
(P W Chapple-Hyam) *trckd ldr: racd keenly: ev ch over 1f out: wknd fnl f* **7/1**
-010 **6** *5* **Balik Pearls**[4] [3841] 3-8-11 **80** ....(b) RichardMullen 7 — 57
(N A Callaghan) *stasrted slowly: hld up: rdn 1/2-way: wknd 3f out* **25/1**

1m 38.39s (-2.04) **Going Correction** -0.15s/f (Firm) **6** Ran SP% **102.2**
Speed ratings (Par 104):104,102,97,95,94 89
CSF £26.60 TOTE £3.10: £1.80, £4.80; EX 39.60.
Owner Budget Stable **Bred** L Jones **Trained** Newmarket, Suffolk
■ Brave Fight (12/1) was withdrawn (loose before start). R4 applies, deduct 5p in the £.
FOCUS
An interesting little handicap, run at a sound enough pace, and the first two, who could be very well handicapped, came clear.
NOTEBOOK
Bosset(USA) ◆ got back to winning ways under a well judged ride from Dettori and did not have to be fully extended to take this. She has now won twice from her three career outings, is versatile as regards underfoot conditions, and is one to follow in this sphere. (op 9-4)
Leningrad(IRE) posted a much more encouraging effort in defeat and, on this evidence, looks to have found his level. He can build on this when reverting to a stiffer test. (tchd 14-1)
South Cape had his chance before being put in his place by the first two. He is proving hard to catch right from this sort of mark. (tchd 9-2)
Minister Of State, bidding for the hat-trick, faded rather tamely once headed and has to rate disappointing. It would be a surprise were he not to prove capable of defying this mark in due course, but he has it to prove now all the same. (op 9-4 tchd 5-2)
Demon Docker(IRE), making his turf debut, ultimately paid for refusing to settle and is capable of better than this. (op 11-2)

3979 NSPCC MEDIAN AUCTION MAIDEN STKS — 6f
4:00 (4:00) (Class 5) 2-Y-O — **£3,886** (£1,156; £577; £288) **Stalls** Low

Form — RPR
1 **Bid For Glory** 2-9-3 .... RichardHughes 10 — 73
(H J Collingridge) *s.i.s: sn prom: swtchd lft over 1f out: rdn to ld ins fnl f: r.o* **16/1**
40 **2** *3/4* **Victory Spirit**[31] [3005] 2-9-3 .... SebSanders 3 — 71
(J L Dunlop) *plld hrd and prom: rdn to ld over 1f out: hdd ins fnl f: styd on* **11/2**[3]
0 **3** *hd* **Popolo (IRE)**[13] [3588] 2-8-12 .... LDettori 6 — 65
(M L W Bell) *led over 4f: styd on* **2/1**[1]
50 **4** *1/2* **Kindlelight Blue (IRE)**[36] [2844] 2-9-3 .... RichardMullen 4 — 69
(N P Littmoden) *chsd ldrs: rdn and ev ch over 1f out: sn hung lft: styd on* **8/1**
5 *2 1/2* **Winged Farasi** 2-9-3 .... MickyFenton 5 — 61
(Miss J Feilden) *s.s: outpcd: r.o ins fnl f: nrst fin* **33/1**
6 *3/4* **Tifernati** 2-9-3 .... JimmyFortune 1 — 59+
(W J Haggas) *chsd ldrs: rdn and ev ch over 1f out: hmpd and wknd 1f out* **5/1**[2]
05 **7** *nk* **Spirited Speedfit (IRE)**[44] [2610] 2-9-3 .... PhilipRobinson 12 — 58
(G G Margarson) *chsd ldrs: rdn over 2f out: wknd over 1f out* **11/2**[3]
6 **8** *4* **The Graig**[9] [3713] 2-9-3 .... RobertHavlin 13 — 46
(C Drew) *chsd ldr over 2f: rdn and wknd over 1f out* **50/1**
9 *2* **Xalted** 2-8-12 .... J-PGuillambert 9 — 35
(S C Williams) *s.s: outpcd* **14/1**
00 **10** *4* **Cavendish**[18] [3408] 2-8-12 .... StephenDonohoe(5) 7 — 28
(J M P Eustace) *mid-div: lost pl 4f out: sn bhd* **66/1**
11 *7* **Ronannis** 2-9-3 .... DerekMcGaffin 8 — 7
(J Jay) *s.s: outpcd* **33/1**
0 **12** *5* **Tafis Beach**[27] [3148] 2-8-12 .... PaulDoe 14 — —
(J R Jenkins) *chsd ldrs over 4f* **66/1**
060 **13** *17* **Joint Expectations (IRE)**[44] [2610] 2-9-3 .... HayleyTurner 11 — —
(Mrs C A Dunnett) *prom: rdn and lost pl 4f out: sn bhd* **66/1**

1m 14.1s (0.75) **Going Correction** -0.15s/f (Firm) **13** Ran SP% **116.8**
Speed ratings (Par 94):89,88,87,87,83 82,82,77,74,69 59,53,30
CSF £96.51 TOTE £17.50: £3.80, £1.80, £1.20; EX 109.50.
Owner Harraton Court One **Bred** Llety Stud **Trained** Exning, Suffolk
FOCUS
A moderate juvenile maiden for the track which saw the first four come clear. It could have been rated 4lb lower.
NOTEBOOK
Bid For Glory, who cost 17,000gns and is half-brother to four winners, overcame a sluggish start and mowed down his rivals in the closing stages to make a winning debut. He ought to have no trouble with an extra furlong in due course, is entitled to improve for the experience, and was a very welcome winner for his yard.
Victory Spirit put a bitterly disappointing effort at Leicester last time behind him, yet did not help his rider by refusing to settle early on, and is clearly not all that straightforward. (op 5-1 tchd 6-1)
Popolo(IRE) improved on the level of her recent Windsor debut and shaped as though she may need a stiffer test. (tchd 15-8 and 9-4)
Kindlelight Blue(IRE) enjoyed the drop back in class and showed his true colours in defeat. He may just be better off stepping back up to a seventh furlong on this evidence and looks a likely sort for nurseries now.
Winged Farasi, bred to appreciate further and representing last year's winning stable, caught the eye staying on after missing the break and looks sure to improve a bundle for the experience.

Tifernati, who cost 42,000gns, was starting to tread water prior to being hampered, but would still have been closer with a clear run. Another furlong ought to play to his strengths before too long. (op 6-1)

3980 BALLYGALLON STUD H'CAP 1m 2f
4:35 (4:36) (Class 3) (0-95,95) 3-Y-0+
£11,217 (£3,358; £1,679; £840; £419; £210) Stalls Low

Form RPR
5-00 **1** **Group Captain**[62] 2079 4-9-2 **88** RichardKingscote(5) 9 98
(R Charlton) *hld up in tch: edgd rt and led over 1f out: r.o* **11/2**[3]
4525 **2** 2 **Mutawaffer**[15] 3549 5-9-5 **86** LDettori 6 94+
(R A Fahey) *trckd ldrs: racd keenly: edgd rt 2f out: nt clr run over 1f out: r.o ins fnl f: no ch w wnr* **4/1**[2]
6160 **3** 1 **Balanced Budget**[37] 2805 3-8-13 **90** SebSanders 8 94+
(J Noseda) *hld up: swtchd lft and hdwy over 1f out: nt rch ldrs* **6/1**
3015 **4** nk **Snowed Under**[16] 3497 5-9-0 **81** PhilipRobinson 5 85
(J D Bethell) *led: rdn and hdd over 1f out: styd on same pce* **7/1**
/-04 **5** ¾ **Russian Consort (IRE)**[32] 2989 4-9-1 **82** RichardHughes 1 84
(A King) *trckd ldr: racd keenly: rdn over 1f out: no ex ins fnl f* **10/1**
0-1 **6** nk **Corum (IRE)**[43] 2655 3-8-8 **85** RobertHavlin 7 87
(J H M Gosden) *chsd ldrs: rdn over 2f out: no ex fnl f* **2/1**[1]
6250 **7** nk **Wellington Hall (GER)**[16] 3497 8-8-11 **78** RichardMullen 2 79
(P W Chapple-Hyam) *hld up: rdn over 1f out: nvr trbld ldrs* **20/1**
-205 **8** 16 **Press Express (IRE)**[22] 3309 4-8-9 **76** HayleyTurner 10 47
(M L W Bell) *prom: rdn 3f out: hmpd and wknd 2f out* **40/1**
5-65 **9** ½ **Im Spartacus**[36] 2872 4-10-0 **95** TomEaves 4 65
(D W Barker) *plld hrd and prom: rdn over 3f out: wknd 2f out* **25/1**

2m 5.10s (-1.34) **Going Correction** -0.15s/f (Firm)
WFA 3 from 4yo+ 10lb 9 Ran SP% **115.6**
Speed ratings (Par 107):99,97,96,96,95 95,95,82,82
CSF £27.16 CT £136.82 TOTE £6.80: £2.10, £1.90, £2.10; EX 36.60.
Owner Peter Webb **Bred** Hascombe And Valiant Studs **Trained** Beckhampton, Wilts

FOCUS
A fair handicap for the class, run at an average pace, and the winner, who ran to form, is value for further.

NOTEBOOK
Group Captain put the race quickly to bed when hitting the front against the stands'-side rail approaching the final furlong and, considering he looked to be doing little in front late on, is probably value for a good deal further than the winning margin. He has clearly benefited from a recent break and would have to be of interest if turning out under a penalty. (op 6-1)
Mutawaffer, taking another step up in trip, rather spoilt his chances by running freely and is a little flattered by his proximity to the winner. However, while he may have been one of the most frustrating horses currently in training , he got home over the trip and is running consistently at present. (tchd 9-2 in places)
Balanced Budget got going all too late after having to switch for his effort, but still posted a much more encouraging run on this drop in grade. He is well worth riding more prominently over this distance in the future and has a little more to offer. (op 8-1)
Snowed Under ran his usual race from the front and was not disgraced. He does look held by the Handicapper now, however. (op 8-1)
Corum(IRE) ran below expectations on this handicap bow and has to rate disappointing. This was just his third outing to date, and he may leave this effort behind as he becomes more streetwise, yet he still has a deal to prove now nevertheless. (op 9-4 and tchd 5-2 in places)
Wellington Hall(GER) would have likely been closer with a more positive ride and is a little better than the bare form suggests.

3981 JOIN THE RACING UK CLUB H'CAP 1m 6f 175y
5:05 (5:05) (Class 4) (0-85,86) 3-Y-0+ £6,477 (£1,927; £963; £481) Stalls Centre

Form RPR
3311 **1** **Cape Secret (IRE)**[23] 3249 3-8-1 **73** NelsonDeSouza(3) 2 91
(R M Beckett) *mde all: styd on strly* **13/8**[2]
2111 **2** 11 **Warsaw Pact (IRE)**[10] 3686 3-9-3 **86** SebSanders 5 93+
(Sir Mark Prescott) *prom: chsd wnr over 5f out: sn rdn: outpcd fnl 2f* **5/4**[1]
4 **3** 14 **Dzesmin (POL)**[29] 3081 4-9-9 **82** StephenDonohoe(5) 7 68
(R C Guest) *hld up: wnt mod 3rd over 2f out: n.d* **16/1**
2411 **4** 6 **Souffleur**[61] 2117 3-8-7 **76** HayleyTurner 4 54
(M L W Bell) *hld up: rdn over 5f out: wknd 4f out* **9/2**[3]
-000 **5** 16 **Domenico (IRE)**[30] 3035 8-8-13 **67** oh10 PaulDoe 6 24
(J R Jenkins) *chsd wnr over 9f: wknd over 3f out* **40/1**

3m 5.19s (-5.85) **Going Correction** -0.15s/f (Firm)
WFA 3 from 4yo+ 15lb 5 Ran SP% **109.0**
Speed ratings (Par 105):109,103,95,92,83
CSF £3.93 TOTE £2.80: £1.60, £1.40; EX 3.70 Place 6 £15.66, Place 5 £13.80..
Owner Larkin, Legge And Milner **Bred** Declan And Catherine Macpartlin **Trained** Whitsbury, Hants

FOCUS
A fair staying handicap which saw the progressive winner run his rivals ragged from the front. Decent form for the grade. The first two are likely to stay ahead of the handicapper.
Souffleur Official explanation: jockey said colt had been unsuited by the good to firm ground
T/Plt: £18.20 to a £1 stake. Pool £66,952.20. 2,673.90 winning tickets. T/Qpdt: £10.20 to a £1 stake. Pool: £3,201.30. 230.70 winning tickets. CR

3713 PONTEFRACT (L-H)
Sunday, July 30

OFFICIAL GOING: Good to firm
The racecourse had missed most of the rainstorms and after light watering the ground was reckoned 'firm but no jar'. The outside of the track was 'very firm'
Wind: Light, half against Weather: Fine and sunny

3982 TOLENT CONSTRUCTION MAIDEN STKS 5f
2:00 (2:01) (Class 4) 2-Y-0 £5,181 (£1,541; £770; £384) Stalls Low

Form RPR
1 **Smart Instinct (USA)** 2-9-3 TonyHamilton 3 86
(R A Fahey) *sn prom: effrt over 2f out: joind ldr 1f out: carried bdly rt: led nr fin* **33/1**
3 **2** ½ **Palo Verde**[13] 3581 2-9-3 KDarley 7 84
(M Johnston) *led: rdn and wnt bdly rt fnl f: hdd towards fin* **5/4**[1]
3 3 ½ **Lucky Bee (IRE)** 2-8-12 MartinDwyer 10 67
(G A Swinbank) *mid-div: hdwy over 2f out: carried rt 1f out: kpt on same pce* **22/1**
65 **4** 3 ½ **Mazin Lady**[8] 3745 2-8-12 RoystonFfrench 4 54
(Miss J A Camacho) *chsd ldrs: rdn and wnt rt 1f out: sn wknd* **20/1**
04 **5** ½ **Bid For Gold**[32] 2973 2-9-3 RobertWinston 5 57+
(Jedd O'Keeffe) *mid-div: hdwy over 2f out: keeping on same pce whn hmpd 1f out* **9/4**[2]
5 **6** 3 ½ **Obe Royal**[16] 3498 2-9-3 TonyCulhane 9 45
(M R Channon) *sn in rr and drvn along: kpt on fnl 2f: nvr on terms* **11/2**[3]
653 **7** ¾ **Wanchai Night**[9] 3693 2-9-3 DavidAllan 2 42
(T D Easterby) *w ldrs: wknd over 1f out* **10/1**
8 1 **Musical Mirage (USA)** 2-8-12 DeanMcKeown 11 33
(G A Swinbank) *prom on outside: rn green and outpcd over 2f out: no threat after* **40/1**
9 nk **Princess Ellis** 2-8-12 FrancisNorton 6 32
(E J Alston) *chsd ldrs: lost pl over 1f out* **66/1**
0 **10** 5 **Wilde Jasmine (IRE)**[8] 3745 2-8-12 PhillipMakin 1 14
(J R Weymes) *s.s: a in rr* **125/1**
0 **11** 1 **Bidders Itch**[70] 1863 2-8-12 TPQueally 8 11
(A Berry) *s.i.s: a bhd* **125/1**

63.10 secs (-0.70) **Going Correction** -0.05s/f (Good) 11 Ran SP% **117.3**
Speed ratings (Par 96):103,102,96,91,90 84,83,81,81,73 71
CSF £73.19 TOTE £17.20: £4.10, £1.30, £2.70; EX 94.40.
Owner David And Jackie Knaggs **Bred** Fair Way Equine, Llc **Trained** Musley Bank, N Yorks
■ Stewards' Enquiry : K Darley five-day ban: careless riding (Aug 10-14)

FOCUS
Just modest form but a nice enough debut by the winner and the first two came clear. Plenty of deadwood behind them.

NOTEBOOK
Smart Instinct(USA), a robust newcomer, was carried very wide by the runner-up but showed the right attitude to force his head in front near the line. It was a tough introduction but he looks a street fighter. (op 22-1)
Palo Verde, back in trip, took them along but despite his rider using his whip in his right hand, he veered right across the track, taking the winner with him. He has plenty of toe and can surely go one better. (op 6-4 tchd 13-8 in places)
Lucky Bee(IRE), on her toes in the paddock and continually swishing her tail, made light of being pushed off a straight line to secure a modest third spot. An April foal, she is quite stoutly bred. (op 16-1)
Mazin Lady, having her third run, shied away from the running rail a furlong out. She still looks on the weak side but nurseries now beckon. (op 16-1)
Bid For Gold, trying for a run between horses, was badly buffetted and looked third best on the day. (op 11-4 tchd 3-1)
Obe Royal, who made his debut two weeks earlier over seven, could never go the pace. (op 7-2)

3983 L & J WINDOWS H'CAP 1m 4f 8y
2:30 (2:32) (Class 5) (0-70,68) 3-Y-0+ £4,533 (£1,348; £674; £336) Stalls Low

Form RPR
0261 **1** **Aimee Vibert**[18] 3412 4-10-0 **68** StephenCarson 12 76
(W R Swinburn) *trckd ldrs: jnd ldr over 4f out: rdn over 1f out: styd on to ld nr fin* **11/1**
3152 **2** nk **Shekan Star**[23] 3243 4-8-13 **53** MartinDwyer 2 60
(K G Reveley) *s.i.s: hdwy to ld 6f out: kpt on wl fnl 2f: hdd nr fin* **11/2**[2]
5522 **3** 1 ½ **Melvino**[17] 3431 4-9-8 **62** PhillipMakin 11 67
(T D Barron) *hld up in rr: drvn 4f out: hdwy over 2f out: styd on wl fnl f* **13/2**[3]
0006 **4** ½ **Sea Grain (IRE)**[22] 3303 3-8-0 **52** CatherineGannon 9 56
(Robert Gray) *chsd ldrs: one pce fnl 2f* **50/1**
0232 **5** ¾ **San Deng**[40] 2736 4-9-11 **65** RobertWinston 14 68
(Micky Hammond) *prom: effrt over 2f out: one pce* **11/2**[2]
4361 **6** 1 ½ **I'll Do It Today**[121] 825 5-9-2 **61** MarkLawson(5) 4 61
(J M Jefferson) *prom: rdn 3f out: one pce* **9/1**
5054 **7** 1 ½ **Turner**[15] 3522 5-8-10 **55** LiamJones(5) 3 53
(W M Brisbourne) *hld up towards rr: drvn over 5f out: kpt on fnl 2f: nvr nr ldrs* **9/1**
0060 **8** 1 ¼ **Rajam**[10] 3674 8-9-4 **58** DO'Donohoe 6 54
(G A Harker) *prom: outpcd and drvn over 5f out: kpt on fnl 2f* **50/1**
1050 **9** shd **Tallyhobye**[8] 3303 3-8-1 **53** oh2 ow3 RoystonFfrench 13 49
(M E Sowersby) *bhd: styd on wl fnl 2f: nrst fin* **50/1**
-161 **10** 1 ¾ **The Pen**[10] 3675 4-8-12 **59** DeanWilliams(7) 5 52
(C W Fairhurst) *t.k.h in rr: hdwy 3f out: nvr nr ldrs* **10/1**
033 **11** 1 ½ **Fairlight Express (IRE)**[23] 3258 6-9-6 **60** FrancisNorton 8 51
(Stef Liddiard) *chsd ldrs: lost pl 3f out* **16/1**
-603 **12** 2 ½ **Tayman (IRE)**[37] 2822 4-9-9 **63** TPQueally 7 50
(G Wragg) *mid-div on outer: effrt over 4f out: lost pl over 2f out* **4/1**[1]
1040 **13** 15 **Zarova (IRE)**[19] 3377 4-8-8 **55** AdeleRothery(7) 15 18
(M W Easterby) *bhd: sme hdwy on wd outside over 4f out: lost pl over 2f out: sn bhd and eased* **33/1**
0-00 **14** 16 **Piccolomini**[37] 2832 4-9-3 **57** TonyHamilton 10 —
(E W Tuer) *led tl 6f out: lost pl 3f out: bhd and eased over 1f out* **66/1**

2m 41.56s (1.26) **Going Correction** -0.05s/f (Good)
WFA 3 from 4yo+ 12lb 14 Ran SP% **117.7**
Speed ratings (Par 103):93,92,91,91,90 89,88,88,88,86 85,84,74,63
CSF £67.30 CT £433.31 TOTE £11.10: £3.30, £2.10, £2.50; EX 82.40.
Owner Mrs P W Harris **Bred** Pendley Farm **Trained** Aldbury, Herts

FOCUS
A modest handicap, the finish dominated by prominent racers. Slight improvement from the first two, with the fourth running to this year's form.
The Pen Official explanation: jockey said saddle slipped
Tayman(IRE) Official explanation: jockey said gelding never travelled
Zarova(IRE) Official explanation: jockey said, regarding running and riding, her orders were to drop the colt in, get him settled and push out to the line to do her best, adding she was unable to switch colt off in order to get the position she wished, and asked for an effort 2f out with little response; trainer's rep added that the colt is ungenuine

3984 GRAHAM ROCK MEMORIAL H'CAP 1m 2f 6y
3:00 (3:02) (Class 4) (0-85,81) 3-Y-0 £6,477 (£1,927; £963; £481) Stalls Low

Form RPR
-336 **1** **Luna Landing**[19] 3375 3-8-11 **71** DaleGibson 1 78
(Jedd O'Keeffe) *trckd ldrs: wnt 2nd 2f out: styd on to ld towards fin* **20/1**
1440 **2** hd **Bin Rahy (IRE)**[22] 3318 3-9-7 **81** TonyCulhane 3 88
(M R Channon) *led: shkn up over 4f out: hung rt: hrd rdn over 1f out: hdd towards fin* **7/2**[3]
-041 **3** 2 ½ **Tawaafud**[20] 3362 3-9-1 **75** MartinDwyer 7 77
(B W Hills) *chsd ldrs: pushed along 7f out: outpcd 3f out: hdwy over 1f out: styd on to take 3rd last 100yds* **4/1**
4041 **4** 1 ½ **Truly Fruitful (IRE)**[19] 3375 3-9-1 **75** RobertWinston 5 74
(K R Burke) *hld up: hdwy to trck ldrs 7f out: wnt 3rd over 1f out: wknd last 150yds* **5/2**[1]
-221 **5** 5 **Otelcalifornia (USA)**[31] 3001 3-9-4 **78** TPQueally 2 68
(J Noseda) *hld up in rr: effrt 3f out: edgd lft and lost pl over 1f out* **10/3**[2]

0100 **6** 3½ **Sir Arthur (IRE)**[8] 3737 3-9-5 **79**............................(b[1]) RoystonFfrench 6 62
(M Johnston) *dwlt: sn trcking ldr: chal 3f out: sn rdn and lost pl* **13/2**

2m 12.04s (-2.04) **Going Correction** -0.05s/f (Good) **6** Ran SP% **112.0**
Speed ratings (Par 102):106,105,103,102,98 95
CSF £86.81 TOTE £15.60: £3.80, £2.80; EX 72.40.
Owner W R B Racing 47 (wrbracing.com) **Bred** Chippenham Lodge Stud Ltd **Trained** Middleham Moor, N Yorks

■ Stewards' Enquiry : Tony Culhane caution: used whip with excessive frequency

FOCUS
A tactical affiair wound up from the front by the runner-up. It was hard to make ground from off the pace. Ordinary form for the grade, and sound enough.

3985 POMFRET H'CAP 1m 4y
3:35 (3:36) (Class 2) (0-100,94) 3-Y-**£12,464** (£3,732; £1,866; £934; £466) **Stalls** Low

Form RPR
4344 **1** **Jubilee Street (IRE)**[5] 3812 7-9-0 **80**............................ RoystonFfrench 5 89
(Mrs A Duffield) *mde all: rdn and hung rt over 1f out: styd on wl* **8/1**[3]
0-10 **2** 1¾ **Namroud (USA)**[8] 3733 7-9-5 **85**............................ TonyHamilton 3 90
(R A Fahey) *trckd ldrs: effrt over 2f out: wnt 2nd over 1f out: kpt on same pce* **9/1**
4400 **3** 2 **El Coto**[15] 3552 6-9-10 **90**............................ DO'Donohoe 2 90
(K A Ryan) *hld up in tch: effrt over 2f out: kpt on to take 3rd appr fnl f: nvr a threat* **5/2**[2]
2015 **4** 3½ **Goodbye Mr Bond**[23] 3255 6-9-9 **89**............................ FrancisNorton 9 81
(E J Alston) *hld up in tch: hdwy over 3f out: drvn over 2f out: wknd over 1f out* **9/4**[1]
2050 **5** ½ **Regal Royale**[16] 3491 3-9-6 **94**............................(v[1]) RobertWinston 6 85
(Sir Michael Stoute) *chsd wnr: rdn and wknd over 1f out* **5/2**[2]

1m 43.18s (-2.52) **Going Correction** -0.05s/f (Good)
WFA 3 from 4yo+ 8lb **5** Ran SP% **109.0**
Speed ratings (Par 109):110,108,106,102,102
CSF £64.38 TOTE £8.50: £2.80, £2.40; EX 27.70.
Owner D W Holdsworth & J A McMahon **Bred** My Firebird Syndicate **Trained** Constable Burton, N Yorks

■ Calcutta (11/2) was withdrawn on vet's advice. R4 applies to board prices prior to w/d, deduct 15p in the £. New market formed.

FOCUS
A depleted field with the actual topweight 10lb below the race ceiling. The winner made sure there was no hanging about, and it is doubtful if he improved as he was granted the run of the race. The second also ran to form.

NOTEBOOK
Jubilee Street(IRE) is as tough as sold boots and, making every yard, recorded his tenth career success. He hung out into the centre in the home straight and ended up racing on the unwatered stands' side. (new market op 15-2 tchd 7-1)
Namroud(USA), only allowed to take his chance after connections had checked the ground, went in pursuit of the winner. Sticking to the watered far side, at one point he looked like making a race of it but he was firmly outpointed in the end. (new market op 8-1)
El Coto, happy to sit off the pace, made laboured headway coming off the final bend and never looked like taking a hand. This trip looks his bare minimum now. (new market op 7-2 tchd 9-4)
Goodbye Mr Bond, racing off a career high-mark, saw plenty of daylight on the outer and soon dropped away once in line for home. (new market op 3-1 tchd 10-3)
Regal Royale, fifth in the Britannia, looks to have gone the wrong way since and the visor fitted here had a negligible effect. (old market tchd 11-4 new market op 3-1 tchd 10-3)

3986 ST. JOHNS AMBULANCE H'CAP 6f
4:10 (4:11) (Class 3) (0-90,90) 3-Y-0+
£8,101 (£2,425; £1,212; £607; £302; £152) **Stalls** Low

Form RPR
1001 **1** **Mr Wolf**[9] 3715 5-9-9 **90**............................(p) MarkLawson[(5)] 2 99
(D W Barker) *mde all: rdn over 1f out: edgd rt ins last: hld on gamely* **15/8**[1]
0040 **2** *hd* **High Ridge**[14] 3567 7-8-11 **73**............................(p) TonyCulhane 8 81+
(J M Bradley) *prom: hdwy over 1f out: styd on ins last* **28/1**
-226 **3** *nk* **Lake Garda**[22] 3281 5-8-13 **75**............................(b[1]) DO'Donohoe 4 82
(K A Ryan) *chsd wnr: edgd rt over 1f out: styd on strly towards fin* **11/1**
4356 **4** ½ **Titinius (IRE)**[19] 3374 6-8-9 **71** oh2............................ DeanMcKeown 3 77
(Micky Hammond) *prom: effrt over 2f out: kpt on wl ins last* **28/1**
0015 **5** ½ **Grazeon Gold Blend**[7] 3761 3-9-6 **87**............................ GrahamGibbons 1 90
(J J Quinn) *chsd ldrs: wnt 2nd over 1f out: no ex ins last* **16/1**
0502 **6** 1 **Currency**[14] 3567 9-8-9 **71** oh2............................ KDarley 5 72
(J M Bradley) *s.i.s: hdwy over 1f out: styd on ins last* **16/1**
0346 **7** *shd* **Red Romeo**[24] 3223 5-9-6 **82**............................ RobertWinston 6 83
(G A Swinbank) *chsd ldrs: kpt on same pce appr fnl f* **9/2**[2]
-110 **8** 2½ **Balakiref**[16] 3471 7-9-1 **77**............................ PhillipMakin 12 70
(M Dods) *in rr: effrt on outer 2f out: kpt on fnl f: nvr nr ldrs* **20/1**
6-10 **9** ¾ **Algharb**[29] 3077 4-9-12 **88**............................ MartinDwyer 9 79
(W J Haggas) *in rr: effrt over 2f out: nvr a threat* **15/2**
2-53 **10** 5 **Sir Nod**[14] 3567 4-9-1 **77**............................ DavidAllan 11 53
(Miss J A Camacho) *chsd ldrs on outer: drvn over 2f out: wknd over 1f out* **7/1**[3]
0060 **11** 5 **Happy As Larry (USA)**[3] 3880 4-8-9 **71**............................(vt[1]) FrancisNorton 10 32
(T J Pitt) *chsd ldrs: lost pl over 2f out: bhd whn eased ins last* **14/1**

1m 16.03s (-1.37) **Going Correction** -0.05s/f (Good)
WFA 3 from 4yo+ 5lb **11** Ran SP% **115.7**
Speed ratings (Par 107):107,106,106,105,105 103,103,100,99,92 85
CSF £68.62 CT £462.03 TOTE £2.40: £1.50, £6.30, £3.60; EX 85.30.
Owner P Asquith **Bred** P Asquith **Trained** Scorton, N Yorks

■ Stewards' Enquiry : Tony Culhane one-day ban: used whip without giving gelding time to respond (Aug 10)

FOCUS
A highly-competitive 71-90 handicap run at an end-to-end gallop. The form looks rock solid.

NOTEBOOK
Mr Wolf, a standing dish here, made it five wins from six visits. He is all speed and, ideally drawn, in the end did just enough. He will not be resting on his laurels either. (op 9-4 tchd 7-4 tchd 5-2 in a place)
High Ridge, usually at his best in the first half of the year, had plenty of cover this time. His rider threw everything at him but he could not quite get there.
Lake Garda, in first-time blinkers, was seeking his first win for over two years. He ended up on the outer and, edging right, ended up with the advantage of racing close to the unwatered ground. At the line he was coming back for more. (tchd 12-1)
Titinius(IRE), without a win for over three years, stuck on really well especially considering he was racing bang on the inside in the home straight and almost certainly on the slower part of the track. (tchd 25-1)
Grazeon Gold Blend, 3lb higher than when winning at Ripon, was against his elders for the first time and went down fighting.
Currency missed the break slightly but was staying on in his own time at the finish. He has never won at this level. (tchd 14-1)
Red Romeo ran better but it is just possible that these days seven suits him better. (op 5-1 tchd 11-2)
Sir Nod Official explanation: jockey said gelding never travelled
Happy As Larry(USA) Official explanation: jockey said colt had no more to give

3987 KEITH HAMMILL MEMORIAL MAIDEN STKS 1m 4y
4:45 (4:46) (Class 5) 3-4-Y-0 **£4,533** (£1,348; £674; £336) **Stalls** Low

Form RPR
05 **1** **Final Esteem**[31] 3001 3-9-3............................ TonyHamilton 1 68
(I Semple) *led after 1f: hdd 4f out: rallied over 1f out: led ins last* **16/1**[3]
0- **2** *nk* **Lucidus**[298] 5699 4-9-11............................ RobertWinston 5 69
(W J Haggas) *w ldrs: t.k.h: led 4f out: rdn and put hd in air over 1f out: hdd ins last* **14/1**[2]
3322 **3** 2½ **Alhaajes (USA)**[43] 2655 3-9-3 95............................ MartinDwyer 6 62
(B W Hills) *reluctant to load: trckd ldrs: chal over 2f out: rdn and wnt rt over 1f out: reluctant and wnt lft ins last* **1/7**[1]
50-0 **4** 5 **Star Sign**[66] 1947 4-9-1 40............................ MarkLawson[(5)] 3 47
(D W Barker) *chsd ldrs: drvn over 3f out: one pce* **25/1**
5 7 **Tagart** 3-9-3............................ GrahamGibbons 4 34
(J J Quinn) *s.s: sn prom: lost pl over 1f out* **25/1**
00 **6** 8 **Birbalini**[11] 3647 3-8-12............................ DaleGibson 2 11
(P J McBride) *led 1f: chsd ldrs: pushed along over 4f out: lost pl over 2f out* **66/1**

1m 47.04s (1.34) **Going Correction** -0.05s/f (Good)
WFA 3 from 4yo 8lb **6** Ran SP% **109.2**
Speed ratings (Par 103):91,90,88,83,76 68
CSF £158.95 TOTE £12.10: £2.90, £2.90; EX 70.10.
Owner The Greens Committee **Bred** Juddmonte Farms Ltd **Trained** Carluke, S Lanarks

FOCUS
A weak maiden run in a pedestrian time and very much a case of the winner wanting it more than the two behind him at the line. The third is officially rated 95, the fourth just 40.

3988 ALEX LAYTON 4 MENINGITIS UK H'CAP 5f
5:15 (5:16) (Class 5) (0-70,68) 3-Y-0+ **£4,533** (£1,348; £674; £336) **Stalls** Low

Form RPR
4132 **1** **Blessed Place**[4] 3846 6-9-4 **66**............................(t) AshleyHamblett[(7)] 11 75
(D J S Ffrench Davis) *mde all: kpt on wl fnl f: jst hld on* **7/1**[3]
1401 **2** *shd* **Namir (IRE)**[22] 3306 4-9-5 **63**............................(vt) AmirQuinn[(3)] 3 72
(S R Bowring) *mid-div: hdwy 2f out: styd on wl ins last: jst failed* **13/2**[2]
6520 **3** *nk* **Henry Hall (IRE)**[12] 3622 10-9-12 **67**............................ KimTinkler 1 75
(N Tinkler) *sn chsng ldr: kpt onwl fnl 2f: no ex wl ins last* **10/1**
3460 **4** 1 **Talcen Gwyn (IRE)**[10] 3683 4-9-2 **57**............................(v) PhillipMakin 2 61
(M F Harris) *chsd ldrs: kpt on same pce fnl f* **20/1**
0006 **5** 1¾ **Brigadore**[1] 3936 7-9-9 **64**............................ TonyCulhane 4 62+
(J G Given) *sn bhd: hdwy 2f out: styd on: nt rch ldrs* **9/2**[1]
0060 **6** 1¾ **Salviati (USA)**[4] 3855 9-9-0 **62**............................ PietroRomeo[(7)] 14 54+
(J M Bradley) *s.s: hdwy 2f out: nvr nr ldrs* **33/1**
0-06 **7** 3 **Fancy You (IRE)**[8] 3750 3-7-13 **49** oh4............................ LiamJones[(5)] 5 30
(A W Carroll) *bhd: sme hdwy 2f out: nvr nr ldrs* **40/1**
0034 **8** 2 **Flying Tackle**[6] 3781 8-8-8 **49** oh1............................(v) RoystonFfrench 10 23
(I W McInnes) *lost pl over 3f out: hdwy on outer over 1f out: nvr on terms* **8/1**
000- **9** *nk* **Hout Bay**[271] 6217 9-9-0 **55**............................ TonyHamilton 6 28
(R A Fahey) *mid-div: nvr nrr* **25/1**
0305 **10** 1¾ **Moon Forest (IRE)**[44] 2611 4-8-9 **50**............................(p) KDarley 17 16
(J M Bradley) *mid-div: sme hdwy on outer over 1f out: n.d* **12/1**
0600 **11** 2 **Jahia (NZ)**[22] 3297 7-8-8 **49** oh1............................ LeeEnstone 15 8
(P T Midgley) *w ldrs: wknd over 1f out* **28/1**
2505 **12** *nk* **Whinhill House**[13] 3584 6-9-13 **68**............................(p) RobertWinston 18 26
(D W Barker) *chsd ldrs on outer: wknd over 1f out* **16/1**
0200 **13** *shd* **Percy Douglas**[2] 3913 6-8-4 **52**............................(bt) AnnStokell[(7)] 7 10
(Miss A Stokell) *n.m.r and lost pl over 3f out: nvr on terms after* **33/1**
-000 **14** *shd* **Rectangle (IRE)**[23] 3245 6-8-9 **50**............................ DeanMcKeown 16 7
(Micky Hammond) *reminders after s: bhd whn stmbld after 100yds: nvr on terms* **33/1**
246 **15** ½ **Trick Cyclist**[9] 3699 5-9-6 **61**............................ DaleGibson 12 17
(M W Easterby) *in tch: hmpd and lost pl over 3f out: bhd after* **8/1**
2060 **16** 1 **Catch The Cat (IRE)**[2] 3913 7-9-2 **64**............................(v) DeanWilliams[(7)] 13 16
(Robert Gray) *a in rr* **22/1**
0004 **17** 8 **Flur Na H Alba**[16] 3503 7-9-8 **63**............................(v) GrahamGibbons 8 —
(J J Quinn) *prom: lost pl over 2f out: bhd whn eased ins last* **14/1**

62.73 secs (-1.07) **Going Correction** -0.05s/f (Good)
WFA 3 from 4yo+ 4lb **17** Ran SP% **123.2**
Speed ratings (Par 103):106,105,105,103,100 98,93,90,89,86 83,83,83,82,82 80,67
CSF £46.57 CT £483.60 TOTE £7.30: £1.80, £2.10, £2.80, £4.00; EX 48.20 Place 6 £6,043.94, Place 5 £2,763.00..
Owner S J Edwards **Bred** Mrs W H Gibson Fleming **Trained** Lambourn, Berks

FOCUS
The winner was never headed and the first four were in the leading quintet at halfway. A modest sprint handicap but the form looks reliable, rated through the second and third.
Jahia(NZ) Official explanation: trainer said mare was found to have bled from the nose
Percy Douglas Official explanation: jockey said horse hung right-handed and saddle slipped
T/Plt: £4,953.40 to a £1 stake. Pool: £56,319.85. 8.30 winning tickets. T/Qpdt: £701.60 to a £1 stake. Pool: £3,129.00. 3.30 winning tickets. WG

3968 DEAUVILLE (R-H)
Sunday, July 30

OFFICIAL GOING: Turf course - soft; all-weather - standard

3990a PRIX DE CABOURG (GROUP 3) 6f
2:05 (2:06) 2-Y-0 **£27,586** (£11,034; £8,276; £5,517; £2,759)

RPR
1 **Out Of Time (FR)**[17] 2-8-8............................ OPeslier 7 100
(J-M Sauve, France) *made all, driven out* **20/1**
2 *shd* **Beta**[57] 2-8-8............................ TGillet 5 99
(J E Pease, France) *pressed winner throughout, ridden over 1f out, challenged final f, ran on under strong pressure* **32/10**[2]
3 ½ **Optari (USA)**[30] 2-8-11............................ IMendizabal 8 101
(J-C Rouget, France) *tracked winner on outside, ridden and every chance approaching final f, no extra final 100y* **5/2**[1]

4 snk **Charlotte O Fraise (IRE)**[17] 2-8-8 .... SMaillot 3 98
(Rod Collet, France) *bandaged both forelegs, held up on rails, 6th approaching final f, stayed on final f, nearest at finish* **6/1**

5 1 1/2 **Take Blood (FR)**[28] 3132 2-8-8 .... TJarnet 6 93
(Mlle S-V Tarrou, France) *tracked leaders, kept on at one pace, never able to challenge* **11/1**

6 nse **Beauty Is Truth**[7] 3777 2-8-8 .... CSoumillon 4 93
(Robert Collet, France) *hld up in rr, hdwy 3f out, edged right from 2f out, hard ridden and every chance well over 1f out, no extra final f* **4/1[3]**

7 8 **Pertinence (IRE)**[15] 2-8-8 .... YLerner 2 69
(C Lerner, France) *in touch on rails disputing 4th, beaten 2f out* **7/1**

8 5 **Katina (FR)**[8] 2-8-8 .... FSpanu 1 54
(G Lellouche, France) *last throughout, well behind from well over 1f out* **33/1**

1m 10.8s 8 Ran SP% **115.2**
PARI-MUTUEL: WIN 14.30; PL 2.30, 1.60, 1.40; DF 33.70.
Owner M Jarlan **Bred** M Jarlan **Trained** France

NOTEBOOK
Out Of Time(FR), always well to the fore, was asked to make a final effort from one and a half out and she ran on bravely, beating the runner-up by a matter of inches. She has now won four of her six races and her provincial trainer is now looking at the Prix Morny.
Beta, always well up there, was given every possible chance, but she appeared to get outpaced at the furlong marker and then ran on again close home. She would have won in another couple of strides and connections feel she needs a longer trip, so the Prix Calvados is now on the cards.
Optari(USA) ran a little free early on and she was brought with a challenge up the centre of the track. He looked like taking the lead but hung a little right as the race came to an end. It was the first time he has run in this kind of company and he looks sure to improve.
Charlotte O Fraise(IRE) appeared to be outpaced when things quickened up before running on well inside the final furlong. She was not beaten by far and is certainly one to note for the future.

3991a PRIX D'ASTARTE (GROUP 1) (F&M) (STRAIGHT COURSE) 1m (R)
3:05 (3:08) 3-Y-0+ **£98,517** (£39,414; £19,707; £9,845; £4,931)

RPR

1 **Mandesha (FR)**[28] 3133 3-8-7 .... CSoumillon 5 115
(A De Royer-Dupre, France) *held up, edged left from outside before halfway, challenged on rails side well over 1f out, driven to lead 100y out* **13/2**

2 1/2 **Impressionnante**[21] 3342 3-8-7 .... OPeslier 11 114
(C Laffon-Parias, France) *tracked leader on outside, led well over 1f out, hard ridden distance, headed 100 yards out, ran on* **4/1[2]**

3 1 1/2 **Tie Black (IRE)**[77] 1719 3-8-7 .... J-BEyquem 1 111
(F Rohaut, France) *always prominent, disputed 2nd over 2f out, ridden and every chance approaching final f, one pace* **4/1[2]**

4 hd **In Clover**[62] 2092 4-9-0 .... C-PLemaire 2 110
(F Head, France) *held up in rear, headway behind winner 2f out, ran on under pressure final 1 1/2f, nearest at finish* **16/1**

5 1/2 **Price Tag**[37] 2802 3-8-7 .... TThulliez 9 110
(P Bary, France) *tracked Impressionnante, disputed 3rd approaching final f, kept on same pace* **11/4[1]**

6 3/4 **Grigorieva (IRE)**[28] 3133 3-8-7 .... MJKinane 7 108
(A Fabre, France) *always in touch, effort 1 1/2f out, soon one pace* **12/1**

7 3/4 **Grand Vadla (FR)**[22] 3327 3-8-7 .... JVictoire 10 107
(A Fabre, France) *midfield towards outside, hard ridden 1 12/f out, one pace* **11/2[3]**

8 1 1/2 **Together (FR)**[7] 3779 6-9-0 ....(b) SMaillot 3 103
(Mme C Vergne, France) *held up in rear, last 2f out, stayed on, never a factor* **40/1**

9 1 1/2 **Lolita (GER)**[37] 2802 3-8-7 .... DBoeuf 4 101
(Andreas Lowe, Germany) *in touch, ridden well over 1f out, soon one pace* **12/1**

10 10 **Indian Fun**[22] 3327 3-8-7 ....(b) GBenoist 8 81
(F Head, France) *led to well over 1f out* **66/1**

1m 36.4s
WFA 3 from 4yo+ 8lb 10 Ran SP% **120.6**
PARI-MUTUEL: WIN 3.50; PL 1.60, 1.90, 1.60; DF 15.20.
Owner Princess Zahra Aga Khan **Bred** Princes Zahra Aga Khan **Trained** Chantilly, France

NOTEBOOK
Mandesha(FR), behind early on but always going well within herself, she was switched towards the stands to make a challenge from two out. She hit the front a furlong later and then stayed on to win finally with a little in hand. She had previously been disqualified from a Group 3 so this victory was well deserved and further improvement can definitely be expected. Her principal target now will be the Prix de l'Opera on Arc day.
Impressionnante, given every possible chance, was settled behind her lead horse up the middle of the track. Her effort started one and a half out and she battled on gamely to the line. There are no plans for her at the moment, but she will stay in training as a four-year-old.
Tie Black(IRE), whose connections were not happy by the way the race went, could never be covered up as hoped. She did stay on, but never looked liked troubling the first two. She looked extremely well in the paddock and the long-term plan is the Prix de la Foret, with a campaign in the States likely afterwards.
In Clover, held up in rear early on, she started her effort from one and a half out up the stands' rail. She did not quicken and just stayed on at the same pace.

2912 MUNICH (L-H)
Sunday, July 30

OFFICIAL GOING: Good

3992a ETZEL-RENNEN (RIEMER STEHER-TROPHY 2006) (LISTED RACE) 1m 6f
3:05 (3:12) 3-Y-0+ **£8,276** (£3,034; £1,655; £828)

RPR

1 **Kiswahili**[15] 3551 4-9-1 .... AStarke 2 99
(Sir Mark Prescott) *held up in rear off slow pace, switched outside and ridden over 1f out, stayed on to lead last 100 yards (11/10F)* **11/10[1]**

2 3/4 **Amoroso (GER)**[287] 5-8-13 .... ASuborics 4 96
(P Rau, Germany)

3 nk **Kiton (GER)**[28] 5-8-13 .... ABest 3 96
(P Rau, Germany)

4 1 1/2 **Le Marquis (GER)**[399] 5-8-13 .... MBlancpain 1 94
(Frau Jutta Mayer, Germany)

5 1 1/2 **Frankly Dancing (HUN)** 4-9-2 .... KKerekes 5 95
(I Papp, Hungary)

3m 6.31s 5 Ran SP% **47.6**
(including 10 Euro stake): WIN 21; PL 13, 13; SF 44.
Owner Miss K Rausing **Bred** Miss K Rausing **Trained** Newmarket, Suffolk

NOTEBOOK
Kiswahili was found a soft opportunity and landed the spoils very readily, quickening up off a slow pace to lead 100 yards out. Gaining black type, this was a case of 'mission accomplished' and her retirement to the breeding paddocks may not be far away.

3993a GROSSER DALLMAYR-PREIS (BAYERISCHES ZUCHTRENNEN) (GROUP 1) 1m 2f
3:40 (3:50) 3-Y-0+ **£62,759** (£24,828; £12,414; £6,897)

RPR

1 **Lord Of England (GER)**[49] 2492 3-8-9 .... AStarke 1 117
(Mario Hofer, Germany) *raced in 2nd, hard ridden to lead 150 yards out, driven out* **33/10[3]**

2 1 **Laverock (IRE)**[35] 2914 4-9-6 .... MBlancpain 3 116
(C Laffon-Parias, France) *raced in 4th, headway to press leaders over 1f out, stayed on to take 2nd final 50 yards* **21/10[2]**

3 1/2 **Almerita (GER)**[56] 2279 3-8-5 .... AlanMunro 2 110
(W Hickst, Germany) *set slow pace, quickened 2 lengths clear entering straight, headed 150 yards out, one pace, just held on for 3rd* **61/10**

4 nk **Fight Club (GER)**[63] 2061 5-9-6 .... WMongil 5 114
(A Trybuhl, Germany) *raced in 3rd, ridden well over 1f out, stayed on* **83/10**

5 1 1/2 **Arcadio (GER)**[42] 2692 4-9-6 .... ASuborics 4 112
(P Schiergen, Germany) *last throughout, switched outside and effort 1 1/2f out, unable to quicken* **4/5[1]**

2m 14.46s
WFA 3 from 4yo+ 10lb 5 Ran SP% **135.9**
WIN 43; PL 21, 19; SF 188.
Owner Stall Lucky Owner **Bred** Stall Pontresini **Trained** Germany

NOTEBOOK
Lord Of England(GER) benefited from racing close to a pedestrian pace and quickened up well in the closing stages. This was a tactical affair and three-year-olds are favoured by the race conditions, but he did it well and, with a dearth of opportunities over this trip in Germany, foreign targets are on his agenda.

3378 SOUTHWELL (L-H)
Monday, July 31

OFFICIAL GOING: Standard
Wind: Slight, half-across

3994 EBF GALA CASINO BRIDLESMITH GATE NOTTINGHAM MAIDEN STKS 5f (F)
2:45 (2:46) (Class 5) 2-Y-0 **£3,886** (£1,156; £577; £288) **Stalls** High

Form RPR

05 1 **Stevie Gee (IRE)**[11] 3685 2-9-3 .... DeanMcKeown 6 80+
(G A Swinbank) *trckd ldrs: hdwy 1/2-way: rdn to ld 1f out: sn clr* **8/1**

56 2 4 **Pavlovia**[24] 3247 2-8-12 .... DavidAllan 5 61
(T D Easterby) *a.p:rdn wl over 1f out: kpt on same pce ins last* **3/1[2]**

3 1 1/4 **Venetian Dancer (IRE)** 2-9-3 .... TedDurcan 10 62
(M J Wallace) *dwlt and towards rr: hdwy 2f out: sn rdn and kpt on ins last nrst fin: fin 4th, plcd 3rd* **7/1**

4 hd **Hidden Ace (IRE)** 2-8-12 ....(b[1]) PaulMulrennan 1 56
(M W Easterby) *dwlt and towards rr: hdwy 1/2-way: rdn wl over 1f out: kpt on ins last: nrst fin: fin 5th, plcd 4th* **33/1**

22 5 4 **Impromptu**[29] 3110 2-9-3 .... SebSanders 13 46
(R M Beckett) *chsd ldrs: rdn along 1/2-way: sn outpcd: fin 6th; plcd 5th* **11/4[1]**

0000 6 1/2 **Homes By Woodford**[82] 1588 2-8-10 .... AdeleRothery[(7)] 3 45
(M W Easterby) *s.i.s: towards rr tl sme late hdwy: fin 7th, plcd 6th* **50/1**

00 7 1 3/4 **Julatten (IRE)**[14] 3596 2-8-7 .... StephenDonohoe[(5)] 9 33
(G A Swinbank) *a towards rr: fin 8th, plcd 7th* **16/1**

60 8 1 **Foxies Firstglance**[23] 3307 2-8-12 .... RoystonFfrench 2 30
(R D E Woodhouse) *bhd: hdwy 1/2-way: rdn wl over 1f out and sn no imp: fin 9th, plcd 8th* **66/1**

00 9 shd **Suntan Lady (IRE)**[80] 1647 2-8-12 .... MickyFenton 8 29
(Miss V Haigh) *a towards rr: fin 10th, plcd 9th* **100/1**

10 6 **Josr's Bank** 2-8-12 .... DaleGibson 7 8
(M W Easterby) *a towards rr: fin 11th, plcd 10th* **25/1**

66 11 3 1/2 **Windjammer**[39] 2783 2-9-3 .... NCallan 11 —
(T D Easterby) *a towards rr: fin 12th, plcd 11th* **16/1**

00 12 1/2 **Imperial Style (IRE)**[7] 3787 2-9-0 .... PatrickMathers[(3)] 4 —
(D Shaw) *sn rdn along: a outpcd in rr: fin 13th, plcd 12th* **100/1**

423 13 3/4 **Joseph Locke (IRE)**[87] 1454 2-9-3 .... KDarley 12 —
(M Dods) *slowly away: a bhd: fin 14th, plcd 13th* **5/1[3]**

0530 D 1 **Bookiesindex Boy**[9] 3734 2-9-3 ....(b) RobertHavlin 14 62
(J R Jenkins) *led: rdn 2f out: drvn and hdd 1f out: wknd: fin 3rd, 4l & 1l: disq: rider failed to weigh in* **11/1**

59.35 secs (-0.95) **Going Correction** -0.325s/f (Stan) 14 Ran SP% **124.3**
Speed ratings (Par 94):94,87,84,83,77 76,73,72,71,62 56,55,54,86
CSF £32.41 TOTE £9.60: £2.30, £1.70, £3.50; EX 44.40.
Owner Steve Gray **Bred** Irish National Stud **Trained** Melsonby, N Yorks
■ Stewards' Enquiry : Robert Havlin seven-day ban: failed to weigh in (Aug 11-17)

FOCUS
A big field and a wide range of abilities, which resulted in them finishing well spread out, and as usual the middle of the track was the place to be. It has been rated through the third and fifth.

NOTEBOOK
Stevie Gee(IRE), who ran better than it might have seemed against previous winners in a Wolverhampton novice event last time, was backed off the boards here. Always to the fore and racing down the favoured centre of the track, he made no mistake and dotted up. He is entitled to improve a bit more yet and much will now depend on what nursery mark he gets. (op 25-1)
Pavlovia ran her race on this switch to sand and though she never had a prayer with the winner, still emerges with credit. She looks worth another try over six, possibly on an easy surface, and she also now qualifies for a nursery mark. (op 10-3 tchd 7-2)
Venetian Dancer(IRE) ♦, a 70,000gns half-brother to a useful two-year-old winner in France, was attempting to overcome an established track bias over this straight five in trying to come from so far off the pace, so he deserves a lot of credit for finishing where he did. Improvement can be expected. (op 11-2)

Hidden Ace(IRE), a half-sister to Unicorn Reward and to a winner in Belgium, was blinkered for this debut which suggests she is not straightforward. Probably finding herself closer to the deeper far rail than ideal in the early stages having started from the number one stall, she did plug on to reach her final position and there should be a small race in her in due course.
Impromptu, runner-up in two turf maidens, failed to cope with this different surface and sticking close to the stands' rail from his high draw would not have done him any favours. (op 7-2)
Windjammer Official explanation: jockey said colt had no more to give
Bookiesindex Boy, berthed in the dreaded stands' rail stall, broke well which enabled him to shift left in front of those drawn closest to him and take a route more towards the centre of the track. He was therefore able to run his race on this return to sand despite his jockey's subsequent brainstorm in failing to weigh in, but is more exposed than most and may need a drop in class or switch to nurseries to gave him a chance of winning. (op 12-1 tchd 9-1)

3995 GALA CASINO - JOIN TODAY PLAY TODAY CLAIMING STKS 6f (F)

3:15 (3:17) (Class 6) 3-Y-O+ **£2,730** (£806; £403) **Stalls** Low

Form RPR

4111 **1** **Further Outlook (USA)**[31] 3033 12-8-13 68......... StephenDonohoe(5) 5 71
(D Carroll) *mde all: rdn wl over 1f out: drvn and edgd rt ins last: hld on gamely* **7/1**

3320 **2** *nk* **Sweet Pickle**[18] 3434 5-9-2 64.......................................(e) AmirQuinn(3) 11 71
(J R Boyle) *hld up in tch gng wl: n.m.r 3f out: effrt and nt clr run 2f out: swtchd lft and rdn over 1f out: styd on wl: jst hld* **11/2**[2]

0530 **3** *3/4* **Mill By The Stream**[13] 3617 4-8-3 54........................... RoryMoore(5) 12 58
(P T Midgley) *in tch: wd st: gd hdwy on outer 2f out: rdn to chal wl over 1f out: ev ch tl drvn and no ex last 75 yds* **14/1**

0000 **4** *5* **Kingsmaite**[13] 3608 5-9-1 70...(b) MSemple(7) 10 57
(S R Bowring) *cl up: challnged 2f out and ev ch: sn rdn and wknd over 1f out* **9/1**

1434 **5** *2* **Soba Jones**[23] 3297 9-9-5 63.................................. JasonEdmunds(3) 14 51
(J Balding) *chsd ldrs: rdn 2f out: drvn and wknd wl over 1f out* **6/1**[3]

140/ **6** *1/2* **Roman Boy (ARG)**[814] 7-9-12 70................................. MickyFenton 13 53
(Stef Liddiard) *racd wd and bhd tl sme late hdwy* **40/1**

5300 **7** *1/2* **Far Note (USA)**[31] 3052 8-8-12 52...................................(bt) PaulEddery 2 38
(S R Bowring) *cl up on inner: rdn along over 2f out and sn wknd* **25/1**

3065 **8** *2* **The City Kid (IRE)**[20] 3381 3-8-12 66...................................(v) NCallan 7 37
(P D Evans) *prom: rdn over 2f out: grad wknd* **11/2**[2]

0024 **9** *2 1/2* **Sarah's Prince (IRE)**[24] 3257 3-8-10 52................... JamesMillman(7) 9 34
(D K Ivory) *a towards rr* **25/1**

6056 **10** *1* **Danehill Stroller (IRE)**[11] 3682 6-8-10 62....................(p) SebSanders 1 19
(R M Beckett) *a rr* **4/1**[1]

0052 **11** *2 1/2* **Mind Alert**[20] 3389 5-9-8 54...(v) ShaneKelly 4 24
(S R Bowring) *dwlt: sn chsng ldrs: rdn over 2f out and sn wknd* **12/1**

5004 **12** *2* **Majik**[90] 1388 7-8-9 63..(p) KevinGhunowa(7) 3 12
(P A Blockley) *a bhd* **9/1**

1m 16.55s (-0.35) **Going Correction** -0.025s/f (Stan)
WFA 3 from 4yo+ 5lb **12** Ran SP% **122.0**
Speed ratings (Par 101):101,100,99,92,90 89,88,86,82,81 78,75
CSF £45.85 TOTE £6.30: £2.00, £2.60, £5.80; EX 39.30.The winner was claimed by Miss Gay Kelleway for £8,000. Danehill Stroller was claimed by Gary P. Martin for £4,000. Mill By The Stream was claimed by Roy Brotherton for £3,000.
Owner Diamond Racing Ltd **Bred** Gainsborough Farm Inc **Trained** Warthill, N Yorks

FOCUS

A routine Fibresand claimer in which those that came down the middle of the track were favoured as normal and the front three pulled well clear. The form is pretty sound amongst the first three.
Danehill Stroller(IRE) Official explanation: jockey said gelding would not face the kickback

3996 GALA CASINO MAID MARIAN WAY NOTTINGHAM H'CAP 6f (F)

3:45 (3:46) (Class 5) (0-75,71) 3-Y-O+ **£3,562** (£1,059; £529; £264) **Stalls** Low

Form RPR

0104 **1** **Scuba (IRE)**[14] 3598 4-9-1 63.......................................(b) TravisBlock(5) 4 72
(H Morrison) *trckd ldrs: hdwy 2f out: rdn over 1f out: styd on ins last to ld last strides* **7/1**

1062 **2** *shd* **Rosein**[18] 3459 4-9-10 67... SebSanders 13 76
(Mrs G S Rees) *in tch on outer: hdwy 2f out: rdn to ld wl over 1f out: drvn ins last: hdd and no ex nr line* **15/2**

0050 **3** *2 1/2* **Devonia Plains (IRE)**[32] 3013 4-8-12 62..............(v) JamesMillman(7) 12 64
(Mrs P N Dutfield) *hmpd s and bhd: hdwy 2f out: sn rdn and styd on strly ins last: nrst fin* **40/1**

-332 **4** *shd* **Gracie's Gift (IRE)**[39] 2792 4-8-9 57..................... StephenDonohoe(5) 9 58
(A G Newcombe) *bhd: hdwy 2f out: sn rdn and kpt on ins last: nrst fin* **6/1**[3]

0030 **5** *2* **Kennington**[39] 2784 6-9-8 65....................................(b) HayleyTurner 7 60
(Mrs C A Dunnett) *prom: rdn along 2f out: drvn over 1f out and kpt on same pce* **16/1**

5002 **6** *3/4* **Tilly's Dream**[20] 3381 3-9-4 66.. ShaneKelly 3 59
(G C H Chung) *cl up: rdn along 2f out: grad wknd* **8/1**

6126 **7** *1/2* **Rancho Cucamonga (IRE)**[5] 3835 4-8-12 55.....................(b) KDarley 6 46
(T D Barron) *outpcd and bhd: rdn along and hdwy wl over 1f out: kpt on ins last: nvr nrr* **9/2**[1]

0-12 **8** *1/2* **Apply Dapply**[80] 1642 3-9-8 70.. SteveDrowne 1 60
(H Morrison) *dwlt and bhd: hdwy on inner 1/2-way: rdn 2f out: no imp appr last* **5/1**[2]

5103 **9** *2* **Union Jack Jackson (IRE)**[27] 3171 4-8-12 55...........(b) DaleGibson 10 39
(J G Given) *trckd ldrs: rdn 2f out: sn drvn and wknd* **12/1**

5406 **10** *2* **Apex**[24] 3262 5-9-7 64.. KimTinkler 5 42
(N Tinkler) *sn outpcd and a towards rr* **7/1**

20-0 **11** *14* **Turn Around**[18] 3459 6-9-3 60.................................... DeanMcKeown 14 —
(J Pearce) *racd wd: a bhd* **25/1**

010- **12** *3/4* **Golband**[275] 6157 4-9-7 71.. AshleyHamblett(7) 2 5
(R F Marvin) *led: rdn along over 2f out: sn hdd & wknd* **66/1**

-004 **13** *3 1/2* **Bold Haze**[11] 3670 4-9-3 60... RobertWinston 11 —
(Miss S E Hall) *chsd ldrs: rdn wl over 2f out: sn wknd* **14/1**

1m 16.44s (-0.46) **Going Correction** -0.025s/f (Stan)
WFA 3 from 4yo+ 5lb **13** Ran SP% **125.0**
Speed ratings (Par 103):102,101,98,98,95 94,94,93,90,88 69,68,63
CSF £60.94 CT £2069.06 TOTE £11.70: £3.40, £3.20, £10.20; EX 97.20.
Owner Graham Doyle & Partners **Bred** Mountarmstrong Stud **Trained** East Ilsley, Berks

FOCUS

A solid pace for this ordinary sprint handicap and the action was all centre to stands' side in the home straight. The winning time was marginally faster than the preceding claimer. The race has been rated positively through the runner-up.
Rancho Cucamonga(IRE) Official explanation: trainer's rep had no explanation for the poor form shown
Apply Dapply Official explanation: jockey said filly never travelled
Turn Around Official explanation: jockey said gelding would not face the kickback

3997 GALA CASINO ANYONE CAN BE A PLAYER NURSERY 7f (F)

4:15 (4:18) (Class 5) 2-Y-O **£3,562** (£1,059; £529; £264) **Stalls** Low

Form RPR

6364 **1** **Silca Soprano**[25] 3210 2-8-7 67............................ EdwardCreighton(3) 8 72
(M R Channon) *hld up in midfield: hdwy 2f out: hdwy on outer wl over 1f out: rdn to chal ins last: styd on to ld nr line* **13/2**[2]

010 **2** *nk* **Easy Lover**[17] 3496 2-9-7 78.. ShaneKelly 10 82
(J A Osborne) *prom: hdwy to ld 2f out: rdn and hung rt ent last: sn drvn: hdd and no ex nr line* **4/1**[1]

645 **3** *3* **Tarif (IRE)**[37] 2857 2-8-7 64 ow2... MickyFenton 4 61
(Mrs P Sly) *s.i.s and outpcd in rr: hdwy 2f out: styd on u.p appr last: nrst fin* **4/1**[1]

0203 **4** *nk* **La Marmotte (IRE)**[19] 3408 2-8-9 66.............................. NickyMackay 6 62
(J W Hills) *chsd ldrs: rdn along 2f out: styd on u.p ent last* **12/1**

3454 **5** *1 1/2* **Nicada (IRE)**[7] 3800 2-8-8 65.. AdrianMcCarthy 3 57
(Miss Gay Kelleway) *cl up: led 1/2-way: rdn and hdd 2f out: grad wknd appr last* **7/1**[3]

0246 **6** *1 1/4* **Montemayorprincess (IRE)**[29] 3117 2-8-4 61........ FrankieMcDonald 1 50
(D Haydn Jones) *chsd ldrs on inner: rdn along 2f out: kpt on same pce* **15/2**

0002 **7** *1 1/2* **Gibsons**[20] 3380 2-7-12 55.. JamieMackay 5 40
(Mrs P N Dutfield) *s.i.s and bhd: hdwy 2f out:s witched lft and rdn over 1f out: no imp* **16/1**

4404 **8** *3* **Urban Warrior**[9] 3727 2-8-12 69...................................... StephenCarson 7 47
(J R Best) *a rr* **11/1**

1150 **9** *2* **Emma Told Lies**[20] 3372 2-8-3 60...................................... DaleGibson 11 33
(M W Easterby) *rrd s: in tch on outer tl rdn along 1/2-way and sn wknd* **20/1**

003 **10** *1/2* **Pirner's Brig**[53] 2382 2-8-2 59.................................... RoystonFfrench 2 31
(M W Easterby) *led to 1/2-way: sn rdn along and wknd* **33/1**

2123 **11** *2* **Tokyo Jo (IRE)**[45] 2626 2-7-11 59 ow1.......................(v) AndrewElliott(5) 9 26
(K R Burke) *cl up: rdn along wl over 2f out: sn wknd* **7/1**[3]

1m 32.6s (1.80) **Going Correction** -0.025s/f (Stan) **11** Ran SP% **119.7**
Speed ratings (Par 94):88,87,84,83,82 80,79,75,73,72 70
CSF £33.30 CT £121.91 TOTE £6.30: £1.60, £2.00, £2.10; EX 35.10.
Owner Aldridge Racing Partnership **Bred** Michael E Broughton **Trained** West Ilsley, Berks

FOCUS

A decent early pace for this nursery with four battling for the early lead, but this proved quite a test for these juveniles and they seemed to finish tired, with the winning time looking modest. The form looks sound. The official ratings shown next to each horse are estimated and for information purposes only.

NOTEBOOK

Silca Soprano was beginning to look regressive, but this switch to Fibresand proved the key and she ground out a very game victory. This performance suggests she is a stayer, as might be expected of a half-sister to the smart chaser Keltic Bard. (op 7-1 tchd 6-1)
Easy Lover was given a positive ride and was unfortunate to be nailed given how gamely she battled on when challenged by the winner. So far her performances on sand have been way above her efforts on turf. (tchd 9-2)
Tarif(IRE) did himself few favours by missing the break on this nursery debut, especially on this track, so he did well to finish in the frame. He probably does not want the ground too fast and has the ability to win a race under suitable conditions if breaking on terms. (op 11-2 tchd 6-1)
La Marmotte(IRE), taking another step up in trip, did not seem to be beaten through lack of stamina.
Nicada(IRE) did not see the trip out so well on this more testing surface and is starting to look exposed now. (op 9-1 after early 12-1 in a place)

3998 GALA CASINO NOTTINGHAM PLAY AND PARTY H'CAP 1m 4f (F)

4:45 (4:48) (Class 6) (0-55,55) 3-Y-O+ **£2,730** (£806; £403) **Stalls** Low

Form RPR

0-55 **1** **Bienheureux**[25] 3221 5-9-9 53..(vt) NCallan 5 63
(Miss Gay Kelleway) *trckd ldrs: hdwy to ld 2f out: sn rdn: hung bdly lft over 1f out: drvn out* **11/2**[3]

-026 **2** *nk* **Swords**[181] 257 4-9-6 50.. DeanMcKeown 12 60
(Heather Dalton) *bmpd s: hld up in rr: hdwy 1/2-way: cl up 2f out: snrdn hmpd and swtchd lft over 1f out: drvn and styd on wl* **25/1**

540 **3** *3* **Agilete**[25] 3232 4-9-0 44.. RoystonFfrench 7 49
(J R Boyle) *hld up: stdy hdwy over 4f out: trckd ldrs 2f out: rdn over 1f out: kpt on same pce* **7/1**

-265 **4** *5* **Pee Jay's Dream**[77] 1745 4-9-11 55..........................(b[1]) PaulMulrennan 8 52
(M W Easterby) *led: rdn along and hdd 3f out: sn drvn and one pce fnl 2f* **5/1**[2]

0300 **5** *nk* **Sorbiesharry (IRE)**[54] 2345 7-8-10 43....................(p) DanielTudhope(3) 3 40
(Mrs N Macauley) *trckd ldrs: hdwy to ld 3f out: rdn and hdd 2f out: sn drvn and grad wknd* **16/1**

3523 **6** *1 1/2* **Romil Star (GER)**[20] 3382 9-9-1 52............................ KevinGhunowa(7) 6 46
(M J Attwater) *prom: sn pushed along: rdn over 5f out: drvn 3f out: sn wknd* **4/1**[1]

2336 **7** *nk* **Bulberry Hill**[139] 635 5-8-10 43.................................. EdwardCreighton(3) 11 37
(R W Price) *hedl up and bhd: hdwy and in tch 4f out: rdn wl over 2f out: sn no imp* **11/2**[3]

-005 **8** *25* **Perfectionist**[14] 3594 4-8-8 43.. AndrewElliott(5) 1 —
(Mrs C A Dunnett) *prom: rdn along over 4f out: sn wknd* **25/1**

0000 **9** *2* **Kentuckian**[42] 2707 4-9-1 45.. StephenCarson 9 —
(P W Hiatt) *a rr* **50/1**

1443 **10** *3/4* **Royal Axminster**[50] 2481 11-9-0 51.............................. JamesMillman(7) 13 —
(Mrs P N Dutfield) *wnt lft s: a towards rr* **15/2**

3-03 **11** *3/4* **Food For Thought**[20] 3379 3-8-10 55 ow1.........................(v) DNolan(3) 10 3
(J J Quinn) *chsd ldrs: rdn along 4f out: sn wknd* **10/1**

0000 **12** *1/2* **Cool Bathwick (IRE)**[58] 2219 7-8-8 43............(b) MichaelJStainton(5) 14 —
(G H Yardley) *midfield: rdn along and lost pl 1/2-way: sn bhd* **100/1**

0605 **13** *15* **Ashwell Rose**[14] 3597 4-8-13 43.. J-PGuillambert 4 —
(R T Phillips) *in tch: rdn along over 4f out: sn wknd* **25/1**

2m 41.03s (-1.06) **Going Correction** -0.025s/f (Stan)
WFA 3 from 4yo+ 12lb **13** Ran SP% **121.2**
Speed ratings (Par 101):102,101,99,96,96 95,95,78,77,76 76,75,65
CSF £145.16 CT £988.60 TOTE £8.70: £2.40, £4.80, £2.50; EX 145.50.
Owner Mr & Mrs I Henderson **Bred** N R Shields **Trained** Exning, Suffolk

FOCUS

A modest handicap, but a solid pace, which at least made it a true test. Pretty solid form for the grade.
Royal Axminster Official explanation: jockey said gelding never travelled
Food For Thought Official explanation: jockey said filly had no more to give
Cool Bathwick(IRE) Official explanation: jockey said gelding was unsuited by the fibresand surface

3999 GALA CASINO CARD ROOM H'CAP 1m (F)
5:15 (5:16) (Class 6) (0-55,56) 3-Y-0+ £2,730 (£806; £403) Stalls Low

Form RPR

060 1 **Im Ova Ere Dad (IRE)**[30] [3090] 3-8-12 **54**.......................... DaleGibson 2 67
(D E Cantillon) *a.p: effrt over 2f out: rdn to ld 11/2f out: drvn ins last and hld on wl* **8/1**

6024 2 ½ **Band**[14] [3599] 6-8-13 **54**.......................... RussellKennemore(7) 3 66
(E S McMahon) *hld up in tch: smooth hdwy 3f out: chal 2f out: sn rdn and ev ch: drvn ins last: no ex towards fin* **3/1**[1]

0603 3 5 **Damburger Xpress**[33] [2978] 4-8-11 **52**.......................... KirstyMilczarek(7) 1 54+
(D M Simcock) *chsd ldrs on inner: rdn along after 2f: sn outpcd and bhd: hdwy 2f out: kpt on u.p appr last* **7/1**

0/00 4 1 **Benny The Ball (USA)**[35] [2936] 5-9-7 **55**.......................... NCallan 14 55
(N P Littmoden) *a cl up: rdn to ld over 2f out: drvn and hdd 11/2f out: wknd* **9/2**[2]

0000 5 3½ **Mujelle**[19] [3410] 3-8-7 **56** ow1..........................(be[1]) JamesMillman(7) 12 49
(D K Ivory) *led: rdn along and hdd 3f out: drvn and wknd over 2f out* **33/1**

0502 6 ½ **Welcome Releaf**[20] [3378] 3-8-13 **55**..........................(v) ShaneKelly 9 47
(G C H Chung) *prominent: led over 3f out: rdn and hdd over 2f out: sn drvn and wknd* **13/2**[3]

-400 7 hd **Southern Tide (USA)**[38] [2820] 4-8-12 **46**.......................... DeanMcKeown 13 38
(J Pearce) *chsd ldrs: rdn wl over 2f out: sn wknd* **10/1**

00U0 8 4 **Subsidise (IRE)**[31] [2282] 3-8-8 **55**..........................(v) MarkLawson(5) 7 39
(F P Murtagh) *rrd s: a towards rr* **33/1**

P-00 9 1¾ **Cavan Gael (FR)**[38] [2820] 4-9-4 **52**.......................... J-PGuillambert 11 33
(P Howling) *midfield: rdn along on outer 3f out: sn wknd* **7/1**

40-0 10 ½ **The Wizard Mul**[83] [1560] 6-8-8 **47**..........................(t) AndrewElliott(5) 8 27
(W Storey) *a rr* **25/1**

0006 11 2 **Monte Mayor Boy**[20] [3388] 4-9-4 **52**..........................(p) FrankieMcDonald 4 28
(D Haydn Jones) *a rr* **12/1**

5000 12 ¾ **Downland (IRE)**[14] [3599] 10-9-4 **52**.......................... KimTinkler 5 26
(N Tinkler) *midfield: effrt and in tch 3f out: sn rdn and btn* **20/1**

005- 13 19 **Compton Micky**[406] [2765] 5-8-8 **49**.......................... AshleyHamblett(7) 10 —
(R F Marvin) *a rr: bhd fr 1/2-way* **25/1**

0-05 14 16 **Wolf Pack**[20] [3383] 4-8-9 **46**.......................... EdwardCreighton(3) 6 —
(R W Price) *a rr: bhd fr 1/2-way* **33/1**

1m 43.8s (-0.80) **Going Correction** -0.025s/f (Stan)
WFA 3 from 4yo+ 8lb **14** Ran SP% **130.7**
Speed ratings (Par 101):103,102,97,96,93 92,92,88,86,86 84,83,64,48
CSF £32.47 CT £165.52 TOTE £9.00: £2.10, £1.60, £3.00; EX 60.60 Place 6 £415.66, Place 5 £179.07.
Owner Allan Milton **Bred** Golden Vale Stud **Trained** Newmarket, Suffolk
■ Stewards' Enquiry : Russell Kennemore one-day ban: used whip with excessive frequency (Aug 11)

FOCUS
A decent pace for this modest handicap and the front pair came well clear. The winner is unexposed and the runner-up has become well handicapped. The form looks solid.
Im Ova Ere Dad(IRE) ◆ Official explanation: trainer said, regarding the improved form shown, the gelding was having its first run on the all-weather and had benefited from today's step up in trip
Compton Micky Official explanation: jockey said gelding became unbalanced round the bend
Wolf Pack Official explanation: jockey said gelding lost its action
T/Jkpt: Not won. T/Plt: £122.30 to a £1 stake. Pool: £76,761.75. 173.85 winning tickets. T/Qpdt: £43.30 to a £1 stake. Pool: £5,169.10. 88.20 winning tickets. JR

3793 WINDSOR (R-H)
Monday, July 31

OFFICIAL GOING: Good to firm (firm in places)
The ground was lightning quick and it may pay to forgive certain horses below-par runs.
Wind: Blustery, behind

4000 MONDAY NIGHTS WITH VC CASINO.COM MAIDEN STKS 6f
6:00 (6:04) (Class 4) 2-Y-0 £5,181 (£1,541; £770; £384) Stalls High

Form RPR

2 1 **Si Foo (USA)**[18] [3457] 2-9-3 .... MartinDwyer 3 76
(A M Balding) *t.k.h: chsd ldr tl led over 2f out: hrd drvn 1 out: styd on gamely: all out* **4/1**[2]

3 2 nk **Callwood Dancer (IRE)**[42] [2710] 2-8-12 .... MichaelHills 5 70
(B W Hills) *led tl over 2f out: rdn 2f out: hung lft u.p fnl f: no ex last 50 yds* **11/2**[3]

40 3 shd **Vitznau (IRE)**[35] [2930] 2-9-3 .... RichardHughes 9 75
(R Hannon) *towards rr: pushed along and hdwy 1/2-way: rdn wl over 1f out: swtchd rt ins fnl f: r.o wl last 100 yds: nrst fin* **13/2**

664 4 ¾ **Marine Parade**[26] [3193] 2-9-3 .... RyanMoore 2 73
(R Hannon) *prom: swtchd rt onto rail 2f out: kpt on same pce u.p fnl f* **7/2**[1]

00 5 1¾ **Spinning Crystal (IRE)**[21] [3363] 2-8-9 .... AdamKirby(3) 6 62
(B W Hills) *chsd ldrs: rdn over 2f out: kpt on same pce fnl f* **50/1**

6 hd **Sohraab** 2-9-3 .... LPKeniry 10 67
(H Morrison) *racd in midfield: swtchd lft 2f out: rdn over 1f out: styd on ins fnl f: nrst fin* **33/1**

005 7 ½ **King Charles**[24] [3242] 2-9-3 .... RichardMullen 7 65
(E A L Dunlop) *bhd: swtchd to outer over 2f out: kpt on: ins fnl f: nt trble ldrs* **14/1**

65 8 1 **The Illies (IRE)**[85] [1510] 2-9-3 .... GeorgeBaker 14 62
(B W Hills) *slowly away: sn in tch: rdn over 2f out: kpt on same pce* **12/1**

9 ¾ **Doyles Lodge** 2-9-3 .... DaneO'Neill 4 60
(H Candy) *slowly away: behind on outer: hdwy into midfield over 2f out: no prog fnl f* **33/1**

0 10 13 **Princess Zada**[51] [2456] 2-8-12 .... RichardThomas 11 16
(B R Millman) *chsd ldrs tl rdn 1/2-way: sn lost pl: eased last 2f: t.o* **25/1**

00 11 6 **Master Golfer (USA)**[19] [3417] 2-9-3 .... FrancisNorton 13 3
(B W Hills) *sn outpcd: t.o last 2f* **66/1**

12 nk **Beaumont (IRE)** 2-9-3 .... PhilipRobinson 15 2
(M A Jarvis) *chsd ldrs: sn rdn along: lost pl after 2f: sn wl bhd: t.o over 2f out* **6/1**

1m 10.93s (-2.74) **Going Correction** -0.475s/f (Firm) **12** Ran SP% **112.8**
Speed ratings (Par 96):99,98,98,97,95 94,94,92,91,74 66,66
CSF £23.64 TOTE £4.80: £2.00, £1.70, £2.00; EX 16.00.
Owner Norman Cheng **Bred** N Cheng **Trained** Kingsclere, Hants

FOCUS
The bare form of this maiden looks fair at best, but there were some interesting runners in behind the principals and it ought to produce some winners in time.

NOTEBOOK
Si Foo(USA) confirmed the promise he showed when runner-up on his debut at Wolverhampton. He was forced to work pretty hard to hold on and was not very convincing, appearing to struggle to let himself down on the quick ground under pressure. However, his trainer thinks he is a decent horse and said he has a race in mind for him in September. (op 9-2 tchd 7-2)
Callwood Dancer(IRE) improved on the modest level of form she showed when third over five furlongs here on her debut. She was just held and an ordinary race should come her way. (op 4-1)
Vitznau(IRE), a beaten favourite on his first two starts, probably showed improved form but was never really seen with a winning chance, having struggled to hold a position early before running on. He may benefit from a step up to seven furlongs. (op 8-1)
Marine Parade did not run badly but is beginning to look exposed. Connections may now be hoping he improves when stepped up in trip. (op 4-1 tchd 5-1)
Spinning Crystal(IRE) had every chance but weakened in the last furlong. She should find things easier when switched to handicap company. (tchd 66-1)
Sohraab ◆, a half-brother to the stable's multiple seven-furlong/mile winner Pango, caught the eye staying on nicely in the latter stages and this must rate as a pleasing introduction. He is open to improvement, and may well be up to winning a maiden, but in the longer term he could develop into a nice handicapper.
The Illies(IRE), who was well beaten behind Cav Okay on his debut at Newbury but showed plenty of ability in a reasonable Newmarket maiden next time, did not look particularly fancied on his return from a 85-day break and was well held. Judged on the form of his previous run, he might be worth taking a chance on when sent handicapping.
Doyles Lodge, a 4,200gns half-brother to a three-year-old winner in Spain, out of a mare placed over 12 to 15 furlongs, was keeping on quite nicely in the closing stages and should be capable of better in time.
Princess Zada Official explanation: jockey said filly lost its action
Beaumont(IRE), a 260,000euros brother to Tsaroxy, a dual seven-furlong/mile winner at two and three, and half-brother to high-class triple seven-furlong/mile scorer Killybegs, showed some early speed but quickly went backwards when coming under pressure a fair way out. He is surely better than this and may benefit from easier ground. Official explanation: trainer said colt was unsuited by the good to firm (firm in places) ground (op 9-2 tchd 4-1)

4001 PLAY AT VC CASINO.COM H'CAP 1m 2f 7y
6:30 (6:31) (Class 5) (0-75,75) 3-Y-0+ £3,238 (£963; £481; £240) Stalls Low

Form RPR

035 1 **William's Way**[12] [3647] 4-9-4 **65**.......................... RyanMoore 5 73
(I A Wood) *t.k.h: chsd ldrs: rdn over 3f out: chal over 1f out: chsd ldr ins fnl f: r.o wl to ld last strides* **8/1**

0104 2 nk **Della Salute**[10] [3703] 4-9-13 **74**.......................... LPKeniry 6 81
(Miss E C Lavelle) *taken down early: hld up bhd: gd hdwy 2f out: rdn to ld 1f out: hdd last strides* **9/2**[3]

6465 3 3 **Mexican Bob**[23] [3311] 3-8-8 **65**.......................... DaneO'Neill 7 66+
(Heather Dalton) *hld up in last: rn wd bnd over 5f out: hdwy on outer 3f out: ev ch over 1f out: wknd ins fnl f* **6/1**

5-20 4 ½ **Cape Diamond (IRE)**[93] [1291] 3-9-0 **71**.......................... AlanMunro 1 71
(W R Swinburn) *hld up bhd: effrt and rdn over 2f out: kpt on same pce ins f* **4/1**[2]

2452 5 2 **Ermine Grey**[23] [3305] 5-8-10 **60**.......................... JamesDoyle(3) 2 57
(A W Carroll) *hld up in tch: hdwy and rdn over 2f out: kpt on same pce* **7/2**[1]

6210 6 ¾ **Nuit Sombre (IRE)**[30] [3068] 6-9-11 **75**.......................... AdamKirby(3) 8 70
(J G M O'Shea) *led: clr 6f out: rdn over 2f out: hdd 1f out: wknd fnl f* **16/1**

0600 7 1¼ **Hayyani (IRE)**[10] [3704] 4-9-12 **73**..........................(be) RichardHughes 3 66
(K McAuliffe) *chsd ldr: rdn over 2f out: wknd over 1f out:* **10/1**

0 8 2½ **Black Chief (SWE)**[16] [3532] 5-9-9 **70**..........................(vt) FJohansson 9 58
(R A Kvisla) *slowly away: sn rcvrd and chsng ldng pair: rdn 4f out: wknd 2f out* **50/1**

45/3 9 1¾ **Tudor Bell (IRE)**[66] [1987] 5-9-13 **74**.......................... RichardMullen 4 59
(J G M O'Shea) *hld up in midfield: rdn and shortlived effrt wl over 2f out: no ch last 2f* **6/1**

2m 4.38s (-3.92) **Going Correction** -0.475s/f (Firm)
WFA 3 from 4yo+ 10lb **9** Ran SP% **117.0**
Speed ratings (Par 103):96,95,93,92,91 90,89,87,86
CSF £44.49 CT £234.90 TOTE £7.80: £2.00, £1.70, £2.50; EX 44.20.
Owner Lewis Caterers **Bred** Lewis Caterers **Trained** Upper Lambourn, Berks

FOCUS
Just a modest handicap, but they went a good pace throughout. Not strong form, with the winner an improver and the second running to the form of her course-and-distance win last month.
Ermine Grey Official explanation: jockey said gelding was unsuited by the good to firm (firm in places) ground
Nuit Sombre(IRE) Official explanation: jockey said gelding hung left closing stages

4002 VC CASINO.COM MAIDEN STKS 5f 10y
7:00 (7:00) (Class 4) 2-Y-0 £5,181 (£1,541; £770; £384) Stalls High

Form RPR

0 1 **Another True Story**[4] [3872] 2-9-3 .... RichardHughes 1 84+
(R Hannon) *chsd ldr: led and edgd lft over 1f out: sn in command: eased nr fin* **11/2**[3]

605 2 2½ **Candyland (IRE)**[18] [3457] 2-8-12 .... TedDurcan 2 70
(M R Channon) *led tl hdd over 1f out: btn and squeezed 1f out: no ch w wnr* **8/1**

6 3 3½ **Equuleus Pictor**[21] [3344] 2-9-3 .... FrancisNorton 4 62
(J L Spearing) *chsd ldrs: hmpd after 1f: sn hung lft: kpt on but no ch w ldrs after* **5/2**[2]

032 4 1¾ **Silver Hotspur**[30] [3070] 2-9-3 ....(b[1]) AlanMunro 6 56
(P W Chapple-Hyam) *chsd ldrs: rdn wl over 2f out: no prog and wl btn after* **13/8**[1]

5 1 **Ranavalona** 2-8-12 .... MartinDwyer 7 48
(A M Balding) *slowly away: rn green in last pl: kpt on and hung lft ins fnl f: n.d* **16/1**

00 6 1½ **Grimes Glory**[10] [3701] 2-9-3 .... RyanMoore 5 47
(R Hannon) *a last trio: wl outpcd after 2f* **20/1**

7 ½ **Time For Change (IRE)** 2-9-3 .... MichaelHills 3 45
(B W Hills) *slowly away: rn green in rr: edgd lft and sme hdwy over 1f out: n.d* **7/1**

59.25 secs (-1.85) **Going Correction** -0.475s/f (Firm) **7** Ran SP% **116.3**
Speed ratings (Par 96):95,91,85,82,81 78,77
CSF £48.84 TOTE £8.10: £2.70, £3.00; EX 60.50.
Owner Fairway Racing **Bred** Miss Alison Wiggins **Trained** East Everleigh, Wilts
■ Stewards' Enquiry : Richard Hughes one-day ban: careless riding (Aug 11)

FOCUS
Just the seven runners and an uncompetitive sprint maiden. There is better to come from the winner.

NOTEBOOK
Another True Story ◆ did not show a great deal on his debut at Sandown just four days earlier, but the run clearly sharpened him no end and, well backed, he ran out a ready winner. This was by no means a strong race, but he looks capable of continuing his progression. (op 12-1 tchd 5-1)

Candyland(IRE), returned to the minimum trip, got the run of the race out in front and can have no excuses - she was beaten when slightly squeezed up by the eventual winner. She may do better in nursery company. (op 7-1)
Equuleus Pictor, who attracted support on his debut at Bath but met with trouble in running and could not show his best, looked to be feeling this extra-quick ground from some way out and can do better. Official explanation: jockey said colt hung left-handed (tchd 11-4, 3-1 in places)
Silver Hotspur failed to run to form in first-time blinkers and does not seem to be progressing. (op 6-4 tchd 11-8 and 7-4, 15-8 in places)
Ranavalona, a 22,000gns half-sister to Sham Sharif, and to Sargon, a 10-furlong scorer who was also a multiple hurdles/chase winner, is out of a winner over ten furlongs who was a half-sister to 1000 Guineas runner-up Kerrera and high-class sprint juvenile Rock City. She looked in need of this experience and can do better over further in time.
Time For Change(IRE), a 38,000gns first foal of a half-sister to very smart Gothenburg, a multiple five- to eight-furlong winner, did not look happy on the fast ground and can do better. (op 8-1)

4003 VC CASINO.COM FILLIES' H'CAP — 6f
7:30 (7:30) (Class 4) (0-80,78) 3-Y-0+ — £6,477 (£1,927; £963; £481) Stalls High

Form — RPR
6310 **1** — **Rosapenna (IRE)**[25] 3217 4-10-0 **74** ... AlanMunro 7 — 83
(C F Wall) *hld up in midfield: hdwy on outer 2f out: chal 1f out: rdn ins fnl f: r.o wl to ld last 50 yds* **7/1**[3]
6344 **2** *nk* **Linda Green**[7] 3783 5-9-6 **66** ... TedDurcan 2 — 74
(M R Channon) *bhd: rdn over 3f out: hdwy on outer over 2f out: hrd rdn to ld ins fnl f: hdd and no ex last 50 yds* **5/1**[2]
4111 **3** *1 3/4* **Aahgowangowan (IRE)**[3] 3912 7-9-6 **71** 6ex ... (t) LiamJones(5) 3 — 74+
(M Dods) *t.k.h: pressed ldr tl led over 3f out: rdn and hung rt over 1f out: hdd ins fnl f: no ex* **7/4**[1]
-414 **4** *1/2* **Mimiteh (USA)**[38] 2818 3-9-13 **78** ... SebSanders 5 — 78
(R M Beckett) *hld up bhd: hdwy on inner over 2f out: ev ch and n.m.r 1f out: kpt on same pce* **9/1**
21- **5** *3* **Rochesis**[286] 5961 3-9-11 **76** ... JimmyFortune 11 — 67
(Miss K B Boutflower) *slowly away: sn rdn and racd in midfield: swtchd lft and effrt over 2f out: no imp over 1f out* **14/1**
2410 **6** *1 1/2* **Hello Roberto**[18] 3447 5-9-11 **74** ... (p) AmirQuinn(3) 6 — 62+
(R A Harris) *chsd ldrs: rdn over 2f out: ev ch over 1f out: sn wknd* **12/1**
00-0 **7** *1 3/4* **Speed Of Sound**[24] 3267 4-9-0 **60** ... LPKeniry 8 — 43
(A M Balding) *racd in midfield: effrt and rdn over 2f out: no imp over 1f out* **33/1**
0100 **8** *2* **Moon Bird**[5] 3845 4-8-10 **61** ... TravisBlock(5) 1 — 38
(C A Cyzer) *slowly away: outpcd in last: nvr on terms* **25/1**
0005 **9** *1 3/4* **Extremely Rare (IRE)**[14] 3593 5-9-0 **60** ... MickyFenton 9 — 31+
(M S Saunders) *led tl over 3f out: rdn 2f out: wkng whn hmpd over 1f out* **7/1**[3]
1350 **10** *1 1/2* **Bens Georgie (IRE)**[21] 3368 4-9-6 **66** ... RyanMoore 10 — 33+
(D K Ivory) *sn drvn along: chsd ldrs tl wknd over 2f out: no ch after* **7/1**[3]
1m 10.9s (-2.77) **Going Correction** -0.475s/f (Firm)
WFA 3 from 4yo+ 5lb — **10** Ran SP% **121.7**
Speed ratings (Par 102):99,98,96,95,91 89,87,84,82,80
CSF £43.90 CT £90.03 TOTE £7.90: £2.20, £1.70, £1.30; EX 38.70.
Owner Thoroughbred Farms Ltd **Bred** Epona Bloodstock Ltd **Trained** Newmarket, Suffolk
■ Stewards' Enquiry : Liam Jones one-day ban: careless riding (Aug 11)

FOCUS
Not a bad fillies' handicap, but it could have been better considering the top weight was rated 6lb below the ceiling of 80. The winning time was only just faster than the earlier juvenile maiden and the leaders may well have gone off too fast. The form makes sense, rated through the second and fourth.
Rochesis ◆ Official explanation: trainer said filly was subsequently found to be lame
Bens Georgie(IRE) Official explanation: jockey said filly was unsuited by the good to firm (firm in places) ground

4004 VC CASINO.COM MAIDEN STKS — 1m 67y
8:00 (8:00) (Class 5) 3-4-Y-0 — £3,238 (£963; £481; £240) Stalls High

Form — RPR
-325 **1** — **Danski**[23] 3301 3-9-3 78 ... RyanMoore 5 — 87+
(P J Makin) *chsd ldr tl rdn to ld over 3f out: clr 1f out: r.o strly: easily* **6/4**[1]
3330 **2** *7* **Montpellier (IRE)**[19] 3419 3-9-3 84 ... RichardMullen 1 — 71
(E A L Dunlop) *w.w in tch: hdwy on outer over 3f out: rdn to chse wnr over 2f out: wl outpcd by wnr over 1f out* **10/3**[2]
0002 **3** *3/4* **Esteem**[20] 3387 3-9-3 73 ... AlanMunro 3 — 69
(W Jarvis) *t.k.h: chsd ldrs: rdn wl over 3f out: kpt on same pce and no ch w ldrs after: wnt 3rd ins fnl f* **7/1**
5 **4** *1 1/4* **Dixieland Boy (IRE)**[17] 3488 3-9-0 ... AmirQuinn(3) 2 — 66
(P J Makin) *w.w in rr: hung lft and rn wd bnd over 5f out: hdwy but stl hanging lft over 3f out: ev ch of 3rd fnl f:no ex* **50/1**
5 *2* **Pagano (IRE)** 3-9-3 ... SebSanders 9 — 62+
(W R Swinburn) *sn rdn along in rr: wl outpcd over 4f out: styd on fnl f: nvr on terms* **14/1**
6 *1/2* **Grand Silence (IRE)** 3-9-3 ... TedDurcan 13 — 60+
(W R Swinburn) *bhd: pushed along over 6f out: rdn and wl outpcd over 4f out: kpt on past btn horses ins fnl f: nvr on terms* **12/1**
0 **7** *nk* **Squiffy**[7] 3794 3-9-3 ... LPKeniry 14 — 60
(P D Cundell) *slowly away: racd in last: lost tch wl over 4f out: kpt on past btn horses wl ins fnl f: nvr nrr* **33/1**
5-0 **8** *1/2* **Sessile (USA)**[52] 2406 3-8-12 ... JimmyFortune 11 — 54
(J H M Gosden) *led tl hdd over 3f out: chsd wnr tl over 2f out: sn wknd* **11/2**[3]
0- **9** *nk* **Grand Court (IRE)**[300] 5688 3-8-9 ... JamesDoyle(3) 7 — 53?
(A W Carroll) *chsd ldrs tl rdn wl over 3f out: sn struggling: no ch whn hung lft over 1f out* **66/1**
0 **10** *shd* **Marina Gamba (IRE)**[54] 2366 3-8-12 ... MartinDwyer 6 — 53
(E A L Dunlop) *t.k.h: hld up in tch: rdn and lost pl 4f out: no ch after* **25/1**
0 **11** *shd* **Star Berry**[12] 3647 3-8-5 ... KMay(7) 4 — 52
(B J Meehan) *hld up in rr: rdn over 4f out: sn no ch* **66/1**
0- **12** *1* **True Ruby**[248] 6424 3-8-12 ... PatDobbs 8 — 50
(S Kirk) *chsd ldrs: rdn 4f out: sn struggling and no ch after* **33/1**
1m 41.6s (-4.00) **Going Correction** -0.475s/f (Firm) — **12** Ran SP% **120.0**
Speed ratings (Par 103):101,94,93,92,90 89,89,88,88,88 88,87
CSF £6.02 TOTE £2.30: £1.10, £1.70, £2.50; EX 9.80.
Owner Camamile Hessert Scott Partnership **Bred** Charlock Farm Stud **Trained** Ogbourne Maisey, Wilts

FOCUS
An ordinary maiden and it would probably be folly to suggest the runner-up ran to his official mark of 84. An improved effort from the winner, and the race has been rated through the third.
Marina Gamba(IRE) Official explanation: jockey said filly was unsuited by the good to firm (firm in places) ground
Star Berry Official explanation: jockey said filly hung left-handed

4005 SLOUGH TRADING ESTATES H'CAP — 1m 3f 135y
8:30 (8:30) (Class 5) (0-70,75) 3-Y-0+ — £3,238 (£963; £481; £240) Stalls Low

Form — RPR
06-0 **1** — **Sendinpost**[170] 373 3-8-3 **56** ... RichardThomas 3 — 66+
(S C Williams) *hld up in midfield: hdwy 4f out: rdn and edgd lft over 2f out: sn chsng ldr: carried lft fnl f: led last 100 yds:readily* **10/1**
6011 **2** *hd* **Kapellmeister (IRE)**[6] 3819 3-9-8 **75** 6ex ... (p) MickyFenton 13 — 85
(M S Saunders) *led: jnd and rdn along over 5f out: battled on gamely:hung lft fnl f: hdd last 100 yds: no ex* **9/4**[1]
5-21 **3** *2 1/2* **Looks The Business (IRE)**[10] 3232 5-9-0 **62** ... PJBenson(7) 7 — 68
(W G M Turner) *w.w in tch: hdwy over 3f out: rdn over 2f out: kpt on same pce u.p* **10/1**
U202 **4** *shd* **Hatch A Plan (IRE)**[10] 3704 5-9-4 **64** ... TravisBlock(5) 12 — 70
(Mrs A J Hamilton-Fairley) *hld up bhd: gd hdwy on outer over 3f out: bmpd over 2f out: sn ev ch: no ex ins fnl f* **9/1**[3]
4622 **5** *1* **Meelup (IRE)**[13] 3616 6-9-2 **60** ... (p) AmirQuinn(3) 15 — 64
(P G Murphy) *chsd ldr for 2f: chsd ldrs after: rdn 3f out: no prog u.p fr over 1f out* **9/1**[3]
3044 **6** *3/4* **Ariodante**[13] 3628 4-9-3 **63** ... StephenDonohoe(5) 4 — 66
(J M P Eustace) *chsd ldrs: effrt u.p on outer over 2f out: kpt on but nt pce to rch ldrs* **12/1**
0000 **7** *hd* **Scottish River (USA)**[7] 3798 7-9-11 **66** ... HayleyTurner 1 — 69
(M D I Usher) *stdd s: hld up in rr: hdwy on outer over 2f out: no hdwy u.p fnl f* **20/1**
0463 **8** *shd* **Eastborough (IRE)**[7] 3798 7-9-10 **65** ... RyanMoore 16 — 68
(B G Powell) *slowly away: wl bhd: rdn 2f out: styd on ins fnl f: nrst fin* **10/1**
4114 **9** *1 1/4* **Bob's Your Uncle**[18] 3439 3-8-11 **64** ... AlanMunro 10 — 65
(J G Portman) *bhd whn hmpd bnd over 6f out: rdn over 4f out: nvr trbld ldrs* **7/1**[2]
50-4 **10** *shd* **Overlook**[68] 1942 3-8-4 **60** ... NeilChalmers(3) 8 — 62+
(A M Balding) *w.w in rr: effrt and rdn 4f out: nt pce to trble ldrs: no ch whn hmpd 1f out* **33/1**
0505 **11** *1 1/2* **Cantrip**[19] 3412 6-8-11 **52** ... SebSanders 6 — 50
(Miss B Sanders) *chsd ldrs rdn and ev ch over 2f out: wknd qckly over 1f out* **12/1**
3503 **12** *7* **Double Spectre (IRE)**[25] 3209 4-9-9 **64** ... VinceSlattery 14 — 51
(Jean-Rene Auvray) *hld up: hmpd and lost pl bnd over 6f out: no ch after* **20/1**
00-0 **13** *15* **Proud Scholar (USA)**[18] 3440 4-9-3 **58** ... (tp) FJohansson 11 — 21
(R A Kvisla) *chsd ldrs: losing pl whn slipped bnd over 6f out: rdn over 4f out: sn wl bhd: t.o* **66/1**
000 **14** *6* **Wilderness Bay (IRE)**[9] 3731 4-9-4 **59** ... GeorgeBaker 2 — 12
(M R Bosley) *prom: chsd ldr after 2f: jnd ldr over 5f out tl over 3f out: sn rdn and lost pl: no ch last 2f: t.o* **66/1**
2m 24.6s (-5.50) **Going Correction** -0.475s/f (Firm)
WFA 3 from 4yo+ 12lb — **14** Ran SP% **121.4**
Speed ratings (Par 103):99,98,97,97,96 95,95,95,94,94 93,89,79,75
CSF £31.30 CT £242.38 TOTE £11.50: £3.90, £1.80, £2.80; EX 44.30 Place 6 £105.38, Place 5 £51.85.
Owner The Tipsy Fountain Partnership **Bred** K G Powter **Trained** Newmarket, Suffolk

FOCUS
A modest handicap, but they went a strong pace throughout and first two home look capable of rating higher. Rated through the third, the form looks solid and should prove reliable.
Sendinpost Official explanation: trainer said, regarding the improved form shown, the filly was returning from a long break and had benefited from today's step up in trip and drop in class
Wilderness Bay(IRE) Official explanation: jockey said filly ran too free
T/Plt: £131.30 to a £1 stake. Pool: £87,407.00. 485.60 winning tickets. T/Qpdt: £28.20 to a £1 stake. Pool: £6,077.80. 159.10 winning tickets. SP

3822 YARMOUTH (L-H)
Monday, July 31

OFFICIAL GOING: Firm
Wind: Fresh, across Weather: Cloudy

4006 FRONTLINE COMPLETE BATHROOM NOVICE FILLIES' AUCTION STKS — 5f 43y
2:30 (2:30) (Class 6) 2-Y-0 — £2,331 (£693; £346; £173) Stalls High

Form — RPR
41 **1** — **Frontline In Focus (IRE)**[21] 3358 2-8-10 ... PatCosgrave 1 — 85
(K R Burke) *a.p: chsd ldr 1/2-way: shkn up to ld over 1f out: rdn out* **5/4**[1]
6233 **2** *1* **Cosmopolitan Lady**[18] 3430 2-8-10 ... ChrisCatlin 3 — 81
(D M Simcock) *led: rdn and hdd over 1f out: styd on same pce* **3/1**[3]
120 **3** *1 1/2* **Marmaida (IRE)**[30] 3084 2-9-0 ... PaulDoe 5 — 80
(W J Knight) *racd keenly: trckd ldr to 1/2-way: rdn over 1f out: styd on same pce* **2/1**[2]
0323 **4** *3* **Hester Brook (IRE)**[27] 3160 2-8-1 ... DominicFox(3) 4 — 59
(J G M O'Shea) *dwlt: hdwy 1/2-way: rdn and wknd over 1f out* **20/1**
0042 **5** *1 3/4* **Caj (IRE)**[23] 3300 2-8-7 ... EddieAhern 2 — 56
(M Quinn) *chsd ldrs over 3f* **28/1**
63.07 secs (0.27) **Going Correction** 0.0s/f (Good) — **5** Ran SP% **111.0**
Speed ratings (Par 89):97,95,93,88,85
CSF £5.46 TOTE £2.30: £1.20, £1.80; EX 7.00.
Owner Frontline Bathrooms **Bred** Christan Syndicate **Trained** Middleham Moor, N Yorks

FOCUS
A moderate event of its type, confined to fillies, and the form is fair rated through the runner-up.

NOTEBOOK
Frontline In Focus(IRE), owned by the race sponsors, knuckled down when asked to win her race and followed up her Ripon maiden success in ready fashion. She is clearly progressing, enjoys a quick surface, and looks best kept to this trip for the short term. (op 13-8)
Cosmopolitan Lady had her chance, only to again find one too good. While she is looking exposed now, she can be considered a little unlucky not to have opened her account yet. Official explanation: jockey said filly hung left at start (op 7-2 tchd 4-1)
Marmaida(IRE), markedly down in class, ultimately paid for running freely through the early parts and was well held under top weight. She is probably better off reverting to a sixth furlong on this evidence. (op 13-8)
Hester Brook(IRE) was unable to race up with the pace as a result of being sluggish from the gates and never seriously figured. (op 18-1)
Caj(IRE), whose stable won this last term with a progressive filly, failed to raise her game for this step up in grade and was always chasing shadows. (op 25-1)

The Form Book, Raceform Ltd, Compton, RG20 6NL

4007 B.I.T.C. (S) STKS 6f 3y
3:00 (3:00) (Class 6) 2-Y-O **£2,266** (£674; £337; £168) **Stalls** High

Form RPR
5 **1** **Distant Flash**[6] [3822] 2-8-6 .... EddieAhern 6 54
(M J Wallace) *prom: reminders over 4f out: rdn to ld and hung lft wl ins fnl f: r.o* **4/1**[3]
2006 **2** ½ **Emergency Services**[13] [3613] 2-8-11 ....(p) JimmyQuinn 7 58
(Tom Dascombe) *chsd ldrs: outpcd over 4f out: hdwy over 1f out: r.o* **22/1**
2042 **3** *nk* **Meru Camp (IRE)**[7] [3801] 2-8-11 .... JohnEgan 1 57
(P Winkworth) *led to 1/2-way: rdn to ld and hung rt over 1f out: hdd wl ins fnl f* **9/2**
02 **4** 1½ **Soffooh (USA)**[5] [3830] 2-8-11 .... TonyCulhane 3 52
(M R Channon) *chsd ldr tl led 1/2-way: rdn and hdd over 1f out: no ex ins fnl f* **9/4**[1]
1202 **5** 2½ **Peggys Flower**[13] [3624] 2-8-11 ....(p) DO'Donohoe 2 45
(N A Callaghan) *plld hrd and prom: jnd ldr 1/2-way: rdn and nt clr run over 1f out: wknd ins fnl f* **5/2**[2]
0632 **6** 1¼ **Loch Clutha (IRE)**[9] [3746] 2-8-6 ....(p) ChrisCatlin 4 36
(K R Burke) *chsd ldrs: rdn over 1f out: sn wknd* **10/1**

1m 15.56s (1.86) **Going Correction** 0.0s/f (Good) **6** Ran SP% **111.0**
Speed ratings (Par 92):87,86,85,83,80 78
CSF £69.34 TOTE £4.50: £1.50, £7.40; EX 63.50.The winner was sold to Mr D Hague for 8,800gns. Meru Camp was the subject of a friendly claim. Soffooh was claimed by W. J. Musson for £6,000.
Owner Clive Dennett **Bred** C Dennett **Trained** Newmarket, Suffolk

FOCUS
An average seller, in which the winner did not need to run to his previous form.

NOTEBOOK
Distant Flash, last of five in a maiden at this venue six days previously, showed the benefit of that experience and got off the mark at the second time of asking. The drop to this class was clearly of benefit, but she saw out the extra furlong well and remains open to further improvement, so deserves her place back at a higher level now. (op 5-2)
Emergency Services, equipped with first-time cheekpieces, struggled to go the early pace and was doing all of his best work towards the finish. The return to this more conventional track was to his liking and, on this evidence, he is well worth another chance back over seven furlongs in this grade. (tchd 25-1)
Meru Camp(IRE) helped force the early pace and ran close to his recent level in defeat. His turn in this grade does not look too far off. Official explanation: jockey said colt hung right (op 11-2)
Soffooh(USA), down in class, had his chance yet did not look at all straightforward when push came to shove. (op 11-4)
Peggys Flower was beaten a fair way out and, even though she has disappointed in the past, this was a very poor effort by her own standards. (tchd 3-1)

4008 VISITNORFOLK.CO.UK MAIDEN AUCTION STKS 7f 3y
3:30 (3:31) (Class 6) 2-Y-O **£2,331** (£693; £346; £173) **Stalls** High

Form RPR
033 **1** **Sweet Lilly**[11] [3663] 2-8-10 .... ChrisCatlin 4 70
(M R Channon) *disp ld over 2f: chsd ldr tl led over 2f out: hung rt and swished tail ins fnl f: hld on reluctantly* **10/11**[1]
00 **2** *shd* **Persian Fox (IRE)**[79] [1688] 2-9-1 .... DO'Donohoe 2 74
(G A Huffer) *chsd ldrs: outpcd 2f out: rallied fnl f: r.o* **7/2**[2]
0 **3** 3 **Glorious Prince (IRE)**[31] [3031] 2-9-1 .... EddieAhern 5 67
(M G Quinlan) *disp ld tl led over 4f out: rdn and hdd over 2f out: no ex fnl f* **7/1**
54 **4** 6 **Three No Trumps**[31] [3031] 2-8-4 .... DerekMcGaffin 3 40
(D Morris) *s.s: hld up: rdn and wknd over 1f out* **16/1**
5 2 **Lay The Cash (USA)** 2-8-9 .... JohnEgan 1 40
(J S Moore) *chsd ldrs: j. path and outpcd over 5f out: hung lft and wknd over 2f out* **5/1**[3]
5 **6** 8 **Hocinail (FR)**[31] [3031] 2-9-1 .... TonyCulhane 6 25
(P Winkworth) *prom over 4f* **28/1**

1m 27.48s (0.88) **Going Correction** 0.0s/f (Good) **6** Ran SP% **113.1**
Speed ratings (Par 92):94,93,90,83,81 72
CSF £4.44 TOTE £1.60: £1.10, £2.20; EX 5.90.
Owner Jaber Abdullah **Bred** Red House Stud **Trained** West Ilsley, Berks

FOCUS
A modest juvenile maiden, which saw the first two come clear, and the form is not easy to assess.

NOTEBOOK
Sweet Lilly, unsuited by the undulations when third at Epsom last time, was rightly given a much more positive ride by Catlin on this return to a more conventional track and just did enough to get off the mark at the fourth attempt. She does have a high head carriage, and is clearly tricky, but probably has more to offer all the same. (op 5-6 tchd Evens)
Persian Fox(IRE), returning from a 79-day break, was flying at the finish and only just failed. This was by far his best effort to date, he looks to have improved for the recent time off, and now qualifies for nurseries. (tchd 3-1)
Glorious Prince(IRE) showed up well enough under a positive ride, but was firmly put in his place by the first two when it mattered. He probably needs more time and it would be a big surprise if we have seen the best of him to date. (op 12-1)
Three No Trumps failed to confirm her Folkestone form with the third horse and never threatened.
Lay The Cash(USA), related to numerous winners at around this trip, ran distinctly green through the early parts and ought to be a lot sharper with this experience under his belt. Official explanation: jockey said colt jumped the crossing at 5f pole and ran green (op 11-2)

4009 MARTIN FOULGER MEMORIAL H'CAP 7f 3y
4:00 (4:00) (Class 5) (0-70,67) 3-Y-O+ **£3,627** (£1,079; £539; £269) **Stalls** High

Form RPR
2223 **1** **Border Artist**[11] [3664] 7-9-2 **55** .... JimmyQuinn 7 63
(J Pearce) *hld up: racd keenly: hdwy over 1f out: led and edgd ins fnl f: r.o* **4/1**[3]
0656 **2** 1 **Crimson Flame (IRE)**[9] [3725] 3-9-0 **60** .... TonyCulhane 6 63
(M R Channon) *hld up: hdwy over 1f out: r.o* **8/1**
0541 **3** *nk* **Linda's Colin (IRE)**[10] [3705] 4-9-7 **67** .... TolleyDean(7) 9 72
(R A Harris) *s.i.s: sn prom: rdn and hung lft fr over 1f out: ev ch ins fnl f: styd on same pce* **11/4**[1]
-603 **4** 1 **Ciccone**[30] [3072] 3-9-4 **64** .... PaulDoe 3 65+
(W Jarvis) *dwlt: hdwy over 5f out: rdn and ev ch whn carried lft over 1f out: styng on same pce whn nt clr run nr fin* **8/1**
0000 **5** *nk* **Wodhill Be**[58] [2248] 6-8-9 **40** oh7 .... DerekMcGaffin 4 50
(D Morris) *hld up: hdwy over 1f out: styd on* **50/1**
0000 **6** 1¼ **Warden Warren**[6] [3827] 8-8-6 **50** ....(b) MarcHalford(5) 1 48
(Mrs C A Dunnett) *led: rdn and hung lft over 1f out: hdd and no ex ins fnl f* **20/1**
4431 **7** ½ **Life's A Whirl**[6] [3828] 4-9-7 **60** 6ex ....(p) JohnEgan 10 57
(Mrs C A Dunnett) *w ldr tl rdn over 2f out: styng on same pce whn hmpd 1f out* **7/2**[2]
2005 **8** 2 **Poker Player (IRE)**[23] [3304] 4-9-12 **65** .... EddieAhern 5 57
(G C Bravery) *chsd ldrs: rdn over 2f out: wknd over 1f out* **13/2**
0000 **9** 4 **Royal Sailor (IRE)**[2] [3933] 4-8-9 **48** .... MichaelTebbutt 2 29
(J Ryan) *hld up: rdn over 2f out: sn wknd* **50/1**

1m 26.52s (-0.08) **Going Correction** 0.0s/f (Good)
WFA 3 from 4yo+ 7lb **9** Ran SP% **113.1**
Speed ratings (Par 103):100,98,98,97,97 95,95,92,88
CSF £34.23 CT £100.08 TOTE £4.60: £1.30, £2.30, £1.60; EX 31.10 Trifecta £177.80 Pool: £991.91 - 3.96 winning tickets..
Owner Jeff Pearce **Bred** Chippenham Lodge Stud Ltd **Trained** Newmarket, Suffolk
■ Stewards' Enquiry : Tolley Dean five-day ban: careless riding (Aug 11-15)

FOCUS
A modest handicap and the form looks sound enough, with the winner, third and fifth running to form.
Life's A Whirl Official explanation: jockey said filly suffered interference

4010 AVENUES FILLIES' H'CAP 1m 2f 21y
4:30 (4:30) (Class 5) (0-70,68) 3-Y-O+ **£3,497** (£1,040; £520; £259) **Stalls** Low

Form RPR
1001 **1** **Gambling Spirit**[18] [3440] 4-10-0 **66** .... FergusSweeney 4 80+
(H Candy) *chsd ldr 8f out: led over 2f out: rdn clr over 1f out* **11/4**[1]
1600 **2** 1¾ **Tata Naka**[13] [3627] 6-9-3 **55** .... JohnEgan 5 66
(Mrs C A Dunnett) *hld up: hdwy over 2f out: nt rch wnr* **6/1**[3]
0142 **3** 4 **Bavarica**[6] [3828] 4-9-1 **60** .... SladeO'Hara(7) 1 63
(Miss J Feilden) *hld up: hdwy over 3f out: rdn over 1f out: no ex* **5/1**[2]
2013 **4** 5 **Al Rayanah**[6] [3828] 3-9-1 **63** .... TonyCulhane 3 57
(G Prodromou) *prom: rdn over 2f out: wknd over 1f out* **7/1**
2350 **5** 5 **Fiore Di Bosco (IRE)**[13] [3610] 5-8-12 **50** .... PhillipMakin 6 34
(T D Barron) *s.s: hld up: effrt over 2f out: hung lft and wknd over 1f out* **7/1**
0-00 **6** 18 **River Mist Image (USA)**[10] [3706] 4-9-12 **64** ....(v[1]) OscarUrbina 7 14
(J R Fanshawe) *s.i.s: sn rcvrd to ld: rdn and hdd over 2f out: sn wknd* **22/1**
523 **7** 2 **Beldon Hill (USA)**[20] [3376] 3-9-6 **68** .... KerrinMcEvoy 2 14
(C E Brittain) *led early: chsd ldrs: rdn over 3f out: sn wknd* **11/4**[1]

2m 6.93s (-1.17) **Going Correction** -0.10s/f (Good)
WFA 3 from 4yo+ 10lb **7** Ran SP% **113.6**
Speed ratings (Par 100):100,98,95,91,87 73,71
CSF £19.52 TOTE £3.80: £2.00, £3.30; EX 25.10.
Owner Simon Broke And Partners **Bred** Beech Park Bloodstock Ltd **Trained** Kingston Warren, Oxon

FOCUS
A modest handicap, run at a sound pace, and the first two came clear. It has been rated around the third.
Beldon Hill(USA) Official explanation: jockey said filly never travelled, lost her action and was unsuited by the firm ground

4011 NORFOLK NELSON MUSEUM H'CAP 2m
5:00 (5:00) (Class 6) (0-55,55) 4-Y-O+ **£2,590** (£770; £385; £192) **Stalls** High

Form RPR
0602 **1** **Lysander's Quest (IRE)**[18] [3437] 8-8-7 **40** .... FergusSweeney 9 51
(R Ingram) *hld up: hdwy 6f out: led over 1f out: rdn out* **6/1**
0000 **2** 2½ **Jadeeron**[25] [3232] 7-8-8 **41** ....(p) ChrisCatlin 7 49
(Miss D A McHale) *hld up: hdwy 6f out: rdn over 2f out: chsd wnr over 1f out: stayed on* **22/1**
3604 **3** 1½ **Lenwade**[7] [3803] 5-8-9 **42** .... EddieAhern 5 48
(G G Margarson) *hld up: hdwy and hung lft over 1f out: nt rch ldrs* **11/2**[3]
1610 **4** 2½ **Lefonic**[13] [3628] 4-9-8 **55** .... OscarUrbina 8 58
(G C H Chung) *chsd ldrs: led 7f out: rdn and hdd over 1f out: wknd ins fnl f* **4/1**[1]
404- **5** 1½ **Rajayoga**[357] [3809] 5-8-12 **52** .... PatrickHills(7) 10 53
(M H Tompkins) *hld up: hdwy over 2f out: nt trble ldrs* **6/1**
2066 **6** 6 **Redspin (IRE)**[13] [3628] 6-8-7 **40** .... JimmyQuinn 6 34
(J S Moore) *prom over 11f* **13/2**
3230 **7** *nk* **Iamback**[7] [3803] 6-8-12 **45** ....(t) BrianReilly 11 39
(Miss D A McHale) *hld up: hdwy 10f out: chsd ldr 6f out: rdn and wknd over 2f out* **20/1**
0042 **8** ¾ **Trials 'n Tribs**[24] [3269] 4-8-13 **46** .... TonyCulhane 4 39
(C A Cyzer) *hld up: rdn 5f out: sme hdwy over 2f out: sn wknd* **5/1**[2]
0-00 **9** ½ **Liameliss**[7] [3803] 4-8-9 **45** ....(v[1]) DeanCorby(3) 1 37
(M A Allen) *chsd ldr 10f: wknd over 4f out* **66/1**
000- **10** 19 **Emma Lilley (USA)**[222] [6652] 4-8-1 **37** .... DominicFox(3) 3 6
(J G M O'Shea) *chsd ldrs: rdn 1/2-way: wknd 5f out* **50/1**
050- **11** 31 **Given A Chance**[8] [2338] 5-9-0 **47** .... JohnEgan 2 —
(T J Pitt) *led 9f: wknd and eased over 4f out* **8/1**

3m 28.58s (-2.83) **Going Correction** -0.10s/f (Good) **11** Ran SP% **117.6**
Speed ratings (Par 101):103,101,101,99,99 96,95,95,95,85 70
CSF £133.24 CT £771.27 TOTE £8.10: £2.00, £6.30, £2.50; EX 119.40 TRIFECTA Not won. Place 6 £97.65, Place 5 £62.40.
Owner Mrs E N Nield **Bred** J M Ryan **Trained** Epsom, Surrey

FOCUS
A very weak handicap, run at a solid pace, and the field came home fairly strung out. The form looks decent for the grade.
T/Plt: £113.50 to a £1 stake. Pool: £64,782.85. 416.60 winning tickets. T/Qpdt: £11.40 to a £1 stake. Pool: £4,616.30. 298.20 winning tickets. CR

4012 - 4015a (Foreign Racing) - See Raceform Interactive

3787 BEVERLEY (R-H)
Tuesday, August 1

OFFICIAL GOING: Good changing to good to soft after race 3 (2.55) and to soft after race 6 (4.40)
Monsoon-like rain quickly changed the going from good at the start of the day to soft and the last race went ahead after a crossing inspection.
Wind: Moderate, half against Weather: Persistent heavy showers

4016 NATIONAL FESTIVAL CIRCUS (S) H'CAP 1m 4f 16y
1:50 (1:51) (Class 6) (0-55,47) 3-Y-O **£3,238** (£963; £481; £240) **Stalls** High

Form RPR
0260 **1** **Alwaysforsale (IRE)**[15] [3592] 3-9-1 **40** .... LPKeniry 5 47
(J S Moore) *in tch: stdy hdwy over 3f out: led over 1f out: edgd rt ins last: styd on* **9/2**[2]

4500 **2** 1 ½ **El Dee (IRE)**[32] [2539] 3-8-13 **41** .... DanielTudhope(3) 1 46
(D Carroll) *bhd: hdwy over 4f out: led over 2f out: hdd over 1f out: kpt on same pce* **9/1**

-000 **3** 1 **The Preacher**[49] [2529] 3-9-8 **47** .... RobertWinston 7 50
(J G Given) *hld up: hdwy on outer over 2f out: kpt on same pce fnl f* **10/1**

0034 **4** 3 ½ **Wensleydale Star**[8] [3785] 3-8-8 **40** .... DeanHeslop(7) 11 38
(T D Barron) *sn trcking ldrs: n.m.r and swtchd outside over 1f out: no imp* **5/2**[1]

5023 **5** 1 ½ **Simplified**[7] [3824] 3-9-6 **45** .... JimmyQuinn 10 40
(J Pearce) *trckd ldrs: chal over 2f out: wknd fnl f* **11/2**[3]

0-00 **6** 6 **Fairytale Of York (IRE)**[24] [3303] 3-8-5 **37** .... KellyHarrison(7) 4 23
(D Carroll) *hdwy on outer to trck ldrs 7f out: wknd over 1f out* **100/1**

0036 **7** 1 ¼ **Ebony Lady**[22] [3357] 3-8-11 **36** .... DeanMcKeown 3 20
(R M Whitaker) *restless in stalls: trckd ldrs: led 3f out: sn hdd: wknd over 1f out* **7/1**

0000 **8** ¾ **Tiptoeing**[7] [3823] 3-9-5 **47** .... SaleemGolam(3) 8 30
(M H Tompkins) *hld up in rr: hrd drvn over 3f out: nvr nr ldrs* **12/1**

050- **9** 3 **Plough Maite**[16] [3402] 3-9-8 **47** .... (b[1]) DaleGibson 6 25
(D E Cantillon) *bhd: pushed along 7f out: nvr on terms* **14/1**

0506 **10** 2 ½ **Cortina**[6] [3836] 3-8-10 **35** .... (t) DerekMcGaffin 2 9
(J Jay) *mid-div: drvn 4f out: nvr a factor* **40/1**

0-00 **11** 22 **Prince Richard**[22] [3357] 3-8-10 **40** .... (p) MarkLawson(5) 12 —
(B Smart) *t.k.h: led tl 3f out: sn lost pl: bhd and eased fnl f* **33/1**

0006 **12** 23 **Frank Cartwright (IRE)**[72] [1868] 3-9-1 **40** .... FrancisNorton 9 —
(A Berry) *chsd ldrs: lost pl over 4f out: t.o 2f out: virtually p.u* **100/1**

2m 47.66s (7.45) **Going Correction** +0.55s/f (Yiel) 12 Ran SP% **115.4**
Speed ratings (Par 98):97,96,95,93,92 88,87,86,84,83 68,53
CSF £42.80 CT £383.03 TOTE £6.80: £2.00, £3.50, £3.30; EX 89.10.The winner was bought in for 7,000gns. The Preacher (no.3) was claimed by J. S. Wainwright for £6,000.
Owner John Wells **Bred** John Williams **Trained** Upper Lambourn, Berks
■ Stewards' Enquiry : L P Keniry two-day ban: careless riding (Aug 12-13)

FOCUS
A bad race even by selling race standards, run at a steady pace for the first mile. The winner did not need to improve and the runner-up ran to form.

4017 MALCOLM KIRK LIFETIME IN RACING MAIDEN AUCTION FILLIES' STKS 5f
2:20 (2:20) (Class 5) 2-Y-O **£3,886** (£1,156; £577; £288) **Stalls** High

Form RPR

00 **1** **Inflagranti**[39] [2816] 2-8-11 .... TPQueally 10 69
(J G Portman) *chsd ldrs: edgd lft over 1f out: kpt on to ld last 75yds: jst hld on* **14/1**

3 **2** hd **Gap Princess (IRE)**[59] [2241] 2-8-7 .... TonyHamilton 4 64
(R A Fahey) *sn outpcd and in rr: hdwy 2f out: styd on wl last 75yds: jst hld* **7/2**[2]

33 **3** ¾ **Wicked Wilma (IRE)**[17] [3521] 2-8-4 .... PaulQuinn 5 59
(A Berry) *chsd ldrs: wandered and led last 100yds: sn hdd and no ex* **8/1**

2506 **4** 1 ½ **The Italian Job**[10] [3720] 2-8-7 .... DavidAllan 8 56
(T D Easterby) *chsd ldr: led 2f out: wknd and hdd 100yds out* **5/1**

645 **5** 3 **Mickleberry (IRE)**[22] [3358] 2-8-7 .... GrahamGibbons 3 45+
(J D Bethell) *hld up in mid-div: hmpd over 2f out: no threat after* **4/1**[3]

56 **6** 1 ¼ **Namarian (IRE)**[24] [3307] 2-8-6 .... DuranFentiman(5) 7 45
(T D Easterby) *dwlt: sn drvn along in rr: sme hdwy fnl 2f: nvr on terms* **14/1**

00 **7** shd **Lost Inheritance**[11] [3713] 2-8-7 .... PaulMulrennan 6 41
(P T Midgley) *w ldrs: rdn and hung lft over 2f out: wknd over 1f out* **100/1**

8 1 ½ **Dazzling Olivia (IRE)** 2-8-4 .... DaleGibson 1 32
(R A Fahey) *dwlt: swtchd rt after s: in rr tl sme hdwy fnl 2f: nvr a factor* **20/1**

43 **9** 2 ½ **Fly So Free (IRE)**[94] [1295] 2-8-11 .... AdrianTNicholls 9 30+
(D Nicholls) *led tl 2f out: wknd over 1f out: eased* **11/4**[1]

67.85 secs (3.85) **Going Correction** +0.425s/f (Yiel) 9 Ran SP% **115.8**
Speed ratings (Par 91):86,85,84,82,77 75,75,72,68
CSF £62.82 TOTE £22.00: £4.40, £1.20, £2.30; EX 89.70.
Owner Berkeley Racing **Bred** Snailwell Stud Co Ltd **Trained** Compton, Berks

FOCUS
A weak event and a slow time. The leaders seemed to be treading water in the closing stages.

NOTEBOOK
Inflagranti, who is not very big, was reported to have suffered from sore shins after her debut and needed her second outing. The rain had got into the ground and she justified the morning support with a narrow victory. Official explanation: trainer's rep said, regarding the apparent improvement in form, filly had possibly needed the run at Goodwood last time, having suffered from sore shins following her racecourse debut (op 16-1)
Gap Princess(IRE) struggled to keep up. With the leaders coming back to her, in the end she was just held. She will be much happier over six. (op 6-1)
Wicked Wilma(IRE), much better suited by this track than Chester, proved very hard to keep straight and, after showing ahead for a few strides inside the last, she missed out in the dash to the line. (op 10-1)
The Italian Job showed bags of toe and looked to have taken a winning lead, but the uphill track and deteriorating ground in the end found her out. She looks a likely sort for a five-furlong nursery. (op 4-1)
Mickleberry(IRE), drawn on the outer, was quite keen and couldn't pick up again after being left short of room at halfway. This is best overlooked. Official explanation: jockey said filly was unsuited by the good ground (tchd 9-2)
Namarian(IRE), having her third outing, was run off her feet until staying on late in the day. She will appreciate seven furlongs in nursery company.
Fly So Free(IRE), quite keen, took them along, but fell in a heap and in the end completed in her own time. The ground had turned against this speedy sort. Official explanation: jockey said filly was unsuited by the good ground (op 9-4)

4018 EUROPEAN BREEDERS FUND MAIDEN STKS 7f 100y
2:55 (2:58) (Class 5) 2-Y-O **£4,533** (£1,348; £674; £336) **Stalls** High

Form RPR

1 **Weld Il Balad (IRE)** 2-9-3 .... J-PGuillambert 3 72
(M Johnston) *chsd ldrs: effrt 3f out: styd on to ld last 50yds* **6/1**[3]

00 **2** nk **Security Tiger (IRE)**[11] [3707] 2-8-12 .... FrancisNorton 10 66
(M R Channon) *led: edgd lft over 2f out: hdd and no ex wl ins last* **9/1**

4 **3** 4 **King's Causeway (USA)**[14] [3623] 2-9-3 .... RobertWinston 7 62
(W J Haggas) *trckd ldrs: chal on inner over 2f out: kpt on same pce appr fnl f* **6/5**[1]

5 **4** 3 ½ **Arabellas Homer**[29] [3157] 2-8-12 .... JimmyQuinn 9 49
(Miss J A Camacho) *hld up in rr: effrt over 2f out: edgd rt and kpt on* **33/1**

00 **5** ½ **Go Red**[18] [3498] 2-9-3 .... PaulMulrennan 4 52
(M W Easterby) *w ldr: wknd appr fnl f* **66/1**

6 **6** 2 **Bollin Felix**[9] [3758] 2-9-3 .... DavidAllan 12 48
(T D Easterby) *in rr: sme hdwy 2f out: nvr on terms* **25/1**

44 **7** nk **Musical Land (IRE)**[23] [3328] 2-9-3 .... PhillipMakin 6 47
(J R Weymes) *prom: outpcd over 3f out: do threat after* **20/1**

8 hd **Sonar Sound (GER)** 2-9-3 .... TPQueally 1 47
(T P Tate) *dwlt: in rr: sme hdwy on outer over 2f out: nvr a factor* **50/1**

9 2 **Until When (USA)** 2-9-3 .... PaulEddery 11 42+
(B Smart) *s.s: drvn and sn in tch: edgd lft 2f out: sn wknd: eased ins last* **3/1**[2]

10 2 ½ **Cadwell** 2-9-3 .... AdrianTNicholls 5 36
(D Nicholls) *s.i.s: hdwy and in tch over 5f out: lost pl 3f out* **25/1**

11 ¾ **Miss Havisham (IRE)** 2-8-12 .... TonyHamilton 8 29
(J R Weymes) *s.s: sme hdwy on ins 3f out: lost pl over 1f out* **66/1**

12 28 **Will Doo** 2-8-12 .... MarkLawson(5) 2 —
(M E Sowersby) *s.i.s: a bhd: lost tch fnl 2f* **200/1**

1m 38.91s (4.60) **Going Correction** +0.55s/f (Yiel) **12** Ran SP% **115.6**
Speed ratings (Par 94):95,94,90,86,85 83,82,82,80,77 76,44
CSF £51.81 TOTE £6.40: £1.70, £2.70, £1.30; EX 53.90.
Owner Hamad Suhail **Bred** P Byrne Mrs E Mulhern And Brian Grassick **Trained** Middleham Moor, N Yorks

FOCUS
Probably just an average maiden, run in deteriorating conditions, but the winner looks the big improver. The first two finished clear, but the likes of the fifth temper enthusiasm for the form.

NOTEBOOK
Weld Il Balad(IRE), a lengthy January foal, was very green to post. His rider was at pains not to pick up his whip and he gained the upper hand near the line. He looks essentially a stayer and will go on from here. (op 11-2 tchd 5-1)
Security Tiger(IRE), backed at long odds, made this a real test but in the end the winner was just too good. She has a willing attitude and deserves to go one better. (op 20-1)
King's Causeway(USA) made his effort on the inner and was upsides coming to the final quarter mile, but in the end did not see it out anywhere near as well as the first two. The ground had possibly turned against him. (op 11-10 tchd 11-8)
Arabellas Homer, a close-coupled filly, stayed on in her own time from the rear despite tending to edge right. She needs another run to qualify for a nursery mark.
Go Red showed a bit more on his third start and looks a longer-term nursery type.
Bollin Felix showed a bit more than on his debut a week earlier but his breeding suggests he will not come into his own until tackling middle-distances at three. (op 50-1)
Until When(USA), who had two handlers and was a bit of a handful in the paddock, proved very inexperienced and the conditions seemed all against him. He is capable of a lot better than he showed here. Official explanation: jockey said colt was unsuited by the good ground (op 5-2 tchd 9-4 and 10-3)

4019 GRAHAM AND ROSEN SOLICITORS H'CAP 5f
3:30 (3:30) (Class 5) (0-75,72) 3-Y-O+ **£3,886** (£1,156; £577; £288) **Stalls** High

Form RPR

5212 **1** **Paddywack (IRE)**[4] [3913] 9-8-7 **53** oh1 .... (b) PaulQuinn 4 67
(D W Chapman) *in rr: gd hdwy over 1f out: led jst ins last: sn clr* **9/2**[2]

4300 **2** 2 ½ **Divine Spirit**[14] [3622] 5-9-6 **66** .... JimmyQuinn 9 71
(M Dods) *mid-div: hdwy 2f out: styd on to take 2nd ins last: no ch w wnr* **5/1**[3]

3053 **3** 4 **Trombone Tom**[9] [3759] 3-8-7 **56** .... PaulMulrennan 2 47
(J R Norton) *chsd ldrs: kpt on same pce fnl f* **20/1**

4205 **4** ¾ **Winthorpe (IRE)**[54] [2380] 6-9-5 **65** .... GrahamGibbons 3 53
(J J Quinn) *hld up in rr: hdwy over 1f out: styd on ins last: tk modest 4th nr line* **10/1**

0503 **5** nk **Betsen (IRE)**[6] [3835] 4-9-5 **65** .... AdrianTNicholls 13 52
(D Nicholls) *led: hdd jst ins last: wknd rapidly towards fin* **4/1**[1]

0600 **6** ½ **Catch The Cat (IRE)**[2] [3988] 7-9-1 **64** .... (b) SaleemGolam(3) 5 49
(Robert Gray) *mid-div: kpt on fnl 2f: nvr a threat* **25/1**

5200 **7** ¾ **Financial Times (USA)**[19] [3447] 4-9-12 **72** .... (t) FrancisNorton 11 54
(Stef Liddiard) *chsd ldrs: one pce fnl 2f* **7/1**

6050 **8** 1 ¼ **Whistler**[19] [3449] 9-8-13 **59** .... (p) PaulFitzsimons 10 37
(Miss J R Tooth) *mid-div: drvn over 2f out: nvr on terms* **12/1**

460 **9** ½ **Trick Cyclist**[2] [3988] 5-9-1 **61** .... DaleGibson 8 37
(M W Easterby) *sn in rr: sme hdwy and hung rt 2f out: nvr on terms* **17/2**

0040 **10** ¾ **Beyond The Clouds (IRE)**[11] [3699] 10-8-9 **55** ow2 .... (p) RobertWinston 7 28
(J S Wainwright) *prom: lost pl over 1f out* **16/1**

6500 **11** ¾ **Zap Attack**[8] [3781] 6-8-7 **53** oh16 .... DavidAllan 1 24
(J Parkes) *swvd lft s: sme hdwy on wd outside 2f out: sn lost pl* **66/1**

0340 **12** 1 ½ **Kashtanka (IRE)**[10] [3749] 4-8-4 **53** oh16 .... (p) JasonEdmunds(3) 12 18
(J Balding) *chsd ldrs on inner: lost pl 2f out* **50/1**

65.64 secs (1.64) **Going Correction** +0.425s/f (Yiel)
WFA 3 from 4yo+ 3lb 12 Ran SP% **112.6**
Speed ratings (Par 103):103,99,92,91,90 90,88,86,86,84 83,81
CSF £24.73 CT £406.34 TOTE £4.20: £1.90, £2.30, £5.40; EX 28.30.
Owner David W Chapman **Bred** Colm McEvoy **Trained** Stillington, N Yorks

FOCUS
In the rain-soaked ground they seemed to congregate towards the middle. Just ordinary form with the winner once again excelling here.

4020 OLD GRAVEL PITS ALLERTHORPE STKS (H'CAP) 1m 100y
4:05 (4:07) (Class 4) (0-85,78) 3-Y-O+ **£6,477** (£1,927; £963; £481) **Stalls** High

Form RPR

0431 **1** **Apsara**[11] [3716] 5-8-11 **61** .... PhillipMakin 4 74
(G M Moore) *chsd ldrs: rdn and outpcd 3f out: styd on down wd outside to ld 1f out: styd on wl* **4/1**[2]

5104 **2** 3 ½ **Nevada Desert (IRE)**[25] [3241] 6-9-5 **69** .... DeanMcKeown 3 75
(R M Whitaker) *trckd ldrs on outer: kpt on to chal 1f out: no ex* **4/1**[2]

35-5 **3** 3 ½ **Baileys Encore**[67] [1999] 3-8-13 **70** .... J-PGuillambert 5 67
(M Johnston) *trckd ldrs: rdn and outpcd over 2f out: kpt on towards fin* **11/2**

21-5 **4** shd **Scotland The Brave**[34] [2977] 6-9-1 **65** .... (v) GrahamGibbons 6 63
(J D Bethell) *led: hdd 1f out: wknd towards fin* **9/2**[3]

4110 **5** 2 **Inside Story (IRE)**[5] [3883] 4-9-1 **65** .... (b) PaulMulrennan 1 59
(M W Easterby) *trckd ldrs: rdn and hung rt 2f out: sn wknd* **10/1**

0216 **6** 1 ½ **Claret And Amber**[12] [3688] 4-10-0 **78** .... TonyHamilton 7 69
(R A Fahey) *trckd ldrs: effrt on inner over 2f out: wknd over 1f out* **7/2**[1]

3500 **7** 23 **Screwdriver**[158] [504] 4-9-3 **67** .... (b) PaulFitzsimons 2 9
(Miss J R Tooth) *in tch: lost pl 4f out: t.o 2f out* **20/1**

1m 51.92s (4.52) **Going Correction** +0.625s/f (Yiel)
WFA 3 from 4yo+ 7lb 7 Ran SP% **109.6**
Speed ratings (Par 105):102,98,95,94,92 91,68
CSF £18.54 TOTE £4.40: £2.10, £2.70; EX 20.50.
Owner Mrs Mary And Miss Susan Hatfield **Bred** St Clare Hall Stud **Trained** Middleham Moor, N Yorks

FOCUS
Very ordinary form rated through the runner-up, but sound enough and the winner deserves credit overcoming conditions that in the past she seemed unable to handle.

The Form Book, Raceform Ltd, Compton, RG20 6NL

4021 DOROTHY LAIRD MEMORIAL TROPHY LADIES STKS (H'CAP) 1m 1f 207y

4:40 (4:40) (Class 5) (0-75,73) 3-Y-0+ £3,578 (£1,050; £525; £262) Stalls High

Form				RPR
4110	1		**Gala Sunday (USA)**[3] [3939] 6-9-11 **60**..................(bt) MissSBrotherton 1 (M W Easterby) *racd wd: in tch: hdwy on wd outside to ld over 1f out: sn drew clr* **5/1**[3]	76
0000	2	6	**Emperor's Well**[14] [3610] 7-9-1 **55**........................ MissJoannaMason(5) 7 (M W Easterby) *w ldr: c wd and led 2f out: sn hdd: no ch w wnr* **14/1**	60
0400	3	3	**Zarova (IRE)**[2] [3983] 4-9-1 **55**.. AdeleRothery(5) 9 (M W Easterby) *hld up: hdwy on outside over 2f out: kpt on same pce: snatched 3rd on line* **16/1**	55+
3622	4	shd	**Parchment (IRE)**[9] [3762] 4-9-5 **54** oh2............................ MissADeniel 10 (A J Lockwood) *chsd ldrs: one pce whn wnt lft ins last: wknd towards fin* **5/1**[3]	53
0505	5	3	**Kylkenny**[35] [2956] 11-10-0 **68**....................................(t) MissVCartmel(5) 4 (P D Cundell) *in tch: effrt over 2f out: kpt on same pce* **7/2**[1]	62
-300	6	3 1/2	**Chapter (IRE)**[29] [3147] 4-10-3 **66**....................................(b[1]) MissLEllison 8 (Mrs A L M King) *led tl 2f out: sn wknd* **12/1**	54
0032	7	1/2	**Tangarita**[8] [3804] 3-8-8 **57**........................... MissMSowerby(5) 11 (A M Balding) *hld up in rr: styd far side in st: kpt on fnl 3f: nvr nr to chal* **9/2**[2]	44+
3314	8	1	**Silverhay**[10] [3724] 5-10-10 **73**..(p) MrsCBartley 5 (T D Barron) *trckd ldrs: edgd rt 2f out: sn wknd* **11/2**	58
10-0	9	22	**Wahchi (IRE)**[29] [3141] 7-9-7 **61** ow1............................ MissJCoward(5) 3 (M W Easterby) *dwlt: sme hdwy 4f out: lost pl over 2f out: sn bhd* **25/1**	6
-000	10	11	**Kalush**[11] [3716] 5-9-5 **54** oh22...(bt[1]) AnnStokell 6 (J Hetherton) *dwlt: hdwy 6f out: lost pl over 3f out: sn bhd* **100/1**	—
0/0-	11	62	**Fusillade (IRE)**[398] [3015] 6-9-0 **54** oh19...................... MissWGibson(5) 2 (A J Lockwood) *mid-div: lost pl over 5f out: t.o whn virtually p.u over 1f out: btn 62 l* **100/1**	—

2m 14.92s (7.62) **Going Correction** +0.625s/f (Yiel)
WFA 3 from 4yo+ 9lb **11** Ran SP% **115.2**
Speed ratings (Par 103):94,89,86,86,84 81,81,80,62,53 4
CSF £70.31 CT £1035.15 TOTE £4.90: £1.90, £3.70, £5.20; EX 59.80.
Owner M W Easterby **Bred** Juddmonte Farms Inc **Trained** Sheriff Hutton, N Yorks
■ A one-two-three for Mick Easterby who had two granddaughters riding in this.
■ Stewards' Enquiry : Miss S Brotherton one-day ban: careless riding (Aug 15)

FOCUS
The stands' side was the place to be and the bare result almost certainly flatters the winner. Modest form, and not rock solid.
Silverhay Official explanation: jockey said gelding was unsuited by the good to soft ground

4022 WESTWOOD H'CAP 1m 4f 16y

5:15 (5:15) (Class 5) (0-70,67) 3-Y-0+ £3,562 (£1,059; £529; £264) Stalls High

Form				RPR
11-5	1		**Halla San**[94] [1288] 4-10-0 **67**... TonyHamilton 6 (R A Fahey) *hld up: effrt over 2f out: chal 1f out: r.o u.p to ld nr fin* **15/8**[2]	74
4004	2	shd	**Red River Rebel**[25] [3243] 8-8-9 **48** oh2........................ PaulMulrennan 5 (J R Norton) *led: rdn and hung rt over 2f out: kpt on: hdd towards fin* **6/1**	55
5223	3	8	**Melvino**[2] [3983] 4-9-9 **62**... PhillipMakin 2 (T D Barron) *trckd ldrs: effrt 3f out: sn rdn: wknd appr fnl f* **13/8**[1]	58
2626	4	21	**Noble Edge**[32] [2124] 3-8-5 **58**...................................... SaleemGolam(3) 1 (Robert Gray) *trckd ldrs: drvn over 3f out: lost pl over 1f out: eased* **5/1**[3]	24+
1-63	5	6	**Fenners (USA)**[13] [3637] 3-8-8 **65**..............................(t) AdeleRothery(7) 7 (G P Kelly) *a last: struggling to keep up after 3f: lost pl over 3f out: sn bhd* **16/1**	23

2m 51.0s (10.79) **Going Correction** +0.70s/f (Yiel)
WFA 3 from 4yo+ 11lb **5** Ran SP% **109.7**
Speed ratings (Par 103):92,91,86,72,68
CSF £12.78 TOTE £2.40: £1.30, £2.70; EX 13.00 Place 6 £201.54, Place 5 £67.35..
Owner Mrs Catherine Reynard **Bred** Hascombe And Valiant Studs **Trained** Musley Bank, N Yorks

FOCUS
A modest handicap, run on the worst ground of the day. It has been rated through the winner, who is a horse of some potential and did not have to be at his very best to take this.
Fenners(USA) Official explanation: jockey said colt was unsuited by the soft ground
T/Plt: £816.20 to a £1 stake. Pool: £46,461.65. 41.55 winning tickets. T/Qpdt: £32.20 to a £1 stake. Pool: £4,560.20. 104.60 winning tickets. WG

2813 GOODWOOD (R-H)

Tuesday, August 1

OFFICIAL GOING: Good (good to firm in places)
Wind: Fresh, against Weather: Fine but cloudy

4023 THE SPORTSMAN NEWSPAPER STKS (HERITAGE H'CAP) 1m 1f 192y

2:05 (2:05) (Class 2) 4-Y-0+ £31,160 (£9,330; £4,665; £2,335; £1,165; £585) Stalls High

Form				RPR
0344	1		**Crosspeace (IRE)**[19] [3432] 4-9-10 **108**........................ RoystonFfrench 9 (M Johnston) *hld up in midfield: pushed along and prog 2f out: swtchd rt jst over 1f out: str run to ld last strides* **12/1**	116
-102	2	nk	**Tabadul (IRE)**[35] [2341] 5-8-4 **88**... RHills 13 (E A L Dunlop) *lw: trckd ldrs: led gng strly jst over 2f out: rdn over 1f out: styd on: collared last strides* **7/1**[2]	95
2214	3	1/2	**Folio (IRE)**[22] [3366] 6-7-13 **83**... NickyMackay 12 (W J Musson) *trckd ldrs: rdn and effrt to chse ldr over 1f out: styd on but a hld fnl f* **25/1**	89
0612	4	shd	**Magic Sting**[19] [3429] 5-7-12 **82**... HayleyTurner 4 (M L W Bell) *dwlt: hld up wl in rr: prog on outer over 2f out: r.o wl fnl f: nrst fin* **25/1**	88
0123	5	shd	**Lucayan Dancer**[10] [3748] 6-7-12 **82** oh1......................... DavidKinsella 3 (D Nicholls) *hld up in last pair: nt clr run jst over 2f out: swtchd to outer over 1f out: flew home but too late* **25/1**	88+
1-00	6	nk	**Pagan Sword**[38] [2848] 4-8-4 **88**.. KerrinMcEvoy 1 (Mrs A J Perrett) *t.k.h: hld up towards rr: threaded through on bridle fr 2f out: shkn up fnl f: r.o but no hope of catching ldrs* **25/1**	95+
3133	7	1	**Active Asset (IRE)**[10] [3747] 4-8-0 **84**................................ ChrisCatlin 14 (M R Channon) *dwlt: hld up wl in rr: pushed along and sme prog over 1f out: rdn and r.o wl last 150yds: nvr nrr* **14/1**	87
0103	8	nk	**Humble Opinion**[10] [3737] 4-8-3 **87**.................................... JohnEgan 7 (B J Meehan) *hld up in midfield: prog over 2f out: rdn to chse ldrs over 1f out: one pce and lost pls nr fin* **12/1**	90
0043	9	1 1/2	**Coup D'Etat**[25] [3255] 4-8-0 **84**.. JamieMackay 18 (J L Dunlop) *trckd ldng pair: pushed along over 2f out: hanging and nt qckn over 1f out: hld whn n.m.r ins fnl f: fdd* **7/1**[2]	84
-525	10	nk	**Jack Of Trumps (IRE)**[20] [3401] 6-8-1 **85**........................ MartinDwyer 10 (G Wragg) *trckd ldrs: effrt on outer over 2f out: no imp over 1f out: wknd ins fnl f* **16/1**	84
5510	11	nk	**I'm So Lucky**[17] [3552] 4-9-5 **103**.. JoeFanning 17 (M Johnston) *b: led to jst over 2f out: hld over 1f out: wknd ins fnl f* **13/2**[1]	102
1155	12	3/4	**Dancing Lyra**[45] [2657] 5-7-12 **82**....................................... PaulHanagan 16 (R A Fahey) *b: dwlt: t.k.h and sn rcvrd to chse ldrs: effrt over 2f out: one pce and hld whn n.m.r over 1f out: fdd* **7/1**[2]	79
3-01	13	nk	**Salinja (USA)**[10] [3733] 4-8-12 **96**.. RyanMoore 2 (Mrs A J Perrett) *lw: a towards rr: rdn 2f out: one pce and no imp* **10/1**[3]	93
5104	14	hd	**Impeller (IRE)**[3] [3929] 7-8-10 **94**.. EddieAhern 8 (W R Muir) *racd on outer: hld up: prog and cl up 4f out: rdn and wknd wl over 1f out: eased ins fnl f* **14/1**	90
5360	15	1	**Salamanca**[39] [2803] 4-8-13 **97**.. JimmyFortune 6 (S Kirk) *a in rr: rdn and struggling 3f out: n.d after* **20/1**	91
-100	16	7	**All That And More (IRE)**[38] [2848] 4-8-10 **94**.................. MichaelHills 11 (B W Hills) *swtg: mostly chsd ldr: upsides over 2f out: sn wknd rapidly* **20/1**	75

2m 7.25s (-0.50) **Going Correction** +0.075s/f (Good) **16** Ran SP% **119.4**
Speed ratings (Par 109):105,104,104,104,104 103,103,102,101,101 101,100,100,100,99 93
CSF £81.69 CT £2045.70 TOTE £14.50: £3.20, £2.20, £7.00, £6.30; EX 105.90 TRIFECTA Not won..
Owner Favourites Racing **Bred** Patrick Jones **Trained** Middleham Moor, N Yorks

FOCUS
A high-class handicap and they went a strong pace from the start, but there were still the usual Goodwood hard-luck stories. The principals raced towards the middle of the track in the straight.

NOTEBOOK
Crosspeace(IRE) was beginning to prove pretty frustrating this season, failing to take advantage of what looked a good opportunity in a four-runner conditions race Epsom on his previous start but, returned to handicap company, he was back at his very best to gain his first success since landing a Listed race at Doncaster towards the end of last year. He may bid for a quick follow-up at this meeting in the Listed Glorious Stakes, and in the longer term has the option of going for the Irish St Leger. (op 14-1)

Tabadul(IRE) ◆ had looked a better horse on Polytrack so far this season, but was able to race off a 7lb lower turf mark as a result and very nearly took advantage. He looked all over the winner when hitting the front, but probably found himself there too soon and was just denied by one of the many strong finishers. This effort suggest he is probably every bit as effective on turf as he is on sand, and he may still look on a reasonable mark once reassessed. He could be a Cambridgeshire horse. (op 13-2)

Folio(IRE) kept on well to the line having travelled nicely throughout and proved well suited by the strong pace. He is in cracking form.

Magic Sting, a winner at Epsom two starts back and then just denied the follow-up by a horse racing on better ground at the same track next time, continued his good run of form with a decent effort. He caught the eye flashing home on the outside, but had actually been in the clear for a little while and did not look that unlucky.

Lucayan Dancer ◆ has a style of running which requires a bit of luck at the best of times, let alone at a place like Goodwood, and things did not fall right for him. Still right out the back two furlongs out, he flew home when switched to the outside and would have gone very close indeed with one continuous run. (op 33-1)

Pagan Sword ◆, without the visor he wore when beating only one home in the Duke of Edinburgh at Royal Ascot on his previous start, looked back to his best and has to be considered very unlucky. He was keeping on as well as anything in the closing stages from well off the pace without being subjected to a hard ride - his jockey presumably thinking he had little chance of getting there in time - and may well have won with more luck. He is not the most reliable, however, and one should not take too short a price about him confirming this next time. Official explanation: jockey said gelding was denied a clear run

Active Asset(IRE), like the two who finished immediately in front of him, got going all too late and is also better than the bare form.

Coup D'Etat was not at his best and has to be considered disappointing. (tchd 15-2 in a place)

I'm So Lucky, successful in the Listed Wolferton Handicap at Royal Ascot but well below his best in the John Smith's Cup at York on his previous start, looked to get his own way in front, and kicked into a clear lead as the field rounded for home, but he offered little when seriously challenged and had probably gone off a little too fast. (op 7-1)

Dancing Lyra was nowhere near his best and was very disappointing. (op 13-2)

4024 BGC STKS (REGISTERED AS THE GORDON STAKES) (GROUP 3) 1m 4f

2:40 (2:42) (Class 1) 3-Y-O £28,390 (£10,760; £5,385; £2,685; £1,345; £675) Stalls Low

Form				RPR
6103	1		**Sixties Icon**[39] [2801] 3-9-0 110...................................... LDettori 1 (J Noseda) *settled in 4th: smooth prog on outer 3f out: shkn up to ld wl over 1f out: sn wl in command: pushed out* **7/4**[1]	119+
1-52	2	1 3/4	**Jadalee (IRE)**[19] [3441] 3-9-0 105.................................. MartinDwyer 2 (M P Tregoning) *hld up in 6th: rdn wl over 2f out: styd on fnl 2f to take 2nd last 75yds* **9/1**[3]	113
2111	3	1/2	**Linas Selection**[17] [3551] 3-9-0 110.. KDarley 4 (M Johnston) *lw: trckd ldr: rdn to chal over 3f out: led jst over 2f out to wl over 1f out: no ch w wnr: lost 2nd last 75yds* **2/1**[2]	112
1203	4	2	**Hazeymm (IRE)**[40] [2775] 3-9-0 107...................................... ChrisCatlin 6 (M R Channon) *hld up in 5th: rdn and effrt over 2f out: one pce and no imp* **10/1**	109
5411	5	2 1/2	**Luberon**[18] [3501] 3-9-0 106.. JoeFanning 5 (M Johnston) *led: rdn and pressed 3f out: hdd jst over 2f out: wknd over 1f out* **10/1**	105
	6	1 1/4	**Savannah**[20] [3426] 3-9-0 .... MJKinane 7 (A P O'Brien, Ire) *lw: trckd ldng pair: rdn over 3f out: lost pl and struggling in last over 2f out* **20/1**	103
3-10	7	hd	**Classic Punch (IRE)**[30] [3127] 3-9-0 104............................... JohnEgan 3 (D R C Elsworth) *lw: hld up in last: effrt on inner 3f out: floundering 2f out: wknd* **11/1**	103

2m 36.85s (-2.07) **Going Correction** +0.075s/f (Good) **7** Ran SP% **111.0**
Speed ratings (Par 110):109,107,107,106,104 103,103
CSF £16.99 TOTE £2.90: £1.70, £3.60; EX 21.40.
Owner Mrs Susan Roy **Bred** Lordship Stud **Trained** Newmarket, Suffolk

FOCUS
This looked like a good renewal of the Gordon Stakes, but the pace appeared just ordinary. The form looks solid and the winner was value for extra.

NOTEBOOK

Sixties Icon, seventh in the Derby before running third in the King Edward VII Stakes at Royal Ascot, found this a good opportunity to gain his first success since landing a Windsor maiden earlier in the season. Despite getting a bit warm beforehand, he was always travelling well within himself just off the leaders, and nothing could go with him when he kicked for home. He was basically too good for this lot and his long-term aim is now the St Leger. Several firms promoted him to favourite off the back of this success, but prices of around 7/2 do not appear to offer value at this stage, not least because he will have to reverse placings with Papal Bull, who beat him a neck and two and a half lengths at Ascot and is around double the price. He may well win the Leger - he is certainly progressing into a high-class individual - but, while the trip should not be a problem on breeding, he is not exactly crying out for a mile six and it remains to be seen whether he will be suited by the demands that will be placed on him at York. We should learn more before then, though, as he is likely to have a prep run in either the Great Voltigeur or Geoffrey Freer. (op 15-8 tchd 2-1)

Jadalee(IRE), who was warm and edgy beforehand, was a little unlucky in a Listed race over a mile five at the Newmarket July meeting on his previous start, and probably ran about as well as could have been expected dropped back in trip and stepped up in grade. He was no match whatsoever for the winner, but the ordinary pace would not have suited and he was doing his best work late on. He looks almost sure to be suited to the test the St Leger is likely to offer and fully deserves to continue on that path. Before then, should connections opt to take him to York, he has the option of either the Great Voltigeur or the Ebor. (op 12-1)

Linas Selection has progressed into a very smart middle-distance stayer this season, winning both the King George V Handicap at Royal Ascot and a Listed race at York on his previous start, but he was probably unable to show his very best this time. Dropped in trip, the early pace set by his stablemate was probably nowhere near as strong as he would have liked, and he was outpaced by the eventual winner in the closing stages. On this evidence, he is going to benefit from a return to further and a more strongly-run race. He is also in the St Leger. (op 13-8 tchd 9-4 in places)

Hazeymm(IRE), stepped up to a mile and a half for the first time, ran creditably in fourth but was never a danger. He is not going to be easy to place and his connections may need to look abroad. (tchd 12-1)

Luberon, upped significantly in class following a couple of comfortable victories in handicap company, the first at Windsor off 89 and the latest off a mark of 98 at York, had the run of the race out in front but was put in his place when it mattered. He does not look up to this level at the moment. (op 8-1)

Savannah won over ten furlongs at Naas recently but that form did not amount to much and he was well held. (op 14-1)

Classic Punch(IRE), off the mark on his reappearance in a maiden at Windsor before finishing ninth of 13 in the Irish Derby, never got a look in. A stronger pace would probably have suited, but he still has to prove he is up to this class at this stage of his career. (op 20-1 tchd 10-1)

4025 BETFAIR CUP (REGISTERED AS THE LENNOX STKS) (GROUP 2) 7f

3:15 (3:16) (Class 1) 3-Y-O+

£85,170 (£32,280; £16,155; £8,055; £4,035; £2,025) **Stalls** High

Form				RPR
0-02	**1**		**Iffraaj**[18] 3494 5-9-4 117 ... LDettori 10 (Saeed Bin Suroor) *lw: trckd ldr: led jst over 2f out and kicked clr: r.o strly fnl f: impressive* **6/4**[1]	125+
3161	**2**	4	**Jedburgh**[16] 3572 5-9-0 105 ...(b) TedDurcan 1 (J L Dunlop) *lw: hld up in last: prog on outer fr 2f out: drvn to take 2nd last 100yds: no ch w wnr* **40/1**	109
1204	**3**	hd	**Assertive**[41] 2739 3-8-8 106 ... RyanMoore 2 (R Hannon) *lw: hld up in last trio: pushed along over 2f out: prog on outer over 1f out: disp 2nd last 100yds: kpt on* **33/1**	107
3414	**4**	nk	**Nayyir**[31] 3086 8-9-0 110 ... JohnEgan 6 (G A Butler) *b.hind: hld up in rr: nt clr run 2f out: hmpd over 1f out and lost all ch: swtchd lft and r.o last 150yds* **7/1**[3]	113+
1010	**5**	¾	**Etlaala**[38] 2846 4-9-0 112 ... RHills 3 (B W Hills) *b.hind: lw: hld up in rr: trapped on inner fr over 2f out: hanging over 1f out: plld out and r.o ins fnl f: no ch* **11/1**	112+
-211	**6**	shd	**Jeremy (USA)**[41] 2739 3-8-8 112 ... MJKinane 9 (Sir Michael Stoute) *hld up in midfield: prog over 2f out: rdn to chse wnr over 1f out: hung rt and no imp: wknd last 100yds* **5/2**[2]	104
2323	**7**	½	**Mac Love**[17] 3518 5-9-0 107 ... SteveDrowne 8 (R Charlton) *t.k.h: hld up bhd ldrs: effrt 2f out: squeezed through over 1f out: one pce and no imp after* **25/1**	104
4616	**8**	1 ¾	**Suggestive**[17] 3534 8-9-0 108 ...(b) NickyMackay 4 (W J Haggas) *lw: led at decent pce: hdd jst over 2f out: wknd jst over 1f out* **66/1**	100
5-21	**9**	shd	**Prince Of Light (IRE)**[17] 3518 3-8-8 109 ... JoeFanning 5 (M Johnston) *trckd ldng pair: rdn over 2f out: wknd over 1f out* **9/1**	98
2106	**10**	3 ½	**Quito (IRE)**[18] 3494 9-9-0 112 ...(b) TonyCulhane 7 (D W Chapman) *t.k.h: hld up in midfield: rdn over 2f out: struggling whn bdly hmpd over 1f out: no ch after* **20/1**	91

1m 25.58s (-2.46) **Going Correction** +0.075s/f (Good)
WFA 3 from 4yo+ 6lb **10** Ran SP% **114.9**
Speed ratings (Par 115):117,112,112,111,111 110,110,108,108,104
CSF £81.26 TOTE £2.50: £1.20, £5.50, £6.40; EX 84.70 Trifecta £1662.20 Part won. Pool £2,341.26 - 0.30 winning units..
Owner Godolphin **Bred** Darley **Trained** Newmarket, Suffolk

FOCUS

This looked like a good renewal of the Lennox Stakes and they went a good pace from the start resulting in a solid winning time, but Iffraaj totally outclassed his nine rivals having been well placed throughout. Iffraaj apart, the form is not that strong for the grade.

NOTEBOOK

Iffraaj ◆ would surely have won the July Cup with a clear run at Newmarket on his previous start, but this was some compensation. He got a near-perfect lead off Suggestive for much of the way and found plenty when that one weakened to sustain his effort right the way to the line, allowing none of the closers to get anywhere near him to defy his 4lb penalty in tremendous style. A fine looker, he has an equally impressive attitude and deserves to win at the highest level. Although as yet unproven beyond this trip, he shapes as though he will stay a mile and his connections will have plenty of options. It would be no surprise to see him turn up at Churchill Downs for the Breeders' Cup Mile. (op 15-8 tchd 2-1 in places)

Jedburgh, as good as ever this season, including when winning a three-runner Group 3 at the Curragh on his previous start, stayed on well from well out he back to take second, but was no match whatsoever for the winner. The Challenge Stakes at Newmarket in October looks a worthwhile target. (op 50-1)

Assertive ran a tremendous race in third and reversed Jersey Stakes form with Jeremy. He may be a touch flattered considering the likes of Nayyir and Etlaala were denied clear runs, but he is holding his form well and could turn out again quickly in the Maurice de Gheest. (op 40-1)

Nayyir, the winner of this race in 2002 and 2003, relies quite heavily on luck in running but things did not fall right for him this time and he is quite a bit better than his finishing position suggests. Official explanation: jockey said gelding suffered interference in running (op 6-1)

Etlaala had to be switched after trying to go for a run up the rail and got going far too late. He remains unable to pull it off on the big day. (op 10-1)

Jeremy(USA) ◆, the Jersey Stakes winner, could not confirm Ascot form with Assertive and was below his best. He made good headway to move into a challenging position, but hung to his right under maximum pressure and did not appear to handle the track. He can definitely be given another chance. (tchd 3-1)

Mac Love, on his toes beforehand, is a very hard horse to catch right and remains winless since 2004.

Suggestive ended up setting the race up for his rivals.

Prince Of Light(IRE) had no chance of dominating considering how fast Suggestive went off and was below form. He can surely do better, but it remains to be seen if he will reach this sort of level. (op 15-2)

Quito(IRE), another who was on his toes beforehand, was not his best.

4026 BETFAIR MOLECOMB STKS (GROUP 3) 5f

3:50 (3:51) (Class 1) 2-Y-O

£28,390 (£10,760; £5,385; £2,685; £1,345; £675) **Stalls** Low

Form				RPR
11	**1**		**Enticing (IRE)**[12] 3684 2-8-11 ... MichaelHills 6 (W J Haggas) *lw: taken down early: trckd ldrs gng wl: effrt to dispute ld wl over 1f out: narrowly hdd ins fnl f: rallied: won on the nod* **3/1**[1]	104+
1	**2**	shd	**Wi Dud**[46] 2623 2-9-0 ... NCallan 11 (K A Ryan) *trckd ldrs gng wl: effrt to dispute ld wl over 1f out: narrow ld ins fnl f: pipped last stride* **9/2**[3]	107+
1161	**3**	¾	**Bahama Mama (IRE)**[25] 3252 2-8-11 ... ShaneKelly 2 (J Noseda) *lw: hld up bhd ldrs: nt clr run briefly on inner 2f out: effrt over 1f out: r.o fnl f: nt rch ldng pair* **10/3**[2]	104+
621	**4**	½	**Siren's Gift**[25] 3239 2-8-11 ... MartinDwyer 13 (A M Balding) *hld up bhd ldrs: gng wl 2f out: rdn and kpt on same pce fr over 1f out* **20/1**	99
1514	**5**	1 ½	**Dazed And Amazed**[19] 3442 2-9-0 ... RyanMoore 3 (R Hannon) *b.hind: towards rr and sn pushed along: drvn and effrt over 1f out: styd on fnl f: nt pce to reaach ldrs* **13/2**	97
0310	**6**	hd	**Scented Present**[10] 3734 2-9-0 ... AlanMunro 9 (B J Meehan) *lw: hld up in midfield: effrt on outer 2f out: one pce and no imp over 1f out* **33/1**	96
6410	**7**	shd	**Gold Spirit (IRE)**[10] 3734 2-9-0 ... RichardMullen 5 (E J O'Neill) *jst off the pce in midfield: pushed along 1/2-way: rdn whn nt clr run briefly over 1f out: kpt on: n.d* **40/1**	96
26	**8**	1 ¾	**King Of Swords (IRE)**[16] 3574 2-9-0 ... PShanahan 1 (C Collins, Ire) *neat: racd against nr side rail: nt on terms w ldrs: outpcd over 1f out: n.d after* **20/1**	89
16	**9**	1	**Narrjoo (USA)**[19] 3442 2-9-0 ... TonyCulhane 4 (M R Channon) *swtg: taken down early: wl in rr: drvn and effrt whn nt clr run briefly 2f out: no real prog* **12/1**	86
2300	**10**	1	**Cav Okay (IRE)**[10] 3734 2-9-0 ...(b[1]) JimmyFortune 8 (R Hannon) *disp ld to wl over 1f out: wknd* **16/1**	82
3231	**11**	6	**Winning Spirit (IRE)**[39] 2827 2-9-0 ... LDettori 7 (J Noseda) *lw: disp ld to wl over 1f out: wknd rapidly* **10/1**	61
2313	**12**	2	**Racing Stripes (IRE)**[18] 3468 2-9-0 ... PatDobbs 12 (A B Haynes) *s.i.s: in tch on outer to 1/2-way: wknd rapidly over 1f out* **100/1**	53
23	**P**		**Fast Freddie**[120] 849 2-9-0 ... JohnEgan 10 (T J Pitt) *a in rr: no ch whn lost action over 1f out: p.u ins fnl f* **40/1**	—

59.19 secs (0.14) **Going Correction** +0.075s/f (Good) **13** Ran SP% **120.6**
Speed ratings (Par 104):101,100,99,98,96 96,95,93,91,89 80,77,—
CSF £15.47 TOTE £4.50: £1.80, £2.10, £1.90; EX 23.40 Trifecta £67.00 Pool £2,494.16 - 26.40 winning units..
Owner Lael Stable **Bred** Lael Stables **Trained** Newmarket, Suffolk

FOCUS

A good, competitive renewal of the Molecomb Stakes. Strong form, which should prove reliable, with the front two the least exposed in the field.

NOTEBOOK

Enticing(IRE) ◆, the winner of a Salisbury maiden before following up with an easy win in minor company on the Polytrack at Wolverhampton, coped with the step up to Group 3 company and was just good enough. She had the benefit of the rail to run against in the closing stages, while the eventual runner-up was on her outside, but she won on merit and her effort is all the more creditable considering she lost her off-fore shoe off in the last furlong. She may now go for the Flying Childers at York, and if she wins that well her connections will consider taking on the older horses in the Prix de l'Abbaye. Her dam won the former before finishing second in France. (op 11-4 tchd 100-30 and 7-2 in places)

Wi Dud ◆, the comfortable winner of a five-furlong maiden at York on his debut, ran a fine race stepped up significantly in class and was just denied. His effort is all the more creditable considering he was drawn wide and did not have the benefit of the rail in the closing stages. There should be more to come and he will now be aimed at the Gimcrack. (op 13-2)

Bahama Mama(IRE), the winner of three of her four career starts, including a Listed race at Sandown on her previous outing, did not get the run of things in behind Enticing, and is probably a little better than the bare form, although it is hard to say she would have beaten the front two. Her trainer will now consider races like the Flying Childers, the Cornwallis and the Lowther. (op 5-2 tchd 7-2)

Siren's Gift, on her toes beforehand, was second to Enticing in a Salisbury maiden before winning a Beverley novice event, and she ran about as well as expected. She is clearly improving and could have even more to offer.

Dazed And Amazed, the winner of a Newbury Listed event before running fourth in the July Stakes, did not appear suited by this quick five furlongs and got going too late. (op 7-1)

Scented Present ran much better than in the Super Sprint on his previous start, keeping on well towards the middle of the track. (op 50-1)

Gold Spirit(IRE), who got a bit warm beforehand, would have found this tougher than the Super Sprint, and could not confirm form with Scented Present. This was by no means a bad effort, though. (op 50-1)

Narrjoo(USA) had shaped as though worth a try over this trip when sixth of nine in the July Stakes on his previous start, but he was well held. (op 14-1)

Winning Spirit(IRE) ran well below the form he showed when winning at Redcar and has not progressed as one might have hoped. Official explanation: jockey said colt ran too free and lost its action (op 12-1 tchd 9-1)

Fast Freddie Official explanation: vet said gelding pulled up lame right behind

4027 TATLER SUMMER SEASON STKS (H'CAP) 1m 6f

4:25 (4:25) (Class 2) (0-105,104) 3-Y-O+

£15,580 (£4,665; £2,332; £1,167; £582; £292) **Stalls** High

Form				RPR
12-1	**1**		**Soulacroix**[45] 2656 5-9-7 97 ... KerrinMcEvoy 11 (L M Cumani) *settled midfield: pushed along over 3f out: lost pl bhd wall of horses 2f out: rallied over 1f out: r.o to ld last 150yds: readily* **10/3**[1]	108+
6031	**2**	1 ¼	**Wunderwood (USA)**[39] 2817 7-10-0 104 ... JohnEgan 5 (D R C Elsworth) *lw: hld up in last trio: effrt on wd outside 3f out: prog to ld jst over 1f out: hdd and one pce last 150yds* **6/1**[3]	110

2320 **3** *hd* **Lets Roll**[24] [3294] 5-9-0 **90** ... NCallan 4 96
(C W Thornton) *trckd ldrs: hrd rdn over 2f out: effrt to chal and upsides over 1f out: one pce ins fnl f* **20/1**

1020 **4** *nk* **Solent (IRE)**[17] [3533] 4-9-5 **95** ... RyanMoore 2 101
(R Hannon) *hld up in last pair: stdy prog on inner fr 3f out: rdn to chal over 1f out: one pce fnl f* **11/1**

5 *3/4* **Swordsman (GER)**[57] 4-9-0 **90** ... MickyFenton 3 95
(M L W Bell) *w'like: settled midfield: prog 3f out: hrd rdn to chal and upsides over 1f out: wknd last 75yds* **50/1**

4224 **6** *1* **Nawamees (IRE)**[45] [2656] 8-8-13 **89** ... (p) JimmyFortune 7 92
(G L Moore) *b.nr hind: hld up in rr: rdn fr 3f out: plugged on fnl 2f: nt pce to rch ldrs* **14/1**

24 **7** *3/4* **Castle Howard (IRE)**[38] [2850] 4-8-8 **89** ... StephenDonohoe(5) 6 93+
(W J Musson) *hld up towards rr: effrt whn nt clr run and stmbld jst over 2f out: no ch after: keeping on nr fin* **14/1**

0220 **8** *1/2* **Michabo (IRE)**[42] [2723] 5-8-12 **88** ... SteveDrowne 8 89
(H Morrison) *led at decent pce: hrd pressed 5f out: hdd over 3f out: kpt on wl and disp ld over 2f out to jst over 1f out: wknd* **12/1**

6521 **9** *nk* **Doctor Scott**[5] [3877] 3-8-1 **90** 6ex ... JoeFanning 10 91
(M Johnston) *trckd ldr after 4f: rdn to ld over 3f out: hdd over 2f out but stl ev ch tl wknd jst over 1f out* **7/2**[2]

4-00 **10** *hd* **Kerashan (IRE)**[18] [3501] 4-9-7 **97** ... LDettori 12 98
(Saeed Bin Suroor) *trckd ldrs: cl up over 2f out: shkn up and wknd over 1f out* **12/1**

0420 **11** *nk* **Top Seed (IRE)**[10] [3748] 5-8-11 **87** ... TonyCulhane 1 87
(M R Channon) *hld up in last: prog on wd outside 3f out: drvn to press ldrs over 1f out: sn wknd* **25/1**

-331 **12** *2 1/2* **Nobelix (IRE)**[26] [3220] 4-8-10 **86** ... MartinDwyer 9 83
(J R Fanshawe) *trckd ldr for 4f: styd prom to 2f out: wkng whn n.m.r over 1f out: eased* **8/1**

3m 0.82s (-3.15) **Going Correction** +0.075s/f (Good)
WFA 3 from 4yo+ 13lb **12** Ran SP% **118.3**
Speed ratings (Par 109):112,111,111,111,110 110,109,109,109,109 108,107
CSF £22.89 CT £350.37 TOTE £4.10: £1.80, £2.20, £4.30; EX 18.30 Trifecta £745.90 Pool £2,206.42 - 2.10 winning units..
Owner P Makin **Bred** D Bunn **Trained** Newmarket, Suffolk

FOCUS
A competitve handicap run at a decent pace in a solid time, in which quite a number were still in with a chance a furlong out. The form looks rock solid, and the winner was value for a bit extra.

NOTEBOOK
Soulacroix did not enjoy the clearest of runs, but picked up well once finding a gap a furlong out and ran out a comfortable winner in the end. He has improved for a change of stable and looks very progressive. Mephisto, trained by Cumani to win the 2004 Ebor, won a lady riders' handicap at York and this event prior to success on the Knavesmire in August, and it is probably no coincidence that Soulacroix has followed the same path. Things are a touch more complicated this time around, however, as the owner already has the ante-post favourite for the Ebor in the shape of Glistening, and it remains to be seen whether both will run. The hint should be taken if he is allowed to take his chance. Longer term, the Melbourne Cup is the target. (tchd 3-1 and 7-2)
Wunderwood(USA), having his first outing for new connections, was ridden more patiently this time. While he could not match the winner's pace late on, he still ran on well for second, posting a very good effort off top weight, 6lb higher than when successful over the course and distance in June. He too has the Melbourne Cup as a long-term aim. (op 8-1)
Lets Roll was unlucky in running at Haydock last time but he is largely consistent and it was no great surprise to see him bounce back to form. It is not as if he has anything in hand of the Handicapper off a mark of 90, though. (op 25-1)
Solent(IRE), runner-up behind Wunderwood here in June, was 6lb better off at the weights with him for a two-and-a-half-length beating. The turnaround in the weights helped him get closer to that rival this time. (op 12-1 tchd 10-1)
Swordsman(GER), who was previously trained in the US and France, was another having his first outing for a new trainer and he looked a bit dull in his coat beforehand. This longer trip was a bit of an unknown for him and, while he ran with plenty of promise, it would not be a surprise to see him drop back to a mile and a half next time.
Nawamees(IRE) could never really muster the pace to challenge in the closing stages. Easier ground might have helped but he is always going to be vulnerable to younger, less exposed rivals off this sort of mark. (op 12-1)
Castle Howard(IRE) was squeezed for room and stumbled approaching the two-furlong marker and, while he stayed on well next to the far rail, he lacked the pace to get any closer on this ground. He could be a different proposition over this sort of trip when he can get his toe in. (op 16-1)
Michabo(IRE) burnt himself out setting a decent pace. (op 16-1)
Doctor Scott was another who paid for racing prominently in a race that was run at a good pace. (op 11-4 tchd 4-1 in places)
Kerashan(IRE) was hit over the head by a rival rider's whip approaching the final two furlongs.
Top Seed(IRE) looked about to take a hand two furlongs out but he did not find a lot under pressure and the suspicion is that the distance stretched his stamina. (op 33-1)
Nobelix(IRE) Official explanation: jockey said gelding lost its action when struck into behind

4028 TURF CLUB EBF MAIDEN STKS (C&G) 6f
5:00 (5:01) (Class 3) 2-Y-O **£8,258** (£2,456; £1,227; £613) **Stalls** Low

Form RPR

3 **1** **Chataway**[26] [3222] 2-9-0 ... LDettori 2 87+
(B J Meehan) *lw: racd against nr side rail: trckd ldrs: effrt to ld over 1f out: swished tail but r.o wl fnl f: readily* **4/1**[3]

2 *1* **Brave Tin Soldier (USA)** 2-9-0 ... MJKinane 5 84
(A P O'Brien, Ire) *w'like: scope: lw: hld up bhd ldrs: taken to wd outside and effrt 2f out: chsd wnr fnl f: styd on wl but no imp* **7/2**[2]

2 **3** *2 1/2* **Makshoof (IRE)**[25] [3242] 2-9-0 ... RHills 8 77
(M A Jarvis) *unf: trckd ldrs: effrt 2f out: outpcd fnl f but kpt on steadily* **6/1**

2 **4** *nk* **Smirfys Diamond**[92] [1342] 2-9-0 ... PaulHanagan 3 76
(D Nicholls) *w'like: led: hanging fr 1/2-way: hdd and outpcd over 1f out* **11/1**

5 *2 1/2* **Ireland Dancer (IRE)** 2-9-0 ... MartinDwyer 10 68
(W R Muir) *w'like: bit bkwd: hld up in last trio and off the pce: shkn up and styd on steadily fnl 2f: n.d* **40/1**

32 **6** *1 1/2* **Benchmark**[92] [1333] 2-9-0 ... RyanMoore 6 64
(R Hannon) *trckd ldrs: rdn over 2f out: wknd over 1f out* **3/1**[1]

7 *hd* **Aegis (IRE)** 2-9-0 ... MichaelHills 7 63
(B W Hills) *unf: dwlt: hld up in last pair and off the pce: no prog tl pushed along and styd on last 150yds* **25/1**

6 **8** *hd* **Dumas (IRE)**[66] [2009] 2-9-0 ... AlanMunro 4 62
(A P Jarvis) *presssed ldrs tl wknd rapidly over 1f out* **5/1**

9 *1 3/4* **Kings Art (IRE)** 2-9-0 ... TonyCulhane 9 57
(B W Hills) *w'like: bit bkwd: dwlt: a in last pair and off the pce: n.d fnl 2f* **25/1**

0 **10** *7* **Bad Habit**[3] [3923] 2-9-0 ... ChrisCatlin 1 36
(M R Channon) *in tch to 1/2-way: sn wknd u.p and bhd* **33/1**

1m 13.71s (0.86) **Going Correction** +0.075s/f (Good) **10** Ran SP% **119.6**
Speed ratings (Par 98):97,95,92,91,88 86,86,86,83,74
CSF £18.25 TOTE £5.30: £1.70, £1.80, £1.90; EX 22.60 Trifecta £303.60 Pool £1,539.78 - 3.60 winning units..
Owner Kennett Valley Thoroughbreds II **Bred** Whitsbury Manor Stud And Pigeon House Stud **Trained** Manton, Wilts

FOCUS
A decent maiden featuring three or four who had run well in this type of company already and one or two interesting newcomers. The form should work out.

NOTEBOOK
Chataway, who travelled well and enjoyed a dream run up the stands'-side rail, won without having to be put under any serious pressure. He has entries in the Shergar Cup Juvenile over seven furlongs and the Royal Lodge Stakes over a mile, but looks much more of a speedy type, so races over sprint distances like the Redcar Two-Year-Old Trophy might suit him better. (op 11-4 tchd 9-2)
Brave Tin Soldier(USA) ◆, whose dam is a sister to Kentucky Derby winner Fusaichi Pegasus, put up a highly encouraging performance on his debut. Forced to switch and challenge on the wide outside, he ran on well for second, and, in finishing clear of the more experienced third and fourth, he signalled that he should not have any trouble going one better soon. (op 4-1)
Makshoof(IRE), who had run with promise on his debut at Beverley, was another who challenged wide. He could not deal with the pace shown by the winner but again posted a decent effort in defeat, and he remains capable of winning a maiden, but perhaps at a lesser track. (tchd 13-2)
Smirfys Diamond had shaped with promise on his debut over five furlongs and he showed a good deal of pace here over six, but he was hanging from a fair way out and perhaps he needs some cut in the ground to be seen at his best. (op 14-1 tchd 16-1 and 10-1)
Ireland Dancer(IRE), a fairly cheap purchase, is a half-brother to Icenaslice, a dual five-furlong winner at three, and to Uhuru Dawn, who won between five and a half furlongs and seven furlongs. Unfancied in the market and from a stable that rarely sends out juveniles to win first time, he stayed on quite well from off the pace and can be expected to step up on this when next seen. (op 33-1)
Benchmark had been off the track for three months since last seen getting turned over at odds-on in a Kempton maiden, and although his coat did not look great he looked very fit for this return and was supported into favouritism. He was beaten with over a furlong and a half to run, though, and now has a few questions to answer. (op 7-2 tchd 11-4)
Aegis(IRE), a half-brother to a triple sprint juvenile winner in Italy, looked fit enough, but he was friendless in the market beforehand and ran as though the experience would do him some good. (op 20-1)
Dumas(IRE) looked fit for this return from a two-month absence but he weakened quickly once the tempo increased. (op 6-1)

4029 COLIN INGLEBY-MACKENZIE MEMORIAL STKS (H'CAP) 1m
5:35 (5:36) (Class 3) (0-90,90) 3-Y-0+ **£9,715** (£2,890; £1,444; £721) **Stalls** High

Form RPR

3351 **1** **Illustrious Blue**[26] [3224] 3-9-4 **87** ... PaulDoe 19 101
(W J Knight) *lw: hld up wl in rr: prog on outer fr over 2f out: str run to ld last 150yds: wandered but sn clr* **7/1**[3]

5304 **2** *1 3/4* **Press The Button (GER)**[13] [3644] 3-8-2 **71** oh1 ... NickyMackay 18 81
(J R Boyle) *cl up: trckd ldr over 2f out: led wl over 1f out and kicked on: hdd and outpcd last 150yds* **33/1**

3300 **3** *1/2* **Binanti**[3] [3926] 6-9-9 **85** ... GeorgeBaker 5 94+
(P R Chamings) *dropped in fr wd draw and hld up in detached last pair: swtchd to outer wl over 1f out: r.o wl fnl f: nrst fin* **20/1**

4256 **4** *hd* **Serieux**[12] [3664] 7-8-10 **72** ... (p) TedDurcan 4 81
(D Nicholls) *hld up in rr: prog on outer 2f out: r.o fnl f: nrst fin* **33/1**

0541 **5** *nk* **Joseph Henry**[7] [3812] 4-9-10 **86** 6ex ... JoeFanning 20 94+
(M Johnston) *lw: wl plcd: prog over 2f out: chsd ldr over 1f out: one pce ins fnl f* **9/2**[1]

4023 **6** *nk* **Dry Ice (IRE)**[20] [3413] 4-9-5 **81** ... FergusSweeney 15 89+
(H Candy) *hld up towards rr: effrt on inner fr over 2f out: nt clr run over 1f out: styd on: nt rch ldrs* **5/1**[2]

0660 **7** *1* **Diktatorial**[10] [3733] 4-9-1 **80** ... (t) AdamKirby(3) 2 85+
(G A Butler) *lw: dropped in fr wd draw and hld up in detached last pair: stl last over 2f out: drvn and r.o wl fnl f: no ch* **25/1**

2615 **8** *1/2* **Tempsford Flyer (IRE)**[17] [3546] 3-9-1 **84** ... EddieAhern 14 87
(J W Hills) *cl up: effrt on inner 2f out: chsd ldrs over 1f out: one pce and no imp after* **25/1**

21-0 **9** *shd* **Ordnance Row**[4] [3889] 3-9-7 **90** ... RyanMoore 8 93+
(R Hannon) *hld up wl in rr: stl in rr whn nudged on outer wl over 1f out: styd on ins fnl f: n.d* **10/1**

0056 **10** *hd* **Guest Connections**[10] [3740] 3-9-3 **86** ... (v[1]) TonyCulhane 3 88
(M R Channon) *wl in tch: trckd ldrs over 2f out: drvn and cl up over 1f out : wknd fnl f* **40/1**

0210 **11** *nk* **Desert Dreamer (IRE)**[17] [3532] 5-9-6 **82** ... AlanMunro 16 85+
(P R Chamings) *dwlt: hld up in last trio: effrt on inner over 2f out: nt clr run over 1f out: kpt on: no ch* **20/1**

6420 **12** *nk* **Glencalvie (IRE)**[17] [3532] 5-9-2 **78** ... (v) MartinDwyer 10 80
(J Akehurst) *led at gd pce: hdd wl over 1f out: wknd fnl f* **20/1**

2530 **13** *1* **Shot To Fame (USA)**[41] [2742] 7-10-0 **90** ... PaulHanagan 6 90+
(D Nicholls) *swtg: wl plcd: effrt and nt clr run wl over 2f out: no imp on ldrs over 1f out: hld whn hmpd last 100yds* **20/1**

113- **14** *7* **High Bray (GER)**[276] [6149] 5-9-8 **84** ... JohnEgan 13 68+
(D R C Elsworth) *wl plcd: effrt to press ldrs 2f out: sn rdn and no rspnse: wknd and eased fnl f* **9/2**[1]

5003 **15** *1/2* **Wahoo Sam (USA)**[17] [3528] 6-8-11 **73** ... NCallan 12 56
(K A Ryan) *chsd ldr to over 2f out: wkng whn n.m.r over 1f out* **14/1**

3101 **16** *hd* **Irony (IRE)**[18] [3470] 7-9-12 **88** ... (p) SteveDrowne 11 70+
(A M Balding) *swtg: racd keenly: prom tl wknd over 2f out* **16/1**

1006 **17** *13* **Trans Sonic**[18] [3473] 3-8-8 **77** ... KDarley 9 29+
(A P Jarvis) *chsd ldrs tl wknd rapidly over 2f out: eased: t.o* **50/1**

0005 **18** *shd* **In On The Act (IRE)**[55] [2349] 3-8-2 **71** oh3 ... FrankieMcDonald 17 23+
(Jamie Poulton) *nvr beyond midfield: drvn and losing pl 1/2-way: eased whn t.o fnl f* **66/1**

1m 38.05s (-2.22) **Going Correction** +0.075s/f (Good)
WFA 3 from 4yo+ 7lb **18** Ran SP% **125.7**
Speed ratings (Par 107):114,112,111,111,111 110,109,109,109,109 108,108,107,100,100 99,86,86
CSF £227.79 CT £4525.09 TOTE £8.50: £2.00, £6.90, £4.60, £6.10; EX 357.10 TRIFECTA Not won. Place 6 £84.18, Place 5 £13.49..
Owner Mr & Mrs I H Bendelow **Bred** B J And Mrs Crangle **Trained** Patching, W Sussex

FOCUS
A typical big-field Goodwood handicap in which a high draw proved an advantage and trouble in running played its part. The time was decent and the form looks fairly solid rated around the third and fourth.

NOTEBOOK

Illustrious Blue, 7lb higher than when successful at Newbury on his debut for his new stable, won here in the spring so clearly likes the place, and he was gifted a good draw in stall 19. He was switched wide entering the straight, though, which proved a good decision as he avoided the trouble near the far-side rail, and ran out a clear winner. He has clearly improved for a change of scenery and may well be capable of defying the Handicapper again. (op 6-1)
Press The Button(GER), who ran quite well here in a maiden in June, made the best of his high draw, chasing the pace on the inside for most of the way before switching to challenge in the straight. This was a personal best but whether he can build on this on a more conventional track remains to be seen. (tchd 40-1)
Binanti fared best of those drawn low and saw his race out really well having been dropped in from his unfavourable stall position, allowing him to hug the rail for much of the way before switching out wide approaching the final two furlongs. It was a good ride from Baker.
Serieux, who was beaten in a claimer last time, raced wide most of the way from his poor low draw, and in the circumstances he deserves plenty of credit for managing to finish fourth.
Joseph Henry, saddled with a 6lb penalty for his Ayr success, had the consolation of being drawn best of all in stall 20. He did not get the best of runs but it is difficult to argue he would have done much better had he got into the clear earlier. (op 4-1 tchd 5-1 in places)
Dry Ice(IRE) looked the most unlucky horse in the race as he was travelling well behind horses next to the far-side rail a furlong out but a gap just did not open up for him. He remains one to be interested in for a similar handicap. Official explanation: jockey said gelding was denied a clear run (op 11-2 tchd 6-1 in a place)
Diktatorial, who has dropped 15lb in the handicap since the beginning of the season, had a difficult draw to overcome and, like the third, was dropped in. Weaving between horses in the closing stages, he made up quite a lot of ground, and this may well be the first sign of a return to form for a horse who was a one-time Classic hope. (tchd 28-1)
Ordnance Row, on his toes beforehand, did not run too badly given that he was making a quick reappearance following a lengthy absence. (op 12-1)
Desert Dreamer(IRE) was continually denied a clear run and this run is probably best forgotten. Official explanation: jockey said gelding suffered interference in running
Glencalvie(IRE) was on his toes beforehand and burnt himself out at the head of affairs in the race itself. Official explanation: jockey said gelding ran too free
Shot To Fame(USA), denied a clear run throughout the final two furlongs, eventually had to be snatched up when squeezed for room inside the final furlong.
High Bray(GER) travelled well for a long way and was brought to have every chance two furlongs out, but he soon emptied. Seven furlongs might suit him better these days, but he should still really have done better than this. (tchd 5-1)
Wahoo Sam(USA) looked a bit dull in his coat. Official explanation: jockey said gelding was denied a clear run (op 12-1)
T/Jkpt: £30,610.90 to a £1 stake. Pool: £64,670.98. 1.50 winning tickets. T/Plt: £114.80 to a £1 stake. Pool: £210,564.34. 1,338.60 winning tickets. T/Qpdt: £8.90 to a £1 stake. Pool: £11,325.95. 939.95 winning tickets. JN

4030 - (Foreign Racing) - See Raceform Interactive

4012 GALWAY (R-H)
Tuesday, August 1

OFFICIAL GOING: Good to yielding (good in places on chase course)

4031a TOTE GALWAY MILE EUROPEAN BREEDERS FUND H'CAP (PREMIER HANDICAP) — 1m 100y
7:00 (7:01) 3-Y-0+
£62,620 (£19,758; £9,413; £3,206; £2,172; £1,137)

RPR

1 — **Quinmaster (USA)**[16] [3578] 4-9-0 93 .... JMurtagh 12 — 105+
(M Halford, Ire) *sn led: travelling best fr bef st: sn rdn clr: styd on wl: comf* **8/1**[3]

2 — 2½ — **Absolute Image (IRE)**[30] [3123] 4-9-2 95 .... PJSmullen 18 — 99
(D K Weld, Ire) *a.p: no imp u.p in 2nd st: kpt on same pce fnl f* **3/1**[1]

3 — ½ — **Taqseem (IRE)**[9] [3770] 3-8-11 100 .... CDHayes(3) 5 — 103
(Kevin Prendergast, Ire) *chsd ldrs: 5th into st: kpt on wout threatening in 3rd fnl f* **14/1**

4 — 1¾ — **Latino Magic (IRE)**[3] [3964] 6-10-1 108 .... RMBurke 17 — 108
(R J Osborne, Ire) *trckd ldrs: mainly 4th: no imp u.p and kpt on same pce st* **14/1**

5 — ½ — **Master Marvel (IRE)**[16] [3578] 5-8-5 84 .... WMLordan 3 — 83
(T J O'Mara, Ire) *mid div: 8th and rdn bef st: kpt on wout threatening fnl f* **20/1**

6 — ¾ — **Shayrazan (IRE)**[30] [3123] 5-8-6 88 .... (t) DMGrant(3) 15 — 85
(James Leavy, Ire) *chsd ldrs: rdn in 5th over 3f out: 6th into st: kpt on same pce* **20/1**

7 — shd — **Amourallis (IRE)**[30] [3123] 5-8-9 88 .... (t) WSupple 10 — 85
(H Rogers, Ire) *chsd ldrs: 9th bef st: rdn and kpt on wout threatening* **50/1**

8 — shd — **Back To Paris (IRE)**[352] [4405] 4-9-9 102 .... DPMcDonogh 11 — 99
(Eoin Griffin, Ire) *chsd ldrs: rdn in 6th over 3f out: sn no imp u.p: kpt on same pce* **16/1**

9 — 1¼ — **Dashing Home (IRE)**[13] [3657] 7-8-7 89 .... RPCleary(3) 14 — 83
(Noel Meade, Ire) *towards rr: kpt on same pce u.p fr over 3f out* **20/1**

10 — nk — **Bricks And Porter (IRE)**[16] [3578] 6-8-2 88 .... (bt) SMLevey(7) 9 — 82
(John A Quinn, Ire) *mid div best: kpt on same pce u.p fr 3f out* **14/1**

11 — shd — **Fremen (USA)**[17] [3549] 6-8-10 89 .... KJManning 16 — 82
(D Nicholls) *prom: 3rd and no ex u.p fr bef st* **8/1**[3]

12 — 1½ — **Christavelli**[9] [3773] 7-8-10 89 .... (b[1]) FMBerry 7 — 79
(David Marnane, Ire) *towards rr: sme hdwy but no imp u.p fr 3f out* **20/1**

13 — 2½ — **Sandie (IRE)**[66] [2040] 3-8-5 96 .... DJMoran(5) 2 — 81
(J S Bolger, Ire) *mid div best: nvr a factor* **20/1**

14 — shd — **Bobs Pride (IRE)**[18] [3504] 4-9-8 101 .... DJCasey 6 — 86
(D K Weld, Ire) *towards rr thrght: nvr a factor* **7/1**[2]

15 — ¾ — **Ask Carol (IRE)**[16] [3576] 5-8-12 96 .... (p) JamieMoriarty(5) 8 — 80
(Joseph G Murphy, Ire) *dwlt: sn mid div: no ex u.p fr 3f out* **33/1**

16 — hd — **Emmpat (IRE)**[13] [3657] 8-8-8 87 .... KFallon 1 — 70
(C F Swan, Ire) *mid div best: nvr a factor* **9/1**

17 — 3 — **Arturius (IRE)**[38] [2848] 4-9-9 102 .... JAHeffernan 13 — 79
(P J Rothwell, Ire) *s.i.s and a bhd* **25/1**

18 — hd — **Rockazar**[6] [3123] 5-8-5 89 .... PBBeggy(5) 4 — 66
(G M Lyons, Ire) *mid div best: nvr a factor* **20/1**

1m 48.0s
WFA 3 from 4yo+ 7lb — **18** Ran SP% **132.9**
CSF £29.36 CT £368.53 TOTE £9.80: £2.50, £1.50, £3.40, £2.90; DF 36.30.
Owner William Durkan **Bred** Farish And Farish Llc **Trained** the Curragh, Co Kildare

NOTEBOOK

Fremen(USA) could not defy a 7lb higher mark than when winning at York on his previous start and may be better suited by decent ground. (op 9/1 tchd 10/1)

4034a TOTE EUROPEAN BREEDERS FUND MAIDEN — 7f
8:40 (8:43) 3-Y-0 — **£8,979** (£2,634; £1,255; £427)

RPR

1 — **Yellow Ridge (IRE)**[1] [4015] 3-9-3 69 .... FranciscoDaSilva 11 — 69
(Luke Comer, Ire) *sn led: strly pressed fnl f: styd on wl* **20/1**

2 — ¾ — **Diman (IRE)** 3-9-3 .... PJSmullen 5 — 67+
(D K Weld, Ire) *chsd ldrs: clsr in 3rd into st: rdn to chal in 2nd ins fnl f: kpt on same pce* **1/1**[1]

3 — 2½ — **Carlowsantana (IRE)**[19] [3463] 3-9-3 .... JAHeffernan 1 — 60
(Adrian Sexton, Ire) *chsd ldrs: rdn to chal in 2nd bef st: dropped to 3rd and kpt on same pce ins fnl f* **14/1**

4 — 1¼ — **Mystery Cat (IRE)**[88] [1468] 3-9-3 .... (t) WSupple 15 — 57
(Miss S Collins, Ire) *trckd ldrs: dropped to 6th into st: sn no imp u.p: kpt on wout threatening* **10/1**

5 — 1½ — **Original Empire (IRE)**[5] [3885] 3-9-3 49 .... CO'Donoghue 12 — 53
(F Costello, Ire) *chsd ldrs: 6th early st: kpt on same pce u.p fnl f* **100/1**

6 — nk — **Forbidden (IRE)**[9] [3771] 3-9-3 .... (t) FMBerry 9 — 52
(Daniel Mark Loughnane, Ire) *rr of mid div: rdn and kpt on wout threatening st* **20/1**

7 — nk — **Wakita (IRE)**[9] [3768] 3-8-12 .... MCHussey 7 — 46
(Gerard Keane, Ire) *mid div: hdwy on outer bef st: kpt on same pce u.p* **33/1**

8 — shd — **Gulf To Bay (IRE)** 3-9-3 .... DPMcDonogh 4 — 51
(Edward Lynam, Ire) *dwlt: towards rr: kpt on wout threatening u.p st* **20/1**

9 — 1½ — **Hucklebuck (IRE)**[13] [3659] 3-9-3 76 .... (b[1]) WMLordan 8 — 47
(T J O'Mara, Ire) *prom: dropped to 5th into st: sn no ex u.p* **5/1**[2]

10 — nk — **Roslea Lady (IRE)**[242] [6477] 3-8-12 .... VRDeSouza 14 — 41
(Liam McAteer, Ire) *mid div: hdwy st: checked and no ex ins fnl f* **25/1**

11 — ¾ — **Alone It Stands (IRE)** 3-9-3 .... KFallon 10 — 44
(D Nicholls) *trckd ldrs: 4th into st: sn no ex u.p: eased ins fnl f* **11/2**[3]

12 — 1¼ — **Kitmaah**[18] [3512] 3-8-7 45 .... SMGorey(5) 16 — 36
(R McGlinchey, Ire) *mid div: no imp u.p and kpt on same pce fr bef st* **100/1**

13 — 1¼ — **Tsini**[298] [5710] 3-8-5 .... KTMaher(7) 3 — 32
(Patrick J Flynn, Ire) *mid div: no imp u.p fr bef st* **50/1**

14 — 6 — **Timore Tiger (IRE)**[13] [3659] 3-9-0 .... RPCleary(3) 13 — 21
(Martin Browne, Ire) *mid div: lost pl and no ex fr bef st* **20/1**

15 — 12 — **Tartu (IRE)** 3-8-9 .... DMGrant(3) 2 — —
(Patrick J Flynn, Ire) *a towards rr* **40/1**

16 — 7 — **Carmens Girl (IRE)**[10] [3754] 3-8-12 .... NGMcCullagh 6 — —
(Daniel Mark Loughnane, Ire) *a bhd: sn trailing: nvr a factor* **50/1**

1m 29.7s — **16** Ran SP% **132.0**
CSF £40.22 TOTE £42.30: £5.40, £1.30, £2.10, £1.80; DF 197.60.
Owner Luke Comer **Bred** Mrs Margaret Comer **Trained** Dunboyne, Co Meath

NOTEBOOK

Alone It Stands(IRE), a 15,000euros half-brother to amongst others Golden Turk, a useful multiple sprint scoreri at two, out of a winner at two and three in Italy, was well held on his racecourse debut but should know a lot more next time. (op 5/1 tchd 6/1)
T/Jkpt: @2,727.70. Pool of @58,193.00 - 16 winning units. T/Plt: @65.80. Pool of @11,503.50 - 31 winning units. II

3989 DEAUVILLE (R-H)
Tuesday, August 1

OFFICIAL GOING: Turf course - good to soft; all-weather - standard

4035a PRIX DE PSYCHE (GROUP 3) (FILLIES) — 1m 2f
3:05 (3:07) 3-Y-0 — **£27,586** (£11,034; £8,276; £5,517; £2,759)

RPR

1 — **Chaibia (IRE)**[51] [2491] 3-8-12 .... DBoeuf 10 — 108
(D Smaga, France) *hld up, hdwy on outside 3f out, 8th str, led just inside final f on outside, ridden out, ran on well* **134/10**

2 — hd — **Lahudood**[37] [2913] 3-8-12 .... FSpanu 9 — 108
(J E Hammond, France) *held up in rear, last straight, tracked winer from 2f out, switched right 1f out, ran on but being held last 50yds* **39/10**[2]

3 — 1 — **Mauralakana (FR)**[51] [2491] 3-8-12 .... IMendizabal 6 — 106
(J-C Rouget, France) *a prom, disp 2nd before half-way, 2nd straight, led well over 1f out to just inside final f, no extra last 100yds* **42/10**[3]

4 — 2 — **Summer's Eve**[30] [3133] 3-8-12 .... DaneO'Neill 1 — 102
(H Candy) *a prom, disp 2nd half-way, 4th straight, disputed 2nd over 1f out, kept on one pace under pressure* **19/1**

5 — 1½ — **Alloway**[51] [2491] 3-9-2 .... JVictoire 7 — 104
(A Fabre, France) *always prominent, 3rd straight, disputed 2nd over 1f out, one pace final f* **82/10**

6 — hd — **Sandglass**[47] [2580] 3-8-12 .... RichardHughes 8 — 99
(Mrs A J Perrett) *held up, 10th straight, effort towards inside from well over 1f out, no extra final f* **61/10**

7 — snk — **Zayafa (FR)**[113] 3-8-12 .... CSoumillon 3 — 99
(A De Royer-Dupre, France) *mid-division, 6th straight, never able to challenge* **84/10**

8 — 2½ — **Sirene Doloise (FR)**[51] [2491] 3-8-12 .... TThulliez 11 — 95
(A Bonin, France) *hld up in mid-div, closed up on outside 3f out, 5th straight, disp 2nd 1 1/2f out, gradually wknd* **22/1**

9 — 1½ — **Mussoorie (FR)**[51] [2491] 3-8-12 .... OPeslier 5 — 92
(R Gibson, France) *held up, 7th straight, ridden & beaten well over 1f out* **27/10**[1]

10 — 3 — **Penchee**[37] [2913] 3-8-12 .... C-PLemaire 2 — 86
(Mme C Head-Maarek, France) *led to well over 1f out* **61/10**

11 — **Shamarkanda (FR)**[42] 3-8-12 .... MBlancpain 4 — —
(Y De Nicolay, France) *mid-division, 8th straight on inside, weakened quickly 1 1/2f out* **33/1**

2m 7.50s — **11** Ran SP% **135.6**
PARI-MUTUEL: WIN 14.40; PL 3.30, 1.90, 1.80; DF 41.30.
Owner M Parrish **Bred** Shadwell Estate Company Ltd **Trained** Lamorlaye, France

NOTEBOOK

Chaibia(IRE), last rounding the final turn, was brought wide in the straight and quickened impressively to take the lead at the furlong marker. She deserved her Group 3 victory as she has been unlucky all season, and she will now be prepared for the Prix de L'Opera in October.

Lahudood, another held up for a late run, took a little time to quicken in the straight and was slightly hampered two furlongs out by the winner. Switched towards the far rail, she accelerated impressively from a furlong out and only failed by a head. She is still a maiden and probably the best one trained in France, and if she recovers well she will go for the Prix Minerve later in the month.
Mauralakana(FR) raced in second place for much of the ten and a half furlongs and, while she appeared to be outpaced when things quickened up in the straight, she ran on again at the finish like a filly who will prefer a longer trip.
Summer's Eve, given every possible chance, was settled on the rail behind the leaders. Under pressure from two out, she stayed on bravely but was rather one-paced as the race drew to a close.
Sandglass never really looked likely to take a hand in the finish. Towards the tail of the field early on, she did make some late progress up the far rail but without being a real threat.

4023 GOODWOOD (R-H)

Wednesday, August 2

OFFICIAL GOING: Good to firm

Wind: Moderate becoming strong, half-against Weather: Fine but cloudy

4036 INVESCO PERPETUAL GOODWOOD STKS (H'CAP) 2m 5f

2:05 (2:05) (Class 2) (0-95,90) 3-Y-0+

£31,160 (£9,330; £4,665; £2,335; £1,165; £585)

Form / RPR

2111 **1** **Key Time (IRE)**[12] [3696] 4-9-1 **81** ..... SebSanders 17 — 90
(Sir Mark Prescott) *racd in 4th and sn clr of rest: clsd to ld over 3f out and kicked on: hrd drvn fnl 2f: hld on* **5/1**[1]

6543 **2** *nk* **Theatre (USA)**[14] [3649] 7-8-7 **73** ..... JohnEgan 16 — 81
(Jamie Poulton) *hld up in rr: prog 7f out: rdn over 4f out: outpcd over 3f out: styd on wl to chse wnr last 100yds: clsd but nt quite get up* **16/1**

-401 **3** *1 1/4* **Master Cobbler (IRE)**[34] [3028] 4-8-8 **74** ..... (p) TPQueally 18 — 81
(J Akehurst) *hld up in rr: prog 1/2-way: chsd ldrs 4f out: rdn to dispute 2nd fr 3f out: hanging rt over 1f out: kpt on same pce* **12/1**

2505 **4** *shd* **Mceldowney**[5] [3888] 4-9-1 **86** ..... GregFairley(5) 3 — 93
(M Johnston) *towards rr: pushed along 8f out: prog u.p on outer fr 4f out: styd on dourly: nrst fin* **14/1**

1-10 **5** *1* **Sir Monty (USA)**[34] [3028] 4-8-11 **77** ..... RyanMoore 14 — 83
(Mrs A J Perrett) *swtg: hld up wl in rr: prog 8f out to chse ldrs 5f out: chsd wnr 3f out: tried to cl but one pce fr over 1f out* **14/1**

/646 **6** *3/4* **Dorothy's Friend**[18] [3533] 6-9-10 **90** ..... SteveDrowne 8 — 95
(R Charlton) *lw: wl plcd in chsng pack: effrt over 4f out: drvn and styd on fr over 2f out: nvr quite able to rch ldrs* **5/1**[1]

5033 **7** *5* **Kristensen**[29] [3177] 7-8-1 **67** ..... (p) FrankieMcDonald 9 — 67
(Karen McLintock) *hld up in rr: prog to midfield 6f out: effrt on outer over 3f out: chsng ldrs 2f out: wknd over 1f out* **33/1**

0210 **8** *1/2* **Ski Jump (USA)**[18] [3533] 6-9-1 **81** ..... (v) PaulHanagan 5 — 81
(R A Fahey) *settled in midfield: effrt over 4f out: outpcd by ldrs over 3f out: one pce and no imp after* **16/1**

0122 **9** *1 3/4* **Our Monogram**[20] [3446] 10-8-7 **76** ..... NelsonDeSouza(3) 6 — 74
(R M Beckett) *rdn after s to chse ldr's str pce: drvn and lost pl 4f out: grad fdd* **10/1**[3]

0/53 **10** *3 1/2* **Almah (SAF)**[18] [3522] 8-8-8 **74** ..... (b) AlanMunro 4 — 69
(Miss Venetia Williams) *lw: prom in chsng gp: effrt and cl up over 5f out: wknd over 2f out* **20/1**

3311 **11** *4* **Mersey Sound (IRE)**[11] [3743] 8-8-8 **79** ..... MarcHalford(5) 15 — 70
(D R C Elsworth) *hld up wl in rr: outpcd and rdn over 3f out: no ch whn nt clr run and swtchd lft over 2f out: no real prog* **7/1**[2]

0403 **12** *2 1/2* **Ten Carat**[21] [3396] 6-8-11 **77** ..... KDarley 2 — 65
(M Todhunter) *settled wl in rr: rdn and struggling over 3f out: no ch after* **16/1**

5105 **13** *3/4* **Salute (IRE)**[28] [3203] 7-9-0 **80** ..... RobertHavlin 20 — 67
(P G Murphy) *lw: a wl in rr: rdn and no prog 3f out* **50/1**

40-0 **14** *4* **Distant Prospect (IRE)**[43] [2723] 9-9-2 **82** ..... MartinDwyer 10 — 65
(A M Balding) *swtg: nvr on terms: wl in rr and no ch whn nt clr run over 2f out: wknd* **16/1**

0060 **15** *13* **Fortune Island (IRE)**[28] [3203] 7-9-2 **82** ..... (vt) JimmyFortune 7 — 52
(D E Pipe) *nvr beyond midfield: drvn and no prog over 3f out: wknd and eased 2f out: t.o* **33/1**

4630 **16** *1/2* **Eastborough (IRE)**[2] [4005] 7-8-4 **70** ow5 ..... EddieAhern 11 — 40
(B G Powell) *swtg: hld up wl in rr: last of main gp and struggling over 3f out: t.o* **66/1**

3231 **17** *5* **Oddsmaker (IRE)**[11] [3723] 5-8-5 **71** ow1 ..... (t) PhilipRobinson 12 — 37
(M A Barnes) *led at furious pce: hdd & wknd over 3f out: eased fnl 2f: t.o* **16/1**

0305 **18** *2 1/2* **Paradise Flight (IRE)**[25] [3284] 5-7-12 **64** oh1 ..... (b) CatherineGannon 13 — 26
(K A Ryan) *prom in chsng gp to 1/2-way: struggling in rr over 4f out: t.o* **33/1**

4-50 **19** *8* **Darasim (IRE)**[28] [3203] 8-9-0 **80** ..... (v) JoeFanning 19 — 34
(M Johnston) *chsd ldng pair tl wknd u.p over 4f out: t.o* **25/1**

4003 **20** *6* **Ocean Of Storms (IRE)**[4] [3952] 11-7-13 **72** ow7 ..... MarkCoumbe(7) 1 — 20
(N I M Rossiter) *b: hld up in detached last: t.o after 8f: pushed along 9f out: no prog* **66/1**

4m 27.9s (-5.20) **Going Correction** -0.10s/f (Good) **20** Ran SP% **127.7**
Speed ratings (Par 109):105,104,104,104,103 103,101,101,100,99 98,97,96,95,90 90,88,87,84,81
CSF £81.73 CT £941.10 TOTE £4.90: £1.80, £3.40, £4.10, £4.50; EX 106.50 TRIFECTA Not won..
Owner G Moore - Osborne House **Bred** Airlie Stud **Trained** Newmarket, Suffolk

FOCUS
Flip start. A decent marathon handicap, run at a searching gallop, and the form looks solid. The winner is highly progressive and looks an ideal Cesarewitch type.

NOTEBOOK
Key Time(IRE), 7lb higher than winning at Carlisle 12 days previously, was given an astute tactical ride by Sanders and just did enough to register his fifth success from his six outings to date since resuming this season. The longer trip proved well within his compass, his rider's decision to kick for home nearing three out proved decisive, and he probably won with a little up his sleeve. This must rate a career-best effort and, while opportunities over this sort of trip are few and far between nowadays, the Cesarewitch in October would appeal as a very realistic target, and he should not go up too much in the weights for this. In the longer term, he also greatly appeals as the type to make his mark as a hurdler. (op 9-2 tchd 11-2)
Theatre(USA), third in this event last term, was doing all of his best work towards the finish and only just failed to reel in the winner. This was his best effort of the current Flat season, he does like this venue, and is a fair benchmark for the form. However, he is not one for win-only purposes.
Master Cobbler(IRE), up 4lb for breaking his duck at Salisbury 34 days previously, stayed on dourly from off the pace over this extra distance and ran very close to his recent level in defeat. He remains in decent form. (op 14-1)
Mceldowney, as had been the case at Ascot five days previously, required all of his rider's strength from an early stage but still kept on stoutly for pressure and clearly got the longer trip. This must rate a near career-best effort in defeat.
Sir Monty(USA), who got very warm beforehand, emerged to have his chance at the top of the straight before finding just the same pace when it mattered. This was a much more encouraging effort, but he is probably happier over a shorter trip. (op 12-1)
Dorothy's Friend, very well backed, turned in an improved effort on this return to turf and got home over the longer trip. This was a respectable effort under top weight, but he is proving hard to catch right this year all the same. (op 7-1)
Mersey Sound(IRE), raised a stone in the handicap for winning on his last two outings, both at Newmarket, never really got into it from off the pace and has to rate disappointing in this bid for the hat-trick.
Fortune Island(IRE) was on his toes beforehand. Official explanation: jockey said gelding ran too free (op 40-1)

4037 VEUVE CLICQUOT VINTAGE STKS (GROUP 2) 7f

2:40 (2:42) (Class 1) 2-Y-O

£39,746 (£15,064; £7,539; £3,759; £1,883; £945) **Stalls** High

Form / RPR

151 **1** **Strategic Prince**[20] [3442] 2-9-3 ..... EddieAhern 1 — 114
(P F I Cole) *trckd ldr: led 2f out: drvn and styd on wl fnl f: a holding on* **6/1**

2 *nk* **Duke Of Marmalade (IRE)**[33] [3057] 2-9-0 ..... MJKinane 6 — 110
(A P O'Brien, Ire) *lw: w'like: scope: str: trckd ldrs: effrt 2f out: drvn to chse wnr ins fnl f: clsd but a jst hld* **11/4**[1]

21 **3** *2* **Kirklees (IRE)**[28] [3187] 2-9-0 ..... JoeFanning 5 — 105
(M Johnston) *lw: w'like: scope: str: led to 2f out: rdn and kpt on same pce after* **10/1**

11 **4** *3/4* **Silent Waves (USA)**[9] [3788] 2-9-0 ..... KDarley 10 — 103
(M Johnston) *w'like: trckd ldrs: rdn over 2f out: hung lft over 1f out: kpt on same pce* **10/3**[2]

1 **5** *1 1/4* **Medicine Path**[19] [3498] 2-9-0 ..... RichardMullen 7 — 100
(E J O'Neill) *trckd ldr: effrt on inner to chal over 2f out: btn over 1f out: wknd ins fnl f* **5/1**[3]

46 **6** *1 3/4* **Eager Lover (USA)**[12] [3701] 2-9-0 ..... MichaelHills 9 — 95
(B W Hills) *stdd s: hld up in last: wl off the pce over 2f out: shuffled along and kpt on steadily* **100/1**

541 **7** *3 1/2* **Kalgoorlie (USA)**[21] [3417] 2-9-0 ..... LDettori 4 — 86
(J Noseda) *lw: pushed along in rr after 2f: sme prog into midfield over 2f out: hanging and no imp after: wknd over 1f out* **7/1**

251 **8** *1 3/4* **Jo'Burg (USA)**[23] [3363] 2-9-0 ..... RyanMoore 3 — 82
(Mrs A J Perrett) *hld up in rr: rdn and struggling 1/2-way: no ch after* **14/1**

01 **9** *1 3/4* **Nur Tau (IRE)**[26] [3253] 2-9-0 ..... MartinDwyer 2 — 77
(M P Tregoning) *t.k.h: hld up in midfield: rdn and steadily wknd fr over 2f out* **33/1**

0 **10** *3* **Habalwatan (IRE)**[20] [3445] 2-9-0 ..... KerrinMcEvoy 8 — 69
(C E Brittain) *in tch in midfield to 3f out: sn wknd* **100/1**

1m 26.02s (-2.02) **Going Correction** -0.10s/f (Good) **10** Ran SP% **113.9**
Speed ratings (Par 106):107,106,104,103,102 100,96,94,92,88
CSF £22.21 TOTE £7.20: £2.20, £1.50, £2.90; EX 22.80 Trifecta £211.20 Pool: £1,487.68 - 5.00 winning tickets..
Owner H R H Sultan Ahmad Shah **Bred** The Ausherra Partnership **Trained** Whatcombe, Oxon

FOCUS
A decent renewal of this Group 2, which has been responsible for many top class juveniles in the past, including this year's Derby hero Sir Percy, and the form looks solid with the first two coming clear.

NOTEBOOK
Strategic Prince ◆, under a penalty for landing the July Stakes at Newmarket, showed a great attitude to hold off the late challenge of Duke Of Marmalade and follow up with a career-best effort over the extra furlong. He was given a positive ride by Ahern, clearly enjoys racing on a quick surface, and is probably value for further as he appeared to idle somewhat when in front. Considering he is a half-brother to dour stayers Yorkshire and Riyadh amongst others, he can be expected to stay much further as a three-year-old, but he also possesses a decent turn of foot and is fast developing into a very exciting colt with next year's Classics in mind. He was immediately promoted to near the top of the ante-post market for next year's 2000 Guineas, and his trainer indicated he was likely to follow a similar path as last season's winner of this event and subsequent 2000 Guineas runner-up and Derby hero, Sir Percy, and head next to the Dewhurst. (op 5-1)
Duke Of Marmalade(IRE) ◆, off the mark at the second attempt over this trip at the Curragh a month ago, threw down a strong challenge to the winner inside the final furlong but could not get past that rival try as he might. He took time to hit full stride in the straight, indeed he still looked green, and it may be that he is already in need of a mile. He was a clear second best, clearly has a race of this class within his compass before the year is out, and should really improve again with this experience under his belt. Like the winner, he too was promoted to near the top of the ante-post betting for the 2000 Guineas next year. (op 9-4 tchd 2-1)
Kirklees(IRE), comfortably off the mark at Catterick over this trip, posted a solid effort from the front on this marked step up in class. He clearly stays well, appears to have the right attitude - like so many from his stable - and is on an upwards curve. He looks a likely sort for the Royal Lodge at Ascot next month. (op 12-1 tchd 14-1 in a place)
Silent Waves(USA), who made it two wins from as many starts when landing a novice event at Beverley over slightly further nine days previously, was denied a clear run when trying to improve turning for home and ran slightly better than the bare form suggests. He may also have found this coming too soon and looks well worth another chance in Group company. (op 7-2 tchd 4-1)
Medicine Path, well backed when winning readily on his debut at York last time, was given a positive ride and had his chance. This was a big step up in class and, while he was not disgraced, he may be better off dropping to Group 3 or Listed company in the short term. (op 11-2)
Eager Lover(USA), who had shown just fair form in two maidens to date, proved a little free under restraint through the early stages before keeping on without threatening in the home straight. This must still rate a vastly-improved effort and a maiden in the coming weeks should really be his for the taking.
Kalgoorlie(USA) was never really travelling out the back and failed to raise his game on this step back up in class. (op 8-1)
Jo'Burg(USA), who made heavy weather of landing the odds in a Windsor maiden 23 days previously, was another to disappoint on this return to Group company and has it to prove now.
Nur Tau(IRE), representing last year's winning stable, ultimately paid for refusing to settle on this big step up in grade. (op 50-1)

4038 CANTOR SPREADFAIR SUSSEX STKS (GROUP 1) 1m

3:15 (3:17) (Class 1) 3-Y-O+

£180,134 (£68,272; £34,167; £17,036; £8,534; £4,282) **Stalls** High

Form / RPR

-632 **1** **Court Masterpiece**[43] [2722] 6-9-7 115 ..... JimmyFortune 5 — 124
(E A L Dunlop) *lw: sn hld up in 5th and off the pce: prog over 2f out: swtchd ins and qcknd to ld over 1f out: sn clr: drvn out* **15/2**

-416 **2** *2* **Soviet Song (IRE)**[21] 3416 6-9-4 119 JMurtagh 1 116
(J R Fanshawe) *swtg: hld up: prog to chse ldng pair over 3f out: rdn to chal over 1f out: wnt 2nd jst ins fnl f but no ch w wnr* **11/2**[3]

0-16 **3** *½* **Rob Roy (USA)**[74] 1840 4-9-7 111 RyanMoore 6 118
(Sir Michael Stoute) *lw: hld up in last: outpcd and rdn 3f out: styd on fr over 1f out on inner to press for 2nd nr fin* **12/1**

4104 **4** *½* **Aussie Rules (USA)**[25] 3314 3-9-0 MJKinane 7 116
(A P O'Brien, Ire) *hld up in 6th: effrt on outer wl over 2f out: rdn to chse ldrs over 1f out: hanging rt and nt qckn* **8/1**

-411 **5** *½* **Araafa (IRE)**[43] 2721 3-9-0 120 AlanMunro 2 115
(J Noseda) *trckd ldr over 5f out: led over 2f out: hdd and nt qckn over 1f out: wknd ins fnl f* **11/10**[1]

10-1 **6** *4* **Echo Of Light**[18] 3534 4-9-7 116 LDettori 4 107
(Saeed Bin Suroor) *taken early and steadily to post: led at decent pce: hdd over 2f out: wknd wl over 1f out* **9/2**[2]

-152 **7** *18* **Vanderlin**[18] 3518 7-9-7 112 MartinDwyer 3 65
(A M Balding) *lw: chsd ldr to over 5f out: sn pushed along: wknd rapidly 3f out: t.o* **100/1**

1m 36.1s (-4.17) **Going Correction** -0.10s/f (Good)
WFA 3 from 4yo+ 7lb **7** Ran SP% **112.7**
Speed ratings (Par 117):116,114,113,113,112 108,90
CSF £46.20 TOTE £6.30: £2.50, £3.00; EX 36.00.

Owner Gainsborough Stud **Bred** Gainsborough Stud Management Ltd **Trained** Newmarket, Suffolk

FOCUS
This looked an up-to-scratch renewal of this Group 1 event, with four previous Group 1 winners and two Classic-winning three-year-olds in attendance. It was run at a strong early pace and those racing off the pace were at a distinct advantage. The winning time was about right for a Group 1 in the conditions.

NOTEBOOK
Court Masterpiece, an unfortunate second in the Queen Anne at Royal Ascot last time, found the generous early pace right up his street and he made amends with a comfortable success. Having been ridden with restraint through the early stages, he found the gap on the inside rail coming at just the right time, and duly produced a telling turn of foot to take full advantage. This confirms he is fully effective over this trip, he is evidently better than ever this term, and does love this venue. His future options are numerous, but a trip to the Breeders' Cup Mile in America later in the year must surely come under strong consideration, with his versatility as regards underfoot conditions a big advantage. However, his trainer stated he could well drop back in trip for the Haydock Sprint Cup over six furlongs in September, with the strong possibility of a soft surface in that thought likely to play into his hands. (op 8-1)
Soviet Song(IRE), winner of this event in 2004 and a narrow runner-up to Proclamation last year, bounced back to form and was another who enjoyed racing off the strong early pace. She was put in her place by the winner, but she still has a host of options available to her this season, with the Group 1 Matron Stakes and Sun Chariot - both back against her own sex - likely to be on her agenda.
Rob Roy(USA), last seen running below-par in the Lockinge in May, took the same route as the winner up the inside rail and produced a career-best effort in defeat. He is still lightly-raced, clearly appreciates a sound surface, and the manner in which he stayed on suggested he could be ready to tackle ten furlongs again now. The Irish Champion Stakes looks a viable option. (op 16-1)
Aussie Rules(USA) kept on from off the pace down the middle of the track, but tended to hang under pressure, and was never a serious threat. He might just be best on easier ground and would probably be more effective when ridden more positively over this trip in the future. (op 10-1)
Araafa(IRE), taking on his elders for the first time, paid for chasing the strong early pace and ran below his best on this totally different track. He should not be written off on the back of this display. (tchd 5-4 and 11-8 in places)
Echo Of Light, supplemented for this after his recent Group 3 win on the All-Weather, was allowed to be taken to the start early and moved very quietly to post. He ultimately went off too fast for his own good and set the race up for the closers. The suspicion remains that he has the talent to be effective at this level, but he is clearly headstrong, and this effort again leaves him with plenty to prove. Official explanation: jockey said colt lost its action
Vanderlin Official explanation: vet said gelding was stiff behind

4039 CANTORSPREADFAIR.COM STKS (HERITAGE H'CAP) 1m 4f
3:50 (3:51) (Class 2) (0-105,100) 3-Y-O

£52,972 (£15,861; £7,930; £3,969; £1,980; £994) **Stalls** Low

Form RPR

2411 **1** **Strategic Mount**[18] 3539 3-8-6 85 EddieAhern 7 98
(P F I Cole) *led after 2f: mde rest: drvn and clr fr over 1f out: styd on stoutly* **6/1**[2]

3113 **2** *1 ¾* **Bandama (IRE)**[40] 2805 3-9-0 93 MJKinane 12 103
(Mrs A J Perrett) *lw: chsd ldrs: rdn 3f out: prog u.p to take 2nd jst over 1f out: styd on but nvr able to chal* **8/1**[3]

1434 **3** *2 ½* **King's Head (IRE)**[20] 3443 3-9-4 97 (p) PhilipRobinson 5 103
(M A Jarvis) *swtg: chsd ldrs: rdn over 3f out: kpt on u.p to take 3rd wl ins fnl f* **11/1**

4052 **4** *½* **London Express (IRE)**[3] 3971 3-8-11 90 StanleyChin 10 95+
(M Johnston) *sn in rr: rdn and struggling 4f out: no prog and stl only 11th over 1f out: r.o wl after: nrst fin* **12/1**

4-42 **5** *nk* **Gordonsville**[22] 3376 3-8-4 83 MartinDwyer 2 88
(A M Balding) *swtg: dwlt: rapid prog to chse ldng pair after 2f: rdn and no imp 3f out: plugged on same pce* **33/1**

-512 **6** *nk* **Enjoy The Moment**[40] 2805 3-8-10 89 ShaneKelly 9 96+
(J A Osborne) *b.hind: hld up wl in rr: rdn 3f out: prog 2f out: styng on and ch of a pl whn nt clr run 1f out and ins fnl f* **11/1**

1114 **7** *1* **Gower Song**[11] 3739 3-9-0 93 JohnEgan 4 96
(D R C Elsworth) *settled in midfield: effrt and rdn on outer over 3f out: no prog and btn over 2f out: kpt on fnl f* **16/1**

6330 **8** *shd* **Baan (USA)**[40] 2801 3-9-7 100 KDarley 8 102
(M Johnston) *led for 2f: chsd wnr and clr of rest: drvn over 3f out: btn wl over 1f out: wknd fnl f* **28/1**

9 *shd* **Magicalmysterytour (IRE)**[32] 3106 3-8-12 91 JMurtagh 1 93+
(A P O'Brien, Ire) *w'like: str: settled in midfield: effrt on outer over 3f out: drvn and no real prog over 2f out: wknd and eased fnl f* **12/1**

0051 **10** *nk* **Nihal (IRE)**[6] 3882 3-8-9 88 5ex JoeFanning 11 90
(M Johnston) *b.hind: swtg: chsd ldrs: rdn and no imp over 3f out: fdd fnl 2f* **14/1**

321 **11** *hd* **Ask**[37] 2917 3-8-11 90 RyanMoore 16 92
(Sir Michael Stoute) *lw: settled in midfield: pushed along 4f out: rdn and no prog 3f out: btn after* **2/1**[1]

-401 **12** *nk* **Kaylianni**[48] 2578 3-8-10 89 TonyCulhane 3 90
(M R Channon) *hld up wl in rr: rdn on outer over 3f out: hung rt to rail fr over 2f out: plugged on: n.d* **20/1**

1346 **13** *½* **Lake Poet (IRE)**[20] 3443 3-8-11 90 KerrinMcEvoy 13 90
(C E Brittain) *hld up in last pair: rdn and struggling wl over 3f out: kpt on fnl 2f: no ch* **16/1**

3012 **14** *40* **Prowess (IRE)**[25] 3292 3-8-13 92 MichaelHills 14 28
(B W Hills) *sn midfield: struggling over 4f out: sn wknd and eased: t.o* **14/1**

-101 **15** *2 ½* **Oh Glory Be (USA)**[35] 2986 3-8-8 87 RichardHughes 15 19
(R Hannon) *a wl in rr: wknd u.p 3f out: virtually p.u fnl f* **16/1**

2m 34.66s (-4.26) **Going Correction** -0.10s/f (Good) **15** Ran SP% **132.9**
Speed ratings (Par 106):110,108,107,106,106 106,105,105,105,105 105,105,104,78,76
CSF £57.84 CT £544.34 TOTE £6.70: £2.20, £2.90, £4.10; EX 65.20 Trifecta £778.70 Pool: £2,522.74 - 2.30 winning tickets..

Owner Ben & Sir Martyn Arbib **Bred** Arbib Bloodstock Partnership **Trained** Whatcombe, Oxon

FOCUS
A highly competitive handicap run at just a steady gallop, but while there is no doubt Strategic Mount was suited in being out in front, he galloped on remorselessly and would probably have picked up again had something got to him. This is strong form and the race should produce its share of winners, and is likely to have a bearing on the outcome of York's Melrose Handicap later in the month.

NOTEBOOK
Strategic Mount ◆, a highly progressive son of Montjeu who destroyed his field over 1m6f at Nottingham last time, went on after two furlongs and was able to lead at just a steady gallop. He gradually wound it up and really started to pour the pressure on from three out, galloping his rivals into the ground for an impressive display. Yes he had the race run to suit, but the switch to positive tactics on a sound surface has transformed the colt and if he continues to progress at this rate he will soon be mixing it at Group level, as his high-class brother Strategic Choice did so effectively. The Melrose Handicap is on the agenda first however and, although he will go up a fair bit for this, he looks progressive enough to handle it and will be well suited to the demands of the track at York. He should make a smashing older horse. (op 13-2 tchd 7-1)
Bandama(IRE), a progressive sort who came from behind to claim a creditable third behind Linas Selection at Royal Ascot, looked to hold strong claims off just a 2lb higher mark in what looked an open race. Always towards the head of the chasing pack, he was outpaced when the winner kicked, but kept on well in the closing stages and finished nicely ahead of the third. He may need to progress to win a race of this nature, but is in good hands and may even get a little further in time. (op 11-1)
King's Head(IRE), who again hinted that a rise to this distance would suit when a keeping-on fourth behind Formal Decree at Newmarket, found improvement for the fitting of cheekpieces and he was coming home better than most at the finish. He clearly saw the trip out well, but is not well enough handicapped to win a race of this nature and may continue to struggle to get his head in front. (op 10-1 tchd 12-1)
London Express(IRE) ◆, who found only stablemate Road To Love too good at Ascot four days previously, was given a lot to do in a steadily-run race and the way he finished suggested he would have at least been placed had his jockey been more aware. His earlier effort behind another stablemate Linas Selection at Royal Ascot confirmed this is his distance and he may not yet have done improving, especially once getting his favoured slow surface. He is another Melrose possible. (op 14-1)
Gordonsville ◆ has looked paceless in three maidens and he stepped up massively on anything he had previously achieved on this handicap debut, keeping on right the way to the line having been prominent on the outside of the chasing pack throughout. As a relation of top-class stayer Turgeon he is obviously going to appreciate trips in excess of this and the fine-looking son of Generous is one to keep on side. (tchd 40-1)
Enjoy The Moment, another to come from the Linas Selection Ascot race, ran so well that day when claiming second, but he was not as well in at the weights on this occasion and, like London Express, he got caught up at the back and then blocked when trying to come through for the places. He should probably have been fourth and remains capable of scoring off this mark. Official explanation: jockey said gelding was denied a clear run (op 12-1)
Gower Song, a highly progressive filly who has shot up 29lb in under two months, winning four handicaps before being beaten just a length in a muddling Listed affair at Newmarket last time, ran well on this return to handicap company, but she was unable to match several better-handicapped rivals and it may well be any further success she gains this season comes in uncompetitive fillies' Listed events.
Baan(USA) is not the biggest, but he has largely run well in small-field Group events this season and this was another good effort on his return to handicaps. Always likely to struggle under top weight, he tracked the winner for most of the way having led early, but was readily brushed aside inside the final quarter mile. This was as a good an effort as could have been expected, but he is going to remain very hard to place and Sheikh Hamdan has probably made a wise decision in offloading him. (op 25-1)
Magicalmysterytour(IRE), unsuited by the drop back to 1m2f at the Curragh last time for his handicap debut, was expected to be much better suited by the return to this distance, but having briefly made a move insdie the four pole, his effort tailed off and he proved most disappointing, extending his trainer's poor run at Glorious Goodwood which stretches back to Rock Of Gibraltar's 2002 Sussex win. Although exceptionally well bred, he is evidently no star. (tchd 14-1 and 16-1 in a place)
Nihal(IRE), a battling winner of a competitive four-runner affair at York last week, looked one of the more obvious winners under a 5lb penalty, but she was a big negative on the exchanges throughout the day and never really featured. She was not the first quickly turned out from the yard to disappoint this week, and probably deserves another chance. (tchd 16-1)
Ask, the big gamble of the race, had to step up on his maiden efforts off a mark of 90, but he never really had a chance to show what he could do as he was reported to have finished lame. The run can be ignored and he remains open to improvement. Official explanation: vet said colt was lame in front (op 11-4 tchd 3-1)
Kaylianni, finally off the mark at Newbury last time, hung under pressure and looked to be feeling something.
Lake Poet(IRE), a tough sort who contests most of these big three-year-old handicaps, never got out of the rear and is likely to remain vulnerable off this sort of mark.
Prowess(IRE) looked to hold nothing more than outside claims, but she was reported to have lost her action. Official explanation: jockey said filly lost its action (tchd 16-1)
Oh Glory Be(USA) has looked progressive, but she ran too bad to be true and was reported to have hated the ground. Official explanation: trainer said filly was unsuited by the good to firm ground

4040 WEATHERBYS BANK FILLIES' STKS (H'CAP) 1m 1f
4:25 (4:25) (Class 3) (0-90,86) 3-Y-O+

£10,906 (£3,265; £1,632; £817; £407; £204) **Stalls** High

Form RPR

3242 **1** **Nice Tune**[19] 3489 4-10-0 86 RyanMoore 2 97
(C E Brittain) *settled in midfield: plld to outer and effrt over 1f out: r.o to ld last 150yds: sn wl in command* **10/1**

1221 **2** *1* **Princess Cocoa (IRE)**[9] 3790 3-8-5 71 6ex PaulHanagan 11 80
(R A Fahey) *prom: rdn to chse ldr over 2f out: led ent fnl f: sn hdd: styd on but readily outpcd by wnr* **6/1**[2]

3 *1 ¼* **Lily Elsie (IRE)**[6] 3885 3-8-12 78 MJKinane 3 85
(A P O'Brien, Ire) *hld up in midfield: prog to chse ldrs 2f out: rdn and nt qckn over 1f out: styd on fnl f to take 3rd last stride* **6/1**[2]

0213 **4** *shd* **Babcary**[36] 2961 3-9-2 82 MartinDwyer 13 89
(M P Tregoning) *led at decent pce: rdn 2f out: collared ent fnl f: fdd last 100yds* **13/2**[3]

0531 **5** 3/4 **Dame Hester (IRE)**[6] 3871 3-9-5 **85** 6ex................................ JMurtagh 9 90
(E J O'Neill) *wl plcd bhd ldrs: rdn and nt qckn 2f out: styd on again ins fnl f: unable to chal* **8/1**

1220 **6** 1/2 **Solva**[25] 3292 3-9-0 **80**.. LDettori 8 84
(B J Meehan) *prom: disp 2nd over 2f out: chal and upsides jst over 1f out: wknd ins fnl f* **7/1**

1623 **7** 1 1/4 **Sharplaw Autumn (USA)**[18] 3546 3-8-7 **78**.................. LiamJones(5) 14 80
(W J Haggas) *settled in midfield: rdn on inner wl over 2f out: kpt on but no real imp on ldrs* **14/1**

441 **8** nk **Millistar**[28] 3200 3-8-9 **75**.. PhilipRobinson 10 76
(M A Jarvis) *hld up towards rr: gng wl enough on outer 3f out: rdn and nt qckn 2f out: edgd rt and btn after* **4/1**[1]

1142 **9** 5 **Night Storm**[38] 2900 5-9-3 **75**.. JohnEgan 7 66
(S Dow) *s.s: t.k.h and sn in tch in rr: nt clr run over 2f out: n.d after: eased whn btn jst over 1f out* **16/1**

216 **10** 3 **Miss McGuire**[13] 3667 3-8-12 **78**.. IanMongan 6 63
(G L Moore) *a towards rr: rdn and struggling over 3f out: no ch after* **50/1**

5060 **11** 1 **Uig**[12] 3703 5-8-9 **67** oh3.. AlanMunro 1 50
(H S Howe) *chsd ldr tl wknd over 2f out* **66/1**

0163 **12** 12 **Dream Rose (IRE)**[9] 3793 3-8-9 **75**.................................. TonyCulhane 5 34
(M R Channon) *lw: a wl in rr and nvr gng wl: lost tch 3f out: t.o* **25/1**

2023 **13** 1 **Tafiya**[6] 3865 3-8-4 **70**.. AliAlSaffar 4 27
(G A Butler) *lw: s.v.s: in tch on wd outside after 2f: bmpd along and wknd over 3f out: t.o* **25/1**

1m 53.56s (-3.30) **Going Correction** -0.10s/f (Good)
WFA 3 from 4yo+ 8lb **13** Ran SP% **118.3**
Speed ratings (Par 104):110,109,108,107,107 106,105,105,100,98 97,86,85
CSF £66.31 CT £410.57 TOTE £13.30: £4.00, £2.20, £2.10; EX 90.00 Trifecta £234.70 Pool: £1,289.44 - 3.90 winning tickets..
Owner Saeed Manana **Bred** Bricklow Ltd **Trained** Newmarket, Suffolk

FOCUS
A fair handicap and sound form. A decent winning time for a race like this and a smashing effort from top weight Nice Tune.

NOTEBOOK
Nice Tune, although somewhat exposed, is as tough as nails and she was always likely to be thereabouts. Recent all-weather runs behind Fairmile and Grain Of Truth suggested she was still capable of winning off this sort of mark and in defying 10st this has to go down as a personal best. She picked up well under pressure to win with a bit to spare and she is likely to return to Listed events in search of winning black type. (op 8-1)
Princess Cocoa(IRE), a progressive filly who won with tons in hand at Beverley last time, ran well under her 6lb penalty and could have done with more of a test. Her two defeats at 1m4f have come against progressive sorts in Liberate and Scotland Yard, but she is just as effective at 1m2f and there should be more to come off what will remain a decent mark. (tchd 13-2 in a place)
Lily Elsie(IRE), narrowly denied back-to-back wins at Limerick last week, was suited by the return to further, but she still found it an inadequate test on this track and she rallied well to snatch third on the line. She is a well-bred sort from a top yard capable of better at 1m2f plus. (op 9-2)
Babcary goes extremely well here, being a speedy sort who often races keenly, and she could easily be fancied to reverse recent Newbury form with Solva, despite being 1lb worse off at the weights. She went a decent gallop in front and had a couple of lengths on her field over two out, but her rider failed to press on, instead waiting until she had been joined before he got stuck in. A good effort nonetheless, and she remains capable of scoring off this mark when things go her way. (op 6-1 tchd 7-1)
Dame Hester(IRE), a cosy winner on her first try beyond a mile at Folkestone, looked unsuited by the slight drop in trip, but it was still a fair effort under a penalty and she remains capable of better back up in distance.
Solva, nominated by her trainer as one of his better chances this week, should have finsished pretty much where Babcary did, but she faded disappointingly under pressure and her improvement may have levelled out for the time being. (op 9-1 tchd 10-1)
Sharplaw Autumn(USA) has on the whole performed well since going handicapping and this was another reasonable effort.
Millistar was the main disappointment of the race, failing to pick up having travelled well into contention. She may require further. (op 11-2 tchd 6-1)

4041 FINDON MAIDEN FILLIES' STKS 6f
5:00 (5:03) (Class 2) 2-Y-O **£10,363** (£3,083; £1,540; £769) **Stalls** Low

Form RPR

5 **1** **Sacre Coeur**[16] 3588 2-9-0 .... EddieAhern 10 83+
(J L Dunlop) *lw: w'like: str: w ldr: led 1/2-way and gng wl: drvn and hrd pressed fnl f: hld on* **5/1**[3]

2 nk **Rahiyah (USA)** 2-9-0 .... LDettori 1 85+
(J Noseda) *w'like: str: lw: hld up in last pair: effrt 2f out: nt clr run and taken to outer over 1f out: r.o to chal last 150yds: clsd but jst hld* **7/2**[1]

2 **3** 2 **Queen Noverre (IRE)**[32] 3096 2-9-0 .... RichardMullen 8 76
(E J O'Neill) *sn pushed along to go prom: rdn to chse wnr over 2f out tl ent fnl f: one pce* **4/1**[2]

2 **4** 2 **To Party (IRE)**[35] 2980 2-9-0 .... MartinDwyer 6 70
(M P Tregoning) *prom: disp 2nd over 2f out to over 1f out: fdd ins fnl f* **6/1**

5 shd **Suppose (USA)**[18] 3556 2-9-0 .... MJKinane 3 70
(A P O'Brien, Ire) *w'like: scope: str: trckd ldrs: shkn up whn carried rt over 1f out: one pce after* **14/1**

6 1 **Lady Lafitte (USA)** 2-9-0 .... MichaelHills 11 67+
(B W Hills) *w'like: bit bkwd: s.s: hld up in last: shuffled along over 1f out: kpt on steadily fnl f: bttr for experience* **33/1**

7 shd **Miss Phuket** 2-9-0 .... RyanMoore 9 67+
(G Wragg) *leggy: bit bkwd: dwlt: rn green in rr: no prog tl kpt on ins fnl f* **20/1**

2 **8** hd **Empress Olga (USA)**[14] 3645 2-9-0 .... ShaneKelly 5 66
(E A L Dunlop) *lw: trckd ldng pair: hanging rt fr 1/2-way: fdd fr over 1f out* **7/1**

9 1/2 **Sylvan (IRE)** 2-9-0 .... JimmyFortune 14 65+
(S Kirk) *leggy: s.s: sn in tch: taken to wd outside and rdn 2f out: rn green and wknd fnl f* **80/1**

10 1/2 **Samdaniya** 2-9-0 .... KerrinMcEvoy 7 63
(C E Brittain) *w'like: bit bkwd: led to 1/2-way: lost pl steadily fr over 2f out: rn green fnl f* **25/1**

4 **11** 3/4 **Freedom At Last (IRE)**[19] 3495 2-9-0 .... AlanMunro 2 61
(W Jarvis) *settled towards rr: shkn up and no real prog fr 2f out* **16/1**

0 **12** 7 **Show Trial (IRE)**[18] 3537 2-9-0 .... TonyCulhane 13 40
(M R Channon) *w'like: dwlt: t.k.h and racd on wd outside: sn prom: cl up 2f out: wknd rapidly over 1f out* **100/1**

1m 12.89s (0.04) **Going Correction** -0.10s/f (Good) **12** Ran SP% **112.0**
Speed ratings (Par 97):95,94,91,89,89 87,87,87,86,86 85,75
CSF £18.77 TOTE £6.30: £2.10, £1.50, £1.70; EX 23.90 Trifecta £213.20 Pool: £925.00 - 3.08 winning tickets..
Owner William Armitage **Bred** Whitsbury Manor Stud **Trained** Arundel, W Sussex
■ Shantina's Dream (12/1, unruly in stalls) & Millisecond (14/1, uns rdr at s) were withdrawn. R4 applies, deduct 10p in the £.

FOCUS
A decent maiden likely to produce winners. The winner was an improver and the third and fourth ran to their sand marks.

NOTEBOOK
Sacre Coeur, whose trainer has a fine record in this race and a good line on the juvenile fillies with the likes of Sudoor and Princess Margaret winner Scarlet Runner in the stable, looked one of the more obvious winners following a pleasing debut at Windsor - mixed form - and she travelled sweetly throughout. She just did enough to hold the late challenge of favourite Rahiyah and may prove just as effective back at the minimum, but she was later reported to have returned with an injury and may be out for some time. (op 7-1 tchd 8-1)
Rahiyah(USA) is related to several useful sorts and she looked to have a good draw in one, but that was assuming she did not get behind, and unfortunately for her supporters she did. Dettori, having been blocked, ended up having to move to the outside, but by the time she hit top stride it was too late and she failed to get there in time. On this evidence she should have little trouble winning races. (op 10-3 tchd 11-4)
Queen Noverre(IRE), although looking to hold claims, finished second in just an average race on her debut at Wolverhampton and it would have been slightly disappointing had she won this. She can probably win a maiden, but her future lies in handicaps. (op 9-2 tchd 5-1)
To Party(IRE) is bred for speed and she looked one of the more likely winners following a promising debut at Kempton. She showed up well for a long way, but did not see her race out as well as the principals and is another for whom a drop to the minimum distance may suit. (op 11-2 tchd 13-2)
Suppose(USA), neglected by Fallon when down the field on her debut at the Curragh, is exceptionally well bred, being by Danehill out of the stable's high-class filly Sophisticat, and looked a reasonable price to build on that debut run. She lacks size though and, although running well enough, it is debatable what, if any, improvement she has in her. (op 10-1)
Lady Lafitte(USA) ♦, another whose trainer has done well in this race in the past, was a negative in the betting and never really featured, not being given a hard time after a slow start before making some late headway. She is almost certain to benefit from the experience and looks sure to benefit from a rise in distance.
Miss Phuket, whose dam is a half-sister to Asian Heights and St Expedit, is understandably going to require further in time, but she should be effective at around seven furlongs this season and, considering she ran green, this has to go down as a pleasing debut effort.
Empress Olga(USA), a sister to top-class mare Russian Rhythm who shaped so encouragingly on her debut at Lingfield, failed to build on that and hung away her chance. She may have been feeling something and deserves another chance, but now has a little bit to prove. (op 8-1)
Sylvan(IRE), whose stables juveniles often benefit from a run, looks no exception as she was green throughout and was unable to get into it. (op 100-1)
Samdaniya ♦, out of high-class mare Cloud Castle and relation of Luso, Warrsan and Needle Gun, showed good early speed and appeared to know her job, but she became outpaced inside the final quarter mile and was unsure of what was required of her once put under pressure. This was a pleasing initial effort and much better can be expected once upped to seven furlongs. Official explanation: jockey said filly hung right in closing stages
Freedom At Last(IRE) looked well drawn, but she failed to build on her debut effort and may be more of a nursery type. (op 14-1)
Show Trial(IRE) has shown little on either start, but it would not surprise to see her do much better once contesting handicaps, albeit it was disconcerting the way she stopped so quickly under pressure here.

4042 LINKS OF LONDON E B F CLASSIFIED STKS 7f
5:35 (5:35) (Class 2) 3-Y-O+
£12,464 (£3,732; £1,866; £934; £466; £234) **Stalls** High

Form RPR

1-10 **1** **Minority Report**[42] 2742 6-9-4 92....................................... NickyMackay 1 106
(L M Cumani) *dwlt: hld up in rr: prog on outer and rdn 2f out: disp ld 1f out: edgd rt fnl f but a jst in command last 100yds* **9/4**[1]

1300 **2** hd **Kalankari (IRE)**[20] 3443 3-8-12 93....................................... MartinDwyer 7 103
(A M Balding) *lw: hld up: nt looking happy on trck: prog over 2f out: edgd lft over 1f out: disp ld 1f out: carried rt and a hld last 100yds* **4/1**[2]

1104 **3** 1 3/4 **Song Of Passion (IRE)**[13] 3687 3-8-9 92............................ RyanMoore 4 96
(R Hannon) *trckd ldr: led 2f out: hdd and outpcd 1f out* **7/1**

2106 **4** 2 1/2 **Kostar**[19] 3493 5-9-4 93.. AdamKirby 8 94
(C G Cox) *hld up in tch: rdn 2f out: sn outpcd and btn* **5/1**[3]

3361 **5** 1 1/4 **The Snatcher (IRE)**[25] 3317 3-8-12 94.......................... RichardHughes 2 89
(R Hannon) *trckd ldrs: rdn and cl up over 2f out: outpcd over 1f out: wknd ins fnl f* **5/1**[3]

1-14 **6** hd **Spinning Ruby**[75] 1834 3-8-9 90.. SebSanders 6 86
(R M Beckett) *hld up in last: rdn and strugglingt 3f out: sn no ch: r.o last 150yds* **12/1**

2502 **7** 1 1/4 **Material Witness (IRE)**[19] 3470 9-9-4 88......................... KerrinMcEvoy 3 89+
(W R Muir) *dwlt: sn rcvrd to ld: hdd 2f out: wknd and eased over 1f out* **9/1**

1m 25.52s (-2.52) **Going Correction** -0.10s/f (Good)
WFA 3 from 5yo+ 6lb **7** Ran SP% **114.3**
Speed ratings (Par 109):110,109,107,104,103 103,101
CSF £11.36 TOTE £3.10: £1.50, £2.90; EX 13.40 Trifecta £296.10 Pool: £834.22 - 2.00 winning tickets. Place 6 £264.54, Place 5 £96.19.
Owner G Shiel **Bred** Fittocks Stud **Trained** Newmarket, Suffolk
■ Stewards' Enquiry : Nicky Mackay two-day ban: careless riding (Aug 13-14)

FOCUS
A tight contest fought out by a couple of progressive sorts. The form is not rock solid.

NOTEBOOK
Minority Report, a progressive and usually most consistent sort who is lightly raced for a six-year-old, bombed out badly from a good draw when fancied for the Hunt Cup, but he had been given a bit of time off to get himself back together and, although not particularly well in at the weights, he narrowly prevailed from three-year-old Kalankari. He made good headway on the outside before knuckling down under pressure and, although edging across the runner-up, it was right that he kept the race. He may yet be capable of further improvement and could return to Ascot for a race at the Shergar Cup meeting. (tchd 5-2 in places)
Kalankari(IRE), a non-stayer over 1m2f at Newmarket recently, ran mightily well considering he looked uneasy on the track and he went down fighting. He seems just as effective at this trip as a mile, but remains 14lb higher than when last winning. (op 7-1)
Song Of Passion(IRE) has struggled off marks in the 90s the last twice and she looked more at home in this type of event. She appeared to run her race, but is going to remain hard to win with. (op 13-2)
Kostar, who recently ran well in the Bunbury Cup, could have been expected to do a little better on a track that should have suited this speedy sort. He might have benefited from a more positive ride. (op 4-1)
The Snatcher(IRE), back to form at Sandown last time, came through to hold every chance, but he did not see the race as one would have hoped and was a bit disappointing. (op 9-2)
Spinning Ruby was the only one who looked likely to struggle and she never got into it. She probably needs a slower surface. (op 10-1 tchd 14-1)
Material Witness(IRE) would have taken the beating in a race like this a few years ago, but he is past his best now and likely to continue to struggle. Official explanation: trainer said gelding lost both front shoes (op 10-1)
T/Jkpt: Not won. T/Plt: £361.40 to a £1 stake. Pool: £214,579.60. 433.35 winning tickets. T/Qpdt: £46.90 to a £1 stake. Pool: £8,930.75. 140.80 winning tickets. JN

3639 KEMPTON (A.W) (R-H)

Wednesday, August 2

OFFICIAL GOING: Standard

Wind: Moderate, half-against

4043 BYRNE BROS NURSERY 5f (P)

7:00 (7:01) (Class 4) 2-Y-O **£4,533** (£1,348; £674; £336) **Stalls** High

Form RPR

1554 **1** **Down The Well (IRE)**[5] 3917 2-8-9 **73** ShaneKelly 7 77+
(J A Osborne) *mde all: rdn clr 1f out: readily* **10/3**[2]

5400 **2** 1 ½ **Weyba Downs (IRE)**[44] 2710 2-7-13 **66** oh2 ow4 JamesDoyle(3) 2 65
(J R Best) *in tch: rdn and hdwy to chse wnr fnl f: r.o* **11/1**

014 **3** *hd* **Northern Fling**[32] 3064 2-9-6 **84** JoeFanning 5 82
(D Nicholls) *a in tch on ins: ridde over 2f out: styd on fnl f* **11/4**[1]

410 **4** ½ **Hucking Hope (IRE)**[31] 3120 2-8-6 **70** JohnEgan 4 66
(J R Best) *hld up: rdn 2f out: kpt on one pce fnl f* **9/1**

6400 **5** ¾ **Mac Gille Eoin**[16] 3588 2-8-0 **64** ow1 FrankieMcDonald 3 57
(J Gallagher) *outpcd early: in tch after 2f: wknd fnl f* **20/1**

011 **6** 1 ½ **Kyshanty**[18] 3544 2-9-4 **82** RichardHughes 6 70
(R Hannon) *trckd wnr tl rdn and wknd approachin fnl f* **9/2**

5101 **7** ½ **Il Palio (IRE)**[21] 3409 2-9-0 **85** JamesMillman(7) 1 71
(B R Millman) *s.i.s: in tch over 3f out: rdn to go 2nd briefly over 1f out: wknd ins fnl f* **7/2**[3]

61.12 secs (0.72) **Going Correction** -0.025s/f (Stan) **7** Ran SP% **113.2**
Speed ratings (Par 96):93,90,90,89,88 85,85
CSF £37.34 TOTE £4.50: £2.40, £5.70; EX 41.40.
Owner Danny Durkan **Bred** Rathasker Stud **Trained** Upper Lambourn, Berks

FOCUS
A small field, but a competitive little nursery nonetheless. The winner ran to his best and the form looks quite solid. The official ratings shown next to each horse are estimated and for information purposes only.

NOTEBOOK
Down The Well(IRE) had gained her only previous win over this trip on turf and appreciated the drop back to the minimum for the first time on her third outing on sand. Given a positive ride from the inside stall, she quickened from the front soon after reaching the home straight and never looked in much danger from then on. She is likely to contest similar events in the near future and can win again over this trip. (op 4-1 tchd 5-1 in a place and 9-2 in places)
Weyba Downs(IRE), 2lb out of the handicap and carrying 4lb overweight, ran his best race so far on this nursery debut and could well find a similar race off this sort of mark. (tchd 12-1)
Northern Fling, whose three previous outings had all been around Chester's sharp left-hand turns, did not look happy on the sharp right-hand turn here so did well to finish third under the circumstances. (op 10-3 tchd 5-2)
Hucking Hope(IRE), winner of her only previous start on sand and a stable-companion of the runner-up, seemed to have every chance and may need an extra furlong now. (op 8-1)
Mac Gille Eoin, making his nursery debut, may need to drop in class if he is to get off the mark.
Kyshanty, bidding for a hat-trick, was disappointing on this switch to sand and drop in trip. (op 7-2 tchd 10-3)
Il Palio(IRE), who had scored on both of his previous starts on sand, dropped away very tamely after holding every chance and was disappointing. (op 4-1 tchd 5-1)

4044 BETBROKERS BETTING JUST GOT BETTER H'CAP 1m 2f (P)

7:28 (7:31) (Class 5) (0-70,70) 3-Y-O **£3,238** (£963; £481; £240) **Stalls** High

Form RPR

322 **1** **Dear Gracie (IRE)**[49] 2542 3-9-7 **70** OscarUrbina 8 77
(J R Fanshawe) *trckd ldrs: rdn to ld ins fnl f: kpt on wl* **5/1**[2]

3102 **2** ¾ **Lester Leaps In (USA)**[8] 3816 3-9-7 **70** RyanMoore 7 76
(R Hannon) *trckd ldrs: rdn to ld over 1f out: hdd ins fnl f: kpt on* **6/1**[3]

5-52 **3** 1 **Lunar River (FR)**[11] 3731 3-9-3 **66** (t) RichardMullen 3 70
(E A L Dunlop) *mid-div: rdn over 1f out: styd on fnl f: nvr nrr* **7/1**

0336 **4** ½ **Kinvara Lass (IRE)**[12] 3703 3-9-5 **68** NickyMackay 1 71
(L M Cumani) *s.i.s: sn mid-div: styd on ins fnl 2f* **8/1**

0-06 **5** ½ **Sonny Mac**[34] 3029 3-9-7 **70** (t) RichardHughes 5 72
(B J Meehan) *led tl rdn and hdd over 1f out: one pce fnl f* **20/1**

3001 **6** 1 ¾ **Follow The Colours (IRE)**[14] 3639 3-9-0 **70** PatrickHills(7) 11 69+
(J W Hills) *slowly away: in rr: hdwy 2f out: nvr nr to chal* **9/2**[1]

5405 **7** ½ **Vodkatini**[25] 3310 3-9-2 **65** (v) SebSanders 6 63
(P J Makin) *hld up in mid-div: no hdwy fnl 2f* **16/1**

0-00 **8** 2 **Snowberry Hill (USA)**[73] 1867 3-9-1 **64** (p) DO'Donohoe 4 58
(K A Ryan) *trckd ldrs tl rdn and wknd wl over 1f out* **50/1**

0234 **9** *shd* **Digger Boy**[22] 3388 3-9-4 **67** JimmyFortune 13 61
(M A Jarvis) *t.k.h in mid-div: no hdwy fnl 2f* **6/1**[3]

004 **10** 1 ¼ **Mr Wiseguy**[32] 3073 3-9-5 **68** AlanMunro 14 59
(G C Bravery) *rwards rr: rdn over 2f out: nvr on terms* **33/1**

060 **11** 1 ½ **Project Sunshine (GER)**[70] 1940 3-8-13 **62** ShaneKelly 9 51
(J A Osborne) *stdd s: a bhd* **50/1**

-233 **12** ½ **Ruffie (IRE)**[22] 3378 3-9-0 **66** AdamKirby(3) 12 54
(Miss Gay Kelleway) *a bhd* **11/1**

0030 **13** 3 **Bride To Be (USA)**[11] 3731 3-9-4 **67** TedDurcan 2 49
(C E Brittain) *trckd ldr tl c wd into strt: wknd qckly* **33/1**

0500 **14** 6 **Rose Briar (IRE)**[58] 2301 3-9-2 **65** SteveDrowne 10 36
(R Charlton) *in tch tl wknd 4f out* **20/1**

2m 8.75s (-0.25) **Going Correction** -0.025s/f (Stan) **14** Ran SP% **120.6**
Speed ratings (Par 100):100,99,98,98,97 96,96,94,94,93 92,91,89,84
CSF £32.36 CT £213.26 TOTE £5.40: £2.10, £2.80, £3.20; EX 33.70.
Owner Mrs C C Regalado-Gonzalez **Bred** Holborn Trust Co **Trained** Newmarket, Suffolk

FOCUS
A competitive little handicap, but it was not strongly run and very few ever got into this. Rated through the third, the form does not look rock solid.
Ruffie(IRE) Official explanation: jockey said filly didn't handle the right-handed track
Bride To Be(USA) Official explanation: jockey said filly hung badly left in home straight
Rose Briar(IRE) Official explanation: jockey said filly hung right throughout

4045 BYRNE BROS MAIDEN STKS 6f (P)

7:56 (7:59) (Class 4) 3-Y-O+ **£5,505** (£1,637; £818; £408) **Stalls** High

Form RPR

-405 **1** **Dama'A (IRE)**[48] 2587 3-8-12 78 JimmyFortune 5 79+
(J H M Gosden) *led for 1f: led again wl over 1f out: rdn clr: comf* **6/5**[1]

06-0 **2** 2 ½ **Blues In The Night (IRE)**[74] 1844 3-9-3 68 SebSanders 2 76
(P J Makin) *mid-div: rdn and qcknd to chse wnr over 1f out: no imp ins fnl f* **9/1**

-054 **3** 5 **Kineta (USA)**[20] 3453 3-8-12 62 RichardMullen 4 56
(W R Muir) *prom on ins: styd on one pce fr over 1f out* **12/1**

05- **4** 1 ¼ **White Ladder (IRE)**[434] 2004 3-9-3 RyanMoore 9 57+
(P F I Cole) *hld up: rdn 2f out: styd on but nvr nr to chal* **6/1**[2]

00 **5** *hd* **Granakey (IRE)**[5] 3914 3-8-9 EdwardCreighton(3) 3 52
(M G Quinlan) *prom tl rdn 2f out: one pce after* **66/1**

0030 **6** 1 ½ **Cabriole**[25] 3299 3-8-12 63 RichardHughes 1 47
(H R A Cecil) *led after 1f: hdd wl over 1f out: sn wknd* **13/2**[3]

5 **7** 1 ¼ **Perfect Cover (IRE)**[97] 1261 3-8-12 AlanMunro 11 43
(J A R Toller) *hld up: rdn over 2f out: wknd over 1f out* **9/1**

8 *nk* **Dhurwah (IRE)** 3-8-12 TedDurcan 7 43
(T Keddy) *mid-div: effrt over 1f out: sn btn* **12/1**

-000 **9** 1 **Grand Parrot**[38] 2897 3-9-3 50 RobertHavlin 6 45
(W De Best-Turner) *mid-div: rdn over 2f out: sn btn* **40/1**

0 **10** 2 **Petite Boulangere (IRE)**[35] 2985 3-8-12 JohnEgan 10 34+
(S Kirk) *rrd up leaving stalls: a bhd* **50/1**

0 **11** *nk* **Sophie James**[91] 1417 3-8-9 ow2 JerryO'Dwyer(5) 12 35
(M G Quinlan) *a bhd* **50/1**

00- **12** 15 **Kentavr's Dream**[306] 5584 3-8-12 ShaneKelly 8 —
(P Howling) *a bhd: lost tch 3f out* **66/1**

1m 12.91s (-0.79) **Going Correction** -0.025s/f (Stan) **12** Ran SP% **117.8**
Speed ratings (Par 105):104,100,94,92,92 90,88,88,86,84 83,63
CSF £12.50 TOTE £2.30: £1.30, £3.40, £3.60; EX 16.40.
Owner H R H Princess Haya Of Jordan **Bred** Lodge Park Stud **Trained** Newmarket, Suffolk

FOCUS
A valuable race of its type, but only a handful could be seriously considered in this maiden. The form is ordinary but sound, rated around the fifth.

4046 IRISH NIGHT H'CAP 2m (P)

8:24 (8:27) (Class 5) (0-75,75) 4-Y-O+ **£3,238** (£963; £481; £240) **Stalls** High

Form RPR

3020 **1** **High Point (IRE)**[43] 2723 8-9-0 **73** RobynBrisland(5) 1 81
(G P Enright) *a in tch: wnt 2nd over 3f out: led 2f out: rdn and hld on gamely fnl f* **9/1**

1442 **2** ¾ **Dark Parade (ARG)**[14] 3649 5-8-4 **65** JamieJones(7) 11 72
(G L Moore) *hld up: hdwy over 3f out: styd on to press wnr fins fnl f* **11/2**[2]

3004 **3** *nk* **Establishment**[20] 3446 9-9-7 **75** TedDurcan 10 82
(C A Cyzer) *wl in rr tl hdwy o0ver 2f out: styd on wl fnl f: nvr nrr* **7/1**[3]

3600 **4** ¾ **Papeete (GER)**[7] 3853 5-8-9 **63** ow1 SebSanders 6 69
(Miss B Sanders) *mid-div: chsd ldrs over 2f out: kpt on u.p fnl f* **12/1**

1401 **5** *shd* **Madiba**[20] 3454 7-8-9 **63** ShaneKelly 3 69
(P Howling) *prom: led after 7f: rdn and hdd 2f out: no ex fnl f* **12/1**

0012 **6** 3 **Montage (IRE)**[5] 3919 4-8-0 **57** JamesDoyle(3) 13 59
(J Akehurst) *in tch tl rdn and wknd 2f out* **11/4**[1]

1215 **7** ¾ **Kayf Aramis**[38] 2894 4-8-11 **65** PaulQuinn 4 66+
(J L Spearing) *slowly away but sn led: faltered on bnd after 7f: hdd sn after: nvr on terms after though sme late hdwy* **8/1**

-004 **8** ¾ **Karlu (GER)**[20] 3452 4-9-7 **75** PaulEddery 2 76
(Pat Eddery) *towards rr: rdn and hdwy over 3f out: wknd over 1f out* **25/1**

0036 **9** 12 **Bukit Fraser (IRE)**[19] 3467 5-8-4 **58** ow1 (t) JohnEgan 5 44
(P F I Cole) *hld up: a bhd* **9/1**

1010 **10** 16 **Galantos (GER)**[22] 3382 5-8-2 **56** oh2 RichardMullen 8 23
(G L Moore) *a bhd: lost tch over 3f out* **12/1**

0000 **11** 5 **Shingle Street (IRE)**[16] 3597 4-8-2 **56** oh4 (tp) JoeFanning 12 17
(I A Wood) *trckd ldr tl hmpd on bnd after 7f: sn bhd* **50/1**

6-00 **12** 5 **Yankeedoodledandy (IRE)**[36] 2176 5-8-9 **70** LukeMorris(7) 7 25
(C Roberts) *a bhd: lost tch over 4f out* **16/1**

3m 29.28s (-2.12) **Going Correction** -0.025s/f (Stan) **12** Ran SP% **120.4**
Speed ratings (Par 103):104,103,103,103,103 101,101,100,94,86 84,81
CSF £58.84 CT £375.73 TOTE £13.00: £4.10, £3.00, £2.60; EX 52.20.
Owner The Aedean Partnership **Bred** Ballymacoll Stud Farm Ltd **Trained** Lewes, E Sussex

FOCUS
This may have been a test of stamina, but there were several still in with a chance passing the two-furlong pole and only a couple of lengths covered the front five at the line. Solid but unexceptional form in this tight handicap.
Montage(IRE) Official explanation: jockey said gelding was never travelling

4047 MARTIN COLLINS ENTERPRISES H'CAP (LONDON MILE QUALIFIER) 1m (P)

8:52 (8:56) (Class 3) (0-90,87) 3-Y-O+

£7,790 (£2,332; £1,166; £583; £291; £146) **Stalls** High

Form RPR

01-0 **1** **Ninth House (USA)**[21] 3413 4-9-13 **81** (t) ShaneKelly 5 91
(D J Daly) *in rr tl hdwy 2f out: squeezed though fnl f to ld cl home* **33/1**

2451 **2** *hd* **Cross The Line (IRE)**[28] 3202 4-9-7 **75** AlanMunro 7 85
(A P Jarvis) *mid-div: hdwy 3f out: rdn to ld ins fnl f: hdd cl home* **7/1**[3]

0031 **3** 2 **Logsdail**[14] 3642 6-9-0 **68** (p) RyanMoore 6 73
(G L Moore) *hld up in rr: rdn and hdwy ins fnl 2f: nvr nrr* **4/1**[2]

-010 **4** *shd* **Top Mark**[53] 2443 4-9-9 **77** SteveDrowne 2 82
(H Morrison) *a.p: wnt 2nd over 3f out: led 1f out: rdn and hdd ins fnl f: no ex* **16/1**

0605 **5** *nk* **Trifti**[7] 3850 5-9-5 **80** AshleyHamblett(7) 4 84
(C A Cyzer) *racd wd: effrt over 2f out: no imp fnl f* **33/1**

352 **6** 1 **Star Crowned (USA)**[23] 3346 3-9-8 **83** (bt) JimmyFortune 1 91+
(B J Meehan) *led for 2f: styd prom tl wknd ins fnl f* **11/1**

0525 **7** *hd* **Outer Hebrides**[35] 2983 5-10-0 **82** (vt) NickyMackay 10 83
(Stef Liddiard) *mid-div: hdwy 2f out: wknd ent fnl f* **25/1**

312 **8** ½ **Our Putra**[21] 3404 3-9-6 **81** (t) PhilipRobinson 9 81
(M A Jarvis) *prom: rdn 3f out: no hdwy fnl 2f* **11/8**[1]

2055 **9** ½ **Moi Aussi (USA)**[14] 3648 3-9-8 **83** (b) SebSanders 3 82
(Sir Mark Prescott) *s.i.s: led after 2f: rdn and hdd 1f out: wknd ins fnl f* **14/1**

2-41 **10** 1 **Muzher (IRE)**[67] 2034 3-9-12 **87** RHills 8 84
(B W Hills) *a bhd* **8/1**

3-60 **11** 2 ½ **Kingdom Of Dreams (IRE)**[21] 3413 4-9-11 **79** (t) TedDurcan 11 70
(J Noseda) *a struggling in rr* **14/1**

1m 39.76s (-1.04) **Going Correction** -0.025s/f (Stan)
WFA 3 from 4yo+ 7lb **11** Ran SP% **123.0**
Speed ratings (Par 107):104,103,101,101,101 100,100,99,99,98 95
CSF £256.94 CT £1150.42 TOTE £50.90: £10.00, £2.30, £1.80; EX 446.90.
Owner Gold Ace Racing **Bred** Juddmonte Farms Inc **Trained** Newmarket, Suffolk
■ Stewards' Enquiry : Alan Munro caution: used whip without allowing sufficient time for response

FOCUS
The classiest contest of the evening and a thrilling finish. The form looks sound, with the winner improving by 10lb.

The Form Book, Raceform Ltd, Compton, RG20 6NL

NOTEBOOK

Ninth House(USA) ◆ came from nowhere to snatch the race near the line. Winner of a Wolverhampton maiden on his only previous sand start last December, he had obviously benefited from his reappearance effort at Newmarket last month. He has had his problems, but if staying sound he has the ability to win more races.

Cross The Line(IRE), raised 4lb for his narrow win over course and distance last time, did nothing wrong and was only just caught. He should soon be winning again. (op 10-1)

Logsdail, another course-and-distance winner last time and now 2lb higher, was never quite getting there in time but ran another solid race nonetheless. (op 3-1 tchd 9-2 and 5-1 in a place)

Top Mark had every chance, but may be better suited by seven.

Trifti also had every chance, but he has not been at his very best on sand this year.

Star Crowned(USA) ◆ was stopped in his tracks when trying for a run up the inside of the weakening Moi Aussi over a furlong from home and then had nowhere to go once switched outside. He passed the post with his rider standing up in the irons and that overdue first win cannot be too far away. Official explanation: jockey said colt was denied a clear run (op 12-1 tchd 14-1)

Our Putra came off the bridle just after halfway, but found nothing and was very disappointing. He is better than this and is worth another chance. (op 6-4 tchd 13-8 in a place)

4048 WEATHERBYS BANK APPRENTICE H'CAP (ROUND 8) — 1m (P)
9:20 (9:21) (Class 5) (0-70,70) 3-Y-0+ — **£3,238** (£963; £481; £240) Stalls High

Form — RPR

0415 **1** — **Captain Darling (IRE)**[16] 3599 6-9-6 **60**........ EdwardCreighton 4 — 72
(R W Price) *mde all: rdn out fnl f* — **14/1**

3032 **2** 1 ¼ **Redeye Special**[34] 3014 4-9-3 **62**........ LukeMorris(5) 11 — 71
(M L W Bell) *a.p: rdn to chse wnr fnl 2f* — **7/2**[1]

0102 **3** 1 ¾ **October Ben**[14] 3643 3-9-0 **66**........ FrankiePickard(5) 3 — 70
(M D I Usher) *hld up in rr: hdwy over 2f out: kpt on to chse first 2 fr over 1f out* — **10/1**

0-04 **4** ¾ **Mohawk Star (IRE)**[14] 3642 5-10-0 **68**........ JamesDoyle 10 — 71+
(I A Wood) *bhd: rdn 3f out: mde late hdwy nvr nr to chal* — **12/1**

3652 **5** 1 ¾ **Takes Tutu (USA)**[14] 3642 7-9-10 **64**........(p) AdamKirby 9 — 63+
(C R Dore) *in rr: hdwy on ins in fnl 2f: nvr nr to chal* — **5/1**[2]

3152 **6** ½ **Terenzium (IRE)**[35] 2978 4-8-11 **54**........ AshleyHamblett(3) 8 — 52
(L M Cumani) *chsd ldrs: rdn over 2f out: no further hdwy* — **7/2**[1]

0233 **7** ½ **Emily's Place (IRE)**[44] 2699 3-9-2 **68**........ PatrickHills(5) 12 — 64
(M H Tompkins) *bhd: effrt on ins 2f out: n.d* — **7/1**[3]

4453 **8** ¾ **Rakata (USA)**[16] 3590 4-9-9 **68**........ PJBenson(5) 7 — 63
(P F I Cole) *prom: chsd wnr 3f out to 2f out: rdn and no ex ent fnl f* — **7/1**[3]

5100 **9** nk **Luckylover**[40] 2823 3-9-9 **70**........ JerryO'Dwyer 6 — 64
(M G Quinlan) *t.k.h: chsd ldrs: rdn 3f out: wknd 2f out* — **20/1**

2-50 **10** 18 **Dalpe**[53] 2460 5-9-3 **57**........ TravisBlock 5 — 10
(A J Lidderdale) *prom on outside tl wknd 3f out* — **25/1**

00 **11** 16 **Bold Finch (FR)**[133] 692 4-9-5 **59**........ NeilChalmers 2 — —
(K O Cunningham-Brown) *s.i.s: a bhd: losst tch over 3f out* — **100/1**

1m 39.46s (-1.34) **Going Correction** -0.025s/f (Stan)
WFA 3 from 4yo+ 7lb — **11** Ran SP% **119.2**
Speed ratings (Par 103):105,103,102,101,99 99,98,97,97,79 63
CSF £62.49 CT £539.75 TOTE £16.00: £4.30, £2.50, £1.80; EX 68.10 Place 6 £218.12, Place 5 £68.02.
Owner Phil Pearce **Bred** Knocktoran Stud **Trained** Newmarket, Suffolk

FOCUS

A decent pace for this apprentice handicap and the winning time was 0.3 seconds faster than the preceding 71-90 handicap. the winner was right back to his best, with the second and third just a length off form.

Takes Tutu(USA) Official explanation: jockey said gelding was never travelling

Bold Finch(FR) Official explanation: jockey said gelding was never travelling

T/Plt: £302.60 to a £1 stake. Pool: £61,061.40. 147.30 winning tickets. T/Qpdt: £18.90 to a £1 stake. Pool: £4,311.50. 168.70 winning tickets. JS

3837 LEICESTER (R-H)
Wednesday, August 2

OFFICIAL GOING: Good

Wind: Fresh, behind Weather: Raining

4049 EUROPEAN BREEDERS FUND TWYFORD MAIDEN STKS — 5f 218y
6:10 (6:11) (Class 4) 2-Y-0 — **£5,181** (£1,541; £770; £384) Stalls Low

Form — RPR

1 — **Doctor Brown** 2-9-3........ NCallan 8 — 93+
(B J Meehan) *mde all: clr over 1f out: r.o wl* — **7/4**[1]

2252 **2** 5 **Dowlleh**[13] 3685 2-9-3........ ChrisCatlin 5 — 78
(M R Channon) *chsd wnr: rdn over 1f out: sn outpcd* — **2/1**[2]

3 5 **Sir Sandicliffe (IRE)** 2-8-12........ AurelioMedeiros(5) 7 — 63
(B W Hills) *prom: rdn over 2f out: sn outpcd* — **18/1**

0 **4** ½ **Mister Lucky (FR)**[16] 3591 2-9-3........ RobertWinston 6 — 62
(Sir Michael Stoute) *prom 4f* — **7/2**[3]

5 5 **Black Mogul** 2-9-3........ DaneO'Neill 3 — 47
(W R Muir) *prom over 3f* — **18/1**

6 11 **Inchigeelagh (IRE)** 2-8-7........ TravisBlock(5) 1 — 9
(H Morrison) *bhd fr 1/2-way* — **12/1**

0 **7** hd **Sweet Soul Diva**[14] 3640 2-8-9........ DominicFox(3) 4 — 8
(Miss V Haigh) *mid-div: wknd over 2f out* — **100/1**

00 **8** 3 ½ **Iced Tango**[21] 3407 2-9-3........ JimmyQuinn 2 — —
(F Jordan) *prom over 3f* — **50/1**

1m 12.66s (-0.54) **Going Correction** -0.175s/f (Firm) — **8** Ran SP% **113.1**
Speed ratings (Par 96):96,89,82,82,75 60,60,55
CSF £5.33 TOTE £2.90: £1.10, £1.10, £5.30; EX 6.60.
Owner J S Threadwell **Bred** Lostford Manor Stud **Trained** Manton, Wilts

FOCUS

Just an average maiden and the runners finished well strung out. The winner made a fine start to his career and could be Listed class.

NOTEBOOK

Doctor Brown, a speedily-bred juvenile whose trainer is more than capable of readying one first time up, was strong in the market throughout the day and he knew his job, soon getting out in front. He showed a nice change of gear to go clear and ran on strongly to win with any amount in hand, suggesting he has enough pace to cope with the minimum distance. He fully deserves a rise in class. (tchd 6-4 and 15-8)

Dowlleh undoubtedly set the standard, but he was always going to be vulnerable to something with a touch of class and he was readily outpointed. He will no doubt find a race eventually, but it is not a good idea to start backing him now. (op 15-8 tchd 3-1)

Sir Sandicliffe(IRE), another already gelded, ran above market expectation on this racecourse debut and, although well held by the winner, he is very much going to benefit from a step up to seven furlongs. (tchd 20-1)

Mister Lucky(FR), whose trainer has yet to get started with his juveniles, failed to build on his initial effort and was woefully outpaced by the front pair. He is clearly nothing special, but may be capable of better in handicaps over seven furlongs plus in time. (op 9-2 tchd 3-1)

Black Mogul comes from a stable whose juveniles often need their first run and he looks no exception. The encouraging thing though was that he was clear of the remainder and better can be expected in time. (op 16-1)

4050 A.R. EDWARDS FAMILY BUTCHERS OF LEICESTER CLAIMING STKS — 7f 9y
6:40 (6:40) (Class 5) 3-Y-0 — **£3,238** (£963; £481; £240) Stalls Low

Form — RPR

0000 **1** — **Bold Love**[61] 2192 3-7-13 37........ AndrewElliott(5) 10 — 48
(J D Bethell) *keen early: cl up: led over 2f out to ent fnl f: rallied to regain ld wl ins last* — **12/1**

2264 **2** nk **Mucho Loco (IRE)**[23] 3364 3-9-3 62........(b) TPQueally 7 — 60
(J G Portman) *keen in tch: smooth hdwy to ld ent fnl f: sn rdn: hdd wl ins last: hld towards fin* — **2/1**[1]

0 **3** ¾ **Top Level (IRE)**[95] 1306 3-8-7........ DominicFox(3) 8 — 51
(M G Quinlan) *midfield on outside: drvn and outpcd over 2f out: rallied over 1f out: kpt on ins last: nt rch first two* — **40/1**

4004 **4** 1 ¼ **Under Fire (IRE)**[7] 3839 3-9-3 47........ FrancisNorton 5 — 55
(A W Carroll) *midfield: outpcd after 3f: rallied over 1f out: nrst fin* — **14/1**

-000 **5** 2 ½ **Knickerless (IRE)**[15] 3604 3-8-1 43 ow1........ ChrisCatlin 6 — 33
(N P Littmoden) *bhd and sn outpcd: hdwy over 1f out: styd on ins fnl f: no imp* — **14/1**

-606 **6** ¾ **Prince Duval (IRE)**[24] 3329 3-8-11 50........ DanielTudhope 11 — 41
(D Carroll) *trckd ldrs tl rdn and no ex over 1f out* — **5/1**[3]

0030 **7** 1 ¾ **Bertie Bear**[18] 3541 3-8-6 39 ow1........(v) BrianReilly 1 — 31
(G G Margarson) *sn wl bhd: hdwy over 1f out: n.d* — **20/1**

6000 **8** 1 ¼ **Saxon Star (IRE)**[9] 3804 3-8-5 40........ HayleyTurner 9 — 27
(M D I Usher) *trckd ldrs tl rdn and wknd fr 2f out* — **33/1**

0000 **9** 1 **Woolfall King (IRE)**[9] 3804 3-8-9 42........ JimmyQuinn 3 — 28
(G G Margarson) *hld up: rdn 3f out: nvr rchd ldrs* — **40/1**

0000 **10** 4 **Night Reveller (IRE)**[81] 1687 3-7-13 30........ JohnMcAuley(3) 2 — 11
(M C Chapman) *dwlt: bhd and sn rdn along: nvr on terms* — **80/1**

6000 **11** 6 **Dispol Valentine**[18] 3538 3-8-0 38........(p) FrancisFerris 14 — —
(P T Midgley) *keen: led to over 2f out: sn rdn and btn* — **20/1**

3440 **12** 2 ½ **Danish Blues (IRE)**[6] 3866 3-9-1 61........(p) NCallan 13 — 2
(N P Littmoden) *plld hrd: chsd ldrs tl rdn and wknd over 2f out* — **4/1**[2]

-006 **13** 5 **Lyrical Blues (IRE)**[20] 3453 3-9-1 60........ DaneO'Neill 12 — —
(B R Millman) *in tch on outside: rdn over 2f out: sn wknd* — **8/1**

0000 **14** 12 **Canvas (IRE)**[29] 3161 3-8-0 40........ AdrianMcCarthy 4 — —
(Miss Z C Davison) *towards rr: drvn 1/2-way: sn btn* — **66/1**

1m 27.13s (1.03) **Going Correction** -0.05s/f (Good) — **14** Ran SP% **122.2**
Speed ratings (Par 100):92,91,90,89,86 85,83,82,81,76 69,66,61,47
CSF £34.75 TOTE £17.30: £4.50, £1.10, £35.90; EX 79.50.The winner was subject to a friendly claim.
Owner Grant Mercer & R G Toes **Bred** P Balding **Trained** Middleham Moor, N Yorks

FOCUS

A weak claimer unlikely to produce many winners.

Danish Blues(IRE) Official explanation: jockey said gelding ran to free

4051 CADEBY HOMES H'CAP — 1m 1f 218y
7:10 (7:11) (Class 4) (0-80,80) 3-Y-0+
£6,232 (£1,866; £933; £467; £233; £117) Stalls High

Form — RPR

2156 **1** — **Custodian (IRE)**[21] 3401 4-9-4 **67**........ EddieAhern 6 — 78
(H R A Cecil) *led 4f: rdn to ld 3f out: hung rt over 1f out: r.o* — **15/2**

5043 **2** 2 **Augustine**[9] 3792 5-9-5 **73**........ LiamTreadwell(5) 3 — 80
(P W Hiatt) *chsd ldrs: rdn over 3f out: hung rt over 1f out: styd on same pce fnl f* — **13/2**

0023 **3** ½ **Shogun Prince (IRE)**[27] 3224 3-9-8 **80**........ NCallan 8 — 86
(A King) *chsd ldrs: rdn over 2f out: styd on same pce fnl f* — **5/1**[2]

0005 **4** 1 ¾ **Gracechurch (IRE)**[11] 3737 3-9-4 **76**........ ChrisCatlin 2 — 79
(M R Channon) *hld up: hdwy over 2f out: sn rdn: styd on same pce fnl f* — **6/1**[3]

256- **5** 5 **Del Mar Sunset**[264] 6314 7-10-0 **77**........ RobertWinston 5 — 74+
(W J Haggas) *hld up: hdwy over 3f out: rdn over 2f out: wknd fnl f* — **11/1**

0661 **6** 5 **Gizmondo**[9] 3804 3-8-0 **58** 6ex........ HayleyTurner 4 — 42
(M L W Bell) *hld up: plld hrd: hdwy 3f out: sn rdn: wknd 2f out* — **9/2**[1]

6100 **7** ¾ **Winners Delight**[23] 3365 5-9-13 **76**........ GeorgeBaker 7 — 58
(C F Wall) *dwlt: hld up: wknd over 2f out* — **8/1**

2-36 **8** 5 **Pigeon Island**[51] 2502 3-9-4 **76**........ DaneO'Neill 1 — 49
(H Candy) *trckd ldr: plld hrd: led 6f out: rdn and hdd 3f out: sn wknd* — **9/2**[1]

2m 9.27s (0.97) **Going Correction** +0.225s/f (Good)
WFA 3 from 4yo+ 9lb — **8** Ran SP% **111.9**
Speed ratings (Par 105):105,103,103,101,97 93,93,89
CSF £52.58 CT £264.22 TOTE £9.10: £1.90, £1.90, £2.10; EX 66.20.
Owner Robert Lanigan & Mrs John Magnier **Bred** Tullamaine Castle Stud And Partners **Trained** Newmarket, Suffolk

FOCUS

Modest but sound handicap form, rated around the second and third.

Gizmondo Official explanation: jockey said gelding found the good ground to be too soft

4052 MULHEARN CONTRACTS LTD H'CAP — 1m 60y
7:40 (7:41) (Class 5) (0-70,70) 3-Y-0 **£5,362** (£1,604; £802; £401; £199) Stalls High

Form — RPR

2-40 **1** — **Munaa (IRE)**[26] 3250 3-9-2 **65**........ FrancisNorton 9 — 71
(K R Burke) *mde all: rdn over 1f out: r.o* — **13/2**

1106 **2** 1 ¾ **Emotive**[14] 3650 3-9-1 **64**........ NCallan 8 — 66
(I A Wood) *chsd wnr to 1/2-way: rdn to go 2nd again over 1f out: no imp ins fnl f* — **11/4**[1]

-004 **3** 4 **Never Say Deya**[8] 3815 3-8-2 **51**........ ChrisCatlin 3 — 44
(M R Channon) *prom: chsd wnr 1/2-way tl rdn over 1f out: no ex* — **7/2**[2]

-641 **4** 1 **Dado Mush**[11] 3750 3-9-1 **64**........ TPQueally 1 — 55
(T T Clement) *chsd ldrs: rdn over 2f out: sn outpcd* — **11/2**[3]

5-00 **5** 1 ¾ **Buckle And Hyde**[44] 2704 3-8-4 **53**........ HayleyTurner 7 — 39
(Mrs A L M King) *s.i.s: hld up: effrt over 2f out: nt trble ldrs* — **25/1**

0000 **6** nk **Earth Master (IRE)**[34] 3016 3-8-1 **53**........(b) StephaneBreux(3) 6 — 39
(S Kirk) *prom: rdn over 2f out: wknd over 1f out* — **15/2**

2225 **7** 3 **Royal Tavira Girl (IRE)**[6] 3869 3-8-7 **59**........ DominicFox(3) 2 — 38
(M G Quinlan) *hld up: hdwy over 2f out: sn hung lft and wknd* — **6/1**

630- **8** 18 **Lady Synthia**[236] 6529 3-9-4 **67**........ FrancisFerris 5 — 4
(B Palling) *hld up: plld hrd: rdn over 3f out: sn wknd* — **22/1**

1m 49.42s (4.12) **Going Correction** +0.525s/f (Yiel) — **8** Ran SP% **111.9**
Speed ratings (Par 100):100,98,94,93,91 91,88,70
CSF £23.63 CT £71.68 TOTE £7.90: £2.30, £1.40, £1.30; EX 23.50.

Owner John A Duffy **Bred** John Malone **Trained** Middleham Moor, N Yorks

FOCUS

A weak handicap, run at an average pace, and the first two came clear.

Munaa(IRE) Official explanation: trainer's representative said, regarding the improved form shown, filly had been better suited by today's good ground and was able to dominate

4053 E B F COPT OAK MEDIAN AUCTION MAIDEN FILLIES' STKS 5f 218y

8:10 (8:12) (Class 5) 2-Y-O **£3,886** (£1,156; £577; £288) **Stalls** Low

Form RPR

0 **1** **Roshanak (IRE)**[12] 3700 2-9-0 .... RobertWinston 4 81
(B J Meehan) *s.i.s: sn chsng ldrs: led over 2f out: rdn out* **7/2**[3]

4 **2** ½ **Russian Rosie (IRE)**[12] 3700 2-9-0 .... TPQueally 8 80
(J G Portman) *hld up: hdwy over 3f out: rdn to chse wnr over 1f out: r.o* **8/1**

4360 **3** ½ **Cassiara**[40] 2800 2-9-0 .... JimmyQuinn 3 78
(J Pearce) *chsd ldrs: outpcd 2f out: rallied fnl f: r.o* **13/8**[1]

62 **4** 1 ¼ **Lady Lily (IRE)**[54] 2388 2-9-0 .... EddieAhern 11 74
(H R A Cecil) *plld hrd: trckd ldrs: rdn over 1f out: no ex ins fnl f* **2/1**[2]

5 1 ¾ **Distant Stars (IRE)** 2-9-0 .... ChrisCatlin 9 69
(E S McMahon) *s.s: in rr whn hmpd over 3f out: styd on appr fnl f: nrst fin* **40/1**

3 **6** ½ **Game Lady**[66] 2045 2-9-0 .... DanielTudhope 6 68
(I A Wood) *hld up: hdwy over 3f out: sn rdn: wkng whn hung lft fnl f* **22/1**

4 **7** 5 **Newport Lass (IRE)**[32] 3096 2-9-0 .... FrancisNorton 2 53
(K R Burke) *led over 3f: rdn and wknd over 1f out* **40/1**

00 **8** 5 **Blue Mistral (IRE)**[12] 3700 2-9-0 .... PaulDoe 1 38
(W J Knight) *prom to 1/2-way* **33/1**

0 **9** ½ **Morning Song (IRE)**[30] 3148 2-9-0 .... NCallan 5 36
(N P Littmoden) *prom to 1/2-way* **66/1**

10 43 **Sparky Vixen** 2-9-0 .... FrancisFerris 7 —
(S Parr) *s.s: outpcd* **100/1**

1m 14.7s (1.50) **Going Correction** +0.10s/f (Good) **10** Ran SP% **119.4**

Speed ratings (Par 91):94,93,92,91,88 88,81,74,74,16

CSF £29.50 TOTE £4.50: £1.70, £2.90, £1.10; EX 41.50.

Owner Ballymacoll Stud **Bred** Ballymacoll Stud Farm Ltd **Trained** Manton, Wilts

FOCUS

A decent juvenile fillies' maiden, run at an average pace, and the form looks sound enough.

NOTEBOOK

Roshanak(IRE), seventh on her debut at Newbury 12 days previously, was again sluggish from the gates but she soon recovered to adopt a handy position and ultimately did enough to get off the mark at the second attempt. The dam's side of her pedigree suggests she ought to really come into her own when racing over further as a three-year-old, but she clearly has a bit more improvement in her this year, and it will be interesting to see where she is pitched in next. (op 11-4 tchd 5-2)

Russian Rosie(IRE), in front of the winner when fourth at Newbury on her debut, was again doing her best work towards the finish and posted an improved effort, even allowing for the fact she failed to confirm her debut form with the winner. She is going the right way and ought to appreciate another furlong in due course. (op 12-1)

Cassiara, not disgraced in the Albany Stakes at Royal Ascot last time, hit a flat spot at a crucial stage and was coming back at the leaders all too late. She is proving frustrating to follow, but helps to set the level of this form all the same. (op 10-3)

Lady Lily(IRE), easy to back, proved too free through the early parts on this return from a 54-day break and ultimately paid the price. She is capable of a little better than this and now qualifies for nurseries. (op 6-4)

Distant Stars(IRE), a half-sister to a couple of juvenile sprint winners amongst others, spoilt her chance by missing the break and never threatened. However, she finished her race in a pleasing fashion and really ought to be plenty sharper for this debut experience. (op 33-1)

Morning Song(IRE) Official explanation: jockey said filly suffered interference in running

4054 HUNCOTE H'CAP 5f 218y

8:40 (8:42) (Class 5) (0-70,67) 3-Y-O+ **£3,886** (£1,156; £577; £288) **Stalls** Low

Form RPR

4-51 **1** **The Cayterers**[8] 3817 4-9-2 **56** 6ex........ MickyFenton 3 68+
(J M Bradley) *chsd ldrs: led over 2f out: rdn and hung rt fr over 1f out: r.o* **5/1**[2]

0265 **2** 1 ½ **Sir Don (IRE)**[13] 3682 7-8-12 **52**........(p) DaneO'Neill 7 59
(E S McMahon) *led over 3f: rdn over 1f out: styd on same pce ins fnl f* **12/1**

3410 **3** ¾ **Stamford Blue**[17] 3565 5-9-1 **62**........(b) TolleyDean(7) 4 67
(R A Harris) *dwlt: outpcd: hdwy over 1f out: r.o* **9/2**[1]

6100 **4** 2 **Norcroft**[12] 3709 4-9-11 **65**........(p) HayleyTurner 13 64
(Mrs C A Dunnett) *chsd ldrs: rdn over 1f out: styd on same pce* **20/1**

0040 **5** ½ **Blue Knight (IRE)**[8] 3817 7-9-4 **58**........(vt) DanielTudhope 15 55
(D Carroll) *hld up: hdwy 1/2-way: rdn over 1f out: styd on same pce* **20/1**

-332 **6** ½ **Inka Dancer (IRE)**[23] 3368 4-9-4 **58**........ FrancisFerris 16 56+
(B Palling) *w ldrs: rdn over 1f out: wknd and eased ins fnl f* **6/1**[3]

0044 **7** ½ **Siraj**[7] 3835 7-8-8 **48** oh1........(p) JimmyQuinn 6 42
(J Ryan) *mid-div: hdwy 1/2-way: rdn over 1f out: wknd fnl f* **6/1**[3]

0033 **8** 1 ½ **Musical Script (USA)**[6] 3866 3-9-0 **58**........ NCallan 10 48
(Mrs A J Hamilton-Fairley) *plld hrd and prom: rdn over 2f out: wknd over 1f out* **9/1**

0001 **9** ½ **Tadlil**[11] 3749 4-9-5 **59**........ GeorgeBaker 14 47
(J M Bradley) *chsd ldrs: rdn over 1f out: wknd fnl f* **13/2**

2126 **10** ¾ **Million Percent**[7] 3846 7-9-8 **62**........ EddieAhern 11 48
(C R Dore) *hld up: nvr trbld ldrs* **11/1**

0/00 **11** 2 ½ **Miss Sudbrook (IRE)**[11] 3749 4-8-8 **48** oh3........(v[1]) FrancisNorton 12 27
(A W Carroll) *mid-div: rdn 1/2-way: wknd 2f out* **80/1**

00-0 **12** ¾ **Spinetail Rufous (IRE)**[20] 3438 8-8-8 **48** oh3........ AdrianMcCarthy 5 24
(Miss Z C Davison) *prom 4f* **50/1**

0065 **13** 1 ¾ **Kallista's Pride**[7] 3855 6-9-6 **67**........ KylieManser(7) 9 38
(J R Best) *sn pushed along: a in rr* **16/1**

-503 **14** nk **Black Oval**[5] 3912 5-8-1 **48** oh9........ MarkCoumbe(7) 2 18
(S Parr) *chsd ldrs over 3f* **25/1**

04/0 **15** 3 ½ **Aegean Mist**[92] 1396 6-8-1 **48** oh7........ SoniaEaton(7) 8 8
(B P J Baugh) *sn outpcd* **66/1**

1m 14.3s (1.10) **Going Correction** +0.275s/f (Good)

WFA 3 from 4yo+ 4lb **15** Ran SP% **126.7**

Speed ratings (Par 103):103,101,100,97,96 96,95,93,92,91 88,87,85,84,79

CSF £62.47 CT £300.58 TOTE £5.50: £2.20, £4.20, £2.70; EX 82.10 Place 6 £27.21, Place 5 £19.29.

Owner R D Willis and M C Watts **Bred** Acrum Lodge Stud **Trained** Sedbury, Gloucs

FOCUS

A moderate handicap, run at a sound pace, and the winner is progressive. The runner-up ran to this year's form.

Black Oval Official explanation: jockey said gelding found the good ground to be too soft

T/Plt: £64.70 to a £1 stake. Pool: £57,854.60. 652.20 winning tickets. T/Qpdt: £20.90 to a £1 stake. Pool: £4,525.20. 160.10 winning tickets. CR

[3350] MUSSELBURGH (R-H)

Wednesday, August 2

OFFICIAL GOING: Good (good to soft in places)

Wind: Slight, across

4055 MUSSELBURGH NEWS MAIDEN AUCTION STKS 7f 30y

2:15 (2:16) (Class 6) 2-Y-O **£3,238** (£963; £481; £240) **Stalls** Low

Form RPR

4422 **1** **Persian Peril**[26] 3259 2-8-11 .... DeanMcKeown 7 63+
(G A Swinbank) *trckd ldr on inner: hdwy to chal 2f out: led ins last: kpt on* **4/9**[1]

50 **2** 1 ¼ **Keep Your Distance**[29] 3175 2-8-11 .... PatCosgrave 2 60
(K R Burke) *led: rdn along over 2f out: drvn and edgd lft over 1f out: hdd and one pce ins last* **20/1**

43 **3** 1 ¾ **Ingleby Flame (IRE)**[14] 3633 2-8-10 .... PaulFessey 4 55
(T D Barron) *chsd ldng pair: rdn along over 2f out: drvn over 1f out: sn one pce* **9/2**[2]

4 2 **Rockfonic** 2-8-12 .... PhillipMakin 5 52
(J R Weymes) *dwlt: in tch: hdwy 3f out: rdn 2f out and sn no imp* **20/1**

00 **5** 17 **Perilore (IRE)**[72] 1884 2-7-13 .... DuranFentiman(5) 6 1
(A Berry) *s.i.s: a rr* **100/1**

03 **6** 25 **Mandurah (IRE)**[7] 3830 2-8-11 .... AdrianTNicholls 3 —
(D Nicholls) *chsd ldrs: rdn 3f out: sn wknd and eased fnl 2f* **8/1**[3]

1m 34.91s (4.97) **Going Correction** +0.375s/f (Good) **6** Ran SP% **109.1**

Speed ratings (Par 92):86,84,82,80,60 32

CSF £12.19 TOTE £1.40: £1.10, £8.50; EX 11.80.

Owner Mrs J Porter **Bred** Mrs P Lewis **Trained** Melsonby, N Yorks

FOCUS

Just an ordinary maiden run in a modest time. Not easy to rate, the winner 4lb off his previous best.

NOTEBOOK

Persian Peril found an ordinary maiden to finally get off the mark in at the fifth time of asking. The step up to seven furlongs suited this son of Erhaab, and he should pay his way in nurseries this season and get a mile in time. (op 8-15)

Keep Your Distance had not shown much on his first two starts but the easier ground brought about improvement. He is bred to need a good deal further in time and the greater emphasis on stamina helped. (op 14-1)

Ingleby Flame(IRE) was a bit below the form he showed at Catterick last time but he is now eligible for a handicap mark and nurseries should present him with a better chance of breaking his duck. (op 4-1)

Rockfonic, whose dam was placed over seven to ten furlongs, was weak in the market beforehand but shaped with some promise. This was a fair effort considering he was giving weight all round on his debut. (op 12-1)

Mandurah(IRE) Official explanation: jockey said colt was unsuited by the good (good to soft in places) ground

4056 TARTANTURFDIRECTORY.CO.UK H'CAP 5f

2:50 (2:50) (Class 6) (0-60,60) 3-Y-O **£2,914** (£867; £433; £216) **Stalls** Low

Form RPR

0042 **1** **Alugat (IRE)**[7] 3833 3-9-0 **53**........(p) RoystonFfrench 4 65+
(Mrs A Duffield) *squeezed out after s and bhd: swtchd rt and gd hdwy 2f out: rdn over 1f out: styd on to ld ins last* **11/4**[1]

-030 **2** 2 **Malelane (IRE)**[11] 3749 3-8-5 **44** ow2........ DavidAllan 10 44
(A Dickman) *hld up: hdwy 1/2-way: rdn to ld briefly over 1f out: drvn and hdd ins last: kpt on same pce* **8/1**

5020 **3** ¾ **Signor Whippee**[7] 3833 3-8-10 **52**........(b) StephenDonohoe(3) 8 49
(A Berry) *rr and pushed along after 1f: hdwy wl over 1f out: styd on ins last: nrst fin* **25/1**

6544 **4** 2 **Howards Prince**[19] 3479 3-9-7 **60**........(p) TonyHamilton 12 50
(I Semple) *cl up: rdn to ld wl over 1f out: hdd aappr last: sn drvn and wknd* **8/1**

0000 **5** 2 **She's Our Beauty (IRE)**[15] 3608 3-8-13 **52**........(v) SilvestreDeSousa 9 35
(D Nicholls) *chsd ldrs: rdn along wl over 1f out: sn btn* **14/1**

6005 **6** 2 **Networker**[10] 3759 3-8-2 **41** oh1........ JamieMackay 6 17
(K G Reveley) *prom: rdn along over 2f out and sn wknd* **6/1**[2]

-246 **7** nk **Slipperfoot**[18] 3526 3-9-2 **55**........ GrahamGibbons 11 30
(J J Quinn) *prom: rdn along 2f out: sn wknd* **6/1**[2]

3063 **8** 1 ¼ **Egyptian Lord**[19] 3479 3-9-3 **56**........(b) RobbieFitzpatrick 3 26
(Peter Grayson) *chsd ldrs: edgd lft 1/2-way: effrt on inner whn nt clr run wl over 1f out: sn eased* **13/2**[3]

2000 **9** 1 ½ **Soviet Legend (IRE)**[8] 3821 3-8-11 **53** ow4........(vt) DNolan(3) 1 18
(T J Etherington) *chsd ldrs on inner tl hmpd and lost pl 1/2-way: swtchd rt and rdn 2f out: no prog* **14/1**

0-06 **10** 1 ¾ **Pensata**[90] 1437 3-8-0 **44** ow1........ AndrewMullen(5) 2 2
(Miss L A Perratt) *chsd ldrs tl hmpd after 2f and sn lost pl: swtchd rt and rdn 2f out: sn no imp* **40/1**

050 **11** 2 **Compton Lad**[18] 3526 3-8-9 **48** ow2........ PatCosgrave 7 —
(D A Nolan) *led: rdn along over 2f out: hdd wl over 1f out and sn wknd* **100/1**

62.83 secs (2.33) **Going Correction** +0.375s/f (Good) **11** Ran SP% **111.4**

Speed ratings (Par 98):96,92,91,88,85 82,81,79,77,74 71

CSF £23.15 CT £440.24 TOTE £2.60: £1.40, £2.40, £5.70; EX 33.50.

Owner Ian West & Partners **Bred** Rathbarry Stud **Trained** Constable Burton, N Yorks

■ Stewards' Enquiry : D Nolan three-day ban: made abusive remark to clerk of the scales (Aug 13-15)

FOCUS

A moderate handicap featuring few in-form contenders. It is unlikely to throw up many future winners. A weak race, the second and third to form.

Networker Official explanation: jockey said gelding hung left throughout

4057 ROSSLEIGH LANDROVER (S) STKS 1m

3:25 (3:25) (Class 6) 3-Y-O+ **£2,730** (£806; £403) **Stalls** Low

Form RPR

0-50 **1** **Zendaro**[39] 2853 4-9-4 **60**........ DavidAllan 8 68
(W M Brisbourne) *keen: trckd ldrs: hdwy 3f out: rdn to ld over 2f out: drvn out* **6/1**

4151 **2** 2 ½ **Sawwaah (IRE)**[23] 3353 9-9-9 **65**........(p) AdrianTNicholls 10 67
(D Nicholls) *hld up towards rr: hdwy 3f out: rdn 2f out: styd on to chse wnr ent last: sn drvn and no imp* **3/1**[2]

2034 **3** 2 ½ **Desert Lightning (IRE)**[18] 3541 4-9-4 **50**........ PatCosgrave 6 56
(K R Burke) *trckd ldrs: hdwy 3f out: rdn to chse wnr wl over 1f out: sn one pce* **9/2**[3]

5232 **4** ½ **Burnley Al (IRE)**[23] 3353 4-9-9 57..............................(b) TonyHamilton 13 60
(R A Fahey) *led: rdn along and hdd over 2f out: grad wknd* **11/4**[1]

4003 **5** 4 **Spring Time Girl**[18] 3541 4-8-10 43....................(b) StephenDonohoe(3) 5 41
(B Ellison) *hld up in rr: hdwy over 2f out: sn rdn and no imp appr last* **11/2**

5620 **6** 7 **Roman History (IRE)**[10] 3762 3-8-11 46............................ GylesParkin 9 30
(Miss Tracy Waggott) *in tch: hdwy on outer to chse ldrs 3f out: rdn along over 2f out and sn btn* **33/1**

0500 **7** shd **Frimley's Matterry**[26] 3240 6-8-13 44...................... MarkLawson(5) 12 30
(R E Barr) *chsd ldrs: rdn over 2f out: sn wknd* **25/1**

-050 **8** nk **Tinian**[17] 1073 8-9-1 43..(b) BenSwarbrick(3) 3 29
(Miss Tracy Waggott) *prom on outer: rdn along 3f out: sn wknd* **25/1**

06/0 **9** hd **Phoenix Nights (IRE)**[13] 3675 6-9-4 46...................... DeanMcKeown 7 28
(A Berry) *a towards rr* **100/1**

-000 **10** 11 **Wood Dalling (USA)**[23] 3353 8-8-13 29................. AndrewMullen(5) 14 3
(Mrs J C McGregor) *dwlt: a rr* **100/1**

0-00 **11** 7 **King Henrik (USA)**[14] 3635 4-9-4 37............................. RoystonFfrench 1 —
(A Crook) *cl up: rdn along over 3f out: sn wknd* **100/1**

5050 **12** 5 **Bold Tiger (IRE)**[10] 3759 3-8-11 50............................... J-PGuillambert 11 —
(Miss Tracy Waggott) *a towards rr* **40/1**

1m 44.15s (1.65) **Going Correction** +0.375s/f (Good)
WFA 3 from 4yo+ 7lb **12** Ran SP% **115.6**
Speed ratings (Par 101):106,103,101,100,96 89,89,89,88,77 70,65
CSF £22.71 TOTE £6.00: £1.80, £1.50, £1.70; EX 37.50.There was no bid for the winner.
Owner Zen Racing **Bred** Lady Juliet Tadgell **Trained** Great Ness, Shropshire

FOCUS
A fair seller in which less than half the field could be given a chance, but it was run in a creditable winning time for the grade. Solid form for the grade.

4058 GERRARD INVESTMENT MANAGEMENT H'CAP 7f 30y
4:00 (4:00) (Class 5) (0-80,76) 3-Y-O **£6,477** (£1,927; £963; £481) **Stalls** Low

Form RPR

3545 **1** **Secret Liaison**[13] 3688 3-9-1 70.. JamieMackay 8 83+
(Sir Mark Prescott) *mde most: rdn along 2f out: styd on strly appr last* **6/4**[1]

0210 **2** 4 **Elegant Times (IRE)**[22] 3381 3-8-8 63................................ DavidAllan 7 63
(T D Easterby) *hld up towards rr: hdwy over 2f out: sn rdn and kpt on ins last: tk 2nd nr line* **12/1**

1605 **3** ½ **La Matanza**[34] 3023 3-9-0 72.. BenSwarbrick(3) 4 71
(T D Barron) *trckd ldrs: hdwy 3f out: rdn to chse wnr wl over 1f out: sn drvn and one pce* **16/1**

-350 **4** hd **Choreography**[57] 2324 3-8-8 63.................................... AdrianTNicholls 2 61
(D Nicholls) *keen:cl up: rdn along to chal 2f out: sn drvn and wknd* **11/2**[3]

-600 **5** 3 **Mr Rooney (IRE)**[21] 3404 3-9-7 76.............................. RoystonFfrench 6 67
(M Johnston) *cl up: rdn along 3f out: drvn over 2f out and sn btn* **9/1**

2641 **6** 12 **Garstang**[14] 3646 3-8-13 68.......................................(b) RobbieFitzpatrick 3 27+
(Peter Grayson) *hld up: a rr* **5/2**[2]

0600 **7** 15 **Laith (IRE)**[4] 3937 3-9-5 74.. TonyHamilton 1 —
(Miss V Haigh) *rrd s: a rr* **20/1**

1m 32.77s (2.83) **Going Correction** +0.375s/f (Good) **7** Ran SP% **112.3**
Speed ratings (Par 100):98,93,92,92,89 75,58
CSF £20.11 CT £204.50 TOTE £2.60: £1.60, £3.70; EX 17.00.
Owner W E Sturt - Osborne House **Bred** Cheveley Park Stud Ltd **Trained** Newmarket, Suffolk

FOCUS
No messing about here despite the rain-softened ground and again the field edged over to the nearside rail on reaching the home straight. The conditions seemed to find a few out and the winner handled them much the best. Just a modest event, rated around the second and fourth.
Garstang Official explanation: jockey said gelding ran too free

4059 EAST LOTHIAN NEWS H'CAP 7f 30y
4:35 (4:35) (Class 6) (0-60,58) 3-Y-O+ **£3,071** (£906; £453) **Stalls** Low

Form RPR

0050 **1** **Sentiero Rosso (USA)**[18] 3543 4-9-11 58..........(t) StephenDonohoe(3) 1 68
(B Ellison) *a.p: hdwy to ld 2 1/2f out: rdn wl over 1f out: styd on wl* **13/2**[3]

00-0 **2** 1¼ **Choreographic (IRE)**[24] 3334 4-8-9 39 oh3.................. TonyHamilton 9 47+
(R A Fahey) *hld up in midfield: hdwy over 2f out: rdn over 1f out: styd on strly ins last* **10/1**

0461 **3** nk **Motu (IRE)**[9] 3786 5-9-10 54 5ex.............................(v) RoystonFfrench 11 60+
(I W McInnes) *trckd ldrs: hdwy 3f out: nt clr run wl over 1f out: swtchd rt: rdn and styd on ent last* **11/2**[1]

0006 **4** hd **Borodinsky**[12] 3697 5-9-3 47.. DavidAllan 14 52
(R E Barr) *chsd ldrs: rdn along over 2f out: drvn and ch over 1f out: one pce ins last* **7/1**

0041 **5** 1 **Drury Lane (IRE)**[7] 3835 6-8-11 44 5ex...................(p) BenSwarbrick(3) 6 47
(D W Chapman) *midfield: hdwy and n.m.r 2f out: sn rdn and kpt on ins last: nt rch ldrs* **7/1**

6 1¾ **Silent Willow (IRE)**[22] 3393 5-8-10 40......................(b[1]) DeanMcKeown 5 38
(Thomas O'Neill, Ire) *hld up in rr: hdwy 3f out: swtchd rt 2f out: sn rdn and ch over 1f out: wknd ent last* **40/1**

0005 **7** 5 **Kabis Amigos**[23] 3361 4-9-9 53.................................... AdrianTNicholls 12 38
(D Nicholls) *prom: rdn along wl over 2f out: sn drvn and wknd* **6/1**[2]

3030 **8** ½ **High Swainston**[44] 2696 5-8-12 45....................................... DNolan(3) 3 29
(R Craggs) *cl up: rdn along and wandered 2f out: sn wknd* **10/1**

3461 **9** hd **Drink To Me Only**[30] 3138 3-9-2 52.................................. PhillipMakin 7 35
(J R Weymes) *a towards rr* **13/2**[3]

0002 **10** 4 **Obe Bold (IRE)**[9] 3783 5-9-3 52............................ NataliaGemelova(5) 2 25
(A Berry) *led: rdn along 3f out: sn hdd & wknd* **12/1**

0006 **11** 4 **Mandarin Grand (IRE)**[8] 3814 3-7-12 39 oh3.....(p) DuranFentiman(5) 10 —
(Miss L A Perratt) *a towards rr* **33/1**

00-0 **12** 2 **Ochil Hills Dancer (IRE)**[18] 3554 4-8-10 40.................. PatCosgrave 4 —
(A Crook) *a towards rr* **66/1**

0500 **13** 10 **Glenviews Oldport (USA)**[21] 3411 4-8-9 39 oh3.(b) RobbieFitzpatrick 8 —
(Peter Grayson) *s.i.s: a b ehind* **33/1**

0-00 **14** 18 **Borsch (IRE)**[69] 1946 4-8-4 39 oh9.........................(b[1]) AndrewMullen(5) 13 —
(Miss L A Perratt) *s.i.s: a bhd* **100/1**

1m 32.98s (3.04) **Going Correction** +0.375s/f (Good)
WFA 3 from 4yo+ 6lb **14** Ran SP% **118.0**
Speed ratings (Par 101):97,95,95,95,93 91,86,85,85,80 76,73,62,41
CSF £66.56 CT £394.96 TOTE £8.30: £2.80, £4.40, £1.90; EX 103.00.
Owner Black and White Diamond Partnership **Bred** Thomas And Lakin **Trained** Norton, N Yorks

FOCUS
A low-grade handicap, but competitive enough. Again the field came stands' side in the home straight. Sound form, rated around the third.

4060 RECTANGLE GROUP H'CAP 1m 1f
5:10 (5:11) (Class 6) (0-65,65) 3-Y-O **£3,238** (£963; £481; £240) **Stalls** Low

Form RPR

2062 **1** **Superior Star**[11] 3725 3-9-2 60..(v) TonyHamilton 9 76+
(R A Fahey) *trckd ldrs: smooth hdwy to ld 2f out: rdn clr ent last: easily* **13/2**[3]

1141 **2** 6 **Touch Of Ivory (IRE)**[15] 3604 3-8-12 61...................(p) MarkLawson(5) 3 62+
(P Monteith) *hld up in rr: hdwy over 2f out: rdn wl over 1f out: styd on ins last: no ch w wnr* **5/1**[2]

0004 **3** ¾ **Twilight Avenger (IRE)**[15] 3609 3-8-4 48............. SilvestreDeSousa 13 48
(W M Brisbourne) *trckd ldrs: hdwy 3f out: rdn to chse wnr over 1f out: sn drvn and one pce* **14/1**

0016 **4** 1½ **The Great Delaney**[60] 2243 3-9-2 60......................... RobbieFitzpatrick 6 57
(T J Pitt) *cl up: led over 3f out: rdn: edgd lfta nd hdd 2f out: sn drvn and wknd* **9/2**[1]

0046 **5** 1 **Coalpark (IRE)**[11] 3724 3-9-7 65................................(t) J-PGuillambert 11 60
(M Johnston) *led: rdn along and hdd over 3f out: plugged on same pce fnl 2f* **8/1**

4556 **6** hd **Ellesappelle**[58] 2283 3-9-6 64... PatCosgrave 2 58
(K R Burke) *chsd ldrs: effrt and ev ch whn hmpd 2f out: sn wknd* **10/1**

0-56 **7** 1¾ **Princess Of Aeneas (IRE)**[29] 3167 3-9-1 59............ PaulMulrennan 10 50
(I Semple) *towards rr tl sme late hdwy* **12/1**

605 **8** 1 **Hill Billy Rock (IRE)**[26] 3261 3-9-4 62.......................... DeanMcKeown 5 51+
(G A Swinbank) *hld up and bhd tl sme late hdwy* **10/1**

05-0 **9** ½ **Dream Mountain**[30] 3147 3-9-6 64................................ RoystonFfrench 4 52
(M Johnston) *prom: rdn along 4f out: sn wknd* **14/1**

5000 **10** hd **English Archer**[24] 3329 3-8-8 52.. DavidAllan 12 39
(J R Weymes) *in tch: rdn along 3f out: sn wknd* **25/1**

0434 **11** 10 **Strong Approach (IRE)**[14] 3638 3-9-7 65......................... PhillipMakin 8 32
(T D Barron) *a rr* **11/1**

-500 **12** 12 **Find It Out (USA)**[14] 3634 3-9-1 59.......................................(t) PaulFessey 7 —
(T D Barron) *a bhd* **25/1**

1m 57.54s (1.54) **Going Correction** +0.375s/f (Good) **12** Ran SP% **114.5**
Speed ratings (Par 98):108,102,102,100,99 99,98,97,96,96 87,76
CSF £37.54 CT £441.16 TOTE £8.40: £3.10, £1.60, £3.50; EX 36.50 Place 6 £60.16, Place 5 £44.28.
Owner J C Parsons **Bred** R F And Mrs Knipe **Trained** Musley Bank, N Yorks

FOCUS
A fairly competitive if modest handicap, but ultimately a one-horse race. The winning time was very decent for a race like this and the form should prove sound.
Hill Billy Rock(IRE) Official explanation: jockey said gelding was unsuited by the good (good to soft in places) ground
T/Plt: £75.60 to a £1 stake. Pool: £38,110.35. 367.80 winning tickets. T/Qpdt: £27.30 to a £1 stake. Pool: £2,169.60. 58.60 winning tickets. JR

4061 - 4065a (Foreign Racing) - See Raceform Interactive

[3693]CARLISLE (R-H)
Thursday, August 3

OFFICIAL GOING: Good (good to soft in places)
The fields came centre to stands side in the straight in all races with those nearest the stands rail holding the edge. Those held up were at a disadvantage.
Wind: Breezy, half-against.

4066 BOWNESS MAIDEN AUCTION STKS 5f 193y
1:55 (1:56) (Class 5) 2-Y-O **£3,238** (£963; £481; £240) **Stalls** High

Form RPR

0 **1** **Terry Molloy (IRE)**[27] 3247 2-8-11 .... PatCosgrave 3 72
(K R Burke) *mde all: c w rest of field to stands side ent st: sn rdn: hld on gamely fnl f* **6/1**[2]

02 **2** ½ **Sir Charles**[35] 3018 2-8-9 .... PhillipMakin 1 68+
(M Dods) *cl up: effrt whn checked 2f out: effrt over 1f out: edgd rt: kpt on fnl f* **7/2**[1]

3 1¾ **Expensive Detour (IRE)** 2-8-11 .... TomEaves 7 65+
(Mrs L Stubbs) *rn green in rr: hdwy and cl up whn n.m.r 2f out: sn rdn: kpt on same pce ins fnl f* **20/1**

4 1½ **First Mate (IRE)** 2-8-11 .... RoystonFfrench 5 60
(M Johnston) *sn rdn in midfield: hdwy and cl up 2f out: kpt on same pce ins fnl f* **7/2**[1]

55 **5** 3 **Muncaster Castle (IRE)**[40] 2854 2-8-11 .... DanielTudhope 11 51
(R F Fisher) *bhd: hdwy outside over 2f out: kpt on: nvr rchd ldrs* **16/1**

4 **6** 1¾ **Milliegait**[68] 2026 2-8-1 .... DuranFentiman(5) 13 41
(T D Easterby) *prom tl rdn and outpcd fr 2f out* **7/2**[1]

7 1½ **Pretty Game** 2-8-9 .... DO'Donohoe 12 39+
(K A Ryan) *sn outpcd and drvn along: sme late hdwy: nvr rchd ldrs* **8/1**[3]

8 shd **Interest (USA)** 2-8-9 .... PaulFessey 8 39
(T D Barron) *bhd and drvn along: nvr rchd ldrs* **20/1**

00 **9** 2 **Silly Gilly (IRE)**[27] 3247 2-8-4 .... FrancisNorton 9 28
(A Berry) *chsd ldrs tl wknd over 2f out* **66/1**

10 hd **Monsieur Dumas (IRE)** 2-8-11 .... PaulMulrennan 4 34
(T P Tate) *sn prom: rdn over 2f out: sn btn* **16/1**

0 **11** ½ **Mambomoon**[33] 3080 2-8-11 ....(t) TonyHamilton 2 33
(T D Easterby) *chsd ldrs tl wknd fr 1/2-way* **33/1**

1m 13.97s (0.36) **Going Correction** -0.05s/f (Good) **11** Ran SP% **117.8**
Speed ratings (Par 94):95,94,92,90,86 83,81,81,78,78 77
CSF £26.19 TOTE £6.90: £2.20, £1.40, £6.40; EX 31.20.
Owner U N Syndicate & Mrs E Burke **Bred** Roland H Alder **Trained** Middleham Moor, N Yorks
■ Stewards' Enquiry : Pat Cosgrave two-day ban: careless riding (Aug 14,15)

FOCUS
An ordinary bunch on looks and almost certainly ordinary form. The pace seemed sound.

NOTEBOOK
Terry Molloy(IRE) looked in good shape and fully confirmed the promise shown on his debut at Haydock in a race that has thrown up winners. He showed a decent attitude for pressure, should stay seven furlongs and may be capable of better. (op 8-1)
Sir Charles has improved with every outing and turned in his best effort yet. Whether he would have won had he not suffered interference at a crucial stage is debatable, but he is now qualified for a handicap mark, should stay seven furlongs and be able to win a small event.
Expensive Detour(IRE) ◆, the first foal of a multiple middle-distance winner, took the eye in the paddock despite looking in need of the race and shaped well over a trip that is sure to be a bare minimum on this racecourse debut. He is open to plenty of improvement and looks capable of winning a similar event. (op 25-1)
First Mate(IRE), a half-brother to winners at up to seven furlongs, ran creditably, despite his apparent greenness on this racecourse debut. He should be suited by the step up to seven furlongs, is in good hands and may do better. (tchd 4-1)

Muncaster Castle(IRE), who has shown ability at a modest level, was not disgraced but his proximity confirms this form is nothing special. He may do better in modest nursery company over further. (op 14-1)
Milliegait failed to build on her encouraging debut display on this much quicker ground. However, more testing conditions or a much stiffer test of stamina should suit and she would not be one to write off just yet. (op 100-30)

4067 FAMILY DAY CLAIMING STKS 5f 193y
2:30 (2:30) (Class 6) 3-Y-0+ **£2,730** (£806; £403) **Stalls** High

Form RPR
3534 **1** **Atlantic Viking (IRE)**[8] 3832 11-9-5 66 PhillipMakin 8 70
(D Nicholls) *in tch: rdn to ld 1f out: edgd rt: r.o strly* **7/2**[2]
0030 **2** *1 ¾* **Val De Maal (IRE)**[27] 3245 6-9-5 58 (v) TomEaves 14 65
(Miss J A Camacho) *in tch: effrt and ev ch appr fnl f: kpt on ins last* **7/1**
0405 **3** *hd* **Blue Knight (IRE)**[1] 4054 7-9-5 58 (vt) DanielTudhope 6 64
(D Carroll) *midfield: hdwy to chse ldrs whn n.m.r over 1f out: kpt on ins fnl f* **5/1**[3]
0530 **4** *2* **Fox Covert (IRE)**[8] 3835 5-8-8 43 (p) CatherineGannon 5 47
(D W Barker) *prom: effrt over 2f out: one pce fnl f* **25/1**
4060 **5** *½* **Apex**[3] 3996 5-9-5 64 KimTinkler 10 57
(N Tinkler) *towards rr: drvn over 2f out: kpt on fnl f: no imp* **10/3**[1]
3200 **6** *2* **Weakest Link**[19] 3524 5-9-9 47 (v[1]) FrancisNorton 1 55
(E J Alston) *mde most to 1f out: sn outpcd* **12/1**
000- **7** *2* **Shinko Femme (IRE)**[205] 5828 5-8-7 42 JamesO'Reilly(7) 4 40
(J O'Reilly) *s.i.s: bhd tl sme late hdwy: n.d* **20/1**
0016 **8** *hd* **The London Gang**[5] 3959 3-9-2 60 (v) StephenDonohoe(3) 13 48
(P D Evans) *bhd: effrt outside over 2f out: sn no imp* **11/2**
0004 **9** *1 ½* **Zantero**[13] 3698 4-9-3 45 PaulMulrennan 2 38
(W M Brisbourne) *w ldr tl wknd appr fnl f* **50/1**
506 **10** *2 ½* **Telepathic (IRE)**[14] 3670 6-9-5 47 TPQueally 9 32
(A Berry) *s.i.s: nvr rchd ldrs* **66/1**
0 **11** *6* **Longy The Lash**[26] 3285 3-8-11 DeanMcKeown 3 10
(K G Reveley) *bhd and sn outpcd: no ch fr 1/2-way* **66/1**
0050 **12** *7* **Valhar**[51] 2535 3-8-2 48 PaulHanagan 11 —
(D W Thompson) *a bhd* **33/1**

1m 12.73s (-0.88) **Going Correction** -0.05s/f (Good)
WFA 3 from 4yo+ 4lb **12 Ran SP% 114.0**
Speed ratings (Par 101):103,100,100,97,97 94,91,91,89,86 78,68
CSF £25.01 TOTE £3.50: £1.50, £2.60, £2.70; EX 24.50.Atlantic Viking was claimed by P. D. Evans for £8,000. Fox Covert was claimed by A. C. Whillans for £2,500.
Owner David Faulkner **Bred** Kilcarn Stud **Trained** Sessay, N Yorks

FOCUS
An ordinary event but one in which the pace was sound throughout and the form looks reliable, rated through the third.
Telepathic(IRE) Official explanation: jockey said gelding missed the break

4068 RACING UK ON SKY 432 H'CAP 1m 1f 61y
3:05 (3:05) (Class 5) (0-70,69) 3-Y-0+ **£3,238** (£963; £481; £240) **Stalls** High

Form RPR
-634 **1** **Lauro**[43] 2747 6-8-9 58 DawnRankin(7) 13 71+
(Miss J A Camacho) *prom: smooth hdwy to ld 2f out: rdn and r.o strly fnl f* **16/1**
225 **2** *2* **Middlemarch (IRE)**[30] 3168 6-9-13 69 (p) DaleGibson 2 78
(J S Goldie) *chsd ldr: effrt and ev ch 2f out: kpt on fnl f: nt rch wnr* **7/1**
4100 **3** *shd* **Scotty's Future (IRE)**[19] 3519 8-9-3 59 FrancisNorton 7 68
(A Berry) *bhd and sn pushed along: hdwy 3f out: swtchd rt over 1f out: kpt on ins fnl f* **12/1**
3621 **4** *1 ½* **Donna's Double**[25] 3333 11-8-10 52 (p) TonyHamilton 10 58
(Karen McLintock) *hld up in tch: smooth hdwy 3f out: effrt over 1f out: kpt on same pce* **8/1**
-454 **5** *5* **Shy Glance (USA)**[30] 3168 4-9-7 63 (t) DeanMcKeown 4 59
(G A Swinbank) *hld up: hdwy and in tch over 1f out: outpcd whn blkd ins fnl f* **7/1**
1213 **6** *nk* **Cottingham (IRE)**[10] 3784 5-9-8 67 BenSwarbrick(3) 3 62
(T D Barron) *cl up: effrt and ch 2f out: sn outpcd* **5/1**[1]
0043 **7** *nk* **Royal Indulgence**[5] 3947 6-8-7 54 LiamJones(5) 12 49
(W M Brisbourne) *led: styd centre in st: hdd 2f out: sn btn* **11/2**[2]
0002 **8** *½* **Silver Court**[10] 3798 4-8-5 50 oh8 JamesDoyle(3) 14 44
(A W Carroll) *missed break: bhd: rdn 1/2-way: nvr on terms* **16/1**
2130 **9** *hd* **Sir Bond (IRE)**[27] 3262 5-9-1 62 MarkLawson(5) 1 55
(B Smart) *dwlt: hld up: effrt and in tch over 1f out: wknd fnl f* **9/1**
1403 **10** *19* **Bridgewater Boys**[31] 3159 5-9-11 67 (b) DO'Donohoe 6 22
(K A Ryan) *bhd: struggling 1/2-way: nvr on terms* **6/1**[3]
500/ **11** *nk* **Medalla (FR)**[662] 6096 6-9-4 60 TomEaves 11 15
(M Brittain) *towards rr: drvn 1/2-way: sn wknd* **40/1**
0 **12** *1 ¼* **Barry The Brave**[22] 3398 4-9-4 60 PatCosgrave 9 12
(Micky Hammond) *in tch to 1/2-way: sn lost pl* **50/1**

1m 56.09s (-1.47) **Going Correction** -0.05s/f (Good) **12 Ran SP% 116.3**
Speed ratings (Par 103):104,102,102,100,96 96,95,95,95,78 78,76
CSF £121.66 CT £1404.32 TOTE £21.20: £6.40, £2.30, £4.30; EX 162.40.
Owner Miss Julie Camacho **Bred** Mrs S Camacho **Trained** Norton, N Yorks

FOCUS
Another ordinary handicap but, although the pace was sound, those racing prominently held the edge. The form appears solid enough, rated around the runner-up and fourth.
Bridgewater Boys Official explanation: jockey said gelding lost its action

4069 VIACOM OUTDOOR H'CAP 7f 200y
3:35 (3:38) (Class 6) (0-60,60) 3-Y-0 **£2,730** (£806; £403) **Stalls** High

Form RPR
3330 **1** **William John**[31] 3145 3-8-13 52 (t) TomEaves 4 61
(B Ellison) *prom: led stands side over 2f out: hrd pressed over 1f out: hld on wl* **4/1**[1]
0000 **2** *1 ¾* **Atwirl**[15] 3650 3-8-11 50 (b) RoystonFfrench 2 55
(D J Daly) *hld up in tch: hdwy over 2f out: ev ch appr fnl f: kpt on ins last* **22/1**
0263 **3** *1 ¾* **Ours (IRE)**[17] 3582 3-9-7 60 FrancisNorton 8 61+
(J D Bethell) *stdd s: hld up: smooth hdwy over 2f out: rdn and edgd lft over 1f out: kpt on ins fnl f* **11/2**
1034 **4** *nk* **Apache Nation (IRE)**[11] 3760 3-9-4 60 StephenDonohoe(3) 10 60
(M Dods) *chsd ldrs: effrt over 2f out: kpt on same pce appr fnl f* **5/1**[3]
1040 **5** *hd* **They All Laughed**[18] 3030 3-9-3 56 PhillipMakin 13 56
(P W Hiatt) *bhd: hdwy centre over 2f out: kpt on fnl f: no imp* **14/1**
60 **6** *5* **Petross**[39] 2896 3-9-5 58 DeanMcKeown 12 46
(R M Whitaker) *in tch: effrt and rdn over 2f out: edgd lft and no ex over 1f out* **33/1**
0202 **7** *3* **Crush On You**[8] 3839 3-8-4 50 RussellKennemore(7) 11 31
(R Hollinshead) *hld up: hdwy over 2f out: wknd over 1f out* **8/1**
0420 **8** *1 ¾* **Artie's Son (IRE)**[31] 3154 3-9-6 59 PaulHanagan 3 36
(T D Easterby) *keen: hld up: rdn over 2f out: nvr rchd ldrs* **9/1**
600- **9** *9* **Bright Sparky (GER)**[316] 5408 3-8-11 50 (t) DaleGibson 5 7
(M W Easterby) *in tch: sn pushed along: wknd fr 3f out* **9/2**[2]
660 **10** *1* **Tip Top Style**[157] 536 3-8-12 51 DO'Donohoe 6 5
(J Mackie) *chsd ldrs: rdn whn n.m.r over 2f out: sn btn* **25/1**
-006 **11** *3* **Katsumoto (IRE)**[30] 3169 3-8-11 50 (p) TPQueally 7 —
(N P Littmoden) *keen: led to over 2f out: sn wknd* **25/1**
6000 **12** *7* **Dzhani**[25] 3329 3-8-11 50 (t) PaulMulrennan 9 —
(Jedd O'Keeffe) *bhd: rdn 3f out: nvr on terms* **28/1**

1m 39.61s (-0.48) **Going Correction** -0.05s/f (Good) **12 Ran SP% 116.4**
Speed ratings (Par 98):100,98,96,96,96 91,88,86,77,76 73,66
CSF £97.39 CT £494.48 TOTE £5.50: £2.20, £5.30, £1.80; EX 124.70.
Owner Gallant Marketing Consultants Ltd **Bred** Bearstone Stud **Trained** Norton, N Yorks

FOCUS
Another run-of-the-mill handicap in which the winner raced next to the favoured stands' rail. The form looks reasonable with the winner and fifth the best guides.

4070 NORTHERN SECURITY LTD FILLIES' H'CAP 6f 192y
4:10 (4:13) (Class 5) (0-70,67) 3-Y-0+ **£3,238** (£963; £361; £361) **Stalls** High

Form RPR
0351 **1** **Celtic Spa (IRE)**[6] 3897 4-9-8 65 6ex StephenDonohoe(3) 7 76
(P D Evans) *prom: led stands rail over 1f out: kpt on strly* **15/8**[1]
0050 **2** *1 ¼* **Royal Pardon**[10] 3786 4-8-8 48 oh1 (v[1]) PaulEddery 9 56
(R C Guest) *s.i.s: hdwy over 2f out: chsd wnr ins fnl f: no imp* **33/1**
6404 **3** *1* **Cut Ridge (IRE)**[6] 3912 7-8-8 48 oh6 TonyHamilton 6 53
(J S Wainwright) *chsd ldrs: effrt and ev ch over 1f out: one pce fnl f* **10/1**
0000 **3** *dht* **Missperon (IRE)**[30] 3172 4-8-13 53 (b) DO'Donohoe 13 58
(K A Ryan) *keen: led: styd centre in st: hdd over 1f out: kpt on same pce* **25/1**
1400 **5** *shd* **Dispol Isle (IRE)**[33] 3089 4-9-10 67 BenSwarbrick(3) 1 72
(T D Barron) *cl up: effrt and ev ch 2f out: one pce fnl f* **10/1**
2000 **6** *1 ¾* **Tequila Sheila (IRE)**[41] 2811 4-8-8 48 oh5 PatCosgrave 12 48
(K R Burke) *prom: effrt over 2f out: no ex over 1f out* **20/1**
40-4 **7** *2 ½* **Guadaloup**[55] 2418 4-8-12 52 DeanMcKeown 2 46
(M Brittain) *chsd ldrs: rdn stands rail over 2f out: wknd over 1f out* **10/1**
635 **8** *nk* **Scylla Cadeaux (IRE)**[36] 2985 3-9-3 63 TomEaves 11 56
(Sir Michael Stoute) *midfield: effrt centre over 2f out: edgd lft: btn over 1f out* **9/2**[2]
0130 **9** *2* **First Rhapsody (IRE)**[40] 2856 4-8-13 56 SaleemGolam(3) 8 44
(T J Etherington) *s.i.s: rdn 1/2-way: n.d* **8/1**
6600 **10** *nk* **Lady Edge (IRE)**[12] 3749 4-8-7 50 (v) JamesDoyle(3) 10 37
(A W Carroll) *towards rr: rdn 3f out: nvr on terms* **12/1**
0004 **11** *1* **Tiber Tilly**[27] 3250 3-9-5 65 TPQueally 4 49
(N P Littmoden) *prom: effrt over 2f out: btn over 1f out* **7/1**[3]
0-00 **12** *2 ½* **Make Us Flush**[85] 1594 4-8-8 48 oh7 FrancisNorton 14 26
(A Berry) *bhdd: rdn 1/2-way: nvr on terms* **66/1**
600- **13** *3* **Zahara Joy**[318] 5355 3-8-9 55 GylesParkin 3 25
(D W Thompson) *racd wd in midfield: rdn 3f out: sn btn* **100/1**

1m 27.24s (0.14) **Going Correction** -0.05s/f (Good)
WFA 3 from 4yo+ 6lb **13 Ran SP% 125.6**
Speed ratings (Par 100):97,95,94,94,94 92,89,89,86,86 85,82,79
(TOTE) PL: Missperon £4.20, Cut Ridge £1.50; TC: Celtic Spa, Royal Pardon, Missperon £662.46; Celtic Spa, Royal Pardon, Cut Ridge £271.35. CSF £91.27 TOTE £2.70: £1.40, £9.60; EX 54.90.
Owner Derek Buckley **Bred** Miss A R Byrne **Trained** Pandy, Abergavenny
■ Stewards' Enquiry : Paul Eddery caution: careless riding

FOCUS
Few progressive types in this low-grade event. The pace was again sound and the form looks straightforward.

4071 NEWS & STAR H'CAP 5f 193y
4:45 (4:45) (Class 6) (0-60,60) 3-Y-0 **£2,730** (£806; £403) **Stalls** High

Form RPR
6042 **1** **Fortress**[12] 3749 3-9-2 55 (b) FrancisNorton 14 63
(E J Alston) *chsd ldrs: led and crossed over to stands rail 3f out: rdn and edgd rt ins fnl f: hld on wl* **4/1**[1]
3510 **2** *nk* **Boy Dancer (IRE)**[39] 2896 3-9-2 60 MarkLawson(5) 2 67
(D W Barker) *bhd: hdwy stands side over 1f out: hrd rdn: kpt on wl fnl f* **4/1**[1]
0-00 **3** *2 ½* **Briery Blaze**[45] 2699 3-9-2 55 PhillipMakin 7 55+
(Mrs K Walton) *s.i.s: bhd: effrt stands side whn nt clr run 2f out: kpt on fnl f: no imp* **7/1**
3000 **4** *½* **Our Mary (IRE)**[6] 3912 3-9-1 54 CatherineGannon 5 52
(Robert Gray) *midfield: drvn over 2f out: kpt on fnl f: no imp* **33/1**
1503 **5** *2 ½* **Money Mate (IRE)**[9] 3821 3-8-7 53 JamesO'Reilly(7) 3 44
(J O'Reilly) *w ldrs tl rdn and no ex over 1f out* **8/1**
0000 **6** *1 ½* **Nilsatisoptimum (USA)**[9] 3821 3-8-5 49 LiamJones(5) 11 35
(M Mullineaux) *chsd ldrs tl rdn and no ex wl over 1f out* **20/1**
0000 **7** *¾* **The Thrifty Bear**[22] 3395 3-9-0 60 KellyHarrison(7) 12 44
(C W Fairhurst) *prom: effrt centre over 2f out: wknd over 1f out* **12/1**
0046 **8** *shd* **Active Audience (IRE)**[13] 3698 3-8-11 50 TonyHamilton 13 34
(A Berry) *bhd: rdn centre over 2f out: n.d* **33/1**
5333 **9** *1 ½* **Myths And Verses**[12] 3725 3-9-7 60 (p) DO'Donohoe 4 39
(K A Ryan) *w ldrs tl wknd fr 2f out* **9/2**[2]
3505 **10** *1 ¼* **Optical Seclusion (IRE)**[8] 3842 3-8-12 54 (t) SaleemGolam(3) 6 29
(T J Etherington) *bhd: drvn centre over 2f out: nvr on terms* **20/1**
0406 **11** *6* **Honor Me (IRE)**[17] 3586 3-9-0 53 GrahamGibbons 8 10
(J J Quinn) *slt ld to 1/2-way: wknd 2f out* **6/1**[3]

1m 13.87s (0.26) **Going Correction** -0.05s/f (Good) **11 Ran SP% 119.2**
Speed ratings (Par 98):96,95,92,91,88 86,85,85,83,81 73
CSF £19.12 CT £110.39 TOTE £3.70: £1.20, £1.90, £2.80; EX 17.50.
Owner Mr & Mrs G Middlebrook **Bred** G And Mrs Middlebrook **Trained** Longton, Lancs

FOCUS
An ordinary event in which the stands' rail was again the place to be. The pace was sound.

4072 BROOKE COURSES FOR HORSES APPRENTICE H'CAP 1m 6f 32y
5:20 (5:20) (Class 6) (0-60,59) 4-Y-0+ **£2,730** (£806; £403) **Stalls** High

Form RPR
4150 **1** **Rare Coincidence**[21] 3454 5-9-0 52 (p) KevinGhunowa(3) 3 62
(R F Fisher) *led: styd centre in st: hdd over 2f out: led again 1f out: edgd lft ins fnl f: hld on wl* **10/1**
0002 **2** *½* **Jazrawy**[14] 3680 4-8-10 50 WilliamCarson(5) 7 59
(P W Hiatt) *pressed wnr: led and c stands side over 2f out: hdd 1f out: kpt on towards fin* **20/1**

0541 **3** *3* **Hugs Destiny (IRE)**[8] [3836] 5-9-0 **54** 6ex........................ MCGeran(5) 13 59
(M A Barnes) *chsd ldrs: effrt centre over 2f out: one pce appr fnl f* **5/1**[2]
4-03 **4** *1 1/4* **Onyergo (IRE)**[24] [3352] 4-9-3 **52**.......................... LiamJones 9 55
(J R Weymes) *in tch: rdn 3f out: one pce over 1f out* **12/1**
0410 **5** *1 1/4* **Dayoff (IRE)**[6] [3894] 5-9-5 **54** 6ex.................(v) LiamTreadwell 8 55
(P D Evans) *bhd: hdwy centre 3f out: kpt on fnl f: no imp* **13/2**[3]
1245 **6** *3/4* **Compton Eclaire (IRE)**[12] [3723] 6-9-7 **59**.........(v) MichaelJStainton(3) 2 59+
(B Ellison) *hld up: rdn over 3f out: hdwy centre over 1f out: no imp* **9/2**[1]
-200 **7** *3/4* **Scurra**[56] [2381] 7-8-10 **45**.................................... MarkLawson 14 44
(A C Whillans) *prom: effrt stands side 3f out: no ex fr 2f out* **12/1**
5005 **8** *3/4* **Kaluana Court**[6] [3919] 10-8-5 **45**.............................. FrankiePickard(5) 10 43
(A W Carroll) *midfield: c stands side and rdn 3f out: sn outpcd* **14/1**
-030 **9** *nk* **Saluscraggie**[41] [2808] 4-8-8 **48**.................................. JamesReveley(5) 1 46
(K G Reveley) *hld up: shkn up over 4f out: outpcd fr over 2f out* **12/1**
2304 **10** *2* **Toss The Caber (IRE)**[11] [3763] 4-9-5 **59**...............(t) NeilBrown(5) 4 54
(K G Reveley) *in tch: rdn on stands side over 2f out: sn btn* **7/1**
0306 **11** *1 1/2* **Millennium Hall**[14] [3674] 7-9-4 **56**.............................. PJMcDonald(3) 6 49
(Miss Lucinda V Russell) *bhd: rdn 4f out: sn btn* **25/1**
0-00 **12** *6* **Grandma's Girl**[26] [3291] 4-8-11 **46**.................................(p) RoryMoore 12 30
(Robert Gray) *bhd: drvn over 4f out: sn btn* **20/1**
-000 **13** *2 1/2* **Arctic Cove**[34] [2871] 5-9-0 **54**................................. PJBenson(5) 11 35
(Micky Hammond) *hld up: rdn over 3f out: sn btn* **12/1**
0200 **14** *18* **Tipu Sultan**[15] [3637] 6-8-8 **46**............................. ThomasO'Brien(3) 5 2
(Micky Hammond) *bhd: hdwy over 4f out: wknd 3f out* **50/1**

3m 7.07s (-0.23) **Going Correction** -0.05s/f (Good) **14** Ran SP% **122.5**
Speed ratings (Par 101):98,97,96,95,94 94,93,93,93,91 91,87,86,75
CSF £203.32 CT £1132.19 TOTE £13.70: £3.90, £4.80, £1.70; EX 159.60 Place 6 £209.58, Place 5 £83.28..
Owner A Kerr **Bred** D R Tucker **Trained** Ulverston, Cumbria

FOCUS
A low-grade contest but, although the pace was sound, the first four stayed in that order throughout. The runner-up and fourth set the standard.
T/Plt: £289.90 to a £1 stake. Pool: £42,930.05. 108.10 winning tickets. T/Qpdt: £28.30 to a £1 stake. Pool: £2,668.50. 69.70 winning tickets. RY

3663 EPSOM (L-H)
Thursday, August 3

OFFICIAL GOING: Good (good to firm in places)
Wind: Virtually nil

4073 THE BROOKE HOSPITAL FOR ANIMALS APPRENTICE H'CAP 1m 2f 18y
5:55 (5:56) (Class 5) (0-70,68) 4-Y-0+ **£3,886** (£1,156; £577; £288) **Stalls** Low

Form RPR
3205 **1** **Jackie Kiely**[37] [2953] 5-9-2 **60**.................................(t) AmirQuinn 3 69
(Stef Liddiard) *trckd ldrs: rdn to chal 2f out: led ins fnl f: kpt on gamely last 100 yds* **12/1**
1063 **2** *hd* **Burgundy**[15] [3639] 9-9-7 **68**.................................(b) AshleyHamblett(3) 6 77
(P Mitchell) *hld up in rr: rdn over 2f out: hdwy on outer to join wnr ins fnl f: nt qckn nr fin* **11/2**[2]
40-0 **3** *1* **Take A Mile (IRE)**[16] [3615] 4-8-9 **58**.................. PatrickHills(5) 7 65
(B G Powell) *racd in midfield: hdwy over 2f out: rdn and edgd lft ins fnl f: kpt on* **6/1**[3]
0213 **4** *nk* **Otranto (USA)**[5] [3960] 4-9-6 **64**..................................(t) GregFairley 9 70
(M Johnston) *trckd ldng pair: rdn to ld 2f out: hdd ins fnl f: no ex* **1/1**[1]
0404 **5** *4* **Mixing**[28] [3221] 4-8-9 **58**.. BRoper(5) 4 57
(W Jarvis) *t.k.h: hld up in rr: rdn over 2f out: styd on past btn horses fnl f: nt rch ldrs* **14/1**
5646 **6** *3/4* **Jools**[17] [3599] 8-9-0 **61**.. JamesMillman(3) 10 58
(D K Ivory) *hld up: in tch: rdn and effrt 2f out: edgd lft fnl f: nt pce to rch ldrs* **10/1**
6620 **7** *1 1/4* **Danzare**[10] [3798] 4-8-10 **54**.. NeilChalmers 5 49
(Mrs A J Hamilton-Fairley) *chsd ldr tl jst over 2f out: rdn and wknd over 1f out* **16/1**
0050 **8** *1/2* **Zinging**[16] [3614] 7-8-5 **49** oh4...(v) MarcHalford 2 43
(J J Bridger) *hld up in tch: rdn and effrt over 2f out: no prog* **40/1**
05-0 **P** **Suivez Moi (IRE)**[5] [3948] 4-9-2 **65**.............................(v[1]) JosephWalsh(5) 8 —
(M F Harris) *sn led: clr tl over 4f out: rdn and hdd 2f out: sn btn: p.u and dismntd over 1f out* **40/1**

2m 10.3s (1.26) **Going Correction** +0.05s/f (Good) **9** Ran SP% **113.9**
Speed ratings (Par 103):96,95,95,94,91 91,90,89,—
CSF £75.40 CT £436.66 TOTE £13.50: £2.30, £1.70, £2.20; EX 92.80.
Owner P S J Croft **Bred** Mrs M Chaworth Musters **Trained** Great Shefford, Berks
■ Stewards' Enquiry : Greg Fairley caution: careless riding

FOCUS
An ordinary handicap run at just a fair gallop, but a modest winning time for the grade.

4074 EUROPEAN BREEDERS FUND MAIDEN STKS 7f
6:25 (6:27) (Class 5) 2-Y-0 **£4,533** (£1,348; £674; £336) **Stalls** Low

Form RPR
42 **1** **White Deer (USA)**[11] [3758] 2-9-3 .... KDarley 8 82+
(M Johnston) *mde all: rdn over 2f out: clr over 1f out: styd on strly* **9/4**[2]
5 **2** *1 3/4* **Streets Ahead**[19] [3545] 2-9-3 .... FergusSweeney 10 77
(A M Balding) *s.i.s: sn in midfield: rdn over 2f out: chsd wnr 1f out: kpt on but no imp after* **8/1**
06 **3** *2* **Recruit**[54] [2432] 2-9-3 .... RyanMoore 3 72
(R Hannon) *pressed wnr: rdn over 3f out: outpcd by wnr over 1f out: lost 2nd 1f out* **12/1**
3 **4** *3/4* **Blithe**[39] [2890] 2-8-12 .... NickyMackay 5 65
(W J Haggas) *bhd: short of room and dropped to rr over 5f out: swtchd to outer and hdwy over 2f out: kpt on u.p: nt rch ldrs* **11/8**[1]
0 **5** *5* **Vodka Luge**[15] [3640] 2-8-9 .... DeanCorby(3) 1 52
(J W Hills) *racd in midfield: rdn over 2f out: no ch w ldrs after* **66/1**
0 **6** *nk* **Tiburon**[17] [3591] 2-9-3 .... SteveDrowne 11 57
(H Morrison) *chsd ldrs: rdn over 2f out: wknd wl over 1f out* **25/1**
0 **7** *1* **Greek God**[27] [3253] 2-9-3 .... AlanMunro 6 54
(W Jarvis) *chsd ldrs: effrt and rdn over 2f out: sn struggling* **16/1**
00 **8** *nk* **Alnwick**[13] [3701] 2-9-3 .... LPKeniry 9 53
(P D Cundell) *dwlt: a bhd: rdn wl over 3f out: no prog* **50/1**
4 **9** *shd* **Jawaab (IRE)**[20] [3485] 2-9-3 .... MartinDwyer 2 53
(E A L Dunlop) *chsd ldrs for over 2f: lost pl over 3f out: no ch after* **7/1**[3]
10 *1 3/4* **Medici Code** 2-9-3 .... MickyFenton 4 48
(H Morrison) *wnt lft and slowly away: rn green and a last* **33/1**

1m 25.08s (1.13) **Going Correction** +0.05s/f (Good) **10** Ran SP% **120.3**
Speed ratings (Par 94):95,93,90,89,84 83,82,82,82,80
CSF £20.96 TOTE £2.90: £1.40, £2.40, £2.70; EX 25.70.
Owner Jaber Abdullah **Bred** Fleetwood Bloodstock Et Al **Trained** Middleham Moor, N Yorks

FOCUS
Probably no more than an ordinary maiden rated around the winner, and the first four finished clear of the rest.

NOTEBOOK
White Deer(USA) showed at Redcar that there was a race such as this in him, and he won well, striding clear from two furlongs out. Although his sire is an influence for speed, there is plenty of stamina on his dam's side, and he should get a mile in time. Nurseries beckon. (tchd 2-1 and 5-2)
Streets Ahead did not have a great draw and was again slowly away, but he came home well and built on his debut effort. He should make a nursery type in time and should stay another furlong. (op 6-1 tchd 10-1)
Recruit, who has been gelded since his last run, was smartly away and up with the pace throughout, in contrast to his previous two starts. Although he hung, this was an encouraging effort and he can now contest nurseries. Official explanation: jockey said gelding hung left throughout
Blithe, who was squeezed up at the start, did not handle the track as well as some of her main rivals and failed to build on her promising debut effort. She should be given another chance on a more conventional course. (op 2-1)
Vodka Luge, whose dam was unraced but is a half-sister to a high-class filly in Fabulous Hostess, a multiple winner over middle distances, finished adrift of the first four but this was a better effort than she put up on her debut. She should come into her own at three. (tchd 100-1)
Tiburon, a half-brother to Nelson's Column, a winner over a mile at three, is bred to do better with time. (op 20-1)
Jawaab(IRE) had run with modest promise on his debut and came in for some support, but he never really threatened in the race itself. (op 10-1)

4075 WOODFORD RESERVE BOURBON FILLIES' H'CAP 1m 114y
6:55 (6:57) (Class 5) (0-75,79) 3-Y-0+ **£5,181** (£1,541; £770; £384) **Stalls** Low

Form RPR
1301 **1** **Wagtail**[10] [3793] 3-9-11 **79** 6ex..(t) RyanMoore 6 88+
(E A L Dunlop) *led after 1f: mde rest: rdn clr 2f out: in command fnl f: rdn out* **9/4**[1]
3024 **2** *3/4* **Starboard Light**[20] [3472] 3-8-1 **55**.................................... NickyMackay 5 62
(R M Beckett) *led for 1f: chsd ldrs: wnt 2nd again wl over 1f out: no imp tl kpt on u.p last 100 yds* **15/2**
0015 **3** *1* **Golden Applause (FR)**[13] [3703] 4-9-10 **73**...................... AmirQuinn(3) 2 78
(Mrs A L M King) *hld up in midfield on inner: plld out and hdwy 2f out: edgd lft but kpt on u.p fnl f: nrst fin* **8/1**
5215 **4** *1/2* **Missed A Beat**[13] [3712] 4-9-11 **71**....................................... OscarUrbina 8 75
(M Blanshard) *w.w in tch: prog to chse ldrs over 3f out: outpcd 2f out: kpt on again ins fnl f* **8/1**
0042 **5** *8* **Toffee Vodka (IRE)**[14] [3687] 4-9-11 **71**.............................. EddieAhern 9 58
(J W Hills) *prom: chsd wnr after 2f: rdn and upsides over 3f out: wknd wl over 1f out* **5/1**[3]
2230 **6** *1 1/2* **Keep Bacckinhit (IRE)**[25] [3337] 4-8-12 **58**......................... TedDurcan 1 42
(G L Moore) *hld up in rr: rdn over 2f out: no imp* **12/1**
6066 **7** *1/2* **Cape Maya**[21] [3433] 3-8-13 **67**... SteveDrowne 7 50
(B J Meehan) *racd in midfield: rdn wl over 3f out: no ch last 2f* **33/1**
000- **8** *1 1/4* **Seejay**[313] [5447] 6-8-5 **54** oh13.................................... NeilChalmers(3) 3 34
(B R Johnson) *hld up in tch: rdn and effrt over 3f out: sn outpcd and no ch* **100/1**
1162 **9** *9* **Diamond De Triano (USA)**[10] [3793] 3-9-7 **75**.................... AlanMunro 4 36
(P W Chapple-Hyam) *nvr gng wl: a last: lost tch 2f out: eased ins fnl f: t.o* **3/1**[2]

1m 45.3s (-0.44) **Going Correction** +0.05s/f (Good)
WFA 3 from 4yo+ 8lb **9** Ran SP% **118.0**
Speed ratings (Par 100):103,102,101,101,93 92,92,91,83
CSF £20.61 CT £118.65 TOTE £3.20: £1.40, £2.10, £3.00; EX 19.00.
Owner Hesmonds Stud **Bred** Jeremy Gompertz **Trained** Newmarket, Suffolk

FOCUS
A fair fillies' handicap in which the first four finished well clear. The form looks solid enough and the winner progressive.
Golden Applause(FR) Official explanation: jockey said filly hung left throughout
Diamond De Triano(USA) Official explanation: jockey said filly didn't act on the track

4076 BUTLINS BINGO JACKPOT H'CAP 1m 114y
7:30 (7:32) (Class 4) (0-80,76) 3-Y-0 **£7,772** (£2,312; £1,155; £577) **Stalls** Low

Form RPR
3042 **1** **Press The Button (GER)**[2] [4029] 3-9-1 **70**...................... NickyMackay 2 88+
(J R Boyle) *chsd ldng pair: clsd 4f out: led wl over 2f out: sn clr: rdn out* **4/1**[3]
0354 **2** *5* **Mujood**[6] [3906] 3-9-6 **75**.. StephenCarson 6 81
(R F Johnson Houghton) *w.w in midfield: hdwy 4f out: ev 3f out: sn outpcd by wnr: kpt on to go 2nd nr fin* **9/1**
0505 **3** *shd* **Blu Manruna**[14] [3667] 3-8-4 **59**..(p) PaulDoe 5 65
(J Akehurst) *hmpd after 1f: hdwy on outer over 3f out: chsd wnr 2f out tl 1f out: kpt on: no ch w wnr* **16/1**
-451 **4** *1/2* **Ebert**[19] [3546] 3-9-7 **76**... SebSanders 8 81
(P J Makin) *bhd: hdwy and nt clr run over 3f out: effrt u.p and edgd lft 2f out: wnt 2nd 1f out: no imp: lost 2 pl cl home* **15/8**[1]
6530 **5** *nk* **Salvestro**[15] [3650] 3-8-5 **60**.. AlanMunro 1 64
(Mrs A J Perrett) *hld up bhd: hdwy on inner over 2f out: nt clr run and swtchd rt 2f out: kpt on fnl f: no ch w wnr* **20/1**
4-14 **6** *17* **It's Unbelievable (USA)**[26] [3282] 3-9-4 **73**........................ NCallan 7 42
(B J Meehan) *squeezed s: swtchd lft after 1f: hdwy to trck ldrs and hmpd over 3f out: sn rdn and outpcd: eased: t.o* **12/1**
4221 **7** *8* **Carloman**[14] [3668] 3-8-12 **67**..(b) RyanMoore 4 19
(R M Beckett) *sn led: clr w rival 6f out: hdd wl over 2f out: sn btn: t.o* **3/1**[2]
0-40 **8** *24* **King's Ransom**[15] [3644] 3-9-3 **72**.. MartinDwyer 3 —
(A M Balding) *jnd ldr after 1f: clr of remainder 6f out: edgd rt and wknd rapidly: over 3f out: eased: t.o* **14/1**

1m 45.14s (-0.60) **Going Correction** +0.05s/f (Good) **8** Ran SP% **114.8**
Speed ratings (Par 102):104,99,99,99,98 83,76,55
CSF £39.44 CT £521.41 TOTE £5.20: £1.80, £2.60, £3.20; EX 34.20.
Owner Brian McAtavey **Bred** Gestut Sommerberg **Trained** Epsom, Surrey
■ Stewards' Enquiry : Seb Sanders caution: careless riding

FOCUS
Carloman and King's Ransom ensured a strong pace in this modest handicap and the form looks solid rated around the consistent runner-up.
It's Unbelievable(USA) Official explanation: jockey said gelding didn't handle the track
King's Ransom Official explanation: jockey said gelding ran too free

4077 MULLER AMORE CLAIMING STKS 7f
8:00 (8:02) (Class 5) 3-Y-O+ **£4,533** (£1,348; £674; £336) **Stalls** Low

Form RPR

3202 **1** **Sweet Pickle**^{3} [3995] 5-8-10 64..(e) AmirQuinn$^{(3)}$ 5 60
(J R Boyle) *t.k.h: hld up midfield: hdwy gng wl over 2f out: jnd ldr 1f out: led last 100 yds: rdn out* **4/1^{2}**

2500 **2** *shd* **Sensuous**^{36} [2987] 3-8-7 63 ow1.. DaneO'Neill 2 57
(R Hannon) *t.k.h: prom: rdn to ld over 1f out: hdd 100 yds out : kpt on u.p* **12/1**

6000 **3** *3* **Muscari**^{13} [3703] 4-8-12 65.. AlanMunro 1 51
(A P Jarvis) *sn bhd: hdwy 2f out: styd on wl fnl f: wnt 3rd on line: nvr nrr* **10/1**

1064 **4** *hd* **Renegade (IRE)**^{14} [3664] 5-9-4 46.. IanMongan 7 56
(Mrs L J Mongan) *led for 1f: led again over 3f out tl over 1f out: one pced u.p fnl f* **25/1**

0440 **5** *3/4* **Hadath (IRE)**^{5} [3933] 9-8-12 50..(b) OscarUrbina 8 48
(B G Powell) *bhd: hdwy u.p wl over 2f out: kpt on fnl f: nt pce to rch ldrs* **14/1**

5320 **6** *1 1/4* **La Fanciulla**^{36} [2987] 3-8-8 63.. RyanMoore 10 45
(R Hannon) *t.k.h: racd in midfield: rdn and effrt over 2f out: wknd over 1f out: hung rt fnl f* **4/1^{2}**

000- **7** *1 3/4* **Forest Air (IRE)**^{393} [3240] 6-8-6 35 ow1........................ AdamKirby$^{(3)}$ 11 37
(B R Johnson) *chsd ldrs tl led after 1f tl over 3f out: hung rt u.p 2f out: wknd* **66/1**

0566 **8** *1* **Vegas Boys**^{16} [3612] 3-9-2 73.. ChrisCatlin 9 46
(N A Callaghan) *dwlt: a bhd: n.d* **6/1^{3}**

0-05 **9** *2 1/2* **Parisi Princess**^{14} [3664] 5-8-4 40........................ NeilChalmers$^{(3)}$ 12 26
(D L Williams) *a towards rr: rdn over 3f out: no prog* **50/1**

2150 **10** *hd* **Curtain Bluff**^{13} [3712] 4-9-7 75..(v) TedDurcan 4 40
(M R Channon) *chsd ldrs: rdn 2f out: sn wknd* **5/2^{1}**

000 **11** *18* **Hollie Dellamore**^{49} [2575] 4-8-10 35........................(v^{1}) NickyMackay 6 —
(A P Jarvis) *t.k.h: chsd ldrs tl hung rt bnd over 3f out: sn wl bhd: eased: t.o* **66/1**

1m 24.24s (0.29) **Going Correction** +0.05s/f (Good)
WFA 3 from 4yo+ 6lb **11** Ran SP% **115.1**
Speed ratings (Par 103):100,99,96,96,95 93,91,90,87,87 67
CSF £48.58 TOTE £3.50: £1.20, £3.10, £4.20; EX 43.80.La Fanciulla was claimed by Paul Thorman for £12,000. Sweet Pickle was the subject of a friendly claim.
Owner M Khan X2 **Bred** C T Van Hoorn **Trained** Epsom, Surrey

FOCUS
An ordinary claimer run at a modest early pace and rated through the fourth to his best recent form. The form is not solid.
Renegade(IRE) Official explanation: jockey said gelding hung right
Forest Air(IRE) Official explanation: jockey said mare had no more to give
Vegas Boys Official explanation: jockey said gelding was unsuited by the track
Hollie Dellamore Official explanation: jockey said filly hung right

4078 BETFRED H'CAP 6f
8:30 (8:32) (Class 4) (0-80,78) 3-Y-O **£6,477** (£1,927; £963; £481) **Stalls** High

Form RPR

0-06 **1** **Sun Catcher (IRE)**^{15} [3644] 3-9-2 **73**.. DaneO'Neill 5 81
(R Hannon) *led tl hdd and rdn over 3f out: led again ins fnl f: r.o gamely* **7/1**

0260 **2** *1 1/4* **Lipizza (IRE)**^{6} [3904] 3-9-5 **76**.. ChrisCatlin 4 80
(N A Callaghan) *hld up bhd: gd hdwy on outer over 2f out: ev ch 1f out: kpt on same pce* **5/1^{3}**

0061 **3** *nk* **Wheelavit (IRE)**^{19} [3538] 3-9-0 **71**.. GeorgeBaker 2 74+
(B G Powell) *trckd ldrs on inner: n.m.r over 2f out: rdn and unbalanced wl over 1f out: r.o wl last 100 yds: nt rch ldrs* **8/1**

5442 **4** *nk* **Scarlet Flyer (USA)**^{20} [3487] 3-9-6 **77**........................(b^{1}) RyanMoore 6 79
(G L Moore) *pressed ldr tl led over 3f out: edgd rt u.p and hdd ins fnl: no ex* **9/4^{1}**

6220 **5** *1* **Mango Music**^{38} [2931] 3-9-7 **78**.. TedDurcan 7 79+
(M R Channon) *chsd ldr: wnt 2nd 2f out tl ins fnl f: hld whn n.m.r wl ins fnl f* **6/1**

2663 **6** *1/2* **Mister Benedictine**^{14} [3667] 3-9-6 **77**........................ MartinDwyer 1 79+
(W R Muir) *hld up bhd: rdn and effrt over 2f out: keeping on whn n.m.r wl ins fnl f* **5/2^{2}**

0-00 **7** *6* **Sofinella (IRE)**^{41} [2826] 3-8-7 **64** ow1.. NCallan 8 44+
(A W Carroll) *t.k.h: hld up in midfield: rdn over 2f out: wknd 1f out: eased wl ins fnl f* **33/1**

1m 10.1s (-0.53) **Going Correction** +0.05s/f (Good) **7** Ran SP% **116.8**
Speed ratings (Par 102):105,103,102,102,101 100,92
CSF £42.79 CT £289.17 TOTE £8.30: £3.30, £3.70; EX 33.90 Place 6 £604.48, Place 5 £218.27..
Owner A F Merritt **Bred** Johnston King **Trained** East Everleigh, Wilts

FOCUS
A competitive sprint handicap but ordinary form rated around the first two.
Wheelavit(IRE) Official explanation: jockey said gelding was denied a clear run
Mister Benedictine Official explanation: jockey said gelding was denied a clear run
T/Plt: £844.40 to a £1 stake. Pool: £56,800.85. 49.10 winning tickets. T/Qpdt: £137.20 to a £1 stake. Pool: £5,212.10. 28.10 winning tickets. SP

4036 GOODWOOD (R-H)
Thursday, August 3

OFFICIAL GOING: Good to firm
8mm of watering overnight, and jockeys reported the ground to be nearer good than firm after the first. A fresh strip was opened against the inside rail.
Wind: Strong, across towards stands Weather: Sunny

4079 LILLIE LANGTRY FILLIES' STKS (GROUP 3) 1m 6f
2:05 (2:05) (Class 1) 3-Y-O+
£28,390 (£10,760; £5,385; £2,685; £1,345; £675) **Stalls** Low

Form RPR

4-14 **1** **Tartouche**^{75} [1860] 5-9-6 103.. SebSanders 6 104
(Lady Herries) *lw: led: jnd 6f out: rdn over 2f out: hdd over 1f out: rallied to ld ent fnl f: hld on gamely* **7/2^{2}**

-425 **2** *nk* **Art Eyes (USA)**^{33} [3085] 4-9-6 105.. JohnEgan 2 103
(D R C Elsworth) *trckd wnr to 6f out: styd cl up: drvn to chal over 2f out: led over 1f out: hdd ent fnl f: kpt on wl* **11/2^{3}**

3141 **3** *hd* **Sirce (IRE)**^{54} [2453] 4-9-6 102..(v) JimmyQuinn 1 103
(D J Coakley) *lw: hld up in last: plenty to do 3f out: drvn and rapid prog fr 2f out : r.o wl fnl f: gaining fast at fin* **12/1**

1142 **4** *3/4* **Cresta Gold**^{12} [3739] 3-8-7 95.. MartinDwyer 7 102
(A Bailey) *chsd ldr to 6f out: styd cl up: rdn 3f out: outpcd 2f out: styd on again fnl f* **12/1**

-122 **5** *3/4* **Scottish Stage (IRE)**^{18} [3575] 3-8-7 109.. MJKinane 5 102+
(Sir Michael Stoute) *hld up midfield: awkward bnd 5f out and lost pl: gd prog to chal and upsides 2f out: nt qckn over 1f out: fdd fnl f* **6/4^{1}**

3-16 **6** *3 1/2* **Power Girl (GER)**^{12} [3739] 4-9-6 95.. RyanMoore 10 96
(P F I Cole) *lw: hld up towards rr: rdn 3f out: sn outpcd: no imp after* **18/1**

10 **7** *1/2* **Novellara**^{42} [2772] 3-8-7 98.. RichardHughes 9 97+
(H R A Cecil) *hld up bhd ldrs: rapid prog to join wnr 6f out tl 3f out: wknd* **10/1**

0144 **8** *2 1/2* **Pine Cone (IRE)**^{16} [3627] 4-9-6 92.. DaneO'Neill 3 92
(A King) *hld up in rr: rdn and struggling over 3f out: no prog after* **66/1**

-645 **9** *3* **Tarandot (IRE)**^{33} [3078] 5-9-6 93.. AlanMunro 4 88
(G G Margarson) *dwlt: hld up in last pair: rdn over 3f out: no prog* **40/1**

1500 **10** *22* **Kassiopeia (IRE)**^{41} [2804] 3-8-7 90.. TonyCulhane 8 57
(M R Channon) *in tch tl rdn and wknd 4f out: t.o* **33/1**

3m 0.70s (-3.27) **Going Correction** -0.225s/f (Firm)
WFA 3 from 4yo+ 13lb **10** Ran SP% **114.2**
Speed ratings (Par 110):100,99,99,99,98 96,96,95,93,80
CSF £22.35 TOTE £4.80: £1.60, £2.00, £2.10; EX 24.10 Trifecta £119.20 Pool £1,780.01 - 10.60 winning units..
Owner Lady Herries and Friends **Bred** Angmering Park Stud **Trained** Patching, W Sussex

FOCUS
A very moderate winning time for a race like this given the conditions. Not strong form for the grade, and the winner did not need to repeat last year's winning form.

NOTEBOOK
Tartouche, successful in this event 12 months ago, was running over this trip for the first time since. Suited by the watered ground, she adopted different tactics, making most of the running at a decent pace and battling on willingly to assert. (op 5-1 tchd 11-2 in places)
Art Eyes(USA), well below par last time, was back up in trip. Unable to lead but never far away, she did show narrowly ahead with over a furlong to run but the winner fought back. She could go for the Ebor, in which she has 9st 5lb. (tchd 6-1 in places)
Sirce(IRE), an admirably progressive mare, was running in Group company for the first time. Unable to go with the leaders halfway up the straight, she was switched outside before running on strongly inside the last, needing a few more strides. (tchd 11-1)
Cresta Gold, who has progressed really well, did best of the three-year-olds, keeping on at the end over this longer trip. This was a fine effort especially considering she would have preferred genuine fast ground. (tchd 14-1)
Scottish Stage(IRE), who looked very fit, was tackling this trip for the first time having been runner-up in the Irish Oaks on her latest start. Losing her pitch when taking the top bend awkwardly, once on an even keel she loomed up going well, but her stamina petered out in the latter stages and she was relegated two places near the finish. (op 5-4 tchd 13-8 and 6-5)
Power Girl(GER), having her first try in this grade and over a trip this far, was never able to play a significant role. (op 20-1)
Novellara was expected to stay this trip, as her sister Modesta did, but after making rapid progress to match strides with the eventual winner at the top of the hill, she faded away in the home straight. (op 11-1)
Tarandot(IRE) was on her toes beforehand. (tchd 50-1)

4080 AUDI STKS (REGISTERED AS THE KING GEORGE STAKES) (GROUP 3) 5f
2:40 (2:41) (Class 1) 3-Y-O+
£28,390 (£10,760; £5,385; £2,685; £1,345; £675) **Stalls** Low

Form RPR

2-00 **1** **La Cucaracha**^{20} [3494] 5-8-11 111.. MichaelHills 2 115+
(B W Hills) *lw: racd nr side: hld up wl in rr: gd prog jst over 1f out: r.o to ld last 75yds: won gng away* **7/2^{1}**

0512 **2** *3/4* **Desert Lord**^{19} [3520] 6-9-0 103..(b) NCallan 3 115
(K A Ryan) *b: swtg: racd against nr side rail: led: gng strly over 1f out: hdd and outpcd last 75yds* **20/1**

2530 **3** *1* **Pivotal Flame**^{26} [3312] 4-9-0 105..(p) SebSanders 15 111
(E S McMahon) *hld up bhd ldrs in centre: prog 2f out: drvn and styd on fnl f* **8/1^{3}**

0066 **4** *shd* **The Tatling (IRE)**^{26} [3312] 9-9-5 110.. RyanMoore 16 116
(J M Bradley) *hld up wl in rr in centre: swtchd to outer and gd prog jst over 1f out: r.o fnl f: nrst fin* **9/1**

0101 **5** *hd* **Fayr Jag (IRE)**^{12} [3732] 7-9-5 111.. DavidAllan 10 115
(T D Easterby) *lw: prom in centre: disp 2nd over 1f out: styd on same pce fnl f* **20/1**

0021 **6** *3/4* **Donna Blini**^{13} [3709] 3-8-8 106.. LDettori 6 104
(B J Meehan) *taken down early: mostly chsd ldr nr side to 1f out: edgd rt and no ex* **13/2^{2}**

-051 **7** *3/4* **Tournedos (IRE)**^{19} [3520] 4-9-0 105.. SteveDrowne 13 105
(R Charlton) *swtg: hld up in midfield towards centre: effrt 2f out: kpt on same pce fnl f* **14/1**

2430 **8** *shd* **Sierra Vista**^{19} [3520] 6-8-11 100.. RobertWinston 5 102
(D W Barker) *a midfield: rdn whn n.m.r over 1f out: kpt on: n.d* **33/1**

2561 **9** *hd* **Green Manalishi**^{19} [3535] 5-9-0 104.. AlanMunro 17 104
(D W P Arbuthnot) *prom in centre: stl pressing for a pl 1f out: fdd* **25/1**

3304 **10** *1 1/4* **Strike Up The Band**^{19} [3520] 3-8-11 105.. AdrianTNicholls 4 98
(D Nicholls) *chsd ldrs nr side: rdn 2f out: sn outpcd: n.d after* **13/2^{2}**

45-0 **11** *nk* **Maltese Falcon**^{4} [3972] 6-9-0 108..(t) EddieAhern 18 98
(P F I Cole) *racd centre: hld up: effrt over 1f out: no prog* **33/1**

-002 **12** *shd* **Majestic Missile (IRE)**^{13} [3709] 5-9-0 108..(t) TonyCulhane 1 98
(W J Haggas) *chsd nr side ldrs: rdn over 2f out: outpcd and btn over 1f out* **9/1**

05-0 **13** *1 1/2* **Dream Impact (USA)**^{18} 5-9-0..(t) GMarcelli 11 93
(L Riccardi, Italy) *swtg: dwlt: a wl in rr: bmpd along and struggling over 2f out* **50/1**

3000 **14** *hd* **Corridor Creeper (FR)**^{26} [3312] 9-9-0 106........................(p) ShaneKelly 14 92
(J M Bradley) *lw: prom in centre tl wknd jst over 1f out* **50/1**

0042 **15** *1 1/2* **Beauty Bright (IRE)**^{5} [3967] 3-8-8.. MJKinane 7 82+
(A P O'Brien, Ire) *swtg: prom to 1/2-way: losing pl whn n.m.r over 1f out* **20/1**

-000 **16** *2* **Ajigolo**^{12} [3732] 3-8-11 100.. TedDurcan 9 78
(M R Channon) *prom to 1/2-way: sn wknd* **50/1**

0011 **17** *3/4* **The Lord**^{70} [1952] 6-9-0 102.. JohnEgan 12 77
(W G M Turner) *nvr on terms struggling in rr fr 1/2-way* **25/1**

1106 **18** ¾ **Empress Jain**[34] 3047 3-8-8 99 PhilipRobinson 8 70+
(M A Jarvis) *taken down early: blindfold stl on as stalls opened and lost all ch: a bhd* **50/1**

56.83 secs (-2.22) **Going Correction** -0.225s/f (Firm)
WFA 3 from 4yo+ 3lb **18** Ran SP% **122.4**
Speed ratings (Par 113):108,106,105,105,104 103,102,102,101,99 99,99,96,96,94 90,89,88
CSF £79.10 TOTE £4.20: £2.00, £6.40, £3.90; EX 96.50 Trifecta £2031.00 Part won. Pool £2,860.64 - 0.70 winning units..
Owner Guy Reed **Bred** G Reed **Trained** Lambourn, Berks
■ La Cucaracha is the tenth filly or mare to win this race since 1991.

FOCUS
An ordinary winning time for a Group 3 sprint, only 0.19 seconds faster than the later 70-85 handicap over the same trip. The form does not look rock solid, with the low numbers favoured and the runner-up showing big improvement, but the others finishing in the first five all ran to within a pound of their marks.

NOTEBOOK
La Cucaracha ◆, unpenalised for her Nunthorpe Stakes win last year as it came before the cut-off date, bounced back to form after a couple of below-par displays. Travelling well at the rear of the field on the stands' side, the gap came for her at the right time and she took full advantage, bursting through to win readily. She will now go to York with an excellent chance of another Nunthorpe victory, especially if the ground rides fast. In the long term, she could go for the Hong Kong Sprint in December, although the distance of that race has been increased to six furlongs this year. (tchd 4-1 in places)
Desert Lord showed excellent pace and tried to make all against the rail, but he edged away from the fence in the latter stages, probably because he lost his near-fore shoe, and was mown down by the mare. This was a fine effort on his first try at this level. (op 16-1)
Pivotal Flame, who came in for plenty of support, ran a fine race from an unfavourable draw which meant he raced towards the centre of the track. He will get it right one of these days. (op 12-1 tchd 14-1 in a place)
The Tatling(IRE), giving 5lb to the whole field except for Fayr Jag, ran well from his high draw and, finishing strongly, would have been third in another stride. He has now made the frame in the last four renewals of this race, winning it in 2003. (op 11-1 tchd 12-1)
Fayr Jag(IRE), saddled with a Group 3 penalty, ran another solid race and did not find the sharp five furlongs inconveniencing him too much.
Donna Blini, who has been reinvented as a sprinter, did best of the five three-year-olds in the line-up. Official explanation: jockey said filly hung right-handed (tchd 6-1 in places)
Tournedos(IRE), successful off a strong pace in the Molecomb here two years ago, could not repeat the trick but ran perfectly respectably. (op 11-1)
Sierra Vista, winner of a handicap off 86 at this meeting a year ago, is proving hard to place now but was not disgraced on her first try at this level.
Strike Up The Band, one of three former Molecomb winners in the line-up, was representing the connections of Fire Up The Band, successful in this last year. He was favourably drawn but, having got warm beforehand, he could not get into the action. (op 8-1)
Majestic Missile(IRE) has become expensive to follow and he was unable to capitalise on his plum draw. He looked to hang away from the rail when the pressure was on. (op 7-1)
Empress Jain, who was on her toes in the paddock, lost all chance at the start. Official explanation: jockey said filly missed the break due to her becoming unsettled and putting her head down with the blinds on

4081 ABN AMRO GOODWOOD CUP (GROUP 2) 2m
3:15 (3:15) (Class 1) 3-Y-O+

£56,780 (£21,520; £10,770; £5,370; £2,690; £1,350) **Stalls** Low

Form RPR
46-1 **1** **Yeats (IRE)**[42] 2773 5-9-10 MJKinane 8 126+
(A P O'Brien, Ire) *lw: hld up midfield: smooth prog 4f out: led over 2f out: galloped on strly: impressive* **10/11**[1]
-404 **2** 5 **Geordieland (FR)**[60] 2277 5-9-5 108 LDettori 6 116+
(J A Osborne) *w'like: hld up in rr: stdy prog fr 4f out: chsd wnr over 1f out: drew clr of rest but no imp* **16/1**
-210 **3** 3½ **Tungsten Strike (USA)**[42] 2773 5-9-8 113 MartinDwyer 1 113
(Mrs A J Perrett) *lw: prom: chsd ldr over 5f out: led over 3f out to 2f out: one pce after* **25/1**
4252 **4** 1½ **Sergeant Cecil**[26] 3315 7-9-5 110 AlanMunro 3 109+
(B R Millman) *hld up towards rr: effrt on inner whn no room over 2f out: no ch after but styd on wl fnl f* **10/1**
5011 **5** nk **Baddam**[40] 2849 4-9-5 99 IanMongan 9 108
(M R Channon) *lw: settled in rr: rdn on outer over 4f out: prog u.p 3f out: no ch w ldrs* **33/1**
5551 **6** hd **Land 'n Stars**[26] 3315 6-9-5 111 PaulDoe 12 108
(Jamie Poulton) *prom: rdn over 3f out: sn outpcd: plugged on* **25/1**
-332 **7** ¾ **Reefscape**[42] 2773 5-9-10 RichardHughes 2 112
(A Fabre, France) *lw: rn in snatches in midfield: struggling 4f out: styd on fnl 2f* **11/2**[2]
6103 **8** shd **Bulwark (IRE)**[19] 3533 4-9-5 98 (be) KerrinMcEvoy 7 108+
(Mrs A J Perrett) *lw: hld up wl in rr: prog on wd outside over 2f out: hung lft then veered sharply rt 1f out whn in w ch of 4th* **25/1**
2102 **9** 3 **Balkan Knight**[19] 3551 6-9-5 108 JohnEgan 15 105+
(D R C Elsworth) *lw: wl in rr: rdn and prog on outer over 3f out: ch of 4th whn bdly hmpd ent fnl f: nt rcvr* **20/1**
-102 **10** 3 **Cover Up (IRE)**[40] 2849 9-9-5 108 RyanMoore 13 100
(Sir Michael Stoute) *lw: drvn leaving stalls to rch chsng position: rdn 5f out: steadily wknd fnl 3f* **20/1**
212- **11** 3½ **Golden Quest**[371] 3879 5-9-5 112 JoeFanning 14 96
(M Johnston) *settled midfield: nt clr run on inner 4f out: no prog 3f out: btn after* **9/1**[3]
0-54 **12** 1 **High Action (USA)**[42] 2773 6-9-5 110 EddieAhern 11 94
(Ian Williams) *chsd ldng trio: u.p 5f out: wknd over 3f out* **25/1**
4154 **13** 2½ **Ebtikaar (IRE)**[40] 2849 4-9-5 97 RHills 16 91
(J L Dunlop) *dwlt: hld up in last: detached fr rest 4f out: no ch* **25/1**
0203 **14** 1½ **Winged D'Argent (IRE)**[26] 3315 5-9-5 107 KDarley 10 90+
(M Johnston) *lw: chsd ldr and sn pushed along: u.p 5f out: wknd over 3f out* **66/1**
5311 **15** 20 **Foreign Affairs**[15] 3660 8-9-5 111 SebSanders 5 66+
(Sir Mark Prescott) *led at furious pce and sn clr: wknd rapidly and hdd over 3f out : t.o* **16/1**

3m 21.55s (-9.24) **Going Correction** -0.225s/f (Firm) course record **15** Ran SP% **129.9**
Speed ratings (Par 115):114,111,109,109,108 108,108,108,106,105 103,103,101,101,91
CSF £16.94 TOTE £1.90: £1.20, £3.50, £7.70; EX 24.10 Trifecta £666.60 Pool £2,816.99 - 3.00 winning units..
Owner Mrs John Magnier & Mrs David Nagle **Bred** Barronstown Stud & Orpendale **Trained** Ballydoyle, Co Tipperary

FOCUS
This was a strong renewal and Yeats showed top-class form, up 2lb on last year's Coronation Cup win. The pace was strong and produced a winning time that was about right for a Group 2 given the conditions, and the form looks solid behind him.

NOTEBOOK
Yeats(IRE) put up a top-class performance under the Group 1 penalty for his Gold Cup victory and is clearly one of the best stayers of recent years. Always going easily, he moved to the front with over two furlongs to run and it was plain sailing from then on. He will go next for the Irish St Leger - a race his trainer needs to win to complete the set of British and Irish Classics - before a decision will be made regarding his participation in the Melbourne Cup. (op 11-8 tchd 6-4 in places)
Geordieland(FR), previously with Jean-Marie Beguigne in France, had never run on fast ground or over a trip beyond 12 furlongs. He made smooth headway to move into second place with half a mile to run but found the top-class winner much too strong. He will probably take his chance in the Ebor, in which he would be of considerable interest off 9st 8lb, before a journey to Australia to contest the Caulfield and Melbourne Cups.
Tungsten Strike(USA) failed to stay in the Gold Cup but this was more like it. Always to the fore in the chasing group, he got to the front in the straight and kept on willingly once headed by the winner. (op 20-1)
Sergeant Cecil, much better suited by the strong pace of this race, met with trouble on the fence when attempting to improve. He flew in the latter stages to snatch fourth close home. (op 9-1 tchd 12-1)
Baddam, who completed a memorable double at the Royal meeting, ran a thoroughly respectable race over a trip on the short side for him. (op 40-1)
Land 'n Stars is a smart stayer and he was close to form again. He is another who could go for the Melbourne Cup.
Reefscape, who was struggling towards the rear with half a mile to run and was short of room when trying to improve approaching the two pole, came home quite well but in truth was never in the hunt. He will be suited by the return to a more galloping track and easier ground. Official explanation: jockey said horse was unsuited by the track (op 13-2)
Bulwark(IRE), stepping out of handicaps, was in with a chance of fourth when the quirky side to his nature was revealed at around the furlong pole. (tchd 33-1)
Balkan Knight ran well and held a chance of squeezing into the frame when he was was bumped by the errant Bulwark with a furlong or so to run. This trip probably just stretches his stamina. (tchd 22-1)
Golden Quest, who fractured his knee when runner-up to Distinction in this race last year, looked fit for this first run since. After travelling quite well for the first mile and a half, he was short of room early in the straight and was not given a hard time once held. (tchd 8-1, 10-1 in a place)
Ebtikaar(IRE) Official explanation: jockey said horse was unsuited by the track

4082 LADBROKES.COM STKS (HERITAGE H'CAP) 1m 1f 192y
3:50 (3:52) (Class 2) 3-Y-O

£62,320 (£18,660; £9,330; £4,670; £2,330; £1,170) **Stalls** High

Form RPR
0101 **1** **Road To Love (IRE)**[4] 3971 3-9-3 98 5ex RHills 2 115+
(M Johnston) *lw: led after 1 1/2f: mde rest at gd pce: drew rt away fr 2f out: rdn out: impressive* **11/4**[1]
0022 **2** 5 **Desert Realm (IRE)**[5] 3929 3-9-0 95 JoeFanning 6 102
(M Johnston) *hld up wl in rr: gd prog on outer over 2f out: wnt 2nd over 1f out: no ch w wnr* **16/1**
1110 **3** 1 **Pearly King (USA)**[41] 2805 3-9-2 97 RobertWinston 5 102
(Sir Michael Stoute) *hld up towards rr: prog on inner 3f out: rdn and styd on fnl 2f* **5/1**[2]
132- **4** 1½ **Familiar Territory**[286] 6005 3-8-13 94 LDettori 3 96+
(Saeed Bin Suroor) *slipped s: given time to rcvr and hld up in detached last pair: gd prog 2f out: impossible position 2f out: nrst fin* **7/1**
-032 **5** 1¾ **Humungous (IRE)**[14] 3681 3-9-3 98 SteveDrowne 12 97+
(C R Egerton) *led for 1 1/f: trckd wnr: tried to chal 3f out: sn brushed aside: fdd over 1f out* **20/1**
041 **6** 1¼ **Zaif (IRE)**[22] 3419 3-8-7 88 JohnEgan 8 85
(D R C Elsworth) *lw: hld up in rr: effrt 3f out: kpt on same pce: n.d* **10/1**
4-14 **7** hd **Kyoto Summit**[36] 2986 3-8-9 90 NickyMackay 16 86
(L M Cumani) *lw: wl in rr: drvn 3f out: no prog tl styd on fnl f: no ch* **6/1**[3]
1304 **8** 1¼ **High Command**[13] 3710 3-8-7 88 KerrinMcEvoy 4 82
(E A L Dunlop) *wl in rr: rdn over 3f out: kpt on u.p over 1f out: no ch* **16/1**
1320 **9** 1¼ **Awatuki (IRE)**[78] 1781 3-8-1 82 ChrisCatlin 7 73
(A P Jarvis) *settled in midfield: rdn and no real prog 3f out: hanging and btn 2f out* **25/1**
-410 **10** 2½ **Hopeful Purchase (IRE)**[42] 2775 3-9-7 102 TonyCulhane 18 89
(W J Haggas) *hld up in midfield: effrt on inner over 3f out: no imp ldrs 2f out: wknd* **20/1**
0120 **11** 2½ **Salute Him (IRE)**[21] 3443 3-8-7 88 TedDurcan 17 70
(M R Channon) *lw: in tch: effrt to chse ldrs over 3f out: no imp over 2f out: wknd* **33/1**
0025 **12** 3½ **Porters (USA)**[13] 3710 3-8-9 90 (p) RichardHughes 14 65
(R Hannon) *a in rr: rdn and brief effrt 3f out: sn btn* **25/1**
5300 **13** 1¼ **Genari**[36] 2988 3-8-4 85 JosedeSouza 9 58
(P F I Cole) *prom: rdn over 3f out: wknd rapidly over 2f out* **66/1**
3421 **14** 2½ **Areyoutalkingtome**[30] 3162 3-9-2 97 EddieAhern 11 65
(C A Cyzer) *prom tl wknd 3f out* **40/1**
1-03 **15** 4 **Salt Man**[47] 2654 3-8-6 87 MartinDwyer 10 48
(M P Tregoning) *prom tl wknd 3f out* **9/1**
20 **16** 18 **Rumsfeld (ITY)**[74] 1872 3-9-0 95 OscarUrbina 1 21+
(M Botti) *v awkward s and lost 10l: a detached in last* **33/1**

2m 2.81s (-4.94) **Going Correction** -0.225s/f (Firm) course record **16** Ran SP% **128.0**
Speed ratings (Par 106):110,106,105,104,102 101,101,100,99,97 95,92,91,89,86 72
CSF £48.56 CT £225.61 TOTE £3.20: £1.40, £3.50, £2.00, £2.10; EX 44.00 Trifecta £181.80 Pool £2,613.16 - 10.20 winning units..
Owner Grant Mercer **Bred** South House Stud **Trained** Middleham Moor, N Yorks
■ A 1-2 for trainer Mark Johnston.

FOCUS
A strong handicap run at a good pace, and this is solid form with the second to fifth horses inclusive running to within a pound of their marks. The winner can prove better still.

NOTEBOOK
Road To Love(IRE) ◆, so impressive at Ascot at the weekend, repeated the dose under his penalty. Soon getting over from his low stall to set a strong pace, he was given a breather at the top of the hill before powering clear of his pursuers in the last quarter-mile, lowering the track record. Handicaps will probably be out when he is reassessed, but this progressive gelding should have no problem making the transition to Listed company at least. (op 7-2 tchd 5-2)
Desert Realm(IRE), making a quick reappearance, made good progress through the pack to move into second place but his stablemate was in a different league. He is well capable of winning a nice race at this trip. (op 14-1)
Pearly King(USA), off the same mark as when seventh in the King George V Handicap at Ascot, had been expected to benefit from this drop back in trip but if anything found this a shade sharp and could never get in a blow. Official explanation: jockey said gelding missed the break (tchd 11-2)
Familiar Territory ◆ looked fit for this first run since October, when he finished ahead of Road To Love, giving him 8lb, in a Doncaster nursery. Forced to race at the back of the field after slipping coming out of the stalls, he made eyecatching progress through the last two furlongs without having a prayer of troubling the winner. He handles easier ground and should be in for a profitable autumn. Official explanation: jockey said colt slipped leaving stalls (tchd 8-1)

Humungous(IRE), making his debut in handicap company having been running in Listed and conditions events, was the only one who could keep tabs on the winner and even tried to challenge him in the straight before being brushed aside. (op 16-1)
Zaif(IRE), who landed a warm maiden at the Newmarket July Festival, ran a respectable race on this handicap debut, staying on from the rear of the field. (op 11-1 tchd 12-1)
Kyoto Summit ran a decent race but gave the impression that the drop from a mile and a half was not what he wanted. (op 13-2 tchd 7-1 in places)
Hopeful Purchase(IRE) faced a very stiff task indeed off topweight on his handicap bow. (op 16-1)
Genari looked dull in his coat. (op 50-1)
Salt Man Official explanation: jockey said colt pulled too hard early
Rumsfeld(ITY) Official explanation: jockey said colt stumbled badly coming out the stalls

4083 DE BOER STKS (H'CAP) 7f
4:25 (4:26) (Class 2) (0-100,100) 3-Y-O

£24,928 (£7,464; £3,732; £1,868; £932; £468) **Stalls** High

Form RPR
3-16 **1** **Dream Theme**[88] 1505 3-8-6 **85** ..... RichardHughes 15 95+
(B W Hills) *trckd ldrs: effrt on inner 2f out: lft w ev ch ent fnl f: hung lft but led last 100yds* **13/2**[2]
0230 **2** *nk* **High Curragh**[22] 3414 3-8-8 **87** ..... NCallan 9 96
(K A Ryan) *lw: led at fast pce: clr w one rival 2f out: hung bdly lft over 1f out: hdd last 100yds: kpt on* **9/1**
1561 **3** *1 ½* **Heaven Sent**[22] 3418 3-8-8 **87** ..... LDettori 13 92
(Sir Michael Stoute) *chsd ldrs: rdn 2f out: styd on fnl f: nt pce to chal* **11/4**[1]
3220 **4** *½* **Multakka (IRE)**[20] 3491 3-8-4 **83** .....(b[1]) RHills 6 87+
(M P Tregoning) *t.k.h early: hld up towards rr: prog on outer 2f out: r.o fnl f: nvr nrr* **14/1**
2251 **5** *½* **Creative Mind (IRE)**[20] 3487 3-8-3 **82** ..... RichardMullen 14 84
(E J O'Neill) *chsd ldr: clr of rest 2f out: cl enough 1f out: fdd* **8/1**[3]
-033 **6** *¾* **Blades Girl**[22] 3418 3-7-13 **83** .....(p) AndrewMullen(5) 8 83
(K A Ryan) *chsd ldng pair: rdn 3f out: sn outpcd: plugged on u.p* **16/1**
5206 **7** *1* **Carmenero (GER)**[20] 3487 3-8-2 **81** oh1 ..... MartinDwyer 11 79
(W R Muir) *settled midfield: effrt 3f out: no imp ldrs 2f out: btn after* **33/1**
2413 **8** *½* **Namid Reprobate (IRE)**[69] 1986 3-8-8 **87** ..... EddieAhern 2 84
(P F I Cole) *hld up wl in rr: rdn 3f out: kpt on same pce: n.d* **25/1**
2124 **9** *shd* **Obe Brave**[68] 2032 3-9-7 **100** ..... TonyCulhane 3 96+
(M R Channon) *t.k.h: hld up in midfield: effrt on inner whn nt clr run over 2f out: no prog over 1f out* **10/1**
3- **10** *½* **Rol'Over Beethoven (FR)**[8] 3856 3-9-1 **94** 6ex ..... MJKinane 7 92+
(A P O'Brien, Ire) *w'like: scope: wl in rr: pushed along 3f out: no ch after: kpt on fnl f* **8/1**[3]
4635 **11** *nk* **Orpsie Boy (IRE)**[4] 3970 3-8-5 **84** ..... JoeFanning 5 78
(N P Littmoden) *dwlt: hld up wl in rr: shuffled along and sme prog over 1f out: nvr nr ldrs* **14/1**
2200 **12** *4* **Pearly Wey**[22] 3414 3-8-11 **93** ..... AdamKirby(3) 12 77+
(C G Cox) *s.v.s and lost all ch: a bhd* **12/1**
-045 **13** *shd* **Oceans Apart**[8] 3852 3-8-9 **88** .....(b) SebSanders 10 72
(P F I Cole) *chsd ldrs and racd wd: rdn and effrt 3f out: wknd rapidly 2f out* **16/1**
1420 **14** *8* **Song Of Silence (USA)**[103] 1130 3-9-3 **96** ..... SteveDrowne 4 59
(E A L Dunlop) *chsd ldrs tl wknd rapidly over 2f out: eased over 1f out* **50/1**
5104 **15** *8* **Orchard Supreme**[8] 3852 3-8-6 **85** ..... RyanMoore 1 27
(R Hannon) *a wl in rr: wknd over 2f out* **20/1**

1m 24.95s (-3.09) **Going Correction** -0.225s/f (Firm) **15** Ran SP% **127.6**
Speed ratings (Par 106):108,107,105,105,104 103,102,102,102,101 101,96,96,87,78
CSF £65.05 CT £209.65 TOTE £9.00: £3.00, £4.10, £1.70; EX 127.90 Trifecta £1020.10 Part won. Pool £1,436.84 - 0.60 winning units..
Owner K Abdulla **Bred** Juddmonte Farms Ltd **Trained** Lambourn, Berks

FOCUS
A decent handicap in which it paid to be on the pace and not many got into it. The race has been rated through the runner-up.

NOTEBOOK
Dream Theme, off the track with niggling problems since flopping on soft ground on his handicap debut in May, got warm beforehand. Travelling well, he came through to challenge when the leader hung into the centre of the track but then hung off the rail himself before winning with a bit more in hand than the margin of a neck. (op 8-1)
High Curragh, upped to this trip for the first time, set out to make every yard, but hung over into the centre of the track when the pressure was on and let the winner in. Continuing a frustrating run for his stable at the meeting, he is edging up the handicap without winning. (op 10-1 tchd 11-1)
Heaven Sent, raised 6lb after her win on the July course, ran well, but the way she was keeping on at the end suggested she could have done with a stronger pace. (op 9-4 tchd 3-1 in a place)
Multakka(IRE), back down in trip, wore blinkers for the first time. Running on strongly inside the last, but too late to get to the leaders, he was the only one of the first six to come from off the pace. He needs a truly-run race at this trip. (op 11-1 tchd 16-1)
Creative Mind(IRE), who went up 3lb after her Lingfield win, is a pretty consistent filly and this was another sound effort. Chasing the leader, she was still disputing second with a furlong to run before running out of steam. (tchd 9-1)
Blades Girl, a stablemate of the runner-up, ran respectably but the Handicapper has her about right.
Rol'Over Beethoven(FR), penalised for his Fairyhouse win, has since been beaten at Naas. Stepping up in trip, he could never get into a race in which it paid to race close to the pace. (op 14-1)
Orchard Supreme Official explanation: jockey said colt was unsuited by the good to firm ground

4084 EUROPEAN BREEDERS FUND NEW HAM MAIDEN FILLIES' STKS 7f
5:00 (5:03) (Class 2) 2-Y-O **£10,363** (£3,083; £1,540; £769) **Stalls** High

Form RPR
262 **1** **Cumin (USA)**[20] 3498 2-9-0 ..... MichaelHills 11 97
(B W Hills) *mde all: drew rt away fr 3f out: rdn out: impressive* **7/2**[1]
2 *7* **Perfect Star** 2-9-0 ..... PhilipRobinson 9 79
(C G Cox) *w'like: medium-sized: a chsng wnr: lft bhd fr 3f out: hld on for 2nd nr fin* **25/1**
32 **3** *nk* **Laureldean Express**[29] 3201 2-9-0 ..... RichardMullen 12 78
(E J O'Neill) *prom: chsd ldng pair fr 4f out: wl outpcd by wnr fr 3f out: kpt on* **10/1**
362 **4** *¾* **Party (IRE)**[13] 3700 2-9-0 ..... RyanMoore 8 76
(R Hannon) *hld up in midfield and off the pce: prog over 2f out: kpt on but no ch* **7/1**[3]
2 **5** *1* **Snake's Head**[19] 3545 2-9-0 ..... SebSanders 13 73
(J L Dunlop) *lw: chsd ldrs: outpcd by wnr fr 3f out: rdn to dispute 3rd over 1f out: one pce after* **4/1**[2]
02 **6** *½* **Bright Moon**[22] 3402 2-9-0 ..... DaneO'Neill 6 72
(R Hannon) *hld up in midfield: sme prog on outer over 2f out: kpt on same pce over 1f out* **50/1**
6 **7** *3 ½* **Regal Quest (IRE)**[13] 3700 2-9-0 ..... GeorgeBaker 5 63
(S Kirk) *rn green and wl bhd in last gp: hanging over 2f out: styd on fnl 2f: bttr for experience* **16/1**
8 *nk* **Mozayada (USA)** 2-9-0 ..... RHills 1 62
(M Johnston) *w'like: bit bkwd: awkward s: hld up towards rr: effrt on outer over 2f out: plugged on: no ch* **16/1**
9 *2* **Fashion Statement** 2-9-0 ..... NCallan 10 57
(M A Jarvis) *w'like: leggy: chsd ldrs: u.p fr 1/2-way: wknd 2f out* **12/1**
10 *6* **Change Course** 2-9-0 ..... RichardHughes 2 41
(Sir Michael Stoute) *w'like: nvr beyond midfield: no ch fr over 2f out: wknd* **10/1**
11 *1* **Ainamaa (USA)** 2-9-0 ..... MartinDwyer 7 39
(E A L Dunlop) *w'like: bit bkwd: wl off the pce in rr gp: nvr a factor* **33/1**
0 **12** *4* **Zoorina**[29] 3201 2-9-0 .....(t) JosedeSouza 16 28
(M P Tregoning) *a wl off the pce in rr gp: wl bhd fnl 2f* **50/1**
00 **13** *hd* **Boogie Dancer**[19] 3545 2-9-0 ..... VinceSlattery 4 28
(H S Howe) *sn struggling in last pair and wl bhd* **100/1**
14 *1* **Crystal Plum (IRE)** 2-9-0 ..... TonyCulhane 3 25
(B W Hills) *unf: lw: s.s: a wl bhd in last pair* **50/1**
0 **15** *1* **Swiftly Addicted (IRE)**[54] 2456 2-9-0 ..... EddieAhern 17 23
(A King) *chsd ldng pair for 3f: wknd rapidly 3f out* **40/1**

1m 25.24s (-2.80) **Going Correction** -0.225s/f (Firm) **15** Ran SP% **108.5**
Speed ratings (Par 97):107,99,98,97,96 96,92,91,89,82 81,76,76,75,74
CSF £69.63 TOTE £3.80: £1.60, £7.00, £3.40; EX 129.20 TRIFECTA Not won..
Owner Lady Bamford **Bred** Nakamura Chikusan Ltd **Trained** Lambourn, Berks

FOCUS
A decent maiden and a very smart winning time for a race of its type, just 0.29 seconds slower than the preceding 81-100 handicap for three-year-olds over the same trip. Very few got into this but the form looks solid.

NOTEBOOK
Cumin(USA) ◆, who showed a useful level of form in her first three runs, got off the mark in impressive fashion. Making all, she was never seriously challenged and careered away for a wide-margin victory. Races like the May Hill and the Fillies' Mile will be on the agenda now. (tchd 4-1)
Perfect Star is out of a mare who was placed at Listed level. Chasing the winner throughout, she was no match whatsoever but kept going to hold on for second. This was a promising debut and she should have no problem going one better in an ordinary maiden. (op 20-1)
Laureldean Express, placed twice on the Kempton Polytrack, on the second occasion in a race that is working out well, was in third place before halfway and filled that position to the line, nearly getting up for second but always having a distant view of the winner. Her turn should not be long in coming. (tchd 9-1)
Party(IRE), reverting to seven furlongs, did best of those to come from off the pace. (op 8-1)
Snake's Head, who had been very green on her debut, ran a respectable race but was running on the spot in the latter stages. (op 9-2 tchd 5-1 in places)
Bright Moon, runner-up to a stablemate on her debut on sand, was unable to get into the hunt on this turf bow over an extra furlong. (tchd 66-1)
Regal Quest(IRE), upped in trip on this second run, was keeping on at the end and the experience should not be lost on her. (op 20-1)
Fashion Statement, whose dam, a sister to Oaks winner Casual Look, was smart over ten furlongs in France, holds a Fillies' Mile entry but is going to need more time. (op 20-1 tchd 22-1)
Change Course, a good-bodied filly out of a mare who has produced the useful performers Weightless and Home Affairs, looked green in the paddock and could be one for next year. (op 8-1)

4085 AUDI Q7 STKS (H'CAP) (PREVIOUSLY KNOWN AS THE CHARLTON STAKES) 5f
5:35 (5:37) (Class 3) (0-90,85) 4-Y-0+ **£10,363** (£3,083; £1,540; £769) **Stalls** Low

Form RPR
-505 **1** **Holbeck Ghyll (IRE)**[62] 2189 4-8-7 **71** ..... JohnEgan 12 88+
(A M Balding) *w nr side ldr: led gp 2f out and sn clr: unchal* **7/1**[2]
5000 **2** *2 ½* **Smokin Beau**[33] 3069 9-8-8 **79** ..... VictoriaBehan(7) 14 87
(D Nicholls) *b: lw: w far side ldr: led gp 2f out: styd on wl: no ch w wnr* **20/1**
0200 **3** *½* **Night Prospector**[35] 3027 6-9-3 **81** ..... RichardHughes 2 87+
(G L Moore) *hld up at bk of nr side gp: effrt jst over 1f out: r.o strly last 150yds: hopeless task: 2nd of 13 that side* **11/1**
4215 **4** *1 ¼* **Bluebok**[5] 3938 5-9-6 **84** ..... DaneO'Neill 19 86
(J M Bradley) *swtg: led far side gp to 2f out: hld by ldr after: kpt on: 2nd of 6 that side* **10/1**
1304 **5** *shd* **Bond Boy**[18] 3567 9-9-5 **83** .....(b) RobertWinston 7 84+
(B Smart) *lw: hld up in rr of nr side gp: nt clr run over 2f out and swtchd rt: r.o fnl f: nrst fin: 3rd of 13 that side* **12/1**
015- **6** *shd* **Semenovskii**[278] 6157 6-8-6 **70** .....(t) RichardThomas 11 71
(Miss B Sanders) *off the pce in midfield nr side: rdn and styd on fnl 2f: nvr pce to rch ldrs: 4th of 13 that side* **66/1**
3242 **7** *shd* **Nautical**[29] 3204 8-9-1 **79** ..... PhilipRobinson 15 80
(A W Carroll) *swtg: s.i.s: hld up in last pair far side: rdn and nt qckn 2f out: styd on fnl f: 3rd of 6 that side* **14/1**
3201 **8** *shd* **Oranmore Castle (IRE)**[26] 3281 4-9-3 **81** ..... AdrianTNicholls 17 81
(D Nicholls) *trckd far side ldrs: rdn and nt qckn over 1f out: kpt on same pce: 4th of 6 that side* **11/2**[1]
0104 **9** *hd* **Pomfret Lad**[14] 3673 8-8-6 **70** .....(v[1]) JimmyQuinn 8 70
(J J Quinn) *lw: chsd nr side ldrs: drvn 2f out: one pce after: 5th of 13 that side* **33/1**
006 **10** *nk* **Spanish Ace**[16] 3625 5-9-1 **79** ..... GeorgeBaker 18 77
(J M Bradley) *trckd far side ldrs gng wl: rdn and no rspnse over 1f out: one pce after: 5th of 6 that side* **12/1**
5000 **11** *½* **Cornus**[167] 441 4-9-0 **78** ..... ShaneKelly 3 75
(J A Osborne) *swtg: chsd nr side ldrs: hrd rdn 2f out: one pce and btn over 1f out: 6th of 13 that side* **25/1**
0066 **12** *nk* **The Jobber (IRE)**[12] 3744 5-9-5 **83** ..... SebSanders 10 84+
(M Blanshard) *lw: hld up in rr nr side: nt clr run over 2f out: effrt but no ch whn hmpd jst ins fnl f: 7th of 13 that side* **20/1**
2536 **13** *hd* **Quality Street**[13] 3715 4-8-11 **75** ..... KerrinMcEvoy 16 70
(P Butler) *taken down early: hld up in last pair far side: rdn and no prog over 1f out: last of 6 that side* **8/1**[3]
4106 **14** *nk* **Hello Roberto**[3] 4003 5-8-10 **74** .....(p) AdrianMcCarthy 4 68
(R A Harris) *lw: chsd nr side ldrs: rdn over 2f out: fdd fnl f: 8th of 13 that side* **25/1**
3600 **15** *¾* **Fizzlephut (IRE)**[4] 3972 4-8-10 **74** ..... PaulFitzsimons 6 65
(Miss J R Tooth) *taken down early: chsd nr side ldrs: rdn 2f out: wknd fnl f: 9th of 13 that side* **33/1**

The Form Book, Raceform Ltd, Compton, RG20 6NL

3414 **16** *1* **Blackheath (IRE)**[30] 3170 10-8-9 **73** .... JoeFanning 1 60
(D Nicholls) *taken down early: chsd nr side ldrs for 3f: wkng whn n.m.r 1f out: 10th of 13 that side* **14/1**

0106 **17** *¾* **One Way Ticket**[8] 3832 6-9-7 **85** ....(p) NCallan 13 70
(J M Bradley) *swtg: led nr side to 2f out: wknd: 11th of 13 in gp* **50/1**

1242 **18** *1* **Malapropism**[5] 3938 6-9-5 **83** .... TonyCulhane 9 64
(M R Channon) *lw: prom nr side but sn rdn: wknd wl over 1f out: 12th of 13 in gp* **7/1**[2]

1040 **19** *17* **Cashel Mead**[27] 3251 6-8-13 **80** .... RichardKingscote[(3)] 5 —
(J L Spearing) *completely missed break: a t.o* **25/1**

57.02 secs (-2.03) **Going Correction** -0.225s/f (Firm) **19** Ran SP% **128.0**
Speed ratings (Par 107):107,103,102,100,100 99,99,99,99,98 97,97,97,96,95 93,92,91,63
CSF £149.87 CT £1595.53 TOTE £9.80: £3.00, £3.80, £3.60, £3.90; EX 277.50 TRIFECTA Not won. Place 6 £49.97, Place 5 £16.16..
Owner Holbeck Ghyll Partnership **Bred** David Brickley **Trained** Kingsclere, Hants

FOCUS
A fair sprint handicap in which the field split into two, a group of six racing up the far side, but there seemed little in the draw. The time was good and the race has been rated positively, with the unexposed winner sure to do better.

NOTEBOOK
Holbeck Ghyll(IRE) ◆, who had become very well handicapped, looked very fit on this return from a two-month break. Brought over to race with the larger stands'-side group, although Egan could have elected to go far side, he showed ahead with a quarter of a mile to run and came away to win with plenty in hand. He will be in for a hefty rise after this, and although he is probably up to defying it his connections will be looking to run him under a penalty. (op 8-1 tchd 6-1 in places)
Smokin Beau, who was having his first run since leaving Nick Littmoden, has a fine record at this course. Coming home on top of the six to race down the far side, there is plenty of mileage in him yet for his new yard to exploit.
Night Prospector ◆ went up to a mark of 105 after landing a substandard Temple Stakes at Epsom in 2004, but has steadily dropped to a very attractive mark during a long losing run since. After having to wait for a gap, he ran on really strongly but the winner had flown. (op 10-1)
Bluebok, finished runner-up in the far-side sextet and fourth overall, although he was wilting in the last half-furlong and would have been an also-ran with a bit further to go.
Bond Boy, running off the same mark as when landing the Stewards' Cup here four years ago, was doing some good late work having been hampered just after halfway.
Semenovskii looked fit on this first run after a nine-month break and debut for this yard. This was an encouraging effort and easier ground will suit him. (tchd 50-1)
Oranmore Castle(IRE), sold out of Barry Hills's yard for 25,000gns since his win at Beverley, was without the regular tongue strap. One of half a dozen to race on the far side, including a stablemate who finished second overall, he was disappointing off a 5lb higher mark.
Spanish Ace Official explanation: jockey said gelding hung left throughout
The Jobber(IRE) can be rated as having finished closer as he was hampered twice.
One Way Ticket Official explanation: jockey said horse was upset in stalls
Cashel Mead Official explanation: jockey said mare reared as stalls opened
T/Jkpt: £4,844.00 to a £1 stake. Pool: £30,701.50. 4.50 winning tickets. T/Plt: £67.80 to a £1 stake. Pool: £215,158.50. 2,313.65 winning tickets. T/Qpdt: £5.40 to a £1 stake. Pool: £10,696.30. 1,456.60 winning tickets. JN

4055 MUSSELBURGH (R-H)

Thursday, August 3

OFFICIAL GOING: Good (good to soft in places on straight course)
Wind: Slight, half-behind

4086 SHOPSPA.CO.UK AMATEUR RIDERS' H'CAP — 1m 5f
6:10 (6:10) (Class 6) (0-60,60) 4-Y-0+ — **£3,296** (£1,014; £507) **Stalls** High

Form RPR

0305 **1** **Danzatrice**[24] 3352 4-10-9 **48** .... MrSDobson 1 55
(C W Thornton) *rel to r and wl bhd: hdwy 1/2-way: wd st and gd prog over 3f out: rdn 2f out: styd on to ld nr fin* **14/1**

0645 **2** *nk* **Kristiansand**[9] 3810 6-10-10 **49** .... MrSWalker 11 56
(P Monteith) *led: clr over 4f out: rdn wl over 2f out: drvn over 1f out: hdd and no ex towards fin* **5/1**[3]

5522 **3** *¾* **Regency Red (IRE)**[13] 3694 8-10-7 **51** .... MrBenBrisbourne[(5)] 2 57
(W M Brisbourne) *s.i.s and bhd: hdwy over 4f out: swtchd lft and rdn wl over 1f out: styd on ins last* **7/1**

6354 **4** *nk* **Transit**[6] 3919 7-10-9 **48** ....(p) MissLEllison 12 53
(B Ellison) *trckd ldng pair: effrt to chse ldr over 4f out: rdn 3f out: drvn last 2f and kpt on same pce* **4/1**[2]

-006 **5** *½* **Tojoneski**[15] 3637 7-10-2 **41** oh1 .... MissSBrotherton 7 46+
(I W McInnes) *hld up: hdwy over 5f out: effrt on inner to chse ldrs over 2f out: rdn and sddle slipped 2f out: kpt on same pce ins last* **12/1**

6023 **6** *6* **Platinum Charmer (IRE)**[11] 3763 6-10-12 **56** ......(p) MissKellyBurke[(5)] 6 52
(K R Burke) *chased ldr: rdn along 4f out: drvn wl over 2f out and grad wknd* **3/1**[1]

10-0 **7** *shd* **Michaels Dream (IRE)**[12] 1199 7-9-10 **42** ....(b) MissWGibson[(7)] 9 38
(N Wilson) *a towards rr* **10/1**

-100 **8** *7* **Cumbrian Knight (IRE)**[141] 643 8-11-2 **60** .... MissNJefferson[(5)] 3 45
(J M Jefferson) *dwlt: a rr* **7/1**

50-0 **9** *¾* **Peter's Imp (IRE)**[35] 2998 11-10-2 **41** oh1 .... MrsCBartley 10 25
(A Berry) *dwlt: midfield: hdwy over 4f out: sn rdn along: drvn 3f out and sn wknd* **33/1**

405- **10** *29* **Orangino**[312] 5487 8-10-1 **47** oh4 ow6 .... MrJBewley[(7)] 8 —
(J S Haldane) *in tch to 1/2-way: sn wknd* **66/1**

2m 52.81s (-1.19) **Going Correction** -0.05s/f (Good) **10** Ran SP% **114.6**
Speed ratings (Par 101):101,100,100,100,99 96,96,91,91,73
CSF £81.15 CT £538.83 TOTE £15.50: £5.10, £2.10, £2.00; EX 46.30.
Owner 980 Racing **Bred** G G A Gregson **Trained** Middleham Moor, N Yorks
■ Stewards' Enquiry : Mr S Walker two-day ban: used whip with excessive frequency (Aug 15,17)

FOCUS
A very moderate contest, but a decent pace and sound enough form, rated around the placed horses. The evidence was that the centre of the track was faster than elsewhere.
Tojoneski Official explanation: jockey said saddle slipped

4087 TARTANTURFDIRECTORY.CO.UK CLAIMING STKS — 1m
6:40 (6:40) (Class 5) 4-Y-0+ — **£3,238** (£963; £481; £240) **Stalls** Low

Form RPR

-021 **1** **Baby Barry**[20] 3480 9-8-8 **56** .... PaulHanagan 3 60
(R A Fahey) *trckd ldrs: hdwy over 2f out: rdn to chse ldr over 1f out: styd on u.p to ld last 100 yds* **7/2**[2]

1512 **2** *1¼* **Sawwaah (IRE)**[1] 4057 9-9-10 **65** ....(p) SilvestreDeSousa 4 73
(D Nicholls) *in tch: pushed along over 3f out: gd hdwy to ld wl over 1f out: hung lft and drvn: hdd and no ex last 100yd* **7/2**[2]

3502 **3** *½* **Bailieborough (IRE)**[5] 3959 7-9-11 **77** .... StephenDonohoe[(3)] 1 76
(B Ellison) *hld up in tch: hdwy 2f out: rdn ent last: drvn and kpt on same pce towards fin* **6/4**[1]

2/00 **4** *5* **Atlantic Story (USA)**[12] 3747 4-10-0 **75** ....(t) DaleGibson 7 64
(M W Easterby) *led: pushed along 3f out: rdn over 2f out: hdd wl over 1f out and sn wknd* **14/1**

0343 **5** *1½* **Desert Lightning (IRE)**[1] 4057 4-9-2 **50** ....(t) PatCosgrave 5 49
(K R Burke) *chsd ldr: effrt 3f out: sn rdn and wknd wl over 1f out* **9/1**[3]

0053 **6** *3½* **Shamwari Fire (IRE)**[5] 3941 6-8-6 **36** ....(b) RoystonFfrench 10 31
(I W McInnes) *chsd ldng pair: rdn along 3f out: wkng whn n.m.r 2f out* **14/1**

4360 **7** *5* **Fit To Fly (IRE)**[61] 2240 5-8-4 **41** ....(p) PaulEddery 11 17
(R C Guest) *a bhd* **33/1**

1m 40.75s (-1.75) **Going Correction** -0.05s/f (Good) **7** Ran SP% **110.7**
Speed ratings (Par 103):106,104,104,99,97 94,89
CSF £15.06 TOTE £3.80: £2.10, £1.70; EX 9.00.
Owner Mrs Annette C Barlow **Bred** Capt J H Wilson **Trained** Musley Bank, N Yorks
■ Stewards' Enquiry : Silvestre De Sousa caution: careless riding

FOCUS
A modest claimer weakened further by four non-runners three of whom were because of the ground. The pace was decent though and with some decent margins between the seven runners at the line the form looks solid for the grade.

4088 JOHN SMITH'S EXTRA SMOOTH NURSERY — 5f
7:10 (7:10) (Class 5) 2-Y-O — **£3,886** (£1,156; £577; £288) **Stalls** Low

Form RPR

0551 **1** **Onenightinlisbon (IRE)**[10] 3787 2-8-11 **75** 6ex .... LeeEnstone 8 81
(K R Burke) *hld up: hdwy on outer 1/2-way: rdn to chal over 1f out: led and hung lft ent last f: styd on* **11/2**[2]

10 **2** *1¾* **Aahayson**[44] 2724 2-9-0 **78** .... PatCosgrave 4 78
(K R Burke) *led: rdn wl over 1f out: drvn and hdd ent last: kpt on same pce* **2/1**[1]

6433 **3** *¾* **Ishibee (IRE)**[10] 3787 2-8-1 **65** ....(p) RoystonFfrench 10 62
(Mrs A Duffield) *bhd: hdwy wl over 1f out: sn swtchd rt and rdn: styd on wl fnl f: nrst fin* **12/1**

034 **4** *1¾* **Sister Etienne (IRE)**[12] 3745 2-8-6 **70** .... PaulFessey 11 61
(T D Barron) *prom: effrt 2f out: rdn to chal over 1f out and ev ch tl drvn and wknd ins last* **10/1**

3110 **5** *1* **Top Tier**[22] 3409 2-7-12 **65** .... PatrickMathers[(3)] 7 52
(Peter Grayson) *chsd ldrs: rdn along 2f out: wknd appr last* **8/1**

5215 **6** *1¼* **Bollin Franny**[20] 3476 2-8-8 **77** .... DuranFentiman[(5)] 6 60
(T D Easterby) *cl up: rdn 2f out: sn wknd* **14/1**

0300 **7** *hd* **Storm Mission (USA)**[10] 3800 2-8-5 **72** .... DominicFox[(3)] 5 54
(Miss V Haigh) *outpcd and bhd: hdwy 2f out: rdn and kpt on ins last* **66/1**

0315 **8** *3* **Stir Crazy (IRE)**[6] 3917 2-8-6 **73** .... EdwardCreighton[(3)] 1 44
(M R Channon) *chsd ldrs: rdn along over 2f out: sn wknd* **13/2**

0530 **9** *1* **Hawaii Prince**[19] 3555 2-8-8 **72** .... SilvestreDeSousa 3 39
(D Nicholls) *keen: chsd ldrs: rdn along over 2f out: sn wandered and btn* **6/1**[3]

4004 **10** *1¼* **Minnie Magician**[22] 3394 2-7-9 **65** oh17 ow2.......... LeanneKershaw[(5)] 2 27
(C Grant) *dwlt: a rr* **100/1**

59.30 secs (-1.20) **Going Correction** -0.30s/f (Firm) **10** Ran SP% **113.4**
Speed ratings (Par 94):97,94,93,90,88 86,86,81,79,77
CSF £16.32 CT £127.24 TOTE £8.90: £3.20, £1.50, £3.20; EX 17.20.
Owner Nigel Shields **Bred** Stephen Moloney **Trained** Middleham Moor, N Yorks
■ A one-two for trainer Karl Burke.

FOCUS
Probably a fair nursery with the pace a sound one from the start. Although the stalls were against the stands' rail, the field shifted out into the centre of the track which on the evidence of the first two races was the fastest strip. As a result those drawn high seemed to hold the advantage. The official ratings shown next to each horse are estimated and for information purposes only.

NOTEBOOK
Onenightinlisbon(IRE), carrying a 6lb penalty after breaking her duck in a Beverley claimer last time and making her debut for new connections, followed up in great style from her stable companion and her highish draw meant that she was able to take the quicker route down the centre of the track rather than having to manoeuvre there. On this evidence she would not mind the return to six and the hat-trick must be a real possibility. (op 9-2)
Aahayson, dropping in class after finishing down the field in the Windsor Castle, was the better fancied of the stable's pair according to the market, but after making much of the running he found his stable companion too strong. He still did best of those drawn low, and as this was only his third outing he still does have some scope for improvement. (op 5-2)
Ishibee(IRE), 5lb better off with Onenightinlisbon compared with their recent meeting, was given a more patient ride than she was at Beverley and managed to narrow the gap without looking likely to win. (op 14-1)
Sister Etienne(IRE), making her nursery debut, held every chance from what turned out to be a favourable draw but failed to see her race out. She is still relatively lightly raced so is by no means without hope. (op 17-2)
Top Tier, returning to the scene of her two previous victories, showed up for a while but seemed to have no excuses this time.
Stir Crazy(IRE), on the face of it was disappointing, but he started from the lowest stall and the evidence at this meeting was that the stands' side was not the place to be. (op 6-1)

4089 EUROPEAN BREEDERS FUND MEDIAN AUCTION MAIDEN FILLIES' STKS — 5f
7:40 (7:40) (Class 5) 2-Y-0 — **£4,210** (£1,252; £625; £312) **Stalls** Low

Form RPR

333 **1** **Wicked Wilma (IRE)**[2] 4017 2-9-0 .... FrancisNorton 7 63
(A Berry) *cl up: rdn to ld wl over 1f out: styd on* **6/1**[2]

0456 **2** *1* **Almora Guru**[20] 3476 2-9-0 .... PaulMulrennan 3 59
(W M Brisbourne) *cl up: ev ch 2f out: sn rdn and edgd lft ent last: kpt on* **12/1**

5222 **3** *1* **Durova (IRE)**[12] 3745 2-8-9 .... DuranFentiman[(5)] 1 56
(T D Easterby) *led: rdn along 2f out: sn hung lft and hdd: drvn and one pce fnl f* **2/5**[1]

0 **4** *1¾* **Its Moon (IRE)**[10] 3796 2-8-11 .... EdwardCreighton[(3)] 5 50
(M R Channon) *s.i.s and bhd: hdwy 1/2-way: rdn and kpt on appr last: nrst fin* **7/1**[3]

055 **5** *½* **The Brat**[12] 3721 2-8-11 .... PatrickMathers[(3)] 6 48
(James Moffatt) *chsd ldrs: rdn along 2f out: sn drvn and one pce* **50/1**

00 **6** *11* **Bidders Itch**[4] 3982 2-8-11 .... StephenDonohoe[(3)] 2 8
(A Berry) *in tch: rdn along and outpcd fr 1/2-way* **66/1**

60.05 secs (-0.45) **Going Correction** -0.30s/f (Firm) **6** Ran SP% **109.4**
Speed ratings (Par 91):91,89,87,85,84 66
CSF £63.89 TOTE £6.10: £1.80, £3.10; EX 74.90.

Owner Auldyn Stud Ltd **Bred** Gerry O'Sullivan **Trained** Cockerham, Lancs

FOCUS

A modest fillies' maiden and with the long odds-on favourite running so poorly, this may not have taken much winning.

NOTEBOOK

Wicked Wilma(IRE), third in all three of her previous starts, went two better but she was surely helped by the red-hot favourite blowing out and also that she kept running down the favoured middle of the track whilst her two nearest rivals hung towards the slower stands' side. Much will now depend on how the Handicapper assesses this. (op 11-2)

Almora Guru had every chance but she did herself few favours by hanging over towards the stands' rail into what looked the slower ground. She appears exposed now and she looks to be the best guide to the form. (op 14-1)

Durova(IRE), bidding to end a run of three consecutive second places, managed to do so but not in the way her supporters would have hoped. Having made the early running, she then started to look very uncomfortable and ended up hanging over to the stands' rail and forfeiting her chance. She is better than this and something may emerge to explain this effort, but it does leave her with a lot of questions to answer. Official explanation: vet said filly was found to be in season (op 4-11 tchd 4-9 in places)

Its Moon(IRE) did not appreciate the drop in trip from her debut and was never going to get there in time. There is plenty of stamina on the dam's side so better can be expected when she goes back up in trip. (op 15-2 tchd 8-1)

The Brat has already been beaten in selling company and achieved little here. (tchd 66-1)

4090 JOHN SMITH'S EXTRA COLD H'CAP — 7f 30y

8:10 (8:10) (Class 4) (0-80,82) 4-Y-O+ — **£6,477** (£1,927; £963; £481) **Stalls** Low

Form / RPR

0064 **1** — **Stoic Leader (IRE)**[5] 3937 6-9-7 **78** ... PaulHanagan 5 — 87
(R F Fisher) *hld up: hdwy over 2f out: rdn to chal ent last: sn drvn and edgd lft: styd on to ld last 50 yds* **8/1**

300 **2** *hd* **Dakota Rain (IRE)**[39] 2900 4-9-1 **72** ... (e[1]) PaulEddery 4 — 81
(R C Guest) *led: rdn over 2f out: drvn ent last: hdd and no ex last 50 yds* **20/1**

0501 **3** *1 1/4* **Sentiero Rosso (USA)**[1] 4059 4-8-6 **66** 6ex ow2(t) StephenDonohoe(3) 7 — 72+
(B Ellison) *chsd ldrs: hdwy over 2f out: rdn to chal over 1f out and ev ch tl squeezed out ins last and no ex after* **7/2**[1]

3426 **4** *shd* **Stellite**[33] 3101 6-8-10 **70** ... EdwardCreighton(3) 9 — 75
(J S Goldie) *hld up in rr: hdwy over 2f out: rdn to chse ldrs over 1f out: drvn and kpt on ins last: nrst fin* **7/1**

4300 **5** *3/4* **H Harrison (IRE)**[29] 3191 6-8-13 **70** ... RoystonFfrench 11 — 73
(I W McInnes) *chsd ldr: rdn along over 2f out: wknd appr last* **12/1**

1605 **6** *3/4* **True Night**[13] 3718 9-8-12 **69** ... SilvestreDeSousa 10 — 70
(D Nicholls) *chsd ldr: rdn along and edgd lft wl over 2f out: sn wknd* **16/1**

0415 **7** *nk* **Passion Fruit**[17] 3598 5-9-4 **75** ... DeanMcKeown 6 — 75
(C W Fairhurst) *hld up in rr: hdwy 1/2-way: effrt and n.m.r 2f out: sn rdn and kpt on ins last: nrst fin* **5/1**[2]

0405 **8** *hd* **Breaking Shadow (IRE)**[5] 3937 4-9-5 **76** ... (p) FrancisNorton 3 — 76
(T D Barron) *hld up: hdwy over 2f out: rdn to chse ldrs wl over 1f out: sn drvn and no imp* **5/1**[2]

5052 **9** *5* **Bessemer (JPN)**[14] 3664 5-9-3 **74** ... (v) DanielTudhope 2 — 61
(D Carroll) *chsd ldrs: rdn along over 2f out: sn wknd* **6/1**[3]

0000 **10** *6* **Local Poet**[31] 3158 5-8-6 **63** ... (b) TomEaves 1 — 34
(I Semple) *in tch on outer: effrt 3f out: sn rdn along and wknd fnl 2f* **25/1**

1m 29.18s (-0.76) **Going Correction** -0.05s/f (Good) — **10** Ran SP% **115.6**

Speed ratings (Par 105):102,101,100,100,99 98,98,97,92,85

CSF £152.21 CT £661.55 TOTE £6.80: £2.30, £4.30, £2.10; EX 232.00.

Owner Alan Willoughby **Bred** P J Higgins **Trained** Ulverston, Cumbria

■ Stewards' Enquiry : Paul Hanagan one-day ban: careless riding (Aug 14)

FOCUS

A fair handicap run at an even pace, but the track bias played its part as the field spun wide turning into the straight and the first three home raced furthest from the nearside rail.

4091 JOHN SMITH'S NO NONSENSE H'CAP — 5f

8:40 (8:40) (Class 5) (0-70,65) 3-Y-O+ — **£3,886** (£1,156; £577; £288) **Stalls** Low

Form / RPR

-242 **1** — **Smiddy Hill**[9] 3825 4-9-7 **60** ... RoystonFfrench 5 — 74
(R Bastiman) *mde all: rdn over 1f out: styd on strly ins last* **11/2**[3]

3041 **2** *1 3/4* **Bond Becks (IRE)**[10] 3781 6-8-10 **56** 6ex ... PJBenson(7) 8 — 64
(B Smart) *a.p: effrt to chal 2f out and ev ch tl rdn and one pce ent last* **11/4**[2]

0421 **3** *3* **Alugat (IRE)**[1] 4056 3-9-3 **59** 6ex ... (p) TPQueally 9 — 56
(Mrs A Duffield) *towards rr and sn pushed along: hdwy 1/2-wy: rdn to chse ldng pair and swtchd lft ent last: sn drvn and no imp* **5/2**[1]

5120 **4** *nk* **Strawberry Patch (IRE)**[10] 3781 7-9-3 **56** ... (p) DanielTudhope 3 — 52+
(J S Goldie) *towards rr: pshd along and hdwy 2f out: sn rdn and kpt on ins last: nt rch ldrs* **8/1**

00 **5** *1 1/4* **Oeuf A La Neige**[87] 1528 6-8-8 **47** ... PaulHanagan 6 — 38
(Miss L A Perratt) *sn outpcd and rdn along in rr: hdwy 2f out: styd on u.p appr last: nvr nr ldrs* **25/1**

0000 **6** *1 1/4* **Northern Svengali (IRE)**[20] 3482 10-8-7 **46** oh9 ... (t) TomEaves 10 — 33
(D A Nolan) *chsd ldrs: rdn along 1/2-way: sn wknd* **100/1**

6513 **7** *hd* **Lady Bahia (IRE)**[24] 3354 5-9-9 **65** ... (b) PatrickMathers(3) 2 — 51
(Peter Grayson) *s.i.s: a rr* **8/1**

1435 **8** *nk* **Sharp Hat**[10] 3781 12-8-13 **52** ... PaulQuinn 1 — 37
(D W Chapman) *chsd ldrs: rdn along 1/2-way: sn wknd* **8/1**

0000 **9** *2* **Mutayam**[10] 3781 6-8-2 **48** oh5 ow2 ... (t) AnnStokell(7) 7 — 26
(D A Nolan) *chsd ldrs: rdn along 1/2-way: sn wknd* **100/1**

000 **10** *1/2* **Oceanico Dot Com (IRE)**[42] 2784 4-9-0 **53** ... FrancisNorton 4 — 29
(A Berry) *cl up: rdn along over 2f out: sn wknd* **28/1**

58.57 secs (-1.93) **Going Correction** -0.30s/f (Firm)

WFA 3 from 4yo+ 3lb — **10** Ran SP% **113.2**

Speed ratings (Par 103):103,100,95,94,92 90,90,90,86,86

CSF £19.94 CT £46.03 TOTE £6.90: £2.00, £2.30, £1.40; EX 19.60 Place 6 £190.05, Place 5 £53.56..

Owner I B Barker **Bred** I B Barker **Trained** Cowthorpe, N Yorks

■ Stewards' Enquiry : T P Queally one-day ban: used whip with excessive force and frequency (Aug 14)

FOCUS

A decent pace for this moderate sprint and again the field came down the centre of the track. The first two came clear and the form looks sound.

Lady Bahia(IRE) Official explanation: jockey said mare missed the break

T/Plt: £254.40 to a £1 stake. Pool: £47,127.15. 135.20 winning tickets. T/Qpdt: £60.10 to a £1 stake. Pool: £4,023.00. 49.50 winning tickets. JR

4092 - 4095a (Foreign Racing) - See Raceform Interactive

4079 GOODWOOD (R-H)

Friday, August 4

OFFICIAL GOING: Good to firm

Wind: Moderate, across

4096 COUTTS GLORIOUS STKS (LISTED RACE) — 1m 4f

2:05 (2:05) (Class 1) 4-Y-O+

£17,034 (£6,456; £3,231; £1,611; £807; £405) **Stalls** Low

Form / RPR

3441 **1** — **Crosspeace (IRE)**[3] 4023 4-9-4 108 ... RoystonFfrench 3 — 112+
(M Johnston) *lw: trckd ldrs: rdn to ld 2f out: styd on gamely fnl f* **10/3**[2]

51-6 **2** *nk* **Foxhaven**[28] 3255 4-9-1 98 ... MartinDwyer 6 — 108
(P R Chamings) *lw: trckd ldr: led over 4f out: hdd 2f out: styd on u.p fnl f* **9/1**

6141 **3** *1* **Admiral's Cruise (USA)**[34] 3085 4-9-4 107 ... JimmyFortune 1 — 110+
(B J Meehan) *hld up: hdwy and rdn 3f out: kpt on fnl f* **2/1**[1]

00-4 **4** *3* **Orange Touch (GER)**[55] 2430 6-9-1 101 ... RyanMoore 5 — 102
(Mrs A J Perrett) *mid-div: rdn 3f out: one pce ins fnl 2f* **33/1**

0-3 **5** *3/4* **Asian Heights**[83] 1677 8-9-1 100 ... AlanMunro 7 — 101
(G Wragg) *trckd ldrs: outpcd 3f out: styd on wl again fnl f* **25/1**

1561 **6** *1/2* **Kandidate**[28] 3254 4-9-4 114 ... (t) SebSanders 4 — 103
(C E Brittain) *hld up: rdn and effrt over 2f out but nvr nr to chal* **4/1**[3]

7 *3* **Honduras (SWI)**[365] 5-9-1 ... TPQueally 8 — 95
(G L Moore) *a in rr* **100/1**

316- **8** *64* **Melrose Avenue (USA)**[353] 4453 4-9-1 107 ... LDettori 2 — —
(Saeed Bin Suroor) *swtg: stmbld leaving stalls but sn led: hdd over 4f out: sn wknd and wl bhd: t.o: dismntd after line: b.b.v* **9/2**

2m 36.64s **Going Correction** -0.225s/f (Firm) — **8** Ran SP% **112.4**

Speed ratings (Par 111):98,97,97,95,94 94,92,49

CSF £31.13 TOTE £4.20: £1.50, £2.20, £1.30; EX 36.20 Trifecta £89.00 Pool £1,931.38 - 15.40 winning units..

Owner Favourites Racing **Bred** Patrick Jones **Trained** Middleham Moor, N Yorks

FOCUS

A reasonable Listed event, but the pace could have been stronger in the early stages and the time was very moderate. As a result the form has been rated conservatively.

NOTEBOOK

Crosspeace(IRE), the winner of a very competitive handicap off a mark of 108 over ten furlongs at the beginning of the meeting, was able to follow up in this higher grade returned to a longer trip just three days later. The ordinary early pace would probably not have been to his liking, so his rider did the right thing in committing for home a long way out and he stayed on strongest of all. He deserves another chance back in Group company. (op 7-2 tchd 4-1 in a place)

Foxhaven was always well placed given the way the race was run and kept on to the line. This was a fine effort considering he already had 7lb to find with the winner at the weights before that one had been reassessed for his win earlier in the week. He could look on a very fair mark if taking his chance in the Ebor, although he has never previously raced beyond this distance. (op 11-1 tchd 12-1)

Admiral's Cruise(USA), the winner of a very suspect Listed race over this trip at Newmarket on his previous start, is not the most consistent and was below the pick of his form. The steady early pace would not have suited and he can do better when things fall right. (op 9-4 tchd 5-2 in places)

Orange Touch(GER) ◆ will surely have pleased connections with this effort considering he is probably a better horse over further on easier ground, and was having just his second run of the season. He could be a live player in the Ebor if conditions are suitable, and it might be worth taking a chance at around the 33/1 mark. (op 25-1)

Asian Heights was a little short of room but basically lacked the pace to go with the principals in the straight. He stayed on again near the line and could do better in a stronger-run race, probably over further.

Kandidate, a ten-furlong Listed winner at Sandown on his previous start, seemed unsuited by the step up to his furthest trip to date. (op 3-1)

Honduras(SWI), formerly trained in Scandinavia, was well held on his British debut off the back of a year-long break, but did not run that badly.

Melrose Avenue(USA), last of six in the Great Voltigeur when last seen nearly a year previously, seemed to recover well enough to lead after stumbling coming out the stalls, but he stopped quickly when asked for an effort in the straight. It turned out he broke a blood-vessel. Official explanation: vet said colt bled from the nose (tchd 5-1 in places)

4097 OAK TREE STKS (GROUP 3) (F&M) — 7f

2:40 (2:41) (Class 1) 3-Y-O+

£28,390 (£10,760; £5,385; £2,685; £1,345; £675) **Stalls** High

Form / RPR

1111 **1** — **Red Evie (IRE)**[44] 2744 3-8-9 105 ... LDettori 9 — 102+
(M L W Bell) *hld up in rr: swtchd lft over 2f out: mde sustained run but edgd rt bef ld ins fnl f: readily* **15/8**[1]

-133 **2** *1/2* **Makderah (IRE)**[44] 2744 3-8-9 99 ... RHills 1 — 100
(M P Tregoning) *lw: trckd ldr: rdn to ld 1f out: nt qckn and hdd ins fnl f* **10/3**[2]

22-2 **3** *1* **Cantabria**[104] 1130 3-8-9 103 ... RichardHughes 6 — 100+
(Sir Michael Stoute) *trckd ldrs: swtchd lft appr fnl f rdn and nt qckn ins fnl f* **10/1**

-310 **4** *1* **Short Dance (USA)**[68] 2054 3-8-9 109 ... RyanMoore 4 — 95
(B W Hills) *led tl rdn and hdd 1f out: one pce after* **7/1**

6311 **5** *1 1/2* **Spinning Queen**[27] 3322 3-8-12 107 ... MichaelHills 5 — 94+
(B W Hills) *mid-div: hdwy 2f out: n.m.r and hmpd ins fnl f: nt rcvr* **7/2**[3]

1566 **6** *3/4* **Illuminise (IRE)**[27] 3316 3-8-9 88 ... RichardMullen 3 — 89
(E A L Dunlop) *in tch tl rdn 2f out: one pce after* **100/1**

5-20 **7** *1* **Nidhaal (IRE)**[21] 3499 3-8-9 100 ... MartinDwyer 7 — 86
(E A L Dunlop) *hld up in tch: wknd over 1f out* **16/1**

00-4 **8** *1 3/4* **She's My Outsider**[13] 3737 4-9-1 76 ... NCallan 2 — 82
(I A Wood) *hmpd sn after s but rcvrd to chse ldrs: wknd appr fnl f* **66/1**

4221 **9** *3 1/2* **Dark Missile**[23] 3414 3-8-9 89 ... LPKeniry 8 — 72
(A M Balding) *t.k.h: mid-div: wknd wl over 1f out* **20/1**

1m 24.94s (-3.10) **Going Correction** -0.225s/f (Firm)

WFA 3 from 4yo 6lb — **9** Ran SP% **114.8**

Speed ratings (Par 113):108,107,106,105,103 102,101,99,95

CSF £8.00 TOTE £2.70: £1.30, £1.50, £2.30; EX 9.60 Trifecta £50.00 Pool £2,099.84 - 29.78 winning units..

Owner Terry Neill **Bred** Dermot Cantillon And Forenaghts Stud **Trained** Newmarket, Suffolk

■ Stewards' Enquiry : L Dettori one-day ban: careless riding (Aug 15)

FOCUS

This looked a good, competitive fillies & mares' Group 3 beforehand. The pace was by no means frantic through the first couple of furlongs as the runners tried to organise themselves, but they were soon going a reasonable clip and there can be no excuses on that front. The third is the best guide to the level but the form is limitedby the sixth and eighth.

NOTEBOOK

Red Evie(IRE) has improved considerably this season and, upped to Group company for the first time, she followed up her success in the Listed Sandringham Handicap at Royal Ascot to complete a magnificent six-timer. She was still last two and a half furlongs out, but picked up in good style when switched toward the middle of the track and always looked like getting there, despite edging to her right with Dettori persisting in using his whip in his left hand. She may now go the Group 1 Matron Stakes, but she will find that a lot tougher and we should find out just how good she is. (op 9-4 tchd 5-2 in places)

Makderah(IRE) probably hit the front too soon when just over a length and a half behind Red Evie in the Sandringham Stakes at Royal Ascot on her previous start, and again the race could have panned out better for her. Drawn out wide in stall one, she found herself racing much closer than was probably ideal and could not resist the winner's late challenge - that one had been held up last. A very strong traveller but not such a great finisher, she promises to be see at her best when held up off a decent pace. She may be aimed at something like the Park Stakes or Hungerford Stakes. (op 7-2)

Cantabria, beaten a short-head by Nasheej in the Fred Darling on her only previous start this season, was a little short of room twice in the closing stages and can be rated a little bit better than the bare form. (op 8-1 tchd 11-1)

Short Dance(USA), the impressive winner of a York Listed race before disappointing in the Irish Guineas, ran better but could not reverse earlier Newbury form with Cantabria. She got warm beforehand and may be capable of better. (op 13-2 tchd 6-1)

Spinning Queen, a Listed winner at Warwick before following up in a Group 3 at Leopardstown, received a bump around a furlong out but was not unlucky. (tchd 10-3)

Illuminise(IRE), dropped in trip, had it all to do at the weights and ran as well as could have been expected.

Nidhaal(IRE) did not improve for the step up to seven furlongs.

Dark Missile Official explanation: trainer said filly was unsuited by the track

4098 TOTESPORT MILE (HERITAGE H'CAP) (FORMERLY KNOWN AS THE GOLDEN MILE) 1m

3:15 (3:16) (Class 2) 3-Y-O+

£93,480 (£27,990; £13,995; £7,005; £3,495; £1,755) **Stalls** High

Form	Pos	Btn	Horse	Jockey	RPR	Trainer / comment	SP
-125	**1**		**Spectait**[20] 3534 4-8-9 **95**	SebSanders 16	109	(Sir Mark Prescott) *lw: a in tch: rdn over 1f out: r.o to ld nr fin*	**9/2**[2]
1021	**2**	½	**Dunelight (IRE)**[7] 3889 3-8-4 **97** 3ex	(v) PhilipRobinson 15	110+	(C G Cox) *lw: a.p: led after 5f: rdn over 2f out: kpt on u.p: hdd nr fin*	**7/2**[1]
2300	**3**	1	**Prince Of Thebes (IRE)**[21] 3493 5-8-8 **94**	JimmyQuinn 11	105	(J Akehurst) *chsd ldrs: rdn over 2f out: kpt on fnl f*	**66/1**
-121	**4**	1 ¾	**Sir Gerard**[43] 2774 3-8-8 **101**	OscarUrbina 1	108+	(J R Fanshawe) *swtg: hld up: hdwy 2f out: r.o: nvr nrr*	**13/2**[3]
4200	**5**	1	**Red Spell (IRE)**[37] 2988 5-8-6 **92**	(p) RichardHughes 14	97	(R Hannon) *in tch: swtchd lft over 1f out: nt qckn ins fnl f*	**12/1**
0043	**6**	½	**Capable Guest (IRE)**[13] 3733 4-8-7 **93**	JohnEgan 12	99+	(M R Channon) *mid-div: n.m.r 2f out: swtchd lft over 1f out: nt qckn ins fnl f*	**12/1**
3530	**7**	½	**My Paris**[27] 3313 5-8-13 **99**	NCallan 4	101+	(K A Ryan) *trckd ldrs: rdn over 2f out: wknd ins fnl f*	**50/1**
2350	**8**	½	**Spirit Of France (IRE)**[13] 3733 4-8-8 **94**	RichardMullen 20	95	(Christian Wroe, UAE) *lw: trckd ldrs tl rdn and one pce appr fnl f*	**66/1**
50-0	**9**	½	**Wise Dennis**[104] 1129 4-8-13 **99**	AlanMunro 17	99	(A P Jarvis) *mid-div: nt clr run 2f out: nvr on terms after*	**20/1**
3400	**10**	½	**Kings Quay**[27] 3313 4-8-8 **94**	GrahamGibbons 7	93	(J J Quinn) *swtg: in tch: rdn 3f out: wknd appr fnl f*	**50/1**
5300	**11**	*nk*	**Shot To Fame (USA)**[3] 4029 7-8-4 **90**	AdrianTNicholls 13	88	(D Nicholls) *lw: led for 5f: rdn and wknd ent fnl f*	**25/1**
4215	**12**	*hd*	**Kelucia (IRE)**[13] 3733 5-8-1 **90**	NelsonDeSouza(3) 10	92+	(R M Beckett) *slowly away: hdwy whn nt clr run over 1f out: nt rcvr*	**25/1**
4144	**13**	1 ¼	**Nayyir**[3] 4025 8-9-10 **110**	LDettori 3	105	(G A Butler) *lw: hld up: nt clr run over 1f out and nvr on terms*	**9/1**
4-20	**14**	3	**Rohaani (USA)**[98] 1267 4-8-13 **99**	RHills 2	87	(Sir Michael Stoute) *lw: a in rr*	**18/1**
3050	**15**	3 ½	**Langford**[27] 3313 6-8-10 **96**	TPQueally 19	76	(M H Tompkins) *slowly away: in rr tl hdwy 1/2-way: wknd over 1f out*	**16/1**
0-55	**16**	1 ¾	**Eden Rock (IRE)**[43] 2776 5-8-8 **94**	RyanMoore 9	70	(Pat Eddery) *mid-div: rdn over 2f out: wkng whn hmpd 1f out*	**8/1**
0501	**17**	2 ½	**Paper Talk (USA)**[29] 3223 4-8-9 **95**	MichaelHills 8	65	(B W Hills) *a in rr*	**25/1**

1m 35.61s (-4.66) **Going Correction** -0.225s/f (Firm) course record
WFA 3 from 4yo+ 7lb **17** Ran SP% **124.6**
Speed ratings (Par 109):114,113,112,110,109 109,108,108,107,107 106,106,105,102,99 97,94
CSF £19.08 CT £945.76 TOTE £6.00: £2.00, £1.60, £9.00, £1.80; EX 24.80 Trifecta £3814.10 Part won. Pool £5,372.00 - 0.70 winning units..
Owner Edward S A Belcher **Bred** B Tait **Trained** Newmarket, Suffolk

FOCUS

A cracking renewal of this valuable mile handicap run in a decent time and the form looks solid, but the huge draw bias over this trip was evident once again with the double-figure stalls dominating. It also proved very difficult to make up ground from off the pace, despite the gallop appearing pretty strong throughout.

NOTEBOOK

Spectait ◆ had his All-Weather rating raised to 108 following his fifth in a Group 3 at Lingfield on his previous start, so he potentially had a fair amount in hand off a mark of 95 if able to run near that level of form back on turf. Well drawn in stall 16, Sanders always had him in a good position, if a touch wider than was ideal, and he travelled strongly throughout. When asked to go and reel in Dunelight in the last quarter, he looked like getting there from a little way out, but lugged to his left under pressure and carried his head a little awkwardly, presumably feeling the fast ground, which he was encountering for the first time. He looks well up to taking his place back in Pattern company, especially with the likelihood of him improving again when returned to easier ground. (tchd 5-1)

Dunelight(IRE) ◆, carrying a penalty for his success in a very decent handicap at Ascot just a week previously, was racing off just a 2lb higher mark and was 9lb lower than in future. Well drawn, he was soon in a good rhythm on the pace and had every chance; he was just unable to hold off the equally progressive and year-older Spectait. He is likely to find things harder from now on, but remains highly progressive. (op 4-1 tchd 9-2 in places)

Prince Of Thebes(IRE), due to be dropped 1lb, was always well positioned under a fine ride by Quinn, and kept on to the line to post a fantastic effort behind two highly-progressive sorts.

Sir Gerard, 10lb higher than when winning the Britannia Stakes, looked to face a near-impossible task from stall one, especially with Spectait and Dunelight drawn so favourably, and that is the way it proved. He did well to even grab fourth having had to be dropped right out the back early, and remains most progressive. It is probably just a matter of time before he is contesting Group races. (op 6-1 tchd 7-1 in places)

Red Spell(IRE), with cheekpieces replacing blinkers, had a fair draw and ran a respectable race. He has been running well on turf lately without managing to get his head in front and should come into his own when returned to sand. (op 14-1 tchd 16-1 in a place)

Capable Guest(IRE) seemed to run his race and, although slightly short of room around two furlongs out, he did not look unlucky.

My Paris ◆ would have had to use a fair amount of energy up to adopt a handy position from stall four and is clearly in good form.

Spirit Of France(IRE) had the best draw of all and ran with credit.

Wise Dennis ◆, having just his second start of the season, would probably have finished quite a bit closer with a clear run and could be one to keep an eye on.

Kelucia(IRE) met with trouble in running and is quite a bit better than the bare form.

Nayyir, fourth in the Lennox Stakes three days earlier, never looked like getting involved. (op 10-1 tchd 11-1 in places)

Rohaani(USA) ◆, last of ten in the Group 3 Gordon Richards Stakes when last seen 98 days previously, was caught wide almost throughout from stall two and is much better than the bare form. Things have not gone his way this season, but he can show what he is capable of when things fall right for him, probably when returned to a galloping track. (op 16-1 tchd 20-1)

Eden Rock(IRE), fifth in the Buckingham Palace Stakes on his previous start, looked beaten when finding trouble and was a major disappointment. (op 9-1)

4099 STERLING INSURANCE RICHMOND STKS (GROUP 2) (C&G) 6f

3:50 (3:50) (Class 1) 2-Y-O

£39,746 (£15,064; £7,539; £3,759; £1,883; £945) **Stalls** Low

Form	Pos	Btn	Horse	Jockey	RPR	Trainer / comment	SP
1	**1**		**Hamoody (USA)**[22] 3445 2-9-0	AlanMunro 6	104	(P W Chapple-Hyam) *lw: t.k.h: alwys in tch: wnt 2nd over 2f out: rdn and kpt on to ld nr fin*	**5/6**[1]
5411	**2**	*hd*	**Bodes Galaxy (IRE)**[24] 3372 2-9-0 93	MickyFenton 7	103	(N P Littmoden) *led: hrd rdn appr fnl f: hdd nr fin*	**12/1**
4113	**3**	1 ¼	**Dubai's Touch**[22] 3442 2-9-0 100	JoeFanning 3	100	(M Johnston) *trckd ldrs: rdn 2f out: nt qckn ins fnl f*	**9/2**[2]
6440	**4**	¾	**La Neige**[13] 3734 2-9-0 98	TonyCulhane 2	97	(M R Channon) *towards rr: rdn and mde sme late hdwy*	**33/1**
15	**5**	1 ½	**Danebury Hill**[22] 3442 2-9-0	LDettori 1	93	(B J Meehan) *trckd ldr to over 2f out: sn rdn: wknd ins fnl f*	**7/1**[3]
1262	**6**	¾	**Mood Music**[28] 3252 2-9-0 100	RichardMullen 4	91	(E J O'Neill) *hld up: rdn over 1f out: no ex fnl f*	**9/1**
5145	**7**	4	**Dazed And Amazed**[3] 4026 2-9-0 100	RichardHughes 5	79	(R Hannon) *in tch on outside tl wknd over 1f out*	**8/1**

1m 10.68s (-2.17) **Going Correction** -0.225s/f (Firm) **7** Ran SP% **117.0**
Speed ratings (Par 106):105,104,103,102,100 99,93
CSF £13.37 TOTE £2.00: £1.40, £4.40; EX 11.60.
Owner Saleh Al Homaizi & Imad Al Sagar **Bred** Ragged Mountain Farm **Trained** Newmarket, Suffolk

FOCUS

The looked like a weak renewal of the Richmond Stakes, although Hamoody appears capable of much better than he was able to show. He was the only one able to get to the positively-ridden Bodes Galaxy, despite having raced very keenly with no cover for most of the way. The winning time was about par for a race like this in the conditions and the third and fourth were close to their marks.

NOTEBOOK

Hamoody(USA) ◆, the impressive winner of a decent Class 2 novice event on his debut at Newmarket's July course, is held in very high regard and was strongly supported to follow up in this much higher grade. He did not make things easy for himself, racing very keenly with little cover towards the outside, but had just enough in reserve to reel in the front-running Bodes Galaxy. The bare form does not look anything special, but he did well to get up and win considering how the race panned out, especially as the eventual runner-up enjoyed the run of things against the possibly favoured near-side rail, and his connections are adamant he can do better when covered up early on. He will now be aimed at the Dewhurst, but really will be required to settle in the early stages if he is to see out seven furlongs at Newmarket, whereas the Middle Park looks made for him. (op 4-5 tchd 10-11 and evens in places)

Bodes Galaxy(IRE), the winner of a Bath maiden before following up in good style off an estimated handicap mark of 81 in a Pontefract nursery on his latest start, soon grabbed the near-side rail under a very enterprising ride, leading at a decent pace and seemingly in a good rhythm, and very nearly clung on. A tough sort, this was a fine effort and he is clearly progressing fast, but he does look a touch flattered to get so close to Hamoody, as that one raced keenly with no cover for much of the way. Still, he was nicely clear of the remainder and deserves to keep taking his chance in similar company, particularly when the emphasis is on speed.

Dubai's Touch, third in the July Stakes on his previous start, ran another respectable race without ever really looking likely to pick up and pose a serious threat. He may be worth a try over seven furlongs. (op 7-1)

La Neige, returned to six furlongs, kept on from the back to pass beaten horses and looks flattered. He may find things easier abroad.

Danebury Hill, who got a little warm beforehand, could not reverse July Stakes form with Dubai's Touch (although he did manage to with Dazed And Amazed) and could be considered disappointing. He got a lovely lead off Bodes Galaxy but found little when let down.

Mood Music, runner-up in a five-furlong Listed race at Sandown on his previous start, was well held upped in trip and grade. (op 11-1)

Dazed And Amazed, fifth in the Molecomb just three days earlier, soon weakened when switched to the outside and probably found this coming too soon.

4100 SCOTTISH EQUITABLE/JOCKEYS ASSOCIATION OF GREAT BRITAIN NURSERY STKS (H'CAP) 7f

4:25 (4:25) (Class 3) 2-Y-O **£11,010** (£3,275; £1,637; £817) **Stalls** High

Form	Pos	Btn	Horse	Jockey	RPR	Trainer / comment	SP
1411	**1**		**Just Dust**[17] 3619 2-7-13 **73**	MarcHalford(5) 4	82	(D R C Elsworth) *mde all: shkn up 2f out: sn in command*	**10/1**
0511	**2**	1 ½	**Eddie Jock (IRE)**[21] 3496 2-9-7 **90**	LDettori 2	95	(M L W Bell) *lw: hld up: hdwy and swtchd lft 2f out: chsd wnr appr fnl f but no imp ins*	**3/1**[1]
332	**3**	2 ½	**Follow The Flag (IRE)**[21] 3485 2-8-0 **72**	JamesDoyle(3) 10	71	(N P Littmoden) *in tch on ins: rdn 1/2-way: kpt on fnl f but no ch w first 2*	**7/1**
2212	**4**	6	**Tencendur (IRE)**[9] 3834 2-8-7 **76**	AdrianTNicholls 9	59	(D Nicholls) *chsd wnr for 3f: wknd over 1f out*	**14/1**
033	**5**	¾	**Global Guest**[35] 3031 2-8-7 **76**	TonyCulhane 8	57	(M R Channon) *s.i.s: stl detchd last 3f out, styd on fnl 2f: nvr on terms*	**33/1**
0613	**6**	¾	**Disco Dan**[7] 3902 2-8-8 **77**	DaneO'Neill 5	56	(D M Simcock) *bhd and nvr on terms*	**13/2**
043	**7**	5	**Star Strider**[25] 3344 2-8-3 **72**	MartinDwyer 7	38	(A M Balding) *t.k.h: mid-div: hdwy and n.c.r. over 2f out to over 1f out: eased when no ch*	**5/1**[3]
5636	**8**	3 ½	**Atheneum (IRE)**[17] 3623 2-8-6 **75**	JoeFanning 6	32	(M Johnston) *in tch tl wknd over 2f out*	**8/1**
61	**9**	3	**Soviet Palace (IRE)**[60] 2287 2-9-6 **89**	NCallan 1	38	(K A Ryan) *lw: t.k.h: prom tl wknd wl over 1f out*	**4/1**[2]

1m 25.29s (-2.75) **Going Correction** -0.225s/f (Firm) **9** Ran SP% **117.3**
Speed ratings (Par 98):106,104,101,94,93 92,87,83,79
CSF £40.84 CT £231.53 TOTE £14.80: £2.60, £1.70, £2.70; EX 49.20 Trifecta £187.10 Pool £,1871.46 - 7.10 winning units..

Owner Matthew Green **Bred** T O C S Ltd And W G M Turner **Trained** Newmarket, Suffolk

FOCUS

Not an easy race to work out, but only two of the nine-strong field were rated over 80, suggesting it was probably just an ordinary nursery for the grade. A strong pace soon put a few of these in their place and the time was decent, suggesting the form is solid.

NOTEBOOK

Just Dust did not look anything special when winning a seller and most recently two claimers for Bill Turner, but he had his optimum conditions on his debut for David Elsworth and, able to sneak into this valuable nursery off a light weight, he ran out a ready winner. Racing without the usual cheekpieces, he ensured this was a good test right from the start and maintained his effort all the way to the line. The £10,000 his new connections laid out to claim has been retrieved in one hit, so anything from now on can be considered a bonus, but there could well be more to come in similar events when he gets his conditions. (op 20-1 tchd 22-1)

Eddie Jock(IRE), an estimated 7lb higher than when winning a similar event on Newmarket's July course on his previous start, stayed on well for second but could not get to the enterprisingly-ridden winner. (op 2-1 tchd 10-3 in places and 7-2 in a place)

Follow The Flag(IRE), upped in trip on his nursery debut following three modest runs in maiden company, never looked totally at ease and just kept on at the one pace. He may prefer slightly easier ground. (tchd 8-1)

Tencendur(IRE) is a Mark Johnston cast-off, and not many of them progress. (op 11-1)

Global Guest stayed on from a mile off the pace to take fifth and was never seen with a chance. A more galloping, or stiffer track should suit better and he may also benefit from a bit of cut in the ground.

Disco Dan was below the form he showed when third in a small-field nursery at Newmarket on his previous start and was disappointing. (op 7-1 tchd 15-2 in a place)

Star Strider ◆, upped in trip on his nursery debut following three modest runs over five furlongs at Bath, is much better than the bare form as he was denied a clear run when trying to make his challenge, and his rider soon accepted the situation. He can do better. (op 6-1 tchd 13-2)

Soviet Palace(IRE) ran nowhere near the form he showed when winning a Leicester maiden on his previous start. (tchd 7-2)

4101 STEWARDS' SPRINT STKS (H'CAP) 6f

5:00 (5:01) (Class 2) 3-Y-0+

£12,464 (£3,732; £1,866; £934; £466; £234) **Stalls** Low

Form					RPR
3140	1		**Fantasy Believer**[6] 3956 8-9-2 **83** 3ex	JimmyFortune 12	97
			(J J Quinn) *w.w on stands' side: hdwy over 1f out: rdn and r.o strly to ld ins fnl f: won gng away*	9/1[3]	
4025	2	1 ½	**Idle Power (IRE)**[21] 3486 8-9-6 **90**	AmirQuinn(3) 21	100
			(J R Boyle) *lw: racd far side: hld up in tch: r.o strly fnl f to go 2nd cl home: 1st of 12 in grp*	12/1	
0002	3	hd	**Smokin Beau**[1] 4085 9-8-12 **79**	JoeFanning 15	88
			(D Nicholls) *lw: a.p far side: led over 2f out tl ins fnl f*	11/1	
2302	4	½	**Circuit Dancer (IRE)**[7] 3904 6-8-6 **73**	AdrianTNicholls 25	81
			(D Nicholls) *racd far side: swtchd lft 2f out: r.o fnl f*	5/1[2]	
6152	5	hd	**Harry Up**[18] 3585 5-9-1 **82**	NCallan 7	89
			(K A Ryan) *lw: led stands side tl hdd and no ex ins fnl f*	16/1	
4260	6	shd	**Handsome Cross (IRE)**[5] 3972 5-9-4 **85**	SilvestreDeSousa 22	92
			(D Nicholls) *prom far side tl no ex ins fnl f*	14/1	
1123	7	hd	**Blue Tomato**[6] 3956 5-9-4 **85** 3ex	LDettori 11	91
			(J M Bradley) *lw: towards rr stands' side: hdwy 2f out: nt qckn ins fnl f*	9/2[1]	
0402	8	hd	**High Ridge**[5] 3986 7-8-8 **75**	(p) TonyCulhane 23	81+
			(J M Bradley) *mid-div far side: kpt on fnl f*	20/1	
2003	9	½	**Golden Dixie (USA)**[5] 3972 7-9-10 **91**	AdrianMcCarthy 6	95
			(R A Harris) *prom stands' side tl nt qckn fnl ff*	20/1	
0000	10	½	**Traytonic**[21] 3493 5-8-11 **85**	VictoriaBehan(7) 27	88+
			(D Nicholls) *in rr far side tl nt clr run over 2f out: swtchd lft: r.o wl fnl f*	20/1	
0510	11	nk	**Gallantry**[6] 3926 4-9-4 **85** 3ex	JimmyQuinn 9	87
			(D W Barker) *lw: racd stands' side: rdn over 2f out: one pce fnl f*	10/1	
0362	12	1	**Chinalea (IRE)**[9] 3855 4-8-6 **73**	(p) LPKeniry 24	72
			(C G Cox) *swtg: led far side gp for over 2f: wknd over 1f out*	25/1	
3142	13	shd	**Caribbean Coral**[14] 3715 7-9-2 **83** 3ex	(p) GrahamGibbons 1	81
			(J J Quinn) *hld up stands' side: sme hdwy over 1f out: nvr nr to chal*	14/1	
54	14	hd	**First Order**[20] 3550 5-9-6 **87**	JohnEgan 18	85
			(Ernst Oertel) *nvr bttr than mid-div on far side*	20/1	
0345	15	nk	**Summer Recluse (USA)**[22] 3434 7-8-1 **68** ow1	RoystonFfrench 16	65
			(J M Bradley) *racd far side: kpt on fnl f but nvr nr to chal*	100/1	
2420	16	shd	**Nautical**[1] 4085 8-8-9 **79**	(p) JamesDoyle(3) 8	76
			(A W Carroll) *racd stands' side: slowly away: a bhd*	16/1	
4030	17	½	**Mine Behind**[6] 3928 6-8-12 **86**	KylieManser(7) 14	81
			(J R Best) *racd stands' side: slowly away: hdwy 2f out: wknd fnl f*	33/1	
0150	18	½	**Prince Cyrano**[7] 3904 7-8-6 **73**	TPQueally 10	67
			(W J Musson) *chsd ldrs stands' side for 4f*	33/1	
0205	19	1 ¼	**Plateau**[5] 3972 7-8-11 **78**	FrancisFerris 17	68
			(D Nicholls) *racd far side in tch tl wknd over 1f out*	33/1	
0053	20	nk	**High Reach**[13] 3744 6-9-9 **90**	MartinDwyer 20	79
			(W R Muir) *racd far side: rdn and wknd over 1f out*	14/1	
0040	21	2	**Pachello (IRE)**[15] 3682 4-8-8 **75**	AlanMunro 3	58
			(J M Bradley) *chsd ldrs stands' side tl rdn and wknd sn after 1/2-way*	66/1	
0006	22	1 ¼	**Goodwood Spirit**[15] 3679 4-8-13 **80**	(p) DaneO'Neill 26	59
			(J M Bradley) *hld up on far side: bhd fnl 2f*	66/1	
0005	23	¾	**Hypnotic**[20] 3523 4-8-0 **70** ow3	StephaneBreux(3) 13	47
			(D Nicholls) *racd far side in mid-div: wknd over 1f out*	66/1	
4430	24	5	**Kempsey**[46] 2711 4-7-11 **69** ow2	(v) MarcHalford(5) 4	31
			(J J Bridger) *a bhd on stands' side*	100/1	

69.74 secs (-3.11) **Going Correction** -0.225s/f (Firm) **24** Ran SP% **139.9**

Speed ratings (Par 109):111,109,108,108,107 107,107,107,106,105 105,104,103,103,103 103,102,101,100,99 97,95,94,87

CSF £109.32 CT £1267.88 TOTE £13.40: £3.10, £3.90, £3.40, £1.80; EX 158.50 Trifecta £1194.40 Pool £2,859.96 - 1.70 winning units..

Owner The Fantasy Fellowship B **Bred** John Khan **Trained** Settrington, N Yorks

FOCUS

A very satisfactory renewal of the Stewards' Cup consolation race - the field split into two groups, with the 12 drawn nearest to the stands' rail racing stands' side, and remainder going far side but, the winner apart, there was next to nothing separating either side at the line. The form looks solid and reliable with the time good and the majority of the first eight close to form.

NOTEBOOK

Fantasy Believer returned to his very best having run slightly below form at York on his previous start, taking advantage of racing off a mark 6lb lower than when third in the Stewards' Cup itself last year. The Handicapper will hit him hard for this, but he will always be worthy of respect when granted these sort of conditions. He may well be aimed at the Ayr Gold Cup. (op 8-1 tchd 10-1)

Idle Power(IRE) ran a blinder to win his race on the far side of the track, especially considering he was 6lb higher than when successful in this race last year and the ground was probably a little faster than he cares for these days. (op 14-1)

Smokin Beau ◆, second over five furlongs here the previous day, ran another fine race in defeat, taking second on the far side. He looks well up to finding a race or two for his current connections. (op 9-1 tchd 12-1)

Circuit Dancer(IRE) had to be switched with run and kept on well to post a very creditable effort in defeat. (op 15-2 tchd 8-1)

Harry Up ensured they went a good clip on the stands' side and can have few excuses. (op 25-1 tchd 33-1)

Handsome Cross(IRE) ran well considering he seems better over the minimum trip at the moment. (op 16-1)

Blue Tomato had conditions in his favour, but never quite looked like getting there having been well off the pace on the stands' side. (op 4-1 tchd 5-1 in places)

Traytonic finished well having met with some trouble.

Nautical Official explanation: vet said gelding was struck into in front

4102 RACINGUK.TV STKS (H'CAP) 5f

5:35 (5:36) (Class 3) (0-95,89) 3-Y-0

£9,971 (£2,985; £1,492; £747; £372; £187) **Stalls** Low

Form					RPR
-115	1		**Terentia**[48] 2639 3-9-6 **88**	JimmyFortune 14	99
			(E S McMahon) *a prom on outside: led 1f out: drvn out*	14/1	
2-11	2	nk	**Buachaill Dona (IRE)**[16] 3636 3-9-4 **86**	AdrianTNicholls 9	102+
			(D Nicholls) *lw: s.i.s and bumped start: rr tl hdwy and n.m.r over 2f out to over 1f out: swtchd rt and r.o strly ins fnl f: unlucky*	2/1[1]	
3121	3	hd	**Loch Verdi**[36] 3000 3-9-1 **83**	MartinDwyer 4	92
			(A M Balding) *led for 1f: styd prom: rdn 2f out: kpt on fnl f*	11/4[2]	
2140	4	¾	**Leopoldine**[21] 3499 3-9-6 **88**	LDettori 5	94
			(H Morrison) *chsd ldrs early: outpcd 1/2-way: swtchd rt over 1f out: styd on fnl f*	8/1	
5440	5	shd	**Total Impact**[23] 3414 3-9-5 **87**	EddieAhern 2	93
			(C A Cyzer) *a abt same pl but styd on fnl f*	9/1	
1050	6	1	**Devine Dancer**[22] 3449 3-8-7 **75**	DaneO'Neill 10	77
			(H Candy) *prom on outside tl wknd ins fnl f*	16/1	
3314	7	½	**Azygous**[13] 3744 3-8-13 **84**	JamesDoyle(3) 11	85
			(J Akehurst) *t.k.h: chsd ldrs tl wknd fnl f*	16/1	
1060	8	½	**Glenviews Youngone (IRE)**[18] 3585 3-9-1 **83**	GrahamGibbons 8	82+
			(Peter Grayson) *hmpd s: in rr: kpt on fnl f: nvr nrr*	50/1	
1-10	9	1	**Rare Breed**[48] 2651 3-9-4 **86**	TPQueally 13	81
			(Mrs L Stubbs) *led after 1f: hdd 1f out: wknd ins fnl f*	50/1	
1510	10	shd	**Glasshoughton**[21] 3475 3-8-13 **81**	PhillipMakin 1	76
			(M Dods) *prom early: bhd fnl 2f*	16/1	
0050	11	1 ¾	**Triskaidekaphobia**[13] 3744 3-8-7 **75**	PaulFitzsimons 12	64
			(Miss J R Tooth) *chsd ldrs tl wknd over 1f out*	33/1	
3243	12	2	**Matuza (IRE)**[11] 3795 3-8-12 **80**	(b[1]) TonyCulhane 6	61
			(W R Muir) *hmpd s but sn mid-div: wknd over 1f out*	6/1[3]	

57.52 secs (-1.53) **Going Correction** -0.225s/f (Firm) **12** Ran SP% **126.6**

Speed ratings (Par 104):103,102,102,101,100 99,98,97,96,95 93,89

CSF £44.76 CT £110.04 TOTE £19.30: £4.00, £1.50, £1.50; EX 73.50 Trifecta £97.90 Pool £2,206.30 - 16.00 winning units. Place 6 £27.30, Place 5 £18.87..

Owner Dr Hugh Jones **Bred** Mrs F S Williams **Trained** Hopwas, Staffs

■ Stewards' Enquiry : Adrian T Nicholls one-day ban: careless riding (Aug 15).

FOCUS

A decent sprint handicap in which they all raced towards the near side of the track and the form looks solid underpinned by the fifth and sixth.

NOTEBOOK

Terentia ◆ was not at her best when racing on fast ground for the first time at Leicester on her previous start, but she handled quick conditions just fine this time and gamely held off the unlucky in-running Buachaill Dona. She is most progressive and it may be unwise to assume the runner-up would definitely have beaten her with a clear run. She is very much one to keep on the right side of. (tchd 16-1)

Buachaill Dona(IRE) ◆, the winner of a maiden at Thirsk and a handicap at Catterick off a mark 79 so far this season, can probably be considered unlucky not to have completed the hat-trick. Bumped at the start, he dropped right out the back in the early stages, and was then denied a clear run when beginning to pick up. He finally got in the clear inside the final furlong, and looked as if he would get up near the line, but he could not go by the eventual winner. There are two ways to look at this; either he was very unlucky, or he got the in the clear in enough time but was just held off by a better horse on the day. Time will tell, but whatever the case he remains lightly raced and capable of rating quite a bit higher. (op 9-4 tchd 5-2)

Loch Verdi ◆, 7lb higher than when winning at Hamilton on her previous start, ran a good race tight against the near-side rail but did not look totally happy, possibly feeling the fast ground, despite having won twice before under similar conditions. She could be one to have on your side when there is a bit of give underfoot. (op 9-4 tchd 3-1 in places)

Leopoldine looked on a stiff mark for her handicap debut, but this was a fine effort in defeat. (op 10-1)

Total Impact ran a good race behind some progressive sprinters. (op 12-1 tchd 14-1)

Matuza(IRE) did not look an obvious candidate for blinkers and was well beaten. (op 7-1 tchd 15-2)

T/Jkpt: Not won. T/Plt: £29.60 to a £1 stake. Pool: £220,007.75. 5,412.25 winning tickets. T/Qpdt: £13.30 to a £1 stake. Pool: £8,655.10. 481.20 winning tickets. JS

3976

NEWMARKET (JULY) (R-H)

Friday, August 4

OFFICIAL GOING: Good to firm (good in places)

Wind: Almost nil Weather: Cloudy with sunny spells

4103 NEWMARKET NIGHTS MEDIAN AUCTION MAIDEN STKS 7f

5:50 (5:53) (Class 5) 2-Y-0 **£3,886** (£1,156; £577; £288) **Stalls** High

Form					RPR
	1		**Hanging On** 2-8-12	StephenCarson 5	74+
			(W R Swinburn) *wlike: scope: s.i.s: hld up: swtchd lft and hdwy over 1f out: rdn to ld wl ins fnl f: r.o*	25/1	
23	2	¾	**Cape Schanck**[24] 3385 2-9-3	RobertHavlin 4	77
			(Jane Chapple-Hyam) *chsd ldrs: rdn to ld and edgd rt over 1f out: hdd wl ins fnl f*	9/2[2]	
	3	shd	**Lady Alize (USA)** 2-8-12	(t) FJohansson 8	72
			(R A Kvisla) *leggy: scope: hld up: hdwy over 1f out: rdn and ev ch ins fnl f: styd on*	33/1	
	4	1 ½	**View From The Top** 2-9-3	SebSanders 13	73
			(W J Knight) *leggy: unf: hld up intch: rdn over 1f out: r.o*	16/1	
	5	shd	**Benny The Bat** 2-9-3	TedDurcan 6	73+
			(H Morrison) *neat: led: hdd over 5f out: remained handy: rdn 1/2-way: hung lft and hmpd over 1f out: styd on*	25/1	

The Form Book, Raceform Ltd, Compton, RG20 6NL

6 shd **Rabbit Fighter (IRE)** 2-9-3 .... FergusSweeney 10 72
(P A Blockley) *w'like: scope: b.bkwd: w ldrs: rdn and ev ch over 1f out: no ex wl ins fnl f* **20/1**

0 7 nk **Bold Abbott (USA)**[14] 3701 2-9-0 .... AdamKirby(3) 9 72
(Mrs A J Perrett) *trckd ldrs: rdn over 1f out: no ex ins fnl f* **9/1**

8 ½ **Gold Option** 2-9-3 .... RichardHughes 7 70
(J H M Gosden) *chsd ldrs: led over 5f out: hdd over 4f out: rdn over 1f out: styd on same pce* **5/4**[1]

00 9 ½ **Safari Sundowner (IRE)**[39] 2930 2-9-3 .... RichardSmith 12 69
(P Winkworth) *lw: w ldrs: led over 4f out: rdn and hdd over 1f out: wknd ins fnl f* **33/1**

10 1 **Musical Award (IRE)** 2-9-3 .... RichardMullen 15 66
(M G Quinlan) *leggy: unf: prom over 5f* **20/1**

11 8 **Berkeley Castle (USA)** 2-9-3 .... ShaneKelly 3 46
(Sir Michael Stoute) *w'like: scope: b.bkwd: chsd ldrs: lost pl over 5f out: wknd over 1f out* **15/2**[3]

12 ½ **Into Action** 2-9-3 .... PatDobbs 11 44
(R Hannon) *cmpt: scope: lw: s.i.s: hld up: rdn and wknd 2f out* **12/1**

13 nk **Speedfit World** 2-9-3 .... JDSmith 2 44
(G G Margarson) *w'like: leggy: s.i.s: wknd 2f out* **25/1**

0 14 12 **Diverse Forecast (IRE)**[34] 3083 2-9-3 .... MickyFenton 1 12
(Mrs P Sly) *swvd lft s: hdwy 4f out: rdn and wknd over 2f out* **50/1**

1m 26.88s (0.10) **Going Correction** -0.15s/f (Firm) **14 Ran SP% 126.9**
Speed ratings (Par 94):93,92,92,90,90 90,89,89,88,87 78,77,77,63
CSF £130.78 TOTE £23.30: £5.90, £1.80, £8.90; EX 187.50.
Owner Mrs P W Harris **Bred** Pendley Farm **Trained** Aldbury, Herts
■ Stewards' Enquiry : Stephen Carson one-day ban: careless riding (August 15)

FOCUS
A drying day meant the going description was changed just before racing from 'Good' to 'Good to firm, Good in places'. The jockeys, returning from the opener, concurred with one reporting 'lovely ground'. The form is fair with the runner-up the best guide.

NOTEBOOK
Hanging On, a half-brother to six winners including Barolo, showed a good turn of foot to cut through the field late on after being held up towards the rear through the opening strides. As could be expected from a debutant, there were hints of greenness - she missed the break - and it would be no surprise if her handler drew significant improvement from her over the rest of the season.
Cape Schanck once again made the frame after placed efforts on the All-Weather on his only other two starts, but this looked to represent a step up on what he had previously achieved. He is now eligible for nurseries where he should be capable of winning a race. (tchd 4-1)
Lady Alize(USA), who fetched 160,000gns as a two-year-old, is a half-sister to six winners. She shaped well enough on her debut and can be expected to build on this.
View From The Top ◆, a half-brother to four winners at up to 12 furlongs, stayed on eyecatchingly and was doing all his best work in the latter stages. This run suggested that staying a mile will not present a problem later in the season.
Benny The Bat ◆, a half-brother to two winners at up to 12 furlongs, holds a Derby entry and comes from a stable whose juveniles can often find a fair amount of improvement as they grow in terms of experience. He certainly caught the eye with a nice introduction as he stuck on in good style after he appeared to be temporarily outpaced.
Gold Option, a half-brother to six winners including Skipping and Innocent Air, has a Royal Lodge entry and was sent off a well-backed favourite for his debut, but the writing was on the wall over a furlong out and he failed to live up to market expectations. (op 6-4 tchd 13-8 and 7-4 in places)

4104 SEE MORE ON RACING UK FILLIES' H'CAP 1m 4f
6:20 (6:25) (Class 5) (0-70,70) 4-Y-0+ £3,886 (£1,156; £577; £288) Stalls Centre

Form RPR

1213 1 **Celtique**[7] 3900 4-9-5 68 .... RyanMoore 4 77
(M Wigham) *lw: hld up: hdwy over 3f out: rdn to ld over 1f out: r.o* **5/2**[1]

4042 2 2½ **Ardea Brave (IRE)**[50] 2577 4-8-11 60 ....(p) OscarUrbina 7 65
(M Botti) *chsd ldrs: led 10f out: rdn and hdd over 1f out: styd on same pce* **8/1**

4432 3 ¾ **Maystock**[13] 3743 6-9-7 70 .... TedDurcan 9 74
(B G Powell) *lw: chsd ldrs: rdn over 3f out: styd on same pce fnl f* **9/2**[2]

2052 4 1¾ **Star Rising**[18] 3597 4-8-2 51 .... TPO'Shea 10 52
(W J Musson) *hld up: hdwy over 3f out: rdn and edgd lft over 1f out: styng on same pce whn swtchd rt ins fnl f* **10/1**

0050 5 1 **Perfectionist**[4] 3998 4-7-9 51 oh8 ....(p) KirstyMilczarek(7) 12 50
(Mrs C A Dunnett) *hld up: hung lft and hdwy over 2f out: sn rdn and swvd rt: hung lft ins fnl f: nt trble ldrs* **66/1**

0-05 6 3 **Authenticate**[12] 3762 4-8-11 60 .... RichardMullen 1 55
(E J O'Neill) *prom: chsd ldr over 5f out: rdn and hung lft over 1f out: sn wknd* **20/1**

6034 7 2½ **So Elegant (IRE)**[9] 3836 4-8-3 52 oh1 ow1 .... RichardSmith 6 43
(J Jay) *hld up: nvr trbld ldrs* **50/1**

1145 8 1¾ **Another Con (IRE)**[17] 3615 5-7-9 51 oh2 .... ManavNem(7) 13 39
(P A Blockley) *hld up: hdwy over 4f out: wknd 2f out* **12/1**

/00- 9 nk **Dalriath**[14] 3691 7-7-13 51 oh21 .... JohnMcAuley(3) 14 38
(M C Chapman) *s.i.s: hld up: rdn over 3f out: n.d* **100/1**

0423 10 3½ **Bowled Out (GER)**[15] 3686 4-9-0 63 .... SebSanders 2 45
(P J McBride) *prom: rdn over 2f out: wknd over 1f out* **8/1**

1212 11 8 **Madhavi**[15] 3666 4-9-4 67 .... RichardHughes 3 36
(R Hannon) *lw: led: hdd 10f out: chsd ldrs tl wknd over 1f out* **7/1**[3]

2620 12 7 **Plain Champagne (IRE)**[17] 3616 4-8-5 54 .... RichardThomas 11 12
(Dr J R J Naylor) *s.i.s: hld up: hdwy over 4f out: wknd over 2f out* **20/1**

45 13 9 **Mawazeen (IRE)**[52] 2533 5-8-10 62 .... AdamKirby(3) 5 5
(N I M Rossiter) *chsd ldrs 8f* **33/1**

3344 14 2½ **Sweet Medicine**[29] 3231 4-9-6 69 .... ShaneKelly 8 8
(P Howling) *hld up: rdn over 3f out: wknd and eased fnl 2f* **10/1**

2m 30.38s (-2.53) **Going Correction** -0.15s/f (Firm) **14 Ran SP% 124.3**
Speed ratings (Par 100):102,100,99,98,98 96,94,93,92,90 85,80,74,72
CSF £22.31 CT £90.78 TOTE £3.70: £1.70, £3.50, £2.20; EX 33.90.
Owner D T L Limited **Bred** Wretham Stud **Trained** Newmarket, Suffolk

FOCUS
A modest handicap and there did not appear to be much pace on early, but the form is straightforward and sound, although anchored by the fifth.
Madhavi Official explanation: jockey said filly had no more to give
Sweet Medicine Official explanation: jockey said filly hung right

4105 EUROPEAN BREEDERS FUND MAIDEN STKS 6f
6:50 (6:52) (Class 5) 2-Y-O £4,533 (£1,348; £674; £336) Stalls High

Form RPR

1 **Ready For Spring (USA)** 2-9-3 .... ShaneKelly 4 86+
(J Noseda) *gd sort: leggy: scope: s.i.s: sn chsng ldrs: shkn up over 1f out: led ins fnl f: r.o* **3/1**[2]

2 ¾ **Leopard King (USA)** 2-9-3 .... RyanMoore 9 84+
(Sir Michael Stoute) *w'like: scope: chsd ldrs: shkn up over 1f out: r.o* **7/2**[3]

3 1 **Shamhoota (USA)** 2-9-3 .... RHills 6 81+
(Sir Michael Stoute) *gd sort: chsd ldr: led over 2f out: sn rdn: hdd and unable qckn ins fnl f* **11/4**[1]

4 1½ **Curzon Prince (IRE)** 2-9-3 .... AlanMunro 2 76
(C F Wall) *w'like: scope: chsd ldrs: outpcd over 2f out: styd on ins fnl f* **16/1**

5 shd **Racing Times** 2-9-3 .... NCallan 3 76
(B J Meehan) *w'like: b.bkwd: chsd ldrs: rdn and ev ch whn hung lft over 1f out: wknd ins fnl f* **10/1**

6 ¾ **Rudry Dragon (IRE)** 2-9-3 .... TPO'Shea 5 74
(P A Blockley) *w'like: scope: lw: dwlt: sn in tch: outpcd 1/2-way: styd on ins fnl f* **28/1**

7 1¾ **Lap Of Honour (IRE)** 2-9-3 .... OscarUrbina 1 68
(N A Callaghan) *w'like: wnt lft s: hld up: nvr trbld ldrs* **8/1**

06 8 1¼ **Mighty Missouri (IRE)**[6] 3949 2-9-3 .... StephenCarson 7 65
(W R Swinburn) *led: rdn and hdd over 2f out: wknd over 1f out* **12/1**

9 7 **Torver** 2-8-12 .... MickyFenton 8 39
(Dr J D Scargill) *w'like: hld up: rdn 1/2-way: sn wknd* **16/1**

1m 13.59s (0.24) **Going Correction** -0.15s/f (Firm) **9 Ran SP% 117.0**
Speed ratings (Par 94):92,91,89,87,87 86,84,82,73
CSF £14.21 TOTE £4.50: £1.50, £1.60, £1.50; EX 13.00.
Owner B J McElroy **Bred** J J Pletcher **Trained** Newmarket, Suffolk

FOCUS
Only one of these had seen the race-track prior to this, but on paper the race contained some smart-looking prospects from top yards. The form is difficult to assess and could rate higher.

NOTEBOOK
Ready For Spring(USA) ◆, a brother to one and half-brother to another winner on turf in the US, missed the break but still managed to triumph and he will have learnt plenty from this to stand him in good stead for future engagements. He really did quicken up nicely and it would be no surprise if he proved good enough to make his mark on grander stages. (op 4-1)
Leopard King(USA) ◆, $400,000 colt out of a smart multiple winner in the US, ran a very promising race in second. A Middle Park Stakes entry, he ran on with purpose in the final furlong and a step up to seven furlongs may see him in an even better light. A maiden success looks a formality. (op 9-2)
Shamhoota(USA) ◆, like his stable companion the runner-up a $400,000 purchase and Middle Park entry, is out of a winning half-sister to a smart multiple winner in the US. He showed plenty of ability on this debut and should find an opportunity before long. (op 2-1 tchd 10-3)
Curzon Prince(IRE), a half-brother to five winners in the US, did a lot right here and should build on this.
Racing Times ◆, a half-brother to three winners including Il Castagno, looked very much in need of the experience and will benefit a good deal from this. (tchd 11-1)
Rudry Dragon(IRE), a half-brother to the smart Jazz Princess, missed the break and will doubtless know more next time. (op 33-1)

4106 HUGO AND THE HUGUENOTES H'CAP 6f
7:25 (7:25) (Class 3) (0-90,88) 3-Y-0+ £8,096 (£2,408; £1,203; £601) Stalls High

Form RPR

3510 1 **Guildenstern (IRE)**[29] 3217 4-9-2 77 ....(t) RyanMoore 10 85
(H Morrison) *lw: chsd ldrs: led over 1f out: rdn out* **9/2**[3]

0240 2 ¾ **Romany Nights (IRE)**[7] 3904 6-9-9 84 ....(b) RichardHughes 8 90
(Miss Gay Kelleway) *a.p: rdn over 1f out: edgd rt ins fnl f: r.o* **8/1**

2312 3 nk **Burning Incense (IRE)**[27] 3296 3-9-8 87 .... SebSanders 6 92+
(R Charlton) *lw: hld up: plld hrd: swtchd lft and hdwy over 1f out: sn rdn: kpt on* **10/3**[2]

5000 4 1 **Hidden Dragon (USA)**[34] 3077 7-9-10 85 .... NCallan 12 87
(J Pearce) *hld up: racd keenly: hdwy and swtchd rt over 1f out: sn rdn: styng on same pce whn n.m.r wl ins fnl f* **18/1**

6413 5 shd **Who's Winning (IRE)**[9] 3855 5-8-7 71 .... RichardKingscote(3) 7 73
(B G Powell) *led over 4f: no ex wl ins fnl f* **7/1**

0200 6 2½ **Goodenough Mover**[21] 3486 10-9-8 83 .... RobertHavlin 5 77
(Andrew Turnell) *w ldr: rdn over 1f out: no ex fnl f* **33/1**

0064 7 1¾ **Swinbrook (USA)**[21] 3493 5-9-13 88 ....(v) AlanMunro 4 77
(J A R Toller) *lw: chsd ldrs: rdn whn hmpd over 1f out: wknd ins fnl f* **11/4**[1]

0004 8 nk **Lord Mayor**[15] 3692 5-9-7 82 .... TedDurcan 9 70
(R M H Cowell) *s.i.s: hld up: rdn over 1f out: n.d* **25/1**

0005 9 1 **Figaro Flyer (IRE)**[17] 3625 3-9-3 82 .... ShaneKelly 2 67
(P Howling) *wnt lft s: hld up: hdwy over 2f out: rdn and hmpd over 1f out: sn wknd* **50/1**

0006 10 1¼ **Emilio**[6] 3928 5-9-10 85 ....(t) FJohansson 3 66
(R A Kvisla) *chsd ldrs 4f* **40/1**

0543 11 3 **Buy On The Red**[22] 3434 5-8-12 73 ....(b) RichardMullen 1 45
(W R Muir) *s.i.s and hmpd s: sn prom: rdn over 2f out: hmpd over 1f out: sn wknd and eased* **8/1**

1m 11.85s (-1.50) **Going Correction** -0.15s/f (Firm)
WFA 3 from 4yo+ 4lb **11 Ran SP% 119.1**
Speed ratings (Par 107):104,103,102,101,101 97,95,95,93,92 88
CSF £39.58 CT £136.99 TOTE £6.10: £2.00, £2.30, £1.80; EX 37.70.
Owner Scott-Barrett,Tufnell,Kerr-Dineen,Burley **Bred** Peter E Daly **Trained** East Ilsley, Berks

FOCUS
This decent handicap was run over two seconds quicker than the juvenile maiden that preceded it. The form is sound rated through the fourth, but could have been stronger.

NOTEBOOK
Guildenstern(IRE) came into this still fairly well treated on his best form. Racing off a mark 3lb lower than he has won off in the past, he battled well after hitting the front over a furlong out and was a deserved winner. The Handicapper may have his say, but he is clearly in fine fettle and merits respect when he runs next. (op 11-2)
Romany Nights(IRE) produced another fine effort in defeat. Rated 7lb higher than his best winning mark, he stuck on inside the final furlong but the winner had first run on him, which proved decisive. (op 10-1)
Burning Incense(IRE) suffered a short-head reverse at Haydock a month earlier for which he was raised 5lb. Taking on his elders for the first time, he performed well enough but may be seen at his best with some ease underfoot. His sole success to date came with cut in the ground. (op 3-1 tchd 7-2)
Hidden Dragon(USA) produced his most encouraging performance in a long while and may have been slightly tightened up by Romany Nights inside the last. (op 16-1 tchd 20-1)
Who's Winning(IRE) was another with winning form off a higher mark than he was racing from here. He came into this off the back of a string of consistent efforts and merited respect. He showed up prominently for much of the race but had nothing in reserve late on. (op 13-2)
Goodenough Mover ran better than he has of late but was well held and may be worth a return to Polytrack.
Swinbrook(USA) had run very well on his two previous starts, including a fourth-placed effort in the Bunbury Cup. Shouldering top-weight, he looked beaten when hampered over a furlong out. (op 3-1 tchd 7-2)

4107 SHARP NUTRITION CONDITIONS STKS 7f
7:55 (7:55) (Class 3) 2-Y-O £6,855 (£2,052; £1,026; £513) Stalls High

Form RPR
01 1 Tobosa[17] [3623] 2-9-1 77 .... AlanMunro 4 93+
(W Jarvis) *s.s: sn chsng ldrs: led over 2f out: rdn and hung lft fr over 1f out: wnt clr ins fnl f* 2/5[1]
2 8 Audit (IRE) 2-8-9 .... RyanMoore 2 66+
(Sir Michael Stoute) *gd sort: lw: s.s: outpcd: hung lft over 1f out: wnt 2nd ins fnl f: no ch w wnr* 10/3[2]
55 3 ¾ Fares (IRE)[9] [3844] 2-8-11 .... SebSanders 1 66
(C E Brittain) *chsd ldr: rdn over 2f out: wknd fnl f* 8/1[3]
2301 4 14 Minimum Fuss (IRE)[24] [3380] 2-8-7 52 ow1 ....(b) BrianReilly 3 26
(M C Chapman) *led: plld hrd: hdd over 2f out: wknd over 1f out* 25/1

1m 26.16s (-0.62) **Going Correction** -0.15s/f (Firm) 4 Ran SP% 109.5
Speed ratings (Par 98):97,87,87,71
CSF £2.09 TOTE £1.50; EX 2.10.
Owner Collins, Randall, Rich & Turnbull **Bred** G S Shropshire **Trained** Newmarket, Suffolk

FOCUS
An ordinary conditions event in which they went an unusually strong early gallop for a small field and the winner sets the standard.

NOTEBOOK
Tobosa, a progressive colt, did the job easily enough, although he was noted hanging left late on. His trainer feels he will get a mile so the early pace will have suited him, and plans are likely to depend on how the Handicapper assesses this effort. (tchd 4-9)
Audit(IRE) can be expected to come on significantly for this first start. The experience will really benefit this Derby entry, who was green enough. (op 7-2)
Fares(IRE) is now qualified for nurseries and that appears to where his future lies. (tchd 10-1)
Minimum Fuss(IRE) set a fierce early gallop and folded quickly. She won a seller last month and needs to be dropped back in grade to become competitive again. (op 20-1)

4108 NEWMARKETRACECOURSES.CO.UK H'CAP 1m
8:25 (8:25) (Class 4) (0-80,80) 3-Y-O+ £5,505 (£1,637; £818; £408) Stalls High

Form RPR
-063 1 Sonny Parkin[14] [3712] 4-9-1 70 ....(v) AdamKirby(3) 6 83
(G A Huffer) *lw: hld up: hdwy over 2f out: led over 1f out: sn hung rt: drvn clr* 11/4[1]
0304 2 3½ Puya[21] [3470] 4-9-12 78 .... FergusSweeney 12 83
(H Candy) *b.hind: chsd ldr tl led over 1f out: sn hdd: styd on same pce* 9/1
4335 3 ½ European Dream (IRE)[34] [3082] 3-9-7 80 .... PaulEddery 1 84
(R C Guest) *hld up: hdwy over 1f out: sn rdn and no imp ins fnl f* 7/1[2]
00-4 4 hd Leoballero[30] [3202] 6-9-11 77 ....(t) MichaelTebbutt 4 82+
(D J Daly) *lw: s.i.s: hld up: nt clr run over 1f out: r.o ins fnl f: nrst fin* 16/1
1160 5 1½ Bold Diktator[14] [3712] 4-9-8 74 ....(b) RichardMullen 5 74
(W R Muir) *chsd ldrs: rdn over 2f out: styd on same pce fnl f* 11/1
3004 6 hd Ali D[14] [3712] 8-8-9 61 ....(p) JimmyQuinn 10 60
(G Woodward) *lw: hld up: hdwy u.p over 1f out: no ex fnl f* 25/1
0006 7 shd Kareeb (FR)[14] [3705] 9-8-9 61 .... TPQueally 2 60
(W J Musson) *hld up: hdwy over 2f out: wknd ins fnl f* 12/1
1000 8 1 Rain Stops Play (IRE)[23] [3413] 4-10-0 80 ....(v[1]) SebSanders 13 77
(M Quinn) *led over 6f: wknd ins fnl f* 8/1[3]
02-3 9 1 Peruvian Prince (USA)[99] [1265] 4-9-0 66 .... AlanMunro 11 61+
(J A R Toller) *lw: hld up in tch: nt clr run fr over 1f out: nvr able to chal* 8/1[3]
0030 10 2½ Boreana[35] [3044] 3-8-11 70 .... RyanMoore 14 59
(N A Callaghan) *chsd ldrs: rdn over 2f out: wknd fnl f* 16/1
0013 11 2½ Tidy (IRE)[42] [2810] 6-9-1 67 .... ShaneKelly 8 50
(Micky Hammond) *hld up: hdwy over 2f out: wkng whn n.m.r over 1f out* 7/1[2]

1m 38.49s (-1.94) **Going Correction** -0.15s/f (Firm)
WFA 3 from 4yo+ 7lb 11 Ran SP% 124.2
Speed ratings (Par 105):103,99,99,98,97 97,97,96,95,92 90
CSF £30.14 CT £169.28 TOTE £3.50: £1.70, £3.40, £2.60; EX 39.50 Place 6 £47.61, Place 5 £6.82..
Owner G A Huffer **Bred** Blenheim Bloodstock **Trained** Newmarket, Suffolk

FOCUS
A fair handicap and straightforward form, that looks sound enough with the time reasonable.
T/Plt: £23.90 to a £1 stake. Pool £53,821.85. 1,637.55 winning tickets. T/Qpdt: £5.00 to a £1 stake. Pool £3,684.60. 537.50 winning tickets. CR

3942 NOTTINGHAM (L-H)
Friday, August 4

OFFICIAL GOING: Good (good to firm in places)
After 10mm rain two days earlier the ground was described as 'near perfect, just on the quick side of good with an excellent cover of grass'.
Wind: Almost nil Weather: Fine and sunny

4109 EUROPEAN BREEDERS FUND MEDIAN AUCTION MAIDEN STKS 6f 15y
6:05 (6:07) (Class 5) 2-Y-O £4,533 (£1,348; £674; £336) Stalls High

Form RPR
4 1 Fish Called Johnny[7] [3895] 2-9-3 .... KDarley 10 92+
(B J Meehan) *mde all: shkn up over 1f out: wnt clr ins last: readily* 3/1[2]
542 2 5 Vaunt[37] [2967] 2-9-3 85 ....(b[1]) SteveDrowne 8 77
(R Charlton) *w wnr: rdn over 1f out: hung rt and sn wl outpcd* 5/2[1]
5 3 1¾ Inspirina (IRE)[20] [3553] 2-9-3 .... NickyMackay 9 72
(T R George) *chsd ldrs: effrt over 2f out: styd on fnl f* 7/1
4 ¾ Mayor Of London (USA) 2-9-3 .... StanleyChin 13 70
(M Johnston) *chsd ldrs: outpcd over 2f out: kpt on wl fnl f: will improve* 14/1
5 ½ Artimino 2-9-3 .... IanMongan 2 68
(J R Fanshawe) *towards rr on outer: hdwy over 2f out: kpt on: bttr for experience* 6/1
3 6 6 Froissee[42] [2821] 2-8-12 .... PatCosgrave 3 45
(N A Callaghan) *sn outpcd and pushed along: hdwy over 2f out: nvr on terms* 4/1[3]
04 7 nk Blakeshall Rose[15] [3684] 2-8-12 .... DeanMcKeown 6 44
(A J Chamberlain) *unruly beforehand: dwlt: in rr tl sme hdwy fnl 2f* 80/1
00 8 nk Vizionary[58] [2354] 2-8-9 .... SaleemGolam(3) 12 43
(Mrs P Sly) *t.k.h in mid-div: nvr a factor* 100/1
9 nk Ten Black 2-8-10 .... FrankiePickard(7) 4 47
(J A Osborne) *a outpcd and in rr* 20/1
10 3½ Danaos 2-9-3 .... GeorgeBaker 5 37
(J A Osborne) *chsd ldrs: lost pl 2f out* 25/1
11 1¾ Buds Dilemma 2-8-9 .... PatrickMathers(3) 11 27
(I W McInnes) *s.i.s: sn in tch on outer: hung lft thrght: lost pl over 2f out* 80/1
12 10 A Foot In Front 2-9-3 .... KimTinkler 1 2
(N Tinkler) *s.s: a in rr: detached fnl 2f* 100/1
5 U Munster Mountain (IRE)[43] [2778] 2-8-10 .... KevinGhunowa(7) 7 —
(P A Blockley) *s.i.s: in rr: uns rdr after 1f* 66/1

1m 13.82s (-1.18) **Going Correction** -0.225s/f (Firm) 13 Ran SP% 121.6
Speed ratings (Par 94):98,91,89,88,87 79,78,78,78,73 71,57,—
CSF £10.76 TOTE £3.30: £2.30, £1.30, £1.90; EX 14.10.
Owner The Fifth Pheasant Inn Partnership **Bred** Mrs D O Joly **Trained** Manton, Wilts

FOCUS
Probably a fair median auction maiden race, the first five well clear and quite an easy winner, with the standard behind reasonable.

NOTEBOOK
Fish Called Johnny had clearly learnt plenty first time and, bagging the plum stands' rail position, he came right away to score with plenty in hand. He is being aimed at the valuable St Leger Yearling Sales race, this year run at York, which his trainer captured last year. (op 10-3 tchd 7-2)
Vaunt, beaten by a good yardstick at Bath five weeks earlier, has been gelded in the meantime. Blinkered for the first time, he took on the winner but was put in his place in a matter of strides. (op 7-2)
Inspirina(IRE), caught flat-footed, was staying on in his own time at the finish and will appreciate a step up to seven. (op 9-1)
Mayor Of London(USA) ◆, on the leg and noisy, shaped nicely. Sure to have learnt plenty and likely to prove suited by a step up to seven, he looks sure to find a race. (op 12-1)
Artimino ◆, a late-April foal, is a robust, round-barrelled individual. Noisy in the paddock and carrying plenty of condition, he found himself rather marooned on the outside. Picking up in his own time, he can do a fair bit better in due course. (op 4-1)
Froissee, a negative on the exchanges, is a moderate walker and poor mover. She never went a yard. (op 9-2 tchd 11-2)
Buds Dilemma Official explanation: trainer said filly ran green and was unsuited by the good (good to firm in places) ground

4110 60'S MUSIC NIGHT H'CAP 5f 13y
6:35 (6:36) (Class 5) (0-75,75) 3-Y-O+ £3,238 (£963; £481; £240) Stalls High

Form RPR
5203 1 Henry Hall (IRE)[5] [3988] 10-9-4 67 .... KimTinkler 12 78
(N Tinkler) *chsd ldrs on ins: styd on to ld ins last: r.o* 4/1[2]
4604 2 1¼ Talcen Gwyn (IRE)[5] [3988] 4-8-8 57 ....(v) DavidKinsella 4 64
(M F Harris) *hmpd s: hdwy over 1f out: tk 2nd ins last: r.o* 5/1[3]
0201 3 nk Bahamian Ballet[18] [3593] 4-9-3 73 .... RussellKennemore(7) 11 78
(E S McMahon) *led tl ins last: no ex* 3/1[1]
0400 4 nk No Time (IRE)[73] [1928] 6-8-13 62 .... IanMongan 9 66
(J A Osborne) *sn chsng ldrs: kpt on same pce fnl f* 7/1
0305 5 1¼ Kennington[4] [3996] 6-8-13 65 ....(b) NeilChalmers(3) 7 65
(Mrs C A Dunnett) *w ldrs: kpt on same pce fnl f* 15/2
0641 6 ½ Silver Dane (IRE)[11] [3802] 4-9-9 75 6ex ....(v) SaleemGolam(3) 2 73
(Mrs C A Dunnett) *in rr: hdwy on outer over 2f out: nvr rchd ldrs* 8/1
0240 7 shd Parkside Pursuit[7] [3899] 8-9-3 66 .... GeorgeBaker 1 64
(J M Bradley) *in rr: hung lft and hdwy over 1f out: kpt on ins last* 16/1
6056 8 1¾ Town House[27] [3297] 4-8-0 56 oh11 .... SoniaEaton(7) 10 47
(B P J Baugh) *t.k.h: w ldr: wknd appr fnl f* 40/1
0000 9 hd Meikle Barfil[9] [3855] 4-9-0 63 .... KDarley 3 54
(J M Bradley) *chsd ldrs on outer: drvn over 2f out: lost pl over 1f out* 16/1
0066 10 3 Niteowl Lad (IRE)[17] [3622] 4-9-9 72 ....(t) DeanMcKeown 6 52
(J Balding) *wnt lft s: t.k.h: sn trcking ldrs: lost pl over 2f out* 10/1

60.12 secs (-1.68) **Going Correction** -0.225s/f (Firm) 10 Ran SP% 120.3
Speed ratings (Par 103):104,102,101,101,99 98,98,95,94,90
CSF £25.31 CT £70.98 TOTE £5.10: £1.90, £2.00, £1.50; EX 38.10.
Owner James Marshall & Mrs Susan Marshall **Bred** Newberry Stud Company **Trained** Langton, N Yorks

FOCUS
A modest sprint handicap in which the stands'-side rail held sway in the end. Overall the form has a sound look about it.

4111 BUY YOUR TICKETS ONLINE @NOTTINGHAMRACECOURSE.CO.UK H'CAP 2m 9y
7:05 (7:06) (Class 6) (0-60,59) 3-Y-O £2,730 (£806; £403) Stalls Low

Form RPR
0461 1 Leo McGarry (IRE)[11] [3791] 3-8-12 53 5ex .... SaleemGolam(3) 11 67+
(S C Williams) *mid-div: hdwy on ins to trck ldrs 4f out: led over 2f out: shkn up and wnt clr over 1f out: readily* 11/8[1]
0252 2 4 Vice Admiral[11] [3791] 3-9-0 52 .... DaleGibson 1 57
(M W Easterby) *chsd ldrs: chal over 3f out: kpt on: no ch w wnr* 8/1[3]
0600 3 nk Synonymy[25] [3347] 3-9-6 58 .... DeanMcKeown 2 63+
(M Blanshard) *chsd ldrs: n.m.r over 3f out: kpt on wl fnl f* 25/1
0-50 4 7 Persian Conqueror (IRE)[67] [2082] 3-8-11 49 .... IanMongan 6 45
(J L Dunlop) *bhd: hdwy over 3f out: styd on wl fnl 2f* 15/2[2]
5320 5 ¾ Bramcote Lorne[32] [3145] 3-9-7 59 .... KDarley 8 54
(S Parr) *hld up in rr: hdwy 6f out: sn chsng ldrs: led over 3f out: hdd over 2f out: wknd appr fnl f* 15/2[2]
6000 6 2½ Silver Mont (IRE)[11] [3791] 3-9-0 52 ....(v) AlanDaly 7 44
(Mrs A Duffield) *mid-div: hdwy to chse ldrs over 4f out: wknd 3f out* 40/1
0-04 7 3 Sara Mana Mou[28] [3258] 3-8-4 45 .... NeilChalmers(3) 16 34
(J G Portman) *swvd rt s: sn chsng ldrs: lost pl 3f out* 66/1
0-04 8 1 Monashee Grey (IRE)[11] [3791] 3-8-2 40 oh2 .... PaulHanagan 12 28
(R A Fahey) *mid-div: drvn over 3f out: nvr nr ldrs* 12/1
6000 9 10 Sunbolt (IRE)[14] [3695] 3-9-1 53 .... PaulFessey 14 29
(T D Barron) *in rr: nvr on terms* 33/1
040 10 1¼ Naval Hero (IRE)[56] [2412] 3-8-12 50 .... DavidKinsella 5 24
(Mrs L Williamson) *s.i.s: hdwy into mid-div 6f out: lost pl over 3f out* 80/1
-064 11 5 Gettysburg (IRE)[23] [3399] 3-8-11 49 .... PaulMulrennan 10 17
(J Howard Johnson) *trckd ldrs: hung lft and lost pl over 3f out* 33/1
4033 12 9 Myrtle Bay (IRE)[11] [3791] 3-9-3 55 ....(p) PatCosgrave 15 12
(K R Burke) *led: rdn 4f out: sn hdd: hung rt and lost pl: eased fnl 2f* 11/1
0506 13 3 Loch Awe[28] [3249] 3-8-12 50 .... SteveDrowne 13 4
(J G Given) *mid-div: drvn along 8f out: lost pl over 5f out* 66/1
0-03 14 hd Lolla's Spirit (IRE)[16] [3634] 3-9-5 57 .... RobertWinston 4 10
(M L W Bell) *chsd ldrs: lost pl 3f out* 8/1[3]
00 15 3 Bu-Ali (USA)[12] [2933] 3-8-6 47 ....(b[1]) EdwardCreighton(3) 9 —
(B W Duke) *s.i.s: a bhd* 80/1

0-00 **16** *8* **Sunny Disposition (IRE)**[84] 1648 3-8-4 42 ChrisCatlin 3 —
(E F Vaughan) *chsd ldrs: drvn along 8f out: lost pl over 3f out: sn bhd* **25/1**

3m 30.29s (-3.21) **Going Correction** -0.225s/f (Firm) **16** Ran SP% **125.4**
Speed ratings (Par 98):99,97,96,93,92 91,90,89,84,84 81,77,75,75,74 70
CSF £11.98 CT £209.62 TOTE £2.50: £1.20, £2.00, £6.90, £2.20; EX 13.10.
Owner E Murphy Racing **Bred** Sugar Puss Corporation **Trained** Newmarket, Suffolk

FOCUS
A moderate staying event in which the winner, the only previous scorer in the field, was all the rage and enjoyed a dream run up the inside once in line for home. The second again looks the key, backed up by the third.
Gettysburg(IRE) Official explanation: jockey said gelding hung left
Myrtle Bay(IRE) Official explanation: jockey said gelding hung right
Lolla's Spirit(IRE) Official explanation: jockey said filly had no more to give

4112 BODEGAS FAUSTINO H'CAP — 1m 1f 213y
7:40 (7:40) (Class 4) (0-85,85) 3-Y-O+ **£6,477** (£1,927; £963; £481) **Stalls** Low

Form RPR
-251 **1** **Zaafran**[18] 3590 3-8-11 **77** PhilipRobinson 7 — 84
(M A Jarvis) *led: qcknd over 3f out: rdn over 1f out: jst hld on* **15/8**[1]
4202 **2** *shd* **Cripsey Brook**[6] 3939 8-8-13 **77** (t) JamesReveley(7) 5 — 84
(K G Reveley) *trckd ldrs: chal 3f out: styd on fnl f: jst failed* **8/1**
-400 **3** *nk* **Solo Flight**[47] 2672 9-9-13 **84** SteveDrowne 3 — 90
(H Morrison) *hld up in rr: hdwy over 3f out: effrt on ins over 1f out: no ex last 75yds* **20/1**
0031 **4** *2 ½* **Transvestite (IRE)**[9] 3850 4-9-1 **75** DeanCorby(3) 6 — 77
(J W Hills) *trckd ldrs: effrt 3f out: rdr lost whip over 1f out: kpt on same pce* **3/1**[2]
3130 **5** *1 ¼* **Dragon Slayer (IRE)**[13] 3747 4-9-8 **79** ChrisCatlin 4 — 78
(M J Attwater) *sn trcking ldrs: effrt on outside 3f out: kpt on same pce fnl 2f* **15/2**
0-06 **6** *¾* **Prime Number (IRE)**[90] 1484 4-10-0 **85** NickyMackay 8 — 83
(G A Butler) *sn trcking ldrs: drvn over 3f out: outpcd over 1f out* **10/1**
-200 **7** *shd* **Master Of The Race**[23] 3401 4-9-8 **79** RobertWinston 2 — 77
(Sir Michael Stoute) *hld up in last: effrt on outside 3f out: nvr a threat* **9/2**[3]

2m 12.06s (2.36) **Going Correction** -0.225s/f (Firm)
WFA 3 from 4yo+ 9lb **7** Ran SP% **114.7**
Speed ratings (Par 105):81,80,80,78,77 77,77
CSF £17.88 CT £226.93 TOTE £2.60: £1.90, £4.10; EX 15.20.
Owner Sheikh Ahmed Al Maktoum **Bred** Darley **Trained** Newmarket, Suffolk

FOCUS
A fair handicap but a pedestrian winning time for a race like this. The winner was handed a soft lead, but in the end she just lasted home. Overall the form is weak, ratred around the placed horses.

4113 VISITNOTTINGHAM.COM MEDIAN AUCTION MAIDEN STKS — 1m 54y
8:10 (8:11) (Class 6) 3-4-Y-O **£2,730** (£806; £403) **Stalls** Centre

Form RPR
4 **1** **Shumookh (IRE)**[15] 3676 3-9-3 PhilipRobinson 9 — 81+
(M A Jarvis) *led qcknd over 4f out: drvn clr over 1f out: unchal* **10/3**[2]
623 **2** *2 ½* **Uno**[41] 2868 3-8-12 80 PaulHanagan 7 — 68
(B W Hills) *t.k.h: trckd ldrs: wnt 2nd over 2f out: no imp* **1/1**[1]
46 **3** *1 ½* **Casual Affair**[26] 3336 3-9-3 ChrisCatlin 8 — 70
(E J O'Neill) *trckd ldrs: kpt on same pce fnl 2f* **25/1**
6-4 **4** *hd* **Ruse**[92] 1445 3-8-12 IanMongan 4 — 64+
(J R Fanshawe) *hld up in rr: hdwy over 6f out: kpt on same pce appr fnl f* **11/2**[3]
0400 **5** *4* **Sorrel Point**[23] 3410 3-9-3 60 KDarley 3 — 60
(H J Collingridge) *trckd ldrs: wknd over 1f out* **50/1**
5640 **6** *1 ¼* **Pop Music (IRE)**[24] 3387 3-9-0 67 (b[1]) DeanCorby(3) 11 — 57
(Miss J Feilden) *trckd ldrs: outpcd over 3f out: no threat after* **40/1**
4540 **7** *5* **Aristofilia**[11] 3793 3-8-12 63 SteveDrowne 2 — 41
(P F I Cole) *rn in snatches: in tch: shkn up over 5f out: rdn and btn over 3f out* **7/1**
00 **8** *4* **Pickwick Miss (USA)**[24] 3387 3-8-9 SaleemGolam(3) 6 — 31
(D M Simcock) *s.i.s: t.k.h in rr: drvn over 4f out: nvr on terms* **100/1**
00 **9** *nk* **Winning Connection (IRE)**[25] 3346 3-8-10 KevinGhunowa(7) 10 — 36
(P A Blockley) *chsd ldrs: lost pl over 2f out* **100/1**
3506 **10** *1 ¾* **Kissi Kissi**[17] 3609 3-8-9 46 DominicFox(3) 5 — 27
(M J Attwater) *in rr: drvn 4f out: nvr on terms* **50/1**
0000 **11** *2 ½* **Diamond Heritage**[6] 3931 4-9-3 48 (b) MarkCoumbe(7) 1 — 26
(S Parr) *hld up in rr: drvn over 3f out: nvr on terms* **50/1**

1m 43.72s (14.60) **Going Correction** -0.225s/f (Firm)
WFA 3 from 4yo 7lb **11** Ran SP% **115.1**
Speed ratings (Par 101):104,101,100,99,95 94,89,85,85,83 81
CSF £6.63 TOTE £3.90: £1.80, £1.10, £2.60; EX 8.10.
Owner Hamdan Al Maktoum **Bred** Shadwell Estate Company Limited **Trained** Newmarket, Suffolk

FOCUS
A fair maiden but a tactical affair with Philip Robinson again allowed to set his own pace. This time he was on very much the best horse in the race and the winning time was 1.39 seconds faster than the following handicap. The form is limited by the fifth.
Diamond Heritage Official explanation: jockey said gelding changed its leading leg throughout

4114 SWINGING 60'S H'CAP — 1m 54y
8:40 (8:42) (Class 5) (0-75,75) 3-Y-O+ **£3,238** (£963; £481; £240) **Stalls** Centre

Form RPR
1 **Coleridge (AUS)**[177] 7-10-0 **72** GeorgeBaker 5 — 79
(B G Powell) *trckd ldrs: effrt on inner over 3f out: swtchd rt over 2f out: rdn to chal over 1f out: styd on to ld last strides* **11/1**
2106 **2** *nk* **Sake (IRE)**[20] 3549 4-10-0 **72** KimTinkler 8 — 78
(N Tinkler) *trckd ldr: chal 4f out: led over 2f out: jst ct* **9/4**[2]
-001 **3** *2* **Certain Justice (USA)**[27] 3304 8-9-13 **71** HayleyTurner 7 — 72
(Stef Liddiard) *trckd ldrs: effrt on outer over 2f out: kpt on same pce* **4/1**[3]
0-21 **4** *2* **Grand Entrance (IRE)**[13] 3742 3-9-10 **75** SteveDrowne 3 — 72
(C R Egerton) *bmpd s: sn led: hdd over 2f out: wknd over 1f out* **1/1**[1]
-006 **5** *1 ¾* **Sea Frolic (IRE)**[87] 1574 5-8-4 **53** oh8 (v) RoryMoore(5) 1 — 46
(Jennie Candlish) *wnt rt s: led eraly: chsd ldrs: drvn over 3f out: one pce* **28/1**
-000 **6** *nk* **Red Lantern**[15] 3679 5-8-9 **53** oh17 PaulHanagan 6 — 45
(M J Attwater) *hld up in rr: effrt over 3f out: nvr a threat* **33/1**
5-00 **7** *9* **Star Fern**[43] 2789 5-8-9 **53** oh9 ChrisCatlin 2 — 24
(M J Attwater) *dwlt and hmpd s: hld up in rr: rdn over 3f out: sn btn* **18/1**

1m 45.11s (-1.29) **Going Correction** -0.225s/f (Firm)
WFA 3 from 4yo+ 7lb **7** Ran SP% **120.8**
Speed ratings (Par 103):97,96,94,92,90 90,81
CSF £38.69 CT £122.71 TOTE £9.90: £3.00, £1.10; EX 50.30 Place 6 £14.41, Place 5 £9.39..
Owner Global Racing **Bred** I R Nelson **Trained** Morestead, Hants

FOCUS
A fair handicap run at a moderate gallop and weakish form rated through the runner-up.
T/Plt: £38.10 to a £1 stake. Pool £52,177.90. 999.70 winning tickets. T/Qpdt: £17.20 to a £1 stake. Pool £3,385.40. 145.60 winning tickets. WG

3907 THIRSK (L-H)
Friday, August 4

OFFICIAL GOING: Good
Wind: Virtually nil

4115 PICKERING CASTLE CLAIMING STKS — 7f
2:30 (2:38) (Class 5) 2-Y-O **£3,886** (£1,156; £577; £288) **Stalls** Low

Form RPR
4066 **1** **Suhayl Star (IRE)**[9] 3834 2-8-11 75 EdwardCreighton(3) 10 — 68
(M R Channon) *mde all: clr 1/2-way: styd on wl appr last* **7/2**[2]
505 **2** *3 ½* **Dansilver**[15] 3677 2-8-3 JosephWalsh(7) 5 — 55
(D J Wintle) *chsd wnr: rdn along 3f out: drvn wl over 1f out: kpt on ins last* **14/1**
0601 **3** *hd* **Colditz (IRE)**[9] 3831 2-9-0 68 MarkLawson(5) 11 — 64
(D W Barker) *hld up in midfield: hdwy on outer 3f out: rdn wl over 1f out: kpt on same pce* **11/4**[1]
0503 **4** *¾* **The Dandy Fox**[9] 3831 2-8-2 PaulQuinn 4 — 45
(D Nicholls) *chsd ldrs on inner: hdwy 3f out: rdn along over 2f out: sn drvn and one pce* **8/1**
526 **5** *1* **Burlington Fayr (IRE)**[60] 2294 2-8-4 52 KimTinkler 7 — 44
(N Tinkler) *chsd ldrs: hdwy 3f out: rdn over 2f out: drvn and wknd over 1f out* **15/2**[3]
3000 **6** *¾* **Bonny Scotland (IRE)**[11] 3801 2-7-11 55 LiamJones(5) 15 — 41
(Miss V Haigh) *towards rr: hdwy wl over 2f out: swtchd ins and rdn wl over 1f out: no imp appr last* **28/1**
060 **7** *1 ½* **Gold Response**[14] 3713 2-8-9 PatrickMathers(3) 6 — 47
(D Shaw) *towards rr: sme hdwy wl over 2f out: sn rdn and kpt on appr last: nrst fin* **40/1**
4364 **8** *1* **Providence Farm**[9] 3831 2-8-12 62 (b) PaulMulrennan 3 — 44
(M W Easterby) *s.i.s: sn chsng ldrs: rdn wl over 2f out and sn btn* **12/1**
3655 **9** *3 ½* **Elizabeth Garrett**[11] 3801 2-8-4 53 (p) ChrisCatlin 12 — 28
(R M H Cowell) *chsd ldrs: rdn along wl over 2f out: sn wknd* **12/1**
00 **10** *2 ½* **Blue Mak**[22] 3457 2-8-10 (v[1]) HayleyTurner 16 — 27
(D Shaw) *a towards rr* **100/1**
006 **11** *½* **Little Tiny Tom**[9] 3831 2-8-3 (b) PaulPickard(7) 1 — 26
(C N Kellett) *s.i.s: a bhd* **80/1**
0000 **12** *¾* **Soundasapound**[40] 2890 2-8-0 (b[1]) AndrewMullen(5) 8 — 19
(I W McInnes) *in tch: rdn along 3f out: sn drvn and wknd* **16/1**
0000 **13** *1 ¾* **Dispol Moonlight (IRE)**[9] 3831 2-8-7 PaulFessey 14 — 17
(T D Barron) *stdd s: a rr* **28/1**
14 *¾* **Iron Dancer (IRE)** 2-8-9 KevinGhunowa(7) 9 — 24
(P A Blockley) *s.i.s: a bhd* **10/1**

1m 27.77s (0.67) **Going Correction** +0.05s/f (Good) **14** Ran SP% **120.3**
Speed ratings (Par 94):98,94,93,92,91 90,89,88,84,81 80,79,77,76
CSF £50.18 TOTE £4.70: £1.90, £3.80, £1.60; EX 61.20.Suhayl Star (no.4) was claimed by W J Musson for £10,000. The Dandy Fox (no.16) was claimed by Naughty Diesel Ltd for £3,000.
Owner Box 41 **Bred** John Mulhern **Trained** West Ilsley, Berks

FOCUS
A very weak affair, which saw the highest-rated BHB runner score as he was entitled to. The form is sound but limited.

NOTEBOOK
Suhayl Star(IRE) benefited from this drop in class and duly made all the running to win very much as he liked. He will be high on confidence now, but further improvement will be required if he is to hold his own back at a higher grade. (op 5-1 tchd 6-1)
Dansilver, who looked well beforehand, came out best of the rest, but was no match for the winner. (op 12-1)
Colditz(IRE), a stable-mate of the winner until changing hands for 12,500gns after winning a seller last week, was not ideally drawn, and did not get going until too late. He kept on towards the finish, but lacked the pace to pose a threat. (op 3-1 tchd 10-3)
The Dandy Fox had no apparent excuses and ran close to her recent level in defeat. (op 15-2)
Burlington Fayr(IRE) had every chance until fading nearing the final furlong on her first start for two months. (tchd 17-2)
Soundasapound Official explanation: jockey said filly had no more to give

4116 WEATHERBYS BANK H'CAP — 7f
3:05 (3:06) (Class 5) (0-70,70) 3-Y-O+ **£3,886** (£1,156; £577; £288) **Stalls** Low

Form RPR
0000 **1** **Hiccups**[45] 2732 6-9-12 **69** RobertWinston 4 — 77
(M Dods) *dwlt: sn in tch on inner: gd hdwy over 2f out: rdn to ld 1f out: drvn out* **25/1**
2620 **2** *¾* **Saxon Lil (IRE)**[15] 3679 4-9-11 **68** FrancisNorton 1 — 74
(J L Spearing) *trckd ldrs: hdwy 3f out: rdn to chal 2f out and ev ch: drvn and kpt on wl fnl f* **14/1**
2024 **3** *½* **Bond Diamond**[11] 3789 9-9-2 **64** RoryMoore(5) 13 — 69
(P T Midgley) *hld up: hdwy on inner over 2f out: rdn and edgd lft over 1f out: styd on u.p ins last* **20/1**
4542 **4** *shd* **Patavium Prince (IRE)**[8] 3866 3-9-5 **68** KerrinMcEvoy 10 — 71
(J R Best) *hld up in midfield: hdwy over 2f out: rdn over 1f out: styd on ins last* **5/1**[2]
0000 **5** *nk* **Mystic Man (FR)**[27] 3298 8-9-4 **66** MarkLawson(5) 9 — 73+
(I W McInnes) *hld up in rr: hdwy on inner over 2f out: effrt and nt clr run over 1f out: swvd rt and nt clr run ins last: kpt on* **50/1**
12 **6** *½* **Dancing Deano (IRE)**[69] 2020 4-9-0 **62** (v) MichaelJStainton(5) 2 — 65
(R M Whitaker) *led: rdn along over 2f out: drvn appr last: sn hdd & wknd* **6/1**[3]
5453 **7** *¾* **No Grouse**[29] 3217 6-9-1 **61** StephenDonohoe(3) 3 — 62
(E J Alston) *in tch: hdwy to trck ldrs 3f out: rdn along 2f out: drvn over 1f out and no imp* **3/1**[1]
2640 **8** *shd* **Dudley Docker (IRE)**[10] 3820 4-9-6 **63** DanielTudhope 8 — 63
(D Carroll) *s.i.s and bhd: hdwy 3f out: rdn and in tch over 1f out: sn drvn and one pce* **20/1**
6520 **9** *1* **Petite Mac**[7] 3912 6-8-10 **60** SuzzanneFrance(7) 11 — 58
(N Bycroft) *bhd: hdwy on outer over 2f out: sn rdn and no imp appr last* **16/1**
4630 **10** *nk* **Iced Diamond (IRE)**[10] 3817 7-8-8 **56** LiamJones(5) 16 — 53
(W M Brisbourne) *s.i.s and bhd: hdwy over 2f out: swtchd rt and rdn over 1f out: nt rch ldrs* **20/1**

2102 **11** *shd* **Elegant Times (IRE)**^{2} [4058] 3-9-0 **63** .... DavidAllan 7 58
(T D Easterby) *prom: rdn along over 2f out: sn drvn and grad wknd* **9/1**

4646 **12** *3/4* **Franksalot (IRE)**^{11} [3789] 6-9-7 **67** .... (b^{1}) PatrickMathers$^{(3)}$ 6 62
(I W McInnes) *chsd ldrs: hdwy over 2f out: rdn wl over 1f out and sn wknd* **20/1**

0643 **13** *shd* **Elkhorn**^{13} [3749] 4-8-12 **55** .... (p) PaulMulrennan 15 50+
(Miss J A Camacho) *bhd: hdwy wl over 3f out: n.m.r and rdn wl over 1f out: sn wknd* **14/1**

-060 **14** *1 1/4* **King Harson**^{47} [2681] 7-9-13 **70** .... ChrisCatlin 12 61
(J D Bethell) *prom on outer: rdn along over 2f out: grad wknd* **11/1**

0-06 **15** *1* **Tom Forest**^{45} [2737] 4-9-9 **66** .... DO'Donohoe 5 55
(K A Ryan) *cl up: rdn along 3f out: wknd over 2f out* **14/1**

1m 26.68s (-0.42) **Going Correction** +0.05s/f (Good)
WFA 3 from 4yo+ 6lb **15** Ran SP% **125.0**
Speed ratings (Par 103):104,103,102,102,102 101,100,100,99,99 98,98,98,96,95
CSF £323.97 CT £7129.17 TOTE £26.30: £6.10, £4.60, £5.20; EX 222.80.
Owner J M & Mrs E E Ranson **Bred** Mrs Susan Corbett **Trained** Denton, Co Durham
■ Stewards' Enquiry : Rory Moore caution: used whip with excessive frequency

FOCUS
A modest handicap, run at an average pace, and this form looks straightforward enough and sound.
Mystic Man(FR) Official explanation: jockey said gelding was denied a clear run

4117 SCARBOROUGH CASTLE MAIDEN STKS 1m
3:40 (3:41) (Class 4) 3-Y-0+ **£6,477** (£1,927; £963; £481) **Stalls** Low

Form RPR

02 **1** **Somersault**^{14} [3711] 3-8-12 .... RobertWinston 1 67+
(Sir Michael Stoute) *trckd ldng pair: hdwy 2f out: rdn to ld appr last: styd on strly* **7/1**^{3}

2 *1 1/2* **Hunters' Glen (USA)** 3-9-3 .... (t) KerrinMcEvoy 6 69+
(Saeed Bin Suroor) *trckd ldrs on outer: hdwy over 2f out: rdn and ev ch over 1f out: kpt on same pce ins last* **8/15**^{1}

-006 **3** *1 1/4* **Sinner Or Saint (IRE)**^{46} [2698] 3-9-3 65 .... DavidAllan 11 66
(T D Easterby) *cl up: led wl over 2f out: rdn wl over 1f out: drvn and hdd appr last: kpt on same pce* **100/1**

0 **4** *3* **Another Gladiator (USA)**^{13} [3742] 3-9-3 .... DO'Donohoe 4 59
(K A Ryan) *trckd ldrs: effrt wl over 2f out: sn rdn and wknd over 1f out* **33/1**

4 **5** *3* **Bayberry King (USA)**^{35} [3050] 3-9-3 .... DanielTudhope 10 52
(J S Goldie) *bhd: hdwy 3f out: sn rdn and no imp fnl 2f* **80/1**

04-2 **6** *shd* **Rodeo**^{104} [1134] 3-9-3 82 .... DeanMcKeown 2 52
(B W Hills) *chsd ldrs: sn pushed along: rdn on inner 3f out: drvn over 2f out and sn btn* **3/1**^{2}

56 **7** *3 1/2* **Counterfactual (IRE)**^{45} [2734] 3-9-3 .... DerekMcGaffin 5 44
(B Smart) *in tch: pushed along wl over 2f out: sn rdn and wknd wl over 1f out* **66/1**

55 **8** *shd* **Chrisjen**^{13} [3750] 4-9-5 .... PaulMulrennan 3 39
(M W Easterby) *a rr* **100/1**

6 **9** *18* **Talisker Rock (IRE)**^{56} [2398] 6-9-10 .... PaulHanagan 8 2
(B Storey) *led: rdn along over 3f out: hdd wl over 2f out and sn wknd* **200/1**

10 *9* **Dukes Bond** 3-8-12 .... MarkLawson$^{(5)}$ 9 —
(M E Sowersby) *s.i.s: a bhd* **100/1**

1m 39.22s (-0.48) **Going Correction** +0.05s/f (Good)
WFA 3 from 4yo+ 7lb **10** Ran SP% **111.9**
Speed ratings (Par 105):104,102,101,98,95 95,91,91,73,64
CSF £10.82 TOTE £4.60: £1.10, £1.40, £7.70; EX 15.70.
Owner Cheveley Park Stud **Bred** Cheveley Park Stud Ltd **Trained** Newmarket, Suffolk

FOCUS
Just an ordinary maiden, which saw the first three come clear, rated through the third-placed horse, who also limits the form.
Chrisjen Official explanation: jockey said filly hung right throughout
Talisker Rock(IRE) Official explanation: jockey said gelding had a breathing problem
Dukes Bond Official explanation: jockey said gelding missed the break

4118 ANTHONY FAWCETT MEMORIAL FILLIES' H'CAP 1m 4f
4:15 (4:16) (Class 5) (0-70,70) 3-Y-0 **£3,886** (£1,156; £577; £288) **Stalls** Low

Form RPR

-411 **1** **Trick Or Treat**^{14} [3714] 3-9-4 **67** .... JamieMackay 7 77+
(J G Given) *trckd ldrs: smooth hdwy over 2f out: swtchd rt wl over 1f out: rdn and qcknd to ld appr last: kpt on wl* **15/8**^{1}

5220 **2** *1 3/4* **Squirtle (IRE)**^{65} [2124] 3-8-9 **63** .... LiamJones$^{(5)}$ 5 68
(W M Brisbourne) *hld up: hdwy 3f out: rdn over 1f out: chsd wnr ins last: no imp* **20/1**

-562 **3** *1 1/4* **Bollin Dolly**^{14} [3714] 3-9-7 **70** .... DavidAllan 3 73
(T D Easterby) *led: pushed along 3f out: rdn 2f out: hdd appr last: drvn and kpt on same pce* **11/1**^{3}

-603 **4** *1* **Westering Home (IRE)**^{10} [3816] 3-9-2 **65** .... RobertWinston 11 66
(J Mackie) *trckd ldrs: hdwy over 3f out: rdn 2f out and ev ch tl drvn and one pce appr last* **20/1**

046 **5** *1/2* **Dream Shared**^{22} [3451] 3-9-5 **68** .... KerrinMcEvoy 12 69
(E A L Dunlop) *trckd ldng pair: effrt on inner whn hmpd 2f out: sn rdn and n.m.r over 1f out: kpt on same pce ins last* **5/1**^{2}

0043 **6** *nk* **Lady Georgette (IRE)**^{11} [3803] 3-8-8 **57** .... ChrisCatlin 8 57
(E J O'Neill) *hld up in rr: hdwy on outer wl over 2f out: rdn wl over 1f out: kpt on ins last: nrst fin* **5/1**^{2}

3110 **7** *4* **Unique Moment**^{5} [3974] 3-9-2 **70** .... GregFairley$^{(5)}$ 2 64
(D J S Ffrench Davis) *trckd ldr: effrt to chal over 2f out: sn rdn and hung lft 2f out: sn drvn and wknd* **11/1**^{3}

006 **8** *2 1/2* **Salonga (IRE)**^{34} [3073] 3-8-13 **62** .... J-PGuillambert 9 52
(C F Wall) *hld up: a rr* **12/1**

6202 **9** *hd* **Fonic Rock (IRE)**^{11} [3803] 3-8-7 **56** .... HayleyTurner 10 45
(M L W Bell) *hld up in rr: effrt and sme hdwy 3f out: rdn along over 2f out and sn wknd* **5/1**^{2}

6-00 **10** *6* **Lucidity Light (IRE)**^{46} [2699] 3-8-11 **60** .... FrancisNorton 4 40
(J D Bethell) *midfield: rdn along 3f out: wknd over 2f out* **100/1**

2m 36.83s (1.63) **Going Correction** +0.05s/f (Good) **10** Ran SP% **119.7**
Speed ratings (Par 97):96,94,94,93,93 92,90,88,88,84
CSF £49.00 CT £343.64 TOTE £2.50: £1.50, £3.90, £2.80.
Owner Peter Onslow **Bred** P Onslow **Trained** Willoughton, Lincs
■ Stewards' Enquiry : Jamie Mackay three-day ban: careless riding (Aug 15-17)

FOCUS
A modest three-year-old handicap run at an ordinary pace and the form is not strong, although the winner is progressive.

4119 PETER BELL MEMORIAL H'CAP 6f
4:50 (4:50) (Class 4) (0-80,76) 3-Y-0+ **£6,477** (£1,927; £963; £481) **Stalls** High

Form RPR

1113 **1** **Aahgowangowan (IRE)**^{4} [4003] 7-9-2 **71** 6ex .... (t) LiamJones$^{(5)}$ 11 87
(M Dods) *sn overall ldr stands side: rdn clr over 1f out: styd on strly* **11/4**^{1}

4614 **2** *2* **Ellens Academy (IRE)**^{6} [3936] 11-9-8 **72** .... FrancisNorton 7 82
(E J Alston) *in tch stands side: hdwy 2f out: rdn to chse wnr over 1f out: kpt on* **10/1**^{3}

3350 **3** *1* **Dorn Dancer (IRE)**^{6} [3936] 4-8-9 **64** .... AndrewMullen$^{(5)}$ 18 71
(D W Barker) *a.p stands side: rdn over 2f out: drvn and one pce fr over 1f out* **11/1**

3400 **4** *1* **Ryedale Ovation (IRE)**^{27} [3296] 3-9-8 **76** .... DavidAllan 19 80
(T D Easterby) *dwlt: in tch stands side: hdwy 2f out: swtchd lft and rdn over 1f out: kpt on ins last: nrst fin* **16/1**

2221 **5** *hd* **Geojimali**^{10} [3811] 4-9-12 **76** 6ex .... DanielTudhope 17 79+
(J S Goldie) *s.i.s and bhd stands side: hdwy 2f out: rdn and kpt on ins last: nrst fin* **4/1**^{2}

5026 **6** *1/2* **Currency**^{5} [3986] 9-9-2 **69** .... StephenDonohoe$^{(3)}$ 10 71
(J M Bradley) *towards rr stands side: haadway 2f out: rdn and kpt on wl fnl f: nrst fin* **11/1**

0003 **7** *3/4* **Trojan Flight**^{11} [3789] 5-9-3 **70** .... (p) BenSwarbrick$^{(3)}$ 1 70
(D W Chapman) *trckd ldr far side: rdn along to ld that gp 2f out: sn drvn and kpt on: no ch w stands side gp* **12/1**

0006 **8** *nk* **Big Bradford**^{10} [3811] 5-8-10 **60** .... TonyHamilton 8 59
(R A Fahey) *hld up towards rr stands side: effrt and sme hdwy 2f out: sn rdn: edgd lft and no imp* **28/1**

2263 **9** *3 1/2* **Lake Garda**^{5} [3986] 5-9-11 **75** .... (b) DO'Donohoe 4 63
(K A Ryan) *led far side gp: rdn along 1/2-way: hdd 2f out and sn wknd* **4/1**^{2}

000 **10** *2* **Dunn Deal (IRE)**^{6} [3936] 6-9-2 **66** .... PaulQuinn 6 48
(W M Brisbourne) *a rr stands side* **25/1**

00/0 **11** *2 1/2* **Smirfys Systems**^{104} [1151] 7-8-10 **65** .... GregFairley$^{(5)}$ 2 40
(W M Brisbourne) *swtchd to r stands side: in tch to 1/2-way: sn rdn and wknd* **50/1**

0-50 **12** *nk* **Minimum Bid**^{7} [3912] 5-8-10 **65** .... (v) MarkLawson$^{(5)}$ 5 39
(B Smart) *chsd ldrs stands side: rdn along wl over 2f out: sn wknd* **50/1**

0-00 **13** *3* **Vanadium**^{21} [3500] 4-9-11 **75** .... JamieMackay 9 40
(J G Given) *prom stands side: rdn along 1/2-way: sn wknd* **20/1**

5002 **14** *3/4* **The History Man (IRE)**^{8} [3879] 3-8-9 **70** .... (b) AdeleRothery$^{(7)}$ 3 33
(M W Easterby) *racd far side: a rr* **25/1**

1m 11.59s (-0.91) **Going Correction** +0.05s/f (Good)
WFA 3 from 4yo+ 4lb **14** Ran SP% **125.8**
Speed ratings (Par 105):108,105,104,102,102 101,100,100,95,93 89,89,85,84
CSF £30.65 CT £281.85 TOTE £3.40: £1.90, £3.30, £4.40; EX 48.30.
Owner Les Waugh **Bred** Seamus Phelan **Trained** Denton, Co Durham

FOCUS
A fair sprint, in which the three to race on the far side were at a disadvantage, and the winner continues on an upward curve. The form looks solid rated through the third.
Smirfys Systems Official explanation: jockey said gelding stumbled leaving stalls

4120 HELMSLEY APPRENTICE MAIDEN H'CAP 6f
5:20 (5:23) (Class 5) (0-70,67) 3-Y-0+ **£3,886** (£1,156; £577; £288) **Stalls** High

Form RPR

0365 **1** **Dazzler Mac**^{7} [3913] 5-9-1 **51** .... AlanRutter 10 64+
(N Bycroft) *midfield: hdwy 2f out: n.m.r and swtchd rt over 1f out: sn rdn and hung rt ins last: kpt on wl to ld nr line* **3/1**^{1}

2040 **2** *nk* **Mostanad**^{13} [3749] 4-8-6 **50** .... BarrySavage$^{(8)}$ 17 59
(J M Bradley) *hld up: gd hdwy 2f out: rdn: edgd lft and led over 1f out: drvn ins last: hdd nr fin* **13/2**^{2}

-600 **3** *1* **Tartan Special**^{20} [3524] 4-8-5 **44** oh2 .... PatrickDonaghy$^{(3)}$ 12 50
(K R Burke) *hld up and bhd on stands rail: hdwy 2f out: carried rt and n.m.r ent last: swtchd lft and rdn:kpt on towards fin* **8/1**

5000 **4** *nk* **Montana**^{23} [3398] 6-8-8 **44** oh3 .... JosephWalsh 15 49
(C W Fairhurst) *chsd ldrs on stands rail: rdn 2f out: styd on ins last* **8/1**

4630 **5** *1* **The Salwick Flyer (IRE)**^{10} [3814] 3-8-7 **50** .... ChristopherEly$^{(3)}$ 16 51
(A Berry) *bhd: gd hdwy wl over 1f out: styd on strly ins last: nrst fin* **40/1**

3026 **6** *nk* **Butterfly Bud (IRE)**^{12} [3759] 3-9-13 **67** .... MarkCoumbe 3 67+
(J O'Reilly) *trckd ldrs: hdwy to chal 2f out: sn rdn and ev ch tl drvn and wknd ent last* **12/1**

6060 **7** *1/2* **Harrington Bates**^{13} [3749] 5-8-3 **44** oh3 .... (v) PaulPickard$^{(5)}$ 7 44
(R M Whitaker) *sn led: jnd and rdn 2f out: hdd over 1f out and grad wknd* **14/1**

40-0 **8** *1 1/2* **Caribbean Nights (IRE)**^{7} [3910] 3-9-5 **59** .... WilliamCarson 9 53
(T D Easterby) *in tch: rdn along over 2f out: kpt on ins last* **33/1**

0006 **9** *shd* **Cate Washington**^{21} [3478] 3-8-5 **45** .... JemmaMarshall 14 39
(Mrs L Williamson) *in tch: rdn along 2f out: sn no imp* **25/1**

-606 **10** *nk* **Athena's Dream**^{6} [3931] 3-9-3 **65** .... JonjoMilczarek$^{(8)}$ 6 58+
(C F Wall) *wnt rt s and towards rr tl styd on fnl 2f: nvr a factor* **12/1**

0502 **11** *3/4* **Cape Sydney (IRE)**^{35} [3039] 3-8-5 **45** .... BRoper 11 36
(D W Barker) *towards rr: swtchd lft and effrt on outer 1/2-way: sn rdn along and plugged on same pce* **9/1**

0500 **12** *4* **North Fleet**^{59} [2316] 3-8-10 **58** .... PietroRomeo$^{(8)}$ 2 37
(J M Bradley) *cl up: rdn along 1/2-way: wknd over 2f out* **25/1**

3323 **13** *2* **Naval Attache**^{14} [3698] 4-9-7 **57** .... SophieDoyle 4 31
(P A Blockley) *cl up: rdn over 2f out: sn wknd* **15/2**^{3}

00-0 **14** *4* **Magical World**^{20} [3538] 3-8-4 **44** oh9 .... DanielleMcCreery 1 6
(J M Bradley) *racd wd: a towards rr* **100/1**

5000 **15** *1/2* **Decider (USA)**^{20} [3538] 3-8-5 **45** .... MarkWaite 5 5
(J M Bradley) *cl up: rdn along wl over 2f out: sn wknd* **40/1**

405- **16** *26* **Tempestuous Sea (IRE)**^{388} [3412] 3-9-8 **65** .... DeanHeslop$^{(3)}$ 8 —
(T D Barron) *chsd ldrs to 1/2-way: sn lost pl and bhd* **16/1**

1m 13.95s (1.45) **Going Correction** +0.05s/f (Good)
WFA 3 from 4yo+ 4lb **16** Ran SP% **126.8**
Speed ratings (Par 103):92,91,90,89,88 88,87,85,85,84 83,78,75,70,69 35
CSF £20.76 CT £151.11 TOTE £3.30: £1.50, £2.50, £1.60, £2.10; EX 34.40 Place 6 £197.31, Place 5 £116.53..
Owner Barrie Abbott **Bred** N Bycroft **Trained** Brandsby, N Yorks
■ Stewards' Enquiry : Paul Pickard caution: careless riding
Alan Rutter caution: careless riding

FOCUS
A typically weak maiden handicap, in which it paid to be drawn high, and the first two came clear. The form is moderate.
T/Plt: £474.80 to a £1 stake. Pool: £53,896.80. 82.85 winning tickets. T/Qpdt: £15.50 to a £1 stake. Pool: £3,282.20. 156.00 winning tickets. JR

The Form Book, Raceform Ltd, Compton, RG20 6NL

[4030] GALWAY (R-H)

Friday, August 4

OFFICIAL GOING: Good to firm

4121a ST. JAMES'S GATE RACE 1m 6f

5:40 (5:40) 4-Y-0+ **£9,877** (£2,897; £1,380; £470)

RPR

1 **Elusive Dream**[12] [3775] 5-9-6 .... DPMcDonogh 5 110
(Sir Mark Prescott) *mde virtually all: drvn along over 4f out: rdn clr 2 1/2f out: styd on strly: eased cl home* **4/9**[1]

2 *14* **Peak Of Perfection (IRE)**[4] [4013] 5-9-2 82 .... FMBerry 10 85
(P Hughes, Ire) *hld up: prog 1/2-way: 3rd 5f out: 4th and rdn over 3f out: mod 2nd into st: kpt on same pce* **12/1**[3]

3 *5 1/2* **Keel Castle Maine (IRE)**[17] [3630] 5-8-13 .... CDHayes(3) 6 77
(Patrick Joseph Hayes, Ire) *towards rr: prog into 5th 5f out: 2nd and rdn under 4f out: outpcd 3f out: mod 3rd and no ex st* **50/1**

4 *16* **Muntami (IRE)**[103] [98] 5-9-2 65 .... JAHeffernan 8 53
(S Donohoe, Ire) *trckd ldrs: 3rd bef 1/2-way: 4th 5f out: 5th and no imp 4f out: kpt on same pce* **50/1**

5 *27* **Impartial**[4] [4013] 5-9-6 70 .... CO'Donoghue 1 17
(S J Mahon, Ire) *chsd ldrs: 5th and rdn 1/2-way: wknd over 4f out: eased st: t.o* **50/1**

6 *4* **Statute**[28] [3273] 4-8-10 44 ow1 .... (t) SJGray(7) 7 8
(F J Bowles, Ire) *nvr a factor: t.o* **100/1**

7 *1 1/2* **Salford City (IRE)**[307] 5-9-9 108 .... (t) JMurtagh 9 11
(Noel Meade, Ire) *prom: 2nd 1/2-way: 3rd and rdn under 4f out: 4th and no ex bef st: virtually p.u fnl f: t.o* **5/2**[2]

8 *dist* **Pretty In Pink (IRE)**[782] [2916] 7-8-8 .... WJLee(3) 4 —
(Anthony Moloney, Ire) *cl up early: wknd fr 1/2-way: completely t.o* **100/1**

3m 2.20s **8** Ran SP% **113.4**

CSF £7.29 TOTE £1.60: £1.10, £1.30, £2.40; DF 7.10.

Owner Cheveley Park Stud **Bred** Cheveley Park Stud Ltd **Trained** Newmarket, Suffolk

NOTEBOOK

Elusive Dream proved far too strong for his rivals. A prolific sort, whose most recent success came in a two-mile Listed event in Germany last month, he made much of the running and had his rivals in trouble with nearly half a mile to run. He stretched right away over the final two furlongs for a wide-margin success. A tough, durable and honest performer, he will continue to win his share of races. (op 2/5)

Salford City(IRE) was an intriguing runner on his first start since last October. A former winner of the Greenham Stakes, he also ran well in the 2000 Guineasand the Derby when last seen in action in Europe. He was returning here from a spell in America where he had run quite respectably at both Grade 1 and Grade 2 level. This trip represented a step into the unknown for him and he was in trouble with half a mile to run, eventually weakening right out of contention and being eased in the straight. He was reported to have choked in running. Official explanation: jockey said gelding blew hard post race (op 9/4)

Pretty In Pink(IRE) Official explanation: trainer said mare was found to have a nasal discharge post race

4124a ARTHUR GUINNESS H'CAP 1m 100y

7:55 (7:56) (50-70,70) 3-Y-O **£7,148** (£1,665; £734; £424)

RPR

1 **Careless Abandon (IRE)**[4] [4014] 3-9-7 63 .... WSupple 3 74
(Andrew Oliver, Ire) *trckd ldrs: 5th 1/2-way: 3rd and hdwy 2 1/2f out: sn chal: led early st: kpt on wl u.p: all out* **10/1**

2 *hd* **Cabo (FR)**[4] [4015] 3-10-0 70 .... FMBerry 16 81
(C F Swan, Ire) *settled 2nd: led 2 1/2f out: sn strly pressed: hdd early st: rallied u.p: no ex nr fin* **5/2**[1]

3 *2* **Sue Princesse (IRE)**[7] [3920] 3-8-13 60 .... (p) JamieMoriarty(5) 12 67
(K J Condon, Ire) *towards rr: hdwy 2 1/2f out: 5th itno st: r.o wl fnl f* **16/1**

4 *1 1/2* **Sky High Guy (IRE)**[37] [2990] 3-9-11 67 .... DPMcDonogh 6 71
(S Kirk) *mid-div: prog into 4th over 2f out: sn rdn: no imp st: kpt on same pce* **6/1**[2]

5 *4 1/2* **Flexline (IRE)**[4] [4014] 3-8-12 61 .... (b) SJGray(7) 4 56
(Daniel Mark Loughnane, Ire) *chsd ldrs: 4th u.p 1/2-way: impr into 2nd and chal over 2f out: cl 3rd into st: sn no ex* **14/1**

6 *1 1/4* **Paddy's Day (IRE)**[27] [3319] 3-9-8 64 .... CO'Donoghue 8 57
(T J O'Mara, Ire) *towards rr: rdn and kpt on st* **33/1**

7 *1 3/4* **Delivered (IRE)**[16] [3654] 3-9-1 62 .... PBBeggy(5) 9 51
(Kevin Prendergast, Ire) *mid-div: 6th u.p over 2f out: no imp st* **12/1**

8 *3/4* **Glazier Mist (IRE)**[16] [3653] 3-9-7 70 .... MJLane(7) 15 58
(Ms F M Crowley, Ire) *chsd ldrs: 6th 1/2-way:* **7/1**[3]

9 *1* **Blackriver Boy**[70] [2002] 3-9-7 63 .... (t) JMurtagh 18 49
(Niall Moran, Ire) *towards rr early: prog into mid-div 1/2-way: no imp fr over 2f out* **12/1**

10 *shd* **Squire Street (USA)**[43] [2797] 3-9-6 62 .... PShanahan 13 47
(C Collins, Ire) *towards rr: kpt on same pce fr 3f out* **16/1**

11 *1* **Ribald**[11] [3806] 3-9-5 61 .... (p) KFallon 5 44
(T Hogan, Ire) *prom: 3rd 1/2-way: rdn and wknd fr 3f out* **6/1**[2]

12 *2* **Lothian Lass (IRE)**[51] [2561] 3-9-6 62 .... (b[1]) PJSmullen 11 41
(D K Weld, Ire) *nvr a factor* **12/1**

13 *3/4* **Tullyorior Promise (IRE)**[20] [3558] 3-9-8 67 .... RPCleary(3) 7 45
(Emmanuel Hughes, Ire) *hld up: prog into mid-div and rdn over 2f out: no ex st* **50/1**

14 *4* **News At Ten (IRE)**[96] [1327] 3-9-6 62 .... (b[1]) DJCondon 17 32
(Declan Gillespie, Ire) *a bhd* **20/1**

15 *2 1/2* **Grand Slam Maria (FR)**[16] [3653] 3-9-1 60 .... WJLee(3) 10 25
(A J McNamara, Ire) *trckd ldrs: 6th 1/2-way: sn wknd* **33/1**

16 *8* **Queen's Entry (IRE)**[43] [2798] 3-9-2 58 .... JAHeffernan 14 7
(Patrick Carey, Ire) *nvr a factor* **40/1**

17 *6* **Hello Man (IRE)**[23] [3421] 3-9-10 66 .... MCHussey 1 3
(Eamon Tyrrell, Ire) *led: hdd & wknd 2 1/2f out: virtually p.u st* **16/1**

1m 48.2s **17** Ran SP% **141.2**

CSF £38.77 CT £459.86 TOTE £9.60: £2.00, £1.20, £3.80, £1.40; DF 28.90.

Owner Mrs M P Oliver **Bred** K And Mrs Cullen **Trained** Caledon, Co. Tyrone

NOTEBOOK

Sky High Guy(IRE) lacked a change of pace and remains a maiden. He may do better ridden from the front. (op 5/1)

4122 - 4124a (Foreign Racing) - See Raceform Interactive

[4096] GOODWOOD (R-H)

Saturday, August 5

OFFICIAL GOING: Good to firm

Wind: Light, half-against Weather: Fine and warm

4125 VODAFONE STKS (H'CAP) 1m 3f

1:30 (1:32) (Class 3) (0-90,90) 3-Y-O

£11,217 (£3,358; £1,679; £840; £419; £210) **Stalls** Low

Form RPR

1403 **1** **Numeric (GER)**[28] [3292] 3-9-2 **85** .... (b) JimmyFortune 2 95
(J H M Gosden) *swtg: dwlt: hld up in last trio: stdy prog on inner fr 3f out: rdn and swtchd lft jst over 1f out: led last 100yds: drvn out* **8/1**

2231 **2** *nk* **New Guinea**[29] [3258] 3-9-3 **86** .... PhilipRobinson 4 95
(M A Jarvis) *pressed ldr: rdn to ld wl over 1f out: hdd last 100yds: styd on but a hld* **7/2**[1]

5500 **3** *1/2* **Beau Nash (USA)**[23] [3443] 3-8-13 **82** .... MJKinane 9 91
(P W Chapple-Hyam) *trckd ldrs: poised to chal 2f out: rdn jst over 1f out: nt qckn and a jst hld fnl f* **14/1**

1221 **4** *3/4* **Cool Customer (USA)**[19] [3589] 3-9-7 **90** .... LDettori 13 97
(E A L Dunlop) *lw: hld up in midfield: effrt over 2f out: prog to press ldrs 1f out: kpt on but no imp last 100yds* **9/2**[2]

0222 **5** *1 1/4* **Fire Two**[13] [3760] 3-8-7 **76** .... JohnEgan 5 81
(M R Channon) *lw: stmbld s: settled in last trio: rdn 3f out: no prog tl r.o jst over 1f out: nrst fin* **12/1**

51 **6** *1/2* **Majaales (USA)**[37] [3029] 3-9-1 **84** .... RHills 8 88
(M P Tregoning) *racd wd: hld up towards rr: shkn up 3f out: no prog tl styd on fr over 1f out: n.d* **6/1**[3]

1200 **7** *nk* **Idarah (USA)**[28] [3292] 3-9-5 **88** .... MartinDwyer 6 92
(W J Haggas) *led: rdn and hdd wl over 1f out: styd w ev ch tl wknd ins fnl f* **22/1**

2130 **8** *1 1/4* **Mystic Storm**[28] [3318] 3-8-5 **74** .... JoeFanning 1 75
(Lady Herries) *trckd ldng pair: rdn to chal 2f out: wknd over 1f out* **14/1**

10 **9** *4* **Simondiun**[38] [2986] 3-9-6 **89** .... KDarley 3 83
(Mrs A J Perrett) *dwlt: a in last trio: outpcd and btn over 2f out: plugged on* **20/1**

-334 **10** *1 1/2* **Monets Masterpiece (USA)**[43] [2825] 3-8-9 **78** .... TPQueally 12 70
(G L Moore) *settled in midfield: rdn 3f out: wknd fr 2f out* **25/1**

21 **11** *shd* **Candle**[45] [2753] 3-8-11 **80** .... DaneO'Neill 11 72
(H Candy) *lw: dwlt: sn midfield: rdn over 2f out: sn wknd* **15/2**

5-62 **12** *9* **Ned Ludd (IRE)**[16] [3665] 3-8-11 **80** .... RyanMoore 7 56
(R Hannon) *nvr bttr than midfield: rdn 3f out: wknd rapidly 2f out* **16/1**

2m 24.25s (-2.96) **Going Correction** -0.10s/f (Good) **12** Ran SP% **117.4**

Speed ratings (Par 104):106,105,105,104,103 103,103,102,99,98 98,91

CSF £34.69 CT £393.29 TOTE £10.60: £2.80, £1.60, £5.50; EX 41.60 Trifecta £855.60 Part won. Pool: £1,205.16 - 0.30 winning units..

Owner Highclere Thoroughbred Racing XXX **Bred** Dr Chr Berglar **Trained** Newmarket, Suffolk

FOCUS

A decent handicap run at a steady pace, and ending with the first four covered by just a length and a half. The form looks sound with the placed horses to form.

NOTEBOOK

Numeric(GER) stays at least a furlong more than this, and it was his stamina that eventually won the day. Raised 3lb for finishing third last time out, he continues to improve bit by bit, with the headgear looking likely to stay on for the foreseeable future because he is known to be lazy. (op 7-1)

New Guinea ◆ made the winner fight for victory, so this goes down as a good start to his handicap career. He can win off his current mark, and should improve further too, with All-Weather races a viable option following his win on sand last time out. (op 4-1 tchd 9-2 in places)

Beau Nash(USA), who ran particularly well on soft ground earlier in the season, bounced back to form following two lack-lustre efforts on fast ground. However, he won on good to firm as a juvenile and still acts well on it, as he proved here with a solid effort that sets him up nicely for the remainder of the summer.

Cool Customer(USA) found an 8lb rise in this better company a little too much to overcome, but he still ran well. (op 4-1 tchd 5-1 in a place)

Fire Two got the longer trip really well, and might even stay a bit farther on this evidence. Official explanation: jockey said colt stumbled leaving stalls (op 16-1)

Majaales(USA), taking a big step up from maiden company, ran with credit. Even better can be expected from this sort of handicap mark as he strengthens up. (op 11-2)

Idarah(USA)'s best trip is probably ten furlongs. (op 20-1 tchd 25-1)

4126 VODAFONE THOROUGHBRED STKS (LISTED RACE) 1m

2:00 (2:03) (Class 1) 3-Y-O

£19,873 (£7,532; £3,769; £1,879; £941; £472) **Stalls** High

Form RPR

-210 **1** **Prince Of Light (IRE)**[4] [4025] 3-9-0 109 .... JoeFanning 1 109
(M Johnston) *mde virtually all: fnd ex whn jnd 3f out: edgd lft fnl f: drvn and kpt on wl* **9/2**[2]

2251 **2** *3/4* **Metropolitan Man**[16] [3671] 3-9-0 108 .... MartinDwyer 5 107
(D M Simcock) *warm: t.k.h: trckd ldrs: jnd wnr wl over 2f out: sn rdn and unable qckn: drifted lft 1f out: kpt on but a hld* **15/2**

4-04 **3** *nk* **City Of Troy**[85] [1627] 3-9-0 100 .... (t) RyanMoore 8 106
(Sir Michael Stoute) *t.k.h: hld up in rr: rdn over 2f out and sn outpcd: carried hd high but styd on fr over 1f out* **15/2**

301 **4** *1 1/2* **Dark Islander (IRE)**[22] [3491] 3-9-0 98 .... RHills 9 103
(J W Hills) *t.k.h: trckd ldrs: cl up over 2f out: sn rdn and outpcd: kpt on same pce after* **4/1**[1]

15-2 **5** *hd* **True Cause (USA)**[23] [3432] 3-9-0 105 .... (v) LDettori 3 102+
(Saeed Bin Suroor) *taken down early: t.k.h: hld up in last pair: rdn over 2f out: no prog tl styd on ins fnl f* **6/1**[3]

4600 **6** *1* **Yarqus**[8] [3889] 3-9-0 100 .... JimmyFortune 7 100
(C E Brittain) *pressed wnr: upsides over 3f out: sn rdn and lost pl: no prog over 1f out* **33/1**

3016 **7** *nk* **Snoqualmie Boy**[28] [3314] 3-9-4 111 .... JohnEgan 2 103
(D R C Elsworth) *lw: in tch: rdn and prog on outer to press ldrs 2f out: wknd rapidly jst over 1f out* **6/1**[3]

11 **8** *shd* **Multidimensional (IRE)**[14] [3740] 3-9-0 101 .... TedDurcan 6 99
(H R A Cecil) *lw: trckd ldrs: lost pl and rdn 3f out: hanging bdly rt fnl 2f and no prog* **4/1**[1]

1m 38.27s (-2.00) **Going Correction** -0.10s/f (Good) **8** Ran SP% **113.2**

Speed ratings (Par 108):106,105,104,103,103 102,101,101

CSF £36.98 TOTE £5.90: £1.80, £2.10, £2.30; EX 46.70 Trifecta £234.60 Pool: £1,427.48 - 4.32 winning units..

Owner Claire Riordan And Kieran Coughlan **Bred** High Bramley Grange Stud Ltd **Trained** Middleham Moor, N Yorks

FOCUS

A decent Listed race, but run at a muddling pace with the winner getting a largely uncontested lead. The form is fair for the grade with the fourth the best guide.

NOTEBOOK

Prince Of Light(IRE) had run here in a better race four days earlier, and seemed to enjoy himself more dominating these rivals, who allowed him to do his own thing. Though carrying his head rather strangely, his battling qualities could not be faulted, with this trip appearing to suit him well these days. (tchd 5-1)

Metropolitan Man found another rival to make the running this time, but that turned out to be the winner, who proved to be impossible to pass. However, he did his level best, and remains a useful customer at Listed and Group 3 level. (tchd 7-1)

City Of Troy, dropped from Group level, looks capable of winning a Listed contest, with this trip looking more suitable than ten furlongs at present, but he does not look a straightforward ride. (op 8-1)

Dark Islander(IRE) made a decent attempt to make the step up from handicaps into Listed company, only to fall slightly short. However, he had a fair crack at it and is worth another chance. (op 9-2 tchd 5-1 in places)

True Cause(USA) may be more effective at slightly longer trips than this, though he is becoming something of a character and needs to be ridden accordingly. (op 13-2 tchd 7-1)

Yarqus gave it his best shot at a big price, but was not quite good enough. He has been campaigned highly in several races this season, but his performance in a valuable handicap last time out was nothing special, so there seems no harm in having another go in Listed company.

Snoqualmie Boy's form is at ten furlongs and farther, so this seemed an odd choice of race for him. In the circumstances, he did not run badly, but he can do much better at longer trips. (op 9-2)

Multidimensional(IRE) has shown a tendency to hang in all three races to date, so a galloping track ought to be more suitable for him. (tchd 9-2)

4127 VODAFONE NASSAU STKS (GROUP 1) (F&M) 1m 1f 192y

2:30 (2:37) (Class 1) 3-Y-O+

£113,560 (£43,040; £21,540; £10,740; £5,380; £2,700) **Stalls** High

Form				RPR
3215	1		**Ouija Board**[28] [3314] 5-9-5 120 ... LDettori 7 (E A L Dunlop) *trckd ldr: led over 3f out: narrowly hdd and rdn wl over 1f out: rallied gamely fnl f: led post* **1/1**[1]	124
-521	2	shd	**Alexander Goldrun (IRE)**[35] [3105] 5-9-5 ... KJManning 5 (J S Bolger, Ire) *lw: hld up in last: smooth prog to join wnr over 2f out: led narrowly wl over 1f out: r.o bravely fnl f: hdd post* **9/2**[3]	123
-012	3	2	**Nannina**[24] [3416] 3-8-10 117 ... JimmyFortune 4 (J H M Gosden) *hld up: rdn and outpcd over 2f out: styd on to take 3rd 1f out: nvr able to chal* **4/1**[2]	119
-422	4	2 ½	**Chelsea Rose (IRE)**[35] [3105] 4-9-5 ... PShanahan 1 (C Collins, Ire) *led to over 3f out: grad outpcd over 2f out: wknd fnl f* **12/1**	115
-112	5	2	**Echelon**[45] [2740] 4-9-5 107 ... KDarley 3 (Sir Michael Stoute) *lw: hld up in tch: nvr looked happy: rdn 3f out: struggling after* **16/1**	111
-044	6	1 ½	**Race For The Stars (USA)**[43] [2802] 3-8-10 ... MJKinane 2 (A P O'Brien, Ire) *trckd ldr: upsides over 3f out to wl over 2f out: wknd tamely sn after* **10/1**	108
3035	7	5	**Nasheej (USA)**[24] [3416] 3-8-10 111 ... RyanMoore 6 (R Hannon) *rdn in rr over 3f out: sn wl btn* **20/1**	99

2m 4.47s (-3.28) **Going Correction** -0.10s/f (Good)
WFA 3 from 4yo+ 9lb **7** Ran SP% **115.6**
Speed ratings (Par 117):109,108,107,105,103 102,98
CSF £6.01 TOTE £2.00: £1.60, £1.70; EX 4.80.

Owner Lord Derby **Bred** Stanley Estate & Stud Co **Trained** Newmarket, Suffolk

FOCUS

A cracking renewal, contested by the winners of 13 Group Ones, though run at a modest pace until Dettori seized the initiative on the winner early in the straight. The form looks solid, rated around the first two.

NOTEBOOK

Ouija Board just got back up in an epic race which had the crowd on its feet throughout the last two furlongs. Her movements for the rest of the season are undecided at present, but this may have been her last appearance in Britain, with her reputation as an all-time great already secure. (op 5-4 tchd 11-8 in places)

Alexander Goldrun(IRE), the winner twelve months earlier, played a magnificent part in one of the greatest races even seen at Goodwood - or anywhere else for that matter. Like the winner, she is a genuine Group 1 performer, and deserves all the plaudits that come her way for a splendid effort. She is now likely to go for the Irish Champion Stakes. (tchd 5-1)

Nannina got the extra two furlongs really well, which opens up several new options for the rest of the season. To finish just a couple of lengths behind two terrific mares, who had already achieved plenty at the distance, should be regarded as an achievement rather than a failure. (tchd 9-2)

Chelsea Rose(IRE) is very versatile, and looks capable of winning in Group company from a mile to a mile and a half, but this race was something special and she was not quite up to it. However, it was another honourable effort. (tchd 10-1)

Echelon was not only stepping into Group 1 company, but into one of the best-ever fields lined up for this race, and her starting price reflected the task she faced. In the event, she was always finding things a bit too hot once the race began in earnest, with a return to a mile now looking likely. (op 14-1)

Race For The Stars(USA) has looked a little below the best this season, and this extremely hot race was not the ideal vehicle in which to expect a renaissance of her winning juvenile form. In any case, she probably failed to stay the extra two furlongs. (op 8-1)

Nasheej(USA) had an uphill task, but ran below her capabilities over a trip which may be too far for her anyway. (op 25-1)

4128 VODAFONE STEWARDS' CUP (HERITAGE H'CAP) 6f

3:05 (3:11) (Class 2) 3-Y-O+

£62,320 (£18,660; £9,330; £4,670; £2,330; £1,170) **Stalls** Low

Form				RPR
-142	1		**Borderlescott**[13] [3767] 4-9-5 102 ... RoystonFfrench 19 (R Bastiman) *trckd far side ldrs: effrt over 1f out: rdn to ld last 150yds: styd on wl* **10/1**	114
1100	2	nk	**Mutamared (USA)**[42] [2847] 6-8-13 96 ... NCallan 26 (K A Ryan) *pressed far side ldr: nt clr run over 1f out: swtchd rt and rdn to chal ins fnl f: styd on: a jst hld* **12/1**	109+
-312	3	nk	**Firenze**[42] [2847] 5-9-1 98 ... LDettori 22 (J R Fanshawe) *lw: towards rr far side: rdn and struggling over 2f out: prog over 1f out: r.o fnl f: nrst fin* **5/1**[1]	109
402	4	hd	**Excusez Moi (USA)**[28] [3295] 4-9-0 97 ... RyanMoore 28 (C E Brittain) *trckd far side ldrs: nt clr run jst over 1f out and swtchd sharply lft: r.o wl last 100yds: gaining at fin* **12/1**	111+
-330	5	shd	**Tax Free (IRE)**[46] [2720] 4-9-10 107 ... AdrianTNicholls 27 (D Nicholls) *led far side gp: hanging lft fr over 1f out: hdd and nt qckn last 150yds* **11/2**[2]	117
4335	6	shd	**Bahamian Pirate (USA)**[28] [3295] 11-9-2 99 ... SilvestreDeSousa 25 (D Nicholls) *settled midfield of far side gp: effrt over 1f out: r.o against far rail fnl f: nrst fin* **66/1**	108
3622	7	shd	**Woodcote (IRE)**[22] [3471] 4-8-7 93 ... (p) AdamKirby(3) 4 (C G Cox) *taken down early: hld up in rr nr side: prog 1/2-way: led gp over 1f out: hung bdly rt and ended on far side: styd on* **25/1**	102
0400	8	1	**Obe Gold**[7] [3956] 4-9-3 100 ... JohnEgan 14 (M R Channon) *s.i.s: hld up in rr nr side: prog over 2f out: hung rt over 1f out: kpt on: n.d* **80/1**	106
-200	9	shd	**Munaddam (USA)**[44] [2776] 4-8-13 96 ... RHills 21 (E A L Dunlop) *dwlt: hld up in last pair far side: nt clr run briefly 2f out: styng on wl but no ch whn rn out of room last 50yds* **33/1**	102
2005	10	nk	**Bond City (IRE)**[21] [3520] 4-9-3 100 ... TedDurcan 5 (B Smart) *trckd nr side ldrs: effrt 2f out: nt on terms over 1f out: kpt on* **100/1**	105
-602	11	shd	**Intrepid Jack**[22] [3493] 4-8-13 96 ... (v[1]) SteveDrowne 18 (H Morrison) *lw: hld up in midfield far side: no real prog over 1f out: kpt on same pce* **10/1**	101
0012	12	shd	**One More Round (USA)**[6] [3972] 8-8-11 97 ... (b) JamesDoyle(3) 23 (N P Littmoden) *hld up wl in rr far side: rdn 2f out: styd on ins fnl f: nt pce to rch ldrs* **14/1**	101
0020	13	½	**Texas Gold**[6] [3972] 8-8-12 98 ... RichardKingscote(3) 2 (W R Muir) *trckd nr side ldrs: effrt and cl up over 1f out but nt on terms w far gp: kpt on* **25/1**	101
0300	14	shd	**Out After Dark**[48] [2675] 5-9-4 101 ... (p) KDarley 12 (C G Cox) *racd on outer of nr side gp: pressed ldrs: upsides wl over 1f out: edgd rt and fdd* **66/1**	103
1100	15	nk	**One Putra (IRE)**[28] [3312] 4-9-9 106 ... PhilipRobinson 3 (M A Jarvis) *racd against nr side rail: hld up in tch: no ch fnl f: running on at fin* **40/1**	108
0340	16	shd	**Continent**[22] [3482] 9-8-8 91 ... JoeFanning 1 (D Nicholls) *taken down early: hld up last of nr side gp: no ch fr over 1f out: running on at fin* **33/1**	92
0146	17	¾	**Peace Offering (IRE)**[6] [3972] 6-8-10 100 ... VictoriaBehan(7) 13 (D Nicholls) *taken down early: awkward s but led nr side gp to over 1f out: wknd* **100/1**	99
2101	18	hd	**Bentong (IRE)**[13] [3761] 3-8-9 99 3ex ... NelsonDeSouza(3) 20 (P F I Cole) *swtg: pressed far side ldrs: cl up whn hmpd jst over 1f out: wknd* **6/1**[3]	97
0030	19	nk	**Connect**[6] [3972] 9-8-10 93 ... (b) TPQueally 8 (M H Tompkins) *hld up in last trio nr side: nt clr run 2f out: no ch after: kpt on fnl f* **100/1**	90
4020	20	nk	**Talbot Avenue**[21] [3520] 8-8-13 96 ... JimmyFortune 9 (M Mullineaux) *b.hind: t.k.h: trckd nr side ldrs for 4f: fdd* **66/1**	93
1101	21	½	**Folga**[14] [3741] 4-8-9 92 5ex ... JamieMackay 7 (J G Given) *chsd nr side ldrs: no ch fr over 1f out* **40/1**	87
12-0	22	1 ¾	**Musadif (USA)**[28] [3312] 8-9-9 106 ... (t) FJohansson 24 (R A Kvisla) *taken down early: chsd far side ldrs tl wknd over 1f out* **100/1**	96
-630	23	½	**Gimasha**[22] [3499] 4-8-9 92 ... AlanMunro 6 (W Jarvis) *taken down early: cl up nr side for 4f: wknd* **33/1**	80
0420	24	1 ¼	**Beaver Patrol (IRE)**[7] [3926] 4-8-10 93 ... StephenCarson 17 (R F Johnson Houghton) *lw: racd far side: nvr on terms: struggling 2f out* **33/1**	78
3000	25	½	**If Paradise**[6] [3972] 5-8-11 94 ... DaneO'Neill 10 (R Hannon) *cl up nr side over 3f: wknd* **100/1**	77
/101	26	¾	**Desert Commander (IRE)**[60] [2323] 4-9-0 97 ... MJKinane 16 (K A Ryan) *racd on outer of nr side gp: in tch: wknd rapidly and eased jst over 1f out* **9/1**	78
0400	27	½	**Merlin's Dancer**[36] [3038] 6-8-12 95 ... KJManning 11 (D Nicholls) *w nr side ldr tl wknd rapidly wl over 1f out* **66/1**	74

69.93 secs (-2.92) **Going Correction** -0.10s/f (Good)
WFA 3 from 4yo+ 4lb **27** Ran SP% **133.1**
Speed ratings (Par 109):115,114,114,113,113 113,113,112,112,111 111,111,110,110,110 110,109,108,108,108 107,105,104,10
CSF £115.69 CT £696.78 TOTE £14.10: £3.90, £4.40, £2.10, £3.10; EX 314.90 Trifecta £1850.60 Pool: £59,951.94 - 23.00 winning units..

Owner Border Rail & Plant Limited **Bred** James Clark **Trained** Cowthorpe, N Yorks

FOCUS

A good renewal of this major sprint handicap. The stands'-side runners (low stalls) led early on, but the far side (high stalls) eventually did best. Other races earlier in the week suggested no draw bias. The winning time was well up to standard for the grade and the form looks solid.

NOTEBOOK

Borderlescott is on a smart upward curve and may eventually have to switch permanently from handicaps into Pattern company. However, this progressive sort looks capable of making his mark at that level, as a number of winners of this race have in the past. (op 9-1)

Mutamared(USA) ran a fine race despite sweating up badly and not getting the best of runs. He is a likely sort for similarly valuable sprint handicaps during the rest of the season. (tchd 14-1 in a place)

Firenze, up 5lb since the Wokingham, got going to too late after struggling to go the pace down the hill. However, she remains a very smart sprinter, with connections keen to find a suitable Listed or Pattern race for her in the coming months. (op 9-2 tchd 11-2 in places)

Excusez Moi(USA), who got warm beforehand, rattled home after being blocked in his run, and can be rated a bit better than this. A decent sprint should be his by the end of the season, though to date he has won only a maiden.

Tax Free(IRE) made a brave effort to make all in the far-side group - never easy at the sort of pace at which this race is invariably run - and deserves credit for going so close. (op 6-1)

Bahamian Pirate(USA) somehow found a way through on the far rail, belying his odds with a sterling effort. (op 50-1)

Woodcote(IRE) was the first home of the low-drawn horses, though he ended up with the far-side group after drifting across the track. He did well on ground that may have been faster than ideal. Official explanation: jockey said gelding hung right-handed inside final furlong

Obe Gold is doing his best to defy the Handicapper, but good efforts like this will not encourage the assessor to drop him down the weights. (op 100-1)

Munaddam(USA) came from a long way back, and should be worth keeping an eye on in future engagements.

Bond City(IRE) did best of those that raced stands' side all the way and, in being beaten barely two lengths, was hardly disgraced. However, previous big-field races over the straight track earlier in the week suggested no obvious draw bias this year.

One Putra(IRE) got warm beforehand, but he kept on well inside the final furlong without ever threatening.

Bentong(IRE) would have finished closer but for being snatched up and eased when meeting trouble in running. (tchd 7-1 in a place and 11-2 in places)

4129 VODAFONE EUROPEAN BREEDERS FUND MAIDEN STKS (C&G) 7f
3:40 (3:46) (Class 2) 2-Y-O £10,363 (£3,083; £1,540; £769) Stalls High

Form RPR

30 **1** **Kilburn**[30] 3222 2-9-0 PhilipRobinson 1 84
(C G Cox) *fast away and crossed fr outside draw: mde all: rdn and hld on wl fnl f* **25/1**

2 1/2 **Mariotto (USA)** 2-9-0 JoeFanning 10 83
(M Johnston) *lw: sn chsd wnr: rdn 2f out: styd on to chal fnl f: a hld* **20/1**

3 1 1/2 **Red Rock Canyon (IRE)**[20] 3573 2-9-0 MJKinane 16 79
(A P O'Brien, Ire) *str: sn trckd ldng pair: rdn over 2f out: nt qckn and hld over 1f out: kpt on* **4/7**[1]

4 1 3/4 **Don't Panic (IRE)** 2-9-0 AlanMunro 14 74
(P W Chapple-Hyam) *unf: swtg: hld up in midfield: effrt on outer 2f out: hanging rt over 1f out: styd on* **16/1**[3]

0 **5** 1 **My Learned Friend (IRE)**[24] 3417 2-9-0 SteveDrowne 11 72
(A M Balding) *trckd ldrs: rdn over 2f out: kpt on same pce and no imp ldrs* **50/1**

2 **6** 3/4 **Sahrati**[18] 3623 2-9-0 TPQueally 2 70
(C E Brittain) *trckd ldrs: effrt over 2f out: one pce and btn over 1f out* **20/1**

2 **7** nk **Romanov Dynasty (IRE)**[23] 3445 2-9-0 RyanMoore 8 69
(R Hannon) *dwlt: wl in rr: sme prog into midfield over 2f out: rn green and no imp over 1f out* **9/2**[2]

0 **8** shd **Italian Stallion (IRE)**[24] 3417 2-9-0 RichardSmith 17 69
(R Hannon) *hld up in midfield: pushed along on inner 2f out: one pce* **66/1**

0 **9** 1 **Grand Heights (IRE)**[42] 2867 2-9-0 NCallan 13 66+
(J L Dunlop) *in tch towards rr: rdn and outpcd 2f out: styng on stoutly whn hmpd and snatched up last 100yds* **100/1**

10 nk **Lunces Lad (IRE)** 2-9-0 TedDurcan 5 65
(M R Channon) *unf: lw: nvr bttr than midfield: shkn up and btn 2f out: wknd* **33/1**

6 **11** 3/4 **Buckie Massa**[30] 3222 2-9-0 JimmyFortune 15 63+
(S Kirk) *lw: t.k.h: cl up: n.m.r 5f out: no prog 2f out: btn whn hmpd ins fnl f* **16/1**[3]

12 1 1/2 **El Dececy (USA)** 2-9-0 RHills 6 59
(J L Dunlop) *w'like: lw: hld up wl in rr: shuffled along and no real prog 2f out* **16/1**[3]

0 **13** 1/2 **Majestas (IRE)**[31] 3193 2-9-0 DaneO'Neill 7 58
(J G M O'Shea) *sn struggling in rr: rdn over 4f out: nvr a factor* **100/1**

36 **14** 1/2 **Raffaas**[21] 3545 2-9-0 NelsonDeSouza 4 57
(M P Tregoning) *hld up wl in rr and racd wd: reminder over 1f out: no ch* **25/1**

15 nk **Rikochet** 2-9-0 LDettori 12 56
(Mrs A J Perrett) *lengthy: lw: sn struggling: a wl in rr* **25/1**

00 **16** 32 **Umpa Loompa (IRE)**[53] 2523 2-9-0 AdrianTNicholls 9 —
(D Nicholls) *t.o fr 1/2-way* **100/1**

1m 26.66s (-1.38) **Going Correction** -0.10s/f (Good) **16** Ran SP% **129.9**
Speed ratings (Par 100):103,102,100,98,97 96,96,96,95,94 93,92,91,91,90 54
CSF £443.13 TOTE £41.60: £6.60, £4.70, £1.20; EX 707.20 TRIFECTA Not won..
Owner Dennis Shaw **Bred** B Walters **Trained** Lambourn, Berks

FOCUS
An above average, though not outstanding, maiden run in a good time which should throw up a number of future winners. Amazingly, the winner got across to the rail from the outside stall, and then dictated a tempo which enabled him to make all.

NOTEBOOK
Kilburn had a difficult task from the lowest draw, but Robinson skilfully got him across to the rail without using up too much early energy, and the extra furlong proved to be well within his range. Always just in charge, he looks a game, battling type who will make the grade in handicaps, and his trainer expects him to stay a mile. (op 20-1)
Mariotto(USA) ◆, a Swain debutant whose dam won over a mile and a half, looks a promising recruit. A Derby entry, he should improve greatly with racing and looks a ready-made maiden winner before going on to better things.
Red Rock Canyon(IRE) had a good draw, unlike the winner, but was still unable to land the odds. Having been beaten in both his first two races, this blue-blooded Rock Of Gibraltar colt, out of the Irish 1000 Guineas and Oaks winner Imagine, has a lot to live up to, though a maiden victory is surely a formality before greater targets are considered. (op 4-6 tchd 8-11 in places)
Don't Panic(IRE), a 40,000gns newcomer from a good Italian family, should be effective at trips up to a mile. Whether he will stay far enough to justify his Derby entry is debatable, but this was a satisfactory debut from which he should learn plenty. (op 33-1)
My Learned Friend(IRE) stepped up a bit on his debut performance, and should pick up a race before long, whether it be a maiden or a nursery after one more run. He ought to stay at least a mile in due course.
Sahrati found this race a bit hotter than the Yarmouth maiden in which he had made his debut, but he ran well enough to keep connections optimistic. (op 25-1)
Romanov Dynasty(IRE) gave himself too much ground to make up. Whether this, or six furlongs, is his trip, he can do much better, judged on his excellent debut performance - the winner there Hamoody having taken the Group 2 Richmond Stakes here the day before. (tchd 5-1)
Italian Stallion(IRE) is showing enough to look a fair nursery prospect after one more run. (op 100-1)
Grand Heights(IRE) will be qualified for nurseries after one more run, and looks a likely improver over longer trips as he matures.

4130 VODAFONE NURSERY STKS (H'CAP) 6f
4:15 (4:15) (Class 3) 2-Y-O £10,687 (£3,179; £1,588; £793) Stalls Low

Form RPR

0143 **1** **Northern Fling**[3] 4043 2-8-10 **84** AdrianTNicholls 6 85
(D Nicholls) *hung rt thrght: chsd ldr: led 2f out: hld on wl fnl f* **7/1**[3]

31 **2** 1 1/4 **Oi Vay Joe (IRE)**[40] 2930 2-8-7 **81** AlanMunro 5 78
(W Jarvis) *lw: chsd ldrs: rdn to chal over 1f out: nt qckn fnl f* **7/2**[2]

513 **3** shd **Part Timer (IRE)**[8] 3903 2-8-11 **85** TedDurcan 7 82
(M R Channon) *dwlt: pushed along and bhd: hdwy to dispute 2nd fnl f: one pce fnl 100 yds* **7/2**[2]

1300 **4** 1 1/4 **Beckenham's Secret**[21] 3530 2-7-12 **75** DominicFox[(3)] 1 68
(B R Millman) *led tl 2f out: hrd rdn and btn over 1f out* **10/1**

3412 **5** 3 1/2 **Argentine (IRE)**[16] 3678 2-8-13 **87** JoeFanning 4 70
(M Johnston) *lw: dwlt: in tch: rdn to join ldrs 2f out: wknd 1f out* **7/4**[1]

0445 **6** 3 **Sparkling Eyes**[29] 3259 2-9-7 **95** RyanMoore 3 69
(C E Brittain) *chsd ldrs: rdn 1/2-way: wknd 2f out* **10/1**

1m 12.29s (-0.56) **Going Correction** -0.10s/f (Good) **6** Ran SP% **111.5**
Speed ratings (Par 98):99,97,97,95,90 86
CSF £30.84 TOTE £8.50: £2.80, £2.40; EX 44.20.
Owner Jim Dale/Jason Berry **Bred** Lady Juliet Tadgell **Trained** Sessay, N Yorks

FOCUS
An ordinary nursery for the track, but run at a solid clip down the hill and the form looks sound.

NOTEBOOK
Northern Fling continues to want to go right-handed, something that should be considered in future engagements. However, he got the extra furlong really well and looks worth campaigning at this trip for the time being. (op 8-1)
Oi Vay Joe(IRE) proved he can handle fast ground with a creditable effort. This was only his third run, his first in a nursery, and he looks the probable winner of a similar event. (op 11-4)
Part Timer(IRE) finally proved he gets this trip, though he found the downhill track too sharp early on and, having made headway, was making no impression up the final incline. The flatter track at Haydock seemed to suit him better. (op 4-1)
Beckenham's Secret looks better on turf than sand, and this was a fair effort. He should stay a bit further as the season progresses. (op 20-1)
Argentine(IRE), having worked his way into contention following a sluggish start, dropped out alarmingly near the centre of the course at the furlong pole. This was not his true form. (op 13-8 tchd 15-8)
Sparkling Eyes looks more of a five-furlong filly at present, but she may not have found this downhill track ideal either. (op 9-1 tchd 8-1)

4131 VODAFONE APPRENTICE STKS (H'CAP) 1m 1f
4:50 (4:50) (Class 3) (0-90,87) 3-Y-O+ £9,715 (£2,890; £1,444; £721) Stalls High

Form RPR

1235 **1** **Lucayan Dancer**[4] 4023 6-9-4 **81** VictoriaBehan[(5)] 7 89
(D Nicholls) *hld up in 4th: smooth hdwy on rail to ld ins fnl 2f: wnt 2l ahd: drvn along fnl f: jst hld on* **11/2**

6600 **2** shd **Diktatorial**[4] 4029 4-9-8 **80** (t) AdamKirby 5 88
(G A Butler) *lw: towards rr: hrd rdn and styd on wl fnl 2f: jst failed* **6/1**

3163 **3** 2 **The Gaikwar (IRE)**[10] 3854 7-8-11 **72** (b) RichardKingscote[(3)] 2 76
(R A Harris) *chsd clr ldng pair: effrt 3f out: wandered fnl 2f: styd on same pce* **14/1**

5415 **4** hd **Joseph Henry**[4] 4029 4-9-9 **84** GregFairley[(3)] 8 88
(M Johnston) *hld up in 5th: effrt over 2f out: styd on same pce appr fnl f* **9/4**[1]

1121 **5** 2 1/2 **Waterside (IRE)**[43] 2819 7-10-0 **86** JamesDoyle 9 85
(G L Moore) *lw: t.k.h: disp ld tl ins fnl 2f: sn outpcd* **5/1**[3]

0430 **6** 1 1/4 **Coup D'Etat**[4] 4023 4-9-12 **84** StephaneBreux 3 80
(J L Dunlop) *s.s: modest last most of way: nvr trbld ldrs* **4/1**[2]

4124 **7** 3 **Deeper In Debt**[23] 3433 8-8-12 **70** DeanCorby 6 60
(J Akehurst) *disp ld tl wknd ins fnl 2f* **13/2**

1m 55.16s (-1.70) **Going Correction** -0.10s/f (Good)
WFA 3 from 4yo+ 8lb **7** Ran SP% **117.1**
Speed ratings (Par 107):103,102,101,100,98 97,94
CSF £39.18 CT £441.84 TOTE £6.90: £3.00, £3.40; EX 44.30 Trifecta £847.70 Part won. Pool: £1,193.95 - 0.80 winning units. Place 6 £103.59. Place 5 £45.30..
Owner James E Greaves **Bred** The National Stud Owner Breeders Club Ltd **Trained** Sessay, N Yorks

FOCUS
An above-average field for a race of this type, and run at a strong gallop. The runner-up is the best guide to the level.

NOTEBOOK
Lucayan Dancer, suited by the strong gallop set by the two front-runners, got a dream run up the inside rail and his rider won the race by dashing him into the lead while he was still full of running. Ideally, he needs farther than this, so victory here was a bonus. (op 6-1 tchd 13-2 and 5-1, 7-1 in places)
Diktatorial, winner of a Group 3 two years ago, has been showing signs of a revival of late, and nearly pulled this off - with the extra furlong being in his favour. He is capable of winning when he finally gets his timing right, though he does not look the most predictable of conveyances these days. (op 5-1 tchd 7-1)
The Gaikwar(IRE), never one to have the mortgage on, plodded away but did not look entirely convincing in his finishing effort.
Joseph Henry, a runner here over a mile four days earlier, got the extra furlong alright, but he is now 4lb higher than his last winning mark. (tchd 11-4)
Waterside(IRE) did not have things his own way in front, and finally gave way after he and Deeper In Debt had disputed it at a good pace seven lengths clear of the rest. (tchd 9-2 and 11-2)
Coup D'Etat, who was on his toes beforehand, probably needs at least ten furlongs these days, and this was much too sharp. Missing the break did not help, but he needs more of a stamina test over a stiffer track. (tchd 9-2)
Deeper In Debt got warm beforehand and could not dominate with fellow front-runner Waterside taking him on, and they both paid the penalty. (op 12-1)
T/Jkpt: Not won. T/Plt: £133.00 to a £1 stake. Pool: £189,967.80. 1,042.50 winning tickets. T/Qpdt: £18.30 to a £1 stake. Pool: £8,382.20. 338.80 winning tickets. JN

3669 HAMILTON (R-H)
Saturday, August 5

OFFICIAL GOING: Good to firm
Wind: Light, across

4132 VARIETY CLUB H'CAP 1m 3f 16y
6:10 (6:10) (Class 6) (0-60,56) 3-Y-O+ £2,590 (£770; £385; £192) Stalls High

Form RPR

1331 **1** **River Logic (IRE)**[12] 3785 3-9-4 **56** StanleyChin 12 64
(A D Brown) *trckd ldrs: led over 2f out: drvn out* **4/1**[2]

0503 **2** 1 **Hurry Up Helen (IRE)**[11] 3823 3-8-12 **50** RobbieFitzpatrick 5 56
(Mrs L Stubbs) *led 1f: cl up: ev ch over 2f out: kpt on same pce ins fnl f* **5/1**[3]

1362 **3** 1/2 **Kyle Of Lochalsh**[16] 3675 6-9-9 **54** DNolan[(3)] 11 59
(J S Goldie) *hld up in tch: rdn and outpcd 3f out: rallied over 1f out: kpt on wl fnl f: nrst fin* **7/2**[1]

3432 **4** 1/2 **Nakwa (IRE)**[11] 3810 8-9-3 **45** PaulEddery 8 49
(E J Alston) *hld up: rdn and outpcd 4f out: gd hdwy over 1f out: kpt on wl fnl f* **8/1**

2344 **5** 1 **Friends Hope**[18] 3610 5-9-4 **53** KevinGhunowa[(7)] 10 56
(P A Blockley) *hld up midfield: rdn and effrt over 2f out: kpt on fnl f: no imp* **4/1**[2]

6-53 **6** 1 3/4 **Neil's Legacy (IRE)**[22] 3480 4-9-8 **50** TonyHamilton 1 50
(Miss L A Perratt) *prom: drvn over 3f out: one pce fr 2f out* **16/1**

3556 **7** 2 **Linton Dancer (IRE)**[12] 3785 3-8-9 **50** (t) BenSwarbrick[(3)] 3 47
(J R Weymes) *keen: led after 1f to over 2f out: sn outpcd* **10/1**

0-00 **8** shd **Montara (IRE)**[13] 3769 7-9-9 **51** (v[1]) CatherineGannon 7 48
(Barry Potts, Ire) *hld up in tch on outside: rdn and edgd rt 3f out: sn outpcd* **14/1**

0000 **9** shd **The Dunion**[45] 2746 3-7-8 **37** LeanneKershaw[(5)] 2 33
(Miss L A Perratt) *bhd: outpcd over 4f out: sme late hdwy: nvr on terms* **100/1**

06-0 **10** 16 **Charlie George**[11] 3815 5-8-9 **37** oh1 LeeEnstone 4 8
(P Monteith) *keen: cl up tl wknd over 3f out* **40/1**

0-05 **11** *6* **Taili**[16] [3675] 5-8-2 **37** oh22 .... NBazeley(7) 9 —
(D A Nolan) *s.i.s: bhd: lost tch fr over 4f out* **100/1**

2m 23.21s (-3.05) **Going Correction** -0.225s/f (Firm)
WFA 3 from 4yo+ 10lb **11** Ran SP% **116.1**
Speed ratings (Par 101):102,101,100,100,99 98,97,97,96,85 80
CSF £23.96 CT £75.98 TOTE £5.90: £2.20, £1.90, £1.30; EX 38.00.
Owner R G Fell **Bred** J K Beckitt And Son **Trained** Pickering, York

FOCUS
An ordinary event in which the moderate gallop meant those racing closest to the pace held the edge. The form looks solid rated around the placed horses.

4133 SUPER SIX CLAIMING STKS — 1m 65y

6:40 (6:40) (Class 6) 3-4-Y-0 — **£2,730** (£806; £403) **Stalls** High

Form — RPR

4051 **1** **Defi (IRE)**[16] [3672] 4-10-0 **69** .... (b) TomEaves 4 — 78
(I Semple) *keen: mde all: rdn clr fr 2f out* **1/1**[1]

2324 **2** *4* **Burnley Al (IRE)**[3] [4057] 4-8-13 **57** .... (b) PaulHanagan 5 — 54
(R A Fahey) *chsd wnr: drvn 3f out: kpt on fnl 2f: nt rch wnr* **11/8**[2]

3530 **3** *5* **Primarily**[37] [3003] 4-9-8 **58** .... TonyHamilton 1 — 52
(A Berry) *in tch: drvn and outpcd 3f out: no imp fr 2f out* **16/1**

-005 **4** *2 ½* **Knock Bridge (IRE)**[19] [3583] 4-8-6 **64** .... KellyHarrison(7) 2 — 37
(D Carroll) *chsd ldrs: hdwy over 3f out: edgd rt and wknd over 1f out* **9/1**[3]

000 **5** *2 ½* **Enjoy The Magic**[102] [1212] 4-8-13 **40** .... PaulEddery 3 — 31
(E J Alston) *in tch: struggling over 3f out: sn btn* **40/1**

1m 45.95s (-3.35) **Going Correction** -0.225s/f (Firm) **5** Ran SP% **110.4**
Speed ratings (Par 101):107,103,98,95,93
CSF £2.64 TOTE £2.00: £1.30, £1.10; EX 2.90.Burnley Al was claimed by Alan Berry for £5,000.
Owner Gordon McDowall **Bred** Skymarc Farm Inc And Dr A J O'Reilly **Trained** Carluke, S Lanarks

FOCUS
An uncompetitive event in which the winner had the run of the race.

4134 FRESH 'N' LO AUCTION NURSERY (A QUALIFIER FOR THE HAMILTON PARK 2-Y-O SERIES FINAL) — 6f 5y

7:10 (7:11) (Class 4) 2-Y-O — **£5,181** (£1,541; £770; £384) **Stalls** Low

Form — RPR

114 **1** **Ingleby Princess**[22] [3496] 2-8-12 **74** .... PaulFessey 5 — 79
(T D Barron) *chsd ldrs: effrt over 2f out: hung rt and ev ch over 1f out: led ins fnl f: styd on wl u.p* **13/8**[1]

120 **2** *1 ¼* **Fathom Five (IRE)**[46] [2724] 2-9-7 **83** .... PaulEddery 3 — 85
(B Smart) *hmpd s: in tch: hdwy to ld over 1f out: hdd ins fnl f: kpt on same pce* **3/1**[3]

001 **3** *2 ½* **Movethegoalposts**[16] [3669] 2-8-11 **73** .... StanleyChin 1 — 67
(M Johnston) *pressed ldr: led briefly 2f out: outpcd fnl f* **5/2**[2]

0601 **4** *shd* **Shes Millie**[16] [3677] 2-7-12 **60** oh5 .... PaulHanagan 6 — 54
(J G M O'Shea) *in tch: outpcd 1/2-way: kpt on fnl f: n.d* **10/1**

001 **5** *¾* **Mundo's Magic**[15] [3713] 2-9-1 **82** .... MarkLawson(5) 4 — 73
(D W Barker) *keen: led to 2f out: sn outpcd* **7/1**

1m 12.36s (-0.74) **Going Correction** -0.225s/f (Firm) **5** Ran SP% **113.3**
Speed ratings (Par 96):95,93,90,89,88
CSF £7.08 TOTE £2.60: £1.20, £1.90; EX 7.00.
Owner Dave Scott **Bred** Wheelersland Stud **Trained** Maunby, N Yorks

FOCUS
Not the most competitive of races but a sound pace throughout and this bare form should stand up at a similar level.

NOTEBOOK
Ingleby Princess ◆, a progressive sort, was not inconvenienced by the return to six furlongs and, despite hanging into the centre of the track, showed a good attitude to record her third win from four starts. She will not mind the return to seven furlongs and remains capable of better. (op 6-4 tchd 2-1)
Fathom Five(IRE), back to a more suitable grade and having his first run over six furlongs, ran right up to his best. On this evidence he should win another race but may continue to look vulnerable to progressive sorts. (op 9-2)
Movethegoalposts, who showed improved form to win a maiden over this course and distance on his previous start, had the run of the race and was not disgraced. He looks ready for the step up to seven furlongs now. (op 11-4 tchd 3-1)
Shes Millie, who gave trouble before the start, was not disgraced on this nursery debut but left the impression that she would be worth a try over seven furlongs. (op 8-1)
Mundo's Magic, who showed much improved form on his first start since being gelded when winning at Pontefract last time, was far too keen to do himself justice on this nursery debut. He should prove effective over five but will have to settle better if he is to progress. (op 13-2 tchd 6-1)

4135 DAILY RECORD E B F FILLIES' H'CAP — 5f 4y

7:40 (7:42) (Class 4) (0-85,78) 3-Y-O+ — **£7,772** (£2,312; £1,155; £577) **Stalls** Low

Form — RPR

5130 **1** **Lady Bahia (IRE)**[2] [4091] 5-9-1 **65** .... (b) RobbieFitzpatrick 1 — 78
(Peter Grayson) *hld up: hdwy stands rail to ld over 1f out: r.o strly fnl f* **8/1**[3]

2021 **2** *2 ½* **Shes Minnie**[20] [3568] 3-9-11 **78** .... PaulHanagan 6 — 81
(J G M O'Shea) *bhd: hdwy to ld briefly over 1f out: kpt on fnl f: nt pce of wnr* **9/2**[1]

4100 **3** *2* **Bonne De Fleur**[64] [2194] 5-9-5 **76** .... (b) PJBenson(7) 2 — 73
(B Smart) *chsd ldrs: drvn and outpcd 2f out: kpt on fnl f: no imp* **10/1**

3212 **4** *nk* **Rothesay Dancer**[17] [3636] 3-9-4 **71** .... (p) DanielTudhope 10 — 66+
(J S Goldie) *hld up bhd ldrs on outside: hdwy and ev ch over 1f out: outpcd fnl f* **6/1**[2]

1130 **5** *¾* **Our Little Secret (IRE)**[15] [3715] 4-8-11 **68** .... KevinGhunowa(7) 7 — 61
(A Berry) *led at str pce to over 1f out: no ex* **12/1**

4502 **6** *2 ½* **Lyndalee (IRE)**[13] [3759] 3-9-0 **67** .... PaulFessey 5 — 50
(T D Easterby) *w ldrs tl wknd over 1f out* **14/1**

-406 **7** *½* **Vondova**[12] [3783] 4-8-12 **62** .... CatherineGannon 9 — 44
(D A Nolan) *dwlt: a bhd* **66/1**

3202 **8** *nk* **Howards Princess**[16] [3673] 4-8-12 **62** .... (b[1]) TomEaves 3 — 43
(I Semple) *sn w ldrs: rdn whn blkd 2f out: sn btn* **9/2**[1]

4234 **9** *2* **Riquewihr**[11] [3811] 6-9-6 **70** .... (p) TonyHamilton 4 — 44
(J S Wainwright) *chsd ldrs to 1/2-way: sn rdn and wknd* **6/1**[2]

59.27 secs (-1.93) **Going Correction** -0.225s/f (Firm)
WFA 3 from 4yo+ 3lb **9** Ran SP% **101.0**
Speed ratings (Par 102):106,102,98,98,97 93,92,91,88
CSF £34.03 CT £253.16 TOTE £9.40: £2.20, £1.60, £2.70; EX 33.80.
Owner Peter Grayson Racing Clubs Limited **Bred** Piercetown Stud **Trained** Formby, Lancs

FOCUS
An overly strong pace set things up for those held up and this bare form does not look reliable with the runner-up the best guide.
Howards Princess Official explanation: jockey said filly had run too freely due to first time blinkers

4136 JIM AND JACKIE MAIDEN STKS — 6f 5y

8:10 (8:11) (Class 5) 3-Y-O+ — **£3,238** (£963; £481; £240) **Stalls** Low

Form — RPR

2343 **1** **Chanteuse Noire (USA)**[28] [3285] 3-8-12 **61** .... (v) PaulHanagan 9 — 65
(J Noseda) *mde virtually all: drvn over 2f out: drew clr fr over 1f out* **1/1**[1]

-262 **2** *5* **Dulce Sueno**[19] [3587] 3-8-12 **58** .... TomEaves 5 — 50
(I Semple) *prom: drvn over 2f out: chsd wnr ins fnl f: no imp* **6/5**[2]

0-0 **3** *2* **Miacarla**[25] [3383] 3-8-7 .... MarkLawson(5) 1 — 44
(A Berry) *prom: effrt over 2f out: outpcd fr over 1f out* **100/1**

0040 **4** *2* **Zantero**[2] [4067] 4-9-4 **45** .... DNolan(3) 2 — 43
(W M Brisbourne) *w ldrs tl wknd over 1f out* **20/1**[3]

0 **5** *6* **Vibrato (USA)**[25] [3384] 4-9-7 .... RobbieFitzpatrick 7 — 25
(C J Teague) *hld up in tch: outpcd over 2f out: n.d after* **25/1**

-060 **6** *¾* **Pensata**[3] [4056] 3-8-12 **43** .... DanielTudhope 8 — 18
(Miss L A Perratt) *chsd ldrs tl wknd over 2f out* **33/1**

06-0 **7** *6* **Seallarain**[40] [2928] 3-8-6 **37** ow1 .... KevinGhunowa(7) 6 — 1
(A Berry) *disp ld to 1/2-way: sn rdn and wknd* **100/1**

0 **8** *1 ¼* **Deer Park Countess**[22] [3480] 5-9-2 .... CatherineGannon 4 —
(D A Nolan) *missed break: nvr on terms* **100/1**

04 **P** **Carabinieri (IRE)**[18] [3620] 3-9-3 .... TonyHamilton 3 —
(J Barclay) *dwlt: outpcd whn broke down and p.u over 4f out* **33/1**

1m 11.6s (-1.50) **Going Correction** -0.225s/f (Firm)
WFA 3 from 4yo+ 4lb **9** Ran SP% **112.9**
Speed ratings (Par 103):101,94,91,89,81 80,72,70,—
CSF £2.18 TOTE £2.30: £1.10, £1.10, £13.50; EX 1.60.
Owner Sir Robert Ogden **Bred** North Wales Farm Llc **Trained** Newmarket, Suffolk

FOCUS
An uncompetitive maiden in which the pace seemed sound throughout but the form is moderate, limited by the fourth.

4137 RACING UK ON SKY 432 H'CAP (A QUALIFIER FOR THE HAMILTON PARK HANDICAP SERIES FINAL) — 1m 1f 36y

8:40 (8:40) (Class 5) (0-75,79) 3-Y-O+ — **£3,886** (£1,156; £577; £288) **Stalls** High

Form — RPR

4221 **1** **Wind Star**[12] [3782] 3-9-13 **79** .... DeanMcKeown 4 — 94+
(G A Swinbank) *prom: smooth hdwy to ld over 1f out: sn shkn up: readily* **4/5**[1]

0662 **2** *2 ½* **Paparaazi (IRE)**[9] [3883] 4-10-0 **72** .... PaulHanagan 2 — 77
(R A Fahey) *cl up: rdn to ld over 2f out: hdd over 1f out: no ch w wnr* **3/1**[2]

1301 **3** *nk* **Seattle Robber**[9] [3862] 4-9-5 **63** .... (p) RobbieFitzpatrick 5 — 67
(P A Blockley) *chsd ldrs: outpcd over 3f out: rallied over 1f out: nrst fin* **8/1**[3]

0-64 **4** *1 ½* **Tetragon (IRE)**[12] [3797] 6-8-13 **60** .... DNolan(3) 3 — 61
(D Carroll) *set stdy pce: rdn and hdd over 2f out: sn one pce* **20/1**

2015 **5** *½* **Insubordinate**[16] [3672] 5-9-2 **60** .... DanielTudhope 6 — 60
(J S Goldie) *stdd in tch: effrt over 2f out: btn over 1f out* **9/1**

1664 **6** *shd* **Ulysees (IRE)**[22] [3484] 7-9-9 **67** .... TomEaves 1 — 67
(I Semple) *hld up last but in tch: rdn and outpcd over 3f out: n.d after* **8/1**[3]

1m 58.76s (-0.90) **Going Correction** -0.225s/f (Firm)
WFA 3 from 4yo+ 8lb **6** Ran SP% **117.5**
Speed ratings (Par 103):95,92,92,91,90 90
CSF £3.74 TOTE £1.90: £1.30, £3.10; EX 3.80 Place 6 £4.14, Place 5 £2.67.
Owner D G Williams **Bred** Mrs N F M Sampson **Trained** Melsonby, N Yorks
■ Stewards' Enquiry : Paul Hanagan caution: careless riding

FOCUS
A muddling gallop to this ordinary event but another step in the right direction for Wind Star, who won with more in hand than the official margin suggests. The form looks sound rated through the third and fourth.
T/Plt: £4.70 to a £1 stake. Pool: £54,963.35. 8,422.00 winning tickets. T/Qpdt: £3.90 to a £1 stake. Pool: £3,114.70. 577.40 winning tickets. RY

3930 LINGFIELD (L-H)

Saturday, August 5

OFFICIAL GOING: Turf course - good to firm; all-weather - standard
Wind: Nil Weather: Fine and warm

4138 EUROPEAN BREEDERS FUND MAIDEN STKS — 5f (P)

5:55 (5:55) (Class 5) 2-Y-O — **£3,886** (£1,156; £577; £288) **Stalls** High

Form — RPR

1 **Resplendent Alpha** 2-9-3 .... IanMongan 3 — 76+
(T G Mills) *w'like: scope: lw: rn green and off the pce in 6th: storming run over 1f out: led ins fnl f: sn wl clr* **10/3**[2]

2 *4* **Beauchamp Viceroy** 2-9-3 .... FJohansson 1 — 62
(G A Butler) *cmpt: str: chsd ldr: hanging lft and green over 1f out: easily outpcd by wnr fnl f but kpt on for 2nd* **16/1**

6 **3** *1* **Daddy Cool**[16] [3685] 2-8-12 .... LiamJones(5) 8 — 58
(W G M Turner) *led and sn 3l clr: rdn over 1f out: wknd and hdd last 150yds* **14/1**

0 **4** *1* **Nou Camp**[14] [3738] 2-9-3 .... SteveDrowne 7 — 54
(N A Callaghan) *chsd ldrs: rdn over 2f out: outpcd fnl f: fdd* **8/1**

5 *nk* **Bajeel (IRE)** 2-9-3 .... DaneO'Neill 10 — 53
(G A Butler) *lengthy: str: scope: dwlt: sn chsd ldrs: pushed along and green fr 3f out: n.m.r on inner briefly 2f out: fdd fnl f* **7/1**[3]

6 *2* **Brightling (IRE)** 2-8-12 .... JohnEgan 9 — 41
(Jamie Poulton) *neat: swtg: s.s: outpcd in last trio: sme prog over 1f out: styng on whn eased last 75yds* **3/1**[1]

0 **7** *¾* **Peggy's Pearl**[12] [3796] 2-8-5 .... StevenGibson(7) 6 — 38
(J S Moore) *v s.i.s: outpcd and looking awkward ride: a bhd* **50/1**

04 **8** *hd* **Avoid The Cat**[21] [3544] 2-9-3 .... RyanMoore 4 — 43
(Mrs A J Perrett) *sn outpcd and scrubbed along: wl bhd fr 1/2-way* **3/1**[1]

00 **9** *5* **Rubber Duck (IRE)**[17] [3645] 2-8-5 .... RonanKeogh(7) 5 — 20
(Peter Grayson) *chsd ldrs to 2f out: wkd v rapidly over 1f out* **50/1**

61.01 secs (1.23) **Going Correction** +0.10s/f (Slow) **9** Ran SP% **113.2**
Speed ratings (Par 94):94,87,86,84,83 80,79,79,71
CSF £53.46 TOTE £4.70: £1.60, £5.40, £2.40; EX 65.10.
Owner Resplendent Racing Limited **Bred** Sunley Stud **Trained** Headley, Surrey

FOCUS
A modest sprint maiden and although the winner was impressive it is difficult to assess the value of the form.

NOTEBOOK
Resplendent Alpha ◆, a 38,000gns first foal of a triple six to seven-furlong winner, made an impressive racecourse debut. Having looked as though he was very much learning his job in the early stages, he got the hang of things in the second half of the contest and picked up in good style to run out a most emphatic winner. He has probably not beaten a great deal, but deserves his chance in better company. (op 4-1 tchd 3-1)
Beauchamp Viceroy, a brother to Beauchamp Utopia, placed over six furlongs on her only start at two, ran green and was no match for the impressive winner. He should improve for the experience. (op 14-1)
Daddy Cool offered very little on his debut over six furlongs at Wolverhampton so, while this was clearly much better, his proximity does not do much for the form as things stand. (op 12-1)
Nou Camp, a well beaten last of seven on his debut over six furlongs at Newmarket, ran better but is probably likely to be seen at his best when handicapped. (op 9-1)
Bajeel(IRE), a 58,000gns half-brother to Calypso Dancer, a five-furlong winner in France, out of a smart dual mile scorer, can improve with the benefit of this experience. (op 11-2)
Brightling(IRE), a half-sister to high-class Hong Kong miler Dave's Best, out of a mile juvenile winner, must have been showing something at home to be sent off joint favourite on her racecourse debut, but this Lowther Stakes entry was soon in trouble after starting slowly. She can do better. (op 5-2)
Avoid The Cat, dropped in trip, was never going and failed to build on the form he showed when fourth at Salisbury on his previous start. He is better than this and will have more options now he is eligible for a handicap mark. (op 4-1)

4139 LADIES EVENING NEXT SATURDAY H'CAP — 1m 2f (P)
6:25 (6:26) (Class 6) (0-55,55) 3-Y-0+ — **£3,238** (£963; £481; £240) **Stalls** Low

Form — RPR
0060 **1** **Hallings Overture (USA)**[57] [2401] 7-9-5 **50** .... JohnEgan 14 — 60
(C A Horgan) *lw: t.k.h: hld up: last 1/2-way: prog gng easily over 3f out: swtchd to inner over 1f out: led last 200yds: idled and rdn o* **25/1**
-000 **2** *3/4* **Cavan Gael (FR)**[5] [3999] 4-9-7 **52** .... ShaneKelly 12 — 61
(P Howling) *prom: trckd ldr 4f out: led wl over 2f out and kicked on: hdd last 200yds: nt qckn* **16/1**
6526 **3** *3* **Ganymede**[12] [3797] 5-9-6 **51** .... IanMongan 9 — 54
(Mrs L J Mongan) *sn pushed along in rr: drvn and struggling 1/2-way: stl wl in rr over 2f out: styd on fr over 1f out to take 3rd nr fin* **9/1**
0000 **4** *1* **Dubai Sunday (JPN)**[8] [3900] 5-9-3 **48** .... BrianReilly 10 — 49
(P S McEntee) *settled in midfield: rdn and prog over 3f out: chsd ldr over 2f out to over 1f out: one pce* **16/1**
2304 **5** *1/2* **Jomus**[42] [2862] 5-9-10 **55** ....(b[1]) AdrianTNicholls 1 — 55
(L Montague Hall) *lw: mounted on crse: s.v.s: hld up in last: prog on wd outside over 3f out: chsd ldrs over 2f out: rel over 1f out* **5/1**[1]
4-36 **6** *3* **Kernel Dowery (IRE)**[18] [3616] 6-9-1 **53** ....(p) JamieHamblett[(7)] 13 — 47
(W R Swinburn) *settled midfield: prog to trck ldrs 5f out: lost pl over 2f out: bmpd along and no imp over 1f out* **8/1**
3235 **7** *shd* **Frank's Quest (IRE)**[25] [3386] 6-9-4 **49** .... RyanMoore 6 — 43
(A B Haynes) *swtg: in tch in midfield: lost pl and rr of main gp over 2f out: rdn and one pce after* **11/2**[2]
0506 **8** *1* **Busy Man (IRE)**[7] [3934] 7-9-3 **48** .... SteveDrowne 11 — 40
(J R Jenkins) *hld up wl in rr: prog on outer over 3f out: gng wl enough over 2f out: wknd over 1f out* **14/1**
0500 **9** *3/4* **Height Of Spirits**[17] [3642] 4-9-4 **54** .... LiamJones[(5)] 3 — 45
(T D McCarthy) *lw: hld up in midfield: trapped bhd wkng rival and dropped to last pair over 3f out: struggling after* **6/1**[3]
100 **10** *3* **Primed Up (IRE)**[46] [2725] 4-9-0 **48** ....(b) NelsonDeSouza[(3)] 5 — 33
(R M Beckett) *sn restrained bhd ldrs: rdn over 3f out: struggling and btn over 2f out* **14/1**
0000 **11** *1* **Tricky Venture**[97] [833] 6-9-2 **47** .... DaneO'Neill 4 — 30
(Mrs L C Jewell) *chsd ldr to 4f out: wknd over 2f out* **16/1**
-303 **12** *11* **Bamzooki**[181] [301] 4-9-2 **47** .... TPQueally 7 — 9
(Mrs C A Dunnett) *swtg: blazed off in front: hdd wl over 2f out: wknd v rapidly over 1f out* **14/1**
0001 **13** *2* **Aberdeen Park**[25] [3379] 4-9-7 **52** ....(b) GeorgeBaker 2 — 11
(Mrs H Sweeting) *dwlt: sn chsd ldrs: wknd 1/2-way: t.o over 2f out* **13/2**

2m 8.34s (0.55) **Going Correction** +0.10s/f (Slow) — **13** Ran SP% **122.3**
Speed ratings (Par 101):101,100,98,97,96 94,94,93,92,90 89,80,79
CSF £387.86 CT £3862.33 TOTE £32.40: £7.20, £9.60, £3.00; EX 419.20.
Owner Mrs B Sumner **Bred** Spectrum Bloodstock S A And Partners **Trained** Uffcott, Wilts

FOCUS
A very moderate handicap, not solid form and certainly not worth dwelling on.

4140 SPECIALIST LIABILITY SERVICES MEDIAN AUCTION MAIDEN STKS — 7f 140y
6:55 (6:59) (Class 5) 2-Y-0 — **£3,238** (£963; £481; £240) **Stalls** Centre

Form — RPR
23 **1** **Spanish Hidalgo (IRE)**[21] [3545] 2-9-3 .... IanMongan 12 — 80+
(J L Dunlop) *lw: racd nr side: trckd ldrs gng wl: wnt 2nd jst over 2f out: rdn to ld 1f out: grad forged clr* **4/5**[1]
2 *1 1/2* **Shebang (IRE)** 2-8-12 .... TPQueally 6 — 71
(M G Quinlan) *lengthy: lw: rced against nr side rail: led: rdn and hrd pressed 2f out: kpt on wl: hdd 1f out: clr of rest but readily hld* **9/1**
025 **3** *5* **Law Of The Land (IRE)**[27] [3335] 2-9-3 71 .... DaneO'Neill 10 — 65
(W R Muir) *t.k.h: hld up bhd ldrs: effrt to chse ldng pair over 1f out: sn outpcd* **16/1**
03 **4** *3* **Zelos (IRE)**[33] [3157] 2-9-3 .... ShaneKelly 5 — 58
(J A Osborne) *pressed ldrs and racd towards outer: rdn 3f out: wknd wl over 1f out* **12/1**
0 **5** *1 1/2* **Bright Dance**[17] [3640] 2-8-12 .... NickyMackay 8 — 49
(L M Cumani) *s.s: wl off the pce and rn green: kpt on steadily fnl 2f: n.d* **25/1**
6 *1 1/4* **Pairumani Princess (IRE)** 2-8-12 .... SteveDrowne 2 — 46
(E A L Dunlop) *neat: s.s: wl off the pce in rr: nudged along and kpt on steadily fnl 2f* **33/1**
2 **7** *hd* **Rambo Honours (IRE)**[21] [3544] 2-9-3 .... SebSanders 4 — 51
(R M Beckett) *racd on outer: pressed ldrs: rdn and struggling 3f out: sn btn* **5/1**[2]
8 *shd* **Redcliff (GER)** 2-9-3 .... RyanMoore 7 — 51
(Mrs A J Perrett) *neat: b.bkwd: mostly chsd ldr to jst over 2f out: sn wknd* **20/1**
0 **9** *1 1/2* **Field Sport (FR)**[33] [3157] 2-9-3 .... ChrisCatlin 11 — 47
(C E Brittain) *sn off the pce towards rr: shkn up and no prog 3f out: no ch after* **66/1**
10 *8* **Muhannak (IRE)** 2-9-3 .... JohnEgan 3 — 28
(G A Butler) *tall: strong: scope: lw: dwlt: rn v green and wl off the pce: nvr a factor* **8/1**[3]
11 *20* **Deep Cover (IRE)** 2-9-0 .... JamesDoyle[(3)] 9 — —
(R M Flower) *strong: bkwd: s.s: all at sea and sn t.o* **50/1**

1m 30.08s (-1.38) **Going Correction** -0.225s/f (Firm) — **11** Ran SP% **121.9**
Speed ratings (Par 94):97,95,90,87,86 84,84,84,82,74 54
CSF £8.87 TOTE £1.80: £1.10, £2.00, £3.00; EX 14.10.
Owner Windflower Overseas Holdings Inc **Bred** Windflower Overseas Holdings Inc **Trained** Arundel, W Sussex

FOCUS
The bare form of this maiden looks just ordinary with the third to his mark.

NOTEBOOK
Spanish Hidalgo(IRE) confirmed the promise of his two previous efforts to get off the mark at the third attempt. The bare form looks just ordinary, but he is progressing and looks one to keep on the right side of. (op 11-8 tchd 6-4)
Shebang(IRE), a 17,000gns half-sister to Lilly Be, who was placed over six furlongs at two and three, out of a winner in the UAE, made a pleasing debut, pulling well clear of all bar the experienced winner. She should be winning before too much longer.
Law Of The Land(IRE) returned to form having disappointed at Brighton on his previous start, but he was readily held by the front two.
Zelos(IRE) was beaten nine and a half lengths in fourth, but is open to improvement when sent down the handicap route.
Bright Dance, well held on her debut at Kempton, stepped up a little on that effort but is likely to come into her own when handicapped.
Pairumani Princess(IRE), a half-sister to Persian Lightning, a useful multiple mile to 12-furlong winner, out of a dual 12-furlong scorer, is going to be seen at her best in middle-distance handicaps from next season onwards. (tchd 28-1)
Rambo Honours(IRE) was below the form he showed when second on his debut over six furlongs at Salisbury and has to be considered disappointing. (op 4-1)
Deep Cover(IRE) Official explanation: jockey said colt ran very green

4141 LINGFIELDPARK.CO.UK H'CAP — 6f
7:25 (7:26) (Class 6) (0-60,60) 3-Y-0+ — **£2,388** (£705; £352) **Stalls** High

Form — RPR
0021 **1** **Ballybunion (IRE)**[8] [3899] 7-9-3 **53** .... RichardKingscote[(3)] 3 — 61
(R A Harris) *lw: taken down early: prom in centre: chsd ldr 2f out: chal and upsides fnl f: won on the nod* **10/1**
2322 **2** *shd* **Millfields Dreams**[7] [3936] 7-9-8 **55** .... RyanMoore 1 — 63
(M G Quinlan) *racd centre: mde most: edgd rt and jnd ins fnl f: pipped on the post* **9/2**[1]
0440 **3** *1 1/4* **Siraj**[3] [4054] 7-9-3 **50** ....(p) MichaelTebbutt 2 — 54
(J Ryan) *lw: racd on wd outside: hld up bhd ldrs: rdn and effrt 2f out: styd on fnl f: unable to chal* **16/1**
6544 **4** *1/2* **Mountain Pass (USA)**[11] [3825] 4-9-8 **55** ....(p) EddieAhern 7 — 57
(M J Wallace) *racd on wd outside: hld up in rr: prog and drvn over 2f out: styd on: nrst fin* **16/1**
143 **5** *1/2* **Diamond Josh**[14] [3728] 4-9-5 **55** .... StephenDonohoe[(3)] 16 — 56
(P D Evans) *led nr side gp but racd away fr rail and nt on terms w centre: drvn and kpt on same pce fnl 2f* **9/2**[1]
0143 **6** *nk* **Vibe**[24] [3405] 5-8-13 **49** .... JamesDoyle[(3)] 18 — 49
(A W Carroll) *hld up and last of nr side gp: taken towards centre and prog over 2f out: hanging lft fnl 2f but styd on* **9/1**
0461 **7** *hd* **Davids Mark**[11] [3825] 6-9-2 **49** .... NickyMackay 15 — 48
(J R Jenkins) *hld up nr side: rdn and prog 2f out: one pce and no hdwy fnl f* **8/1**[3]
-600 **8** *nk* **Stokesies Wish**[23] [3434] 6-9-7 **54** .... AdrianTNicholls 11 — 53
(J L Spearing) *towards rr nr side: rdn and struggling over 2f out: styd on ins fnl f* **25/1**
4026 **9** *3/4* **Beverley Beau**[11] [3825] 4-8-9 **49** .... KristinStubbs[(7)] 5 — 45
(Mrs L Stubbs) *w ldr in centre to 2f out: bmpd along and wknd* **33/1**
6322 **10** *hd* **Cree**[10] [3835] 4-9-9 **56** .... SteveDrowne 9 — 52
(W R Muir) *chsd nr side ldrs: rdn over 2f out: no prog and btn over 1f out* **8/1**[3]
40-0 **11** *1 1/2* **Pinafore**[14] [3728] 4-9-2 **49** .... AdrianMcCarthy 8 — 40
(P Winkworth) *chsd ldrs in centre: rdn over 2f out: wknd over 1f out* **50/1**
4051 **12** *hd* **Banjo Bay (IRE)**[14] [3728] 8-9-10 **60** .... AdamKirby[(3)] 12 — 51
(Miss Gay Kelleway) *lw: racd nr side: hld up wl in rr: last over 2f out: hrd rdn over 1f out: no ch* **7/1**[2]
5035 **13** *3/4* **A Teen**[21] [3536] 8-8-10 **50** .... JPFeatherstone[(7)] 17 — 38
(P Howling) *lw: hld up in rr nr side: rdn whn nt clr run 2f out: no prog after* **33/1**
0-00 **14** *1 1/2* **Firework**[38] [2971] 8-9-3 **50** .... StephenCarson 6 — 34
(E A Wheeler) *taken down early: chsd ldrs in centre 4f: wknd* **50/1**
4052 **15** *1* **Danny The Dip**[9] [3873] 3-9-2 **58** .... MarcHalford[(5)] 14 — 39
(J J Bridger) *s.s: wl in rr nr side: taken to centre and effrt over 2f out: wknd rapidly over 1f out* **25/1**
5036 **16** *1 1/2* **Alwariah**[11] [3821] 3-9-6 **57** .... SebSanders 10 — 33
(C E Brittain) *chsd ldrs to 1/2-way: wkng and moving bdly wl over 1f out* **10/1**
006 **17** *18* **Burnt Orange (IRE)**[36] [3034] 3-8-13 **55** .... LiamJones[(5)] 4 — —
(T D McCarthy) *racd centre: nvr on terms w ldrs: struggling whn hmpd over 2f out: wknd rapidly: t.o* **40/1**

69.86 secs (-1.81) **Going Correction** -0.225s/f (Firm)
WFA 3 from 4yo+ 4lb — **17** Ran SP% **131.0**
Speed ratings (Par 101):103,102,101,100,99 99,99,98,97,97 95,95,94,92,90 88,64
CSF £55.08 CT £541.48 TOTE £9.70: £2.00, £1.90, £6.80, £5.70; EX 56.60.
Owner The Over The Bridge Partnership **Bred** La Pescaia S A S Di Miuta Pontello **Trained** Earlswood, Monmouths

FOCUS
A moderate sprint handicap in which the principals raced towards the centre of the track, and those drawn low dominated. The trime was reasonable and the form looks sound, rated around the placed horses.
Vibe Official explanation: jockey said gelding hung left
Banjo Bay(IRE) Official explanation: trainer said gelding was distressed
Danny The Dip Official explanation: jockey said gelding hung left

4142 BOOK ONLINE FOR A £2 DISCOUNT MAIDEN STKS — 6f
7:55 (7:57) (Class 5) 3-Y-0+ — **£3,238** (£963; £481; £240) **Stalls** High

Form — RPR
63 **1** **Mail Express (IRE)**[21] [3554] 3-8-12 .... NickyMackay 1 — 87+
(L M Cumani) *lw: dwlt: prog fr rr to trck ldr over 3f out: led wl over 1f out : shkn up to go clr 1f out: comf* **1/3**[1]
3204 **2** *4* **Discotheque (USA)**[21] [3538] 3-8-12 64 .... ShaneKelly 3 — 65
(P Howling) *lw: in tch: outpcd 2f out: rdn and styd on to take 2nd 1f out: kpt on but no ch w wnr* **7/1**[3]
3 *1 3/4* **Tumpuluna (IRE)** 3-8-12 .... MichaelTebbutt 2 — 60
(G Prodromou) *lw: w'like: t.k.h and rn green: hld up: prog but outpcd 2f out: disp 2nd 1f out: shkn up briefly and one pce* **25/1**

6 **4** *2* **Tetrode (USA)**[25] 3384 4-9-7 ... EddieAhern 7 59
(R M H Cowell) *led and sn clr: hdd wl over 1f out: wknd rapidly ins fnl f* **25/1**

5-00 **5** *shd* **Rembrandt Quality (USA)**[42] 2863 3-9-3 70 ... ChrisCatlin 5 58
(N A Callaghan) *lw: hld up in tch: outpcd and shkn up 2f out: fdd* **5/1**[2]

00 **6** *3 ½* **All About Him (USA)**[35] 3090 3-8-10 ... MarkCoumbe(7) 6 48
(N I M Rossiter) *chsd ldr to over 3f out: wknd 2f out* **50/1**

0-0 **7** *14* **Saint Nick**[203] 112 3-9-3 ... SteveDrowne 4 6
(J J Bridger) *chsd ldrs to 1/2-way: wknd: t.o* **66/1**

1m 10.15s (-1.52) **Going Correction** -0.225s/f (Firm)
WFA 3 from 4yo 4lb **7 Ran SP% 115.3**
Speed ratings (Par 103):101,95,93,90,90 85,67
CSF £3.32 TOTE £1.10: £1.10, £2.50; EX 2.10.
Owner JMC Breed & Race Limited **Bred** Scuderia Archi Romani **Trained** Newmarket, Suffolk
FOCUS
A modest, weak sprint maiden and the form is not solid.
Discotheque(USA) Official explanation: jockey said filly was denied a clear run

4143 LINGFIELD PARK 0870 2200022 H'CAP 7f
8:25 (8:26) (Class 5) (0-75,76) 3-Y-O **£3,238** (£963; £481; £240) **Stalls** High

Form RPR
4-1 **1** **Macedon**[23] 3436 3-9-5 **73** ... JohnEgan 8 87+
(J S Moore) *h.d.w: lw: t.k.h: hld up bhd ldrs: hanging 3f out and looked in trble: chsd ldr 2f out: styd on to ld ins fnl f* **11/10**[1]

5006 **2** *¾* **Halfwaytoparadise**[51] 2574 3-8-0 **59** ...(p) MarcHalford(5) 3 66
(W G M Turner) *led and sn at least 2 l clr: hung bdly lft fr over 2f out and ended on far rail: hdd ins fnl f: kpt on* **33/1**

2050 **3** *2* **Valentino Swing (IRE)**[7] 3943 3-9-1 **69** ...(b[1]) AdrianTNicholls 2 71
(J L Spearing) *mostly chsd ldr to 2f out: kpt on same pce u.p* **16/1**

1000 **4** *hd* **Fratt'n Park (IRE)**[10] 3852 3-8-12 **66** ... SteveDrowne 5 67
(J J Bridger) *hld up in last pair: rdn over 2f out: styd on fr wl over 1f out: nt pce to rch ldrs* **20/1**

1000 **5** *hd* **Sands Of Barra (IRE)**[16] 3679 3-9-7 **75** ... ChrisCatlin 1 76
(N A Callaghan) *dwlt: hld up in last pair: prog and drvn over 2f out: kpt on but nt pce to rch ldrs* **16/1**

3251 **6** *1* **Imperial Gain (USA)**[7] 3932 3-9-5 **76** ...(v) AdamKirby(3) 14 74
(W R Swinburn) *hld up wl in rr and racd towards nr side: effrt 2f out: kpt on over 1f out: no ch* **3/1**[2]

3560 **7** *3 ½* **Broken Spur (FR)**[17] 3644 3-9-1 **69** ...(t) EddieAhern 4 58
(B W Hills) *in tch: drifted towards far side u.p fr 2f out: wknd over 1f out* **10/1**

5600 **8** *1 ½* **Simpsons Ross (IRE)**[9] 3869 3-8-1 **58** oh2 ow2...(b[1]) JamesDoyle(3) 12 43
(R M Flower) *chsd ldr to over 2f out: sn wknd* **20/1**

0-00 **9** *5* **Compton Express**[17] 3647 3-8-2 **56** oh6 ... AdrianMcCarthy 9 27
(Jamie Poulton) *hld up in rr: rdn and struggling 3f out* **66/1**

4665 **10** *½* **Cool Sting (IRE)**[15] 3708 3-9-0 **68** ...(p) RyanMoore 11 38
(A M Balding) *lw: dwlt: rcvrd to chse ldrs after 3f: hrd rdn 3f out: sn wknd* **5/1**[3]

00-0 **11** *2* **Savannah Pride (IRE)**[52] 2554 3-8-6 **63** ... NelsonDeSouza(3) 13 27
(Ernst Oertel) *chsd ldrs: hrd rdn 3f out: sn wknd* **66/1**

1m 22.32s (-1.89) **Going Correction** -0.225s/f (Firm) **11 Ran SP% 125.6**
Speed ratings (Par 100):101,100,97,97,97 96,92,90,84,84 81
CSF £61.90 CT £442.61 TOTE £2.30: £1.10, £3.80, £3.80; EX 77.80 Place 6 £284.69, Place 5 £59.93.
Owner Mrs Fitri Hay **Bred** Cheveley Park Stud Ltd **Trained** Upper Lambourn, Berks
FOCUS
Just an ordinary handicap and the form looks sound with the third, fourth and sixth close to recent form.
Halfwaytoparadise Official explanation: jockey said filly hung left final 2f
Cool Sting(IRE) Official explanation: jockey said gelding had no more to give
T/Plt: £394.90 to a £1 stake. Pool: £56,045.80. 103.60 winning tickets. T/Qpdt: £5.30 to a £1 stake. Pool: £4,711.40. 851.70 winning tickets. JN

4103
NEWMARKET (JULY) (R-H)
Saturday, August 5

OFFICIAL GOING: Good to firm
Wind: Nil Weather: Fine and sunny

4144 BLUE SQUARE EXCLUSIVE PRICES H'CAP 7f
2:05 (2:06) (Class 4) (0-85,85) 3-Y-O **£6,477** (£1,927; £963; £481) **Stalls** High

Form RPR
11 **1** **Bustin Justin (USA)**[15] 3708 3-9-4 **82** ... ShaneKelly 7 94
(J Noseda) *lw: chsd ldr: led over 5f out: rdn and edgd rt over 1f out: r.o* **11/8**[1]

1 **2** *1 ½* **Ceremonial Jade (UAE)**[39] 2948 3-9-2 **80** ... OscarUrbina 8 88+
(M Botti) *b. hld up in tch: plld hrd: n.m.r and lost pl 1/2-way: swtchd rt and hdwy over 1f out: r.o* **14/1**

0163 **3** *hd* **Louie Louie (IRE)**[15] 3708 3-9-7 **85** ... KerrinMcEvoy 14 92
(N A Callaghan) *b.hind: lw: hld up: hdwy 2f out: n.m.r over 1f out: r.o* **7/1**[2]

6532 **4** *hd* **Neardown Beauty (IRE)**[16] 3667 3-8-11 **75** ... EddieAhern 2 81
(I A Wood) *lw: hld up: hdwy over 2f out: rdn over 1f out: styd on* **10/1**

0020 **5** *2 ½* **Kings Heir (IRE)**[27] 3337 3-9-0 **78** ... SebSanders 6 78
(R M Beckett) *led: hdd over 5f out: rdn over 1f out: styd on same pce* **25/1**

4201 **6** *½* **Final Tune (IRE)**[10] 3839 3-7-13 **66** ... PatrickMathers(3) 5 64
(Miss M E Rowland) *trckd ldrs: racd keenly: rdn over 1f out: styd on same pce* **40/1**

1-1 **7** *¾* **Fast Bowler**[12] 3795 3-9-2 **83** ... StephenDonohoe(3) 12 79
(J M P Eustace) *hld up: hdwy and hmpd over 1f out: nt trble ldrs* **7/1**[2]

441- **8** *¾* **Misphire**[292] 5944 3-9-7 **85** ... DavidAllan 11 79
(T D Easterby) *hld up in tch: rdn and nt clr run over 1f out: wknd ins fnl f* **25/1**

6-12 **9** *1 ½* **Mataram (USA)**[17] 3644 3-8-5 **69** ... JimmyQuinn 9 59
(W Jarvis) *swtg: plld hrd and prom: rdn over 2f out: wkng whn hmpd over 1f out* **8/1**[3]

1200 **10** *½* **Smart Ass (IRE)**[8] 3906 3-8-2 **66** ... TPO'Shea 10 55
(J S Moore) *lw: s.s: rdn over 2f out: n.d* **25/1**

0100 **11** *2* **Savernake Blue**[14] 3722 3-9-3 **81** ... TonyCulhane 1 65
(M R Channon) *dwlt: hld up: effrt over 2f out: n.d* **33/1**

4-34 **12** *¾* **Lindenburgh Way (IRE)**[63] 2244 3-9-7 **85** ... RobertWinston 3 66
(B J Meehan) *chsd ldrs: rdn over 2f out: wknd fnl f* **14/1**

1m 24.78s (-2.00) **Going Correction** -0.20s/f (Firm) **12 Ran SP% 117.6**
Speed ratings (Par 102):103,101,101,100,97 97,96,95,93,93 91,90
CSF £20.91 CT £108.91 TOTE £2.30: £1.30, £3.90, £1.80; EX 28.30.
Owner Zayat Stables Ltd **Bred** A U Jones & Marie D Jones **Trained** Newmarket, Suffolk
■ Stewards' Enquiry : Stephen Donohoe two-day ban: careless riding (Aug 16-17)
Oscar Urbina one-day ban: careless riding (Aug 16)
FOCUS
A good three-year-old handicap in which a pair of unexposed and progressive sorts claimed the first two places. The form looks sound with the third to form.
Lindenburgh Way(IRE) Official explanation: trainer said colt was unsuited by the good to firm ground

4145 GET BETTER SHOW PRICES WITH BLUE SQUARE EBF CONDITIONS STKS 1m
2:35 (2:36) (Class 2) 4-Y-0+ **£12,464** (£3,732; £1,866; £934; £466) **Stalls** High

Form RPR
322- **1** **Belenus (IRE)**[385] 3538 4-8-9 105 ...(t) KerrinMcEvoy 7 113+
(Saeed Bin Suroor) *h.d.w: led: hdd over 5f out: hmpd sn after: chsd ldr tl led over 1f out: r.o wl* **6/5**[1]

2026 **2** *1 ¾* **Ace Of Hearts**[14] 3733 7-8-9 102 ... EddieAhern 6 106+
(C F Wall) *lw: chsd ldrs: rdn and hung lft 2f out: nt clr run over 1f out: r.o: no ch w wnr* **4/1**[2]

6-41 **3** *shd* **Polar Ben**[71] 1979 7-9-6 109 ... OscarUrbina 2 116
(J R Fanshawe) *lw: hld up: hdwy over 2f out: rdn over 1f out: edgd rt: styd on same pce* **9/1**

6403 **4** *1 ¾* **Rocamadour**[9] 3881 4-8-9 110 ... TonyCulhane 1 101
(M R Channon) *lw: w ldr tl led over 5f out: sn edgd rt: rdn and hdd over 1f out: no ex ins fnl f* **9/2**[3]

4031 **5** *2* **Momtic (IRE)**[9] 3881 5-9-6 106 ... SebSanders 3 107
(W Jarvis) *lw: chsd ldrs: rdn over 2f out: wknd fnl f* **9/2**[3]

1m 37.12s (-3.31) **Going Correction** -0.20s/f (Firm) **5 Ran SP% 111.8**
Speed ratings (Par 109):108,106,106,104,102
CSF £6.44 TOTE £2.10: £1.40, £2.20; EX 7.10.
Owner Godolphin **Bred** Gainsborough Stud Management Ltd **Trained** Newmarket, Suffolk
FOCUS
A tight conditions event on paper, but Belenus proved a class apart. The form is decent for the grade with the third to last year's mark.
NOTEBOOK
Belenus(IRE) ◆, who was on standby for pacemaking duties in the previous weekend's King George, is a smart performer in his own right and this drop back to a mile for his seasonal reappearance looked a good move. Sporting a tongue tie for the first time since last year's Predominate Stakes, he was settled well in front by McEvoy and seemed happy enough to take a lead when Rocamadour went on, getting slightly checked in the process. It was clear from quarter of a mile out though that he was travelling by far the best and he readily came clear. Twice placed at Listed level, he looks up to Group standard and, with further improvement likely at this distance, he is very much one to keep on the right side of. (op 13-8)
Ace Of Hearts is a tough handicapper who runs his race more often than not and, although officially the worst horse in the race here, he came home well to just snatch second. He remains 6lb higher than when last winning mark however, and may continue to struggle to get his head in front. (op 9-2 tchd 5-1)
Polar Ben ran well considering it was his first start since winning at Goodwood in May on ground faster than ideal and, although getting a little long in the tooth, he remains capable of winning this type of race when the ground is in his favour. (op 8-1)
Rocamadour, who ran well back from a short break at York last time, again found the mile on the short side and was always likely to be vulnerable to something with a turn of pace. He is a smart colt capable of further success back at ten furlongs. (op 3-1 tchd 5-1)
Momtic(IRE), 11lb worse off for his recent defeat of Rocamadour at York, held every chance and was simply outclassed by the winner. He was not that well in at the weights, but is generally consistent and should bounce back from this. (tchd 5-1)

4146 BET@BLUESQ.COM FOR EXCLUSIVE LIVE SHOW PRICES NURSERY 6f
3:10 (3:11) (Class 2) 2-Y-O **£12,954** (£3,854; £1,926; £962) **Stalls** High

Form RPR
211 **1** **Ponty Rossa (IRE)**[16] 3685 2-8-7 82 ... DavidAllan 3 88
(T D Easterby) *lw: chsd ldrs: led wl over 1f out: rdn out* **10/1**

242 **2** *¾* **Gremlin**[8] 3895 2-7-12 73 ... JimmyQuinn 8 77
(A King) *chsd ldrs: rdn over 1f out: r.o* **7/2**[2]

241 **3** *hd* **Pretty Majestic (IRE)**[54] 2500 2-8-13 88 ... TonyCulhane 5 91
(M R Channon) *lw: hld up: hdwy over 1f out: r.o* **10/1**

6211 **4** *2* **Market Day**[21] 3530 2-9-6 95 ... KerrinMcEvoy 6 92
(L M Cumani) *lw: hld up: hdwy over 2f out: no ex ins fnl f* **9/4**[1]

2100 **5** *hd* **Everymanforhimself (IRE)**[14] 3734 2-9-5 94 ... EddieAhern 9 91
(J G Given) *hld up: outpcd 1/2-way: r.o ins fnl f: nt rch ldrs* **12/1**

12 **6** *nk* **Ela Aleka Mou**[30] 3216 2-8-11 86 ... SebSanders 7 82
(M A Jarvis) *mid-div: hdwy over 2f out: rdn over 1f out: styd on same pce* **7/1**[3]

01 **7** *shd* **Addictive**[23] 3430 2-7-7 73 ... LiamJones(5) 11 68
(S C Williams) *s.i.s: hld up: nt clr run over 2f out: r.o ins fnl f: nvr able to chal* **12/1**

1300 **8** *nk* **Nina Blini**[14] 3734 2-8-13 95 ... KMay(7) 10 89
(B J Meehan) *chsd ldr: rdn and hung lft over 1f out: wknd ins fnl f* **33/1**

014 **9** *nk* **El Bosque (IRE)**[14] 3734 2-9-0 96 ... JamesMillman(7) 2 90
(B R Millman) *lw: led: hdd wl over 1f out: wknd ins fnl f* **9/1**

1402 **10** *½* **Dickie Le Davoir**[8] 3903 2-9-4 93 ...(v[1]) RobertWinston 4 85
(K R Burke) *hld up in tch: rdn over 1f out: wknd ins fnl f* **25/1**

1532 **11** *1* **King's Bastion (IRE)**[14] 3727 2-9-1 90 ... HayleyTurner 1 79
(M L W Bell) *chsd ldrs: rdn over 2f out: wknd over 1f out* **25/1**

1m 11.98s (-1.37) **Going Correction** -0.20s/f (Firm) **11 Ran SP% 119.7**
Speed ratings (Par 100):101,100,99,97,96 96,96,95,95,94 93
CSF £44.92 CT £378.94 TOTE £7.60: £2.30, £1.90, £3.30; EX 91.60.
Owner The Lapin Blanc Racing Partnership **Bred** Jim McDonald **Trained** Great Habton, N Yorks
FOCUS
A good, competitive nursery that should work out well and likely to produce winners.
NOTEBOOK
Ponty Rossa(IRE), on a hat-trick following wins at Carlisle and Wolverhampton - the latter a novice stakes - was ridden more prominently on this occasion and showed a tidy change of gear to go into a clear lead over a furlong out. She stayed on strongly under pressure and was always holding the placed horses. Evidently progressive, she deserves a crack at something a bit better now and has the Shergar Cup juvenile and/or the Redcar Two-Year-Trophy next month as options. (op 12-1)
Gremlin, twice placed in maiden company, comes from a stable that is more than capable with its juveniles and he raised his game again for this nursery debut, but the winner possessed too much speed for him and he was forced to settle for second once more. (op 9-2)
Pretty Majestic(IRE) looked to be starting out handicap life off a stiffish mark, mainly thanks to her debut second to Gilded, but she flashed home to just miss out on second and is clearly capable of winning off this sort of mark. She is likely to stay further in time, but was ridden more positively when winning her maiden at Pontefract last time and a return to slightly more aggressive tactics in future may help. (tchd 11-1)

Market Day, an easy winner on her nursery debut in a modest contest at Lingfield last month, had been raised a hefty 11lb for that success and, although made favourite in the hope of further progression, she looked vulnerable to a lighter-weighted rival. She made her move with quarter of a mile to run, but found the winner had flown and in the end could make no impression, although forced to challenge wide. She may struggle to score off this sort of mark. (tchd 2-1 and 5-2)
Everymanforhimself(IRE), back down to a more realistic level having contested the Coventry and Super Sprint on his two most recent starts, was struggling for pace from quite a way out, but he did finish well, as was the case at Newbury. He either requires softer ground or could be worth a try at seven furlongs. (op 11-1)
Ela Aleka Mou has not really built on a tidy winning debut and, although far from disgraced on either start since, she has not done enough to suggest she is ready to win off this sort of mark. That said, she is bred to appreciate upwards of this distance and may be capable of better at seven furlongs.
Addictive, quite an impressive winner of her maiden at Epsom last time, looked to be on a fair mark for this handicap debut, but she never had a chance to get involved, a slow start leading to her being unable to get a clear run when trying to come through and challenge. She remains a good prospect and compensation may await. (op 10-1)
El Bosque(IRE), beaten just two lengths into fourth in the Super Sprint, took them along for most of the way, but he did not see his race out as well as could have been expected and was disappointing.

4147 CHECK BLUESQ.COM BEFORE EVERY H'CAP 1m 2f

3:45 (3:45) (Class 3) (0-90,87) 3-Y-O+ **£9,067** (£2,697; £1,348; £673) **Stalls** Centre

Form				RPR
2315	**1**		**Blue Bajan (IRE)**[35] [3093] 4-10-0 **86** MichaelHills 5 (Andrew Turnell) *lw: hld up: hdwy over 1f out: led ins fnl f: r.o* **4/1**[3]	97+
033	**2**	*1*	**Star Magnitude (USA)**[38] [2989] 5-9-4 **76** JimmyQuinn 6 (S Dow) *chsd ldr: led over 1f out: rdn: edgd lft and hdd ins fnl f: kpt on* **9/1**	85
0066	**3**	*4*	**Rawdon (IRE)**[26] [3366] 5-9-7 **79** (v) HayleyTurner 7 (M L W Bell) *led: clr 1/2-way: rdn and hdd over 1f out: no ex fnl f* **5/1**	80
1422	**4**	*2 1/2*	**Black Beauty**[9] [3871] 3-8-13 **80** EddieAhern 8 (M G Quinlan) *lw: chsd ldrs: rdn over 2f out: wknd fnl f* **13/8**[1]	77
0145	**5**	*19*	**Great Hawk (USA)**[49] [2659] 3-9-5 **86** RobertWinston 3 (Sir Michael Stoute) *hld up: hdwy over 2f out: sn rdn: wknd over 1f out: eased ins fnl f* **11/4**[2]	47+

2m 5.37s (-1.07) **Going Correction** -0.20s/f (Firm)
WFA 3 from 4yo+ 9lb **5** Ran SP% **111.4**
Speed ratings (Par 107):96,95,92,90,74
CSF £34.65 TOTE £5.30: £1.80, £3.80; EX 38.80.
Owner Dr John Hollowood **Bred** Dr J Hollowood **Trained** Broad Hinton, Wilts

FOCUS
A tricky five-runner affair in which the fancied three-year-old pair trailed in at the rear. The winning time was modest for the grade and this form may prove on the weak side for the level.

NOTEBOOK
Blue Bajan(IRE), in good form until meeting a highly-progressive Johnston runner at Windsor last time, was not inconvenienced by this drop in trip and he appreciated the decent gallop set by Rawdon. He led inside the final furlong and ran on too strongly for the runner-up, confirming his improvement this season, and he should continue to go well in similar contests. (op 3-1)
Star Magnitude(USA), third to a couple of useful sorts in Great Plains and subsequent John Smith's winner Fairmile at Salisbury last time, had slipped back down to just a 1lb higher mark than when last successful and he took it up off Rawdon over a furlong out, but Blue Bajan soon swept by and he was again forced to settle for a place. (op 6-1)
Rawdon(IRE), a winner over course and distance last June, has been creeping back to form and looked a leading player off a 2lb lower mark than when last winning. Soon in front, he had established a nice lead as they raced inside the final half mile, but his rider failed to act on it and allowed him to come back to the pack before really asking him. He is nearing a win, but this was a good opportunity missed. (op 11-2 tchd 6-1)
Black Beauty, a progressive three-year-old, albeit he was racing off a 10lb higher mark than when last winning at Beverley in May, proved most disappointing and faded tamely under pressure. He is better than this, but may now begin to struggle off this mark. (op 5-2 tchd 11-4 in places)
Great Hawk(USA), who looked a typically progressive sort from his yard when winning his maiden at Haydock in May, followed that with a fair handicap debut fourth on slow ground, but his York effort was disappointing and this was disasterous, dropping right away and being reported to have lost his action. He may be the sort who does not come into his own until he is four or five. Official explanation: jockey said colt lost its action (op 3-1)

4148 BLUE SQUARE POKER E B F MAIDEN FILLIES' STKS 7f

4:20 (4:21) (Class 5) 2-Y-O **£4,533** (£1,348; £674; £336) **Stalls** High

Form				RPR
6	**1**		**So Sweet (IRE)**[10] [3851] 2-9-0 TonyCulhane 8 (M R Channon) *chsd ldrs: rdn over 1f out: r.o to ld wl ins fnl f* **15/2**[3]	83
02	**2**	*shd*	**Zonta Zitkala**[21] [3537] 2-9-0 SebSanders 5 (R M Beckett) *lw: led: rdn: edgd lft and hdd wl ins fnl f: r.o* **2/1**[1]	83
	3	*3/4*	**Brisk Breeze (GER)** 2-9-0 EddieAhern 13 (H R A Cecil) *gd sort: hld up: hdwy over 2f out: nt clr run over 1f out: r.o: nvr able to chal* **10/1**	81+
	4	*shd*	**Cliche (IRE)** 2-9-0 RobertWinston 14 (Sir Michael Stoute) *w'like: scope: s.i.s: hld up: swtchd lft and r.o wl ins fnl f: nrst fin* **8/1**	81
	5	*hd*	**Inquisitress** 2-8-11 StephenDonohoe(3) 15 (J M P Eustace) *neat: hld up: r.o ins fnl f: nt rch ldrs* **12/1**	80+
	6	*3*	**Princess Taylor** 2-9-0 OscarUrbina 7 (M Botti) *w'like: b.hind: chsd ldrs: rdn over 2f out: styng on same pce whn nt clr run ins fnl f* **16/1**	72+
	7	*3/4*	**Folly Lodge** 2-9-0 MichaelHills 1 (B W Hills) *w'like: scope: s.i.s: sn prom: shkn up over 1f out: wknd ins fnl f* **11/2**[2]	70
	8	*1*	**Tarteel (USA)** 2-9-0 MatthewHenry 2 (J L Dunlop) *w'like: scope: s.i.s: sn chsng ldr: rdn and ev ch over 1f out: wknd ins fnl f* **25/1**	68
	9	*hd*	**Lost In Wonder (USA)** 2-9-0 KerrinMcEvoy 9 (Sir Michael Stoute) *gd sort: b.bkwd: hld up: r.o ins fnl f: nrst fin* **8/1**	67
	10	*7*	**Clytha** 2-9-0 ShaneKelly 4 (M L W Bell) *cmpt: b.bkwd: prom 5f* **33/1**	49
	11	*1/2*	**She's So Pretty (IRE)** 2-9-0 HayleyTurner 12 (W R Swinburn) *leggy: scope: s.i.s: outpcd* **20/1**	48
00	**12**	*1 1/2*	**Wickedish**[24] [3417] 2-9-0 DavidAllan 3 (P Howling) *mid-div: rdn over 2f out: sn wknd* **66/1**	44
0	**13**	*2*	**Breezeway (IRE)**[12] [3796] 2-9-0 TPO'Shea 6 (B J Meehan) *chsd ldrs: rdn 1/2-way: sn lost pl* **20/1**	39
	14	*hd*	**Sky Beam (USA)** 2-9-0 JimmyQuinn 11 (J L Dunlop) *leggy: unf: lw: hld up: wknd over 2f out* **20/1**	38

1m 25.88s (-0.90) **Going Correction** -0.20s/f (Firm) **14** Ran SP% **127.9**
Speed ratings (Par 91):97,96,96,95,95 92,91,90,90,82 81,79,77,77
CSF £22.21 TOTE £8.50: £2.30, £1.30, £3.50; EX 31.00.
Owner Sheikh Ahmed Al Maktoum **Bred** Patrick Jones **Trained** West Ilsley, Berks

FOCUS
A good fillies' maiden, with half of the 14 runners holding Group 1 entries, and the front five put three lengths between themselves and the remainder. The form looks sound with the runner-up the best guide.

NOTEBOOK
So Sweet(IRE), who lost all chance in a decent race on debut with a very slow start, was well supported in the market beforehand and had no trouble at the gate on this occasion. Always holding good position, she came through to challenge the winner inside the final furlong and edged her out in the dying strides. This was clearly not unexpected and the daughter of Cape Cross, who should have little trouble staying a mile, is open to further improvement in nurseries. (op 14-1)
Zonta Zitkala stepped up on her debut effort when just touched off at Nottingham last time and she was a strongly-supported favourite to make it third time lucky. Soon in front on the rail, she ran on strongly right the way to the line, but So Sweet denied her on the nod. She is now qualified for a nursery mark, but her Fillies' Mile entry suggests connections think she is better than a handicapper and she is likely to try and win her maiden before anything else. (op 7-2)
Brisk Breeze(GER) ◆, who holds entries in both the Group 1 Moyglare Stud and Fillies' Mile in the coming weeks, is clearly held in some regard and she would have joined the front two in a three-way photo finish had she not been kept in on the rail. For a filly bred to appreciate ten furlongs in time, it was no surprise to see she could not quicken instantly once getting a run, but she should have no trouble winning her maiden before going on to better things. (op 8-1)
Cliche(IRE) ◆, whose trainer introduced four juveniles at the course the night before, has yet to really get going with them and she looked set to finish well beaten having been slowly away and niggled from an early stage. However, once switched to the outside and seeing a bit of daylight, she picked up well and was finishing better than most towards the middle of the track. This was a highly-pleasing debut from the Fillies' Mile entrant and she is another for whom winning a maiden should prove a formality. (op 10-1)
Inquisitress, a cheap purchase at just 9,000gns also entered in the Fillies' Mile, is a half-sister to useful sprinter Caribbean Coral and she made a highly-pleasing debut. Held up early, she made a little headway before really finding her stride and came home strongly. There is no reason why she should not come on for this and an ordinary maiden can come her way. (tchd 10-1)
Princess Taylor, who is related to high-class middle-distance performers in Give The Slip and Stowaway, was always likely to find this an inadequate test on her debut and she finished a bit adrift of the fifth, but should have been closer with a clear run and is another capable of winning an average maiden. She holds no entires of note at this stage and is clearly viewed as more of a three-year-old prospect. (op 12-1)
Folly Lodge, a Cheveley Park Stakes entrant, showed good early speed towards the outside from her low draw, but could not go on inside the final furlong and faded out of it. This was slightly disappointing, but she was a drifter in the market beforehand and maybe today was not the day. (op 3-1)
Tarteel(USA), whose handler appears to have a strong hand in the juvenile fillies' department this term, Wid, Sudoor and Princess Margaret winner Scarlet Runner being the pick at present, was dismissed in the betting, but she showed up well for a long way and it was only her early exertions - raced over-enthusiastically - that prevented her from going on inside the final furlong. She can be expected to come on for the outing, but lacks any big-race entries. Official explanation: jockey said filly ran very green and got tired
Lost In Wonder(USA), a Fillies' Mile entrant by Derby winner Galileo, like almost all of her stable's juveniles to debut so far, looked badly in need of the experience and the penny did not drop until the race was all over. She is going to appreciate a mile and significant improvement can be expected next time. (op 10-1)
Clytha, a half-sister to a high-class miler abroad, should be effective at around this sort of distance and she showed up well to a point, but dropped away in the end and it is safe to assume the run was needed.
She's So Pretty(IRE), whose stable introduced a big-priced first-time-up winner at the course the previous evening, is yet another with the Fillies' Mile entry, but she was struggling from an early stage and looked far too green to do herself justice. She should come on appreciably or the outing. (op 25-1)
Wickedish has thus far contested three good maidens, out of her league each time, and she will not be capable of winning until tackling low-grade nurseries. (op 80-1)
Breezeway(IRE), a 340,000 euros purchase who was never in the hunt over an inadequate six furlongs on debut, failed to progress as one may have expected on this rise in distance and is clearly more of a nursery type.
Sky Beam(USA), although well bred and related to several smart performers, lacks any big-race entries, but she travelled well until a point and, although dropping right away, may have needed the outing. (op 33-1)

4149 BLUE SQUARE PRICES V THE REST H'CAP 1m 4f

4:55 (4:58) (Class 4) (0-85,82) 4-Y-O+ **£5,505** (£1,637; £818; £408) **Stalls** Centre

Form				RPR
5116	**1**		**Our Teddy (IRE)**[14] [3748] 6-9-5 **80** TonyCulhane 12 (P A Blockley) *hld up: hdwy over 4f out: rdn to ld and hung lft fr over 1f out : styd on* **8/1**	91
4-64	**2**	*3/4*	**Buster Hyvonen (IRE)**[24] [3401] 4-8-9 **70** OscarUrbina 6 (J R Fanshawe) *led: rdn and hdd over 1f out: carried lft ins fnl f: styd on* **4/1**[2]	80
1123	**3**	*1*	**Ti Adora (IRE)**[23] [3446] 4-9-4 **79** RobertWinston 10 (P W D'Arcy) *swtg: dwlt: hld up: hdwy over 2f out: rdn and ev ch over 1f out: styng on same pce whn nt clr run ins fnl f* **6/1**[3]	87
2-00	**4**	*1 1/4*	**Self Respect (USA)**[65] [2176] 4-9-7 **82** EddieAhern 5 (A King) *lw: chsd ldrs: rdn over 3f out: styd on same pce fnl f* **14/1**	88
12-3	**5**	*2 1/2*	**Authority (IRE)**[71] [1995] 6-8-13 **74** KerrinMcEvoy 9 (Lady Herries) *lw: chsd ldr over 3f: remined handy: rdn and hung lft over 1f out: no ex* **11/4**[1]	76
-006	**6**	*2*	**Mutamaasek (USA)**[26] [3365] 4-8-2 **63** JimmyQuinn 4 (Lady Herries) *prom: rdn over 2f out: wknd over 1f out* **16/1**	62
2500	**7**	*hd*	**Wellington Hall (GER)**[6] [3980] 8-8-10 **78** MCGeran(7) 8 (P W Chapple-Hyam) *hld up: hdwy over 4f out: rdn and ev ch over 2f out: wknd over 1f out* **20/1**	76
4340	**8**	*2 1/2*	**Tcherina (IRE)**[38] [2975] 4-9-2 **77** DavidAllan 7 (T D Easterby) *chsd ldr over 8f out: rdn over 2f out: sn wknd* **8/1**	71
0005	**9**	*7*	**The Violin Player (USA)**[30] [3209] 5-8-9 **70** (p) MichaelHills 11 (H J Collingridge) *lw: hld up: a in rr* **12/1**	53
040	**10**	*1 1/4*	**Smooth Jazz**[26] [3365] 4-9-0 **75** SebSanders 2 (R M Beckett) *chsd ldrs over 9f* **12/1**	56
0-55	**11**	*hd*	**Mayadeen (IRE)**[21] [3528] 4-8-10 **74** (p) StephenDonohoe(3) 3 (J G M O'Shea) *hld up: lost pl over 5f out: bhd fnl 3f* **25/1**	55
0-00	**12**	*12*	**Anousa (IRE)**[56] [2437] 5-8-9 **70** HayleyTurner 14 (P Howling) *b. hld up: hdwy over 4f out: rdn: hung lft and wknd 3f out* **66/1**	32

2m 30.17s (-2.74) **Going Correction** -0.20s/f (Firm) **12** Ran SP% **121.2**
Speed ratings (Par 105):101,100,99,99,97 96,95,94,89,88 88,80
CSF £40.18 CT £212.51 TOTE £9.40: £2.40, £2.00, £2.10; EX 47.00.
Owner The Beare Family **Bred** Vizcaya Ag **Trained** Lambourn, Berks

FOCUS
A competitive handicap and the form seems sound enough, rated around the third and fourth.
Mayadeen(IRE) Official explanation: jockey said gelding hung left throughout

4150 BLUE SQUARE CASINO H'CAP — 1m 4f

5:25 (5:32) (Class 5) (0-70,69) 3-Y-O — **£3,886** (£1,156; £577; £288) **Stalls** Centre

Form — RPR

0534 **1** **Plemont Bay**[29] [3249] 3-8-8 **56**....(v[1]) HayleyTurner 14 — 73+
(M L W Bell) *hld up: hdwy over 8f out: led 3f out: rdn clr and hung rt over 1f out: eased ins fnl f* **5/1**[3]

0242 **2** *5* **Osolomio (IRE)**[17] [3634] 3-8-12 **60**.... RobertWinston 7 — 67
(J G Given) *led 1f: chsd ldr: rdn to chse wnr over 2f out: no imp appr fnl f* **10/3**[2]

00-3 **3** *7* **Trafalgar Day**[35] [3065] 3-9-2 **64**.... DavidAllan 13 — 60
(W M Brisbourne) *hld up: hdwy over 3f out: rdn and wknd over 1f out* **9/1**

000 **4** *5* **Himba**[61] [2304] 3-9-6 **68**.... KerrinMcEvoy 4 — 56
(Mrs A J Perrett) *chsd ldrs: rdn over 3f out: wknd over 2f out* **12/1**

-630 **5** *1 ½* **Canyouwin**[39] [2961] 3-8-12 **60**.... DavidKinsella 1 — 45
(J H M Gosden) *b.hind: s.i.s: sn pushed along in rr: sme hdwy u.p over 2f out: n.d* **16/1**

6-05 **6** *2 ½* **Height Of Fury (IRE)**[38] [2990] 3-9-7 **69**.... EddieAhern 11 — 50
(J L Dunlop) *s.i.s: hld up: rdn 1/2-way: wknd over 2f out* **3/1**[1]

-550 **7** *12* **Machhapuchhare**[43] [2814] 3-8-2 **50**.... MatthewHenry 2 — 12
(W M Brisbourne) *lw: s.i.s: drvn to ld after 1f: clr 8f out: hdd 3f out: wknd 2f out* **33/1**

03-0 **8** *1* **India Run (IRE)**[43] [2825] 3-9-6 **68**.... JimmyQuinn 5 — 29
(J L Dunlop) *s.i.s: hld up: rdn and wknd over 3f out: eased* **7/1**

0040 **9** *½* **Delorain (IRE)**[23] [3439] 3-8-4 **52**....(v) TPO'Shea 9 — 12
(J A R Toller) *mid-div: rdn 1/2-way: wknd over 3f out* **33/1**

0000 **10** *31* **El Faro (FR)**[10] [3848] 3-8-11 **59**.... TonyCulhane 10 — —
(M R Channon) *lw: chsd ldrs over 8f* **16/1**

6035 **11** *86* **Shardia (IRE)**[85] [1648] 3-8-0 **51**.... PatrickMathers(3) 6 — —
(J Jay) *hld up: wknd over 3f out: virtually p.u fnl f* **25/1**

2m 30.34s (-2.57) **Going Correction** -0.20s/f (Firm) — **11** Ran SP% **116.4**
Speed ratings (Par 100):100,96,92,88,87 86,78,77,77,56 —
CSF £21.34 CT £144.07 TOTE £6.20: £2.00, £1.70, £2.20 Place 6 £119.72, Place 5 £80.92..
Owner Bryan & Philippa Burrough **Bred** B Burrough **Trained** Newmarket, Suffolk

FOCUS
They finished well strung out in what was just a modest handicap and the form has been rated positively, although it is not that strong.
Height Of Fury(IRE) Official explanation: jockey said colt was too keen and was unsuited by the good to firm ground
India Run(IRE) Official explanation: jockey said colt had no more to give
El Faro(FR) Official explanation: jockey said colt had no more to give
T/Plt: £143.40 to a £1 stake. Pool: £91,867.25. 467.40 winning tickets. T/Qpdt: £39.40 to a £1 stake. Pool: £3,338.50. 62.60 winning tickets. CR

4115 THIRSK (L-H)

Saturday, August 5

OFFICIAL GOING: Straight course - good; round course - good to firm
Wind: Slight, behind

4151 EUROPEAN BREEDERS FUND MCCARTHY & STONE MAIDEN STKS — 5f

2:15 (2:16) (Class 4) 2-Y-O — **£6,477** (£1,927; £963; £481) **Stalls** High

Form — RPR

32 **1** **Palo Verde**[6] [3982] 2-9-3.... J-PGuillambert 3 — 78+
(M Johnston) *mde all: rdn and hung lft over 1f out: styd on strly ins last: comf* **4/6**[1]

2 *1* **Hurricane Flyer** 2-9-3.... RichardMullen 6 — 74
(E J O'Neill) *trckd ldrs: hdwy 2f out: effrt and n.m.r over 1f out: rdn and kpt on ins last* **13/2**[3]

2324 **3** *nk* **Perlachy**[7] [3958] 2-9-3 75.... PaulHanagan 1 — 73
(T D Easterby) *cl up: rdn along wl over 1f out: kpt on u.p ins last* **5/1**[2]

0 **4** *1 ½* **Mambo Spirit (IRE)**[50] [2623] 2-9-3.... MickyFenton 7 — 68
(J G Given) *chsd ldrs: rdn along 2f out: kpt on same pce appr last* **25/1**

5 *1 ¼* **Solwind (USA)** 2-8-12.... TomEaves 9 — 58
(B Smart) *hld up: hdwy 2f out: kpt on ins last: bttr for r* **9/1**

6 *1 ½* **Beaumont Boy** 2-9-3.... DeanMcKeown 2 — 58
(G A Swinbank) *s.i.s and bhd tl kpt on fnl 2f* **25/1**

56 **7** *1 ¾* **Obe Royal**[6] [3982] 2-9-0.... EdwardCreighton(3) 8 — 52
(M R Channon) *hld up: swtchd lft and effrt wl over 1f out: sn rdn and no imp* **14/1**

6 **8** *58* **Miss Capricorn**[21] [3521] 2-8-12.... DO'Donohoe 4 — —
(K A Ryan) *prom on outer: pushed along whn stmbld over 2f out: sn wknd: lost action and virtually p.u fnl f* **50/1**

59.96 secs (0.06) **Going Correction** -0.15s/f (Firm) — **8** Ran SP% **116.3**
Speed ratings (Par 96):93,91,90,88,86 84,81,—
CSF £5.61 TOTE £1.70: £1.10, £2.10, £1.50; EX 7.60.
Owner Jumeirah Racing **Bred** Darley **Trained** Middleham Moor, N Yorks
■ Stewards' Enquiry : Paul Hanagan one-day ban: failed to keep straight from stalls (Aug 16)

FOCUS
An average maiden, but Perlachy can be used as a reliable benchmark.

NOTEBOOK
Palo Verde, smartly away, crossed to the stands' rail and dictated the race. He wandered slightly approaching the last, but he was soon back on an even keel and he won with something to spare. He looks as though six furlongs might suit him even better and there should be more to come from hims in nurseries. (op 8-11 tchd 4-5)
Hurricane Flyer, although not the biggest of horses, is strongly made and he kept on well to get second, despite not getting the clearest of runs. This was a pleasing debut and, provided he progresses with experience, he should win something similar. (tchd 7-1)
Perlachy, who was content to get a lead, ran another respectable race, but was unable to quicken when the chips were down. He is well exposed, but will winh one of these eventually if he continues to hold his form. (op 11-2 tchd 6-1)
Mambo Spirit(IRE), who was full of himself beforehand, stepped up on his debut effort and momentarily threatened to play a part in the finish. He could not quicken in the end though and looks sure to be helped by a rise to six furlongs. (op 20-1)
Solwind(USA), a filly by Johannesburg, made a little late headway and looks sure to be capable of better with the experience under her belt, probably up to six furlongs. (op 15-2 tchd 7-1)
Miss Capricorn Official explanation: jockey said filly lost its action

4152 HERTEL NURSERY — 5f

2:45 (2:46) (Class 3) 2-Y-O — **£9,067** (£2,697; £1,348; £673) **Stalls** High

Form — RPR

211 **1** **Vale Of Belvoir (IRE)**[22] [3476] 2-8-13 **83**.... PatCosgrave 10 — 88+
(K R Burke) *trckd ldrs: smooth hdwy 2f out: rdn and qcknd to ld ent last: comf* **7/2**[2]

4120 **2** *1 ¼* **Frisky Talk (IRE)**[14] [3734] 2-8-6 **76**.... MickyFenton 9 — 77
(B W Hills) *led: rdn along 2f out: hdd and drvn ent last: kpt on* **11/1**

1305 **3** *1* **Mr Klick (IRE)**[21] [3555] 2-8-11 **81**.... GrahamGibbons 11 — 78+
(N Wilson) *trckd ldrs on stands rail: swtchd lft and effrt whn n.m.r over 1f out: swtchd rt and rdn ins last: styd on* **33/1**

2131 **4** *¾* **My Valerina (IRE)**[14] [3720] 2-8-5 **75**.... PaulHanagan 4 — 69+
(Mrs A Duffield) *hld up: hdwy on stands rail and n.m.r over 1f out:swtchd markedly lft and rdn ent last: kpt on: nrst fin* **12/1**

5210 **5** *nk* **Naayla (IRE)**[7] [3925] 2-8-8 **83**.... MichaelJStainton(5) 2 — 76
(B J Meehan) *chsd ldrs on outer: rdn along wl over 1f out: kpt on same pce ins last* **13/2**

0631 **6** *1* **Danger Alley**[18] [3624] 2-8-2 **72**....(b) RichardMullen 5 — 62
(E J O'Neill) *cl up: ev ch 2f out: sn rdn and grad wknd* **40/1**

6452 **7** *1 ¾* **Danum Dancer**[21] [3555] 2-8-5 **75** ow1.... DeanMcKeown 1 — 58
(N Bycroft) *chsd ldrs on outer: rdn along 2f out: sn wknd* **40/1**

4100 **8** *½* **Riverside Dancer (USA)**[14] [3734] 2-9-3 **87**.... DO'Donohoe 12 — 68+
(K A Ryan) *s.i.s and bhd: swtchd lft over 2f out: sn rdn and edgd lft whn n.m.r over 1f out: nvr nrr* **11/4**[1]

1453 **9** *½* **Kerry's Dream**[22] [3474] 2-9-1 **85**.... PaulMulrennan 6 — 65
(T D Easterby) *towards rr: effrt and hdwy over 2f out: sn rdn and no imp* **14/1**

3150 **10** *4* **Stir Crazy (IRE)**[2] [4088] 2-8-0 **73**.... EdwardCreighton(3) 8 — 38
(M R Channon) *prom: rdn along 1/2-way: sn wknd* **16/1**

15 **11** *1 ½* **Ingleby Image**[14] [3734] 2-8-11 **81**.... PaulFessey 7 — 41
(T D Barron) *s.i.s: sn chsng ldrs: rdn over 2f out and sn wknd* **11/2**[3]

0210 **12** *5* **Ice Mountain**[14] [3734] 2-9-2 **91**.... MarkLawson(5) 3 — 33
(B Smart) *a rr* **10/1**

58.94 secs (-0.96) **Going Correction** -0.15s/f (Firm) — **12** Ran SP% **123.1**
Speed ratings (Par 98):101,99,97,96,95 94,91,90,89,83 80,72
CSF £43.34 CT £835.78 TOTE £5.70: £2.60, £3.80, £4.50; EX 65.50.
Owner S Marley & Tweenhills Racing IX **Bred** Denis And Mrs Teresa Bergin **Trained** Middleham Moor, N Yorks

FOCUS
A good nursery; the form is sound and likely to produce winners.

NOTEBOOK
Vale Of Belvoir(IRE), on a hat-trick following wins at Catterick and Chester, produced an impressive burst of speed to cut down the leaders and win with something in hand. She will now step up to Listed company at Newbury later this month in the St Hugh's Stakes and looks well worth her place, as speed is her most potent weapon. (op 4-1 tchd 9-2)
Frisky Talk(IRE) ran well in defeat, showing her customary early speed before being cut down by the winner. (op 12-1)
Mr Klick(IRE) took advantage of his favourable draw and ran a sound race, staying on well having been a bit squeezed for room over a furlong out.
My Valerina(IRE), up 5lb for her Haydock win, ran well from an unfavourable draw and was probably unlucky not to finish closer, being forced to switch before finishing well. (tchd 11-1)
Naayla(IRE), back down to a more realistic level, was forced to use up plenty of early speed from a wide draw and ran well considering. (op 15-2 tchd 6-1)
Danger Alley was not disgraced against this stronger opposition and looks an improved performer for the fitting of blinkers.
Riverside Dancer(USA) ran better than her finishing position might suggest, given that she missed the break, and also met a little trouble in running. (op 10-3 tchd 7-2)
Ingleby Imagewho ran so well in the Super Sprint a fortnight ago, got very warm in the preliminaries, exited awkwardly from the stalls and never played a part. Official explanation: jockey said filly missed the break (op 7-2 tchd 6-1 tchd 13-2 in a place)

4153 EKOS CONSULTING H'CAP — 1m

3:20 (3:20) (Class 3) (0-90,88) 3-Y-O+ — **£9,067** (£2,697; £1,348; £673) **Stalls** Low

Form — RPR

5025 **1** **Granston (IRE)**[28] [3313] 5-9-12 **86**.... GrahamGibbons 4 — 96
(J D Bethell) *trckd ldrs: hdwy to chse ldr 3f out: rdn to chal 2f out: led over 1f out: edgd lft ins last: drvn and jst hld on* **9/4**[1]

0030 **2** *shd* **Wahoo Sam (USA)**[4] [4029] 6-8-13 **73**....(p) DO'Donohoe 1 — 83
(K A Ryan) *led: clr 1/2-way: rdn along and jnd 2f out: drvn and hdd over 1f out: drvn and ch whn bmpd ins last: styd on wl* **8/1**

5343 **3** *hd* **Hula Ballew**[11] [3812] 6-9-1 **75**.... PhillipMakin 8 — 85+
(M Dods) *midfield: hdwy wl over 2f out: rdn to chse elading pair over 1f out: styd on strly ins last* **7/1**[3]

1004 **4** *3 ½* **Commitment Lecture**[27] [3331] 6-8-9 **69** oh1....(t) PaulFessey 3 — 70
(M Dods) *dwlt and bhd: hdwy wl over 2f out: styd on ins last: nrst fin* **16/1**

0602 **5** *¾* **Mezuzah**[7] [3937] 6-9-2 **76**.... PaulMulrennan 11 — 76
(M W Easterby) *chsd ldrs: rdn along 3f out: drvn 2f out and sn wknd* **10/1**

3030 **6** *2 ½* **Tough Love**[12] [3789] 7-8-13 **73**....(p) MickyFenton 10 — 67
(T D Easterby) *outpcd and bhd tl sme late hdwy* **16/1**

1042 **7** *½* **Nevada Desert (IRE)**[4] [4020] 6-8-9 **69**.... DeanMcKeown 7 — 62
(R M Whitaker) *prom: pushed along over 3f out: rdn wl over 2f out and sn btn* **9/2**[2]

0133 **8** *nk* **Queen's Composer (IRE)**[11] [3813] 3-8-5 **77** ow1.... MarkLawson(5) 6 — 69
(B Smart) *prom: rdn along 3f out: drvn 2f out and sn wknd* **10/1**

2461 **9** *1 ¾* **Aperitif**[88] [1561] 5-8-11 **71**.... PaulQuinn 9 — 59
(D Nicholls) *hld up towards rr: effrt and sme hdwy over 2f out: sn btn* **9/1**

0-36 **10** *5* **Tsaroxy (IRE)**[43] [2810] 4-9-3 **77**.... PatCosgrave 5 — 54
(J Howard Johnson) *in tch: hdwy to chse ldrs 1/2-way: rdn along 3f out and sn wknd* **20/1**

1m 37.79s (-1.91) **Going Correction** 0.0s/f (Good)
WFA 3 from 4yo+ 7lb — **10** Ran SP% **117.3**
Speed ratings (Par 107):109,108,108,105,104 101,101,101,99,94
CSF £20.94 CT £113.54 TOTE £3.30: £1.40, £1.90, £1.90; EX 29.80.
Owner The Four Players Partnership **Bred** Yeomanstown Stud **Trained** Middleham Moor, N Yorks

FOCUS
A fair handicap and ordinary form.

NOTEBOOK
Granston(IRE), a horse who does only the bare minimum, took plenty of hard driving to get home. He is, reportedly, better going right-handed than left and will now return to Ripon to bid for a second successive win in the Ripon Rowels. (op 11-4 tchd 3-1)
Wahoo Sam(USA), who adopted his usual front-running tactics, battled home in tremendous style and did not get a great deal of room when tackled by the winner. (op 6-1)
Hula Ballew picked up in great style entering the last and was only just denied. She looks on excellent terms with herself. (op 15-2)
Commitment Lecture ran a sound race on ground which was beginning to go against her. (op 14-1)
Mezuzah ran well for a long way on ground that would have been a little lively for him. (op 9-1)

4154 RACING UK H'CAP — 1m
3:55 (3:55) (Class 5) (0-70,70) 3-Y-O+ — £3,238 (£963; £481; £240) Stalls Low

Form — RPR

5441 **1** **Champain Sands (IRE)**[15] [3697] 7-9-1 **61**............ MichaelJStainton(5) 1 — 70
(E J Alston) *hld up in rr: stdy hdwy on inner over 2f out: rdn to chal and edgd rt ins last: led last 100 yds* **5/1**[3]

3142 **2** 1 ¼ **Joshua's Gold (IRE)**[20] [3565] 5-9-10 **65**....................(v) DanielTudhope 8 — 71
(D Carroll) *in tch: gd hdwy on outer 3f out: chal over 1f out: rdn to ld jst ins last: sn edgd lft: hdd and no ex last 100 yds* **9/4**[1]

0022 **3** 1 ¾ **Major Magpie (IRE)**[19] [3583] 4-10-0 **69**.......................... PhillipMakin 13 — 71
(M Dods) *dwlt and bhd: hdwy on wd outside over 2f out: rdn and styd on ins last: nrst fin* **4/1**[2]

0040 **4** hd **Mozakhraf (USA)**[21] [3543] 4-9-3 **58**.................................. DO'Donohoe 5 — 60
(K A Ryan) *cl up: led after 2f: rdn clr 2f out: drvn and hdd ins jst ins last: wknd towards fin* **10/1**

303 **5** nk **Can Can Star**[17] [3638] 3-9-5 **67**.. MickyFenton 11 — 67
(J G Given) *chsd ldng pair: rdn along over 2f out: drvn wl over 1f out and kpt on same pce* **25/1**

0-16 **6** ½ **Jordan's Light (USA)**[72] [1950] 3-8-8 **63**...................... JamesO'Reilly(7) 6 — 63+
(T J Pitt) *hld up and bhd: hdwy on bit 3f out: swtchd rt 2f out: swtchd lft and rt ent last: tenderly rdn: styd on: nrst fin* **14/1**

5366 **7** shd **Efidium**[20] [3565] 8-9-10 **65**.. DeanMcKeown 7 — 65
(N Bycroft) *in tch: hdwy to chse ldrs 3f out: rdn 2f out:kpt on same pce* **13/2**

0043 **8** ¾ **Flashing Floozie**[29] [3264] 3-7-13 **50** oh6................ EdwardCreighton(3) 4 — 47
(M F Harris) *chsd ldrs: rdn along over 2f out: drvn wl over 1f out and grad wknd* **33/1**

6000 **9** 2 ½ **Frogs' Gift (IRE)**[18] [3610] 4-8-9 **50** oh12.............................. PaulQuinn 9 — 42
(G M Moore) *towards rr: hdwy over 2f out: sn rdn: edgd lft and no imp* **66/1**

6000 **10** nk **Wayward Shot (IRE)**[33] [3147] 4-9-0 **55**........................... DaleGibson 10 — 46
(M W Easterby) *led 2f: prom tl rdn along wl over 2f out and sn wknd* **40/1**

5-64 **11** 26 **Pepper Road**[102] [1227] 7-8-9 **50** oh1............................. J-PGuillambert 12 — —
(R Bastiman) *hld up: hdwy on outer 1/2-way: rdn to chse ldrs 3f out: wknd 2f out and sn eased* **16/1**

-556 **12** 11 **Thistle**[29] [3241] 5-9-10 **65**.. PaulMulrennan 3 — —
(J Howard Johnson) *chsd ldrs: rdn along over 3f out and sn wknd* **10/1**

1m 39.17s (-0.53) **Going Correction** 0.0s/f (Good)
WFA 3 from 4yo+ 7lb — **12** Ran SP% **122.2**
Speed ratings (Par 103):102,100,99,98,98 98,97,97,94,94 68,57
CSF £16.72 CT £52.29 TOTE £7.70: £2.60, £1.70, £1.80; EX 26.40.
Owner Geoff & Astrid Long **Bred** Gerrardstown House Stud **Trained** Longton, Lancs
■ Stewards' Enq : James O'Reilly 30-day ban: in breach of rule 157 (Aug 16-Sep 14) Pitt fined £600.

FOCUS
Modest handicap form and not that strong, rated through the runner-up.
Jordan's Light(USA) Official explanation: 40-day ban (Aug 8-Sep 16); jockey said his orders were to ride gelding mid-division but he had been unable to do so, adding that his saddle slipped in the straight; trainer added that gelding had had muscular problems since its last run
Pepper Road Official explanation: jockey said gelding ran too free

4155 HYGICARE WORKPLACE SOLUTIONS MAIDEN FILLIES' STKS — 7f
4:30 (4:33) (Class 4) 3-Y-O+ — £6,477 (£1,927; £963; £481) Stalls Low

Form — RPR

1 **Quaich** 3-9-0 .... DO'Donohoe 15 — 69+
(Saeed Bin Suroor) *trckd ldrs: smooth hdwy wl over 2f out: led 1 1/2f out: sn pushed clr* **10/3**[3]

3 **2** 5 **Shiitake**[46] [2734] 3-8-11 .... EdwardCreighton(3) 2 — 56+
(Miss L A Perratt) *s.i.s and bhd: hdwy on inner whn hmpd wl over 2f out: swtchd rt and rdn: styd on strly fr over 1f out* **11/2**

-204 **3** ¾ **Angel Voices (IRE)**[78] [1836] 3-9-0 77................................ PatCosgrave 8 — 54
(K R Burke) *trckd ldrs: hdwy over 3f out: rdn and hung lft wl over 1f out: sn drvn and kpt on ins last* **5/2**[2]

06 **4** nk **Bond Free Spirit (IRE)**[8] [3909] 3-9-0 .... GylesParkin 10 — 53
(G R Oldroyd) *cl up: rdn to ld wl over 2f out: drvn and hdd 1 1/2f out: wknd ent last* **66/1**

205 **5** nk **Another Genepi (USA)**[21] [3554] 3-9-0 69............................ J-PGuillambert 6 — 52
(J W Hills) *hld up: hdwy on outer wl over 2f out: rdn wl over 1f out: kpt on same pce* **9/4**[1]

0U **6** 1 **Miss Imperious**[8] [3916] 3-8-9 .... DuranFentiman(5) 7 — 49+
(B Smart) *towards rr: hdwy over 2f out: sn rdn and kpt on ins last: nrst fin* **100/1**

-005 **7** shd **Quintin**[29] [3244] 3-9-0 43.. GrahamGibbons 1 — 49
(T D Easterby) *led: rdn along 3f out: sn hdd and grad wknd* **33/1**

4 **8** ½ **How's She Cuttin' (IRE)**[8] [3916] 3-9-0 .... PhillipMakin 16 — 48+
(T D Barron) *hld up in rr: sme hdwy 3f out: rdn and edgd lft 2f out: no prog* **10/1**

4 **9** 1 ¾ **Mrs Quince**[36] [3039] 4-9-6 .... DeanMcKeown 9 — 43
(F Watson) *dwlt: a rr* **100/1**

-000 **10** nk **Bottomless Wallet**[15] [3698] 5-9-6 40...................................... PaulQuinn 4 — 42
(F Watson) *prom: rdn along 3f out: wknd fnl 2f* **100/1**

6 **11** 4 **Agnes Pearl**[120] [907] 3-9-0 .... DerekMcGaffin 3 — 31
(B Smart) *chsd ldrs: rdn along 1/2-way: sn lost pl and bhd* **50/1**

12 ¾ **Gigi Glamor** 4-9-6 .... PaulMulrennan 13 — 29
(W M Brisbourne) *rr: rdn and hung lft wl over 2f out: nvr a factor* **33/1**

-306 **13** 4 **Sister Gee (IRE)**[25] [3379] 4-8-13 41..................... RussellKennemore(7) 5 — 18
(R Hollinshead) *chsd ldrs: rdn along 1/2-way: sn wknd* **50/1**

1m 26.79s (-0.31) **Going Correction** 0.0s/f (Good)
WFA 3 from 4yo+ 6lb — **13** Ran SP% **121.2**
Speed ratings (Par 102):101,95,94,94,93 92,92,91,89,89 85,84,79
CSF £21.76 TOTE £3.80: £2.00, £1.70, £1.50; EX 21.60.
Owner Godolphin **Bred** Gainsborough Stud Management Ltd **Trained** Newmarket, Suffolk

FOCUS
A race lacking strength in depth and it was pleasing to see the Godolphin newcomer score. The form is limited by the seventh.

4156 POLAR FORD H'CAP — 2m
5:00 (5:02) (Class 5) (0-75,71) 4-Y-O+ — £3,886 (£1,156; £577; £288) Stalls Low

Form — RPR

0043 **1** **Dancer's Serenade (IRE)**[14] [3723] 4-9-5 **69**.................... MickyFenton 8 — 76
(T P Tate) *trckd ldr: effrt 3f out: rdn to ld wl over 1f out: drvn ins last: styd on gamely* **7/1**[3]

4064 **2** ½ **The Grey Man**[28] [3284] 5-8-13 **63**.................................. RichardMullen 1 — 69
(E S McMahon) *led: pushed along and qcknd 3f out: jnd and rdn 2f out: drvn and hdd wl over 1f out: rallied ins last: no ex towards fin* **12/1**

21 **3** nk **Riodan (IRE)**[45] [2750] 4-9-7 **71**...................................... GrahamGibbons 6 — 77
(J J Quinn) *hld up: hdwy over 4f out: rdn along wl over 2f out: drvn over 1f out: styd on ins last: nrst fin* **9/4**[1]

0320 **4** 1 ½ **Thewhirlingdervish (IRE)**[7] [3955] 8-8-10 **65**.......... DuranFentiman(5) 9 — 69
(T D Easterby) *rr: pushed along and hdwy 4f out: rdn along on outer over 2f out: sn drvn and kpt on fnl f: nrst fin* **8/1**

3434 **5** 5 **Cotton Eyed Joe (IRE)**[38] [2975] 5-9-6 **70**.................... DeanMcKeown 7 — 68
(G A Swinbank) *hld up: hdwy and in tch over 4f out: rdn along 3f out: drvn 2f out and sn btn* **11/4**[2]

0130 **6** ½ **Whoopsie**[68] [2078] 4-8-4 **54**.. JosedeSouza 3 — 51
(S Parr) *trckd ldrs: hdwy 4f out: rdn along 3f out: drvn over 2f out and sn btn* **16/1**

0-01 **7** 3 **Sharp N Frosty**[57] [2408] 4-8-6 **56**.................................. PaulMulrennan 2 — 50
(W M Brisbourne) *trckd ldng pair: rdn along over 3f out: sn drvn and wknd over 2f out* **8/1**

3200 **8** 44 **Step Perfect (USA)**[96] [975] 5-8-2 **52** oh6............................ PaulQuinn 5 — —
(G M Moore) *a rr: bhd fnl 3f* **50/1**

5055 **9** nk **Rule For Ever**[15] [3696] 4-8-7 **57**....................................(t) J-PGuillambert 4 — —
(M Johnston) *chsd ldrs: rdn along after 3f: rn in snatches: lost pl over 6f out: sn bhd* **7/1**[3]

3m 29.39s (-1.81) **Going Correction** 0.0s/f (Good) — **9** Ran SP% **120.2**
Speed ratings (Par 103):104,103,103,102,100 100,98,76,76
CSF £90.05 CT £251.75 TOTE £10.80: £2.30, £2.80, £2.00; EX 114.30.
Owner S M Racing **Bred** Dunderry Stud **Trained** Tadcaster, N Yorks
■ Stewards' Enquiry : Richard Mullen one-day ban: used whip with excessive frequency (Aug 16)

FOCUS
A modest staying handicap but run at a fair gallop and rated through the winner.
Cotton Eyed Joe(IRE) Official explanation: jockey said gelding hung left and was unsuited by the good to firm ground
Rule For Ever Official explanation: jockey said gelding had a breathing problem

4157 WHITBY H'CAP (LADIES' RACE) — 6f
5:35 (5:37) (Class 6) (0-55,61) 3-Y-O+ — £3,123 (£968; £484; £242) Stalls High

Form — RPR

0000 **1** **Compton Plume**[44] [2785] 6-9-13 **51**............................ MissJCoward(7) 19 — 64
(M W Easterby) *a.p stands rail: hdwy to ld wl over 1f out: rdn and kpt on strly ins last* **28/1**

5000 **2** 2 **Frimley's Matterry**[3] [4057] 6-9-8 **44**....................(v) MissMSowerby(5) 18 — 51
(R E Barr) *hld up stands rail: hdwy 2f out: swtchd lft and rdn top chse wnr ent last: kpt on* **25/1**

0200 **3** 3 **Hamaasy**[18] [3617] 5-9-9 **47**.. MissERamstrom(7) 14 — 45+
(D Nicholls) *trckd ldrs: hdwy 2f out: sn rdn and kpt on ins last* **33/1**

00-0 **4** 1 **Hout Bay**[6] [3988] 9-10-5 **55**..................................(p) MissVTunnicliffe(5) 16 — 50
(R A Fahey) *dwlt and bhd stands rail: hdwy 2f out: styd on ent last: nrst fin* **33/1**

0020 **5** 1 **Obe Bold (IRE)**[3] [4059] 5-10-7 **52**...................................... MrsCBartley 13 — 44
(A Berry) *a.p: rdn wl over 1f out: kpt on one pce* **16/1**

6004 **6** ¾ **Outrageous Flirt (IRE)**[12] [3786] 4-10-5 **50**............... MissSBrotherton 20 — 40
(A Dickman) *outpcd and bhd stands rail tl styd on fr wl over 1f out: nt rch ldrs* **4/1**[3]

6005 **7** 2 **Sundried Tomato**[21] [3524] 7-9-6 **42**...........................(p) MissJRiding(5) 17 — 26
(D W Chapman) *chsd ldrs: rdn along 2f out: wknd over 1f out* **16/1**

0064 **8** nk **Borodinsky**[3] [4059] 5-9-11 **47**.............................. MissHCuthbert(5) 6 — 30+
(R E Barr) *towards rr: hdwy over 2f out: sn rdn and no imp fnl f* **10/1**

0605 **9** shd **Crystal Mystic (IRE)**[40] [2920] 4-9-10 **48**...................... MrsJMBerry(7) 10 — 31
(B Palling) *led: rdn along and hdd wl over 2f out: grad wknd* **40/1**

0062 **10** 1 **Tuscan Flyer**[18] [3617] 8-9-8 **44**...........................(b) MissRBastiman(5) 15 — 24
(R Bastiman) *dwlt: a towards rr* **14/1**

6003 **11** 1 **Tartan Special**[1] [4120] 4-9-6 **42**...........................(p) MissKellyBurke(5) 11 — 19
(K R Burke) *a towards rr* **14/1**

606 **12** ½ **Diamond Katie (IRE)**[10] [3855] 4-10-4 **52**............. MissFayeBramley(3) 8 — 27
(N Tinkler) *midfield: rdn along over 2f out: sn wknd* **14/1**

3050 **13** 1 ¾ **Moon Forest (IRE)**[6] [3988] 4-9-12 **50**..................(p) MissSBradley(7) 5 — 20
(J M Bradley) *chsd ldrs: rdn over 2f out: sn drvn: hung lft and wknd* **50/1**

0003 **14** ½ **Fairgame Man**[11] [3811] 8-10-1 **46**.................................... MissLEllison 2 — 14
(J S Wainwright) *racd wd: nvr nr ldrs* **33/1**

0-40 **15** hd **Elisha (IRE)**[8] [3912] 4-10-2 **52**.....................................(b) MissARyan(5) 12 — 20
(K A Ryan) *cl up: led over 2f out: sn rdn: hdd wl over 1f out and wknd appr last* **50/1**

511 **16** 2 **The Cayterers**[3] [4054] 4-10-9 **61** 5ex.............................. MissHDavies(7) 4 — 23
(J M Bradley) *racd wd: prom: rdn over 2f out: sn drvn and wknd* **3/1**[1]

2121 **17** 1 ¼ **Paddywack (IRE)**[4] [4019] 9-11-2 **61** 5ex.........................(b) MissADeniel 9 — 19
(D W Chapman) *s.i.s and bhd: hdwy wl over 1f out: sn swtchd lft: rdn and wknd* **7/2**[2]

0220 **18** 2 **Beau Marche**[7] [3933] 4-9-8 **46**...............................(b) MissSGoldsmith(7) 7 — —
(G G Margarson) *racd wd: a bhd* **25/1**

5510 **19** shd **Grand View**[82] [1728] 10-9-10 **48**................................(p) MissCParrish(7) 3 — —
(J R Weymes) *racd wd: bhd fr 1/2-way* **50/1**

0006 **20** 2 ½ **Straffan (IRE)**[93] [1447] 4-9-5 **43**..................................(p) MissWGibson(7) 1 — —
(J Hetherton) *prom on outer: rdn along 1/2-way: sn wknd* **66/1**

1m 11.76s (-0.74) **Going Correction** -0.15s/f (Firm) — **20** Ran SP% **137.9**
Speed ratings (Par 101):98,95,91,90,88 87,85,84,84,83 81,81,78,78,77 75,73,70,70,67
CSF £626.22 CT £20565.69 TOTE £44.10: £7.70, £7.30, £8.10, £6.80; EX 290.70 Place 6 £26.76, Place 5 £23.92.
Owner W H & Mrs J A Tinning **Bred** Mrs D A La Trobe **Trained** Sheriff Hutton, N Yorks

FOCUS
A moderate but highly-competitive handicap in which the high draws dominated. The runner-up sets the standard.
Compton Plume Official explanation: trainer's representative had no explanation for the improved form shown
T/Plt: £20.10 to a £1 stake. Pool: £52,683.95. 1,911.45 winning tickets. T/Qpdt: £11.10 to a £1 stake. Pool: £1,939.10. 128.60 winning tickets. JR

4000 WINDSOR (R-H)
Saturday, August 5

OFFICIAL GOING: Good to firm
Wind: Almost nil

4158 INTERCASINO.CO.UK CONDITIONS STKS — 6f
2:20 (2:20) (Class 3) 3-Y-O+ — £8,724 (£2,612; £1,306; £653; £326) Stalls High

Form — RPR

0340 **1** **Celtic Mill**[6] [3972] 8-9-4 104..(p) NickyMackay 3 — 112
(D W Barker) *mde all: shkn up over 2f out: kpt up to work fnl f but a in command* **1/2**[1]

30 **2** *1 ¼* **Andronikos**[61] [2303] 4-8-13 105..................(t) RichardHughes 1 103
(P F I Cole) *wnt to stands' side s: swtchd lft and hdwy on outside over 2f out: rdn to chse wnr over 1f out* **11/4**[2]

4552 **3** *7* **Peter Island (FR)**[7] [3943] 3-8-9 72..................(v) LPKeniry 4 81
(J Gallagher) *t.k.h: trckd wnr tl wknd over 1f out* **7/1**[3]

5360 **4** *1 ¼* **Quality Street**[2] [4085] 4-8-8 75.................. FergusSweeney 2 73
(P Butler) *a in rr* **12/1**

6000 **5** *nk* **Jayanjay**[30] [3211] 7-8-13 85.................. RichardThomas 5 77
(Miss B Sanders) *racd 3rd tl rdn and wknd wl over 1f out* **10/1**

1m 10.43s (-3.24) **Going Correction** -0.35s/f (Firm)
WFA 3 from 4yo+ 4lb **5** Ran SP% **122.6**
Speed ratings (Par 107):107,105,96,94,93
CSF £2.73 TOTE £1.50: £1.10, £1.80; EX 2.40.
Owner P Asquith **Bred** P Asquith **Trained** Scorton, N Yorks

FOCUS
An uncompetitive conditions race but much the fastest of the four races over the trip on the day. The first two came clear.

NOTEBOOK
Celtic Mill, who finished well ahead of the runner-up in a Listed race over course and distance in June, was 5lb worse off but was strong in the market and justified the support by making all. It was not that easy however, as although he never looked like being beaten, he was made to work by the runner-up. This win should have restored some confidence and it will be no surprise to see him back in Pattern company before long. (tchd 4-7)
Andronikos, who was officially rated 1lb higher than the winner and was getting 5lb, did his best to make a race of it but was always being held. Although he handles fast ground, his wins have all been on softer and, with his stable in such good form, he will be interesting if we get some rain. (op 7-2)
Peter Island(FR), narrowly beaten in a 0-75 handicap last time and rated just 72, hand a mountain to climb on official figures and ran as well as could have been expected. (op 8-1)
Quality Street, another with no chance on official ratings, was held up at the back and never got involved. (op 10-1)
Jayanjay, who should have been third judged on offical ratings, is on the downgrade but is better off on switchback tracks like Epsom and Brighton, and prefers more cut in the ground. (op 9-1)

4159 INTERCASINO.CO.UK FILLIES' H'CAP 1m 3f 135y
2:50 (2:51) (Class 4) (0-85,81) 3-Y-0 **£6,477** (£1,927; £963; £481) **Stalls** Low

Form RPR

3262 **1** **My Petra**[40] [2917] 3-9-0 74.................. FergusSweeney 1 82
(A King) *mde all: rdn over 3f out: kpt on wl fnl f* **8/1**[3]

321 **2** *1 ¼* **Kibara**[10] [3849] 3-9-4 78.................. NickyMackay 8 84+
(L M Cumani) *trckd ldrs: rdn 2f out: rdn 2f out: kpt on to go 2nd wl ins fnl f* **11/10**[1]

-231 **3** *1 ½* **Fleeting Memory**[26] [3346] 3-9-7 81..................(t) RichardHughes 5 85
(Sir Michael Stoute) *trckd wnr tl rdn and lost 2nd wl ins fnl f* **15/8**[2]

4310 **4** *nk* **Generosia**[15] [3703] 3-8-6 66..................(t) FrancisNorton 3 70
(A M Balding) *hld up in rr: rdn and hdwy over 2f out: no imp ins fnl f* **8/1**[3]

-315 **5** *7* **And Again (USA)**[44] [2781] 3-8-9 74.................. RoryMoore(5) 4 66
(J R Fanshawe) *stdd s: hld up: rdn over 3f out: wknd 2f out* **12/1**

-016 **6** *3* **Fear To Tread (USA)**[19] [3589] 3-9-2 76.................. IanMongan 6 64
(J L Dunlop) *prom: rdn over 3f out: sn outpcd* **14/1**

6-20 **7** *5* **Dubai Melody (USA)**[33] [3146] 3-9-3 77.................. RobertHavlin 7 57
(J H M Gosden) *hld up: rdn and effrt over 3f out: sn wknd* **33/1**

1136 **8** *6* **Spring Dream (IRE)**[16] [3666] 3-8-13 73.................. ChrisCatlin 2 43
(M R Channon) *w.w: rdn 5f out: sn wl bhd* **20/1**

2m 26.55s (-3.55) **Going Correction** -0.225s/f (Firm) **8** Ran SP% **126.7**
Speed ratings (Par 99):102,101,100,99,95 93,89,85
CSF £19.27 CT £26.59 TOTE £13.70: £2.30, £1.10, £1.40; EX 37.10 Trifecta £16.40 Pool: £258.76 - 11.20 winning units..
Owner Mrs P S Wallace **Bred** W Wilkinson **Trained** Barbury Castle, Wilts

FOCUS
A fair fillies' handicap in which the winner dictated the pace.

4160 INTERCASINO.CO.UK H'CAP 1m 2f 7y
3:25 (3:25) (Class 4) (0-85,88) 3-Y-0+ **£16,192** (£4,817; £2,407; £1,202) **Stalls** Low

Form RPR

0313 **1** **Urban Tiger (GER)**[26] [3366] 3-8-7 77.................. RichardHughes 10 87
(A King) *hld up in mid-div: rdn and hdwy over 2f out: edgd rt and led ins fnl f* **7/2**[2]

0030 **2** *1 ¼* **Krugerrand (USA)**[24] [3413] 7-9-10 85.................. FergusSweeney 13 94+
(W J Musson) *slowly away: hdwy 3f out: swtchd rt over 2f out: running on whn hmpd ins fnl f: nt rcvr* **10/1**

-536 **3** *nk* **Cactus King**[42] [2863] 3-8-13 83.................. RobertHavlin 12 90
(J H M Gosden) *led tl hmpd and hdd ins fnl f: swtchd lft and kpt on* **6/1**[3]

0231 **4** *nk* **Pevensey (IRE)**[10] [3840] 4-9-10 88.................. SaleemGolam(3) 4 94
(M A Buckley) *mid-div: chsd ldrs over 3f out: kpt on one pce fnl f* **9/1**

0000 **5** *shd* **Scottish River (USA)**[5] [4005] 7-8-1 62.................. FrancisFerris 8 68
(M D I Usher) *slowly away: hld up in rr: hdwy over 2f out: r.o: nvr nrr* **20/1**

/02- **6** *3* **Kuster**[425] [2347] 10-9-2 84.................. HeatherMcGee(7) 9 84
(L M Cumani) *hld up: hdwy on outside over 3f out: edgd lft over 1f out: kpt on fnl f* **25/1**

1155 **7** *nk* **Olimpo (FR)**[9] [3876] 5-9-1 76.................. AdrianMcCarthy 5 76
(B R Millman) *prom: rdn over 4f out: wknd ins fnl 2f* **25/1**

-231 **8** *1 ½* **Cusoon**[33] [3151] 4-9-0 75.................. GeorgeBaker 1 72
(G L Moore) *in tch: wknd 3f out* **7/1**

-631 **9** *¾* **I Have Dreamed (IRE)**[9] [3876] 4-9-11 86.................. IanMongan 2 81
(T G Mills) *in tch: chsd ldr 5f out: rdn 3f out: wknd over 1f out* **6/4**[1]

4021 **10** *1 ½* **Daring Affair**[14] [3724] 5-9-0 75.................. FrancisNorton 7 67
(K R Burke) *chsd ldrs: rdn 4f out: wknd 2f out* **9/1**

6/0- **11** *5* **Deep Purple**[309] [5594] 5-9-8 83.................. LPKeniry 3 66
(A M Balding) *a in rr* **25/1**

0655 **12** *5* **Night Spot**[10] [3854] 5-8-10 71..................(p) ChrisCatlin 6 44
(B R Millman) *towards rr: short-lived effrt 3f out* **16/1**

-000 **13** *2 ½* **Cape Presto (IRE)**[30] [3223] 3-8-9 84.................. MarcHalford(5) 11 53
(Mrs C A Dunnett) *chsd ldr to 5f out: wknd over 2f out* **50/1**

2m 4.93s (-3.37) **Going Correction** -0.225s/f (Firm)
WFA 3 from 4yo+ 9lb **13** Ran SP% **142.2**
Speed ratings (Par 105):104,103,102,102,102 100,99,98,98,96 92,88,86
CSF £44.36 CT £227.75 TOTE £6.00: £2.20, £3.30, £2.70; EX 73.70 Trifecta £513.40 Pool: £737.68 - 1.02 winning units.
Owner Four Mile Racing **Bred** Gestut Gorlsdorf **Trained** Barbury Castle, Wilts
■ A first double on the Flat for trainer Alan King.
■ Stewards' Enquiry : Richard Hughes caution: careless riding

FOCUS
A decent handicap that produced a close finish.

4161 INTERCASINO.CO.UK E B F MEDIAN AUCTION MAIDEN STKS (DIV I) 6f
4:00 (4:00) (Class 4) 2-Y-0 **£3,886** (£867; £867; £288) **Stalls** High

Form RPR

0324 **1** **Cheap Street**[9] [3872] 2-9-3 81.................. NickyMackay 7 73
(J G Portman) *a in tch: rdn 1/2-way: drvn out to ld ins fnl f* **5/2**[1]

00 **2** *½* **Wilmington**[10] [3844] 2-9-3.................. PatDobbs 10 72
(R Hannon) *led to 1/2-way: led again over 2f out: rdn and hdd ins: kpt on but jnd for 2nd on line* **12/1**

2 *dht* **Event Music (IRE)** 2-8-12.................. ChrisCatlin 1 67
(M R Channon) *slowly away: hdwy over 3f out: sn chsd ldrs: r.o to dead-heat for 2nd line* **6/1**[3]

6400 **4** *1 ¼* **Fort Worth (IRE)**[17] [3641] 2-9-3 64.................. FergusSweeney 8 68
(B Gubby) *in rr tl mde gd late hdwy* **20/1**

04 **5** *1* **Masai Moon**[26] [3363] 2-9-3.................. AdrianMcCarthy 9 65
(B R Millman) *prom and t.k.h: rdn over 2f out: hmpd over 1f out: wnt lft and no ex ins fnl f* **3/1**[2]

6 *½* **Show House (USA)** 2-8-12.................. RichardHughes 11 58
(Mrs A J Perrett) *chsd ldrs: lost pl on bnd over 3f out: edgd lft but kpt on ins fnl f* **5/2**[1]

5 **7** *2* **Ranavalona**[5] [4002] 2-8-9.................. NeilChalmers(3) 3 52
(A M Balding) *trckd ldrs on outside: rdn and wknd appr fnl f* **20/1**

00 **8** *½* **Hoh Me Hoh You (IRE)**[10] [3851] 2-9-3.................. GeorgeBaker 6 56
(S Kirk) *in rr tl mde sme late hdwy* **16/1**

04 **9** *3 ½* **Oedipuss (IRE)**[10] [3838] 2-8-12.................. EmmettStack(5) 5 45
(K J Burke) *led 1/2-way: hdd over 2f out: sn wknd* **40/1**

10 *1 ¼* **Distiller (IRE)** 2-9-3.................. IanMongan 4 42
(W R Muir) *in tch: jnd ldrs over 2f out: wknd over 1f out* **16/1**

U **Dolcello (IRE)** 2-8-12.................. RobertHavlin 2 —
(Mrs P N Dutfield) *wnt lft s: bhd whn broke leg and uns rdr over 2f out: dead* **33/1**

1m 12.63s (-6.83) **Going Correction** -0.35s/f (Firm) **11** Ran SP% **130.8**
Speed ratings (Par 96):92,91,91,89,88 87,85,84,79,78 —
WIN: Cheap Street £4.10. PL: £1.40, Wilmington £3.90, Event Music £1.60. EX: CS/W £21.90, CS/EM £15.40. CSF: CS/W £18.75, CS/EM £9.94. TRIF: CS/W/EM £73.00, CS/EM/W £73.00 Pool: £220.40 - 2.20 winning units..
Owner A S B Portman **Bred** Catridge Farm Stud Ltd **Trained** Compton, Berks

FOCUS
Just a fair maiden but fractionally faster than the second division.

NOTEBOOK
Cheap Street, stepping back up to the trip over which he chased home Jo'Burg over this course last month, duly got off the mark in straightforward fashion. His rating may flatter him, and he will not find things easy in handicaps unless the assessor drops him a little. (tchd 11-4 and 3-1 in places)
Wilmington, returning to turf and dropping in trip, got a lot closer to the winner than he had on his debut. He seemed to appreciate setting the pace and, now qualified for a handicap mark, may be best campaigned in that sphere.
Event Music(IRE) ◆, a speedily-bred newcomer from a good German family, ran on really well having missed the break. She should come on a fair amount for the experience and can win her maiden.
Fort Worth(IRE), along with the winner the most experienced in the field, ran his best race yet on this first encounter with fast turf and looks a fair guide to the form.
Masai Moon, who finished a length behind the winner over course and distance last month, finished a little further back this time but helps set the level for the form. He will do better once qualified for a mark. (op 7-2)
Show House(USA), a half-sister to Chatshow from a family of good fillies, had the rail draw but could not hold her place having raced prominently early. She will know more next time. (tchd 9-4 tchd 11-4 in a place)

4162 OSSIE&HUTCH MEMORIAL RACE SPONSORED BY INTERCASINO.CO.UK MAIDEN STKS 6f
4:35 (4:36) (Class 5) 3-4-Y-0 **£3,238** (£963; £481; £240) **Stalls** High

Form RPR

-444 **1** **Call Me Waki (USA)**[7] [3950] 3-8-12 69.................. RichardHughes 7 73
(A M Balding) *mde all: edgd lft whn clr over 1f out but won unchal* **10/11**[1]

2 *3* **Bachelor Party (USA)** 3-9-3.................. ChrisCatlin 2 69+
(J Noseda) *a.p: chsd ldrs: wnt 2nd over 2f out: kpt on but no ch w wnr* **9/4**[2]

2023 **3** *2 ½* **Balian**[9] [3873] 3-9-3 66..................(p) GeorgeBaker 8 62
(G L Moore) *chsd wnr tl over 2f out: kpt on one pce after* **4/1**[3]

04 **4** *¾* **Royal Senga**[35] [3090] 3-8-12.................. FergusSweeney 3 54
(C A Horgan) *sn in tch: rdn over 1f out: no ex* **14/1**

0 **5** *5* **Always A Story**[11] [3826] 4-9-4.................. SaleemGolam(3) 5 44
(Miss D Mountain) *a bhd* **50/1**

6 *2* **Golden Surf (IRE)** 3-8-12.................. PatDobbs 6 33
(R Hannon) *a bhd* **8/1**

00-0 **7** *20* **Martian Mystery**[35] [3090] 3-8-12 40.................. LPKeniry 4 —
(M Madgwick) *mid-div to 1/2-way: sn bhd* **66/1**

1m 11.6s (-6.24) **Going Correction** -0.35s/f (Firm)
WFA 3 from 4yo 4lb **7** Ran SP% **124.4**
Speed ratings (Par 103):99,95,91,90,84 81,54
CSF £3.72 TOTE £1.90: £1.10, £2.10; EX 5.50 Trifecta £15.60 Pool: £168.00 - 7.60 winning units.
Owner D H Caslon **Bred** A Fried Jr **Trained** Kingsclere, Hants

FOCUS
A modest sprint maiden run 1.27sec slower than the earlier conditions race but faster than both divisions of the juvenile race and the first three held those positions throughout.
Balian Official explanation: jockey said gelding hung left under pressure
Martian Mystery Official explanation: jockey said filly had a breathing problem

4163 INTERCASINO.CO.UK EBF MEDIAN AUCTION MAIDEN STKS (DIV II) 6f
5:05 (5:06) (Class 4) 2-Y-0 **£3,886** (£1,156; £577; £288) **Stalls** High

Form RPR

0 **1** **Jack Oliver**[56] [2432] 2-9-3.................. MichaelTebbutt 3 71
(B J Meehan) *a.p: led appr fnl f: drvn out* **7/2**[2]

0600 **2** *hd* **Linkslade Lad**[9] [3860] 2-9-3 50..................(b) FrancisNorton 4 70
(W R Muir) *hld up: rdn over 2f out: r.o fnl f to go cl 2nd nr fin* **33/1**

06 **3** *1 ½* **My Tiger Lilly**[17] [3645] 2-8-12.................. FergusSweeney 7 61
(W J Knight) *hld up in tch: rdn over 2f out: styd on one pce fnl f* **5/2**[1]

4 *hd* **Sunquest** 2-9-3.................. PatDobbs 6 65
(R Hannon) *s.i.s: in rr tl rdn and hdwy 2f out: styd on one pce ins fnl f* **5/1**[3]

0 5 3/4 **Mamalini**[123] 877 2-8-12 .... LPKeniry 1 58
(P D Cundell) *t.k.h: led tl rdn and hdd appr fnl f: one pce after* **100/1**

6 6 hd **Sherjawy (IRE)**[14] 3721 2-9-3 .... NickyMackay 5 62
(L M Cumani) *s.i.s: in rr and hdwy 2f out: wknd fnl f* **7/1**

0655 7 1 1/2 **It's No Problem (IRE)**[9] 3868 2-8-12 65........ RobertHavlin 8 53
(Jean-Rene Auvray) *chsd ldrs on ins: one pce appr fnl f* **5/1**[3]

00 8 1 **Distant Sunset (IRE)**[10] 3844 2-9-3 .... RichardHughes 9 55
(B W Hills) *s.i.s: sn in tch: hdwy ins fnl 2f: nvr nr to chal* **6/1**

9 3 **Fun Thai** 2-8-12 .... ChrisCatlin 2 41
(M R Channon) *rdn 1/2-way: a bhd* **8/1**

10 9 **Maskaraid** 2-9-3 .... AdrianMcCarthy 10 19
(B R Millman) *a bhd* **25/1**

1m 12.91s (-0.76) **Going Correction** -0.35s/f (Firm) **10** Ran SP% **129.8**
Speed ratings (Par 96):91,90,88,88,87 87,85,83,79,67
CSF £123.52 TOTE £4.10: £2.20, £4.40, £1.50; EX 242.80 TRIFECTA Not won..
Owner Alan Merritt&Aldridge Racing Partnership **Bred** R And Mrs Mitchell And Natton House Thoroughbreds **Trained** Manton, Wilts

FOCUS
This second division was fractionally slower than the first and the slowest of the four races over the trip on the day.

NOTEBOOK
Jack Oliver, a speedily-bred colt, came on from his debut to take this modest maiden despite running green. He is nothing special but looks open to improvement if going the right way from this, and has entries in a couple of sales races later in the season. (tchd 9-2)
Linkslade Lad, who had the blinkers re-applied having been reluctant to race last time, appeared to turn over a new leaf and was only just held. If he is able to build on this, he could be well treated in handicaps off his current mark. (tchd 40-1 in a place)
My Tiger Lilly, a well-backed favourite, performed well enough on this return to turf, but had every chance and failed to find an extra gear. She is now qualified for nurseries and may do better in that sphere, possibly over further. (op 4-1)
Sunquest ◆, a debutant from the family of Divine Danse and Pursuit of Love, was doing his best work at the finish having missed the break. He could well progress past those that finished ahead of him next time and should be capable of picking up a maiden. (op 4-1)
Mamalini, a cheaply-bought first foal who finished last in a seller on her debut, had clearly learnt a lot for that outing as she broke quickly and got over to the stands' rail from her outside stall. She kept battling away once headed by the winner and could prove a bargain. However, along with the runner-up she holds the form down. (op 50-1)
Sherjawy(IRE), from the family of the useful Royal Storm, showed up until fading late on. he is likely to do better once handicapped.
It's No Problem(IRE), dropping back in trip having failed to stay seven furlongs last time, is likely to having his rating adjusted downwards following this effort, as he was close enough a quarter mile out if good enough. (tchd 11-2)

4164 PLAY BLACKJACK AT INTERCASINO.CO.UK H'CAP 5f 10y
5:40 (5:42) (Class 5) (0-70,68) 3-Y-O **£3,238** (£963; £481; £240) Stalls High

Form RPR

05-0 1 **That's Blue Chip**[28] 3285 3-8-8 **55**........ PatDobbs 4 67+
(P W D'Arcy) *in rr: qcknd 2f out: sn carried lft: edgd rt bef led ins fnl f* **33/1**

5441 2 1 1/4 **Gwilym (GER)**[9] 3873 3-9-6 **67**........ RobertHavlin 8 74
(D Haydn Jones) *in rr: hdwy on ins whn hmpd 2f out: swtchd rt over 1f out: r.o strly fnl f to go 2nd: unlucky* **3/1**[1]

0502 3 1 1/4 **Jucebabe**[9] 3864 3-8-7 **54**........ FrancisNorton 10 61+
(J L Spearing) *mid-div: hdwy 2f out: edgd lft over 1f out: nt clr run whn hmpd and stmbld ins fnl f: nt rcvr* **9/2**[2]

0450 4 1 3/4 **Supreme Kiss**[49] 2652 3-8-12 **59**........(b[1]) RichardThomas 12 55
(Miss B Sanders) *trckd ldrs: led over 2f out: wnt lft bef fnl f: hung rt and hdd ins fnl f* **14/1**

0031 5 nk **Montzando**[9] 3864 3-8-7 **57**........(v) SaleemGolam(3) 7 52
(B R Millman) *mid-div: rdn over 2f out: one pce ins fnl 2f* **9/2**[2]

0000 6 nk **Jessica Wigmo**[22] 3472 3-7-12 **52** oh4 ow3........ MarkCoumbe(7) 13 46
(A W Carroll) *in rr: mde sme late hdwy* **66/1**

6603 7 nk **Matterofact (IRE)**[9] 3864 3-8-13 **65**........ TravisBlock(5) 2 58
(Mrs P N Dutfield) *trckd ldr tl rdn 2f out: one pce after* **9/1**

4200 8 nk **Succeed (IRE)**[10] 3847 3-8-5 **55**........ NeilChalmers(3) 1 47
(Mrs H Sweeting) *prom on outside: wknd over 1f out* **33/1**

0612 9 1 **Glenargo (USA)**[11] 3821 3-9-3 **64**........(p) AdrianMcCarthy 11 52
(R A Harris) *mid-div: rdn 1/2-way: wknd over 1f out* **13/2**[3]

0000 10 3/4 **Forces Sweetheart**[9] 3866 3-7-9 **49**........ LukeMorris(7) 5 35
(M L W Bell) *bhd: effrt over 2f out: wknd over 1f out* **8/1**

6-13 11 1/2 **Safari Mischief**[26] 3349 3-9-2 **68**........ MarcHalford(5) 3 52
(P Winkworth) *in tch on outside: wknd over 1f out* **7/1**

0600 12 1 3/4 **African Concerto (IRE)**[17] 3646 3-8-8 **55**........ LPKeniry 9 32
(S Kirk) *a bhd* **14/1**

0004 13 2 **Jackie Francis (IRE)**[11] 3821 3-8-2 **49** oh5........ FrancisFerris 14 19
(R Brotherton) *led tl hdd over 2f out: wknd qckly* **33/1**

59.40 secs (-1.70) **Going Correction** -0.35s/f (Firm) **13** Ran SP% **132.0**
Speed ratings (Par 100):99,97,95,92,91 91,90,90,88,87 86,83,80
CSF £141.30 CT £575.05 TOTE £31.70: £6.40, £2.00, £1.80; EX 254.10 TRIFECTA Not won. Place 6 £11.21, Place 5 £10.08.
Owner Blue Chip Feed Ltd **Bred** J E Jackson **Trained** Newmarket, Suffolk

FOCUS
A moderate sprint handicap and something of a rough race, with horses running around in front and causing interference to those behind.
That's Blue Chip Official explanation: trainer's rep said, regarding the improved form shown, the gelding had been fitted with a new bit and also may have benefited from being covered up today
Safari Mischief Official explanation: jockey said gelding was hampered inside first furlong
T/Plt: £21.60 to a £1 stake. Pool: £58,250.00. 1,964.45 winning tickets. T/Qpdt: £14.60 to a £1 stake. Pool: £2,364.50. 119.20 winning tickets. JS

4165 - (Foreign Racing) - See Raceform Interactive

4121 GALWAY (R-H)
Saturday, August 5
OFFICIAL GOING: Good to firm

4166a CHEESTRINGS H'CAP 2m
4:20 (4:20) (40-70,68) 4-Y-O+ **£7,148** (£1,665; £734; £424)

RPR

1 **Always The Groom (IRE)**[10] 3859 4-8-11 54........ DMGrant(3) 14 70+
(Patrick J Flynn, Ire) *trckd ldrs on inner: 8th 5f out: 6th travelling wl 3f out: 4th 2f out: chal ent st: led 1f out: styd on wl: comf* **11/2**[2]

2 2 **Baileysunice (IRE)**[24] 3426 4-9-5 62........ WJLee(3) 16 71
(Seamus Fahey, Ire) *mid-div: 10th 1/2-way: 7th 2 1/2f out: styd on wl st* **20/1**

3 1 1/4 **Amarjit (IRE)**[24] 3425 5-9-7 61........ RMBurke 8 69
(R J Osborne, Ire) *mid-div: 10th 5f out: 9th appr st: 5th 1f out: kpt on* **10/1**

4 1 **Ashlawn (IRE)**[16] 3691 6-9-2 56........(bt) WSupple 5 63
(H Rogers, Ire) *mid-div: 7th 5f out: rdn and kpt on wl fr 2f out* **16/1**

5 3/4 **Monahullan Prince**[16] 3691 5-9-0 57........(t) CDHayes(3) 10 63
(Gerard Keane, Ire) *hld up towards rr: hdwy over 2f out: 10th into st: kpt on u.p* **11/1**

6 hd **Karramalu (IRE)**[4] 4030 5-9-5 66........ SJGray(7) 1 72
(Daniel Mark Loughnane, Ire) *mid-div on outer: 9th and rdn over 4f out: 7th into st: kpt on* **25/1**

7 2 1/2 **Thunder Road (IRE)**[5] 3603 6-9-11 65........ DPMcDonogh 4 69
(P A Fahy, Ire) *trckd ldrs in 4th: 6th 5f out: rdn 3f out: 3rd briefly 2f out: no ex st* **5/1**[1]

8 3/4 **Hawkwind (USA)**[59] 2372 7-9-2 56........ CO'Donoghue 7 59
(Patrick O Brady, Ire) *rr of mid-div: 11th 4f out: kpt on fr bef st* **25/1**

9 nk **Lagniappe (IRE)**[23] 3462 6-8-9 54........ DJMoran(5) 19 57
(R P Burns, Ire) *led: rdn and strly pressed 2 1/2f out: hdd ent st: sn wknd* **11/1**

10 2 **Balakan (IRE)**[4] 2514 5-9-9 63........ JMurtagh 3 64
(M Halford, Ire) *sn 2nd: rdn to chal 2 1/2f out: led ent st: hdd 1f out: sn no ex* **7/1**

11 nk **Blue Away (IRE)**[56] 2460 8-9-10 64........ KFallon 2 64
(S Kirk) *hld up: 11th into st: kpt on same pce* **6/1**[3]

12 1 1/4 **Luxi River (USA)**[23] 3462 6-8-8 53........ PBBeggy(5) 13 52
(Michael McElhone, Ire) *mid-div: 8th 1/2-way: no ex fr 4f out* **20/1**

13 1/2 **Strike**[34] 3130 5-9-8 62........(b) PACarberry 15 60
(John Charles McConnell, Ire) *hld up in rr: nvr a factor* **33/1**

14 2 1/2 **Ebony Shades (IRE)**[4] 4030 5-10-0 68........(t) DJCondon 20 64
(W P Mullins, Ire) *s.i.s and a bhd* **16/1**

15 1 3/4 **Proper Article (IRE)**[115] 999 4-9-7 61........(b) PJSmullen 6 55
(D K Weld, Ire) *trckd ldrs in 3rd: 4th 3f out: rdn and wknd 2f out: eased st* **10/1**

16 2 **Belinkin**[16] 3691 6-9-1 58........ RPCleary(3) 9 50
(W P Mullins, Ire) *in tch: 7th 1/2-way: impr into 4th 6f out: 3rd 3f out: sn rdn and wknd* **20/1**

17 hd **The Alamo**[19] 3603 8-9-6 60........ NGMcCullagh 11 52
(Malachy J Ryan, Ire) *trckd ldrs on outer: 5th 1/2-way: 3rd 5f out: sn wknd* **25/1**

18 shd **Adjudication (IRE)**[29] 3273 4-9-0 54........ JAHeffernan 17 46
(P Hughes, Ire) *a bhd* **16/1**

19 15 **Reve De Rose**[205] 3785 7-8-12 52........(t) MCHussey 12 29
(W P Mullins, Ire) *a towards rr* **20/1**

3m 35.1s **20** Ran SP% **144.9**
CSF £127.04 CT £1147.72 TOTE £6.50: £2.00, £7.30, £2.00, £7.30; DF 362.40.
Owner Alexander Stafford **Bred** Irish National Stud **Trained** Carrick-On-Suir, Co Waterford

NOTEBOOK
Blue Away(IRE), back up in trip, was well held and proved disappointing. (op 6/1 tchd 7/1)

4095 DEAUVILLE (R-H)
Saturday, August 5
OFFICIAL GOING: Turf course - good to soft; all-weather - standard

4168a PRIX DE TOURGEVILLE (LISTED RACE) (C&G) (ROUND) 1m (R)
3:00 (3:01) 3-Y-O **£17,241** (£6,897; £5,172; £3,448; £1,724)

RPR

1 **Kersimon (FR)**[32] 3186 3-8-12 .... TThulliez 4 100
(J De Roualle, France)

2 shd **Carlotamix (FR)**[104] 1178 3-8-12 .... CSoumillon 6 100
(A Fabre, France)

3 shd **Tell**[16] 3681 3-8-12 .... GMosse 5 100
(J L Dunlop) *raced in 3rd to straight, ridden 2f out, every chance final f, ran on well but lost 2nd on line (15/1)*

4 3/4 **El Capitano (FR)**[21] 3-8-12 .... YLerner 3 99
(C Lerner, France)

5 1/2 **Major Grace (FR)**[32] 3186 3-8-12 .... JVictoire 2 98
(Mme J Laurent-Joye Rossi, France)

6 1 1/2 **Mezel (USA)**[93] 3-8-12 .... IMendizabal 1 95
(J-C Rouget, France)

7 nk **Strive**[12] 3-8-12 .... DBoeuf 9 94
(D Smaga, France)

8 1/2 **Salsalava (FR)**[27] 3341 3-9-2 .... C-PLemaire 8 97
(P Demercastel, France)

9 2 **Fastmambo (USA)**[32] 3186 3-8-12 .... OPeslier 10 89
(F Head, France)

10 3 **Chief Commander (FR)**[73] 1944 3-8-12 .... DBonilla 7 83
(Jane Chapple-Hyam) *held up, 7th straight, ridden well over 1f out, soon beaten (19/1)*

1m 42.1s **10** Ran
PARI-MUTUEL: WIN 7.10; PL 2.00, 1.50, 3.60; DF 9.10.
Owner P N Rossier **Bred** Scea Des Prairies & Patrick Kienlen **Trained** France

NOTEBOOK
Tell, who was well beaten in two previous attempts at this level, ran much better and handled the easier ground, being narrowly held in a finish of heads. He continues to run well in defeat and deserves a change of fortune.
Chief Commander(FR) ran below best form on ground that suits on this return from a break and never figured.

4169a PRIX DE REUX (LISTED RACE) 1m 4f 110y
3:30 (3:30) 3-Y-O+ **£17,241** (£6,897; £5,172; £3,448; £1,724)

RPR

1 **Magadino (FR)**[161] 523 5-9-7 .... BrigitteRenk 2 107
(Brigitte Renk, Switzerland)

2 1 1/2 **Vendangeur (IRE)**[27] 3341 3-8-7 ow1........ OPeslier 9 103
(E Lellouche, France)

3 shd **Kocab**[293] 5932 4-9-4 .... CSoumillon 6 102
(A Fabre, France)

4 1 1/2 **Marend (FR)**[62] 2277 5-9-4 .... DBoeuf 7 100
(D Sepulchre, France)

5 1 **Barolo**[28] 3315 7-9-7 .... DBonilla 5 101
(W R Swinburn) *tracked leader til led 4f out, headed well over 1f out, one pace (62/10)*

6 8 **Lord Sunshine (FR)**[22] 3516 4-9-4 .... FSpanu 4 86
(A Spanu, France)
7 shd **Farouge (FR)**[9] 3887 5-9-4 .... IMendizabal 1 86
(Mme Pia Brandt, France)
8 1 **The Devil (GER)**[74] 1929 4-9-4 .... TJarnet 8 85
(U Suter, France)
9 2 **Belle Suisse (FR)**[22] 3516 4-9-1 .... JVictoire 3 79
(Y De Nicolay, France)

2m 39.7s
WFA 3 from 4yo+ 11lb **9** Ran
PARI-MUTUEL: WIN 5.70; PL 1.40, 1.30, 1.40; DF 7.60.
Owner A Renk **Bred** Adolf Renk **Trained** Switzerland

NOTEBOOK
Barolo, dropping in trip and back on ground that he handles, was ridden to make use of his stamina but could not quicken in the straight.

3518 CHESTER (L-H)
Sunday, August 6

OFFICIAL GOING: Good to firm
The ground was described as 'fast but no jar and an excellent cover of grass'.
Wind: Light, half-against. Weather: Fine, sunny and warm

4170 WOODS OF WINDSOR NURSERY 6f 18y
2:20 (2:21) (Class 4) 2-Y-O **£4,728** (£1,406; £702; £351) **Stalls** Low

Form RPR
2114 1 **Invincible Force (IRE)**[23] 3474 2-9-7 **86** .... EddieAhern 1 88
(Ms Deborah J Evans) *mde all: hld on gamely* **1/1**[1]
0214 2 ½ **Rainbow Fox**[17] 3685 2-9-0 **79** .... PaulHanagan 2 80
(R A Fahey) *chsd ldrs: sn drvn along: chal 1f out: no ex towards fin* **4/1**[2]
4324 3 shd **Yerevan**[15] 3720 2-8-5 **70** ow1 .... JohnEgan 6 70
(R T Phillips) *hld up in tch: hdwy 2f out: sn chsng ldrs: nt qckn ins last* **9/1**
3003 4 1 **Bazroy (IRE)**[15] 3720 2-8-12 **80** .... (b) StephenDonohoe(3) 5 77
(P D Evans) *chsd ldrs: rdn 2f out: kpt on ins last* **8/1**
1406 5 nk **Cheshire Prince**[23] 3481 2-7-12 **63** oh1 .... PaulQuinn 4 59
(W M Brisbourne) *hld up in tch: effrt on inner and nt clr run 2f out: kpt on same pce fnl f* **25/1**
3140 6 ½ **Proper (IRE)**[15] 3734 2-8-9 **74** .... ChrisCatlin 3 69
(M R Channon) *sn chsng ldrs: kpt on same pce fnl 2f* **6/1**[3]
3031 7 6 **Ensign's Trick**[15] 3746 2-8-10 **80** .... LiamJones(5) 7 57
(W M Brisbourne) *dwlt: sn in tch: outpcd and lost pl over 1f out* **25/1**

1m 14.91s (-0.74) **Going Correction** -0.225s/f (Firm) 7 Ran SP% **113.1**
Speed ratings (Par 96):95,94,94,92,92 91,83
CSF £5.07 TOTE £1.80: £1.20, £2.20; EX 4.00.
Owner Terry Cummins **Bred** Robert Wilson **Trained** Lydiate, Merseyside

FOCUS
A tight-knit nursery with the first two home lowest drawn and little between the first six at the line. The form looks fairly strong.

NOTEBOOK
Invincible Force(IRE), who is thriving, controlled things from the front and showed a very willing attitude. He is an admirable type. (op 6-4)
Rainbow Fox, noisy in the paddock, hassled the winner all the way but had to be driven along to do so. He never gave up the fight and will be even more effective on a more orthodox track. (op 7-2)
Yerevan, already beaten in selling company, was in no hurry to join issue. Tightened up for a stride or two coming off the bend, she challenged strongly all the way to the line. This was a much better effort. (op 13-2)
Bazroy(IRE), again fitted with blinkers, appreciated the step up to six and deserves credit for this.
Cheshire Prince, 1lb out of the handicap, was messed about when trying for a run up the inner on the turn for home. This seemed to represent improved form from him. (op 16-1)
Proper(IRE), very warm beforehand, proved suited by the return to six but he has started life in handicap company rated to the very limit. (op 8-1)

4171 CHESHIRE COUNTY COUNCIL FOSTER CARE EBF MAIDEN STKS 7f 2y
2:50 (2:51) (Class 4) 2-Y-O **£4,792** (£1,425; £712; £355) **Stalls** Low

Form RPR
353 1 **Gweebarra**[23] 3498 2-9-3 90 .... DO'Donohoe 7 85
(K A Ryan) *chsd ldrs: led 2f out: rdn and r.o wl* **4/6**[1]
33 2 1¾ **Silkie Smooth (IRE)**[23] 3495 2-8-12 .... JoeFanning 4 75
(B W Hills) *trckd ldrs: wnt 2nd over 1f out: no ex ins last* **5/2**[2]
45 3 7 **Snowflight**[12] 3809 2-9-3 .... PaulHanagan 2 62
(R A Fahey) *sn in tch: hdwy 3f out: one pce fnl 2f* **7/1**[3]
003 4 ¾ **Just Oscar (GER)**[58] 2416 2-9-3 67 .... DavidAllan 6 60
(W M Brisbourne) *led tl 2f out: one pce* **33/1**
0 5 3 **Pace Telecom Flyer (IRE)**[65] 2185 2-9-3 .... EddieAhern 9 53
(J W Hills) *in tch: hdwy u.p 3f out: wknd over 1f out* **40/1**
4 6 1 **Mick Is Back**[15] 3721 2-9-0 .... StephenDonohoe(3) 13 50+
(P D Evans) *hld up in rr: kpt on fnl 2f: nvr nr ldrs* **33/1**
0 7 hd **Dee Valley Boy (IRE)**[39] 2972 2-9-3 .... GrahamGibbons 8 49
(J D Bethell) *mid-div: kpt on fnl 2f: nvr on terms* **100/1**
006 8 5 **Taran Tregarth**[9] 3915 2-8-12 .... FergusSweeney 10 31
(A Bailey) *in rr: nvr a factor* **200/1**
06 9 ½ **Salto Chico**[28] 3328 2-9-3 .... JohnEgan 1 35
(W M Brisbourne) *s.i.s: a in rr* **66/1**
06 10 1 **Bowman's Boy (IRE)**[22] 3553 2-9-3 .... DaleGibson 12 32
(M W Easterby) *a towards rr* **100/1**
00 11 5 **Cadi May**[56] 2166 2-8-12 .... PaulMulrennan 11 14
(W M Brisbourne) *w ldr: rdn 3f out: sn lost pl* **100/1**
0 12 57 **Tullythered (IRE)**[72] 1982 2-9-3 .... FrancisNorton 5 —
(A Berry) *sn bhd: t.o 2f out: virtually p.u* **200/1**

1m 26.39s (-2.08) **Going Correction** -0.225s/f (Firm) 12 Ran SP% **114.8**
Speed ratings (Par 96):102,100,92,91,87 86,86,80,80,78 73,8
CSF £2.23 TOTE £1.70: £1.10, £1.20, £1.70; EX 2.90.
Owner J Duddy,B McDonald,A Heeney,M McMenamin **Bred** The Complimentary Pass Partnership **Trained** Hambleton, N Yorks

FOCUS
A decent winning time for a race like this. The betting suggested a two-horse race with plenty of dead wood and so it proved, but the form behind looks reliable enough.

NOTEBOOK
Gweebarra, highly-tried, made no mistake always looking in control. (op 4-5)
Silkie Smooth(IRE), a lengthy filly, went in pursuit of the winner but was never going to finish anything but second best. She deserves to go one better. (op 2-1)
Snowflight, helped by the turning track, settled better and is now primed for nurseries. (op 9-1)
Just Oscar(GER), having his fourth start, took them along but was left for dead by the first two coming off the bend. Nurseries are surely a better option.
Pace Telecom Flyer(IRE), having just his second outing, was rousted along to keep tabs on the leaders. He looks to lack basic speed. (op 33-1)
Mick Is Back, given a quiet ride, stayed on steadily and looks capable of better. (tchd 28-1)

4172 HALLIWELL JONES BMW - MILE (H'CAP) 7f 122y
3:25 (3:26) (Class 3) (0-90,89) 3-Y-O+ **£10,039** (£2,986; £1,492; £745) **Stalls** Low

Form RPR
1022 1 **Chicken Soup**[16] 3716 4-8-10 **70** .... JohnEgan 6 87
(T J Pitt) *trckd ldrs: qcknd to ld 2f out: sn rdn clr* **9/4**[1]
6143 2 5 **Waterline Twenty (IRE)**[23] 3487 3-8-11 **81** .... StephenDonohoe(3) 10 84
(P D Evans) *chsd ldrs: styd on to take 2nd ins last: no ch w wnr* **18/1**
4063 3 nk **Roman Maze**[8] 3928 6-9-12 **86** .... DavidAllan 9 89
(W M Brisbourne) *in tch: hdwy over 2f out: styd on fnl f* **8/1**[3]
4464 4 nk **Heureux (USA)**[32] 3191 3-8-10 **77** .... TomEaves 3 79
(J Howard Johnson) *chsd ldrs: kpt on same pce fnl 2f* **16/1**
0010 5 ½ **Kindlelight Debut**[8] 3928 6-9-8 **85** .... JamesDoyle(3) 15 86
(N P Littmoden) *in tch: hdwy over 2f out: kpt on same pce* **33/1**
5100 6 nk **Adeje Park (IRE)**[46] 2744 3-9-8 **89** .... EddieAhern 13 89+
(P W Chapple-Hyam) *in rr: hdwy over 2f out: styd on fnl f* **16/1**
2013 7 shd **Caustic Wit (IRE)**[9] 3898 8-9-0 **74** .... FergusSweeney 4 74
(M S Saunders) *chsd ldrs: one pce fnl 2f* **6/1**[2]
4060 8 1½ **Fiefdom (IRE)**[8] 3937 4-9-8 **85** .... (b[1]) PatrickMathers(3) 12 82
(I W McInnes) *hld up in rr: hdwy over 2f out: nvr nr ldrs* **50/1**
0000 9 hd **Millennium Force**[8] 3937 8-9-5 **79** .... ChrisCatlin 18 75
(M R Channon) *in rr: sn drvn along: kpt on fnl 2f: nvr on terms* **40/1**
0520 10 nk **Bessemer (JPN)**[3] 4090 5-9-0 **74** .... (p) DanielTudhope 17 69
(D Carroll) *s.i.s: bhd tl sme hdwy fnl 2f* **33/1**
0200 11 ½ **Tanforan**[70] 2047 4-9-6 **80** .... PaulHanagan 8 74
(K G Reveley) *in tch: effrt over 2f out: fdd over 1f out* **25/1**
3005 12 1¾ **H Harrison (IRE)**[3] 4090 6-8-5 **70** .... AndrewElliott(5) 2 60
(I W McInnes) *w ldr: wknd over 1f out* **9/1**
5065 13 1¼ **Will He Wish**[22] 3518 10-10-0 **88** .... DO'Donohoe 5 75
(S Gollings) *dwlt: a in rr* **20/1**
1106 14 2½ **Imperial Echo (USA)**[8] 3937 5-9-9 **83** .... PaulFessey 14 63
(T D Barron) *s.i.s: a towards rr* **9/1**
1000 15 1¼ **Baylaw Star**[31] 3218 5-9-12 **86** .... JoeFanning 1 63
(K A Ryan) *led tl 2f out: sn wknd* **10/1**
400 16 nk **Top Dirham**[22] 3549 8-9-1 **75** .... PaulMulrennan 16 51
(M W Easterby) *swtchd lft s: a bhd* **50/1**
4066 17 3½ **Kirstys Lad**[22] 3523 4-8-4 **69** oh29 .... (b) LiamJones(5) 7 37
(M Mullineaux) *a bhd: detached 2f out* **200/1**

1m 31.82s (-2.93) **Going Correction** -0.225s/f (Firm)
WFA 3 from 4yo+ 7lb 17 Ran SP% **123.6**
Speed ratings (Par 107):105,100,99,99,98 98,98,97,96,96 96,94,93,90,89 88,85
CSF £44.93 CT £295.44 TOTE £2.90: £1.20, £4.50, £2.00, £3.20; EX 67.90 Trifecta £577.20 Part won. Pool £813.02 - 0.40 winning units..
Owner Fishlake Commercial Motors Ltd **Bred** Limestone Stud **Trained** Bawtry, S Yorks

FOCUS
An ordinary handicap in which the two pacesetters went off very fast and soon had the field strung out. The form looks sound with the runner-up, fourth and sixth to form.

NOTEBOOK
Chicken Soup, who looked very fit indeed, swept to the front and had this won in a matter of strides. He will be very interesting if turning out under a penalty. (op 5-2 tchd 11-4)
Waterline Twenty(IRE), 5lb higher than for her win here, stayed on in willing fashion to snatch second spot but the winner had flown.
Roman Maze, just 1lb higher than for his win here a year ago, had an outside draw to overcome and is clearly right back on song. (op 15-2 tchd 7-1)
Heureux(USA), with the blinkers left off, again gave a good account of himself but he still looks high in the handicap. (tchd 20-1 in a place)
Kindlelight Debut, whose last seven wins have been on the All-Weather, showed that she is at least as good on turf, doing as well as could be expected from her outside draw.
Adeje Park(IRE), 5lb higher than Warwick, has been highly tried since. On her toes beforehand, she did well coming from off the pace and will be suited by a return to the full mile.
Fiefdom(IRE) Official explanation: jockey said gelding was denied a clear run

4173 ACCUMA H'CAP 1m 2f 75y
4:00 (4:00) (Class 5) (0-75,73) 3-Y-O **£4,095** (£1,209; £604) **Stalls** High

Form RPR
0426 1 **Dream Of Paradise (USA)**[13] 3804 3-8-1 **58** .... LiamJones(5) 8 66
(Mrs L Williamson) *mde all: kpt on wl fnl 2f: hld on towards fin* **25/1**
4011 2 ¾ **Benbrook**[12] 3816 3-9-3 **69** .... EddieAhern 2 75
(J L Dunlop) *trckd ldrs: effrt over 2f out: no ex towards fin* **9/4**[1]
0403 3 hd **Floodlight Fantasy**[18] 3650 3-8-13 **65** .... (p) RichardMullen 10 71
(E S McMahon) *sn chsng ldrs: styd on fnl f: no ex ins last* **8/1**
4320 4 1 **Conservation (FR)**[27] 3347 3-9-7 **73** .... RobertWinston 7 77
(P W Chapple-Hyam) *trckd ldrs: effrt over 2f out: kpt on same pce fnl f* **7/1**[3]
3321 5 5 **Markington**[14] 3760 3-9-7 **73** .... (b[1]) GrahamGibbons 12 68
(J D Bethell) *s.i.s: bhd tl sme hdwy over 2f out: nvr on terms* **12/1**
1026 6 hd **Norman Beckett**[23] 3483 3-9-4 **70** .... (p) TomEaves 6 64
(I Semple) *s.i.s: hdwy 3f out: nvr nr ldrs* **16/1**
6131 7 1¼ **Maidford (IRE)**[18] 3650 3-8-7 **59** .... FergusSweeney 4 51
(M Meade) *trckd ldrs: wknd over 1f out* **7/1**[3]
0042 8 2½ **Evening**[8] 3934 3-9-3 **69** .... MartinDwyer 1 56
(B W Hills) *stdd s: hld up in mid-field: effrt over 2f out: wknd over 1f out* **9/2**[2]
-540 9 5 **Gamesters Lady**[23] 3477 3-9-4 **70** .... DavidAllan 3 48
(W M Brisbourne) *chsd ldrs: sn drvn along: lost pl over 4f out* **50/1**
6104 10 1¼ **Peephole**[46] 2746 3-8-7 **59** .... MickyFenton 9 34
(A Bailey) *chsd ldrs: drvn along 5f out: lost pl over 2f out* **33/1**
6023 11 5 **Shaydreambeliever**[14] 3760 3-9-3 **69** .... PaulHanagan 5 35
(R A Fahey) *in rr: drvn 5f out: sn lost tch* **9/1**

2m 10.05s (-3.09) **Going Correction** -0.225s/f (Firm) 11 Ran SP% **117.4**
Speed ratings (Par 100):103,102,102,101,97 97,96,94,90,89 85
CSF £80.06 CT £517.71 TOTE £37.10: £6.40, £1.30, £3.20; EX 220.20.
Owner Eatonfield Racing Limited **Bred** R N Clay **Trained** Saighton, Cheshire

FOCUS
An end-to-end gallop set by the winner who thoroughly deserved this first career success. The form looks sound enough, rated through the third and fourth.
Dream Of Paradise(USA) Official explanation: trainer's representative said, regarding the improved form shown, filly was better suited by being able to make the running today

4174 RED CORNER EVENTS QUEENSFERRY STKS (LISTED RACE) 6f 18y
4:35 (4:35) (Class 1) 3-Y-O+
£15,898 (£6,025; £3,015; £1,503; £753; £378) **Stalls** Low

Form RPR
062 **1** **The Kiddykid (IRE)**[36] 3092 6-9-0 103 .... StephenDonohoe 5 107
(P D Evans) *chsd ldrs: led 1f out: hld on towards fin* **9/1**
0204 **2** ½ **Beckermet (IRE)**[22] 3518 4-9-0 105 .... MartinDwyer 8 106+
(R F Fisher) *hld up in rr: hdwy and swtchd outside over 1f out: styd on: nt quite rch wnr* **9/2**[2]
2661 **3** *hd* **Indian Maiden (IRE)**[8] 3967 6-8-13 102 .... RobertWinston 7 104+
(M S Saunders) *hld up in rr: effrt on wd outside over 1f out: styd on wl ins last* **7/2**[1]
5060 **4** *1* **Moone Cross (IRE)**[11] 3856 3-8-5 .... EddieAhern 2 96
(Mrs John Harrington, Ire) *trckd ldr: led over 3f out: hdd 1f out: no ex* **9/2**[2]
2-50 **5** 1 ¼ **Masta Plasta (IRE)**[20] 3585 3-8-10 103 .... TomEaves 3 97
(J Howard Johnson) *chsd ldrs: outpcd over 2f out: kpt on same pce fnl f* **25/1**
-610 **6** ½ **Racer Forever (USA)**[46] 2739 3-9-0 106 .... RobertHavlin 9 100
(J H M Gosden) *hld up in rr: effrt on outer 2f out: nvr trbld ldrs* **16/1**
0011 **7** *shd* **Mr Wolf**[7] 3986 5-9-0 90 ....(p) AdrianTNicholls 4 96
(D W Barker) *led over 2f: chsd ldrs: fdd fnl f* **9/1**
1013 **8** *1* **Paradise Isle**[23] 3499 5-8-13 105 .... KDarley 11 92
(C F Wall) *charged gate: s.s: hdwy to chse ldrs 3f out: wknd jst ins last* **11/2**[3]
0363 **9** *10* **Ooh Aah Camara (IRE)**[22] 3520 3-8-5 97 .... JohnEgan 10 58+
(T J Pitt) *sn in tch: rdn over 2f out: lost pl over 1f out: eased and sn bhd* **10/1**

1m 13.37s (-2.28) **Going Correction** -0.225s/f (Firm)
WFA 3 from 4yo+ 4lb **9** Ran SP% **112.8**
Speed ratings (Par 111):106,105,105,103,102 101,101,99,86
CSF £47.96 TOTE £11.10: £2.70, £2.20, £1.70; EX 46.70.
Owner Mrs Claire Massey **Bred** Knocklong House Stud **Trained** Pandy, Abergavenny

FOCUS
A fair Listed event run at a breakneck early gallop and rated around the fourth.

NOTEBOOK
The Kiddykid(IRE), whose rider was unable to draw his 3lb claim, looked at his very best. He travelled strongly and richly deserved this first success since taking the Group 2 Duke of York in May last year. He would not want the ground any quicker and the Ayr Gold Cup is the backend target. (tchd 10-1)
Beckermet(IRE), who has a good record here, was back sprinting but had a high draw to overcome. Forced into being given a much more patient ride, he was pulled wide off the turn and was closing the winner down all the way to the line.
Indian Maiden(IRE), who took this last year, was bidding for her seventh Listed win. Despite fears about the fast ground she was allowed to take her chance and, making her effort widest of all in the straight, she went down fighting, closing on the winner all the way to the line. She has the heart of a lion. (tchd 10-3 in a place)
Moone Cross(IRE), a natural front-runner, was at the head of affairs before halfway and to her credit, stuck on all the way to the line, gaining valuable black type. (op 4-1 tchd 5-1 in a place and 7-2 in another)
Masta Plasta(IRE), the 2005 Norfolk winner, put two moderate efforts behind him but, rated 103, opportunities will be thin on the ground.
Racer Forever(USA), with his 4lb penalty, seemed to find this trip on this track too sharp and from his outside draw, never figured.
Mr Wolf took them along but could not dominate and in the end found this much too tough. (tchd 8-1)
Paradise Isle, who looked her very best, was worst drawn. She seemed to anticipate the stalls opening and was last away. She did well to get on terms but the exertions soon took their toll. This is best overlooked. Official explanation: jockey said mare missed the break (op 7-1)
Ooh Aah Camara(IRE) Official explanation: trainer said filly may have been feeling the effects of a long season

4175 WARWICK INTERNATIONAL H'CAP 1m 4f 66y
5:05 (5:06) (Class 4) (0-85,83) 3-Y-O+ **£5,829** (£1,734; £866; £216) **Stalls** Low

Form RPR
0415 **1** **Mr Aitch (IRE)**[15] 3724 4-9-3 72 ....(t) JohnEgan 9 81
(R T Phillips) *hld up in tch: effrt over 2f out: led over 1f out: hld on towards fin* **10/1**
323 **2** ½ **Mobaasher (USA)**[44] 2829 3-9-1 81 .... MartinDwyer 4 89
(Sir Michael Stoute) *trckd ldrs: drvn over 3f out: rallied over 1f out: no ex wl ins last* **3/1**[1]
5604 **3** *2* **Sporting Gesture**[8] 3960 9-9-4 73 .... PaulMulrennan 10 78
(M W Easterby) *led: hdd over 1f out: kpt on same pce* **13/2**
6126 **4** ½ **Hawkit (USA)**[28] 3331 5-9-2 71 .... RobertWinston 1 75
(A Bailey) *hld up in tch: effrt 3f out: one pce fnl 2f* **6/1**[3]
1000 **4** *dht* **Cool Hunter**[25] 3401 5-10-0 83 .... EddieAhern 6 87
(W R Swinburn) *hld up in rr: hdwy over 7f out: effrt on outer over 2f out: kpt on fnl f* **14/1**
6010 **6** ½ **Merrymaker**[8] 3955 6-9-2 74 .... PatrickMathers(3) 7 77
(W M Brisbourne) *s.i.s: drvn 5f out: hdwy on outside 2f out: kpt on: nt rch ldrs* **9/1**
1065 **7** 1 ¼ **Stretton (IRE)**[15] 3748 8-9-7 81 .... AndrewElliott(5) 2 82+
(J D Bethell) *s.i.s: bhd: hdwy and swtchd outside over 1f out: kpt on: nvr nr ldrs* **4/1**[2]
-230 **8** *shd* **Toshi (USA)**[25] 3413 4-9-11 80 .... TomEaves 3 81
(I Semple) *t.k.h: trckd ldrs: one pce fnl 2f* **9/1**
/0-0 **9** *4* **Tycoon Hall (IRE)**[15] 3256 6-9-1 70 .... VinceSlattery 8 65
(P Bowen) *chsd ldrs: drvn over 4f out: lost pl over 1f out* **10/1**
0540 **10** *2* **Turner**[7] 3983 5-8-4 64 oh10 .... LiamJones(5) 5 56
(W M Brisbourne) *mid-div: drvn and lost pl over 4f out: in rr after* **20/1**

2m 37.64s (-3.01) **Going Correction** -0.225s/f (Firm)
WFA 3 from 4yo+ 11lb **10** Ran SP% **122.2**
Speed ratings (Par 105):101,100,99,99,99 98,97,97,95,93
CSF £42.16 CT £220.08 TOTE £11.70: £2.70, £1.70, £2.30; EX 43.40 Place 6 £10.05, Place 5 £8.55..
Owner Bellflower Racing Ltd **Bred** Mount Coote Stud **Trained** Adlestrop, Gloucs

FOCUS
A fair handicap run at a staccato pace with the first eight stacked up at the line. The third is the best guide to the level.
Stretton(IRE) Official explanation: jockey said gelding missed the break
T/Jkpt: Not won. T/Plt: £10.10 to a £1 stake. Pool: £93,421.20. 6,737.90 winning tickets. T/Qpdt: £9.20 to a £1 stake. Pool: £3,346.00. 267.50 winning tickets. WG

3732 NEWBURY (L-H)
Sunday, August 6

OFFICIAL GOING: Good to firm
Wind: Nil.

4176 CANTORSPREADFAIR.COM LADIES INVITATION FEGENTRI H'CAP (LADY AMATEUR RIDERS) 1m 2f 6y
2:00 (2:01) (Class 5) (0-70,70) 3-Y-O+ **£3,747** (£1,162; £580; £290) **Stalls** Centre

Form RPR
3511 **1** **Luis Melendez (USA)**[9] 3914 4-10-9 69 ....(t) MissAnnikaKallse 8 76
(Tom Dascombe) *lw: mde all: pushed out fnl f: readily* **3/1**[1]
0430 **2** *1* **Shosolosa (IRE)**[34] 3142 4-10-0 60 .... MissFayeBramley 3 65
(Mrs A L M King) *hld up in rr: hdwy 3f out: styd on to chse wnr ins last and gng on cl home but a hld* **10/1**
-320 **3** 2 ½ **Compton Court**[58] 2401 4-10-10 70 .... MrsCBartley 1 70
(A M Balding) *lw: disp 2nd: hit rail after 2f: rdn and effrt 2f out: nvr quite gng pce to chal: one pce ins last* **3/1**[1]
0030 **4** *nk* **Haiti Dancer**[25] 3400 3-9-0 55 ....(p) MrsSMoore 9 55
(C G Cox) *swtg: disp 2nd: rdn and effrt over 2f out: nvr quite gng pce to chal: one pce ins last* **4/1**[2]
0064 **5** ½ **Garston Star**[9] 3894 5-9-5 51 oh5 .... MmeCatherineRieb-Menard 4 50
(J S Moore) *bhd: pushed along over 2f out: hdwy over 1f out and kpt on ins last: nvr gng pce to trble ldrs* **5/1**[3]
0-60 **6** *2* **Emily's Pet (IRE)**[56] 2479 3-8-10 51 oh6 .... MissSHofer 6 46
(B W Duke) *chsd ldrs: rdn and outpcd 3f out: styd on again fnl f but nvr a danger* **33/1**
000/ **7** 1 ¼ **Billy Bathwick (IRE)**[665] 6083 9-9-5 51 oh3 .... MissSBrotherton 2 44
(J M Bradley) *hit rail after 2f: nvr bttr than mid-div: no ch fr over 2f out* **50/1**
4300 **8** 2 ½ **Itcanbedone Again (IRE)**[67] 2149 7-9-6 52 .... MissSZapico 10 40
(Ian Williams) *in tch on outer: chsd ldrs 4f out: sn rdn: n.d after* **10/1**
000- **9** *4* **Twist Bookie (IRE)**[115] 4091 6-9-9 55 .... MissEDoyle 12 35
(J S Moore) *racd towards outer: a in rr* **25/1**
10/ **10** *10* **Zorn (GER)**[1437] 7-10-10 70 .... MissRDavidson 7 31
(M F Harris) *slowly away: sme hdwy 4f out: nvr in contention and sn bhd* **25/1**
0600 **11** 1 ¼ **Monkstown Road**[28] 1058 4-9-11 57 ....(b) MissKHof 5 16
(C N Kellett) *s.i.s: bhd: sme prog over 4f out: sn rr* **50/1**

2m 7.48s (-1.23) **Going Correction** -0.25s/f (Firm)
WFA 3 from 4yo+ 9lb **11** Ran SP% **119.4**
Speed ratings (Par 103):94,93,91,90,90 88,87,85,82,74 73
CSF £33.35 CT £98.29 TOTE £3.80: £1.60, £3.10, £1.50; EX 48.10.
Owner Oneway **Bred** Bloomsbury Stud **Trained** Lambourn, Berks
■ Stewards' Enquiry : Miss E Doyle caution: used whip when out of contention

FOCUS
A moderate contest and ordinary form, limited by the fifth and sixth.

4177 FIRST GREAT WESTERN EUROPEAN BREEDERS FUND MAIDEN STKS 6f 8y
2:30 (2:32) (Class 4) 2-Y-O **£6,477** (£1,927; £963; £481) **Stalls** Centre

Form RPR
1 **Astronomer Royal (USA)**[11] 3858 2-9-3 .... CO'Donoghue 9 85+
(A P O'Brien, Ire) *w'like: str: scope: gd sort: lw: trckd ldrs: led appr fnl f: rdn ins last: clr whn veered bdly lft u.p nr fin* **4/7**[1]
3 **2** 2 ½ **Maker's Mark (IRE)**[20] 3591 2-9-3 .... DaneO'Neill 3 78
(H Candy) *trckd ldr: led over 2f out: rdn: hdd and edgd lft appr fnl f: styd on same pce* **4/1**[2]
3 3 ½ **Lights Of Vegas** 2-9-3 .... LDettori 4 67
(B J Meehan) *w'like: bit bkwd: chsd ldrs: rdn and one pce fnl 2f* **14/1**
4 *1* **Bachnagairn** 2-9-3 .... SteveDrowne 5 64+
(R Charlton) *w'like: bit bkwd: s.i.s: pushed along and hdwy over 2f out: kpt on ins last but nvr gng pce to rch ldrs* **25/1**
5 *nk* **Christalini** 2-9-3 .... PatDobbs 6 63
(J C Fox) *str: chsd ldrs: shkn up and one pce fnl 2f* **100/1**
6 3 ½ **Wadnagin (IRE)** 2-8-12 .... LPKeniry 8 48+
(I A Wood) *w'like: bit bkwd: bhd: hdwy 3f out: kpt on fnl f but nvr in contention* **80/1**
7 ¾ **Golan Way** 2-9-3 .... SebSanders 7 50
(I A Wood) *chsd ldrs: pushed along 3f out: outpcd fnl 2f* **40/1**
8 1 ¾ **Fistral** 2-9-3 .... TonyCulhane 10 45
(M R Channon) *unf: swtg: bhd: sme prog fnl 2f but nvr in contention* **25/1**
9 *nk* **Duke Of Tuscany** 2-9-3 .... RyanMoore 11 44
(R Hannon) *w'like: scope: bit bkwd: a outpcd* **6/1**[3]
10 1 ½ **Anthill** 2-8-9 .... AdamKirby(3) 12 35
(I A Wood) *leggy: s.i.s: a bhd* **66/1**
0 **11** ½ **Beat The Bully**[97] 1333 2-9-3 .... IanMongan 1 38
(I A Wood) *led tl hdd over 2f out: wknd over 1f out* **66/1**
12 2 ½ **My Jeanie (IRE)** 2-8-9 .... StephaneBreux(3) 13 26
(J C Fox) *neat: slowly away: a in rr* **100/1**
04 **13** *17* **Straw Boy**[10] 3860 2-9-0 .... EdwardCreighton(3) 2 —
(M R Channon) *leggy: unf: lw: racd alone far side: nvr travelling and a wl bhd* **25/1**

1m 12.74s (-1.58) **Going Correction** -0.25s/f (Firm) **13** Ran SP% **124.8**
Speed ratings (Par 96):100,96,92,90,90 85,84,82,81,79 79,75,53
CSF £2.98 TOTE £1.40: £1.10, £1.60, £2.40; EX 3.90.
Owner D Smith, Mrs J Magnier & M Tabor **Bred** Classicstar **Trained** Ballydoyle, Co Tipperary

FOCUS
Just an average maiden for the course, with only two of the runners holding engagements in Group races. However, the time was reasonable and the form should work out.

NOTEBOOK
Astronomer Royal(USA), whose trainer has had a few reversals with his short-price juveniles this season, most recently Red Rock Canyon at Goodwood the previous day, made no mistake in landed cramped odds, getting well on top inside the final furlong and winning with a fair bit in hand, considering he swerved badly to his left under pressure. He holds entries in almost all the big remaining juvenile events and will doubtlessly take his chance in at least one of them, but there are surely several better at Ballydoyle. (op 4-6)
Maker's Mark(IRE), a keeping-on third in a fair race at Windsor on debut, looked the main danger to the favourite and he was able to match him until the over a furlong out, at which point he became outpaced and outclassed. He should have little trouble finding a maiden. (tchd 9-2)
Lights Of Vegas, a relation of the stable's formerly smart King's Ironbridge, layed up well early, but he began to struggle as the front pair quickened it up and could only keep on at the one pace. This was a most pleasing introduction and, given the vast majority of two-year-olds from the yard need their debut, it is reasonable to expect improvement on this. He will require further in time. (op 10-1)

Bachnagairn, from the family of Height Of Fasion, was being niggled from an early stage following a slow start and he looked very much in need of the education. Already gelded, he was not given a hard time and can be expected to show significant improvement for a rise in distance. (op 20-1)
Christalini, whose yard is not known for its blistering success with juveniles, defied his odds to make a promising debut and raise a few eyebrows in the process. It could be argued he holds the form down, but he deserves a chance to show this was not a fluke.
Wadnagin(IRE), related to several sprinters and one of four in the race for her trainer, comes from a yard whose two-year-olds often need a run, so it was pleasing to see her going on nicely at the end. She can find a race at a lesser track. (op 66-1)
Golan Way, a half-brother to recent scorer William's Way, was the shortest priced runner of his trainer's quartet. However, he is going to require further than this and, having showed up well early, he began to struggle as soon as the pace quickened. There were many positives to take from the run and he too should improve for the outing. (op 33-1)
Duke Of Tuscany, well supported in the market beforehand, holds a Royal Lodge entry, but he showed next to nothing and the support beforehand was clearly misplaced. He is sure to be capable of better in time, but needs to leave this behind. (op 9-1)
Anthill, who looked on the weak side, is going to improve for time and distance. Official explanation: jockey said filly ran very green (op 50-1)
Beat The Bully put his previous experience to good use and made the running until over two furlongs out, but he stopped quickly under pressure and dropped right away. He may be more of a nursery type.
Straw Boy Official explanation: jockey said gelding hung left-handed

4178 GRUNDON RECYCLE NURSERY 7f (S)

3:05 (3:05) (Class 4) 2-Y-O **£5,181** (£1,541; £770; £384) **Stalls** Centre

Form RPR
0063 **1** **Cesc**[22] [3544] 2-8-6 **68** .... JimmyQuinn 13 79+
(P J Makin) *stdd s: hld up in rear and t.k.h: hdwy on rails 2f out: qckind to ld appr fnl f: sn in command: comf* **16/1**
6431 **2** 3 **Bobbish**[9] [3902] 2-8-13 **75** .... LDettori 12 78
(N A Callaghan) *chsd ldrs: rdn over 2f out: chsd wnr ins last but a comf hld* **9/4**[1]
0421 **3** ½ **Stagehand (IRE)**[18] [3641] 2-8-12 **74** .... AdrianMcCarthy 14 76
(B R Millman) *lw: plld hrd: led: rdn 2f out: hdd appr fnl f: styd on same pce ins last* **9/2**[3]
414 **4** hd **Princeton (IRE)**[15] [3735] 2-9-7 **83** .... TonyCulhane 8 84
(M R Channon) *lw: chsd ldrs: rdn and effrt over 2f out: styd on same pce fr over 1f out* **13/2**
234 **5** 3 **Buddies Girl (IRE)**[57] [2456] 2-8-13 **75** .... RyanMoore 10 69
(R Hannon) *lw: in tch: hdwy 2f out: nver gng pce to rch ldrs: wknd ins last* **4/1**[2]
1005 **6** hd **Hephaestus**[10] [3861] 2-8-10 **72** .... TPO'Shea 3 65
(M R Channon) *bhd: swtchd lft and hdwy on outside over 2f out: chsd ldrs but nvr in contention over 1f out: sn one pce* **33/1**
3122 **7** shd **Relkida**[10] [3861] 2-9-0 **79** .... EdwardCreighton(3) 5 72
(M R Channon) *slowly away: bhd: hday 2f out: nvr gng pce to be competitive and one pce fnl f* **8/1**
0200 **8** 1½ **Peppin's Gold (IRE)**[39] [2980] 2-8-0 **65** .... DominicFox(3) 2 54
(B R Millman) *bhd: mod prog fr over 1f out* **50/1**
0036 **9** hd **Regal Ovation**[23] [3496] 2-8-4 **66** .... NickyMackay 1 54
(W R Muir) *prssed ldrs: rdn over 2f out: wknd fnl f* **16/1**
16 **10** ¾ **Fuji (IRE)**[22] [3531] 2-9-0 **76** .... DaneO'Neill 6 62
(M L W Bell) *chsd ldrs: rdn over 2f out: wknd over 1f out* **16/1**
0310 **11** 3 **Party Palace**[17] [3678] 2-8-1 **63** ow1 .... RoystonFfrench 7 42
(J A Osborne) *swtg: pressed ldrs over 4f* **20/1**
5553 **12** 1½ **Mr Mini Scule**[19] [3613] 2-7-8 **61** .... AurelioMedeiros(5) 11 36
(A B Haynes) *chsd ldrs: rdn and wknd qckly 2f out* **66/1**

1m 25.29s (-1.71) **Going Correction** -0.25s/f (Firm) **12** Ran SP% **122.2**
Speed ratings (Par 96):99,95,95,94,91 91,91,89,88,88 84,83
CSF £52.49 CT £192.53 TOTE £19.00: £4.30, £1.40, £1.60; EX 66.50.
Owner Keith And Brian Brackpool **Bred** H J P Farr **Trained** Ogbourne Maisey, Wilts

FOCUS
Just a fair nursery but the form looks solid rated around the runner-up and should work out.

NOTEBOOK
Cesc has been running well in maidens at shorter and this step up in trip for his nursery debut proved the answer. Bred to stay, he was ridden with restraint and, despite taking a grip, he showed a telling burst to seal it a furlong out. Winning here off a mark of 68, he is sure to go up a bit, but should remain capable of following up if the rise is not too severe, with further improvement quite possible.
Bobbish, up 5lb for his Newmarket win, stayed on to take second inside the final furlong, but was firmly put in his place. He is going to stay further in time and could be one to look out for in mile nurseries when they come into effect. Official explanation: jockey said saddle slipped (tchd 2-1)
Stagehand(IRE), raised 8lb for his all-the-way Kempton success, again attempted to lead throughout, but he pulled too hard in the early stages and could only plug on once headed by the winner. He can find a race off this mark, but needs to settle better. (op 11-2)
Princeton(IRE), fourth behind three potentially smart sorts in a conditions race at the course last month, had to give upward of 7lb to all his rivals and ran as well as could have been expected. He is likely to remain vulnerable off this sort of mark. (op 8-1)
Buddies Girl(IRE) was the subject of support throughout the day, but she never really looked like landing the bets and was disappointing. She may be regressive. (op 11-2)
Hephaestus, who got a bit warm beforehand, has not shown much since coming back from a break, but this was slightly better. He may need some assistance from the Handicapper. (op 25-1)
Relkida looked one of the likelier winners, but she never recovered from a slow start and was unable to get into it. She deserves another chance. (tchd 9-1)

4179 EUROPEAN BREEDERS FUND CHALICE STKS (LISTED RACE) (F&M) 1m 4f 5y

3:40 (3:40) (Class 1) 3-Y-0+

£15,898 (£6,025; £3,015; £1,503; £753; £378) **Stalls** Centre

Form RPR
0- **1** **Fermion (IRE)**[21] [3576] 3-8-5 .... CO'Donoghue 3 107+
(A P O'Brien, Ire) *w'like: lengthy: lw: hld up rr: hdwy on ins and n.m.r over 2f out: drvn and qcknd over 1f out: led last half f: readily* **14/1**
-151 **2** 1¼ **Reunite (IRE)**[19] [3627] 3-8-8 107 .... LDettori 10 108
(Saeed Bin Suroor) *lw: racd wd early and led after 2f: rdn over 2f out: kpt on tl hdd and outpcd last half f* **4/6**[1]
14/3 **3** 1½ **Intrigued**[71] [2023] 4-9-2 109 .... SebSanders 4 102
(Sir Mark Prescott) *chsd ldrs: rdn and effrt fr 2f out: styd on same pce fnl f* **5/1**[2]
0-55 **4** 1½ **Idealistic (IRE)**[48] [2706] 5-9-2 90 .... NickyMackay 8 100
(L M Cumani) *lw: chsd ldrs: rdn over 2f out: nvr gng pce to chal: wknd ins last* **25/1**
50-3 **5** ½ **Ruby Wine**[19] [3627] 4-9-2 100 .... TonyCulhane 6 99
(J M P Eustace) *bhd: rdn and hdwy fr 3f out: kpt on same pce fr over 1f out* **20/1**
-105 **6** 1¼ **Sindirana (IRE)**[15] [3739] 3-8-8 95 .... RyanMoore 11 100
(Sir Michael Stoute) *swtg: chsd ldrs: rdn fr 4f out: effrt over 2f out: nvr gng pce to chal: wknd fnl f* **12/1**
3122 **7** nk **Local Spirit (USA)**[19] [3627] 3-8-5 102 .... TPQueally 1 97
(C E Brittain) *chsd ldrs: rdn and flashed tail 2f out: wknd fnl f* **20/1**
12-2 **8** 1¾ **Bunood (IRE)**[91] [1509] 3-8-5 96 .... RHills 9 94
(J L Dunlop) *lw: keen hold: in tch: rdn 3f out: nvr gng pce to chal: wknd fnl f* **15/2**[3]
10-2 **9** 1¾ **Giving**[107] [1108] 3-8-5 84 .... SteveDrowne 7 91
(G Wragg) *swtg: bhd: sme hdwy 3f out: nvr in contention and no ch fnl 2f* **16/1**
2-56 **10** hd **Littletown Bridge (USA)**[57] [2430] 4-9-2 .... TPO'Shea 5 91
(Christian Wroe, UAE) *swtg: rrd stalls: bhd most of way* **100/1**
0120 **11** hd **Prowess (IRE)**[4] [4039] 3-8-5 92 .... MichaelHills 2 90
(B W Hills) *led 2f: styd chsng ldr to 3f out: wknd ins fnl 2f* **40/1**
12 25 **Sterling Moll** 3-8-5 .... AdrianMcCarthy 12 50
(W De Best-Turner) *rangy: slowly away: a in rr* **100/1**

2m 31.14s (-4.85) **Going Correction** -0.25s/f (Firm)
WFA 3 from 4yo+ 11lb **12** Ran SP% **126.4**
Speed ratings (Par 111):106,105,104,103,102 102,101,100,99,99 99,82
CSF £24.28 TOTE £17.70: £3.40, £1.30, £1.50; EX 42.90.
Owner D Smith, Mrs J Magnier & M Tabor **Bred** Quay Bldst,Luna Wells Syn & H **Trained** Ballydoyle, Co Tipperary
■ Stewards' Enquiry : C O'Donoghue one-day ban: used whip without giving filly time to respond (Aug 17)

FOCUS
A fair fillies and mares' Listed race in which three progressive and potentially Group-class fillies filled the first three places. The form looks sound behind, with the next three home close to form.

NOTEBOOK
Fermion(IRE) ◆, a nice type to look at, has showed improved form the last twice since being switched to fast ground, and she raised her game once more on this rise in distance. Ridden with plenty of confidence, she came with a well-timed challenge and showed a decent change of gear once asked to go and win the race. This was a smart effort from a filly who is beginning to fulfill her potential and she looks more than capable of making her mark at Group level.
Reunite(IRE), whose only prior defeat to this came in the Ribblesdale at Royal Ascot - beaten just a length after tiring late on - was ridden positively by Dettori and kept on well under prssure, but not as well as the winner. She clearly stays this distance and was unfortunate to bump into an improved filly, but gives the impression she is best kept to ten furlongs for the time being. (op 10-11)
Intrigued, turned over at odds-on in a Listed event on her return from a long lay-off in May, came out top of the older horses, keeping on stoutly under pressure, and this lightly-raced filly, who was beaten only two lengths in the Marcel Boussac as a juvenile, looks a winner waiting to happen at this level. She remains a filly of potential. (op 9-2)
Idealistic(IRE), a progressive filly last term, has not been at her best thus far in 2006, seeming to fall short at this level, but this was a better and she is worth returning to handicaps. (tchd 33-1)
Ruby Wine, a Listed winner at the course last season, ran well over an inadequate distance behind Reunite on her seasonal debut at Yarmouth and appreciated the return to further. She was going on at the end and may have benefited from a more positive ride though, as stamina is her strong suit. (op 16-1)
Sindirana(IRE), who scraped home in a weak renewal of the Lingfield Oaks trial on her return, has been unable to build on that in three starts since and she does not look up to this grade. (tchd 14-1)
Bunood(IRE), second to the smart Riyalma in the Pretty Polly on her seasonal debut, has been off since, but looked well beforehand. Keen early, she was unable to pick up under pressure and proved to be most disappointing. She got a little warm beforehand though, and this was he fastest ground she has tackled to date, so could be worth another chance. Official explanation: jockey said filly was unsuited by the good to firm ground (op 8-1 tchd 9-1)

4180 FIRST GREAT WESTERN H'CAP 5f 34y

4:15 (4:16) (Class 4) (0-85,86) 3-Y-0+ **£5,505** (£1,637; £818; £408) **Stalls** Centre

Form RPR
0660 **1** **The Jobber (IRE)**[3] [4085] 5-9-10 **83** .... SebSanders 2 98
(M Blanshard) *lw: stdd s: hld up in tch: hdwy and qcknd to ld jst ins last: drvn out* **6/1**
1014 **2** 1 **Didn't We (IRE)**[13] [3795] 3-9-9 **85** .... (b[1]) IanMongan 10 96
(T G Mills) *lw: w ldr tl def advantage 3f out: rdn 2f out: hdd jst ins last: kpt on but nt pce of wnr* **7/1**
0400 **3** 2 **Cashel Mead**[3] [4085] 6-9-4 **80** .... AdamKirby(3) 6 84+
(J L Spearing) *bhd: sn rdn and outpcd: hdwy over 1f out: kpt on wl fnl f but nvr gng pce to rch ldrs* **16/1**
0352 **4** nk **Conjecture**[13] [3802] 4-9-0 **73** .... RoystonFfrench 4 76
(R Bastiman) *lw: broke wl: sn drvn along to chse ldrs: nvr gng pce to chal and one pce fnl f* **9/2**[2]
2420 **5** ½ **Malapropism**[3] [4085] 6-9-10 **86** .... EdwardCreighton(3) 14 87
(M R Channon) *sn slt ld tl hdd 3f out: styd w ldr and sn rdn: wknd ins fnl f* **8/1**
3030 **6** 1¼ **Desperate Dan**[8] [3956] 5-9-0 **80** .... (b) FrankiePickard(7) 1 77
(J A Osborne) *trckd ldrs: shkn up 2f out: wknd over 1f out* **14/1**
31-2 **7** 3 **Shade Cozy (USA)**[213] [47] 4-8-9 **68** .... (t) LPKeniry 7 54
(A M Balding) *s.i.s: sn in tch: outpcd fr 1/2-way* **4/1**[1]
2136 **8** ¾ **Cheney Hill**[31] [3226] 3-8-6 **68** .... DaneO'Neill 11 51
(H Candy) *lw: chsd ldrs: shkn up 2f out: wknd fnl f* **5/1**[3]
0500 **9** ½ **Whistler**[5] [4019] 9-8-0 **66** oh7 .... (p) JosephWalsh(7) 8 48
(Miss J R Tooth) *a outpcd* **40/1**
100- **10** 10 **Great Fox (IRE)**[288] [6021] 5-9-4 **77** .... BrianReilly 13 23
(P L Gilligan) *spd to 1/2-way* **9/1**

60.46 secs (-2.10) **Going Correction** -0.25s/f (Firm)
WFA 3 from 4yo+ 3lb **10** Ran SP% **117.7**
Speed ratings (Par 105):106,104,101,100,99 97,93,91,91,75
CSF £48.13 CT £658.48 TOTE £7.90: £2.30, £2.80, £4.50; EX 56.80 Trifecta £416.30 Part won. Pool £586.40 - 0.70 winning units..
Owner Mrs R Wilkerson, Mrs J Breton & Partners **Bred** Dr T J Molony **Trained** Upper Lambourn, Berks

FOCUS
A fair sprint handicap run at a fair pace but ordinary form for the grade.
Cheney Hill Official explanation: jockey said gelding was unsuited by the good to firm ground

4181 SPILLERS FILLIES' H'CAP 1m 2f 6y

4:45 (4:45) (Class 5) (0-75,73) 3-Y-0 **£3,886** (£1,156; £577; £288) **Stalls** Centre

Form RPR
0621 **1** **Hanella (IRE)**[10] [3865] 3-9-5 **71** .... SebSanders 4 72+
(R M Beckett) *trckd ldrs: rdn 3f out: styd on u.p to ld cl home* **15/8**[1]
5434 **2** ¾ **Regent's Park**[27] [3347] 3-9-7 **73** .... SteveDrowne 5 73
(R Charlton) *lw: sn led: rdn 3f out: hdd over 1f out: ld again ins last: ct cl home* **4/1**[3]

0000 **3** *nk* **Vinska (USA)**[24] 3440 3-8-2 **54** oh8..............................(p) NickyMackay 9 53
(J W Hills) *t.k.h: hld up in rr: swtchd to outside and rapid hdwy fnl f: fin wl but nt quite get up* **50/1**

0-30 **4** *shd* **Persian Express (USA)**[37] 3046 3-9-5 **71**........................ MichaelHills 7 70
(B W Hills) *chsd ldrs: chal fr 3f out tl led over 1f out: hdd ins last: styd upsides tl no ex nr fin* **20/1**

6352 **5** *hd* **Theatre Royal**[10] 3865 3-8-10 **62**... LPKeniry 2 63+
(A M Balding) *lw: chsd ldrs: n.m.r appr fnl f: kpt on ins last: styng on cl home* **3/1**[2]

3601 **6** *2* **Odessa Star (USA)**[25] 3400 3-9-6 **72**............................ RyanMoore 1 67
(J G Portman) *in tch: chsd ldrs 3f out: sn pushed along: one pce fnl f* **7/1**

3-34 **7** *nk* **Gouranga**[50] 2646 3-9-4 **70**.. DaneO'Neill 3 64
(H Candy) *chsd ldr: chal 3f out: sn rdn: wkng whn hmpd jst ins last* **10/1**

0600 **8** *1* **Jabbara (IRE)**[13] 3793 3-8-12 **64**.. TPQueally 6 56
(C E Brittain) *lw: rr but in tch: effrt over 2f out: one pce fnl 2f* **14/1**

-000 **9** *7* **Laqataat (IRE)**[36] 3072 3-8-13 **65**...(t) RHills 8 44
(J L Dunlop) *a in rr* **20/1**

2m 6.86s (-1.85) **Going Correction** -0.25s/f (Firm) **9** Ran SP% **119.5**
Speed ratings (Par 97):97,96,96,96,95 94,94,93,87
CSF £9.77 CT £281.30 TOTE £2.70: £1.20, £1.90, £10.30; EX 16.60 Place 6 £20.33, Place 5 £12.31..
Owner Frank Brady **Bred** Cathal Ryan **Trained** Whitsbury, Hants

FOCUS
A competitive fillies' handicap in which any one of five was in with a chance inside the final furlong. The form is modest rated around the fourth.
Laqataat(IRE) Official explanation: jockey said filly had a breathing problem
T/Plt: £16.40 to a £1 stake. Pool £68,533.45. 3045.60 winning tickets. T/Qpdt: £13.30 to a £1 stake. Pool £3,020.60. 168.00 winning tickets. ST

4182 - 4185a (Foreign Racing) - See Raceform Interactive

4165 GALWAY (R-H)
Sunday, August 6

OFFICIAL GOING: Good

4186a GALWAY FAIRGREEN HOTEL H'CAP 7f
3:50 (3:51) (50-70,70) 3-Y-0+ **£7,148** (£1,665; £734; £424)

RPR

1 **Kuwait Tower (IRE)**[13] 3807 4-9-3 59................................ DJCondon 2 68
(Joseph Quinn, Ire) *mid-div: 8th bef 1/2-way: 6th appr st: mod 2nd under 1f out: r.o wl to ld nr fin* **20/1**

2 *hd* **Incline (IRE)**[4] 4064 7-9-12 68... PJSmullen 4 76
(R McGlinchey, Ire) *trckd ldrs: 5th 1/2-way: 3rd and chal 2f out: led ent st: 3 l clr under 1f out: strly pressed cl home: hdd nr fin* **12/1**

3 *½* **Bolton Hall (IRE)**[28] 3331 4-9-3 59................................ DPMcDonogh 3 66
(R A Fahey) *towards rr: hdwy over 2f out: 5th early st: 3rd ins fnl f: styd on wl* **5/1**[2]

4 *3 ½* **No Frontier (IRE)**[8] 3966 8-8-12 59...............................(tp) PBBeggy[(5)] 6 56
(T Hogan, Ire) *towards rr: 13th into st: styd on wl* **20/1**

5 *1* **Sweet Emily**[29] 3304 4-9-10 66... KJManning 1 61
(Patrick J Flynn, Ire) *mid-div: 8th 1/2-way: 7th 2f out: kpt on st* **12/1**

6 *nk* **Dart Along (USA)**[19] 3631 4-10-0 70.................................(b[1]) JMurtagh 15 64
(Michael McCullagh, Ire) *chsd ldrs on inner: 8th 1/2-way: rdn and no imp fr over 2f out* **9/1**

7 *½* **Togher Castle (IRE)**[17] 3690 6-9-1 60.............................. RPCleary[(3)] 11 52
(T J O'Mara, Ire) *towards rr: kpt on fr 2f out* **20/1**

8 *nk* **Zakfree (IRE)**[3] 4092 5-9-9 65......................................(b) VRDeSouza 12 57
(Liam McAteer, Ire) *chsd ldrs: 6th 1/2-way: rdn and no imp fr over 2f out* **20/1**

9 *1 ½* **Noble Purpose (IRE)**[62] 2310 3-9-7 69............................ NPMadden 9 56
(J C Hayden, Ire) *towards rr: kpt on one pce fr 2 1/2f out* **25/1**

10 *½* **Pretty Posh (IRE)**[19] 3631 5-9-3 59..............................(b[1]) WSupple 13 45
(Timothy Doyle, Ire) *led: rdn and strly pressed over 2f out: hdd appr st: sn wknd* **14/1**

11 *½* **Moon At Midnight**[5] 4033 6-10-0 70 5ex............................ RMBurke 16 55
(R J Osborne, Ire) *settled 3rd: 4th 1/2-way: wknd over 2f out* **6/1**[3]

12 *¾* **Jazabelle (IRE)**[10] 3885 3-9-7 69.................................(p) PShanahan 8 52
(C Collins, Ire) *settled 2nd: rdn to chal over 2f out: led briefly appr st: sn wknd* **7/1**

13 *¾* **Foxy Gwynne**[4] 4064 4-9-5 64.. DMGrant[(3)] 7 45
(Patrick J Flynn, Ire) *prom: 3rd 1/2-way: rdn to chal over 2f out: sn wknd* **12/1**

14 *1* **Dollars Rock (IRE)**[4] 4064 6-9-13 69.................................(b) KFallon 14 47
(T J O'Mara, Ire) *mid-div on inner: 10th 2f out: effrt whn nt clr run early st: eased fnl f* **10/3**[1]

15 *1* **Danehill Chancer (IRE)**[25] 3421 5-9-3 62...................... CDHayes[(3)] 5 37
(D J Ryan, Ire) *a bhd* **20/1**

16 *dist* **Toberogan (IRE)**[111] 1062 5-9-6 62..................................... FMBerry 10 —
(W A Murphy, Ire) *a bhd: virtually p.u st: t.o* **20/1**

1m 29.6s
WFA 3 from 4yo+ 6lb **16** Ran SP% **138.7**
CSF £249.55 CT £978.54 TOTE £75.80: £11.50, £3.30, £2.40, £3.80; DF 1400.10.
Owner Miss Aine Brodbin **Bred** Philip Carroll **Trained** Sixmilebridge, Co. Clare

NOTEBOOK
Bolton Hall(IRE), racing off a career-low mark, ran on well for pressure late on this was probably his best effort of the season so far. (op 3/1)

4187a MICHAEL MCNAMARA & CO. BUILDERS DUBLIN & GALWAY H'CAP (PREMIER HANDICAP) 7f
4:20 (4:22) 3-Y-0+ **£44,896** (£13,172; £6,275; £2,137)

RPR

1 **Bolodenka (IRE)**[3] 4094 4-8-12 86 5ex........................ DPMcDonogh 10 98+
(R A Fahey) *mid-div: 8th 1/2-way: 7th and hdwy on outer 2f out: 4th and chal 1f out: sn led: styd on wl* **9/2**[2]

2 *2* **Dynamo Dancer (IRE)**[14] 3773 3-9-3 97..........................(p) JMurtagh 14 104
(G M Lyons, Ire) *chsd ldrs: 6th 1/2-way: hdwy 2f out: 3rd and chal under 1f out: kpt on* **9/1**

3 *shd* **King Of Tory (IRE)**[19] 3629 4-8-6 83.............................(b) CDHayes[(3)] 13 90
(Edward Lynam, Ire) *trckd ldrs in 4th: cl up 2f out: chal early st: kpt on fnl f* **33/1**

4 *¾* **Uhoomagoo**[8] 3926 8-9-11 99..(b) KFallon 4 104
(K A Ryan) *hld up in rr: last and trailing over 2f out: r.o wl st: nvr nrr* **3/1**[1]

5 *1 ¼* **Crooked Throw (IRE)**[35] 3125 7-8-3 80.............................. DMGrant[(3)] 3 81
(C F Swan, Ire) *rr of mid-div: wl fr 2f out* **16/1**

6 *½* **Cheyenne Star (IRE)**[39] 2991 3-8-10 90........................... PShanahan 7 90
(Ms F M Crowley, Ire) *chsd ldrs on outer: 7th 1/2-way: hdwy into 2nd 2f out: sn chal: led early st: hdd ins fnl f: no ex* **14/1**

7 *2* **Amourallis (IRE)**[5] 4031 5-9-0 88..................................... WSupple 6 83
(H Rogers, Ire) *mid-div: 10th appr 1/2-way: kpt on fr 2f out* **16/1**

8 *hd* **Orpailleur**[29] 3321 5-9-4 92.. KJManning 16 86
(Ms Joanna Morgan, Ire) *led: rdn and strly pressed over 2f out: hdd early st: sn no ex* **9/1**

9 *nk* **Bricks And Porter (IRE)**[5] 4031 6-8-7 88.....................(bt) SMLevey[(7)] 2 81
(John A Quinn, Ire) *towards rr: kpt on st* **20/1**

10 *¾* **Chained Emotion (IRE)**[23] 3504 5-9-2 95...................... PBBeggy[(5)] 11 86
(Kevin Prendergast, Ire) *prom: 2nd over 2f out: 5th appr st: sn no ex* **16/1**

11 *1* **Senator's Alibi**[3] 4094 8-8-5 82... RPCleary[(3)] 9 71
(T J O'Mara, Ire) *mid-div: no imp fr 2f out* **10/1**

12 *¾* **Alone He Stands (IRE)**[35] 3125 6-9-9 97........................ NPMadden 12 83
(J C Hayden, Ire) *cl 2nd: rdn and wknd fr 2 1/2f out* **33/1**

13 *1* **Sheer Tenby (IRE)**[18] 3657 9-8-8 82..............................(bt) RMBurke 8 66
(Paul A Roche, Ire) *chsd ldrs: 5th 1/2-way: rdn and wknd fr 2 1/2f out* **20/1**

14 *5 ½* **Keen Look (IRE)**[18] 3657 7-8-10 84....................................... FMBerry 15 53
(Gerard Keane, Ire) *mid-div on inner: no ex over 2f out: eased fnl f* **14/1**

15 *2 ½* **Bobs Pride (IRE)**[5] 4031 4-9-13 101.................................(b) PJSmullen 5 63
(D K Weld, Ire) *towards rr: effrt and no imp 2f out: virtually p.u st* **8/1**[3]

16 *12* **Noplacelikehome (IRE)**[24] 3464 3-8-8 88..........................(t) MJKinane 1 18
(Thomas Mullins, Ire) *rr of mid-div: wknd fr over 2f out: eased st* **14/1**

1m 28.4s
WFA 3 from 4yo+ 6lb **16** Ran SP% **136.4**
CSF £48.62 CT £1266.05 TOTE £7.60: £1.90, £1.90, £7.80, £1.40; DF 76.00.
Owner Enda Hunston **Bred** Kildaragh Stud **Trained** Musley Bank, N Yorks

NOTEBOOK
Bolodenka(IRE) ◆, successful over a mile here on Thursday, followed up here under a mandatory 5lb penalty. In what was a competitive renewal of this valuable handicap, he coped well with the drop in trip and won going away after closing into the straight and hitting the front well inside the final furlong. He is improving and although the Handicapper will make it harder for him in future there may well be more to come. (op 9/2 tchd 5/1)
Uhoomagoo, who overcame a poor draw and swept home from behind to win this race on good to firm ground a year ago, went into this renewal on a high after his win at Royal Ascot and his good second to Dabbers Ridge at Ascot eight days previously. However, the rain overnight did nothing for his chance and, again drawn low, he was last and clearly struggling starting downhill. Driven along and going nowhere starting the climb, he had only one rival behind him into the straight before producing a strong late burst which this time was never going to be a winning one. (op 5/2 tchd 100/30)

4188 - (Foreign Racing) - See Raceform Interactive

COPENHAGEN (L-H)
Sunday, August 6

OFFICIAL GOING: Good

4189a SCANDINAVIAN OPEN CHAMPIONSHIP (GROUP 3) 1m 4f
3:20 (12:00) 3-Y-0+ **£27,771** (£9,257; £4,629; £2,277; £1,851)

RPR

1 **Halfsong (SWE)**[266] 6340 6-8-11 .... SaraSlot 2 98
(K P Andersen, Sweden) *raced in 2nd behind clear leader to straight, led 1 1/2f out, ran on well* **119/10**

2 *½* **Zenato (GER)**[171] 437 5-9-2 .... MMartinez 9 102
(F Reuterskiold, Sweden) *mid-division, 4th straight, challenged 1f out, every chance til no extra in final 50y* **52/10**[3]

3 *2* **Alpino Chileno (ARG)**[114] 1014 7-9-4 .... CLopez 5 101
(Rune Haugen, Norway) *clear leader to straight, headed 1 1/2f out, one pace* **9/10**[1]

4 *1 ½* **Crimson And Gold**[291] 4-9-2 .... FDiaz 3 97
(L Reuterskiold, Sweden) *mid-division, 6th straight, effort on outside final 2f, never able to challenge* **92/10**

5 *½* **Mick Jerome (IRE)**[114] 1014 5-9-2 .... YvonneDurant 7 96
(Rune Haugen, Norway) *last to straight, headway final 2f, nearest at finish* **10/1**

6 *shd* **Alnitak (USA)**[49] 5-9-2 .... LHammer-Hansen 6 96
(B Olsen, Norway) *reaced in 7th to straight, stayed on but never able to challenge* **14/1**

7 *shd* **Bongo Bello (DEN)** 5-9-2 .... JJohansen 4 96
(T Christensen, Denmark) *in rear til headway & 3rd straight, soon faded* **21/1**

8 *3 ½* **Mambo King (DEN)**[42] 4-9-2 .... MSantos 8 90
(L Kelp, Sweden) *raced in 3rd, close 5th straight, brief effort 2f out, beaten approaching final f* **48/10**[2]

9 *9* **The Khamsin (DEN)**[371] 3988 7-9-2 .... KAndersen 1 77
(Ms C Erichsen, Norway) *mid-division, 8th straight, eased when beaten over 1f out* **26/1**

2m 28.9s **9** Ran SP% **127.6**
(including 1DKr stakes): WIN 12.94; PL 2.32, 1.95, 1.37; DF 310.05.
Owner Stall Australia **Bred** Gerda Rebsdorf **Trained** Sweden

3131 COLOGNE (R-H)
Sunday, August 6

OFFICIAL GOING: Soft

4190a OPPENHEIM PRAMERICA MEILE (GROUP 3) 1m
4:00 (4:11) 3-Y-0+ **£22,069** (£6,897; £3,448; £2,069)

RPR

1 **Lateral**[22] 3563 3-9-0 .... WMongil 2 113
(P Schiergen, Germany) *raced in 3rd, pushed along straight, ridden and went 2nd over 2f out, challenged final furlong, led final strides* **2/5**[1]

2 *nk* **Willingly (GER)**[22] 3563 7-9-2 .... ADeVries 3 108
(M Trybuhl, Germany) *led, ridden and ran on 2f out, kept on and looked definite winner til headed final strides* **104/10**

3 *2 ½* **Common World (USA)**[68] 2116 7-9-4 .... THellier 4 110
(T Hogan, Ire) *raced in 2nd, ridden entering straight, kept on at same pace to line, never challenged for lead* **43/10**[3]

4 3 **Santiago (GER)**[392] 3384 4-9-0 .... ABoschert 5 106
(U Ostmann, Germany) *raced in 4th, shaken up 2 1/2f out, no impression on leading trio* **4/1**[2]

5 5 **Shapira (GER)**[46] 2740 5-8-12 .... AHelfenbein 6 104
(Andreas Lowe, Germany) *last, ridden straight, beaten 2f out* **82/10**

1m 36.31s
WFA 3 from 4yo+ 7lb **5** Ran SP% **129.9**
(Including 10 Euros stake): WIN 14; PL 12, 18; SF 48.
Owner Stiftung Gestut Fahrhof **Bred** Stiftung Gestut Fahrhof **Trained** Germany

NOTEBOOK
Common World(USA), returning from a break, had conditions to suit but could never land a blow.

4168 DEAUVILLE (R-H)
Sunday, August 6
OFFICIAL GOING: Turf course - good; all-weather - standard

4191a PRIX MAURICE DE GHEEST (GROUP 1) 6f 110y(S)
3:20 (3:24) 3-Y-0+ **£98,517** (£39,414; £19,707; £9,845; £4,931)

RPR

1 **Marchand D'Or (FR)**[22] 3564 3-8-11 .... DBonilla 12 121
(F Head, France) *held up, headway on stands side over 2f out, ran on strongly to lead 1f out, driven clear final 100y* **13/1**

2 2 **Satri (IRE)**[22] 3564 4-9-2 .... C-PLemaire 7 114
(J-M Beguigne, France) *held up towards outside, ridden & ran on 1 1/2f out, stayed on well final f to take 2nd close home* **26/10**[1]

3 1/2 **Amadeus Wolf**[23] 3494 3-8-11 .... NCallan 14 114
(K A Ryan) *close up, 3rd half-way, ridden to lead 2f out to 1f out, stayed on under pressure, lost 2nd close home* **12/1**

4 snk **Kodiac**[15] 3732 5-9-2 .... (b) GMosse 6 112
(J L Dunlop) *always close up, disputed 4th half-way, ridden & disputing lead 1 1/2f out, ran on at same pace to line* **86/10**

5 3/4 **Quiet Royal (USA)**[105] 1177 3-8-8 .... OPeslier 4 108
(Mme C Head-Maarek, France) *last, shaken up 2f out, ridden & finished well from 1f out, nearest at finish* **10/1**

6 nse **Linngari (IRE)**[134] 742 4-9-2 .... YTake 16 110
(Diego Lowther, France) *mid-division, 7th half-way, ridden over 1f out, ran on steadily to line* **20/1**

7 shd **Eisteddfod**[43] 2846 5-9-2 .... DBoeuf 3 110
(P F I Cole) *held up, 16th half-way, ridden 1 1/2f out, ran on steadily on stands rail, nearest at finish* **21/1**

8 1 1/2 **Ashdown Express (IRE)**[15] 3732 7-9-2 .... AlanMunro 8 105
(C F Wall) *mid-division, disputing close 4th at half-way, driven & ran on 1 1/2f out til no extra final 100y* **48/1**

9 3/4 **Assertive**[5] 4025 3-8-11 .... TThulliez 1 104
(R Hannon) *held up, some headway under pressure from over 1f out* **24/1**

10 nse **Presto Shinko (IRE)**[22] 3564 5-9-2 .... RichardHughes 15 103
(R Hannon) *mid-division, ridden to chase leaders over 1f out, ran on one pace, never dangerous* **21/1**

11 1 1/2 **La Chunga (USA)**[23] 3499 3-8-8 .... ShaneKelly 2 96
(J Noseda) *mid-division, ridden to dispute lead on stands rail 2f out, weakened from 1f out* **39/1**

12 hd **New Girlfriend (IRE)**[63] 2275 3-8-8 .... CSoumillon 5 96
(Robert Collet, France) *tracked leaders in mid-division, disputing close 4th half-way, ridden to challenge 2f out, ran on til weakened final 150y* **58/10**[2]

13 1 **Somnus**[29] 3295 6-9-2 .... TedDurcan 10 95
(T D Easterby) *tracked leaders in mid-division, effort 2f out, no impression* **13/1**

14 nk **Baltic King**[15] 3732 6-9-2 .... JimmyFortune 13 94
(H Morrison) *held up on outside, never a factor* **58/1**

15 snk **Balthazaar's Gift (IRE)**[15] 3732 3-8-11 .... KerrinMcEvoy 11 95
(T R George) *held up on outside, driven 1 1/2f out, never dangerous* **62/10**[3]

16 15 **Biniou (IRE)**[3] 4095 3-8-11 .... TGillet 9 51
(Robert Collet, France) *disputed lead til 2nd half-way, weakened 1 1/2f out* **58/10**[2]

17 10 **Tycoon's Hill (IRE)**[22] 3564 7-9-2 .... JAuge 17 21
(Robert Collet, France) *disputed lead til narrow leader at half-way, ridden & headed 2f out, weakened, eased final f* **58/10**[2]

1m 15.9s **Going Correction** -0.025s/f (Good)
WFA 3 from 4yo+ 4lb **17** Ran SP% **151.4**
Speed ratings: 117,114,114,113,113 113,112,111,110,110 108,108,107,106,106 89,78
PARI-MUTUEL: WIN 14.00; PL 3.50, 1.70, 3.30; DF 28.50.
Owner Mme J-L Giral **Bred** Mme J-L Giral **Trained** France

NOTEBOOK
Marchand D'Or(FR) having been held up early on when towards the tail of the field, moved to the stands' rail over two furlongs out before quickening and taking the lead at the furlong marker. He ultimately drew away impressively in the final stages and the waiting tactics on this occasion paid dividends. This was by far his best effort to date and he will now have the Prix de la Foret as a long-term objective.
Satri(IRE), a well-backed favourite, was outpaced in the early stages but made good progress from the half way stage. He was bought with his run up the middle of the track, yet never looked like pegging back the winner. He looks like another tailor-made for the Foret later in the season.
Amadeus Wolf, fourth in the July Cup last time, was always up with the pace and had his chance. He did not see out the race as well as the front pair, but is running consistently well at present, and will now be aimed at the Betfair Sprint at Haydock in September.
Kodiac made a promising effort and had every possible chance at the furlong marker. He looks to be in the form of his life at present and would take some beating on this form if found an opportunity at Group 3 level again before too long.
Quiet Royal(USA) looked distinctly unlucky, having been hampered several times when looking for a run and finished really well. Having her first run since April, she looks one to bear in mind for the rest of the campaign.
Eisteddfod was running on at the end, having endured a troubled passage, and looks to be coming back to near his best again now. He is likely to be back at Deauville for the Prix de Meautry later in the month.
Ashdown Express(IRE) looked to have an excellent chance of being in the frame as the field passed the furlong marker. However, he was another ultimately one paced towards to the end.
Assertive, third in the Lennox Stakes five days previously, was thereabouts for much of the race but never looked a danger when things warmed up.
Presto Shinko(IRE) did not make much of a show on this occasion and was never seen with a chance of finishing in the frame.
La Chunga(USA) had her limitations exposed and was a spent force by the furlong marker.
Somnus was always mid-division and merely stayed on at the one pace.
Baltic King tried to quicken and join the leaders one and a half out but his effort was short-lived.
Balthazaar's Gift(IRE) was disappointing and made no show. He was well-backed and only one paced when things quickened up.

4192a PRIX DE POMONE (GROUP 2) (F&M) 1m 4f 110y
3:50 (3:56) 3-Y-0+ **£51,103** (£19,724; £9,414; £6,276; £3,138)

RPR

1 **Freedonia**[56] 4-9-4 .... TGillet 5 115
(J E Hammond, France) *s.i.s, held up in rear, 7th straight, stayed near far rail & soon prominent, led 1f out, driven clear, ran on well* **14/1**

2 2 **Montare (IRE)**[23] 3516 4-9-4 .... C-PLemaire 8 112
(J E Pease, France) *broke well, restrained in rear, 8th straight, ridden & hung right over 1f out, ran on well closing stages* **3/1**[1]

3 1 1/2 **Exhibit One (USA)**[63] 2280 4-9-4 .... EBotti 4 110
(V Valiani, Italy) *raced in 3rd, 3rd straight, ridden well over 1f out, kept on under pressure* **20/1**

4 snk **Royal Highness (GER)**[63] 2277 4-9-4 .... TThulliez 1 110
(P Bary, France) *held up, headway & 4th straight, reached 2nd inside final f, one pace last 150y* **3/1**[1]

5 nk **Histoire De Moeurs (FR)**[21] 3-8-6 .... DBoeuf 6 109
(Y De Nicolay, France) *mid-division, 5th straight, disputed 3rd 1f out, ran on steadily* **33/1**

6 2 **Quenched**[15] 3739 3-8-6 .... RichardHughes 3 106
(J H M Gosden) *mid-division, headway to go 2nd well over 3f out, hard ridden 1 1/2f out, gradually weakened* **13/2**[3]

7 1/2 **Time On**[42] 2913 3-8-10 .... OPeslier 9 109
(J L Dunlop) *tracked leader, led over 4f out, headed & weakened 1f out* **3/1**[1]

8 15 **Celebre Vadala (FR)**[60] 2374 3-8-6 .... CSoumillon 7 83
(A Fabre, France) *mid-division, 6th straight, brought wide, soon outpaced, eased* **6/1**[2]

9 20 **Virginia Key (IRE)**[21] 3-8-6 .... DBonilla 2 53
(F Head, France) *led to over 4f out, tailed off* **66/1**

2m 39.2s **Going Correction** -0.40s/f (Firm)
WFA 3 from 4yo 11lb **9** Ran SP% **118.5**
Speed ratings: 107,105,104,104,104 103,103,93,81
PARI-MUTUEL: WIN 10.20; PL 2.70, 1.70, 6.80; DF 17.70.
Owner Niarchos Family **Bred** The Niarchos Family **Trained** France

NOTEBOOK
Freedonia posted much-improved form and dominated the final stages of this Group 2 event. She was for a long time at the tail of the field but moved up in the straight to challenge at the furlong and a half marker. She quickened impressively and ultimately looked in a class of her own on this occasion. Injury kept her off the track last year, but she has always been rated by her trainer, who is now looking at the Prix Vermeille.
Montare(IRE) was bought with a run up the centre of the track and she put in her best work at the finish. She held her head high when challenging and may be fitted with cheek pieces next time to keep her mind on the job. She is entered in the Yorkshire Oaks, but could also be another for the Vermeille.
Exhibit One(USA) was always well placed, and battled well throughout the straight, but could only find the one pace inside the final furlong.
Royal Highness(GER) came with a promising run two out but could not fully go through with her effort. This outing will have brought her on nicely as she had been off the track for two months.
Quenched attempted to take the lead half way up the straight, but was dominated soon after. This was still arguably an improved effort in defeat.
Time On took over the lead coming out of the final turn. She kept up the good work until one and a half out and then gradually dropped out of contention. This filly is at her best when able to dominate.

4066 CARLISLE (R-H)
Monday, August 7
OFFICIAL GOING: Good to firm (good in places)
The second meeting within a week where it proved an advantage to be racing up with the pace.
Wind: Light, across

4194 DOBIES VAUXHALL LADY AMATEUR RIDERS' H'CAP 7f 200y
6:10 (6:11) (Class 5) (0-70,70) 3-Y-0+ **£3,123** (£968; £484; £242) **Stalls** High

Form RPR

0004 **1** **Uhuru Peak**[17] 3697 5-9-5 **51** oh1 .... (bt) MissSBrotherton 8 62
(M W Easterby) *keen: chsd ldrs: led stands rail over 2f out: styd on strly* **9/2**[2]

5032 **2** 2 **Able Mind**[13] 3815 6-9-0 **51** oh5 .... MissHCuthbert(5) 11 57
(D W Thompson) *hld up: smooth hdwy centre over 2f out: chsd wnr over 1f out: edgd rt: kpt on same pce fnl f* **4/1**[1]

6056 **3** 3 1/2 **True Night**[4] 4090 9-10-2 **69** .... MissERamstrom(7) 7 67
(D Nicholls) *keen: led to over 2f out: nt qckn over 1f out* **13/2**

1003 **4** nk **Scotty's Future (IRE)**[4] 4068 8-9-13 **59** .... MrsCBartley 2 57
(A Berry) *s.i.s: sn outpcd: styd far side w one other and hdwy 3f out: no imp over 1f out* **6/1**[3]

6500 **5** 3 **Son Of Thunder (IRE)**[13] 3815 5-8-12 **51** .... (v) MissTMasefield(7) 1 42
(M Dods) *keen: prom on outside: effrt stands rail over 2f out: btn over 1f out* **7/1**

0010 **6** 1 3/4 **Legal Dram**[14] 3786 5-9-0 **51** oh3 .... MissKellyBurke(5) 4 38
(M Dods) *midfield: effrt over 2f out: btn over 1f out* **12/1**

-532 **7** hd **Gifted Flame**[35] 3147 7-10-10 **70** .... MissADeniel 9 56
(J J Quinn) *missed break: bhd: hdwy and in tch 3f out: rdn and wknd over 1f out* **4/1**[1]

4000 **8** 3/4 **King Nicholas (USA)**[9] 3944 7-9-5 **51** oh14 .... (bt) MissLEllison 12 36
(J Parkes) *in tch tl wknd over 2f out* **100/1**

0-00 **9** 4 **Wahchi (IRE)**[6] 4021 7-9-9 **62** ow2 .... MissJCoward(7) 5 37
(M W Easterby) *hld up: rdn over 3f out: n.d* **33/1**

6000 **10** 50 **Annals**[7] 3353 4-9-0 **51** oh13 .... (v) MissJRiding(5) 6 —
(R C Guest) *chsd ldrs: styd far side w one other ent st: wknd qckly: t.o* **100/1**

1m 39.44s (-0.65) **Going Correction** 0.0s/f (Good) **10** Ran SP% **110.9**
Speed ratings (Par 103): 103,101,97,97,94 92,92,91,87,37
CSF £21.41 CT £109.79 TOTE £5.90: £1.80, £1.50, £2.90; EX 30.30.
Owner K Hodgson & Mrs J Hodgson **Bred** M W Easterby And K Hodgson **Trained** Sheriff Hutton, N Yorks

FOCUS
An ordinary event in which the pace was sound and the bulk of the runners came centre to stands' side. The form is somewhat messy.

4195 BEADLE AND HILL CLAIMING STKS 1m 1f 61y
6:40 (6:44) (Class 6) 3-Y-O £2,730 (£806; £403) Stalls High

Form RPR

4000 1 **Lewis Lloyd (IRE)**[11] 3870 3-8-12 42 PaulHanagan 10 52
(I A Wood) *cl up: led after 3f: mde rest: c to stands side w rest of field and kicked clr over 2f out: hld on wl fnl f* **9/1**

0451 2 nk **Mister Maq**[10] 3910 3-8-12 61 (b) PaulFessey 8 51
(M Dods) *hld up: hdwy 4f out: effrt and chsd wnr over 1f out: edgd rt: kpt on ins fnl f* **7/4**[1]

6506 3 1 3/4 **Makai**[10] 3914 3-8-11 65 StanleyChin 5 47
(M Johnston) *prom: effrt 3f out: edgd rt: no ex over 1f out* **5/2**[2]

4554 4 1 1/4 **Elite Land**[10] 3910 3-8-3 45 SuzzanneFrance(7) 7 43
(N Bycroft) *bhd tl hdwy centre 2f out: nvr rchd ldrs* **8/1**[3]

-406 5 12 **Stanley Bay (IRE)**[10] 3910 3-8-6 50 ow1 DavidAllan 6 15
(T D Easterby) *prom: outpcd 1/2-way: rallied 2f out: no imp* **8/1**[3]

5035 6 8 **Coronation Flight**[14] 3785 3-8-2 40 AndrewMullen(5) 2 —
(F P Murtagh) *bhd tl hdwy 2f out: nvr rchd ldrs* **11/1**

5000 7 3/4 **Boumsong (IRE)**[30] 3288 3-8-5 36 (e[1]) PaulEddery 9 —
(R C Guest) *keen early: cl up: carried lft bnd after 1f: wknd fr over 3f out* **40/1**

-000 8 1 **Arisea (IRE)**[81] 1792 3-8-0 40 (v) JamieMackay 1 —
(R C Guest) *chsd ldrs tl wknd over 3f out* **50/1**

005 9 12 **Smoke It (IRE)**[37] 3066 3-8-12 35 FrancisNorton 4 —
(A Berry) *bhd: rdn over 4f out: nvr on terms* **66/1**

0 10 1 **Westcourt Phoenix**[31] 3261 3-8-7 PaulMulrennan 3 —
(M W Easterby) *uns rdr and loose bef s: a bhd* **80/1**

0-00 11 15 **Flick N Flack**[30] 3288 3-8-9 33 GylesParkin 11 —
(D W Thompson) *keen: led: hung lft bnd after 1f: hdd after 3f: wknd over 3f out* **100/1**

1m 57.3s (-0.26) **Going Correction** 0.0s/f (Good) 11 Ran SP% **113.6**
Speed ratings (Par 98):101,100,99,98,87 80,79,78,68,67 53
CSF £24.11 TOTE £11.90: £3.30, £1.10, £1.60; EX 39.00.
Owner Brian Morton **Bred** Brian Delahunt **Trained** Upper Lambourn, Berks
■ Stewards' Enquiry : Paul Fessey two-day ban: used whip with excessive frequency (Aug 18-19)

FOCUS
A modest event in which the pace was sound and the form is rated through the winner, and the field again came centre to stands' side in the straight.
Flick N Flack Official explanation: jockey said gelding hung left throughout

4196 WBX.COM WORLD BET EXCHANGE MAIDEN AUCTION STKS 5f
7:10 (7:12) (Class 5) 2-Y-O £3,238 (£963; £481; £240) Stalls High

Form RPR

3452 1 **Josr's Magic (IRE)**[12] 3834 2-8-11 74 (b) RoystonFfrench 9 69
(Mrs A Duffield) *chsd ldrs: rdn to ld appr fnl f: edgd rt: hld on wl* **5/4**[1]

0 2 1/2 **Princess Ellis**[8] 3982 2-8-4 FrancisNorton 2 60
(E J Alston) *led: rdn stands rail 2f out: hdd appr fnl f: kpt on fnl f: hld nr fin* **28/1**

0 3 2 1/2 **Lafontaine Bleu**[10] 3907 2-8-5 PaulHanagan 3 52
(R A Fahey) *in tch: rdn 1/2-way: kpt on fnl f: no imp* **20/1**

4 1 3/4 **Arena's Dream (USA)** 2-8-11 TonyHamilton 10 52
(R A Fahey) *missed break: outpcd tl hdwy over 1f out: nrst fin* **25/1**

000 5 hd **Silly Gilly (IRE)**[4] 4066 2-8-4 PaulQuinn 5 44
(A Berry) *bhd and outpcd: hdwy fnl f: n.d* **66/1**

6 1 1/4 **Inspainagain (USA)** 2-8-10 PaulFessey 1 46
(T D Barron) *dwlt: sn in tch: rdn and wknd over 1f out* **12/1**

5403 7 1 1/2 **Pernomente (IRE)**[10] 3907 2-8-10 75 (t) LPKeniry 6 40
(J S Moore) *disp ld: rdn and edgd rt over 1f out: wknd fnl f* **7/4**[2]

6530 8 hd **Wanchai Night**[8] 3982 2-8-13 65 DavidAllan 7 43
(T D Easterby) *towards rr: drvn 1/2-way: n.d* **10/1**[3]

9 1 3/4 **Uace Mac** 2-7-11 SuzzanneFrance(7) 8 27
(N Bycroft) *s.i.s: a bhd* **25/1**

61.01 secs (-0.49) **Going Correction** -0.175s/f (Firm) 9 Ran SP% **115.0**
Speed ratings (Par 94):96,95,91,88,88 86,83,83,80
CSF £46.36 TOTE £2.00: £1.10, £4.10, £2.90; EX 55.40.
Owner Jon Carter **Bred** Bryan Ryan **Trained** Constable Burton, N Yorks

FOCUS
A race that took little winning with the second favourite disappointing and one in which the majority again raced centre to stands' side.

NOTEBOOK
Josr's Magic(IRE), with the blinkers on again, was not inconvenienced by the drop in trip at this stiff course and did not have to improve to get off the mark. He will not mind the return to further and, although this was not a competitive event, should continue to give a good account. (op 6-4)
Princess Ellis, soundly beaten on her debut at Pontefract just over a week ago, turned in a much-improved effort and, although having the run of the race against the stands' rail, showed a decent attitude and looks capable of winning a small event. (op 25-1)
Lafontaine Bleu, another well beaten on her debut in recent times, turned in a much-improved display. She should have no problems with an extra furlong and appeals the type to win in modest handicap company in due course. (tchd 25-1)
Arena's Dream(USA), a half-brother to three winners in the US, looked in need of the race but hinted at ability in this modest event on his racecourse debut. He will be suited by the step up to six furlongs plus and may be capable of winning a small contest. (op 22-1 tchd 20-1)
Silly Gilly(IRE) turned in her best effort to date but, while shaping as though a much stiffer test of stamina would have suited, she is likely to continue to look vulnerable in this type of event.
Inspainagain(USA) proved easy to back and, although ultimately well beaten, showed up for a long way. He is in good hands and is likely to leave this bare form behind in due course. (tchd 11-1)
Pernomente(IRE), whose best efforts have been on sharp courses when the emphasis has been on speed, dropped out very tamely having travelled well for a long way. He has had plenty of chances and, although the return to a quicker track will suit, he is likely to remain vulnerable in this type of event. (op 15-8 tchd 2-1)

4197 WBX.COM WORLD BET EXCHANGE H'CAP 1m 3f 107y
7:40 (7:40) (Class 4) (0-80,80) 3-Y-O £6,477 (£1,927; £963; £481) Stalls Low

Form RPR

0644 1 **Regal Connection (USA)**[14] 3784 3-8-5 64 (b) JoeFanning 8 75
(M Johnston) *mde all: styd centre ent st: hld on gamely fnl f* **10/1**

2232 2 hd **Kerriemuir Lass (IRE)**[8] 3977 3-9-0 73 PhilipRobinson 3 84
(M A Jarvis) *keen: chsd wnr: c stands rail and ev ch over 2f out: kpt on wl fnl f: jst hld* **7/2**[2]

1211 3 2 **Bauer (IRE)**[24] 3502 3-9-7 80 NickyMackay 7 87+
(L M Cumani) *chsd ldrs: sddle slipped forward 1/2-way but wnt bk over 3f out: effrt over 2f out: one pce appr fnl f* **4/7**[1]

5213 4 11 **Mull Of Dubai**[21] 3589 3-8-6 65 LPKeniry 4 55
(J S Moore) *hld up: effrt 4f out: outpcd fr 3f out* **8/1**[3]

-542 5 shd **Moonhawk**[69] 2111 3-8-11 70 TomEaves 1 60
(J Howard Johnson) *chsd ldrs tl edgd rt and wknd over 2f out* **20/1**

200 6 5 **Stolen Glance**[45] 2809 3-8-9 68 PaulMulrennan 5 50
(M W Easterby) *hld up: rdn over 4f out: sn btn* **33/1**

2m 22.46s (-5.54) **Going Correction** 0.0s/f (Good) 6 Ran SP% **113.8**
Speed ratings (Par 102):101,100,99,91,91 87
CSF £45.17 CT £51.87 TOTE £8.80: £2.90, £2.00; EX 33.30.
Owner Claire Riordan And Kieran Coughlan **Bred** Lantern Hill Farm Llc **Trained** Middleham Moor, N Yorks

FOCUS
A fair handicap but not the most competitive of races and just an ordinary pace, although the form appears solid enough. The first three remained pretty much in that order throughout and the field again came centre to stands' side in the straight.

4198 DOBIES VAUXHALL H'CAP 6f 192y
8:10 (8:11) (Class 6) (0-60,58) 3-Y-O+ £2,730 (£806; £403) Stalls High

Form RPR

0455 1 **Ayam Jantan**[49] 2698 3-9-4 54 JoeFanning 13 63
(M Johnston) *w ldr: led 1/2-way: styd on strly in centre fr 2f out* **14/1**

0322 2 1/2 **Sedge (USA)**[13] 3817 6-9-9 58 (p) RoryMoore(5) 14 68
(P T Midgley) *hld up in tch: effrt over 2f out: kpt on fnl f: hld towards fin* **11/4**[1]

0502 3 shd **Royal Pardon**[4] 4070 4-9-0 44 (v) PaulEddery 11 53
(R C Guest) *s.i.s: bhd tl hdwy 2f out: kpt on fnl f: no ex towards fin* **7/1**

3406 4 1 1/4 **Attacca**[14] 3786 5-9-9 53 PhilipRobinson 4 59
(J R Weymes) *trckd ldrs: effrt over 1f out: kpt on same pce ins fnl f* **5/1**[2]

0506 5 3/4 **Peters Delite**[9] 3947 4-9-6 50 PaulHanagan 10 54
(R A Fahey) *sn towards rr: drvn 1/2-way: no imp tl hdwy appr fnl f: nrst fin* **12/1**

-230 6 1 1/4 **Riverhill (IRE)**[26] 3398 3-9-5 55 TomEaves 15 54
(J Howard Johnson) *towards rr: drvn 1/2-way: hdwy 2f out: no imp ins fnl f* **25/1**

0046 7 3 **Outrageous Flirt (IRE)**[2] 4157 4-9-6 50 RobertWinston 8 43
(A Dickman) *in tch tl rdn and outpcd fr 2f out* **13/2**[3]

4550 8 1/2 **Eternal Legacy (IRE)**[27] 3379 4-9-6 50 DavidAllan 3 42
(J Parkes) *bhd tl hdwy over 1f out: nvr rchd ldrs* **33/1**

2104 9 1 **Gem Bien (USA)**[10] 3914 8-9-5 49 (p) PaulQuinn 9 38
(D W Chapman) *s.i.s: bhd: hdwy far rail over 2f out: sn no imp* **16/1**

0460 10 nk **El Rey Royale**[13] 3815 4-8-10 45 GregFairley(5) 12 33
(Micky Hammond) *chsd ldrs tl wknd over 2f out* **16/1**

00-0 11 1 1/4 **Shinko Femme (IRE)**[4] 4067 5-8-5 42 JamesO'Reilly(7) 2 27
(J O'Reilly) *dwlt: rdn towards stands side over 2f out: nvr on terms* **40/1**

0130 12 nk **Bodden Bay**[18] 3682 4-9-12 56 DanielTudhope 6 40
(D Carroll) *keen: prom: rdn and hung lft 2f out: sn btn* **10/1**

4660 13 1/2 **Desertina (IRE)**[47] 2758 4-8-8 43 MichaelJStainton(5) 5 26
(R M Whitaker) *towards rr: drvn 1/2-way: sn btn* **16/1**

0-05 14 2 1/2 **Compton Bay**[10] 3909 6-9-1 45 DeanMcKeown 7 21
(M Brittain) *slt ld to 1/2-way: wknd over 2f out* **100/1**

55-0 15 hd **Zafarilla (IRE)**[20] 3614 3-8-8 49 EmmettStack(5) 1 23
(Pat Eddery) *midfield: rdn and hung to stands rail over 2f out: sn btn* **25/1**

1m 27.02s (-0.08) **Going Correction** 0.0s/f (Good)
WFA 3 from 4yo+ 6lb 15 Ran SP% **124.3**
Speed ratings (Par 101):100,99,99,97,97 95,92,91,90,90 88,88,87,84,84
CSF £51.56 CT £267.21 TOTE £11.60: £4.20, £1.30, £2.70; EX 53.40.
Owner Mrs I Bird **Bred** M P B Bloodstock Ltd **Trained** Middleham Moor, N Yorks
■ Stewards' Enquiry : Rory Moore four-day ban: used whip with excessive frequency (Aug 18-21)
Paul Eddery one-day ban: used whip with excessive frequency (Aug 18)

FOCUS
An ordinary event in which the pace was sound but it paid to race prominently. The form looks sound enough rated around the winner and fourth and the field fanned across the course in the home straight.

4199 CARLING H'CAP 5f 193y
8:40 (8:41) (Class 6) (0-60,60) 3-Y-O £2,730 (£806; £403) Stalls High

Form RPR

2030 1 **Markestino**[14] 3785 3-8-8 47 DavidAllan 17 54
(T D Easterby) *cl up: led 1/2-way: rdn and hld on gamely fnl f* **25/1**

0000 2 nk **Megalo Maniac**[21] 3586 3-8-4 43 PaulHanagan 3 49
(R A Fahey) *in tch: rdn over 2f out: ev ch fnl f: hld towards fin* **25/1**

006 3 2 **Littledodayno (IRE)**[22] 3569 3-9-6 59 JamieMackay 12 62+
(M Wigham) *prom: n.m.r and lost pl after 2f: rallied 2f out: kpt on same pce fnl f* **11/4**[2]

-605 4 hd **Gifted Glori**[13] 3814 3-8-4 43 RoystonFfrench 14 42
(J J Quinn) *blkd s: chsd ldrs: rdn over 2f out: one pce over 1f out* **25/1**

4200 5 1 1/4 **Artie's Son (IRE)**[4] 4069 3-9-6 59 GrahamGibbons 9 54
(T D Easterby) *sn towards rr: hdwy over 1f out: nrst fin* **16/1**

5042 6 nk **Suhezy (IRE)**[21] 3582 3-8-9 48 TonyHamilton 16 42
(J S Wainwright) *led to 1/2-way: one pce fr 2f out* **9/1**

5310 7 1/2 **Desert Hunter (IRE)**[13] 3814 3-8-13 52 DeanMcKeown 2 45
(Micky Hammond) *bhd: drvn 1/2-way: effrt 2f out: nvr rchd ldrs* **12/1**

5102 8 1 **Boy Dancer (IRE)**[4] 4071 3-9-2 60 MarkLawson(5) 5 50
(D W Barker) *towards rr: drvn and effrt over 2f out: nvr rchd ldrs* **9/4**[1]

005 9 1 **Mister Jingles**[38] 3050 3-8-3 47 MichaelJStainton(5) 7 34
(R M Whitaker) *chsd ldrs tl rdn and outpcd fr 2f out* **25/1**

0-05 10 3/4 **Heads Turn (IRE)**[21] 3582 3-8-3 42 FrancisNorton 11 27
(E J Alston) *towards rr: drvn 1/2-way: n.d* **33/1**

0000 11 1/2 **Rainbow Prince**[48] 2734 3-8-7 46 DanielTudhope 15 29
(A Dickman) *bmpd s: hdwy and prom 1/2-way: hung rt over 1f out: sn wknd* **40/1**

-000 12 1 1/4 **Sprouston (FR)**[11] 3869 3-8-11 50 (p) LPKeniry 6 29
(J S Moore) *bhd: drvn 1/2-way: nvr on terms* **14/1**

4-01 13 1 **Fen Guest**[10] 3916 3-9-5 58 RobertWinston 8 34
(Rae Guest) *chsd ldrs: drvn 1/2-way: wknd wl over 1f out* **8/1**[3]

0000 14 8 **Trumpita**[23] 3538 3-8-4 43 PaulQuinn 10 —
(T D Easterby) *dwlt: sn prom: rdn and wknd fr 2f out* **50/1**

650 15 3 1/2 **Eurana**[30] 3288 3-8-3 42 oh2 ow1 JoeFanning 13 —
(Jedd O'Keeffe) *stmbld and wnt rt s: sn t.o* **20/1**

00-0 16 13 **Beverley Hills (IRE)**[47] 2763 3-8-8 47 oh2 ow6 TomEaves 1 —
(J Howard Johnson) *bhd: drvn 1/2-way: edgd rt and sn wknd* **66/1**

1m 13.1s (-0.51) **Going Correction** -0.175s/f (Firm) 16 Ran SP% **127.8**
Speed ratings (Par 98):96,95,92,92,91 90,89,88,87,86 85,83,82,71,67 49
CSF £531.16 CT £2366.18 TOTE £26.90: £3.60, £7.50, £1.30, £4.20; EX 596.20 Place 6 £1,278.21, Place 5 £230.69.
Owner Mrs Jennifer E Pallister **Bred** Deerfield Farm **Trained** Great Habton, N Yorks
■ Stewards' Enquiry : Paul Hanagan three-day ban: used whip with excessive frequency (Aug 19-21)

FOCUS
Another run-of-the-mill handicap in which the pace was sound and the field again fanned nearly the width of the track in the home straight. The form is weak rated through the fourth.
Markestino ◆ Official explanation: trainer said, regarding the improved form shown, gelding was suited by the drop back in trip
Fen Guest Official explanation: jockey said filly ran too free
Eurana Official explanation: jockey said filly stumbled leaving stalls
T/Plt: £90.80 to a £1 stake. Pool: £63,506.00. 510.15 winning tickets. T/Qpdt: £37.80 to a £1 stake. Pool: £3,408.70. 66.70 winning tickets. RY

3745 RIPON (R-H)

Monday, August 7

OFFICIAL GOING: Good (good to soft in places)
Wind: Virtually nil

4200 BBC RADIO YORK 103.7FM & 104.3FM EBF NOVICE STKS — 6f
2:20 (2:20) (Class 5) 2-Y-O — **£4,533** (£1,348; £674; £336) **Stalls** Low

Form — RPR
1 **1** **Big Timer (USA)**[21] 3581 2-9-10 .... TomEaves 1 — 102+
(I Semple) *trckd ldrs gng wl: hdwy on bit 2f out: squeezed through to ld ent last: qcknd clr* **7/1**
41 **2** *4* **Fool Me (IRE)**[100] 1284 2-9-7 87 .... RichardMullen 4 — 87
(E S McMahon) *cl up: rdn along 2f out: ev ch whn edgd lft entering last: sn drvn and one pce* **20/1**
41 **3** *½* **Fish Called Johnny**[3] 4109 2-9-7 .... KDarley 2 — 86
(B J Meehan) *led: rdn along wl over 1f out: hdd ent last: sn drvn and one pce* **2/1**[2]
1 **4** *3 ½* **Codeword (IRE)**[23] 3553 2-9-10 .... JoeFanning 5 — 78
(M Johnston) *cl up: on outer: rdn along 2f out: drvn and wknd appr last* **6/4**[1]
414 **5** *½* **Top Bid**[25] 3445 2-9-7 92 .... DavidAllan 3 — 74
(T D Easterby) *keen: cl up tl n.m.r and checked after 1 1/2f: rdn along 1/2-way and sn btn* **5/1**[3]

1m 14.4s (1.40) **Going Correction** +0.20s/f (Good) — **5** Ran SP% **107.3**
Speed ratings (Par 94):98,92,92,87,86
CSF £89.73 TOTE £7.50: £2.40, £5.80; EX 66.10.
Owner David McKenzie **Bred** Mt Brilliant Farm Llc **Trained** Carluke, S Lanarks
■ Stewards' Enquiry : Tom Eaves two-day ban: careless riding (Aug 18-19)

FOCUS
A good little novice stakes won in impressive fashion by Big Timer.

NOTEBOOK
Big Timer(USA), an impressive winner on his debut at Ayr, travelled strongly before coming away, looked to face no easy task in this better contest, but he again travelled in the style of a good horse and quickened smartly once getting the gap. His trainer has clearly got a smart prospect on his hands and he fully deserves to take his chance in a better class of contest, with next month's Mill Reef looking the likeliest target. (op 8-1 tchd 6-1)
Fool Me(IRE), a winner at the second attempt at Leicester back in April, had been off since and his price of 20/1 looked about right. He ran above those odds however, holding a prominent position throughout and keeping on well to hold second. He has clearly progressed and remains open to a little further improvement.
Fish Called Johnny, an all-the-way winner at Nottingham three days previously, again attempted to make all, but he was found out in this better race and could only plug on for third. It is possible the race came too soon though, and as a result he can be given another chance, with a move into nurseries likely to see him in a better light. (op 9-4 tchd 5-2)
Codeword(IRE), who overcame inexperience to make a winning debut at York, looked the likeliest winner with his trainer's juveniles going well, and the fact he had been switched from the Jumeriah Racing colours to the Sheikh Mohammed silks was a good sign. Drawn on the outside though, he could never quite get settled into the race and was struggling to keep up from halfway. (op 10-11)
Top Bidlooked likely to be thereabouts, but he was never really going having been checked after almost two furlongs and can probably be granted another chance. (op 8-1 tchd 9-2)

4201 RBS INVOICE FINANCE (S) H'CAP — 5f
2:50 (2:51) (Class 6) (0-65,60) 3-Y-O — **£2,590** (£770; £385; £192) **Stalls** Low

Form — RPR
0-20 **1** **Epineuse**[28] 3348 3-8-9 48 .... MartinDwyer 1 — 53
(J R Best) *trckd ldrs stands side: swtchd rt and hdwy wl over 1f out: rdn to ld ins last: hung rt and kpt on wl* **10/1**
2460 **2** *hd* **Slipperfoot**[5] 4056 3-9-2 55 .... (v[1]) GrahamGibbons 9 — 59
(J J Quinn) *led far side gp: rdn wl over 1f out: drvn and ev ch whn hung lft wl ins last: nt qckn towards fin* **8/1**
0005 **3** *nk* **She's Our Beauty (IRE)**[5] 4056 3-8-13 52 .... (v) AdrianTNicholls 2 — 55
(D Nicholls) *overall ldr stands side: rdn wl over 1f out: drvn and hdd ins last: kpt on* **14/1**
-000 **4** *1* **Martharum**[15] 3759 3-8-2 41 oh1 .... (p) JimmyQuinn 11 — 40
(J J Quinn) *cl up far side: rdn and ev ch over 1f out tl drvn and one pce ins last* **25/1**
-043 **5** *1* **Turn Me On (IRE)**[11] 3867 3-9-5 58 .... (t) HayleyTurner 12 — 54
(M L W Bell) *chsd ldng pair far side: rdn along 2f out: sn drvn and edgd lft: kpt on same pce* **6/1**[3]
6600 **6** *1 ½* **First Among Equals**[30] 3306 3-8-6 45 .... PaulFitzsimons 5 — 35+
(Miss J R Tooth) *dwlt and hmpd s: bhd stands side tl hdwy 2f out: sn rdn and no imp appr last* **25/1**
0631 **7** *nk* **Miss Mujahid Times**[31] 3257 3-8-7 46 .... (b) SilvestreDeSousa 3 — 35
(A D Brown) *chsd ldr stands side: rdn along 2f out: grad wknd* **5/1**[2]
-003 **8** *1 ½* **Sweetly Sharp (IRE)**[81] 1791 3-8-4 43 .... PaulHanagan 8 — 27
(A Berry) *in tch stands side: rdn along over 2f out: n.d* **15/2**
160 **9** *¾* **Mullady Penelope**[20] 3608 3-9-5 58 .... RoystonFfrench 4 — 39
(Mrs A Duffield) *chsd ldrs stands side: rdn along over 2f out: sn wknd* **4/1**[1]
0050 **10** *hd* **Nautico**[13] 3814 3-8-0 44 oh1 ow3 .... (b) AndrewMullen[(5)] 6 — 24
(Miss L A Perratt) *a towards rr stands side* **25/1**
-000 **11** *1 ½* **Maayafushi**[26] 3397 3-8-2 41 .... DaleGibson 14 — 16
(Micky Hammond) *a rr far side* **66/1**
436 **12** *hd* **Spirit Of Coniston**[11] 3864 3-9-7 60 .... (b) RobbieFitzpatrick 7 — 34
(Peter Grayson) *chsd ldrs stands side: rdn along over 2f out: sn wknd* **5/1**[2]

61.37 secs (1.17) **Going Correction** +0.20s/f (Good) — **12** Ran SP% **119.3**
Speed ratings (Par 98):98,97,97,95,94 91,91,88,87,87 84,84
CSF £84.88 CT £1148.14 TOTE £11.40: £2.90, £2.30, £4.20; EX 55.00 Trifecta £335.40 Part won. Pool: £472.40 - 0.34 winning units..There was no bid for the winner. Turn Me On was claimed by Timothy Walford for £6,000.
Owner Dr A N Howard **Bred** R W Huggins **Trained** Hucking, Kent
■ Stewards' Enquiry : Jimmy Quinn one-day ban: failed to keep straight from the stalls (Aug 18)
Graham Gibbons one-day ban: failed to keep straight from the stalls (Aug 18); two-day ban: used whip with excessive force (Aug 19-20); caution: careless riding

FOCUS
A moderate handicap and there was not a great deal of difference in the draw. The time was modest and the form is not solid.
Turn Me On(IRE) Official explanation: jockey said gelding hung left
Spirit Of Coniston Official explanation: jockey said colt hung left

4202 ARMSTRONG MEMORIAL H'CAP — 6f
3:20 (3:21) (Class 3) (0-95,94) 3-Y-O+
£11,217 (£3,358; £1,679; £840; £419; £210) **Stalls** Low

Form — RPR
2006 **1** **Rising Shadow (IRE)**[24] 3471 5-9-6 87 .... PaulFessey 6 — 98+
(T D Barron) *in tch stands side: hdwy wl over 1f out: rdn ins last: kpt on to ld on line* **15/2**[3]
00-5 **2** *shd* **Rainbow Rising (IRE)**[72] 2017 4-9-0 81 .... TomEaves 4 — 92
(J Howard Johnson) *cl up stands side: led that gp and overall ldr wl over 1f out: rdn ent last: snd drvn: hdd and no ex nr line* **20/1**
3214 **3** *1 ¼* **Knot In Wood (IRE)**[9] 3956 4-9-1 82 .... PaulHanagan 13 — 89
(R A Fahey) *led far side gp: hdd over 2f out: rdn wl over 1f out: styd on ins last* **4/1**[2]
5352 **4** *shd* **Ice Planet**[9] 3956 5-9-9 90 .... RobertWinston 8 — 97
(D Nicholls) *chsd ldrs stands side: rdn along wl over 1f out: kpt on same pce ent last* **3/1**[1]
5051 **5** *½* **Fullandby (IRE)**[10] 3904 4-9-5 86 .... NickyMackay 7 — 91
(T J Etherington) *towards rr stands side: swtchd rt and hdwy over 2f out: rdn over 1f out: kpt on ins last* **9/1**
6000 **6** *1 ¾* **Josh**[80] 1835 4-9-7 88 .... NCallan 9 — 88
(K A Ryan) *cl up far side: hdwy to ld that gp over 2f out: rdn and ev ch over 1f out: wknd ins last* **16/1**
1000 **7** *1* **Zomerlust**[24] 3482 4-9-11 92 .... GrahamGibbons 12 — 89
(J J Quinn) *in tch far side: hdwy 2f out: sn rdn and kpt on same pce ent last* **11/1**
0000 **8** *nk* **Prince Tum Tum (USA)**[22] 3567 6-8-10 77 .... JimmyQuinn 11 — 73
(D W Barker) *hld up far side: hdwy 2f out: rdn ent last: wknd* **33/1**
3205 **9** *1 ¼* **King's Gait**[81] 1803 4-9-13 94 .... (b) RichardMullen 3 — 87
(T D Easterby) *dwlt and hmpd s: a rr stands side* **22/1**
0160 **10** *1 ¼* **Johnston's Diamond (IRE)**[37] 3077 8-9-2 83 .... FrancisNorton 2 — 72
(E J Alston) *wnt rt s: sn overall ldr stands side: rdn along 2f out: sn hdd & wknd* **16/1**
03/3 **11** *shd* **Crimson Silk**[110] 1076 6-9-8 89 .... PaulEddery 14 — 78+
(B Smart) *prom far side: rdn along over 2f out: sn wknd* **20/1**
-340 **12** *2 ½* **Game Lad**[72] 2012 4-9-10 91 .... KDarley 1 — 72
(T D Easterby) *in tch stands side: rdn along 1/2-way: sn wknd* **8/1**
-160 **13** *6* **Dazzling Bay**[9] 3956 6-9-9 90 .... (b) DavidAllan 5 — 53
(T D Easterby) *chsd ldrs stands side: rdn along 1/2-way: sn wknd* **33/1**

1m 13.04s (0.04) **Going Correction** +0.20s/f (Good) — **13** Ran SP% **117.7**
Speed ratings (Par 107):107,106,105,105,104 102,100,100,98,97 96,93,85
CSF £153.42 CT £709.79 TOTE £9.00: £3.10, £8.40, £1.60; EX 160.00 TRIFECTA Not won..
Owner G Morrill **Bred** 6c Stallions Ltd **Trained** Maunby, N Yorks
■ Stewards' Enquiry : Paul Eddery one-day ban: failed to keep straight from the stalls (Aug 30)
Paul Hanagan one-day ban: failed to keep straight from the stalls (Aug 18)

FOCUS
A competitive sprint handicap in which those who raced on the stands' side emerged on top. The form is good for the grade, backed up by a decent time, with the first two to form.

NOTEBOOK
Rising Shadow(IRE) has been a bit below par of late, mainly on firm ground, but the slight ease in the ground enabled him to return to his best and he rallied strongly to get up in the final stride. A very useful sort when conditions are in his favour, he will need to progress to defy a higher mark, but that is possible and he should continue to pay his way. (op 8-1)
Rainbow Rising(IRE) claimed the scalp of group-class sprinter Reverence when winning his maiden at Thirsk last year, but he had been off since reappearing over seven furlongs in May and looked to have a bit to prove. He allayed those fears though with a smashing effort, looking the winner entering the final furlong, only to be nailed late on. He is probably on a fair mark now and is capable of winning a similar race. (op 16-1)
Knot In Wood(IRE) has been in really good form of late, albeit winning just once, and he came out best of the far-side group, leading throughout and keeping on well but finding himself a little behind the stands' side. (tchd 9-2)
Ice Planet is a pretty consistent sort who often runs his race and this was another good effort, but he continues to find winning hard and is likely to remain vulnerable. (tchd 11-4)
Fullandby(IRE), up 3lb for last month's Newmarket win, came with his challenge more towards the centre of the track, but was never quite getting on terms and may have benefited from being ridden more positively. (op 17-2 tchd 10-1)
Josh has been struggling for form, but this was better and he is on a mark now that should enable him to win. He likes a bit of cut in the ground and is one to keep on-side. (tchd 20-1 in places)
Dazzling Bay Official explanation: trainer said gelding bled from the nose

4203 WEATHERBYS INSURANCE H'CAP — 1m 1f 170y
3:50 (3:51) (Class 4) (0-85,82) 3-Y-O+ **£6,309** (£1,888; £944; £472; £235) **Stalls** High

Form — RPR
2311 **1** **Nelsons Column (IRE)**[16] 3747 3-9-4 81 .... PaulMulrennan 2 — 94
(G M Moore) *mde all: rdn and qcknd 2f out: styd on strly* **4/1**[1]
343 **2** *2* **My Arch**[28] 3362 4-9-7 75 .... NCallan 9 — 84
(K A Ryan) *hld up: hdwy on inner and pushed along 3f out: swtchd lft over 2f out: rdn to chse wnr ent last: sn drvn and no imp* **9/1**
6124 **3** *2 ½* **Magic Sting**[6] 4023 5-10-0 82 .... HayleyTurner 7 — 86
(M L W Bell) *dwlt and hld up in rr: gd hdwy on outer over 3f out: chsd wnr 2f out: sn rdn and kpt on same pce appr last* **4/1**[1]
2136 **4** *¾* **Trouble Mountain (USA)**[22] 3566 9-9-1 69 .... (t) DaleGibson 1 — 72
(M W Easterby) *hld up in rr: hdwy 3f out: rdn over 2f out: swtchd lft over 1f out and styd on wl fnl f: nrst fin* **12/1**
-045 **5** *nk* **Torrens (IRE)**[55] 2519 4-9-11 79 .... PaulHanagan 6 — 81
(R A Fahey) *hld up in midfield: hdwy 3f out: rdn along to chse ldrs wl over 1f out: wknd appr last* **13/2**
0541 **6** *hd* **Chief Scout**[34] 3168 4-9-9 77 .... TomEaves 10 — 79
(I Semple) *chsd ldrs on inner: rdn along 3f out: drvn 2f out and sn wknd* **5/1**[2]
6244 **7** *5* **Bright Sun (IRE)**[11] 3883 5-9-2 70 .... (t) KimTinkler 8 — 62
(N Tinkler) *keen: prom: rdn along wl over 2f out: grad wknd* **14/1**
0034 **8** *7* **Lady Disdain**[50] 2679 3-8-2 65 ow1 .... RoystonFfrench 4 — 44
(G M Moore) *midfield: effrt and sme hdwy 4f out: rdn along and nty much room wl over 2f out: sn wknd* **22/1**
6006 **9** *½* **Motafarred (IRE)**[9] 3960 4-8-13 67 .... DeanMcKeown 5 — 45
(Micky Hammond) *chsd ldrs on outer: pushed along over 4f out: wknd over 3f out* **20/1**

0232 **10** *13* **Nesno (USA)**[27] 3375 3-9-4 **81** .... KDarley 11 34
(J D Bethell) *chsd ldrs on inner: rdn along over 3f out: wknd wl over 2f out* **6/1**[3]

2m 3.26s (-1.74) **Going Correction** -0.025s/f (Good)
WFA 3 from 4yo+ 9lb **10** Ran SP% **117.8**
Speed ratings (Par 105):105,103,101,100,100 100,96,90,90,80
CSF £41.11 CT £154.58 TOTE £5.30: £2.10, £2.00, £1.70; EX 25.20 Trifecta £69.70 Pool: £740.95 - 7.54 winning units..
Owner Ean Muller Associates **Bred** E A C Muller **Trained** Middleham Moor, N Yorks
■ Stewards' Enquiry : N Callan two-day ban: careless riding (Aug 18-19)

FOCUS
A fair handicap and a race dominated from the front by Nelsons Column. The third represents a solid marker for the form.

4204 BLACK SHEEP BREWERY MAIDEN STKS 1m 4f 10y
4:20 (4:21) (Class 5) 3-Y-0+ **£4,533** (£1,348; £674; £336) **Stalls** High

Form RPR

44-2 **1** **Raucous (GER)**[18] 3676 3-9-3 76 .... MickyFenton 8 82+
(T P Tate) *cl up: led 1/2-way: rdn over 2f out: drvn ent last and styd on wl* **8/1**

32 **2** *nk* **Behlaya (IRE)**[23] 3522 5-9-9 75 .... DavidAllan 3 77
(T D Easterby) *hld up in rr: hdwy over 3f out: nt clr run and swtchd lft over 1f out: rdn to chse wnr ins last: edgd rt and styd on wl* **7/1**[3]

4-5 **3** *1 3/4* **Adelfia (IRE)**[53] 2578 3-8-12 .... RobertWinston 11 74
(Sir Michael Stoute) *trckd ldrs: hdwy over 3f out: rdn along 2f out: kpt on same pce appr last* **7/1**[3]

4 **4** *2 1/2* **Burnt Oak (UAE)**[31] 3261 4-10-0 .... TomEaves 9 75
(C W Fairhurst) *dwlt: sn in midfield: hdfway on outer over 4f out: rdn to chse ldrs over 2f out: drvn and one pce fr over 1f out* **18/1**

632 **5** *3* **Miss Trinidad (USA)**[14] 3794 3-8-12 77 .... NCallan 2 65
(B J Meehan) *trckd ldrs: hdwy over 4f out: chsd wnr 3f out: rdn and ch 2f out: sn drvn and wknd over 1f out* **6/1**[2]

4 **6** *1 1/2* **Phebe**[14] 3794 3-8-12 .... NickyMackay 6 63
(L M Cumani) *trckd ldrs: hdwy over 3f out: rdn and ch 2f out: sn drvn and btn* **5/4**[1]

2422 **7** *4* **Phone In**[13] 3819 3-9-3 65 .... RoystonFfrench 10 62
(R Brotherton) *prom: hdwy to chse wnr 5f out: rdn along 3f out: grad wknd fnl 2f* **10/1**

8 *2* **Intersky High (USA)**[51] 4-9-9 .... DeanMcKeown 4 53
(K A Ryan) *dwlt: a rr* **40/1**

0-0 **9** *shd* **Celtic Empire (IRE)**[31] 3258 3-9-3 .... DaleGibson 5 58
(Jedd O'Keeffe) *hld up: hdwy and in tch over 4f out rdn along and wknd over 3f out* **250/1**

6 **10** *1 3/4* **Kitabaat (IRE)**[53] 2578 3-8-12 .... MartinDwyer 7 50
(E A L Dunlop) *a towards rr* **14/1**

00- **11** *69* **Shake The Spear (IRE)**[300] 5817 3-9-3 .... PaulFitzsimons 12 —
(Miss J R Tooth) *led to 1/2-way: rdn along over 4f out and sn wknd* **200/1**

2m 35.7s (-1.30) **Going Correction** -0.025s/f (Good)
WFA 3 from 4yo+ 11lb **34** Ran SP% **119.2**
Speed ratings (Par 103):103,102,101,99,97 96,94,92,92,91 45
CSF £63.95 TOTE £9.50: £2.30, £2.20, £2.50; EX 67.00 Trifecta £373.00 Pool: £609.45 - 1.16 winning units..
Owner The Ivy Syndicate **Bred** Gestut Graditz **Trained** Tadcaster, N Yorks

FOCUS
Average maiden form, but solid enough rated through the runner-up.

4205 BBC.CO.UK/NORTHYORKSHIRE WEBSITE H'CAP 1m 4f 10y
4:50 (4:51) (Class 5) (0-70,66) 3-Y-0+ **£3,886** (£1,156; £577; £288) **Stalls** High

Form RPR

6142 **1** **Fossgate**[20] 3621 5-9-9 **66** .... AndrewElliott(5) 10 77
(J D Bethell) *hld up towards rr: gd hdwy on outer over 3f out: rdn 2f out and hung rt: led over 1f out: hung rt: drvn and styd on* **9/1**

00-6 **2** *2 1/2* **Jumeirah Scarer**[35] 3147 5-9-8 **60** .... NCallan 8 67
(K A Ryan) *cl up: led over 3f out: rdn along over 2f out: drvn and hdd over 1f out: kpt on wl u.p ins last* **20/1**

1610 **3** *1/2* **The Pen**[8] 3983 4-9-7 **59** .... DeanMcKeown 5 65
(C W Fairhurst) *hld up in tch: stdy hdwy over 3f out: rdn 2f out: drvn and edgd rt ent last: kpt on same pce* **16/1**

0212 **4** *1 1/4* **Sudden Impulse**[28] 3352 5-8-10 **48** .... SilvestreDeSousa 1 52
(A D Brown) *trckd ldrs: hdwy 3f out: rdn along 2f out: drvn and kpt on same pce fnl f* **4/1**[2]

6516 **5** *shd* **Brief Statement (IRE)**[29] 3333 4-9-2 **59** .... LiamJones(5) 12 63
(W M Brisbourne) *hld up towards rr on inner: hdwy over 3f out: swtchd outside and rdn 2f out: styd on wl appr last: nrst fin* **8/1**

1422 **6** *1* **Gigs Magic (USA)**[13] 3823 3-8-3 **52** .... JoeFanning 11 54
(M Johnston) *trckd ldrs: hdwy to chse ldng pair 3f out: rdn over 2f out: drvn wl over 1f out and sn wknd* **7/4**[1]

5066 **7** *2* **Just Waz (USA)**[66] 2193 4-8-8 **51** .... MichaelJStainton(5) 2 50
(R M Whitaker) *chsd ldrs: rdn along over 3f out: drvn over 2f out and sn wknd* **25/1**

0044 **8** *5* **Thorny Mandate**[39] 3024 4-9-9 **61** .... StephenCarson 9 52
(R F Johnson Houghton) *dwlt: a rr* **16/1**

2221 **9** *hd* **Intavac Boy**[31] 3243 5-9-7 **59** .... DanielTudhope 7 50
(C W Thornton) *led: rdn along 4f out: hdd over 3f out and sn wknd* **7/1**[3]

2325 **10** *23* **San Deng**[8] 3983 4-9-13 **65** .... RobertWinston 3 19+
(Micky Hammond) *trckd ldng pair: rdn along over 3f out: wknd over 2f out* **11/1**

/00- **11** *4* **Swinton**[310] 5621 5-8-9 **47** oh11 .... DaleGibson 4 —
(M Brittain) *a rr* **150/1**

0-00 **12** *3* **Melodian**[105] 1187 11-9-3 **55** ....(b) KDarley 6 —
(M Brittain) *a towards rr* **40/1**

2m 36.33s (-0.67) **Going Correction** -0.025s/f (Good)
WFA 3 from 4yo+ 11lb **12** Ran SP% **121.8**
Speed ratings (Par 103):101,99,99,98,98 97,96,92,92,77 74,72
CSF £181.35 CT £2838.31 TOTE £10.80: £2.70, £4.80, £4.20; EX 234.60 TRIFECTA Not won. Place 6 £10,711.47, Place 5 £643.90.
Owner Mrs James Bethell **Bred** Mrs P A Clark **Trained** Middleham Moor, N Yorks

FOCUS
Ordinary handicap form, but solid enough with the first four all close to form.

San Deng Official explanation: jockey said gelding had no more to give
T/Jkpt: Not won. T/Plt: £7,908.00 to a £1 stake. Pool: £81,247.40. 7.50 winning tickets. T/Qpdt: £76.10 to a £1 stake. Pool: £7,162.20. 69.60 winning tickets. JR

4158 WINDSOR (R-H)
Monday, August 7

OFFICIAL GOING: Good
Wind: Light, against Weather: Overcast becoming fine

4206 BOLLINGER CHAMPAGNE CHALLENGE SERIES H'CAP (FOR GENTLEMAN AMATEUR RIDERS) 1m 3f 135y
5:55 (5:55) (Class 5) (0-75,75) 3-Y-0+ **£3,123** (£968; £484; £242) **Stalls** Low

Form RPR

4362 **1** **Undeterred**[9] 3948 10-11-0 **70** .... MrPCollington(5) 6 77
(K J Burke) *hld up in last: prog fr 3f out: hrd rdn to ld jst over 1f out : kpt on u.p* **8/1**

040- **2** *1/2* **Bay Hawk**[87] 5220 4-11-2 **70** .... MrSPJones(3) 3 76
(B G Powell) *hld up in last pair: prog to chse ldng pair over 3f out: led 2f out to jst over 1f out: kpt on fnl f but a hld* **20/1**

46-3 **3** *5* **Bucks**[32] 3220 9-10-12 **70** .... MrHSensoy(7) 8 68
(Ian Williams) *hld up in 6th: c wd fr 3f out: pushed along and kpt on: n.d to ldng pair* **6/1**

0643 **4** *3* **Zilcash**[12] 3848 3-10-9 **71** .... GerardTumelty 4 64
(A King) *pressed ldr: rdn to chal 3f out: fdd fr over 2f out* **5/2**[2]

0040 **5** *2* **Karrnak**[22] 1911 4-9-12 **56** oh14 ....(tp) MrRBirkett(7) 2 46
(Miss J Feilden) *led to 7f out: sn lost pl: nt qckn 3f out: n.d fnl 2f* **50/1**

-010 **6** *1/2* **Three Ships**[22] 3232 5-10-5 **59** oh3 ow3 .... MrMatthewSmith(3) 5 48
(Miss J Feilden) *trckd ldrs: rdn and struggling over 3f out: sn wknd* **16/1**

521- **7** *1/2* **Kyles Prince (IRE)**[247] 6485 4-11-10 **75** .... MrSWalker 9 63
(P J Makin) *cl up: led 7f out: hdd & wknd 2f out* **9/4**[1]

430- **8** *3 1/2* **War Pennant**[46] 1758 4-10-6 **62** ....(b[1]) MrDHutchison(5) 1 45
(G L Moore) *in tch in midfield: u.p 5f out: sn btn* **11/2**[3]

2m 31.1s (1.00) **Going Correction** -0.075s/f (Good)
WFA 3 from 4yo+ 11lb **8** Ran SP% **112.7**
Speed ratings (Par 103):93,92,89,87,86 85,85,83
CSF £141.71 CT £1020.35 TOTE £7.60: £1.50, £6.20, £1.80; EX 260.30.
Owner Peter Valentine **Bred** Deerfield Farm **Trained** Bourton-on-the-Water, Gloucs
■ Stewards' Enquiry : Mr P Collington one-day ban: used whip with excessive frquency (Aug 18)

FOCUS
A modest amateur riders' handicap and not a very strong race for the grade, with the fifth anchoring the form.

4207 EUROPEAN BREEDERS FUND MAIDEN FILLIES' STKS 6f
6:25 (6:25) (Class 4) 2-Y-0 **£5,181** (£1,541; £770; £384) **Stalls** High

Form RPR

1 **Suki Bear** 2-9-0 .... KerrinMcEvoy 5 72+
(W R Muir) *dwlt: off the pce in last trio: prog and swtchd lft over 2f out: swtchd lft over 1f out: str run to ld last 100yds* **50/1**

2 **2** *3/4* **Abbotts Ann**[12] 3843 2-9-0 .... MichaelHills 7 70
(B W Hills) *trckd ldr: shkn up to ld wl over 1f out: hdd and outpcd last 100yds* **11/8**[1]

3 *1/2* **Mimisel** 2-8-7 .... RobbieMills(7) 4 68
(Rae Guest) *wl in rr and off the pce: gd prog on outer fr over 2f out: rdn along to chal ins fnl f: kpt on* **50/1**

4 *1 3/4* **Shustraya** 2-9-0 .... FergusSweeney 10 63
(P J Makin) *trckd ldrs: gng wl 2f out: c to nr side rail 1f out: outpcd fnl f* **12/1**

4 **5** *nk* **Russian Gift (IRE)**[62] 2328 2-8-11 .... AdamKirby(3) 1 62
(C G Cox) *s.i.s: rcvrd to join ldrs on outer: stl pressing 1f out: fdd* **13/2**[3]

0 **6** *nk* **Blue Bamboo**[41] 2957 2-9-0 .... JimCrowley 3 61
(Mrs A J Perrett) *trckd ldrs: shkn up over 1f out: one pce fnl f* **12/1**

7 *1 1/2* **Juncea** 2-9-0 .... SteveDrowne 14 57
(H Morrison) *trckd ldrs: rdn and wl in tch over 1f out: wknd fnl f* **25/1**

8 *hd* **Rumbled** 2-9-0 .... TedDurcan 13 56+
(J A Geake) *wore net-muzzle: dwlt: hld up in midfield: nt clr run on inner 2f out: swtchd lft: nudged along and kpt on steadily* **66/1**

64 **9** *nk* **Eastern Princess**[14] 3796 2-9-0 .... RichardThomas 12 55
(J A Geake) *settled midfield: pushed along and no imp 2f out: wknd fnl f* **20/1**

10 *3/4* **A Nod And A Wink (IRE)** 2-9-0 .... RichardHughes 11 53
(R Hannon) *s.s: in tch in rr: shkn up 2f out: no real prog* **5/1**[2]

06 **11** *1/2* **Maid Of Ale (IRE)**[45] 2816 2-9-0 .... RyanMoore 2 51
(B J Meehan) *towards rr: rdn and sme prog 2f out: wknd fnl f* **14/1**

5 **12** *3 1/2* **Sahara Crystal**[23] 3537 2-9-0 .... DaneO'Neill 16 41
(H Candy) *mde most to wl over 1f out: wknd rapidly* **8/1**

0 **13** *1/2* **Koffiefontein (USA)**[23] 3537 2-9-0 .... EddieAhern 6 39+
(L M Cumani) *sn in midfield: rdn and no prog against nr side rail whn nt clr run over 1f out: wknd* **25/1**

14 *3/4* **Pickled Again** 2-9-0 .... ChrisCatlin 9 37
(S Dow) *outpcd and sn wl bhd: nvr a factor* **66/1**

15 *1/2* **Hot Cherry** 2-8-11 .... StephenDonohoe(3) 8 36
(J M P Eustace) *sn outpcd and detached: a struggling* **25/1**

0 **16** *16* **Delaporte**[9] 3942 2-9-0 .... ShaneKelly 15 —
(M A Buckley) *chsd ldrs to 1/2-way: wknd rapidly: t.o* **100/1**

1m 14.35s (0.68) **Going Correction** +0.025s/f (Good) **16** Ran SP% **129.5**
Speed ratings (Par 93):96,95,94,92,91 91,89,88,88,87 86,82,81,80,79 58
CSF £120.35 TOTE £57.80: £7.70, £1.40, £9.40; EX 195.20.
Owner Joe Bear Racing **Bred** Foursome Thoroughbreds **Trained** Lambourn, Berks

FOCUS
An average maiden in which the bare form, rated through the runner-up, looks just ordinary. However, as is often the case in Windsor maidens, a few of these are open to plenty of improvement.

NOTEBOOK
Suki Bear, a 22,000gns first foal of the stable's seven-furlong four-year-old winner Dominion Rose, made a most pleasing introduction. Well off the pace for much of the way, she began to stay on when switched to her left in the last third, and really got going when pulled to the wide outside, sustaining her challenge right the way to the line. Her trainer's horses do not win first-time out very often, so she should be open to improvement and deserves her chance in better company.
Abbotts Ann was the one to beat having run second on her debut over seven furlongs on Lingfield's Polytrack, but that form did not look anything special and she was again just held. She did not do much wrong, and should find a race, but will be vulnerable to anything above-average. (tchd 6-4)
Mimisel ◆, a half-sister to Conrad, placed over seven-furlongs/mile at two and three, out of an unraced daughter of high-class sprinter Millyant, made a most encouraging debut. Considering she was sent off 50/1 and ridden by a 7lb claimer, it is probably safe to assume that she was not particularly fancied and better can be expected with the benefit of this experience.

Shustraya, a 7,000gns first foal of a mare whose dam was a smart sort in the US, made a highly-satisfactory introduction. Her stable is going quite well at the moment and she could find a race with normal improvement.

Russian Gift(IRE) did not seem to improve on the form she showed when fourth over course and distance on her debut two months previously. (tchd 7-1)

Blue Bamboo, who offered promise on her debut in a Newbury maiden that has produced winners, again showed ability and is likely to come into her own when handicapped. (op 10-1 tchd 14-1)

Juncea, closely related to six-furlong juvenile winner Orange Dancer, out of a useful ten-furlong scorer in South Africa, offered plenty of encouragement and should do better in time.

Rumbled ◆, out of an unraced half-sister to She's Classy, high-class at two and three in the US, caught the eye and is one to keep in mind. It is remains to be seen if she will win a maiden, or improve when eligible for handicaps.

A Nod And A Wink(IRE), a half-sister to Inchloss, a dual six-furlong/mile winner at three, was sent off a short enough price on her debut considering she has been entered in selling company. She was never seen with a chance after starting very slowly. (op 20-1)

Maid Of Ale(IRE) Official explanation: jockey said filly was denied a clear run

4208 TOTESPORT 0800 221 221 H'CAP — 5f 10y

6:55 (6:55) (Class 5) (0-75,75) 3-Y-0+ **£3,238** (£963; £481; £240) **Stalls** High

Form RPR

-500 **1** **Bold Minstrel (IRE)**[16] 3744 4-9-12 **75** ChrisCatlin 3 — 83
(M Quinn) *trckd ldr: rdn to ld over 1f out: styd on fnl f: drvn out* **16/1**

414 **2** *1* **King Egbert (FR)**[10] 3899 5-8-0 **56** oh3 TolleyDean(7) 7 — 60+
(A W Carroll) *trckd ldrs and racd against nr side rail: effrt over 1f out: rdn and styd on to chse wnr last 100yds: no imp* **7/1**[3]

0205 **3** *½* **Fisola (IRE)**[14] 3802 3-9-5 **74** (p) AdamKirby(3) 8 — 76
(C G Cox) *fast away: led against nr side rail: hdd over 1f out: hrd rdn and one pce* **8/1**

3133 **4** *1 ½* **Forest Dane**[33] 3199 6-8-11 **60** OscarUrbina 5 — 57
(Mrs N Smith) *t.k.h: trckd ldrs: plld out and effrt over 1f out: nt qckn* **4/1**[2]

0336 **5** *½* **Harrison's Flyer (IRE)**[10] 3899 5-9-4 **67** (p) RyanMoore 1 — 62
(J M Bradley) *sn trckd ldrs: rdn on outer over 1f out: hanging lft and fnd nil* **4/1**[2]

3150 **6** *1 ¼* **Pititana (IRE)**[11] 3873 3-9-6 **72** RichardHughes 4 — 63
(R Hannon) *pushed along in last pair: edgd lft to centre 1/2-way: effrt u.p over 1f out: sn btn* **17/2**

3113 **7** *2 ½* **Heavens Walk**[20] 3625 5-9-1 **64** (t) FergusSweeney 6 — 46
(P J Makin) *rrd s: hld up in last: rdn wl over 1f out: sn no prog and btn* **5/2**[1]

2000 **8** *1 ½* **Financial Times (USA)**[6] 4019 4-9-9 **72** (t) SteveDrowne 2 — 48
(Stef Liddiard) *in tch: taken towards centre 2f out: btn over 1f out: eased ins fnl f* **12/1**

60.70 secs (-0.40) **Going Correction** +0.025s/f (Good)
WFA 3 from 4yo+ 3lb — **8** Ran SP% **116.3**
Speed ratings (Par 103):104,102,101,99,98 96,92,90
CSF £123.79 CT £981.41 TOTE £13.70: £3.00, £3.00, £1.80; EX 206.00.
Owner The Boys From The Shed Partnership **Bred** John & Denis Dunne **Trained** Newmarket, Suffolk

FOCUS
An ordinary sprint handicap rated around the principals.
Financial Times(USA) Official explanation: jockey said gelding had no more to give

4209 TOTESPORT.COM H'CAP — 1m 67y

7:25 (7:25) (Class 4) (0-85,84) 3-Y-0+ **£6,477** (£1,927; £963; £481) **Stalls** High

Form RPR

5322 **1** **Bold Act (IRE)**[38] 3048 4-9-6 **76** DaneO'Neill 7 — 87
(H Candy) *trckd ldrs on outer: rdn to ld 2f out: edgd rt over 1f out: drvn and styd on wl* **4/1**[2]

2511 **2** *1 ¼* **Habshan (USA)**[12] 3854 6-10-0 **84** AlanMunro 5 — 92
(C F Wall) *trckd ldrs: lost pl 1/2-way: effrt on nr side over 2f out: chsd wnr over 1f out: nt qckn fnl f* **9/2**[3]

5110 **3** *½* **Aggravation**[38] 3044 4-9-0 **70** JohnEgan 6 — 77
(D R C Elsworth) *hld up in rr: effrt on outer over 2f out: drvn and styd on fr over 1f out: unable to chal* **8/1**

5216 **4** *1 ¾* **Tumbleweed Glory (IRE)**[10] 3889 3-9-4 **81** TedDurcan 4 — 83
(B J Meehan) *hld up in last: stl last 2f out: rdn and n.m.r briefly over 1f out: styd on but no ch* **7/1**

2004 **5** *¾* **Merrymadcap (IRE)**[12] 3854 4-9-4 **74** ChrisCatlin 3 — 75
(M Blanshard) *hld up in last pair: effrt on wd outside over 2f out: prog wl over 1f out: one pce sn after* **20/1**

-504 **6** *shd* **Nanton (USA)**[9] 3951 4-9-5 **75** EddieAhern 8 — 76
(P F I Cole) *chsd ldr to 3f out: wnt to centre over 2f out: hrd rdn and btn over 1f out* **16/1**

1045 **7** *¾* **Full Victory (IRE)**[25] 3459 4-9-5 **75** SteveDrowne 1 — 74
(R A Farrant) *hld up in midfield: hrd rdn and edgd lft 2f out: nt qckn and btn over 1f out* **20/1**

1221 **8** *5* **Billy One Punch**[11] 3883 4-9-0 **70** TonyCulhane 10 — 58
(G G Margarson) *led: edgd lft and hdd 2f out: sn wknd* **7/2**[1]

2104 **9** *1* **Magic Peak (IRE)**[37] 3088 3-8-12 **75** RyanMoore 9 — 59
(Sir Michael Stoute) *sn trckd ldrs: rdn over 3f out: stl cl up on nr side 2f out: wknd sn after* **6/1**

6-00 **10** *10* **Go Mo (IRE)**[75] 1932 4-9-3 **73** RichardHughes 2 — 35
(S Kirk) *trckd ldrs: rdn 3f out: wknd 2f out: t.o* **14/1**

1m 43.82s (-1.78) **Going Correction** -0.075s/f (Good)
WFA 3 from 4yo+ 7lb — **10** Ran SP% **120.4**
Speed ratings (Par 105):105,103,103,101,100 100,99,94,93,83
CSF £23.26 CT £137.02 TOTE £5.70: £1.80, £2.30, £2.00; EX 37.90.
Owner Mrs C M Poland **Bred** Tally-Ho Stud **Trained** Kingston Warren, Oxon

FOCUS
A fair handicap for the grade and very competitive. The form looks sound rated around the runner-up and fifth.
Go Mo(IRE) Official explanation: jockey said gelding had no more to give

4210 TOTE TEXT BETTING 60021 MAIDEN STKS — 1m 2f 7y

7:55 (7:56) (Class 5) 3-4-Y-0 **£3,886** (£1,156; £577; £288) **Stalls** Low

Form RPR

00-3 **1** **Prince Ary**[130] 802 3-9-3 71 MichaelHills 11 — 66+
(B W Hills) *led after 2f: mde rest: shkn up and drew clr fr 2f out: comf* **8/1**[3]

42 **2** *5* **Valverde (IRE)**[80] 1822 3-9-3 RyanMoore 10 — 56
(J L Dunlop) *trckd ldrs: rdn and nt qckn 3f out: chsd wnr over 2f out: hanging and sn no imp* **8/13**[1]

00 **3** *nk* **Moon Empress (FR)**[28] 3367 3-8-12 KerrinMcEvoy 1 — 51
(W R Muir) *prom: chsd wnr jst over 3f out to over 2f out: sn outpcd: one pce after* **7/1**[2]

0-66 **4** *¾* **Acknowledgement**[12] 3850 4-9-12 65 JohnEgan 5 — 54
(D R C Elsworth) *prog fr midfield and prom over 4f out: outpcd by wnr over 2f out: one pce after* **9/1**

0 **5** *shd* **You Live And Learn**[14] 3794 3-8-12 SteveDrowne 2 — 49+
(H Morrison) *hld up in midfield: shkn up over 2f out: running green and hanging but kpt on steadily fr over 1f out* **20/1**

00 **6** *3 ½* **Star Berry**[7] 4004 3-8-5 KMay(7) 12 — 42
(B J Meehan) *hld up in midfield: rdn over 3f out: outpcd and btn 2f out: fdd* **66/1**

00 **7** *1* **Klassen (USA)**[39] 3029 3-9-3 DaneO'Neill 4 — 46
(A King) *rdn in midfield over 4f out: struggling and btn over 2f out* **50/1**

00 **8** *nk* **Camp Attack**[49] 2712 3-9-3 ChrisCatlin 9 — 45+
(S Dow) *t.k.h: hld up in last: shuffled along over 3f out: nt clr run briefly 2f out: fin wl last 100yds: do bttr* **66/1**

00 **9** *hd* **Suzuki (IRE)**[31] 3258 3-8-12 TedDurcan 3 — 40
(H Morrison) *led for 2f: chsd wnr to over 3f out: sn btn* **25/1**

0000 **10** *nk* **Kentuckian**[7] 3998 4-9-12 45 JimCrowley 6 — 44
(P W Hiatt) *trckd ldrs: gng wl enough over 3f out: rdn and wknd wl over 2f out* **100/1**

0 **11** *1 ¾* **Persian Warrior (IRE)**[14] 3794 3-9-3 AlanMunro 7 — 41+
(W R Swinburn) *hld up towards rr: pushed along 4f out: no real prog: wl btn fnl 2f* **12/1**

0- **12** *11* **Mr Bilbo Baggins**[259] 6395 3-9-3 FergusSweeney 8 — 20
(J S Moore) *dwlt: a towards rr: t.o* **33/1**

13 *5* **Forever Thine** 3-8-12 RichardThomas 13 — 5
(J A Geake) *s.s: sn rdn: a in last trio: wknd 4f out: t.o* **33/1**

2m 9.89s (1.59) **Going Correction** -0.075s/f (Good)
WFA 3 from 4yo 9lb — **13** Ran SP% **123.6**
Speed ratings (Par 103):90,86,85,85,85 82,81,81,81,80 79,70,66
CSF £13.06 TOTE £9.00: £1.90, £1.20, £2.00; EX 11.70.
Owner Mrs Belinda Harvey & Cavendish Inv Ltd **Bred** Mrs V E Hughes **Trained** Lambourn, Berks

FOCUS
A weak maiden run in a slow time, which is probably to be expected for the time of year, and Prince Ary set a stop-start gallop before clearing away in the straight. The time was slow and the form is dubious.

4211 EXPRESS COLIN BIRCH MEMORIAL H'CAP — 6f

8:25 (8:28) (Class 5) (0-70,70) 3-Y-0+ **£3,238** (£963; £481; £240) **Stalls** High

Form RPR

6564 **1** **Mirasol Princess**[12] 3847 5-8-8 **51** oh4 ChrisCatlin 2 — 58
(D K Ivory) *hld up in rr: prog on outer 2f out: drvn to ld 1f out: styd on wl* **25/1**

3303 **2** *1* **Monashee Prince (IRE)**[130] 806 4-9-6 **63** GeorgeBaker 8 — 67
(J R Best) *cl up: rdn to dispute ld over 1f out: nt qckn w wnr fnl f* **16/1**

2002 **3** *nk* **Whitbarrow (IRE)**[10] 3899 7-8-12 **62** (v) JamesMillman(7) 12 — 65
(B R Millman) *mde most to 1/2-way: styd cl up: upsides again over 1f out: one pce* **10/1**

3442 **4** *½* **Linda Green**[7] 4003 5-9-8 **65** TedDurcan 5 — 67
(M R Channon) *hld up in last trio: effrt 2f out: rdn and styd on fnl f: nt rch ldrs* **5/2**[1]

5500 **5** *shd* **Marker**[37] 3094 6-9-10 **67** SteveDrowne 14 — 68
(J A Geake) *racd against nr side rail: pressed ldrs: disp ld 1/2-way to 1f out: fdd* **12/1**

15-6 **6** *shd* **Semenovskii**[4] 4085 6-9-13 **70** (t) KerrinMcEvoy 13 — 71
(Miss B Sanders) *pressed ldr: disp ld 1/2-way to 1f out: fdd* **7/2**[2]

1065 **7** *nk* **Full Spate**[11] 3867 11-8-13 **59** AdamKirby(3) 9 — 59+
(J M Bradley) *hld up in last trio: nt clr run on inner 2f out: styd on ins fnl f: nrst fin* **25/1**

-000 **8** *½* **The Crooked Ring**[23] 3543 4-9-10 **70** (v) StephenDonohoe(3) 1 — 69
(P D Evans) *pressed ldrs: upsides 2f out to 1f out: wknd* **11/1**

2312 **9** *½* **Endless Summer**[21] 3593 9-9-9 **66** TonyCulhane 6 — 65+
(A W Carroll) *racd against nr side rail in midfield: chsd ldrs and nt clr run briefly over 1f out: wknd ins fnl f* **5/1**[3]

1436 **10** *nk* **Vibe**[2] 4141 5-8-8 **51** oh2 ShaneKelly 3 — 47
(A W Carroll) *hld up in midfield: rdn 2f out: hanging lft and fnd nil 1f out* **14/1**

0303 **11** *3* **Convince (USA)**[10] 3899 5-9-8 **65** RyanMoore 10 — 52
(J M Bradley) *chsd ldrs but sn pushed along: struggling over 2f out: wknd over 1f out* **9/1**

0600 **12** *2 ½* **Mount Sinai**[19] 3644 3-9-3 **64** JohnEgan 7 — 44
(W J Knight) *nvr on terms w ldrs: struggling 2f out: eased whn no ch fnl f* **33/1**

1m 14.13s (0.46) **Going Correction** +0.025s/f (Good)
WFA 3 from 4yo+ 4lb — **12** Ran SP% **125.8**
Speed ratings (Par 103):97,95,95,94,94 94,93,93,92,92 88,84
CSF £392.16 CT £4295.23 TOTE £36.00: £5.70, £6.30, £3.10; EX 211.30 Place 6 £94.99, Place 5 £53.79.
Owner Mrs D P Ivory **Bred** Bearstone Stud **Trained** Radlett, Herts

FOCUS
A modest event and a moderate time, but still a typically competitive sprint handicap and sound enough, rated around the first two.
Full Spate Official explanation: jockey said gelding was denied a clear run
T/Plt: £626.00 to a £1 stake. Pool: £76,458.35. 89.15 winning tickets. T/Qpdt: £42.50 to a £1 stake. Pool: £6,326.80. 110.15 winning tickets. JN

4182 CORK (R-H)

Monday, August 7

OFFICIAL GOING: Good to firm

4212a IRISH STALLION FARMS EUROPEAN BREEDERS FUND GIVE THANKS STKS (LISTED RACE) (FILLIES) — 1m 4f

3:45 (3:48) 3-Y-0+ **£31,427** (£9,220; £4,393; £1,496)

RPR

1 **Reform Act (USA)**[45] 2840 3-8-12 95 PJSmullen 6 — 107
(D K Weld, Ire) *trckd ldrs in 4th: 3rd appr st: rdn to chal and ld fr 2f out: styd on wl u.p fnl f* **12/1**

2 *1* **Sina Cova (IRE)**[50] 2689 4-9-12 102 JMurtagh 5 — 108
(Peter Casey, Ire) *chsd ldrs in 5th: 4th over 2f out: rdn to chal in 2nd fr over 1f out: kpt on same pce ins fnl f* **7/1**[3]

3 3 **Souvenance**[24] 3515 3-8-12 .... SebSanders 2 100
(Sir Mark Prescott) *trckd ldr in 2nd: rdn over 4f out: led 2 1/2f out: hdd fr 2f out: dropped to 3rd and kpt on same pce fr wl over 1f out* **4/1**[2]
4 2 ½ **Ayla (IRE)**[59] 2425 3-8-12 .... MJKinane 4 96
(John M Oxx, Ire) *towards rr: clsr in 8th appr st: kpt on wout threatening u.p fr over 2f out* **12/1**
5 1 ¼ **Arosa (IRE)**[43] 2908 3-8-9 .... WJLee(3) 10 94
(David Wachman, Ire) *trckd ldrs in 3rd: dropped to 5th over 2f out: sn no imp: kpt on same pce* **8/1**
6 ½ **Clara Allen (IRE)**[19] 3651 8-9-9 95 .... TPO'Shea 8 93
(John E Kiely, Ire) *towards rr: 10th appr st: sn no imp u.p: kpt on same pce* **7/1**[3]
7 ¾ **Sacrosanct (IRE)**[22] 3576 3-8-12 95 .... KFallon 11 92
(A P O'Brien, Ire) *mid div: no imp u.p in 7th and kpt on same pce fr over 2f out* **7/1**[3]
8 nk **Kushnarenkovo**[22] 3576 3-8-12 97 .... CO'Donoghue 1 92
(A P O'Brien, Ire) *dwlt: sn mid div: 6th appr st: sn no imp u.p* **14/1**
9 1 ½ **Tropical Lady (IRE)**[37] 3105 6-10-0 110 .... DJMoran 3 94
(J S Bolger, Ire) *dwlt: in rr: sme hdwy into 9th appr st: sn no imp u.p* **5/2**[1]
10 9 **Malt Lios (IRE)**[38] 3058 3-8-12 65 .... PShanahan 7 75?
(John Joseph Murphy, Ire) *chsd ldrs in 6th: 7th 5f out: sn lost pl and no ex u.p* **100/1**
P **Ice Princess (IRE)**[19] 3660 3-8-12 88 .... DMGrant 9 —
(David Wachman, Ire) *led: strly pressed and hdd 2 1/2f out: p.u bdly injured under 2f out* **25/1**

2m 31.7s
WFA 3 from 4yo+ 11lb **11** Ran SP% **124.1**
CSF £98.74 TOTE £17.50: £4.30, £2.40, £1.90; DF 142.80.
Owner J Higgins **Bred** Ws Farish & Kilroy Thbred Prtn **Trained** The Curragh, Co Kildare

NOTEBOOK
Reform Act(USA) quickened up well to go to the front over two furlongs out before sticking out her head and running on gamely to secure her first stakes race success having finished in the frame in similar type events on her two previous starts. She had run over just short of this trip at Limerick in June and she got the distance well here to earn a possible tilt at the Galtres Stakes. (op 10/1)
Sina Cova(IRE), carrying a 3lb Group 3 penalty for her course and distance win in June, produced another good effort. Never far off the leaders, she threw down her challenge from a furlong and a half out and kept on well without ever looking like pegging back the winner.
Souvenance had finished in the frame in Group 1, Group 2 and Listed events in Italy, Germany and France respectively in recent months. She had every chance and disputed the lead early in the straight before failing to raise her effort from over one furlong out. (op 5/2 tchd 9/2)

4213 - 4220a (Foreign Racing) - See Raceform Interactive

3860 BATH (L-H)
Tuesday, August 8

OFFICIAL GOING: Firm
Wind: Moderate, against Weather: Sunny

4221 DRIVE BRISTOL ACCIDENT REPAIR CENTRE MAIDEN AUCTION FILLIES' STKS 5f 161y
2:45 (2:46) (Class 6) 2-Y-0 **£2,590** (£770; £385; £192) **Stalls** Low

Form RPR
1 **Ficoma** 2-8-6 ow3 .... AdamKirby(3) 5 76+
(C G Cox) *hld up and bhd: rdn over 3f out: hdwy over 2f out: swtchd rt over 1f out: led wl ins fnl f: r.o wl* **9/1**
34 2 1 ½ **Reem Al Fallah (IRE)**[50] 2703 2-8-10 .... TedDurcan 6 72
(M R Channon) *a.p: led over 2f out: rdn and hdd jst over 1f out: nt qckn ins fnl f* **11/8**[1]
62 3 hd **Foxy Games**[59] 2442 2-7-13 .... JamesDoyle(3) 7 63
(D J S Ffrench Davis) *s.i.s: hdwy over 2f out: rdn to ld jst over 1f out: edgd lft and hdd wl ins fnl f: nt qckn* **13/2**
4 3 **Aussie Cricket (FR)** 2-8-12 .... TPQueally 8 63+
(D J Coakley) *outpcd and bhd: hdwy over 1f out: nvr nr to chal* **20/1**
0 5 1 ¾ **Lake Pontchartrain (IRE)**[18] 3700 2-8-8 .... RyanMoore 9 53
(S Kirk) *chsd ldrs: rdn and ev ch over 1f out: wknd ins fnl f* **14/1**
00 6 1 ¼ **Princess Zada**[8] 4000 2-8-2 .... TPO'Shea 3 43
(B R Millman) *hld up in tch: rdn over 3f out: wknd over 2f out* **20/1**
6 7 5 **Cantique (IRE)**[24] 3544 2-8-7 ow1 .... SebSanders 4 32
(R M Beckett) *w ldr: rdn over 2f out: wknd wl over 1f out* **6/1**[3]
553 8 3 ½ **Retaliate**[14] 3822 2-8-4 69 .... ChrisCatlin 1 17
(M Quinn) *led: rdn and hdd over 2f out: wknd wl over 1f out* **11/2**[2]
9 6 **Yearning (IRE)** 2-8-3 .... NeilChalmers(3) 2 —
(J G Portman) *s.s: a in rr* **40/1**

1m 11.88s (0.68) **Going Correction** -0.075s/f (Good) **9** Ran SP% **113.7**
Speed ratings (Par 89):92,90,89,85,83 81,75,70,62
CSF £20.98 TOTE £8.70: £2.60, £1.20, £1.80; EX 21.00 Trifecta £112.20 Pool: £749.54 - 4.74 winning units..
Owner P G Jacobs & Partners **Bred** P G Jacobs, J Osborne And A Briam **Trained** Lambourn, Berks

FOCUS
An ordinary maiden but this could turn out to be fair form for the grade.

NOTEBOOK
Ficoma, a half-sister to Premier Fantasy, was nibbled at in the ring on this debut. Taking a while for the penny to drop, she did it nicely in the end and is likely to go for the Watership Down sales race at Ascot next month. (op 11-1 tchd 8-1)
Reem Al Fallah(IRE) did not do a lot wrong over this slightly longer trip and kept on to secure second. (op 2-1)
Foxy Games could not quite hold the runner-up let alone the winner on this slight drop back in distance. Official explanation: jockey said filly hung right-handed (op 6-1 tchd 7-1)
Aussie Cricket(FR) ◆, out of a French mile and a half winner, seems sure to improve on this debut when tackling further. (op 12-1)
Lake Pontchartrain(IRE) lasted a lot longer than when making her debut in better company at Newbury. (op 12-1)
Yearning(IRE) Official explanation: jockey said filly missed the break

4222 WBX.COM - WORLD BET EXCHANGE (S) STKS 5f 11y
3:15 (3:15) (Class 6) 2-Y-0 **£2,266** (£674; £337; £168) **Stalls** Low

Form RPR
3063 1 **Diminuto**[15] 3801 2-8-11 52 .... HayleyTurner 7 56
(M D I Usher) *hld up in tch: n.m.r and lost pl over 2f out: hdwy over 1f out: rdn to ld wl ins fnl f: r.o* **11/2**[3]
3222 2 ½ **House Arrest**[21] 3613 2-8-11 56 .... RyanMoore 4 54
(I A Wood) *led: hdd over 2f out: rdn to ld over 1f out: hdd wl ins fnl f: nt qckn* **5/2**[2]
50 3 1 **Ten For Tosca (IRE)**[63] 2315 2-9-2 .... ShaneKelly 3 55
(J A Osborne) *w ldr: led over 2f out: rdn and hdd over 1f out: nt qckn ins fnl f* **8/1**
6106 4 1 ½ **Suzieblue (IRE)**[21] 3624 2-9-2 52 .... (p) LPKeniry 8 49
(J S Moore) *hld up: hdwy over 2f out: rdn over 1f out: one pce fnl f* **22/1**
00 5 2 ½ **King Of Tricks**[22] 3591 2-9-2 .... RichardSmith 2 40
(M D I Usher) *prom: rdn over 2f out: wknd over 1f out* **33/1**
2436 6 ¾ **Dotty's Daughter**[11] 3907 2-8-11 57 .... (b) SebSanders 6 32
(Mrs A Duffield) *prom: rdn over 2f out: wknd over 1f out* **7/1**
4034 7 1 ¾ **Alittleriskie (IRE)**[31] 3300 2-8-9 55 .... (b) JosephWalsh(7) 5 31
(J S Moore) *s.i.s: hld up: rdn over 2f out: sn bhd* **33/1**
4301 8 8 **Pat Will (IRE)**[31] 3300 2-8-13 63 .... StephenDonohoe(3) 1 1
(P D Evans) *bhd fnl 3f* **7/4**[1]

64.14 secs (1.64) **Going Correction** -0.075s/f (Good) **8** Ran SP% **114.2**
Speed ratings (Par 92):83,82,80,78,74 73,70,57
CSF £19.27 TOTE £6.70: £1.90, £1.20, £2.60; EX 24.80 Trifecta £111.80 Pool: £1,121.84 - 7.12 winning units..The winner was bought in for 3,200gns.
Owner M D I Usher **Bred** B Minty **Trained** Upper Lambourn, Berks

FOCUS
An average juvenile seller but a very moderate winning time, even for a race like this, with most of the runners well exposed and the favourite a flop.

NOTEBOOK
Diminuto got a good run through on the inside in the closing stages and managed to get away with the drop back from six furlongs. (op 15-2)
House Arrest found one too good on her first start over the minimum distance after twice finishing second over as far as seven furlongs. (op 11-4 tchd 3-1)
Ten For Tosca(IRE) could not quite take full advantage of a drop into selling company. (op 7-1)
Suzieblue(IRE) had the ground on the soft side when landing a similar event in first-time cheekpieces at Chepstow in June. (op 14-1)
King Of Tricks did not find a drop in grade the answer. (tchd 40-1)
Dotty's Daughter was another rather disappointing on this descent into a seller. (op 11-2)
Pat Will(IRE) may have been feeling the ground and was reported by her rider to have lost her action. Official explanation: jockey said filly lost its action (op 9-4)

4223 WBX.COM - WORLD BET EXCHANGE CLAIMING STKS 5f 161y
3:45 (3:45) (Class 6) 3-Y-O+ **£2,331** (£693; £346; £173) **Stalls** Low

Form RPR
0426 1 **Peruvian Style (IRE)**[28] 3389 5-9-1 52 .... SteveDrowne 13 66
(J M Bradley) *hld up in mid-div: hdwy over 2f out: led over 1f out: edgd lft and drvn clr ins fnl f* **11/1**
5001 2 4 **Carcinetto (IRE)**[12] 3863 4-8-9 47 .... (p) FrancisFerris 11 47
(B Palling) *chsd ldrs: rdn 3f out: ev ch over 1f out: one pce* **8/1**[3]
0560 3 nk **Danehill Stroller (IRE)**[8] 3995 6-9-1 62 .... DaneO'Neill 9 52
(A M Hales) *hld up in mid-div: rdn over 2f out: hdwy and swtchd rt over 1f out: kpt on same pce fnl f* **8/1**[3]
4405 4 4 **Flying Dancer**[22] 3595 4-8-2 50 .... (p) TolleyDean(7) 12 33
(R A Harris) *s.i.s: bhd: rdn over 2f out: hdwy over 1f out: nvr trbld ldrs* **50/1**
5354 5 ½ **Tomthevic**[12] 3863 8-8-11 44 .... (p) NelsonDeSouza(3) 5 37
(J M Bradley) *led: hdd over 2f out: wknd over 1f out* **12/1**
2140 6 shd **Devon Flame**[25] 3471 7-9-5 80 .... JimCrowley 10 50+
(R J Hodges) *hld up towards rr: rdn over 2f out: no real prog whn hmpd over 1f out: fin lame* **6/5**[1]
6006 7 2 ½ **Jinksonthehouse**[12] 3863 5-8-6 41 .... HayleyTurner 2 21
(M D I Usher) *chsd ldrs over 2f out: wknd over 2f out* **40/1**
0000 8 hd **Bare Rambler**[17] 3729 3-8-6 37 ow2 .... (v) AdamKirby(3) 3 26
(Stef Liddiard) *sn rdn along: a bhd* **100/1**
0030 9 2 ½ **Rag Tag (IRE)**[15] 3802 3-9-5 77 .... (t) LPKeniry 8 28
(A M Balding) *w ldr: led over 2f out: rdn and hdd over 1f out: sn wknd* **6/1**[2]
0020 10 6 **Neardown Queen**[22] 3595 3-8-1 50 .... JamesDoyle(3) 7 —
(I A Wood) *s.i.s: a bhd* **40/1**
45-0 11 3 **Indian Bazaar (IRE)**[12] 3863 10-8-11 41 .... AmirQuinn(3) 4 —
(R A Harris) *prom: rdn over 3f out: wknd over 2f out* **40/1**
0320 12 1 **Smokincanon**[12] 3867 4-8-9 47 .... LiamJones(5) 1 —
(W G M Turner) *s.s: a in rr* **20/1**
4600 13 8 **Bahhmirage (IRE)**[11] 3897 3-8-2 50 .... (be) ChrisCatlin 6 —
(Stef Liddiard) *s.i.s: a in rr* **40/1**

1m 10.26s (-0.94) **Going Correction** -0.075s/f (Good)
WFA 3 from 4yo+ 4lb **13** Ran SP% **115.5**
Speed ratings (Par 101):103,97,97,91,91 91,87,87,84,76 72,70,60
CSF £87.97 TOTE £12.40: £2.70, £2.50, £2.90; EX 93.50 Trifecta £602.40 Part won. Pool: £848.46 - 0.54 winning units..Carcinetto was claimed by David Evans for £6,000.
Owner Clifton Hunt **Bred** Forenaghts Stud **Trained** Sedbury, Gloucs

FOCUS
Not many got into this modest claimer with the hot favourite disappointing. The form is not rock solid, but has been rated fairly positively.
Devon Flame Official explanation: vet said gelding was lame on the left fore
Indian Bazaar(IRE) Official explanation: jockey said gelding had no more to give

4224 WBX.COM - WORLD BET EXCHANGE H'CAP 1m 3f 144y
4:15 (4:15) (Class 5) (0-75,75) 3-Y-0 **£4,210** (£1,252; £625; £312) **Stalls** Low

Form RPR
2122 1 **Ollie George (IRE)**[9] 3974 3-9-3 **71** .... (v) LPKeniry 4 83+
(A M Balding) *t.k.h: a.p: led over 2f out: rdn over 1f out: clr ins fnl f: eased cl home* **6/5**[1]
1641 2 2 ½ **Rahy's Crown (USA)**[40] 3017 3-8-10 **64** .... RyanMoore 2 70
(G L Moore) *hld up: hdwy over 2f out: rdn to chse wnr over 1f out: no imp* **11/2**[3]
4-14 3 2 **Balloura (USA)**[42] 2961 3-9-7 **75** .... MartinDwyer 3 78
(W J Haggas) *t.k.h: a.p: rdn and one pce fnl 2f* **10/1**
0461 4 ¾ **Spaceman**[14] 3823 3-8-6 **60** .... (v) NickyMackay 5 62
(L M Cumani) *hld up: hdwy over 3f out: rdn over 2f out: edgd rt jst ins fnl f: one pce* **11/4**[2]
4145 5 2 **Stellenbosch (USA)**[24] 3547 3-9-0 **68** .... EddieAhern 7 67
(J W Hills) *hld up in rr: rdn over 2f out: no rspnse* **8/1**
5626 6 5 **Rajaall**[18] 3704 3-9-5 **73** .... (v[1]) TedDurcan 6 64
(M R Channon) *led: rdn and hdd over 2f out: wknd wl over 1f out* **20/1**

2m 28.14s (-2.16) **Going Correction** -0.075s/f (Good) **6** Ran SP% **112.5**
Speed ratings (Par 100):104,102,101,100,99 95
CSF £8.41 TOTE £1.90: £1.30, £2.30; EX 9.30.
Owner Peter R Grubb **Bred** Lawrence Walsh **Trained** Kingsclere, Hants

FOCUS
A modest handicap and the time was below standard despite what appeared to be a muddling pace. The form looks sound enough with the placed horses to recent form.

4225 WORLD BET EXCHANGE - WBX.COM H'CAP — 1m 5y
4:45 (4:45) (Class 5) (0-75,73) 3-Y-O — £4,210 (£1,252; £625; £312) Stalls Low

Form — RPR

3541 **1** **Cool Ebony**[23] 3569 3-9-5 71 .... JimmyQuinn 5 — 82
(M Dods) *w ldr: led over 2f out: rdn over 1f out: drvn out* — 3/1[1]

6-24 **2** 1 **Signal Hill**[22] 3586 3-8-6 63 .... LiamJones(5) 3 — 72
(W J Haggas) *a.p: edgd rt 2f out: rdn and ev ch over 1f out: nt qckn ins fnl f* — 4/1[2]

0226 **3** 2½ **High Octave (IRE)**[10] 3932 3-9-0 66 .... DaneO'Neill 6 — 69
(B G Powell) *hld up in mid-div: hdwy 3f out: rdn and ev ch over 1f out: one pce fnl f* — 9/1

4654 **4** 2 **Star Of The Desert (IRE)**[33] 3224 3-9-4 73 .... AdamKirby(3) 7 — 72
(C G Cox) *hld up: hdwy on outside 3f out: sn rdn: no imp fnl f* — 5/1[3]

5400 **5** 1¾ **You Call That Art (USA)**[20] 3644 3-9-6 72 ....(b) RichardHughes 2 — 67
(R Hannon) *led: hdd over 2f out: sn rdn: wknd over 1f out* — 25/1

0232 **6** 1 **Sgt Schultz (IRE)**[23] 3569 3-9-0 66 .... LPKeniry 9 — 58+
(J S Moore) *hld up and bhd: rdn and sme hdwy whn hmpd wl over 1f out: n.d after* — 11/2

660 **7** 3 **Monmouthshire**[74] 1994 3-9-0 66 .... RyanMoore 10 — 51
(M L W Bell) *hld up and bhd: rdn over 3f out: no rspnse* — 20/1

000- **8** 1½ **Tecktal (FR)**[325] 5315 3-9-0 66 .... NickyMackay 1 — 48
(L M Cumani) *t.k.h: sn prom: rdn over 3f out: wknd over 2f out* — 16/1

0605 **9** nk **Lady Cree (IRE)**[15] 3793 3-8-12 64 ....(b) MartinDwyer 8 — 52+
(W R Muir) *bhd: rdn over 3f out: hmpd wl over 1f out* — 14/1

4612 **U** **Piano Player (IRE)**[10] 3951 3-9-5 71 .... ShaneKelly 11 — —
(J A Osborne) *prom: rdn over 2f out: hmpd and uns rdr wl over 1f out* — 9/1

1m 39.91s (-1.19) **Going Correction** -0.075s/f (Good) — **10** Ran SP% **118.2**
Speed ratings (Par 100):102,101,98,96,94 93,90,89,88,—
CSF £15.00 CT £97.64 TOTE £4.00: £1.60, £1.90, £2.50; EX 21.10 Trifecta £177.60 Pool: £728.26 - 2.91 winning units..
Owner Wedgewood Estates **Bred** Wedgewood Estates **Trained** Denton, Co Durham
■ Stewards' Enquiry : Liam Jones five-day ban: careless riding (Aug 19-23)

FOCUS
An ordinary handicap with several coming into the race in reasonable form. The form is straightforward, rated through the runner-up.

4226 WBX.COM - WORLD BET EXCHANGE EBF FILLIES' H'CAP — 5f 11y
5:15 (5:15) (Class 5) (0-75,75) 3-Y-O+ — £4,210 (£1,252; £625; £312) Stalls Low

Form — RPR

4346 **1** **Overwing (IRE)**[12] 3866 3-9-0 65 .... EddieAhern 5 — 72
(R M H Cowell) *a.p: rdn over 1f out: led wl ins fnl f: r.o* — 3/1[1]

0146 **2** ½ **Musical Romance (IRE)**[12] 3873 3-9-5 70 ....(b) RyanMoore 7 — 75
(B J Meehan) *hld up: hdwy over 1f out: sn edgd lft: rdn and ev ch ins fnl f: nt qckn* — 4/1[2]

0506 **3** 1 **Devine Dancer**[4] 4102 3-9-10 75 .... DaneO'Neill 8 — 76
(H Candy) *hld up: hdwy over 3f out: rdn to ld over 1f out: sn edgd lft: hdd wl ins fnl f* — 3/1[1]

0065 **4** 1½ **Zimbali**[17] 3728 4-8-7 55 oh10 .... JosedeSouza 2 — 52
(J M Bradley) *chsd ldrs: swtchd rt over 1f out: swtchd rt ent fnl f: one pce* — 16/1

1060 **5** 3 **Hello Roberto**[5] 4085 5-9-9 74 ....(p) AmirQuinn(3) 6 — 60
(R A Harris) *a.p: led 2f out: rdn and hdd whn sltly hampd over 1f out: wknd fnl f* — 4/1[2]

1600 **6** 3½ **Mullady Penelope**[1] 4201 3-8-7 58 .... TPQueally 3 — 31
(Mrs A Duffield) *hld up: rdn and hdwy over 1f out: hmpd ent fnl f: wknd* — 9/1[3]

5650 **7** ½ **Pro Tempore**[11] 3899 4-8-0 55 oh8 .... TolleyDean(7) 1 — 27
(David Pinder) *chsd ldrs: rdn over 2f out: sn wknd* — 25/1

/000 **8** 3½ **Royal Supremacy (IRE)**[29] 3348 5-8-7 58 oh16 ow3.... AdamKirby(3) 4 — 17
(J M Bradley) *led: rdn and hdd 2f out: sn wknd* — 40/1

62.22 secs (-0.28) **Going Correction** -0.075s/f (Good)
WFA 3 from 4yo+ 3lb — **8** Ran SP% **112.2**
Speed ratings (Par 100):99,98,96,94,89 83,83,77
CSF £14.56 CT £37.23 TOTE £4.30: £1.60, £1.40, £1.10; EX 13.30 Trifecta £36.40 Pool: £923.64 - 17.99 winning units. Place 6 £33.84, Place 5 £21.03.
Owner Keith Robinson & Ian Robinson **Bred** Noel Finegan And Noel Cogan **Trained** Six Mile Bottom, Cambs
■ Stewards' Enquiry : Dane O'Neill one-day ban: careless riding (Aug 19)

FOCUS
A competitive little sprint despite the fact that three of the runners were out of the handicap. The form appears sound enough with the first three close to recent form.
Devine Dancer Official explanation: jockey said filly hung right handed
T/Plt: £62.20 to a £1 stake. Pool: £82,122.75. 963.05 winning tickets. T/Qpdt: £14.90 to a £1 stake. Pool: £4,411.20. 218.10 winning tickets. KH

3830 CATTERICK (L-H)
Tuesday, August 8

OFFICIAL GOING: Good to firm (good in places)
Wind: Virtually nil

4227 "JANADRIYAH" (S) STKS — 1m 7f 177y
2:30 (2:31) (Class 6) 3-5-Y-O — £2,730 (£806; £403) Stalls Low

Form — RPR

3100 **1** **True (IRE)**[10] 3944 5-9-9 41 .... PaulFessey 13 — 53
(Mrs S Lamyman) *in tch: hdwy over 5f out: led over 2f out: sn rdn clr and kpt on wl* — 5/1[1]

0-00 **2** 7 **Dimashq**[62] 2362 4-9-3 40 .... PhillipMakin 5 — 39
(Ronald Thompson) *hld up in rr: hdwy over 3f out: rdn 2f out: sn drvn and styd on to take 2nd nr line* — 5/1[1]

0440 **3** shd **King Forever**[20] 3635 4-9-8 47 .... DaleGibson 8 — 43
(D E Cantillon) *hld up in rr: hdwy 5f out: rdn to chse wnr wl over 1f out: sn drvn and no imp: lost 2nd nr fin* — 7/1[2]

6400 **4** 7 **Esquillon**[16] 3763 4-8-10 42 .... CharlotteKerton(7) 14 — 30
(S Parr) *cl up: led over 7f out: rdn along over 3f out: hdd over 2f out and sn wknd* — 9/1

5 1 **Hialeah**[95] 5-9-3 .... AndrewMullen(5) 6 — 34
(Robert Gray) *hld up in rr: hdwy over 3f out: sn rdn and no imp fnl 2f* — 10/1

-000 **6** 4 **Grandma's Girl**[5] 4072 4-9-3 46 ....(p) CatherineGannon 10 — 24
(Robert Gray) *chsd ldrs: rdn along 4f out: drvn 3f out and sn wknd* — 8/1[3]

0000 **7** 1 **Kalush**[7] 4021 5-9-1 32 .... AnnStokell(7) 11 — 28
(J Hetherton) *hld up: a rr* — 40/1

0015 **8** ½ **Kristalchen**[13] 3836 4-9-9 39 .... GylesParkin 3 — 28
(D W Thompson) *prom: rdn along over 3f out: wknd over 2f out* — 7/1[2]

0000 **9** 3 **Night Reveller (IRE)**[6] 4050 3-8-2 30 .... RoystonFfrench 9 — 19
(M C Chapman) *a rr* — 50/1

0000 **10** hd **Tammy**[70] 2107 3-8-2 40 .... JoeFanning 1 — 18
(C W Thornton) *midfield: pushed along over 4f out: sn wknd* — 12/1

600- **11** nk **Trickstep**[7] 526 5-9-8 55 .... LeeEnstone 4 — 23
(D McCain Jnr) *chsd ldrs: rdn along over 4f out: sn wknd* — 12/1

0 **12** 34 **One And Only (GER)**[19] 469 5-9-0 35 ....(v[1]) DNolan(3) 12 — —
(D W Thompson) *led: hdd over 7f out: rdn along and lost pl over 5f out* — 16/1

-060 **P** **Vincent Vegas**[55] 2542 3-8-7 25 .... PaulMulrennan 7 — —
(Mrs S Lamyman) *sn outpcd and bhd: t.o whn p.u over 7f out* — 40/1

3m 28.42s (-2.98) **Going Correction** -0.175s/f (Firm)
WFA 3 from 4yo+ 15lb — **13** Ran SP% **116.6**
Speed ratings (Par 101):100,96,96,92,92 90,89,89,88,88 87,70,—
CSF £27.16 TOTE £6.70: £2.20, £1.90, £2.30; EX 34.90.The winner was bought in for 4,200gns.
Owner The Underlaws **Bred** Philip Newton **Trained** Ruckland, Lincs

FOCUS
A very weak event which saw a wide-margin winner and the time was reasonable.

4228 GO RACING AT PONTEFRACT TOMORROW MAIDEN STKS — 7f
3:00 (3:02) (Class 5) 2-Y-O — £3,886 (£1,156; £577; £288) Stalls Low

Form — RPR

43 **1** **Coconut Queen (IRE)**[15] 3788 2-8-12 .... RoystonFfrench 2 — 70
(Mrs A Duffield) *trckd ldng pair: swtchd rt and hdwy over 2f out: rdn to chal over 1f out: led ent last and kpt on* — 5/1[2]

2 **2** 1½ **Carillon (IRE)**[15] 3780 2-8-12 .... KDarley 7 — 66
(M Johnston) *sn led: rdn along over 2f out: drvn and hdd ent last: kpt on same pce* — 5/6[1]

3 ½ **Dilwin (IRE)** 2-9-3 .... JoeFanning 3 — 70
(D Nicholls) *chsd ldng pair: hdwy over 2f out: sn rdn and ev ch over 1f out: kpt on same pce fnl f* — 33/1

4 nk **Pagan Starprincess** 2-8-12 .... DanielTudhope 5 — 64
(G M Moore) *towards rr: hdwy over 2f out: kpt on wl appr last: nrst fin* — 66/1

4 **5** ½ **Fadeyev (IRE)**[18] 3713 2-9-3 .... NCallan 10 — 68
(K A Ryan) *cl up: ev ch 2f out: sn rdn and wknd appr last* — 6/1[3]

4 **6** ½ **Kunte Kinteh**[95] 1454 2-9-3 .... AdrianTNicholls 6 — 66
(D Nicholls) *chsd ldrs: rdn along over 2f out: kpt on same pce appr last* — 11/1

7 6 **Love On The Rocks** 2-9-3 .... DO'Donohoe 8 — 51
(K A Ryan) *in tch: rdn along 3f out: sn outpcd* — 20/1

04 **8** ½ **Bellapais Boy**[22] 3596 2-9-3 .... DavidAllan 1 — 50
(T D Easterby) *midfield and rdn along 1/2-way: sn wknd* — 20/1

004 **9** 23 **Micky Mac (IRE)**[13] 3830 2-9-0 59 ....(b) PatrickMathers(3) 9 — —
(I W McInnes) *sn outpcd: a bhd* — 40/1

R **Mageniken (USA)** 2-9-3 .... TomEaves 4 — —
(J Howard Johnson) *dwlt: sn pushed along in rr: ref to r after 1f* — 10/1

1m 27.08s (-0.28) **Going Correction** -0.175s/f (Firm) — **10** Ran SP% **119.3**
Speed ratings (Par 94):94,92,91,91,90 90,83,82,56,—
CSF £9.29 TOTE £5.60: £1.40, £1.10, £9.90; EX 11.30.
Owner Middleham Park Racing Xi **Bred** Bakewell Bloodstock **Trained** Constable Burton, N Yorks
■ Stewards' Enquiry : Adrian T Nicholls caution: allowed colt to coast home with no assistance

FOCUS
A modest maiden, run at a decent early pace and sound enough, and it should produce its share of future winners.

NOTEBOOK
Coconut Queen(IRE) got off the mark at the third time of asking with a gritty display. She dug deep when hitting the front nearing the final furlong and proved game thereafter. Her future now lies with the Handicapper and she probably has a little more to offer. (op 6-1)
Carillon(IRE), runner-up on debut at Ayr 15 days previously, was unsuited by being taken on for the early lead and paid for her early exertions nearing the final furlong. She got all of this longer trip, indeed it may be that she already requires an even stiffer test, and a more galloping track in the future should see her in a better light. (tchd 4-5 after early evens and 11-10 in places)
Dilwin(IRE), a 38,000euros purchase, turned in a pleasing debut effort and looked well suited by this trip. He is entitled to improve for the experience and has a future.
Pagan Starprincess, who has just an ordinary pedigree, caught the eye staying on late after running green through the early parts. She will be better suited by a more galloping track in the future and looks up to finding a race before the year is out. (op 50-1)
Fadeyev(IRE), fourth on debut at Pontefract 18 days previously, failed to really improve for this extra furlong and would have probably been better off under a more patient ride. He looks the type to fare better when switching to nurseries in due course. (op 13-2 tchd 7-1)
Kunte Kinteh, fourth over the minimum trip on debut 95 days previously, did not look all that suited by the undulations of this track and shaped as though the run was needed. (tchd 12-1)
Micky Mac(IRE) Official explanation: jockey said gelding hung left-handed
Mageniken(USA), who cost 150,000gns and is the first foal of a smart juvenile sprint winner, was taken quietly to post and then produced a mulish effort through the race itself. He is clearly one to have serious reservations about and, while this was his first-ever outing, he already looks like proving expensive. (op 8-1)

4229 "WETHERBY STEEPLECHASES" CLAIMING STKS — 1m 3f 214y
3:30 (3:30) (Class 6) 3-Y-O+ — £3,412 (£1,007; £504) Stalls Low

Form — RPR

3001 **1** **Tedstale (USA)**[19] 3680 8-9-9 75 ....(b) NCallan 10 — 69
(K A Ryan) *trckd ldrs: hdwy over 2f out: sn rdn: drvn over 1f out: styd on to ld ins last* — 13/8[1]

6224 **2** 1 **Parchment (IRE)**[7] 4021 4-9-4 52 ....(b[1]) MarkLawson(5) 8 — 67
(A J Lockwood) *hld up: hdwy 4f out: rdn and hung bdly lft wl over 1f out: drvn and kpt on wl fnl f* — 16/1

5003 **3** nk **Khanjar (USA)**[19] 3680 6-9-2 70 .... AndrewElliott(5) 1 — 65
(K R Burke) *led: rdn along over 3f out: drvn wl over 1f out: hdd and no ex ins last* — 7/2[3]

1415 **4** 1¾ **Court Of Appeal**[37] 3116 9-9-7 64 ....(tp) TomEaves 2 — 62
(B Ellison) *a.p: effrt to chal 3f out: rdn along and ev ch tl drvn and wknd ent last* — 2/1[2]

563 **5** 7 **Mr Maxim**[42] 2944 4-9-2 53 ....(v) MichaelJStainton(5) 5 — 51
(R M Whitaker) *midfield: effrt over 4f out: sn rdn along and nvr nr ldrs* — 12/1

2040 **6** 6 **Fiddlers Creek (IRE)**[7] 3352 7-9-7 53 ....(t) PaulMulrennan 6 — 41
(R Allan) *chsd ldrs: rdn along over 4f out: sn wknd* — 20/1

-000 **7** 6 **Piccolomini**[9] 3983 4-9-7 57 .... TonyHamilton 3 — 31
(E W Tuer) *chsd ldrs: rdn along over 3f out: drvn and wknd over 2f out* — 50/1

000- **8** 5 **Southern Bazaar (USA)**[12] 3428 5-9-3 48 ow1...... TomMessenger(5) 7 — 24
(M C Chapman) *a rr* — 50/1

000/ 9 shd **Luferton Lane (IRE)**[1054] 5048 9-8-4 26................. AshleyHamblett(7) 4 13
(R F Marvin) *a rr* **100/1**
2m 37.97s (-1.03) **Going Correction** -0.175s/f (Firm) 9 Ran SP% **116.9**
Speed ratings (Par 101):96,95,95,93,89 85,81,77,77
CSF £28.71 TOTE £2.90: £1.50, £2.40, £1.40; EX 18.10.
Owner Yorkshire Racing Club & Derek Blackhurst **Bred** Gainesway Thoroughbreds Limited **Trained** Hambleton, N Yorks

FOCUS
A modest time, even for a claimer, and the form is limited rated through the runner-up.
Piccolomini Official explanation: jockey said gelding had no more to give

4230 NEXT FRIDAY'S DURHAM CHESHIRE HOME CHARITY NIGHT H'CAP 5f 212y
4:00 (4:03) (Class 5) (0-75,72) 3-Y-0+ **£5,181** (£1,541; £770; £384) **Stalls** Low

Form RPR
0342 1 **Flying Edge (IRE)**[14] 3811 6-9-6 65................................ FrancisNorton 8 76
(E J Alston) *trckd ldrs: hdwy 2f out: rdn over 1f out: led jst ins last: kpt on wl* **10/1**
0505 2 1 ¼ **Mandarin Spirit (IRE)**[13] 3846 6-9-8 67........................(b) OscarUrbina 5 74
(G C H Chung) *midfield: hdwy 2f out: rdn over 1f out: kpt on ins last: nrst fin* **12/1**
0030 3 ½ **Trojan Flight**[4] 4119 5-9-11 70..(p) TonyCulhane 9 76
(D W Chapman) *midfield: hdwy on outer 3f out: rdn wl over 1f out: styd on ins last: nrst fin* **6/1**[3]
0001 4 hd **Compton Plume**[3] 4157 6-8-12 57 6ex................................ DaleGibson 1 62
(M W Easterby) *cl up: effrt 2f out: swtchd rt and rdn over 1f out: sn challenegd and ev ch tl no ex ins last* **7/2**[1]
2564 5 ½ **Serieux**[7] 4029 7-9-13 72..(p) AdrianTNicholls 10 80+
(D Nicholls) *midfield: hdwy on outer 3f out: rdn and squeezed out wl over 1f out: swtchd rt and kpt on u.p ins last: nrst fin* **8/1**
2350 6 nk **Safranine (IRE)**[11] 3912 9-8-3 55...................................... AnnStokell(7) 7 58
(Miss A Stokell) *cl up: rdn 2f out: led briefly 1f out: hdd just ins last: wknd* **33/1**
3000 7 ½ **Hit's Only Money (IRE)**[11] 3899 6-8-10 58.......... RichardKingscote(3) 3 59
(R A Harris) *bhd tl styd on fnl 2f: nt rch ldrs* **12/1**
3002 8 1 ½ **Divine Spirit**[7] 4019 5-9-7 66... TomEaves 14 63
(M Dods) *hld up and bhd: hdwy on inner 2f out: swtchd rt and rdn over 1f out: kpt on ins last: nt rch ldrs* **8/1**
5104 9 nk **Never Without Me**[11] 3913 6-9-5 64.............................. MickyFenton 11 60
(J F Coupland) *in tch: rdn along and edgd rt wl over 1f out: sn drvn and no imp* **25/1**
2600 10 1 **Dispol Katie**[11] 3913 5-9-4 70... DeanHeslop(7) 2 63
(T D Barron) *in tch on inner: rdn along 1/2-way: sn drvn and wknd* **12/1**
5040 11 ½ **Angelofthenorth**[19] 3683 4-8-12 57........................ RobbieFitzpatrick 13 48
(C J Teague) *a towards rr* **33/1**
0332 12 3 **Special Gold**[31] 3306 4-8-9 54...(b) DavidAllan 6 36
(T D Easterby) *cl up: rdn along over 2f out: sn wknd* **16/1**
10-0 13 hd **Golband**[8] 3996 4-9-5 71.. AshleyHamblett(7) 12 53
(R F Marvin) *led: rdn along 2f out: drvn and hdd 1f out: wknd qckly* **66/1**
0-04 14 nk **High Voltage**[22] 3584 5-9-9 68.......................................(t) PatCosgrave 4 49
(K R Burke) *in tch and sn rdn along: lost pl 1/2-way and sn bhd* **5/1**[2]
1m 12.54s (-1.46) **Going Correction** -0.175s/f (Firm) 14 Ran SP% **124.7**
Speed ratings (Par 103):102,100,99,99,98 98,97,95,95,93 93,89,89,88
CSF £125.46 CT £800.07 TOTE £9.30: £2.60, £3.60, £2.50; EX 113.70.
Owner The Eric Alston Partnership **Bred** Michael Shefflin **Trained** Longton, Lancs

FOCUS
A modest sprint that was run at a strong early pace and the form looks reliable, rated through the placed horses. Those to be held up proved at an advantage.

4231 BOOK TICKETS ON-LINE AT CATTERICKBRIDGE.CO.UK H'CAP 1m 5f 175y
4:30 (4:30) (Class 4) (0-85,84) 3-Y-0+ **£7,772** (£2,312; £1,155; £577) **Stalls** Low

Form RPR
2513 1 **Bronze Dancer (IRE)**[19] 3674 4-8-12 68....................... RobertWinston 6 78+
(G A Swinbank) *trckd ldrs: rdn along 3f out: hdwy 2f out: rdn wl over 1f out: drvn and styd on ins last to ld last 50 yds* **10/3**[1]
310 2 ½ **Aspasias Tizzy (USA)**[54] 2584 3-8-8 77.................. RoystonFfrench 10 86
(M Johnston) *led: rdn along and qckned wl over 2f out: drvn over 1f out: hdd and no ex last 50 yds* **5/1**[3]
5205 3 shd **Incursion**[35] 3177 5-8-12 68.. AdrianTNicholls 5 77
(D Nicholls) *hld up: hdwy 3f out: rdn wl over 1f out: styd on strly ins last* **20/1**
6-20 4 2 ½ **Valance (IRE)**[59] 2437 6-9-5 75...(t) NCallan 1 81
(C R Egerton) *trckd ldng pair: hdwy 3f out: sn rdn along and one pce fr over 1f out* **13/2**
0410 5 ¾ **Maneki Neko (IRE)**[10] 3960 4-9-3 73............................. TonyHamilton 2 78
(E W Tuer) *cl up: rdn along over 2f out and ev ch tl drvn and wknd over 1f out* **20/1**
6000 6 1 **Most Definitely (IRE)**[17] 3748 6-9-9 79.............................. DavidAllan 4 82
(T D Easterby) *hld up in rr: hdwy 4f out: sn rdn along and nvr nr ldrs* **5/1**[3]
-115 7 ½ **Silvertown**[45] 2850 11-10-0 84.. PaulHanagan 8 87
(L Lungo) *trckd ldrs: rdn along over 3f out: drvn over 2f out and sn one pce* **6/1**
2-40 8 5 **Tarabut**[49] 2723 4-9-8 78... RHills 9 74+
(E A L Dunlop) *in tch: rdn along over 3f out: sn wknd* **4/1**[2]
300/ 9 1 ¼ **Zibeline (IRE)**[242] 5435 9-9-10 80.. TomEaves 3 74
(B Ellison) *a rr* **33/1**
3m 0.10s (-20.50) **Going Correction** -0.175s/f (Firm)
WFA 3 from 4yo+ 13lb 9 Ran SP% **116.5**
Speed ratings (Par 105):105,104,104,103,102 102,101,99,98
CSF £19.81 CT £288.17 TOTE £3.20: £1.60, £1.70, £4.60; EX 19.10.
Owner Mrs I Gibson **Bred** Lisieux Stud **Trained** Melsonby, N Yorks

FOCUS
A fair staying handicap, run at an uneven pace, and the winner is value for slightly further. The form should be treated with a degree of caution.

4232 "REDCAR" H'CAP 5f
5:00 (5:01) (Class 6) (0-55,59) 3-Y-0+ **£3,412** (£1,007; £504) **Stalls** Low

Form RPR
0150 1 **Multahab**[14] 3825 7-9-8 52...(t) NCallan 3 72
(Miss D A McHale) *sn led: edgd rt and rdn 2f out: clr under stands rail over 1f out: kpt on strly* **7/1**[3]
0153 2 4 **Estoille**[55] 2543 5-9-7 51.. PaulHanagan 17 57
(Mrs S Lamyman) *chsd ldrs: hdwy 2f out: rdn over 1f out: kpt on ins last* **12/1**
2531 3 shd **Chairman Bobby**[13] 3833 8-9-1 50...........................(p) MarkLawson(5) 9 56
(D W Barker) *sn rdn along towards rr: hdwy halfway: rdn wl over 1f out: kpt on ins last: nrst fin* **8/1**
0601 4 1 ¼ **Compton Classic**[30] 3334 4-8-13 50......................(p) KellyHarrison(7) 12 51
(J S Goldie) *towards rr: hdwy 2f out: styng on whn hit in face by opponents whip: kpt on ins last: nrst fin* **10/1**
0533 5 shd **Trombone Tom**[7] 4019 3-9-8 55.................................. PaulMulrennan 16 56
(J R Norton) *chsd ldrs: rdn 2f out: kpt on same pce* **16/1**
0211 6 1 ½ **Ballybunion (IRE)**[3] 4141 7-9-12 59 6ex.............. RichardKingscote(3) 7 54
(R A Harris) *towards rr: hdwy 2f out: sn rdn and kpt on: nt rch ldrs* **11/4**[1]
4350 7 shd **Sharp Hat**[5] 4091 12-9-6 50.. TonyCulhane 2 45
(D W Chapman) *prom: rdn along and edgd rt 2f out: drvn over 1f out: sn wknd* **9/1**
3063 8 1 ¼ **Seven No Trumps**[12] 3863 9-9-8 52..................................... TomEaves 6 43
(J M Bradley) *towards rr: hdwy 2f out: sn rdn and no imp appr last* **11/2**[2]
-000 9 nk **My Rascal (IRE)**[21] 3608 4-9-5 49.......................(b[1]) RoystonFfrench 4 38
(J Balding) *prom: rdn along 2f out: grad wknd* **25/1**
0406 10 shd **Waggledance (IRE)**[15] 3781 4-9-2 46......................... DanielTudhope 8 35
(D Carroll) *nvr nr ldrs* **25/1**
0301 11 2 ½ **Sir Loin**[19] 3683 5-9-2 53...................................(v) DanielleMcCreery(7) 15 33
(N Tinkler) *n.d* **14/1**
6000 12 ¾ **Coalite (IRE)**[21] 3604 3-9-4 51................................ SilvestreDeSousa 13 28
(A D Brown) *a midfield* **33/1**
0400 13 nk **Beyond The Clouds (IRE)**[7] 4019 10-9-9 53.........(v) RobertWinston 11 29
(J S Wainwright) *a rr* **22/1**
0000 14 nk **Amanda's Lad (IRE)**[11] 3913 6-9-5 49........................... BrianReilly 5 24
(M C Chapman) *chsd ldrs to 1/2-way: sn wknd* **20/1**
0500 15 5 **Tombalina**[104] 1234 3-9-2 49............................... RobbieFitzpatrick 10 6
(C J Teague) *cl up: rdn along 1/2-way: sn wknd* **66/1**
58.80 secs (-1.80) **Going Correction** -0.325s/f (Firm)
WFA 3 from 4yo+ 3lb 15 Ran SP% **126.2**
Speed ratings (Par 101):101,94,94,92,92 89,89,87,87,87 83,81,81,80,72
CSF £84.27 CT £720.93 TOTE £9.30: £3.20, £3.50, £2.70; EX 147.20.
Owner P J Burke and Dave Anderson **Bred** Shadwell Estate Company Limited **Trained** Newmarket, Suffolk

FOCUS
A weak handicap which saw those coming over the stands' side favoured. The winner is full value for his winning margin and the form has been rated positively.
Beyond The Clouds(IRE) Official explanation: jockey said gelding was unsuited by the undulating track

4233 "CATTERICK BRIDGE" H'CAP 7f
5:30 (5:31) (Class 6) (0-55,55) 3-Y-0+ **£3,412** (£1,007; £504) **Stalls** Low

Form RPR
0050 1 **Kabis Amigos**[6] 4059 4-9-9 53....................................(t) RobertWinston 8 62
(D Nicholls) *mde virtually all: c wd to stands rail: rdn wl over 1f out: kpt on gamely* **9/1**
4613 2 ¾ **Motu (IRE)**[6] 4059 5-9-10 54......................................(v) RoystonFfrench 9 61
(I W McInnes) *trckd ldrs: gd hdwy 2f out: rdn to chal over 1f out and ev ch tl drvn and no ex last 50 yds* **9/2**[1]
2003 3 ½ **Hamaasy**[3] 4157 5-9-3 47... AdrianTNicholls 5 53
(D Nicholls) *a.p: effrt 2f out: sn rdn and ev ch tl drvn and no ex wl ins last* **8/1**[2]
-431 4 ¾ **The Old Soldier**[20] 3635 8-9-10 54... DavidAllan 4 58
(A Dickman) *towards rr: gd hdwy over 2f out: rdn over 1f out: styd on ins last: nrst fin* **9/2**[1]
5350 5 1 ¾ **Pride Of Kinloch**[15] 3786 6-9-4 51.....................................(p) DNolan(3) 14 51
(N Wilson) *midfield: hdwy over 2f out: rdn to chse ldrs over 1f out: kpt on same pce ins last* **20/1**
5055 6 ½ **Cayman Breeze**[13] 3835 6-9-7 51... TomEaves 3 49
(J M Bradley) *midfield: hdwy over 2f out: rdn over 1f out and kpt on in side last* **8/1**[2]
4230 7 3 **Second Reef**[15] 3786 4-9-11 55.. FrancisNorton 1 49+
(E J Alston) *chsd ldrs: effrt 2f out and ch tl rdn and wknd over 1f out* **8/1**[2]
0-3P 8 nk **Smirfys Night**[19] 3682 7-9-8 52... JoeFanning 11 47+
(E S McMahon) *cl up: rdn over 2f out: grad wknd* **17/2**[3]
0415 9 ¾ **Drury Lane (IRE)**[6] 4059 6-9-6 50.....................................(p) TonyCulhane 6 38
(D W Chapman) *nvr nr ldrs* **10/1**
05-0 10 ½ **Compton Micky**[8] 3999 5-8-12 49......................... AshleyHamblett(7) 17 35
(R F Marvin) *a towards rr* **66/1**
0600 11 shd **Yorkie**[14] 3817 7-9-6 50.. DeanMcKeown 2 36+
(J Pearce) *a rr* **12/1**
0006 12 1 **Warden Warren**[8] 4009 8-8-11 46.............................(p) MarcHalford(5) 13 30+
(Mrs C A Dunnett) *a rr* **16/1**
0400 13 11 **Bahrain Gold (IRE)**[21] 3617 6-9-8 52.............................(b) DaleGibson 15 7
(N P McCormack) *cl up: on outer rdn along wl over 2f out: sn wknd* **33/1**
1m 25.67s (-1.69) **Going Correction** -0.175s/f (Firm) 13 Ran SP% **122.1**
Speed ratings (Par 101):102,101,100,99,97 97,93,93,92,91 91,90,78
CSF £49.53 CT £349.04 TOTE £9.00: £4.00, £1.70, £4.00; EX 61.30 Place 6 £92.76, Place 5 £51.55.
Owner Ian W Glenton & D Faulkner **Bred** Cheveley Park Stud Ltd **Trained** Sessay, N Yorks

FOCUS
A moderate handicap which was run at a fair gallop and the form appears sound enough with the first four close to their marks. Those racing on the stands' rail in the home straight proved to be at an advantage.
Kabis Amigos Official explanation: trainer had no explanation for the improved form shown
T/Jkpt: £28,392.30 to a £1 stake. Pool: £79,978.50. 2.00 winning tickets. T/Plt: £54.30 to a £1 stake. Pool: £79,280.65. 1,064.60 winning tickets. T/Qpdt: £31.30 to a £1 stake. Pool: £3,808.00. 89.80 winning tickets. JR

4234 - 4237a (Foreign Racing) - See Raceform Interactive

3611 BRIGHTON (L-H)
Wednesday, August 9

OFFICIAL GOING: Firm
Wind: Nil

4238 KING'S HEAD AT BURGESS HILL EBF MEDIAN AUCTION MAIDEN FILLIES' STKS 6f 209y
2:40 (2:41) (Class 5) 2-Y-O **£3,886** (£1,156; £577; £288) **Stalls** Low

Form RPR
4 1 **Free Offer**[19] 3707 2-9-0 .... EddieAhern 1 73+
(J L Dunlop) *sn led: hdd 3f out tl 2f out: sn in command: drifted rt ins fnl f: readily* **1/5**[1]

3 **2** *5* **Belvedere Vixen**[14] 3838 2-9-0 KerrinMcEvoy 6 56
(J A Osborne) *prom: led 3f out tl 2f out: sn rdn: hung lft ins fnl f: no ch w wnr* **11/2**[2]

3 *2 ½* **Valeesha** 2-8-9 LiamJones(5) 5 49
(W G M Turner) *squeezed out sn after s: chsd ldrs: jnd ldrs after 3f: sn rdn: outpcd wl over 2f out: wnt 3rd cl home* **40/1**

0 **4** *hd* **Fun Thai**[4] 4163 2-8-11 EdwardCreighton(3) 4 49
(M R Channon) *chsd ldrs: effrt 2f out: wknd fnl f* **20/1**[3]

1m 22.78s (0.08) **Going Correction** -0.125s/f (Firm) **4** Ran SP% **105.9**
Speed ratings (Par 91):94,88,85,85
CSF £1.55 TOTE £1.10; EX 1.50.
Owner The Earl Cadogan **Bred** The Earl Cadogan **Trained** Arundel, W Sussex

FOCUS
Just the four runners for this fillies' maiden and a straightforward success for Free Offer, who did not need to step up on her debut to score.

NOTEBOOK
Free Offer, an encouraging fourth on her debut over seven furlongs at Newmarket, found this a lot less competitive and ran out a comfortable winner. It looked for a split second as though she might have to work to see off the eventual runner-up, and this ground will have been fast enough for her, but she soon cleared away and was eased near the finish. A Fillies' Mile entry, she is bred to do better over further and her connections may now look for a novice event. (op 2-9)
Belvedere Vixen, sent off joint favourite but only third in a pretty modest maiden over seven furlongs at Leicester on her debut, was no match for the winner and probably failed to improve a great deal. She may benefit from a drop back to six furlongs and is likely to come into her own when handicapped. (op 5-1)
Valeesha, a half-sister to Deletia, a ten-furlong winner who was later successful over hurdles, as well as Anna Panna, who also won over obstacles, made a respectable racecourse debut and is open to improvement. (op 50-1)
Fun Thai, well beaten on her debut over six furlongs at Windsor just four days earlier, offered little. She may be more of a handicap prospect.

4239 JACK SANDHU PUB GROUP (S) H'CAP — 1m 3f 196y
3:10 (3:11) (Class 6) (0-55,50) 3-Y-0+ **£2,590** (£770; £385; £192) **Stalls** High

Form RPR
0-00 **1** **Our Glenard**[46] 2861 7-8-8 **35** NataliaGemelova(3) 3 41
(J E Long) *s.i.s: towards rr: hdwy 5f out: shkn up to ld over 3f out: edgd rt over 2f out: styd on: rdn out* **16/1**

0454 **2** *1* **Arabian Moon (IRE)**[12] 3896 10-10-0 **50** GeorgeBaker 4 54
(R Brotherton) *hld up in tch: rdn and stdy prog fr 3f out: styd on wl ins fnl f: wnt 2nd fnl 50yds: nt rch wnr* **9/4**[2]

0250 **3** *1 ¾* **Chocolate Boy (IRE)**[16] 3797 7-9-7 **43** (be) RyanMoore 5 44
(G L Moore) *hld up towards rr: hdwy over 4f out: rdn and ev ch 2f out: one pce fnl f: lost 2nd fnl 50yds* **2/1**[1]

6000 **4** *5* **Skelligs Rock (IRE)**[12] 3896 6-9-6 **45** JamesDoyle(3) 6 38
(A W Carroll) *hld up bhd: rdn and hdwy over 2f out: styd on to go 4th 1f out: nvr trbld ldrs* **20/1**

-005 **5** *½* **Tuscany Rose**[14] 3839 3-8-11 **44** KerrinMcEvoy 1 36
(W R Muir) *chsd ldr: rdn to chal 3f out: one pce fr 2f out* **5/1**[3]

0500 **6** *10* **Skin Sure Thing**[16] 3797 3-8-8 **41** (p) MickyFenton 7 17
(D G Bridgwater) *led tl over 3f out: sn btn* **10/1**

-000 **7** *7* **Liameliss**[9] 4011 4-9-1 **42** (v) JerryO'Dwyer(5) 2 7
(M A Allen) *s.i.s: sn drvn along to chse ldrs: wknd over 3f out* **33/1**

05 **8** *16* **Boysie Brigador (USA)**[27] 3436 3-8-12 **45** (vt[1]) FJohansson 8 —
(R A Kvisla) *chsd ldr: rdn 5f out: wknd over 3f out: t.o* **33/1**

R **Mount George (IRE)**[24] 4734 8-8-11 **33** (tp) ChrisCatlin 9 —
(Evan Williams) *ref to r* **10/1**

2m 32.13s (-0.07) **Going Correction** -0.125s/f (Firm)
WFA 3 from 4yo+ 11lb **9** Ran SP% **115.5**
Speed ratings (Par 101):95,94,93,89,89 82,78,67,—
CSF £51.38 CT £105.90 TOTE £20.40: £3.30, £1.50, £1.20; EX 66.30.There was no bid for the winner.
Owner P Saxon **Bred** Floors Farming **Trained** Caterham, Surrey

FOCUS
As is to be expected in a 0-55 selling handicap, a very moderate race but sound enough for the level.
Arabian Moon(IRE) Official explanation: vet said gelding had lost a shoe

4240 CUBAN H'CAP — 1m 1f 209y
3:40 (3:41) (Class 5) (0-70,69) 3-Y-0+ **£5,181** (£1,541; £770; £384) **Stalls** High

Form RPR
2030 **1** **Fantasy Crusader**[11] 3934 7-8-11 **52** AdamKirby(3) 1 61
(R M H Cowell) *chsd ldng pair: tk clsr order over 3f out: sn rdn: styd on wl fnl f: led cl home* **6/1**[3]

3406 **2** *nk* **Wester Lodge (IRE)**[14] 3840 4-10-0 **66** (b[1]) MickyFenton 2 74
(J M P Eustace) *sn pushed along to ld after 1f: rdn over 2f out: no ex whn hdd cl home* **6/1**[3]

466 **3** *6* **Will Be (IRE)**[14] 3848 3-9-8 **69** (tp) FJohansson 6 66
(R A Kvisla) *hld up: rdn 3f out: styd on to go 3rd wl ins f: nvr trbld ldng pair* **33/1**

0001 **4** *½* **Factual Lad**[22] 3615 8-9-8 **60** GeorgeBaker 5 56
(B R Millman) *hld up in 4th: outpcd 3f out: kpt on ins fnl f* **6/4**[1]

5136 **5** *nk* **Fortune Point (IRE)**[17] 3615 8-9-5 **57** (v) ChrisCatlin 4 53
(A W Carroll) *led for over 1f: chsd ldr: rdn over 2f out: wknd ins fnl: lost 3rd cl home* **12/1**

0-03 **6** *2 ½* **Take A Mile (IRE)**[6] 4073 4-9-6 **58** RyanMoore 3 49
(B G Powell) *s.i.s: racd in 5th: rdn over 3f out: no imp* **9/4**[2]

2m 0.80s (-1.80) **Going Correction** -0.125s/f (Firm)
WFA 3 from 4yo+ 9lb **6** Ran SP% **110.0**
Speed ratings (Par 103):102,101,96,96,96 94
CSF £38.40 TOTE £8.20: £2.40, £2.40; EX 39.00.
Owner The Fantasy Fellowship **Bred** J R C And Mrs Wren **Trained** Six Mile Bottom, Cambs

FOCUS
Just the six runners and a pretty modest handicap. The pacen was reasonable and the first two are the best guides to the level.
Take A Mile(IRE) Official explanation: trainer said gelding ran flat

4241 JOHN SMITH'S BRIGHTON MILE CHALLENGE TROPHY (H'CAP) — 7f 214y
4:10 (4:11) (Class 4) (0-80,80) 3-Y-0+
£21,812 (£6,531; £3,265; £1,634; £815; £409) **Stalls** Low

Form RPR
1135 **1** **Bee Stinger**[10] 3973 4-9-6 **76** RyanMoore 2 89
(I A Wood) *t.k.h trcking ldrs: swtchd rt over 1f out: r.o to ld ins fnl f: drifted rt: drvn out* **9/2**[2]

6620 **2** *1 ¼* **Katiypour (IRE)**[11] 3928 9-9-7 **80** AdamKirby(3) 13 90
(Miss B Sanders) *hld up bhd: hdwy and nt clr run over 3f out: swtchd lft wl over 1f out: r.o strly to go 2nd ins fnl f: hld cl home* **11/1**[3]

0404 **3** *1 ¾* **Voice Mail**[14] 3850 7-8-11 **67** (b) LPKeniry 3 73
(A M Balding) *mid-div: hdwy over 2f out: sn rdn: swtchd rt over 1f out: styd on* **12/1**

3542 **4** *½* **Mujood**[6] 4076 3-8-12 **75** StephenCarson 9 79
(R F Johnson Houghton) *prom: led over 5f out tl over 4f out: led again 3f out: sn rdn :no ex whn hdd ins fnl f* **20/1**

1420 **5** *1 ¼* **Night Storm**[7] 4040 5-9-5 **75** ChrisCatlin 4 79+
(S Dow) *s.i.s: bhd: nt clr run and swtchd rt wl over 1f out: r.o: nrst fin* **25/1**

1526 **6** *hd* **Samuel Charles**[10] 3973 8-9-8 **78** EddieAhern 8 80
(C R Dore) *mid-div: outpcd 3f out: styd on ins fnl f* **14/1**

2001 **7** *1 ¾* **Given A Choice (IRE)**[20] 3688 4-9-7 **77** (v[1]) AlanMunro 1 75
(J G Given) *prom: led over 4f out tl 3f out: sn rdn: one pce fnl f* **11/1**[3]

0062 **8** *1 ½* **Pillars Of Wisdom**[20] 3679 4-9-8 **78** (t) KerrinMcEvoy 12 72
(J L Dunlop) *led tl over 5f out: styd prom: ev ch over 2f out: one pce fr over 1f out* **7/2**[1]

0551 **9** *1 ¼* **Deira (USA)**[14] 3841 3-8-9 **72** HayleyTurner 6 62
(C E Brittain) *bhd: hdwy on rails 3f out: sn rdn: wknd ins fnl f* **20/1**

2154 **10** *½* **Missed A Beat**[6] 4075 4-9-1 **71** OscarUrbina 10 61
(M Blanshard) *mid-div: effrt over 2f out: wknd over 1f out* **14/1**

6525 **11** *1 ¼* **Takes Tutu (USA)**[7] 4048 7-9-0 **70** (p) SteveDrowne 15 57
(C R Dore) *a towards rr* **25/1**

2202 **12** *hd* **Gaelic Princess**[11] 3953 6-9-9 **79** FergusSweeney 11 66
(A G Newcombe) *in tch: rdn over 3f out: wknd over 1f out* **14/1**

6565 **13** *2* **Landucci**[31] 3337 5-9-8 **78** MichaelHills 14 60
(J W Hills) *mid-div: hdwy 3f out: effrt 2f out: sn btn* **9/2**[2]

1500 **14** *4* **Boundless Prospect (USA)**[11] 3928 7-9-10 **80** (p) MickyFenton 7 53
(Miss Gay Kelleway) *s.i.s: a bhd* **16/1**

1m 32.75s (-2.29) **Going Correction** -0.125s/f (Firm)
WFA 3 from 4yo+ 7lb **14** Ran SP% **126.0**
Speed ratings (Par 105):106,104,103,102,101 101,99,97,96,96 94,94,92,88
CSF £53.13 CT £582.87 TOTE £5.00: £2.20, £4.30, £3.30; EX 85.00.
Owner Sporting Occasions No 11 **Bred** Templeton Stud **Trained** Upper Lambourn, Berks

FOCUS
An added prize fund of £35,000 attracted a strong field for the latest renewal of the Brighton Mile. The time was decent and the form looks sound enough, rated around the fourth.
Gaelic Princess Official explanation: jockey said mare lost her action in the final furlong

4242 PULSE BAR SPRINT H'CAP — 5f 213y
4:40 (4:41) (Class 4) (0-80,78) 3-Y-0 **£8,096** (£2,408; £1,203; £601) **Stalls** Low

Form RPR
2205 **1** **Mango Music**[6] 4078 3-9-7 **78** ChrisCatlin 2 85
(M R Channon) *a.p: led 2f out: r.o wl: rdn out* **8/1**

5130 **2** *1 ½* **Perfect Treasure (IRE)**[42] 2987 3-8-13 **70** (t) AlanMunro 6 73
(J A R Toller) *pushed along bhd ldng quintet: swtchd rt over 1f out: r.o but drifted lft fr 1f out: wnt 2nd fnl 75yds: nt rch wnr* **14/1**

3020 **3** *1 ¾* **Make My Dream**[11] 3936 3-8-5 **62** ow2 JimCrowley 1 59
(J Gallagher) *led: rdn and hdd 2f out: kpt on same pce* **15/2**

4144 **4** *½* **Mimiteh (USA)**[9] 4003 3-9-7 **78** GeorgeBaker 3 74
(R M Beckett) *wnt rt s: trckd ldrs: rdn over 2f out: kpt on same pce* **4/1**[3]

4424 **5** *hd* **Scarlet Flyer (USA)**[6] 4078 3-9-6 **77** (p) RyanMoore 4 72
(G L Moore) *trckd ldrs: effrt over 2f out: kpt on same pce* **6/4**[1]

1613 **6** *3 ½* **Namu**[11] 3943 3-8-7 **71** SladeO'Hara(7) 5 56
(B W Hills) *trckd ldrs: effrt over 2f out: wknd over 1f out* **3/1**[2]

68.17 secs (-1.93) **Going Correction** -0.125s/f (Firm) **6** Ran SP% **114.5**
Speed ratings (Par 102):107,105,102,102,101 97
CSF £100.64 TOTE £6.40: £3.30, £3.90; EX 40.40.
Owner Antoniades Family **Bred** A G Antoniades **Trained** West Ilsley, Berks

FOCUS
A disappointing turnout considering there was £12,500 in added prizemoney up for grabs, and the form looks just ordinary for the grade but solid enough.

4243 FOSTERS TWIST H'CAP — 7f 214y
5:10 (5:10) (Class 5) (0-70,70) 3-Y-0 **£4,015** (£1,194; £597; £298) **Stalls** Low

Form RPR
6420 **1** **High Class Problem (IRE)**[24] 3569 3-9-2 **65** EddieAhern 6 71
(P F I Cole) *mde virtually all: hrd pressed fr over 2f out: kpt on u.p: all out* **7/2**[1]

5305 **2** *nk* **Salvestro**[6] 4076 3-8-11 **60** AlanMunro 7 65
(Mrs A J Perrett) *chsd ldrs: rdn over 2f out: kpt on to press wnr ins fnl f* **7/2**[1]

2165 **3** *1* **Murrumbidgee (IRE)**[12] 3906 3-9-1 **64** MichaelHills 2 67
(J W Hills) *hld up bhd ldrs: hdwy over 2f out: rdn over 1f out: ev ch ins fnl f: no ex cl home* **7/2**[1]

0-25 **4** *nk* **Snow Symphony (IRE)**[20] 3668 3-9-0 **63** ChrisCatlin 1 65?
(D M Simcock) *racd freely: prom: rdn 2f out: ev ch ins fnl f: no ex cl home* **12/1**

4666 **5** *2* **Dalima (IRE)**[26] 3477 3-9-2 **65** RyanMoore 3 62
(C E Brittain) *chsd ldrs: rdn wl over 2f out: kpt on same pce* **6/1**[2]

5340 **6** *5* **Merchant Bankes**[42] 2990 3-9-4 **67** GeorgeBaker 5 53
(W G M Turner) *rrd leaving stalls: bhd: tk clsr order over 3f out: wknd 1f out* **7/1**[3]

3260 **7** *10* **My Lovely Lady (IRE)**[15] 3828 3-9-7 **70** HayleyTurner 4 33
(M L W Bell) *s.i.s: sn in tch: rdn 4f out: sn btn* **7/1**[3]

1m 34.48s (-0.56) **Going Correction** -0.125s/f (Firm) **7** Ran SP% **113.6**
Speed ratings (Par 100):97,96,95,95,93 88,78
CSF £15.41 TOTE £3.90: £1.80, £3.30; EX 17.90 Place 6 £1,168.85, Place 5 £941.65.
Owner M Tabor & Philip Green **Bred** Mrs Clare McGinn **Trained** Whatcombe, Oxon

FOCUS
The seven-strong field had won just two races between them from a total of 69 starts coming into this, so this was obviously not a particularly strong handicap. However, there were at least four runners still in with a shout at the furlong pole and they provided a cracking finish. The runner-up and fourth set the standard.
Merchant Bankes Official explanation: jockey said colt reared up leaving the gates

T/Plt: £549.80 to a £1 stake. Pool: £59,388.95. 78.85 winning tickets. T/Qpdt: £181.80 to a £1 stake. Pool: £2,579.90. 10.50 winning tickets. TM

[4043]KEMPTON (A.W) (R-H)

Wednesday, August 9

OFFICIAL GOING: Standard

Wind: Nil

4244 WEATHERBYS FINANCE APPRENTICE H'CAP (ROUND 9) 1m 2f (P)

7:00 (7:01) (Class 4) (0-85,83) 3-Y-0+ £5,505 (£1,637; £818; £408) Stalls High

Form RPR

5-61 1 **Strawberry Lolly**[27] [3458] 3-8-8 75 JamieHamblett(3) 8 87+
(Sir Michael Stoute) *trckd ldrs: led jst ins fnl f: pushed out: comf* 11/4[1]

2551 2 3 **Katchit (IRE)**[42] [2990] 3-8-13 82 JosephWalsh(5) 6 88
(A King) *lw: chsd ldr: chal over 3f out tl slt ld 2f out: sn rdn: hdd jst ins last: kpt on but nt pce of wnr* 9/1

0632 3 1 1/4 **Burgundy**[6] [4073] 9-9-0 69 (b) AshleyHamblett 1 73
(P Mitchell) *hld up in rr: hdwy on outside over 3f out: styd on fr over 1f out but nvr gng pce to rch ldrs* 7/1[3]

0545 4 1/2 **Sky Quest (IRE)**[14] [3840] 8-9-3 75 (tp) KMay(3) 9 78+
(W R Swinburn) *bhd: drvn along 2f out: hdwy over 1f out: r.o wl cl home but nt rch ldrs* 15/2

1456 5 hd **Secretary General (IRE)**[20] [3686] 5-9-7 76 (b) TolleyDean 5 78
(P F I Cole) *s.i.s: sn in tch: drvn along fr 4f out: styd on same pce fnl 2f* 9/1

0034 6 3/4 **King's Thought**[21] [3639] 7-9-7 76 JamieJones 7 77
(S Gollings) *t.k.h early: led: hdd 2f out: wknd ins fnl f* 14/1

2410 7 1/2 **Le Colombier (IRE)**[42] [2986] 3-8-12 81 PatrickHills(5) 3 81
(J W Hills) *bhd: hdwy on outside fr 3f out: one pce and no imp fr over 1f out* 8/1

060- 8 1/2 **Babe Maccool (IRE)**[336] [5048] 4-10-0 83 SladeO'Hara 10 82
(B W Hills) *in tch tl lost position 1/2-way: rdn over 2f out: kpt on again ins last but n.d* 14/1

00/3 9 3 1/2 **Rapscallion (GER)**[50] [600] 7-9-5 77 PJBenson(3) 4 69
(Heather Dalton) *chsd ldrs: rdn fr 4f out: wknd 2f out* 14/1

0000 10 nk **Stagbury Hill (USA)**[34] [3218] 4-9-13 82 ThomasO'Brien 11 74
(J W Hills) *s.i.s: nvr beyond mid-div* 33/1

5111 11 2 **Prime Powered (IRE)**[42] [2982] 5-9-8 77 JamesMillman 2 65
(R M Beckett) *s.i.s: sn chsng ldrs on outside: wknd 2f out* 5/1[2]

2m 7.93s (-1.07) **Going Correction** -0.075s/f (Stan)
WFA 3 from 4yo+ 9lb 11 Ran SP% **121.7**
Speed ratings (Par 105):101,98,97,97,97 96,96,95,92,92 91
CSF £29.48 CT £163.54 TOTE £3.10: £1.60, £3.30, £1.60; EX 36.80.
Owner Mrs R J Jacobs **Bred** Newsells Park Stud Limited **Trained** Newmarket, Suffolk

FOCUS
A fair handicap and ordinary form, but sound enough for the grade.
Prime Powered(IRE) Official explanation: jockey said gelding lost its action

4245 PLATINUM SECURITY SERVICES H'CAP 1m 2f (P)

7:28 (7:29) (Class 6) (0-65,65) 3-Y-0 £3,238 (£963; £481; £240) Stalls High

Form RPR

5525 1 **Wee Charlie Castle (IRE)**[40] [3045] 3-9-1 59 OscarUrbina 13 66
(G C H Chung) *trckd ldrs: drvn to chal jst ins last: led fnl 75yds: rdn out* 9/2[1]

2 nk **No Recollection (IRE)**[287] [6115] 3-9-3 61 (p) EddieAhern 6 67
(M J Wallace) *chsd ldrs: drvn along 4f out: chal between horses bnd 2f out: sn led: kpt slt advantage tl hdd and no ex fnl 75yds* 7/1[3]

6-00 3 1/2 **Hazelnut**[30] [3367] 3-9-0 58 ChrisCatlin 11 63+
(J R Fanshawe) *bhd: hdwy over 2f out: styd on u.p fr over 1f out: gng on cl home but nt pce to chal* 8/1

0625 4 3/4 **Siakira**[14] [3848] 3-9-2 63 JamesDoyle(3) 2 67
(I A Wood) *bhd: hdwy and pushed wd bnd 2f out: styd on fnl f but nvr gng pce to chal* 10/1

6100 5 nk **Raise The Heights (IRE)**[71] [2102] 3-8-13 60 EdwardCreighton(3) 10 63
(C Tinkler) *s.i.s: bhd: hdwy on ins over 1f out: kpt on ins last but nvr gng pce to rch ldrs* 8/1

4600 6 3/4 **Tranos (USA)**[18] [3725] 3-9-5 63 (v1) NickyMackay 14 65+
(L M Cumani) *s.i.s: bhd: hdwy whn pushed wd bnd 2f out: kpt on again fnl f: gng on nr fin* 16/1

0-52 7 3/4 **Irish Whispers (IRE)**[13] [3870] 3-9-2 60 RichardHughes 8 60
(B G Powell) *chsd ldrs: rdn over 2f out: styd on same pce over 1f out* 5/1[2]

0000 8 5 **Super Frank (IRE)**[21] [3650] 3-9-2 60 JimmyFortune 7 55+
(G A Butler) *led: rdn over 3f out: kpt slt advantage tl hdd ins fnl 2f: wknd appr fnl f* 7/1[3]

2500 9 6 **Marcello**[102] [1291] 3-9-7 65 SteveDrowne 9 44
(P F I Cole) *chsd ldrs: rdn over 3f out: wknd 2f out* 16/1

0-40 10 3 **Gnillah**[28] [3419] 3-8-13 57 MichaelHills 1 31+
(B W Hills) *chsd ldrs: chalng whn veered bdly lft bnd 2f out: nt rcvr* 10/1

0000 11 1/2 **Cativo Cavallino**[11] [3932] 3-9-0 58 IanMongan 12 31+
(Jamie Poulton) *in tch: stl prom whn carried bdly lft bnd 2f out: nt rcvr* 16/1

06-0 12 12 **Mayden Dawn**[14] [3849] 3-9-2 60 MickyFenton 4 10
(Miss E C Lavelle) *bhd most of way: no ch fnl 3f* 33/1

2m 8.54s (-0.46) **Going Correction** -0.075s/f (Stan) 12 Ran SP% **120.8**
Speed ratings (Par 98):98,97,97,96,96 95,95,91,86,84 83,74
CSF £36.45 CT £250.75 TOTE £4.20: £2.20, £1.50, £3.70; EX 19.30.
Owner The Maybe This Time Partnership **Bred** Bryan Ryan **Trained** Newmarket, Suffolk

FOCUS
A modest but competitive handicap and the form looks ordinary.
Raise The Heights(IRE) Official explanation: jockey said gelding jumped slowly and was reluctant to race in the early stages
Super Frank(IRE) Official explanation: jockey said colt hung left
Gnillah Official explanation: jockey said filly was taken wide on the home bend
Cativo Cavallino Official explanation: jockey said gelding suffered interference on the home bend

4246 BETBROKERS OPEN AN ACCOUNT ON 0844 855 2111 NURSERY 6f (P)

7:56 (7:59) (Class 4) 2-Y-0 £4,533 (£1,348; £674; £336) Stalls High

Form RPR

3642 1 **High Style**[25] [3530] 2-9-2 78 RyanMoore 8 83+
(R Hannon) *lw: in tch: gd hdwy fr 2f out: qckdn to ld appr fnl f: sn in command: comf* 7/2[3]

4556 2 3 1/2 **Vadinka**[21] [3641] 2-8-6 68 JimCrowley 10 63
(P Winkworth) *bhdm: hdwy and n.m.r 2f out: styd on wl fnl f: wnt 2nd cl home but no ch w wnr* 20/1

3063 3 nk **Mogok Ruby**[11] [3930] 2-8-8 70 ow1 MickyFenton 4 64
(L Montague Hall) *prom: rdn to chse wnr 1f out: sn no ch: no ex and ct for 2nd cl home* 16/1

040 4 1 1/4 **Cadeaux Du Monde**[61] [2416] 2-8-10 72 ChrisCatlin 3 62
(E J O'Neill) *lw: sltly hmpd after 1f: rdn and hdwy 2f out: styd on u.p fnl f but nvr gng pce to chal* 6/1

4051 5 shd **Sweet Candy**[12] [3917] 2-9-1 77 DO'Donohoe 7 67
(K A Ryan) *chsd ldr: led ins fnl 3f: rdn 2f out: hdd appr fnl f wknd ins last* 10/3[2]

6063 6 3/4 **Hucking Hill (IRE)**[18] [3727] 2-8-13 75 SteveDrowne 9 62
(J R Best) *chsd ldrs: rdn over 2f out: wknd fnl f* 20/1

052 7 3/4 **Seaflower Reef (IRE)**[20] [3684] 2-8-7 69 FergusSweeney 2 54
(A M Balding) *in tch: rdn and outpcd 1/2-way: nvr in contention after* 10/1

3130 8 1 **Racing Stripes (IRE)**[8] [4026] 2-9-7 83 PatDobbs 6 65
(A B Haynes) *sn ld: hdd ins fnl 3f: wknd wl over 1f out* 11/1

0241 9 6 **Okikoki**[12] [3895] 2-9-2 78 KerrinMcEvoy 1 42
(W R Muir) *nvr travelling and a in rr* 3/1[1]

040 10 5 **Pas De Trois**[27] [3448] 2-7-12 60 oh4 HayleyTurner 5 9
(R F Johnson Houghton) *slowly away: no ch whn rn v wd bnd over 3f out* 50/1

1m 13.51s (-0.19) **Going Correction** -0.075s/f (Stan) 10 Ran SP% **119.4**
Speed ratings (Par 96):98,93,92,91,91 90,89,87,79,73
CSF £74.75 CT £1024.81 TOTE £3.90: £1.80, £3.50, £3.00; EX 80.70.
Owner The Queen **Bred** The Queen **Trained** East Everleigh, Wilts

FOCUS
A competitive nursery won in taking style by the progressive High Style and the placed horses set a solid standard.

NOTEBOOK
High Style showed improved form at Lingfield last time behind Market Day and he produced a tidy turn of pace to quickly settle the issue. He seems to be progressing with racing and it looks as though he was suited by this slower surface. (op 6-1)
Vadinka, who appeared not to last out the seven-furlong trip here last time, finished strongly on this drop in distance and would have been closer had he had more of a clear run through. He can find a similar race on this evidence.
Mogok Ruby shaped pleasingly on this nursery debut and seemed suited by the step up in trip, but was well held by the winner and just got run out of second close home.
Cadeaux Du Monde looked in need of further in maidens and could not get going in time, finding himself outpaced from some way out. The step up to seven furlongs is going to suit and he has a race in him off this mark. (tchd 13-2)
Sweet Candy, a ready winner on his nursery debut at Wolverhampton, faced a stiffer task off a 9lb higher mark and, having gone on well over two furlongs out, he dropped away under pressure. He may remain vulnerable off this sort of mark. (op 3-1 tchd 11-4)
Hucking Hill(IRE) ran well, but is well exposed now and likely to remain vulnerable to anything progressing. (op 25-1)
Seaflower Reef(IRE), whose stable is not in the best of form at present, finished a well-beaten second behind subsequent group scorer Enticing at Wolverhampton last time, but she failed to improve for this move into handicaps and it may take a step up to seven furlongs before she is winning.
Okikoki, off the mark at Chepstow last time, was always likely to be up against it from stall one and he was struggling in rear from an early stage. This was clearly not his form. Official explanation: jockey said colt did not face the kickback (op 5-2 tchd 10-3 in aplace)
Pas De Trois Official explanation: jockey said colt missed the break and hung left throughout

4247 TFM NETWORKS MAIDEN STKS 1m (P)

8:24 (8:31) (Class 5) 3-Y-0+ £3,238 (£963; £481; £240) Stalls High

Form RPR

1 **Changing Wind (USA)** 3-9-3 KerrinMcEvoy 4 77+
(Saeed Bin Suroor) *w'like: scope: towards rr tl stdy hdwy fr 1/2-way: drvn and qcknd over 1f out: led last half f: readily* 13/2[3]

3 2 1 1/4 **Country Escape**[114] [1055] 3-9-3 AlanMunro 14 75
(C F Wall) *bhd: drvn along 3f out: stl plenty to do 2f out: hdwy over 1f out: r.o strly fnl f: tk 2nd cl home but a hld* 12/1

2 3 3/4 **Mosharref (IRE)**[112] [1087] 3-9-3 RHills 10 73
(B W Hills) *lw: disp ld tl narrow but def advantage 5f out: rdn over 1f out: hdd and no ex last half f: lost 2nd nr fin* 10/11[1]

4 4 **Reload (IRE)** 3-9-3 SteveDrowne 9 69+
(J Noseda) *unf: scope: bit bkwd: bhd: pushed along: hdwy and swtchd rt 2f out: kpt on ins last but nvr in contention* 20/1

04 5 nk **Tiz Timely (USA)**[27] [3458] 3-8-12 FergusSweeney 13 58
(A M Balding) *chsd ldrs: pushed along over 3f out: wknd fnl f* 33/1

4 6 1 1/4 **Aryaamm (IRE)**[30] [3367] 3-8-12 PhilipRobinson 6 55
(M A Jarvis) *unf: disp ld 3f: chsd ldr ins fnl 3f: sn rdn: wknd appr fnl f* 5/2[2]

7 4 **Agnes Gift** 3-8-12 IanMongan 3 46
(Jamie Poulton) *unf: bit bkwd: bhd: sme hday on outside over 2f out: nvr gng pce to rch ldrs and wknd fnl f* 66/1

8 4 **Mantolini** 3-8-12 EmmettStack(5) 8 42
(Pat Eddery) *w'like: bit bkwd: disp ld 3f: rdn 3f out: wknd 2f out* 66/1

5 9 3 1/2 **Cool Tiger**[19] [3711] 3-9-0 DeanCorby(3) 2 34
(P Howling) *chsd ldrs: chal 4f out tl c wd over 3f and sn wknd* 66/1

10 nk **Calming Waters** 3-9-3 EddieAhern 12 33
(D W P Arbuthnot) *w'like: scope: bit bkwd: chsd ldrs over 5f* 66/1

02 11 6 **Dik Dik**[32] [3303] 3-9-3 NickyMackay 1 19
(C N Allen) *nvr travelling an a in rr* 25/1

1m 39.88s (-0.92) **Going Correction** -0.075s/f (Stan) 11 Ran SP% **119.5**
Speed ratings (Par 103):101,99,99,95,94 93,89,85,81,81 75
CSF £19.08 TOTE £6.80: £2.00, £2.20, £1.20; EX 70.50.
Owner Godolphin **Bred** Stonerside Stable **Trained** Newmarket, Suffolk
■ Outsiders My Mum Mary, Crystal Annie and Spinning Reel were withdrawn after refusing to go in the stalls.

FOCUS
An ordinary maiden. However, the front three pulled well clear of the rest and each probably has a future, with the fifth running to form.

4248 TFM NETWORKS H'CAP 1m (P)

8:52 (8:58) (Class 6) (0-65,65) 3-Y-0+ £3,238 (£963; £481; £240) Stalls High

Form RPR

4134 1 **Magic Warrior**[15] [3820] 6-9-9 60 PatDobbs 5 69
(J C Fox) *mid-div: drvn and hdwy 2f out:hrd rdn and rdr dropped rein 1f out: led ins last: hld on all out* 13/2[2]

3045 2 hd **Jomus**[4] [4139] 5-9-4 55 (b) MickyFenton 3 64
(L Montague Hall) *lw: hld up rr: hdwy on outside 2f out: str run fnl f: fin wl: nt quite get up* 15/2[3]

0322 3 1/2 **Redeye Special**[7] [4048] 4-9-6 62 LiamJones(5) 4 69
(M L W Bell) *lw: chsd ldrs: led ins fnl 3f: rdn 2f out: hdd ins last: one pce cl home* 6/4[1]

-054 **4** *shd* **Musical Echo**[28] [3410] 3-9-7 **65** .... OscarUrbina 2 71
(G C H Chung) *chsd ldrs: rdn and kpt on wl fnl 2f but nvr quite gng pce to chal* **11/1**

0060 **5** *½* **Bridegroom**[30] [3366] 4-9-1 **55** .... AntonyProcter(3) 8 61
(D R C Elsworth) *bhd: hdwy on outside over 1f out: kpt on wl cl home but nvr gng pce to chal* **25/1**

0300 **6** *½* **Possessed**[11] [3932] 3-9-2 **60** .... JimmyQuinn 1 65
(T D McCarthy) *chsd ldrs: rdn over 2f out: styd on fnl f: one pce cl home* **33/1**

1500 **7** *hd* **Brave Dane (IRE)**[12] [3900] 8-9-9 **60** .... JimmyFortune 12 64
(A W Carroll) *slowly away: bhd: rdn over 2f oout: swtchd lft to outside over 1f out: kpt on wl cl home but nvr in contention* **10/1**

/004 **8** *2½* **Benny The Ball (USA)**[9] [3999] 5-9-4 **55** .... RyanMoore 6 54
(N P Littmoden) *b.hind: bhd: swtchd rt to ins and hdwy ins fnl 2f: one pce ins last* **8/1**

0-00 **9** *1* **Lifted Way**[21] [3642] 7-9-9 **60** .... JimCrowley 14 56
(P R Chamings) *chsd ldrs: rdn 3f out: wknd over 1f out* **40/1**

5-04 **10** *1* **Future Deal**[41] [3014] 5-9-8 **59** .... SteveDrowne 10 53
(C A Horgan) *s.i.s: sn rcvrd to chse ldrs: wknd over 1f out* **16/1**

13-0 **11** *shd* **King After**[15] [3820] 4-9-10 **61** .... GeorgeBaker 11 55
(J R Best) *a towards rr and nvr in contention* **12/1**

0060 **12** *9* **Must Be Keen**[89] [1644] 7-9-1 **55** .... AdamKirby(3) 7 28
(Ernst Oertel) *led tl hdd ins fnl 3f: wknd ins fnl 2f* **50/1**

-000 **13** *14* **Morgan Lewis (IRE)**[14] [3845] 5-9-8 **59** ....(v¹) StephenCarson 13 —
(J A Geake) *lw: chsd ldrs 5f* **16/1**

1m 40.24s (-0.56) **Going Correction** -0.075s/f (Stan)
WFA 3 from 4yo+ 7lb **13 Ran SP% 124.3**
Speed ratings (Par 101):99,98,98,98,97 97,97,94,93,92 92,83,69
CSF £55.42 CT £113.51 TOTE £8.40: £2.30, £3.30, £1.40; EX 56.20.
Owner Miss H J Flower **Bred** Patrick Eddery Ltd **Trained** Collingbourne Ducis, Wilts

FOCUS
A modest handicap run at a moderate pace and the slowest of the three races run over the trip on the night. However, the form rated around the first two appears solid and should prove reliable.
Brave Dane(IRE) Official explanation: jockey said gelding missed the break and hung right in the straight
Must Be Keen Official explanation: jockey said gelding had no more to give

4249 MARTIN COLLINS ENTERPRISES H'CAP (LONDON MILE QUALIFIER) 1m (P)
9:20 (9:24) (Class 4) (0-80,80) 3-Y-O **£5,505** (£1,637; £818; £408) **Stalls** High

Form RPR

6261 **1** **Mcnairobi**[21] [3647] 3-8-13 **72** .... JimmyFortune 2 82
(P D Cundell) *trckd ldrs: slt ld 2f out: hrd drvn fnl f: hld on all out* **20/1**

0131 **2** *½* **Dancing Guest (IRE)**[21] [3643] 3-9-1 **74** .... EddieAhern 6 86+
(G G Margarson) *hld up in rr: n.m.r ins fnl 3f: hdwy 2f out: str run over 1f out: chsd wnr ins last but nvr quite gng pce to get up* **5/1²**

1060 **3** *2½* **Magical Music**[47] [2823] 3-9-0 **73** .... JimmyQuinn 8 76+
(J Pearce) *s.i.s and stmbld sn after s: plenty to do 3f out: hdwy on outside 2f out: str run ins last: gng on cl home* **25/1**

1661 **4** *1* **Lii Najma**[15] [3827] 3-8-9 **68** .... KerrinMcEvoy 5 69
(C E Brittain) *led tl narrowly hdd 2f out: wknd fnl f* **8/1**

43-4 **5** *½* **Tennis Star (IRE)**[99] [1374] 3-9-2 **78** .... RichardKingscote(3) 7 78
(R Charlton) *chsd ldrs: chal 3f out to 2f out: wknd fnl f* **16/1**

0100 **6** *hd* **Royal Amnesty**[10] [3973] 3-9-5 **78** .... OscarUrbina 10 77
(G C H Chung) *mid-div: pushed along over 2f out: nvr gng pce to trble ldrs* **8/1**

045 **7** *2* **Dance Spirit (IRE)**[33] [3266] 3-8-11 **70** .... RichardHughes 4 65
(B J Meehan) *lw: b.hind: chsd ldrs: rdn 3f out: wknd fnl f* **25/1**

623 **8** *hd* **Silent Applause**[15] [3826] 3-9-0 **73** .... MickyFenton 11 67
(Dr J D Scargill) *sn mid-div: drvn over 2f out: styd on fnl f but n.d* **14/1**

6-02 **9** *nk* **Brave Fight**[35] [3202] 3-9-4 **77** .... FergusSweeney 12 71
(A King) *lw: chsd ldrs: rdn 3f out: wknd fnl f* **11/2³**

-200 **10** *1¼* **Cloud Atlas (IRE)**[88] [1681] 3-8-13 **72** .... PatDobbs 9 63
(S Kirk) *bhd: styd on fr over 1f out: nvr in contention* **50/1**

4511 **11** *8* **Opera Writer (IRE)**[18] [3729] 3-8-9 **68** ....(e) AlanMunro 14 40
(J R Boyle) *lw: chsd ldrs 5f* **11/2³**

12 *11* **Versatile**[135] 3-9-7 **80** .... SteveDrowne 3 27
(G A Ham) *bhd: effrt 3f out: nvr bttr than mid-div: sn bhd* **50/1**

-301 **13** *13* **Sicilian (IRE)**[44] [2932] 3-9-5 **78** .... MichaelHills 13 —
(B W Hills) *sn bhd and nvr travelling* **9/2¹**

1m 39.57s (-1.23) **Going Correction** -0.075s/f (Stan) **13 Ran SP% 116.8**
Speed ratings (Par 102):103,102,100,99,98 98,96,96,95,94 86,75,62
CSF £110.05 CT £2595.57 TOTE £32.00: £4.90, £2.30, £7.20; EX 219.10 Place 6 £120.66, Place 5 £27.10.
Owner Ian M Brown **Bred** Roden House Stud **Trained** Compton, Berks

FOCUS
The fastest of the three races run over the trip at the meeting, but also the classiest and the form looks sound. The winner and the fourth were both at the front end throughout, whilst the second and third came from well back, suggesting no bias.
Magical Music Official explanation: jockey said filly was hampered at the start
Sicilian(IRE) Official explanation: jockey said gelding did not face the kickback
T/Plt: £152.30 to a £1 stake. Pool: £56,960.80. 272.95 winning tickets. T/Qpdt: £27.10 to a £1 stake. Pool: £3,145.90. 85.70 winning tickets. ST

3936 NEWCASTLE (L-H)
Wednesday, August 9
OFFICIAL GOING: Good to firm (good in places)
Wind: Fairly strong, against

4250 J & G ARCHIBALD BUILDERS MERCHANT NURSERY 7f
2:30 (2:30) (Class 5) 2-Y-O **£3,238** (£963; £481; £240) **Stalls** High

Form RPR

3513 **1** **Monkey Glas (IRE)**[29] [3372] 2-8-9 **73** .... PatCosgrave 2 74
(K R Burke) *keen: prom: smooth hdwy over 1f out: led ins fnl f: pushed out* **7/1³**

015 **2** *½* **Moonwalking**[26] [3481] 2-9-2 **80** .... DaleGibson 4 80
(Jedd O'Keeffe) *keen: hld up: hdwy over 1f out: chsd wnr ins fnl f: r.o* **8/1**

532 **3** *¾* **Centenary (IRE)**[22] [3619] 2-8-11 **75** .... TonyHamilton 7 73
(J S Wainwright) *trckd ldrs: effrt over 2f out: kpt on ins fnl f* **11/1**

2505 **4** *1* **Nota Liberata**[29] [3372] 2-8-2 **66** .... FrancisNorton 5 61
(G M Moore) *hld up: effrt whn nt clr run fr 2f out tl ins fnl f: swtchd lft and kpt on: no imp* **25/1**

3251 **5** *shd* **Domino Dancer (IRE)**[42] [2972] 2-9-10 **88** .... TomEaves 3 83
(J Howard Johnson) *cl up: led briefly 1f out: wknd wl ins fnl f* **4/1²**

0531 **6** *1¼* **Heywood**[14] [3843] 2-9-0 **78** .... RichardMullen 8 70
(M R Channon) *led tl hdd 1f out: sn no ex* **5/2¹**

6013 **7** *1½* **Colditz (IRE)**[5] [4115] 2-8-1 **70** .... AndrewMullen(5) 1 58
(D W Barker) *hld up outside: rdn fr 1/2-way: wknd appr fnl f* **20/1**

U01 **8** *3½* **Always Best**[14] [3838] 2-8-4 **68** .... JoeFanning 9 47
(M Johnston) *w ldr: rdn over 2f out: wknd over 1f out* **4/1²**

1m 28.29s (0.87) **Going Correction** -0.10s/f (Good) **8 Ran SP% 109.1**
Speed ratings (Par 94):94,93,92,91,91 89,88,84
CSF £55.38 CT £556.38 TOTE £9.80: £2.40, £2.10, £2.00; EX 79.60 Trifecta £373.30 Part won. Pool: £525.87 - 0.10 winning tickets..
Owner Denis Fehan **Bred** D Bourke And Yuriy Meduedyev **Trained** Middleham Moor, N Yorks

FOCUS
A fair event in which the pace was only moderate but a reasonable test as the runners were racing into a blustery headwind and the form appears sound enough with the first three close to their marks. The field raced stands' side.

NOTEBOOK
Monkey Glas(IRE), third to the Richmond Stakes runner-up at Pontefract last time, proved suited by the step up to this trip and turned in his best effort yet. His tendency to race keenly does not detract from his performances and he is the type to continue to give a good account. (op 6-1 tchd 8-1 in a place)
Moonwalking took the eye in the paddock and, although still racing a shade keenly, showed his Hamilton form to be all wrong upped to this more suitable trip. A better end-to-end gallop would have suited and he appeals as the type to win another race. (op 10-1 tchd 11-1)
Centenary(IRE), who chased home subsequent Goodwood nursery winner Just Dust in a course and distance claimer on his previous start, shaped well on his first start for new connections but again left the strong impression that the step up to a mile will be in his favour. (op 9-1)
Nota Liberata ◆ has not proved entirely reliable so far but caught the eye on his first run over a trip that his pedigree suggested he would relish. He was denied room as the leaders were getting first run and, on this evidence, looks sure to win an ordinary event around this trip.
Domino Dancer(IRE), who turned in a much-improved effort to win at Carlisle last time, had his limitations exposed from this mark on this nursery debut over this longer trip. He will be worth another chance from this sort of mark back over six furlongs. (op 5-1)
Heywood, who had the run of the race when getting off the mark in ordinary maiden company last time, found things tougher back on turf in this more competitive event after being harried for the lead throughout. He may be best when allowed to do his own thing in front. (op 9-4)

4251 ROBERT MUCKLE MEDIAN AUCTION MAIDEN STKS 6f
3:00 (3:01) (Class 6) 2-Y-O **£2,590** (£770; £385; £192) **Stalls** High

Form RPR

0 **1** **Flying Valentino**[35] [3188] 2-8-12 .... DeanMcKeown 5 74+
(G A Swinbank) *keen: hld up: smooth hdwy over 1f out: led on bit ins fnl f: hrd hld* **25/1**

2 *nk* **Cedarlea (IRE)** 2-9-3 .... TonyHamilton 4 70
(R A Fahey) *hld up: hdwy whn nt clr run and stmbld over 1f out: chsd wnr ins fnl f: kpt on towards fin* **14/1**

5 **3** *½* **Grand Art (IRE)**[41] [3018] 2-9-0 .... SaleemGolam(3) 8 69
(M H Tompkins) *trckd ldrs: effrt over 1f out: kpt on ins fnl f: nrst fin* **9/2³**

4 *¾* **Tawnybrack (IRE)** 2-9-3 .... RichardMullen 10 66
(E J O'Neill) *missed break: keen in rr: hdwy over 1f out: nvr rchd ldrs* **7/2¹**

036 **5** *1¼* **Seaton Snooks**[64] [2321] 2-9-3 **68** .... JoeFanning 9 63
(T D Easterby) *keen: mde most to ins fnl f: sn outpcd* **7/1**

6 *1* **Aitutaki (IRE)** 2-9-3 .... DavidAllan 11 60
(T D Easterby) *hld up midfield: effrt over 1f out: no imp fnl f* **20/1**

0244 **7** *2* **Ronnie Howe**[12] [3907] 2-9-3 **73** .... TomEaves 12 54
(M Dods) *in tch gng wl: effrt and shkn up appr fnl f: sn outpcd* **4/1²**

63 **8** *¾* **Bert's Memory**[32] [3307] 2-8-7 .... AndrewMullen(5) 2 46
(K A Ryan) *keen: trckd ldrs tl wknd over 1f out* **11/2**

0 **9** *1¼* **By The Edge (IRE)**[13] [3878] 2-8-12 .... DaleGibson 13 43
(T D Barron) *keen: w ldrs tl wknd over 1f out* **16/1**

10 *1¼* **Irish Relative (IRE)** 2-9-0 .... BenSwarbrick(3) 6 44
(T D Barron) *bhd: drvn and outpcd 1/2-way: nvr on terms* **16/1**

0 **11** *½* **Dazzling Olivia (IRE)**[8] [4017] 2-8-12 .... GylesParkin 1 37
(R A Fahey) *w ldrs tl wknd over 2f out* **40/1**

00 **12** *hd* **Wilde Jasmine (IRE)**[10] [3982] 2-8-12 .... PatCosgrave 3 37
(J R Weymes) *dwlt: sn midfield: effrt wl over 1f out: sn wknd* **100/1**

0 **13** *9* **Semahs Holly**[12] [3908] 2-8-5 .... JamesO'Reilly(7) 7 10
(J O'Reilly) *trckd ldrs: outpcd after 2f: n.d after* **66/1**

1m 16.4s (1.31) **Going Correction** -0.10s/f (Good) **13 Ran SP% 120.2**
Speed ratings (Par 92):87,86,85,84,83 81,79,78,76,74 74,74,62
CSF £330.38 TOTE £27.30: £4.50, £5.00, £1.60; EX 441.80 TRIFECTA Not won..
Owner A Butler **Bred** Helshaw Grange Stud Ltd **Trained** Melsonby, N Yorks

FOCUS
In all probability an ordinary event but one in which the winner turned in an eyecatching performance. The pace was just fair, but the time was modest and the field converged in the centre. This race was hand-timed.

NOTEBOOK
Flying Valentino ◆, well beaten over five on her debut, turned in a vastly-improved effort and won without her rider having to move a muscle. Although this bare form may not be anything special, she won with much more in hand than the margin suggests and left the impression that she can hold her own in slightly stronger company. (op 22-1)
Cedarlea(IRE) ◆, a 13,500euros half-brother to three winners at up to a mile and a quarter, shaped well on this racecourse debut, despite appearing to stumble when asked for an effort. While flattered by his proximity to the winner, he will stay further and looks the sort to win a similar event. (op 12-1)
Grand Art(IRE), who shaped better than the bare form over this course and distance on his debut at the end of June, confirmed that promise but left the impression the step up to seven furlongs would be in his favour. (op 10-3)
Tawnybrack(IRE), a 40,000 euro half-brother to winners from six furlongs to middle distances, shaped well after missing the break on this racecourse debut. He will be suited by the step up to seven furlongs and appeals as the type to win a similar event. (op 11-2)
Seaton Snooks, back up in trip, had the run of the race and ran creditably. However, he is starting to appear exposed and is likely to continue to look vulnerable in this type of event. (op 17-2)
Aitutaki(IRE), a half-brother to several winners over a variety of distances, hinted at ability on this racecourse debut. He should be suited by the step up to seven furlongs but may do better in ordinary nursery company in due course.
Ronnie Howe, the most experienced of these with four previous runs, travelled strongly for a long way but found disappointingly little when let down. The return to five may suit but, as he has had plenty of chances, would not be one to place maximum faith in. (op 9-2)

4252 ESH CHARITABLE TRUST H'CAP 2m 19y
3:30 (3:30) (Class 5) (0-70,70) 3-Y-O+ **£3,886** (£1,156; £577; £288) **Stalls** Centre

Form RPR

-033 **1** **Indonesia**[52] [2684] 4-10-0 **70** .... TomEaves 4 80
(T D Walford) *prom: effrt over 2f out: led 1f out: styd on wl* **14/1³**

1234 **2** *2* **Mister Arjay (USA)**[11] [3955] 6-9-4 **60** .... TonyHamilton 7 68
(B Ellison) *chsd ldrs: rdn to ld 3f out: hdd 1f out: kpt on same pce* **13/2²**

-420 **3** 1 ½ **Calatagan (IRE)**[18] 2628 7-9-6 **67** .... AndrewMullen(5) 1 73
(J M Jefferson) *set decent pce: hdd 3f out: rallied: one pce fr 1f out* **25/1**

4611 **4** ½ **Leo McGarry (IRE)**[5] 4111 3-8-2 **62** 6ex.................... SaleemGolam(3) 5 69+
(S C Williams) *hld up and bhd: hdwy over 2f out: hung lft: hrd rdn in 4th whn veered bdly lft ins fnl f: no imp* **8/15**[1]

4015 **5** 4 **Madiba**[7] 4046 7-8-13 **55** oh2.. JoeFanning 8 56
(P Howling) *hld up: hdwy over 5f out: rdn and outpcd 3f out: n.d after* **16/1**

1664 **6** ¾ **Mulligan's Pride (IRE)**[19] 3696 5-8-13 **55**.................... DeanMcKeown 6 55
(G A Swinbank) *midfield: drvn over 4f out: outpcd fr 3f out* **25/1**

04-5 **7** ¾ **Rajayoga**[9] 4011 5-8-13 **55** oh3.. RichardMullen 3 54
(M H Tompkins) *hld up in tch: outpcd over 3f out: sn btn* **20/1**

4122 **8** 17 **Lodgician (IRE)**[11] 3955 4-9-9 **65**.............................. GrahamGibbons 9 44
(J J Quinn) *cl up tl rdn and wknd fr over 2f out* **13/2**[2]

5-00 **9** *dist* **Rockpiler**[35] 3192 4-8-13 **55** oh11................................ GylesParkin 2 —
(D W Thompson) *bhd: struggling 6f out: t.o* **100/1**

3m 32.68s (-2.52) **Going Correction** -0.025s/f (Good)
WFA 3 from 4yo+ 15lb **9 Ran SP% 117.9**
Speed ratings (Par 103):105,104,103,103,101 100,100,91,—
CSF £98.28 CT £2266.94 TOTE £21.50: £2.60, £2.30, £6.50; EX 92.90 TRIFECTA Not won..
Owner G E Dempsey **Bred** Darley **Trained** Sheriff Hutton, N Yorks
■ Tim Walford's first Flat winner.

FOCUS
A run-of-the-mill handicap but, with the hot favourite looking anything but straightforward having been set plenty to do, this race did not take as much winning as seemed likely beforehand. The placed horses suggest the form is reasonable.
Lodgician(IRE) Official explanation: trainer was unable to explain the poor form shown

4253 TARMAC H'CAP 7f
4:00 (4:00) (Class 5) (0-75,74) 3-Y-0+ **£5,181** (£1,541; £770; £384) **Stalls** High

Form RPR

5-13 **1** **Carnivore**[19] 3697 4-9-0 **61**... GrahamGibbons 5 74+
(T D Barron) *prom: effrt 2f out: led ins fnl f: hung lft: comf* **5/1**[2]

0223 **2** ¾ **Kool Ovation**[11] 3936 4-9-9 **70**.. DavidAllan 10 81+
(A Dickman) *blindfold stl on and s.s: hld up: hdwy over 2f out: chsd wnr ins fnl f: r.o* **15/2**

0021 **3** 1 ¼ **Neon Blue**[11] 3959 5-9-10 **71**..(p) DeanMcKeown 7 79
(R M Whitaker) *prom: effrt and ev ch over 1f out: one pce ins fnl f* **7/1**[3]

1231 **4** 1 **Lincolneurocruiser**[11] 3928 4-9-6 **74**................. RussellKennemore(7) 2 79
(Mrs N Macauley) *chsd ldrs: led over 1f out to ins fnl f: nt qckn* **4/1**[1]

-U05 **5** ½ **Flying Bantam (IRE)**[15] 3813 5-9-9 **70**............................ GylesParkin 6 74
(R A Fahey) *hld up: hdwy to chse ldrs over 1f out: no ex ins fnl f* **25/1**

0000 **6** 2 ½ **Harvest Warrior**[26] 3500 4-9-10 **71**...............................(b) JoeFanning 8 68
(T D Easterby) *hld up: effrt over 2f out: effrt and cl up over 1f out: outpcd fnl f* **11/1**

0056 **7** 1 **Red Chairman**[22] 3621 4-8-10 **62** ow2..................(t) DeclanMcGann(5) 13 56
(R Johnson) *dwlt: hld up: rdn 3f out: sme late hdwy: n.d* **25/1**

0606 **8** ½ **George The Best (IRE)**[31] 3330 5-8-6 **58**.......................... GregFairley(5) 9 51
(Micky Hammond) *set decent pce to over 1f out: sn btn* **25/1**

6104 **9** ¾ **Snow Bunting**[15] 3817 8-8-4 **56**............................... LeanneKershaw(5) 3 47
(Jedd O'Keeffe) *hld up: effrt over 2f out: nvr rchd ldrs* **12/1**

6150 **10** 4 **Elusive Warrior (USA)**[13] 3879 3-8-8 **61**........................ TonyHamilton 1 39
(R A Fahey) *hld up: rdn over 2f out: nvr on terms* **20/1**

035 **11** 5 **Final Award (IRE)**[30] 3362 3-8-5 **58**............................. FrancisNorton 14 22
(G M Moore) *in tch tl wknd over 2f out* **16/1**

0335 **12** 1 ½ **Society Music (IRE)**[47] 2810 4-9-10 **71**........................(p) TomEaves 16 33
(M Dods) *chsd ldrs tl wknd over 2f out* **14/1**

002 **13** 2 **Dakota Rain (IRE)**[6] 4090 4-9-11 **72**................................(e) PaulEddery 12 29
(R C Guest) *cl up: rdn 3f out: wknd 2f out* **7/1**[3]

3045 **14** 1 ¾ **Fair Shake (IRE)**[31] 3331 6-9-1 **67**.......................(v) AndrewMullen(5) 15 19
(Karen McLintock) *missed break: sn rdn along: nvr on terms* **14/1**

1m 25.61s (-2.41) **Going Correction** -0.10s/f (Good)
WFA 3 from 4yo+ 6lb **14 Ran SP% 125.0**
Speed ratings (Par 103):109,108,106,105,105 102,101,100,99,95 89,87,85,83
CSF £41.89 CT £264.90 TOTE £5.90: £2.40, £2.60, £2.20; EX 36.30 Trifecta £109.10 Pool: £309.13 - 2.01 winning tickets..
Owner The Meat Eaters **Bred** Lord Halifax **Trained** Maunby, N Yorks

FOCUS
An ordinary race in which the pace seemed sound and the form looks solid; the field converged in the centre. This race was hand-timed.
Dakota Rain(IRE) Official explanation: trainer said, regarding the poor form shown, that the race may have come too soon for the gelding having run six days earlier
Fair Shake(IRE) Official explanation: jockey said gelding missed the break

4254 PLUMBING TRADE SUPPLIES RATING RELATED MAIDEN STKS 1m 1f 9y
4:30 (4:32) (Class 5) 3-Y-0+ **£3,886** (£1,156; £577; £288) **Stalls** Centre

Form RPR

0342 **1** **Teide Lady**[21] 3650 3-8-12 57... FrancisFerris 1 65
(Rae Guest) *hld up: hdwy and cl up whn hmpd appr fnl f: ev ch whn hmpd ins last: kpt on: fin 2nd, nk: awrdd r* **7/1**

-053 **2** *nk* **Summer Lodge**[76] 1946 3-8-12 68.................................(b[1]) SaleemGolam(3) 7 68
(M H Tompkins) *cl up: effrt whn hung lft and blkd appr fnl f: hung lft ins last: led last 75yds: kpt on wl: fin 1st, nk: plcd 2nd* **9/2**[3]

0063 **3** ½ **Sinner Or Saint (IRE)**[5] 4117 3-9-1 65................................. DavidAllan 3 67
(T D Easterby) *cl up: led over 2f out tl last 75yds: no ex* **8/1**

054 **4** 2 **Hassaad**[30] 3362 3-9-1 69..(b) RichardMullen 5 63
(W J Haggas) *s.s: plld hrd and sn chsng ldrs: rdn and hung lft over 2f out: one pce over 1f out* **11/4**[1]

0344 **5** *nk* **Blacktoft (USA)**[32] 3301 3-9-1 65.................................. J-PGuillambert 6 62
(S C Williams) *slowly away: plld hrd in rr: effrt over 2f out: kpt on fnl f: no imp* **7/2**[2]

4344 **6** 3 ½ **Imperial Harry**[15] 3826 3-9-1 70.. JoeFanning 2 55
(M R Channon) *set modest pce to over 2f out: wknd over 1f out* **7/2**[2]

00-0 **7** ½ **Little Britain (USA)**[92] 1564 3-9-1 56.................................. TomEaves 4 54
(J Howard Johnson) *keen: hld up in tch: rdn over 2f out: sn btn* **20/1**

1m 58.1s (0.29) **Going Correction** -0.025s/f (Good) **7 Ran SP% 117.7**
Speed ratings (Par 103):96,97,96,94,94 91,90
CSF £39.77 TOTE £7.40: £2.60, £3.30; EX 30.80.
Owner E P Duggan **Bred** Wrottesley Limited **Trained** Newmarket, Suffolk
■ Stewards' Enquiry : Saleem Golam three-day ban: careless riding (Aug 20-21,25)

FOCUS
A modest event run at just an ordinary gallop but a rough race late on, which saw the positions of the first two reversed in the Stewards' room. The form looks sound enough rated around the first two and seventh.

4255 KPMG APPRENTICE H'CAP 1m 2f 32y
5:00 (5:00) (Class 6) (0-60,60) 3-Y-O **£2,357** (£701; £350; £175) **Stalls** Centre

Form RPR

0513 **1** **Moonlight Fantasy (IRE)**[16] 3785 3-8-7 **47**......... DanielleMcCreery(5) 4 52
(N Tinkler) *keen: led after 2f: clr over 2f out: hld on wl* **8/1**

3-03 **2** ¾ **Knight Valliant**[22] 3620 3-9-3 **55**.. NeilBrown(3) 2 62+
(J Howard Johnson) *hld up: hdwy 2f out: kpt on wl fnl f* **20/1**

6462 **3** ½ **Dubai Around (IRE)**[16] 3785 3-9-4 **53**........................ LeanneKershaw 8 56
(Micky Hammond) *keen: hld up in tch: effrt over 2f out: kpt on ins fnl f* **8/1**

4433 **4** 1 ¼ **English City (IRE)**[16] 3790 3-8-13 **55**...................... DanielRobinson(7) 7 56
(B Smart) *hld up: hdwy outside 3f out: chsd wnr over 1f out to ins last: no ex towards fin* **9/2**[2]

-002 **5** 3 **Carrietau**[30] 3357 3-8-11 **46**.................................... RussellKennemore 11 41
(J G Given) *cl up tl rdn and wknd over 1f out* **16/1**

0043 **6** ½ **Twilight Avenger (IRE)**[7] 4060 3-8-10 **48**.................. CharlotteKerton(3) 3 42
(W M Brisbourne) *in tch: rdn over 2f out: sn outpcd* **25/1**

0601 **7** *nk* **Im Ova Ere Dad (IRE)**[9] 3999 3-9-11 **60** 6ex............. TomMessenger 9 53
(D E Cantillon) *plld hrd: chsd ldrs tl rdn and wknd wl over 1f out* **2/1**[1]

0364 **8** *hd* **Peas 'n Beans (IRE)**[13] 3870 3-9-4 **58**........................ LukeMorris(5) 10 51
(M L W Bell) *midfield: rdn 3f out: btn over 1f out* **5/1**[3]

0344 **9** ½ **Apache Nation (IRE)**[6] 4069 3-9-10 **59**.......................... PJMcDonald 1 51
(M Dods) *disp ld 2f: cl up tl wknd fr 2f out* **15/2**

6-36 **10** 20 **Distant Vision (IRE)**[34] 3219 3-8-0 **40**..............................(t) NSLawes(5) 5 —
(A Berry) *disp ld 2f: cl up tl wknd over 2f out* **40/1**

-006 **11** 34 **Fairytale Of York (IRE)**[8] 4016 3-8-5 **40** oh3.................. KellyHarrison 6 —
(D Carroll) *bhd: lost tch fr 1/2-way: t.o* **66/1**

2m 12.6s (0.80) **Going Correction** -0.025s/f (Good) **11 Ran SP% 120.6**
Speed ratings (Par 98):95,94,94,93,90 90,89,89,89,73 46
CSF £160.23 CT £1332.64 TOTE £11.10: £3.40, £4.90, £3.20; EX 164.50 TRIFECTA Not won.
Place 6 £8,598.94, Place 5 £1,752.01.
Owner Mount Pleasant Farm Racing Partnership **Bred** Rockhart Trading Ltd **Trained** Langton, N Yorks

FOCUS
A modest event but an enterprising ride on Moonlight Fantasy. The form looks weak, rated around the placed horses.
T/Plt: £2,214.10 to a £1 stake. Pool: £54,898.10. 18.10 winning tickets. T/Qpdt: £131.20 to a £1 stake. Pool: £3,947.70. 22.25 winning tickets. RY

3982 PONTEFRACT (L-H)
Wednesday, August 9

OFFICIAL GOING: Good to firm
Wind: Moderate, behind

4256 BOLLINGER CHAMPAGNE CHALLENGE SERIES H'CAP (IN ASSOCIATION WITH THE DAILY TELEGRAPH) 1m 2f 6y
2:20 (2:21) (Class 5) (0-75,75) 3-Y-0+ **£4,372** (£1,355; £677; £338) **Stalls** Low

Form RPR

5224 **1** **Dark Charm (FR)**[12] 3900 7-10-13 **69**........................... MrBMcHugh(5) 9 77
(R A Fahey) *hld up: stdy hdwy over 3f out: effrt over 1f out: rdn and squeezed through to ld ins last: edgd lft: r.o* **9/2**[2]

3504 **2** 2 **Barbirolli**[25] 3519 4-10-5 **61**................................... MrBenBrisbourne(5) 7 65
(W M Brisbourne) *trckd ldrs gng wl: hdwy on inner 2f out: rdn and ev ch whn bmpd ins last: kpt on same pce* **7/1**[3]

2-64 **3** 1 **Hilltime (IRE)**[18] 3377 6-10-0 **56** oh5.............................. MrTierney(5) 1 58
(J S Wainwright) *led: rdn along over 2f out: drvn over 1f vout: hdd jst ins last and kpt on same pce* **15/2**

06-4 **4** 5 **Planters Punch (IRE)**[11] 3939 5-10-4 **60**...................... MrSFMagee(5) 2 53
(G M Moore) *a.p: effrt over 3f out: rdn and ev ch over 1f out: edgd lft and wknd ins last* **9/1**

3003 **5** 4 **Ransom Strip (USA)**[11] 3939 3-10-7 **67**............................... MrWHogg 6 52
(M Johnston) *hld up: hdwy over 4f out: rdn along wl over 2f out: sn no imp* **7/1**[3]

0105 **6** 1 **Splodger Mac (IRE)**[19] 3716 7-10-0 **56** oh5............. MrPCollington(5) 4 39
(N Bycroft) *cl up: rdn along 3f out: drvn wl over 1f out: sn wknd* **10/1**

3600 **7** ½ **Fit To Fly (IRE)**[6] 4087 5-10-0 **56** oh15.....................(p) JackMitchell(5) 5 38
(R C Guest) *a towards rr* **150/1**

2425 **8** ¾ **Top Spec (IRE)**[19] 3706 5-11-0 **70**...................................... MrSPearce(5) 3 51
(J Pearce) *dwlt and bhd: hdwy 1/2-way: pushed along over 3f out: sn drvn and btn* **3/1**[1]

-050 **9** 26 **El Chaparral (IRE)**[37] 3141 6-10-9 **65**............................... CJCallow(5) 8 —
(F P Murtagh) *dwlt: a bhd* **25/1**

0/0- **10** 10 **Castleshane (IRE)**[291] 2361 9-11-10 **75**......................... MrSWalker 10 —
(S Gollings) *prom: rdn along over 4f out: wknd over 3f out* **14/1**

2m 13.67s (-0.41) **Going Correction** -0.20s/f (Firm)
WFA 3 from 4yo+ 9lb **10 Ran SP% 110.2**
Speed ratings (Par 103):93,91,90,86,83 82,82,81,60,52
CSF £33.43 CT £214.59 TOTE £4.60: £1.50, £2.50, £2.40; EX 25.40.
Owner R A Fahey **Bred** Cyril Humphris **Trained** Musley Bank, N Yorks

FOCUS
A modest amateurs' handicap but they went a decent gallop early and not many managed to get into this from off the pace apart from the winner. The form is straightforward, rated around the winner and third.

4257 POLAR BRADFORD NEW RANGER H'CAP 1m 4y
2:50 (2:51) (Class 5) (0-70,67) 3-Y-O **£3,886** (£1,156; £577; £288) **Stalls** Low

Form RPR

-600 **1** **Colton**[31] 3329 3-8-9 **55**... NCallan 7 71
(J M P Eustace) *trckd ldrs: hdwy 1/2-way: swtchd rt and effrt to chse ldr over 1f out: rdn to ld ent last: kpt on* **33/1**

0000 **2** 1 **Light Dreams**[28] 3412 3-9-0 **60**....................................(v) JimmyQuinn 8 73
(W J Knight) *chsd ldr: hdwy to ld 2f out: sn rdn and edgd lft: drvn and hdd ent last: kpt on u.p* **33/1**

6022 **3** 6 **Jenny Soba**[12] 3910 3-8-1 **52**................................ MichaelJStainton(5) 3 51
(R M Whitaker) *prom: rdn along and sltly outpcd over 2f out: styd on u.p appr last* **10/1**

2432 **4** *shd* **Spinning**[19] 3698 3-9-7 **67**... PaulFessey 1 66+
(T D Barron) *chsd ldrs: effrt 3f out: sn rdn along and kpt on appr last* **10/1**

3454 **5** *shd* **Feelin Irie (IRE)**[18] 3725 3-9-0 **60**.................................... KimTinkler 2 59
(N Tinkler) *led: rdn along 3f out: hdd 2f out: sn drvn and wknd fr over 1f out* **10/1**

6562 **6** 2 ½ **Crimson Flame (IRE)**[9] 4009 3-9-0 **60**............................ TonyCulhane 9 53+
(M R Channon) *hld up in rr: hdwy over 3f out: sn rdn along and nvr nr ldrs* **7/1**[2]

0621 **7** *9* **Superior Star**[7] 4060 3-9-6 **66** 6ex..............................(v) PaulHanagan 13 39
(R A Fahey) *in tch: pushed along over 3f out: rdn over 2f out and sn btn* **11/8**[1]

4214 **8** *3 ½* **Farne Island**[19] 3695 3-8-13 **62**.. DNolan(3) 10 27
(J J Quinn) *midfield: effrt and sme hdwy 3f out: rdn over 2f out: sn drvn and nvr a factor* **8/1**[3]

5166 **9** *¾* **Decree Nisi**[19] 3695 3-9-3 **63**...................................... RoystonFfrench 11 26
(Mrs A Duffield) *a rr* **16/1**

4530 **10** *1 ½* **Royal Composer (IRE)**[22] 3606 3-9-6 **66**..........................(v[1]) KDarley 4 25
(T D Easterby) *bhd fr 1/2-way* **11/1**

6006 **11** *45* **Baileys Polka**[15] 3828 3-8-11 **57**.............................(b[1]) RobertWinston 12 —
(J G Given) *prom: rdn along over 3f out: drvn: wknd and hung rt over 2f out: sn bhd and virtually p.u fnl f* **50/1**

1m 43.79s (-1.91) **Going Correction** -0.20s/f (Firm) **11** Ran SP% **115.0**
Speed ratings (Par 100):101,100,94,93,93 91,82,78,78,76 31
CSF £799.08 CT £11104.11 TOTE £34.10: £7.60, £6.00, £2.20; EX 747.80.
Owner Park Lodge Racing **Bred** Dunchurch Lodge Stud Co **Trained** Newmarket, Suffolk

FOCUS
Another ordinary handicap but they went a decent pace and again few ever managed to get into it. The front pair pulled well clear and, though neither of them had previously made the frame, the form still looks solid for the grade.
Colton Official explanation: trainer's rep said, regarding the improved form shown, the gelding had taken time to mature and had benefited from being ridden more patiently today

4258 CHAPLINS CLUB H'CAP 5f
3:20 (3:21) (Class 5) (0-75,75) 3-Y-0+ **£4,533** (£1,348; £674; £336) **Stalls** Low

Form RPR

6511 **1** **Blue Maeve**[19] 3718 6-9-1 **64**.................................... SilvestreDeSousa 13 81
(A D Brown) *qckly away: mde all: rdn wl over 1f out and styd on strly* **8/1**[3]

1423 **2** *2 ½* **Kings College Boy**[11] 3938 6-9-5 **75**......................(v) JamesReveley(7) 3 83
(R A Fahey) *keen: trckd ldrs: hdwy wl over 1f out: styd on to chse wnr ins last: no imp* **9/1**

6042 **3** *1* **Talcen Gwyn (IRE)**[5] 4110 4-8-8 **57**.............................(v) DavidKinsella 9 61
(M F Harris) *prom: hdwy 2f out: rdn to chal wl over 1f out: sn drvn and one pce* **9/1**

4012 **4** *¾* **Namir (IRE)**[10] 3988 4-8-11 **63**....................................(vt) AmirQuinn(3) 10 64
(S R Bowring) *chsd ldrs: hdwy 2f out: sn rdn and no imp appr last* **6/1**[2]

4053 **5** *¾* **Blue Knight (IRE)**[6] 4067 7-8-8 **57**..............................(vt) DanielTudhope 5 56
(D Carroll) *hld up: hdwy whn n.m.r 2f out: swtchd rt and rdn over 1f out: kpt on ins last* **25/1**

1210 **6** *nk* **Paddywack (IRE)**[4] 4157 9-9-0 **63** 7ex..........................(b) TonyCulhane 6 61
(D W Chapman) *towards rr: hdwy 2f out: sn rdn and kpt on: nt rch ldrs* **10/1**

0020 **7** *1 ¾* **Divine Spirit**[1] 4230 5-9-3 **66**.. JimmyQuinn 8 57
(M Dods) *towards rr: hdwy wl over 1f out: sn rdn and no imp* **8/1**[3]

0065 **8** *1 ½* **Brigadore**[10] 3988 7-8-13 **62**... RobertWinston 14 48
(J G Given) *s.i.s: sme hdwy over 2f out: nvr a factor* **8/1**[3]

4631 **9** *nk* **Witchry**[27] 3438 4-9-11 **74**.. NCallan 4 59
(A G Newcombe) *nvr nr ldrs* **9/1**

0000 **10** *nk* **Rectangle (IRE)**[10] 3988 6-8-7 **56** oh6............................. PaulHanagan 1 40
(Micky Hammond) *chsd ldrs on inner: rdn along over 2f out and sn wknd* **100/1**

1200 **11** *¾* **Glencairn Star**[10] 3972 5-9-9 **75**.. DNolan(3) 12 56
(J S Goldie) *in tch on outer: rdn along over 2f out: sn wknd* **5/1**[1]

0035 **12** *1 ¾* **Brut**[14] 3832 4-9-3 **66**.. RoystonFfrench 7 41
(D W Barker) *a towards rr* **25/1**

6330 **13** *2* **Raccoon (IRE)**[11] 3938 6-9-1 **64**..(v) KDarley 15 31
(D W Chapman) *prom: rdn along over 2f out: sn wknd* **20/1**

62.05 secs (-1.75) **Going Correction** -0.20s/f (Firm)
WFA 3 from 4yo+ 3lb **13** Ran SP% **116.8**
Speed ratings (Par 103):106,102,100,99,98 97,94,92,91,91 90,87,84
CSF £73.16 CT £686.47 TOTE £9.20: £2.80, £2.60, £3.70; EX 55.50.
Owner R G Fell **Bred** P J And Mrs Nolan **Trained** Pickering, York

FOCUS
A decent sprint handicap run at a good pace and yet again very few ever figured.
Divine Spirit Official explanation: jockey said gelding was denied a clear run

4259 POLAR CASTLEFORD CONNECT H'CAP 1m 4f 8y
3:50 (3:50) (Class 3) (0-90,87) 3-Y-0+
£9,348 (£2,799; £1,399; £700; £349; £175) **Stalls** Low

Form RPR

2133 **1** **Go Solo**[25] 3519 5-9-4 **77**.. RobertWinston 9 86
(G A Swinbank) *hld up in tch: smooth hdwy 3f out: rdn to ld over 1f out: drvn ins last: edgd lft and kpt on wl* **5/1**[3]

2333 **2** *½* **Gee Dee Nen**[71] 2117 3-8-10 **80**.. NCallan 5 88
(M H Tompkins) *hld up in rr: gd hdwy 4f out: led over 2f out: rdn and hdd over 1f out: edgd rt and rallied ins last: no ex towards fin* **9/2**[2]

0000 **3** *1 ¾* **Crow Wood**[32] 3294 7-9-11 **87**... DNolan(3) 3 92
(J J Quinn) *chsd ldrs: rdn along 3f out: kpt on u.p appr last* **8/1**

0501 **4** *2* **Best Prospect (IRE)**[26] 3497 4-9-12 **85**............................ PhillipMakin 4 87
(M Dods) *hld up in tch: hdwy over 3f out: swtchd rt 2f out and rdn to chal wl over 1f out: ch tl drvn and wknd ent last* **6/1**

-000 **5** *8* **Jeepstar**[41] 3028 6-9-2 **75**.. RoystonFfrench 8 64
(S C Williams) *sn led: rdn along over 3f out: hdd over 2f out and sn wknd* **10/1**

0001 **6** *32* **Highest Regard**[11] 3939 4-8-9 **68**..................................... DanielTudhope 6 —
(N P McCormack) *cl up: rdn along over 3f out: sn wknd and eased* **14/1**

-052 **7** *76* **Royal Jet**[12] 3890 4-9-13 **86**... TonyCulhane 7 —
(M R Channon) *hld up towards rr: hdwy 4f out: rdn along and in tch whn stmbld 2f out: sn wknd and virtually p.u fnl f* **2/1**[1]

2m 36.28s (-4.02) **Going Correction** -0.20s/f (Firm)
WFA 3 from 4yo+ 11lb **7** Ran SP% **109.3**
Speed ratings (Par 107):105,104,103,102,96 75,24
CSF £25.04 CT £159.47 TOTE £5.10: £2.60, £2.10; EX 21.10.
Owner B Valentine **Bred** G Reed **Trained** Melsonby, N Yorks

FOCUS
A competitive handicap and sound form rated around the first three.

NOTEBOOK
Go Solo, trying this distance for the first time, has been shaping over slightly shorter as though it was required and, having been held up early on, he made stylish headway to reach a challenging position and kept on strongly from the persistent Gee Dee Nen. There is probably further improvement in him and he deserves a crack at something a bit better on this evidence. (tchd 9-2)
Gee Dee Nen, not for the first time this season, ran with great credit in defeat, but he again found one too good and was unable to stay on as strongly as the winner. He will doubtlessly find a race, but continues to creep up the handicap without winning. (op 5-1 tchd 11-2, 6-1 in places)
Crow Wood has been running in hotly-contested handicaps and the less-competitive nature of this enabled him to produce an improved performance. He probably remains too high in the weights to win at present though. (op 10-1 tchd 11-1)
Best Prospect(IRE), who showed improved form for the step up to this distance when winning at Newmarket last time, came through to hold every chance, but he appeared to be found out by the 4lb rise and faded under his big weight. (op 4-1)
Jeepstar, backed in the morning, drifted right out on course and today was clearly not the day. Almost all of his wins have been at around this time of year and a return to winning form cannot be far away, with a step back up in trip likely to suit. Official explanation: jockey said gelding hung right handed throughout (op 6-1)
Highest Regard, a surprise winner at Newcastle last time, was unable to build on that, but was beaten too far for this to be his true form. (op 10-1 tchd 16-1)
Royal Jet, back to his best at Ascot recently, was rightly made favourite to confirm that promise, but he was already struggling when stumbling and he quickly stopped afterwards. He deserves another chance. Official explanation: jockey said gelding stumbled and lost its action on the final bend (op 3-1)

4260 POLAR FORD VAN CENTRE MAIDEN STKS 6f
4:20 (4:23) (Class 4) 2-Y-O **£5,181** (£1,541; £770; £384) **Stalls** Low

Form RPR

0242 **1** **Ebn Reem**[26] 3496 2-9-3 **84**... PhilipRobinson 6 88
(M A Jarvis) *mde all: rdn wl over 1f out: styd on wl* **6/4**[1]

23 **2** *1 ½* **Gentleman Pirate**[18] 3738 2-9-3 .... JimmyQuinn 7 84
(M H Tompkins) *trckd ldrs: hdwy to chse wnr over 1f out: sn rdn and kpt on fnl f* **12/1**

5 **3** *2 ½* **Karoo Blue (IRE)**[33] 3253 2-9-3 .... StanleyChin 12 76+
(C E Brittain) *a.p: rdn along 2f out: kpt on same pce appr last* **9/1**

4 *5* **Captain Jacksparra (IRE)** 2-9-3 .... NCallan 13 61+
(K A Ryan) *dwlt: sn in tch towards outer: rdn along 2f out: sn one pce* **4/1**[2]

5 *1 ¼* **Denbera Dancer (USA)** 2-9-3 .... KDarley 11 57+
(M Johnston) *chsd ldrs: rdn along over 2f out: sn one pce* **6/1**[3]

6 *1* **King's Apostle (IRE)** 2-9-3 .... AdrianTNicholls 5 54
(W J Haggas) *towards rr: sltly hmpd iover 3f out: styd on fnl 2f: nrst fin* **33/1**

45 **7** *7* **Alberts Story (USA)**[14] 3830 2-9-3 .... PaulHanagan 1 33
(R A Fahey) *a towards rr* **50/1**

6 **8** *2* **Monet's Lady (IRE)**[14] 3830 2-8-12 .... RoystonFfrench 2 22
(R A Fahey) *a towards rr* **66/1**

9 *1 ¼* **Prince Noel** 2-9-0 .... DNolan(3) 3 24
(N Wilson) *a rr* **100/1**

10 *7* **Hits Only Vic (USA)** 2-9-3 .... PaulQuinn 8 —
(J Pearce) *a bhd* **100/1**

11 *7* **Glorious View** 2-9-3 .... PhillipMakin 9 —
(M W Easterby) *a rr* **150/1**

12 *5* **Bad Boy Al (IRE)** 2-8-12 .... MarkLawson(5) 4 —
(D W Barker) *s.i.s: a bhd* **100/1**

0 **B** **Packers Hill (IRE)**[42] 2972 2-9-3 .... RobertWinston 15 —
(G A Swinbank) *in tch towards outer whn b.d over 3f out* **25/1**

U **Watch Out** 2-9-3 .... DanielTudhope 14 —
(M W Easterby) *wnt bdly rt s: in rr whn hmpd and uns rdr over 3f out* **125/1**

64 **F** **Roclette (USA)**[43] 2958 2-8-12 .... TonyCulhane 10 —
(B W Hills) *chsd ldrs: sddle slipped: stmbld and fell over 3f out* **6/1**[3]

1m 16.43s (-0.97) **Going Correction** -0.20s/f (Firm) **15** Ran SP% **120.9**
Speed ratings (Par 96):98,96,92,86,84 83,73,71,69,60 50,44,—,—,—
CSF £22.04 TOTE £2.40: £1.40, £2.60, £2.40; EX 21.30.
Owner Sheikh Ahmed Al Maktoum **Bred** Darley **Trained** Newmarket, Suffolk

FOCUS
Probably a decent maiden that is likely to produce future winners, although the winner is arguably a bit exposed. None of the principals were hampered by the fall of Roclette, who came down on the run to the straight.

NOTEBOOK
Ebn Reem finally put his head in front in an incident-packed race. He will probably have to try his luck back in nurseries now, unless connections believe he is worth a try in a higher grade, off what could be a stiff-enough mark. (op 11-4 tchd 3-1 in a place)
Gentleman Pirate, who was a beaten favourite last time, stayed on nicely up the hill to give the winner some minor scares in the latter stages. Six or seven furlongs looks ideal for him. (op 16-1)
Karoo Blue(IRE) once again showed enough promise to suggest he is capable of winning races. He will be of serious interest in handicap company if he fails to land a maiden next time. (op 11-1 tchd 12-1)
Captain Jacksparra(IRE) ◆, a Danehill newcomer that cost 90,000gns earlier in the year, caught the eye just behind the places and could be the nicest horse to come out of the race. Entries in the Champagne Stakes (Group 2) and Middle Park Stakes (Group 1) suggest he is well thought of, and an ordinary maiden is well within his scope before connections possibly raise their sights. (op 10-3)
Denbera Dancer(USA), a $170,000 brother to last season's top filly Rumplestiltskin, was arguably slightly disappointing on his debut considering the calibre of opposition he was taking on. Clearly held in some regard given his big-race entries (he holds three Group 1 entries,) one would presume he is capable of much better. (op 9-2)
King's Apostle(IRE) was not helped by the melee that surrounded the fall of Roclette and showed enough promise to suggest he can win races at two. (op 50-1)
Watch Out, a newcomer by Observatory, was clearly not fancied to go close but failed to get around after getting involved in melee that surrounded the fall of Roclette. (tchd 28-1)
Roclette(USA) was being held up in the middle of the pack when her saddle slipped, causing her to buck and kick, which contributed to her coming down. One hopes her confidence has not been too badly affected by the experience. (tchd 28-1)
Packers Hill(IRE) had nowhere to go when Roclette came down, depositing himself and the jockey on the turf. He will, obviously, need to prove the experience did not sour his opinion of racing. (tchd 28-1)

4261 MATTY BOWN MEMORIAL MAIDEN STKS 1m 4y
4:50 (5:00) (Class 5) 3-Y-0+ **£3,886** (£1,156; £577; £288) **Stalls** Low

Form RPR

-322 **1** **O'Tara (IRE)**[53] 2662 3-9-3 **80**... NCallan 1 76
(M H Tompkins) *trckd ldr: effrt to chal 2f out: rdn wl over 1f out: edgd rt and drvn ins last: kpt on to ld nr line* **2/1**[2]

0403 **2** *hd* **Alhaitham (USA)**[19] 3711 3-9-3 **85**...(t) KDarley 7 75
(J L Dunlop) *led: rdn along and jnd 2f out: drvn and hung bdly rt ins last: hdd nr fin* **1/2**[1]

0-04 **3** *5* **Star Sign**[10] 3987 4-9-0 **40**....................................... MarkLawson(5) 4 57
(D W Barker) *trckd ldng pair: rdn along wl over 2f out: kpt on same pce* **100/1**

4 *7* **Zamhrear** 3-8-12 .... StanleyChin 8 41
(C E Brittain) *in tch: pushed along over 3f out: sn rdn and outpcd fr over 2f out* **20/1**[3]

 The Form Book, Raceform Ltd, Compton, RG20 6NL

45 **5** *8* **Bayberry King (USA)**^{5} [4117] 3-9-3 PaulHanagan 6 28
(J S Goldie) *hld up: a rr* **25/1**

5 **6** *8* **Tagart**^{10} [3987] 3-9-3 JimmyQuinn 9 9
(J J Quinn) *wnt rt s: a rr* **100/1**

0-00 **7** *1¾* **Earthling**^{33} [3258] 5-9-10 37 PaulQuinn 3 —
(D W Chapman) *a rr* **200/1**

1m 44.09s (-1.61) **Going Correction** -0.20s/f (Firm)
WFA 3 from 4yo+ 7lb **7** Ran SP% **111.1**
Speed ratings (Par 103):100,99,94,87,79 71,70
CSF £3.17 TOTE £2.90: £1.20, £1.10; EX 4.00.
Owner The Tara Syndicate **Bred** Mrs Brid Cosgrove **Trained** Newmarket, Suffolk

FOCUS
An uncompetitive maiden and it would have been nicer to see the front two pull more than five lengths clear of a 40-rated rival, who limits the form. Alhaitham again found a way to get beat.

4262 POLAR BARNSLEY NEW TRANSIT H'CAP 6f
5:20 (5:27) (Class 5) (0-75,73) 3-Y-O **£3,886** (£1,156; £577; £288) **Stalls** Low

Form RPR

305 **1** **Conrad**^{32} [3285] 3-9-2 **68** PaulHanagan 3 75
(R A Fahey) *trckd ldrs on inner: hdwy to chse ldr wl over 1f out: rdn to ld ent last: styd on* **8/1**

0055 **2** *1¼* **Greek Secret**^{11} [3943] 3-9-0 **66** NCallan 2 70
(T D Easterby) *hld up in rr: hdwy over 2f out: rdn over 1f out: styd on ins last: nrst fin* **8/1**

0014 **3** *½* **Hotham**^{17} [3759] 3-9-0 **69** DNolan(3) 4 71
(N Wilson) *led: rdn along over 2f out: drvn over 1f out: hdd ent last: kpt on same pce* **12/1**

0331 **4** *5* **Soto**^{11} [3936] 3-9-6 **72** DaleGibson 7 59
(M W Easterby) *sn cl up: effrt and ev ch over 2f out: sn rdn and wknd over 1f out* **9/4**^{1}

0650 **5** *3* **Josarty**^{18} [3749] 3-8-2 **54** oh3 JimmyQuinn 10 32
(J J Quinn) *wnt rt s: a towards rr* **12/1**

2321 **6** *1¼* **Lucksin (IRE)**^{14} [3842] 3-9-3 **69** RoystonFfrench 9 43
(N Tinkler) *sn cl up on outer: pushed along and ev ch over 2f out: sn rdn and wknd over 1f out* **4/1**^{2}

-310 **7** *¾* **Charles Parnell (IRE)**^{17} [3761] 3-9-7 **73** KDarley 8 45
(M Dods) *hmpd s: a rr* **9/2**^{3}

0-00 **8** *10* **Caribbean Nights (IRE)**^{5} [4120] 3-8-5 **57** (b^{1}) PaulQuinn 6 —
(T D Easterby) *in tch: rdn along wl over 2f out: sn wknd* **20/1**

1m 15.8s (-1.60) **Going Correction** -0.20s/f (Firm) **8** Ran SP% **111.3**
Speed ratings (Par 100):102,100,99,93,89 87,86,73
CSF £65.64 CT £550.52 TOTE £9.50: £2.30, £2.10, £3.50; EX 38.70 Place 6 £474.74, Place 5 £216.34.
Owner Cathal M Ryan **Bred** C J Mills **Trained** Musley Bank, N Yorks

FOCUS
A modest sprint handicap and not that strong form.
T/Jkpt: Not won. T/Plt: £278.00 to a £1 stake. Pool: £59,935.10. 157.35 winning tickets. T/Qpdt: £16.30 to a £1 stake. Pool: £3,743.40. 169.50 winning tickets. JR

4006 YARMOUTH (L-H)
Wednesday, August 9

OFFICIAL GOING: Good to firm
Wind: Light, half-behind Weather: Cloudy with sunny spells

4263 AVENUES CLAIMING STKS 1m 2f 21y
5:45 (5:48) (Class 6) 3-Y-O **£2,266** (£674; £337; £168) **Stalls** Low

Form RPR

0206 **1** **Coffin Dodger**^{15} [3823] 3-7-13 45 KirstyMilczarek(7) 1 49
(C N Allen) *s.s: hld up: racd keenly: hdwy and hung lft fr over 2f out: styd on to ld post* **7/1**

2046 **2** *shd* **Keisha Kayleigh (IRE)**^{33} [3244] 3-8-10 58 TedDurcan 3 53
(B Ellison) *trckd ldrs: rdn to ld over 1f out: hung rt ins fnl f: hdd post* **11/8**^{1}

006 **3** *2½* **Deserted Prince (IRE)**^{15} [3827] 3-9-0 50 TPO'Shea 6 52
(M J Wallace) *hld up in tch: rdn over 1f out: no ex ins fnl f* **16/1**

0303 **4** *hd* **Penmara**^{16} [3804] 3-8-10 54 TPQueally 11 51+
(M H Tompkins) *hld up: hdwy over 2f out: nt clr run 1f out: styd on* **5/1**^{3}

0000 **5** *2* **Rockatorri**^{13} [3870] 3-8-0 36 (b^{1}) DominicFox(3) 4 37
(G G Margarson) *chsd ldr: led over 3f out: rdn and hdd over 1f out: wknd ins fnl f* **66/1**

553 **6** *1¾* **Matinee Idol**^{32} [3303] 3-8-10 53 DaneO'Neill 8 41
(H Candy) *s.i.s: sn chsng ldrs: rdn and hung lft over 2f out: styd on same pce* **9/4**^{2}

50-0 **7** *2½* **Plough Maite**^{8} [4016] 3-8-12 47 (p) MichaelTebbutt 9 38
(D E Cantillon) *led: hdd over 7f out: led over 4f out: rdn and hdd over 3f out: wknd over 1f out* **33/1**

0000 **8** *5* **Teddy Monty (IRE)**^{15} [3821] 3-8-7 42 ow5 ChrisCavanagh(7) 2 30
(M Quinn) *hld up: in rr whn hmpd over 4f out: hung lft 3f out: n.d* **50/1**

0 **9** *9* **Lady Suffragette (IRE)**^{18} [3742] 3-8-9 FrankiePickard(7) 5 15
(John Berry) *hld up: edgd lft over 4f out: sn wknd* **40/1**

000 **10** *6* **Sansel**^{66} [2261] 3-7-12 20 MarcHalford(5) 10 —
(J Ryan) *hld up: rdn and wknd over 3f out* **100/1**

00 **11** *19* **Solomans Prospect**^{137} [735] 3-9-3 BrianReilly 7 —
(Miss D A McHale) *plld hrd and prom: led over 7f out: hdd over 4f out: wknd 3f out* **100/1**

2m 10.47s (2.37) **Going Correction** +0.15s/f (Good) **11** Ran SP% **118.7**
Speed ratings (Par 98):96,95,93,93,92 90,88,84,77,72 57
CSF £17.06 TOTE £5.50: £1.60, £1.20, £4.70; EX 25.00.
Owner Mrs C N Allen **Bred** Larkwood Stud **Trained** Newmarket, Suffolk

FOCUS
A very ordinary race, where long-time maiden Coffin Dodger finally got off the mark and the formis weak, limited by the fifth and seventh.
Lady Suffragette(IRE) Official explanation: trainer said filly was found to have pulled muscles in her hindquarters

4264 BBC RADIO NORFOLK NOVICE AUCTION STKS 7f 3y
6:15 (6:15) (Class 6) 2-Y-O **£2,331** (£693; £346; £173) **Stalls** High

Form RPR

0331 **1** **Sweet Lilly**^{9} [4008] 2-8-10 71 TedDurcan 5 76
(M R Channon) *chsd ldr: shkn up to ld 1f out: styd on* **9/4**^{1}

1235 **2** *1¼* **Hart Of Gold**^{16} [3800] 2-9-5 80 DaneO'Neill 1 82
(M J Wallace) *plld hrd: hld up: hdwy over 2f out: rdn and nt clr run over 1f out: swtchd rt: styd on* **4/1**^{2}

1425 **3** *3* **Ten Dollars More (IRE)**^{21} [3641] 2-9-1 78 SebSanders 4 70
(J A Osborne) *led: rdn and hdd 1f out: sn btn* **9/4**^{1}

2 **4** *9* **Novista (IRE)**^{54} [2604] 2-8-12 TPQueally 2 44
(M H Tompkins) *chsd ldrs: rdn over 2f out: sn wknd* **9/4**^{1}

1m 26.97s (0.37) **Going Correction** 0.0s/f (Good) **4** Ran SP% **112.3**
Speed ratings (Par 92):97,95,92,81
CSF £11.33 TOTE £2.80; EX 9.10.
Owner Jaber Abdullah **Bred** Red House Stud **Trained** West Ilsley, Berks

FOCUS
A modest-looking affair but a sound little race, with the winner to form.

NOTEBOOK
Sweet Lilly showed much more determination in victory, after giving the impression last time that she was a hard ride. Beating colts is no mean feat, and the race was won last year by a decent sort, so it would be no surprise to see her improve again. (tchd 5-2)
Hart Of Gold, who was unruly in the stalls before the off, sat off the pace early, pulling hard, before throwing down a challenge to the eventual winner throughout the final furlongs. He was never going to get on terms and, consistent though he is, is looking a bit exposed. (op 5-1 tchd 6-1)
Ten Dollars More(IRE) set the early pace and tried to steal it from the front. However, he was collared before the final furlong before coming home at the one pace. A drop in trip might suit him. (op 11-4)
Novista(IRE), returning from a break, failed to improve on his debut effort and has something to prove now. (op 7-4 tchd 5-2)

4265 YOUR MORTGAGE SOLUTIONS FILLIES' H'CAP 7f 3y
6:45 (6:46) (Class 5) (0-70,70) 3-Y-O+ **£3,497** (£1,040; £520; £259) **Stalls** High

Form RPR

0040 **1** **Tiber Tilly**^{6} [4070] 3-9-3 **65** RichardThomas 8 72
(N P Littmoden) *mde all: rdn and hung lft fr over 1f out: r.o* **11/1**

1105 **2** *1* **Whistleupthewind**^{15} [3828] 3-8-12 **60** (b) DaneO'Neill 1 64
(J M P Eustace) *mid-div: hdwy 1/2-way: rdn and ev ch fr over 1f out tl no ex wl ins fnl f* **11/2**^{3}

410/ **3** *hd* **Charlottebutterfly**^{627} [6696] 6-8-6 **51** oh1 NeilChalmers(3) 3 56
(P J McBride) *trckd wnr: racd keenly: rdn and ev ch over 1f out: styd on* **18/1**

6000 **4** *½* **Prettilini**^{12} [3897] 3-9-2 **64** TPQueally 2 66
(Stef Liddiard) *hld up: hdwy over 2f out: rdn and ev ch over 1f out: no ex ins fnl f* **14/1**

0134 **5** *1¼* **Al Rayanah**^{9} [4010] 3-9-1 **63** MichaelTebbutt 5 62
(G Prodromou) *s.i.s: hld up: hdwy over 2f out: rdn over 1f out: styd on same pce* **8/1**

/5-2 **6** *½* **Villarosi (IRE)**^{19} [3705] 4-10-0 **70** TedDurcan 4 69
(J R Best) *hld up in tch: outpcd over 2f out: styd on ins fnl f* **5/1**^{2}

5046 **7** *¾* **Whisper Inthe Wind (IRE)**^{20} [3668] 3-8-2 **53** DominicFox(3) 9 48
(Miss J Feilden) *prom: rdn over 1f out: no ex* **25/1**

-600 **8** *hd* **Mugeba**^{55} [2590] 5-9-0 **56** (t) SebSanders 7 53
(Miss Gay Kelleway) *chsd ldrs: rdn over 1f out: wknd ins fnl f* **13/2**

0-40 **9** *¾* **Sam's Secret**^{13} [3883] 4-9-9 **70** RoryMoore(5) 10 65
(S Parr) *s.s: hld up: rdn over 1f out: n.d* **9/1**

0005 **10** *¾* **Wodhill Be**^{9} [4009] 6-8-9 **51** oh10 DerekMcGaffin 11 44
(D Morris) *hld up: rdn over 2f out: a in rr* **25/1**

4203 **11** *10* **Foreplay (IRE)**^{39} [3099] 3-9-5 **70** NelsonDeSouza(3) 6 34+
(E A L Dunlop) *trckd ldrs: plld hrd: lost pl 3f out: sn rdn and wknd* **11/4**^{1}

1m 26.18s (-0.42) **Going Correction** 0.0s/f (Good)
WFA 3 from 4yo+ 6lb **11** Ran SP% **121.1**
Speed ratings (Par 100):102,100,100,100,98 98,97,96,96,95 83
CSF £72.62 CT £1115.77 TOTE £14.60: £4.00, £2.60, £6.40; EX 100.50.
Owner Mark Harniman **Bred** Mill House Stud **Trained** Newmarket, Suffolk

FOCUS
A race that took little winning after Foreplay disappointed badly. The winner was well handicapped on her best form and took advantage in a weak race, with the runner-up the best guide to the level.
Tiber Tilly ◆ Official explanation: trainers representative said, regarding the improved form, filly needs to dominate her races, and had been able to do so on this occasion
Charlottebutterfly Official explanation: jockey said mare had been hampered 2f out
Foreplay(IRE) Official explanation: trainer's representative said filly had run too free early on

4266 GARDLINE GROUP (S) H'CAP 1m 3y
7:15 (7:17) (Class 6) (0-55,52) 4-Y-O+ **£2,266** (£674; £337; £168) **Stalls** High

Form RPR

2200 **1** **Beau Marche**^{4} [4157] 4-9-2 **46** (b) SebSanders 7 58
(G G Margarson) *racd centre: chsd ldrs: rdn over 1f out: styd on u.p to ld wl ins fnl f* **7/1**^{2}

0660 **2** *hd* **Panshir (FR)**^{15} [3817] 5-8-11 **41** TPQueally 6 53
(Mrs C A Dunnett) *racd centre: hld up: hdwy 1/2-way: led over 1f out: rdn and hdd wl ins fnl f* **8/1**^{3}

050- **3** *1* **Frenchgate**^{374} [3191] 5-8-0 **35** NataliaGemelova(5) 9 44
(I W McInnes) *racd centre: chsd ldrs tl led 1/2-way: rdn and hdd over 1f out: styd on same pce ins fnl f* **40/1**

0035 **4** *1¼* **Spring Time Girl**^{7} [4057] 4-8-13 **43** DaneO'Neill 1 49
(B Ellison) *racd centre: chsd ldrs: rdn over 1f out: styd on same pce* **8/1**^{3}

0536 **5** *1¾* **Shamwari Fire (IRE)**^{6} [4087] 6-8-3 **36** (b) NelsonDeSouza(3) 2 38
(I W McInnes) *racd centre: hld up: hdwy over 2f out: styd on* **14/1**

0665 **6** *1* **Sriology (IRE)**^{78} [1915] 5-9-2 **46** (t) MichaelTebbutt 5 46
(G Prodromou) *racd centre: hld up: hdwy u.p 2f out: styd on same pce fnl f* **8/1**^{3}

0005 **7** *nk* **Kalani Star (IRE)**^{11} [3944] 6-8-7 **40** PatrickMathers(3) 14 39
(I W McInnes) *racd centre: s.i.s: hld up: hdwy over 2f out: rdn over 1f out: nt trble ldrs* **12/1**

0003 **8** *nk* **Hows That**^{49} [2758] 4-8-1 **36** AndrewElliott(5) 11 35
(K R Burke) *racd centre: chsd ldrs: rdn and hung lft over 1f out: styd on same pce* **10/1**

4600 **9** *shd* **Viscount Rossini**^{11} [3944] 4-8-5 **35** RobbieFitzpatrick 4 33
(A W Carroll) *racd centre: chsd ldrs: rdn over 2f out: wknd over 1f out* **33/1**

0-00 **10** *4* **Pragmatica**^{22} [3614] 5-8-7 **37** (p) TPO'Shea 12 26
(R M H Cowell) *racd centre: led to 1/2-way: rdn and wknd over 1f out* **20/1**

0105 **11** *1* **Wodhill Gold**^{22} [3626] 5-8-13 **43** (v) DerekMcGaffin 16 30
(D Morris) *racd centre: s.i.s: hld up: n.d* **16/1**

0000 **12** *1½* **Royal Sailor (IRE)**^{9} [4009] 4-8-8 **43** MarcHalford(5) 8 26
(J Ryan) *racd centre: chsd ldrs 6f* **50/1**

6033 **13** *2½* **Damburger Xpress**^{9} [3999] 4-9-1 **52** KirstyMilczarek(7) 10 30
(D M Simcock) *racd centre: chsd ldrs over 5f* **6/1**^{1}

0400 **14** *2½* **Whatatodo**^{15} [3827] 4-9-4 **48** (v^{1}) TedDurcan 3 20
(M L W Bell) *racd centre: chsd ldrs: rdn over 2f out: sn wknd* **6/1**^{1}

0010 **15** *¾* **Silver Visage (IRE)**^{25} [3541] 4-9-1 **45** (p) BrianReilly 15 15
(Miss J Feilden) *racd alone stands' side: chsd ldrs 6f* **16/1**

5003 **16** *11* **Angel River**[18] [3729] 4-8-7 **42**.......................................(b) RoryMoore(5) 13 —
(J Ryan) *racd centre: dwlt: a in rr* **33/1**

1m 39.39s (-0.51) **Going Correction** 0.0s/f (Good) **16** Ran SP% **124.7**
Speed ratings (Par 101):102,101,100,99,97 96,96,96,96,92 91,89,87,84,83 72
CSF £60.36 CT £2130.34 TOTE £8.60: £1.40, £2.60, £13.20, £1.70; EX 90.70.There was no bid for the winner.
Owner E P Stibbe and D Brookes **Bred** Alan Spargo Ltd **Trained** Newmarket, Suffolk

FOCUS
A pretty ordinary seller, average for the grade and sound enough.
Damburger Xpress Official explanation: trainer had no explanation for the poor form shown

4267 BANHAM POULTRY H'CAP 6f 3y
7:45 (7:46) (Class 5) (0-75,71) 3-Y-0+ **£3,691** (£1,098; £548; £274) **Stalls** High

Form RPR
1004 **1** **Norcroft**[7] [4054] 4-9-7 **65**.......................................(p) TPQueally 4 78
(Mrs C A Dunnett) *chsd ldrs: rdn to ld over 1f out: hung rt ins fnl f : r.o* **9/1**
3055 **2** *2 ½* **Kennington**[5] [4110] 6-9-7 **65**.......................................(b) RobbieFitzpatrick 7 71+
(Mrs C A Dunnett) *a.p: rdn to chse wnr fnl f: sn nt clr run: styd on same pce* **15/2**
4004 **3** *1 ¾* **No Time (IRE)**[5] [4110] 6-9-1 **62**....................................... NelsonDeSouza(3) 9 62
(J A Osborne) *hld up: hdwy over 1f out: nt trble ldrs* **9/2**[2]
3450 **4** *hd* **Regal Dream (IRE)**[22] [3612] 4-9-13 **71**.......................................(t) FrankieMcDonald 2 71
(J W Hills) *hld up: hdwy over 1f out: nt trble ldrs* **11/1**
3003 **5** *¾* **Gone'N'Dunnett (IRE)**[14] [3846] 7-9-4 **62**.......................................(v) SebSanders 6 59
(Mrs C A Dunnett) *led 1f: chsd ldr: rdn over 1f out: no ex ins fnl f* **7/2**[1]
0000 **6** *¾* **Kool Acclaim**[15] [3825] 5-8-12 **56**....................................... TedDurcan 1 51
(S C Williams) *hld up: hdwy over 2f out: rdn over 1f out: wknd ins fnl f* **6/1**
0000 **7** *¾* **Titian Saga (IRE)**[14] [3841] 3-9-3 **65**.......................................(b[1]) TPO'Shea 8 57
(C N Allen) *hld up: rdn over 2f out: n.d* **14/1**
5030 **8** *shd* **Black Oval**[7] [4054] 5-8-3 **52** oh8....................................... RoryMoore(5) 5 45
(S Parr) *hld up: rdn over 2f out: n.d* **33/1**
4034 **9** *1 ¾* **Vindication**[16] [3802] 6-9-3 **61**.......................................(b[1]) DaneO'Neill 10 48
(R M H Cowell) *racd alone towards stands' side: led 5f out: rdn and hdd over 1f out: wknd ins fnl f* **5/1**[3]
5005 **10** *18* **Malinsa Blue (IRE)**[16] [3789] 4-9-12 **70**.......................................(b) MichaelTebbutt 3 3
(S Parr) *chsd ldrs over 3f* **18/1**

1m 13.4s (-0.30) **Going Correction** 0.0s/f (Good)
WFA 3 from 4yo+ 4lb **10** Ran SP% **116.3**
Speed ratings (Par 103):102,98,96,96,95 94,93,92,90,66
CSF £74.57 CT £354.96 TOTE £8.50: £2.40, £3.20, £2.60; EX 36.70.
Owner Mrs Christine Dunnett **Bred** Norcroft Park Stud **Trained** Hingham, Norfolk

FOCUS
A modest sprint handicap and rated at face value with the first two to form.

4268 PKF (UK) LLP H'CAP 1m 6f 17y
8:15 (8:15) (Class 5) (0-75,71) 3-Y-0+ **£3,497** (£1,040; £520; £259) **Stalls** Low

Form RPR
1111 **1** **Alambic**[20] [3674] 3-8-6 **62** ow1....................................... SebSanders 4 77+
(Sir Mark Prescott) *chsd ldr 12f out: led over 3f out: rdn and edgd lft over 1f out: styd on u.p* **8/13**[1]
-052 **2** *½* **Boxhall (IRE)**[14] [3853] 4-9-12 **69**.......................................(t) TedDurcan 5 78
(W R Swinburn) *led 13f out: hdd over 3f out: sn rdn: styd on u.p* **6/1**[3]
0123 **3** *2 ½* **Shore Thing (IRE)**[26] [3502] 3-9-0 **70**....................................... TPQueally 3 76
(M H Tompkins) *hld up in tch: rdn and hung lft over 2f out: styd on same pce fnl f* **3/1**[2]
0005 **4** *8* **Domenico (IRE)**[10] [3981] 8-8-11 **57**....................................... NelsonDeSouza(3) 6 51
(J R Jenkins) *prom 11f* **40/1**
0260 **5** *5* **Dovedon Hero**[18] [3748] 6-9-10 **67**.......................................(b) DerekMcGaffin 9 54
(P J McBride) *hld up: rdn over 3f out: sn wknd* **20/1**
5000 **6** *8* **Meantime (USA)**[44] [2933] 3-8-9 **65**....................................... MichaelTebbutt 1 41
(G Prodromou) *led 1f: remained handy tl wknd over 3f out* **33/1**
1034 **7** *5* **Haatmey**[18] [3743] 4-10-0 **71**.......................................(v) TPO'Shea 7 40
(M R Channon) *hld up: rdn over 4f out: sn hung lft and wknd* **16/1**

3m 5.61s (0.31) **Going Correction** +0.15s/f (Good)
WFA 3 from 4yo+ 13lb **7** Ran SP% **117.2**
Speed ratings (Par 103):105,104,103,98,95 91,88
CSF £5.23 CT £7.47 TOTE £1.80: £1.50, £2.00; EX 6.40 Place 6 £281.49, Place 5 £163.66.
Owner Lady O'Reilly **Bred** Miss K Rausing And Mrs S M Rogers **Trained** Newmarket, Suffolk

FOCUS
A modest staying handicap in which Alambic gained her fifth consecutive success. The runner-up sets the standard.
T/Plt: £307.00 to a £ stake. Pool: £51,800.10. 123.15 winning tickets. T/Qpdt: £99.60 to a £1 stake. Pool: £3,850.30. 28.60 winning tickets. CR

4269 - 4275a (Foreign Racing) - See Raceform Interactive

4238 BRIGHTON (L-H)
Thursday, August 10

OFFICIAL GOING: Firm
Wind: Moderate, half-behind. Weather: Cloudy

4276 TOTEPLACEPOT APPRENTICE H'CAP 7f 214y
5:40 (5:40) (Class 6) (0-55,55) 3-Y-0+ **£2,590** (£770; £385; £192) **Stalls** Low

Form RPR
4405 **1** **Hadath (IRE)**[7] [4077] 9-9-2 **48**.......................................(b) PatrickHills(5) 9 55
(B G Powell) *hld up towards rr: gd hdwy on ins rail to ld ins fnl 2f: rdn out fnl f: jst hld on* **11/2**
1503 **2** *shd* **Diamond Dan (IRE)**[12] [3933] 4-9-7 **53**....................................... JamieHamblett(5) 1 60+
(P D Evans) *chsd ldrs: nt clr run over 2f out: r.o wl fnl f: jst failed* **5/1**[3]
0500 **3** *1 ¾* **Zinging**[7] [4073] 7-9-4 **45**.......................................(v) MarcHalford 3 48
(J J Bridger) *in tch: rdn to chal 2f out: styd on same pce* **16/1**
0003 **4** *2 ½* **At The Helm (IRE)**[19] [3730] 4-8-13 **47**....................................... RichardRowe(7) 8 44
(W J Knight) *in tch: rdn over 2f out: styd on fnl f: nt pce to chal* **10/1**
3301 **5** *5* **Start Of Authority**[23] [3614] 5-9-3 **47**....................................... AshleyHamblett(3) 5 33+
(J Gallagher) *plld hrd: sn w ldr: wknd wl over 1f out* **7/4**[1]
5000 **6** *hd* **Virginia Plain**[16] [3823] 3-8-4 **41**....................................... NicolPolli(3) 2 26
(Miss Diana Weeden) *chsd ldrs: hrd rdn over 2f out: sn wknd* **33/1**
6351 **7** *½* **Fantasy Defender (IRE)**[12] [3933] 4-9-6 **50**.......................................(v) JamesMillman(3) 6 34
(Ernst Oertel) *hld up in rr: hmpd on ins rail over 3f out: sn rdn and nvr nr ldrs after* **7/2**[2]
00-0 **8** *nk* **Keon (IRE)**[12] [3944] 4-9-11 **55**....................................... RussellKennemore(3) 4 38
(R Hollinshead) *led and restrained in front: hdd 2f out: wkng whn n.m.r wl over 1f out* **25/1**

4446 **9** *7* **Queue Up**[54] [2636] 4-8-5 **37**.......................................(p) JosephWalsh(5) 7 4
(A G Newcombe) *s.s: rdn 1/2-way: a bhd* **12/1**

1m 36.12s (1.08) **Going Correction** +0.075s/f (Good)
WFA 3 from 4yo+ 7lb **9** Ran SP% **120.1**
Speed ratings (Par 101):97,96,95,92,87 87,86,86,79
CSF £34.58 CT £426.62 TOTE £5.30: £2.20, £1.80, £4.00; EX 31.00.
Owner Wooden Tops Partnership **Bred** Shadwell Estate Company Limited **Trained** Morestead, Hants

FOCUS
A low-grade event run at an ordinary pace rated around the principals.
Virginia Plain Official explanation: trainer said filly lost a front shoe
Keon(IRE) Official explanation: jockey said gelding hung right

4277 TOTEEXACTA MEDIAN AUCTION MAIDEN STKS 7f 214y
6:10 (6:10) (Class 5) 3-5-Y-0 **£3,886** (£1,156; £577) **Stalls** Low

Form RPR
0-34 **1** **Distant Drums (IRE)**[12] [3931] 3-8-12 62....................................... SebSanders 4 56+
(B W Hills) *sn led: narrow ld most of way: drvn along and swished tail fnl 2f: rdr briefly dropped rein fnl 50 yds: jst on top nr fin* **2/5**[1]
0043 **2** *nk* **Never Say Deya**[8] [4052] 3-8-12 50....................................... RyanMoore 1 55
(M R Channon) *sn w wnr: str chal fnl 3f: hrd rdn and kpt on wl fnl f: jst hld* **11/4**[2]
050 **3** *12* **Norakit**[31] [3367] 3-8-5 52....................................... ThomasO'Brien(7) 3 27
(M R Channon) *stdd s: pressed ldng pair and plld hrd: rdn 3f out: wknd 2f out* **16/1**[3]

1m 36.45s (1.41) **Going Correction** +0.075s/f (Good) **3** Ran SP% **104.0**
Speed ratings (Par 103):95,94,82
CSF £1.64 TOTE £1.30; EX 1.40.
Owner N N Browne **Bred** Yeomanstown Stud **Trained** Lambourn, Berks

FOCUS
A weak maiden, suffering from lack of numbers as well as quality, run at an average pace and rated through the runner-up.

4278 CLASSIC EVENT MARQUEES (S) H'CAP 5f 213y
6:40 (6:40) (Class 6) (0-55,51) 3-Y-0+ **£2,388** (£529; £529) **Stalls** Low

Form RPR
0620 **1** **Tuscan Flyer**[5] [4157] 8-9-5 **44**.......................................(b) SebSanders 4 52
(R Bastiman) *chsd ldr: slt ld over 2f out: hrd drvn and kpt on: all out* **9/4**[1]
40-0 **2** *½* **Tiny Tim (IRE)**[128] [876] 8-8-5 **37**.......................................(b) WilliamBuick(7) 2 44
(A M Balding) *chsd ldrs: rdn over 2f out: edgd rt over 1f out: kpt on wl fnl f: clsng at fin* **16/1**
0600 **2** *dht* **Noble Mount**[107] [1228] 5-8-11 **41**.......................................(p) EmmettStack(5) 10 48
(A B Haynes) *towards rr: hrd rdn and hdwy fnl 3f: edgd lft: styd on wl fnl f: clsng at fin* **10/1**
50-0 **4** *½* **Saintly Place**[79] [1909] 5-9-1 **40**....................................... OscarUrbina 3 45
(A W Carroll) *led tl over 2f out: hrd rdn over 1f out: nt qckn ins fnl f* **9/1**[3]
0650 **5** *1* **Salinger (USA)**[19] [3730] 4-9-1 **43**.......................................(b) AmirQuinn(3) 6 45
(Mrs L J Mongan) *dwlt: bhd: hrd rdn over 2f out: nrst fin* **5/1**[2]
0554 **6** *3 ½* **Snow Wolf**[14] [3867] 5-9-5 **51**....................................... BarrySavage(7) 5 43
(J M Bradley) *dwlt: bhd: pushed along after 2f: sme hdwy on rail 2f out: no further prog* **5/1**[2]
00-0 **7** *2 ½* **Forest Air (IRE)**[7] [4077] 6-8-10 **35**....................................... DavidKinsella 11 19
(B R Johnson) *bhd: rdn over 2f out: nvr rchd ldrs* **10/1**
0000 **8** *nk* **Saxon Star (IRE)**[8] [4050] 3-8-9 **38**....................................... HayleyTurner 1 21
(M D I Usher) *mid-div: hrd rdn and btn 2f out* **16/1**
0004 **9** *¾* **Song Huntress**[32] [3340] 3-9-0 **43**....................................... JamieMackay 13 24
(A G Newcombe) *sn stdd bk into midfield: wknd over 2f out* **12/1**
0P50 **10** *1* **Look Here's May**[34] [3266] 4-8-8 **40**....................................... RussellKennemore(7) 7 18
(R Hollinshead) *dwlt: sn chsng ldrs: wknd over 2f out* **33/1**
0000 **11** *2 ½* **Ameliore (IRE)**[12] [3932] 3-8-7 **43**....................................... AshleyHamblett(3) 9 13
(S Woodman) *prom: drvn along over 2f out: sn wknd* **50/1**

1m 10.26s (0.16) **Going Correction** +0.075s/f (Good)
WFA 3 from 4yo+ 4lb **11** Ran SP% **116.6**
Speed ratings (Par 101):101,100,100,99,98 93,90,89,88,87 84
Pl: Noble Mount £4.70, Tiny Tim £4.60.Ex: TF/NM £21.30, TF/TT £17.30.CSF: TF/NM £12.94, TF/TT £21.34.Tri: TF/NM/TT £149.83, TF/TT/NM £156.08 TOTE £3.40: £1.70.There was no bid for the winner.
Owner John Endersby **Bred** F Hines **Trained** Cowthorpe, N Yorks

FOCUS
A routine seller, run at a decent tempo, and straightforward form for the grade, rated around the winner and fourth.

4279 TOTESPORT.COM FILLIES' H'CAP 1m 1f 209y
7:10 (7:11) (Class 5) (0-70,70) 3-Y-0+ **£4,210** (£1,252; £625; £312) **Stalls** High

Form RPR
3445 **1** **Friends Hope**[5] [4132] 5-9-2 **53**....................................... SebSanders 1 61+
(P A Blockley) *s.s: towards rr: effrt and nt clr run over 2f out: led 1f out: drvn clr* **7/2**[2]
6-33 **2** *1 ¾* **Bracklinn**[20] [3703] 4-10-0 **65**....................................... OscarUrbina 4 70
(J R Fanshawe) *blindfold removed after stalls opened and wnt rt s: in tch: led 2f out tl over 1f out: nt pce of wnr* **11/10**[1]
0430 **3** *3* **Flashing Floozie**[5] [4154] 3-8-0 **46** oh2....................................... DavidKinsella 3 45
(M F Harris) *chsd ldrs: led briefly over 1f out: no ex fnl f* **25/1**
1320 **4** *¾* **Miss Monica (IRE)**[33] [3305] 5-8-9 **46** oh3....................................... HayleyTurner 5 44
(P W Hiatt) *dwlt: bhd: rdn 3f out: nrst fin* **8/1**
0446 **5** *hd* **Polish Welcome**[14] [3870] 3-8-6 **52**....................................... JamieMackay 2 49
(S C Williams) *w ldrs tl no ex 1f out* **12/1**
3044 **6** *3 ½* **Didoe**[14] [3862] 7-8-4 **46** oh5....................................... MarcHalford(5) 8 37
(P W Hiatt) *s.i.s: sn led and set modest pce: qcknd over 4f out: hdd 2f out: btn whn sltly hmpd over 1f out* **14/1**
0004 **7** *½* **Cunegonde**[21] [3668] 3-7-10 **47**....................................... RobynBrisland(5) 7 37
(G L Moore) *towards rr: rdn 3f out: n.d after* **16/1**
3534 **8** *1 ¼* **Moonlight Music (IRE)**[15] [3848] 3-9-10 **70**....................................... RyanMoore 6 58
(E J O'Neill) *bmpd s: trckd ldng pair tl wknd 2f out* **6/1**[3]

2m 1.84s (-0.76) **Going Correction** +0.075s/f (Good)
WFA 3 from 4yo+ 9lb **8** Ran SP% **119.3**
Speed ratings (Par 100):106,104,102,101,101 98,98,97
CSF £8.11 CT £82.90 TOTE £5.30: £1.50, £1.10, £4.00; EX 10.00.
Owner M J Wiley **Bred** Huish Bloodstock **Trained** Lambourn, Berks
■ Stewards' Enquiry : Oscar Urbina caution: used whip down shoulder in forehand position

FOCUS
A moderate fillies' handicap, run at a modest pace until halfway, and the form is sound enough.

The Form Book, Raceform Ltd, Compton, RG20 6NL

4280 TOTE TEXT BETTING 60021 CLAIMING STKS 1m 3f 196y
7:40 (7:40) (Class 5) 3-4-Y-0 **£3,562** (£1,059; £529; £264) **Stalls** High

Form RPR

0304 **1** **Mighty Dancer (IRE)**[17] 3804 3-8-9 58 .... RyanMoore 5 61
(S Kirk) *chsd ldrs: wnt 2nd over 2f out: drvn to ld ins fnl f* **7/4**[1]

4052 **2** ¾ **Shaheer (IRE)**[14] 3862 4-9-2 47 ....(b) OscarUrbina 6 56
(J Gallagher) *chsd ldr: led over 2f out tl ins fnl f: hrd rdn: kpt on* **7/2**[2]

-003 **3** 3 ½ **Park Lane Princess (IRE)**[24] 3594 3-7-11 52 .... MarcHalford(5) 4 47
(D M Simcock) *hld up in rr: hdwy whn hmpd 3f out: fnd gap 2f out: one pce appr fnl f* **9/2**[3]

0000 **4** nk **Dream Witness (FR)**[17] 3791 3-8-4 52 .... HayleyTurner 1 49
(W R Muir) *in tch: outpcd over 2f out: kpt on fnl f* **8/1**

0502 **5** 1 ¾ **Cool Isle**[16] 3824 3-7-11 46 ....(b) JohnMcAuley(3) 8 42
(P Howling) *prom tl wknd 2f out* **12/1**

3534 **6** 11 **Macho Dancer (IRE)**[28] 3456 3-8-5 50 ....(p) EmmettStack(5) 3 35
(K J Burke) *led tl over 2f out: sn wknd* **7/1**

5666 **7** 8 **Elms Schoolboy**[45] 2935 4-8-9 42 .... JPFeatherstone(7) 7 17
(P Howling) *dwlt: bhd tl hdwy over 3f out: wknd over 2f out: bhd and eased over 1f out* **20/1**

600- **8** dist **Woodlands Belle**[320] 5446 3-7-13 35 .... JamieMackay 2 —
(B G Powell) *sn wl bhd and moving poorly: t.o and virtually p.u fr 1/2-way* **33/1**

2m 32.08s (-0.12) **Going Correction** +0.075s/f (Good)
WFA 3 from 4yo 11lb **8** Ran SP% **115.8**
Speed ratings (Par 103):103,102,100,99,98 91,86,—
CSF £8.03 TOTE £3.20: £1.40, £1.30, £1.80; EX 10.70.
Owner Sylvester Kirk **Bred** Kiyoshi Takada **Trained** Upper Lambourn, Berks

FOCUS
A weak claimer and the form is sound but modest.
Woodlands Belle Official explanation: jockey said filly moved badly throughout

4281 TOTESPORTCASINO.COM H'CAP 6f 209y
8:10 (8:10) (Class 5) (0-75,76) 3-Y-0+ **£4,210** (£1,252; £625; £312) **Stalls** Low

Form RPR

5451 **1** **Secret Liaison**[8] 4058 3-9-13 **76** 6ex .... SebSanders 3 85+
(Sir Mark Prescott) *chsd ldr: led and edgd lft 2f out: drvn out* **5/4**[1]

0425 **2** ¾ **Toffee Vodka (IRE)**[7] 4075 4-10-0 **71** .... RyanMoore 2 80
(J W Hills) *hld up in tch: drvn to chse wnr over 1f out: styd on wl fnl f: clsng at fin* **5/2**[2]

6650 **3** 2 **Cool Sting (IRE)**[5] 4143 3-9-2 **68** .... NeilChalmers(3) 5 70
(A M Balding) *hld up in tch: effrt and hung lft fnl 2f: one pce* **10/1**

2306 **4** 4 **Keep Bacckinhit (IRE)**[7] 4075 4-9-1 **58** .... HayleyTurner 1 51
(G L Moore) *last most of wy: outpcd over 2f out: n.d after* **9/1**

0002 **5** 2 **Golden Square**[13] 3898 4-8-13 **56** .... OscarUrbina 4 44
(A W Carroll) *led tl 2f out: hung bdly lft and wknd over 1f out* **6/1**[3]

1m 22.1s (-0.60) **Going Correction** +0.075s/f (Good)
WFA 3 from 4yo 6lb **5** Ran SP% **106.4**
Speed ratings (Par 103):106,105,102,98,96
CSF £4.19 TOTE £2.20: £1.80, £1.10; EX 3.30 Place 6 £12.78, Place 5 £2.91.
Owner W E Sturt - Osborne House **Bred** Cheveley Park Stud Ltd **Trained** Newmarket, Suffolk

FOCUS
A fair handicap, but lacking in numbers and the form is not strong, rated through the runner-up.
Golden Square Official explanation: jockey said gelding hung right
T/Plt: £17.70 to a £1 stake. Pool: £48,518.70. 1,990.05 winning tickets. T/Qpdt: £3.30 to a £1 stake. Pool: £4,491.70. 998.50 winning tickets. LM

3894 CHEPSTOW (L-H)
Thursday, August 10

OFFICIAL GOING: Good to firm
Wind: Light, across. Weather: Fine.

4282 32RED H'CAP 1m 4f 23y
2:20 (2:20) (Class 6) (0-60,58) 3-Y-0+ **£2,590** (£770; £385; £192) **Stalls** Low

Form RPR

6542 **1** **Equilibria (USA)**[13] 3894 4-9-5 **49** .... RichardHughes 9 57
(G L Moore) *a.p: led over 4f out: rdn over 2f out: hdd jst over 1f out: led ins fnl f: r.o* **7/2**[1]

6503 **2** 1 **Nina Fontenail (FR)**[19] 3731 5-10-0 **58** .... JimCrowley 11 64
(B R Millman) *hld up in mid-div: hdwy over 3f out: rdn to ld jst over 1f out: hdd ins fnl f: nt qckn* **6/1**[3]

0242 **3** 1 ¼ **Guadiana (GER)**[12] 3944 4-9-0 **44** ....(v) FrancisNorton 5 48
(A W Carroll) *hld up and bhd: rdn and hdwy 3f out: one pce fnl f* **10/1**

5511 **4** nk **Joy In The Guild (IRE)**[14] 3870 3-9-0 **55** .... FergusSweeney 16 59
(W S Kittow) *plld hrd in rr: hdwy 3f out: rdn over 1f out: one pce fnl f* **11/2**[2]

2410 **5** 1 **Opera Knight**[54] 2636 6-9-1 **45** .... SteveDrowne 13 47
(A W Carroll) *t.k.h in mid-div: rdn and hdwy over 2f out: one pce fnl f* **12/1**

0605 **6** 3 **Bobsleigh**[12] 3952 7-9-10 **54** .... VinceSlattery 14 51
(H S Howe) *sn w ldr: led over 9f out tl over 4f out: wknd over 1f out* **12/1**

0120 **7** 1 ¼ **Padre Nostro (IRE)**[15] 3850 7-9-6 **57** .... ChrisGlenister(7) 1 52
(J R Holt) *hld up in mid-div: rdn over 4f out: sme hdwy on ins over 2f out: nvr trbld ldrs* **7/1**

60-0 **8** ½ **Ben Kenobi**[52] 2707 8-8-7 **42** .... GregFairley(5) 4 36
(Mrs P Ford) *plld hrd in rr: rdn and hdwy over 2f out: wknd fnl f* **33/1**

5515 **9** 2 **Bold Trump**[30] 3382 5-9-4 **48** ....(p) FrancisFerris 2 39
(Mrs N S Evans) *sn led: hdd over 9f out: rdn over 3f out: wknd wl over 1f out* **20/1**

6544 **10** 6 **Chookie Windsor**[29] 3411 3-8-8 **49** .... StephenCarson 8 31
(R M Stronge) *t.k.h: a bhd* **16/1**

0066 **11** 2 **Bubbling Fun**[24] 3597 5-9-3 **47** .... DaneO'Neill 6 25
(T Wall) *hld up in tch: wkng whn n.m.r over 2f out* **28/1**

0120 **12** 2 **Major Blade (GER)**[24] 3597 8-9-3 **47** .... ChrisCatlin 7 22
(Heather Dalton) *led early: hld up in tch: wknd 4f out* **16/1**

0060 **13** 10 **Ballymena**[13] 3919 5-8-5 **42** .... TolleyDean(7) 10 1
(R A Harris) *prom: rdn 4f out: wknd over 2f out* **40/1**

2m 36.95s (-1.77) **Going Correction** -0.10s/f (Good)
WFA 3 from 4yo+ 11lb **13** Ran SP% **114.2**
Speed ratings (Par 101):101,100,99,99,98 96,95,95,94,90 88,87,80
CSF £21.12 CT £189.76 TOTE £4.40: £2.30, £1.80, £3.10; EX 20.30 Trifecta £88.50 Pool £279.34. - 2.24 winning units..
Owner Dr C A Barnett **Bred** Calumet Farm **Trained** Woodingdean, E Sussex

FOCUS
An open-looking low-grade affair but straightforward form with the third to his latest mark.
Joy In The Guild(IRE) Official explanation: jockey said filly hung left-handed

4283 32RED.COM MEDIAN AUCTION MAIDEN FILLIES' STKS 5f 16y
2:50 (2:51) (Class 5) 2-Y-0 **£3,562** (£1,059; £529; £264) **Stalls** High

Form RPR

2 **1** **Fanlight Fanny (USA)**[38] 3148 2-9-0 .... JimCrowley 2 74
(P Winkworth) *led: rdn and hdd over 1f out: edgd lft ins fnl f: led last strides* **3/1**[3]

0 **2** shd **Pretty Miss**[24] 3588 2-9-0 .... DaneO'Neill 1 74
(H Candy) *chsd ldrs: rdn to ld over 1f out: hdd last strides* **5/2**[2]

03 **3** 2 ½ **Popolo (IRE)**[11] 3979 2-9-0 .... RichardHughes 5 65
(M L W Bell) *w wnr: rdn 2f out: one pce fnl f* **5/4**[1]

4 6 **Lady Chastity** 2-9-0 .... VinceSlattery 6 43
(Mrs L J Young) *dwlt: outpcd: nvr nrr* **50/1**

5023 **5** 2 **Fly Time**[14] 3860 2-9-0 54 .... ChrisCatlin 3 36
(H J Manners) *prom over 2f* **16/1**

6 1 ½ **One White Sock** 2-9-0 .... SteveDrowne 4 30
(J L Spearing) *dwlt: outpcd* **25/1**

58.95 secs (-0.65) **Going Correction** -0.225s/f (Firm) **6** Ran SP% **109.7**
Speed ratings (Par 91):96,95,91,82,79 76
CSF £10.39 TOTE £3.40: £2.00, £1.40; EX 9.20.
Owner Badger's Set **Bred** Harold Harrison **Trained** Chiddingfold, Surrey

FOCUS
An ordinary contest rated through the winner and the form looks sound.

NOTEBOOK
Fanlight Fanny(USA) ◆ built on the promise of her debut at Warwick despite connections' concerns about her ability to handle the undulations of the course. She is going the right way. (op 2-1)
Pretty Miss ◆ had obviously learnt a lot from her Windsor debut where she had finished a length and a half behind Popolo. Just touched off, she can be considered as good as a winner without a penalty. (op 4-1)
Popolo(IRE) ◆ had finished a length and a half ahead of Pretty Miss on her debut prior to shaping as though she may need even further when upped to six at Newmarket. It was a shade surprising to see her back at the minimum trip. Official explanation: jockey said filly was unsuited by the good to firm ground (op 11-8 tchd 6-4)
Lady Chastity is a half-sister to five-furlong winner Sea Salt. (op 40-1)
One White Sock Official explanation: jockey said filly had run green

4284 32RED ONLINE CASINO NURSERY 6f 16y
3:20 (3:20) (Class 5) 2-Y-0 **£4,533** (£1,348; £674; £336) **Stalls** High

Form RPR

315 **1** **Diamond Hurricane (IRE)**[83] 1824 2-9-0 **74** .... SteveDrowne 7 74
(P D Evans) *hld up in tch: rdn over 2f out: led wl ins fnl f: r.o* **9/2**[3]

0116 **2** ½ **Kyshanty**[8] 4043 2-9-7 **81** .... RichardHughes 4 80
(R Hannon) *led: rdn and hdd wl over 1f out: kpt on ins fnl f* **10/3**[2]

051 **3** nk **Jost Van Dyke**[17] 3801 2-8-7 **67** .... DaneO'Neill 2 65
(B R Millman) *s.i.s: sn w ldr: rdn to ld wl over 1f out: hdd and nt qckn wl ins fnl f* **5/1**

1205 **4** hd **Mrs Crossy (IRE)**[15] 3837 2-8-0 **60** .... FrancisNorton 1 57
(A W Carroll) *hld up: hdwy over 2f out: sn rdn: ev ch ins fnl f: nt qckn* **18/1**

0331 **5** 1 ½ **Tom Paris**[15] 3837 2-8-12 **72** ....(b) ChrisCatlin 6 65
(W R Muir) *t.k.h in rr: rdn over 2f out: nvr able to chal* **15/8**[1]

004 **6** hd **Mulvany (IRE)**[12] 3949 2-7-12 **65** ....(b) KMay(7) 3 57
(B J Meehan) *hld up in tch: rdn 2f out: one pce* **10/1**

3330 **7** 3 **Bush Breakfast**[12] 3930 2-8-13 **73** .... StephenCarson 5 56
(P Winkworth) *w ldrs: rdn over 2f out: wknd over 1f out* **28/1**

1m 11.55s (-0.85) **Going Correction** -0.225s/f (Firm) **7** Ran SP% **110.5**
Speed ratings (Par 94):96,95,94,94,92 92,88
CSF £18.45 TOTE £5.70: £3.10, £1.30; EX 22.90.
Owner Diamond Racing Ltd **Bred** Rathasker Stud **Trained** Pandy, Abergavenny

FOCUS
A competitive little nursery with the first three close to their marks.

NOTEBOOK
Diamond Hurricane(IRE) had benefited from being given a break since being beaten in some very soft ground at Nottingham in May, according to his trainer. He came through to justify support in the ring. (op 7-1)
Kyshanty appreciated being back up to six and may now be ready to tackle even further. (op 11-4)
Jost Van Dyke had been given a realistic mark after winning a Yarmouth seller and gave a good account of himself. (op 9-2 tchd 6-1)
Mrs Crossy(IRE), dropped 4lb, put a couple of lacklustre efforts in nurseries since leaving Richard Hannon behind her. (op 16-1)
Tom Paris could never land a blow off a 5lb higher mark. Official explanation: trainer said gelding had been unsuited by the track (op 2-1)
Mulvany(IRE) did not seem to be that well treated based on what he has actually achieved. (op 14-1)

4285 32REDPOKER.COM (S) STKS 1m 14y
3:50 (3:52) (Class 6) 3-Y-0+ **£2,266** (£674; £337; £168) **Stalls** High

Form RPR

300/ **1** **Todlea (IRE)**[638] 6617 6-9-2 68 .... NelsonDeSouza(3) 4 60+
(J A Osborne) *hld up: nt clr run whn swtchd rt and hdwy 2f out: led on bit over 1f out: shkn up ins fnl f: r.o wl* **15/2**

0343 **2** 2 ½ **Zafarshah (IRE)**[16] 3817 7-8-12 45 ....(b) TolleyDean(7) 7 54
(R A Harris) *s.i.s: sn struggling and detached: gd hdwy fnl 2f: fin wl: nt trble wnr* **5/1**[2]

1400 **3** 2 **Thornfield Clo (IRE)**[14] 3869 3-8-12 52 .... DaneO'Neill 11 49
(R Hannon) *led: rdn and hdd over 1f out: one pce* **14/1**

0000 **4** ¾ **Hawridge Sensation**[12] 3933 4-9-5 52 ....(t) FergusSweeney 2 48
(W S Kittow) *wnt rt s: hld up: rdn and hdwy 2f out: sn ev ch: one pce* **11/1**

-146 **5** 1 ½ **It's Unbelievable (USA)**[7] 4076 3-9-3 73 .... RichardHughes 6 49
(B J Meehan) *prom: rdn and ev ch over 1f out: wknd ins fnl f* **11/10**[1]

4005 **6** 4 **Balearic Star (IRE)**[12] 3947 5-9-5 52 ....(v[1]) ChrisCatlin 3 35
(B R Millman) *prom: rdn and ev ch 2f out: wknd over 1f out* **6/1**[3]

0-00 **7** shd **King Faz (IRE)**[72] 2109 3-8-12 57 .... FrancisNorton 5 35
(P A Blockley) *t.k.h: prom: rdn and ev ch 2f out: wknd over 1f out: eased whn btn ins fnl f* **40/1**

5020 **8** ¾ **Emperor Cat (IRE)**[13] 3894 5-9-5 45 .... FrancisFerris 10 33
(Mrs N S Evans) *hld up in tch: rdn over 2f out: wknd wl over 1f out* **20/1**

6000 **9** 2 **Grandos (IRE)**[69] 2198 4-9-5 51 .... VinceSlattery 9 28
(Karen George) *hld up in tch: rdn and wknd over 2f out* **40/1**

000- **10** *8* **Indian Sky (IRE)**[464] 1452 4-9-5 .... PaulFitzsimons 8 10
(B R Millman) *hld up: rdn and hung rt 3f out: sn bhd* **66/1**

1m 34.21s (-1.79) **Going Correction** -0.225s/f (Firm)
WFA 3 from 4yo+ 7lb **10** Ran SP% **116.5**
Speed ratings (Par 101):99,96,94,93,92 88,88,87,85,77
CSF £43.40 TOTE £9.00: £2.30, £1.70, £3.60; EX 51.60 Trifecta £369.00 Part won. Pool £519.81.- 0.34 winning units..The winner was sold to Jene-Rene Auvray for 10,500gns. It's Unbelievable (USA) was claimed by Mr P. T. Midgley for £6,000.
Owner J A Osborne **Bred** Irish National Stud **Trained** Upper Lambourn, Berks

FOCUS
There were doubts hanging over most of the principals in this seller and the proximity of the runner-up limits the form.
Indian Sky(IRE) Official explanation: jockey said gelding had hung right-handed

4286 32RED ONLINE POKER ROOM FILLIES' H'CAP 1m 14y
4:20 (4:22) (Class 5) (0-75,74) 3-Y-0+ **£3,886** (£1,156; £577; £288) **Stalls** High

Form RPR
4530 **1** **Rakata (USA)**[8] 4048 4-10-0 **68** .... RichardHughes 9 79
(P F I Cole) *mde all: hrd rdn over 1f out: r.o wl* **4/1**[2]
0054 **2** *2 ½* **Tuscarora (IRE)**[13] 3897 7-9-5 **59** .... FrancisNorton 10 64
(A W Carroll) *t.k.h in tch: rdn and chsd wnr over 2f out: no imp* **6/1**[3]
3511 **3** *hd* **Celtic Spa (IRE)**[7] 4070 4-9-10 **71** 6ex.......................... JamieJones(7) 2 76
(P D Evans) *hld up: rdn and hdwy 3f out: one pce fnl f* **11/4**[1]
2-64 **4** *3 ½* **With Style**[32] 3336 3-9-11 **72** .... SteveDrowne 3 69+
(E A L Dunlop) *hld up and bhd: rdn and hdwy 2f out: wknd ins fnl f* **10/1**
460 **5** *3* **Over Ice**[50] 2753 3-9-5 **66** .... VinceSlattery 8 56
(Karen George) *prom: rdn over 3f out: wknd over 2f out* **40/1**
4300 **6** *1* **Reflecting (IRE)**[19] 3731 3-9-6 **67** .... ChrisCatlin 1 55
(J W Hills) *hld up: rdn over 2f out: short-lived effrt over 1f out* **16/1**
003 **7** *¾* **Sprinkle**[12] 3950 3-8-12 **62** .... NelsonDeSouza(3) 4 48
(R M Beckett) *t.k.h in tch: rdn 3f out: wknd wl over 1f out* **4/1**[2]
5150 **8** *1* **Right Ted (IRE)**[12] 3945 3-9-13 **74** .... DaneO'Neill 6 58
(T Wall) *prom: rdn 3f out: sn wknd* **15/2**
0005 **9** *2 ½* **Waiting For Mary (IRE)**[13] 3897 3-8-2 **49** .... FrancisFerris 5 27
(J G M O'Shea) *s.s: hdwy over 3f out: rdn and wknd over 2f out* **20/1**

1m 34.06s (-1.94) **Going Correction** -0.225s/f (Firm)
WFA 3 from 4yo+ 7lb **9** Ran SP% **114.9**
Speed ratings (Par 100):100,97,97,93,90 89,89,88,85
CSF £28.09 CT £76.47 TOTE £5.50: £1.50, £1.60, £2.10; EX 31.80 Trifecta £125.30 Pool £882.40. - 5.00 winning units..
Owner A H Robinson **Bred** Mike G Rutherford Sr **Trained** Whatcombe, Oxon

FOCUS
A modest fillies' handicap rated through the winner to previous best.
Waiting For Mary(IRE) Official explanation: vet said filly had lost a shoe

4287 32RED.COM MAIDEN STKS 7f 16y
4:50 (4:50) (Class 5) 3-Y-0+ **£3,368** (£1,002; £500; £250) **Stalls** High

Form RPR
6346 **1** **Nightstrike (IRE)**[12] 3950 3-8-12 60.................................. DaneO'Neill 4 70
(H Candy) *a.p: rdn to ld jst over 2f out: edgd lft 1f out: r.o wl* **9/2**[3]
4-33 **2** *1 ½* **Mashaair (IRE)**[13] 3909 3-9-3 79.................................. RichardHughes 2 71
(B W Hills) *led: rdn and hdd jst over 2f out: kpt on same pce fnl f* **6/5**[1]
046 **3** *2* **Mambonow (USA)**[19] 3742 3-9-3 73.................................. SteveDrowne 6 69+
(J Noseda) *hld up: hdwy over 2f out: sn rdn: one pce fnl f* **7/4**[2]
0-0 **4** *5* **Grand Court (IRE)**[10] 4004 3-8-12 .... FrancisNorton 5 48
(A W Carroll) *hld up and bhd: pushed along over 3f out: n.d* **50/1**
-000 **5** *3 ½* **Task Complete**[52] 2704 3-8-12 48..........................(b[1]) VinceSlattery 3 39
(Jean-Rene Auvray) *t.k.h: prom: rdn over 2f out: sn wknd* **80/1**
0460 **6** *1 ¼* **Measured Response**[56] 2567 4-9-9 59...................... FergusSweeney 1 41
(J G M O'Shea) *hld up in tch: rdn over 2f out: sn wknd* **16/1**

1m 21.96s (-1.34) **Going Correction** -0.225s/f (Firm)
WFA 3 from 4yo 6lb **6** Ran SP% **109.1**
Speed ratings (Par 103):98,96,94,88,84 82
CSF £9.76 TOTE £4.90: £2.30, £1.10; EX 8.00.
Owner Henry Candy & Partners **Bred** Philip Brady **Trained** Kingston Warren, Oxon

FOCUS
A weak maiden but far from solid, with the placed horses well below form.

4288 CHEPSTOW SUNDAY MARKET H'CAP (LADIES RACE) 1m 14y
5:25 (5:28) (Class 5) (0-70,68) 3-Y-0+ **£3,247** (£1,007; £503; £251) **Stalls** High

Form RPR
4000 **1** **Wind Chime (IRE)**[16] 3820 9-9-8 **52**.......................... MissCHannaford 12 62
(A G Newcombe) *a.p on stands' rail: led over 1f out: r.o* **5/1**[3]
4200 **2** *½* **Tiber Tiger (IRE)**[20] 3712 6-10-5 **63**...............(b) MrsEmmaLittmoden 11 72
(N P Littmoden) *hld up on stands' rail: rdn and hdwy over 2f out: ev ch fnl f: r.o* **5/2**[2]
3006 **3** *3 ½* **Chapter (IRE)**[9] 4021 4-10-8 **66**..................................(b) MissLEllison 4 67
(Mrs A L M King) *t.k.h: prom: swtchd to stands' side over 3f out: rdn and edgd lft 2f out: one pce* **12/1**
-000 **4** *½* **Elidore**[43] 2969 6-9-9 **60**.................................. MrsJMBerry(7) 2 60+
(B Palling) *racd centre: led: hdd over 2f out: no ex fnl f* **16/1**
2046 **5** *2* **Molem**[20] 3706 4-10-8 **66**..................................(vt) MsKWalsh 1 61
(Lady Herries) *racd centre: prom: wnt 2nd after 2f: led over 2f out tl over 1f out: wknd ins fnl f* **2/1**[1]
00/5 **6** *3 ½* **Johannian**[12] 3948 8-10-2 **67**.................................. MissHDavies(7) 9 54
(J M Bradley) *hld up in centre: rdn over 3f out: hdwy over 2f out: hung bdly lft and wknd over 1f out* **12/1**
6000 **7** *¾* **Lord Chamberlain**[12] 3948 13-9-4 **55**......................(b) MissSBradley(7) 7 40
(J M Bradley) *s.s: nvr nr ldrs* **10/1**
0035 **8** *6* **Comeintothespace (IRE)**[26] 3541 4-8-13 **48** oh3 MissAshleighHorton(5) 6 19
(Miss Victoria Roberts) *racd centre: hld up in mid-div: rdn over 3f out: sme hdwy over 2f out: edgd lft and wknd over 1f out* **12/1**
2-30 **9** *12* **Korikancha (IRE)**[193] 234 3-9-12 **68**......... MissGDGracey-Davison(5) 8 12
(Miss Z C Davison) *s.i.s: a bhd* **33/1**
0460 **10** *3 ½* **Legal Call**[36] 3195 3-9-6 **64** oh8 ow16.......................... MrsSDutton(7) 3 —
(M Appleby) *chsd ldr 2f: wknd 5f out* **100/1**
04-0 **11** *13* **Monashee Express (IRE)**[41] 3056 4-9-8 **52**................. MissEJJones 5 —
(G H Yardley) *s.i.s: a bhd* **100/1**

1m 34.08s (-1.92) **Going Correction** -0.225s/f (Firm)
WFA 3 from 4yo+ 7lb **11** Ran SP% **121.5**
Speed ratings (Par 103):100,99,96,95,93 90,89,83,71,67 54
CSF £18.49 CT £148.82 TOTE £6.60: £2.40, £1.70, £4.00; EX 24.60 Trifecta £246.40 Pool £558.79. - 1.61 winning units. Place 6 £70.86, Place 5 £42.84..
Owner M K F Seymour **Bred** Saeed Manana **Trained** Yarnscombe, Devon

FOCUS
The first two raced under the stands' rail and the third eventually came to join them. The principals set the standard.
T/Plt: £61.10 to a £1 stake. Pool: £55,951.70. 668.45 winning tickets. T/Qpdt: £24.80 to a £1 stake. Pool: £2,713.10. 80.85 winning tickets. KH

3866 FOLKESTONE (R-H)
Thursday, August 10

OFFICIAL GOING: Good to firm (firm in places)
Wind: Nil. Weather: Fine but cloudy, shower race 4.

4289 DEBENHAMS AT FOLKESTONE FILLIES' H'CAP 1m 1f 149y
5:30 (5:31) (Class 6) (0-60,60) 3-Y-0+ **£2,730** (£806; £403) **Stalls** Low

Form RPR
0046 **1** **Greenmeadow**[28] 3440 4-9-4 **55**.......................... MichaelJStainton(5) 14 62
(S Kirk) *cl up: effrt on inner 2f out: led over 1f out: rdn and hld on wl* **13/2**[3]
6060 **2** *¾* **Princess Danah (IRE)**[22] 3650 3-9-0 **58**....................(t) AdamKirby(3) 11 64
(W R Swinburn) *led: kicked on over 2f out: hung lft and hdd over 1f out: styd on but a hld fnl f* **14/1**
6232 **3** *shd* **Granary Girl**[15] 3836 4-9-2 **48**.................................. JimmyQuinn 1 53
(J Pearce) *hld up in midfield: prog on inner 2f out: drvn to chal fnl f: kpt on but a hld* **4/1**[2]
0003 **4** *2* **Glory Be (ITY)**[24] 3592 4-8-9 **41** oh1.................................. MickyFenton 9 43
(J L Spearing) *chsd ldr: rdn and nt qckn 2f out: one pce after* **13/2**[3]
6200 **5** *hd* **Danzare**[7] 4073 4-9-5 **54**.................................. NeilChalmers(3) 7 55
(Mrs A J Hamilton-Fairley) *taken down early: trckd ldrs: chal 2f out: rdn and fnd nil over 1f out* **20/1**
-000 **6** *½* **Saucy**[19] 3731 5-8-8 **45**.................................. LiamJones(5) 3 45+
(A W Carroll) *rrd s: t.k.h: hld up in last pair: rdn over 2f out: styd on fnl f: nvr rchd ldrs* **10/1**
0001 **7** *1 ¼* **Baboosh (IRE)**[17] 3803 5-10-0 **60**.................................. MichaelTebbutt 5 58
(M Wigham) *hld up: prog on outer 5f out: trckd ldrs 3f out: shkn up and nt qckn 2f out: n.d fnl f* **6/4**[1]
6000 **8** *1 ½* **Romanova (IRE)**[17] 3798 4-9-4 **50**..........................(b) RichardThomas 10 45
(Dr J R J Naylor) *s.i.s: wl in rr tl sme prog 4f out: no hdwy and btn over 1f out* **66/1**
0044 **9** *¾* **Grecianette (IRE)**[101] 1352 3-8-11 **52**.................................. JDSmith 12 46
(W J Musson) *hld up: last 4f out: stl gng wl enough 3f out: pushed along fnl 2f : nvr nr ldrs* **16/1**
000 **10** *5* **Silk Purse**[17] 3794 3-9-0 **55**.................................. LPKeniry 13 39
(M Madgwick) *nvr beyond midfield: rr and struggling over 2f out* **50/1**
-0P0 **11** *4* **Shibumi**[40] 3099 5-8-11 **43**.................................. PaulEddery 4 20
(P A Trueman) *taken down early: t.k.h and sn prom: wknd rapidly 3f out* **66/1**

2m 3.88s (-1.35) **Going Correction** -0.175s/f (Firm)
WFA 3 from 4yo+ 9lb **11** Ran SP% **118.0**
Speed ratings (Par 98):98,97,97,95,95 95,94,92,92,88 85
CSF £90.28 CT £411.98 TOTE £9.20: £3.30, £2.00, £1.20; EX 127.60.
Owner Miss Amanda Rawding **Bred** Green Meadow Stud **Trained** Upper Lambourn, Berks

FOCUS
A weak fillies' handicap, run at a fair pace, and the first three came clear. The third is the best guide to the level.

4290 ALAN LIPTROTT'S 60TH BIRTHDAY CELEBRATION MEDIAN AUCTION MAIDEN STKS 7f (S)
6:00 (6:01) (Class 5) 2-Y-0 **£3,238** (£963; £481; £240) **Stalls** Low

Form RPR
0 **1** **Majuro (IRE)**[13] 3892 2-9-0 .... EdwardCreighton(3) 10 81+
(M R Channon) *dwlt: racd wd: hld up: prog 3f out: led wl over 1f out: pushed out* **17/2**
05 **2** *¾* **Little Miss Tara (IRE)**[19] 3735 2-8-12 .... LPKeniry 9 74
(A B Haynes) *disp ld to wl over 1f out: styd on but a readily hld by wnr fnl f* **6/1**[3]
2 **3** *2* **Wait Watcher (IRE)**[50] 2745 2-8-12 .... TPO'Shea 2 69
(P A Blockley) *dwlt: hld up bhd ldrs: effrt 2f out: rdn and nt qckn over 1f out: one pce after* **5/2**[2]
2630 **4** *1 ¾* **Straight Face (IRE)**[22] 3641 2-9-3 76.............................. JimmyQuinn 4 69
(W J Knight) *dwlt: last tl rdn and prog 2f out: one pce and no imp fnl f* **9/4**[1]
0 **5** *5* **Toggle**[20] 3701 2-9-3 .... PatDobbs 8 56
(R Hannon) *disp ld to 2f out: wknd rapidly* **13/2**
000 **6** *hd* **Numerical (IRE)**[21] 3663 2-9-3 58..................................(b[1]) IanMongan 5 56
(J L Dunlop) *chsd ldrs: rdn 3f out: brief effrt 2f out: sn wknd rapidly* **12/1**
0 **7** *3 ½* **Six Shots**[82] 1838 2-9-3 .... PaulEddery 7 47+
(J A Osborne) *disp ld to 2f out: wknd rapidly and eased* **16/1**
66 **8** *5* **Flushed**[84] 1807 2-9-0 .... RichardKingscote(3) 3 34
(J A Osborne) *chsd ldrs: rdn 3f out: sn struggling and btn* **33/1**

1m 26.3s (-1.60) **Going Correction** -0.325s/f (Firm) **8** Ran SP% **114.0**
Speed ratings (Par 94):96,95,92,90,85 84,80,75
CSF £57.87 TOTE £10.30: £1.70, £1.60, £1.70; EX 97.10.
Owner Capital **Bred** Tally-Ho Stud **Trained** West Ilsley, Berks

FOCUS
No more than a fair juvenile maiden and the first two came clear. The form looks sound enough through the runner-up.

NOTEBOOK
Majuro(IRE), eighth on his debut at Ascot over this trip 13 days previously, was again sluggish at the start yet ultimately still had enough class to get off the mark in workmanlike fashion. He looks to type to improve again with this experience under his belt, and should get a mile before the season's end, yet his future does appear to lie with the Handicapper. (op 11-1)
Little Miss Tara(IRE), a notable market drifter, appeared to give her all in defeat and finished nicely clear of the rest. She can pick up a similar event over this trip. (op 11-4)
Wait Watcher(IRE), runner-up on debut at Hamilton 50 days previously, lacked the required change of gear when it mattered yet still posted another sound effort in defeat. She got the extra furlong well, still looked in need of the experience, and appeals strongly as the type to come into her own when eligible for nurseries after her next assignment. (tchd 11-4)
Straight Face(IRE), very well backed on this return to maiden company, was always playing catch-up after a sluggish start and ultimately proved disappointing. (op 4-1)

4291 DENNIS WRIGHT 60TH BIRTHDAY H'CAP 7f (S)
6:30 (6:30) (Class 5) (0-70,69) 3-Y-O £3,886 (£1,156; £577; £288) Stalls Low

Form RPR
1001 1 **Takitwo**[14] [3869] 3-9-3 **65** LPKeniry 3 74
(P D Cundell) *trckd ldrs: pushed along 3f out: prog to ld jst over 1f out: drvn out* **4/1**[3]
3423 2 *nk* **Young Bertie**[20] [3705] 3-8-8 **61** (p) TravisBlock(5) 1 69
(H Morrison) *bmpd s: chsd ldng pair: rdn and effrt to ld briefly over 1f out: pressed wnr after: nt qckn and hld nr fin* **9/4**[1]
4005 3 ½ **Chia (IRE)**[31] [3364] 3-8-8 **56** MickyFenton 2 63
(D Haydn Jones) *mounted on crse: bmpd s: hld up in tch nr side: effrt over 1f out: drvn and styd on fnl f: jst unable to chal* **9/1**
5424 4 1 ½ **Patavium Prince (IRE)**[6] [4116] 3-9-7 **69** GeorgeBaker 7 72+
(J R Best) *racd on outer: hld up in tch: prog to chal over 1f out: nrly upsides ent fnl f: nt qckn* **3/1**[2]
5402 5 1 ½ **Dab Hand (IRE)**[12] [3931] 3-9-1 **66** AdamKirby(3) 4 65
(D M Simcock) *led to over 1f out: wandering and wknd fnl f* **11/2**
-000 6 7 **Madame Constanze (IRE)**[13] [3906] 3-8-3 **51** JimmyQuinn 5 32
(Miss Gay Kelleway) *dwlt: a in last pair: wknd 2f out* **33/1**
0603 7 *nk* **Mid Valley**[12] [3932] 3-8-2 **50** (v) RichardThomas 6 30
(J R Jenkins) *chsd ldr to over 1f out: wknd rapidly* **11/1**

1m 24.75s (-3.15) **Going Correction** -0.325s/f (Firm) 7 Ran SP% **112.4**
Speed ratings (Par 100):105,104,104,102,100 92,92
CSF £12.97 TOTE £5.40: £2.70, £1.80; EX 15.80.
Owner Miss M C Fraser **Bred** Roden House Stud **Trained** Compton, Berks

FOCUS
A modest handicap for three-year-olds, run at an average pace, and sound neough rated around the third and fifth.
Dab Hand(IRE) Official explanation: trainers representative said gelding was unsuited by the track

4292 GET AHEAD HATS MAIDEN STKS 6f
7:00 (7:00) (Class 5) 2-Y-O £4,210 (£1,252; £625; £312) Stalls Low

Form RPR
4 1 **College Scholar (GER)**[19] [3738] 2-9-3 TPO'Shea 5 76
(M R Channon) *hld up in tch: prog to trck ldr 2f out: rdn and styd on wl to ld last 75yds* **3/1**[2]
343 2 *nk* **Malaaq**[36] [3188] 2-8-12 74 MatthewHenry 7 70
(M A Jarvis) *t.k.h: w ldrs: led over 3f out: drvn over 1f out: worn down last 75yds* **7/2**[3]
0 3 1 ½ **L'Oiseau De Feu (USA)**[31] [3363] 2-9-3 PatDobbs 6 71
(E A L Dunlop) *stdd s: hld up in last: stdy prog on outer over 2f out: rdn over 1f out: one pce fnl f* **11/10**[1]
00 4 2 ½ **Hucking Heat (IRE)**[14] [3872] 2-9-3 GeorgeBaker 1 63
(J R Best) *led to over 3f out: hanging rt after: outpcd 2f out: nudged along and one pce after* **40/1**
5 5 1 ¼ **Orange Pekoe (USA)**[26] [3531] 2-9-3 JimmyQuinn 3 59
(P Mitchell) *in tch: rdn and no prog over 1f out: wknd fnl f* **12/1**
00 6 1 ¾ **Poor Nelly**[26] [3537] 2-8-12 IanMongan 4 49
(J L Dunlop) *w ldrs: hanging rt fr 1/2-way: wknd wl over 1f out* **33/1**
7 9 **Priceless Melody (USA)** 2-9-3 JimCrowley 2 27
(Mrs A J Perrett) *dwlt: sn pushed along and struggling: t.o fnl 2f* **20/1**

1m 12.7s (-0.90) **Going Correction** -0.325s/f (Firm) 7 Ran SP% **112.7**
Speed ratings (Par 94):93,92,90,87,85 83,71
CSF £13.35 TOTE £4.70: £2.10, £2.30; EX 14.60.
Owner Mohammed Jaber **Bred** Stiftung Gestut Fahrhof **Trained** West Ilsley, Berks
■ The first winner in Britain for Tadhg O'Shea, former champion apprentice in Ireland.

FOCUS
A fair juvenile maiden, run at a solid pace, and the first two came clear. The winner can rate higher with the placed horses close to their marks.

NOTEBOOK
College Scholar(GER) showed the clear benefit of his recent Newmarket debut and was always going to get up in the closing stages. There was a fair bit to like about the manner in which he travelled until asked to win his race, he will get further before the season's end, and looks a nice handicapper in the making. (op 9-2)
Malaaq ultimately paid for running too freely through the early parts and, while she may have been racing on slower ground up the stands' rail late on, she always looked a sitting duck for the winner. She was clear of the rest and, while she undoubtedly has a small race within her compass, she is proving frustrating to follow nevetheless. (op 3-1)
L'Oiseau De Feu(USA) ran distinctly green when asked to make up his ground and was never a serious threat to the first pair. This was still a step in the right direction, however, and he ought to improve again for the experience. (tchd 5-4)
Hucking Heat(IRE) showed decent early pace and posted his best effort to date in defeat. He is a scopey individual, who probably needs more time, and ought to fare better when switching to nurseries in due course.
Orange Pekoe(USA) ran too freely under restraint and is another who still looked to need the experience. (op 11-1 tchd 10-1)

4293 KMFM LISA BRITNELL MEDIAN AUCTION MAIDEN STKS 6f
7:30 (7:30) (Class 5) 3-4-Y-O £3,238 (£963; £481; £240) Stalls Low

Form RPR
00-0 1 **Hotchpotch (USA)**[34] [3257] 3-9-3 46 GeorgeBaker 4 58
(J R Best) *mde all: hanging rt and wandering fr over 1f out: rdn out* **11/1**
6060 2 1 ¼ **Athena's Dream**[6] [4120] 3-8-12 60 JimmyQuinn 1 49
(C F Wall) *pressed wnr: rdn over 1f out: fnd nil and hld fnl f* **9/4**[2]
0233 3 1 ¾ **Balian**[5] [4162] 3-9-3 66 (be) IanMongan 2 49
(G L Moore) *hld up in 4th: rdn and no rspnse over 1f out: snatched 3rd nr fin* **5/4**[1]
3350 4 *nk* **Shinko (IRE)**[21] [3668] 3-8-12 54 (b[1]) MickyFenton 5 43
(Miss J Feilden) *racd on outer: cl up: rdn and nt qckn over 1f out: wknd ins fnl f* **4/1**[3]
3400 5 4 **Kashtanka (IRE)**[9] [4019] 4-9-4 37 (p) JasonEdmunds(3) 3 36
(J Balding) *stdd s: a last: btn 2f out* **20/1**

1m 12.16s (-1.44) **Going Correction** -0.325s/f (Firm)
WFA 3 from 4yo 4lb 5 Ran SP% **108.3**
Speed ratings (Par 103):96,94,92,91,86
CSF £34.55 TOTE £8.40: £3.20, £1.80; EX 30.50.
Owner Miss Vanessa Church **Bred** Runnymeade Farm Inc & Catesby W Clay **Trained** Hucking, Kent

FOCUS
A moderate maiden which was run at a solid pace.

4294 HAPPY BIRTHDAY NITA FILLIES' H'CAP 6f
8:00 (8:00) (Class 5) (0-70,71) 3-Y-O+ £3,886 (£1,156; £577; £288) Stalls Low

Form RPR
0601 1 **Piddies Pride (IRE)**[14] [3867] 4-8-13 **56** (v) JimmyQuinn 9 63
(Miss Gay Kelleway) *pressed ldrs: rdn wl over 1f out: styd on u.p to ld nr fin* **11/2**[3]
0101 2 *nk* **Limonia (GER)**[21] [3673] 4-8-5 **51** JamesDoyle(3) 7 57
(N P Littmoden) *t.k.h: led for 1f: pressed ldr: led again u.p over 1f out: hdd nr fin* **7/1**
5643 3 *shd* **Highland Cascade**[16] [3827] 4-9-10 **70** AdamKirby(3) 1 76
(J M P Eustace) *led after 1f to over 1f out: styd pressing ldr: hung rt ins fnl f: nt qckn nr fin* **4/1**[2]
0650 4 2 ½ **Kallista's Pride**[8] [4054] 6-9-3 **67** KylieManser(7) 3 65+
(J R Best) *hld up: prog to trck ldrs 1/2-way: urged along and no imp over 1f out* **9/1**
000- 5 1 ½ **Chilly Cracker**[227] [6664] 4-9-0 **57** MickyFenton 10 51
(John Berry) *fractious to post: hld up in rr: prog on outer over 2f out: chsd ldrs over 1f out: wknd fnl f* **20/1**
6026 6 *nk* **Miss Porcia**[13] [3897] 5-8-11 **54** TPO'Shea 8 47
(P A Blockley) *t.k.h: hld up: struggling over 2f out: n.d after* **6/1**
4424 7 1 **Linda Green**[3] [4211] 5-9-5 **65** EdwardCreighton(3) 2 55+
(M R Channon) *hld up in tch: dropped away tamely 2f out* **5/2**[1]
-055 8 2 ½ **Nephetriti Way (IRE)**[12] [3953] 5-9-12 **69** GeorgeBaker 5 51
(P R Chamings) *hld up: prog to chse ldrs 2f out: hanging and wknd over 1f out* **11/1**

1m 12.14s (-1.46) **Going Correction** -0.325s/f (Firm)
WFA 3 from 4yo+ 4lb 8 Ran SP% **113.8**
Speed ratings (Par 100):96,95,95,92,90 89,88,85
CSF £42.87 CT £170.67 TOTE £5.00: £1.60, £2.30, £1.50; EX 30.30 Place 6 £95.40, Place 5 £40.36..
Owner Countrywide Classics Limited **Bred** B Kennedy **Trained** Exning, Suffolk

FOCUS
A moderate fillies' handicap, run at a fair pace, and the first three were in a blanket finish but came clear. The form is ordinary, rated around the placed horses.
Nephetriti Way(IRE) Official explanation: jockey said mare hung right under pressure
T/Plt: £132.90 to a £1 stake. Pool: £44,015.55. 241.75 winning tickets. T/Qpdt: £29.30 to a £1 stake. Pool: £3,890.20. 98.20 winning tickets. JN

3720 HAYDOCK (L-H)
Thursday, August 10

OFFICIAL GOING: Good to firm
Wind: Fresh, against. Weather: Overcast, shower for race 6.

4295 RACINGUK.TV MAIDEN AUCTION STKS 6f
2:10 (2:12) (Class 5) 2-Y-O £3,238 (£963; £481; £240) Stalls Centre

Form RPR
2 1 **Fishforcompliments**[19] [3721] 2-8-13 PaulHanagan 5 84+
(R A Fahey) *midfield: rdn 1/2-way: edgd rt 2f out: hdwy over 1f out: led ins fnl f: sn hung lft: r.o* **11/8**[1]
32 2 1 ¼ **Mason Ette**[17] [3796] 2-8-4 PhilipRobinson 15 71
(C G Cox) *a.p: led wl over 1f out: sn rdn: hdd ins fnl f: carried sltly lft and nt qckn towards fin* **2/1**[2]
32 3 *nk* **Smokey Oakey (IRE)**[29] [3407] 2-8-9 NCallan 13 75
(M H Tompkins) *chsd ldrs: rdn and ev ch over 1f out: carried sltly lft whn hld towards fin* **16/1**
00 4 1 ¼ **Wool Mart**[24] [3596] 2-8-9 TedDurcan 6 71
(M Blanshard) *chsd ldrs: rdn over 2f out: styd on same pce ins fnl f: carried sltly lft towards fin* **100/1**
3 5 ¾ **Sir Sandicliffe (IRE)**[8] [4049] 2-8-13 RHills 10 73
(B W Hills) *midfield: rdn over 2f out: edgd rt over 1f out: styd on fnl f: nt rch ldrs* **14/1**
6 1 ½ **Five Wishes** 2-8-8 TomEaves 11 64
(M Dods) *unruly in stalls: s.i.s: bhd: styd on wl fnl f: nrst fin* **100/1**
7 *nk* **Brean Dot Com (IRE)** 2-8-9 RichardMullen 12 64
(Mrs P N Dutfield) *unruly in stalls: s.s: bhd: rdn 1/2-way: hdwy and hung lft 2f out: styd on fnl f* **100/1**
50 8 ¾ **Green Day Packer (IRE)**[47] [2844] 2-8-13 DeanMcKeown 14 65
(P C Haslam) *midfield: rdn whn sltly hmpd over 2f out: kpt on fnl f* **66/1**
0 9 3 **Aegis (IRE)**[9] [4028] 2-8-13 MichaelHills 3 56+
(B W Hills) *in rr: rn green: swtchd rt ins fnl f: kpt on: nt trble ldrs* **33/1**
05 10 ½ **Todwick Owl**[57] [2552] 2-8-9 PaulFessey 8 51
(J G Given) *prom: rdn 2f out: wknd over 1f out* **100/1**
0 11 ¾ **Bold Adventure**[11] [3976] 2-8-9 TPQueally 1 49
(W J Musson) *bhd: rdn over 2f out: nvr on terms* **100/1**
22 12 1 ¾ **Beautiful Madness (IRE)**[33] [3307] 2-8-1 DominicFox(3) 16 38
(M G Quinlan) *led: rdn 2f out: hdd and edgd lft wl over 1f out: sn wknd* **20/1**
0 13 2 **Nordic Light (USA)**[55] [2623] 2-8-11 AlanMunro 9 39
(P W Chapple-Hyam) *s.i.s: towards rr: rdn 1/2-way: no imp* **8/1**[3]
04 14 1 ¼ **Sahara Dawn (IRE)**[12] [3942] 2-8-6 DaleGibson 2 31
(C G Cox) *prom: lost pl after 1f: bhd over 2f out* **100/1**
15 ½ **Woodland Traveller (USA)** 2-8-11 JimmyFortune 17 34
(N Tinkler) *s.i.s: sn in midfield: rdn and wknd over 2f out* **80/1**

1m 15.14s (0.24) **Going Correction** -0.05s/f (Good) 15 Ran SP% **115.5**
Speed ratings (Par 94):96,94,93,92,91 89,88,87,83,83 82,79,77,75,74
CSF £3.61 TOTE £2.30: £1.20, £1.30, £3.00; EX 5.00.
Owner Mel Roberts and Ms Nicola Meese **Bred** Dunchurch Lodge Stud Co **Trained** Musley Bank, N Yorks

FOCUS
Probably just an ordinary maiden, but several of these are likely to improve, especially the winner. The third sets the standard.

NOTEBOOK
Fishforcompliments ◆, so promising though showing inexperience on his debut here last month, was every bit as green here and his chances of winning looked remote as he was going nowhere and was under severe pressure a long way out. The fact that he still eventually produced enough to score, despite hanging all over the track, suggests he could be decent when finally shaking off his immaturity. (op 13-8 tchd 7-4,15-8 in places)
Mason Ette did nothing wrong under a positive ride and just ran into a decent prospect on the day. She has already shown that he has the ability to win a race, with nurseries now also open to her, and it is merely a question of when. (tchd 9-4 in places)
Smokey Oakey(IRE) had every chance and ran another solid race on this return to turf. He has an ordinary maiden in him and also now has the added option of nurseries. (op 14-1 after 12-1 in places)

Wool Mart ran a huge race at massive odds and improved a great deal on his two previous efforts. His proximity could be seen as holding the form down, but the front three all had previous placed form to their names so it is probably best to give him the benefit of the doubt. He also now qualifies for nurseries. (op 80-1)

Sir Sandicliffe(IRE) probably improved on the form of his Leicester debut despite the inferior placing. His pedigree is all about speed, but he shapes as though he needs further than this. (op 8-1)

Five Wishes ◆, a 25,000gns filly, did best of the newcomers and the way she came home was encouraging for the future. (op 66-1)

Brean Dot Com(IRE) ◆, a relatively cheap yearling and the first foal of the Irish Listed-race winner Anna Elise, performed with credit on this debut as he gave his rivals a start. There should be better to come. (op 66-1)

4296 SEE MORE ON RACING UK H'CAP — 6f

2:40 (2:43) (Class 5) (0-70,70) 3-Y-O — **£3,238** (£963; £481; £240) **Stalls** Centre

Form				RPR
6-02	**1**		**Blues In The Night (IRE)**[8] [4045] 3-9-5 **68** .... JimmyFortune 13 (P J Makin) *in tch: rdn and edgd lft fr over 1f out: led ins fnl f: r.o* **5/1**[2]	76+
5600	**2**	*1 ¼*	**Flylowflylong (IRE)**[29] [3395] 3-9-2 **65** .... TomEaves 7 (I Semple) *midfield: rdn and hdwy over 1f out: sn chalng: nt qckn cl home* **12/1**	69
4000	**3**	*hd*	**Glenbuck (IRE)**[74] [2050] 3-8-13 **62** .... NCallan 16 (A Bailey) *a.p: rdn to ld over 1f out: hdd ins fnl f: hld cl home* **10/1**	65
4410	**4**	*nk*	**Falmassim**[22] [3646] 3-9-6 **69** .... NickyMackay 14 (L M Cumani) *s.i.s: sn in midfield: rdn over 2f out: swtchd rt and hdwy 1f out: sn edgd lft: r.o towards fin* **11/2**[3]	72+
2200	**5**	*1 ¾*	**Maison Dieu**[14] [3879] 3-8-13 **62** ....(p) TedDurcan 9 (E J Alston) *in tch: rdn over 1f out: kpt on same pce ins fnl f* **8/1**	59
3221	**6**	*1*	**Kansas Gold**[12] [3950] 3-9-7 **70** .... EddieAhern 11 (W R Muir) *led: rdn and hdd over 1f out: wknd ins fnl f* **7/2**[1]	64
6000	**7**	*2 ½*	**Laith (IRE)**[8] [4058] 3-9-4 **70** .... DominicFox(3) 12 (Miss V Haigh) *unruly in stalls: midfield: rdn over 2f out: one pce* **16/1**	57
6303	**8**	*nk*	**Night In (IRE)**[14] [3879] 3-9-7 **70** ....(t) KimTinkler 6 (N Tinkler) *prom: rdn over 1f out: wknd ins fnl f* **8/1**	56
6000	**9**	*nk*	**Rondo**[12] [3943] 3-9-0 **63** .... PaulFessey 2 (T D Barron) *s.i.s: bhd: sme hdwy over 1f out: nvr able to chal* **33/1**	48
0203	**10**	*4*	**Signor Whippee**[8] [4056] 3-8-2 **51** oh1 .... PaulQuinn 8 (A Berry) *chsd ldrs tl rdn and wknd over 1f out* **20/1**	24
0000	**11**	*7*	**Bellsbank (IRE)**[24] [3582] 3-9-2 **65** .... PaulHanagan 4 (A Bailey) *s.i.s: a bhd* **33/1**	17
0006	**12**	*1 ¾*	**Nilsatisoptimum (USA)**[7] [4071] 3-8-2 **51** oh3 .... SilvestreDeSousa 3 (M Mullineaux) *broke wl: dropped to midfield after 2f: wknd over 2f out* **50/1**	—
5-00	**13**	*2 ½*	**Felin Gruvy (IRE)**[70] [2167] 3-9-7 **70** .... RHills 15 (R F Johnson Houghton) *a bhd: sn hung lft: eased whn btn fnl f* **20/1**	9

1m 14.94s (0.04) **Going Correction** -0.05s/f (Good) **13** Ran SP% **116.5**
Speed ratings (Par 100):97,95,95,94,92 91,87,87,86,81 72,69,66
CSF £57.45 CT £600.91 TOTE £5.10: £1.80, £4.30, £3.80; EX 71.30.
Owner Martin Holland John Gale T Wellard **Bred** Fergus Cousins **Trained** Ogbourne Maisey, Wilts

FOCUS
This was probably not a great race overall, but the form looks pretty solid. The winner looks to be on the upgrade and should prove better than this.
Rondo Official explanation: jockey said gelding lost its action
Signor Whippee Official explanation: jockey said gelding was unsuited by the good to firm ground
Felin Gruvy(IRE) Official explanation: jockey said filly had been lame on her off-fore

4297 JOIN THE RACING UK CLUB MAIDEN CLAIMING STKS — 1m 30y

3:10 (3:15) (Class 6) 3-Y-O — **£2,388** (£705; £352) **Stalls** Low

Form				RPR
2330	**1**		**Emily's Place (IRE)**[8] [4048] 3-8-9 68 .... TPQueally 12 (M H Tompkins) *midfield: hdwy over 2f out: led over 1f out: edgd lft ins fnl f: drvn out* **7/4**[1]	63
5566	**2**	*nk*	**Ellesappelle**[8] [4060] 3-8-9 64 .... PatCosgrave 1 (K R Burke) *chsd ldrs: rdn over 1f out: ev ch fnl f: styd on* **6/1**[3]	62
0040	**3**	*4*	**Dream Forest (IRE)**[15] [3854] 3-8-12 62 .... RichardMullen 2 (Mrs P N Dutfield) *in tch: rdn and ev ch over 1f out: eased whn one pce wl ins fnl f* **14/1**	56
3500	**4**	*1 ¾*	**Dancing Flame**[20] [3695] 3-8-11 51 ....(p) DavidAllan 13 (E J Alston) *prom: led over 5f out: rdn and hdd over 2f out: no ex fnl f* **25/1**	51
-606	**5**	*1 ¾*	**Emily's Pet (IRE)**[4] [4176] 3-8-10 45 .... JimmyFortune 3 (B W Duke) *sn led: hdd over 5f out: remained cl up: rdn and outpcd over 2f out: no imp after* **14/1**	46
5305	**6**	*shd*	**Bolckow**[17] [3790] 3-8-12 56 .... NCallan 6 (K A Ryan) *cl up: led over 2f out: hdd over 1f out: sn hmpd whn n.m.r: btn after* **12/1**	51+
000	**7**	*hd*	**Woolsey**[42] [3029] 3-8-13 55 .... TedDurcan 8 (M Blanshard) *midfield: rdn over 2f out: no imp* **33/1**	48
03	**8**	*1 ¼*	**Top Level (IRE)**[8] [4050] 3-8-5 .... DominicFox(3) 16 (M G Quinlan) *swtchd lft s: hld up: rdn and hdwy 3f out: nvr able to chal* **12/1**	40
2642	**9**	*nk*	**Mucho Loco (IRE)**[8] [4050] 3-9-0 62 ....(b) EddieAhern 10 (J G Portman) *chsd ldrs tl rdn and wknd over 1f out* **7/2**[2]	46
0-05	**10**	*10*	**Double Oh Seven (IRE)**[16] [3816] 3-8-12 53 ....(t) MichaelHills 7 (J W Unett) *a bhd* **50/1**	21
00	**11**	*3*	**Longy The Lash**[7] [4067] 3-8-10 .... DeanMcKeown 14 (K G Reveley) *a bhd* **100/1**	12
00	**12**	*¾*	**Madame Diktatit**[15] [3839] 3-8-4 .... PaulFessey 4 (Ms Deborah J Evans) *in tch: rdn 3f out: wknd over 2f out* **100/1**	4
0000	**13**	*1 ½*	**Our Serendipity**[33] [3288] 3-8-4 35 .... PaulHanagan 11 (K G Reveley) *midfield tl wknd over 3f out* **66/1**	1
0620	**14**	*17*	**The Flying Peach**[13] [3910] 3-8-2 39 .... PaulQuinn 15 (W M Brisbourne) *s.s: a wl bhd* **33/1**	—
0-06	**15**	*22*	**Isharram (IRE)**[26] [3529] 3-8-6 34 ....(b) TonyHamilton 5 (A Berry) *s.i.s: a wl bhd* **150/1**	—

1m 44.45s (-1.06) **Going Correction** -0.125s/f (Firm) **15** Ran SP% **117.4**
Speed ratings (Par 98):100,99,95,93,92 92,91,90,90,80 77,76,75,58,36
CSF £11.14 TOTE £2.80: £1.30, £2.20, £4.40; EX 14.00.
Owner Barry Brewster **Bred** Bryan Ryan **Trained** Newmarket, Suffolk
■ Stewards' Enquiry : T P Queally two-day ban: careless riding (Aug 21, 25)

FOCUS
A modest race but a big field and a wide range of abilities, but probably not that competitive and the front pair pulled well clear. Those first, second and third best in at the weights finished one-two-three.
Longy The Lash Official explanation: jockey said gelding hung right throughout
Madame Diktatit Official explanation: jockey said filly did not handle the bend

4298 SUBSCRIBE TO RACING UK ON 08700 506957 H'CAP — 1m 30y

3:40 (3:43) (Class 3) (0-95,94) 3-Y-O — **£11,334** (£3,372; £1,685; £841) **Stalls** Low

Form				RPR
10-3	**1**		**Charlie Cool**[27] [3491] 3-9-7 **94** .... AlanMunro 2 (W J Haggas) *hld up: hdwy over 2f out: qcknd and edgd lft on outside 1f out: r.o to ld towards fin* **5/2**[1]	103+
0-13	**2**	*½*	**Count Trevisio (IRE)**[39] [3119] 3-9-7 **94** .... KerrinMcEvoy 8 (Saeed Bin Suroor) *led at stdy pce: rdn over 1f out: tail flashed u.p: hdd towards fin* **9/2**[3]	102
4002	**3**	*nk*	**Leningrad (IRE)**[11] [3978] 3-9-3 **90** .... JimmyFortune 5 (M L W Bell) *hld up: hdwy over 1f out: carried hd high: r.o towards fin* **6/1**	97+
-450	**4**	*1 ½*	**Bonnie Prince Blue**[49] [2774] 3-8-12 **85** .... MichaelHills 6 (B W Hills) *midfield: pushed along and hdwy over 2f out: carried lft sltly 1f out: nt qckn ins fnl f* **40/1**	89
1136	**5**	*2 ½*	**Electric Warrior (IRE)**[15] [3852] 3-8-7 **80** .... PatCosgrave 10 (K R Burke) *hld up: hld up: rdn over 1f out: kpt on ins fnl f: nvr able to chal* **20/1**	78
2-10	**6**	*hd*	**Master Pegasus**[49] [2774] 3-8-13 **86** .... EddieAhern 7 (C F Wall) *midfield: effrt whn edgd lft over 1f out: looking hld whn n.m.r and hmpd 1f out: no imp after* **11/2**	84
3353	**7**	*4*	**European Dream (IRE)**[6] [4108] 3-8-7 **80** .... PhilipRobinson 3 (R C Guest) *prom: rdn whn n.m.r and hmpd 1f out: lost pl qckly: n.d after* **14/1**	69+
2211	**8**	*1 ¼*	**Wind Star**[5] [4137] 3-8-12 **85** 6ex .... DeanMcKeown 4 (G A Swinbank) *racd keenly: prom tl rdn and wknd over 1f out* **4/1**[2]	71
0-00	**9**	*4*	**Playtotheaudience**[13] [3889] 3-8-12 **85** .... PaulHanagan 1 (R A Fahey) *midfield: rdn 2f out: n.m.r and hmpd over 1f out: n.d after* **66/1**	62

1m 43.18s (-2.33) **Going Correction** -0.125s/f (Firm) **9** Ran SP% **111.8**
Speed ratings (Par 104):106,105,105,103,101 101,97,95,91
CSF £13.04 CT £58.36 TOTE £3.30: £1.50, £1.60, £2.00; EX 12.20.
Owner W J Gredley **Bred** Middle Park Stud Ltd **Trained** Newmarket, Suffolk
■ Stewards' Enquiry : Eddie Ahern two-day ban: careless riding (Aug 21, 25)

FOCUS
A decent handicap, but not a strong pace early and eventually a rough race with a few hampered in the sprint for home. The form looks reasonable though, with those in the frame close to their marks.

NOTEBOOK
Charlie Cool ◆, all the better for his belated reappearance in a red-hot handicap at Newmarket last month, was produced with his effort widest of all which was probably a wise move as things turned out and, despite edging to his left, found enough to nail the leader. He is still relatively lightly raced and looks destined for even better things. (op 3-1 tchd 10-3 in places)
Count Trevisio(IRE) was given a canny front-running ride over this shorter trip and, quickening from the front inside the last couple of furlongs, the tactic very nearly paid off. He may not be one of the stable stars, but is capable of winning races like this. (op 5-1)
Leningrad(IRE), who was held up, did not have a lot of room to play with for much of the home straight but eventually put in a power-packed run against the inside rail to finish right alongside the front pair. This was a fair effort over a trip probably on the sharp side for him now and run at a modest early pace to boot, but although his head-carriage is not the most attractive he does look genuine enough. (op 4-1)
Bonnie Prince Blue, very disappointing in his last two outings, ran better but would probably have preferred a more end-to-end gallop and getting brushed by the winner as he went past made no difference to the result. (op 50-1)
Electric Warrior(IRE) tried to come from off the pace, but because of the way the race was run early his finishing effort was completely ineffective. He remains 5lb above his last winning mark and looks held. (op 16-1)
Master Pegasus ◆, far from disgraced in the Britannia, was trying to stay on from off the pace when completely shut out against the inside rail. He is still unexposed and there are more races to be won with him. (op 8-1)
European Dream(IRE), the most exposed in the line-up, already looked to have run his race when badly squeezed out a furlong from home. Official explanation: jockey said gelding suffered interference in running (op 16-1)
Wind Star, bidding for a hat-trick under a 6lb penalty, was totally unsuited by the way the race was run and pulled his chance away early. (op 10-3 tchd 3-1 in places)

4299 ST HELENS H'CAP — 1m 3f 200y

4:10 (4:11) (Class 4) (0-80,80) 3-Y-O+ — **£6,477** (£1,927; £963; £481) **Stalls** High

Form				RPR
2310	**1**		**Oddsmaker (IRE)**[8] [4036] 5-9-4 **70** ....(t) DeanMcKeown 1 (M A Barnes) *mde all: sn clr: rdn over 1f out: jst hld on* **6/1**	77
-254	**2**	*nk*	**Mandatum**[19] [3723] 5-10-0 **80** .... NickyMackay 4 (L M Cumani) *chsd clr ldr (wnr): rdn over 2f out: clsd ins fnl f: styd on wl towards fin* **3/1**[1]	87
4151	**3**	*1 ½*	**Mr Aitch (IRE)**[4] [4175] 4-9-12 **78** 6ex ....(t) AlanMunro 3 (R T Phillips) *hld up: hdwy 3f out: clsd ins fnl f: no ex towards fin* **4/1**[2]	84+
00-0	**4**	*1*	**Neutrino**[34] [3248] 4-9-4 **70** .... NCallan 7 (P C Haslam) *hld up: rdn and hung lft over 2f out: kpt on ins fnl f: nvr able to chal* **25/1**	73
1650	**5**	*nk*	**Count Kristo**[15] [3840] 4-9-7 **73** .... PhilipRobinson 5 (C G Cox) *hld up in rr: rdn over 1f out: kpt on ins fnl f: nvr able to chal* **8/1**	76
4341	**6**	*10*	**Darghan (IRE)**[20] [3704] 6-8-11 **63** .... TPQueally 2 (W J Musson) *chsd ldrs: rdn 2f out: wknd over 1f out* **9/2**[3]	50
0163	**7**	*31*	**The Composer**[34] [3248] 4-9-5 **71** .... TedDurcan 6 (M Blanshard) *chsd ldrs: rdn 3f out: wknd over 2f out: eased whn btn over 1f out: t.o* **9/2**[3]	8

2m 32.85s (-2.14) **Going Correction** -0.125s/f (Firm) **7** Ran SP% **110.6**
Speed ratings (Par 105):102,101,100,100,99 93,72
CSF £22.68 TOTE £6.10: £2.70, £2.00; EX 19.60.
Owner D Maloney **Bred** Margaret Conlon **Trained** Farlam, Cumbria

FOCUS
A fair handicap but this was a race totally decided by tactics, with the eventual winner quickly being sent into a clear lead, setting the tempo he wanted, and then just holding on. The form is not rock solid, with the placed horses close to form.
The Composer Official explanation: jockey said gelding was unsuited by the good to firm ground

4300 RACING UK TV MAIDEN STKS — 1m 2f 120y

4:40 (4:42) (Class 5) 3-Y-O+ — **£3,238** (£963; £481; £240) **Stalls** High

Form				RPR
0-2	**1**		**Mulaazem**[14] [3875] 3-9-0 .... RHills 1 (M P Tregoning) *a.p: led 5f out: rdn over 1f out: hld on wl* **5/6**[1]	83
02	**2**	*nk*	**Accompanist**[72] [2118] 3-9-0 .... JimmyFortune 5 (J H M Gosden) *trckd ldrs: rdn and ev ch fr over 1f out: hld last strides* **13/8**[2]	82

3 nk **Falpiase (IRE)** 4-9-10 ....(b[1]) NickyMackay 4 81
(L M Cumani) *trckd ldrs: rdn 2f out: eevry ch fr over 1f out: hung lft ins fnl f: nt qckn last strides* **10/1[3]**

6-0 4 15 **Satisfaction (IRE)**[40] 3100 3-9-0 .... RichardMullen 3 54
(E J O'Neill) *led: hdd 5f out: rdn and wknd over 2f out* **33/1**

0 5 nk **Thunder S (USA)**[28] 3458 3-8-9 .... EddieAhern 6 49
(L M Cumani) *hld up: rdn over 2f out: wknd over 1f out* **50/1**

6 9 **Daylesford** 3-8-9 .... TomEaves 2 33
(I Semple) *s.i.s: pushed along over 4f out: a bhd* **40/1**

2m 15.36s (-2.37) **Going Correction** -0.125s/f (Firm)
WFA 3 from 4yo 10lb 6 Ran SP% **109.1**
Speed ratings (Par 103):103,102,102,91,91 84
CSF £2.20 TOTE £1.80: £1.10, £1.50; EX 2.60.
Owner Hamdan Al Maktoum **Bred** Shadwell Estate Company Limited **Trained** Lambourn, Berks
■ Stewards' Enquiry : Jimmy Fortune two-day ban: used whip down shoulder and not giving colt time to respond (Aug 21,25)

FOCUS
Not a very competitive maiden, but at least the pace was solid and there was little to separate the front three at the line. The form is rated fairly positively around the winner.

4301 RACING UK ON SKY 432 H'CAP 1m 2f 120y
5:10 (5:10) (Class 5) (0-70,70) 3-Y-0+ **£3,238** (£963; £481; £240) **Stalls High**

Form RPR

2345 1 **Sforzando**[41] 3037 5-9-6 **62** .... TomEaves 4 70+
(Mrs L Stubbs) *midfield: hdwy and swtchd rt over 2f out: led ins fnl f: r.o* **7/2[1]**

0-35 2 1 1/4 **United Nations**[13] 3918 5-9-11 **70** .... DNolan(3) 9 76
(N Wilson) *a.p: rdn to ld over 1f out: hdd ins fnl f: nt qckn towards fin* **9/2[3]**

4545 3 1 **Shy Glance (USA)**[7] 4068 4-9-7 **63** ....(t) DaleGibson 3 67
(G A Swinbank) *cl up: rdn over 2f out: ev ch 1f out: one pce towards fin* **11/2**

0100 4 1/2 **Mae Cigan (FR)**[22] 3650 3-8-11 **63** .... TedDurcan 5 66+
(M Blanshard) *hld up: nt clr run and hmpd over 2f out: hdwy and swtchd rt over 1f out: edgd lft ins fnl f: styd on wl towards fin* **8/1**

0063 5 3 **Evolution Ex (USA)**[20] 3694 4-9-10 **66** .... NCallan 1 64
(K R Burke) *led: rdn over 2f out: hdd over 1f out: wknd and eased ins fnl f* **4/1[2]**

2415 6 6 **Ruby Legend**[12] 3941 8-9-1 **57** ....(b) DavidAllan 10 44
(K G Reveley) *hld up: effrt 4f out: wknd fnl f* **5/1**

50-0 7 14 **Kamari Gold**[41] 3053 3-7-13 **51** oh11 .... PaulQuinn 2 13
(M Mullineaux) *a bhd* **66/1**

50-0 8 6 **Norwegian**[64] 2360 5-8-9 **51** oh6 .... NickyMackay 8 2
(Ian Williams) *in tch: rdn 3f out: wknd 2f out: eased over 1f out* **16/1**

2m 18.66s (0.93) **Going Correction** -0.125s/f (Firm)
WFA 3 from 4yo+ 10lb 8 Ran SP% **110.9**
Speed ratings (Par 103):91,90,89,89,86 82,72,67
CSF £18.19 CT £79.48 TOTE £4.60: £1.70, £1.90, £1.90; EX 15.70 Place 6 £17.60, Place 5 £14.48..
Owner Mrs L Stubbs **Bred** M E Wates **Trained** Norton, N. Yorks
■ Stewards' Enquiry : Tom Eaves one-day ban: careless riding (Aug 21)
Ted Durcan caution: careless riding

FOCUS
This modest handicap was run at a dawdle for much of the way and it developed into a sprint. Not surprisingly a very moderate winning time for a race like this, 3.3 seconds slower than the preceding maiden. the form is not strong with the placed horses to recent form.
T/Jkpt: £354.30 to a £1 stake. Pool: £11,480.50. 23.00 winning tickets. T/Plt: £18.90 to a £1 stake. Pool: £66,276.05. 2,554.35 winning tickets. T/Qpdt: £5.80 to a £1 stake. Pool: £2,944.40. 374.90 winning tickets. DO

4263 YARMOUTH (L-H)
Thursday, August 10

OFFICIAL GOING: Good to firm
Wind: Fresh, across Weather: Overcast

4302 EUROPEAN BREEDERS FUND MAIDEN STKS 6f 3y
2:30 (2:30) (Class 5) 2-Y-0 **£4,210** (£1,252; £625; £312) **Stalls High**

Form RPR

3 1 **Winged Flight (USA)**[12] 3923 2-9-3 .... JoeFanning 7 84+
(M Johnston) *s.i.s: sn rcvrd to ld: clr over 1f out: comf* **1/3[1]**

2 3 1/2 **Swift Image** 2-8-9 .... SaleemGolam(3) 1 69
(S C Williams) *prom: rdn to chse wnr over 1f out: no imp* **40/1**

3 1/2 **Northern Jem** 2-9-3 .... BrianReilly 8 72
(G G Margarson) *dwlt: hld up: hdwy u.p over 1f out: hung lft ins fnl f: nrst fin* **14/1[3]**

4 2 1/2 **Rabshih (IRE)** 2-8-12 .... J-PGuillambert 4 60
(Sir Michael Stoute) *led early: chsd wnr: rdn over 2f out: wknd over 1f out* **7/1[2]**

03 5 8 **Glorious Prince (IRE)**[10] 4008 2-9-3 .... DO'Donohoe 6 41
(M G Quinlan) *hld up: rdn and wknd over 2f out* **14/1[3]**

4605 6 2 1/2 **Breckland Boy**[13] 3903 2-9-3 68 ....(p) RoystonFfrench 2 33
(Mrs C A Dunnett) *chsd ldrs: rdn 1/2-way: sn hung lft: wknd over 1f out* **50/1**

7 3 **Awe** 2-9-3 .... RobbieFitzpatrick 5 24
(Mrs C A Dunnett) *chsd ldrs 4f* **66/1**

0 8 4 **Loose Canon**[13] 3908 2-8-7 .... AndrewElliott(5) 3 7
(Mrs C A Dunnett) *hld up: wknd over 2f out* **50/1**

1m 12.93s (-0.77) **Going Correction** -0.075s/f (Good) 8 Ran SP% **108.7**
Speed ratings (Par 94):102,97,96,93,82 79,75,70
CSF £22.69 TOTE £1.20: £1.02, £7.00, £2.20; EX 16.80.
Owner J Barson **Bred** ClassicStar LLC **Trained** Middleham Moor, N Yorks

FOCUS
An uncompetitive maiden that played out pretty much as expected. The winning time was very decent for a race like this, 0.55 seconds quicker than the later maiden for older horses, and although not easy to rate, the form could work out.

NOTEBOOK
Winged Flight(USA) ◆, who put up a bold showing on his recent debut at Ascot, did not have to improve on that to win this significantly lesser race and, despite starting slowly, he was soon tanking along up on the pace. He went clear with the minimum of fuss and could have doubled the winning margin had Fanning got serious with him. Further will see him in a better light in time, but he seems happy at this trip for the moment and it will be interesting to see what sort of mark he gets for nurseries. (op 4-11 after 2-5 in places)
Swift Image, who is bred to be effective at around this sort of distance at this stage of her career, was weak in the market and clearly not expected to get involved, but she appeared to know her job and, although no match for the easy winner, she kept on well for second. Natural progression should see her landing an average maiden. (tchd 50-1)
Northern Jem, who holds entries in the Champagne Stakes and Royal Lodge - both Group 2s - kept on well having been behind early and was going on well at the finish. He is clearly thought highly of and, as a relation of several middle-distance performers, it is reasonable to expect him to benefit from a rise in distance. (op 12-1)
Rabshih(IRE), a 200,000gns purchase, comes from a stable whose two-year-olds have been slow to come to hand but, unlike many of her young stable companions, she actually seemed to know her job. Although fading away in the end, she showed promise and her breeding points to her requiring further. (op 11-2)
Glorious Prince(IRE) showed his debut running to be all wrong when third at the course last time, but this was not such a good effort and he dropped away disappointingly. On the plus side, he is now qualified for nurseries. (tchd 12-1)
Loose Canon Official explanation: jockey said filly hung right

4303 ONE RAILWAY TAKING PEOPLE PLACES MAIDEN AUCTION STKS 1m 3y
3:00 (3:00) (Class 5) 2-Y-0 **£3,238** (£963; £481; £240) **Stalls High**

Form RPR

002 1 **Persian Fox (IRE)**[10] 4008 2-8-11 .... DO'Donohoe 1 71+
(G A Huffer) *prom: jnd ldr 6f out: led over 2f out: rdn out* **4/5[1]**

0 2 2 **Kingsmead (USA)**[11] 3976 2-8-7 .... SaleemGolam(3) 2 65
(Miss J Feilden) *a.p: rdn to chse wnr ins fnl f: no imp* **28/1**

4 3 3/4 **Petrosian**[17] 3788 2-9-1 .... JoeFanning 3 69
(M Johnston) *led: rdn and hdd over 2f out: edgd lft fnl f: styd on same pce* **7/2[2]**

0 4 nk **Daylami Dreams**[13] 3892 2-8-11 .... J-PGuillambert 4 64
(J S Moore) *hld up in tch: rdn over 3f out: styd on same pce fnl f* **11/2[3]**

500 5 1 3/4 **Right Option (IRE)**[55] 2619 2-8-10 68 .... FrankieMcDonald 5 59
(A P Jarvis) *chsd ldrs: rdn over 3f out: styd on same pce fnl 2f* **7/1**

1m 40.35s (0.45) **Going Correction** -0.075s/f (Good) 5 Ran SP% **109.1**
Speed ratings (Par 94):94,92,91,90,89
CSF £21.86 TOTE £1.70: £1.10, £6.70; EX 23.50.
Owner C and H Racing **Bred** William P Fogarty **Trained** Newmarket, Suffolk

FOCUS
A race that took little winning and not easy to rate.

NOTEBOOK
Persian Fox(IRE), just touched off by yesterday's course scorer Sweet Lily at the last meeting here, was the clear form pick and did not have to perform to a very high level to win. Always travelling strongly, he found what was required and may be capable of further progression in nurseries. (op 10-11 tchd Evens)
Kingsmead(USA), always struggling to stay in touch on his debut in a good race at Newmarket, showed improved form in what was a lesser race and stayed on again for second. There is evidently a little race in him and he is another who may prefer life in handicaps.
Petrosian, ultimately well held on his debut behind smart stablemate Silent Waves at Beverley, did not look comfortable on the track that day and this straight, galloping mile was much more to his liking. He still showed signs of greeness and was outpaced when the winner kicked for home, but there should be a small race in him on this evidence and he will be one to watch out for when the ten furlongs races come into effect. (op 4-1)
Daylami Dreams did not shape badly in a better race on debut at Ascot, and this extra furlong helped, but he does not look blessed with pace and is another ten-furlong nursery type. (op 4-1)
Right Option(IRE) has been contesting better maidens and this was disappointing, but it is likely low-grade nurseries will present him with better opportunities. (op 15-2 tchd 8-1)

4304 CONSTITUTION MOTORS NORWICH ISUZU (S) H'CAP 1m 3y
3:30 (3:30) (Class 6) (0-55,52) 3-Y-0 **£2,266** (£674; £337; £168) **Stalls High**

Form RPR

0004 1 **Apres Ski (IRE)**[30] 3378 3-9-5 **52** .... DeanCorby(3) 4 60
(J W Hills) *mid-div: hdwy over 2f out: rdn to ld ins fnl f: styd on* **17/2**

50-0 2 nk **By Storm**[87] 1726 3-8-3 **40** .... KirstyMilczarek(7) 3 47
(John Berry) *mid-div: hdwy over 3f out: rdn and ev ch ins fnl f: styd on* **25/1**

-600 3 1 3/4 **Marvin Gardens**[30] 3378 3-8-10 **40** .... BrianReilly 6 43
(P S McEntee) *chsd ldrs: rdn to ld over 1f out: hdd and unable qckn ins fnl f* **33/1**

0060 4 2 1/2 **Lady Duxyana**[21] 3668 3-9-0 **44** .... RichardSmith 11 45+
(M D I Usher) *hld up: hdwy 1/2-way: led over 2f out: rdn and hdd whn hung lft over 1f out: hung rt and lft ins fnl f: nt run on* **16/1**

0060 5 3/4 **Kings Cavalier (USA)**[13] 3910 3-8-12 **45** ....(b[1]) PatrickMathers(3) 9 41
(I W McInnes) *led to 1/2-way: rdn over 2f out: wknd over 1f out* **18/1**

0036 6 2 1/2 **Is**[16] 3824 3-8-9 **39** .... J-PGuillambert 7 29
(Rae Guest) *prom: rdn and lost pl over 3f out: n.d after* **6/1[3]**

0000 7 1 **Woolfall King (IRE)**[8] 4050 3-8-7 **37** .... JoeFanning 5 25
(G G Margarson) *hld up: rdn over 2f out: n.d* **9/1**

-003 8 1/2 **Great Composer (IRE)**[67] 2260 3-9-1 **45** .... RobbieFitzpatrick 8 32
(M J Attwater) *s.i.s: hdwy over 6f out: rdn 1/2-way: sn lost pl* **11/4[1]**

0500 9 3 **Salisbury World (IRE)**[13] 3910 3-8-12 **42** .... RoystonFfrench 1 22
(J F Coupland) *chsd ldrs: led 1/2-way: hdd over 2f out: wknd over 1f out* **12/1**

0060 10 1 3/4 **Katsumoto (IRE)**[7] 4069 3-8-13 **50** .... JemmaMarshall(7) 10 26
(N P Littmoden) *s.i.s: outpcd* **18/1**

0005 11 12 **Canary Girl**[13] 3910 3-8-3 **38** .... AndrewElliott(5) 2 —
(Mrs C A Dunnett) *chsd ldrs over 5f* **10/1**

0000 12 5 **Night Reveller (IRE)**[2] 4227 3-7-11 **34** oh2 ow2 .... KristinStubbs(7) 12 —
(M C Chapman) *mid-div: rdn and lost pl 1/2-way: sn bhd* **40/1**

0063 13 1/2 **Deserted Prince (IRE)**[1] 4263 3-9-6 **50** .... DO'Donohoe 13 —
(M J Wallace) *hld up: rdn and wknd over 2f out* **9/2[2]**

1m 40.54s (0.64) **Going Correction** -0.075s/f (Good) 13 Ran SP% **122.1**
Speed ratings (Par 98):93,92,90,88,87 85,84,83,80,78 66,61,61
CSF £210.70 CT £6538.53 TOTE £11.10: £3.00, £9.40, £9.00; EX 265.40.The winner was sold to John Coupland for 5,800gns.
Owner G Woodward **Bred** Edward Kelly **Trained** Upper Lambourn, Berks
■ Stewards' Enquiry : Kirsty Milczarek four-day ban: used whip with excessive frequency (Aug 21,25,26-27)

FOCUS
A weak selling handicap rated negatively through the winner and below average for the grade.

4305 PARKLANDS LEISURE HOLIDAY CARAVANS FILLIES' H'CAP 7f 3y
4:00 (4:01) (Class 5) (0-75,75) 3-Y-0 **£3,562** (£1,059; £529; £264) **Stalls High**

Form RPR

1152 1 **Inaminute (IRE)**[15] 3841 3-8-13 **72** .... AndrewElliott(5) 4 80
(K R Burke) *led over 5f: rdn to ld over 1f out: r.o wl* **11/4[2]**

5324 2 4 **Neardown Beauty (IRE)**[5] 4144 3-9-7 **75** .... JoeFanning 7 73+
(I A Wood) *s.s: hld up: rdn over 3f out: styd on ins fnl f : no ch w wnr* **5/2[1]**

2055 3 1/2 **Arculinge**[12] 3950 3-8-2 **56** oh1 .... RoystonFfrench 2 52
(M Blanshard) *chsd ldrs: rdn over 2f out: no ex fnl f* **9/1**

0500 4 2 **Precautionary**[14] 3869 3-7-9 **56** oh2 .... LukeMorris(7) 3 47
(Miss J Feilden) *chsd ldrs: rdn over 2f out: wknd fnl f* **20/1**

6405 **5** *1 1/4* **Spectacular Show (IRE)**[19] [3741] 3-9-0 **68**................ J-PGuillambert 6 56
(M Quinn) *w ldr tl led over 2f out: rdn and hdd over 1f out: wknd ins fnl f*
9/1

6034 **6** *nk* **Ciccone**[10] [4009] 3-8-10 **64**...(p) DO'Donohoe 1 51
(W Jarvis) *prom: rdn over 2f out: wknd over 1f out* **7/1**[3]

1m 25.2s (-1.40) **Going Correction** -0.075s/f (Good) **6** Ran SP% **92.5**
Speed ratings (Par 97):105,100,99,97,96 95
CSF £6.70 TOTE £2.70: £1.50, £1.40; EX 4.90.

Owner Ray Bailey **Bred** R Bailey **Trained** Middleham Moor, N Yorks
■ Whistleupthewind was withdrawn (100/30, unruly in stalls). R4, deduct 20p in the £.

FOCUS
A decent winning time for a race like this but the form is somewhat suspect, although the winner is rated to the best of his previous form.

4306 GREAT YARMOUTH GLASS MAIDEN H'CAP 6f 3y
4:30 (4:32) (Class 6) (0-55,55) 3-Y-0+ **£2,590** (£770; £385; £192) **Stalls** High

Form RPR

0000 **1** **Great Belief (IRE)**[26] [3536] 4-9-7 **48**....................... RobbieFitzpatrick 11 58
(T D McCarthy) *led: hdd over 4f out: led over 2f out: rdn and hung lft fr over 1f out: r.o* **33/1**

-003 **2** *3/4* **Knead The Dough**[16] [3825] 5-8-9 **41**..................... NataliaGemelova(5) 6 48
(A E Price) *chsd ldrs: rdn over 1f out: r.o* **11/1**

5060 **3** *1 3/4* **Dora's Green**[14] [3869] 3-9-5 **50**... DO'Donohoe 1 51
(M Blanshard) *chsd ldrs: rdn over 1f out: styd on same pce ins fnl f* **33/1**

/553 **4** *nk* **Limit Down (IRE)**[54] [2645] 5-8-10 **42**......................... AndrewElliott(5) 10 43
(John Berry) *chsd ldrs: rdn over 1f out: edgd lft: styd on* **11/2**[2]

2500 **5** *3/4* **For Life (IRE)**[12] [3933] 4-9-7 **48**.............................(v¹) FrankieMcDonald 7 47+
(A P Jarvis) *s.s: hdwy over 4f out: rdn over 1f out: styd on* **8/1**

4030 **6** *1 3/4* **Riolo (IRE)**[19] [3728] 4-9-7 **55**...................................(b) KevinGhunowa(7) 5 49+
(K F Clutterbuck) *s.i.s: outpcd: r.o ins fnl f: nrst fin* **16/1**

2652 **7** *hd* **Yorke's Folly (USA)**[13] [3912] 5-8-13 **45**.............(b) LeanneKershaw(5) 12 38
(C W Fairhurst) *chsd ldrs: rdn over 2f out: wknd ins fnl f* **7/2**[1]

0030 **8** *hd* **Immaculate Red**[19] [3749] 3-9-5 **50**..........................(b) RoystonFfrench 4 41
(R Bastiman) *chsd ldrs: rdn over 2f out: wknd over 1f out* **11/1**

0600 **9** *1 1/2* **Chillin Out**[136] [766] 4-9-1 **42**.. JoeFanning 2 30
(W Jarvis) *hld up: effrt over 1f out: nvr trbld ldrs* **14/1**

2050 **10** *hd* **Penny Glitters**[12] [3933] 3-9-8 **53**.................................... J-PGuillambert 3 39
(S Parr) *chsd ldrs over 4f* **20/1**

0600 **11** *1/2* **Miss Redactive**[40] [3072] 3-9-1 **46**.................................. RichardSmith 8 31
(M D I Usher) *sn outpcd* **33/1**

0060 **12** *hd* **Franky'N'Jonny**[13] [3910] 3-8-10 **48**.......................(v¹) KirstyMilczarek(7) 9 32
(Mrs C A Dunnett) *dwlt: hdwy to ld over 4f out: hdd over 2f out: rdn and wknd over 1f out* **11/1**

0060 **13** *1* **Attila The Hun**[22] [3635] 7-8-10 **42**............................... MarkLawson(5) 16 24
(F Watson) *s.i.s: outpcd* **20/1**

5005 **14** *1* **Detonate**[16] [3825] 4-9-8 **49**...(v) BrianReilly 13 28
(Mrs C A Dunnett) *hld up in tch: rdn over 2f out: wknd over 1f out* **7/1**[3]

36-0 **15** *1* **Swallow Senora (IRE)**[22] [3635] 4-8-7 **41**................. KristinStubbs(7) 15 17
(M C Chapman) *s.i.s: hdwy over 4f out: wknd over 2f out* **33/1**

1m 13.48s (-0.22) **Going Correction** -0.075s/f (Good) **15** Ran SP% **120.1**
WFA 3 from 4yo+ 4lb
Speed ratings (Par 101):98,97,94,94,93 90,90,90,88,88 87,87,85,84,83
CSF £338.14 CT £11732.85 TOTE £64.20: £13.90, £3.80, £8.10; EX 566.00.

Owner A D Spence **Bred** David Fitzgerald **Trained** Godstone, Surrey

FOCUS
A poor, yet competitive maiden handicap and the form appears sound enough with the third to form.

Yorke's Folly(USA) Official explanation: jockey said mare had run flat

4307 ROY AND JOAN TANNER MEMORIAL LADY RIDERS' H'CAP 1m 2f 21y
5:00 (5:01) (Class 6) (0-65,66) 3-Y-0+ **£2,186** (£677; £338; £169) **Stalls** Low

Form RPR

1101 **1** **Gala Sunday (USA)**[9] [4021] 6-10-11 **66** 6ex..........(bt) MissSBrotherton 1 74
(M W Easterby) *chsd clr ldr: led over 2f out: rdn out* **7/4**[1]

5005 **2** *nk* **Blue Hedges**[12] [3934] 4-9-8 **54**............................ MissALHutchinson(5) 9 61
(H J Collingridge) *hld up: hdwy over 2f out: rdn over 1f out: r.o* **16/1**

4610 **3** *1/2* **Siena Star (IRE)**[39] [3115] 8-10-1 **61**............................ MrsSLiddiard(5) 3 67
(Stef Liddiard) *hld up: hdwy over 2f out: rdn over 1f out: r.o* **7/1**

-005 **4** *2 1/2* **Oh Danny Boy**[13] [3914] 5-10-3 **58**... MrsSMoore 8 59
(Jane Chapple-Hyam) *chsd ldrs: rdn and ev ch over 1f out: no ex ins fnl f* **9/1**

0004 **5** *2 1/2* **Dubai Sunday (JPN)**[5] [4139] 5-9-4 **48**............... MissFayeBramley(3) 11 45
(P S McEntee) *chsd ldrs: rdn over 2f out: wknd fnl f* **9/1**

403 **6** *hd* **Agilete**[10] [3998] 4-9-0 **46** oh2... MissARyan(5) 10 42
(J R Boyle) *hld up: hdwy over 2f out: rdn over 1f out: wknd fnl f* **13/2**[3]

5430 **7** *2* **Love You Always (USA)**[13] [3900] 6-9-12 **53**..................(t) MrsACooke 6 45
(Miss J Feilden) *s.i.s: hld up: rdn over 2f out: n.d* **5/1**[2]

-000 **8** *3* **Wahchi (IRE)**[3] [4194] 7-10-0 **60**..............................(b¹) MissJCoward(5) 2 47
(M W Easterby) *s.s: hdwy 8f out: rdn and wknd over 2f out* **25/1**

000/ **9** *1 1/4* **Sea Holly (IRE)**[614] [6805] 6-10-3 **65**...................... MissKMargarson(7) 4 49
(G G Margarson) *s.s: a bhd* **40/1**

0-03 **10** *18* **On Every Street**[86] [1767] 5-9-3 **49** oh4 ow3............. MissRBastiman(5) 7 —
(R Bastiman) *chsd ldrs 6f* **20/1**

3030 **11** *3* **Bamzooki**[5] [4139] 4-10-0 **62** ow15................................ MrsSFarnese(7) 5 6
(Mrs C A Dunnett) *led and sn clr: hung rt 7f out: wknd and hdd over 2f out* **28/1**

00-0 **12** *10* **Herninski**[22] [3634] 3-9-5 **60**... MissMSowerby(5) 12 —
(M C Chapman) *hld up: wknd over 4f out* **66/1**

2m 8.85s (0.75) **Going Correction** -0.075s/f (Good)
WFA 3 from 4yo+ 9lb **12** Ran SP% **120.7**
Speed ratings (Par 101):94,93,93,91,89 89,87,85,84,69 67,59
CSF £32.96 CT £169.81 TOTE £2.80: £1.70, £4.60, £2.30; EX 50.60 Place 6 £537.90, Place 5 £435.57..

Owner M W Easterby **Bred** Juddmonte Farms Inc **Trained** Sheriff Hutton, N Yorks

FOCUS
Moderate handicap form, as one would expect for a race of this nature, rated around the placed horses.

T/Plt: £446.00 to a £1 stake. Pool: £47,229.15. 77.30 winning tickets. T/Qpdt: £398.40 to a £1 stake. Pool: £2,638.70. 4.90 winning tickets. CR

4316 - 4319a (Foreign Racing) - See Raceform Interactive

4295 HAYDOCK (L-H)
Friday, August 11

OFFICIAL GOING: Good to firm (firm in places)
Wind: Almost nil Weather: Overcast

4320 MTB GROUP H'CAP 1m 6f
6:00 (6:00) (Class 5) (0-70,70) 4-Y-0+ **£3,238** (£963; £481; £240) **Stalls** Low

Form RPR

5054 **1** **Linden Lime**[13] [3935] 4-8-7 **56**... FrancisNorton 4 68+
(Jamie Poulton) *in tch: rdn to ld over 2f out: styd on wl: eased towards fin* **11/2**[3]

5330 **2** *2* **Red Forest (IRE)**[13] [3952] 7-8-5 **54**..................................(t) DaleGibson 7 61
(J Mackie) *chsd ldrs: wnt 2nd over 3f out: rdn over 2f out: kpt on u.p fnl f: no ch w wnr* **7/1**

5146 **3** *hd* **Let It Be**[20] [3723] 5-8-11 **60**... DavidAllan 3 69+
(K G Reveley) *in tch: n.m.r over 3f out: sn swtchd rt and outpcd: nt clr run over 2f out: styd on ins fnl f* **5/1**[2]

6030 **4** *shd* **Plenty Cried Wolf**[22] [3686] 4-8-9 **58**............................... PaulHanagan 2 65
(R A Fahey) *chsd ldr to over 3f out: sn rdn and nt qckn: styd on ins fnl f* **8/1**

1432 **5** *1 1/4* **Eldorado**[13] [3952] 5-9-7 **70**... DeanMcKeown 1 75
(S Kirk) *hld up: rdn and hung lft fr 3f out: hdwy over 2f out: kpt on ins fnl f: no ex cl home* **7/2**[1]

4324 **6** *3 1/2* **Nakwa (IRE)**[6] [4132] 8-8-2 **51** oh6.. PaulQuinn 6 51
(E J Alston) *led: rdn and hdd over 2f out: wknd fnl f* **12/1**

006P **7** *15* **Spanish Ridge (IRE)**[20] [3743] 4-9-7 **70**.........................(t) JimmyQuinn 9 49
(J L Dunlop) *s.s and wnt rt: t.k.h: hld up: hdwy over 3f out: hung rt and wknd over 1f out* **20/1**

0000 **8** *1/2* **Golden Boot**[59] [2522] 7-8-10 **59**...(v) TomEaves 8 37
(A Bailey) *s.s: hld up: rdn and nt keen over 3f out: nvr on terms* **11/1**

-010 **9** *nk* **Sharp N Frosty**[6] [4156] 4-8-7 **56**................................ PaulMulrennan 5 34
(W M Brisbourne) *midfield: lost pl after 6f: struggling 5f out: n.d* **6/1**

3m 3.11s (-3.18) **Going Correction** -0.20s/f (Firm) **9** Ran SP% **113.0**
Speed ratings (Par 103):101,99,99,99,98 96,88,88,87
CSF £42.56 CT £202.84 TOTE £7.60: £2.10, £2.90, £1.80; EX 59.50.

Owner R C Moules **Bred** R C Moules **Trained** Telscombe, E Sussex

FOCUS
Modest form but sound enough rated around the runner-up, fourth and fifth.

Spanish Ridge(IRE) Official explanation: jockey said gelding missed the break and had no more to give in closing stages

4321 COUNTRYWIDE FREIGHT NURSERY 5f
6:30 (6:33) (Class 5) 2-Y-0 **£3,238** (£963; £481; £240) **Stalls** Centre

Form RPR

1205 **1** **Just Joey**[28] [3474] 2-9-7 **81**... PaulHanagan 14 85
(J R Weymes) *chsd ldrs: led over 1f out: drvn out* **12/1**

0053 **2** *1/2* **Emefdream**[24] [3605] 2-8-0 **60**.................................. CatherineGannon 8 62
(K A Ryan) *in tch: swtchd lft 1/2-way: rdn over 1f out: ev ch ins fnl f: styd on u.p: hld cl home* **28/1**

345 **3** *shd* **Davaye**[32] [3351] 2-8-5 **65**... FrancisNorton 1 67
(K R Burke) *towards rr: hdwy 1/2-way: rdn and ev ch ins fnl f: nt qckn cl home* **9/1**

2332 **4** *1* **Cosmopolitan Lady**[11] [4006] 2-9-1 **75**.......................... PaulMulrennan 3 73
(D M Simcock) *led: rdn 2f out: hdd over 1f out: no ex ins fnl f* **11/2**[2]

033 **5** *1/2* **Proud**[13] [3942] 2-8-11 **71**.. JimmyQuinn 2 67
(M L W Bell) *in rr: rdn and hdwy over 1f out: styd on ins fnl f* **7/1**[3]

3053 **6** *hd* **Mr Klick (IRE)**[6] [4152] 2-9-4 **81**.. DNolan(3) 12 77
(N Wilson) *s.i.s: in rr: hdwy over 1f out: kpt on ins fnl f: nt pce to trble ldrs* **7/1**[3]

524 **7** *3/4* **Ghost Dancer**[29] [3457] 2-8-12 **72**................................... NickyMackay 13 65
(L M Cumani) *hld up: rdn and hdwy over 1f out: kpt on ins fnl f: nvr able to chal* **4/1**[1]

6536 **8** *2 1/2* **The Nifty Fox**[27] [3555] 2-8-12 **72**...................................... DavidAllan 9 56
(T D Easterby) *hld up: nt clr run 1/2-way: sn rdn: nt pce to chal* **12/1**

5042 **9** *1/2* **Violet's Pride**[17] [3818] 2-8-12 **72**............................... DeanMcKeown 11 54
(S Parr) *prom: rdn 2f out: edgd lft and wknd fnl f* **20/1**

5000 **10** *1 3/4* **Smirfy's Silver**[14] [3917] 2-8-0 **60**............................... SilvestreDeSousa 7 36
(W M Brisbourne) *towards rr: sn pushed along: nvr trbld ldrs* **66/1**

6106 **11** *2 1/2* **Major Third (IRE)**[39] [3136] 2-8-5 **70**......................... DuranFentiman(5) 10 37
(T D Easterby) *prom tl rdn 1/2-way: sn wknd* **33/1**

5401 **12** *3 1/2* **Loves Bidding**[18] [3799] 2-9-5 **79**.. NCallan 4 33
(R Ingram) *prom: rdn 1/2-way: wknd wl over 1f out* **8/1**

0504 **13** *47* **Poniard (IRE)**[20] [3746] 2-8-1 **61**.. DaleGibson 5 —
(D W Barker) *a bhd: t.o 1/2-way* **66/1**

61.41 secs (-0.66) **Going Correction** -0.20s/f (Firm) **13** Ran SP% **111.0**
Speed ratings (Par 94):97,96,96,94,93 93,92,88,87,84 80,74,—
CSF £287.39 CT £2771.26 TOTE £14.10: £3.40, £5.80, £2.70; EX 683.50.

Owner Rosemary's Racing **Bred** Mrs D O Joly **Trained** Middleham Moor, N Yorks
■ Bazroy was withdrawn (12/1, upset in stalls). R4 applies, deduct 5p in the pound.

FOCUS
Just a fair nursery but sound form rated around the placed horses.

NOTEBOOK
Just Joey, outclassed in better races at Royal Ascot and Chester the last twice, confirmed herself a fairly useful juvenile with this success off a mark of 81, leading just over a furlong out and running on well. She may progress further, but will need to if she is to defy a higher mark. (op 14-1)
Emefdream took a step in the right direction when third at Beverley last time and he was able to progress again on this nursery debut, staying on well to claim second. He can find a race off this sort of mark. (op 25-1 tchd 33-1)
Davaye showed marginally improved form on this nursery debut, especially as she may have been at a slight disadvantage in racing on the stands' side of the track. (op 8-1)
Cosmopolitan Lady is pretty well exposed and as a result this was a fair effort. She is likely to remain vulnerable however. (op 7-2)
Proud was slightly disappointing on this handicap debut, lacking the basic speed for this distance. She is in good hands though and will benefit for a step back up in trip. Official explanation: jockey said filly slipped leaving stalls (op 13-2)
Mr Klick(IRE) would have challenged for a place had he got away and been able to take up a better position. He has generally been progressing, but is likely to remain vulnerable off this mark. (op 10-1)
Ghost Dancer was the main disappointment of the race, failing to build on his efforts in maidens and shaping as though the minimum trip was on the short side. He deserves a chance to show he is capable of better back up in trip. (op 5-1)
Poniard(IRE) Official explanation: jockey said gelding lost its action

4322 EUROPEAN BREEDERS FUND NOVICE FILLIES' STKS 6f
7:00 (7:01) (Class 5) 2-Y-O £3,886 (£1,156; £577; £288) Stalls Centre

Form RPR
1 **1** **Wid (USA)**[42] 3043 2-9-4 .... RHills 3 90+
(J L Dunlop) *racd keenly: w ldr: led over 2f out: rdn 1f out: r.o: in command towards fin* **11/10**[1]
2 ½ **La Presse (USA)** 2-8-7 .... MichaelHills 2 78
(B W Hills) *racd keenly: hld up: hdwy over 1f out: ev ch ins fnl f: hld towards fin: promising* **10/1**
1 **3** 3 **Boreal Applause**[27] 3537 2-9-4 .... PaulHanagan 4 80
(E A L Dunlop) *racd keenly bhd ldrs: rdn 2f out: nt pce of front pair fnl f* **9/4**[2]
31 **4** 2½ **Chervil**[23] 3645 2-9-4 83 .... PhilipRobinson 6 72
(Mrs A J Perrett) *racd keenly: cl up: swtchd stand side over 2f out: btn fnl f* **10/1**
1 **5** 2½ **Crumbs Of Comfort (USA)**[25] 3596 2-9-1 .... NickyMackay 5 62
(L M Cumani) *racd keenly: sn led: rdn and hdd over 2f out: wknd 1f out* **7/1**[3]

1m 15.08s (0.18) **Going Correction** -0.20s/f (Firm) 5 Ran SP% **109.1**
Speed ratings (Par 91):90,89,85,82,78
CSF £12.20 TOTE £2.10: £1.60, £2.70; EX 11.50.
Owner Hamdan Al Maktoum **Bred** Shadwell Farm LLC **Trained** Arundel, W Sussex

FOCUS
A decent novice event restricted to fillies and it was pleasing to see the highly-rated winner pull clear with the newcomer.

NOTEBOOK
Wid(USA), who did it nicely on her debut at Newmarket - just a fair maiden - comes from a stable who house some smart juvenile fillies this term and, despite racing keenly early on, she had a little too much class for her rivals. She has Lowther and Cheveley Park Stakes entries and looks worth the rise in grade, albeit, she will need to raise her game again. (op Evens tchd 5-4)
La Presse(USA), a Cheveley Park entrant, made a highly pleasing debut against four previous winners and, although the highly-rated winner proved too strong in the end, she pulled nicely clear of the third. Winning an ordinary maiden should be a formality on this evidence. (op 8-1 tchd 11-1)
Boreal Applause, narrow winner from a fair sort on debut, took a good pull early on and took a while to pick up, ultimately getting nowhere near the front two. This was just an average effort, but she may improve for the step up to seven furlongs in nurseries. (op 3-1)
Chervil, who recorded a fair effort when winning on the polytrack at Lingfield, was switched to the stands' side coming down towards the two pole, but it made no difference and she ended up well held. She is another likely nursery type. Official explanation: jockey said filly hung right (op 9-1 tchd 8-1 and 11-1)
Crumbs Of Comfort(USA), who created a good impression when winning on debut at Wolverhampton, raced keenly in front and was readily brushed aside, failing to confirm the promise of that initial effort. She is probably beter than this and deserves another chance. (tchd 6-1 and 15-2)

4323 EBF JOHN GOOD MEMORIAL MAIDEN STKS 6f
7:30 (7:32) (Class 5) 2-Y-O £3,886 (£1,156; £577; £288) Stalls Centre

Form RPR
1 **Blue Rocket (IRE)** 2-8-12 .... RobbieFitzpatrick 8 84+
(T J Pitt) *trckd ldrs: rdn whn n.m.r and hmpd over 1f out: r.o to ld ins fnl f: rdn out* **6/1**[3]
3022 **2** ¾ **Tudor Prince (IRE)**[23] 3641 2-9-3 88 .... NCallan 2 87
(B J Meehan) *racd keenly: a.p: led 2f out: edgd rt over 1f out: hdd ins fnl f: nt qckn cl home* **2/1**[1]
3 2½ **Manchurian** 2-9-3 .... DO'Donohoe 12 79
(M J Wallace) *s.i.s: hld up in midfield: rdn and hdwy 2f out: edgd lft and styd on ins fnl f* **9/1**
0 **4** 2 **What A Treasure (IRE)**[27] 3537 2-8-12 .... NickyMackay 11 68
(L M Cumani) *in tch: led over 2f out: sn hdd: rdn over 1f out: no ex ins fnl f* **25/1**
5 2 **Tredegar** 2-9-3 .... PhilipRobinson 7 67
(C G Cox) *led: rdn and hdd over 2f out: wknd fnl f* **5/2**[2]
6 1½ **College Land Boy** 2-9-3 .... GrahamGibbons 1 63
(J J Quinn) *towards rr: pushed along over 2f out: kpt on fnl f: nvr able to chal* **66/1**
7 ½ **Danetime Panther (IRE)** 2-9-3 .... MickyFenton 4 61
(Carl Llewellyn) *towards rr: sme hdwy over 2f out: wknd over 1f out* **50/1**
8 2 **Sweet Seville (FR)** 2-8-12 .... JimmyQuinn 10 50
(Mrs G S Rees) *in tch early: outpcd fr 1/2-way* **66/1**
00 **9** 4 **Better Off Red (USA)**[35] 3247 2-8-12 .... MichaelHills 6 38
(B J Meehan) *rdn 1/2-way: a bhd* **33/1**
46 **10** 7 **Mick Is Back**[5] 4171 2-9-3 .... J-PGuillambert 9 22
(P D Evans) *prom tl rdn and wknd over 2f out* **20/1**
11 3 **John Stanley (IRE)** 2-8-12 .... MichaelJStainton(5) 3 13
(D Carroll) *a bhd* **100/1**
33 **P** **Astronomic View**[16] 3844 2-9-3 .... PaulHanagan 5 —
(E A L Dunlop) *in tch: rdn over 2f out: close up when broke down over 1f out: sn p.u* **6/1**[3]

1m 14.9s **Going Correction** -0.20s/f (Firm) 12 Ran SP% **118.0**
Speed ratings (Par 94):92,91,87,85,82 80,79,77,71,62 58,—
CSF £17.45 TOTE £7.40: £1.90, £1.70, £2.80; EX 21.50.
Owner Joey Barton & Willie Mckay **Bred** Mrs John McEnery **Trained** Bawtry, S Yorks

FOCUS
An ordinary maiden, but it should produce winners.

NOTEBOOK
Blue Rocket(IRE), a 96,000euros purchase by Rock Of Gibraltar and relation to smart sprint handicapper Halmahera, looked a fascinating contender on this racecourse debut and he put the frustrating Tudor Prince firmly in his place close home. Overcoming greeness and the fact he was hampered over a furlong out, it was a smart debut effort and Cheveley Part entrant looks well worth her place in a better class of contest. (op 7-1 tchd 8-1 in places)
Tudor Prince(IRE), who travelled up strongly before finding nothing at Kempton last time, again travelled with great fluency on this drop in trip and he pulled away with the winner, but proved no match for her close home. He will no doubt find a race eventually, but only a fool would start backing him now. (op 15-8 tchd 9-4 in places)
Manchurian, a half-brother to smart spirnter Tadeo, made some good late headway following a slow start and came through for third close home. He will stay further in time, but can be expected to benefit for the experience and should find a race. (tchd 10-1)
What A Treasure(IRE), beaten a long way on her debut at Nottingham, stepped up significantly on that and, although fading out of it late on, she showed more than enough to suggest she can find a race once contesting nurseries. (op 20-1)
Tredegar, a half-brother to Brecon Beacon and Eisteddfod, comes from a stable who generally do well with their juveniles and he knew his job, being sent straight to the front. However, he floundered once coming under pressure and was quickly headed, dropping away under pressure. He can probably find a race, but is is debatable how much improvement there is to come on this. (op 10-3)

4324 RICHARD BOLTON INSURANCE GROUP SILVER JUBILEE CLAIMING STKS 6f
8:00 (8:01) (Class 6) 3-Y-O+ £2,730 (£806; £403) Stalls Centre

Form RPR
3120 **1** **Endless Summer**[4] 4211 9-9-6 66 .... FrancisNorton 5 71
(A W Carroll) *hld up: hdwy 2f out: led 1f out: pushed out towards fin* **10/3**[1]
4261 **2** 2½ **Peruvian Style (IRE)**[3] 4223 5-9-6 52 .... JimmyQuinn 14 64
(J M Bradley) *midfield: hdwy 2f out: led over 1f out: sn hdd: nt pce of wnr ins fnl f* **10/3**[1]
0006 **3** 2 **Throw The Dice**[21] 3718 4-9-9 66 ....(p) MarkLawson(5) 6 66
(D W Barker) *sn led: rdn 1/2-way: hdd over 1f out: no ex ins fnl f* **20/1**
005 **4** ½ **Teyaar**[126] 907 10-8-10 40 .... MickyFenton 8 46
(M Wellings) *in tch: rdn 2f out: one pce fr over 1f out* **50/1**
0650 **5** nk **Full Spate**[4] 4211 11-9-6 59 .... TomEaves 10 55+
(J M Bradley) *s.i.s: bhd: hdwy over 1f out: kpt on ins fnl f* **8/1**
0535 **6** 1 **Blue Knight (IRE)**[2] 4258 7-8-13 57 ....(vt) MichaelJStainton(5) 13 50
(D Carroll) *midfield: rdn over 2f out: no hdwy* **11/2**[2]
5660 **7** nk **Vegas Boys**[8] 4077 3-9-2 73 .... NCallan 3 51
(N A Callaghan) *midfield: rdn and hdwy 2f out: ev ch over 1f out: wknd ins fnl f* **11/2**[2]
3320 **8** 3½ **Special Gold**[3] 4230 4-9-2 54 ....(b) DavidAllan 11 37
(T D Easterby) *chsd ldrs: rdn 2f out: wknd over 1f out* **15/2**[3]
0050 **9** shd **Rapid Flow**[72] 2148 4-9-2 44 .... RobbieFitzpatrick 1 36
(J W Unett) *in rr after 1f: effrt and hdwy over 2f out: wknd 1f out: eased whn btn ins fnl f* **66/1**
0600 **10** 1¾ **Revien (IRE)**[16] 3833 4-8-12 42 .... PaulFitzsimons 2 27
(Miss J R Tooth) *prom: rdn 2f out: wknd over 1f out* **100/1**
0020 **11** 4 **Graceful Flight**[14] 3912 4-8-5 35 .... StanleyChin 9 8
(P T Midgley) *broke wl: prom tl rdn and wknd over 2f out* **100/1**
0030 **12** 2½ **Sweetly Sharp (IRE)**[4] 4201 3-8-5 43 .... PaulHanagan 7 5
(A Berry) *a bhd* **25/1**

1m 13.75s (-1.15) **Going Correction** -0.20s/f (Firm)
WFA 3 from 4yo+ 4lb 12 Ran SP% **113.8**
Speed ratings (Par 101):99,95,93,92,91 90,90,85,85,83 77,74
CSF £12.53 TOTE £4.00: £1.60, £1.50, £4.70; EX 13.30.
Owner Seasons Holidays **Bred** Juddmonte Farms **Trained** Cropthorne, Worcs

FOCUS
A ready win for Endless Summer.
Sweetly Sharp(IRE) Official explanation: jockey said filly was unsuited by the good to firm (firm in places) ground

4325 WILMSLOW H'CAP 1m 30y
8:30 (8:30) (Class 5) (0-70,76) 3-Y-O+ £3,238 (£963; £481; £240) Stalls Low

Form RPR
000 **1** **Bucharest**[48] 2864 3-8-7 56 .... FrancisNorton 10 68
(M Wigham) *a.p: led 4f out: rdn over 2f out: r.o ins fnl f* **16/1**
1422 **2** 1¾ **Joshua's Gold (IRE)**[6] 4154 5-9-4 65 ....(v) MichaelJStainton(5) 6 73
(D Carroll) *in tch: rdn to chse wnr 2f out: one pce towards fin* **9/2**[2]
4304 **3** 1½ **Treasure House (IRE)**[29] 3459 5-9-11 67 .... DeanMcKeown 13 72
(M Blanshard) *s.i.s: sn trckd ldrs: rdn 2f out: kpt on same pce fnl f* **16/1**
0003 **4** 4 **Will The Till**[13] 3948 4-8-11 53 .... TomEaves 3 48+
(J M Bradley) *hld up in rr: rdn and hung lft fr 2f out: hdwy 1f out: one pce ins fnl f* **8/1**[3]
4226 **5** 2 **Musicmaestroplease (IRE)**[14] 3906 3-9-1 64 .... MickyFenton 7 55
(S Parr) *hld up: rdn and hdwy over 2f out: wknd ins fnl f* **14/1**
6300 **6** 2 **Time To Regret**[73] 2108 6-8-11 53 .... RoystonFfrench 4 39
(I W McInnes) *led: hdd 4f out: rdn over 3f out: wknd 2f out* **16/1**
0221 **7** 1 **Chicken Soup**[5] 4172 4-10-1 76 6ex .... GregFairley(5) 8 60
(T J Pitt) *s.i.s: racd keenly: hld up: effrt over 2f out: wknd fnl f* **8/11**[1]
0-00 **8** 2½ **Raul Sahara**[22] 3680 4-8-9 51 oh7 .... RobbieFitzpatrick 11 29
(J W Unett) *midfield: rdn 2f out: sn wknd* **100/1**
-000 **9** 7 **Palatinate (FR)**[22] 3679 4-9-11 67 .... PhilipRobinson 9 29
(C G Cox) *a bhd* **20/1**
050- **10** 11 **Indian Dawn (IRE)**[343] 4916 3-7-11 51 oh1 .... DuranFentiman(5) 12 —
(T H Caldwell) *midfield: rdn over 3f out: sn wknd* **100/1**

1m 42.95s (-2.56) **Going Correction** -0.20s/f (Firm)
WFA 3 from 4yo+ 7lb 10 Ran SP% **118.3**
Speed ratings (Par 103):104,102,100,96,94 92,91,89,82,71
CSF £87.18 CT £1235.72 TOTE £14.50: £2.90, £1.30, £3.50; EX 171.60 Place 6 £348.67, Place 5 £157.50.
Owner D T L Limited **Bred** Juddmonte Farms Ltd **Trained** Newmarket, Suffolk

FOCUS
Modest handicap form.
Chicken Soup Official explanation: jockey said gelding suffered interference shortly after the start
T/Plt: £347.10 to a £1 stake. Pool: £68,112.80. 143.25 winning tickets. T/Qpdt: £16.70 to a £1 stake. Pool: £4,694.00. 207.50 winning tickets. DO

4138 LINGFIELD (L-H)
Friday, August 11

OFFICIAL GOING: Turf course - good to firm (firm in places); all-weather - standard
Wind: Moderate, against Weather: Fine but cloudy

4326 CELEBRATE YOUR WEDDING AT LINGFIELD RACECOURSE NOVICE STKS 5f (P)
2:10 (2:10) (Class 5) 2-Y-O £3,238 (£963; £481; £240) Stalls High

Form RPR
101 **1** **Holdin Foldin (IRE)**[24] 3618 2-9-4 100 .... PatCosgrave 5 86+
(K R Burke) *lw: disp ld tl rdn and drew clr over 1f out: drvn out* **4/9**[1]
060 **2** 1¾ **Chingford (IRE)**[25] 3588 2-8-7 52 .... FrankieMcDonald 4 69
(D W P Arbuthnot) *chsd ldng pair: outpcd after 2f: styd on fr over 1f out to take 2nd last 150yds* **100/1**
5206 **3** 3 **Fairfield Princess**[35] 3252 2-9-0 86 .... DaneO'Neill 3 65
(N A Callaghan) *w wnr to over 1f out: wknd rapidly* **3/1**[2]
1314 **4** shd **My Valerina (IRE)**[6] 4152 2-9-1 75 .... RoystonFfrench 2 66
(Mrs A Duffield) *drvn and outpcd in last over 3f out: no ch fr 1/2-way: kpt on fnl f* **7/1**[3]

60.33 secs (0.55) **Going Correction** +0.025s/f (Slow) 4 Ran SP% **107.7**
Speed ratings (Par 94):96,93,88,88
CSF £23.02 TOTE £1.40; EX 16.60.

Owner Tweenhills Racing & P Timmins J Rhodes **Bred** Paul Starr **Trained** Middleham Moor, N Yorks

FOCUS

No strength in depth to this novice event, which was run at a brisk early pace, and the winner scored as he was entitled to. The fourth sets the standard.

NOTEBOOK

Holdin Foldin(IRE), making his All-Weather debut, eventually stamped his class on the race and followed up his Newcastle success in ready fashion. He was probably not all that suited by the drop back to this trip, and should prove happier when reverting to a stiffer test, but on this evidence he is flattered by his official rating. (op 1-2 tchd 8-15, 4-7 in places)

Chingford(IRE) was staying on nicely towards the finish on this All-Weather debut, without seriously threatening the winner, and posted her best effort to date. She is most probably flattered, but still appeals as the type to do better when switching to nurseries, providing the Handicapper does not react literally to this form.

Fairfield Princess eventually paid for trying to go with the winner through the early stages and can be rated a touch better than the bare form. She is still another who looks flattered by her current official rating, however. (op 5-2)

My Valerina(IRE), making her All-Weather bow, struggled to go the early pace and was keeping on all too late in the day. She ought to prove happier again when reverting to a stiffer track. (op 8-1 tchd 9-1)

4327 GOLF AND GAMBLE FILLIES' (S) STKS — 6f (P)

2:40 (2:41) (Class 6) 2-Y-O — £2,388 (£705; £352) Stalls Low

Form — RPR

4333 **1** **Ishibee (IRE)**[8] 4088 2-8-12 65 (p) RoystonFfrench 4 — 62
(Mrs A Duffield) *lw: pushed up to chse ldng pair after 1f: wnt 2nd over 2f out: rdn to ld over 1f out: sn clr* **9/4**[1]

06 **2** 3 **Sepia Print (IRE)**[33] 3335 2-8-12 ChrisCatlin 5 — 53
(W J Knight) *s.s: outpcd in last and wl off the pce: sme prog on outer over 2f out: styd on wl fr over 1f out to take 2nd last 75yds* **16/1**

5 **3** 2 **Porjenski**[14] 3915 2-8-12 FergusSweeney 6 — 47
(A B Haynes) *s.s: outpcd in rr: prog on outer over 2f out: chsd ldng pair 1f out: one pce* **14/1**

000 **4** ¾ **Suntan Lady (IRE)**[11] 3994 2-8-9 EdwardCreighton(3) 9 — 45
(Miss V Haigh) *b: led after 1f: all at sea bnd 2f out: hdd over 1f out: wknd rapidly ins fnl f* **66/1**

03 **5** nk **Marist Madame**[14] 3915 2-8-6 ow1 JamesMillman(7) 8 — 45
(D K Ivory) *lw: nvr beyond midfield: rdn and struggling over 2f out: no ch after* **15/2**[2]

0555 **6** ¾ **Dancing Daisy (IRE)**[15] 3860 2-8-9 60 JamesDoyle(3) 7 — 42
(Mrs P N Dutfield) *wl in rr: shkn up 1/2-way: n.d after: plugged on fnl f* **8/1**[3]

7 1 ¾ **Prima Luna** 2-8-12 RichardMullen 2 — 36
(K R Burke) *neat: lw: chsd ldrs: rdn bef 1/2-way: wknd rapidly jst over 1f out* **8/1**[3]

05 **8** shd **Mamalini**[6] 4163 2-8-12 LPKeniry 3 — 36
(P D Cundell) *lw: led for 1f: chsd ldr to over 2f out: sn wknd* **9/4**[1]

0 **9** 13 **Flying Namid (IRE)**[58] 2552 2-8-12 TPO'Shea 1 — —
(P A Blockley) *dwlt: n.m.r after 1f: nvr on terms: wknd over 2f out: t.o* **33/1**

1m 13.94s (1.13) **Going Correction** +0.025s/f (Slow) **9** Ran SP% **112.5**

Speed ratings (Par 89):93,89,86,85,84 83,81,81,64

CSF £42.76 TOTE £2.60: £1.20, £4.60, £2.90; EX 34.90 TRIFECTA Not won..The winner was bought in for 8,000gns.

Owner D K Barker,L Bolingbroke & N Gravett **Bred** Ambersham Stud **Trained** Constable Burton, N Yorks

FOCUS

A dire fillies' event which was run at a sound pace. The 65-rated winner did job readily and sets the standard.

NOTEBOOK

Ishibee(IRE) eventually came home to score in good style and belatedly broke her duck at the eighth attempt. The drop to this class clearly worked the oracle for this consistent filly, yet while she will be high on confidence after this, she does appeal as one to take on again when stepping back up in grade. (op 2-1 tchd 15-8)

Sepia Print(IRE) got squeezed at the start, and then markedly outpaced through the early parts, so deserves credit in the circumstances on this All-Weather debut. She looks to have found her level now, and the way in which she finished her race suggests she can be found an opening in this class when reverting to seven furlongs. Official explanation: jockey said filly suffered interference leaving stalls

Porjenski was another doing all of her best work towards the finish and did not prove at all suited by the drop to this trip. She is entitled to improve a little again for the experience. (op 16-1)

Suntan Lady(IRE), down in class, proved a sitting duck for the principals and failed to see out this first attempt over a sixth furlong under such a positive ride.

Mamalini, back down in grade, dropped out tamely once push came to shove and proved disappointing on this All-Weather bow. She has it all to prove now. (op 3-1 tchd 7-2 in a place)

4328 LADIES EVENING TOMORROW H'CAP — 6f (P)

3:10 (3:10) (Class 4) (0-80,77) 3-Y-O — £5,505 (£1,637; £818; £408) Stalls Low

Form — RPR

-212 **1** **Stonecrabstomorrow (IRE)**[163] 550 3-9-5 77 JoeFanning 8 — 86
(P F I Cole) *lw: cl up: effrt on outer over 1f out: drvn to ld narrowly last 100yds: styd on wl* **7/1**

2215 **2** nk **Libor (IRE)**[20] 3722 3-9-4 76 EddieAhern 1 — 84
(L M Cumani) *lw: trckd ldng pair: effrt on inner over 1f out: drvn and upsides last 100yds: jst hld* **7/2**[2]

3301 **3** nk **Sant Elena**[30] 3403 3-9-5 77 SteveDrowne 3 — 84
(G Wragg) *trckd ldr: hrd rdn to chal over 1f out: upsides 100yds out: nt qckn* **3/1**[1]

0051 **4** 1 ¼ **His Master's Voice (IRE)**[16] 3845 3-9-2 74 AlanMunro 2 — 77
(D W P Arbuthnot) *lw: led: drvn over 1f out: hdd & wknd last 100yds* **9/2**[3]

0414 **5** shd **Sleeping Storm (IRE)**[20] 3741 3-8-10 75 KMay(7) 5 — 78
(B J Meehan) *hld up in last trio: prog on wd outside 2f out: nt qckn over 1f out: styd on wl last 150yds: nrst fin* **14/1**

2123 **6** ½ **Xaluna Bay (IRE)**[16] 3841 3-9-3 75 RichardMullen 6 — 77
(W R Muir) *hld up in last trio: rdn and outpcd over 1f out: styd on ins fnl f* **9/1**

4430 **7** 3 ½ **Hypocrisy**[16] 3841 3-9-1 76 AdamKirby(3) 7 — 67
(S C Williams) *dwlt: a in last trio: rdn and no prog 2f out* **7/1**

1463 **8** shd **Charlie Delta**[23] 3646 3-8-12 77 KellyHarrison(7) 4 — 68
(D Carroll) *trckd ldrs tl wknd wl over 1f out* **9/1**

1m 12.74s (-0.07) **Going Correction** +0.025s/f (Slow) **8** Ran SP% **117.1**

Speed ratings (Par 102):101,100,100,98,98 97,93,92

CSF £32.54 CT £90.94 TOTE £7.50: £2.30, £1.50, £1.40; EX 27.60 Trifecta £69.90 Pool: £694.65 - 7.05 winning tickets..

Owner Team Havana **Bred** P Dillon **Trained** Whatcombe, Oxon

FOCUS

A tight handicap in which it paid to race handily. The first three came clear and the next two give the form a sound look.

Hypocrisy Official explanation: jockey said filly ran flat

4329 BOOK ONLINE FOR A £2 DISCOUNT FILLIES' H'CAP — 7f (P)

3:40 (3:40) (Class 6) (0-55,55) 3-Y-O+ — £2,388 (£705; £352) Stalls Low

Form — RPR

0040 **1** **Elrafa Mujahid**[20] 3731 4-9-7 54 (t) AdamKirby(3) 6 — 66
(Ernst Oertel) *lw: b.hind: trckd ldr: led wl over 2f out: sn kicked 2l clr: hung rt over 1f out: drvn and kpt on wl fnl f* **10/1**

2460 **2** 1 ½ **Miskina**[28] 3478 5-9-11 55 ChrisCatlin 14 — 63
(W M Brisbourne) *trckd ldrs: poised to chal over 2f out: rdn to chse wnr over 1f out: sn clsd: fnd nil and hld fnl f* **10/1**

6-04 **3** 1 **Pearl Farm**[13] 3933 5-9-5 49 SteveDrowne 5 — 54
(C A Horgan) *lw: trckd ldrs: outpcd over 2f out: drvn to chse ldng pair fnl f: one pce* **9/2**[1]

-005 **4** ¾ **Buckle And Hyde**[9] 4052 3-9-0 53 JamesDoyle(3) 10 — 54
(Mrs A L M King) *s.i.s: settled in rr: effrt over 2f out: kpt on fr over 1f out: nvr rchd ldrs* **25/1**

6056 **5** shd **Grezie**[17] 3817 4-9-0 47 EdwardCreighton(3) 1 — 50
(T D McCarthy) *dwlt: sn in tch: outpcd over 2f out: effrt over 1f out: kpt on same pce* **5/1**[2]

3402 **6** ¾ **Divine White**[14] 3897 3-9-5 55 (p) JimCrowley 4 — 54
(Mrs A J Perrett) *lw: led to wl over 2f out: fdd on inner over 1f out* **5/1**[2]

1005 **7** shd **Jennverse**[16] 3847 4-8-9 46 JamesMillman(7) 13 — 47
(D K Ivory) *hld up wl in rr and racd wd: prog over 1f out: styd on: no ch* **10/1**

0500 **8** hd **Free Silver (IRE)**[13] 3933 3-9-3 53 AlanMunro 2 — 51
(Miss K B Boutflower) *trckd ldrs: rdn and lost pl over 2f out: tried to renew effrt over 1f out: one pce* **25/1**

4063 **9** nk **Red Vixen (IRE)**[15] 3869 3-8-10 53 KirstyMilczarek(7) 11 — 51+
(C N Allen) *hld up wl in rr: last of main gp over 1f out: styd on: no ch* **15/2**

5010 **10** shd **Tuscany Queen (IRE)**[30] 3410 3-9-2 52 DaneO'Neill 8 — 49
(R Hannon) *wl in tch: outpcd over 2f out: grad fdd fnl f* **10/1**

4532 **11** 6 **Blakeshall Quest**[16] 3847 6-9-6 50 (b) GeorgeBaker 7 — 34
(R Brotherton) *b.hind: hld up wl in rr: struggling fr 1/2-way: no ch fnl 2f* **7/1**[3]

003 **12** 23 **Little Miss Verity**[15] 3875 3-9-2 52 RichardThomas 3 — —
(J A Geake) *t.k.h early: prom 3f: wknd rapidly: sn t.o* **40/1**

1m 26.32s (0.43) **Going Correction** +0.025s/f (Slow)

WFA 3 from 4yo+ 6lb **12** Ran SP% **122.3**

Speed ratings (Par 98):98,96,95,94,94 93,93,92,92,92 85,59

CSF £107.37 CT £530.85 TOTE £12.30: £3.60, £3.70, £1.80; EX 143.20 TRIFECTA Not won..

Owner Giovanni Favarulo **Bred** R S A Urquhart **Trained** Newmarket, Suffolk

FOCUS

A weak fillies' handicap run at just a modest pace with hte placed horses to recent form.

Blakeshall Quest Official explanation: trainer said mare lost a front shoe and hung right throughout

Little Miss Verity Official explanation: trainer said filly had tied up post race

4330 LINGFIELD PARK GOLF CLUB MAIDEN STKS — 1m 6f

4:10 (4:10) (Class 5) 3-Y-O+ — £3,238 (£963; £481; £240) Stalls Low

Form — RPR

5640 **1** **Riff Raff**[12] 3974 3-8-9 72 AlanMunro 3 — 60
(W Jarvis) *lw: mde virtually all: pushed along bnd after 2f: jnd over 2f out: drvn and kpt on wl fnl f* **3/1**[2]

0- **2** 1 ¼ **Land Of Light**[316] 5574 3-9-0 JimCrowley 8 — 63
(G L Moore) *sn trckd wnr: rdn to chal 2f out: hanging and fnd little: hld fnl f* **16/1**

05 **3** 1 ¼ **Noddies Way**[16] 3849 3-9-0 DaneO'Neill 2 — 61
(J F Panvert) *lw: trckd ldrs: rdn and nt qckn over 2f out: plugged on same pce* **8/1**[3]

006 **4** nk **Naini Tal**[18] 3794 3-8-9 73 JohnEgan 6 — 56
(D R C Elsworth) *lw: hld up: prog 1/2-way to trck ldrs: rdn 3f out: flashing tail and nt looking keen: plugged on* **1/1**[1]

0 **5** 3 ½ **Gallileo Figaro (USA)**[35] 3261 3-8-6 JamesDoyle(3) 1 — 51
(W M Brisbourne) *in tch: rdn and outpcd over 3f out: nvr on terms after* **40/1**

4322 **6** 2 **Tip Toes (IRE)**[14] 3896 4-9-5 46 DeanCorby(3) 5 — 48
(P Howling) *dwlt: hld up: rapid prog to join ldrs over 3f out: wknd rapidly over 1f out* **10/1**

0-40 **7** 5 **Overlook**[11] 4005 3-8-9 60 LPKeniry 4 — 41
(A M Balding) *in tch: outpcd over 3f out: steadily wknd* **9/1**

8 12 **Curved Air (IRE)**[19] 4-9-8 SteveDrowne 7 — 24
(Stef Liddiard) *s.s: a last: wknd 3f out* **28/1**

3m 9.50s (2.58) **Going Correction** +0.125s/f (Good)

WFA 3 from 4yo 13lb **8** Ran SP% **117.0**

Speed ratings (Par 103):97,96,95,95,93 92,89,82

CSF £49.81 TOTE £5.10: £1.30, £4.20, £2.60; EX 47.70 TRIFECTA Not won..

Owner Anthony Foster **Bred** Darley **Trained** Newmarket, Suffolk

FOCUS

A modest maiden, run at an uneven pace, and the form is ordinary, limited by the sixth.

4331 LINGFIELDPARK.CO.UK H'CAP — 1m 3f 106y

4:40 (4:40) (Class 5) (0-70,69) 3-Y-O+ — £3,238 (£963; £481; £240) Stalls High

Form — RPR

0422 **1** **Ardea Brave (IRE)**[7] 4104 4-9-5 60 (p) OscarUrbina 7 — 74
(M Botti) *mde virtually all and set gd pce: jnd 2f out: cajoled along and limited response: jst hld on* **9/4**[1]

000 **2** shd **Altilhar (USA)**[25] 3589 3-8-13 64 (b[1]) SteveDrowne 2 — 78
(G L Moore) *lw: prom: trckd wnr 3f out gng easily: chal and upsides fr 2f out: fnd little u.p: jst hld* **11/2**[2]

3303 **3** 4 **Serramanna**[28] 3467 5-8-6 50 JamesDoyle(3) 6 — 57
(Ms J S Doyle) *settled in rr: rdn and struggling over 4f out: prog u.p to chse ldng pair over 2f out: one pce and no imp* **11/2**[2]

4004 **4** 3 **Stolen Hours (USA)**[16] 3840 6-9-12 67 ChrisCatlin 3 — 69
(J Akehurst) *hld up in last: rdn over 4f out: sn struggling: kpt on u.p fr over 2f out: no imp over 1f out* **6/1**[3]

0360 **5** 1 ¼ **Bukit Fraser (IRE)**[9] 4046 5-8-13 57 NelsonDeSouza(3) 1 — 57
(P F I Cole) *in tch in rr: rdn 5f out: struggling 4f out: plugged on fnl 2f* **9/1**

3634 **6** 1 ¼ **Kalatime (IRE)**[20] 3731 3-9-3 68 LPKeniry 5 — 66
(A M Balding) *trckd ldrs: rdn to chse ldng trio over 2f out: wknd over 1f out* **17/2**

020 **7** 3 ½ **Quel Ange (FR)**[28] 3469 4-10-0 69 JimCrowley 4 — 61
(R J Hodges) *in tch: dropped to rr and rdn 1/2-way: a struggling after* **20/1**

0020 **8** 1 **King's Fable (USA)**[15] 3870 3-8-3 54 JoeFanning 9 — 44
(M Johnston) *lw: chsd wnr to 3f out: hanging and nt keen after: sn wknd* **13/2**

40-0 **9** *7* **Beaufort**[13] 3952 4-9-9 **64** GeorgeBaker 8 43
(D K Ivory) *chsd ldrs: pushed along 5f out: wknd 3f out* **40/1**

2m 28.82s (-1.10) **Going Correction** +0.125s/f (Good)
WFA 3 from 4yo+ 10lb **9** Ran SP% **116.9**
Speed ratings (Par 103):109,108,106,103,102 102,99,98,93
CSF £14.84 CT £61.21 TOTE £2.80: £1.10, £2.60, £2.00; EX 20.10 Trifecta £98.20 Pool: £456.73 - 3.30 winning tickets..
Owner Dioscuri Srl **Bred** Scuderia San Pancrazio Sas **Trained** Newmarket, Suffolk

FOCUS
A modest handicap that saw the first two come clear. The time was decent so the form looks sound enough for the class.
Beaufort Official explanation: vet said gelding was struck into

4332 LINGFIELD PARK LEISURE CLUB H'CAP 1m 2f
5:10 (5:12) (Class 6) (0-60,60) 3-Y-0+ **£2,388** (£705; £352) **Stalls** Low

Form RPR
0314 **1** **Good Article (IRE)**[20] 3730 5-9-3 **46** GeorgeBaker 6 56
(D K Ivory) *hld up: prog fr 1/2-way: trckd ldr gng easily 3f out: rdn to chal wl over 1f out: forced ahd last 100yds* **4/1**[1]
4002 **2** *1/2* **Alqaayid**[28] 3580 5-9-2 **52** JamesMillman(7) 2 61
(P W Hiatt) *trckd ldrs: lft in ld bnd over 3f out: drvn and hdd last 100yds* **20/1**
3500 **3** *nk* **Choristar**[55] 2641 5-9-2 **48** NelsonDeSouza(3) 10 56
(J Mackie) *t.k.h: hld up in rr: outpcd over 3f out: rdn and prog fr 2f out: r.o fnl f: gaining at fin* **7/1**[3]
06-0 **4** *1/2* **Storm Prospect**[74] 2063 3-9-8 **60** (b[1]) ChrisCatlin 11 67
(C Tinkler) *lw: t.k.h: trckd ldrs: rdn and nt qckn over 2f out: rallied over 1f out: styd on: nvr able to chal* **16/1**
5053 **5** *2* **Blu Manruna**[8] 4076 3-9-7 **59** (p) FrancisFerris 4 62
(J Akehurst) *lw: trckd ldrs: rdn and cl enough 2f out: fnd nil over 1f out: fdd fnl f* **11/2**[2]
3005 **6** *1 3/4* **Postmaster**[13] 3933 4-9-7 **50** StephenCarson 3 50
(R Ingram) *hld up in last pair: gd prog on inner 3f out: rdn 2f out: wknd over 1f out* **11/1**
0010 **7** *1 1/4* **Bishops Finger**[20] 3730 6-9-7 **57** (b) HarryPoulton(7) 7 55
(Jamie Poulton) *b: settled in midfield: prog 3f out: pressing ldrs 2f out: hung rt and sn wknd* **10/1**
0005 **8** *hd* **Oakley Absolute**[14] 3900 4-9-11 **57** (v) StephaneBreux(3) 1 54
(R Hannon) *lw: trckd ldr: followed her wd bnd over 3f out and lost pl: rdn and steadily wknd* **12/1**
4403 **9** *1 3/4* **Captain Bolsh**[15] 3870 3-9-2 **54** SteveDrowne 12 48
(J Pearce) *settled in rr: rdn over 2f out: no rspnse and btn after* **9/1**
6060 **10** *nk* **Simplify**[17] 3820 4-9-5 **48** (p) PatDobbs 13 41
(T M Jones) *racd wd: hld up in rr: rdn over 2f out: sn btn* **33/1**
0160 **11** *3 1/2* **Wild Lass**[17] 3817 5-9-4 **47** (p) LPKeniry 14 34
(J C Fox) *led: hung rt and wd bnd over 3f out: hdd & wknd* **66/1**
2/0- **12** *15* **Noble Calling (FR)**[180] 4219 9-9-12 **55** JimCrowley 9 13
(R J Hodges) *s.v.s: in tch in rr to 4f out: sn wknd: t.o* **66/1**

2m 10.54s (0.82) **Going Correction** +0.125s/f (Good)
WFA 3 from 4yo+ 9lb **12** Ran SP% **99.6**
Speed ratings (Par 101):101,100,100,99,98 96,95,95,94,94 91,79
CSF £59.97 CT £282.69 TOTE £3.20: £1.50, £5.40, £2.30; EX 86.20 Trifecta £70.40 Part won. Pool: £99.18 - 0.34 winning tickets..
Owner T G N Burrage **Bred** T G N Burrage **Trained** Radlett, Herts

FOCUS
A moderate handicap that was run at a sound pace, and rated negatively though the runner-up and fourth.
T/Jkpt: Not won. T/Plt: £76.30 to a £1 stake. Pool: £56,134.15. 536.95 winning tickets. T/Qpdt: £25.10 to a £1 stake. Pool: £3,655.60. 107.80 winning tickets. JN

4144
NEWMARKET (JULY) (R-H)
Friday, August 11

OFFICIAL GOING: Good to firm
Wind: Fresh, across Weather: Cloudy with the occasional shower

4333 JOOLS HOLLAND 10TH ANNIVERSARY MAIDEN STKS 7f
5:45 (5:47) (Class 4) 2-Y-0 **£4,533** (£1,348; £674; £336) **Stalls** High

Form RPR
1 **Furnace (IRE)** 2-9-3 JamieSpencer 3 82+
(M L W Bell) *gd sort: leggy: hld up: hdwy over 2f out: led ins fnl f: r.o* **10/1**
00 **2** *1/2* **Bold Abbott (USA)**[7] 4103 2-9-3 RyanMoore 8 81
(Mrs A J Perrett) *lw: chsd ldr: led 2f out: rdn and hdd ins fnl f: styd on* **18/1**
3 *1 3/4* **Hazzard County (USA)** 2-9-3 DaneO'Neill 11 76+
(D M Simcock) *wl grwn: lw: dwlt: hld up: hdwy over 1f out: sn swtchd lft: r.o* **33/1**
4 **4** *1 1/2* **Stark Contrast (USA)**[28] 3498 2-9-3 LDettori 12 73
(G A Butler) *lw: led 5f: styd on same pce fnl f* **4/1**[2]
4 **5** *1/2* **Kid Mambo (USA)**[16] 3844 2-9-3 IanMongan 13 71
(T G Mills) *chsd ldrs: rdn over 2f out: edgd lft 1f out: styd on same pce* **5/1**[3]
6 *shd* **Ea (USA)** 2-9-3 RobertWinston 6 71+
(Sir Michael Stoute) *gd sort: scope: prom: rdn 1/2-way: outpcd over 2f out: nt clr run over 1f out: styd on ins fnl f* **3/1**[1]
0 **7** *3/4* **Leonide**[21] 3701 2-9-3 GMosse 15 69
(B J Meehan) *chsd ldrs: rdn and n.m.r over 1f out: wknd ins fnl f* **16/1**
8 *3/4* **Titan Triumph** 2-9-3 SebSanders 17 67
(W J Knight) *w'like: leggy: dwlt: hld up: hdwy 1/2-way: rdn over 1f out: wknd ins fnl f* **20/1**
03 **9** *1/2* **Dubai Builder**[14] 3895 2-9-3 JohnEgan 1 66
(J S Moore) *lw: plld hrd and prom: rdn whn bmpd 1f out: sn wknd* **13/2**
10 *1/2* **Style Sunday (IRE)** 2-9-3 JimmyFortune 9 64
(B W Hills) *w'like: mid-div: effrt over 2f out: nvr trbld ldrs* **33/1**
11 *1* **Mutadarrej (IRE)** 2-9-3 KerrinMcEvoy 4 62
(J L Dunlop) *w'like: scope: lw: prom: hmpd and lost pl 6f out: bhd tl r.o ins fnl f* **14/1**
0 **12** *2 1/2* **Musical Award (IRE)**[7] 4103 2-9-3 TPQueally 14 55
(M G Quinlan) *mid-div: rdn over 2f out: sn wknd* **66/1**
00 **13** *3* **Diggs Lane (IRE)**[12] 3976 2-9-3 PaulEddery 10 48
(N A Callaghan) *a in rr* **66/1**
14 *shd* **King's Attitude** 2-9-3 TPO'Shea 5 47
(B J Meehan) *w'like: scope: s.i.s: n.d* **66/1**
15 *3/4* **Seeking The Buck (USA)** 2-9-3 EddieAhern 2 45
(M A Magnusson) *gd sort: bkwd: s.i.s: hld up: n.d* **25/1**
16 *nk* **Alpes Maritimes** 2-9-3 AlanMunro 7 45
(G Wragg) *w'like: unf: bkwd: a in rr* **33/1**
17 *5* **Storm Path (IRE)** 2-9-3 TedDurcan 16 32
(C E Brittain) *cmpt: scope: s.s: hdwy over 4f out: wknd 3f out* **50/1**

1m 25.49s (-1.29) **Going Correction** -0.20s/f (Firm) **17** Ran SP% **125.8**
Speed ratings (Par 96):99,98,96,94,94 94,93,92,91,91 90,87,83,83,82 82,76
CSF £166.60 TOTE £13.40: £3.90, £4.40, £10.20; EX 239.20.
Owner Highclere Thoroughbred Racing XXXV **Bred** Barouche Stud Ireland Ltd **Trained** Newmarket, Suffolk

FOCUS
A fair-looking maiden despite a twice-raced horse, who had only shown limited form prior to the race, finishing second. Along with the fourth he helps set the standard and winners look sure to come from the race, however.

NOTEBOOK
Furnace(IRE), a late foal who holds an entry in the Royal Lodge Stakes later in the season, took a while to get the hang of things but finished to good purpose up the incline. Presumably he was not overly fancied for his debut, considering his starting price, and more improvement can be expected. (op 11-1 tchd 12-1)
Bold Abbott(USA), who had experience on his side, showed his best form to date - which might hold the overall form down slightly - keeping on well all the way to the line after taking the lead with a quarter of a mile to go. He has the option of nurseries now but will probably win any ordinary maiden. (op 16-1 tchd 20-1)
Hazzard County(USA) ◆ finished to good effect from off the pace and certainly caught the eye. With normal progression, he should go very close next time.
Stark Contrast(USA), whose debut run has worked out well, was arguably a bit disappointing after leading early. However, considering the way his York run has worked out, he is certainly worth another chance next time if kept to a realistic level. (op 10-3 tchd 11-4 5-1 in a place)
Kid Mambo(USA) was always thereabouts but failed to quicken when the race started to take shape. He was not given a hard time by his jockey in the final furlong and looks like a horse that needs a bit futher than seven furlongs. (op 7-1 tchd 15-2 in places)
Ea(USA) ◆, who holds entries in the Royal Lodge and Derby, was niggled along early before realising what was required, picking up steadily when meeting the rising ground. He was badly impeded at about the furlong marker, and that ended any chance he had of being placed at the very least, but showed enough to make him of some interest next time (op 5-2)
Leonide was far from disgraced and is not without ability. He appeals as the sort to do better in handicap company at either two or three, and is definitely one to keep in mind when a suitable opportunity arises.
Dubai Builder was far too keen in the early stages to have anything left for the finish of the race. He is likely to be better suited by six furlongs. He is the sort for handicaps. (op 9-1)
Mutadarrej(IRE) was completely clueless early but caught the eye, staying on late under a typically considerate ride by the jockey. He is better than his final position suggests. (op 16-1)
Musical Award(IRE)was probably out of her depth in this company but does not seem without ability. She is one to keep an eye on when she is eligible for nurseries.
Seeking The Buck(USA) is nowhere near as bad as his finishing postion suggests and was not given a hard time from off the pace. He is sure to do better.
Alpes Maritimes was pushed along from the outset and never looked like making any progress. (op 40-1)

4334 HEADLAND INTERNATIONAL (S) STKS 7f
6:15 (6:17) (Class 5) 2-Y-0 **£3,886** (£1,156; £577; £288) **Stalls** High

Form RPR
2034 **1** **La Marmotte (IRE)**[11] 3997 2-8-8 66 EddieAhern 1 63+
(J W Hills) *chsd ldr 6f out: led over 2f out: hung rt ins fnl f: drvn clr* **9/2**[1]
3234 **2** *3 1/2* **Hester Brook (IRE)**[11] 4006 2-8-8 68 RobertWinston 13 54
(J G M O'Shea) *b: hld up: hdwy 1/2-way: rdn over 1f out: no ex ins fnl f* **13/2**[3]
0414 **3** *nk* **Sunstroke (IRE)**[18] 3801 2-8-13 60 TPQueally 12 58
(M G Quinlan) *led 1f: chsd ldrs: rdn and ev ch over 1f out: styd on same pce* **6/1**[2]
6443 **4** *nk* **Generist**[38] 3175 2-8-5 57 DominicFox(3) 7 52
(M J Attwater) *lw: s.s: hld up: hdwy over 1f out: styd on* **12/1**
0062 **5** *2* **Emergency Services**[11] 4007 2-8-13 54 (p) SebSanders 6 52
(Tom Dascombe) *chsd ldrs: rdn over 2f out: hung lft and wknd over 1f out* **13/2**[3]
006 **6** *1 1/4* **Grimes Glory**[11] 4002 2-8-13 RyanMoore 8 49
(R Hannon) *hld up: rdn 1/2-way: styd on ins fnl f: nvr nrr* **8/1**
40 **7** *shd* **Equal And Approved**[25] 3588 2-8-13 JimmyFortune 3 49
(R Hannon) *hld up: hrd rdn fr over 2f out: n.d* **6/1**[2]
0006 **8** *2* **Bonny Scotland (IRE)**[7] 4115 2-8-8 48 AlanMunro 5 38
(Miss V Haigh) *s.s: nvr nrr* **25/1**
34 **9** *1/2* **Cookies Quiff (IRE)**[18] 3799 2-8-13 JohnEgan 4 42
(J S Moore) *lw: hld up in tch: plld hrd: rdn over 2f out: sn wknd* **10/1**
000 **10** *4* **Roxy Singer**[14] 3915 2-8-8 40 FergusSweeney 10 27
(W J Musson) *lw: hld up: wknd over 2f out* **33/1**
006 **11** *shd* **Take My Turn**[35] 3246 2-8-13 60 TedDurcan 11 31
(M Blanshard) *mid-div: rdn 1/2-way: wknd over 2f out* **10/1**
50 **12** *5* **Eastern Playboy (IRE)**[20] 3746 2-8-13 DerekMcGaffin 9 18
(J Jay) *s.i.s: rcvrd to ld 6f out: hdd over 2f out: sn rdn and wknd* **66/1**
00 **13** *13* **Bronco's Filly (IRE)**[22] 3677 2-8-8 TPO'Shea 2 —
(J G M O'Shea) *unf: hld up: wknd 3f out* **66/1**

1m 26.35s (-0.43) **Going Correction** -0.20s/f (Firm) **13** Ran SP% **120.2**
Speed ratings (Par 94):94,90,89,89,87 85,85,83,82,78 77,72,57
CSF £32.57 TOTE £4.30: £2.00, £3.00, £2.20; EX 29.50.The winner was bought in for 7,500gns
Owner Gary And Linnet Woodward **Bred** Rathasker Stud **Trained** Upper Lambourn, Berks
■ Stewards' Enquiry : T P Queally one-day ban: failed to keep straight from stalls (Aug 26)

FOCUS
A decent race for a seller, dominated by the highest-rated horses. The time, as you would expect, was the slowest of the three races run over the trip on the night and the form looks solid.

NOTEBOOK
La Marmotte(IRE), who had to be led for a half a furlong when on the way to the start, did the job nicely when getting to the front. She is not one to trust implicitly, given her antics before the race, but might handle a return to nursery company. (op 7-2 tchd 5-1)
Hester Brook(IRE), who was top-rated on official figures, is a model of consistency and once again ran up to her best. However, the step up in trip did not obviously suit. (op 5-1 tchd 7-1)
Sunstroke(IRE) had something to find at the weights on official figures and came up just short. This is her level and she should remain relatively effective in it. (op 9-2)
Generist was not the best away but kept on well in the final stages. She is clearly moderate and selling grade is her level. (op 14-1)
Emergency Services, who was very well supported in the market, threw away any chance he had by hanging under pressure. He is already very exposed. (op 12-1)
Grimes Glory, dropped to this class for the first time, was never going with any fluency early and only picked up late on. It was far from a promising effort. (op 10-1)
Equal And Approved does at least look like a horse that tries his best and probably has enough ability to pick up a similar race in time. (op 8-1)
Bronco's Filly(IRE) Official explanation: jockey said filly hung badly left

4335 FIRESTONE BUILDING PRODUCTS NURSERY 7f
6:45 (6:45) (Class 4) 2-Y-O **£5,181** (£1,541; £770; £384) **Stalls** High

Form					RPR
011	**1**		**Tobosa**[7] [4107] 2-9-13 **83** 6ex. AlanMunro 1 (W Jarvis) *lw: a.p: racd keenly: chsd ldr 1/2-way: rdn over 2f out: hung lft over 1f out: led ins fnl f: r.o wl* **11/8**[1]		94
4111	**2**	*1 ¼*	**Just Dust**[7] [4100] 2-9-4 **79** 6ex. MarcHalford(5) 5 (D R C Elsworth) *sn led at stdy pce: qcknd 1/2-way: rdn and hung lft fr over 2f out: hdd and unable qckn ins fnl f* **3/1**[2]		87
4314	**3**	*1 ¾*	**Capannina**[16] [3834] 2-9-4 **74**. TPQueally 4 (J Noseda) *lw: hld up: rdn over 2f out: hung lft over 1f out: styd on ins fnl f: nt rch ldrs* **9/1**		77
3521	**4**	*nk*	**Little Miss Wizzy**[18] [3800] 2-8-11 **67**. HayleyTurner 3 (M L W Bell) *prom: rdn over 2f out: hung lft over 1f out: styd on same pce* **7/1**		70
01	**5**	*¾*	**Strike Force**[62] [2442] 2-9-1 **71**. JimmyFortune 2 (J H M Gosden) *chsd ldr tl rdn 1/2-way: hung lft and no ex fnl f* **4/1**[3]		72

1m 24.83s (-1.95) **Going Correction** -0.20s/f (Firm) **5** Ran SP% **109.6**
Speed ratings (Par 96):103,101,99,99,98
CSF £5.66 TOTE £2.10: £1.30, £2.00; EX 4.80.
Owner Collins, Randall, Rich & Turnbull **Bred** G S Shropshire **Trained** Newmarket, Suffolk

FOCUS
A smart performance by the winner, who looks well up to trying his hand in better company. The runner-up is a solid marker to the form and the race should work out. The winning time was decent for a race like this and the fastest of the three juvenile races over the trip.

NOTEBOOK
Tobosa ◆ has not looked back since making a fair debut, and completed the hat-trick in good style. A nice big sort with more scope for improvement, he stretched away from his main rival inside the final furlong to win convincingly under top weight. He is ready for a rise in class and has the makings of a smart juvenile. (tchd 6-4 and 13-8 in places)
Just Dustwas outclassed inside the final furlong by Tobosa and could not hold the winner despite receiving a nice chunk of weight. A useful sort in his own right, he comfortably held the rest of the field and can win another race before the end of the season. (tchd 10-3 in places)
Capannina never got to the front two and was not good enough on the day. Tobosa and Just Dust are above-average juveniles, so she was probably facing a impossible task off her current handicap mark. (op 7-1)
Little Miss Wizzy seemed to run up to her very best but was not in the same class as the first two. She will find much easier opportunities in the future and is capable of going close next time. (op 8-1)
Strike Force was rolling around inside the final two furlongs and gave the impression he still needed the experience, despite already winning a race. As long as it was inexperience that made him hang both ways under pressure, he can be given another chance. (op 11-2)

4336 MYKAL INDUSTRIES LTD H'CAP 1m 2f
7:15 (7:16) (Class 5) (0-75,76) 3-Y-O+ **£3,886** (£1,156; £577; £288) **Stalls** Centre

Form				RPR
0011	**1**		**Gambling Spirit**[11] [4010] 4-9-11 **72** 6ex. DaneO'Neill 2 (H Candy) *chsd ldrs: rdn to ld and hung rt ins fnl f: r.o* **9/2**[1]	81
206-	**2**	*½*	**Art Modern (IRE)**[64] [5799] 4-10-0 **75**. RyanMoore 6 (G L Moore) *b.hind: led: qcknd over 3f out: rdn: edgd lft and hdd ins fnl f: styd on* **12/1**	83
2542	**3**	*½*	**Qualitair Wings**[14] [3900] 7-8-12 **59**. DerekMcGaffin 4 (J Hetherton) *s.i.s: hld up: swtchd lft over 2f out: hdwy over 1f out : r.o* **13/2**	66
0631	**4**	*hd*	**Sonny Parkin**[7] [4108] 4-9-12 **76** 6ex. (v) AdamKirby(3) 1 (G A Huffer) *lw: hld up: racd keenly: outpcd 3f out: nt clr run over 1f out: r.o u.p ins fnl f: nrst fin* **5/1**[2]	83
-240	**5**	*1*	**Villa Sonata**[34] [3301] 3-9-1 **71**. JamieSpencer 8 (J R Fanshawe) *chsd ldrs: rdn and swtchd lft 1f out: sn bdly hmpd: nt rcvr* **5/1**[2]	80+
6002	**6**	*nk*	**Tata Naka**[11] [4010] 6-8-9 **56** oh1. JohnEgan 9 (Mrs C A Dunnett) *hld up: hdwy over 1f out: styng on whn hmpd ins fnl f: nt trble ldrs* **6/1**	61
-300	**7**	*2*	**Fen Game (IRE)**[78] [1958] 4-9-7 **68**. JimmyFortune 7 (J H M Gosden) *lw: s.i.s: hld up: rdn over 2f out: nt clr run over 1f out: hmpd ins fnl f: nt trble ldrs* **11/2**[3]	73+
503	**8**	*3*	**True West (USA)**[33] [3336] 3-8-11 **67**. OscarUrbina 5 (G C H Chung) *chsd ldr: rdn and ev ch over 1f out: hmpd 1f out: eased* **22/1**	62+
4066	**9**	*2 ½*	**Firesong**[23] [3642] 4-9-7 **68**. EddieAhern 3 (Pat Eddery) *hld up: racd keenly: hrd rdn over 1f out: wknd fnl f* **9/1**	58

2m 8.43s (1.99) **Going Correction** -0.20s/f (Firm)
WFA 3 from 4yo+ 9lb **9** Ran SP% **116.6**
Speed ratings (Par 103):84,83,83,83,82 82,80,78,76
CSF £58.92 CT £351.65 TOTE £3.50: £1.70, £4.90, £2.30; EX 66.60.
Owner Simon Broke And Partners **Bred** Beech Park Bloodstock Ltd **Trained** Kingston Warren, Oxon

FOCUS
A rough race run in a very moderate time and questionable form, even with the runner-up and fourth to form.

4337 TRAVELEX CONDITIONS STKS 1m 2f
7:45 (7:45) (Class 3) 3-Y-O+
£8,724 (£2,612; £1,306; £653; £326; £163) **Stalls** Centre

Form				RPR
3-22	**1**		**Windsor Knot (IRE)**[20] [3736] 4-8-13 106. LDettori 1 (Saeed Bin Suroor) *lw: chsd ldr: swtchd to ld 5 rivals centre 6f out: overall ldr over 2f out: rdn and hung lft fr over 1f out: styd on: eased* **4/5**[1]	110
21-3	**2**	*½*	**Khyber Kim**[20] [3736] 4-8-13 104. DaneO'Neill 4 (H Candy) *lw: prom: swtchd to chse wnr centre 6f out: rdn over 2f out: carried lft fnl f: styd on* **3/1**[2]	109
6365	**3**	*6*	**Morghim (IRE)**[29] [3441] 3-8-4 97. (b[1]) KerrinMcEvoy 7 (J L Dunlop) *lw: led: lft alone stands' side 6f out: hdd and hung lft fr over 2f out: wknd over 1f out* **18/1**	98
1243	**4**	*3*	**Degas Art (IRE)**[29] [3441] 3-8-7 107. JohnEgan 3 (D R C Elsworth) *hld up: racd keenly: swtchd centre 6f out: rdn over 3f out: wknd 2f out* **7/1**[3]	95
610	**5**	*¾*	**Invention (USA)**[50] [2775] 3-8-7 96. RyanMoore 5 (J H M Gosden) *hld up: swtchd centre 6f out: rdn and wknd 2f out: sn hung lft* **8/1**	93
	6	*24*	**First Friend (IRE)**[124] 5-9-2. TPQueally 6 (P Mitchell) *hld up: swtchd centre 6f out: wknd over 2f out* **50/1**	48

2m 2.03s (-4.41) **Going Correction** -0.20s/f (Firm)
WFA 3 from 4yo+ 9lb **6** Ran SP% **111.4**
Speed ratings (Par 107):109,108,103,101,100 81
CSF £3.34 TOTE £1.70: £1.20, £1.90; EX 3.60.
Owner Godolphin **Bred** Tally-Ho Stud **Trained** Newmarket, Suffolk

FOCUS
A conditions race but up to Listed standard. Only two horses counted in the latter stages and they can be rated some way clear of their rivals.

NOTEBOOK
Windsor Knot(IRE) confirmed placings with Khyber Kim on their recent meeting, and won with a little bit in hand, despite drifting from the middle of the course to the far side. This was his second success on the July course from two attempts, and will probably be tried in Listed company again. He should stay further than ten furlongs. (op 11-10 tchd 6-5)
Khyber Kim, who was more-or-less forced to go towards the far-side by the winner, is probably getting sick of the sight of Windsor Knot, after finishing behind him on his last two runs. However, he has shown more than enough already this season to suggest he is running close to the form he showed last year, and should pick up a race or two before the end of the season if not continually bumping into other smart sorts in similar races. He gives the impression that he could stay further. (op 9-4)
Morghim(IRE), with blinkers fitted for the first time and dropped in trip, tried a different route to his rivals that did not pay off. It is fair to say that he has become a little bit disappointing, although he did reverse placings with Degas Art, who seemed to run well below his best. (op 16-1)
Degas Art(IRE), dropping back in trip, ran a long way below his best and the run can be ignored. It is hard to say with any certainty why he performed so badly, but it was his worst effort for a long time. (op 6-1)
Invention(USA) has found things very difficult since landing his maiden and was a long way below the required class. It is possible that he will be better suited by soft ground, but, even so, there was little in the run to suggest he will be winning next time. Official explanation: jockey said colt hung left (op 9-1 tchd 15-2 and 10-1 in a place)
First Friend(IRE) did not show a great deal on his first run in Britain after winning a couple of races in Brazil last year. (op 66-1)

4338 MINERAL STAR H'CAP 6f
8:15 (8:15) (Class 4) (0-85,85) 3-Y-O+ **£5,505** (£1,637; £818; £408) **Stalls** High

Form				RPR
4506	**1**		**Spearit (IRE)**[14] [3904] 3-8-9 **71**. JohnEgan 6 (D R C Elsworth) *lw: hld up: swtchd rt and hdwy over 1f out: rdn and hung lft ins fnl f: r.o to ld post* **9/1**	78
3564	**2**	*nk*	**Titinius (IRE)**[12] [3986] 6-8-11 **69**. RobertWinston 1 (Micky Hammond) *chsd ldrs: rdn and edgd lft over 1f out: led wl ins fnl f: hdd post* **13/2**	76
10-0	**3**	*nk*	**Calabaza**[74] [2074] 4-8-9 **67**. (p) AlanMunro 12 (W Jarvis) *trckd ldrs: racd keenly: rdn over 1f out: hung lft and r.o ins fnl f* **25/1**	73
5634	**4**	*nk*	**Seamus Shindig**[14] [3904] 4-9-8 **81**. DaneO'Neill 7 (H Candy) *b.hind: w ldr tl led over 2f out: hung lft over 1f out: edgd rt and hdd wl ins fnl f* **4/1**[1]	86
3300	**5**	*1*	**Bobski (IRE)**[72] [2147] 4-9-10 **82**. RyanMoore 5 (G A Huffer) *lw: chsd ldrs: rdn over 1f out: styng on same pce whn hmpd wl ins fnl f* **11/2**[3]	85+
0506	**6**	*nk*	**Polish Emperor (USA)**[18] [3802] 6-9-4 **76**. (p) JimmyFortune 8 (W R Swinburn) *sn led: hdd over 2f out: rdn and ev ch ins fnl f: hld whn hmpd sn after* **12/1**	77+
0050	**7**	*1 ¼*	**Figaro Flyer (IRE)**[7] [4106] 3-9-3 **82**. DeanCorby(3) 10 (P Howling) *s.i.s: hld up: rdn over 1f out: nt trble ldrs* **28/1**	79
4003	**8**	*1*	**Kingscross**[14] [3904] 8-9-8 **80**. FergusSweeney 3 (M Blanshard) *hld up: n.d* **5/1**[2]	75
0004	**9**	*nk*	**Hidden Dragon (USA)**[7] [4106] 7-9-13 **85**. (v[1]) EddieAhern 2 (J Pearce) *hld up: racd keenly: rdn over 1f out: sn btn* **6/1**	79
6044	**10**	*5*	**Critic (IRE)**[22] [3667] 3-9-1 **77**. (v) JamieSpencer 11 (M L W Bell) *lw: prom: rdn over 2f out: wknd over 1f out* **7/1**	55

1m 12.24s (-1.11) **Going Correction** -0.20s/f (Firm)
WFA 3 from 4yo+ 4lb **10** Ran SP% **117.2**
Speed ratings (Par 105):99,98,98,97,96 96,94,93,92,86
CSF £66.70 CT £1454.11 TOTE £14.00: £3.60, £2.40, £6.60; EX 142.50 Place 6 £633.65, Place 5 £34.94.
Owner Raymond Tooth **Bred** Raymond Clive Tooth **Trained** Newmarket, Suffolk
■ Stewards' Enquiry : Alan Munro one-day ban: careless riding (Aug 25)
John Egan caution: careless riding

FOCUS
A fair sprint-handicap, which resulted in a very close finish. The form is somewhat shaky, with the runner-up to recent form.
T/Plt: £561.90 to a £1 stake. Pool: £65,350.40. 84.90 winning tickets. T/Qpdt: £19.60 to a £1 stake. Pool: £5,231.80. 197.20 winning tickets. CR

4339 - 4342a (Foreign Racing) - See Raceform Interactive

3970 ASCOT (R-H)
Saturday, August 12

OFFICIAL GOING: Good to firm
Following watering and some light rain, the ground looked loose on top and easier than the official description, an assessment agreed with by the jockeys.
Wind: Moderate, across.

4343 SODEXHO PRESTIGE SHERGAR CUP DISTAFF (H'CAP) (F&M) 6f
1:20 (1:27) (Class 2) (0-100,100) 3-Y-O+
£14,772 (£5,172; £2,364; £1,845; £1,626; £1,182) **Stalls** Centre

Form				RPR
2210	**1**		**Dark Missile**[8] [4097] 3-8-13 **89**. RyanMoore 7 (A M Balding) *trckd ldrs: led 2f out: kpt on wl: rdn out* **4/1**[2]	99
-010	**2**	*1 ½*	**Lady Livius (IRE)**[31] [3418] 3-9-2 **92**. LDettori 2 (R Hannon) *lw: trckd ldrs: rdn 2f out: r.o to chse wnr jst ins fnl f: kpt on but a hld* **12/1**	97
30-5	**3**	*1*	**Sling Back (IRE)**[3] [4272] 5-8-9 **81** oh2. GBoss 9 (Eamon Tyrrell, Ire) *lw: trckd ldrs: ev ch 2f out: sn rdn: kpt on same pce* **10/1**	84
1015	**4**	*1*	**Tagula Sunrise (IRE)**[29] [3499] 4-9-6 **92**. JamieSpencer 10 (R A Fahey) *hld up: hdwy over 2f out: sn rdn: kpt on same pce fnl f: snatched 4th fnl stride* **7/2**[1]	92
3523	**5**	*hd*	**Secret Night**[21] [3741] 3-8-8 **84**. EmmaJayneWilson 4 (J A R Toller) *in tch: rdn and effrt over 2f out: one pce fnl f: lost 4th fnl stride* **22/1**	82
611	**6**	*1 ¼*	**Meditation**[14] [3953] 4-8-10 **80** 3ex ow1. GMosse 5 (I A Wood) *lw: led tl 2f out: sn one pce* **6/1**[3]	78
-520	**7**	*1*	**Bouboulina**[49] [2880] 3-9-4 **94**. SebSanders 3 (E A L Dunlop) *s.i.s: towards rr: rdn over 2f out: hdwy over 1f out: wknd ins fnl f* **14/1**	86
4300	**8**	*3 ½*	**Sierra Vista**[9] [4080] 6-10-0 **100**. HayleyTurner 6 (D W Barker) *prom: rdn over 2f out: wknd over 1f out* **8/1**	82

1010 **9** ½ **Folga**[7] 4128 4-9-10 **96** YFukunaga 8 77
(J G Given) *in tch: effrt over 2f out: wknd over 1f out* **11/1**

1530 **10** 3 **Auwitesweetheart**[36] 3251 4-8-9 **81** oh1 MJKinane 1 53
(B R Millman) *lw: hld up: rdn over 2f out: sn btn* **10/1**

1m 14.89s (-0.01) **Going Correction** +0.125s/f (Good)
WFA 3 from 4yo+ 4lb **10** Ran SP% **112.8**
Speed ratings (Par 109):105,103,101,100,100 98,97,92,91,87
CSF £49.36 CT £454.01 TOTE £5.00: £1.80, £2.30, £2.50; EX 36.30 Trifecta £556.70 Pool: £1,262.40 - 1.61 winning units..
Owner J C Smith **Bred** Littleton Stud **Trained** Kingsclere, Hants

FOCUS
The runners raced mid-track. The pace was only steady and nothing got into it from behind. The winner improved again but the overall form is unconvincing.

NOTEBOOK
Dark Missile was back down in trip after a try over seven in a Group 3 at Goodwood, where the undulating track did not suit her. Improving on the form which saw her land a competitive handicap at Newmarket the time before, she came clear in the last two furlongs for a decisive victory. (op 10-3)
Lady Livius(IRE), like the winner, was reverting to this trip after a run over seven. Racing on the stands' side of the bunch, she kept on to secure second inside the last but the winner was too good. (tchd 11-1)
Sling Back(IRE), who has been performing with credit in Ireland, mainly over seven furlongs, was always up with the pace but lost second place inside the last. She looks high enough in the weights. (op 11-1 tchd 12-1)
Tagula Sunrise(IRE) ran on late from the rear in a race in which it paid to race prominently. She was not raised for finishing fifth in a Group 3 last time but does look vulnerable off this career-high mark. (op 4-1 tchd 9-2)
Secret Night, a consistent filly, turned around Newmarket form with Folga but lacked the pace to get involved. Her Canadian jockey picked up a caution for her use of the whip on this first ride in Britain. (op 18-1 tchd 25-1)
Meditation has had a fine season, but all her four wins have come over seven furlongs on genuine fast ground and, including the overweight, she was 4lb higher here than for the latest of them. After setting a moderate pace, she could not counter when headed by the winner two furlongs from home. (op 7-1)

4344 PORTHAULT SHERGAR CUP JUVENILE (AUCTION STKS) 7f
1:55 (2:00) (Class 2) 2-Y-O
£14,772 (£5,172; £2,364; £1,845; £1,626; £1,182) **Stalls** Centre

Form RPR

5112 **1** **Eddie Jock (IRE)**[8] 4100 2-8-12 90 RobertWinston 10 105+
(M L W Bell) *lw: s.i.s: in rr: hdwy over 2f out: shkn up to ld over 1f out: sn drifted rt but in command: readily* **10/3**[2]

1 **2** 4 **Doctor Brown**[10] 4049 2-9-1 LDettori 2 98
(B J Meehan) *lw: prom: led 5f out tl over 1f out: sn rdn: nt pce of wnr* **11/8**[1]

0102 **3** 5 **Johannesburg Jack (IRE)**[28] 3531 2-9-4 92 JamieSpencer 4 88
(H Morrison) *lw: trckd ldrs: rdn and ev ch 2f out: one pce fr over 1f out* **12/1**

5300 **4** 6 **Slipasearcher (IRE)**[16] 3874 2-8-7 92 MJKinane 5 61
(P D Evans) *s.i.s: bhd: rdn 3f out: wnt mod 4th ins fnl f: n.d* **25/1**

2224 **5** 2 **Armigerent (IRE)**[14] 3924 2-8-12 105 DJWhyte 1 61
(M Johnston) *lw: trckd ldrs: rdn and ev ch over 2f out: sn hung lft: wknd ins fnl f* **4/1**[3]

232 **6** ½ **Cape Schanck**[8] 4103 2-8-12 SebSanders 3 60
(Jane Chapple-Hyam) *chsd ldrs: rdn 3f out: grad fdd* **33/1**

1005 **7** 1¼ **Zafonical Storm (USA)**[29] 3496 2-9-1 80 HayleyTurner 9 59
(B W Duke) *hld up: rdn and sme hdwy over 2f out: wknd over 1f out* **66/1**

2114 **8** 7 **Grand Prix**[44] 3026 2-9-1 89 GMosse 8 41
(R Hannon) *hld up: effrt wl over 2f out: sn wknd* **16/1**

3104 **9** 6 **Hythe Bay**[28] 3530 2-8-7 80 EmmaJayneWilson 6 17
(R T Phillips) *led for 2f: chsd ldrs tl wknd over 2f out* **33/1**

0212 **10** 3½ **Going Straight (IRE)**[70] 2225 2-8-7 93 YFukunaga 7 8
(I A Wood) *in tch: rdn over 3f out: sn wknd* **16/1**

1m 28.71s (0.61) **Going Correction** +0.125s/f (Good) **10** Ran SP% **115.9**
Speed ratings (Par 100):101,96,90,83,81 81,79,71,64,60
CSF £7.95 TOTE £4.70: £1.70, £1.20, £2.30; EX 10.60 Trifecta £67.20 Pool: £1,509.29 - 15.94 winning units..
Owner C A Gershinson **Bred** J Egan, J Corcoran And J Judd **Trained** Newmarket, Suffolk

FOCUS
They raced down the centre of the track again. Not many were able to get involved and the field came home at wide intervals.

NOTEBOOK
Eddie Jock(IRE) came into this in fine form, having landed a nursery at the Newmarket July festival before finishing second in a similar event at Goodwood. Improving from the rear to track the leading pair down the centre of the track before coming right away in the final furlong and a half, he is set to step into Group 3 company now. (op 3-1 tchd 7-2)
Doctor Brown travelled well but could not match the winner in the latter stages on this loose surface. He finished clear of the remainder and, while he stayed this longer trip, he would not be inconvenienced by a drop back to six furlongs. (op 7-4)
Johannesburg Jack(IRE), attempting to successfully concede weight all round, disputed the lead with the eventual runner-up two furlongs out but was soon left floundering. The return to genuine fast ground will suit him. Official explanation: trainer said colt was unsuited by the going, which he believed to be softer than the official good to firm ground (op 14-1)
Slipasearcher(IRE), upped in trip, looked like being left well behind at halfway and merely plugged on late to claim a remote fourth place.
Armigerent(IRE) was the form pick on his second to Strategic Prince in the July Stakes, but he did not get home in this rain-affected ground. He remains a maiden, albeit a talented one. (op 7-2)

4345 SODEXHO PRESTIGE SHERGAR CUP SPRINT (H'CAP) 6f
2:30 (2:32) (Class 2) (0-100,100) 3-Y-O
£14,772 (£5,172; £2,364; £1,845; £1,626; £1,182) **Stalls** Centre

Form RPR

4020 **1** **Come Out Fighting**[26] 3585 3-9-1 **89** RyanMoore 1 102
(P A Blockley) *hld up in tch: smooth prog to ld over 1f out: sn drifted rt: r.o: rdn out* **8/1**

0142 **2** 2 **Didn't We (IRE)**[6] 4180 3-8-11 **85** (b) DJWhyte 4 92
(T G Mills) *lw: trckd ldr: rdn and ev ch over 1f out: kpt on but nt pce of wnr* **13/2**[3]

2100 **3** hd **Phantom Whisper**[31] 3414 3-9-0 **88** HayleyTurner 2 94
(B R Millman) *hld up: rdn over 2f out: no imp tl styd on wl ins fnl f: nrst fin* **20/1**

1050 **4** 1 **Ingleby Arch (USA)**[31] 3414 3-9-9 **97** RobertWinston 6 100
(T D Barron) *pushed along in mid-div: rdn over 2f out: styd on fnl f: wnt 4th fnl strides* **13/2**[3]

0021 **5** nk **King Orchisios (IRE)**[35] 3296 3-9-8 **96** GBoss 10 98
(K A Ryan) *lw: sn led: rdn and hdd over 1f out:one pce fnl f* **7/1**

-053 **6** ¾ **Grantley Adams**[13] 3970 3-9-5 **93** MJKinane 7 93
(M R Channon) *mid-div: rdn over 2f out: kpt on same pce* **10/3**[1]

0630 **7** 1 **Gamble In Gold (IRE)**[49] 2880 3-9-2 **90** GMosse 8 87
(R Hannon) *pushed along towards rr: n.d* **16/1**

-000 **8** 2 **Curtail (IRE)**[13] 3970 3-9-10 **98** JamieSpencer 9 89
(I Semple) *hld up: nt clr run and swtchd rt over 2f out: hdwy over 1f out: wknd ins fnl f* **22/1**

5046 **9** 2½ **Sweet Afton (IRE)**[14] 3967 3-9-4 **92** YFukunaga 5 75
(Eamon Tyrrell, Ire) *trckd ldrs: rdn over 2f out: wknd over 1f out* **9/1**

5010 **10** 3½ **Angus Newz**[31] 3414 3-9-12 **100** (v) LDettori 3 73
(M Quinn) *lw: trckd ldrs: rdn over 2f out: wknd over 1f out* **6/1**[2]

1m 14.68s (-0.22) **Going Correction** +0.125s/f (Good) **10** Ran SP% **112.6**
Speed ratings (Par 106):106,103,103,101,101 100,99,96,93,88
CSF £57.07 CT £720.12 TOTE £11.10: £3.00, £2.00, £7.10; EX 89.20 TRIFECTA Not won..
Owner M J Wiley **Bred** G J Hamer **Trained** Lambourn, Berks

FOCUS
The runners again kept to the centre of the track. The form is not rock solid, but the winner is less exposed than most and the second and third ran pretty much to form.

NOTEBOOK
Come Out Fighting belied stamina doubts with a clear-cut victory, coming away in good style after making up his ground towards the stands' side of the bunch. Some juice in the ground suits him well. (op 9-1)
Didn't We(IRE), runner-up over five furlongs at Newbury recently, ran another sound race on the return to this trip but found one too good. (op 6-1)
Phantom Whisper made late gains after appearing to be well held. All his wins have been at five furlongs but he is certainly effective at this trip. (tchd 25-1 in a place)
Ingleby Arch(USA) was under pressure by the halfway stage and eventually kept on to snatch fourth. He just looks high enough in the handicap. (op 6-1 tchd 7-1)
King Orchisios(IRE), reportedly gelded since his Haydock win, was 6lb higher here and the cheekpieces were left off. Bustled along leaving the stalls to secure an early lead, he was rather free in front and did not have much left when tackled. (tchd 13-2)
Grantley Adams was unable to reach a challenging position on this loose ground. (op 3-1 tchd 7-2 in places)

4346 CARVILL SHERGAR CUP STAYERS (H'CAP) 2m
3:00 (3:02) (Class 2) (0-100,99) 4-Y-O+
£14,772 (£5,172; £2,364; £1,845; £1,626; £1,182) **Stalls** High

Form RPR

6466 **1** **Dorothy's Friend**[10] 4036 6-9-3 **90** SebSanders 7 103
(R Charlton) *lw: in tch: tk clsr order 4f out: wnt 2nd 3f out: rdn to ld over 1f out: styd on strly* **5/2**[1]

5054 **2** 4 **Mceldowney**[10] 4036 4-8-13 **86** RyanMoore 3 94
(M Johnston) *led: rdn and hdd over 1f out: kpt on but no ch w wnr fnl f* **9/2**[2]

-050 **3** 1½ **Casual Glance**[53] 2723 4-8-12 **85** JamieSpencer 5 91
(A M Balding) *s.i.s: sn mid-div: hdwy 4f out: rdn to chse ldng pair 2f out: kpt on same pce* **10/1**

4466 **4** nk **Rehearsal**[29] 3501 5-9-4 **91** MJKinane 1 97
(L Lungo) *hld up bhd: swtchd lft and hdwy wl over 2f out: sn rdn: styd on* **7/1**

2654 **5** 3½ **Wise Owl**[15] 3888 4-8-10 **83** DJWhyte 2 84
(J Pearce) *lw: in tch: tk clsr order 7f out: rdn 3f out: sn one pce* **13/2**[3]

3020 **6** 3 **Trance (IRE)**[30] 3446 6-8-9 **82** (p) EmmaJayneWilson 9 80
(T D Barron) *hld up towards rr: nvr a factor* **16/1**

0- **7** ¾ **Cavallino (USA)**[303] 6-9-12 **99** (t) YFukunaga 4 96
(R A Kvisla) *a towards rr* **33/1**

5 **8** 1¾ **Swordsman (GER)**[11] 4027 4-9-3 **90** (b) GBoss 8 85
(M L W Bell) *t.k.h: trckd ldr: jnd ldr 7f out: rdn 3f out: sn wknd* **10/1**

6450 **9** 18 **Tarandot (IRE)**[9] 4079 5-9-6 **93** RobertWinston 6 66
(G G Margarson) *b.hind: trckd ldrs: rdn over 3f out: sn wknd: eased fnl f* **8/1**

3m 30.16s (-6.34) **10** Ran SP% **110.7**
CSF £12.46 CT £87.61 TOTE £3.00: £1.50, £2.00, £3.20; EX 11.30 Trifecta £112.00 Pool: £1,633.84 - 10.35 winning units..
Owner Mountgrange Stud **Bred** Floors Farming And Christopher J Heath **Trained** Beckhampton, Wilts

FOCUS
The runner-up set only a steady pace before winding it up from about the seven pole. The form, set through the second and fourth, does not look all that strong, but the winner is generally progressive.

NOTEBOOK
Dorothy's Friend gained his first victory since landing the last running of this event two years ago. Only 2lb higher than for that win, he had no problem with ground that was easier than the official assessment and did it nicely. He could go for the Ebor but his trainer has the Cesarewitch more in mind for him. (op 9-4)
Mceldowney finished in front of Dorothy's Friend in the Goodwood Stakes last time but could not confirm the form on the same terms. Setting only a steady pace before quickening up when challenged for the lead with about seven furlongs to run, he was put in his place by the favourite in the straight but held on for second. He is 10lb higher than when gaining his last victory in June and has now been found wanting five times from this mark . (op 4-1 tchd 5-1)
Casual Glance, having her first run since finishing in midfield in the Ascot Stakes at the Royal meeting, plugged on for third and something like the Cesarewitch could suit her. (tchd 11-1)
Rehearsal, ridden to get this longer trip, stayed it well enough but continues to struggle with the handicapper. (op 13-2)
Wise Owl, a consistent performer, ran respectably again and was still disputing third with a furlong and a half to run. (op 7-1)
Trance(IRE), held up in last place, did pass a few rivals in the home straight but was faced with a hopeless task. (op 14-1)
Swordsman(GER), having his second run in this country, ran freely in the reapplied blinkers and failed to see out the trip, the longest he has tackled. (op 17-2)
Tarandot(IRE) Official explanation: jockey said mare ran too free early and had no more to give

4347 MICHAEL PAGE INTERNATIONAL SHERGAR CUP CHALLENGE (H'CAP) 1m 4f
3:35 (3:36) (Class 2) (0-100,96) 4-Y-O+
£19,696 (£6,896; £3,152; £2,460; £2,168; £1,576) **Stalls** High

Form RPR

6161 **1** **Young Mick**[15] 3890 4-9-13 **96** 3ex (v) GMosse 6 106
(G G Margarson) *hld up mid-div: tk clsr order over 3f out: nt clr run tl over 1f out: led jst ins fnl f: comf* **9/4**[1]

1233 **2** 1 **Ti Adora (IRE)**[7] 4149 4-8-10 **79** RyanMoore 7 87
(P W D'Arcy) *hld up towards rr: rdn and hdwy fr 2f out: styd on but drifted lft ins fnl f: wnt 2nd cl home* **12/1**

1006 **3** *1 ¼* **Mikao (IRE)**[15] [3888] 5-9-3 **86**.. JamieSpencer 9 92
(M H Tompkins) *lw: trckd ldr: rdn to ld wl over 2f out: hdd jst ins fnl f: no ex* **9/1**

2314 **4** *¾* **Pevensey (IRE)**[7] [4160] 4-9-3 **86** 3ex.. LDettori 4 94+
(M A Buckley) *hld up: hdwy and nt clr run 2f out: gradually swtchd lft: styd on fnl f: nrst fin* **5/1**[2]

0522 **5** *1* **Nero's Return (IRE)**[17] [3840] 5-8-11 **80**.. GBoss 1 83
(M Johnston) *mid-div: rdn over 3f out: kpt on same pce fnl 2f* **15/2**

5012 **6** *1* **Isidore Bonheur (IRE)**[49] [2872] 5-9-2 **85**.............. EmmaJayneWilson 3 87
(G A Swinbank) *trckd ldr: rdn 3f out: one pce fr over 1f out* **8/1**

1005 **7** *hd* **Chantaco (USA)**[28] [3552] 4-9-12 **95**.. HayleyTurner 2 96
(A M Balding) *lw: sn led: rdn and hdd wl over 2f out: one pce after* **7/1**[3]

4200 **8** *½* **Top Seed (IRE)**[11] [4027] 5-9-4 **87**.. RobertWinston 5 87
(M R Channon) *hld up bhd: n.m.r and stmbld on bnd over 3 out: sn rdn: swtchd lft 2f out: styd on: n.d* **16/1**

2246 **9** *½* **Nawamees (IRE)**[11] [4027] 8-9-6 **89**..............................(p) SebSanders 10 89
(G L Moore) *mid-div: tk clsr order 3f out: sn rdn: wknd ins fnl f* **14/1**

5540 **10** *3* **Wingman (IRE)**[15] [3890] 4-9-2 **85**..............................(p) DJWhyte 8 80
(J W Hills) *trckd ldrs: effrt wl over 2f out: wknd fnl f* **16/1**

2m 31.47s (-1.53) **Going Correction** +0.05s/f (Good) **10** Ran SP% **118.9**
Speed ratings (Par 109):107,106,105,105,104 103,103,103,102,100
CSF £32.36 CT £211.76 TOTE £2.50: £1.70, £2.50, £2.80; EX 29.60 Trifecta £371.50 Pool: £34,851.96 - 66.60 winning units..
Owner M F Kentish **Bred** M F Kentish **Trained** Newmarket, Suffolk

FOCUS
This was run at a sound pace. Another improved effort from the winner, and sound form with the second, third and fourth all within a pound of their marks.

NOTEBOOK
Young Mick, one of the season's success stories, gained his third big prize over course and distance and his ninth win of the year in all. It was a fluent victory too, as he travelled well before putting his seal on the race once the gap came. He is now likely to take his chance in the Ebor, for which he picks up a further 3lb penalty, and he will have a leading chance if he stays the extra two furlongs. (op 5-2 tchd 11-4)
Ti Adora(IRE) stayed on well for second despite running around a bit in the latter stages. A return to 14 furlongs could see her add to her two victories so far this season.
Mikao(IRE) has been campaigned over further since winning over this trip at the Craven meeting in April. He went on early in the home straight but was put in his place by the winner and could not hold on to second.
Pevensey(IRE), back up in trip, had to wait for a run but came home in good style once switched out. He is capable of winning off this mark when things drop for him. (op 11-2)
Nero's Return(IRE) kept on down the outer without quite getting to the leaders. He is running well since being stepped up to this trip and remains 7lb lower than for his last victory just under a year ago. (op 7-1)
Isidore Bonheur(IRE) did not quite get home over this longer trip after racing prominently. (op 11-1)
Wingman(IRE) Official explanation: jockey said gelding made a noise

4348 SONY SHERGAR CUP MILE (H'CAP) 1m (R)
4:10 (4:11) (Class 2) (0-100,100) 4-Y-0+
£19,696 (£6,896; £3,152; £2,460; £2,168; £1,576) **Stalls** High

Form RPR

3003 **1** **Prince Of Thebes (IRE)**[8] [4098] 5-9-5 **93**.......................... SebSanders 3 103
(J Akehurst) *lw: trckd ldr: rdn to chal over 2f out: battled on to ld narrowly jst ins fnl f: all out* **9/2**[3]

5030 **2** *shd* **Tucker**[52] [2742] 4-9-10 **98**..............................(p) HayleyTurner 6 108
(W R Swinburn) *sn led: rdn and hrd pressed fr over 2f out: narrowly hdd ins fnl f: rallied gamely: jst failed* **16/1**

0204 **3** *½* **Appalachian Trail (IRE)**[14] [3926] 5-9-11 **99**.......................(b) GMosse 2 108
(I Semple) *hld up: rdn and hdwy fr 2f out: r.o fnl f: nrst fin* **7/2**[1]

2060 **4** *1 ¼* **Bustan (IRE)**[13] [3971] 7-9-9 **97**.. DJWhyte 10 103
(G C Bravery) *trckd ldrs: rdn wl over 2f out: kpt on* **20/1**

0311 **5** *shd* **Hartshead**[14] [3937] 7-9-8 **96** 3ex.. YFukunaga 4 102
(G A Swinbank) *in tch: rdn 2f out: kpt on* **7/1**

0050 **6** *½* **Pentecost**[35] [3313] 7-9-12 **100**.. MJKinane 5 105
(A M Balding) *hld up: hdwy 2f out: sn rdn: kpt on same pce fnl f* **4/1**[2]

2005 **7** *shd* **Red Spell (IRE)**[8] [4098] 5-9-4 **92**..............................(p) GBoss 1 97
(R Hannon) *lw: hld up: rdn over 2f out: kpt on fnl f* **8/1**

2000 **8** *½* **Royal Island (IRE)**[71] [2200] 4-9-12 **100**.......................... RyanMoore 8 103
(M Johnston) *hld up: rdn over 2f out: styd on ins fnl f: nvr trbld ldrs* **11/2**

0006 **9** *5* **Jalamid (IRE)**[56] [2649] 4-9-5 **93**..............................(t) RobertWinston 9 85
(G C Bravery) *in tch: rdn over 2f out: wknd fnl f* **14/1**

1m 40.29s (-1.81) **Going Correction** +0.05s/f (Good) **10** Ran SP% **116.7**
Speed ratings (Par 109):111,110,110,109,109 108,108,107,102
CSF £73.33 CT £283.27 TOTE £4.30: £1.50, £4.40, £2.00; EX 92.90 Trifecta £355.90 Pool: £2,702.55 - 5.39 winning units. Place 6 £106.74, Place 5 £26.31..
Owner Canisbay Bloodstock **Bred** Mrs A Rothschild And London Thoroughbred Services **Trained** Epsom, Surrey
■ A comfortable victory for the British and Irish jockeys over the Rest of the World team in the Shergar Cup.
■ Stewards' Enquiry : Seb Sanders one-day ban: used whip with excessive frequency (Aug 25)
Hayley Turner caution: used whip with excessive frequency

FOCUS
This was run at just an average pace and the first two were always prominent. The form looks sound.

NOTEBOOK
Prince Of Thebes(IRE) fought back inside the last to get the better of a great scrap with the second up the straight. He was already due to race off 6lb higher in future following his fine run at Goodwood and might be found wanting off what will be a career-high mark.
Tucker, having his first run since leaving David Elsworth, was without the cheekpieces he wore in the Royal Hunt Cup on his latest start. Setting a moderate pace, he was tackled early in the home straight and, after a fine duel, just missed out. (op 12-1)
Appalachian Trail(IRE) was stepped up to a mile for the first time on turf this year. Making good progress from the rear of the field down the outside in the straight, it looked as if he would claw back the duelling leaders but he could not quite get to them. (op 4-1 tchd 9-2 in places)
Bustan(IRE), who has run a couple of decent races from favourable draws this year, ran respectably but remains hard to win with. (op 16-1)
Hartshead, under a 3lb penalty on this quest for a hat-trick, was not best served by this step back up to a mile on loose ground. (op 9-2)
Pentecost had won the last two runnings of this event in 2003 and 2004 but never really looked like making it a hat-trick. (op 9-2)
Royal Island(IRE) got going too late in a race run at only a moderate pace but was only beaten around three lengths in the end. Official explanation: jockey said colt stumbled leaving stalls (op 9-1)
T/Jkpt: Not won. T/Plt: £116.00 to a £1 stake. Pool: £116,940.25. 735.75 winning tickets. T/Qpdt: £34.10 to a £1 stake. Pool: £6,506.50. 141.10 winning tickets. TM

[3809] AYR (L-H)
Saturday, August 12

OFFICIAL GOING: Good to firm
Wind: Slight across

4349 UNITED UTILITIES EBF MAIDEN STKS 6f
5:45 (5:45) (Class 5) 2-Y-O **£4,533** (£1,348; £674; £336) **Stalls** Low

Form RPR

4 **1** **First Mate (IRE)**[9] [4066] 2-9-3 .... J-PGuillambert 5 82
(M Johnston) *wnt rt s: sn w ldrs: led 2f out: drvn over 1f out: edgd lft ins fnl f: styd on wl* **7/2**[3]

6 **2** *2* **Rabbit Fighter (IRE)**[8] [4103] 2-8-10 .... KevinGhunowa[(7)] 1 76+
(P A Blockley) *led to over 2f out: rallied: one pce whn hmpd ins fnl f: no ex* **7/4**[1]

64 **3** *4* **Stay Active (USA)**[23] [3669] 2-9-3 .... PaulMulrennan 4 64
(I Semple) *wnt rt s: sn prom: outpcd over 2f out: rallied over 1f out: no ch w first two* **7/2**[3]

2 **4** *6* **Go On Green (IRE)**[70] [2234] 2-9-3 .... MichaelTebbutt 3 46
(E A L Dunlop) *w ldrs tl outpcd over 2f out: wkng whn hung lft over 1f out* **11/4**[2]

6326 **5** *¾* **Loch Clutha (IRE)**[12] [4007] 2-8-12 57.. LeeEnstone 2 39
(K R Burke) *chsd ldrs tl wknd over 2f out: btn whn hmpd over 1f out* **50/1**

1m 13.24s (-0.43) **Going Correction** -0.225s/f (Firm) **5** Ran SP% **109.4**
Speed ratings (Par 94):93,90,85,77,76
CSF £9.95 TOTE £4.80: £2.70, £1.50; EX 13.70.
Owner Claire Riordan And Kieran Coughlan **Bred** Kieran Coughlan And Miss Claire Riordan **Trained** Middleham Moor, N Yorks
■ Stewards' Enquiry : J-P Guillambert two-day ban: careless riding (Aug 25-26)

FOCUS
An ordinary event but a fair pace and the winner may be capable of a bit better. The placed horses set the standard.

NOTEBOOK
First Mate(IRE), turned out fairly quickly after a fair debut effort at Carlisle, seemed to have benefited a good deal from that experience and turned in an improved effort. He remains likely to do better over seven furlongs and appeals as the type to win another race. (op 5-1tchd 11-2 in places)
Rabbit Fighter(IRE), who shaped well on his debut at Newmarket over seven furlongs, confirmed that promise despite dropping in distance. Although hampered late on, it made little difference to the result and he looks capable of winning a similar event. (tchd 13-8)
Stay Active(USA) ◆ again showed ability and again left the impression that the step up to seven furlongs plus in ordinary nursery company will be in his favour. He looks the type to win a race for his capable trainer. (op 6-1 tchd 13-2 tchd 7-1 in a place)
Go On Green(IRE), who shaped well on his debut in June, failed to build on that effort on his first run since and did not impress with the way he hung off a true line under pressure. He has the ability to win a small race but will have to show more before he is worth a bet. Official explanation: trainer's representative said colt had a breathing problem (op 11-8)
Loch Clutha(IRE), a modest maiden, again had her limitations firmly exposed in this grade. (tchd 66-1)

4350 RACING TO MAKE POVERTY HISTORY CLAIMING STKS 7f 50y
6:15 (6:17) (Class 5) 3-Y-0+ **£3,238** (£963; £481; £240) **Stalls** Low

Form RPR

6206 **1** **Roman History (IRE)**[10] [4057] 3-8-8 44.................(p) SilvestreDeSousa 2 54
(Miss Tracy Waggott) *in tch: effrt over 2f out: kpt on wl fnl f to ld towards fin* **25/1**

6460 **2** *nk* **Franksalot (IRE)**[8] [4116] 6-9-3 65.. MarkLawson[(5)] 1 63
(I W McInnes) *hld up bhd: gd hdwy centre to ld over 1f out: hdd and no ex towards fin* **6/1**

-060 **3** *2* **Tom Forest**[8] [4116] 4-8-13 62..............................(p) AndrewMullen[(5)] 13 54
(K A Ryan) *slowly away: bhd tl hdwy over 2f out: kpt on fnl f: nt rch first two* **8/1**

000/ **4** *¾* **Ho Pang Yau**[43] [4546] 8-9-2 .... LeeEnstone 12 50
(J S Goldie) *bhd: rdn and hung lft fr 3f out: kpt on fr 2f out: no imp* **66/1**

3054 **5** *1 ½* **Alfonso**[18] [3813] 5-9-5 71..............................(b) TomEaves 8 54+
(I Semple) *hld up ins: effrt whn repeatedly blkd over 2f out: hmpd and outpcd wl over 1f out: kpt on ins fnl f* **7/4**[1]

4000 **6** *½* **Top Dirham**[6] [4172] 8-9-8 75.. PaulMulrennan 9 51
(M W Easterby) *hld up ins: hdwy whn blkd repeatedly over 2f out: n.m.r but effrt over 1f out: no ex ins fnl f* **7/2**[2]

-501 **7** *2* **Zendaro**[10] [4057] 4-9-2 63 ow3.. PJBenson[(7)] 10 47
(W M Brisbourne) *hld up in tch: hdwy to ld over 2f out: hdd over 1f out: sn btn* **5/1**[3]

0000 **8** *2* **Nebraska City**[100] [1443] 5-8-8 38 ow2.......................... JamesO'Reilly[(7)] 3 33
(D W Thompson) *mde most tl hdd over 2f out: sn rdn and wknd* **100/1**

000 **9** *1 ½* **Wood Dalling (USA)**[10] [4057] 8-9-0 29.......................... RichardThomas 11 29
(Mrs J C McGregor) *s.v.s: wl bhd tl sme late hdwy: nvr on terms* **100/1**

4100 **10** *1 ¼* **Bellini Star**[57] [2599] 3-8-8 55..............................(b) J-PGuillambert 7 23
(P D Evans) *w ldrs: rdn and hung lft 2f out: sn wknd* **16/1**

0060 **11** *1 ½* **Mandarin Grand (IRE)**[10] [4059] 3-7-11 36...........(p) DuranFentiman[(5)] 5 13
(Miss L A Perratt) *chsd ldrs: drvn 1/2-way: wknd over 2f out* **33/1**

0-00 **12** *20* **Four Kings**[19] [3781] 5-9-0 34.. PaulHanagan 4 —
(R Allan) *w ldrs tl wknd over 2f out: eased whn no ch over 1f out* **50/1**

-000 **13** *2* **Borsch (IRE)**[10] [4059] 4-8-13 30..............................(b) RoystonFfrench 6 —
(Miss L A Perratt) *in tch: drvn 1/2-way: wknd over 2f out* **100/1**

1m 31.92s (-0.80) **Going Correction** -0.225s/f (Firm)
WFA 3 from 4yo+ 6lb **13** Ran SP% **119.7**
Speed ratings (Par 103):95,94,92,91,89 89,86,84,82,81 79,56,54
CSF £167.00 TOTE £38.40: £6.20, £2.60, £3.00; EX 410.60.
Owner B Douglas **Bred** Lodge Park Stud **Trained** Spennymoor, Co Durham
■ Stewards' Enquiry : J-P Guillambert three-day ban: careless riding (Aug 27-29)

FOCUS
A modest event and the winner, who raced prominently and sets the level, may be a bit better than the bare form.
Roman History(IRE) Official explanation: trainer's representative said, regarding the improved form shown, gelding was better suited by the re-application of cheekpieces and the faster ground
Wood Dalling(USA) Official explanation: jockey said gelding missed the break

4351 ALFRED MCALPINE H'CAP 1m 7f
6:45 (6:45) (Class 6) (0-60,60) 4-Y-0+ **£3,238** (£963; £481; £240) **Stalls** Low

Form RPR

3051 **1** **Danzatrice**[9] [4086] 4-8-12 **51**.. J-PGuillambert 6 59
(C W Thornton) *hld up and bhd: stdy hdwy over 5f out: effrt and hung lft over 2f out: no imp tl rallied over 1f out: led ins last: styd on* **7/1**[3]

1501 2 3/4 **Rare Coincidence**[9] 4072 5-8-13 **59**....................(p) KevinGhunowa(7) 11 66
(R F Fisher) *cl up: led 3f out: edgd lft over 1f out: hdd ins fnl f: r.o* **7/1**[3]

4105 3 1/2 **Dayoff (IRE)**[9] 4072 5-8-13 **52**....................(b) PaulMulrennan 4 58
(P D Evans) *hld up: stdy hdwy 6f out: effrt and ev ch over 1f out: kpt on same pce ins fnl f* **3/1**[1]

0/06 4 1 1/2 **Culcabock (IRE)**[18] 3810 6-8-2 **41**.................... PaulHanagan 7 45
(Miss Lucinda V Russell) *prom: rdn 3f out: kpt on ins fnl f* **8/1**

0404 5 hd **Lennel**[18] 3810 8-8-3 **49**....................(b) RussellKennemore(7) 10 53
(A Bailey) *missed break: bhd and drvn 1/2-way: hdwy and wandered over 2f out: r.o fnl f: nvr nrr* **10/1**

3403 6 3/4 **Caymans Gift**[18] 3810 6-8-11 **55**....................(p) AndrewMullen(5) 5 58
(A C Whillans) *prom: effrt over 2f out: hung lft: no ex over 1f out* **9/1**

0065 7 3 **Tojoneski**[9] 4086 7-8-2 **41**.................... RoystonFfrench 3 40
(I W McInnes) *in tch tl rdn and outpcd over 2f out: n.d after* **8/1**

6452 8 1 **Kristiansand**[9] 4086 6-8-6 **50**.................... MarkLawson(5) 8 48
(P Monteith) *led to 3f out: wknd 2f out* **5/1**[2]

2064 9 1 1/2 **Keshya**[23] 3686 5-9-7 **60**.................... RichardThomas 9 56
(N P Littmoden) *keen: hld up: rdn 6f out: sn n.d* **14/1**

-050 10 46 **Taili**[7] 4132 5-8-2 **41** oh26....................(v[1]) SilvestreDeSousa 1 —
(D A Nolan) *chsd ldrs to 1/2-way: sn lost pl: t.o* **100/1**

06-0 11 3 1/2 **Acceleration (IRE)**[62] 414 6-9-1 **54**....................(t) TomEaves 2 —
(R Allan) *hld up: drvn over 5f out: sn wknd: t.o* **20/1**

3m 19.22s (-3.25) **Going Correction** -0.225s/f (Firm) **11** Ran SP% **120.4**
Speed ratings (Par 101):99,98,98,97,97 97,95,94,94,69 67
CSF £56.79 CT £181.67 TOTE £9.10: £3.00, £2.40, £1.80; EX 51.80.
Owner 980 Racing **Bred** G G A Gregson **Trained** Middleham Moor, N Yorks

FOCUS
A run-of-the-mill handicap but one run at a fair pace throughout and sound enough, with the third and fifth to recent course form.

4352 WATERAID SILVER ANNIVERSARY H'CAP 6f
7:15 (7:16) (Class 5) (0-70,70) 3-Y-O+ **£3,886** (£1,156; £577; £288) **Stalls** Low

Form RPR

5111 1 **Blue Maeve**[3] 4258 6-10-0 **70** 6ex.................... SilvestreDeSousa 11 81
(A D Brown) *cl up: led over 2f out: rdn and edgd rt ins fnl f: hdd wl ins last: rallied to ld post* **11/10**[1]

4264 2 shd **Stellite**[9] 4090 6-9-13 **69**.................... LeeEnstone 4 80
(J S Goldie) *hld up: gd hdwy over 1f out: led wl ins fnl f: ct post* **9/1**

2313 3 3/4 **Viewforth**[19] 3781 8-9-5 **61**....................(b) TomEaves 5 70
(I Semple) *in tch: effrt over 2f out: swtchd lft over 1f out: nt qckn ins fnl f* **7/1**[3]

0003 4 3 1/2 **Glenbuck (IRE)**[2] 4296 3-9-2 **62**....................(v) PaulHanagan 8 60
(A Bailey) *midfield: reminders after 2f: effrt and chsng ldrs over 1f out: nt qckn ins last* **11/2**[2]

1260 5 2 **Rancho Cucamonga (IRE)**[12] 3996 4-8-12 **54**.......(b) RoystonFfrench 7 46
(T D Barron) *bhd: hdwy and prom over 1f out: rdn and outpcd fnl f* **7/1**[3]

1204 6 3/4 **Strawberry Patch (IRE)**[9] 4091 7-8-13 **55**.................... J-PGuillambert 6 45
(J S Goldie) *chsd ldrs: rdn over 2f out: wknd over 1f out* **10/1**

3215 7 2 1/2 **Prospect Court**[18] 3811 4-8-6 **53**.................... AndrewMullen(5) 1 36
(A C Whillans) *chsd ldrs: rdn whn n.m.r and lost pl 1/2-way: n.d after* **9/1**

060 8 5 **Telepathic (IRE)**[9] 4067 6-8-8 **50** oh5....................(b) PaulMulrennan 10 18
(A Berry) *led to over 2f out: sn wknd* **40/1**

4060 9 5 **Vondova**[7] 4135 4-8-13 **60**.................... MarkLawson(5) 3 13
(D A Nolan) *missed break: sn in tch: rdn 1/2-way: wknd 2f out* **50/1**

1m 11.7s (-1.97) **Going Correction** -0.225s/f (Firm)
WFA 3 from 4yo+ 4lb **9** Ran SP% **119.1**
Speed ratings (Par 103):104,103,102,98,95 94,91,84,77
CSF £12.80 CT £52.29 TOTE £2.40: £1.20, £3.40, £2.10; EX 25.20.
Owner R G Fell **Bred** P J And Mrs Nolan **Trained** Pickering, York

FOCUS
An ordinary event in which the field raced centre to far side with the third the best guide to the level.

4353 MORRISON PURAC H'CAP 1m 2f
7:45 (7:45) (Class 5) (0-70,68) 3-Y-O+ **£4,533** (£1,348; £674; £336) **Stalls** Low

Form RPR

3550 1 **Wing Commander**[22] 3716 7-9-9 **63**....................(b) RoystonFfrench 7 74
(I W McInnes) *hld up midfield: rdn over 3f out: hdwy over 1f out: hung rt and led wl ins fnl f: kpt on* **12/1**

1412 2 1 1/4 **Touch Of Ivory (IRE)**[10] 4060 3-8-7 **61**....................(p) MarkLawson(5) 4 70
(P Monteith) *hld up midfield: hdwy to ld over 1f out: hdd wl ins fnl f: r.o* **6/1**[2]

1232 3 3 **Esoterica (IRE)**[25] 3604 3-9-5 **68**.................... PaulFessey 8 71
(T D Barron) *keen: prom chsng gp: effrt over 2f out: ev ch over 1f out: no ex ins fnl f* **8/1**[3]

3311 4 1 3/4 **River Logic (IRE)**[7] 4132 3-8-11 **60**.................... SilvestreDeSousa 11 60
(A D Brown) *cl up chsng gp: effrt and hung lft over 2f out: no ex appr fnl f* **7/2**[1]

434 5 4 **Ballyhurry (USA)**[27] 3353 9-9-8 **62**.................... LeeEnstone 3 54
(J S Goldie) *hld up: effrt centre over 2f out: hung lft: nvr rchd ldrs* **12/1**

4003 6 4 **Zarova (IRE)**[11] 4021 4-8-13 **53**.................... PaulMulrennan 2 37
(M W Easterby) *hld up: rdn over 3f out: nvr rchd ldrs* **14/1**

003- 7 hd **Oulan Bator (FR)**[87] 5509 6-9-3 **57**.................... PaulHanagan 5 41
(R A Fahey) *hld up: pushed along over 3f out: nvr on terms* **12/1**

6401 8 3 1/2 **Jordans Elect**[19] 3784 6-9-7 **68**....................(v) JamesO'Reilly(7) 10 45
(T J Pitt) *set str pce: sn clr: wknd and hdd over 1f out* **7/2**[1]

1-05 9 1 **Roscommon**[19] 3782 3-9-2 **65**.................... TomEaves 1 40
(I Semple) *hld up: rdn and hung lft over 3f out: nvr on terms* **25/1**

0001 10 7 **Terminate (GER)**[19] 3792 4-9-8 **62**....................(b) RichardThomas 6 24
(N P Littmoden) *sn chsng clr ldr: rdn and wknd over 2f out* **6/1**[2]

2m 8.33s (-3.39) **Going Correction** -0.225s/f (Firm)
WFA 3 from 4yo+ 9lb **10** Ran SP% **117.7**
Speed ratings (Par 103):104,103,100,99,96 92,92,89,89,83
CSF £83.07 CT £620.93 TOTE £13.00: £3.10, £2.10, £3.00; EX 151.80.
Owner Steve Ryan **Bred** P And Mrs Venner **Trained** Catwick, E Yorks

FOCUS
A run-of-the-mill handicap but a strong pace teed things up for a finisher. This bare form looks reasonable, rated around the principals, but may not be totally reliable.
Wing Commander Official explanation: trainer said, regarding the improved form shown, gelding had run several times in a short period and appreciated the three week rest before today's run

4354 WATERAID H'CAP 5f
8:15 (8:16) (Class 6) (0-65,64) 3-Y-O **£2,914** (£867; £433; £216) **Stalls** Low

Form RPR

0300 1 **Highland Song (IRE)**[20] 3759 3-9-0 **64**.................... KevinGhunowa(7) 5 72
(R F Fisher) *prom: drvn 1/2-way: rallied over 1f out: led wl ins fnl f: styd on wl* **9/2**[3]

0002 2 3/4 **Megalo Maniac**[5] 4199 3-8-2 **45** oh2.................... PaulHanagan 6 50+
(R A Fahey) *towards rr and sn drvn along: hdwy over 1f out: kpt on fnl f: nt rch wnr* **11/4**[1]

0500 3 shd **Compton Lad**[10] 4056 3-8-2 **45** oh2.................... PaulFessey 1 50
(D A Nolan) *w ldr: led over 1f out to wl ins fnl f: no ex* **66/1**

0421 4 1 **Fortress**[9] 4071 3-9-3 **60**....................(b) J-PGuillambert 4 61
(E J Alston) *chsd ldrs: effrt and drvn 2f out: one pce fnl f* **11/4**[1]

3052 5 1/2 **Newkeylets**[18] 3814 3-8-12 **55**....................(b) TomEaves 7 55
(I Semple) *dwlt: outpcd: hdwy and hung lft over 1f out: nrst fin* **7/2**[2]

3360 6 3 1/2 **Stoneacre Fred (IRE)**[15] 3916 3-8-7 **50**..............(b) RobbieFitzpatrick 3 37
(Peter Grayson) *chsd ldrs: effrt over 2f out: hung lft over 1f out: no ex fnl f* **8/1**

0606 7 3/4 **Pensata**[7] 4136 3-7-11 **45** oh6.................... DuranFentiman(5) 2 29
(Miss L A Perratt) *outpcd and bhd: no imp fr 2f out* **50/1**

0046 8 5 **Mytton's Pride**[26] 3587 3-8-3 **53** ow1..............(b[1]) RussellKennemore(7) 8 19
(A Bailey) *set str pce to over 1f out: hung lft and sn btn* **16/1**

59.45 secs (-0.99) **Going Correction** -0.225s/f (Firm) **8** Ran SP% **114.2**
Speed ratings (Par 98):98,96,96,95,94 88,87,79
CSF £17.25 CT £711.48 TOTE £6.60: £2.20, £1.10, £5.30; EX 24.90.
Owner A Kerr **Bred** John Grogan **Trained** Ulverston, Cumbria

FOCUS
A modest event but a race run at a strong gallop throughout and suited those coming from just behind the pace. The winner ran to his recent best but the third raises doubts.

4355 UNITED UTILITIES H'CAP 1m 1f 20y
8:45 (8:45) (Class 6) (0-60,58) 3-Y-O+ **£2,866** (£846; £423) **Stalls** Low

Form RPR

6051 1 **Jordans Spark**[18] 3815 5-9-1 **50**.................... MarkLawson(5) 7 59
(P Monteith) *hld up: hdwy over 2f out: led ins fnl f: jst hld on* **4/1**[2]

4110 2 shd **Bijou Dan**[23] 3688 5-9-3 **52**....................(b) DuranFentiman(5) 2 61
(W G Harrison) *prom: effrt 2f out: kpt on wl fnl f: jst hld* **9/2**[3]

0606 3 2 1/2 **Whittinghamvillage**[18] 3815 5-9-8 **52**.................... TomEaves 3 56
(D W Whillans) *in tch: hdwy to ld briefly 1f out: kpt on same pce* **16/1**

0430 4 shd **Royal Indulgence**[9] 4068 6-9-9 **53**.................... RobbieFitzpatrick 9 57
(W M Brisbourne) *s.i.s: rdn 3f out: kpt on fnl f: nrst fin* **13/2**

0343 5 1/2 **Anthemion (IRE)**[18] 3815 9-9-0 **49**.................... AndrewMullen(5) 4 52
(Mrs J C McGregor) *led tl hdd 1f out: sn outpcd* **6/1**

5335 6 5 **Inch High**[19] 3784 8-9-6 **50**.................... PaulHanagan 11 43
(J S Goldie) *keen: chsd ldrs: effrt and hung lft over 2f out: sn outpcd* **7/2**[1]

4231 7 2 **Thornaby Green**[14] 3941 5-8-10 **47**.................... DeanHeslop(7) 10 36
(T D Barron) *chsd ldr: drvn over 2f out: wknd wl over 1f out* **4/1**[2]

00-0 8 18 **Diktatit**[16] 1885 4-9-1 **45**.................... PaulFessey 8 —
(R C Guest) *s.v.s: nvr on terms* **25/1**

1m 56.57s (0.73) **Going Correction** -0.225s/f (Firm)
WFA 3 from 4yo+ 8lb **8** Ran SP% **117.8**
Speed ratings (Par 101):106,105,103,103,103 98,96,80
CSF £23.12 CT £262.00 TOTE £4.90: £2.00, £1.90, £4.10; EX 22.60 Place 6 £238.54, Place 5 £79.46.
Owner B A Jordan **Bred** Egerton Stud Farms **Trained** Rosewell, Midlothian

FOCUS
Another run-of-the-mill handicap but a decent pace throughout and this bare form should stand up at a similar level, with the fourth the best guide.
Diktatit Official explanation: jockey said filly missed the break and would not face the cross nose band
T/Plt: £297.40 to a £1 stake. Pool: £46,229.35. 113.45 winning tickets. T/Qpdt: £29.60 to a £1 stake. Pool: £4,273.50. 106.80 winning tickets. RY

4320 HAYDOCK (L-H)
Saturday, August 12

OFFICIAL GOING: Good to firm (firm in places)
There were 22 non-runners on the card, all bar one because the forecast rain failed to materialise.
Wind: Almost nil. Weather: Fine.

4356 MALCOLM PRESCOTT 60TH BIRTHDAY H'CAP 1m 30y
1:40 (1:40) (Class 2) (0-100,98) 3-Y-O+ **£16,192** (£4,817; £2,407; £1,202) **Stalls** Low

Form RPR

0332 1 **Audience**[21] 3733 6-9-5 **89**.................... JimmyQuinn 12 98
(J Akehurst) *a.p: led over 2f out: sn rdn: r.o ins fnl f* **7/1**

201 2 1 1/4 **Banknote**[37] 3218 4-9-8 **92**.................... FrancisNorton 8 98+
(A M Balding) *lw: racd keenly: in tch: rdn over 2f out: ev ch ent fnl f: nt qckn towards fin* **5/2**[1]

2053 3 3/4 **Military Cross**[15] 3889 3-9-4 **95**.................... NickyMackay 15 99
(W J Haggas) *lw: hld up in midfield: rdr dropped rein whn rdn and hung lft over 2f out: hdwy over 1f out: styd on ins fnl f* **3/1**[2]

0-00 4 nk **Wise Dennis**[8] 4098 4-10-0 **98**.................... AlanMunro 13 102
(A P Jarvis) *hld up: rdn 2f out: hdwy over 1f out: styd on ins fnl f* **20/1**

6600 5 1 **Bahar Shumaal (IRE)**[15] 3890 4-9-5 **89**..................(b[1]) PhilipRobinson 6 91
(C E Brittain) *led: rdn and hdd over 2f out: kpt on same pce fnl f* **33/1**

3126 6 1/2 **Regent's Secret (USA)**[13] 3971 6-8-10 **82** ow1.................... DNolan(3) 10 84+
(J S Goldie) *in rr: pushed along over 3f out: effrt whn nt clr run over 1f out: styd on ins fnl f: nt rch ldrs* **12/1**

0154 7 1 **Goodbye Mr Bond**[13] 3985 6-9-2 **89**.................... StephenDonohoe(3) 4 87
(E J Alston) *lw: midfield: rdn 3f out: swtchd rt over 1f out: one pce ins fnl f* **15/2**

6243 8 1 1/2 **In Full Cry**[22] 3710 3-8-8 **85**.................... RoystonFfrench 11 79
(M Johnston) *lw: prom: rdn over 3f out: wknd over 1f out* **11/2**[3]

2120 9 9 **Paraguay (USA)**[14] 3928 3-8-8 **85**.................... AdrianMcCarthy 7 58
(Miss V Haigh) *trckd ldrs: rdn 3f out: wknd over 1f out* **16/1**

1m 42.51s (-3.00) **Going Correction** -0.225s/f (Firm)
WFA 3 from 4yo+ 7lb **9** Ran SP% **114.5**
Speed ratings (Par 109):106,104,104,103,102 102,101,99,90
CSF £24.63 CT £64.47 TOTE £8.10: £2.20, £1.70, £1.60; EX 22.30.

Owner Canisbay Bloodstock **Bred** Whitsbury Manor Stud And Gerald W Leigh **Trained** Epsom, Surrey

FOCUS

A fair handicap, run at a decent pace, and the form looks ordinary for the grade, with the runner-up to form.

NOTEBOOK

Audience, a narrow runner-up at Newbury last time, was ridden more prominently than has often been the case in the past and duly went one better in resolute fashion. Without the usual cheekpieces, he showed a great attitude when pressed by the eventual runner-up inside the final furlong and and this success was greatly deserved. A future weight rise may well scupper a follow-up bid, however. (op 8-1)

Banknote, upped 5lb for scoring over course and distance last month, emerged to throw down a late challenge to the winner, but he ultimately paid for refusing to settle through the early parts and in the end was well held by that rival. He remains in good form, clearly loves this venue, and does have another race in him from this new mark. (op 3-1)

Military Cross took too long to find his full stride from off the pace and was never a serious threat to the first two. He is capable of slightly better than this, and is a decent benchmark for the form, but still looks very much in the Handicapper's grip at present nevertheless. (op 9-4 tchd 10-3)

Wise Dennis, on his toes beforehand, ran an improved race, indeed his best for some time, and was not at all disgraced under top weight. He can build on this, but is very much the type who needs all to fall right in his races.

Bahar Shumaal(IRE), on his toes and edgy, showed more enthusiasm in the first-time blinkers and was given an aggressive ride. He really wants a stiffer test.

Regent's Secret(USA) tended to run in snatches through the early parts and then met trouble when finally hitting his full stride nearing the final furlong. He can be rated a little better than the bare form. (op 14-1)

In Full Cry appeared to use up too much energy in attaining a handy early position from his wide draw and proved disappointing. (op 7-1)

Paraguay(USA) looked rather 'tucked up' in the paddock and may need a break now.

4357 HANNAH FAYE JOHNSON MEMORIAL H'CAP — 6f

2:15 (2:21) (Class 3) (0-90,90) 3-Y-0+ **£11,334** (£3,372; £1,685; £841) **Stalls** Centre

Form				RPR
6142	1		**Ellens Academy (IRE)**[8] [4119] 11-8-10 **72**........ JimmyQuinn 9 (E J Alston) *lw: hld up: hdwy whn nt clr run and swtchd lft over 1f out: sn led: rdn out: in command towards fin* **6/1**[3]	85
005	2	1	**Countdown**[37] [3217] 4-8-11 **73**........ AlanMunro 13 (T D Easterby) *midfield: hdwy 2f out: chsd wnr and ev ch 1f out: nt qckn towards fin* **7/1**	83
2215	3	2	**Geojimali**[8] [4119] 4-8-10 **75**........ DNolan(3) 11 (J S Goldie) *s.i.s: in rr: hdwy 1/2-way: sn rdn: ev ch 1f out: one pce ins fnl f* **8/1**	79
2630	4	nk	**Lake Garda**[8] [4119] 5-8-13 **75**........ NCallan 12 (K A Ryan) *w ldr: rdn and ev ch over 1f out: kpt on same pce after* **11/2**[2]	78
1510	5	1 3/4	**Adantino**[22] [3715] 7-8-13 **82**........(b) JamesMillman(7) 8 (B R Millman) *chsd ldrs: rdn and hung lft whn outpcd over 2f out: no imp after* **12/1**	80
0301	6	1	**Rochdale**[21] [3722] 3-9-10 **90**........ PhilipRobinson 3 (M A Jarvis) *lw: led: rdn over 1f out: sn hdd: wknd ins fnl f* **7/2**[1]	85
1301	7	3 1/2	**Lady Bahia (IRE)**[7] [4135] 5-8-11 **73**........(b) RobbieFitzpatrick 6 (Peter Grayson) *s.i.s: in rr: hdwy 2f out: wknd fnl f* **16/1**	57
0530	8	1	**High Reach**[8] [4101] 6-9-13 **89**........ RichardHughes 7 (W R Muir) *chsd ldrs: rdn whn nt clr run and swtchd lft over 1f out: wknd ins fnl f* **16/1**	70
1000	9	6	**Don Pele (IRE)**[15] [3904] 4-9-11 **87**........ CatherineGannon 2 (K A Ryan) *b: chsd ldrs: rdn over 2f out: wknd over 1f out* **25/1**	50

1m 13.57s (-1.33) **Going Correction** -0.225s/f (Firm)

WFA 3 from 4yo+ 4lb **9** Ran SP% **98.8**

Speed ratings (Par 107):99,97,95,94,92 90,86,84,76

CSF £34.78 CT £206.04 TOTE £5.60: £1.70, £2.40, £2.20; EX 46.00.

Owner K Lee And I Davies **Bred** Mrs Chris Harrington **Trained** Longton, Lancs

■ My Gacho (11/2, broke out of stalls) was withdrawn. R4 applies, deduct 15p in the £.

FOCUS

A fair sprint which was run at a generous early pace. Ordinary form. The field elected to race down the middle of the track.

NOTEBOOK

Ellens Academy(IRE) relished the decent early clip and came home to score with a deal up his sleeve. He has now been successful on both occasions that he has been ridden by today's jockey, and is clearly still very much at the top of his game despite his veteran status. (tchd 5-1)

Countdown, with the blinkers left off on this debut for his new stable, posted a solid effort in defeat, holding every chance, yet could not match the winner's speed towards the finish. He looks to be on a fair mark now and could well be placed to go one better in the coming weeks on this evidence. (op 10-1)

Geojimali had every chance, and was not at all disgraced in defeat, but he nearly always seems to find an excuse or two in his races. (op 10-1)

Lake Garda, well backed, had his chance and turned in an improved effort. He is capable of winning from this mark, but is an unpredictable sprinter all the same. (op 9-1)

Rochdale, easy to back, was given an aggressive ride and found little when push came to shove. He may well be weighted to the hilt now. Official explanation: jockey said gelding stumbled at start and lost its action in closing stages (op 5-2)

High Reach Official explanation: jockey said gelding stumbled at start and lost its action in closing stages

4358 PETROS ROSE OF LANCASTER STKS (GROUP 3) — 1m 2f 120y

2:45 (2:47) (Class 1) 3-Y-0+

£42,585 (£16,140; £8,077; £4,027; £2,017; £1,012) **Stalls** High

Form				RPR
0454	1		**Mulaqat**[21] [3736] 3-8-7 109........(b[1]) NCallan 5 (M P Tregoning) *s.i.s: hld up: hdwy 4f out: rdn whn nt clr run and swtchd rt 2f out: led over 1f out: r.o* **25/1**	119
-250	2	1 3/4	**Notable Guest (USA)**[35] [3314] 5-9-3 112........ RichardHughes 6 (Sir Michael Stoute) *lw: trckd ldrs: effrt 3f out: hung lft and led over 2f out: hdd over 1f out: no ex towards fin* **4/1**[3]	116
3402	3	1 1/2	**Hattan (IRE)**[14] [3957] 4-9-3 106........ JimmyQuinn 4 (C E Brittain) *hld up: rdn over 2f out: hdwy and edgd lft over 1f out: styd on ins fnl f: nt rch ldrs* **16/1**	113
220	4	shd	**Cougar Bay (IRE)**[41] [3127] 3-8-7 ....(b) DPMcDonogh 2 (David Wachman, Ire) *str: lw: a.p: rdn and ev ch wl over 1f out: no ex ins fnl f* **25/1**	113
1410	5	2 1/2	**Hinterland (IRE)**[14] [3926] 4-9-3 105........ PhilipRobinson 3 (M A Jarvis) *racd keenly: midfield: rdn over 2f out: btn over 1f out* **7/2**[2]	108
1011	6	1 3/4	**Road To Love (IRE)**[9] [4082] 3-8-7 93........ RoystonFfrench 7 (M Johnston) *led: rdn 3f out: hdd over 2f out: wknd over 1f out* **11/8**[1]	105
0-33	7	28	**Vol De Nuit**[55] [2693] 5-9-3 111........(v[1]) NickyMackay 8 (L M Cumani) *hld up: hung bdly rt on bnd over 5f out: struggling after* **6/1**	55
-134	8	1	**Markovitch**[20] [3778] 3-8-7 105........ AlanMunro 1 (P W Chapple-Hyam) *plld hrd: prom tl wknd over 3f out: eased over 1f out* **33/1**	53

2m 10.29s (-7.44) **Going Correction** -0.225s/f (Firm)

WFA 3 from 4yo+ 10lb **8** Ran SP% **115.1**

Speed ratings (Par 113):118,116,115,115,113 112,92,91

CSF £120.92 TOTE £32.50: £6.00, £1.80, £3.10; EX 202.70.

Owner Sheikh Ahmed Al Maktoum **Bred** Darley **Trained** Lambourn, Berks

FOCUS

A fair renewal of this Group 3 which was run at a solid pace and the winning time was 3.48 seconds quicker than the valuable handicap which followed. The field came home fairly strung out.

NOTEBOOK

Mulaqat, whose trainer had won this event twice in the last six years with Ekraar and Nayef, bounced back to his best in the first-time blinkers and came home to win with a deal up his sleeve. His last two runs had been almost too bad to be true, but on the form of his effort at Royal Ascot he could have been given every chance in this, and the headgear clearly worked the oracle. It is possible he has more to offer, but whether the blinkers have the same effect next time remains to be seen.

Notable Guest(USA), who landed this event in 2005, enjoyed this drop back from the top level and showed his true colours in defeat. He helps to set the level for this form, but is clearly vulnerable under his penalty in this grade. (op 7-2)

Hattan(IRE) was another who enjoyed the drop in class, but may have been better served by a more positive ride over this trip. He is a little better than this, but is a very hard horse to win with nevertheless.

Cougar Bay(IRE), out the back in the Irish Derby last time, showed that this is really his level at present yet failed to raise his game that much for the drop back in trip. (op 20-1)

Hinterland(IRE) was put in his place on this debut in Group company and did not help his chances by running freely through the early parts. He could do better with further experience in this class. Official explanation: jockey said colt was unsuited by the good to firm (firm in places) ground (op 5-1)

Road To Love(IRE), very well backed for this first venture into Group company, had his chance from the front yet found disappointingly little when pressed approaching the two-furlong marker. He may have found this coming too soon however, and is not one to write off in this sort of company just yet. (tchd 6-4 and 13-8 in places)

Vol De Nuit, equipped with a first-time visor, failed to handle the bend on the turn for home and was never in the hunt thereafter. (tchd 11-2)

Markovitch, down in grade, proved far too keen and not surprisingly paid the price before two out. (op 40-1 tchd 50-1)

4359 TOTESPORT.COM STKS (HERITAGE H'CAP) — 1m 2f 120y

3:20 (3:21) (Class 2) (0-105,102) 3-Y-0+

£49,856 (£14,928; £7,464; £3,736; £1,864; £936) **Stalls** High

Form				RPR
0101	1		**Dansili Dancer**[36] [3255] 4-9-2 **94**........ PhilipRobinson 5 (C G Cox) *racd keenly: trckd ldrs: rdn to ld over 1f out: edgd lft ins fnl f: r.o* **8/1**	104
0121	2	1 1/2	**Fairmile**[28] [3552] 4-9-2 **97**........ AdamKirby(3) 15 (W R Swinburn) *hld up: nt clr run over 2f out: hdwy and swtchd rt over 1f out: r.o ins fnl f: gaining at fin* **7/2**[1]	107+
0602	3	hd	**Bravo Maestro (USA)**[28] [3552] 5-9-2 **94**........ NCallan 3 (N P Littmoden) *hld up: hdwy whn nt clr run and swtchd rt over 2f out: hung lft over 1f out: styd on ins fnl fnl* **7/1**[3]	101
6510	4	3/4	**Great Plains**[28] [3552] 4-9-5 **97**........ RichardHughes 7 (Mrs A J Perrett) *led: rdn 2f out: hdd over 1f out: kpt on same pce ins fnl f* **12/1**	103
-006	5	1	**Pagan Sword**[11] [4023] 4-8-11 **89**........ JimCrowley 11 (Mrs A J Perrett) *lw: midfield: hdwy over 2f out: rdn over 1f out: one pce wl ins fnl f* **10/1**	93
2143	6	1/2	**Folio (IRE)**[11] [4023] 6-8-6 **84**........ NickyMackay 2 (W J Musson) *midfield: hdwy over 2f out: rdn over 1f out: one pce ins fnl f* **16/1**	88+
5-64	7	3/4	**Premier Dane (IRE)**[29] [3501] 4-8-11 **89**........ TomEaves 14 (N G Richards) *hld up: rdn and hdwy over 1f out: kpt on ins fnl f: nt trble ldrs* **33/1**	91+
0035	8	1	**Boo**[14] [3929] 4-8-9 **92**........ AndrewElliott(5) 1 (K R Burke) *prom: rdn over 3f out: one pce over 1f out* **14/1**	92
3300	9	1/2	**Baan (USA)**[10] [4039] 3-8-10 **98**........ J-PGuillambert 12 (M Johnston) *w ldr: rdn over 3f out: hmpd whn wkng over 1f out* **12/1**	97
0302	10	3/4	**Krugerrand (USA)**[7] [4160] 7-8-6 **87**........ StephenDonohoe(3) 10 (W J Musson) *hld up: rdn over 2f out: no imp* **12/1**	85
5100	11	3 1/2	**I'm So Lucky**[11] [4023] 4-9-10 **102**........ RoystonFfrench 13 (M Johnston) *b: midfield: pushed along over 3f out: edgd lft whn wkng 2f out* **10/1**	93
3530	12	1/2	**Star Of Light**[28] [3552] 5-9-8 **100**........ AlanMunro 16 (B J Meehan) *cl up: rdn over 3f out: wknd over 2f out* **6/1**[2]	90

2m 13.77s (-3.96) **Going Correction** -0.225s/f (Firm)

WFA 3 from 4yo+ 10lb **12** Ran SP% **116.9**

Speed ratings (Par 109):105,103,103,103,102 102,101,100,100,99 97,97

CSF £35.49 CT £209.41 TOTE £8.70: £2.50, £1.70, £3.00; EX 28.50 Trifecta £53.70 Pool: £908.78 - 12.00 winning units..

Owner The Troupers **Bred** The Magic Slipper Partnership **Trained** Lambourn, Berks

FOCUS

A decent handicap which was run at just a modest early pace. Those to be held up proved at a disadvantage and the form should be treated with a degree of caution. The runner-up is rated as having finished upsides the winner and the fourth ran to form.

NOTEBOOK

Dansili Dancer, 4lb higher than when scoring at Sandown last time, fully proved he stays this trip and followed up in good style. He had the run of the race, but still did well considering he ran freely through the early stages, and is clearly now very much at the top of his game. The Cambridgeshire looks the obvious target for him now, but he would probably require a fastish surface to show his best in that.

Fairmile ◆, raised 6lb for his recent York success, was warm in the paddock and proved unsuited by being held up off the average pace and ultimately got going all too late in the day after being denied a clear run on several occasions. He has to rate as unfortunate, and is clearly better than the bare form, so it would be no surprise to see this consistent gelding make amends next time.

Bravo Maestro(USA) ◆ was another who would have been seen to better effect off a stronger early gallop and was doing his best work towards the finish. He failed to reverse his recent York form with the runner-up, but remains in good heart, and is another who can be rated better than the bare form. (op 6-1)

Great Plains was made to look one-paced when pressed after passing the two-furlong marker and has to rate a touch flattered by this form, as he had very much the run of the race out in front.

Premier Dane(IRE) shaped better than his finishing position suggests, as he ideally needs a stronger early pace, and was not given too hard a time of things. This looks to be his optimum trip and he may well have a race in him from this sort of mark before the season's end. (tchd 40-1)

Star Of Light, warm in the paddock, ran well below expectations and may just be in need of a break now. (op 8-1)

4360 **CORAL "BOOKMAKER OF THE YEAR" H'CAP** **5f**
3:50 (3:51) (Class 2) (0-100,100) 3-Y-O+**£16,192** (£4,817; £2,407; £1,202) **Stalls** Centre

Form RPR
6601 **1** **The Jobber (IRE)**[6] 4180 5-9-1 **89** 6ex.................................... NCallan 17 103
(M Blanshard) *hld up: hdwy and swtchd lft over 1f out: led wl ins fnl: r.o* **15/2**
6-00 **2** ¾ **Pivotal's Princess (IRE)**[77] 2021 4-9-4 **92**................ PhilipRobinson 12 103
(E S McMahon) *led: rdn ins fnl f: sn hdd: hld cl home* **14/1**
0200 **3** 1 **Texas Gold**[7] 4128 8-9-11 **99**.. RichardHughes 10 106+
(W R Muir) *lw: hld up: rdn and hdwy over 1f out: r.o ins fnl f: nt rch ldrs* **7/1**[3]
6050 **4** nk **Cape Royal**[21] 3744 6-9-0 **91**.............................(bt) StephenDonohoe(3) 14 97
(J M Bradley) *in tch: rdn and ev ch ent fnl f: sn nt qckn* **20/1**
2154 **5** nk **Bluebok**[9] 4085 5-8-9 **83**..(t) AlanMunro 11 88
(J M Bradley) *chsd ldrs: rdn and outpcd over 1f out: styd on ins fnl f* **11/1**
1430 **6** hd **Bo McGinty (IRE)**[13] 3972 5-8-10 **84**............................(b) PaulHanagan 5 89
(R A Fahey) *lw: chsd ldrs: rdn whn n.m.r over 1f out: styd on ins fnl f* **7/1**[3]
3020 **7** ½ **Treasure Cay**[28] 3520 5-9-6 **97**.................................(t) AdamKirby(3) 16 100
(P W D'Arcy) *in tch: effrt over 1f out: sn ev ch: no ex ins fnl f* **25/1**
5051 **8** ½ **Holbeck Ghyll (IRE)**[9] 4085 4-8-7 **81** oh1..................... FrancisNorton 7 82
(A M Balding) *chsd ldrs: rdn over 1f out: wknd ins fnl f* **5/2**[1]
2031 **9** hd **Grigorovitch (IRE)**[14] 3938 4-9-0 **88**.............................. TomEaves 3 88
(I Semple) *racd keenly: hld up: rdn 1f out: kpt on ins fnl f: nvr able to chal* **13/2**[2]
6060 **10** 1¼ **Kay Two (IRE)**[13] 3972 4-8-9 **86**.................................... JamesDoyle(3) 9 82
(R J Price) *prom tl rdn and wknd over 1f out* **25/1**
0200 **11** shd **Talbot Avenue**[7] 4128 8-9-7 **95**... JimCrowley 2 90
(M Mullineaux) *b: b.hind: prom: rdn over 1f out: wknd ins fnl f* **18/1**
1060 **12** 4 **Graze On**[13] 3972 4-9-3 **91**...................................(b) AdrianMcCarthy 15 72
(R A Harris) *prom tl rdn and wknd over 1f out: b.b.v* **40/1**
2010 **13** 13 **Stoneacre Lad (IRE)**[29] 3475 3-8-13 **90**................(b) RobbieFitzpatrick 4 24
(Peter Grayson) *prom 1f: racd alone on far rail: rdn over 2f out: wknd over 1f out* **28/1**

59.84 secs (-2.23) **Going Correction** -0.225s/f (Firm) **13** Ran SP% **117.3**
WFA 3 from 4yo+ 3lb
Speed ratings (Par 109):108,106,105,104,104 103,103,102,102,100 99,93,72
CSF £97.53 CT £795.21 TOTE £8.20: £2.80, £4.10, £2.30; EX 113.50.
Owner Mrs Rosemary Wilkerson & Partners **Bred** Dr T J Molony **Trained** Upper Lambourn, Berks

FOCUS
A decent sprint handicap and the form looks solid, with the first two posting personal bests and the third pretty much back to form.

NOTEBOOK
The Jobber(IRE), under a penalty for resuming winning ways at Newbury six days previously, knuckled down to get the better of the runner-up late on and followed up in ready fashion. He is back at the top of his game now and, while he will still have a bit to prove from a likely higher mark, further improvement cannot be ruled out. He reportedly heads for the Portland Handicap at York (switched from Doncaster) now. (op 8-1)
Pivotal's Princess(IRE) gave her all from the front, but had no more to offer when the winner asserted late on. This was by far her best effort for some time, she looks to have improved for her recent break, and would have claims of reversing form with the winner if also going for the Portland Handicap at York next month.
Texas Gold, winner of this event last term from a 2lb lower mark, finished fast but all too late. While this was no disgrace, he is proving hard to catch right this term. (op 15-2 tchd 8-1)
Cape Royal had his chance, yet failed to find the required turn of foot when it mattered, and looks held by the Handicapper at present. (op 16-1)
Bluebok, with the tongue tie back on, shaped as though he may be ready to tackle another furlong again now and remains in good form. (tchd 10-1)
Bo McGinty(IRE) was another who finished his race all too late in the day. He could do with a little respite in the weights on recent evidence. (op 8-1)
Holbeck Ghyll(IRE) was found out by his latest 10lb rise in the weights for winning at Goodwood last time. Official explanation: jockey said gelding became upset in stalls and ran too free early (op 11-4 tchd 3-1)
Graze On Official explanation: jockey said gelding bled from the nose
Stoneacre Lad(IRE) Official explanation: jockey said colt wouldn't let himself down on the ground

4361 **RACING UK ON SKY 432 H'CAP** **6f**
4:25 (4:27) (Class 5) (0-70,68) 4-Y-0+ **£3,238** (£722; £722; £240) **Stalls** Centre

Form RPR
0010 **1** **Tadlil**[10] 4054 4-8-12 **59**.. NCallan 12 77
(J M Bradley) *lw: hld up: hdwy over 2f out: led over 1f out: sn hung lft: r.o wl and drew clr ins fnl f* **11/2**[3]
2006 **2** 4 **Weakest Link**[9] 4067 5-8-2 **49** oh2....................................(p) PaulQuinn 10 55
(E J Alston) *lw: a.p: led 2f out: sn rdn and hung lft: hdd over 1f out: kpt on same pce ins fnl f* **20/1**
0040 **2** dht **Bold Haze**[12] 3996 4-8-10 **57**.......................................(v[1]) DeanMcKeown 3 63
(Miss S E Hall) *hld up: hdwy after 2f: rdn and ev ch over 1f out: sn hung lft: kpt on same pce ins fnl f* **20/1**
0060 **4** ¾ **Coranglais**[42] 3094 6-8-3 **50**...(p) FrancisNorton 6 54
(J M Bradley) *b: midfield: rdn and hdwy over 1f out: edgd lft and styd on ins fnl f* **13/2**
0266 **5** 1½ **Currency**[8] 4119 9-9-4 **68**.. StephenDonohoe(3) 1 67
(J M Bradley) *b: lw: in tch: dropped to rr after 2f: renewed effrt over 2f out: one pce ins fnl f* **13/2**
0023 **6** shd **Whitbarrow (IRE)**[5] 4211 7-8-8 **62**.........................(v) JamesMillman(7) 5 61
(B R Millman) *led: rdn and edgd rt over 2f out: sn hdd: wknd ins fnl f* **9/2**[2]
2652 **7** 3 **Sir Don (IRE)**[10] 4054 7-8-6 **53**...(p) JimmyQuinn 2 43
(E S McMahon) *prom: rdn over 2f out: wknd over 1f out* **4/1**[1]
6620 **8** 3½ **Smirfys Party**[28] 3524 8-8-2 **49** oh5.......................(v) CatherineGannon 11 28
(W M Brisbourne) *hld up: rdn over 2f out: no imp* **16/1**
0000 **9** 10 **Navigation (IRE)**[31] 3398 4-8-7 **54**.................................(t) NickyMackay 9 3
(T J Etherington) *a bhd: eased whn btn fnl f* **10/1**
0020 **10** 1 **Gavioli (IRE)**[21] 3728 4-8-5 **52**... AlanMunro 7 —
(J M Bradley) *chsd ldrs: wkng whn hmpd over 2f out: eased over 1f out* **9/1**

1m 13.25s (-1.65) **Going Correction** -0.225s/f (Firm) **10** Ran SP% **114.7**
Speed ratings (Par 103):102,96,96,95,93 93,89,84,71,70
Pl: Bold Haze £4.90, Weak Link £5.20. Ex: T/BH £83.10, T/WL £59.50. CSF: T/BH £53.01, T/WL £53.01. Tri: T/BH/WL £1,037.29, T/WL/BH £1,037.29 TOTE £7.20: £2.20.
Owner E A Hayward **Bred** Wheelersland Stud **Trained** Sedbury, Gloucs

FOCUS
A modest sprint, but the form looks solid. The winner was value for slightly further than the winning margin and looks progressive.
Whitbarrow(IRE) Official explanation: jockey said gelding had no more to give
Sir Don(IRE) Official explanation: trainer's representative said bridle slipped
Navigation(IRE) Official explanation: jockey said gelding hit its leg on stall and was never travelling thereafter

4362 **LEVY BOARD H'CAP** **1m 6f**
4:55 (4:56) (Class 5) (0-70,67) 3-Y-0 **£3,238** (£963; £481; £240) **Stalls** Low

Form RPR
2202 **1** **Squirtle (IRE)**[8] 4118 3-9-4 **65**................................ StephenDonohoe(3) 8 74
(W M Brisbourne) *hld up: hdwy after 6f: effrt on outside on bnd over 4f out: rdn to ld narrowly 2f out: edgd lft 1f out: styd on wl* **6/1**[3]
2422 **2** ½ **Osolomio (IRE)**[7] 4150 3-9-2 **60**.. PhilipRobinson 9 70+
(J G Given) *led: hdd narrowly 2f out: cl 2nd whn rdn and unbalanced jst over 1f out: rallied wl ins fnl f: hld cl home* **9/2**[2]
1111 **3** 2½ **Alambic**[3] 4268 3-9-9 **67** 6ex.. JamieMackay 4 72
(Sir Mark Prescott) *lw: upset in stalls: trckd ldrs: rdn and hung lft over 3 out: outpcd by front pair over 2f out: kpt on ins fnl f* **8/13**[1]
6003 **4** 8 **Synonymy**[8] 4111 3-9-3 **61**.. DeanMcKeown 6 55
(M Blanshard) *in tch: rdn over 4f out: wknd over 3f out* **16/1**
-600 **5** hd **Sunny Parkes**[21] 3725 3-8-3 **47**.. JimmyQuinn 1 41
(M Mullineaux) *hld up: rdn over 3f out: edgd rt over 2f out: nvr on terms* **50/1**
6020 **6** 8 **Virginia Rose (IRE)**[19] 3791 3-8-9 **53**.. NCallan 2 35
(J G Given) *in tch: lost pl after 6f: rdn 4f out: n.d whn n.m.r and hung lft wl over 2f out* **16/1**
6264 **7** 16 **Noble Edge**[11] 4022 3-8-12 **56**.................................(p) CatherineGannon 7 16
(Robert Gray) *prom: rdn and wknd over 3f out: n.d whn edgd lft wl over 2f out* **25/1**
0-04 **8** 7 **Skit**[42] 3066 3-8-2 **46** oh6.. PaulQuinn 5 —
(W M Brisbourne) *hld up: rdn over 4f out: nvr on terms* **33/1**

3m 3.64s (-2.65) **Going Correction** -0.225s/f (Firm) **8** Ran SP% **114.9**
Speed ratings (Par 100):98,97,96,91,91 87,77,73
CSF £32.58 CT £39.07 TOTE £7.50: £1.40, £1.70, £1.10; EX 47.90 Place 6 £378.97, Place 5 £259.57..
Owner J Jones Racing Ltd **Bred** Ballygallon Stud **Trained** Great Ness, Shropshire
■ Stewards' Enquiry : Stephen Donohoe two-day ban: careless riding (Aug 25-26)

FOCUS
A moderate handicap which saw the first two come clear. The form is not strong with the favourite disappointing, but seems sound enough with the first three clear.
Virginia Rose(IRE) Official explanation: jockey said filly hung right-handed
Skit Official explanation: jockey said gelding was unsuited by the good to firm (firm in places) ground
T/Plt: £1,109.10 to a £1 stake. Pool: £96,101.10. 63.25 winning tickets. T/Qpdt: £193.60 to a £1 stake. Pool: £4,710.85. 18.00 winning tickets. DO

4326 LINGFIELD (L-H)
Saturday, August 12

OFFICIAL GOING: Turf course - good to firm (good in places); all-weather - standard
Wind: Moderate, against Weather: Overcast

4363 **LADIES NIGHT H'CAP** **7f 140y**
5:25 (5:25) (Class 6) (0-55,55) 3-Y-0+ **£2,388** (£705; £352) **Stalls** Centre

Form RPR
6503 **1** **Dark Moon**[55] 2676 3-9-0 **51**.. NeilChalmers(3) 15 59
(A M Balding) *t.k.h: hld up in midfield: prog 2f out: rdn and r.o to ld last 75yds* **12/1**
5265 **2** nk **Only If I Laugh**[47] 2936 5-9-11 **52**.................................... PatCosgrave 18 60
(M J Attwater) *hld up bhd ldrs: gng easily over 2f out: effrt to ld jst over 1f out: idled in front and hdd last 75yds* **7/2**[2]
0300 **3** nk **Margaret's Dream (IRE)**[19] 3786 5-9-4 **45**................ StephenCarson 17 52
(D Carroll) *racd against nr side rail: mde most: drvn and hdd jst over 1f out : kpt on: a jst hld* **14/1**
3432 **4** 1 **Zafarshah (IRE)**[2] 4285 7-9-1 **45**........................(b) RichardKingscote(3) 7 50+
(R A Harris) *hld up in midfield and racd towards outer: stdy prog over 2f out: pressed ldrs over 1f out: kpt on same pce after* **11/4**[1]
-000 **5** 1 **Seldemosa**[71] 2186 5-9-8 **49**.. FergusSweeney 16 51
(M S Saunders) *hld up wl in rr against nr side rail: plenty to do over 2f out: prog and swtchd lft over 1f out: drvn and r.o: nvr nrr* **33/1**
0004 **6** 2½ **Bollywood (IRE)**[14] 3932 3-9-0 **53**.................................. MarcHalford(5) 14 48
(J J Bridger) *trckd ldrs: rdn over 2f out: no imp over 1f out: wknd ins fnl f* **25/1**
1400 **7** hd **Trevian**[18] 3820 5-9-8 **52**.. NelsonDeSouza(3) 10 48+
(J M Bradley) *hld up wl in rr and racd on outer: effrt 2f out: plugged on one pce : n.d* **15/2**
000/ **8** 1¾ **Over Tipsy**[662] 6282 4-9-4 **45**.. PatDobbs 2 36
(R Hannon) *dwlt: sn trckd ldrs: rdn and lost pl over 2f out: n.d over 1f out* **25/1**
4400 **9** 1½ **Blue Line**[14] 3933 4-9-5 **51**...(v) TravisBlock(5) 9 38
(M Madgwick) *hld up wl in rr: stdy prog on outer over 2f out: pushed along and no imp over 1f out: wknd and eased fnl f* **8/1**
0034 **10** 1½ **Fateful Attraction**[16] 3869 3-9-4 **55**.............................. SaleemGolam(3) 5 38
(I A Wood) *sn chsd ldrs: hrd rdn fr 3f out: wknd over 1f out* **7/1**[3]
1606 **11** 1 **Inescapable (USA)**[21] 3729 5-8-8 **42**...................... ThomasO'Brien(7) 11 23
(A W Carroll) *dwlt: t.k.h: hld up wl in rr: rdn and no real prog over 2f out* **16/1**
0030 **12** 7 **Angel River**[3] 4266 4-9-1 **42**..(b) BrianReilly 8 6
(J Ryan) *w ldr: hrd rdn over 2f out: sn wknd* **50/1**
6430 **13** 2½ **Ace Club**[117] 1054 5-8-13 **43**.. DominicFox(3) 1 —
(M J Attwater) *pressed ldrs: rdn over 3f out: wknd over 2f out* **20/1**
3/00 **14** 17 **Love Academy**[59] 2551 11-9-1 **42**.................................... RobertMiles 3 —
(Luke Comer, Ire) *racd alone far side: sn wl off the pce: t.o* **50/1**
0500 **15** 5 **Ronaldo**[93] 1616 3-9-5 **53**.. FrancisFerris 12 —
(A M Hales) *hld up wl in rr: hmpd 5f out: nvr gng wl after: t.o fnl 2f* **28/1**

1m 33.74s (2.28) **Going Correction** +0.325s/f (Good)
WFA 3 from 4yo+ 7lb **15** Ran SP% **127.3**
Speed ratings (Par 101):101,100,100,99,98 95,95,93,92,90 89,82,80,63,58
CSF £52.72 CT £478.84 TOTE £13.60: £3.40, £2.30, £3.90; EX 95.70.
Owner M E Wates **Bred** Langton Stud And G E M Wates **Trained** Kingsclere, Hants

FOCUS
An ordinary handicap in which the draw played its part as usual with the four highest drawn finishing in the first five. The form looks sound enough on paper, rated through the placed horses.

4364 SARAH WRIGHT PHOTOGRAPHY H'CAP 6f
5:55 (5:55) (Class 5) (0-75,74) 3-Y-O+ £3,238 (£963; £481; £240) Stalls High

Form RPR
-454 1 Inch By Inch[25] 3612 7-9-7 71 (b) AmirQuinn(3) 3 80
(P J Makin) *racd against nr side rail: mde all: rdn over 1f out: wandered but in no real danger fnl f* 6/1
0130 2 1 1/4 Caustic Wit (IRE)[6] 4172 8-9-13 74 (p) FergusSweeney 8 79
(M S Saunders) *wnt lft s: hld up in tch: effrt 2f out: drvn to chse wnr ins fnl f: kpt on but nvr able to chal* 5/2[1]
4103 3 1 1/2 Stamford Blue[10] 4054 5-8-12 62 (b) RichardKingscote(3) 1 63
(R A Harris) *dwlt: hld up in last pair: prog on outer 1/2-way: chsd wnr 2f out: hanging and nt qckn ins fnl f* 7/1
5430 4 2 Buy On The Red[8] 4106 5-9-11 72 (b) RobertMiles 6 67
(W R Muir) *t.k.h: hld up in last pair: struggling over 2f out on wd outside: plugged on fr over 1f out* 11/2
4020 5 nk High Ridge[8] 4101 7-9-10 74 (p) NelsonDeSouza(3) 7 68
(J M Bradley) *bmpd s: t.k.h: prom: rdn and fnd nil 2f out: sn btn* 4/1[2]
0434 6 2 1/2 Colonel Cotton (IRE)[25] 3622 7-9-10 71 PatCosgrave 5 57
(R A Fahey) *prom: hrd rdn and wknd 2f out* 5/1[3]
3220 7 1 Cree[7] 4141 4-8-8 55 oh1 (b) StephenCarson 4 38
(W R Muir) *racd on outer: mostly chsd wnr to 2f out: wknd* 14/1
1m 13.71s (2.04) **Going Correction** +0.325s/f (Good)
WFA 3 from 4yo+ 4lb 7 Ran SP% 114.1
Speed ratings (Par 103):99,97,95,92,92 88,87
CSF £21.30 CT £107.01 TOTE £5.80: £2.80, £2.00; EX 25.60.
Owner Mrs Anna L Sanders **Bred** Mrs Anna L Sanders **Trained** Ogbourne Maisey, Wilts
FOCUS
An ordinary handicap in which the stands' rail was again the place to be and the form is modest.

4365 FURLONGS & FAIRWAYS H'CAP 6f
6:25 (6:25) (Class 6) (0-65,69) 3-Y-O+ £2,388 (£705; £352) Stalls High

Form RPR
0510 1 Banjo Bay (IRE)[7] 4141 8-9-6 60 (t) NeilChalmers(3) 15 71
(Miss Gay Kelleway) *hld up in midfield: nt clr run 2f out: got through and prog to ld jst over 1f out: rdn and in command fnl f* 15/2[3]
/00- 2 1 1/2 Tapau (IRE)[579] 73 8-8-3 47 BarrySavage(7) 13 54
(J M Bradley) *hld up wl in rr: nt clr run 2f out: followed wnr through 1f out: r.o wl nr fin: nvr able to chal* 66/1
-000 3 1/2 Firework[7] 4141 8-8-8 45 StephenCarson 2 50+
(E A Wheeler) *taken down early: hld up wl in rr: prog on wd outside 2f out: styd on fnl f: unable to chal* 33/1
2400 4 1/2 Parkside Pursuit[8] 4110 8-9-9 63 NelsonDeSouza(3) 11 67+
(J M Bradley) *hld up wl in rr: nt clr run over 2f out to 1f out: styd on wl last 100yds: nrst fin* 16/1
4403 5 1/2 Siraj[7] 4141 7-8-9 49 (p) SaleemGolam(3) 1 51+
(J Ryan) *racd towards outer: wl in tch: effrt and upsides over 1f out: one pce after* 10/1
5641 6 hd Mirasol Princess[5] 4211 5-9-2 53 6ex SebSanders 9 54
(D K Ivory) *chsd ldrs: pushed along bef 1/2-way: effrt and upsides over 1f out : fdd ins fnl f* 6/1[2]
0556 7 hd Cayman Breeze[4] 4233 6-9-0 51 EddieAhern 8 52
(J M Bradley) *fast away but restrained to rr: nt clr run 2f out: pushed along over 1f out: styd on ins fnl f: nvr nr ldrs* 15/2[3]
-000 8 1 1/4 Arfinnit (IRE)[44] 3004 5-8-5 45 RichardKingscote(3) 5 42
(Mrs A L M King) *pressed ldrs: rdn and upsides over 1f out: wknd fnl f* 33/1
0330 9 nk Musical Script (USA)[10] 4054 3-8-11 57 TravisBlock(5) 7 53
(Mrs A J Hamilton-Fairley) *taken down early: dwlt: wl in rr: prog on wd outside 2f out: no imp 1f out: wknd* 20/1
00-0 10 1/2 King Of Diamonds[22] 3712 5-9-6 64 KylieManser(7) 4 62+
(J R Best) *taken down early: dwlt: hld up wl in rr: shkn up 2f out: styng on but no ch whn hmpd and snatched up ins fnl f* 33/1
0035 11 shd Gone'N'Dunnett (IRE)[3] 4267 7-9-11 62 (v) BrianReilly 10 56
(Mrs C A Dunnett) *w ldrs: led briefly over 1f out: wknd fnl f* 9/1
6000 12 1 Stokesies Wish[7] 4141 6-8-8 52 JamieHamblett(7) 14 43
(J L Spearing) *trckd ldrs: rdn 2f out: wknd over 1f out* 14/1
0000 13 hd Indian Lady (IRE)[17] 3846 3-8-11 55 (b[1]) AmirQuinn(3) 16 46+
(Mrs A L M King) *t.k.h: hld up bhd ldrs: gng strly but nowhere to go fr 1/2-way: no ch to rcvr* 20/1
0041 14 3/4 Norcroft[3] 4267 4-9-13 69 6ex (p) MarcHalford(5) 17 58
(Mrs C A Dunnett) *w ldrs: upsides wl over 1f out: wknd sn after* 10/3[1]
4020 15 nk Chantelle's Dream[50] 2813 4-8-6 50 SophieDoyle(7) 18 38
(Ms J S Doyle) *taken down early: racd against nr side rail: led to over 1f out: wknd* 12/1
0620 16 4 Lady Algarhoud (FR)[15] 3899 4-9-4 55 AlanDaly 3 31
(M Appleby) *prom on outer tl wknd 2f out* 20/1
1m 13.34s (1.67) **Going Correction** +0.325s/f (Good)
WFA 3 from 4yo+ 4lb 16 Ran SP% 124.8
Speed ratings (Par 101):101,99,98,97,97 96,96,94,94,93 93,92,92,91,90 85
CSF £455.51 CT £15039.10 TOTE £11.10: £2.70, £13.40, £5.20, £6.10; EX 548.70.
Owner Miss Zora Fakirmohamed **Bred** Yeomanstown Stud **Trained** Exning, Suffolk
FOCUS
A modest handicap, but a very competitive event of its type and the third appears better than the bare form.
Arfinnit(IRE) Official explanation: jockey said gelding hung badly right
Indian Lady(IRE) Official explanation: jockey said filly was denied a clear run

4366 HOLLIWELL SEED & GRAIN 40TH ANNIVERSARY MAIDEN STKS 1m (P)
6:55 (6:56) (Class 5) 2-Y-O £3,238 (£963; £481; £240) Stalls High

Form RPR
55 1 Sri Pekan Two[33] 3363 2-9-3 EddieAhern 3 81
(P F I Cole) *hld up: prog to trck ldrs 1/2-way: shkn up 3f out: chsd ldr over 1f out: hanging but r.o to ld last 150yds: sn clr* 11/8[1]
5 2 1 3/4 Beverly Hill Billy[17] 3843 2-9-3 DaneO'Neill 11 77
(A King) *t.k.h: racd wd: hld up: prog over 3f out: led over 2f out and kicked 2l clr: hdd and outpcd last 150yds* 8/1
4 3 5 Laish Ya Hajar (IRE)[36] 3253 2-9-3 TedDurcan 8 65
(M R Channon) *t.k.h: cl up: led 3f out to over 2f out: sn drvn and outpcd* 3/1[2]
6 4 1 3/4 Satyricon[17] 3843 2-9-0 NelsonDeSouza(3) 6 61
(M Botti) *chsd ldrs: rdn and wl outpcd over 2f out: modest 4th fr over 1f out* 12/1
00 5 5 Hemispear[24] 3645 2-8-12 PaulFitzsimons 7 45
(Miss J R Tooth) *hld up in rr: wl outpcd fr 3f out: shkn up and kpt on one pce fr over 1f out* 100/1
6 1 3/4 Sonovishi 2-9-3 RichardMullen 10 46
(E J O'Neill) *sn drvn in rr: effrt u.p to chse ldrs over 3f out: wkng whn rn wd bnd 2f out* 16/1
0 7 7 Garrya[17] 3851 2-9-0 StephaneBreux(3) 4 30
(R Hannon) *sn outpcd in last: t.o 3f out* 66/1
55 8 3/4 Mastership (IRE)[45] 2979 2-9-3 SebSanders 2 28
(C E Brittain) *pushed up to ld and sn set gd pce: hrd rdn and hdd 3f out: wknd rapidly fnl 2f* 22/1
0 9 7 Jafaru[31] 3417 2-9-3 TPQueally 9 12
(G A Butler) *sn struggling in rr: t.o sn after 1/2-way* 20/1
03 10 5 Perfect Courtesy (IRE)[17] 3851 2-9-3 (b[1]) FergusSweeney 12 1
(P W Chapple-Hyam) *sn crossed to outside draw to press ldr: rdn and wknd rapidly over 3f out: t.o* 9/2[3]
11 nk Jeer (IRE) 2-9-3 SteveDrowne 1 —
(E A L Dunlop) *chsd ldrs for 3f: wknd rapidly 1/2-way: t.o* 20/1
1m 37.77s (-1.66) **Going Correction** -0.025s/f (Stan) 11 Ran SP% 126.3
Speed ratings (Par 94):107,105,100,98,93 91,84,84,77,72 71
CSF £14.19 TOTE £2.50: £1.30, £2.30, £1.50; EX 20.60.
Owner H R H Sultan Ahmad Shah **Bred** B Walters **Trained** Whatcombe, Oxon
FOCUS
This looked a very decent maiden and was run at a scorching pace. A very smart winning time for a race like this and the form looks sound, with the fourth running to his debut mark.
NOTEBOOK
Sri Pekan Two ◆, stepping up two furlongs in trip, was caught for a bit of speed coming down the hill but there was a lot to like about the way he put some decent rivals to the sword at the business end. He still looks inexperienced and may be capable of more. (op 2-1 tchd 5-4)
Beverly Hill Billy, a springer in the market, looked for a few strides when grabbing Laish Ya Hajar that he would reward that support. He had improved a good deal from his promising debut, and should be able to pick up a maiden without any trouble. (op 10-1 tchd 15-2)
Laish Ya Hajar(IRE) was keen to get an early position and held every chance, but the principals pulled away from him in the straight. (op 11-4)
Satyricon showed marked improvement for a step up in trip - like the winner and runner-up - and is one to bear in mind for a small race. (op 10-1)
Hemispear appeared to run her best race yet at a massive price, but she was well held and may not have achieved that much. She can now be handicapped. (op 66-1)
Perfect Courtesy(IRE) Official explanation: jockey said colt had no more to give

4367 WHIPS & TEES MEDIAN AUCTION MAIDEN STKS 1m 2f (P)
7:25 (7:26) (Class 5) 3-4-Y-O £3,238 (£963; £481; £240) Stalls Low

Form RPR
6 1 Pothos Way (GR)[32] 3387 3-9-0 NelsonDeSouza(3) 11 59
(P R Chamings) *plld hrd: w ldr: pushed into ld over 2f out: rdn over 1f out: jst hld on* 11/1
0565 2 shd Pactolos Way[24] 3650 3-9-3 53 SebSanders 1 59
(P R Chamings) *prom: rdn to chse wnr over 1f out: clsd fnl f: jst failed* 7/1
3 1 1/4 Nando's Dream 3-8-12 TPQueally 7 63+
(J Noseda) *dwlt: hld up towards rr: prog and nt clr run 2f out: green over 1f out: nt clr run fnl f: r.o nr fin: nt rcvr* 11/4[1]
6- 4 1 1/4 Dan Buoy (FR)[344] 4916 3-9-3 DaneO'Neill 12 54
(A King) *wl in tch: prog over 2f out: disp 2nd over 1f out: sn rdn and nt qckn* 3/1[2]
00- 5 shd You're My Son[351] 4727 4-9-12 FergusSweeney 10 54
(A B Haynes) *t.k.h: hld up in rr: prog on wd outside fr 3f out: chsd ldrs and hanging lft over 1f out: nt qckn* 50/1
0 6 3/4 Mookerr (IRE)[115] 1088 3-9-3 EddieAhern 2 53
(M P Tregoning) *trckd ldrs: pushed along over 3f out: rdn and flashed tail 2f out: looked reluctant over 1f out* 6/1[3]
0050 7 3 Helen Wood[14] 3932 3-8-5 43 FrankiePickard(7) 9 42
(M D I Usher) *dwlt: hld up in rr: gng wl enough 3f out: lost tch w ldng gp over 2f out: shkn up over 1f out: nvr on terms* 33/1
00 8 2 Sunley Song[30] 3451 3-8-12 RobertMiles 13 38
(B G Powell) *prom: pushed along 4f out: wknd over 2f out* 40/1
9 1 1/2 Sky Walk 3-9-3 SteveDrowne 4 40
(Jamie Poulton) *unruly stalls: hld up wl in rr: pushed along and lost tch w ldng gp over 2f out* 16/1
0 10 nk Goodenough Prince[41] 3112 3-9-0 RichardKingscote(3) 6 40
(Andrew Turnell) *wl in tch tl rdn and struggling 3f out* 20/1
06 11 1 3/4 Special Place[58] 2575 3-9-3 IanMongan 3 36
(J A R Toller) *t.k.h: led at v stdy pce: hdd over 2f out: wknd rapidly over 1f out* 10/1
0050 12 1 1/4 Go Amwell[18] 3823 3-9-3 48 StephenCarson 14 34
(J R Jenkins) *hld up in last: nvr a factor* 40/1
6550 13 shd Sky At Night (IRE)[19] 3797 3-9-3 47 (p) PatDobbs 8 34
(P Mitchell) *chsd ldrs for 4f: lost pl and struggling in rr over 4f out* 20/1
2m 9.56s (1.77) **Going Correction** -0.025s/f (Stan)
WFA 3 from 4yo 9lb 13 Ran SP% 121.1
Speed ratings (Par 103):91,90,89,88,88 88,85,84,83,82 81,80,80
CSF £80.74 TOTE £14.40: £3.90, £1.80, £1.50; EX 51.70.
Owner Mrs Alexandra J Chandris **Bred** Ippotour Stud **Trained** Baughurst, Hants
■ A 1-2 for trainer Patrick Chamings and owner Alexandra Chandris.
FOCUS
A very modest winning time for the grade, but few ever got into contention and the form looks unreliable.
Nando's Dream ◆ Official explanation: jockey said filly was denied a clear run on final bend
You're My Son Official explanation: jockey said gelding hung left
Mookerr(IRE) Official explanation: jockey said gelding ran very green
Go Amwell Official explanation: jockey said gelding hung right

4368 LINGFIELD PARK GOLF COURSE H'CAP 7f (P)
7:55 (7:58) (Class 5) (0-70,70) 3-Y-O+ £3,238 (£963; £481; £240) Stalls Low

Form RPR
30-0 1 James Street (IRE)[17] 3850 3-9-2 65 DaneO'Neill 4 74
(J R Best) *prom: chsd ldr 2f out: rdn to ld over 1f out: jst hld on* 8/1
4104 2 hd Sovereignty (JPN)[17] 3845 4-9-2 59 SebSanders 1 70
(D K Ivory) *fractious to post: trckd ldrs: effrt over 2f out: chsd wnr ent fnl f: clsng fin: jst failed* 11/2[2]
0303 3 1 1/2 Hollow Jo[17] 3845 6-9-7 64 MickyFenton 8 71
(J R Jenkins) *reluctant to enter stalls: trckd ldrs: prog 2f out: rdn to dispute 2nd ent fnl f: nt qckn* 6/1[3]
3440 4 nk Guilded Warrior[33] 3349 3-9-4 67 FergusSweeney 11 71
(W S Kittow) *hld up wl in rr: prog on wd outside wl over 1f out: r.o fnl f: nrst fin* 16/1
2030 5 nk Foreplay (IRE)[3] 4265 3-9-7 70 RichardMullen 7 73
(E A L Dunlop) *settled in midfield: effrt 2f out: rdn and r.o fnl f: nvr rchd ldrs* 12/1

4151 **6** *1 1/2* **Captain Darling (IRE)**[10] 4048 6-9-8 **65**.............................. TedDurcan 5 67
(R W Price) *mde most: kicked on 2f out: hdd over 1f out: wknd ins fnl f* **5/1**[1]

5561 **7** *nk* **What-A-Dancer (IRE)**[15] 3898 9-9-8 **68**......................(b) AmirQuinn(3) 12 69
(R A Harris) *hld up wl in rr: plenty to do 2f out: urged along and styd on fnl f: no ch* **9/1**

-255 **8** *1/2* **Antigoni (IRE)**[28] 3548 3-9-6 **69**....................................... SteveDrowne 6 66
(A M Balding) *rrd s: wl in rr: n.m.r 5f out: effrt on inner 2f out: one pce over 1f out* **7/1**

0-00 **9** *1* **Khalidia (USA)**[17] 3846 5-9-6 **63**......................................(t) EddieAhern 9 60
(M A Magnusson) *prom: chsd ldr 4f out to 2f out: wknd fnl f* **12/1**

0600 **10** *3/4* **Happy As Larry (USA)**[13] 3986 4-9-10 **67**.......................... JohnEgan 3 62
(T J Pitt) *chsd ldr for 3f: styd prom on inner tl wknd over 1f out* **7/1**

2240 **11** *1/2* **Doctor Dennis (IRE)**[131] 862 9-8-10 **60**...........(v) StevenCorrigan(7) 14 54
(J Pearce) *stdd s and dropped in fr wd draw: effrt on wd outside again 3f out: no prog fnl 2f* **20/1**

0000 **12** *1* **Western Roots**[15] 3918 5-9-8 **65**.. AlanDaly 10 56
(M Appleby) *hld up wl in rr: last 2f out: shuffled along and nvr nr ldrs after* **50/1**

0000 **13** *2* **Jonny Ebeneezer**[17] 3845 7-9-0 **60**......................(v) NelsonDeSouza(3) 2 46
(M Wellings) *taken down early: t.k.h: hld up in rr: rdn over 2f out: no prog* **20/1**

1m 25.02s (-0.87) **Going Correction** -0.025s/f (Stan)
WFA 3 from 4yo+ 6lb **13** Ran SP% **125.2**
Speed ratings (Par 103):103,102,101,100,100 98,98,97,96,95 95,94,91
CSF £53.00 CT £303.26 TOTE £9.00: £2.30, £3.30, £2.60; EX 72.70 Place 6 £207.54, Place 5 £115.57.
Owner John Mayne **Bred** Thoroughbred Trust **Trained** Hucking, Kent
■ Stewards' Enquiry : Dane O'Neill caution: used whip with excessive frequency

FOCUS
An ordinary handicap of its type though the pace was sound and the third sets the standard.
What-A-Dancer(IRE) Official explanation: jockey said gelding was slowly away
Antigoni(IRE) Official explanation: jockey said filly missed the break
T/Plt: £313.20 to a £1 stake. Pool: £48,339.65. 112.65 winning tickets. T/Qpdt: £31.00 to a £1 stake. Pool: £4,160.10. 99.30 winning tickets. JN

4333

NEWMARKET (JULY) (R-H)

Saturday, August 12

OFFICIAL GOING: Soft (good to soft in places)
Wind: Strong, behind Weather: Rain clearing

4369 THOROUGHBRED HOTELS H'CAP 2m 24y

2:05 (2:06) (Class 3) (0-90,83) 3-Y-O+ **£9,067** (£2,697; £1,348; £673) **Stalls** Centre

Form RPR

-105 **1** **Sir Monty (USA)**[10] 4036 4-9-8 **77**.................................. KerrinMcEvoy 4 86
(Mrs A J Perrett) *chsd ldrs: led over 4f out: hung lft and hdd over 1f out: rallied to ld ins fnl f: drvn out* **5/2**[1]

3110 **2** *3/4* **Mersey Sound (IRE)**[10] 4036 8-9-4 **78**.......................... MarcHalford(5) 3 86
(D R C Elsworth) *hld up: hdwy over 2f out: rdn and hung lft over 1f out: styd on ins fnl f: hmpd nr fin: nt rch wnr* **7/2**[2]

505/ **3** *1/2* **Laggan Bay (IRE)**[558] 6798 6-8-10 **65**..................................(b) JohnEgan 7 72
(J S Moore) *hld up in tch: rdn to ld over 1f out: hdd ins fnl f: styng on same pce whn edgd lft nr fin* **16/1**

/530 **4** *5* **Almah (SAF)**[10] 4036 8-9-2 **71**..(b) JoeFanning 6 72
(Miss Venetia Williams) *led: hdd over 4f out: sn rdn: styd on same pce fnl 2f* **13/2**

3060 **5** *4* **Escayola (IRE)**[15] 3888 6-9-9 **83**...................................(b) LiamJones(5) 1 80
(W J Haggas) *s.s: hld up: rdn over 5f out: n.d* **9/2**

5214 **6** *1 1/2* **Takafu (USA)**[17] 3853 4-9-7 **76**.. SteveDrowne 2 71
(W S Kittow) *chsd ldr tl rdn 4f out: wknd 2f out* **4/1**[3]

3m 31.12s (4.13) **Going Correction** +0.125s/f (Good) **6** Ran SP% **108.2**
Speed ratings (Par 107):94,93,93,90,88 88
CSF £10.52 TOTE £3.10: £1.60, £2.10; EX 10.00.
Owner Lingfield Breakfast Club **Bred** D Holt And Dana Holt **Trained** Pulborough, W Sussex

FOCUS
A fair staying race, run on very tacky ground. The winning time was modest and the form is not strong, but should prove sound.

NOTEBOOK
Sir Monty(USA), who is a decent staying handicapper on his day, battled back bravely after being headed by Laggan Bay in the last two furlongs. His courage saw him home and he could just be improving at a two-mile and further trip - although he possibly does not get home over extremes. The Cesarewitch would seem a logical race for him towards the end of the season, but there is a race here later in the month, over a mile and seven on August 25th, which could be within his scope before. (tchd 11-4 tchd 3-1 in a place)
Mersey Sound(IRE), who was caught out by the leaders quickening the modest tempo, did really well to bridge the gap to the winner in ground that looked very tacky. Behind Sir Monty last time at Goodwood, he is starting to look high in the weights, but nothing in this effort suggested he was not capable of going close next time as long as the pace is strong. One would think he may take on the winner again back here later in the month. (op 3-1)
Laggan Bay(IRE) performed really well after such a long absence, but, as is the case with all horses returning from a long layoff, whether the effort can be reproduced next time is questionable. (op 20-1)
Almah(SAF) set the early gallop before being passed by the winner over half a mile from home. There was no obvious reason why she capitulated so quickly, and was allowed to come home in her own time. (op 7-1 tchd 6-1)
Escayola(IRE) failed to get involved at any stage after starting slowly, looking far from co-operative during the race. It does seem strange that a horse that has run his best recent races with a tongue strap, does not always have one fitted. However, it should be pointed out that all of his wins have come without one - the last being back in 2004. (op 5-1)
Takafu(USA) was readily left behind when the race took shape. His jockey was not hard on him when his chance was gone. All of his worst efforts have come on ground with ease in it.

4370 SOLBERGE HALL HOTEL H'CAP 1m 2f

2:35 (2:36) (Class 3) (0-95,92) 3-Y-O+ **£9,067** (£2,697; £1,348; £673) **Stalls** Centre

Form RPR

4-22 **1** **Noble Gent (IRE)**[22] 3710 3-9-10 **92**............................... KerrinMcEvoy 5 104+
(Saeed Bin Suroor) *mde all: rdn and hung lft fr over 1f out: styd on* **13/8**[1]

2000 **2** *1* **Crime Scene (IRE)**[15] 3890 3-9-9 **91**................................ JoeFanning 6 97
(M Johnston) *chsd wnr: rdn and ev ch over 2f out: styd on u.p* **6/1**[3]

1401 **3** *1/2* **Steppe Dancer (IRE)**[22] 3710 3-9-10 **92**............................ EddieAhern 8 97
(D J Coakley) *chsd ldrs: rdn and hung lft fnl 2f: styd on* **4/1**[2]

2-40 **4** *1 1/2* **True Companion**[29] 3490 7-9-3 **76**.................................. RichardMullen 1 78
(N P Littmoden) *prom: rdn over 3f out: outpcd over 2f out: nt clr run over 1f out: no imp ins fnl f* **16/1**

1603 **5** *3* **Balanced Budget**[13] 3980 3-9-8 **90**.................................... TPQueally 4 87
(J Noseda) *hld up: hdwy over 3f out: rdn and wknd over 1f out* **6/1**[3]

2013 **6** *5* **Brief Goodbye**[16] 3876 6-9-7 **80**...................................... MickyFenton 2 68
(John Berry) *hld up: hung lft and wknd 2f out* **16/1**

51-6 **7** *5* **All The Good (IRE)**[109] 1205 3-9-0 **82**.......................... SteveDrowne 10 61
(G A Butler) *hld up: rdn and wknd over 2f out* **18/1**

1330 **8** *1 3/4* **Active Asset (IRE)**[11] 4023 4-9-11 **84**............................... TedDurcan 9 60
(M R Channon) *hld up: rdn and wknd over 2f out* **12/1**

2m 7.47s (1.03) **Going Correction** +0.125s/f (Good)
WFA 3 from 4yo+ 9lb **8** Ran SP% **111.4**
Speed ratings (Par 107):100,99,98,97,95 91,87,85
CSF £11.00 CT £31.50 TOTE £2.40: £1.10, £2.10, £1.80; EX 14.10.
Owner Godolphin **Bred** Swettenham Stud And Hugo Lascelles **Trained** Newmarket, Suffolk

FOCUS
This was the quickest time over seven furlongs on the card. It paid to be up with the pace and the first four were always about in the same position from the off. Those with held up in their in-running comments never featured. The form seems sound enough, with the winner and third progressive and the second running to earlier form.

NOTEBOOK
Noble Gent(IRE) was given an intelligent ride from the front on the prevailing ground, and just about had enough left to keep going to the line - although he possibly idled in front during the last furlong. He was fully entitled to go close on all of his previous form and could easily improve again. The ground was not a problem, but it might be that he is better suited to a quicker surface. (tchd 7-4)
Crime Scene(IRE), who was awash with sweat, had every chance and was closing in on Noble Gent in the final stages of the race, after the winner had quickened away from him at about the two-furlong marker. He was not good enough at the weights to throw down a serious challenge to the winner, but did shape as though worth a try over slightly further.
Steppe Dancer(IRE), who beat Noble Gent last time, moved nicely during the race but started to flounder when put under pressure. He did stay on well enough when getting to the far rail but all the evidence suggests he needs much better ground.
True Companion did really well to come off the pace when it was not an advantage to do so. It was a solid effort against some talented youngsters, but he still remains high enough in the weights.
Balanced Budget shaped like a horse who did not handle the going. It would be dangerous to write him off for a very moderate effort in ground he almost certainly did not like. (op 7-1)
Brief Goodbye Official explanation: trainer said gelding had been unsuited by the soft ground
All The Good(IRE) was one of a few that probably did not appreciate the underfoot conditions. (op 16-1)

4371 SWYNFORD PADDOCKS HOTEL SWEET SOLERA STKS (GROUP 3) (FILLIES) 7f

3:10 (3:10) (Class 1) 2-Y-O

£22,712 (£8,608; £4,308; £2,148; £1,076; £540) **Stalls** Low

Form RPR

1 **1** **English Ballet (IRE)**[19] 3796 2-8-12 .... MichaelHills 9 103+
(B W Hills) *s.s: hdwy over 4f out: led over 2f out: rdn over 1f out: r.o: eased nr fin* **7/2**[2]

1 **2** *1* **Princess Taise (USA)**[22] 3707 2-8-12 .... JoeFanning 7 99
(M Johnston) *chsd ldr: rdn and ev ch 2f out: styd on same pce ins fnl f* **15/8**[1]

5201 **3** *1 3/4* **Satulagi (USA)**[14] 3924 2-8-12 98... JohnEgan 8 95
(J S Moore) *hld up: hdwy over 2f out: rdn and edgd lft over 1f out: styd on same pce* **9/2**[3]

5112 **4** *2* **Precocious Star (IRE)**[16] 3874 2-8-12 93........................ PatCosgrave 3 90
(K R Burke) *chsd ldrs: rdn and nt clr run over 2f out: swtchd rt: no ex fnl f* **6/1**

211 **5** *nk* **Sans Reward (IRE)**[36] 3265 2-8-12 82............................ SteveDrowne 6 89
(B J Meehan) *prom: rdn and hung lft over 1f out: no ex* **6/1**

515 **6** *1* **Dora Explora**[16] 3874 2-8-12 90....................................... EddieAhern 4 87
(P W Chapple-Hyam) *led over 4f: wknd fnl f* **14/1**

1m 25.96s (-0.82) **Going Correction** +0.125s/f (Good) **6** Ran SP% **110.4**
Speed ratings (Par 101):109,107,105,103,103 102
CSF £10.14 TOTE £3.90: £1.90, £1.70; EX 9.20.
Owner David Reid Scott & Sangster Family **Bred** Swettenham Stud **Trained** Lambourn, Berks
■ Stewards' Enquiry : Eddie Ahern two-day ban: dropped hands and lost 5th place (Aug 26-27)

FOCUS
A fair-looking renewal of the race, with the unexposed front two looking the classiest prospects. The third, as ever, is a solid marker to the form, but the first two home have scope for improvement. The time compared favourably with the all-age handicap on the card and is very decent for the type of contest.

NOTEBOOK
English Ballet(IRE) was not the best away but came home strongly to land a prize that has produced some very good horses in recent years, Nasheej, Maids Causeway and Soviet Song amongst others. One could not fail but be impressed by the manner of success and she looks well worth her 25/1 quote for next season's 1000 Guineas in what, to date, had been an ordinary year for juvenile fillies. A strict line through the third suggests she does not have much to find with Sander Camillo, the best two-year-old filly seen so far, and it is to be hoped they will meet before the end of the season. Wherever she runs next, she is entitled to the utmost respect. (op 4-1 tchd 3-1)
Princess Taise(USA) did not quicken as well as English Ballet but, to her credit, kept on really well all the way to the line. She has the substance to keep on improving and it would be little surprise to see her make up into a nice three-year-old. However, before that, she will hold her own in some decent races at two, and could take on the winner again in the Fillies' Mile at Ascot in late September. (op 7-4 tchd 2-1)
Satulagi(USA) is an absolute credit to all concerned with her, and she ran right up to her best again. Holding a lot of top-grade entries, she has not shirked a challenge all season and will give her all wherever she runs next. (tchd 5-1)
Precocious Star(IRE) was not in any way disgraced but fell a bit short of the required class for the race. It is a shame for connections that they could not get her placed in a Group 3, and it may be that she is best at six furlongs, although seven is well within her compass. (op 5-1)
Sans Reward(IRE) was starting to stay on again when she was slightly hampered, but it would have made no difference to her chances of winning the race. She is a useful sort and stays seven well. Official explanation: jockey said filly suffered interference in running (op 9-1)
Dora Explora had her moment of glory in front but was easily brushed aside when the race took shape. Official explanation: jockey said filly was unsuited by the soft (good to soft in places) ground

4372 THE SPORTSMAN NEWSPAPER SILVER SALVER STKS (H'CAP) 7f

3:40 (3:40) (Class 2) (0-105,97) 3-Y-O+

£18,696 (£5,598; £2,799; £1,401; £699; £351) **Stalls** Low

Form RPR

5010 **1** **Paper Talk (USA)**[8] 4098 4-9-11 **95**.................................. MichaelHills 10 104
(B W Hills) *mde all: rdn clr 2f out: all out* **9/1**

0020 **2** *shd* **Compton's Eleven**[29] 3493 5-9-11 **95** TedDurcan 5 104
(M R Channon) *hld up: hdwy over 2f out: rdn to chse wnr ins fnl f: r.o* **9/1**

12-2 **3** *1* **Cross My Mind**[13] 3973 4-9-1 **85** EddieAhern 1 91
(T Keddy) *hld up: hdwy over 1f out: styng on whn n.m.r nr fin* **5/1**[2]

13-0 **4** *nk* **High Bray (GER)**[11] 4029 5-9-0 **84** JohnEgan 6 90
(D R C Elsworth) *s.s: hld up: r.o ins fnl f: nrst fin* **13/2**[3]

/000 **5** *shd* **Seulement (USA)**[21] 3733 4-9-9 **93** KerrinMcEvoy 8 98
(L M Cumani) *hld up: racd keenly: hdwy 5f out: rdn to chse wnr over 1f out: hung lft ins fnl f: styd on same pce* **5/1**[2]

0105 **6** *2* **Kindlelight Debut**[6] 4172 6-9-1 **85** RichardMullen 9 85
(N P Littmoden) *chsd ldrs: rdn over 2f out: no ex fnl f* **25/1**

6020 **7** *1 1/4* **Intrepid Jack**[7] 4128 4-9-13 **97** (v) SteveDrowne 4 94
(H Morrison) *prom: rdn over 2f out: nt clr run over 1f out: wknd ins fnl f* **4/1**[1]

3003 **8** *hd* **Binanti**[11] 4029 6-9-1 **85** JoeFanning 2 81
(P R Chamings) *prom: nt clr run and lost pl over 1f out: nvr able to chal* **11/1**

0050 **9** *1* **Cool Panic (IRE)**[77] 2012 4-9-6 **90** MickyFenton 11 84
(M L W Bell) *racd keenly: trckd ldr over 5f out tl rdn over 1f out: wknd ins fnl f* **10/1**

6030 **10** *44* **Banjo Patterson**[15] 3904 4-8-13 **83** IanMongan 3 —
(G A Huffer) *hld up: rdn and wknd over 2f out* **25/1**

1m 25.7s (-1.08) **Going Correction** +0.125s/f (Good) **10** Ran SP% **111.8**
Speed ratings (Par 109):111,110,109,109,109 107,105,105,104,53
CSF £83.46 CT £455.98 TOTE £10.60: £3.10, £3.20, £1.50; EX 106.00 Trifecta £366.50 Part won. Pool: £516.24 - 0.50 winning units..
Owner Gainsborough Stud **Bred** Gainsborough Farm Llc **Trained** Lambourn, Berks

FOCUS
A competitive handicap run at a good pace, considering the ground. The form looks sound enough overall, although the winner was trying new tactics and possibly stole the race, while the runner-up is not the easiest to win with.

NOTEBOOK
Paper Talk(USA) thoroughly deserved his success after just about making every yard of the running. However, it is not hard to argue that he nicked the race from the front - which was a new tactic - and he is going to find things very tough when reassessed. Official explanation: trainer said, regarding the improved form shown, colt was inconvenienced by his draw at Goodwood last time and could never get into the race whereas today he was able to dominate (op 10-1)
Compton's Eleven always looked as if he was going to pick up the winner inside the final furlong, but never quite got his nose in front. He is never the easiest to predict but is on a fair handicap mark at the moment. (tchd 10-1 in places)
Cross My Mind is a really consistent horse for his small yard, and was arguably a bit unlucky not to have won. He is sure to serve connections well and still has scope for some improvement, as he was unraced at two. (op 9-2)
High Bray(GER) ran much better than he did at Glorious Goodwood, which was his seasonal reappearance, and was close to something near his best of last season. That said, he will need to find some more improvement from somewhere, as he is plenty high enough in the weights on all known form. (op 6-1)
Seulement(USA) again travelled well for much of the race before finding less than looked likely when asked to quicken. He was not beaten a long way and is worth one more chance before he can be counted as being disappointing. His pedigree shouts fast ground, which makes him an interesting horse for next season if he fails to find a quicker surface or get his head in front before next summer. (op 6-1)
Intrepid Jack floundered in the ground a touch when asked to quicken and was not given a hard time by his jockey when the leaders had gone beyond recall. He has no form on an easy surface, and it is easy to excuse the effort. (op 7-2)
Binanti Official explanation: jockey said gelding was denied a clear run
Banjo Patterson Official explanation: jockey said colt was never travelling

4373 WYCK HALL STUD MAIDEN FILLIES' STKS 7f
4:15 (4:17) (Class 4) 2-Y-O £4,533 (£1,348; £674; £336) **Stalls** Low

Form RPR

5 **1** **Passage Of Time**[25] 3623 2-9-0 TedDurcan 13 86
(H R A Cecil) *chsd ldrs: led over 1f out: rdn out* **4/1**[1]

2 *hd* **Fretwork** 2-9-0 DaneO'Neill 17 86
(R Hannon) *hld up: hdwy 1/2-way: ev ch fr over 1f out: r.o* **9/1**

0 **3** *3 1/2* **Nadawat (USA)**[22] 3700 2-9-0 RHills 12 77
(J L Dunlop) *chsd ldr: rdn and ev ch over 1f out: wknd ins fnl f* **5/1**[3]

4 *1/2* **La Spezia (IRE)** 2-9-0 MickyFenton 10 76
(M L W Bell) *chsd ldrs: outpcd 2f out: r.o ins fnl f* **12/1**

00 **5** *1 1/4* **Split Briefs (IRE)**[22] 3707 2-9-0 JoeFanning 2 72
(D J Daly) *chsd ldrs: rdn over 1f out: wknd fnl f* **25/1**

6 *hd* **Malyana** 2-9-0 MatthewHenry 4 72
(M A Jarvis) *led: rdn and hdd over 1f out: wknd ins fnl f* **14/1**

7 *2* **Usk Melody** 2-9-0 TPQueally 16 67
(B J Meehan) *s.i.s: hld up: rdn and edgd lft over 2f out: nt trble ldrs* **18/1**

8 *nk* **Rosie's Glory (USA)** 2-9-0 EddieAhern 7 66
(B J Meehan) *dwlt: hld up: nvr nrr* **18/1**

9 *nk* **Feolin** 2-9-0 SteveDrowne 1 65
(H Morrison) *sn pushed along in rr: sme hdwy over 1f out: nvr trbld ldrs* **50/1**

10 *2* **Rose Of Petra (IRE)** 2-9-0 KerrinMcEvoy 9 60
(Sir Michael Stoute) *mid-div: rdn and wknd over 2f out* **12/1**

11 *1* **Orange** 2-9-0 JohnEgan 8 58
(W J Haggas) *hld up: effrt over 2f out: sn wknd* **8/1**

12 *hd* **Wateera (IRE)** 2-9-0 IanMongan 11 57
(J L Dunlop) *hld up: rdn over 2f out: a in rr* **20/1**

13 *1/2* **Indigo Rose (IRE)** 2-9-0 JimmyFortune 6 56
(J H M Gosden) *s.i.s: hld up: a in rr* **9/2**[2]

14 *5* **Memphis Marie** 2-8-7 KirstyMilczarek(7) 3 44
(C N Allen) *prom over 4f* **50/1**

15 *3 1/2* **Stringsofmyheart** 2-9-0 MichaelHills 5 35
(Sir Michael Stoute) *sn outpcd* **12/1**

1m 26.63s (-0.15) **Going Correction** +0.125s/f (Good) **15** Ran SP% **128.8**
Speed ratings (Par 93):105,104,100,100,98 98,96,95,95,93 92,91,91,85,81
CSF £41.45 TOTE £4.80: £2.20, £3.80, £2.40; EX 62.70.Aaron's Way was withdrawn. Price at time of withdrawal 66/1. Rule 4 does not apply.
Owner K Abdulla **Bred** Juddmonte Farms Ltd **Trained** Newmarket, Suffolk

FOCUS
Probably just an ordinary fillies' maiden but the time was decent, just 0.67 seconds slower than the Sweet Solera. Winners are likely to come from the race, but there were no obvious stars on show, and most will be better over middle-distances next season.

NOTEBOOK
Passage Of Time, who in hindsight ran in an above-average maiden on her debut, put her experience to good use, staying on stoutly to the line under maximum pressure. She has physical scope for improvement and can build on her success if kept to a realistic level. (op 5-1)
Fretwork ◆ made Passage Of Time fight all the way to the line, showing a splendid attitude in the process. A similar maiden should be a formality for her, as long as a strong gallop is assured, and she could make up into a fair middle-distance performer next season. (op 12-1)
Nadawat(USA), who was well supported for her debut at Newbury before becoming upset in the stalls, improved for her initial run and should find a race before the end of the season. She did not fully convince she saw the seventh furlong out, and would be susceptible to a stronger stayer over the trip. (op 4-1)
La Spezia(IRE) caught the eye in no uncertain terms and relished the uphill finish. She is bred to stay and is likely to be very effective over ten furlongs plus next season.
Split Briefs(IRE) is progressing with racing and would be very interesting if tried in handicap company next time.
Malyana ran a fine race on this debut and can be reasonably expected to improve for the run. She is well-related and holds a Group 1 entry, so presumably she will be capable of more in time. (op 16-1)
Usk Melody kept on steadily from the rear, shaping with some promise after racing green. She holds an entry in the Group 1 Moyglare Stud Stakes, so must have been showing something at home, but middle distances are likely to show her in a good light next season. (op 16-1)
Rosie's Glory(USA) is bred for fast ground and would have not enjoyed the underfoot conditions. She is worth a look if tried on a quicker surface next time, as she was far from disgraced. (op 25-1)
Feolin did not run quite as badly as her finishing position suggested, but gave the impression she may need more time.
Rose Of Petra(IRE) ran a very ordinary race and is not an obvious candidate to go close next time.
Indigo Rose(IRE) failed to get involved after being away slowly. She is almost certainly much better than she showed. (op 5-1)

4374 JOIN THE RACING UK CLUB MAIDEN STKS 1m 4f
4:50 (4:50) (Class 5) 3-Y-O+ £5,181 (£1,541; £770; £384) **Stalls** Centre

Form RPR

35 **1** **Well Hidden**[37] 3225 3-8-10 KerrinMcEvoy 3 88+
(Sir Michael Stoute) *mde virtually all: rdn out* **7/1**

2623 **2** *4* **Nimra (USA)**[41] 3122 3-8-10 79 SteveDrowne 4 82
(G A Butler) *a.p: chsd wnr over 3f out: rdn over 1f out: edgd lft and styd on same pce* **8/1**

4 **3** *10* **Shahmina (IRE)**[14] 3946 3-8-10 JimmyFortune 1 68
(J H M Gosden) *hld up in tch: rdn over 3f out: wknd 2f out* **7/2**[2]

-425 **4** *1/2* **Gordonsville**[10] 4039 3-9-1 83 TedDurcan 6 72
(A M Balding) *dwlt: sn chsng ldrs: rdn over 2f out: wknd over 1f out* **7/4**[1]

53-6 **5** *5* **Art Investor**[15] 3901 3-9-1 78 JohnEgan 7 65
(D R C Elsworth) *hld up: hdwy over 4f out: rdn and wknd over 1f out* **9/1**

6 *20* **Sunset Boulevard (IRE)** 3-9-1 TPQueally 5 37
(J Noseda) *s.i.s: hld up: rdn and wknd over 3f out* **16/1**

4 **7** *33* **Last Warrior**[41] 3122 3-9-1 RHills 2 —
(J H M Gosden) *chsd wnr tl rdn and wknd over 3f out* **11/2**[3]

2m 33.35s (0.44) **Going Correction** +0.125s/f (Good) **7** Ran SP% **113.5**
Speed ratings (Par 103):103,100,93,93,90 76,54
CSF £58.77 TOTE £6.10: £3.00, £3.60; EX 58.60.
Owner The Queen **Bred** The Queen **Trained** Newmarket, Suffolk

FOCUS
A modest maiden, rated at face value, but the winner could be alright. Plenty of the runners ran badly and were beaten too far for it to be their true running.
Last Warrior Official explanation: jockey said colt lost its action; vet said colt was distressed

4375 EUROPEAN BREEDERS FUND FILLIES' H'CAP 1m
5:20 (5:20) (Class 4) (0-80,80) 3-Y-O+ £6,477 (£1,927; £963; £481) **Stalls** Low

Form RPR

0-05 **1** **Ginger Spice (IRE)**[23] 3687 4-9-7 **71** LiamJones(5) 3 79
(W J Haggas) *mde all: rdn and edgd rt over 2f out: styd on* **7/1**

2-1 **2** *3/4* **Dash To The Front**[32] 3387 3-10-0 **80** OscarUrbina 4 86+
(J R Fanshawe) *hld up: rdn over 2f out: hdwy over 1f out: sn chsng wnr: styd on* **9/4**[2]

2312 **3** *1 3/4* **Usk Poppy**[28] 3548 3-9-11 **77** JohnEgan 2 79
(D R C Elsworth) *hld up: rdn over 2f out: styd on fnl f: nt rch ldrs* **2/1**[1]

4202 **4** *nk* **Panic Stations**[14] 3947 3-8-8 **60** MickyFenton 1 61
(M L W Bell) *chsd ldrs: rdn over 2f out: no ex ins fnl f* **6/1**[3]

-303 **5** *hd* **Materialize (USA)**[30] 3451 3-9-6 **72** RHills 8 73
(H R A Cecil) *chsd wnr: rdn over 1f out: styd on same pce* **10/1**

0-04 **6** *10* **Goodwood March**[21] 3742 3-9-0 **66** JoeFanning 5 44
(J L Dunlop) *hld up: plld hrd: hdwy 1/2-way: hung rt and wknd over 1f out* **8/1**

1m 40.31s (-0.12) **Going Correction** +0.125s/f (Good)
WFA 3 from 4yo 7lb **6** Ran SP% **111.1**
Speed ratings (Par 102):105,104,102,102,102 92
CSF £22.65 CT £41.24 TOTE £8.90: £3.30, £1.80; EX 25.20 Place 6 £114.36, Place 5 £73.57.
Owner B Trew/R Shead/D Scott/W Haggas **Bred** Ballymacoll Stud Farm Ltd **Trained** Newmarket, Suffolk

FOCUS
An ordinary handicap won by a horse who had tasted success in soft ground - none of the others had - and may have stole it from the front. The winner may follow up in similar ground, while the runner-up has more scope for improvement. Panic Stations is only rated 60 and was not beaten very far by horses with marks of 71 and above, making the form a bit dubious.
Goodwood March Official explanation: jockey said filly hung badly right
T/Plt: £61.40 to a £1 stake. Pool: £81,219.60. 964.30 winning tickets. T/Qpdt: £31.60 to a £1 stake. Pool: £3,566.40. 83.50 winning tickets. CR

3758 REDCAR (L-H)
Saturday, August 12

OFFICIAL GOING: Good to firm
Wind: Strong, against

4376 COMMUNITY UNION FOR SAFER BETTING SHOPS (S) STKS 6f
1:50 (1:51) (Class 6) 2-Y-O £2,730 (£806; £403) **Stalls** Centre

Form RPR

2424 **1** **Fractured Foxy**[19] 3787 2-8-6 65 GrahamGibbons 1 59
(J J Quinn) *hld up in tch: hdwy on outer 2f out: rdn and edgd rt ins last: styd on to ld last 100 yds* **9/4**[2]

00 **2** *hd* **Grazie Mille**[15] 3908 2-8-6 DavidAllan 2 59
(T D Easterby) *rr and pushed along after 2f out: swtchd rt and hdwy over 2f out: rdn to appr last: hdd and no ex last 100 yds* **33/1**

6 **3** *2* **Birdie Birdie**[19] 3787 2-8-6 TonyHamilton 7 53
(R A Fahey) *dwlt: hdwy 1/2-way: rdn to chse ldrs wl over 1f out: drvn and kpt on fnl f* **11/2**[3]

000 **4** *1 1/2* **Rue Soleil**[20] 3758 2-8-2 45 ow1 .... MichaelJStainton(5) 11 49
(J R Weymes) *trckd ldrs: effrt 2f out: pushed along whn stmbld bdly wl over 1f out: sn rdn: styd on ins last: nrst fin* **33/1**

0300 **5** *1/2* **Abdu**[15] 3917 2-8-11 50 .... DaleGibson 6 52
(M W Easterby) *hld up towards rr: hdwy over 2f out: rdn over 1f out: kpt on ins last: nrst fin* **33/1**

5350 **6** *3/4* **Flamestone**[25] 3619 2-8-11 61 .... (b[1]) ChrisCatlin 10 49
(J D Bethell) *chsd ldrs: rdn along over 2f out: kpt on same pce* **8/1**

5265 **7** *3/4* **Burlington Fayr (IRE)**[8] 4115 2-8-6 52 .... KimTinkler 12 42
(N Tinkler) *dwlt: sn prom: rdn along over 2f out and gradually wknd* **8/1**

06 **8** *nk* **Ellies Faith**[39] 3174 2-8-1 ow2 .... SuzzanneFrance(7) 3 43
(N Bycroft) *led: pushed along and hdd 1/2-way: sn rdn and wknd fnl 2f* **50/1**

000 **9** *hd* **Lost Inheritance**[11] 4017 2-8-1 .... RoryMoore(5) 9 41
(P T Midgley) *chsd ldrs: rdn along over 2f out: swtchd lft wl over 1f out: sn no imp* **40/1**

1122 **10** *4* **Granny Peel (IRE)**[19] 3787 2-8-12 67 .... DO'Donohoe 14 35+
(K A Ryan) *prom: led 1/2-way: rdn and hung lft wl over 1f out: hdd appr last and sn wknd: fin lame* **2/1**[1]

0000 **11** *1 1/4* **Rose Court**[25] 3619 2-8-6 47 .... PaulFessey 4 25
(K G Reveley) *bhd fr 1/2-way* **25/1**

0455 **12** *3/4* **Wakeys Wizzard**[17] 3831 2-8-4 47 ow1 .... JasonEdmunds(3) 13 24
(M E Sowersby) *cl up: rdn along 1/2-way: hung bdly lft over 2f out and sn wknd* **33/1**

13 *2 1/2* **Heidi Hi** 2-8-6 .... FrankieMcDonald 15 15
(J R Turner) *s.i.s: a bhd* **50/1**

1m 15.64s (3.94) **Going Correction** +0.40s/f (Good) **13** Ran SP% **123.7**
Speed ratings (Par 92):89,88,86,84,83 82,81,81,80,75 73,72,69
CSF £86.70 TOTE £3.90: £1.80, £6.20, £2.20; EX 83.80.There was no bid for the winner. Granny Peel was claimed by Mel Brittain for £6,000. Grazie Mille was claimed by Roy Brotherton for £6,000.
Owner Mrs E Wright **Bred** Bearstone Stud **Trained** Settrington, N Yorks

FOCUS
A competitive enough seller with favourite Granny Peel finishing lame and the form is about standard for the grade.

NOTEBOOK
Fractured Foxy, who failed to capitalise on the drop into claiming company at Beverley last time, seemed well suited by the step up to six furlongs was not winning out of turn. Although of limited ability, hence why she is running in this grade, she has a good attitude and may have more to offer at this distance. (op 5-2)
Grazie Mille, dropped into a seller for the first time, was struggling in rear from an early stage, but picked up strongly inside the final quarter mile and was just run out of it close home. She should win something similar.
Birdie Birdie, too green to do herself justice on her debut, was helped by the step up to six furlongs and, although unable to get in a telling blow at the first two, she showed enough to suggest she can win a similar race. (op 6-1 tchd 7-1)
Rue Soleil, who had previously shown little, was the eyecatcher, staying on well and looking likely to challenge for a place when stumbling badly over a furlong. There may be a little race in her. (op 50-1)
Abdu ran one of his better races and can find a race at this sort of level, possibly at seven furlongs. (op 28-1)
Granny Peel(IRE) has had a brilliant season, winning four times, but she failed to run her race on this occasion and was reported to be lame. She was still claimed after the race, and can bounce back from this. Official explanation: vet said filly was lame on left fore (op 15-8 tchd 9-4)
Wakeys Wizzard Official explanation: jockey said filly lost its action

4377 DURHAM CIU NURSERY 6f
2:20 (2:20) (Class 3) 2-Y-O **£9,715** (£2,890; £1,444; £721) **Stalls** Centre

Form RPR

051 **1** **Stevie Gee (IRE)**[12] 3994 2-9-7 **85** .... TPO'Shea 2 93+
(G A Swinbank) *trckd ldrs gng wl: smooth hdwy 2f out: led over 1f out: rdn clr ins last* **4/1**[2]

2613 **2** *1 3/4* **Voodoo Moon**[17] 3837 2-8-11 **80** .... GregFairley(5) 4 81
(M Johnston) *led: rdn along 2f out: drvn and hdd over 1f out: kpt on u.p* **6/1**

0414 **3** *nk* **Valley Of The Moon (IRE)**[28] 3555 2-8-10 **74** .... DaleGibson 1 74
(R A Fahey) *in tch on outer: pushed along and sltly outpcd 2f out: sn rdn and styd on u.p ins last: nrst fin* **8/1**

2142 **4** *1/2* **Rainbow Fox**[6] 4170 2-9-0 **78** .... TonyHamilton 8 77
(R A Fahey) *trckd ldrs: effrt 2f out: sn rdn and ev ch tl edgd rt over 1f out and kpt on same pce* **6/1**

333 **5** *1 1/2* **Karma Llama (IRE)**[20] 3758 2-8-10 **74** .... PaulEddery 6 68
(B Smart) *dwlt: hdwy over 2f out: nt clr run and swtchd lft over 1f out: sn rdn and kpt on same pce* **14/1**

2156 **6** *1/2* **Bollin Franny**[9] 4088 2-8-8 **72** .... DavidAllan 9 65
(T D Easterby) *trckd ldrs: hdwy on outer to chal 2f out and ev ch tl rdn: edgd lft and wknd over 1f out* **11/1**

0344 **7** *hd* **Sister Etienne (IRE)**[9] 4088 2-8-3 **67** .... PaulFessey 3 59
(T D Barron) *cl up: rdn along 2f out: grad wknd* **16/1**

003 **8** *4* **Blackwater Stream (IRE)**[16] 3872 2-8-6 **70** .... AdrianTNicholls 7 50
(Mrs P N Dutfield) *dwlt: hdwy on wd outside over 2f out: rdn to chse ldrs wl over 1f out: sn wknd* **5/1**[3]

01 **9** *1* **Bateleur**[16] 3860 2-8-12 **76** .... ChrisCatlin 5 53
(M R Channon) *chsd ldrs: rdn along over 2f out: sn wknd* **7/2**[1]

1m 14.35s (2.65) **Going Correction** +0.40s/f (Good) **9** Ran SP% **119.5**
Speed ratings (Par 98):98,95,95,94,92 91,91,86,85
CSF £29.38 CT £186.86 TOTE £4.00: £2.40, £2.30, £2.20; EX 19.60.
Owner Steve Gray **Bred** Irish National Stud **Trained** Melsonby, N Yorks

FOCUS
A good nursery won quite tidily by the progressive Stevie Gee and the form looks solid, with the placed horses setting the standard.

NOTEBOOK
Stevie Gee(IRE), who was confidently ridden from off the pace, came there still on the bridle over a furlong out and he was ridden clear inside the last to score in decisive style. His previous success, when well backed at Southwell, was over five furlongs, and this step up to six proved no problem to this pacey horse. He should be kept on the right side and looks well worth his place in a nursery at the better tracks. (op 9-2 tchd 7-2)
Voodoo Moon, easy winner of her maiden at Ayr last month, has now run well on both starts in nurseries and, having taken them along from the front, she fought off all bar the cosy winner. She is going to stay further and is one to watch out for upped to seven furlongs. (op 13-2)
Valley Of The Moon(IRE) appreciated the extra furlong and was going on well close home, herself looking as though seven furlongs could bring about a fair bit of improvement. (op 7-1 tchd 9-1)
Rainbow Fox, a keen-going sort, saw his race out well enough but lacked a turn of foot when it mattered. He may continue to struggle off this sort of mark. (op 8-1)
Karma Llama(IRE), who was a bit sluggish coming out of the stalls, had to switch to make her challenge, and she lacked the speed to pose a threat over this distance. (op 10-1)
Bollin Franny, stepped up a furlong, could not make his presence felt when the race began in earnest and may require a drop in class. (op 14-1)
Bateleur, a recent maiden winner at Bath, looked to hold a favourite's chance, but he ran too bad to be true and dropped right out in the final furlong or so. (op 9-2)

4378 TRANSMORE VAN HIRE LTD H'CAP 7f
2:50 (2:51) (Class 4) (0-80,80) 3-Y-O+ **£6,477** (£1,927; £963; £481) **Stalls** Centre

Form RPR

0000 **1** **Traytonic**[8] 4101 5-9-8 **80** .... MichaelJStainton(5) 11 95
(D Nicholls) *hld up: hdwy 2f out: rdn to ld appr last: kpt on wl* **9/1**[3]

-131 **2** *3/4* **Carnivore**[3] 4253 4-9-0 **67** 6ex .... PaulFessey 7 81+
(T D Barron) *trckd ldrs: hdwy 2f out: swed lft wl over 1f out: sn rdn and chsd wnr ins last: kpt on* **2/1**[1]

4004 **3** *3* **Ryedale Ovation (IRE)**[8] 4119 3-9-1 **74** .... DavidAllan 14 80
(T D Easterby) *rr and pushed along 1/2-way: hdwy 2f out: sn rdn and kpt on ins last: nrst fin* **16/1**

3660 **4** *3/4* **Efidium**[7] 4154 8-8-10 **63** .... (b) ChrisCatlin 6 67
(N Bycroft) *hld up in rr: swtchd lft and gd hdwy on outer 2f out: sn rdn and kpt on appr last: nrst fin* **25/1**

1062 **5** *nk* **Sake (IRE)**[8] 4114 4-9-8 **75** .... KimTinkler 12 78
(N Tinkler) *cl up: rdn and ev ch 2f out: drvn and one pce appr last* **12/1**

3050 **6** *3/4* **Looks Could Kill (USA)**[14] 3928 4-9-13 **80** .... AdrianTNicholls 13 81
(E J Alston) *hld up towards rr: gd hdwy 2f out: rdn over 1f out: kpt on ins last: nrst fin* **18/1**

1241 **7** *nk* **Confide (IRE)**[18] 3813 4-9-2 **69** .... TPO'Shea 5 69
(G A Swinbank) *hld up: hdwy over 2f out: nt clr run wl over 1f out: swtchd lft and sn rdn: no imp* **5/1**[2]

2135 **8** *nk* **Yorkshire Blue**[14] 3936 7-9-11 **78** .... PhillipMakin 2 77
(J S Goldie) *midfield: hdwy over 2f out: in tch over 1f out: sn rdn and btn* **10/1**

3035 **9** *hd* **Suits Me**[16] 3883 3-8-10 **69** .... PaulEddery 17 68
(J J Quinn) *hld up towards rr: gd hdwy on wd outside wl over 2f out: rdn over 1f out: no imp ent last* **20/1**

2000 **10** *2* **Tanforan**[6] 4172 4-9-6 **80** .... JamesReveley(7) 10 74
(K G Reveley) *led: rdn along over 2f out: drvn and hdd over 1f out: sn wknd* **40/1**

2016 **11** *2* **Bold Argument (IRE)**[19] 3795 3-8-11 **73** .... BenSwarbrick(3) 9 62
(Mrs P N Dutfield) *chsd ldrs: rdn along over 2f out: grad wknd* **25/1**

0-40 **12** *3/4* **Keyaki (IRE)**[37] 3229 5-9-7 **74** .... GeorgeBaker 16 61
(C F Wall) *nvr nr ldrs* **12/1**

6400 **13** *1/2* **Dudley Docker (IRE)**[8] 4116 4-8-2 **62** .... KellyHarrison(7) 1 47
(D Carroll) *in tch: rdn along over 2f out: sn wknd* **33/1**

-056 **14** *1/2* **Millfield (IRE)**[26] 3584 3-9-0 **73** .... TonyHamilton 8 57
(J Howard Johnson) *prom: rdn along and wkng whn n.m.r wl over 1f out* **25/1**

4512 **15** *3* **Cross The Line (IRE)**[10] 4047 4-9-11 **78** .... FrankieMcDonald 3 54
(A P Jarvis) *chsd ldrs: rdn along over 2f out: sn wknd* **10/1**

-063 **16** *2* **Categorical**[77] 2033 3-9-4 **77** .... DO'Donohoe 15 48
(K G Reveley) *in tch: rdn along over 2f out: sn wknd* **22/1**

1m 25.92s (1.02) **Going Correction** +0.40s/f (Good)
WFA 3 from 4yo+ 6lb **16** Ran SP% **130.7**
Speed ratings (Par 105):110,109,105,104,104 103,103,102,102,100 98,97,96,96,92 90
CSF £26.72 CT £325.12 TOTE £10.20: £2.40, £1.30, £3.80, £4.10; EX 45.60.
Owner Clipper Group Holdings **Bred** Col J L Parkes **Trained** Sessay, N Yorks

FOCUS
A competitive handicap, run in a fair time, and above average form for the grade.
Chicken Soup Official explanation: jockey said gelding suffered interference shortly after start

4379 JOHN SMITH'S REDCAR STRAIGHT-MILE CHAMPIONSHIP H'CAP (QUALIFIER) 1m
3:25 (3:27) (Class 3) (0-90,90) 3-Y-O+ **£9,715** (£2,890; £1,444; £721) **Stalls** Centre

Form RPR

5023 **1** **Baileborough (IRE)**[9] 4087 7-8-9 **73** .... GregFairley(5) 6 85
(B Ellison) *trckd ldrs: effrt wl over 1f out: rdn ent last: qcknd to ld last 100 yds* **8/1**[3]

6500 **2** *3/4* **Freeloader (IRE)**[45] 2974 6-9-1 **74** .... TonyHamilton 2 84
(R A Fahey) *prom: ld over 1f out: shkn up wl ins last: hdd and nt qckn last 100 yds* **5/1**[1]

3460 **3** *1* **Red Romeo**[13] 3986 5-9-7 **80** .... DaleGibson 5 88
(G A Swinbank) *in tch: hdwy wl over 1f out: rdn ent last and kpt on* **8/1**[3]

1100 **4** *3/4* **Kaymich Perfecto**[18] 3812 6-8-11 **75** .... MichaelJStainton(5) 4 81
(R M Whitaker) *hld up in rr: hdwy on outer wl over 1f out: rdn and kpt on same pce ins last* **14/1**

252 **5** *hd* **Middlemarch (IRE)**[9] 4068 6-8-10 **69** .... (p) PhillipMakin 3 75
(J S Goldie) *hld up in rr: hdwy wl over 1f out: sn rdn and kpt on ins last: nrst fin* **5/1**[1]

1630 **6** *1 3/4* **Royal Dignitary (USA)**[14] 3928 6-9-9 **82** .... AdrianTNicholls 9 84
(D Nicholls) *set stdy pce: qcknd over 2f out: sn rdn and hdd over 1f out: wknd ent last* **14/1**

0433 **7** *1/2* **South Cape**[13] 3978 3-9-10 **90** .... ChrisCatlin 10 91
(M R Channon) *trckd ldrs: rdn along over 2f out: grad wknd* **8/1**[3]

2356 **8** *2* **Spring Goddess (IRE)**[42] 3088 5-9-6 **79** .... FrankieMcDonald 12 75
(A P Jarvis) *in tch: effrt over 2f out: sn rdn and gradually wknd* **20/1**

1-01 **9** *1 1/2* **Ninth House (USA)**[10] 4047 4-9-12 **85** .... (t) VinceSlattery 1 78
(D J Daly) *hld up: a towards rr* **14/1**

0100 **10** *2* **Along The Nile**[14] 3937 4-9-6 **79** .... (t) DavidAllan 7 67+
(K G Reveley) *prom: effrt and ch 2f out: sn rdn and wknd over 1f out* **6/1**[2]

0600 **11** *3* **Fiefdom (IRE)**[6] 4172 4-9-9 **85** .... (b) PatrickMathers(3) 11 66
(I W McInnes) *prom: rdn along wl over 2f out: sn wknd* **25/1**

1m 40.58s (2.78) **Going Correction** +0.40s/f (Good)
WFA 3 from 4yo+ 7lb **11** Ran SP% **109.6**
Speed ratings (Par 107):102,101,100,99,99 97,97,95,93,91 88
CSF £38.65 CT £214.35 TOTE £10.30: £2.20, £2.00, £4.10; EX 67.50.Jubilee Street was withdrawn. Price at time of withdrawal 11/2. Rule 4 applies to all bets - deduction 15p in the pound.
Owner Naughty Diesel Ltd **Bred** Churchtown Stud **Trained** Norton, N Yorks
■ Jubilee Street (11/2, upset in stalls) was withdrawn. R4 applies, deduct 15p in the £.

FOCUS
A fair, competitive handicap likely to produce the odd winner.

NOTEBOOK
Baileborough(IRE), who has been frustrating this season, bounced back here and got on top close home. He has worn headgear in the past, but it was left off on this occasion and trainer Brian Ellison also revealed that the horse has benefited from being treated for a back problem. Now that he has got his head in front again, he may be able to build on this and score again. (tchd 9-1)
Freeloader(IRE), who came in for support, was produced to win his race, but the winner then got first run on him and he was unable to fight back in time. His turn will come. (op 11-2 tchd 6-1)

Red Romeo seemed suited by this step back up to a mile and ran well in third. He is on a fair enough mark and his in-form yard can get another win out of him sooner rather than later. (op 10-1 tchd 15-2)
Kaymich Perfecto has been a bit below his best off this sort of mark the last twice, but this was better and he was going on well close home. He may need some assistance from the Handicapper before being ready to win again however.
Middlemarch(IRE) ran well on this drop in distance and, as was to be expected, he was doing his best work late. He has not won since his three-year-old days with Aidan O'Brien and, although on a decent mark, he remains hard to win with. (op 6-1)
Spring Goddess(IRE) Official explanation: jockey said mare was denied a clear run
Along The Nile Official explanation: jockey said gelding lost its action

4380 SAM HALL MEMORIAL H'CAP — 1m 6f 19y
4:00 (4:01) (Class 6) (0-60,57) 3-Y-0+ — **£2,590** (£770; £385; £192) **Stalls** Low

Form				RPR
2-62	**1**		**Master Nimbus**[14] 3941 6-9-3 **46** .... GrahamGibbons 14 (J J Quinn) *trckd ldrs gng wl: smooth hdwy to ld wl over 1f out: rdn and edgd lft ent last: drvn and jst hld on* **8/1**	52
/20-	**2**	*shd*	**Danebank (IRE)**[16] 4122 6-9-6 **54** .... (p) GregFairley(5) 4 (J Mackie) *hld up in tch: hdwy 3f out: rdn over 1f out: drvn and styd on strly ins last: jst failed* **20/1**	60
0300	**3**	*½*	**Saluscraggie**[9] 4072 4-9-3 **46** .... DavidAllan 2 (K G Reveley) *in tch: hdwy 3f out: rdn along 2f out: styd on u.p ins last: nrst fin* **14/1**	51
0-05	**4**	*nk*	**Sun King**[21] 3022 9-9-1 **51** .... (t) JamesReveley(7) 9 (K G Reveley) *hld up: hdwy on outer 3f out: rdn wl over 1f out: styd on ins last: nrst fin* **10/1**	56
0002	**5**	*hd*	**Jadeeron**[12] 4011 7-9-0 **43** .... (p) ChrisCatlin 10 (Miss D A McHale) *hld up towards rr: pushed along 3f out: rdn over 2f out: swtchd rt and hdwy over 1f out: styd on strly ins last* **9/1**	47
0006	**6**	*½*	**Silver Mont (IRE)**[8] 4111 3-8-7 **49** .... (v) TPO'Shea 6 (Mrs A Duffield) *in tch on inner: hdwy 3f out: rdn along wl over 1f out: kpt on ins last* **20/1**	53
5413	**7**	*½*	**Hugs Destiny (IRE)**[9] 4072 5-9-10 **53** .... TonyHamilton 1 (M A Barnes) *prom: rdn along over 2f out: drvn and wknd over 1f out* **13/2**[3]	56
5045	**8**	*¾*	**Three Boars**[23] 3680 4-9-0 **50** .... (b) AshleyHamblett(7) 8 (S Gollings) *bhd tl styd on fnl 2f: nrst fin* **50/1**	52
-000	**9**	*hd*	**William Tell (IRE)**[75] 1562 4-9-9 **57** .... MichaelJStainton(5) 15 (Micky Hammond) *hld up towards rr: hdwy on outer wl over 2f out: rdn wl over 1f out: kpt on same pce ins last* **66/1**	59
0005	**10**	*nk*	**Sa Nau**[16] 3870 3-8-4 **46** .... FrankieMcDonald 5 (T Keddy) *hld up in rr: hdwy on inner over 2f out: rdn along over 1f out: no imp* **40/1**	47
0/45	**11**	*shd*	**Dear Sir (IRE)**[15] 3896 6-8-12 **44** .... BenSwarbrick(3) 7 (Mrs P N Dutfield) *towards rr: hdwy on outer 3f out: rdn along 2f out and kpt on same pce* **33/1**	45
2124	**12**	*hd*	**Sudden Impulse**[5] 4205 5-9-5 **48** .... DO'Donohoe 13 (A D Brown) *trckd ldr: hdwy to ld wl over 2f out: sn rdn: hdd wl over 1f out: sn drvn and wknd* **7/2**[1]	49
6002	**13**	*nk*	**Best Port (IRE)**[20] 3763 10-9-5 **53** .... RoryMoore(5) 3 (J Parkes) *hld up: hdwy 3f out: rdn to chse ldrs wl over 1f out: kpt on same pce fnl f* **6/1**[2]	53
0-00	**14**	*1 ¼*	**Michaels Dream (IRE)**[9] 4086 7-8-11 **40** .... (b) VHalliday 16 (N Wilson) *trckd ldrs: effrt 3f out: sn rdn along and wknd fnl 2f* **28/1**	39
00-3	**15**	*¾*	**Comical Errors (USA)**[17] 3836 4-9-3 **46** .... (p) AdrianTNicholls 12 (P C Haslam) *a towards rr* **25/1**	44
2522	**16**	*¾*	**Vice Admiral**[8] 4111 3-8-13 **55** .... DaleGibson 11 (M W Easterby) *led: rdn along over 3f out: hdd wl over 2f out and grad wknd fnl 2f* **13/2**[3]	51

3m 11.62s (6.60) **Going Correction** +0.40s/f (Good)
WFA 3 from 4yo+ 13lb — **16** Ran SP% **125.7**
Speed ratings (Par 101):97,96,96,96,96 96,95,95,95,95 95,94,94,94,93 93
CSF £166.77 CT £2232.04 TOTE £12.70: £3.20, £3.30, £3.00, £2.40; EX 283.90.
Owner J H Hewitt **Bred** A H Bennett **Trained** Settrington, N Yorks
■ Stewards' Enquiry : Chris Catlin caution: used whip without giving gelding time to respond

FOCUS
A low-grade staying handicap run at a modest early pace and the form looks weak.
Sa Nau Official explanation: jockey said gelding was denied a clear run

4381 CELEBRATING MO MOWLAM CLAIMING STKS — 1m 1f
4:35 (4:36) (Class 6) 4-Y-0+ — **£2,730** (£806; £403) **Stalls** Low

Form				RPR
6300	**1**		**Everest (IRE)**[14] 3928 9-9-6 79 .... GregFairley(5) 10 (B Ellison) *hld up towards rr: stdy hdwy on outer 3f out: rdn to ld over 1f out: styd on* **5/2**[1]	78
0211	**2**	*1*	**Baby Barry**[9] 4087 9-8-5 56 .... TonyHamilton 9 (R A Fahey) *trckd ldng pair: hdwy to ld 2f out: rdn and hdd over 1f out kpt on u.p ins last* **11/4**[2]	56
4351	**3**	*¾*	**Apache Point (IRE)**[20] 3762 9-8-11 59 .... KimTinkler 2 (N Tinkler) *trckd ldrs on inner: hdwy 3f out: rdn and n.m.r 2f out: sn swtchd rt and drvn: kpt on ins last* **10/3**[3]	66+
4603	**4**	*¾*	**Rudaki**[14] 3944 4-8-6 49 .... JasonEdmunds(3) 8 (M E Sowersby) *hld up in tch: hdwy 3f out: rdn to chse ldrs wl over 1f out: drvn and edgd lft ent last: kpt on* **16/1**	57
2000	**5**	*1 ½*	**Cardinal Venture (IRE)**[42] 3068 8-9-12 82 .... DO'Donohoe 3 (K A Ryan) *led: rdn along 3f out: hdd 2f out: wkng whn n.m.r ent last* **7/1**	71
0003	**6**	*3*	**Muscari**[9] 4077 4-9-0 63 .... FrankieMcDonald 4 (A P Jarvis) *in tch: rdn along 3f out: sn drvn and wknd over 2f out* **8/1**	53
0000	**7**	*1 ¾*	**Aqua**[21] 3749 4-8-0 36 ow3 .... RoryMoore(5) 11 (P T Midgley) *in tch: effrt and hdwy on outer 3f out: rdn over 2f out and sn btn* **80/1**	41
-005	**8**	*nk*	**Filey Buoy**[36] 3240 4-8-6 38 .... MichaelJStainton(5) 7 (R M Whitaker) *cl up: rdn along 3f out: sn wknd* **25/1**	46
622-	**9**	*3 ½*	**Time Marches On**[212] 3180 8-8-12 46 .... JamesReveley(7) 1 (K G Reveley) *hld up: a rr* **20/1**	47
0/60	**10**	*dist*	**Villa Chigi (IRE)**[32] 3384 4-8-9 36 .... (p) GylesParkin 6 (G R Oldroyd) *a rr: wl bhd fnl 3f* **100/1**	—

1m 54.95s (1.55) **Going Correction** +0.40s/f (Good) — **10** Ran SP% **118.6**
Speed ratings (Par 101):109,108,107,106,105 102,101,100,97,—
CSF £9.50 TOTE £3.50: £1.70, £1.50, £1.50; EX 11.20.Baby Barry was claimed by Michael Attwater for £5,000.
Owner Black and White Diamond Partnership **Bred** Sir Eric Parker **Trained** Norton, N Yorks

FOCUS
A modest claimer in which few could be fancied and, although pretty sound, the fourth and eighth limit the form.
Villa Chigi(IRE) Official explanation: jockey said gelding hung right-handed throughout

4382 FREECLAIM IDC MEDIAN AUCTION MAIDEN STKS — 1m 1f
5:05 (5:07) (Class 5) 3-4-Y-0 — **£3,238** (£963; £481; £240) **Stalls** Low

Form				RPR
-043	**1**		**Star Sign**[3] 4261 4-9-6 40 .... DO'Donohoe 4 (D W Barker) *trckd ldrs on outer: hdwy 3f out: swtchd ins over 1f out: rdn to ld jst ins last: kpt on* **13/2**	61
6	**2**	*1 ¼*	**Maud's Cat (IRE)**[52] 2753 3-8-12 .... FrankieMcDonald 2 (A P Jarvis) *led: rdn along 2f out: hdd and hung rt jst ins last: kpt on same pce* **4/1**[3]	59
032	**3**	*1 ¾*	**Giverny Spring**[21] 3750 3-8-5 57 .... PatrickHills(7) 3 (J W Hills) *hld up: hdwy 3f out: rdn to chse ldng pair over 1f out: sn one pce* **13/8**[1]	55
063	**4**	*6*	**Silk Topper (IRE)**[21] 3750 3-9-3 60 .... TonyHamilton 9 (R A Fahey) *chsd ldr: rdn along over 2f out: sn drvn and wknd* **5/2**[2]	48
00	**5**	*5*	**Jiminor Mack**[71] 2188 3-8-7 .... GregFairley(5) 1 (W J H Ratcliffe) *chsd ldrs: rdn along 3f out: drvn and wknd 2f out* **25/1**	33
0-50	**6**	*1*	**Xenia**[40] 3146 3-8-12 42 .... (b) DavidAllan 6 (T J Etherington) *in tch: rdn along over 3f out: sn wknd* **40/1**	31
-000	**7**	*9*	**Dancing Moonlight (IRE)**[32] 3383 4-8-13 27 .... AnnStokell(7) 5 (Mrs N Macauley) *plld hrd: chsd ldrs tl rdn along 3f out and sn wknd* **100/1**	13
0-0	**8**	*10*	**Newcastles Owen (IRE)**[22] 3698 3-8-13 ow1 .... DeclanMcGann(5) 8 (R Johnson) *s.i.s: bhd tl hdwy on outer and in tch 3f out: sn rdn and wknd* **40/1**	—
0-	**F**		**Zell (IRE)**[307] 5768 3-8-12 .... AdrianTNicholls 7 (E J Alston) *s.i.s: plld hrd and sn in midfield: slipped and fell over 5f out* **20/1**	—

1m 56.61s (3.21) **Going Correction** +0.40s/f (Good)
WFA 3 from 4yo 8lb — **9** Ran SP% **114.5**
Speed ratings (Par 103):101,99,98,93,88 87,79,70,—
CSF £30.51 TOTE £9.20: £1.70, £1.40, £1.10; EX 41.80 Place 6 £109.32, Place 5 £48.44.
Owner G N Parker **Bred** Burns Farm Stud **Trained** Scorton, N Yorks

FOCUS
A very poor maiden, selling grade at best, best rated through the runner-up.
Dancing Moonlight(IRE) Official explanation: jockey said filly ran too free
T/Plt: £215.70 to a £1 stake. Pool: £59,602.10. 201.70 winning tickets. T/Qpdt: £56.00 to a £1 stake. Pool: £2,719.00. 35.90 winning tickets. JR

2910 DUSSELDORF (R-H)
Saturday, August 12

OFFICIAL GOING: Soft

4383a BMW PREIS DUSSELDORF (LISTED RACE) (F&M) — 1m 110y
4:10 (4:34) 3-Y-0+ — **£8,276** (£3,034; £1,655; £828)

			RPR
1		**Molly Art (GER)**[24] 3661 4-9-6 .... (b) ABoschert 10 (U Ostmann, Germany)	110
2	*2 ½*	**Flor Y Nata (USA)**[48] 2912 3-8-6 .... FilipMinarik 6 (Sir Mark Prescott) *unruly beforehand, missed break, sn rousted along, 8th str, swtchd outside over 1f out, styd on to take 2nd on line* **64/10**[1]	99
3	*hd*	**River Melody (GER)**[97] 4-9-2 .... AStarke 4 (Mario Hofer, Germany)	101
4	*1 ½*	**Directa (GER)**[69] 2279 3-8-8 .... AHelfenbein 1 (Andreas Lowe, Germany)	98
5	*1 ½*	**Ruby Hill (GER)**[79] 1974 4-9-6 .... ADeVries 8 (W Baltromei, Germany)	99
6	*11*	**New Inspiration (GER)**[25] 5-9-0 .... THellier 2 (W Kujath, Germany)	71
7	*2*	**Lasira (GER)**[69] 2279 3-8-10 .... WMongil 5 (P Schiergen, Germany)	71
8	*¾*	**Mellanie Surprise (HOL)**[77] 2059 3-8-6 .... CarolinLippert 3 (J Pubben, Holland)	65
9	*nk*	**Norwegian Pride (FR)**[24] 3661 4-9-4 .... AGoritz 9 (P Schiergen, Germany)	69
10	*1 ¾*	**Desert Dabby (GER)** 3-8-10 .... ASuborics 7 (J Kozlowski, Sweden)	65

1m 47.46s
WFA 3 from 4yo+ 7lb — **10** Ran SP% **13.5**
(including 10 Euro stake): WIN 25; PL 14, 20, 24; SF 118.
Owner Gestut Auenquelle **Bred** Gestut Auenquelle **Trained** Germany

NOTEBOOK
Flor Y Nata(USA) was up to her usual tricks, bucking and kicking in the paddock and missing the break, and in the circumstances did well to come from last to get up for second on the line. She is capable of winning a race of this nature if her temperament can be controlled.

SARATOGA (R-H)
Saturday, August 12

OFFICIAL GOING: Firm

4384a ALFRED G VANDERBILT H'CAP (GRADE 2) — 6f
11:07 (11:07) 3-Y-0+
£72,627 (£24,209; £12,104; £6,052; £3,631; £2,420)

			RPR
1		**War Front (USA)**[27] 4-8-3 .... JSantos 5 (H A Jerkens, U.S.A) **7/4**[1]	112
2	*2 ½*	**Judiths Wild Rush (USA)**[105] 5-8-4 .... (b) KDesormeaux 1 (Reade Baker, Canada) **56/10**	106
3	*1 ½*	**Mass Media (USA)**[75] 2093 5-8-5 .... (b) JCastellano 2 (R J Frankel, U.S.A) **61/20**[3]	102
4	*4 ¾*	**Afrashad (USA)**[759] 3847 4-8-3 .... RMigliore 3 (Saeed Bin Suroor) **9/4**[2]	86
5	*1*	**Bishop Court Hill (USA)**[91] 6-8-5 .... RBejarano 6 (T Pletcher, U.S.A) **115/10**	85
6	*5 ¼*	**Thunder Touch (USA)**[41] 3134 5-8-1 .... FJara 4 (K McLaughlin, U.S.A) **298/10**	65

1m 10.21s — **6** Ran SP% **118.2**

Owner Joseph Allen **Bred** Joseph Allen **Trained** USA

NOTEBOOK
Afrashad(USA), formerly trained in Britain, was stepping up in grade after racing in allowance company. He was comfortably held at this level.

3756 ARLINGTON (L-H)
Saturday, August 12

OFFICIAL GOING: Firm

4385a BEVERLY D STKS (GRADE 1) (F&M) 1m 1f 110y(T)
9:42 (9:43) 3-Y-0+

£261,628 (£87,209; £43,605; £21,802; £13,081; £8,721)

RPR
1 **Gorella (FR)**[63] 4-8-11 .... JRLeparoux 1 119
(P L Biancone, U.S.A) *held up in rear, last til headway on outside from well over 2f out, 8th st, strong run to lead inside final f, ran on well* **13/10**[1]
2 1 3/4 **Film Maker (USA)**[49] 6-8-11 ....(b) RADominguez 10 116
(H G Motion, U.S.A) *held up, headway & 6th straight, strong run to take 2nd close home* **33/10**[2]
3 1/2 **Live Life (FR)**[21] 4-8-11 .... VEspinoza 6 115
(N Drysdale, U.S.A) *led to inside final f, lost 2nd close home* **14/1**
4 nse **Honey Ryder (USA)**[28] 5-8-11 ....(b) JRVelazquez 5 115
(T Pletcher, U.S.A) *always in touch, 4th straight, 3rd inside final f, ran on same pace* **33/10**[2]
5 2 1/4 **Rich In Spirit (USA)**[28] 4-8-11 .... MGuidry 9 111
(T Proctor, U.S.A) *prominent, close 7th straight on outside, one pace* **219/10**
6 nk **Royal Copenhagen (FR)**[21] 4-8-11 .... RRDouglas 8 110
(Laura De Seroux, U.S.A) *mid-division, 5th straight, kept on one pace* **64/1**
7 1/2 **Sharp Lisa (USA)**[41] 4-8-11 .... EPrado 2 110
(Doug O'Neill, U.S.A) *tracked leader to half-way, 3rd & under pressure straight, weakened final furlong* **223/10**
8 1 **Wend (USA)**[49] 5-8-11 .... GKGomez 4 108
(W Mott, U.S.A) *went 2nd half-way, ridden over 1f out, weakened final f* **92/10**[3]
9 hd **Minge Cove (USA)**[21] 5-8-11 .... SBridgmohan 7 107
(S Blasi, U.S.A) *last straight, always in rear* **68/1**
10 1 1/4 **Rising Cross**[27] [3575] 3-8-5 .... MartinDwyer 3 108
(J R Best) *mid-division, 6th & pushed along over 3f out, 9th & beaten straight* **24/1**

1m 53.71s
WFA 3 from 4yo+ 8lb **10** Ran SP% **122.1**
PARI-MUTUEL (including $2 stakes): WIN 4.60; PL (1-2) 3.00, 3.60; SHOW (1-2-3) 2.40, 3.40, 5.60; SF 17.20.
Owner M Schwartz **Bred** E A R L Eleveage De La Source **Trained** USA

NOTEBOOK
Gorella(FR) simply trounced these rivals, circling the field having been virtually last on the home turn, and producing an electric burst of speed. She needs to be held up for a late run, but if her stamina can be stretched to 1m 3f she looks a worthy opponent for Ouija Board in the Breeders' Cup Filly & Mare Turf.
Rising Cross held a good position on the inside in fourth until she came under pressure and was readily outpaced in the final half mile. She needs further.

4386a ARLINGTON MILLION (GRADE 1) 1m 2f
10:42 (10:44) 3-Y-0+

£348,837 (£116,279; £58,140; £29,070; £17,442; £11,628)

RPR
1 **The Tin Man (USA)**[41] 8-9-0 .... VEspinoza 2 122
(Richard E Mandella, U.S.A) *made all, driven out & ran on well* **11/2**
2 1 **Cacique (IRE)**[35] 5-9-0 .... EPrado 9 120
(R J Frankel, U.S.A) *tracked winner throughout, pressing him 3f out, 2nd straight, ran on steadily final f* **39/10**[3]
3 1 1/4 **Soldier Hollow**[55] [2692] 6-9-0 .... RRDouglas 5 118
(P Schiergen, Germany) *went right start, raced in 5th, 4th straight, ran on under pressure final f* **139/10**
4 hd **English Channel (USA)**[35] 4-9-0 .... JRVelazquez 10 117
(T Pletcher, U.S.A) *disputed 3rd, 3rd straight, one pace* **21/10**[1]
5 nk **Cosmonaut (USA)**[21] 4-9-0 .... JRLeparoux 7 117
(P L Biancone, U.S.A) *mid-division, 6th straight, kept on one pace* **22/1**
6 nk **Ace (IRE)**[28] [3559] 5-9-0 .... GKGomez 3 116
(A P O'Brien, Ire) *mid-division, 7th straight, never able to challenge* **37/10**[2]
7 1 **Better Talk Now (USA)**[35] 7-9-0 ....(b) RADominguez 8 115
(H G Motion, U.S.A) *held up in rear, 8th on inside straight, never a factor* **94/10**
8 nse **Touch Of Land (FR)**[24] [3662] 6-9-0 .... C-PLemaire 4 114
(H-A Pantall, France) *held up, 9th straight, never a factor* **254/10**
9 1 3/4 **Major Rhythm (USA)**[41] 7-9-0 ....(b) EFires 1 111
(Ed Beam, U.S.A) *disputed 3rd, 5th straight, weakened 1f out* **39/1**
10 6 **Phoenix Reach (IRE)**[385] [3733] 6-9-0 .... MartinDwyer 6 100
(A M Balding) *carried right start, settled towards rear, last & beaten straight* **16/1**

2m 1.35s **10** Ran SP% **122.2**
PARI-MUTUEL: WIN 13.00; PL (1-2) 6.00, 5.40; SHOW (1-2-3) 4.60, 3.80, 6.80; SF 70.60.
Owner R & A Todd **Bred** Ralph & Aury Todd **Trained** USA

NOTEBOOK
The Tin Man(USA) proved he was no slouch when handed an uncontested lead in the Dubai Duty Free and, again allowed to dawdle at the head of affairs, found more when pressed by the runner-up on the home turn. He is getting better with age but will not always have things so easy up front.
Cacique(IRE) was in the right place to strike throughout, but the winner picked up too well for him once in line for home.
Soldier Hollow posted a solid effort but is one of many that would have preferred a stronger pace.
Ace(IRE) raced in seventh and was always going to struggle to come from there given the slow tempo.
Touch Of Land(FR) was always at the back in a race that was not run to suit, especially given the short home straight.
Phoenix Reach(IRE) pulled very hard and threw his head around in the early stages. He stays further, so the lack of pace was a major problem and, mindful of his injury problems and the firm ground, Dwyer let him coast home in the final furlong. It remains to be seen if he can get back to his best.

4387a SECRETARIAT STKS (GRADE 1) 1m 2f
11:58 (12:00) 3-Y-0

£139,535 (£46,512; £23,256; £11,628; £6,977; £4,651)

RPR
1 **Showing Up (USA)**[49] 3-9-0 .... CVelasquez 1 122
(B Tagg, U.S.A) *made all, clear 1f out, ran on* **1/2**[1]
2 1 1/2 **Ivan Denisovich (IRE)**[34] [3342] 3-8-7 .... JRVelazquez 5 112
(A P O'Brien, Ire) *held up in 5th, headway on outside & 4th straight, chased winner from distance, no impression* **58/10**[3]
3 4 1/2 **Primary (USA)**[56] [2671] 3-8-7 .... RAlbarado 4 104
(W J Haggas) *went right start, raced in 4th, 3rd & ridden straight, one pace final f* **97/10**
4 3/4 **Proudinsky (GER)**[28] 3-8-7 .... EPrado 2 103
(R J Frankel, U.S.A) *pressed winner early, settled in 3rd, went 2nd again 3f out, weakened approaching final f* **87/10**
5 1/2 **Niagara Causeway (USA)**[21] [3756] 3-8-7 .... CEmigh 6 102
(Ron Sticka, U.S.A) *held up in rear, 5th straight, never a factor* **44/1**
6 8 3/4 **Go Between (USA)**[28] 3-9-0 .... GKGomez 3 93
(W Mott, U.S.A) *pressed winner after 2f, ridden & weakened 3f out, last straight* **37/10**[2]

2m 0.09s **6** Ran SP% **124.5**
PARI-MUTUEL: WIN 3.00; PL (1-2) 2.60, 6.00; SHOW (1-2-3) 2.40, 4.80, 4.40; SF 19.40.
Owner Lael Stable **Bred** Nellie M Cox & Rose Retreat Farm **Trained** USA

NOTEBOOK
Showing Up(USA) had things all his own way up front and, quickening nicely into the straight, soon had matters in hand. He is proving as good on grass as he is on the dirt (where his only defeat was behind his ill-fated entrymate, Barbaro, in the Kentucky Derby) and may go on to give America the worthy turf champion that it has been lacking for some time.
Ivan Denisovich(IRE) was forced to come around three horses on the final turn and, getting into overdrive, did well to eat into the winner's advantage a furlong out, but was making no further headway in the closing stages.
Primary(USA) launched his bid around the outside three furlongs from home and briefly made it into second place. But he did not negotiate the turn too smoothly and, having dropped back to fifth approaching the furlong marker, did well to rally and regain third.

4049 LEICESTER (R-H)
Sunday, August 13

OFFICIAL GOING: Good (good to soft in places)
Wind: Fresh, against Weather: Raining

4388 EBF COOZE MAIDEN STKS 7f 9y
2:20 (2:21) (Class 4) 2-Y-0 £5,047 (£1,510; £755; £377; £188) Stalls Low

Form RPR
02 1 **Nightinshining (IRE)**[18] [3844] 2-9-3 .... RichardHughes 1 82
(A King) *hld up in tch: rdn to chse ldr fnl f: edgd rt and styd on to ld wl ins fnl f* **6/1**[3]
4 2 hd **Hadahoo (USA)**[14] [3976] 2-9-3 .... PhilipRobinson 5 81
(M A Jarvis) *led: rdn and hdd wl ins fnl f* **13/8**[1]
43 3 3 **King's Causeway (USA)**[12] [4018] 2-9-3 .... JoeFanning 8 74
(W J Haggas) *w ldr: rdn over 2f out: no ex fnl f* **11/4**[2]
40 4 1/2 **Jawaab (IRE)**[10] [4074] 2-9-3 .... ChrisCatlin 4 72
(E A L Dunlop) *s.i.s: hld up: rdn over 1f out: styd on ins fnl f: nrst fin* **40/1**
5 hd **Polish Red** 2-9-0 .... AdamKirby[(3)] 6 72
(G G Margarson) *s.i.s: hld up: hung rt 1/2-way: styd on ins fnl f: nrst fin* **40/1**
0 6 1 **Wind Flow**[18] [3843] 2-9-3 .... DO'Donohoe 9 69
(E A L Dunlop) *mid-div: rdn 1/2-way: wknd ins fnl f* **8/1**
7 1/2 **Kalasam** 2-9-3 .... FrancisNorton 10 68
(W R Muir) *s.i.s: hld up: effrt over 1f out: n.d* **25/1**
8 1 **Spume (IRE)** 2-9-3 .... RobertWinston 2 66
(Sir Michael Stoute) *s.i.s: sn chsng ldrs: rdn over 2f out: wknd fnl f* **9/1**
0 9 1/2 **Furmigadelagiusta**[26] [3623] 2-8-10 .... AshleyHamblett[(7)] 11 64
(L M Cumani) *s.i.s: hdwy over 5f out: rdn 1/2-way: wknd fnl f* **33/1**

1m 27.83s (1.73) **Going Correction** +0.15s/f (Good) **9** Ran SP% **111.8**
Speed ratings (Par 96): 96,95,92,91,91 90,89,88,88
CSF £15.18 TOTE £8.00: £2.40, £1.10, £1.10; EX 24.10.
Owner Nigel Bunter **Bred** M Stewkesbury **Trained** Barbury Castle, Wilts

FOCUS
A fair juvenile maiden which was run at a sound pace. The first two came clear and the form looks sound, rated through the runner-up.

NOTEBOOK
Nightinshining(IRE) got off the mark at the third time of asking with a hard-fought display. He enjoyed the softened ground, showed a decent attitude under pressure, and is clearly improving. A mile will be within his compass before too long. (op 7-1)
Hadahoo(USA), fourth at Newmarket on his debut a fortnight previously, gave his all from the front and was only just denied. He handled the easier ground well enough, and is clearly up to going one better before too long, yet may already be in need of a stiffer test. (op 15-8)
King's Causeway(USA) had his chance and appeared to run close to his recent level in defeat. He helps set the standard for this form, and now qualifies for a nursery mark, but at this stage his Group entries appear ambitious. (op 9-4 tchd 3-1)
Jawaab(IRE) was doing all of his best work towards the finish, having been slow to break, and proved his previous effort at Epsom to be all wrong. He still looks to be learning his trade and is clearly best kept to a galloping track. (op 33-1)
Polish Red, whose pedigree suggests a mix of speed and stamina, fell out the gates and took time to get the hang of things. The manner in which he finished his race bodes well for his future however, and he can be expected to get closer next time out.
Wind Flow, a well-beaten favourite on his debut on Lingfield's Polytrack 18 days previously, was again nibbled at in the betting ring yet once more ran well below expectations on this first outing on turf. He already looks more of a nursery type and is presumably thought capable of better. (op 10-1)
Spume(IRE), whose dam was a winner over this trip as a juvenile, showed up well enough until running green and finding just the same pace when it mattered. His stable's juveniles are suprisingly yet to find their feet this term and it will come as little surprise to see this well-named colt leave this debut form behind as he becomes more streetwise. (op 7-1)

4389 LEICESTERSHIRE AND RUTLAND LIFE (S) STKS 7f 9y
2:50 (2:50) (Class 5) 3-4-Y-0 £3,238 (£963; £481; £240) Stalls Low

Form RPR
0005 1 **Enjoy The Magic**[8] [4133] 4-8-11 40 .... FrancisNorton 15 54
(E J Alston) *chsd ldrs: led wl over 1f out: pushed out* **20/1**
2001 2 3 **Beau Marche**[4] [4266] 4-9-7 45 ....(b) RobertWinston 5 56
(G G Margarson) *sn outpcd: hdwy over 1f out: nt rch wnr* **9/2**[2]

0052 **3** 2 **Princely Vale (IRE)**[17] 3867 4-8-11 51......................(p) LiamJones(5) 1 46
(W G M Turner) *chsd ldrs: led over 2f out: rdn and hdd wl over 1f out: wknd ins fnl f* **11/2**[3]

0000 **4** ¾ **Bogaz (IRE)**[89] 1753 4-8-13 45......................(v) RichardKingscote(3) 8 44
(Mrs H Sweeting) *outpcd: hdwy over 1f out: nt rch ldrs* **16/1**

0060 **5** ½ **Ronsard (IRE)**[15] 3947 4-9-2 58...................... JohnEgan 3 43
(T J Pitt) *dwlt: hld up: hdwy u.p over 1f out: nt rch ldrs* **7/4**[1]

5250 **6** 1 ¾ **Pontefract Glory**[19] 3814 3-8-7 39......................(p) StephenDonohoe(3) 9 38
(M Dods) *sn led: hdd over 2f out: wknd fnl f* **10/1**

4430 **7** 5 **Noorain**[37] 3263 4-8-11 40......................(t) MickyFenton 18 20
(Stef Liddiard) *chsd ldrs: rdn over 2f out: wknd over 1f out* **11/1**

-050 **8** ½ **Tay Bridge (IRE)**[37] 3264 3-8-7 38......................(b[1]) DominicFox(3) 13 24
(G F Bridgwater) *prom: rdn 1/2-way: wknd over 2f out* **80/1**

0000 **9** 2 **Shortbread**[20] 3797 4-8-9 45......................(p) WilliamCarson(7) 11 19
(M Salaman) *s.s: hdwy 1/2-way: rdn and wknd over 2f out* **40/1**

0020 **10** *shd* **Baytown Valentina**[29] 3541 3-8-2 40......................(p) NelsonDeSouza(3) 6 13
(R Brotherton) *chsd ldrs: lost pl over 4f out: sn bhd* **40/1**

2660 **11** *hd* **Fallal Parc**[39] 3195 3-8-10 39...................... DavidKinsella 17 18
(M F Harris) *mid-div: rdn 1/2-way: wknd over 2f out* **66/1**

4000 **12** 1 ¼ **Roko**[27] 3595 4-8-9 37......................(t) MSemple(7) 16 14
(S R Bowring) *chsd ldrs 4f* **50/1**

5303 **13** 33 **Mill By The Stream**[13] 3995 4-9-2 42...................... DO'Donohoe 2 —
(R Brotherton) *s.i.s: hdwy 5f out: wknd over 2f out: eased* **15/2**

1m 28.48s (2.38) **Going Correction** +0.375s/f (Good)
WFA 3 from 4yo 6lb **13** Ran SP% **119.3**
Speed ratings (Par 103):101,97,95,94,93 91,86,85,83,83 82,81,43
CSF £104.89 TOTE £27.60: £6.50, £1.80, £2.10; EX 230.90.The winner was bought in for 3,200gns.
Owner Miss F Fenley **Bred** Southern Seafoods **Trained** Longton, Lancs

FOCUS
A weak affair that produced a ready winner who is value for further than the winning margin, with the second running to his previous mark.

4390 COALVILLE GLASS & GLAZING H'CAP 1m 60y
3:20 (3:21) (Class 5) (0-75,75) 3-Y-O+ **£4,533** (£1,348; £674; £336) **Stalls** High

Form RPR

30B4 **1** **Surwaki (USA)**[15] 3928 4-10-0 **75**...................... PhilipRobinson 10 84
(C G Cox) *led: hdd over 6f out: chsd ldr tl led over 3f out: hdd 1f out: rallied to ld nr fin* **7/2**[1]

3132 **2** ¾ **Barons Spy (IRE)**[19] 3820 5-9-1 **65**...................... JamesDoyle(3) 4 73
(R J Price) *a.p: chsd wnr over 2f out: led 1f out: rdn and hdd nr fin* **9/2**[3]

0041 **3** 2 **Cantarna (IRE)**[19] 3820 5-8-12 **59**...................... MickyFenton 7 62
(J Mackie) *hld up: outpcd 3f out: hdwy and hung rt over 1f out: nt rch ldrs* **4/1**[2]

4411 **4** ½ **Champain Sands (IRE)**[8] 4154 7-9-4 **68**...................... StephenDonohoe(3) 8 70
(E J Alston) *hld up: hdwy over 2f out: rdn over 1f out: styd on same pce* **13/2**

1633 **5** *nk* **The Gaikwar (IRE)**[8] 4131 7-9-8 **72**......................(b) RichardKingscote(3) 2 73
(R A Harris) *s.i.s: plld hrd: hdwy 5f out: rdn and hung rt 2f out: styd on same pce fnl f* **7/1**

06-0 **6** 3 **Wotchalike (IRE)**[209] 125 4-8-8 **60**...................... LiamJones(5) 11 54
(R J Price) *hld up: hdwy 1/2-way: rdn over 2f out: wknd over 1f out* **16/1**

-000 **7** 5 **Komreyev Star**[27] 3597 4-8-9 **56** oh6...................... JohnEgan 6 39
(M Mullineaux) *chsd ldrs: rdn whn n.m.r and wknd 2f out* **25/1**

6431 **8** 32 **Blue Empire (IRE)**[15] 3947 5-9-2 **63**...................... RobertWinston 3 —
(C R Dore) *racd keenly: led over 6f out: hdd over 3f out: wknd 2f out: eased* **11/2**

6000 **9** 7 **Monkstown Road**[7] 4176 4-8-10 **57**......................(p) FrancisNorton 1 —
(C N Kellett) *sn outpcd and bhd* **50/1**

1m 47.39s (2.09) **Going Correction** +0.25s/f (Good)
WFA 3 from 4yo+ 7lb **9** Ran SP% **113.3**
Speed ratings (Par 103):99,98,96,95,95 92,87,55,48
CSF £18.93 CT £64.42 TOTE £4.30: £1.50, £1.80, £1.60; EX 24.40.
Owner Dennis Shaw **Bred** Airlie Stud **Trained** Lambourn, Berks
■ Stewards' Enquiry : James Doyle two-day ban: used whip with excessive frequency (Aug 25,26)
Philip Robinson one-day ban: used whip with excessive frequency (Aug 25)

FOCUS
A modest handicap and the form looks sound and fair for the class.
Blue Empire(IRE) Official explanation: jockey said gelding slipped on the bend
Monkstown Road Official explanation: jockey said gelding slipped on the bend

4391 LEICESTER MERCURY FAMILY DAY H'CAP 7f 9y
3:50 (3:51) (Class 2) (0-100,95) 3-Y-O
£12,464 (£3,732; £1,866; £934; £466; £234) **Stalls** Low

Form RPR

-161 **1** **Dream Theme**[10] 4083 3-9-2 **90**...................... RichardHughes 10 106+
(B W Hills) *hld up: hdwy over 1f out: shkn up to ld ins fnl f: r.o wl* **13/8**[1]

2544 **2** 3 **Jimmy The Guesser**[14] 3970 3-8-2 **79**...................... JamesDoyle(3) 7 84
(N P Littmoden) *chsd ldrs: rdn over 1f out: sn ev ch: outpcd ins fnl f* **7/2**[2]

0560 **3** *hd* **Guest Connections**[12] 4029 3-8-10 **84**...................... JohnEgan 5 88
(M R Channon) *s.i.s: hld up: rdn over 2f out: hdwy over 1f out: styd on same pce ins fnl f* **9/2**[3]

2000 **4** 1 ¼ **Pearly Wey**[10] 4083 3-9-0 **91**...................... AdamKirby(3) 9 92
(C G Cox) *led: clr 1/2-way: hdd and no ex ins fnl f* **5/1**

0100 **5** 3 ½ **Red Cape (FR)**[32] 3414 3-9-1 **89**...................... RobertWinston 3 81
(Jane Chapple-Hyam) *chsd ldr: rdn over 2f out: ev ch 1f out: sn wknd* **9/1**

-040 **6** 2 ½ **Art Market (CAN)**[52] 2774 3-9-7 **95**......................(t) JoeFanning 2 81
(P F I Cole) *hld up: rdn 1/2-way: wknd 2f out* **12/1**

1m 27.5s (1.40) **Going Correction** +0.375s/f (Good) **6** Ran SP% **112.9**
Speed ratings (Par 106):107,103,103,101,97 95
CSF £7.61 CT £20.04 TOTE £1.90: £1.60, £1.90; EX 6.80.
Owner K Abdulla **Bred** Juddmonte Farms Ltd **Trained** Lambourn, Berks

FOCUS
A fair handicap that was decimated by non-runners, and the progressive winner is value for further than the winning margin, although the form behind looks far from solid.

NOTEBOOK
Dream Theme ◆, raised 5lb for winning at Goodwood ten days previously, allayed any fears about not handling the easier ground and came through to follow up with a deal left up his sleeve at the finish. He is still a much better performer on fast ground, but he is clearly progressing fast at present, and a bold bid for the hat-trick can now be expected. (tchd 11-8 and 7-4)
Jimmy The Guesser turned in another solid effort in defeat without posing a serious threat to the winner. He really does deserve a change of fortune, but is not going to get any respite from the Handicapper with efforts like this. (op 4-1 tchd 9-2)
Guest Connections, with the visor abandoned, was never really in the hunt after missing the break, but he kept on well enough towards the finish and looks to have slipped to a more realistic mark now. (op 11-2)
Pearly Wey had his chance from the front and is just struggling for form at present. (op 11-2 tchd 6-1)
Red Cape(FR), making his debut for a new yard, had his chance yet failed to quicken on the easy surface. He looks high enough in the weights at present, but could get closer when reverting to faster ground. (op 8-1)
Art Market(CAN) proved unsuited by the softened ground and is probably best forgiven this form. However, he is another who is likely to continue to find life hard until slipping down the handicap. (op 10-1)

4392 SANDRA LEESON 60TH BIRTHDAY CELEBRATION H'CAP 1m 1f 218y
4:20 (4:20) (Class 4) (0-85,84) 3-Y-O+
£6,232 (£1,866; £933; £467; £233; £117) **Stalls** High

Form RPR

5531 **1** **Rationale (IRE)**[36] 3301 3-8-7 **68**...................... HayleyTurner 5 80+
(S C Williams) *chsd ldr: led 2f out: rdn and edgd rt over 1f out: r.o: eased nr fin* **3/1**[2]

1324 **2** 1 **Fabrian**[14] 3973 8-9-4 **73**...................... JamesDoyle(3) 6 81
(R J Price) *led 8f: rdn and nt clr run over 1f out: styd on* **9/2**[3]

0-1 **3** 11 **Farringdon**[20] 3794 3-9-6 **84**...................... NelsonDeSouza(3) 3 71
(M P Tregoning) *hld up: rdn 1/2-way: wnt centre 4f out: hung rt and wknd over 2f out* **3/1**[2]

2022 **4** 2 ½ **Cripsey Brook**[9] 4112 8-9-5 **78**......................(t) JamesReveley(7) 1 60
(K G Reveley) *hld up and bhd: wnt centre 4f out: n.d* **8/1**

-615 **5** 10 **Swains Bridge (USA)**[33] 3377 4-10-0 **80**...................... RichardHughes 2 43
(L M Cumani) *chsd ldrs: wnt centre 4f out: hung rt and wknd over 2f out* **6/1**

0154 **6** 8 **Snowed Under**[14] 3980 5-10-0 **80**...................... PhilipRobinson 4 28
(J D Bethell) *chsd ldrs: wnt centre 4f out: hung rt and wknd 3f out* **11/4**[1]

2m 9.53s (1.23) **Going Correction** +0.25s/f (Good)
WFA 3 from 4yo+ 9lb **6** Ran SP% **120.2**
Speed ratings (Par 105):105,104,95,93,85 79
CSF £18.15 TOTE £4.00: £2.40, £3.00; EX 18.00.
Owner Alasdair Simpson **Bred** Middle Park Stud Ltd **Trained** Newmarket, Suffolk

FOCUS
A fair handicap which saw the first two come well clear. The winner is value for further, but the overall form should be treated with a little caution.
Swains Bridge(USA) Official explanation: jockey said colt was unsuited by the good (good to soft in places) ground
Snowed Under Official explanation: jockey said gelding was unsuited by the good (good to soft in places) ground

4393 CAPITA IT SERVICES H'CAP 1m 3f 183y
4:50 (4:51) (Class 5) (0-75,71) 4-Y-O+ **£5,505** (£1,637; £818; £408) **Stalls** High

Form RPR

2-03 **1** **Spectral Star**[76] 2067 4-9-6 **70**...................... JoeFanning 2 79
(J R Fanshawe) *led 1f: chsd ldr tl led over 2f out: rdn out* **8/1**

1522 **2** 1 ¼ **Shekan Star**[14] 3983 4-8-5 **55**...................... FrancisNorton 5 62
(K G Reveley) *s.i.s: hld up: hdwy over 2f out: rdn to chse wnr over 1f out: no ex nr fin* **7/1**

-332 **3** 2 **Hawridge King**[38] 3209 4-9-4 **68**...................... MickyFenton 3 72
(W S Kittow) *chsd ldrs: rdn over 1f out: styd on same pce* **7/2**[2]

1215 **4** 1 ½ **Taxman (IRE)**[22] 3743 4-9-6 **70**......................(p) PhilipRobinson 8 72
(C E Brittain) *chsd ldrs: rdn over 2f out: styd on same pce fnl f* **7/2**[2]

3320 **5** 3 **Shamrock Bay**[7] 2078 4-8-6 **61**...................... LiamJones(5) 6 58
(C R Dore) *hld up: rdn over 3f out: wknd fnl f* **10/1**

4553 **6** 12 **Gobi King**[22] 3724 4-9-2 **66**...................... RichardHughes 4 44
(L M Cumani) *led after 1f: rdn and hdd over 2f out: wknd over 1f out* **10/3**[1]

00/0 **7** 2 **Sharmy (IRE)**[29] 3547 10-9-7 **71**...................... ChrisCatlin 7 45
(Ian Williams) *hld up: rdn over 3f out: sn wknd* **25/1**

3611 **8** 10 **Monash Lad (IRE)**[20] 3797 4-8-9 **66**...................... PatrickHills(7) 1 24
(Mrs K Waldron) *hld up: plld hrd: hdwy over 4f out: hung rt and wknd over 2f out* **6/1**[3]

2m 36.6s (2.10) **Going Correction** +0.25s/f (Good) **8** Ran SP% **118.4**
Speed ratings (Par 103):103,102,100,99,97 89,88,81
CSF £64.40 CT £234.81 TOTE £8.50: £3.90, £3.20, £1.20; EX 21.00 Place 6 £38.62, Place 5 £32.89..
Owner Helena Springfield Ltd **Bred** Meon Valley Stud **Trained** Newmarket, Suffolk

FOCUS
A modest handicap which was run at a sound enough pace. The winner may rate higher in due course with the third setting the standard.
T/Plt: £40.20 to a £1 stake. Pool £64,667.70. 1,171.85 winning tickets. T/Qpdt: £13.00 to a £1 stake. Pool £3,650.60. 207.80 winning tickets. CR

4363 LINGFIELD (L-H)
Sunday, August 13

OFFICIAL GOING: Turf course - good to soft (good in places); all-weather - standard
Wind: Virtually nil Weather: Overcast

4394 LINGFIELDPARK.CO.UK MAIDEN AUCTION FILLIES' STKS 1m (P)
2:30 (2:30) (Class 6) 2-Y-O **£2,730** (£806; £403) **Stalls** High

Form RPR

2 **1** **Steam Cuisine**[35] 3328 2-8-10...................... TPQueally 5 74
(M G Quinlan) *chsd ldr: rdn to ld over 2f out: styd on wl u.p* **5/4**[1]

02 **2** 2 ½ **Anthea**[31] 3448 2-8-8...................... DaneO'Neill 8 66
(B R Millman) *chsd ldrs: wnt 2nd over 2f out: no ex u.p ins fnl f* **15/8**[2]

0200 **3** *hd* **Bathwick Style**[34] 3345 2-8-6 52...................... AdrianMcCarthy 9 64
(B R Millman) *chsd ldrs: rdn over 2f out: wnt 3rd over 1f out: kpt on* **20/1**

05 **4** 5 **Grand Lucre**[36] 3307 2-8-10...................... RichardMullen 6 56
(E J O'Neill) *taken down early: stirrup leather broke leaving stalls: led on wd outside: hdd over 2f out: wknd over 1f out* **14/1**

05 **5** ¾ **Mayireneyrbel**[18] 3851 2-8-4...................... JamieMackay 3 49
(R Ingram) *sn outpcd in rr: drvn over 4f out: n.d* **8/1**[3]

55 **6** 8 **Poyle Kiera**[18] 3838 2-8-6...................... FergusSweeney 1 32
(M Blanshard) *sn outpcd in last pair: n.d* **14/1**

6 **7** *shd* **Group Force (IRE)**[38] 3227 2-8-5...................... SaleemGolam(3) 10 34
(M H Tompkins) *slowly away: sn racing in midfield: drvn over 3f out: sn struggling* **16/1**

8 1 ½ **Gutter Press (IRE)** 2-8-8...................... PatDobbs 2 30
(J S Moore) *sn outpcd in last pair: n.d* **14/1**

05 **9** *2* **Vodka Luge**[10] 4074 2-8-8 .... RHills 4 26
(J W Hills) *chsd ldrs to 1/2-way: sn rdn and struggling* **16/1**

1m 39.29s **Going Correction** -0.25s/f (Stan) **9** Ran SP% **126.9**
Speed ratings (Par 89):90,87,87,82,81 73,73,71,69
CSF £4.22 TOTE £2.00: £1.10, £1.10, £6.80; EX 6.60 Trifecta £62.10 Pool: £131.20 - 1.50 winning units..
Owner Burns Farm Racing **Bred** Burns Farm Stud **Trained** Newmarket, Suffolk

FOCUS
Modest maiden form anchored by the performance of the third.

NOTEBOOK
Steam Cuisine could not cope with a Mark Johnston-trained colt at Ayr on her debut but, against this weaker opposition from her own sex, she proved much the strongest with that experience under her belt. She is likely to go the nursery route now. (op 11-8 tchd 6-4)
Anthea, making her All-Weather debut, probably ran to a similar level as she had done on her first two starts. The extra furlong did not seem to cause her any bother and she is now eligible for nurseries, too. (op 5-2)
Bathwick Style was well beaten in a seller last time out but that was over five furlongs and she ran a better race stepped up to this mile trip. She had performed with credit on her only previous start on Polytrack and clearly the surface suits her. (op 25-1 tchd 33-1)
Grand Lucre, stepping up to a mile for the first time, ran well considering a stirrup leather broke as the stalls opened and her rider was unable to assist her during the race. Official explanation: jockey said he lost an iron (op 12-1)
Mayireneyrbel, despite the step up in trip, again struggled to go the early pace and never got competitive.

4395 LINGFIELD PARK LEISURE CLUB H'CAP 1m (P)
3:00 (3:00) (Class 4) (0-80,79) 3-Y-O **£5,505** (£1,637; £818; £408) **Stalls** High

Form RPR

2611 **1** **Mcnairobi**[4] 4249 3-9-6 **78** 6ex .... DaneO'Neill 7 88
(P D Cundell) *t.k.h: stdd into midfield after 2f: hdwy 3f out: rdn to ld wl over 1f out: styd on wl* **9/4**[1]

423 **2** *1* **Benandonner (USA)**[16] 3906 3-9-0 **72** .... SteveDrowne 11 80
(E A L Dunlop) *led for 1f: led again over 2f out tl wl over 1f out: kpt on same pce wl ins fnl f* **7/2**[2]

0600 **3** *5* **Doctor David**[39] 3202 3-8-6 **64** .... PatDobbs 10 61
(Ernst Oertel) *hld up in rr on outer: hdwy 3f out: chsd ldng pair over 2f out: no imp* **33/1**

-050 **4** *nk* **Cinematic (IRE)**[48] 2931 3-9-0 **75** .... AmirQuinn(3) 5 71
(J R Boyle) *trckd ldrs: rdn 3f out: outpcd 2f out: no ch after* **12/1**

5146 **5** *1 3/4* **Scroll**[132] 855 3-8-8 **73** .... (v) JPFeatherstone(7) 6 65
(P Howling) *hld up on inner: plld out and rdn over 2f out: kpt on fnl f: nt trble ldrs* **16/1**

0003 **6** *1/2* **Air Biscuit (IRE)**[32] 3410 3-8-2 **60** .... (t) JimmyQuinn 4 51+
(C F Wall) *trckd ldrs on inner: nt clr run over 2f out tl over 1f out: shkn up and no imp after* **9/2**[3]

2016 **7** *2* **Empire Dancer (IRE)**[17] 3871 3-8-9 **74** .... KirstyMilczarek(7) 8 60
(C N Allen) *t.k.h: w ldr: rdn 3f out: wknd qckly 2f out* **14/1**

0050 **8** *2* **In On The Act (IRE)**[12] 4029 3-8-10 **68** .... RichardMullen 9 50
(Jamie Poulton) *bhd: in tch: rdn 3f out: sn struggling* **33/1**

016 **9** *2 1/2* **Josie Marcus (USA)**[15] 3953 3-9-7 **79** .... TPQueally 2 55
(J Noseda) *sn prom: led after 1f tl over 2f out: sn wknd* **9/2**[3]

1m 37.5s **Going Correction** -0.25s/f (Stan) **9** Ran SP% **115.5**
Speed ratings (Par 102):99,98,93,92,90 90,88,86,83
CSF £10.08 CT £192.30 TOTE £3.60: £1.30, £1.60, £4.90; EX 10.50 Trifecta £149.80 Part won. Pool £211.10 - 0.10 winning units..
Owner Ian M Brown **Bred** Roden House Stud **Trained** Compton, Berks
■ The 500th career success, Flat and jumps, for Peter Cundell.

FOCUS
A fair handicap but not that competitive as it turned out. The form looks solid rated around the third and fourth.
Air Biscuit(IRE) Official explanation: jockey said filly was denied a clear run
Empire Dancer(IRE) Official explanation: trainer said gelding finished lame and was found to have an infected corn

4396 LINGFIELD PARK GOLF CLUB MAIDEN FILLIES' STKS 1m 2f (P)
3:30 (3:34) (Class 5) 3-Y-O+ **£3,238** (£963; £481; £240) **Stalls** Low

Form RPR

550 **1** **Spirit Of The Fen (IRE)**[15] 3946 3-8-12 70 .... DaneO'Neill 10 67
(J H M Gosden) *s.i.s: bhd: hdwy on outer over 3f out: rdn to chal 2f out: led 1f out: r.o strly and drew clr fnl f* **6/1**

232 **2** *3* **Majestic Halo**[15] 3946 3-8-12 77 .... SteveDrowne 11 61
(E A L Dunlop) *trckd ldrs: rdn to ld 2f out: hdd 1f out: outpcd by wnr after* **10/3**[2]

62 **3** *2* **Pochard**[23] 3717 3-8-12 .... JimmyQuinn 12 58
(J M P Eustace) *t.k.h: hld up in midfield: rdn 3f out: outpcd over 2f out: styd on ins fnl f: nt rch ldrs* **14/1**

0 **4** *3/4* **Seeking Kali (IRE)**[106] 1290 3-8-12 .... RHills 9 56
(Sir Michael Stoute) *w.w in midfield: hdwy and rdn 2f out: one pce whn hung lft over 1f out: no imp* **7/4**[1]

5 *nk* **Theologicum** 3-8-9 .... EdwardCreighton(3) 7 56
(Miss J R Gibney) *unruly in stalls: slowly away: bhd: hdwy on outer over 2f out: kpt on ins fnl f: nt rch ldrs* **33/1**

544 **6** *3 1/2* **Aegean Pearl (USA)**[16] 3901 3-8-12 75 .... PatDobbs 1 49
(J H M Gosden) *led 2f: led again over 5f out: hdd 2f out: wknd qckly over 1f out* **7/2**[3]

7 *2* **Dancing Diamonds**[48] 3-8-12 .... FergusSweeney 2 45
(D M Simcock) *bhd: rdn 4f out: nvr on terms* **20/1**

4 **8** *10* **Zamhrear**[4] 4261 3-8-12 .... TPQueally 5 26
(C E Brittain) *t.k.h: prom: rdn 3f out: wknd qckly over 2f out: t.o* **14/1**

00 **9** *1 1/2* **Sophie James**[11] 4045 3-8-12 .... RichardMullen 6 23
(M G Quinlan) *w.w in tch: lost pl 4f out: rdn wl over 2f out: sn wl bhd: t.o* **33/1**

0-0 **10** *7* **Florida Legend (IRE)**[92] 1674 3-8-9 .... SaleemGolam(3) 13 10
(Miss J Feilden) *w ldrs: led after 2f tl over 5f out: wknd 3f out: t.o* **33/1**

00 **11** *nk* **Queen Of Song**[42] 3122 4-9-2 .... RobynBrisland(5) 3 9
(G L Moore) *chsd ldrs tl over 5f out: sn rdn and lost pl: t.o* **50/1**

0 **12** *20* **Forementor**[25] 3647 3-8-6 ow1 .... JamesMillman(7) 8 —
(D K Ivory) *bhd: lost tch 6f out: t.o* **50/1**

2m 6.24s **Going Correction** -0.25s/f (Stan)
WFA 3 from 4yo 9lb **12** Ran SP% **126.8**
Speed ratings (Par 100):96,93,92,91,91 88,86,78,77,71 71,55
CSF £26.73 TOTE £8.80: £2.00, £1.60, £4.50; EX 29.40 Trifecta £139.30 Part won. Pool: £196.30 - 0.60 winning units..
Owner C J Murfitt **Bred** Marston Stud **Trained** Newmarket, Suffolk

FOCUS
An ordinary maiden and probably sound, but no better than fair form.

4397 DEREK BURRIDGE RACING & GOLF TROPHIES CONDITIONS STKS 6f
4:00 (4:01) (Class 4) 2-Y-O **£4,533** (£1,348; £674; £336) **Stalls** High

Form RPR

4100 **1** **Gold Spirit (IRE)**[12] 4026 2-8-10 86 .... RichardMullen 2 87
(E J O'Neill) *wnt lft s: chsd ldr tl led over 2f out: styd on wl u.p* **11/10**[2]

4315 **2** *3/4* **The Old Fella**[31] 3445 2-8-12 95 .... DaneO'Neill 3 87
(R Hannon) *trckd ldrs: swtchd lft over 2f out: ev ch wl over 1f out: no ex last 100yds* **5/6**[1]

60 **3** *9* **Prince Of Charm (USA)**[18] 3851 2-8-10 .... TPQueally 4 58
(P Mitchell) *hld up in last: effrt over 2f out: sn ev ch: wknd over 1f out* **33/1**

1355 **4** *3* **Mind The Style**[43] 3064 2-8-9 88 .... AmirQuinn(3) 1 51
(W G M Turner) *sn led: hdd over 2f out: sn rdn and wknd* **12/1**[3]

1m 12.76s **Going Correction** +0.10s/f (Good) **4** Ran SP% **112.8**
Speed ratings (Par 96):96,95,83,79
CSF £2.49 TOTE £2.20; EX 2.80.
Owner Roadmate Racing **Bred** Norelands Bloodstock **Trained** Averham Park, Notts

FOCUS
A small field but featuring a couple of useful performers. The race effectively turned into a match but looks sound with the second the guide.

NOTEBOOK
Gold Spirit(IRE) had not disgraced himself in tougher contests on his last two starts and confirmed himself to be a very useful performer on this drop in grade. A winner now on good to firm ground and good to soft, he got the extra furlong well, and the Doncaster Sales race at York later this month is the target. (op 11-8 tchd 6-4 in places)
The Old Fella, made favourite over Gold Spirit, had to give 2lb to that rival and, in theory, they ran to the same level. He is a very useful performer but is not going to be the easiest to place. (op 10-11 tchd 4-5)
Prince Of Charm(USA) was out of his depth but picked up a few hundred pounds in prizemoney for beating one home.
Mind The Style, who would have probably preferred quicker ground, appears to be going the wrong way. His rating gave him a chance in this company but he has not shown a lot since finishing third in the Lily Agnes back in May. Official explanation: jockey said gelding was unsuited by the good to soft (good in places) ground (op 8-1)

4398 FAMILY FUN DAY H'CAP 5f
4:30 (4:30) (Class 5) (0-75,75) 3-Y-O **£3,238** (£963; £481; £240) **Stalls** High

Form RPR

2615 **1** **Diane's Choice**[132] 851 3-9-4 **72** .... DaneO'Neill 8 78
(J Akehurst) *mde all on stands' rail: rdn 2f out: hld on gamely ins fnl f* **9/2**[3]

0005 **2** *3/4* **Be My Charm**[17] 3866 3-7-9 **56** oh9 .... LauraReynolds(7) 6 59
(M Blanshard) *taken down early: slowly away: hld up: hdwy wl over 1f out: wnt 2nd jst ins fnl f: kpt on* **16/1**

5023 **3** *1/2* **Jucebabe**[6] 4164 3-8-2 **56** oh2 .... JimmyQuinn 5 57
(J L Spearing) *restless in stalls: t.k.h: hld up: rdn over 2f out: styd on ins fnl f: nt rch ldrs* **3/1**[2]

1-33 **4** *nk* **Queen Cobra (IRE)**[37] 3268 3-9-7 **75** .... SteveDrowne 2 75+
(H Morrison) *chsd ldrs: drvn and ev ch wl over 1f out: hung lft and no ex ins fnl f* **9/4**[1]

000 **5** *1 3/4* **Phinerine**[19] 3821 3-8-5 **59** .... (b) TPQueally 1 53
(R A Harris) *prom on outer: rdn and hung lft 2f out: wknd ins fnl f* **10/1**

6120 **6** *1/2* **Glenargo (USA)**[8] 4164 3-8-10 **64** .... (p) AdrianMcCarthy 7 56
(R A Harris) *w wnr: rdn 2f out: wknd ins fnl f* **7/1**

4504 **7** *3 1/2* **Supreme Kiss**[8] 4164 3-8-3 **57** .... (bt) RichardThomas 4 36
(Miss B Sanders) *slowly away: chsd ldrs: rdn 2f out: btn whn hung lft ins fnl f* **7/1**

59.25 secs **Going Correction** +0.10s/f (Good) **7** Ran SP% **113.9**
Speed ratings (Par 100):101,99,99,98,95 94,89
CSF £67.43 CT £247.72 TOTE £5.70: £3.40, £2.80; EX 57.40 Trifecta £130.60 Part won. Pool: £184.00 - 0.20 winning units..
Owner The Grass Is Greener Partnership Ii **Bred** Green Pastures Farm **Trained** Epsom, Surrey

FOCUS
A modest handicap and the form looks reasonable, with the third the best guide.
Queen Cobra(IRE) Official explanation: jockey said filly hung left
Supreme Kiss Official explanation: jockey said filly hung left

4399 LINGFIELD PARK 0870 2200022 H'CAP 7f 140y
5:00 (5:00) (Class 5) (0-75,75) 3-Y-O+ **£3,238** (£963; £481; £240) **Stalls** Centre

Form RPR

2525 **1** **Taranaki**[23] 3705 8-8-4 **58** .... JamieHamblett(7) 4 66
(P D Cundell) *swtchd to stands' rail sn after s and racd alone: rdn over 2f out: overall ldr 1f out: drvn out* **7/1**

5413 **2** *1 1/4* **Linda's Colin (IRE)**[13] 4009 4-9-6 **67** .... (p) AdrianMcCarthy 2 72
(R A Harris) *t.k.h: swtchd in bhd centre gp 5f out: hdwy over 1f out: wnt 2nd ins fnl f: kpt on* **8/1**

4225 **3** *nk* **Grizedale (IRE)**[15] 3928 7-10-0 **75** .... (t) MichaelTebbutt 3 81+
(J Akehurst) *t.k.h: hld up: rdn to ld centre gp over 2f out: sn hung rt and hdd 1f out: no ex last 100yds* **3/1**[1]

5431 **4** *hd* **Charlie Bear**[15] 3948 5-8-8 **58** .... SaleemGolam(3) 1 62
(Miss Z C Davison) *rrd leaving stalls: cl up in centre: ev ch and rdn 2f out: one pce* **5/1**[3]

3042 **5** *2* **Mina A Salem**[29] 3532 4-9-12 **73** .... RichardMullen 5 72
(C E Brittain) *led centre gp: rdn and hdd over 2f out: one pce* **4/1**[2]

6202 **6** *shd* **Saxon Lil (IRE)**[9] 4116 4-9-8 **69** .... SteveDrowne 8 67
(J L Spearing) *trckd ldrs in centre: rdn and ev ch 2f out: wknd ins fnl f* **4/1**[2]

1146 **7** *3 1/2* **Le Chiffre (IRE)**[16] 3898 4-9-9 **70** .... (p) TPQueally 7 60
(R A Harris) *hld up in centre: rdn 3f out: wknd over 1f out* **12/1**

3360 **8** *3 1/2* **Veronica's Girl**[18] 3848 3-9-1 **69** .... DaneO'Neill 6 50
(W J Knight) *trckd ldrs in centre: rdn 3f out: wknd over 1f out* **16/1**

1m 33.43s **Going Correction** +0.10s/f (Good)
WFA 3 from 4yo+ 7lb **8** Ran SP% **118.9**
Speed ratings (Par 103):94,92,92,92,90 90,86,83
CSF £63.38 CT £206.36 TOTE £8.90: £2.70, £2.90, £1.80; EX 63.00 Trifecta £66.10 Pool: £195.72 - 2.10 winning units. Place 6 £191.56, Place 5 £143.98..
Owner Miss M C Fraser **Bred** D W Evers **Trained** Compton, Berks
■ Stewards' Enquiry : Jamie Hamblett two-day ban: used whip with excessive frequency (Aug 25-26)

FOCUS
A modest handicap in which the winning rider's decision to switch his mount to the stands'-side rail proved decisive.
T/Plt: £166.00 to a £1 stake. Pool: £52,808.20. 232.10 winning tickets. T/Qpdt: £105.50 to a £1 stake. Pool: £2,511.00. 17.60 winning tickets. SP

4376 REDCAR (L-H)

Sunday, August 13

OFFICIAL GOING: Good to firm (good in places) changing to good after race 2 (3.10) and to good to soft after race 4 (4.10)

After 8mm rain before racing and more to come the ground was reckoned good to soft at the start and soft in the end. The official version was always behind

Wind: Fresh; half-against Weather: Cool, blustery and persistent heavy rain

4400 EUROPEAN BREEDERS FUND MAIDEN FILLIES' STKS 7f
2:40 (2:44) (Class 5) 2-Y-O £3,886 (£1,156; £577; £288) Stalls Centre

Form RPR

0 **1** **Musical Mirage (USA)**14 [3982] 2-9-0 .... RobbieFitzpatrick 9 80+
(G A Swinbank) *hld up in mid-field: hdwy over 2f out: led 1f out: drew clr* **25/1**

2 4 **Starbougg** 2-9-0 .... PaulEddery 11 70
(B Smart) *chsd ldrs: sn drvn along: kpt on same pce fnl f* **16/1**

3 1 1/2 **Golden Dagger (IRE)** 2-9-0 .... NCallan 13 66+
(K A Ryan) *trckd ldrs: led over 5f out: edgd lft and hdd 1f out: kpt on same pce* **6/1**2

0 **4** 1 **Pret A Porter (UAE)**20 [3796] 2-9-0 .... PaulHanagan 3 64
(M R Channon) *mid-div: hdwy over 2f out: kpt on same pce* **16/1**

5 1 **Chasing Memories (IRE)** 2-8-9 .... MarkLawson(5) 10 61
(B Smart) *sn in rr and drvn along: hdwy 3f out: kpt on: nvr rchd ldrs* **50/1**

36 **6** 1 **Love On Sight**15 [3925] 2-9-0 .... FrankieMcDonald 2 59
(A P Jarvis) *trckd ldrs: rdn and wknd appr fnl f* **8/15**1

03 **7** 1 **Falimar**17 [3878] 2-9-0 .... TomEaves 8 56
(Miss J A Camacho) *sn in rr and pushed along: styd on fnl 2f: nvr nr ldrs* **11/1**3

00 **8** 3 1/2 **Featherlight**23 [3707] 2-9-0 .... PatCosgrave 5 48
(N A Callaghan) *s.i.s: sn detached in rr: swvd rt over 2f out: sme late hdwy* **100/1**

9 1/2 **Montjeu's Melody (IRE)** 2-9-0 .... PhillipMakin 12 46
(E J O'Neill) *chsd ldrs: wknd over 2f out* **16/1**

0 **10** 2 **Xaar Too Busy**57 [2638] 2-9-0 .... TPO'Shea 4 41
(Mrs A Duffield) *prom early: lost pl and in rr after 2f* **40/1**

0 **11** 9 **Amaretto Venture**34 [3358] 2-9-0 .... GrahamGibbons 1 19
(J J Quinn) *swvd lft s: a bhd* **80/1**

0 **12** 5 **Double Precedent**17 [3878] 2-9-0 .... J-PGuillambert 6 6
(M Johnston) *led over 1f: lost pl over 2f out: sn bhd* **16/1**

0 **13** 12 **Star Of Night**16 [3908] 2-9-0 .... TonyHamilton 7 —
(C Grant) *sn outpcd and bhd* **100/1**

1m 28.47s (3.57) **Going Correction** +0.375s/f (Good) **13** Ran SP% **122.8**

Speed ratings (Par 91):94,89,87,86,85 84,83,79,78,76 66,60,46

CSF £376.60 TOTE £28.70: £4.40, £3.50, £2.20; EX 779.90.

Owner Elsa Crankshaw & G Allan Ii **Bred** Budget Stables **Trained** Melsonby, N Yorks

■ The ground was described as 'good to soft', a lot easier than the official version.

FOCUS

A fair maiden with the favourite flopping it probably did not take a deal of winning but the winner looks to have further improvement in her especially when stepped up to a mile.

NOTEBOOK

Musical Mirage(USA), much better suited by the seven rather than the five she ran over on her debut, in the end won going right away and there may be even better to come, especially over a mile.

Starbougg, a March foal, is out of a prolific winner. She needs to furnish and was quite green but, after working her way upsides, in the end like the rest, found the winner much too strong. This will have taught her a fair amount. (op 14-1)

Golden Dagger(IRE), a close-coupled newcomer, travelled strongly in the lead and kept going all the way to the line. She is bred to do better over middle distances at three. (op 13-2)

Pret A Porter(UAE), who is not that big, showed more than on her debut and will be better suited by a mile.

Chasing Memories(IRE), a cheap purchase, is on the leg and narrow. She stuck on in her own time and should be wiser as a result.

Love On Sight, a sharp sort, is a good mover. She seemed to flounder in the rain-softened ground and was a long way below the form she showed in a Group 3 event at Ascot. (op 4-6 tchd 8-11 tchd 4-5 in places)

4401 WEDDINGS AT REDCAR RACECOURSE H'CAP 6f
3:10 (3:12) (Class 6) (0-65,60) 3-Y-O+ £2,730 (£806; £403) Stalls Centre

Form RPR

0002 **1** **Frimley's Matterry**8 [4157] 6-8-8 **46** .... MichaelJStainton(5) 12 55
(R E Barr) *mid-div: hdwy over 2f out: led ins fnl f: r.o* **8/1**

0003 **2** nk **Missperon (IRE)**10 [4070] 4-9-4 **51** ....(b) NCallan 8 59
(K A Ryan) *led after 1f: edgd rt and hdd ins last: no ex towards fin* **7/1**3

5200 **3** 1 1/2 **Petite Mac**9 [4116] 6-9-5 **59** .... SuzzanneFrance(7) 5 63
(N Bycroft) *bhd: hdwy over 2f out: styd on wl fnl f* **8/1**

5356 **4** 1 1/2 **Blue Knight (IRE)**2 [4324] 7-9-9 **56** ....(vt) StephenCarson 1 55
(D Carroll) *bhd and drvn along: hdwy on wd outside over 2f out: styd on same pce appr fnl f* **14/1**

0560 **5** nk **Red Chairman**4 [4253] 4-9-8 **60** ....(p) DeclanMcGann(5) 17 58
(R Johnson) *hld up in rr: hdwy on ins over 2f out: kpt on wl fnl f* **20/1**

6000 **6** nk **Jahia (NZ)**14 [3988] 7-9-0 **47** .... RobbieFitzpatrick 14 44
(P T Midgley) *w ldr: one pce appr fnl f* **25/1**

0040 **7** 3/4 **Flur Na H Alba**14 [3988] 7-9-13 **60** ....(b) GrahamGibbons 13 55
(J J Quinn) *chsd ldrs: outpcd over 2f out: kpt on fnl f* **16/1**

1066 **8** 1 **Dark Champion**16 [3913] 6-9-9 **56** ....(b) PatCosgrave 16 48
(R E Barr) *chsd ldrs: one pce fnl 2f* **14/1**

0003 **9** nk **Quantica (IRE)**20 [3786] 7-8-13 **46** ....(t) KimTinkler 3 37
(N Tinkler) *bhd and drvn along: hdwy on outer over 2f out: nvr nr ldrs* **7/1**3

004U **10** 1 1/4 **Sounds Simla (IRE)**16 [3912] 3-9-9 **60** .... PaulFessey 10 47
(J F Coupland) *prom: one pce fnl 2f* **33/1**

1260 **11** nk **Million Percent**11 [4054] 7-9-8 **60** .... AndrewMullen(5) 15 47
(C R Dore) *led 1f: chsd ldrs: wknd over 1f out* **12/1**

-000 **12** 1/2 **Quote Unquote**21 [3759] 3-8-12 **54** .... MarkLawson(5) 11 39
(J Parkes) *in rr and sn drvn along: nvr on terms* **66/1**

3506 **13** shd **Safranine (IRE)**5 [4230] 9-9-1 **55** .... AnnStokell(7) 18 40
(Miss A Stokell) *in rr: sme hdwy 2f out: nvr on terms* **20/1**

0302 **14** 1 3/4 **Val De Maal (IRE)**10 [4067] 6-9-10 **57** ....(v) TomEaves 7 36
(Miss J A Camacho) *mid-div: lost pl over 2f out* **5/1**1

0-04 **15** 3 1/2 **Hout Bay**8 [4157] 9-9-6 **53** ....(p) PaulHanagan 2 22
(R A Fahey) *a in rr* **13/2**2

4000 **16** 1 1/2 **Bahrain Gold (IRE)**5 [4233] 6-9-5 **52** .... DaleGibson 6 16
(N P McCormack) *a bhd* **20/1**

0-00 **17** 2 1/2 **Stokesies Luck (IRE)**50 [2881] 3-8-8 **45** .... PaulQuinn 9 2
(J L Spearing) *s.i.s: a bhd* **50/1**

1m 16.38s (4.68) **Going Correction** +0.70s/f (Yiel)

WFA 3 from 4yo+ 4lb **17** Ran SP% **128.7**

Speed ratings (Par 101):96,95,93,91,91 90,89,88,88,86 86,85,85,82,78 76,72

CSF £60.87 CT £496.61 TOTE £10.40: £4.00, £1.70, £2.90, £3.30; EX 103.10.

Owner Mrs R E Barr **Bred** T P Lyons **Trained** Seamer, N Yorks

FOCUS

A low-grade handicap and those towards the far side seemed to be at a disadvantage. The form is straightforward with the first two setting the level.

Safranine(IRE) Official explanation: jockey said mare found the good ground too soft

Val De Maal(IRE) Official explanation: trainer said, regarding the poor form shown, gelding was unsuited by the loose ground

4402 BREAKTHROUGH BREAST CANCER MAIDEN H'CAP 1m 2f
3:40 (3:41) (Class 5) (0-75,70) 3-Y-O+ £3,238 (£963; £481; £240) Stalls Low

Form RPR

5-53 **1** **Baileys Encore**12 [4020] 3-9-13 **69** .... J-PGuillambert 2 75
(M Johnston) *trckd ldr: led 3f out: kpt on fnl f: hld on towards fin* **7/4**1

4653 **2** hd **Mexican Bob**13 [4001] 3-9-9 **65** .... DaleGibson 7 71
(Heather Dalton) *sn trcking ldrs: t.k.h: chal over 2f out: rallied ins last: jst hld* **9/2**

5623 **3** 1 1/2 **Bollin Dolly**9 [4118] 3-10-0 **70** .... PaulHanagan 1 73
(T D Easterby) *led tl 3f out: kpt on same pce appr fnl f* **11/4**2

-400 **4** 2 1/2 **Bond Angel Eyes**49 [2896] 3-9-3 **59** .... GylesParkin 5 57
(G R Oldroyd) *hld up: hdwy on ins to chse ldrs 4f out: fdd fnl f* **25/1**

4055 **5** 2 **Airbound (USA)**26 [3621] 3-9-0 **61** .... GregFairley(5) 4 56
(M Johnston) *chsd ldrs: drvn over 4f out: outpcd fnl 2f* **3/1**3

/0-0 **6** 73 **Attack Minded**41 [3141] 5-8-9 **42** oh18 .... TonyHamilton 3 —
(L R James) *stdd s: detached in last: t.o 3f out* **66/1**

2m 13.54s (6.74) **Going Correction** +0.75s/f (Yiel)

WFA 3 from 5yo 9lb **6** Ran SP% **111.6**

Speed ratings (Par 103):103,102,101,99,98 39

CSF £10.01 TOTE £2.20: £1.10, £2.50; EX 11.70.

Owner G R Bailey Ltd (baileys Horse Feeds) **Bred** P And Mrs Venner **Trained** Middleham Moor, N Yorks

■ The official going description had been changed to good but it was still misleading.

FOCUS

A modest maiden handicap and, although sound enough, the form is not strong.

4403 MARY REVELEY RACING CLUB H'CAP 6f
4:10 (4:10) (Class 4) (0-85,84) 3-Y-O £6,477 (£1,927; £963; £481) Stalls Centre

Form RPR

2203 **1** **Damika (IRE)**21 [3761] 3-9-2 **84** .... MichaelJStainton(5) 11 94
(R M Whitaker) *hld up: smooth hdwy on ins to ld 2f out: r.o strly: readily* **2/1**1

4630 **2** 2 1/2 **Charlie Delta**2 [4328] 3-8-11 **81** .... KellyHarrison(7) 10 84
(D Carroll) *sn trcking ldrs: kpt on fnl f: tk 2nd nr fin* **16/1**

3033 **3** shd **The Terrier**23 [3718] 3-8-7 **70** .... DaleGibson 6 73
(G A Swinbank) *chsd ldrs: outpcd over 2f out: kpt on wl fnl f* **7/1**3

5426 **4** hd **Mulligan's Gold (IRE)**17 [3879] 3-8-7 **70** .... PaulMulrennan 7 72
(T D Easterby) *unruly in stalls: hld up: smooth hdwy over 2f out: kpt on fnl f* **10/1**

3504 **5** 1 **Choreography**11 [4058] 3-8-2 **65** oh3 .... AdrianTNicholls 4 66+
(D Nicholls) *v free to post: hld up in rr: hdwy over 2f out: nt clr run 1f out: kpt on ins last* **10/1**

-000 **6** nk **Colorus (IRE)**21 [3761] 3-9-3 **80** ....(p) PaulHanagan 5 78
(R A Fahey) *w ldrs: kpt on same pce appr fnl f* **15/2**

1220 **7** 2 **Angaric (IRE)**15 [3937] 3-8-9 **77** .... MarkLawson(5) 9 69
(B Smart) *chsd ldrs: wknd 1f out* **4/1**2

0000 **8** 8 **Crosby Hall**36 [3296] 3-8-2 **65** ....(t) KimTinkler 3 33
(N Tinkler) *s.i.s: hdwy to chse ldrs over 4f out: lost pl over 2f out* **33/1**

1556 **9** 1/2 **Spiritual Peace (IRE)**32 [3403] 3-9-0 **77** ....(p) NCallan 8 44
(K A Ryan) *led tl 2f out: edgd lft and sn wknd: eased* **8/1**

003- **10** 6 **Nell Tupp**334 [5202] 3-7-12 **66** oh5 ow1 .... AndrewElliott(5) 1 15
(G Woodward) *s.i.s: sn chsng ldrs on outer: lost pl over 2f out: sn bhd* **66/1**

1m 15.91s (4.21) **Going Correction** +0.75s/f (Yiel) **10** Ran SP% **117.2**

Speed ratings (Par 102):101,97,97,97,95 95,92,82,81,73

CSF £38.49 CT £198.47 TOTE £2.50: £1.20, £4.70, £2.70; EX 57.60.

Owner G B Bedford **Bred** Patrick J Monahan **Trained** Scarcroft, W Yorks

FOCUS

A fair contest and a smooth success from the progressive winner. The form looks sound enough with those in the frame behind the winner close to their marks, but it is not that strong.

Spiritual Peace(IRE) Official explanation: jockey said colt had no more to give

4404 REDCAR CRICKET CLUB (S) STKS 1m 3f
4:40 (4:48) (Class 6) 3-5-Y-O £2,730 (£806; £403) Stalls Low

Form RPR

-006 **1** **Rock Haven (IRE)**15 [3944] 4-9-2 52 .... AndrewElliott(5) 14 52
(J Mackie) *w ldrs: t.k.h: led over 3f out: shkn up 1f out: drvn out* **8/1**

5544 **2** 2 **Elite Land**6 [4195] 3-8-4 45 .... SuzzanneFrance(7) 8 49
(N Bycroft) *bhd: hdwy on outside over 3f out: styd on to take 2nd nr line* **7/1**3

3546 **3** shd **Alisdanza**21 [3762] 4-9-2 48 .... DaleGibson 9 44
(G A Swinbank) *mid-div: stdy hdwy over 2f out: rdn over 1f out: kpt on same pce* **5/2**1

5466 **4** 1 1/4 **Campbells Lad**24 [3672] 5-9-4 40 .... PatrickMathers(3) 13 47
(Mrs G S Rees) *swtchd lft s: hd up in rr: hdwy and swtchd ins over 2f out: one pce fnl f* **33/1**

5002 **5** 2 1/2 **El Dee (IRE)**12 [4016] 3-8-4 43 .... KellyHarrison(7) 5 43
(D Carroll) *prom: effrt over 2f out: one pce* **10/1**

6061 **6** nk **Ming Vase**15 [3944] 4-9-13 46 .... RobbieFitzpatrick 3 48
(P T Midgley) *trckd ldrs: hung lft over 2f out: fdd over 1f out* **15/2**

0360 **7** 4 **Ebony Lady**12 [4016] 3-8-1 32 ....(p) NataliaGemelova(5) 12 31
(R M Whitaker) *chsd ldrs: wknd over 1f out* **50/1**

0034 **8** 2 1/2 **Glory Be (ITY)**3 [4289] 4-9-2 40 .... AdrianTNicholls 1 27
(J L Spearing) *led: hdd over 3f out: lost pl over 1f out* **13/2**2

0060 **9** 5 **Fairytale Of York (IRE)**4 [4255] 3-8-1 34 .... MichaelJStainton(5) 11 19
(D Carroll) *chsd ldrs: effrt 4f out: lost pl over 1f out* **50/1**

6-60 **10** 2 **Sebaaq (USA)**61 [2535] 3-8-11 52 .... TomEaves 10 21
(M E Sowersby) *hdwy and in tch after 3f: lost pl over 2f out* **16/1**

0-00 **11** 14 **Broadway Calling**197 [217] 3-8-6 60 .... GregFairley(5) 4 —
(M E Sowersby) *chsd ldrs: lost pl over 3f out: sn bhd* **25/1**

0500 **12** *7* **Tallyhobye**[14] 3983 3-9-3 48 PaulHanagan 2 —
(M E Sowersby) *hld up in rr: hdwy on inner 4f out: lost pl over 2f out: sn bhd* **12/1**

-250 **13** *6* **Bint Il Sultan (IRE)**[41] 3140 4-9-2 41 PaulMulrennan 7 —
(W M Brisbourne) *stmbld s: a bhd* **14/1**

2m 29.49s (8.49) **Going Correction** +0.80s/f (Soft)
WFA 3 from 4yo+ 10lb **13** Ran SP% **117.3**
Speed ratings (Par 101):101,99,99,98,96 96,93,91,88,86 76,71,67
CSF £60.16 TOTE £11.00: £2.50, £3.10, £1.80; EX 69.20.There was no bid for the winner.
Owner Mrs Sue Adams **Bred** Joe Crowley And Mr And Mrs A P O'Brien **Trained** Church Broughton , Derbys

■ The ground was officially changed to good to soft ahead of this but by now the riders thought it was genuinely soft.

FOCUS
A poor race even by selling race standards but the winner always looked in control and along with the fourth sets the level.

4405 HOT CHOCOLATE PLAYS REDCAR 24TH AUGUST H'CAP 1m

5:10 (5:16) (Class 6) (0-60,60) 3-Y-0+ **£2,730** (£806; £403) **Stalls** Centre

Form RPR

0000 **1** **Typhoon Ginger (IRE)**[17] 3883 11-9-3 **54** AndrewElliott(5) 13 70
(G Woodward) *hld up in rr: hdwy over 2f out: styd on to ld jst ins last: drvn out* **8/1**

3651 **2** *1* **Dazzler Mac**[9] 4120 5-9-1 **54** SuzzanneFrance(7) 14 68
(N Bycroft) *hld up in rr: smooth hdwy on ins over 2f out: led over 1f out: hdd and no ex jst ins last* **5/1**[2]

0065 **3** *7* **Sea Frolic (IRE)**[9] 4114 5-8-8 **45** (v) RoryMoore(5) 16 44
(Jennie Candlish) *trckd ldrs: hung lft over 1f out: one pce* **16/1**

03-3 **4** *3* **Primo Gold**[25] 3642 3-9-5 **58** StephenCarson 2 50
(W R Swinburn) *chsd ldrs: drvn over 2f out: one pce* **11/4**[1]

0-00 **5** *½* **Etijahaat (IRE)**[81] 1233 4-9-11 **60** NeilMulholland(3) 17 52
(C W Fairhurst) *led tl hdd & wknd over 1f out* **33/1**

0004 **6** *hd* **Stormingmichaelori**[16] 3909 3-8-6 **45** (p) VHalliday 11 36
(N Wilson) *chsd ldrs: lost pl over 1f out* **33/1**

-100 **7** *nk* **Sonderborg**[15] 3947 5-9-1 **47** (p) DaleGibson 18 38
(J Mackie) *hld up in rr: effrt on inner over 2f out: nvr nr ldrs* **12/1**

0164 **8** *16* **The Great Delaney**[11] 4060 3-9-6 **59** RobbieFitzpatrick 12 15
(T J Pitt) *mid-div: sn drvn along: lost pl over 2f out: sn bhd* **5/1**[2]

6004 **9** *2* **Pauline's Prince**[15] 3947 4-9-4 **57** RussellKennemore(7) 1 10
(R Hollinshead) *in tch on outer: lost pl 2f out* **8/1**

1120 **10** *2* **Pay Time**[16] 3912 7-9-7 **58** MichaelJStainton(5) 10 7
(R E Barr) *in tch on outer: drvn over 3f out: edgd lft and lost pl 2f out* **6/1**[3]

0-00 **11** *10* **Beacon Rambler**[23] 3698 4-8-6 **43** oh1 ow2 MarkLawson(5) 8 —
(F Watson) *s.i.s: sn drvn along: a bhd: t.o 3f out* **66/1**

0000 **12** *3½* **Bottomless Wallet**[8] 4155 5-8-9 **41** oh1 (v[1]) PaulHanagan 5 —
(F Watson) *mid-div: lost pl over 2f out: sn wl bhd* **66/1**

1m 43.85s (6.05) **Going Correction** +0.80s/f (Soft)
WFA 3 from 4yo+ 7lb **12** Ran SP% **119.0**
Speed ratings (Par 101):101,100,93,90,89 89,89,73,71,69 59,55
CSF £47.10 CT £632.91 TOTE £12.10: £3.20, £2.40, £3.80; EX 63.00 Place 6 £265.11, Place 5 £46.95..
Owner Garry Woodward **Bred** Pat And Mary Dillon **Trained** Conisbrough, S Yorks

FOCUS
Just two ultimately mattered in this low-grade handicap and they came home well strung out, with the runner-up to recent form. Those that raced towards the far side were at a disadvantage.
The Great Delaney Official explanation: jockey said gelding ran flat
T/Jkpt: Not won. T/Plt: £1,010.20 to a £1 stake. Pool £57,504.05. 41.55 winning tickets. T/Qpdt: £33.50 to a £1 stake. Pool £3,752.40. 82.70 winning tickets. WG

4406 - (Foreign Racing) - See Raceform Interactive

3571 CURRAGH (R-H)
Sunday, August 13

OFFICIAL GOING: Good to firm

4407a UNITED ARAB EMIRATES RACING AND EQUESTRIAN FEDERATION ROYAL WHIP STKS (GROUP 2) 1m 2f

2:45 (2:45) 3-Y-0+ **£56,034** (£16,379; £7,758; £2,586)

RPR

1 **Mustameet (USA)**[29] 3559 5-9-9 115 DPMcDonogh 3 121+
(Kevin Prendergast, Ire) *settled 3rd: cl up travelling wl st: qcknd to ld over 1f out: sn clr: easily* **3/1**[3]

2 *3* **Chelsea Rose (IRE)**[8] 4127 4-9-6 113 PShanahan 1 113
(C Collins, Ire) *cl 2nd: disp ld fr 1/2-way: rdn and slt advantage st: hdd over 1f out: kpt on same pce* **7/4**[1]

3 *1½* **Soar With Eagles (USA)**[29] 3562 3-9-0 KFallon 4 113
(A P O'Brien, Ire) *hld up in tch: rdn and outpcd over 3f out: kpt on u.p fr 2f out* **7/1**

4 *1¾* **Heliostatic (IRE)**[15] 3964 3-9-0 114 KJManning 2 110
(J S Bolger, Ire) *led: jnd 1/2-way: rdn and narrowly hdd early st: no ex fr over 1f out* **2/1**[2]

2m 7.03s **Going Correction** +0.175s/f (Good)
WFA 3 from 4yo+ 9lb **4** Ran SP% **107.2**
Speed ratings: 115,112,111,110
CSF £8.46 TOTE £2.80; DF 11.40.
Owner Hamdan Al Maktoum **Bred** Shadwell Farm LLC **Trained** Friarstown, Co Kildare

FOCUS
A quality line-up for this Group 2, and solid form for the grade.

NOTEBOOK
Mustameet(USA) has been in terrific form this season and had struck four times at stakes level, including when landing the International Stakes here last month. The five-year-old, who relishes quick ground, had his stamina to prove over this trip but provided conclusive evidence that a mile and a quarter is within his range. Settled just off the front pair, he was travelling strongly with two furlongs to run and, once switched out to deliver his challenge, he picked up well and soon put the result beyond doubt. The Irish Champion Stakes will be next for him. (op 5/2)
Chelsea Rose(IRE) ran another honest race just eight days after her fourth place behind Ouija Board and Alexander Goldrun in the Nassau Stakes. She helped to force the pace with Heliostatic and had a spell in the lead before the winner took over. She stuck to her task once headed and should add to her stakes-race haul. (op 2/1)
Soar With Eagles(USA) was taking a big step up in class from his maiden victory - the form of which has been working out well - over course and distance last month. He appeared to be struggling at the rear nearing the straight but stayed on well under pressure from over a furlong out. This was only his third run and there should be more to come from him. A step up to a mile and a half might also be in his favour. (op 6/1)
Heliostatic(IRE) won the Meld Stakes over this trip last month and had previously run well when seventh in the Irish Derby, but he was not at his best here. He cut out the running until headed by Chelsea Rose early in the straight and was fighting a losing battle from over a furlong out. (op 7/4)

4409a INDEPENDENT WATERFORD WEDGWOOD PHOENIX STKS (GROUP 1) (ENTIRE COLTS & FILLIES) 6f

3:45 (3:45) 2-Y-O **£122,482** (£39,724; £19,034; £6,620; £4,551; £2,482)

RPR

1 **Holy Roman Emperor (IRE)**[42] 3126 2-9-1 KFallon 4 118+
(A P O'Brien, Ire) *trckd ldrs: 5th 2f out: impr to chal over 1f out: led under 1f out: qcknd clr: v easily* **13/8**[1]

2 *1¾* **Hellvelyn**[54] 2719 2-9-1 TedDurcan 6 111
(B Smart) *cl up: 2nd 1/2-way: led 1 1/2f out: hdd under 1f out: kpt on: no ch w wnr* **13/8**[1]

3 *½* **Miss Beatrix (IRE)**[25] 3658 2-8-12 WSupple 3 107
(Kevin Prendergast, Ire) *hld up: 6th 1/2-way: rdn and kpt on fr 1 1/2f out* **50/1**

4 *hd* **Brazilian Bride (IRE)**[69] 2309 2-8-12 DPMcDonogh 7 106
(Kevin Prendergast, Ire) *sn chsd ldrs in 4th: rdn over 2f out: kpt on same pce u.p fr over 1f out* **7/1**[2]

5 *shd* **Drayton (IRE)**[42] 3126 2-9-1 WMLordan 5 109
(T Stack, Ire) *led: rdn and hdd 1 1/2f out: kpt on same pce fnl f* **7/1**[2]

6 *1¼* **Rabatash (USA)**[22] 3751 2-9-1 MJKinane 1 105
(David Wachman, Ire) *hld up in rr: kpt on wout threatening fr 1 1/2f out* **14/1**[3]

7 *6* **King Of Swords (IRE)**[12] 4026 2-9-1 PShanahan 2 87
(C Collins, Ire) *prom: cl 3rd to 2f out: wknd 1 1/2f out: eased ins fnl f* **100/1**

1m 11.06s **Going Correction** -0.25s/f (Firm) **7** Ran SP% **110.8**
Speed ratings: 112,109,109,108,108 106,98
CSF £3.91 TOTE £2.50: £1.50, £1.80; DF 5.10.
Owner Mrs John Magnier **Bred** Tower Bloodstock **Trained** Ballydoyle, Co Tipperary

FOCUS
An impressive performance from the winner, who gave his trainer his eighth win in this event.

NOTEBOOK
Holy Roman Emperor(IRE) moved through smoothly approaching the final furlong and, after quickening up and leading under a furlong out, he settled the outcome in a hurry before winning comfortably. A quick reappearance in the Prix Morny next Sunday is being considered, while plans for later in the season will depend on what develops with some of his fellow Ballydoyle juveniles, including Duke Of Marmalade and Trinity College, one of whom will be the trainer's main contender for the Futurity Stakes at the Curragh on August 26. He is now 8-1 favourite for the 2000 Guineas. (op Evs)
Hellvelyn raced a bit keenly early but was soon settled on the pace. He went to the front under two furlongs out but had no answer when the winner quickened past him. To his credit, he kept on to the line but the winner appeared to have plenty in hand in the closing stages. The reality is probably that Holy Roman Emperor is now a much better and experienced horse than when they last met. (op 9/4)
Miss Beatrix(IRE) had been a bit keen in some of her previous races but she settled well here and produced her best effort, running on from over a furlong out, having had only one rival behind her two furlongs out. She is eligible for the Shelbourne Hotel Goffs Million and the Fillies Five Hundred here next month, but the Moyglare Stud Stakes here on August 27 may be her next target.
Brazilian Bride(IRE), winner of a Group 3 fillies' event at Naas and unbeaten in two starts, ran a good race. After coming under pressure two furlongs out, she kept on quite well inside the final furlong. (op 8/1)
Drayton(IRE), beaten three-quarters of a length when second to Holy Roman Emperor in the Railway Stakes here last month, again made the running. He was headed under two furlongs out and only weakened out of the first three near the finish. It is difficult to say he does not stay the trip, although five furlongs, over which he has twice won at Listed level, probably suits him better (op 6/1)
Rabatash(USA), unlucky not to have run into the money in the Windsor Castle Stakes at Royal Ascot where he was badly hampered at the start, had won his maiden over five furlongs with some ease at Tipperary last month. However, he failed to make any impact here, although he did make some headway from behind over the final furlong. (op 16/1)

4410a PATRICK P.O'LEARY MEMORIAL PHOENIX SPRINT STKS (GROUP 3) 6f

4:15 (4:15) 3-Y-O+ **£33,620** (£9,827; £4,655; £1,551)

RPR

1 **Moss Vale (IRE)**[30] 3494 5-9-10 KFallon 5 123+
(D Nicholls) *cl 2nd: led shortly after 1/2-way: r.o wl fr over 1f out: comf* **7/4**[1]

2 *1¾* **Red Clubs (IRE)**[30] 3494 3-9-4 MichaelHills 8 116
(B W Hills) *trckd ldrs in 5th: prog 1/2-way: 2nd 2f out: kpt on u.p wout troubling wnr* **6/1**[3]

3 *1½* **Pivotal Point**[30] 3494 6-9-8 SebSanders 1 112
(P J Makin) *hld up towards rr: 5th and hdwy after 1/2-way: 3rd 2f out: kpt on* **9/2**[2]

4 *nk* **The Trader (IRE)**[23] 3709 8-9-5 (b) TedDurcan 3 108
(M Blanshard) *hld up: 5th 2f out: kpt on fr over 1f out* **12/1**

5 *1½* **Fayr Jag (IRE)**[10] 4080 7-9-10 DavidAllan 7 108
(T D Easterby) *chsd ldrs: 3rd and rdn 1/2-way: 4th 2f out: one pce* **11/1**

6 *hd* **Miss Sally (IRE)**[67] 2369 4-9-5 109 (t) JMurtagh 4 103
(M Halford, Ire) *led: hdd after 1/2-way: sn lost pl: last 1 1/2f out: kpt on same pce u.p fnl f* **7/1**

7 *shd* **Beckermet (IRE)**[7] 4174 4-9-5 DPMcDonogh 2 102
(R F Fisher) *hld up in tch: 6th 2f out: kpt on same pce u.p* **8/1**

8 *1¾* **Indian Maiden (IRE)**[7] 4174 6-9-2 FMBerry 6 94
(M S Saunders) *towards rr: rdn and no imp fr 2f out* **14/1**

1m 11.09s **Going Correction** -0.25s/f (Firm)
WFA 3 from 4yo+ 4lb **8** Ran SP% **115.1**
Speed ratings: 112,109,107,107,105 105,104,102
CSF £12.66 TOTE £2.50: £1.50, £2.30, £1.60; DF 12.70.
Owner Lady O'Reilly **Bred** Derek Veitch **Trained** Sessay, N Yorks

FOCUS
A decent renewal of this Group 3 rated around the second back to his best.

NOTEBOOK
Moss Vale(IRE) led home the powerful British challenge in good style to book his place in the Nunthorpe Stakes at York this month. Successful in a Group 3 over the course and distance in May, he had gone on to strike at Group 2 level in France and was a good fifth in the July Cup last time. Initially settled close to the pace, he took over in front passing halfway and soon opened up a useful lead. He was still going well enough when Red Clubs and Pivotal Point moved into challenging positions and asserted inside the final furlong once asked to raise his effort. He has looked better than ever this season and should continue to do well when moving back up in grade. (op 9/4)

Red Clubs(IRE) finished much closer to the winner than when they met in the July Cup and produced his best effort since winning the Greenham Stakes in the spring. He looked a big threat to the winner with over a furlong to run but just could not quite get on terms. This was an encouraging effort and he looks to have a good future at this level. (op 5/1)
Pivotal Point was another to come here off a July Cup outing, where he finished a respectable eighth. He started a forward move when Moss Vale struck the front and kept on without getting to the front two. A Group 3 winner this season, he should continue to be a force at this level. (op 4/1)
The Trader(IRE) kept on over the final two furlongs but could not land a telling blow. He finished closer to Pivotal Point than when they met in a Group 3 at Sandown last month, though, and probably remains capable of further stakes-race success. (op 10/1)
Fayr Jag(IRE), who had recently won a Group 3 at Newbury and also run well in a similar contest at Goodwood last time, did not seem to match that level of form and is capable of better. (op 10/1)
Miss Sally(IRE) was running for the first time in two months. She made the early running but gradually faded after Moss Vale took over in front. She is better than this and would probably prefer an easier surface. (op 6/1)

4408 - 4413a (Foreign Racing) - See Raceform Interactive

4190 COLOGNE (R-H)

Sunday, August 13

OFFICIAL GOING: Good

4414a RHEINLAND-POKAL DER SPARKASSE KOLNBONN (GROUP 1) 1m 4f

3:30 (3:32) 3-Y-O+ **£65,517** (£24,138; £11,724; £5,517)

			RPR
1		**Cherry Mix (FR)**^{15} [3927] 5-9-6 ... KerrinMcEvoy 5 (Saeed Bin Suroor) *tracked leader and soon 8l clear of remainder, led over 2f out, still 6l clear over 1 1/2f out, ridden out* **38/10**^{3}	121
2	*4*	**Fracas (IRE)**^{413} [2961] 4-9-6 ... JimmyFortune 2 (David Wachman, Ire) *raced in 4th, disputing 3rd straight, ridden 2f out, stayed on determinedly under pressure to take 2nd close home* **71/10**	114
3	*shd*	**Collier Hill**^{43} [3107] 8-9-6 ... DeanMcKeown 1 (G A Swinbank) *rcd in 3rd 8l bhd leading pair, rdn over 2f out, went 2nd over 1 1/2f out, styd on gamely tl no ex and lost 2nd cl hme* **22/10**^{1}	114
4	*2*	**Egerton (GER)**^{28} [3579] 5-9-6 ... THellier 3 (P Rau, Germany) *raced in 5th, n.m.r and switched outside over 1f out, n.m.r again inside final f, stayed on at same pace* **5/2**^{2}	111
5	*1 1/4*	**Song Writer (GER)**^{28} [3579] 6-9-6 ... ABoschert 4 (Carmen Bocskai, Switzerland) *raced in 7th early, 6th straight, kept on same pace final 2f* **99/10**	109
6	*6*	**All Spirit (GER)**^{28} [3579] 4-9-6 ... EPedroza 7 (N Sauer, Germany) *held up in last, never a factor* **263/10**	99
7	*1 1/4*	**Donaldson (GER)**^{28} [3579] 4-9-6 ... TMundry 8 (P Rau, Germany) *raced in 6th early, 8th straight, beaten 2f out* **64/10**	97
8	*1*	**El Tango (GER)**^{21} [3775] 4-9-6 ... WMongil 6 (P Schiergen, Germany) *held up in 8th, never a factor* **139/10**	96
9	*3 1/2*	**Academy Reward (IRE)**^{42} 6-9-6 ... AStarke 9 (Mario Hofer, Germany) *set strong pace til headed over 2f out, weakened* **203/10**	90

2m 28.25s (-4.65) **9** Ran SP% **130.8**
(including 10 Euro stake): WIN 48; PL 19, 27, 14; SF 338.
Owner Godolphin **Bred** S N C Lagardere Elevage **Trained** Newmarket, Suffolk

NOTEBOOK
Cherry Mix(FR) could be named the winner half a mile from home, as Donaldson's pacemaker, Academy Reward, gave him a beautiful lead, clear of the pack. Allowed such a lot of rope without doing too much, he was never going to be caught. Things are unlikely to pan out quite so perfectly for him again, but he is finally beginning to reveal the talent that saw him take second in the 2004 Arc. The Grosser Preis von Baden looks a suitable next target.
Fracas(IRE) made a pleasing return from injury, getting the better of a long battle with Collier Hill to take second on the line.
Collier Hill was unable to go the early pace, allowing Cherry Mix to build up an unassailable lead. The first off the bridle, he showed all his usual fighting qualities to only relinquish second in the last strides. He ideally needs faster ground and a longer trip, conditions that may well prevail when he defends his Irish St Leger crown.

4191 DEAUVILLE (R-H)

Sunday, August 13

OFFICIAL GOING: Turf course - very soft; all-weather - standard

4415a PRIX FRANCOIS BOUTIN (LISTED RACE) (STRAIGHT) 7f (S)

2:50 (2:48) 2-Y-O **£17,241** (£6,897; £5,172; £3,448; £1,724)

			RPR
1		**Visionario (IRE)**^{29} 2-9-2 ... LDettori 3 (A Fabre, France) **4/5**^{1}	106+
2	*2 1/2*	**Striving Storm (USA)**^{22} [3735] 2-9-2 ... AlanMunro 7 (P W Chapple-Hyam) *pressed leader after 2f, led over 2f out til approaching final f, kept on same pace (12/1)* **12/1**^{2}	100
3	*1*	**Ikat (IRE)**^{36} 2-8-13 ... C-PLemaire 5 (D Sepulchre, France) **16/1**^{3}	94
4	*2*	**Kahyasola (FR)** 2-8-13 ... FSpanu 6 (G Doleuze, France)	89
5	*4*	**Beta**^{14} [3990] 2-8-13 ... TGillet 8 (J E Pease, France)	79
6	*4*	**Neuf Trois (FR)**^{17} 2-8-13 ... JAuge 1 (Robert Collet, France)	69
7	*nk*	**Lac Majeur (FR)**^{12} 2-9-2 ... OPeslier 4 (Robert Collet, France)	72
8	*8*	**Luxstar (FR)**^{20} 2-9-2 ... DBoeuf 9 (Mme I T Oakes-Cottin, France)	52
9	*1 1/2*	**Flyng Teapot (IRE)** 2-9-2 ... GMosse 2 (J Heloury, Italy)	48

1m 31.5s **Going Correction** +0.45s/f (Yiel) **9** Ran SP% **69.1**
Speed ratings: 94,91,90,87,83 78,78,69,67
PARI-MUTUEL: WIN 1.80; PL 1.40, 2.50, 2.30; DF 10.40.
Owner H H Aga Khan **Bred** Snc Lagardere Elevage **Trained** Chantilly, France

NOTEBOOK
Striving Storm(USA) was given every possible chance and raced in second place until one and a half out where he took up the running. He had nothing in hand to hold off the winner, who scored with authority and is thought to be a Classic prospect. Nevertheless, this was a very promising effort and it should not be long before the colt visits the winners' enclosure.

4416a PRIX DU HARAS DE FRESNAY-LE-BUFFARD JACQUES LE MAROIS (GROUP 1) (C&F) (STRAIGHT) 1m

3:25 (3:26) 3-Y-O+ **£236,441** (£94,593; £47,297; £23,628; £11,834)

			RPR
1		**Librettist (USA)**^{21} [3779] 4-9-4 ... LDettori 4 (Saeed Bin Suroor) *always close up, led over 1f out, driven out* **7/2**^{2}	123
2	*nk*	**Manduro (GER)**^{21} [3779] 4-9-4 ... OPeslier 11 (A Fabre, France) *disputed 2nd on outside, 2nd over 2f out, every chance over 1f out, ran on to regain 2nd last strides* **5/1**	122
3	*hd*	**Peeress**^{32} [3416] 5-9-1 ... RyanMoore 6 (Sir Michael Stoute) *held up in mid-division, headway over 1f out, went 2nd inside final f, no extra last strides* **4/1**^{3}	119
4	*1 1/2*	**Stormy River (FR)**^{35} [3342] 3-8-11 ... TThulliez 1 (N Clement, France) *held up in rear, headway on rails side over 2f out, disputed 2nd over 1f out, one pace final f* **11/4**^{1}	119
5	*2 1/2*	**Ad Valorem (USA)**^{54} [2722] 4-9-4 ... JamieSpencer 10 (A P O'Brien, Ire) *mid-division, headway on outside 2f out, hard ridden & every chance 1 1/2f out, soon weakened* **13/2**	114
6	*2*	**Special Kaldoun (IRE)**^{21} [3779] 7-9-4 ... DBoeuf 7 (D Smaga, France) *held up in rear, never a factor* **50/1**	110
7	*1 1/2*	**Ramonti (FR)**^{72} [2217] 4-9-4 ... EBotti 8 (A Botti, Italy) *led after 2f til headed over 1f out, soon weakened* **14/1**	107
8	*2 1/2*	**New Girlfriend (IRE)**^{7} [4191] 3-8-8 ... JAuge 9 (Robert Collet, France) *held up in rear, pulling early, never a factor* **40/1**	99
9	*snk*	**Helios Quercus (FR)**^{21} [3779] 4-9-4 ... IMendizabal 3 (C Diard, France) *mid-division, beaten 2f out* **25/1**	101
10	*15*	**Kendargent (FR)**^{35} [3342] 3-8-11 ... RMarchelli 5 (Y Fouin, France) *led 2f, weakened over 2f out, eased* **100/1**	71

1m 43.1s **Going Correction** +0.45s/f (Yiel)
WFA 3 from 4yo+ 7lb **10** Ran SP% **114.8**
Speed ratings: 117,116,116,115,112 110,109,106,106,91
PARI-MUTUEL: WIN 3.90; PL 1.80, 1.90, 3.40; DF 9.70.
Owner Godolphin **Bred** Calumet Farm **Trained** Newmarket, Suffolk
■ Godolphin's first European Group 1 winner of the year. Minutes later Cherry Mix made it two when winning at Cologne.

NOTEBOOK
Librettist(USA) looked in great shape and had a fine action going down to the start. He was well up with the pace early on and challenged for the lead at the furlong and a half marker. He took control one out and stayed on bravely to hold the fast-finishing runner-up. He acted well on the very soft ground and appears to still be improving. If he comes out of the race well the Prix du Moulin is next on the cards, probably followed by the Queen Elizabeth II Stakes at Ascot.
Manduro(GER), for whom the overnight change in the ground to very soft was not in his favour, was smartly into his stride and always well placed. Outpaced when things quickened up at the two-furlong marker, he rallied 50 yards from the line and was finishing best of all. The Moulin is also a possibility for this colt.
Peeress, in mid-division early on, ran a little free as the leaders slowed things down around the halfway stage. She came with a promising run from two out and was given every chance before going under by under half a length. A very genuine and consistent mare, she would have been better suited by an even and stronger pace.
Stormy River(FR) was behind early on and made his challenge from one and a half out on the stands' side. He looked very dangerous at the furlong marker but did not go through with his effort. He was meeting older horses for the first time on very testing ground, so can be given a chance to atone.
Ad Valorem(USA), who won the queen Anne on a much faster surface, had every chance but was unable to pick up in this soft ground.

4417a PRIX GONTAUT-BIRON (GROUP 3) 1m 2f

4:05 (4:06) 4-Y-O+ **£27,586** (£11,034; £8,276; £5,517; £2,759)

			RPR
1		**Atlantic Air (FR)**^{26} 4-8-9 ... TThulliez 5 (Y De Nicolay, France) *held up in 6th to straight, headway over 1f out, ran on to lead last strides* **20/1**	107
2	*hd*	**Musketier (GER)**^{46} 4-8-9 ... C-PLemaire 3 (P Bary, France) *always in touch, 4th st, bumped well over 1f out, switched & ridden 1f out, fin well, fin 3rd, shd and hd, placed 2nd* **14/1**	107
3	*1 1/2*	**Annenkov (IRE)**^{59} [2597] 4-8-11 ... OPeslier 8 (E Lellouche, France) *a prom, tracked leader halfway, slightly hampered 2f out, ridden & one pace final f, fin 4th, shd, hd and 1 1/2l, plcd 3rd* **9/2**^{3}	106
4	*1*	**Green Girl (FR)**^{35} 4-8-6 ... YTake 6 (J E Hammond, France) *held up, last straight, some headway from over 1f out, never nearer, finished 5th, placed 4th* **13/2**	100
5	*hd*	**Blip**^{46} 4-8-9 ... DBoeuf 7 (D Smaga, France) *held up, 7th straight, slightly hampered well over 1f out, never dangerous, finished sixth, placed 5th* **20/1**	102
6	*shd*	**Mango Mischief (IRE)**^{55} [2706] 5-8-8 ... RyanMoore 4 (J L Dunlop) *led, edged left 2f out, ridden approaching final furlong, caught last strides, finished 2nd, shd disq & placed 6th* **15/2**	106
7	*1/2*	**Ruwi**^{25} [3662] 4-8-11 ... IMendizabal 1 (J-C Rouget, France) *broke well, settled in 5th, 5th on inside straight, ridden & beaten over 1f out* **15/8**^{1}	103
8	*2 1/2*	**Crosspeace (IRE)**^{9} [4096] 4-8-11 ... RoystonFfrench 2 (M Johnston) *close up, 3rd half-way, ridden & weakened well over 1f out* **4/1**^{2}	99

2m 12.4s **Going Correction** +0.45s/f (Yiel) **8** Ran SP% **114.3**
Speed ratings: 111,110,109,108,108 110,108,106
PARI-MUTUEL: WIN 29.70; PL 5.30, 3.50, 2.00; DF 89.60.
Owner Mme H Devin **Bred** Mme H Devin **Trained** France

NOTEBOOK
Atlantic Air(FR), held up for much of this race, had a wall of horses to pass early in the straight. Taken to the far rail, he quickened impressively to get up on the line. His trainer was surprised he acted so well on the testing ground and he is now likely to turn out for the Prix Dollar at Longchamp on September 30.
Musketier(GER), always thereabouts, started his challenge from two out and was slightly hampered at the one and a half furlong point. He kept up the good work until the end and finally only went under by inches.
Annenkov(IRE) raced in second place for much of this event, but hung left after being slightly hampered one and a half out. He ran on again to take fourth and was moved up after the Stewards changed the order. The overnight change to very soft ground certainly was not in his favour.

Green Girl(FR), dropped out last for the early part of the race, was still in the same place at the entrance to the straight. She did make some late progress but never really looked dangerous.
Mango Mischief(IRE), tried to lead from pillar to post and was very courageous in the straight. Unfortunately she hung slightly left and caused some problems for two other runners. One nearly came down and she was demoted from second place to sixth.
Crosspeace(IRE), third in the early part of the race and still in the same position at the entrance to the straight, was soon a beaten force. He dropped back to finish last and his jockey felt that he was not his normal self. He is another that prefers faster ground.

HANOVER (L-H)
Sunday, August 13

OFFICIAL GOING: Good

4418a PFERDEWETTEN.DE-PREIS (EX GROSSER PREIS VON BERLIN) (GROUP 3) 6f 110y
2:35 (2:36) 3-Y-0+ £22,069 (£6,897; £3,448; £2,069)

			RPR
1		**Shinko's Best (IRE)**[80] [1973] 5-9-5 ..... MTimpelan 3	107
		(A Kleinkorres, Germany) *close 2nd til led approaching straight, hard ridden 1 1/2f out, just held on* **39/10**[3]	
2	hd	**Lucky Strike**[22] [3755] 8-9-5 ..... ADeVries 2	106
		(A Trybuhl, Germany) *disputed 4th, ran on down stands side from over 1 1/2f out, challenged close home, just failed* **7/10**[1]	
3	4	**Lord Areion (GER)**[29] [3563] 4-9-5 ..... FilipMinarik 4	94
		(H J Groschel, Germany) *disputed 4th, 3rd straight, one pace final 2f* **67/10**	
4	½	**Austrian (GER)**[22] [3755] 5-9-5 ..... WPanov 6	93
		(M Sowa, Germany) *last straight, never a factor* **20/1**	
5	½	**Austriaco (GER)**[104] 4-9-5 ..... StanleyChin 5	92
		(R Suerland, Germany) *led til headed approaching straight, soon outpaced* **52/10**	
6	5	**Marabout Directa (GER)**[48] [2941] 5-9-5 ..... AHelfenbein 1	77
		(Andreas Lowe, Germany) *held up in last, hard ridden to dispute 4th entering straight, soon beaten* **33/10**[2]	

1m 18.94s **6** Ran SP% **136.4**
(including 10 Euro stake): WIN 49; PL 16, 12; SF 120.
Owner Stall Ampuria **Bred** R Ernst & M Amdree **Trained** Germany

3326 JAGERSRO (R-H)
Sunday, August 13

OFFICIAL GOING: Standard

4419a MEC-COM KLIPPAN AB SOFIEROLOPNING (DIRT) 1m 143y(D)
1:50 (1:50) 3-Y-0 £17,753 (£8,166; £3,551; £2,485; £1,775; £1,065)

			RPR
1		**Icaros (SWE)**[27] 3-9-2 ..... EddieAhern 12	—
		(Wido Neuroth, Norway)	
2	1½	**Macleod's (SWE)**[27] 3-9-2 ..... (b) FDiaz 6	—
		(L Reuterskiold, Sweden)	
3	4	**Be My Wings (SWE)**[255] 3-9-2 ..... MMartinez 1	—
		(F Castro, Sweden)	
4	nse	**Smart Guy (DEN)** 3-9-2 ..... KAndersen 3	—
		(B Olsen, Norway)	
5	hd	**Crossoffissio (SWE)** 3-9-2 ..... (b) P-AGraberg 8	—
		(L Reuterskiold, Sweden)	
6	½	**Rockbranglen (USA)** 3-9-2 ..... MSantos 4	—
		(F Reuterskiold, Sweden)	
7	½	**Omoto Sando (FR)** 3-9-2 ..... LHammer-Hansen 5	—
		(A Lund, Norway)	
8	6	**Xaara (SWE)**[37] [3326] 3-8-12 ..... YvonneDurant 9	—
		(M Kahn, Sweden)	
9	½	**Major Gunn's (SWE)**[301] 3-9-2 ..... JJohansen 2	—
		(L Reuterskiold, Sweden)	
10	28	**Valuta (USA)**[18] [3849] 3-9-2 ..... FJohansson 10	—
		(R A Kvisla) *raced in 8th on outside, under pressure 3f out, soon weakened* **12/1**[1]	

1m 50.5s **10** Ran SP% **7.7**
(Including 1SKr stake): WIN 1.44; PL 1.08, 1,45, 1.29; DF 11.57.
Owner Stall Eos **Bred** Stall Eos **Trained** Norway

NOTEBOOK
Valuta(USA) was runner-up in a modest maiden on fast ground at Lingfield on her previous run. She has a dirt pedigree but appeared to struggle on the surface on this evidence.

4420a SVENSKT DERBY (LISTED RACE) (DIRT) 1m 4f
3:45 (3:45) 3-Y-0 £62,152 (£28,590; £12,430; £8,701; £6,215; £3,729)

			RPR
1		**Mad Dog Slew (USA)**[301] 3-9-2 ..... MMartinez 15	101
		(F Reuterskiold, Sweden)	
2	1	**Nobileo**[21] [3776] 3-9-2 ..... EddieAhern 14	100
		(Wido Neuroth, Norway)	
3	2½	**Highway (IRE)** 3-9-2 ..... (b) RVaras 8	96
		(F Castro, Sweden)	
4	nk	**Dream Catcher (SWE)**[27] 3-9-2 ..... KAndersen 5	95
		(R A Kvisla) *raced freely early, led after 1f, headed 7f out, chased winner til tired inside final furlong, lost 3rd post* **157/10**[1]	
5	5	**Django (SWE)** 3-9-2 ..... MLarsen 12	88
		(Caroline Stromberg)	
6	1	**Double It (IRE)** 3-9-2 ..... NCordrey 10	86
		(P Wahl, Sweden)	
7	1	**Peintre Modern (FR)**[70] 3-9-2 ..... FSanchez 11	85
		(R Gibson, France)	
8	21	**Negra Del Oro (GER)**[37] [3326] 3-8-12 ..... LHammer-Hansen 6	49
		(A Lund, Norway)	
9	2½	**Flying Fraam (SWE)**[42] 3-9-2 ..... (b) P-AGraberg 2	50
		(Mme Pia Brandt, France)	
10	2½	**Half Sadlers (SWE)** 3-9-2 ..... MSantos 13	46
		(K P Andersen, Sweden)	
11	3	**Gilmore (GER)**[73] 3-9-2 ..... (b) FJohansson 9	41
		(Mme Pia Brandt, France)	
12	1½	**El Gallo (IRE)** 3-9-2 ..... (b) ESki 4	39
		(F Castro, Sweden)	
13	1	**Dreamshower (IRE)**[234] 3-9-2 ..... (b) SaraSlot 3	38
		(Kerstin Helander, Sweden)	

2m 35.2s **13** Ran SP% **6.0**
WIN 6.54; PL 1.99, 1.60, 3.73; DF 28.80.
Owner Stall Mec-Com Klippan AB **Bred** Hot Foot Inc **Trained** Sweden

NOTEBOOK
Dream Catcher(SWE), who had winning form at up to a mile in this country in 2005, was taking a big step up in trip. He probably ran too free, but stayed in contention until fading late on.

4151 THIRSK (L-H)
Monday, August 14

OFFICIAL GOING: Good to soft
After 17mm rain the previous day and overnight after a drying day the ground was described as 'just on the easy side of good'.
Wind: Light, half against Weather: Cool, overcast but dry

4421 EBF OSWALDS RESTAURANT WITH ROOMS MEDIAN AUCTION MAIDEN STKS 5f
5:55 (5:56) (Class 5) 2-Y-0 £3,886 (£1,156; £577; £288) Stalls High

Form				RPR
24	1		**Smirfys Diamond**[13] [4028] 2-9-3 ..... AdrianTNicholls 5	76
			(D Nicholls) *edgd rt after s: sn chsng ldrs: swtchd lft over 1f out: hung lft and led last 75yds* **4/1**[2]	
04	2	1½	**Mambo Spirit (IRE)**[9] [4151] 2-9-3 ..... J-PGuillambert 7	71
			(J G Given) *sn outpcd and in rr: hdwy 2f out: hung lft and styd on fnl f* **10/1**	
3630	3	¾	**Feelin Foxy**[54] [2743] 2-8-12 76 ..... JamieSpencer 13	63
			(D Shaw) *led: hung bdly lft and hdd ins last* **11/4**[1]	
4	4	nk	**Catlivius (IRE)**[35] [3358] 2-8-12 ..... DO'Donohoe 8	62+
			(K A Ryan) *chsd ldrs: edgd lft and kpt on same pce fnl f* **4/1**[2]	
6	5	2½	**Beaumont Boy**[9] [4151] 2-9-3 ..... DavidAllan 11	58
			(G A Swinbank) *chsd ldrs: outpcd fnl 2f* **6/1**[3]	
6	6	¾	**Minnow**[32] [3435] 2-8-9 ..... SaleemGolam(3) 3	50
			(S C Williams) *mid-div: kpt on fnl 2f: nvr trbld ldrs* **14/1**	
	7	shd	**Jenny Geddes (IRE)** 2-8-12 ..... TonyHamilton 10	50
			(R A Fahey) *dwlt: outpcd and bhd tl kpt on fnl 2f* **20/1**	
6	8	2	**Back In The Red (IRE)**[51] [2878] 2-8-10 ..... KevinGhunowa(7) 2	48
			(M Wellings) *s.i.s: nvr nr ldrs* **100/1**	
00	9	1¼	**Soviet Sound (IRE)**[46] [3018] 2-9-3 ..... TomEaves 6	43
			(Jedd O'Keeffe) *dwlt: nvr on terms* **50/1**	
65	10	¾	**My Two Girls (IRE)**[17] [3907] 2-8-12 ..... MickyFenton 9	35
			(P T Midgley) *chsd ldrs: lost pl over 1f out* **25/1**	
4	11	1½	**Shotley Mac**[70] [2281] 2-8-10 ..... SuzzanneFrance(7) 4	35
			(N Bycroft) *mid-div: lost pl 2f out* **20/1**	
	12	6	**Le Masque** 2-9-3 ..... RoystonFfrench 1	13
			(B Smart) *swvd lft s: wl bhd fnl 2f* **16/1**	

61.72 secs (1.82) **Going Correction** +0.225s/f (Good) **12** Ran SP% **118.9**
Speed ratings (Par 94):94,91,90,89,85 84,84,81,79,78 75,66
CSF £40.92 TOTE £4.90: £1.70, £3.50, £1.70; EX 42.60.
Owner Mrs Dian Plant **Bred** Green Meadow Stud **Trained** Sessay, N Yorks

FOCUS
The stands'-side rail was the place to be but all the first four tended to go towards the centre in the closing stages. It looked a fair median auction maiden race and could have been rated a bit higher than it has been.

NOTEBOOK
Smirfys Diamond, switched after the start to overcome his outside draw, hung left as he took charge but in the end ran out a decisive winner. Nurseries now beckon. (op 10-3)
Mambo Spirit(IRE) struggled to go the pace but despite hanging put in some solid late work. A step up to six and nurseries beckon. (op 11-1 tchd 8-1)
Feelin Foxy, highly tried, had the plum stands'-side draw but she proved almost unrideable. A change of bit and bridle looks likely. Official explanation: jockey said filly hung both ways (tchd 3-1 tchd 10-3 in places)
Catlivius(IRE) raced on the outer of the leading group and deserves credit for this effort. Her inexperience still showed and there should be even better to come. (op 9-2)
Beaumont Boy improved on his debut effort but seems to need six already. (op 8-1)

4422 BEATRICE STEPHENSON H'CAP 5f
6:25 (6:25) (Class 4) (0-85,84) 3-Y-0 £6,477 (£1,927; £963; £481) Stalls High

Form				RPR
652	1		**Tender Process (IRE)**[84] [1877] 3-8-3 66 ..... RoystonFfrench 11	77
			(E S McMahon) *chsd ldrs: styd on to ld ins last* **7/1**[2]	
5560	2	1	**Spiritual Peace (IRE)**[1] [4403] 3-9-0 77 ..... (p) DO'Donohoe 10	85
			(K A Ryan) *chsd ldrs: sn drvn along: styd on to take 2nd wl ins last* **9/1**[3]	
1000	3	1	**Bel Cantor**[24] [3718] 3-8-0 68 ..... AndrewElliott(5) 13	72
			(W J H Ratcliffe) *led: hung lft thrght: hdd and no ex ins last* **7/1**[2]	
5141	4	½	**River Kirov (IRE)**[16] [3943] 3-9-2 79 ..... JamieSpencer 6	81
			(P W Chapple-Hyam) *sn drvn along in rr: bmpd over 1f out: styd on wl fnl f* **13/8**[1]	
5440	5	hd	**City For Conquest (IRE)**[18] [3873] 3-8-6 69 ..... (b) FrancisNorton 2	70
			(K R Burke) *s.i.s: effrt and bmpd over 1f out: nt clr run and swtchd ins: styd on wl* **20/1**	
4415	6	½	**Moorhouse Lad**[31] [3475] 3-9-7 84 ..... JimmyQuinn 4	84
			(G Woodward) *chsd ldrs: kpt on same pce fnl 2f* **12/1**	
6-	7	1¾	**Ascot Lady (IRE)**[56] 3-8-12 78 ..... JasonEdmunds(3) 7	71
			(J Balding) *stdd s: t.k.h in rr: sme hdwy on ins 2f out: nvr trbld ldrs* **20/1**	
-100	8	nk	**Rare Breed**[10] [4102] 3-9-6 83 ..... TomEaves 9	75
			(Mrs L Stubbs) *chsd ldr: wknd appr fnl f* **11/1**	
1124	9	1¼	**Toy Top (USA)**[26] [3636] 3-9-5 82 ..... (b) PhillipMakin 5	70
			(M Dods) *sn in rr and drvn along: nvr on terms* **10/1**	
0044	10	½	**Rainbow Bay**[23] [3722] 3-8-10 73 ..... (p) TonyHamilton 3	59
			(R A Fahey) *chsd ldrs on outer: outpcd 2f out: no threat after* **9/1**[3]	

60.66 secs (0.76) **Going Correction** +0.225s/f (Good) **10** Ran SP% **117.7**
Speed ratings (Par 102):102,100,98,98,97 96,94,93,91,90
CSF £69.05 CT £352.64 TOTE £6.00: £1.60, £3.00, £2.60; EX 49.90.

Owner J J Staunton **Bred** Timothy Coughlan **Trained** Hopwas, Staffs
FOCUS
The first three home had the best of the draw even though in the end they raced towards the centre. An ordinary event, which has been rated through the third.
City For Conquest(IRE) Official explanation: jockey said filly was denied a clear run

4423 BLACK SHEEP BREWERY H'CAP 2m
6:55 (6:55) (Class 6) (0-60,60) 4-Y-O+ **£3,238** (£963; £481; £240) **Stalls** Low

Form RPR
00-0 **1** **Sharaab (USA)**[13] 2345 5-8-6 **45**........(t) DaleGibson 3 52
(D E Cantillon) *hld up in rr: hdwy 7f out: led over 2f out: hdd over 1f out: kpt on to ld nr fin* **9/1**
0-30 **2** *nk* **Comical Errors (USA)**[2] 4380 4-8-2 **46**........(p) LeanneKershaw(5) 2 53
(P C Haslam) *hld up in mid-field: hdwy on ins over 3f out: led over 1f out: hdd towards fin* **25/1**
-023 **3** *½* **Primondo (IRE)**[16] 3935 4-9-6 **59**........ JamieSpencer 9 65
(J R Fanshawe) *chsd ldrs: wnt 2nd after 4f: hrd drvn over 4f out: led 3f out: sn hdd: kpt on same pce ins last* **6/4**[1]
6043 **4** *1* **Lenwade**[14] 4011 5-8-3 **42**........ JimmyQuinn 4 47
(G G Margarson) *s.i.s: rn in snatches: kpt on fnl 3f: nvr able chal* **5/1**[2]
0-62 **5** *½* **Jumeirah Scarer**[7] 4205 5-9-7 **60**........ DO'Donohoe 5 65
(K A Ryan) *led 2f: lost pl after 4f: hdwy 4f out: sn chsng ldrs: kpt one same pce fnl 2f* **11/2**[3]
0660 **6** *1 ½* **Just Waz (USA)**[7] 4205 4-8-7 **51**........(p) MichaelJStainton(5) 6 54
(R M Whitaker) *trckd ldrs: outpcde over 3f out: kpt on same pce fnl 2f* **12/1**
2300 **7** *11* **Iamback**[14] 4011 6-8-3 **42**........(t) RoystonFfrench 11 32
(Miss D A McHale) *led after 2f: qcknd over 5f out: hdd 3f out: lost pl over 1f out* **16/1**
0123 **8** *10* **High Frequency (IRE)**[17] 3919 5-8-7 **46**........(p) MickyFenton 7 24
(A Crook) *chsd ldrs: drvn over 5f out: lost pl over 3f out: sn bhd* **13/2**
3m 35.0s (3.80) **Going Correction** +0.325s/f (Good) 8 Ran SP% **112.8**
Speed ratings (Par 101):103,102,102,102,101 101,95,90
CSF £188.32 CT £518.87 TOTE £12.10: £3.00, £5.60, £1.10; EX 217.70.
Owner Mrs J Hart & Mrs C Reed **Bred** Shadwell Farm LLC **Trained** Newmarket, Suffolk
FOCUS
A low-grade stayers' handicap run at a very steady pace and the first six home finished in a heap. The form is not strong.
Iamback Official explanation: jockey said mare hung right-handed throughout
High Frequency(IRE) Official explanation: jockey said gelding was unsuited by the good to soft ground

4424 RACING AT BEVERLEY ON WEDNESDAY MAIDEN AUCTION STKS 7f
7:25 (7:26) (Class 5) 2-Y-O **£3,886** (£1,156; £577; £288) **Stalls** Low

Form RPR
32 **1** **Kay Gee Be (IRE)**[52] 2821 2-8-12........ JamieSpencer 5 77
(D J Daly) *trckd ldrs: led 1f out: styd on* **8/11**[1]
432 **2** *1 ½* **Cassie's Choice (IRE)**[24] 3713 2-8-7 71........ DerekMcGaffin 2 68
(B Smart) *trckd ldrs: chal 2f out: no ex ins last* **7/1**[2]
3 *1* **Espejo (IRE)** 2-8-12........ TomEaves 1 71
(K R Burke) *s.i.s: hdwy on ins 4f out: led 2f out: hdd 1f out: kpt on same pce* **8/1**[3]
4 *nk* **Celtic Change (IRE)** 2-9-1........ PhillipMakin 10 73
(M Dods) *chsd ldrs: hung rt bnd over 3f out: rdn and edgd rt: styd on wl fnl 2f* **10/1**
34 **5** *¾* **Cape Dancer (IRE)**[18] 3878 2-8-10........ PaulMulrennan 3 66
(J S Wainwright) *trckd ldrs: chal 3f out: kpt on same pce fnl f* **20/1**
6 *2 ½* **Lets Get Cracking (FR)** 2-9-1........ DO'Donohoe 7 65
(K A Ryan) *in rr and sn drvn along: styd on fnl 2f: nvr nr ldrs* **14/1**
0 **7** *1 ¼* **Speedfit World**[10] 4103 2-9-1........ RobertWinston 12 62
(G G Margarson) *w ldrs on outer: led over 4f out tl 2f out: sn wknd* **20/1**
600 **8** *1 ¾* **Nihil Petere (IRE)**[18] 3878 2-8-4........(p) FrancisNorton 6 46
(P T Midgley) *s.s: nvr a factor* **100/1**
9 *1 ¼* **Amanda Carter** 2-8-7........ TonyHamilton 11 46
(R A Fahey) *s.i.s: sn drvn along: nvr on terms* **33/1**
2 **10** *nk* **Lady Best (IRE)**[21] 3788 2-8-7........ DavidAllan 8 45
(J R Weymes) *in tch: outpcd and lost pl 5f out: no threat after* **14/1**
63 **11** *1 ½* **Silver Appraisal**[53] 2783 2-8-7........ PaulEddery 9 42
(B Smart) *led tl over 4f out: lost pl 2f out* **33/1**
1m 30.35s (3.25) **Going Correction** +0.325s/f (Good) 11 Ran SP% **120.3**
Speed ratings (Par 94):94,92,91,90,89 87,85,83,82,81 80
CSF £5.83 TOTE £1.80: £1.10, £2.00, £2.10; EX 8.10.
Owner Par Jeu Partnership **Bred** Pursuit Of Truth Syndicate **Trained** Newmarket, Suffolk
■ Stewards' Enquiry : Derek McGaffin two-day ban: used whip with excessive frequency (Aug 25,26)
FOCUS
Just a steady pace and the winner, who had easily the best credentials, made hard work of it. The form looks essentially sound but the proximity of the eighth strikes a note of caution.
NOTEBOOK
Kay Gee Be(IRE), a decent type and a fluent mover, made hard work of it but was firmly in command at the line. He is the type to make an even better three-year-old. (op 5-6 tchd 10-11)
Cassie's Choice(IRE) appreciated the step up to seven but in the end simply met one too good. (op 8-1)
Espejo(IRE), who looked ready, was nibbled at in the morning. After a tardy start, he worked his way to the front but his inexperience showed and he was run out of it. He should be a fair bit wiser next time. (tchd 9-1)
Celtic Change(IRE), a gelded son of Celtic Swing, has plenty of size and scope. He hung badly right coming off the home turn and edged further towards the centre before putting in some solid work. He looks a fair longer-term prospect. Official explanation: jockey said gelding hung right on bend (op 17-2)
Cape Dancer(IRE) mixed it from the start but this may be as good as she is. (op 25-1)
Lets Get Cracking(FR), a medium-sized, good-bodied individual, was fairly clueless but he showed promise, picking up in his own time late in the day. He will know a lot more next time. (op 16-1)
Silver Appraisal Official explanation: jockey said filly was unsuited by the good to soft ground

4425 HAMBLETON INN SUTTON BANK (S) H'CAP 1m
7:55 (7:56) (Class 6) (0-60,57) 3-Y-O+ **£3,238** (£963; £481; £240) **Stalls** Low

Form RPR
0006 **1** **Tequila Sheila (IRE)**[11] 4070 4-8-9 **43**........ AndrewElliott(5) 2 54
(K R Burke) *chsd ldrs: led 1f out: kpt on* **13/2**[3]
50-3 **2** *1 ¼* **Frenchgate**[5] 4266 5-8-4 **38** oh3........ NataliaGemelova(5) 15 46
(I W McInnes) *trckd ldrs: styd on fnl f: no real imp* **8/1**
-000 **3** *shd* **Gypsy Royal (IRE)**[17] 3909 4-8-9 **38**........ PaulFessey 16 46
(G Woodward) *in tch: hdwy over 2f out: kpt on same pce fnl f* **40/1**
3540 **4** *3 ½* **Go Garuda**[17] 3914 5-10-0 **57**........ JamieSpencer 10 57
(Miss Gay Kelleway) *hld up in mid-div: hdwy on ins and hrd rdn over 2f out: nvr rchd ldrs* **6/1**[2]
4043 **5** *¾* **Cut Ridge (IRE)**[11] 4070 7-9-3 **46**........ TonyHamilton 12 44
(J S Wainwright) *led tl 1f out: sn wknd* **6/1**[2]
0000 **6** *3 ½* **Downland (IRE)**[14] 3999 10-9-1 **44**........ KimTinkler 3 34
(N Tinkler) *chsd ldrs: sn drvn along: one pce fnl 2f* **9/1**
0106 **7** *1* **Legal Dram**[7] 4194 5-9-5 **48**........ TomEaves 14 36
(M Dods) *trckd ldrs: t.k.h: one pce fnl 2f* **17/2**
1056 **8** *1 ½* **Splodger Mac (IRE)**[5] 4256 7-9-1 **51**........ SuzzanneFrance(7) 8 35
(N Bycroft) *s.i.s: bhd tl hdwy on outside over 2f out: nvr on terms* **11/2**[1]
0006 **9** *3 ½* **Dorn Hill**[59] 2599 4-8-6 **40**........(p) RoryMoore(5) 17 16
(D G Bridgwater) *t.k.h on outer: nvr nr ldrs* **33/1**
20/0 **10** *hd* **Explode**[37] 3298 9-8-12 **48**........ DawnRankin(7) 7 24
(Miss L C Siddall) *s.s: wl bhd tl kpt on fnl 2f: nvr on terms* **40/1**
0500 **11** *8* **Keyalzao (IRE)**[16] 3941 4-8-9 **38** oh8........(b[1]) JimmyQuinn 5 —
(A Crook) *dwlt: a in rr* **100/1**
2650 **12** *10* **Spanish Law**[35] 3361 4-9-8 **51**........(b) PhillipMakin 1 —
(M Dods) *s.i.s: sme hdwy 3f out: lost pl and eased over 1f out* **11/2**[1]
00-0 **13** *1 ¾* **Zahara Joy**[11] 4070 3-9-0 **50**........ GylesParkin 13 —
(D W Thompson) *a in rr: bhd fnl 2f* **100/1**
4300 **14** *33* **Headland (USA)**[101] 1465 8-8-10 **39**........(be) PaulQuinn 4 —
(D W Chapman) *unruly in stalls: s.s: a bhd: t.o:* **40/1**
1m 41.94s (2.24) **Going Correction** +0.325s/f (Good)
WFA 3 from 4yo+ 7lb 14 Ran SP% **116.5**
Speed ratings (Par 101):101,99,99,96,95 91,90,89,85,85 77,67,65,32
CSF £53.77 CT £1969.29 TOTE £5.50: £2.10, £2.40, £10.40; EX 61.20.There was no bid for the winner.
Owner Lee Westwood **Bred** Martyn J McEnery **Trained** Middleham Moor, N Yorks
FOCUS
A run-of-the-mill selling handicap but run at a very strong pace. The form is sound for the level, rated through the third.
Keyalzao(IRE) Official explanation: jockey said filly had a breathing problem
Spanish Law Official explanation: jockey said gelding had no more to give
Zahara Joy Official explanation: jockey said filly was unsuited by the good to soft ground

4426 FAIRFAX ARMS GILLING EAST H'CAP 1m
8:25 (8:25) (Class 5) (0-75,77) 3-Y-O **£3,886** (£1,156; £577; £288) **Stalls** Low

Form RPR
0023 **1** **Esteem**[14] 4004 3-9-4 **70**........ RobertWinston 12 77+
(W Jarvis) *hld up: hdwy on outer over 3f out: styd on fnl f: led nr fin* **13/2**[3]
5411 **2** *hd* **Cool Ebony**[6] 4225 3-9-6 **77** 6ex........ MarkLawson(5) 8 83
(M Dods) *trckd ldrs: drvn over 2f out: led over 1f out: hdd and no ex towards fin* **11/4**[1]
4611 **3** *1 ½* **Just Lille (IRE)**[23] 3725 3-9-6 **72**........ RoystonFfrench 7 75+
(Mrs A Duffield) *trckd ldrs: kpt on same pce fnl f* **4/1**[2]
-401 **4** *hd* **Munaa (IRE)**[12] 4052 3-9-4 **70**........ FrancisNorton 3 72
(K R Burke) *trckd ldrs: led on ins over 4f out: hdd over 1f out: one pce* **9/1**
6353 **5** *nk* **Stainley (IRE)**[31] 3473 3-8-6 **63**........ AndrewElliott(5) 10 65
(J D Bethell) *led tl over 4f out: cl up: kpt on same pce fnl f* **4/1**[2]
450 **6** *2* **Gattuso**[117] 1078 3-8-9 **61**........ JimmyQuinn 2 58
(Ms Deborah J Evans) *tk fierce hold in rr: hdwy over 2f out: nvr trbld ldrs* **20/1**
2140 **7** *2 ½* **Farne Island**[5] 4257 3-8-10 **62**........ JamieSpencer 1 53
(J J Quinn) *chsd ldrs: hrd rdn over 1f out: sn wknd* **9/1**
560 **8** *3* **Counterfactual (IRE)**[10] 4117 3-8-5 **57**........ DerekMcGaffin 9 41
(B Smart) *hld up: effrt over 2f out: sn outpcd* **22/1**
0450 **9** *shd* **Rainbow's Classic**[44] 3082 3-8-13 **65**........ DO'Donohoe 4 49
(K A Ryan) *hld up: hdwy on ins over 3f out: nt clr run over 1f out: sn wknd* **12/1**
0-06 **10** *16* **Royal Song**[132] 874 3-8-2 **54** oh14........ DaleGibson 11 —
(D Shaw) *hld up in rr: lost pl over 2f out: sn bhd* **150/1**
1m 43.05s (3.35) **Going Correction** +0.325s/f (Good) 10 Ran SP% **117.5**
Speed ratings (Par 100):96,95,94,94,93 91,89,86,86,70
CSF £24.48 CT £84.67 TOTE £7.80: £2.20, £1.70, £1.40; EX 40.30 Place 6 £73.65, Place 5 £44.10.
Owner The L E H Partnership **Bred** Larkwood Stud **Trained** Newmarket, Suffolk
FOCUS
Just a steady pace and not strong form, although it seems solid rated through the runner-up and the fourth.
Counterfactual(IRE) Official explanation: jockey said gelding had a breathing problem
T/Plt: £137.00 to a £1 stake. Pool: £57,525.35. 306.35 winning tickets. T/Qpdt: £20.90 to a £1 stake. Pool: £4,266.20. 151.00 winning tickets. WG

4206 WINDSOR (R-H)
Monday, August 14
OFFICIAL GOING: Good (good to soft in places)
Wind: Nil

4427 COME RACING AT SANTA ROSA (TRINIDAD & TOBAGO) FILLIES' AUCTION NURSERY 6f
5:45 (5:46) (Class 5) 2-Y-O **£3,886** (£1,156; £577; £288) **Stalls** High

Form RPR
3243 **1** **Yerevan**[8] 4170 2-8-6 **69**........ JohnEgan 7 71
(R T Phillips) *chsd ldr: chal fr 2f out: led 1f out: rdn out* **11/2**[2]
5004 **2** *¾* **Whipchord (IRE)**[32] 3435 2-7-13 **62** oh1 ow1........ FrankieMcDonald 6 62
(R Hannon) *chsd ldrs: drvn to chal fr 2f out: stl ev ch jst ins last: no ex nr fin* **12/1**
0432 **3** *nk* **Angeletta**[63] 2500 2-8-11 **74**........ DaneO'Neill 9 73
(E S McMahon) *pressed ldr: slt advantage fr 3f out tl hdd 1f out: kpt on same pce* **8/1**
4224 **4** *shd* **Dolly Coughdrop (IRE)**[19] 3837 2-8-7 **70**........ LPKeniry 2 69
(K R Burke) *chsd ldrs: ev chnce fr 2f out utnil one pce ins last* **12/1**
1203 **5** *1 ¾* **Marmaida (IRE)**[14] 4006 2-9-7 **84**........ PaulDoe 1 77
(W J Knight) *bhd: t.k.h: swtchd lft to outside and hdwy over 1f out: kpt on same pce u.p ins last* **12/1**
0450 **6** *¾* **Ask Don't Tell (IRE)**[30] 3530 2-7-13 **62**........ DavidKinsella 3 53
(Tom Dascombe) *bhd: hdwy over 2f out: kpt on fnl firlong but nvr gng pce to rch ldrs* **33/1**
2522 **7** *½* **Drifting Gold**[17] 3917 2-8-5 **71**........ AdamKirby(3) 4 61
(C G Cox) *bhd: pushed along 1/2-way: styd on fnl f but nvr gng pce to rch ldrs* **6/1**[3]

521 **8** *1 ¼* **Top Royelle**[76] 2100 2-9-1 **78**...................................... RichardHughes 11 64
(R Hannon) *s.i.s: sn rcvrd to chse ldrs: rdn over 2f out: wknd fnl f* **9/4**[1]

460 **9** *1* **Rosie Cross (IRE)**[40] 3201 2-7-13 **65**.......................... JamesDoyle(3) 8 48
(R F Johnson Houghton) *bhd: rdn 1/2-way: mod prog fnl f but nvr in contention* **12/1**

001 **10** *3 ½* **Inflagranti**[13] 4017 2-8-10 **73**.. RyanMoore 5 45
(J G Portman) *a outpcd* **12/1**

040 **11** *1* **Kerswell**[19] 3844 2-8-7 **70**.. KerrinMcEvoy 10 39
(B R Millman) *in tch 4f* **14/1**

1m 13.9s (0.23) **Going Correction** -0.225s/f (Firm) **11** Ran SP% **119.6**
Speed ratings (Par 91):89,88,87,87,85 84,83,81,80,75 74
CSF £71.07 CT £533.63 TOTE £7.30: £2.20, £4.00, £2.50; EX 107.30.
Owner Bellflower Racing Ltd **Bred** Jenny Hall Bloodstock Ltd **Trained** Adlestrop, Gloucs

FOCUS
A reasonable and very competitive fillies' nursery, but the winning time was 1.7 seconds slower than the following maiden. Solid form, the winner well in on her Nottingham win in June.

NOTEBOOK
Yerevan has held her form well since being picked up out of Mick Channon's yard after running second in a seller earlier in the season, and ran out a game winner. She is particularly tough and should continue to go well in this sort of company. (op 6-1)
Whipchord(IRE) clearly benefited from the drop back in trip and switch to nursery company and ran a good race in second. She is at the right end of the handicap and could find a small race. (op 14-1)
Angeletta had been running well in maiden company and showed herself on a fair mark switched to handicaps for the first time. (op 10-1)
Dolly Coughdrop(IRE) was disappointing in a similar event at Leicester on her previous start, but this was better.
Marmaida(IRE) has struggled a touch since winning a maiden on her debut but, switched to nursery company for the first time, she ran a good race conceding upwards of 6lb all around.
Drifting Gold was not at her best and probably wants better ground. (op 13-2)
Top Royelle would have found this a tougher than the three-runner five-furlong Leicester maiden she won last time and was well beaten. (op 2-1 tchd 5-2)
Rosie Cross(IRE) Official explanation: jockey said filly was unsuited by the good (good to soft in places) ground
Kerswell Official explanation: jockey said filly became unbalanced approaching 1f out

4428 VC CASINO.COM MAIDEN STKS 6f
6:15 (6:16) (Class 4) 2-Y-O **£5,181** (£1,541; £770; £384) **Stalls** High

Form RPR

3 **1** **Sakhee's Secret**[35] 3363 2-9-3 .... SteveDrowne 5 94+
(H Morrison) *racd stands side and led after 1f: wnt sharply to far side over 2f out: led over 1f out: sn clr: easily* **5/6**[1]

0 **2** *6* **Oldjoesaid**[17] 3895 2-9-3 .... DaneO'Neill 4 76
(H Candy) *in tch centre crse: styd on fr over 1f out: tk 2nd ins last but no ch w wnr* **25/1**

3 *½* **Manhasset Indian (USA)** 2-9-3 .... LDettori 3 75
(J Noseda) *racd far side and possibly overall ldr after 1f: hdd over 1f out: sn outpaed and lost 2nd ins last* **8/1**[3]

326 **4** *2 ½* **Benchmark**[13] 4028 2-9-3 80.. RichardHughes 2 67
(R Hannon) *chsd ldrs: racd in centre crse after 2f: kpt on same pce fnl f* **4/1**[2]

5 *1 ¼* **Oakley Heffert (IRE)** 2-9-3 .... RyanMoore 9 63
(R Hannon) *bhd: racd iddle to stands side after 2f: kpt on fr over 1f out but nvr in contention* **33/1**

04 **6** *3* **Bertoliver**[28] 3591 2-9-3 .... JohnEgan 15 54
(D K Ivory) *chsd ldrs towards stands side 2f: c towards middle over 2f out: sn one pce* **16/1**

7 *2* **Dance Of Dreams** 2-9-0 .... JamesDoyle(3) 1 48
(N P Littmoden) *unruly stalls and re-entered: chsd ldr far side: rdn 1/2-way: wknd over 1f out* **33/1**

0 **8** *hd* **Dan Tucker**[24] 3701 2-9-3 .... EddieAhern 13 48
(B J Meehan) *chsd ldrs stands side: moved centre 1/2-way: wknd over 1f out* **25/1**

60 **9** *1 ½* **Purple Sands (IRE)**[28] 3591 2-9-3 .... TPO'Shea 7 43
(B J Meehan) *nvr bttr than mid-div* **66/1**

0 **10** *½* **Time For Change (IRE)**[14] 4002 2-9-3 .... GeorgeBaker 8 42
(B W Hills) *chsd ldrs towards centre crse 4f* **33/1**

04 **11** *2 ½* **Nou Camp**[9] 4138 2-9-3 .... JimmyFortune 11 34
(N A Callaghan) *chsd ldrs towards centre crse: wknd ins fnl 2f* **50/1**

12 *1* **Woqoodd** 2-9-3 .... PhilipRobinson 12 31
(M A Jarvis) *led stands side 1f: chsd ldrs and edgd twoards centre crse 1/2-way: wknd fr 2f out* **14/1**

13 *1 ½* **Nellie Soprano (IRE)** 2-8-12 .... LPKeniry 14 22
(K R Burke) *slowly into striude: a in rr* **33/1**

14 *hd* **Lagoon Royale** 2-9-0 .... DeanCorby(3) 6 26
(B W Duke) *a in rr* **100/1**

15 *3 ½* **Rajeef Ashog** 2-9-3 .... KerrinMcEvoy 10 16
(L M Cumani) *a in rr* **20/1**

1m 12.2s (-1.47) **Going Correction** -0.225s/f (Firm) **15** Ran SP% **126.9**
Speed ratings (Par 96):100,92,91,88,86 82,79,79,77,76 73,72,70,69,65
CSF £35.30 TOTE £2.00: £1.10, £5.60, £2.50; EX 35.10.
Owner Miss B Swire **Bred** Miss B Swire **Trained** East Ilsley, Berks

FOCUS
This looked a fair maiden beforehand, but the bare form may be a touch unreliable with the easy ground playing a big part. The majority of the field raced towards the stands' side before drifting across the track inside the last furlong, while eventual third Manhasset Indian and Dance Of Dreams raced far side throughout; a pretty messy race on the eye. The race has been rated at face value.

NOTEBOOK
Sakhee's Secret ◆ shaped very encouragingly when third in a good course-and-distance maiden on his debut just over a month previously and confirmed that promise with an impressive success. He probably handled the ground better than many of these, and distances can often be exaggerated in these types of conditions, but he won in the style of an above-average sort. He is entered in the Gimcrack, Mill Reef and Middle Park Stakes, and could well be a Group horse. (tchd Evens)
Oldjoesaid did not seem suited by fast ground when well beaten on his debut at Chepstow, so these conditions would have been much more suitable and he ran a good race behind a potentially smart sort.
Manhasset Indian(USA), a 160,000gns half-brother to three winners, all at a mile plus, out of a dual six- to eight-furlong winner at three in the US, made a bold bid racing with one other horse on the far side of the track and only appeared to be put in his place late on. He should improve.
Benchmark ran better than when a beaten favourite at Goodwood on his previous start, but was still well held and is not currently progressing. (tchd 9-2)
Oakley Heffert(IRE), a 60,000euros half-brother to Golden Island, a useful mile winner, made a pleasing introduction and should improve.
Rajeef Ashog Official explanation: jockey said colt missed the break

4429 VC CASINO.COM H'CAP 1m 67y
6:45 (6:45) (Class 4) (0-85,82) 3-Y-O+ **£6,477** (£1,927; £963; £481) **Stalls** High

Form RPR

4111 **1** **Envision**[16] 3951 3-9-2 **79**... RyanMoore 1 92
(R Hannon) *in tch: pushed along and hdwy over 3f out: led jst ins fnl 2f: drvn and styd on strly fnl f* **7/2**[2]

0450 **2** *1 ½* **Full Victory (IRE)**[7] 4209 4-9-5 **75**............................... SteveDrowne 6 86
(R A Farrant) *chsd ldrs: rdn 3f out: chsd wnr appr fnl f: kpt on ins last but a hld* **13/2**

310 **3** *2 ½* **Abwaab**[15] 3973 3-9-5 **82**.. LDettori 7 86
(R F Johnson Houghton) *bhd: rdn over 2f out: kpt on fr over 1f out to go 3rd ins last but nvr gng pce to rch ldrs* **10/1**

4200 **4** *½* **Glencalvie (IRE)**[13] 4029 5-9-6 **76**...............................(p) DaneO'Neill 5 80
(J Akehurst) *sn narrow advantage: drvn along 1/2-way: hdd jst ins fnl 3f: one pce fr over 1f out* **4/1**[3]

0153 **5** *2* **Golden Applause (FR)**[11] 4075 4-9-3 **73**......................... EddieAhern 3 72
(Mrs A L M King) *chsd ldrs: led ins fnl 3f: hdd jst ins fnl 2f: wknd fnl f* **15/2**

0-44 **6** *nk* **Leoballero**[10] 4108 6-9-7 **77**......................................(t) MichaelTebbutt 2 75
(D J Daly) *a outpcd in rr but styd on fnl f* **12/1**

3120 **7** *63* **Our Putra**[12] 4047 3-9-4 **81**..(t) PhilipRobinson 8 —
(M A Jarvis) *prssed ldr to halway: sn rdn: lost action and wknd qckly over 2f out: t.o and virtually p.u* **9/4**[1]

1m 43.58s (-2.02) **Going Correction** -0.10s/f (Good)
WFA 3 from 4yo+ 7lb **7** Ran SP% **114.9**
Speed ratings (Par 105):106,104,102,101,99 99,36
CSF £26.35 CT £206.60 TOTE £4.40: £2.30, £4.80; EX 39.70.
Owner Mrs J Wood **Bred** Cheveley Park Stud Ltd **Trained** East Everleigh, Wilts
■ Stewards' Enquiry : Michael Tebbutt caution: allowed gelding to caost home with no assistance

FOCUS
Just an ordinary handicap for the grade, but they went a good pace and the form looks solid. They all raced towards the far side in the straight.
Our Putra Official explanation: vet said colt had an irregular heart beat

4430 PLAY AT VC CASINO.COM H'CAP 6f
7:15 (7:15) (Class 2) (0-100,97) 3-Y-O+ **£11,658** (£3,468; £1,733; £865) **Stalls** High

Form RPR

0252 **1** **Idle Power (IRE)**[10] 4101 8-9-3 **90**.................................. AmirQuinn(3) 6 99
(J R Boyle) *in tch: hdwy 2f out: qcknd ins last: pushed out to ld last strides* **7/2**[2]

1064 **2** *hd* **Kostar**[12] 4042 5-9-8 **92**.. PhilipRobinson 1 100
(C G Cox) *chsd ldr: rdn over 2f out: slt ld over 1f out: kpt on tl ct last strides* **4/1**[3]

-010 **3** *hd* **Greenslades**[51] 2847 7-9-13 **97**.. SebSanders 5 104
(P J Makin) *led: rdn over 2f out: hdd over 1f out: styd chalng thrght fnl f tl no ex last strides* **9/4**[1]

4000 **4** *2 ½* **Obe Gold**[9] 4128 4-9-13 **97**... JohnEgan 4 97
(M R Channon) *rr and sn drvn along: hdwy over 2f out: styd on u.p fnl f but nvr in contention* **4/1**[3]

1230 **5** *2 ½* **Blue Tomato**[10] 4101 5-9-2 **89**................................ StephenDonohoe(3) 3 81
(J M Bradley) *hld up rr but in tch: rdn appr fnl 2f and no imp on ldrs* **13/2**

2330 **6** *3* **Grimes Faith**[21] 3795 3-8-8 **82**.. RichardHughes 2 65
(R Hannon) *chsd ldrs: ev ch 2f out: wknd qckly fnl f* **20/1**

1m 11.78s (-1.89) **Going Correction** -0.10s/f (Good)
WFA 3 from 4yo+ 4lb **6** Ran SP% **111.1**
Speed ratings (Par 109):108,107,107,104,100 96
CSF £17.27 TOTE £3.90: £2.20, £2.50; EX 17.00.
Owner The Idle B's **Bred** Mountarmstrong Stud **Trained** Epsom, Surrey

FOCUS
Some decent sprinters on show, but one would have expected more runners for the money. The form looks pretty sound.

NOTEBOOK
Idle Power(IRE) would have been well suited by the cut in the ground and produced an effort right up there with his very best, this being the highest mark he has ever won off. If conditions are suitable in the Ayr Gold Cup, he should give a very good account of himself. (op 3-1 tchd 4-1)
Kostar was well suited by the drop back from seven furlongs and was just denied. He should continue to go well over this trip, or an easy seven. (op 7-2)
Greenslades, 22nd of 28 in the Wokingham when last seen in June, ran a good race and can have few excuses. (op 3-1 tchd 10-3 in places)
Obe Gold, eighth of 27 in the Stewards' Cup on his previous start, should have found this less competitve but was still well held. (tchd 9-2)
Blue Tomato might want better ground, but he could just have reached his level for the time being. (op 11-2 tchd 7-1 in places)

4431 PLAY BLACKJACK AT VC CASINO.COM MAIDEN STKS 1m 67y
7:45 (7:45) (Class 5) 3-Y-O+ **£3,238** (£963; £481; £240) **Stalls** High

Form RPR

1 **Very Far (USA)** 3-9-3 ....(t) LDettori 2 81+
(Saeed Bin Suroor) *trckd ldrs: shkn up over 2f out: led over 1f out: styd on strly* **7/4**[1]

05- **2** *2* **Birkside**[287] 6200 3-9-3 .... StephenCarson 8 73
(W R Swinburn) *hld up in rr: gd hdwy over 2f out: kpt on strly fnl f to take 2nd nr fin but no ch w wnr* **33/1**

3 *nk* **Duke Of Milan (IRE)**[73] 2214 3-8-12 .... DerekNolan(5) 3 73
(G C Bravery) *led 1f: styd chsng ldrs tl led 3f out: hdd over 1f out: styd on but no ch w wnr ins last: lost 2nd cl home* **20/1**

0-0 **4** *¾* **Towerofcharlemagne (IRE)**[86] 1845 3-9-3 .... GeorgeBaker 11 71
(Miss Gay Kelleway) *mid-div: hdwy 3f out: one pce 2f out: kpt on again ins last but nt rch ldrs* **25/1**

2- **5** *½* **Well Guarded (IRE)**[275] 6332 3-9-3 .... JohnEgan 10 70+
(C R Egerton) *chsd ldrs: pushed along over 2f out: one pce ins last whn n.m.r: eased cl home* **3/1**[2]

6 *1 ¾* **Pikaboo** 3-8-12 .... JimmyFortune 7 61
(J H M Gosden) *chsd ldrs: drvn to chal over 2f out: wknd ins last* **9/2**[3]

05 **7** *¾* **You Live And Learn**[7] 4210 3-8-12 .... SteveDrowne 13 59+
(H Morrison) *chsd ldrs: outpcd 3f out: styd on again fnl f* **16/1**

5 **8** *shd* **Pagano (IRE)**[14] 4004 3-9-3 .... SebSanders 14 64
(W R Swinburn) *trckd ldrs: sltly hmpd 4f out: shkn up and kpt on fnl but nvr gng pce to be competitive* **10/1**

00 **9** *3* **Squiffy**[14] 4004 3-9-3 .... LPKeniry 12 57
(P D Cundell) *in tch: pushed along over 2f out and sn one pce* **33/1**

10 *1 ¼* **Debutante** 3-8-12 .... KerrinMcEvoy 4 49
(L M Cumani) *bhd: pushed along over 2f out: kpt on ins last but nvr in contention* **10/1**

11 *1 ¼* **Cut To (USA)** 3-9-0 .... DeanCorby(3) 6 51
(J Akehurst) *bhd: sme hdwy 3f out: nvr in contention* **40/1**

12 2 **Ath Tiomain (IRE)** 3-9-0 .... AdamKirby(3) 1 47
(D J S Ffrench Davis) *a in rr* **66/1**

6 **13** *17* **Master Pip**[100] 1492 4-9-10 .... TPO'Shea 5 7
(T H Caldwell) *led after 1f: hdd 3f out and sn wknd* **100/1**

1m 47.03s (1.43) **Going Correction** +0.075s/f (Good)
WFA 3 from 4yo 7lb **13** Ran SP% **123.0**
Speed ratings (Par 103):95,93,92,91,91 89,88,88,85,84 83,81,64
CSF £80.31 TOTE £2.60: £1.60, £9.40, £3.20; EX 78.50.
Owner Godolphin **Bred** A I Appleton **Trained** Newmarket, Suffolk
■ Stewards' Enquiry : John Egan one-day ban: careless riding (Aug 25)

FOCUS
An ordinary maiden in which they raced far side in the straight. Not strong form but the winner was value for extra and can improve.
Well Guarded(IRE) Official explanation: jockey said he dropped hands shortly before the winning post for fear of clipping heels

4432 MONDAY NIGHT RACING WITH VC CASINO.COM H'CAP 1m 3f 135y
8:15 (8:15) (Class 5) (0-70,70) 3-Y-O+ **£3,238** (£963; £481; £240) **Stalls** Low

Form RPR

2024 **1** **Hatch A Plan (IRE)**[14] 4005 5-9-4 **65** .... TravisBlock(5) 8 72
(Mrs A J Hamilton-Fairley) *in tch: hdwy over 3f out far side: led over 1f out: edgd lft cl home and jst hld on* **7/1**

1140 **2** *hd* **Bob's Your Uncle**[14] 4005 3-8-11 **64** .... RyanMoore 5 71
(J G Portman) *bhd: hdwy far side over 2f out: styd on u.p to chse wnr fnl f: str chal cl home: nt quite get up* **9/4**[1]

-213 **3** *1 1/4* **Looks The Business (IRE)**[14] 4005 5-9-0 **63** .... PJBenson(7) 2 68
(W G M Turner) *chsd ldrs: led 3f out and styd centre crse: hdd over 1f out: kpt on same pce* **9/2**[3]

0000 **4** *2 1/2* **Love Angel (USA)**[19] 3853 4-8-10 **57** .... MarcHalford(5) 3 58
(J J Bridger) *led: hdd 3f out: styd centre crse: one pce fnl 2f* **16/1**

40-2 **5** *nk* **Bay Hawk**[7] 4206 4-10-0 **70** .... JimmyFortune 6 71
(B G Powell) *chsd ldrs: wnt far side and chal fr over 2f out: wknd fnl f* **4/1**[2]

/1-0 **6** *2* **Dark Society**[17] 3900 8-8-11 **53** .... RichardHughes 9 50
(A W Carroll) *hld up in rr: hdwy and wnt far side over 3f out: chsd ldrs 2f out: sn one pce* **10/1**

0005 **7** *5* **Scottish River (USA)**[9] 4160 7-9-6 **62** .... HayleyTurner 7 51
(M D I Usher) *hld up in rr: t.k.h: nvr gng pce to trble ldrs* **9/2**[3]

00 **8** *8* **Black Chief (SWE)**[14] 4001 5-9-8 **64** .... (t) FJohansson 1 41
(R A Kvisla) *prom early: bhd fr 1/2-way* **50/1**

2m 31.99s (1.89) **Going Correction** +0.075s/f (Good)
WFA 3 from 4yo+ 11lb **8** Ran SP% **116.6**
Speed ratings (Par 103):96,95,95,93,93 91,88,83
CSF £23.67 CT £80.26 TOTE £8.00: £2.30, £1.40, £1.70; EX 24.10 Place 6 £113.84, Place 5 £35.43.
Owner Hamilton-Fairley Racing **Bred** Camogue Stud Ltd **Trained** Bramshill, Hants

FOCUS
A modest race and the form does not look worth a great deal, although it seems sound enough. They raced towards the far side in the straight.
Scottish River(USA) Official explanation: jockey said gelding ran too free
T/Plt: £98.70 to a £1 stake. Pool: £75,539.95. 558.20 winning tickets. T/Qpdt: £14.00 to a £1 stake. Pool: £5,476.50. 288.40 winning tickets. ST

3914 WOLVERHAMPTON (A.W) (L-H)
Monday, August 14

OFFICIAL GOING: Standard
Wind: Light, across Weather: Cloudy with sunny spells

4433 WBX.COM WORLD BET EXCHANGE EBF MEDIAN AUCTION MAIDEN STKS (DIV I) 5f 216y(P)
2:00 (2:02) (Class 5) 2-Y-O **£3,238** (£963; £481; £240) **Stalls** Low

Form RPR

1 **Social Rhythm** 2-8-12 .... JimmyQuinn 3 71
(H J Collingridge) *s.i.s: hdwy over 4f out: led 1f out: rdn out* **6/1**

0 **2** *1 1/2* **Call Me Rosy (IRE)**[45] 3043 2-8-12 .... SebSanders 6 66
(C F Wall) *s.i.s: hdwy over 4f out: hung rt over 2f out: rdn to chse ldr over 1f out: styd on* **5/1**[3]

45 **3** *shd* **Madam Gaffer**[26] 3640 2-8-5 .... KMay(7) 11 66
(B J Meehan) *chsd ldrs: led over 2f out: rdn and hdd 1f out: styd on same pce* **9/2**[2]

23 **4** *3 1/2* **Tipsy Prince**[20] 3818 2-9-0 .... JasonEdmunds(3) 7 61
(Mrs G S Rees) *chsd ldrs: rdn over 1f out: no ex* **5/1**[3]

006 **5** *2 1/2* **Perfect Style (IRE)**[18] 3872 2-8-12 .... FergusSweeney 4 48
(M Blanshard) *chsd ldrs: rdn over 2f out: sn outpcd* **10/1**

50 **6** *1/2* **Avoncreek**[103] 1420 2-9-3 .... DeanMcKeown 8 52
(B P J Baugh) *mid-div: rdn over 2f out: no imp* **25/1**

000 **7** *hd* **Pertemps Networks**[19] 3830 2-9-3 .... PaulMulrennan 2 51
(M W Easterby) *plld hrd and prom: outpcd over 2f out: no ch whn nt clr run over 1f out* **12/1**

65 **8** *2* **Only A Splash**[21] 3780 2-9-3 .... PaulQuinn 9 45
(D W Chapman) *led over 3f: wknd over 1f out* **66/1**

0 **9** *1/2* **Iron Dancer (IRE)**[10] 4115 2-9-3 .... TPO'Shea 1 43
(P A Blockley) *s.s: a in rr* **33/1**

10 *1/2* **Mister Always** 2-8-12 .... LiamJones(5) 10 42
(C R Dore) *s.i.s: outpcd* **33/1**

40 **11** *1/2* **Fen Dream**[15] 3976 2-9-3 .... ChrisCatlin 5 40
(E F Vaughan) *sn outpcd* **4/1**[1]

1m 14.47s (-1.34) **Going Correction** -0.375s/f (Stan) **11** Ran SP% **113.8**
Speed ratings (Par 94):93,91,90,86,82 82,81,79,78,77 77
CSF £33.70 TOTE £5.80: £2.20, £1.70, £2.10; EX 33.30 Trifecta £198.30 Pool: £433.03 - 1.55 winning units..
Owner A Fairfield **Bred** And Mrs A Fairfields **Trained** Exning, Suffolk

FOCUS
A moderate juvenile maiden rated through the third-placed horse.

NOTEBOOK
Social Rhythm, whose pedigree suggests a mix of speed and stamina, overcame a sluggish start and showed a good attitude to make a winning debut. She had a little up her sleeve at the finish, is entitled to be sharper for the experience, and ought to get another furlong before the year is out. (op 7-1 tchd 5-1)
Call Me Rosy(IRE), as on her Newmarket debut 45 days previously, was slow to break and ran green under pressure. This was a definite step in the right direction, however, and she appeals as the type to fare better when switching to nurseries in due course. (op 7-2)
Madam Gaffer eventually paid for using up energy in attaining a handy early position from her wide draw and was not disgraced. She now qualifies for a nursery mark and looks best kept to this trip for the short term. (op 10-3 tchd 3-1)
Tipsy Prince had his chance, but failed to see out the extra furlong as well as the principals. He is another who is now eligible for nurseries. (op 4-1 tchd 11-2)
Perfect Style(IRE) was never a factor on this All-Weather debut and has it to prove after this display. (op 12-1)
Mister Always Official explanation: jockey said gelding wouldn't face the kick-back
Fen Dream Official explanation: jockey said colt wouldn't face the kick-back

4434 WBX.COM WORLD BET EXCHANGE EBF MEDIAN AUCTION MAIDEN STKS (DIV II) 5f 216y(P)
2:30 (2:30) (Class 5) 2-Y-O **£3,238** (£963; £481; £240) **Stalls** Low

Form RPR

2 **1** **Beauchamp Viceroy**[9] 4138 2-9-3 .... LDettori 9 76
(G A Butler) *mid-div: hdwy and swtchd lft over 2f out: swtchd lft over 1f out: rdn to ld ins fnl f: r.o* **5/2**[1]

3 **2** *1 1/4* **Baylini**[26] 3645 2-8-9 .... JamesDoyle(3) 5 67
(Ms J S Doyle) *led: rdn and edgd rt over 1f out: hdd and unable qck ins fnl f* **7/2**[2]

6 **3** *3* **Convivial Spirit**[16] 3930 2-9-3 .... TedDurcan 7 63
(E F Vaughan) *mid-div: hdwy 1/2-way: sn rdn: styd on same pce fnl 2f* **7/1**[3]

4 *nk* **Final Dynasty** 2-8-12 .... SebSanders 4 57
(Mrs G S Rees) *chsd ldr: rdn and hung lft fr over 1f out: wknd ins fnl f* **9/1**

5 **5** *1/2* **Hidden Ace (IRE)**[14] 3994 2-8-12 .... (b) PaulMulrennan 10 56
(M W Easterby) *sn outpcd: hmpd 3f out: styd on ins fnl f: nrst fin* **8/1**

02 **6** *1/2* **Nepos**[18] 3860 2-9-0 .... RichardKingscote(3) 2 59
(J A Osborne) *chsd ldrs: rdn 1/2-way: hmpd over 2f out: sn outpcd* **7/2**[2]

7 *5* **Brave Quest (IRE)** 2-9-3 .... IanMongan 3 44
(C J Down) *s.i.s: a in rr* **12/1**

3330 **8** *2 1/2* **Aggbag**[25] 3678 2-9-3 54 .... RobbieFitzpatrick 6 37
(B P J Baugh) *chsd ldrs 4f* **25/1**

1m 13.93s (-1.88) **Going Correction** -0.375s/f (Stan) **8** Ran SP% **118.2**
Speed ratings (Par 94):97,95,91,90,90 89,82,79
CSF £11.82 TOTE £2.60: £1.10, £1.80, £2.40; EX 12.90 Trifecta £59.60 Pool: £668.82 - 7.96 winning units..
Owner Erik Penser **Bred** E Penser **Trained** Blewbury, Oxon
■ Stewards' Enquiry : James Doyle one-day ban: failed to keep straight from the stalls (Aug 27)

FOCUS
A modest juvenile maiden which as run at a sound pace. Fair form, and the winner can rate higher.

NOTEBOOK
Beauchamp Viceroy, runner-up on his debut at Lingfield nine days previously, required all of his rider's strength to get on top in the home straight yet still had enough class to break his duck. He clearly appreciates this surface and shaped as though he really ought to find further improvement when stepping up to seven furlongs in due course. (tchd 11-4)
Baylini, third over this trip at Lingfield on her debut, momentarily appeared set to score nearing the final furlong, yet she ultimately failed to cope with the winner's late challenge. This was another solid effort and she looks well up to winning something similar in the coming weeks. Official explanation: jockey said filly hung right-handed in home straight (op 9-4 tchd 4-1)
Convivial Spirit, who shaped a little better than the bare form on his debut at Lingfield last time, kept to his task under pressure, albeit at the same pace, and showed improved form on this step up in trip. He is entitled to improve a little again for the experience. (op 9-1)
Final Dynasty, bred to make her mark as a juvenile, showed up encouragingly until fading approaching the final furlong and looks sure to benefit for this debut experience. She may well be worth dropping to the minimum trip next time. (op 14-1)
Hidden Ace(IRE) was doing all of her best work towards the finish having again run green through the early parts. She looks the type to improve with further experience. (op 9-1 tchd 10-1)
Nepos, making his All-Weather debut, was beaten a fair way out and proved disappointing. He may not have appreciated the surface, however, and should not be written off now that he becomes eligible for a nursery mark. (op 4-1)

4435 WBX.COM WORLD BET EXCHANGE (S) STKS 1m 4f 50y(P)
3:00 (3:02) (Class 6) 3-Y-O+ **£2,388** (£705; £352) **Stalls** Low

Form RPR

0020 **1** **He's A Star**[65] 2455 4-9-9 65 .... StephenDonohoe(3) 2 67
(P D Evans) *a.p: chsd ldr over 3f out: led over 2f out: rdn clr appr fnl f* **13/8**[1]

-052 **2** *5* **Woolly Back (IRE)**[42] 3159 5-9-7 58 .... JimCrowley 9 54
(A C Whillans) *plld hrd: led after 1f: rdn and hdd over 2f out: styd on same pce* **11/4**[2]

0055 **3** *1 1/2* **Tuscany Rose**[5] 4239 3-8-5 44 .... HayleyTurner 5 47
(W R Muir) *plld hrd and prom: trckd ldr 8f out tl over 3f out: styd on same pce fnl 2f* **14/1**

3602 **4** *2 1/2* **Molly's Secret**[28] 3594 8-8-13 42 .... (p) EdwardCreighton(3) 8 43
(Miss S J Wilton) *hld up: hdwy u.p over 3f out: no imp fnl 2f* **11/2**[3]

0-05 **5** *14* **Mr Strowger**[3] 788 5-9-7 37 .... (p) TedDurcan 6 26
(S Curran) *hld up: rdn over 4f out: sn wknd* **40/1**

001/ **6** *3* **Lord Of Methley**[19] 4825 7-9-7 45 .... (t) ChrisCatlin 1 21
(S Lycett) *hld up: rdn 7f out: sn wknd* **9/1**

5006 **7** *7* **Skin Sure Thing**[5] 4239 3-8-6 41 ow1 .... (v) RobbieFitzpatrick 4 6
(D G Bridgwater) *led 1f: chsd ldrs: rdn over 6f out: wknd over 3f out* **25/1**

2m 37.72s (-4.70) **Going Correction** -0.375s/f (Stan)
WFA 3 from 4yo+ 11lb **7** Ran SP% **103.1**
Speed ratings (Par 101):100,96,95,94,84 82,78
CSF £4.97 TOTE £2.60: £1.60, £1.90; EX 6.50 Trifecta £31.90 Pool: £417.16 - 9.26 winning units..The winner was sold to Barry Leavy for 8,200gns.
Owner W Clifford **Bred** Arnfin Lund And John James **Trained** Pandy, Abergavenny
■ Dubonai (5/1) was withdrawn on vet's advice. Rule 4 applies, deduct 15p in the pound.

FOCUS
A very weak affair in which the winner was full value for his winning margin. The third limits the form.

4436 WORLD BET EXCHANGE WBX.COM NURSERY 7f 32y(P)
3:30 (3:31) (Class 5) 2-Y-O **£3,238** (£963; £481; £240) **Stalls** High

Form RPR

622 **1** **Billy Dane (IRE)**[25] 3663 2-9-5 **80** .... LDettori 7 87
(B J Meehan) *a.p: hung lft and hit over hd by rival's whip over 1f out: rdn to ld and hung rt ins fnl f: r.o* **9/4**[2]

0631 **2** *1/2* **Cesc**[8] 4178 2-8-13 **74** 6ex .... SebSanders 3 80+
(P J Makin) *s.i.s: hld up: hdwy over 2f out: nt clr run over 1f out tl r.o ins fnl f: nt rch wnr* **2/1**[1]

0102 **3** *1 3/4* **Easy Lover**[14] 3997 2-9-4 **82** .... RichardKingscote(3) 5 83
(J A Osborne) *chsd ldr over 5f out: rdn to ld over 1f out: hdd and no ex ins fnl f* **5/1**[3]

0346 **4** *3/4* **Goose Green (IRE)**[17] 3902 2-8-1 **65** .... EdwardCreighton(3) 2 64
(M R Channon) *chsd ldrs: nt clr run ins fnl f: swtchd rt: r.o* **8/1**

2444 **5** *1* **Intersky Sports (USA)**[16] 3940 2-8-6 **67** .... DeanMcKeown 1 64
(K A Ryan) *led: rdn and hdd over 1f out: no ex ins fnl f* **7/1**

13 **6** *11* **Beau Sancy**[27] 3619 2-8-11 **72**....................(p) AdrianMcCarthy 8 41
(R A Harris) *s.i.s: rdn 1/2-way: wknd over 2f out* **16/1**
024 **7** *1 ¼* **Soffooh (USA)**[14] 4007 2-7-12 **59** oh2.................... HayleyTurner 4 25
(W J Musson) *hld up: plld hrd: hdwy 4f out: wknd over 2f out* **20/1**
0046 **8** *½* **Fasuby (IRE)**[32] 3448 2-7-9 **59** oh4.................... DominicFox(3) 6 24
(P D Evans) *chsd ldrs: rdn 1/2-way: n.m.r and wknd over 2f out* **40/1**
0540 **9** *2 ½* **Everyman**[25] 3678 2-7-9 **61** oh2 ow2.................... LiamJones(5) 9 19
(P D Evans) *sn outpcd and bhd* **33/1**
5600 **10** *nk* **Spinning Game**[17] 3917 2-7-12 **59** oh9.................... PaulQuinn 10 17
(D W Chapman) *chsd ldrs over 4f* **66/1**

1m 27.7s (-2.70) **Going Correction** -0.375s/f (Stan) **10** Ran SP% **121.9**
Speed ratings (Par 94):100,99,97,96,95 82,81,80,78,77
CSF £7.33 CT £20.73 TOTE £3.70: £1.30, £1.30, £1.30; EX 8.00 Trifecta £22.00 Pool: £1,012.12 - 32.62 winning units..
Owner The Comic Strip Heroes **Bred** Brian Killeen **Trained** Manton, Wilts

FOCUS
A fair nursery run in a good time. The winner has to rate a little fortunate as the runner-up endured a luckless passge when it mattered.

NOTEBOOK
Billy Dane(IRE), making his handicap debut after the mandatory three previous outings, came home to score under a strong ride from Dettori and break his duck on this All-Weather bow. He pulled out a little more when threatened by the runner-up close home and probably has more to offer in this sphere. (op 11-4 tchd 3-1)
Cesc, under a penalty for winning at Newbury eight days previously, endured a troubled passage at a crucial stage and has to be considered an unfortunate loser. It would be little surprise to see him out again quickly, before the Handicapper can reassess him, in a bid to gain compensation. (tchd 7-4)
Easy Lover had her chance under top weight and ran another sound race in defeat. She is a decent benchmark for this form, but is clearly vulnerable from her current official mark. (op 3-1)
Goose Green(IRE), popular in the betting ring, was a little short of room at the top of the straight and can be rated a touch better than the bare form. This must rate a more encouraging effort. (op 11-1 tchd 12-1)
Intersky Sports(USA) failed to raise his game on this handicap bow and does not appear all that straightforward. (tchd 6-1)

4437 WBX.COM WORLD BET EXCHANGE H'CAP 7f 32y(P)
4:00 (4:00) (Class 5) (0-75,75) 3-Y-O+ **£3,238** (£963; £481; £240) **Stalls** High

Form RPR
323 **1** **Magic Rush**[16] 3931 4-9-10 **75**.................... EdwardCreighton(3) 6 88
(Mrs Norma Pook) *mde all: edgd rt ins fnl f: pushed out* **7/1**[2]
260P **2** *1 ½* **Lord Of The East**[20] 3813 7-9-7 **72**.................... PatrickMathers(3) 12 81
(I W McInnes) *chsd wnr over 4f: rdn to chse wnr fnl f: styd on* **20/1**
2410 **3** *1 ½* **Vienna's Boy (IRE)**[28] 3598 5-9-6 **71**.................... StephenDonohoe(3) 7 76
(W J Musson) *hld up: hdwy over 2f out: nt rch ldrs* **7/1**[2]
0135 **4** *hd* **Joyeaux**[19] 3845 4-9-1 **63**....................(v) DerekMcGaffin 5 67
(J Hetherton) *hld up: hdwy over 1f out: nrst fin* **14/1**
0622 **5** *¾* **Rosein**[14] 3996 4-9-8 **70**.................... SebSanders 9 73
(Mrs G S Rees) *hld up: hdwy 1/2-way: chsd wnr over 2f out to 1f out: hung lft and wknd ins fnl f* **5/1**[1]
5200 **6** *hd* **Bessemer (JPN)**[8] 4172 5-9-13 **75**....................(p) TedDurcan 2 77
(D Carroll) *chsd ldrs: rdn 1/2-way: styd on same pce appr fnl f* **7/1**[2]
0302 **7** *¾* **Golden Alchemist**[28] 3598 3-9-6 **74**....................(v[1]) IanMongan 3 72
(M D I Usher) *s.i.s: rdn 1/2-way: r.o ins fnl f: nvr nrr* **5/1**[1]
0000 **8** *½* **The Crooked Ring**[7] 4211 4-9-3 **70**.................... MichaelJStainton(5) 1 69
(P D Evans) *hld up: hdwy u.p over 1f out: nt trble ldrs* **12/1**[3]
5-06 **9** *1* **Pommes Frites**[26] 3643 3-9-7 **75**.................... RichardMullen 10 69
(W R Muir) *hld up: rdn over 1f out: n.d* **25/1**
5603 **10** *¾* **Underscore (USA)**[17] 3914 4-9-6 **68**....................(p) AdrianMcCarthy 4 62
(R A Harris) *chsd ldrs: rdn over 2f out: wknd over 1f out* **7/1**[2]
0006 **11** *1 ¼* **Thunderwing (IRE)**[17] 3918 4-9-8 **70**.................... RobbieFitzpatrick 11 61
(K R Burke) *sn pushed along in rr: rdn 1/2-way: sn wknd* **7/1**[2]
0204 **12** *6* **Mistral Sky**[20] 3827 7-9-3 **65**....................(v) HayleyTurner 8 40
(Stef Liddiard) *chsd ldrs 5f* **14/1**

1m 27.46s (-2.94) **Going Correction** -0.375s/f (Stan)
WFA 3 from 4yo+ 6lb **12** Ran SP% **125.5**
Speed ratings (Par 103):101,99,97,97,96 96,95,94,93,92 91,84
CSF £146.21 CT £1051.13 TOTE £5.70: £2.20, £13.10, £3.10; EX 199.80 Trifecta £352.70 Part won. Pool: £496.80 - 0.53 winning units..
Owner R Stuart A Taylor J Ambler A Najeeb **Bred** J Baker **Trained** Wanborough, Wilts
■ Norma Pook's first winner from her new base at Stan Mellor's old yard.

FOCUS
A fair handicap which was run at an uneven pace. The winner made all readily and the form could be a shade above average for the grade.
Golden Alchemist Official explanation: jockey said gelding was unsuited by first-time visor

4438 TAKE CONTROL WITH WBX.COM H'CAP 2m 119y(P)
4:30 (4:30) (Class 6) (0-55,53) 4-Y-O+ **£2,730** (£806; £403) **Stalls** Low

Form RPR
0262 **1** **Swords**[14] 3998 4-9-8 **53**.................... DeanMcKeown 2 64
(Heather Dalton) *hld up: hdwy over 2f out: led and hung lft ins fnl f: rdn out* **7/1**[3]
0030 **2** *hd* **Irish Ballad**[16] 3952 4-9-7 **52**....................(t) SebSanders 13 63
(W R Swinburn) *a.p: led 3f out: rdn and hdd ins fnl f: styd on* **6/1**[2]
0524 **3** *3 ½* **Star Rising**[10] 4104 4-9-2 **50**.................... StephenDonohoe(3) 8 57
(W J Musson) *hld up: hdwy over 2f out: rdn and hung lft over 1f out: styd on same pce* **6/1**[2]
333- **4** *2* **Johnny Alljays (IRE)**[67] 1255 5-9-1 **46**.................... ChrisCatlin 9 51
(S Lycett) *chsd ldrs: rdn over 2f out: wknd fnl f* **12/1**
2000 **5** *1* **Step Perfect (USA)**[9] 4156 5-9-1 **46**....................(p) JoeFanning 5 49
(G M Moore) *led 1f: chsd ldrs: rdn over 5f out: wknd over 1f out* **14/1**
0420 **6** *1 ½* **Trials 'n Tribs**[14] 4011 4-9-0 **45**.................... TedDurcan 12 47
(C A Cyzer) *dwlt: swtchd lft after s: hld up: rdn over 2f out: n.d* **7/1**[3]
0050 **7** *1* **Aristi (IRE)**[17] 3919 5-9-3 **48**.................... RobbieFitzpatrick 10 48
(M Quinn) *led after 1f: hdd 14f out: chsd ldrs: led over 3f out: sn hdd: rdn and wknd over 1f out* **9/1**
2000 **8** *5* **Scurra**[11] 4072 7-8-12 **43**.................... JimCrowley 4 37
(A C Whillans) *hld up: nvr trbld ldrs* **33/1**
5441 **9** *nk* **Ice And Fire**[17] 3919 7-8-13 **51**....................(b) AshleyHamblett(7) 6 45
(J T Stimpson) *hld up: hdwy over 3f out: rdn and wknd over 2f out* **7/1**[3]
6021 **10** *nk* **Lysander's Quest (IRE)**[14] 4011 8-9-1 **46**.................... FergusSweeney 1 40
(R Ingram) *hld up: rdn over 4f out: wknd over 2f out* **5/1**[1]
5006 **11** *shd* **Lets Try Again (IRE)**[17] 3894 9-9-0 **45**.................... VinceSlattery 11 39
(R A Farrant) *hld up: rdn over 3f out* **40/1**
0000 **12** *9* **Shingle Street (IRE)**[12] 4046 4-9-5 **50**....................(vt[1]) RichardMullen 7 33
(I A Wood) *s.i.s: sn chsng ldrs: led 14f out: rdn and hdd over 3f out: sn wknd* **33/1**
0000 **13** *4* **Indian Chase**[17] 3919 9-9-3 **48**.................... RichardThomas 3 26
(Dr J R J Naylor) *plld hrd and prom: rdn over 4f out: wknd 3f out: eased* **33/1**

3m 38.04s (-5.09) **Going Correction** -0.375s/f (Stan) **13** Ran SP% **118.4**
Speed ratings (Par 101):96,95,94,93,92 92,91,89,89,89 88,84,82
CSF £46.73 CT £270.97 TOTE £7.80: £2.20, £2.20, £2.30; EX 37.00 Trifecta £337.90 Part won. Pool: £475.97 - 0.67 winning units..
Owner Ms Heather Dalton **Bred** Mrs A Yearley **Trained** Norton, Shropshire

FOCUS
A weak staying handicap run in a modest time which saw the first pair come clear. The form looks sound enough at face value.

4439 WBX.COM WORLD BET EXCHANGE APPRENTICE H'CAP 1m 1f 103y(P)
5:00 (5:00) (Class 6) (0-55,55) 3-Y-O+ **£2,730** (£806; £403) **Stalls** Low

Form RPR
3430 **1** **Harare**[17] 3894 5-9-0 **47**....................(b) WilliamCarson(5) 10 58+
(R J Price) *chsd ldrs: nt clr run and swtchd rt over 1f out: r.o to ld towards fin* **6/1**[1]
1203 **2** *½* **Scamperdale**[28] 3599 4-9-8 **55**....................(p) SoniaEaton(5) 1 63
(B P J Baugh) *hld up: hdwy over 3f out: led ins fnl f: hdd towards fin* **7/1**[3]
40-5 **3** *1 ½* **Rem Time (IRE)**[20] 3817 6-9-6 **48**.................... JamieHamblett 13 53
(John Berry) *chsd ldrs: rdn to ld over 1f out: hdd and unable qck ins fnl f* **6/1**[1]
0010 **4** *nk* **Aberdeen Park**[9] 4139 4-9-10 **52**....................(b) KylieManser 2 56+
(Mrs H Sweeting) *s.s: hld up: hdwy over 1f out: nt trble ldrs* **33/1**
0002 **5** *2 ½* **Cavan Gael (FR)**[9] 4139 4-9-8 **55**.................... JPFeatherstone(5) 3 55
(P Howling) *hld up: hdwy over 3f out: rdn and hung lft over 1f out: styd on same pce* **13/2**[2]
1040 **6** *1* **Gem Bien (USA)**[7] 4198 8-9-10 **55**....................(b) LukeMorris(3) 9 53
(D W Chapman) *hld up: rdn over 2f out: nvr nrr* **9/1**
1040 **7** *1* **Abbeygate**[52] 2820 5-9-8 **50**....................(p) PatrickHills 7 46
(T Keddy) *hld up: effrt over 3f out: n.d* **7/1**[3]
3505 **8** *¾* **Fiore Di Bosco (IRE)**[14] 4010 5-9-0 **47**.................... DeanHeslop(5) 6 41
(T D Barron) *s.i.s: nvr nrr* **7/1**[3]
0005 **9** *½* **Windy Prospect**[55] 2728 4-9-4 **51**.................... JosephWalsh(5) 8 45
(P A Blockley) *chsd ldr: led 6f out: rdn and hdd over 1f out: wknd ins fnl f* **7/1**[3]
-000 **10** *½* **Raul Sahara**[3] 4325 4-9-2 **44**.................... CharlotteKerton 5 37
(J W Unett) *a in rr* **25/1**
400- **11** *1* **Channel Crossing**[286] 6215 4-9-8 **50**.................... PJBenson 12 41
(W M Brisbourne) *led: hdd 6f out: rdn and hung rt over 2f out: wknd over 1f out : eased* **12/1**
/60- **12** *11* **Trusted Mole (IRE)**[343] 5008 8-9-6 **48**.................... AlanRutter 4 18
(W M Brisbourne) *chsd ldrs: rdn over 3f out: wknd over 2f out* **20/1**

2m 1.03s (-1.59) **Going Correction** -0.375s/f (Stan) **12** Ran SP% **121.1**
Speed ratings (Par 101):92,91,90,89,87 86,85,85,84,84 83,73
CSF £47.33 CT £269.03 TOTE £9.40: £2.10, £2.00, £2.00; EX 62.90 Trifecta £90.30 Pool: £459.32 - 3.61 winning units. Place 6 £39.91, Place 5 £19.31.
Owner Mrs P A Wallis **Bred** Limestone Stud **Trained** Ullingswick, H'fords
■ Stewards' Enquiry : Jamie Hamblett three-day ban: used whip with excessive frequency (Aug 27,28, Oct 19)

FOCUS
A decidedly weak handicap run in a very moderate time and the form should be treated with caution. The winner was back to the pick of his sand form.
T/Jkpt: Not won. T/Plt: £25.90 to a £1 stake. Pool: £62,431.85. 1,753.55 winning tickets. T/Qpdt: £7.90 to a £1 stake. Pool: £4,402.20. 408.10 winning tickets. CR

4440 - 4443a (Foreign Racing) - See Raceform Interactive

4276 BRIGHTON (L-H)
Tuesday, August 15

OFFICIAL GOING: Firm
Wind: Moderate, half against

4444 TOTEPLACEPOT NURSERY 5f 59y
2:00 (2:00) (Class 4) 2-Y-O **£5,505** (£1,637; £818) **Stalls** Low

Form RPR
4225 **1** **Inflight (IRE)**[24] 3720 2-7-13 **69** oh1 ow4.................... NelsonDeSouza(3) 3 72
(R M Beckett) *hld up in 3rd pl: qcknd to ld wl over 1f out: pushed out: easily* **7/4**[2]
6052 **2** *4* **Candyland (IRE)**[15] 4002 2-8-1 **68**.................... ChrisCatlin 5 56
(M R Channon) *trckd ldr: chal over 2f out: hung lft: one pce ins fnl f* **8/13**[1]
3554 **3** *1 ½* **Mind The Style**[2] 4397 2-9-4 **88**.................... AmirQuinn(3) 2 71
(W G M Turner) *led tl rdn and hdd wl over 1f out: wknd fnl f* **10/1**[3]

63.37 secs (1.07) **Going Correction** +0.15s/f (Good) **3** Ran SP% **107.4**
Speed ratings (Par 96):97,90,88
CSF £3.28 TOTE £2.80; EX 3.70.
Owner The Millennium Madness Partnership **Bred** M Munnelly **Trained** Whitsbury, Hants
■ Stewards' Enquiry : Amir Quinn caution: used whip down the shoulder in the forehand position

FOCUS
A weakly contested event and not a race to place much faith in. The winner basically ran to form.

NOTEBOOK
Inflight(IRE) adopted different tactics and was held up rather than blazing a trail. Cruising into the lead, she won this weak event very comfortably despite the overweight.
Candyland(IRE), on her nursery bow, got the better of a tussle with the third despite looking less than happy on the track's undulations, but the winner proved much too good. (op 8-11)
Mind The Style, back down in trip for this nursery debut, could never shake off the attentions of the eventual runner-up and finished up well held. She is proving disapppointing. (op 8-1)

4445 TOTECOURSE TO COURSE MAIDEN AUCTION STKS 6f 209y
2:30 (2:31) (Class 5) 2-Y-O **£3,238** (£963; £481; £240) **Stalls** Low

Form RPR
0 **1** **Redcliff (GER)**[10] 4140 2-9-0.................... JimCrowley 5 73
(Mrs A J Perrett) *sn disp 2nd pl: rdn to ld jst ins fnl f: r.o wl* **16/1**
32 **2** *1 ½* **Belvedere Vixen**[6] 4238 2-8-8.................... SteveDrowne 3 63
(J A Osborne) *trckd ldr: hung lft over 1f out: rallied to run on and regained 2nd ins fnl f* **6/1**[2]
22 **3** *2 ½* **Brenin Gwalia**[26] 3669 2-8-9.................... ChrisCatlin 7 57
(D M Simcock) *led tl rdn and hdd jst ins fnl f: one pce and lost 2nd sn after* **15/8**[1]
0 **4** *1 ¼* **Cape Runaway (IRE)**[27] 3645 2-8-9.................... NickyMackay 1 54
(L M Cumani) *in rr: rdn 1/2-way: styd on fnl f: nvr nrr* **10/1**
0 **5** *3* **Ten Black**[11] 4109 2-9-2.................... TPQueally 6 53
(J A Osborne) *a outpcd in rr* **20/1**
4 **6** *hd* **Sunquest**[10] 4163 2-8-13.................... RyanMoore 2 49
(R Hannon) *chsd ldrs: rdn and hung lft 2f out: sn btn* **15/8**[1]

6002 **L** **Linkslade Lad**[10] 4163 2-9-0 70 (b) FrancisNorton 4 —
(W R Muir) *ref to r* **9/1**[3]

1m 24.24s (1.54) **Going Correction** +0.15s/f (Good) **7** Ran SP% **113.6**
Speed ratings (Par 94):97,95,92,91,87 87,—
CSF £104.74 TOTE £19.30: £7.10, £2.50; EX 81.60.
Owner Exterior Profiles & & Mrs Bovingdon **Bred** Gestut Am Schlossgarten **Trained** Pulborough, W Sussex

FOCUS
A modest maiden in which the third was below form and the sixth failed to run his race.

NOTEBOOK
Redcliff(GER), who hinted at ability on his Lingfield debut, showed the benefit of that experience and won decisively. He will not mind a return to a bit further and looks a nursery type.
Belvedere Vixen, runner-up over course and distance last time, filled the same position despite looking less happy on the track this time. She can find a race on a more conventional track. (op 9-2 tchd 13-2)
Brenin Gwalia, back up in trip, travelled well in front but could not counter when headed. (op 2-1 tchd 9-4 in a place)
Cape Runaway(IRE), well held on Polytrack on her debut, made late progress without being knocked about. Out of an unraced half-sister to July Cup winner Mr Brooks, she is a sister to Gibraltar Bay and half-sister to Double Ransom, both multiple winners, and should come into her own over a bit further next year. (op 12-1)
Sunquest had made a promising debut and had been expected to improve for this longer trip, but he did not act on the track. Official explanation: jockey said colt was unsuited by the track and firm going (op 2-1 tchd 9-4)
Linkslade Lad has shown mulish tendencies before and is not one to trust. (op 10-1)

4446 TOTEQUADPOT H'CAP 7f 214y
3:00 (3:00) (Class 6) (0-60,64) 3-Y-O+ **£3,238** (£963; £481; £240) **Stalls** Low

Form RPR
2212 **1** **Prince Valentine**[28] 3614 5-9-6 **50** (p) RyanMoore 3 59
(G L Moore) *hld up: hdwy 2f out: hung lft enter ing fnl f: sn r.o and led ins: won gng away* **7/2**[1]
5032 **2** *1 1/4* **Diamond Dan (IRE)**[5] 4276 4-9-2 **53** JamieHamblett(7) 8 59
(P D Evans) *chsd ldr: led 2f out: hdd 1f out: kpt on one pce: hdd ins fnl f* **5/1**[2]
0600 **3** *shd* **Perfect Order (USA)**[26] 3668 3-8-10 **47** (p) ChrisCatlin 13 52
(N A Callaghan) *slowly away: hld up: hdwy on ins 2f out: led 1f out: rdn and hdd ins fnl f: lost 2nd cl home* **33/1**
4324 **4** *shd* **Zafarshah (IRE)**[3] 4363 7-9-1 **45** (b) AdrianMcCarthy 4 51
(R A Harris) *a in tch: kpt on u.p fnl f* **15/2**
00 **5** *shd* **Connotation**[50] 2936 4-9-11 **55** (b) FergusSweeney 1 60
(A G Newcombe) *a.p on ins: hrd rdn 2f out: kpt on one pce ins fnl f* **9/1**
2005 **6** *nk* **Danzare**[5] 4289 4-9-5 **52** NeilChalmers(3) 10 57
(Mrs A J Hamilton-Fairley) *prom on outside: rdn over 2f out: kpt on fnl f* **33/1**
0400 **7** *nk* **Border Edge**[17] 3928 8-10-0 **58** (v) J-PGuillambert 5 62
(J J Bridger) *t.k.h: in tch: rdn over 3f out: no ex ins fnl f* **12/1**
0350 **8** *1 3/4* **Comeintothespace (IRE)**[5] 4288 4-8-12 **45** AdamKirby(3) 11 45
(Miss Victoria Roberts) *racd wd: in rr: rdn and hdwy 3f out: eased whn btn ins fnl f* **25/1**
1526 **9** *1 1/2* **Terenzium (IRE)**[13] 4048 4-9-9 **53** NickyMackay 6 49
(L M Cumani) *hld up in rr: rdn and effrt 2f out: sn btn: eaased ins fnl f* **5/1**[2]
5003 **10** *3/4* **Zinging**[5] 4276 7-8-10 **45** (b) MarcHalford(5) 7 40
(J J Bridger) *chsd ldrs tl rdn and wknd wl over 1f out* **33/1**
5251 **11** *3* **Taranaki**[2] 4399 8-10-1 **64** 6ex TravisBlock(5) 12 52+
(P D Cundell) *hld up on outside: c over to r alone stands' side over 3f out: lost tch over 1f out* **7/1**[3]
2000 **12** *11* **It's Basil**[22] 3797 3-8-9 **46** (b) PaulDoe 2 8
(R M Flower) *led: sn clr: rdn and hdd 2f out: sn wknd: eased fnl f* **66/1**
6466 **13** *7* **Jools**[12] 4073 8-9-7 **58** JamesMillman(7) 9 4
(D K Ivory) *t.k.h: in tch: rdn over 3f out: wknd wl over 1f out: eased ins fnl f* **14/1**

1m 36.6s (1.56) **Going Correction** +0.15s/f (Good)
WFA 3 from 4yo+ 7lb **13** Ran SP% **118.3**
Speed ratings (Par 101):98,96,96,96,96 96,95,94,92,91 88,77,70
CSF £19.06 CT £516.96 TOTE £3.60: £1.60, £2.10, £10.30; EX 16.60 Trifecta £450.90 Part won. Pool: £635.21 - 0.69 winning units.
Owner D R Hunnisett **Bred** Mrs E Y Hunnisett **Trained** Woodingdean, E Sussex

FOCUS
This was hand-timed. A modest handicap, and ordinary if sound form.
Comeintothespace(IRE) Official explanation: jockey said gelding was never travelling
Terenzium(IRE) Official explanation: vet said colt finished lame
Jools Official explanation: vet said gelding had bled from the nose

4447 TOTE TEXT BETTING 60021 FILLIES' H'CAP 6f 209y
3:30 (3:30) (Class 5) (0-70,70) 3-Y-O+ **£4,857** (£1,445; £722; £360) **Stalls** Low

Form RPR
4252 **1** **Toffee Vodka (IRE)**[5] 4281 4-9-7 **70** PatrickHills(7) 3 77+
(J W Hills) *hld up: hdwy to ld 2f out: sn clr: pushed out fnl f* **5/4**[1]
0000 **2** *5* **Tilsworth Charlie**[19] 3865 3-8-3 **51** oh9 (v[1]) NickyMackay 2 43
(J R Jenkins) *in tch: wnt 2nd 4f out: hung lft over 2f out: styd on one pce fnl f* **66/1**
6500 **3** *1 1/2* **Miss Madame (IRE)**[24] 3728 5-8-9 **51** oh1 IanMongan 4 41
(T G Mills) *t.k.h: led after 1f: hdd 2f out: rdn and no hdwy fr over 1f out* **5/1**
4 *9* **Sotanna (IRE)**[659] 6407 4-8-11 **53** DaneO'Neill 5 20
(P R Webber) *t.k.h: in tch: rdn 3f out: sn btn* **9/2**[3]
6324 **5** *shd* **My Princess (IRE)**[21] 3828 4-10-0 **70** RyanMoore 1 36
(N A Callaghan) *led for 1f: hmpd over 2f out: sn btn* **9/4**[2]

1m 23.66s (0.96) **Going Correction** +0.15s/f (Good)
WFA 3 from 4yo+ 6lb **5** Ran SP% **111.6**
Speed ratings (Par 100):100,94,92,82,82
CSF £46.34 TOTE £2.00: £1.40, £4.60; EX 32.40.
Owner Gary And Linnet Woodward **Bred** Mrs K Smyth **Trained** Upper Lambourn, Berks
■ Stewards' Enquiry : Nicky Mackay one-day ban: careless riding (Aug 26)

FOCUS
A weak handicap in which the winner did not need to improve.

4448 TOTESPORT.COM BRIGHTON CHALLENGE CUP (H'CAP) 1m 3f 196y
4:00 (4:01) (Class 4) (0-80,80) 3-Y-O+
£18,696 (£5,598; £2,799; £1,401; £699; £351) **Stalls** High

Form RPR
0446 **1** **Ariodante**[15] 4005 4-8-6 **62** RyanMoore 14 72
(J M P Eustace) *chsd ldrs: led appr fnl fnl f: rdn and hdd briefly ins: battled bk: hld on gamely* **13/2**[3]
0314 **2** *nk* **Transvestite (IRE)**[11] 4112 4-9-3 **80** PatrickHills(7) 5 90
(J W Hills) *mid-div: hdwy 2f out: swtchd lft over 1f out: led briefly ins fnl f: kpt on to line* **8/1**
4614 **3** *4* **Blackmail (USA)**[26] 3666 8-8-2 **61** (b) NelsonDeSouza(3) 8 64
(Miss B Sanders) *mid-div: hdwy on outside over 1f out: styd on fnl f: nvr nrr* **12/1**
5100 **4** *3* **Love Always**[20] 3853 4-9-0 **70** PatDobbs 9 68
(S Dow) *in rr: styd on one pce fr over 1f out* **12/1**
0050 **5** *1/2* **The Violin Player (USA)**[10] 4149 5-8-7 **66** (p) JamesDoyle(3) 13 64
(H J Collingridge) *mid-div: rdn over 3f out: nt qckn ins fnl 2f* **16/1**
6020 **6** *2 1/2* **Boot 'n Toot**[20] 3853 5-9-0 **70** J-PGuillambert 11 64
(C A Cyzer) *disp 2nd pl tl wknd wl over 1f out* **9/1**
6225 **7** *3* **Meelup (IRE)**[15] 4005 6-8-3 **59** (p) RoystonFfrench 10 48
(P G Murphy) *chsd ldrs: rdn 4f out: wknd over 2f out* **8/1**
3101 **8** *2 1/2* **Oddsmaker (IRE)**[5] 4299 5-9-6 **76** 6ex (t) DeanMcKeown 3 61
(M A Barnes) *led tl rdn and hdd over 1f out: wknd qckly* **6/1**[2]
6412 **9** *1 3/4* **Rahy's Crown (USA)**[7] 4224 3-7-12 **65** oh1 NickyMackay 4 47
(G L Moore) *in tch: rdn 4f out: eased whn btn fnl f* **15/8**[1]
254- **10** *13* **Jack Dawson (IRE)**[451] 1898 9-9-2 **72** GeorgeBaker 12 33
(John Berry) *hld up in rr: lost tch over 2f out* **16/1**
35/6 **L** **Kalambari (IRE)**[111] 1238 7-9-9 **79** ChrisCatlin 7 —
(S Dow) *ref to r* **50/1**

2m 30.95s (-1.25) **Going Correction** +0.15s/f (Good)
WFA 3 from 4yo+ 11lb **11** Ran SP% **123.7**
Speed ratings (Par 105):110,109,107,105,104 103,101,99,98,89 —
CSF £60.94 CT £626.46 TOTE £8.60: £2.90, £2.70, £3.50; EX 98.30 Trifecta £503.00 Part won. Pool: £708.57 - 0.35 winning units.
Owner The Macdougall Partnership **Bred** Bishop's Down Farm **Trained** Newmarket, Suffolk

FOCUS
A big prize for the grade. This was run at a strong gallop and the field was soon stretched out. The winning time was very creditable for a race like this and the form is solid, rated through the runner-up.
Rahy's Crown(USA) Official explanation: trainer said colt was unsuited by the firm ground
Jack Dawson(IRE) Official explanation: jockey said gelding failed to handle the rough/firm ground

4449 TOTESPORT 0800 221 221 BRIGHTON DASH (H'CAP) 5f 213y
4:30 (4:30) (Class 4) (0-80,80) 3-Y-O+ **£6,477** (£1,927; £963; £481) **Stalls** Low

Form RPR
6133 **1** **Ivory Lace**[28] 3612 5-9-10 **76** JamesDoyle(3) 2 85
(S Woodman) *a.p: rdn to ld jst ins fnl f: drvn out* **4/1**[1]
2021 **2** *nk* **Sweet Pickle**[12] 4077 5-9-1 **64** (e) GeorgeBaker 7 72
(J R Boyle) *hld in rr on outside: hdwy over 1f out: r.o to go 2nd ins fnl f* **11/2**[3]
3450 **3** *2* **Summer Recluse (USA)**[11] 4101 7-9-3 **66** (t) RyanMoore 6 71+
(J M Bradley) *s.i.s: making hdwy whn bdly hmpd on ins wl over 1f out: r.o wl whn clr run ins fnl f* **5/1**[2]
4304 **4** *1* **Buy On The Red**[3] 4364 5-9-9 **72** (b) DaneO'Neill 3 71
(W R Muir) *sn chsd ldrs: rdn 1/2-way: ev ch ent fnl f: nt qckn ins* **5/1**[2]
0050 **5** *nk* **H Harrison (IRE)**[9] 4172 6-9-5 **68** RoystonFfrench 8 66
(I W McInnes) *chsd ldrs on outside: rdn over 2f out: hung bdly both ways fr 2f out tl r.o ins fnl f* **9/1**
5300 **6** *nk* **Willhewiz**[20] 3855 6-9-7 **70** SebSanders 1 67
(M S Saunders) *led tl rdn and hdd jst ins fnl f: wknd qckly* **13/2**
1000 **7** *2* **Savernake Blue**[10] 4144 3-9-6 **80** ThomasO'Brien(7) 4 71
(M R Channon) *chsd ldrs tl rdn and wknd 2f out* **20/1**
4541 **8** *2* **Inch By Inch**[3] 4364 7-9-11 **77** 6ex (b) AmirQuinn(3) 5 62
(P J Makin) *t.k.h: chsd ldr tl wknd over 1f out* **4/1**[1]

69.87 secs (-0.23) **Going Correction** +0.15s/f (Good)
WFA 3 from 5yo+ 4lb **8** Ran SP% **116.8**
Speed ratings (Par 105):107,106,103,102,102 101,99,96
CSF £26.79 CT £113.29 TOTE £5.60: £1.10, £2.90, £2.20; EX 29.60 Trifecta £300.50 Pool: £698.56 - 1.65 winning units..
Owner Christopher J Halpin **Bred** D R Tucker **Trained** East Lavant, W Sussex

FOCUS
A competitive sprint handicap and the form should prove reliable.
Buy On The Red Official explanation: jockey said he dropped his whip 2f out
Inch By Inch Official explanation: jockey said mare ran flat

4450 CLASSICEVENTMARQUEES.CO.UK MAIDEN H'CAP 6f 209y
5:00 (5:01) (Class 6) (0-55,54) 3-Y-O+ **£2,590** (£770; £385; £192) **Stalls** Low

Form RPR
3504 **1** **Shinko (IRE)**[5] 4293 3-9-9 **54** DeanCorby(3) 4 62
(Miss J Feilden) *a in tch: rdn to ld ins fnl f: won gng away* **5/1**[3]
3636 **2** *1 1/4* **Three Feathers**[28] 3614 3-8-9 **42** LiamJones(5) 1 47
(M Salaman) *led tl hdd and hmpd over 4f out: swtchd rt over 1f out: r.o to go 2nd ins fnl f* **4/1**[2]
0543 **3** *1* **Sunset Ridge (IRE)**[42] 3164 3-9-10 **52** ChrisCatlin 6 54
(Rae Guest) *a.p: chal 2f out: no ex and lost 2nd ins fnl f* **7/4**[1]
4000 **4** *1 3/4* **Megalala (IRE)**[17] 3933 5-9-9 **45** (p) J-PGuillambert 3 45
(J J Bridger) *slowly away: racd wd: prom after 1f: led over 2f out: rdn and hdd ins fnl f: sn btn* **12/1**
-050 **5** *1 1/4* **Parisi Princess**[12] 4077 5-9-1 **40** NelsonDeSouza(3) 10 36
(D L Williams) *chsd ldrs on outside: rdn over 2f out: no further hdwy* **14/1**
0065 **6** *1 1/4* **Opera Belle**[35] 3379 4-9-4 **43** (bt[1]) AdamKirby(3) 9 36
(Miss Gay Kelleway) *a in rr* **5/1**[3]
4054 **7** *1 1/4* **Flying Dancer**[7] 4223 4-10-0 **50** (p) AdrianMcCarthy 8 40
(R A Harris) *chsd ldrs: effrt on outside over 2f out:wknd over 1f out* **6/1**
0000 **8** *hd* **Flying Visitor**[32] 3472 3-8-6 **41** (b) KirstyMilczarek(7) 2 28
(J M P Eustace) *in rr whn hmpd over 4f out: nvr on terms after* **12/1**

1m 24.59s (1.89) **Going Correction** +0.15s/f (Good)
WFA 3 from 4yo+ 6lb **8** Ran SP% **126.0**
Speed ratings (Par 101):95,93,92,90,89 87,86,85
CSF £28.17 CT £51.27 TOTE £7.20: £1.80, £1.40, £1.20; EX 44.80 Trifecta £29.20 Pool: £596.52 - 14.46 winning units. Place 6 £804.05, Place 5 £237.90.
Owner DD & N Associates **Bred** Lodge Park Stud **Trained** Exning, Suffolk
■ Stewards' Enquiry : J-P Guillambert five-day ban (increased from four after an appeal): careless riding (Aug 30-Sep 3)

FOCUS
A weak maiden handicap in which the winner is rated to the best of this year's form.
T/Jkpt: Not won. T/Plt: £434.30 to a £1 stake. Pool: £70,707.85. 118.85 winning tickets. T/Qpdt: £21.60 to a £1 stake. Pool: £6,328.80. 216.40 winning tickets. JS

^{4194}CARLISLE (R-H)

Tuesday, August 15

OFFICIAL GOING: Good to firm (firm in places)

The latest meeting at this track that saw the prominent racers enjoy a big advantage over those held up.

Wind: Almost nil

4451 RACING UK ON SKY 432 AMATEUR RIDERS' H'CAP — 1m 6f 32y

6:00 (6:00) (Class 6) (0-65,65) 3-Y-0+ — **£2,637** (£811; £405) **Stalls** High

Form — RPR

4063 **1** **Montosari**^{18} [3894] 7-10-3 **52** .... JackMitchell$^{(5)}$ 9 — 65+
(P Mitchell) *hld up: hdwy over 5f out: led centre over 2f out: sn clr* **7/1**

3204 **2** 5 **Thewhirlingdervish (IRE)**^{10} [4156] 8-11-2 **65** .... MissJCoward$^{(5)}$ 2 — 71
(T D Easterby) *hld up: hdwy to chse wnr over 1f out: kpt on ins fnl f: no imp* **5/1**^{1}

5223 **3** 5 **Regency Red (IRE)**^{12} [4086] 8-10-2 **51** .... MrBenBrisbourne$^{(5)}$ 8 — 50
(W M Brisbourne) *s.i.s: hld up: faltered 1/2-way: effrt stands rail 2f out: kpt on fnl f: no imp* **11/2**^{2}

1000 **4** ½ **Cumbrian Knight (IRE)**^{12} [4086] 8-10-6 **55** .... MissNJefferson$^{(5)}$ 7 — 53
(J M Jefferson) *s.i.s: hld up: hdwy towards stands side over 1f out: r.o ins fnl f* **14/1**

30-2 **5** 3½ **Front Rank (IRE)**^{14} [2998] 6-10-13 **62** .... MissJSayer$^{(5)}$ 4 — 55
(Mrs Dianne Sayer) *prom chsng gp: outpcd over 3f out: hung rt and rallied over 1f out: no imp* **8/1**

4004 **6** 1¼ **Esquillon**^{7} [4227] 4-9-9 **46** oh4 .... MrRRamloll$^{(7)}$ 5 — 38
(S Parr) *led and sn clr: hdd over 3f out: wknd wl over 1f out* **33/1**

3544 **7** 3 **Transit**^{12} [4086] 7-10-4 **48** .... (p) MissLEllison 1 — 35
(B Ellison) *hld up outside: rdn over 3f out: edgd rt and outpcd fr 2f out* **13/2**

1030 **8** 2 **Richtee (IRE)**^{17} [3960] 5-11-2 **65** .... MrBMcHugh$^{(5)}$ 10 — 50
(R A Fahey) *chsd clr ldr: led over 3f out to over 2f out: sn rdn and outpcd* **6/1**^{3}

0-00 **9** hd **Peter's Imp (IRE)**^{12} [4086] 11-10-2 **46** oh8 .... MrsCBartley 12 — 30
(A Berry) *hld up: pushed along over 4f out: nvr on terms* **50/1**

3200 **10** shd **Our Choice (IRE)**^{53} [2822] 4-11-3 **61** .... MrsEmmaLittmoden 3 — 45
(N P Littmoden) *prom chsng gp tl wknd fr 4f out* **11/2**^{2}

3m 7.96s (0.66) **Going Correction** +0.05s/f (Good)
WFA 3 from 4yo+ 13lb — **10** Ran SP% **110.2**
Speed ratings (Par 101):100,97,94,94,92 91,89,88,88,88
CSF £39.00 CT £193.84 TOTE £8.90: £2.20, £2.10, £2.30; EX 46.00.
Owner Mrs S Sheldon **Bred** S Gollogly **Trained** Epsom, Surrey

FOCUS
An ordinary event but a decent gallop and this form should prove reliable, although it is not strong.
Regency Red(IRE) Official explanation: jockey said saddle slipped
Our Choice(IRE) Official explanation: jockey said gelding was unsuited by the track

4452 TAPAS EBF MEDIAN AUCTION MAIDEN STKS — 5f

6:30 (6:31) (Class 6) 2-Y-0 — **£2,730** (£806; £403) **Stalls** High

Form — RPR

6 **1** **Sunnyside Tom (IRE)**^{17} [3958] 2-9-3 .... PaulHanagan 4 — 78
(R A Fahey) *trckd ldrs: effrt and edgd lft over 1f out: led wl ins fnl f: styd on* **5/1**

2223 **2** nk **Durova (IRE)**^{12} [4089] 2-8-12 72 .... DavidAllan 8 — 72
(T D Easterby) *led: rdn over 1f out: hdd wl ins fnl f: kpt on* **3/1**^{2}

633 **3** 2 **Howards Tipple**^{55} [2745] 2-9-3 78 .... TomEaves 6 — 70
(I Semple) *cl up: effrt over 2f out: one pce fnl f* **7/2**^{3}

045 **4** ½ **Bid For Gold**^{16} [3982] 2-9-3 80 .... PaulMulrennan 3 — 68
(Jedd O'Keeffe) *prom: drvn 1/2-way: hung lft over 1f out: sn one pce* **6/5**^{1}

5 4 **Forest Machine** 2-9-3 .... TonyHamilton 2 — 54
(J S Wainwright) *s.i.s: rn green and outpcd: no imp fr 1/2-way* **66/1**

0555 **6** 55 **The Brat**^{12} [4089] 2-8-12 .... PaulFessey 1 — —
(James Moffatt) *racd wd: in tch tl wknd qckly fr 1/2-way: t.o* **50/1**

61.04 secs (-0.46) **Going Correction** -0.225s/f (Firm) — **6** Ran SP% **112.8**
Speed ratings (Par 92):94,93,90,89,83 —
CSF £20.45 TOTE £6.10: £2.80, £1.50; EX 15.10.
Owner The Sunnyside Racing Partnership **Bred** S W D McIlveen **Trained** Musley Bank, N Yorks

FOCUS
Not the most competitive race and the market leader disappointed. The second and third set the standard. The pace was sound throughout.

NOTEBOOK
Sunnyside Tom(IRE) ◆, dropped in trip, bettered his debut effort and showed a good attitude to beat a fairly reliable yardstick. He should prove equally effective back over six furlongs and appeals as the type to win another race. (tchd 11-2)
Durova(IRE) had disappointed on rain-softened ground at Musselburgh on her previous outing but returned to her best on a sound surface. Although starting to look exposed, she is a reliable yardstick who is capable of picking up a small event. (op 11-4 tchd 10-3)
Howards Tipple had the run of the race and ran creditably dropped in distance. The return to six furlongs will suit but he may find life tough in nursery company from his current mark of 78. (tchd 4-1)
Bid For Gold looked the one to beat following efforts over this course and distance and when an unlucky-in-running fifth at Pontefract. He turned in a laboured effort and, although the return to six furlongs will suit, he may continue to look vulnerable in this type of event. (op 6-4 tchd 13-8, 7-4 in places)
Forest Machine had few supporters and was too green to do himself justice on this racecourse debut. A stiffer test of stamina will suit but he is likely to continue to look vulnerable in this type of event. (op 40-1)
The Brat, exposed as poor, was soundly beaten and will have to have her sights lowered considerably if she is to get off the mark. Official explanation: jockey said filly lost its action (op 40-1)

4453 ELITE RACING CLUB H'CAP — 5f

7:00 (7:00) (Class 4) (0-80,79) 3-Y-0+ — **£6,477** (£1,927; £963; £481) **Stalls** High

Form — RPR

2214 **1** **Aegean Dancer**^{17} [3938] 4-9-0 **72** .... MarkLawson$^{(5)}$ 13 — 85
(B Smart) *mde all: c centre w rest of field st: edgd to stands rail fr over 1f out: hld on wl* **10/1**

0023 **2** ¾ **Smokin Beau**^{11} [4101] 9-9-12 **79** .... SilvestreDeSousa 7 — 89
(D Nicholls) *chsd ldrs: effrt and edgd rt over 1f out: chsd wnr ins fnl f: kpt on towards fin* **5/2**^{1}

5050 **3** 1¼ **Whinhill House**^{16} [3988] 6-8-11 **64** .... (p) RobertWinston 10 — 70
(D W Barker) *chsd ldrs: effrt over 2f out: kpt on same pce fnl f* **15/2**

0220 **4** hd **True Magic**^{18} [3912] 5-9-3 **70** .... TomEaves 5 — 75
(J D Bethell) *s.i.s: bhd tl hdwy over 1f out: nrst fin* **16/1**

4232 **5** 1½ **Kings College Boy**^{5} [4258] 6-9-1 **75** .... (v) JamesReveley$^{(7)}$ 9 — 74
(R A Fahey) *hld up midfield: effrt over 2f out: sn no imp* **9/2**^{2}

1103 **6** 1 **Ryedane (IRE)**^{20} [3832] 4-9-6 **73** .... DavidAllan 4 — 69
(T D Easterby) *midfield: drvn 1/2-way: nvr rchd ldrs* **18/1**

2520 **7** hd **Coconut Moon**^{16} [3972] 4-9-1 **71** .... StephenDonohoe$^{(3)}$ 12 — 66
(E J Alston) *w wnr tl rdn and outpcd fr 2f out* **7/1**^{3}

0430 **8** 1 **Bold Marc (IRE)**^{52} [2852] 4-9-0 **72** .... AndrewElliott$^{(5)}$ 3 — 63
(K R Burke) *midfield: drvn 1/2-way: sn no ex* **10/1**

6516 **9** ¾ **Strensall**^{17} [3938] 9-9-3 **70** .... PaulHanagan 1 — 59
(R E Barr) *racd wd in midfield: edgd rt and wknd fr 1/2-way* **33/1**

4346 **10** nk **Colonel Cotton (IRE)**^{3} [4364] 7-9-4 **71** .... (v) TonyHamilton 11 — 59
(R A Fahey) *s.i.s: bhd and hung rt 1/2-way: nvr on terms* **10/1**

60.03 secs (-1.47) **Going Correction** -0.225s/f (Firm)
WFA 3 from 4yo+ 3lb — **10** Ran SP% **112.4**
Speed ratings (Par 105):102,100,98,98,96 94,94,92,91,90
CSF £33.89 CT £206.21 TOTE £10.00: £2.50, £1.50, £2.50; EX 45.60.
Owner Pinnacle Piccolo Partnership **Bred** Theobalds Stud **Trained** Hambleton, N Yorks

FOCUS
A fair handicap for the grade and the form should prove solid. Although the pace was sound throughout, those racing prominently held the edge.
Colonel Cotton(IRE) Official explanation: jockey said gelding missed the break

4454 AZURE H'CAP — 1m 1f 61y

7:30 (7:30) (Class 5) (0-70,70) 3-Y-0+ — **£3,238** (£963; £481; £240) **Stalls** High

Form — RPR

5501 **1** **Wing Commander**^{3} [4353] 7-9-8 **69** 6ex .... (b) MarkLawson$^{(5)}$ 4 — 76
(I W McInnes) *dwlt: led after 1f: rdn and hung rt over 1f out: hld on wl fnl f* **11/2**^{3}

0003 **2** hd **Bolton Hall (IRE)**^{9} [4186] 4-9-3 **59** .... PaulHanagan 6 — 66
(R A Fahey) *keen early: chsd ldrs: effrt over 2f out: ev ch fnl f: kpt on: jst hld* **5/4**^{1}

3301 **3** 1½ **William John**^{12} [4069] 3-8-7 **57** .... (t) TomEaves 3 — 61
(B Ellison) *led 1f: cl up: effrt 2f out: kpt on same pce ins fnl f* **4/1**^{2}

5320 **4** 2½ **Gifted Flame**^{8} [4194] 7-10-0 **70** .... GrahamGibbons 2 — 69
(J J Quinn) *prom: effrt over 2f out: no ex over 1f out* **10/1**

5114 **5** shd **Awaken**^{23} [3762] 5-9-1 **57** .... PhillipMakin 1 — 56
(Miss Tracy Waggott) *in tch: drvn over 2f out: no imp over 1f out* **11/2**^{3}

5060 **6** 1 **Tedsdale Mac**^{19} [3883] 7-8-10 **59** .... SuzzanneFrance$^{(7)}$ 7 — 56
(N Bycroft) *dwlt: hld up: rdn over 2f out: nvr rchd ldrs* **14/1**

0000 **7** nk **Reaching Out (IRE)**^{18} [3900] 4-9-3 **59** .... RichardThomas 8 — 55
(N P Littmoden) *missed break: hld up: rdn 3f out: nvr a factor* **20/1**

1m 58.48s (0.92) **Going Correction** +0.05s/f (Good)
WFA 3 from 4yo+ 8lb — **7** Ran SP% **115.7**
Speed ratings (Par 103):97,96,95,93,93 92,92
CSF £13.17 CT £30.63 TOTE £8.20: £2.50, £1.60; EX 19.10.
Owner Steve Ryan **Bred** P And Mrs Venner **Trained** Catwick, E Yorks

FOCUS
A muddling gallop in this ordinary event not surprisingly resulted in a modest winning time for the grade. The winner ran to the best of his form of the last twelve months.
Reaching Out(IRE) Official explanation: jockey said gelding missed the break

4455 CARLING FILLIES' H'CAP — 7f 200y

8:00 (8:01) (Class 5) (0-70,70) 3-Y-0+ — **£3,238** (£963; £481; £240) **Stalls** High

Form — RPR

0465 **1** **Coalpark (IRE)**^{13} [4060] 3-9-0 **63** .... (t) KDarley 2 — 71
(M Johnston) *chsd ldr: drvn over 2f out: led 1f out: edgd lft ins fnl f: styd on strly* **7/2**^{2}

24 **2** 1¼ **Westcourt Dream**^{43} [3142] 6-8-9 **51** .... PaulMulrennan 1 — 57
(M W Easterby) *set stdy pce: rdn 2f out: hdd 1f out: kpt on ins fnl f* **11/4**^{1}

4303 **3** 1¼ **Flashing Floozie**^{5} [4279] 3-8-2 **51** oh7 .... RichardThomas 9 — 53
(M F Harris) *in tch: effrt over 2f out: edgd rt over 1f out: kpt on ins fnl f* **12/1**

0020 **4** 1¼ **Hansomelle (IRE)**^{32} [3484] 4-9-0 **56** .... DaleGibson 4 — 56
(B Mactaggart) *chsd ldrs: drvn over 2f out: one pce over 1f out* **9/1**

0424 **5** 3 **Lysandra (IRE)**^{17} [3954] 4-10-0 **70** .... KimTinkler 3 — 63
(N Tinkler) *dwlt: bhd: hdwy and hung rt fr over 2f out: nvr rchd ldrs* **7/2**^{2}

005- **6** 5 **Dream Of Dubai (IRE)**^{229} [6684] 5-8-9 **51** oh11 .... PaulHanagan 7 — 33
(P Mitchell) *hld up: hmpd over 5f out: n.d after* **25/1**

0000 **7** ½ **Ellens Princess (IRE)**^{17} [3947] 4-8-9 **51** oh5 .... TonyHamilton 6 — 32
(J S Wainwright) *in tch: drvn 3f out: sn btn* **33/1**

5023 **8** 12 **Royal Pardon**^{8} [4198] 4-8-9 **51** oh3 .... (v) PaulEddery 5 — 4
(R C Guest) *stmbld s: hld up: rdn over 3f out: sn wknd* **5/1**^{3}

1m 39.58s (-0.51) **Going Correction** +0.05s/f (Good)
WFA 3 from 4yo+ 7lb — **8** Ran SP% **112.3**
Speed ratings (Par 100):104,102,101,100,97 92,91,79
CSF £13.03 CT £100.27 TOTE £3.80: £1.70, £1.10, £2.40; EX 10.80.
Owner Joy And Valentine Feerick **Bred** Rathasker Stud **Trained** Middleham Moor, N Yorks
■ Mark Johnston's 100th winner of the year, and his 13th consecutive century.

FOCUS
Another modest handicap, but a steady gallop meant it again paid to race right up with the pace. The form seems sound.
Royal Pardon Official explanation: jockey said filly stumbled on leaving stalls and suffered interference in running

4456 SUBSCRIBE TO RACING UK ON 087005 50 69 57 H'CAP — 6f 192y

8:30 (8:32) (Class 6) (0-65,65) 3-Y-0+ — **£2,590** (£770; £385; £192) **Stalls** High

Form — RPR

0050 **1** **Hypnotic**^{11} [4101] 4-9-11 **63** .... (t) RobertWinston 14 — 78
(D Nicholls) *in tch: drvn over 2f out: hdwy to ld ins fnl f: sn clr* **9/2**^{3}

00 **2** 3½ **Barry The Brave**^{12} [4068] 4-8-12 **55** .... GregFairley$^{(5)}$ 11 — 61
(Micky Hammond) *chsd str pce: led over 2f out to ins fnl f: no ch w wnr* **66/1**

2002 **3** 2½ **Tiber Tiger (IRE)**^{5} [4288] 6-9-11 **63** .... (b) RichardThomas 4 — 63+
(N P Littmoden) *bhd: hdwy stands rail over 1f out: kpt on wl fnl f: nrst fin* **4/1**^{2}

0060 **4** nk **Big Bradford**^{11} [4119] 5-9-5 **57** .... PaulHanagan 7 — 56
(R A Fahey) *in tch: drvn and outpcd over 2f out: r.o fnl f: no imp* **9/1**

6300 **5** 1 **Iced Diamond (IRE)**^{11} [4116] 7-9-2 **54** .... PaulMulrennan 13 — 50
(W M Brisbourne) *hld up midfield: drvn over 2f out: no imp over 1f out* **16/1**

2061 **6** shd **Roman History (IRE)**^{3} [4350] 3-8-6 **50** 6ex .... (p) SilvestreDeSousa 15 — 44
(Miss Tracy Waggott) *hld up: effrt outside over 2f out: sn no imp* **7/1**

0-20 **7** ½ **Bandos**^{22} [3786] 6-9-1 **53** .... TomEaves 3 — 48
(I Semple) *set str pce: hdd over 2f out: hung rt and wknd over 1f out* **16/1**

4530 **8** *shd* **No Grouse**[11] 4116 6-9-9 **61**............ DavidAllan 6 55
(E J Alston) *bhd: rdn over 3f out: hdwy over 1f out: no imp fnl f* **5/1**
-000 **9** *2 ½* **Luke After Me (IRE)**[74] 2198 6-8-9 **47** oh1 ow1............ PhillipMakin 10 35
(Miss Tracy Waggott) *bhd: rdn 3f out: hung rt and sn btn* **100/1**
5303 **10** *1 ¾* **Primarily**[10] 4133 4-9-3 **55**............(p) KDarley 5 38
(A Berry) *chsd ldrs tl edgd rt and wknd 2f out* **28/1**
0640 **11** *3 ½* **Borodinsky**[10] 4157 5-8-3 **46**............ AndrewElliott(5) 9 20
(R E Barr) *missed break: rdn rr over 3f out: edgd rt: sn btn* **7/2**[1]

1m 26.38s (-0.72) **Going Correction** +0.05s/f (Good)
WFA 3 from 4yo+ 6lb **11** Ran SP% **117.3**
Speed ratings (Par 101):106,102,99,98,97 97,96,96,94,92 88
CSF £270.09 CT £1311.86 TOTE £5.40: £2.20, £11.80, £1.90; EX 201.00 Place 6 £55.65, Place 5 £31.33.
Owner Bill Wallace/Gary Butters **Bred** Cheveley Park Stud Ltd **Trained** Sessay, N Yorks
■ Stewards' Enquiry : Silvestre De Sousa four-day ban: used whip with excessive frequency (Aug 26-29)

FOCUS
An overly strong pace throughout and a decent winning time for the grade, but those held up were still at a disadvantage. Just a modest handicap, but the form seems sound.
Borodinsky Official explanation: jockey said gelding finished distressed
T/Plt: £63.10 to a £1 stake. Pool: £51,491.30. 594.85 winning tickets. T/Qpdt: £11.10 to a £1 stake. Pool: £4,112.70. 274.10 winning tickets RY

4109 NOTTINGHAM (L-H)
Tuesday, August 15

OFFICIAL GOING: Good (good to firm in places)
Wind: Nil Weather: Cloudy with sunny spells

4457 BETFAIR APPRENTICE H'CAP (PART OF THE BETFAIR "APPRENTICE TRAINING RACE" SERIES) 1m 1f 213y
5:45 (5:45) (Class 5) (0-75,75) 4-Y-0+ **£3,238** (£963; £481; £240) **Stalls** Low

Form RPR
3451 **1** **Sforzando**[5] 4301 5-9-3 **68** 6ex............ KristinStubbs 5 75
(Mrs L Stubbs) *hld up in tch: rdn over 1f out: rdr dropped whip wl ins fnl f: styd on to ld post* **11/1**
0432 **2** *hd* **Augustine**[13] 4051 5-9-6 **74**............ PJBenson(3) 4 81
(P W Hiatt) *broke wl: stdd to trck ldrs: ridden over 2f out: chsd ldr over 1f out: led ins fnl f: hdd post* **11/4**[2]
-340 **3** *2 ½* **Rowan Lodge (IRE)**[34] 3404 4-9-10 **75**............ AshleyHamblett 1 77
(M H Tompkins) *hld up: hdwy u.p over 2f out: hung lft over 1f out: styd on: nt rch ldrs* **10/1**
0300 **4** *nk* **Viable**[43] 3141 4-8-6 **62**............ JosephWalsh(5) 3 64
(Mrs P Sly) *led 9f out: clr 3f out: rdn over 1f out: hdd and no ex ins fnl f* **28/1**
3250 **5** *3 ½* **Santando**[32] 3490 6-8-3 **59**............(b) WilliamCarson(5) 2 54
(C E Brittain) *sn pushed along in rr: effrt over 2f out: nvr trbld ldrs* **9/2**
0400 **6** *¾* **Sharp Reply (USA)**[24] 3748 4-9-9 **74**............(v) MichaelJStainton 6 68
(R M Whitaker) *chsd ldrs: rdn over 3f out: wknd over 1f out* **4/1**[3]
5111 **7** *5* **Luis Melendez (USA)**[9] 4176 4-9-10 **75** 6ex............(t) KevinGhunowa 7 59
(Tom Dascombe) *chsd ldrs: rdn 1/2-way: edgd rt over 4f out: sn wknd* **5/2**[1]
0000 **8** *½* **Monkstown Road**[2] 4390 4-8-6 **57**............(p) RussellKennemore 8 40
(C N Kellett) *sn led: hdd 9f out: chsd ldrs tl hung lft 4f out: sn rdn and wknd* **100/1**

2m 9.64s (-0.06) **Going Correction** +0.075s/f (Good) **8** Ran SP% **115.3**
Speed ratings (Par 103):103,102,100,100,97 97,93,92
CSF £41.85 CT £319.44 TOTE £21.30: £4.90, £1.10, £5.80; EX 52.90.
Owner Mrs L Stubbs **Bred** M E Wates **Trained** Norton, N. Yorks
■ Stewards' Enquiry : P J Benson five-day ban: used whip with excessive frequency (Aug 26-30)

FOCUS
A modest apprentice handicap run at a reasonable pace. Weakish form, but a personal best from the winner under her penalty.

4458 EUROPEAN BREEDERS FUND COLWICK PARK NOVICE STKS 1m 54y
6:15 (6:17) (Class 5) 2-Y-0 **£4,533** (£1,348; £674; £336) **Stalls** Centre

Form RPR
1 **1** **Sesmen**[41] 3201 2-8-13............ KerrinMcEvoy 5 89+
(M Botti) *mde all: styd on wl* **5/1**
1 **2** *3 ½* **Five A Side**[26] 3663 2-9-2............ JoeFanning 1 84
(M Johnston) *chsd wnr: rdn and ev ch over 2f out: hung lft over 1f out: wknd ins fnl f* **11/4**[3]
52 **3** *nk* **Eglevski (IRE)**[16] 3976 2-8-12............ TedDurcan 2 79
(J L Dunlop) *chsd ldrs: rdn and hung rt over 2f out: styd on same pce* **5/2**[2]
0 **4** *nk* **Sonar Sound (GER)**[14] 4018 2-8-12............ MickyFenton 4 79?
(T P Tate) *s.i.s: hld up: outpcd 1/2-way: r.o ins fnl f: nt trble ldrs* **16/1**
5 **5** *¾* **Maslak (IRE)**[34] 3417 2-8-12............ RHills 6 77
(E A L Dunlop) *chsd ldrs: rdn over 2f out: styd on same pce* **2/1**[1]

1m 46.12s (-0.28) **Going Correction** +0.075s/f (Good) **5** Ran SP% **111.1**
Speed ratings (Par 94):104,100,100,99,99
CSF £18.99 TOTE £6.90: £2.80, £2.20; EX 12.20.
Owner Scuderia Rencati Srl **Bred** Peter Ebdon Racing **Trained** Newmarket, Suffolk

FOCUS
A decent conditions race run in a smart time for a race like this. The winner impressed and could rate in three figures.

NOTEBOOK
Sesmen ◆, who defied the widest draw of all when making a winning debut over seven furlongs at Kempton, a race that has produced winners, showed improved form to follow up on her first start on turf over this longer trip. She got the run of the race out in front, but was properly tested by Five A Side in the closing stages and there was plenty to like about the way she kept responding to pressure, eventually drawing well clear. This was a fine effort against the colts and she may now be stepped up to Listed or Group company. (op 11-2 tchd 6-1)
Five A Side, who looked to have a tough enough race when overcoming his inexperience to make a winning debut over seven furlongs at Epsom first time up, seemed to have his chance but found the winner far too strong in the closing stages. (op 2-1)
Eglevski(IRE), upped to a mile for the first time, ran a respectable race but would possibly have found an easier opportunity in maiden company. (op 11-4)
Sonar Sound(GER) ◆, well held on his debut over an extended seven furlongs at Beverley, caught the eye staying on very nicely late on and this represented improvement. There should be more to come and he is well worth keeping in mind, especially when there is cut in the ground. (op 25-1 tchd 14-1)
Maslak(IRE) did not confirm the promise he showed on his debut at Newmarket and was a little disappointing. (op 9-4 tchd 5-2)

4459 RACING UK ON SKY 432 H'CAP 1m 6f 15y
6:45 (6:45) (Class 3) (0-90,89) 3-Y-0 **£8,096** (£2,408; £1,203; £601) **Stalls** Low

Form RPR
2-55 **1** **Zurbaran (IRE)**[71] 2290 3-8-7 **75**............ MickyFenton 6 84
(B J Meehan) *led 2f: chsd ldr tl led 4f out: drvn out* **20/1**
100 **2** *½* **Simondiun**[10] 4125 3-9-4 **86**............ PhilipRobinson 7 95
(Mrs A J Perrett) *hld up: hdwy and hung lft fr over 1f out: styd on u.p* **14/1**
-156 **3** *2 ½* **Power Of Future (GER)**[46] 3046 3-8-8 **76**............ TedDurcan 1 81
(H R A Cecil) *chsd ldrs: rdn and swtchd rt 2f out: styd on same pce fnl f* **14/1**
-626 **4** *3* **Los Cabos (IRE)**[19] 3877 3-8-11 **79** ow1............ JamieSpencer 5 81+
(J H M Gosden) *hld up: hdwy and hung lft fr over 2f out: hmpd 2f out: wknd fnl f* **11/2**[3]
5126 **5** *½* **Enjoy The Moment**[13] 4039 3-9-7 **89**............ KerrinMcEvoy 4 89
(J A Osborne) *chsd ldrs: rdn over 3f out: carried rt 2f out: wknd fnl f* **5/4**[1]
5210 **6** *3 ½* **Doctor Scott**[14] 4027 3-9-5 **87**............ JoeFanning 3 82
(M Johnston) *w ldr tl led after 2f: hdd 4f out: sn rdn: wknd over 1f out* **3/1**[2]
4002 **7** *2* **Twill (IRE)**[19] 3877 3-8-11 **79**............ SteveDrowne 8 71
(H Morrison) *chsd ldrs: rdn whn hmpd over 2f out: sn lost pl* **7/1**

3m 8.52s (1.42) **Going Correction** +0.075s/f (Good) **7** Ran SP% **115.4**
Speed ratings (Par 104):98,97,96,94,94 92,91
CSF £254.05 CT £4002.04 TOTE £28.10: £10.00, £5.60; EX 131.90.
Owner Mrs C C Regalado-Gonzalez **Bred** Mount Coote Stud **Trained** Manton, Wilts
■ Stewards' Enquiry : Ted Durcan three-day ban: careless riding (Aug 26-28)

FOCUS
This looked a decent staying handicap beforehand, but some of the principals disappointed and the bare form looks just ordinary for the grade. An improved effort from the winner, with the third running to form.

NOTEBOOK
Zurbaran(IRE) had shown ability in both maiden and handicap company without suggesting he was about to win but, upped fully four furlongs in trip, he showed improved form. He could progress over staying trips. (op 16-1)
Simondiun benefited from the step up in trip and was clear of the remainder in second. He looks high enough in the weights, but will have more options now he has proven his stamina. (op 8-1)
Power Of Future(GER) had to force her way into the clear and could find only the one pace thereafter. (op 10-1 tchd 16-1)
Los Cabos(IRE), unproven over this trip, completely blew his chance by continually hanging to his left in the straight and was almost asking to be hampered. (op 13-2)
Enjoy The Moment, unlucky in-running in a decent handicap at Goodwood on his previous start, was below form this time and may want better ground. (op 11-8 tchd 6-4, 13-8 in places)
Doctor Scott is another who may want better ground. (op 4-1)

4460 TRENT NURSERY 6f 15y
7:15 (7:15) (Class 5) 2-Y-0 **£3,238** (£963; £481; £240) **Stalls** High

Form RPR
1005 **1** **Everymanforhimself (IRE)**[10] 4146 2-9-12 **92**............ PhilipRobinson 1 92
(J G Given) *chsd ldrs: rdn to ld ins fnl f: r.o* **9/2**[3]
321 **2** *½* **Palo Verde**[10] 4151 2-9-6 **86**............ JoeFanning 7 84
(M Johnston) *led: rdn and hdd ins fnl f: kpt on* **9/4**[1]
0430 **3** *shd* **Star Strider**[11] 4100 2-8-2 **68**............ FrancisNorton 9 66
(A M Balding) *plld hrd and prom: outpcd 2f out: r.o ins fnl f* **11/2**
2105 **4** *1 ¾* **Naayla (IRE)**[10] 4152 2-9-2 **82**............ JamieSpencer 4 75
(B J Meehan) *chsd ldrs: rdn and edgd rt over 1f out: no ex ins fnl f* **4/1**[2]
4404 **5** *½* **Indian Song (IRE)**[17] 3930 2-7-12 **64** oh1............ HayleyTurner 2 55
(R F Johnson Houghton) *hld up: plld hrd: rdn over 1f out: nt trble ldrs* **16/1**
0056 **6** *1 ½* **Hephaestus**[9] 4178 2-8-3 **72**............ EdwardCreighton(3) 3 59
(M R Channon) *slwly into stride: hld up: rdn over 1f out: n.d* **25/1**
4004 **7** *5* **Fort Worth (IRE)**[10] 4161 2-8-8 **74** ow5............ EddieAhern 8 46
(B Gubby) *w ldr 4f: wknd over 1f out* **11/2**

1m 15.06s (0.06) **Going Correction** -0.20s/f (Firm) **7** Ran SP% **109.4**
Speed ratings (Par 94):91,90,90,87,87 85,78
CSF £13.72 CT £49.97 TOTE £5.50: £2.80, £1.80; EX 10.90.
Owner Cavan Pickering & Stewart Whitehead **Bred** Denis McDonnell **Trained** Willoughton, Lincs

FOCUS
A decent little nursery, but the pace was not great and it suited those that raced handily. Despite the stalls being against the stands' rail, the field took a route more towards the centre of the track. The form looks solid.

NOTEBOOK
Everymanforhimself(IRE) was ridden much closer to the pace than at Newmarket and that did the trick. He did this nicely under a big weight for a two-year-old and, though he has twice been held at a much higher level, does look capable of winning another nursery at least. (op 5-1)
Palo Verde tried to dictate from the front, but although he managed to keep the majority of his rivals at bay he was unable to hold the winner's late effort. He still has to convince that he truly stays this far. (op 11-4)
Star Strider could have been renamed Star Gazer given the way he pulled in the first couple of furlongs, but when he did eventually settle he put in some decent late work. He looks worth another try over seven, but will need to settle better. (tchd 5-1)
Naayla(IRE) had every chance but failed to pick up to any great degree. She would probably have preferred a stronger gallop, but looks fairly exposed now. (op 11-4)
Indian Song(IRE), trying this trip for the first time on her nursery debut, pulled hard at the back in a moderately-run race which was not ideal, and she failed to get competitive. (op 14-1)
Hephaestus was another to fail to get competitive from off the pace in a moderately-run race. He does not seem to be progressing.
Fort Worth(IRE), carrying 5lb overweight, showed up for a while before fading. (op 7-1 tchd 15-2)

4461 LADY BAY BRIDGE CONDITIONS STKS 5f 13y
7:45 (7:46) (Class 4) 3-Y-0+
£6,232 (£1,866; £933; £467; £233; £117) **Stalls** High

Form RPR
1460 **1** **Peace Offering (IRE)**[10] 4128 6-8-4 **100**............ VictoriaBehan(7) 9 108
(D Nicholls) *mde all: racd keenly: pushed out* **11/2**[3]
010- **2** *1 ¾* **Fictional**[332] 5288 5-8-11 **94**............ RichardMullen 10 102+
(E J O'Neill) *a.p: chsd wnr over 1f out: sn rdn and ev ch: no ex towards fin* **14/1**
0004 **3** *1* **Fyodor (IRE)**[16] 3972 5-8-11 **100**............ JamieSpencer 7 98+
(W J Haggas) *trckd ldrs: rdn and swtchd rt over 1f out: styng on same pce whn slipped nr fin* **6/1**
5610 **4** *2* **Green Manalishi**[12] 4080 5-8-11 **104**............ KerrinMcEvoy 6 91
(D W P Arbuthnot) *chsd ldr: rdn over 1f out: wknd ins fnl f* **3/1**[1]
0300 **5** *nk* **Connect**[10] 4128 9-8-11 **90**............(b) TPQueally 4 90+
(M H Tompkins) *outpcd: styd on ins fnl f: nt rch ldrs* **25/1**

-025 **6** *hd* **Dixie Belle**[37] 3332 3-8-0 93 ....(t) DominicFox(3) 8 84
(M G Quinlan) *s.i.s: hld up: rdn over 1f out: nvr trbld ldrs* **22/1**

3356 **7** *5* **Bahamian Pirate (USA)**[10] 4128 11-8-11 99 .... JoeFanning 1 71
(D Nicholls) *outpcd* **11/2**[3]

5-00 **8** *1 ½* **Maltese Falcon**[12] 4080 6-9-0 106 ....(t) EddieAhern 3 69
(P F I Cole) *chsd ldrs over 3f* **7/2**[2]

0000 **9** *1* **Ajigolo**[12] 4080 3-9-5 98 ....(v) TedDurcan 2 73
(M R Channon) *prom 3f* **20/1**

59.48 secs (-2.32) **Going Correction** -0.20s/f (Firm)
WFA 3 from 5yo+ 3lb **9** Ran SP% **111.9**
Speed ratings (Par 105):110,107,105,102,101 101,93,91,89
CSF £72.19 TOTE £6.60: £2.10, £3.80, £2.50; EX 96.80.
Owner Lady O'Reilly **Bred** Chevington Stud **Trained** Sessay, N Yorks

FOCUS
A fair contest and a very creditable winning time for the grade. Unlike in the previous race the field stayed on the nearside and the first three home started from the four highest stalls. The first two dominated on the rail and it might be best not to take the form at face value.
Maltese Falcon Official explanation: jockey said gelding was unsuited by the good (good to firm in places) ground

4462 NOTTINGHAMRACECOURSE.CO.UK H'CAP 5f 13y
8:15 (8:15) (Class 5) (0-70,67) 3-Y-0+ **£3,238** (£963; £481; £240) **Stalls** High

Form RPR

5000 **1** **Whistler**[9] 4180 9-9-2 57 ....(b) PaulFitzsimons 4 68
(Miss J R Tooth) *a.p: rdn to ld ins fnl f: r.o* **28/1**

0200 **2** *¾* **Desert Opal**[20] 3846 6-9-5 60 .... PhilipRobinson 10 68
(C R Dore) *mid-div: hdwy over 1f out: r.o* **5/1**[3]

3365 **3** *shd* **Harrison's Flyer (IRE)**[8] 4208 5-9-12 67 ....(p) FrancisNorton 2 75
(J M Bradley) *hld up: hdwy over 1f out: r.o* **8/1**

3010 **4** *½* **Sir Loin**[7] 4232 5-8-12 53 ....(v) EddieAhern 3 59
(N Tinkler) *led: rdn: edgd rt and hdd ins fnl f: no ex* **9/1**

4142 **5** *½* **King Egbert (FR)**[8] 4208 5-8-12 53 .... JamieSpencer 1 57
(A W Carroll) *swtchd rt sn after s: hld up: swtchd rt and hdwy over 1f out: nt rch ldrs* **10/3**[2]

0000 **6** *1* **Sweetest Revenge (IRE)**[36] 3368 5-9-1 56 .... HayleyTurner 8 57
(M D I Usher) *sn outpcd: r.o ins fnl f: nrst fin* **15/2**

0000 **7** *nk* **Meikle Barfil**[11] 4110 4-9-4 59 ....(p) TedDurcan 7 59
(J M Bradley) *hmpd sn after s: hld up: r.o ins fnl f: nvr nrr* **16/1**

5035 **8** *¾* **Betsen (IRE)**[14] 4019 4-9-10 65 .... JoeFanning 9 62
(D Nicholls) *w ldr over 3f: wknd ins fnl f* **3/1**[1]

0-00 **9** *shd* **Spinetail Rufous (IRE)**[13] 4054 8-8-7 48 oh8 .... TPQueally 6 44
(Miss Z C Davison) *s.i.s: sn chsng ldrs: wknd fnl f* **66/1**

0000 **10** *7* **New Options**[36] 3356 9-8-7 48 oh8 ....(b) RobbieFitzpatrick 11 19
(Peter Grayson) *chsd ldrs 3f* **28/1**

0405 **11** *hd* **Master Malarkey**[21] 3821 3-8-1 48 oh3 ....(b) DominicFox(3) 5 19
(Mrs C A Dunnett) *s.i.s: sn w ldrs: rdn and wknd over 1f out* **40/1**

60.98 secs (-0.82) **Going Correction** -0.20s/f (Firm)
WFA 3 from 4yo+ 3lb **11** Ran SP% **114.3**
Speed ratings (Par 103):98,96,96,95,95 93,92,91,91,80 80
CSF £155.70 CT £1261.11 TOTE £15.70: £3.40, £2.50, £3.60; EX 101.00 Place 6 £5,064.33, Place 5 £1,815.25.
Owner Warwick Racing Partnership **Bred** Raymond Clive Tooth **Trained** Lowsonford, Warwickshire

FOCUS
A modest winning time, 1.5 seconds slower than the preceding conditions event. The runners reverted to taking a route more towards the centre of the track, just as they had done in the nursery, despite the advantage that seemed to be held by racing tight against the stands' rail in the previous race. Modest form, but solid.
T/Plt: £2,211.60 to a £1 stake. Pool: £46,354.60. 15.30 winning tickets. T/Qpdt: £588.60 to a £1 stake. Pool: £3,738.50. 4.70 winning tickets. CR

4415 DEAUVILLE (R-H)
Tuesday, August 15

OFFICIAL GOING: Turf course - soft; all-weather - standard

4464a GRAND PRIX BECHCOMBER HOTEL (PRIX DE LA VALLEE D'AUGE) (LISTED RACE) 5f
3:05 (3:05) 2-Y-0 **£17,241** (£6,897; £5,172; £3,448; £1,724)

RPR

1 **Numerieus (FR)**[32] 3514 2-8-8 .... OPeslier 9 97
(Y De Nicolay, France)

2 *¾* **Maka (FR)**[19] 2-8-8 .... JVictoire 5 94
(F Cohen, France)

3 *2* **Jailamigraine (IRE)**[64] 2-8-8 .... C-PLemaire 3 87
(P Bary, France)

4 *1* **Palin**[44] 3132 2-8-11 .... FBranca 2 87
(F Folco, Italy)

5 *½* **Mr Klick (IRE)**[4] 4321 2-8-11 .... JimmyFortune 4 85
(N Wilson) *pressed leader til hard driven and one pace final 1 1/2f*

6 *¾* **Candelabro (USA)**[24] 2-8-11 .... IMendizabal 7 82
(J-C Rouget, France)

7 *1 ½* **Finikas**[31] 2-8-11 .... MBlancpain 10 77
(C Laffon-Parias, France)

8 *¾* **Parched (IRE)** 2-8-8 .... JAuge 6 71
(Robert Collet, France)

9 *1* **Hitra (USA)**[16] 2-8-8 .... DBoeuf 8 67
(Mme C Head-Maarek, France)

60.10 secs **9** Ran
PARI-MUTUEL: WIN 7.50; PL 2.70, 5.70, 2.90; DF 99.50.
Owner J P J Dubois **Bred** Jean-Pierre Dubois **Trained** France

NOTEBOOK
Mr Klick(IRE), smartly into his stride, was settled in second place behind the favourite and was going very easily early on. He was one of the leaders a furlong and a half out and then gradually dropped out of contention. His trainer felt that a longer trip and better ground would be an advantage in the future.

4465a GRAND PRIX BEACHCOMBER HOTELS LE PARADIS (LISTED RACE) 1m 7f
3:35 (3:34) 3-Y-0 **£17,241** (£6,897; £5,172; £3,448; £1,724)

RPR

1 **Getaway (GER)**[48] 3-8-11 .... OPeslier 5 99
(A Fabre, France)

2 *nk* **Grey Mystique (IRE)**[16] 3-8-8 .... IMendizabal 4 95
(J-C Rouget, France)

3 *2* **Shazand (FR)**[34] 3-8-11 .... CSoumillon 2 96
(A De Royer-Dupre, France)

4 *¾* **Varevees**[123] 3-8-8 .... TJarnet 6 93
(J Boisnard, France)

5 *½* **Ermine Sea**[40] 3225 3-8-11 .... JimmyFortune 3 95
(J H M Gosden) *led to 2f out, one pace*

6 *5* **Elvard (FR)**[22] 3-8-11 .... DBoeuf 1 90
(D Smaga, France)

7 *½* **Herboriste**[23] 3-8-8 .... C-PLemaire 7 87
(P Bary, France)

3m 19.1s **7** Ran
PARI-MUTUEL: WIN 3.40; PL 1.80, 2.90; SF 23.30.
Owner Baron G Von Ullmann **Bred** Baron G Von Ullmann **Trained** Chantilly, France

NOTEBOOK
Ermine Sea made a brave effort to lead from pillar to post. Still in front at the entrance to the straight, he could not quicken as well as his rivals, and his rider felt that the colt did not appreciate the soft ground.

4016 BEVERLEY (R-H)
Wednesday, August 16

OFFICIAL GOING: Good
After rain three days earlier the ground was reckoned to be'good but loose on top'.
Wind: Light, half against Weather: Mostly fine

4466 EBF HULL DAILY MAIL MAIDEN STKS 7f 100y
2:10 (2:12) (Class 4) 2-Y-0 **£5,829** (£1,734; £866; £432) **Stalls** High

Form RPR

46 **1** **Mesbaah (IRE)**[19] 3892 2-9-3 ....(p) MartinDwyer 6 92
(M A Jarvis) *mde all: clr over 1f out: drvn out* **9/4**[2]

4 **2** *6* **Emerald Wilderness (IRE)**[53] 2867 2-9-3 .... RobertWinston 3 78
(M R Channon) *chsd ldrs: drvn over 4f out: wnt 2nd over 3f out: no imp* **2/1**[1]

3 **3** *8* **Pennyrock (IRE)**[39] 3280 2-9-3 .... DO'Donohoe 8 59
(K A Ryan) *wnt rt s: chsd ldrs: one pce fnl 2f* **13/2**

4 *3 ½* **Inasus (GER)** 2-9-3 .... JoeFanning 4 51
(M Johnston) *in tch: effrt and chse ldrs over 3f out: hung rt and wknd over 1f out* **9/2**[3]

4 **5** *2* **Firestorm (IRE)**[24] 3758 2-9-3 .... LeeEnstone 9 46
(C W Fairhurst) *sltly hmpd s: in rr: kpt on fnl 2f: nvr on terms* **20/1**

54 **6** *hd* **Arabellas Homer**[15] 4018 2-8-12 .... TonyHamilton 5 41
(Miss J A Camacho) *s.i.s: t.k.h: n.m.r and lost pl over 5f out: kpt on fnl 2f* **20/1**

005 **7** *2* **Go Red**[15] 4018 2-9-3 .... PaulMulrennan 7 41
(M W Easterby) *t.k.h: trckd ldrs: lost pl over 4f out* **25/1**

4 **8** *shd* **Admiral Savannah (IRE)**[28] 3633 2-9-3 .... PaulQuinn 2 41
(T D Easterby) *dwlt: a in rr* **80/1**

04 **9** *½* **Bollin Freddie**[42] 3187 2-9-3 .... DavidAllan 10 40
(T D Easterby) *chsd wnr over 4f: lost pl over 2f out* **40/1**

1m 33.59s (-0.72) **Going Correction** +0.025s/f (Good) **9** Ran SP% **112.7**
Speed ratings (Par 96):105,98,89,85,82 82,80,80,79
CSF £6.42 TOTE £3.40: £1.70, £1.20, £1.70; EX 9.80.
Owner Hamdan Al Maktoum **Bred** Shadwell Estate Company Limited **Trained** Newmarket, Suffolk

FOCUS
A very decent winning time for a race like this. No strength in depth and in the end very much a one-horse race, but the form looks solid.

NOTEBOOK
Mesbaah(IRE), fitted with cheekpieces, was a shade above himself and needed two handlers in the paddock. Dominating throughout, in the end he quickened right away. He certainly has the ability. (op 3-1)
Emerald Wilderness(IRE), driven along some way out, went in pursuit of the winner but was never going to get anywhere near him. (op 9-4)
Pennyrock(IRE), who is not that big, failed to improve on his debut effort.
Inasus(GER), who stands over plenty of ground, is narrow and was inclined to misbehave in the paddock. He showed a glimmer of ability on his debut but looks some way short of the finished article just yet. (op 10-3)
Firestorm(IRE), a moderate walker, was never in the contest. (tchd 16-1)
Arabellas Homer, keen to get on with it, was knocked back leaving the back stretch. At least this opens up the nursery route for her. (tchd 22-1)

4467 JOURNAL CLAIMING STKS 1m 100y
2:40 (2:41) (Class 5) 3-Y-0+ **£3,562** (£1,059; £529; £264) **Stalls** High

Form RPR

3513 **1** **Apache Point (IRE)**[4] 4381 9-9-8 59 .... KimTinkler 16 64
(N Tinkler) *hld up towards rr: hdwy on ins over 5f out: led jst ins last: styd on* **9/2**[2]

0000 **2** *½* **Flaxby**[26] 3697 4-9-4 46 ....(b) JamieSpencer 5 59
(J D Bethell) *hld up in mid-div: hdwy over 2f out: styd on ins last: no ex towards fin* **14/1**

5122 **3** *¾* **Sawwaah (IRE)**[13] 4087 9-9-12 69 ....(p) AdrianTNicholls 10 65
(D Nicholls) *hld up towards rr: hdwy on outside over 2f out: styd on ins last* **4/1**[1]

/004 **4** *2* **Atlantic Story (USA)**[13] 4087 4-9-12 67 ....(t) DaleGibson 3 61
(M W Easterby) *trckd ldr: led over 1f out: hdd jst ins last: sn fdd* **25/1**

0462 **5** *½* **Keisha Kayleigh (IRE)**[7] 4263 3-9-1 58 ....(v[1]) RobertWinston 14 55
(B Ellison) *in tch: effrt and nt clr run 2f out: styd on appr fnl f* **9/2**[2]

6034 **6** *hd* **Rudaki**[4] 4381 4-9-3 49 .... JasonEdmunds(3) 8 54
(M E Sowersby) *chsd ldrs: one pce fnl 2f* **20/1**

1105 **7** *nk* **Inside Story (IRE)**[15] 4020 4-9-8 64 ....(b) SebSanders 9 55
(M W Easterby) *hld up in rr: hdwy and nt clr run 2f out: kpt on appr fnl f* **5/1**[3]

20-5 **8** *½* **Lottie**[25] 3749 5-8-10 36 .... MickyFenton 6 42
(G Woodward) *chsd ldrs: one pce fnl 2f* **25/1**

0050 **9** *2* **Filey Buoy**[4] 4381 4-9-4 38 .... DanielTudhope 1 46
(R M Whitaker) *trckd ldrs: effrt over 2f out: wknd over 1f out* **66/1**

-100 **10** *1 ½* **Mobane Flyer**[55] 2790 6-9-0 58 .... TonyHamilton 11 39
(R A Fahey) *in tch: effrt over 2f out: wknd appr fnl f* **15/2**

3660 **11** *hd* **Prince Of Gold**[107] 1353 6-9-3 46 .... RussellKennemore(7) 7 48
(R Hollinshead) *s.s: nvr on terms* **25/1**

0050 **12** *2* **Eddies Jewel**[22] 3815 6-8-9 35 .... PatrickMathers(3) 4 32
(I W McInnes) *led tl hdd over 1f out: sn wknd* **66/1**

000- **13** 1 1/2 **Alpine Hideaway (IRE)**[272] [5246] 13-8-12 45................(p) DavidAllan 2 29
(J S Wainwright) *chsd ldrs: lost pl 2f out* **50/1**
6000 **14** 1 1/4 **Ronnies Lad**[24] [3762] 4-9-2 38................................(v) PaulMulrennan 15 30
(J R Norton) *t.k.h: trckd ldrs: lost pl 2f out* **66/1**
-000 **15** *hd* **Paris Heights**[79] [2077] 4-8-13 49.......................(p) MichaelJStainton(5) 13 32
(R M Whitaker) *a in rr* **25/1**
3000 **16** 9 **Headland (USA)**[2] [4425] 8-8-10 39.................................(be) PaulQuinn 12 5
(D W Chapman) *dwlt: a in rr: bhd fnl 2f* **50/1**

1m 47.89s (0.49) **Going Correction** +0.025s/f (Good)
WFA 3 from 4yo+ 6lb **16** Ran SP% **120.0**
Speed ratings (Par 103):98,97,96,94,94 94,93,93,91,89 89,87,86,84,84 75
CSF £57.70 TOTE £7.50: £2.00, £3.70, £1.90; EX 101.40.
Owner Bull Boys Syndicate I **Bred** Newgate Stud Co **Trained** Langton, N Yorks
FOCUS
An ordinary claimer but reasonably sound, rated through the runner-up to form.
Ronnies Lad Official explanation: jockey said gelding had spread a front plate

4468 CORPORATE SPORT YOU WEAR IT WELL H'CAP 5f
3:10 (3:10) (Class 4) (0-85,85) 3-Y-0+ **£7,772** (£2,312; £1,155; £577) **Stalls** High

Form RPR
2450 **1** **Pawan (IRE)**[18] [3937] 6-8-5 72.........................(b) AnnStokell(7) 6 83+
(Miss A Stokell) *in rr: hdwy in centre over 1f out: styd on wl to ld post* **33/1**
410 **2** *shd* **Steel Blue**[18] [3956] 6-9-0 79.................................. MichaelJStainton(5) 15 90
(R M Whitaker) *led 1f: chsd ldrs: led over 1f out: hdd last stride* **9/2**[1]
1100 **3** 1 **Balakiref**[17] [3986] 7-9-2 76... JamieSpencer 13 83+
(M Dods) *s.i.s: gd hdwy on inner and nt clr run 1f out: styd on last 100yds* **8/1**
2031 **4** 1 **Henry Hall (IRE)**[12] [4110] 10-8-12 72.............................. KimTinkler 11 75
(N Tinkler) *bmpd s: in tch: effrt on inner over 1f out: kpt on same pce* **10/1**
2606 **5** *hd* **Handsome Cross (IRE)**[12] [4101] 5-9-11 85 SilvestreDeSousa 10 88
(D Nicholls) *in tch on outer: styd on same pce fnl f* **5/1**[2]
1420 **6** *hd* **Caribbean Coral**[12] [4101] 7-9-11 85...................(p) GrahamGibbons 14 87
(J J Quinn) *bhd: hdwy 2f out: kpt on: nt rch ldrs* **11/2**[3]
4306 **7** 1 **Bo McGinty (IRE)**[4] [4360] 5-9-3 84.......................(b) JamesReveley(7) 9 82
(R A Fahey) *chsd ldrs: kpt on same pce appr fnl f* **9/2**[1]
2325 **8** *hd* **Kings College Boy**[1] [4453] 6-9-1 75...........................(b) TonyHamilton 2 73+
(R A Fahey) *in tch on outer: carried wd to stands' side over 2f out: kpt on fnl f* **14/1**
3524 **9** 3/4 **Conjecture**[10] [4180] 4-8-13 73.................................. RobertWinston 1 68+
(R Bastiman) *in tch on outer: c stands' side over 2f out: kpt on same pce appr fnl f* **16/1**
4003 **10** 1 3/4 **Cashel Mead**[10] [4180] 6-9-6 80.................................. AdrianTNicholls 8 69
(J L Spearing) *mid-div on outer: nvr nr ldrs* **18/1**
1003 **11** 1 3/4 **Bonne De Fleur**[11] [4135] 5-9-0 74..............................(b) JoeFanning 3 61+
(B Smart) *chsd ldrs on outer: lost pl over 1f out* **40/1**
0410 **12** 3 **Maktavish**[116] [1150] 7-9-3 80...(b) DNolan(3) 4 52
(R Brotherton) *led after 1f: hdd & wknd over 1f out* **66/1**
1016 **13** 1/2 **Mormeatmic**[31] [3568] 3-9-2 78.................................. PaulMulrennan 12 48
(M W Easterby) *wnt lft s: chsd ldrs: lost pl over 1f out* **22/1**
530 **14** 3/4 **Bowness**[27] [3687] 4-9-11 85.. SebSanders 7 52
(J G Given) *a towards rr* **16/1**
3004 **15** *hd* **Mimi Mouse**[20] [3880] 4-9-6 80.. DavidAllan 5 46
(T D Easterby) *mid-div on outer: lost pl over 2f out* **20/1**

63.31 secs (-0.69) **Going Correction** +0.025s/f (Good)
WFA 3 from 4yo+ 2lb **15** Ran SP% **128.3**
Speed ratings (Par 105):106,105,104,102,102 102,100,100,98,96 93,88,87,86,86
CSF £179.53 CT £1393.30 TOTE £38.30: £7.30, £2.90, £3.10; EX 353.40.
Owner Ms Caron Stokell **Bred** Hadi Al Tajir **Trained** Brompton-on-Swale, N Yorks
FOCUS
A fair handicap but could have been stronger and rated around the fourth.
Caribbean Coral Official explanation: jockey said gelding missed the break

4469 CHARLES ELSEY MEMORIAL H'CAP 2m 35y
3:40 (3:41) (Class 4) (0-85,84) 3-Y-0+ **£5,505** (£1,637; £818; £408) **Stalls** High

Form RPR
4144 **1** **Som Tala**[20] [3877] 3-8-8 78.. RobertWinston 1 90
(M R Channon) *chsd ldrs: styd on fnl 2f: led towards fin* **11/2**[3]
1111 **2** 3/4 **Key Time (IRE)**[14] [4036] 4-10-0 84.................................. SebSanders 6 95
(Sir Mark Prescott) *led after 1f: rdn 3f out: hdd and no ex wl ins last* **8/11**[1]
6-23 **3** 6 **Gandalf**[46] [3098] 4-9-8 78... JamieSpencer 4 82
(J R Fanshawe) *hld up: hdwy to chse ldrs 7f out: effrt and wnt lft over 2f out: hung rt over 1f out: one pce* **4/1**[2]
213 **4** 1/2 **Riodan (IRE)**[11] [4156] 4-9-0 73.. DNolan(3) 2 76
(J J Quinn) *chsd ldrs: drvn along 7f out: outpcd fnl 2f* **9/1**
0304 **5** 4 **Double Obsession**[35] [3396] 6-9-5 75.........................(v) AdrianTNicholls 5 74
(D Nicholls) *led 1f: chsd ldrs: drvn over 6f out: one pce* **16/1**
0-00 **6** 10 **Vicious Prince (IRE)**[138] [816] 7-9-0 70............................ DeanMcKeown 7 57
(R M Whitaker) *s.i.s: hld up detached in last: pushed along 6f out: nvr on terms* **33/1**
43 **7** 8 **Dzesmin (POL)**[17] [3981] 4-9-10 80..................................(p) JoeFanning 3 57
(R C Guest) *t.k.h: trckd ldrs: lost pl over 2f out: eased ins last* **20/1**

3m 37.26s (-2.24) **Going Correction** +0.025s/f (Good)
WFA 3 from 4yo+ 14lb **7** Ran SP% **116.9**
Speed ratings (Par 105):106,105,102,102,100 95,91
CSF £10.31 TOTE £6.90: £2.60, £1.30; EX 14.70.
Owner Sheikh Ahmed Al Maktoum **Bred** Usk Valley Stud **Trained** West Ilsley, Berks
FOCUS
An end-to-end gallop in this fair staying handicap, and more solid than similar contests.
Dzesmin(POL) Official explanation: jockey said colt had no more to give

4470 EAST RIDING MAIL H'CAP 1m 1f 207y
4:10 (4:14) (Class 5) (0-70,70) 3-Y-0 **£4,210** (£1,252; £625; £312) **Stalls** High

Form RPR
5020 **1** **Sanctity**[35] [3410] 3-8-10 59 ow1.. JamieSpencer 11 66+
(J R Fanshawe) *chsd ldrs: rdn and outpcd 3f out: sn swtchd wd: styd on wl appr fnl f: led nr fin* **8/1**[3]
0531 **2** *nk* **Summer Lodge**[7] [4254] 3-9-5 68.......................................(b) JoeFanning 9 74
(M H Tompkins) *chsd ldrs: led 1f out: hdd and no ex towards fin* **7/1**[2]
03 **3** 1 **Malakiya (IRE)**[37] [3347] 3-9-5 68.. KerrinMcEvoy 1 72
(G A Butler) *hld up in rr: effrt on outside over 2f out: hung rt: gd hdwy over 1f out: fin strly* **13/2**[1]
6034 **4** *nk* **Westering Home (IRE)**[12] [4118] 3-9-0 63.......................... MickyFenton 5 67
(J Mackie) *chsd ldrs: kpt on same pce appr fnl f* **16/1**
6214 **5** 1 1/4 **Cantabilly (IRE)**[17] [3974] 3-9-7 70.................................... RobertWinston 2 71
(M R Channon) *mid-div: hdwy on outer 4f out: one pce fnl 2f* **8/1**[3]
3035 **6** 3 1/2 **Can Can Star**[11] [4154] 3-9-3 66.. SebSanders 14 61+
(J G Given) *led 2f: led over 2f out: hdd 1f out: sn wknd* **17/2**
P204 **7** 1 1/4 **Dimelight**[20] [3865] 3-9-4 67.. MartinDwyer 7 59
(D R C Elsworth) *hld up in rr: hdwy on outer over 2f out: nvr nr ldrs* **17/2**
002- **8** 1 1/2 **Royle Dancer**[264] [6423] 3-8-13 62.................................... GrahamGibbons 10 51
(R Hollinshead) *hld up in rr: hdwy 4f out: nvr nr ldrs* **50/1**
050 **9** 1 **Golden Groom**[19] [3909] 3-8-2 51 oh6...................................... PaulQuinn 6 38
(C W Fairhurst) *in rr: detached 3f out: sme late hdwy* **66/1**
3102 **10** *nk* **Three Strings (USA)**[23] [3790] 3-8-8 57..........................(p) PatCosgrave 4 44
(P D Niven) *a in rr* **14/1**
040 **11** 2 1/2 **Beautiful Summer (IRE)**[19] [3909] 3-8-11 60.............. TonyHamilton 13 42
(R A Fahey) *mid-div: pushed along 6f out: sn lost pl* **20/1**
5401 **12** *shd* **Peak Seasons (IRE)**[22] [3824] 3-8-1 57.................(b) JamieHamblett(7) 12 39
(M C Chapman) *t.k.h: trckd ldrs: led after 2f: hdd over 2f out: sn wknd and bhd* **16/1**
0-00 **13** 3 **Grandad Bill (IRE)**[61] [2622] 3-9-3 66.................................. DavidAllan 15 42
(T D Easterby) *chsd ldrs: lost pl over 1f out* **11/1**

2m 6.95s (-0.35) **Going Correction** +0.025s/f (Good) **13** Ran SP% **104.1**
Speed ratings (Par 100):102,101,100,100,99 96,95,94,93,93 91,91,89
CSF £46.51 CT £244.39 TOTE £6.80: £2.50, £2.10, £2.50.
Owner Cheveley Park Stud **Bred** Cheveley Park Stud **Trained** Newmarket, Suffolk
■ Mister Fizzbomb (15/2) and Carlton Scroop (12/1) were withdrawn after refusing to enter the stalls. R4, deduct 15p in the £.
FOCUS
A modest handicap in which the leader went off very fast and soon had them strung out. The form looks sound enough rated around the fourth and fifth.

4471 MAIL PUBLICATIONS MAIDEN STKS 1m 1f 207y
4:40 (4:42) (Class 5) 3-Y-0+ **£3,886** (£1,156; £433; £433) **Stalls** High

Form RPR
2 **1** **Hunters' Glen (USA)**[12] [4117] 3-9-3 ....(t) KerrinMcEvoy 3 88+
(Saeed Bin Suroor) *led: qcknd over 6f out: clr over 1f out: v easily* **1/2**[1]
5 **2** 11 **Darenjan (IRE)**[78] [2118] 3-9-3 .... RobertWinston 4 67
(Sir Michael Stoute) *chsd wnr: outpcd over 2f out: stuck on to take modest 2nd 1f out* **11/4**[2]
3 1/2 **Brocatello (IRE)** 3-9-3 ....(b[1]) JoeFanning 7 66
(M Johnston) *dwlt: rn in snatched: sn in tch: hung rt over 1f out: kpt on ins last* **14/1**[3]
60 **3** *dht* **Aphorism**[18] [3946] 3-8-12 .... JamieSpencer 1 61
(J R Fanshawe) *hld up: hdwy to chse ldrs over 5f out: one pce fnl 2f* **16/1**
0 **5** *shd* **Arabian Tiger**[23] [3794] 3-9-3 .... MartinDwyer 2 66
(P W Chapple-Hyam) *dwlt: pushed along and sn chsng ldrs: kpt on fnl f* **40/1**
04 **6** 9 **Sweet Lavinia**[37] [3357] 3-8-12 .... SebSanders 5 44
(J D Bethell) *chsd ldrs: lost pl over 4f out: sn bhd* **50/1**
0-00 **7** 2 **Herninski**[6] [4307] 3-8-5 60.. JamieHamblett(7) 6 40
(M C Chapman) *hld up in rr: sme hewady over 3f out: lost pl over 2f out: sn bhd* **80/1**

2m 7.60s (-41.39) **Going Correction** +0.025s/f (Good) **7** Ran SP% **111.5**
Speed ratings (Par 103):99,90,89,89,89 82,80
CSF £1.93 TOTE £1.50: £1.30, £1.40; EX 2.60.
Owner Godolphin **Bred** Darley **Trained** Newmarket, Suffolk
FOCUS
There was a problem with the stalls and the race had to be hand-timed. The winner was in total command throughout and while those behind were no great shakes, he could hardly have won more easily. The runner-up and fourth set the standard.

4472 MAILHOMES.CO.UK H'CAP 1m 4f 16y
5:10 (5:10) (Class 6) (0-65,65) 3-Y-0+ **£3,238** (£963; £481; £240) **Stalls** High

Form RPR
2242 **1** **Parchment (IRE)**[8] [4229] 4-9-0 51.................................(b) RobertWinston 1 61+
(A J Lockwood) *hld up in rr: hdwy over 4f out: styd on wl to ld ins last: drvn out* **4/1**[1]
-644 **2** 1 1/2 **Tetragon (IRE)**[11] [4137] 6-9-7 58.................................... DanielTudhope 2 66
(D Carroll) *chsd ldrs: styd on to ld 1f out: sn hdd and no ex* **22/1**
0061 **3** 1 1/4 **Dance A Daydream**[48] [3016] 3-8-12 59.............................. JamieSpencer 5 65
(J R Fanshawe) *hld up in rr: hdwy over 4f out: chsng ldrs whn n.m.r 1f out: kpt on same pce* **5/1**[2]
0330 **4** 1 3/4 **Leslingtaylor (IRE)**[18] [3960] 4-9-13 64.......................... GrahamGibbons 11 67
(J J Quinn) *chsd ldrs: chal over 3f out: hung rt and led over 1f out: sn hdd and nt qckn* **9/1**
5416 **5** 1 3/4 **Acuzio**[24] [3763] 5-9-4 55.. DavidAllan 9 55
(W M Brisbourne) *trckd ldrs: one pce appr fnl f* **8/1**
0042 **6** *shd* **Red River Rebel**[15] [4022] 8-9-0 51.................................. PaulMulrennan 13 51
(J R Norton) *led tl over 1f out: wknd ins last* **5/1**[2]
5015 **7** 1 **Abstract Folly (IRE)**[27] [3674] 4-9-8 59.................................. SebSanders 10 57
(J D Bethell) *in tch: effrt over 3f out: one pce* **7/1**
6103 **8** 2 1/2 **The Pen**[9] [4205] 4-9-8 59.. DeanMcKeown 12 53
(C W Fairhurst) *trckd ldrs: pushed along over 4f out: wknd over 1f out* **6/1**[3]
306- **9** *nk* **Turn Of Phrase (IRE)**[326] [4892] 7-9-5 56......................... PatCosgrave 8 50
(B Ellison) *mid-div: effrt on outer 3f out: wknd over 1f out* **22/1**
0600 **10** 3/4 **Rajam**[17] [3983] 8-9-4 55.. DO'Donohoe 4 48+
(G A Harker) *hld up in rr: kpt on fnl 2f: nvr on terms* **14/1**
-664 **11** 3 **Acknowledgement**[9] [4210] 4-10-0 65................................ AntonyProcter 6 53
(D R C Elsworth) *in tch: effrt on outside over 3f out: lost pl and eased over 1f out* **20/1**
-635 **12** 16 **Fenners (USA)**[15] [4022] 3-8-8 62.................................(t) AdeleRothery(7) 14 24
(G P Kelly) *in tch: lost pl after 2f: swvd lft 3f out: sn bhd* **33/1**

2m 39.92s (-0.29) **Going Correction** +0.025s/f (Good)
WFA 3 from 4yo+ 10lb **12** Ran SP% **124.3**
Speed ratings (Par 101):101,100,99,98,96 96,96,94,94,93 91,81
CSF £102.93 CT £464.66 TOTE £5.10: £1.80, £5.50, £1.90; EX 107.40 Place 6 £9.98, Place 5 £7.70.
Owner A J Lockwood **Bred** Wickfield Farm Partnership **Trained** Brawby, N Yorks
FOCUS
A modest handicap run at a steady pace but the form looks sound enough.
Fenners(USA) Official explanation: jockey said colt had a breathing problem
T/Plt: £19.70 to a £1 stake. Pool: £54,723.65. 2,019.90 winning tickets. T/Qpdt: £11.10 to a £1 stake. Pool: £2,285.00. 151.80 winning tickets. WG

[4132]HAMILTON (R-H)

Wednesday, August 16

OFFICIAL GOING: Good to firm

Wind: Light, half across.

4473 TELETEXT "HANDS AND HEELS" APPRENTICE H'CAP (ROUND 4 OF HAMILTON PARK APPRENTICE RIDER SERIES) 6f 5y

5:45 (5:45) (Class 6) (0-60,54) 3-Y-0+ **£2,914** (£867; £433; £216) **Stalls** Low

Form — RPR

2605 **1** **Rancho Cucamonga (IRE)**[4] 4352 4-9-9 **54**..............(b) NeilBrown(3) 1 — 63
(T D Barron) *hld up in rr: smooth hdwy over 2f out: swtchd rt over 1f out: styd on to ld ent last: pushed clr* **11/8**[1]

0004 **2** *2* **Our Mary (IRE)**[13] 4071 3-9-2 **50**..............................(t) RobbieMills(3) 7 — 53
(Robert Gray) *cl up: led wl over 1f out: sn rdn: hdd ent last and kpt on same pce* **7/1**[3]

0060 **3** *nk* **Straffan (IRE)**[11] 4157 4-8-6 **41**..............................(p) PaulPickard(7) 3 — 43
(J Hetherton) *dwlt: hdwy to trck ldrs over 3f out: rdn wl over 1f out: kpt on same pce* **12/1**

0-05 **4** *3 ½* **Whoopee (USA)**[22] 3826 3-9-1 **49**........................ PJBenson(3) 2 — 41
(M Johnston) *cl up: rdn along wl over 2f out and sn outpcd* **8/1**

0060 **5** *½* **Geordie Dancer (IRE)**[21] 3835 4-8-11 **39**...............(p) KevinGhunowa 4 — 29
(A Berry) *cl up: rdn along wl over 2f out: grad wknd* **25/1**

0002 **6** *1* **Dematraf (IRE)**[56] 2758 4-8-8 **41**..................... JohnCavanagh(5) 6 — 28
(Ms Deborah J Evans) *led: rdn along over 2f out: hdd wl over 1f out and sn wknd* **5/2**[2]

1m 12.15s (-0.95) **Going Correction** -0.15s/f (Firm)
WFA 3 from 4yo+ 3lb — 6 Ran SP% **105.8**
Speed ratings (Par 101):100,97,96,92,91 90
CSF £10.07 CT £60.72 TOTE £2.10: £1.50, £2.30; EX 8.70.
Owner P D Savill **Bred** P D Savill **Trained** Maunby, N Yorks

FOCUS
A weak event limited by the third.
Dematraf(IRE) Official explanation: jockey said filly was unsuited by the track

4474 AZURE EBF NOVICE STKS (A QUALIFIER FOR THE HAMILTON PARK 2-Y-O SERIES FINAL) 1m 65y

6:15 (6:15) (Class 4) 2-Y-O **£5,181** (£1,541; £770; £384) **Stalls** High

Form — RPR

41 **1** **Old Romney**[21] 3851 2-9-5 87... KDarley 2 — 88
(M Johnston) *cl up: led over 3f out: pushed along 2f out: rdn ins last: kpt on* **1/4**[1]

4144 **2** *nk* **Princeton (IRE)**[10] 4178 2-9-2 83............................ PhillipMakin 4 — 84
(M R Channon) *hld up: hdwy 4f out: rdn to chse wnr over 1f out: drvn and kpt on wl fnl f* **9/2**[2]

04 **3** *8* **Chookie Hamilton**[22] 3809 2-8-12........................ TomEaves 5 — 62
(I Semple) *pushed along in rr: hdwy over 2f out: styd on appr last: nvr nr ldng pair* **66/1**

00 **4** *3* **Greek God**[13] 4074 2-8-12.................................. PaulFessey 3 — 55
(W Jarvis) *chsd ldng pair: effrt over 3f out: sn rdn along and wknd fnl 2f* **16/1**[3]

6 **5** *14* **Danni Di Guerra (IRE)**[101] 1499 2-8-7 .... GregFairley(5) 6 — 23
(P C Haslam) *led: rdn along and hdd over 3f out: sn drvn and wknd* **66/1**

1m 45.92s (-3.38) **Going Correction** -0.40s/f (Firm) — 5 Ran SP% **107.0**
Speed ratings (Par 96):100,99,91,88,74
CSF £1.56 TOTE £1.30: £1.10, £1.20; EX 1.50.
Owner Gainsborough Stud **Bred** Gainsborough Stud Management Ltd **Trained** Middleham Moor, N Yorks

FOCUS
Solid form, the front pair finishing well clear of the no-hopers. They went a decent pace.

NOTEBOOK
Old Romney made slightly heavy weather of following up his Sandown win. Always up with the strong pace and leading with three to run, he had to fight off a strong challenge from the runner-up inside the last but found sufficient. Racing a little lazily in front, he should be capable of a bit better and a drop back to seven furlongs would not inconvenience him. (op 1-3 tchd 4-11 in a place)
Princeton(IRE) was entitled to finish close to the favourite on official figures and duly did so but, after throwing down a spirited challenge to his rival - a much bigger individual than himself - he was held near the line. He handled the longer trip well and this was a solid effort. (op 7-2 tchd 5-1 in places)
Chookie Hamilton, upped in trip for this third run, looked set to trail in last at one stage but he stayed on in the final furlong. He should do better in nurseries. (op 33-1)
Greek God ran a bit green when the pressure was on and lost third place inside the last. He can now run in nurseries. (tchd 12-1)
Danni Di Guerra(IRE) had not been seen since his debut over five furlongs here in May. He set a decent pace, but when headed by the eventual winner he dropped right away. (op 40-1 tchd 33-1)

4475 EXTRA CLAIMING STKS 1m 65y

6:45 (6:45) (Class 6) 3-Y-O+ **£2,730** (£806; £403) **Stalls** High

Form — RPR

3242 **1** **Burnley Al (IRE)**[11] 4133 4-8-13 55....................................(b) KDarley 5 — 66
(A Berry) *chsd clr ldr: hdwy 3f out: rdn to chal ent last: drvn and styd on to ld last 75 yds* **8/1**

6000 **2** *1 ¼* **Redwood Rocks (IRE)**[39] 3289 5-8-12 65.................. MarkLawson(5) 3 — 67
(B Smart) *led and sn clr: rdn 2f out: jnd ent last and sn drvn: hdd and no ex last 75 yds* **8/1**

3001 **3** *1 ¼* **Everest (IRE)**[4] 4381 9-9-8 79.. GregFairley(5) 1 — 74
(B Ellison) *hld up in tch: hdwy 4f out: rdn and ch whn hung rt wl over 1f out: sn drvn and one pce* **11/8**[1]

0011 **4** *6* **Tedstale (USA)**[8] 4229 8-9-2 75.............................(b) AndrewMullen(5) 4 — 54
(K A Ryan) *towards rr: hdwy on inner over 3f out: rdn along wl over 2f out and sn outpcd* **10/3**[2]

6646 **5** *nk* **Ulysees (IRE)**[11] 4137 7-8-13 66.. TomEaves 7 — 46
(I Semple) *in tch: hdwy 4f out: rdn along wl over 2f out and sn wknd* **7/2**[3]

000 **6** *18* **Wood Dalling (USA)**[4] 4350 8-8-6 29 ow3...................... NeilBrown(7) 6 — 4
(Mrs J C McGregor) *a bhd* **100/1**

1m 45.42s (-3.88) **Going Correction** -0.40s/f (Firm)
WFA 3 from 4yo+ 6lb — 6 Ran SP% **110.6**
Speed ratings (Par 101):103,101,100,94,94 76
CSF £63.58 TOTE £7.60: £3.00, £4.00; EX 57.70.
Owner Thomas & Susan Blane **Bred** James Mahon **Trained** Cockerham, Lancs

FOCUS
A fair claimer run at a strong pace and rated around the principals.

4476 CAPTAIN J. C. STEWART H'CAP 1m 1f 36y

7:20 (7:20) (Class 4) (0-80,80) 3-Y-0+ **£6,477** (£1,927; £963; £481) **Stalls** High

Form — RPR

0032 **1** **Bolton Hall (IRE)**[1] 4454 4-8-9 **61** oh2............................. DaleGibson 4 — 70+
(R A Fahey) *trckd ldrs: smooth hdwy 3f out: led wl over 1f out: rdn clr ent last: styd on wl* **9/2**[2]

3435 **2** *3* **Anthemion (IRE)**[4] 4355 9-8-4 **61** oh12..................... AndrewMullen(5) 9 — 64
(Mrs J C McGregor) *led: rdn along 3f out: hdd wl over 1f out: drvn and kpt on fnl f* **25/1**

4311 **3** *1* **Apsara**[15] 4020 5-9-2 **68**.. PhillipMakin 7 — 69
(G M Moore) *a.p: effrt and ev ch over 2f out: sn rdn and kpt on same pce* **9/2**[2]

1264 **4** *½* **Hawkit (USA)**[10] 4175 5-9-5 **71**.. LeeEnstone 8 — 71
(A Bailey) *chsd ldrs on inner: rdn along wl over 2f out: drvn over 1f out: kpt on same pce* **10/1**

0-60 **5** *¾* **Wasalat (USA)**[81] 2018 4-9-0 **71**........................ MarkLawson(5) 10 — 70
(D W Barker) *s.i.s and bhd: stdy hdwy over 4f out: rdn to chse ldrs over 2f out: drvn and one pce appr last* **28/1**

0112 **6** *hd* **Mistress Twister**[18] 3954 5-9-8 **74**................................. PaulFessey 6 — 72
(T D Barron) *hld up in rr: stdy hdwy on outer over 3f out: rdn 2f out: sn edgd rt and no imp* **9/2**[2]

4122 **7** *nk* **Touch Of Ivory (IRE)**[4] 4353 3-8-4 **63** ow2.........................(p) KDarley 3 — 61
(P Monteith) *hld up in rr: hdwy 4f out: rdn wl over 2f out: sn drvn and no imp* **7/2**[1]

2300 **8** *2* **Toshi (USA)**[10] 4175 4-10-0 **80**.. TomEaves 2 — 74
(I Semple) *prom: rdn along 3f out: drvn: wandered and put hd in air 2f out sn hung rt and wknd* **13/2**[3]

0155 **9** *hd* **Insubordinate**[11] 4137 5-8-4 **61** oh2........................ KevinGhunowa(5) 11 — 54
(J S Goldie) *hld up towards rr: hdwy on inner whn nt clr run over 3f out: swtchd lft and sn rdn: no further prog* **14/1**

5015 **10** *1 ¼* **Dispol Peto**[40] 3263 6-8-4 **61** oh9...........................(b) DuranFentiman(5) 1 — 52
(R Johnson) *keen: in tch on outer: rdn along over 3f out: sn wknd* **66/1**

1m 55.49s (-4.17) **Going Correction** -0.40s/f (Firm)
WFA 3 from 4yo+ 7lb — 10 Ran SP% **114.6**
Speed ratings (Par 105):102,99,98,98,97 97,96,95,94,93
CSF £109.55 CT £533.55 TOTE £6.00: £2.40, £6.00, £2.20; EX 109.20.
Owner J J Staunton **Bred** M Duffy **Trained** Musley Bank, N Yorks

FOCUS
An ordinary but competitive handicap and the form looks above average for the grade.
Wasalat(USA) Official explanation: jockey said filly missed the break
Toshi(USA) Official explanation: jockey said gelding hung right-handed

4477 ALL AMERICAN H'CAP 5f 4y

7:50 (7:51) (Class 5) (0-70,68) 3-Y-0+ **£3,238** (£963; £481; £240) **Stalls** Low

Form — RPR

6006 **1** **Catch The Cat (IRE)**[15] 4019 7-8-12 **60**......................(b) GregFairley(5) 7 — 71
(Robert Gray) *prom: hdwy wl over 1f out: rdn to ld ins last: drvn out* **14/1**

5313 **2** *¾* **Chairman Bobby**[8] 4232 8-8-5 **53** ow3...................(p) MarkLawson(5) 9 — 61
(D W Barker) *prom on outer: hdwy wl over 1f out: sn rdn and ev ch tl drvn ins last and no ex last 50 yds* **3/1**[2]

3133 **3** *½* **Viewforth**[4] 4352 8-9-4 **61**..(b) TomEaves 10 — 67+
(I Semple) *in tch: hdwy 2f out: swtchd lft and rdn over 1f out: styd on u.p ins last: nrst fin* **9/4**[1]

0030 **4** *2 ½* **The Leather Wedge (IRE)**[74] 2237 7-9-6 **68**.......... DeclanMcGann(5) 5 — 65
(R Johnson) *led: rdn wl over 1f out: hdd & wknd ins last* **12/1**

2622 **5** *1 ½* **Dulce Sueno**[11] 4136 3-8-12 **57**.. PaulFessey 2 — 49
(I Semple) *sn pushed along towards rr: hdwy on outer 2f out: rdn and edgd rt over 1f out: kpt on ins last: nt rch ldrs* **7/1**

3062 **6** *hd* **Rosie's Result**[23] 3781 6-8-1 **49** oh5..................... AndrewMullen(5) 8 — 40
(M Todhunter) *in tch: effrt 2f out: sn rdn and no imp* **6/1**[3]

6014 **7** *3* **Compton Classic**[8] 4232 4-8-0 **50**.........................(p) KellyHarrison(7) 1 — 30
(J S Goldie) *a rr* **7/1**

0600 **8** *½* **Vondova**[4] 4352 4-9-3 **60**...(p) DaleGibson 3 — 38
(D A Nolan) *chsd ldrs: rdn along over 2f out: sn drvn and wknd* **66/1**

59.94 secs (-1.26) **Going Correction** -0.15s/f (Firm)
WFA 3 from 4yo+ 2lb — 8 Ran SP% **110.9**
Speed ratings (Par 103):104,102,102,98,95 95,90,89
CSF £52.61 CT £127.11 TOTE £14.10: £2.70, £1.40, £1.30; EX 32.30.
Owner T W Heseltine **Bred** Mrs Jill M Harley **Trained** Malton, N Yorks

FOCUS
A low-grade sprint handicap rated through the runner-up to recent form.
Catch The Cat(IRE) Official explanation: trainer had no explanation for the apparent improvement in form

4478 RACING UK ON SKY 432 AUTUMN FINALE H'CAP 1m 4f 17y

8:20 (8:20) (Class 5) (0-70,70) 3-Y-0+ **£3,238** (£963; £481; £240) **Stalls** High

Form — RPR

3623 **1** **Kyle Of Lochalsh**[11] 4132 6-8-11 **54**........................ KevinGhunowa(5) 6 — 62
(J S Goldie) *trckd ldrs on inner: hdwy 3f out: rdn to ld 2f out: drvn and edgd lft ins last: hld on gamely* **11/4**[2]

4226 **2** *shd* **Gigs Magic (USA)**[9] 4205 3-8-4 **52**.. KDarley 3 — 60
(M Johnston) *chsd ldr: hdwy over 3f out: rdn to chal over 2f out: drvn over 1f out: kpt on gamely u.p ins last: jst hld* **9/4**[1]

2233 **3** *1* **Melvino**[15] 4022 4-9-10 **62**.. PhillipMakin 7 — 68+
(T D Barron) *hld up in rr: hdwy on inner wl over 2f out: rdn over 1f out: kpt on ins last* **4/1**[3]

3444 **4** *2 ½* **Easibet Dot Net**[15] 3674 6-10-0 **66**................................(tp) PaulFessey 2 — 68
(I Semple) *led: rdn along 3f out: hdd 2f out: sn drvn and grad wknd appr last* **6/1**

051 **5** *2 ½* **Final Esteem**[17] 3987 3-9-8 **70**... TomEaves 4 — 68
(I Semple) *hld up in tch: hdwy over 3f out: rdn to chse ldrs over 2f out: wknd wl over 1f out* **7/1**

000 **6** *3 ½* **The Dunion**[11] 4132 3-7-8 **47** oh14........................... DuranFentiman(5) 1 — 40
(Miss L A Perratt) *prom: rdn along over 3f out: wknd over 2f out* **80/1**

3060 **7** *½* **Millennium Hall**[13] 4072 7-8-11 **54**.............................. MarkLawson(5) 5 — 46
(Miss Lucinda V Russell) *hld up: hdwy on outer over 3f out: rdn over 2f out and sn btn* **18/1**

2m 38.67s (-0.51) **Going Correction** -0.40s/f (Firm)
WFA 3 from 4yo+ 10lb — 7 Ran SP% **110.7**
Speed ratings (Par 103):85,84,84,82,80 78,78
CSF £8.73 TOTE £2.70: £1.90, £2.60; EX 7.60 Place 6 £74.81, Place 5 £44.05.
Owner Loch Ness Racing Club **Bred** Terry Minahan **Trained** Uplawmoor, E Renfrews

FOCUS
A tight handicap run in a pedestrian winning time for the type of contest and the form is not strong.
T/Plt: £102.60 to a £1 stake. Pool: £43,255.00. 307.75 winning tickets. T/Qpdt: £43.70 to a £1 stake. Pool: £3,059.40. 51.70 winning tickets. JR

3948 SALISBURY (R-H)

Wednesday, August 16

OFFICIAL GOING: Good to firm

Wind: Nil

4479 CARMEN WINES EBF MAIDEN STKS — 6f

2:30 (2:32) (Class 4) 2-Y-O — **£4,857** (£1,445; £722; £360) **Stalls** High

Form — RPR

2 **1** **St Philip (USA)**[18] 3949 2-9-3 .... GeorgeBaker 2 — 76
(R M Beckett) *scope: lw: s.i.s: sn rcvrd to trck ldr: led 2f out: pushed clr ins last: easily* **3/1**[2]

2 1 ¾ **Opera Music** 2-9-3 .... JohnEgan 8 — 71
(S Kirk) *w'like: scope: lw: trckd ldrs: pushed along over 2f out: styd on to chse wnr ins last: no imp but kpt on wl* **10/1**[3]

3 ½ **Fine Ruler (IRE)** 2-9-3 .... TedDurcan 6 — 69
(M R Channon) *unf: scope: s.i.s: bhd: pushed along over 2f out: hdwy over 1f out: styd on wl fnl f but nvr gng pce to trble wnr* **20/1**

004 **4** 1 **Bertie Swift**[22] 3822 2-9-3 69 .... JimCrowley 4 — 66
(J Gallagher) *sn led: hdd 2f out: no chnace w wnr over 1f out: wknd ins last* **33/1**

5 ½ **Leptis Magna** 2-9-3 .... PaulDoe 10 — 65
(W J Knight) *str: bit bkwd: s.i.s: bhd: stl plenty to do 2f out: swtchd to outside: rdn and kpt on fnl f but nvr in contention* **25/1**

6 2 **Moorlander (USA)** 2-9-3 .... RyanMoore 3 — 59
(Mrs A J Perrett) *athletic: scope: s.i.s: towards rr but in tch: pushed along after 2f: sme prog 1/2-way: one pce fnl 2f* **3/1**[2]

20 **7** nk **Romanov Dynasty (IRE)**[11] 4129 2-9-3 .... RichardHughes 7 — 58
(R Hannon) *chsd ldrs: rdn and n.m.r 2f out: n.d after* **6/4**[1]

0 **8** shd **Golden Desert (IRE)**[49] 2979 2-9-3 .... IanMongan 1 — 58
(T G Mills) *s.i.s: sn chsng ldrs: wknd over 1f out* **33/1**

9 15 **Dancing Reva (IRE)** 2-9-3 .... SteveDrowne 5 — 13
(J J Bridger) *w'like: plain: s.i.s: a in rr* **80/1**

1m 14.91s (-0.07) **Going Correction** -0.025s/f (Good) — **9** Ran SP% **114.8**

Speed ratings (Par 96):99,96,96,94,94 91,90,90,70

CSF £28.97 TOTE £4.30: £1.50, £2.50, £3.00; EX 35.20.

Owner R A Pegum **Bred** Foxfield **Trained** Whitsbury, Hants

FOCUS

Probably a fair maiden in which the pace was sound and there were some eye-catching performances behind the winner. The form looks solid enough rated around the winner and fourth.

NOTEBOOK

St Philip(USA) confirmed the promise he showed here on his debut. Always in the ideal place to strike, he found plenty when asked to go and win his race and there is no reason why he should not continue to progress. (tchd 11-4, 10-3 in a place)

Opera Music ◆, a half-brother to five very smart performers including Opera Cape, Grey Shot and Night Shot, showed enough on this debut to suggest he will not let the family down. Never far away, he kept on all the way to the line without offering a threat to the race-fit winner. He shapes as though he will get further. (op 15-2)

Fine Ruler(IRE) ◆, out of an unraced half-sister to three winners including Material Witness, was a bit edgy beforehand and gave his rivals a start, but grasped what was required as the race progressed and finished nicely. Improvement seems assured as he gains experience and his breeding suggests he will appreciate further. (op 25-1)

Bertie Swift, on his toes beforehand, was the most experienced in the field and used it to quickly bag the rail in front, but was eventually firmly outpointed by the front three. He would probably be better off in nurseries. (op 25-1)

Leptis Magna ◆, a 52,000gns half-brother to four winning two-year-old sprinters, was clueless early but stayed on well down the outside later on to offer promise for the future. His pedigree suggests he will not get much further than this.

Moorlander(USA) ◆, a full-brother to three winners overseas including the top-class US performer Gaviola, fetched $340,000 as a foal and $190,000 as a yearling. Rather surprisingly well backed considering the stable's juveniles usually improve for a run, he duly ran as though very much in need of the experience. Obviously highly regarded, he is very much one to watch out for next time. (op 7-1)

Romanov Dynasty(IRE) was already in trouble even before meeting interference and has not built on his promising debut effort. (op 11-10)

4480 CASTLEPOINT SHOPPING PARK, A3060 BOURNEMOUTH NURSERY — 6f 212y

3:00 (3:00) (Class 5) 2-Y-O — **£3,886** (£1,156; £577; £288) **Stalls** Centre

Form — RPR

026 **1** **Bright Moon**[13] 4084 2-9-1 76 .... RichardHughes 13 — 78
(R Hannon) *hld up in rr: stdy hdwy over 2f out: rdn to ld 1f out: styd on strly u.p ins last* **13/2**[3]

0335 **2** 1 ¼ **Global Guest**[12] 4100 2-8-11 72 .... TedDurcan 6 — 71
(M R Channon) *s.i.s: bhd: hdwy over 2f out: drvn to chal 1f out: styd on same pce ins last* **12/1**

1112 **3** 1 **Just Dust**[5] 4335 2-9-2 82 .... MarcHalford(5) 7 — 78
(D R C Elsworth) *lw: led: rdn 2f out: hdd ins fnl 2f: stl upsides 1f out: styd on same pce ins last* **10/3**[2]

3642 **4** 1 ¾ **Diamond Light (USA)**[19] 3902 2-8-9 70 .... LDettori 4 — 62
(J L Dunlop) *hld up in rr: swtchd lft and hdwy fr 3f out: slt ld ins fnl 2f: hdd 1f out: wknd ins last* **5/2**[1]

630 **5** 1 ½ **Down The Brick (IRE)**[21] 3844 2-9-0 75 .... DaneO'Neill 10 — 63
(B R Millman) *s.i.s: bhd: hdwy 2f out: pushed along and kpt on fr over 1f out: no ex ins last* **18/1**

063 **6** 6 **My Tiger Lilly**[11] 4163 2-8-1 62 .... NickyMackay 8 — 34
(W J Knight) *chsd ldrs: rdn over 2f out: wknd fnl f: eased whn no ch nr fin* **9/1**

0040 **7** 1 **Queensgate**[44] 3148 2-8-0 61 ow1 .... FrankieMcDonald 14 — 31+
(M Blanshard) *s.i.s: bhd and t.k.h: pushed along over 2f out: sme hdwy whn n.m.r wl over 1f out: nvr in contention* **50/1**

040 **8** 1 ½ **Private Peachey (IRE)**[21] 3843 2-7-10 60 .... DominicFox(3) 11 — 26
(B R Millman) *in tch: sn drvn along: wknd over 2f out* **66/1**

0355 **9** 3 ½ **Tres Hombres**[19] 3902 2-7-12 59 oh2 .... DavidKinsella 2 — 16
(Tom Dascombe) *lw: drvn to chse ldrs after 2f: wknd 3f out* **28/1**

603 **10** nk **Ron In Ernest**[33] 3485 2-8-8 69 .... StephenCarson 3 — 25
(J A Geake) *chsd ldrs 4f* **12/1**

0052 **11** ½ **Gifted Heir (IRE)**[21] 3838 2-7-13 60 .... FrancisFerris 12 — 14
(I A Wood) *chsd ldrs: rdn over 3f out: wknd over 2f out* **10/1**

1m 28.34s (-0.72) **Going Correction** -0.025s/f (Good) — **11** Ran SP% **111.6**

Speed ratings (Par 94):103,101,100,98,96 89,88,87,83,82 82

CSF £76.26 CT £304.61 TOTE £9.30: £2.90, £2.90, £1.30; EX 100.60.

Owner Coriolan Links Partnership VIII **Bred** Mrs J M F Dibben And Mrs Amanda Brudenell **Trained** East Everleigh, Wilts

FOCUS

A decent pace and a very smart winning time for the type of contest. The field finished well spread out and the form looks solid with the third rated to pre-Newmarket form.

NOTEBOOK

Bright Moon ◆, making her nursery debut, seemed to be well suited by the way the race was run and she came from well off the pace to eventually score comfortably. Though by a sprinter, there is stamina on the dam's side and she shaped here as though a mile will be no problem. (op 7-1 tchd 6-1)

Global Guest, beaten just under 11 lengths by Just Dust at Goodwood last time, comprehensively turned the form around on 13lb better terms. Suited by the strong pace, he came from well off the pace to hold every chance and just lacked finishing speed where it mattered. Like the winner, he is by a sprinter but the dam's side is all about stamina and he should relish the step up to a mile. (op 16-1 tchd 18-1)

Just Dust, bumped up another 3lb, travelled well in front more towards the centre of the track, but may have been set alight sooner than ideal as it gave his rivals plenty of time to get back at him. They duly did so, but to his credit he did not capitulate completely once caught and he should be capable of winning off this sort of mark if held on to a little longer. (op 9-4)

Diamond Light(USA), off the bridle a fair way out, managed to get herself into a position where she held every chance but the effort of getting her there seemed to find her out. (op 9-4)

Down The Brick(IRE) stayed on from off the pace over the last couple of furlongs without managing to land a blow. There should be a race in him, but he may appreciate easier ground. (op 16-1 tchd 20-1)

My Tiger Lilly, making her nursery debut, had every chance but did not see out the extra furlong as well as might have been expected. (op 10-1 tchd 8-1)

Tres Hombres Official explanation: jockey said colt was unsuited by the good to firm ground

4481 GOLDRING SECURITY SERVICES PEMBROKE CUP (H'CAP) — 1m

3:30 (3:32) (Class 4) (0-85,84) 3-Y-O — **£6,477** (£1,927; £963; £481) **Stalls** High

Form — RPR

5310 **1** **Hill Spirit**[62] 2581 3-9-2 79 .... JohnEgan 6 — 88
(D R C Elsworth) *lw: trckd ldrs: led ins fnl 2f: hrd drvn fnl f: jst hld on* **7/2**[2]

4514 **2** shd **Ebert**[13] 4076 3-8-13 76 .... LDettori 8 — 85+
(P J Makin) *hld up in rr: hdwy and n.m.r appr fnl 2f: styng on whn sltly hmpd 1f out: fin strly: jst failed* **5/2**[1]

4036 **3** 3 **Polliwilline (IRE)**[35] 3418 3-9-3 80 .... SteveDrowne 7 — 82
(R Hannon) *in tch: hdwy 2f out: chsd ldrs 1f out: kpt on one pce* **25/1**

0043 **4** ¾ **Ahmedy (IRE)**[17] 3977 3-8-6 72 .... EdwardCreighton(3) 4 — 72
(M R Channon) *slowly away: bhd: swtchd to outside 2f out: kpt on fr over 1f out but nvr gng pce to rch ldrs* **7/1**

0102 **5** 2 ½ **Lyrical Sound (IRE)**[26] 3708 3-9-2 79 .... MichaelHills 3 — 74
(B W Hills) *chsd ldrs: wkng whn hmpd 1f out* **5/1**

-400 **6** 8 **Bertie Southstreet**[24] 3761 3-9-2 79 .... DaneO'Neill 2 — 55
(J R Best) *t.k.h: chsd ldr to 2f out: sn wknd: no ch whn hmpd 1f out* **20/1**

0000 **7** 3 **Charlton**[51] 2932 3-9-0 77 ....(v) IanMongan 5 — 46
(T G Mills) *chsd ldrs to 2f out: no ch whn hmpd 1f out* **20/1**

1-33 **U** **Alfie Tupper (IRE)**[21] 3852 3-9-7 84 .... GeorgeBaker 1 — 88
(S Kirk) *lw: led tl hdd ins fnl 2f: stl chsng wnr and 1l down whn sddle slipped and uns rdr 1f out* **9/2**[3]

1m 42.48s (-0.61) **Going Correction** -0.025s/f (Good) — **8** Ran SP% **111.5**

Speed ratings (Par 102):102,101,98,98,95 87,84,—

CSF £11.90 CT £168.01 TOTE £4.10: £1.70, £1.70, £5.50; EX 13.70.

Owner Chimera Racing **Bred** Gestut Goerlsdorf **Trained** Newmarket, Suffolk

FOCUS

A dramatic race in which the early pace was modest and it developed into something of a sprint. The third sets the level which is average for the grade.

4482 EUROPEAN BREEDERS FUND UPAVON FILLIES' STKS (LISTED RACE) — 1m 1f 198y

4:00 (4:02) (Class 1) 3-Y-O+

£23,847 (£9,038; £4,523; £2,255; £1,129; £567) **Stalls** High

Form — RPR

2-13 **1** **Pictavia (IRE)**[25] 3739 4-9-4 107 .... LDettori 5 — 114+
(Saeed Bin Suroor) *lw: mde virtually all: shkn up 2f out: forged clr fnl f: easily* **10/11**[1]

3144 **2** 4 **Summer's Eve**[15] 4035 3-8-6 102 .... DaneO'Neill 6 — 100
(H Candy) *chsd ldrs: drvn to chal 2f out: outpcd by wnr fnl f but hld on wl for 2nd* **9/1**

-113 **3** 1 ½ **Princess Nada**[39] 3293 3-8-10 101 .... NickyMackay 1 — 102
(L M Cumani) *rr but in tch: hdwy 3f out: chsd ldrs ovr 1f out: one pce ins last* **9/2**[2]

1311 **4** 1 **Kahlua Kiss**[18] 3954 3-8-6 91 .... RichardKingscote 8 — 96
(W R Muir) *lw: chsd ldrs: drvn to chal 3f out: lost 2nd 2f out: wknd ins last* **8/1**[3]

-542 **5** ¾ **Jaish (USA)**[62] 2582 3-8-6 97 .... RHills 7 — 94
(J L Dunlop) *chsd ldrs: rdn 3f out: wknd ins fnl 2f* **16/1**

-621 **6** nk **Acts Of Grace (USA)**[44] 3146 3-8-6 90 .... EddieAhern 3 — 94
(J L Dunlop) *lw: rr but in tch: drvn along 3f out: nvr gng pce to be competitive* **28/1**

2206 **7** nk **Solva**[14] 4040 3-8-6 79 .... TedDurcan 4 — 93?
(B J Meehan) *lw: rr but in tch: rdn and effrt 3f out: nvr gng pce to rch ldrs* **66/1**

-040 **8** 6 **Bon Nuit (IRE)**[56] 2740 4-9-0 100 .... SteveDrowne 2 — 82
(G Wragg) *in tch: rdn 3f out: sn edgd lft and btn* **8/1**[3]

2m 6.07s (-2.39) **Going Correction** -0.025s/f (Good)

WFA 3 from 4yo 8lb — **8** Ran SP% **113.6**

Speed ratings (Par 108):108,104,103,102,102 101,101,96

CSF £10.06 TOTE £1.70: £1.10, £2.40, £1.70; EX 11.30.

Owner Godolphin **Bred** Gainsborough Stud Management L **Trained** Newmarket, Suffolk

FOCUS

A fair Listed race and the winning time was bang on par for a race like this and 3.8sec faster than the following handicap. The winner is above average for the grade but the form is not totally rock solid.

NOTEBOOK

Pictavia(IRE), dropped back to this trip after possibly not staying a mile and a half last time, was given a positive ride and fought off a couple of challenges before drawing away in the last furlong. Although third in last season's Oaks, she has yet to win above this level, and the next target will presumably to win a Group race. Connections have suggested she could go for the Breeders' Cup Filly and Mare Turf, if she goes the right way from this. (op 11-10)

Summer's Eve, a consistent sort who has been progressing steadily this season, ran a fine race on this return to fast ground, taking on the winner a quarter of a mile out and holding on for second once that rival drew away. She looks capable of winning in Pattern company, possibly on an easier surface. (op 8-1 tchd 10-1)

Princess Nada, dropping in trip after finishing third in the Lancashire Oaks, never got to the leaders but appeared to stumble crossing a path early in the straight which may not have helped. However, she ran close to previous form with Jaish, and this may be as good as she is. (op 4-1 tchd 5-1)

Kahlua Kiss has progressed quickly in handicaps this summer, having been rated just 73 in late June. She travelled well and came through to challenge the winner early in the straight, but faded in the closing stages. She could well earn black type back on a flatter track, and the John Musker Stakes at Yarmouth next month looks a suitable target, providing the ground does not go against her. (op 15-2 tchd 17-2)

Jaish(USA) ran close to previous form with the third, and will do well to find a race at this level. (tchd 20-1)

Bon Nuit(IRE), dropping in grade, was disappointing and dropped out tamely in the closing stages.

4483 MANOR FARM MEATS H'CAP — 1m 1f 198y

4:30 (4:30) (Class 5) (0-70,70) 3-Y-O+ **£3,886** (£1,156; £577; £288) **Stalls** High

Form				RPR
50-0	**1**		**Al Hazim (IRE)**[20] [3871] 3-9-8 **69** .... NickyMackay 14 (L M Cumani) *trckd ldrs: drvn to chal ins fnl 2f: led appr fnl f: drvn out* **11/2**[3]	78
5030	**2**	*1*	**Double Spectre (IRE)**[16] [4005] 4-9-9 **62** .... VinceSlattery 12 (Jean-Rene Auvray) *rr: hdwy whn bmpd 3f out: hdwy and nt clr run 2f out and over 1f out: n.m.r ins last: fin wl but nt rcvr* **7/1**	71+
0604	**3**	*½*	**Henchman**[28] [3650] 3-8-8 **58** .... (b) RichardKingscote(3) 9 (Lady Herries) *t.k.h: led after 1f: rdn 3f out: kpt slt advantage tl hdd appr fnl f: styd on same pce u.p* **4/1**[2]	64
0400	**4**	*2*	**River Gypsy**[65] [2507] 5-8-9 **53** .... MarcHalford(5) 11 (D R C Elsworth) *chsd ldrs: wnt 2nd 3f out: rdn 2f out: hung rt u.p and wknd ins last* **7/1**	55
4043	**5**	*1 ¼*	**Voice Mail**[7] [4241] 7-10-0 **67** .... (b) LPKeniry 3 (A M Balding) *hld up in tch: hdwy to chse ldrs 3f out: wknd appr fnl f* **10/3**[1]	67
040	**6**	*1 ¼*	**Future Deal**[7] [4248] 5-9-6 **59** .... SteveDrowne 1 (C A Horgan) *stdd s and swtchd to ins rail: bhd: hdwy 2f out:swtchd rt to ins 1f out: styng on whn hmpd: ins last: nt rcvr* **8/1**	60+
0060	**7**	*nk*	**Louise Dupin (IRE)**[18] [3947] 3-8-7 **57** .... NelsonDeSouza(3) 7 (R M Beckett) *chsd ldrs: rdn over 2f out: wknd over 1f out* **10/1**	54
000-	**8**	*3*	**Prince Of Medina**[355] [4725] 3-8-10 **57** .... StephenCarson 5 (J R Best) *bhd: rdn 4f out: nvr gng pce to be competitive* **25/1**	48
6-60	**9**	*2 ½*	**Pelham Crescent (IRE)**[42] [3197] 3-9-9 **70** .... FrancisFerris 10 (B Palling) *led 1f: styd chsng ldr to 3f out: wknd 2f out* **25/1**	56
60-0	**10**	*4*	**The Rip**[67] [2455] 5-9-0 **53** .... DaneO'Neill 8 (R M Stronge) *bit bkwd: mid-div 1/2-way: rdn 4f out: sn btn* **25/1**	32

2m 9.87s (1.41) **Going Correction** -0.025s/f (Good)
WFA 3 from 4yo+ 8lb **10** Ran SP% **115.2**
Speed ratings (Par 103):93,92,91,90,89 88,87,85,83,80
CSF £41.98 CT £168.35 TOTE £5.60: £2.00, £3.10, £2.00; EX 43.70.

Owner Sheikh Mohammed Obaid Al Maktoum **Bred** Premier Bloodstock **Trained** Newmarket, Suffolk

■ Stewards' Enquiry : Marc Halford one-day ban: careless riding (Aug 27)

FOCUS
A modest handicap and, despite a fast early pace, a very moderate winning time for the grade, 3.8 seconds slower than the preceding Listed event. The placed horses set the standard.

Al Hazim(IRE) Official explanation: trainer's rep said, regarding the improvement in form, he had no explanation other than that the colt had had problems with splints and may have needed its previous run

4484 PLAY FREE & WIN CASH AT 123RACING.COM FILLIES' H'CAP — 6f

5:00 (5:00) (Class 5) (0-70,70) 3-Y-O+ **£3,886** (£1,156; £577; £288) **Stalls** High

Form				RPR
3124	**1**		**China Cherub**[21] [3841] 3-9-8 **69** .... DaneO'Neill 6 (H Candy) *lw: trckd ldr: led appr fnl 2f: drvn and styd on strly fnl f* **3/1**[1]	78
00-2	**2**	*1*	**Tapau (IRE)**[4] [4365] 8-8-0 **51** oh4 .... BarrySavage(7) 3 (J M Bradley) *rr but in tch: n.m.r on rail ins fnl 2f: swtchd lft and qcknd to chse wnr ins last but a hld* **9/1**	57+
6433	**3**	*shd*	**Highland Cascade**[6] [4294] 4-9-12 **70** .... TedDurcan 2 (J M P Eustace) *bhd: hdwy on outside whn edgd rt over 1f out: styd on to press for 2nd ins last but nt pce to rch wnr* **4/1**[2]	76
0232	**4**	*1 ¼*	**Rogue**[18] [3950] 4-9-5 **63** .... SteveDrowne 4 (Jane Southcombe) *bhd: hdwy 2f out: swtchd rt and styd on fnl f: nt rch ldrs* **9/2**[3]	65
0443	**5**	*2 ½*	**Pink Bay**[19] [3897] 4-8-8 **52** .... (v) LPKeniry 10 (W S Kittow) *lw: chsd ldrs: hmpd and lost plcd jst ins last: nt rcvr* **4/1**[2]	47
3006	**6**	*2*	**My Girl Pearl (IRE)**[20] [3867] 6-8-7 **51** oh4 .... NickyMackay 1 (M S Saunders) *chsd ldrs: rdn and one pce whn hmpd over 1f out: sn btn* **12/1**	40
1200	**7**	*nk*	**Ruby's Dream**[19] [3897] 4-8-7 **54** .... (p) NelsonDeSouza(3) 7 (J M Bradley) *in tch: rdn and hdwy fr 2f out: one pce whn edgd lft over 1f out: sn btn* **9/1**	42
-006	**8**	*10*	**Exmoor Dancer (IRE)**[21] [3842] 3-8-4 **51** oh11 .... DavidKinsella 8 (H S Howe) *led tl hdd appr fnl 2f: sn wknd* **66/1**	9

1m 14.43s (-0.55) **Going Correction** -0.025s/f (Good)
WFA 3 from 4yo+ 3lb **8** Ran SP% **112.4**
Speed ratings (Par 100):102,100,100,98,95 92,92,79
CSF £29.69 CT £107.03 TOTE £3.60: £1.50, £3.50, £1.90; EX 36.50 Place 6 £45.20, Place 5 £14.31.

Owner Wayne And Hilary Thornton **Bred** Wayne And Hilary Thornton **Trained** Kingston Warren, Oxon

■ Stewards' Enquiry : Nelson De Souza caution: careless riding

FOCUS
A moderate fillies' sprint, run just under half a second faster than the opening juvenile maiden. The form is modest but sound.

T/Jkpt: £17,842.10 to a £1 stake. Pool: £75,389.50. 3.00 winning tickets. T/Plt: £77.70 to a £1 stake. Pool: £70,377.25. 660.85 winning tickets. T/Qpdt: £11.80 to a £1 stake. Pool: £4,035.30. 252.30 winning tickets. ST

3872 SANDOWN (R-H)

Wednesday, August 16

OFFICIAL GOING: Good to firm
Wind: Nil Weather: Fine

4485 TONY O'CONNOR MEMORIAL MEDIAN AUCTION MAIDEN STKS — 5f 6y

5:30 (5:31) (Class 5) 2-Y-O **£3,238** (£963; £481; £240) **Stalls** High

Form				RPR
4456	**1**		**Sparkling Eyes**[11] [4130] 2-8-12 **90** .... AlanMunro 6 (C E Brittain) *lw: mde all: drew clr fr 2f out: easily* **7/4**[2]	82+
2524	**2**	*4*	**Dee Jay Wells**[27] [3663] 2-9-3 **75** .... RyanMoore 1 (R Hannon) *swtg: chsd wnr: outpcd clr of rest 2f out but sn outpcd* **6/4**[1]	73
0	**3**	*3*	**Wachiwi (IRE)**[46] [3096] 2-8-12 .... RoystonFfrench 2 (A P Jarvis) *chsd ldng pair: outpcd and rdn 1/2-way: no ch after: jst hld on for 3rd* **16/1**	57
06	**4**	*shd*	**Tiburon**[13] [4074] 2-9-3 .... JimCrowley 4 (H Morrison) *lw: dwlt: a off the pce: nt clr run 1/2-way: plugged on to chal for modest 3rd nr fin* **12/1**	62
000	**5**	*8*	**Countyourblessings**[19] [3915] 2-8-12 .... PaulDoe 3 (I A Wood) *a in last trio: rdn and struggling 1/2-way: sn bhd* **50/1**	28
	6	*3 ½*	**Master Of Destiny (IRE)** 2-9-3 .... RichardHughes 5 (H J Collingridge) *str: lw: dwlt: a in last trio: struggling bef 1/2-way: sn bhd* **4/1**[3]	20

61.86 secs (-0.35) **Going Correction** -0.25s/f (Firm) **6** Ran SP% **111.9**
Speed ratings (Par 94):92,85,80,80,67 62
CSF £4.72 TOTE £2.90: £1.50, £1.30; EX 4.40.

Owner A J Richards **Bred** Sarl Ewar Stud Farms France **Trained** Newmarket, Suffolk

FOCUS
Just an ordinary maiden to start the evening, with the threat of rain looming large over the course. With a couple in the race already looking exposed and somewhat modest, the market centred on only half the field. The race has been rated through the runner-up.

NOTEBOOK
Sparkling Eyes ◆ had not really progressed since her fourth in the Queen Mary at Royal Ascot in June. Down the field in an ordinary maiden on the Fibresand at Southwell on her next start, she then finished last in a nursery at Goodwood. However, the drop down to the minimum distance worked the oracle, and she could be called the winner some way out. Five furlongs would appear her preferred trip and she can win again. (op 6-4 tchd 15-8, 2-1 in places)
Dee Jay Wells, representing a trainer with a fine record in the race, was also dropped in trip after racing over seven furlongs last time, a race that has worked out very well. Beaten just over ten lengths by dual Group 2 winner Strategic Prince on his debut, another race that has worked out very nicely, he certainly deserved to land a race but again found one too good for him. He will surely have his day soon. (op 2-1)
Wachiwi(IRE) kept on inside the final stages to just snatch third, but did not display too much obvious potential for this grade. (op 14-1)
Tiburon, stepping down from seven furlongs, lacks the pace for this trip. (op 14-1)
Countyourblessings is modest and never got into things.
Master Of Destiny(IRE) failed to build on the impressive record this season of the stable's two-year-olds. (tchd 9-2)

4486 DAIKIN AIRCONDITIONING (THE ENGINEERS CHOICE) H'CAP — 5f 6y

6:00 (6:02) (Class 4) (0-80,80) 4-Y-O+ **£5,505** (£1,637; £818; £408) **Stalls** High

Form				RPR
1334	**1**		**Forest Dane**[9] [4208] 6-8-2 **61** oh1 .... RoystonFfrench 12 (Mrs N Smith) *trckd ldrs: swtchd to inner over 2f out: prog to ld over 1f out: clr fnl f: unchal* **11/1**	73
136U	**2**	*2*	**Matsunosuke**[17] [3972] 4-9-0 **78** .... LiamJones(5) 11 (A B Coogan) *s.s: hld up in last: swtchd to wd outside and rapid prog over 1f out: wnt 2nd nr fin: no ch w wnr* **7/1**[2]	83
0510	**3**	*½*	**Holbeck Ghyll (IRE)**[4] [4360] 4-9-7 **80** .... JohnEgan 10 (A M Balding) *lw: dwlt: sn in midfield on inner: nt clr run over 2f out: prog over 1f out: chsd wnr briefly ins fnl f: no imp* **2/1**[1]	83+
4135	**4**	*nk*	**Who's Winning (IRE)**[12] [4106] 5-9-2 **75** .... RobertMiles 2 (B G Powell) *towards rr: prog on outer fr 2f out: hanging rt and kpt on same pce fnl f* **14/1**	77+
1321	**5**	*¾*	**Blessed Place**[17] [3988] 6-8-4 **70** .... (t) AshleyHamblett(7) 9 (D J S Ffrench Davis) *taken down early: led to over 1f out: sn no ch w wnr: lost 2nd ins fnl f* **8/1**[3]	69
0200	**6**	*shd*	**Divine Spirit**[7] [4258] 5-8-7 **66** .... AlanMunro 4 (M Dods) *lw: settled wl in rr: rdn and prog on outer fr 2f out: one pce fnl f* **10/1**	65+
060-	**7**	*1 ½*	**Sundance (IRE)**[322] [5558] 4-9-6 **79** .... RichardHughes 8 (H J Collingridge) *settled wl in rr: rdn over 1f out: styd on same pce fnl f: n.d* **33/1**	73
0060	**8**	*hd*	**Spanish Ace**[13] [4085] 5-9-3 **76** .... RyanMoore 6 (J M Bradley) *b: settled midfield: rdn and nt qckn 2f out: no prog after* **11/1**	69
00-1	**9**	*1*	**Little Edward**[21] [3855] 8-9-5 **78** .... JimCrowley 7 (R J Hodges) *pressed ldr to 2f out: wknd fnl f* **12/1**	67
3620	**10**	*shd*	**Chinalea (IRE)**[12] [4101] 4-8-13 **75** .... (p) AdamKirby(3) 5 (C G Cox) *lw: hld up on inner: hmpd jst over 2f out: effrt over 1f out: nvr on terms* **10/1**	64
3222	**11**	*1 ½*	**Millfields Dreams**[11] [4141] 7-7-13 **61** oh3 .... DominicFox(3) 3 (M G Quinlan) *prom for 3f: steadily wknd* **14/1**	45
0000	**12**	*1 ¾*	**Cornus**[13] [4085] 4-9-2 **75** .... PaulDoe 13 (J A Osborne) *lw: prom: hmpd jst over 2f out: wknd over 1f out* **14/1**	52
0400	**13**	*5*	**Pachello (IRE)**[12] [4101] 4-8-8 **70** .... (t) NeilChalmers(3) 1 (J M Bradley) *pressed ldrs on outer: wknd rapidly over 1f out* **25/1**	29

60.08 secs (-2.13) **Going Correction** -0.25s/f (Firm) **13** Ran SP% **126.3**
Speed ratings (Par 105):107,103,103,102,101 101,98,98,96,96 94,91,83
CSF £91.00 CT £211.86 TOTE £15.30: £4.20, £2.30, £1.70; EX 93.10.

Owner The Ember Partnership **Bred** Loan And Development Corporation **Trained** Bury, W Sussex

FOCUS
A few of these had met during the season, which made it an intricate puzzle to solve. As usual, the draw played its part in the result, with high-numbered stalls predictably having the edge in these handicaps for older sprinters. The form looks straightforward and sound.

4487 123RACING.COM MEDIAN AUCTION MAIDEN STKS — 7f 16y

6:30 (6:33) (Class 4) 2-Y-O **£4,533** (£1,348; £674; £336) **Stalls** High

Form				RPR
5	**1**		**Overturn (IRE)**[17] [3976] 2-9-3 .... AlanMunro 4 (W R Swinburn) *trckd ldrs: prog to ld over 2f out: rdn and pressed 1f out: styd on wl to draw clr fnl f* **9/4**[1]	91+

2	3	**Murbek (IRE)** 2-9-3 .... RHills 3 (M A Jarvis) *cmpt: lw: hld up in last trio: prog 3f out: chsd wnr 2f out: clsd to chal 1f out: sn no ex and btn* **13/2**	83
3	4	**Plane Painter (IRE)** 2-9-3 .... RoystonFfrench 6 (M Johnston) *neat: hld up in last trio: rdn and efofrt over 2f out: styd on to chse ldng pair over 1f out: no imp* **8/1**	73
4	3	**Spirit Of The Mist (IRE)** 2-9-3 .... JohnEgan 10 (T J Pitt) *unf: scope: lw: dwlt: sn chsd ldrs: rdn over 2f out: no imp wl over 1f out: fdd* **15/2**	65
4	5 shd	**Messiah Garvey**[32] 3545 2-9-3 .... IanMongan 12 (M R Channon) *chsd ldr to 3f out: rdn and wknd over 1f out* **6/1**[3]	65
	6 ¾	**Seven Steps (IRE)** 2-8-12 .... EddieAhern 5 (J W Hills) *neat: hld up in last: nt clr run briefly over 2f out: shkn up over 1f out: kpt on steadily: nvr nr ldrs* **20/1**	58
0	7 5	**Rikochet**[11] 4129 2-9-3 .... JimCrowley 2 (Mrs A J Perrett) *nvr beyond midfield: rdn 3f out: sn struggling and btn* **10/1**	50
0	8 6	**Ceris Star (IRE)**[81] 2009 2-8-10 .... JamesMillman(7) 8 (B R Millman) *h.d.w: lw: mde most to over 2f out: wknd rapidly over 1f out* **20/1**	34
4	9 6	**View From The Top**[12] 4103 2-9-3 .... PaulDoe 9 (W J Knight) *chsd ldrs: wknd whn squeezed out over 2f out* **4/1**[2]	19
00	10 7	**The Grey Bam Bam**[18] 3949 2-8-9 .... EdwardCreighton(3) 7 (R J Hodges) *taken down early: t.k.h: hld up in midfield: sltly hmpd and rn wd bnd over 3f out: sn wknd* **66/1**	—

1m 29.93s (-1.16) **Going Correction** -0.175s/f (Firm) **10** Ran SP% **121.4**
Speed ratings (Par 96):99,95,91,87,87 86,80,74,67,59
CSF £17.81 TOTE £3.20: £1.20, £2.00, £2.40; EX 13.20.
Owner Mrs P W Harris **Bred** Pendley Farm **Trained** Aldbury, Herts

FOCUS
This maiden last season produced plenty of winners, in fact the runner-up down to the ninth all went on to win afterwards. Horses such as Dunelight, Jadalee and Gracechurch emerged as the most prominent performers from the race, but Suzy Bliss landed that race and the same connections repeated the feat. THe time was reasonable but the form is difficult to assess.

NOTEBOOK
Overturn(IRE) ◆ moved ominously well at the top of the home straight, moving smoothly into the lead just over two out, before facing a real fight from the runner-up. Progression has been made from his first run and he looks a very promising sort. (tchd 2-1 and 5-2)
Murbek(IRE) ◆, who cost 78,000gns at two, holds a couple of high-profile entries later in the season and threw down a big challenge to the winner inside the last quarter of a mile. Given a fine introductory ride by his jockey, he looks sure to go one better in due course. (op 6-1 tchd 7-1)
Plane Painter(IRE), out of a dam that stayed ten furlongs, was far from disgraced on his debut and looks the sort to do better over a mile at two. (op 9-1)
Spirit Of The Mist(IRE) ◆, a half-brother to nine individual winners, including the top-class pair Almushtarak and Tiber, is a nice big sort and raced a bit green during the race. He has plenty of scope for improvement and should do better with time. Official explanation: jockey said colt hung left (op 11-2 tchd 8-1)
Messiah Garvey was a bit keen early and only kept on at one pace. (op 13-2)
Seven Steps(IRE) can be rated slightly better than her finishing position, as she encountered a bit of interference when making her bid up the home straight.
Rikochet gives the impression he will improve with experience. By Generous out of a Nashwan mare, he is almost certain to stay middle distances at three and is one to keep an eye out for in handicaps. (op 20-1)
View From The Top was rushed up to help force the pace early but dropped right out of contention once the pressure was applied. (op 9-2)

4488 XL INSURANCE H'CAP — 7f 16y
7:05 (7:05) (Class 3) (0-90,86) 3-Y-O **£8,096** (£2,408; £1,203; £601) **Stalls** High

Form			RPR
-323	1	**Signor Peltro**[49] 2981 3-9-3 **82** .... FergusSweeney 12 (H Candy) *lw: hld up bhd ldrs: n.m.r over 2f out: chsd ldr over 1f out: chal fnl f: hrd rdn to ld last strides* **4/1**[1]	91+
0336	2 hd	**Blades Girl**[13] 4083 3-9-3 **82** .... (p) CatherineGannon 9 (K A Ryan) *mde most: kicked 2l clr wl over 1f out: hrd pressed fnl f: kpt on wl u.p: hdd last strides* **10/1**	90
-060	3 4	**River Kintyre**[41] 3226 3-8-9 **74** .... MichaelHills 2 (B W Hills) *stdd s and swtchd to inner: hld up in last pair: prog on outer 2f out: styd on to take 3rd last strides* **20/1**	72
2430	4 shd	**Zennerman (IRE)**[18] 3945 3-8-11 **81** .... LiamJones(5) 6 (W M Brisbourne) *hld up in last pair: n.m.r over 2f out: weaved through fr over 1f out: disp 3rd ins fnl f: no ch w ldng pair* **20/1**	78
2060	5 nk	**Carmenero (GER)**[13] 4083 3-8-13 **78** .... SteveDrowne 8 (W R Muir) *lw: hld up in rr: n.m.r over 2f out: prog over 1f out: styd on fnl f: n.d* **16/1**	75
0220	6 1¼	**Woodcote Place**[21] 3852 3-8-7 **72** .... AlanMunro 5 (P R Chamings) *lw: hld up in rr: nt clr run over 2f out: hmpd twice wl over 1f out : no ch after: fin w plenty lft* **4/1**[1]	65+
221-	7 1½	**Magadar (USA)**[313] 5710 3-8-13 **78** .... RichardHughes 3 (C E Brittain) *lw: hld up in rr: smoooth prog on outer to press ldrs 2f out: rdn and nt qckn over 1f out: wknd fnl f* **14/1**	67
4130	8 shd	**Namid Reprobate (IRE)**[13] 4083 3-9-7 **86** .... EddieAhern 10 (P F I Cole) *trckd ldrs: n.m.r over 2f out: rdn whn squeezed out sn after: no ch after* **8/1**[3]	75
1633	9 1¾	**Louie Louie (IRE)**[11] 4144 3-9-3 **85** .... AdamKirby(3) 4 (N A Callaghan) *b.hind: prom: chsd ldr briefly wl over 1f out: wknd rapidly fnl f* **4/1**[1]	70
0060	10 1¼	**Trans Sonic**[15] 4029 3-8-9 **74** .... TPQueally 11 (A P Jarvis) *lw: pressed ldr for 3f: trbld passage on inner fr 1/2-way: no ch whn nt clr run over 1f out: wknd* **25/1**	55
-214	11 7	**Grand Entrance (IRE)**[12] 4114 3-8-10 **75** .... JohnEgan 1 (C R Egerton) *plld hrd: pressed ldr after 3f to wl over 1f out: wknd rapidly* **6/1**[2]	38+

1m 28.64s (-2.45) **Going Correction** -0.175s/f (Firm) **11** Ran SP% **120.4**
Speed ratings (Par 104):107,106,102,102,101 100,98,98,96,95 87
CSF £45.38 CT £740.01 TOTE £5.10: £2.00, £3.40, £6.40; EX 52.10.
Owner First Of Many Partnership **Bred** R D And J S Chugg And The Overbury Partnership **Trained** Kingston Warren, Oxon
■ Stewards' Enquiry : Liam Jones one-day ban: careless riding (Aug 27)
Catherine Gannon one-day ban: used whip with excessive frequency (Aug 27)

FOCUS
A decent handicap in which there did not seem a great deal of pace on in the early stages, which may have contributed to one or two horses not getting the best of runs. The principals set the standard.

NOTEBOOK
Signor Peltro, one of the least exposed runners in the line-up, was being asked to try seven furlongs for the first time, after he was noted staying on under pressure over six last time. He was a bit keen early, but found plenty under pressure and caught the runner-up close to the line. There can be little doubt he gets the trip and more options are available to connections now.
Blades Girl, a very useful two-year-old last year, has acquitted herself well so far this season and almost returned north with a nice prize. She gave her all and is very tough. (op 12-1)
River Kintyre was well held by the principals but was doing his best work late on. He appeared to be purposely restrained leaving the stalls and was never really getting to the leaders quickly enough to cause them any worries when making his challenge down the centre of the track. (op 16-1)
Zennerman(IRE) had not been beaten more than six lengths all season, which means no respite from the Handicapper, even though his form figures do not look overly inspiring. He was under pressure quite early, but stayed on fairly well after meeting a little interference on his way through.
Carmenero(GER) got caught up in a bit of scrimmaging but basically had every chance.
Woodcote Place can add another unlucky run to his growing collection. He had plenty left when passing the post but is becoming expensive to follow. (tchd 9-2)
Magadar(USA), having her first run of the year, did not find a great deal when asked to quicken but can be expected to come on for the race. (op 16-1)
Namid Reprobate(IRE) dropped out disappointingly when the tempo quickened, and although he was short of room at one stage he was in the process of going backwards at the time.
Louie Louie(IRE) was close up early, but was another that dropped out tamely when the tempo quickened. (op 9-2 tchd 5-1)
Trans Sonic was very keen early and dropped out quickly, although he did not have the greatest of runs up the rail when making a challenge. (op 33-1)

4489 THE COLONY CLUB MAIDEN FILLIES' STKS — 1m 14y
7:35 (7:35) (Class 5) 3-Y-O+ **£3,886** (£1,156; £577; £288) **Stalls** High

Form			RPR
4223	1	**Pirouetting**[41] 3219 3-8-12 72 .... MichaelHills 6 (B W Hills) *lw: trckd ldrs: prog to chal 2f out: led over 1f out: drvn out to hold on nr fin* **3/1**[3]	71
4-36	2 nk	**Regal Velvet**[17] 3975 3-8-12 77 .... RyanMoore 8 (J H M Gosden) *hld up towards rr: prog over 2f out: chal and upsides over 1f out: nt qckn and looked hld: rallied and clsng nr fin* **2/1**[2]	70
032	3 ½	**Muntada**[54] 2815 3-8-12 75 .... RHills 5 (M P Tregoning) *lw: mde most and dictated stdy pce: jnd but looked to be gng wl 2f out: hdd and nt qckn over 1f out: hld after* **15/8**[1]	69
62	4 6	**Maud's Cat (IRE)**[4] 4382 3-8-12 .... TPQueally 4 (A P Jarvis) *heavily restrained s: hld up in last pair: swtchd to inner and hanging rt over 2f out: outpcd by ldng trio and no ch* **8/1**	55
3-00	5 1½	**Divisive**[169] 538 3-8-12 52 .... SteveDrowne 7 (G Wragg) *sn pushed along in last: nvr a factor: plugged on* **25/1**	52
0	6 3½	**Kindallachan**[25] 3742 3-8-12 .... EddieAhern 2 (G C Bravery) *t.k.h: trckd ldrs tl wknd wl over 2f out* **40/1**	44
-000	7 hd	**Prima Markova**[25] 3742 3-8-12 45 .... (t) RoystonFfrench 3 (D J Daly) *trckd ldrs tl rdn and wknd over 2f out* **50/1**	43
5	8 2½	**Hello Deauville (FR)**[20] 3875 3-8-12 .... AlanMunro 1 (J Akehurst) *bit bkwd: t.k.h: w ldr tl wknd rapidly over 2f out* **25/1**	37

1m 44.37s (0.42) **Going Correction** -0.175s/f (Firm) **8** Ran SP% **116.3**
Speed ratings (Par 100):90,89,89,83,81 78,78,75
CSF £9.33 TOTE £4.60: £1.60, £1.40, £1.10; EX 11.70.
Owner Hon Mrs J M Corbett,C Wright,P Hills **Bred** Mrs A J Brudenell **Trained** Lambourn, Berks

FOCUS
This was far from a strong fillies' maiden, and they did not go particularly quickly early and the race turned into a sprint up the straight, resulting in a moderate winning time for the type of contest and the fiftha nd seventh anchor the form.

4490 CORPORATE CREDIT MEDIA H'CAP — 1m 2f 7y
8:05 (8:07) (Class 4) (0-80,76) 3-Y-O **£5,505** (£1,637; £818; £408) **Stalls** High

Form			RPR
1215	1	**Pagan Crest**[27] 3665 3-9-0 **69** .... RyanMoore 2 (Mrs A J Perrett) *lw: trckd ldng pair: squeezed through on inner 2f out and sn led: drvn and looked in command fnl f: jst hld on nr fin* **4/1**[2]	78+
1-42	2 nk	**Whatizzit**[46] 3095 3-9-7 **76** .... SteveDrowne 8 (E A L Dunlop) *b: lw: trckd ldr: chal 3f out: led briefly 2f out: chsd wnr after: rallied and clsng nr fin* **7/2**[1]	83
2102	3 2½	**Don Pietro**[19] 3918 3-9-2 **74** .... EdwardCreighton(3) 1 (D J Coakley) *stdd s: hld up in last pair: rdn and prog over 2f out: chsd ldng pair over 1f out: no imp after* **7/1**	76
1341	4 hd	**Bon Viveur**[23] 3798 3-9-4 **73** .... (p) RichardHughes 7 (R Hannon) *lw: led at fast pce: breather 1/2-way: tried to kick on again over 3f out: hdd 2f out: sn outpcd: keeping on again nr fin* **9/2**[3]	75
0054	5 6	**Gracechurch (IRE)**[14] 4051 3-9-6 **75** .... TedDurcan 3 (M R Channon) *hld up in last pair: effrt but hanging over 2f out: no imp: wknd over 1f out* **9/2**[3]	65
-650	6 1½	**Semi Detached (IRE)**[68] 2403 3-9-0 **72** .... (t) AmirQuinn(3) 6 (J R Boyle) *chsd ldng trio to 1/2-way: rdn and in tch over 2f out: wknd wl over 1f out* **10/1**	60
4103	7 shd	**Nefski Alexander (USA)**[27] 3665 3-9-5 **74** .... EddieAhern 5 (P F I Cole) *swtg: hld up: chsd ldng trio 1/2-way: rdn and no imp over 2f out: wknd wl over 1f out* **9/1**	61

2m 10.01s (-0.23) **Going Correction** -0.175s/f (Firm) **7** Ran SP% **110.2**
Speed ratings (Par 102):93,92,90,90,85 84,84
CSF £16.95 CT £86.48 TOTE £4.40: £2.40, £2.50; EX 10.70 Place 6 £11.47, Place 5 £9.79.
Owner The Gap Partnership **Bred** Fonthill Stud **Trained** Pulborough, W Sussex
■ Tower Hill (20/1) refused to enter the stalls, Rule 4 does not apply.

FOCUS
A fair handicap but a very moderate winning time for the grade. Nevertheless the form looks solid with those in the frame behind the winner close to their marks.
T/Plt: £21.40 to a £1 stake. Pool: £47,947.00. 1,633.95 winning tickets. T/Qpdt: £7.90 to a £1 stake. Pool: £4,083.90. 382.35 winning tickets. JN

4302 YARMOUTH (L-H)
Wednesday, August 16

OFFICIAL GOING: Good
Wind: Variable Weather: Sunny

4491 BBC RADIO NORFOLK CLAIMING STKS — 1m 2f 21y
2:20 (2:22) (Class 6) 3-Y-O **£2,266** (£674; £337; £168) **Stalls** Low

Form			RPR
5025	1	**Cool Isle**[6] 4280 3-7-13 46 .... (b) JohnMcAuley(3) 1 (P Howling) *pressed ldr: rdn ahd 2f out: a holding rival fnl f* **10/1**	43
2340	2 1	**Digger Boy**[14] 4044 3-9-11 60 .... PhilipRobinson 3 (M A Jarvis) *led: drvn 3f out: hdd 2f out: one pce and no imp fnl f* **7/2**[1]	64

The Form Book, Raceform Ltd, Compton, RG20 6NL

0235 **3** *1* **Simplified**[15] 4016 3-8-0 44 ... JimmyQuinn 2 37
(J Pearce) *chsd ldrs: rdn 3f out: styd on same pce fnl 2f* **4/1**[2]

0005 **4** *shd* **Rockatorri**[7] 4263 3-8-0 36 ... (b) HayleyTurner 8 37
(G G Margarson) *a pressing ldrs: rdn over 2f out: hld whn hung rt over 1f out* **33/1**

030 **5** *4* **Top Level (IRE)**[6] 4297 3-8-10 ... TPQueally 7 39
(M G Quinlan) *towards rr: rdn over 3f out: nvr looked like chalng after* **17/2**[3]

0005 **6** *½* **Mujelle**[16] 3999 3-8-13 51 ... JimmyFortune 6 41
(D K Ivory) *towards rr: rdn over 3f out: fnd nothing fnl 2f* **14/1**

2061 **7** *½* **Coffin Dodger**[7] 4263 3-7-13 45 ... KirstyMilczarek(7) 4 34
(C N Allen) *dwlt: bhd: rdn over 3f out: sn no rspnse* **4/1**[2]

2330 **8** *3* **Ruffie (IRE)**[14] 4044 3-9-0 65 ... (v[1]) ChrisCatlin 5 36
(Miss Gay Kelleway) *bhd: u.p 3f out: no rspnse: wl btn over 2f out* **7/2**[1]

05-5 **U** **Zastra's Pride**[141] 786 3-7-7 35 ... BRoper(7) 9 —
(W G M Turner) *2nd early but sddle sn slipped: uns rdr after 4f* **33/1**

2m 10.88s (2.78) **Going Correction** +0.225s/f (Good) **9** Ran SP% **116.6**
Speed ratings (Par 98):97,96,95,95,92 91,91,88,—
CSF £45.47 TOTE £10.80: £2.90, £1.70, £1.20; EX 50.30 Trifecta £104.20 Pool £422.99, 2.88 w/u.
Owner Rory Murphy **Bred** The C H F Partnership **Trained** Newmarket, Suffolk
■ Stewards' Enquiry : Hayley Turner one-day ban: careless riding (Aug 27)

FOCUS
A weak claimer limited by the fourth and unlikely to produce winners.

4492 EUROPEAN BREEDERS FUND MAIDEN STKS 6f 3y
2:50 (2:50) (Class 5) 2-Y-O **£3,562** (£1,059; £529; £264) **Stalls** High

Form RPR

4 **1** **Curzon Prince (IRE)**[12] 4105 2-9-3 ... TPQueally 3 73
(C F Wall) *pressed ldr: drvn 2f out: styd on gamely and sustained run to ld fnl 50 yds* **6/1**[3]

4 **2** *¾* **Dodge City (USA)**[18] 3923 2-9-3 ... PhilipRobinson 7 71
(J Noseda) *set brisk pce: clr early: rdn over 1f out: hdd and nt qckn fnl 50 yds* **2/5**[1]

3 *4* **Nabra** 2-8-12 ... JimmyFortune 5 54
(J H M Gosden) *dwlt: bhd: rdn 1/2-way: kpt on to go 3rd 1f out: no ch w ldrs* **9/2**[2]

0 **4** *1½* **The Light Fandango**[60] 2631 2-8-12 ... AdrianMcCarthy 4 49
(R A Harris) *chsd ldng pair: pushed along 1/2-way: outpcd wl over 1f out* **80/1**

0 **5** *3* **Hot Cherry**[9] 4207 2-8-12 ... HayleyTurner 6 40
(J M P Eustace) *hrd drvn over 3f out: struggling after* **33/1**

6 *9* **Tibinta** 2-8-12 ... ChrisCatlin 2 13
(Rae Guest) *chsd ldrs: rdn 1/2-way: wknd over 2f out: eased ins fnl f* **50/1**

1m 15.62s (1.92) **Going Correction** +0.175s/f (Good) **6** Ran SP% **110.0**
Speed ratings (Par 94):94,93,87,85,81 69
CSF £8.67 TOTE £10.10: £2.50, £1.10; EX 13.80.
Owner Arkland International (uk) Ltd **Bred** Scuderia San Pancrazio **Trained** Newmarket, Suffolk

FOCUS
A decent maiden likely to produce winners. Not an easy race to rate at this stage.

NOTEBOOK
Curzon Prince(IRE), a close-up fourth in a decent maiden on his debut at Newmarket, received a nice tow from hot favourite Dodge City and stayed on too strongly for him inside the final furlong. Held in high regard by connections who can get a smart juvenile, as seen last season with Wake Up Maggie, he is heading the right way and reportedly has the £250,000 Newmarket Tattersalls Sales Stakes in October as his main aim. (op 7-1 tchd 8-1)
Dodge City(USA), a pleasing fourth on his debut at Ascot - the third has third won since - was made a hot favourite to build on that promise and Robinson was evidently keen for it not to turn into a sprint. However, in setting such a good clip, he left himself vulnerable to anything that was able to lay up and the winner ultimately outstayed him. He can win a maiden before going handicapping. (op 8-15 tchd 4-7 in places)
Nabra, bred to be effective at this distance at two, holds an entry in the Group 1 Cheveley Park Stakes, but she was conceding experience to the front pair and was never quite in the hunt. She can be expected to improve for this and can win a maiden before possibly stepping up in trip. (op 3-1 tchd 5-1)
The Light Fandango stepped up on her debut effort and seemed better suited by this extra furlong. She is the type to do better in low-grade nurseries. (op 66-1)
Hot Cherry still looks in need of the experience, and this half-sister to smart middle-distance mare Red Wine looks sure to improve once tackling further in nurseries. (tchd 28-1)
Tibinta, a 4,000gns purchase by Averti, showed up early on, but she dropped right away inside the final quarter-mile and it is likely she will benefit from the experience. (op 33-1)

4493 NORFOLK NELSON MUSEUM (S) STKS 5f 43y
3:20 (3:20) (Class 6) 2-Y-O **£2,266** (£674; £337; £168) **Stalls** High

Form RPR

6316 **1** **Danger Alley**[11] 4152 2-9-4 70 ... (b) ChrisCatlin 5 62
(E J O'Neill) *led: hrd drvn over 1f out: ears flat and hdd 100 yds out: led u.p fnl stride* **5/4**[1]

2222 **2** *hd* **House Arrest**[8] 4222 2-8-4 56 ... JamesDoyle(3) 7 50
(I A Wood) *t.k.h: chsd ldrs: n.m.r 2f out: edgd lft to chal 1f out: led 100 yds out: pipped post* **7/2**[2]

0425 **3** *1½* **Caj (IRE)**[16] 4006 2-8-7 58 ... JimmyQuinn 2 45
(M Quinn) *cl up on outer: rdn over 2f out: edgd sltly rt over 1f out: ev ch tl outpcd ins fnl f* **17/2**

1105 **4** *2* **Top Tier**[13] 4088 2-8-13 64 ... RobbieFitzpatrick 3 44
(Peter Grayson) *cl up: rdn over 2f out: wkng whn squeezed out over 1f out* **4/1**[3]

2025 **5** *5* **Peggys Flower**[16] 4007 2-8-13 68 ... JimmyFortune 4 26
(N A Callaghan) *dwlt: plld hrd in last: lost tch wl over 1f out* **11/2**

65.42 secs (2.62) **Going Correction** +0.175s/f (Good) **5** Ran SP% **112.6**
Speed ratings (Par 92):86,85,83,80,72
CSF £6.08 TOTE £1.90: £1.20, £2.20; EX 6.10.The winner was bought in for 4,000gns. House Arrest was claimed by A. J. McCabe for £6,000
Owner Scholes,Kirkham & Fretwell **Bred** J S Middleton And Miss K S Buckley **Trained** Averham Park, Notts

FOCUS
A modest time, even for a juvenile seller, but the form looks solid and the winner is better than the grade.

NOTEBOOK
Danger Alley, winner of a selling nursery over course and distance on his penultimate outing, ran well behind a useful type in Vale Of Belvoir last time and he was right at home on this drop back down in grade. He made hard enough work of winning, outbattling the runner-up late on, but is a tough sort likely to win again at the right sort of level. (op 2-1)
House Arrest has developed a nasty habit of finishing second - this the fifth consecutive occasion - and although she appears to do little wrong, there is a strong suspicion she does not have the biggest of hearts. That said, she will probably find a race eventually if continuing to perform consistently. (op 10-3)
Caj(IRE) travelled strongly on the outer and held every chance, but the front two pulled away from her inside the final furlong. She may benefit from a step up to six furlongs. (op 7-1 tchd 9-1)
Top Tier was the disappointment of the race as she had looked a useful sort for the grade earlier in the season and had won a nursery at Musselburgh in July. She was already beaten when being squeezed for room and may be ready for a return to six furlongs. (op 7-2)
Peggys Flower, without the cheekpieces this time, was unable to reproduce last month's course form and could not pick up having pulled so hard early on. (op 9-2)

4494 GREAT YARMOUTH & GORLESTON ADVERTISER FILLIES' H'CAP 6f 3y
3:50 (3:51) (Class 5) (0-70,69) 3-Y-O **£3,562** (£1,059; £529; £264) **Stalls** High

Form RPR

0000 **1** **Forces Sweetheart**[11] 4164 3-8-3 **47** ... (v[1]) HayleyTurner 5 62
(M L W Bell) *prom: led over 2f out: clr and in command fnl 100 yds: pushed out* **20/1**

0026 **2** *2½* **Tilly's Dream**[16] 3996 3-9-7 **65** ... PhilipRobinson 3 72
(G C H Chung) *handy: chsd wnr and clr of rest wl over 1f out: one pce and no imp fnl 100 yds* **11/2**[3]

0401 **3** *3½* **Tiber Tilly**[7] 4265 3-9-11 **69** 6ex ... RichardThomas 13 66
(N P Littmoden) *drvn and outpcd 1/2-way: passed btn horses fr wl over 1f out: nvr able to chal* **11/4**[1]

40 **4** *hd* **Mandarin Lady**[56] 2763 3-8-10 **54** ... JimmyQuinn 10 50
(Miss J A Camacho) *last away: bhd: r.o stoutly ins fnl f: too much to do* **11/1**

2042 **5** *1¼* **Discotheque (USA)**[11] 4142 3-9-5 **63** ... J-PGuillambert 7 55
(P Howling) *towards rr: rdn 2f out: kpt on ins fnl f but no ch w ldrs* **8/1**

-004 **6** *1* **Fun Time**[20] 3866 3-8-4 **48** ... ChrisCatlin 2 37
(M R Channon) *bhd: effrt 1/2-way: rdn 2f out: btn over 1f out* **13/2**

-060 **7** *1¾* **Fancy You (IRE)**[17] 3988 3-8-2 **46** oh1 ... FrancisNorton 9 30
(A W Carroll) *chsd ldrs: rdn 2f out: sn no ch but kpt on nicely ins fnl f* **16/1**

0543 **8** *shd* **Kineta (USA)**[14] 4045 3-9-2 **60** ... JimmyFortune 1 44
(W R Muir) *cl up on outside tl rdn and wknd over 2f out* **17/2**

0460 **9** *5* **Whisper Inthe Wind (IRE)**[7] 4265 3-8-2 **53** ... LukeMorris(7) 8 22
(Miss J Feilden) *cl up over 3f: lost pl qckly* **20/1**

0062 **10** *2½* **Halfwaytoparadise**[11] 4143 3-9-1 **62** ... (p) SaleemGolam(3) 12 23
(W G M Turner) *drvn 1/2-way: racing awkwardly after and sn btn* **5/1**[2]

0-00 **11** *7* **Savannah Pride (IRE)**[11] 4143 3-8-11 **55** ... (v[1]) TPO'Shea 6 —
(Ernst Oertel) *led tl rdn and hdd over 2f out: fdd rapidly: t.o and eased* **40/1**

1m 14.09s (0.39) **Going Correction** +0.175s/f (Good) **11** Ran SP% **119.9**
Speed ratings (Par 97):104,100,96,95,94 92,90,90,83,80 70
CSF £126.37 CT £413.85 TOTE £25.00: £4.80, £2.30, £2.30; EX 220.70 TRIFECTA Not won. Pool of £398.51 carried over to 19th August.
Owner Richard I Morris Jr **Bred** Barton Stud Partnership **Trained** Newmarket, Suffolk

FOCUS
Moderate sprint form, but solid enough for the grade with a reasonable time.
Kineta(USA) Official explanation: vet said filly finished sore behind the saddle
Halfwaytoparadise Official explanation: trainer said filly suffered a breathing problem

4495 GREATER YARMOUTH TOURIST AUTHORITY MAIDEN FILLIES' STKS 6f 3y
4:20 (4:23) (Class 5) 3-Y-O **£3,238** (£963; £481; £240) **Stalls** High

Form RPR

2232 **1** **Madame Medusa (IRE)**[22] 3826 3-9-0 72 ... (v) PhilipRobinson 8 72
(J A R Toller) *mde all: drvn clr over 1f out: kpt rt up to work* **6/5**[1]

2 *4* **Jodrell Bank (IRE)**[396] 3554 3-9-0 ... JimmyQuinn 6 60
(W Jarvis) *keen chsng ldrs: rdn to chse wnr wl over 1f out: in vain pursuit after* **10/1**[3]

3 *1* **Dorelia (IRE)** 3-9-0 ... JimmyFortune 9 57
(J H M Gosden) *slowly away and swished tail leaving stalls: bhd tl prog 2f out: wnt 3rd 1f out: unable to chal and looked green* **9/4**[2]

00 **4** *2½* **Mozie Cat (IRE)**[95] 1680 3-9-0 ... TPO'Shea 1 50
(John Berry) *towards rr: rdn and btn 2f out: snatched mod 4th* **12/1**

-000 **5** *nk* **Wendals**[62] 2589 3-9-0 61 ... ChrisCatlin 7 49
(Rae Guest) *mounted crse and taken down early: chsd wnr: rdn over 2f out: lost pl qckly fnl f* **10/1**[3]

0- **6** *1¼* **Prinquet (USA)**[375] 4163 3-9-0 ... HayleyTurner 3 45
(C E Brittain) *taken down early: chsd ldrs: drvn over 2f out: fdd wl over 1f out* **16/1**

0460 **7** *12* **Kellys Dream (IRE)**[51] 2939 3-8-7 56 ... ChrisCavanagh(7) 10 9
(M Quinn) *racd alone stands side w rest in centre: struggling over 2f out: hung lft ins fnl f* **12/1**

1m 14.37s (0.67) **Going Correction** +0.175s/f (Good) **7** Ran SP% **115.7**
Speed ratings (Par 97):102,96,95,92,91 89,73
CSF £15.07 TOTE £2.20: £1.30, £5.70; EX 14.70 Trifecta £61.40 Pool £426.96, 4.93 w/u.
Owner N R M Williams **Bred** Barronstown And Orpendale **Trained** Newmarket, Suffolk
■ Tumpuluna (15/2, unseated rider and bolted before start) was withdrawn. R4, deduct 10p in the £.

FOCUS
An uncompetitive sprint maiden, but it may produce the occasional winner.

4496 DRONSFIELDS MERCEDES H'CAP 7f 3y
4:50 (4:52) (Class 5) (0-70,70) 3-Y-O+ **£3,562** (£1,059; £529; £264) **Stalls** High

Form RPR

2231 **1** **Border Artist**[16] 4009 7-9-1 **59** ... JimmyQuinn 12 70+
(J Pearce) *hld up: prog gng wl to ld wl over 1f out: rdn out: comf* **10/3**[1]

1500 **2** *1¾* **Curtain Bluff**[13] 4077 4-9-12 **70** ... (v) JimmyFortune 2 76
(M R Channon) *t.k.h: sn chsng ldrs: drvn over 1f out: wl hld ins fnl f* **13/2**[3]

0302 **3** *hd* **Silent Storm**[22] 3827 6-9-9 **67** ... J-PGuillambert 3 73
(C A Cyzer) *chsd ldrs: rdn 3f out: racd awkwardly: no imp fr over 1f out* **7/2**[2]

1050 **4** *nk* **Polish Index**[28] 3642 4-9-7 **65** ... (p) PhilipRobinson 6 70
(J R Jenkins) *led: drvn and hdd wl over 1f out: wknd nr fin and jst lost 3rd* **9/1**

0005 **5** *½* **Mystic Man (FR)**[12] 4116 8-9-8 **66** ... RobbieFitzpatrick 10 70
(I W McInnes) *hld up and bhd: drvn and outpcd over 3f out: kpt on ins fnl f but unable to chal* **7/1**

0000 **6** *shd* **Hit's Only Money (IRE)**[8] 4230 6-9-0 **58** ... AdrianMcCarthy 11 62
(R A Harris) *plld hrd early and hld up: drvn wl over 2f out: one pce and n.d after* **10/1**

0040 **7** *½* **Benny The Ball (USA)**[7] 4248 5-8-6 **53** ... JamesDoyle(3) 9 55
(N P Littmoden) *jnd ldr briefly 1/2-way: rdn and no ex fnl 2f* **8/1**

0060 **8** *nk* **Warden Warren**[8] 4233 8-8-8 **52** oh5 ow1 ... (p) BrianReilly 8 54?
(Mrs C A Dunnett) *chsd ldrs: rdn 2f out: no imp* **20/1**

0503 **9** *6* **Valentino Swing (IRE)**[11] 4143 3-9-5 **68** ... (b) FrancisNorton 13 54
(J L Spearing) *drvn and struggling over 2f out: eased fnl f* **10/1**

-000 **10** *6* **Star Fern**[12] 4114 5-8-7 **51** oh12 .... TPO'Shea 1 21
(M J Attwater) *s.s: bhd: struggling 3f out: eased 1f out* **28/1**

1m 27.55s (0.95) **Going Correction** +0.175s/f (Good)
WFA 3 from 4yo+ 5lb **10** Ran SP% **118.6**
Speed ratings (Par 103):101,99,98,98,97 97,97,96,89,83
CSF £25.87 CT £83.20 TOTE £3.70: £1.50, £3.30, £2.20; EX 22.70 Trifecta £64.30 Pool £313.64, 3.46 w/u.
Owner Kevin Pattinson **Bred** Chippenham Lodge Stud Ltd **Trained** Newmarket, Suffolk
FOCUS
A modest handicap that looks sound enough rated through the runner-up and third.

4497 VISITNORFOLK.COM H'CAP 1m 2f 21y
5:20 (5:21) (Class 6) (0-55,61) 3-Y-O+ **£2,331** (£693; £346; £173) **Stalls** Low

Form RPR

6001 **1** **Colton**[7] 4257 3-9-13 **61** 6ex .... PhilipRobinson 11 73+
(J M P Eustace) *hld up last for over 5f: smooth prog after: led over 1f out: sn in command: rdn out* **7/2**[1]

0054 **2** *1 1/4* **Ruling Reef**[18] 3944 4-9-5 **45** .... HayleyTurner 7 53
(M D I Usher) *bhd: l0th and pushed along st: hdwy over 2f out: kpt on ins fnl f: snatched 2nd but no ch w wnr* **8/1**

0000 **3** *nk* **Diktatorship (IRE)**[71] 2316 3-9-1 **52** .... JamesDoyle(3) 8 59
(Ernst Oertel) *hld up towards rr: hdwy 4f out: led 2f out tl over 1f out: drvn and one pced: lost 2nd nr fin* **28/1**

4064 **4** *5* **Prince Of The May**[18] 3948 4-9-12 **52** .... JimmyFortune 5 50+
(H Morrison) *led: hdd over 5f out: led again 3f out tl 2f out: racd w v awkward hd carriage and btn over 1f out: hung lft* **5/1**[2]

0020 **5** *1/2* **Silver Court**[13] 4068 4-9-8 **48** .... FrancisNorton 4 45
(A W Carroll) *t.k.h in rr: effrt 4f out: rdn and n.d fnl 3f* **12/1**

0006 **6** *1 1/4* **Native American**[23] 3798 4-10-0 **54** .... RobbieFitzpatrick 3 49
(T D McCarthy) *midfield: rdn 4f out: btn over 2f out* **16/1**

000 **7** *1/2* **Miss Ruby**[36] 3387 4-9-6 **46** .... JimmyQuinn 6 40
(Rae Guest) *cl up: chal briefly 3f out: rdn and wknd 2f out* **40/1**

3063 **8** *nk* **Tacid**[40] 3263 4-9-6 **46** .... TPO'Shea 13 39
(Dr J D Scargill) *pressed ldrs: rdn 4f out: fdd over 2f out* **14/1**

4266 **9** *3* **Wood Fern (UAE)**[29] 3610 6-8-10 **41** .... RoryMoore(5) 2 28
(W M Brisbourne) *bhd: rdn over 4f out: nvr on terms after* **6/1**[3]

-366 **10** *7* **Kernel Dowery (IRE)**[11] 4139 6-9-6 **49** ....(p) SaleemGolam(3) 9 23
(W R Swinburn) *prom: led over 5f out tl 3f out: rdn and dropped out rapidly: eased fnl f* **7/1**

11 *9* **All Rise (GER)**[88] 4-9-5 **45** .... ChrisCatlin 1 2
(Ian Williams) *prom: rdn over 4f out: wknd wl over 2f out: eased and t.o fnl f* **6/1**[3]

2m 9.90s (1.80) **Going Correction** +0.225s/f (Good)
WFA 3 from 4yo+ 8lb **11** Ran SP% **117.2**
Speed ratings (Par 101):101,100,99,95,95 94,93,93,91,85 78
CSF £31.69 CT £679.24 TOTE £3.60: £2.00, £2.20, £8.70; EX 43.00 Trifecta £279.00 Part won. 0.20 winning units. Pool of 314.40 carried over to 19th August. Place 6 £6.40, Place 5 £3.22.
Owner Park Lodge Racing **Bred** Dunchurch Lodge Stud Co **Trained** Newmarket, Suffolk
FOCUS
A moderate handicap but the winner is lightly raced and progressive, while the first three pulled clear of the rest and the form looks solid enough with the runner-up to this year's form.
T/Plt: £13.60 to a £1 stake. Pool: £49,048.80. 2,622.20 winning tickets. T/Qpdt: £4.60 to a £1 stake. Pool: £2,676.80. 427.50 winning tickets. IM

4498 - 4501a (Foreign Racing) - See Raceform Interactive

4269 GOWRAN PARK (R-H)
Wednesday, August 16

OFFICIAL GOING: Good to yielding

4502a DENNY CORDELL EUROPEAN BREEDERS FUND FILLIES STKS (GROUP 3) 1m 1f 100y
6:50 (6:50) 3-Y-O+ **£44,827** (£13,103; £6,206; £2,068)

RPR

1 **Race For The Stars (USA)**[11] 4127 3-8-12 110 .... KFallon 5 106+
(A P O'Brien, Ire) *trckd ldrs: 5th 1/2-way: rdn to chal 2f out: 2nd over 1f out: led ins fnl f: kpt on wl* **5/4**[1]

2 *1/2* **Blessyourpinksox (IRE)**[31] 3576 5-9-5 98 .... JMurtagh 8 103
(Peter Casey, Ire) *a.p: 3rd 1/2-way: chal early st: 3rd and kpt on ins fnl f* **5/2**[2]

3 *1* **Ardbrae Lady**[46] 3105 3-8-12 105 .... FMBerry 10 101
(Joseph G Murphy, Ire) *hld up in tch: 6th 1/2-way: smooth hdwy early st: led over 1 1/2f out: hdd ins fnl f: kpt on u.p* **11/2**[3]

4 *1* **Be My Queen (IRE)**[9] 4219 3-8-12 100 .... JAHeffernan 1 100
(A P O'Brien, Ire) *hld up towards rr: plld hrd early: prog into 6th 2f out: 4th and kpt on fnl f* **8/1**

5 *1/2* **Mrs Snaffles (IRE)**[31] 3576 3-8-12 95 .... WSupple 3 99
(Francis Ennis, Ire) *hld up in tch: 7th appr st: kpt on same pce fr 2f out* **20/1**

6 *1 1/2* **Poetical (IRE)**[54] 2824 5-9-5 .... MJKinane 2 96
(D J Daly) *cl up in 2nd: rdn st: led briefly over 1 1/2f out: sn no ex* **50/1**

7 *2* **Lily Elsie (IRE)**[7] 4272 3-8-12 78 .... CO'Donoghue 9 92
(A P O'Brien, Ire) *chsd ldrs: 4th 1/2-way: 5th into st: sn wknd* **20/1**

8 *2 1/2* **Sweet Petite (IRE)**[6] 4312 3-8-12 84 ....(b) PJSmullen 6 88
(Kevin F O'Donnell, Ire) *led: rdn and hdd over 1 1/2f out: sn wknd* **40/1**

9 *3 1/2* **Aunty Euro (IRE)**[31] 3578 4-9-5 84 .... DJCondon 7 82
(Patrick Morris, Ire) *a towards rr: wknd st* **50/1**

2m 4.00s
WFA 3 from 4yo+ 7lb **10** Ran SP% **115.4**
CSF £4.13 TOTE £1.80: £1.10, £1.80, £1.90; DF 4.80.
Owner Mrs John Magnier **Bred** Strategy Bloodstock **Trained** Ballydoyle, Co Tipperary
■ The first Group race to be run at Gowran Park.

NOTEBOOK
Race For The Stars(USA), who has been finding life tough in the very top fillies' races so far this season, appreciated the drop in grade and, although she was made to work hard for her victory, got the confidence booster connections were looking for. Although not quite up to Group One class, there are more decent races to be won with her. (op Evens tchd 11/8)
Blessyourpinksox(IRE), who has made the step up into Pattern company this season after a spell over hurdles, gave the winner a race. She looks capable of scoring again at Listed level, and on this evidence might even win a Group race. (op 3/1 tchd 9/4)
Ardbrae Lady, who finished a distant runner-up in the Irish 1000 Guineas, travelled well into the race, but could not find another gear in the closing stages. She may be better back at a mile. (op 5/1 tchd 6/1)
Be My Queen(IRE), a stable-companion of the winner, was too keen early on this step up in trip and could not pick up in the closing stages. (op 7/1)

4503 - 4505a (Foreign Racing) - See Raceform Interactive

4466 BEVERLEY (R-H)
Thursday, August 17

OFFICIAL GOING: Good
The ground had dried out slightly since the previous day and was described as 'genuine good'.
Wind: Light, half-behind Weather: Fine but overcast and cool

4506 HULL TRUCK THEATRE "LADIES DAY" PRODUCTION (S) H'CAP 2m 35y
2:10 (2:10) (Class 6) (0-60,55) 4-Y-O+ **£3,238** (£963; £481; £240) **Stalls** High

Form RPR

-002 **1** **Dimashq**[9] 4227 4-8-6 **40** .... DaleGibson 7 49+
(Ronald Thompson) *hld up: hdwy to chse ldr over 6f out: led over 2f out: styd on strly: readily* **11/2**

5635 **2** *3* **Mr Maxim**[9] 4229 4-9-5 **53** ....(v) DeanMcKeown 3 57
(R M Whitaker) *chsd ldrs: effrt over 3f out: wnt 2nd over 2f out: no imp* **5/1**[3]

6646 **3** *3/4* **Mulligan's Pride (IRE)**[8] 4252 5-9-7 **55** .... RobertWinston 4 58
(G A Swinbank) *hld up: hdwy 5f out: wnt 3rd over 1f out: kpt on same pce* **15/8**[1]

0020 **4** *9* **Best Port (IRE)**[5] 4380 10-9-5 **53** .... DavidAllan 6 45
(J Parkes) *mid-div: drvn 5f out: one pce fnl 3f* **5/2**[2]

00/4 **5** *9* **Protocol (IRE)**[39] 2395 12-8-2 **36** oh6 ....(tp) RoystonFfrench 2 18
(Mrs S Lamyman) *s.i.s: drvn and sme hdwy 7f out: lost pl over 4f out* **16/1**

00/0 **6** *5* **Luferton Lane (IRE)**[9] 4229 9-7-11 **36** oh10 .... NataliaGemelova(5) 1 12
(R F Marvin) *hld up in rr: hdwy on outside 7f out: lost pl over 3f out* **66/1**

0-60 **7** *6* **Ivana Illyich (IRE)**[11] 3944 4-8-2 **36** oh2 ....(p) PaulHanagan 8 4
(J S Wainwright) *chsd ldrs: lost pl over 2f out* **16/1**

-060 **8** *1/2* **Starmix**[45] 3140 5-8-7 **41** ....(b) PaulMulrennan 5 9
(G A Harker) *led: hung rt and hdd over 2f out: nt run on* **22/1**

3m 39.81s (0.31) **Going Correction** +0.05s/f (Good) **8** Ran SP% **113.0**
Speed ratings (Par 101):101,99,99,94,90 87,84,84
CSF £32.20 CT £69.38 TOTE £4.60: £1.40, £2.00, £1.10; EX 23.80.There was no bid for the winner. Mr Maxim was claimed by G. Doel for £6,000.
Owner B Bruce **Bred** Darley **Trained** Stainforth, S Yorks
FOCUS
As bad a seller as you will find and the genuine winner made the most of a golden opportunity.

4507 ST JOHN EXIT COLLECTION FILLIES' H'CAP 5f
2:45 (2:46) (Class 5) (0-70,70) 3-Y-O+ **£3,562** (£1,059; £529; £264) **Stalls** High

Form RPR

-110 **1** **Bahamian Bay**[30] 3608 4-8-6 **49** oh4 .... RoystonFfrench 15 59
(M Brittain) *mde virtually all: hld on gamely* **11/2**[2]

060 **2** *hd* **Diamond Katie (IRE)**[12] 4157 4-8-6 **49** .... KimTinkler 10 59
(N Tinkler) *chsd ldrs on ins: upsides 1f out: no ex towards fin* **8/1**

1532 **3** *1* **Estoille**[9] 4232 5-8-8 **51** .... PaulHanagan 9 57
(Mrs S Lamyman) *chsd ldrs: kpt on same pce ins last* **7/2**[1]

340 **4** *nk* **Riquewihr**[12] 4135 6-9-10 **67** ....(p) RobertWinston 7 72
(J S Wainwright) *mid-div: hdwy 2f out: styd on ins last* **7/1**[3]

-040 **5** *3/4* **Princess Cleo**[47] 3087 3-9-11 **70** .... PaulMulrennan 4 72
(T D Easterby) *sn chsng ldrs: nt qckn appr fnl f* **25/1**

3366 **6** *1/2* **Making Music**[20] 3912 3-9-6 **65** ....(p) DavidAllan 2 65+
(T D Easterby) *mid-div: hdwy over 1f out: styd on towards fin* **16/1**

-400 **7** *shd* **Elisha (IRE)**[12] 4157 4-8-6 **49** oh2 ....(p) CatherineGannon 13 49
(K A Ryan) *chsd ldrs: kpt on same pce appr fnl f* **11/1**

2040 **8** *1* **Sahara Silk (IRE)**[41] 3267 5-9-2 **62** ....(v) PatrickMathers(3) 12 58
(D Shaw) *rr-div: hdwy 2f out: styd on ins last* **8/1**

0005 **9** *2* **Westlake Bond (IRE)**[20] 3912 4-8-6 **49** oh11 ....(p) GylesParkin 3 38
(G R Oldroyd) *in rr: sme hdwy 2f out: nvr on terms* **66/1**

3400 **10** *1* **Quadrophenia**[53] 2896 3-8-10 **55** .... J-PGuillambert 11 41
(J G Given) *bhd: hdwy on inner 2f out: nvr nr ldrs* **10/1**

006 **11** *1* **Fayr Sky (IRE)**[19] 3943 3-9-4 **63** .... MickyFenton 5 45
(J J Quinn) *mid-div on outer: nvr a factor* **20/1**

0-00 **12** *nk* **Golband**[9] 4230 4-9-3 **65** .... MichaelJStainton(5) 14 46
(R F Marvin) *chsd ldrs: lost pl appr fnl f* **16/1**

6600 **13** *1* **Desertina (IRE)**[10] 4198 4-8-1 **49** oh6 .... NataliaGemelova(5) 6 26
(R M Whitaker) *s.i.s: a in rr* **33/1**

6-00 **14** *3/4* **Swallow Senora (IRE)**[7] 4306 4-8-6 **49** oh8 ....(b) HayleyTurner 1 24
(M C Chapman) *s.i.s: a in rr* **100/1**

0-00 **15** *9* **Millsy**[78] 2136 4-8-10 **53** .... AdrianTNicholls 8 —
(J L Spearing) *mid-div: lost pl over 2f out: sn bhd and eased* **20/1**

62.33 secs (-1.67) **Going Correction** -0.30s/f (Firm)
WFA 3 from 4yo+ 2lb **15** Ran SP% **120.3**
Speed ratings (Par 100):101,100,99,98,97 96,96,94,91,90 88,87,86,85,70
CSF £44.98 CT £183.06 TOTE £7.40: £2.50, £2.40, £1.70; EX 53.40.
Owner Mel Brittain **Bred** The National Stud **Trained** Warthill, N Yorks
FOCUS
A moderate handicap and as usual here the draw was vital. Ordinary form rated through the runner-up.
Swallow Senora(IRE) Official explanation: jockey said saddle slipped

4508 NICK WILMOT-SMITH MEMORIAL H'CAP 1m 1f 207y
3:15 (3:15) (Class 3) (0-90,89) 3-Y-O+ **£9,067** (£2,697; £1,348; £673) **Stalls** High

Form RPR

603/ **1** **Altay**[652] 6533 9-8-13 **72** .... TonyHamilton 2 81
(R A Fahey) *chsd ldrs: led over 1f out: hld on towards fin* **50/1**

1000 **2** *1* **Along The Nile**[5] 4379 4-9-6 **79** ....(t) DO'Donohoe 10 91+
(K G Reveley) *t.k.h in rr: nt clr run over 2f out: swtchd outside over 1f out: fin fast: nt quite rch wnr* **22/1**

01-4 **3** *nk* **Dynacam (USA)**[99] 1586 3-8-13 **80** .... RobertWinston 3 87
(Sir Michael Stoute) *chsd ldrs: effrt over 3f out: kpt on same pce ins last* **11/2**[2]

4125 **4** *1* **Mount Usher**[26] 3747 4-8-13 **72** .... DeanMcKeown 7 77
(G A Swinbank) *trckd ldrs: chal and hung rt 1f out: kpt on same pce* **7/1**[3]

6002 **5** *1 1/4* **Diktatorial**[12] 4131 4-9-10 **83** ....(t) TPO'Shea 9 85+
(G A Butler) *t.k.h in rr: hdwy and in tch after 3f: effrt 3f out: kpt on same pce appr fnl f* **8/1**

6622 **6** *nk* **Paparaazi (IRE)**[12] 4137 4-8-13 **72** .... PaulHanagan 8 76+
(R A Fahey) *trckd ldrs: nt clr run and dropped bk over 1f out: styd on wl ins last* **12/1**

5-01 **7** *1 3/4* **Rhinebird**[55] 2825 3-9-8 **89** .... OscarUrbina 4 87
(J R Fanshawe) *s.i.s: hdwy and in tch over 5f out: one pce fnl 2f* **8/1**

3111 **8** *shd* **Nelsons Column (IRE)**[10] 4203 3-9-6 **87** 6ex .... PaulMulrennan 6 85
(G M Moore) *mde most tl 2f out: one pce* **3/1**[1]

2351 **9** *½* **Lucayan Dancer**[12] 4131 6-9-12 **85** .... AdrianTNicholls 12 82
(D Nicholls) *hld up in rr: effrt 3f out: swtchd outside over 1f out: nvr on terms* **14/1**

0010 **10** *nk* **Go Tech**[33] 3552 6-9-12 **85** .... DavidAllan 11 82
(T D Easterby) *sn w ldr: led 2f out: sn hdd and fdd* **9/1**

1224 **11** *3 ½* **Riley Boys (IRE)**[21] 3876 5-9-12 **85** .... J-PGuillambert 5 75
(J G Given) *t.k.h in rr: stdy hdwy on ins over 2f out: n.m.r over 1f out: sn wknd* **10/1**

2m 5.93s (-1.37) **Going Correction** +0.05s/f (Good)
WFA 3 from 4yo+ 8lb **11** Ran SP% **114.9**
Speed ratings (Par 107):107,106,105,105,104 103,102,102,102,101 99
CSF £870.23 CT £6856.51 TOTE £61.30: £14.00, £8.30, £2.50; EX 529.60.
Owner R M Jeffs & J Potter **Bred** Exors Of The Late J T Robson **Trained** Musley Bank, N Yorks

FOCUS
A decent handicap but a very steady pace resulted in a surprise winner and an unlucky runner-up, who is rated the clear winner.

NOTEBOOK
Altay, absent for almost two years, proved very game but he had luck on his side. The plan is to send him novice chasing this autumn.
Along The Nile ◆, only 1lb higher than his last win, was a very unlucky loser. Suited by the easier ground, he found himself locked behind a wall of horses early in the straight. Eventually making his way to the outside, he only needed a few more strides. He can surely gain compensation. (tchd 20-1)
Dynacam(USA), a solidly-made filly, stuck to her guns and was only found wanting inside the last. She should add to her record on easy ground. (op 5-1)
Mount Usher, 11lb higher than his last win, ran right up to his very best. (op 8-1)
Diktatorial, who looked really well, took a fierce grip. He kept on without ever really threatening and this may be as good as he is.
Paparaazi(IRE) found himself trapped between horses and dropped back several places. Sticking on at the finish, he is clearly in very good heart. Official explanation: jockey said gelding was denied a clear run (op 16-1)
Rhinebird, harshly handicapped on his maiden win, never got competitive and needs to be dropped several pounds if he is to get competitive. (tchd 17-2)
Nelsons Column(IRE), under his penalty, did not really force the pace and was comfortably run out of it in the final quarter mile. (op 5-2)
Riley Boys(IRE) Official explanation: jockey said gelding was denied a clear run

4509 BP DIMLINGTON NURSERY 7f 100y
3:50 (3:51) (Class 5) 2-Y-O **£3,562** (£1,059; £529; £264) **Stalls** High

Form RPR

553 **1** **Lemon Silk (IRE)**[28] 3669 2-8-13 **70** .... MickyFenton 6 72
(T P Tate) *chsd ldrs: led 1f out: kpt on wl* **8/1**[3]

652 **2** *1* **Al Raahi**[23] 3809 2-9-3 **74** .... RobertWinston 7 73+
(M R Channon) *bhd: gd hdwy on outer 2f out: edgd rt jst ins last: fin strly* **13/2**[2]

2124 **3** *hd* **Tencendur (IRE)**[13] 4100 2-9-5 **76** .... AdrianTNicholls 4 75
(D Nicholls) *trckd ldrs: hung rt and led 2f out: hdd 1f out: no ex* **8/1**[3]

553 **4** *nk* **Fares (IRE)**[13] 4107 2-8-13 **70** .... HayleyTurner 3 68
(C E Brittain) *prom: hung rt 2f out: styd on fnl f: no ex ins last* **18/1**

6453 **5** *nk* **Tarif (IRE)**[17] 3997 2-8-0 **62** .... RoryMoore(5) 2 60
(Mrs P Sly) *dwlt: hdwy on outside over 4f out: styd on fnl 2f* **14/1**

5323 **6** *2* **Centenary (IRE)**[8] 4250 2-9-4 **75** .... PaulHanagan 11 68
(J S Wainwright) *sn chsng ldrs: keeping on same pce whn carried rt jst ins last* **17/2**

0152 **7** *1 ¼* **Moonwalking**[8] 4250 2-9-7 **78** .... DaleGibson 9 68
(Jedd O'Keeffe) *in rr: kpt on fnl 2f: nvr nr ldrs* **11/2**[1]

5052 **8** *½* **Dansilver**[13] 4115 2-8-6 **63** ow2 .... PaulMulrennan 1 52
(D J Wintle) *chsd ldrs on outer: one pce fnl 2f* **25/1**

4352 **9** *hd* **Fongs Gazelle**[19] 3940 2-8-11 **68** .... RoystonFfrench 8 56
(M Johnston) *in rr: sn drvn along: kpt on fnl 3f: nvr nr ldrs* **11/2**[1]

2016 **10** *1 ¾* **Merry Moon (IRE)**[20] 3917 2-8-4 **61** .... DavidAllan 14 45
(M Dods) *prom: effrt over 2f out: one pce* **8/1**[3]

0602 **11** *2* **Only A Grand**[22] 3831 2-7-12 **60** ....(b) AurelioMedeiros(5) 13 39
(R Bastiman) *chsd ldrs: lost pl over 1f out* **20/1**

004 **12** *3 ½* **Devilfishpoker Com**[24] 3780 2-7-12 **55** oh7 ....(be[1]) DavidKinsella 10 26
(R C Guest) *led tl 2f out: sn wknd* **80/1**

524 **13** *16* **Kaladar (IRE)**[45] 3157 2-8-8 **65** .... DO'Donohoe 5 —
(K A Ryan) *in rr and drvn along: lost tch over 1f out: eased* **14/1**

1m 34.49s (0.18) **Going Correction** +0.05s/f (Good) **13** Ran SP% **116.4**
Speed ratings (Par 94):100,98,98,98,97 95,94,93,93,91 89,85,66
CSF £56.52 CT £433.35 TOTE £10.40: £2.50, £2.40, £3.20; EX 50.90.
Owner A S Helaissi **Bred** Duncan Grimley **Trained** Tadcaster, N Yorks

FOCUS
A fair nursery with a game winner but a somewhat unlucky runner-up. The third is the best guide to the level.

NOTEBOOK
Lemon Silk(IRE), a lean sort, proved suited by the step up in trip and he showed a very willing attitude. (op 7-1)
Al Raahi, on his toes and swishing his tail in the paddock, was interfered with at the start and had to bide his time at the back on this occasion. Forced to come wide for a run, he was eating up ground at the finish and would have won with a bit further to go. He richly deserves compensation. Official explanation: jockey said colt was hampered at start (op 7-1)
Tencendur(IRE) is running well in his new yard and after hanging when he hit the front, in the end he was just found lacking.
Fares(IRE) tended to hang under pressure but he was sticking on at the finish and will be suited by the full mile. (op 16-1)
Tarif(IRE), drawn wide, missed a beat at the start and was always having to travel wide. That first success cannot be far away. (op 12-1)
Centenary(IRE) was going nowhere when taken off a straight line just inside the last. (op 9-1)
Moonwalking, 2lb lower, never got competitive. (tchd 5-1)
Fongs Gazelle was soon making hard work of this and never really figured. (tchd 5-1)
Devilfishpoker Com Official explanation: jockey said gelding had no more to give
Kaladar(IRE) Official explanation: vet said gelding finished lame

4510 EBF HOLDERNESS PONY CLUB MAIDEN FILLIES' STKS 5f
4:25 (4:27) (Class 4) 2-Y-O **£5,181** (£1,541; £770; £384) **Stalls** High

Form RPR

3 **1** **Lucky Bee (IRE)**[18] 3982 2-9-0 .... RobertWinston 7 76
(G A Swinbank) *chsd ldrs: lft 2nd over 1f out: styd on to ld nr fin* **15/8**[2]

02 **2** *½* **Pretty Miss**[7] 4283 2-9-0 .... DO'Donohoe 2 74
(H Candy) *led: edgd rt over 1f out: hdd and no ex towards fin* **7/4**[1]

32 **3** *5* **Gap Princess (IRE)**[16] 4017 2-9-0 .... PaulHanagan 5 56
(R A Fahey) *chsd ldrs: lft mod 3rd over 1f out* **11/2**[3]

4 *1 ¾* **Glen Avon Girl (IRE)** 2-9-0 .... DavidAllan 10 50+
(T D Easterby) *mid-div: hdwy over 2f out: keeping on one pce whn hmpd over 1f out* **16/1**

5 *¾* **Bond Casino** 2-9-0 .... GylesParkin 1 47
(G R Oldroyd) *dwlt: bhd tl hdwy on outside fnl 2f* **66/1**

000 **6** *1 ¼* **Vizionary**[13] 4109 2-9-0 .... MickyFenton 9 43+
(Mrs P Sly) *sn outpcd: hdwy and mid-field over 2f out: hmpd over 1f out* **50/1**

7 *1* **Galway Girl (IRE)** 2-9-0 .... J-PGuillambert 8 39
(T D Easterby) *s.i.s: kpt on fnl 2f on outer: nvr on terms* **33/1**

8 *1 ¾* **Cranworth Blaze** 2-9-0 .... RoystonFfrench 13 33
(T J Etherington) *sn outpcd and in rr: nvr on terms* **33/1**

0 **9** *10* **Clappers (IRE)**[19] 3942 2-9-0 .... PaulMulrennan 6 —
(T D Easterby) *sn outpcd and bhd* **100/1**

0 **10** *nk* **Josr's Bank**[17] 3994 2-9-0 .... DaleGibson 11 —
(M W Easterby) *chsd ldrs: 5th and wkng whn hmpd over 1f out: bhd whn bdly hmpd ins last* **33/1**

11 *9* **Molto Duro (IRE)** 2-9-0 .... VHalliday 3 —
(N Wilson) *s.i.s: a bhd* **100/1**

02 **U** **Princess Ellis**[10] 4196 2-8-9 .... MichaelJStainton(5) 4 60+
(E J Alston) *w ldr: 1l down whn n.m.r on inner: stmbld and uns rdr over 1f out* **10/1**

62.67 secs (-1.33) **Going Correction** -0.30s/f (Firm) **12** Ran SP% **115.8**
Speed ratings (Par 93):98,97,89,86,85 83,81,78,62,62 47,—
CSF £5.12 TOTE £2.40: £1.50, £1.30, £1.70; EX 7.10.
Owner Mrs J Bellwood **Bred** Sean Madigan **Trained** Melsonby, N Yorks

FOCUS
A fair winning time for a race like this and the form looks sound for the grade.

NOTEBOOK
Lucky Bee(IRE) knew her job this time and stuck on under a most determined ride to show ahead near the line. Six will suit her better in nursery company. (tchd 13-8)
Pretty Miss, drawn one from the outside, travelled strongly in front only to be worn down near the line. A half-sister to Kyllachy, she lacks size and scope and an easier track will be in her favour. (op 13-8 tchd 15-8)
Gap Princess(IRE), drawn wide, could never get competeitive and a modest nursery or a claimer looks a better option. (tchd 6-1)
Glen Avon Girl(IRE), a tall newcomer, was very inexperienced and was only making limited headway when forced to take a side step. This will have opened her eyes. (op 20-1)
Bond Casino, who has size and scope, was very green to post. Drawn widest of all, she was very inexperienced but there was plenty to like about the way she was going about her work in the second half of the race. (op 80-1)
Vizionary, unsighted in three previous outing, was very keen to post. She was going nowhere when put out of her stride.
Princess Ellis, drawn wide, was soon upsides the leader on her inside. Left short of room as she edged across to the rail, she was getting the worst of the argument when he stumbled and gave her rider no chance. Fortunately neither was any the worse. (op 11-1)

4511 EAST RIDING H'CAP (FOR AMATEUR RIDERS) 1m 100y
5:00 (5:01) (Class 6) (0-55,55) 3-Y-O+ **£3,123** (£726; £726; £242) **Stalls** High

Form RPR

6000 **1** **Jewel Of India**[108] 1353 7-11-2 **50** ....(p) MissLEllison 6 57
(Mrs A L M King) *trckd ldrs: led over 1f out: hrd rdn and hld on* **33/1**

0-20 **2** *nk* **Wizard Of Us**[26] 3724 6-11-2 **55** .... MissMMullineaux(5) 8 61
(M Mullineaux) *chsd ldrs: chal over 1f out: no ex wl ins last* **18/1**

6656 **2** *dht* **Sriology (IRE)**[8] 4266 5-10-5 **46** ....(t) MrDarylChinn(7) 4 52+
(G Prodromou) *in rr: hdwy and swtchd to stands' side over 2f out: hrd rdn and styd on strly fnl f* **22/1**

0010 **4** *1 ½* **Sol Rojo**[19] 3948 4-11-2 **55** ....(v) MrSPearce(5) 16 58
(J Pearce) *mid-div: hdwy on ins over 2f out: kpt on same pce ins last* **4/1**[1]

0405 **5** *1* **They All Laughed**[14] 4069 3-10-10 **55** .... MrsMarieKing(5) 11 56
(P W Hiatt) *in rr: hdwy and c towards stands' side 3f out: kpt on fnl 2f* **8/1**

0400 **6** *¾* **Fairy Monarch (IRE)**[27] 3716 7-10-12 **49** ....(b) MissFayeBramley(3) 1 48
(P T Midgley) *stmbld s: hdwy over 5f out: edgd lft over 2f out: kpt on* **20/1**

0230 **7** *3* **Airedale Lad (IRE)**[73] 2286 5-11-1 **49** .... MissSBrotherton 12 42
(R M Whitaker) *hld up towards rr: effrt on inner over 2f out: nvr nr ldrs* **9/2**[2]

0002 **8** *2 ½* **Emperor's Well**[16] 4021 7-11-2 **55** ....(b) MissJCoward(5) 3 43
(M W Easterby) *mde most tl hdd & wknd over 1f out* **9/2**[2]

5-00 **9** *1 ½* **Compton Micky**[9] 4233 5-10-3 **44** .... MissAColley(7) 13 28
(R F Marvin) *t.k.h: in tch: lost pl over 1f out* **66/1**

-640 **10** *2 ½* **Pepper Road**[12] 4154 7-10-8 **47** .... MissRBastiman(5) 14 26
(R Bastiman) *hld up in rr: hdwy and c towards stands' side 3f out: wknd fnl 2f* **25/1**

/00- **11** *¾* **Rust En Vrede**[25] 4975 7-11-0 **48** .... MissADeniel 10 26
(J J Quinn) *in tch: effrt 3f out: sn btn* **6/1**[3]

0033 **12** *nk* **Hamaasy**[9] 4233 5-10-4 **45** .... MrJNewman(7) 5 22
(D Nicholls) *t.k.h: w ldr: edgd lft and lost pl over 1f out* **8/1**

13 *5* **Urban Freeway (IRE)**[808] 4895 7-10-12 **53** .... MrMLurcock(7) 7 20
(Robert Gray) *chsd ldrs: edgd lft and lost pl 2f out* **33/1**

00/0 **14** *7* **Oh Golly Gosh**[48] 3056 5-11-5 **53** ....(p) MrsEmmaLittmoden 15 5
(N P Littmoden) *sn bhd: t.o 3f out* **22/1**

/00- **15** *6* **Land Sun's Legacy (IRE)**[284] 4920 5-10-11 **52** ow4....(p) MrMDHill(7) 9 —
(J S Wainwright) *s.s: a bhd: t.o 3f out* **80/1**

1m 49.16s (1.76) **Going Correction** +0.05s/f (Good)
WFA 3 from 4yo+ 6lb **15** Ran SP% **124.0**
Speed ratings (Par 101):93,92,92,91,90 89,86,83,82,79 79,78,73,66,60
WIN: Jewel Of India £38.30. PL: £9.20, Wizard Of Us £5.90, Sriology £5.90. EX: JOI/WOU £310.80, JOI/S £345.90. CSF: JOI/WOU £256.22, JOI/S £304.43. TRIC: JOI/WOU/S £6,297.59, JOI/S/WOU £6,343.83. Place 6 £1,048.42, Place 5 £668.22.
Owner Touchwood Racing **Bred** Baldernock Bloodstock Ltd **Trained** Wilmcote, Warwicks
■ Stewards' Enquiry : Mr Daryl Chinn three-day ban: used whip with excessive frequency (Sep 10, Nov 6,13)

FOCUS
Worse than a seller and they ended up all over the track with a multiplicity of riding styles - some of them not pretty. the form is rated around the principals.
T/Jkpt: Not won. T/Plt: £1,410.30 to a £1 stake. Pool: £42,695.55. 22.10 winning tickets. T/Qpdt: £448.30 to a £1 stake. Pool: £2,726.50. 4.50 winning tickets. WG

4282 CHEPSTOW (L-H)

Thursday, August 17 (Evening)

4512 Meeting Abandoned - Waterlogged

4086 MUSSELBURGH (R-H)

Thursday, August 17

OFFICIAL GOING: Good to firm (good in places)

Wind: Moderate, half-behind

4518 EDINBURGH EVENING NEWS APPRENTICE H'CAP 1m
5:30 (5:31) (Class 6) (0-65,65) 4-Y-0+ **£3,412** (£1,007; £504) **Stalls** Low

Form RPR
4352 **1** **Anthemion (IRE)**[1] 4476 9-8-5 **49** ... AndrewMullen 8 60
(Mrs J C McGregor) *chsd ldr: hdwy 2f out: rdn to ld over 1f out: drvn ins last and styd on* **12/1**

345 **2** ½ **Ballyhurry (USA)**[5] 4353 9-9-1 **62** ... KevinGhunowa(3) 11 72
(J S Goldie) *towards rr on inner: bmpd home turn: hdwy wl over 2f out: rdn over 1f out: styd on wl fnl f* **12/1**

2421 **3** ½ **Burnley Al (IRE)**[1] 4475 4-9-3 **61** 6ex ... (b) GregFairley 2 69
(A Berry) *chsd ldrs: hdwy over 2f out: rdn and ch over 1f out: kpt on u.p ins last* **15/2**[3]

0321 **4** *hd* **Bolton Hall (IRE)**[1] 4476 4-9-2 **65** 6ex ... JamesReveley(5) 12 73
(R A Fahey) *chsd ldrs: smooth hdwy over 2f out: effrt over 1f out and ev ch tl rdn and no ex wl ins last* **9/4**[1]

0501 **5** *3* **Kabis Amigos**[9] 4233 4-8-9 **58** 6ex ... (t) VictoriaBehan(5) 3 59
(D Nicholls) *led and set str pce: rdn 2f out: hdd and drvn over 1f out: wknd ins last* **8/1**

0431 **6** ½ **Star Sign**[5] 4382 4-8-5 **49** 6ex ow3 ... MarkLawson 9 49
(D W Barker) *midfield: effrt and sme hdwy wl over 2f out: sn rdn and no imp* **4/1**[2]

4005 **7** *hd* **Dispol Isle (IRE)**[14] 4070 4-9-4 **65** ... PJMcDonald(3) 5 64
(T D Barron) *rr tl hdwy over 2f out: swtchd lft and rdn no further prog* **16/1**

-000 **8** 3½ **Earthling**[8] 4261 5-7-13 **46** oh9 ... (p) KellyHarrison(3) 1 37
(D W Chapman) *bhd tl sme late hdwy* **100/1**

0600 **9** *nk* **Adobe**[23] 3820 11-8-12 **56** ... LiamJones 6 47
(W M Brisbourne) *bhd tl sme late hdwy* **33/1**

1300 **10** *1* **Sir Bond (IRE)**[14] 4068 5-8-11 **60** ... PJBenson(5) 4 48
(B Smart) *chsd ldrs: rdn over 2f out: sn drvn and wknd* **10/1**

0-00 **11** *17* **Diktatit**[5] 4355 4-7-13 **46** oh1 ... LeanneKershaw(3) 10 —
(R C Guest) *s.i.s: carried wd home bnd and a bhd* **100/1**

500- **12** *19* **The Terminator (IRE)**[325] 5515 4-8-2 **46** oh5 ... (p) DuranFentiman 7 —
(R Johnson) *towards rr whn carried wd home bnd and bhd after* **100/1**

/3-0 **13** *3* **Jabraan (USA)**[154] 653 4-8-6 **50** ... AndrewElliott 13 —
(D W Chapman) *plld hrd: chsd ldrs tl hung lft turn bnd after 3f: hung bdly lft on home turn: sn bhd* **33/1**

1m 40.06s (-2.44) **Going Correction** -0.175s/f (Firm) **13** Ran SP% **112.9**
Speed ratings (Par 101):105,104,104,103,100 100,100,96,96,95 78,59,56
CSF £136.73 CT £1181.78 TOTE £16.40: £3.20, £3.80, £2.80; EX 117.70.
Owner Tillyrie Racing Club **Bred** C And R O'Brien **Trained** Milnathort, Perth & Kinross
■ Stewards' Enquiry : Mark Lawson two-day ban: careless riding (Sep 28, Oct 19)

FOCUS
The ground had been well-watered, but, on a drying day, was getting quicker by the hour. A moderate handicap but sound form with four recent winners taking part and best rated through the placed horses.
Sir Bond(IRE) Official explanation: jockey said gelding had no more to give
Diktatit Official explanation: jockey said filly was carried wide on bend turning in
The Terminator(IRE) Official explanation: jockey said gelding was carried wide on bend turning in
Jabraan(USA) Official explanation: jockey said colt cocked its jaw and failed to handle bend turning in

4519 SCOTTISH EQUITABLE/JOCKEY'S ASSOCIATION NURSERY 5f
6:00 (6:01) (Class 4) 2-Y-0 **£6,477** (£1,927; £963; £481) **Stalls** Low

Form RPR
102 **1** **Aahayson**[14] 4088 2-9-0 **79** ... PatCosgrave 6 79
(K R Burke) *cl up: rdn over 1f out: styd on u.p ins last to ld last 75 yds* **6/4**[1]

654 **2** *hd* **Mazin Lady**[18] 3982 2-7-13 **64** ... PaulFessey 2 63
(Miss J A Camacho) *pushed along in rr: swtchd lft and hdwy wl over 1f out: rdn to chal and hung rt ins last: sn drvn and no ex nr fin* **7/1**

3301 **3** *nk* **Startolini**[27] 3693 2-8-6 **71** ... PaulEddery 1 69
(B Smart) *cl up: led wl over 1f out: sn rdn: drvn ins last: hdd and no ex last 75 yds* **7/1**

4002 **4** 3½ **Weyba Downs (IRE)**[15] 4043 2-7-12 **63** ... SilvestreDeSousa 4 49
(J R Best) *chsd ldrs: rdn along 2f out: wknd over 1f out* **5/1**[3]

4223 **5** *shd* **Riotous (IRE)**[34] 3476 2-8-6 **71** ow1 ... TomEaves 3 56
(A Dickman) *sn led: rdn along 2f out: sn hdd and grad wknd* **4/1**[2]

4562 **6** *1* **Almora Guru**[14] 4089 2-7-9 **65** oh2 ow2 ... LiamJones(5) 7 47
(W M Brisbourne) *cl up on outer: rdn along 2f out: grad wknd* **10/1**

59.31 secs (-1.19) **Going Correction** -0.275s/f (Firm) **6** Ran SP% **110.8**
Speed ratings (Par 96):98,97,97,91,91 89
CSF £12.21 TOTE £2.50: £1.40, £4.60; EX 13.40.
Owner Mrs M Gittins **Bred** Whitsbury Manor Stud And Mrs M E Slade **Trained** Middleham Moor, N Yorks

FOCUS
A tight little nursery, and a close finish with the first three clear of the remainder and near their form.

NOTEBOOK
Aahayson won in gritty style having had a fight on his hands inside the last. He fulfilled the promise of his latest runner-up effort on this track and looks the type to continue to prove competitive in this grade. (op 13-8 tchd 2-1)
Mazin Lady, who was making her handicap debut, picked-up well more than a furlong out, and came to win her race, but looked as though she was hanging to her right towards the finish. The ability is there and she should be able to find a similar contest. (op 13-2 tchd 8-1 in places)
Startolini, attempting to follow up his Carlisle maiden success, ran a blinder, being prominent throughout and only being denied in the shadow of the post. (op 6-1 tchd 11-2)
Weyba Downs(IRE) lacked the speed to get in a telling blow late on. (tchd 9-2)
Riotous(IRE) did plenty early on, but failed to see out his race. (op 9-2 tchd 5-1 in places)

4520 CRUISE CLAIMING STKS 1m
6:30 (6:30) (Class 5) 2-Y-0 **£3,886** (£1,156; £577; £288) **Stalls** Low

Form RPR
3464 **1** **Goose Green (IRE)**[3] 4436 2-9-3 65 ... TomEaves 3 62
(M R Channon) *trckd ldr: cl up 1/2-way: led wl over 2f out: rdn clr ent last* **1/4**[1]

U **2** *5* **Watch Out**[8] 4260 2-9-0 ... PhillipMakin 4 48
(M W Easterby) *s.i.s and bhd: hdwy and rn green over 2f out: sn rdn and styd on ins last to take 2nd nr fin* **20/1**[3]

3640 **3** ½ **Providence Farm**[13] 4115 2-8-10 57 ... PatCosgrave 1 42
(M W Easterby) *led: rdn along over 3f out: sn hdd: drvn and one pce appr last: lost 2nd nr fin* **4/1**[2]

005 **4** *6* **Perilore (IRE)**[15] 4055 2-8-4 ... PaulFessey 2 23
(A Berry) *s.i.s: sn trcking ldng pair: rdn along over 3f out: outpcd over 2f out* **50/1**

1m 44.11s (1.61) **Going Correction** -0.175s/f (Firm) **4** Ran SP% **106.7**
Speed ratings (Par 94):84,79,78,72
CSF £6.38 TOTE £1.20; EX 4.90.
Owner Box 41 **Bred** Liam Queally **Trained** West Ilsley, Berks

FOCUS
An uncompetitive contest and a very moderate winning time, even for a race like this.

NOTEBOOK
Goose Green(IRE) was sent off at prohibitive odds to beat his three rivals and duly did so with the minimum of fuss. Sent clear entering the final furlong, he was never in any danger of being denied. He clearly stays well, admittedly in modest company, but the time was very slow. (op 1-3 tchd 2-5 in a place)
Watch Out, who failed to complete on his debut, having lost his rider in last week's Pontefract pile-up, ran green at the rear before staying on late in the day; there could be some improvement to come from him. Official explanation: jockey said gelding missed the break (op 16-1)
Providence Farm, who made the running, carried his head high under pressure and failed to see out his race. (op 7-2)

4521 CHAMPAGNE POMMERY H'CAP 7f 30y
7:00 (7:00) (Class 4) (0-85,85) 3-Y-0+ **£8,096** (£2,408; £1,203; £601) **Stalls** Low

Form RPR
0600 **1** **King Harson**[13] 4116 7-8-11 **68** ... PatCosgrave 3 81
(J D Bethell) *chsd ldng pair: hdwy over 2f out: rdn to ld ent last: sn drvn and kpt on gamely* **16/1**

1312 **2** *nk* **Carnivore**[5] 4378 4-8-10 **67** 6ex ... PaulFessey 7 80
(T D Barron) *in tch: gd hdwy on inner wl over 1f out: rdn to chal ins last: ev ch tl drvn and nt qckn nr fin* **6/4**[1]

0641 **3** 2½ **Stoic Leader (IRE)**[14] 4090 6-9-4 **80** ... KevinGhunowa(5) 9 86
(R F Fisher) *led: rdn along over 2f out: drvn and hdd ent last: kpt on same pce* **10/1**

/300 **4** *nk* **Tajaathub (USA)**[54] 2851 4-9-2 **78** ... GregFairley(5) 1 83
(M Johnston) *chsd ldrs: rdn along over 2f out: sn drvn and one pce appr last* **14/1**

0001 **5** *3* **Hiccups**[13] 4116 6-8-10 **74** ow1 ... PJBenson(7) 4 71
(M Dods) *hld up in tch: smooth hdwy 3f out: swtchd outside and rdn wl over 1f out: sn drvn: wandered and no imp* **11/1**

2166 **6** *nk* **Claret And Amber**[16] 4020 4-8-13 **77** ... JamesReveley(7) 2 74
(R A Fahey) *towards rr: rdn along and sme hdwy over 2f out: nvr nr ldrs* **11/1**

0511 **7** *3* **Defi (IRE)**[12] 4133 4-9-1 **72** ... (b) TomEaves 8 61
(I Semple) *chsd ldr: hdwy to chal over 2f out: sn rdn and ev ch tl wknd appr last* **7/1**[3]

5100 **8** *5* **Gallantry**[13] 4101 4-10-0 **85** ... GrahamGibbons 6 61
(D W Barker) *in tch: rdn along 3f out: sn btn* **5/1**[2]

4630 **9** *12* **Fast Heart**[22] 3832 5-10-0 **85** ... (t) PhillipMakin 5 30
(D Nicholls) *dwlt: a rr* **25/1**

1m 28.26s (-1.68) **Going Correction** -0.175s/f (Firm) **9** Ran SP% **111.3**
Speed ratings (Par 105):102,101,98,98,95 94,91,85,71
CSF £38.43 CT £256.74 TOTE £20.50: £4.00, £1.10, £2.70; EX 60.90.
Owner C J Burley **Bred** Mrs Anne Bell **Trained** Middleham Moor, N Yorks

FOCUS
A modest handicap but the form looks sound rated through the third.
Fast Heart Official explanation: jockey said gelding never travelled

4522 SCOTTISH EQUITABLE/JOCKEY'S ASSOCIATION H'CAP 1m 6f
7:30 (7:36) (Class 6) (0-65,65) 4-Y-0+ **£3,238** (£963; £481; £240) **Stalls** High

Form RPR
-034 **1** **Onyergo (IRE)**[14] 4072 4-8-8 **52** ... PhillipMakin 5 59
(J R Weymes) *hld up in tch: smooth hdwy 4f out: chal over 1f out: sn rdn: drvn to ld and edgd lft ins last: styd on wl* **7/1**

0330 **2** *nk* **Kristensen**[15] 4036 7-9-2 **65** ... (v) GregFairley(5) 1 72
(Karen McLintock) *a.p: effrt 3f out: rdn to ld jst over 1f out: drvn and hdd ins last: kpt on gamely* **9/2**[2]

3-36 **3** *6* **Gone Too Far**[26] 1758 8-8-9 **58** ... (v) MarkLawson(5) 4 56
(P Monteith) *prom: effrt to ld wl over 2f out and sn rdn: drvn and hdd jst over 1f out: sn wknd* **6/1**

3313 **4** *1* **York Cliff**[49] 2998 8-8-7 **56** ... LiamJones(5) 6 53
(W M Brisbourne) *hld up in rr: pushed along over 4f out: rdn 3f out: styd on fnl 2f: nrst fin* **7/1**

5012 **5** *6* **Rare Coincidence**[5] 4351 5-8-10 **59** ... (p) KevinGhunowa(5) 3 47
(R F Fisher) *led: rdn along 3f out: sn hdd & wknd* **11/4**[1]

4045 **6** *10* **Lennel**[5] 4351 8-8-6 **50** ow1 ... (b) TomEaves 2 24
(A Bailey) *sn rdn along: a rr* **12/1**

3616 **7** 1¼ **I'll Do It Today**[18] 3983 5-8-11 **60** ... AndrewMullen(5) 7 33
(J M Jefferson) *chsd ldrs: rdn along 4f out: sn wknd* **11/2**[3]

3m 0.72s (-4.98) **Going Correction** -0.175s/f (Firm) **7** Ran SP% **107.2**
Speed ratings (Par 101):107,106,103,102,99 93,92
CSF £33.39 TOTE £8.20: £4.00, £2.60; EX 45.90.
Owner Mrs N Napier **Bred** Lord Halifax **Trained** Middleham Moor, N Yorks

FOCUS
The rails on the home turn were slightly adjusted before this race at the request of jockeys, who felt the bend was not riding as well as it should. A moderate handicap but run at a good pace and rated around the winner with the first two clear.

4523 BELMONT SUZUKI STYLE H'CAP 5f
8:00 (8:01) (Class 6) (0-60,58) 3-Y-0+ **£3,412** (£1,007; £504) **Stalls** Low

Form RPR
0626 **1** **Rosie's Result**[1] 4477 6-8-6 **44** ... AndrewMullen(5) 1 53
(M Todhunter) *chsd ldrs: rdn along 1/2-way: hdwy over 1f out: styd on u.p ins last to ld last stride* **13/2**

2046 **2** *shd* **Strawberry Patch (IRE)**[5] 4352 7-9-8 **55**...............(p) DanielTudhope 12 64
(J S Goldie) *stall opened early and sn cl up: led 2f out: rdn and edgd rt ent last: sn drvn and hdd last stride* **11/1**

3132 **3** *1 ½* **Chairman Bobby**[1] 4477 8-8-12 **50**...........................(p) MarkLawson(5) 7 53
(D W Barker) *chsd ldrs: rdn along over 2f out: drvn and kpt on wl fnl f* **4/1**[2]

0005 **4** *1 ¼* **On The Trail**[22] 3833 9-8-7 **40**...(p) PaulQuinn 5 39
(D W Chapman) *towards rr: gd hdwy on outer wl over 1f out: sn rdn and kpt on ins last: nrst fin* **33/1**

0053 **5** *¾* **She's Our Beauty (IRE)**[10] 4201 3-9-0 **49**..........(v) SilvestreDeSousa 13 45
(D Nicholls) *chsd ldrs: swtchd lft and rdn wl over 1f out: kpt on same pce* **12/1**

0404 **6** *nk* **Zantero**[12] 4136 4-8-9 **45**.. DNolan(3) 11 40
(W M Brisbourne) *cl up: rdn along 2f out: grad wknd over 1f out* **50/1**

3500 **7** *shd* **Sharp Hat**[9] 4232 12-9-0 **50**... BenSwarbrick(3) 6 45
(D W Chapman) *stall opened sltly early: prom: rdn along 2f out: one pce appr last* **14/1**

0260 **8** *2* **Beverley Beau**[12] 4141 4-8-8 **48**.. KristinStubbs(7) 8 35
(Mrs L Stubbs) *a towards rr* **16/1**

0412 **9** *1 ½* **Bond Becks (IRE)**[14] 4091 6-9-4 **58**.. PJBenson(7) 3 40
(B Smart) *sn led: rdn 2f out: sn hdd & wknd* **3/1**[1]

/00- **10** *1* **John O'Groats (IRE)**[271] 6385 8-8-7 **45**.................... DuranFentiman(5) 4 23
(W G Harrison) *a rr* **33/1**

4600 **11** *6* **Trick Cyclist**[16] 4019 5-9-11 **58**.. PhillipMakin 10 15
(M W Easterby) *blindfold removed late: slowly away and a bhd* **11/2**[3]

5444 **12** *3* **Howards Prince**[15] 4056 3-9-9 **58**................................(b[1]) TomEaves 14 4
(I Semple) *wnt rt s: a rr* **25/1**

59.24 secs (-1.26) **Going Correction** -0.275s/f (Firm)
WFA 3 from 4yo+ 2lb **12** Ran SP% **114.0**
Speed ratings (Par 101):99,98,96,94,93 92,92,89,87,85 75,71
CSF £70.07 CT £326.52 TOTE £8.10: £2.10, £2.90, £2.10; EX 82.30.
Owner Mrs J Mandle **Bred** P G Airey And R R Whitton **Trained** Orton, Cumbria
■ Stewards' Enquiry : Phillip Makin caution: failed to take all reasonable and permissible measures to obtain best possible placing

FOCUS
A banded-class sprint handicap but the form looks sound enough, rated around the winner and third.
Trick Cyclist Official explanation: jockey said gelding missed the break

4524 BANK OF SCOTLAND BUSINESS BANKING H'CAP 7f 30y
8:30 (8:30) (Class 6) (0-65,65) 3-Y-O **£3,412** (£1,007; £504) **Stalls** Low

Form RPR

5045 **1** **Choreography**[4] 4403 3-9-4 **62**.................................. SilvestreDeSousa 7 69
(D Nicholls) *trckd ldrs on inner gng wl: swtchd lft and hdwy 2f out: led wl over 1f out: sn rdn and styd on wl fnl f* **7/2**[1]

5626 **2** *1 ½* **Crimson Flame (IRE)**[8] 4257 3-8-12 **61**.......................(v) GregFairley(5) 6 64
(M R Channon) *trckd ldrs: hdwy to ld over 3f out: rdn 2f out and sn hdd: drvn and kpt on last* **4/1**[2]

1020 **3** *1 ¼* **Elegant Times (IRE)**[13] 4116 3-8-13 **62**..................(b[1]) MarkLawson(5) 2 62+
(T D Easterby) *stdd s: hld up in rr: hdwy on outer over 2f out: rdn to chse ldrs over 1f out: sn edgd lft and kpt on same pce* **6/1**

6002 **4** *3 ½* **Flylowflylong (IRE)**[7] 4296 3-9-7 **65**.. TomEaves 1 56
(I Semple) *hld up towards rr: hdwy 3f out: rdn to chse ldrs wl over 1f out: sn drvn and hld whn n.m.r over 1f out* **5/1**[3]

0-01 **5** *2* **Hotchpotch (USA)**[7] 4293 3-8-8 **52** 6ex............................. PhillipMakin 3 38
(J R Best) *keen: chsd ldrs: rdn along over 2f out: drvn and btn wl over 1f out* **7/2**[1]

6050 **6** *nk* **Beginners Luck (IRE)**[23] 3814 3-8-2 **46** oh8............................ PaulQuinn 9 31
(D Carroll) *dwlt: hdwy over 3f out: in tch and rdn over 2f out: sn wknd* **50/1**

4060 **7** *3* **Honor Me (IRE)**[14] 4071 3-8-6 **50**............................(v[1]) GrahamGibbons 11 27
(J J Quinn) *led: rdn along and hdd over 3f out: sn wknd* **16/1**

0500 **8** *nk* **Nautico**[10] 4201 3-8-2 **46** oh6.. PaulFessey 4 22
(Miss L A Perratt) *prom: rdn along over 3f out: sn wknd* **66/1**

1000 **9** *1 ½* **Miss Lopez (IRE)**[40] 3290 3-9-2 **60**.. PatCosgrave 8 46+
(K R Burke) *s.i.s and bhd: hdwy 2f out: sn rdn and n.m.r whn stmbld bdly over 1f out* **22/1**

0600 **10** *¾* **Mandarin Grand (IRE)**[5] 4350 3-7-11 **46** oh10....(p) DuranFentiman(5) 5 16
(Miss L A Perratt) *a towards rr* **66/1**

1m 29.39s (-0.55) **Going Correction** -0.175s/f (Firm) **10** Ran SP% **110.6**
Speed ratings (Par 98):96,94,92,88,86 86,82,82,80,79
CSF £16.16 CT £76.63 TOTE £5.50: £2.10, £2.30, £1.80; EX 24.60 Place 6 £121.46, Place 5 £28.35.
Owner Bill Wallace/Gary Butters **Bred** Cheveley Park Stud Ltd **Trained** Sessay, N Yorks

FOCUS
A low-grade handicap rated around the placed horses.
Miss Lopez(IRE) Official explanation: jockey said filly clipped heels final furlong
T/Plt: £201.00 to a £1 stake. Pool: £43,634.20. 158.40 winning tickets. T/Qpdt: £18.40 to a £1 stake. Pool: £6,225.00. 249.50 winning tickets. JR

4479 SALISBURY (R-H)
Thursday, August 17

OFFICIAL GOING: Good to soft (good in places)
Wind: Virtually nil

4525 STELLA ARTOIS MAIDEN AUCTION STKS (DIV I) 6f 212y
2:00 (2:06) (Class 5) 2-Y-O **£3,238** (£963; £481; £240) **Stalls** Centre

Form RPR

24 **1** **Caldra (IRE)**[75] 2234 2-8-11 .... JamieSpencer 2 82
(S Kirk) *in tch: swtchd rt over 2f out: sn pushed along and drifted lft: swtchd rt jst ins fnl f: r.o to ld cl home* **5/1**[3]

0 **2** *½* **Duke Of Tuscany**[11] 4177 2-8-13 .... DaneO'Neill 4 83
(R Hannon) *a.p: rdn wl over 1f out: led jst ins fnl f: no ex whn hdd cl home* **12/1**

4 **3** *1 ½* **Flying Encore (IRE)**[29] 3640 2-8-8 .... SebSanders 12 74
(W R Swinburn) *trckd ldrs: rdn over 2f out: wnt 2nd briefly jst ins fnl f: kpt on* **5/1**[3]

5 **4** *3* **Racing Times**[13] 4105 2-8-13 .... LDettori 6 72
(B J Meehan) *scope: led: rdn 2f out: hdd jst ins fnl f: wknd* **7/2**[1]

0 **5** *5* **Balnagore**[18] 3976 2-8-9 .... JimmyQuinn 3 55
(J L Dunlop) *lw: rrd and stmbld leaving stalls: sn rcvrd: trckd ldrs: rdn over 2f out: wknd 1f out* **5/1**[3]

3 **6** *nk* **Cool Box (USA)**[19] 3949 2-9-2 .... JimmyFortune 14 61
(Mrs A J Perrett) *lw: mid-div: hdwy over 3f out to trck ldrs: sn rdn: wknd fnl f* **9/2**[2]

5 **7** *5* **Lay The Cash (USA)**[17] 4008 2-8-9 .... JohnEgan 7 42
(J S Moore) *str: bit bkwd: in tch: rdn over 2f out: wknd over 1f out* **20/1**

0 **8** *1* **Falcon Flyer**[36] 3408 2-8-6 .... JoeFanning 1 36
(J R Best) *trckd ldrs for 4f* **33/1**

9 *1 ½* **First To Call** 2-8-9 .... ChrisCatlin 8 36
(P J Makin) *cmpt: bit bkwd: a towards rr* **40/1**

0 **10** *½* **Homecroft Boy**[19] 3958 2-8-11 .... SteveDrowne 9 36
(J A Osborne) *a towards rr* **50/1**

11 *1 ½* **Is It Time (IRE)** 2-8-4 .... PaulDoe 11 26
(Mrs P N Dutfield) *w'like: bit bkwd: mid div for over 4f* **66/1**

12 *1* **Disintegration (IRE)** 2-8-8 .... RichardKingscote(3) 13 30
(A King) *w'like: lw: s.i.s: a bhd* **33/1**

13 *19* **Hard As Iron** 2-8-9 .... TedDurcan 5 —
(M Blanshard) *w'like: bit bkwd: s.i.s: a bhd* **100/1**

14 *dist* **Twenty Percent** 2-8-11 .... AlanMunro 10 —
(P R Chamings) *w'like: fit: s.i.s: a wl bhd: t.o* **50/1**

1m 29.14s (0.08) **Going Correction** +0.075s/f (Good) **14** Ran SP% **117.6**
Speed ratings (Par 94):102,101,99,96,90 90,84,83,81,81 79,78,56,—
CSF £57.42 TOTE £6.20: £2.20, £4.10, £1.50; EX 100.10.
Owner Norman Ormiston **Bred** S J Macdonald **Trained** Upper Lambourn, Berks

FOCUS
A fair maiden in which the easing of the ground led to the riders bringing their mounts stands' side, setting a trend for the day. It was run in a time 0.84sec quicker than the second division.

NOTEBOOK
Caldra(IRE), gelded since his last run, was bred to appreciate the step up to seven furlongs and he really came into his own in the final furlong. It was a cosy win in the end and he looks an interesting prospect for nurseries, with better ground likely to suit him according to his rider. (op 7-1)
Duke Of Tuscany, who looked just in need of the run, was well backed on his debut before disappointing in the race itself, but he showed here that his supporters that day were not too far wide of the mark. He has the ability to win a maiden but one more run will see him qualify for nurseries.
Flying Encore(IRE), who shaped with plenty of promise on her debut at Kempton, was disadvantaged by a wide draw and did not run too badly in the circumstances. She looked very fit beforehand and will find things easier back against her own sex. (op 10-3)
Racing Times, stepping up from six furlongs on easier ground, did not see the trip out. He should get this distance in time, but will probably need faster ground to do so. (op 9-2)
Balnagore, who was a bit keen early, failed to build on his debut effort. Official explanation: jockey said colt reared on leaving stalls (tchd 11-2)
Cool Box(USA) was poorly drawn and failed to improve for the step up in trip. Perhaps he needs quicker ground. (op 5-1)

4526 STELLA ARTOIS MAIDEN AUCTION STKS (DIV II) 6f 212y
2:30 (2:34) (Class 5) 2-Y-O **£3,238** (£963; £481; £240) **Stalls** Centre

Form RPR

52 **1** **Streets Ahead**[14] 4074 2-8-11 .... JamieSpencer 6 80+
(A M Balding) *trckd ldrs: nt clr run and swtchd rt to chal jst under 2f out: led 1f out: r.o: rdn out* **7/4**[1]

2 *nk* **Worldly** 2-8-9 .... JohnEgan 1 77+
(S Kirk) *w'like: scope: lw: s.i.s: hld up towards rr: hdwy fr over 2f out: steadily swtchd rt:r.o to go cl 2nd wl ins fnl f: nrst fi* **8/1**[3]

3 *3* **Mount Hermon (IRE)** 2-8-13 .... SteveDrowne 11 74+
(H Morrison) *w'like: bit bkwd: mid-div: hdwy to trck ldrs 3f out: sn rdn: kpt on fnl f* **9/1**

4 *hd* **Actodos (IRE)** 2-8-9 .... AlanMunro 10 69
(B R Millman) *w'like: bit bkwd: trckd ldrs: rdn over 2f out: ev ch 1f out: nt qckn* **25/1**

002 **5** *shd* **Security Tiger (IRE)**[16] 4018 2-8-6 **73**.............................. TedDurcan 9 66
(M R Channon) *led: rdn over 2f out: hdd 1f out: no ex* **11/4**[2]

6 *3* **Chant De Guerre (USA)** 2-8-6 .... NickyMackay 7 59
(P Mitchell) *w'like: bit bkwd: in tch: rdn over 2f out: one pce fnl f* **25/1**

00 **7** *½* **Six Shots**[7] 4290 2-8-10 .... RichardKingscote(3) 5 64
(J A Osborne) *trckd ldrs: rdn over 2f out: sn one pce* **33/1**

0 **8** *1 ¾* **Extractor**[26] 3726 2-8-11 .... JimmyQuinn 8 58
(J L Dunlop) *hld up in tch: rdn over 1f out: one pce fnl f* **33/1**

9 *1 ½* **Franchoek (IRE)** 2-8-13 .... DaneO'Neill 4 56
(A King) *w'like: s.i.s: bhd hdwy into mid-div 4f out: rdn over 2f out: wknd over 1f out* **10/1**

10 *6* **Acosta** 2-8-9 .... RichardThomas 3 37
(Dr J R J Naylor) *unf: bit bkwd: a towards rr* **100/1**

0 **11** *2* **Priceless Melody (USA)**[7] 4292 2-9-2 .... JimmyFortune 13 39
(Mrs A J Perrett) *bit bkwd: mid-div: effrt 2f out: sn wknd* **40/1**

12 *¾* **Shouldntbethere (IRE)** 2-8-9 .... SebSanders 12 30
(Mrs P N Dutfield) *leggy: bit bkwd: towards rr: short-lived effrt over 2f out: sn hung rt and wknd* **20/1**

0060 **13** *3 ½* **Take My Turn**[6] 4334 2-8-9 ....(b[1]) ChrisCatlin 2 22
(M Blanshard) *lw: a towads rr* **66/1**

1m 29.98s (0.92) **Going Correction** +0.075s/f (Good) **13** Ran SP% **116.5**
Speed ratings (Par 94):97,96,93,93,92 89,88,86,85,78 76,75,71
CSF £14.41 TOTE £2.70: £1.30, £2.80, £2.90; EX 18.80.
Owner John Dwyer & Mrs J R Ramsden **Bred** Deerpark Stud **Trained** Kingsclere, Hants

FOCUS
Another fair maiden but the slower of the two divisions by 0.84sec.

NOTEBOOK
Streets Ahead has shown steady improvement with every run and got off the mark at the third time of asking. He picked up well in the closing stages to put daylight between himself and the pack, and looks an ideal type for nurseries. (op 9-4 tchd 5-2)
Worldly, a half-brother to Day To Remember, a triple winner between a mile and ten furlongs, and Tasdeed, a winner over seven furlongs at two, shaped with a good deal of promise on his debut, finishing well from off the pace to come home clear of the rest of the field. He was probably aided by the rain-softened ground as his siblings showed a preference for give. (op 9-1)
Mount Hermon(IRE), drawn wide, carried his head to one side. A half-brother to Rightprice Premier, a five-furlong winner at two, he is from a stable whose two-year-olds invariably improve for their debut outings. (op 8-1)
Actodos(IRE), whose dam is an unraced half-sister to Nell Gwyn Stakes winner Misterah, was to the fore for much of the race and posted a promising effort. He was green in the paddock and the market suggested he was not particularly fancied on this debut so he should come on for the run.
Security Tiger(IRE), the most experienced runner in the line-up, put that to good use, getting to the front and attempting to make all. She might have found the ground softer than ideal, though, as she did not get home. (op 9-4 tchd 3-1)
Chant De Guerre(USA), a May foal out of a mare who was a smart six-furlong winner at three, is likely to do better with time and experience.
Extractor looked very fit beforehand. (op 20-1)
Franchoek(IRE) was very green going to post. (op 14-1 tchd 8-1)

4527 MARY WORT MEMORIAL MAIDEN STKS — 6f 212y
3:05 (3:07) (Class 4) 3-4-Y-O — £5,505 (£1,637; £818; £408) Stalls Centre

Form — RPR
0-43 **1** **Vino**[50] 2985 3-8-12 67 ... MichaelHills 2 — 72
(B W Hills) *lengthy: bit bkwd: trckd ldr: rdn to chal wl over 1f out: led wl ins fnl f: drvn out* **7/2**[3]
0- **2** *hd* **Highland Blaze (USA)**[363] 4550 3-9-3 ... LDettori 5 — 80+
(Saeed Bin Suroor) *hld up towards rr: nt clr run 2f out: swtchd lft and styd on fr 1f out: wnt cl 2nd wl ins fnl f: jst failed* **9/4**[2]
3-00 **3** *1* **Rose Of Inchinor**[48] 3055 3-8-12 65 ... RHills 1 — 69
(M P Tregoning) *led: rdn 2f out: no ex whn hdd wl ins fnl f* **20/1**
54 **4** *4* **Dixieland Boy (IRE)**[17] 4004 3-9-0 ... AmirQuinn(3) 9 — 64
(P J Makin) *lw: in tch: rdn and effrt 2f out: kpt on same pce* **16/1**
000 **5** *1 ½* **Warden Rose**[26] 3742 3-8-12 58 ... JohnEgan 7 — 55
(D R C Elsworth) *lw: trckd ldrs: rdn to chal 2f out: one pce fnl f* **20/1**
02 **6** *2* **Whistle Away**[20] 3916 3-9-3 ... StephenCarson 10 — 55
(W R Swinburn) *trckd ldrs: rdn 2f out: wknd fnl f* **25/1**
-300 **7** *¾* **Bellanora**[43] 3204 3-8-12 60 ... JimmyFortune 3 — 48
(R F Johnson Houghton) *towards rr: rdn over 2f out: sme late hdwy: n.d* **33/1**
4225 **8** *1 ¾* **Quintrell**[18] 3975 3-8-12 74 ... DaneO'Neill 6 — 43
(H Candy) *lw: sn struggling in rr: nvr a factor* **2/1**[1]
9 *5* **Summer Celebrity (IRE)** 3-8-12 ... AntonyProcter 11 — 30
(D R C Elsworth) *s.i.s: t.k.h and sn trcking ldrs: rdn 2f out : wknd 1f out* **50/1**
4-5 **10** *shd* **Pertemps Green**[26] 3742 3-9-3 ... SteveDrowne 8 — 35
(Stef Liddiard) *s.i.s: stmbld 4f out: nvr bttr than mid div* **16/1**
0000 **11** *16* **Catabound (USA)**[38] 3349 3-9-3 47 ... TedDurcan 4 — —
(B R Millman) *in tch: short lived effrt 3f out* **100/1**

1m 28.88s (-0.18) **Going Correction** +0.075s/f (Good) — 11 Ran SP% **117.4**
Speed ratings (Par 105):104,103,102,98,96 94,93,91,85,85 67
CSF £10.83 TOTE £4.70: £1.50, £1.60, £5.60; EX 16.40.
Owner Guy Reed **Bred** G Reed **Trained** Lambourn, Berks

FOCUS
A modest maiden in which few could be fancied. It has been rated through the third, fifth and sixth.
Dixieland Boy(IRE) Official explanation: jockey said gelding stumbled approx 3 1/2f out
Quintrell Official explanation: trainer said filly was in season
Pertemps Green Official explanation: jockey said gelding stumbled approx 3 1/2f out

4528 EUROPEAN BREEDERS FUND FILLIES' H'CAP — 1m 4f
3:40 (3:43) (Class 4) (0-80,78) 3-Y-0+ — £7,772 (£2,312; £1,155; £577) Stalls High

Form — RPR
4111 **1** **Trick Or Treat**[13] 4118 3-9-1 74 ... LDettori 9 — 89+
(J G Given) *lw: hld up: tk clsr order 4f out: drew upsides over 2f out: shkn up to ld over 1f out: sn forged clr: comf* **15/8**[1]
210 **2** *3 ½* **Candle**[12] 4125 3-9-3 76 ... DaneO'Neill 6 — 83
(H Candy) *warm: hld up: rdn and stdy hdwy fr over 2f out: wnt 2nd ins fnl f: no ch w wnr* **10/1**
2621 **3** *2 ½* **My Petra**[12] 4159 3-9-5 78 ... TedDurcan 4 — 81
(A King) *led: rdn and hdd wl over 2f out: rallied: kpt on same pce fr over 1f out* **5/1**[2]
6534 **4** *1 ½* **Spinning Coin**[27] 3714 4-9-12 75 ... (p) SebSanders 1 — 76
(J G Portman) *in tch: tk clsr order 5f out: effrt 3f out: one pce fnl 2f* **9/1**
54-1 **5** *nk* **Vale De Lobo**[47] 3068 4-10-0 77 ... AlanMunro 2 — 77
(B R Millman) *trckd ldr: led wl over 2f out: sn rdn: hdd over 1f out: wknd ins fnl f* **8/1**
2611 **6** *10* **Aimee Vibert**[18] 3983 4-9-8 71 ... StephenCarson 7 — 55
(W R Swinburn) *in tch: hdwy over 3f out: effrt over 2f out: wknd over 1f out* **9/1**
2120 **7** *nk* **Madhavi**[13] 4104 4-9-4 67 ... JimmyFortune 8 — 51
(R Hannon) *trckd ldrs: jnd ldrs briefly over 3f out: sn rdn: wknd wl over 2f out* **18/1**
-213 **8** *11* **Fyvie**[34] 3489 3-9-4 77 ... JamieSpencer 5 — 43
(E A L Dunlop) *warm: hld up and a in rr* **11/2**[3]
450 **9** *16* **Mawazeen (IRE)**[13] 4104 5-8-9 58 ... JohnEgan 3 — —
(N I M Rossiter) *b: in tch: rdn over 4f out: wknd over 2f out* **100/1**

2m 37.47s (1.11) **Going Correction** +0.075s/f (Good)
WFA 3 from 4yo+ 10lb — 9 Ran SP% **113.3**
Speed ratings (Par 102):99,96,95,94,93 87,86,79,68
CSF £21.68 CT £80.55 TOTE £2.40: £1.10, £3.30, £1.80; EX 25.70.
Owner Peter Onslow **Bred** P Onslow **Trained** Willoughton, Lincs

FOCUS
A fair handicap won by a progressive type and the form looks sound enough rated through the second and third.

4529 TOTESPORT.COM SOVEREIGN STKS (GROUP 3) (C&G) — 1m
4:15 (4:17) (Class 1) 3-Y-0+
£39,746 (£15,064; £7,539; £3,759; £1,883; £945) Stalls High

Form — RPR
22-1 **1** **Belenus (IRE)**[12] 4145 4-9-0 106 ... (t) LDettori 8 — 115+
(Saeed Bin Suroor) *h.d.w: trckd ldrs: shkn up wl over 1f out: sn hung lft: led ins fnl f: kpt on wl to assert cl home* **11/10**[1]
-603 **2** *1 ¼* **Notability (IRE)**[33] 3534 4-9-0 100 ... PhilipRobinson 2 — 112
(M A Jarvis) *warm: trckd ldr: tk narrow advantage over 4f out: rdn over 2f out: hdd ins fnl f: kpt on but sn hld* **9/2**[2]
6602 **3** *1 ¼* **Kings Point (IRE)**[21] 3881 5-9-0 105 ... DaneO'Neill 7 — 109
(R A Fahey) *in tch: rdn wl over 2f out: kpt on ins fnl f* **50/1**
0315 **4** *nk* **Momtic (IRE)**[12] 4145 5-9-0 106 ... AlanMunro 1 — 108
(W Jarvis) *trckd ldrs: rdn 3f out: kpt on ins fnl f* **16/1**
2033 **5** *2* **Marching Song**[19] 3926 4-9-0 94 ... JimmyFortune 5 — 104
(R Hannon) *lw: in tch: n.m.r and lost pl 3f out: sn rdn: styd on fnl f* **25/1**
2450 **6** *½* **Grand Passion (IRE)**[55] 2803 6-9-0 101 ... SteveDrowne 6 — 103
(G Wragg) *towards rr: rdn 3f out: no imp tl styd on fnl f* **66/1**
200 **7** *1* **Babodana**[33] 3534 6-9-0 110 ... RHills 9 — 100
(M H Tompkins) *lw: mid-div: effrt over 2f out: one pce fnl f* **12/1**
5501 **8** *1* **Champions Gallery**[18] 3973 3-8-8 95 ... JohnEgan 13 — 97
(D R C Elsworth) *lw: towards rr: swtchd rt over 3f out: sn rdn: no imp* **14/1**
2101 **9** *hd* **Prince Of Light (IRE)**[12] 4126 3-8-8 109 ... JoeFanning 3 — 97
(M Johnston) *warm: led: hdd narrowly over 4f out: styd prom: rdn wl over 2f out : wknd over 1f out* **17/2**
-104 **10** *nk* **Killybegs (IRE)**[33] 3559 3-8-11 110 ... MichaelHills 4 — 99+
(B W Hills) *trckd ldrs: rdn over 3f out: wknd 1f out* **13/2**[3]
-303 **11** *5* **St Andrews (IRE)**[75] 2236 6-9-0 106 ... TedDurcan 11 — 85
(M A Jarvis) *lw: mid-div: effrt over 2f out: wknd over 1f out* **20/1**

1m 41.39s (-1.70) **Going Correction** +0.075s/f (Good)
WFA 3 from 4yo+ 6lb — 11 Ran SP% **122.0**
Speed ratings: 111,109,108,108,106 105,104,103,103,103 98
CSF £6.03 TOTE £2.10: £1.20, £2.00, £8.10; EX 8.50 Trifecta £336.40 Pool: £995.06 - 2.10 winning tickets..
Owner Godolphin **Bred** Gainsborough Stud Management Ltd **Trained** Newmarket, Suffolk

FOCUS
Just a fair pace for this Group 3 resulting in an unspectacular time and it suited those that raced close to the pace, so the form is only fair for the grade. More evidence of the Godolphin resurgence and another black mark against the three-year-old colts against their elders.

NOTEBOOK
Belenus(IRE), who had never run on anything but fast ground before this, had no problem with the easier conditions and ran out an authoritative winner in the end. He may not be the most straightforward but, considering he had a bit to find with a few of these on official ratings, this was a good effort and he is still comparatively lightly raced. This trip seems to suit him well and he should be able to win again at this level at the very least. (op 5-4 tchd 6-4 in a place)
Notability(IRE) never stopped trying and kept on to finish a clear second best. This was the second time at this level that he has split horses officially rated higher than him and he deserves to win in Pattern company. (op 6-1)
Kings Point(IRE) managed to reverse York form with Momtic on 3lb better terms and did very well to plug on and make the frame at this level, but it is still hard to see him winning a race like this. (op 40-1)
Momtic(IRE) was not disgraced and finished a bit closer to Belenus than he did at Newmarket, but could have done without the rain and failed to confirm York form with Kings Point on 3lb worse terms. (op 14-1 tchd 20-1)
Marching Song, tried over a mile for the first time, did not appear to be beaten through lack of stamina and ran with credit considering he was the lowest rated in the field, but he has only managed one win from 19 attempts which has to be a worry.
Grand Passion(IRE) would have preferred the ground to have remained on the quick side and was up against it in trying to come from off the pace in a race that suited those that raced handily. This was a fair effort under the circumstances, but he does seem to reserve his best for Polytrack these days.
Champions Gallery, who would not have appreciated the easing of the ground, still emerged best of the three-year-olds but that is not saying much. (op 16-1)
Killybegs(IRE), winner of the Craven earlier in the season and as a result the only penalised runner in the field, raced up with the pace in the early stages but eventually dropped tamely away. The softer ground may not have helped, but this hardly advertised the strength of the three-year-olds. (op 11-2 tchd 7-1)

4530 BLACKTHORN CIDER H'CAP — 1m 6f 15y
4:50 (4:51) (Class 5) (0-70,70) 3-Y-0+ — £3,886 (£1,156; £577; £288)

Form — RPR
43-4 **1** **Fair Along (GER)**[26] 3431 4-9-9 65 ... DaneO'Neill 8 — 80+
(P J Hobbs) *mde all: qcknd pce 5f out: rdn wl over 2f out:styd on strly: readily* **7/1**
1233 **2** *5* **Shore Thing (IRE)**[8] 4268 3-9-2 70 ... RHills 1 — 78
(M H Tompkins) *hld up in tch: smooth prog fr 4f: trcking wnr and travelling wl over 2f out: sn rdn for effrt: fnd little* **5/2**[1]
4501 **3** *1 ½* **Rehearsed (IRE)**[19] 3952 3-8-7 64 ... EdwardCreighton(3) 11 — 70
(H Morrison) *hld up bhd: gd hdwy fr 4f out: rdn to chse ldng pair 2f out: kpt on but no further impression* **5/1**[2]
4323 **4** *7* **Maystock**[13] 4104 6-10-0 70 ... TedDurcan 4 — 66
(B G Powell) *trckd wnr: rdn over 4f out: one pce fr 2f out* **7/1**
0044 **5** *½* **Grey Paint (USA)**[19] 3952 3-8-12 66 ... (t) JimmyFortune 13 — 62
(R Hannon) *in tch: hdwy 4f out: jnd wnr 3f out: sn rdn: one pce fnl 2f* **6/1**[3]
-055 **6** *2* **The Spread**[35] 3439 3-7-12 52 oh1 ... NickyMackay 3 — 45
(M Blanshard) *mid-div tl wknd 2f out* **25/1**
6056 **7** *2* **Bobsleigh**[7] 4282 7-8-12 54 ... AlanMunro 7 — 44
(H S Howe) *in tch: outpcd 5f out: nt a danger after* **10/1**
5050 **8** *5* **Cantrip**[17] 4005 6-8-10 52 oh2 ... JoeFanning 6 — 35
(Miss B Sanders) *trckd wnr: rdn over 4f out: wknd over 2f out* **25/1**
0000 **9** *26* **Tilla**[6] 2935 6-8-5 52 oh2 ... (v) TravisBlock(5) 10 — —
(Mrs A J Hamilton-Fairley) *a towards rr* **50/1**
6004 **10** *3 ½* **Papeete (GER)**[15] 4046 5-9-6 62 ... MichaelHills 14 — 4
(Miss B Sanders) *hld up towards rr: short-lived effrt over 3f out: eased whn btn* **10/1**
06 **11** *21* **The Iron Giant (IRE)**[19] 3952 4-8-12 57 ... RichardKingscote(3) 12 — —
(B G Powell) *a towards rr: eased whn btn* **33/1**
0030 **12** *112* **Ocean Of Storms (IRE)**[15] 4036 11-9-4 65 ... EmmettStack(5) 2 — —
(N I M Rossiter) *virtually ref to r: a 2f adrift* **33/1**

3m 4.55s (-1.68) **Going Correction** +0.075s/f (Good)
WFA 3 from 4yo+ 12lb — 12 Ran SP% **118.2**
Speed ratings (Par 103):107,104,103,99,99 97,96,93,79,77 65,—
CSF £23.47 CT £98.02 TOTE £8.40: £3.80, £1.80, £1.80; EX 43.00.
Owner Alan Peterson **Bred** Gestut Harzburg **Trained** Withycombe, Somerset

FOCUS
A fair handicap and a decent pace set by the eventual winner made it a proper test. The runners finished well spread out as a result and the form looks solid, rated around the placed horses.
Papeete(GER) Official explanation: trainer's rep said mare was struck into
The Iron Giant(IRE) Official explanation: jockey said gelding was unsuited by the good to soft (good in places) ground

4531 AXMINSTER CARPETS APPRENTICE H'CAP — 6f 212y
5:20 (5:27) (Class 5) (0-70,69) 3-Y-0+ — £3,886 (£1,156; £577; £288) Stalls Centre

Form — RPR
2056 **1** **Stormy Monday**[22] 3845 3-9-9 69 ... PatrickHills(5) 4 — 76
(J W Hills) *mid-div: swtchd rt and hdwy wl over 1f out: sn rdn: styd on ins fnl f: led fnl stride* **5/1**[2]
0-60 **2** *shd* **Moyoko (IRE)**[49] 3016 3-7-13 48 ... LauraReynolds(8) 9 — 55
(M Blanshard) *s.i.s: towards rr: hdwy over 2f out: led jst over 1f out : ct fnl stride* **25/1**
5404 **3** *1 ¾* **Palais Polaire**[68] 2459 4-9-1 56 ... WilliamCarson(5) 6 — 60
(J A Geake) *lw: mid-div: rdn and hdwy 3f out: led jst under 2f out: hdd jst over 1f out: kpt on but no ex* **9/2**[1]
3324 **4** *shd* **Gracie's Gift (IRE)**[17] 3996 4-9-2 57 ... JosephWalsh(5) 5 — 61+
(A G Newcombe) *s.i.s: bhd on rails: nt clr run over 1f out: rdn and r.o ins fnl f: nrst fin* **5/1**[2]
0060 **5** *3* **Kareeb (FR)**[13] 4108 9-9-1 59 ... AlanRutter(8) 3 — 55
(W J Musson) *s.i.s: towards rr: stdy prog fr over 2f out: rdn over 1f out: no further imp* **7/1**[3]
3000 **6** *¾* **Catherines Cafe (IRE)**[35] 3450 3-9-2 60 ... JamesMillman(3) 11 — 52
(Mrs P N Dutfield) *racd alone in centre: nvr bttr than mid-div* **14/1**
0043 **7** *5* **No Time (IRE)**[8] 4267 6-9-3 61 ... FrankiePickard(8) 1 — 42
(J A Osborne) *led tl jst over 2f out: sn btn* **10/1**

-500 **8** *hd* **Spanish Story**[35] 3458 3-7-11 **48**...(p) WilliamBuick[(10)] 7 — 27
(A M Balding) *keen early: trckd ldr: rdn 2f out: sn wknd* **8/1**

/6-0 **9** *4* **Red Apache (IRE)**[77] 2182 4-8-11 **50**... SladeO'Hara[(3)] 2 — 21
(H J Collingridge) *trckd ldr: rdn over 2f out: sn wknd* **40/1**

0032 **10** *2* **Endless Night**[19] 3932 3-9-4 **62**...(v[1]) TravisBlock[(3)] 8 — 25
(H Morrison) *mid-div: rdn 3f out: sn wknd* **9/2**[1]

-000 **11** *13* **Yorkies Boy**[33] 3543 11-8-4 **45** oh10...(p) JamieHamblett[(5)] 10 — —
(N E Berry) *bhd fnl 3f* **66/1**

1m 30.02s (0.96) **Going Correction** +0.075s/f (Good)
WFA 3 from 4yo+ 5lb **11** Ran SP% **116.8**
Speed ratings (Par 103):97,96,94,94,91 90,84,84,79,77 62
CSF £123.24 CT £617.54 TOTE £6.90: £2.60, £7.70, £1.70; EX 170.00 Place 6 £24.15, Place 5 £6.19.
Owner Christopher Wright & Mrs J A Wright **Bred** Sir Eric Parker **Trained** Upper Lambourn, Berks

FOCUS
A moderate race and a modest pace, resulting in the slowest of the four races over the trip on the day, including both divisions of the two-year-old maiden. The form looks weak.
T/Plt: £27.10 to a £1 stake. Pool: £49,732.40. 1,336.30 winning tickets. T/Qpdt: £6.40 to a £1 stake. Pool: £3,676.60. 421.30 winning tickets. TM

4485 SANDOWN (R-H)

Thursday, August 17

OFFICIAL GOING: Good to firm (firm in places)
Wind: Light, across

4532 FLYERS H'CAP — 5f 6y

2:20 (2:22) (Class 5) (0-75,73) 3-Y-O — **£3,238** (£963; £481; £240) **Stalls** High

Form — RPR

-036 **1** **Tamino (IRE)**[46] 3118 3-8-6 **58**... MartinDwyer 9 — 66
(H Morrison) *lw: mde all: rdn clr wl over 1f out: hld on wl ins fnl f* **11/2**[3]

-130 **2** *½* **Safari Mischief**[12] 4164 3-9-0 **66**... JimCrowley 10 — 72
(P Winkworth) *chsd ldng pair: rdn wl over 1f out: chsd wnr jst over 1f out: kpt on* **10/1**

0233 **3** *¾* **Jucebabe**[4] 4398 3-8-2 **54**... FrancisNorton 6 — 61+
(J L Spearing) *chsd ldng trio: rdn wl over 1f out: styng on whn nt clr run wl ins fnl f* **5/1**[2]

2333 **4** *½* **Balian**[7] 4293 3-8-13 **65**...(be) RyanMoore 8 — 67
(G L Moore) *towards rr: rdn 2f out: styd on fnl f: nt rch ldrs* **13/2**

4412 **5** *1* **Gwilym (GER)**[12] 4164 3-9-2 **68**... RichardHughes 4 — 66
(D Haydn Jones) *lw: hld up in rr: hdwy and rdn 2f out: no imp ins fnl f* **5/2**[1]

0315 **6** *2* **Montzando**[12] 4164 3-8-2 **57**...(v) SaleemGolam[(3)] 11 — 48
(B R Millman) *pressed wnr: rdn over 2f out: wknd over 1f out* **6/1**

0520 **7** *¾* **Danny The Dip**[12] 4141 3-8-0 **57**... MarcHalford[(5)] 2 — 45
(J J Bridger) *racd alone in centre: rdn and hung lft 1/2-way: no ch after* **16/1**

0404 **8** *1* **Supercast (IRE)**[41] 3268 3-9-7 **73**...(b) LPKeniry 3 — 57
(J S Moore) *racd in midfield: rdn 1/2-way: sn struggling* **25/1**

-000 **9** *nk* **Eversden (USA)**[21] 3873 3-9-2 **71**... AdamKirby[(3)] 5 — 54
(C G Cox) *lw: sn outpcd: virtually t.o after 2f: styd on fnl f: nvr nrr* **10/1**

61.88 secs (-0.33) **Going Correction** -0.05s/f (Good) **9** Ran SP% **116.2**
Speed ratings (Par 100):100,99,98,97,95 92,91,89,89
CSF £59.20 CT £293.43 TOTE £7.30: £3.50, £4.40, £1.40; EX 69.40.
Owner H Scott-Barrett & Lord Margadale **Bred** Century Bloodstock **Trained** East Ilsley, Berks

FOCUS
This was just an average affair, but it was run at a solid pace, and the form looks fair for the class. The form is rated at face value through the runner-up and looks sound.
Jucebabe Official explanation: jockey said filly was denied a clear run
Eversden(USA) Official explanation: jockey said colt was never travelling

4533 ELMBRIDGE CLAIMING STKS — 1m 14y

2:50 (2:51) (Class 5) 3-Y-O — **£3,238** (£963; £481; £240) **Stalls** High

Form — RPR

3301 **1** **Emily's Place (IRE)**[7] 4297 3-8-6 68... TPQueally 7 — 60
(M H Tompkins) *lw: hld up: hdwy 3f out: plld out and rdn 2f out: str run fnl f: led last 75 yds* **6/5**[1]

5054 **2** *¾* **Roya**[22] 3849 3-8-11 65... RyanMoore 4 — 63
(R Hannon) *lw: led: rdn and hdd 2f out: led again ins jst ins fnl f: hdd and no ex last 75 yds* **4/1**[2]

-060 **3** *¾* **El Capitan (FR)**[29] 3644 3-8-11 60... AdamKirby[(3)] 1 — 64
(Miss Gay Kelleway) *b: chsd ldr: rdn to ld 2f out: hdd jst over 1f out: nt qckn fnl f* **33/1**

4512 **4** *¾* **Mister Maq**[10] 4195 3-8-9 61...(b) JimCrowley 3 — 58
(M Dods) *lw: chsd ldrs: rdn wl over 2f out: edgd lft over 1f out: kpt on onepced ins fnl f* **10/1**

5110 **5** *3 ½* **Opera Writer (IRE)**[8] 4249 3-9-0 68...(e) MartinDwyer 5 — 55
(J R Boyle) *lw: stdd s: t.k.h in rr: rdn 3f out: no imp* **6/1**[3]

6420 **6** *¾* **Mucho Loco (IRE)**[7] 4297 3-8-4 60...(b) NeilChalmers[(3)] 8 — 46
(J G Portman) *b: t.k.h: hld up in rr: rdn 2f out: nvr trbld ldrs* **9/1**

-000 **7** *13* **Solicitude**[47] 3101 3-8-4 55... FrancisNorton 6 — 13
(D Haydn Jones) *plld v hrd: chsd ldrs: rdn over 2f out: btn whn lost action over 1f out: eased* **20/1**

00-1 **8** *5* **Maid In England**[49] 3006 3-8-3 45... NelsonDeSouza[(3)] 2 — 3
(G A Ham) *slowly away: hld up in last: rdn and lost tch over 3f out: t.o* **25/1**

1m 45.24s (1.29) **Going Correction** -0.025s/f (Good) **8** Ran SP% **110.4**
Speed ratings (Par 100):92,91,90,89,86 85,72,67
CSF £5.40 TOTE £2.10: £1.10, £1.60, £11.30; EX 7.00.The winner was claimed by Jeff Pearce for £12,000. Roya was subject to a friendly claim.
Owner Barry Brewster **Bred** Bryan Ryan **Trained** Newmarket, Suffolk

FOCUS
A very moderate winning time, around half a second slower than the two-year-old maiden, due to the steady early gallop. The first four came clear but the race has been rated negatively.
Solicitude Official explanation: jockey said filly lost her action

4534 EUROPEAN BREEDERS FUND MAIDEN STKS — 1m 14y

3:25 (3:26) (Class 5) 2-Y-O — **£4,533** (£1,348; £674; £336) **Stalls** High

Form — RPR

2 **1** **Mariotto (USA)**[12] 4129 2-9-3... MartinDwyer 5 — 87+
(M Johnston) *lw: sn led: shkn up and qcknd clr over 2f out: eased last 100 yds* **2/5**[1]

2 *7* **Teslin (IRE)** 2-9-3... KDarley 6 — 67+
(M Johnston) *cmpt: bit bkwd: s.i.s: rr: hdwy over 3f out: rdn and chsd wnr 2f out: no ch w wnr but kpt on* **13/2**[3]

3 **3** *1* **Fever**[22] 3843 2-9-3... RyanMoore 3 — 65
(R Hannon) *chsd wnr: rdn over 3f out: lost 2nd 2f out: no ch after* **6/1**[2]

4 *3* **Nothing Is Forever (IRE)** 2-9-3... JimCrowley 4 — 58
(Mrs A J Perrett) *str: scope: bit bkwd: t.k.h: trckd ldrs: rdn over 2f out: sn outpcd* **20/1**

5 *5* **Countrywide Style (IRE)** 2-9-0... JamesDoyle[(3)] 2 — 46
(N P Littmoden) *w'like: chsd ldrs tl rdn and lost pl 4f out: no ch after* **25/1**

1m 44.76s (0.81) **Going Correction** -0.025s/f (Good) **5** Ran SP% **107.7**
Speed ratings (Par 94):94,87,86,83,78
CSF £3.27 TOTE £1.40: £1.10, £2.00; EX 3.50.
Owner Sheikh Mohammed **Bred** Darley **Trained** Middleham Moor, N Yorks

FOCUS
Despite the small field this interesting juvenile maiden was run at sound pace throughout and the field came home strung out behind the impressive winner.

NOTEBOOK
Mariotto(USA) ◆ had proved green when finishing runner-up on his debut at Goodwood 12 days previously and still looked in need of this experience, but the step up to this longer trip was right up his street and he ultimately proved in a different league his rivals. He has an abundance of scope, looks suited by a decent surface, and is clearly an exciting middle-distance prospect for next season. However, he looks well worth his place in Pattern company now and, while currently holding no fancy entries apart from the 2007 Derby, he will surely be seen out again this season before too long. Something like the Royal Lodge at Ascot next month would seem a viable target, but he would need to be supplemented for that all the same. (op 4-9)
Teslin(IRE) ◆, a half-brother to the high-class filly Independence, looked much in need of this debut experience and ran distinctly green through the early parts. He did emerge to have a chance around two out, but his effort proved short-lived and he was ultimately firmly put in his place by his winning stable companion. He has numerous Group entries and, on this evidence, should soon be placed to get off the mark. (op 5-1)
Fever, third on Lingfield's Polytrack on debut 22 days previously, failed to really improve as expected for this step up in trip yet was not disgraced all the same. He looks in need of further experience, and is probably going to prove happier when reverting to a sharper test in the short term, but time may also tell he faced an impossible task. (tchd 13-2 in a place)
Nothing Is Forever(IRE), an 80,000gns half-brother to the high-class miler Decorated Hero, ran a little freely through the early parts and his fate was sealed a fair way from home. He is entitled to improve for the experience. (op 16-1)
Countrywide Style(IRE), who cost 80,000gns as a two-year-old, found this all too hot and looked in need of the outing. He will stay further next year without fuss.

4535 VARIETY CLUB DAY ON 26TH AUGUST H'CAP — 7f 16y

4:00 (4:00) (Class 3) (0-90,90) 3-Y-O+ — **£8,096** (£2,408; £1,203; £601) **Stalls** High

Form — RPR

1215 **1** **Waterside (IRE)**[12] 4131 7-9-10 **86**... RyanMoore 9 — 96
(G L Moore) *lw: in tch: hdwy 3f out: led 2f out: styd on wl u.p* **15/2**

0030 **2** *¾* **Binanti**[5] 4372 6-9-9 **85**... JimCrowley 2 — 93
(P R Chamings) *w.w in midfield: hdwy over 2f out: chsd wnr 1f out: a hld* **15/2**

2100 **3** *1* **Desert Dreamer (IRE)**[16] 4029 5-9-6 **82**... RichardHughes 14 — 87+
(P R Chamings) *hld up bhd: swtchd lft and hdwy over 1f out: r.o wl fnl f: nrst fin* **14/1**

2141 **4** *nk* **Phluke**[24] 3789 5-9-5 **84**... NelsonDeSouza[(3)] 12 — 89
(R F Johnson Houghton) *t.k.h: chsd ldrs: rdn wl over 2f out: sltly outpcd over 1f out: kpt on again last 100 yds* **6/1**[3]

1010 **5** *½* **Irony (IRE)**[16] 4029 7-9-9 **88**...(p) NeilChalmers[(3)] 5 — 91
(A M Balding) *prom: chsd ldr 4f out tl over 2f out: kpt on one pced after* **25/1**

14-0 **6** *nk* **Unshakable (IRE)**[57] 2742 7-10-0 **90**... FrancisNorton 1 — 93+
(Bob Jones) *b: b.hind: hld up bhd: rdn and effrt on outer over 2f out: kpt on ins fnl f: nt rch ldrs* **10/1**

3005 **7** *hd* **Bobski (IRE)**[6] 4338 4-9-6 **82**... KDarley 4 — 84
(G A Huffer) *lw: bhd: rdn 3f out: hung lft and nt qckn over 1f out: kpt on last 100 yds* **12/1**

0236 **8** *hd* **Dry Ice (IRE)**[16] 4029 4-9-5 **81**... FergusSweeney 8 — 83
(H Candy) *lw: slowly away: hld up in rr: rdn over 1f out: kpt on but nvr pce to rch ldrs* **3/1**[1]

5020 **9** *nk* **Material Witness (IRE)**[15] 4042 9-9-12 **88**... MartinDwyer 7 — 89
(W R Muir) *lw: slowly away: sn rcvrd and led after 1f: hdd 2f out: wknd last 100 yds* **25/1**

0650 **10** *½* **Will He Wish**[11] 4172 10-9-12 **88**... IanMongan 11 — 87
(S Gollings) *chsd ldrs: rdn wl over 2f out: kpt on one pce* **25/1**

4513 **11** *¾* **Blue Trojan (IRE)**[18] 3973 6-9-9 **85**... GeorgeBaker 6 — 82
(S Kirk) *hld up in last: shkn up 3f out: swtchd lft over 1f out: n.d* **9/2**[2]

0060 **12** *2* **Emilio**[13] 4106 5-9-7 **83**...(t) FJohansson 13 — 75
(R A Kvisla) *lw: led for 1f: chsd ldrs tl rdn over 2f out: wknd fnl f* **50/1**

1m 29.34s (-1.75) **Going Correction** -0.025s/f (Good) **12** Ran SP% **117.9**
Speed ratings (Par 107):109,108,107,106,106 105,105,105,104,104 103,101
CSF £59.83 CT £791.52 TOTE £7.70: £2.30, £2.50, £4.90; EX 49.90.
Owner Nigel Shields **Bred** Yeomanstown Stud **Trained** Woodingdean, E Sussex

FOCUS
A fair handicap for the class which was run at no more than a modest early pace. The form looks straightforward enough with the first four close to their marks.

NOTEBOOK
Waterside(IRE) showed a decent attitude under pressure and got back to winning ways under a typically strong ride from Moore. He has held his form very well all year, indeed this was his fifth success to date in 2006, and he is well suited by the stiff finish over this trip. He ought to continue to be competitive despite a future weight rise.
Binanti, better than his finishing position suggested at Newmarket five days previously, ran one of his better races and showed his true colours in defeat. He is a fair benchmark for this form, but remains on a lengthy losing run all the same. (op 7-1)
Desert Dreamer(IRE) travelled sweetly off the pace and the manner in which he finished suggested he would have been seen to better effect off the stronger early gallop. He is the type who needs things to fall right, but on this evidence he looks capable of winning another race from this mark.
Phluke, raised 4lb for his recent Beverley success, turned in a solid effort in defeat and remains in good heart at present. (op 13-2)
Irony(IRE) was handy throughout and, while lacking a change of pace when push came to shove, turned in an improved effort in defeat.
Dry Ice(IRE) never looked a serious threat from off the pace and is becoming frustrating to follow now. (op 10-3 tchd 7-2 in a place)
Blue Trojan(IRE) was given a lot to do from off the pace and proved disappointing. Official explanation: jockey said gelding was denied a clear run

4536 N.E.C. HARLEQUINS OF LONDON H'CAP 1m 1f

4:35 (4:35) (Class 4) (0-80,78) 3-Y-O+ **£5,505** (£1,228; £1,228; £408) **Stalls** High

Form RPR

3230 1 **South O'The Border**[38] [3366] 4-9-13 **76** .... IanMongan 7 83
(T G Mills) *swtg: chsd ldrs: wnt 2nd 3f out: rdn to ld 2f out: wandered u.p after: hld on cl home* **7/2**[1]

3242 2 *shd* **Fabrian**[4] [4392] 8-9-7 **73** .... JamesDoyle(3) 11 80
(R J Price) *led tl 1/2-way: rdn and outpcd 3f out: rallied u.p over 1f out: styd on wl: jst hld* **4/1**[2]

0012 2 *dht* **Personify**[34] [3469] 4-9-5 **71** ....(p) AdamKirby(3) 9 78
(C G Cox) *chsd ldrs: rdn 3f out: hdwy 2f out: ev ch and carried lft ins fnl f: no ex cl home* **11/2**

2310 4 *½* **Cusoon**[12] [4160] 4-9-12 **75** .... RyanMoore 10 81
(G L Moore) *lw: hld up bhd: rdn and hdwy on inner 2f out: ev ch wl ins fnl f: no ex last 50 yds* **9/2**[3]

1042 5 *3* **Della Salute**[17] [4001] 4-9-13 **76** .... LPKeniry 8 76
(Miss E C Lavelle) *hld up in tch: rdn and outpcd 3f out: swtchd lft over 1f out: kpt on one pced fnl f* **14/1**

4205 6 *½* **Night Storm**[8] [4241] 5-9-12 **75** .... KerrinMcEvoy 6 74
(S Dow) *slowly away: hld up in last: effrt on outer 3f out: nvr pce to rch ldrs* **8/1**

3305 7 *1 ½* **Barathea Dreams (IRE)**[29] [3642] 5-10-0 **77** .... MartinDwyer 1 73
(J S Moore) *lw: chsd ldr tl led 1/2-way: hdd 2f out: wknd fnl f* **7/1**

0063 8 *1 ¾* **Chapter (IRE)**[7] [4288] 4-8-12 **64** ....(b) NeilChalmers(3) 5 57
(Mrs A L M King) *slowly away: in tch: stmbld bnd 4f out: rdn over 2f out: sn struggling* **16/1**

1m 55.06s (-1.05) **Going Correction** -0.025s/f (Good)
WFA 3 from 4yo+ 7lb **8** Ran SP% **111.9**
Speed ratings (Par 105):103,102,102,102,99 99,98,96
WIN: South O'The Border £3.40. PL: £1.40, Fabrian £1.90, Personify £2.00. EX: SOTB/F £7.90, SOTB/P £13.00. CSF: SOTB/F £8.39, SOTB/P £10.95. TRIC: SOTB/F/P £36.74, SOTB/P/F £39.17..

Owner T G Mills **Bred** Summertree Stud **Trained** Headley, Surrey

FOCUS
This was a modest handicap, which was run at a fair pace, and the first four came clear in a thrilling finish. The form looks sound and should prove reliable.

4537 OXSHOTT H'CAP 1m 6f

5:10 (5:10) (Class 4) (0-80,76) 3-Y-O **£5,505** (£1,637; £818; £408) **Stalls** Centre

Form RPR

1233 1 **Meadow Mischief (FR)**[33] [3539] 3-9-7 **76** ....(b) RyanMoore 4 90+
(E A L Dunlop) *lw: w.w in midfield: hdwy 4f out: rdn to ld 2f out: sn clr: rdn out* **11/4**[1]

0004 2 *11* **Himba**[12] [4150] 3-8-10 **65** .... JimCrowley 2 64
(Mrs A J Perrett) *lw: chsd ldrs: wnt 2nd over 4f out tl over 2f out: sn outpcd: wnt poor 2nd on line* **16/1**

0334 3 *nk* **Reinstated (IRE)**[42] [3225] 3-9-3 **72** .... RichardHughes 6 71
(B W Hills) *swtg: led: clr after 2f: rdn and hdd 2f out: no ch w wnr after: lost 2nd on line* **5/1**[3]

4321 4 *½* **La Via Ferrata (IRE)**[35] [3456] 3-8-10 **65** .... LPKeniry 1 63
(A G Newcombe) *hld up in rr: rdn and effrt over 3f out: nvr on terms* **11/2**

-545 5 *¾* **Impostor (IRE)**[83] [1975] 3-9-7 **76** .... KerrinMcEvoy 5 73
(J R Fanshawe) *bit bkwd: hld up in rr: rdn over 4f out: sn lost tch* **5/1**[3]

5105 6 *11* **Brigadore (USA)**[21] [3877] 3-9-6 **75** .... MartinDwyer 7 56
(W R Muir) *chsd ldr tl over 4f out: wknd 3f out: eased fnl f: t.o* **7/2**[2]

4000 7 *12* **Soubriquet (IRE)**[19] [3935] 3-8-13 **68** .... IanMongan 8 33
(T G Mills) *lw: hld up in rr: rdn and lost tch wl over 3f out: eased over 1f out: t.o* **11/1**

3m 2.68s (-1.83) **Going Correction** -0.025s/f (Good) **7** Ran SP% **111.8**
Speed ratings (Par 102):104,97,97,97,96 90,83
CSF £43.62 CT £205.39 TOTE £2.90: £2.20, £4.60; EX 49.10 Place 6 £70.18, Place 5 £21.37.
Owner Gainsborough Stud **Bred** Gainsborough Stud Management Ltd **Trained** Newmarket, Suffolk

FOCUS
This staying handicap represented a decent test for these three-year-olds and the strong early pace ensured the field was fairly strung out from an early stage. The third and fourth set the level for the form.
Brigadore(USA) Official explanation: jockey said colt hung right in straight
T/Plt: £91.30 to a £1 stake. Pool: £55,106.35. 440.50 winning tickets. T/Qpdt: £16.90 to a £1 stake. Pool: £3,344.60. 145.80 winning tickets. SP

4538 - 4541a (Foreign Racing) - See Raceform Interactive

4463 DEAUVILLE (R-H)

Thursday, August 17

OFFICIAL GOING: Turf course - soft; all-weather - standard

4542a PRIX DE LIEUREY-SHADWELL (LISTED RACE) (FILLIES) (ROUND) 1m (R)

2:20 (12:00) 3-Y-O **£17,241** (£6,897; £5,172; £3,448; £1,724)

RPR

1 **Gwenseb (FR)**[40] [3327] 3-8-12 .... OPeslier 98
(C Laffon-Parias, France) **10/1**[1]

2 *1 ½* **Tonic Star (FR)**[35] 3-8-12 .... GFaucon 95
(E Lellouche, France)

3 *1* **Sabana Perdida (IRE)**[60] [2694] 3-9-2 .... C-PLemaire 97
(A De Royer-Dupre, France)

4 *snk* **Dancing Guest (IRE)**[8] [4249] 3-8-12 .... MBlancpain 93
(G G Margarson) *prominent, led after 2f, pushed along entering straight, ridden and headed approaching final furlong, no extra inside last*

5 *hd* **Grigorieva (IRE)**[18] [3991] 3-9-2 .... CSoumillon 96
(A Fabre, France)

6 *1 ½* **Sirene Doloise (FR)**[16] [4035] 3-8-12 .... TThulliez 89
(A Bonin, France)

7 *½* **Samsa (FR)**[319] [5649] 3-8-12 .... FSpanu 88
(R Gibson, France)

8 *1* **Deauville (GER)**[29] [3661] 3-8-12 .... DBonilla 86
(Frau E Mader, Germany)

9 *2* **Triennale (FR)**[59] 3-8-12 .... DBoeuf 82
(Mme C Head-Maarek, France)

10 *2* **Travel Team (USA)**[19] [3968] 3-8-12 .... IMendizabal 78
(J-C Rouget, France)

11 **Highway To Glory (IRE)**[20] [3891] 3-8-12 .... EBotti 78
(M Botti) *never a factor*

12 **Madura (GER)**[29] [3661] 3-8-12 .... ASuborics 78
(Mario Hofer, Germany)

1m 43.8s **12** Ran SP% **9.1**
PARI-MUTUEL: WIN 11.00; PL 3.10, 3.20, 2.30; DF 71.30.
Owner Wertheimer Et Frere **Bred** Mme M-T & G Geffrelot **Trained** Chantilly, France

NOTEBOOK
Dancing Guest(IRE) made a brave effort in this Listed race and was always one of the leaders. She battled on well in the straight but could not quicken like several of her rivals. She could be back in France next time out when different tactics will be employed.
Highway To Glory(IRE) ran very freely and was a spent force before the straight.

4543a PRIX MINERVE-SHADWELL (GROUP 3) (FILLIES) 1m 4f 110y

2:50 (3:08) 3-Y-O **£27,586** (£11,034; £8,276; £5,517; £2,759)

RPR

1 **Maroussies Wings (IRE)**[56] [2772] 3-8-9 .... OPeslier 4 106
(P C Haslam) *always with leaders, narrow leader after 2f & tried to slow it down, headed after 4f, led again over 3f out, driven out* **59/10**[3]

2 *½* **Mary Louhana**[34] [3515] 3-8-9 .... SMaillot 8 105
(M Delzangles, France) *held up in rear, 8th straight, headway on inside from 2f out, hard ridden to chase winner final 150y, kept on one pace* **35/1**

3 *½* **Ponte Tresa (FR)**[34] [3515] 3-8-9 .... DBonilla 3 105
(Y De Nicolay, France) *held up, last straight, headway on outside final 1 1/2f, nearest at finish* **83/10**

4 *1 ½* **Sanaya (IRE)**[67] [2491] 3-8-9 .... CSoumillon 7 102
(A De Royer-Dupre, France) *always close up, 3rd straight, chased winner well over 1f out, every cahnace 150y out, one pace* **8/5**[1]

5 *1 ½* **Anna Mona (GER)**[75] [2257] 3-8-9 .... TThulliez 5 100
(N Clement, France) *reluctant to load, raced in mid-division, 5th straight, ridden well over 1f out, one pace* **12/1**

6 *2 ½* **Litalia (IRE)**[27] [3719] 3-8-9 .... C-PLemaire 9 96
(P Schiergen, Germany) *first to show, with leaders til led after 4f, headed over 3f out, 2nd straight, weakened over 1f out* **13/1**

7 *nk* **Village Fete**[34] [3515] 3-8-9 .... DBoeuf 2 96
(D Smaga, France) *held up, 7th & pushed along straight, never a factor* **44/10**[2]

8 *5* **Penne (FR)**[34] [3515] 3-8-9 .... IMendizabal 6 88
(J-C Rouget, France) *mid-division, headway & 4th on inside straight, ridden & beaten 1 1/2f out* **67/10**

9 *6* **Softlanding (IRE)**[35] 3-8-9 .... TGillet 1 79
(J E Hammond, France) *narrow leader til headed after 2f, close up to 3f out, 6th & weakening straight, eased* **10/1**

2m 50.0s **9** Ran SP% **121.9**
PARI-MUTUEL: WIN 6.90; PL 2.40, 5.40, 2.80; DF 121.70.
Owner Mrs R J Jacobs **Bred** Newsells Park Stud Limited **Trained** Middleham Moor, N Yorks

NOTEBOOK
Maroussies Wings(IRE) was kicked on before the straight and then stayed on extremely bravely in the final stages. She looked like being caught at the furlong marker, but found a little extra to hold off the runner-up. There are no firm plans for this filly at the moment.
Mary Louhana still had a lot to do in the straight. She made her challenge up the far rail and was fairly flying at the finish. It should be noted that she was not obviously fancied, however, and is yet to win a race to date.
Ponte Tresa(FR) did not appear on the scene until inside the final furlong. The filly then ran on well up the centre of the track and finished best of all.
Sanaya(IRE) was always well placed and dropped in behind the leading group. Two furlongs out she looked extremely dangerous, but she did not go through with her challenge, and this distance looked a little extreme for her.

4227 CATTERICK (L-H)

Friday, August 18

OFFICIAL GOING: Soft
The ground having gone soft exposed one of the negative aspects of 48-hour decs. Of the 16 non-runners, 13 were due to the ground.
Wind: Light, half against Weather: Persistent heavy showers

4544 I.R.M. AMATEUR RIDERS' H'CAP 1m 3f 214y

5:40 (5:40) (Class 5) (0-75,73) 3-Y-O+ **£3,747** (£1,162; £580; £290) **Stalls** Low

Form RPR

5412 1 **Champagne Shadow (IRE)**[48] [3074] 5-10-5 **60** .... MissARyan(5) 6 71
(K A Ryan) *hld up: stdy hdwy over 2f out: racd centre: led ins last: styd on* **6/1**[2]

4154 2 *1* **Court Of Appeal**[10] [4229] 9-11-0 **64** ....(tp) MissLEllison 1 73
(B Ellison) *led 1f: chsd ldrs: led over 2f out: hung rt and hdd ins last: no ex* **13/2**[3]

1340 3 *3* **Ramsgill (USA)**[21] [3900] 4-10-9 **64** .... MrSPearce(5) 9 68
(J Pearce) *sn chsng ldrs: rdn over 2f out: kpt on same pce* **10/1**

1-51 4 *¾* **Halla San**[17] [4022] 4-11-2 **71** .... MrBMcHugh(5) 5 74
(R A Fahey) *hld up in last: hdwy over 3f out: rdn over 1f out: nvr rchd ldrs* **5/6**[1]

666 5 *2 ½* **Edas**[20] [3939] 4-10-13 **68** .... MrMWalford(5) 4 67
(J J Quinn) *hld up: effrt over 2f out: one pce* **20/1**

0033 6 *nk* **Khanjar (USA)**[10] [4229] 6-11-1 **70** .... MissKellyBurke(5) 7 69
(K R Burke) *trckd ldrs: jnd ldr 7f out: led over 5f out tl over 2f out: one pce* **12/1**

0004 7 *8* **Cumbrian Knight (IRE)**[3] [4451] 8-10-0 **55** .... MissNJefferson(5) 11 41
(J M Jefferson) *led after 1f: hdd over 5f out: wknd over 1f out* **11/1**

-030 8 *26* **On Every Street**[8] [4307] 5-9-11 **52** oh10 .... MissRBastiman(5) 3 —
(R Bastiman) *hld up: drvn over 5f out: sn lost pl: styd far side in home st* **100/1**

40-0 9 *1* **Poirot**[199] [258] 4-9-11 **52** oh7 .... CJCallow(5) 2 —
(J Howard Johnson) *t.k.h in rr: lost pl over 3f out: sn bhd: styd far side in home st* **66/1**

2m 45.6s (6.60) **Going Correction** +0.35s/f (Good)
WFA 3 from 4yo+ 10lb **9** Ran SP% **114.5**
Speed ratings (Par 103):92,91,89,88,87 86,81,64,63
CSF £43.49 CT £382.99 TOTE £7.70: £1.90, £1.70, £2.20; EX 42.50.
Owner John Duddy **Bred** Mrs Kate Watson **Trained** Hambleton, N Yorks

FOCUS
No pace on at all early, though it picked up after a couple of furlongs. These amateurs had very much a difference of opinion as to where to go on reaching the home straight - three came stands' side, two stayed inside and the other four, including the winner, came down the middle. Despite that the form seems sound enough.
On Every Street Official explanation: jockey said the gelding was unsuited by the soft ground

The Form Book, Raceform Ltd, Compton, RG20 6NL

4545 SIMON BAILES PEUGEOT207 (S) STKS — 7f

6:10 (6:13) (Class 6) 2-Y-O — £2,730 (£806; £403) Stalls Low

Form — RPR

4241 **1** **Fractured Foxy**[6] 4376 2-8-6 65 ... RoystonFfrench 9 — 50
(J J Quinn) *chsd ldrs: styd on centre to ld jst ins last: drvn out* **2/1**[1]

650 **2** *1* **Only A Splash**[4] 4433 2-8-11 ... PaulQuinn 3 — 53
(D W Chapman) *chsd ldr: led over 1f out: hdd jst ins last: no ex* **50/1**

0060 **3** *nk* **Little Tiny Tom**[14] 4115 2-8-4 ... (p) PaulPickard(7) 10 — 52
(C N Kellett) *in tch: hdwy over 2f out: styd on centre to take 2nd wl ins last: eased towards fin* **100/1**

04 **4** *½* **Fun Thai**[9] 4238 2-8-6 ... CatherineGannon 2 — 46
(M R Channon) *s.i.s: hdwy over 2f out: styd on same pce ins last* **12/1**

0335 **5** *1* **Denton Hawk**[25] 3787 2-8-11 60 ... PhillipMakin 12 — 48
(M Dods) *hld up in tch: hdwy on outer 3f out: chsng ldrs on wd outside 1f out: one pce* **8/1**

4434 **6** *½* **Generist**[7] 4334 2-8-3 57 ... DominicFox(3) 4 — 42
(M J Attwater) *chsd ldrs: sn drvn along: edgd rt appr fnl f: one pce* **5/1**[3]

0500 **7** *5* **Delta Queen**[59] 2731 2-8-6 ... AdrianTNicholls 7 — 29
(C N Kellett) *led tl over 1f out: sn wknd* **100/1**

0 **8** *2½* **Strathmore (IRE)**[74] 2281 2-8-11 ... RichardMullen 6 — 28+
(E J O'Neill) *chsd ldrs: drvn along over 4f out: wknd appr fnl f: eased* **5/2**[2]

005 **9** *2½* **Stunningjo**[39] 3345 2-8-6 ... (b) FrancisNorton 8 — 17
(J L Spearing) *s.s: nvr on terms* **6/1**

5556 **10** *9* **The Brat**[3] 4452 2-8-1 ow2 ... GemmaAnderson(7) 5 — —
(James Moffatt) *chsd ldrs: lost pl over 2f out: sn bhd* **66/1**

000 **11** *nk* **Makeusabuck**[89] 1862 2-8-2 ow1 ... KevinGhunowa(5) 11 — —
(A Berry) *chsd ldrs: lost pl 3f out: sn bhd* **80/1**

0 **12** *15* **Herons Kiss (IRE)**[89] 1862 2-8-3 ... JohnMcAuley(3) 1 — —
(B S Rothwell) *hld up in rr: lost tch over 2f out: sn bhd* **100/1**

1m 32.99s (5.63) **Going Correction** +0.35s/f (Good) — **12** Ran SP% **119.3**
Speed ratings (Par 92):81,79,79,78,77 77,71,68,65,55 55,38
CSF £117.38 TOTE £3.70: £2.20, £13.40, £9.30; EX 120.80.There was no bid for the winner. Strathmore was claimed by Richard Fahey for £6,000.
Owner Mrs E Wright **Bred** Bearstone Stud **Trained** Settrington, N Yorks
■ Stewards' Enquiry : Paul Pickard seven-day ban: dropped hands and lost 2nd place (Aug 29-Sep 4)

FOCUS
This looked a poor seller, as the odds of the placed horses might suggest, and there was not much covering the first six home at the line. As in the first race, the winner came down the centre of the track in the home straight. The winning time was very slow, even for a race like this and allowing for the conditions and the form is weak.

NOTEBOOK
Fractured Foxy, best in on adjusted official ratings and the only previous winner in the field having landed a similar event on faster ground at Redcar last time, appreciated this further step up in trip and proved very game down the centre of the track in the home straight. She had already shown that she can handle these conditions and is now likely to find herself in nurseries. (op 15-8 tchd 7-4 and 9-4 in places)
Only A Splash, well beaten in all three of his outings to date, improved a good deal for this drop in class and had every chance. The longer trip did not seem to be a problem, but this was a poor seller and he will need to find one just as bad if he is to break his duck.
Little Tiny Tom, beaten out of sight in all four of his outings to date including in a seller, made his effort furthest from the stands' rail and arguably might have finished second had his rider not gone easy on him in he dying strides. Given the slow winning time, this may not have been the improvement on previous efforts that it may have looked and his proximity does nothing for the form.
Fun Thai, who had only beaten one horse in her two previous outings, was encountering very different conditions but although she came closer to winning she probably improved little in terms of performance. She looks very moderate indeed. (op 17-2)
Denton Hawk, whose five previous outings have all been on fast ground, tried to put in an effort against the stands' rail in the latter stages, but it came to little. Perhaps the longer trip or easier ground did not suit him. (op 9-1)
Generist stepped down on recent efforts, but this was her first try on soft ground and it may not have suited. (tchd 11-2)
Strathmore(IRE), up two furlongs from his debut here in June and on much easier ground, was all the rage in the market in this lower grade but failed to pick up at all. The ground seems to be the most likely excuse. (op 5-1)

4546 BOOK ON-LINE AT CATTERICKBRIDGE.CO.UK CLAIMING STKS — 5f

6:45 (6:45) (Class 6) 3-Y-O+ — £2,730 (£806; £403) Stalls Low

Form — RPR

1030 **1** **Trinculo (IRE)**[19] 3972 9-9-7 92 ... AdrianTNicholls 9 — 79
(D Nicholls) *trckd ldrs: c wd and racd stands' side after 1f: rdn over 1f out: styd on to ld ins last: drvn rt out* **1/2**[1]

04U0 **2** *nk* **Sounds Simla (IRE)**[5] 4401 3-8-5 60 ... PaulQuinn 10 — 64
(J F Coupland) *swtchd wd after 1f to r stands's side: hdwy over 1f out: kpt on to take 2nd nr fin: no ex* **12/1**

1305 **3** *¾* **Our Little Secret (IRE)**[13] 4135 4-8-6 65 ... KevinGhunowa(5) 1 — 65
(A Berry) *w ldr: led over 3f out: hung rt and hdd ins last: no ex* **9/2**[2]

4213 **4** *6* **Alugat (IRE)**[15] 4091 3-8-11 59 ... (v[1]) RoystonFfrench 12 — 47
(Mrs A Duffield) *led over 1f: chsd ldr: wknd fnl f* **6/1**[3]

-000 **5** *8* **Four Kings**[6] 4350 5-8-10 34 ... CatherineGannon 2 — 16
(R Allan) *racd towards far side: outpcd and lost pl after 1f: sn bhd* **80/1**

0000 **6** *12* **Torrent**[23] 3833 11-8-1 40 ow1 ... (p) KevinMachent(7) 8 — —
(J M Saville) *racd towards far side: sn outpcd and bhd* **50/1**

61.19 secs (0.59) **Going Correction** +0.15s/f (Good)
WFA 3 from 4yo+ 2lb — **6** Ran SP% **110.0**
Speed ratings (Par 101):101,100,99,89,76 57
CSF £7.58 TOTE £1.50: £1.10, £4.20; EX 9.60.Sounds Simla was claimed by Ron Harris for £7,000.
Owner Nigel Shields **Bred** Humphrey Okeke **Trained** Sessay, N Yorks

FOCUS
A race decimated by six non-runners and although the odds-on favourite won, it was a very close-run thing. The first two came up the nearside of the track, but for a long time it seemed that the leading pair down the middle would take some catching. The third sets the level for the form.

4547 CEMEX MATERIALS NURSERY — 5f 212y

7:15 (7:15) (Class 4) 2-Y-O — £6,477 (£1,927; £963; £481) Stalls Low

Form — RPR

2244 **1** **Dolly Coughdrop (IRE)**[4] 4427 2-8-6 70 ... FrancisNorton 8 — 74
(K R Burke) *chsd ldrs: led on stands' side over 2f out: kpt on wl ins last* **8/1**

6421 **2** *1¼* **High Style**[9] 4246 2-9-6 84 6ex ... RobertWinston 1 — 84
(R Hannon) *hld up: hdwy 3f out: chal over 1f out: no ex ins last* **3/1**[1]

1424 **3** *2* **Rainbow Fox**[6] 4377 2-9-0 78 ... TonyHamilton 2 — 72
(R A Fahey) *chsd ldrs: outpcd over 2f out: kpt on wl fnl f* **6/1**[3]

042 **4** *2* **Astroangel**[25] 3799 2-8-7 71 ... RichardMullen 3 — 59
(M H Tompkins) *s.i.s: hdwy over 2f out: one pce fnl f* **8/1**

5360 **5** *nk* **The Nifty Fox**[7] 4321 2-8-8 72 ... DavidAllan 7 — 59
(T D Easterby) *led 1f: chsd ldrs: kpt on same pce fnl 2f* **17/2**

1202 **6** *nk* **Fathom Five (IRE)**[13] 4134 2-9-2 85 ... MarkLawson(5) 4 — 71
(B Smart) *trckd ldrs: effrt over 2f out: kpt on same pce* **7/2**[2]

1364 **7** *¾* **The Mighty Ogmore**[35] 3481 2-8-2 66 ... (p) PaulQuinn 5 — 50
(R C Guest) *s.i.s: hdwy over 2f out: kpt on: nvr nr ldrs* **18/1**

0013 **8** *4* **Movethegoalposts**[13] 4134 2-8-7 71 ... RoystonFfrench 9 — 43
(M Johnston) *chsd ldrs: drvn over 3f out: lost pl over 1f out* **8/1**

0015 **9** *½* **Mundo's Magic**[13] 4134 2-9-1 79 ... AdrianTNicholls 6 — 49
(D W Barker) *led after 1f: hdd over 2f out: lost pl over 1f out* **25/1**

5034 **10** *3* **The Dandy Fox**[14] 4115 2-7-7 62 oh7 ... DuranFentiman(5) 10 — 23
(R Bastiman) *prom on outer: lost pl over 2f out* **40/1**

1m 16.4s (2.40) **Going Correction** +0.35s/f (Good) — **10** Ran SP% **116.9**
Speed ratings (Par 96):98,96,93,91,90 90,89,83,83,79
CSF £32.33 CT £160.33 TOTE £9.50: £2.70, £1.50, £3.00.
Owner Bega Racing **Bred** Gisella Dettoni **Trained** Middleham Moor, N Yorks
■ Stewards' Enquiry : David Allan caution: careless riding

FOCUS
A fair little nursery in which the pace was decent and the whole field came over to the stands' rail as a group. The form looks sound rated around the first two.

NOTEBOOK
Dolly Coughdrop(IRE), never far away, was brought right over to bag the stands' rail slot turning for home and that may have been crucial in the battle to the line with the favourite. This was her first try on soft ground and it obviously suited. (op 15-2)
High Style, carrying a 6lb penalty for his Kempton Polytrack victory, was also encountering soft ground for the first time. He was brought through to hold every chance, but the winner had the rail and saw it out that much better. (op 7-2)
Rainbow Fox had every chance and was not disgraced, but shapes as though an extra furlong would not come amiss. (op 13-2)
Astroangel, making her nursery debut and on very different ground to anything she had encountered before, had a real problem going the pace and then made her effort furthest from the stands' rail. Under the circumstances, she probably did well to finish fourth and there appeared none of the tail-swishing antics that marked her last outing. On this evidence, a step up to seven might be in order. (tchd 13-2)
The Nifty Fox was given a positive ride, but this first try at six furlongs and softer ground did not bring about any improvement. (op 14-1 tchd 8-1)
Fathom Five(IRE), up 2lb, showed that he handled cut when winning on this debut, but lacked pace where it mattered this time. He looks plenty high enough in the weights. (op 4-1 tchd 10-3)
Mundo's Magic Official explanation: jockey said the gelding was unsuited by the track

4548 TENNANTS ANTIQUE AND FINE ART AUCTIONEERS H'CAP — 7f

7:50 (7:51) (Class 6) (0-65,65) 3-Y-O+ — £2,730 (£806; £403) Stalls Low

Form — RPR

0061 **1** **Tequila Sheila (IRE)**[4] 4425 4-8-7 49 6ex ... AndrewElliott(5) 16 — 61
(K R Burke) *racd wd: led: rdn and edgd lft wl ins last: hld on towards fin* **10/3**[2]

5013 **2** *¾* **Sentiero Rosso (USA)**[15] 4090 4-9-11 65 ... (t) StephenDonohoe(3) 15 — 75
(B Ellison) *chsd ldrs: styd on down wd outside fnl 2f: tk 2nd nr line* **9/4**[1]

0426 **3** *¾* **Suhezy (IRE)**[11] 4199 3-8-6 48 ... RoystonFfrench 13 — 54
(J S Wainwright) *w wnr: keeping on same pce whn hmpd last 75yds* **9/1**

1300 **4** *3* **First Rhapsody (IRE)**[15] 4070 4-9-3 54 ... PaulMulrennan 8 — 54
(T J Etherington) *chsd ldrs: drvn 4f out: one pce fnl 2f* **13/2**

-015 **5** *½* **Hotchpotch (USA)**[1] 4524 3-8-10 52 6ex ... CatherineGannon 6 — 49
(J R Best) *hld up and bhd: effrt over 2f out: kpt on: nvr rchd ldrs* **5/1**[3]

-050 **6** *6* **Compton Bay**[11] 4198 6-8-9 46 oh1 ... DaleGibson 11 — 29
(M Brittain) *chsd ldrs: n.m.r and lost pl over 2f out* **33/1**

5-06 **7** *3½* **Jenise (IRE)**[53] 2940 3-8-3 50 ... DuranFentiman(5) 2 — 22
(Mark Campion) *a in rr* **33/1**

5000 **8** *3* **Rosthwaite (IRE)**[66] 2525 3-9-4 60 ... DeanMcKeown 9 — 24
(Ronald Thompson) *hld up in mid-div: effrt over 2f out: sn lost pl* **33/1**

3505 **9** *5* **Pride Of Kinloch**[10] 4233 6-9-0 51 ... (p) TonyHamilton 4 — 4
(N Wilson) *chsd ldrs: sn drvn along: lost pl over 4f out: sn bhd* **8/1**

1m 29.7s (2.34) **Going Correction** +0.35s/f (Good)
WFA 3 from 4yo+ 5lb — **9** Ran SP% **113.8**
Speed ratings (Par 101):100,99,98,94,94 87,83,80,74
CSF £10.87 CT £58.05 TOTE £3.90: £1.20, £1.60, £2.60; EX 12.20.
Owner Lee Westwood **Bred** Martyn J McEnery **Trained** Middleham Moor, N Yorks
■ Stewards' Enquiry : Andrew Elliott one-day ban: careless riding (Aug 29)

FOCUS
No less than eight non-runners for this handicap. The pace was sound and very few ever got into it, with the pair that were sent into a clear lead eventually finishing first and third. The front three started from the three outside stalls and with the ground becoming ever more poached on the inside in the back straight, that may have been another factor.

4549 TRANSCENDBLOODSTOCK.COM MAIDEN STKS — 1m 3f 214y

8:20 (8:21) (Class 5) 3-Y-O+ — £3,886 (£1,156; £577; £288) Stalls Low

Form — RPR

44 **1** **Burnt Oak (UAE)**[11] 4204 4-9-12 ... DeanMcKeown 3 — 91
(C W Fairhurst) *trckd ldrs: wnt 2nd over 2f out: styd on to ld ins last* **6/1**[3]

0- **2** *1* **Melpomene**[290] 6213 3-8-11 ... RoystonFfrench 2 — 84
(M Johnston) *w ldr: led after 2f: qcknd over 6f out: c stands' side in st: hdd and no ex ins last* **16/1**

322 **3** *11* **Behlaya (IRE)**[11] 4204 5-9-7 74 ... DavidAllan 8 — 69
(T D Easterby) *hld up: effrt over 3f out: wnt mod 3rd 2f out: one pce* **5/4**[1]

00 **4** *5* **Greek Well (IRE)**[60] 2712 3-9-2 ... (t) RobertWinston 7 — 67
(Sir Michael Stoute) *trckd ldrs: wnt 2nd 7f out: hrd drvn over 2f out: wknd over 1f out* **7/4**[2]

5 *9* **The Music Queen**[123] 5-9-7 ... PaulQuinn 5 — 49
(G A Swinbank) *dwlt: in rr: outpcd over 3f out: kpt on fnl 2f* **14/1**

6 *6* **Benny The Rascal (IRE)** 4-9-12 ... J-PGuillambert 9 — 46
(J Pearce) *chsd ldrs: drvn over 6f out: lost pl over 4f out* **33/1**

44 **7** *½* **Greyside (USA)**[61] 2682 3-9-2 ... PaulMulrennan 4 — 45
(J Howard Johnson) *chsd ldrs: drvn over 5f out: lost pl over 3f out: sn bhd* **9/1**

04-0 **8** *5* **Full As A Rocket (IRE)**[53] 2927 5-9-12 52 ... AdrianTNicholls 6 — 38
(D Nicholls) *t.k.h: led 2f: hung rt thrght: lost pl and eased 3f out: sn bhd* **33/1**

9 *1¼* **Mister Jungle (FR)**[112] 4-9-7 ... AndrewElliott(5) 1 — 37
(Mrs S C Bradburne) *s.s: a last: detached 5f out* **80/1**

2m 44.75s (5.75) **Going Correction** +0.35s/f (Good)
WFA 3 from 4yo+ 10lb — **9** Ran SP% **124.8**
Speed ratings (Par 103):94,93,86,82,76 72,72,69,68
CSF £99.44 TOTE £8.20: £2.10, £6.10, £1.10; EX 182.80 Place 6 £31.55, Place 5 £8.16.

Owner Glasgow House Racing Syndicate **Bred** Darley **Trained** Middleham Moor, N Yorks
FOCUS
Few could be given much chance in this maiden and, despite a very moderate early pace, they still finished well spread out. There is little solid form to go on.
Full As A Rocket(IRE) Official explanation: jockey said the gelding hung badly right throughout
T/Plt: £19.20 to a £1 stake. Pool: £44,262.55. 1,677.25 winning tickets. T/Qpdt: £4.20 to a £1 stake. Pool: £4,537.60. 791.40 winning tickets. WG

4289 FOLKESTONE (R-H)
Friday, August 18

OFFICIAL GOING: Good to soft (good in places)
Wind: Strong, half-against Weather: Sunshine and showers

4550 WIN A MILLION WITH LADBROKES FOOTBALL COUPONS MAIDEN AUCTION STKS — 5f
1:20 (1:21) (Class 5) 2-Y-O — **£3,238** (£963; £481; £240) **Stalls** Low

Form — RPR
5 **1** **Honest Danger**[22] 3872 2-8-11 .... DaneO'Neill 1 — 80
(J R Best) *chsd ldng pair: wnt 2nd wl over 1f out: rdn to ld last 100yds: shade cleverly* **4/1**[2]
3324 **2** *nk* **Cosmopolitan Lady**[7] 4321 2-8-10 84 .... ChrisCatlin 4 — 78
(D M Simcock) *led: rdn and hrd pressed over 1f out: hdd last 100yds: kpt on but readily hld by wnr* **11/10**[1]
05 **3** *6* **Oh So Saucy**[25] 3796 2-8-10 .... SebSanders 6 — 56
(C F Wall) *dwlt: chsd ldng trio: rdn over 2f out: wl outpcd and btn over 1f out* **4/1**[2]
00 **4** *½* **Beat The Bully**[12] 4177 2-8-11 .... PaulDoe 2 — 55
(I A Wood) *w ldr to 2f out: u.p and sn btn* **33/1**
0 **5** *3 ½* **A Nod And A Wink (IRE)**[11] 4207 2-8-4 .... RichardSmith 7 — 36
(R Hannon) *dwlt: nvr on terms: rdn and struggling fr 1/2-way: wknd over 1f out* **15/2**[3]
6 *4* **Festive Tipple (IRE)** 2-8-9 .... JimCrowley 3 — 26
(P Winkworth) *dwlt: outpcd in last pair after 1f: bhd rest of way* **14/1**
7 *10* **Foreland Sands (IRE)** 2-9-1 .... MartinDwyer 5 — —
(J R Best) *s.s: a outpcd and bhd: t.o* **16/1**

60.65 secs (-0.15) **Going Correction** -0.05s/f (Good) — 7 Ran SP% **114.9**
Speed ratings (Par 94):99,98,88,88,82 76,60
CSF £8.90 TOTE £5.80: £2.90, £1.20; EX 11.00.
Owner Keith C Bennett **Bred** Wickfield Farm Partnership **Trained** Hucking, Kent

FOCUS
A modest maiden run in a fair winning time for a race like this, and solid enough rated around the runner-up.

NOTEBOOK
Honest Danger was better leaving the stalls this time and showed the benefit of his debut outing to run out a narrow, albeit slightly cosy, winner of this modest affair. He is bred to get further and it would not be a surprise to see him step up to six furlongs next time. (op 11-2)
Cosmopolitan Lady looked to have been found a good opportunity to finally get off the mark but she once again found one too good. She has the ability to win a race - she did after all finish well clear of the rest - but will continue to look vulnerable to something with a bit more scope for improvement. (op 5-4 tchd 11-8 in a place)
Oh So Saucy, who ran quite well in a Windsor maiden won by subsequent Sweet Solera winner English Ballet last time, was disappointing, especially as the drop back to the minimum trip had looked unlikely to be a problem for her. Nurseries are now an option and perhaps quicker ground will see her in a better light. (op 7-2)
Beat The Bully showed early speed again and was not disgraced. He probably needs dropping in class, though.
A Nod And A Wink(IRE), a half-sister to Inchloss, who has a couple of wins to his name over six and eight furlongs, and to three prolific sprint winners in Italy, never got competitive. (tchd 7-1)
Festive Tipple(IRE), a cheap purchase bred to be effective over this trip, looked to need his debut outing.

4551 EASTWELL MANOR H'CAP — 5f
1:50 (1:50) (Class 6) (0-65,58) 3-Y-0+ — **£3,238** (£963; £481; £240) **Stalls** Low

Form — RPR
6060 **1** **Lady Hopeful (IRE)**[39] 3356 4-8-11 43 .... (b) LiamJones(5) 13 — 57
(Peter Grayson) *racd alone far side: wl on terms: def advantage over 1f out: rdn out and in n.d fnl f* **9/1**
0-55 **2** *3* **Fern House (IRE)**[39] 3356 4-9-4 45 .... TPQueally 8 — 48
(Peter Grayson) *hld up in last pair nr side: prog fr 2f out: kpt on to ld gp nr fin: no ch w wnr* **4/1**[2]
0-04 **3** *hd* **Saintly Place**[8] 4278 5-8-6 40 .... MarkCoumbe(7) 4 — 42
(A W Carroll) *chsd nr side ldrs: prog to chal 1f out: kpt on fnl f: no ch w wnr* **8/1**[3]
0000 **4** *nk* **College Queen**[52] 2949 8-9-2 43 .... TPO'Shea 6 — 44
(S Gollings) *racd on outer of nr side gp: chsd ldr 3f out: led over 1f out to nr fin: no ch w wnr* **20/1**
3545 **5** *nk* **Tomthevic**[10] 4223 8-9-3 44 .... (p) DaneO'Neill 2 — 44
(J M Bradley) *led nr side gp to over 1f out: hanging rt and nt qckn* **8/1**[3]
-201 **6** *nk* **Epineuse**[11] 4201 3-9-11 54 6ex .... MartinDwyer 5 — 53
(J R Best) *chsd nr side ldr for 2f: lost pl and struggling sn after: kpt on again fnl f* **8/1**[3]
04-0 **7** *nk* **Vlasta Weiner**[221] 74 6-8-13 40 .... (b) NickyMackay 11 — 38
(J M Bradley) *wl in rr nr side and racd on outer: kpt on fr over 1f out: no ch* **10/1**
/000 **8** *1 ¼* **Galloway Boy (IRE)**[27] 3728 9-8-11 43 .... (t) EmmettStack(5) 1 — 37
(J F Panvert) *chsd nr side ldrs for 2f: sn outpcd and struggling* **20/1**
2612 **9** *½* **Peruvian Style (IRE)**[7] 4324 5-10-3 58 6ex .... SebSanders 12 — 50
(J M Bradley) *racd on outer of nr side gp: chsd ldrs: hld ent fnl f: wknd rapidly last 100yds* **9/4**[1]
0000 **10** *2* **New Options**[3] 4462 9-8-13 40 .... (b) JimCrowley 10 — 25
(Peter Grayson) *dwlt: hld up in last pair nr side: no prog 2f out* **10/1**

61.10 secs (0.30) **Going Correction** -0.05s/f (Good)
WFA 3 from 4yo+ 2lb — 10 Ran SP% **121.8**
Speed ratings (Par 101):95,90,89,89,88 88,87,85,85,81
CSF £47.05 CT £312.21 TOTE £13.10: £3.40, £1.70, £3.00; EX 63.00 TRIFECTA Not won..
Owner Peter Grayson Racing Clubs Limited **Bred** Raymond P Doyle **Trained** Formby, Lancs

FOCUS
A low-grade contest run in a modest winning time, 0.45 seconds slower than the preceding two-year-old maiden. The form looks somewhat complicated and is best rated around the winner to sand form.
Tomthevic Official explanation: jockey said gelding hung right throughout

4552 EUROPEAN BREEDERS FUND MAIDEN FILLIES' STKS (DIV I) — 7f (S)
2:20 (2:21) (Class 4) 2-Y-O — **£3,886** (£1,156; £577; £288) **Stalls** Low

Form — RPR
3 **1** **Farley Star**[30] 3640 2-9-0 .... MartinDwyer 7 — 77
(R Charlton) *settled midfield: prog over 2f out: effrt to chse ldr ins fnl f: styd on wl to ld last 50yds* **10/3**[3]
34 **2** *nk* **Blithe**[15] 4074 2-9-0 .... NickyMackay 8 — 77
(W J Haggas) *wl plcd: prog to trck ldr wl over 2f out: shkn up to ld over 1f out: idled fnl f: hdd last 50yds* **11/4**[2]
23 **3** *1 ½* **Queen Noverre (IRE)**[16] 4041 2-9-0 .... ChrisCatlin 12 — 73
(E J O'Neill) *led against far side rail: rdn and hdd over 1f out: one pce* **15/8**[1]
0 **4** *3 ½* **Irish Dancer**[28] 3701 2-9-0 .... TPQueally 1 — 64
(J L Dunlop) *dwlt: wl in rr and racd on outer: prog fr 2f out: kpt on fnl f: n.d* **16/1**
5 *1 ¼* **Roca Redonda (IRE)** 2-9-0 .... DaneO'Neill 3 — 61
(D J Daly) *dwlt: wl in rr and racd on outer: prog 2f out: rn green and hung rt 1f out: kpt on* **16/1**
6 *shd* **Fiumicino** 2-8-11 .... EdwardCreighton(3) 9 — 61
(M R Channon) *dwlt: rn green in last pair and wl off the pce: sme prog over 2f out: kpt on: n.d* **20/1**
60 **7** *1 ½* **Our Ruby**[84] 1989 2-9-0 .... AdrianMcCarthy 5 — 57
(P W Chapple-Hyam) *chsd ldrs: pushed along 3f out: steadily fdd fnl 2f* **10/1**
06 **8** *1 ¾* **Killer Heels**[22] 3868 2-9-0 .... PatDobbs 2 — 53
(S Kirk) *racd on outer: nvr on terms w ldrs: no real prog fnl 2f* **50/1**
0 **9** *1 ¼* **On The Go**[28] 3707 2-9-0 .... PhilipRobinson 11 — 49
(M A Jarvis) *dwlt: settled in rr: rn green over 2f out: wknd and eased* **12/1**
40 **10** *9* **Check Tou**[95] 1743 2-9-0 .... TPO'Shea 6 — 27
(P A Blockley) *chsd ldr to wl over 2f out: reluctant and wknd rapidly* **66/1**
3 **11** *9* **Valeesha**[9] 4238 2-8-9 .... LiamJones(5) 4 — 4
(W G M Turner) *prom to 1/2-way: wknd rapidly: t.o* **40/1**

1m 27.35s (-0.55) **Going Correction** -0.05s/f (Good) — 11 Ran SP% **123.7**
Speed ratings (Par 93):101,100,98,94,93 93,91,89,88,77 67
CSF £13.39 TOTE £4.10: £1.40, £1.70, £1.30; EX 14.70 Trifecta £34.30 Pool £490.90, 10.16 w/u.
Owner A Parker (London) **Bred** A Parker **Trained** Beckhampton, Wilts

FOCUS
Not a bad maiden. The whole field raced towards the far-side rail and the winning time was fair for a race of its type and almost a second faster than the second division.

NOTEBOOK
Farley Star had shaped with plenty of promise on the Polytrack on her debut, seeing her race out well from off the pace, and it was a similar scenario here, in that she finished strongly to collar Blithe, who was idling in front. She looks capable of better again and should not have any trouble getting a mile in time. (op 11-4)
Blithe travelled well in behind the leader and looked likely to be difficult to catch once switched out to challenge, but she idled in front and was mugged close home. She certainly has the ability to win a race but it is likely that her challenge will have to be delayed a touch longer next time. (op 3-1 tchd 7-2)
Queen Noverre(IRE) had a good draw to make the most of the advantage of the far-side rail, and she was soon making the running there. Given every chance, she once again had to settle for a place, but at least she now has the option of going the nursery route. (op 9-4 tchd 11-4)
Irish Dancer was suited by the decent pace set by the favourite and kept on for a pleasing fourth. She is bred to come into her own over middle distances next season. (tchd 20-1)
Roca Redonda(IRE), a half-sister to Dawning, who was placed over five furlongs at two, and to a triple juvenile winner in Turkey, hails from a stable that does not send out many juveniles to win first time out. Green on her debut, she should improve for the outing.
Fiumicino, who cost 85,000gns, is out of a mare who was unplaced in two starts over seven furlongs, albeit in Group 3 company both times. Too green to do herself justice on her debut, her Fillies' Mile entry suggests she is thought capable of better in time. (op 25-1)
Valeesha Official explanation: jockey said filly had no more to give

4553 EUROPEAN BREEDERS FUND MAIDEN FILLIES' STKS (DIV II) — 7f (S)
2:50 (2:51) (Class 4) 2-Y-O — **£3,886** (£1,156; £577; £288) **Stalls** Low

Form — RPR
4 **1** **Veenwouden**[30] 3645 2-9-0 .... OscarUrbina 3 — 76
(J R Fanshawe) *settled in rr of gp in centre: pushed along 1/2-way: prog and overall ldr wl over 1f out: sn clr* **5/2**[1]
62 **2** *1 ¾* **Ronaldsay**[22] 3868 2-9-0 .... MartinDwyer 2 — 72
(R Hannon) *trckd ldrs in centre: effrt whn veered bdly lft over 1f out: r.o against nr side rail last 150yds* **7/2**[3]
3 *hd* **Silca Key** 2-8-11 .... EdwardCreighton(3) 6 — 71+
(M R Channon) *hld up in last pair of gp in centre: prog over 2f out: styng on whn sltly hmpd 1f out: kpt on fnl f* **20/1**
02 **4** *2* **Avina Laugh**[21] 3908 2-9-0 .... PaulDoe 11 — 66
(P W Chapple-Hyam) *led trio on far side: hung bdly lft fr 3f out: stl jst in front whn gps merged 2f out: continued to hang and sn btn* **11/1**
6 **5** *2 ½* **Rowan River**[62] 2643 2-9-0 .... ChrisCatlin 8 — 60
(M H Tompkins) *hld up in last pair in centre: plugged on fnl 2f: nt pce to trble ldrs* **25/1**
6 *7* **Kashmir Lady (FR)** 2-9-0 .... DaneO'Neill 1 — 42
(H Candy) *prom in centre: led gp 1/2-way to 2f out: wknd rapidly* **6/1**
3 **7** *1 ½* **Serene Highness (IRE)**[27] 3726 2-9-0 .... SebSanders 7 — 39
(J L Dunlop) *dwlt: chsd far side ldr: edgd lft fr 3f out: stl upsides whn gps merged 2f out: wknd rapidly* **3/1**[2]
05 **8** *5* **Bright Dance**[13] 4140 2-9-0 .... NickyMackay 10 — 26
(L M Cumani) *v fractious in stalls: last of trio on far side: nvr a factor* **20/1**
9 *nk* **Teratai (IRE)** 2-9-0 .... PhilipRobinson 5 — 25
(M A Jarvis) *led main gp and tk it up centre of trck: hdd 1/2-way: sn wknd* **20/1**
6 **10** *shd* **Show House (USA)**[13] 4161 2-9-0 .... JimCrowley 4 — 25
(Mrs A J Perrett) *trckd ldrs in centre: wknd rapidly fr over 2f out* **12/1**

1m 28.3s (0.40) **Going Correction** -0.05s/f (Good) — 10 Ran SP% **124.2**
Speed ratings (Par 93):95,93,92,90,87 79,77,72,71,71
CSF £11.57 TOTE £4.00: £1.40, £1.90, £3.80; EX 16.70 Trifecta £89.90 Pool £366.32, 2.89 w/u.
Owner Wood Hall Stud Limited **Bred** Wood Hall Stud **Trained** Newmarket, Suffolk

FOCUS
Not as strong a maiden as the first division, and the winning time was almost a second slower. The runner-up helps set the standard.

NOTEBOOK
Veenwouden came from off the pace to win fairly comfortably. She appreciated the extra furlong and, while the form appears modest in comparison with the first division, she looks the type to progress with racing. (op 3-1 tchd 4-1)

Ronaldsay, runner-up over the course and distance last month on quicker ground, did not do herself many favours when jinking towards the rail inside the final quarter mile (opposite the racecourse stables), but she would not have caught the winner anyway. She is now eligible for nurseries and should pay her way in that sphere. Official explanation: jockey said filly hung left (op 4-1 tchd 10-3)
Silca Key, a half-sister to Cross The Line, a dual winner over a mile, shaped with some promise on her debut, staying on well for the minor placing and clear of the rest. She should get another furlong alright. (op 25-1)
Avina Laugh initially went over to race next to the far-side rail, but she hung badly left towards the centre group from halfway and compromised her chance. She is another now eligible for nurseries. Official explanation: jockey said filly hung left (op 12-1)
Rowan River, off the track for a couple of months since her debut, looked as though she might go far side to begin with, but her rider changed his mind and switched back to race with ther group up the centre. Not given a hard time, she kept on without ever mounting a serious threat, and handicaps will be her game in time.
Kashmir Lady(FR), a half-sister to the very useful handicapper Prince of Thebes and to smart hurdler Royal Shakespeare, showed speed on her debut but dropped out tamely in the closing stages. She should do better in time, perhaps on quicker ground. (op 5-1)
Serene Highness(IRE) hung left from halfway and failed to build on the promise of her debut effort, which came on faster ground. Official explanation: jockey said filly hung left (op 7-2)

4554 LADBROKES OFFER XTRA VIRTUAL RACING FILLIES H'CAP 6f
3:25 (3:25) (Class 6) (0-55,55) 3-Y-0+ **£2,730** (£806; £403) **Stalls** Low

Form RPR
1012 **1** **Limonia (GER)**[8] 4294 4-9-5 **51** .... JamesDoyle(3) 12 60
(N P Littmoden) *racd towards far side: mde most: def advantage over 1f out: kpt on wl* **2/1**[1]
630- **2** *1 1/4* **Tipsy Lillie**[247] 6580 4-9-2 **45** .... OscarUrbina 8 50
(P S McEntee) *wl in rr towards far side: prog 2f out: r.o to take 2nd nr fin* **33/1**
0050 **3** *nk* **Jennverse**[7] 4329 4-9-3 **46** .... MartinDwyer 5 50
(D K Ivory) *dwlt: wl in rr of gp towards far side: rdn and prog on outer 2f out: chsd ldrs ins fnl f: kpt on same pce* **6/1**[3]
060- **4** *hd* **Phlaunt**[283] 6292 4-9-2 **45** .... StephenCarson 7 49
(R F Johnson Houghton) *wl in rr gp towards far side: rdn 1/2-way: prog wl over 1f out: chsd ldrs and kpt on fnl f: nvr able to chal* **28/1**
0066 **5** *nk* **My Girl Pearl (IRE)**[2] 4484 6-9-4 **47** .... JimCrowley 11 50
(M S Saunders) *racd against far side rail: trckd ldrs: effrt and looked dangerous over 1f out: no imp fnl f: lost 3 pls nr fin* **12/1**
0266 **6** *1 3/4* **Miss Porcia**[8] 4294 5-9-11 **54** .... TPO'Shea 2 52
(P A Blockley) *disp ld nr side but nvr on terms: clr of two rivals fnl 2f but no ch* **9/1**
10/3 **7** *1/2* **Charlottebutterfly**[9] 4265 6-9-7 **50** .... DaneO'Neill 10 46
(P J McBride) *racd towards far side and off the pce: effrt u.p 2f out: chsd ldrs 1f out: wknd ins fnl f* **5/1**[2]
0654 **8** *5* **Zimbali**[10] 4226 4-9-2 **45** .... ChrisCatlin 4 26
(J M Bradley) *chsd ldrs towards far side: rdn over 2f out: wknd over 1f out* **8/1**
6515 **9** *3/4* **Titus Wonder (IRE)**[127] 1003 3-9-0 **53** .... ManavNem(7) 6 32
(P A Blockley) *racd in centre: w wnr to 2f out: wknd rapidly u.p* **66/1**
0062 **10** *3/4* **Attitude Annie**[23] 3847 3-9-3 **49** .... PaulDoe 9 26
(S Dow) *w ldrs towards far side over 3f: sn wknd* **16/1**
0350 **11** *shd* **Tiviski (IRE)**[109] 1348 4-9-5 **55** .... NathanHitchcock(7) 3 31
(Miss Gay Kelleway) *last of nr side trio and sn wl off the pce: nvr a factor* **14/1**
0603 **12** *7* **Dora's Green**[8] 4306 3-9-4 **50** .... SebSanders 1 5
(M Blanshard) *w nr side ldr to over 2f out: wknd rapidly* **14/1**

1m 13.51s (-0.09) **Going Correction** -0.05s/f (Good)
WFA 3 from 4yo+ 3lb **12** Ran SP% **120.2**
Speed ratings (Par 101):98,96,95,95,95 92,92,85,84,83 83,74
CSF £89.45 CT £363.54 TOTE £2.80: £1.20, £6.60, £2.20; EX 87.70 Trifecta £242.70 Part won. 0.68 winning units.
Owner M Murphy **Bred** D Furstin Zu Oettingen-Wallerstein **Trained** Newmarket, Suffolk

FOCUS
A moderate handicap in which the majority of the field went far side. That group provided the first five home and the form looks sound.
Attitude Annie Official explanation: jockey said filly lost its near-hind and near-front shoes

4555 EUROPEAN BREEDERS FUND FILLIES' H'CAP 1m 1f 149y
4:00 (4:00) (Class 3) (0-90,87) 3-Y-0+
£11,217 (£3,358; £1,679; £840; £419; £210) **Stalls** Low

Form RPR
-221 **1** **Early Evening**[20] 3946 3-9-2 **77** .... DaneO'Neill 5 82
(H Candy) *trckd ldr: led over 2f out: drvn and hrd pressed fnl f: hld on wl* **11/2**[2]
454 **2** *3/4* **Penfection (IRE)**[34] 3548 3-9-9 **84** .... OscarUrbina 6 88
(M Botti) *trckd ldng pair: rdn over 2f out: chsd wnr over 1f out: str chal ins fnl f: nt qckn and hld last 100yds* **16/1**
5315 **3** *1* **Dame Hester (IRE)**[16] 4040 3-9-10 **85** .... ChrisCatlin 4 87+
(E J O'Neill) *hld up in 5th: sltly outpcd and pushed along over 2f out: drvn and r.o to chse ldng pair ins fnl f: too much to do* **8/1**[3]
4-05 **4** *1 3/4* **Psychic Star**[47] 3119 3-9-12 **87** .... SebSanders 7 86
(W R Swinburn) *led: kicked on 3f out: hdd over 2f out: grad fdd* **20/1**
1 **5** *2* **Quaich**[13] 4155 3-9-3 **78** .... LDettori 3 73
(Saeed Bin Suroor) *trckd ldng trio: pushed along 4f out: drvn and nt qckn 2f out: btn after* **4/6**[1]
41 **6** *1* **Adraaj (USA)**[94] 1759 3-9-12 **87** .... MartinDwyer 1 80+
(E A L Dunlop) *s.s: hld up in 6th: outpcd and detached 2f out: shkn up and no prog after* **20/1**
6252 **7** *1 1/4* **Noora (IRE)**[28] 3703 5-9-11 **78** .... (v) PhilipRobinson 2 69
(C G Cox) *s.v.s: a last: outpcd and detached fr over 2f out: no ch* **11/2**[2]

2m 5.37s (0.14) **Going Correction** -0.05s/f (Good)
WFA 3 from 5yo 8lb **7** Ran SP% **117.3**
Speed ratings (Par 104):97,96,95,94,92 91,90
CSF £84.99 TOTE £7.10: £2.90, £5.30; EX 101.50.
Owner Sarah Lakin & Tony Solomons **Bred** Lakin Bloodstock, Hillard Bloodstock And Trading L **Trained** Kingston Warren, Oxon

FOCUS
Not a bad fillies' handicap but the pace was not particularly strong and it turned into a bit of a sprint. The form appears ordinary.

NOTEBOOK
Early Evening, who had solid form in maiden company, raced prominently throughout in a race that was not run at a strong gallop, and she ground out the win in workmanlike fashion. She may not have much in the way of scope but she is a consistent filly. (tchd 7-1)
Penfection(IRE) benefited from a 9lb turnaround in the weights with Dame Hester compared with when they met at Salisbury last month, and that was enough to see her reverse form. The extra two furlongs was in her favour but once again a lack of a decent pace was not.
Dame Hester(IRE) could not confirm Salisbury form with Penfection on 9lb worse terms, but the way the race was run did not suit her as the leader set a modest tempo which resulted in something of a sprint to the line. Being held up off the pace, she was left with a lot of catching up to do when those in front kicked for home. (op 12-1 tchd 14-1)
Psychic Star enjoyed the run of the race in front but could not take advantage. She remains high in the handicap. (op 16-1)
Quaich, weak in the market prior to running out a five-length winner of a Thirsk maiden on her debut, did not look to have been too harshly treated in being given a mark of 78. Well backed this time and stepping up in distance, she let her supporters down badly as she was in trouble as far out as the turn into the straight. Neither the track nor the ground appeared to suit her. Official explanation: jockey said filly did not handle the track (op 8-11 tchd 8-13)
Adraaj(USA), off the track for three months following her maiden win at Newcastle in May, appeared to face a stiff task off a mark of 87 on her handicap debut, and she was never competitive. It would be dangerous to write her off completely but she needs some help from the assessor. (op 25-1)
Noora(IRE) Official explanation: trainer said the mare was unsuited by the good to soft (good in places) ground

4556 FOLKESTONE-RACECOURSE.CO.UK H'CAP 1m 4f
4:30 (4:30) (Class 6) (0-60,59) 3-Y-0 **£2,730** (£806; £403) **Stalls** Low

Form RPR
2065 **1** **Wise Choice**[25] 3791 3-8-10 **51** .... JamesDoyle(3) 10 57
(N P Littmoden) *led for 3f: trckd ldr: led again over 2f out: rdn 3l clr over 1f out: unchal after* **7/2**[1]
0033 **2** *1 1/4* **Park Lane Princess (IRE)**[8] 4280 3-8-7 **52** .... KirstyMilczarek(7) 6 56
(D M Simcock) *hld up in last trio: wl off the pce 4f out: prog on inner 2f out: r.o to take 2nd last 75yds and clsng: hopeless task* **10/1**
0436 **3** *3/4* **Lady Georgette (IRE)**[14] 4118 3-9-5 **57** .... ChrisCatlin 8 60
(E J O'Neill) *settled in midfield: effrt over 2f out: rdn and prog to chse wnr over 1f out: no imp: lost 2nd last 75yds* **4/1**[2]
060 **4** *3* **Sasetti (IRE)**[20] 3946 3-9-7 **59** .... (t) OscarUrbina 7 57
(J R Fanshawe) *s.s: sn midfield: prog 5f out: wnt 3rd over 3f out and 2nd briefly wl over 1f out: nt qckn: wknd fnl f* **9/2**[3]
-040 **5** *3* **Sara Mana Mou**[14] 4111 3-8-4 **42** .... NickyMackay 5 35
(J G Portman) *trckd ldng pair: reminder 5f out: lost 3rd over 3f out: steadily fdd* **16/1**
0333 **6** *7* **Macs Ransom (USA)**[23] 3839 3-8-10 **48** .... SebSanders 11 30
(S C Williams) *led after 3f: rdn and hdd over 2f out: sn wknd* **7/2**[1]
006 **7** *20* **Birbalini**[19] 3987 3-7-13 **40** oh2 .... EdwardCreighton(3) 4 —
(P J McBride) *chsd ldrs: rdn 5f out: wknd 4f out: t.o* **33/1**
-000 **8** *6* **Archivist (IRE)**[38] 3388 3-9-1 **53** .... DaneO'Neill 3 —
(M Blanshard) *chsd ldng trio: rdn over 5f out: sn wknd: t.o* **11/1**
5500 **9** *shd* **Sky At Night (IRE)**[6] 4367 3-8-9 **47** .... (b) MartinDwyer 2 —
(P Mitchell) *a in last pair: lost tch over 4f out: sn t.o* **16/1**
0000 **10** *1 1/4* **Eastlands (IRE)**[20] 3934 3-9-7 **59** .... PaulDoe 1 —
(Jamie Poulton) *s.s: rn wd and reluctant bnd over 9f out: a in last pair: t.o* **10/1**

2m 40.19s (-0.31) **Going Correction** -0.05s/f (Good) **10** Ran SP% **123.8**
Speed ratings (Par 98):99,98,97,95,93 89,75,71,71,70
CSF £42.36 CT £151.66 TOTE £7.00: £2.00, £2.30, £1.30; EX 51.90 Trifecta £339.20 Pool £516.04, 1.08 w/u.
Owner A A Goodman **Bred** Loughtown Stud Ltd **Trained** Newmarket, Suffolk

FOCUS
Moderate handicap form and a steady pace to boot, rated around the second to recent form.
Sky At Night(IRE) Official explanation: jockey said the gelding hung left

4557 REGISTER TODAY FOR LADBROKES TBS ACCOUNT H'CAP 7f (S)
5:05 (5:05) (Class 5) (0-75,75) 3-Y-0+ **£4,533** (£1,348; £674; £336) **Stalls** Low

Form RPR
5424 **1** **Mujood**[9] 4241 3-9-8 **75** .... StephenCarson 4 82
(R F Johnson Houghton) *trckd ldr: disp ld fr 2f out: styd on wl fnl f: hld on nr fin* **10/3**[3]
6-00 **2** *shd* **Sincerely**[37] 3398 4-8-10 **58** .... OscarUrbina 3 65
(B W Hills) *t.k.h: cl up: jnd wnr gng easily wl over 1f out: upsides fnl f: nt qckn nr fin* **13/2**
1302 **3** *3* **Caustic Wit (IRE)**[6] 4364 8-9-5 **74** .... (p) TolleyDean(7) 6 73
(M S Saunders) *trckd ldrs: upsides and gng wl 2f out: rdn over 1f out: wknd fnl f* **3/1**[2]
0004 **4** *6* **Wrighty Almighty (IRE)**[21] 3898 4-9-12 **74** .... SebSanders 2 57
(P R Chamings) *s.s: reminders in last over 4f out: struggling fr 1/2-way: plugged on fnl 2f* **5/1**
3461 **5** *5* **Nightstrike (IRE)**[8] 4287 3-8-13 **66** 6ex .... DaneO'Neill 5 36
(H Candy) *mde most to 2f out: wknd rapidly* **2/1**[1]
0060 **6** *9* **Goodwood Spirit**[14] 4101 4-9-11 **73** .... (b1) JimCrowley 1 20
(J M Bradley) *plld hrd: sn prom: wknd rapidly over 2f out* **16/1**

1m 26.86s (-1.04) **Going Correction** -0.05s/f (Good)
WFA 3 from 4yo+ 5lb **6** Ran SP% **117.3**
Speed ratings (Par 103):103,102,99,92,86 76
CSF £25.69 TOTE £4.50: £2.30, £3.20; EX 42.60 Place 6 £70.70, Place 5 £49.45.
Owner Eden Racing **Bred** Bloomsbury Stud And The Hon Sir David Sieff **Trained** Blewbury, Oxon

FOCUS
All six runners immediately went far side. An ordinary pace for this handicap, though they still finished well spread out behind the front pair, who set the standard. The winning time was the fastest of the three races over the trip on the day, though that was to be expected as the other two were for juveniles.
T/Plt: £123.90 to a £1 stake. Pool: £43,277.00. 254.80 winning tickets. T/Qpdt: £19.90 to a £1 stake. Pool: £3,287.10. 122.10 winning tickets. JN

4176 NEWBURY (L-H)
Friday, August 18

OFFICIAL GOING: Good
Wind: Nil

4558 TERENCE O'ROURKE EUROPEAN BREEDERS FUND MAIDEN FILLIES' STKS (DIV I) 6f 8y
2:10 (2:11) (Class 4) 2-Y-0 **£5,829** (£1,734; £866; £432) **Stalls** High

Form RPR
42 **1** **Russian Rosie (IRE)**[16] 4053 2-9-0 .... EddieAhern 3 86+
(J G Portman) *warm: trckd ldr: led ins fnl 2f: c clr ins last: easily* **7/2**[2]
2 *3 1/2* **Dragon Flower (USA)** 2-9-0 .... MichaelHills 7 76+
(B W Hills) *w'like: stdd towards rr: hdwy 2f out: pushed along and kpt on wl fnl f: tk 2nd cl home but no ch w wnr* **8/1**
6 **3** *nk* **Selinka**[21] 3893 2-9-0 .... RichardHughes 10 75
(R Hannon) *sn led: hdd ins fnl 2f: outpcd fnl f and lost 2nd cl home* **8/1**

4 **4** *3 ½* **Shustraya**[11] 4207 2-9-0 .... FergusSweeney 11 64
(P J Makin) *s.i.s: sn chsng ldrs: rdn over 2f out: wknd fnl f* **5/1**[3]
5 *¾* **Sophia Gardens** 2-9-0 .... FrankieMcDonald 4 62+
(D W P Arbuthnot) *leggy: bhd: pushed along over 2f out: swtchd lft to outside over 1f out: r.o ins last: nvr gng pce to rch ldrs* **66/1**
5 **6** *1 ½* **Shantina's Dream (USA)**[44] 3193 2-9-0 .... SteveDrowne 1 57
(H Morrison) *lw: chsd ldrs: drvn along over 2f out: wknd fnl f* **9/4**[1]
623 **7** *1 ¾* **Foxy Games**[10] 4221 2-9-0 .... LPKeniry 5 52
(D J S Ffrench Davis) *t.k.h: chsd ldrs: rdn over 2f out: wknd fnl f* **25/1**
8 *½* **Armillary** 2-9-0 .... TedDurcan 8 51
(Mrs A J Perrett) *unf: scope: bhd: sn pushed along: kpt on fnl f but nvr in contention* **25/1**
9 *2 ½* **Mystery River (USA)** 2-9-0 .... JamieSpencer 6 43+
(B J Meehan) *unf: scope: bit bkwd: chsd ldrs: rdn over 2f out: wknd appr fnl f* **14/1**
10 *½* **What Budget** 2-9-0 .... JimmyFortune 9 42
(B J Meehan) *unf: scope: lengthy: bit bkwd: s.i.s: outpcd* **25/1**
500 **11** *½* **Splendored Love (USA)**[28] 3700 2-9-0 .... RyanMoore 2 40
(R Hannon) *a outpcd* **16/1**

1m 14.68s (0.36) **Going Correction** +0.125s/f (Good) **11 Ran SP% 117.5**
Speed ratings (Par 93):102,97,96,92,91 89,86,86,82,82 81
CSF £30.27 TOTE £4.10: £1.40, £2.70, £2.90; EX 17.40.
Owner The Traditionalists **Bred** C J Foy **Trained** Compton, Berks

FOCUS
The first division of this juvenile fillies' maiden looked a reasonable contest and was run in a very decent winning time for a race of its nature, over half a second quicker than the division two. This was an improved effort by the winner, and a taking debut from the runner-up. A race that should work out.

NOTEBOOK
Russian Rosie(IRE), who has progressed steadily from her debut on this track last month, was always travelling well. She drew away in good style for an easy success and looks capable of going on to better things. The Watership Down sales race at Ascot has been mentioned as a target. (tchd 10-3)
Dragon Flower(USA) ◆ was the eyecatcher of the race. A sister to the Dewhurst winner In Command, she ran on well once she got the hang of things despite not troubling the winner. She should not be too long in getting off the mark. (tchd 15-2)
Selinka, the first foal of the dual Listed winner Lady Links, showed the benefit of her debut with a better effort, but after making the running was brushed aside by the winner. (op 10-1)
Shustraya was well backed but did not really build on her debut effort, although this may prove to have been a better contest. (op 7-1 tchd 15-2)
Sophia Gardens, the rank outsider, came from virtually last at the quarter-mile pole, and posted quite a promising effort. This 34,000gns half-sister to Jeanmaire should come on for the experience.
Shantina's Dream(USA), made favourite after a promising and somewhat unlucky debut, had to race on the outside of the field and was in trouble before the winner went for home. (op 5-2)
Mystery River(USA), a 120,000gns sister to Fong's Thong, showed early speed and was allowed to come home in her own time once beaten. (op 11-1)

4559 TERENCE O'ROURKE EUROPEAN BREEDERS FUND MAIDEN FILLIES' STKS (DIV II) 6f 8y

2:40 (2:42) (Class 4) 2-Y-O **£5,829** (£1,734; £866; £432) **Stalls** High

Form RPR
3 **1** **Silca Chiave**[21] 3893 2-9-0 .... TedDurcan 9 78
(M R Channon) *lw: chsd ldrs: rdn and styd on fnl f: led fnl 75yds: kpt on wl* **8/15**[1]
6 **2** *¾* **Miss Jenny (IRE)**[46] 3148 2-9-0 .... JimmyFortune 5 76
(B J Meehan) *str: chsd ldrs: drvn to ld wl over 1f out: kpt on u.p: edgd rt and hdd fnl 75yds* **9/1**[3]
3 **3** *¾* **Mimisel**[11] 4207 2-8-7 .... RobbieMills(7) 7 74
(Rae Guest) *leggy: chsd ldrs: shkn up 2f out: swtchd lft and kpt on strly cl home but nt pce to chal* **11/1**
4 *½* **Laurentina** 2-9-0 .... JamieSpencer 4 75+
(B J Meehan) *w'like: scope: bit bkwd: s.s: t.k.h in rr: hdwy fr 2f out styng on whn nt clr run ins last & again whn shkn up cl home: nt* **20/1**
0 **5** *1 ¼* **Ocean Blaze**[52] 2957 2-8-7 .... JamesMillman(7) 11 68
(B R Millman) *chsd ldrs: rdn over 2f out and sn one pce: kpt on again u.p ins last but nvr gng pce to chal* **66/1**
6 *shd* **Fustaan (IRE)** 2-9-0 .... RHills 6 68
(M P Tregoning) *w'like: in tch: drvn to chse ldrs 2f out: sn no imp: one pce fnl f* **8/1**[2]
0 **7** *hd* **Bluebelle Dancer (IRE)**[88] 1896 2-9-0 .... SteveDrowne 8 67
(W R Muir) *str: w ldr: led over 2f out: sn rdn: hdd wl over 1f out: wknd ins last* **20/1**
8 *2 ½* **Cape Velvet (IRE)** 2-9-0 .... EddieAhern 2 60
(J W Hills) *w'like: s.i.s: t.k.h: hung lft over 3f out: hdwy over 1f out: kpt on fnl f but nvr in contention* **50/1**
9 *1* **Kyloe Belle (USA)** 2-9-0 .... RyanMoore 3 57
(Mrs A J Perrett) *w'like: lw: chsd ldrs: pushed along 1/2-way: wknd fnl f* **20/1**
10 *12* **Goodbye** 2-8-9 .... AurelioMedeiros(5) 1 21
(B W Hills) *w'like: bit bkwd: wnt lft s and slowly away: swtchd to stands rail after 2f: a in rr* **33/1**
0 **11** *6* **Queen Of Fools (IRE)**[28] 3700 2-9-0 .... RichardHughes 10 3
(R Hannon) *lw: slt ld tl hdd over 2f out: sn wknd* **28/1**

1m 15.27s (0.95) **Going Correction** +0.125s/f (Good) **11 Ran SP% 118.8**
Speed ratings (Par 93):98,97,96,95,93 93,93,89,88,72 64
CSF £5.10 TOTE £1.50: £1.10, £2.00, £2.20; EX 7.00.
Owner Aldridge Racing Partnership **Bred** E Aldridge **Trained** West Ilsley, Berks

FOCUS
A much closer affair than division one. The winning time was still creditable for a race of its type, despite being over half a second slower, and the form looks solid enough.

NOTEBOOK
Silca Chiave was a beaten favourite on her debut at Ascot and had to work hard to justify her odds-on status on this occasion. She looked likely to be held by the runner-up until getting to the front well inside the last. She may not prove as good as her half-sister Silca's Sister, but her value is assured and she may improve with this under her belt. Connections are looking at the Cheveley Park or Rockfel Stakes for her. (op 4-6 tchd 1-2 in places)
Miss Jenny(IRE) ◆, a half-sister to the useful Autumnal, built on her debut and ran well in defeat despite still looking as if in need of the experience. She looks capable of gaining compensation in a similar contest. (op 7-1 tchd 10-1)
Mimisel ran another sound race under her inexperienced rider, and this speedily-bred filly can win a race before long, possibly once handicapped. (tchd 12-1)
Laurentina ◆ was the eye-catcher. She missed the break but finished on the heels of the principals despite running green. Although by Cadeaux Genereux, she had stamina on the dam's side and may appreciate a little further.
Ocean Blaze did considerably better than on her debut here in June, and this half-sister to Maktavish and Phantom Whisper among others should be winning once she gets into handicaps.
Fustaan(IRE), who is attractive and speedily-bred, did best of the other newcomers and should come on for the run.
Bluebelle Dancer(IRE), who had been absent since her first run in May, showed up for a long way and should come on for the outing. (tchd 25-1)

4560 STUART MICHAEL ASSOCIATES H'CAP 1m 5f 61y

3:15 (3:15) (Class 3) (0-90,90) 3-Y-O+ **£8,096** (£2,408; £1,203; £601) **Stalls** Centre

Form RPR
-300 **1** **Stoop To Conquer**[78] 2176 6-9-4 77 .... JamieSpencer 11 91
(J L Dunlop) *in tch: hdwy to chse ldr 2f out: hrd rdn to chal fnl f: led last 110yds: drvn out* **15/2**
551 **2** *1* **Zurbaran (IRE)**[3] 4459 3-8-11 81 6ex .... MickyFenton 10 93
(B J Meehan) *chsd ldrs: wnt 2nd over 1m out: chal fr 4f out tl rdn to ld appr fnl 2f: hdd and no ex fnl 110yds* **7/1**[3]
2325 **3** *4* **Altenburg (FR)**[23] 3853 4-9-7 80 .... HayleyTurner 7 86+
(Mrs N Smith) *warm: hld up in rr: stl plenty to do whn swtchd rt to outside 2f out: kpt on fr over 1f out to take 3rd ins last: nvr a dan* **25/1**
-214 **4** *¾* **Duty (IRE)**[69] 2436 3-9-4 88 .... RyanMoore 4 93
(Sir Michael Stoute) *lw: bhd: hrd drvn fr over 3f out: styd on and edgd lft 2f out: nvr gng pce to rch ldrs* **5/1**[2]
-021 **5** *1* **Rayhani (USA)**[19] 3974 3-9-6 90 .... JosedeSouza 15 93
(M P Tregoning) *lw: s.i.s: rr but in tch: rdn: hd high and hung lft fr 3f out: kpt on fr over 1f out but nt keen* **9/4**[1]
2200 **6** *1 ¼* **Michabo (IRE)**[17] 4027 5-9-12 85 .... SteveDrowne 1 87+
(H Morrison) *led 1f: styd chsng ldrs: rdn 3f out: styd on same pce fnl 2f* **12/1**
-236 **7** *¾* **Prince Vector**[50] 3028 4-9-9 82 .... (v[1]) EddieAhern 5 82
(A King) *in tch: drvn to chse ldrs 2f out: no imp: wknd fnl f* **16/1**
1102 **8** *1* **Mersey Sound (IRE)**[6] 4369 8-9-0 78 .... MarcHalford(5) 14 77
(D R C Elsworth) *lw: stdd rr after 3f: pushed along on outside 3f out: nvr gng pce to rch ldrs* **10/1**
0-00 **9** *¾* **Cavallini (USA)**[42] 3255 4-9-7 80 .... GeorgeBaker 12 78
(G L Moore) *led after 1f: hdd over 1m out: styd chsng ldrs tl wknd and hmpd 2f out* **66/1**
2032 **10** *6* **Ocean Avenue (IRE)**[39] 3365 7-9-4 77 .... RHills 2 66
(C A Horgan) *chsd ldrs: led over 1m out: hdd over 2f out and wknd qckly* **16/1**
6400 **11** *25* **Cruise Director**[19] 3971 6-9-9 82 .... TedDurcan 3 33
(Ian Williams) *in tch tl rdn and wknd qckly over 3f out* **28/1**
5114 **P** **Sphinx (FR)**[83] 2035 8-9-10 83 .... (b) IanMongan 8 —
(Jamie Poulton) *bhd: lost tch and p.u fnl 2f* **10/1**

2m 50.07s (-0.92) **Going Correction** +0.125s/f (Good)
WFA 3 from 4yo+ 11lb **12 Ran SP% 118.1**
Speed ratings (Par 107):107,106,103,103,102 102,101,101,100,96 81,—
CSF £58.07 CT £1257.76 TOTE £10.30: £3.00, £2.50, £5.80; EX 94.70.
Owner Seasons Holidays **Bred** I Stewart-Brown And M Meacock **Trained** Arundel, W Sussex

FOCUS
A decent staying handicap run at steady pace until Ocean Avenue kicked on with a mile to go. He stretched the field out and very few got into contention afterwards. Personal bests from the first two, and the third and fourth both ran to form.

NOTEBOOK
Stoop To Conquer had dropped to within a pound of his previous winning mark, when scoring over two miles on this track, and he picked up well to get the better of Zurbaran inside the final furlong. His trainer won three times with him two years ago and so there may be more to come, with the Cesarewitch a possible end-of-season target. (tchd 8-1)
Zurbaran(IRE) ◆ is a progressive three-year-old and, after collaring Ocean Avenue early in the straight, resisted the winner's efforts until inside the final furlong. The step up to staying trips has brought out the best in him and he should be winning again before long. (op 8-1)
Altenburg(FR), who has been steadily upped in trip since returning to the Flat, ran on from the rear without ever threatening.
Duty(IRE), trying his longest trip to date, was keeping on steadily under pressure but it appears as if the Handicapper may have overrated him. (op 9-2 tchd 11-2)
Rayhani(USA) had looked to be progressing steadily in recent outings, but hung left most of the way up the straight and did not appear keen. It would be no surprise to see headgear fitted sooner rather than later. (tchd 2-1, 5-2 in places)
Michabo(IRE) Official explanation: jockey said gelding never travelled
Ocean Avenue(IRE) went on and upped the tempo after a modest early gallop, but was in trouble as soon as he was taken on early in the straight. Official explanation: jockey said gelding ran too free (op 20-1)
Cruise Director Official explanation: jockey said gelding stopped very quickly
Sphinx(FR) Official explanation: jockey said gelding lost its action

4561 LINDA ALEXANDER STKS (REGISTERED AS WASHINGTON SINGER STAKES) (LISTED RACE) 7f (S)

3:50 (3:52) (Class 1) 2-Y-O
£13,343 (£5,057; £2,530; £1,261; £632; £317) **Stalls** High

Form RPR
1133 **1** **Dubai's Touch**[14] 4099 2-9-0 102 .... JoeFanning 5 100
(M Johnston) *lw: pressed wnr tl led jst ins fnl 2f: drvn and hld on wl fnl f* **9/4**[1]
1 **2** *1 ¼* **Valiance (USA)**[23] 3844 2-9-0 .... JimmyFortune 2 97
(J H M Gosden) *chsd ldrs: rdn 2f out: chsd wnr fnl f but a hld* **4/1**[2]
21 **3** *½* **Celtic Sultan (IRE)**[27] 3721 2-9-0 .... KDarley 1 96
(T P Tate) *chsd ldrs: rdn 2f out: styd on fnl f but nvr quite gng pce to chal* **9/4**[1]
4 *nk* **Dubai Twilight** 2-8-11 .... MichaelHills 3 92+
(B W Hills) *unf: slowly away: bhd: pushed along and green 4f out: hdwy over 2f out: styd on wl fnl f but nt rch ldrs* **20/1**
4212 **5** *1 ¼* **Pires**[20] 3924 2-9-0 100 .... TedDurcan 8 92
(M R Channon) *lw: sn slt ld: rdn fr 3f out: hdd jst ins fnl 2 fs: kpt on one pce fnl f* **7/1**[3]
6 *nk* **Tastahil (IRE)** 2-8-11 .... RHills 6 88+
(B W Hills) *w'like: str: bit bkwd: outpcd in rr: pushed along over 2f out: kpt ins last but nt rch ldrs* **25/1**
41 **7** *nk* **Valdan (IRE)**[20] 3958 2-9-0 80 .... JamieSpencer 4 90
(P D Evans) *plld hrd early: stdd in tch: pushed along 2f out: kpt on same pce fnl f* **14/1**
0 **8** *½* **Cry Presto (USA)**[28] 3701 2-9-0 .... RichardHughes 7 89?
(R Hannon) *chsd ldrs: rdn 3f out: wknd fnl f* **33/1**

1m 28.34s (1.34) **Going Correction** +0.125s/f (Good) **8 Ran SP% 112.3**
Speed ratings (Par 102):97,95,95,94,93 92,92,91
CSF £10.94 TOTE £2.80: £1.50, £1.70, £1.10; EX 17.30.
Owner Salem Suhail **Bred** Miss S N Ralphs **Trained** Middleham Moor, N Yorks

FOCUS
A fair renewal of this Listed contest, better known as the Washington Singer Stakes, but a fairly modest time for a race of its stature.

NOTEBOOK

Dubai's Touch came into this with solid form at Group 2 level, having been placed in both the July Stakes and Richmond Stakes, and ultimately ran out a decisive winner on this first try over seven furlongs. He is likely to be competing back in Group company soon, with next month's Champagne Stakes a likely target. (op 2-1 tchd 11-4)

Valiance(USA), a narrow winner on Polytrack on his debut, stepped up on that effort in chasing home the winner and can build on this decent effort. (op 5-1)

Celtic Sultan(IRE), who beat a subsequent winner when taking his maiden, failed to find an extra gear after having every chance. (tchd 15-8)

Dubai Twilight ◆ made a cracking debut and ran with plenty of promise. This 110,000 guineas son of Alhaarth should come on for the run and ultimately will appreciate a little further. (tchd 22-1)

Pires seemed to run his race once again and helps set the standard for the form, but he is exposed at this level, (op 15-2)

Tastahil(IRE) ◆, making his debut like his stable companion in fourth, looked in need of the experience and ran well considering the nature of the task he faced, even though it was to some extemnt a question of running on past beaten rivals. He will need much further eventually, but he has already shown enough to win most maidens and can be expected to know more next time. (op 20-1)

Valdan(IRE) found the step up in grade too much but was not knocked about when beaten and can repay the kindness in lesser company. (op 12-1)

Cry Presto(USA) faced a stiff task and appeared to step up considerably on his debut effort, despite finishing last.

4562 CHRISTOPHER SMITH ASSOCIATES H'CAP — 6f 8y

4:20 (4:21) (Class 4) (0-80,79) 3-Y-O — **£6,477** (£1,927; £963; £481) **Stalls** High

Form					RPR
4604	**1**		**Stanley Goodspeed**^{21} [3918] 3-9-2 **74** (J W Hills) *lw: s.i.s: rr: hdwy over 2f out: led appr fnl f: pushed along and kpt on strly ins last*	(t) EddieAhern 3 **14/1**	86
4244	**2**	½	**Patavium Prince (IRE)**^{8} [4291] 3-8-10 **68** (J R Best) *chsd ldrs: n.m.r 2f out: drvn and qcknd to chse wnr fnl f kpt on but a hld*	JoeFanning 6 **6/1**^{3}	78
4145	**3**	2 ½	**Sleeping Storm (IRE)**^{7} [4328] 3-8-10 **75** (B J Meehan) *bhd: hdwy over 2f out: drvn and styd on to chse ldrs ins last but nvr gng pce to chal*	KMay$^{(7)}$ 7 **8/1**	78
0500	**4**	hd	**Figaro Flyer (IRE)**^{7} [4338] 3-9-4 **79** (P Howling) *lw: bhd: rdn 3f out: swtchd lft to outside and hdwy over 1f out: kpt on ins last but nvr gng pce to chal*	DeanCorby$^{(3)}$ 13 **25/1**	81
0205	**5**	2 ½	**Kings Heir (IRE)**^{13} [4144] 3-9-1 **76** (R M Beckett) *pressed ldrs over 3f: stl wl there 2f out: wknd fnl f*	AdamKirby$^{(3)}$ 2 **10/1**	70
3205	**6**	1 ½	**Tous Les Deux**^{67} [2509] 3-9-3 **75** (R F Johnson Houghton) *lw: bhd: rdn 1/2-way: sme prog fnl f but nvr in contention*	MichaelHills 14 **5/1**^{1}	65
1353	**7**	½	**Mannikko (IRE)**^{25} [3802] 3-9-4 **76** (G Wragg) *lw: drvn and lost pl in rr over 3f out: n.m.r whn shkn up 2f out: kpt on ins last: nvr in contention*	SteveDrowne 15 **11/2**^{2}	64
0024	**8**	½	**Even Bolder**^{22} [3873] 3-8-6 **67** (S Kirk) *warm: chsd ldrs: ev chnace 2f out: wknd fnl f*	StephaneBreux$^{(3)}$ 10 **28/1**	54
6416	**9**	2	**Garstang**^{16} [4058] 3-8-10 **68** (Peter Grayson) *chsd ldrs: rdn 1/2-way: wknd 2f out*	(b) RobbieFitzpatrick 1 **11/1**	49
1010	**10**	nk	**George The Second**^{50} [3011] 3-8-2 **63** (Mrs H Sweeting) *chsd ldrs: rdn 1/2-way: wknd 2f out*	RichardKingscote$^{(3)}$ 12 **16/1**	43
0500	**11**	shd	**Triskaidekaphobia**^{14} [4102] 3-9-0 **72** (Miss J R Tooth) *chsd ldrs over 3f*	PaulFitzsimons 4 **28/1**	52
264-	**12**	½	**Johnny Alpha (IRE)**^{305} [5945] 3-9-4 **76** (P W Chapple-Hyam) *pressed ldrs: led 2f out: hdd appr fnl f: eased whn hld ins last*	KDarley 5 **7/1**	54
0103	**13**	3	**Catspraddle (USA)**^{46} [3150] 3-9-0 **72** (R Hannon) *sn slt ld: hdd 2f out: sn wknd*	RichardHughes 8 **10/1**	41

1m 14.36s (0.04) **Going Correction** +0.125s/f (Good) **13** Ran SP% **119.8**
Speed ratings (Par 102):104,103,100,99,96 94,93,93,90,90 89,89,85
CSF £94.11 CT £728.11 TOTE £17.80: £4.30, £2.30, £2.30; EX 135.40.
Owner R J Tufft **Bred** Burton Agnes Stud Co Ltd **Trained** Upper Lambourn, Berks

FOCUS

An ordinary sprint handicap featuring little that was progressive, and an open betting market, but in the end they finished fairly well strung out behind Stanley Goodspeed, who had also won his only previous race at this trip.

Johnny Alpha(IRE) Official explanation: jockey said gelding lost its action; vet said gelding finished lame right-fore

4563 SPORTING INDEX MAIDEN FILLIES' STKS — 7f (S)

4:55 (4:56) (Class 5) 3-Y-O+ — **£3,886** (£1,156; £577; £288) **Stalls** High

Form					RPR
	1		**Lady Stardust** 3-8-12 (J R Fanshawe) *w'like: scope: lengthy: lw: hld up in rr: stdy hdwy over 2f out to ld 1f out: sn in command: comf*	JamieSpencer 5 **8/1**	77
	2	2 ½	**Indication** 3-8-12 (J H M Gosden) *w'like: scope: s.i.s: hld up rr but in tch: hdwy to chal 2f out: chsd wnr fnl f but a readily hld*	RichardHughes 2 **7/4**^{1}	71
	3	hd	**Yandina (IRE)** 3-8-12 (B W Hills) *w'like: small: warm: s.i.s: sn in tch: slt ld: green and led jst ins fnl 2f: hdd 1f out: kpt on same pce*	MichaelHills 7 **11/4**^{2}	70
3-6	**4**	2	**Miss Thailand**^{107} [1417] 3-8-12 (G Wragg) *lw: chsd ldrs: pushed along 2f out: kpt on fnl f but nvr a danger*	SteveDrowne 4 **13/2**^{3}	65
	5	½	**Wax Eloquent** 3-8-9 (C G Cox) *unf: scope: rr and sn pushed along: rdn 3f out: hdwy to chse ldrs 2f out: wknd fnl f*	AdamKirby$^{(3)}$ 8 **22/1**	64
-360	**6**	1	**Namoos (USA)**^{64} [2583] 3-8-12 68 (J L Dunlop) *led tl hdd jst ins fnl 2f: wknd fnl f*	(b^{1}) RHills 9 **12/1**	61
30	**7**	¾	**Wild Academy (IRE)**^{64} [2587] 3-8-12 (G C Bravery) *in tch: wkng whn hmpd 2f out*	EddieAhern 6 **8/1**	59
06-0	**8**	5	**Pertemps Heroine**^{165} [595] 3-8-12 47 (A D Smith) *chsd ldrs: ev chnace over 2f out: sn btn*	FergusSweeney 3 **100/1**	46

1m 27.9s (0.90) **Going Correction** +0.125s/f (Good) **8** Ran SP% **111.6**
Speed ratings (Par 100):99,96,95,93,93 91,91,85
CSF £21.36 TOTE £10.90: £2.20, £1.40, £1.30; EX 28.20.
Owner Mrs Martin Armstrong **Bred** Newsells Park Stud Limited **Trained** Newmarket, Suffolk

FOCUS

On paper just a modest-looking fillies' maiden, but it featured a couple of well-bred newcomers at the head of the market. Unlike the earlier races, in which they raced up the stands' rail, this time the field came up the centre of the track. The form has been rated arouund the sixth.

4564 PETER BRETT ASSOCIATES H'CAP — 6f 8y

5:30 (5:31) (Class 5) (0-70,70) 4-Y-O+ — **£3,238** (£963; £481; £240) **Stalls** High

Form					RPR
2020	**1**		**Zazous**^{48} [3071] 5-8-2 **56** (J J Bridger) *chsd ldrs: led 1f out: drvn out*	MarcHalford$^{(5)}$ 7 **16/1**	65
524/	**2**	1	**Small Stakes (IRE)**^{623} [6796] 4-8-12 **61** (P J Makin) *in tch: hdwy over 2f out: drvn to chal 1f out: kpt on but nt pce of wnr ins last*	(t) FergusSweeney 2 **25/1**	67
2402	**3**	hd	**Cesar Manrique (IRE)**^{52} [2962] 4-9-6 **69** (B W Hills) *warm: hld up in rr: hdwy over 1f out: kpt on ins last but nvr quite gng pce to rch ldrs*	MichaelHills 9 **9/2**^{1}	74
0-03	**4**	½	**Calabaza**^{7} [4338] 4-9-4 **67** (W Jarvis) *s.i.s: bhd: hdwy fr 2f out: chsd ldrs ins last: kpt on same pce cl home*	(p) LPKeniry 16 **8/1**^{3}	71
3030	**5**	¾	**Convince (USA)**^{11} [4211] 5-8-9 **65** (J M Bradley) *w ldrs: stl upsides 1f out: nt qckn ins last*	BarrySavage$^{(7)}$ 8 **25/1**	67
3020	**6**	¾	**Roman Quintet (IRE)**^{35} [3486] 6-9-7 **70** (D W P Arbuthnot) *swtg: sn slt ld: rdn 2f out :hdd 1f out: wknd ins last*	(v^{1}) FrankieMcDonald 11 **16/1**	69
5005	**7**	½	**Marker**^{11} [4211] 6-9-4 **67** (J A Geake) *stdd s: bhd: hdwy over 1f out: kpt on ins last: nt rch ldrs*	(v) RichardHughes 3 **8/1**^{3}	65
2604	**8**	hd	**Aastral Magic**^{52} [2954] 4-9-3 **69** (R Hannon) *bhd: rdn: hdwy and n.m.r 1f out: kpt on ins last but nvr gng pce to trble ldrs*	StephaneBreux$^{(3)}$ 14 **25/1**	66
2665	**9**	½	**Currency**^{6} [4361] 9-9-5 **68** (J M Bradley) *behid: styd on fr over 1f out: kpt on cl home but nt rch ldrs*	JoeFanning 12 **9/1**	64
3032	**10**	½	**Monashee Prince (IRE)**^{11} [4211] 4-9-0 **63** (J R Best) *chsd ldrs: rdn over 2f out: wknd fnl f*	SteveDrowne 13 **9/1**	57
5444	**11**	shd	**Mountain Pass (USA)**^{13} [4141] 4-8-4 **53** (M J Wallace) *in tch: rdn and hung lft 2f out: n.d after*	(p) DavidKinsella 5 **16/1**	47
2220	**12**	2 ½	**Millfields Dreams**^{2} [4486] 7-8-9 **58** (M G Quinlan) *chsd ldrs 4f*	PatDobbs 15 **6/1**^{2}	45
2041	**13**	¾	**Kahlua Bear**^{31} [3611] 4-8-6 **58** ow4 (Miss K B Boutflower) *chsd ldrs: ev ch 2f out: wknd over 1f out*	(v) AdamKirby$^{(3)}$ 4 **20/1**	42
5101	**14**	shd	**Banjo Bay (IRE)**^{6} [4365] 8-9-0 **66** 6ex (Miss Gay Kelleway) *lw: in tch: wkng whn carried lft 2f out*	(t) NeilChalmers$^{(3)}$ 6 **8/1**^{3}	50
0644	**15**	10	**Renegade (IRE)**^{15} [4077] 5-8-11 **60** (Mrs L J Mongan) *disp ld tl wknd and carried lft 2f out*	(b) IanMongan 1 **33/1**	14

1m 13.93s (-0.39) **Going Correction** +0.125s/f (Good) **15** Ran SP% **122.7**
Speed ratings (Par 103):107,105,105,104,103 102,102,101,101,100 100,97,96,95,82
CSF £380.59 CT £2154.46 TOTE £22.70: £5.90, £8.10, £2.40; EX 377.90.
Owner J J Bridger **Bred** Lordship Stud **Trained** Liphook, Hants

FOCUS

Just a modest sprint handicap, but decent form for the grade. It was run in a time 0.43 sec faster than the earlier handicap for three-year-olds. As in the previous race, they came up the centre of the track.

Kahlua Bear Official explanation: jockey said gelding was unsuited by the good ground
Renegade(IRE) Official explanation: jockey said gelding suffered interference

4565 JACK COLLING POLAR JEST APPRENTICE H'CAP — 1m 1f

6:05 (6:07) (Class 5) (0-70,70) 3-Y-O+ — **£3,238** (£963; £481; £240) **Stalls** Centre

Form					RPR
4304	**1**		**Royal Indulgence**^{6} [4355] 6-8-11 **53** (W M Brisbourne) *bhd: hdwy 2f out: styd u.p fnl f to ld last stride*	LiamJones 8 **8/1**	61
4000	**2**	shd	**Border Edge**^{3} [4446] 8-9-2 **58** (J J Bridger) *lw: led tl hdd ins fnl 3f: styd pressing ldrs tl drvn to take slt advantage fnl 110yds: ct last stride*	MarcHalford 2 **11/1**	66
0230	**3**	½	**Consonant (IRE)**^{20} [3948] 9-9-5 **66** (D G Bridgwater) *chsd ldrs: slt ld 2f out: rdn fr over 1f out: hdd and no ex fnl 110yds*	MarkCoumbe$^{(5)}$ 5 **16/1**	73
1103	**4**	¾	**Aggravation**^{11} [4209] 4-9-11 **70** (D R C Elsworth) *b.hind: swtg: bhd: stdy hdwy on outside fr 2f out: styd on to chse ldrs ins last but nt qckn fnl 110yds*	StephanieHollinshead$^{(3)}$ 10 **11/2**^{3}	75
0016	**5**	1 ½	**Follow The Colours (IRE)**^{16} [4044] 3-9-2 **70** (J W Hills) *swtg: t.k.h in rr: hdwy 4f out to ld jst ins fnl 3f: hdd 2f out: styd challening tl wknd ins last*	PatrickHills$^{(5)}$ 7 **5/1**^{2}	72
0322	**6**	1 ¼	**Diamond Dan (IRE)**^{3} [4446] 4-8-6 **53** (P D Evans) *lw: t.k.h in rr: hdwy 4f out: chsd ldrs 2f out: wknd ins last*	JamieHamblett$^{(5)}$ 6 **4/1**^{1}	53
6003	**7**	¾	**Christmas Truce (IRE)**^{23} [3850] 7-9-1 **60** (Ms J S Doyle) *in tch: hrd drvn to press ldrs 2f out: wknd fnl f*	(v) JamieJones$^{(3)}$ 4 **9/1**	58
4045	**8**	1 ¾	**Mixing**^{15} [4073] 4-8-9 **56** (W Jarvis) *chsd ldsrs utnil wknd 2f out*	BRoper$^{(5)}$ 3 **9/1**	51
3422	**9**	nk	**Teide Lady**^{9} [4254] 3-8-9 **63** 6ex (Rae Guest) *chsd ldrs over 5f*	RobbieMills$^{(5)}$ 1 **13/2**	57
1230	**10**	17	**New England**^{21} [3918] 4-9-3 **64** (W M Brisbourne) *unruly stalls and virtually ref to r: a wl bhd*	PJBenson$^{(5)}$ 9 **14/1**	24

1m 56.86s (2.27) **Going Correction** +0.125s/f (Good)
WFA 3 from 4yo+ 7lb **10** Ran SP% **117.4**
Speed ratings (Par 103):94,93,93,92,91 90,89,88,87,72
CSF £92.86 CT £1409.91 TOTE £10.10: £3.10, £2.10, £4.50; EX 102.60 Place 6 £60.70, Place 5 £22.55.
Owner P G Evans **Bred** P V And J P Jackson **Trained** Great Ness, Shropshire
■ Stewards' Enquiry : P J Benson jockey said gelding got upset in stalls and was reluctant to race

FOCUS

A modest apprentice race, run in pouring rain. It produced the best finish of the day, but it was a moderate winning time, even for the grade.

New England Official explanation: jockey said gelding got upset in stalls and was reluctant to race
T/Jkpt: Not won. T/Plt: £94.60 to a £1 stake. Pool: £65,424.45. 504.80 winning tickets. T/Qpdt: £30.80 to a £1 stake. Pool: £3,846.80. 92.20 winning tickets. ST

4250 NEWCASTLE (L-H)

Friday, August 18

OFFICIAL GOING: Soft (good to soft in places)
Wind: Light, behind

4566 J N BENTLEY/E.B.F. MEDIAN AUCTION MAIDEN STKS — 7f

2:30 (2:33) (Class 6) 2-Y-O — **£2,590** (£770; £385; £192) **Stalls** High

Form					RPR
4	**1**		**Mayor Of London (USA)**^{14} [4109] 2-9-3 (M Johnston) *led to over 1f out: rallied to regain ld ins fnl f: styd on wl*	RoystonFfrench 3 **5/2**^{1}	80

4 **2** *nk* **Arch Of Titus (IRE)**[38] [3385] 2-9-3 RobertWinston 8 79
(M L W Bell) *keen: trckd ldrs: led over 1f out to ins fnl f: hld nr fin* **11/4**[2]

3 *7* **Akiyama (IRE)** 2-9-3 PaulMulrennan 4 62
(J Howard Johnson) *hld up in tch: hdwy 1/2-way: rdn and outpcd fr 2f out* **25/1**

4 *3* **The Diamond Bond** 2-9-3 GylesParkin 6 54
(G R Oldroyd) *towards rr: hdwy over 2f out: rdn and kpt on: no imp* **66/1**

0 **5** *1 ¾* **Baarrij**[25] [3796] 2-8-12 FrancisNorton 14 45
(M R Channon) *midfield: pushed along 1/2-way: no imp fr 2f out* **9/1**

66 **6** *hd* **Bollin Felix**[17] [4018] 2-9-3 DavidAllan 7 49
(T D Easterby) *s.i.s: bhd tl sme late hdwy: nvr rchd ldrs* **11/1**

0 **7** *10* **Pretty Game**[15] [4066] 2-9-3 CatherineGannon 2 24
(K A Ryan) *cl up: rdn 1/2-way: wknd over 2f out* **20/1**

0 **8** *1 ½* **Miss Havisham (IRE)**[17] [4018] 2-8-12 PhillipMakin 10 16
(J R Weymes) *sn midfield: drvn 1/2-way: wknd fr 2f out* **50/1**

9 *7* **Myfrenchconnection (IRE)** 2-9-3 LeeEnstone 15 3
(P T Midgley) *midfield: drvn 1/2-way: sn btn* **100/1**

03 **10** *shd* **Smugglers Bay (IRE)**[20] [3940] 2-9-3 TonyHamilton 5 3
(T D Easterby) *s.i.s: bhd and drvn along: nvr on terms* **9/2**[3]

11 *1 ½* **Bret Maverick (IRE)** 2-9-3 DeanMcKeown 1 —
(J R Weymes) *missed break: sn rdn along: nvr on terms* **50/1**

0 **12** *2 ½* **Hunting Call**[100] [1595] 2-9-3 DO'Donohoe 11 —
(K A Ryan) *midfield: drvn after 3f: sn btn* **20/1**

05 **13** *6* **Pace Telecom Flyer (IRE)**[12] [4171] 2-9-3 J-PGuillambert 12 —
(J W Hills) *cl up 3f: sn rdn and wknd* **12/1**

14 *2 ½* **Shandelight (IRE)** 2-8-12 VHalliday 13 —
(Mrs A Duffield) *bhd and drvn along: no ch fr 1/2-way* **50/1**

0 **15** *29* **Swan Of Raunds**[38] [3385] 2-9-3 (v[1]) PatCosgrave 9 —
(J R Norton) *chsd ldrs to 1/2-way: sn rdn and btn* **100/1**

1m 28.98s (0.98) **Going Correction** +0.175s/f (Good) **15** Ran SP% **122.2**
Speed ratings (Par 92):101,100,92,89,87 87,75,73,65,65 64,61,54,51,18
CSF £8.62 TOTE £4.10: £1.80, £2.10, £11.70; EX 13.90.
Owner Jumeirah Racing **Bred** Darley **Trained** Middleham Moor, N Yorks

FOCUS
The field raced in the centre and a race where the market leaders pulled clear in the last quarter mile and the form could be rated higher. This race lacked strength but it was a very decent winning time for a race like this allowing for the conditions.

NOTEBOOK
Mayor Of London(USA) ◆ fully confirmed debut promise in these softer conditions and over this longer trip. As is usually the case of one from this stable, he showed a determined attitude under pressure and he will stay a mile. He is sure to win more races. (op 3-1 tchd 10-3)
Arch Of Titus(IRE) ◆ fully confirmed debut promise on this first run on turf and pulled clear of the rest in the closing stages. He showed more than enough, despite failing to settle in the first half of the race, to suggest a similar race can be found. (op 3-1 tchd 7-2)
Akiyama(IRE), out of a juvenile six-furlong winner, took the eye in the preliminaries and shaped well without being knocked about on this racecourse debut. He looks sure to win a modest event in due course. (op 20-1)
The Diamond Bond is related to several winners and was not disgraced on this racecourse debut. He left the impression that a stiffer test of stamina in ordinary handicap company would enable him to get off the mark at some point.
Baarrij, encountering a much stiffer test of stamina than on her debut, again only hinted at ability and is likely to remain vulnerable in this grade but appeals as the type to fare better in ordinary handicap company over middle distances next term. (op 15-2)
Bollin Felix, having his first run on easy ground, again underlined his vulnerability in this type of race but again showed enough to suggest he should be a different proposition in ordinary handicap company over middle distances next year. (op 25-1)
Miss Havisham(IRE) Official explanation: jockey said filly lost her action
Smugglers Bay(IRE) had shown ability in maidens on a sound surface but was all at sea in these much softer conditions. He is worth another chance back on more suitable ground in modest handicaps. (tchd 7-2)

4567 NORTHUMBRIAN WATER FILLIES' H'CAP — 1m 3y(S)
3:00 (3:03) (Class 5) (0-75,75) 3-Y-O **£3,562** (£1,059; £529; £264) **Stalls** High

Form RPR
5662 **1** **Ellesappelle**[8] [4297] 3-8-9 **63** PatCosgrave 6 73
(K R Burke) *cl up: led over 1f out: styd on strly to go clr fnl f* **8/1**

3233 **2** *4* **Tour D'Amour (IRE)**[51] [2977] 3-8-11 **68** StephenDonohoe[(3)] 7 70
(R Craggs) *led to over 1f out: kpt on: no ch w wnr* **9/2**[2]

5-05 **3** *2* **Lady Lochinver (IRE)**[74] [2283] 3-8-2 **56** oh4 DaleGibson 3 54
(Micky Hammond) *towards rr: hdwy over 2f out: kpt on fnl f: nrst fin* **33/1**

4-10 **4** *nk* **Amy Louise (IRE)**[37] [3418] 3-9-7 **75** RobertWinston 2 72
(T D Barron) *in tch gng wl: effrt over 1f out: no ex ins fnl f* **8/1**

3636 **5** *2* **Damelza (IRE)**[29] [3687] 3-9-4 **72** (t) DavidAllan 8 65
(T D Easterby) *bhd: rdn 1/2-way: kpt on fnl 2f: nrst fin* **7/1**[3]

0223 **6** *2 ½* **Jenny Soba**[9] [4257] 3-7-11 **56** oh4 NataliaGemelova[(5)] 1 44
(R M Whitaker) *chsd ldrs tl wknd over 1f out* **14/1**

5540 **7** *½* **Choysia**[27] [3722] 3-9-2 **75** MarkLawson[(5)] 4 62
(D W Barker) *hmpd s: bhd and rdn along: hdwy u.p over 2f out: wknd over 1f out* **16/1**

6113 **8** *1 ½* **Just Lille (IRE)**[4] [4426] 3-9-4 **72** RoystonFfrench 11 56
(Mrs A Duffield) *towards rr: drvn 1/2-way: effrt over 2f out: sn no imp* **11/4**[1]

4-10 **9** *43* **Hazelhurst (IRE)**[51] [2977] 3-9-3 **71** PaulMulrennan 9 —
(J Howard Johnson) *plld hrd: chsd ldrs: rdn wl over 2f out: wknd qckly* **15/2**

100- **10** *¾* **Korolieva (IRE)**[336] [5265] 3-8-13 **67** DO'Donohoe 12 —
(K A Ryan) *bhd: drvn 1/2-way: sn btn* **50/1**

0-30 **11** *hd* **Ravish**[64] [2589] 3-8-3 **57** (t) AdrianTNicholls 10 —
(W J Haggas) *hld up: rdn 3f out: sn wknd* **12/1**

260- **12** *hd* **High Meadow Girl**[405] [3362] 3-9-0 **68** FrancisNorton 5 —
(J D Bethell) *hmpd s: sn chsng ldrs: drvn 1/2-way: wknd* **25/1**

1m 43.09s (1.19) **Going Correction** +0.175s/f (Good) **12** Ran SP% **120.3**
Speed ratings (Par 97):101,97,95,94,92 90,89,88,45,44 44,44
CSF £43.92 CT £1149.85 TOTE £9.90: £2.20, £2.40, £10.10; EX 59.40.
Owner A Rhodes Haulage and P Timmins 2 **Bred** N R Shields **Trained** Middleham Moor, N Yorks

FOCUS
An ordinary event in which the field converged in the centre of the track. The pace seemed fair but nothing got into the race from off the pace, but the form appears sound rated around those in the frame behind the winner.
Just Lille(IRE) Official explanation: jockey said filly was unsuited by the soft (good to soft in places) ground

4568 LUMSDEN & CARROLL (S) STKS — 1m 2f 32y
3:35 (3:36) (Class 6) 3-Y-O+ **£2,388** (£705; £352) **Stalls** Centre

Form RPR
005 **1** **Son Of Thunder (IRE)**[11] [4194] 5-9-5 51 (b[1]) PhillipMakin 4 61
(M Dods) *hld up in tch: hdwy to ld centre over 1f out: hung rt and sn clr: kpt on u.p fnl f: all out* **13/2**[3]

3435 **2** *nk* **Desert Lightning (IRE)**[15] [4087] 4-9-5 50 PatCosgrave 6 60
(K R Burke) *prom: effrt over 2f out: chsd wnr and drifted to stands rail fr over 1f out: kpt on wl fnl f: jst hld* **4/1**[1]

0050 **3** *5* **Lambency (IRE)**[24] [3823] 3-8-8 43 ow2 J-PGuillambert 2 48
(J G Given) *in tch: outpcd over 2f out: rallied over 1f out: kpt on fnl f: nt rch first two* **8/1**

3204 **4** *1 ¼* **Miss Monica (IRE)**[8] [4279] 5-9-2 43 StephenDonohoe[(3)] 5 49
(P W Hiatt) *in tch: effrt over 2f out: outpcd fnl f* **6/1**[2]

05/0 **5** *1 ½* **Blushing Prince (IRE)**[39] [3352] 8-9-5 37 (t) DeanMcKeown 3 46
(R C Guest) *hld up: hdwy towards stands side to ld over 2f out: hdd over 1f out: sn btn* **50/1**

0616 **6** *½* **Ming Vase**[5] [4404] 4-9-10 46 LeeEnstone 9 50
(P T Midgley) *sn led: c centre w majority and hdd over 2f out: no ex over 1f out* **6/1**[2]

22-0 **7** *2* **Time Marches On**[6] [4381] 8-8-12 46 JamesReveley[(7)] 10 42
(K G Reveley) *cl up: rdn and swtchd to r alone far rail fr 2f out: sn no imp* **9/1**

0030 **8** *7* **Great Composer (IRE)**[8] [4304] 3-8-11 45 (v[1]) DaleGibson 1 29
(M J Attwater) *plld hrd in rr: drvn over 3f out: nvr on terms* **14/1**

6/00 **9** *7* **Phoenix Nights (IRE)**[16] [4057] 6-9-5 42 TonyHamilton 7 16
(A Berry) *early ldr: chsd ldrs tl wknd fr over 2f out* **50/1**

4156 **U** **Ruby Legend**[8] [4301] 8-9-10 57 (b) DavidAllan 8 —
(K G Reveley) *rrd and uns rdr as stalls opened* **4/1**[1]

2m 18.21s (6.41) **Going Correction** +0.525s/f (Yiel)
WFA 3 from 4yo+ 8lb **10** Ran SP% **113.6**
Speed ratings (Par 101):95,94,90,89,88 88,86,80,75,—
CSF £31.78 TOTE £7.20: £2.00, £1.90, £3.20; EX 16.10.There wa no bid for the winner.
Owner Russ Mould **Bred** Sentinel Bloodstock And B Stewart **Trained** Denton, Co Durham
■ Stewards' Enquiry : James Reveley two-day ban: careless riding (Aug 29+1)

FOCUS
A low-grade event in which the bulk of the field raced in the centre in the last quarter mile but the winner and runner-up edged to the stands' side in the closing stages. The pace was ordinary but the form makes sense.

4569 UTS H'CAP — 7f
4:10 (4:10) (Class 4) (0-80,75) 3-Y-O+ **£5,505** (£1,637; £818; £408) **Stalls** High

Form RPR
2642 **1** **Stellite**[6] [4352] 6-9-8 **69** LeeEnstone 5 83
(J S Goldie) *hld up in tch: hdwy to ld appr fnl f: r.o strly* **4/1**[2]

2231 **2** *1 ¼* **Daaweitza**[21] [3918] 3-9-1 **70** StephenDonohoe[(3)] 7 79
(B Ellison) *hld up midfield: effrt over 2f out: rallied over 1f out: chsd wnr ins fnl f: kpt on* **4/1**[2]

0563 **3** *1 ¼* **True Night**[11] [4194] 9-9-6 **67** AdrianTNicholls 3 75
(D Nicholls) *cl up: led over 2f out to appr fnl f: lost 2nd and no ex ins fnl f* **12/1**

4050 **4** *3 ½* **Breaking Shadow (IRE)**[15] [4090] 4-9-13 **74** PhillipMakin 12 72
(T D Barron) *bhd: hdwy over 1f out: no imp ins fnl f* **7/1**

4400 **5** *4* **Danzig River (IRE)**[62] [2661] 5-9-4 **72** VictoriaBehan[(7)] 9 60
(D Nicholls) *prom tl rdn and wknd over 1f out* **16/1**

5605 **6** *2 ½* **Red Chairman**[5] [4401] 4-8-8 **60** (b[1]) DeclanMcGann[(5)] 11 42
(R Johnson) *keen: led tl hung lft and hdd over 2f out: sn btn* **16/1**

1-54 **7** *5* **Scotland The Brave**[17] [4020] 6-9-3 **64** (v) FrancisNorton 6 33
(J D Bethell) *cl up: effrt whn carried to far rail and hmpd over 2f out: n.d after* **6/1**[3]

0450 **8** *5* **Fair Shake (IRE)**[9] [4253] 6-9-6 **67** (v) TonyHamilton 15 23
(Karen McLintock) *prom: lost pl and struggling after 3f: n.d after* **12/1**

1500 **9** *6* **Elusive Warrior (USA)**[9] [4253] 3-8-9 **61** PatCosgrave 4 —
(R A Fahey) *bhd: effrt u.p 3f out: btn over 1f out* **25/1**

2232 **10** *13* **Kool Ovation**[9] [4253] 4-9-9 **70** RobertWinston 13 —
(A Dickman) *racd alone stands rail: hung lft thrght: wknd fr 3f out* **7/2**[1]

1m 28.66s (0.66) **Going Correction** +0.175s/f (Good)
WFA 3 from 4yo+ 5lb **10** Ran SP% **120.0**
Speed ratings (Par 105):103,101,100,96,91 88,83,77,70,55
CSF £21.12 CT £180.44 TOTE £5.00: £1.60, £2.10, £3.50; EX 22.50.
Owner S Bruce **Bred** Cheveley Park Stud Ltd **Trained** Uplawmoor, E Renfrews

FOCUS
An open handicap run at a fair pace in which the bulk of the field raced centre to far side in the last three furlongs. The form looks sound and a shade above average.
Red Chairman Official explanation: jockey said gelding hung left and saddle slipped
Scotland The Brave Official explanation: jockey said mare suffered interference in running approximately 2f out
Fair Shake(IRE) Official explanation: trainer said gelding was found to have mucus on its lungs
Kool Ovation Official explanation: jockey said gelding was unsuited by the soft (good to soft in places) going

4570 NPOWER H'CAP — 1m 2f 32y
4:40 (4:40) (Class 5) (0-70,69) 3-Y-O+ **£3,886** (£1,156; £577; £288) **Stalls** Centre

Form RPR
5402 **1** **Rotuma (IRE)**[25] [3784] 7-8-11 **52** (b) RobertWinston 7 60
(M Dods) *hld up in tch: smooth hdwy to ld over 2f out: rdn and hld on wl fnl f* **7/2**[1]

1166 **2** *nk* **Dium Mac**[51] [2975] 5-9-7 **69** SuzzanneFrance[(7)] 11 76
(N Bycroft) *keen: hld up: hdwy over 2f out: effrt and ch over 1f out: hung lft: kpt on fnl f: jst hld* **6/1**[3]

-000 **3** *3* **Melodian**[11] [4205] 11-8-9 **55** (b) MarkLawson[(5)] 1 57
(M Brittain) *chsd ldrs: drvn 3f out: rallied: no ex over 1f out* **25/1**

6214 **4** *7* **Donna's Double**[15] [4068] 11-8-11 **52** (p) TonyHamilton 6 41
(Karen McLintock) *hld up: hdwy over 2f out: no imp fnl f* **7/1**

1364 **5** *2 ½* **Trouble Mountain (USA)**[11] [4203] 9-10-0 **69** (t) DaleGibson 4 54
(M W Easterby) *in tch: outpcd 4f out: rallied appr fnl f: no imp* **4/1**[2]

6341 **6** *1* **Lauro**[15] [4068] 6-9-0 **62** DawnRankin[(7)] 2 45
(Miss J A Camacho) *in tch: pushed along 3f out: wknd 2f out* **7/1**

3040 **7** *1 ¼* **Toss The Caber (IRE)**[15] [4072] 4-9-0 **55** (t) DavidAllan 3 36
(K G Reveley) *rdr slow to remove blindfold: missed break: hld up: effrt and hung lft over 2f out: wknd wl over 1f out* **8/1**

2310 **8** *1 ¼* **Thornaby Green**[6] [4355] 5-8-2 **50** oh3 DeanHeslop[(7)] 9 29
(T D Barron) *keen: led after 2f: hdd over 2f out: sn wknd* **12/1**

0533 9 2 **Hill Of Almhuim (IRE)**[35] 3477 3-9-5 **68**......................(v) PatCosgrave 5 43
(K R Burke) *led 2f: w ldr: ev ch over 2f out: wknd wl over 1f out* **10/1**

2m 16.23s (4.43) **Going Correction** +0.525s/f (Yiel)
WFA 3 from 4yo+ 8lb 9 Ran SP% **113.2**
Speed ratings (Par 103):103,102,100,94,92 91,90,89,88
CSF £24.09 CT £445.35 TOTE £3.80: £1.50, £2.40, £7.20; EX 37.60.
Owner Denton Hall Racing Ltd **Bred** Sean Twomey **Trained** Denton, Co Durham

FOCUS
A modest handicap run at just an ordinary pace and best rated around the first two.
Toss The Caber(IRE) Official explanation: jockey said gelding missed the break due to the blindfold getting stuck on the bridle

4571 NALCO H'CAP 6f
5:15 (5:15) (Class 6) (0-65,62) 3-Y-0+ **£3,071** (£906; £453) **Stalls** High

Form RPR

2003 1 **Petite Mac**[5] 4401 6-9-2 **59**...................................... SuzzanneFrance(7) 11 68
(N Bycroft) *hld up midfield: hdwy over 1f out: led ins fnl f: styd on wl* **8/1**

0-40 2 ½ **Guadaloup**[15] 4070 4-8-11 **50**...(b¹) DNolan(3) 12 58
(M Brittain) *hld up in tch: hdwy to ld over 1f out: hdd ins fnl f: kpt on fin* **33/1**

0140 3 1 **Briery Lane (IRE)**[59] 2737 5-9-7 **62**...............................(p) GregFairley(5) 9 67
(Mrs K Walton) *prom: led over 2f to over 1f out: kpt on same pce fnl f* **33/1**

1505 4 2½ **Piccolo Prince**[45] 3171 5-9-4 **57**.............................. JasonEdmunds(3) 16 54+
(E J Alston) *racd alone stands rail: rdn over 2f out: kpt on ins fnl f* **14/1**

6060 5 shd **George The Best (IRE)**[9] 4253 5-9-8 **58**..................... DeanMcKeown 7 55
(Micky Hammond) *led to over 2f out: rdn and edgd lft: kpt on same pce fnl f* **20/1**

6430 6 1¼ **Elkhorn**[14] 4116 4-9-4 **54**..(p) PaulMulrennan 14 47
(Miss J A Camacho) *s.i.s: hdwy over 2f out: rdn and no imp fnl f* **10/1**

0605 7 1½ **Apex**[15] 4067 5-9-9 **59**...(p) KimTinkler 6 47
(N Tinkler) *prom tl rdn and no ex wl over 1f out* **12/1**

3503 8 ½ **Dorn Dancer (IRE)**[14] 4119 4-9-7 **62**.......................... MarkLawson(5) 1 49
(D W Barker) *chsd ldrs: effrt over 2f out: no ex over 1f out* **9/2**[1]

4233 9 2½ **Drum Dance (IRE)**[74] 2288 4-8-7 **50**................. DanielleMcCreery(7) 10 29
(N Tinkler) *in tch tl wknd fr 2f out* **20/1**

040 10 shd **Hout Bay**[5] 4401 9-9-3 **53**..(p) TonyHamilton 13 32
(R A Fahey) *hld up: effrt over 2f out: sn btn* **20/1**

126 11 ½ **Dancing Deano (IRE)**[14] 4116 4-9-11 **61**.................(v) J-PGuillambert 3 39
(R M Whitaker) *prom tl wknd fr 2f out* **7/1**[3]

2002 12 4 **Desert Opal**[3] 4462 6-9-10 **60**... DO'Donohoe 5 26
(C R Dore) *in tch: drvn over 2f out: btn over 1f out* **8/1**

0032 13 nk **Missperon (IRE)**[5] 4401 4-8-10 **51**.......................(b) AndrewMullen(5) 15 16
(K A Ryan) *sn outpcd and drvn along: no ch fr 1/2-way* **6/1**[2]

6210 14 1¼ **Celtic Thunder**[31] 3617 5-9-8 **58**...................................(b) GylesParkin 4 19
(T J Etherington) *bhd and sn struggling: no ch fr 1/2-way* **25/1**

4064 15 39 **Attacca**[11] 4198 5-9-3 **53**.. RobertWinston 17 —
(J R Weymes) *chsd ldrs to 1/2-way: sn lost pl: virtually p.u fnl f* **8/1**

1m 16.13s (1.04) **Going Correction** +0.175s/f (Good) 15 Ran SP% **125.8**
Speed ratings (Par 101):100,99,98,94,94 92,90,90,86,86 86,80,80,78,26
CSF £266.05 CT £8055.92 TOTE £10.80: £2.70, £8.50, £7.80; EX 394.70 Place 6 £514.18, Place 5 £322.09.
Owner N Bycroft **Bred** T Umpleby **Trained** Brandsby, N Yorks

FOCUS
A modest event run at a decent gallop but, although the bulk of runners raced in the centre, the proximity of Piccolo Prince showed that the stands' rail could not have been much slower than the rest of the track. The form looks sound rated around the first three.
Attacca Official explanation: jockey said gelding felt wrong
RY

4369 **NEWMARKET (JULY)** (R-H)
Friday, August 18

OFFICIAL GOING: Good
Wind: Light, across Weather: Cloudy with sunny periods

4572 NEWMARKETNIGHTS.CO.UK MEDIAN AUCTION MAIDEN STKS 7f
5:25 (5:28) (Class 5) 2-Y-0 **£3,886** (£1,156; £577; £288) **Stalls** Low

Form RPR

0 1 **Gold Option**[14] 4103 2-9-3 .... JimmyFortune 13 88+
(J H M Gosden) *trckd ldrs: led 2f out: hung lft ins fnl f: drvn out* **11/4**[1]

52 2 1½ **Farleigh House (USA)**[48] 3083 2-9-3 .... TPQueally 10 84
(M H Tompkins) *hld up in tch: racd keenly: rdn and ev ch over 1f out: styd on same pce ins fnl f* **13/2**[3]

002 3 2½ **Bold Abbott (USA)**[7] 4333 2-9-3 .... RyanMoore 4 78
(Mrs A J Perrett) *disp ld 5f: sn rdn: wknd ins fnl f* **3/1**[2]

4 1½ **Aaim To Prosper (IRE)** 2-9-3 .... TedDurcan 8 74
(M R Channon) *s.i.s: sn pushed along in rr: styd on fnl 2f: nt trble ldrs* **16/1**

06 5 1¼ **Look Who's Dancing**[28] 3707 2-8-12 .... KerrinMcEvoy 12 66
(J L Dunlop) *disp ld 5f: wknd fnl f* **12/1**

5500 6 8 **Mint State**[37] 3417 2-9-3 .... JohnEgan 2 51
(D R C Elsworth) *prom: nt clr run and lost pl over 2f out: n.d after* **8/1**

7 1¾ **River Deuce** 2-9-0 .... SaleemGolam(3) 5 47
(M H Tompkins) *sed lsowly: hld up: rdn over 2f out: sn wknd* **50/1**

8 5 **New Beginning (IRE)** 2-8-10 .... AshleyHamblett(7) 1 34
(Mrs S Lamyman) *sn chsng ldrs: hung lft and wknd 2f out* **50/1**

0 9 shd **Torver**[14] 4105 2-8-12 .... RobertHavlin 6 29
(Dr J D Scargill) *prom: rdn 1/2-way: wknd 2f out* **50/1**

0 10 2½ **Beaumont (IRE)**[18] 4000 2-9-3 .... MatthewHenry 3 28
(M A Jarvis) *chsd ldrs: rdn 1/2-way: wknd 2f out* **33/1**

11 5 **Miss Taboo (IRE)** 2-8-12 .... JamieMackay 9 —
(Miss V Haigh) *s.s: outpcd* **50/1**

12 7 **Ballyshane Spirit (IRE)** 2-9-3 .... AlanMunro 7 —
(N A Callaghan) *racd keenly: hdwy over 5f out: lost pl 1/2-way: sn bhd* **33/1**

13 3½ **Man Of Fortune (IRE)** 2-9-0 .... PatrickMathers(3) 11 —
(D Shaw) *s.s: a in rr: hung rt fnl 3f* **50/1**

1m 28.07s (1.29) **Going Correction** +0.175s/f (Good) 13 Ran SP% **105.4**
Speed ratings (Par 94):99,97,94,92,91 82,80,74,74,71 65,57,53
CSF £14.88 TOTE £3.10: £1.10, £2.00, £1.40; EX 16.90.
Owner K Abdulla **Bred** Juddmonte Farms Ltd **Trained** Newmarket, Suffolk
■ Benny The Bat (9/2) withdrawn reared up and got fore legs caught over the side of the stalls. Rule 4 deduct 15p in £.

FOCUS
Although the going was given as 'good', the jockeys felt it was on the easier side of that description. This looked a good maiden and the third and fifth given a good guide to the level of the form.

NOTEBOOK
Gold Option did well to remain calm in the next-door box when Benny The Bat reared up, and he came out to win his race nicely. He was a beaten favourite over course and distance on his only other start, but travelled like a useful prospect and came to lead over two furlongs out. He ran on up the hill in eyecatching fashion and a mile conditions race looks like the next port of call. (op 7-2)
Farleigh House(USA), second at Newmarket on his only other start a six weeks earlier, again had to settle for the runner-up berth. This was another solid performance and a maiden should come his way soon enough. (op 7-1)
Bold Abbott(USA), making his third consecutive course-and-distance appearance, was bidding to build on a second-place finish a week earlier. Having come there with every chance, he weakened inside the final furlong. On his previous form, he shapes as if capable of winning a slightly less competitive race but, off a mark of 85, he could be difficult to place in nurseries. (tchd 10-3)
Aaim To Prosper(IRE) ◆, a half-brother to Hurricane Alan, made a most promising debut. He is entitled to go even closer next time.
Look Who's Dancing is now qualified for a handicap mark and it will be interesting to see how the assessor evaluates her.
Man Of Fortune(IRE) Official explanation: jockey said gelding hung right from 2f out

4573 MERVYN LAMBERT PLANT LTD H'CAP 6f
5:55 (5:56) (Class 4) (0-85,81) 3-Y-0+ **£5,505** (£1,637; £818; £408) **Stalls** Low

Form RPR

0-00 1 **Gold Express**[27] 3742 3-8-5 **63**... AlanMunro 3 74+
(W A O'Gorman) *racd far side: hld up: swtchd centre over 2f out: hdwy over 1f out: rdn to ld ins fnl f: all out* **9/1**[3]

611 2 shd **Al Qasi (IRE)**[22] 3879 3-9-9 **81**................................... AdrianMcCarthy 7 92
(P W Chapple-Hyam) *racd centre: plld hrd and prom: led over 1f out: rdn and hdd ins fnl f: r.o* **15/8**[1]

3042 3 1¼ **Greenwood**[20] 3928 8-9-3 **72**... RobertHavlin 8 79
(P G Murphy) *racd centre: chsd ldrs: rdn over 1f out: r.o* **9/1**[3]

1353 4 nk **Marmooq**[43] 3212 3-8-13 **74**....................................... SaleemGolam(3) 5 80
(S C Williams) *racd centre: w ldr tl led and overall ldr over 3f out: rdn and hdd over 1f out: styd on same pce ins fnl f* **12/1**

0600 5 hd **Nistaki (USA)**[23] 3846 5-8-6 **64**................................ PatrickMathers(3) 10 70
(D Shaw) *racd centre: hld up: hdwy over 1f out: r.o* **25/1**

5101 6 4 **Guildenstern (IRE)**[14] 4106 4-9-12 **81**..............................(t) RyanMoore 2 75
(H Morrison) *racd far side: led that gp over 4f out and on terms w centre gp tl over 2f out: sn rdn: wknd fnl f* **5/2**[2]

-000 7 ½ **Siena Gold**[29] 3687 4-9-8 **77**... JimmyFortune 6 69
(J G Given) *racd centre: prom: rdn over 2f out: wknd over 1f out* **50/1**

2503 8 1½ **Flint River**[176] 489 8-9-4 **73**... MickyFenton 9 61
(H Morrison) *led centre gp and overall ldr: hdd over 3f out: rdn and wknd over 1f out* **12/1**

0040 9 5 **Lord Mayor**[14] 4106 5-9-9 **78**... TedDurcan 1 51
(R M H Cowell) *racd far side: prom 4f* **20/1**

0001 10 25 **Anfield Dream**[183] 426 4-9-9 **78**... JohnEgan 4 —
(J R Jenkins) *led far side: hdd that gp over 4f out: hung rt and wknd wl over 1f out* **16/1**

1m 13.89s (0.54) **Going Correction** +0.175s/f (Good)
WFA 3 from 4yo+ 3lb 10 Ran SP% **115.2**
Speed ratings (Par 105):103,102,101,100,100 95,94,92,85,52
CSF £25.40 CT £163.34 TOTE £10.60: £2.90, £1.40, £2.40; EX 31.10.
Owner N S Yong **Bred** Deerfield Farm **Trained** Newmarket, Suffolk
■ Stewards' Enquiry : Alan Munro two-day ban: used whip with excessive frequency and without allowing sufficient time to respond (Aug 29-30)

FOCUS
A fair handicap but the pace was just moderate early on and field split into two groups. The form is sound enough rated around the third and fourth.
Gold Express Official explanation: trainer said, regarding the improved form shown, the colt was big and green and has matured and may have benefited from today's drop in trip to 6f

4574 EUROPEAN BREEDERS FUND MAIDEN STKS 1m
6:30 (6:32) (Class 5) 2-Y-0 **£4,533** (£1,348; £674; £336) **Stalls** Low

Form RPR

1 **Yazamaan** 2-9-3 .... RHills 8 83+
(J H M Gosden) *hld up: racd keenly: hdwy to ld over 1f out: shkn up and edgd lft ins fnl f: r.o wl* **5/2**[2]

00 2 3 **Italian Stallion (IRE)**[13] 4129 2-9-3 .... RyanMoore 2 76
(R Hannon) *w ldr tl led over 3f out: rdn and hdd over 1f out: no ex ins fnl f* **2/1**[1]

3 2 **Dansimar** 2-8-12 .... TedDurcan 3 67
(M R Channon) *prom: rdn over 1f out: sn outpcd* **6/1**[3]

4 5 **Regime (IRE)** 2-9-3 .... JamieSpencer 1 61
(M L W Bell) *dwlt: sn chsng ldrs: rdn over 1f out: wknd qckly* **5/2**[2]

0 5 3½ **Ski For Luck (IRE)**[19] 3976 2-9-3 .... EddieAhern 6 53
(J L Dunlop) *led over 4f: rdn and wknd over 1f out* **6/1**[3]

1m 43.59s (3.16) **Going Correction** +0.175s/f (Good) 5 Ran SP% **119.0**
Speed ratings (Par 94):91,88,86,81,77
CSF £8.71 TOTE £4.00: £2.10, £1.40; EX 11.60.
Owner Hamdan Al Maktoum **Bred** Shadwell Estate Company Limited **Trained** Newmarket, Suffolk
■ Desert Vision was withdrawn (5/1, vet's advice). R4 applies, deduct 15p in the £.

FOCUS
Only two of these had previous racecourse experience, and the time was unexceptional. The runner-up is the best guide to the level.

NOTEBOOK
Yazamaan, a Derby entry from the family of Kingmambo and Miesque, won this in taking fashion. The lack of gallop would not have been ideal for this Galileo colt, but he picked up nicely to lead over a furlong out before scoring in style. He will go for a conditions race next and, likely to stay further in time, and looks a nice prospect. (op 11-4 tchd 3-1)
Italian Stallion(IRE) was upped to a mile after finishing well held over seven on his previous start. He tried to give the winner a fight but may have come up against a useful sort. (op 4-1)
Dansimar ran reasonably on this debut and this stoutly bred half-sister to a number of winners is likely to improve over time and with a longer trip. (op 12-1)
Regime(IRE), a 120,000 euros half-brother to the useful Salut D'Amour, never threatened but will likely have benefited from the experience. (op 2-1 tchd 7-2)
Ski For Luck(IRE) needs his sights lowered if he is to win a maiden, but he may be the type who is seen to better effect in handicaps. (op 16-1)

4575 PORTLAND PLACE PROPERTIES H'CAP 1m
7:05 (7:06) (Class 5) (0-75,74) 3-Y-0+ £3,886 (£1,156; £577; £288) Stalls Low

Form RPR

2143 1 **She's Our Lass (IRE)**22 3883 5-9-8 69 DanielTudhope 9 79
(D Carroll) *chsd ldrs: led over 1f out: sn rdn: hung rt ins fnl f: r.o* 6/1²

313 2 1 **Logsdail**16 4047 6-9-9 70 (p) RyanMoore 10 77
(G L Moore) *hld up: hdwy over 1f out: sn rdn and hung lft: hung rt ins fnl f: styd on u.p* 9/2¹

0045 3 shd **Merrymadcap (IRE)**11 4209 4-9-13 74 TedDurcan 13 81
(M Blanshard) *hld up: hdwy over 1f out: r.o* 11/1

-044 4 ½ **Mohawk Star (IRE)**16 4048 5-9-7 68 KerrinMcEvoy 14 74
(I A Wood) *chsd ldr: led over 4f out: rdn and hdd over 1f out: no ex ins fnl f* 8/1³

0000 5 1¼ **Parnassian**84 1993 6-9-7 68 RichardThomas 8 71
(J A Geake) *chsd ldrs: rdn over 1f out: styd on same pce* 8/1³

0003 6 4 **Crail**21 3918 6-9-4 65 GeorgeBaker 1 59
(C F Wall) *hld up: hdwy u.p over 1f out: hung rt and wknd ins fnl f* 6/1²

1306 7 nk **Catskill**21 3900 4-9-6 67 (p) JimmyFortune 15 60
(E F Vaughan) *chsd ldrs: rdn over 2f out: wknd over 1f out* 9/1

226- 8 1¼ **Smart John**315 5720 6-9-5 69 PatrickMathers(3) 12 59+
(D Shaw) *s.i.s: hld up: nt clr run fr over 2f out tl 1f out: n.d* 16/1

0025 9 nk **Cavan Gael (FR)**4 4439 4-8-8 55 JohnEgan 7 45
(P Howling) *hld up in tch: racd keenly: rdn and wknd over 1f out* 20/1

62/0 10 2 **Cadeaux Des Mages**21 3918 6-9-12 73 JamieMackay 17 58
(J G Given) *chsd ldrs: rdn over 3f out: wknd over 1f out* 25/1

P000 11 1¼ **Halcyon Magic**28 3712 8-8-3 57 oh7 ow2 (b) JPFeatherstone(7) 11 39
(M Wigham) *w ldrs: rdn over 2f out: wknd over 1f out* 33/1

0245 12 5 **Malech (IRE)**19 3977 3-9-3 70 JamieSpencer 16 41
(M L W Bell) *hld up: swtchd rt and hdwy over 2f out: rdn and wknd over 1f out* 9/1

40 13 5 **Midshipman**102 1553 8-8-8 55 oh2 (tp) TPQueally 6 14
(T Keddy) *chsd ldrs: rdn over 2f out: wknd over 1f out* 16/1

0660 14 10 **Unprecedented (IRE)**95 1727 5-8-5 55 oh18 SaleemGolam(3) 19 —
(T T Clement) *led: hdd over 4f out: wknd 2f out* 100/1

1m 41.09s (0.66) **Going Correction** +0.175s/f (Good)
WFA 3 from 4yo+ 6lb 14 Ran SP% 121.6
Speed ratings (Par 103):103,102,101,101,100 96,95,94,94,92 91,86,81,71
CSF £32.27 CT £298.52 TOTE £5.00: £1.90, £2.40, £4.70; EX 16.00.
Owner We-Know Partnership **Bred** Illuminatus Investments **Trained** Warthill, N Yorks

FOCUS
This modest handicap was run over two seconds quicker than the preceding juvenile maiden and the form looks solid rated around the placed horses.

4576 STABLECARE CONDITIONS STKS 1m 4f
7:35 (7:36) (Class 2) 3-Y-0+ £11,217 (£3,358; £1,679; £840; £419) Stalls Centre

Form RPR

0/5- 1 **Perfectperformance (USA)**377 4148 4-9-0 109 LDettori 5 106
(Saeed Bin Suroor) *chsd ldrs: nt clr run fr over 3f out tl led over 2f out: sn edgd rt: rdn out* 7/4²

-252 2 ¾ **Camrose**54 2893 5-9-0 99 (b) JimmyFortune 2 105
(J L Dunlop) *hld up in tch: ev ch fr over 2f out: hrd rdn over 1f out: no ex wl ins fnl f* 4/1³

0-35 3 5 **Asian Heights**14 4096 8-9-0 100 AlanMunro 3 97
(G Wragg) *hld up: hdwy u.p over 2f out: hung rt over 1f out: styd on same pce* 13/2

4115 4 8 **Luberon**17 4024 3-8-4 106 KDarley 1 84
(M Johnston) *chsd ldr tl led over 3f out: sn edgd rt: n.m.r and hdd over 2f out: wknd over 1f out: eased* 13/8¹

0045 5 9 **Dubai Sunday (JPN)**8 4307 5-9-0 47 BrianReilly 4 70?
(P S McEntee) *led over 8f: sn wknd* 66/1

2m 32.97s (0.06) **Going Correction** +0.175s/f (Good)
WFA 3 from 4yo+ 10lb 5 Ran SP% 109.3
Speed ratings (Par 109):106,105,102,96,90
CSF £8.86 TOTE £2.30: £1.50, £2.40; EX 10.00.
Owner Godolphin **Bred** Brushwood Stable **Trained** Newmarket, Suffolk

FOCUS
A fair conditions race and a good effort by the winner on his return from over a year off. The runner-up is the best guide to the form.

NOTEBOOK
Perfectperformance(USA), after an absence of over a year, returned to winning ways with a hard-fought success. Connections explained that the horse sustained a fracture behind on his sole start at three, ruling him out for the rest of the year. However, their patience has been rewarded as he still retains the sort of ability that took him to a Royal Lodge success at two. He is likely to step up in grade for his next start and could be one to follow this autumn. (op 11-8 tchd 15-8 in places)
Camrose had a lot to do based on official ratings but ran a fine race, although he did not carry his head in the most attractive manner in the closing stages. He is hard to place off his mark but at least he showed he is in good heart at present. (op 11-2)
Asian Heights is a shadow of his former self and never got into contention. (op 6-1 tchd 7-1)
Luberon seems better on genuinely fast ground, but this was some way below what he is capable of. (op 7-4 tchd 15-8 in places)

4577 JOIN THE RACING UK CLUB FILLIES' H'CAP 7f
8:05 (8:05) (Class 3) (0-95,88) 3-Y-0+ £8,096 (£2,408; £1,203; £601) Stalls Low

Form RPR

3042 1 **Puya**14 4108 4-9-4 78 DaneO'Neill 8 90
(H Candy) *chsd ldrs: led over 2f out: rdn and hung lft fr over 1f out: styd on* 11/4¹

-200 2 1¾ **Arm Candy (IRE)**41 3316 3-9-9 88 AlanMunro 5 93
(J A R Toller) *led over 4f: rdn over 1f out: styd on same pce* 7/1³

0530 3 2 **Local Fancy**72 2344 3-8-11 76 MickyFenton 4 76
(J M P Eustace) *s.i.s: sn chsng ldrs: rdn over 1f out: styd on same pce* 10/1

1306 4 2½ **Kaveri (USA)**20 3945 3-9-4 83 KerrinMcEvoy 2 76
(C E Brittain) *chsd ldrs: rdn over 2f out: wknd over 1f out* 10/1

6-0 5 nk **Indian's Feather (IRE)**123 1043 5-10-0 88 (b) LDettori 1 83
(N Tinkler) *s.i.s: sn prom: rdn 3f out: wknd over 1f out* 7/1³

2602 6 hd **Lipizza (IRE)**15 4078 3-8-11 76 ChrisCatlin 3 68
(N A Callaghan) *hld up: racd keenly: hdwy over 1f out: wknd fnl f* 8/1

1-0 7 5 **Queen's Pudding (IRE)**56 2824 3-9-5 84 JamieSpencer 9 63
(J R Fanshawe) *hld up: sme hdwy over 1f out: sn wknd* 3/1²

-000 8 3 **I'm In Love (USA)**19 3973 3-9-0 79 EddieAhern 10 50
(M A Magnusson) *hld up: rdn and wknd over 1f out* 14/1

0-00 9 1½ **Love Thirty**83 2011 4-9-11 85 TedDurcan 6 54
(M R Channon) *prom: rdn over 2f out: wknd over 1f out* 20/1

1m 26.0s (-0.78) **Going Correction** +0.175s/f (Good)
WFA 3 from 4yo+ 5lb 9 Ran SP% 117.4
Speed ratings (Par 104):111,109,106,103,103 103,97,94,92
CSF £22.97 CT £169.84 TOTE £3.90: £1.60, £2.90, £3.30; EX 26.90 Place 6 £19.09, Place 5 £15.76.
Owner Girsonfield Ltd **Bred** Girsonfield Ltd **Trained** Kingston Warren, Oxon

FOCUS
A decent fillies' handicap run in a smart winning time for a race of its type. The form looks solid rated around the placed horses.

NOTEBOOK
Puya has generally been running well on fast ground this season, including when second over a mile here a fortnight ago and scored well despite hanging left. Both of her career victories have come in August over seven and that certainly looks like her best trip. (tchd 3-1 in places)
Arm Candy(IRE) was dropping into handicaps after unsuccessfully chasing black type at Sandown and Newbury. She produced a decent effort but was never able to peg back the winner. She is up to winning a similar race.
Local Fancy had shown some form in the soft at Sandown in May but subsequently finished last at Kempton, where she was not suited by the surface. This was more encouraging, however and she is worth bearing in mind.
Kaveri(USA) was more competitive back at seven furlongs, racing prominently without seriously threatening a third career win.
Indian's Feather(IRE), whose sole win in Ireland was over this trip on soft ground, missed the break but soon got into contention, only to fade up the hill.
Lipizza(IRE), returning to this trip for the first time since last October, has been having a decent time at sprint distances. She was probably too keen and it cost her late on. (op 7-1)
Queen's Pudding(IRE) having only her third run and first since disappointing in June, again failed to make an impression. She may not have trained on or possibly does not like this track, in any case she has something to prove now. Official explanation: jockey said filly had lost her action (op 4-1)
T/Plt: £16.10 to a £1 stake. Pool: £50,775.30. 2,302.00 winning tickets. T/Qpdt: £11.30 to a £1 stake. Pool: £3,855.50. 250.95 winning tickets. CR

4578 - 4584a (Foreign Racing) - See Raceform Interactive

4125 GOODWOOD (R-H)
Saturday, August 19

OFFICIAL GOING: Good to firm (good in places)
Wind: Moderate, half-against

4585 BOLLINGER CHAMPAGNE CHALLENGE SERIES H'CAP (FOR GENTLEMAN AMATEUR RIDERS) 1m
4:50 (4:51) (Class 6) (0-55,53) 3-Y-0+ £3,123 (£968; £484; £242) Stalls High

Form RPR

1 **Dannabelle (IRE)**35 3558 6-10-6 40 JackMitchell(5) 18 60
(John A Quinn, Ire) *a in tch: hdwy on outside 2f out: sn clr: readily* 9/1

5000 2 8 **Height Of Spirits**14 4139 4-11-3 46 MrSWalker 11 48
(T D McCarthy) *a in tch: rdn 2f out: hdwy to go 2nd ins fnl f but no ch w wnr* 9/1

6004 3 2 **The Job**88 1915 5-10-10 46 (v) MrMDavies(7) 9 43
(A D Smith) *a.p: rdn to ld 2f out: sn hdd: one pce and lost 2nd ins fnl f* 16/1

000- 4 1 **Bowl Of Cherries**306 5944 3-10-8 48 MrCRNelson(5) 13 43
(I A Wood) *a in tch: rdn 2f out: one pce after* 33/1

5065 5 1¼ **Peters Delite**12 4198 4-11-1 49 MrBMcHugh(5) 15 41
(R A Fahey) *mid-div: rdn 2f out: one pce after* 4/1¹

0005 6 ½ **Seldemosa**7 4363 5-11-6 49 MrWHogg 10 40
(M S Saunders) *in tch: rdn and ever ch 2f out: wknd fnl f* 12/1

0030 7 shd **Zinging**4 4446 7-10-9 45 (v) RyanBird(7) 19 36
(J J Bridger) *mid-div: one pce fr over 2f out* 12/1

00-0 8 ½ **Dream Alive**16 3797 5-10-12 46 (t) MrFelixDeGiles(5) 1 36
(S Curran) *mid-div: lost tch fnl 2f* 50/1

00/0 9 2 **Billy Bathwick (IRE)**13 4176 9-11-0 48 MrNPearce(5) 17 33
(J M Bradley) *a.p: led 2f out: sn hdd & wknd qckly* 20/1

3510 10 ½ **Fantasy Defender (IRE)**9 4276 4-11-2 50 (v) MrDavidTurner(5) 14 34
(Ernst Oertel) *w ldr: led over 3f out: rdn and hdd over 2f out: sn wknd* 13/2²

0000 11 hd **Carpet Ride**16 3592 4-10-13 45 (b¹) MrSPJones(3) 2 28
(B G Powell) *led tl hdd over 3f out: wknd over 1f out* 25/1

0004 12 1¼ **Bogaz (IRE)**6 4389 4-10-9 45 (v) MrAMerriam(7) 5 26
(Mrs H Sweeting) *nvr bttr than mid-div* 16/1

0043 13 1¾ **Gran Clicquot**26 3797 11-10-11 45 MrSPearce(5) 7 21
(G P Enright) *a towards rr* 8/1³

5600 14 3 **Ms Rainbow Runner**111 1314 3-11-1 50 GerardTumelty 16 20
(P Butler) *a in rr* 25/1

0046 15 9 **Samson Quest**28 3730 4-11-0 50 (v) MrJGoss(7) 3 —
(G F Bridgwater) *slowly away fr outside draw: swtchd to ins but a struggling in rr* 25/1

0060 16 1½ **Jinksonthehouse**11 4223 5-10-12 41 MrLeeNewnes 8 —
(M D I Usher) *mid-div tl wknd 2f out* 50/1

0000 17 2 **Smoking Star**20 3975 3-10-8 50 MrCHughes(7) 6 —
(N I M Rossiter) *in tch tl wknd 3f out* 66/1

1-06 18 hd **Dark Society**5 4432 8-11-5 53 MrMJJSmith(5) 20 —
(A W Carroll) *v.s.a: a wl bhd* 9/1

1m 41.83s (1.56) **Going Correction** +0.10s/f (Good)
WFA 3 from 4yo+ 6lb 18 Ran SP% 126.2
Speed ratings (Par 101):96,88,86,85,83 83,83,82,80,80 79,78,76,73,64 63,61,61
CSF £82.05 CT £1343.75 TOTE £12.90: £3.90, £3.30, £5.40, £6.90; EX 244.90.
Owner P F Kilmartin **Bred** Frank Kilmartin **Trained** Blackmiller Hill, Co. Kildare

FOCUS
A moderate amateur riders' handicap, but they did at least go a good pace. The form is very limited.
Jinksonthehouse Official explanation: vet said mare bled from the nose
Dark Society Official explanation: jockey said gelding reared leaving stalls

4586 HOUSE PARTY STKS (H'CAP) 1m 3f
5:25 (5:33) (Class 5) (0-75,74) 3-Y-0+ £4,857 (£1,445; £722; £360) Stalls Low

Form RPR

-642 1 **Buster Hyvonen (IRE)**14 4149 4-10-0 72 JamieSpencer 6 78
(J R Fanshawe) *led: hdd over 1f out: rdn and battled on again to ld cl home* 2/1¹

3204 2 hd **Conservation (FR)**13 4173 3-9-4 71 MartinDwyer 2 77
(P W Chapple-Hyam) *trckd wnr: tk narrow ld over 1f out: edgd rt: kpt on u.p: hdd cl home* 7/1³

The Form Book, Raceform Ltd, Compton, RG20 6NL

0414 **3** *1 ¼* **Truly Fruitful (IRE)**[20] [3984] 3-9-7 **74**.......... PatCosgrave 3 77
(K R Burke) *a.p: rdn 2f out: one pce ent fnl f* **8/1**
033 **4** *5* **Malakiya (IRE)**[3] [4470] 3-8-12 **68**.......... AdamKirby(3) 1 63
(G A Butler) *s.i.s: nvr on terms* **3/1**[2]
0004 **5** *5* **Love Angel (USA)**[5] [4432] 4-8-8 **57**.......... MarcHalford(5) 7 44
(J J Bridger) *hld up: lost tch over 2f out* **16/1**
0351 **6** *9* **William's Way**[19] [4001] 4-9-11 **69**.......... ChrisCatlin 4 40
(I A Wood) *bhd: effrt over 3f out: sn btn* **8/1**
0000 **7** *47* **Fortunes Favourite**[103] [1541] 6-8-4 **53** oh8.......... NataliaGemelova(5) 5 —
(J E Long) *chsd ldrs tl wknd over 3f out: t.o* **50/1**

2m 26.89s (-0.32) **Going Correction** +0.10s/f (Good)
WFA 3 from 4yo+ 9lb **7** Ran SP% **100.9**
Speed ratings (Par 103):105,104,103,100,96 90,55
CSF £12.45 CT £57.90 TOTE £2.50: £1.90, £2.10; EX 12.20.
Owner Simon Gibson **Bred** Hollington Stud **Trained** Newmarket, Suffolk
■ Garston Star was withdrawn (8/1, ins rdr & bolted bef s). R4 applies, deduct 10p in the £.

FOCUS
Just a fair handicap and the form looks relatively weak for the grade..
Conservation(FR) Official explanation: jockey said colt hung badly right throughout

4587 SEASON STKS (H'CAP) 5f
5:55 (6:01) (Class 5) (0-70,65) 3-Y-0+ **£4,210** (£1,252; £625; £312) **Stalls** Low

Form RPR
1130 **1** **Heavens Walk**[12] [4208] 5-9-11 **63**.......... (t) MartinDwyer 9 77
(P J Makin) *s.i.s: strly rdn and hdwy over 1f out: battled on gamely to ld nr fin* **7/2**[2]
5000 **2** *½* **Dancing Mystery**[33] [3593] 12-9-7 **59**.......... (b) StephenCarson 1 71
(E A Wheeler) *led: rdn ent fnl f: kpt on but hdd nr fin* **12/1**
0423 **3** *3* **Talcen Gwyn (IRE)**[10] [4258] 4-9-4 **56**.......... (v) JamieSpencer 5 57
(M F Harris) *a in tch: rdn over 1f out: kpt on one pce fnl f* **7/4**[1]
-000 **4** *shd* **Sofinella (IRE)**[16] [4078] 3-9-6 **60**.......... FrancisFerris 2 61
(A W Carroll) *chsd ldr tl rdn and one pce fnl f* **20/1**
0000 **5** *2 ½* **Meikle Barfil**[4] [4462] 4-9-0 **59**.......... (p) BarrySavage(7) 8 51
(J M Bradley) *prom on outside: rdn over 1f out: wknd fnl f* **9/1**
0001 **6** *1 ¾* **Shank On Fourteen (IRE)**[22] [3913] 5-9-10 **62**.......... PatCosgrave 6 48
(K R Burke) *outpcd thrght* **6/1**[3]
-506 **7** *1 ¼* **Titus Maximus (IRE)**[76] [2263] 3-9-8 **65**.......... AdamKirby(3) 4 46
(G A Butler) *t.k.h: chsd ldrs: rdn over 2f out: wknd wl over 1f out* **8/1**
006 **8** *2* **All About Him (USA)**[14] [4142] 3-8-6 **51**.......... EmmettStack(5) 3 25
(N I M Rossiter) *chsd ldrs tl wknd sn after 1/2-way* **66/1**
00-6 **9** *5* **Free Wheelin (IRE)**[85] [1981] 6-8-12 **50**.......... ChrisCatlin 7 6
(T M Jones) *in tch tl wknd qckly wl over 1f out* **9/1**

58.39 secs (-0.66) **Going Correction** -0.05s/f (Good)
WFA 3 from 4yo+ 2lb **9** Ran SP% **117.9**
Speed ratings (Par 103):103,102,97,97,93 90,88,85,77
CSF £45.80 CT £98.26 TOTE £4.30: £1.40, £2.40, £1.30; EX 47.30.
Owner Mrs P J Makin **Bred** Mrs P J Makin **Trained** Ogbourne Maisey, Wilts

FOCUS
A modest sprint handicap run in a fair time and the form could prove reasonable.
Sofinella(IRE) Official explanation: jockey said saddle slipped
Titus Maximus(IRE) Official explanation: jockey said gelding never travelled
Free Wheelin(IRE) Official explanation: jockey said gelding was unsuited by the good to firm (good in places) ground

4588 EUROPEAN BREEDERS FUND CHICHESTER CITY MEDIAN AUCTION MAIDEN STKS 6f
6:25 (6:26) (Class 5) 2-Y-0 **£4,048** (£1,204; £601; £300) **Stalls** Low

Form RPR
2 **1** **Rahiyah (USA)**[17] [4041] 2-8-12.......... LDettori 2 83+
(J Noseda) *trckd ldr: led over 2f out: sn in command: v easily* **1/7**[1]
00 **2** *2* **Leonide**[8] [4333] 2-9-3.......... RichardHughes 4 73
(B J Meehan) *chsd ldrs: rdn 2f out: kpt on to go 2nd ins fnl f: no ch w wnr* **14/1**[3]
3 *½* **Spriggan** 2-9-0.......... AdamKirby(3) 5 72
(C G Cox) *s.i.s: sn trckd ldrs: rdn over 1f out: kpt on one pce* **25/1**
000 **4** *2 ½* **Blue Mistral (IRE)**[17] [4053] 2-8-12.......... PaulDoe 6 59
(W J Knight) *t.k.h: rdn 1/2-way: in tch tl wknd ins fnl f* **40/1**
5 **5** *1 ½* **Ireland Dancer (IRE)**[18] [4028] 2-9-3.......... MartinDwyer 1 60
(W R Muir) *led tl hdd over 2f out: wknd ent fnl f* **9/1**[2]
60 **6** *26* **The Graig**[20] [3979] 2-9-3.......... ChrisCatlin 3 —
(C Drew) *a outpcd in rr* **50/1**

1m 12.51s (-0.34) **Going Correction** -0.05s/f (Good) **6** Ran SP% **112.4**
Speed ratings (Par 94):100,97,96,93,91 56
CSF £3.38 TOTE £1.10: £1.10, £3.20; EX 5.30.
Owner H E Sheikh Rashid Bin Mohammed **Bred** Darley **Trained** Newmarket, Suffolk

FOCUS
An uncompetitive maiden, but by no means a bad contest and, although the winner did not need to run to her debut mark, the form should not be underestimated.

NOTEBOOK
Rahiyah(USA) ◆, a promising second over course and distance on her debut, found this easier and hardly had to come off the bridle to win impressively. Although this was not a competitive race, they were not totally rubbish in behind and this must rate as a most encouraging success. She does not have any Group-race entries, but is well worth her place in better company.
Leonide had shown ability on his two previous starts, and this was again encouraging, but he was no match for the winner. (tchd 16-1)
Spriggan ◆, a half-brother to dual sprint-juvenile winner Lotto, and mile scorer Liberty Royal, ran green on his racecourse debut but should know much more next time and could be one to be with.
Blue Mistral(IRE) is now eligible for a handicap mark and could do better. (op 33-1)
Ireland Dancer(IRE) faded disappointingly and failed to build on the promise he showed on his debut over course and distance. He might want easier ground and is not one to give up on just yet. (op 8-1 tchd 10-1)
The Graig Official explanation: trainer said the colt was unsuited by the good to firm (good in places) ground

4589 EUROPEAN BREEDERS FUND PANAMA HAT FILLIES' STKS (H'CAP) 6f
7:00 (7:00) (Class 4) (0-85,83) 3-Y-0+ **£6,477** (£1,927; £963; £481) **Stalls** Low

Form RPR
0450 **1** **Tara Too (IRE)**[24] [3852] 3-9-10 **80**.......... RyanMoore 2 93
(D W P Arbuthnot) *hld up: swtchd rt over 2f out:: rdn and hdwy to ld 1f out: drvn out* **9/1**
1131 **2** *2* **Aahgowangowan (IRE)**[15] [4119] 7-9-10 **77**.......... (t) JamieSpencer 5 84
(M Dods) *led: rdn and hdd 1f out: no ex ins fnl f* **2/1**[1]
1236 **3** *1 ½* **Xaluna Bay (IRE)**[8] [4328] 3-9-4 **74**.......... LDettori 3 76
(W R Muir) *a.p: rdn over 1f out: fdd ins fnl f* **8/1**
0212 **4** *1 ½* **Sweet Pickle**[4] [4449] 5-8-8 **64**.......... (e) AmirQuinn(3) 6 62
(J R Boyle) *in tch: rdn over 1f out: wknd ins fnl f* **9/2**[2]
3100 **5** *nk* **Rydal Mount (IRE)**[28] [3722] 3-9-10 **80**.......... FergusSweeney 1 77+
(W S Kittow) *bhd: nt clr run fr over 2f out: swtchd rt over 1f out: nvr on terms* **20/1**
1331 **6** *½* **Ivory Lace**[4] [4449] 5-9-13 **83** 7ex.......... JamesDoyle(3) 7 78
(S Woodman) *prom tl wknd ins fnl f* **10/1**
2051 **7** *hd* **Mango Music**[10] [4242] 3-9-5 **82**.......... ThomasO'Brien(7) 4 77
(M R Channon) *trckd ldrs tl wknd over 1f out* **10/1**
0046 **8** *¾* **Qusoor (IRE)**[28] [3741] 3-9-10 **80**.......... MartinDwyer 8 72
(J L Dunlop) *prom tl rdn and wknd ent fnl f* **14/1**
0412 **9** *5* **Daniella**[28] [3741] 4-9-10 **77**.......... (p) FrancisFerris 9 54
(Rae Guest) *s.i.s: wnt rt and racd alone far side tl wnt lft 2f out: sn btn* **7/1**[3]

1m 12.22s (-0.63) **Going Correction** -0.05s/f (Good)
WFA 3 from 4yo+ 3lb **9** Ran SP% **114.7**
Speed ratings (Par 102):102,99,97,95,94 94,94,93,86
CSF £27.19 CT £153.31 TOTE £11.00: £3.20, £1.40, £2.50; EX 34.90.
Owner Prof C D Green **Bred** Tally-Ho Stud **Trained** Upper Lambourn, Berks

FOCUS
A good fillies' handicap and the form seems sound enough, rated around the runner-up and third.
Xaluna Bay(IRE) Official explanation: jockey said filly lost its action final furlong
Sweet Pickle Official explanation: trainer said mare lost a front shoe

4590 EBF ALICE KEPPEL STKS (FILLIES' H'CAP) (LISTED RACE) 1m 1f 192y
7:30 (7:33) (Class 1) (0-110,99) 3-Y-0+
£15,898 (£6,025; £3,015; £1,503; £753; £378) **Stalls** High

Form RPR
1-13 **1** **Portal**[21] [3929] 3-8-12 **93**.......... JamieSpencer 7 103+
(J R Fanshawe) *hld up in rr: short of room on ins fr over 2f out: swtchd lft appr fnl f: r.o strly to ld nr fin* **10/3**[1]
1621 **2** *hd* **Grain Of Truth**[36] [3489] 3-8-10 **91**.......... RyanMoore 11 100
(Sir Michael Stoute) *hld up: hdwy over 4f out: led jst ins fnl f: hdd nr fin* **5/1**[2]
1-34 **3** *1 ¾* **Play Me**[42] [3293] 4-9-5 **92**.......... AlanMunro 1 98
(P W Chapple-Hyam) *a.p: led 6f out: rdn and hdd jst ins fnl f: no ex nr fin* **20/1**
50 **4** *nk* **Astronomia (NZ)**[59] [2740] 4-9-11 **99**.......... LDettori 5 103
(Saeed Bin Suroor) *a.p: led wl over 1f out: hde jst ins fnl f: kpt on one pce* **8/1**
0310 **5** *½* **Tanzanite (IRE)**[48] [3123] 4-9-6 **93**.......... PatDobbs 3 97
(D W P Arbuthnot) *led tl hdd 6f out: styd prom: one pce ins fnl f* **16/1**
2421 **6** *nk* **Nice Tune**[17] [4040] 4-9-4 **91**.......... TedDurcan 10 95
(C E Brittain) *mid-div: rdn and one pce fr over 1f out* **9/1**
2-12 **7** *¾* **Dash To The Front**[7] [4375] 3-8-3 **84**.......... MartinDwyer 2 86
(J R Fanshawe) *towards rr: mde sme late prog* **6/1**[3]
-554 **8** *½* **Idealistic (IRE)**[13] [4179] 5-9-8 **95**.......... NickyMackay 6 97
(L M Cumani) *mid-div: nt clr tun over 2f out: sn btn* **20/1**
3600 **9** *3* **Salamanca**[18] [4023] 4-9-8 **95**.......... SteveDrowne 4 91
(S Kirk) *a struggling in rr* **12/1**
3153 **10** *5* **Dame Hester (IRE)**[1] [4555] 3-8-4 **85**.......... ChrisCatlin 12 71
(E J O'Neill) *trckd ldr: rdn over 1f out: wknd qckly* **25/1**
-104 **11** *16* **Shortest Day**[59] [2744] 3-9-0 **95**.......... (t) RichardHughes 8 51
(Sir Michael Stoute) *s.i.s: trckd ldrs after 2f out: rdn over 2f out: sn wknd* **5/1**[2]

2m 6.46s (-1.29) **Going Correction** +0.10s/f (Good)
WFA 3 from 4yo+ 8lb **11** Ran SP% **118.8**
Speed ratings (Par 108):109,108,107,107,106 106,105,105,103,99 86
CSF £19.07 CT £292.35 TOTE £4.60: £1.90, £2.30, £3.20; EX 20.30.
Owner Cheveley Park Stud **Bred** Cheveley Park Stud Ltd **Trained** Newmarket, Suffolk

FOCUS
A good fillies' Listed handicap, although the pace was only steady for much of the way. The form is not rock solid although the time was reasonable.

NOTEBOOK
Portal ◆ was given too much to do in a steadily-run race at Ascot on her previous start but, despite the pace again not being as strong as she would have liked, she bounced back with what has to rate as a career-best effort. She only got in the clear about a furlong out having been buried away towards the inside rail for much of the way, and displayed a smart change of pace to pick up off the steady gallop. She can probably be rated better than the bare form and, progressing into a smart filly, will not look out of place in Group company. (op 4-1)
Grain Of Truth ran a fine race off a 7lb higher mark than when winning a lesser race on Lingfield's Polytrack on her previous start. She had to wait for a gap, but the winner got in the clear after her and she basically bumped into a smart sort in the making. There should be more to come. (tchd 6-1)
Play Me, a ten-length fourth in the Group 2 Lancashire Oaks at Haydock on her previous start, had the run of the race and ran respectably. Time may show she had a very tough task indeed conceding 7lb to Portal. (op 22-1)
Astronomia(NZ) had it all to do under top weight but improved considerably on the form of her two previous efforts since transferring from Australia. She could build on this.
Tanzanite(IRE) ran a good race off the back of a 48-day break, but is better suited by easy ground. (op 14-1)
Nice Tune, 5lb higher than when winning over nine furlongs here on her previous start, could not reverse form with Grain Of Truth from two starts back. (op 10-1 tchd 11-1)
Dash To The Front, upped to her furthest trip to date and returned to fast ground, never looked like picking up and appeared totally unsuited by the way the race was run. (op 5-1)
Shortest Day, not seen since running fourth in the Sandringham Stakes at Royal Ascot, proved a major disappointment and this was not her running. Official explanation: jockey said filly stopped quickly (op 11-2 tchd 6-1)

4591 TWILIGHT STKS (H'CAP) 1m
8:00 (8:01) (Class 4) (0-80,80) 3-Y-0 **£5,829** (£1,734; £866; £432) **Stalls** High

Form RPR
3006 **1** **Kavachi (IRE)**[41] [3338] 3-8-6 **63**.......... AlanMunro 3 71+
(G L Moore) *hld up: hdwy over 1f out: strly rdn to ld nr fin* **16/1**
00-5 **2** *nk* **Veiled Applause**[25] [3820] 3-8-2 **62**.......... JamesDoyle(3) 2 67
(R M Beckett) *mid-div: hdwy over 2f out: sn swtchd lft: rdn to ld ins fnl f: hdd nr fin* **8/1**
0505 **3** *shd* **Scarlet Knight**[51] [3015] 3-9-7 **78**.......... RyanMoore 4 82
(P Mitchell) *in rr: rdn over 3f out: hdwy over 1f out: r.o strly fnl f* **14/1**
0535 **4** *hd* **Blu Manruna**[8] [4332] 3-8-4 **61** oh2.......... (p) PaulDoe 8 65
(J Akehurst) *t.k.h: in tch: rdn over 2f out: ev ch ins fnl f: no ex cl home* **7/1**[3]
-304 **5** *½* **Persian Express (USA)**[13] [4181] 3-9-0 **71**.......... MartinDwyer 7 78+
(B W Hills) *mid-div: n.m.r over 1f out: r.o ins fnl f* **12/1**

3000 **6** *1 ½* **Genari**[16] [4082] 3-9-9 **80**...(b[1]) SteveDrowne 9 79
(P F I Cole) *led to 1/2-way: n.m.r fr over 2f out: wknd ins fnl f* **13/2**[2]
-360 **7** *1 ½* **Pigeon Island**[17] [4051] 3-9-2 **73**.................................... FergusSweeney 1 69
(H Candy) *a towards rr* **9/1**
0460 **8** *6* **What Do You Know**[31] [3646] 3-8-11 **71**.......................... AdamKirby(3) 6 53
(G A Butler) *nvr on terms* **22/1**
02-2 **9** *½* **Dynamic Rhythm (USA)**[44] [3219] 3-9-7 **78**........................... LDettori 10 59
(J Noseda) *trckd ldrs: short of room over 1f out on ins: sn wknd* **13/8**[1]
0254 **10** *nk* **Way To The Stars**[21] [3953] 3-8-13 **70**........................... RichardHughes 5 50
(A M Balding) *trckd ldrs tl wknd over 1f out* **10/1**
0000 **11** *2* **Cativo Cavallino**[10] [4245] 3-7-13 **61** oh3................... EmmettStack(5) 11 37+
(Jamie Poulton) *plld hrd: led 1/2-way: hdd over 2f out: wkng whn hmpd on ins over 1f out: nt rcvr* **50/1**

1m 39.95s (-0.32) **Going Correction** +0.10s/f (Good) **11** Ran SP% **120.7**
Speed ratings (Par 102):105,104,104,104,103 102,100,94,94,94 92
CSF £141.88 CT £1237.36 TOTE £20.90: £3.80, £3.70, £2.20; EX 127.60 Place 6 £28.31, Place 5 £5.12.
Owner G L Moore **Bred** Gainsborough Stud Management Ltd **Trained** Woodingdean, E Sussex
■ Stewards' Enquiry : Alan Munro one-day ban: used whip without giving gelding time to respond (Aug 31)

FOCUS
A fair handicap, but a bizarre finish with the winner looking sure to come from Veiled Applause, Scarlet Runner or Blu Manruna inside the last furlong, only for Kavachi to swoop late and take advantage of those three perhaps not doing a great deal under pressure. The pace was just ordinary and the form is rated around the third and fourth.
Dynamic Rhythm(USA) Official explanation: jockey said the colt was unsuited by the good to firm (good in places) ground and hung right
T/Plt: £91.70 to a £1 stake. Pool: £40,765.40. 324.20 winning tickets. T/Qpdt: £5.10 to a £1 stake. Pool: £4,120.40. 597.05 winning tickets. JS

4558 NEWBURY (L-H)
Saturday, August 19

OFFICIAL GOING: Good to soft (good in places) changing to good to soft after race 1 (1.40) and good to soft (soft in places) after race 2 (2.10)
Wind: Slight, ahead

4592 THE SPORTSMAN NEWSPAPER EBF MAIDEN STKS (DIV I) 7f (S)
1:40 (1:42) (Class 4) 2-Y-O **£5,829** (£1,734; £866; £432) **Stalls** Centre

Form RPR
1 **Prince Forever (IRE)** 2-9-3 .... PhilipRobinson 3 88+
(M A Jarvis) *unf: scope: lw: w ldr tl slt ld 2f out: rdn and styd on wl fnl f* **3/1**[2]
2 *1 ¼* **Thabaat** 2-9-3 .... RHills 4 85+
(B W Hills) *cmpt: str: lw: chsd ldrs: upsides 2f out: chsd wnr thrght fnl f but a hld* **11/4**[1]
3 *1 ½* **Ravi River (IRE)** 2-9-3 .... MJKinane 8 81
(B W Hills) *str: scope: bit bkwd: sn slt ld: narrowly hdd 2f out: kpt on same pce ins last* **9/1**
4 *½* **History Boy** 2-9-3 .... TedDurcan 1 80
(D J Coakley) *neat: lw: plld hrd: trckd ldrs: upsides 2f out: kpt on same pce fnl f* **16/1**
5 *3* **Traditionalist (IRE)** 2-9-3 .... NickyMackay 5 72
(G A Butler) *wl grwn: bit bkwd: t.k.h early: chsd ldrs: rdn over 1f out: wknd fnl f* **33/1**
6 *1 ¼* **Patavian (IRE)** 2-9-3 .... ChrisCatlin 9 69
(M R Channon) *lt-f: s.i.s: bhd: stl plenty to do over 1f out: kpt on nr fin* **25/1**
3 **7** *1 ¼* **Lights Of Vegas**[13] [4177] 2-9-3 .... LDettori 10 66
(B J Meehan) *lw: chsd ldrs: rdn over 2f out: wknd fnl f* **10/3**[3]
8 *5* **Mujahaz (IRE)** 2-9-3 .... MartinDwyer 11 54
(J L Dunlop) *leggy: s.i.s: outpcd* **12/1**
9 *¾* **Private Reason (USA)** 2-9-3 .... RichardHughes 7 52
(R Hannon) *cmpt: str: lw: s.i.s: sn chsng ldrs: rdn over 2f out: wknd over 1f out* **9/1**

1m 29.05s (2.05) **Going Correction** +0.20s/f (Good) **9** Ran SP% **115.1**
Speed ratings (Par 96):96,94,92,92,88 87,86,80,79
CSF £11.65 TOTE £4.10: £1.70, £1.30, £2.40; EX 14.10.
Owner H R H Sultan Ahmad Shah **Bred** Longueville Bloodstock **Trained** Newmarket, Suffolk

FOCUS
A maiden in which only one of the runners had seen a racecourse previously, run in a time 0.49sec faster than the later second division, but 1.39sec slower than the following all-aged handicap. The going was changed from good to soft (good in places) to good to soft after this race.

NOTEBOOK
Prince Forever(IRE) ♦, a half-brother to five winners, including successful juveniles, clearly knew his job on this debut and, breaking quickly, was always in the firing line. He picked up well when asked for more and looks the sort who can win decent races. He is likely to be aimed at a Listed race next. (op 11-4 tchd 9-2)
Thabaat ♦, a half-brother to numerous winners, including Khasayl and Muklah, was made favourite. He tracked the leader before keeping on well in the final furlong and, looking more in need of the experience than the winner, can be expected to improve for the outing. He should pick up his maiden before long. (op 3-1 tchd 5-2)
Ravi River(IRE), out of a high-class juvenile, looked sure to benefit from the run and in the circumstances did well. He put up a decent challenge to the winner before fading in the final furlong and should do better with the experience behind him. (op 12-1)
History Boy, out of a mare who won on her racecourse debut, was very keen early on this debut and that counted against\n\x\x him late on. He does not have the substance of those that finished ahead of him, but he should be capable of winning races on this evidence. (op 25-1)
Traditionalist(IRE)looked less furnished than a lot of these, but showed ability until outpaced in the last furlong and a half. Given time to develop he could make up into a nice sort.
Patavian(IRE), who is already gelded, was loaded with the aid of a blanket. He was held up at the back before making late progress and should have learnt from the outing.
Lights Of Vegas, the only one with a previous outing, having made his debut over six furlongs here, was somewhat disappointing. In mitigation though, this ground was quite different from the fast ground he handled well there, and it may not have suited. (op 9-4)

4593 HEBRIDEAN INTERNATIONAL CRUISES H'CAP 7f (S)
2:10 (2:15) (Class 2) (0-100,99) 3-Y-O+ **£12,464** (£3,732; £1,866; £934; £466; £234) **Stalls** Centre

Form RPR
-044 **1** **Jamieson Gold (IRE)**[22] [3889] 3-8-11 **88**................................. RHills 13 97+
(B W Hills) *sn trcking ldrs: drvn along over 1f out: styd on wl to ld fnl 100yds: all out* **20/1**
-146 **2** *hd* **Polar Magic**[21] [3926] 5-9-12 **98**.. JamieSpencer 8 106
(J R Fanshawe) *lw: s.i.s: sn in tch: hdwy over 1f out: str run u.p ins last: fin wl but nt quite get up* **5/2**[1]
121 **3** *½* **Bosset (USA)**[20] [3978] 3-9-5 **96**.. LDettori 12 102
(J Noseda) *lw: chsd ldrs: drvn along over 2f out: str run to chal ins fnl f: upsides fnl 100yds: no ex nr fin* **10/3**[2]
116 **4** *¾* **Meditation**[7] [4343] 4-8-6 **81** ow1.................................... AdamKirby(3) 11 86
(I A Wood) *lw: led: rdn 2f out: kpt slt advantage tl hdd fnl 110yds* **25/1**
3306 **5** *1* **Grimes Faith**[5] [4430] 3-8-2 **82**.. StephaneBreux(3) 9 82
(R Hannon) *bhd: swtchd rt 2f out: hdwy fnl f: kpt on ins last but nt rch ldrs* **150/1**
3150 **6** *nk* **Trafalgar Bay (IRE)**[38] [3414] 3-9-4 **95**................................. PatDobbs 10 95
(S Kirk) *in tch: pushed along 2f out: styd on fnl f but nvr gng pce to rch ldrs* **7/1**[3]
1240 **7** *½* **Obe Brave**[16] [4083] 3-9-8 **99**.. ChrisCatlin 6 97
(M R Channon) *chsd ldr: rdn over 2f out: wknd ins last* **20/1**
3000 **8** *½* **Bahiano (IRE)**[21] [3926] 5-9-11 **97**.................................... RichardHughes 7 99+
(C E Brittain) *hld up in rr: shkn up over 1f out: sme prog ins last but nvr in contention* **11/1**
1060 **9** *2* **Imperial Echo (USA)**[13] [4172] 5-8-10 **82**.......................... RyanMoore 1 76
(T D Barron) *chsd ldrs: rdn over 2f out: wknd fnl f* **16/1**
0030 **10** *nk* **Kingscross**[8] [4338] 8-8-8 **80**... AlanMunro 4 73
(M Blanshard) *bhd: swtchd lft and rdn over 1f out: nvr in contention* **16/1**
0200 **11** *1 ¼* **Intrepid Jack**[7] [4372] 4-9-10 **96**...................................... TedDurcan 5 86
(H Morrison) *stdd rr: rdn over 2f out: n.d* **8/1**
0500 **12** *11* **Cool Panic (IRE)**[7] [4372] 4-8-13 **85**................................ MartinDwyer 3 46
(M L W Bell) *lw: rr: hdwy over 2f out: sn rdn and wknd* **12/1**

1m 26.66s (-0.34) **Going Correction** +0.20s/f (Good)
WFA 3 from 4yo+ 5lb **12** Ran SP% **117.1**
Speed ratings (Par 109):109,108,108,107,106 105,105,104,102,102 100,88
CSF £66.79 CT £221.54 TOTE £19.60: £4.30, £1.60, £1.80; EX 59.60.
Owner John C Grant & D M James **Bred** Yeomanstown Stud **Trained** Lambourn, Berks

FOCUS
A decent handicap run 0.10 sec faster than the opening juvenile maiden. Solid form, rated thrugh a best view of fourth-placed Meditation. After this race the going was adjusted again, from good to soft to good to soft (soft in places).

NOTEBOOK
Jamieson Gold(IRE), who has gradually been running into form, handled this softening ground really well and, always close up, found extra to forge ahead inside the last and then resist the late run of the favourite. He had looked high enough in the weights beforehand and will have to continue the improvement to score off his new mark.
Polar Magic loves cut in the ground and was backed in to favourite. He came from off the pace but the winner got first run and the line came too soon. He may be able to gain compensation if the rains continue. (op 11-4)
Bosset(USA), a lightly-raced filly who won her maiden on soft ground here, was ridden positively and delivered her challenge at the right time, only to find the winner too strong. She is open to further improvement, but off her current\n\x\x rating may be worth aiming for a fillies' Listed race. (op 3-1 tchd 7-2)
Meditation whose good form this season has all been on much faster ground and in lower-grade contests, ran really well. She tried to make all, and it was only in the last furlong that she was collared. On this evidence there may be more to come.
Grimes Faith was held up out the back and only ran on past beaten horses late on, never looking like reaching the front rank. (op 100-1)
Trafalgar Bay(IRE), whose form this year has been at six furlongs on fast ground, was in the right place most of the way, but in the conditions looked to find the extra furlong beyond him, although he won over the trip last year. (op 8-1)
Obe Brave is another who may be better over six on ground as easy as this. (op 25-1)
Imperial Echo(USA) raced up with the pace, but has gone off the boil since his two wins earlier in the summer. (op 20-1)

4594 NEWVOICEMEDIA ST HUGH'S STKS (LISTED RACE) (FILLIES) 5f 34y
2:40 (2:44) (Class 1) 2-Y-O
£13,343 (£5,057; £2,530; £1,261; £632; £317) **Stalls** Centre

Form RPR
241 **1** **Abby Road (IRE)**[28] [3745] 2-8-12 **88**.. LDettori 5 101
(B J Meehan) *lw: mde all: drvn and edgd lft fnl f: hld on wl* **9/2**[3]
2111 **2** *1* **Vale Of Belvoir (IRE)**[14] [4152] 2-8-12 **91**.......................... PatCosgrave 6 97
(K R Burke) *lw: prom: chsd wnr fnl f but a hld* **10/3**[2]
3125 **3** *1* **Alzerra (UAE)**[21] [3925] 2-8-12 **104**.. TedDurcan 1 94
(M R Channon) *chsd wnr to 1f out: outpcd ins last* **7/4**[1]
4152 **4** *½* **Bridge It Jo**[36] [3474] 2-8-12 **92**.. AlanMunro 2 92
(Miss J Feilden) *chsd ldrs: rdn over 2f out: kpt on same pce fnl f* **20/1**
10 **5** *4* **Pelican Key (IRE)**[21] [3925] 2-9-1 .... RyanMoore 8 81
(D M Simcock) *in tch: rdn 1/2-way: wknd appr fnl f* **16/1**
6303 **6** *1 ½* **Feelin Foxy**[5] [4421] 2-8-12 **76**.. PatrickMathers 3 72
(D Shaw) *s.i.s: outpcd tl mod prog fnl f* **80/1**
624 **7** *1* **Lady Lily (IRE)**[17] [4053] 2-8-12 **76**................................ RichardHughes 9 69
(H R A Cecil) *lw: sn in tch: rdn and effrt 1/2-way: n.d: sn wknd* **12/1**
1 **8** *1 ¾* **Fabuleux Millie (IRE)**[33] [3588] 2-8-12 .... MJKinane 10 62
(R M Beckett) *h.d.w: lw: s.i.s: sn rdn: a outpcd* **11/1**
1 **9** *6* **Danetime Music (IRE)**[21] [3942] 2-8-12 .... JamieSpencer 4 41
(M J Wallace) *s.i.s: bhd: no ch whn hung lft fr 1/2-way* **25/1**
2120 **10** *2* **Going Straight (IRE)**[7] [4344] 2-8-12 **93**............................. ChrisCatlin 7 34
(I A Wood) *chsd ldrs to 1/2-way* **66/1**

62.13 secs (-0.43) **Going Correction** +0.20s/f (Good) **10** Ran SP% **110.9**
Speed ratings (Par 99):111,109,107,107,100 98,96,93,84,81
CSF £18.15 TOTE £4.90: £2.00, £1.40, £1.50; EX 19.80.
Owner Andrew Rosen **Bred** Western Bloodstock **Trained** Manton, Wilts

FOCUS
A decent Listed event, run in a very good time, 0.69 sec faster than the later all-aged handicap.

NOTEBOOK
Abby Road(IRE) ♦, all of whose previous form was on fast ground, handled this surface well and made all to score in cosy fashion. She is progressing well now and the fast time she recorded here suggests she is well up to taking her chance in the Flying Childers at York next month, her next intended target. (tchd 4-1)
Vale Of Belvoir(IRE), whose only previous defeat was on an easy surface, has been very progressive in nursery company and handled this step up in grade well. She gave the winner a race, but may have encountered a useful sprinter in the making and lost nothing in defeat. The Roses Stakes at York next week is a possibility if she recovers quickly enough from this, with the Harry Rosebery at Ayr next month an alternative. (op 7-2)
Alzerra(UAE), who was dropping in trip and grade, having been runner-up in the Cherry Hinton and fifth in the Princess Margaret, ran a sound enough race and had every chance, but came up against a couple of progressive sorts. She can win a Listed race, but possibly back over six, and the Dick Poole Stakes at the end of the month may provide a suitable opportunity. (op 13-8 tchd 15-8 and 6-4 in places)

Bridge It Jo, encountering easy ground for the first time, nevertheless ran her race and went close to earning black type. She looks a fair guide to the level of the form and it will be no surprise to see her taking on those that finished ahead of her again.
Pelican Key(IRE), whose maiden win has not really worked out, finished distressed when tailed off last time. This was a much better effort but she was well held. She now qualifies for a handicap mark. (tchd 14-1)

4595 THE SPORTSMAN NEWSPAPER GEOFFREY FREER STKS (GROUP 3) 1m 5f 61y

3:10 (3:11) (Class 1) 3-Y-O+ **£28,390** (£10,760; £5,385; £2,685; £1,345) **Stalls** Centre

Form				RPR
1413	**1**		**Admiral's Cruise (USA)**[15] [4096] 4-9-3 107 .... RyanMoore 4 (B J Meehan) *lw: hld up rr but in tch: hdwy 3f out: led 2f out and hung rt: then wnt lft: hung bdly rt again ins last: hld on all out* **8/1**	118
3-61	**2**	½	**Guadalajara (GER)**[22] [3905] 5-9-0 111 .... LDettori 6 (Saeed Bin Suroor) *b: b.hind: led: hdd over 10f out: styd chsng wnr tl led ins fnl 4f: hdd 2f out: styd on ins last but a jst hld* **10/11**[1]	114
-220	**3**	*nk*	**Munsef**[76] [2277] 4-9-3 112 .... RHills 2 (J L Dunlop) *hld up rr but in tch: rdn and hdwy over fr 2f out: styd on wl fnl f but a jst hld* **5/2**[2]	117
-456	**4**	2	**Self Defense**[56] [2845] 9-9-3 110 .... AlanMunro 3 (Miss E C Lavelle) *chsd ldrs: rdn over 3f out: styd on same pce u.p fnl 2f* **25/1**	114
-112	**5**	5	**Galient (IRE)**[57] [2804] 3-8-6 94 .... PhilipRobinson 7 (M A Jarvis) *fly j. stalls and s.i.s: sn rcvrd: led over 10f out: hdd ins fnl 4f: wknd over 2f out* **11/2**[3]	107

2m 52.42s (1.43) **Going Correction** +0.30s/f (Good)
WFA 3 from 4yo+ 11lb **5** Ran SP% **111.3**
Speed ratings (Par 113):107,106,106,105,102
CSF £16.26 TOTE £8.80: £3.30, £1.30; EX 15.80.
Owner Joe L Allbritton **Bred** Lazy Lane Stables Inc **Trained** Manton, Wilts

FOCUS
Just a fair renewal of this Group 3, which has been downgraded from Group 2. The time was ordinary for a race of its status, but the runners raced down the far rail in the back straight, which may have contributed to that.

NOTEBOOK
Admiral's Cruise(USA), who may not have been suited by the steady early pace and the track when a beaten favourite at Goodwood, has form on soft ground and gained his first Group win. He travelled well before taking the advantage halfway up the straight, but then tended to hang right and it was only when he reached the stands' rail that he was able to settle the issue. His rider felt he had got to the front too soon, and he should make an even better five-year-old. In the meantime the Dubai Arc Trial, the Cumberland Lodge and the St Simon Stakes all look suitable targets. (op 11-1)
Guadalajara(GER), who made all to gain her first victory in this country on similar ground at Newmarket, did not really settle in front with Galient pressing her. She regained the lead early in the straight, but could not respond immediately once taken on by the winner. However, she kept battling, doing little wrong in defeat, and will have Group-winning prospects against her own sex in something like the Park Hill. (op Evens tchd 11-10, 5-4 in places and 6-5 in places)
Munsef has run some good races in Group company since winning a Listed race last season, particularly on this track, and handles cut in the ground. He ran well again and it would be no surprise to see him return here for the Dubai Arc Trial before another crack at the St Simon Stakes. (op 9-4 tchd 2-1 and 11-4)
Self Defense, who has never won on the Flat in this country despite numerous good efforts, could not find an extra gear and may be worth another try over further. However, his likely target is the Cumberland Lodge, in which he has been runner-up for the last two seasons. (tchd 20-1)
Galient(IRE), who progressed from handicap company to run second in the Queen's Vase, had a difficult task taking on his elders on ground softer than he prefers, and he made it more so by banging his head and losing ground at the start when trying to anticipate the stalls opening. He recovered to lead after 3f but was unable to stretch his field and was in trouble early in the straight, although on paper this was his best form yet. This was his first outing for two months and things did not go right for him, so he can be given another chance against his own age group. He remains a possible for the St Leger, although the Noel Murless Stakes at Newmarket would represent easier pickings. Official explanation: jockey said colt banged its head in stalls (op 9-2 tchd 6-1)

4596 THE SPORTSMAN NEWSPAPER HUNGERFORD STKS (GROUP 2) 7f (S)

3:45 (3:46) (Class 1) 3-Y-O+
£51,102 (£19,368; £9,693; £4,833; £2,421; £1,215) **Stalls** Centre

Form				RPR
2-10	**1**		**Welsh Emperor (IRE)**[94] [1778] 7-9-3 110 .... JamieSpencer 8 (T P Tate) *lw: mde all: hrd rdn fnl f: hld on gamely: all out* **13/2**[3]	115
2116	**2**	½	**Jeremy (USA)**[18] [4025] 3-8-12 112 .... MJKinane 2 (Sir Michael Stoute) *lw: chsd ldrs: rdn to go 2nd over 1f out: styd on wl u.p fnl f but a hld by wnr* **10/3**[2]	113
12-1	**3**	1	**Caradak (IRE)**[29] [3702] 5-9-3 114 .... LDettori 5 (Saeed Bin Suroor) *lw: chsd ldrs: rdn 2f out: styd on same pce u.p fnl f* **5/6**[1]	111
3230	**4**	1 ½	**Mac Love**[18] [4025] 5-9-3 105 .... RichardHughes 1 (R Charlton) *s.i.s: hdwy to chse ldrs over 2f out: hrd drvn and nt qckn fr over 1f out* **20/1**	107
2100	**5**	*hd*	**Royal Power (IRE)**[41] [3342] 3-9-0 107 .... RyanMoore 6 (M R Channon) *chsd ldr: rdn over 2f out: hdd appr fnl f: wknd fnl 110yds* **25/1**	107
0105	**6**	1 ¼	**Etlaala**[18] [4025] 4-9-3 112 .... RHills 3 (B W Hills) *lw: b.hind: s.i.s: bhd: hdwy 2f out: sn rdn: nvr gng pce to rch ldrs and styd on same pce* **9/1**	103
-025	**7**	13	**Sir Xaar (IRE)**[49] [3086] 3-8-12 107 .... PhilipRobinson 7 (B Smart) *lw: s.i.s: rr but in tch: rdn 3f out: wknd over 2f out* **40/1**	69

1m 26.76s (-0.24) **Going Correction** +0.20s/f (Good)
WFA 3 from 4yo+ 5lb **7** Ran SP% **112.0**
Speed ratings (Par 115):109,108,107,105,105 103,89
CSF £26.90 TOTE £7.30: £2.70, £1.80; EX 22.20.
Owner Mrs Sylvia Clegg **Bred** Times Of Wigan Ltd **Trained** Tadcaster, N Yorks

FOCUS
A competitive renewal of this Group 2, upgraded from Group 3 this year. The time was fractionally slower than the earlier handicap over the same trip, although the earlier rain may have got into the ground.

NOTEBOOK
Welsh Emperor(IRE), who loves soft ground and making the running, gained his tenth win and first at Group 2 level with a game display. He has been a fine servant for connections and will presumably go wherever ground conditions suit, with the Betfred Sprint Cup at Haydock and the Prix de la Foret at Longchamp both possibilities. (op 8-1 tchd 9-1 and 6-1)
Jeremy(USA), who did not appear to handle the Goodwood track on his first try at this level, bounced back on this more conventional course and on ground that he handles, but bumped into a tough and determined rival. He lost little in defeat and it would be no surprise to see him gaining compensation before long. He should make an even better four-year-old. (op 3-1 tchd 7-2)
Caradak(IRE) was Godolphin's second successive beaten odds-on favourite on the day. He seemed to be in the right place but started to struggle as the race began in earnest soon after halfway and, despite running on, never looked a serious threat from that point. He handles this soft ground but all his wins have been on a fast surface and, although he may have another crack at the Prix de la Foret on Arc weekend, the Group 2 Daniel Wildenstein over an extra furlong may prove a better option. (op 10-11 tchd 1-1 in places)
Mac Love has not raced much on soft ground but seemed to handle it well enough. He has not scored for nearly two years and his best chance of ending that sequence may be in the Fortune Stakes at Epsom early next month, as he seems to appreciate the undulating nature of that track. (tchd 25-1)
Royal Power(IRE), second in the Premio Parioli and winner of the German 2000 Guineas in the spring, has been held in the highest grade in two subsequent runs. He performed creditably against mainly older rivals, and it will be no surprise if he is aimed at the Europa-Meile in Cologne at the end of next month. (tchd 33-1)
Etlaala ran well enough despite missing the break, but he has yet to win on ground softer than good in five attempts now and will be better off back on a sound surface. (op 7-1 tchd 13-2)
Sir Xaar(IRE), who has yet to score above Listed level, like many that have been good juveniles has been really struggling to make his mark in this second season. It might pay connections to draw stumps and bring him back fresh next year. Official explanation: jockey said colt was unsuited by the good to soft (soft in places) ground (op 33-1)

4597 THE SPORTSMAN NEWSPAPER EBF MAIDEN STKS (DIV II) 7f (S)

4:15 (4:16) (Class 4) 2-Y-O **£5,829** (£1,734; £866; £432) **Stalls** Centre

Form				RPR
0	**1**		**Lunces Lad (IRE)**[14] [4129] 2-9-3 .... TedDurcan 1 (M R Channon) *bit bkwd: in tch: hdwy 3f out: slt ld jst ins fnl 2f: drvn and hld on wl thrght fnl f* **6/1**[3]	79
	2	*nk*	**Amazing Request** 2-9-3 .... RichardHughes 4 (R Charlton) *gd sort: scope: lw: in tch: pushed along to chal 2f out: outpcd over 1f out: styd on wl fnl f: fin strly: nt quite get up* **7/1**	78+
	3	1 ¼	**Aqaleem** 2-9-3 .... RHills 8 (M P Tregoning) *rangy: bit bkwd: rr but in tch: hdwy fr 2f out: drvn and kpt on wl fnl f but nvr gng pce to rch ldrs* **13/2**	75+
5	**4**	½	**Paceman (USA)**[21] [3923] 2-9-3 .... JamieSpencer 2 (R Hannon) *h.d.w: lw: rr but in tch: drvn and hdwy fr 2f out: chsd ldrs over 1f out: kpt on same pce ins last* **5/2**[2]	74
03	**5**	½	**King Joshua (IRE)**[22] [3892] 2-9-3 ....(t) LDettori 5 (G A Butler) *trckd ldrs: shkn up over 1f out and kpt on same pce* **2/1**[1]	73
	6	5	**Salient** 2-9-3 .... PaulDoe 6 (W J Knight) *w'like: bkwd: rr but in tch: wnt sharply rt 2f out: hung lft fr over 1f out: nvr rchd ldrs* **20/1**	60
	7	5	**Like To Golf (USA)** 2-9-3 .... JimCrowley 3 (Mrs A J Perrett) *rangy: scope: bit bkwd: s.i.s: hdwy over 3f out: rdn over 2f out: sn btn* **25/1**	48
00	**8**	*nk*	**Garrya**[7] [4366] 2-9-3 .... PatDobbs 7 (R Hannon) *led: hdd jst ins fnl 2f and wknd qckly* **66/1**	47
	9	3 ½	**Lord Orpheus** 2-9-3 .... PhilipRobinson 11 (B W Hills) *cmpt: lw: w ldr after 1f to 3f out: wknd fr 2f out* **14/1**	38

1m 29.51s (2.51) **Going Correction** +0.20s/f (Good) **9** Ran SP% **118.8**
Speed ratings (Par 96):93,92,91,90,90 84,78,78,74
CSF £47.64 TOTE £8.70: £1.90, £2.30, £2.30; EX 51.50.
Owner Jon and Julia Aisbitt **Bred** Fortbarrington Stud **Trained** West Ilsley, Berks

FOCUS
The second division of this maiden was the slowest of the four races over the trip on the day and 0.49 sec slower than the first division, although the rain during the afternoon had affected the ground.

NOTEBOOK
Lunces Lad(IRE), who finished well beaten on his Goodwood debut, had clearly come on for the experience and battled on well after racing close to the pace. Related to juvenile winners, he upheld the family tradition and has entries in the Champagne and Royal Lodge stakes, but that may be aiming a bit high at this stage. (tchd 11-2 and 13-2, 7-1 in a place and 5-1 in a place)
Amazing Request ◆, a half-brother to Roman Maze but with a fair amount of stamina in his pedigree, ran really well on this debut and looks capable of winning his maiden this season, although he may do better next year. (op 8-1)
Aqaleem ◆, by Sinndar out of an unraced half-sister to Alhaarth, caught the eye with a decent debut despite appearing to run green and look at the crowd in the stands. A Dewhurst and Derby entry, he is clearly though a lot of and will come on a good deal for the outing. He looks to have a good future. (op 11-2)
Paceman(USA), well backed beforehand, improved on his debut effort, doing his best work in the closing stages. He looks capable of winning a maiden. (op 4-1)
King Joshua(IRE), one of the most experienced in the line-up, had run well in a maiden that has already produced two subsequent winners and was made favourite. He had every chance but may have found this easy ground against him, as he could not sustain the effort. Now qualified for a handicap mark, he was well clear of the rest and looks capable of winning races. Official explanation: jockey said colt was unsuited by the good to soft (soft in places) ground (op 15-8 tchd 7-4)
Salient, who has both speed and stamina in his pedigree, showed promise on this debut but tended to wander around when asked for an effort and should know more next time. (op 16-1)

4598 THESPORTSMAN.COM H'CAP 5f 34y

4:45 (4:45) (Class 4) (0-85,83) 3-Y-O+ **£5,829** (£1,734; £866; £432) **Stalls** Centre

Form				RPR
0030	**1**		**Cashel Mead**[3] [4468] 6-9-7 79 .... PhilipRobinson 5 (J L Spearing) *lw: trckd ldrs: swtchd lft and qckd fnl f: led fnl 50yds: readily* **9/2**[2]	89
5066	**2**	*hd*	**Polish Emperor (USA)**[8] [4338] 6-9-3 75 ....(p) TedDurcan 2 (W R Swinburn) *chsd ldrs: drvn to take slt ld jst ins last: hdd and outpcd fnl 50yds* **4/1**[1]	84
3215	**3**	3	**Blessed Place**[3] [4486] 6-8-5 70 ....(t) AshleyHamblett(7) 3 (D J S Ffrench Davis) *lw: led: hdd jst ins last and sn btn* **9/2**[2]	68
0-0	**4**	1 ¾	**Matty Tun**[50] [3038] 7-9-8 80 .... PatDobbs 11 (J Balding) *s.i.s: rr but in tch: rdn 1/2-way: kpt on fnl f but nvr in contention* **9/1**	72
4501	**5**	*nk*	**Pawan (IRE)**[3] [4468] 6-9-0 79 7ex ....(b) AnnStokell(7) 6 (Miss A Stokell) *s.i.s: bhd: shkn up and hdwy on outside over 1f out nvr gng pce to rch ldrs* **5/1**[3]	70
5300	**6**	¾	**Auwitesweetheart**[7] [4343] 4-9-7 79 .... AlanMunro 8 (B R Millman) *chsd ldrs: rdn 1/2-way: sn one pce* **6/1**	67
0-40	**7**	1	**Westbrook Blue**[122] [1076] 4-9-4 83 .... JackDean(7) 4 (W G M Turner) *lw: chsd ldrs over 3f* **10/1**	68
-000	**8**	10	**Tartatartufata**[150] [699] 4-8-10 71 ....(v) PatrickMathers(3) 12 (D Shaw) *spd to 1/2-way* **16/1**	20

62.82 secs (0.26) **Going Correction** +0.20s/f (Good) **8** Ran SP% **112.3**
Speed ratings (Par 105):105,104,99,97,96 95,93,77
CSF £21.97 CT £83.64 TOTE £5.70: £1.90, £1.60, £1.70; EX 26.50.

Owner Masonaires **Bred** D R Tucker **Trained** Kinnersley, Worcs

FOCUS

A fair sprint handicap, though weakened by four non-runners. The winning time 0.69 sec slower than the earlier juvenile fillies' Listed race, though still reasonable in the deteriorating ground.

Pawan(IRE) Official explanation: jockey said gelding hung left-handed

4599 THE SPORTSMAN NEWSPAPER H'CAP — 1m 2f 6y

5:20 (5:21) (Class 4) (0-85,87) 3-Y-O — £5,829 (£1,734; £866; £432) Stalls Centre

Form			Horse	Jockey	RPR
4410	1		**Millistar**[17] 4040 3-8-11 **75** (M A Jarvis) *trckd ldrs: wnt 2nd 3f out: hrd drvn to ld fnl 110yds: kpt on wl* **4/1**[2]	PhilipRobinson 1	85
0-31	2	¾	**Prince Ary**[12] 4210 3-9-0 **78** (B W Hills) *led: rdn and kpt on fr over 2f out: hdd: rdr dropped whip and one pce fnl 110yds* **5/1**[3]	RHills 8	87
6511	3	1 ½	**Stotsfold**[36] 3477 3-9-3 **81** (W R Swinburn) *lw: t.k.h: chsd ldrs: rdn and kpt on fnl 2f but nt qckn ins last* **5/2**[1]	AlanMunro 9	87
4-10	4	3	**Oscillator**[68] 2502 3-8-13 **77** (G A Butler) *lw: bhd: hdwy 3f out: chsd ldrs 2f out: sn outpcd* **8/1**	NickyMackay 3	77
0233	5	4	**Shogun Prince (IRE)**[17] 4051 3-8-13 **80** (v[1]) (A King) *chsd ldrs: rdn 3f out: edgd lft over 2f out and sn btn* **4/1**[2]	RichardKingscote(3) 4	73
-400	6	1 ½	**Silver Chariot**[79] 2177 3-8-4 **68** (B W Hills) *lw: rr: rdn 3f out: n.d* **16/1**	FrankieMcDonald 5	58
4036	7	hd	**Herring (IRE)**[20] 3974 3-8-11 **75** (v[1]) (D J Coakley) *lw: s.i.s: t.k.h: chsd ldrs: wknd over 2f out* **10/1**	JimCrowley 11	64
4-13	8	2	**De La Rue (USA)**[166] 592 3-9-2 **80** (M G Quinlan) *stdd rr: rdn and effrt over 2f out: nvr nr ldrs and sn btn* **11/1**	TPQueally 6	66

2m 9.81s (1.10) **Going Correction** +0.30s/f (Good) **8 Ran SP% 119.7**

Speed ratings (Par 102):107,106,105,102,99 98,98,96

CSF £25.58 CT £60.64 TOTE £6.10: £2.10, £1.70, £1.70; EX 28.10 Place 6 £40.48, Place 5 £25.47.

Owner Helena Springfield Ltd **Bred** Meon Valley Stud **Trained** Newmarket, Suffolk

■ A treble for jockey Philip Robinson

FOCUS

A fair handicap which was run at just a reasonable gallop and the first three held the first three places throughout, with nothing figuring from behind.

Herring(IRE) Official explanation: jockey said saddle slipped

T/Plt: £92.10 to a £1 stake. Pool: £110,353.85. 873.90 winning tickets. T/Qpdt: £38.90 to a £1 stake. Pool: £4,906.70. 93.15 winning tickets. ST

4572 NEWMARKET (JULY) (R-H)

Saturday, August 19

OFFICIAL GOING: Good

Wind: Light, across Weather: Cloudy with sunny periods; heavy shower during Race 7 (5.05)

4600 EBF BBC RADIO SUFFOLK MAIDEN STKS — 6f

1:50 (1:50) (Class 5) 2-Y-O — £4,533 (£1,348; £674; £336) Stalls High

Form			Horse	Jockey	RPR
23	1		**Wait Watcher (IRE)**[9] 4290 2-8-12 (P A Blockley) *mid-div: hdwy 2f out: rdn to ld and carried lft wl ins fnl f: r.o* **15/2**	TPO'Shea 1	78
	2	¾	**Diysem (USA)** 2-9-3 (B J Meehan) *trckd ldrs: led over 1f out: sn rdn: hung lft and hdd wl ins fnl f: styd on* **6/1**[3]	JimmyFortune 11	81
	3	1 ¼	**Emaara** 2-8-12 (J L Dunlop) *s.i.s: hld up: swtchd rt and hdwy over 1f out: r.o* **8/1**	EddieAhern 7	72+
	4	1 ¾	**Benfleet Boy** 2-9-3 (B J Meehan) *s.i.s: hld up: hdwy over 1f out: nt rch ldrs* **20/1**	SteveDrowne 8	72+
6644	5	2 ½	**Marine Parade**[19] 4000 2-9-3 **74** (R Hannon) *led: hung lft and hdd over 1f out: wknd ins fnl f* **4/1**[2]	FrancisNorton 9	64
	6	1	**Highland Harvest** 2-9-3 (D R C Elsworth) *hld up: styd on fnl f: nvr trbld ldrs* **25/1**	AntonyProcter 12	61
	7	shd	**Ben Chorley** 2-9-3 (P W Chapple-Hyam) *s.i.s: outpcd: styd on ins fnl f: nrst fin* **16/1**	DanielTudhope 2	61
	8	1 ¼	**Radical Views** 2-9-3 (B W Hills) *chsd ldrs: rdn and ev ch 2f out: wknd fnl f* **3/1**[1]	MichaelHills 3	57
	9	2	**Forced Upon Us** 2-9-3 (P J McBride) *chsd ldrs over 4f* **66/1**	RichardMullen 10	51
	10	¾	**Kon Tiki** 2-8-12 (M Johnston) *prom: sn drvn along: lost pl over 3f out: sn bhd* **7/1**	RoystonFfrench 4	44
	11	2	**Dee Burgh** 2-8-12 (J Pearce) *s.i.s and hmpd s: sn outpcd* **33/1**	JimmyQuinn 6	38
	12	shd	**Gilded Youth** 2-9-3 (H Candy) *chsd ldr: rdn and ev ch 2f out: sn wknd* **9/1**	FergusSweeney 5	43

1m 13.8s (0.45) **Going Correction** +0.025s/f (Good) **12 Ran SP% 123.6**

Speed ratings (Par 94):98,97,95,93,89 88,88,86,83,82 80,80

CSF £52.47 TOTE £8.40: £2.40, £2.00, £3.00; EX 51.70.

Owner M J Wiley **Bred** Rathasker Stud **Trained** Lambourn, Berks

FOCUS

The field raced down the centre early, despite the stalls being against the stands' rail, and gradually drifted towards the far side of the track. This rather set the trend for the day. This looked a fair maiden and several of these are likely to improve from this.

NOTEBOOK

Wait Watcher(IRE), back to six after her reasonable effort over seven at Folkestone last time, was produced with her effort towards the far side of the track and became involved in a dour battle to the line with the runner-up. She had the benefit of previous experience which was probably crucial, and despite her rival carrying her over to the far rail she still found enough to score. Nurseries look her best option for adding to this victory, but she would be very unlikely to confirm the placings with the placed horses if they met again. (tchd 7-1)

Diysem(USA) ◆, who fetched 30,000gns as a two-year-old, is a half-brother to a dual turf winner in the US. Very well backed to make a winning debut, he was produced to win his race a furlong out and looked like justifying the support, but he then tended to hang right through greenness and that gave his more-experienced rival the chance she needed. He will be a short price to go one better next time. Official explanation: jockey said colt ran green (op 14-1)

Emaara ◆, out of a winning half-sister to several winners including Volanchine, Khatan and Ghataas, was brought through to hold every chance and stayed on well up the final hill. She should come on for this and is likely to appreciate further. (tchd 15-2)

Benfleet Boy ◆, a 38,000gns yearling, is out of a dam who won over two miles so it was no surprise to see him doing his best work late after fluffing the start. He is well worth keeping an eye on, especially when stepped up in trip.

Marine Parade, by far the most experienced in the field, tried to make it count under a positive ride but did not get home. He is not progressing and will always be vulnerable to improvers in races like this. (op 7-2)

Highland Harvest, out of a half-sister to Freya's Dream and Jilly Why, showed a bit on this debut and should improve with experience.

Radical Views, a full-brother to three winners including the triple Group-race winner No Excuse Needed, was well supported in the market but faded rather tamely after showing up for a while. He is probably capable of better. (op 4-1 tchd 9-2 in places)

4601 NGK SPARK PLUGS H'CAP — 6f

2:25 (2:25) (Class 2) (0-105,102) 3-Y-O

£18,696 (£5,598; £2,799; £1,401; £699; £351) Stalls High

Form			Horse	Jockey	RPR
3123	1		**Burning Incense (IRE)**[15] 4106 3-8-6 **87** (b[1]) (R Charlton) *hld up: hdwy over 1f out: sn hung rt: rdn to ld ins fnl f: r.o* **5/1**[1]	SteveDrowne 1	102
0120	2	1 ¼	**Mutamarres**[27] 3761 3-8-9 **90** (v) (Sir Michael Stoute) *chsd ldr: led over 4f out: rdn over 1f out: hdd and unable qck ins fnl f* **13/2**[2]	MichaelHills 10	101
0201	3	1 ¼	**Come Out Fighting**[7] 4345 3-9-0 **95** (P A Blockley) *s.i.s: hld up: racd keenly: hdwy over 1f out: r.o* **8/1**[3]	TPO'Shea 5	102
0504	4	1	**Ingleby Arch (USA)**[7] 4345 3-9-1 **96** (v[1]) (T D Barron) *s.i.s: sn prom: outpcd 1/2-way: hdwy and nt clr run over 1f out: r.o: nt rch ldrs* **14/1**	JimmyFortune 7	100
3021	5	nk	**Charles Darwin (IRE)**[20] 3970 3-8-8 **89** (M Blanshard) *chsd ldrs: rdn over 2f out: styd on same pce fnl f* **12/1**	FrancisNorton 8	92
6000	6	1 ½	**Green Park (IRE)**[27] 3761 3-8-10 **91** (R A Fahey) *hld up: hdwy and nt clr run over 1f out: wknd ins fnl f* **25/1**	RichardMullen 2	90
2302	7	1 ¾	**High Curragh**[16] 4083 3-8-9 **90** (K A Ryan) *led: hdd over 4f out: chsd ldr tl rdn 2f out: nt clr run and edgd rt over 1f out: wknd fnl f* **5/1**[1]	CatherineGannon 6	83
-521	8	¾	**Skilling Spirit**[84] 2022 3-9-0 **98** (T D Barron) *hld up: hdwy 1/2-way: rdn and wknd over 1f out* **8/1**[3]	BenSwarbrick(3) 11	89+
1010	9	nk	**Bentong (IRE)**[14] 4128 3-9-7 **102** (P F I Cole) *trckd ldrs: rdn over 1f out: sn wknd* **13/2**[2]	EddieAhern 4	92
0-00	10	hd	**River Thames**[92] 1818 3-8-12 **93** (J A R Toller) *chsd ldrs: rdn over 1f out: sn wknd* **20/1**	RoystonFfrench 3	83
6350	11	1	**Orpsie Boy (IRE)**[16] 4083 3-8-0 **84** oh1 ow1 (t) (N P Littmoden) *hld up: effrt over 2f out: wknd over 1f out* **12/1**	JamesDoyle(3) 12	71+
41-0	12	9	**Misphire**[14] 4144 3-8-2 **83** oh1 (T D Easterby) *s.s: sn prom: rdn over 2f out: sn wknd* **20/1**	JimmyQuinn 9	43+

1m 11.78s (-1.57) **Going Correction** +0.025s/f (Good) **12 Ran SP% 117.6**

Speed ratings (Par 106):111,109,107,106,105 103,101,100,100,99 98,86

CSF £35.14 CT £262.39 TOTE £5.00: £2.00, £2.10, £3.00; EX 26.90.

Owner Thurloe Thoroughbreds XV **Bred** Pier House Stud **Trained** Beckhampton, Wilts

FOCUS

This looked a decent handicap. The pace was solid and the form seems likely to work out.

NOTEBOOK

Burning Incense(IRE) ◆, back against his own age-group and blinkered for the first time, was settled right at the back and was still last with under two furlongs left, but he demonstrated a potent turn of foot to sluice through the entire field and was well on top at the line. This slightly easier ground proved ideal and there should be much more to come from him. (op 4-1)

Mutamarres was always up there and hardly did anything wrong, but ran into a decent sort on the day who saw his race out that much better. He is versatile when it comes to ground and there should be other races for him over this trip. (op 7-1 tchd 6-1 in a place)

Come Out Fighting, raised 6lb for his Ascot victory, stayed on well over the last couple of furlongs but the front pair had already gone beyond recall. He looks to be on a stiff mark now. Official explanation: jockey said colt was fractious in stalls

Ingleby Arch(USA), visored for the first time and 7lb better off with Come Out Fighting for a beating of just over three lengths at Ascot the previous week, received something of a buffeting when trying for a run between Charles Darwin and High Curragh over a furlong out. He would probably have finished a little closer otherwise.

Charles Darwin(IRE), raised 3lb for his Ascot victory, had every chance but lacked finishing pace when it mattered.

Green Park(IRE) ran a bit better than in recent outings, but is still to convince over this trip.

High Curragh, rather harshly up another 3lb despite not winning, was given a positive ride as usual but had already run his race when receiving a few bumps from Ingleby Arch over a furlong from home. (op 6-1)

Bentong(IRE) travelled well, but did not find much off the bridle. He will remain very hard to place off this mark. Official explanation: jockey said colt was unsuited by the good ground (op 8-1)

4602 SKYBET.COM GREY HORSE H'CAP — 6f

2:55 (2:56) (Class 4) (0-85,81) 3-Y-O+

£12,464 (£3,732; £1,866; £934; £466; £234) Stalls High

Form			Horse	Jockey	RPR
0230	1		**Clearing Sky (IRE)**[49] 3071 5-8-0 **54** (J R Boyle) *w ldr: rdn to ld over 1f out: jst hld on* **50/1**	MatthewHenry 1	62
0013	2	nk	**Certain Justice (USA)**[15] 4114 8-9-3 **71** (Stef Liddiard) *hld up: hdwy over 1f out: rdn and hung lft ins fnl f: r.o* **14/1**	HayleyTurner 12	78+
4200	3	nk	**Nautical**[15] 4101 8-9-9 **77** (A W Carroll) *hld up: hdwy over 1f out: sn rdn: r.o* **6/1**[2]	JimmyFortune 10	83
0000	4	hd	**Middleton Grey**[37] 3434 8-9-0 **68** (b) (A G Newcombe) *trckd ldrs: rdn over 1f out: styd on* **11/1**	FergusSweeney 2	74
1111	5	nk	**Further Outlook (USA)**[19] 3995 12-8-12 **66** (t) (Miss Gay Kelleway) *led: rdn and hdd over 1f out: edgd rt ins fnl f: styd on* **11/2**[1]	JimmyQuinn 4	71
0161	6	½	**Finsbury**[31] 3644 3-9-6 **77** (C F Wall) *hld up: hdwy over 1f out: rdn and nt clr run ins fnl f : kpt on* **6/1**[2]	GeorgeBaker 8	80
6005	7	nk	**Paris Bell**[57] 2830 4-9-6 **74** (T D Easterby) *s.i.s: hld up: hdwy and nt clr run over 1f out: styd on* **17/2**	PaulQuinn 5	76
0006	8	½	**Harvest Warrior**[10] 4253 4-9-0 **68** (b) (T D Easterby) *sn pushed along in rr: rdn over 2f out: outpcd over 1f out: r.o u.p ins fnl f* **10/1**	RichardMullen 3	69
0-00	9	1 ¼	**Milton's Keen**[51] 3011 3-7-10 **60** (P S McEntee) *s.i.s: plld hrd and sn prom: rdn over 1f out: styng on same pce whn hmpd ins fnl f* **50/1**	KirstyMilczarek(7) 9	57
0050	10	1	**Hits Only Jude (IRE)**[54] 2939 3-8-11 **68** (J Pearce) *chsd ldrs: rdn over 2f out: wknd fnl f* **13/2**[3]	DeanMcKeown 11	62
5113	11	nk	**Celtic Spa (IRE)**[9] 4286 4-9-0 **71** (P D Evans) *chsd ldrs: rdn over 2f out: wknd fnl f* **8/1**	StephenDonohoe(3) 13	64
0243	12	1 ¾	**Bond Diamond**[15] 4116 9-8-10 **64** (p) (P T Midgley) *hld up: hdwy over 2f out: wknd over 1f out* **14/1**	DanielTudhope 15	52

0000 **13** 2 ½ **Calypso King**[49] [3067] 3-9-10 **81** .... EddieAhern 14 61
(J W Hills) *hld up: rdn and wknd over 1f out* **14/1**

1m 13.27s (-0.08) **Going Correction** +0.025s/f (Good)
WFA 3 from 4yo+ 3lb **13** Ran SP% **120.3**
Speed ratings (Par 105):101,100,100,99,99 98,98,97,96,94 94,92,88
CSF £647.31 CT £4925.71 TOTE £48.40: £9.80, £4.10, £2.50; EX 667.60.
Owner Clearing Sky Partnership **Bred** C H Wacker Iii **Trained** Epsom, Surrey

FOCUS
As the name suggests a race confined to greys, but a few of them were so dark-skinned that the visual effect was limited. This did not look a great race for the money, however, and both the winning time and the fact that the front eight finished in a heap rather backs that up. The form looks straightforward rated around the first three.
Further Outlook(USA) Official explanation: jockey said gelding hung right
Calypso King Official explanation: jockey said gelding ran too free and had no more to give

4603 SEE MORE ON RACING UK NURSERY 5f
3:25 (3:25) (Class 4) 2-Y-O **£5,181** (£1,541; £770; £384) **Stalls** High

Form RPR
621 **1** **Abunai**[40] [3344] 2-8-8 **72** .... SteveDrowne 1 78
(R Charlton) *trckd ldrs: rdn to ld and hung lft ins fnl f: r.o* **9/4**[1]
41 **2** *shd* **Black Moma (IRE)**[25] [3818] 2-8-6 **70** .... RichardSmith 4 75
(R Hannon) *chsd ldrs: led 2f out: rdn and hung lft fr over 1f out: hdd ins fnl f: r.o* **10/1**
625 **3** 1 ¾ **Pango's Legacy**[22] [3895] 2-8-5 **74** .... TravisBlock(5) 3 73
(H Morrison) *hld up: hdwy and hung lft over 1f out: r.o* **14/1**
430 **4** ¾ **Baytown Paikea**[26] [3801] 2-7-12 **62** oh6 .... CatherineGannon 6 58
(P S McEntee) *led 3f: sn rdn: styd on same pce fnl f* **50/1**
61 **5** ¾ **Nobilissima (IRE)**[21] [3930] 2-8-5 **69** .... FrancisNorton 5 63
(J L Spearing) *chsd ldr: rdn over 1f out: wknd wl ins fnl f* **6/1**[3]
4230 **6** *nk* **Joseph Locke (IRE)**[19] [3994] 2-8-9 **73** .... JimmyQuinn 9 66
(M Dods) *trckd ldrs: rdn and hung lft over 1f out: styd on same pce* **16/1**
01 **7** *hd* **Another True Story**[19] [4002] 2-9-5 **83** .... JimmyFortune 2 75
(R Hannon) *s.i.s: hld up: hdwy 2f out: sn rdn: wknd ins fnl f* **11/4**[2]
0335 **8** 2 ½ **Proud**[8] [4321] 2-8-5 **69** .... HayleyTurner 7 52
(M L W Bell) *s.i.s: outpcd* **6/1**[3]
10 **9** 2 ½ **Supreme Speedster**[80] [2127] 2-9-7 **85** .... EddieAhern 8 59
(T R George) *chsd ldrs over 3f* **12/1**

59.84 secs (0.28) **Going Correction** +0.025s/f (Good) **9** Ran SP% **117.3**
Speed ratings (Par 96):98,97,95,93,92 92,91,87,83
CSF £26.48 CT £260.92 TOTE £3.20: £1.50, £2.30, £3.90; EX 26.20.
Owner A E Oppenheimer **Bred** Hascombe And Valiant Studs **Trained** Beckhampton, Wilts
■ Stewards' Enquiry : Steve Drowne caution: used whip with excessive frequency

FOCUS
A reasonable nursery in which, as in the first race, the field came down the middle early and the front pair migrated towards the far rail in the closing stages. Not many got into this.

NOTEBOOK
Abunai, making her nursery debut, travelled well just behind the leaders on the far side of the field before delivering her effort a furlong from home. She drifted over to the far rail under pressure and, after looking like winning by a reasonably comfortable margin, only just scrambled home in the end. She seems to be improving and with stamina on the dam's side she may get a bit further. (op 11-4)
Black Moma(IRE), having only her third outing, was always up there and rallied really well after the favourite went past her despite edging left under pressure. A step up to six should see her winning again. (tchd 9-1)
Pango's Legacy, making his nursery debut, stayed on to make the frame but may not have been helped by dropping to the minimum trip for the first time. There is a race like this in him back over six.
Baytown Paikea, who has plenty of miles on the clock already, seemed to run well at this level considering she was 6lb wrong and has repeatedly been beaten in sellers since winning a race of that type back in June. However, she was given a positive ride in a contest that suited those that raced up with the pace, so it would be wrong to get too carried away. (op 66-1)
Nobilissima(IRE), another having only her third outing, showed up for a while before calling it a day. She may have been flattered by her Lingfield victory as she probably benefited from a track bias.
Another True Story, another having his third outing after winning his maiden last time, never looked like winning on this easier ground and the value of his Windsor victory may not be as strong as it looked at the time. (tchd 3-1 and 10-3 in places)

4604 ASTAC INTERNATIONAL H'CAP 1m 4f
4:00 (4:02) (Class 4) (0-85,84) 3-Y-O+ **£5,505** (£1,637; £818; £408) **Stalls** Centre

Form RPR
-636 **1** **Sweet Indulgence (IRE)**[36] [3497] 5-9-10 **79** .... StephenDonohoe(3) 4 88
(W J Musson) *hld up: hdwy 1/2-way: led over 1f out: rdn out* **12/1**
0-16 **2** ½ **Corum (IRE)**[20] [3980] 3-9-8 **84** .... JimmyFortune 11 92
(J H M Gosden) *led: rdn and hdd over 1f out: styd on* **13/2**[2]
136 **3** 2 ½ **Madroos**[52] [2986] 3-9-5 **81** .... J-PGuillambert 3 85
(J L Dunlop) *hld up: hdwy 4f out: bmpd 2f out: sn rdn: styd on* **10/1**
5341 **4** *nk* **Plemont Bay**[14] [4150] 3-8-2 **64** .... (v) HayleyTurner 6 68
(M L W Bell) *chsd ldr: rdn and ev ch over 1f out: styd on same pce* **8/1**
6-01 **5** 1 ½ **Sendinpost**[19] [4005] 3-8-0 **62** .... JimmyQuinn 10 63
(S C Williams) *hld up: rdn over 4f out: outpcd 3f out: hdwy and nt clr run 2f out: no imp fnl f* **9/4**[1]
6314 **6** *nk* **Sonny Parkin**[8] [4336] 4-9-11 **77** .... (v) RichardMullen 2 78
(G A Huffer) *s.i.s: hld up: hdwy and hmpd over 2f out: rdn over 1f out: wknd ins fnl f* **20/1**
-205 **7** 1 ½ **Simonda**[77] [2231] 5-10-0 **80** .... EddieAhern 5 78
(Mrs A J Perrett) *prom: rdn over 2f out: wknd fnl f* **16/1**
5-15 **8** ½ **Captain General**[43] [3256] 4-9-0 **66** .... TPO'Shea 8 63
(J A R Toller) *s.i.s: hld up: rdn over 1f out: nt trble ldrs* **25/1**
2-35 **9** *hd* **Authority (IRE)**[14] [4149] 6-9-7 **73** .... SteveDrowne 1 70
(Lady Herries) *chsd ldrs: rdn over 1f out: sn wknd* **8/1**
1041 **10** *shd* **Sualda (IRE)**[29] [3694] 7-9-13 **79** .... DanielTudhope 15 76
(D Carroll) *hld up: racd keenly: nt clr run fr over 2f out to over 1f out: n.d* **20/1**
21-0 **11** 2 ½ **Kyles Prince (IRE)**[12] [4206] 4-9-9 **75** .... FergusSweeney 12 68
(P J Makin) *prom: rdn over 2f out: wknd over 1f out* **33/1**
0/30 **12** *nk* **Rapscallion (GER)**[10] [4244] 7-9-7 **73** .... LPKeniry 9 65
(Heather Dalton) *trckd ldrs: racd keenly: rdn over 2f out: hung rt and wknd over 1f out* **50/1**
4100 **13** 6 **Le Colombier (IRE)**[10] [4244] 3-9-4 **80** .... MichaelHills 14 63
(J W Hills) *hld up: hdwy over 2f out: sn rdn and wknd* **28/1**
2131 **14** 5 **Celtique**[15] [4104] 4-9-8 **74** .... JamieMackay 13 49
(M Wigham) *hld up in tch: racd keenly: wkng whn nt clr run over 1f out* **7/1**[3]

2m 32.7s (-0.21) **Going Correction** +0.025s/f (Good)
WFA 3 from 4yo+ 10lb **14** Ran SP% **123.2**
Speed ratings (Par 105):101,100,99,98,97 97,96,96,96,96 94,94,90,86
CSF £82.63 CT £830.72 TOTE £15.20: £3.30, £2.90, £3.40; EX 102.90.
Owner Broughton Thermal Insulation **Bred** Mrs M Campbell-Andenaes **Trained** Newmarket, Suffolk

FOCUS
A competitive handicap and sound form overall, but the pace was not that strong. Again the field came up the centre in the long home straight.
Plemont Bay Official explanation: jockey said gelding lost a front shoe and pulled up lame
Celtique Official explanation: trainer said, regarding the poor form shown, that perhaps the filly saw too much daylight, and having been short of room a furlong out, then appeared to lose interest

4605 HALF MOON MONTEGO BAY JAMAICA H'CAP 1m
4:35 (4:35) (Class 4) (0-85,85) 3-Y-O **£5,505** (£1,637; £818; £408) **Stalls** High

Form RPR
-134 **1** **Kinsya**[58] [2779] 3-9-1 **79** .... GeorgeBaker 13 92+
(M H Tompkins) *racd centre: hld up: swtchd far side 1/2-way: hdwy over 1f out: rdn and hung lft ins fnl f: r.o to ld nr fin* **4/1**[1]
0421 **2** ½ **Press The Button (GER)**[16] [4076] 3-9-1 **79** .... SteveDrowne 7 91
(J R Boyle) *racd centre: chsd ldrs: swtchd far side 1/2-way: rdn to ld over 1f out: hdd nr fin* **4/1**[1]
1-45 **3** 2 ½ **Demon Docker (IRE)**[20] [3978] 3-9-7 **85** .... EddieAhern 6 91
(P W Chapple-Hyam) *racd alone far side to 1/2-way: overall ldr: rdn and hdd over 1f out: styd on same pce* **9/1**
032- **4** ½ **Sotik Star (IRE)**[313] [5796] 3-8-9 **73** .... RichardMullen 3 78
(P J Makin) *racd centre: s.i.s: hld up: swtchd to far side 1/2-way: hdwy 3f out: rdn over 1f out: styd on* **14/1**
316 **5** 1 ¼ **The Osteopath (IRE)**[64] [2620] 3-8-12 **76** .... (p) JimmyQuinn 4 78+
(M Dods) *racd centre: hld up: plld hrd: swtchd far side 1/2-way: hdwy u.p over 1f out: nt trble ldrs* **13/2**[3]
0000 **6** 2 **Cape Presto (IRE)**[14] [4160] 3-9-2 **80** .... J-PGuillambert 9 78
(Mrs C A Dunnett) *racd centre: led that gp tl swtchd far side 1/2-way: chsd ldr : rdn over 2f out: wknd fnl f* **33/1**
1330 **7** 1 ¾ **King Of The Moors (USA)**[36] [3491] 3-9-5 **83** .... JimmyFortune 2 77
(T D Barron) *racd centre: hld up: swtchd far side 1/2-way: rdn over 2f out: nvr trbld ldrs* **11/1**
6430 **8** 1 ¼ **Zabeel House**[54] [2932] 3-9-1 **79** .... TPO'Shea 8 70
(J A R Toller) *racd centre: chsd ldrs: swtchd far side 1/2-way: rdn over 2f out : wknd over 1f out* **12/1**
1200 **9** 2 ½ **Paraguay (USA)**[7] [4356] 3-9-2 **83** .... EdwardCreighton(3) 1 68
(Miss V Haigh) *racd centre: hld up: swtchd far side 1/2-way: hdwy over 2f out: sn wknd* **14/1**
3010 **10** 9 **Sicilian (IRE)**[10] [4249] 3-9-0 **78** .... MichaelHills 14 42
(B W Hills) *racd centre: in tch: swtchd centre over 3f out: wknd over 1f out* **6/1**[2]
0-60 **11** *shd* **Chris Corsa**[98] [1681] 3-8-4 **68** .... RoystonFfrench 10 32
(M L W Bell) *racd centre: swtchd far side 1/2-way: rdn and wknd over 2f out* **22/1**
1620 **12** 12 **Diamond De Triano (USA)**[16] [4075] 3-9-1 **79** .... DanielTudhope 5 15
(P W Chapple-Hyam) *racd centre: prom: swtchd far side 1/2-way: wknd over 2f out* **14/1**

1m 40.6s (0.17) **Going Correction** +0.025s/f (Good) **12** Ran SP% **120.9**
Speed ratings (Par 102):100,99,97,96,95 93,91,90,87,78 78,66
CSF £19.04 CT £141.53 TOTE £5.20: £2.00, £1.70, £3.20; EX 21.30.
Owner Roalco Limited **Bred** Whitsbury Manor Stud And Clarendon Farms **Trained** Newmarket, Suffolk

FOCUS
Just a fair handicap and the race followed the trend for the day in terms of where the runners went. The bulk of the field came down the centre early, but one went straight over to the far rail. Eventually the others joined him and that is where the finish was fought out. The form is ordinary, rated around the third and fifth.
Diamond De Triano(USA) Official explanation: jockey said filly hung left and never travelled

4606 BRITISH VIRGIN ISLANDS TOURIST BOARD H'CAP 1m 2f
5:05 (5:06) (Class 5) (0-70,69) 3-Y-O+ **£3,886** (£1,156; £577; £288) **Stalls** Centre

Form RPR
0054 **1** **Oh Danny Boy**[9] [4307] 5-9-4 **56** .... RobertHavlin 1 65
(Jane Chapple-Hyam) *hld up: rdn over 3f out: hdwy u.p and nt clr run over 1f out: led ins fnl f: styd on* **16/1**
4230 **2** *shd* **Bowled Out (GER)**[15] [4104] 4-9-10 **62** .... RichardMullen 7 71
(P J McBride) *hld up: hdwy over 1f out: rdn and edgd lft ins fnl f: r.o* **14/1**
-004 **3** ¾ **Lobengula (IRE)**[34] [3566] 4-9-9 **61** .... RoystonFfrench 10 68
(I W McInnes) *led: rdn over 1f out: hdd ins fnl f: styd on* **25/1**
4511 **4** 1 **Sforzando**[4] [4457] 5-9-7 **66** .... KristinStubbs(7) 2 71
(Mrs L Stubbs) *hld up: hdwy over 3f out: styd on same pce ins fnl f* **5/1**[1]
0026 **5** *nk* **Tata Naka**[8] [4336] 6-9-4 **56** .... J-PGuillambert 5 61
(Mrs C A Dunnett) *hld up: hdwy over 3f out: rdn and ev ch over 1f out: no ex ins fnl f* **14/1**
5423 **6** ¾ **Qualitair Wings**[8] [4336] 7-9-8 **60** .... DerekMcGaffin 4 63
(J Hetherton) *hld up: hdwy 3f out: rdn and ev ch over 1f out: no ex ins fnl f* **8/1**
0050 **7** 1 ½ **Scottish River (USA)**[5] [4432] 7-9-10 **62** .... HayleyTurner 16 63
(M D I Usher) *s.s: hld up: hdwy u.p over 1f out: no ex ins fnl f* **16/1**
1004 **8** ½ **Mae Cigan (FR)**[9] [4301] 3-9-3 **63** .... FrancisNorton 6 63
(M Blanshard) *hld up: hdwy over 2f out: wknd ins fnl f* **6/1**[2]
0010 **9** *shd* **Terminate (GER)**[7] [4353] 4-9-10 **62** .... (b) GeorgeBaker 11 62
(N P Littmoden) *s.s: hld up: hdwy over 1f out: wknd ins fnl f* **20/1**
-551 **10** 5 **Bienheureux**[19] [3998] 5-9-2 **57** .... (vt) StephenDonohoe(3) 9 47
(Miss Gay Kelleway) *chsd ldrs: rdn over 2f out: wknd over 1f out* **15/2**[3]
0600 **11** 2 ½ **Your Amount (IRE)**[51] [3015] 3-9-7 **67** .... JDSmith 14 52
(W J Musson) *prom 8f* **33/1**
0324 **12** *shd* **Royal Flynn**[26] [3792] 4-9-5 **57** .... (p) JimmyFortune 3 42
(M Dods) *hld up in tch: rdn and wknd over 1f out* **8/1**
4-03 **13** 1 ¼ **Campanile**[54] [2940] 3-9-9 **69** .... OscarUrbina 13 52
(J R Fanshawe) *plld hrd and prom: wknd over 2f out* **15/2**[3]
5000 **14** 2 ½ **Cheveley Flyer**[23] [3869] 3-8-1 **47** .... JimmyQuinn 12 25
(J Pearce) *prom: rdn over 3f out: wkng whn hung lft wl over 1f out* **33/1**
2-24 **15** 45 **Generator**[79] [2184] 4-9-11 **63** .... TPO'Shea 15 —
(Dr J D Scargill) *hld up: wknd 3f out* **8/1**

2m 7.30s (0.86) **Going Correction** +0.025s/f (Good)
WFA 3 from 4yo+ 8lb **15** Ran SP% **127.4**
Speed ratings (Par 103):97,96,96,95,95 94,93,93,93,89 87,86,85,83,47
CSF £225.57 CT £5510.65 TOTE £16.10: £3.90, £6.00, £6.70; EX 609.20 Place 6 £513.55, Place 5 £158.27.

Owner Danny Berry **Bred** Whitsbury Manor Stud **Trained** Newmarket, Suffolk

■ Stewards' Enquiry : Robert Havlin two-day ban: used whip with excessive frequency (Aug 30-31)

FOCUS

A moderate handicap in which the early pace was modest and something of a messy race too, with the field finishing more spread out across the track than in earlier contests. The form seems sound on paper, rated around the principals. The result was further evidence that the far side of the track was the place to be.

Campanile Official explanation: jockey said filly ran too free

Generator Official explanation: jockey said gelding lost its action

T/Jkpt: Not won. T/Plt: £572.80 to a £1 stake. Pool: £77,493.45. 98.75 winning tickets. T/Qpdt: £73.00 to a £1 stake. Pool: £4,163.30. 42.15 winning tickets. CR

4200 RIPON (R-H)

Saturday, August 19

OFFICIAL GOING: Soft (good to soft on home bend) changing to heavy after race 4 (4.05)

Wind: Light, behind

4607 RIPON HORN BLOWER CONDITIONS STKS 6f

2:30 (2:31) (Class 3) 2-Y-O **£7,478** (£2,239; £1,119; £560; £279) **Stalls** Low

Form RPR

1 **1** **Smart Instinct (USA)**[20] [3982] 2-9-5 .... TonyHamilton 2 98
(R A Fahey) *trckd ldr: swtchd rt and hdwy over 1f out: rdn to chal ent last: styd on wl to ld last 100 yds* **7/2**[3]

1011 **2** *2* **Holdin Foldin (IRE)**[8] [4326] 2-9-8 100 .... RobertWinston 3 95
(K R Burke) *led: rdn along over 1f out: drvn ent last: hdd and no ex last 100 yds* **10/3**[2]

05 **3** *7* **Mandy's Maestro (USA)**[21] [3958] 2-8-9 .... MichaelJStainton(5) 4 66
(R M Whitaker) *trckd ldrs: swtchd rt and rdn to chal over 1f out: sn drvn and one pce* **33/1**

4404 **4** *1 ¾* **La Neige**[15] [4099] 2-9-5 100 .... JohnEgan 5 66
(M R Channon) *dwlt: sn trcking ldrs: hdwy to chse ldr 1/2-way: rdn 2f out and sn btn* **8/11**[1]

006 **5** *dist* **Bidders Itch**[16] [4089] 2-8-9 .... JoeFanning 1 —
(A Berry) *dwlt: a bhd* **200/1**

1m 16.08s (3.08) **Going Correction** +0.45s/f (Yiel) **5** Ran SP% **106.6**

Speed ratings (Par 98):97,94,85,82,—

CSF £14.19 TOTE £4.50: £2.00, £1.40; EX 11.00.

Owner David And Jackie Knaggs **Bred** Fair Way Equine, Llc **Trained** Musley Bank, N Yorks

FOCUS

The testing ground led to them finishing well strung out in this small-field conditions event. The favourite failed to run his race, but this still looks decent form from the winner - bordering on Listed level.

NOTEBOOK

Smart Instinct(USA), despite his American pedigree, handled these testing conditions well and saw the longer trip out strongly on this step up in grade. He looks tough, which will stand him in good stead, and it would not be a surprise to see him progress to Pattern level. (op 11-4)

Holdin Foldin(IRE), a winner of three of his previous four starts, was keen to lead and was in the prime position going into the final two furlongs, but giving 3lb to the potentially very useful winner proved too difficult and he was eventually well held. He may prove difficult to place now. (op 7-2)

Mandy's Maestro(USA) briefly looked as though he might get into the mix inside the final quarter mile, but he weakened from a furlong out. The ground appeared to suit him but the sixth furlong did not, and he should appreciate dropping back to five in maiden company. (tchd 25-1)

La Neige, fourth in the Group 2 Richmond Stakes last time, looked to have been found a race in which to get back to winning ways, but he was never going that well and eventually dropped right out of contention. He had won on his debut in soft ground so that ought not to have been a concern, but for one reason or another he failed to run his race. He is another who is likely to prove difficult to place throughout the rest of the season. Official explanation: trainer's rep had no explanation for the poor form shown (op 4-5 tchd 10-11 and evens in places)

4608 ARK DE TRIUMPH MAIDEN AUCTION STKS 6f

3:00 (3:03) (Class 4) 2-Y-O **£5,181** (£1,541; £770; £384) **Stalls** Low

Form RPR

03 **1** **Lafontaine Bleu**[12] [4196] 2-8-4 .... DaleGibson 13 62
(R A Fahey) *trckd ldr far side: hdwy wl over 1f out: rdn to ld and overall ldr ent last: edgd lft and drvn out: 1st of 6 in gp* **8/1**[3]

45 **2** *½* **Fadeyev (IRE)**[11] [4228] 2-8-13 .... DO'Donohoe 10 70
(K A Ryan) *led far side gp: rdn along wl over 1f out: hdd ent last: kpt on wl u.p: 2nd of 6 in gp* **9/2**[2]

0 **3** *2* **Woodland Traveller (USA)**[9] [4295] 2-8-13 ....(t) KimTinkler 11 64
(N Tinkler) *chsd ldng pair far side: rdn wl over 1f out: kpt on ins last: 3rd of 6 in gp* **40/1**

342 **4** *hd* **Reem Al Fallah (IRE)**[11] [4221] 2-8-6 73.............................. JohnEgan 3 65+
(M R Channon) *chsd ldrs stands side: hdwy 2f out: rdn to ld that gp ent last: sn drvn and kpt on same pce: 1st of 7 in gp* **9/4**[1]

0 **5** *½* **Juvenescent (USA)**[23] [3878] 2-8-8 .... PaulMulrennan 2 65+
(R D E Woodhouse) *overall ldr stands side: rdn along wl over 1f out: drvn and hdd ent last: grad wknd: 2nd of 7 in gp* **20/1**

6 *shd* **Para Siempre** 2-8-8 .... PaulEddery 12 56
(B Smart) *rr far side tl styd on appr last: nrst fin: 4th of 6 in gp* **12/1**

0 **7** *5* **Interest (USA)**[16] [4066] 2-8-9 .... PhillipMakin 14 42
(T D Barron) *in tch far side: rdn along over 2f out: sn wknd: 5th of 6 in gp* **25/1**

6 **8** *2 ½* **Aitutaki (IRE)**[10] [4251] 2-8-4 .... DuranFentiman(5) 7 44+
(T D Easterby) *dwlt and hmpd s: a towards rr stands side: 3rd of 7 in gp* **16/1**

6560 **9** *1 ¼* **First Valentini**[40] [3358] 2-7-13 .... AndrewElliott(5) 9 35+
(N Bycroft) *cl up stands side: rdn along over 2f out and sn wknd: 4th of 7 in gp* **14/1**

0005 **10** *2 ½* **Silly Gilly (IRE)**[12] [4196] 2-8-4 .... AdrianTNicholls 8 18+
(A Berry) *chsd ldrs stands side: rdn over 2f out and sn wknd: 5th of 7 in gp* **22/1**

0 **11** *3 ½* **Hesaguru (IRE)**[51] [3018] 2-8-6 .... MarkLawson(5) 4 15+
(J R Norton) *a rr stands side: 6th of 7 in gp* **80/1**

0 **12** *10* **Finlay's Footsteps**[51] [3018] 2-8-9 .... JoeFanning 6 —
(G M Moore) *a rr stands side: last of 7 in gp* **50/1**

13 *1 ¼* **Surprise Pension (IRE)** 2-8-13 .... WSupple 15 —
(J J Quinn) *a towards rr far side: last of 6 in gp* **16/1**

1m 16.32s (3.32) **Going Correction** +0.45s/f (Yiel) **13** Ran SP% **104.8**

Speed ratings (Par 96):95,94,91,91,90 90,83,80,78,75 70,57,55

CSF £30.15 TOTE £7.30: £2.00, £1.80, £7.50; EX 24.90 TRIFECTA Not won..

Owner The Cosmic Cases **Bred** D R Botterill **Trained** Musley Bank, N Yorks

FOCUS

A modest maiden, dominated by those who raced on the far side. The stands' side runners have provisionally been assessed as being at a three-length disadvantage.

NOTEBOOK

Lafontaine Bleu has progressed with every outing and her latest effort at Carlisle had suggested that she would appreciate this extra furlong. She saw it out well on the favoured far side and, while the form is only modest, she should pay her way in ordinary nursery company. (tchd 15-2)

Fadeyev(IRE), who showed good speed to cross over to the favoured far side from stall ten and make the running, is now eligible to run in nurseries, although on this evidence there might still be an ordinary maiden out there for him. (op 6-1)

Woodland Traveller(USA), a half-brother to Nova Huta, a winner over ten furlongs in France, stepped up greatly on his debut effort when he finished last of 15, and the application of a tongue tie this time might well have been significant.

Reem Al Fallah(IRE) ◆ had already shown enough to suggest that a maiden of this quality was within her ability, and the softer ground did not stop her running another solid race on the unfavoured stands' side. Had she been drawn on the other side she would probably have won. (op 5-2 tchd 7-2)

Juvenescent(USA) stepped up greatly on her debut effort, clearly appreciating the conditions underfoot. She finished miles clear of the third on her side and, given her pedigree - closely related to German 2000 Guineas winners Dupont & Pacino and half-sister to six other winners - it would not be a surprise to see her improve again next time. (op 16-1)

Para Siempre, a half-sister to five winners over the minimum trip, had the advantage of racing on the faster ground towards the far side. She stayed on late from off the pace and is entitled to improve for this racecourse debut. (op 10-1 tchd 14-1)

4609 WILLIAM HILL GREAT ST WILFRID STKS (HERITAGE H'CAP) 6f

3:30 (3:32) (Class 2) (0-105,105) 3-Y-0+

£37,392 (£11,196; £5,598; £2,802; £1,398; £702) **Stalls** Low

Form RPR

024 **1** **Excusez Moi (USA)**[14] [4128] 4-9-4 99.......................... KerrinMcEvoy 12 111
(C E Brittain) *swtchd rt s and sn trcking ldr far side: hdwy to ld over 1f out: rdn and edgd lft ins last: kpt on wl* **10/1**[3]

0515 **2** *1* **Fullandby (IRE)**[12] [4202] 4-8-0 86................................. AndrewElliott(5) 7 95+
(T J Etherington) *swtchd rt s and towards rr far side: gd hdwy 2f out: sn rdn and styd on strly ins last* **28/1**

3524 **3** *hd* **Ice Planet**[12] [4202] 5-8-9 90... RobertWinston 8 98
(D Nicholls) *swtchd rt s and midfield far side: hdwy and edgd rt over 1f out: sn rdn anmd edgd rt ins last: styd on towards fin* **14/1**

0030 **4** *hd* **Pieter Brueghel (USA)**[50] [3038] 7-8-7 88.................... AdrianTNicholls 6 95+
(D Nicholls) *led stands side gp: rdn wl over 1f out: drvn and hung rt ins last: kpt on: clear 1st of 5 in gp* **25/1**

0110 **5** *½* **Mr Wolf**[13] [4174] 5-8-6 92..(p) MarkLawson(5) 16 98
(D W Barker) *overall ldr far side: rdn along 2f out: drvn and hdd over 1f out: kpt on same pce ins last* **25/1**

0004 **6** *hd* **Obe Gold**[5] [4430] 4-9-2 97..(v) JohnEgan 21 102
(M R Channon) *hld up towards rr far side: hdwy whn n.m.r over 1f out and again ins last: kpt on: nrst fin* **14/1**

0000 **7** *½* **Zomerlust**[12] [4202] 4-8-9 90... WSupple 15 94
(J J Quinn) *chsd ldrs far side: rdn along 2f out: kpt on* **10/1**[3]

0154 **8** *1* **Tagula Sunrise (IRE)**[7] [4343] 4-8-10 91........................ TonyHamilton 20 92
(R A Fahey) *in tch far side: effrt 2f out: sn rdn and kpt on same pce appr last* **11/2**[1]

2050 **9** *1 ¾* **King's Gait**[12] [4202] 4-8-11 92..(b) DavidAllan 18 88
(T D Easterby) *dwlt and bhd far side tl styd on appr last: nrst fin* **14/1**

0061 **10** *½* **Rising Shadow (IRE)**[12] [4202] 5-8-10 91......................... PhillipMakin 14 85
(T D Barron) *dwlt and towards rr far side: effrt and sme hdwy wl over 1f out: sn no imp* **12/1**

3400 **11** *1 ¼* **Continent**[14] [4128] 9-8-8 89... MickyFenton 22 79
(D Nicholls) *chsd ldrs far side: rdn along wl over 1f out: wkng whn n.m.r ins last* **14/1**

0001 **12** *¾* **Traytonic**[7] [4378] 5-8-2 88 ow1.............................. MichaelJStainton(5) 11 76
(D Nicholls) *dwlt: swtchd to r far side: bhd tl sme late hdwy* **20/1**

2-50 **13** *2* **Fonthill Road (IRE)**[94] [1778] 6-9-5 100........................... GylesParkin 23 82
(R A Fahey) *a rr far side* **8/1**[2]

0006 **14** *hd* **Josh**[12] [4202] 4-8-5 86.. PaulMulrennan 19 67
(K A Ryan) *chsd ldrs far side: rdn along 2f out: sn wknd* **12/1**

3/30 **15** *¾* **Crimson Silk**[12] [4202] 6-8-6 87.. PaulEddery 1 66
(B Smart) *in tch stands side: rdn along over 2f out: sn wknd* **80/1**

1010 **16** *hd* **Desert Commander (IRE)**[14] [4128] 4-9-2 97.................. DO'Donohoe 4 76
(K A Ryan) *prom stands side: rdn 2f out: wknd ent last* **25/1**

0021 **17** *½* **Machinist (IRE)**[20] [3972] 6-8-11 92.................................. JoeFanning 2 69
(D Nicholls) *racd stands side: a towards rr* **14/1**

401 **18** *1* **Fantasy Believer**[15] [4101] 8-8-8 89... KDarley 9 63
(J J Quinn) *a rr far side* **20/1**

-240 **19** *6* **Coleorton Dancer**[84] [2012] 4-8-10 96......................... AndrewMullen(5) 5 52
(K A Ryan) *stmbld s: sn chsng ldr stands side: rdn along 2f out: wknd over 1f out* **18/1**

1m 13.82s (0.82) **Going Correction** +0.45s/f (Yiel) **19** Ran SP% **124.4**

Speed ratings (Par 109):112,110,110,110,109 109,108,107,104,104 102,101,98,98,97 97,96,95,87

CSF £274.22 CT £3906.33 TOTE £9.90: £3.00, £6.30, £4.40, £7.00; EX 351.20 Trifecta £13930.30 Part won. Pool: £19,620.14 - 0.80 winning tickets..

Owner Sheikh Hamdan Bin Mohammed Al Maktoum **Bred** Lyons Demesne **Trained** Newmarket, Suffolk

■ Stewards' Enquiry : Micky Fenton one-day ban: failed to keep straight from the stalls (Aug 30)
Mark Lawson one-day ban: failed to keep straight from the stalls (Aug 30)

FOCUS

A competitive renewal, but one lacking obviously well-handicapped contenders. The far side came out on top, as is usually the case when the ground rides soft, and the form looks solid.

NOTEBOOK

Excusez Moi(USA) ◆, unlucky in the Stewards' Cup, made up for that with a decisive success here. He showed plenty of early pace to cross over from his awkward middle draw to race up with the pace on the favoured far side and travelled well throughout. Indeed, he was still cruising approaching the final furlong while all his rivals were hard at it. Shaken up by McEvoy to go and win his race, he edged left towards the centre of the course, but he always had plenty in hand and won a lot more easily than the winning margin suggests. He might not be the most straightforward and ideally probably ought to be held up to the last minute, but he has tons of ability and the Ayr Gold Cup looks the obvious target, although it would not be a surprise if his trainer was tempted to shoot for the stars first in the Haydock Sprint Cup. (op 9-1)

Fullandby(IRE) likes to get his toe in, so the soft ground was in his favour, but he is not the easiest to win with and, having crossed over from his low draw, he was forced to race on the outside of the far-side group for most of the race. It was a good effort in the circumstances and he could well win a decent handicap in the coming weeks when things fall right, as this is his time of year.

Ice Planet, who won this race last year from the best draw off a 10lb lower mark, had things much tougher this time from his single-figure stall and, in the circumstances, ran very well. He has run consistently all season in decent handicap company and deserves to win one, but he has little in hand of the Handicapper at present. He should still be of interest if turning out in the Portland, though.

Pieter Brueghel(USA) ◆, another whose consistency does him few favours with the Handicapper, finished a long way clear of his four companions on the stands' side. He has now placed in this race in each of the last three years, twice 'winning' on the wrong side, and is a credit to his stable. (op 20-1)

Mr Wolf, whose style of running is not as suited to straight tracks as it is to turning tracks, is probably happier on quicker ground, too, so he was far from disgraced off a career-high mark.

Obe Gold, who ran a decent race in the Stewards' Cup when drawn on the wrong side, was well berthed this time but did not enjoy the clearest of passages. He still looks held off his current mark, though, a comment that applies to many in this field. (op 16-1)

Zomerlust, another who does not mind getting his feet wet, had the ground to suit and was back down to a reasonable mark, just 2lb higher than when running out a convincing winner at Pontefract in April. He did not look to have too many excuses.

Tagula Sunrise(IRE), supported into favouritism from double-figure prices in the morning, had plenty in her favour on paper, with draw, ground and current form all pointing to a bold show. She proved disappointing, though. (tchd 9-2, 13-2 and 6-1 in places)

King's Gait likes this sort of ground but he remains in the Handicapper's grip. In addition, his form over the minimum trip, which reads 6141225, is superior to his form over this distance, which reads 401003099. (op 12-1)

Fonthill Road(IRE) had the best draw but he never got competitive on his return from a three-month break. The Ayr Gold Cup is his stated objective and he remains one to be interested in for that contest. (op 7-1 tchd 17-2)

Josh is on a reasonable mark now and had shaped with a bit of promise here earlier in the month. He was well backed but never offered his supporters much hope.

Coleorton Dancer Official explanation: jockey said gelding was unsuited by the soft (good to soft in places) ground

4610 EUROPEAN BREEDERS FUND FILLIES' H'CAP — 1m 1f 170y

4:05 (4:05) (Class 4) (0-80,78) 3-Y-O- **£7,886** (£2,360; £1,180; £590; £293) **Stalls** High

Form			Horse	Jockey	RPR
0340	1		**Lady Disdain**[12] 4203 3-8-8 **63** ... JohnEgan 11 *(G M Moore) hld up in tch on inner: swtchd lft and hdwy over 2f out: rdn to ld wl over 1f out: clr ins last* **25/1**		74
3155	2	3 ½	**And Again (USA)**[14] 4159 3-9-4 **73** ... JoeFanning 2 *(J R Fanshawe) cl up: led wl over 2f out: rdn and hdd wl over 1f out: sn drvn and one pce* **13/2**[3]		78
3113	3	shd	**Apsara**[3] 4476 5-9-7 **68** ... PhillipMakin 5 *(G M Moore) a.p: effrt over 2f out: sn rdn and kpt on same pce appr last* **5/1**[2]		73
021	4	7	**Somersault**[15] 4117 3-9-1 **70** ... RobertWinston 8 *(Sir Michael Stoute) trckd ldrs on inner: pushed along over 3f out: rdn over 2f out and sn btn* **5/2**[1]		62
3036	5	2 ½	**Word Perfect**[81] 2095 4-9-2 **63** ... DaleGibson 7 *(M W Easterby) hld up in rr: hdwy wl over 2f out: styd on appr last: nrst fin* **12/1**		51
0321	6	2 ½	**Let Slip**[28] 3731 4-10-0 **75** ... KerrinMcEvoy 10 *(W Jarvis) hld up: smooth hdwy 3f out: rdn 2f out and sn btn* **5/2**[1]		58
2-44	7	5	**Cheviot Heights**[67] 2526 3-8-12 **70** ... SaleemGolam(3) 1 *(S C Williams) led: rdn along over 3f out: hdd wl over 2f out: drvn and grad wknd fnl 2f* **20/1**		44
5126	8	1 ¾	**Gelder**[26] 3793 3-9-4 **73** ... MickyFenton 3 *(H Morrison) in tch: hdwy 3f out: rdn over 2f out and sn wknd* **12/1**		44
-605	9	4	**Wasalat (USA)**[3] 4476 4-9-5 **71** ... MarkLawson(5) 4 *(D W Barker) dwlt: a rr* **33/1**		35

2m 9.35s (4.35) **Going Correction** +0.55s/f (Yiel)
WFA 3 from 4yo+ 8lb — 9 Ran SP% **114.1**
Speed ratings (Par 102):104,101,101,95,93 91,87,86,82
CSF £173.20 CT £956.61 TOTE £33.60: £8.90, £3.30, £2.90; EX 223.10 TRIFECTA Not won..
Owner Mrs D N B Pearson **Bred** Mrs D N B Pearson **Trained** Middleham Moor, N Yorks

FOCUS
Few handled the testing conditions here and there was a shock result. The form is pretty ordinary.
Lady Disdain Official explanation: trainer said, regarding apparent improvement in form, that the filly had benefited from its previous run having been off for seven weeks beforehand
Let Slip Official explanation: jockey said filly was unsuited by the soft (good to soft places) ground
Wasalat(USA) Official explanation: jockey said the filly was unsuited by the soft (good to soft places) ground

4611 E-TECH GROUP GEOFF JEWSON MEMORIAL MAIDEN STKS (DIV I) — 5f

4:40 (4:42) (Class 5) 3-Y-0+ **£4,533** (£1,348; £674; £336) **Stalls** Low

Form			Horse	Jockey	RPR
40	1		**How's She Cuttin' (IRE)**[14] 4155 3-8-12 ... PhillipMakin 10 *(T D Barron) mde all far side: rdn clr wl over 1f out: styd on* **7/1**[3]		56
0062	2	3	**Weakest Link**[7] 4361 5-9-5 46 ... (p) DavidAllan 6 *(E J Alston) chsd ldrs far side: hdwy 2f out: rdn to chse wnr ins last no imp* **3/1**[1]		51
5-	3	hd	**Glamaraazi (IRE)**[423] 2813 3-8-12 ... TonyHamilton 2 *(R A Fahey) prom centre: rdn along 2f out: sn one pce* **15/2**		46
0600	4	¾	**Harrington Bates**[15] 4120 5-9-0 41 ... (v) MichaelJStainton(5) 9 *(R M Whitaker) chsd ldrs far side: rdn along 2f out: kpt on same pce appr last* **11/1**		48
2030	5	3	**Signor Whippee**[9] 4296 3-9-3 49 ... (b) JoeFanning 3 *(A Berry) towards rr centre tl styd on appr last* **16/1**		38
0600	6	1	**Born For Diamonds (IRE)**[22] 3909 4-8-9 40 ... MarkLawson(5) 4 *(R E Barr) prom centre: rdn along 1/2-way: sn wknd* **28/1**		29
3350	7	3 ½	**All Clued Up (IRE)**[30] 3683 3-8-12 52 ... JohnEgan 1 *(Rae Guest) racd stands side: prom tl rdn along and wknd fnl* **14/1**		18
0	8	2	**Alone It Stands (IRE)**[18] 4034 3-9-3 ... AdrianTNicholls 7 *(D Nicholls) in tch far side: rdn along 2f out: no imp* **7/1**[3]		16
	9	nk	**Bond Sea Breeze (IRE)** 3-8-12 ... GylesParkin 11 *(G R Oldroyd) wnt rt s: a rr* **14/1**		10
4602	10	3 ½	**Slipperfoot**[12] 4201 3-8-12 56 ... (v) WSupple 8 *(J J Quinn) chsd ldrs far side: rdn along over 2f out: sn wknd* **7/2**[2]		—
	11	shd	**Game Bertie** 3-8-10 ... SuzzanneFrance(7) 13 *(N Bycroft) unruly s: a rr far side* **28/1**		—
/0-0	12	2 ½	**Hiats**[95] 1764 4-9-5 30 ... PaulEddery 5 *(J O'Reilly) a rr stands side* **100/1**		—
00-	13	7	**Dominello**[339] 5219 3-9-3 ... DaleGibson 12 *(R A Fahey) a rr far side* **25/1**		—

62.00 secs (1.80) **Going Correction** +0.45s/f (Yiel)
WFA 3 from 4yo+ 2lb — 13 Ran SP% **123.3**
Speed ratings (Par 103):103,98,97,96,91 90,84,81,81,75 75,71,60
CSF £28.29 TOTE £9.80: £2.60, £1.80, £2.80; EX 48.40 Trifecta £211.20 Part won. Pool: £297.58 - 0.68 winning tickets..
Owner Christopher McHale **Bred** A M Burke **Trained** Maunby, N Yorks
■ Stewards' Enquiry : Michael J Stainton one-day ban: failed to keep straight from the stalls (Aug 30). caution: careless riding

FOCUS
The quicker of the two divisions by 0.79sec, but no more than moderate, plating-class form.
All Clued Up(IRE) Official explanation: jockey said filly hung right-handed throughoiut
Slipperfoot Official explanation: jockey said filly had no more to give

4612 RIPON CATHEDRAL H'CAP — 1m 4f 10y

5:15 (5:16) (Class 3) (0-90,90) 3-Y-O
£9,348 (£2,799; £1,399; £700; £349; £175) **Stalls** High

Form			Horse	Jockey	RPR
1500	1		**Peppertree Lane (IRE)**[42] 3292 3-9-5 **88** ... KDarley 2 *(M Johnston) trckd ldrs: hdwy to ld over 3f out: rdn clr wl over 1f out: styd on wl* **7/2**[2]		100+
1112	2	3	**Bollin Derek**[81] 2102 3-8-2 **71** ... JoeFanning 5 *(T D Easterby) hld up: hdwy on outer over 3f out: rdn to chse wnr wl over 1f out: sn drvn and no imp* **5/4**[1]		77
1443	3	1 ½	**Flying Clarets (IRE)**[21] 3954 3-8-8 **77** ... TonyHamilton 4 *(R A Fahey) hld up in tch on inner: swtchd lft and hdwy 3f out: rdn wl over 1f out: kpt on same pce* **20/1**		81
-311	4	1 ¼	**Bedouin Blue (IRE)**[47] 3156 3-8-6 **75** ... PaulMulrennan 9 *(P C Haslam) led 2f: prom tl rdn along wl over 2f out and grad wknd* **16/1**		77
231	5	2	**Hernando Royal**[43] 3261 3-8-11 **80** ... MickyFenton 7 *(H Morrison) prom: rdn along 3f out: drvn 2f out and grad wknd* **7/1**[3]		79
02-1	6	8	**Act Friendly (IRE)**[32] 3620 3-9-0 **90** ... PatrickHills(7) 3 *(Saeed Bin Suroor) hld up: hdwy on outside wl over 2f out: sn rdn: hung lft and wknd wl over 1f out* **10/1**		78
2000	7	38	**Idarah (USA)**[14] 4125 3-9-3 **86** ... RobertWinston 6 *(W J Haggas) prom: led after 2f: pushed along and hung lft over 4f out: sn rdn and hdd over 3f out: sn wknd and eased fnl 2f* **8/1**		21
1214	8	2 ½	**Dream Champion**[35] 3539 3-8-10 **79** ... JohnEgan 8 *(M R Channon) prom: rdn along wl over 3f out: sn wknd and eased fnl 2f* **12/1**		11

2m 42.18s (5.18) **Going Correction** +0.55s/f (Yiel) — 8 Ran SP% **117.7**
Speed ratings (Par 104):104,102,101,100,98 93,68,66
CSF £8.53 CT £74.78 TOTE £5.20: £1.90, £1.20, £3.10; EX 12.10 Trifecta £128.40 Pool: £617.15 - 3.41 winning tickets..
Owner P D Savill **Bred** Gestut Wittekindshof **Trained** Middleham Moor, N Yorks

FOCUS
A decent handicap and a welcome return to form for Peppertree Lane, who was impressive and is worth following.

NOTEBOOK
Peppertree Lane(IRE) ◆, who had looked a promising colt on soft ground in the spring but whose form took a dive when reappearing too quickly in the Silver Bowl at Haydock and then failing to perform on fast ground, had been given a six-week break subsequently, and the benefit of that was seen here. Back on his favoured surface, he had his stamina to prove over a mile and a half, but his pedigree gave no cause for concern on that front and he won this very easily indeed. He looks one to keep on side as we move into the autumn, and there is a decent prize to be won with him somewhere. (op 4-1)

Bollin Derek, beaten off a rating of 64 when last seen in May, was reappearing off a 7lb higher mark than that, but he had course and distance form to his name and was proven in the ground. He might have been better off making the running, as he took an age to pick up, but for the second race in succession he was likely beaten by a very well-handicapped rival. (op 2-1 tchd 85-40 in a place)

Flying Clarets(IRE), a steady improver this season as she has been stepped up in distance, got the trip well enough but she is probably at her best on faster ground. This was a decent effort in the circumstances. (op 16-1)

Bedouin Blue(IRE), whose win at Redcar in the spring came on easier ground than the official going description would suggest, was down in the paper as only a runner in the event of sufficient rain. He got his ground, but the hat-trick never looked like being landed on his return from a 47-day break. (op 14-1)

Hernando Royal, another returning from his summer holidays, had run well in similar conditions on his debut and looked fairly rated on a mark of 80, but he was disappointing. It is too early to write him off, though. (op 15-2 tchd 17-2)

Act Friendly(IRE) looked to have been set a stiff task on her handicap debut off a mark of 90 and could not be given away in the ring beforehand. She performed as the market predicted and, although by Sadler's Wells, she might need quicker ground to be seen at her best. (op 6-1)

Idarah(USA) should have been at home in the ground, but he hung in the straight and weakened very tamely. Something may have been amiss. Official explanation: jockey said colt lost its action and hung badly left-handed from 2f out (op 6-1)

Dream Champion Official explanation: trainer's rep had no explanation for the poor form shown

4613 E-TECH GROUP GEOFF JEWSON MEMORIAL MAIDEN STKS (DIV II) — 5f

5:45 (5:47) (Class 5) 3-Y-0+ **£4,533** (£1,348; £674; £336) **Stalls** Low

Form			Horse	Jockey	RPR
00	1		**Orpenlina (IRE)**[73] 2356 3-8-12 ... TonyHamilton 6 *(R A Fahey) qckly away and mde all far side: rdn over 1f out: styd on* **11/1**		51
6305	2	½	**The Salwick Flyer (IRE)**[15] 4120 3-9-3 50 ... JoeFanning 1 *(A Berry) chsd ldr stands side: hdwy to ld that gp over 1f out: sn rdn and kpt on* **10/1**		54
0306	3	2 ½	**Cabriole**[17] 4045 3-8-12 60 ... KDarley 5 *(H R A Cecil) led stands side gp: rdn along 2f out: drvn and hdd over 1f out: one pce* **5/2**[1]		41
4060	4	2	**The Keep**[28] 3749 4-8-9 39 ... (b) MichaelJStainton(5) 8 *(R E Barr) chsd ldrs far side: rdn along 2f out: one pce appr last* **14/1**		34
0004	5	1	**Montana**[15] 4120 6-9-5 41 ... LeeEnstone 12 *(C W Fairhurst) chsd ldrs far side: rdn along 2f out: sn drvn and no imp* **4/1**[2]		36
0-	6	1	**Ponty Carlo (IRE)**[434] 2497 3-9-3 ... DavidAllan 10 *(T D Easterby) chsd wnr far side: rdn along 2f out: sn wknd* **5/1**[3]		32
05	7	4	**Vibrato (USA)**[14] 4136 4-9-5 ... JohnEgan 7 *(C J Teague) chsd ldrs far side: rdn along over 2f out: sn outpcd* **28/1**		19
	8	nk	**Bella Marie** 3-8-12 ... PaulMulrennan 11 *(L R James) a rr far side* **33/1**		13
6664	9	¾	**Musette (IRE)**[35] 3526 3-8-7 42 ... AndrewMullen(5) 9 *(R E Barr) midfield far side: rdn along 1/2-way: sn outpcd* **14/1**		10

10 1 1/4 **Boppys Dancer** 3-9-3 .... MickyFenton 3 11
(P T Midgley) *s.i.s: swtchd to far side: a bhd* **40/1**

11 *nk* **City Miss** 3-8-7 .... GregFairley(5) 13 5
(Miss L A Perratt) *a rr far side* **20/1**

12 2 1/2 **Tyrone Lady (IRE)** 3-8-12 .... WSupple 2 —
(J J Quinn) *a bhd stands side* **7/1**

62.79 secs (2.59) **Going Correction** +0.45s/f (Yiel)
WFA 3 from 4yo+ 2lb **12** Ran SP% **122.1**
Speed ratings (Par 103):97,96,92,89,87 85,79,78,77,75 75,71
CSF £114.87 TOTE £18.00: £4.60, £3.30, £1.50; EX 170.00 Trifecta £320.90 Part won. Pool: £452.11 - 0.10 winning tickets. Place 6 £353.70, Place 5 £144.21.
Owner Mrs Janis Macpherson **Bred** Johnny Kent **Trained** Musley Bank, N Yorks
■ Stewards' Enquiry : Lee Enstone one-day ban: failed to keep straight from the stalls (Aug 30)
Tony Hamilton one-day ban: failed to keep straight from the stalls (Aug 30)

FOCUS
Another moderate maiden and the slower of the two divisions by 0.79sec. The form has been rated loosely around the fourth.
Musette(IRE) Official explanation: jockey said filly was unsuited by the heavy ground
T/Plt: £515.60 to a £1 stake. Pool: £76,923.15. 108.90 winning tickets. T/Qpdt: £80.70 to a £1 stake. Pool: £5,311.10. 48.70 winning tickets. JR

4614 - 4620a (Foreign Racing) - See Raceform Interactive

[4542] DEAUVILLE (R-H)
Saturday, August 19
OFFICIAL GOING: Turf course - soft; all-weather - standard

4621a PRIX DU CALVADOS HARAS DES CAPUCINES (GROUP 3) (FILLIES) (STRAIGHT) 7f
2:20 (2:27) 2-Y-O **£27,586** (£11,034; £8,276; £5,517; £2,759)

RPR

1 **Charlotte O Fraise (IRE)**[20] 3990 2-8-9 .... C-PLemaire 7 103
(Rod Collet, France) *held up in rear, followed 2 others to stands rail after 1f, headway 1 1/2f out, led 140 yards out, ran on well* **39/10**[2]

2 1 1/2 **Poltava (FR)**[28] 2-8-9 .... DBoeuf 3 99
(D Smaga, France) *prominent when brought 2 others to stands rail after 1f, led over 1f out, headed 140 yards out, one pace* **11/1**

3 1 1/2 **Mpumalanga**[23] 2-8-9 .... TThulliez 5 95
(R Gibson, France) *held up in centre, ridden 1 1/2f out, every chance briefly over 1f out, kept on at one pace, took 3rd close home* **12/1**

4 *shd* **Rosamixa (FR)** 2-8-9 .... CSoumillon 1 95
(A Fabre, France) *led in centre of course, headed over 1f out, one pace, lost 3rd close home* **17/10**[1]

5 1/2 **Missvinski (USA)**[20] 2-8-9 .... IMendizabal 8 94
(J-C Rouget, France) *slightly detached in last in centre, good headway to press leaders 1 1/2f out, one pace final f* **69/10**

6 4 **Iron Lips**[37] 2-8-9 .... OPeslier 6 84
(C Laffon-Parias, France) *midfield when came to stands rail after 1f, outpaced final 1 1/2f* **11/1**

7 *nk* **Bellifiore (FR)**[36] 3514 2-8-9 .... TJarnet 2 83
(Mlle S-V Tarrou, France) *pressed leader in centre til weakened 2 1/2f out* **17/1**

8 2 **Afra Tsitsi (FR)**[36] 3514 2-8-9 .... YLerner 4 78
(C Lerner, France) *close up in centre til weakened quickly 1 1/2f out* **51/10**[3]

1m 30.5s **Going Correction** +0.65s/f (Yiel) **8** Ran SP% **116.4**
Speed ratings: 96,94,92,92,91 87,86,84
PARI-MUTUEL: WIN 4.90; PL 2.00, 2.50, 3.00; DF 76.70.
Owner Robert Collet **Bred** Mrs Chris Harrington **Trained** France

NOTEBOOK
Charlotte O Fraise(IRE), behind the leaders early on, made a forward move on the rails before the final furlong and was dominant as the race came to an end. She is now eligible for the Goffs Million and an alternative would be the Prix Marcel Boussac.
Poltava(FR), smartly into her stride, led a group near the rail. She held the lead until passed by the winner and comfortably held second place.
Mpumalanga really got into the race in the dying stages and may well be suited to a longer trip.
Rosamixa(FR) did not show her best form on this occasion and was a disappointing favourite.

4623a PRIX GUILLAUME D'ORNANO (GROUP 2) 1m 2f
3:20 (3:30) 3-Y-O **£51,103** (£19,724; £9,414; £6,276; £3,138)

RPR

1 **Multidimensional (IRE)**[14] 4126 3-8-11 .... C-PLemaire 2 110
(H R A Cecil) *held up in rear, last straight, headway on outside over 1f out, finished strongly to lead close home* **97/10**

2 3/4 **Boris De Deauville (IRE)**[41] 3342 3-8-11 .... YBarberot 6 109
(S Wattel, France) *raced in 3rd til led 6f out, ridden over 1f out, headed and no extra close home* **17/1**

3 1 1/2 **Barastraight**[76] 2278 3-8-11 .... IMendizabal 1 106
(J-C Rouget, France) *prominent on inside, 2nd straight, raced alon up far rail, stayed on steadily under pressure final 1 1/2f* **47/10**

4 1 1/2 **Kachgai (IRE)**[41] 3341 3-8-11 .... OPeslier 4 104
(E Libaud, France) *led til headed after 4f, 3rd straight, one pace final 1 1/2f, weakened close home* **44/10**[3]

5 *shd* **Carlotamix (FR)**[14] 4168 3-8-11 .... CSoumillon 5 103
(A Fabre, France) *raced in 5th, effort over 1f out, unable to quicken* **17/10**[1]

6 6 **Sudan (IRE)**[36] 3517 3-8-11 .... TThulliez 3 93
(E Lellouche, France) *held up, 4th straight, weakened over 1f out* **19/10**[2]

2m 14.3s **Going Correction** +0.65s/f (Yiel) **6** Ran SP% **122.5**
Speed ratings: 112,111,110,109,108 104
PARI-MUTUEL: WIN 10.70; PL 3.90, 4.80; SF 89.60.
Owner Niarchos Family **Bred** The Niarchos Family **Trained** Newmarket, Suffolk
■ Henry Cecil's first Group winner for four years.

NOTEBOOK
Multidimensional(IRE) was given a brilliant ride by his jockey and certainly acted on the rain-soaked turf. Dropped out completely early on, he was brought with a finely-timed challenge up the centre of the track and swept into the lead 50 yards from the post. He will probably be given a rest now but could go for the Champion Stakes at Newmarket later in the season, although he would have to be supplemented.
Boris De Deauville(IRE) ran a very courageous race and tried to make most of the running. He set a good pace and quickened things up early in the straight but could not repel the late challenge of the winner. He was apparently bought to go jumping and will certainly be pretty useful over hurdles.
Barastraight was always well placed and given every possible chance. His run was made up the far rail but he could not quicken late on and is probably better on good ground.
Kachgai(IRE) led for the first two furlongs and battled all the way up the straight, just managing to hold on to fourth place by a short-head.

[4221] BATH (L-H)
Sunday, August 20
OFFICIAL GOING: Good to firm (firm in places)
Wind: Fresh, half against.

4624 SKYBET LIVE ON PREMPLUS CHANNEL 480 MAIDEN AUCTION STKS 5f 11y
2:30 (2:31) (Class 6) 2-Y-O **£2,590** (£770; £385; £192) **Stalls Low**

Form RPR

403 1 **Cuppacocoa**[48] 3148 2-8-5 66 .... AdamKirby(3) 8 67
(C G Cox) *trckd ldr: led 3f out: rdn out fnl f* **6/4**[1]

2 1 **The Cool Sandpiper** 2-8-9 .... JimCrowley 7 64
(P Winkworth) *s.i.s: sn in tch: rdn over 1f out: styd on to go 2nd ins fnl f* **10/1**

60 3 *shd* **Cantique (IRE)**[12] 4221 2-8-6 .... EddieAhern 2 61
(R M Beckett) *in tch: hrd rdn 1/2-way: styd on wl fnl f* **9/2**[3]

503 4 3 **Ten For Tosca (IRE)**[12] 4222 2-8-13 57 .... SteveDrowne 6 57
(J A Osborne) *a.p: chsd wnr 1/2-way: wknd fnl f* **4/1**[2]

0 5 *nk* **Yearning (IRE)**[12] 4221 2-8-5 ow2 .... NeilChalmers(3) 5 51
(J G Portman) *prom tl wknd over 1f out* **22/1**

6 3/4 **Neat 'n Tidy** 2-8-1 .... JamesDoyle(3) 1 44
(C A Cyzer) *s.i.s: effort 1/2-way: one pce after* **10/1**

0406 7 3 **Spirit Rising**[31] 3678 2-8-6 54 .... StephenDonohoe(3) 4 39
(J M Bradley) *t.k.h: in tch tl wknd wl over 1f out* **12/1**

0005 8 4 **Countyourblessings**[4] 4485 2-8-6 .... PaulDoe 3 21
(I A Wood) *led for 2f: wknd wl over 1f out* **40/1**

0400 9 1 1/4 **Lenard Frank (IRE)**[43] 3300 2-8-2 44 ....(v) FrankiePickard(7) 9 20
(M D I Usher) *sn outpcd: a bhd* **33/1**

63.79 secs (1.29) **Going Correction** +0.05s/f (Good) **9** Ran SP% **113.8**
Speed ratings (Par 92):91,89,89,84,83 82,77,71,69
CSF £17.39 TOTE £2.20: £1.20, £3.00, £1.60; EX 16.80 Trifecta £115.80 Pool £409.49 - 2.51 winning units..
Owner John And Anne Soul **Bred** A J Coleing **Trained** Lambourn, Berks

FOCUS
Modest maiden form.

NOTEBOOK
Cuppacocoa, whose two previous starts on turf gave her every chance of winning an ordinary maiden of this type, was up with the pace throughout and held off her pursuers fairly comfortably. She should pay her way in modest nursery company. (op 11-10)
The Cool Sandpiper, whose dam was unraced but is from the family of The Whistling Teal, is by a speedy sire in Piccolo. This was a promising effort on his debut and a little improvement should see him hold every chance in a similarly modest heat. (op 14-1)
Cantique(IRE) appreciated the drop back to the minimum trip and ran her best race to date. She is now eligible for nurseries. (op 11-2)
Ten For Tosca(IRE) looked a threat two furlongs out but found little under pressure. In fairness, he had a fairly tough task at these weights, as he would have been a stone better off at the weights with the winner had this been a nursery. (op 5-1)
Yearning(IRE), last on her debut here 12 days earlier, showed a little improvement, but she probably needs dropping in class. (op 20-1)
Neat 'n Tidy, a half-sister to Boot'N Toot, a triple winner over middle distances, was green and needs more time. (op 12-1)

4625 SKYBET - LIVE ON ALL SKY PREMIERSHIP GAMES MAIDEN STKS 1m 3f 144y
3:00 (3:01) (Class 5) 3-Y-O+ **£3,886** (£1,156; £577; £288) **Stalls Low**

Form RPR

52 1 **Topjeu (IRE)**[23] 3901 3-9-3 .... NickyMackay 5 81+
(L M Cumani) *a in tch: led 2f out: sn clr: pushed out* **10/11**[1]

4- 2 5 **Fisher Bridge (IRE)**[247] 6588 3-9-3 .... SebSanders 6 73
(W R Swinburn) *a in tch: chsd wnr over 2f out: styd on but no imp fnl f* **9/1**[3]

3232 3 *nk* **Mobaasher (USA)**[14] 4175 3-9-3 84 ....(v[1]) MartinDwyer 1 72
(Sir Michael Stoute) *rdn fr s to ld after fnl f: hdd 2f out: rdn and reluctant to run on* **9/4**[2]

53 4 4 **Valart**[25] 3849 3-8-12 .... AlanDaly 3 61
(C Tinkler) *mid-div: plugged on one pce fnl 2f* **20/1**

5 2 **Junior** 3-8-10 .... KMay(7) 7 63
(B J Meehan) *bhd: no ch fnl 2f* **33/1**

00 6 1 1/4 **Montana Sky (IRE)**[55] 2917 3-9-3 .... AdrianMcCarthy 2 61
(R A Harris) *sn trckd ldr: rdn over 2f out: sn wknd* **150/1**

7 19 **Jupiters Moon (IRE)** 3-9-0 .... RichardKingscote(3) 9 30
(R Charlton) *hld up: wl bhd fnl 4f* **14/1**

8 8 **White Wingo (SAF)**[198] 6-9-10 45 ....(v) AdamKirby(3) 10 18
(R Simpson) *led for 1f: rdn over 3f out: sn wknd* **100/1**

2m 28.8s (-1.50) **Going Correction** +0.05s/f (Good)
WFA 3 from 6yo 10lb **8** Ran SP% **109.2**
Speed ratings (Par 103):107,103,103,100,99 98,85,80
CSF £9.02 TOTE £1.80: £1.10, £2.50, £1.10; EX 10.10 Trifecta £17.00 Pool £392.63 - 16.35 winning units..
Owner JMC Breed & Race Limited **Bred** Swettenham Stud **Trained** Newmarket, Suffolk

FOCUS
An uncompetitive maiden, but won by a promising sort.

4626 BATHWICK TYRES LADY RIDERS' DERBY (H'CAP) 1m 3f 144y
3:30 (3:30) (Class 3) (0-90,83) 3-Y-O+
£15,005 (£4,687; £2,342; £1,172; £585; £295) **Stalls Low**

Form RPR

5311 1 **Rationale (IRE)**[7] 4392 3-9-5 74 6ex .... MissAElsey 5 84
(S C Williams) *hld up: stdy hdwy fr 3f out: led ins fnl f: won gng away* **9/2**[1]

2053 2 3/4 **Incursion**[12] 4231 5-9-9 68 .... MrsSBosley 11 77
(D Nicholls) *a.p: rdn to chse wnr fnl f* **11/1**

0020 3 *nk* **Thyolo (IRE)**[50] 3093 5-10-4 82 .... MissJFerguson(5) 13 91
(C G Cox) *a in tch: hdwy on outside 2f out: r.o fnl f* **14/1**

0025 4 1/2 **Diktatorial**[3] 4508 4-10-10 83 ....(t) MissNCarberry 10 91
(G A Butler) *hld up: hdwy over 2f out: kpt on fnl f* **9/1**[3]

2131 5 1/2 **Fort Churchill (IRE)**[22] 3960 5-10-6 79 ....(bt) MissLEllison 6 86
(B Ellison) *a.p: led 3f out: rdn: hdd & wknd fins fnl f* **9/1**[3]

The Form Book, Raceform Ltd, Compton, RG20 6NL

5002 **6** 3/4 **Resonate (IRE)**[25] 3850 8-10-1 **74**.......................... MissCHannaford 14 80
(A G Newcombe) *chsd ldrs: n.m.r 2f out: styd on sme pce* **16/1**
1161 **7** *hd* **Our Teddy (IRE)**[15] 4149 6-10-7 **83**...................... MissFayeBramley(3) 7 88
(P A Blockley) *hld up towards rr: hdwy and styd on fnl f: nvr nrr* **14/1**
05/3 **8** 1/2 **Laggan Bay (IRE)**[8] 4369 6-9-7 **66**..............................(b) MrsSMoore 9 71
(J S Moore) *hld up: passed sme btn horses ins fnl 2f: nvr nr to chal* **25/1**
1221 **9** *hd* **Ollie George (IRE)**[12] 4224 3-9-7 **81**.....................(v) MissMSowerby(5) 3 88+
(A M Balding) *in tch tl lost pl 5f out: hdwy on ins whn hmpd ent fnl f: swtchd rt: r.o but no ch after* **5/1**[2]
1633 **10** *nk* **Mister Right (IRE)**[25] 3853 5-10-3 **76**........................... MissEJJones 2 80
(D J S Ffrench Davis) *trckd ldrs tl wknd appr fnl f* **20/1**
6-33 **11** 2 **Bucks**[13] 4206 9-9-7 **69**....................................... MrsLucindaCrowley(3) 12 70
(Ian Williams) *s.i.s: sn mid-div: one pce fnl 2f* **20/1**
4322 **12** 3/4 **Augustine**[5] 4457 5-9-10 **74**.......................................(b[1]) MrsMarieKing(5) 15 73
(P W Hiatt) *trckd ldr: rdn and wknd over 1f out* **16/1**
6043 **13** 3 1/2 **Sporting Gesture**[14] 4175 9-10-0 **73**........................ MissSBrotherton 1 67
(M W Easterby) *led tl hdd 3f out: sn wknd* **16/1**
02-6 **14** 1 3/4 **Kuster**[15] 4160 10-10-5 **83**...(b) MissFCumani(5) 4 74
(L M Cumani) *hld up: a bhd* **9/1**[3]

2m 28.7s (-34.76) **Going Correction** +0.05s/f (Good)
WFA 3 from 4yo+ 10lb **14** Ran SP% **117.5**
Speed ratings (Par 107):107,106,106,105,105 105,105,104,104,104 103,102,100,99
CSF £50.56 CT £646.29 TOTE £6.20: £2.50, £3.90, £5.40; EX 104.70 TRIFECTA Not won. Pool of £353.36 carried forward to Saturday, August 26th..
Owner Alasdair Simpson **Bred** Middle Park Stud Ltd **Trained** Newmarket, Suffolk
■ Annie Elsey announced her retirement from the saddle after landing this valuable event.

FOCUS
A competitive handicap run at a decent gallop, which led to the race being won by a horse held up well off the pace. Solid form, with plenty of the principals running within a pound or so of their marks.

NOTEBOOK
Rationale(IRE) has been in great form this summer and was not at all inconvenienced by having to race over another two furlongs. Indeed, she saw it out strongly, having been held up off the pace in a race run at a good gallop from the off. This was only her seventh career start and it would be unwise to assume that this improving filly's winning run will come to an end here. (op 4-1)
Incursion took over briefly when the leaders hit the wall but was soon collared by the eventual winner. He has not won for a long time but he is back on a good mark and the race was run to suit. (tchd 10-1)
Thyolo(IRE), another who remains on a long losing run, also had the race run to suit and came from mid-division to throw down a challenge. He has the ability to put in a performance from time to time that makes it difficult for the assessor to drop him much. (op 20-1)
Diktatorial had his stamina to prove over this longer distance, but he was held up as usual in a race run at a good pace and, challenging wide from off the pace, posted a solid effort. This should open up new opportunities for him. (op 11-1)
Fort Churchill(IRE), 6lb higher than at York, was up with the decent pace throughout and he paid the price in the closing stages, tiring and losing not only the lead but a placing, too. Official explanation: jockey said gelding did not handle the track (op 8-1)
Resonate(IRE), third in this race last year, ran well considering he was up with the decent pace for most of the way and was short of room at a crucial stage. (op 14-1)
Kuster, who won this race in 2003, was disappointing but was later found to be lame on his right fore. Official explanation: vet said gelding returned lame right-fore (op 7-1)

4627 SALTWELL SIGNS FILLIES' H'CAP 1m 5y
4:00 (4:01) (Class 5) (0-70,70) 3-Y-O+ **£4,533** (£1,348; £674; £336) **Stalls** Low

Form RPR
0542 **1** **Tuscarora (IRE)**[10] 4286 7-9-0 **59**.............................. JamesDoyle(3) 10 65
(A W Carroll) *hld up in mid-div: hdwy u.p over 1f out: r.o to ld cl home* **6/1**[3]
0242 **2** *nk* **Starboard Light**[17] 4075 3-8-9 **57**................................... SebSanders 15 62
(R M Beckett) *mid-div: hdwy to ld ins fnl f: ct nr fin* **4/1**[2]
3525 **3** 3/4 **Theatre Royal**[14] 4181 3-9-0 **62**.. MartinDwyer 14 65
(A M Balding) *a.p: led over 1f out: rdn and hdd ins fnl f: no ex* **7/2**[1]
0446 **4** 1 1/4 **Didoe**[10] 4279 7-8-9 **51** oh10.. PaulDoe 12 52
(P W Hiatt) *trckd ldr: led wl over 2f out: hdd over 1f out: no ex u.p* **16/1**
6014 **5** *nk* **Dancing Storm**[27] 3793 3-8-10 **58**................................ FergusSweeney 8 57
(W S Kittow) *mid-div: rdn over 2f out: styd on one pce* **6/1**[3]
050 **6** *nk* **Lady Cree (IRE)**[12] 4225 3-9-0 **62**......................................(p) EddieAhern 4 61
(W R Muir) *in rr: styd on ins fnl 2f: nvr nr to chal* **12/1**
5660 **7** 3 1/2 **Bathwick Emma (IRE)**[67] 2554 3-9-1 **63**........................ SteveDrowne 7 54
(P D Evans) *led tl hdd wl over 2f out: wknd fnl f* **16/1**
00-0 **8** 3/4 **Suesam**[27] 3793 3-8-13 **68**.. JamesMillman(7) 9 57
(B R Millman) *mid-div: rdn over 2f out: sn wknd* **10/1**
0505 **9** 2 **Parisi Princess**[5] 4450 5-8-6 **51** oh11......................(v) NeilChalmers(3) 6 36
(D L Williams) *slowly away: a bhd* **66/1**
5-26 **10** 2 **Villarosi (IRE)**[11] 4265 4-10-0 **70**.................................... DaneO'Neill 11 51
(J R Best) *in rr whn rdn over 3f out: sn btn* **10/1**
-006 **11** 1 **Ello Lucky (IRE)**[22] 3941 4-8-2 **51** oh17...................... BarrySavage(7) 5 29
(J M Bradley) *in tch: rdn 3f out: wknd over 2f out* **100/1**
40/5 **12** 1 1/2 **Bathwick Finesse (IRE)**[29] 3729 4-9-11 **70**.......... StephenDonohoe(3) 1 45
(B R Millman) *prom tl wknd 4f out* **66/1**
4430 **13** *hd* **Khyber Knight (IRE)**[31] 3668 3-8-6 **54**........................ AdrianMcCarthy 2 29
(Jane Southcombe) *prom: rdn 4f out: wknd qckly 2f out* **50/1**
2000 **P** **Catherine Medici**[26] 3828 3-8-3 **51** oh1...........................(v) ChrisCatlin 3 —
(R M H Cowell) *hld up: in rr whn hung bdly lft and hit rail over 5f out: sn p.u* **33/1**

1m 41.02s (-0.08) **Going Correction** +0.05s/f (Good)
WFA 3 from 4yo+ 6lb **14** Ran SP% **117.3**
Speed ratings (Par 100):102,101,100,99,99 99,95,94,92,90 89,88,88,—
CSF £28.84 CT £94.52 TOTE £5.70: £1.80, £2.30, £1.90; EX 30.10 Trifecta £32.40 Pool £378.54 - 8.27 winning units..
Owner Oliver Ryan **Bred** Yeomanstown Stud **Trained** Cropthorne, Worcs

FOCUS
A modest handicap for fillies featuring few that had tasted success recently. The fourth, rated to the best of this year's form, was a bit close for comfort.
Suesam Official explanation: jockey said filly failed to handle the bend
Villarosi(IRE) Official explanation: jockey said filly hung right
Catherine Medici Official explanation: jockey said the filly hung badly left and hit the rails

4628 EUROPEAN BREEDERS FUND DICK HERN FILLIES' STKS (LISTED RACE) 1m 5y
4:30 (4:35) (Class 1) 3-Y-O+
£15,898 (£6,025; £3,015; £1,503; £753; £378) **Stalls** Low

Form RPR
-450 **1** **Three Wrens (IRE)**[87] 1974 4-9-0 **85**.............................. NickyMackay 7 94
(D J Daly) *hld up: rdn and hdwy to ld over 1f out: hld on wl cl home* **25/1**
5-25 **2** *nk* **Sweet Treat (IRE)**[85] 2041 4-9-0 **98**.............................. MartinDwyer 10 93
(J R Fanshawe) *s.i.s: hdwy over 1f out: pressed wnr ins fnl f: no imp cl home* **12/1**
-421 **3** 2 **Sabah**[41] 3367 3-8-8 **78**... NeilChalmers 9 87
(A M Balding) *mid-div: rdn to chal 2f out: nt qckn fnl f* **40/1**
3011 **4** *nk* **Wagtail**[17] 4075 3-8-8 **85**..(t) EddieAhern 3 87
(E A L Dunlop) *in tch: rdn over 2f out: kpt on one pce* **9/1**[3]
1432 **5** *nk* **Waterline Twenty (IRE)**[14] 4172 3-8-8 **81**............... StephenDonohoe 5 86
(P D Evans) *hld up in rr: styd on fnl 2f: nvr nr to chal* **66/1**
2-23 **6** 3/4 **Cantabria**[16] 4097 3-8-8 **103**.. RichardHughes 4 84
(Sir Michael Stoute) *in tch: rdn over 2f out: swtchd rt but nvr threatened to get on terms* **4/5**[1]
-146 **7** 1 1/4 **Spinning Ruby**[18] 4042 3-8-9 **88** ow1............................ SebSanders 2 82
(R M Beckett) *s.i.s: nvr on terms* **40/1**
4133 **8** 1 3/4 **Squaw Dance**[23] 3891 4-9-0 **100**.................................... ChrisCatlin 6 78
(W J Haggas) *prom: led over 2f out: hdd over 1f out: wknd fnl f* **3/1**[2]
4420 **9** 2 **Little Miss Gracie**[23] 3891 4-9-0 **95**............................. DaneO'Neill 8 74
(A B Haynes) *led tl hdd over 2f out: rdn and wknd over 1f out* **33/1**
0120 **10** 1 1/2 **Pintle**[37] 3493 6-9-0 **87**... FrancisNorton 1 70
(J L Spearing) *trckd ldr: rdn over 2f out: wknd over 1f out* **25/1**

1m 39.81s (-1.29) **Going Correction** +0.05s/f (Good)
WFA 3 from 4yo+ 6lb **10** Ran SP% **115.3**
Speed ratings (Par 108):108,107,105,105,105 104,103,101,99,97
CSF £265.30 TOTE £25.40: £5.60, £3.00, £3.90; EX 460.00 TRIFECTA Not won. Pool of £775.26 carried forward to Saturday, August 26th..
Owner Mrs James Wigan **Bred** Mrs James Wigan **Trained** Newmarket, Suffolk

FOCUS
They went a good pace in this fillies' Listed race and the principals challenged from off the pace. Dubious form, with two long-priced runners in the frame and the thoroughly exposed fifth limiting the level.

NOTEBOOK
Three Wrens(IRE), despite having plenty to find strictly on the book, was travelling best of all off the pace two furlongs out and the biggest question was whether she would get a run or not. Thankfully the gap came pretty soon and she took full advantage. It was pleasing to see her battle once challenged by the eventual runner-up, and she has now won on both occasions she has encountered good to firm ground.
Sweet Treat(IRE) has done most of her racing on easier ground but she coped with these quicker conditions well. The race was run to suit her as the decent pace played into the hands of the hold-up horses, but it was still a good effort. (op 10-1)
Sabah, a winner on her previous start of a Windsor maiden which has worked out quite well, was handed an official rating of 78 on the back of that and was underestimated by the market as a result. She made a mockery of that mark, though, with a solid staying-on performance in this higher grade, earning herself some valuable black type in the process. (op 33-1)
Wagtail, who had seen her Epsom form boosted slightly by the performance of the runner-up Starboard Light in the preceding handicap, did not enjoy the clearest of runs and was not disgraced in this tougher company. She remains open to further improvement. (op 12-1 tchd 8-1)
Waterline Twenty(IRE), ridden to stay on for some black type, had the race run to suit but was unable to get close enough to realise the objective. (op 50-1)
Cantabria, third in the Oak Tree Stakes last time out, was best in at the weights and understandably made a short-price favourite to win in this lesser grade. She proved very disappointing, though, finding little off the bridle, and perhaps a second race on fast ground in the space of 16 days proved too much. (tchd 5-6 and 10-11 in places)
Squaw Dance went too fast at the head of affairs but her trainer blamed the ground. Official explanation: trainer said filly was unsuited by the good to firm (firm in places) ground (op 10-3 tchd 7-2)

4629 SKYBET - PRESS RED ON SKY SPORTS FOOTBALL H'CAP 5f 161y
5:00 (5:03) (Class 5) (0-75,75) 3-Y-O+ **£4,533** (£1,348; £674; £336) **Stalls** Low

Form RPR
4503 **1** **Summer Recluse (USA)**[5] 4449 7-9-3 **66**..................(t) SteveDrowne 9 74
(J M Bradley) *hld up: hdwy over 1f out: r.o wl to ld ins fnl f* **9/2**[1]
0042 **2** 3/4 **Kitchen Sink (IRE)**[41] 3348 4-8-7 **56** oh4....................(e) MartinDwyer 10 62
(P J Makin) *chsd ldrs on outside: led and hung lft over 1f out: hdd ins fnl f* **6/1**[3]
4004 **3** 3/4 **Parkside Pursuit**[8] 4365 8-8-6 **62**.......................... BarrySavage(7) 13 69+
(J M Bradley) *in rr: nt clr run 2f out: r.o strly fnl f: nvr nrr* **14/1**
3023 **4** 1/2 **Caustic Wit (IRE)**[2] 4557 8-9-3 **73**.............................(p) TolleyDean(7) 12 75
(M S Saunders) *hld up in mid-div: rdn 1/2-way: kpt on u.p fnl f* **5/1**[2]
0010 **5** *shd* **Digital**[83] 2074 9-9-12 **75**.. ChrisCatlin 11 77
(M R Channon) *bhd: hdwy appr fnl f: r.o wl: nvr nrr* **14/1**
5052 **6** 1 **Mandarin Spirit (IRE)**[12] 4230 6-9-5 **68**.........................(b) DaneO'Neill 4 67
(G C H Chung) *hld up in tch: rdn 2f out: kpt on one pce* **8/1**
6504 **7** 1/2 **Kallista's Pride**[10] 4294 6-8-9 **65**................................ KylieManser(7) 5 62
(J R Best) *bolted on way to s: towards rr: kpt on one pce fnl f* **28/1**
5341 **8** *nk* **Atlantic Viking (IRE)**[17] 4067 11-8-13 **65**............. StephenDonohoe(3) 8 61
(P D Evans) *towards rr: sme late hdwy* **7/1**
6006 **9** *nk* **Middle Eastern**[34] 3598 4-8-7 **56** oh8................................. EddieAhern 2 51
(P A Blockley) *hld up: led briefly wl over 1f out: wknd fnl f* **28/1**
3006 **10** 1 1/4 **Willhewiz**[5] 4449 6-9-7 **70**.. SebSanders 6 61
(M S Saunders) *trckd ldrs: rdn over 1f out: wknd fnl f* **9/1**
5124 **11** 2 1/2 **Misaro (GER)**[25] 3855 5-9-10 **73**.................................(b) AdrianMcCarthy 1 56
(R A Harris) *led tl hdd & wknd over 1f out* **7/1**
0200 **12** 1 3/4 **Chantelle's Dream**[8] 4365 4-8-0 **56** oh8.......................... SophieDoyle(7) 7 34
(Ms J S Doyle) *bolted on way to s: hld up mid-div: wknd 2f out* **100/1**
06-0 **13** 4 **Make It Happen Now**[202] 255 4-8-2 **56** oh13......... KevinGhunowa(5) 3 21
(P A Blockley) *in tch tl wknd over 2f out* **100/1**

1m 11.17s (-0.03) **Going Correction** +0.05s/f (Good) **13** Ran SP% **117.5**
Speed ratings (Par 103):102,101,100,99,99 97,97,96,96,94 91,89,83
CSF £29.92 CT £280.70 TOTE £5.30: £1.90, £2.40, £4.00; EX 44.50 Trifecta £200.70 Pool £395.87 - 1.40 winning units. Place 6 £160.09, Place 5 £109.97..
Owner Clifton Hunt **Bred** Juddmonte Farms Inc **Trained** Sedbury, Gloucs
■ Stewards' Enquiry : Martin Dwyer caution: careless riding

FOCUS
A modest handicap, but competitive enough. The winner ran to this year's best and the second improved again on recent form.
Misaro(GER) Official explanation: jockey said saddle slipped
T/Jkpt: Not won. T/Plt: £281.30 to a £1 stake. Pool: £71,831.15. 186.40 winning tickets. T/Qpdt: £189.30 to a £1 stake. Pool: £3,403.85. 13.30 winning tickets. JS

4256 PONTEFRACT (L-H)

Sunday, August 20

OFFICIAL GOING: Last 6f - good; remainder good (good to firm in places)

After 6mm rain over the previous 24 hourse the ground was described as 'just on the easy side of good'. It was much quicker on the outside in the straight.

Wind: Moderate, half behind. Weather: Fine

4630 EUROPEAN BREEDERS FUND SUNDAY PLATE MAIDEN STKS 5f

2:20 (2:21) (Class 4) 2-Y-O **£5,181** (£1,541; £770; £384) **Stalls** Low

Form RPR

1 **Pegasus Dancer (FR)** 2-9-3 ..... DO'Donohoe 5 63+
(K A Ryan) *s.i.s: sn chsng ldrs: hung lft over 1f out: styd on wl to ld fnl strides* **7/1[2]**

2 2 *nk* **Hurricane Flyer**[15] 4151 2-9-3 ..... RobertWinston 2 62
(E J O'Neill) *trckd ldrs: wnt 2nd over 1f out: led last 75 yds: hdd nr fin* **10/11[1]**

3 *nk* **Kilcusnin Queen (IRE)**[10] 4316 2-8-12 ..... TPO'Shea 9 56
(Adrian Sexton, Ire) *sn outpcd: hrd rdn and hdwy on outside 2f: styd on wl ins last* **7/1[2]**

0004 4 *1* **Suntan Lady (IRE)**[9] 4327 2-8-9 50 ..... EdwardCreighton(3) 4 52
(Miss V Haigh) *led: hdd wl ins last: wknd* **33/1**

0000 5 *2 ½* **Lost Inheritance**[8] 4376 2-8-12 ..... TomEaves 10 43
(P T Midgley) *chsd ldrs on wd outside: hung lft over 1f out: one pce* **50/1**

000 6 *2 ½* **Ruthles Philly**[36] 3553 2-8-7 ..... MarkLawson(5) 8 34
(D W Barker) *w ldrs: fdd appr fnl f* **66/1**

5 7 *2 ½* **Emirate Isle**[34] 3581 2-9-3 ..... PaulMulrennan 3 30
(J Wade) *s.i.s: sn in tch: outpcd and lost pl over 2f out* **10/1[3]**

060 8 *hd* **Ellies Faith**[8] 4376 2-8-5 ..... SuzzanneFrance(7) 7 24
(N Bycroft) *w ldrs: lost pl over 1f out* **66/1**

00 9 *2 ½* **Diverse Forecast (IRE)**[16] 4103 2-9-3 ..... MickyFenton 11 20
(Mrs P Sly) *s.s: a in rr* **40/1**

66.09 secs (2.29) **Going Correction** +0.25s/f (Good) 9 Ran SP% **96.8**

Speed ratings (Par 96):91,90,90,88,84 80,76,76,72

CSF £9.69 TOTE £6.80: £1.60, £1.10, £1.70; EX 15.00.

Owner Rievaulx Racing Syndicate **Bred** J C Campos Et Al **Trained** Hambleton, N Yorks

■ Deserted Dane was withdrawn (11/2, vet's advice). R4 applies, deduct 15p in the £.

■ Stewards' Enquiry : Robert Winston caution: used whip without giving horse time to respond

FOCUS

An ordinary maiden with horses beaten in selling company in fourth and fifth place the form is suspect. The placed horses give the best guide to the form.

NOTEBOOK

Pegasus Dancer(FR), an April foal, is long in the back and narrow. Showing a pronounced knee action, he was very keen to post. He really picked up inside the last to lead near the finish and will be even better suited by seven. (op 6-1)

Hurricane Flyer had the leader in his sights. Under a strong ride he put his head in front only to be edged out near the line. He might have been racing on the slightly slower ground on the inside. (op 11-10)

Kilcusnin Queen(IRE), who finished fifth on her debut at Tipperary ten days earlier, struggled to keep up. Making her effort on the wide outside, she finished best of all. The suspicion was that she was racing on the quicker, unwatered ground away from the running rail.

Suntan Lady(IRE), beaten in selling company last time, was on her toes and took them along. She quickened three lengths clear off the bend but could not last home.

Lost Inheritance, beaten further than this in a seller last time, raced wide and is probably flattered.

Ruthles Philly, very keen to post, tired noticeably late on. (op 50-1)

Emirate Isle Official explanation: jockey said gelding never travelled

4631 ENTER TODAY'S RACECARD COMPETITION H'CAP 1m 4f 8y

2:50 (2:53) (Class 3) (0-95,95) 3-Y-0+ **£8,420** (£2,505; £1,251; £625) **Stalls** Low

Form RPR

2312 1 **New Guinea**[15] 4125 3-8-11 88 ..... PhilipRobinson 6 101+
(M A Jarvis) *trckd ldrs: plld wd over 1f out: qcknd to ld 1f out: edgd lft: r.o strly: readily* **9/4[1]**

0006 2 *3* **Most Definitely (IRE)**[12] 4231 6-8-11 78 ..... DavidAllan 3 86
(T D Easterby) *s.i.s: hld up in last: hdwy on ins over 2f out: chal and wnt 2nd 1f out: kpt on same pce* **16/1**

0432 3 *1 ¼* **St Savarin (FR)**[53] 2982 5-8-11 78 ..... TonyHamilton 9 84
(R A Fahey) *trckd ldrs: t.k.h: led over 1f out: sn hdd and no ex* **14/1**

-000 4 *8* **Kerashan (IRE)**[19] 4027 4-10-0 95 ..... (t) KerrinMcEvoy 5 88
(Saeed Bin Suroor) *trckd ldrs: moved upsides on outsider over 5f out: wknd over 1f out* **13/2**

240 5 *½* **Castle Howard (IRE)**[19] 4027 4-9-8 89 ..... TPQueally 4 81
(W J Musson) *trckd ldrs: wknd over 1f out* **6/1[3]**

431 6 *1* **Belanak (IRE)**[40] 3376 3-8-7 84 ..... RobertWinston 2 75
(Sir Michael Stoute) *hld up in tch: drvn over 3f out: lost pl 2f out* **9/2[2]**

5250 7 *nk* **Jack Of Trumps (IRE)**[19] 4023 6-9-3 84 ..... TedDurcan 1 74
(G Wragg) *hld up in rr: hdwy on outer over 3f out: sn chsng ldrs: lost pl over 1f out* **8/1**

3102 8 *5* **Aspasias Tizzy (USA)**[12] 4231 3-8-0 77 ..... RoystonFfrench 8 59
(M Johnston) *led: qcknd over 3f out: hdd over 1f out: sn lost pl* **8/1**

2m 41.85s (1.55) **Going Correction** +0.25s/f (Good)

WFA 3 from 4yo+ 10lb 8 Ran SP% **111.3**

Speed ratings (Par 107):104,102,101,95,95 94,94,91

CSF £38.59 CT £394.72 TOTE £3.00: £1.30, £4.30, £3.00; EX 49.40.

Owner Sheikh Mohammed **Bred** Milton Park Stud Partnership **Trained** Newmarket, Suffolk

FOCUS

A decent handicap but run at just a steady pace. The form should prove reasonable as the first three finished clear and the winner is still improving.

NOTEBOOK

New Guinea, just 2lb higher, had to pull wide coming off the final bend. That took him on to the faster ground and he quickened up in good style. He is still improving and should continue to give a good account of himself. (op 2-1 tchd 5-2)

Most Definitely(IRE), slipping down the ratings, showed a lot more dash but had crossed paths with an improving three-year-old. (op 20-1)

St Savarin(FR), absent for seven weeks, was a bit too keen for his own good. This will have taken the freshness away from him. (tchd 12-1)

Kerashan(IRE), winner of two handicaps last year for Sir Michael Stoute, is not that big and continually swished his tail in the paddock. He came there with every chance but dropped out in a matter of strides once in line for home. (op 7-1)

Castle Howard(IRE) would not settle as a result of the steady pace, and turning in the needle was on empty. The drop back in trip was not the answer. Official explanation: jockey said gelding ran too free in early stages and had no more to give

Belanak(IRE), making his handicap debut, was very warm in the paddock and keen to post. He dropped right out turning in. (op 5-1)

4632 FRONTLINE COMPLETE BATHROOM H'CAP 2m 1f 22y

3:20 (3:20) (Class 5) (0-70,65) 3-Y-0+ **£4,533** (£1,348; £674; £336) **Stalls** Low

Form RPR

2342 1 **Mister Arjay (USA)**[11] 4252 6-9-10 61 ..... TonyHamilton 4 71
(B Ellison) *chsd ldrs: drvn along 6f out: hrd rdn to ld over 2f out: edgd rt and c stands' side: styd on strly ins last* **6/1[3]**

1115 2 *6* **Rose Bien**[22] 3955 4-9-9 63 ..... (p) EdwardCreighton(3) 7 66
(P J McBride) *hld up: hdwy to trck ldrs 8f out: styd on to take 2nd ins last* **6/1[3]**

1001 3 *½* **True (IRE)**[12] 4227 5-8-13 50 ..... PaulFessey 8 52
(Mrs S Lamyman) *s.i.s: hld up in rr: hdwy 5f out: kpt on same pce appr fnl f* **14/1**

6114 4 *7* **Leo McGarry (IRE)**[11] 4252 3-8-10 61 ..... JamieSpencer 3 55
(S C Williams) *hld up towards rr: hdwy to chse ldrs 5f out: sn drvn: wknd over 1f out* **5/2[1]**

2150 5 *½* **Kayf Aramis**[18] 4046 4-10-0 65 ..... PaulQuinn 2 58
(J L Spearing) *hld up in rr: hdwy over 4f out: hung lft and lost pl over 1f out* **5/1[2]**

2456 6 *nk* **Compton Eclaire (IRE)**[17] 4072 6-9-7 58 ..... (v) TomEaves 1 51
(B Ellison) *hld up in mid-div: stdy hdwy to trck ldrs 6f out: lost pl over 2f out* **12/1**

-625 7 *½* **Jumeirah Scarer**[6] 4423 5-9-5 61 ..... AndrewMullen(5) 6 53
(K A Ryan) *trckd ldrs: led over 3f out: hdd over 2f out: lost pl over 1f out* **10/1**

2042 8 *¾* **Thewhirlingdervish (IRE)**[5] 4451 8-9-9 65 ..... DuranFentiman(5) 9 56
(T D Easterby) *in tch: dropped bk 8f out: drvn and sme hdwy over 4f out: lost pl 2f out* **8/1**

0001 9 *21* **Optimum (IRE)**[40] 3382 4-9-9 60 ..... MickyFenton 5 26
(J T Stimpson) *set str pce: pushed along 6f out: hdd over 3f out: lost pl over 2f out: sn bhd* **25/1**

3m 52.07s (1.57) **Going Correction** +0.25s/f (Good)

WFA 3 from 4yo+ 14lb 9 Ran SP% **112.2**

Speed ratings (Par 103):106,103,102,99,99 99,99,98,88

CSF £40.22 CT £477.24 TOTE £5.10: £1.60, £1.80, £3.50; EX 28.80.

Owner Keith Middleton **Bred** Barbara Hunter **Trained** Norton, N Yorks

FOCUS

A modest staying event run at an end-to-end gallop and rated at face value around the winner and third. The winner ended up racing alone on the unwatered stands' side in the home straight and the eventual style of success might well flatter him.

4633 SLATCH FARM STUD FLYING FILLIES' STKS (LISTED RACE) 6f

3:50 (3:52) (Class 1) 3-Y-0+

£25,551 (£9,684; £4,846; £2,416; £1,210; £607) **Stalls** Low

Form RPR

6130 1 **Indian Maiden (IRE)**[7] 4410 6-9-4 102 ..... TedDurcan 12 111
(M S Saunders) *hld up: smooth hdwy on outside over 2f out: led 1f out: r.o strly* **4/1[3]**

1102 2 *3 ½* **Home Sweet Home (IRE)**[27] 3795 3-8-11 84 ..... JimmyFortune 2 97
(P D Evans) *led 1f: w ldrs: hdd over 2f out: hung bdly rt over 1f out: styd on ins last: snatched 2nd last stride* **20/1**

5645 3 *shd* **Ripples Maid**[22] 3967 3-8-11 92 ..... RichardThomas 7 96
(J A Geake) *trckd ldrs: led over 2f out: hdd 1f out: wknd towards fin* **6/1**

4 4 *1* **Absolutelyfabulous (IRE)**[22] 3967 3-8-11 ..... JamieSpencer 6 93+
(David Wachman, Ire) *n.m.r and lost pl sn after s: effrt on outer over 2f out: carried v wd 1f out: kpt on same pce* **3/1[1]**

130 5 *nk* **Lady Orpen (IRE)**[49] 3125 3-8-11 ..... KerrinMcEvoy 10 92
(Patrick Morris, Ire) *chsd ldrs on outer: carried v wd 1f out: kpt on wl* **9/1**

0145 6 *2 ½* **Sunderland Echo (IRE)**[82] 2105 3-8-11 85 ..... TomEaves 5 85
(B Ellison) *chsd ldrs: sn drvn along: outpcd 2f out: styd on ins last* **28/1**

-031 7 *5* **Portmeirion**[25] 3846 5-9-0 67 ..... J-PGuillambert 3 70+
(S C Williams) *dwlt: hdwy on outside over 2f out: c stands' side: lost pl 1f out: eased* **33/1**

0100 8 *2* **Folga**[8] 4343 4-9-0 95 ..... KDarley 4 64
(J G Given) *w ldr: led after 1f: hdd over 2f out: lost pl over 1f out* **9/1**

2101 9 *2 ½* **Dark Missile**[8] 4343 3-8-11 89 ..... JohnEgan 9 56
(A M Balding) *trckd ldrs: effrt over 2f out: lost pl over 1f out* **10/3[2]**

1m 17.13s (-0.27) **Going Correction** +0.25s/f (Good)

WFA 3 from 4yo+ 3lb 9 Ran SP% **113.5**

Speed ratings (Par 108):111,106,106,104,104 101,94,91,88

CSF £79.11 TOTE £5.40: £2.10, £3.40, £2.20; EX 74.90.

Owner Chris Scott & Peter Hall **Bred** Shadwell Estate Co Ltd **Trained** Green Ore, Somerset

■ Stewards' Enquiry : Jimmy Fortune one-day ban: careless riding (Aug 31)

FOCUS

Winner of 37 races in a well up to standard renewal of this Listed Fillies' prize. They ended up racing across the entire width of the track but there was no doubting the winner's performance, although the form is only fair for the grade, rated through the third.

NOTEBOOK

Indian Maiden(IRE), drawn on the wide outside, appreciated getting her toe in and shot clear in a matter of strides when given the office. This was her 14th career win and on her 48th start she seemed better than ever. She is a credit to her trainer. (op 3-1)

Home Sweet Home(IRE), who had a stone to find with the winner hung badly in front but stuck on grimly to snatch second spot on the line. (tchd 16-1)

Ripples Maid, who had something to find with the winner on Leopardstown running, showed clear second inside the last but she was tying up fast at the line. (op 13-2 tchd 7-1)

Absolutelyfabulous(IRE), close up fourth behind the winner at Leopardstown, had no luck in running and in the end did well to finish fourth and gain more black type. (op 7-2)

Lady Orpen(IRE), absent for seven weeks, was pushed very wide in the home straight. It did mean however that she ended up racing on the quicker, unwatered ground on the outside.

Sunderland Echo(IRE), absent for almost three months, needs plenty of driving and she could have done with a lot more rain. (op 25-1)

Portmeirion Official explanation: jockey said mare lost a front shoe

Dark Missile looks to be thriving physically but she ran poorly just a week after her Ascot success for no apparent reason. Official explanation: trainer had no explanation for the poor form shown (op 3-1)

4634 UNISON DEFEND PUBLIC SERVICES H'CAP 1m 4y

4:20 (4:20) (Class 3) (0-90,88) 3-Y-O **£8,420** (£2,505; £1,251; £625) **Stalls** Low

Form RPR

41 1 **Shumookh (IRE)**[16] 4113 3-8-12 79 ..... RHills 8 97+
(M A Jarvis) *mde all: qcknd clr over 1f out: r.o wl* **9/2[1]**

4504 2 *3* **Bonnie Prince Blue**[10] 4298 3-9-2 83 ..... MichaelHills 6 90
(B W Hills) *in rr: sn pushed along: effrt on ins 3f out: wnt 2nd 1f out: kpt on: no imp* **6/1[3]**

21 3 *2* **Speedy Sam**[78] 2244 3-8-13 80 ..... PatCosgrave 2 82
(K R Burke) *chsd ldrs: kpt on same pce fnl 2f* **7/1**

The Form Book, Raceform Ltd, Compton, RG20 6NL

5634 **4** *hd* **Pab Special (IRE)**[35] [3569] 3-7-13 **71** ow1 .... AndrewElliott[(5)] 1 73
(K R Burke) *prom:effrt over 2f out: styd on same pce* **20/1**
-021 **5** *1* **Collateral Damage (IRE)**[93] [1836] 3-9-7 **88** .... DavidAllan 10 88
(T D Easterby) *rr-div: hdwy on wd outside over 1f out: kpt on: nvr rchd ldrs* **5/1**[2]
00-0 **6** *nk* **Skyelady**[110] [1384] 3-8-12 **79** .... TomEaves 7 78
(Miss J A Camacho) *prom: effrt over 2f out: one pce* **50/1**
1300 **7** *2 1/2* **Mystic Storm**[15] [4125] 3-8-5 **72** .... KDarley 3 65
(Lady Herries) *trckd ldrs: t.k.h: hung lft and lost pl over 1f out: eased ins last* **6/1**[3]
2U12 **8** *4* **Advancement**[27] [3789] 3-8-6 **73** .... TonyHamilton 9 57
(R A Fahey) *w wnr: t.k.h: wknd appr fnl f* **10/1**
1- **9** *5* **Snow Crystal (IRE)**[416] [3054] 3-9-5 **86** .... JimmyFortune 4 59
(J H M Gosden) *dwlt: hdwy over 3f out: hung lft and wknd over 1f out: eased ins last* **5/1**[2]
4644 **P** **Heureux (USA)**[14] [4172] 3-8-10 **77** .... RobertWinston 11 —
(J Howard Johnson) *hdwy on outside to chse ldrs over 5f out: lost pl over 2f out: eased and sn t.o: p.u over 1f out* **20/1**

1m 46.33s (0.63) **Going Correction** +0.25s/f (Good) **10** Ran SP% **113.2**
Speed ratings (Par 104):106,103,101,100,99 99,97,93,88,—
CSF £29.60 CT £188.15 TOTE £4.00: £1.60, £2.60, £2.20; EX 23.20.
Owner Hamdan Al Maktoum **Bred** Shadwell Estate Company Limited **Trained** Newmarket, Suffolk

FOCUS
A decent handicap and sound enough form rated through the third.

NOTEBOOK
Shumookh(IRE), a half-brother to the stable's Epsom Oaks winner Eswarah, was allowed to set his own pace on his handicap bow and just his third career start. He went clear once in line for home and, with even better to come, he should continue to give a good account of himself especially going left-handed. (op 7-2)
Bonnie Prince Blue, fitted with a rope halter, has slipped 6lb down the rtaings this year. Appreciating the easier ground, he stuck on in pursuit of the winner but was never going to get in a blow. (op 5-1)
Speedy Sam, raised 3lb after his Southwell maiden race success, has yet to finish out of the first three in five career starts. (op 9-1)
Pab Special(IRE), a maiden after 11 previous starts, continually swished his tail in the paddock but in the race itself he seemed to do nothing wrong.
Collateral Damage(IRE), 7lb higher than York, was back after a three-month break and he would have appreciated much softer ground. (tchd 11-2)
Skyelady, absent since May, ran with credit and is slipping to a more realistic mark. (op 40-1)
Mystic Storm, dropping back in trip, was far too keen for his own good. (op 8-1)
Advancement Official explanation: jockey said gelding ran too free in early stages
Snow Crystal(IRE), winner in maiden company at Yarmouth in June last year, never really threatened and after hanging once in line for home she was eventually allowed to complete in her own time. Bred in the purple, this must have been a huge let-down to connections. (op 8-1)
Heureux(USA) Official explanation: jockey said colt had a breathing problem

4635 UNISON SAVE PONTEFRACT INFIRMARY MAIDEN STKS 1m 4y
4:50 (4:51) (Class 4) 3-Y-O+ **£5,829** (£1,734; £866; £432) **Stalls** Low

Form RPR
23 **1** **Mosharref (IRE)**[11] [4247] 3-9-1 .... RHills 13 88+
(B W Hills) *trckd ldrs: rdn to ld over 1f out: hld on wl towards fin* **8/13**[1]
3432 **2** *3/4* **My Arch**[13] [4203] 4-9-2 78 .... AndrewMullen[(5)] 7 79
(K A Ryan) *chsd ldrs: reminders over 3f out: kpt on fnl f: a hld* **9/4**[2]
3 *shd* **Cooperstown** 3-9-1 .... TomEaves 5 78
(J Howard Johnson) *s.i.s: bhd: gd hdwy on outer over 2f out: hung lft over 1f out: styd on same pce ins last* **20/1**
4060 **4** *12* **Zed Candy (FR)**[59] [2795] 3-9-1 64 .... MickyFenton 10 50
(J T Stimpson) *w ldrs: wknd over 1f out* **20/1**
06 **5** *3/4* **Light Sentence**[106] [1493] 3-9-1 .... DeanMcKeown 6 48
(G A Swinbank) *in rr: kpt on fnl 2f: nvr nr ldrs* **14/1**[3]
00 **6** *2 1/2* **Hippolyte (USA)**[109] [1418] 3-8-10 .... J-PGuillambert 3 38
(J G Given) *w ldrs: led over 3f out: hdd over 2f out: lost pl over 1f out* **100/1**
0-F **7** *3* **Zell (IRE)**[8] [4382] 3-8-10 .... AdrianTNicholls 9 31
(E J Alston) *s.i.s: hdwy over 4f out: led over 2f out: hdd & wknd over 1f out* **66/1**
8 *1 1/2* **Kildare Sun (IRE)**[342] [5191] 4-9-7 .... DaleGibson 8 33
(J Mackie) *in rr: drvn 4f out: nvr a factor* **50/1**
00 **9** *10* **Auburndale**[52] [3022] 4-9-2 .... PJMcDonald[(5)] 2 10
(A Crook) *led tl over 3f out: lost pl over 2f out* **200/1**
0 **10** *2 1/2* **Orchard House (FR)**[23] [3916] 3-9-1 .... DerekMcGaffin 1 4
(J Jay) *prom: lost pl 3f out: sn bhd* **50/1**
06 **11** *nk* **It's Gone**[32] [3638] 3-9-1 .... JamieMackay 12 3
(J G Given) *t.k.h: trckd ldrs: stdd and dropped bk after 2f: bhd fnl 3f* **50/1**
12 *36* **Skodger (IRE)** 3-9-1 .... PhillipMakin 4 —
(G Woodward) *s.i.s: t.o 2f out: virtually p.u: btn 36l* **66/1**

1m 47.99s (2.29) **Going Correction** +0.25s/f (Good)
WFA 3 from 4yo 6lb **12** Ran SP% **119.2**
Speed ratings (Par 105):98,97,97,85,84 81,78,77,67,64 64,28
CSF £1.90 TOTE £1.50: £1.10, £1.40, £3.50; EX 2.40.
Owner Hamdan Al Maktoum **Bred** Shadwell Estate Company Limited **Trained** Lambourn, Berks

FOCUS
An uncompetitive maiden in which they went 20/1 bar three and the first three finished clear of what was mainly dead wood. The form is not rock solid and the runner-up is the best guide.
Skodger(IRE) Official explanation: jockey said colt had a breathing problem

4636 TREVOR WOODS MEMORIAL H'CAP 5f
5:20 (5:20) (Class 5) (0-70,69) 3-Y-O+ **£4,533** (£1,348; £674; £336) **Stalls** Low

Form RPR
0104 **1** **Sir Loin**[5] [4462] 5-8-2 **52** ....(v) DanielleMcCreery[(7)] 11 64
(N Tinkler) *chsd ldrs: c stands' side and led over 1f out: styd on wl* **11/1**
0063 **2** *2* **Throw The Dice**[9] [4324] 4-9-2 **64** ....(p) MarkLawson[(5)] 7 69
(D W Barker) *w ldr: led 2f out: hdd over 1f out: edgd rt and no ex* **14/1**
3200 **3** *1* **Special Gold**[9] [4324] 4-8-10 **53** ....(b) DavidAllan 8 54
(T D Easterby) *chsd ldrs: edgd rt and kpt on same pce fnl f* **20/1**
5060 **4** *1/2* **Safranine (IRE)**[7] [4401] 9-8-6 **54** .... AnnStokell[(5)] 15 53
(Miss A Stokell) *rr-div: hdwy on outer over 1f out: styd on wl ins last* **25/1**
0604 **5** *nk* **Coranglais**[8] [4361] 6-8-6 **49** oh2 ....(p) TomEaves 2 47+
(J M Bradley) *sn in rr and drvn along: hdwy over 1f out: kpt on wl ins last* **10/1**
6 *shd* **Rokocoko (IRE)**[28] [3774] 4-9-6 **63** ....(bt) JamieSpencer 18 61
(John A Quinn, Ire) *s.i.s: hdwy and c stands' side over 1f out: kpt on: nt rch ldrs* **8/1**[3]
0143 **7** *nk* **Hotham**[11] [4262] 3-9-10 **69** .... PatCosgrave 13 66
(N Wilson) *s.i.s: sn chsng ldrs: c stands' side over 1f out: kpt on same pce* **12/1**
0061 **8** *shd* **Catch The Cat (IRE)**[4] [4477] 7-9-4 **66** 6ex ....(b) GregFairley[(5)] 6 63+
(Robert Gray) *led tl 2f out: kpt on same pce fnl f* **10/1**
-000 **9** *3/4* **World At My Feet**[60] [2758] 4-7-13 **49** oh2 ....(t) SuzzanneFrance[(7)] 12 43+
(N Bycroft) *s.i.s: in rr: kpt on fnl 2f: nvr rchd ldrs* **50/1**
1040 **10** *nk* **Pomfret Lad**[17] [4085] 8-9-8 **68** ....(v) DNolan[(3)] 5 61
(J J Quinn) *chsd ldrs: upsides over 1f out: one pce* **12/1**
0124 **11** *3/4* **Namir (IRE)**[11] [4258] 4-9-8 **65** ....(vt) JohnEgan 3 55+
(S R Bowring) *mid-div: effrt over 2f out: nvr trbld ldrs* **9/2**[1]
0622 **12** *1/2* **Weakest Link**[1] [4611] 5-8-6 **49** oh3 ....(p) PaulQuinn 4 37
(E J Alston) *in tch on inner: one pce fnl 2f* **11/1**
00 **13** *1/2* **Alexia Rose (IRE)**[44] [3245] 4-9-0 **57** .... TonyHamilton 1 43
(A Berry) *chsd ldrs on inner: one pce fnl 2f* **33/1**
2045 **14** *1* **Mystery Pips**[47] [3172] 6-9-5 **62** ....(v) KimTinkler 16 45
(N Tinkler) *mid-div: c stands' side over 1f out: nvr a factor* **16/1**
0606 **15** *1* **Salviati (USA)**[21] [3988] 9-9-1 **58** .... TedDurcan 10 37
(J M Bradley) *s.s: nvr on terms* **14/1**
0000 **16** *1 1/4* **Rectangle (IRE)**[11] [4258] 6-8-6 **49** oh3 .... DeanMcKeown 14 24
(Micky Hammond) *mid-div: c stands' side over 1f out: nvr a factor* **66/1**
0503 **17** *4* **Whinhill House**[5] [4453] 6-9-7 **64** ....(p) RobertWinston 9 24
(D W Barker) *mid-div: lost pl over 1f out: eased ins last* **13/2**[2]

64.37 secs (0.57) **Going Correction** +0.25s/f (Good)
WFA 3 from 4yo+ 2lb **17** Ran SP% **127.1**
Speed ratings (Par 103):105,101,100,99,98 98,98,98,96,96 95,94,93,92,90 88,82
CSF £154.60 CT £3063.98 TOTE £14.40: £3.20, £4.50, £5.60, £5.10; EX 307.70 Place 6 £57.17, Place 5 £46.29..
Owner W F Burton **Bred** Britton House Stud And C Gregson **Trained** Langton, N Yorks

FOCUS
A moderate sprint handicap in which they ended up racing all over the track. The winner was the first to swing wide in the straight, Coranglais did best of those that stuck to the far side. The winner is rated as having run to his best.
Salviati(USA) Official explanation: jockey said gelding had no more to give
T/Plt: £28.80 to a £1 stake. Pool: £60,588.90. 1,531.85 winning tickets. T/Qpdt: £17.60 to a £1 stake. Pool: £2,900.60. 121.55 winning tickets. WG

4637 - 4638a (Foreign Racing) - See Raceform Interactive

3961 LEOPARDSTOWN (L-H)
Sunday, August 20

OFFICIAL GOING: Good to yielding

4639a BALLYROAN STKS (LISTED RACE) 1m 4f
3:25 (3:26) 3-Y-O+ **£22,448** (£6,586; £3,137; £1,068)

RPR
1 **Kastoria (IRE)**[50] [3107] 5-9-9 110 ....(t) MJKinane 1 113
(John M Oxx, Ire) *mod 2nd: tk clsr order appr st: led over 1f out: rdn clr: kpt on* **4/5**[1]
2 *3* **Foreign Affairs**[17] [4081] 8-9-10 111 .... DPMcDonough 5 110
(Sir Mark Prescott) *led: sn clr: drvn along fr 1/2-way: reduced advantage u.p ent st: hdd over 1f out: kpt on* **11/4**[2]
3 *1* **Good Surprise**[50] [3107] 5-9-7 106 ....(b) KJManning 4 105
(J S Bolger, Ire) *mod 3rd: 4th and rdn 1 1/2f out: kpt on ins fnl f* **12/1**
4 *shd* **Road To Mandalay (IRE)**[32] [3660] 3-8-11 92 .... KFallon 3 104
(A P O'Brien, Ire) *hld up in rr: tk clsr order after 1/2-way: 4th whn briefly short of room early st: 3rd and no imp over 1f out: one pce* **7/1**[3]
5 *dist* **Power Elite (IRE)**[156] [6210] 6-9-7 103 .... FMBerry 2 —
(Noel Meade, Ire) *chsd ldrs in 4th: dropped to rr after 1/2-way: rdn and wknd fr 3f out: eased fnl f: t.o* **10/1**

2m 33.1s **Going Correction** -0.15s/f (Firm)
WFA 3 from 5yo+ 10lb **5** Ran SP% **111.5**
Speed ratings: 116,114,113,113,—
CSF £3.29 TOTE £1.90: £1.50, £1.50; DF 3.20.
Owner H H Aga Khan **Bred** H H Aga Khan's Stud's S C **Trained** Currabeg, Co Kildare

NOTEBOOK
Kastoria(IRE) cemented her position as a leading contender for the Irish St Leger with a fluent success under the penalty that she picked up for last month's Curragh Cup success. She travelled well throughout and, despite idling in the closing stages, won with plenty to spare. She goes for the Classic with every chance of getting involved. (op 9/10 tchd 1/1)
Foreign Affairs was bidding for his third Listed victory of the season, and he ran an honourable race in defeat. He was bustled along to get to the front and was five lengths clear at halfway. He came under strong pressure before the turn in and despite battling on, could not fend off the winner. There are more races to be won with him at this level on this evidence. (op 5/2)
Good Surprise turned in a creditable effort and finished closer to the winner than when fifth in the Curragh Cup. He looks capable of making his mark at Listed level. (op 10/1)
Road To Mandalay(IRE) had plenty to do on official ratings and ran respectably, only narrowly losing out in the battle for third. He probably needs to improve to win at this level. (op 6/1)

4641a DESMOND STKS (GROUP 3) 1m
4:25 (4:26) 3-Y-O+ **£31,379** (£9,172; £4,344; £1,448)

RPR
1 **King Jock (USA)**[13] [4213] 5-9-7 106 .... PShanahan 4 113
(R J Osborne, Ire) *hld up: prog into 4th 2f out: rdn to ld under 1f out: r.o wl* **20/1**
2 *3/4* **Arch Rebel (USA)**[41] [3371] 5-9-7 110 .... JMurtagh 7 111
(Noel Meade, Ire) *mod 4th: 5th early st: swtchd to inner 1 1/2f out: kpt on wl ins fnl f* **5/2**[1]
3 *1* **Arabian Prince (USA)**[13] [4213] 3-9-1 107 .... KFallon 3 109
(A P O'Brien, Ire) *trckd ldrs in 3rd: swtchd to inner 1 1/2f out: 3rd and kpt on ins fnl f* **3/1**[2]
4 *1/2* **Latino Magic (IRE)**[19] [4031] 6-9-7 106 .... RMBurke 5 108
(R J Osborne, Ire) *hld up: 6th into st: kpt on wl ins fnl f* **14/1**
5 *4 1/2* **Heliostatic (IRE)**[7] [4407] 3-9-4 114 .... KJManning 2 105+
(J S Bolger, Ire) *led: rdn and strly pressed appr st: hdd under 1f out: sn no ex and eased* **10/3**[3]
6 *nk* **Common World (USA)**[14] [4190] 7-9-12 110 .... FMBerry 6 103
(T Hogan, Ire) *dwlt: sn cl up in 2nd: rdn to chal appr st: ev ch 1 1/2f out: no ex and wknd fnl f* **5/1**
7 *12* **Mon Michel (IRE)**[71] [2471] 3-9-1 102 .... DPMcDonough 1 74
(Kevin Prendergast, Ire) *hld up in 5th: dropped to rr ent st: sn no ex: eased fnl f* **10/1**

1m 40.8s **Going Correction** -0.15s/f (Firm)
WFA 3 from 5yo+ 6lb **7** Ran SP% **113.8**
Speed ratings: 112,111,110,109,105 104,92
CSF £69.22 TOTE £43.00: £18.20, £2.40; DF 92.40.

Owner Thistle Bloodstock Limited **Bred** Kenneth L Ramsey & Sarah K Ramsey **Trained** Naas, Co Kildare

NOTEBOOK

King Jock(USA) caused a surprise in this open contest. He had not previously scored outside handicap company, but he had won off a mark of 102 in Dubai in January and had also run well there in a Group 2 event. He had clearly benefited from his run at Cork earlier this month after a break and, normally a fast-ground performer, handled the easy ground well. He will return to Dubai again this winter, but before that he could run in the Concorde Stakes at Tipperary in October, and there are races in England that are under consideration. (op 16/1)

Arch Rebel(USA) was settled in fourth and looked as though he would struggle to get involved heading into the final quarter of a mile, but he did run on well in the closing stages without getting to the winner. This represented a significant improvement on his last run, and he should be able to add to his Stakes race haul in the near future. (op 100/30)

Arabian Prince(USA) had finished four lengths in front of the winner when running second in the Platinum Stakes. He tracked the leaders in third and moved into a challenging position with over a furlong to run, but he could do no more in the closing stages. He looks capable of making his mark at Stakes level and may prefer quicker ground. (op 11/4)

Latino Magic(IRE) looked a possible threat when launching his challenge on the outside with over a furlong to run, but he just could not quite get to the leaders. He is another that would have preferred quicker ground. (op 12/1)

Heliostatic(IRE) was having his first run over amile since contesting the Irish 2000 Guineas, and he set a good pace but could do no more once headed. He won the Meld Stakes over ten furlongs and may need to return to that trip. (op 3/1)

Common World(USA) was somewhat disappointing over a trip and ground that should have suited. (op 11/2 tchd 6/1)

4640 - 4643a (Foreign Racing) - See Raceform Interactive

4621 DEAUVILLE (R-H)

Sunday, August 20

OFFICIAL GOING: Turf course - very soft; all-weather - standard

4644a DARLEY PRIX MORNY (GROUP 1) (C&F) — 6f

2:20 (2:21) 2-Y-O **£137,924** (£55,179; £27,590; £13,783; £6,903)

			RPR
1		**Dutch Art**59 [2771] 2-9-0 ... CSoumillon 8 (P W Chapple-Hyam) *lw: in touch on outside, close 2nd halfway, led 1 1/2f out, ridden final f, ran on well to line, ridden out* **4/1**3	117+
2	1	**Magic America (USA)**28 [3777] 2-8-11 ... C-PLemaire 1 (Mme C Head-Maarek, France) *held up, last halfway, headway on inside over 1 1/2f out, ridden 1f out, stayed on steadily to line, took 2nd post* **14/1**	111
3	hd	**Excellent Art**49 [3126] 2-9-0 ... LDettori 5 (N A Callaghan) *prominent, 3rd halfway, ridden 1 1/2f out, ran on to press winner 100 yards out, no extra close home* **7/2**2	113
4	3	**Sandwaki (USA)**49 [3132] 2-9-0 ... OPeslier 9 (C Laffon-Parias, France) *led to 1 1/2f out, one pace, just held on for 4th* **5/4**1	104
5	nse	**Golden Titus (IRE)**28 [3777] 2-9-0 ... SLandi 3 (A Renzoni, Italy) *towards rear, disputing 5th halfway, ridden approaching final f, stayed on steadily, just missed 4th* **11/1**	104
6	snk	**Beauty Is Truth**21 [3990] 2-8-11 ...(b) TThulliez 7 (Robert Collet, France) *held up, disputing 5th halfway, driven over 1 1/2f out, unable to quicken* **28/1**	101
7	2	**Boccassini (GER)**28 [3777] 2-8-11 ... DBonilla 6 (M Rulec, Germany) *midfield, 4th halfway, ridden on outside over 1 1/2f out, no impression* **7/1**	95

1m 13.6s **Going Correction** +0.30s/f (Good) **7** Ran SP% **117.6**

Speed ratings: 108,106,106,102,102 102,99

PARI-MUTUEL: WIN 5.50; PL 3.70, 4.00; SF 39.10.

Owner Mrs Susan Roy **Bred** Cromlech Bloodstock **Trained** Newmarket, Suffolk

FOCUS

The absence of Holy Roman Emperor on account of the testing conditions robbed this of some of its interest, but it was a highly competitive affair nonetheless and Dutch Art put up one of the juvenile performances of the season so far, a provisional RPR of 116 putting him upsides the filly Sander Camillo at the head of the list.

NOTEBOOK

Dutch Art, who looked well in the paddock, was always travelling well within himself early on and took the advantage one and a half out, before staying on to win with something in hand. He looks likely to improve further and now heads for the Middle Park Stakes. His connections feel he will be even more of a force to be reckoned with on good or faster ground.

Magic America(USA), without blinkers on this occasion, ran an excellent race. Held up in the early stages, she made a forward move just before the final furlong and was running on well at the end. A longer trip should certainly be an advantage, but in the short term she goes for the Cheveley Park Stakes at Newmarket.

Excellent Art, who looked really fit, made his effort at the furlong marker but never made it to the front and was eventually beaten narrowly for second. Connections stated that he stumbled inside the final furlong and this probably cost the colt the runner-up position.

Sandwaki(USA) was a very disappointing favourite. Sent to the front soon after the start, he ran a little freely but was swamped by several other runners at the furlong marker before dropping out of contention. His jockey felt that the very soft ground was against the horse and there are no immediate plans.

4645a DARLEY PRIX DE LA NONETTE (GROUP 3) (FILLIES) — 1m 2f

2:50 (2:54) 3-Y-O **£27,586** (£11,034; £8,276; £5,517; £2,759)

			RPR
1		**Germance (USA)**70 [2491] 3-9-0 ... IMendizabal 3 (J-C Rouget, France) *raced in 4th, ran on 1 1/2f out on far side to lead 1f out, quickened clear final 100 yards, pushed out* **4/9**1	115+
2	3	**Mysterious Lina (FR)**22 [3968] 3-9-0 ... FSpanu 4 (P Demercastel, France) *raced in 3rd, driven to challenge final f, outpaced by winner but stayed on to take 2nd close home* **6/1**3	105
3	snk	**Ballet Pacifica (USA)**35 3-9-0 ... OPeslier 1 (J-C Rouget, France) *raced in 2nd, shaken up entering straight, led 1 1/2f out to 1f out, ridden when headed, no extra and lost 2nd close home* **7/1**	105
4	2	**Alix Road (FR)**70 [2491] 3-9-0 ... TThulliez 5 (Mme M Bollack-Badel, France) *held up in last, never in challenging position* **9/2**2	101
5	8	**Keladora (USA)**70 [2491] 3-9-0 ... SCoffigny 2 (J-C Rouget, France) *led to 1 1/2f out, eased final f* **100/1**	87

2m 11.2s **Going Correction** +0.40s/f (Good) **5** Ran SP% **115.2**

Speed ratings: 114,111,111,109,103

PARI-MUTUEL: WIN 1.40 (coupled with Keladora); PL 1.10, 1.60; SF 6.10.

Owner Nelson Radwan **Bred** Edmund J Loder **Trained** Pau, France

NOTEBOOK

Germance(USA), beaten only by Confidential Lady in the Prix de Diane in five previous starts, posted a very impressive performance, proving in a different class to her four rivals and quickening much the best at the end of a slowly-run contest. Her main target is now the Breeders' Cup Filly and Mare Turf, and either the Prix de L'Opera or Queen Elizabeth II Cup at Keeneland will be taken in before then.

Mysterious Lina(FR) just managed to get second and appears to be still on the upgrade. She can make the breakthrough at this level before the end of the season.

Ballet Pacifica(USA), tucked in behind the leader early on, joined battle with the runner-up at the furlong marker and only lost second place with 50 yards left to run.

Alix Road(FR), last for the early part of this race, was brought with a run up the centre of the track but never looked like threatening the first three past the post.

4646a DARLEY PRIX JEAN ROMANET (GROUP 2) (F&M) — 1m 2f

3:20 (3:21) 4-Y-O+ **£51,103** (£19,724; £9,414; £6,276; £3,138)

			RPR
1		**Satwa Queen (FR)**177 [510] 4-8-11 ... TThulliez 7 (J De Roualle, France) *raced in 3rd, took closer order entering straight, pushed along 1 1/2f out, led 1f out, ridden and ran on well to line* **6/1**	118
2	1 1/2	**Sweet Stream (ITY)**252 [6549] 6-8-11 ... TGillet 5 (J E Hammond, France) *raced in 4th, pushed along approaching straight, driven and ran on from over 1f out, no extra close home* **5/1**3	115
3	1	**Red Bloom**50 [3105] 5-8-11 ... RyanMoore 1 (Sir Michael Stoute) *first to show, raced in 2nd, joined leader entering straight, led 1 1/2f out to 1f out, no extra close home* **13/8**1	113
4	2	**In Clover**21 [3991] 4-8-11 ... DBonilla 4 (F Head, France) *held up in 5th, stayed on from over 1f out to take 4th inside final f* **7/1**	110
5	2	**Strawberry Dale (IRE)**94 [1804] 4-8-11 ... LDettori 2 (J D Bethell) *soon led, joined straight, headed 1 1/2f out, ridden and weakened final f* **11/4**2	106
6	8	**Here She Comes (FR)**5 [4463] 4-8-11 ... CSoumillon 6 (Mme C Martens, France) *raced in last, never a factor* **50/1**	92

2m 11.9s **Going Correction** +0.40s/f (Good) **6** Ran SP% **110.2**

Speed ratings: 111,109,109,107,105 99

PARI-MUTUEL: WIN 6.10; PL 2.60, 2.60; SF 25.50.

Owner The Lamprell Partnership **Bred** Societe Sogir **Trained** France

NOTEBOOK

Satwa Queen(FR) posted a fine effort considering she had not run since finishing second at Nad Al Sheba in February. She was tucked in behind the two English runners before quickening impressively approaching the furlong marker. The Prix de L'Opera and EP Taylor Stakes are now on the cards for this talented individual, who clearly runs well fresh.

Sweet Stream(ITY), off the track since the Hong Kong Vase last December, ran well up to expectations and looks likely to pick up another Group race before the end of the season. By no means given a hard race, she came with a progressive run up the centre of the track from one and a half out. A supplementary entry, she will now be aimed at the Prix Vermeille and should be spot on for that Group 1 contest.

Red Bloom ran on well but was one-paced and did hang a little to the right inside the final furlong. The very soft ground was certainly against her.

In Clover, second-last early on, made some late progress but has been disappointing this season. This was her first run over this distance and she may be better back over a mile

Strawberry Dale(IRE) took the field along at a sensible pace until early in the straight but failed to run on through the final two furlongs. She had not been out since May and her jockey felt that she needed the outing. She is a possible for the Blandford Stakes.

4647a DARLEY PRIX KERGORLAY (GROUP 2) — 1m 7f

3:50 (3:50) 3-Y-O+ **£51,103** (£19,724; £9,414; £6,276; £3,138)

			RPR
1		**Lord Du Sud (FR)**112 [1332] 5-9-4 ... IMendizabal 5 (J-C Rouget, France) *made all, ridden clear 1 1/2f out, easily* **9/4**2	119+
2	5	**Policy Maker (IRE)**56 [2914] 6-9-6 ... OPeslier 4 (E Lellouche, France) *raced in last, headway entering straight, pushed along and ran on to go 2nd over 1f out, kept on, not pace of winner* **15/8**1	116
3	2 1/2	**Le Miracle (GER)**24 [3887] 5-9-4 ... DBoeuf 3 (W Baltromei, Germany) *raced in 3rd, disputing 2nd halfway, 3rd straight, ridden and went 2nd 1 1/2f out, no extra under pressure* **10/1**	112
4	1	**Soledad (IRE)**65 [2629] 6-9-4 ... RonanThomas 1 (G Cherel, France) *raced in 4th, driven entering straight, quickly beaten* **14/1**	111
5	2 1/2	**Reefscape**17 [4081] 5-9-8 ... CSoumillon 2 (A Fabre, France) *raced in 2nd, pushed along over 4f out and struggled to hold place, 2nd straight, one pace from over 1 1/2f out* **5/2**3	112

3m 20.7s **Going Correction** +0.40s/f (Good) **5** Ran SP% **109.9**

Speed ratings: 114,111,110,109,108

PARI-MUTUEL: WIN 2.40; PL 1.30, 1.50; SF 4.60.

Owner Mme B Hermelin **Bred** Alexandre Guerini **Trained** Pau, France

NOTEBOOK

Lord Du Sud(FR) appeared to really enjoy himself on the very soft ground on his return from a three-month break. He passed the post on his own and will probably now go directly for the Prix du Cadran.

Policy Maker(IRE) was given a waiting ride but never got in a blow at the winner. He did make some late progress but was a little disappointing. He might not have stayed and it will be no surprise if he returned to a mile and a half next time out, possibly in a race like the Prix Foy.

Le Miracle(GER) appeared to be going well in second place until the straight, where he could find only the one pace. This was rather disappointing and he may want better ground.

Soledad(IRE), held up at the tail of the field, could not accelerate with the others when things quickened up in the straight and was a little out of his depth.

Reefscape was being niggled a fair way from home and ran a long way below form.

1014 BREMEN

Sunday, August 20

OFFICIAL GOING: Good

4648a WALTHER J JACOBS-STUTENPREIS (GROUP 3) (F&M) — 1m 3f

3:40 (3:51) 3-Y-O+ **£22,069** (£6,897; £3,448; £2,069)

			RPR
1		**Wurfscheibe (GER)**30 [3719] 4-9-5 ... TMundry 3 (P Rau, Germany) *prominent, 2nd straight, ridden to lead 1f out, driven clear final f* **7/2**	112
2	2 1/2	**Quelle Amore (GER)**28 [3776] 3-8-8 ... EPedroza 6 (A Wohler, Germany) *led to 1f out, one pace* **34/10**3	106

3 1 1/4 **Nordtanzerin (GER)**[35] [3579] 3-8-8 .... WMongil 1 104
(P Schiergen, Germany) *prominent, 3rd straight, stayed on at same pace final 2f* **22/10**[1]

4 1 3/4 **Ioannina**[37] [3515] 3-8-8 .... ASuborics 4 101
(P Schiergen, Germany) *raced in 4th, ridden and one pace final 1 1/2f* **27/10**[2]

5 1 **Fair Breeze (GER)**[133] 3-8-8 .... HanaMouchova 7 100
(P Vovcenko, Germany) *held up in rear, never a factor* **274/10**

6 nk **Intrigued**[14] [4179] 4-9-5 .... FilipMinarik 2 101
(Sir Mark Prescott) *raced in 5th on inside, ridden and not quicken from over 1 1/2f out* **37/10**

7 3/4 **Smart Move (GER)**[77] [2280] 4-9-5 .... FGeroux 5 100
(H Blume, Germany) *always in rear* **22/1**

2m 23.15s
WFA 3 from 4yo 9lb **7** Ran SP% **132.4**
(including 10 Euro stake): WIN 45; PL 12, 15, 12; SF 243.
Owner Gestut Ravensberg **Bred** Gestut Ravensberg **Trained** Germany

NOTEBOOK
Wurfscheibe(GER) was driven clear in the closing stages to register her third career victory at this level. The Preis von Europa or a race at Longchamp over Arc weekend are now being considered.
Intrigued simply ran poorly without any obvious explanation. Asked for her effort with two furlongs to run, she did not pick up.

4383 DUSSELDORF (R-H)
Sunday, August 20

OFFICIAL GOING: Soft

4649a GROSSER PREIS DER STADTSPARKASSE DUSSELDORF (LISTED RACE) (F&M) 7f
3:50 (4:02) 3-Y-O+ **£8,966** (£4,138; £2,759; £1,379)

RPR

1 **Delora (GER)**[87] [1974] 5-9-4 .... KKerekes 6 106
(M Weber, Germany)

2 2 1/2 **Priere**[59] [2799] 4-9-0 .... J-MBreux 9 95
(N Clement, France)

3 nk **Heat Of The Night**[106] [1477] 4-9-0 .... THellier 7 94
(P W Chapple-Hyam) *racd in 4th on outside, wnt 2nd halfway, led 1 1/2f out, strongly pressed whn ducked rt ins fnl f, hdd and one pace (44/10)*

4 3 **Quadrupa (GER)**[87] [1974] 4-9-0 .... ADeVries 4 86
(C Von Der Recke, Germany)

5 shd **Neila (GER)**[292] [6219] 3-8-7 .... AStarke 8 84
(W Hickst, Germany)

6 2 **Nebraska Lady (IRE)**[22] [3953] 4-9-0 .... RichardMullen 2 81
(E J O'Neill) *raced in 5th on inside, no progress final 2f (177/10)*

7 shd **Annatira (GER)**[32] [3661] 5-9-2 .... ABoschert 5 83
(E Kurdu, Germany)

8 2 1/2 **Alte Sage (GER)**[100] 3-8-7 .... AngelaRosenbaum 3 72
(P Rau, Germany)

1m 29.67s
WFA 3 from 4yo+ 5lb **8** Ran
TOTE (including 10 Euro stake): WIN 84; PL 22, 22, 22; SF 398.
Owner Stall Tobago **Bred** Frau Dr J Denig **Trained** Germany

NOTEBOOK
Heat Of The Night hit the front with a furlong and a half to run but, having shown a tendency to edge left away from the whip, Hellier pulled his whip through and her reaction to two sharp left-handed cracks was to swerve right. The winner may have prevailed even if she had kept straight, but her waywardness definitely cost her second and connections were lucky that no serious interference was caused.
Nebraska Lady(IRE) had no excuses and does not look up to this class of competition.

4349 AYR (L-H)
Monday, August 21

OFFICIAL GOING: Good to soft (good in places)
Wind: Light, against Weather: Fine

4650 EUROPEAN BREEDERS FUND KIRKOSWALD MAIDEN STKS 7f 50y
2:00 (2:00) (Class 4) 2-Y-O **£5,181** (£1,541; £770; £384) **Stalls** Low

Form RPR

0 1 **Massive (IRE)**[22] [3976] 2-9-3 .... RobertWinston 8 80
(M R Channon) *hld up in tch: rdn 3f out: hdwy over 2f out: led 1f out: r.o and in command towards fin* **7/1**

22 2 2 **Gazboolou**[35] [3581] 2-9-3 .... PatCosgrave 5 75
(K R Burke) *trckd ldrs: led over 2f out: hdd 1f out: nt qckn towards fin* **7/4**[2]

4 3 2 1/2 **Captain Jacksparra (IRE)**[12] [4260] 2-9-3 .... NCallan 1 69
(K A Ryan) *trckd ldrs: effrt and ev ch fr over 2f out tl no ex ins fnl f* **13/8**[1]

3 4 5 **Tartan Tie**[27] [3809] 2-9-3 .... JoeFanning 7 56+
(M Johnston) *led: rdn and hdd over 2f out: wknd over 1f out* **11/2**[3]

0 5 4 **Fire In Cairo (IRE)**[103] [1595] 2-8-12 .... RoystonFfrench 9 41
(P C Haslam) *racd keenly: prom: rdn over 2f out: wknd over 1f out* **33/1**

4 6 3 1/2 **Rockfonic**[19] [4055] 2-9-3 .... PhillipMakin 4 38
(J R Weymes) *racd keenly: hld up: rdn 3f out: nvr on terms* **20/1**

0 7 nk **Bad Boy Al (IRE)**[12] [4260] 2-8-12 .... MarkLawson(5) 3 37
(D W Barker) *dwlt: pushed along over 3f out: a bhd* **100/1**

1m 33.25s (0.53) **Going Correction** -0.075s/f (Good) **7** Ran SP% **111.0**
Speed ratings (Par 96):93,90,87,82,77 73,73
CSF £18.59 TOTE £9.40: £2.50, £1.60; EX 33.20.
Owner Sheikh Ahmed Al Maktoum **Bred** Mrs S Lloyd And Dr M Klay **Trained** West Ilsley, Berks

FOCUS
A fair maiden. Sound form, with the second quite consistent.

NOTEBOOK
Massive(IRE), down the field in a decent maiden on his debut at Newmarket, was nibbled at in the market beforehand and, having travelled well on the outside, he battled his way to the front a furlong out before staying on well. This was obviously a big step forward and the Derby entrant looks sure to improve further for a step up to a mile later in the season. (op 8-1)
Gazboolou had shown fair form in two previous placed efforts and he looked sure to be suited by this step up to seven furlongs. He held every chance and pulled nicely clear of the favourite, but the winner improved past him. (op 13-8 tchd 2-1, 6-4 and 9-4 in places)
Captain Jacksparra(IRE) shaped with promise on his debut at Pontefract, albeit beaten nine lengths, and he was made favourite in the hope he had improved on that effort. Representing a yard with plenty of two-year-old talent this season, he was ultimately disappointing, failing to find much off the bridle. He may be worth another chance, but hardly looks progressive. (op 2-1)
Tartan Tie, a pleasing third at this course on his debut, failed to build on that effort and may be more of a nursery type. (op 7-2)

4651 CAMPBELTOWN BAR STEWART SCOTT MEMORIAL H'CAP 1m 2f
2:30 (2:30) (Class 6) (0-60,60) 3-Y-O **£3,238** (£963; £481; £240) **Stalls** Low

Form RPR

2034 1 **Wednesdays Boy (IRE)**[48] [3167] 3-8-13 **52**........(p) RobertWinston 2 61+
(P D Niven) *hld up: hdwy whn rdn and swtchd lft over 2f out: sn hmpd whn nt clr run: edgd rt and str run ins fnl f to ld cl home* **7/2**[1]

3114 2 nk **River Logic (IRE)**[9] [4353] 3-9-6 **59**........ SilvestreDeSousa 12 64
(A D Brown) *midfield: hdwy over 2f out: sn wnt 2nd and hung lft: led ins fnl f: hdd cl home* **7/2**[1]

-560 3 1 1/4 **Princess Of Aeneas (IRE)**[19] [4060] 3-9-4 **57**........ TonyHamilton 3 60
(I Semple) *s.s: racd keenly in rr: rdn over 3f out: hdwy over 2f out: r.o u.p towards fin* **14/1**

5131 4 1 1/4 **Moonlight Fantasy (IRE)**[12] [4255] 3-8-12 **51**........ KimTinkler 4 52
(N Tinkler) *led: rdn over 1f out: hdd ins fnl f: no ex* **9/1**

0-00 5 3 **Missouri (USA)**[100] [1687] 3-8-10 **49**........ DanielTudhope 7 44
(G M Moore) *in tch: rdn over 2f out: one pce fr over 1f out* **9/1**

1462 6 9 **Hi Dancer**[36] [2379] 3-9-1 **54**........ PaulMulrennan 5 32
(P C Haslam) *prom: rdn 3f out: wknd ent fnl 2f* **6/1**[3]

2262 7 1 **Gigs Magic (USA)**[5] [4478] 3-8-13 **52**........ JoeFanning 11 28
(M Johnston) *stdd s: hld up: hdwy 6f out: rdn and wknd 2f out* **4/1**[2]

-003 8 3/4 **Silver Sail**[35] [3586] 3-8-2 **41**........ RoystonFfrench 9 16
(J S Wainwright) *trckd ldrs: rdn 3f out: wknd 2f out* **16/1**

000- 9 62 **Poutu (FR)**[309] [5921] 3-8-2 **41** oh11........ PaulQuinn 1 —
(A Berry) *trckd ldrs tl lost pl 6f out: bhd after: t.o* **100/1**

2m 12.01s (0.29) **Going Correction** -0.075s/f (Good) **9** Ran SP% **112.3**
Speed ratings (Par 98):95,94,93,92,90 83,82,81,32
CSF £15.13 CT £147.11 TOTE £6.60: £1.40, £1.60, £3.60; EX 24.40.
Owner The Wednesday Club **Bred** Sean Collins **Trained** Barton-le-Street, N Yorks

FOCUS
A modest handicap, but it should produce the odd winner at a similar level. The first three came from off the pace and the winner was value for a bit extra.
Gigs Magic(USA) Official explanation: trainer's rep said, regarding the poor form shown, gelding suffered interference at start and was carried wide on bend leaving the back straight

4652 LADIES DAY ON FRIDAY 15 SEPTEMBER H'CAP 7f 50y
3:05 (3:05) (Class 6) (0-65,65) 3-Y-O+ **£3,238** (£963; £481; £240) **Stalls** Low

Form RPR

6132 1 **Motu (IRE)**[13] [4233] 5-9-4 **55**........(v) RoystonFfrench 11 65
(I W McInnes) *trckd ldrs: led 2f out: edgd rt ins fnl f: drvn out* **6/1**[3]

0000 2 3/4 **Paris Heights**[5] [4467] 4-8-7 **49**........ MichaelJStainton(5) 5 57
(R M Whitaker) *in tch: rdn and hung lft fr over 2f out: impr over 1f out: wnt 2nd and ev ch ins fnl f: hld cl home* **25/1**

1102 3 1 1/4 **Bijou Dan**[9] [4355] 5-9-0 **56**........(b) DuranFentiman(5) 9 61
(W G Harrison) *in tch: rdn over 3f out: ev ch ins fnl f: nt qckn cl home* **6/1**[3]

5615 4 nk **California Laws**[41] [3390] 4-9-7 **61**........ BenSwarbrick(3) 8 65
(T D Barron) *hld up: rdn and hdwy over 2f out: styd on ins fnl f* **7/2**[1]

1020 5 nk **Boy Dancer (IRE)**[14] [4199] 3-9-1 **62**........ MarkLawson(5) 12 63
(D W Barker) *s.i.s: in rr: rdn over 2f out: hdwy over 1f out: styd on wl towards fin* **10/1**

-000 6 2 **Young Mr Grace (IRE)**[87] [1996] 6-9-3 **54**........ PatCosgrave 14 52
(B S Rothwell) *prom: rdn and ev ch 2f out: no ex ins fnl f* **12/1**

4602 7 2 1/2 **Franksalot (IRE)**[9] [4350] 6-9-11 **65**........ PatrickMathers(3) 10 57
(I W McInnes) *hld up: rdn over 2f out: kpt on fnl f: nvr trbld ldrs* **10/1**

3356 8 1 3/4 **Inch High**[9] [4355] 8-8-11 **48**........ DanielTudhope 1 35
(J S Goldie) *tracked ldrs: rdn over 2f out: wknd over 1f out* **4/1**[2]

00/4 9 1 **Ho Pang Yau**[9] [4350] 8-8-11 **48**........ LeeEnstone 7 33
(J S Goldie) *midfield: rdn over 2f out: sn wknd* **20/1**

-050 10 nk **Roscommon**[9] [4353] 3-9-4 **60**........(v[1]) RobertWinston 6 42
(I Semple) *dwlt: hld up: rdn 3f out: nvr on terms* **16/1**

5060 11 1/2 **Ailsa**[73] [2418] 4-8-10 **47**........ DeanMcKeown 4 30
(C W Thornton) *led: rdn and hdd 2f out: wknd over 1f out* **20/1**

3-00 12 3 **Jabraan (USA)**[4] [4518] 4-8-13 **50**........(be[1]) PaulQuinn 13 25
(D W Chapman) *towards rr: psuhed along 4f out: bhd fnl f* **66/1**

1m 31.99s (-0.73) **Going Correction** -0.075s/f (Good)
WFA 3 from 4yo+ 5lb **12** Ran SP% **117.4**
Speed ratings (Par 101):101,100,98,98,98 95,92,90,89,89 88,85
CSF £152.03 CT £957.10 TOTE £4.70: £1.90, £11.90, £2.20; EX 145.00.
Owner G Parkinson **Bred** J Hanly **Trained** Catwick, E Yorks

FOCUS
A moderate affair but the form should prove reliable. The winner returned to the level he showed early last year, and the second was back to form.

4653 TO WATCH RACING UK CALL 08700 506 949 H'CAP 1m
3:35 (3:35) (Class 4) (0-80,77) 3-Y-O+ **£6,477** (£1,927; £963; £481) **Stalls** Low

Form RPR

0000 1 **Anduril**[24] [3918] 5-8-13 **65**........(b) PatrickMathers(3) 5 74
(Miss M E Rowland) *hld up: hdwy over 2f out: led 1f out: kpt on wl* **25/1**

2241 2 1/2 **Dark Charm (FR)**[12] [4256] 7-9-8 **71**........ TonyHamilton 7 79
(R A Fahey) *in tch: rdn and impr over 1f out: wnt 2nd ins fnl f: styd on* **5/1**[3]

2525 3 3/4 **Middlemarch (IRE)**[9] [4379] 6-9-6 **69**........(p) DaleGibson 1 75
(J S Goldie) *in tch: rdn and nt qckn over 2f out: r.o ins fnl f* **9/2**[2]

3433 4 hd **Hula Ballew**[16] [4153] 6-10-0 **77**........ PhillipMakin 4 83
(M Dods) *trckd ldrs: rdn 2f out: ev ch ent fnl f: no ex cl home* **9/2**[2]

0625 5 2 **Sake (IRE)**[9] [4378] 4-9-12 **75**........ KimTinkler 8 76
(N Tinkler) *trckd ldrs: rdn to ld 2f out: hdd 1f out: no ex ins fnl f* **7/1**

0223 6 7 **Major Magpie (IRE)**[16] [4154] 4-9-6 **69**........ PaulFessey 6 54+
(M Dods) *s.s: rdn over 2f out: a bhd* **4/1**[1]

402 7 3 1/2 **Crosby Vision**[28] [3782] 3-9-4 **73**........ RobertWinston 3 50
(J R Weymes) *prom: rdn over 3f out: led over 2f out: sn hdd: wknd fnl f* **12/1**

4010 8 3 **Jordans Elect**[9] [4353] 6-9-0 **68**........(v) MarkLawson(5) 2 38
(T J Pitt) *sn led: rdn and hdd over 2f out: wknd over 1f out* **6/1**

1m 41.1s (-2.39) **Going Correction** -0.075s/f (Good)
WFA 3 from 4yo+ 6lb **8** Ran SP% **111.4**
Speed ratings (Par 105):108,107,106,106,104 97,94,91
CSF £137.31 CT £666.92 TOTE £25.40: £6.80, £1.40, £1.80; EX 236.30.
Owner M Shirley **Bred** Miss K Rausing **Trained** Lower Blidworth, Notts
■ The first Flat winner for Mandy Rowland.

FOCUS
A competitive handicap that went the way of rank outsider Anduril. Sound if unremarkable form.
Major Magpie(IRE) Official explanation: jockey said gelding missed the break

4654 DAWN CONSTRUCTION H'CAP — 1m 2f
4:10 (4:10) (Class 4) (0-85,81) 3-Y-0+

£7,478 (£2,239; £1,119; £560; £279; £140) **Stalls** Low

Form — RPR

1331 **1** — **Go Solo**[12] [4259] 5-10-0 **81** .... RobertWinston 1 — 91
(G A Swinbank) *a.p: rdn to ld over 1f out: kpt on wl* **5/2**[1]

0455 **2** ¾ **Torrens (IRE)**[14] [4203] 4-9-10 **77** .... TonyHamilton 4 — 86
(R A Fahey) *in tch: effrt 2f out: wnt 2nd 1f out: ev ch ins fnl f: nt qckn cl home* **5/1**[2]

4325 **3** 2 **Vicious Warrior**[23] [3939] 7-9-13 **80** .... DeanMcKeown 7 — 85
(R M Whitaker) *led: rdn and hdd over 1f out: styd on same pce fnl f* **13/2**

5416 **4** 1 **Chief Scout**[14] [4203] 4-9-10 **77** .... DanielTudhope 2 — 80
(I Semple) *a.p: rdn 3f out: kpt on same pce fnl f* **6/1**[3]

1126 **5** 1 ¼ **Mistress Twister**[5] [4476] 5-9-7 **74** .... PaulFessey 5 — 75
(T D Barron) *hld up: rdn over 2f out: styd on fnl f: nvr rchd ldrs* **15/2**

5011 **6** 4 **Wing Commander**[6] [4454] 7-9-2 **74** 6ex........(b) MarkLawson(5) 3 — 67
(I W McInnes) *restless in stalls: racd keenly: prom: rdn and ev ch 2f out: wknd ins fnl f* **8/1**

0034 **7** 8 **Scotty's Future (IRE)**[14] [4194] 8-8-9 **62** oh3........ FrancisNorton 6 — 40
(A Berry) *s.i.s: a bhd: eased whn n.d fnl f* **20/1**

0-44 **8** 20 **Always Baileys (IRE)**[32] [3665] 3-8-13 **74** .... JoeFanning 9 — 14
(M Johnston) *in tch: rdn over 3f out: wknd over 2f out* **10/1**

2m 9.12s (-2.60) **Going Correction** -0.075s/f (Good)
WFA 3 from 4yo+ 8lb — **8** Ran SP% **109.6**
Speed ratings (Par 105):107,106,104,104,103 99,93,77
CSF £13.49 CT £64.03 TOTE £3.70: £1.40, £1.90, £1.90; EX 17.40 Trifecta £46.30 Pool: £566.36 - 8.68 winning tickets..
Owner B Valentine **Bred** G Reed **Trained** Melsonby, N Yorks
FOCUS
A decent handicap won by the progressive Go Solo. Fair form for the grade, and sound too, with a personal best from the winner.

4655 KIDZ PLAY H'CAP — 6f
4:40 (4:40) (Class 5) (0-70,68) 3-Y-0+ — **£3,368** (£1,002; £500; £250) **Stalls** Low

Form — RPR

05 **1** — **Oeuf A La Neige**[18] [4091] 6-8-7 **49** oh4........ SilvestreDeSousa 10 — 59
(Miss L A Perratt) *hld up: rdn and hdwy over 2f out: led 1f out: r.o* **8/1**

-040 **2** ½ **High Voltage**[13] [4230] 5-9-10 **66** ....(t) PatCosgrave 7 — 74
(K R Burke) *a.p: rdn 2f out: ev ch ins fnl f: nt qckn cl home* **11/2**[3]

0602 **3** nk **Diamond Katie (IRE)**[4] [4507] 4-8-7 **49** .... KimTinkler 4 — 56
(N Tinkler) *midfield: hdwy over 2f out: sn rdn: ev ch ins fnl f: hld cl home* **5/1**[2]

6000 **4** 1 **Dispol Katie**[13] [4230] 5-9-11 **67** .... PaulFessey 8 — 71
(T D Barron) *in rr: rdn over 2f out: hdwy over 1f out: styd on ins fnl f* **7/1**

0-50 **5** nk **Zhitomir**[104] [1561] 8-9-10 **66** .... PhillipMakin 11 — 69
(M Dods) *in tch: rdn over 2f out: nt qckn over 1f out: styd on ins fnl f* **9/1**

U055 **6** ¾ **Flying Bantam (IRE)**[12] [4253] 5-9-5 **68** .... JamesReveley(7) 9 — 69
(R A Fahey) *midfield: hdwy over 2f out: rdn over 1f out: kpt on same pce ins fnl f* **11/4**[1]

0340 **7** shd **Flying Tackle**[22] [3988] 8-8-7 **49** oh1........(v) RoystonFfrench 2 — 50
(I W McInnes) *prom: rdn to ld over 2f out: hdd 1f out: no ex ins fnl f* **9/1**

0205 **8** ¾ **Obe Bold (IRE)**[16] [4157] 5-8-8 **50** .... FrancisNorton 5 — 48
(A Berry) *prom: rdn over 2f out: outpcd over 1f out* **12/1**

606 **9** 6 **Petross**[18] [4069] 3-8-9 **54** .... DeanMcKeown 3 — 34
(R M Whitaker) *s.i.s: bhd: c stand's side 1/2-way: nvr on terms* **25/1**

0-00 **10** 5 **Ochil Hills Dancer (IRE)**[19] [4059] 4-8-2 **49** oh12........ AndrewMullen(5) 1 — 14
(A Crook) *led: rdn and hdd over 2f out: wknd over 1f out: eased whn btn ins fnl f* **100/1**

1m 14.76s (1.09) **Going Correction** +0.275s/f (Good)
WFA 3 from 4yo+ 3lb — **10** Ran SP% **114.9**
Speed ratings (Par 103):103,102,101,100,100 99,99,98,90,83
CSF £50.78 CT £249.31 TOTE £9.90: £2.30, £1.90, £2.00; EX 87.20.
Owner Peter Tsim **Bred** Gainsborough Stud Management Ltd **Trained** Ayr, S Ayrshire
■ Stewards' Enquiry : Pat Cosgrave one-day ban: failed to keep straight from the stalls (Sep 1)
Kim Tinkler two-day ban: used whip with excessive frequency (Sep 1,3)
FOCUS
Just an average sprint handicap, but it should produce winners. Pretty ordinary form.

4656 RACING UK IS NOW £15 PER MONTH H'CAP — 5f
5:10 (5:11) (Class 6) (0-55,50) 3-Y-0 — **£3,071** (£906; £453) **Stalls** Low

Form — RPR

0000 **1** — **Trumpita**[14] [4199] 3-8-12 **40** .... DavidAllan 4 — 46
(T D Easterby) *a.p: rdn to ld over 1f out: r.o* **16/1**

5000 **2** 1 **Nautico**[4] [4524] 3-8-12 **40** .... RoystonFfrench 15 — 42
(Miss L A Perratt) *towards rr: rdn 2f out: hdwy 1f out: r.o ins fnl f: nrst fin* **16/1**

0060 **3** ¾ **Nilsatisoptimum (USA)**[11] [4296] 3-9-3 **45**........(t) SilvestreDeSousa 13 — 44
(M Mullineaux) *chsd ldrs: rdn 2f out: swtchd lft over 1f out: kpt on same pce ins fnl f* **16/1**

0022 **4** nk **Megalo Maniac**[9] [4354] 3-9-5 **47** .... TonyHamilton 9 — 45
(R A Fahey) *in tch: rdn and outpcd 3f out: styd on ins fnl f* **11/4**[1]

0000 **5** shd **Rainbow Prince**[14] [4199] 3-9-2 **44** .... DanielTudhope 6 — 42
(A Dickman) *hld up: rdn 2f out: hdwy and edgd lft over 1f out: kpt on ins fnl f* **20/1**

0004 **6** hd **Martharum**[14] [4201] 3-8-12 **40** ....(p) GrahamGibbons 12 — 37
(J J Quinn) *led for 1f: remained prom: rdn over 1f out: no ex ins fnl f* **10/1**

0-00 **7** ¾ **Newcastles Owen (IRE)**[9] [4382] 3-8-4 **35** .... PatrickMathers(3) 10 — 29
(R Johnson) *s.i.s: in rr: rdn 1/2-way: hdwy over 1f out: kpt on ins fnl f: nt pce to chal* **33/1**

5003 **8** 3 ½ **Compton Lad**[9] [4354] 3-9-5 **47** .... PaulFessey 3 — 29
(D A Nolan) *prom: led after 1f: rdn and hdd over 1f out: wknd ins fnl f* **14/1**

3052 **9** 3 **The Salwick Flyer (IRE)**[2] [4613] 3-9-1 **50** .... GaryBartley(7) 14 — 21
(A Berry) *upset in stalls: s.s: in rr: rdn 1/2-way: nvr trbld ldrs* **11/2**[2]

0302 **10** 2 **Malelane (IRE)**[19] [4056] 3-9-1 **43** .... RobertWinston 2 — 7
(A Dickman) *rrd up s and slowly away: hdwy 1/2-way: sn rdn: wknd over 1f out* **6/1**[3]

060- **11** nk **Kirkbys Belle (IRE)**[294] [6196] 3-8-7 **35** .... DeanMcKeown 11 — —
(G A Swinbank) *trckd ldrs tl rdn and wknd 1/2-way* **8/1**

3-00 **12** 1 ¼ **Lake Suprima (IRE)**[30] [3749] 3-9-0 **47** .... MichaelJStainton(5) 5 — 5
(R M Whitaker) *a bhd* **20/1**

005 **13** ½ **One More Than Ten**[24] [3916] 3-8-11 **44** .... DuranFentiman(5) 1 — —
(T D Easterby) *in rr: rdn and hdwy 1/2-way: wknd over 1f out* **16/1**

61.95 secs (1.51) **Going Correction** +0.275s/f (Good) — **13** Ran SP% **119.2**
Speed ratings (Par 98):98,96,95,94,94 94,93,87,82,79 78,76,76
CSF £242.74 CT £4260.98 TOTE £23.80: £7.20, £5.10, £6.20; EX 333.20 Place 6 £103.17, Place 5 £47.03.
Owner Jonathan Gill & Jennifer Pallister **Bred** Southill Stud **Trained** Great Habton, N Yorks
FOCUS
A poor handicap, and really weak form.
Trumpita Official explanation: trainer's rep said, regarding the apparent improvement in form, that the gelding was better suited by the drop back to 5f
Malelane(IRE) Official explanation: jockey said filly became upset in stalls
T/Jkpt: Not won. T/Plt: £124.60 to a £1 stake. Pool: £69,777.10. 408.70 winning tickets. T/Qpdt: £21.80 to a £1 stake. Pool: £4,654.60. 157.40 winning tickets. DO

4427 WINDSOR (R-H)
Monday, August 21

OFFICIAL GOING: Good
Wind: Nil

4657 VC CASINO.COM EUROPEAN BREEDERS FUND MAIDEN FILLIES' STKS — 6f
5:30 (5:34) (Class 5) 2-Y-0 — **£4,533** (£1,348; £674; £336) **Stalls** High

Form — RPR

1 — **Alovera (IRE)** 2-9-0 .... TedDurcan 15 — 82
(M R Channon) *towards rr tl hdwy fr 3f out: drvn and qcknd in centre crse fr over 2f out: str run fnl f: led last stride* **5/1**[3]

5 **2** shd **Blue Echo**[72] [2439] 2-9-0 .... PhilipRobinson 13 — 82
(M A Jarvis) *sn slt advantage in centre of crse: rdn 2f out: kpt on wl: ct last stride* **10/1**

5 **3** ½ **Ms Victoria (IRE)**[54] [2984] 2-9-0 .... JamieSpencer 5 — 80
(B J Meehan) *in tch: hrd drvn and hdwy over 1f out: str chal ins last: no ex last strides* **9/2**[2]

63 **4** 3 ½ **Temtation (IRE)**[72] [2461] 2-8-11 .... AmirQuinn(3) 3 — 70
(J R Boyle) *chsd ldrs:chal on far side fr 3f out: stl ev ch over 1f out: wknd ins last* **40/1**

22 **5** 2 **Abbotts Ann**[14] [4207] 2-9-0 .... MichaelHills 16 — 64
(B W Hills) *chsd ldsrs towards centre of crse: wknd fnl f* **7/2**[1]

5 **6** ¾ **Distant Stars (IRE)**[19] [4053] 2-9-0 .... DaneO'Neill 8 — 61
(E S McMahon) *chsd ldrs towards far side: rdn over 2f out: wknd fnl f* **11/2**

7 3 **Nashharry (IRE)** 2-9-0 .... RichardHughes 10 — 52
(R Hannon) *s.i.s: sn rcvrd to chse ldrs towards centre crse: wknd appr fnl f* **25/1**

8 1 ¾ **Izabela Hannah** 2-9-0 .... JosedeSouza 6 — 47
(R M Beckett) *s.i.s: bhd pushed along 1/2-way: kpt on fnl f but nvr in contention* **16/1**

3 **9** nk **Naughty Thoughts (IRE)**[30] [3721] 2-9-0 .... DO'Donohoe 9 — 46
(K A Ryan) *chsd ldrs towards middle crse: wknd over 1f out* **11/1**

0 **10** shd **Juncea**[14] [4207] 2-9-0 .... SteveDrowne 14 — 46
(H Morrison) *bmpd s: sn in tch: towards middle of crse: rdn 1/2-way: wknd fr 2f out* **25/1**

0 **11** nk **Dubai's Fairy**[100] [1675] 2-9-0 .... RyanMoore 11 — 45
(R Hannon) *chsd ldrs: rdn over 2f out: sn wknd* **16/1**

04 **12** nk **The Light Fandango**[5] [4492] 2-9-0 .... AdrianMcCarthy 1 — 44
(R A Harris) *chsd ldrs towards far side: wknd 2f out* **66/1**

13 ¾ **Little Iris** 2-9-0 .... OscarUrbina 4 — 42
(L M Cumani) *s.i.s: racd towards far side: outpcd tl sme hdwy fnl f* **40/1**

14 3 ½ **Bellehurst** 2-9-0 .... TPO'Shea 2 — 31
(B J Meehan) *a outpcd* **33/1**

15 15 **Just Lovely** 2-9-0 .... MartinDwyer 12 — —
(M P Tregoning) *s.i.s: sn outpcd* **20/1**

0 **16** 17 **Byanita (IRE)**[33] [3640] 2-9-0 .... FrancisFerris 7 — —
(B Palling) *sn wl bhd* **100/1**

1m 12.64s (-1.03) **Going Correction** -0.225s/f (Firm) — **16** Ran SP% **124.4**
Speed ratings (Par 91):97,96,96,91,88 87,83,81,81,81 80,80,79,74,54 31
CSF £51.07 TOTE £7.40: £2.80, £3.90, £2.30; EX 68.70.
Owner Sheikh Ahmed Al Maktoum **Bred** Gerard Callanan **Trained** West Ilsley, Berks
■ Stewards' Enquiry : Philip Robinson one-day ban: used whip with excessive frequency (Sep 1)
FOCUS
This looked a reasonable fillies' maiden and it should produce a few winners.
NOTEBOOK
Alovera(IRE) ◆, a sister to Army Of Angels, a six-furlong juvenile winner, and a half-sister to five-furlong two-year-old winners Seraphima, Alegranza and Brantwood, out of a sprint winner at two, went through the ring for 70,000euros as a foal but sold as a yearling for 320,000euros. Entered in the Group 1 Fillies' Mile, she was well backed on her racecourse debut and justified the support with a very narrow success, getting up literally on the line. She looked sure to get on top about a furlong out, but ran green and just took her time getting there, suggesting she is open to plenty of improvement. She can leave the bare form of this success well behind and deserves her place in better company. (op 8-1)
Blue Echo, supported on her debut in a five-furlong maiden at Haydock but well held in fifth, put her experience to good use on her return from 72 days off and was just denied. One can only guess at this stage just how much improvement there is to come, but she looks up to winning a similar race. (tchd 9-1)
Ms Victoria(IRE), fifth of eight on her debut in a Salisbury maiden that has worked out very well, ran a good race upped a furlong in trip off the back of a two-month break and was not beaten very far. It will be disappointing if she cannot be placed to effect before the season is out. (op 7-2)
Temtation(IRE) still looked in need of the experience when third at Wolverhampton 72 days previously and ran with credit on her return to action. She is now qualified for a handicap mark and should not be underestimated in that sphere. Official explanation: jockey said filly hung right throughout (tchd 50-1)
Abbotts Ann, a beaten favourite when second over course and distance last time, was below that form and does not seem to be progressing. (tchd 3-1 and 4-1)
Distant Stars(IRE) offered plenty of promise on her debut in what looked a reasonable Leicester maiden, but failed to build on that and has to be considered disappointing. (op 7-1 tchd 8-1)
Izabela Hannah ◆, a half-sister to, amongst others, Summer Lightning, a multiple five-furlong winner at two and three, out of a six-furlong winner at two, was not totally unconsidered in the market and made a pleasing enough debut, keeping on after a slow start. (op 14-1)
Naughty Thoughts(IRE) was below the form she showed on her debut at Haydock. (op 10-1 tchd 9-1)
Dubai's Fairy ◆, well held on her debut 100 days earlier, was not given a hard time once held and could be one to keep in mind.

The Form Book, Raceform Ltd, Compton, RG20 6NL

4658 MONDAY NIGHTS WITH VC CASINO.COM PREMIER CLAIMING STKS 6f

6:00 (6:00) (Class 5) 3-Y-O+ **£4,533** (£1,348; £674; £336) **Stalls** High

Form RPR

1003 **1** **Desert Dreamer (IRE)**[4] 4535 5-9-5 82 GeorgeBaker 2 76
(P R Chamings) *hld up last but in tch: qcknd to ld ins fnl 2f: drvn out ins last* **11/4**[2]

0400 **2** *nk* **Just James**[23] 3926 7-8-13 90 RyanMoore 1 70
(D Nicholls) *chsd ldrs: drvn to chal ins fnl 2f: pressed wnr ins last but no ex cl home* **9/4**[1]

5250 **3** *2* **Outer Hebrides**[19] 4047 5-9-1 78 (vt) JamieSpencer 3 66
(Stef Liddiard) *chsd ldr: led over 2f out: hdd ins fnl 2f: sn one pce* **7/2**

0046 **4** *3 ½* **Bollywood (IRE)**[9] 4363 3-8-3 51 MarcHalford(5) 5 51
(J J Bridger) *led and racd alone centre crse over 3f: hdd over 2f out: wknd fnl f* **33/1**

0040 **U** **Funfair Wane**[55] 2946 7-9-1 82 AdrianTNicholls 4 —
(D Nicholls) *charged sing gates and uns rdr in stalls* **3/1**[3]

1m 12.96s (-0.71) **Going Correction** -0.225s/f (Firm)
WFA 3 from 5yo+ 3lb 5 Ran SP% **107.6**
Speed ratings (Par 103):95,94,91,87,—
CSF £8.86 TOTE £4.10: £1.80, £1.80; EX 10.70.
Owner Patrick Chamings Sprint Club **Bred** Gainsborough Stud Management Ltd **Trained** Baughurst, Hants

FOCUS
A fair claimer, but somewhat devalued with Funfair Wane parting company with his jockey as the stalls opened. That one would surely have set the pace, so they ended up going just an ordinary gallop for a sprint and the time was very moderate, slower even than the two-year-old fillies' maiden.

4659 VC CASINO.COM H'CAP 5f 10y

6:30 (6:30) (Class 4) (0-85,83) 3-Y-O **£6,477** (£1,927; £963; £481) **Stalls** High

Form RPR

3050 **1** **Blue Aura (IRE)**[46] 3226 3-8-11 73 (b[1]) SteveDrowne 2 79
(R Charlton) *mde virtually all: hrd drvn and hld on wl thrght fnl f* **4/1**[3]

-334 **2** *nk* **Queen Cobra (IRE)**[8] 4398 3-8-13 75 (v[1]) RobertHavlin 4 80
(H Morrison) *sn w wnr: hrd rdn fr over 1f out: no ex nr fin* **7/1**

4040 **3** *1 ¼* **Supercast (IRE)**[4] 4532 3-8-11 73 (b) LPKeniry 1 74
(J S Moore) *chsd ldrs: rdn fr 2f out: kpt on same pce ins last* **20/1**

0212 **4** *hd* **Shes Minnie**[16] 4135 3-9-2 78 JamieSpencer 6 78+
(J G M O'Shea) *bdly bmpd s and bhd: rdn and effrt fr 2f out: kpt on ins last but nvr gng pce to rch ldrs* **7/2**[2]

1240 **5** *½* **Toy Top (USA)**[7] 4422 3-9-6 82 (b) PhilipRobinson 5 80
(M Dods) *sltly hmpd s: bhd: drvn and sme hdwy fr over 1f out: kpt on ins last but nvr in contention* **8/1**

3140 **6** *2* **Azygous**[17] 4102 3-9-4 83 JamesDoyle(3) 7 74
(J Akehurst) *stmbld s and wnt bdly lft: racd alone stands side and outpcd fr 1/2-way* **9/2**

1525 **7** *2* **Jakeini (IRE)**[25] 3873 3-8-11 73 (p) RyanMoore 3 57
(E S McMahon) *chsd ldrs: rdn 1/2-way: sn btn* **3/1**[1]

59.84 secs (-1.26) **Going Correction** -0.225s/f (Firm) 7 Ran SP% **113.8**
Speed ratings (Par 102):101,100,98,98,97 94,91
CSF £31.10 TOTE £6.50: £2.40, £2.50; EX 29.40.
Owner D & J Newell **Bred** Miss Mary Davison **Trained** Beckhampton, Wilts

FOCUS
This looked like a weak sprint handicap for the grade. The first two ran to form.
Queen Cobra(IRE) Official explanation: jockey said filly lost its action
Azygous Official explanation: jockey said gelding stumbled on leaving stalls

4660 WEATHERBYS INSURANCE FILLIES' H'CAP 1m 67y

7:00 (7:02) (Class 4) (0-85,83) 3-Y-O+
£6,232 (£1,866; £933; £467; £233; £117) **Stalls** High

Form RPR

5301 **1** **Rakata (USA)**[11] 4286 4-9-3 73 JamieSpencer 8 81
(P F I Cole) *mde all: hrd drvn fnl f: hld on all out* **9/2**[1]

1056 **2** *nk* **Kindlelight Debut**[9] 4372 6-9-10 83 JamesDoyle(3) 10 90
(N P Littmoden) *chsd ldrs: wnt 2nd over 2f out: str chal fnl f but a jst hld* **15/2**

5343 **3** *1* **All Quiet**[23] 3953 5-9-8 78 RichardHughes 4 83
(R Hannon) *hld up in rr: hdwy over 2f out: swtchd rt of rails 1f out and str run ins last:gng on cl home: nvr gng pce to chal* **9/2**[1]

-146 **4** *½* **Pleasing**[68] 2554 3-8-3 65 MartinDwyer 3 68
(J L Dunlop) *chsd ldrs: drvn to dispute 2nd over 2f out: nvr gng pce to trble wnr: one pce u.p fnl f* **5/1**[2]

0420 **5** *2 ½* **Evening**[15] 4173 3-8-3 65 MatthewHenry 2 62
(B W Hills) *t.k.h: in tch: drvn along 3f out and styd on same pce* **12/1**

0044 **6** *5* **Commitment Lecture**[16] 4153 6-8-12 68 (t) RyanMoore 1 55
(M Dods) *bhd: pushed along 3f out: nvr in contention* **11/2**[3]

36-0 **7** *hd* **Laugh 'n Cry**[150] 711 5-8-9 65 TedDurcan 5 51
(C A Cyzer) *chsd ldr tl wknd over 2f out: no ch whn stmbld and lost action ins last* **33/1**

4310 **8** *nk* **Lisathedaddy**[75] 2351 4-9-0 70 RobertMiles 7 55
(B G Powell) *stdd s: a in rr* **28/1**

1023 **9** *½* **October Ben**[19] 4048 3-7-11 66 FrankiePickard(7) 6 49
(M D I Usher) *t.k.h: a towards rr* **12/1**

210- **10** *¾* **Congressional (IRE)**[317] 5733 3-8-13 75 PhilipRobinson 9 57
(M A Jarvis) *chsd ldrs: rdn 3f out: sn wknd* **6/1**

1m 45.27s (-0.33) **Going Correction** -0.075s/f (Good)
WFA 3 from 4yo+ 6lb 10 Ran SP% **116.2**
Speed ratings (Par 102):98,97,96,96,93 88,88,88,87,86
CSF £38.27 CT £163.89 TOTE £4.70: £1.80, £3.20, £2.20; EX 33.60.
Owner A H Robinson **Bred** Mike G Rutherford Sr **Trained** Whatcombe, Oxon

FOCUS
An ordinary fillies' handicap for the grade and, with Rakata able to dictate on her own terms, the form looks a little suspect. The third and fourth ran to form.
Congressional(IRE) Official explanation: jockey said filly ran too freely

4661 VC CASINO.COM MAIDEN STKS 1m 67y

7:30 (7:31) (Class 5) 3-4-Y-O **£3,238** (£963; £481; £240) **Stalls** High

Form RPR

3526 **1** **Star Crowned (USA)**[19] 4047 3-9-3 83 (bt) RichardHughes 7 83+
(B J Meehan) *trckd ldr: led gng wl appr fnl 2f: drvn out and kpt on wl fnl f* **2/1**[1]

04 **2** *1 ¼* **Manipulate**[31] 3711 3-9-3 OscarUrbina 12 80
(L M Cumani) *chsd ldrs: rdn and swtchd rt over 1f out: hung lft and r.o ins last to chse wnr fnl 100yds but a hld* **22/1**

-526 **3** *1 ¼* **Great Orator (USA)**[30] 3737 4-9-9 76 DaneO'Neill 1 78
(H Candy) *chsd ldrs: rdn over 2f out: wnt 2nd over 1f out but no imp on wnr: wknd and lost 2nd fnl 100yds* **10/3**[2]

3334 **4** *¾* **Escape Clause (USA)**[25] 3875 3-9-3 84 (v[1]) RyanMoore 9 75
(Sir Michael Stoute) *led: rdn 3f out: hdd appr fnl 2f: wknd fnl f* **11/2**[3]

5 *1 ¼* **Fairdonna** 3-8-12 TedDurcan 4 67
(D J Coakley) *s.i.s: bhd tl stdy hdwy fnl 2f: gng on cl home: nvr in contention* **33/1**

63-3 **6** *1 ¾* **Best Lady (IRE)**[28] 3794 3-8-12 77 MichaelHills 3 63
(B W Hills) *towards rr: hdwy 3f out: nvr rchd ldrs and one pce fnl 2f* **9/1**

224 **7** *3* **Just Logic (IRE)**[163] 630 3-9-3 MartinDwyer 14 61
(J Noseda) *bhd tl styd on fnl 2f: nvr in contention* **6/1**

8 *1* **Tipsy Me** 3-8-12 JamieSpencer 8 60+
(M L W Bell) *s.i.s: bhd: hdwy 3f out: effrt and shkn up 2f out: nvr rchd ldrs and wknd fnl f* **16/1**

2 **9** *1 ¼* **Medieval Maiden**[52] 3045 3-8-12 PhilipRobinson 5 51
(W J Musson) *in tch: pushed along 3f out: wknd fr 2f out* **12/1**

000- **10** *1* **Up At Dawn**[327] 5554 3-8-12 45 SteveDrowne 6 49
(C F Wall) *bhd most of way* **66/1**

0 **11** *24* **Ath Tiomain (IRE)**[7] 4431 3-9-0 AdamKirby(3) 10 —
(D J S Ffrench Davis) *a in rr* **100/1**

3600 **12** *20* **Just Devine (IRE)**[38] 3472 3-8-12 65 FrancisFerris 2 —
(B Palling) *chsd ldrs over 5f* **66/1**

1m 43.68s (-1.92) **Going Correction** -0.075s/f (Good)
WFA 3 from 4yo 6lb 12 Ran SP% **120.9**
Speed ratings (Par 103):106,104,103,102,101 99,96,95,94,93 69,49
CSF £55.97 TOTE £3.00: £1.30, £3.70, £2.00; EX 78.40.
Owner Star Crown Stables **Bred** Carl Rosen Associates **Trained** Manton, Wilts

FOCUS
Not a bad maiden for the time of year, even if a few of these are quite exposed. The form should prove sound, the third setting the standard. Despite the pace appearing strong from the start, it proved hard to make up significant amounts of ground.

4662 PLAY AT VC CASINO.COM H'CAP 1m 2f 7y

8:00 (8:01) (Class 5) (0-75,75) 3-Y-O+ **£3,238** (£963; £481; £240) **Stalls** Low

Form RPR

2405 **1** **Villa Sonata**[10] 4336 3-9-2 71 JamieSpencer 9 80+
(J R Fanshawe) *chsd ldrs: led over 2f out: drvn out fnl f* **2/1**[1]

3516 **2** *½* **William's Way**[2] 4586 4-9-8 69 TedDurcan 6 75
(I A Wood) *in tch: hdwy over 2f out: styd on to chse wnr fnl f but nvr quite gng pce to chal* **12/1**

1251 **3** *½* **High Treason (USA)**[55] 2956 4-9-8 69 PhilipRobinson 2 74+
(W J Musson) *hld up in rr: hdwy over 2f out: kpt on to chse ldrs ins fnl f: one pce nr fin* **3/1**[2]

0241 **4** *3* **Hatch A Plan (IRE)**[7] 4432 5-9-5 71 6ex TravisBlock(5) 8 70
(Mrs A J Hamilton-Fairley) *slowly into stride: bhd: hdwy fr 2f out: rdn and edgd lft over 1f out: kpt on same pce* **7/1**[3]

0036 **5** *1 ¼* **Monte Mayor Junior**[45] 3263 3-8-1 56 (v) FrankieMcDonald 4 53
(D Haydn Jones) *chsd ldrs: rdn over 2f out: hung bdly lft over 1f out and sn btn* **50/1**

2050 **6** *1* **Press Express (IRE)**[22] 3980 4-9-12 73 MartinDwyer 5 68
(M L W Bell) *in tch: drvn to dispute 2nd over 2f out: wknd fnl f* **11/1**

1500 **7** *nk* **Charlie Kennet**[23] 3934 8-9-9 70 GeorgeBaker 10 65
(Mrs H Sweeting) *chsd ldrs: rdn 3f out: wknd fr 2f out* **11/1**

0 **8** *1* **Ma'Am (USA)**[72] 2457 4-9-11 75 JamesDoyle(3) 7 68
(I A Wood) *stdd s: bhd: hdwy on ins over 2f out: sn edgd lft: no ch whn hmpd over 1f out* **16/1**

0040 **9** *nk* **Mr Wiseguy**[19] 4044 3-8-9 67 AdamKirby(3) 3 59
(G C Bravery) *chsd ldr: led 3f out tl over 2f out: sn btn* **50/1**

-630 **10** *½* **Velvet Valley (USA)**[65] 2654 3-9-1 70 RichardHughes 11 61
(Sir Michael Stoute) *hld up in rr: hdwy and rdn over 2f out: btn whn hmpd over 1f out* **9/1**

030- **11** *11* **Earl Kraul (IRE)**[284] 6304 3-9-3 72 RyanMoore 1 42
(G L Moore) *led: hdd 3f out: sn btn* **20/1**

2m 11.94s (3.64) **Going Correction** -0.075s/f (Good)
WFA 3 from 4yo+ 8lb 11 Ran SP% **119.8**
Speed ratings (Par 103):82,81,81,78,77 77,76,75,75,75 66
CSF £28.28 CT £72.89 TOTE £3.30: £1.60, £3.10, £1.70 Place 6 £50.85, Place 5 £17.33.
Owner J H Richmond-Watson **Bred** Lawn Stud **Trained** Newmarket, Suffolk

FOCUS
A fair handicap, but they went no pace and the winning time was very ordinary. The form is not strong but the winner is value for a bit extra.
Hatch A Plan(IRE) Official explanation: jockey said gelding hung left-handed
Velvet Valley(USA) Official explanation: jockey said colt suffered interference
T/Plt: £104.80. Pool £68,730.45, 478.75 winning tickets T/Qpdt: £17.90. Pool £5,346.40, 220.20 winning tickets ST

4491 YARMOUTH (L-H)

Monday, August 21

OFFICIAL GOING: Soft
Wind: Nil

4663 VISITNORFOLK.COM MAIDEN STKS 6f 3y

5:20 (5:20) (Class 5) 3-4-Y-O **£3,238** (£963; £481; £240) **Stalls** High

Form RPR

32- **1** **Felicitous**[353] 4923 3-8-12 LDettori 5 72+
(Saeed Bin Suroor) *taken down early: t.k.h: chsd ldrs: led wl over 1f out: pushed out and in command fnl f* **2/11**[1]

2 *1 ¼* **Conservative** 3-9-3 RHills 1 73
(W J Haggas) *slowly away: hdwy 3f out: chsd wnr over 1f out: kpt on same pce ins fnl f* **12/1**[2]

0-00 **3** *5* **Girandola**[51] 3090 3-9-3 60 StephenCarson 8 58
(R F Johnson Houghton) *hld up in tch: rdn 2f out: chsd ldng pair over 1f out: no imp* **20/1**[3]

64 **4** *9* **Tetrode (USA)**[16] 4142 4-9-6 RichardMullen 6 31
(R M H Cowell) *led tl rdn and hdd wl over 1f out: sn wknd* **33/1**

4050 **5** *5* **Master Malarkey**[6] 4462 3-9-3 45 (b) ChrisCatlin 2 16
(Mrs C A Dunnett) *chsd ldr tl 2f out: sn wknd: t.o* **100/1**

00- **6** *7* **Little Trinket**[287] 6281 3-8-12 HayleyTurner 4 —
(Mrs C A Dunnett) *chsd ldrs: rdn and hung lft over 3f out: sn wl bhd: t.o* **150/1**

50 **7** *hd* **Cool Tiger**[12] 4247 3-9-0 DeanCorby(3) 7 —
(P Howling) *dwlt: hld up in tch: rdn over 2f out: sn wl bhd: t.o* **40/1**

1m 14.7s (1.00) **Going Correction** +0.20s/f (Good)
WFA 3 from 4yo 3lb **7** Ran SP% **104.1**
Speed ratings (Par 103):101,99,92,80,74 64,64
CSF £1.54 TOTE £1.10: £1.02, £3.00; EX 2.90.
Owner Godolphin **Bred** Darley **Trained** Newmarket, Suffolk

FOCUS
Race times suggested that the ground was on the soft side of good without being too testing. The stalls were against the stands' rail, but the runners came down the centre which basically set the trend for the evening. This was an uncompetitive maiden, though the first two look fair prospects. The third has been rated to this year's best.
Cool Tiger Official explanation: jockey said gelding ran too freely to post

4664 EUROPEAN BREEDERS FUND MAIDEN STKS — 5f 43y
5:50 (5:50) (Class 5) 2-Y-0 — **£3,238** (£963; £481) **Stalls** High

Form — RPR

3 **1** **Shamhoota (USA)**[17] 4105 2-9-3 RHills 2 81+
(Sir Michael Stoute) *trckd ldr: led wl over 1f out: shkn up and sn clr: eased nr fin* **1/12**[1]

00 **2** *5* **Show Trial (IRE)**[19] 4041 2-8-12 ChrisCatlin 3 50
(M R Channon) *hld up in last: hdwy to chse wnr over 1f out: sn outpcd* **14/1**[2]

3 *16* **Silver Bolt (IRE)** 2-9-3 MickyFenton 1 —
(N P Littmoden) *led: rdn 1/2-way: hdd wl over 1f out: sn wknd: eased fnl f: t.o* **28/1**[3]

65.10 secs (2.30) **Going Correction** +0.20s/f (Good) **3** Ran SP% **102.5**
Speed ratings (Par 94):89,81,55
CSF £1.46 TOTE £1.10; EX 1.20.
Owner Hamdan Al Maktoum **Bred** Kilcarn Stud **Trained** Newmarket, Suffolk

FOCUS
An even less competitive maiden than the opener and the long odds-on winner had little more than an exercise gallop. He has been rated to his debut form. They came down the middle again.

NOTEBOOK
Shamhoota(USA) probably did not even have to run up to his Newmarket debut to dispose of his two rivals and this told us nothing new about him. Again the runners came down the middle. (tchd 1-9 in a place)
Show Trial(IRE), well beaten in both of her previous starts, was completely outclassed by the winner but does seem to have a little ability and much will depend on what nursery mark she gets. (op 12-1)
Silver Bolt(IRE), a half-brother to a winning chaser, led his two rivals until approaching the last furlong and was then left behind. There is a fair amount of stamina on the dam's side so he may need a lot more time. (op 33-1 tchd 25-1)

4665 CLS OFFSHORE LTD CLAIMING STKS — 6f 3y
6:20 (6:20) (Class 6) 2-Y-0 — **£2,266** (£674; £337; £168) **Stalls** High

Form — RPR

5530 **1** **Retaliate**[13] 4221 2-8-13 67 SebSanders 5 67
(M Quinn) *mde all: rdn over 1f out: clr 1f out: styd on wl* **4/1**[3]

0625 **2** *3* **Emergency Services**[10] 4334 2-8-7 59 (p) JimmyQuinn 3 52
(Tom Dascombe) *in tch: rdn and outpcd 1/2-way: styd on u.p over 1f out: wnt 2nd ins fnl f: nt trble wnr* **7/2**[2]

60 **3** *1 ½* **Group Force (IRE)**[8] 4394 2-8-6 (b[1]) JohnEgan 1 47
(M H Tompkins) *t.k.h: hld up in rr: rdn and hdwy over 2f out: wnt 2nd 1f out: no imp: lost 2nd ins fnl f* **10/1**

1500 **4** *2 ½* **Stir Crazy (IRE)**[16] 4152 2-9-2 70 EdwardCreighton(3) 7 52
(M R Channon) *cl up: chsd wnr 1/2-way: ev ch and rdn 2f out: wknd qckly 1f out* **9/4**[1]

00 **5** *hd* **Sweet Soul Diva**[19] 4049 2-7-12 DominicFox(3) 4 33
(Miss V Haigh) *sn rdn along: in tch in rr: outpcd over 2f out* **33/1**

0400 **6** *1 ½* **Pas De Trois**[12] 4246 2-8-5 53 (b[1]) StephenCarson 6 33
(R F Johnson Houghton) *chsd wnr tl 3f out: sn rdn: no ch wl over 1f out* **15/2**

0050 **7** *13* **Stunningjo**[3] 4545 2-8-2 (b) ChrisCatlin 2 —
(J L Spearing) *chsd ldrs: rdn 2f out: sn wl bhd: t.o* **13/2**

1m 15.76s (2.06) **Going Correction** +0.20s/f (Good) **7** Ran SP% **110.1**
Speed ratings (Par 92):94,90,88,84,84 82,65
CSF £16.93 TOTE £4.90: £2.60, £1.10; EX 12.80.Pas de Trois was claimed by Jeff Pearce for £4,000
Owner M J Quinn **Bred** Helshaw Grange Farm And C J Whiston **Trained** Newmarket, Suffolk

FOCUS
An ordinary juvenile claimer in which the field finished very much in the order adjusted official ratings suggested they should. The form should prove sound, rated through the winner. Once again the field raced down the centre.

NOTEBOOK
Retaliate, just about best in at the weights, had only shown modest ability in her previous outings but this represented a drop in class and she made no mistake under a positive ride. The easier ground obviously suited her, which means that she could find another opportunity at a modest level this autumn. (op 7-2 tchd 3-1)
Emergency Services, exposed and already beaten in sellers, ran as though in need of a return to seven but adjusted official ratings suggest he finished precisely where he was entitled to. (op 4-1)
Group Force(IRE), one of the least exposed in the field but beaten a total of nearly 47 lengths in her two outings to date, performed a little better in this lesser grade in first-time blinkers but it will be a poor race she wins. (op 11-1 tchd 8-1)
Stir Crazy(IRE), one of the most experienced and the only previous winner in the field, was stepping down from nursery company and, even though the ground was probably easier than ideal, he still might have been expected to do a bit better than this. Official explanation: trainer's rep said the gelding was not suited by the soft ground (op 15-8 tchd 5-2)
Sweet Soul Diva, beaten a total of more than 52 lengths in her two outings to date, was dropping in class but this was hardly an improvement. (op 25-1)
Stunningjo Official explanation: jockey said filly was not suited by the soft ground

4666 REGGIE HOLE SENIOR MEMORIAL H'CAP — 7f 3y
6:50 (6:50) (Class 5) (0-70,70) 3-Y-O — **£3,562** (£1,059; £529; £264) **Stalls** High

Form — RPR

4612 **1** **Mocha Java**[25] 3869 3-9-0 63 IanMongan 4 74
(Mrs L J Mongan) *mde all: rdn over 2f out: styd on strly and wnt clr ins fnl f* **8/1**

0302 **2** *3* **Kasumi**[44] 3290 3-9-1 64 MickyFenton 9 67
(H Morrison) *bhd: rdn and outpcd over 4f out: styd on under presssure over 1f out: wnt 2nd nr fin: n.d* **9/2**

4005 **3** *¾* **Sorrel Point**[17] 4113 3-8-11 60 JimmyQuinn 1 61
(H J Collingridge) *trckd ldrs: rdn to chse wnr 2f out: kpt on same pce ins fnl f: lost 2nd nr fin* **20/1**

3222 **4** *½* **Mr Cellophane**[57] 2896 3-8-13 62 LDettori 3 62
(J R Jenkins) *wnt lft s: plld hrd: chsd wnr tl 4f out: rdn over 2f out: onepced ins fnl f* **5/2**[1]

6614 **5** *3* **Lil Najma**[12] 4249 3-9-5 68 KerrinMcEvoy 10 60
(C E Brittain) *bhd: pushed along 4f out: n.d after: kpt on ins fnl f* **3/1**[2]

4104 **6** *nk* **Falmassim**[11] 4296 3-9-5 68 NickyMackay 2 59
(L M Cumani) *hmpd s: t.k.h: chsd wnr 4f out tl 2f out: wknd 1f out* **4/1**[3]

0000 **7** *4* **Crosby Hall**[8] 4403 3-9-2 65 (t) HayleyTurner 7 46
(N Tinkler) *t.k.h: hld up in tch: rdn over 2f out: wknd over 1f out* **33/1**

3000 **8** *¾* **Bellanora**[4] 4527 3-8-11 60 (b[1]) StephenCarson 8 39
(R F Johnson Houghton) *chsd ldrs: rdn over 2f out: wknd u.p 1f out* **25/1**

1m 27.31s (0.71) **Going Correction** +0.20s/f (Good) **8** Ran SP% **114.4**
Speed ratings (Par 100):103,99,98,98,94 94,89,88
CSF £42.55 CT £699.24 TOTE £10.00: £2.80, £1.40, £3.10.
Owner D Turner **Bred** A H And C E Robinson Partnership **Trained** Epsom, Surrey

FOCUS
The pace was quite decent in this handicap and the field raced more towards the nearside of the track than in the previous contests. The winner has been rated to the best view of his previous run, with the third to his maiden form.

4667 PKF (UK) LLP H'CAP — 1m 3y
7:20 (7:21) (Class 6) (0-55,55) 3-Y-0+ — **£2,461** (£732; £365; £182) **Stalls** High

Form — RPR

6602 **1** **Panshir (FR)**[12] 4266 5-9-2 43 SebSanders 11 56+
(Mrs C A Dunnett) *t.k.h: trckd ldrs: wnt 2nd 2f out: rdn to ld jst over 1f out: drvn clr* **9/2**[1]

0354 **2** *3* **Spring Time Girl**[12] 4266 4-9-1 42 (p) KerrinMcEvoy 15 49
(B Ellison) *wl bhd: rdn 1/2-way: styd on wl over 1f out: wnt 2nd last 50 yds: no ch w wnr* **11/2**[2]

3015 **3** *1 ¼* **Start Of Authority**[11] 4276 5-9-6 47 JimCrowley 4 52
(J Gallagher) *prom: chsd ldr over 3f out: led over 2f out tl hdd jst over 1f out: nt pce of wnr: lost 2nd last 50 yds* **12/1**

0002 **4** *5* **Balerno**[23] 3933 7-10-0 55 PaulEddery 9 50
(Mrs L J Mongan) *hld up: hdwy over 3f out: no hdwy u.p over 1f out* **12/1**

1600 **5** *1* **Wild Lass**[10] 4332 5-9-4 45 (p) MickyFenton 1 38
(J C Fox) *chsd ldrs on outer: rdn 3f out: chsd ldng pair over 1f out: wknd u.p fnl f* **33/1**

0656 **6** *shd* **Opera Belle**[6] 4450 4-8-13 43 (bt) StephenDonohoe(3) 8 35
(Miss Gay Kelleway) *led tl over 2f out: wknd wl over 1f out* **22/1**

0-53 **7** *5* **Rem Time (IRE)**[7] 4439 6-9-0 48 JamieHamblett(7) 7 30
(John Berry) *hld up in tch: rdn over 2f out: sn struggling* **15/2**

0300 **8** *3* **Bamzooki**[11] 4307 4-9-6 47 JimmyQuinn 12 23
(Mrs C A Dunnett) *plld hrd: chsd ldr tl over 3f out: rdn and wknd over 2f out* **25/1**

0000 **9** *3* **Royal Sailor (IRE)**[12] 4266 4-8-13 40 BrianReilly 14 10
(J Ryan) *in tch in midfield: rdn wl over 2f out: sn struggling: t.o* **100/1**

5534 **10** *1 ¾* **Limit Down (IRE)**[11] 4306 5-9-0 41 NickyMackay 2 8
(John Berry) *chsd ldrs tl rdn wl over 2f out: sn wl btn: t.o* **8/1**

0056 **11** *5* **Postmaster**[10] 4332 4-9-8 49 ChrisCatlin 16 6
(R Ingram) *a bhd: nvr on terms: t.o* **14/1**

2250 **12** *2 ½* **Expected Bonus (USA)**[15] 3115 7-9-1 42 JohnEgan 6 —
(Jamie Poulton) *racd in midfield: reminders 6f out: rdn over 4f out: sn no ch: t.o* **7/1**

6003 **13** *1 ½* **Perfect Order (USA)**[6] 4446 3-9-0 47 (p) LDettori 10 —
(N A Callaghan) *slowly away: a bhd: t.o* **13/2**[3]

1m 41.32s (1.42) **Going Correction** +0.20s/f (Good)
WFA 3 from 4yo+ 6lb **13** Ran SP% **116.5**
Speed ratings (Par 101):100,97,95,90,89 89,84,81,78,76 71,69,67
CSF £26.50 CT £287.78 TOTE £5.80: £2.30, £2.00, £4.50; EX 32.10.
Owner Suffolk Racing **Bred** Curtasse S A S **Trained** Hingham, Norfolk

FOCUS
A very low-grade handicap if probably the most competitive race on the card, but ultimately another easy winner. Sound form for the grade. Normal service was resumed with the runners coming down the centre of the track.
Rem Time(IRE) Official explanation: trainer said gelding had not been suited by the soft ground
Bamzooki Official explanation: jockey said filly ran too keenly
Limit Down(IRE) Official explanation: trainer said gelding had not been suited by the soft ground
Perfect Order(USA) Official explanation: jockey said filly never travelled and lost its action

4668 GREAT YARMOUTH MERCURY MAIDEN H'CAP — 1m 6f 17y
7:50 (7:52) (Class 5) (0-70,69) 3-Y-0+ — **£3,432** (£1,021; £510; £254) **Stalls** High

Form — RPR

3-62 **1** **Born Wild (GER)**[45] 3261 3-9-0 67 LDettori 10 84+
(Sir Michael Stoute) *w.w in tch: hdwy over 4f out: rdn to led over 3f out: sn clr: eased nr fin* **4/1**[2]

5243 **2** *4* **Star Rising**[7] 4438 4-8-7 51 oh2 StephenDonohoe(3) 1 59
(W J Musson) *hld up in rr: hdwy 4f out: sn rdn: chsd wnr over 2f out: no imp* **4/1**[2]

0400 **3** *3 ½* **Delorain (IRE)**[16] 4150 3-7-12 51 oh1 (v) JimmyQuinn 4 54
(J A R Toller) *trckd ldrs: hdwy 4f out: rdn over 3f out: kpt on but no ch w wnr after* **20/1**

4222 **4** *5* **Osolomio (IRE)**[9] 4362 3-8-7 60 MickyFenton 5 56
(J G Given) *led tl rdn and hdd over 3f out: sn no ch w wnr* **11/10**[1]

0505 **5** *16* **Perfectionist**[17] 4104 4-8-10 51 oh5 (p) ChrisCatlin 8 25
(Mrs C A Dunnett) *hld up in tch: pushed along 6f out: sn lost tch: t.o* **20/1**

0-00 **6** *1 ½* **Plough Maite**[12] 4263 3-7-8 52 oh7 ow1 (p) AurelioMedeiros(5) 11 24
(D E Cantillon) *chsd ldr tl 8f out: rdn and wknd over 4f out: t.o* **80/1**

0405 **7** *12* **Kiama**[31] 3714 4-9-0 55 J-PGuillambert 6 10
(M Johnston) *chsd ldrs: wnt 2nd 8f out tl 4f out: sn wknd: t.o* **9/1**[3]

0000 **8** *11* **Kalush**[13] 4227 5-8-5 51 oh19 AnnStokell(5) 2 —
(Miss A Stokell) *rrd in stalls and v.s.a: a wl bhd: t.o last 4f* **100/1**

00-0 **9** *133* **Cetshwayo**[28] 3794 4-10-0 69 SebSanders 9 —
(J M P Eustace) *stmbld s: hld up in rr: rdn over 5f out: sn lost tch and t.o* **14/1**

3m 9.96s (4.66) **Going Correction** +0.425s/f (Yiel)
WFA 3 from 4yo+ 12lb **9** Ran SP% **116.0**
Speed ratings (Par 103):103,100,98,95,86 85,79,72,—
CSF £19.78 CT £284.43 TOTE £3.40: £1.60, £1.60, £5.50 Place 6 £54.59, Place 5 £46.97.
Owner Ammerland Verwaltung GmbH & Co KG **Bred** Gestut Ammerland **Trained** Newmarket, Suffolk

FOCUS
This was a modest race, but at least the pace was good and it provided a true test of stamina, hence the field finishing spread out all over Norfolk. The unexposed winner was a big improver but the form is not strong with the favourite well below form.
Kiama Official explanation: jockey said filly hung right
Cetshwayo Official explanation: vet said gelding bled from the nose

T/Plt: £35.30. Pool £41,284.15. 852.50 winning tickets T/Qpdt: £23.60. Pool £3,921.60. 122.70 winning tickets SP

4444 BRIGHTON (L-H)

Tuesday, August 22

OFFICIAL GOING: Good to firm (firm in places)

Wind: Moderate, half-against

4669 EUROPEAN BREEDERS FUND MAIDEN STKS 6f 209y

2:00 (2:00) (Class 5) 2-Y-O **£4,210** (£1,252; £625; £312) **Stalls** Low

Form RPR

2522 **1** **Dowlleh**[20] 4049 2-9-3 82 ChrisCatlin 3 74
(M R Channon) *broke wl: sn hdd but cl 2nd tl led wl over 2f out: pushed out fnl f* **4/5**[1]

3 **2** ¾ **Quiddity (IRE)**[33] 3685 2-8-12 RichardMullen 4 67
(E J O'Neill) *in tch: rdn over 1f out: r.o to go 2nd ins fnl f* **12/1**

00 **3** *nk* **Grand Heights (IRE)**[17] 4129 2-9-3 SebSanders 1 71
(J L Dunlop) *hld up in tch: chsd wnr over 1f out tl one pce and lost 2nd ins fnl f* **3/1**[2]

04 **4** 5 **Mister Lucky (FR)**[20] 4049 2-9-3 (v[1]) DaneO'Neill 2 58
(Sir Michael Stoute) *sn led: rdn and hdd wl over 2f out: wknd over 1f out* **9/2**[3]

1m 23.48s (0.78) **Going Correction** +0.075s/f (Good) 4 Ran SP% **106.4**

Speed ratings (Par 94):98,97,96,91

CSF £9.63 TOTE £1.70; EX 6.70.

Owner Sheikh Ahmed Al Maktoum **Bred** C R Mason **Trained** West Ilsley, Berks

FOCUS

A fair maiden. The winner had some reasonable earlier form and was clear top-rated.

NOTEBOOK

Dowlleh had developed a habit of finishing second, but proved there was nothing wrong with his resolution, scoring readily. The step up from six to seven furlongs proved no problem, and he can now be campaigned over either trip in handicaps. (op 10-11 tchd evens in places)

Quiddity(IRE), whose only other run was on Polytrack, looks capable of winning a little maiden on either surface. (op 9-1 tchd 8-1)

Grand Heights(IRE) is now qualified for handicaps, which is where he has always looked likely to be more effective. In due course, he should stay well beyond a mile. (op 9-2 tchd 11-4)

Mister Lucky(FR) is not one of the stable stars, and the application of a visor on only his third run was not a good sign. He looks a handicapper now he is qualified, and a modest one at that. (op 11-4)

4670 C BREWER AND SONS SUPPORT THE A.B.F. (S) STKS 6f 209y

2:35 (2:37) (Class 6) 3-Y-O+ **£2,388** (£705; £352) **Stalls** Low

Form RPR

4440 **1** **Mountain Pass (USA)**[4] 4564 4-9-6 53 (p) DaneO'Neill 9 58
(M J Wallace) *hld up in tch: rdn over 1f out: r.o to ld nr fin* **9/2**[2]

0012 **2** *hd* **Beau Marche**[9] 4389 4-9-6 49 (b) SebSanders 8 57
(G G Margarson) *a.p: led 2f out: rdn and kpt on fnl f but hdd nr fin* **7/2**[1]

6505 **3** ¾ **Salinger (USA)**[12] 4278 4-8-12 42 (b) AmirQuinn(3) 6 50
(Mrs L J Mongan) *s.i.s: in rr tl rdn and hdwy over 1f out: r.o fnl f: nvr nrr* **12/1**

3244 **4** *hd* **Zafarshah (IRE)**[7] 4446 7-8-8 48 (b) TolleyDean(7) 3 50
(R A Harris) *in rr: rdn over 1f out: r.o fnl f: nvr nrr* **9/2**[2]

0060 **5** 2 **Dorn Hill**[8] 4425 4-8-10 40 (p) MickyFenton 2 39
(D G Bridgwater) *a.p on ins: ev ch 2f out: wknd ins fnl f* **16/1**

0100 **6** 1½ **Silver Visage (IRE)**[13] 4266 4-9-6 45 (p) BrianReilly 14 45
(Miss J Feilden) *chsd ldr: c over to r alone stands' side 1/2-way: no imp on ldrs fr over 1f out* **16/1**

0-00 **7** 1 **Sham Ruby**[45] 3306 4-8-10 42 (t) LPKeniry 5 33
(M R Bosley) *in tch on outside: rdn 2f out: no further hdwy* **66/1**

6040 **8** ½ **Reality Time (IRE)**[26] 3867 3-8-5 42 PaulDoe 12 32
(W J Knight) *prom on outside: rdn 2f out: wknd appr fnl f* **20/1**

1600 **9** *hd* **Stagnite**[24] 3948 6-9-6 55 (p) TPO'Shea 10 41
(P A Blockley) *led tl hdd 2f out: wknd over 1f out* **7/1**[3]

0 **10** *shd* **Littleton Aldor (IRE)**[50] 3158 6-9-1 AlanDaly 13 36
(W G M Turner) *a towards rr* **66/1**

00-0 **11** ½ **Seejay**[8] 4075 6-8-7 41 (p) NeilChalmers(3) 1 29
(B R Johnson) *in rr: sme hdwy on ins whn hmpd over 1f out: nt rcvr* **33/1**

0-02 **12** 1¾ **Tiny Tim (IRE)**[12] 4278 8-8-8 38 (b) WilliamBuick(7) 4 30
(A M Balding) *nvr bttr than mid-div* **14/1**

5260 **13** 1¾ **Princess Kai (IRE)**[33] 3664 5-8-10 40 ChrisCatlin 15 20
(R Ingram) *a in rr* **16/1**

0000 **14** 1¼ **Binty**[34] 3635 4-8-3 41 MarkCoumbe(7) 7 17
(A J Chamberlain) *s.i.s: a bhd* **25/1**

1406 **15** 2½ **Dexileos (IRE)**[24] 3933 7-9-6 44 (t) FergusSweeney 11 21
(David Pinder) *chsd ldrs: rdn over 2f out: sn wknd* **15/2**

1m 23.2s (0.50) **Going Correction** +0.075s/f (Good)
WFA 3 from 4yo+ 5lb 15 Ran SP% **126.4**

Speed ratings (Par 101):100,99,98,98,96 94,93,92,92,92 92,90,88,86,83

CSF £20.21 TOTE £6.40: £2.20, £1.60, £4.90; EX 26.60 Trifecta £322.70 Part won. Pool: £454.54 - 0.44 winning tickets..There was no bid for the winner.

Owner B Walsh **Bred** Marablue Farm **Trained** Newmarket, Suffolk

FOCUS

A routine but competitive seller. The form looks sound.

Binty Official explanation: jockey said filly was in season

4671 ARMY BENEVOLENT FUND FILLIES' H'CAP 7f 214y

3:05 (3:05) (Class 6) (0-60,60) 3-Y-O **£2,590** (£770; £385; £192) **Stalls** Low

Form RPR

0036 **1** **Air Biscuit (IRE)**[9] 4395 3-9-7 60 (t) GeorgeBaker 9 66+
(C F Wall) *hld up: hdwy on outside oer 2f out: r.o u.p to ld wl ins fnl f* **3/1**[1]

0040 **2** 1¼ **Cunegonde**[12] 4279 3-8-6 45 JimCrowley 5 48
(G L Moore) *hld up in tch: hdwy on outside over 1f out: r.o fnl f to go 2nd nr fin* **14/1**

5031 **3** ¾ **Dark Moon**[10] 4363 3-8-12 54 NeilChalmers(3) 2 57+
(A M Balding) *t.k.h: hld up in rr: hdwy fr 2f out but hung lft tl r.o ins fnl f: nvr nrr* **5/1**[2]

4040 **4** *nk* **On Air (USA)**[43] 3347 3-9-7 60 RichardMullen 10 61
(E J O'Neill) *trckd ldrs: rdn over 1f out: nt qckn ins fnl f* **15/2**

6000 **5** *shd* **Jabbara (IRE)**[16] 4181 3-9-7 60 SebSanders 1 60
(C E Brittain) *trckd ldr: led 5f out: rdn: hdd & wknd wl ins fnl f* **15/2**

0650 **6** 2 **Cape Latina**[119] 1226 3-8-2 41 AdrianMcCarthy 4 37
(J R Best) *mid-div: rdn and wknd over 1f out* **33/1**

0432 **7** ½ **Never Say Deya**[12] 4277 3-8-12 51 ChrisCatlin 7 46
(M R Channon) *led tl hdd 5f out: wknd over 1f out* **11/2**[3]

5041 **8** 1¼ **Shinko (IRE)**[7] 4450 3-9-0 56 6ex DeanCorby(3) 8 48
(Miss J Feilden) *in tch on outside: rdn 3f out: wknd wl over 1f out* **9/1**

0450 **9** 2 **Zafantage**[29] 3793 3-9-7 60 DaneO'Neill 6 47
(S Kirk) *mid-div: rdn and hdwy 2f out: wknd qckly fnl f* **7/1**

0-02 **10** 27 **By Storm**[12] 4304 3-8-3 42 TPO'Shea 3 —
(John Berry) *chsd ldrs to 1/2-way: sn bhd: t.o* **16/1**

1m 37.17s (2.13) **Going Correction** +0.075s/f (Good) 10 Ran SP% **118.6**

Speed ratings (Par 95):92,90,90,89,89 87,87,85,83,56

CSF £49.04 CT £212.33 TOTE £4.80: £1.60, £3.80, £1.90; EX 83.10 Trifecta £371.80 Part won. Pool of £523.72 - 0.20 winning tickets..

Owner M Sinclair **Bred** Farmers Hill Stud **Trained** Newmarket, Suffolk

FOCUS

A modest race for fillies. The form seems to make sense but is pretty weak.

By Storm Official explanation: jockey said filly lost its action

4672 BOB DALEY MEMORIAL H'CAP 1m 3f 196y

3:40 (3:40) (Class 5) (0-70,68) 3-Y-O **£3,562** (£1,059; £529; £264) **Stalls** High

Form RPR

00-0 **1** **Mighty Splash**[28] 3823 3-8-3 53 RichardKingscote(3) 5 59+
(R Charlton) *sn trckd ldr: rdn to ld but hung lft appr fnl f: r.o ins fnl f* **7/2**[2]

2134 **2** 2 **Mull Of Dubai**[15] 4197 3-9-4 65 LPKeniry 1 68
(J S Moore) *racd in 3rd pl: in cl tch whn short of room appr fnl f: squeezed through to go 2nd jst ins fnl f* **4/1**[3]

6441 **3** 3½ **Regal Connection (USA)**[15] 4197 3-9-2 68 (b) GregFairley(5) 4 65
(M Johnston) *led: rdn over 2f out: hdd appr fnl f: wknd ins* **4/7**[1]

5000 **4** 88 **Ronaldo**[10] 4363 3-8-2 49 oh1 ChrisCatlin 3 —
(A M Hales) *hld up: lost tch 1/2-way* **33/1**

2m 32.78s (0.58) **Going Correction** +0.075s/f (Good) 4 Ran SP% **108.8**

Speed ratings (Par 100):101,99,97,38

CSF £16.04 TOTE £4.50; EX 15.90.

Owner Mrs M D Low **Bred** Hollington Stud **Trained** Beckhampton, Wilts

FOCUS

A modest handicap won by an unexposed filly from a good yard. Not strong form with the favourite running poorly, but the winner is unexposed and the second ran up to her best.

Mighty Splash Official explanation: trainer's rep said, regarding the improved form shown, the filly had been disappointing and very green on its previous runs and may have just come to herself

Ronaldo Official explanation: jockey said gelding was unsuited by the good to firm (firm in places) ground

4673 JIMMY HEAL MEMORIAL H'CAP 1m 1f 209y

4:15 (4:16) (Class 5) (0-70,70) 3-Y-O+ **£3,238** (£963; £481; £240) **Stalls** High

Form RPR

0002 **1** **Altilhar (USA)**[11] 4331 3-9-7 70 (b) GeorgeBaker 9 81
(G L Moore) *hld up in rr: hdwy on outside over 1f out: hung lft but led ins fnl f* **4/1**[2]

2-30 **2** 2½ **Peruvian Prince (USA)**[18] 4108 4-9-10 65 TPO'Shea 4 71
(J A R Toller) *mid-div: rdn and hdwy to ld over 1f out: hdd ins fnl f* **12/1**

2051 **3** *nk* **Jackie Kiely**[19] 4073 5-9-7 62 (t) RobertHavlin 10 67
(Stef Liddiard) *hld up: hdwy 2f out: hung lft: swtchd rt over 1f out: r.o ins fnl f: nvr nrr* **12/1**

2044 **4** 4 **Miss Monica (IRE)**[4] 4568 5-8-9 50 oh7 ChrisCatlin 1 48
(P W Hiatt) *hld up: hdwy on ins over 2f out: rdn and ev ch over 1f out: wknd ins fnl f* **25/1**

2250 **5** 1¼ **Meelup (IRE)**[7] 4448 6-9-1 59 (p) AmirQuinn(3) 11 54
(P G Murphy) *in tch: rdn 2f out: no hdwy fr over 1f out* **8/1**

4451 **6** *shd* **Friends Hope**[12] 4279 5-9-2 57 SebSanders 7 52
(P A Blockley) *hld up: effrt over 3f out: wknd appr fnl f* **3/1**[1]

4062 **7** *nk* **Wester Lodge (IRE)**[13] 4240 4-10-0 69 (v[1]) MickyFenton 2 64
(J M P Eustace) *led tl rdn and hdd over 1f out: sn wknd* **6/1**[3]

0435 **8** *hd* **Voice Mail**[6] 4483 7-9-11 66 (b) LPKeniry 6 60
(A M Balding) *prom on ins tl rdn and wknd fnl f* **8/1**

0014 **9** 5 **Factual Lad**[13] 4240 8-9-5 60 DaneO'Neill 3 45
(B R Millman) *trckd ldr: rdn 3f out: wknd wl over 1f out* **10/1**

5030 **10** 11 **True West (USA)**[11] 4336 3-9-4 67 OscarUrbina 8 31
(G C H Chung) *a towards rr: lost tch 2f out* **8/1**

2m 2.16s (-0.44) **Going Correction** +0.075s/f (Good)
WFA 3 from 4yo+ 8lb 10 Ran SP% **120.9**

Speed ratings (Par 103):104,102,101,98,97 97,97,97,93,84

CSF £53.38 CT £542.51 TOTE £5.30: £2.00, £3.10, £3.10; EX 66.70 Trifecta £385.90 Part won. Pool: £543.58 - 0.68 winning tickets..

Owner H R Hunt **Bred** Grapestock Llc & Westwood Thoroughbreds Llc **Trained** Woodingdean, E Sussex

FOCUS

A moderate handicap, but with an improving winner. The form looks pretty solid with plenty coming into it in good form.

Factual Lad Official explanation: jockey said gelding hung right

4674 KERI DAVIES & KRISTINA MILLER APEX MEMORIAL H'CAP 6f 209y

4:50 (4:51) (Class 5) (0-70,69) 3-Y-O+ **£3,886** (£1,156; £577; £288) **Stalls** Low

Form RPR

0306 **1** **Riolo (IRE)**[12] 4306 4-8-5 53 (b) KevinGhunowa(5) 3 61
(K F Clutterbuck) *trckd ldr: hung lft 2f out and sn lost 2nd: rallied again ins fnl f to ld last strides* **16/1**

4051 **2** *nk* **Hadath (IRE)**[12] 4276 9-8-9 52 (b) SebSanders 1 59+
(B G Powell) *a in tch on ins: rdn to ld 1f out: hdd last strides* **4/1**[1]

5610 **3** ¾ **What-A-Dancer (IRE)**[10] 4368 9-9-6 63 (b) AdrianMcCarthy 5 68
(R A Harris) *hld up: hdwy on outside over 1f out: r.o fnl f: nvr nrr* **6/1**[3]

0340 **4** 4 **Vindication**[13] 4267 6-9-1 58 (t) OscarUrbina 2 53
(R M H Cowell) *led tl rdn and hdd 1f out: wknd ins fnl f* **5/1**[2]

3023 **5** 1 **Silent Storm**[6] 4496 6-9-10 67 RobertHavlin 6 59
(C A Cyzer) *hld up: rdn 1/2-way: no hdwy fnl 2f* **4/1**[1]

6503 **6** *shd* **Cool Sting (IRE)**[12] 4281 3-9-4 66 LPKeniry 4 58
(A M Balding) *in tch: rdn over 2f out: sn btn* **9/1**

5003 **7** 2½ **Miss Madame (IRE)**[7] 4447 5-8-7 50 (e[1]) ChrisCatlin 7 35
(T G Mills) *t.k.h: prom tl rdn over 2f out: sn wknd* **6/1**[3]

4504 **8** *nk* **Regal Dream (IRE)**[13] 4267 4-9-12 69 (t) FrankieMcDonald 9 53
(J W Hills) *hld up in tch on outside: bhd fnl 2f* **8/1**

1m 23.49s (0.79) **Going Correction** +0.075s/f (Good)
WFA 3 from 4yo+ 5lb 8 Ran SP% **112.2**

Speed ratings (Par 103):98,97,96,92,91 90,88,87

CSF £75.95 CT £436.10 TOTE £29.10: £5.10, £1.40, £2.30; EX 100.10 Trifecta £364.90 Part won. Pool: £513.96 - 0.88 winning tickets..

Owner K F Clutterbuck **Bred** E Kopica And M Rosenfeld **Trained** Exning, Suffolk

FOCUS

An ordinary handicap and the winning time was slower than the seller. Weak form.

Silent Storm Official explanation: jockey said gelding did not act coming down the hill

4675 THE A.B.F. H'CAP — 5f 59y

5:20 (5:20) (Class 6) (0-65,60) 3-Y-0+ £2,590 (£770; £385; £192) Stalls Low

Form — RPR

1501 **1** **Multahab**14 4232 7-9-11 **60**..................(t) BrianReilly 2 — 71
(Miss D A McHale) *trckd ldr: c over to stands' side 3f out: led 2f out: r.o wl fnl f* **3/1**1

4233 **2** ¾ **Talcen Gwyn (IRE)**3 4587 4-9-7 **56**..................(v) DavidKinsella 8 — 64
(M F Harris) *hld up: hdwy over 1f out: r.o to go 2nd ins fnl f* **3/1**1

0012 **3** ¾ **Imperium**56 2955 5-9-2 **51**..................(p) MickyFenton 4 — 56
(Stef Liddiard) *in rr: hdwy appr fnl f: r.o to go 3rd ins fnl f* **11/2**2

5455 **4** ¾ **Tomthevic**4 4551 8-8-9 **44**..................(p) DaneO'Neill 7 — 47
(J M Bradley) *led tl hdd 2f out: kpt on but no ex ins fnl f* **10/1**

2116 **5** 1½ **Ballybunion (IRE)**14 4232 7-9-5 **57**.................. RichardKingscote(3) 9 — 54
(R A Harris) *in tch: hung lft and no hdwy fr over 1f out* **8/1**3

6540 **6** 1 **Zimball**4 4554 4-9-1 **50**.................. JosedeSouza 6 — 44
(J M Bradley) *in tch tl rdn over 1f out: sn wknd* **11/1**

05-0 **7** 1¼ **Turibius**216 136 7-9-8 **60**.................. AmirQuinn(3) 5 — 49
(T E Powell) *hld up on ins: hdwy 2f out: wknd fnl f* **9/1**

0100 **8** 3½ **Ardkeel Lass (IRE)**26 3863 5-8-6 **41**.................. AdrianMcCarthy 3 — 18
(R A Harris) *chsd ldrs: rdn over 2f out: wknd over 1f out* **20/1**

6500 **9** ¾ **Pro Tempore**14 4226 4-8-12 **47**..................(v1) FergusSweeney 1 — 21
(David Pinder) *in tch tl rdn and wknd 2f out* **16/1**

0000 **10** 1½ **Royal Supremacy (IRE)**14 4226 5-8-6 **41** oh2..................(t) ChrisCatlin 10 — 9
(J M Bradley) *chsd ldrs: rdn 2f out: sn btn* **33/1**

62.06 secs (-0.24) **Going Correction** +0.075s/f (Good) **10** Ran SP% **117.5**
Speed ratings (Par 101):104,102,101,100,98 96,94,88,87,85
CSF £11.28 CT £47.99 TOTE £4.20: £2.00, £1.10, £2.40; EX 11.50 Trifecta £37.60 Pool: £417.86 - 7.88 winning tickets. Place 6 £234.85, Place 5 £143.58.
Owner P J Burke and Dave Anderson **Bred** Shadwell Estate Company Limited **Trained** Newmarket, Suffolk

FOCUS
A typical Brighton sprint handicap.
Ballybunion(IRE) Official explanation: jockey said gelding was unsuited by the track
T/Plt: £448.20 to a £1 stake. Pool: £50,131.25. 81.65 winning tickets. T/Qpdt: £63.40 to a £1 stake. Pool: £3,187.70. 37.20 winning tickets. JS

3954 YORK (L-H)
Tuesday, August 22

OFFICIAL GOING: Good to soft
After 40mm rain over the previous four days the ground was described as 'dead, slow and quite hard work'.
Wind: Light, half-against Weather: Fine and sunny

4676 THE SPORTSMAN RACING STKS (H'CAP) — 1m 4f

1:45 (1:45) (Class 2) (0-100,99) 3-Y-0+ £19,431 (£5,781; £2,889; £1,443) Stalls Centre

Form — RPR

0524 **1** **London Express (IRE)**20 4039 3-8-12 **90**.................. RobertWinston 11 — 99+
(M Johnston) *lw: in tch: hdwy over 3f out: rdn to ld over 2f out: rdn and edgd rt wl over 1f out: rdr dropped whip: edgd lft ins last: kpt on* **7/2**1

0650 **2** hd **Stretton (IRE)**16 4175 8-8-12 **80**.................. LDettori 9 — 88
(J D Bethell) *hld up: hdwy 4f out: swtchd lft and effrt to chal ent last and sn ev ch: carried lft and no ex towards fin* **16/1**

2332 **3** 1¼ **Ti Adora (IRE)**10 4347 4-8-12 **80**.................. JohnEgan 8 — 86
(P W D'Arcy) *rrd s and bhd: hdwy on inner wl over 2f out: rdn and ev ch ent last: sn drvn and kpt on same pce* **16/1**

1126 **4** nk **Gringo**25 3890 4-9-2 **84**.................. MichaelHills 1 — 90
(B W Hills) *midfield: hdwy 3f out: rdn and ev ch over 1f out: drvn and one pce ins last* **8/1**2

-004 **5** nk **Self Respect (USA)**17 4149 4-9-0 **82**..................(v) EddieAhern 17 — 87
(A King) *lw: in tch: hdwy to chse ldrs 4f out: rdn over 2f out and kpt on same pce appr last* **16/1**

141 **6** nk **Inchloch**31 3737 4-9-4 **86**.................. RichardHughes 6 — 91
(B G Powell) *hld up towards rr: hdwy 3f out: pushed along 2f out: sn rdn and kpt on ins last: nrst fin* **12/1**

5014 **7** 1 **Best Prospect (IRE)**13 4259 4-9-2 **84**.................. JamieSpencer 20 — 87+
(M Dods) *hld up: gd hdwy on outer 3f out: rdn and ev ch over 1f out: wknd ins last* **25/1**

1315 **8** 1 **Fort Churchill (IRE)**2 4626 5-8-11 **79**..................(bt) TomEaves 14 — 81
(B Ellison) *midfield: hdwy on outer over 4f out: chsd ldrs 3f out: sn rdn and wknd over 1f out* **16/1**

00/0 **9** shd **Zibeline (IRE)**14 4231 9-8-9 **77**..................(b) KerrinMcEvoy 16 — 79
(B Ellison) *dwlt and bhd: effrt and rdn along 3f out: styd on u.p appr last: nrst fin* **100/1**

5004 **10** nk **Tiger Tiger (FR)**88 1976 5-9-13 **95**.................. IanMongan 2 — 96
(Jamie Poulton) *lw: chsd ldrs: rdn along 3f out: grad wknd fnl 2f* **33/1**

120 **11** 1¼ **Purple Moon (IRE)**61 2775 3-9-7 **99**.................. RyanMoore 18 — 98
(Sir Michael Stoute) *towards rr: pushed along over 3f out: drvn 2f out: nvr nr ldrs* **10/1**3

1530 **12** ½ **Miss Provvidence (IRE)**46 3255 4-9-5 **90**.................. AdamKirby(3) 19 — 88
(W R Swinburn) *bhd tl sme late hdwy* **25/1**

0062 **13** 2 **Most Definitely (IRE)**2 4631 6-8-10 **78**.................. DavidAllan 10 — 73+
(T D Easterby) *a towards rr* **20/1**

0063 **14** shd **Mikao (IRE)**10 4347 5-9-4 **86**.................. NCallan 13 — 81
(M H Tompkins) *lw: wnt rt s: sn prom: rdn along 3f out: drvn and wkng whn n.m.r wl over 1f out* **16/1**

2100 **15** ½ **Ski Jump (USA)**20 4036 6-8-12 **80**..................(v) PaulHanagan 12 — 74
(R A Fahey) *cl up: rdn along 4f out: sn wknd* **20/1**

0002 **16** 2½ **Crime Scene (IRE)**10 4370 3-9-0 **92**.................. KDarley 3 — 82
(M Johnston) *prom: rdn along 4f out: sn wknd* **12/1**

2000 **17** 7 **Top Seed (IRE)**10 4347 5-9-3 **85**.................. TedDurcan 4 — 64
(M R Channon) *a rr* **33/1**

620 **18** 1¼ **Quizzene (USA)**82 2176 4-9-2 **84**.................. RoystonFfrench 5 — 61
(M Johnston) *led: rdn along over 3f out: drvn and hdd over 2f out: sn wknd* **14/1**

3-13 **19** 1¼ **Millville**52 3093 6-10-0 **96**.................. PhilipRobinson 7 — 71
(M A Jarvis) *lw: trckd ldrs: effrt over 3f out: sn rdn along and wknd 2f out* **10/1**3

2m 34.6s (2.20) **Going Correction** +0.475s/f (Yiel)
WFA 3 from 4yo+ 10lb **19** Ran SP% **127.1**
Speed ratings (Par 109):111,110,110,109,109 109,108,108,108,107 107,106,105,105,104 103,98,97,96
CSF £57.59 CT £832.48 TOTE £4.20: £1.70, £3.60, £2.60, £2.10; EX 89.00 Trifecta £1448.60 Part won. Pool: £2,040.42 - 0.50 winning tickets..

Owner Leung Kai Fai & Vincent Leung **Bred** Denis McDonnell **Trained** Middleham Moor, N Yorks
■ Stewards' Enquiry : Robert Winston caution: careless riding

FOCUS
A typically competitive handicap to start the meeting and, as has become the trend here, the field came down the middle of the track in the home straight. The early pace was solid, but those that helped set it ended up well beaten. The form looks rock solid.

NOTEBOOK
London Express(IRE), one of only three three-year-olds in the line-up, was a solidly backed favourite and the market got it right. He was off the bridle a fair way out and his rider eventually lost his whip, but the stable's representatives know how to battle even without the assistance of one and he showed typical gameness to hold off the runner-up. The ground had come right for him and there is no reason why he cannot continue to progress. (op 4-1 tchd 9-2)
Stretton(IRE), for whom the easier ground would not have been a problem, was given his usual patient ride and was produced to win his race at just the right time. Had he been involved in a battle with a rival from just about any other yard he may well have carried the day, but he was just unable to go past and getting carried left by the winner in the dying strides probably made little difference. This was a cracking effort against his younger rivals.
Ti Adora(IRE) ◆, suited by the strong pace, made her effort closest to the inside rail and stayed on really well without ever quite getting to the front pair. This was a fine effort considering her four turf wins have all been on fast ground and she is still 4lb above her highest winning mark. She deserves another win on consistency alone.
Gringo, suited by the strong pace, was brought through to hold every chance and was just found wanting for pace where it mattered. He is another that would have preferred faster ground and lost little in defeat of a mark 8lb higher than for his last win. (op 10-1)
Self Respect(USA), for whom the ground had come right, had gained his only previous turf win in similar conditions on this track. He had every chance here, confirming his recent revival with another solid effort, and remains an interesting prospect for the winter game.
Inchloch ◆, raised 4lb for his Newbury win, was trying this trip for the first time on the level and, given the solid pace, he indicated strongly that he stayed every yard of it. The easier ground did not seem to bother him and there should be another opportunity for him this autumn. (op 11-1)
Best Prospect(IRE) looked a possible winner when moving up strongly on the nearside halfway up the home straight, but his effort then flattened out. He appeared not to see out the trip in the conditions.
Fort Churchill(IRE) had every chance halfway up the home straight, but failed to last home. His only win in soft ground came in a claimer when favoured by the weights, but a race like this was a different ball game off this sort of mark.
Tiger Tiger(FR) Official explanation: jockey said gelding hung both ways
Miss Provvidence(IRE) Official explanation: jockey said filly hung badly right-handed
Crime Scene(IRE) showed to the fore for a mile or so before tiring and still has it to prove over this trip.
Quizzene(USA) should have relished the softer ground, but after making much of the running he fell in a hole. He lost his form in the second half of last season after running well in the spring and it is becoming a similar story this year.
Millville, a winner in similar conditions over course and distance at the Dante Meeting, might have faced a stiff task under top weight but this was too bad to be true. (tchd 11-1)

4677 WEATHERBYS INSURANCE LONSDALE CUP (GROUP 2) — 1m 7f 198y

2:15 (2:16) (Class 1) 3-Y-0+
£70,975 (£26,900; £13,462; £6,712; £3,362; £1,687) Stalls Low

Form — RPR

2524 **1** **Sergeant Cecil**19 4081 7-9-1 **111**.................. LDettori 7 — 117
(B R Millman) *lw: bhd: hdwy over 3f out: pushed along over 2f out: rdnto chal and edgd rt ent last: sn drvn and styd on to ld 100 yds* **11/4**1

600- **2** ½ **Franklins Gardens**294 6223 6-9-1 **107**.................. NCallan 3 — 116
(M H Tompkins) *trckd ldr: led 4f out: pushed clr over 2f out: rdn and edgd rt over 1f out: drvn ent last: hdd and no ex last 100 yds* **17/2**

-516 **3** 5 **The Whistling Teal**39 3516 10-9-1 **110**.................. SteveDrowne 2 — 110
(G Wragg) *hld up towards rr: stdy hdwy 4f out: rdn to chse ldr whn n.m.r and swtchd lft over 1f out: kpt on same pce* **16/1**

1030 **4** 4 **Bulwark (IRE)**19 4081 4-9-1 **105**..................(be) KerrinMcEvoy 5 — 106
(Mrs A J Perrett) *in tch: hdwy to trck ldrs 1/2-way: effrt to chse ldr wl over 2f out: sn rdn and wknd wl over 1f out* **12/1**

0115 **5** 2½ **Baddam**19 4081 4-9-1 **105**.................. IanMongan 9 — 103
(M R Channon) *hld up in rr: hdwy 4f out: rdn along 3f out and sn no imp* **12/1**

12-0 **6** 3 **Golden Quest**19 4081 5-9-1 **110**.................. JoeFanning 1 — 99
(M Johnston) *chsd ldrs: rdn along 3f out: drvn and wknd over 2f out* **9/2**3

2103 **7** 8 **Tungsten Strike (USA)**19 4081 5-9-4 **112**.................. MartinDwyer 8 — 95+
(Mrs A J Perrett) *lw: cl up: rdn along over 3f out: drvn and wknd over 2f out* **4/1**2

2030 **8** 20 **Winged D'Argent (IRE)**19 4081 5-9-1 **105**.................. KDarley 4 — 65
(M Johnston) *midfield: rdn along 1/2-way: sn wknd* **20/1**

1540 **9** 7 **Ebtikaar (IRE)**19 4081 4-9-1 **96**.................. RHills 11 — 57
(J L Dunlop) *lw: midfield: rdn along over 5f out: wknd 4f out* **16/1**

-540 **10** 10 **High Action (USA)**19 4081 6-9-1 **109**.................. RichardHughes 6 — 45
(Ian Williams) *led: rdn along over 4f out: sn hdd & wknd* **40/1**

/03- **11** 5 **Kasthari (IRE)**122 5068 7-9-1 **108**.................. TomEaves 10 — 39
(J Howard Johnson) *chsd ldrs: rdn along over 6f out: sn wknd* **28/1**

3m 28.47s (5.22) **11** Ran SP% **113.2**
CSF £24.90 TOTE £3.10: £1.40, £2.30, £3.00; EX 26.40 Trifecta £163.20 Pool: £1,259.86 - 5.48 winning tickets..
Owner Terry Cooper **Bred** D E Hazzard **Trained** Kentisbeare, Devon
■ The first running of this race on the new round course.
■ Stewards' Enquiry : L Dettori one-day ban: used whip without allowing time to respond and down the shoulder in forehand position (Sep 3)

FOCUS
This looked a competitive renewal and, with the pace solid throughout, the field finished well spread out. The form looks sound. Again the runners moved to the centre of the track turning for home, but eventually migrated right over to the stands' rail. Due to the contest being run on a new track, it is not possible to produce speed figures for this race.

NOTEBOOK
Sergeant Cecil, who was without the services of Alan Munro for the first time in 13 appearances, was marginally best in at the weights and crucially got the strong pace he needs. His prospects did not look that rosy coming to the last quarter-mile, as although he was travelling adequately the leader was going much better and looked as though he would take a deal of catching. However, toughness has never been a problem for the gelding and he dourly managed to wear his rival down and gain a richly-deserved first success at Group level. (op 10-3 tchd 7-2 in places)
Franklins Gardens has a fine record fresh, so it was no surprise to see him put up such a big effort on this first run since being injured in the Melbourne Cup nine months ago. Sent into a clear lead halfway up the home straight, it looked as though his rider's enterprise might pay off as he was still going better than his rivals passing the two-furlong pole, but his tendency to hang towards the stands' rail a furlong out was the first hint that he was getting tired and that gave the ultra-tough favourite the chance he needed. He still has what it takes to be successful a this sort of level. (op 8-1 tchd 9-1 in a place)

The Whistling Teal had the ground come in his favour, but this was his first try at the trip. He was produced with what looked a dangerous effort under severe pressure entering the last quarter-mile, but his stamina then appeared to give out. This was still a decent effort at this level over a trip beyond his best. (op 14-1)

Bulwark(IRE) had a bit to find with a few of these on official ratings and the ground was probably a bit softer than ideal, but the strong pace helped him and he still had every chance passing the two-furlong pole before finding the demands too great. His new inflated mark means that he will have to stay in races like this from now on.

Baddam is in a similar position to Bulwark, a successful handicapper plying his trade in Pattern company, and he is also finding things tough though even this was probably an insufficient test for him.

Golden Quest, for whom the ground had come right, might have been expected to bounce after his recent return in the Goodwood Cup following a 13-month break, but this performance did not really prove whether he did or not. Either way, he still has to prove that he is as good as he was. (tchd 5-1)

Tungsten Strike(USA), the only penalised runner in the field having won a Group 2 back in May, faded tamely, and the fact that his Sandown victim Winged D'Argent finished even further behind him here and no winners have come out of that race suggests this year's Henry II Stakes was a particularly poor renewal. (op 7-2)

High Action(USA) Official explanation: jockey said gelding had no more to give

4678 LADBROKES GREAT VOLTIGEUR STKS (GROUP 2) (C&G) 1m 4f

2:50 (2:51) (Class 1) 3-Y-O

£76,653 (£29,052; £14,539; £7,249; £3,631; £1,822) **Stalls** Centre

Form				RPR
1301	**1**		**Youmzain (IRE)**[40] 3441 3-8-12 107 RichardHughes 3 (M R Channon) *stdd s and bhd: hdwy 3f out: rdn over 1f out: str run ent last: led last 50 yds* **12/1**	119+
1122	**2**	*hd*	**Red Rocks (IRE)**[39] 3517 3-8-12 114 LDettori 2 (B J Meehan) *lw: trckd ldrs: hdwy to ld over 2f out: rdn and edgd rt over 1f out: drvn ins last: hdd and no ex last 50 yds* **10/3**[2]	119
100	**3**	*3*	**Puerto Rico (IRE)**[39] 3517 3-8-12 JAHeffernan 1 (A P O'Brien, Ire) *hld up towards rr: hdwy over 3f out: rdn to chse ldrs over 1f out: kpt on same pce* **40/1**	114
1250	**4**	*1*	**The Last Drop (IRE)**[60] 2805 3-8-12 100 (t) MichaelHills 10 (B W Hills) *hld up in rr: hdwy 3f out: rdn to chse ldrs and swtchd lft over 1f out: no imp ins last* **100/1**	112
2111	**5**	*hd*	**Soapy Danger**[40] 3444 3-9-1 119 KDarley 4 (M Johnston) *lw: led: rdn along 3f out: edgd rt: drvn and hdd over 2f out: wknd over 1f out: finshed lame* **4/1**[3]	115+
1-	**6**	*2 1/2*	**Fire And Rain (FR)**[327] 5574 3-8-12 MJKinane 6 (A P O'Brien, Ire) *prom: rdn along over 3f out: sn wknd* **8/1**	108
-111	**7**	*10*	**Stage Gift (IRE)**[80] 2224 3-8-12 107 RobertWinston 9 (Sir Michael Stoute) *lw: trckd ldrs: hdwy over 4f out: chal 3f out and ev ch whn hmpd over 2f out: sn rdn and wknd* **8/1**	92+
1101	**8**	*4*	**Papal Bull**[60] 2801 3-9-1 115 RyanMoore 7 (Sir Michael Stoute) *lw: in tch: pushed along over 3f out: rdn wl over 2f out and sn btn* **11/4**[1]	89+
2-10	**9**	*10*	**Championship Point (IRE)**[80] 2228 3-8-12 110 TedDurcan 5 (M R Channon) *keen: chsd ldrs: rdn along over 3f out: sn wknd* **8/1**	70
-320	**10**	*16*	**Sienna Storm (IRE)**[80] 2228 3-8-12 99 NCallan 8 (M H Tompkins) *chsd ldrs: rdn along over 3f out: sn wknd* **100/1**	44

2m 34.93s (2.53) **Going Correction** +0.475s/f (Yiel) 10 Ran SP% **115.2**

Speed ratings (Par 112):110,109,107,107,107 105,98,96,89,78

CSF £51.27 TOTE £18.00: £3.80, £1.60, £6.50; EX 78.50 Trifecta £1276.60 Pool: £1,798.10 - 1.00 winning ticket..

Owner Jaber Abdullah **Bred** Frank Dunne **Trained** West Ilsley, Berks

FOCUS

The early pace was only fair and resulted in just an acceptable winning time for a race of its status, 0.33 seconds slower than the earlier handicap. Again the field came right over to the stands' rail in the home straight. A few of these ran below form for one reason or another and a couple of big outsiders finished close up, putting a question mark over the form which has not been rated as positively as it might have been.

NOTEBOOK

Youmzain(IRE) gave his rivals a couple of lengths' lead at the start, but that was probably by design. Given a waiting ride, he sliced his way through the field up the home straight and found a decent turn of speed to nail the leader close to the line. The ground appeared to be no problem and he has not looked back since his unfortunate experience behind Papal Bull at Royal Ascot, but he looks the sort for whom things need to fall right and that will be the key if he returns here for the St Leger.

Red Rocks(IRE) was not asked to lead this time, but it took nothing away from his performance and he looked likely to score when sent to the front a quarter of a mile out. However, that gave the eventual winner a target to aim at and the race was snatched from him near the line. He has now finished runner-up three times in a row and deserves to win a Group race. (op 4-1)

Puerto Rico(IRE), suited by the softer ground, improved on a couple of moderate performances at the highest level and had every chance, but he still looks to have a few questions to answer.

The Last Drop(IRE), very disappointing in two outings since his narrow defeat in the Sandown Classic Trial, had no chance on official ratings but ran a blinder at a monster price. The short break since his last outing and the first-time tongue tie may have been contributory factors, but it may also have been a case of him handling the ground rather better than some of the big guns so it would be a mistake to get too carried away.

Soapy Danger, given a typically positive ride in a bid to maintain his terrific run this season, did his best to keep his rivals at bay in the home straight but, despite giving it his all, he finally had to succumb. It transpired that he had fractured a pastern. Official explanation: jockey said colt finished lame (op 3-1)

Fire And Rain(FR), not seen since making a successful racecourse debut 11 months ago and taking a half-mile step up in trip, was in trouble some way out but it is too early to write him off. (op 10-1)

Stage Gift(IRE) had a chance halfway up the home straight, but was soon on the retreat. The longer trip and softer ground were probably more to blame than the step up in class. (tchd 15-2)

Papal Bull, who had the front pair behind him when winning the King Edward VII Stakes at Royal Ascot, never looked happy on this softer ground and ran well below form. Official explanation: jockey said colt was unsuited by the good to soft ground (op 3-1 tchd 7-2 and 5-2 in a place)

Championship Point(IRE) pulled far too hard to give himself any chance of seeing out the trip in this ground. (op 10-1)

4679 JUDDMONTE INTERNATIONAL STKS (GROUP 1) 1m 2f 88y

3:25 (3:25) (Class 1) 3-Y-O+

£283,900 (£107,600; £53,850; £26,850; £13,450; £6,750) **Stalls** Low

Form				RPR
1152	**1**		**Notnowcato**[45] 3314 4-9-5 118 RyanMoore 5 (Sir Michael Stoute) *trckd ldrs: hdwy 3f out: led 2f out: sn rdn: drvn ins last: hdd last 100 yds: rallied to ld on line* **8/1**	125
3115	**2**	*shd*	**Maraahel (IRE)**[24] 3927 5-9-5 120 (v) RHills 3 (Sir Michael Stoute) *lw: hld up: pushed along and hdwy 3f out: rdn to chal ins last: drvn to ld last 100 yds: hdd on line* **9/1**	125
1143	**3**	*3*	**Blue Monday**[45] 3314 5-9-5 117 SteveDrowne 8 (R Charlton) *lw: trckd ldng pair: hdwy over 2f out: sn rdn and kpt on same pce fnl f* **11/2**[2]	119
-131	**4**	*3/4*	**Dylan Thomas (IRE)**[51] 3127 3-8-11 MJKinane 2 (A P O'Brien, Ire) *trckd ldrs: effrt on outer over 2f out: sn rdn and btn* **5/6**[1]	118
0132	**5**	*1/2*	**Laverock (IRE)**[23] 3993 4-9-5 (t) DBonilla 4 (C Laffon-Parias, France) *hld up: effrt over 3f out: sn rdn along and no imp fnl 2f* **12/1**	117
0661	**6**	*1/2*	**Cherry Mix (FR)**[9] 4414 5-9-5 115 (t) LDettori 1 (Saeed Bin Suroor) *led: rdn over 2f out and sn hdd: drvn and wknd over 1f out* **7/1**[3]	116
0160	**7**	*8*	**Snoqualmie Boy**[17] 4126 3-8-11 111 JohnEgan 6 (D R C Elsworth) *a rr* **66/1**	100

2m 12.32s (1.84) **Going Correction** +0.475s/f (Yiel)

WFA 3 from 4yo+ 8lb 7 Ran SP% **112.7**

Speed ratings (Par 117):111,110,108,107,107 107,100

CSF £72.40 TOTE £10.00: £3.60, £3.60; EX 78.20 Trifecta £37.60 Pool: £1,806.84 - 34.10 winning tickets..

Owner Anthony & David de Rothschild **Bred** Southcourt Stud **Trained** Newmarket, Suffolk

■ A one-two for the Stoute yard and a first Group 1 win for jockey Ryan Moore, still well clear in the race to be champion jockey.

FOCUS

The early pace was not at all strong, resulting in a couple taking a stronger hold than ideal, and the winning time was modest for such a prestigious race. The field again came centre to stands' side. This is not championship form, but a solid Group 1 with the winner progressing by 5lb and the runner-up reproducing last year's figure.

NOTEBOOK

Notnowcato was always in a good position in a moderately-run race, but did not appear to be going as well as a few of his rivals starting up the home straight. However, he responded extremely well to pressure and, in what eventually became a war of attrition with his stable companion, just forced his head back in front on the line. The way the race was run, the ground, and the winning time all raise questions over the form, but he is the sort of improver his trainer works magic with year after year and it would be no surprise if he was an even better horse if returning at the age of five. (op 6-1)

Maraahel(IRE), beaten less than half a length into third in this race last year, was given his usual patient ride before being asked to take closer order halfway up the home straight. Asked for everything in the last furlong, it looked just a few yards from the line as though his effort had been timed just right and after the post his rider thought he had won, but on the line itself it was proved that he had once again fallen agonisingly short at Group 1 level. He obviously has the ability to win a race like this when everything goes right for him, but how many more chances he will get remains to be seen. (op 11-1 tchd 12-1 in a place)

Blue Monday, for whom the easing of the ground would have been most welcome, had every chance but could not produce a turn of foot where it mattered. He ran very close to Eclipse form with Notnowcato, however, and is more than capable of winning another lesser Group race. (op 7-1 tchd 15-2)

Dylan Thomas(IRE), all the rage for this after his convincing success in the Irish Derby, did himself few favours by taking a strong hold early, and when he was finally asked for his effort the response was laboured. The softer ground may have been the reason, despite his having won a couple of times on yielding ground in Ireland, but this was still yet another reverse for the Classic generation against their elders at Group 1 level this season. (op 10-11 tchd Evens)

Laverock(IRE), suited by the ground, was switched off out the back before coming under strong pressure soon after turning for home, but he never looked like getting to the leaders. The form of the Prix d'Ispahan, which he won back in May, has not worked out at all. (op 11-1)

Cherry Mix(FR) was allowed an uncontested lead and seemed to be going particularly well starting up the home straight, but once losing the advantage a quarter of a mile out he then dropped away rather tamely. The ground should not have been a problem and perhaps his victory in a Group 1 in Germany last time was a false dawn. (tchd 15-2)

Snoqualmie Boy took a keen hold early, but even so he is not up to this level. (op 50-1)

4680 SYMPHONY GROUP ACOMB STKS (GROUP 3) 7f

4:00 (4:01) (Class 1) 2-Y-O **£23,708** (£8,964; £4,480; £2,240) **Stalls** Low

Form				RPR
11	**1**		**Big Timer (USA)**[15] 4200 2-9-0 TomEaves 5 (I Semple) *lw: trckd ldrs: t.k.h: shkn up to ld over 1f out: r.o strly* **5/4**[1]	105+
3531	**2**	*2 1/2*	**Gweebarra**[16] 4171 2-9-0 91 NCallan 6 (K A Ryan) *lw: chsd ldrs: hmpd over 1f out: styd on to take 2nd nr fin* **9/1**	99
1	**3**	*shd*	**Ready For Spring (USA)**[18] 4105 2-9-0 LDettori 7 (J Noseda) *trckd ldrs: effrt and edgd lft over 1f out: kpt on same pce* **7/1**	99
2	**4**	*3 1/2*	**Putra Square**[32] 3701 2-9-0 EddieAhern 2 (P F I Cole) *hld up in tch: outpcd over 3f out: kpt on fnl f* **7/1**	90
	5	*nk*	**Celestial Halo (IRE)** 2-9-0 MichaelHills 1 (B W Hills) *wl grwn: dwlt: outpcd over 3f out: kpt on fnl f* **25/1**	89
411	**6**	*3*	**Old Romney**[6] 4474 2-9-0 87 KDarley 4 (M Johnston) *led tl over 1f out: sn wknd* **9/2**[2]	82
31	**7**	*2 1/2*	**Winged Flight (USA)**[12] 4302 2-9-0 JoeFanning 3 (M Johnston) *w ldrs: wknd appr fnl f* **6/1**[3]	76

1m 27.28s (1.88) **Going Correction** +0.25s/f (Good) 7 Ran SP% **115.8**

Speed ratings (Par 104):99,96,96,92,91 88,85

CSF £14.17 TOTE £2.40: £1.50, £4.90; EX 17.80.

Owner David McKenzie **Bred** Mt Brilliant Farm Llc **Trained** Carluke, S Lanarks

■ Previously a Listed race, but upgraded to Group 3 this time. A first Group winner for both Ian Semple and Tom Eaves.

FOCUS

A solid renewal of a race won last year by subsequent Racing Post Trophy winner Palace Episode from Araafa. The winning time was modest for a race like this, but the decisive and unbeaten winner has plenty of untapped potential yet.

NOTEBOOK

Big Timer(USA) made it three from three, travelling strongly, if a shade keen early on. He scored in most decisive fashion and is still learning, but being a gelding his targets are limited. Unless he is sold connections are contemplating supplementing him for the Champagne Stakes over this course and distance in two weeks time. (op 6-4 tchd 13-8)

Gweebarra, who really took the eye in the paddock, would have finished clear second but for being knocked out of his stride. He is crying out for a mile. (op 11-1 tchd 12-1)

Ready For Spring(USA), a moderate mover, came off a straight line for a stride or two, getting in the way of the runner-up. He is still on the weak side and should make a better three-year-old. (op 9-2)

Putra Square, a heavy-topped individual, couldn't keep up when the pace increased. Staying on in his own time at the death, a mile will suit him much better. (tchd 8-1)

Celestial Halo(IRE), a well-made individual, has a round action. He was very inexperienced but there was much to like about the way he picked up late on. He can surely find an ordinary maiden at the very least.

Old Romney took them along but, on his first try on easy ground, it was disappointing the way he fell in a heap. (tchd 5-1 in places)

Winged Flight(USA), stepping up in trip and trying easy ground for the first time, was another to disappoint. (op 8-1 tchd 9-1)

4681 IRWIN MITCHELL SOLICITORS STKS (NURSERY) 6f

4:35 (4:35) (Class 2) 2-Y-O £16,192 (£4,817; £2,407; £1,202) **Stalls** Centre

Form RPR

030 **1** **Dubai Builder**[11] [4333] 2-8-7 **75** JohnEgan 12 97+
(J S Moore) *in rr: hdwy over 2f out: led over 1f out: r.o wl* **7/1**[3]

232 **2** *1 ½* **Gentleman Pirate**[13] [4260] 2-8-11 **79** JimmyQuinn 13 93
(M H Tompkins) *hld up in mid-div: hdwy over 2f out: styd on to go 2nd ins last: kpt on wl* **8/1**

41 **3** *4* **First Mate (IRE)**[10] [4349] 2-8-10 **78** J-PGuillambert 11 80
(M Johnston) *w ldrs: kpt on same pce appr fnl f* **7/1**[3]

5511 **4** *1* **Onenightinlisbon (IRE)**[19] [4088] 2-9-1 **83** LeeEnstone 10 82
(K R Burke) *w ldrs: edgd lft over 1f out: kpt on same pce* **25/1**

411 **5** *shd* **Frontline In Focus (IRE)**[22] [4006] 2-9-5 **87** PatCosgrave 15 86
(K R Burke) *mid-div: hdwy over 3f out: outpcd 2f out: kpt on fnl f* **14/1**

403 **6** *nk* **Vitznau (IRE)**[22] [4000] 2-8-7 **75** RyanMoore 17 73
(R Hannon) *in rr: hdwy over 2f out: kpt on fnl f* **12/1**

105 **7** *2* **Prospect Place**[54] [3026] 2-8-9 **77** JamieSpencer 4 69+
(M Dods) *lw: trckd ldrs: effrt whn hmpd over 1f out: kpt on same pce* **16/1**

4520 **8** *nk* **Danum Dancer**[17] [4152] 2-8-5 **73** NickyMackay 9 64
(N Bycroft) *mid-div: effrt over 2f out: nvr nr ldrs* **33/1**

4243 **9** *1 ¼* **Rainbow Fox**[4] [4547] 2-8-12 **80** PaulHanagan 5 67
(R A Fahey) *rr-div: hdwy 3f out: nvr nr ldrs* **25/1**

2111 **10** *1 ¼* **Ponty Rossa (IRE)**[17] [4146] 2-9-6 **88** DavidAllan 2 71
(T D Easterby) *w ldrs: chal 2f out: sn wknd* **6/1**[1]

4143 **11** *3* **Valley Of The Moon (IRE)**[10] [4377] 2-8-7 **75** TonyHamilton 19 49
(R A Fahey) *racd stands' side: led other pair that side over 1f out: no ch w main gp* **33/1**

3212 **12** *nk* **Palo Verde**[7] [4460] 2-9-4 **86** JoeFanning 8 60
(M Johnston) *led: hung lft and hdd over 1f out: sn lost pl* **10/1**

210 **13** *2 ½* **Prince Rossi (IRE)**[56] [2960] 2-9-1 **83** LDettori 14 49
(J D Bethell) *mid-div: effrt over 2f out: sn lost pl* **12/1**

153 **14** *1 ½* **Opal Noir**[46] [3239] 2-9-5 **87** TomEaves 3 49
(J Howard Johnson) *w ldrs: lost pl over 1f out* **25/1**

002 **15** *6* **Wilmington**[17] [4161] 2-8-4 **72** MartinDwyer 20 16
(R Hannon) *racd stands' side: led that pair 2f: no ch fnl 2f* **25/1**

5130 **16** *½* **As One Does**[31] [3735] 2-9-7 **89** NCallan 6 31
(K A Ryan) *lw: w ldrs: lost pl over 1f out* **25/1**

3000 **17** *2* **Storm Mission (USA)**[19] [4088] 2-7-9 **66** oh2 DominicFox(3) 16 —
(Miss V Haigh) *w ldrs: rdn 3f out: lost pl over 1f out* **100/1**

220 **18** *½* **Folio (USA)**[32] [3701] 2-9-1 **83** RichardHughes 18 18
(B W Hills) *swtchd rt after s and racd w 2 others stands' side: led that pair 4f out tl over 1f out: sn wknd* **13/2**[2]

1m 13.04s (0.48) **Going Correction** +0.25s/f (Good) 18 Ran SP% **126.9**
Speed ratings (Par 100):106,104,98,97,97 96,94,93,92,90 86,86,82,80,72 72,69,68
CSF £57.73 CT £421.79 TOTE £9.10: £2.90, £2.20, £2.30, £3.90; EX 89.50 Trifecta £1275.60 Part won. Pool: £1,796.74 - 0.70 winning tickets..
Owner Uplands Acquisitions Limited **Bred** Theakston Stud **Trained** Upper Lambourn, Berks

FOCUS
A highly competitive nursery, the first two clear and likely to go on to better things. The gallop was very strong, the time was smart, and they finished well strung out. Solid form which should work out well.

NOTEBOOK
Dubai Builder ◆, quite a big type, settled much better and came through strongly to take charge, justifying strong support. This was only his fourth start and there looks to be even better to come, so it will be hard for the Handicapper to catch up with next time. (tchd 8-1)
Gentleman Pirate, a good-bodied individual, travelled strongly and in the end finished clear second best. He can surely break his duck either in another nursery or if returned to maiden company. (op 10-1)
First Mate(IRE), in the thick of things in a race run at a very strong pace, looks on the weak side and can do even better in time. (tchd 15-2)
Onenightinlisbon(IRE), 8lb higher after accounting for two subsequent winners at Musselburgh, was in the thick of things from the off and has proved a shrewd claim.
Frontline In Focus(IRE), on her toes beforehand, was stepping up from the minimum trip. Surprisingly tapped for toe soon after the halfway mark, she was going on at the finish. (tchd 16-1)
Vitznau(IRE), put to sleep at the rear, kept on in his own time and has finally learned to relax in his races.
Prospect Place, absent for over seven weeks, was messed about at a crucial stage otherwise he would have finished a bit closer. Official explanation: jockey said colt was denied a clear run (op 14-1)
Ponty Rossa(IRE), who looked very fit, took them along at a strong gallop but on this easy ground he wavered and dropped away. (op 5-1 tchd 7-1)
Valley Of The Moon(IRE) did best of the three who raced isolated down the stands'-side rail.
Prince Rossi(IRE) Official explanation: jockey said colt ran flat
Folio(USA), one of three to race hard against the stands'-side rail, took charge of that group but they were never on terms with the main body of the field and in the end his rider gave up. Official explanation: jockey said colt had no more to give (op 7-1)

4682 PATRINGTON HAVEN LEISURE PARK STKS (H'CAP) 6f

5:10 (5:11) (Class 2) (0-100,98) 3-Y-O+ **£16,192** (£4,817; £2,407; £1,202) **Stalls** Centre

Form RPR

2143 **1** **Knot In Wood (IRE)**[15] [4202] 4-8-8 **82** PaulHanagan 3 93
(R A Fahey) *chsd ldrs: sn drvn along: styd on fnl f: led nr fin* **4/1**[1]

-350 **2** *nk* **Pacific Pride**[52] [3079] 3-9-5 **96** (b[1]) JamieSpencer 13 106
(J Howard Johnson) *s.i.s: hdwy far side over 2f out: led 1f out: hdd and no ex towards fin* **33/1**

3005 **3** *nk* **Connect**[7] [4461] 9-8-9 **90** (b) PatrickHills(3) 18 99
(M H Tompkins) *hld up in rr: hdwy over 2f out: upsides ins last: no ex nr fin* **20/1**

0610 **4** *1 ¼* **Rising Shadow (IRE)**[3] [4609] 5-9-3 **91** PaulFessey 8 96
(T D Barron) *in rr: hdwy over 2f out: kpt on same pce fnl f* **6/1**[2]

102 **5** *¾* **Steel Blue**[6] [4468] 6-8-5 **79** HayleyTurner 2 82
(R M Whitaker) *chsd ldrs: kpt on same pce fnl f* **9/1**

00-2 **6** *shd* **River Falcon**[122] [1145] 6-9-4 **92** DanielTudhope 16 95
(J S Goldie) *hld up in rr: hdwy on ins 2f out: styd on ins last: nt rch ldrs* **8/1**

4000 **7** *2* **Continent**[3] [4609] 9-9-1 **89** AdrianTNicholls 12 86
(D Nicholls) *mid-div: nt clr run over 2f out: kpt on fnl f* **14/1**

0155 **8** *¾* **Grazeon Gold Blend**[23] [3986] 3-8-10 **87** GrahamGibbons 19 82
(J J Quinn) *in rr: hdwy and hung lft over 2f out: nvr nr ldrs* **50/1**

2400 **9** *¾* **Coleorton Dancer**[3] [4609] 4-9-3 **96** AndrewMullen(5) 15 88
(K A Ryan) *led tl hdd & wknd 1f out* **16/1**

6055 **10** *½* **Tony The Tap**[31] [3744] 5-8-11 **85** FrancisFerris 9 76
(B Palling) *in rr: sn pushed along: styd on appr fnl f* **20/1**

615- **11** *2 ½* **Special Lad**[296] [6182] 4-8-6 **80** EddieAhern 4 63
(P F I Cole) *chsd ldrs: wknd over 1f out* **20/1**

2000 **12** *¾* **Munaddam (USA)**[17] [4128] 4-9-8 **96** RHills 10 77
(E A L Dunlop) *mid-div: wkng whn n.m.r over 1f out* **13/2**[3]

3045 **13** *¾* **Bond Boy**[19] [4085] 9-8-8 **82** (b) TedDurcan 6 61
(B Smart) *chsd ldrs: hung lft and lost pl over 1f out* **7/1**

6011 **14** *¾* **Pic Up Sticks**[31] [3744] 7-9-3 **91** RyanMoore 14 68
(B G Powell) *rrd s: hdwy and mid-div 3f out: nvr nr ldrs* **14/1**

0300 **15** *shd* **Malcheek (IRE)**[24] [3937] 4-8-10 **84** DavidAllan 11 60
(T D Easterby) *chsd ldrs: lost pl 2f out* **50/1**

104- **16** *3 ½* **Foreign Edition (IRE)**[478] [1388] 4-8-11 **85** TomEaves 17 51
(Miss J A Camacho) *chsd ldrs: lost pl over 1f out* **50/1**

0100 **17** *11* **Desert Commander (IRE)**[3] [4609] 4-9-9 **97** NCallan 20 30
(K A Ryan) *chsd ldrs: lost pl and heavily eased over 1f out* **20/1**

1m 12.66s (0.10) **Going Correction** +0.25s/f (Good)
WFA 3 from 4yo+ 3lb 17 Ran SP% **128.3**
Speed ratings (Par 109):109,108,108,106,105 105,102,101,100,100 96,95,94,93,93 88,74
CSF £160.30 CT £2487.65 TOTE £5.00: £1.60, £5.60, £4.20, £2.40; EX 210.60 Trifecta £1657.90 Part won. Pool: £2,335.14 - 0.10 winning tickets. Place 6 £1,352.77, Place 5 £534.82.
Owner Rhodes, Kenyon & Gill **Bred** Rathbarry Stud **Trained** Musley Bank, N Yorks

FOCUS
A sound gallop and those that raced in the firing line paid the price in the end. This was a strong handicap and the form looks solid, the winner progressing by another 6lb.

NOTEBOOK
Knot In Wood(IRE), on ground that suits him, improved again and gamely defied a mark 8lb above that of his last win. He is most consistent and appeals as the type to reach even greater heights next season. (op 11-2 tchd 6-1 in a place)
Pacific Pride, runner-up in the Coventry Stakes here at two, wore blinkers for the first time. After a sluggish start he made his effort on the far side but, after taking a narrow advantage, he was edged out near the line. He may prove a tricky customer.
Connect, whose last success was here from the same mark just over a year ago, came through from the back to hold every chance only to just miss out near the line. He seems to barely see out the six. (op 25-1)
Rising Shadow(IRE), just 4lb higher than when ending a lengthy losing run at Ripon two outings ago, takes time to warm to his task but he deserves credit for the way he knuckled down here. (op 8-1)
Steel Blue, reunited with Hayley Turner who has won twice on him, did well considering he raced up with what was a strong pace towards the wide outside. (op 8-1)
River Falcon, absent since April, was set an impossible task. He was going about his business in really pleasing fashion at the end and looks set for a lucrative backend campaign on the soft ground he loves.
Tony The Tap stayed on from the rear when it was all over but it transpired that he had been struck into during the course of the race.
Bond Boy Official explanation: jockey said gelding hung right-handed
T/Jkpt: Not won. T/Plt: £617.40 to a £1 stake. Pool: £207,803.75. 245.70 winning tickets. T/Qpdt: £95.80 to a £1 stake. Pool: £8,364.90. 64.65 winning tickets. JR

4683 - 4685a (Foreign Racing) - See Raceform Interactive

4550 FOLKESTONE (R-H)

Wednesday, August 23

OFFICIAL GOING: Good to soft
Wind: Nil Weather: Heavy rain before racing becoming overcast

4686 ARENA LEISURE PLC MAIDEN STKS 1m 1f 149y

5:15 (5:15) (Class 5) 3-Y-O+ **£3,238** (£963; £481; £240) **Stalls** Low

Form RPR

0-22 **1** **Dayrose**[75] [2398] 3-8-12 **84** DaneO'Neill 5 82+
(Sir Michael Stoute) *sn trckd ldr: rdn to chal over 2f out: led narrowly over 1f out: asserted last 100yds* **5/4**[1]

4342 **2** *1 ¾* **Regent's Park**[17] [4181] 3-8-12 **74** ChrisCatlin 3 78
(R Charlton) *led: shkn up and jnd over 2f out: narrowly hdd over 1f out: no ex last 100yds* **11/8**[2]

3 *½* **Clear Sailing** 3-9-3 OscarUrbina 2 82
(Mrs A J Perrett) *dwlt: settled in 4th: chsd ldng pair over 2f out: sn shkn up and rn green: styd on last 150yds: nrst fin* **8/1**[3]

0300 **4** *19* **Bride To Be (USA)**[21] [4044] 3-8-12 **70** StephenCarson 6 39
(C E Brittain) *chsd ldng pair tl wknd over 2f out: t.o* **20/1**

5 *8* **Pearl Of Esteem** 3-8-9 AdamKirby(3) 4 23
(J Pearce) *s.s: a last and rn green: in tch tl wknd 4f out: t.o* **20/1**

2m 4.77s (-0.46) **Going Correction** +0.125s/f (Good) 5 Ran SP% **107.2**
Speed ratings (Par 103):106,104,104,89,82
CSF £3.04 TOTE £1.80: £1.10, £1.20; EX 2.90.
Owner Sir Evelyn De Rothschild **Bred** Southcourt Stud **Trained** Newmarket, Suffolk

FOCUS
An uncompetitive maiden in which the front three pulled clear of the no-hopers. The form is of a fair standard but on the weak side, rated through the runner-up.

4687 GERRY COTTER MEMORIAL H'CAP 1m 4f

5:45 (5:45) (Class 5) (0-70,71) 3-Y-O+ **£3,238** (£963; £481; £240) **Stalls** Low

Form RPR

6030 **1** **Tayman (IRE)**[24] [3983] 4-9-11 **62** SebSanders 7 70
(G Wragg) *hld up in 4th: effrt over 2f out: chsd ldr jst over 1f out: hrd rdn and r.o to ld last stride* **11/4**[2]

1245 **2** *hd* **Icannshift (IRE)**[36] [3616] 6-8-10 **50** NeilChalmers(3) 2 58
(T M Jones) *led: kicked on 3f out: drvn and kpt on wl fnl 2f: collared on post* **5/1**[3]

-340 **3** *3 ½* **Gouranga**[17] [4181] 3-9-7 **68** DaneO'Neill 1 70
(H Candy) *trckd ldng pair: wnt 2nd 4f out: rdn and no imp 2f out: wknd jst over 1f out* **13/2**

2302 **4** *1 ¼* **Bowled Out (GER)**[4] [4606] 4-9-8 **62** AdamKirby(3) 8 62
(P J McBride) *hld up in 5th: effrt on outer 3f out: rdn 2f out: no imp: fdd fnl f* **6/4**[1]

0100 **5** *1* **Arsad (IRE)**[47] [3249] 3-8-10 **57** OscarUrbina 9 55
(C E Brittain) *chsd ldr to 4f out: sn rdn: grad wknd fr over 2f out* **12/1**

000 **6** *11* **Sunley Song**[11] [4367] 3-8-1 **48** ow2 ChrisCatlin 4 29
(B G Powell) *a in last pair: detached fr main gp 4f out: sn no ch* **25/1**

10/0 **7** *22* **Zorn (GER)**[17] [4176] 7-9-9 **63** RichardKingscote(3) 3 9
(M F Harris) *s.s: a in last pair: lost tch 4f out: t.o* **33/1**

2m 42.66s (2.16) **Going Correction** +0.125s/f (Good)
WFA 3 from 4yo+ 10lb 7 Ran SP% **111.1**
Speed ratings (Par 103):97,96,94,93,93 85,71
CSF £15.84 CT £76.46 TOTE £4.40: £2.10, £1.90; EX 13.10.

Owner Mollers Racing **Bred** J Hanly, A Stroud And T Stewart **Trained** Newmarket, Suffolk

FOCUS

A modest handicap in which the winner showed slight improvement and the second ran to recent course-and-distance form.

Bowled Out(GER) Official explanation: jockey said filly ran flat

Zorn(GER) Official explanation: jockey said gelding lost its action

4688 WIN A MILLION WITH LADBROKES FOOTBALL COUPONS MAIDEN AUCTION STKS 7f (S)

6:15 (6:15) (Class 5) 2-Y-O **£3,238** (£963; £481; £240) **Stalls** Low

Form RPR

1 **Big Player** 2-8-13 .... OscarUrbina 4 77+
(W J Haggas) *trckd rival nr side: shkn up over 1f out: led the pair and in overall charge last 150yds: readily* **25/1**

2 **2** 3/4 **Shebang (IRE)**[18] 4140 2-8-8 .... TPO'Shea 2 70
(M G Quinlan) *led nr side pair and looked to have def advantage over other side: rdn 2f out: hdd last 150yds: kpt on but readily hld* **11/10**[1]

5 **3** 1 **Winged Farasi**[24] 3979 2-8-6 .... SaleemGolam(3) 7 69
(Miss J Feilden) *cl up far side: chsd ldr over 2f out: styd on fnl f to ld gp nr fin but nvr quite on terms w pair on other side* **16/1**

002 **4** nk **Up In Arms (IRE)**[32] 3726 2-9-2 74 .... StephenCarson 6 75
(P Winkworth) *led far side gp but a appeared to be bhd nr side pair: rdn over 2f out: kpt on: hdd nr fin* **10/1**[3]

53 **5** 6 **Grand Art (IRE)**[14] 4251 2-8-13 .... SebSanders 3 57
(M H Tompkins) *dwlt: hld up far side: prog 1/2-way: chsd ldng pair over 2f out: wknd over 1f out* **5/2**[2]

0 **6** 2 **Fistral**[17] 4177 2-8-13 .... ChrisCatlin 1 52
(M R Channon) *chsd far side ldr tl wknd over 2f out* **10/1**[3]

500 **7** shd **Fine Leg**[35] 3645 2-7-13 ....(t) RoryMoore(5) 8 43
(P J McBride) *dwlt: racd far side: hld up in last: shuffled along 3f out: wknd over 1f out* **66/1**

0253 **8** 3/4 **Law Of The Land (IRE)**[18] 4140 2-8-13 70 .... DaneO'Neill 5 50
(W R Muir) *dwlt: hld up far side: no prog 3f out: wknd 2f out* **10/1**[3]

1m 29.39s (1.49) **Going Correction** +0.125s/f (Good) 8 Ran SP% **114.7**

Speed ratings (Par 94):96,95,94,93,86 84,84,83

CSF £53.67 TOTE £21.70: £6.00, £1.10, £2.40; EX 76.20.

Owner W J Gredley **Bred** P D And Mrs Player **Trained** Newmarket, Suffolk

FOCUS

A fair juvenile maiden, which saw the two racing on the stands' side at a slight advantage this time, though there was little between the two sides. The form looks straightforward enough.

NOTEBOOK

Big Player, a 15,000gns purchase, tracked the runner-up on the favoured stands'-side rail and showed a decent attitude to get on top of that rival late on and register a winning debut. He acted well on the easy surface and, considering he was seemingly unfancied for this, ought to improve a deal for the experience. (op 20-1 tchd 28-1)

Shebang(IRE), runner-up on her debut at Lingfield on fast ground, did nothing wrong in defeat but failed to see out her race as well as the winner. She certainly has a race in her before too long and will be suited by the return to faster ground in due course. (op Evens tchd 5-4)

Winged Farasi, stepping up in trip, showed the clear benefit of his recent Newmarket debut and emerged the best of those to race on the far side. He looks best kept to this trip, may just prefer faster ground than this, and does have a future. (tchd 18-1)

Up In Arms(IRE) showed up well on the far side until his big weight found him out. He is another who ideally needs faster ground and with an official rating of 74 he helps to set the standard of this form. (tchd 12-1)

Grand Art(IRE), well backed, eventually failed to see out the extra furlong on this easing surface. He can be given another chance over this trip on a quicker surface and may fare better when switching to nurseries. (op 7-2)

4689 LADBROKES OFFER XTRA VIRTUAL RACING H'CAP 7f (S)

6:45 (6:47) (Class 4) (0-80,79) 3-Y-O **£5,505** (£1,637; £818; £408) **Stalls** Low

Form RPR

4511 **1** **Secret Liaison**[13] 4281 3-9-7 79 .... SebSanders 2 87+
(Sir Mark Prescott) *trckd ldrs: effrt 2f out: drvn and r.o to ld last 150yds: sn in command* **11/10**[1]

5241 **2** 3/4 **Secret Assassin (IRE)**[35] 3638 3-9-1 73 .... ChrisCatlin 3 77
(W R Muir) *hld up in last trio: gng wl enough 2f out: rdn ent fnl f: r.o to take 2nd last 75yds: gaining on wnr: too much to do* **20/1**

5031 **3** 1 **Trimlestown (IRE)**[25] 3931 3-9-1 73 .... DaneO'Neill 7 74
(H Candy) *w ldr: led 2f out: drvn over 1f out: hdd and one pce last 150yds* **7/1**[3]

0011 **4** nk **Takitwo**[13] 4291 3-8-9 67 .... LPKeniry 5 67
(P D Cundell) *chsd ldrs: pushed along bef 1/2-way: effrt u.p to chal over 1f out: one pce ins fnl f* **9/2**[2]

4-40 **5** 2 **Waddon (IRE)**[102] 1672 3-8-7 68 ....(p) AdamKirby(3) 4 63
(C G Cox) *mde most to 2f out: losing pl whn sltly hmpd over 1f out: no ch after* **20/1**

5510 **6** 4 **Deira (USA)**[14] 4241 3-9-0 72 .... StephenCarson 1 57
(C E Brittain) *uns rdr leaving paddock: dwlt: a in last pair: urged along 4f out: no prog and btn 2f out* **16/1**

3351 **7** 8 **Southport Star (IRE)**[47] 3266 3-9-4 76 .... OscarUrbina 6 40
(J R Fanshawe) *settled in rr on outer: pushed along 4f out: struggling and wl btn over 2f out* **9/2**[2]

1m 28.52s (0.62) **Going Correction** +0.125s/f (Good) 7 Ran SP% **111.9**

Speed ratings (Par 102):101,100,99,98,96 91,82

CSF £25.19 TOTE £1.70: £1.20, £7.60; EX 11.70.

Owner W E Sturt - Osborne House **Bred** Cheveley Park Stud Ltd **Trained** Newmarket, Suffolk

■ Stewards' Enquiry : Dane O'Neill caution: careless riding

FOCUS

A modest three-year-old handicap which was run at sound pace. The winner is progressing well, but the overall form is not strong and is worth treating with a degree of caution.

Trimlestown(IRE) Official explanation: jockey said gelding hung left

Waddon(IRE) Official explanation: jockey said gelding suffered interference in running

Deira(USA) Official explanation: jockey said filly never travelled

4690 REGISTER TODAY FOR LADBROKES TBS ACCOUNT H'CAP 6f

7:15 (7:15) (Class 6) (0-55,55) 3-Y-O **£2,730** (£806; £403) **Stalls** Low

Form RPR

0001 **1** **Forces Sweetheart**[7] 4494 3-9-0 54 7ex........(v) LukeMorris(7) 6 62
(M L W Bell) *racd nr side: led after 1f: mde rest and grabbed rail 2f out: urged along over 1f out: holding on whn veered rt last 75yds* **7/2**[2]

-054 **2** 1/2 **Hot Agnes**[43] 3383 3-9-8 55 .... MichaelTebbutt 1 61
(H J Collingridge) *trckd ldrs nr side: rdn and effrt 2f out: got through to chse wnr last 100yds: looked hld whn carried rt nr fin* **9/1**

0360 **3** shd **Alwariah**[18] 4141 3-9-8 55 .... OscarUrbina 13 61
(C E Brittain) *trckd far side ldr: led gp 1/2-way: hung lft sn after and nrly on terms w other side: hld whn bmpd nr fin* **14/1**

3606 **4** 1 **Stoneacre Fred (IRE)**[11] 4354 3-9-1 48 .... TPO'Shea 11 51
(Peter Grayson) *chsd far side ldrs: pressed ldr wl over 1f out and hung lft after: nvr quite on terms* **20/1**

-445 **5** 1 **Gift Aid**[44] 3349 3-9-4 51 .... SebSanders 5 54+
(P J Makin) *chsd wnr nr side 3f out: drvn 2f out: lost pl and hld whn squeezed out nr fin* **9/4**[1]

0000 **6** shd **Indian Lady (IRE)**[11] 4365 3-9-5 55 ....(b) AdamKirby(3) 7 55
(Mrs A L M King) *settled in rr of nr side gp: rdn and effrt 2f out: pressed ldrs 1f out: hld whn carried rt nr fin* **12/1**

5000 **7** 1 1/2 **North Fleet**[19] 4120 3-9-6 53 .... DaneO'Neill 14 48
(J M Bradley) *taken down early: racd far side and in last pair: outpcd 2f out: hung lft fnl f: nvr on terms* **20/1**

0300 **8** nk **Immaculate Red**[13] 4306 3-8-11 47 .... SaleemGolam(3) 9 41
(R Bastiman) *prog on outer of nr side gp to go prom 3f out: rdn 2f out: wknd 1f out* **12/1**

0464 **9** 1 3/4 **Bollywood (IRE)**[2] 4658 3-8-13 51 .... MarcHalford(5) 12 40
(J J Bridger) *led far side gp to 1/2-way: edgd lft and wknd over 1f out* **14/1**

0553 **10** 1 1/2 **Arculinge**[13] 4305 3-9-7 54 .... ChrisCatlin 8 39
(M Blanshard) *chsd nr side ldrs: rdn and struggling 2f out* **6/1**[3]

-000 **11** 8 **Charles Street Lad (IRE)**[92] 1923 3-9-1 48 .... LPKeniry 10 9
(M R Bosley) *racd far side: a in last pair: wknd over 1f out* **50/1**

0060 **12** 5 **Burnt Orange (IRE)**[18] 4141 3-8-12 50 .... RoryMoore(5) 4 —
(T D McCarthy) *dwlt: struggling nr side after 2f: sn wl bhd* **33/1**

0000 **13** 10 **Young Flavio**[29] 3821 3-8-7 47 ....(p) BarrySavage(7) 2 —
(J M Bradley) *led nr side for 1f: wknd rapidly after 2f: t.o* **100/1**

1m 14.51s (0.91) **Going Correction** +0.125s/f (Good) 13 Ran SP% **121.4**

Speed ratings (Par 98):98,97,97,95,94 94,92,92,89,87 77,70,57

CSF £33.78 CT £417.35 TOTE £5.40: £1.20, £4.80, £7.90; EX 33.90.

Owner Richard I Morris Jr **Bred** Barton Stud Partnership **Trained** Newmarket, Suffolk

FOCUS

A modest handicap but the form looks sound. The field spilt after leaving the stalls, but joined together inside the final furlong. There was also some trouble close to the line, although the winner, who caused most of it, did it well enough.

Alwariah Official explanation: jockey said filly hung left

North Fleet Official explanation: jockey said gelding hung left

4691 FOLKESTONE-RACECOURSE.CO.UK FILLIES' H'CAP 5f

7:45 (7:45) (Class 5) (0-75,75) 3-Y-0+ **£3,886** (£1,156; £577; £288) **Stalls** Low

Form RPR

0262 **1** **Tilly's Dream**[7] 4494 3-8-12 65 .... SaleemGolam(3) 13 77
(G C H Chung) *hld up off the pce: gd prog on outer fr 2f out to ld over 1f out: sn clr: rdn out* **3/1**[2]

3461 **2** 2 **Overwing (IRE)**[15] 4226 3-9-6 70 .... OscarUrbina 5 75
(R M H Cowell) *trckd ldn trio: effrt over 1f out: chsd wnr jst over 1f out but sn outpcd: styd on* **5/1**[3]

3200 **3** 3 **Red Sovereign**[82] 2207 5-8-10 65 .... MarkCoumbe(7) 2 59
(D G Bridgwater) *pressed ldng pair: nt qckn and lost pl over 1f out: n.d after: plugged on against nr side rail* **20/1**

5040 **4** nk **Kallista's Pride**[3] 4629 6-8-10 65 .... KylieManser(7) 7 58
(J R Best) *dwlt and bmpd s: outpcd in last trio: urged along and r.o fr over 1f out: nvr nrr* **13/2**

00-5 **5** 3/4 **Chilly Cracker**[13] 4294 4-8-6 54 oh1 .... LPKeniry 10 44
(John Berry) *fractious to post: w ldr at fast pce: upsides but hanging over 1f out: sn wknd* **12/1**

2421 **6** nk **Smiddy Hill**[20] 4091 4-9-5 67 .... SebSanders 3 56
(R Bastiman) *mde most at str pce: hdd & wknd over 1f out* **13/8**[1]

-010 **7** 1 1/2 **Fen Guest**[16] 4199 3-8-6 56 .... ChrisCatlin 9 40
(Rae Guest) *son outpcd and rdn in last trio: nvr on terms* **16/1**

/00- **8** 6 **Globe Trekker (USA)**[461] 1838 4-8-7 55 .... TPO'Shea 4 17
(Peter Grayson) *a last trio and sn struggling: wl bhd over 1f out* **25/1**

61.54 secs (0.74) **Going Correction** +0.125s/f (Good)

WFA 3 from 4yo+ 2lb 8 Ran SP% **115.3**

Speed ratings (Par 100):99,95,91,90,89 88,86,76

CSF £18.63 CT £253.70 TOTE £4.90: £1.10, £2.10, £3.80; EX 15.60 Place 6 £61.19, Place 5 £48.96.

Owner Richard Withers And Meddler Bloodstock **Bred** Southill Stud **Trained** Newmarket, Suffolk

FOCUS

Not a great race, with three runners appearing to go off too fast in front, setting it up for a finisher. The winner has been rated to the best view of her previous form.

T/Plt: £58.80 to a £1 stake. Pool: £39,524.00. 490.05 winning tickets. T/Qpdt: £16.80 to a £1 stake. Pool: £3,518.70. 154.60 winning tickets. JN

4473 HAMILTON (R-H)

Wednesday, August 23

OFFICIAL GOING: Good (good to soft in places)

Wind: Light, half across

4692 PHOTOFUN UK CLAIMING STKS 1m 1f 36y

2:00 (2:00) (Class 6) 3-Y-0+ **£2,730** (£806; £403) **Stalls** High

Form RPR

4213 **1** **Burnley Al (IRE)**[6] 4518 4-9-4 55 ....(b) FrancisNorton 9 69
(A Berry) *chsd ldrs: rdn 3f out: wnt 2nd over 1f out: styd on wl to ld towards fin* **11/2**

-536 **2** 3 **Neil's Legacy (IRE)**[18] 4132 4-8-7 50 .... GregFairley(5) 8 55
(Miss L A Perratt) *hld up: rdn and hdwy over 2f out: chsd ldng pair 1f out: kpt on: nvr able to chal: fin 3rd, 1l & 3l: plcd 2nd* **10/1**

0545 **3** 7 **Alfonso**[11] 4350 5-9-6 69 ....(b) TomEaves 4 49
(I Semple) *midfield: rdn over 3f out: no imp: fin 4th: plcd 3rd* **4/1**[3]

1550 **4** 2 1/2 **Insubordinate**[7] 4476 5-9-0 59 .... DNolan(3) 1 41
(J S Goldie) *hld up: rdn over 2f out: nvr trbld ldrs: fin 5th: plcd 4th* **20/1**

5010 **5** 3 **Double Ransom**[79] 2282 7-9-1 48 ....(b) PhillipMakin 2 33
(Mrs L Stubbs) *hld up: rdn over 2f out: nvr on terms: fin 6th: plcd 5th* **16/1**

03-0 **6** 3 1/2 **Oulan Bator (FR)**[11] 4353 6-9-3 56 .... DaleGibson 7 28
(R A Fahey) *midfield: rdn 4f out: wknd 2f out: fin 7th: plcd 6th* **11/1**

1223 **7** 1 **Sawwaah (IRE)**[7] 4467 9-8-12 69 ....(v) VictoriaBehan(7) 3 28
(D Nicholls) *prom: chsd ldr over 6f out: rdn 3f out: wknd over 1f out: fin 8th: plcd 7th* **10/3**[1]

0-00 **8** nk **The Wizard Mul**[23] 3999 6-8-12 42 ....(t) AndrewElliott(5) 5 25
(W Storey) *cl up: rdn over 2f out: sn wknd: fin 9th: plcd 8th* **66/1**

0000 **D** *1* **Baylaw Star**[17] [4172] 5-9-8 83 ... AndrewMullen(5) 6 76
(K A Ryan) *led: rdn 2f out: hdd and no ex towards fin: fin 2nd, 1l: disq & plcd last* **7/2**[2]

1m 57.53s (-2.13) **Going Correction** -0.05s/f (Good) **9** Ran SP% **110.2**
Speed ratings (Par 101):107,103,97,95,92 89,88,88,106
CSF £54.63 TOTE £5.90: £1.20, £2.90, £2.10; EX 56.80.Baylaw Star was subject to a friendly claim.
Owner Thomas & Susan Blane **Bred** James Mahon **Trained** Cockerham, Lancs

FOCUS
An ordinary claimer, and sound form. A decent winning time for a race of its type. There was controversy as original runner-up Baylaw Star weighed in 14lb light, his rider claiming that he had not lost his weight cloth and must have weighted out light.

4693 RACING UK AND SETANTA FOR £15 MAIDEN AUCTION STKS (QUALIFIER FOR THE HAMILTON PARK 2-Y-O FINAL) 5f 4y
2:35 (2:35) (Class 6) 2-Y-O **£3,071** (£906; £453) **Stalls** Low

Form RPR
0 **1** **Triple Shadow**[46] [3286] 2-8-13 ... PhillipMakin 1 73
(T D Barron) *racd keenly: in tch: hung rt and led ent fnl f: r.o* **7/1**
2 **2** *¾* **Cedarlea (IRE)**[14] [4251] 2-8-13 ... DaleGibson 3 70
(R A Fahey) *a.p: led over 2f out: rdn whn hung rt and hdd ent fnl f: hld towards fin* **1/1**[1]
0004 **3** *hd* **Rue Soleil**[11] [4376] 2-8-0 53 ow1 ... AndrewMullen(5) 5 62
(J R Weymes) *in rr: pushed along after 2f: effrt whn swtchd lft ins fnl f: r.o towards fin* **25/1**
02U **4** *½* **Princess Ellis**[6] [4510] 2-8-4 ... FrancisNorton 2 59
(E J Alston) *led: rdn and hdd over 2f out: continued to chal: kpt on u.p fnl f* **9/2**[3]
2306 **5** *2* **Joseph Locke (IRE)**[4] [4603] 2-8-13 73 ... (p) TomEaves 4 61
(M Dods) *prom: rdn and ev ch over 1f out: fdd fnl f* **7/2**[2]

61.12 secs (-0.08) **Going Correction** -0.05s/f (Good) **5** Ran SP% **106.8**
Speed ratings (Par 92):98,96,96,95,92
CSF £13.81 TOTE £9.30: £2.90, £1.10; EX 18.60.
Owner G Morrill **Bred** D & S Horn **Trained** Maunby, N Yorks

FOCUS
A modest maiden, with 53-rated Rue Soleil being beaten under a length and only a length and a quarter covering the first four, but Triple Shadow did it well and may be capable of better back on a faster surface.

NOTEBOOK
Triple Shadow, nibbled at in the market when disappointing on his debut at Carlisle in early July, had been off since and has clearly benefited from the experience, travelling best throughout and finding what was required under pressure. There may be even more to come from him on a faster surface and he looks a bright nursery prospect. (op 8-1 tchd 9-1)
Cedarlea(IRE), runner-up on his debut at Newcastle, looked the one to beat and was up there throughout, but he hung under pressure and was always being held inside the final furlong. He should find a race on this evidence. (op 4-5 tchd 11-10 in a place)
Rue Soleil, fourth in a seller at Redcar last time, appeared to run above herself in third and was going on close home. She does little for the form, but evidently has a small race in her. (op 20-1)
Princess Ellis, still in with a chance when unseating at Beverley last time, took them along until past halfway and tried her best to cling on when challenged, but found herself outpaced inside the final furlong. (tchd 7-2)
Joseph Locke(IRE), although not beaten far, is not really progressing and the first-time cheekpieces failed to bring about any improvement. (op 4-1)

4694 DM HALL H'CAP 6f 5y
3:10 (3:10) (Class 5) (0-70,67) 3-Y-O+ **£3,238** (£963; £481; £240) **Stalls** Low

Form RPR
1041 **1** **Scuba (IRE)**[23] [3996] 4-9-3 63 ... (b) TravisBlock(5) 1 72
(H Morrison) *midfield: rdn 1/2-way: hdwy over 1f out: led wl ins fnl f: r.o* **9/2**[3]
2054 **2** *½* **Winthorpe (IRE)**[22] [4019] 6-9-4 62 ... DNolan(3) 2 70
(J J Quinn) *in tch: rdn and ev ch ins fnl f: hld cl home* **8/1**
6051 **3** *shd* **Rancho Cucamonga (IRE)**[7] [4473] 4-8-11 52 ... (b) PhillipMakin 5 59
(T D Barron) *hld up: hdwy over 1f out: styd on ins fnl f* **7/2**[1]
04 **4** *shd* **Dechiper (IRE)**[36] [3617] 4-8-7 48 oh1 ... (p) PaulEddery 3 55
(R Johnson) *a.p: rdn 2f out: ev ch ins fnl f: nt qckn* **22/1**
1354 **5** *1* **Joyeaux**[9] [4437] 4-9-8 63 ... (v) DerekMcGaffin 9 67
(J Hetherton) *hld up: hdwy 1/2-way: rdn 2f out: led over 1f out: hdd wl ins fnl f: no ex* **10/1**
5054 **6** *2 ½* **Piccolo Prince**[5] [4571] 5-9-2 57 ... FrancisNorton 6 54
(E J Alston) *towards rr: effrt whn bmpd over 1f out: nvr trbld ldrs* **4/1**[2]
1333 **7** *2* **Viewforth**[7] [4477] 8-9-7 62 ... (b) TomEaves 10 53
(I Semple) *trckd ldrs: rdn 2f out: wknd fnl f* **6/1**
0021 **8** *1 ¼* **Frimley's Mattery**[10] [4401] 6-8-6 52 6ex ... MichaelJStainton(5) 8 39
(R E Barr) *a towards rr* **7/1**
6 **9** *1 ¾* **Silent Willow (IRE)**[21] [4059] 5-8-2 48 oh10 ... (b) HMuya(5) 4 30
(D Nicholls) *led: rdn and hdd over 1f out: sn wknd* **50/1**
0604 **10** *½* **The Keep**[4] [4613] 4-8-2 48 oh9 ... (b) AndrewMullen(5) 11 28
(R E Barr) *prom: rdn over 2f out: wknd over 1f out* **40/1**

1m 12.97s (-0.13) **Going Correction** -0.05s/f (Good) **10** Ran SP% **116.1**
Speed ratings (Par 103):98,97,97,97,95 92,89,88,85,85
CSF £39.40 CT £140.43 TOTE £7.90: £2.00, £2.20, £1.80; EX 61.10.
Owner Graham Doyle & Partners **Bred** Mountarmstrong Stud **Trained** East Ilsley, Berks
■ Stewards' Enquiry : Derek McGaffin five-day ban: used whip with excessive frequency (Sep 3-7)

FOCUS
A competitive handicap, but sound form and a straightforward race to rate.
Viewforth Official explanation: trainer said gelding ran too freely early on

4695 SITE SERVICES (PLANT) LTD H'CAP 6f 5y
3:45 (3:47) (Class 6) (0-65,68) 3-Y-O **£2,730** (£806; £403) **Stalls** Low

Form RPR
0451 **1** **Choreography**[6] [4524] 3-9-6 68 6ex ... VictoriaBehan(7) 3 79+
(D Nicholls) *a.p: led 1f out: edgd lft ins fnl f: r.o wl* **11/4**[1]
0525 **2** *1 ¾* **Newkeylets**[11] [4354] 3-8-8 54 ... (p) MarkLawson(5) 9 60
(I Semple) *led: rdn 2f out: hdd 1f out: nt pce of wnr ins fnl f* **9/1**
0301 **3** *1 ½* **Markestino**[16] [4199] 3-8-9 50 ... (t) PaulEddery 2 52
(T D Easterby) *a.p: rdn 2f out: nt qckn ins fnl f* **4/1**[2]
0000 **4** *½* **Rondo**[13] [4296] 3-9-4 59 ... PhillipMakin 6 59
(T D Barron) *in tch: rdn and hdwy over 1f out: kpt on ins fnl f* **8/1**
6054 **5** *½* **Gifted Glori**[16] [4199] 3-7-13 45 oh1 ow2 ... AndrewMullen(5) 1 44
(J J Quinn) *prom: rdn over 2f out: styd on same pce fnl f* **10/1**
2506 **6** *nk* **Pontefract Glory**[10] [4389] 3-8-2 43 oh4 ... (b[1]) DaleGibson 5 41
(M Dods) *in rr: rdn over 2f out: styd on fnl f: nt pce to chal* **22/1**
0050 **7** *shd* **Mister Jingles**[16] [4199] 3-7-13 45 ... AndrewElliott(5) 8 42
(R M Whitaker) *prom: rdn 2f out: no ex ins fnl f* **33/1**
1044 **8** *1 ¾* **Seesawmilu (IRE)**[29] [3814] 3-8-10 51 ... FrancisNorton 11 43
(E J Alston) *hld up: rdn 2f out: no imp* **7/1**[3]
6225 **9** *nk* **Dulce Sueno**[7] [4477] 3-9-2 57 ... TomEaves 7 48
(I Semple) *cl up: rdn 2f out: fdd ins fnl f* **9/1**
0-06 **10** *19* **Bitter Chill**[43] [3381] 3-9-2 62 ... TravisBlock(5) 10 —
(H Morrison) *a bhd* **9/1**

1m 13.16s (0.06) **Going Correction** -0.05s/f (Good) **10** Ran SP% **116.7**
Speed ratings (Par 98):97,94,92,92,91 90,90,88,88,62
CSF £28.39 CT £101.31 TOTE £3.20: £1.70, £2.10, £1.90; EX 31.30.
Owner Bill Wallace/Gary Butters **Bred** Cheveley Park Stud Ltd **Trained** Sessay, N Yorks

FOCUS
A moderate handicap, which saw those drawn low at an advantage, and the form looks sound for the class.
Bitter Chill Official explanation: trainer had no explanation for the poor form shown

4696 RBS SCOTTISH TROPHY H'CAP 1m 65y
4:20 (4:20) (Class 4) (0-85,85) 3-Y-O+ **£6,477** (£1,927; £963; £481) **Stalls** High

Form RPR
5253 **1** **Middlemarch (IRE)**[2] [4653] 6-8-13 69 ... PhillipMakin 5 78
(J S Goldie) *in tch: rdn and outpcd 3f out: rallied over 1f out: led ins fnl f: r.o* **7/2**[1]
0420 **2** *½* **Nevada Desert (IRE)**[18] [4153] 6-8-7 68 ... MichaelJStainton(5) 4 76
(R M Whitaker) *a.p: rdn 2f out: ev ch ins fnl f: styd on* **5/1**[2]
3330 **3** *½* **Speed Dial Harry (IRE)**[67] [2657] 4-9-1 76 ... (v) AndrewElliott(5) 7 83
(K R Burke) *a.p: rdn over 2f out: ev ch ins fnl f: nt qckn* **6/1**[3]
5002 **4** *1 ½* **Freeloader (IRE)**[11] [4379] 6-9-6 76 ... DaleGibson 1 79
(R A Fahey) *in tch: effrt 3f out: rdn and ev ch over 1f out: kpt on u.p ins fnl f* **7/2**[1]
6024 **5** *shd* **Byron Bay**[27] [3881] 4-10-0 84 ... TomEaves 2 87
(I Semple) *led: rdn 2f out: hdd ins fnl f: no ex cl home* **9/1**
13-0 **6** *1 ¾* **Startori**[25] [3945] 3-9-9 85 ... PaulEddery 3 83
(B Smart) *hld up: hdwy over 2f out: sn rdn: one pce ins fnl f* **20/1**
1266 **7** *1 ½* **Regent's Secret (USA)**[11] [4356] 6-9-8 81 ... DNolan(3) 6 77
(J S Goldie) *hld up: effrt over 2f out: no imp fr over 1f out* **7/1**
2644 **8** *½* **Hawkit (USA)**[7] [4476] 5-8-10 71 ... MarkLawson(5) 8 65
(A Bailey) *hld up: effrt over 2f out: no imp fr over 1f out* **7/1**

1m 48.31s (-0.99) **Going Correction** -0.05s/f (Good)
WFA 3 from 4yo+ 6lb **8** Ran SP% **115.2**
Speed ratings (Par 105):102,101,101,99,99 97,96,95
CSF £21.26 CT £100.99 TOTE £4.20: £1.40, £1.60, £2.70; EX 22.80.
Owner W M Johnstone **Bred** Swettenham Stud And Hugo Lascelles **Trained** Uplawmoor, E Renfrews
■ Stewards' Enquiry : Phillip Makin caution: used whip down the shoulder in forehand position

FOCUS
A modest handicap which saw the first three come clear. Very ordinary form for the grade, but sound enough.

4697 RACING UK FOR £15 CALL 08700 506949 RATING RELATED MAIDEN STKS 1m 3f 16y
4:55 (4:55) (Class 6) 3-4-Y-O **£2,388** (£705; £352) **Stalls** High

Form RPR
-030 **1** **Lolla's Spirit (IRE)**[19] [4111] 3-8-7 58 ... AndrewElliott(5) 9 64
(M L W Bell) *a.p: rdn over 1f out: r.o to ld wl ins fnl f* **4/1**[3]
5032 **2** *½* **Hurry Up Helen (IRE)**[18] [4132] 3-8-12 51 ... TomEaves 5 63
(Mrs L Stubbs) *in tch: clsd 4f out: led over 2f out: rdn over 1f out: hdd wl ins fnl f: styd on* **7/2**[2]
4043 **3** *3* **Musical Magic**[39] [3540] 3-8-7 60 ... GregFairley(5) 7 58
(J Noseda) *s.i.s: in tch: rdn over 4f out: kpt on fnl f: nvr able to chal* **3/1**[1]
6056 **4** *2 ½* **Red Chairman**[5] [4569] 4-9-5 57 ... DeclanMcGann(5) 2 57
(R Johnson) *racd keenly: hld up: hdwy 6f out: led 4f out: rdn and hdd over 2f out: wknd fnl f* **14/1**
0040 **5** *¾* **Nassar (IRE)**[30] [3804] 3-9-1 58 ... PhillipMakin 1 56
(G Prodromou) *hld up: hdwy 4f out: rdn and edgd lft over 3f out: wknd over 1f out* **7/1**
-002 **6** *14* **Fadansil**[12] [3620] 3-8-10 52 ... MarkLawson(5) 8 32
(J Wade) *led: hdd 4f out: rdn 3f out: wknd over 2f out* **20/1**
-004 **7** *5* **Orange Stravinsky**[50] [3169] 3-9-1 60 ... DaleGibson 6 24
(P C Haslam) *racd keenly: in tch: lost pl 6f out: n.d after* **7/1**
-050 **8** *5* **Heads Turn (IRE)**[16] [4199] 3-8-12 40 ... FrancisNorton 3 12
(E J Alston) *hld up: rdn over 2f out: nvr on terms* **33/1**
00-0 **9** *14* **Nona**[62] [2795] 3-8-7 60 ... TravisBlock(5) 4 —
(Jedd O'Keeffe) *prom: rdn 4f out: sn wknd: eased whn btn wl over 1f out* **20/1**

2m 24.77s (-1.49) **Going Correction** -0.05s/f (Good)
WFA 3 from 4yo 9lb **9** Ran SP% **111.4**
Speed ratings (Par 101):103,102,100,98,98 87,84,80,70
CSF £17.11 TOTE £5.00: £1.60, £1.70, £1.60; EX 23.20.
Owner Brett Palos **Bred** Barouche Stud Ireland Ltd **Trained** Newmarket, Suffolk

FOCUS
A very weak maiden, run at a sound pace, and the first two pulled clear. It has been rated through the runner-up.
Nassar(IRE) Official explanation: jockey said colt hung left in straight

4698 TOTESPORT AUTUMN FINALE H'CAP 1m 4f 17y
5:30 (5:30) (Class 5) (0-70,69) 3-Y-O+ **£3,238** (£963; £481; £240) **Stalls** High

Form RPR
4436 **1** **Kentucky Warbler (IRE)**[32] [3731] 3-8-8 64 ... TravisBlock(5) 4 75+
(H Morrison) *trckd ldrs: led over 3f out: r.o ins fnl f: comf* **9/1**
0-04 **2** *¾* **Neutrino**[13] [4299] 4-10-0 69 ... FrancisNorton 6 78
(P C Haslam) *in tch: rdn over 2f out: sn chsd wnr: nt qckn ins fnl f* **8/1**
5222 **3** *3* **Shekan Star**[10] [4393] 4-9-0 55 ... TomEaves 2 59
(K G Reveley) *midfield: hdwy 3f out: sn rdn: hung rt over 1f out: styd on same pce ins fnl f* **5/1**[1]
0004 **4** *nk* **Cleaver**[56] [2982] 5-9-2 62 ... AndrewElliott(5) 7 66
(Lady Herries) *hld up: hdwy over 1f out: styd on ins fnl f: nvr nrr* **11/2**[2]
-223 **5** *½* **Minthare (IRE)**[50] [3169] 3-8-6 62 ... (p) MarkLawson(5) 8 65
(C Grant) *midfield: rdn and outpcd over 3f out: styd on fr over 1f out* **25/1**
453 **6** *¾* **Shy Glance (USA)**[13] [4301] 4-9-7 62 ... (t) DaleGibson 5 64
(G A Swinbank) *trckd ldrs: rdn and lost pl over 3f out: kpt on fr over 1f out: one pce ins fnl f* **13/2**
0446 **7** *1 ¾* **Balwearie (IRE)**[30] [3784] 5-8-10 58 ... NeilBrown(7) 11 57
(Miss L A Perratt) *hld up: rdn over 2f out: nvr able to chal* **10/1**
6606 **8** *hd* **Just Waz (USA)**[9] [4423] 4-8-4 50 ... (p) MichaelJStainton(5) 3 49
(R M Whitaker) *led: hdd over 3f out: rdn over 2f out: wknd over 1f out* **7/1**
2333 **9** *1* **Melvino**[7] [4478] 4-9-7 62 ... PhillipMakin 9 59
(T D Barron) *hld up: hdwy 6f out: rdn and wknd over 2f out* **6/1**[3]

The Form Book, Raceform Ltd, Compton, RG20 6NL

0600 **10** *nk* **Millennium Hall**[7] 4478 7-8-8 **54**.................................. GregFairley(5) 10 51
(Miss Lucinda V Russell) *s.i.s: sn in midfield: hdwy over 5f out: ev ch 3f out: rdn and wknd 2f out* **14/1**

0204 **11** *3* **Hansomelle (IRE)**[8] 4455 4-8-10 **56**.......................... AndrewMullen(5) 1 48
(B Mactaggart) *prom: rdn 3f out: wknd over 1f out* **20/1**

2m 38.82s (-0.36) **Going Correction** -0.05s/f (Good)
WFA 3 from 4yo+ 10lb **11** Ran SP% **117.6**
Speed ratings (Par 103):99,98,96,96,95 95,94,94,93,93 91
CSF £79.15 CT £404.78 TOTE £13.60: £3.60, £2.40, £1.60; EX 121.90 Place 6 £16.83, Place 5 £5.02.
Owner Sir Thomas Pilkington **Bred** Airlie Stud And Sir Thomas Pilkington **Trained** East Ilsley, Berks

FOCUS
A moderate handicap which was run at no more than an average pace. The winner can be rated value for a little further.
T/Plt: £33.80 to a £1 stake. Pool: £38,324.60. 825.80 winning tickets. T/Qpdt: £6.90 to a £1 stake. Pool: £2,518.70. 269.20 winning tickets. DO

4244 KEMPTON (A.W) (R-H)
Wednesday, August 23

OFFICIAL GOING: Standard
Rain got into the track and the surface appeared to be riding very quick.
Wind: Nil

4699 BETBROKERS NEW FOOTBALL SEASON NEW ACCOUNT NURSERY 5f (P)
7:00 (7:03) (Class 5) 2-Y-O **£3,238** (£963; £481; £240) **Stalls** High

Form RPR

2251 **1** **Inflight (IRE)**[8] 4444 2-9-1 **72** 6ex...................................... TedDurcan 11 73
(R M Beckett) *trckd ldrs: rdn and hdwy over 1f out: led fnl 110yds: kpt on strly* **9/2**[3]

4104 **2** *nk* **Hucking Hope (IRE)**[21] 4043 2-8-12 **69**........................... RobertMiles 9 69
(J R Best) *chsd ldrs: drvn over 2f out and outpcd: rallied and styd on strly fr over 1f out: fin wl but a jst hld* **10/1**

0633 **3** *¾* **Mogok Ruby**[14] 4246 2-9-0 **71**... MickyFenton 10 68
(L Montague Hall) *drvn to ld: kpt slt advantage u.p tl hdd fnl 110yds and no ex* **11/2**

322 **4** *hd* **Dress To Impress (IRE)**[61] 2827 2-9-4 **78**...................... AmirQuinn(3) 6 75
(J R Boyle) *t.k.h: sn w ldr: travelling wl appr fnl f: sn rdn: no ex fnl 110yds* **5/2**[1]

0024 **5** *1 ½* **Weyba Downs (IRE)**[6] 4519 2-8-7 **67**........................... JamesDoyle(3) 4 58
(J R Best) *in tch: rdn over 2f out: styd on fnl f but nvr gng pce to rch ldrs* **14/1**

5240 **6** *½* **Ghost Dancer**[12] 4321 2-9-1 **72**.. NickyMackay 3 61
(L M Cumani) *sn in tch: rdn and outpcd 1/2-way: kpt on again fnl f* **4/1**[2]

0631 **7** *shd* **Diminuto**[15] 4222 2-7-7 **57**... NicolPolli(7) 2 46
(M D I Usher) *outpcd in rr: rdn 1/2-way: kpt on fr over 1f out and styd on cl home but nvr gng pce to get competitive* **16/1**

0602 **8** *2* **Chingford (IRE)**[12] 4326 2-8-7 **71**................................... PatrickHills(7) 8 53
(D W P Arbuthnot) *s.i.s: outpcd most of way but styd on fnl f* **10/1**

530 **9** *nk* **Aggresive**[77] 2342 2-8-3 **60**... RoystonFfrench 1 41
(Ernst Oertel) *outpcd: wd into st 2f out* **25/1**

60.29 secs (-0.11) **Going Correction** -0.20s/f (Stan) **9** Ran SP% **116.7**
Speed ratings (Par 94):92,91,90,90,87 86,86,83,82
CSF £49.13 CT £215.38 TOTE £4.80: £1.90, £2.20, £2.20; EX 27.90.
Owner The Millennium Madness Partnership **Bred** M Munnelly **Trained** Whitsbury, Hants
■ Stewards' Enquiry : Amir Quinn one-day ban: used whip without allowing sufficient time to respond (Sep 3)
Ted Durcan one-day ban: used whip with excessive frequency (Sep 3)

FOCUS
Just an ordinary nursery - the top weight ran off 78 - but a case could be made for several of these beforehand and it was certainly competitive enough. The form looks solid, the winner confirming Brighton form. A new juvenile course record, but the rain had got in and quickened up the track.

NOTEBOOK
Inflight(IRE) ◆ is a really likeable filly and proved good enough to defy the 6lb penalty she picked up for winning a three-runner nursery over an extended five furlongs at Brighton on her previous start. There should be more to come and she will have every chance of completing the hat-trick in similar company. (op 10-3)
Hucking Hope(IRE), fourth in a slightly less competitive nursery over course and distance on her previous start, stepped up on that form and reversed placings with her stablemate Weyba Downs. Her effort is all the more creditable considering she appeared slightly short of room rounding the bend and she looks capable of finding a similar event. (op 9-1)
Mogok Ruby, a four-length third on his nursery debut over six furlongs here on his previous outing, ran another creditable race and is holding his form. (op 8-1)
Dress To Impress(IRE), a creditable but distant third in a four-runner Listed event on his debut before showing fair form in a couple of maidens, was returning from a two-month break and making his Polytrack debut. He seemed well enough placed, but raced keenly and seemed a bit fresh following his short lay-off. (op 10-3 tchd 7-2)
Weyba Downs(IRE), below form at Musselburgh last time, again failed to run to his best and could not confirm placings with Hucking Hope from two starts back. (op 12-1)
Ghost Dancer failed to justify favouritism when dropped back to this trip on his nursery debut at Haydock last time and, switched to Polytrack, he was again well held. He looks in need of a return to further. (tchd 9-2)

4700 TFM H'CAP 1m 2f (P)
7:28 (7:32) (Class 6) (0-65,65) 3-Y-O **£3,238** (£963; £481; £240) **Stalls** High

Form RPR

0544 **1** **Musical Echo**[14] 4248 3-9-0 **65**...................................... DeanWilliams(7) 3 74+
(G C H Chung) *t.k.h: trckd ldr tl led ins fnl 4f: drvn 4l clr 2f out: nvr in danger after and kpt on wl* **6/1**[3]

4663 **2** *1 ¾* **Will Be (IRE)**[14] 4240 3-9-7 **65**.......................................(tp) FJohansson 7 71
(R A Kvisla) *bhd: hdwy on outside fr 4f out: sn rdn: styd on to chse wnr ins last and kpt on cl home but a hld* **40/1**

0060 **3** *1 ½* **Salonga (IRE)**[19] 4118 3-9-2 **60**...................................... GeorgeBaker 5 63
(C F Wall) *s.i.s and sn drvn: chsd ldrs after 2f: wnt 2nd over 2f out but nvr nr wnr: no ex and lost 2nd ins last* **9/1**

61 **4** *shd* **Pothos Way (GR)**[11] 4367 3-9-6 **64**................................. JimCrowley 2 67
(P R Chamings) *chsd ldrs tl n.m.r and outpcd bnd appr fnl 2f: styd on again fr over 1f out: kpt on cl home* **9/1**

2 **5** *2 ½* **No Recollection (IRE)**[14] 4245 3-9-6 **64**......................(v[1]) TedDurcan 14 62
(M J Wallace) *drvn fr stalls to chse ldrs: t.k.h: rdn over 3f out: wknd appr fnl f* **5/1**[2]

3006 **6** *½* **Possessed**[14] 4248 3-9-1 **59**... RobertMiles 8 56
(T D McCarthy) *bhd: hdwy 6f out: pressed ldrs over 3f out: rdn over 2f out: wknd over 1f out* **10/1**

000 **7** *1 ½* **Camp Attack**[16] 4210 3-9-1 **59**...................................... NickyMackay 13 53
(S Dow) *in tch: rdn over 4f out: sme prog fr over 2f out but nvr in contention* **14/1**

6000 **8** *5* **Lanfredo**[86] 2070 3-8-8 **52**.. FrankieMcDonald 4 37
(D W P Arbuthnot) *bhd: mod hdwy fnl 2f* **33/1**

4030 **9** *1 ½* **Captain Bolsh**[12] 4332 3-8-9 **53**..................................... MickyFenton 10 35
(J Pearce) *bhd: sme hdwy 4f out: sn rdn: wknd fr3f out* **12/1**

1062 **10** *1* **Emotive**[21] 4052 3-9-1 **62**... JamesDoyle(3) 12 42
(I A Wood) *sn led: hdd ins fnl 4f: wknd qckly fr 2f out* **4/1**[1]

0365 **11** *1 ½* **Cape Of Storms**[32] 3725 3-9-2 **60**.................................. RoystonFfrench 1 37
(R Brotherton) *chsd ldrs to 4f out: sn btn* **10/1**

-000 **12** *½* **Snowberry Hill (USA)**[21] 4044 3-8-9 **60**.....................(p) NSLawes(7) 9 36
(K A Ryan) *in tch: rdn 1/2-way: sn bhd* **16/1**

21-0 **13** *6* **Pip's Baby**[58] 2933 3-9-5 **63**... JohnEgan 11 28
(S Kirk) *rr on outside: sme prog whn hmpd and stmbld jst ins fnl 4f: n.d after* **10/1**

2m 6.18s (-2.82) **Going Correction** -0.20s/f (Stan) **13** Ran SP% **123.8**
Speed ratings (Par 98):103,101,100,100,98 97,96,92,91,90 89,89,84
CSF £227.97 CT £2172.90 TOTE £8.70: £2.60, £7.80, £3.10; EX 129.40.
Owner The Headquarters Partnership Ltd **Bred** Southill Stud **Trained** Newmarket, Suffolk
■ Stewards' Enquiry : N S Lawes two-day ban: careless riding (Sep 3-4)

FOCUS
A modest handicap and the form is not strong.
Captain Bolsh Official explanation: jockey said gelding suffered interference shortly after start

4701 AUGUST EVENING MAIDEN FILLIES' STKS 1m 4f (P)
7:56 (7:59) (Class 4) 3-Y-O+ **£5,505** (£1,637; £818; £408) **Stalls** Centre

Form RPR

4-53 **1** **Adelfia (IRE)**[16] 4204 3-8-9 73.................................... RoystonFfrench 10 77
(Sir Michael Stoute) *chsd ldrs: pushed along fr over 3f out: styd on u.p fnl 2f to ld fnl 110yds: kpt on wl* **4/1**[3]

6232 **2** *1 ¾* **Nimra (USA)**[11] 4374 3-8-9 80.. SteveDrowne 3 74
(G A Butler) *sn led: drvn along whn chal fr 3f out: narrowly hdd 2f out: slt ld again jst ins last: hdd and no ex fnl 110yds* **6/4**[1]

43 **3** *1* **Shahmina (IRE)**[11] 4374 3-8-9 .... RobertHavlin 7 73
(J H M Gosden) *in tch: hdwy to chse ldrs 4f out: rdn and one pce 2f out: kpt on again ins last but nvr gng pce to chal* **10/3**[2]

043 **4** *1* **Izadore (IRE)**[25] 3946 3-8-9 73..................................... DO'Donohoe 2 71
(E A L Dunlop) *chsd ldr after 2f: chal fr 3f out tl slt ld 2f out: sn hrd drvn: hdd jst ins last and sn wknd* **7/1**

0064 **5** *1 ½* **Naini Tal**[12] 4330 3-8-9 70.. JohnEgan 1 69
(D R C Elsworth) *bhd: hdwy 4f out: rdn to chse ldrs and flashed tail fr 2f out nt keen and sn btn* **9/1**

6 *11* **Aberlady Bay (IRE)** 3-8-2 .... AshleyHamblett(7) 8 51
(T T Clement) *bhd: hdwy over 4f out: chsd ldrs 3f out and sn rdn: wknd and hung bdly lft over 1f out: eased* **50/1**

0-0 **7** *31* **Alice Amelia**[214] 165 3-8-9 .... MickyFenton 9 —
(C R Egerton) *in tch: rdn 1/2-way and sn wknd: t.o* **50/1**

0-00 **8** *nk* **The Lady Mandarin**[25] 3946 3-8-9 38.............................. TedDurcan 6 —
(G Wragg) *rdn 1/2-way and sn lost tch: t.o* **66/1**

-40 **9** *62* **Valdemosa**[66] 2673 3-8-9 .... JimCrowley 5 —
(B I Case) *chsd ldrs tl wknd qckly 5f out: t.o* **33/1**

2m 33.3s (-3.60) **Going Correction** -0.20s/f (Stan)
WFA 3 from 4yo 10lb **9** Ran SP% **113.9**
Speed ratings (Par 102):104,102,102,101,100 93,—,—,—
CSF £10.12 TOTE £4.40: £1.60, £1.20, £1.40; EX 9.10.
Owner H H Aga Khan **Bred** His Highness The Aga Khan's Studs S C **Trained** Newmarket, Suffolk

FOCUS
A 12-furlong fillies' maiden is never going to be a great race at this stage of the season, and this looked ordinary, despite some decent stables being represented. The course record was broken, but they had actually not gone that fast early on and the rain appeared to be quickening up the track.
Alice Amelia Official explanation: jockey said filly had a breathing problem
Valdemosa Official explanation: trainer said filly finished distressed

4702 TFM NETWORKS H'CAP 1m 4f (P)
8:24 (8:30) (Class 6) (0-65,65) 3-Y-O+ **£3,238** (£963; £481; £240) **Stalls** Centre

Form RPR

5510 **1** **Bienheureux**[4] 4606 5-9-6 **57**...(vt) JohnEgan 7 66
(Miss Gay Kelleway) *mid-div: hdwy and wd into st: str run fr 2f out to ld jst ins last: comf* **15/2**[3]

5300 **2** *nk* **Missie Baileys**[25] 3935 4-9-0 **54**...................................(p) AmirQuinn(3) 9 63
(Mrs L J Mongan) *bhd: hdwy 3f out: chsd ldrs and n.m.r over 2f out: styd on u.p fnl f: no ex cl home* **33/1**

060 **3** *1 ¼* **The Iron Giant (IRE)**[6] 4530 4-9-6 **57**............................. RobertMiles 11 64
(B G Powell) *led: hdd 3f out: led agsin ins fnl 2f: hdd jst ins last and kpt on same pce* **25/1**

0605 **4** *1* **Bridegroom**[14] 4248 4-9-4 **55**... AntonyProcter 3 60
(D R C Elsworth) *s.i.s: bhd: wd into st 3f out: stl plenty to do over 1f out: str run ins last: nt rch ldrs* **14/1**

5263 **5** *shd* **Ganymede**[18] 4139 5-9-0 **51**... IanMongan 8 56
(Mrs L J Mongan) *bhd: wd into st 3f out: hdwy fr 2f out: kpt on fnl f but nt rch ldrs* **16/1**

3034 **6** *1 ¾* **Amwell Brave**[26] 3905 5-9-12 **63**..................................... NickyMackay 10 65
(J R Jenkins) *in tch: hdwy and n.m.r 2f out: hdwy over 1f out: styng on but nt pce to rch ldrs and hmpd ins last: eased cl home* **14/1**

3033 **7** *shd* **Serramanna**[12] 4331 5-8-10 **50**....................................... JamesDoyle(3) 2 52
(Ms J S Doyle) *chsd ldrs: led 3f out: hdd ins fnl 2f: wknd fnl f* **11/1**

1025 **8** *shd* **Birthday Star (IRE)**[34] 3686 4-9-7 **61**................... StephenDonohoe(3) 12 63
(W J Musson) *chsd ldrs: rdn over 2f out: wknd fnl f and hung rt u.p* **7/2**[1]

2621 **9** *1 ½* **Cemgraft**[26] 3894 5-8-13 **50**...(tp) RichardThomas 4 52+
(A J Lidderdale) *bhd: rdn and sme hdwy into mid-div 4f out: styng on one pce whn hmpd ins last* **12/1**

4422 **10** *1 ¾* **Dark Parade (ARG)**[21] 4046 5-9-7 **65**............................... JamieJones(7) 6 62
(G L Moore) *chsd ldrs: rdn 3f out: wknd fr 2f out* **4/1**[2]

1300 **11** *shd* **Dinner Date**[25] 3934 4-9-9 **60**... TedDurcan 1 57
(T Keddy) *bhd:sme hdwy whn nt clr run and swtchd lft over 2f out: n.d after* **12/1**

0066 **12** *7* **Mutamaasek (USA)**[18] 4149 4-9-10 **61**...........................(vt[1]) SteveDrowne 5 47
(Lady Herries) *s.i.s: sn in tch: chsd ldrs and wd into st 3f out: sn wknd* **16/1**

1402 **13** *2 ½* **Bob's Your Uncle**[9] 4432 3-9-0 **64**................................. NeilChalmers(3) 13 46
(J G Portman) *in tch: rdn 3f out: wknd over 2f out* **10/1**

5251 **14** *3* **Wee Charlie Castle (IRE)**[14] 4245 3-8-9 **63**........... DeanWilliams(7) 14 40
(G C H Chung) *chsd ldrs: t.k.h: rdn 3f out: n.m.r and wknd over 2f out* **9/1**

2m 33.3s (-3.60) **Going Correction** -0.20s/f (Stan)
WFA 3 from 4yo+ 10lb **14** Ran SP% **128.7**
Speed ratings (Par 101):104,103,102,102,102 101,101,100,99,98 98,94,92,90
CSF £246.22 CT £5851.98 TOTE £9.50: £3.50, £8.90, £9.70; EX 223.10.
Owner Mr & Mrs I Henderson **Bred** N R Shields **Trained** Exning, Suffolk

FOCUS
Just a modest middle-distance handicap but, despite the pace appearing ordinary early, the winning time equalled the new course record set by Adelfia in the earlier maiden. The form looks solid and should prove reliable.
Dinner Date Official explanation: jockey said gelding ran flat
Bob's Your Uncle Official explanation: jockey said gelding did not face the kickback

4703 RELAY TECHNICAL TRANSPORT H'CAP 6f (P)
8:52 (8:59) (Class 4) (0-80,78) 3-Y-0
£7,790 (£2,332; £1,166; £583; £291; £146) **Stalls** High

Form RPR
5523 **1** **Peter Island (FR)**[18] 4158 3-9-4 **75**................................(v) JimCrowley 4 82
(J Gallagher) *led after 1f: drvn along over 2f out: a in command fnl f* **6/1[3]**
5061 **2** *1* **Spearit (IRE)**[12] 4338 3-9-3 **74**.................................... JohnEgan 5 78
(D R C Elsworth) *rr but in tch: rdn over 2f out: styd on fr over 1f out to chse wnr ins last but a readily hld* **7/2[2]**
-054 **3** *1 ½* **Violet Ballerina (IRE)**[35] 3646 3-9-2 **73**...............(b[1]) IanMongan 2 73
(B J Meehan) *chsd ldrs: rdn to go 2nd 2f out: hd high and one pce u.p fnl f* **14/1**
6350 **4** *½* **Scylla Cadeaux (IRE)**[20] 4070 3-8-4 **61**................(v[1]) RoystonFfrench 1 59
(Sir Michael Stoute) *bhd: rdn and hung rt 2f out: swtchd lft to outside over 1f out and r.o cl home but nvr in contention* **12/1**
001 **5** *1* **Indian Sabre (IRE)**[43] 3384 3-9-5 **76**.................................. TedDurcan 9 71+
(J Noseda) *bhd: rdn 3f out: styd on fr over 1f out but nvr in contention* **10/1**
0100 **6** *½* **George The Second**[5] 4562 3-8-3 **63**.................. RichardKingscote(3) 8 57
(Mrs H Sweeting) *ld 1f: styd chsng wnr to 2f out: sn wknd* **12/1**
0000 **7** *1* **Titian Saga (IRE)**[14] 4267 3-8-5 **62**...............................(b) NickyMackay 10 53
(C N Allen) *chsd ldrs: rdn 1/2-way: wknd over 1f out* **33/1**
-061 **8** *½* **Sun Catcher (IRE)**[20] 4078 3-9-6 **77**................................. SteveDrowne 7 66
(R Hannon) *wd into st: bhd tl mod late hdwy fnl f* **7/1**
0113 **9** *7* **Hillbilly Cat (USA)**[58] 2937 3-8-8 **65** ow1......................... MickyFenton 3 33
(R Ingram) *chsd ldrs 4f* **20/1**
4051 **10** *1 ¼* **Dama'A (IRE)**[21] 4045 3-9-7 **78**..................................... RobertHavlin 6 42
(J H M Gosden) *s.i.s: bhd: hdwy 1/2-way: wknd over 2f out* **5/2[1]**

1m 12.23s (-1.47) **Going Correction** -0.20s/f (Stan) **10** Ran SP% **116.4**
Speed ratings (Par 102):101,99,97,97,95 95,93,93,83,82
CSF £27.25 CT £284.24 TOTE £8.30: £2.10, £1.50, £3.40; EX 33.30.
Owner C R Marks (banbury) **Bred** E A R L Elevage De La Source **Trained** Chastleton, Oxon
■ Stewards' Enquiry : Richard Kingscote one-day ban: dropped hands and failed to ride out for 5th place (Sep 3)

FOCUS
A reasonable little sprint handicap restricted to three-year-olds, featuring four last-time out winners, but few could get involved from off the pace and the track again seemed to be riding on the fast side. Ordinary form for the grade.
Sun Catcher(IRE) Official explanation: jockey said gelding never travelled
Dama'A(IRE) Official explanation: trainer had no explanation for the poor form shown

4704 WEATHERBYS PRINTING APPRENTICE H'CAP (ROUND 10) 1m (P)
9:20 (9:22) (Class 5) (0-75,75) 3-Y-0+ **£5,505** (£1,637; £818; £408) **Stalls** High

Form RPR
2000 **1** **Cloud Atlas (IRE)**[14] 4249 3-9-3 **68**.. NicolPolli 2 76
(S Kirk) *mde virtually all: drvn and hld on wl whn chal thrght fnl f* **10/1**
0452 **2** *½* **Jomus**[14] 4248 5-8-11 **56**..(b) JamesMillman 1 64
(L Montague Hall) *hld up and trckd ldrs: gng wl and cl 2nd over 1f out: shkn up ins last and sn no ex* **4/1[2]**
612U **3** *1* **Piano Player (IRE)**[15] 4225 3-9-5 **75**........................ FrankiePickard(5) 8 80
(J A Osborne) *chsd ldrs: rdn and effrt on ins fnl f: kpt on but nvr quite gng pce to chal* **9/2[3]**
-600 **4** *¾* **Colinca's Lad (IRE)**[72] 2508 4-9-0 **59**......................... AshleyHamblett 6 63
(T T Clement) *chsd ldrs: outpcd 3f out: styd on again fnl f: gng on cl home* **12/1**
6564 **5** *1 ¾* **Kingsholm**[34] 3688 4-9-9 **73**...................................... WilliamCarson(5) 5 73
(A M Balding) *chsd ldr: chal 4f out to 3f out: stl upsides 2f out: wknd fnl f* **3/1[1]**
6143 **6** *2 ½* **Blackmail (USA)**[8] 4448 8-9-2 **61**.................................(b) JamieJones 4 55
(Miss B Sanders) *sltly hmpd after 2f: nvr in contention after* **5/1**
2063 **7** *14* **Scutch Mill (IRE)**[25] 3951 4-9-5 **67**........................... JamieHamblett(3) 7 29
(Karen George) *hmpd after 2f: a in rr after* **9/1**
3006 **U** **Reflecting (IRE)**[13] 4286 3-9-2 **70**.............................. PatrickHills(3) 3 —
(J W Hills) *trcking ldrs whn stmbld and uns rdr after 2f* **10/1**

1m 40.82s (0.02) **Going Correction** -0.20s/f (Stan)
WFA 3 from 4yo+ 6lb **8** Ran SP% **115.7**
Speed ratings (Par 103):91,90,89,88,87 84,70,—
CSF £50.34 CT £210.58 TOTE £11.70: £1.80, £2.00, £1.80; EX 121.10 Place 6 £323.43, Place 5 £132.74.
Owner Martin White & Partners **Bred** Patrick Ryan **Trained** Upper Lambourn, Berks

FOCUS
A modest apprentice handicap run at just a steady pace early on, and the time was very slow for the grade. Very ordinary form.
T/Plt: £524.40 to a £1 stake. Pool: £54,420.30. 75.75 winning tickets. T/Qpdt: £56.60 to a £1 stake. Pool: £3,235.20. 42.25 winning tickets. ST

4388 LEICESTER (R-H)
Wednesday, August 23

OFFICIAL GOING: Good to soft (good in places)
Wind: Light, behind Weather: Overcast, turning to rain for race 4

4705 LADBROKES.COM MAIDEN STKS 7f 9y
2:25 (2:28) (Class 3) 2-Y-0
£7,790 (£2,332; £1,166; £583; £291; £146) **Stalls** Low

Form RPR
1 **Cold Quest (USA)** 2-9-3 .... RobertHavlin 5 82+
(J H M Gosden) *mid-div: hdwy over 2f out: rdn to ld ins fnl f: comf* **7/2[1]**
2 *¾* **The Wizened Apple (USA)** 2-9-3 .... JamieMackay 12 80
(N A Callaghan) *dwlt: hld up: hdwy over 1f out: r.o* **40/1**
3 *3* **Stanley George (IRE)** 2-9-3 .... MatthewHenry 18 72
(M A Jarvis) *chsd ldrs: rdn to ld over 1f out: hdd and no ex ins fnl f* **28/1**
35 **4** *1 ¾* **Sir Sandicliffe (IRE)**[13] 4295 2-9-3 .... DavidKinsella 1 68
(B W Hills) *led 4f: sn rdn: styd on same pce appr fnl f* **6/1**
0 **5** *¾* **Crystal Plum (IRE)**[20] 4084 2-8-5 .... SladeO'Hara(7) 2 61
(B W Hills) *chsd ldrs: led 3f out: rdn and hdd over 1f out: wknd fnl f* **66/1**
4 **6** *2 ½* **Venetian Dancer (IRE)**[23] 3994 2-9-3 .... TedDurcan 16 60
(M J Wallace) *chsd ldrs: rdn over 2f out: wknd over 1f out* **5/1[3]**
4 **7** *nk* **Bachnagairn**[17] 4177 2-9-3 .... FergusSweeney 10 59
(R Charlton) *mid-div: pushed along 1/2-way: hdwy over 2f out: wknd over 1f out* **4/1[2]**
0 **8** *1* **Kings Art (IRE)**[22] 4028 2-9-3 .... FrankieMcDonald 3 57
(B W Hills) *chsd ldrs: rdn 2f out: wknd fnl f* **14/1**
9 *¾* **Joyful Tears (IRE)** 2-8-12 .... RichardMullen 13 50
(E A L Dunlop) *s.i.s: hdwy 1/2-way: rdn and wknd 2f out* **25/1**
0 **10** *1 ¾* **Present**[60] 2867 2-8-12 .... HayleyTurner 8 45
(D Morris) *hld up: hdwy 3f out: rdn and wknd over 1f out* **66/1**
11 *2 ½* **Abbotts Account (USA)** 2-9-3 .... JimCrowley 14 44
(Mrs A J Perrett) *s.s: outpcd* **33/1**
12 *4* **Lisselan Dancer (USA)** 2-8-12 .... JimmyQuinn 17 29
(Mrs A J Perrett) *chsd ldrs: rdn over 2f out: sn wknd* **33/1**
13 *3* **Ladies Best** 2-9-3 .... RoystonFfrench 15 27
(Sir Michael Stoute) *sn outpcd* **9/1**
14 *1 ¼* **Bronzo Di Riace (IRE)** 2-9-3 .... CatherineGannon 7 24
(K A Ryan) *chsd ldrs over 4f* **33/1**
0 **15** *2* **Ma Ridge**[78] 2315 2-9-3 .... RobertMiles 6 19
(T D McCarthy) *chsd ldrs: rdn whn nt much roon 1/2-way: sn wknd* **100/1**
16 *33* **Apache Chant (USA)** 2-9-3 .... GeorgeBaker 11 —
(E A L Dunlop) *s.s: outpcd* **16/1**
17 *1 ¾* **Capahouse** 2-9-3 .... FrancisFerris 4 —
(B Palling) *sn outpcd* **66/1**

1m 26.02s (-0.08) **Going Correction** -0.125s/f (Firm) **17** Ran SP% **119.7**
Speed ratings (Par 98):95,94,90,88,87 85,84,83,82,80 77,73,69,68,66 28,26
CSF £157.35 TOTE £3.30: £1.60, £9.80, £11.00; EX 343.80 TRIFECTA Not won..
Owner Carwell Equities Ltd **Bred** G Tanaka **Trained** Newmarket, Suffolk

FOCUS
Not easy to assess with few of these having run before, but the standard looks pretty good overall.

NOTEBOOK
Cold Quest(USA) is out of a high-class winner at up to ten furlongs. He showed signs of greenness on this debut and was under pressure not long after passing the three pole, but came through to win tidily in the end. He should improve for the experience and will appreciate the chance to race on some better ground. (tchd 3-1 and 4-1)
The Wizened Apple(USA) had work to do at halfway following a slow start but came home in good style, if held by the favourite. This was an encouraging debut. (op 50-1)
Stanley George(IRE), whose dam was unraced, made a promising debut from his wide draw but had to give best inside the final furlong.
Sir Sandicliffe(IRE), the only runner in the field to have had two previous outings, made the running against the stands' fence and kept on when headed, suggesting he stayed this longer trip. He should make his mark in nurseries. (op 8-1)
Crystal Plum(IRE) showed much more than when beating just one home on her debut at Goodwood but faded in the latter stages.
Venetian Dancer(IRE), stepping up two furlongs in trip for this turf debut, confirmed that he has ability. (op 4-1)
Bachnagairn, unable to confirm debut promise on this much slower going, shaped as if in need of another step up in trip. (op 3-1 tchd 11-4)
Ladies Best Official explanation: jockey said colt clipped heels approx 5f out
Ma Ridge Official explanation: jockey said colt was unsuited by the good to soft (good in places) ground

4706 LADBROKESCASINO.COM H'CAP 7f 9y
3:00 (3:00) (Class 4) (0-80,77) 4-Y-0+
£7,790 (£2,332; £1,166; £583; £291; £146) **Stalls** Low

Form RPR
1322 **1** **Barons Spy (IRE)**[10] 4390 5-8-6 **65**................................ JamesDoyle(3) 3 76
(R J Price) *hld up: hdwy over 2f out: led ins fnl f: r.o* **11/2[1]**
4502 **2** *1* **Full Victory (IRE)**[9] 4429 4-9-5 **75**................................... RobertHavlin 5 83
(R A Farrant) *chsd ldrs: led over 4f out: rdn and hdd over 1f out: ev ch ins fnl f: styd on same pce* **15/2[3]**
0132 **3** *nk* **Certain Justice (USA)**[4] 4602 8-9-1 **71**.......................... HayleyTurner 15 78+
(Stef Liddiard) *hld up: hdwy over 1f out: r.o* **6/1[2]**
1410 **4** *hd* **Blue Java**[25] 3928 5-9-3 **76**................................... EdwardCreighton(3) 16 83
(H Morrison) *chsd ldrs: rdn to ld over 1f out: hung lft and hdd ins fnl f: styd on same pce* **8/1**
4103 **5** *1 ½* **Vienna's Boy (IRE)**[9] 4437 5-8-12 **71**..................... StephenDonohoe(3) 8 74
(W J Musson) *mid-div: hdwy over 2f out: styd on same pce fnl f* **14/1**
0060 **6** *1 ¼* **Harvest Warrior**[4] 4602 4-8-12 **68**..............................(b) RichardMullen 6 68
(T D Easterby) *s.s: outpcd: r.o ins fnl f: nrst fin* **12/1**
0000 **7** *1 ¼* **Mineral Star (IRE)**[56] 2974 4-9-7 **77**.............................. GeorgeBaker 12 73
(M H Tompkins) *led: hdd over 4f out: wknd fnl f* **15/2[3]**
2/6- **8** *2 ¼* **Climate (IRE)**[437] 2514 7-9-3 **73**............................ CatherineGannon 2 63
(K A Ryan) *mid-div: rdn 1/2-way: nvr trbld ldrs* **50/1**
0000 **9** *hd* **Millennium Force**[17] 4172 8-9-7 **77**.................................. IanMongan 11 67
(M R Channon) *dwlt: hdwy u.p over 2f out: wknd fnl f* **12/1**
0504 **10** *1 ½* **Breaking Shadow (IRE)**[5] 4569 4-9-4 **74**.................(b[1]) PaulFessey 10 60
(T D Barron) *hld up: hdwy 1/2-way: rdn and wknd over 1f out* **9/1**
2253 **11** *¾* **Grizedale (IRE)**[10] 4399 7-9-5 **75**......................................(t) PaulDoe 14 59
(J Akehurst) *hld up: nt clr run over 2f out: hdwy u.p over 1f out: wknd fnl f* **9/1**
0045 **12** *1 ½* **Lizarazu (GER)**[40] 3470 7-8-12 **75**................................(p) TolleyDean(7) 4 55
(R A Harris) *chsd ldrs over 5f* **40/1**
0320 **13** *10* **Danielle's Lad**[37] 3599 10-8-6 **62**................................... FrancisFerris 17 16
(B Palling) *chsd ldrs: rdn over 2f out: sn wknd* **33/1**
020- **14** *1* **Grand Show**[368] 4588 4-9-5 **75**... TedDurcan 9 27
(W R Swinburn) *plld hrd and prom: hung rt 4f out: wknd over 1f out* **20/1**
4132 **15** *1* **Linda's Colin (IRE)**[10] 4399 4-8-11 **67**....................... AdrianMcCarthy 1 16
(R A Harris) *chsd ldrs: rdn over 2f out: sn wknd* **12/1**

1m 24.73s (-1.37) **Going Correction** -0.125s/f (Firm) **15** Ran SP% **126.2**
Speed ratings (Par 105):102,100,100,100,98 97,95,93,92,91 90,88,77,76,74
CSF £46.32 CT £271.33 TOTE £7.40: £2.10, £4.40, £4.10; EX 78.20 TRIFECTA Not won..
Owner Barry Veasey **Bred** Tally-Ho Stud **Trained** Ullingswick, H'fords

FOCUS
A fair handicap and solid form for the grade.
Certain Justice(USA) Official explanation: jockey said gelding was denied a clear run
Grand Show Official explanation: jockey said gelding ran too freely
Linda's Colin(IRE) Official explanation: jockey said gelding finished distressed

The Form Book, Raceform Ltd, Compton, RG20 6NL

4707 LADBROKES.COM H'CAP 5f 218y
3:35 (3:35) (Class 3) (0-95,95) 3-Y-O

£11,217 (£3,358; £1,679; £840; £419; £210) Stalls Low

Form RPR

0-06 **1** **Dizzy Dreamer (IRE)**[33] [3709] 3-9-2 **90** RobertHavlin 6 104
(P W Chapple-Hyam) *led 5f out: hung rt fnl 4f: rdn out* **16/1**

-021 **2** *2* **Blues In The Night (IRE)**[13] [4296] 3-8-2 **76** oh2 JimmyQuinn 7 84
(P J Makin) *chsd ldrs: rdn over 1f out: styd on same pce fnl f* **13/2**

3615 **3** *2* **The Snatcher (IRE)**[21] [4042] 3-9-6 **94** RichardSmith 4 96
(R Hannon) *chsd ldrs: rdn over 1f out: wknd ins fnl f* **6/1**[3]

1160 **4** *3/4* **Gavarnie Beau (IRE)**[46] [3296] 3-8-11 **85** TedDurcan 1 85
(M Blanshard) *hld up: rdn and nt clr run over 1f out: nvr nrr* **12/1**

1423 **5** *1* **Antica (IRE)**[90] [1953] 3-9-2 **90** GeorgeBaker 5 87
(M H Tompkins) *s.i.s: hld up: swtchd rt and hdwy over 2f out: wknd ins fnl f* **11/4**[1]

2105 **6** *1/2* **Westport**[44] [3360] 3-8-3 **77** CatherineGannon 2 72
(K A Ryan) *hld up: rdn over 2f out: nvr trbld ldrs* **14/1**

2200 **7** *shd* **Imperial Sword**[31] [3761] 3-8-11 **85** PaulFessey 3 80
(T D Barron) *led 1f: chsd ldrs tl wknd over 1f out* **7/2**[2]

6302 **8** *1* **Charlie Delta**[10] [4403] 3-8-7 **81** DanielTudhope 10 73
(D Carroll) *prom: rdn over 1f out: wknd fnl f* **16/1**

-560 **9** *hd* **Campbeltown (IRE)**[88] [2022] 3-9-7 **95** AdrianMcCarthy 9 86
(R A Harris) *chsd ldrs: rdn and ev ch over 2f out: wknd fnl f* **40/1**

3051 **10** *2* **Conrad**[14] [4262] 3-8-2 **76** oh2 RoystonFfrench 8 61
(R A Fahey) *mid-div: rdn 1/2-way: wknd over 1f out* **10/1**

1m 10.95s (-2.25) **Going Correction** -0.125s/f (Firm) **10** Ran SP% **114.2**
Speed ratings (Par 104):110,107,104,103,102 101,101,100,99,97
CSF £113.90 CT £702.03 TOTE £12.20: £2.50, £2.90, £2.70; EX 127.20 Trifecta £189.00 Part won. Pool: £266.25 - 0.20 winning tickets..
Owner P W Chapple-Hyam **Bred** Albert Sherwood **Trained** Newmarket, Suffolk

FOCUS
A fair handicap but the form does not have a rock-solid feel to it. A decent winning time for a race like this. The winner confirmed that the stands' side was favoured.

NOTEBOOK
Dizzy Dreamer(IRE) was dropping in grade for only her third run of the campaign. In front after a furlong and with the rail to race against, she was hanging a little through the remainder of the contest but nonetheless ran on strongly. (op 14-1)
Blues In The Night(IRE), out of the handicap and in effect 8lb higher than when winning at Haydock, produced a decent effort on this different ground and continues on the upgrade. (op 6-1 tchd 5-1)
The Snatcher(IRE), proven on this ground, ran respectably dropped back in trip but looks high enough in the weights now. (op 5-1)
Gavarnie Beau(IRE), only 2lb higher than when scoring here in May, was putting in some good late work. (op 14-1 tchd 16-1)
Antica(IRE) was down in both class and trip on this first run in three months. After a slow start, she was switched to the centre to try and get involved but the effort flattened out inside the last. Official explanation: jockey said filly hung right from halfway (tchd 9-4 and 3-1 in places)

4708 LADBROKESCASINO.COM MEDIAN AUCTION MAIDEN STKS 1m 60y
4:10 (4:12) (Class 5) 3-4-Y-O £4,533 (£1,348; £674; £336) Stalls High

Form RPR

34 **1** **Our Faye**[35] [3647] 3-8-12 FrankieMcDonald 9 53
(S Kirk) *plld hrd: trckd ldrs: led over 2f out: rdn clr over 1f out* **5/1**[3]

6-4 **2** *2* **Dan Buoy (FR)**[11] [4367] 3-9-3 RobertHavlin 2 54+
(A King) *chsd ldrs: rdn over 3f out: styd on* **10/1**

0 **3** *1* **Arabian Breeze**[26] [3916] 3-8-12 AdrianMcCarthy 8 46
(M Mullineaux) *led over 5f: sn rdn: no ex fnl f* **100/1**

3203 **4** *1* **Compton Court**[17] [4176] 4-9-9 68 FergusSweeney 10 49
(A M Balding) *hld up in tch: n.m.r over 5f out: effrt over 1f out: nt run on* **15/8**[1]

505 **5** *1/2* **Stumped**[43] [3387] 3-9-3 69 JimCrowley 12 48
(W J Haggas) *plld hrd and prom: nt clr run over 5f out: rdn over 2f out: styd on same pce appr fnl f* **10/1**

0 **6** *nk* **City Minx**[26] [3914] 4-9-4 HayleyTurner 1 42
(D Morris) *prom: chsd ldr 5f out: rdn over 3f out: hung rt over 1f out : no ex* **66/1**

0 **7** *1 3/4* **Cosmic Messenger (FR)**[79] [2292] 3-9-0 StephaneBreux[(3)] 6 43
(L A Dace) *s.i.s: hld up: hdwy u.p over 1f out: nvr trbld ldrs* **50/1**

0- **8** *1/2* **Leprechaun's Maite**[17] [1015] 4-9-4 TomMessenger[(5)] 7 42?
(B N Pollock) *hld up: rdn 1/2-way: nvr trbld ldrs* **100/1**

0-04 **9** *nk* **Towerofcharlemagne (IRE)**[9] [4431] 3-9-3 GeorgeBaker 3 41
(Miss Gay Kelleway) *hld up: shkn up and edgd rt over 1f out: nvr trbld ldrs* **6/1**

10 *10* **Ektimaal** 3-9-3 RichardMullen 4 18
(E A L Dunlop) *s.i.s: hdwy 6f out: rdn over 3f out: wknd over 1f out* **7/2**[2]

0 **11** *10* **Elsie Alderman**[81] [2220] 4-9-4 RichardSmith 5 —
(J C Fox) *hld up: wknd over 3f out* **80/1**

12 *1 1/2* **Pagan Island** 3-9-3 JimmyQuinn 13 —
(J A R Toller) *s.s: outpcd* **12/1**

1m 47.05s (1.75) **Going Correction** 0.0s/f (Good)
WFA 3 from 4yo 6lb **12** Ran SP% **120.5**
Speed ratings (Par 103):91,89,88,87,86 86,84,83,83,73 63,62
CSF £54.59 TOTE £5.70: £2.00, £1.70, £11.90; EX 46.50 Trifecta £173.70 Part won. Pool: £244.67 - 0.34 winning tickets..
Owner J B J Richards **Bred** J B J Richards **Trained** Upper Lambourn, Berks
■ Stewards' Enquiry : Tom Messenger one-day ban: used whip with excessive frequency and on a horse showing no response (Sep 3)

FOCUS
A weak maiden run at a dawdle early, resulting in several pulling too hard, and it suited those that raced handily. Not surprisingly a very moderate winning time for the class, and the form is decidely dodgy with the third, sixth and eighth too close for comfort.
Ektimaal Official explanation: jockey said gelding had a breathing problem

4709 LADBROKES.COM ROTHERBY H'CAP 1m 1f 218y
4:45 (4:45) (Class 6) (0-60,60) 4-Y-O+ £3,238 (£963; £481; £240) Stalls High

Form RPR

1240 **1** **Sudden Impulse**[11] [4380] 5-8-8 **47** SilvestreDeSousa 12 57+
(A D Brown) *broke wl: plld hrd: stdd and lost pl over 8f out: hmpd sn after: hdwy over 2f out: led over 1f out: rdn out* **7/2**[1]

-005 **2** *1 1/4* **Montjeu Baby (IRE)**[68] [2601] 4-9-6 **59** IanMongan 6 67
(B J Meehan) *hld up: hdwy over 2f out: rdn and edgd rt fr over 1f out: styd on* **6/1**[3]

3240 **3** *1 1/4* **Royal Flynn**[4] [4606] 4-9-4 **57** PaulFessey 7 63
(M Dods) *s.i.s: hld up: hdwy 2f out: sn rdn: styd on same pce ins fnl f* **15/2**

6442 **4** *2* **Tetragon (IRE)**[7] [4472] 6-9-5 **58** DanielTudhope 10 60
(D Carroll) *a.p: rdn over 3f out: styng on same pce whn nt clr run ins fnl f* **11/2**[2]

0605 **5** *1/2* **Ronsard (IRE)**[10] [4389] 4-9-5 **58** RobertHavlin 3 59
(T J Pitt) *hld up in tch: rdn over 3f out: outpcd 2f out: styd on ins fnl f* **10/1**

0066 **6** *1* **Native American**[7] [4497] 4-9-1 **54** FergusSweeney 14 53
(T D McCarthy) *hld up: hdwy over 3f out: rdn over 1f out: wknd ins fnl f* **14/1**

1341 **7** *2 1/2* **Magic Warrior**[14] [4248] 6-9-6 **59** RichardSmith 13 53+
(J C Fox) *broke wl: stdd and lost pl over 8f out: hdwy over 2f out: nt trble ldrs* **8/1**

0444 **8** *1/2* **Miss Monica (IRE)**[1] [4673] 5-8-1 **43** EdwardCreighton[(3)] 4 36
(P W Hiatt) *chsd ldr tl led over 3f out: rdn and hdd over 1f out: wknd fnl f* **12/1**

0660 **9** *2* **Bubbling Fun**[13] [4282] 5-8-5 **51** ow5 SladeO'Hara[(7)] 11 40
(T Wall) *hld up: hdwy over 3f out: wknd fnl f* **33/1**

5050 **10** *1/2* **Fiore Di Bosco (IRE)**[9] [4439] 5-8-8 **47** JamieMackay 15 36
(T D Barron) *s.i.s: hld up: plld hrd: hdwy over 2f out: rdn and wknd over 1f out* **18/1**

000- **11** *3/4* **Moonshine Bill**[331] [5518] 7-8-4 **43** MatthewHenry 9 30
(P W Hiatt) *sn led: hdd over 3f out: n.m.r and wknd over 1f out* **28/1**

0005 **12** *1 3/4* **Malibu (IRE)**[154] [694] 5-9-4 **60** StephenDonohoe[(3)] 1 44
(S R Bowring) *hld up: n.d* **33/1**

0/00 **13** *3/4* **Explode**[9] [4425] 9-8-6 **48** JasonEdmunds[(3)] 16 30
(Miss L C Siddall) *sn outpcd* **66/1**

0000 **14** *1* **Kentuckian**[16] [4210] 4-8-4 **43** ow1 PaulDoe 17 23
(P W Hiatt) *chsd ldrs: lost pl 8f out: sme hdwy over 2f out: sn wknd* **40/1**

0061 **15** *nk* **Rock Haven (IRE)**[10] [4404] 4-8-12 **58** 6ex RussellKennemore[(7)] 8 38
(J Mackie) *chsd ldrs over 7f* **12/1**

400- **16** *6* **Sheriff's Deputy**[329] [5545] 6-9-2 **55** AdrianMcCarthy 2 23
(C N Kellett) *hld up in tch: rdn and wknd over 2f out* **25/1**

0000 **17** *nk* **Komreyev Star**[10] [4390] 4-8-11 **50** JimmyQuinn 5 18
(M Mullineaux) *chsd ldrs 7f* **33/1**

2m 7.91s (-0.39) **Going Correction** 0.0s/f (Good) **17** Ran SP% **131.2**
Speed ratings (Par 101):101,100,99,97,97 96,94,93,92,91 91,89,89,88,88 83,83
CSF £23.59 CT £160.42 TOTE £5.70: £2.70, £1.90, £4.70, £1.60; EX 32.80 Trifecta £97.60 Part won. Pool: £137.60 - 0.68 winning tickets..
Owner Mrs S L Salt **Bred** Sagittarius Bloodstock Associates Ltd **Trained** Pickering, York

FOCUS
A moderate handicap, but competitive enough in view of the size of the field and the form looks sound. Unlike in the previous contest, a solid pace here suited those that were held up. Sudden Impulse was helped by the decent pace over this shorter trip and scored in good style.
Sheriff's Deputy Official explanation: jockey said gelding was unsuited by the good to soft (good in places) ground

4710 LADBROKESCASINO.COM SPRINT H'CAP 5f 2y
5:20 (5:20) (Class 6) (0-60,57) 3-Y-O £3,238 (£963; £481; £240) Stalls Low

Form RPR

6310 **1** **Miss Mujahid Times**[16] [4201] 3-8-9 **45** (b) SilvestreDeSousa 2 52
(A D Brown) *mde all: rdn over 1f out: r.o: eased nr fin* **8/1**

0000 **2** *2* **Desert Dust**[60] [2876] 3-8-7 **43** ow1 (b[1]) FergusSweeney 12 43
(R M H Cowell) *chsd wnr: rdn over 1f out: styd on same pce ins fnl f* **20/1**

0052 **3** *shd* **Be My Charm**[10] [4398] 3-8-4 **47** LauraReynolds[(7)] 9 46
(M Blanshard) *s.s: outpcd: hmpd 2f out: hdwy over 1f out: r.o: nt rch ldrs* **9/2**[2]

4000 **4** *1 1/4* **Quadrophenia**[6] [4507] 3-9-5 **55** JamieMackay 7 50
(J G Given) *s.i.s: outpcd: hung rt fr over 3f out: hdwy 2f out: sn rdn: no ex ins fnl f* **11/1**

6006 **5** *2* **First Among Equals**[16] [4201] 3-8-7 **43** PaulFitzsimons 8 31
(Miss J R Tooth) *chsd ldrs: rdn over 1f out: wknd fnl f* **40/1**

6343 **6** *1/2* **Crusader's Gold (FR)**[26] [3916] 3-9-0 **50** (v) RichardMullen 3 36
(T D Easterby) *s.i.s: sn pushed along in mid-div: rdn and hung lft 2f out: nvr trbld ldrs* **7/2**[1]

0603 **7** *1/2* **Nilsatisoptimum (USA)**[2] [4656] 3-8-9 **45** (t) AdrianMcCarthy 1 29
(M Mullineaux) *sn outpcd: hdwy 2f out: wknd fnl f* **13/2**[3]

-404 **8** *3 1/2* **No Inkling (IRE)**[197] [335] 3-8-0 **43** ow1 TolleyDean[(7)] 4 15
(John A Harris) *prom: rdn 1/2-way: wknd over 1f out* **25/1**

5035 **9** *1* **Money Mate (IRE)**[20] [4071] 3-9-4 **54** IanMongan 10 22
(J O'Reilly) *chsd ldrs over 3f* **7/1**

6430 **10** *10* **Night Rainbow (IRE)**[32] [3728] 3-9-4 **57** EdwardCreighton[(3)] 6 —
(C Tinkler) *sn outpcd: effrt and hmpd over 1f out: eased* **7/1**

0300 **11** *3* **The Lady Caster**[27] [3866] 3-8-13 **49** (b[1]) JimmyQuinn 11 —
(R M Beckett) *trckd ldrs: rdn and wknd over 1f out* **7/1**

60.40 secs (-0.50) **Going Correction** -0.125s/f (Firm) **11** Ran SP% **121.7**
Speed ratings (Par 98):99,95,95,93,90 89,88,83,81,65 60
CSF £161.35 CT £830.18 TOTE £9.60: £2.50, £7.40, £2.20; EX 271.30 TRIFECTA Not won. Place 6 £517.57, Place 5 £164.20.
Owner John Wills **Bred** John Wills And Gordon Kendrick **Trained** Pickering, York
■ This completed a 39.5-1 double for jockey Silvestre de Sousa and trainer Alan Brown.

FOCUS
A sprint run at a decent pace, but another case of a horse making full use of the 'golden highway' tight against the stands' rail. It looked a weak race on paper but the time was quite good. Nothing got involved from the rear.
Night Rainbow(IRE) Official explanation: jockey said filly moved poorly and hung left
T/Plt: £315.20 to a £1 stake. Pool: £45,835.15. 106.15 winning tickets. T/Qpdt: £31.40 to a £1 stake. Pool: £3,039.20. 71.50 winning tickets. CR

4676 YORK (L-H)
Wednesday, August 23

OFFICIAL GOING: Good to soft
There had been no rain since the previous day and the ground remained the same.
Wind: Light, half-behind Weather: Mainly fine but overcast and humid ahead of heavy thunder rain race 7

4711 MOTABILITY SUPPORTED BY ROYAL & SUNALLIANCE STKS (H'CAP) 1m 2f 88y
1:45 (1:45) (Class 2) (0-105,101) 3-Y-O+£19,431 (£5,781; £2,889; £1,443) Stalls Low

Form RPR

2410 **1** **Topatoo**[61] [2810] 4-8-9 **83** MichaelHills 14 95
(M H Tompkins) *hld up in rr: stdy hdwy 4f out: swtchd rt 2f out: rdn to chal ent last: sn drvn and edgd lft: led last 100 yds* **14/1**

0300 **2** *1 ¼* **Dunaskin (IRE)**39 3552 6-9-4 **92**...................................... MartinDwyer 3 102
(Karen McLintock) *led: rdn over 2f out: drvn over 1f out: edgd lft ins last: hdd and no ex last 100 yds* **28/1**

-001 **3** *¾* **Group Captain**24 3980 4-9-7 **95**.................................. RichardHughes 1 105+
(R Charlton) *trckd ldrs gng wl: hdwy over 3f out: rdn over 1f out: styng on and ev ch whn hmpd ins last* **15/2**3

2034 **4** *3 ½* **Palomar (USA)**39 3551 4-9-13 **101**.................................. SteveDrowne 18 103
(R Charlton) *bhd: pushed along 4f out: swtchd ins and hdwy over 2f out: sn rdn and styd on ins last: nrst fin* **12/1**

6003 **5** *½* **Kamanda Laugh**24 3971 5-9-4 **92**... NCallan 5 93
(K A Ryan) *trckd ldrs: hdwy to chse ldr oevr 2f out: sn rdn and wknd appr last* **11/1**

-350 **6** *4* **Thunder Rock (IRE)**46 3294 4-9-2 **90**........................ RobertWinston 10 84
(Sir Michael Stoute) *lw: towards rr: hdwy on outer 3f out: rdn along 2f out: edgd lft wl over 1f out: sn no imp* **8/1**

1212 **7** *1 ¾* **Futun**27 3882 3-9-3 **99**..(t) NickyMackay 4 90
(L M Cumani) *lw: t.k.h: midfield: hdwy over 3f out: sn rdn along and no imp fnl 2f* **4/1**1

3100 **8** *2* **Blue Spinnaker (IRE)**39 3552 7-9-10 **98**.................. PaulMulrennan 19 85
(M W Easterby) *hld up towards rr: hdwy over 2f out: sn rdn and nvr nr ldrs* **11/1**

00-0 **9** *½* **Invasian (IRE)**24 3971 5-8-10 **87**................................ JohnMcAuley(3) 16 73
(B J McMath) *nvr nr ldrs* **100/1**

5252 **10** *¾* **Mutawaffer**24 3980 5-9-0 **88**... PaulHanagan 7 73
(R A Fahey) *in tch: rdn along over 3f out: sn drvn and btn* **12/1**

/01- **11** *3* **Leo's Luckyman (USA)**111 5106 7-9-12 **100**................. JoeFanning 17 80
(M Johnston) *lw: chsd ldrs: rdn along 4f out: grad wknd* **33/1**

650 **12** *1 ¼* **Im Spartacus**24 3980 4-8-11 **85**.................................... JamieSpencer 2 62
(D W Barker) *in tch: hdwy 4f out: rdn along over 2f out: sn drvn and btn* **20/1**

-040 **13** *13* **Ofaraby**86 2079 6-9-11 **99**.. PhilipRobinson 6 53
(M A Jarvis) *hld up towards rr:hdwy 3f out: rdn to chse ldrs wl over 1f out: sn wknd and heavily eased fnl f* **7/1**2

-010 **14** *16* **Salinja (USA)**22 4023 4-9-8 **96**... RyanMoore 11 21
(Mrs A J Perrett) *lw: a towards rr* **16/1**

0222 **15** *shd* **Desert Realm (IRE)**20 4082 3-9-2 **98**.............................. KDarley 8 23
(M Johnston) *in tch: rdn along over 3f out: sn wknd* **11/1**

6-10 **16** *½* **Abbondanza (IRE)**67 2659 3-8-4 **86** ow2.......................... JohnEgan 12 10
(J Howard Johnson) *prom: rdn along 4f out: sn wknd* **66/1**

6005 **17** *24* **Bahar Shumaal (IRE)**11 4356 4-8-13 **87**......................(b) SebSanders 13 —
(C E Brittain) *chsd ldng pair: rdn along over 4f out: sn wknd* **33/1**

2m 11.21s (0.73) **Going Correction** +0.30s/f (Good)
WFA 3 from 4yo+ 8lb **17** Ran SP% **124.9**
Speed ratings (Par 109):109,108,107,104,104 101,99,98,97,97 94,93,83,70,70 69,50
CSF £380.76 CT £3164.21 TOTE £20.90: £4.30, £7.00, £2.30, £3.60; EX 637.10 Trifecta £1798.90 Part won. Pool £2,533.74 - 0.10 winning tickets..
Owner Mrs P R Bowring **Bred** M P Bowring **Trained** Newmarket, Suffolk

FOCUS

A high-class handicap and solid-looking on paper, but holes can be picked in the form. The winner has a fine record at the track and was winning off her highest-winning mark, Group Captain, Palomar and Thunder Rock seem to need further while Kamanda Laugh did not see out the trip.

NOTEBOOK

Topatoo, who looked very fit indeed, has a tremendous record at York and got the better of the runner-up in a tight finish after scything through the pack. Winning off her highest-ever handicap mark, she will need to find significant improvement to hold her own next time in similar company. Connections suggested that the Cambridgeshire is now in their plans although they also feel she is better around a bend. (tchd 16-1 in a place)

Dunaskin(IRE), very keen to post, was given a fine front-running ride and looked the most likely winner at the three-furlong marker. Understandably he tired towards the end of the race, but he never gave up and harried Topatoo throughout much of the final furlong. He is high enough in the handicap and will struggle to reproduce the effort next time if raised in the weights. (tchd 33-1 in a place)

Group Captain was keeping on well inside the final furlong when hampered by the winner and the runner-up. He almost certainly would not have won, but it was a fine effort and he would be suited by a step back up in trip. (tchd 8-1)

Palomar(USA), who was fitted with ear plugs, kept on strongly in the final stages up the far-side rail, a route he followed alone. The drop in trip was against him, considering all of his best form, so it was a fine effort, especially as he was last entering the home straight. A return to a mile and a half plus will be to his advantage. (tchd 14-1 in a place)

Kamanda Laugh was bang there until the final furlong before not getting home. All of his best form has been at up to a mile and it seems clear that he does not stay much further. A drop down in trip will obviously suit him.

Thunder Rock(IRE) kept on really well from the two-furlong marker, suggesting he will be much better suited by further. He ought to get dropped a couple of pounds for the run, which would make him of some interest next time if stepped up in distance again. (tchd 17-2 and 9-1 in a place)

Futun, fitted with a tongue tie, was too keen early to have anything left for the business end of the race. If learning to settle better, he can return to the form he showed at Haydock in July and progress into a very good handicapper. (tchd 9-2 in places)

Im Spartacus Official explanation: jockey said gelding had no more to give

Ofaraby was staying on quite well when something appeared to go amiss at the furlong pole. He was not going to be involved in the finish but showed some promise, and is not one to dismiss lightly next time if a reason for the effort can be found. (op 10-1)

Salinja(USA) Official explanation: jockey said gelding hung right-handed

Bahar Shumaal(IRE) Official explanation: jockey said colt had no more to give

4712 SCOTTISH EQUITABLE GIMCRACK STKS (GROUP 2) (C&G) 6f

2:15 (2:15) (Class 1) 2-Y-0

£80,570 (£30,536; £15,282; £7,620; £3,817; £1,915) **Stalls** Centre

Form RPR

2521 **1** **Conquest (IRE)**46 3308 2-8-12 102.........................(b) JimmyFortune 3 114
(W J Haggas) *hld up: hdwy and swtchd rt over 2f out: swtchd lft and rdn over 1f out: drvn and styd on ins last to ld last 50 yds* **9/2**3

12 **2** *¾* **Wi Dud**22 4026 2-8-12 .... DO'Donohoe 2 112
(K A Ryan) *hld up: hdwy on outer 1/2-way: rdn to chal and edgd rt 2f out: led over 1f out: drvn ins last: hdd and no ex last 50 yds* **5/1**

4112 **3** *2 ½* **Bodes Galaxy (IRE)**19 4099 2-8-12 105......................... MickyFenton 5 104
(N P Littmoden) *lw: led: rdn and edgd lft over 2f out: sn drvn and hdd over 1f out: wknd ins last* **7/1**

1611 **4** *2* **Elhamri**32 3734 2-8-12 111.. DPMcDonogh 1 98
(S Kirk) *lw: sn cl up: rdn and wkng whn bmpd over 2f out: kpt on same pce* **11/4**2

1 **5** *7* **He's A Humbug (IRE)**50 3173 2-8-12 .... NCallan 6 77
(K A Ryan) *chsd ldrs: rdn along over 2f out: sn btn* **5/2**1

2245 **6** *½* **Armigerent (IRE)**11 4344 2-8-12 103...................................... KDarley 4 76
(M Johnston) *chsd ldng pair: rdn along over 3f out: sn drvn and wknd* **11/1**

1m 11.81s (-0.75) **Going Correction** 0.0s/f (Good) **6** Ran SP% **110.9**
Speed ratings (Par 106):105,104,100,98,88 88
CSF £25.84 TOTE £6.00: £2.40, £2.10; EX 26.50.
Owner Highclere Thoroughbred Racing XXXVIII **Bred** Gerrardstown House Stud **Trained** Newmarket, Suffolk

FOCUS

This did not look a great renewal of the Gimcrack beforehand, but the winner posted a near-average figure of the race, with the runner-up to form. The first two look decent prospects over sprint distances, while the rest have something to find, although Elhamri can be given another chance. The winning time was close to par for a race of its stature.

NOTEBOOK

Conquest(IRE), an edgy individual, travelled with plenty of zest throughout the race and overcame trouble in running, mostly of his own making, to win going away. Looking every inch a sprinter, although his pedigree suggests he could get further, he has quite a few options open to him now ranging from a speculative entry in the Prix de l'Abbaye to races such as the Mill Reef and Middle Park, the first and last-named races being Group 1s. (tchd 5-1)

Wi Dud was quite keen early and became slightly outpaced as the tempo increased. However, once straightened out, he really found his stride and powered through to lead about a furlong from home. He always looked to be covered by Conquest throughout the final stages but ran right up to his very best. The Middle Park looks the obvious target for him, following in the footsteps of his stablemate Amadeus Wolf. (op 7-2)

Bodes Galaxy(IRE), who was supplemented for the race, continues to run with real credit in Group races, but it is hard to forget the fact he was beaten twice in maiden company early in his career, which gives the form a slight doubt. Connections cannot be faulted by the way they have campaigned the horse, and have done a great job with him, but he does not look up to Group 2 company. (op 15-2)

Elhamri had every chance but was not good enough on the day. He had beaten Conquest at Royal Ascot so the suggestion must be that that horse has improved past him, although the sixth furlong on easy ground could also have found him out. (op 7-2)

He's A Humbug(IRE), who was ridden by the stable jockey instead of Wi Dud, moved well in the early stages but was readily put in his place when the race took shape. He has physical scope for improvement but he is not up to Group 2 company yet. The trainer reported that the horse did not handle the ground. (op 3-1)

Armigerent(IRE) is on the small side and dropped out quickly when the pace increased. He is sure to win a maiden in due course but he lacks any physical scope. (op 10-1 tchd 12-1)

4713 TOTESPORT EBOR (HERITAGE H'CAP) 1m 5f 197y

2:50 (2:53) (Class 2) 3-Y-0+

£124,640 (£37,320; £18,660; £9,340; £4,660; £2,340) **Stalls** Low

Form RPR

310 **1** **Mudawin (IRE)**26 3888 5-8-4 **88**... JohnEgan 14 99
(Jane Chapple-Hyam) *bhd: hdwy on outer wl over 2f out: sn rdn and hung lft wl over 1f out: drvn ent last: styd on wl to ld last strides* **100/1**

-623 **2** *hd* **Glistening**26 3890 4-9-0 **98**.. JamieSpencer 6 109
(L M Cumani) *hld up: gd hdwy over 3f out: rdn to chse ldrs wl over 1f out: led jst ins last and sn drvn: ct last strides* **13/2**2

1611 **3** *shd* **Young Mick**11 4347 4-9-2 **100** 7ex............................(v) RobertWinston 12 111
(G G Margarson) *lw: trckd ldrs: hdwy 4f out: chsd ldr over 2f out: drvn and led briefly 1f out: kpt on gamely u.p* **12/1**

4042 **4** *1 ¾* **Geordieland (FR)**20 4081 5-9-10 **108**..................................... LDettori 11 116
(J A Osborne) *hld up: hdwy 3f out: effrt to chse ldrs wel over 1f out: sn rdn and kpt on same pce ins last* **8/1**

2422 **5** *1 ½* **River Alhaarth (IRE)**53 3078 4-8-8 **92** ow1................(v1) CSoumillon 10 98
(P W Chapple-Hyam) *led 1f: chsd ldr tl led again over 3f out: pushed clr over 2f out: drvn and edgd lft over 1f out: hdd jst ins last and wknd* **12/1**

1-62 **7** *¾* **Foxhaven**19 4096 4-9-0 **98**.. MartinDwyer 3 99
(P R Chamings) *in tch on inner: gd hdwy over 3f out: rdn 2f out and wknd appr last* **7/1**3

3203 **8** *nk* **Lets Roll**22 4027 5-8-6 **90**.. DeanMcKeown 17 91
(C W Thornton) *lw: chsd ldrs: rdn wl over 2f out: drvn and kpt on same pce fr wl over 1f out* **20/1**

0-50 **9** *1 ¼* **Red Lancer**46 3294 5-8-9 **93**... TonyHamilton 13 92
(R A Fahey) *towards rr tl hdwy wl over 2f out: kpt on u.p appr last: nrst fin* **25/1**

-304 **10** *10* **Odiham**39 3533 5-8-11 **95**...(v) EddieAhern 9 80
(H Morrison) *towards rr tl styd on fnl 2f* **33/1**

4661 **11** *3* **Dorothy's Friend**11 4346 6-8-10 **94** 4ex...................(b1) SteveDrowne 18 75
(R Charlton) *a midfield* **25/1**

3014 **12** *5* **Consular**26 3890 4-8-12 **96**... PhilipRobinson 1 70
(M A Jarvis) *chsd ldrs: rdn along 4f out: sn wknd* **22/1**

1313 **13** *hd* **Greenwich Meantime**53 3078 6-8-10 **94**........................ PaulHanagan 4 68
(R A Fahey) *lw: midfield: hdwy and in tch over 3f out: sn rdn and wknd over 2f out* **9/1**

-100 **14** *21* **Public Forum**39 3552 4-8-12 **96**.................................... RichardHughes 5 40
(Sir Michael Stoute) *hld up: hdwy over 3f out: rdn and wknd over 2f out* **25/1**

-130 **15** *2* **Hearthstead Wings**39 3551 4-9-4 **102**...........................(v) JoeFanning 2 44
(M Johnston) *prom: rdn along 4f out: sn wknd* **50/1**

33-0 **16** *½* **Desert Move (IRE)**32 3739 4-8-13 **97**................................ KDarley 7 38
(M R Channon) *a rr* **100/1**

6023 **17** *3* **Bravo Maestro (USA)**11 4359 5-8-10 **94**............................. NCallan 19 31
(N P Littmoden) *bhd fr 1/2-way* **33/1**

0211 **18** *2* **Elusive Dream**19 4121 5-9-4 **102** 7ex...........................(b1) SebSanders 8 36
(Sir Mark Prescott) *cl up: led after 1f: rdn along 4f out: hdd over 3f out and sn wknd* **7/1**3

2-14 **19** *17* **Signatory (USA)**46 3294 4-8-13 **97**................................ JimmyFortune 15 7
(J H M Gosden) *stmbld s: racd wd and in tch tl rdn along 4f out and sn wknd* **11/2**1

2m 57.78s (-0.66) **Going Correction** +0.30s/f (Good) **20** Ran SP% **124.5**
Speed ratings (Par 109):113,112,112,111,110 109,109,108,108,102 100,97,97,85,84 84,82,81,71
CSF £621.78 CT £8273.31 TOTE £124.20: £18.90, £2.10, £2.90, £2.10; EX 790.70 Trifecta £4526.30 Part won. Pool £6,375.18 - 0.10 winning tickets..
Owner Franconson Partners **Bred** Shadwell Estate Company Limited **Trained** Newmarket, Suffolk

■ The biggest-priced winner ever of the Ebor, which was first run in 1843, and only his trainer's fifth winner.

■ Stewards' Enquiry : Jamie Spencer three-day ban: used whip without allowing mount time to respond, and with whip arm above shoulder height down the shoulder in forehand position (Sep 3-5)

John Egan four-day ban: used whip with excessive force (Sep 3-6)

FOCUS

The winning time was more than creditable for such a prestigious race. A shock winner, and the race lacked really progressive types, but the form looks solid with the 2nd, 3rd, 4th and 5th all capable of running well next time.

NOTEBOOK
Mudawin(IRE), who was well beaten on his last run after a similar last-ditch success at Sandown, ground out victory after looking booked for a place only at the furlong marker. He shapes as though another run over two miles is definitely worth a try and he will probably get further than that in time, so a tilt at the Cesarewitch could come into the reckoning later in the season.
Glistening, whose connections' other fancied candidate Soulacroix had to miss the race, did almost everything right and was mugged only yards from the line. The step back up in trip seemed to suit him well and a race such as the Doncaster Cup, which will be run at York this season, might be the race for him next. (tchd 7-1 in places)
Young Mick again ran right up to his very best and gives the form some shape. Trying further than a mile and a half for the first time, he saw the trip out well and the Melbourne Cup dream remains alive. He has all the attributes needed for that rough race and would give a good account of himself if getting to Flemington in one piece. (op 14-1)
Geordieland(FR) ran a great race under his huge weight, but that burden ultimately made the difference between being involved in the finish and an honourable effort in defeat. He will struggle in handicaps giving weight away and will probably be tried in Group company again. The Doncaster Cup, run at York next month, would seem a logical race for him next. (tchd 9-1 in a place)
River Alhaarth(IRE) ◆, wearing a first-time visor, travelled really well in the early stages of the race and probably hit the front too soon, finding himself at the head of affairs fully three furlongs from home when Elusive Dream weakened. It looked as though he got bored in front and he was joined and passed around a furlong from home, but he did not drop away, although edging to the left under pressure, and he can be given another chance as long as he can be held up for longer.
Solent(IRE) was not good enough but strongly suggested that he needs further, staying on really well throughout the final furlong. (tchd 28-1)
Foxhaven was going well early in the home straight but found very little under pressure, giving the impression that he did not see out the trip. A drop back in trip would make him far more interesting next time. (tchd 8-1 and 15-2 in a place)
Red Lancer kept on well from quite a way off the pace but never threatened to take a hand in the finish at any stage.
Greenwich Meantime, who was amazingly weak in the market and on the exchanges prior to the off, never got out of midfield and was really disappointing. (op 15-2)
Desert Move(IRE) Official explanation: jockey said filly lost its action
Elusive Dream, lit up and very warm in first-time blinkers, was too keen early and never had a chance of being involved at the end. He has yet to win a race in which there were more than ten runners. (op 9-1)
Signatory(USA) was struggling off the home bend and dropped right out up the home straight. There did not seem an obvious excuse for the poor effort. Official explanation: trainer had no explanation for the poor form shown (op 7-1)

4714 DARLEY YORKSHIRE OAKS (GROUP 1) (F&M) 1m 4f
3:25 (3:26) (Class 1) 3-Y-O+
£156,145 (£59,180; £29,617; £14,767; £7,397; £3,712) **Stalls** Centre

Form RPR
-211 **1** **Alexandrova (IRE)**[38] 3575 3-8-11 .... MJKinane 4 121+
(A P O'Brien, Ire) *lw: hld up in last pl: smooth hdwy over 3f out: shkn up to ld over 1f out: pushed clr* **4/9**[1]
0-13 **2** *3 ½* **Short Skirt**[82] 2203 3-8-11 105 .... RobertWinston 5 112
(Sir Michael Stoute) *lw: t.k.h: led after 1f: wnt lft over 2f out: hdd over 1f out: no ch w wnr* **11/2**[2]
-611 **3** *¾* **Allegretto (IRE)**[46] 3293 3-8-11 107 .... RyanMoore 6 110
(Sir Michael Stoute) *trckd ldrs: pushed along 6f out: kpt on same pce fnl 2f* **12/1**
1-13 **4** *nk* **Exhibit One (USA)**[17] 4192 4-9-7 70 .... EBotti 2 110
(V Valiani, Italy) *lw: led 1f: chsd ldrs: hung lft over 1f out: one pce* **66/1**
-212 **5** *9* **Sina Cova (IRE)**[16] 4212 4-9-7 .... JMurtagh 1 96
(Peter Casey, Ire) *hld up: effrt over 3f out: sn chsng ldrs: lost pl over 1f out* **50/1**
4114 **6** *27* **Shamdala (IRE)**[40] 3516 4-9-7 .... CSoumillon 3 52
(A De Royer-Dupre, France) *lw: hld up in rr: effrt over 3f out: lost pl over 2f out: heavily eased* **6/1**[3]

2m 32.41s (0.01) **Going Correction** +0.30s/f (Good)
WFA 3 from 4yo 10lb 6 Ran SP% **110.1**
Speed ratings (Par 117):111,108,108,107,101 83
CSF £3.19 TOTE £1.70: £1.10, £2.70; EX 4.20.
Owner Mrs John Magnier, M Tabor & D Smith **Bred** Quay Bloodstock **Trained** Ballydoyle, Co Tipperary
■ Alexandrova was the first filly to complete the Oaks, Irish Oaks, Yorkshire Oaks hat-trick since Ramruna in 1999.
■ Stewards' Enquiry : E Botti three-day ban: used whip with excessive frequency (Sep 3-5)

FOCUS
A weakish renewal of the Yorkshire Oaks but the form looks sound enough. Just a steady gallop but the winner, who came from last to first, could hardly have been more impressive and rates the leading three-year-old filly, although just how good she is is hard to know until she meets something comparable.

NOTEBOOK
Alexandrova(IRE), ridden with incredible confidence, cut through the field like a knife through butter and had only to be kept up to her work to pull clear. She is a top-class filly and thankfully will stay in training next year. The clash with the older fillies and mares at the Breeders' Cup should be a mouth-watering prospect. (op 8-13 tchd 4-6 in places)
Short Skirt, conqueror of the winner in the Musidora here in May in the mud, was the reluctant pacesetter. She dug deep under pressure but this time the Epsom and Irish Oaks winner was much too good. She deserves another good prize. (op 9-2)
Allegretto(IRE), who looked on the light side, had her trainer alongside her in the parade. She hit a flat spot on the home turn but stuck to her task in willing fashion and in the end was just held for second spot. She will stay further and should make a better four-year-old. (op 10-1)
Exhibit One(USA), winner of a poor maiden at Catterick a year ago for Sir Michael Stoute, has thrived in Italy and excelled herself here on ground softer than she truly prefers. The Stewards took a dim view though of her rider's use of his whip. (tchd 50-1)
Sina Cova(IRE) was biting off more than she could chew. (op 66-1)
Shamdala(IRE) looked at her best beforehand but ran poorly for no obvious reason. Official explanation: trainer had no explanation for the poor form shown (op 11-2 tchd 13-2 in a place)

4715 JULIA GRAVES ROSES STKS (LISTED RACE) 5f
4:00 (4:00) (Class 1) 2-Y-O
£17,781 (£6,723; £3,360; £1,680) **Stalls** Centre

Form RPR
2115 **1** **Not For Me (IRE)**[31] 3777 2-9-0 101 .... JohnEgan 6 101
(T J Pitt) *trckd ldrs: shkn up to ld over 1f out: r.o wl* **7/2**[2]
21 **2** *1 ¾* **Fanlight Fanny (USA)**[13] 4283 2-8-9 70 .... EddieAhern 4 90
(P Winkworth) *led: hung lft and hdd over 1f out: kpt on same pce* **20/1**
11 **3** *1* **Smart Instinct (USA)**[4] 4607 2-9-0 .... PaulHanagan 2 91+
(R A Fahey) *lw: wnt lft s: drvn along and sn outpcd: hdwy over 1f out: kpt on to take 3rd ins last* **2/1**[1]
6100 **4** *1* **Resignation (IRE)**[32] 3734 2-9-0 95 .... RichardHughes 5 88
(R Hannon) *hld up: effrt over 2f out: hrd rdn over 1f out: edgd lft and one pce* **5/1**[3]
41 **5** *3* **Zanida (IRE)**[61] 2806 2-8-9 85 .... PatCosgrave 3 72
(K R Burke) *chsd wnr: rdn and edgd lft over 1f out: sn wknd* **5/1**[3]
0112 **6** *16* **Holdin Foldin (IRE)**[4] 4607 2-9-0 95 .... RobertWinston 1 19
(K R Burke) *hung lft thrght: nvr wnt pce: wknd and eased over 1f out* **5/1**[3]

58.78 secs (-0.54) **Going Correction** 0.0s/f (Good) 6 Ran SP% **110.3**
Speed ratings (Par 102):104,101,99,98,93 67
CSF £56.97 TOTE £4.60: £2.70, £2.50; EX 58.70.
Owner Ms K O'Hare **Bred** Floral Partnership **Trained** Bawtry, S Yorks

FOCUS
Not strong form for a Listed race and the winner probably did not have to improve on his previous efforts. The winner ran roughly to form.

NOTEBOOK
Not For Me(IRE), a real speedball, took this Listed race in convincing fashion and a return here for the Flying Childers next month looks on the agenda. (op 4-1 tchd 9-2 in a place)
Fanlight Fanny(USA) stepped up considerably on her Chepstow maiden win but in the end the winner proved much too good. She would have an obvious chance if back in action in a nursery before she is reassesed. (op 14-1 tchd 22-1)
Smart Instinct(USA), asked to make a quick return to action, looked at his best but did not run as well. Never happy, he deserves full marks for the way he stuck to his task and he looks ready for a step up to six. (op 6-4 tchd 9-4 and 5-4 and 11-8 in a place)
Resignation(IRE), a keen type, was dropped in at the start. He was simply not up to the task and his sights need lowering. (op 7-1)
Zanida(IRE), absent for two months, was not up to this task at this stage. (op 7-1 tchd 15-2)
Holdin Foldin(IRE) did not impress at all going to post and after missing a beat at the start he was on one rein throughout, ending up racing virtually alone on the far rail. He looks to have had enough for the time being. Official explanation: jockey said colt missed kick and hung left-handed from halfway (op 9-2 tchd 11-2)

4716 NEWITTS.COM CONVIVIAL MAIDEN STKS 6f
4:35 (4:35) (Class 2) 2-Y-O
£16,192 (£4,817; £2,407; £1,202) **Stalls** Centre

Form RPR
2 **1** **La Presse (USA)**[12] 4322 2-8-12 .... MichaelHills 3 90+
(B W Hills) *hld up: smooth hdwy over 2f out: shkn up to ld over 1f out: pushed out* **9/2**[2]
2 **2** *1* **Brave Tin Soldier (USA)**[22] 4028 2-9-3 .... MJKinane 2 92+
(A P O'Brien, Ire) *lw: led 1f: w ldrs: led over 2f out: hdd over 1f out: kpt on wl* **6/5**[1]
3 *½* **Love Dubai (USA)** 2-9-3 .... JoeFanning 5 91?
(M Johnston) *rangy: scope: w ldrs: led after 1f: hdd over 2f out: kpt on same pce appr fnl f* **25/1**
4 *7* **Black Rock (IRE)** 2-9-3 .... PhilipRobinson 9 70+
(M A Jarvis) *wl grwn: wth ldrs: edgd lft and wknd fnl f* **9/2**[2]
5 *½* **Fushe Jo** 2-9-3 .... RobertWinston 7 68
(J Howard Johnson) *lenghy: scope: w ldrs: wknd over 1f out* **33/1**
6 *nk* **Deadline (UAE)** 2-9-3 .... KDarley 4 67
(M Johnston) *s.i.s: sn drvn along: hdwy 3f out: sn wl outpcd* **22/1**
7 *2 ½* **Delta Shuttle (IRE)** 2-9-3 .... PatCosgrave 1 60
(K R Burke) *rangy: s.i.s: nvr on terms* **100/1**
8 *2 ½* **Double Bill (USA)** 2-9-3 .... EddieAhern 10 52+
(P F I Cole) *lengthy: scope: trckd ldrs: hung lft and wknd over 1f out* **6/1**[3]
9 *½* **Zayyir (IRE)** 2-9-3 .... LDettori 8 51
(G A Butler) *rangy: unf: dwlt: outpcd after 2f: nvr on terms* **10/1**
10 *5* **Tomorrow's Dancer** 2-9-3 .... NCallan 6 36
(K A Ryan) *lengthy: unf: scope: t.k.h: hdwy to trck ldrs over 2f out: sn wknd* **33/1**

1m 12.59s (0.03) **Going Correction** 0.0s/f (Good) 10 Ran SP% **120.3**
Speed ratings (Par 100):99,97,97,87,87 86,83,79,79,72
CSF £10.20 TOTE £6.40: £1.80, £1.20, £4.50; EX 10.60 Trifecta £89.30 Pool: £981.96 - 7.80 winning tickets.
Owner Gainsborough Stud **Bred** Gainsborough Farm Llc **Trained** Lambourn, Berks

FOCUS
Historically a strong maiden and the time compared well with the previous Listed race. The first three finished well clear and plenty of winners should come out of this.

NOTEBOOK
La Presse(USA), the only filly in the field, travelled smoothly and had this won the second she hit the front. She must be worth a chance in Listed company now. (tchd 4-1 and 5-1)
Brave Tin Soldier(USA), who stands over plenty of ground, looked in good nick. After regaining the lead, he was coming back for more at the line and looks sure to make his mark, especially on better ground than he encountered here. (op 6-4 tchd 13-8 and 11-10, tchd 7-4 in a place)
Love Dubai(USA) ◆, a February foal, has size and scope. He mixed it from the start and, sure to have learnt from the experience, is surely a ready-made winner. (op 20-1)
Black Rock(IRE) ◆, a late-May Foal, is a solidly-made type. He showed plenty of toe down the stands' side until tiring in the final furlong. He may not have appreciated the ground and is sure to step up markedly on this debut effort. (op 4-1 tchd 5-1)
Fushe Jo, a half-brother to the stable's smart hurdler Arcalis, looks an immature type who will appreciate being given a fair bit more time. (op 3-1)
Deadline(UAE), colty and noisy in the paddock, will need to keep his mind on racing rather than extra-curricular activities if he is to show his true worth on the racetrack. (tchd 20-1)
Double Bill(USA), a lazy walker, showed ability but hung and dropped away as if not appreciating the ground. Official explanation: jockey said colt hung left and had no more to give (op 7-1, tchd 8-1 in places)

4717 EVENTMASTERS STKS (H'CAP) 5f
5:10 (5:11) (Class 2) (0-100,99) 3-Y-O
£16,192 (£4,817; £2,407; £1,202) **Stalls** Centre

Form RPR
-112 **1** **Buachaill Dona (IRE)**[19] 4102 3-8-13 91 .... AdrianTNicholls 13 106
(D Nicholls) *lw: hld up: hdwy 2f out: led jst ins last: hld on towards fin* **13/8**[1]
1151 **2** *hd* **Terentia**[19] 4102 3-9-1 93 .... JimmyFortune 10 107
(E S McMahon) *chsd ldrs: hrd rdn and styd on ins last: jst hld* **13/2**[3]
2111 **3** *1 ½* **Fantasy Explorer**[37] 3585 3-8-12 90 .... GrahamGibbons 6 99
(J J Quinn) *lw: trckd ldrs: upsides 1f out: no ex* **11/2**[2]
2226 **4** *3* **Blazing Heights**[31] 3761 3-7-12 81 .... DuranFentiman(5) 14 79
(J S Goldie) *hld up in rr: hdwy 2f out: styd on ins last* **16/1**
1213 **5** *½* **Loch Verdi**[19] 4102 3-8-8 86 .... MartinDwyer 5 82
(A M Balding) *led tl hdd & wknd jst ins last* **8/1**
0200 **6** *nk* **Guto**[24] 3970 3-9-3 95 .... NCallan 8 90
(K A Ryan) *w ldrs: upsides 1f out: sn fdd* **20/1**
0006 **7** *1 ¾* **Colorus (IRE)**[10] 4403 3-8-2 80 .... (b[1]) PaulHanagan 11 69
(R A Fahey) *sn chsng ldrs: edgd lft over 1f out: sn wknd* **33/1**
0042 **8** *1* **Gallery Girl (IRE)**[31] 3761 3-8-12 90 .... DavidAllan 3 75
(T D Easterby) *lw: wnt lft s: chsd ldrs: hrd drvn 2f out: wknd appr last* **8/1**

0100 **9** *nk* **Stoneacre Lad (IRE)**[11] 4360 3-8-10 **88**...............(b) RobbieFitzpatrick 1 72
(Peter Grayson) *hung lft and racd alone far side: nvr rchd ldrs* **40/1**
0552 **10** *nk* **Greek Secret**[14] 4262 3-8-2 **80** oh13.................................... PaulQuinn 4 63
(J O'Reilly) *sn outpcd and in rr* **33/1**
0000 **11** *hd* **Godfrey Street**[24] 3970 3-9-2 **94**... RyanMoore 7 76
(R Hannon) *hld up in mid-div: effrt over 2f out: hung lft and sn wknd* **12/1**
0-00 **12** *nk* **Classic Encounter (IRE)**[39] 3535 3-9-7 **99**............... RichardHughes 9 80
(D M Simcock) *t.k.h in mid-div: effrt 2f out: sn btn* **50/1**

58.38 secs (-0.94) **Going Correction** 0.0s/f (Good) **12** Ran SP% **117.7**
Speed ratings (Par 106):107,106,104,99,98 98,95,93,93,92 92,92
CSF £11.24 CT £49.29 TOTE £2.50: £1.40, £2.40, £2.20; EX 11.20 Trifecta £61.00 Pool: £1,894.72 - 22.02 winning tickets. Place 6 £260.64, Place 5 £67.75.
Owner Mike Browne **Bred** John O Browne **Trained** Sessay, N Yorks
■ Stewards' Enquiry : Jimmy Fortune two-day ban: used whip with excessive force (Sep 3-4)

FOCUS
Strong three-year-old sprint handicap form and a race to take a positive view about. The first three continue to progress and they finished clear.

NOTEBOOK
Buachaill Dona(IRE), out of luck at Goodwood, defied a 5lb hike in the ratings. He travelled strongly off what was a strong pace and though it was a close call in the end, he always looked like pulling it off. He will continue on the upgrade and will make a smart sprinter at four. (tchd 7-4)
Terentia, 5lb higher, was meeting the unlucky Goodwood runner-up on the same terms. She had everything thrown at her inside the last but could not quite make it. (op 8-1)
Fantasy Explorer, up 31lb this season, looked in tip-top condition. He travelled strongly and in the end was just found wanting. He is at his very best on quicker ground than he encountered here and there may well be even more success for him this term. (op 5-1)
Blazing Heights, patiently ridden, picked up in his own time late on but the first three had flown. He is proving hard to win with this time. (op 22-1)
Loch Verdi, who is not that big, took them along, but in the end the two who finished just ahead of her at Goodwood had her well beaten off this time on this much easier ground. Official explanation: jockey said filly lost its action (op 7-1)
Guto is still 7lb higher than his last winning mark. (op 25-1)
Classic Encounter(IRE) Official explanation: jockey said colt was unbalanced throughout
T/Jkpt: Not won. T/Plt: £336.90 to a £1 stake. Pool: £207,483.66. 449.50 winning tickets. T/Qpdt: £25.60 to a £1 stake. Pool: £12,544.00. 361.65 winning tickets. JR

4722 - (Foreign Racing) - See Raceform Interactive

4518 MUSSELBURGH (R-H)
Thursday, August 24

OFFICIAL GOING: Good to firm (good in places)
Wind: Almost nil

4723 RACING UK FOR £15 PER MONTH APPRENTICE H'CAP 1m 6f
2:05 (2:05) (Class 5) (0-70,66) 3-Y-O+ **£3,886** (£1,156; £577; £288) **Stalls** High

Form RPR
3302 **1** **Kristensen**[7] 4522 7-9-13 **65**.......................................(v) PaulMulrennan 7 73
(Karen McLintock) *hld up: hdwy over 3f out: rdn and hung lft fr over 2f out: styd on to ld wl ins fnl f* **4/1**[1]
-001 **2** *½* **Mighty Moon**[27] 3900 3-9-0 **64**.................................(bt) AndrewElliott 2 71
(Lady Herries) *hld up: hdwy 1/2-way: led and edgd lft over 1f out: rdn and hdd wl ins fnl f* **5/1**[2]
4130 **3** *¾* **Hugs Destiny (IRE)**[12] 4380 5-8-10 **53**........................ MCGeran(5) 8 59
(M A Barnes) *a.p: rdn to ld and hung lft over 2f out: hdd over 1f out: styd on* **13/2**[3]
0511 **4** *hd* **Danzatrice**[12] 4351 4-9-1 **53**... DanielTudhope 9 59
(C W Thornton) *hld up: hdwy over 2f out: nt clr run over 1f out: hung lft ins fnl f: styd on* **4/1**[1]
3330 **5** *6* **Melvino**[1] 4698 4-9-10 **62**... BenSwarbrick 5 60
(T D Barron) *hld up: hdwy 5f out: rdn whn hmpd over 2f out: wknd over 1f out* **8/1**
5440 **6** *1* **Transit**[9] 4451 7-8-10 **48**..(bt) AndrewMullen 1 44
(B Ellison) *s.i.s: hdwy over 5f out: rdn over 3f out: wknd over 1f out* **14/1**
-363 **7** *4* **Gone Too Far**[7] 4522 8-9-6 **58**..................................(v) MarkLawson 4 49
(P Monteith) *chsd ldr: rdn to ld over 3f out: hdd over 2f out: sn hung rt: wknd over 1f out* **10/1**
4036 **8** *3½* **Caymans Gift**[12] 4351 6-9-2 **54**................................(p) GregFairley 3 40
(A C Whillans) *chsd ldrs: rdn over 3f out: wkng whn n.m.r over 2f out* **14/1**
4444 **9** *12* **Easibet Dot Net**[8] 4478 6-10-0 **66**.......................(tp) EdwardCreighton 10 35
(I Semple) *sn led: rdn and hdd over 3f out: wknd over 2f out: eased* **16/1**
400- **10** *79* **Procrastinate (IRE)**[349] 4445 4-8-7 **48** oh3............ KevinGhunowa(3) 6 —
(R F Fisher) *chsd ldrs: lost pl 1/2-way: bhd fnl 5f: sddle slipped* **66/1**

3m 2.23s (-3.47) **Going Correction** -0.10s/f (Good)
WFA 3 from 4yo+ 12lb **10** Ran SP% **110.9**
Speed ratings (Par 103):105,104,104,104,100 100,97,95,89,43
CSF £22.21 CT £119.84 TOTE £5.30: £1.80, £2.30, £2.20; EX 25.40.
Owner Equiname Ltd **Bred** Lordship Stud Limited **Trained** Ingoe, Northumberland
■ Stewards' Enquiry : Mark Lawson two-day ban: careless riding (Sep 4-5)

FOCUS
A modest apprentice handicap but run at a sound gallop. The form is ordinary rated around the third and fourth.
Procrastinate(IRE) Official explanation: jockey said saddle slipped

4724 RACING UK AND SETANTA FOR £15 (S) STKS 7f 30y
2:35 (2:36) (Class 6) 2-Y-O **£3,238** (£963; £481; £240) **Stalls** Low

Form RPR
4143 **1** **Sunstroke (IRE)**[13] 4334 2-8-8 60..................................... DominicFox(3) 4 60
(M G Quinlan) *mde virtually all: rdn clr fnl f: eased towards fin* **9/2**[3]
555 **2** *2* **Muncaster Castle (IRE)**[21] 4066 2-8-11 .... DanielTudhope 10 55
(R F Fisher) *prom: rdn and hung lft fr over 2f out: outpcd over 1f out* **4/1**[2]
006 **3** *shd* **Hair Of The Dog**[66] 2695 2-8-11 .... MickyFenton 11 55
(J G Given) *chsd ldrs: rdn and ev ch over 1f out: sn outpcd* **40/1**
3355 **4** *2* **Denton Hawk**[6] 4545 2-8-11 60..................................... PhillipMakin 9 49
(M Dods) *hld up: hdwy over 2f out: sn rdn: styd on same pce appr fnl f* **10/1**
2650 **5** *1½* **Burlington Fayr (IRE)**[12] 4376 2-8-6 49......................... KimTinkler 5 40
(N Tinkler) *hld up: plld hrd: hdwy over 1f out: n.d* **16/1**
433 **6** *5* **Ingleby Flame (IRE)**[22] 4055 2-8-11 63......................... PaulFessey 3 32
(T D Barron) *chsd ldrs: rdn over 2f out: wknd over 1f out* **11/8**[1]
044 **7** *shd* **Fun Thai**[6] 4545 2-8-6 .... TomEaves 8 27
(M R Channon) *hld up: hdwy over 2f out: wknd over 1f out* **10/1**
6340 **8** *3* **Moist**[37] 3613 2-8-6 48.. PaulMulrennan 1 19
(Jedd O'Keeffe) *w wnr tl rdn over 2f out: wknd over 1f out* **25/1**
0054 **9** *7* **Perilore (IRE)**[7] 4520 2-8-6 .... GylesParkin 6 1
(A Berry) *s.s: outpcd: hdwy over 2f out: sn rdn and wknd* **100/1**
0 **10** *¾* **Wingsinmotion (IRE)**[27] 3915 2-8-7 ow1...................... PatCosgrave 7 —
(K R Burke) *sn outpcd* **50/1**
0000 **11** *55* **Makeusabuck**[6] 4545 2-8-6 ....(b[1]) RoystonFfrench 2 —
(A Berry) *hung lft and rn v wd over 5f out: sn t.o* **100/1**

1m 31.01s (1.07) **Going Correction** -0.10s/f (Good) **11** Ran SP% **114.6**
Speed ratings (Par 92):89,86,86,84,82 76,76,73,65,64 1
CSF £21.64 TOTE £5.60: £1.60, £1.90, £3.70; EX 30.90.The winner was bought in for 5,000gns.
Owner The Afternoon Syndicate **Bred** Peter Savill **Trained** Newmarket, Suffolk
■ Stewards' Enquiry : Dominic Fox two-day ban: careless riding (Sep 4-5)

FOCUS
Modest fare, and Sunstroke simply looked better class.

NOTEBOOK
Sunstroke(IRE), third in a better race of this type at Newmarket last time, won in taking style and was value for further. She will not be able to run in any more sellers this year but she should be able to hold her own in minor nurseries while the ground remains fast. (op 4-1)
Muncaster Castle(IRE), dropped in grade, was back up in trip and encountering fast ground for the first time. Hanging badly over towards the stands' side in the straight, he kept on for second but had no chance with the comfortable winner. (op 5-1 tchd 7-2)
Hair Of The Dog, tackling this trip for the first time, saw it out well and if anything might benefit from a bit further still.
Denton Hawk is an exposed performer and he ran his race back on this faster ground. (op 9-1)
Burlington Fayr(IRE), having her second try over this far, was ridden to get the trip and connections can revert to more positive tactics now she has proved she stays. (op 12-1)
Ingleby Flame(IRE) was proven over this trip and seemed to hold sound claims on this drop in grade, but he proved disappointing with no obvious excuses. Official explanation: jockey said gelding hung right-handed in straight (op 6-4 tchd 13-8 in a place)
Makeusabuck Official explanation: jockey said filly hung violently left throughout

4725 DM HALL H'CAP 5f
3:10 (3:10) (Class 4) (0-80,80) 3-Y-O+
£6,232 (£1,866; £933; £467; £233; £117) **Stalls** Low

Form RPR
0232 **1** **Smokin Beau**[9] 4453 9-9-4 **79**.................................... VictoriaBehan(7) 10 94+
(D Nicholls) *chsd ldr: led 1/2-way: rdn out* **6/4**[1]
2403 **2** *¾* **Millinsky (USA)**[27] 3913 5-8-9 **70**........................... RobbieMills(7) 13 80
(Rae Guest) *chsd ldrs: rdn over 1f out: r.o* **13/2**[3]
4200 **3** *3½* **Ptarmigan Ridge**[38] 3585 10-8-13 **72**...................... AndrewMullen(5) 6 69
(Miss L A Perratt) *hdwy 1/2-way: rdn over 1f out: no ex ins fnl f* **6/1**[2]
5160 **4** *3* **Strensall**[9] 4453 9-9-2 **70**... PhillipMakin 7 57
(R E Barr) *chsd ldrs: rdn and ev ch 2f out: wknd fnl f* **16/1**
00P0 **5** *1* **Wanchai Lad**[25] 3972 5-9-8 **76**...................................... PaulQuinn 9 59
(T D Easterby) *chsd ldrs over 3f* **14/1**
0314 **6** *1* **Henry Hall (IRE)**[8] 4468 10-9-4 **72**............................ KimTinkler 4 51
(N Tinkler) *s.i.s: hdwy 1/2-way: wknd over 1f out* **8/1**
2124 **7** *hd* **Rothesay Dancer**[19] 4135 3-9-0 **70**.........................(p) DanielTudhope 5 49
(J S Goldie) *chsd ldrs: rdn and ev ch over 1f out: wknd fnl f* **10/1**
530- **8** *2½* **Island Prince (IRE)**[295] 6226 3-9-2 **72**........................ RoystonFfrench 8 42
(Mrs A Duffield) *s.i.s: outpcd* **16/1**
2550 **9** *2* **John Keats**[77] 2385 3-9-10 **80**....................................... TomEaves 11 42
(I Semple) *prom: lost pl over 3f out: sn bhd* **20/1**
0030 **10** *shd* **Compton Lad**[3] 4656 3-8-4 **60** oh13............................ PaulFessey 12 22
(D A Nolan) *led to 1/2-way: wknd over 1f out* **66/1**
0304 **11** *¾* **The Leather Wedge (IRE)**[8] 4477 7-8-9 **68**............ DeclanMcGann(5) 1 27
(R Johnson) *s.s: hdwy over 3f out: hung rt and wknd over 1f out* **16/1**

59.87 secs (-0.63) **Going Correction** -0.10s/f (Good)
WFA 3 from 4yo+ 2lb **11** Ran SP% **118.4**
Speed ratings (Par 105):101,99,94,89,87 86,85,81,78,78 77
CSF £11.28 CT £48.41 TOTE £2.20: £1.10, £3.10, £2.80; EX 14.60.
Owner Miss Vanessa Church **Bred** Alan Spargo **Trained** Sessay, N Yorks
■ Stewards' Enquiry : Daniel Tudhope one-day ban: dropped hands and lost 6th place (Sep 4)

FOCUS
A fair handicap in which the runners raced against the far rail and they finished spread out behind the winner who sets the standard based on last year's form.
Compton Lad Official explanation: jockey said nose band slipped impairing gelding's vision

4726 RACING UK FOR £15 CALL 08700 506949 CLAIMING STKS 1m 1f
3:45 (3:45) (Class 5) 3-Y-O+ **£3,238** (£963; £481; £240) **Stalls** Low

Form RPR
0002 **1** **Baylaw Star**[1] 4692 5-9-7 83.................................... AndrewMullen(5) 4 73
(K A Ryan) *sn led: rdn clr over 1f out: styd on* **6/1**[2]
2131 **2** *2* **Burnley Al (IRE)**[1] 4692 4-8-12 55............................(b) MarkLawson(5) 3 60
(A Berry) *plld hrd: trckd wnr over 2f: remained handy: rdn to chse wnr over 1f out: styd on* **7/1**[3]
4006 **3** *3* **Fairy Monarch (IRE)**[7] 4511 7-9-4 49..........................(b) MickyFenton 5 55
(P T Midgley) *hld up: hdwy over 2f out: sn rdn: edgd rt and no imp ins fnl f* **50/1**
3000 **4** *2½* **Toshi (USA)**[8] 4476 4-9-10 78.. TomEaves 6 56
(I Semple) *chsd wnr over 6f out: rdn over 2f out: wknd over 1f out* **8/1**
0110 **5** *4* **Fremen (USA)**[23] 4031 6-9-7 87.................................... VictoriaBehan(7) 8 52
(D Nicholls) *broke wl: stdd and lost pl after 1f: hdwy over 3f out: wknd over 1f out* **4/7**[1]
2P20 **6** *1½* **La Viola**[27] 3914 4-8-9 51..(v) PatCosgrave 2 30
(K R Burke) *prom: rdn and lost pl over 3f out: wknd over 2f out* **33/1**
0-00 **7** *28* **Move On (IRE)**[117] 1293 3-8-4 45.................................(t) RoystonFfrench 1 —
(B Ellison) *hld up: wknd 4f out* **66/1**

1m 52.07s (-3.93) **Going Correction** -0.10s/f (Good)
WFA 3 from 4yo+ 7lb **7** Ran SP% **107.9**
Speed ratings (Par 103):103,101,98,96,92 91,66
CSF £40.04 TOTE £6.20: £2.20, £2.00; EX 26.00.The winner was claimed by Ian McInnes for £18,000. Fremen was the subject of a friendly claim.
Owner T C Racing Partnership **Bred** John Wilkinson Bloodstock **Trained** Hambleton, N Yorks

FOCUS
A moderately-run race in which the winner turned around Hamilton form from the previous day with the runner-up. Not a bad claimer, but the third does limit the form.
Fremen(USA) Official explanation: trainer had no explanation for the poor form shown

4727 SUBSCRIBE ONLINE @ RACINGUK.TV NURSERY 5f
4:20 (4:22) (Class 4) 2-Y-O **£5,181** (£1,541; £770; £384) **Stalls** Low

Form RPR
3453 **1** **Davaye**[13] 4321 2-8-7 **66**.. PatCosgrave 6 67
(K R Burke) *chsd ldrs: swtchd lft over 1f out: r.o to ld towards fin* **9/2**[2]
3605 **2** *nk* **The Nifty Fox**[6] 4547 2-8-11 **70**................................... TomEaves 5 70
(T D Easterby) *chsd ldr: led 2f out: rdn and hdd towards fin* **8/1**
150 **3** *nk* **Ingleby Image**[19] 4152 2-9-6 **79**..............................(e[1]) PaulFessey 7 78
(T D Barron) *led 3f: sn rdn and edgd lft: r.o* **6/1**[3]

3013 **4** 3 ½ **Startolini**[7] 4519 2-8-12 **71**.................... PaulEddery 1 56
(B Smart) *hmpd s: hdwy 1/2-way: rdn over 1f out: hung rt and wknd ins fnl f* **7/2**[1]

3331 **5** 1 **Ishibee (IRE)**[13] 4327 2-8-5 **64**....................(p) RoystonFfrench 2 45
(Mrs A Duffield) *hmpd s: outpcd: hdwy u.p over 1f out: wknd ins fnl f* **7/2**[1]

2416 **6** 7 **Minaash (USA)**[41] 3474 2-9-7 **80**.................... MickyFenton 3 33
(J Noseda) *wnt lft s: sn chsng ldrs: rdn 1/2-way: hung rt and wknd over 1f out* **7/2**[1]

0044 **7** 6 **Suntan Lady (IRE)**[4] 4630 2-8-0 **62** oh7 ow5........ EdwardCreighton(3) 4 —
(Miss V Haigh) *chsd ldrs over 3f* **14/1**

61.71 secs (1.21) **Going Correction** -0.10s/f (Good) **7** Ran SP% **116.9**
Speed ratings (Par 96):86,85,85,79,77 66,57
CSF £40.58 TOTE £5.90: £2.90, £3.30; EX 47.00.
Owner The Baltika Partnership **Bred** D Simpson **Trained** Middleham Moor, N Yorks

FOCUS
A fair nursery but the form is posssibly muddied by scrimmaging between the three co-favourites leaving the stalls and it was run 1.84 sec slower than the earlier all-aged handicap over the same trip.

NOTEBOOK
Davaye, a maiden coming into this, had run well on her nursery debut last time and responded really well to pressure to get up near the finish. She should not go up much for this and could well follow up. (op 5-1 tchd 4-1)
The Nifty Fox, back on a fast surface, ran his best race since finishing third to the useful Wi Dud back in June. He did nothing wrong in defeat and looks capable of winning a similar contest. (op 9-1 tchd 15-2)
Ingleby Image, who won her debut over course and distance on heavy ground, ran well in the Newbury Super Sprint, but disappointed last time and had the eyeshield fitted. She ran much better and only just lost out, despite giving weight to both those who beat her. (op 7-1)
Startolini, who came into this in good form, had his chance spoilt by the antics of Minaash leaving the stalls. (op 11-2 tchd 6-1)
Ishibee(IRE), dropping in trip following her win in a Polytrack seller, was the worst sufferer in the barging between the market leaders coming out of the stalls. Official explanation: jockey said filly suffered interference leaving stalls (op 9-2)
Minaash(USA) went badly left leaving the stalls hampering the chances of the other co-favourites, but also spoiling his own. (op 9-4)

4728 RECRUITMENT ZONE LTD H'CAP 7f 30y
4:55 (4:56) (Class 6) (0-60,59) 3-Y-O £2,914 (£867; £433; £216) **Stalls** Low

Form RPR
3103 **1** **Sapphire Storm (IRE)**[37] 3604 3-8-7 **50**.................... RoryMoore(5) 14 59
(P T Midgley) *chsd ldrs: rdn over 1f out: r.o to ld wl ins fnl f* **20/1**

4545 **2** 1 **Feelin Irie (IRE)**[15] 4257 3-9-7 **59**.................... KimTinkler 1 66
(N Tinkler) *led: rdn over 1f out: sn edgd lft: hdd wl ins fnl f* **8/1**

0130 **3** 1 **Walnut Grove**[31] 3786 3-9-2 **54**.................... PhillipMakin 8 58
(T D Barron) *a.p: racd keenly: rdn over 1f out: styd on same pce ins fnl f* **20/1**

4263 **4** ½ **Suhezy (IRE)**[6] 4548 3-8-9 **47**.................... DanielTudhope 13 50
(J S Wainwright) *chsd ldr: rdn over 2f out: nt clr run over 1f out: styd on same pce* **6/1**[3]

3330 **5** nk **Myths And Verses**[21] 4071 3-9-1 **58**....................(p) AndrewMullen(5) 5 60
(K A Ryan) *chsd ldrs: rdn and ev ch 2f out: no ex fnl f* **16/1**

0042 **6** 1 ¾ **Our Mary (IRE)**[8] 4473 3-8-12 **50**....................(t) TomEaves 9 47
(Robert Gray) *hld up in tch: rdn over 3f out: hung rt over 1f out: no ex* **16/1**

0050 **7** ¾ **Quintin**[19] 4155 3-8-7 **45**.................... PaulFessey 10 40
(T D Easterby) *hld up: hdwy over 2f out: sn rdn: nt clr run over 1f out: no imp fnl f* **16/1**

4610 **8** nk **Drink To Me Only**[22] 4059 3-9-0 **52**.................... PatCosgrave 3 47
(J R Weymes) *hld up: hdwy over 2f out: sn rdn: nt trble ldrs* **18/1**

5063 **9** 1 **Makai**[17] 4195 3-9-5 **57**.................... RoystonFfrench 6 49
(M Johnston) *hld up: rdn over 3f out: n.d* **5/1**[2]

0460 **10** ¾ **Active Audience (IRE)**[21] 4071 3-8-3 **46**.................... KevinGhunowa(5) 12 36
(A Berry) *hld up: rdn over 3f out: a in rr* **50/1**

0046 **11** 2 **Fun Time**[8] 4494 3-8-7 **48**.................... EdwardCreighton(3) 7 33
(M R Channon) *outpcd* **12/1**

0-00 **12** nk **Zahara Joy**[10] 4425 3-8-12 **50**.................... GylesParkin 11 34
(D W Thompson) *dwlt: outpcd* **50/1**

-052 **13** 5 **Taranis**[38] 3586 3-9-0 **52**.................... MickyFenton 2 23
(Sir Mark Prescott) *mid-div: rdn 1/2-way: wknd over 1f out* **3/1**[1]

0000 **14** 15 **English Archer**[22] 4060 3-8-6 **49** ow2....................(p) MarkLawson(5) 4 —
(J R Weymes) *dwlt: outpcd* **33/1**

1m 29.23s (-0.71) **Going Correction** -0.10s/f (Good) **14** Ran SP% **114.1**
Speed ratings (Par 98):100,98,97,97,96 94,93,93,92,91 89,88,83,66
CSF £156.92 CT £3300.87 TOTE £30.10: £4.90, £3.60, £5.30; EX 191.60.
Owner J F Wright **Bred** Dermot Farrington **Trained** Westow, N Yorks

FOCUS
A pretty weak handicap although the form seems sound. They went a fair gallop and nothing got into it from the rear.
Myths And Verses Official explanation: jockey said filly finished distressed
Taranis Official explanation: jockey said gelding lost a front shoe
English Archer Official explanation: jockey said gelding hung badly left on turning in

4729 SUBSCRIBE TO RACING UK ON 08700 506949 H'CAP 7f 30y
5:25 (5:27) (Class 6) (0-65,65) 4-Y-O+ £3,238 (£963; £481; £240) **Stalls** Low

Form RPR
1040 **1** **Snow Bunting**[15] 4253 8-8-11 **55**.................... MickyFenton 7 64+
(Jedd O'Keeffe) *hld up: nt clr run over 1f out: swtchd rt and r.o wl ins fnl f to ld nr fin* **11/1**

1321 **2** nk **Motu (IRE)**[3] 4652 5-9-3 **61** 6ex....................(v) DanielTudhope 5 69
(I W McInnes) *hld up: hdwy 4f out: rdn over 2f out: ev ch ins fnl f: r.o* **7/2**[1]

-200 **3** shd **Bandos**[9] 4456 6-8-9 **53**.................... TomEaves 9 61
(I Semple) *chsd ldr: led over 5f out: rdn and edgd lft fr over 1f out: hdd nr fin* **14/1**

0640 **4** 1 ¼ **Attacca**[6] 4571 5-8-9 **53**.................... PhillipMakin 2 57
(J R Weymes) *hld up: hdwy u.p over 1f out: styd on* **12/1**

0 **5** 1 **Linden's Lady**[31] 3786 6-8-0 **49** oh1 ow3....................(v) AndrewMullen(5) 14 51
(J R Weymes) *s.i.s: hdwy over 5f out: rdn over 2f out: styd on* **15/2**[3]

6020 **6** ¾ **Franksalot (IRE)**[3] 4652 6-9-2 **65**....................(p) MarkLawson(5) 1 65+
(I W McInnes) *s.i.s: hld up: nt clr run over 1f out: r.o ins fnl f: nrst fin* **14/1**

2150 **7** shd **Prospect Court**[12] 4352 4-8-8 **52**.................... PaulFessey 4 52
(A C Whillans) *led: hdd over 5f out: rdn over 2f out: no ex ins fnl f* **16/1**

6063 **8** hd **Whittinghamvillage**[12] 4355 5-8-5 **52**.................... EdwardCreighton(3) 3 51
(D W Whillans) *hld up: hdwy over 1f out: nt trble ldrs* **16/1**

0435 **9** nk **Cut Ridge (IRE)**[10] 4425 7-8-0 **49** ow3.................... KevinGhunowa(5) 6 47
(J S Wainwright) *hld up in tch: plld hrd: rdn over 1f out: nt trble ldrs* **12/1**

6400 **10** ½ **Pepper Road**[7] 4511 7-8-3 **47**.................... RoystonFfrench 13 44
(R Bastiman) *hld up: hdwy u.p over 1f out: no ex ins fnl f* **16/1**

0050 **11** 2 **Dispol Isle (IRE)**[7] 4518 4-9-4 **65**.................... BenSwarbrick(3) 11 57
(T D Barron) *hld up in tch: rdn over 2f out: wknd ins fnl f* **13/2**[2]

0603 **12** 1 ¼ **Straffan (IRE)**[8] 4473 4-8-2 **46** oh5....................(p) SilvestreDeSousa 12 35
(J Hetherton) *chsd ldrs: rdn over 2f out: wknd ins fnl f* **20/1**

0000 **13** ½ **Mis Chicaf (IRE)**[27] 3912 5-8-0 **49** oh6 ow3....................(t) RoryMoore(5) 10 36
(Robert Gray) *s.i.s: hld up: n.d* **50/1**

0006 **14** ½ **Young Mr Grace (IRE)**[3] 4652 6-8-10 **54**.................... PatCosgrave 8 40
(B S Rothwell) *chsd ldrs: rdn over 2f out: wknd over 1f out* **9/1**

1m 28.43s (-1.51) **Going Correction** -0.10s/f (Good) **14** Ran SP% **118.7**
Speed ratings (Par 101):104,103,103,102,100 100,100,99,99,98 96,95,94,94
CSF £48.43 CT £558.07 TOTE £13.80: £3.40, £1.70, £5.50; EX 45.20 Place 6 £991.38, Place 5 £556.53.
Owner W R B Racing 49 (wrbracingcom) **Bred** The Queen **Trained** Middleham Moor, N Yorks

FOCUS
A moderate handicap that developed into a battle in the straight but pretty solid form rated through the third.
Snow Bunting Official explanation: trainer had no explanation for the apparent improvement in form
Franksalot(IRE) Official explanation: jockey said gelding lost its action on bend turning in
T/Plt: £587.40 to a £1 stake. Pool: £36,936.15. 45.90 winning tickets. T/Qpdt: £471.60 to a £1 stake. Pool: £2,676.90. 4.20 winning tickets. CR

4400 REDCAR (L-H)
Thursday, August 24
OFFICIAL GOING: Good (good to firm in places)
Wind: Virtually nil

4730 AJA 14TH OCTOBER DANCE RAMADA WETHERBY LADY RIDERS' H'CAP 1m 2f
5:30 (5:31) (Class 5) (0-75,75) 3-Y-O+ £3,123 (£968; £484; £242) **Stalls** Low

Form RPR
3140 **1** **Silverhay**[23] 4021 5-10-3 **72**....................(p) MissARyan(5) 7 79
(T D Barron) *trckd ldng pair: hdwy to chse ldr wl over 2f out: rdn to ld wl over 1f out: kpt on ins last* **8/1**

0020 **2** nk **Emperor's Well**[7] 4511 7-9-6 **56** oh1....................(b) MissSBrotherton 5 62
(M W Easterby) *keen: trckd ldrs: hdwy 3f out: rdn 2f out: styd on wl fnl f* **6/1**[3]

2326 **3** 2 **Sgt Schultz (IRE)**[16] 4225 3-9-8 **66**.................... MrsSMoore 8 69
(J S Moore) *dwlt: hld up in rr: hdwy over 3f out: rdn 2f out: styd on appr last: nrst fin* **6/1**[3]

1011 **4** nk **Gala Sunday (USA)**[14] 4307 6-9-13 **68**....................(bt) MissJCoward(5) 9 70
(M W Easterby) *chsd ldrs: pushed along and sltly outpcd 3f out: kpt on u.p fnl 2f* **8/1**

2412 **5** ¾ **Dark Charm (FR)**[3] 4653 7-10-2 **71**.................... MissVTunnicliffe(5) 11 72
(R A Fahey) *wnt rt s: keen and sn prom: effrt to ld over 3f out and pushed clr: rdn and hdd wl over 1f out: wknd ent last* **5/2**[1]

0340 **6** 5 **Scotty's Future (IRE)**[3] 4654 8-9-9 **59**.................... MrsCBartley 1 50
(A Berry) *hld up in rr: pushed along and hdwy 3f out: rdn over 2f out: kpt on ins last: nvr rch ldrs* **17/2**

4302 **7** 1 ½ **Shosolosa (IRE)**[18] 4176 4-9-10 **60**.................... MissLEllison 2 48
(Mrs A L M King) *bhd tl sme late hdwy* **5/1**[2]

0000 **8** shd **Komreyev Star**[1] 4709 4-9-1 **56** oh6.................... MissMMullineaux(5) 10 44
(M Mullineaux) *led: rdn along over 3f out: sn hdd & wknd* **33/1**

0000 **9** 5 **Jonny Ebeneezer**[12] 4368 7-10-8 **75**.................... MissFayeBramley(3) 4 54
(M Wellings) *in tch on inner: rdn along over 3f out: sn wknd* **25/1**

0000 **10** 13 **Wahchi (IRE)**[14] 4307 7-9-1 **58**....................(b) MissJoannaMason(7) 6 12
(M W Easterby) *chsd ldrs: rdn along 4f out: sn wknd* **40/1**

2m 8.29s (1.49) **Going Correction** +0.125s/f (Good)
WFA 3 from 4yo+ 8lb **10** Ran SP% **115.8**
Speed ratings (Par 103):99,98,97,96,96 92,91,91,87,76
CSF £53.96 CT £310.86 TOTE £10.60: £3.30, £2.30, £1.70; EX 75.30.
Owner D C Rutter P J Huntbach **Bred** Major W R Hern And W H Carson **Trained** Maunby, N Yorks
■ Stewards' Enquiry : Miss Faye Bramley one-day ban: used whip with excessive force (Sep 10)

FOCUS
Ordinary form, rated around the principals.

4731 GISBOROUGH HALL HOTEL MEDIAN AUCTION MAIDEN STKS 6f
6:00 (6:00) (Class 5) 2-Y-O £3,238 (£963; £481; £240) **Stalls** Centre

Form RPR
2 **1** **Event Music (IRE)**[19] 4161 2-8-12.................... ChrisCatlin 5 70
(M R Channon) *trckd ldrs: hdwy on outer 2f out: rdn to chse ldr ent last: styd on wl to ld last 100 yds* **6/1**[2]

2 **2** ½ **Cavalry Guard (USA)**[33] 3738 2-9-3.................... NCallan 16 73
(H R A Cecil) *sn trcking ldrs: effrt to ld wl over 1f out: sn edgd lft: rdn and wandered ins last: hdd and nt qckn last 100 yds* **1/4**[1]

00 **3** 3 ½ **Xaar Too Busy**[11] 4400 2-8-12....................(v[1]) TPO'Shea 3 58
(Mrs A Duffield) *hld up towards rr: hdwy 2f out: rdn and kpt on wl fnl f: nrst fin* **33/1**

0 **4** 1 **Prince Noel**[15] 4260 2-9-3.................... GrahamGibbons 9 60
(N Wilson) *cl up: led 1/2-way: rdn and hdd wl over 1f out: grad wknd* **66/1**

65 **5** ½ **Beaumont Boy**[10] 4421 2-9-3.................... DeanMcKeown 7 58
(G A Swinbank) *trckd ldrs: effrt 2f out: sn rdn and kpt on same pce* **14/1**[3]

0 **6** hd **Heidi Hi**[12] 4376 2-8-7.................... GregFairley(5) 2 52
(J R Turner) *led: pushed along and hdd 1/2-way: rdn over 2f out: grad wknd* **100/1**

0 **7** hd **Le Masque**[10] 4421 2-9-3.................... DerekMcGaffin 17 57
(B Smart) *hld up towards rr: swtchd rt and hdwy over 2f oiut: sn rdn and kpt on ins last: nrst fin* **33/1**

8 ½ **Miss Percy** 2-8-12.................... TonyHamilton 6 50
(R A Fahey) *hld up towards rr: hdwy over 2f out: edging lft whn n.m.r over 1f out: kpt on same pce ins last* **20/1**

9 nk **Bonnet O'Bonnie** 2-8-12.................... DaleGibson 1 49
(J Mackie) *towards rr: hdwy on outer 2f out: sn rdn and kpt on ins last: nrst fin* **50/1**

10 1 ¾ **Orotund** 2-9-3.................... DavidAllan 12 49
(T D Easterby) *chsd ldrs: rdn along over 2f out: sn wknd* **40/1**

0 **11** ½ **Shandelight (IRE)**[6] 4566 2-8-12.................... VHalliday 8 43
(Mrs A Duffield) *chsd ldrs: pushed along 1/2-way: rdn and wknd over 2f out* **100/1**

12 ¾ **Crosby Jemma** 2-8-12.................... JimmyQuinn 13 40
(J R Weymes) *dwlt: a towards rr* **50/1**

0 **13** *2* **Hits Only Vic (USA)**[15] [4260] 2-9-3 .... FrancisNorton 4 39
(J Pearce) *s.i.s: a rr* **66/1**

0 **14** *5* **Molto Duro (IRE)**[7] [4510] 2-8-12 .... CatherineGannon 10 19
(N Wilson) *dwlt: sn cl up: rdn along 1/2-way: wknd over 2f out* **100/1**

15 *1 1/4* **Forzarzi (IRE)** 2-9-3 .... AdrianTNicholls 14 21
(A Berry) *a rr* **66/1**

40 **16** *5* **Shotley Mac**[10] [4421] 2-8-10 .... SuzzanneFrance(7) 18 6
(N Bycroft) *a rr* **66/1**

0 **17** *1 1/2* **Frill A Minute**[26] [3942] 2-8-5 .... DawnRankin(7) 11 —
(Miss L C Siddall) *chsd ldrs to 1/2-way: sn wknd* **100/1**

1m 13.07s (1.37) **Going Correction** +0.125s/f (Good) **17** Ran SP% **127.9**
Speed ratings (Par 94):95,94,89,88,87 87,87,86,86,83 83,82,79,72,71 64,62
CSF £7.68 TOTE £6.10: £1.20, £1.02, £8.20; EX 14.70.
Owner Jaber Abdullah **Bred** Gestut Wittekindshof **Trained** West Ilsley, Berks

FOCUS
A fair maiden for the track in which the front two pulled clear.

NOTEBOOK
Event Music(IRE), runner-up in a reasonable maiden at Windsor on her debut, looked the one serious threat to the hot favourite and, having tracked him through, she produced the greater turn of speed. It was encouraging to see the pair draw clear, and the daughter of Distant Music fully deserves her place in a better class of contest now. (op 5-1)
Cavalry Guard(USA), whose debut second had been given a significant boost when the winner, Cockney Rebel, finished second in the valuable sales race at York earlier in the day, was rightly made a hot favourite to get off the mark, but having given the winner a nice tow through he ultimately lacked her speed. This was disappointing, but he is likely to appreciate further than this and it may be that he bumped into a useful filly. (op 2-5 tchd 4-9 in a place)
Xaar Too Busy had previously shown little, but the application of a visor sparked her into life and she showed greatly-improved form. The front two were in a different league, but a little further progression could see her winning a small race.
Prince Noel stepped up massively on his debut effort and certainly knew his job better on this occasion. He showed plenty of pace and is another for whom nurseries will present better opportunities.
Beaumont Boy has run to a similar level on each of his three outings and failed to improve as anticipated for the step up to six furlongs. He may find life easier in handicaps. (op 12-1)
Heidi Hi is clearly modest, but she showed some ability and did at least improve on her initial effort.
Le Masque made a little late headway, improving for the sixth furlong, and he could be one to look out for in nurseries. (op 40-1)
Miss Percy, bred to stay further in time, made a pleasing debut considering she did not get the clearest of runs, and an ordinary maiden should be within her grasp. (op 16-1)

4732 RACING UK ON SKY 432 NOVICE MEDIAN AUCTION STKS 7f
6:30 (6:31) (Class 5) 2-Y-O **£3,238** (£963; £481; £240) **Stalls** Centre

Form RPR

1 **Greek Envoy** 2-8-8 .... MichaelJStainton(5) 6 78
(T P Tate) *prom: effrt 2f out: rdn along over 1f out: styd on wl to ld nr line* **20/1**

01 **2** *shd* **Majuro (IRE)**[14] [4290] 2-9-5 82 .... TedDurcan 1 84
(M R Channon) *led. rdn 2f out: drvn ins last: hdd nr line* **2/1**[2]

0 **3** *6* **Monsieur Dumas (IRE)**[21] [4066] 2-8-13 .... PaulMulrennan 3 62
(T P Tate) *chsd ldrs: hdwy over 2f out: sn rdn and kpt on same pce appr last* **20/1**

01 **4** *nk* **Musical Mirage (USA)**[11] [4400] 2-9-2 .... DeanMcKeown 5 65
(G A Swinbank) *keen: trckd ldrs: pushed along 3f out: rdn 2f out and sn btn* **4/6**[1]

0 **5** *21* **Scarlet Baby**[76] [2409] 2-8-13 .... NCallan 4 7
(K A Ryan) *cl up: rdn along wl over 2f out: sn wknd* **16/1**[3]

1m 26.02s (1.12) **Going Correction** +0.125s/f (Good) **5** Ran SP% **108.7**
Speed ratings (Par 94):98,97,91,90,66
CSF £58.39 TOTE £10.30: £3.70, £1.10; EX 40.30.
Owner T P Tate **Bred** Worksop Manor Stud **Trained** Tadcaster, N Yorks

FOCUS
Difficult form to be confident about, but Majuro did well to beat previous winner Majuro first time out.

NOTEBOOK
Greek Envoy, a 15,000gns son of Diktat, looked to be here for the experience with his rider, although very useful for his allowance, pointing to him being the second string. However, he knew his job and responded gamely when asked, getting up to collar Majuro close home. His stable house a very useful juvenile in Celtic Sultan and he too may develop into a useful type. (tchd 16-1)
Majuro(IRE) won tidily at Folkestone last time and looked a leading player in what at first appeared to be an uncompetitive race. Soon in front, he made them all go and pulled right away from the third, but the newcomer, in receipt of 11lb, wore him down. He should continue to pay his way in nurseries. (op 9-4 tchd 15-8)
Monsieur Dumas(IRE), a stablemate of the winner, looked the first string on jockey bookings and he stepped up on his initial effort, but the front pair were too classy. He looks sure to benefit from further in time and is a likely nursery type. (op 16-1)
Musical Mirage(USA), easy winner of a maiden at the course last time, looked the one to beat with her stable's juveniles going so well, but she raced keenly early on and it told at the business end as she dropped away without putting up much of a fight. (op 8-13 tchd 4-5)
Scarlet Baby has beaten just the one home in two starts now and he looks in need of more time. (op 20-1)

4733 MARKET CROSS JEWELLERS H'CAP 1m
7:00 (7:00) (Class 4) (0-80,77) 3-Y-O+ **£6,477** (£1,927; £963; £481) **Stalls** Centre

Form RPR

0231 **1** **Bailieborough (IRE)**[12] [4379] 7-9-8 77 .... GregFairley(5) 4 91
(B Ellison) *in tch: hdwy on outer 3f out: rdn to ld 1f out: sn clr* **5/1**[2]

-352 **2** *3 1/2* **United Nations**[14] [4301] 5-9-7 71 .... TonyHamilton 2 77
(N Wilson) *led: rdn along 3f out: rein broke and hung bdly rt 2f out: hdd 1f out: kpt on one pce* **10/1**

2332 **3** *1 1/4* **Tour D'Amour (IRE)**[6] [4567] 3-8-9 68 .... StephenDonohoe(3) 3 70
(R Craggs) *chsd ldrs: rdn along 2f out: kpt on same pce appr last* **7/1**[3]

1004 **4** *nk* **Kaymich Perfecto**[12] [4379] 6-9-5 74 .... MichaelJStainton(5) 10 76
(R M Whitaker) *hld up towards rr: hdwy and nt clr run 2f out: rdn and kpt on same pce appr last* **17/2**

0001 **5** *1/2* **Typhoon Ginger (IRE)**[11] [4405] 11-8-5 60 6ex .... AndrewElliott(5) 6 61+
(G Woodward) *hld up towards rr: hdwy 2f out: nt clr run 1f out: kpt on ins last: nrst fin* **8/1**

0130 **6** *nk* **Tidy (IRE)**[20] [4108] 6-9-2 66 .... PaulHanagan 1 67
(Micky Hammond) *hld up in rr: hdwy 2f out: n.m.r and swtchd lft over 1f out: kpt on u.p ins last* **9/1**

0501 **7** *3/4* **Hypnotic**[9] [4456] 4-9-5 69 6ex ....(t) AdrianTNicholls 7 68
(D Nicholls) *keen: prom: rdn along over 2f out: grad wknd* **7/2**[1]

0-00 **8** *1/2* **Kudbeme**[58] [2947] 4-8-5 62 .... SuzzanneFrance(7) 12 60
(N Bycroft) *prom: rdn along whn hmpd 2f out: nt rcvr* **40/1**

0306 **9** *1 3/4* **Tough Love**[19] [4153] 7-9-7 71 ....(p) DavidAllan 5 65
(T D Easterby) *keen in midfield: pushed along wl over 2f out and sn btn* **11/1**

6604 **10** *1 1/4* **Efidium**[12] [4378] 8-8-12 62 ....(b) ChrisCatlin 11 53
(N Bycroft) *hld up: a towards rr* **7/1**[3]

6201 **11** *1* **Perez (IRE)**[76] [2413] 4-8-10 65 ....(v) EmmettStack(5) 9 54
(W Storey) *keen: cl up: rdn along whn hmpd 2f out: nt rcvr* **20/1**

1m 38.3s (0.50) **Going Correction** +0.125s/f (Good)
WFA 3 from 4yo+ 6lb **11** Ran SP% **120.2**
Speed ratings (Par 105):102,98,97,96,96 96,95,94,93,91 90
CSF £55.64 CT £285.39 TOTE £6.10: £1.80, £3.60, £2.50; EX 86.00.
Owner Naughty Diesel Ltd **Bred** Churchtown Stud **Trained** Norton, N Yorks
■ Stewards' Enquiry : Adrian T Nicholls one-day ban: improper riding - unintentionally struck Kudbeme with whip and failed to moderate use of whip (Sep 4)

FOCUS
A competitive handicap won in good style by Bailieborough, but United Nations would have given him much more to think about had his rein not broke. The form seems sound, rated around the placed horses.
Tough Love Official explanation: jockey said gelding ran too free

4734 ARYM FLOWERS H'CAP 1m 6f 19y
7:30 (7:30) (Class 6) (0-55,55) 3-Y-O **£2,590** (£770; £385; £192) **Stalls** Low

Form RPR

0050 **1** **Sa Nau**[12] [4380] 3-8-12 45 .... FrancisNorton 14 53
(T Keddy) *trckd ldrs: hdwy over 3f out: rdn to ld over 2f out: drvn clr ent last: styd on wl* **7/1**[3]

6-00 **2** *1 3/4* **That Look**[20] [2591] 3-9-5 52 .... DaleGibson 8 58
(D E Cantillon) *towards rr: hdwy 3f out: rdn 2f out: styd on u.p ent last: nrst fin* **8/1**

0500 **3** *1/2* **Golden Groom**[8] [4470] 3-8-12 45 .... DeanMcKeown 2 50
(C W Fairhurst) *prom: hdwy to chal over 3f out and ev ch tl rdn and one pce fr over 1f out* **16/1**

3640 **4** *3 1/2* **Peas 'n Beans (IRE)**[15] [4255] 3-9-8 55 .... HayleyTurner 10 55
(M L W Bell) *midfield: hdwy and in tch 5f out: rdn along to chse ldrs over 2f out: sn drvn and no imp* **9/2**[1]

0066 **5** *3/4* **Silver Mont (IRE)**[12] [4380] 3-9-2 49 ....(v) TPO'Shea 15 48
(Mrs A Duffield) *prom: hdwy to ld after 4f: rdn clr over 4f out: jnd 3f out: sn drvn and hdd: grad wknd* **8/1**

0206 **6** *2 1/2* **Virginia Rose (IRE)**[12] [4362] 3-9-4 51 .... PaulHanagan 5 47
(J G Given) *hld up in mikdfield: hdwy 3f out: sn rdn along and no imp fnl 2f* **12/1**

0405 **7** *1/2* **Sara Mana Mou**[6] [4556] 3-8-9 42 .... TedDurcan 7 37
(J G Portman) *in tch: hdwy 4f out: rdn along wl over 2f out and sn btn* **9/1**

-000 **8** *1* **Andorran (GER)**[31] [3785] 3-9-3 50 .... DavidAllan 4 44
(A Dickman) *a towards rr* **25/1**

5536 **9** *3/4* **Matinee Idol**[15] [4263] 3-9-3 50 .... TonyHamilton 12 43
(Mrs S Lamyman) *a towards rr* **20/1**

0200 **10** *1/2* **King's Fable (USA)**[13] [4331] 3-9-0 52 .... GregFairley(5) 3 44
(M Johnston) *prom: rdn along 4f out: sn wknd* **11/2**[2]

6005 **11** *1 3/4* **Sunny Parkes**[12] [4362] 3-8-12 45 .... JimmyQuinn 9 35
(M Mullineaux) *a towards rr* **20/1**

5442 **12** *1 3/4* **Elite Land**[11] [4404] 3-8-5 45 .... SuzzanneFrance(7) 11 32
(N Bycroft) *a towards rr* **8/1**

00-0 **13** *3 1/2* **Bright Sparky (GER)**[21] [4069] 3-9-0 47 ....(t) PaulMulrennan 1 29
(M W Easterby) *a towards rr* **22/1**

-000 **14** *1 3/4* **Meddle**[72] [2529] 3-8-12 45 .... DerekMcGaffin 13 25
(J Jay) *a bhd* **66/1**

-000 **15** *35* **Allouette**[26] [3941] 3-8-3 43 .... AdeleRothery(7) 16 —
(W J H Ratcliffe) *led 4f: prom tl rdn along over 4f out and sn wknd* **100/1**

3m 7.63s (2.61) **Going Correction** +0.125s/f (Good) **15** Ran SP% **123.2**
Speed ratings (Par 98):97,96,95,93,93 91,91,91,90,90 89,88,86,85,65
CSF £58.06 CT £885.28 TOTE £5.70: £1.30, £3.30, £5.60; EX 47.40.
Owner Howard Fielding **Bred** Juddmonte Farms Ltd **Trained** Newmarket, Suffolk

FOCUS
Moderate handicap form rated around the placed horses.
Sa Nau Official explanation: trainer said, regarding the improved form shown, the gelding had been denied a clear run on its previous start at Redcar
Virginia Rose(IRE) Official explanation: jockey said filly hung right-handed throughout

4735 BEST DRESSED LADY H'CAP 6f
8:00 (8:00) (Class 6) (0-65,63) 3-Y-O+ **£2,730** (£806; £403) **Stalls** Centre

Form RPR

4306 **1** **Elkhorn**[6] [4571] 4-9-3 54 ....(b[1]) TonyHamilton 9 62+
(Miss J A Camacho) *hld up and bhd: hdwy whn nt clr run wl over 1f out: rdn and str run ent last to ld nr fin* **7/1**[3]

1403 **2** *nk* **Briery Lane (IRE)**[6] [4571] 5-9-6 62 ....(p) AndrewElliott(5) 17 69
(Mrs K Walton) *in tch: hdwy 2f out: swtchd rt and rdn over 1f out: drvn to ld ins last: hdd and nt qckn nr fin* **8/1**

0020 **3** *hd* **Desert Opal**[6] [4571] 6-9-9 60 .... JimmyQuinn 16 66
(C R Dore) *prom: rdn and ev ch over 1f out tl drvn and nt qckn wl ins last* **10/1**

2330 **4** *shd* **Drum Dance (IRE)**[6] [4571] 4-8-13 50 ....(p) AdrianTNicholls 18 56
(N Tinkler) *prom: led over 2f out and sn rdn:drvn 1f out: hdd ins last and no ex towards fin* **16/1**

6512 **5** *1 1/2* **Dazzler Mac**[11] [4405] 5-8-10 54 .... SuzzanneFrance(7) 15 56+
(N Bycroft) *hld up: hdwy and n.m.r wl over 1f out: sn rdn and kpt on ins last: nrst fin* **7/2**[1]

0364 **6** *nk* **Tagula Bay (IRE)**[86] [2112] 4-9-0 56 .... DuranFentiman(5) 12 57
(T D Easterby) *dwlt and bhd: gd hdwy 2f out: rdn to chse ldrs over 1f out: drvn and one pce ins last* **14/1**

0000 **7** *1* **Observatory Star (IRE)**[41] [3473] 3-9-8 62 .... DavidAllan 7 60
(T D Easterby) *prom: rdn along and ev ch 2f out: drvn and wknd ent last* **25/1**

-000 **8** *3/4* **Khalidia (USA)**[12] [4368] 5-9-12 63 ....(t) TedDurcan 4 58
(M A Magnusson) *chsd ldrs on outer: rdn along 2f out: kpt on same pce ent last* **10/1**

0400 **9** *shd* **Flur Na H Alba**[11] [4401] 7-9-9 60 ....(b) GrahamGibbons 3 55
(J J Quinn) *led: rdn and edgd rt 1/2-way: hdd over 2f out: drvn and wknd ent last* **20/1**

0400 **10** *3/4* **Angelofthenorth**[16] [4230] 4-9-3 54 .... ChrisCatlin 5 47
(C J Teague) *chsd ldrs: rdn along 2f out: wknd appr last* **25/1**

0/00 **11** *1/2* **Smirfys Systems**[20] [4119] 7-9-9 60 .... PaulMulrennan 6 51
(W M Brisbourne) *prom: rdn along over 2f out: sn wknd* **33/1**

0660 **12** *1/2* **Dark Champion**[11] [4401] 6-9-2 56 .... StephenDonohoe(3) 10 46
(R E Barr) *prom: rdn along 2f out: wknd over 1f out* **18/1**

0605 **13** ½ **George The Best (IRE)**6 4571 5-9-0 **56**...................... GregFairley(5) 14 44
(Micky Hammond) *a towards rr* **14/1**

5323 **14** *nk* **Estoille**7 4507 5-8-13 **50**.. PaulHanagan 13 37
(Mrs S Lamyman) *prom: rdn along over 2f out: sn wknd* **5/1**2

6050 **15** 3½ **Apex**6 4571 5-9-1 **59**...(p) DanielleMcCreery(7) 2 36
(N Tinkler) *v.s.a: a bhd* **16/1**

0-00 **16** 2 **Turn Around**24 3996 6-9-4 **55**...................................... DeanMcKeown 11 26
(J Pearce) *a rr* **33/1**

1m 12.19s (0.49) **Going Correction** +0.125s/f (Good)
WFA 3 from 4yo+ 3lb **16** Ran SP% **129.4**
Speed ratings (Par 101):101,100,100,100,98 97,96,95,95,94 93,93,92,91,87 84
CSF £61.84 CT £599.74 TOTE £9.60: £2.40, £2.40, £3.60, £3.90; EX 101.00 Place 6 £197.38, Place 5 £77.27.
Owner Lee Bolingbroke & Partners VI **Bred** George Strawbridge **Trained** Norton, N Yorks
■ Stewards' Enquiry : Adrian T Nicholls caution: careless riding

FOCUS
Moderate handicap form but sound rated through the runner-up.
T/Plt: £284.10 to a £1 stake. Pool: £40,680.35. 104.50 winning tickets. T/Qpdt: £90.90 to a £1 stake. Pool: £4,534.30. 36.90 winning tickets. JR

4711 YORK (L-H)
Thursday, August 24

OFFICIAL GOING: Soft
After 10mm rain after racing the previous day the ground was described as 'generally soft'.
Wind: Light, half against Weather: Fine and mainly sunny

4736 £300000 ST LEGER YEARLING STKS 6f
1:45 (1:46) (Class 2) 2-Y-O
£159,126 (£63,650; £31,825; £15,896; £7,948; £7,948) **Stalls** Centre

Form RPR

12 **1** **Doctor Brown**12 4344 2-8-11 .... LDettori 11 107
(B J Meehan) *lw: chsd ldr: led over 1f out: rdn and hung rt ins fnl f: r.o* **4/1**1

1 **2** 1½ **Cockney Rebel (IRE)**33 3738 2-8-11 .... DO'Donohoe 9 103
(G A Huffer) *lw: hld up: hdwy over 2f out: rdn over 1f out: styd on* **6/1**3

21 **3** *nk* **Prime Defender**28 3872 2-8-11 .... MichaelHills 16 105+
(B W Hills) *lw: hld up: hdwy over 1f out: sn rdn: running on whn nt clr run wl ins fnl f: swtchd lft: nvr able to chal* **11/2**2

2163 **4** ¾ **We'll Confer**33 3734 2-8-11 95.................................... JamieSpencer 7 99
(K A Ryan) *outpcd: hdwy over 1f out: r.o: nrst fin* **12/1**

012 **5** 1¾ **Dhanyata (IRE)**44 3372 2-8-7 86 ow1.......................... RobertWinston 3 90
(B J Meehan) *led over 4f: wknd wl ins fnl f* **10/1**

2321 **6** ¾ **Lipocco**35 3678 2-8-11 83.. SebSanders 17 92
(R M Beckett) *chsd ldrs: rdn over 1f out: wknd fnl f* **40/1**

6221 **7** 3½ **Billy Dane (IRE)**10 4436 2-8-11 .... JimmyFortune 12 81
(B J Meehan) *hld up in tch: rdn over 1f out: wknd fnl f* **50/1**

432 **8** ½ **Transpique (IRE)**28 3872 2-8-11 .... PhilipRobinson 20 80
(C G Cox) *hld up: hmpd over 3f out: nvr trbld ldrs* **33/1**

413 **9** *hd* **Fish Called Johnny**17 4200 2-8-11 .... KDarley 19 79
(B J Meehan) *hld up: hmpd over 3f out: hdwy over 2f out: sn rdn: wknd over 1f out* **25/1**

3152 **10** *hd* **The Old Fella**11 4397 2-8-11 .... EddieAhern 13 79
(R Hannon) *hld up: rdn 1/2-way: sme hdwy over 1f out: n.d* **22/1**

21 **11** *hd* **Fishforcompliments**14 4295 2-8-11 .... PaulHanagan 8 78
(R A Fahey) *lw: mid-div: rdn 1/2-way: wknd over 1f out: hung rt ins fnl f* **12/1**

3631 **12** *nk* **Golden Balls (IRE)**40 3545 2-8-11 .... RyanMoore 2 77
(R Hannon) *hld up: rdn over 2f out: nvr trbld ldrs* **22/1**

1102 **13** 4 **Sadeek**39 3574 2-9-2 100.. NCallan 18 70
(K A Ryan) *prom: rdn and lost pl 1/2-way: wknd over 1f out* **6/1**3

4530 **14** 2 **Kerry's Dream**19 4152 2-8-6 89... DavidAllan 6 54
(T D Easterby) *hld up: n.d* **50/1**

1000 **15** *hd* **Riverside Dancer (USA)**19 4152 2-8-6 87........... CatherineGannon 14 54
(K A Ryan) *s.i.s: sn pushed along: a in rr* **50/1**

2515 **16** 3 **Domino Dancer (IRE)**15 4250 2-8-11 90........................... JohnEgan 10 50
(J Howard Johnson) *chsd ldrs over 3f* **50/1**

422 **17** 6 **Ishi Adiva**33 3734 2-8-6 .... SteveDrowne 15 27
(Tom Dascombe) *prom: rdn 1/2-way: wknd over 1f out* **33/1**

1450 **18** 3 **Dazed And Amazed**20 4099 2-9-2 101...................... RichardHughes 4 28
(R Hannon) *chsd ldrs over 4f* **20/1**

0210 **19** 3 **Avertuoso**33 3734 2-8-11 85.. TedDurcan 1 14
(B Smart) *swtg: chsd ldrs: rdn 1/2-way: wknd wl over 1f out* **66/1**

1m 14.67s (2.11) **Going Correction** +0.475s/f (Yiel) **19** Ran SP% **123.4**
Speed ratings (Par 100):104,102,101,100,98 97,92,91,91,91 91,90,85,82,82 78,70,66,62
CSF £22.69 TOTE £5.00: £2.20, £3.10, £2.60; EX 38.70 Trifecta £198.50 Pool: £1,482.00 - 5.30 winning units..
Owner J S Threadwell **Bred** Lostford Manor Stud **Trained** Manton, Wilts
■ Stewards' Enquiry : L Dettori three-day ban: careless riding (Sep 4-6)

FOCUS
The usual mix of ability in this sales race, and the field headed towards the stands'-side rail. The first three were all among the least exposed in the race and clearly well fancied, and the three that chased them home give the form a solid look.

NOTEBOOK
Doctor Brown, who provided his stable with a third win in the last four years in this race, gradually made his way over to race next to the stands'-side rail, and there appeared to be an advantage in racing there. He edged off the rail as he got tired in the final furlong, before hanging back into it and hampering the eventual third in the process, but he was a worthy winner and the drop back to six suited him. His trainer reckons the gelding will get a mile in time but that he needs to strengthen up.
Cockney Rebel(IRE), who was thought to need to have a bit of give prior to his winning debut on good to firm ground, handled conditions well and came with a strong late run down the outside of his field, towards the middle of the track. He would have only been third had Prime Defender enjoyed a clear run, but may not have been favoured by where he raced, so he deserves plenty of credit. (tchd 5-1 in a place)
Prime Defender, who won his maiden in good style, had softer ground to deal with this time but that did not cause him any bother. Staying on strongly in the closing stages, he tried to take a gap which had opened up between the favourite and the stands' rail inside the final furlong, only for the Brian Meehan-trained gelding to hang back towards the rail and chop his run off. He would have gone close with a clear passage. (op 7-1)
We'll Confer was third in the Weatherbys Super Sprint last time out so clearly has the speed for the minimum trip, but he ran as though he will get a bit further than six, as he was doing his best work at the finish. (tchd 14-1)
Dhanyata(IRE) was turned over at odds-on for a nursery off 83 last time out, but that performance does not look as disappointing as it did at the time in light of the winner going on to place in Group 2 company. She showed good speed to lead from her disadvantageous low draw and seemed to handle the softer ground. (op 9-1)
Lipocco, a winner of a nursery last time out, finished nicely clear of the rest from what looked a decent draw given the way the race panned out. (op 50-1)
Billy Dane(IRE), the biggest priced of the Brian Meehan-trained quartet, had more to do in this company than when successful in a Polytrack nursery last time out, but he fared quite well, bringing home the second group of six at a respectful distance.
Transpique(IRE), runner-up to and well held by Prime Defender last time out, never looked like reversing that form, although he would have finished a bit closer had he not been hampered.
Fish Called Johnny, who trailed in third behind subsequent Acomb Stakes winner Big Timer at Ripon last time, was another who met some trouble in running.
Fishforcompliments may have found this too much of a task at this stage of his career, but he remains a potential improver and quicker ground might suit him better, too.
Sadeek, previously successful in Listed company and runner-up in a Group 3 race last time out, was disappointing, even allowing for him having to carry a 5lb penalty, as he had trip and ground to suit, and appeared well berthed in stall 18. (op 13-2)

4737 JAGUAR CARS LOWTHER STKS (GROUP 2) (FILLIES) 6f
2:15 (2:17) (Class 1) 2-Y-O **£50,379** (£19,048; £9,520; £4,760) **Stalls** Centre

Form RPR

126 **1** **Silk Blossom (IRE)**43 3415 2-8-12 103............................ MichaelHills 4 110
(B W Hills) *chsd ldrs: wnt 2nd 1f out: styd on wl to ld nr fin* **3/1**3

014 **2** ½ **Indian Ink (IRE)**26 3925 2-8-12 104.............................. RichardHughes 1 109+
(R Hannon) *led: edgd rt after s: qcknd over 1f out: hdd nr fin* **11/4**2

652 **3** 2½ **Darrfonah (IRE)**27 3893 2-8-12 80...................................... RyanMoore 5 101
(C E Brittain) *sn outpcd: hdwy over 2f out: styd on to take 3rd ins last* **16/1**

6214 **4** 1½ **Siren's Gift**23 4026 2-8-12 88... MartinDwyer 3 97
(A M Balding) *trckd ldrs: effrt over 2f out: wknd wl ins last* **10/1**

0131 **5** *nk* **Scarlet Runner**26 3925 2-8-12 107................................ KerrinMcEvoy 2 96
(J L Dunlop) *lw: chsd ldrs: n.m.r on inner over 2f out: one pce* **9/4**1

62 **6** 4 **Miss Jenny (IRE)**6 4559 2-8-12 .... JimmyFortune 7 84
(B J Meehan) *dwlt: hld up: effrt over 2f out: wknd over 1f out* **8/1**

455 **7** 2½ **Miss Ippolita**43 3402 2-8-12 71.. EddieAhern 6 76
(J R Jenkins) *prom: lost pl over 2f out* **66/1**

1m 14.82s (2.26) **Going Correction** +0.475s/f (Yiel) **7** Ran SP% **110.0**
Speed ratings (Par 103):103,102,99,97,96 91,87
CSF £10.74 TOTE £4.00: £2.10, £2.00; EX 12.00.
Owner E D Kessly **Bred** Richard F Barnes **Trained** Lambourn, Berks
■ Stewards' Enquiry : Richard Hughes two-day ban: used whip from above shoulder height (Sep 4,5)
Michael Hills one-day ban: used whip with excessive frequency (Sep 4)

FOCUS
A below-average renewal in which the performances of 80-rated Darrfonah and 88-rate Siren's Gift in finishing third and fourth respectively underline the relatively modest level of the form.

NOTEBOOK
Silk Blossom(IRE) deserved to finish closer than she did in the Cherry Hinton last time and on her Royal Ascot form she had the edge over the favourite Scarlet Runner. A daughter of Barathea, she was suited by the soft ground and saw the trip out just that bit better than the runner-up. She will stay a mile next year and should get seven this season, but the Goffs Million over an extended six at the Curragh looks likely to be her next target. (tchd 10-3)
Indian Ink(IRE) enjoyed the run of the race next to the stands'-side rail and looked to have the race in the bag entering the final furlong, but she got tired and was eventually worn down by the winner near the finish. As a daughter of Indian Ridge it was not a great surprise that she proved well suited by the soft ground. The Watership Down Stakes is her next target. (op 3-1)
Darrfonah(IRE) had not done enough in her first three starts to suggest she was likely to trouble the judge in this company, but the soft ground made it more of a test of stamina and, as the filly with the stoutest pedigree in the line-up, she was able to pick up places late on from off the pace. She is going to be a middle-distance performer next season so it is highly encouraging that she has been able to record a third place at this level at two, and it would be a surprise if she was not stepped up in trip next time. (tchd 20-1)
Siren's Gift found the step up to six furlongs for the first time combined with the soft ground placing too much of an emphasis on stamina, and she did not get home. She is worth another try at this distance, but on a quicker surface. (op 8-1)
Scarlet Runner, whose two wins to date, including the Princess Margaret Stakes, have come on fast ground, failed to cope with these more demanding conditions and did not run anywhere near her best. She will be worthy of consideration again in similar company if the ground is on the fast side. (op 5-2)
Miss Jenny(IRE), making a fairly quick reappearance after finishing runner-up in a Newbury maiden six days earlier, was not unfancied but failed to cut much ice on this step up in grade. She will win races in time, though. (op 9-1 tchd 15-2)
Miss Ippolita was out of her depth in this company. (op 50-1)

4738 VC BET NUNTHORPE STKS (GROUP 1) 5f
2:50 (2:51) (Class 1) 2-Y-O+
£147,400 (£55,865; £27,958; £13,940; £6,983; £3,504) **Stalls** Centre

Form RPR

4105 **1** **Reverence**47 3312 5-9-11 111.. KDarley 6 122
(E J Alston) *lw: mde virtually all: rdn clr fnl f: hung lft towards fin* **5/1**3

0543 **2** 2 **Amadeus Wolf**18 4191 3-9-9 115.. NCallan 16 116
(K A Ryan) *lw: chsd wnr: rdn and ev ch over 1f out: styd on same pce ins fnl f* **5/1**3

5303 **3** *hd* **Pivotal Flame**21 4080 4-9-11 105...................................(p) SebSanders 2 115
(E S McMahon) *lw: chsd ldrs: rdn and ev ch over 1f out: styd on same pce ins fnl f* **14/1**

0334 **4** ¾ **The Trader (IRE)**11 4410 8-9-11 108................................(b) TedDurcan 4 112
(M Blanshard) *mid-div: hdwy u.p over 1f out: styd on same pce ins fnl f* **33/1**

0602 **5** ¾ **Red Clubs (IRE)**11 4410 3-9-9 111.................................. MichaelHills 17 110
(B W Hills) *hld up: hdwy 1/2-way: rdn over 1f out: edgd lft: styd on same pce* **22/1**

0664 **6** 1¼ **The Tatling (IRE)**21 4080 9-9-11 110.............................. RyanMoore 8 106
(J M Bradley) *mid-div: hdwy u.p over 1f out: styd on same pce fnl f* **20/1**

-551 **7** *shd* **Steenberg (IRE)**99 1778 7-9-11 112.................................. TPQueally 11 105+
(M H Tompkins) *hmpd s: sn outpcd: r.o ins fnl f: nrst fin* **16/1**

4B30 **8** *shd* **Orientor**25 3972 8-9-11 106.. JohnEgan 15 105
(J S Goldie) *hld up in tch: rdn over 1f out: styd on same pce* **33/1**

0155 **9** *nk* **Fayr Jag (IRE)**11 4410 7-9-11 111...................................... DavidAllan 10 104+
(T D Easterby) *hmpd s: chsd ldrs: rdn whn nt clr run over 1f out: wknd fnl f* **50/1**

3306 **10** *nk* **Mecca's Mate**54 3076 5-9-8 100.................................. RobertWinston 13 100
(D W Barker) *hld up in tch: n.m.r and lost pl over 3f out: n.d after* **50/1**

-500 **11** ½ **Gift Horse**[41] [3494] 6-9-11 106 .... EddieAhern 3 101
(D Nicholls) *hld up: swtchd rt sn after s: stmbld 1/2-way: nt clr run over 1f out: nvr trbld ldrs* **14/1**

2141 **12** 1 **Dandy Man (IRE)**[53] [3124] 3-9-9 .... PShanahan 14 98+
(C Collins, Ire) *lw: plld hrd and prom: rdn over 1f out: wknd ins fnl f* **4/1**[1]

111 **13** 1 **Enticing (IRE)**[23] [4026] 2-7-12 105 .... NickyMackay 9 91
(W J Haggas) *wnt rt s: sn chsng ldrs: rdn over 1f out: wknd fnl f* **11/1**

1051 **14** ½ **Moss Vale (IRE)**[11] [4410] 5-9-11 114 .... AdrianTNicholls 12 93+
(D Nicholls) *lw: hld up in tch: shkn up and n.m.r from over 1f out: eased ins fnl f* **9/2**[2]

60.68 secs (1.36) **Going Correction** +0.475s/f (Yiel)
WFA 2 from 3yo 24lb 3 from 4yo+ 2lb **14** Ran SP% **118.0**
Speed ratings: 108,104,104,103,102 100,99,99,99,98 98,96,94,94
CSF £27.18 TOTE £7.50: £2.70, £2.10, £4.50; EX 30.40 Trifecta £508.20 Pool: £4,008.82 - 5.60 winning units..
Owner Mr & Mrs G Middlebrook **Bred** G And Mrs Middlebrook **Trained** Longton, Lancs

FOCUS
Not the greatest renewal on paper, a moderate time for a race like this, and the lack of a strong pace counted against those who were held up, but Reverence won with authority and remains unbeaten in seven starts over five furlongs on easy ground. The form is rated around the placed horses.

NOTEBOOK
Reverence loves to get his toe in, and making the running in a race not run at a furious gallop also gave him a tactical advantage. He stamped his authority on the race inside the final furlong, clearing away from his rivals in impressive style, and he looks sure to take plenty of stopping in the Prix de l'Abbaye, ground conditions permitting. Things might be tougher for him back over six in the Betfred Sprint Cup, as he looks a pure speedball, but he is still likely to be a leading contender. With victory here he took his record over five furlongs on ground officially described as good to soft or softer to an impressive seven wins from seven starts. (tchd 11-2)
Amadeus Wolf did not lack for speed on the drop back to the minimum trip, but it was also to his advantage that the pace he helped set was not that strong, making it difficult for challengers from off the pace to get competitive. He will not mind returning to six in the Betfred Sprint Cup and would have fair claims of reversing the form with the winner over an extra furlong. (op 7-1 tchd 8-1 in places)
Pivotal Flame has not won since 2004 but he had his ground for the first time since finishing one place behind Reverence on his seasonal reappearance at Redcar, and he put up a personal best. He was definitely suited by racing close to the pace, though, and the bare form may flatter him as a result.
The Trader(IRE), runner-up to Reverence in the Temple Stakes earlier in the season, is at his best finishing strongly from off a decent pace. He did not get this race run to suit but still put up a fine effort. He still has the ability to pop up in a Group race somewhere when things fall right.
Red Clubs(IRE) finished in front of The Trader in Ireland last time but the drop in trip was perhaps more in that rival's favour. He stayed on well next to the stands' rail and, curiously, matched his Gimcrack and Middle Park form with Amadeus Wolf almost to the pound. (op 25-1)
The Tatling(IRE), the oldest in the line-up and runner-up in this race for the past three years, would have appreciated a stronger pace, but he still ran a sound race. He has not hit the target yet this season but he certainly retains a fair degree of his ability.
Steenberg(IRE) likes this sort of ground but he has done his winning over six and seven furlongs and he struggled to go the pace on this first start over the minimum trip. A stronger pace would have seen him do better, but the same could be said for one or two of the others. (op 18-1)
Orientor is a capable if frustrating performer at his level, but this is not it. The softer ground helped him improve his last place in this race last year to a respectable eighth this time around.
Fayr Jag(IRE), who has only recorded one of his 11 wins over the minimum trip (his maiden success), has always preferred a sound surface so conditions were hardly ideal for him. Bumped leaving the stalls, he was also hampered as he weakened in the latter part of the race.
Mecca's Mate looked likely to be up against it in this grade, despite having seen the ground come her way, and she was predictably outclassed.
Gift Horse had never before run over the minimum trip but he travelled well enough towards the rear off this fairly steady pace. Denied a clear run in a race not run to suit the hold-up horses, he deserves rating a bit better than his finishing position suggests. (op 12-1)
Dandy Man(IRE), about whom there were concerns on this soft ground, did not give himself a chance of getting home as he pulled so hard in the early stages. He has the ability to win at this level, but he probably needs fast ground and a decent pace to run off, as his weapon is a turn of foot. Official explanation: jockey said colt ran too free early stages (op 7-2 tchd 9-2)
Enticing(IRE) is by Pivotal so she should have liked the ground, but it takes a top-class horse to win this race at two despite the huge receipt of weight, and she was not up to the task. Connections were presumably encouraged to run on the basis that her dam was runner-up in the Abbaye as a juvenile. (op 8-1)
Moss Vale(IRE) ◆ suffered a luckless run as he always had a wall of horses in front of him and every gap his rider went for closed in his face. He could never get a run and was eventually eased off to finish last. His finishing position does not reflect his performance and he remains one to be interested in for the Betfred Sprint Cup and the Abbaye. Official explanation: jockey said horse was denied a clear run

4739 ADDLESHAW GODDARD STKS (H'CAP) 1m
3:25 (3:26) (Class 2) (0-105,105) 3-Y-0+ **£25,908** (£7,708; £3,852; £1,924) **Stalls** Low

Form RPR

2141 **1** **Smart Enough**[43] [3413] 3-8-12 96 .... KerrinMcEvoy 12 111+
(M A Magnusson) *hdw: lw: mde all: shkn up and qcknd over 1f out: r.o wl* **6/1**[2]

2011 **2** 2½ **Bolodenka (IRE)**[18] [4187] 4-9-3 95 .... PaulHanagan 19 105
(R A Fahey) *lw: mid-div: hdwy over 2f out: styd on to take 2nd ins last* **20/1**

-110 **3** ¾ **Pride Of Nation (IRE)**[64] [2742] 4-9-4 96 .... NickyMackay 3 104+
(L M Cumani) *lw: hld up in mid-div: effrt on inner and n.m.r 3f out: styd on same pce ins last* **2/1**[1]

0340 **4** ½ **Blythe Knight (IRE)**[64] [2742] 6-9-7 99 .... GrahamGibbons 17 106
(J J Quinn) *trckd ldrs: effrt over 2f out: hung lft: styd on same pce fnl f* **20/1**

520- **5** ½ **St Petersburg**[278] [6378] 6-9-5 97 .... TPQueally 14 103+
(M H Tompkins) *hld up in rr: nt clr run and swtchd lft over 2f out: nt clr run over 1f out: styd on wl* **16/1**

3511 **6** nk **Illustrious Blue**[23] [4029] 3-8-9 93 .... PaulDoe 16 102+
(W J Knight) *lw: hld up in rr: hdwy and nt clr run over 1f out: styd on strly ins last* **12/1**

-200 **7** ½ **Rohaani (USA)**[20] [4098] 4-9-6 98 .... RHills 8 102
(Sir Michael Stoute) *lw: s.i.s: hdwy on ins to chse ldrs 3f out: wknd ins last* **16/1**

3225 **8** shd **Skidrow**[57] [2988] 4-8-12 90 .... MartinDwyer 13 94
(M L W Bell) *mid-div: effrt over 2f out: nvr nr ldrs* **20/1**

1000 **9** ½ **I'm So Lucky**[12] [4359] 4-9-8 100 .... JoeFanning 11 103
(M Johnston) *chsd ldrs: wknd over 1f out* **33/1**

0150 **10** ½ **Zero Tolerance (IRE)**[53] [3123] 6-9-13 105 .... JamieSpencer 10 107
(T D Barron) *chsd ldrs: one pce fnl 2f* **8/1**[3]

-004 **11** 1¼ **Wise Dennis**[12] [4356] 4-9-5 97 .... RyanMoore 15 96
(A P Jarvis) *swtchd lft s: bhd: kpt on fnl 2f: nvr nr ldrs* **10/1**

0000 **12** ¾ **Royal Island (IRE)**[12] [4348] 4-9-6 98 .... KDarley 6 96
(M Johnston) *in rr: stmbld over 5f out: styd on fnl 3f* **14/1**

-000 **13** ½ **Spanish Don**[64] [2742] 8-8-13 91 .... LPKeniry 22 88
(D R C Elsworth) *hld up in rr: nvr a factor* **50/1**

3321 **14** nk **Audience**[12] [4356] 6-9-0 92 .... JimmyQuinn 20 88
(J Akehurst) *prom: lost pl over 1f out* **20/1**

0262 **15** 3½ **Ace Of Hearts**[19] [4145] 7-9-10 102 .... GeorgeBaker 5 91
(C F Wall) *lw: prom: wknd fnl f* **25/1**

3000 **16** 2 **Shot To Fame (USA)**[20] [4098] 7-8-10 88 .... (t) AdrianTNicholls 7 73
(D Nicholls) *chsd ldrs: lost pl over 1f out* **33/1**

6006 **17** nk **Yarqus**[19] [4126] 3-9-0 98 .... SebSanders 2 82
(C E Brittain) *prom: lost pl over 1f out* **40/1**

1m 40.73s (1.23) **Going Correction** +0.55s/f (Yiel)
WFA 3 from 4yo+ 6lb **17** Ran SP% **127.1**
Speed ratings (Par 109):115,112,111,111,110 110,109,109,109,108 107,106,106,106,102 100,100
CSF £128.91 CT £342.98 TOTE £7.70: £2.00, £4.30, £1.50, £5.00; EX 302.20 Trifecta £617.80 Pool: £2,871.84 - 3.30 winning units..
Owner East Wind Racing Ltd **Bred** Whitsbury Manor Stud And Mrs M E Slade **Trained** Upper Lambourn, Berks

FOCUS
A highly-competitive handicap run at a strong gallop in a smart time and strong form rated through the fourth. A much-improved effort from the unexposed winner, one of just three three-year-olds in the field. They all came middle to stands' side resulting in traffic problems.

NOTEBOOK
Smart Enough, who is thriving and has quickly made up into a high-class performer since winning his maiden in May, defied a 7lb higher mark, enjoying himself in front and making light of the soft ground. Unsurprisingly the Cambridgeshire is on the agenda now and he should make his mark in Pattern company at four. (tchd 11-2 and 13-2 in places)
Bolodenka(IRE), a stone higher than when he ran in handicap company here before his dual victories at Galway, had an outside draw ro overcome. He stayed on in willing fashion to snatch second spot inside the last and the easy ground did not seem to be a problem.
Pride Of Nation(IRE), 9lb higher than Haydock, had the ground to suit and was well backed. Looking his very best, he seemed to lie a fraction too far off the pace and did not have the smoothest of runs through. His effort faded near the line but there is clearly another good prize to be picked up with him this backend. (op 5-2 tchd 11-4 in places)
Blythe Knight(IRE), now just 4lb higher than for his Lincoln success, was back after a break and had the ground to suit. He gave a good account of himself from his outside draw and should be spot-on next time.
St Petersburg, third in this two years ago, looked very fit on his first outing since November. Trying to improve from the rear, he met plenty of traffic problems but was staying on in fine style at the death.
Illustrious Blue, 6lb higher, had a wide draw and was encountering much easier ground. He had no luck in running but was scything them down at the line. (tchd 11-1)
Rohaani(USA), a grand stamp of horse, fluffed his lines at the start. He moved up on the inner to join contention once in line for home but was treading water in the closing stages. He remains unexposed and would prefer quicker ground than he encountered here. (op 18-1)
Ace Of Hearts Official explanation: jockey said gelding had no more to give

4740 SKF CITY OF YORK STKS (LISTED RACE) 7f
4:00 (4:00) (Class 1) 3-Y-0+ **£20,744** (£7,843; £3,920; £1,960) **Stalls** Low

Form RPR

1060 **1** **Quito (IRE)**[23] [4025] 9-9-5 112 .... (b) RobertWinston 6 116
(D W Chapman) *lw: hld up: hdwy and nt clr run over 2f out: led jst ins last: r.o strly* **4/1**[2]

1-1 **2** 1 **Lightning Flash**[36] [3648] 4-9-0 98 .... JamieSpencer 4 108
(J R Fanshawe) *lw: hld up in rr: nt clr run and swtchd ins over 2f out: squeezed through on inner to chse wnr jst ins last: no ex* **7/1**[3]

1-30 **3** 3 **Arminius (IRE)**[90] [1990] 3-8-9 88 .... RichardHughes 8 99
(R Hannon) *hld up in rr: nt clr run and swtchd lft over 1f out: styd on to take 3rd wl ins last* **66/1**

3510 **4** 1¾ **Somnus**[18] [4191] 6-9-0 107 .... NCallan 5 96
(T D Easterby) *chsd ldrs: upsides 1f out: one pce* **4/1**[2]

1301 **5** 2½ **Dabbers Ridge (IRE)**[26] [3926] 4-9-0 102 .... MichaelHills 9 90
(B W Hills) *trckd ldrs: led over 2f out: hdd & wknd jst ins last* **2/1**[1]

1303 **6** ½ **Azarole (IRE)**[40] [3563] 5-9-0 105 .... JohnEgan 11 88
(J S Moore) *chsd ldrs: drvn over 2f out: one pce* **12/1**

356- **7** 2 **Swing The Ring (IRE)**[43] 3-8-9 .... SteveDrowne 2 81
(Bruce Hellier, Germany) *in tch: outpcd and lost pl over 4f out: no imp whn hmpd over 1f out* **50/1**

1-44 **8** 9 **Mostashaar (FR)**[75] [2431] 4-9-0 105 .... RHills 1 60
(Sir Michael Stoute) *w ldrs: wkng whn n.m.r appr fnl f: lost pl and eased* **8/1**

-102 **9** 2 **Saville Road**[34] [3702] 3-8-9 97 .... KerrinMcEvoy 3 52
(D J Daly) *led tl over 2f out: lost pl and eased over 1f out* **20/1**

2430 **10** 7 **Chief Commander (FR)**[19] [4168] 3-8-9 102 .... RyanMoore 7 34
(Jane Chapple-Hyam) *chsd ldrs: outpcd over 2f out: wkng whn hmpd over 1f out: eased* **50/1**

1m 26.3s (0.90) **Going Correction** +0.475s/f (Yiel)
WFA 3 from 4yo+ 5lb **10** Ran SP% **114.8**
Speed ratings (Par 111):113,111,108,106,103 103,100,90,88,80
CSF £30.54 TOTE £4.70: £1.70, £1.90, £12.00; EX 40.90 TRIFECTA Not won..
Owner Michael Hill **Bred** Sheikh Mohammed Bin Rashid Al Maktoum **Trained** Stillington, N Yorks
■ Stewards' Enquiry : N Callan two-day ban: careless riding (Sep 19-20)
Richard Hughes one-day ban: careless riding (Sep 6)

FOCUS
A high-class renewal of this Listed race but the pace was not that strong. The winner is a model professional and sets the standard, with the runner-up unexposed.

NOTEBOOK
Quito(IRE), a credit to his trainer, defied the 5lb penalty. He came with a well-timed effort and once he had his head in front he would simply not be denied. This was his 19th career win and he seems better than ever. (op 7-2)
Lightning Flash, having just his third career start, had 9lb to find with the winner on official ratings. Loaded with the help of a rug, he had to search long and hard for a run. Eventually making his effort hard against the stands'-side rail, he looked a major threat inside the last but was safely held at the line. This was a notable effort for one so inexperienced and if all remains well with him he should have a bright future. A return here in two weeks is on the cards. (op 13-2 tchd 6-1)
Arminius(IRE), absent since May, has been gelded and had the headgear dispensed with. He had to switch for a run but stuck on well to snatch third place near the line. Hopefully the operation has helped him turn the corner. (op 100-1)
Somnus, a Group 1 winner at four, seems to have lost some of his sparkle and this may be as good as he is now. In all he has three Group 1 races to his credit and it must be said he owes connections nothing. (op 9-2)
Dabbers Ridge(IRE), up in grade, had 5lb to find with the winner on official ratings. He went on but had no more to give when tackled by Quito. Official explanation: trainer had no explanation for the poor form shown (op 5-2 tchd 11-4 in places)
Azarole(IRE) ran respectably without ever posing a potent threat. (op 14-1 tchd 11-1)

Saville Road Official explanation: jockey said colt ran too keenly

4741 EUROPEAN BREEDERS FUND GALTRES STKS (LISTED RACE) (F&M) 1m 4f

4:35 (4:36) (Class 1) 3-Y-0+ **£20,744** (£7,843; £3,920; £1,960) **Stalls** Centre

Form RPR

16 **1** **Anna Pavlova**[70] 2582 3-8-8 97........................ PaulHanagan 2 107+
(R A Fahey) *mid-div: hdwy on outside 3f out: wnt lft and led over 1f out: drvn out* **4/1**[2]

2-20 **2** *3* **Bunood (IRE)**[18] 4179 3-8-8 96........................ RHills 6 102
(J L Dunlop) *mid-div: hdwy over 5f out: c wd: styd on fnl 2f: tk 2nd nr fin* **15/2**

1140 **3** *3/4* **Gower Song**[22] 4039 3-8-8 93........................ JohnEgan 3 101
(D R C Elsworth) *hld up: hdwy 6f out: c wd: chsng ldrs over 2f out: lost 2nd nr fin* **14/1**

1424 **4** *1 1/2* **Cresta Gold**[21] 4079 3-8-8 101........................ MartinDwyer 9 99+
(A Bailey) *trckd ldrs: qcknd to ld over 7f out: styd far side: hdd over 1f out: one pce* **7/1**

-166 **5** *nk* **Power Girl (GER)**[21] 4079 4-9-10 95........................ JamieSpencer 11 104
(P F I Cole) *hld up in rr: hdwy over 5f out: c wd: kpt on fnl 2f* **28/1**

6 *5* **Zarwala (IRE)**[90] 2007 3-8-8........................ MJKinane 7 90+
(John M Oxx, Ire) *rangy: unf: swtchd lft after s: lost pl and bhd after 3f: drvn over 5f out: styd towards far side: nvr a factor* **5/2**[1]

-365 **7** *1 1/2* **Valentina Guest (IRE)**[26] 3964 5-9-4........................ RyanMoore 8 88
(Peter Casey, Ire) *hld up in rr: effrt on outside 3f out: nvr nr ldrs* **25/1**

351 **8** *5* **Well Hidden**[12] 4374 3-8-8 86........................ KerrinMcEvoy 4 80
(Sir Michael Stoute) *led tl over 7f out: c wd: wknd fnl 2f* **13/2**[3]

0-10 **9** *18* **Cortesia (IRE)**[106] 1583 3-8-8 83........................ EddieAhern 5 51
(P W Chapple-Hyam) *prom: racd centre: lost pl 4f out: sn bhd* **40/1**

2-16 **10** *45* **Sandglass**[23] 4035 3-8-8 99........................ RichardHughes 1 —
(Mrs A J Perrett) *trckd ldrs: racd centre: lost pl and eased over 2f out: virtually p.u: t.o* **11/1**

0-35 **P** **Ruby Wine**[18] 4179 4-9-4 98........................ TedDurcan 10 —
(J M P Eustace) *trckd ldrs: wnt 2nd over 4f out: p.u and dismntd 3f out* **14/1**

2m 36.6s (4.20) **Going Correction** +0.55s/f (Yiel)
WFA 3 from 4yo+ 10lb **11 Ran SP% 117.6**
Speed ratings (Par 111):108,106,105,104,104 100,99,96,84,54 —
CSF £33.47 TOTE £5.00: £1.80, £3.00, £4.40; EX 50.10 Trifecta £962.10 Part won. Pool: £1,355.10 - 0.90 winning units..
Owner Galaxy Racing **Bred** Raymond Cowie **Trained** Musley Bank, N Yorks

FOCUS
A sub-standard renewal and the pace was just steady for the first half-mile. They raced all over the track in the straight and the third and fifth, along with the runner-up, set the standard.

NOTEBOOK
Anna Pavlova, conqueror of Sir Gerard in a handicap at Haydock in May, was back after a ten-week break. Suited by the give, she made her effort on the outer but swerved left and ended up towards the far side. Firmly in command at the line, a mile six will be no problem and the Park Hill could be next on the agenda. Still not the finished article, hopefully she will make an even better four-year-old. (op 7-2 tchd 9-2 and 5-1 in a place)
Bunood(IRE), much happier on this easy ground, stuck on to snatch second spot. The extra two furlongs certainly suited her. (op 9-1 tchd 10-1 in places)
Gower Song, much improved in handicap company this year, fully justified her place in this Listed race. (op 12-1)
Cresta Gold, who looked very fit indeed, went on and stepped up the pace. She remained alone on the far side in the home straight and, after being matched at odds-on on the exchanges, in the end she was comfortably run out of it. The ground had probably turned against her. (op 13-2 tchd 15-2)
Power Girl(GER) continues to struggle under her Listed race penalty but to her credit she was far from disgraced.
Zarwala(IRE), whose trainer had won the two previous runnings, came here on the back of a maiden race success at Limerick. Soon in the rear and pushed along, she stuck towards the far side in the straight and never entered the argument. In time she might well prove a fair bit better than she was able to show here. (op 3-1 tchd 2-1)
Well Hidden, taking a big step up in class, was simply not up to the task in hand. (op 8-1)
Sandglass dropped out in a matter of strides and allowed to complete in her own time, was reported to have suffered an injury. Official explanation: jockey said filly returned injured (op 12-1)
Ruby Wine was still bang in the firing line when taken out of the contest and dismounted. Hopefully it was not a severe injury. (op 16-1)

4742 BRILLIANT MEDIA MELROSE STKS (H'CAP) 1m 5f 197y

5:10 (5:10) (Class 2) (0-100,98) 3-Y-0 **£16,192** (£4,817; £2,407; £1,202) **Stalls** Low

Form RPR

1111 **1** **Trick Or Treat**[7] 4528 3-8-3 **80** 6ex........................ JamieMackay 1 95
(J G Given) *lw: trckd ldrs: edgd rt over 3f out: chal over 1f out:edgd lft and led wl ins last: all out* **9/2**[3]

3210 **2** *shd* **Ask**[22] 4039 3-8-13 **90**........................(t) RyanMoore 4 104
(Sir Michael Stoute) *lw: trckd ldr: led on bit over 3f out: edgd lft over 1f out: hdd wl ins last: r.o* **5/2**[1]

3332 **3** *6* **Gee Dee Nen**[15] 4259 3-8-5 **82**........................ TPQueally 2 88
(M H Tompkins) *swvd rt s: hld up: hdwy over 3f out: one pce fnl 2f* **8/1**

-313 **4** *nk* **Salesin**[75] 2436 3-8-13 **90**........................ NickyMackay 7 96
(L M Cumani) *hld up in tch: drvn over 3f out: one pce fnl 2f* **6/1**

4031 **5** *7* **Numeric (GER)**[19] 4125 3-8-11 **88**........................(b) JimmyFortune 3 84
(J H M Gosden) *hld up: hdwy on outside over 4f out: sn chsng ldrs: edgd lft and lost pl over 1f out* **7/1**

1132 **6** *31* **Bandama (IRE)**[22] 4039 3-9-7 **98**........................ MJKinane 6 50+
(Mrs A J Perrett) *trckd ldrs: lost pl over 2f out: sn bhd and eased: t.o* **10/1**

3111 **7** *15* **Cape Secret (IRE)**[25] 3981 3-8-8 **85**........................ SebSanders 8 16+
(R M Beckett) *led: hdd over 3f out: sn hmpd and lost pl: sn bhd and eased: t.o* **4/1**[2]

3m 3.88s (5.44) **Going Correction** +0.55s/f (Yiel) **7 Ran SP% 113.7**
Speed ratings (Par 106):106,105,102,102,98 80,72
CSF £16.00 CT £85.70 TOTE £3.40: £2.00, £2.30; EX 13.70 Trifecta £185.00 Pool: £1,146.66 - 4.40 winning units. Place 6 £151.40, Place 5 £73.38.
Owner Peter Onslow **Bred** P Onslow **Trained** Willoughton, Lincs

FOCUS
A decent staying handicap run at a strong gallop and the first two pulled right away. The form looks solid rated around the third and fourth.

NOTEBOOK
Trick Or Treat, raised 12lb after Salisbury carried just a 6lb penalty. Clearly thriving, she went at it hammer and tongs with the runner-up and showed great bravery to edge ahead near the line. She must be worth a try in Listed company now. (op 11-4 tchd 5-2 in places)
Ask, who was clearly a major let-down to the stable at Goodwood, has been left in the St Leger. Turned out in magnificent condition and with his tongue-tied this time, he travelled strongly. After a titanic battle he came off just second best. Trouble is that his handicap rating will shoot up as a result. (op 3-1 tchd 100-30 in a place)
Gee Dee Nen, keen to get on with it, finished a creditable third behind two vastly-improved types. That first handicap win is proving elusive. (op 10-1 tchd 12-1 in places)
Salesin is another maiden winner who is struggling to make a real impact in handicap company. (op 7-1)
Numeric(GER), 3lb higher, was racing on much softer ground and he turned in a lifeless effort. (tchd 8-1)
Bandama(IRE), stepping up in distance, was encountering much softer ground and dropped right away in a matter of strides. It was clearly more than the trip and the ground. (op 12-1 tchd 14-1 in places)
Cape Secret(IRE), forcing a strong pace from a 12lb higher mark, had been swallowed up when the winner knocked her out of her stride. She crossed the line in her own time and her rider reported that she was not suited by the soft ground. Official explanation: trainer's rep said gelding was unsuited by the soft ground (op 11-2)
T/Jkpt: £18,280.70 to a £1 stake. Pool: £180,232.50. 7.00 winning tickets. T/Plt: £118.20 to a £1 stake. Pool: £218,042.50. 1,345.95 winning tickets. T/Qpdt: £26.90 to a £1 stake. Pool: £9,261.00. 254.70 winning tickets. WG

4316 TIPPERARY

Thursday, August 24

OFFICIAL GOING: Good

4747a DANEHILL DANCER TIPPERARY STKS (LISTED RACE) 5f

5:35 (5:35) 2-Y-0 **£26,937** (£7,903; £3,765; £1,282)

RPR

1 **Flash McGahon (IRE)**[14] 4316 2-9-1........................ FMBerry 6 99
(John M Oxx, Ire) *trckd ldr in 2nd: rdn to chal and ld 1f out: strly pressed and styd on wl cl home* **20/1**

2 *hd* **Spirit Of Pearl (IRE)**[14] 4309 2-8-12........................ WSupple 3 95
(David P Myerscough, Ire) *trckd ldrs in 4th: kpt on wl u.p ins fnl f: nt rch wnr* **14/1**

3 *hd* **Mood Music**[20] 4099 2-9-1........................ RichardMullen 5 98
(E J O'Neill) *racd in mod 6th: r.o wl u.p ins fnl f: nt rch ldrs* **11/2**[3]

4 *nk* **City Of Tribes (IRE)**[63] 2771 2-9-1........................ JMurtagh 8 96
(G M Lyons, Ire) *trckd ldrs in 3rd: no imp u.p and kpt on same pce ins fnl f* **7/2**[2]

5 *1 1/2* **Drayton (IRE)**[11] 4409 2-9-4........................ WMLordan 2 94
(T Stack, Ire) *attempted to make all: strly pressed and hdd 1f out: sn no imp u.p: kpt on same pce* **4/6**[1]

6 *3/4* **Divert (IRE)**[14] 4316 2-8-12........................(t) KFallon 4 85
(Edward Lynam, Ire) *chsd ldrs: mainly 5th: no imp u.p and kpt on same pce fnl f* **20/1**

7 *3 1/2* **Ghostmilk (IRE)**[6] 4580 2-8-12........................ CO'Donoghue 7 73
(P D Deegan, Ire) *racd in mod 7th: no imp u.p and kpt on same pce fr under 2f out* **33/1**

8 *2* **Leathaoibh (IRE)**[43] 3423 2-8-12........................ DPMcDonogh 9 66
(P A Fahy, Ire) *dwlt: a towards rr: nvr a factor* **66/1**

9 *hd* **Friarscourt (USA)**[26] 3962 2-9-1........................ RMBurke 1 68
(R J Osborne, Ire) *sn in rr: nvr a factor* **50/1**

58.09 secs **9 Ran SP% 120.2**
CSF £250.91 TOTE £19.20: £3.00, £1.60, £2.00; DF 106.30.
Owner Dundalk Racing Club **Bred** Barnane Stud **Trained** Currabeg, Co Kildare

NOTEBOOK
Flash McGahon(IRE) improved markedly on the form of his first two runs to break his maiden tag in good style. The winner was edged out by Inourthoughts in a maiden over this course and distance earlier in the month but left that form well behind here. He broke smartly to dispute the lead from the outset and began to edge ahead nearing the final furlong before keeping on well under pressure. Trainer John Oxx felt that his charge was not sharp enough when beaten here the last day but was anxious to try him again at five furlongs. He will now aim him at a six-furlong Listed race at the Curragh later this month.
Spirit Of Pearl(IRE) maintained her recent progress. Successful in a nursery off 77 here last month, she was a clear-cut winner of a Sligo claimer last time and stepped up markedly on that form. This trip seems to suit her well.
Mood Music had some useful placed form to his name in England, including when second to Bahama Mama in a Listed event at Sandown last month. He looked to be labouring at halfway but came home well and looks as though he will appreciate stepping up in trip. (op 4/1 tchd 6/1)
City Of Tribes(IRE), a stylish maiden winner here earlier in the season, was having his first outing since an unplaced run in the Norfolk Stakes at Royal Ascot. He was always close to the pace and kept on under pressure without quite getting on terms with the leaders. (op 7/2 tchd 100/30)
Drayton(IRE), a dual Listed winner over this trip, looked to have an excellent chance following good runs in defeat in both the Railway and Phoenix Stakes. He was disputing the lead from the outset but was starting to struggle nearing the final furlong. He was not at his best here and was possibly feeling the effects of his run behind Holy Roman Emperor at the Curragh ten days ago. (op 4/6 tchd 4/5)
Divert(IRE) finished just half a length off the winner last time out, emphasising the progress made by that rival in the intervening period. She should be able to make her mark when dropping down in grade.

4749a IRISH STALLION FARMS EUROPEAN BREEDERS FUND FAIRY BRIDGE STKS (LISTED RACE) (FILLIES) 7f 100y

6:35 (6:37) 3-Y-0+ **£31,427** (£9,220; £4,393; £1,496)

RPR

1 **Modeeroch (IRE)**[26] 3967 3-8-12 103........................ KJManning 5 105
(J S Bolger, Ire) *sn settled in mid-div: 5th appr st: rdn to go mod 2nd fr 1 1/2f out: r.o wl fnl f to ld fnl stride* **6/1**[3]

2 *shd* **Cheyenne Star (IRE)**[4] 4637 3-8-12 90........................ PJSmullen 9 105
(Ms F M Crowley, Ire) *mid-div: 6th appr st: rdn to cl and ld over 1 1/2f out: sn clr: reduced ld ins fnl f and hdd last stride* **6/1**[3]

3 *1 3/4* **Ugo Fire (IRE)**[47] 3322 3-9-3 102........................ DPMcDonogh 13 106
(Kevin Prendergast, Ire) *chsd ldrs: clsr in 3rd appr st: rdn to chal fr 2f out: no imp and kpt on same pce fr over 1f out* **8/1**

4 *2 1/2* **Ardbrae Lady**[8] 4502 3-8-12 105........................ WMLordan 6 96
(Joseph G Murphy, Ire) *rr of mid-div: dropped to 12th bef st: rdn to go mod 7th 1f out: kpt on wl wout threatening* **7/2**[1]

5 *3/4* **Anna Karenina (IRE)**[21] 4093 3-8-12 86........................ KFallon 12 94
(David Wachman, Ire) *mid-div: 9th bef st: rdn to go mod 6th 1f out: kpt on wout threatening* **7/1**

6 *1/2* **Dani's Girl (IRE)**[21] 4093 3-8-12 82........................ DMGrant 8 93
(P A Fahy, Ire) *prom: rdn to chal 2f out: no imp u.p and kpt on same pce fr over 1f out* **12/1**

7 *1 1/4* **Set Fire (IRE)**[15] 4272 3-8-12 88........................(b) JMurtagh 11 91
(M Halford, Ire) *cl up: led bef 1/2-way: strly pressed and hdd under 2f out: sn no imp: kpt on same pce* **14/1**

8 3 ½ **Amourallis (IRE)**[18] 4187 5-9-3 86 CDHayes 7 83
(H Rogers, Ire) *towards rr: hdwy into 8th bef st: no imp u.p and kpt on same pce fr under 2f out* **33/1**

9 *shd* **Noelani (IRE)**[39] 3572 4-9-8 105 FMBerry 4 88
(John M Oxx, Ire) *cl up: 5th appr st: sn no imp u.p* **5/1**[2]

10 *2* **That's Hot (IRE)**[26] 3967 3-8-12 96 JAHeffernan 1 79
(G M Lyons, Ire) *towards rr: no imp u.p st* **10/1**

11 *2 ½* **Homegrown (IRE)**[109] 1521 5-9-3 102 RMBurke 10 74
(Patrick Tallis, Ire) *sn led: hdd bef 1/2-way: remained cl up: no ex u.p st* **20/1**

12 *1 ¾* **Sweet Afton (IRE)**[12] 4345 3-8-12 95 WSupple 3 70
(Eamon Tyrrell, Ire) *mid-div: lost pl and no imp u.p fr bef st* **10/1**

13 *1 ¾* **Delphie Queen (IRE)**[53] 3125 5-9-3 85 RPCleary 2 66
(M Halford, Ire) *dwlt: a bhd* **50/1**

1m 32.8s
WFA 3 from 4yo+ 5lb **13** Ran SP% **133.3**
CSF £45.20 TOTE £7.10: £2.50, £3.40, £2.80; DF 122.20.
Owner Ballylinch Stud **Bred** Ballylinch Stud **Trained** Coolcullen, Co Carlow
■ Stewards' Enquiry : K J Manning caution: used whip with excessive frequency

NOTEBOOK
Modeeroch(IRE), who had run several fine races in defeat this season, including when second to Queen Cleopatra in a Group 3 at Leopardstown in May and when third behind Mustameet and Ace in the International Stakes at the Curragh last month, was registering her first victory since taking last year's Tyros Stakes. Settled in midfield, she launched her challenge off the final bend and ran on strongly under pressure to grab the lead on the line. The Concorde Stakes back here in October is a possible target and trainer Jim Bolger indicated that his charge could also go on her travels. (op 4/1)
Cheyenne Star(IRE) was making a quick reappearance and was stepping up in grade after winning a six-furlong fillies' handicap at Leopardstown on Sunday. She looked as though she might have done enough for victory when going clear with over a furlong to run and she came up just short. On this evidence she should not have any trouble making her mark at this level. (op 5/1)
Ugo Fire(IRE) produced a solid effort in third and ran to a similar level with the winner as when contesting the Brownstown Stakes at Leopardstown last month. A Group 3 winner last season and also Group 1-placed, she looks capable of further Stakes race success. (op 7/1)
Ardbrae Lady, who has run a number of good races at Stakes level, could never quite land a telling blow. She may be better over a longer trip and deserves to gain a black-type success. (op 4/1)
Anna Karenina(IRE) was having her first run at this level and acquitted herself quite well, improving on the form of her second in a handicap at Galway. A black-type placing may be within her reach. (op 6/1)
Dani's Girl(IRE), who won a Galway handicap off 75 last time, ran respectably having been up with the pace from early on. She has improved with every run lately and further progress could not be ruled out. (op 12/1 tchd 10/1)
Set Fire(IRE) was another to race prominently but she could do no more from early in the straight. (op 10/1)
Noelani(IRE) was well below her best. She was a close second in the Minstrel Stakes last time but could not match that form and is capable of much better. (op 4/1 tchd 11/2)

4748 - 4752a (Foreign Racing) - See Raceform Interactive

4624 BATH (L-H)
Friday, August 25

OFFICIAL GOING: Good to firm
Wind: Almost nil Weather: Showers

4753 BATH ALES HOP POLE MAIDEN AUCTION STKS 5f 161y
5:30 (5:30) (Class 5) 2-Y-O **£3,886** (£1,156; £577; £288) **Stalls** Low

Form RPR

4005 **1** **Mac Gille Eoin**[23] 4043 2-8-8 61 ChrisCatlin 4 65
(J Gallagher) *hld up: rdn and hdwy whn swtchd rt over 2f out: led 1f out: rdn out* **25/1**

3 **2** *½* **Mr Loire**[29] 3861 2-8-12 RichardKingscote(3) 7 70
(R Charlton) *hld up in mid-div: rdn over 2f out: hdwy on outside over 1f out: r.o ins fnl f* **7/4**[1]

5220 **3** *2* **Drifting Gold**[11] 4427 2-8-3 71 JimmyQuinn 8 52
(C G Cox) *bhd: hrd rdn 3f out: hdwy over 1f out: kpt on ins fnl f* **11/4**[2]

03 **4** *¾* **Wachiwi (IRE)**[9] 4485 2-8-8 FergusSweeney 5 54
(A P Jarvis) *a.p: rdn 3f out: ev ch 1f out: one pce* **14/1**

0423 **5** *1 ¼* **Piccolena Boy**[32] 3799 2-8-9 73 JimCrowley 3 51
(P Winkworth) *led: rdn 2f out: hdd 1f out: wknd ins fnl f* **3/1**[3]

650 **6** *hd* **Ambrosiano**[28] 3892 2-8-13 RichardThomas 2 54
(Miss E C Lavelle) *sn chsng ldrs: rdn over 2f out: edgd lft jst ins fnl f: no imp* **12/1**

0 **7** *½* **Golan Way**[19] 4177 2-8-12 DavidKinsella 9 51
(I A Wood) *bhd: rdn over 2f out: sme late prog* **20/1**

60 **8** *2* **Back In The Red (IRE)**[11] 4421 2-8-9 KevinGhunowa(5) 1 47
(M Wellings) *w ldr: rdn over 2f out: wkng whn hmpd on ins jst ins fnl f* **33/1**

9 *2 ½* **Georges Pride** 2-8-10 ow2 PhillipMakin 6 34
(J M Bradley) *hld up: rdn over 2f out: sn bhd* **33/1**

10 *18* **Meerlust** 2-8-3 MatthewHenry 10 —
(E F Vaughan) *a in rr* **33/1**

1m 10.65s (-0.55) **Going Correction** -0.20s/f (Firm) **10** Ran SP% **119.8**
Speed ratings (Par 94):95,94,91,90,89 88,88,85,82,58
CSF £68.17 TOTE £23.90: £5.30, £1.40, £1.20; EX 186.10.
Owner M C S D Racing Partnership **Bred** M C S D Racing Ltd **Trained** Chastleton, Oxon

FOCUS
A moderate juvenile maiden.

NOTEBOOK
Mac Gille Eoin, who had looked well exposed in similar events, was finally getting his head in front and showed improved form. Officially rated 61, he has to prove this was no fluke, but he deserves a chance to do so.
Mr Loire, who made a pleasing debut at the course last month, finished well down the outside and there may be a small contest waiting for him somewhere. He needs one more outing to be eligible for nurseries. (op 2-1 tchd 9-4)
Drifting Gold, another fairly well-exposed type, could not quicken under pressure and was slightly disappointing. She may require a bit further. (tchd 5-2)
Wachiwi(IRE) did not seem inconvenienced by this step up in trip and is now qualified for nurseries. (tchd 12-1)
Piccolena Boy looked to set the standard, but he failed to last out having made the running and was most disappointing. He may be regressing. (tchd 4-1)
Golan Way Official explanation: jockey said colt was unsuited by the good to firm ground
Back In The Red(IRE) Official explanation: jockey said colt suffered interference in running

4754 BATH ALES SALAMANDER/E.B.F. MAIDEN FILLIES' STKS 5f 11y
6:00 (6:06) (Class 5) 2-Y-O **£3,886** (£1,156; £577; £288) **Stalls** Low

Form RPR

1 **Mystery Ocean** 2-9-0 FergusSweeney 7 75
(R M Beckett) *hld up: smooth hdwy over 1f out: shkn up to ld ins fnl f: pushed out* **33/1**

26 **2** *2* **Centreboard (USA)**[32] 3796 2-9-0 JimmyQuinn 6 68
(R Charlton) *trckd ldrs: gng wl: nt clr run over 1f out: swtchd rt ins fnl f: r.o* **7/2**[2]

3324 **3** *¾* **Isobel Rose (IRE)**[69] 2638 2-9-0 76 MatthewHenry 10 65
(E A L Dunlop) *a.p: rdn to ld over 1f out: hdd and nt qckn ins fnl f* **3/1**[1]

45 **4** *½* **Russian Gift (IRE)**[18] 4207 2-8-11 AdamKirby(3) 5 63
(C G Cox) *led: rdn 2f out: hdd over 1f out: no ex ins fnl f* **5/1**

0 **5** *1 ¼* **Ken's Girl**[53] 3148 2-9-0 JimCrowley 4 59
(W S Kittow) *hld up: rdn over 2f out: hdwy over 1f out: n.m.r briefly ins fnl f: nt qckn* **50/1**

04 **6** *¾* **What A Treasure (IRE)**[14] 4323 2-9-0 HayleyTurner 1 56
(L M Cumani) *hld up: effrt on ins jst over 1f out: nvr able to chal* **10/1**

7 *1* **Contentious (IRE)** 2-8-11 RichardKingscote(3) 3 53
(D M Simcock) *w ldr: rdn and ev ch wl over 1f out: wkng whn hmpd on rail ins fnl f* **4/1**[3]

8 *4* **Our Mona (USA)** 2-9-0 ChrisCatlin 8 38
(M R Channon) *a bhd* **5/1**

62.46 secs (-0.04) **Going Correction** -0.20s/f (Firm) **8** Ran SP% **114.5**
Speed ratings (Par 91):92,88,87,86,84 83,82,75
CSF £145.71 TOTE £18.40: £4.00, £1.40, £1.90; EX 142.40.
Owner Turf Club 2004 **Bred** Mill House Stud **Trained** Whitsbury, Hants

FOCUS
An average maiden, but the the shock debut winner Mystery Ocean beat three fillies with previous form and can improve on the bare form.

NOTEBOOK
Mystery Ocean, who holds an engagement in the Redcar Two-Year-Old Trophy, made a highly-promising winning debut, overcoming inexperience and ultimately winning with a fair bit in hand. She gave the impression there was more to come and that another furlong would hold absolutely no terrors as she was going away at the line. Connections stated she was in the valuable Racecall Trophy at Redcar later in the autumn and she could well end up going there. (op 25-1)
Centreboard(USA) did not get the greatest of runs but it made no difference as she would not have beaten the winner in any case. She is now eligible for nurseries but with 76-rated Isobel Rose back in third, she may not get in lightly. (op 11-4 tchd 4-1)
Isobel Rose(IRE) has had a few chances now and her rating looks a bit prohibitive as far as nurseries are concerned. (op 5-2 tchd 7-2)
Russian Gift(IRE) is now qualified for nurseries and can be expected to fare a lot better in that sphere. (op 8-1)
Ken's Girl stepped up on her debut effort and was arguably unlcuky not to get a little closer. She will be qualified for nurseries after one more run. (tchd 25-1)
What A Treasure(IRE) made some late headway and can now get into nurseries. She wants further on this evidence. (tchd 17-2)
Contentious(IRE) ran a little better than her finishing position suggests on this racecourse debut, showing good speed, and she can find a small race is finding a little improvement. (op 5-1 tchd 7-2)
Our Mona(USA), who is related to some useful performers, was struggling from the word go, but the combination of a rise in distance and further experience should see her improve. (op 11-1)

4755 BATH ALES WILD HARE ORGANIC ALE (S) STKS 1m 3f 144y
6:30 (6:31) (Class 6) 3-4-Y-O **£2,266** (£674; £337; £168) **Stalls** Low

Form RPR

2423 **1** **Guadiana (GER)**[15] 4282 4-9-2 44 (v) FrancisNorton 13 49+
(A W Carroll) *bhd: rdn over 3f out: swtchd rt and hdwy over 2f out: led 1f out: drew clr: eased towards fin* **10/3**[1]

0340 **2** *3* **Glory Be (ITY)**[12] 4404 4-9-2 40 (p) JimmyQuinn 3 44
(J L Spearing) *hld up in tch: rdn 3f out: styd on u.p to take 2nd post* **8/1**

036 **3** *shd* **Agilete**[15] 4307 4-9-7 43 MatthewHenry 4 49
(J R Boyle) *hld up and bhd: gd hdwy on ins 3f out: rdn over 1f out: one pce* **9/2**[3]

0004 **4** *nk* **Dream Witness (FR)**[15] 4280 3-8-6 50 HayleyTurner 12 43
(W R Muir) *hld up: hdwy 7f out: led over 2f out: rdn and hdd 1f out: one pce* **13/2**

000 **5** *3 ½* **Primed Up (IRE)**[20] 4139 4-9-9 50 (b) AdamKirby(3) 9 48
(R M Beckett) *hld up and bhd: hdwy on outside 4f out: rdn and ev ch 4f out: wknd ins fnl f* **11/1**

2500 **6** *5* **Bint Il Sultan (IRE)**[12] 4404 4-9-2 41 ChrisCatlin 5 30
(W M Brisbourne) *hld up in mid-div: rdn and hdwy over 2f out: wknd over 1f out* **16/1**

0000 **7** *shd* **Grandos (IRE)**[15] 4285 4-9-4 45 RichardKingscote(3) 15 35
(Karen George) *hld up in mid-div: rdn over 3f out: hdwy over 2f out: wknd over 1f out* **33/1**

0522 **8** *1 ¼* **Shaheer (IRE)**[15] 4280 4-9-12 53 (v[1]) JimCrowley 2 38
(J Gallagher) *hld up in tch: rdn over 2f out: sn wknd* **7/2**[2]

0000 **9** *6* **Romanova (IRE)**[15] 4289 4-9-2 45 (b) RichardThomas 7 18
(Dr J R J Naylor) *t.k.h: prom: slipped on bnd over 4f out: led 3f out: sn hdd: rdn & wknd 2f out* **20/1**

0060 **10** *6* **Ello Lucky (IRE)**[5] 4627 4-9-2 34 PhillipMakin 1 8
(J M Bradley) *hld up in tch: rdn and wknd over 2f out* **33/1**

0000 **11** *5* **Silk Purse**[15] 4289 3-8-6 50 (b[1]) LPKeniry 10 —
(M Madgwick) *s.s: a bhd* **33/1**

0000 **12** *13* **Woolsey**[15] 4297 3-8-11 54 FergusSweeney 11 —
(M Blanshard) *prom: rdn and ev ch 3f out: wknd qckly* **12/1**

000- **13** *1* **Quebecois**[431] 2764 3-8-11 25 RobertHavlin 8 —
(P D Evans) *hld up in tch: lost pl after 2f: bhd fnl 5f* **66/1**

0-00 **14** *27* **Bold Brownie**[44] 3411 4-9-2 31 (p) AdrianMcCarthy 6 —
(Miss Z C Davison) *led: rdn and hdd 3f out: wknd qckly over 2f out: t.o* **66/1**

2m 30.75s (0.45) **Going Correction** +0.075s/f (Good)
WFA 3 from 4yo 10lb **14** Ran SP% **126.4**
Speed ratings (Par 101):101,99,98,98,96 93,93,92,88,84 80,72,71,53
CSF £30.36 TOTE £5.00: £1.80, £2.30, £2.20; EX 46.80.The winner was bought in for 5,000gns. Dream Witness was claimed by B. W. Duke for £6,000.
Owner The Gumley Gropers **Bred** F Oettingen-Wallerstein **Trained** Cropthorne, Worcs

FOCUS
A poor seller, but the winner looked back to her best and the placed horses ran to recent form.
Woolsey Official explanation: jockey said gelding had no more to give

The Form Book, Raceform Ltd, Compton, RG20 6NL

4756 BATH ALES SPA H'CAP — 5f 11y
7:00 (7:02) (Class 5) (0-70,71) 3-Y-O £4,210 (£1,252; £625; £312) Stalls Low

Form				RPR
2333	1		**Jucebabe**[8] 4532 3-8-6 **54**........(p) FrancisNorton 12 (J L Spearing) *a.p: rdn wl over 1f out: led ins fnl f: r.o* **3/1**[1]	65
1302	2	1	**Safari Mischief**[8] 4532 3-9-4 **66**........ JimCrowley 2 (P Winkworth) *chsd ldr: rdn to ld 1f out: hdd ins fnl f: nt qckn cl home* **5/1**[3]	73
040	3	1 ¼	**Supreme Kiss**[12] 4398 3-8-6 **57**........ RichardKingscote(3) 3 (Miss B Sanders) *s.i.s: bhd tl rdn and hdwy on ins over 1f out: hld whn n.m.r towards fin* **16/1**	62+
4125	4	hd	**Gwilym (GER)**[8] 4532 3-9-6 **68**........ RobertHavlin 9 (D Haydn Jones) *hld up: hdwy over 2f out: rdn over 1f out: kpt on towards fin* **9/2**[2]	70
6030	5	½	**Matterofact (IRE)**[20] 4164 3-8-13 **64**........ AdamKirby(3) 14 (Mrs P N Dutfield) *led: rdn and hdd 1f out: one pce* **13/2**	64
0045	6	1	**Twinned (IRE)**[29] 3863 3-8-2 **50**........ JimmyQuinn 7 (Karen George) *bhd: rdn 2f out: hdwy over 1f out: no imp fnl f* **16/1**	46
0001	7	½	**Two Acres (IRE)**[31] 3821 3-8-8 **56**........ FergusSweeney 5 (A G Newcombe) *hld up: hdwy on outside 2f out: sn rdn: fdd ins fnl f* **13/2**	51
00-0	8	2	**Madam Patti**[28] 3897 3-8-6 **54** ow1........ LPKeniry 4 (B Palling) *chsd ldrs: rdn 2f out: wknd jst over 1f out* **33/1**	41
0000	9	1 ¾	**Bermuda Beauty (IRE)**[39] 3595 3-7-10 **51** oh9 ow1... PietroRomeo(7) 1 (J M Bradley) *a bhd* **50/1**	32
4U02	10	1	**Sounds Simla (IRE)**[7] 4546 3-8-12 **60**........ AdrianMcCarthy 11 (R A Harris) *chsd ldrs: rdn over 2f out: wknd over 1f out* **7/1**	37
30-0	11	5	**Lady Synthia**[23] 4052 3-8-12 **60**........ ChrisCatlin 8 (B Palling) *prom over 2f* **50/1**	19

61.40 secs (-1.10) **Going Correction** -0.20s/f (Firm) **11 Ran SP% 117.6**
Speed ratings (Par 100):100,98,96,96,95 93,92,89,86,85 77
CSF £17.61 CT £207.50 TOTE £3.30: £1.70, £2.10, £4.60; EX 19.30.
Owner G M Eales **Bred** G M Eales **Trained** Kinnersley, Worcs

FOCUS
A typically trappy little sprint handicap, but sound enough form, with the first two close to their recent Sandown form.

4757 BATH ALES GEM H'CAP — 1m 5y
7:30 (7:30) (Class 6) (0-65,65) 3-Y-O £2,849 (£847; £423; £211) Stalls Low

Form				RPR
0044	1		**Under Fire (IRE)**[23] 4050 3-8-4 **48**........ FrancisNorton 9 (A W Carroll) *led early: w ldr: rdn to ld jst over 2f out: drvn out* **14/1**	53
2263	2	1	**High Octave (IRE)**[17] 4225 3-9-4 **65**........ AdamKirby(3) 2 (B G Powell) *hld up in mid-div: rdn and hdwy whn swtchd rt 1f out: r.o to take 2nd last strides* **13/2**	68
0002	3	hd	**Light Dreams**[16] 4257 3-9-6 **64**........(v) JimmyQuinn 14 (W J Knight) *a.p: rdn and ev ch over 1f out: nt qckn ins fnl f* **5/1**[3]	66
02-0	4	½	**Royle Dancer**[9] 4470 3-8-11 **62**........ RussellKennemore(7) 13 (R Hollinshead) *a.p: rdn 3f out: kpt on same pce fnl f* **25/1**	63
3052	5	1 ¼	**Salvestro**[16] 4243 3-9-3 **61**........ JimCrowley 4 (Mrs A J Perrett) *plld hrd: sn mid-div: hdwy 2f out: nt clr run over 1f out: kpt on ins fnl f* **13/2**	61+
6414	6	½	**Dado Mush**[23] 4052 3-9-4 **62**........ PhillipMakin 11 (T T Clement) *in rr: rdn 2f out: hdwy fnl f: nt rch ldrs* **16/1**	59
00-4	7	nk	**Bowl Of Cherries**[6] 4585 3-8-4 **48**........ DavidKinsella 5 (I A Wood) *a.p: rdn over 2f out: fdd fnl f* **18/1**	44
6-00	8	½	**Mayden Dawn**[16] 4245 3-8-11 **55**........ AdrianMcCarthy 1 (Miss E C Lavelle) *sn led: hdd jst over 2f out: wknd ins fnl f* **66/1**	50
-600	9	½	**Dancing Melody**[88] 2065 3-8-10 **54**........ RichardThomas 16 (J A Geake) *hld up in mid-div: lost pl 5f out: n.d after* **12/1**	48
1465	10	nk	**Scroll**[12] 4395 3-9-0 **65**........(v) JPFeatherstone(7) 7 (P Howling) *t.k.h in mid-div: rdn an hdwy over 2f out: wknd jst over 1f out* **20/1**	58
1653	11	nk	**Murrumbidgee (IRE)**[16] 4243 3-8-12 **63**........ PatrickHills(7) 6 (J W Hills) *a bhd* **4/1**[1]	56
6262	12	1	**Crimson Flame (IRE)**[8] 4524 3-9-2 **60**........ ChrisCatlin 10 (M R Channon) *a bhd* **9/2**[2]	50
1061	13	12	**Katie Lawson (IRE)**[55] 3099 3-9-4 **62**........(v) RobertHavlin 8 (D Haydn Jones) *hld up in mid-div: rdn over 3f out: bhd fnl 2f* **14/1**	25

1m 41.47s (0.37) **Going Correction** +0.075s/f (Good) **13 Ran SP% 123.8**
Speed ratings (Par 98):101,100,99,99,98 97,97,96,96,95 95,94,82
CSF £104.21 CT £549.02 TOTE £16.20: £3.60, £2.70, £2.20; EX 144.30.
Owner Marita Bayley and Trevor Turner **Bred** Mrs M Bayley **Trained** Cropthorne, Worcs

FOCUS
Pretty ordinary form, and by no means rock-solid, with several of those relatively close-up a bit shaky.

4758 BATH ALES BARNSTORMER H'CAP — 1m 5f 22y
8:00 (8:00) (Class 5) (0-70,66) 3-Y-O £3,886 (£1,156; £577; £288) Stalls High

Form				RPR
-063	1		**Wings Of Dawn**[53] 3145 3-8-6 **51**........ JimmyQuinn 6 (M P Tregoning) *a.p: rdn 3f out: led jst over 1f out: all out* **7/2**[2]	58
4220	2	½	**Phone In**[18] 4204 3-9-4 **63**........ PhillipMakin 4 (R Brotherton) *set slow pce: rdn over 2f out: hdd jst over 1f out: r.o* **9/1**	69
2021	3	1 ½	**Squirtle (IRE)**[13] 4362 3-9-7 **66**........ ChrisCatlin 1 (W M Brisbourne) *hld up in tch: rdn over 4f out: styd on same pce fnl f* **5/2**[1]	70
-520	4	nk	**Irish Whispers (IRE)**[16] 4245 3-8-11 **59**........ AdamKirby(3) 10 (B G Powell) *chsd ldr: rdn over 2f out: ev ch over 1f out: no ex ins fnl f* **8/1**	62
5114	5	7	**Joy In The Guild (IRE)**[15] 4282 3-8-10 **55**........ FergusSweeney 5 (W S Kittow) *hld up in rr: hdwy over 2f out: sn rdn: edgd lft and wknd 1f out* **9/2**[3]	47
1310	6	2 ½	**Maidford (IRE)**[19] 4173 3-8-13 **58**........ RobertHavlin 3 (M Meade) *hld up in tch: rdn 2f out: wknd over 1f out* **10/1**	46
-002	7	3	**Gateland**[34] 3730 3-9-1 **60**........ FrancisNorton 9 (B J Llewellyn) *plld hrd in rr: rdn over 2f out: no rspnse* **6/1**	43
0000	8	½	**King's College (USA)**[56] 2352 3-8-1 **53** ow5........(v¹) JamieJones(7) 2 (P D Evans) *hld up towards rr: rdn over 2f out: sn struggling* **33/1**	36

2m 55.43s (3.93) **Going Correction** +0.075s/f (Good) **8 Ran SP% 116.4**
Speed ratings (Par 100):90,89,88,88,84 82,80,80
CSF £35.31 CT £92.13 TOTE £4.80: £2.10, £1.70, £1.30; EX 45.20 Place 6 £30.93, Place 5 £19.97..
Owner Lady Tennant **Bred** Lady Tennant **Trained** Lambourn, Berks

FOCUS
A moderate winning time for the grade and not many actually got competitive in this handicap, as the leaders dictated matters. Essentially weak form.

T/Plt: £28.20 to a £1 stake. Pool: £57,221.15. 1,479.05 winning tickets. T/Qpdt: £11.80 to a £1 stake. Pool: £4,491.05. 279.80 winning tickets. KH

4170 CHESTER (L-H)
Friday, August 25

OFFICIAL GOING: Good (good to firm places)
Wind: Light, across

4759 DAVID MCLEAN MAIDEN FILLIES' STKS — 1m 2f 75y
2:20 (2:20) (Class 5) 3-Y-O+ £4,048 (£1,204; £601; £300) Stalls High

Form				RPR
4430	1		**Thumpers Dream**[28] 3901 3-8-12 82........ RoystonFfrench 7 (H R A Cecil) *trckd ldrs: hdwy on inner and n.m.r over 2f out: qcknd to ld wl over 1f out: rdn clr and kpt on* **11/4**[2]	73
60	2	2	**Kalandara (IRE)**[28] 3901 3-8-12........ KerrinMcEvoy 5 (Sir Michael Stoute) *hld up: hdwy over 3f out: nt clr run over 2f out: swtchd rt and hdwy over 1f out: rdn to chse wnr ins last: no imp* **9/2**[3]	72+
46	3	1 ½	**Aryaamm (IRE)**[16] 4247 3-8-12........ PaulHanagan 4 (M A Jarvis) *trckd ldrs: unbalanced and lost pl bnd after 3f: sn in tch: effrt and nt clr run over 2f out: swtchd rt: rdn and one pce* **2/1**[1]	73+
05	4	3	**Gallileo Figaro (USA)**[14] 4330 3-8-9........ PatrickMathers(3) 2 (W M Brisbourne) *towards rr whn hmpd after 3f and sn bhd. hdwy 4f out: rdn along over 2f out: kpt on: nrst fin* **33/1**	61+
0230	5	1 ¼	**Tafiya**[23] 4040 3-8-12 70........ TPO'Shea 6 (G A Butler) *hld up: hdwy over 4f out: rdn to chse ldrs 2f out: sn btn* **6/1**	59
5346	6	5	**Macho Dancer (IRE)**[15] 4280 3-8-7 47........ AndrewMullen(5) 8 (K J Burke) *cl up: rdn along 3f out: drvn 2f out and sn wknd* **20/1**	49
0	7	5	**Gigi Glamor**[20] 4155 4-9-6........ DavidAllan 3 (W M Brisbourne) *a rr* **66/1**	40
040	8	2	**Shangazi (USA)**[77] 2406 3-8-12 65........ MichaelHills 1 (B W Hills) *led: rdn along 3f out: hdd wl over 1f out and wknd qckly* **6/1**	36
000-	9	33	**Nee Lemon Left**[293] 6258 4-9-6 35........ PaulQuinn 9 (M Mullineaux) *plld hrd: in tch: rdn along over 3f out and sn wknd* **150/1**	—

2m 10.74s (-2.40) **Going Correction** -0.20s/f (Firm)
WFA 3 from 4yo 8lb **9 Ran SP% 116.6**
Speed ratings (Par 100):101,99,98,95,94 90,86,85,58
CSF £15.35 TOTE £4.00: £1.40, £2.00, £1.20; EX 17.40.
Owner Mrs Ann Morris **Bred** Mrs A Morris **Trained** Newmarket, Suffolk

FOCUS
A modest maiden run at a fair tempo. The usual bunching occurred on the final bend, with the third the worst affected. Second, third and fourth all look capable of landing a race of some description.
Shangazi(USA) Official explanation: jockey said filly had no more to give

4760 GLOBAL TRAVEL H'CAP — 7f 2y
2:55 (2:56) (Class 3) (0-95,92) 3-Y-O **£9,463** (£2,832; £1,416; £708; £352) Stalls Low

Form				RPR
044	1		**Inter Vision (USA)**[66] 2732 6-9-11 **84**........ PaulHanagan 4 (A Dickman) *trckd ldrs: hdwy on inner over 1f out: rdn to ld ins last: drvn and jst hld on* **16/1**	96
210	2	hd	**Areyoutalkingtome**[22] 4082 3-10-0 **92**........ RoystonFfrench 15 (C A Cyzer) *hld up towards rr: hdwy over 2f out: swtchd outside and rdn over 1f out: styd on strly ins last: jst failed* **50/1**	102+
0112	3	1 ¼	**Scrummage**[30] 3852 3-8-10 **74**........(v) KerrinMcEvoy 3 (Sir Michael Stoute) *led: rdn and edgd rt over 1f out: drvn and hdd ins last: one pce* **2/1**[1]	80
1050	4	shd	**Dhaular Dhar (IRE)**[27] 3926 4-9-10 **83**........ DanielTudhope 7 (J S Goldie) *hld up towards rr: hdwy wl over 1f out: rdn and n.m.r ins last: styd on wl towards fin* **10/1**	91
1-00	5	½	**Ordnance Row**[24] 4029 3-9-11 **89**........ PatDobbs 2 (R Hannon) *midfield: hdwy over 2f out: rdn along over 1f out: kpt on ins last: nrst fin* **10/1**	94+
6025	6	¾	**Mezuzah**[20] 4153 6-9-2 **75**........ PaulMulrennan 1 (M W Easterby) *prom: rdn along 2f out: drvn and edgd rt over 1f out: kpt on same pce* **12/1**	80
0633	7	¾	**Roman Maze**[19] 4172 6-9-13 **86**........ DavidAllan 6 (W M Brisbourne) *chsd ldrs: pushed along 2f out: rdn over 1f out and grad wknd* **7/1**[3]	89
6200	8	¾	**Marshman (IRE)**[27] 3926 7-10-0 **87**........ PaulFessey 9 (M H Tompkins) *midfield: hdwy 3f out: rdn to chse ldrs wl over 1f out: wknd ins last* **16/1**	88
5650	9	nk	**Landucci**[16] 4241 5-9-3 **76**........(t) MichaelHills 5 (J W Hills) *s.i.s and bhd: hdwy over 2f out: sn rdn along and kpt on ins last: nt rch ldrs* **16/1**	76
60P2	10	hd	**Lord Of The East**[11] 4437 7-9-7 **83**........ PatrickMathers(3) 8 (I W McInnes) *prom: hdwy and cl up 3f out: rdn along 2f out: grad wknd* **33/1**	83
0506	11	nk	**Looks Could Kill (USA)**[13] 4378 4-9-5 **78**........ TPO'Shea 16 (E J Alston) *stdd and swtchd lft s: a rr* **28/1**	77
0005	12	2 ½	**Kenmore**[28] 3904 4-9-13 **86**........ TomEaves 12 (D Nicholls) *a rr* **9/1**	78+
0000	13	3 ½	**Tanforan**[13] 4378 4-8-12 **78**........ JamesReveley(7) 14 (K G Reveley) *midfield: pushed along 3f out: sn wknd* **50/1**	61
2210	14	5	**Chicken Soup**[14] 4325 4-9-7 **80**........ RobbieFitzpatrick 11 (T J Pitt) *in tch: pushed along over 3f out: wknd fnl 2f* **13/2**[2]	50

1m 24.88s (-3.59) **Going Correction** -0.20s/f (Firm)
WFA 3 from 4yo+ 5lb **14 Ran SP% 123.0**
Speed ratings (Par 107):112,111,110,110,109 108,107,107,106,106 106,103,99,93
CSF £676.61 CT £2347.91 TOTE £23.70: £6.30, £7.60, £1.40; EX 1134.50 Trifecta £633.50 Part won. Pool: £892.26 - 0.30 winning units..
Owner Mrs D Hodgkinson **Bred** W A Carl **Trained** Sandhutton, N Yorks

FOCUS
A fair handicap run at a good tempo - the winning time was decent and the form should prove solid.

NOTEBOOK
Inter Vision(USA), who was on his last-winning handicap mark, travelled well into the straight and found a nice gap open for him up the inside rail, which he took and gained enough of an advantage to just hold off the runner-up. He always goes well at Chester but this was his first success at seven furlongs.
Areyoutalkingtome flew home down the middle of the course but just had too much ground to make up. His draw did not help and probably cost him, as he had a clear run.
Scrummage tried to make all from his favourable draw but could not hold off the finishers. The time of the race was pretty quick, so he may have gone off a bit too fast in front and can be given another chance. (op 5-2 tchd 11-4)
Dhaular Dhar(IRE), who was unbeaten at the track before the race, met a tiny bit of interference off the final bend but appeared to have every chance. (op 9-1)

Ordnance Row, whose form with London Express as a two-year-old gave him every chance, missed the break from an advantageous draw, and was never really able to get into a challenging position during the early part of the race. He did well to finish as close as he did and looks sure to win more races. (op 12-1)
Mezuzah is a bit high in the weights on his winning form, and shaped accordingly. All of his wins have come on easy ground, so is one to watch for in the final months of the season if dropping down the handicap a few pounds.
Landucci ◆, trying a tongue tie for the first time, is back to a winning handicap mark and shaped better than his finishing position suggests. He did not get the clearest of runs throughout the race and was not given a hard time once his chance was gone. Brighton is where he does all of his winning, so will be of obvious interest if returning to that course soon.
Kenmore Official explanation: jockey said gelding never travelled
Chicken Soup Official explanation: jockey said gelding never travelled

4761 SURRENDA-LINK NURSERY 7f 2y
3:30 (3:30) (Class 3) 2-Y-O £8,743 (£2,601; £1,300; £649) Stalls Low

Form RPR
202 1 **Orpen Prince (IRE)**[58] 2972 2-8-0 70 AndrewMullen(5) 6 72
(K A Ryan) *trckd ldr: effrt 2f out and sn pushed along: rdn to chal over 1f out: led wl ins last: drvn and kpt on* 9/2[3]
0661 2 ½ **Suhayl Star (IRE)**[21] 4115 2-8-6 71 KerrinMcEvoy 7 72
(W J Musson) *set stdy pce: qcknd 2f out: rdn over 1f out: hdd wl ins last: kpt on* 10/1
6132 3 shd **Voodoo Moon**[13] 4377 2-9-3 82 RoystonFfrench 1 82
(M Johnston) *chsd ldrs: rdn along 2f out: swtchd lft and drvn ins last: kpt on* 5/2[1]
5133 4 ¾ **Part Timer (IRE)**[20] 4130 2-9-7 86 TPO'Shea 4 84
(M R Channon) *trckd ldrs: hdwy on outer 2f out: rdn to chal ins last and ev ch tl no ex towards fin* 11/2
4065 5 1½ **Cheshire Prince**[19] 4170 2-7-12 63 oh2 PaulQuinn 2 62+
(W M Brisbourne) *hld up: hdwy 2f out: pushed along and styng on along inner whn hmpd ins last: nt rcvr* 16/1
431 6 2½ **Coconut Queen (IRE)**[17] 4228 2-8-7 72 PaulFessey 3 60
(Mrs A Duffield) *hld up: rdn along over 2f out: n.d* 6/1
010 7 hd **Addictive**[20] 4146 2-8-6 71 DavidAllan 5 59
(S C Williams) *a rr* 10/3[2]
1m 26.46s (-2.01) **Going Correction** -0.20s/f (Firm) 7 Ran SP% 114.5
Speed ratings (Par 98):103,102,102,101,99 96,96
CSF £46.89 TOTE £6.10: £2.80, £5.40; EX 47.10.
Owner J Nattrass **Bred** Lodge Park Stud **Trained** Hambleton, N Yorks
■ Stewards' Enquiry : Royston Ffrench three-day ban: careless riding (Sep 5-7)

FOCUS
Just a fair nursery. The winner is improving and saw the trip out well on his first try at it, while the runner-up might have been slightly flattered due to a fine ride by his jockey.

NOTEBOOK
Orpen Prince(IRE) tracked the early leader and was produced with a winning effort inside the final furlong. Trying seven furlongs for the first time and making his handicap debut, he should continue to progress and has scope for improvement. (tchd 4-1 in a place)
Suhayl Star(IRE), bought for 10,000gns after winning a claimer last time, looked like hanging on up the straight but could not resist the late challenge of Orpen Prince. He was given a good ride and might be a touch flattered by the result. (op 9-1 tchd 8-1)
Voodoo Moon was not able to make best use of his stall one position and was under serious pressure early in the race. To his credit, he did stay on but gives the impression that he is a shade high in the weights. (op 7-2)
Part Timer(IRE) moved nicely during the race and made his challenge wide off the bend. He did not find a great deal off the bridle and probably did not see out the seven furlong trip, even around a tight track like Chester. (tchd 5-1 and 6-1)
Cheshire Prince, who was fairly keen at the rear of the field early in the race, did not get the best of runs when making his challenge but appeared to run close to his best. He looks capable of picking up more races at two. (op 14-1 tchd 12-1)
Coconut Queen(IRE) Official explanation: jockey said filly hung right-handed
Addictive was done no favours rounding the bend - she was knocked sideways as Coconut Queen moved away from the rail - and was never sighted with a winning chance afterwards. It is too soon to write her off. Official explanation: jockey said filly suffered interference in running and never travelled thereafter (op 7-2 tchd 4-1)

4762 EUROPEAN BREEDERS FUND COMBERMERE FILLIES' CONDITIONS STKS 6f 18y
4:05 (4:05) (Class 2) 2-Y-O £12,618 (£3,776; £1,888; £944; £470) Stalls Low

Form RPR
2413 1 **Pretty Majestic (IRE)**[20] 4146 2-8-12 91 TPO'Shea 6 85
(M R Channon) *dwlt: hld up in rr: hdwy 2f out: rdn over 1f out: styd on to ld ins last: drvn out* 13/8[2]
1 2 2 **Blue Rocket (IRE)**[14] 4323 2-9-1 RobbieFitzpatrick 5 82
(T J Pitt) *trckd ldrs: hdwy over 2f out: rdn to ld over 1f out: drvn and hdd ins last: one pce* 5/4[1]
3 1 **Whazzis** 2-8-9 KerrinMcEvoy 7 73
(W J Haggas) *hld up on outer: effrt wl over 1f out: kpt on ins last: nrst fin* 10/1
0310 4 1¼ **Ensign's Trick**[19] 4170 2-8-12 73 DavidAllan 3 72
(W M Brisbourne) *cl up: led over 2f out: sn rdn: hdd over 1f out and grad wknd* 50/1
2431 5 1½ **Yerevan**[11] 4427 2-9-1 71 PaulHanagan 4 71
(R T Phillips) *chsd ldrs: rdn along over 2f out: sn one pce* 16/1
2231 6 3 **Crystal Gazer (FR)**[63] 2816 2-9-1 80 PatDobbs 1 62
(R Hannon) *chsd ldrs: rdn along 2f out: sn wknd* 8/1[3]
0050 7 3½ **Silly Gilly (IRE)**[6] 4608 2-8-12 PaulQuinn 2 48
(A Berry) *led: rdn along and hdd over 2f out: sn wknd* 100/1
1m 14.44s (-1.21) **Going Correction** -0.20s/f (Firm) 7 Ran SP% 111.6
Speed ratings (Par 97):100,97,96,94,92 88,83
CSF £3.76 TOTE £2.60: £1.50, £1.50; EX 4.20.
Owner Jaber Abdullah **Bred** Peter Gibbons And Dermot Forde **Trained** West Ilsley, Berks

FOCUS
A decent race that produced a visually impressive winner. Pretty Majestic looks sure to go on to better things, while Blue Rocket had little chance trying to give weight away. Whazzis shaped nicely and will be wiser next time. Ensign's Trick is the only concern about the value of the form.

NOTEBOOK
Pretty Majestic(IRE) ◆ was very impressive despite missing the break badly. She powered down the home straight to win in taking style, justifying her connections high opinion of her - she holds a Group 1 entry. Costing very little at the sales, she looks a shrewd purchase and can win again. (op 2-1)
Blue Rocket(IRE) had the run of the race and was not good enough - the weight concession had little bearing on the final result. The winner looks a smart individual, so can be given another chance to confirm her debut promise. (op Evens tchd 11-8 and 6-4 in a place)
Whazzis was given a nice introductory ride and will be much wiser next time. She was subject of encouraging gallops reports before the race and is bred to make a two-year-old, so should go very close next time if kept to a realistic level. (op 8-1 tchd 15-2)
Ensign's Trick, who is relatively exposed, had plenty to find on official figures and was predictably not good enough, although she was far from disgraced. Her only victory was in selling company - where she was retained for 20,000gns - so the effort was not a bad one considering the distance she was beaten.
Yerevan, who finished in front of Ensign's Trick last time, will find easier tasks in the future. She is a consistent sort and will be suited by a lesser grade again.
Crystal Gazer(FR) had every chance and failed to pick up when asked to quicken, suggesting the Handicapper has her about right already. (tchd 9-1 and 10-1 in a place)

4763 ALEXANDER EVENTS H'CAP 1m 2f 75y
4:40 (4:40) (Class 3) (0-90,86) 3-Y-O £9,348 (£2,799; £1,399; £700; £349; £175) Stalls High

Form RPR
1-12 1 **Heaven Knows**[69] 2654 3-9-7 86 MichaelHills 2 94+
(W J Haggas) *trckd ldrs: pushed along 3f out: swtchd rt 2f out: rdn and qcknd to ld ins last: r.o* 5/6[1]
4402 2 1½ **Bin Rahy (IRE)**[26] 3984 3-9-4 83 TPO'Shea 4 88
(M R Channon) *led: rdn along over 2f out: drvn and hdd ins last: kpt on same pce* 8/1[3]
3221 3 ½ **O'Tara (IRE)**[16] 4261 3-9-1 80 PaulFessey 5 84
(M H Tompkins) *keen: cl up: effrt 2f out: sn rdn and ev ch tl no ex ins last* 11/1
-603 4 1¾ **Punta Galera (IRE)**[44] 3401 3-9-7 86 PatDobbs 8 87
(R Hannon) *trckd ldrs: hdwy on outer 4f out: rdn 2f out and kpt on same pce* 16/1
0413 5 shd **Tawaafud**[26] 3984 3-8-10 75 RoystonFfrench 3 76
(B W Hills) *hld up: effrt on inenr 3f out: sn rdn along: edgd lft and wknd wl over 1f out* 9/1
-611 6 hd **Strawberry Lolly**[16] 4244 3-9-4 83 KerrinMcEvoy 6 83
(Sir Michael Stoute) *in tch: effrt 3f out: rdn along and n.m.r 2f out: sn one pce* 4/1[2]
0630 7 1¼ **Categorical**[13] 4378 3-8-10 75 TomEaves 1 73
(K G Reveley) *hld up: a rr* 33/1
2m 11.6s (-1.54) **Going Correction** -0.20s/f (Firm) 7 Ran SP% 112.8
Speed ratings (Par 104):98,96,96,95,94 94,93
CSF £8.15 CT £42.74 TOTE £1.90: £1.20, £4.20; EX 9.00.
Owner B Haggas **Bred** Southcourt Stud **Trained** Newmarket, Suffolk

FOCUS
A good handicap won by a progressive sort. The form is not that strong but should work out, with runner-up and fifth to recent form.

NOTEBOOK
Heaven Knows ◆, returning from a short break, took a while to warm to his task but did the job nicely by the end of the race. He did not seem ideally suited by the track and can rate a bit higher than the bare result. (op 5-4)
Bin Rahy(IRE) led the field early but did not seem fully at home on the track, tending to hang slightly away from the rail at different stages of the race. He seemed to perfom up to his best and is a decent marker for the form. (op 10-1)
O'Tara(IRE) tried to go with the winner down the home straight, but was always fighting a losing battle. He still looks progressive and is one to consider next time. (op 12-1)
Punta Galera(IRE) was pretty keen in the early stages of the race and failed to quicken when asked. He appears just a bit too high in the weights although not beaten far. (tchd 20-1)
Tawaafud had every chance but was nowhere near good enough. She needs to come down the weights. (op 8-1 tchd 15-2)
Strawberry Lolly ◆, who was on a hat-trick, was hampered on the final bend and lost her chance there. She was going almost as well as Heaven Knows at the time, and the trouble she found may have affected her confidence. Her final position does not tell the whole story. (op 5-2)

4764 BOLLINGER CHAMPAGNE CHALLENGE SERIES H'CAP (FOR GENTLEMAN AMATEUR RIDERS) 1m 4f 66y
5:10 (5:11) (Class 5) (0-75,72) 3-Y-O+ £3,903 (£1,210; £605; £302) Stalls Low

Form RPR
3403 1 **Ramsgill (USA)**[7] 4544 4-10-11 64 MrSPearce(5) 8 72
(J Pearce) *hld up: gd hdwy over 2f out: swtchd rt and rdn over 1f out: styd on ins last to ld nr line* 7/1[3]
3134 2 shd **York Cliff**[8] 4522 8-10-3 56 MrPCollington(5) 2 64
(W M Brisbourne) *hld up in rr: swtchd rt and gd hdwy over 2f out: rdn to ld ent lastr: sn drvn: hdd and no ex nr line* 7/1[3]
00 3 2 **Best Of The Lot (USA)**[37] 3639 4-11-3 70 MrBMcHugh(5) 3 75
(R A Fahey) *chsd ldrs: rdn along 2f out: drvn and kpt on appr last* 10/1
4165 4 shd **Acuzio**[9] 4472 5-10-0 55 MrHSkelton(7) 5 59
(W M Brisbourne) *in tch: hdwy over 4f out: led over 3f out: rdn 2f out: drvn and hdd ent last: one pce* 9/1
5042 5 4 **Barbirolli**[16] 4256 4-10-7 60 MrBenBrisbourne(5) 4 58
(W M Brisbourne) *led: rdn along and hdd over 3f out: drvn 2f out: grad wknd* 3/1[1]
5400 6 4 **Turner**[19] 4175 5-10-5 53 oh1 MrWHogg 9 45
(W M Brisbourne) *hld up in rr: stdy hdwy on inner over 3f out: chsd ldrs whn hmpd 2f out: nt rcvr* 12/1
0-40 7 shd **Fair Spin**[47] 3333 6-10-5 53 oh6 GerardTumelty 1 45
(Micky Hammond) *trckd ldrs on inner: rdn along 3f out: wknd 2f out* 20/1
0405 8 1 **Karrnak**[18] 4206 4-9-12 53 oh8 (tp) MrRBirkett(7) 7 43
(Miss J Feilden) *prom: rdn along over 2f out: sn wknd* 66/1
5/30 9 1¼ **Tudor Bell (IRE)**[25] 4001 5-11-7 72 MrSPJones(3) 11 60
(J G M O'Shea) *chsd ldrs: rdn along 4f out: sn btn* 20/1
0631 10 nk **Montosari**[10] 4451 7-10-5 58 6ex JackMitchell(5) 6 45
(P Mitchell) *hld up towards: gd hdwy on outer to chse ldrs 1/2-way: rdn along over 2f out: wknd wl over 1f out* 7/2[2]
4666 11 5 **Aleron (IRE)**[34] 3081 8-11-3 70 (p) MrMWalford(5) 10 49
(J J Quinn) *chsd ldrs: rdn 3f out: wknd 2f out* 9/1
2m 41.01s (0.36) **Going Correction** -0.20s/f (Firm) 11 Ran SP% 120.0
Speed ratings (Par 103):90,89,88,88,85 83,83,82,81,81 78
CSF £55.27 CT £498.24 TOTE £8.80: £2.30, £2.10, £2.40; EX 56.00 Place 6 £61.37, Place 5 £49.10.
Owner Mrs M Miller **Bred** C L Kidder, J K Griggs And N M Cole **Trained** Newmarket, Suffolk
■ Stewards' Enquiry : Mr S Pearce one-day ban: careless riding (Sep 10)

FOCUS
An ordinary amateur riders' handicap run at a steady gallop and the form, rated around the winner and fourth, is not strong,.
T/Plt: £111.40 to a £1 stake. Pool: £69,153.10. 452.90 winning tickets. T/Qpdt: £37.10 to a £1 stake. Pool: £3,719.80. 74.10 winning tickets. JR

The Form Book, Raceform Ltd, Compton, RG20 6NL

4600 **NEWMARKET (JULY)** (R-H)

Friday, August 25

OFFICIAL GOING: Soft

Wind: Light, across Weather: Fine

4765 DAVID THOM MEMORIAL EBF MAIDEN FILLIES' STKS 7f

1:40 (1:40) (Class 5) 2-Y-O **£4,533** (£1,348; £674; £336) **Stalls** Low

Form RPR

3 **1** **Golden Dagger (IRE)**[12] 4400 2-9-0 .... NCallan 16 85
(K A Ryan) *lw: hld up: hdwy over 2f out: chsd ldr over 1f out: rdn to ld wl ins fnl f* **14/1**

54 **2** *1* **Onida (IRE)**[29] 3874 2-9-0 .... MJKinane 2 83
(C G Cox) *led: rdn over 1f out: hdd wl ins fnl f* **5/2**[2]

4 **3** *1* **Cliche (IRE)**[20] 4148 2-9-0 .... RobertWinston 10 80
(Sir Michael Stoute) *lw: hld up: hdwy over 2f out: swtchd rt over 1f out: r.o* **15/8**[1]

4 *½* **Wishing On A Star** 2-9-0 .... RichardMullen 4 79
(E J O'Neill) *cmpt: scope: s.i.s: sn chsng ldrs: rdn over 1f out: styd on* **33/1**

3 **5** *1* **Brisk Breeze (GER)**[20] 4148 2-9-0 .... TedDurcan 7 76
(H R A Cecil) *chsd ldrs: rdn over 2f out: outpcd over 1f out: styd on ins fnl f* **9/2**[3]

3 **6** *shd* **Lady Alize (USA)**[21] 4103 2-9-0 ....(t) FJohansson 14 76
(R A Kvisla) *a.p: chsd ldr over 2f out tl rdn over 1f out: no ex ins fnl f* **33/1**

7 *shd* **Sister Maria (USA)** 2-9-0 .... JamieSpencer 11 76
(E A L Dunlop) *gd sort: hld up: swtchd rt over 2f out: hdwy over 1f out: nvr nr to chal* **33/1**

8 *½* **Latanazul** 2-9-0 .... RHills 15 75
(J L Dunlop) *w'like: leggy: s.s: sn pushed along in rr: hdwy over 1f out: edgd lft: nt trble ldrs* **16/1**

0 **9** *5* **She's So Pretty (IRE)**[20] 4148 2-9-0 .... StephenCarson 6 62
(W R Swinburn) *lw: hld up: rdn 1/2-way: n.d* **18/1**

10 *1 ½* **Wanessa Tiger (IRE)** 2-9-0 .... JoeFanning 12 58
(M R Channon) *gd sort: s.s: hld up: rdn over 2f out: a in rr* **33/1**

0 **11** *hd* **Dubai Shadow (IRE)**[32] 3796 2-9-0 .... TPQueally 13 58
(C E Brittain) *lw: plld hrd: trckd ldr tl rdn over 2f out: wknd over 1f out* **25/1**

12 *½* **Peppermint Green** 2-9-0 .... NickyMackay 8 57
(L M Cumani) *leggy: scope: bit bkwd: hld up: rdn over 2f out: n.d* **16/1**

0 **13** *1 ¾* **Best Warning**[37] 3640 2-8-9 .... MarcHalford[(5)] 5 52
(J Ryan) *prom: n.m.r and lost pl over 5f out: rdn 1/2-way: wknd wl over 1f out* **100/1**

14 *1* **Mid Ocean** 2-9-0 .... RichardHughes 9 50
(P W D'Arcy) *w'like: hld up: rdn and wknd over 2f out* **25/1**

1m 28.97s (2.19) **Going Correction** +0.275s/f (Good) **14** Ran SP% **125.7**

Speed ratings (Par 91):98,96,95,95,94 93,93,93,87,85 85,84,82,81

CSF £48.53 TOTE £16.60: £3.20, £1.50, £1.20; EX 58.20.

Owner Mr & Mrs K Hughes and Dr J Gozzard **Bred** Niall Farrell **Trained** Hambleton, N Yorks

FOCUS

Those with previous experience dominated, but they set a reasonable standard, and this looked like a good fillies' maiden. They all raced towards the far side.

NOTEBOOK

Golden Dagger(IRE), a five and a half-length third in a fair maiden at Redcar on her debut, showed improved form to get off the mark in this more competitive company. This was a likeable effort and, open to further progression, she has to be respected in better company. (op 16-1 tchd 18-1)

Onida(IRE), who improved on the form she showed in maiden company on her debut when fourth in a Listed race at Sandown on her previous start, could not take advantage of the drop back in grade. Having appeared to get a little warm, she basically ran into a better filly on the day, but her turn should not be too long in coming. (op 3-1 tchd 10-3)

Cliche(IRE) looked a certain future winner when a pleasing fourth over course and distance on her debut, but that run came on faster ground and she did not really show much improvement on this softer surface. (op 13-8 tchd 2-1)

Wishing On A Star, a 60,000euros half-sister to three winners, out of a dual winner in France at two who is a sister to the dam of top-class juvenile One Cool Cat, fared best of the newcomers and this was an encouraging debut. She should be a lot sharper and looks capable of winning this year, although we are unlikely to see the best of her until next season and beyond.

Brisk Breeze(GER), a short-head in front of today's third Cliche on her debut over course and distance, struggled badly when the pace increased, but caught the eye running on near the line. She is almost sure to improve with both time and distance. Official explanation: trainer's rep said filly had been struck into on near-fore knee (op 5-1)

Lady Alize(USA) failed to build on the form she showed over course and distance on her debut, but the soft ground may not have suited.

Sister Maria(USA) ◆, the first foal of the top-class seven to ten-furlong winner Fraulein, was the real eye-catcher of the race. Always too far back to ever pose a serious threat, she kept on very nicely indeed without being given too hard a time and finished on the heels of the principals. She might not be a great price next time, because a few people will have spotted her, but she should not be far away. (tchd 28-1)

Latanazul ◆, whose dam placed over six furlongs as a juvenile, was far too green to do herself justice and is open to any amount of improvement.

4766 DBS ST LEGER YEARLING STKS 6f

2:10 (2:11) (Class 2) 2-Y-O

£24,625 (£9,850; £4,925; £2,460; £1,230; £1,230) **Stalls** Low

Form RPR

3241 **1** **Cheap Street**[20] 4161 2-9-0 .... NickyMackay 9 84
(J G Portman) *racd far side: hld up in tch: swtchd rt over 2f out: rdn to ld wl ins fnl f* **16/1**

0404 **2** *hd* **Cadeaux Du Monde**[16] 4246 2-9-0 72 .... RichardMullen 4 83
(E J O'Neill) *racd far side: led that grp: overall ldr, rdn & and hung rt fr over 1f out: hdd wl ins fnl f: styd on* **33/1**

2422 **3** *5* **Gremlin**[20] 4146 2-9-0 .... RichardHughes 1 68
(A King) *racd far side: hld up in tch: rdn over 1f out: styd on same pce* **9/2**[1]

241 **4** *1* **Smirfys Diamond**[11] 4421 2-9-0 .... AdrianTNicholls 15 65
(D Nicholls) *racd stands' side: hld up: hdwy to ld that gp & overall ldr 2f out: sn rdn & hdd: styd on same pce* **10/1**

062 **5** *hd* **Eager Igor (USA)**[28] 3907 2-9-0 .... StephenCarson 16 65
(R F Johnson Houghton) *racd stands' side: dwlt: hdwy over 2f out: sn rdn: no imp fnl f* **50/1**

1202 **6** *nk* **Frisky Talk (IRE)**[20] 4152 2-8-9 73 .... RHills 19 59
(B W Hills) *lw: led stands' side & overall ldr 4f: no ex appr fnl f* **7/1**[3]

0515 **7** *2 ½* **Sweet Candy**[16] 4246 2-8-9 .... NCallan 2 51
(K A Ryan) *chsd ldrs far side: rdn 2f out: wkng whn hung rt fnl f* **14/1**

2352 **8** *shd* **Hart Of Gold**[16] 4264 2-9-0 82 .... DO'Donohoe 17 56
(M J Wallace) *racd stands' side: chsd ldrs: rdn whn hmpd and lost pl over 2f out: n.d after* **20/1**

10 **9** *1* **Baltimore Jack (IRE)**[66] 2719 2-9-0 85 .... DeanMcKeown 7 53
(R M Whitaker) *racd far side: hld up in tch: rdn over 2f out: n.d* **14/1**

2410 **10** *nk* **Okikoki**[16] 4246 2-9-0 .... JoeFanning 18 52
(W R Muir) *racd stands' side: prom: rdn and edgd rt over 2f out: wknd over 1f out* **12/1**

345 **11** *nk* **Cape Dancer (IRE)**[11] 4424 2-8-9 .... TonyHamilton 6 46
(J S Wainwright) *racd far side: chsd ldrs: rdn over 2f out: wknd over 1f out* **100/1**

3323 **12** *½* **Follow The Flag (IRE)**[21] 4100 2-9-0 .... TedDurcan 8 50
(N P Littmoden) *racd far side: chsd ldrs 4f* **20/1**

042 **13** *¾* **Mambo Spirit (IRE)**[11] 4421 2-9-0 .... JamieMackay 3 48
(J G Given) *lw: racd far side: s.i.s: hld up: nt clr run over 2f out: n.d* **12/1**

312 **14** *1 ¼* **Oi Vay Joe (IRE)**[20] 4130 2-9-0 84 .... LPKeniry 12 44
(W Jarvis) *racd far side: chsd ldrs: rdn over 2f out: sn wknd* **7/1**[3]

2 **15** *2 ½* **Colonel Flay**[30] 3851 2-9-0 .... RobertHavlin 13 36
(Mrs P N Dutfield) *lw: racd far side: hld up: n.d* **33/1**

16 *¾* **Six Mile Bottom (IRE)**[26] 2-8-9 ....(b) MickyFenton 5 29
(Bruce Hellier, Germany) *w'like: racd far side: chsd ldrs to 1/2-way* **25/1**

1 **17** *2* **Arnie's Joint (IRE)**[104] 1688 2-9-0 .... JamieSpencer 10 28
(N P Littmoden) *racd far side: chsd ldrs over 4f* **13/2**[2]

60 **18** *3* **Buckie Massa**[20] 4129 2-9-0 .... TPQueally 20 19
(S Kirk) *lw: racd stands' side: chsd ldrs: edgd lft over 2f out: sn rdn and wknd* **25/1**

3315 **19** *2 ½* **Tom Paris**[15] 4284 2-9-0 68 ....(b) IanMongan 14 12
(W R Muir) *racd far side: chsd ldrs over 4f* **50/1**

2010 **20** *6* **See In The Dark (IRE)**[42] 3496 2-9-0 79 .... RobertWinston 11 —
(B J Meehan) *lw: racd far side: hld up: rdn 1/2-way: sn wknd* **12/1**

1m 14.75s (1.40) **Going Correction** +0.275s/f (Good) **59** Ran SP% **135.9**

Speed ratings (Par 100):101,100,94,92,92 92,88,88,87,86 86,85,84,83,79 78,76,72,68,60

CSF £501.28 TOTE £27.50: £8.10, £16.60, £2.30; EX 914.60.

Owner A S B Portman **Bred** Catridge Farm Stud Ltd **Trained** Compton, Berks

FOCUS

A big field for this consolation sales race, but the form looks pretty ordinary. They split into two groups early on and, although they finished strung out across the track at the end, those who raced in the larger groups towards the far side appeared at an advantage. Fourth-placed Smirfys Diamond fared best of those on the near side.

NOTEBOOK

Cheap Street, who confirmed earlier promise when getting off the mark on fast ground at Windsor on his previous start, coped with both the more competitive contest and the softer ground, and displayed a particularly willing attitude. His chances of completing the hat-trick may depend on how the Handicapper views this, but the runner-up was rated just 72, so he should not be harshly treated.

Cadeaux Du Monde looked in need of seven furlongs when fourth over this trip in a nursery at Kempton on his previous start, so he clearly benefited from having plenty of use made over him on this stiff track, and the easy ground will also have helped. There was a long way back to the remainder, so surely he can be placed to effect before too much longer.

Gremlin seemed to have his chance, but he had never previously raced on ground this soft and he was no match for the front two. (op 7-1)

Smirfys Diamond ◆, off the mark on easy ground over five furlongs at Thirsk on his previous start, fared best of those in the smaller group on the near side of the track and may have been even closer had he had more horses to race with. He seems to be improving. (op 9-1)

Eager Igor(USA) had never previously raced on soft ground, but he seemed to handle it okay and ran well.

Frisky Talk(IRE) finished second in the smaller group on the near side, but is not easy to win with. (op 8-1)

Oi Vay Joe(IRE) should not have minded the ground, but he was well below form and proved a major disappointment. (op 13-2 tchd 8-1)

Arnie's Joint(IRE), not seen since making a winning debut in a Warwick maiden that worked out quite well, did little to justify his Group-race entries. Official explanation: jockey said colt lost its action (op 7-1)

Tom Paris Official explanation: jockey said gelding was unsuited by the soft going

4767 RENAULT VANS NURSERY 1m

2:45 (2:45) (Class 4) 2-Y-O **£4,533** (£1,348; £674; £336) **Stalls** Low

Form RPR

231 **1** **Spanish Hidalgo (IRE)**[20] 4140 2-9-7 **84** .... IanMongan 4 94
(J L Dunlop) *lw: chsd ldr tl led over 3f out: rdn over 1f out: styd on wl* **5/2**[2]

5214 **2** *3* **Little Miss Wizzy**[14] 4335 2-8-3 **66** .... NickyMackay 6 70
(M L W Bell) *dwlt: hld up: hdwy over 3f out: rdn to chse wnr over 1f out: styd on same pce fnl f* **5/1**[3]

604 **3** *3* **Deccan Express (IRE)**[30] 3851 2-8-6 **69** .... RichardHughes 7 67
(R Hannon) *lw: led over 4f: styd on same pce appr fnl f* **10/1**

3641 **4** *nk* **Silca Soprano**[25] 3997 2-8-9 **72** .... TedDurcan 3 69
(M R Channon) *s.i.s: sn prom: outpcd over 3f out: n.d after* **10/1**

030 **5** *1 ¾* **Perfect Courtesy (IRE)**[13] 4366 2-8-13 **76** .... JamieSpencer 8 70
(P W Chapple-Hyam) *hld up: effrt over 2f out: nvr trbld ldrs* **10/1**

0520 **6** *2* **Dansilver**[8] 4509 2-7-12 **61** oh2 .... SilvestreDeSousa 1 51
(D J Wintle) *chsd ldrs: rdn over 3f out: wknd 2f out* **20/1**

0021 **7** *¾* **Persian Fox (IRE)**[15] 4303 2-8-7 **70** .... DO'Donohoe 5 58
(G A Huffer) *trckd ldrs: plld hrd: rdn over 2f out: wknd over 1f out* **2/1**[1]

305 **8** *3* **Su Doku (USA)**[27] 3942 2-8-9 **72** .... NCallan 2 54
(N P Littmoden) *swtg: hld up: rdn over 3f out: wknd wl over 1f out* **11/1**

1m 44.21s (3.78) **Going Correction** +0.275s/f (Good) **8** Ran SP% **118.9**

Speed ratings (Par 96):92,89,86,85,83 81,81,78

CSF £16.32 CT £108.72 TOTE £3.30: £1.40, £1.80, £2.90; EX 16.60.

Owner Windflower Overseas Holdings Inc **Bred** Windflower Overseas Holdings Inc **Trained** Arundel, W Sussex

FOCUS

They raced down the centre of the track. This was just an ordinary nursery and, with the ground testing, the pace was steady for much of the way, but Spanish Hidalgo impressed in galloping clear of a strung-out field.

NOTEBOOK

Spanish Hidalgo(IRE) ◆, off the mark on fast ground over an extended seven furlongs in maiden company at Lingfield on his previous start, was always well placed given the way the race was run and ran out a most emphatic winner, proving well suited by the testing ground, which placed the emphasis on stamina. At this stage of his career, he is perhaps not too dissimilar to Big Bad Bob, who represented this trainer/owner combination and rattled up a sequence at two after taking three attempts to get off the mark, then made a smart older horse. Big Bad Bob won the Autumn Stakes at Ascot, which would be an option, or else he could step up in trip again for the Zetland Stakes on Newmarket's Rowley Mile course. (tchd 11-4)

Little Miss Wizzy had never previously raced over a trip this far or on ground this soft, but she seemed to handle the conditions and ran well off her light weight. (op 11-2)

Deccan Express(IRE), upped in trip and racing on soft ground for the first time on his nursery debut, ran respectably but was ultimately well held. (tchd 9-1)

Silca Soprano, 5lb higher, was below the form she showed when winning over seven furlongs on Southwell's Fibresand on her previous start. (op 8-1)

Perfect Courtesy(IRE), making his nursery debut, was well held and may want better ground. (tchd 11-1)

Persian Fox(IRE) was nowhere near the form he showed when winning a fast-ground maiden over this trip at Yarmouth on his previous start, and this testing ground appeared totally unsuitable. (op 11-4)

4768 RENAULT MASTER EBF MAIDEN STKS (C&G) 7f

3:20 (3:20) (Class 5) 2-Y-O **£4,533** (£1,348; £674; £336) **Stalls** Low

Form RPR

1 **Moudez (IRE)** 2-9-0 JamieSpencer 2 84
(D M Simcock) *w'like: leggy: lw: a.p: rdn to ld ins fnl f: r.o: edgd rt towards fin* **12/1**

2 2 **Strobilus** 2-9-0 NCallan 12 79
(M A Jarvis) *w'like: scope: a.p: rdn to ld over 1f out: sn hung lft: hdd and unable qck ins fnl f* **25/1**

3 1 3/4 **Lion Sands** 2-9-0 NickyMackay 8 75
(L M Cumani) *cmpt: lw: hld up in tch: outpcd over 1f out: r.o ins fnl f* **10/1**[3]

6 4 1 3/4 **Mo (USA)**[27] [3923] 2-9-0 (t) FJohansson 1 70
(R A Kvisla) *lw: led over 5f: wknd ins fnl f* **50/1**

5 hd **Vanquisher (IRE)** 2-9-0 TedDurcan 5 70
(W J Haggas) *w'like: lw: s.s: hld up: r.o ins fnl f: nvr nr to chal* **33/1**

3 6 1 1/4 **Many Volumes (USA)**[44] [3417] 2-9-0 RichardHughes 4 67
(H R A Cecil) *chsd ldr: shkn up over 1f out: wknd ins fnl f* **8/11**[1]

0 7 2 **Style Sunday (IRE)**[14] [4333] 2-9-0 JoeFanning 11 62
(B W Hills) *hld up: rdn over 2f out: nvr nrr* **20/1**

8 shd **Snaafy (USA)** 2-9-0 RHills 14 61
(B W Hills) *gd sort: s.s: hld up: rdn 1/2-way: wknd over 1f out* **11/1**

9 1/2 **Rock Anthem (IRE)** 2-9-0 IanMongan 6 60
(J L Dunlop) *neat: chsd ldrs over 5f* **20/1**

10 5 **Laddies Poker (USA)** 2-9-0 TPQueally 13 48
(J Noseda) *tall: scope: hld up: rdn over 2f out: sn wknd* **16/1**

11 1/2 **Saloon (USA)** 2-9-0 RobertWinston 10 46
(Sir Michael Stoute) *gd sort: dwlt: hld up: rdn 1/2-way: hung lft and wknd 2f out* **7/1**[2]

12 hd **Sonara (IRE)** 2-9-0 MickyFenton 3 46
(M H Tompkins) *w'like: bkwd: scope: mid-div: hdwy over 2f out: sn rdn and wknd* **40/1**

13 3 1/2 **Mandragola** 2-9-0 RichardMullen 9 37
(B W Hills) *w'like: scope: hld up: wknd 2f out* **33/1**

1m 28.82s (2.04) **Going Correction** +0.275s/f (Good) 13 Ran SP% **125.1**
Speed ratings (Par 94):99,96,94,92,92 91,88,88,88,82 81,81,77
CSF £286.40 TOTE £19.20: £3.40, £5.90, £3.10; EX 467.30.

Owner Zayat Stables Ltd **Bred** Sean Murphy **Trained** Newmarket, Suffolk

FOCUS

A good maiden full of decent three-year-old prospects. They raced down the centre of the track.

NOTEBOOK

Moudez(IRE) ◆, an 87,000euros brother to Russian Dreams, who was placed over 12 furlongs at three, out of a mare who was also placed over middle-distances, was the subject of a late jockey change - Adrian Nicholls lost out - and supported into 12/1 from 16s on course. Always travelling well in behind the leaders, he ran green when switched out for a run, taking a little longer than first looked likely to hit full stride, but he responded well to the whip and eventually powered clear to land a bit of a touch. A strong-galloping type, he promises to make a smart three-year-old over further and his trainer, who has had some nice horses in his care in the short time he has held a licence, thinks he is potentially the best he has ever trained. He is likely to have one more run before being put away for the year. (op 16-1)

Strobilus, the first foal of a smart triple winner over ten to 12 furlongs, made a very pleasing introduction. A starting price of 25/1 suggests he was not fancied to go in first time, so there should be plenty of improvement to come. (op 20-1)

Lion Sands ◆, a 300,000gns purchase, who is closely related to Pukka, a quite useful dual middle-distance winner, and to Pongee, who was high class over ten to 12 furlongs, holds entries in the Royal Lodge, Racing Post Trophy and Derby. This was a most encouraging introduction but, while he is clearly capable of winning as a juvenile, he will come into his own over further next year and beyond, and looks a smart prospect.

Mo(USA) had the run of the race and improved significantly on the form he showed on his debut over six furlongs at Ascot.

Vanquisher(IRE), a 30,000gns half-brother to five winners, including high-class Nazirali, a multiple middle-distance winner, out of a ten-furlong scorer at three, made a pleasing start to his career and should make a nice horse over further next year.

Many Volumes(USA) was well below the form he showed on his debut on fast ground over course and distance, and one can only assume he failed to handle these vastly different conditions. (op 5-6 tchd evens in places)

Saloon(USA), a $400,000 brother to Moscow Ballet, a smart dual seven to ten-furlong winner, out of a top-class US miler, did not offer a great deal on his racecourse debut but can surely do better. (op 9-1 tchd 13-2)

4769 RENAULT TRAFIC CLAIMING STKS 7f

3:55 (3:56) (Class 5) 3-Y-O **£3,238** (£963; £481; £240) **Stalls** Low

Form RPR

0034 1 **Glenbuck (IRE)**[13] [4352] 3-9-4 62 (v) MickyFenton 15 73
(A Bailey) *mde virtually all: rdn over 1f out: styd on* **16/1**

0000 2 2 **Charlton**[9] [4481] 3-9-9 77 (v) IanMongan 1 73
(T G Mills) *chsd wnr: rdn over 1f out: styd on same pce* **12/1**

4304 3 1 1/2 **Zennerman (IRE)**[9] [4488] 3-9-2 81 LiamJones(5) 7 67
(W M Brisbourne) *hld up: hdwy 1/2-way: rdn over 1f out: styd on same pce* **11/4**[1]

5002 4 3/4 **Sensuous**[22] [4077] 3-8-10 61 RichardHughes 10 57+
(R Hannon) *hld up: nt clr run fr over 2f out tl r.o ins fnl f: nt trble ldrs* **15/2**[3]

4206 5 1/2 **Mucho Loco (IRE)**[8] [4533] 3-8-13 56 (b) TPQueally 4 56
(J G Portman) *b: hld up in tch: racd keenly: rdn over 1f out: styd on same pce* **22/1**

-003 6 2 1/2 **Girandola**[4] [4663] 3-9-4 60 StephenCarson 13 55
(R F Johnson Houghton) *hld up in tch: rdn over 2f out: wknd fnl f* **33/1**

0005 7 1 **Sands Of Barra (IRE)**[20] [4143] 3-9-7 74 NCallan 19 55
(N A Callaghan) *hld up: rdn over 2f out: nvr trbld ldrs* **8/1**

0600 8 nk **Franky'N'Jonny**[15] [4306] 3-8-2 45 FrancisFerris 11 36
(Mrs C A Dunnett) *hld up: hdwy over 3f out: rdn over 2f out: wknd over 1f out* **50/1**

0005 9 shd **Knickerless (IRE)**[23] [4050] 3-7-9 40 CharlotteKerton(7) 9 35
(N P Littmoden) *b.hind: s.s: hdwy 1/2-way: wknd over 1f out* **66/1**

6621 10 1 1/2 **Ellesappelle**[7] [4567] 3-8-10 63 PatCosgrave 3 40
(K R Burke) *lw: s.i.s: sn chsng ldrs: rdn and wknd over 1f out* **3/1**[2]

0300 11 nk **Bertie Bear**[23] [4050] 3-8-0 37 (v) GMasure(7) 17 36
(G G Margarson) *hld up: hdwy over 2f out: wknd over 1f out* **100/1**

1013 12 8 **Jellytot (USA)**[32] [3782] 3-8-8 64 CatherineGannon 14 17
(K A Ryan) *swtg: s.i.s: hdwy 1/2-way: wknd over 1f out* **10/1**

0001 13 1 3/4 **Bold Love**[23] [4050] 3-8-10 41 JasonEdmunds(3) 8 18
(J Balding) *s.i.s: hld up: plld hrd: hdwy over 3f out: wknd over 2f out* **28/1**

6102 14 39 **Bekoning (IRE)**[101] [1768] 3-8-10 47 RobertWinston 6 —
(M Quinn) *lw: prom over 5f* **33/1**

05-4 15 87 **White Ladder (IRE)**[23] [4045] 3-9-4 64 JamieSpencer 5 —
(P F I Cole) *h.d.w: prom: lost pl 1/2-way: sn eased* **12/1**

1m 28.5s (1.72) **Going Correction** +0.275s/f (Good) 15 Ran SP% **123.0**
Speed ratings (Par 100):101,98,97,96,95 92,91,91,91,89 89,79,77,33,—
CSF £188.83 TOTE £18.90: £6.20, £4.90, £1.50; EX 220.60.

Owner Middleham Park Racing XLII **Bred** Mrs Teresa Monaghan **Trained** Cotebrook, Cheshire

■ Stewards' Enquiry : Ian Mongan one-day ban: failed to keep straight from stalls (Sep 5)

FOCUS

A decent enough claimer in which they all tended to race towards the centre of the track but the form is not strong.

White Ladder(IRE) Official explanation: jockey said colt lost its action

4770 BREHENY H'CAP 1m 6f 175y

4:30 (4:30) (Class 3) (0-95,95) 3-Y-O+ **£8,420** (£2,505; £1,251; £625) **Stalls** Centre

Form RPR

0411 1 **Alessano**[30] [3853] 4-8-12 79 (b) NCallan 7 96
(G L Moore) *chsd ldr tl led 3f out: rdn clr and edgd lft fr over 1f out* **11/2**

2144 2 6 **Duty (IRE)**[7] [4560] 3-8-8 88 RobertWinston 5 98
(Sir Michael Stoute) *chsd ldrs: rdn to chse wnr and edgd rt over 1f out: styd on same pce* **9/4**[1]

2331 3 11 **Meadow Mischief (FR)**[8] [4537] 3-8-1 81 5ex (b) RichardMullen 1 78
(E A L Dunlop) *hld up: hdwy 1/2-way: rdn: hung lft and wknd over 1f out* **5/2**[2]

2121 4 nk **Whispering Death**[27] [3955] 4-8-12 84 (v) LiamJones(5) 9 80
(W J Haggas) *lw: hld up: nvr nr to chal* **4/1**[3]

0-0 5 2 1/2 **Cavallino (USA)**[13] [4346] 6-10-0 95 (t) FJohansson 8 88
(R A Kvisla) *hld up: hdwy u.p over 2f out: sn wknd* **25/1**

400- 6 12 **Gold Ring**[426] [2925] 6-9-9 90 StephenCarson 3 69
(J A Geake) *led: hdd 3f out: wknd 2f out* **14/1**

-040 7 5 **Massif Centrale**[68] [2229] 5-9-6 92 (t) MarcHalford(5) 4 65
(D R C Elsworth) *lw: chsd ldrs: rdn over 3f out: wknd 2f out* **16/1**

3m 16.59s (5.55) **Going Correction** +0.275s/f (Good)
WFA 3 from 4yo+ 13lb 7 Ran SP% **111.1**
Speed ratings (Par 107):96,92,86,86,85 79,76
CSF £17.24 CT £36.37 TOTE £6.50: £3.10, £1.90; EX 18.70.

Owner D J Deer **Bred** D J And Mrs Deer **Trained** Woodingdean, E Sussex

FOCUS

This looked a reasonable staying handicap, but very few of these were suited by the testing conditions and they came home well strung out with only the front pair showing form.

NOTEBOOK

Alessano, chasing the hat-trick off a mark just 1lb higher than when winning on much faster ground at Sandown on his previous start, handled this soft surface well and was a most convincing winner. He is progressing into a useful stayer and could well go in again. (tchd 7-1)

Duty(IRE) had never previously raced on ground with soft in the description, but he handled it well enough to finish upwards of 11 lengths clear of the remainder. (op 11-4)

Meadow Mischief(FR) was 4lb well-in under the penalty he picked up for winning at Sandown on his previous start, but he had never previously raced on soft ground and was not at his best. (op 11-4 tchd 9-4)

Whispering Death, 8lb higher, was below the form he showed when winning over two miles two at York on his previous start, and one has to assume this ground did not suit. (op 3-1 tchd 11-4)

Cavallino(USA) was below the form he showed in the Shergar Cup Stayers on his previous start and may have been unsuited by the ground. (op 33-1 tchd 22-1)

4771 RENAULT KANGOO H'CAP 5f

5:00 (5:00) (Class 4) (0-85,85) 3-Y-O+ **£5,505** (£1,637; £818; £408) **Stalls** Low

Form RPR

0301 1 **Cashel Mead**[6] [4598] 6-9-6 85 6ex MarcHalford(5) 2 94
(J L Spearing) *hld up in tch: led ins fnl f: rdn out* **7/2**[2]

362 2 shd **After The Show**[51] [3199] 5-9-1 75 NCallan 6 83
(Rae Guest) *hld up: hdwy over 1f out: r.o wl* **14/1**

1111 3 1 **Blue Maeve**[13] [4352] 6-9-0 74 SilvestreDeSousa 9 79
(A D Brown) *led: hdd over 3f out: rdn to ld over 1f out: edgd rt and hdd ins fnl f: no ex nr fin* **7/1**

0450 4 1 **Bond Boy**[3] [4682] 9-9-3 82 (v[1]) MarkLawson(5) 11 84
(B Smart) *hld up: rdn over 1f out: r.o ins fnl f: nt rch ldrs* **11/2**[3]

1500 5 hd **Prince Cyrano**[21] [4101] 7-8-12 72 JoeFanning 1 73
(W J Musson) *chsd ldrs: rdn and ev ch over 1f out: no ex ins fnl f* **16/1**

6344 6 3/4 **Seamus Shindig**[14] [4338] 4-9-7 81 CatherineGannon 10 79
(H Candy) *b.hind: chsd ldrs: rdn 1/2-way: styd on same pce fnl f* **3/1**[1]

04 7 1/2 **Matty Tun**[6] [4598] 7-9-6 80 RobertWinston 7 77+
(J Balding) *lw: trckd ldrs: racd keenly: rdn and ev ch over 1f out: wknd ins fnl f* **11/2**[3]

4205 8 4 **Malapropism**[19] [4180] 6-9-11 85 TedDurcan 5 68
(M R Channon) *lw: chsd ldrs: rdn over 1f out: sn btn* **16/1**

0200 9 hd **Hits Only Cash**[39] [3598] 4-8-7 67 DeanMcKeown 3 49
(J Pearce) *lw: sn outpcd* **20/1**

0010 10 1 3/4 **Anfield Dream**[7] [4573] 4-9-4 78 RichardMullen 4 54
(J R Jenkins) *w ldr tl led over 3f out: rdn and hdd over 1f out: wknd fnl f* **50/1**

60.85 secs (1.29) **Going Correction** +0.275s/f (Good) 10 Ran SP% **115.6**
Speed ratings (Par 105):100,99,98,96,96 95,94,87,87,84
CSF £51.18 CT £333.14 TOTE £3.80: £1.60, £2.80, £2.50; EX 44.00 Place 6 £371.87, Place 5 £270.37.

Owner Masonaires **Bred** D R Tucker **Trained** Kinnersley, Worcs

FOCUS

A good sprint handicap rated around the placed horses to their recent best.

T/Jkpt: Not won. T/Plt: £1,318.90 to a £1 stake. Pool: £62,873.90. 34.80 winning tickets. T/Qpdt: £83.10 to a £1 stake. Pool: £3,841.80. 34.20 winning tickets. CR

[4525]SALISBURY (R-H)

Friday, August 25

OFFICIAL GOING: Good (good to soft in places)

Wind: Virtually nil

4772 AXMINSTER CARPETS APPRENTICE H'CAP 6f 212y

4:50 (4:52) (Class 5) (0-70,75) 3-Y-O+ **£3,562** (£1,059; £529; £264) **Stalls** Centre

Form RPR

3022 **1** **Kasumi**[4] [4666] 3-8-11 **64** .... TravisBlock(6) 8 73
(H Morrison) *mde all on far side: rdn clr wl over 1f out: r.o wl* **9/2**[2]

-232 **2** 2 **Red Rudy**[121] [1245] 4-8-11 **63** .... MarkCoumbe(10) 7 67
(A W Carroll) *hld up on far side: swtchd to stand side over 3f out: rdn and hdwy over 1f out: sn edgd lft: kpt on to go 2nd ins fnl f* **4/1**[1]

0561 **3** *nk* **Stormy Monday**[8] [4531] 3-9-9 **75** 6ex .... PatrickHills(5) 4 78
(J W Hills) *hld up on stand side: rdn and hdwy fr 2f out: styd on ins fnl f* **11/2**[3]

-602 **4** *nk* **Moyoko (IRE)**[8] [4531] 3-7-8 **51** oh3 .... LauraReynolds(10) 11 53
(M Blanshard) *wnt lft and blkd s: bhd on far side: edgd lft and hdwy over 2f out: sn rdn: styd on* **10/1**

0-04 **5** *1 1/4* **My Michelle**[44] [3405] 5-8-13 **55** .... NeilChalmers 14 54
(B Palling) *in tch on far side: rdn over 2f out: kpt on same pce* **12/1**

6650 **6** *3/4* **Currency**[7] [4564] 9-8-13 **65** .... BarrySavage(10) 13 62
(J M Bradley) *w wnr on far side: rdn 4f out: chsd wnr wl over 1f out: one pce fnl f* **14/1**

0001 **7** *3/4* **Wind Chime (IRE)**[15] [4288] 9-8-7 **54** .... TolleyDean(5) 3 49
(A G Newcombe) *s.i.s: sn chsng ldrs on stand side: ev ch 2f out : sn one pce* **12/1**

0/50 **8** *2 1/2* **Bathwick Finesse (IRE)**[5] [4627] 4-9-9 **70** .... JamesMillman(5) 5 58
(B R Millman) *led stand side gp tl 4f out: sn rdn: hung rt over 1f out: wknd* **50/1**

0-00 **9** *1* **King Of Diamonds**[13] [4365] 5-8-12 **62** .... KylieManser(8) 1 48
(J R Best) *restrained s: bhd on stand side: short lived effrt 2f out* **33/1**

0403 **10** *1/2* **Dream Forest (IRE)**[15] [4297] 3-8-10 **60** .... JamieJones(3) 16 44
(Mrs P N Dutfield) *keen early: trckd ldrs on far side: rdn over 2f out: wknd over 1f out* **25/1**

0220 **11** *nk* **Dr Synn**[35] [3705] 5-9-7 **66** .... RoryMoore(3) 12 50
(J Akehurst) *trckd ldrs on far side: rdn over 2f out: sn wknd* **11/2**[3]

-000 **12** *1/2* **Go Mo (IRE)**[18] [4209] 4-9-9 **65** .... DominicFox 6 47
(S Kirk) *prom on stand side: rdn 3f out: wknd over 1f out* **16/1**

5002 **13** *nk* **Curtain Bluff**[9] [4496] 4-9-6 **70** .... (v) ThomasO'Brien(8) 10 52
(M R Channon) *blkd s: in tch on far side: rdn over 2f out: sn wknd* **12/1**

1m 29.59s (0.53) **Going Correction** +0.125s/f (Good)
WFA 3 from 4yo+ 5lb **40** Ran SP% **122.4**
Speed ratings (Par 103):101,98,98,98,96 95,94,92,90,90 89,89,89
CSF £23.08 CT £104.69 TOTE £6.90: £1.90, £2.20, £2.10; EX 30.10.
Owner Viscountess Trenchard **Bred** Fonthill Stud **Trained** East Ilsley, Berks

■ Charlie Bear was withdrawn (9/1, bolted before s). R4 applies, deduct 10p in the £. New market formed.

FOCUS
A modest handicap in which the draw appeared to have little influence.
Bathwick Finesse(IRE) Official explanation: jockey said filly hung right throughout

4773 FRAMERSWAREHOUSE.CO.UK NURSERY 1m

5:20 (5:23) (Class 5) 2-Y-O **£3,562** (£1,059; £529; £264) **Stalls** Centre

Form RPR

3311 **1** **Sweet Lilly**[16] [4264] 2-8-12 **74** .... LDettori 11 81
(M R Channon) *stdd sn after s towards rr: hdwy over 2f out: swtchd lft over 1f out: rdn and r.o strly: led post* **15/8**[1]

630 **2** *shd* **Colchium (IRE)**[46] [3344] 2-8-3 **65** .... FrankieMcDonald 8 71
(H Morrison) *mid div: hdwy over 2f out: rdn into narrow advantage over 1f out: ct post* **14/1**

4213 **3** *1 1/2* **Stagehand (IRE)**[19] [4178] 2-8-12 **74** .... GrahamGibbons 4 77
(B R Millman) *chsd ldrs: led 2f out: sn rdn and narrowly hdd: rallied: no ex fnl 20yds* **10/3**[2]

063 **4** *2 1/2* **Recruit**[22] [4074] 2-9-0 **76** .... RichardSmith 13 73
(R Hannon) *s.i.s: towards rr: swtchd lft over 3f out: hdwy to chse ldrs over 1f out: one pce fnl f* **12/1**

2003 **5** *5* **Bathwick Style**[12] [4394] 2-7-9 **60** oh8 .... DominicFox(3) 12 46
(B R Millman) *sn led: rdn 3f out: hdd 2f out: wknd fnl f* **20/1**

025 **6** *nk* **Our Herbie**[36] [3663] 2-8-1 **70** .... PatrickHills(7) 1 55
(J W Hills) *t.k.h in mid div: rdn over 2f out: kpt on same pce* **14/1**

0360 **7** *3/4* **Regal Ovation**[19] [4178] 2-7-13 **64** ow1 .... StephaneBreux(3) 7 47
(W R Muir) *pushed along towards rr: hdwy 3f out: effrt 2f out: wknd fnl f* **25/1**

010 **8** *5* **Nur Tau (IRE)**[23] [4037] 2-9-7 **83** .... DaneO'Neill 3 55
(M P Tregoning) *in tch: edgd lft and rdn 3f out: wknd 2f out* **9/2**[3]

306 **9** *4* **Tension Point**[30] [3844] 2-8-12 **74** .... SteveDrowne 2 37
(J A Osborne) *chsd ldrs: rdn over 3f out: wknd 2f out* **10/1**

640 **10** *13* **Eastern Princess**[18] [4207] 2-7-8 **63** .... LukeMorris(7) 9 —
(J A Geake) *w ldr: rdn over 3f out: wknd 2f out* **20/1**

1m 44.44s (1.35) **Going Correction** +0.125s/f (Good) **10** Ran SP% **119.5**
Speed ratings (Par 94):98,97,96,93,88 88,87,82,78,65
CSF £30.98 CT £86.53 TOTE £2.20: £1.10, £4.20, £1.80; EX 35.00.
Owner Jaber Abdullah **Bred** Red House Stud **Trained** West Ilsley, Berks

FOCUS
A fair nursery and sound enough form.

NOTEBOOK
Sweet Lilly did not look at all badly handicapped for her nursery debut, but she made hard work of things and only got up on the line having looked unlikely to get to the eventual runner-up. On the plus side, the assessor cannot put her up too much for this, and her style of running could see her stay ahead of the Handicapper for a while. (op 9-4 tchd 13-8)
Colchium(IRE), stepping up three furlongs in distance on her handicap debut, ran her best race so far, only getting caught on the line. She beat the rest well enough and can go one better in similar company.
Stagehand(IRE) did not see the extra furlong out as well as the first two and this rather keen colt should be happier back over seven and/or on faster ground. (op 7-2)
Recruit, another stepping up in trip on his handicap debut, carried his head high and hung both ways under pressure once switched out wide to deliver his challenge, and he looks to have his share of temperament. (op 10-1)
Bathwick Style was officially 8lb wrong at the weights but she was 7lb well in based on her new All-Weather mark, so it was not a total surprise that she ran quite well having set a fair gallop in front. Polytrack does seem to suit her better, though.
Our Herbie raced too keenly for his own good, did not enjoy the clearest of runs and failed to improve for an extra furlong on this handicap debut. (op 12-1)

4774 ACORN TAVERNS MAIDEN AUCTION STKS 6f

5:50 (5:55) (Class 5) 2-Y-O **£3,562** (£1,059; £529; £264) **Stalls** Centre

Form RPR

0 **1** **Sylvan (IRE)**[23] [4041] 2-8-1 .... StephaneBreux(3) 5 73
(S Kirk) *hld up towards rr: stdy prog fr 3f out: rdn to chse ldr over 1f out: r.o: led cl home* **10/1**[3]

32 **2** *1/2* **Maker's Mark (IRE)**[19] [4177] 2-8-11 .... DaneO'Neill 10 79
(H Candy) *sn led: rdn and edgd lft over 1f out: drifted rt ins fnl f: no ex whn ct cl home* **8/11**[1]

045 **3** *2* **Masai Moon**[20] [4161] 2-8-9 72 .... GrahamGibbons 2 71
(B R Millman) *chsd ldrs: rdn to chse ldr 2f out: kpt on same pce fnl f* **10/1**[3]

226 **4** *1/2* **Impromptu**[25] [3994] 2-8-8 75 .... NeilChalmers(3) 9 71
(R M Beckett) *in tch tl n.m.r amd lost position over 4f out: rdn and hdwy 2f out: r.o ins fnl f* **6/1**[2]

5 *2 1/2* **Oceana Gold** 2-8-9 .... SteveDrowne 12 62
(A M Balding) *s.i.s: bhd: swtchd lft 2f out: r.o fnl f: nrst fin* **40/1**

6 *3* **Money For Fun** 2-8-4 .... FrankieMcDonald 6 48
(J S Moore) *s.i.s: t.k.h early: towards rr: hdwy 3f out: edgd lft over 2f out: one pce fnl f* **66/1**

0 **7** *1 1/2* **Is It Time (IRE)**[8] [4525] 2-8-4 .... PaulEddery 7 43
(Mrs P N Dutfield) *prom: rdn over 2f out: grad fdd* **100/1**

50 **8** *1 1/4* **Lay The Cash (USA)**[8] [4525] 2-8-2 .... JosephWalsh(7) 8 44
(J S Moore) *chsd ldrs: rdn over 3f out: one pce fnl 2f* **40/1**

0 **9** *5* **Lady Firecracker (IRE)**[109] [1542] 2-8-4 .... PaulFitzsimons 3 24
(J R Best) *in tch: n.m.r over 4f out: wknd over 1f out* **11/1**

00 **10** *2 1/2* **Falcon Flyer**[8] [4525] 2-8-6 .... RichardSmith 11 19
(J R Best) *nvr bttr than mid div* **66/1**

5 **11** *1 1/2* **Black Mogul**[23] [4049] 2-8-11 .... LDettori 14 19
(W R Muir) *in tch tl wknd 2f out* **10/1**[3]

12 *1/2* **Nelson Vettori** 2-8-9 .... JosedeSouza 1 16
(R M Beckett) *a towards rr* **33/1**

00 **13** *shd* **Priceless Melody (USA)**[8] [4526] 2-9-2 .... AlanDaly 13 22
(Mrs A J Perrett) *chsd ldrs: rdn 3f out: wknd 2f out* **100/1**

1m 15.96s (0.98) **Going Correction** +0.125s/f (Good) **13** Ran SP% **120.6**
Speed ratings (Par 94):98,97,94,94,90 86,84,83,76,73 71,70,70
CSF £17.53 TOTE £11.60: £2.10, £1.20, £2.60; EX 23.70.
Owner R Gander **Bred** James Doyle **Trained** Upper Lambourn, Berks

FOCUS
A modest maiden rated around the third and fourth.

NOTEBOOK
Sylvan(IRE) came home well down the centre of the track to grab the spoils close home. She had been too green to do herself justice at Goodwood on her debut but she had less to beat here, was receiving weight from most of her rivals and had clearly improved for that initial outing. She shapes as though she will get further. (op 15-2)
Maker's Mark(IRE), who was a well-supported favourite, just could not hold off the strong finish of the eventual winner. Perhaps the ground was not as fast as he would have liked, but he wandered under pressure and might have been better suited to being held up a bit longer. (op Evens tchd 5-4 in a place and 6-5 in places and 11-10 in places)
Masai Moon, whose trainer has a poor record at this track, probably ran close to his mark and helps set the level of the form. (op 8-1)
Impromptu, a beaten favourite on his last two starts, got the sixth furlong well and, not for the first time, gave the impression that a race can be won with him. (op 11-2 tchd 7-1)
Oceana Gold, a half-brother to Snake Skin, a moderate seven-furlong winner at two, got going late in the day and stayed on well from off the pace. His trainer's juveniles usually improve for their debut outings so he could well step up on this next time.
Money For Fun, who is out of a mare who won over a mile, did not shape too badly on her debut. (tchd 80-1)

4775 WEATHERBYS BANK STONEHENGE STKS (LISTED RACE) 1m

6:20 (6:23) (Class 1) 2-Y-O
£14,195 (£5,380; £2,692; £1,342; £672; £337) **Stalls** Centre

Form RPR

521 **1** **Streets Ahead**[8] [4526] 2-8-13 .... LDettori 4 99
(A M Balding) *hld up bhd ldrs: rdn to ld 2f out: kpt on gamely: rdn out* **7/1**[3]

1121 **2** *1* **Eddie Jock (IRE)**[13] [4344] 2-8-13 105 .... JamieSpencer 2 96
(M L W Bell) *trckd ldrs: effrt 2f out: wnt 2nd ins fnl f but a hld by wnr* **10/11**[1]

11 **3** *3/4* **Champery (USA)**[48] [3280] 2-8-13 .... KDarley 5 95
(M Johnston) *led: rdn and narrowly hdd 2f out: battled on: no ex ins fnl f* **2/1**[2]

1023 **4** *nk* **Easy Lover**[11] [4436] 2-8-8 82 .... RyanMoore 1 89
(J A Osborne) *hld up but in tch: slighlty outpcd 3f out: styd on ins fnl f* **33/1**

6310 **5** *3* **La Roca (IRE)**[63] [2800] 2-8-8 90 .... TPQueally 3 82
(R M Beckett) *hld up bhd ldrs: effrt 2f out: kpt on same pce fnl f* **25/1**

1023 **6** *5* **Johannesburg Jack (IRE)**[13] [4344] 2-8-13 93 .... SteveDrowne 6 76
(H Morrison) *t.k.h early: trckd ldr: rdn over 2f out: wknd over 1f out* **14/1**

1m 44.86s (1.77) **Going Correction** +0.125s/f (Good) **6** Ran SP% **111.7**
Speed ratings (Par 102):96,95,94,93,90 85
CSF £13.81 TOTE £6.60: £3.00, £1.20; EX 12.60.
Owner John Dwyer & Mrs J R Ramsden **Bred** Deerpark Stud **Trained** Kingsclere, Hants

FOCUS
Not the strongest Listed race ever run, and the form is held down by the fourth. The soft ground may well have been against the market leaders.

NOTEBOOK
Streets Ahead, who has progressed with every outing, was well backed to follow up his recent course win on this step up in trip and grade. Brought to challenge four or five horse-widths off the rail, he was going best two furlongs out and knuckled down well under pressure to gain the day. The little bit of ease in the ground suited him and connections are now planning to send him out to Canada for the valuable Summer Stakes at Woodbine next month, where they hope he will showcase his talent to potential buyers from the US. (op 11-1 tchd 6-1)
Eddie Jock(IRE), who saw the form of his Shergar Cup success given a boost when the runner-up won a valuable sales race at York the previous day, was not as effective with cut in the ground as the winner and failed to justify his short price in the market. (op 8-11 tchd Evens)
Champery(USA) enjoyed the run of the race in front but he clung to the far-side rail when perhaps the better ground was wide of it. It is also quite possible that the easy surface in general was not in his favour as his previous two wins had come on quick ground. (op 9-4 tchd 5-2)
Easy Lover, stepping up a furlong in distance, ran her best race so far on turf and got the trip well. She is probably a good marker for the level of the form. (tchd 40-1)
La Roca(IRE), running for the first time since finishing in mid-division in the Albany Stakes at Royal Ascot, was stepping up in trip and taking on the colts, and it proved too much for her. (op 20-1)

Johannesburg Jack(IRE) finished nine lengths behind Eddie Jock at Ascot in the Shergar Cup Juvenile and, while he had a 6lb pull at the weights with him this time, it made no difference as he came home nine lengths adrift again. (op 12-1 tchd 16-1)

4776 BEGBIES TRAYNOR MAIDEN STKS — 1m 1f 198y
6:50 (6:52) (Class 5) 3-4-Y-O — **£5,181** (£1,541; £770; £384) **Stalls** High

Form — RPR

2- **1** **Sharpsburg (USA)**[322] 5709 3-9-3 .... LDettori 8 — 82+
(Saeed Bin Suroor) *trckd ldrs: rdn to chal over 3f out: led 1f out: styd on wl to assert fnl 75yds* **1/1**[1]

022 **2** *2 ½* **Accompanist**[15] 4300 3-9-3 84 .... RichardHughes 9 — 77+
(J H M Gosden) *led for over 1f: trckd ldr: led again wl over 2f out: sn rdn: edgd rt ent fnl f and hdd: kpt on but hld fnl 75yds* **9/4**[2]

5- **3** *2 ½* **Gravinsky (USA)**[342] 5306 3-9-3 .... RyanMoore 13 — 72
(Mrs A J Perrett) *chsd ldrs: rdn over 2f out: swtchd lft over 1f out: kpt on* **10/1**

4 *1* **Foreigner (IRE)** 3-9-3 .... SteveDrowne 6 — 70
(B J Meehan) *chsd ldrs: rdn wl over 2f out: kpt on same pce fnl 2f* **20/1**

5 *5* **Kala Dancer** 3-9-3 .... KDarley 7 — 61
(Lady Herries) *towards rr: rdn 3f out: styd on fnl f: nrst fin* **50/1**

6 *1* **Bonnie Belle** 3-8-9 .... AmirQuinn(3) 14 — 54
(J R Boyle) *in tch: rdn over 3f out: one pce fr over 1f out* **100/1**

7 *2* **Well Versed** 3-8-12 .... TPQueally 12 — 50+
(C F Wall) *s.i.s: towards rr: sme late prog: nvr trbld ldrs* **100/1**

5 **8** *¾* **Theologicum**[12] 4396 3-8-9 .... NeilChalmers(3) 3 — 48
(Miss J R Gibney) *mid div: effrt 3f out: wknd fnl f* **25/1**

0 **9** *5* **The Combo**[55] 3100 3-9-3 .... AlanDaly 1 — 44
(M Blanshard) *mid div tl 4f out* **100/1**

52 **10** *1 ¾* **Darenjan (IRE)**[9] 4471 3-9-3 .... JamieSpencer 2 — 41
(Sir Michael Stoute) *led after 1f: reminders over 6f out: rdn 4f out: hdd wl over 2f out: grad fdd* **9/2**[3]

0-0 **11** *5* **Mr Bilbo Baggins**[18] 4210 3-8-10 .... JosephWalsh(7) 4 — 31
(J S Moore) *mid div tl 4f out* **100/1**

12 *1 ¼* **Xeniam (IRE)** 3-9-3 .... DaneO'Neill 11 — 29
(A King) *slowly away: a bhd* **50/1**

0 **13** *14* **Forever Thine**[18] 4210 3-8-7 .... TravisBlock(5) 5 — —
(J A Geake) *a towards rr* **100/1**

14 *½* **Definitely Blue** 3-8-12 .... PaulFitzsimons 10 — —
(C F Wall) *in tch: rdn 3f out: sn wknd* **100/1**

2m 11.19s (2.73) **Going Correction** +0.125s/f (Good) — **14** Ran SP% **126.5**
Speed ratings (Par 103):94,92,90,89,85 84,82,82,78,76 72,71,60,60
CSF £3.39 TOTE £2.10: £1.10, £1.20, £3.10; EX 5.70.
Owner Godolphin **Bred** George Strawbridge Jnr **Trained** Newmarket, Suffolk

FOCUS
A fair maiden on paper, but the winning time was modest.

4777 WESTOVER GROUP H'CAP — 1m 6f 15y
7:20 (7:21) (Class 5) (0-70,71) 3-Y-O+ — **£3,562** (£1,059; £529; £264) **Stalls** Far side

Form — RPR

3-41 **1** **Fair Along (GER)**[8] 4530 4-10-1 71 6ex .... JamieSpencer 3 — 94+
(P J Hobbs) *mde all: shkn up to storm clr 2f out: v easily* **1/1**[1]

5013 **2** *8* **Rehearsed (IRE)**[8] 4530 3-8-9 63 .... SteveDrowne 10 — 70
(H Morrison) *mid div: hdwy 4f out: rdn 3f out: styd on but no ch w wnr fr 2f out* **5/1**[2]

0330 **3** *1* **Ritsi**[37] 3649 3-9-1 69 .... (t) NickyMackay 7 — 75
(Mrs A J Perrett) *hld up mid div: dropped rr over 6f out:hdwy wl over 3f out: sn rdn: styd on to go 3rd ins fnl f* **14/1**

132 **4** *½* **Carlton Scroop (FR)**[57] 3016 3-8-5 59 ow2 .... (b) KDarley 4 — 64
(J Jay) *hld up towards rr: hdwy 7f out: rdn in 3rd over 3f out: kpt on same pce fnl 2f* **10/1**

000 **5** *7* **Blue Away (IRE)**[20] 4166 8-9-7 63 .... RichardHughes 13 — 58
(S Kirk) *hld up towards rr: styd on past btn horses fr 2f out: nvr a danger* **14/1**

0445 **6** *2 ½* **Grey Paint (USA)**[8] 4530 3-8-11 65 .... (t) RyanMoore 1 — 57
(R Hannon) *trckd ldrs: rdn to chse wnr over 3f out: wknd over 1f out* **9/1**[3]

0050 **7** *5* **Kaluana Court**[22] 4072 10-8-3 52 oh11 .... MarkCoumbe(7) 11 — 37
(A W Carroll) *in tch: tk clsr order over 4f out: sn rdn: wknd over 1f out* **50/1**

0541 **8** *6* **Linden Lime**[14] 4320 4-9-4 63 .... AmirQuinn(3) 2 — 39
(Jamie Poulton) *t.k.h in rr early: hdwy over 4f out: sn rdn: wknd 2f out* **11/1**

9 *3 ½* **Salym (FR)**[88] 5-8-10 55 .... NeilChalmers(3) 5 — 26
(D J S Ffrench Davis) *a towards rr* **33/1**

051 **10** *16* **Mustang Ali (IRE)**[43] 3437 5-9-0 56 .... AlanDaly 12 — 5
(Dr J R J Naylor) *mid div tl wknd over 3f out* **20/1**

11 *6* **April Attraction (FR)**[82] 4-9-9 70 .... TomMessenger(5) 8 — 11
(C J Down) *t.k.h trcking wnr: rdn over 3f out: sn wknd* **66/1**

0126 **12** *22* **Montage (IRE)**[23] 4046 4-9-2 58 .... TPQueally 6 — —
(J Akehurst) *trckd ldrs: clipped rails after 4f: wnt 2nd briefly over 6f out: rdn over 4f out: sn btn: eased fnl 2f* **12/1**

3m 6.00s (-0.23) **Going Correction** +0.125s/f (Good)
WFA 3 from 4yo+ 12lb — **37** Ran SP% **126.3**
Speed ratings (Par 103):105,100,99,99,95 94,91,87,85,76 73,60
CSF £6.28 CT £51.32 TOTE £1.90: £1.30, £2.10, £4.30; EX 8.20.
Owner Alan Peterson **Bred** Gestut Harzburg **Trained** Withycombe, Somerset

FOCUS
A modest staying handicap, turned into a procession by the well-handicapped winner.
Linden Lime Official explanation: jockey said filly was unsuited by the good (good to soft in places) ground
Mustang Ali(IRE) Official explanation: jockey said gelding had no more to give

4778 SALISBURY PRINTING COMPANY LTD H'CAP — 1m 4f
7:50 (7:50) (Class 4) (0-85,82) 3-Y-O — **£6,477** (£1,927; £963; £481) **Stalls** High

Form — RPR

2130 **1** **Green Room (FR)**[29] 3877 3-9-7 82 .... RyanMoore 3 — 91
(J L Dunlop) *hld up: hdwy 4f out: sn rdn: led 2f out and drifted rt: styd on wl* **14/1**

3212 **2** *1 ¾* **Juniper Girl (IRE)**[96] 1867 3-8-2 70 .... LukeMorris(7) 6 — 76
(M L W Bell) *hld up bhd ldrs: swtchd to stand side and hdwy u.p fr 3f out: wnt 2nd and veered bdly rt 1f out: no ch after* **13/2**

2225 **3** *1 ¾* **Fire Two**[20] 4125 3-9-1 76 .... RichardHughes 2 — 79
(M R Channon) *trckd ldrs: rdn and ev ch 2f out: hld in 3rd whn squeezed up jst ins fnl f* **9/2**[3]

1-60 **4** *nk* **All The Good (IRE)**[13] 4370 3-9-4 79 .... SteveDrowne 5 — 82
(G A Butler) *prom for 3f: trckd ldr: rdn to ld briefly jst over 2f out: kpt on same pce* **20/1**

-440 **5** *1 ¼* **Island Myth (IRE)**[71] 2584 3-9-1 76 .... (b[1]) DaneO'Neill 7 — 82+
(M P Tregoning) *trckd ldrs: swtchd to stand side over 3f out: sn rdn: styng on w runner up whn carried bdly rt 1f out: nt rcvr* **8/1**

6211 **6** *3 ½* **Hanella (IRE)**[19] 4181 3-9-0 75 .... GeorgeBaker 4 — 70
(R M Beckett) *hld up bhd ldrs: rdn over 3f out: no imp* **7/2**[2]

3212 **7** *7* **Kibara**[20] 4159 3-9-5 80 .... NickyMackay 1 — 64
(L M Cumani) *sn led: rdn over 3f out: hdd jst over 2f out: grad fdd* **11/8**[1]

2m 37.65s (1.29) **Going Correction** +0.125s/f (Good) — **7** Ran SP% **118.4**
Speed ratings (Par 102):100,98,97,97,96 94,89
CSF £103.75 TOTE £15.30: £5.70, £2.70; EX 82.20 Place 6 £4.22, Place 5 £2.62..
Owner Nigel & Carolyn Elwes **Bred** Aylesfield Farms Stud Ltd **Trained** Arundel, W Sussex

FOCUS
A fair handicap but the disappointing runs of the first two in the betting weakens the form.
Juniper Girl(IRE) Official explanation: jockey said filly hung badly right
T/Plt: £4.40 to a £1 stake. Pool: £40,715.70. 6,704.45 winning tickets. T/Qpdt: £2.60 to a £1 stake. Pool: £3,781.90. 1,058.40 winning tickets. TM

4532 SANDOWN (R-H)
Friday, August 25

OFFICIAL GOING: Good (good to firm in places on round course)
Wind: Light, half against

4779 VARIETY CLUB DAY TOMORROW NURSERY — 5f 6y
2:00 (2:02) (Class 4) 2-Y-O — **£4,533** (£1,348; £674; £336) **Stalls** High

Form — RPR

412 **1** **Black Moma (IRE)**[6] 4603 2-8-6 70 .... RichardSmith 1 — 76
(R Hannon) *lw: mde all and sn crossed to far side rail: kicked on over 1f out: in n.d after: comf* **7/2**[2]

6230 **2** *1 ¼* **Foxy Games**[7] 4558 2-8-1 65 .... FrancisNorton 4 — 66
(D J S Ffrench Davis) *s.i.s: sn chsd ldrs: rdn 2f out: wnt 2nd 1f out: kpt on but no imp on wnr* **33/1**

0513 **3** *¾* **Jost Van Dyke**[15] 4284 2-8-3 67 .... ChrisCatlin 3 — 65
(B R Millman) *t.k.h: pressed ldrs: wnt 2nd briefly jst over 1f out: one pce fnl f* **14/1**

1220 **4** *½* **Relkida**[19] 4178 2-8-11 78 .... EdwardCreighton(3) 10 — 75+
(M R Channon) *hld up: hmpd after 150yds and dropped to last: effrt 2f out: styd on ins fnl f: nt rch ldrs* **11/2**[3]

210 **5** *nk* **Alternative**[100] 1780 2-9-7 85 .... GeorgeBaker 7 — 80
(R M Beckett) *lw: t.k.h: hld up: reminder ent fnl f: hanging rt and kpt on same pce* **13/2**

0400 **6** *1 ¼* **Queensgate**[9] 4480 2-8-0 64 oh2 ow2 .... HayleyTurner 2 — 55
(M Blanshard) *t.k.h: pressed wnr tl jst over 1f out: wknd ins fnl f* **66/1**

630 **7** *shd* **Land Ahoy**[46] 3344 2-9-2 80 .... MartinDwyer 5 — 71
(D W P Arbuthnot) *t.k.h early: chsd ldrs: rdn 1/2-way: plugging on at one pce and no ch whn nt clr run fnl f* **12/1**

2054 **8** *1 ¾* **Mrs Crossy (IRE)**[15] 4284 2-7-12 62 oh2 .... JimmyQuinn 8 — 46
(A W Carroll) *racd on outer: nvr on terms w ldrs: rdn and struggling 2f out* **25/1**

5242 **9** *¾* **Dee Jay Wells**[9] 4485 2-8-11 75 .... RyanMoore 6 — 57
(R Hannon) *a towards rr: rdn 2f out: no prog* **13/2**

2511 **10** *2 ½* **Inflight (IRE)**[2] 4699 2-8-6 70 6ex .... JosedeSouza 9 — 43
(R M Beckett) *t.k.h: hld up in rr: rdn and no rspnse over 1f out: wknd* **3/1**[1]

62.63 secs (0.42) **Going Correction** -0.025s/f (Good) — **10** Ran SP% **111.9**
Speed ratings (Par 96):95,93,91,91,90 88,88,85,84,80
CSF £111.08 CT £1055.75 TOTE £3.00: £1.20, £7.50, £3.70; EX 72.50.
Owner B Bull **Bred** Poulton Farm Stud **Trained** East Everleigh, Wilts
■ Stewards' Enquiry : Chris Catlin three-day ban: careless riding (Sep 5-7)

FOCUS
The fast strip down the far rail which gave high numbers an advantage over the sprint track the previous week had effectively been eliminated by moving it in three or four yards, and on this occasion there did not appear to be any great bias. It was a bit messy in behind, but the winner won well.

NOTEBOOK
Black Moma(IRE), who went down by a short head to the progressive Abunai at Newmarket six days previously, was 3lb well-in. Smartly away, she quickly got over from her outside draw to claim the rail and, keeping up the gallop, was never seriously threatened. (op 11-4)
Foxy Games, having her first run over this trip and making her nursery debut, went after the winner at the furlong pole but was never going to get to her.
Jost Van Dyke, having his first run at the bare five furlongs, was away on terms this time. After crossing over to the rail, inconveniencing several opponents as he did so, he kept on without getting within striking distance of the winner. (op 16-1)
Relkida was chopped off against the rail before the end of the first furlong, dropping to the rear of the field, and did well to reach her final position. She was down two furlongs in trip and looks worth another try at six on this evidence. Official explanation: jockey said filly suffered interference in running (op 6-1)
Alternative, a stablemate of the beaten favourite, was not given a hard time when held on this first appearance since May. He is capable of a bit better. (op 7-1 tchd 8-1)
Queensgate, reverting to the minimum trip after a run over seven, showed plenty of pace before fading. (op 50-1)
Land Ahoy Official explanation: jockey said colt suffered interference in running
Mrs Crossy(IRE) Official explanation: jockey said filly suffered interference in running
Dee Jay Wells Official explanation: jockey said colt suffered interference in running
Inflight(IRE), bidding for a quick hat-trick, was able to race from a 2lb lower mark than when winning at Brighton two days earlier. She was unable to take advantage, always at the back of the field after being slightly hampered early on, and this run probably came too soon. Official explanation: jockey said filly suffered interference in running (tchd 10-3, 7-2 in places)

4780 BETFRED H'CAP — 5f 6y
2:35 (2:39) (Class 5) (0-75,74) 3-Y-O+ — **£3,886** (£1,156; £577; £288) **Stalls** High

Form — RPR

0005 **1** **Cerulean Rose**[28] 3899 7-8-8 57 .... FrancisNorton 1 — 65
(A W Carroll) *dwlt: wl in rr: rdn and prog on outer fr 2f out: sustained effrt to ld last 50yds* **12/1**

3653 **2** *hd* **Harrison's Flyer (IRE)**[10] 4462 5-9-3 66 .... (p) RyanMoore 5 — 74
(J M Bradley) *b: chsd ldrs: rdn 2f out: prog over 1f out: r.o ins fnl f: jst hld by wnr* **6/1**[3]

2153 **3** *hd* **Blessed Place**[6] 4598 6-9-0 70 .... (t) AshleyHamblett(7) 9 — 77
(D J S Ffrench Davis) *lw: led: rdn over 1f out: kpt on wl: collared last 50yds* **8/1**

2150 **4** *1 ¼* **Drumming Party (USA)**[43] 3438 4-9-1 64 .... (t) DaneO'Neill 2 — 67
(A M Balding) *s.i.s: towards rr tl prog on outer 2f out: drvn and clsd on ldrs ins fnl f: nt qckn last 100yds* **20/1**

3341 **5** *nk* **Forest Dane**[9] 4486 6-9-2 **65** 6ex OscarUrbina 6 66
(Mrs N Smith) *lw: sn prom: trckd ldr 3f out: rdn and no imp over 1f out: fdd and lost pls ins fnl f* **3/1**[1]

5-66 **6** *3* **Semenovskii**[18] 4211 6-9-5 **68** (t) LDettori 7 59
(Miss B Sanders) *wl in rr: rdn and no prog 2f out: no ch after: plugged on ins fnl f* **9/2**[2]

1115 **7** *2* **Further Outlook (USA)**[6] 4602 12-9-0 **66** AdamKirby(3) 3 49
(Miss Gay Kelleway) *pressed ldr for 2f: sn losing pl u.p: wknd fnl f* **8/1**

3604 **8** *½* **Quality Street**[20] 4158 4-9-11 **74** MartinDwyer 8 56
(P Butler) *settled in rr: rdn and no prog 2f out: wl btn after* **9/1**

000 **9** *nk* **Fizzlephut (IRE)**[22] 4085 4-9-9 **72** RichardSmith 11 53
(Miss J R Tooth) *chsd ldrs to 1/2-way: lost pl rapidly u.p* **16/1**

0001 **10** *1½* **Whistler**[10] 4462 9-9-0 **63** 6ex (b) PaulFitzsimons 10 38
(Miss J R Tooth) *dwlt: hld up in last: plenty to do over 1f out: trapped on inner after and no ch: eased ins fnl f* **12/1**

61.38 secs (-0.83) **Going Correction** -0.025s/f (Good) **10** Ran SP% **115.7**
Speed ratings (Par 103):105,104,104,102,101 97,93,93,92,90
CSF £81.65 CT £636.00 TOTE £11.40: £2.50, £2.20, £3.00; EX 80.80.
Owner Rob Willis **Bred** J And Mrs Bowtell **Trained** Cropthorne, Worcs

FOCUS
A second win for a horse drawn one over the five-furlong track, seemingly confirming that there was no real draw advantage at this meeting. Low level handicap form though.
Whistler Official explanation: jockey said gelding was denied a clear run

4781 EUROPEAN BREEDERS FUND MAIDEN STKS 7f 16y
3:10 (3:16) (Class 5) 2-Y-O **£4,533** (£1,348; £674; £336) **Stalls** High

Form RPR

2 **1** **Big Robert**[28] 3892 2-9-3 MartinDwyer 9 85
(W R Muir) *t.k.h early: trckd ldng pair: effrt 3f out: rdn to ld 2f out: styd on wl fnl f* **7/2**[2]

4 **2** *2* **Regal Flush**[35] 3701 2-9-3 LDettori 5 80
(Sir Michael Stoute) *lw: trckd ldr: chal over 2f out: w wnr sn after: nt qckn over 1f out: outpcd ins fnl f* **4/7**[1]

3 **3** *2* **Hunting Tower**[81] 2287 2-9-3 RyanMoore 3 75
(R Hannon) *w'like: trckd ldrs: effrt 3f out: hanging bdly rt fr over 2f out: kpt on to take 3rd ins fnl f* **10/1**[3]

6 **4** *nk* **Altar (IRE)**[57] 3025 2-9-3 HayleyTurner 2 74
(R Hannon) *t.k.h early: trckd ldrs: effrt over 2f out: kpt on same pce fr over 1f out* **33/1**

4 **5** *2½* **Lady Chastity**[15] 4283 2-8-9 EdwardCreighton(3) 12 63
(Mrs L J Young) *leggy: led: rdn and hdd 2f out: fdd* **66/1**

6 *½* **Murrin (IRE)** 2-9-3 FrancisNorton 11 66
(T G Mills) *unf: scope: hld up in midfield: nt on terms fr 3f out: shuffled along and rn green 2f out: kpt on* **50/1**

7 *1* **Camps Bay (USA)** 2-9-3 OscarUrbina 6 64
(Mrs A J Perrett) *w'like: bit bkwd: s.s: hld up in last pair: shuffled along over 2f out: no prog tl styd on ins fnl f* **40/1**

8 *1* **Professor Twinkle** 2-9-3 PaulDoe 10 61
(W J Knight) *w'like: bit bkwd: hld up wl in rr: nt on terms fr 3f out: nudged along and no prog* **50/1**

9 *½* **Celtic Step** 2-9-3 KDarley 7 60
(M Johnston) *unf: plld hrd early: restrained into midfield: rn green and struggling 3f out* **14/1**

0 **10** *2* **Berkeley Castle (USA)**[21] 4103 2-9-3 DaleGibson 1 55
(Sir Michael Stoute) *w'like: scope: str: dwlt: a wl in rr: pushed along and no prog 3f out* **40/1**

11 *1¼* **Hatherden** 2-9-3 GeorgeBaker 8 51
(Miss E C Lavelle) *w'like: bit bkwd: hld up wl in rr: pushed along 2f out: no prog* **40/1**

12 *1* **Raglan Copenhagen** 2-9-3 DaneO'Neill 4 49
(B R Millman) *w'like: bit bkwd: s.s: rn green in rr: hanging bdly 3f out: sn btn* **25/1**

1m 30.35s (-0.74) **Going Correction** -0.025s/f (Good) **12** Ran SP% **121.2**
Speed ratings (Par 94):103,100,98,98,95 94,93,92,91,89 88,86
CSF £5.62 TOTE £4.20: £1.20, £1.10, £1.90; EX 9.40.
Owner Martin P Graham **Bred** Deerfield Farm **Trained** Lambourn, Berks

FOCUS
They went just an ordinary pace and not many got involved. The form as it stands is nothing special, but there were some nice prospects for later on in the field.

NOTEBOOK
Big Robert ◆ confirmed the promise of his Ascot debut second, fighting off the favourite and well on top at the end. He holds no big-race engagements this year but is a nice prospect for middle distances next term. (tchd 4-1)
Regal Flush had every chance but was outpointed by the winner in the latter stages. He is still immature and needs more time, but the ability is there and he could make a decent three-year-old. (op 8-11 tchd 4-5 in places)
Hunting Tower, off the track since his debut in June, stayed on quite well for third despite hanging. A further step up in trip should suit. (op 9-1)
Altar(IRE), off the track since his debut two months earlier, was never far away and was just denied third by his stablemate.
Lady Chastity, stepped up two furlongs in trip from her debut, set just an ordinary pace and gradually faded after being collared with a quarter of a mile to run.
Murrin(IRE), who cost 26,000gns earlier this year, is a half-brother to a couple of minor winners out of an unraced daughter of Musidora winner Fatah Flare. He looked in need of the race beforehand and kept on without being given a hard time.
Camps Bay(USA), a $130,000 yearling, raced at the back of the field following a sluggish start but was keeping on against the rail in the straight. He can do better. Official explanation: jockey said colt missed the break (op 33-1)
Professor Twinkle, out of a half-sister to the smart Polar Boy, is a half-brother to a couple of winners at around a mile. He was by no means given a hard time on this debut and is capable of better.
Raglan Copenhagen Official explanation: jockey said colt hung right

4782 ATLANTIS CHRISTMAS PARTY NIGHTS AT SANDOWN PARK H'CAP 1m 14y
3:45 (3:46) (Class 3) (0-90,90) 3-Y-O+ **£8,096** (£2,408; £1,203; £601) **Stalls** High

Form RPR

-300 **1** **Killena Boy (IRE)**[26] 3973 4-9-2 **79** PaulDoe 9 92+
(W Jarvis) *trckd ldrs: tried to chal on inner and hmpd over 1f out: rallied ent fnl f: r.o to ld last 75yds* **25/1**

2020 **2** *¾* **Gaelic Princess**[16] 4241 6-9-1 **78** OscarUrbina 6 84+
(A G Newcombe) *hld up in last trio: effrt 2f out: plenty to do whn nt clr run ent fnl f: r.o wl last 150yds: nrst fin* **20/1**

4-06 **3** *shd* **Unshakable (IRE)**[8] 4535 7-9-13 **90** FrancisNorton 8 99+
(Bob Jones) *b: t.k.h: hld up midfield: shkn up and lost pl 3f out: nt clr run over 1f out to last 150yds: r.o wl nr fin* **10/3**[2]

/00- **4** *¾* **Esquire**[386] 4101 4-9-12 **89** LDettori 5 93
(Saeed Bin Suroor) *lw: trckd ldng pair: clsd over 2f out: led over 1f out and looked likely wnr: hdd & wknd last 75yds* **3/1**[1]

1005 **5** *¾* **Red Cape (FR)**[12] 4391 3-9-6 **89** DaneO'Neill 3 91
(Jane Chapple-Hyam) *hld up in last trio: rdn and effrt on outer 2f out: tried to cl 1f out: one pce fnl f* **25/1**

5112 **6** *nk* **Habshan (USA)**[18] 4209 6-9-8 **85** GeorgeBaker 1 87
(C F Wall) *lw: trckd ldrs on outer: effrt over 2f out: hanging rt after: chsd ldng pair over 1f out: fdd ins fnl f* **5/1**[3]

0342 **7** *1* **Titian Dancer**[28] 3906 3-8-4 **73** (t) DaleGibson 10 72
(W R Swinburn) *pushed up to ld and then t.k.h: hdd after 1f: chsd ldr to over 2f out: wknd fnl f* **5/1**[3]

3050 **8** *2* **Barathea Dreams (IRE)**[8] 4536 5-9-0 **77** MartinDwyer 7 72
(J S Moore) *pushed up to ld after 1f and set gd pce: 3 l clr 1/2-way: hdd & wknd over 1f out* **13/2**

0000 **9** *5* **Silver Blue (IRE)**[34] 3737 3-9-4 **87** RyanMoore 2 70
(R Hannon) *a last and nvr gng wl: rdn 1/2-way: wknd 2f out* **14/1**

1m 43.53s (-0.42) **Going Correction** -0.025s/f (Good)
WFA 3 from 4yo+ 6lb **9** Ran SP% **113.9**
Speed ratings (Par 107):101,100,100,99,98 98,97,95,90
CSF £415.38 CT £2091.44 TOTE £27.20: £6.00, £5.00, £1.70; EX 391.90.
Owner Capel (CS) Ltd **Bred** John Malone **Trained** Newmarket, Suffolk
■ Stewards' Enquiry : Martin Dwyer two-day ban: careless riding (Sep 5-6)
Paul Doe two-day ban: careless riding (Sep 5 & 6)

FOCUS
A messy race in which they finished in a bit of a heap, but the first three are all a bit better than the bare form as none of them enjoyed a trouble-free passage.

NOTEBOOK
Killena Boy(IRE) had laboured off this sort of mark since gaining his most recent victory in April last year. He was badly hampered against the rail over a furlong out and deserves plenty of credit - Doe too - for the way he picked himself up to show ahead in the last half-furlong. (op 33-1)
Gaelic Princess was running on easier ground than of late. Held up as usual, she was slightly hampered entering the last when attempting to improve but ran on well up the final climb once in the clear.
Unshakable(IRE), having only his third run of the campaign, was back at his optimum trip. Like the runner-up he met with traffic problems at a crucial stage, but finished strongly when in the clear. Official explanation: jockey said gelding was denied a clear run (op 7-2)
Esquire, sidelined with niggling problems since his last appearance just over a year ago, was having only the fifth run of his life. Always well placed, he moved smoothly to the front approaching the final furlong and the race looked his, but he began to tire up the final hill. His connections' patience should be rewarded before long. (op 11-4 tchd 5-2)
Red Cape(FR) improved to look a threat a furlong from home but the effort flattened out late on. He would have no problem with this trip on an easier track. (op 20-1)
Habshan(USA), raised a further pound and racing from a career-high mark, was in with a chance in the straight but looked to hang under pressure and could never quite get to the front. Official explanation: jockey said gelding hung right under pressure (tchd 6-1)
Barathea Dreams(IRE), who won this event a year ago from the same mark, was three lengths to the good turning into the straight. Headed with over a furlong to run, he was still in second place with 200 yards to go but weakened quickly. He really requires softer ground. (op 5-1 tchd 7-1)

4783 SANDOWN FUTURITY CONDITIONS STKS 1m 14y
4:20 (4:22) (Class 4) 2-Y-O **£6,232** (£1,866) **Stalls** High

Form RPR

01 **1** **Gold Option**[7] 4572 2-8-12 RyanMoore 1 93
(J H M Gosden) *trckd rival: pushed into ld 2f out: rdn out fnl f* **4/7**[1]

41 **2** *1¼* **Frosty Night (IRE)**[47] 3328 2-8-12 **87** MartinDwyer 2 90
(M Johnston) *lw: led: rdn and hdd 2f out: kpt on but readily hld fnl f* **11/8**[2]

1m 45.56s (1.61) **Going Correction** -0.025s/f (Good) **2** Ran SP% **105.8**
Speed ratings (Par 96):90,88
TOTE £1.40.
Owner K Abdulla **Bred** Juddmonte Farms Ltd **Trained** Newmarket, Suffolk

FOCUS
A very disappointing turnout, and this race will not be staged next year. The two of them went a decent pace, though.

NOTEBOOK
Gold Option, stepped up to a mile, tracked his sole opponent before quickening up to lead and was always in command thereafter. This likeable colt is ready for a step up in grade and may go for the Royal Lodge. (op 8-13 tchd 4-6 in places)
Frosty Night(IRE), like his rival coming here off the back of a win in a seven-furlong maiden, set a decent pace until headed at the quarter-mile pole. He tried his best to rally, but was always being held. (op 5-4)

4784 BETFREDPOKER H'CAP 1m 2f 7y
4:55 (4:55) (Class 4) (0-80,78) 3-Y-O **£5,505** (£1,637; £818; £408) **Stalls** High

Form RPR

612 **1** **Celtic Spirit (IRE)**[65] 2754 3-9-4 **75** GeorgeBaker 8 89+
(R M Beckett) *settled off the pce towards rr: prog 3f out: chsd ldr over 1f out: clsd to ld last 100yds: styd on wl* **7/2**[2]

14 **2** *1* **Lake Shabla (USA)**[100] 1777 3-9-7 **78** MartinDwyer 7 90+
(E A L Dunlop) *trckd ldrs: effrt 3f out: led 2f out and kicked on: hrd pressed 1f out: hdd and no ex last 100yds* **15/8**[1]

3361 **3** *1¾* **Luna Landing**[26] 3984 3-9-3 **74** DaleGibson 3 83
(Jedd O'Keeffe) *hld up wl in rr: struggling in last pair 3f out: gd prog on inner fr 2f out: styd on: nrst fin* **14/1**

0112 **4** *5* **Benbrook**[19] 4173 3-8-12 **69** PaulDoe 11 69
(J L Dunlop) *led at str pce for 3f: chsd ldr: led again briefly over 2f out: wknd over 1f out* **7/1**[3]

-204 **5** *3½* **Cape Diamond (IRE)**[25] 4001 3-8-13 **70** OscarUrbina 5 63
(W R Swinburn) *hld up in midfield: effrt over 3f out: no imp 2f out: sn wknd* **12/1**

3414 **6** *3½* **Bon Viveur**[9] 4490 3-9-2 **73** (p) RyanMoore 6 59
(R Hannon) *w ldr: led after 3f and maintained gd pce: hdd over 2f out: sn wknd* **9/1**

4143 **7** *1¼* **Truly Fruitful (IRE)**[6] 4586 3-8-12 **74** AndrewElliott(5) 1 58
(K R Burke) *chsd ldng pair to 3f out: wknd 2f out* **8/1**

0434 **8** *3½* **Ahmedy (IRE)**[9] 4481 3-8-12 **72** EdwardCreighton(3) 12 49
(M R Channon) *s.s: prog fr last pair 5f out: rdn and wknd over 2f out* **10/1**

5062 **9** *3½* **Jebel Ali (IRE)**[30] 3848 3-9-3 **74** MichaelTebbutt 4 45
(B Gubby) *chsd ldrs: rdn and wknd 3f out: no ch whn n.m.r 2f out* **20/1**

0 **10** *88* **Versatile**[16] 4249 3-8-11 **73** EmmettStack(5) 9 —
(G A Ham) *v s.i.s: a in last pair: rdn and wknd 4f out: virtually p.u over 1f out* **66/1**

2m 8.64s (-1.60) **Going Correction** -0.025s/f (Good) **10** Ran SP% **120.3**
Speed ratings (Par 102):105,104,102,98,96 93,92,89,86,16
CSF £10.83 CT £83.24 TOTE £4.70: £1.50, £1.60, £3.20; EX 13.90 Place 6 £101.53, Place 5 £29.79.

Owner Mrs H M Chamberlain **Bred** Genesis Green Stud Ltd **Trained** Whitsbury, Hants
FOCUS
This was run at a fast pace. A fair handicap, and the form looks solid, with the front pair progressive and probably better than the bare form.
Versatile Official explanation: jockey said gelding lost its action 5f out
T/Plt: £135.60 to a £1 stake. Pool: £55,769.45. 300.10 winning tickets. T/Qpdt: £14.30 to a £1 stake. Pool: £2,954.40. 151.90 winning tickets. JN

4785 - 4786a (Foreign Racing) - See Raceform Interactive

4384 SARATOGA (R-H)
Friday, August 25

OFFICIAL GOING: Fast

4787a ALLOWANCE OPTIONAL CLAIMING RACE — 7f
11:07 (11:07) 3-Y-O+ **£18,837**

RPR
1 **Discreet Cat (USA)**[153] [739] 3-8-4 .... GKGomez 123+
(Saeed Bin Suroor) **2/5**[1]
2 *11* **Accountforthegold (USA)**[683] 4-8-7 .... MLuzzi 92
(G Contessa, U.S.A) **35/1**[3]
3 *3/4* **Dark Cheetah (USA)**[104] 4-8-7 .... EPrado 90
(R Dutrow Jr, U.S.A) **51/10**[2]
1m 21.53s
WFA 3 from 4yo 5lb **6** Ran SP% **90.6**

Owner Godolphin Racing Inc **Bred** E Paul Robsham **Trained** Newmarket, Suffolk
FOCUS
Just an Allowance race, but the long-awaited return of Discreet Cat following a five-month break, and he did not disappoint.
NOTEBOOK
Discreet Cat(USA) ◆, purchased privately by Godolphin after winning his maiden here as a juvenile, has since hacked up in two races in Dubai, including in the UAE Derby, where he had subsequent multiple Grade 1 winner Invasor around seven lengths behind in fourth. Returned to the US off the back of a five-month break, he maintained his unbeaten record with a mightily-impressive success. Off the pace in the early stages, he cruised into the lead on the turn into the straight without his jockey having to move a muscle and sustained his challenge in effortless fashion to draw well clear. The winning time was the fastest recorded over this trip at the whole Saratoga meet, despite the apparent ease of his victory, and the trainer's assistant, Rick Mettee, reported him to be "a good two works short of being spot-on fit". He may now be aimed at the Jerome Handicap at Belmont Park in October, but longer-term plans are as yet undecided. He would surely be one of the leading contenders if lining up in the Breeders' Cup Classic, but he is owned by the same connections as current ante-post favourite Bernardini and it is unlikely they would want the pair to clash. Whatever the case, he stays in training as a four-year-old and could be aimed at the Dubai World Cup. He is developing into a top-class performer and it will be fascinating to see him at full throttle.

4759 CHESTER (L-H)
Saturday, August 26

OFFICIAL GOING: Good (good to soft in places)
Wind: Light, across

4788 WILLIAM T CORBETT E B F MAIDEN STKS — 7f 2y
2:15 (2:16) (Class 4) 2-Y-O **£6,800** (£2,023; £1,011; £505) **Stalls** Low

Form RPR
3 **1** **Ravi River (IRE)**[7] [4592] 2-9-3 .... MichaelHills 4 84
(B W Hills) *trckd ldng pair: hdwy 2f out: rdn to ld jst ins last: kpt on* **1/1**[1]
5 **2** *1/2* **Minos (IRE)**[29] [3892] 2-9-3 .... FrancisNorton 3 83
(R Hannon) *dwlt: sn cl up: rdn to ld wl over 1f out: hdd jst ins last: kpt on wl u.p* **7/4**[2]
04 **3** *5* **Its Moon (IRE)**[23] [4089] 2-8-12 .... RobertWinston 6 65
(M R Channon) *hld up in rr: hdwy over 2f out: sn rdn and no imp fr over 1f out* **16/1**
5 **4** *nk* **Sendali (FR)**[34] [3758] 2-9-3 .... KerrinMcEvoy 1 70
(J D Bethell) *trckd ldrs: rdn along over 2f out: sn one pce* **20/1**
0 **5** *3 1/2* **Mozayada (USA)**[23] [4084] 2-8-12 .... RoystonFfrench 2 56
(M Johnston) *led: rdn along over 2f out: hdd wl over 1f out: sn wknd* **8/1**[3]
1m 27.68s (-0.79) **Going Correction** +0.025s/f (Good) **5** Ran SP% **108.1**
Speed ratings (Par 96):105,104,98,98,94
CSF £2.83 TOTE £1.90: £1.30, £1.50; EX 2.20.
Owner Gainsborough Stud **Bred** Gainsborough Stud Management Ltd **Trained** Lambourn, Berks
FOCUS
A good maiden, run in a decent time, in which two useful sorts pulled clear.
NOTEBOOK
Ravi River(IRE), who looked to set the standard on the back of his promising debut third at Newbury the previous weekend, comes from a stable that does exceptionally well with their juveniles here and he produced a good burst close home to win with a bit to spare. The front pair put distance between themselves and the third and the son of Barathea looks worth his place in a better class of contest, although whether he is up to his Group 1 Dewhurst and Racing Post Trophy entries is doubtful. (op 4-5 tchd 11-10)
Minos(IRE), who shaped promisingly on his debut in a warm race at Ascot, always had the pace-setting Mozayada covered and he went on over a furlong out, but the winner had a superior finish. He should find a maiden before stepping into nurseries. (op 11-4)
Its Moon(IRE) has been crying out for this step up in distance and she showed improved form, but the front pair proved superior. She is now qualified for nurseries and can fare much better in that sphere. (tchd 14-1)
Sendali(FR) stepped up on his debut effort and the son of Derby runner-up Daliapour can be expected to improve once tackling a mile plus in nurseries. (op 16-1)
Mozayada(USA) could never get into it from a bad draw on her debut at Goodwood, but she was able to get to the lead here and dictate at just a steady gallop. It was disappointing therefore that she dropped away like she did and, for the time being, she is one to have serious reservations over. (op 7-1)

4789 BETTERBETCORBETT E B F CONDITIONS STKS (C&G) — 6f 18y
2:45 (2:46) (Class 2) 2-Y-O **£9,778** (£2,926; £1,463; £731) **Stalls** Low

Form RPR
1001 **1** **Gold Spirit (IRE)**[13] [4397] 2-9-1 98 .... FrancisNorton 1 101+
(E J O'Neill) *wnt rt s: mde all: rdn clr over 1f out: comf* **4/5**[1]
1205 **2** *3* **Captain Marvelous (IRE)**[28] [3924] 2-9-1 94 .... MichaelHills 3 92
(B W Hills) *fly leapt and hmpd s: hdwy 2f out: rdn to chse wnr ent last: no imp* **3/1**[2]
160 **3** *1 1/2* **Narrjoo (USA)**[25] [4026] 2-9-1 96 .... RobertWinston 2 88
(M R Channon) *hmpd s: sn chsng wnr: effrt to chal wl over 2f out: sn rdn and wknd over 1f out* **4/1**[3]
4020 **4** *3/4* **Dickie Le Davoir**[21] [4146] 2-8-12 90 .... (v) KerrinMcEvoy 5 82
(K R Burke) *sltgly hmpd s. chsd ldng pair: rdn along over 2f out: wknd wl over 1f out* **7/1**
1m 15.35s (-0.30) **Going Correction** +0.025s/f (Good) **4** Ran SP% **113.1**
Speed ratings (Par 100):103,99,97,96
CSF £3.75 TOTE £1.80; EX 3.20.
Owner Roadmate Racing **Bred** Norelands Bloodstock **Trained** Averham Park, Notts
FOCUS
A decent conditions event, but only the winner is progressive and he won tidily.
NOTEBOOK
Gold Spirit(IRE) has progressed extremely well with racing and the step up to six furlongs has really helped of late, with him winning at Lingfield last time. Making the most of stall one on this occasion, he picked up well when asked and won with any amount in hand. He is in both the Group 2 Mill Reef and Redcar Two-Year-Old Trophy, with the latter looking the better option. (op Evens tchd 11-10 in places)
Captain Marvelous(IRE) lost all chance at the start after being hampered and the late headway he made past the weakening Narrjoo was not significant enough to get him near the winner. The drop back to six furlongs helped, but he is not an easy one to place in future. (op 7-2)
Narrjoo(USA) has not been up to it in Group races the last twice, but this drop in grade failed to help and he dropped away disappointingly. He was hampered at the start, but overcame it and is going to be tough to place off this sort of mark. (op 7-2)
Dickie Le Davoir was not disgraced, but the visor he has worn the last twice has failed to make a difference and he is another who is going to be hard to place. (op 13-2)

4790 RAYMOND CORBETT STKS (HERITAGE H'CAP) — 7f 122y
3:25 (3:26) (Class 2) 3-Y-O+
£28,044 (£8,397; £4,198; £2,101; £1,048; £526) **Stalls** Low

Form RPR
-005 **1** **Ordnance Row**[1] [4760] 3-8-8 89 .... MatthewHenry 8 97
(R Hannon) *mde all: qckned 2f out: rdn clr over 1f out: styd on strly* **20/1**
0105 **2** *1* **Irony (IRE)**[9] [4535] 7-8-12 87 .... FrancisNorton 12 93
(A M Balding) *a.p: chsd wnr fr 1/2-way: rdn over 1f out: kpt on ins last* **33/1**
0504 **3** *1* **Dhaular Dhar (IRE)**[1] [4760] 4-8-8 83 .... DanielTudhope 4 87+
(J S Goldie) *hld up towards rr: hdwy 2f out: effrt and edgd lft ent last: sn rdn and kpt on wl towards fin* **9/1**
0060 **4** *1/2* **Josh**[7] [4609] 4-8-3 83 .... (p) AndrewMullen(5) 5 85
(K A Ryan) *chsd ldrs: hdwy 2f out: sn rdn and kpt on same pce ins last* **11/1**
0562 **5** *shd* **Kindlelight Debut**[5] [4660] 6-8-8 83 .... RobbieFitzpatrick 2 85
(N P Littmoden) *a.p: rdn along 2f out: drvn and one pce ent last* **16/1**
0005 **6** *nk* **Seulement (USA)**[14] [4372] 4-9-3 92 .... KerrinMcEvoy 1 93
(L M Cumani) *in tch: effrt 2f out: sn rdn and kpt on same pce ins last* **7/1**[2]
2252 **7** *hd* **Easy Air**[29] [3889] 3-9-0 95 .... RobertWinston 9 95
(E A L Dunlop) *midfield: hdwy on outer over 2f out: rdn to chse ldrs over 1f: drvn and no ex ins last* **7/2**[1]
-102 **8** *hd* **Into The Breeze (IRE)**[74] [2520] 6-8-11 86 .... SebSanders 11 86
(J W Hills) *trckd ldrs: hdwy 3f out: rdn wl over 1f out: wknd ins last* **8/1**[3]
6000 **9** *1 1/2* **Fiefdom (IRE)**[14] [4379] 4-8-7 82 .... RoystonFfrench 14 79
(I W McInnes) *hld up towards rr: pushed along and hdwy 2f out: sn rdn: edgd lft and one pce ins last* **50/1**
102 **10** *hd* **Namroud (USA)**[27] [3985] 7-8-10 85 .... PaulHanagan 7 81
(R A Fahey) *in tch: effrt 2f out: sn rdn and one pce ins last* **10/1**
6330 **11** *shd* **Roman Maze**[1] [4760] 6-8-11 86 .... DavidAllan 10 82
(W M Brisbourne) *keen: hld up in rr: effrt 2f out: sn rdn and kpt on ins last: nt rch ldrs* **12/1**
415 **12** *3/4* **Bayeux (USA)**[28] [3926] 5-9-5 99 .... LiamJones(5) 13 93
(G A Butler) *keen: hld up: a towards rr* **10/1**
3303 **13** *hd* **Speed Dial Harry (IRE)**[3] [4696] 4-7-11 77 ow1 .... (v) AndrewElliott(5) 3 70
(K R Burke) *midfield: whn n.m.r after 1f: rdn along over 2f out: nvr a factor* **12/1**
4325 **14** *2* **Waterline Twenty (IRE)**[6] [4628] 3-8-0 81 .... PaulQuinn 6 68
(P D Evans) *midfield whn hmpd on inner and lost pl after 1f: towards rr after* **20/1**
0P20 **15** *3 1/2* **Lord Of The East**[1] [4760] 7-8-5 83 .... PatrickMathers(3) 15 63
(I W McInnes) *a towards rr* **50/1**
0441 **16** *16* **Jamieson Gold (IRE)**[7] [4593] 3-8-10 91 .... MichaelHills 17 30
(B W Hills) *stdd and swtchd lft s: a rr* **10/1**
1m 34.15s (-0.60) **Going Correction** +0.025s/f (Good)
WFA 3 from 4yo+ 6lb **16** Ran SP% **129.1**
Speed ratings (Par 109):104,103,102,101,101 101,100,100,99,99 98,98,97,95,92 76
CSF £575.13 CT £6488.12 TOTE £29.90: £5.40, £5.80, £3.20, £2.80; EX 622.40 Trifecta £9283.80 Pool: £69,302.26 - 6.30 winning units..
Owner Mrs P Good **Bred** Mrs P Good **Trained** East Everleigh, Wilts
FOCUS
A good, competitive handicap likely to produce winners and best rated through the runner-up.
NOTEBOOK
Ordnance Row, a never-nearer fifth over a half a furlong shorter the previous day, was subject to a late jockey change, but the tactics remained the same and he received a fine ride, leading throughout for a cosy victory. He quickened well off the final bend and his was a welcome return to form, but he was suited by the way the race was run and that is worth bearing in mind off a higher mark in future.
Irony(IRE) ran a huge race from his disadvantageous draw, keeping on well despite having already done a lot of early running and producing probably his best-ever run over this distance. He is not getting any better at the age of seven, but showed here he is still capable of scoring.
Dhaular Dhar(IRE), a dual course winner who finished one spot ahead of Ordnance Row the previous day, finished better than most having been held up, but the winner had the race sewn up. He may soon be ready to win again. (op 8-1)
Josh has been threatening a return to winning ways, but his lack of consistency is usually off-putting with regards to backing him. This was a a decent effort on this step up in distance with the cheekpieces back on, but he cannot be relied up on to repeat it next time. (op 10-1)
Kindlelight Debut, a tough and progressive mare having her 17th outing of the year, ran her race without being good enough to win off this mark and that is likely to continue to be the case. (op 14-1)
Seulement(USA) has in truth proved disappointing since arriving from France and, although having the plum berth here, he could manage no better than sixth. He held the ideal position throughout, but was unable to quicken sufficiently and may be worth stepping back up to ten furlongs. (op 8-1)
Easy Air, a taking winner of his maiden at two, has confirmed that impression this season, developing into a very useful handicapper, but he was a below his best on this occasion and failed to see his race out as strongly as one would have hoped. He was not beaten far in the end and deserves another chance back on a more conventional track. (op 4-1 tchd 9-2 in a place)
Into The Breeze(IRE), who has a good record at the course, was running for the first time since finishing second here in June - behind Dhaular Dhar - and he ran well for a long way considering he had a poor draw. He can be expected to come on for the run.

4791 BETTERBETCORBETT CHESTER H'CAP (LISTED RACE) 1m 5f 89y
4:00 (4:00) (Class 1) (0-110,106) 3-Y-O+

£21,576 (£8,177; £4,092; £2,040; £1,022; £513) Stalls Low

Form				RPR
3121	1		**New Guinea**[6] 4631 3-8-0 **91** 3ex .... MatthewHenry 1 (M A Jarvis) *trckd ldrs: hdwy on inner over 2f out: swtchd rt over 1f out: sn rdn and qcknd to ld ins last: styd on* **11/4**[2]	98+
233-	2	2	**Sunday Symphony**[360] 4870 4-9-3 **98** .... KerrinMcEvoy 6 (Saeed Bin Suroor) *hld up in tch: hdwy and prom after 5f: effrt 3f out: rdn to dispute ld 2f out and ev ch tl drvn and no ex ins last* **7/2**[3]	101
0503	3	shd	**Casual Glance**[14] 4346 4-8-11 **92** oh7 .... FrancisNorton 8 (A M Balding) *a.p: rdn to ld 2f out: drvn over 1f out: hdd and no ex ins last* **20/1**	95
1651	4	3/4	**Kiswahili**[27] 3992 4-9-2 **97** .... SebSanders 2 (Sir Mark Prescott) *in tch: hdwy over 2f out: sn rdn: kpt on u.p ins last* **8/1**	99
0-33	5	hd	**Lost Soldier Three (IRE)**[42] 3551 5-9-11 **106** .... PaulHanagan 9 (L M Cumani) *towards rr: pushed along 1/2-way: rdn along over 4f out: kpt on ins last: nrst fin* **14/1**	107+
1250	6	1 3/4	**Gavroche (IRE)**[49] 3294 5-9-5 **100** .... DavidAllan 4 (J R Boyle) *s.i.s and bhd tl styd on fnl 2f* **25/1**	99
1154	7	1 1/2	**Luberon**[8] 4576 3-8-13 **105** .... RoystonFfrench 7 (M Johnston) *led: rdn along 3f out: drvn and hdd 2f out: sn btn* **20/1**	102
-404	8	3/4	**Private Business (USA)**[44] 3441 3-8-8 **100** ....(b[1]) MichaelHills 5 (B W Hills) *a towards rr* **20/1**	95
1-42	9	1 1/2	**Book Of Music (IRE)**[50] 3255 3-8-7 **99** ow1 .... RobertWinston 3 (Sir Michael Stoute) *in tch: hdwy 3f out pushed along and in tch whn n.m.r wl over 1f out: sn rdn and btn* **9/4**[1]	92

2m 55.07s (-0.35) **Going Correction** +0.025s/f (Good)
WFA 3 from 4yo+ 11lb 9 Ran SP% **115.6**
Speed ratings (Par 111):102,100,100,100,100 99,98,97,96
CSF £11.94 CT £157.21 TOTE £4.10: £1.50, £1.70, £4.30; EX 20.80.
Owner Sheikh Mohammed **Bred** Milton Park Stud Partnership **Trained** Newmarket, Suffolk

FOCUS
A good handicap with a valuable prize but not rated positively with the fourth the best guide.

NOTEBOOK
New Guinea, who showed improved form when winning easily at Pontefract last time, had just a 3lb penalty here and he looked to have the best of the draw for a horse that likes to race prominently. Never far away, he made good headway to challenge and picked up strongly once switched to the outside, coming through to win with a fair bit in hand. On this evidence even further is going to help and he is capable of landing a good back-end handicap on a similarly kind surface. (op 9-4 tchd 3-1, 7-2 and 10-3 in places)
Sunday Symphony, having his first start in almost a year, comes from a yard that is now in top form and he looked set to go close turning in, but the winner stayed on far too strongly for him and he just held on for second. Logic says he will come on for the run and he is the type to continue to run well in similarly good handicaps. (op 4-1 tchd 9-2)
Casual Glance has faced some stiff tasks this season, but she is an honest filly who often runs her race and she put up a cracking effort from 7lb out of the weights. The problem is she is likely to remain too high in the weights to win handicaps and she falls a little short at Listed level.
Kiswahili returned to winning ways in a Listed event at Munich last month, but this was much more competitive and, although running well, she was not up to it off this mark. That is likely to remain the case in handicaps, but her trainer is likely to find her another small race abroad. (op 15-2 tchd 7-1)
Lost Soldier Three(IRE), third to the progressive Linas Selection at York last time, looked vulnerable under top weight and he ran a bit better than expected, not being beaten far at all in fifth. He may be nearing a return to winning form. (tchd 12-1)
Gavroche(IRE) bounced back from a poor effort at Haydock last time, doing well following a slow start. He was racing here off a 6lb higher mark than when last winning and probably needs to drop a few more pounds before winning again. (tchd 33-1)
Luberon, a dual winner in July, ran better than his finishing position suggested in the Gordon Stakes, but his most recent effort at Newmarket was bitterly disappointing and this step up in trip failed to see him in a better light. He may require a break to freshen up. (op 18-1)
Private Business(USA), whose five-length seventh in the Queens Vase gave him a chance, failed to improve for cheekpieces behind Youmzain at Newmarket last time and the first-time blinkers on this occasion also failed to have the desired effect. (tchd 16-1)
Book Of Music(IRE), who was withdrawn as first reserve from the Ebor during the week, is bred to be best at around a mile and, although keeping on when second over ten furlongs at Sandown last time, this substantial rise in distance did not have the desired effect. He is likely to benefit from a drop back in trip. (tchd 5-2, 11-4 in places, 2-1 in a place)

4792 BETTERBETCORBETT "IN RUNNING" H'CAP 1m 7f 195y
4:35 (4:35) (Class 4) (0-85,83) 3-Y-O+ £5,829 (£1,734; £866; £432) Stalls Low

Form				RPR
0043	1		**Establishment**[24] 4046 9-9-6 **75** .... RobertWinston 6 (C A Cyzer) *hld up in rr: rn in snatches: hdwy on outer wl over 1f out: rdn to ld ins last and kpt on wl* **9/1**	83
1062	2	1	**Velvet Heights (IRE)**[52] 3203 4-10-0 **83** .... MichaelHills 7 (J L Dunlop) *hld up: hdwy on bit wl over 2f out: rdn and led briefly 1f out: sn hdd: edgd rt and kpt on* **11/4**[1]	90
3223	3	1 3/4	**Behlaya (IRE)**[8] 4549 5-9-5 **74** .... DavidAllan 2 (T D Easterby) *hld up in tch: pushed along over 3f out: hdwy on inner 2f out: rdn and kpt on fnl f* **9/1**	79
0106	4	1 1/4	**Merrymaker**[20] 4175 6-9-1 **73** .... PatrickMathers[(3)] 4 (W M Brisbourne) *sn pushed along in rr: hdwy over 4f out: rdn along 3f out: kpt on same pce appr last* **8/1**	76
6401	5	hd	**Riff Raff**[15] 4330 3-7-13 **68** .... PaulHanagan 3 (W Jarvis) *cl up: led wl over 2f out: sn rdn: hdd 1f out and grad wknd* **5/1**[3]	71
0522	6	1 1/4	**Boxhall (IRE)**[17] 4268 4-9-4 **73** ....(t) SebSanders 1 (W R Swinburn) *trckd ldrs: effrt and nt clr run wl over 1f out: sn rdn and no imp ins last* **7/2**[2]	78+
0020	7	3 1/2	**Twill (IRE)**[11] 4459 3-8-9 **78** ....(v[1]) FrancisNorton 5 (H Morrison) *led: rdn along over 3f out: hdd wl over 2f out: sn drvn and wknd* **13/2**	75
1/	8	hd	**Fantastic Arts (FR)**[131] 5784 6-9-3 **72** .... RoystonFfrench 8 (Miss Venetia Williams) *chsd ldrs: rdn along over 3f out: sn wknd* **16/1**	69

3m 30.76s (-2.84) **Going Correction** +0.025s/f (Good)
WFA 3 from 4yo+ 14lb 11 Ran SP% **115.9**
Speed ratings (Par 105):108,107,106,106,105 105,103,103
CSF £34.54 CT £234.03 TOTE £10.20: £2.40, £1.60, £2.20; EX 29.20.
Owner Mrs Charles Cyzer **Bred** C A And R M Cyzer **Trained** Maplehurst, W Sussex

FOCUS
Just an average handicap and straightforward form rated around the first three.

4793 BETTERBETCORBETT H'CAP 5f 16y
5:10 (5:11) (Class 4) (0-85,83) 3-Y-O+ £5,829 (£1,734; £866; £432) Stalls Low

Form				RPR
5200	1		**Coconut Moon**[11] 4453 4-8-11 **69** .... DavidAllan 5 (E J Alston) *chsd ldrs: hdwy 2f out: rdn to chal over 1f out: led ins last: drvn out* **17/2**	81
040/	2	1	**Lone Plainsman**[16] 4317 5-9-1 **73** .... DanielTudhope 8 (P F O'Donnell, Ire) *chsd ldrs: hdwy 2f out: rdn to ld briefly over 1f out: hdd and nt qckn ins last* **10/1**	81
3250	3	3/4	**Kings College Boy**[10] 4468 6-9-1 **73** ....(v) PaulHanagan 11 (R A Fahey) *midfield: hdwy wl over 1f out: rdn and edgd lft ins last: kpt on* **11/1**	79+
6065	4	1	**Handsome Cross (IRE)**[10] 4468 5-9-11 **83** .... PaulQuinn 15 (D Nicholls) *towards rr: hdwy on outer 2f out: rdn over 1f out: kpt on ins last: nrst fin* **14/1**	85+
0003	5	1/2	**Bel Cantor**[12] 4422 3-8-4 **67** .... PatrickMathers[(3)] 6 (W J H Ratcliffe) *chsd ldrs: hdwy to ld wl over 1f out: sn rdn: hdd appr last: kpt on same pce* **16/1**	67
1600	6	1/2	**Johnston's Diamond (IRE)**[19] 4202 8-9-9 **81** .... FrancisNorton 3 (E J Alston) *towards rr: hdwy on inner over 1f out: rdn and kpt on ins last* **7/1**[3]	80
0662	7	1/2	**Polish Emperor (USA)**[7] 4598 6-9-7 **79** ....(p) SebSanders 4 (W R Swinburn) *chsd ldrs: rdn wl over 1f out: wknd appr last* **4/1**[1]	76
-400	8	hd	**Westbrook Blue**[7] 4598 4-9-0 **79** .... JackDean[(7)] 14 (W G M Turner) *rr tl styd on wl appr last* **33/1**	75
2050	9	2 1/2	**Plateau**[22] 4101 7-9-8 **80** .... RobertWinston 2 (D Nicholls) *chsd ldrs on inner: rdn along 2f out: sn drvn and wknd* **4/1**[1]	67
1060	10	shd	**One Way Ticket**[23] 4085 6-9-10 **82** ....(p) RoystonFfrench 7 (J M Bradley) *cl up: rdn along 2f out: wknd wl over 1f out* **18/1**	69
1201	11	3/4	**Endless Summer**[15] 4324 9-8-8 **66** .... RobbieFitzpatrick 1 (A W Carroll) *towards rr: n.m.r and hmpd on inner after 1 1/2f: bhd after* **9/2**[2]	50+
4100	12	3/4	**Maktavish**[10] 4468 7-9-0 **75** ....(b) DNolan[(3)] 9 (R Brotherton) *sn led: rdn 2f out: sn hdd & wknd* **33/1**	56

61.65 secs (-0.40) **Going Correction** +0.025s/f (Good)
WFA 3 from 4yo+ 2lb 32 Ran SP% **122.3**
Speed ratings (Par 105):104,102,101,99,98 98,97,96,92,92 91,90
CSF £93.75 CT £962.32 TOTE £10.90: £2.50, £3.60, £3.10; EX 127.90 Place 6 £226.96, Place 5 £207.07.
Owner Valley Paddocks Racing Limited **Bred** Mrs R D Peacock **Trained** Longton, Lancs

FOCUS
Modest handicap form rated through the runner-up.
Plateau Official explanation: jockey said gelding was denied a clear run
T/Plt: £434.30 to a £1 stake. Pool: £67,644.20. 113.70 winning tickets. T/Qpdt: £289.70 to a £1 stake. Pool: £2,976.20. 7.60 winning tickets. JR

4585 GOODWOOD (R-H)
Saturday, August 26

OFFICIAL GOING: Good
Wind: Light across Weather: Changeable

4794 SEABEACH MAIDEN AUCTION STKS 1m
2:00 (2:11) (Class 5) 2-Y-O £3,238 (£963; £481; £240) Stalls High

Form				RPR
02	1		**Duke Of Tuscany**[9] 4525 2-9-1 .... RyanMoore 4 (R Hannon) *lw: mde all: shkn up over 2f out: hung lft but drvn clr fnl f* **4/6**[1]	82
	2	3	**Docofthebay (IRE)** 2-9-0 .... JohnEgan 6 (J A Osborne) *cmpt: lw: dwlt: sn in tch: plld out and effrt over 2f out: rdn to chse wnr over 1f out: outpcd fnl f* **20/1**	74
05	3	1 3/4	**Only Hope**[36] 3713 2-8-8 .... KDarley 2 (M R Channon) *chsd ldrs on outer: rdn over 2f out: effrt to dispute 2nd over 1f out: hanging rt and sn one pce* **14/1**	65
06	4	1 1/4	**Bed Fellow (IRE)**[43] 3498 2-8-12 .... AdamKirby[(3)] 1 (A P Jarvis) *mostly chsd wnr: shkn up and nt qckn 2f out: lost 2nd over 1f out: wknd fnl f* **10/1**[3]	69
5	5	1 3/4	**Grand Diamond (IRE)**[71] 2619 2-8-13 .... JimCrowley 9 (Mrs A J Perrett) *lw: prom: shkn up 2f out: no rspnse: fdd over 1f out* **7/2**[2]	63
4	6	3/4	**The Skerret**[63] 2857 2-8-10 ow1 .... RobertHavlin 7 (P Winkworth) *chsd ldrs: rdn over 2f out: wknd over 1f out* **16/1**	58
	7	7	**Bajan Pride** 2-8-12 .... RichardSmith 3 (R Hannon) *w'like: str: bit bkwd: restless stalls: s.s: a in last trio: off the pce fr over 3f out* **16/1**	45
	8	1	**Mystical Moon** 2-8-12 .... JimmyQuinn 8 (Lady Herries) *leggy: dwlt: rn green and a in last pair: bhd fr 1/2-way* **20/1**	43
0	9	11	**Dancing Reva (IRE)**[10] 4479 2-8-9 .... DaleGibson 5 (J J Bridger) *lw: hanging and racing awkwardly after 3f: sn lost tch: t.o* **100/1**	16

1m 41.14s (0.87) **Going Correction** +0.025s/f (Good) 9 Ran SP% **120.2**
Speed ratings (Par 94):96,93,91,90,88 87,80,79,68
CSF £21.81 TOTE £1.70: £1.10, £3.30, £2.10; EX 19.40.
Owner Justin Dowley & Michael Pescod **Bred** Cheveley Park Stud Ltd **Trained** East Everleigh, Wilts
■ Laureldean Express withdrawn: (2/1, jockey injured.) Rule 4 applies to board prices only deduction 30p in £. New market formed.

FOCUS
This looked a modest maiden for the course following teh withdrawal of 'form' horse Laureldean Express.

NOTEBOOK
Duke Of Tuscany had a relatively straightforward task following the withdrawal of market rival Laureldean Express, whose jockey was injured in a parade-ring fall. He got the extra furlong alright, but a drop back to seven furlongs should not be a problem either. (new market new market op 7-4 tchd 8-13)
Docofthebay(IRE), related to several winners at up to nine furlongs, made a promising debut. He does not need to improve on this to find a maiden, so the future looks bright. (new market new market op 22-1 tchd 25-1 and 14-1)
Only Hope stayed the mile, but might be worth a try at seven furlongs. She is now qualified for nurseries, and has shown enough to be competitive in that field, though on this evidence she could still find a maiden at one of the lesser tracks. (new market new market op 20-1)
Bed Fellow(IRE) has not quite been getting home in his three races to date, though better can be expected now he is qualified for nurseries as soon as connections have established his ideal trip. (new market new market op 20-1 tchd 9-1)
Grand Diamond(IRE) had been off for more than two months, and looks to be heading for an autumn campaign. Though not living up to his billing as second-favourite, he can step up on this as he matures. (new market new market op 13-2 tchd 7-1)

The Skerret, who looked very fit, was stepping up to a mile from seven furlongs, but the jury is still out on that score. However, he has shown some ability, and looks a nursery type after one more run. (new market new market op 28-1)
Mystical Moon, a half-brother (by the top-class Medicean) to two fine stayers - Sheriff's Star and Moon Madness - is bred to come into his own over longer trips. It may take a little time, and the fact that he has already been gelded is something of a negative, but he is certainly one to monitor. (new market new market op 25-1 tchd 16-1)

4795 PICNIC STKS (H'CAP) 7f
2:30 (2:40) (Class 5) (0-70,70) 3-Y-0+ **£3,238** (£963; £481; £240) **Stalls** High

Form RPR
2510 **1** **Taranaki**[11] 4446 8-8-10 **61** .... AshleyHamblett(7) 4 72
(P D Cundell) *t.k.h: trckd ldrs: wnt 2nd over 2f out: rdn to ld over 1f out: styd on wl* **12/1**
0104 **2** *1* **Torquemada (IRE)**[37] 3679 5-9-3 **61** .... PaulDoe 10 69
(W Jarvis) *dwlt: hld up in last trio: prog on wd outside to chal 2f out: wandered u.p: kpt on to take 2nd ins fnl f* **15/2**
0000 **3** *½* **Morgan Lewis (IRE)**[17] 4248 5-8-11 **55** ....(p) RobertHavlin 6 62
(J A Geake) *lw: led: rdn and hdd over 1f out: one pce fnl f* **25/1**
5633 **4** *1* **True Night**[8] 4569 9-9-4 **67** .... MichaelJStainton(5) 11 71
(D Nicholls) *trckd ldr for 3f: lost pl and hemmed in 3f out: struggling over 1f out: r.o again last 150yds* **5/1**[3]
0141 **5** *1* **Mister Elegant**[45] 3405 4-8-12 **59** .... AdamKirby(3) 8 61
(J L Spearing) *swtg: t.k.h: prom: trckd ldr 4f out to over 2f out: wknd fnl f* **8/1**
4000 **6** *½* **Blue Line**[14] 4363 4-8-7 **51** oh2 .... DaleGibson 7 51
(M Madgwick) *in tch: rdn fr 1/2-way: struggling in rr over 2f out: plugged on* **25/1**
2311 **7** *nk* **Border Artist**[10] 4496 7-9-7 **65** .... JimmyQuinn 12 64+
(J Pearce) *t.k.h: hld up in last trio: nowhere to go 3f out to 2f out: one pce after* **4/1**[2]
3300 **8** *nk* **Mythical Charm**[31] 3854 7-9-0 **58** ....(t) JohnEgan 3 57
(J J Bridger) *lw: t.k.h: hld up towards rr: prog to join ldrs 3f out: nt qckn and lost pl 2f out: n.d after* **20/1**
132 **9** *¾* **Logsdail**[8] 4575 6-9-12 **70** ....(p) RyanMoore 13 67+
(G L Moore) *hld up on inner: rdn whn nt clr run 3f out to 2f out: sn eased* **5/2**[1]
0404 **10** *¾* **Kallista's Pride**[3] 4691 6-9-0 **65** .... KylieManser(7) 9 60+
(J R Best) *dwlt: t.k.h: hld up bhd ldrs: lost pl 1/2-way: terrible run bhd rivals after and no ch* **28/1**

1m 28.05s (0.01) **Going Correction** +0.025s/f (Good) **10** Ran SP% **111.7**
Speed ratings (Par 103):100,98,98,97,96 95,95,94,93,93
CSF £88.97 CT £2218.40 TOTE £14.60: £2.50, £2.10, £5.30; EX 75.00.
Owner Miss M C Fraser **Bred** E D Evers **Trained** Compton, Berks
■ Stewards' Enquiry : Adam Kirby three-day ban: careless riding (Sep 6-8)

FOCUS
A modest handicap for the track, rated around the placed horses. The form is not that convincing.
Border Artist Official explanation: jockey said gelding suffered interference in running
Logsdail Official explanation: jockey said gelding was hampered and felt wrong

4796 SOUTH COAST STKS (H'CAP) 6f
3:05 (3:08) (Class 3) (0-95,95) 3-Y-0+
£11,217 (£3,358; £1,679; £840; £419; £210) **Stalls** Low

Form RPR
010 **1** **Fantasy Believer**[7] 4609 8-9-5 **89** .... JimmyQuinn 9 99
(J J Quinn) *hld up bhd ldrs: prog 1/2-way: pushed along over 2f out: rdn to ld jst over 1f out: styd on gamely* **7/1**
0016 **2** *1* **Hits Only Heaven (IRE)**[42] 3532 4-9-0 **84** ....(e) PaulDoe 2 91
(D Nicholls) *hld up bhd ldrs: swtchd to outer and drvn over 2f out: styd on wl to take 2nd last 100yds: no imp on wnr* **25/1**
100 **3** *nk* **Algharb**[27] 3986 4-9-1 **85** .... KDarley 5 93+
(W J Haggas) *hld up bhd ldrs: effrt over 2f out: nt clr run wl over 1f out: rdn and styd on to take 3rd last 75yds: unable to chal* **14/1**
6220 **4** *½* **Woodcote (IRE)**[21] 4128 4-9-8 **95** ....(p) AdamKirby(3) 8 100
(C G Cox) *lw: led after 2f: mde most after: gng easily 2f out: shkn up and no rspnse over 1f out: sn hdd and btn* **3/1**[1]
5103 **5** *1* **Holbeck Ghyll (IRE)**[10] 4486 4-8-9 **79** .... JohnEgan 7 81
(A M Balding) *w ldr after 2f to 2f out: fdd jst over 1f out* **5/1**[3]
2003 **6** *1 ¼* **Night Prospector**[23] 4085 6-8-11 **81** .... RyanMoore 3 79
(G L Moore) *hld up: last and rdn over 2f out: swtchd to outer and no imp fnl 2f* **8/1**
2521 **7** *nk* **Idle Power (IRE)**[12] 4430 8-9-5 **92** .... AmirQuinn(3) 6 89
(J R Boyle) *disp ld after 2f to 1/2-way: lost pl: struggling 2f out: wknd* **11/2**
0304 **8** *1 ¾* **Pieter Brueghel (USA)**[7] 4609 7-8-13 **88** .... MichaelJStainton(5) 1 80
(D Nicholls) *racd against nr side rail: led for 2f: sn lost pl and struggling: wl btn fnl 2f* **7/2**[2]

1m 11.83s (-1.02) **Going Correction** +0.075s/f (Good) **8** Ran SP% **113.4**
Speed ratings (Par 107):109,107,107,106,105 103,103,100
CSF £150.55 CT £2365.15 TOTE £6.30: £2.00, £3.90, £2.90; EX 106.30.
Owner The Fantasy Fellowship B **Bred** John Khan **Trained** Settrington, N Yorks
■ Stewards' Enquiry : K Darley one-day ban: careless riding (Sep 6)

FOCUS
A fair sprint for the money, the time was good and the form looks straightforward.

NOTEBOOK
Fantasy Believer has been right back to his best in recent months, and took this from a mark only 2lb below his top winning rating. He goes particularly well at Goodwood, and would be one to consider whenever making the long return journey from Yorkshire, though the Ayr Gold Cup is next on the agenda, and he goes there with a sporting chance. Official explanation: trainer's rep said, regarding apparent improvement in form, that the gelding appeared suited by the better ground (op 5-1)
Hits Only Heaven(IRE) ◆ has been running over longer trips on sand, but his trainer is a master at getting horses to adapt to races like this on turf, and on this evidence he is well capable of winning one.
Algharb ◆ had a shocking passage, and is one to note for a similar race. He is capable of winning on sand as well as turf, and this unlucky run suggests there is a decent prize in him.
Woodcote(IRE) has never won a handicap, but he continues to do well from a tough mark. On this occasion he was racing from 2lb higher than when finishing seventh here in the Stewards' Cup. (op 4-1)
Holbeck Ghyll(IRE) is up against it off his higher mark since winning here earlier in the month, and he is more effective over five furlongs anyway. (op 6-1)
Night Prospector, tried over an extra furlong, is inconsistent but capable of finding a race at his best. However, he has not won since 2004, and has been expensive to follow. (op 11-2)
Idle Power(IRE) did not travel as well as he often does, being in trouble a long way out. Official explanation: jockey said gelding ran flat (op 6-1)
Pieter Brueghel(USA) was unable to dominate for long, and ultimately ran well below his best. (op 4-1)

4797 WINDFLOWER MARCH STKS (LISTED RACE) 1m 6f
3:40 (3:40) (Class 1) 3-Y-0+ **£17,034** (£6,456; £3,231; £1,611; £807) **Stalls** High

Form RPR
-522 **1** **Jadalee (IRE)**[25] 4024 3-8-7 110 .... DaleGibson 5 107
(M P Tregoning) *t.k.h: trckd ldng pair: effrt on inner to ld narrowly 4f out: sn rdn: plugged on fnl 3f: a jst holding on* **10/11**[1]
3045 **2** *nk* **Barolo**[21] 4169 7-9-7 104 ....(p) AdamKirby 2 109
(W R Swinburn) *lw: led to 4f out: sn rdn: styd w ev ch: tried to rally fnl f: a jst hld* **13/2**[3]
1104 **3** *¾* **Akarem**[56] 3107 5-9-10 111 .... JimCrowley 3 111
(K R Burke) *s.i.s: hld up in last: effrt over 3f out: chal and upsides 2f out: nt qckn fnl f* **11/1**
4252 **4** *1 ¼* **Art Eyes (USA)**[23] 4079 4-9-5 103 .... JohnEgan 1 104
(D R C Elsworth) *trckd ldr to over 4f out: styd cl up: nt clr run 3f out and over 2f out: one pce fnl 2f* **3/1**[2]
0-44 **5** *30* **Orange Touch (GER)**[22] 4096 6-9-7 101 .... RyanMoore 4 64
(Mrs A J Perrett) *hld up in 4th: brought wd fr 4f out: shkn up and wknd 3f out: heavily eased fnl 2f: t.o* **10/1**

3m 2.37s (-1.60) **Going Correction** +0.025s/f (Good)
WFA 3 from 4yo+ 12lb **5** Ran SP% **108.1**
Speed ratings (Par 111):105,104,104,103,86
CSF £7.01 TOTE £1.80: £1.40, £2.50; EX 8.40.
Owner Sheikh Ahmed Al Maktoum **Bred** Hawthorn Villa Stud **Trained** Lambourn, Berks

FOCUS
A Listed race of reasonable quality, producing a cracking finish between the first three after a prolonged battle. The winning time was only modest for such a contest though and the form is fair with the third the best guide.

NOTEBOOK
Jadalee(IRE), who got warm beforehand, held on bravely under a strong ride from Gibson, who had made a rare trip to Goodwood from Yorkshire. Favoured by the weights here, he also lacks nothing in stamina, and that - plus his commendable tenacity - helped to win the day. He is a possible runner in the St Leger, but more will be required there. (op 11-10)
Barolo gave the winner a tremendous race, refusing to go under during a sustained home-straight battle. He stays two miles, but this trip suits him ideally, and he deserves to get off the mark for the season. (op 9-1)
Akarem has not won beyond a mile-and-a-half, but this determined effort should allay fears that he does not truly stay the extra two furlongs - giving connections a set of alternative options from now on. (op 9-1)
Art Eyes(USA) did not get the best of runs, but it did not cost her victory. However, she is capable of winning a decent prize over this trip. (op 5-2)
Orange Touch(GER) had a tough task at the weights, but is capable of better. Official explanation: jockey said gelding had no more to give (op 15-2)

4798 CARNES SEAT STKS (H'CAP) 7f
4:15 (4:15) (Class 2) (0-105,96) 3-Y-0+
£12,464 (£3,732; £1,866; £934; £466; £234) **Stalls** High

Form RPR
5116 **1** **Illustrious Blue**[2] 4739 3-9-4 **93** .... PaulDoe 6 101+
(W J Knight) *lw: hld up in 6th and wl off the pce: clsd over 2f out: sn rdn and struggling: picked up over 1f out: r.o wl to ld last str* **5/2**[2]
0202 **2** *shd* **Compton's Eleven**[14] 4372 5-9-12 **96** .... RyanMoore 4 106
(M R Channon) *hld up in 5th and wl off the pce: clsd over 2f out: rdn to ld jst over 1f out: r.o fnl f: hdd last stride* **4/1**[3]
-101 **3** *2* **Minority Report**[24] 4042 6-9-12 **96** .... JohnEgan 7 101
(L M Cumani) *settled in 4th and off the pce: chsd clr ldng pair 3f out: clsd and ch over 1f out: one pce fnl f* **2/1**[1]
0200 **4** *1 ¼* **Material Witness (IRE)**[9] 4535 9-8-12 **85** .... AdamKirby(3) 5 87
(W R Muir) *w ldr at str pce: led over 2f out: hdd jst over 1f out: fdd* **14/1**
5235 **5** *2* **Secret Night**[14] 4343 3-8-7 **82** .... JimmyQuinn 3 78
(J A R Toller) *lw: chsd clr ldng pair to 3f out: nt qckn and btn 2f out: wknd fnl f* **20/1**
0010 **6** *½* **Traytonic**[7] 4609 5-8-12 **87** .... MichaelJStainton(5) 1 82
(D Nicholls) *taken down early: dwlt: hld up in last and wl off the pce: rdn and struggling over 2f out: no prog* **9/1**
3410 **7** *hd* **King's Caprice**[28] 3926 5-9-11 **95** ....(t) RichardThomas 2 90
(J A Geake) *taken down early: narrow ld at str pce to over 2f out: wknd rapidly sn after* **14/1**

1m 26.73s (-1.31) **Going Correction** +0.025s/f (Good)
WFA 3 from 5yo+ 5lb **7** Ran SP% **110.0**
Speed ratings (Par 109):108,107,105,104,101 101,101
CSF £11.88 TOTE £3.10: £1.90, £2.10; EX 12.80.
Owner Mr & Mrs I H Bendelow **Bred** B J And Mrs Crangle **Trained** Patching, W Sussex

FOCUS
A decent handicap, run at a furious pace which set things up for the late finishers. The runner-up looks to limit the form.

NOTEBOOK
Illustrious Blue always goes well on this track, and has yet to finish out of the first three here in his five visits. He stays a mile, so the strong early pace helped him over this shorter trip, and his stamina finally kicked in on the run to the final furlong as others began to flag. (op 2-1)
Compton's Eleven came with a smart run from off the strong gallop, and looked sure to win with 100 yards to go, only to be pipped on the line. He is close to victory if able to keep up his current form. (op 11-2)
Minority Report must have appreciated the good early tempo, but the ground was not as fast as he would have liked, and he was not quite at his best. He was 4lb higher than when winning here earlier in the month, but the market suggested he is still on the upgrade, and he remains one to keep in mind. (tchd 9-4)
Material Witness(IRE) helped to set a fast gallop, so did well to finish as close as he did, but he enjoys this track, having won three times over course and distance in the past. (tchd 12-1)
Secret Night put in a fair effort, having chased the strong early gallop, and is not far off a winning mark these days. (op 25-1)
Traytonic ought to have appreciated the strong gallop, but they went so fast he was unable to keep up, and gave himself too much ground to make up. He can do much better on a going day, but they are currently outnumbered by the off-days, and supporters banking on compensation need to be aware of that. (op 8-1 tchd 10-1)
King's Caprice, harried by Material Witness, went off at a frenetic pace, and paid the penalty.

4799 WATERBEACH MEDIAN AUCTION MAIDEN STKS 6f
4:45 (4:45) (Class 4) 3-4-Y-0 **£5,505** (£1,637; £818; £408) **Stalls** Low

Form RPR
002- **1** **Woodsley House (IRE)**[220] 4-9-6 .... PaulDoe 3 74
(W R Muir) *trckd ldrs: prog against nr side rail over 2f out: drvn to ld 1f out: styd on wl* **10/1**
24/2 **2** *1 ¼* **Small Stakes (IRE)**[8] 4564 4-9-3 62 ....(t) AmirQuinn(3) 6 70
(P J Makin) *pressed ldr: rdn 2f out: nt qckn over 1f out: styd on to take 2nd again ins fnl f: no imp on wnr* **3/1**[1]

The Form Book, Raceform Ltd, Compton, RG20 6NL

3 **3** 1 ½ **Dorelia (IRE)**[10] 4495 3-8-12 .... RobertHavlin 5 61+
(J H M Gosden) *pressed ldng pair: rdn over 2f out: sn outpcd: styd on again fnl f* **3/1**[1]

-046 **4** 1 ¼ **Goodwood March**[14] 4375 3-8-12 64........ JimCrowley 4 57
(J L Dunlop) *led: rdn and hanging rt fr wl over 1f out: hdd & wknd 1f out* **15/2**

5653 **5** 1 ¼ **Danawi (IRE)**[39] 3611 3-9-3 62........ RyanMoore 7 58
(R Hannon) *chsd ldrs: rdn over 2f out: hanging rt and nt qckn over 1f out* **5/1**[2]

2 **6** 1 **Jodrell Bank (IRE)**[10] 4495 3-8-12 62........ JimmyQuinn 11 50
(W Jarvis) *racd on wd outside: wl in tch: shkn up 2f out: grad wknd* **6/1**[3]

7 *shd* **Maiden Investor** 3-8-5 .... AshleyHamblett(7) 10 50
(Stef Liddiard) *leggy: hld up in rr: effrt on outer 1/2-way: no imp 2f out: wknd over 1f out* **33/1**

-300 **8** *hd* **Ravish**[8] 4567 3-8-12 54........(bt[1]) DaleGibson 9 49
(W J Haggas) *chsd ldrs: rdn and outpcd over 2f out: n.d after* **14/1**

9 2 **Royal Borough** 3-9-0 .... AdamKirby(3) 2 48
(R M Beckett) *w'like: a wl in rr: struggling fr over 2f out* **14/1**

10 7 **Batchworth Blaise** 3-9-3 .... PaulFitzsimons 8 27
(E A Wheeler) *leggy: dwlt: a in last pair: struggling over 3f out: wknd 2f out* **66/1**

1m 12.75s (-0.10) **Going Correction** +0.075s/f (Good)
WFA 3 from 4yo 3lb **10 Ran SP% 119.6**
Speed ratings (Par 105):103,101,99,97,96 94,94,94,91,82
CSF £41.21 TOTE £14.50: £3.90, £1.70, £1.70; EX 77.80.
Owner Brian Moss **Bred** Roger G English **Trained** Lambourn, Berks

FOCUS
A weak maiden for older horses run at a sound gallop and best rated through the second.

4800 HOLIDAY MAIDEN STKS (H'CAP) 2m
5:20 (5:21) (Class 5) (0-70,70) 3-Y-O £3,238 (£963; £481; £240) Stalls High

Form RPR

0-35 **1** **Picacho (IRE)**[71] 2607 3-9-0 **61**........ JimmyQuinn 10 70+
(J L Dunlop) *hld up in tch: trckd ldrs gng easily 4f out: wnt 2nd wl over 2f out: drvn to ld jst over 1f out: styd on* **5/2**[1]

6305 **2** 2 **Canyouwin**[21] 4150 3-8-8 **55**........ RobertHavlin 5 61
(J H M Gosden) *lw: hld up in midfield: reminders 6f out: prog to ld over 3f out: drvn and hdd jst over 1f out: kpt on same pce* **8/1**

05-0 **3** 6 **Karshaan (FR)**[81] 2332 3-9-9 **70**........ PaulFitzsimons 8 69
(P Winkworth) *dwlt: hld up: drvn and effrt 5f out: plugged on fnl 2f to take 3rd nr fin* **28/1**

0034 **4** ½ **Synonymy**[14] 4362 3-8-12 **59**........ RobertMiles 4 57
(M Blanshard) *settled in rr: reminders 7f out: rdn and struggling over 4f out: kpt on to chse ldng pair over 1f out: lost 3rd nr fin* **6/1**[3]

-566 **5** 3 ½ **Being There**[72] 2569 3-8-8 **55**........ JosedeSouza 9 49
(P F I Cole) *lw: hld up in rr: rdn and lost tch wl over 4f out: n.d after: plugged on fr over 1f out* **12/1**

053 **6** 4 **Noddies Way**[15] 4330 3-9-1 **65**........ AdamKirby(3) 3 54
(J F Panvert) *w ldrs: narrow ld 10f out to over 3f out: sn wknd* **6/1**[3]

0042 **7** 2 ½ **Himba**[9] 4537 3-9-1 **62**........ JimCrowley 11 48
(Mrs A J Perrett) *lw: prom: pressed ldr 10f out to over 3f out: sn wknd* **7/2**[2]

0330 **8** 20 **Zizou (IRE)**[40] 3592 3-8-4 **51** oh10........ RichardThomas 6 13
(J J Bridger) *led for 2f: styd prom tl wknd rapidly u.p 3f out: t.o* **16/1**

0060 **9** 52 **Seal Of Hope**[47] 3347 3-9-1 **62**........(b[1]) DaleGibson 7 —
(M P Tregoning) *drvn in rr bef 1/2-way: sn struggling: t.o 5f out: eased fnl f* **14/1**

0000 **10** 1 ¾ **Cativo Cavallino**[7] 4591 3-8-1 **55**........ NicolPolli(7) 1 —
(Jamie Poulton) *awkward s and rdr lost iron: plld hrd to ld after 2f: hdd 10f out: wknd rapidly over 4f out: t.o whn eased fnl f* **20/1**

3m 28.96s (-1.83) **Going Correction** +0.025s/f (Good) **10 Ran SP% 118.9**
Speed ratings (Par 100):105,104,101,100,99 97,95,85,59,58
CSF £23.88 CT £461.65 TOTE £3.20: £1.50, £2.90, £6.90; EX 32.90 Place 6 £428.51, Place 5 £270.89.
Owner Michael H Watt **Bred** Dr J Hollowood **Trained** Arundel, W Sussex

FOCUS
A weak staying handicap run at a fair pace and rated through the third.
T/Plt: £759.40 to a £1 stake. Pool: £55,710.65. 53.55 winning tickets. T/Qpdt: £51.40 to a £1 stake. Pool: £2,471.15. 35.55 winning tickets. JN

4765
NEWMARKET (JULY) (R-H)
Saturday, August 26

OFFICIAL GOING: Soft
The historic Newmarket Town Plate, not under Rules, was won by Papua ridden by Charlie Duckworth.
Wind: Light, behind

4801 EUROPEAN BREEDERS FUND MAIDEN STKS 6f
1:45 (1:46) (Class 5) 2-Y-O £4,533 (£1,348; £674; £336) Stalls Low

Form RPR

0222 **1** **Tudor Prince (IRE)**[15] 4323 2-9-3 88........ LDettori 2 92
(B J Meehan) *lw: mde all: pushed clr fnl f* **10/11**[1]

2 5 **We'll Come** 2-9-3 .... PhilipRobinson 6 77
(M A Jarvis) *wl grwn: bkwd: hld up: hdwy over 2f out: rdn to chse wnr over 1f out: sn outpcd* **7/1**[2]

3 2 ½ **Deserted Dane (USA)** 2-9-3 .... DeanMcKeown 1 70
(G A Swinbank) *w'like: bit bkwd: trckd wnr: racd keenly: shkn up over 1f out: wknd ins fnl f* **10/1**

4 *nk* **Danehillsundance (IRE)** 2-9-3 .... JimmyFortune 3 69
(R Hannon) *wl grwn: s.i.s: hld up: hdwy 1/2-way: wknd fnl f* **8/1**[3]

5 2 ½ **Royal Rationale (IRE)** 2-9-3 .... MartinDwyer 7 61
(W J Haggas) *gd sort: bit bkwd: s.i.s: sme hdwy over 1f out: n.d* **11/1**

6 *nk* **Edison** 2-9-3 .... TomEaves 10 60
(N P Littmoden) *w'like: bkwd: chsd ldrs: hung lft and wknd over 1f out* **8/1**[3]

7 1 ¼ **World Spirit** 2-8-12 .... FrancisFerris 5 51
(Rae Guest) *neat: bkwd: sn pushed along in rr: hdwy over 2f out: wknd over 1f out* **50/1**

8 7 **Barley Moon** 2-8-12 .... JamieMackay 9 30
(T Keddy) *w'like: s.i.s: a in rr* **40/1**

9 1 ½ **Doctor Ned** 2-9-3 .... OscarUrbina 8 31
(N A Callaghan) *w'like: scope: s.s: a in rr* **20/1**

0 **10** *hd* **Lord Orpheus**[7] 4597 2-8-12 .... AurelioMedeiros(5) 4 30
(B W Hills) *w'like: scope: lw: chsd ldrs over 3f* **33/1**

1m 16.17s (2.82) **Going Correction** +0.525s/f (Yiel) **10 Ran SP% 116.6**
Speed ratings (Par 94):102,95,92,91,88 87,86,76,74,74
CSF £7.29 TOTE £1.80: £1.10, £2.60, £2.40; EX 9.50.
Owner Wyck Hall Stud **Bred** Edmond And Richard Kent **Trained** Manton, Wilts

FOCUS
Only a modest maiden, and the winner was streets ahead of his rivals on the day. The time was quicker, however, than the nursery later on the card, and only slightly slower than the handicap for older horses that ended the day.

NOTEBOOK
Tudor Prince(IRE) simply sauntered away from his rivals after being given a positive ride. Not much more was learnt about how good he is, and he will be given stiffer challenges in the future, but he did conclusively prove that he handles ease in the ground, which could be to his advantage before the end of the turf season. (op 11-8 tchd 6-4 in places)
We'll Come looked almost twice the size of most of his rivals and shaped encouragingly behind the easy winner. The best of him may not been seen until next year, although he is entitled to come on for the run. (op 13-2)
Deserted Dane(USA) did not disgrace himself on his debut and should certainly come on for the run. His sire was a good dirt horse in America who did act on turf as well, so he is likely to do better on a far quicker surface. (op 6-1)
Danehillsundance(IRE), a late foal, showed a glimmer of ability and is entitled to come on for the run. (op 9-1 tchd 7-1)
Royal Rationale(IRE), who has entries in the Group 1 Racing Post Trophy and Dewhurst Stakes, was in need of the experience and showed some promise after starting slowly.
Edison, who holds Group 1 entries, showed up early before fading under pressure. Connections would not have wasted their money on lofty entries if he was not thought capable of better, and is worth considering next time if kept to a realistic level. (op 9-1)

4802 123RACING.COM H'CAP 7f
2:20 (2:21) (Class 3) (0-90,95) 3-Y-O £8,096 (£2,408; £1,203; £601) Stalls Low

Form RPR

-410 **1** **Muzher (IRE)**[24] 4047 3-9-2 **85**........ MartinDwyer 8 92
(B W Hills) *mde all: rdn: hung lft and put hd in air ins fnl f: styd on* **7/1**[3]

3101 **2** *hd* **Hill Spirit**[10] 4481 3-8-9 **83**........ MarcHalford(5) 10 89
(D R C Elsworth) *a.p: rdn over 2f out: ev ch ins fnl f: styd on* **10/1**

5442 **3** 1 **Jimmy The Guesser**[13] 4391 3-8-10 **79**........ LDettori 4 83
(N P Littmoden) *chsd ldrs: rdn over 1f out: no ex towards fin* **9/2**[2]

0514 **4** *hd* **His Master's Voice (IRE)**[15] 4328 3-8-5 **74**........ FergusSweeney 13 77
(D W P Arbuthnot) *hld up: hdwy 1/2-way: rdn over 1f out: styd on same pce ins fnl f* **20/1**

4-11 **5** *hd* **Macedon**[21] 4143 3-8-12 **81**........ LPKeniry 6 84
(J S Moore) *s.i.s: sn chsng ldrs: outpcd 2f out: styd on ins fnl f* **8/1**

1300 **6** 1 **Namid Reprobate (IRE)**[10] 4488 3-9-0 **83**........ JimmyFortune 12 83
(P F I Cole) *lw: hld up: hdwy over 2f out: rdn over 1f out: styd on* **10/1**

3165 **7** *hd* **The Osteopath (IRE)**[7] 4605 3-8-6 **75**........(p) PhillipMakin 5 75
(M Dods) *sn pushed along in rr: styd on appr fnl f: nrst fin* **10/1**

2243 **8** 6 **North Walk (IRE)**[28] 3945 3-8-11 **80**........ PaulMulrennan 11 65
(K A Ryan) *lw: chsd wnr tl rdn over 2f out: wknd over 1f out* **8/1**

-355 **9** 3 ½ **Vacation (IRE)**[87] 2126 3-8-9 **78**........ MichaelTebbutt 3 54
(V Smith) *hld up: a in rr* **25/1**

3124 **10** ½ **Dancing Guest (IRE)**[9] 4542 3-9-12 **95**........ PhilipRobinson 1 70
(G G Margarson) *lw: s.i.s: hld up: wknd over 2f out* **14/1**

12 **11** 4 **Ceremonial Jade (UAE)**[21] 4144 3-8-12 **81**........ OscarUrbina 2 46
(M Botti) *prom: rdn over 2f out: hung lft and wknd over 1f out* **4/1**[1]

1m 29.02s (2.24) **Going Correction** +0.525s/f (Yiel) **11 Ran SP% 115.5**
Speed ratings (Par 104):108,107,106,106,106 105,104,97,93,93 88
CSF £73.64 CT £350.42 TOTE £8.70: £2.50, £4.40, £1.80; EX 116.30 Trifecta £352.20 Part won. Pool: £496.10 - 0.10 winning units..
Owner Hamdan Al Maktoum **Bred** Shadwell Estate Company Limited **Trained** Lambourn, Berks
■ Stewards' Enquiry : Marc Halford three-day ban: used whip with excessive frequency and in an incorrect place (Sep 6-8)

FOCUS
A good race for the class, run at a solid tempo for the ground. The winner did his best to throw it away, but still managed to hang on. The form looks sound with the next three home close to their marks.

NOTEBOOK
Muzher(IRE), described by Dwyer as a very nervous horse, looked to be hating every moment he was under pressure but somehow found enough, despite hanging to the left throughout the final furlong, to hold off the runner-up. He was given a really good ride by his jockey and may be flattered by the bare result, and is not one to trust implicitly next time. (op 8-1)
Hill Spiritwas given every chance to score by the wayward winner, but still managed to not get his head in front. The winner did pull out more when joined, but it still must go down as a slightly disappointing effort considering the lack of visible effort by Muzher.
Jimmy The Guesser was always close to the pace but could not quicken in the ground. He is quite high in the handicap on his winning form. (op 5-1tchd 4-1)
His Master's Voice(IRE), only having his second run on turf after showing good form on Polytrack, did not run too badly but it remains to be seen whether he truly handles soft ground. Nothing in the effort suggested that the going was a problem, so he remains a interesting prospect.
Macedon , who was untried on soft ground, did not get away very well and pulled a bit in the early part of the race, but kept on quite well for pressure to finish on the heels of the placed horses. He can be given another chance on quicker ground or an All-Weather surface, and shapes as though he will get a mile. (op 7-1)
The Osteopath(IRE) only got going when meeting the rising ground and is probably better suited by a mile. (tchd 11-1)
Dancing Guest(IRE) Official explanation: jockey said filly was unsuited by the soft ground
Ceremonial Jade(UAE) had it all to prove on the soft ground and failed by a long way to justify favouritism. He has a worrying tendency of hanging under pressure. (tchd 9-2)

4803 COUNTRYWIDE STEEL AND TUBES HOPEFUL STKS (LISTED RACE) 6f
2:50 (2:50) (Class 1) 3-Y-O+
£15,898 (£6,025; £3,015; £1,503; £753; £378) Stalls Low

Form RPR

2043 **1** **Appalachian Trail (IRE)**[14] 4348 5-9-0 99........(b) TomEaves 1 104
(I Semple) *hld up: hmpd and r.o to ld ins fnl f: rdn out* **4/1**[3]

0430 **2** 2 **Assertive**[20] 4191 3-9-1 106........ JimmyFortune 6 102
(R Hannon) *trckd ldrs: rdn and ev ch ins fnl f: unable qck* **6/1**

1456 **3** ½ **Sunderland Echo (IRE)**[6] 4633 3-8-6 85........ TonyHamilton 5 91
(B Ellison) *chsd ldrs: rdn and ev ch ins fnl f: styd on same pce* **25/1**

302 **4** *nk* **Andronikos**[21] 4158 4-9-0 103........(t) LDettori 3 97+
(P F I Cole) *lw: trckd ldrs: effrt and hmpd ins fnl f: nt rcvr* **7/2**[2]

1000 **5** 1 ¼ **One Putra (IRE)**[21] 4128 4-9-4 105........ PhilipRobinson 4 95
(M A Jarvis) *lw: led: rdn: hung lft and hdd ins fnl f: wknd towards fin* **5/1**

-505 **6** 2 ½ **Masta Plasta (IRE)**[20] 4174 3-8-11 100........ OscarUrbina 2 84
(J Howard Johnson) *chsd ldr: rdn over 1f out: hld whn hmpd ins fnl f* **10/1**

1243 **7** *6* **Tawaassol (USA)**[35] 3732 3-8-11 106............................(t) MartinDwyer 7 66
(Sir Michael Stoute) *hld up in tch: rdn over 2f out: wknd fnl f* **3/1**[1]
1m 15.33s (1.98) **Going Correction** +0.525s/f (Yiel)
WFA 3 from 4yo+ 3lb **7** Ran SP% **111.1**
Speed ratings (Par 111):107,104,103,101,102 98,90
CSF £26.15 TOTE £5.70: £3.00, £2.50; EX 36.30.
Owner G L S Partnership **Bred** Swettenham Stud **Trained** Carluke, S Lanarks
■ Stewards' Enquiry : Philip Robinson caution: careless riding

FOCUS
A solid Listed race won by a horse dropping back in trip. Tawaassol, arguably the form horse coming into the race, did not seem to act on the ground at all and the form does not appear solid, with the third the best guide.

NOTEBOOK
Appalachian Trail(IRE), whose best form is over further, finished really well up the far-side rail, despite getting bumped by a horse hanging towards him, to win nicely. Unproven on ground with so much ease in it, he handled it well and now has the Ayr Gold Cup as his target. He goes there with every chance. (op 5-1)
Assertive is a powerful sort and finished strongly up the hill. Appearing to handle the soft ground without a problem, he had first run on the winner but was unable to hold him. He has an entry in a Group 3 race at the Curragh in mid-September, which would seem the logical next target for him. (op 8-1)
Sunderland Echo(IRE) was proven in the going and kept on really well inside the final furlong, and was catching Appalachian Trail and Assertive again after being passed by them. If the ground remains in her favour, she can pick up another race before the end of the season, although connections would not want the Handicapper to take a literal view of the result.
Andronikos was not helped by One Putra hanging across him when trying to make his challenge, but it is not obvious that he would have won. He can definitely be rated higher than the bare result and will have his chance of revenge on the winner if both take their places in the Ayr Gold Cup as well. (op 11-4)
One Putra(IRE) was demoted to fifth after hampering Andronikos and Master Plasta. Despite drifting left under pressure, he cannot be counted as unlucky and looked to run up to his best. (op 11-2 tchd 6-1 in places)
Masta Plasta(IRE) was going backwards when squeezed out inside the final furlong. (op 12-1)
Tawaassol(USA) had a clear run and was very disappointing. One can only surmise that the ground was far too soft for him and it seems unlikely that his entry in the Group 1 Sprint Cup at Haydock is a realistic target. (op 11-4)

4804 HOME OF HORSE RACING NURSERY 6f
3:20 (3:20) (Class 4) 2-Y-O £4,533 (£1,348; £674; £336) Stalls Low

Form RPR
41 **1** **College Scholar (GER)**[16] 4292 2-9-2 **79**........................ MartinDwyer 4 82
(M R Channon) *chsd ldrs: led over 4f out: rdn out* **5/1**[3]
5210 **2** *1¾* **Top Royelle**[12] 4427 2-9-1 **78**.. JimmyFortune 1 76
(R Hannon) *hld up: hdwy over 1f out: r.o: nt rch wnr* **15/2**
2421 **3** *¾* **Ebn Reem**[17] 4260 2-9-7 **84**.. PhilipRobinson 3 80
(M A Jarvis) *swtg: led: hdd over 4f out: rdn over 1f out: styd on same pce ins fnl f* **7/4**[1]
21 **4** *¾* **Beauchamp Viceroy**[12] 4434 2-9-4 **81**..................................... LDettori 5 75
(G A Butler) *hld up: hdwy over 2f out: rdn over 1f out: no ex ins fnl f* **9/2**[2]
033 **5** *6* **Popolo (IRE)**[16] 4283 2-8-6 **69**.. HayleyTurner 2 45
(M L W Bell) *trckd ldrs: rdn over 2f out: sn wknd* **12/1**
004 **6** *shd* **Wool Mart**[16] 4295 2-8-12 **75**.. FergusSweeney 6 50
(M Blanshard) *lw: chsd ldrs: rdn over 1f out: wknd fnl f* **25/1**
1123 **7** *1* **Just Dust**[10] 4480 2-9-0 **82**.. MarcHalford(5) 8 54
(D R C Elsworth) *chsd ldrs: rdn over 2f out: wknd over 1f out* **7/1**
544 **8** *3½* **Ioweyou**[60] 2943 2-8-4 **67**... FrancisFerris 9 29
(J S Moore) *hld up: rdn and hung lft 2f out: sn wknd* **16/1**
1m 17.15s (3.80) **Going Correction** +0.525s/f (Yiel) **8** Ran SP% **112.9**
Speed ratings (Par 96):95,92,91,90,82 82,81,76
CSF £40.68 CT £89.42 TOTE £6.60: £1.40, £2.10, £1.20.
Owner Mohammed Jaber **Bred** Stiftung Gestut Fahrhof **Trained** West Ilsley, Berks

FOCUS
A useful nursery won by a horse that will stay further in time. The first four should be competitive for the near future.

NOTEBOOK
College Scholar(GER), making his handicap debut, confirmed the impression he had made in his first two races by winning in good style. He has an entry in the Two-Year-Old Trophy at Redcar at the end of September, which could be the ideal race for him. (op 7-1)
Top Royelle got going a bit too late and failed to get on terms with the winner. Seven furlongs will pose no problems to her. (op 17-2 tchd 9-1 and 7-1)
Ebn Reem looks on a stiff mark, even allowing for his form with Eddie Jock, and was found wanting against a couple of lower-weighted rivals. His consistent form will not help him drop down the weights. (op 5-4 tchd 15-8 and 2-1 in a place)
Beauchamp Viceroy easily landed a maiden at Polytrack last time, but found the soft-ground conditions a completely different proposition. He does not look obviously well handicapped on his two maiden efforts but does have scope for improvement. (op 11-2 tchd 6-1)
Popolo(IRE) is either not very quick or hated the ground. She, not for the first time, shaped like she needs a mile already.
Wool Mart (op 22-1 tchd 20-1)
Just Dust has had a good season, but all of his best form has come on much quicker ground and he can be readily excused a below-par effort on a surface he is not proven on. Official explanation: trainer said gelding was unsuited by the soft ground (tchd 13-2 and 15-2)
Ioweyou Official explanation: trainer said filly was unsuited by the soft ground

4805 NEWMARKETRACECOURSES.CO.UK H'CAP 1m 2f
3:55 (3:57) (Class 3) (0-95,95) 3-Y-O+ £8,096 (£2,408; £1,203; £601) Stalls Centre

Form RPR
3404 **1** **Forroger (CAN)**[89] 2069 3-8-6 **73**................................. PhilipRobinson 5 82
(M A Jarvis) *hld up: hdwy over 1f out: rdn to ld ins fnl f: r.o: hung lft nr fin* **7/1**[2]
3146 **2** *1* **Sonny Parkin**[7] 4604 4-9-4 **77**..(v) DO'Donohoe 1 85
(G A Huffer) *sn pushed along in rr: hdwy 3f out: led over 1f out: rdn and hdd ins fnl f: styd on same pce* **14/1**
32-4 **3** *¾* **Familiar Territory**[23] 4082 3-10-0 **95**....................................... LDettori 8 101+
(Saeed Bin Suroor) *chsd ldrs: led 2f out: rdn and hdd over 1f out: no ex ins fnl f* **6/5**[1]
200 **4** *1¾* **Rumsfeld (ITY)**[23] 4082 3-9-12 **93**..................................... OscarUrbina 2 96
(M Botti) *lw: a.p: chsd ldr over 3f out: rdn and ev ch whn hung rt over 1f out: no ex fnl f* **16/1**
314 **5** *5* **Red Somerset (USA)**[93] 1953 3-9-8 **89**........................ JimmyFortune 11 83
(R Hannon) *lw: racd keenly: trckd ldr tl over 3f out: rdn and wknd over 1f out* **12/1**
0-00 **6** *hd* **Blaise Hollow (USA)**[86] 2169 4-9-8 **84**................. RichardKingscote(3) 3 78
(R Charlton) *hld up: swtchd lft over 4f out: sn rdn: nvr trbld ldrs* **18/1**
0126 **7** *5* **Isidore Bonheur (IRE)**[14] 4347 5-9-11 **84**.................. DeanMcKeown 7 69
(G A Swinbank) *hld up: bmpd after 1f: rdn over 2f out: sn wknd* **7/1**[2]
1-10 **8** *3½* **Music Note (IRE)**[51] 3224 3-9-4 **85**.................................. MartinDwyer 6 63
(M R Channon) *b: lw: led 8f: rdn whn hmpd over 1f out: sn wknd* **9/1**
5-54 **9** *1½* **Activo (FR)**[210] 222 5-9-12 **85**... LPKeniry 10 61
(S Dow) *trckd ldrs: rdn and wknd over 2f out* **28/1**
0663 **10** *½* **Rawdon (IRE)**[21] 4147 5-9-4 **77**.....................................(v) HayleyTurner 9 52
(M L W Bell) *hld up: plld hrd: hdwy over 8f out: wknd over 2f out* **8/1**[3]
2m 12.64s (6.20) **Going Correction** +0.525s/f (Yiel)
WFA 3 from 4yo+ 8lb **10** Ran SP% **120.5**
Speed ratings (Par 107):96,95,94,93,89 89,85,82,81,80
CSF £103.17 CT £198.88 TOTE £10.60: £2.40, £4.00, £1.20; EX 146.10.
Owner Stephen Dartnell **Bred** M C Byrne **Trained** Newmarket, Suffolk

FOCUS
A solid handicap despite the modest time. The first two home exceeded their official marks and appeared to run above themselves, so the form should be treated with caution.

NOTEBOOK
Forroger(CAN), having his first run for the Jarvis stable, came home fast and late to deny Sonny Parkin inside the final furlong down the middle of the track. He had looked disappointing last time, but he did have some respectable form in the ground, and may have handled it better than others in the race. (op 8-1 tchd 10-1)
Sonny Parkin, dropping in trip after failing to stay a mile and a half last time, looks a far from enthusiastic individual but could not be faulted for the way he got to the head of affairs a furlong from home, after being slowly away. He could not have seen Forrager finishing fast down the middle of the course, and looked to idle in front on the ground. It was fair performance all the same.
Familiar Territory travelled well enough in the early stages but did not seem to appreciate the ground when asked to quicken - he also flashed his tail when given a smack with the whip. He will probably be suited by better ground. (op 13-8)
Rumsfeld(ITY), who has won at odds of 1/100 in Italy on heavy ground, loves a very soft surface and finally got his chance on it in Britain. Lots of ease in the ground holds no fears for him, and is one to have on your side if the ground stays in his favour during the rest of the season. (op 14-1)
Red Somerset(USA) had not been seen since well beaten in the Listed Heron Stakes at Goodwood in May, where he did not seem at ease on a soft surface. That looked the case again and his pedigree/best form suggests he will be better on quicker ground. (tchd 11-1)
Blaise Hollow(USA) did not run as badly as his finishing position suggests, and looks to be coming back to form. (op 16-1)
Music Note(IRE) was starting to tire when squeezed for a bit of room. Even though he has won in soft ground, he did not seem obviously suited by it. (op 10-1)
Rawdon(IRE) was doing too much early in the race to get home in the conditions. His two worst results before the race came when there was plenty of ease in the ground.

4806 JAPAN RACING ASSOCIATION MAIDEN STKS 1m
4:30 (4:31) (Class 5) 3-Y-O+ £4,533 (£1,348; £674; £336) Stalls Low

Form RPR
0-2 **1** **Highland Blaze (USA)**[9] 4527 3-9-3 .... LDettori 12 86+
(Saeed Bin Suroor) *racd stands' side: mde all: shkn up ins fnl f: eased nr fin* **10/11**[1]
2 *1¾* **Sculastic** 3-9-3 .... DO'Donohoe 4 81
(L M Cumani) *racd stands' side: a.p: rdn over 3f out: styd on to go 2nd ins fnl f: no ch w wnr* **16/1**
65 **3** *1¼* **Rainbow Zest**[45] 3419 3-9-3 .... PhilipRobinson 10 78
(P W Chapple-Hyam) *lw: racd stands' side: chsd wnr: rdn over 1f out: no ex ins fnl f* **10/1**
4-26 **4** *12* **Rodeo**[22] 4117 3-9-3 82.. MartinDwyer 2 48+
(B W Hills) *racd far side: led that pair: rdn over 2f out: wknd over 1f out* **11/4**[2]
20 **5** *1½* **Vampyrus**[61] 2940 3-9-3 .... FergusSweeney 11 44
(H Candy) *racd stands' side: chsd ldrs: rdn over 2f out: wknd over 1f out* **9/1**[3]
00 **6** *¾* **Mustammer**[99] 1823 3-9-3 .... HayleyTurner 8 42
(S R Bowring) *lw: racd stands' side: plld hrd and prom: rdn over 2f out: wknd over 1f out* **33/1**
7 *5* **Penryn** 3-9-3 .... LPKeniry 3 30
(D R C Elsworth) *racd stands' side: dwlt: a in rr* **16/1**
8 *shd* **Dream Master (IRE)** 3-9-3 .... DeanMcKeown 6 30
(J Ryan) *b: b.hind: racd stands' side: s.s: outpcd* **28/1**
00-0 **9** *¾* **Kentavr's Dream**[24] 4045 3-8-5 40.......................... JPFeatherstone(7) 1 23+
(P Howling) *racd far side: chsd ldr: rdn over 2f out: sn wknd* **66/1**
00 **10** *9* **Jiggy Spriggy (IRE)**[131] 1048 3-8-12 .... MichaelTebbutt 5 —
(V Smith) *bkwd: racd stands' side: hld up: wknd over 2f out* **20/1**
1m 43.7s (3.27) **Going Correction** +0.525s/f (Yiel) **10** Ran SP% **122.5**
Speed ratings (Par 103):104,102,101,89,87 86,81,81,80,71
CSF £19.91 TOTE £1.80: £1.20, £3.50, £1.90; EX 23.80.
Owner Godolphin **Bred** Gainsborough Farm Llc **Trained** Newmarket, Suffolk

FOCUS
A very ordinary maiden but the time was decent and the first three were clear.

4807 SEE MORE ON RACING UK H'CAP 6f
5:00 (5:02) (Class 4) (0-85,83) 3-Y-O+ £5,505 (£1,637; £818; £408) Stalls Low

Form RPR
31 **1** **Cape**[86] 2167 3-9-1 **75**.. OscarUrbina 10 92+
(J R Fanshawe) *hld up: hdwy and nt clr run fr over 1f out tl swtchd rt wl ins fnl f: qckned to ld last strides* **4/1**[1]
6041 **2** *hd* **Stanley Goodspeed**[8] 4562 3-8-12 **79**...........................(t) PatrickHills(7) 9 87
(J W Hills) *lw: hld up in tch: nt clr run ins fnl f: swtchd rt: r.o* **16/1**
6304 **3** *nk* **Lake Garda**[14] 4357 5-9-3 **74**...(b) DO'Donohoe 11 81
(K A Ryan) *chsd ldrs: rdn and ev ch ins fnl f: r.o* **10/1**
1003 **4** *shd* **Balakiref**[10] 4468 7-9-5 **76**... PhillipMakin 15 83
(M Dods) *s.i.s: hdwy over 2f out: sn rdn: hung lft and led wl ins fnl f: hdd last stides* **9/2**[2]
3231 **5** *½* **Magic Rush**[12] 4437 4-9-4 **78**.................................. EdwardCreighton(3) 8 83
(Mrs Norma Pook) *sn led: rdn over 1f out: hdd and no ex wl ins fnl f* **11/1**
0300 **6** *1¼* **Kingscross**[7] 4593 8-9-8 **79**... FergusSweeney 13 81
(M Blanshard) *hld up: r.o ins fnl f: nrst fin* **9/1**
4023 **7** *nk* **Cesar Manrique (IRE)**[8] 4564 4-8-13 **70**........................ JimmyFortune 1 71
(B W Hills) *chsd ldr: rdn over 1f out: no ex ins fnl f* **7/1**[3]
0206 **8** *½* **Roman Quintet (IRE)**[8] 4564 6-8-11 **68**......................(v) PhilipRobinson 2 67
(D W P Arbuthnot) *hld up: hdwy over 1f out: no ex fnl f* **16/1**
5030 **9** *2½* **Flint River**[8] 4573 8-9-1 **72**... LPKeniry 7 64
(H Morrison) *chsd ldrs: outpcd over 3f out: hdwy 2f out: wknd ins fnl f* **25/1**
3500 **10** *½* **Orpsie Boy (IRE)**[7] 4601 3-9-1 **80**...............................(t) MarcHalford(5) 6 70
(N P Littmoden) *s.i.s: hld up: n.d* **33/1**
2010 **11** *1¾* **Exmoor**[82] 2302 4-9-5 **79**.. RichardKingscote(3) 3 64
(R Charlton) *b: hld up: rdn over 2f out: a in rr* **15/2**
1015 **12** *½* **Russian Rocket (IRE)**[36] 3709 4-9-9 **80**........................ HayleyTurner 14 63
(Mrs C A Dunnett) *chsd ldr: rdn and edgd rt over 1f out: sn wknd* **22/1**

The Form Book, Raceform Ltd, Compton, RG20 6NL

-005 **13** ½ **Sabrina Brown**[89] 2074 5-8-6 **70**.................................(t) TolleyDean(7) 12 52
(J A Geake) *chsd ldrs: rdn over 2f out: wknd fnl f* **16/1**

0040 **14** *8* **Hidden Dragon (USA)**[15] 4338 7-9-12 **83**.................... DeanMcKeown 5 41
(J Pearce) *chsd ldrs: lost pl over 3f out: sn hung lft and wknd* **33/1**

21-0 **15** *10* **Magadar (USA)**[10] 4488 3-9-2 **76**................................. MichaelTebbutt 4 4
(C E Brittain) *s.i.s: sn chsng ldrs: hmpd and lost pl over 2f out: sn wknd* **33/1**

1m 16.14s (2.79) **Going Correction** +0.525s/f (Yiel)
WFA 3 from 4yo+ 3lb **15** Ran SP% **124.5**
Speed ratings (Par 105):102,101,101,101,100 98,98,97,94,93 91,90,90,79,66
CSF £66.89 CT £606.28 TOTE £4.80: £2.20, £3.60, £3.30; EX 81.30 Place 6 £41.38, Place 5 £30.14.
Owner Wyck Hall Stud **Bred** Wyck Hall Stud Ltd **Trained** Newmarket, Suffolk

FOCUS
A good sprint handicap with a great finish. Cape can be rated far better than the bear result, and the race looks sound rated through the runner-up and fourth to recent marks.
Russian Rocket(IRE) Official explanation: jockey said gelding ran too keen
Magadar(USA) Official explanation: jockey said filly was unsuited by the soft ground
T/Plt: £47.10 to a £1 stake. Pool: £69,232.90. 1,072.80 winning tickets. T/Qpdt: £20.30 to a £1 stake. Pool: £2,586.00. 93.90 winning tickets. CR

4779 SANDOWN (R-H)
Saturday, August 26

OFFICIAL GOING: Good (good to soft in places on round course)
Wind: Moderate across

4808 BLUESQUARE.COM ATALANTA STKS (LISTED RACE) ((FILLIES & MARES) 1m 14y
2:05 (2:07) (Class 1) 3-Y-0+
£15,898 (£6,025; £3,015; £1,503; £753; £378) **Stalls** High

Form RPR

-011 **1** **Wasseema (USA)**[29] 3891 3-8-12 112.. RHills 12 111+
(Sir Michael Stoute) *swtg: mde all: wnt clr 2f out but kpt up to work fnl f* **9/4**[2]

5516 **2** *1 ¼* **Bahia Breeze**[56] 3086 4-9-4 100.. NCallan 3 108
(Rae Guest) *mid-div: hdwy over 2f out: chsd wnr wl over 1f out: faltered nr fin* **25/1**

-124 **3** *3 ½* **La Mottie**[49] 3316 3-8-8 102.. JamieSpencer 9 96
(J Noseda) *in tch on outside: rdn and styd on one pce fnl 2f* **6/4**[1]

1-55 **4** *2* **Innocent Air**[49] 3293 3-8-8 100.................................. RichardHughes 10 91
(J H M Gosden) *lw: chsd ldrs: lost pl 3f out: one pce fnl 2f* **11/1**

013- **5** ½ **Tiana**[329] 5605 3-8-8 98.. DavidKinsella 4 90+
(J H M Gosden) *bit bkwd: in rr: hdwy 2f out: styd on but nvr nr to chal* **25/1**

0354 **6** *4* **Expensive**[29] 3891 3-8-8 99.. DaneO'Neill 5 81
(C F Wall) *mid-div: no hdwy fnl 3f* **20/1**

21-4 **7** *1 ¼* **Rosinka (IRE)**[36] 3702 3-8-8 87.. PatDobbs 7 78
(J L Dunlop) *lw: bhd: rdn over 2f out: nvr on terms* **50/1**

1220 **8** ¾ **Local Spirit (USA)**[20] 4179 3-8-8 102.......................... StephenCarson 13 76
(C E Brittain) *trckd ldrs: rdn 3f out: sn wknd* **25/1**

4160 **9** *1* **Adventuress**[43] 3491 3-8-8 85...(b[1]) TPO'Shea 11 74
(B J Meehan) *hld up in mid-div: rdn 3f out: wknd over 1f out* **66/1**

-510 **10** *3* **After You**[66] 2744 3-8-8 99.. PaulEddery 1 67
(B W Hills) *a towards rr* **33/1**

3105 **11** *2 ½* **Tanzanite (IRE)**[7] 4590 4-9-0 93.. JoeFanning 6 61
(D W P Arbuthnot) *lw: trckd ldrs: chsd wnr over 2f out tl wknd rapidly wl over 1f out* **8/1**[3]

216- **12** *24* **Eilean Ban (USA)**[328] 5649 3-8-8 105.............................. SteveDrowne 8 6
(E A L Dunlop) *s.i.s: a wl in rr and eased whn btn over 2f out* **14/1**

1m 41.08s (-2.87) **Going Correction** -0.125s/f (Firm)
WFA 3 from 4yo+ 6lb **12** Ran SP% **119.6**
Speed ratings (Par 111):109,107,104,102,101 97,96,95,94,91 89,65
CSF £64.28 TOTE £2.90: £1.30, £6.40, £1.20; EX 45.50 Trifecta £86.80 Pool: £599.44 - 4.90 winning units..
Owner Hamdan Al Maktoum **Bred** Swettenham Stud And Ben Sangster **Trained** Newmarket, Suffolk

FOCUS
A good fillies' Listed contest and, although Wasseema was allowed to make all the running, the pace seemed fair. The runner-up sets the standard.

NOTEBOOK
Wasseema(USA) ◆, who made all in impressive fashion in a weaker Listed race than this at Ascot on her previous start, got warm beforehand and proved very easy to back, but she once again enjoyed her own way out in front and was able to follow up. Racing under a 4lb penalty, she was forced to work in the end after looking set for an easy win two out, but she and Bahia Breeze were clear and she looks ready for the step up to Group company now. (op 5-4)
Bahia Breeze found the Criterion Stakes a bit too hot at Newmarket on her previous start, but a strongly-run mile suits her ideally and she ran a fine race, particularly as she too was conceding a Listed win penalty all around. She wandered slightly under pressure, and did not enjoy the clearest runs, but was probably not unlucky. (op 33-1)
La Mottie looked a threat at one stage, but did not find quite as much as had looked likely and failed to justify strong market support. She has been beaten at a short price on her last two starts, but things are just not quite dropping ideally for her and she is not one to write off just yet. (op 9-4)
Innocent Air, a well-beaten fifth over 12 furlongs in the Lancashire Oaks on her previous start, proved better suited by this trip but was still well held. She is taking a bit of working out. (op 14-1)
Tiana ◆, the winner of a Folkestone maiden before running third to Race For The Stars and Scottish Stage in a Listed race at Newmarket as a juvenile, made a pleasing return from her 329-day absence. Held up last of all early, she was never really seen with a winning chance, but kept on nicely and is open to improvement.
Tanzanite(IRE) looks best watched until returned to ground with 'soft' in the description. (op 12-1)
Eilean Ban(USA) Official explanation: jockey said filly lost its action on the bend

4809 IVECO DAILY SOLARIO STKS (GROUP 3) 7f 16y
2:35 (2:38) (Class 1) 2-Y-0
£22,712 (£8,608; £4,308; £2,148; £1,076; £540) **Stalls** High

Form RPR

12 **1** **Drumfire (IRE)**[35] 3735 2-9-0 .... JoeFanning 2 101
(M Johnston) *lw: led tl hdd 2f out: rallied gamely u.p to ld again ins fnl f* **6/4**[1]

241 **2** ½ **Caldra (IRE)**[9] 4525 2-9-0 .... GeorgeBaker 5 100
(S Kirk) *lw: hld up in rr: rdn and hdwy 2f out: styd on to go 2nd nr fin* **8/1**

155 **3** ½ **Danebury Hill**[22] 4099 2-9-0 99.......................................(t) SteveDrowne 6 99
(B J Meehan) *trckd ldr: tk narrow ld 2f out: rdn and hdd ins fnl f: lost 2nd cl home* **12/1**

0113 **4** ½ **Norisan**[28] 3924 2-9-0 100... RichardHughes 8 97
(R Hannon) *chsd ldrs: rdn 2f out: styd on one pce* **15/2**

62 **5** *1 ¾* **Rabbit Fighter (IRE)**[14] 4349 2-9-0 .... TPO'Shea 9 93
(P A Blockley) *t.k.h in mid-div: rdn over 2f out: no hdwy after* **50/1**

021 **6** *nk* **Nightinshining (IRE)**[13] 4388 2-9-0 .... DaneO'Neill 3 92
(A King) *lw: a towards rr: outpcd 2f out: nvr on terms* **20/1**

1 **7** *nk* **Furnace (IRE)**[15] 4333 2-9-0 .... JamieSpencer 7 91
(M L W Bell) *towards rr: rdn 3f out: no ch fnl 2f* **11/4**[2]

410 **8** *7* **Prince Golan (IRE)**[67] 2719 2-9-0 97... NCallan 4 74
(K A Ryan) *prom tl rdn and wknd wl over 1f out* **6/1**[3]

1m 29.18s (-1.91) **Going Correction** -0.125s/f (Firm) **8** Ran SP% **118.2**
Speed ratings (Par 104):105,104,103,103,101 100,100,92
CSF £15.39 TOTE £2.60: £1.20, £2.60, £3.60; EX 16.30 Trifecta £101.20 Pool: £570.22 - 4.00 winning units..
Owner Kennet Valley Thoroughbreds Iv **Bred** Epona Bloodstock Ltd **Trained** Middleham Moor, N Yorks

FOCUS
This looked an ordinary renewal of the Solario Stakes and the first seven home were covered by only around three and a half lengths. Moderate form by Group 3 standards.

NOTEBOOK
Drumfire(IRE), an impressive winner on his debut at Beverley before being beaten only by the highly-regarded Thousand Words when favourite in conditions company at Newbury, coped with the step up to Group company and displayed a particularly game attitude, battling back after being headed by Danebury Hill. The form looks ordinary for the level, but he gives the impression he is very much still learning and may benefit from setting a stronger gallop the next time he is asked to lead. He will be aimed at the Goffs Million at the Curragh. (op 11-8 tchd 13-8 in places)
Caldra(IRE) came into this with a profile not too dissimilar to Opera Cape, who won this race last year for the Kirk yard, and he ran a blinder, showing much improved form. It was a particularly good effort considering he was held up in a race run at no more than an ordinary gallop. (tchd 7-1)
Danebury Hill, upped a furlong in trip and fitted with a tongue-tie for the first time, looked the most likely winner when sent to the front, but he was outstayed and lost two places inside the last furlong. This trip should suit strictly on breeding, but perhaps a flatter track will be more to his liking.
Norisan was strongly supported on course, and ran well, but he never really looked like winning. He has yet to prove he is quite up to this class. (op 12-1 tchd 14-1 in places)
Rabbit Fighter(IRE) was beaten in an ordinary six-furlong maiden at Ayr on his previous start, so his proximity does little for the form. He is probably flattered given the steady pace, but will surely find an opening in maiden company before much longer. (tchd 40-1)
Nightinshining(IRE), off the mark over seven furlongs at Leicester on his previous start, ran well considering he faced a stiff task and the ordinary gallop would not have suited. (op 25-1)
Furnace(IRE) failed to build on the promise he showed when winning on his debut at Newmarket and was a major disappointment. (tchd 7-2)
Prince Golan(IRE) had not been seen since finishing ninth of 21 in the Coventry Stakes over two months previously and ran no sort of race. (op 7-1)

4810 BLUE SQUARE PRICES H'CAP 1m 2f 7y
3:10 (3:12) (Class 3) (0-90,90) 3-Y-0+ **£9,715** (£2,890; £1,444; £721) **Stalls** High

Form RPR

1200 **1** **Salute Him (IRE)**[23] 4082 3-9-3 **87**................................ RichardHughes 10 97
(M R Channon) *mde all: rdn and kpt on gamely whn chal ins fnl f: all out* **20/1**

0-20 **2** *shd* **Giving**[20] 4179 3-9-3 **87**.. SteveDrowne 16 97
(G Wragg) *lw: chsd ldrs: wnt 2nd over 1f out: rdn and pressed wnr to line* **12/1**

3221 **3** *1 ¼* **Bold Act (IRE)**[19] 4209 4-9-5 **81**.. DaneO'Neill 4 88
(H Candy) *mid-div: hdwy over 2f out: styd on but nt qckn ins fnl f* **15/2**[2]

3151 **4** ½ **Blue Bajan (IRE)**[21] 4147 4-10-0 **90**.. RHills 12 96
(Andrew Turnell) *swtg: in rr tl hdwy over 2f out: kpt on one pce fnl f* **9/1**[3]

56-5 **5** *1* **Del Mar Sunset**[24] 4051 7-8-11 **76**............................ SaleemGolam(3) 3 81
(W J Haggas) *b: mid-div: rdn and styd on ins fnl 2f* **33/1**

0136 **6** *nk* **Brief Goodbye**[14] 4370 6-9-4 **80**.................................. MickyFenton 13 84+
(John Berry) *lw: slowly away: hdwy on outside fnl 2f: r.o: nvr nrr* **33/1**

2422 **7** *1* **Fabrian**[9] 4536 8-8-9 **74**.. NeilChalmers(3) 9 76
(R J Price) *chsd ldrs: one pce ins fnl 2f* **11/1**

3422 **8** ½ **Robustian**[29] 3911 3-8-13 **83**..................................... StephenCarson 2 84
(R F Johnson Houghton) *prom tl wknd over 2f out* **20/1**

3020 **9** *1 ¼* **Krugerrand (USA)**[14] 4359 7-9-10 **86**.. NCallan 5 85+
(W J Musson) *nvr bttr than mid-div* **14/1**

-030 **10** *2 ½* **Salt Man**[23] 4082 3-9-3 **87**.. PaulEddery 11 81
(M P Tregoning) *t.k.h in mid-div: no hdwy fr over 2f out* **20/1**

6310 **11** *nk* **I Have Dreamed (IRE)**[21] 4160 4-9-9 **85**............................. IanMongan 17 78
(T G Mills) *swtg: trckd wnr tl wknd over 1f out* **6/1**[1]

0065 **12** *1 ¼* **Pagan Sword**[14] 4359 4-9-13 **89**.. PatDobbs 6 80
(Mrs A J Perrett) *lw: chsd ldrs tl wknd over 1f out* **15/2**[2]

4306 **13** *hd* **Coup D'Etat**[21] 4131 4-9-6 **82**.. JoeFanning 8 73
(J L Dunlop) *mid-div: rdn over 2f out: sn wknd* **9/1**[3]

213- **14** *2 ½* **Dance Partner**[289] 6306 4-9-11 **87**.................................... DavidKinsella 1 73
(J H M Gosden) *lw: prom on outside tl wknd over 2f out* **14/1**

0002 **15** *8* **Along The Nile**[9] 4508 4-9-7 **83**..................................(t) JamieSpencer 15 54
(K G Reveley) *lw: a towards rr* **15/2**[2]

0000 **16** *7* **Stagbury Hill (USA)**[17] 4244 4-8-12 **77**.......................... DeanCorby(3) 14 34
(J W Hills) *b: s.i.s: a in rr* **33/1**

4/0- **17** *1 ½* **Hills Of Aran**[462] 1912 4-9-7 **90**.. JamieJones(7) 7 45
(W K Goldsworthy) *in rr: rdn 3f out: sn lost tch* **50/1**

2m 9.20s (-1.04) **Going Correction** -0.125s/f (Firm)
WFA 3 from 4yo+ 8lb **17** Ran SP% **124.0**
Speed ratings (Par 107):99,98,97,97,96 96,95,95,94,92 92,91,90,88,82 76,75
CSF £230.43 CT £1987.39 TOTE £21.70: £4.80, £3.10, £2.20, £2.70; EX 268.90 Trifecta £856.60 Part won. Pool: £1,206.60 - 0.10 winning units..
Owner Jaber Abdullah **Bred** Drumhass Stud **Trained** West Ilsley, Berks

FOCUS
This did not look a great handicap for the grade and the winning time was moderate. With Salute Him getting his own way in front and setting just an ordinary pace, the bare form wants treating with some caution.

NOTEBOOK
Salute Him(IRE) was below form when unable to dominate in a very good three-year-old handicap at Goodwood on his previous start, but he was able to lead from the start this time and showed what he is capable of with a very game success. This was a fine effort, but recent evidence suggests he has become pretty reliant on front running and he will not always get his own way. (op 16-1)
Giving ◆, dropped in grade having contested a Listed race at Newbury on her previous start, ran a fine race and would have won in another stride. She will go up in the weights, but looks up to finding a similar race. (op 10-1)
Bold Act(IRE) ran well off a 5lb higher mark than when winning over a mile at Windsor on his previous start, but the ordinary early pace would not have suited and he can do better again when getting the race run to suit. (op 8-1)

Blue Bajan(IRE) posted a respectable effort off a 5lb higher mark than when winning at Newmarket on his previous start but is another who would surely have benefited from a stronger gallop. (op 10-1 tchd 11-1)
Del Mar Sunset, having just his second run of the season, ran about as well as could have been expected considering he is another who would have benefited from a stronger gallop. (op 25-1)
Brief Goodbye was yet another who was unsuited by the ordinary pace, although he was perhaps a little more unlucky than most as he had it all to do after missing the break. (op 25-1)
Fabrian could have had more use made of him given the way the race was run. (op 10-1)
I Have Dreamed(IRE), a major disappointment when beaten at 6/4 at Windsor on his previous start, appeared to get pretty wound up beforehand and ran well below his best. He is very talented, but seems quite highly strung and the Terry Mills camp look to have a job on their hands to get the best out of him. (op 7-1 tchd 15-2 and 8-1 in places)
Pagan Sword has looked a little unlucky in recent starts, but he can have few excuses this time. (op 8-1)
Along The Nile looked an unlucky loser at Beverley on his previous start, but he never featured this time. Official explanation: jockey said gelding was unsuited by the ground (op 6-1)

4811 EXCLUSIVEPRICES@BLUESQUARE.COM H'CAP 5f 6y
3:45 (3:47) (Class 2) (0-100,93) 3-Y-O+

£11,217 (£3,358; £1,679; £840; £419; £210) Stalls High

Form RPR
-013 1 **Hogmaneigh (IRE)**[91] 2032 3-9-4 91 .... SaleemGolam(3) 4 106+
(S C Williams) *hw: hld up: rapid hdwy on outside: over 1f out: fin fast and led nr fin: won gng away* **8/1**[3]
6300 2 1 1/4 **Gimasha**[21] 4128 4-9-8 90 .... JamieSpencer 3 100
(W Jarvis) *lw: t.k.h: led 2f out: rdn and hdd nr fin* **9/2**[1]
540 3 1 **First Order**[22] 4101 5-9-3 85 .... PatDobbs 1 91
(Ernst Oertel) *b: mid-div: rdn over 1f out: r.o fnl f: nvr nrr* **14/1**
5300 4 1 **High Reach**[14] 4357 6-9-5 87 .... RichardHughes 7 90
(W R Muir) *in tch: styd on fnl f* **14/1**
545 5 nk **Bluebok**[14] 4360 5-9-0 82 .... (t) NCallan 6 84
(J M Bradley) *led for 2f: rdn and no ex ins fnl f* **9/1**
-000 6 1/2 **Hoh Hoh Hoh**[50] 3251 4-9-0 82 .... DaneO'Neill 2 82
(R J Price) *t.k.h: chsd ldrs tl one pce fnl f* **25/1**
0030 7 1/2 **Golden Dixie (USA)**[22] 4101 7-9-11 93 .... AdrianMcCarthy 11 91
(R A Harris) *b: chsd ldrs: rdn over 1f out: no ex fnl f* **6/1**[2]
36U2 8 1/2 **Matsunosuke**[10] 4486 4-8-2 77 .... LukeMorris(7) 9 73+
(A B Coogan) *lw: mid-div: hdwy on ins 2f out: n.m.r over 1f out: eased* **9/2**[1]
0600 9 hd **Kay Two (IRE)**[14] 4360 4-9-1 83 .... GeorgeBaker 10 83+
(R J Price) *chsd ldrs: short of room 1f out: nt rcvr* **9/1**
0005 10 2 1/2 **Jayanjay**[21] 4158 7-8-12 80 .... JoeFanning 13 67+
(Miss B Sanders) *in tch whn short of room 1/2-way: sn bhd* **8/1**[3]
5-40 11 nk **Angel Sprints**[77] 2429 4-9-4 86 .... DavidKinsella 5 72
(C J Down) *chsd ldrs tl rdn and wknd over 1f out* **20/1**
60-0 12 9 **Dance Night (IRE)**[42] 3535 4-9-5 87 .... (bt[1]) SteveDrowne 12 40
(R Charlton) *s.i.s: a bhd* **16/1**
60.49 secs (-1.72) **Going Correction** -0.125s/f (Firm)
WFA 3 from 4yo+ 2lb 12 Ran SP% **120.7**
Speed ratings (Par 109):108,106,104,102,102 101,100,99,99,95 95,80
CSF £44.69 CT £394.31 TOTE £8.70: £2.80, £2.00, £4.80; EX 38.60 Trifecta £479.90 Part won. Pool: £676.00 - 0.40 winning units..
Owner Mrs Lucille Bone **Bred** John Malone **Trained** Newmarket, Suffolk

FOCUS
Just an ordinary sprint handicap for the grade, the finish of which was dominated by low-drawn horses, but they went a good pace and the time was decent, so the form looks solid. The unexposed Hogmaneigh was produced with a highly impressive late burst to win in style.

NOTEBOOK
Hogmaneigh(IRE) ◆, trying five furlongs for the first time on his return from a three-month break, appreciated the slight ease in the ground and showed a decent turn of foot close home to come from near last to first and win going away. He will start finding things a lot tougher from now on, but has a very progressive profile and will be aimed at the Ayr Gold Cup, for which he has incurred a 5lb penalty. In the meantime, he could take in the Portland, and the five and a half furlong trip should suit. (tchd 17-2)
Gimasha, well down the field in the Stewards' Cup on her previous start, found this less competitive and ran a good race considering she raced very enthusiastically on the pace, whereas the eventual winner came from near last. (tchd 5-1and 4-1 in places)
First Order is not an easy horse to win with, but a strongly-run five furlongs on such a stiff track suits well and he ran a good race. His effort is all the more creditable considering he was reported to have lost a fore and hind shoe. Official explanation: jockey said gelding lost a front and back shoe
High Reach has not been in the best of form lately but, returned to the minimum trip, he ran a reasonable enough race. (op 12-1 tchd 16-1)
Bluebok stuck to his task well when headed, but looks a better horse on fast ground. (op 7-1)
Hoh Hoh Hoh, returning from a 50-day break, is slipping down the handicap and shaped with some promise on his debut for new connections.
Matsunosuke ◆, an unlucky second over course and distance on his previous start, was again denied a clear run and is much better than his finishing position suggests. Official explanation: jockey said gelding was denied a clear run (op 5-1)
Kay Two(IRE) did not enjoy the best of runs. Official explanation: jockey said gelding was denied a clear run (op 12-1)
Dance Night(IRE) Official explanation: jockey said colt suffered interference after the start

4812 BDO STOY HAYWARD H'CAP 5f 6y
4:20 (4:22) (Class 4) (0-85,76) 3-Y-O £5,505 (£1,637; £818; £408) Stalls High

Form RPR
6000 1 **Memphis Man**[71] 2616 3-8-7 62 .... JoeFanning 4 69
(Miss V Haigh) *lw: s.i.s: in rr tl rdn and hdwy over 1f out: r.o to ld ins fnl f* **18/1**
626 2 3/4 **Welcome Approach**[47] 3360 3-9-3 72 .... NCallan 1 76
(J R Weymes) *chsd ldrs: rdn over 1f out: kpt on to go 2nd ins fnl f* **15/2**
1135 3 2 **Bahamian Duke**[30] 3879 3-8-9 64 .... PatCosgrave 3 61
(K R Burke) *mde most tl rdn and hdd ins fnl f: fdd nr fin* **7/2**[3]
0332 4 3/4 **Woodnook**[35] 3744 3-9-7 76 .... JamieSpencer 5 82+
(J A R Toller) *lw: hld up whn hdwy and edgd rt over 1f out: v short of room on ins in fnl f: nt rcvr* **11/8**[1]
1360 5 3/4 **Cheney Hill**[20] 4180 3-8-12 67 .... (v[1]) DaneO'Neill 2 58
(H Candy) *lw: in tch: rdn over 1f out: sn wknd* **10/3**[2]
6066 6 5 **Smooch**[58] 3000 3-9-1 73 .... SaleemGolam(3) 6 46
(R M H Cowell) *w ldr for 2f: wkng whdn bdly hmpd over 1f out: eased ins fnl f* **16/1**
61.33 secs (-0.88) **Going Correction** -0.125s/f (Firm) 6 Ran SP% **110.3**
Speed ratings (Par 102):102,100,97,96,95 87
CSF £131.77 TOTE £23.50: £4.80, £3.40; EX 112.20.
Owner J L Guillambert **Bred** R T And Mrs Watson **Trained** Wiseton, Notts
■ Stewards' Enquiry : Jamie Spencer six-day ban (includes three activated deferred days): careless riding (Sep 6-8,10-12)

FOCUS
Just the six runners and a pretty modest contest for the grade, rated through the runner-up.

4813 FANTASIA CEILING FANS NURSERY 7f 16y
4:50 (4:57) (Class 4) 2-Y-O £4,533 (£1,348; £674; £336) Stalls High

Form RPR
5316 1 **Heywood**[17] 4250 2-9-0 75 .... TPO'Shea 1 82
(M R Channon) *lw: towards rr tl gd hdwy 2f out: led 1f out: styd on wl* **4/1**[1]
404 2 3 **Jawaab (IRE)**[13] 4388 2-8-11 72 .... RHills 7 72
(E A L Dunlop) *lw: slowly away: hld up in rr: n.m.r and swtchd lft over 2f out: styd on to go 2nd ins fnl f: no ch w wnr* **6/1**[3]
0341 3 3/4 **La Marmotte (IRE)**[15] 4334 2-8-3 64 .... JoeFanning 9 62
(J W Hills) *sn led: rdn: edgd rt and hdd 1f out: lost 2nd ins fnl f* **15/2**
2345 4 3 **Buddies Girl (IRE)**[20] 4178 2-8-11 72 .... JamieMackay 11 62
(R Hannon) *lw: broke wl prom but one pce appr fnl f* **9/1**
0123 5 2 **Blue Madeira**[38] 3641 2-9-2 77 .... NCallan 6 62
(Mrs L Stubbs) *lw: mid-div: hdwy on ins when checked over 2f out: one pce fr over 1f out* **9/2**[2]
01 6 hd **Terry Molloy (IRE)**[23] 4066 2-8-13 74 .... PatCosgrave 2 59
(K R Burke) *in tch: rdn 2f out: one pce after* **6/1**[3]
01 7 3/4 **Cavallo Di Ferro (IRE)**[73] 2552 2-8-13 74 .... JamieSpencer 8 57
(J R Boyle) *chsd ldrs tl wknd over 1f out* **8/1**
1162 8 2 **Kyshanty**[16] 4284 2-9-7 82 .... RichardHughes 4 60
(R Hannon) *mid-div: rdn over 2f out: wknd over 1f out* **9/1**
603 9 2 1/2 **Prince Of Charm (USA)**[13] 4397 2-8-4 68 .... SaleemGolam(3) 3 40
(P Mitchell) *slowly away: nt handle bnd over 4f out: a bhd* **50/1**
3004 10 12 **Beckenham's Secret**[21] 4130 2-8-12 73 .... AdrianMcCarthy 5 15
(B R Millman) *a towards rr: lost tch over 2f out* **16/1**
1m 30.55s (-0.54) **Going Correction** -0.125s/f (Firm) 10 Ran SP% **117.5**
Speed ratings (Par 96):98,94,93,90,88 87,86,84,81,68
CSF £28.29 CT £178.62 TOTE £4.60: £2.00, £1.70, £2.50; EX 26.40.
Owner Jumeirah Racing **Bred** R F And S D Knipe **Trained** West Ilsley, Berks

FOCUS
No more than a fair nursery, but it was run at a reasonable gallop, which arguably favoured horses coming from off the pace.

NOTEBOOK
Heywood, 3lb lower than when a beaten favourite on his nursery debut at Newcastle, picked up well from off the pace to run out a convincing winner, despite displaying an awkward head carriage. Things will be tougher once the Handicapper has had his say, but he is clearly progressing. (tchd 9-2)
Jawaab(IRE) ◆, switched to handicap company having shown ability in three runs in maidens, fell out of the stalls and was denied a clear run when trying to pick up. Although the winner scored on merit, he should have been closer, and he ought to win a similar race before long. (op 11-2)
La Marmotte(IRE), the winner of a seller at Newmarket on her previous start, was always just doing too much in front and that cost her on this stiff track. (op 8-1 tchd 17-2)
Buddies Girl(IRE) seemed to have her chance, but was beaten a fair way and does not seem to be progressing at the moment. (op 10-1 tchd 11-1)
Blue Madeira the interference Blue Madeira suffered was of little consequence. He might prove best over shorter. Official explanation: jockey said gelding was hampered (op 5-1)
Terry Molloy(IRE), making his nursery debut, did not build on the form he showed when winning a five and a half furlong maiden at Carlisle on his previous start. (op 7-1 tchd 15-2 and 8-1 in places)
Beckenham's Secret Official explanation: jockey said gelding was unsuited by the ground

4814 VARIETY CLUB MAIDEN FILLIES' STKS 1m 14y
5:25 (5:27) (Class 5) 3-Y-O £3,886 (£1,156; £577; £288) Stalls High

Form RPR
4232 1 **Jewaar (USA)**[27] 3975 3-9-0 78 .... RHills 2 88
(M A Jarvis) *lw: mde all: qcknd clr 2f out: unchal* **5/2**[2]
2 2 5 **Indication**[8] 4563 3-9-0 .... RichardHughes 6 77
(J H M Gosden) *lw: mid-div: hdwy 1/2-way: wnt 2nd over 1f out but no ch w wnr* **13/8**[1]
3 3 3 1/2 **Moon Valley**[27] 3975 3-9-0 .... NCallan 9 68
(M P Tregoning) *s.i.s: sn chsd ldrs: wnt 2nd over 2f out: rdn and lost 2nd over 1f out: wknd ins fnl f* **11/4**[3]
-440 4 2 1/2 **Cheviot Heights**[7] 4610 3-8-11 69 .... SaleemGolam(3) 8 63
(S C Williams) *mid-div: hrd rdn over 1f out: no hdwy* **25/1**
5 1 **Pentatonic** 3-9-0 .... JoeFanning 5 60+
(L M Cumani) *neat: lw: slowly away: in rr: hdwy 1/2-way: one pce fnl 2f* **14/1**
63-0 6 4 **Dawaleeb (IRE)**[106] 1642 3-9-0 67 .... StephenCarson 1 51
(Jane Chapple-Hyam) *trckd wnr to over 2f out: sn wknd* **25/1**
00 7 1 1/4 **Reeling N' Rocking (IRE)**[98] 1844 3-9-0 .... PaulEddery 4 48+
(B W Hills) *bit bkwd: slowly away: outpcd fr 1/2-way* **25/1**
8 7 **Jeu D'Esprit (IRE)** 3-9-0 .... JamieMackay 7 32
(J G Given) *a towards rr* **40/1**
50 9 15 **Hello Deauville (FR)**[10] 4489 3-9-0 .... AlanDaly 3 —
(J Akehurst) *a struggling in rr* **100/1**
1m 42.71s (-1.24) **Going Correction** -0.125s/f (Firm) 9 Ran SP% **115.0**
Speed ratings (Par 97):101,96,92,90,89 85,83,76,61
CSF £6.56 TOTE £3.30: £1.50, £1.10, £1.40; EX 8.10 Place 6 £617.69, Place 5 £472.42.
Owner Hamdan Al Maktoum **Bred** Bohanon-Walden **Trained** Newmarket, Suffolk

FOCUS
Just an ordinary fillies' maiden, but the once well-regarded Jewaar showed improved form in coming home clear after enjoying the run of the race, and the unexposed runner-up also stepped up significantly on her debut effort.
T/Jkpt: Not won. T/Plt: £523.10 to a £1 stake. Pool: £115,915.40. 161.75 winning tickets. T/Qpdt: £279.20 to a £1 stake. Pool: £3,320.60. 8.80 winning tickets. JS

4657 WINDSOR (R-H)
Saturday, August 26

OFFICIAL GOING: Good (good to soft in places)
Wind: Brisk, behind (last 3 races)

4815 READING EVENING POST E B F NOVICE MEDIAN AUCTION STKS 6f
5:05 (5:05) (Class 5) 2-Y-O £4,533 (£1,348; £674; £336) Stalls High

Form RPR
0140 1 **El Bosque (IRE)**[21] 4146 2-9-4 93 .... GrahamGibbons 4 90
(B R Millman) *wnt lft s: sn slt ld: hrd drvn and hld on wl fnl f* **5/4**[1]

1 **2** *1* **Resplendent Alpha**[21] 4138 2-9-6 .... SteveDrowne 6 89
(P Howling) *chsd ldrs: edgd lft 2f out: chsd wnr over 1f out: hung lft and no imp ins last* **11/4**[2]
53 **3** *2 1/2* **Inspirina (IRE)**[22] 4109 2-8-12 .... MickyFenton 1 74
(T R George) *prssed ldrs after 2f: ev ch 2f out: wknd fnl f* **12/1**
000 **4** *3* **Susanna's Prospect (IRE)**[52] 3201 2-8-7 .... TomEaves 5 60
(B J Meehan) *chsd ldrs: rdn: hung lft and wknd fnl f* **15/2**[3]
5 *3* **Earl Compton (IRE)** 2-8-8 .... PatDobbs 8 52
(P F I Cole) *w ldr 2f: wknd 2f out* **16/1**
2035 **6** *1 3/4* **Marmaida (IRE)**[12] 4427 2-8-11 82........ IanMongan 3 49
(W J Knight) *bmpd s: rcvrd to chse ldrs after 2f: hung lft and wknd 2f out* **15/2**[3]
7 *4* **The Geester** 2-8-1 .... MSemple(7) 2 34
(S R Bowring) *wnt rt s and bmpd: chsd ldrs 1/2-way: sn wknd* **50/1**

1m 13.67s **Going Correction** -0.05s/f (Good) 7 Ran SP% **110.2**
Speed ratings (Par 94):98,96,93,89,85 83,77
CSF £4.35 TOTE £2.20: £1.70, £2.60; EX 5.20.
Owner Wessex Racing **Bred** Mrs M Campbell-Andenaes **Trained** Kentisbeare, Devon

FOCUS
Not a great deal of strength in depth, but the bare form looks of a reasonable standard.

NOTEBOOK
El Bosque(IRE) was a little disappointing off a mark of 96 in a nursery at Newmarket last time, but he had previously taken fourth in the Super Sprint and returned to form with a straightforward success. Even so, he will still have something to prove when returned to handicap company. (op 11-8)
Resplendent Alpha, the impressive winner of a weak five-furlong Polytrack maiden at Lingfield on his debut when trained by Terry Mills, ran well on his first start for the Howling yard but basically ran into a better horse on the day. This was only his second outing and there should be more to come. (op 5-2)
Inspirina(IRE) found the front two a bit hot at this stage of his career and will have more options now he eligible to run in nurseries. (op 14-1)
Susanna's Prospect(IRE) was below form on the Polytrack at Kempton last time, but she had previously shown plenty of ability in maiden company over this course and distance. There was not a great deal of promise in this effort, however.
Earl Compton(IRE), a half-brother to dual sprint winner Excalinor, showed good early speed but weakened rather tamely in the latter stages. (op 20-1)
Marmaida(IRE) ran nowhere near her official mark of 82. (op 7-1 tchd 8-1)

4816 PATRICK CHONG (S) STKS 5f 10y
5:35 (5:35) (Class 5) 2-Y-O **£3,238** (£963; £481; £240) **Stalls** High

Form RPR
4304 **1** **Baytown Paikea**[7] 4603 2-8-11 59........ BrianReilly 12 59+
(P S McEntee) *mde all: hrd rdn over 1f out: styd on strly ins last: won readily* **7/2**[2]
0235 **2** *1 3/4* **Fly Time**[16] 4283 2-8-5 52 ow2........ NeilChalmers(3) 4 50
(H J Manners) *chsd wnr thrght: styd on same pce u.p fr over 1f out* **13/2**
6 **3** *1 3/4* **Tibinta**[10] 4492 2-8-6 .... FrancisFerris 6 41
(Rae Guest) *rr but in tch: hdwy 2f out swtchd lft over 1f out: hrd rdn and styd on fnl f but nvr gng pce to rch ldrs* **20/1**
5034 **4** *1 1/4* **Ten For Tosca (IRE)**[6] 4624 2-8-11 57........ PatDobbs 10 42
(J A Osborne) *chsd ldrs: pushed along and outpcd 1/2-way: rdn: edgd lft and styd on fr 2f out: nvr gng pce to be competitive* **3/1**[1]
05 **5** *3/4* **A Nod And A Wink (IRE)**[8] 4550 2-8-3 .... StephaneBreux(3) 9 34
(R Hannon) *sn t.k.h on rails: n.m.r and dropped rr: rdn 1/2-way: kpt on ins last but nvr in contention* **4/1**[3]
0050 **6** *1 1/4* **Countyourblessings**[6] 4624 2-7-13 .... SophieDoyle(7) 2 30
(I A Wood) *chsd ldrs: pushed along over 2f out: wknd over 1f out* **33/1**
005 **7** *nk* **King Of Tricks**[18] 4222 2-8-11 ....(v[1]) RichardSmith 3 34
(M D I Usher) *chsd ldrs: rdn 2f out: sn btn* **16/1**
0600 **8** *7* **Take My Turn**[9] 4526 2-8-11 ....(b) DaneO'Neill 7 8
(M Blanshard) *s.i.s: outpcd most of way* **20/1**
0016 **9** *2* **River Rosie (IRE)**[37] 3677 2-8-11 55........ TomEaves 5 —
(J G Portman) *s.i.s: outpcd most of way* **9/2**

61.87 secs (0.77) **Going Correction** -0.05s/f (Good) 9 Ran SP% **117.1**
Speed ratings (Par 94):91,88,85,83,82 80,79,68,65
CSF £26.08 TOTE £4.90: £1.80, £1.80, £6.90; EX 28.00.There was no bid for the winner.
Owner Eventmaker Partnership **Bred** Launceston Stud **Trained** Newmarket, Suffolk
■ Stewards' Enquiry : Francis Ferris two-day ban: used whip with excessive force (Sep 6-7)

FOCUS
Moderate form, as is to be expected in a seller and very few got involved.

NOTEBOOK
Baytown Paikea, having her 13th start already, hardly saw another horse to gain the second win of her career. She cannot run in sellers again until next year, and will do well to find another race this term. (op 4-1)
Fly Time benefited from the return to selling company and ran well. (op 8-1 tchd 6-1)
Tibinta, a well beaten last of six in a Yarmouth maiden on her debut, proved suited by the drop into selling company and showed some ability. (op 14-1)
Ten For Tosca(IRE) never got involved and was below form. (op 4-1)
A Nod And A Wink(IRE) could not take advantage of the drop into selling company. (op 11-4)
River Rosie(IRE) has not gone on at all since winning a seller at Bath earlier in the season. Official explanation: jockey said filly moved badly (op 4-1)

4817 TOTEPOOL AUGUST STKS (LISTED RACE) 1m 3f 135y
6:05 (6:06) (Class 1) 3-Y-O+
£15,898 (£6,025; £3,015; £1,503; £753; £378) **Stalls** Low

Form RPR
11/3 **1** **Crocodile Dundee (IRE)**[28] 3957 5-9-2 105........ JamieSpencer 3 112
(L M Cumani) *chsd ldrs: pressed ldr fr 2f out tl slt ld jst ins fnl f: hrd rdn and hld on gamely* **6/1**
1-32 **2** *hd* **Khyber Kim**[15] 4337 4-9-2 104........ DaneO'Neill 8 112
(H Candy) *t.k.h:chsd ldr:chal 3f out: slt ld 2f out:narrowly hdd jst ins last: kpt on u.p but a jst hld* **4/1**[2]
2222 **3** *1 1/2* **Ouninpohja (IRE)**[29] 3905 5-9-2 110........(v[1]) TomEaves 4 109+
(I Semple) *hld up in rr: hdwy and edgd lft 2f out: sn pushed along: carried hd high over 1f out and nt keen: styd on for 3rd ins last* **5/1**[3]
-221 **4** *1 1/4* **Windsor Knot (IRE)**[15] 4337 4-9-2 106........ LDettori 2 107
(Saeed Bin Suroor) *set modest pce: pushed along 4f out: drvn 3f out: hdd 2f out: wknd ins fnl f* **11/8**[1]
0-00 **5** *nk* **Hawridge Prince**[29] 3890 6-9-2 90........ MickyFenton 7 107
(B R Millman) *sn chsing ldrs: pushed along 3f out: one pce fnl 2f* **66/1**
4023 **6** *nk* **Hattan (IRE)**[14] 4358 4-9-2 106........ RyanMoore 5 106
(C E Brittain) *rr but in tch: hdwy 4f out: rdn and hung lft 2f out: sn wknd* **5/1**[3]
6-63 **7** *9* **Something Exciting**[29] 3905 4-8-11 105........ JohnEgan 1 86
(D R C Elsworth) *hld up in tch and t.k.h: rdn over 3f out: wknd over 2f out* **16/1**
-000 **8** *33* **Hippodrome (IRE)**[177] 565 4-9-2 90........ SteveDrowne 6 36
(R Simpson) *rr: lost tch fnl 5f: t.o* **66/1**

2m 27.2s (-2.90) **Going Correction** -0.05s/f (Good) 8 Ran SP% **118.6**
Speed ratings (Par 111):107,106,105,105,104 104,98,76
CSF £31.42 TOTE £6.80: £2.40, £1.90, £1.10; EX 39.30.
Owner R C Thompson **Bred** T J Pabst **Trained** Newmarket, Suffolk
■ Stewards' Enquiry : Dane O'Neill five-day ban: used whip with excessive frequency and without giving gelding time to respond (Sep 6-10)

FOCUS
A reasonable renewal of the Listed August Stakes, but they went just a steady pace for much of the way. Hawridge Prince may have finished a little close for comfort in many people's opinion, but it is worth keeping in mind he finished second in this race in 2004.

NOTEBOOK
Crocodile Dundee(IRE) confirmed the promise he showed on his debut for this yard off the back of a 727-day layoff in a Group 2 at York with a narrow success, reaffirming both that he is clearly standing training and retains all of his ability. He very much deserves his chance back in Group company, although the bare form of this success will probably need improving on. (tchd 5-1 and 7-1)
Khyber Kim, half a length behind Windsor Knot in a conditions event at Newmarket on his previous, reversed form with that rival and was just held. He has always promised to develop into a smart sort at this sort of level and is coming along nicely. (op 5-1)
Ouninpohja(IRE), fitted with a visor for the first time on his debut for Ian Semple, displayed an awkward head carriage and looked pretty laboured under pressure, although that was probably exaggerated as he was held up in a race run at just a steady pace. It could be argued he did well to get so close all things considered and, although his attitude is a little suspect, it would be unwise to write him off completely. (op 7-2 tchd 11-8)
Windsor Knot(IRE) had the run of the race out in front, but could not confirm recent Newmarket form with Khyber Kim and has to be considered a little disappointing. (op 2-1)
Hawridge Prince has not been in much form in two runs for his new yard this year since returning from an 11-month absence, but this was much better. It would be unwise to use him to hold down the form too much, as he ran second in this very race in 2004.
Hattan(IRE) would probably have benefited from a stronger pace. (op 9-2)

4818 TOTESPORT.COM WINTER HILL STKS (GROUP 3) 1m 2f 7y
6:35 (6:36) (Class 1) 3-Y-O+
£28,390 (£10,760; £5,385; £2,685; £1,345; £675) **Stalls** High

Form RPR
1151 **1** **Tam Lin**[35] 3736 3-8-6 110........ RyanMoore 1 117+
(Sir Michael Stoute) *trckd ldrs: drvn along 3f out: str run under hand riding to ld fnl 110yds: kpt on wl* **5/2**[1]
1512 **2** *1/2* **Reunite (IRE)**[20] 4179 3-8-3 107........ KerrinMcEvoy 13 113
(Saeed Bin Suroor) *chsd ldr: led ins fnl 2f: styd on u.p tl hdd and nt qckn fnl 110yds* **3/1**[2]
5616 **3** *2* **Kandidate**[22] 4096 4-9-0 114........(t) LDettori 2 112
(C E Brittain) *led: rdn 3f out: hdd ins fnl 2f: one pce fnl f* **5/1**[3]
1-05 **4** *1/2* **Tau Ceti**[92] 1976 7-9-0 105........ JamieSpencer 12 111
(R M Beckett) *bhd: hdwy on ins and rdn over 2f out: styd on ins last but nvr in contention* **20/1**
4541 **5** *3 1/2* **Mulaqat**[14] 4358 3-8-10 112........(b) MartinDwyer 6 109
(M P Tregoning) *hld up in rr: stdy hdwy 3f out: sn trcking ldrs: rdn over 2f out and no rspnse* **11/2**
3114 **6** *3* **Kahlua Kiss**[10] 4482 3-8-6 91 ow3........ TomEaves 3 99
(W R Muir) *in tch: racd on outside: hdwy fr 3f out: wknd fr 2f out* **33/1**
2230 **7** *2* **Kew Green (USA)**[64] 2803 8-9-0 109........(t) DaneO'Neill 11 95
(P R Webber) *in tch: rdn and effrt over 3f out: nvr in contention and wknd 2f out* **12/1**
1140 **8** *3/4* **Before You Go (IRE)**[84] 2228 3-8-6 104........(v[1]) KDarley 8 94
(T G Mills) *chsd ldrs: rdn 3f out: wknd over 2f out* **16/1**
0520 **9** *1* **Counsel's Opinion (IRE)**[85] 2201 9-9-0 102........ GeorgeBaker 7 92
(C F Wall) *stdd s: hld up in rr: rdn 3f out: nvr in contention* **20/1**
4506 **10** *5* **Grand Passion (IRE)**[9] 4529 6-9-0 101........ SteveDrowne 4 82
(G Wragg) *chsd ldrs 7f* **25/1**
0-01 **11** *6* **Chancellor (IRE)**[85] 2201 8-9-0 93........(t) JohnEgan 5 71
(Ernst Oertel) *in tch drvn to chse ldrs over 3f out: sn wknd* **40/1**

2m 6.91s (-1.39) **Going Correction** -0.05s/f (Good)
WFA 3 from 4yo+ 8lb 11 Ran SP% **117.9**
Speed ratings (Par 113):103,102,101,100,97 95,93,93,92,88 83
CSF £9.19 TOTE £3.40: £1.40, £1.80, £2.20; EX 11.50.
Owner Gainsborough Stud **Bred** Gainsborough Stud Management Ltd **Trained** Newmarket, Suffolk

FOCUS
A fair renewal of the Winter Hill Stakes, but they hardly went a frantic pace - the winning time was very moderate winning time for a Group 3 - and the first three home were always handy.

NOTEBOOK
Tam Lin, a dual Listed winner whose only defeat so far this season came in the Group 2 King Edward VII Stakes at Royal Ascot, coped with the step back up in grade and might even have taken this a touch cosily. Not without his quirks, he was given a fine ride by Moore, who resisted the temptation to go for the whip, and looked in control when flashing his tail near the line. His resolution will be more severely tested against better opposition, but he is progressing into a high-class individual and will be worth his place at a higher level. (op 9-4)
Reunite(IRE), turned over at odds on in a 12-furlong fillies' Listed race at Newbury on her previous start, looked better suited by this shorter trip and was just denied. This was a fine effort against the colts and she could be found plenty of opportunities against her won sex. (op 4-1)
Kandidate, returned to a more suitable trip, ran a fine race under a positive ride and his effort is all the more creditable considering he seems better on genuinely fast ground. (op 9-2)
Tau Ceti did not offer much in a couple of runs earlier in the season but, returned from a three-month break, he ran a fine race, faring best of those who raced off the pace early. (op 16-1)
Mulaqat , carrying a 4lb penalty, ran nowhere near the form he showed in first-time blinkers when a shock winner in this grade at Haydock on his previous start and may want better ground. The effect of the headgear may also have worn off. (op 9-2 tchd 13-2)
Kahlua Kiss ran with credit, but will be better off against her own sex.
Kew Green(USA) Official explanation: jockey said gelding lost its action final furlong

4819 TOTEEXACTA H'CAP 1m 67y
7:05 (7:05) (Class 4) (0-85,85) 3-Y-O+
£6,232 (£1,866; £933; £467; £233; £117) **Stalls** High

Form RPR
1111 **1** **Envision**[12] 4429 3-9-6 **83**........ RyanMoore 2 96
(R Hannon) *rr: hdwy on outside 3f out:led jst ins fnl 2f: hung bdly rt u.p fnl f: rdr dropped whip and kpt on cl home* **5/2**[1]
5046 **2** *1 1/4* **Nanton (USA)**[19] 4209 4-9-2 **73**........ JamieSpencer 7 84+
(P F I Cole) *rr: stdy hdwy over 2f out: styng on strly whn bdly hmpd jst ins fnl f: swtchd lft: kpt on: nt rcvr* **9/1**
-106 **3** *1* **Master Pegasus**[16] 4298 3-9-8 **85**........ GeorgeBaker 5 92
(C F Wall) *hld up in tch: hdwy 3f out: kpt on to chse ldrs fnl f but a hld* **3/1**[2]

5050 **4** 1 ½ **Norton (IRE)**[27] 3973 9-9-13 **84** .... IanMongan 8 89
(T G Mills) *chsd ldrs: drvn to ld jst ins fnl 4f: hdd jst ins fnl 2f: wknd fnl f* **8/1**
-410 **5** 1 ½ **Alfridini**[196] 375 5-8-13 **70** .... LPKeniry 6 71
(D R C Elsworth) *chsd ldr to 4f out: rdn 3f out: wknd over 1f out* **25/1**
-33U **6** 1 ¼ **Alfie Tupper (IRE)**[10] 4481 3-9-7 **84** .... RichardHughes 9 81
(S Kirk) *trckd ldrs: rdn over 2f out: sn btn* **7/2**[3]
2004 **7** ½ **Glencalvie (IRE)**[12] 4429 5-9-4 **75** ....(p) DaneO'Neill 11 72
(J Akehurst) *chsd ldrs: rdn 3f out: wknd over 2f out* **13/2**
4660 **8** 3 **San Antonio**[55] 3121 6-9-8 **79** .... MickyFenton 10 69
(Mrs P Sly) *drvn to ld: hdd ins fnl 4f: btn ins fnl 3f* **12/1**

1m 43.26s (-2.34) **Going Correction** -0.05s/f (Good)
WFA 3 from 4yo+ 6lb **8** Ran SP% **121.8**
Speed ratings (Par 105):109,107,106,105,103 102,102,99
CSF £27.96 CT £73.20 TOTE £3.10: £1.50, £2.60, £1.60; EX 20.40.
Owner Mrs J Wood **Bred** Cheveley Park Stud Ltd **Trained** East Everleigh, Wilts
■ Stewards' Enquiry : Ryan Moore two-day ban: careless riding (Sep 6-7)

FOCUS
A decent handicap run at a strong pace and the form looks solid.

4820 TOTESPORTCASINO.COM FILLIES' H'CAP 1m 67y
7:35 (7:36) (Class 5) (0-75,75) 3-Y-0+ **£3,238** (£963; £481; £240) **Stalls** High

Form RPR
-030 **1** **Dansa Queen**[49] 3318 3-9-10 **75** .... AdamKirby(3) 1 85
(W R Swinburn) *hld up in rr: hdwy over 2f out: drvn to ld fnl 110yds: kpt on wl* **8/1**
4014 **2** ½ **Munaa (IRE)**[12] 4426 3-9-3 **70** .... AndrewElliott(5) 8 79
(K R Burke) *chsd ldr after 2f: led 2f out: sn rdn: hdd and no ex fnl 110yds* **9/2**[1]
0461 **3** 1 ¾ **Greenmeadow**[16] 4289 4-8-11 **58** .... MichaelJStainton(5) 3 64
(S Kirk) *bhd: hdwy on outside over 3f out: drvn to chal 2f out: kpt on same pce fnl f* **8/1**
4043 **4** 1 ¾ **Palais Polaire**[9] 4531 4-8-13 **55** .... RichardThomas 7 57
(J A Geake) *in tch: drvn to chse ldrs fr 3f out: one pce fnl 2f* **5/1**[2]
0-00 **5** ½ **Suesam**[6] 4627 3-9-6 **68** .... GeorgeBaker 13 68
(B R Millman) *sn led: rdn and hdd 2f out: hung lft and wknd fnl f* **6/1**[3]
0005 **6** 1 ¼ **Warden Rose**[9] 4527 3-8-7 **55** .... JohnEgan 11 52
(D R C Elsworth) *chsd ldrs: rdn over 3f out: kpt on fnl f but nvr a danger* **7/1**
0030 **7** 10 **Sprinkle**[16] 4286 3-8-12 **60** .... RichardHughes 12 34
(R M Beckett) *chsd ldrs: rdn 3f out: wknd qckly 2f out: eased whn no ch fnl f* **8/1**
0305 **8** 13 **Foreplay (IRE)**[14] 4368 3-9-7 **69** .... SteveDrowne 6 13
(E A L Dunlop) *mid-div: hdwy to chse ldrs 3f out: wknd 2f out: eased whn no ch fnl f* **8/1**
6-00 **9** 1 **Laugh 'n Cry**[5] 4660 5-9-9 **65** .... MickyFenton 5 7
(C A Cyzer) *chsd ldr: rdn 3f out: wknd 2f out: eased whn no ch fnl f* **20/1**
0050 **10** 2 ½ **Nan Jan**[38] 3642 4-8-12 **54** ....(bt[1]) DaneO'Neill 10 —
(R Ingram) *s.i.s: bhd most of way* **16/1**
2-40 **11** 6 **Desert Flair**[59] 2985 3-9-8 **70** .... RyanMoore 9 —
(R Hannon) *bhd: rdn 4f out: nvr bttr than mid-div: lost tch fnl 2f and eased whn no ch* **12/1**

1m 44.55s (-1.05) **Going Correction** -0.05s/f (Good)
WFA 3 from 4yo+ 6lb **11** Ran SP% **124.4**
Speed ratings (Par 100):103,102,100,99,98 97,87,74,73,70 64
CSF £46.60 CT £315.40 TOTE £10.90: £2.80, £1.50, £2.60; EX 92.40 Place 6 £43.25, Place 5 £33.35.
Owner Persistent Partners **Bred** C R Mason **Trained** Aldbury, Herts

FOCUS
This was a fair fillies' handicap and the form looks solid. The winner improved and the second also seems to be on the upgrade.
Sprinkle Official explanation: jockey said filly lost its action
T/Plt: £66.40 to a £1 stake. Pool: £47,289.90. 519.80 winning tickets. T/Qpdt: £5.10 to a £1 stake. Pool: £4,890.40. 709.10 winning tickets. ST

4821 - (Foreign Racing) - See Raceform Interactive

4406 CURRAGH (R-H)
Saturday, August 26

OFFICIAL GOING: Straight course - good; round course - good to firm

4822a CILL DARA SECURITY BALLYCULLEN STKS (LISTED RACE) 1m 6f
2:45 (2:46) 3-Y-0+ **£24,693** (£7,244; £3,451; £1,175)

RPR
1 **Tusculum (IRE)**[56] 3106 3-8-11 96 .... JAHeffernan 4 111+
(A P O'Brien, Ire) *hld up towards rr: 7th travelling wl appr st: hdwy into mod 2nd 1 1/2f out: led under 1f out: wandered abt: kpt on wl* **8/1**[3]
2 2 ½ **Good Surprise**[6] 4639 5-9-9 106 ....(b) KJManning 8 108
(J S Bolger, Ire) *trckd ldr in 2nd: imrpoved to ld appr st: sn rdn clr: hdd under 1f out: kpt on u.p* **11/2**[2]
3 2 **Clara Allen (IRE)**[19] 4212 8-9-6 95 .... TPQueally 6 102
(John E Kiely, Ire) *hld up towards rr: 6th whn swtchd lft 2f out: kpt on wl fr over 1f out* **9/1**
4 1 ¾ **Ayla (IRE)**[19] 4212 3-8-8 .... PJSmullen 2 100
(John M Oxx, Ire) *hld up in 6th: rdn st: kpt on one pce fr 2f out* **16/1**
5 4 **Lounaos (FR)**[8] 4584 3-8-8 89 .... DPMcDonogh 3 95
(Eoin Griffin, Ire) *trckd ldrs in 5th: prog into 4th 1/2-way: rdn to go mod 2nd 2f out: no ex fr over 1f out* **14/1**
6 9 **Savannah**[25] 4024 3-8-11 100 .... KFallon 5 86
(A P O'Brien, Ire) *chsd ldrs in 3rd: rdn appr st: no ex fr 2f out* **8/1**[3]
7 4 ½ **Harrington (IRE)** 4-9-9 .... PShanahan 7 80
(Noel Furlong, Ire) *s.i.s and hld up in rr: no imp fr over 3f out* **20/1**
8 1 ¾ **Mkuzi**[38] 3660 7-9-9 110 .... MJKinane 1 78
(John M Oxx, Ire) *settled 4th: 5th 1/2-way: pushed along 5f out: wknd bef st* **9/10**[1]
9 7 **Virginia Woolf**[38] 3660 4-9-6 98 .... FMBerry 9 66
(John M Oxx, Ire) *sn drvn into ld: hdd & wknd qckly appr st* **12/1**

2m 59.1s **Going Correction** -0.45s/f (Firm)
WFA 3 from 4yo+ 12lb **9** Ran SP% **125.2**
Speed ratings: 91,89,88,87,85 80,77,76,72
CSF £56.01 TOTE £8.80: £2.60, £1.90, £1.90; DF 68.60.
Owner Karin Baronin von Ullmann **Bred** Gestut Schlenderham & Abbey Bl **Trained** Ballydoyle, Co Tipperary

FOCUS
A useful renewal of this Listed event, which has been rated around the third, fourth and fifth all slightly improving on their personal bests.

NOTEBOOK
Tusculum(IRE) delivered his challenge down the outside in the straight and soon moved into second behind Good Surprise. He edged ahead of that rival heading towards the final furlong and was going away towards the finish. He was rated 96 coming into this race and the St Leger will represent an altogether tougher challenge, but he makes considerable appeal for that Classic and could have a big part to play there. This was only the fourth run of his career and there should certainly be better to come from him. (op 7/1)
Good Surprise ran another sound race, six days after taking third behind Kastoria in the Ballyroan Stakes at Leopardstown. He seized command of the race early in the straight but was just unable to fend off the winner. He is certainly good enough to win at this level. (op 4/1)
Clara Allen(IRE), last year's Irish Cesarewitch winner, ran a fine race to pick up a valuable black-type placing. She had only one behind her turning for home but did stay on well in the closing stages. (op 10/1)
Ayla(IRE) finished in front of Clara Allen in a Listed event at Cork last time but was unable to confirm placings with that rival over this longer trip. She posted a sound effort here on what was only her third start and should prove good enough to reach the frame in a Listed race.
Lounaos(FR) was taking a big step up in class from winning a Roscommon maiden and acquitted herself respectably, but more will be needed if she is to reach the frame at this level.
Savannah looked to have plenty to do on form and could make no further impression over the final two furlongs. He may need to drop back in trip.
Mkuzi looked to have an excellent chance of opening his account for the season, but he was the first horse under pressure and was beaten some way out. His rider reported that he was never travelling throughout the race and lost his action with about six furlongs to run. Official explanation: jockey said horse was never travelling and its action at the top of the hill (op 9/10 tchd Evens)

4824a TATTERSALLS IRELAND SALE STKS 6f
3:50 (3:52) 2-Y-0
£101,379 (£39,310; £23,793; £13,448; £4,137; £2,068)

RPR
1 **Invincible Force (IRE)**[20] 4170 2-9-2 .... FMBerry 18 98
(Ms Deborah J Evans) *mde virtually all: rdn clr over 1f out: comf* **9/1**
2 2 ½ **Southandwest (IRE)**[30] 3861 2-9-2 .... KFallon 24 91
(J S Moore) *mid-div: hdwy on outer under 1 1/2f out: 9th over 1f out: styd on wl wout threatening wnr* **11/2**[1]
3 ½ **Bazroy (IRE)**[20] 4170 2-9-2 .... MCHussey 21 89
(P D Evans) *sn trckd ldrs: 4th after 1/2-way: 2nd and chal under 2f out: one pce fnl f* **33/1**
4 1 **Don't Panic (IRE)**[21] 4129 2-9-2 .... MJKinane 9 86
(P W Chapple-Hyam) *prom: 2nd 1/2-way: 3rd and rdn under 2f out: kpt on same pce* **7/1**[3]
5 1 ¾ **Howya Now Kid (IRE)**[21] 4165 2-9-2 .... JMurtagh 6 81
(G M Lyons, Ire) *chsd ldrs: 7th appr 1/2-way: kpt on wout threatening fr over 1f out* **15/2**
6 nk **Goodbye Cash (IRE)**[52] 3193 2-8-11 .... CDHayes 22 75
(P D Evans) *chsd ldrs: 4th over 1f out: kpt on same pce* **20/1**
7 hd **Weekend Escape (IRE)**[31] 3858 2-9-2 .... WSupple 4 79
(K J Condon, Ire) *chsd ldrs: 4th under 1 1/2f out: no ex fnl f* **25/1**
8 1 ¼ **Fabrigas (IRE)**[55] 3126 2-9-2 .... DPMcDonogh 13 76
(Kevin Prendergast, Ire) *chsd ldrs: 5th and rdn 1 1/2f out: no ex fnl f* **6/1**[2]
9 ¾ **Northern Fling**[21] 4130 2-9-2 .... AdrianTNicholls 16 73
(D Nicholls) *chsd ldrs: 6th and effrt under 2f out: kpt on same pce* **10/1**
10 1 ¼ **Simba Sun (IRE)**[63] 2857 2-9-2 .... PJSmullen 8 70
(R M Beckett) *mid-div: rdn and no imp fr 2f out* **8/1**
11 hd **Montalembert (USA)**[63] 2844 2-9-2 .... SMGorey 23 69
(J S Moore) *hld up in tch: kpt on same pce fr 1 1/2f out* **25/1**
12 1 **Dal Cais (IRE)**[21] 4165 2-9-2 .... RPCleary 15 66
(Francis Ennis, Ire) *chsd ldrs: 5th 1 1/2f out: sn no ex and wknd* **14/1**
13 1 **Fadeyev (IRE)**[7] 4608 2-9-2 ....(p) CatherineGannon 5 63
(K A Ryan) *mid-div: kpt on same pce fr 1 1/2f out* **25/1**
14 nk **Tyreless Endeavour (IRE)**[19] 4218 2-9-2 .... KJManning 12 62
(Peter Casey, Ire) *nvr bttr than mid-div* **25/1**
15 1 **Inis Ceithleann (IRE)**[13] 4412 2-8-11 .... JAHeffernan 3 54
(Peter Casey, Ire) *mid-div: no imp fr 2f out* **20/1**
16 ½ **Casco Bay (IRE)**[22] 4193 2-9-2 ....(b[1]) NGMcCullagh 20 58
(P J Prendergast, Ire) *a bhd* **50/1**
17 ½ **Invincible Star (IRE)**[19] 4217 2-8-11 .... OCasey 2 51
(Peter Casey, Ire) *prom on stand's rail: 4th appr 1/2-way: wknd fr 2f out* **20/1**
18 hd **Hoptilludrop (IRE)**[13] 4406 2-8-11 .... FranciscoDaSilva 7 50
(Matthieu Palussiere, Ire) *prom: 3rd appr 1/2-way: sn wknd* **66/1**
19 1 ¼ **Alecia (IRE)**[36] 3700 2-8-11 .... WMLordan 1 47
(C G Cox) *nvr a factor* **20/1**
20 hd **Smokey Oakey (IRE)**[16] 4295 2-9-2 .... TPQueally 10 51
(M H Tompkins) *nvr a factor* **16/1**
21 ¾ **Daring Spirit (IRE)**[20] 4182 2-9-2 .... DMGrant 11 49
(J C Hayden, Ire) *a towards rr* **33/1**
22 ¾ **Rosa Chester (IRE)**[6] 4638 2-8-11 .... RMBurke 17 42
(R J Osborne, Ire) *a bhd* **40/1**
23 ½ **Wishfully Tropical (IRE)** 2-8-11 ....(t) PShanahan 14 40
(C Collins, Ire) *a towards rr* **25/1**
24 16 **Please The King (IRE)** 2-9-2 ....(t) CO'Donoghue 19 —
(T Hogan, Ire) *v.s.a and a bhd* **50/1**

1m 12.2s **Going Correction** -0.35s/f (Firm) **24** Ran SP% **148.7**
Speed ratings: 101,97,97,95,93 92,92,91,90,88 88,86,85,85,83 83,82,82,80,80 79,78,77,56
CSF £55.65 TOTE £13.70: £3.30, £2.20, £12.20, £2.40; DF 59.30.
Owner Terry Cummins **Bred** Robert Wilson **Trained** Lydiate, Merseyside
■ Stewards' Enquiry : M C Hussey one-day ban: used whip with excessive frequency (Sep 4)

FOCUS
The English domination of this race continued, with the first four home all hailing from across the Irish Sea.

NOTEBOOK
Invincible Force(IRE), who won a Chester Nursery off a mark of 86 last time, produced a fine effort to win his fourth race of the season. He showed good early speed to get across towards the stands' side rail and was in the firing line from the outset. Heading into the final two furlongs he had all his rivals hard at work and kept on well for a clear-cut success. A Listed race is likely to be next and this improving gelding looks quite capable of making his mark at that level.
Southandwest(IRE) did well from the widest draw of all. He had plenty to do with over a furlong to run but stayed on well on the outer to secure second. A two-time winner over five furlongs at Bath, he had also run respectably at Listed level at Sandown last month. There are more races to be won with him and he should stay seven furlongs. (op 5/1 tchd 7/1)
Bazroy(IRE) finished fourth behind the winner at Chester last time and had previously run creditably in defeat in a Haydock nursery. On more disadvantageous terms here, he did well to get so close to Invincible Force, looking a big danger with two furlongs to run. He can win again.
Don't Panic(IRE) came here off an encouraging run in what looked a useful Goodwood maiden earlier this month. He was always close to the pace but had no more to give from over a furlong out. He should have little trouble in opening his account. (op 6/1)

Howya Now Kid(IRE), who has been a model of consistency all season, fared best of the home team. He was in midfield heading into the final two furlongs before staying on again. He may now want seven furlongs to be seen at his best. (op 6/1 tchd 8/1)
Goodbye Cash(IRE) was always prominent and ran a sound race. She has already shown up well in a couple of maidens and deserves to get off the mark.
Weekend Escape(IRE) was vying for the placings heading towards the final furlong but had no more to give in the closing stages. He looked a useful sort when winning a maiden at Naas last month and should be able to win again.
Fabrigas(IRE) was under pressure some way from home and took closer order over a furlong out, but he could soon do no more. This did not match the form of his creditable sixth-place finish in the Railway Stakes. (op 6/1 tchd 7/1)
Northern Fling looked as though six furlongs here might have proved beyond him. (op 7/1)
Dal Cais(IRE) began to weaken from a good position with over a furlong to run and may benefit from going back up in trip.
Daring Spirit(IRE) Official explanation: trainer said gelding suffered interference when leaving the stalls

4825a GALILEO EUROPEAN BREEDERS FUND FUTURITY STKS (GROUP 2) 7f

4:25 (4:25) 2-Y-0

£51,724 (£16,379; £7,758; £2,586; £1,724; £862)

			RPR
1		**Teofilo (IRE)**[28] 3962 2-9-1 .... KJManning 3 (J S Bolger, Ire) *cl up in 2nd: led under 2f out: sn rdn clr: strly pressed ins fnl f: styd on wl u.p* **6/4**[1]	112
2	*hd*	**Eagle Mountain**[90] 2052 2-9-1 .... CO'Donoghue 4 (A P O'Brien, Ire) *hld up in rr: 5th and hdwy 1 1/2f out: 2nd and chal ins fnl f: ev ch cl home: jst failed* **16/1**	112
3	*3*	**Ferneley (IRE)**[16] 4318 2-9-1 .... WSupple 8 (Francis Ennis, Ire) *hld up in tch: prog into 4th after 1/2-way: 2nd briefly 1 1/2f out: 3rd and no ex whn edgd lft ins fnl f* **15/2**	104
4	*1 3/4*	**Trinity College (USA)**[19] 4215 2-9-1 .... KFallon 2 (A P O'Brien, Ire) *trckd ldrs in 5th: rdn and outpcd over 2f out: 6th 1f out: styd on* **7/4**[2]	100
5	*1 1/4*	**Regional Counsel**[41] 3574 2-9-1 .... DPMcDonogh 1 (Kevin Prendergast, Ire) *trckd ldrs in 4th: 3rd 2f out: sn rdn and no imp: no ex fnl f* **13/2**[3]	97
6	*1*	**Vorteeva (USA)**[16] 4318 2-9-1 .... MJKinane 6 (John M Oxx, Ire) *led: rdn and strly pressed 3f out: hdd & wknd over 1 1/2f out* **25/1**	94
7	*2 1/2*	**Yellowstone (IRE)**[43] 3505 2-9-1 .... JAHeffernan 7 (A P O'Brien, Ire) *dwlt: sn chsd ldrs in 3rd: wknd fr over 2f out* **33/1**	88

1m 22.6s **Going Correction** -0.45s/f (Firm) 8 Ran SP% **114.1**
Speed ratings: 110,109,106,104,102 101,98
CSF £26.29 TOTE £2.00: £1.60, £5.80; DF 72.20.
Owner Mrs J S Bolger **Bred** J S Bolger **Trained** Coolcullen, Co Carlow

FOCUS
A race that has been won by some top class sorts in recent years with Giant's Causeway, Hawk Wing, Oratorio and Horatio Nelson among those to have appeared on its roll of honour since 1999. This renewal looked well up to standard.

NOTEBOOK
Teofilo(IRE) cemented his position as one of the best juveniles around with a gritty effort that saw him maintain his unbeaten record. A winner over this course and distance last month, he had looked a possible contender for top honours when following up in Listed company at Leopardstown. On this occasion he raced in a close second from early on and was a little keen over the first few furlongs. He only had to be pushed along when going to the front with well over a furlong to run and, when Eagle Mountain seemed poised to collar him, he pulled out that bit more to make sure of victory. Jim Bolger holdsn the colt in the highest regard and it was no surprise to see his price contracting for both next year's 2000 Guineas and Derby. Future targets for this season are undecided, but the National Stakes is one possibility. He looks quite capable of making his mark at the highest level this season. (op 5/4)
Eagle Mountain was the surprise package of the race on his first start since winning a six-furlong maiden on soft ground here in May. Given a patient ride, he started a forward move on the outer heading into the final two furlongs. He picked up well when asked for his all and looked as if he might overhaul the winner inside the final furlong, but his effort came up just short. This was a fine effort on his first start for three months and it will be a surprise if he does not make his mark at Stakes level. There should be more to come from him.
Ferneley(IRE) came here off victories in a Galway maiden and a conditions event at Tipperary. He was taking a marked rise in class and acquitted himself well. With a furlong and a half to run he looked the biggest danger to the winner but could not go with Eagle Mountain when that one quickened up. A likeable sort, he should be able to land a good prize in the coming months. (op 6/1)
Trinity College(USA) looked a horse of considerable potential when winning a Cork maiden on his debut earlier this month but this represented a major rise in class. He lost a couple of places and came under strong pressure with two furlongs to run, but he was staying on again in the closing stages. He should derive significant benefit from this experience and an extra furlong will be in his favour. (op 2/1)
Regional Counsel had a good position from the outset and held third with two furlongs to run, but he could do no more nearing the furlong pole. He turned in a sound effort in a race that looked tougher than the Anglesey. (op 6/1)
Vorteeva(USA) finished the same distance behind Ferneley as when they met at Tipperary.
Yellowstone(IRE) found the step up to this grade too much.

4826 - 4827a (Foreign Racing) - See Raceform Interactive

2060 BADEN-BADEN (L-H)

Saturday, August 26

OFFICIAL GOING: Soft

4828a PREIS DER SPARKASSEN - FINANZGRUPPE (EX SPRETI-RENNEN) (GROUP 3) 1m 2f

4:00 (4:10) 4-Y-0+ £24,138 (£10,345; £4,138; £2,759)

			RPR
1		**White Lightning (GER)** 4-8-9 .... RJuracek 8 (U Stech, Norway) *raced in 6th, stayed on down outside from over 1 1/2f out to lead last 50 yards* **264/10**	107
2	*hd*	**Mohandas (FR)**[38] 3662 5-8-11 .... ASuborics 5 (W Hefter, Germany) *raced in 4th, 3rd straight, disputed lead over 1f out til led just inside final f, headed last 50 yards* **72/10**	109
3	*1 3/4*	**Bailamos (GER)**[62] 2910 6-8-9 .... AStarke 4 (H Hesse, Germany) *held up in 8th, 7th straight, stayed on from over 1f out to take 3rd on line* **114/10**	104
4	*hd*	**Brisant (GER)**[69] 4-8-9 .... AHelfenbein 6 (M Trybuhl, Germany) *held up in 7th, 8th straight, stayed on down outside from over 1f out to take 4th on line* **108/10**	103
5	*hd*	**Fight Club (GER)**[27] 3993 5-9-2 .... ADeVries 2 (A Trybuhl, Germany) *raced in 5th, close 4th straight, disputed lead over 1f out to just inside final f, one pace, lost 3rd on line* **6/4**[1]	110
6	*1 1/4*	**Simonas (IRE)**[41] 3579 7-8-11 ....(b) EPedroza 7 (A Wohler, Germany) *held up in last, stayed on steadily down outside final 1 1/2f, never a factor* **43/10**[3]	103
7	*1*	**Genios (GER)**[76] 2492 5-8-11 .... ABoschert 1 (Dr A Bolte, Germany) *prominent early, close 5th straight, one pace from over 1f out* **22/1**	101
8	*nk*	**Rocamadour**[21] 4145 4-8-11 .... ChrisCatlin 3 (M R Channon) *led, pushed along and strongly pressed well over 2f out, headed over 1f out, weakened* **22/10**[2]	101
9	*nk*	**Spatzolita (GER)**[358] 7-8-5 .... J-PCarvalho 9 (D K Richardson, Germany) *raced in 2nd, pressed leader well over 2f out to over 1f out, weakened* **253/10**	94

2m 5.35s 9 Ran SP% **130.7**
(including 10 Euro stake): WIN 274; PL 45, 24, 39; SF 3532.
Owner P Hanke **Bred** Frau Lore Zieger-Dickerhoff **Trained** Norway

NOTEBOOK
Rocamadour, returning to this trip after three tries over a mile, had to work hard when challenged for his lead on the final elbow and had done enough more than a furlong from home. He faded back through the field but, even so, was beaten less than five lengths. It is nine races and 16 months since he last won - over this distance at Newmarket - and he looks difficult to place.

4506 BEVERLEY (R-H)

Sunday, August 27

OFFICIAL GOING: Good to soft (good in places)
The ground was described as 'on the easy side of good but a bit rough and patchy hard against the running rail'.
Wind: Fresh, half-against. Weather: Mainly fine

4829 E B F BEVERLEY LIONS MEDIAN AUCTION MAIDEN STKS 1m 100y

2:00 (2:01) (Class 4) 2-Y-0 £5,181 (£1,541; £770; £384) Stalls High

Form				RPR
4	1		**Regime (IRE)**[9] 4574 2-9-3 .... MickyFenton 8 (M L W Bell) *chsd ldrs: hmpd 2f out: led jst ins last: r.o strly* **4/1**[2]	83+
44	2	*3*	**Beech Games**[32] 3843 2-9-3 .... FrancisNorton 2 (E J O'Neill) *s.i.s: bhd tl hdwy 3f out: styd on wl ins last: tk 2nd nr fin* **5/1**[3]	76
	3	*1/2*	**Tempelstern (GER)** 2-9-3 .... RHills 10 (H R A Cecil) *s.i.s: sn trcking ldrs: plld wd over 2f out: led 1f out: sn hdd and no ex* **5/1**[3]	75
0B	4	*3*	**Packers Hill (IRE)**[18] 4260 2-9-3 .... DeanMcKeown 13 (G A Swinbank) *led tl 1f out: wknd towards fin* **20/1**	69
00	5	*2*	**Musical Award (IRE)**[16] 4333 2-9-3 .... PatCosgrave 5 (M G Quinlan) *in tch: swtchd wd over 2f out: kpt on* **6/1**	64
	6	*7*	**Bobansheil (IRE)** 2-8-12 .... JohnEgan 6 (J S Wainwright) *s.i.s: sn bhd: styd on fnl 2f* **33/1**	44
550	7	*1 1/2*	**Mastership (IRE)**[15] 4366 2-9-3 ....(b[1]) KerrinMcEvoy 4 (C E Brittain) *chsd ldrs: wknd over 1f out* **16/1**	46
45	8	*6*	**Messiah Garvey**[11] 4487 2-9-3 .... RobertWinston 9 (M R Channon) *trckd ldr: lost pl over 1f out* **7/2**[1]	32
20	9	*5*	**Lady Best (IRE)**[13] 4424 2-8-12 .... DavidAllan 3 (J R Weymes) *mid-div: drvn over 3f out: sn btn* **20/1**	16
00	10	*shd*	**Double Precedent**[14] 4400 2-8-12 .... KDarley 7 (M Johnston) *chsd ldrs: edgd rt 2f out: sn wknd* **25/1**	16
00	11	*1 1/2*	**Dee Valley Boy (IRE)**[21] 4171 2-9-3 .... GrahamGibbons 12 (J D Bethell) *mid-div: sn drvn along: wknd fnl 2f* **25/1**	18
0	12	*14*	**Man Of Fortune (IRE)**[9] 4572 2-9-0 .... PatrickMathers(3) 1 (D Shaw) *s.i.s: sn bhd: t.o 3f out* **100/1**	—
0	13	*8*	**Will Doo**[26] 4018 2-9-3 .... TomEaves 11 (M E Sowersby) *lost pl over 4f out: sn bhd* **100/1**	—

1m 47.64s (0.24) **Going Correction** -0.025s/f (Good) 13 Ran SP% **117.9**
Speed ratings (Par 96):97,94,93,90,88 81,80,74,69,68 67,53,45
CSF £22.00 TOTE £4.70: £1.70, £1.80, £2.20; EX 21.10.
Owner Highclere Thoroughbred Racing XL **Bred** Philip Brady **Trained** Newmarket, Suffolk

FOCUS
A better than average maiden although a severe test of stamina for juveniles. The winner can improve again.

NOTEBOOK
Regime(IRE), a grand type, in the end won going away. He clearly stays well and may now be aimed at the Goffs Million at the Curragh. (op 9-2 tchd 7-2)
Beech Games, making his debut on turf, took an age to get going. He was putting in his best work at the death and looks a real stayer. (op 11-2)
Tempelstern(GER), a rangy, unfurnished type, was soon on the heels of the leaders. Pulled out to make his finishing effort, he had no answer when the winner swept by on his inside. He is bred to make a middle-distance three-year-old. (op 6-1)
Packers Hill(IRE), clearly none-the-worse for Pontefract, took them along but had nothing at all left in reserve near the line. This opens up the nursery route for him and he looks capable of better. (op 14-1)
Musical Award(IRE), stepping up in trip and encountering slower ground, stayed on when it was all over. A May foal, he may be capable of a bit better yet. (op 11-2 tchd 13-2)
Bobansheil(IRE), a February foal, stands over plenty of ground. After a tardy start she seemed all at sea round the bend but was picking up in her own time at the finish. She will benefit from being given a bit more time yet. Official explanation: jockey said filly ran very green early and failed to handle bend (op 28-1)
Messiah Garvey, having his third outing, was disappointing encountering easy ground and a round track for the first time. Official explanation: jockey said colt had no more to give (op 4-1)

4830 E B F BP ACETYLS SALTEND SPECIOSA MAIDEN FILLIES' STKS 7f 100y

2:30 (2:35) (Class 4) 2-Y-0 £5,829 (£1,734; £866; £432) Stalls High

Form				RPR
0	1		**Lost In Wonder (USA)**[22] 4148 2-9-0 .... RobertWinston 9 (Sir Michael Stoute) *trckd ldrs: pushed rt over 1f out: led last 150yds: r.o* **3/1**[2]	80
4	2	*3/4*	**La Spezia (IRE)**[15] 4373 2-9-0 .... MickyFenton 5 (M L W Bell) *trckd ldrs: led over 2f out: rdn and edgd rt over 1f out: hdd and no ex ins last* **11/10**[1]	78
0	3	*3*	**Ainamaa (USA)**[24] 4084 2-9-0 .... RHills 8 (E A L Dunlop) *trckd ldrs: kpt on same pce fnl f* **20/1**	71

63 **4** *3* **Golden Topaz (IRE)**[30] 3908 2-9-0 .... TomEaves 7 64
(J Howard Johnson) *chsd ldrs: wknd appr fnl f* **14/1**
5 *1 1/4* **Celtic Memories (IRE)** 2-9-0 .... PaulMulrennan 4 61
(M W Easterby) *dwlt: hdwy over 3f out: nvr nr ldrs* **40/1**
04 **6** *3/4* **Pret A Porter (UAE)**[14] 4400 2-9-0 .... PaulHanagan 1 59
(M R Channon) *mid-div: hdwy over 3f out: kpt on: nvr trbld ldrs* **9/1**[3]
7 *3/4* **Atlantic Light** 2-9-0 .... KDarley 6 57+
(M Johnston) *led tl over 2f out: wkng whn hmpd over 1f out* **12/1**
8 *2* **Galingale (IRE)** 2-9-0 .... JohnEgan 11 53+
(Mrs P Sly) *s.i.s: hld up towards rr: sltly hmpd over 3f out: nvr trbld ldrs* **18/1**
6 **9** *8* **Olgarena (IRE)**[54] 3175 2-9-0 .... DavidAllan 10 34
(T D Easterby) *sn prom: lost pl over 1f out* **66/1**
10 *1/2* **Neon** 2-9-0 .... KerrinMcEvoy 3 33
(J R Fanshawe) *s.s: a in rr* **11/1**
11 *1/2* **Fairy Slipper** 2-9-0 .... TonyHamilton 2 32
(Jedd O'Keeffe) *s.s: a bhd* **33/1**
6000 **12** *9* **Nihil Petere (IRE)**[13] 4424 2-9-0 .... FrancisNorton 12 10
(P T Midgley) *unruly leaving paddock: s.s: a detached in rr* **100/1**

1m 34.59s (0.28) **Going Correction** -0.025s/f (Good) 12 Ran SP% **123.2**
Speed ratings (Par 93):97,96,92,89,87 87,86,83,74,74 73,63
CSF £6.66 TOTE £4.40: £1.60, £1.20, £5.20; EX 9.30.
Owner The Queen **Bred** The Queen **Trained** Newmarket, Suffolk
■ The 1000 Guineas winner Speciosa opened her account in the corresponding race a year ago.
■ Stewards' Enquiry : Robert Winston two-day ban: careless riding (Sep 7-8)

FOCUS
Probably just an ordinary maiden fillies' race - no Speciosa this time. The form looks fairly solid rated through the runner-up and should work out.

NOTEBOOK
Lost In Wonder(USA) had clearly learnt plenty first time. Leant on by the runner-up, her rider was left with no option but to switch to the rail, hampering the weakening Atlantic Light. She dug deep to take charge near the finish and will be suited by the full mile. (op 7-2 tchd 4-1)
La Spezia(IRE) went on but edged in leaving the winner short of room. In the end she was just worn down but should have little difficulty going one better. (op 5-4 tchd 11-8)
Ainamaa(USA) improved on her debut effort and looks essentially a stayer.
Golden Topaz(IRE) tackling a stiffer test, did not seem to fully see it out. (op 12-1 tchd 16-1)
Celtic Memories(IRE), an April foal, is long in the back and narrow. She stuck on in her own time after a tardy start and should improve a fair amount for the outing. (tchd 33-1)
Pret A Porter(UAE) stayed on in her own time up the final hill but she looks to lack a gear or two. (op 12-1)
Atlantic Light, a rangy daughter of Linamix, looked very inexperienced beforehand. She took them along but had come to the end of her tether when the runner-up forced the winner on to her. Hopefully this will have whetted her appetite. (op 9-1 tchd 15-2)
Galingale(IRE), representing last year's winning stable, was as green as grass going to post. Forced to check turning in, she did at least show a modicum of ability. (op 16-1)

4831 TOTECOURSE TO COURSE H'CAP — 7f 100y
3:05 (3:09) (Class 5) (0-75,78) 3-Y-0+ **£3,886** (£1,156; £577; £288) **Stalls** High

Form RPR
2026 **1** **Saxon Lil (IRE)**[14] 4399 4-9-7 **68** .... FrancisNorton 10 78
(J L Spearing) *trckd ldrs: nt clr run over 2f out: led jst ins last: hld on towards fin* **10/1**
5040 **2** *1/2* **Breaking Shadow (IRE)**[4] 4706 4-9-4 **72** .... DeanHeslop(7) 2 80+
(T D Barron) *swtchd rt after s: hld up in rr: effrt on outside over 2f out: styd on wl ins last* **12/1**
0060 **3** *1/2* **Thunderwing (IRE)**[13] 4437 4-9-7 **68** .... (v[1]) PatCosgrave 12 75
(K R Burke) *in rr: hdwy over 2f out: styd on wl fnl f* **12/1**
3350 **4** *3/4* **Society Music (IRE)**[18] 4253 4-9-7 **68** .... (p) PhillipMakin 14 73
(M Dods) *chsd ldrs: kpt on same pce ins last* **25/1**
4241 **5** *shd* **Mujood**[9] 4557 3-9-12 **78** .... KDarley 5 81
(R F Johnson Houghton) *w ldrs: styd on same pce fnl f* **15/2**[3]
0132 **6** *nk* **Sentiero Rosso (USA)**[9] 4548 4-9-0 **66** .... (t) GregFairley(5) 6 70
(B Ellison) *prom: effrt over 2f out: edgd lft and styd on fnl f* **13/2**[2]
0303 **7** *hd* **Trojan Flight**[19] 4230 5-9-9 **70** .... RobertWinston 15 74
(D W Chapman) *towards rr: hdwy on ins over 2f out: kpt on ins last* **9/2**[1]
3204 **8** *1/2* **Gifted Flame**[12] 4454 7-9-7 **68** .... GrahamGibbons 13 71
(J J Quinn) *prom: effrt on ins over 2f out: nt clr run and swtchd rt ins last: kpt on wl* **12/1**
4310 **9** *1* **Blue Empire (IRE)**[14] 4390 5-9-2 **63** .... JohnEgan 9 63
(C R Dore) *led tl hdd jst ins last: wknd and eased towards fin* **16/1**
0560 **10** *1 3/4* **Millfield (IRE)**[15] 4378 3-9-4 **70** .... TomEaves 16 64
(J Howard Johnson) *hld up in rr: hdwy on ins over 2f out: hung rt: nvr rchd ldrs* **25/1**
0004 **11** *6* **Dispol Katie**[6] 4655 5-9-6 **67** .... PaulMulrennan 4 48
(T D Barron) *w ldrs: wknd appr fnl f* **12/1**
6-00 **12** *6* **Danceinthevalley (IRE)**[37] 3716 4-9-4 **65** .... DeanMcKeown 11 31
(G A Swinbank) *t.k.h in rr: effrt on outside over 2f out: sn lost pl* **22/1**
3022 **13** *1/2* **Up Tempo (IRE)**[32] 3845 8-9-5 **71** .... (b) AndrewMullen(5) 3 35
(C R Dore) *chsd ldrs: wknd over 1f out* **14/1**
5000 **14** *2 1/2* **Loaderfun (IRE)**[41] 3598 4-9-2 **63** .... PaulHanagan 1 21
(N Wilson) *hld up in rr: hdwy on outside over 4f out: lost pl 3f out* **40/1**
0055 **15** *shd* **Mystic Man (FR)**[11] 4496 8-8-13 **65** .... (b) MarkLawson(5) 7 23
(I W McInnes) *bhd: effrt on outer 3f out: sn wknd* **20/1**
540 **16** *3* **Scotland The Brave**[9] 4569 6-9-3 **64** .... (v) KerrinMcEvoy 8 14
(J D Bethell) *hld up in rr: hdwy over 2f out: n.m.r: wknd and eased over 1f out* **8/1**

1m 34.22s (-0.09) **Going Correction** -0.025s/f (Good)
WFA 3 from 4yo+ 5lb 16 Ran SP% **126.0**
Speed ratings (Par 103):99,98,97,97,96 96,96,95,94,92 85,78,78,75,75 71
CSF £120.09 CT £1540.17 TOTE £11.60: £2.40, £4.80, £3.20, £7.20; EX 225.80.
Owner T N Siviter **Bred** David Barry **Trained** Kinnersley, Worcs

FOCUS
A tight-knit handicap and with the field congregating towards the inside running rail there were plenty of traffic problems. The form looks sound with the winner right back to her best.
Sentiero Rosso(USA) Official explanation: jockey said gelding was unsuited by the good to soft (good in places) ground
Gifted Flame Official explanation: jockey said gelding was denied a clear run
Blue Empire(IRE) Official explanation: jockey said gelding had no more to give
Scotland The Brave Official explanation: jockey said mare never travelled

4832 TOTEPOOL BEVERLEY BULLET SPRINT STKS (LISTED RACE) — 5f
3:35 (3:36) (Class 1) 3-Y-0+
£18,169 (£6,886; £3,446; £1,718; £860; £432) **Stalls** High

Form RPR
6150 **1** **Baltic King**[21] 4191 6-9-0 112 .... (t) KDarley 5 110
(H Morrison) *mid-div: hdwy 2f out: styd on wl to ld towards fin* **7/2**[2]
-002 **2** *hd* **Pivotal's Princess (IRE)**[15] 4360 4-8-9 95 .... GrahamGibbons 4 105
(E S McMahon) *trckd ldrs: qcknd to ld 2f out: hdd and no ex towards fin* **28/1**
3560 **3** *1* **Bahamian Pirate (USA)**[12] 4461 11-9-0 99 .... PaulHanagan 9 106
(D Nicholls) *in tch: outpcd over 2f out: hdwy over 1f out: styd on to take 3rd nr line* **22/1**
3305 **4** *nk* **Tax Free (IRE)**[22] 4128 4-9-0 107 .... AdrianTNicholls 8 105
(D Nicholls) *trckd ldrs on ins: chal over 1f out: nt qckn* **2/1**[1]
-440 **5** *1* **Lafi (IRE)**[28] 3972 7-9-0 104 .... MickyFenton 11 101+
(D Nicholls) *hld up towards rr: nt clr run 2f out: styd on steadily fnl f* **16/1**
1105 **6** *3/4* **Mr Wolf**[8] 4609 5-9-0 92 .... (p) KerrinMcEvoy 6 99
(D W Barker) *led tl hdd & wknd 1f out* **20/1**
3060 **7** *2* **Mecca's Mate**[3] 4738 5-8-9 100 .... (p) TomEaves 10 86
(D W Barker) *chsd ldrs: fdd over 1f out* **5/1**[3]
0601 **8** *3/4* **Quito (IRE)**[3] 4740 9-9-4 112 .... (b) RobertWinston 7 93+
(D W Chapman) *s.i.s: hdwy and n.m.r over 2f out: sme hdwy and hung rt jst ins last: sddle slipped: eased towards fin* **7/1**
5123 **9** *1* **Prince Namid**[70] 2683 4-9-0 93 .... RoystonFfrench 12 85
(Mrs A Duffield) *rr-div: hdwy on ins 2f out: nvr rchd ldrs* **9/1**
0100 **10** *1 1/2* **Angus Newz**[15] 4345 3-8-11 98 .... FrancisNorton 2 79
(M Quinn) *in tch on outer: effrt over 2f out: nvr trbld ldrs* **33/1**
0420 **11** *1* **Beckermet (IRE)**[14] 4410 4-9-0 105 .... JohnEgan 3 76
(R F Fisher) *prom: lost pl over 1f out* **20/1**
5015 **12** *1 3/4* **Pawan (IRE)**[8] 4598 6-9-0 72 .... (b) AnnStokell 1 70
(Miss A Stokell) *mid-div: effrt on outside over 2f out: nvr on terms* **100/1**

63.21 secs (-0.79) **Going Correction** +0.125s/f (Good)
WFA 3 from 4yo+ 2lb 12 Ran SP% **121.9**
Speed ratings (Par 111):111,110,109,108,107 105,102,101,99,97 95,93
CSF £108.86 TOTE £5.50: £2.10, £7.00, £5.70; EX 163.60.
Owner Thurloe Thoroughbreds Viii **Bred** R F And Mrs Knipe **Trained** East Ilsley, Berks
■ The third running of this Listed sprint.

FOCUS
A good renewal and the winner certainly deserved his success. The form looks rock solid with the placed horses and sixth close to their marks.

NOTEBOOK
Baltic King, third in 2004 and runner-up last year, was top on official ratings. He showed real spirit to nail the filly near the line and the Diadem Stakes at the end of next month at Ascot looks the logical next step. (tchd 4-1)
Pivotal's Princess(IRE), full of beans, travelled strongly and kicked on at just the right time, only to find the winner too strong near the line. The Portland at York is next on the agenda but unfortunately she will run there from her new mark - here she had 12lb to find with the winner on official figures. (op 25-1)
Bahamian Pirate(USA), without a win since his 2004 Nunthorpe success, had the easy ground he needs and he showed that there is still life in the old dog. (op 20-1)
Tax Free(IRE), happy to take a lead, came through on the inner to look the likely winner but there was a distinct possibility he was racing on the slowest part of the track. (tchd 9-4 and 5-2 in a place)
Lafi(IRE), who finished lame at Ascot, looked in good trim and this leg stretch will have restored his confidence. There is surely another good handicap to be won with him when the ground is in his favour. (op 20-1)
Mr Wolf, who had a lot to find judged on official ratings, showed blinding speed to take these better-class sprinters along at a fierce pace. It is to be hoped his handicap mark does not suffer as a result. (op 16-1)
Mecca's Mate, third last year, was making a quick return to action and did not run up to her best. (op 6-1)
Quito(IRE), hero of the hour at York, was dropping back two furlongs in trip but his weight cloth moved leaving the stalls resulting in the saddle shifting. He will bounce back none the worse.
Official explanation: jockey said saddle slipped (op 6-1)
Prince Namid, with a lot to find, looked just in need of the outing on his first run for 70 days. This will have blown away the cobwebs with a trip to Ayr very much in connections' minds. (op 10-1)

4833 TOTESPORT.COM STKS (HERITAGE H'CAP) — 1m 1f 207y
4:10 (4:11) (Class 2) (0-105,98) 3-Y-0
£31,160 (£9,330; £4,665; £2,335; £1,165; £585) **Stalls** High

Form RPR
5010 **1** **Champions Gallery**[10] 4529 3-9-4 **95** .... JohnEgan 10 104
(D R C Elsworth) *hld up towards rr: hdwy on outer over 2f out: led over 1f out: r.o wl* **10/1**
1103 **2** *1* **Pearly King (USA)**[24] 4082 3-9-7 **98** .... RobertWinston 2 105
(Sir Michael Stoute) *hld up on outer in midfield: effrt and c ins over 2f out: no ex ins last* **9/2**[3]
-221 **3** *1 1/2* **Noble Gent (IRE)**[15] 4370 3-9-6 **97** .... KerrinMcEvoy 12 101
(Saeed Bin Suroor) *chsd ldrs: kpt on same pce fnl f* **3/1**[1]
2111 **4** *3/4* **Formal Decree (GER)**[45] 3443 3-9-6 **97** .... DeanMcKeown 7 100
(G A Swinbank) *hld up in rr: hdwy on outer over 2f out: kpt on same pce ins last* **10/3**[2]
1110 **5** *1* **Nelsons Column (IRE)**[10] 4508 3-8-12 **89** .... TomEaves 13 90
(G M Moore) *chsd ldr: hung rt and one pce fnl f* **16/1**
2-60 **6** *1* **Charlie Tokyo (IRE)**[85] 2224 3-8-1 **78** .... PaulHanagan 3 77
(R A Fahey) *hld up in rr: hdwy over 4f out: nvr rchd ldrs* **10/1**
4224 **7** *nk* **Black Beauty**[22] 4147 3-8-0 **80** .... DominicFox(3) 1 79
(M G Quinlan) *led tl over 1f out: wknd ins last* **25/1**
5210 **8** *7* **Layazaal (IRE)**[66] 2774 3-9-4 **95** .... RHills 8 80+
(J L Dunlop) *chsd ldrs: lost pl over 1f out* **11/1**
0510 **9** *nk* **Nihal (IRE)**[25] 4039 3-8-9 **86** .... RoystonFfrench 9 71
(M Johnston) *s.i.s: in rr and pushed along: nvr on terms* **16/1**
12 **10** *1/2* **Future's Dream**[88] 2142 3-8-3 **80** .... FrancisNorton 5 64
(K R Burke) *in tch: rdr briefly lost iron over 3f out: lost pl over 2f out* **17/2**
1465 **11** *shd* **King's Revenge**[47] 3375 3-8-0 **77** oh4 ow2 .... PaulFessey 6 61
(T D Easterby) *prom: lost pl over 4f out: bhd fnl 2f* **100/1**

2m 5.02s (-2.28) **Going Correction** -0.025s/f (Good) 11 Ran SP% **119.9**
Speed ratings (Par 106):108,107,106,105,104 103,103,97,97,97 97
CSF £55.73 CT £172.68 TOTE £10.90: £3.50, £1.80, £1.90; EX 107.30.
Owner Champions Gallery **Bred** Middle Park Stud Ltd **Trained** Newmarket, Suffolk
■ Stewards' Enquiry : Robert Winston caution: careless riding

FOCUS
A £50,000 added handicap that resulted in a decent field. The first four are all progressive types and the form has been rated positively through the fifth.

NOTEBOOK
Champions Gallery, 7lb higher than Ascot, came wide and showed a willing attitude. This may well prove to have been his swan song here - the intention is to send him out to Hong Kong now. (op 11-1 tchd 12-1 and 9-1)
Pearly King(USA), 11lb higher than his first success in handicap company this year, saw plenty of daylight down the outside in the back straight. Edging towards the far rail, he was on the heels of the winner entering the last but was always just being held. He deserves plenty of credit for this. (op 13-2 tchd 7-1)

Noble Gent(IRE), who looked very fit indeed, was racing from a 5lb higher mark and this might just be as good as he is. (op 7-2 tchd 4-1 and 11-4)

Formal Decree(GER), up 25lb in just three outings, kept on without ever looking likely to riase his game sufficiently. He is ready for a step up to a mile and a half and he really prefers more give than he encountered here. (op 5-2 tchd 7-2)

Nelsons Column(IRE) was feeling the strain when Pearly King came across and gave him a bump on his blind side. The ground had marginally turned against him. (op 20-1 tchd 14-1)

Charlie Tokyo(IRE), given no relief by the Handicapper, ran respectably without ever looking like setting the house on fire. (op 9-1)

Black Beauty, 10lb higher than his last win, took them along but on this easy ground was readily swallowed up.

4834 TOTESPORT 0800 221 221 H'CAP — 5f

4:40 (4:41) (Class 5) (0-75,75) 3-Y-0+ — **£5,505** (£1,637; £818; £408) **Stalls** High

Form — RPR

4005 **1** **Danzig River (IRE)**[9] 4569 5-8-13 **70** ... VictoriaBehan(7) 4 — 81+
(D Nicholls) *hld up in rr: stdy hdwy 2f out: r.o strly ins fnl f: led post* **28/1**

3024 **2** *shd* **Circuit Dancer (IRE)**[23] 4101 6-9-10 **74** ... AdrianTNicholls 15 — 85
(D Nicholls) *hdwy on ins over 3f out: led ins last: hdd post* **5/1**[1]

140 **3** *1 ¼* **Blackheath (IRE)**[24] 4085 10-9-8 **72** ... PhillipMakin 16 — 79
(D Nicholls) *chsd ldr: led over 1f out: hdd and no ex ins last* **11/1**

4300 **4** *1* **Bold Marc (IRE)**[12] 4453 4-9-6 **70** ... (v[1]) PatCosgrave 10 — 73
(K R Burke) *chsd ldrs: styd on fnl f* **10/1**[3]

2106 **5** *1* **Paddywack (IRE)**[18] 4258 9-8-9 **59** ... (b) PaulQuinn 7 — 58+
(D W Chapman) *in rr: hdwy on ins and nt clr run over 1f out: nt clr run ins last: r.o wl towards fin* **8/1**[2]

0632 **6** *hd* **Throw The Dice**[7] 4636 4-8-9 **64** ... (p) MarkLawson(5) 14 — 63
(D W Barker) *in rr: hdwy on ins over 2f out: n.m.r over 1f out: kpt on ins last* **5/1**[1]

0610 **7** *¾* **Catch The Cat (IRE)**[7] 4636 7-8-11 **66** ... (b) GregFairley(5) 6 — 62
(Robert Gray) *mid-div on outer: effrt 2f out: kpt on: nvr rchd ldrs* **18/1**

3001 **8** *½* **Highland Song (IRE)**[15] 4354 3-9-3 **69** ... JohnEgan 19 — 63
(R F Fisher) *chsd ldrs: n.m.r over 1f out: kpt on same pce* **8/1**[2]

0400 **9** *hd* **Hout Bay**[9] 4571 9-8-6 **56** oh6 ... (b) PaulHanagan 11 — 49+
(R A Fahey) *mid-div: keeping on same pce whn bdly hmpd ins last* **20/1**

0000 **10** *nk* **Tartatartufata**[8] 4598 4-8-13 **66** ... (v) PatrickMathers(3) 18 — 58
(D Shaw) *led: hdd over 1f out: edgd lft and wknd ins last* **16/1**

1036 **11** *½* **Ryedane (IRE)**[12] 4453 4-9-6 **70** ... DavidAllan 13 — 60+
(T D Easterby) *chsd ldrs: one pce whn hmpd ins last* **14/1**

3300 **12** *shd* **Raccoon (IRE)**[18] 4258 6-8-12 **62** ... RobertWinston 2 — 52
(D W Chapman) *in rr: effrt on outer 2f out: nvr a factor* **33/1**

6320 **13** *shd* **Zarzu**[59] 3012 7-9-6 **75** ... AndrewMullen(5) 5 — 65
(C R Dore) *towards rr: kpt on fnl 2f: nvr on terms* **25/1**

00 **14** *½* **Alexia Rose (IRE)**[7] 4636 4-8-7 **57** ... FrancisNorton 12 — 45
(A Berry) *in tch: outpcd fnl 2f* **50/1**

2006 **15** *½* **Divine Spirit**[11] 4486 5-9-0 **64** ... TomEaves 9 — 50+
(M Dods) *bhd and drvn along: sme hdwy whn nt clr run ins last* **12/1**

6600 **16** *hd* **Dark Champion**[3] 4735 6-8-6 **56** oh1 ... (v) RoystonFfrench 8 — 41
(R E Barr) *mid-div: one pce whn hmpd ins last* **28/1**

0000 **17** *nk* **World At My Feet**[7] 4636 4-7-13 **56** oh9 ... (t) SuzzanneFrance(7) 20 — 40
(N Bycroft) *mid-div on ins: nvr a factor* **28/1**

0266 **18** *nk* **Butterfly Bud (IRE)**[23] 4120 3-8-13 **65** ... PaulEddery 17 — 48+
(J O'Reilly) *chsd ldrs: one pce whn n.m.r ins last* **16/1**

64.89 secs (0.89) **Going Correction** +0.125s/f (Good)
WFA 3 from 4yo+ 2lb — **18** Ran SP% **128.2**
Speed ratings (Par 103):97,96,94,93,91 91,90,89,89,88 87,87,87,86,85 85,85,84
CSF £159.61 CT £1744.94 TOTE £34.10: £6.00, £1.70, £3.20, £3.30; EX 162.80.
Owner Miss Anna Graves **Bred** Orpendale **Trained** Sessay, N Yorks
■ A one-two-three for David Nicholls.

FOCUS
A fair handicap but a modest winning time, 1.68 seconds slower than the Listed race. Ordinary form and plenty of traffic problems on the inner.
Paddywack(IRE) Official explanation: jockey said gelding was denied a clear run
Highland Song(IRE) Official explanation: jockey said gelding was denied a clear run
Tartatartufata Official explanation: jockey said filly hung left

4835 TELETEXT RACING "HANDS AND HEELS" APPRENTICE MAIDEN H'CAP — 1m 1f 207y

5:15 (5:16) (Class 6) (0-65,65) 3-Y-0+ — **£3,238** (£963; £481; £240) **Stalls** High

Form — RPR

5003 **1** **Choristar**[16] 4332 5-9-6 **49** ... NeilBrown 4 — 54
(J Mackie) *mid-div: effrt on outer over 3f out: edgd rt over 1f out: led last 150yds: styd on wl* **11/4**[1]

0000 **2** *2 ½* **Kentuckian**[4] 4709 4-8-13 **42** ... LukeMorris 9 — 42
(P W Hiatt) *chsd ldr: led over 1f out: hdd and no ex ins last* **12/1**

5345 **3** *hd* **Grey Outlook**[94] 1946 3-10-0 **65** ... AlanRutter 7 — 67+
(Miss L A Perratt) *mid-div: hdwy on outside over 5f out: sn chsng ldrs: hmpd over 1f out: styd on wl towards fin* **9/2**[2]

0630 **4** *2* **Boucheen**[64] 2877 3-8-5 **45** ... JohnCavanagh(3) 11 — 41
(Ms Deborah J Evans) *led tl over 1f out: one pce* **16/1**

2306 **5** *2 ½* **Riverhill (IRE)**[20] 4198 3-9-2 **53** ... JamesMillman 6 — 44
(J Howard Johnson) *trckd ldrs: one pce appr fnl f* **11/4**[1]

000- **6** *nk* **Summer Force**[320] 5828 4-8-5 **40** ... PaulPickard(6) 5 — 31
(C N Kellett) *chsd ldrs: outpcd over 3f out: kpt on fnl 2f* **40/1**

4004 **7** *1 ¾* **Bond Angel Eyes**[14] 4402 3-9-3 **57** ... (p) NSLawes(3) 2 — 45
(G R Oldroyd) *in rr: drvn over 3f out: nvr nr ldrs* **10/1**

550 **8** *21* **Chrisjen**[23] 4117 4-9-6 **52** ... AdeleRothery(3) 10 — —
(M W Easterby) *trckd ldrs: lost pl 3f out: wandered and sn bhd* **16/1**

0-00 **9** *19* **Springwood Blues (IRE)**[63] 2895 3-8-3 **40** ... VictoriaBehan 1 — —
(I W McInnes) *in rr: lost pl 2f out: sn bhd* **8/1**[3]

2m 10.51s (3.21) **Going Correction** -0.025s/f (Good)
WFA 3 from 4yo+ 8lb — **9** Ran SP% **113.6**
Speed ratings (Par 101):86,84,83,82,80 80,78,61,46
CSF £37.45 CT £143.08 TOTE £3.90: £1.60, £3.80, £1.70; EX 61.00 Place 6 £179.40, Place 5 £100.64..
Owner Derbyshire Racing **Bred** Coln Valley Stud **Trained** Church Broughton , Derbys

FOCUS
Arock bottom maiden handicap and a slow winning time, even for a race like this. The form looks near worthless but it does serve a purpose in the greater scheme of things.
Chrisjen Official explanation: jockey said filly hung badly left
T/Plt: £207.20 to a £1 stake. Pool: £58,031.60. 204.45 winning tickets. T/Qpdt: £102.00 to a £1 stake. Pool: £2,977.30. 21.60 winning tickets. WG

[4794] GOODWOOD (R-H)

Sunday, August 27

OFFICIAL GOING: Good
The false running rail that protected 8m of ground the previous day had been taken down overnight to provide a fresh strip. The ground was drying out.
Wind: Moderate; across towards stands Weather: Fine

4836 CEDARS OF LEBANON STKS (H'CAP) — 1m 4f

2:10 (2:10) (Class 5) (0-70,68) 3-Y-0+ — **£3,238** (£963; £481; £240) **Stalls** Low

Form — RPR

5165 **1** **Brief Statement (IRE)**[20] 4205 4-9-5 **59** ... (v[1]) RyanMoore 5 — 65
(W M Brisbourne) *lw: sn led: hdd after 2f: led again over 6f out: rdn over 3f out: kpt on wl u.p and in command fnl f* **5/1**[3]

-523 **2** *¾* **Lunar River (FR)**[25] 4044 3-9-2 **66** ... (t) LDettori 2 — 71+
(E A L Dunlop) *led after 2f to over 6f out: upsides wnr 3f out: clr of rest and gng bttr: rdn and nt qckn wl over 1f out: hld after* **4/1**[2]

0330 **3** *1* **Serramanna**[4] 4702 5-8-10 **50** ... LPKeniry 7 — 53
(Ms J S Doyle) *cl up: chsd ldng pair over 3f out: sn rdn and no imp: styd on ins fnl f: nvr able to chal* **15/2**

0530 **4** *4* **Phoebe Woodstock (IRE)**[29] 3935 4-9-11 **68** ... AdamKirby(3) 10 — 65
(W R Swinburn) *swtg: hld up in last pair: outpcd fr over 3f out: plugged on fnl 2f: no ch* **10/1**

1455 **5** *6* **Stellenbosch (USA)**[19] 4224 3-9-3 **67** ... (t) MichaelHills 6 — 54
(J W Hills) *swtg: hld up in last trio: pushed along and lost tch w ldrs 3f out: wknd 2f out* **7/2**[1]

6254 **6** *3 ½* **Siakira**[18] 4245 3-9-0 **64** ... JoeFanning 3 — 45
(I A Wood) *dwlt: sn prom: rdn 4f out: wknd 3f out* **16/1**

0230 **7** *2 ½* **High Hope (FR)**[29] 3935 8-8-8 **53** ... (b) RobynBrisland(5) 9 — 30
(G L Moore) *t.k.h: hld up in tch: rdn and nt qckn 4f out: steadily wknd* **9/1**

0-50 **8** *12* **Dawn's Last Shot (IRE)**[127] 1138 4-9-7 **61** ... IanMongan 4 — 19
(J L Dunlop) *swtg: hld up in tch: wd bnd 5f out and sn struggling: t.o* **11/2**

2m 38.56s (-0.36) **Going Correction** -0.10s/f (Good)
WFA 3 from 4yo+ 10lb — **8** Ran SP% **111.0**
Speed ratings (Par 103):97,96,95,93,89 86,85,77
CSF £23.75 CT £141.26 TOTE £6.00: £1.90, £1.50, £2.70; EX 20.10.
Owner Midland Racing Partnership **Bred** S Ross **Trained** Great Ness, Shropshire

FOCUS
Just a modest handicap, but sound form although there was not much pace on. The race concerned only the first two in the final three furlongs and the third sets the level.

4837 CHICHESTER OBSERVER FILLIES' STKS (H'CAP) — 7f

2:45 (2:45) (Class 4) (0-85,85) 3-Y-0 — **£6,477** (£1,927; £963; £481) **Stalls** High

Form — RPR

1050 **1** **Silver Dip**[32] 3852 3-9-4 **82** ... MichaelHills 7 — 90
(B W Hills) *hld up in midfield: prog wl over 2f out: chsd ldr wl over 1f out: r.o fnl f to ld last strides* **14/1**

2515 **2** *nk* **Creative Mind (IRE)**[24] 4083 3-9-3 **81** ... DaneO'Neill 8 — 88
(E J O'Neill) *led: drew 2l clr over 1f out: kpt on u.p: collared last strides* **4/1**[2]

0000 **3** *nk* **I'm In Love (USA)**[9] 4577 3-8-10 **74** ... JamieSpencer 3 — 80+
(M A Magnusson) *s.s: hld up in last: prog on outer 2f out: r.o fnl f to take 3rd nr fin: too much to do* **16/1**

1300 **4** *½* **Lavenham (IRE)**[64] 2863 3-8-10 **74** ... RichardHughes 2 — 79
(R Hannon) *hld up in midfield: rdn and effrt over 2f out: chsd ldng pair fnl f: kpt on but lost 3rd nr fin* **25/1**

1022 **5** *¾* **Home Sweet Home (IRE)**[7] 4633 3-9-6 **84** ... MJKinane 9 — 87
(P D Evans) *trckd ldrs: shkn up and nt qckn 2f out: styd on same pce fnl f* **7/2**[1]

0450 **6** *nk* **Oceans Apart**[24] 4083 3-9-7 **85** ... SteveDrowne 13 — 87
(P F I Cole) *lw: hld up in tch on inner: nt clr run over 2f out to 1f out: kpt on same pce whn in the clr fnl f* **14/1**

6230 **7** *½* **Lunar Express (USA)**[30] 3889 3-9-4 **82** ... RyanMoore 11 — 83
(W J Haggas) *hld up in rr: last and u.p over 2f out: styd on fnl f: nt rch ldrs* **7/1**[3]

2550 **8** *shd* **Antigoni (IRE)**[15] 4368 3-8-3 **67** ... MartinDwyer 12 — 70+
(A M Balding) *awkward s: hld up wl in rr: rdn over 2f out: nt clr run over 1f out to ent fnl f: kpt on: no ch* **12/1**

3123 **9** *hd* **Usk Poppy**[15] 4375 3-8-13 **77** ... LPKeniry 6 — 77
(D R C Elsworth) *lw: trckd ldrs: rdn and nt qckn over 2f out: one pce and lost pls fnl f* **7/1**[3]

1521 **10** *1 ¼* **Inaminute (IRE)**[17] 4305 3-8-9 **78** ... AndrewElliott(5) 10 — 75
(K R Burke) *lw: chsd ldrs to 2f out: lost pl rapidly: n.d after* **8/1**

1005 **11** *5* **Rydal Mount (IRE)**[8] 4589 3-9-0 **78** ... FergusSweeney 4 — 62
(W S Kittow) *chsd ldr to wl over 1f out: wknd rapidly* **16/1**

4615 **12** *5* **Nightstrike (IRE)**[9] 4557 3-8-5 **69** ... JoeFanning 1 — 40
(H Candy) *prom tl wknd rapidly 2f out* **33/1**

1m 26.05s (-1.99) **Going Correction** -0.10s/f (Good) — **12** Ran SP% **117.9**
Speed ratings (Par 99):107,106,106,105,104 104,103,103,103,102 96,90
CSF £68.88 CT £927.18 TOTE £14.40: £3.90, £1.90, £5.40; EX 87.90.
Owner Burton Agnes Bloodstock **Bred** Mountgrange Stud Ltd **Trained** Lambourn, Berks

FOCUS
A pretty ordinary handicap, rated around the placed horses. They went a good pace and there were plenty of hard-luck stories.
Oceans Apart Official explanation: jockey said filly was denied a clear run
Antigoni(IRE) Official explanation: jockey said filly was denied a clear run

4838 BEECH STKS (H'CAP) — 1m 1f

3:15 (3:20) (Class 4) (0-85,84) 3-Y-0 — **£6,477** (£1,927; £963; £481) **Stalls** High

Form — RPR

13 **1** **Speedy Sam**[7] 4634 3-8-12 **80** ... AndrewElliott(5) 12 — 92+
(K R Burke) *lw: mde virtually all: kicked clr over 1f out: styd on strly fnl f* **7/1**[2]

2212 **2** *1 ¾* **Safqa**[29] 3945 3-9-6 **83** ... MartinDwyer 11 — 91
(B W Hills) *swtg: hld up wl in rr: effrt 3f out: swtchd to outer and prog 2f out: r.o fnl f to snatch 2nd on post* **7/1**[2]

5142 **3** *shd* **Ebert**[11] 4481 3-9-3 **80** ... LDettori 15 — 88
(P J Makin) *lw: hld up in rr: prog into midfield 1/2-way: effrt and hanging rt 2f out: nt qckn: drvn and styd on fnl f* **11/4**[1]

01- **4** *nk* **Danamour (IRE)**[268] 6484 3-9-2 **79** ... MJKinane 8 — 86
(M P Tregoning) *chsd clr ldrs: prog on outer 3f out: chsd wnr wl over 1f out: no imp: lost 2 pls nr fin* **14/1**

0061 **5** *3* **Kavachi (IRE)**[8] 4591 3-8-0 **66** ow1 EdwardCreighton(3) 4 67
(G L Moore) *lw: hld up in midfield: clsd over 2f out: rdn to dispute 2nd over 1f out: wknd ins fnl f* **16/1**

0004 **6** *hd* **Fratt'n Park (IRE)**[22] 4143 3-8-2 **65** NickyMackay 9 66
(J J Bridger) *wl in rr: shkn up over 3f out: no real prog tl styd on fr over 1f out: no ch* **33/1**

-115 **7** *2* **Starship (IRE)**[29] 3954 3-9-5 **82** JamieSpencer 10 79
(W J Haggas) *s.i.s and pushed along early: prog into midfield 2f out: no imp over 1f out: fdd ins fnl f* **8/1**[3]

1660 **8** *shd* **Divine River**[29] 3928 3-8-13 **76** DaneO'Neill 2 72
(A P Jarvis) *hld up wl in rr: rn v wd bnd 5f out: sme prog 3f out: shkn up and no hdwy 2f out* **66/1**

6544 **9** *1 ½* **Star Of The Desert (IRE)**[19] 4225 3-8-7 **73** ow2 AdamKirby(3) 5 66
(C G Cox) *w wnr and clr of rest tl wknd 2f out* **25/1**

150 **10** *2* **Incidentally (IRE)**[30] 3889 3-9-5 **82** RyanMoore 1 71
(R Hannon) *lw: racd on outer: hld up wl in rr: shkn up and no prog 3f out: no ch after* **16/1**

2145 **11** *shd* **Cantabilly (IRE)**[11] 4470 3-8-7 **70** ow1 RobertHavlin 6 59+
(M R Channon) *swtg: a wl in rr: rdn whn nt clr run briefly 3f out: no ch after* **20/1**

2151 **12** *½* **Pagan Crest**[11] 4490 3-8-10 **73** JimCrowley 14 61
(Mrs A J Perrett) *lw: settled in midfield: effrt on inner 3f out: no prog 2f out: wknd sn after* **7/1**[2]

5253 **13** *½* **Theatre Royal**[7] 4627 3-8-2 **65** oh3 JoeFanning 16 52
(A M Balding) *reluctant to enter stalls: chsd clr ldng pair to over 2f out: sn wknd* **16/1**

3005 **14** *hd* **Beckett Hall (IRE)**[34] 3794 3-8-13 **76** RichardHughes 13 63
(R Hannon) *a towards rr: u.p and struggling 3f out* **33/1**

-415 **15** *3* **Fantastisch (IRE)**[57] 3088 3-9-3 **80** SteveDrowne 7 61
(H R A Cecil) *chsd clr ldng pair to over 2f out: wknd rapidly over 1f out* **16/1**

1m 53.56s (-3.30) **Going Correction** -0.10s/f (Good) **15** Ran SP% **121.5**
Speed ratings (Par 102):110,108,108,108,105 105,103,103,102,100 100,99,99,99,96
CSF £52.39 CT £170.88 TOTE £9.30: £3.10, £2.50, £1.60; EX 74.00.
Owner Mrs M Gittins **Bred** Cheveley Park Stud Ltd **Trained** Middleham Moor, N Yorks

FOCUS
A fair handicap and a decent winning time for a race like this. The first four finished clear, and with the winner and fourth unexposed and the second and fourth going the right way this has been rated positively.
Incidentally(IRE) Official explanation: vet said colt returned lame left-fore

4839 TOTESPORT CELEBRATION MILE (GROUP 2) 1m
3:50 (3:53) (Class 1) 3-Y-O+
£56,780 (£21,520; £10,770; £5,370; £2,690; £1,350) **Stalls** High

Form RPR
2-13 **1** **Caradak (IRE)**[8] 4596 5-9-1 114 LDettori 5 115
(Saeed Bin Suroor) *lw: trckd clr ldr: clsd fr 2f out: led 1f out: drvn fnl f: jst hld on* **6/1**[3]

1040 **2** *shd* **Killybegs (IRE)**[10] 4529 3-8-9 110 MichaelHills 4 114
(B W Hills) *hld up in 3rd: clsd fr 2f out: rdn to chal 1f out: nt qckn sn after: rallied nr fin: jst failed* **50/1**

1-12 **3** *1 ¼* **George Washington (IRE)**[92] 2039 3-9-1 MJKinane 2 117
(A P O'Brien, Ire) *s.s: t.k.h: hld up in detached last: urged along to cl 2f out: hanging and nt keen: r.o fnl f: nrst fin* **5/6**[1]

0 **4** *1 ½* **River Tiber**[92] 2039 3-8-9 DavidMcCabe 6 108?
(A P O'Brien, Ire) *w'like: lw: led: clr after 2f: 10l up over 3f out: collared 1f out: fdd* **100/1**

4162 **5** *hd* **Soviet Song (IRE)**[25] 4038 6-9-1 115 JamieSpencer 1 108
(J R Fanshawe) *hld up in detached 5th: shkn up to cl over 2f out: nt qckn and btn over 1f out* **3/1**[2]

-163 **6** *nk* **Rob Roy (USA)**[25] 4038 4-9-4 114 RyanMoore 3 111
(Sir Michael Stoute) *lw: hld up in 4th and wl off the pce: rdn to try to cl over 2f out: hanging and fnd nil over 1f out* **7/1**

1m 37.26s (-3.01) **Going Correction** -0.10s/f (Good)
WFA 3 from 4yo+ 6lb **6** Ran SP% **109.3**
Speed ratings (Par 115):111,110,109,108,107 107
CSF £156.86 TOTE £6.50: £2.80, £7.70; EX 124.70.
Owner Godolphin **Bred** His Highness The Aga Khan's Studs S C **Trained** Newmarket, Suffolk

FOCUS
This was a fair contest for the grade, although not satisfactory with George Washington a long way below his best on his comeback and the pacemaker not beaten far in fourth. It was a modest winning time for a Group 2, and it is doubtful if Caradak had to produce his best.

NOTEBOOK
Caradak(IRE), beaten favourite in the Hungerford Stakes on easy ground last time, was stepping back up to a mile. Always well placed at the head of the main group, ignoring the pacemaker, he showed narrowly ahead with a furlong to run and just held the renewed challenge of the runner-up. Not needing to produce his best here, he will be aimed at the Hong Kong Mile now. (tchd 15-2)
Killybegs(IRE) shadowed the eventual winner throughout but just hit a bit of a flat spot in the final furlong before knuckling down and reducing the gap near the line. Following a poor effort in easy ground at Salisbury last time, this was his best run to date.
George Washington(IRE), off the track since pulling muscles in the Irish Guineas in May, was as usual a bit edgy beforehand but generally behaved well in the preliminaries. After standing still as the stalls opened, probably by design, he took a keen tug at the back of the field. Once into the straight - the first time he has raced round a bend - he hung to his right, hating the track, but after being pulled off the fence he found his stride inside the last and came home strongly. Considering that he did everything wrong yet still finished third this was a satisfactory return to action and he can show his true colours in the Queen Elizabeth II Stakes at Ascot. (op 4-5 tchd 8-11)
River Tiber was in as pacemaker to George Washington, a role he had carried out in the Irish Guineas. Effectively ignored by the rest of the field, he was clear after a quarter of a mile and was still ten lengths to the good passing the three pole, eventually being picked off with a furlong to run but sticking on for fourth prize.
Soviet Song(IRE) travelled well towards the rear but when the tempo lifted she was unable to pick up. She needs a stronger pace than she got here but has been a bit in and out this season. (tchd 10-3)
Rob Roy(USA), third in the Sussex Stakes over course and distance, was unable to reproduce that form with the lack of a strong gallop a contributory factor. (tchd 8-1)

4840 NORMANDIE STUD PRESTIGE STKS (GROUP 3) (FILLIES) 7f
4:20 (4:25) (Class 1) 2-Y-O
£22,712 (£8,608; £4,308; £2,148; £1,076; £540) **Stalls** High

Form RPR
11 **1** **Sesmen**[12] 4458 2-9-0 OscarUrbina 4 104
(M Botti) *trckd ldng pair: wnt 2nd over 2f out: shkn up to ld jst over 1f out: sn in command: pushed out* **9/1**

210 **2** *nk* **Bicoastal (USA)**[65] 2800 2-9-0 84 (b[1]) LDettori 10 103
(B J Meehan) *chsd ldng trio: rdn 2f out: r.o to take 2nd last 75yds: clsng on wnr fin but nvr able to chal* **14/1**

2621 **3** *1 ½* **Cumin (USA)**[24] 4084 2-9-0 96 MichaelHills 6 99
(B W Hills) *led at decent pce: rdn over 1f out: sn hdd and one pce* **6/4**[1]

1140 **4** *1 ¼* **Hope'N'Charity (USA)**[29] 3925 2-9-0 99 AdamKirby 9 96
(C G Cox) *towards rr: pushed along 1/2-way: styd on u.p fnl 2f: nrst fin* **14/1**

1 **5** *¾* **Italian Girl**[30] 3893 2-9-0 RyanMoore 8 94
(A P Jarvis) *hld up in midfield: rdn and effrt over 2f out: one pce and no imp on ldrs* **5/1**[3]

10 **6** *1 ½* **Princess Iris (IRE)**[67] 2743 2-9-0 85 JamieSpencer 3 90
(E J O'Neill) *hld up in last trio and off the pce early: effrt on outer and sme prog 2f out: no ch w ldrs* **25/1**

4213 **7** *1 ½* **Harvest Joy (IRE)**[31] 3874 2-9-0 91 DaneO'Neill 7 87
(B R Millman) *hld up in last and off the pce early: rdn 3f out: one pce and no real prog* **50/1**

1 **8** *hd* **Hanging On**[23] 4103 2-9-0 StephenCarson 5 86
(W R Swinburn) *lw: hld up in last trio and off the pce early: shkn up and no prog over 2f out* **33/1**

0 **9** *1* **Samdaniya**[25] 4041 2-9-0 SteveDrowne 1 84
(C E Brittain) *nvr beyond midfield: rdn and struggling 2f out* **100/1**

12 **10** *3 ½* **Princess Taise (USA)**[15] 4371 2-9-0 JoeFanning 2 75
(M Johnston) *lw: scope: reluctant to enter stalls: chsd ldr: rdn 3f out: wknd over 2f out* **11/4**[2]

1m 25.76s (-2.28) **Going Correction** -0.10s/f (Good) **10** Ran SP% **116.4**
Speed ratings (Par 101):109,108,106,105,104 102,101,101,99,95
CSF £120.17 TOTE £11.50: £2.30, £2.60, £1.40; EX 114.10 Trifecta £201.50 Pool £937.00 - 3.30 winning units..
Owner Scuderia Rencati Srl **Bred** Peter Ebdon Racing **Trained** Newmarket, Suffolk

FOCUS
A very smart winning time even for a race like this and 0.29 seconds quicker than the earlier Listed race for three-year-old fillies. This looked a strong renewal.

NOTEBOOK
Sesmen ◆, back down in trip, made it three from three with a victory that was more convincing than the narrow margin. Travelling well close to the pace, she quickened past the leader to settle the issue although the runner-up was closing on her at the line. Likely to be put away for the season now, she is a bright prospect. (tchd 11-1)
Bicoastal(USA), off the track since Royal Ascot, ran here in preference to the Moyglare Stud Stakes in Ireland. In first-time blinkers, she came under pressure with two to run and it was only in the last half-furlong that she really found her stride, cutting into the winner's advantage all too late.
Cumin(USA) looked very fit beforehand. Attempting to replicate her all-the-way win in a maiden at the big meeting here, she set a decent pace but had to give best when tackled by the winner approaching the final furlong. (tchd 7-4)
Hope'N'Charity(USA), held in better company since landing a Listed race on her second start, ran her race and stayed on from the rear for fourth. She got the seventh furlong well enough but just falls short at this level.
Italian Girl, sold to Michael Tabor since her winning debut at Ascot, was a little keen in the first part of the race and was never able to get out of midfield, although she was keeping on at the end to suggest that she stayed. (tchd 9-2)
Princess Iris(IRE), off the track since finishing towards the rear in the Queen Mary at Ascot, was held up on this first try over seven furlongs and could never get into the action.
Princess Taise(USA), who gave trouble at the stalls, failed to show the form which saw her finish second in this grade last time. After tracking the favourite, she weakened with over a quarter of a mile still to run. (op 3-1 tchd 10-3)

4841 GG CLUB STKS (H'CAP) 6f
4:55 (4:56) (Class 4) (0-85,87) 3-Y-O **£5,505** (£1,637; £818; £408) **Stalls** Low

Form RPR
5603 **1** **Guest Connections**[14] 4391 3-9-8 **84** (v) JamieSpencer 2 91
(M R Channon) *s.i.s: last tl swtchd to outer and prog 2f out: hrd rdn and sustained chal to ld nr fin* **9/2**[2]

2152 **2** *hd* **Libor (IRE)**[16] 4328 3-9-3 **79** NickyMackay 8 85
(L M Cumani) *lw: hld up bhd ldrs on outer: prog to ld jst over 2f out: edgd lft sn after: hrd rdn fnl f: hdd nr fin* **9/2**[2]

6136 **3** *¾* **Namu**[18] 4242 3-8-8 **70** MichaelHills 1 74
(B W Hills) *hld up bhd ldrs: effrt over 1f out: rdn to press ldrs ins fnl f: a jst hld* **10/1**

1604 **4** *shd* **Gavarnie Beau (IRE)**[4] 4707 3-9-9 **85** SteveDrowne 7 89
(M Blanshard) *hld up bhd ldrs: effrt over 1f out: pressed ldrs ins fnl f: nt qckn* **12/1**

1241 **5** *¾* **China Cherub**[11] 4484 3-8-11 **73** DaneO'Neill 3 74
(H Candy) *w ldr to 1/2-way: sn shkn up: nt qckn 2f out: styd on again ins fnl f* **7/2**[1]

2216 **6** *4* **Kansas Gold**[17] 4296 3-8-7 **69** MartinDwyer 4 58+
(W R Muir) *lw: mde most to jst over 2f out: losing pl whn n.m.r over 1f out* **9/1**[3]

4501 **7** *2 ½* **Tara Too (IRE)**[8] 4589 3-9-11 **87** RyanMoore 6 69+
(D W P Arbuthnot) *trckd ldng pair: lost pl whn bdly hmpd 2f out: nt rcvr and eased* **7/2**[1]

000 **8** *1 ½* **Laith (IRE)**[17] 4296 3-8-4 **66** JoeFanning 5 43+
(Miss V Haigh) *hld up bhd ldrs: effrt and cl up whn bdly hmpd 2f out: nt rcvr* **25/1**

1m 12.64s (-0.21) **Going Correction** +0.025s/f (Good) **8** Ran SP% **111.4**
Speed ratings (Par 102):102,101,100,100,99 94,90,88
CSF £23.68 CT £185.56 TOTE £5.10: £1.60, £1.90, £2.60; EX 29.70.
Owner John Guest **Bred** The Lavington Stud **Trained** West Ilsley, Berks
■ Stewards' Enquiry : Nicky Mackay four-day ban: careless riding (Sep 7-9,11)

FOCUS
A fair handicap, although a bit messy with the last three home all sufferers, but sound form amongst the principals.
Tara Too(IRE) Official explanation: jockey said filly suffered interference in running
Laith(IRE) Official explanation: jockey said gelding suffered interference in running

4842 SILVER BIRCH STKS (H'CAP) 1m 1f 192y
5:30 (5:30) (Class 5) (0-70,69) 3-Y-O+ **£3,238** (£963; £481; £240) **Stalls** High

Form RPR
0000 **1** **Lenoir (GER)**[37] 3706 3-9-1 **56** (v) DaneO'Neill 4 66+
(V Smith) *s.i.s: hld up in 6th: cruising over 2f out: burst through sn after: led jst over 1f out and sn clr: rdn out* **7/1**

-056 **2** *¾* **Height Of Fury (IRE)**[22] 4150 3-9-12 **67** JamieSpencer 6 76
(J L Dunlop) *s.s: hld up in last: prog and squeezed through on inner 2f out: nt pce of wnr 1f out: wnt 2nd last 150yds: r.o but no ch* **4/1**[2]

6346 **3** *4* **Kalatime (IRE)**[16] 4331 3-9-10 **65** MartinDwyer 1 66
(A M Balding) *lw: led: kicked on 1/2-way: drvn 2f out: hdd & wknd jst over 1f out* **6/1**[3]

0425 **4** 1 1/2 **Barbirolli**[2] [4764] 4-9-13 **60** .... RyanMoore 10 — 59
(W M Brisbourne) *wl in tch: rdn to chse ldr over 2f out to wl over 1f out: sn wknd* **7/2**[1]

0600 **5** 4 **Simplify**[16] [4332] 4-8-10 **46** .... (p) AdamKirby(3) 3 — 37
(T M Jones) *hld up in tch: prog on outer 3f out: rdn over 2f out: wknd over 1f out* **20/1**

6532 **6** 1/2 **Mexican Bob**[14] [4402] 3-9-12 **67** .... LPKeniry 5 — 57
(Heather Dalton) *lw: chsd ldr: rdn 3f out: wknd lost pl and btn over 2f out: wknd over 1f out* **4/1**[2]

-065 **7** 37 **Sonny Mac**[25] [4044] 3-10-0 **69** .... (bt1) LDettori 9 — —
(B J Meehan) *chsd ldng pair: rdn 4f out: wknd 3f out: sltly hmpd 2f out and eased: t.o* **4/1**[2]

2m 8.41s (0.66) **Going Correction** -0.10s/f (Good)
WFA 3 from 4yo 8lb — **7** Ran SP% **113.8**
Speed ratings (Par 103):93,92,89,88,84 84,54
CSF £34.50 CT £177.93 TOTE £8.80: £3.50, £2.90; EX 46.70 Place 6 £490.48, Place 5 £259.04..
Owner The Contretemps Partnership **Bred** Graf And Grafin Von Stauffenberg **Trained** Exning, Suffolk

FOCUS
A modest handicap run at a muddling pace and producing a very moderate winning time. The first two finished clear and the form looks sound.
Sonny Mac Official explanation: jockey said colt stopped quickly
T/Jkpt: Not won. T/Plt: £384.30 to a £1 stake. Pool: £93,434.10. 177.45 winning tickets. T/Qpdt: £50.20 to a £1 stake. Pool: £6,179.65. 91.05 winning tickets. JN

4663 YARMOUTH (L-H)
Sunday, August 27

OFFICIAL GOING: Good to firm
Wind: Light, across Weather: Cloudy with sunny spells

4843 EUROPEAN BREEDERS FUND EASTERN DAILY PRESS MAIDEN STKS — 6f 3y
2:20 (2:20) (Class 5) 2-Y-O — **£4,210** (£1,252; £625; £312) **Stalls** High

Form — RPR

2 **1** **Leopard King (USA)**[23] [4105] 2-9-3 .... SebSanders 1 — 77
(Sir Michael Stoute) *chsd ldr: led and hung lft over 2f out: sn rdn: hung rt ins fnl f: styd on* **4/9**[1]

3 **2** 1/2 **Expensive Detour (IRE)**[24] [4066] 2-9-3 .... RobbieFitzpatrick 2 — 75
(Mrs L Stubbs) *led over 3f: sn rdn: styd on* **16/1**

64F **3** 4 **Roclette (USA)**[18] [4260] 2-8-12 .... DaleGibson 6 — 58
(B W Hills) *prom: jnd ldr over 3f out: rdn over 2f out: styd on same pce appr fnl f* **5/1**[2]

0 **4** 1/2 **Until When (USA)**[26] [4018] 2-9-3 .... PhilipRobinson 7 — 62
(B Smart) *prom: effrt over 2f out: styd on same pce appr fnl f* **10/1**[3]

5 7 **Orange Lily** 2-8-12 .... MatthewHenry 4 — 36
(M A Jarvis) *prom: jnd ldr over 3f out: rdn and wknd over 1f out* **14/1**

0 **6** 4 **Ronannis**[28] [3979] 2-9-3 .... DerekMcGaffin 5 — 29
(J Jay) *s.s: sn prom: wknd 2f out* **150/1**

0 **7** 45 **Mister Always**[13] [4433] 2-9-0 .... SaleemGolam(3) 3 — —
(C R Dore) *s.i.s: outpcd* **150/1**

1m 13.23s (-0.47) **Going Correction** -0.10s/f (Good) — **7** Ran SP% **108.9**
Speed ratings (Par 94):99,98,93,92,83 77,17
CSF £8.46 TOTE £1.50: £1.10, £5.30; EX 6.10.
Owner Gainsborough Stud **Bred** Hidden Creek Farm **Trained** Newmarket, Suffolk

FOCUS
This was probably a fair juvenile maiden. The first two came clear.

NOTEBOOK
Leopard King(USA), runner-up on debut at Newmarket last time, duly went one better yet still made hard work of justifying his prohibitive odds. He is probably capable of a lot better, and is clearly still learning his trade, but he will have to improve rapidly if he is to justify his current Group 1 entries. (op 2-5 tchd 1-2)
Expensive Detour(IRE) ◆ showed up well under a positive ride and made the winner pull out all the stops. He already looks to need a stiffer test and should soon be placed to go one better. (tchd 20-1)
Roclette(USA), who fell at Pontefract last time, was again supported in the betting ring yet never really gave any hope to her supporters. This experience should be to her benefit, however, and she may do better when switching to nurseries. (op 7-1)
Until When(USA) improved a touch on his debut effort at Beverley and still looks in need of further experience. (op 15-2)
Mister Always Official explanation: jockey said gelding moved very poorly

4844 NORWICH EVENING NEWS FILLIES' H'CAP — 7f 3y
2:55 (2:55) (Class 5) (0-75,73) 3-Y-0+ — **£3,562** (£1,059; £529; £264) **Stalls** High

Form — RPR

000 **1** **Mugeba**[18] [4265] 5-8-11 **53** .... (t) JimmyQuinn 1 — 62
(Miss Gay Kelleway) *chsd ldrs: led over 1f out: rdn out* **8/1**

2000 **2** 3/4 **Smart Ass (IRE)**[22] [4144] 3-9-2 **63** .... PhilipRobinson 8 — 68
(J S Moore) *hld up: hdwy over 1f out: rdn and hung rt ins fnl f: sn chsng wnr: r.o* **13/2**[3]

0611 **3** 2 1/2 **Tequila Sheila (IRE)**[9] [4548] 4-8-10 **52** .... LeeEnstone 3 — 53
(K R Burke) *led over 5f: no ex ins fnl f* **4/1**[2]

0050 **4** 1 **Wodhill Be**[18] [4265] 6-8-7 **49** oh4 .... DerekMcGaffin 2 — 47
(D Morris) *hld up: hdwy u.p over 1f out: hmpd ins fnl f: no ex* **40/1**

55 **5** nk **Another Genepi (USA)**[22] [4155] 3-9-5 **66** .... PatDobbs 4 — 63
(J W Hills) *chsd ldrs: rdn over 2f out: styd on same pce fnl f* **7/1**

0401 **6** 2 1/2 **Elrafa Mujahid**[16] [4329] 4-8-13 **58** .... (t) SaleemGolam(3) 5 — 49
(Ernst Oertel) *chsd ldrs: rdn over 1f out: sn wknd* **4/1**[2]

-104 **7** 1/2 **Amy Louise (IRE)**[9] [4567] 3-9-12 **73** .... SebSanders 6 — 62
(T D Barron) *hld up: rdn over 2f out: wknd fnl f* **7/2**[1]

0-22 **8** 1 1/4 **Tapau (IRE)**[11] [4484] 8-8-2 **51** .... BarrySavage(7) 9 — 37
(J M Bradley) *s.s: hld up: rdn whn hmpd and wknd over 1f out* **8/1**

1m 26.16s (-0.44) **Going Correction** -0.10s/f (Good)
WFA 3 from 4yo+ 5lb — **8** Ran SP% **112.7**
Speed ratings (Par 100):98,97,94,93,92 89,89,87
CSF £56.86 CT £240.10 TOTE £10.70: £2.80, £1.90, £2.00; EX 90.30 TRIFECTA Not won..
Owner M M Foulger **Bred** Broughton Bloodstock And M Billings **Trained** Exning, Suffolk
■ Stewards' Enquiry : Derek McGaffin one-day ban: careless riding (Sep 8)

FOCUS
A moderate fillies' handicap, run at a strong early pace but resulting in a moderate overall time, and the first two came clear. The form is modest rated through the runner-up.

4845 GREAT YARMOUTH MERCURY H'CAP — 1m 3y
3:25 (3:26) (Class 6) (0-60,60) 3-Y-0+ — **£2,428** (£722; £361; £180) **Stalls** High

Form — RPR

0041 **1** **Apres Ski (IRE)**[17] [4304] 3-9-1 **56** .... DeanCorby(3) 7 — 67
(J F Coupland) *std slowly: hld up: hdwy 1/2-way: jnd ldrs over 2f out: rdn to ld ins fnl f: r.o* **22/1**

1345 **2** 1 1/4 **Al Rayanah**[18] [4265] 3-9-1 **60** .... KirstyMilczarek(7) 8 — 68
(G Prodromou) *chsd ldrs: led over 2f out: rdn and hdd ins fnl f: unable qckn* **11/1**

6021 **3** 1 **Panshir (FR)**[6] [4667] 5-9-3 **49** 6ex .... SebSanders 11 — 56
(Mrs C A Dunnett) *hld up: hdwy over 2f out: hung lft over 1f out: styd on same pce ins fnl f* **5/2**[1]

23-0 **4** 1 **Bank On Benny**[233] [52] 4-9-12 **58** .... PatDobbs 1 — 62
(P W D'Arcy) *hld up: hdwy over 2f out: sn outpcd: r.o u.p ins fnl f* **9/1**

0122 **5** shd **Beau Marche**[5] [4670] 4-9-5 **51** .... (v1) PhilipRobinson 5 — 55
(G G Margarson) *chsd ldrs: ev ch over 2f out: sn rdn: no ex fnl f* **4/1**[2]

2112 **6** nk **Baby Barry**[15] [4381] 9-9-10 **56** .... RobbieFitzpatrick 3 — 59
(M J Attwater) *chsd ldrs: ev ch over 2f out: sn rdn: no ex fnl f* **8/1**

5000 **7** nk **Picture Show (USA)**[34] [3804] 3-9-5 **57** .... JimmyQuinn 2 — 59
(C E Brittain) *hld up: hdwy over 2f out: no ex fnl f* **33/1**

1310 **8** 2 **Orpen Quest (IRE)**[29] [3947] 4-9-7 **58** .... (v) KevinGhunowa(5) 14 — 56
(M J Attwater) *chsd ldrs: rdn and ev ch over 2f out: wknd ins fnl f* **18/1**

3013 **9** 3 **William John**[12] [4454] 3-9-3 **58** .... (t) StephenDonohoe(3) 13 — 48
(B Ellison) *prom: rdn 1/2-way: wknd over 1f out* **11/2**[3]

4046 **10** 2 1/2 **Primeshade Promise**[53] [3197] 5-9-4 **50** .... JamieMackay 15 — 36
(J M Bradley) *hld up: nvr trbld ldrs* **20/1**

3006 **11** 1 3/4 **Time To Regret**[16] [4325] 6-9-1 **50** .... SaleemGolam(3) 6 — 32
(I W McInnes) *led over 5f: wknd over 1f out* **16/1**

00-0 **12** 6 **Channel Crossing**[13] [4439] 4-9-2 **48** .... MatthewHenry 16 — 16
(W M Brisbourne) *a bhd* **40/1**

0600 **13** 3 **Must Be Keen**[18] [4248] 7-9-9 **55** .... AdrianMcCarthy 10 — 16
(Ernst Oertel) *prom over 5f* **40/1**

00-0 **14** 3 1/2 **Twist Bookie (IRE)**[21] [4176] 6-8-13 **52** .... StevenGibson(7) 9 — 5
(J S Moore) *mid-div: rdn and lost pl 1/2-way: bhd whn rdr dropped whip over 3f out* **66/1**

1m 38.55s (-1.35) **Going Correction** -0.10s/f (Good)
WFA 3 from 4yo+ 6lb — **14** Ran SP% **123.0**
Speed ratings (Par 101):102,100,99,98,98 98,98,96,93,90 88,82,79,76
CSF £238.79 CT £832.90 TOTE £19.40: £4.60, £3.40, £1.60; EX 204.70 Trifecta £114.60 Part won. Pool £161.50 - 0.20 winning units..
Owner J F Coupland **Bred** Edward Kelly **Trained** Grimsby, Lincs

FOCUS
A moderate handicap that was run at a sound gallop. The winner is progressive and the form is basically solid.
Must Be Keen Official explanation: trainer said gelding lost a shoe

4846 LOWESTOFT JOURNAL H'CAP — 5f 43y
4:00 (4:01) (Class 5) (0-70,67) 3-Y-0+ — **£3,562** (£1,059; £529; £264) **Stalls** High

Form — RPR

0552 **1** **Kennington**[18] [4267] 6-9-9 **65** .... (b) SebSanders 9 — 75
(Mrs C A Dunnett) *chsd ldr: rdn to ld wl ins fnl f* **9/2**[2]

0050 **2** 1 1/4 **Detonate**[17] [4306] 4-8-6 **48** oh1 .... (p) AdrianMcCarthy 1 — 53
(Mrs C A Dunnett) *led: rdn and hdd wl ins fnl f* **18/1**

6532 **3** 1/2 **Harrison's Flyer (IRE)**[2] [4780] 5-9-11 **67** .... (p) PhilipRobinson 6 — 70
(J M Bradley) *hld up: r.o ins fnl f: nt rch ldrs* **9/4**[1]

0350 **4** 1/2 **Gone'N'Dunnett (IRE)**[15] [4365] 7-8-11 **60** .... (p) KirstyMilczarek(7) 5 — 61
(Mrs C A Dunnett) *chsd ldrs: outpcd 2f out: r.o ins fnl f* **11/1**

4610 **5** 1 1/2 **Davids Mark**[22] [4141] 6-8-2 **51** ow3 .... JamieJones(7) 12 — 47
(J R Jenkins) *s.i.s: hld up: hdwy over 1f out: nt trble ldrs* **15/2**[3]

0305 **6** 1 1/4 **Convince (USA)**[9] [4564] 5-9-1 **64** .... BarrySavage(7) 10 — 56
(J M Bradley) *prom: rdn 1/2-way: styd on same pce fnl 2f* **12/1**

0601 **7** 3 **Lady Hopeful (IRE)**[9] [4551] 4-8-7 **49** .... (b) RobbieFitzpatrick 8 — 30
(Peter Grayson) *s.s: hdwy over 3f out: wknd over 1f out* **11/1**

2600 **8** hd **Million Percent**[14] [4401] 7-9-1 **57** .... JimmyQuinn 3 — 37
(C R Dore) *chsd ldrs over 3f* **16/1**

1040 **9** 2 **Never Without Me**[19] [4230] 6-9-4 **63** .... DeanCorby(3) 7 — 36
(J F Coupland) *s.s: a in rr* **11/1**

4200 **10** 1 3/4 **Tag Team (IRE)**[146] [858] 5-8-10 **52** .... JamieMackay 11 — 18
(John A Harris) *mid-div: rdn and hung lft 1/2-way: sn wknd* **22/1**

0055 **11** nk **Mambazo**[59] [3012] 4-8-7 **52** .... (e) SaleemGolam(3) 13 — 17
(S C Williams) *s.i.s: sn outpcd* **11/1**

62.17 secs (-0.63) **Going Correction** -0.10s/f (Good)
WFA 3 from 4yo+ 2lb — **11** Ran SP% **117.2**
Speed ratings (Par 103):101,99,98,97,95 93,88,87,84,81 81
CSF £82.05 CT £233.53 TOTE £5.10: £2.00, £7.40, £1.20; EX 56.80 Trifecta £121.40 Part won. Pool £171.04 - 0.10 winning units..
Owner Mrs Christine Dunnett **Bred** C J R Trotter **Trained** Hingham, Norfolk

FOCUS
A modest sprint that saw the Dunnett stable fill three of the first four places. The form looks fair for the class with the second the best guide.
Harrison's Flyer(IRE) Official explanation: trainer said gelding was unsuited by the good to firm ground
Million Percent Official explanation: jockey said gelding anticipated start and struck front gate of stalls

4847 EDP24.CO.UK H'CAP — 1m 2f 21y
4:30 (4:30) (Class 6) (0-60,60) 3-Y-0 — **£2,428** (£722; £361; £180) **Stalls** Low

Form — RPR

0322 **1** **Hurry Up Helen (IRE)**[4] [4697] 3-8-12 **51** .... RobbieFitzpatrick 7 — 58
(Mrs L Stubbs) *chsd ldr: led over 3f out: rdn out* **11/4**[1]

0003 **2** 1 **Diktatorship (IRE)**[11] [4497] 3-8-13 **52** .... AdrianMcCarthy 13 — 57
(Ernst Oertel) *a.p: chsd ldr over 3f out: rdn and ev ch 2f out: styd on same pce ins fnl f* **10/1**

0603 **3** 2 **El Capitan (FR)**[10] [4533] 3-9-4 **60** .... StephenDonohoe(3) 5 — 61
(Miss Gay Kelleway) *chsd ldrs: rdn and ev ch 2f out: hung lft over 1f out: styd on same pce* **8/1**

0630 **4** 3/4 **Deserted Prince (IRE)**[17] [4304] 3-8-13 **55** .... DeanCorby(3) 10 — 55
(M J Wallace) *hld up: plld hrd: hdwy 1/2-way: rdn over 2f out: styd on same pce appr fnl f* **33/1**

0440 **5** hd **Grecianette (IRE)**[17] [4289] 3-8-11 **50** .... PhilipRobinson 3 — 49
(W J Musson) *s.i.s: hld up: hdwy over 2f out: no ex fnl f* **6/1**[3]

0405 **6** 1 **Nassar (IRE)**[4] [4697] 3-9-5 **58** .... (p) MichaelTebbutt 8 — 56
(G Prodromou) *s.i.s: hld up: hdwy and hung lft over 1f out: nt trble ldrs* **16/1**

0610 **7** *3* **Coffin Dodger**[11] 4491 3-8-5 **51**..............................(b) KirstyMilczarek(7) 9 43
(C N Allen) *s.s: bhd: hung lft ins fnl f: nvr nrr* **9/1**
5006 **8** *3 ½* **Maximix**[62] 2933 3-9-7 **60**.. DaleGibson 6 45
(B W Hills) *hld up: rdn over 3f out: n.d* **12/1**
0060 **9** *2 ½* **Baileys Polka**[18] 4257 3-9-1 **54**..............................(b) JamieMackay 11 34
(J G Given) *hld up: hdwy over 2f out: sn rdn and wknd* **25/1**
4261 **10** *½* **Dream Of Paradise (USA)**[21] 4173 3-9-4 **60**........... SaleemGolam(3) 2 40
(Mrs L Williamson) *led over 6f: sn rdn and wknd* **4/1**[2]
0300 **11** *6* **Captain Bolsh**[4] 4700 3-9-0 **53**... JimmyQuinn 4 21
(J Pearce) *chsd ldr 6f: sn rdn and wknd* **12/1**

2m 10.27s (2.17) **Going Correction** +0.175s/f (Good) **11** Ran SP% **119.2**
Speed ratings (Par 98):98,97,95,95,94 94,91,88,86,86 81
CSF £31.94 CT £201.61 TOTE £3.10: £1.10, £4.00, £3.40; EX 37.20 Trifecta £106.30 Part won. Pool £149.84 - 0.60 winning units..
Owner Des Thurlby **Bred** G Callanan **Trained** Norton, N. Yorks

FOCUS
A moderate handicap that saw the field finish fairly strung out. The form is modest rated around the runner-up and fourth.

4848 EASTERN DAILY PRESS RISING STARS H'CAP 1m 6f 17y
5:05 (5:05) (Class 5) (0-75,72) 3-Y-0+ **£3,562** (£1,059; £529; £264) **Stalls** High

Form RPR
54-0 **1** **Jack Dawson (IRE)**[12] 4448 9-9-11 **70**................. StephenDonohoe(3) 2 79
(John Berry) *hld up: hdwy over 3f out: rdn 2f out: styd on to ld wl ins fnl f* **7/1**
0606 **2** *1* **Duroob**[65] 2812 4-8-12 **61**.. PatrickDonaghy(7) 5 69
(K R Burke) *s.i.s: sn chsng ldrs: led 5f out: rdn and hdd wl ins fnl f* **3/1**[2]
3416 **3** *9* **Darghan (IRE)**[17] 4299 6-9-7 **63**... PhilipRobinson 3 58
(W J Musson) *hld up: hdwy over 1f out: sn rdn and wknd* **6/4**[1]
5055 **4** *2 ½* **Perfectionist**[6] 4668 4-8-10 **52** oh6................................(p) JimmyQuinn 1 44
(Mrs C A Dunnett) *chsd ldrs: lost pl 7f out: rdn over 3f out: btn whn nt clr run over 1f out* **17/2**
6306 **5** *shd* **Magic Amigo**[59] 3009 5-9-7 **70**....................................... JamieJones(7) 8 61
(J R Jenkins) *hld up: hdwy 1/2-way: hung lft and wknd over 1f out* **13/2**[3]
0-00 **6** *3 ½* **Bendarshaan**[24] 168 6-9-12 **68**..................................(b) JamieMackay 7 54
(C A Dwyer) *led 12f out: hdd 5f out: wknd over 2f out* **12/1**
20-0 **7** *12* **China Pearl**[97] 1898 3-9-1 **72**.. SaleemGolam(3) 6 42
(John Berry) *led 2f: chsd ldrs: rdn over 4f out: wkng whn nt clr run over 2f out* **16/1**

3m 10.14s (4.84) **Going Correction** +0.175s/f (Good)
WFA 3 from 4yo+ 12lb **7** Ran SP% **114.9**
Speed ratings (Par 103):93,92,87,85,85 83,76
CSF £28.55 CT £48.03 TOTE £9.30: £3.60, £2.00; EX 29.90 Trifecta £101.40 Part won. Pool £142.86 - 0.90 winning units. Place 6 £75.55, Place 5 £56.43..
Owner The Premier Cru **Bred** P C Green **Trained** Newmarket, Suffolk

FOCUS
A modest handicap run in a very moderate winning time and the first two came clear. The form is rated around the principals but is not rock-solid.
China Pearl Official explanation: jockey said gelding pulled up lame
T/Plt: £134.10 to a £1 stake. Pool: £57,946.85. 315.35 winning tickets. T/Qpdt: £26.30 to a £1 stake. Pool: £3,314.80. 93.10 winning tickets. CR

4849 - (Foreign Racing) - See Raceform Interactive

4821 CURRAGH (R-H)
Sunday, August 27

OFFICIAL GOING: Round course - good to firm; straight course - good

4850a GO AND GO ROUND TOWER STKS (GROUP 3) 6f
2:40 (2:40) 2-Y-0 **£35,917** (£10,537; £5,020; £1,710)

RPR
1 **Rabatash (USA)**[14] 4409 2-9-1 .... WMLordan 9 108+
(David Wachman, Ire) *3rd early: 2nd 1/2-way: led travelling wl 2f out: rdn clr fr over 1f out: easily* **4/1**[2]
2 *3* **Chivalrous (IRE)**[27] 4012 2-9-1 .... KFallon 3 99
(A P O'Brien, Ire) *trckd ldrs: prog into 3rd after 1/2-way: rdn 2f out: kpt on same pce* **2/1**[1]
3 *nk* **Dushinka (IRE)**[44] 3507 2-8-12 .... WSupple 1 95
(Timothy Doyle, Ire) *hld up: hdwy under 2f out: 5th 1f out: kpt on u.p* **8/1**
4 *2 ½* **Isola Star (IRE)** 2-8-12 .... KJManning 2 88
(David P Myerscough, Ire) *hld up: hdwy on outer 2f out: 5th over 1f out: kpt on same pce* **33/1**
5 *shd* **Saint Andrew (IRE)**[13] 4440 2-9-1 ....(p) PJSmullen 4 90
(Peter Casey, Ire) *led: rdn and hdd 2f out: no ex ins fnl f* **11/1**
6 *hd* **Jopau**[20] 4217 2-9-1 .... JMurtagh 6 90
(G M Lyons, Ire) *towards rr: 7th and rdn over 2f out: kpt on ins fnl f* **10/1**
7 *hd* **Musthav (IRE)**[21] 4182 2-8-12 ....(p) WJLee 10 86
(T Stack, Ire) *in rr: trailing over 2f out: r.o fr over 1f out* **20/1**
8 *2* **Streetofchampions (USA)**[29] 3962 2-9-1 .... MCHussey 8 83
(T J O'Mara, Ire) *chsd ldrs: 4th after 1/2-way: rdn 2f out: wknd ins fnl f* **16/1**
9 *3* **Chin Wag (IRE)**[30] 3903 2-9-1 .... TedDurcan 7 74
(E S McMahon) *2nd early: 3rd and rdn 1/2-way: sn wknd* **5/1**[3]
10 *4 ½* **Johnstown Lad (IRE)**[20] 4217 2-9-1 ....(t) PShanahan 5 61
(Niall Moran, Ire) *chsd ldrs to 1/2-way: sn wknd* **16/1**

1m 11.3s **Going Correction** -0.45s/f (Firm) **10** Ran SP% **118.0**
Speed ratings: 103,99,98,95,95 94,94,91,87,81
CSF £12.54 TOTE £4.60: £1.50, £1.70, £2.40; DF 17.30.
Owner Joseph Joyce **Bred** Desmond Ryan & Paul Saylor **Trained** Goolds Cross, Co Tipperary

FOCUS
The best renewal of this Group 3 event for years and the form, which looks quite solid, gave another boost to Holy Roman Emperor's Phoenix Stakes win.

NOTEBOOK
Rabatash(USA), who had finished sixth of seven behind Holy Roman Emperor in the Group 1 Phoenix Stakes on his previous start, was sent to the front fully two furlongs out and quickened clear in good style. A return to the top level of competition is now on the cards for this dual winner, and his trainer said that the colt is still a bit big and weak and capable of better. (op 7/2)
Chivalrous(IRE), in the frame on all of his three previous attempts, had been placed at a similar level in the Anglesey Stakes before chasing home the smart Fleeting Shadow at the Galway festival. He tracked the leaders and, although unable to quicken when the winner raised the tempo, he kept on best of the rest inside the final furlong. (op 9/4 tchd 5/2)
Dushinka(IRE), placed on her debut in Germany before winning her maiden easily over this trip at Fairyhouse, ran a good race. She made headway from two furlongs out and kept on quite well in the closing stages. (op 7/1)
Isola Star(IRE) performed creditably on what was her debut and, following this good effort, she should be capable of winning a maiden before reverting to Pattern company.
Saint Andrew(IRE), who came good at the seventh time of asking when making all from a bad draw over this trip at Ballinrobe on his previous start, again made the running but could raise no extra when headed by the winner and was run out of the money inside the final furlong. (op 10/1)
Chin Wag(IRE), the sole British challenger, had two wins to his credit over this trip in lesser company and, after chasing the leaders, he was done with soon after passing the two-furlong marker.

4853a MOYGLARE STUD STKS (GROUP 1) (FILLIES) 7f
4:10 (4:13) 2-Y-0
£116,275 (£39,724; £19,034; £6,620; £4,551; £2,482)

RPR
1 **Miss Beatrix (IRE)**[14] 4409 2-8-12 .... WSupple 6 109
(Kevin Prendergast, Ire) *hld up towards rr: smooth hdwy on stand's side under 2f out: 3rd 1f out: styd on wl to ld on line* **14/1**
2 *shd* **Silca Chiave**[9] 4559 2-8-12 .... TedDurcan 8 109
(M R Channon) *hld up in tch: 7th 2 1/2f out: hdwy under 2f out: rdn to ld 1f out: sn strly pressed: kpt on wl: hdd on line* **12/1**
3 *1* **Supposition**[26] 4032 2-8-12 .... PJSmullen 9 106
(D K Weld, Ire) *trckd ldrs in 4th: 5th 2f out: rdn and kpt on fr over 1f out* **7/2**[1]
4 *shd* **Brazilian Bride (IRE)**[14] 4409 2-8-12 .... DPMcDonogh 13 106
(Kevin Prendergast, Ire) *hld up: 7th 2 1/2f out: kpt on fr over 1f out* **11/2**[3]
5 *nk* **Alexander Tango (IRE)**[29] 3963 2-8-12 .... WMLordan 5 105
(T Stack, Ire) *in tch: 5th after 1/2-way: rdn to ld 1 1/2f out: hdd 1f out: no ex cl home* **13/2**
6 *1* **Dimenticata (IRE)**[29] 3963 2-8-12 .... CDHayes 1 103
(Kevin Prendergast, Ire) *mid-div: prog on outer 1/2-way: 4th 2f out: kpt on same pce u.p* **16/1**
7 *nk* **Simply Perfect**[29] 3925 2-8-12 .... KFallon 12 105+
(J Noseda) *hld up in tch: nt clr run over 1f out: kpt on* **4/1**[2]
8 *¾* **Gaudeamus (USA)**[29] 3963 2-8-12 .... KJManning 10 100
(J S Bolger, Ire) *cl 3rd: 2nd and rdn to chal 2f out: no ex fr over 1f out* **8/1**
9 *1 ½* **Silk Dress (IRE)**[14] 4412 2-8-12 .... DMGrant 11 96
(John Joseph Murphy, Ire) *a towards rr* **100/1**
10 *hd* **Diamond Necklace (USA)**[39] 3656 2-8-12 .... JAHeffernan 3 95
(A P O'Brien, Ire) *led: rdn and strly pressed fr over 2f out: hdd 1 1/2f out: sn wknd* **14/1**
11 *2 ½* **Mythical Echo (USA)**[20] 4218 2-8-12 .... JMurtagh 7 89
(David Wachman, Ire) *hld up in tch: wknd fr over 2f out* **16/1**
12 *9* **Simonetta (IRE)**[39] 3658 2-8-12 ....(p) DJMoran 2 65
(J S Bolger, Ire) *chsd ldrs in 2nd: rdn 1/2-way: wknd fr 2 1/2f out* **66/1**

1m 23.1s **Going Correction** -0.45s/f (Firm) **12** Ran SP% **117.3**
Speed ratings: 107,106,105,105,105 104,103,102,101,101 98,87
CSF £170.03 TOTE £13.30: £3.40, £4.30, £1.60; DF 202.60.
Owner William Durkan **Bred** Bill Durkan **Trained** Friarstown, Co Kildare

FOCUS
A typical renewal in many respects, with the fourth, sixth and eighth all helping to set the standard.

NOTEBOOK
Miss Beatrix(IRE) posted a career-best to finish third in the Phoenix Stakes here two weeks ago and improved over this longer trip in a truly-run race to give trainer Kevin Prendergast his third win in this event. She was settled towards the rear but came with a powerful, sweeping run down the outside over the final two furlongs that carried her to the front in the last strides. She has improved with racing and there is every reason to believe that there could be more to come from her. The Shelbourne Hotel Goffs Fillies' 500 over this course and distance next month will be her next target, and she should go on to make a fine three-year-old.
Silca Chiave was having just her third run and was taking a major rise in class from the Newbury maiden that she won earlier this month. She seemed to appreciate the step up to this trip and looked as if she might have done enough for victory inside the final furlong but was just unable to fend off the winner. The well-related daughter of Pivotal will not be long in landing a good race and thoroughly vindicated connections' decision to let her take her chance.
Supposition was also taking a marked rise in class after easily landing a Galway maiden earlier this month. She was never too far off the pace and stuck to her task well over the final furlong. This experience can be expected to bring her on considerably and she looks a ready-made Stakes winner and a good prospect for 2007. (op 5/2 tchd 4/1)
Brazilian Bride(IRE), who was just behind the winner when fourth in the Phoenix Stakes, did not seem to get the clearest of runs and was another staying on towards the finish. Already a Group 3 winner this season, she is probably capable of improving on this form and may also prefer an easier surface. (op 5/1)
Alexander Tango(IRE) reversed Debutante Stakes form with Dimenticata and Gaudeamus. A maiden winner here last month, she looked a likely winner when taking over in front and it was only near the finish that she got run out of the placings. She could be the type to do better over further and this was a good effort on what was only her third start. (op 8/1)
Dimenticata(IRE), the Debutante runner-up, looked to be in with a chance heading into the final two furlongs, but she could not quite match some of those around her. This represented a solid effort on her part. (op 14/1)
Simply Perfect did not enjoy the clearest of runs and would have finished considerably closer only for that. She has already shown some very smart form in Britain this season and is certainly good enough to make her mark in decent company. She will be well worth another try over seven furlongs. (op 7/2)
Gaudeamus(USA) failed to match the form of her Debutante victory. She raced prominently and had every chance with two furlongs to run but soon weakened out of contention. She is capable of better.
Diamond Necklace(USA) made much of the running and only gave best with over a furlong to run. This was only her second start and she did improve appreciably from her maiden run. She performed some way better than her finishing position suggests and remains one to keep an eye on. (op 14/1 tchd 16/1)

4855a NOLAN & BROPHY AUCTIONEERS FLYING FIVE STKS (GROUP 3) 5f
5:10 (5:10) 3-Y-0+ **£33,620** (£9,827; £4,655; £1,551)

RPR
1 **Benbaun (IRE)**[50] 3312 5-9-3 ....(b) PJSmullen 4 118
(M J Wallace) *trckd ldrs in 3rd: 2nd 1/2-way: rdn to chal 2f out: led under 1f out: kpt on wl u.p* **11/10**[1]
2 *hd* **Desert Lord**[24] 4080 6-9-3 ....(b) NCallan 11 118
(K A Ryan) *attempted to make all: rdn and strly pressed 2f out: hdd under 1f out: kpt on wl u.p* **9/2**[2]
3 *5* **Leitra (IRE)**[43] 3561 3-8-12 **102**..(t) JMurtagh 3 97
(M Halford, Ire) *trckd ldrs: prog into 3rd after 1/2-way: rdn and no imp fr under 2f out* **6/1**[3]
4 *hd* **Absolutelyfabulous (IRE)**[7] 4633 3-8-12 **100**................... WMLordan 2 96
(David Wachman, Ire) *hld up: prog 2f out: mod 4th over 1f out: kpt on same pce* **12/1**
5 *¾* **Tournedos (IRE)**[24] 4080 4-9-3 .... TedDurcan 9 96
(R Charlton) *hld up: 7th and nt clr run 1 1/2f out: r.o ins fnl f* **7/1**

6 *hd* **Beauty Bright (IRE)**[24] 4080 3-8-12 97 .... KFallon 5 93
(A P O'Brien, Ire) *chsd ldrs: 6th 1/2-way: 5th under 2f out: kpt on same pce* **12/1**

7 *1* **Fictional**[12] 4461 5-9-3 .... FMBerry 12 92
(E J O'Neill) *chsd ldrs on outer: 6th and rdn over 2f out: no imp* **14/1**

8 *2 1/2* **Free Roses (IRE)**[43] 3561 3-8-12 100 .... DPMcDonogh 6 80
(Edward Lynam, Ire) *chsd ldr in 2nd: 3rd and rdn after 1/2-way: sn wknd* **16/1**

9 *shd* **Shinko Dancer (IRE)**[3] 4746 3-8-12 63 .... (bt) WSupple 10 80
(H Rogers, Ire) *towards rr: no imp fr over 2f out* **40/1**

10 *1 1/4* **Senor Benny (USA)**[92] 2040 7-9-3 104 .... KJManning 8 78
(M McDonagh, Ire) *a towards rr* **16/1**

57.50 secs **Going Correction** -0.45s/f (Firm)
WFA 3 from 4yo+ 2lb 10 Ran SP% **128.8**
Speed ratings: 112,111,103,103,102 101,100,96,96,94
CSF £7.11 TOTE £2.20: £1.20, £1.50, £2.00; DF 6.50.
Owner Ransley, Birks, Hillen **Bred** Dr T A Ryan **Trained** Newmarket, Suffolk

FOCUS
Not that competitive a Group 3, and the race has been rated through the ninth.

NOTEBOOK
Benbaun(IRE), who was not winning out of turn, has been a model of consistency over the minimum trip this year. He did, however, have to dig deep for his third course win after tracking fellow British raider Desert Lord throughout. Despite wandering around under pressure, when asked a serious question he eventually forged to the front inside the final furlong for a narrow success. The likelihood of soft ground could well sway connections away from the Prix de l'Abbaye, but the Betfred Sprint Cup at Haydock or most likely a trip to Japan for a Group 1 sprint on October 1 could be next for the son of Stravinsky. (op 6/4)
Desert Lord broke smartly to lead and lost little in defeat on ground that had eased somewhat following several showers overnight. He has also proved himself an ultra-consistent sort, and had the underfoot conditions been quicker it could well have been a different story. The two principals pulled well clear of the chasing pack. (op 4/1)
Leitra(IRE) was simply outclassed by the visitors. Still only three, this was a fair effort, and improvement is likely over time. (op 11/2)
Absolutelyfabulous(IRE) was dropping back to this shorter trip for the first time in her career and connections can be pleased with this effort, although she is probably more effective over an extra furlong as she showed when winning a couple of Naas handicaps early in the summer.
Tournedos(IRE), who previously landed a Listed sprint from a favourable draw at Chester by half a length from Desert Lord, was struggling at halfway to make any inroads when the runner-up quickened the tempo. (op 6/1)
Fictional, a two-time winner over this trip, struggled to make this step up in class after a pleasing comeback effort when second at Nottingham 12 days previously.

4854 - 4856a (Foreign Racing) - See Raceform Interactive

4828 BADEN-BADEN (L-H)
Sunday, August 27

OFFICIAL GOING: Soft

4857a KRONIMUS-RRENNEN (LISTED RACE) 6f
1:35 (1:40) 2-Y-O **£8,966** (£3,793; £1,724; £690)

RPR

1 **Adamantinos**[21] 2-9-2 .... JVictoire 3 91
(Frau E Mader, Germany) **9/5**[1]

2 *shd* **Taita (GER)** 2-8-7 .... FilipMinarik 5 82
(H J Groschel, Germany) **7/2**[3]

3 *1 3/4* **Gainsbury (GER)** 2-8-11 .... J-PCarvalho 6 80
(P Vovcenko, Germany) **6/1**

4 *3 1/2* **Queen Of Narnia**[76] 2495 2-8-9 .... ChrisCatlin 7 68
(M R Channon) *led and soon five lengths clear, reduced advantage entering straight, headed 1f out, weakened* **32/10**[2]

5 *8* **Qualinka Royale (FR)** 2-8-5 .... AHelfenbein 4 40
(Andreas Lowe, Germany) **29/2**

6 *4 1/2* **Sybelio (FR)** 2-9-2 .... ASuborics 1 37
(W Hefter, Germany) **74/10**

7 *1 1/4* **Johannesburg Cat (USA)**[21] 2-8-9 .... ABoschert 2 27
(A Trybuhl, Germany) **51/10**

1m 13.28s 7 Ran SP% **130.8**
(including ten euro stakes); WIN 28; PL 13, 15, 16; SF 107.
Owner Stall Capricorn **Bred** Capricorn Stud **Trained** Germany

NOTEBOOK
Queen Of Narnia, a narrow winner of a Folkestone seller last time, looked little more than a travelling-companion for the previous day's big-race runner, Rocamadour. She had not raced for 11 weeks, and was trying six furlongs for the first time, so fourth prize was a creditable effort.

4858a BESTWETTEN.DE GOLDENE PEITSCHE (GROUP 2) 6f
4:00 (4:03) 3-Y-O+ **£35,862** (£15,172; £6,897; £4,138)

RPR

1 **Linngari (IRE)**[21] 4191 4-9-2 .... ASuborics 6 113
(Diego Lowther, France) *raced in 3rd, ridden to lead 1f out, ran on well* **2/1**[2]

2 *3/4* **Donatello (GER)**[62] 2941 5-9-2 .... JVictoire 2 111
(W Baltromei, Germany) *held up in last, headway & switched left 1f out, went 2nd inside final f, kept on* **93/10**

3 *nk* **Soave (GER)**[94] 1973 7-9-2 .... ADeVries 3 110
(A Trybuhl, Germany) *held up, headway to press leaders over 1f out, kept on same pace* **13/10**[1]

4 *3/4* **Matrix (GER)**[36] 3755 5-9-2 .... ABoschert 7 108
(W Baltromei, Germany) *led to over 1f out, one pace* **91/10**

5 *2* **Electric Beat**[36] 3755 3-8-12 .... AHelfenbein 5 101
(Andreas Lowe, Germany) *raced in 5th, one pace final 1 1/2f out* **3/1**[3]

6 *3/4* **Zita (GER)** 4-8-12 .... AWhelan 1 96
(P Bradik, Germany) *raced in 4th, effort on inside entering straight, beaten over 1f out* **27/1**

7 *4 1/2* **Omasheriff (IRE)**[36] 3755 4-9-2 .... THellier 4 86
(Bruce Hellier, Germany) *raced in 2nd, weakened 1 1/2f out* **16/1**

1m 11.76s
WFA 3 from 4yo+ 3lb 7 Ran SP% **130.9**
WIN 30; PL 14, 17, 12; SF 216.
Owner Jim Atkinson & P Walraninski **Bred** Hh Aga Khan's Stud **Trained** France

NOTEBOOK
Linngari(IRE), fourth in last year's Lingfield Derby Trial, is picking up speed with age. He was rested from March to August but should enjoy a profitable autumn before returning to Dubai. He is to rejoin Herman Brown, who won two Group races with him at the International Carnival at Nad al Sheba earlier this year.

4644 DEAUVILLE (R-H)
Sunday, August 27

OFFICIAL GOING: Turf course - very soft; all-weather - standard

4859a PRIX DU HARAS DE LA HUDERIE ROYAL BARRIERE (LISTED) (C&G) 7f 110y
1:15 (1:15) 2-Y-O **£17,241** (£6,897; £5,172; £3,448; £1,724)

RPR

1 **Iron Fist (IRE)**[45] 3448 2-8-11 .... CSoumillon 5 100
(E J O'Neill) *mde all, hanging lft fr halfway, brought to stands' rail in str, jinked rt under rt-handed drive 1 1/2f out, pushed out fnl* **51/10**[1]

2 *1* **Lac Majeur (FR)**[8] 4622 2-8-11 .... JAuge 1 98
(Robert Collet, France)

3 *1/2* **Slickly Royal (FR)**[5] 2-8-11 .... RonanThomas 2 96
(P Demercastel, France)

4 *shd* **Tatsuya (FR)** 2-8-11 .... IMendizabal 6 96
(J-C Rouget, France)

5 *hd* **Ilie Nastase (FR)**[18] 2-8-11 .... TThulliez 3 96
(R Gibson, France)

6 *3/4* **Bomber Pilot (IRE)**[69] 2-8-11 .... OPeslier 4 94
(E Lellouche, France)

1m 41.7s 6 Ran SP% **16.4**
PARI-MUTUEL (including 1 Euro stake): WIN 6.10; PL 3.40, 2.50; SF 35.20.
Owner J C Fretwell **Bred** Pier House Stud **Trained** Averham Park, Notts

NOTEBOOK
Iron Fist(IRE) reluctantly made all the running and eventually won with a little in hand. Still very green, he was inclined to hang and eventually found himself coming up the stands' rail where he stumbled a furlong and a half out. This was a very promising effort and he has been entered in another Listed race at Craon next month.

4860a PRIX DE MEAUTRY LUCIEN BARRIERE (GROUP 3) 6f
2:20 (2:22) 3-Y-O+ **£27,586** (£11,034; £8,276; £5,517; £2,759)

RPR

1 **Indian Maiden (IRE)**[7] 4633 6-8-11 .... TThulliez 4 113
(M S Saunders) *held up in 7th, headway on inside to lead over 1f out, ridden out* **9/2**[2]

2 *1* **Eisteddfod**[21] 4191 5-9-1 .... (b) CSoumillon 6 114
(P F I Cole) *held up in 5th, ridden and headway on outside from 1 1/2f out, went 2nd inside final f, not pace of winner* **2/1**[1]

3 *snk* **Ratio**[24] 4095 8-9-1 .... TGillet 1 114
(J E Hammond, France) *held up in last, stayed on well on inside from 1f out to take 3rd on line* **11/2**[3]

4 *shd* **Abundance (USA)**[24] 4095 4-8-11 .... RonanThomas 5 109
(Mme C Head-Maarek, France) *close up, went 2nd briefly 1f out, one pace, lost 3rd on line* **7/1**

5 *1 1/2* **Mednaya (IRE)**[26] 3-8-8 .... FSpanu 7 105
(R Gibson, France) *raced in 5th, never a factor* **13/2**

6 *1/2* **Ricine (IRE)**[24] 4-9-2 .... FXBertras 3 108
(F Rohaut, France) *tracked leader in 3rd, one pace from over 1f out* **12/1**

7 *1* **Tycoon's Hill (IRE)**[21] 4191 7-9-1 .... OPeslier 8 104
(Robert Collet, France) *led to over 1f out, weakened* **7/1**

8 *3* **Protector (SAF)**[28] 5-9-1 .... MBlancpain 9 95
(Diego Lowther, France) *raced in 2nd til weakened 1 1/2f out* **25/1**

1m 13.8s **Going Correction** +0.475s/f (Yiel)
WFA 3 from 4yo+ 3lb 8 Ran SP% **116.8**
Speed ratings: 113,111,111,111,109 108,107,103
PARI-MUTUEL: WIN 7.00; PL 1.80, 1.50, 1.60; DF 8.90.
Owner Chris Scott & Peter Hall **Bred** Shadwell Estate Co Ltd **Trained** Green Ore, Somerset

NOTEBOOK
Indian Maiden(IRE) lifted her first Group race in style. Always going well within herself just behind the leading group, she took the advantage a furlong and a half out and was not put under pressure during the final half furlong. She keeps her form amazingly well and will soon be off to Chester for a Listed event before another trip to Ireland for the Renaissance Stakes at the Curragh. Another target is the Group 1 Prix de la Foret.
Eisteddfod, who raced up the centre of the track behind the leading group, was under pressure from a furlong and a half out but could not quicken in the same style as the winner. He wore blinkers for the first time and his jockey felt the gelding was unsuited by a lack of early pace.
Ratio made his effort late on up the stands' rail. He just failed to make it into second place and this veteran should still be capable of winning a Listed race in the future.
Abundance(USA) made his effort at the furlong marker with the runner-up and was only caught for third place in the final strides.

4861a GRAND PRIX DE DEAUVILLE LUCIEN BARRIERE (GROUP 2) 1m 4f 110y
2:50 (2:53) 3-Y-O+ **£78,621** (£30,345; £14,483; £9,655; £4,828)

RPR

1 **Irish Wells (FR)**[38] 3-8-6 .... DBoeuf 6 120
(F Rohaut, France) *tracked his pacemaker til led 1 1/2f out, ridden out, ran on well* **5/2**[2]

2 *2 1/2* **Groom Tesse**[70] 2693 5-9-3 .... (b) SLandi 8 116
(L Camici, Italy) *disputed 3rd, 3rd straight, chased winner final 1 1/2f, no impression* **6/1**

3 *1 1/2* **Marend (FR)**[22] 4169 5-9-3 .... OPeslier 4 114
(D Sepulchre, France) *held up, 6th straight, stayed on one pace final 1 1/2f* **6/1**

4 *hd* **Bellamy Cay**[44] 3516 4-9-6 .... CSoumillon 5 116
(A Fabre, France) *held up in close 5th to straight, never able to challenge* **13/8**[1]

5 *1/2* **Bannaby (FR)**[41] 3-8-6 .... (b) FXBertras 7 113
(F Rohaut, France) *led to 1 1/2f out, kept on steadily* **25/1**

6 *2 1/2* **Elasos (FR)**[18] 4-9-3 .... DBonilla 3 109
(D Sepulchre, France) *held up, 7th straight, never a factor* **33/1**

7 *8* **Tartouche**[24] 4079 5-9-0 .... IMendizabal 1 94
(Lady Herries) *disputed 3rd, 4th and ridden straight, soon beaten* **5/1**[3]

8 *nk* **Vatori (FR)**[18] 4-9-3 .... TThulliez 2 97
(P Demercastel, France) *last throughout* **8/1**

2m 50.1s **Going Correction** +0.65s/f (Yiel)
WFA 3 from 4yo+ 10lb 8 Ran SP% **129.8**
Speed ratings: 115,113,112,112,112 110,105,105
PARI-MUTUEL: WIN 4.30 (coupled with Bannaby); PL 1.70, 1.90, 1.80; DF 17.30.
Owner B Van Dalfsen **Bred** Eight International Racing Ltd **Trained** Sauvagnon, France

NOTEBOOK

Irish Wells(FR) is going from strength to strength and won this Group 2 event with comparative ease. He settled behind his excellent lead horse early on, took control of the event a furlong and a half out and was never likely to beaten from that point on. Connections will be tempted to run him in the Arc de Triomphe but his trainer would prefer to give him even more time to mature.

Groom Tesse was given every possible chance but could not quicken like the winner in the straight where he hung a little to the right. He always looked like holding second place and his jockey felt that the very soft ground was not an advantage.

Marend(FR) spent most of his time in sixth place before making progress up the centre of the track in the straight. He ran on one-paced but never looked like threatening the winner and runner-up.

Bellamy Cay was a disappointing favourite and never looked like taking a major role in the finish. In mid-division for most of this race, he made a little late progress but it was nevertheless a disappointing effort. His jockey felt that the testing ground was a definite disadvantage.

Tartouche appeared to be going well in third place down the back straight but she was under serious pressure rounding the final turn and was a spent force at the entrance to the straight. Her jockey felt that she might have still had her Goodwood victory in her legs.

4862a PRIX QUINCEY LUCIEN BARRIERE (GROUP 3) (STRAIGHT COURSE) 1m (R)

3:25 (3:24) 3-Y-O+ **£27,586** (£11,034; £8,276; £5,517; £2,759)

RPR

1 **Hello Sunday (FR)**[62] 2942 3-8-10 ..... C-PLemaire 7 111
(Mme C Head-Maarek, France) *raced in 4th on outside, went 2nd 1 1/2f out, joined leader 1f out, led 130 yards out, ran on strongly* **7/1**

2 1 **Racinger (FR)**[35] 3779 3-8-10 ..... DBonilla 2 109
(F Head, France) *pressed leader til led over 1 1/2f out, joined 1f out, headed 130 yards out, one pace* **9/2**[2]

3 2 ½ **Svedov (FR)**[77] 2490 5-9-6 ..... OPeslier 8 108
(E Lellouche, France) *raced in 6th, headway to go 3rd over 1f out, kept on same pace* **10/3**[1]

4 2 ½ **Sculpted (FR)**[29] 5-8-10 ..... CSoumillon 5 93
(H Steguweit, Germany) *raced in 5th, effort over 1 1/2f out, one pace* **11/2**[3]

5 1 ½ **Together (FR)**[28] 3991 6-8-12 .....(b) SMaillot 4 92
(Mme C Vergne, France) *held up in 7th, some headway on outside over 1 1/2f out but never a factor* **18/1**

6 2 **Folk Tune (IRE)**[24] 3-8-8 ..... IMendizabal 6 90
(J-C Rouget, France) *held up in last, always in rear* **7/1**

7 ¾ **Mister Charm (FR)**[29] 3969 6-8-13 ..... SCerdan 1 88
(J-C Rouget, France) *led to over 1 1/2f out, weakened* **9/2**[2]

8 1 **Nid D'Abeilles (IRE)**[83] 2313 4-9-4 ..... TThulliez 3 91
(P Bary, France) *race in 3rd til weakened 2f out* **6/1**

1m 42.3s **Going Correction** +0.475s/f (Yiel)
WFA 3 from 4yo+ 6lb **8** Ran SP% **119.4**
Speed ratings: 113,112,109,107,105 103,102,101
PARI-MUTUEL: WIN 6.80; PL 1.90, 1.50, 1.60; DF 11.60.
Owner Mme M Leurson **Bred** Earl Haras Du Camp Benard **Trained** Chantilly, France

NOTEBOOK

Hello Sunday(FR) made a forward move from a furlong and a half out and ran on gamely to the line. He was being brought back in distance here, and that proved an advantage, as did the cut in the ground. The Prix de Rond-Point (Daniel Wildenstein) is now on the cards for this colt.

Racinger(FR) was in second place virtually throughout the race. He did take the advantage for a short time a furlong and a half out but was then passed by the winner.

Svedov(FR), given a waiting ride, made some good late progress. He was putting in his best work at the finish and this performance bodes well for the future.

Sculpted(FR), given a waiting race, was fifth early on and brought with his run up the stands' rail. He never looked like finishing any closer.

OVREVOLL (R-H)

Sunday, August 27

OFFICIAL GOING: Soft

4863a ERIK O STEENS MEMORIAL (LISTED RACE) (F&M) 1m 4f

1:50 (12:00) 3-Y-O+ **£17,212** (£8,606; £4,131; £2,754; £1,721)

RPR

1 **Miss The Boat**[317] 5877 4-9-0 ..... PPinto 3 97
(A Lund, Norway) **15/4**[2]

2 4 **Souvenance**[20] 4212 3-8-13 ..... FJohansson 9 100
(Sir Mark Prescott) *led tl 5f out: one pce fr 3f out: tiring in fnl f* **1/2**[1]

3 ½ **La Petite Chinoise**[287] 6340 5-9-0 ..... MSantos 4 90
(L Kelp, Sweden) **119/10**

4 7 **Born To Win (CHI)** 4-9-0 ..... CLopez 5 80
(Annike Bye Nunez) **20/1**

5 hd **Lumen (FR)** 4-9-4 ..... DinaDanekilde 1 83
(O Larsen, Sweden) **59/10**[3]

6 24 **Lurifux (SWE)**[1832] 7-9-0 ..... FDiaz 6 43
(Maria ANdersson, Norway) **30/1**

7 10 **Athene (DEN)** 5-9-0 ..... KAndersen 8 28
(S Jensen, Denmark) **27/1**

8 12 **Rue D'Alsace**[723] 5280 4-9-0 ..... LHammer-Hansen 7 10
(B Olsen, Norway) **24/1**

2m 36.5s
WFA 3 from 4yo+ 10lb **8** Ran SP% **125.5**
(including one kroner stakes): WIN 4.75; PL 1.28, 1.18, 1.41; DF 5.66.
Owner Stall Fun Game **Bred** The Lavington Stud **Trained** Norway

NOTEBOOK

Souvenance was no match for the winner, who joined her on the final turn. The only one of her generation in this field, she was receiving only 1lb from her principal rivals. One or two of her efforts have suggested that she would benefit from an even longer trip but she was clearly tired in the final furlong here. Although the going was officially soft, the 5.6 reading on the local penetrometer meant that it was only just bad enough to qualify for that description.

4864a MARIT SVEAAS MINNELOP (GROUP 3) 1m 1f

2:20 (12:00) 3-Y-O+ **£61,962** (£20,654; £10,327; £6,196; £4,131)

RPR

1 **Binary File (USA)**[21] 8-9-4 ..... MSantos 5 102
(L Kelp, Sweden) *hld up in midfield: hdwy 2f out: str run fnl f: led cl home* **169/10**

2 1 **Crimson And Gold**[21] 4189 4-9-4 ..... FDiaz 10 100
(L Reutersköld, Sweden) *racd keenly: a cl up: led wl over 1f out tl no ex and ct cl home* **484/10**

3 1 **Special Envoy (FR)**[39] 3662 4-9-4 ..... J-MBreux 7 98
(N Clement, France) *chsd ldrs: rdn 2f out: r.o again fnl f* **37/10**[2]

4 ½ **Funny Legend (NOR)**[39] 3661 5-9-0 ..... FJohansson 9 93
(Wido Neuroth, Norway) *mid-div: hdwy over 2f out: ev ch ins fnl f: one pce* **97/10**

5 hd **Fly Society (DEN)**[21] 5-9-4 ..... KAndersen 11 97
(S Jensen, Denmark) *mid-div: hdwy over 1f out: nrest at fin* **13/1**

6 2 **Day Walker**[42] 3579 4-9-4 ..... CLopez 14 93
(Rune Haugen, Norway) *hld up in rr: hdwy over 1f out: fin strly but too much to do* **41/1**

7 ½ **Salt Track (ARG)**[24] 6-9-4 ..... ESki 13 92
(Niels Petersen, Norway) *a in tch: kpt on one pce fnl f* **17/1**

8 shd **Tiberius Caesar (FR)**[24] 6-9-4 ..... GSolis 6 92
(F Reutersköld, Sweden) *t.k.h: led tl wl over 1f out* **59/1**

9 2 **Jubilation**[43] 3563 7-9-6 ..... MMartinez 3 90
(F Reutersköld, Sweden) *in tch tl no ex fr wl over 1f out* **21/10**[1]

10 hd **Angel De Madrid (CHI)**[21] 5-9-4 ..... JJohansen 1 88
(R Hagen, Germany) *s.i.s: a bhd* **26/1**

11 5 **Storm Trooper (GER)**[24] 6-9-4 .....(b) AStarke 15 77
(Rune Haugen, Norway) *s.i.s: nvr nrr than mid-div* **13/1**

12 ½ **Firello (NOR)**[70] 6-9-4 ..... TJorgensen 8 76
(W Togersen, Norway) *chsd ldrs tl wknd fr 1/2-way* **16/1**

13 shd **Common World (USA)**[7] 4641 7-9-6 ..... TPO'Shea 4 78
(T Hogan, Ire) *s.i.s: a in rr* **82/10**[3]

14 2 ½ **Pecoiquen (CHI)**[89] 2123 5-9-4 .....(b) YvonneDurant 12 71
(F Castro, Sweden) *hld up early: rapid hdwy to press ldrs after 3f: wknd 4f out* **23/1**

15 7 **Babodana**[10] 4529 6-9-4 .....(v) TPQueally 2 57
(M H Tompkins) *s.s: a bhd* **14/1**

1m 50.8s (0.90) **15** Ran SP% **125.7**
WIN 17.92; PL 4.03, 12.51, 2.18; DF 596.75.
Owner Stald Milo & Light Valley Stud **Bred** Juddmonte Farms **Trained** Sweden

NOTEBOOK

Binary File(USA), three times a winner and Group 2 placed in his days with John Gosden, is enjoying his best season since leaving England. He produced a fine late burst here and has now scored in Sweden, Denmark and Norway this year.

Common World(USA), who disappointed at Leopardstown the previous weekend, again had conditions to suit but never got into the race after a slow start.

Babodana lost his chance at the start and never figured. He was allowed to come home in his own time.

4865 - (Foreign Racing) - See Raceform Interactive

4282 CHEPSTOW (L-H)

Monday, August 28

OFFICIAL GOING: Good

The overnight rain had eased the ground but officially it remained good and the jockeys thought that assessment was about right.
Wind: Moderate, half behind

4866 EBF / STRATSTONE JAGUAR - CARDIFF MAIDEN FILLIES' STKS 1m 14y

2:30 (2:32) (Class 5) 2-Y-O **£3,886** (£1,156; £577; £288) **Stalls** High

Form RPR

1 **Baroness Richter (IRE)** 2-9-0 ..... PatDobbs 1 72
(R Hannon) *s.i.s: hdwy over 2f out: r.o wl to ld ins fnl f* **25/1**

2 2 **Wild Thyme** 2-9-0 ..... RichardSmith 11 67
(R Hannon) *t.k.h in mid-div: styd on wl to go 2nd ins fnl f* **25/1**

000 3 1 **Boogie Dancer**[25] 4084 2-9-0 ..... FrancisNorton 12 65
(H S Howe) *led: rdn edgd lft and hdd ins fnl f* **33/1**

6 4 1 ½ **Fiumicino**[10] 4552 2-9-0 ..... ChrisCatlin 3 62
(M R Channon) *chsd ldrs: rdn and edgd lft appr fnl f: wknd ins* **5/1**[2]

25 5 ½ **Snake's Head**[25] 4084 2-9-0 ..... SebSanders 5 61
(J L Dunlop) *trckd ldrs: wnt 2nd 2f out: rdn and wknd ins fnl f* **1/1**[1]

0460 6 5 **Fasuby (IRE)**[14] 4436 2-9-0 53 ..... LPKeniry 9 49
(P D Evans) *chsd ldrs: rdn 3f out: wknd 2f out* **50/1**

7 shd **Isola Madre** 2-9-0 ..... KDarley 4 49
(M Johnston) *s.i.s: rdn over 3f out: wknd over 2f out* **8/1**[3]

8 1 **Divine Love (IRE)** 2-9-0 ..... RobbieFitzpatrick 8 46
(E J O'Neill) *mid-div: wknd over 2f out* **11/1**

9 hd **Capel Island (USA)** 2-9-0 ..... DaneO'Neill 13 46
(R Hannon) *slowly away: a bhd* **14/1**

10 nk **Polyquest (IRE)** 2-9-0 ..... JosedeSouza 2 45
(P F I Cole) *prom on outside to 1/2-way* **18/1**

0 11 5 **Sky Beam (USA)**[23] 4148 2-9-0 ..... IanMongan 7 34+
(J L Dunlop) *a towards rr: lost tch 2f out: eased* **33/1**

1m 35.73s (-0.27) **Going Correction** -0.15s/f (Firm) **11** Ran SP% **113.6**
Speed ratings (Par 91):95,93,92,90,90 85,84,83,83,83 78
CSF £493.42 TOTE £26.40: £3.80, £3.20, £4.70; EX 432.20.
Owner Richard Morecombe **Bred** Barronstown Stud And Pacelco S A **Trained** East Everleigh, Wilts

FOCUS

A one-two for Richard Hannon. This looked a fair event but the form is held down to an extent by the third and sixth.

NOTEBOOK

Baroness Richter(IRE) scored with a bit in hand on her debut. She managed to win despite being not too well drawn in one and could develop into a nice type for next season, as her breeding suggests she will be suited by further. Connections will not rush her this term, although she could be aimed at something a bit better later this autumn. (op 20-1)

Wild Thyme is a half-sister to several winners, notably the smart Arabian Story. She was staying on with some purpose but never really looked like getting to her stablemate. In a similar event, she could take some beating next time as she is bound to come on for the outing. (op 20-1)

Boogie Dancer casts a slight cloud over the bare form as she had shown next to nothing in three previous outings. In front against the stands' rail until drifting left in the closing stages, this represented an improved showing and she might be getting the hang of things now. Official explanation: jockey said filly hung left-handed (tchd 25-1)

Fiumicino once again ran well enough but she looks a longer-term prospect. (op 13-2 tchd 7-1)

Snake's Head basically had every chance but has not built on her promising debut and this extra furlong seemed to find her out. On the plus side, she is now eligible for handicaps, but a Group 1 Fillies' Mile entry looks fanciful on this showing. (op 5-4)

Fasuby(IRE), who has been beaten in a seller, is exposed and does hold down the form a little.

4867 EUROPEAN BREEDERS FUND/FORESTERS IN SUPPORT OF SPARKLE MAIDEN STKS (C&G) 1m 14y

3:05 (3:13) (Class 5) 2-Y-O £3,886 (£1,156; £577; £288) Stalls High

Form				RPR
0	1		**Mutadarrej (IRE)**[17] 4333 2-9-0 ... IanMongan 10 72 (J L Dunlop) *trckd ldrs: rdn and edgd lft bef led ins fnl f: all out* **7/1**	72
2	2	nk	**Teslin (IRE)**[11] 4534 2-9-0 ... KDarley 2 (M Johnston) *led tl hrd rdn and hdd ins fnl f: kpt on to line* **9/4**[1]	72
4	3	3/4	**Aaim To Prosper (IRE)**[10] 4572 2-9-0 ... ChrisCatlin 3 (M R Channon) *a.p: ev ch 1f out: no ex ins fnl f* **5/2**[2]	70
0	4	2	**Into Action**[24] 4103 2-9-0 ... DaneO'Neill 9 (R Hannon) *sn trckd ldrs: rdn over 1f out: kpt on one pce* **20/1**	66
	5	3/4	**Zoom One** 2-9-0 ... JosedeSouza 11 (M P Tregoning) *s.i.s: sn trckd ldrs: rdn half way: hung lft over 1f out: no ex ins fnl f* **20/1**	64
5	6	1 1/2	**Polish Red**[15] 4388 2-8-11 ... AdamKirby(3) 4 (G G Margarson) *in tch: rdn over 2f out: wknd ent fnl f* **13/2**[3]	61
	7	1 1/4	**Clarricien (IRE)** 2-9-0 ... RobbieFitzpatrick 12 (E J O'Neill) *in tch: rdn over 2f out: wknd ins fnl f* **33/1**	58
	8	2 1/2	**Seteem (USA)** 2-9-0 ... PatDobbs 13 (M P Tregoning) *in rr: mde sme late hdwy* **14/1**	52
0	9	11	**Franchoek (IRE)**[11] 4526 2-9-0 ... RobertHavlin 1 (A King) *mid-div: wknd 2f out* **25/1**	28
	10	3 1/2	**Always Sparkle (CAN)** 2-9-0 ... FrancisFerris 8 (B Palling) *mid-div to 1/2-way: sn bhd* **16/1**	21
	11	6	**Irish Poet (IRE)** 2-9-0 ... FrancisNorton 7 (E J O'Neill) *v.s.a: a bhd* **16/1**	7
00	12	3	**Last Dog Standing (IRE)**[44] 3545 2-9-0 ... RobertMiles 5 (B G Powell) *slowly away: a bhd* **50/1**	1
	13	45	**Almudo (IRE)** 2-9-0 ... AdrianMcCarthy 6 (B Palling) *wnt sharply lft s: sn bhd: t.o* **40/1**	—

1m 35.87s (-0.13) **Going Correction** -0.15s/f (Firm) **13** Ran SP% **124.3**
Speed ratings (Par 94):94,93,92,90,90 88,87,84,73,70 64,61,16
CSF £22.22 TOTE £10.20: £3.70, £1.50, £1.80; EX 39.00.
Owner Hamdan Al Maktoum **Bred** Shadwell Estate Company Limited **Trained** Arundel, W Sussex

FOCUS
This juvenile maiden for colts and geldings was won in a time fractionally slower than the fillies' event, and they looked longer-term prospects. It has been rated through the third.

NOTEBOOK
Mutadarrej(IRE), who is out of an unraced half-sister to Arc winner Sakhee, had shown some promise on his debut at Newmarket and the step up to a mile clearly suited him. Given that his stable's youngsters seem to progress with racing, he can only go on from here. (op 10-1)
Teslin(IRE) filled the same position as on his debut and did not go down without a fight, only headed inside the last and making the winner work all the way to the line. On this showing, he should be placed to go one better shortly. (tchd 5-2 in a place)
Aaim To Prosper(IRE), upped in trip, ran another good race and he can soon be found an opportunity to get his head in front. (op 7-2 tchd 4-1 in a place)
Into Action plugged on and now needs another outing before being eligible for a nursery rating. In time he is likely to need middle distances. (op 33-1)
Zoom One fared best of the newcomers and was doing his best work in the closing stages. He should stay further and can only benefit from the experience. (op 16-1)
Polish Red Official explanation: jockey said colt was very unbalanced
Irish Poet(IRE) Official explanation: jockey said colt stumbled twice
Almudo(IRE) Official explanation: jockey said colt shied away from other runners after start and hung left-handed

4868 V DRINKS RED VODKA SUPPORTS S.I.A. H'CAP 2m 49y

3:40 (3:41) (Class 6) (0-55,55) 3-Y-O £3,238 (£963; £481; £240) Stalls Low

Form				RPR
-040	1		**Skit**[16] 4362 3-8-7 **40** ow1 ... RobbieFitzpatrick 7 (W M Brisbourne) *trckd ldr: led 3f out: drvn out* **16/1**	47
0556	2	2 1/2	**The Spread**[11] 4530 3-9-3 **50** ... FrancisNorton 1 (M Blanshard) *trckd ldrs: rdn over 2f out: chsd wnr fr over 1f out* **13/2**[3]	54
-400	3	3	**Overlook**[17] 4330 3-9-8 **55** ...(v[1]) SebSanders 2 (A M Balding) *hld up in mid-div: hdwy over 4f out: kpt on one pce fnl 3f* **11/2**[2]	55
-504	4	8	**Persian Conqueror (IRE)**[24] 4111 3-9-1 **48** ... IanMongan 11 (J L Dunlop) *slowly away: rdn and wnt mid-div 5f out: sn rdn: no hdwy fnl 3f* **2/1**[1]	43+
0054	5	5	**Rockatorri**[12] 4491 3-8-7 **43** ow3 ...(v[1]) AdamKirby(3) 6 (G G Margarson) *in tch: rdn over 3f out: wknd over 2f out* **8/1**	28
000	6	1	**Suzuki (IRE)**[21] 4210 3-9-5 **52** ... DaneO'Neill 4 (H Morrison) *in rr: effrt 3f out: sn btn* **7/1**	36
0500	7	3	**Indian Girl**[35] 3785 3-9-3 **50** ... ChrisCatlin 5 (M R Channon) *bhd: sme hdwy 4f out: wknd 3f out* **12/1**	30
0000	8	1 1/4	**King's College (USA)**[3] 4758 3-9-1 **48** ...(v) PatDobbs 8 (P D Evans) *sn led: hdd 3f out: wknd qckly* **14/1**	27
400	9	3	**Naval Hero (IRE)**[24] 4111 3-8-8 **46** ... KevinGhunowa(5) 10 (Mrs L Williamson) *slowly away: hdwy 6f out: wknd over 2f out* **22/1**	21
-000	10	16 1/2	**Queen Of Diamonds (IRE)**[108] 1648 3-9-1 **48** ... RobertHavlin 9 (Mrs P N Dutfield) *prom tl rdn and wknd 5f out: t.o* **16/1**	3
0000	11	31	**Flying Penne**[13] 1726 3-8-12 **45** ... LPKeniry 3 (R Curtis) *hld up: a bhd: eased 2f out: t.o* **25/1**	—

3m 43.29s (3.89) **Going Correction** +0.15s/f (Good) **11** Ran SP% **120.0**
Speed ratings (Par 98):96,94,93,89,86 86,84,84,82,74 58
CSF £118.84 CT £660.03 TOTE £23.80: £5.00, £2.50, £1.90; EX 478.70.
Owner A P Burgoyne **Bred** Lord Rothschild **Trained** Great Ness, Shropshire

FOCUS
A very moderate bunch in this weak staying handicap, contested entirely by maidens, and they finished well spread out. A modest winning time too and the race has been rated through the runner-up.

4869 BET365 CALL 08000 322 365 H'CAP 1m 2f 36y

4:15 (4:15) (Class 6) (0-55,54) 3-Y-O+ £3,238 (£963; £481; £240) Stalls Low

Form				RPR
3141	1		**Good Article (IRE)**[17] 4332 5-9-7 **50** ... GeorgeBaker 15 (D K Ivory) *hld up in rr: gd hdwy over 3f out: edgdd lft bef ld over 1f out: rdn out* **4/1**[1]	63+
0666	2	1 1/2	**Native American**[5] 4709 4-9-9 **52** ... RobertHavlin 6 (T D McCarthy) *chsd ldrs: wnt 2nd over 3f out: kpt on one pce fnl f* **12/1**	59
0542	3	1/2	**Ruling Reef**[12] 4497 4-9-3 **46** ... DavidKinsella 7 (M D I Usher) *mid-div: hdwy 3f out: kpt one one pce fnl f* **6/1**[2]	52
0050	4	hd	**Oakley Absolute**[17] 4332 4-9-11 **54** ... DaneO'Neill 5 (R Hannon) *a.p: sltly hmpd and swtchd rt over 1f out: r.o one pce* **12/1**	60
4653	5	2 1/2	**Danish Monarch**[32] 3862 5-9-3 **46** ... ChrisCatlin 12 (David Pinder) *chsd ldr after 2f: led 4f out: hdd over 1f out: no ex* **14/1**	47
6600	6	3/4	**Bubbling Fun**[5] 4709 5-8-10 **46** ... SladeO'Hara(7) 16 (T Wall) *racd wd on outside: in rr tl hdwy and edgd lft over 3f out: wknd appr fnl f* **28/1**	45
6020	7	1/2	**Yenaled**[31] 3894 9-9-7 **50** ... RobertMiles 4 (J M Bradley) *hld up: hdwy on ins 4f out: swtchd rt 2f out: nt qckn appr fnl f* **11/1**	49
0034	8	9	**Will The Till**[17] 4325 4-9-4 **52** ...(p) KevinGhunowa(5) 8 (J M Bradley) *mid-div: wknd wl over 2f out* **8/1**[3]	33
0/00	9	1/2	**Billy Bathwick (IRE)**[9] 4585 9-8-10 **46** ... BarrySavage(7) 13 (J M Bradley) *mid-div tl qckly lost pl 3f out* **33/1**	26
0104	10	1 3/4	**Aberdeen Park**[14] 4439 4-9-6 **52** ...(b) RichardKingscote(3) 3 (Mrs H Sweeting) *v.s.a: sme hdwy after 3f but nvr on terms* **16/1**	29
6003	11	nk	**Weet A Head (IRE)**[85] 1566 5-9-11 **54** ... LPKeniry 9 (R Hollinshead) *in tch tl wknd over 3f out* **14/1**	31
0205	12	4	**Silver Court**[12] 4497 4-9-3 **46** ... FrancisNorton 1 (A W Carroll) *in tch: wkng whn hmpd over 3f out* **12/1**	15
0004	13	1 1/2	**Ronaldo**[6] 4672 3-9-2 **53** ...(b[1]) PatDobbs 2 (A M Hales) *chsd ldr early: wknd qckly over 2f out* **33/1**	19
0056	14	6	**Seldemosa**[9] 4585 5-9-4 **47** ... RobbieFitzpatrick 11 (M S Saunders) *a in rr* **14/1**	2
0304	15	6	**Haiti Dancer**[22] 4176 3-8-13 **53** ...(v) AdamKirby(3) 10 (C G Cox) *led tl hdd 4f out: wkng whn hmpd sn after* **6/1**[2]	—

2m 10.57s (0.67) **Going Correction** +0.15s/f (Good)
WFA 3 from 4yo+ 8lb **15** Ran SP% **126.3**
Speed ratings (Par 101):103,101,101,101,99 98,98,91,90,89 89,85,84,79,75
CSF £54.42 CT £295.30 TOTE £5.70: £2.20, £5.50, £3.10; EX 80.50.
Owner T G N Burrage **Bred** T G N Burrage **Trained** Radlett, Herts

FOCUS
An ordinary handicap. Sound form, rated through the runner-up. The winner was value for a bit extra.
Aberdeen Park Official explanation: jockey said filly was slowly away

4870 ETHEL GOLD MEMORIAL H'CAP (SPONSORED BY PICKWICK BOOKMAKERS) 7f 16y

4:50 (4:50) (Class 6) (0-65,65) 3-Y-O+ £3,238 (£963; £481; £240) Stalls High

Form				RPR
2322	1		**Red Rudy**[3] 4772 4-9-10 **63** ... FrancisNorton 12 (A W Carroll) *a in tch: rdn over 2f out: styd on to ld ins fnl f* **11/4**[1]	75
0024	2	1 1/2	**Unlimited**[67] 2785 4-9-6 **59** ... RobertHavlin 13 (R Simpson) *a.p: ev ch fr 2f out tl nt qckn ins fnl f* **16/1**	67
6600	3	3/4	**Bathwick Emma (IRE)**[8] 4627 3-9-2 **63** ... PatrickMathers(3) 11 (P D Evans) *chsd ldr: rdn and no ex ins fnl f* **25/1**	67
1033	4	1/2	**Stamford Blue**[16] 4364 5-9-0 **60** ...(b) TolleyDean(7) 14 (R A Harris) *mid-div: rdn and hdwy 2f out: styd on one pce* **6/1**[2]	65
045	5	hd	**My Michelle**[3] 4772 5-9-2 **55** ... FrancisFerris 9 (B Palling) *mid-div: rdn and swtchd rt over 2f out: styd on one pce* **12/1**	63+
4314	6	1 1/4	**Charlie Bear**[15] 4399 5-9-5 **58** ... AdrianMcCarthy 8 (Miss Z C Davison) *in tch: rdn and fdd appr fnl f* **7/1**[3]	59
3200	7	shd	**Danielle's Lad**[5] 4706 10-9-2 **62** ... KylieManser(7) 16 (B Palling) *led tl rdn and hdd over 1f out: fdd ins fnl f* **20/1**	63
5000	8	hd	**Tregarron**[126] 1201 5-9-0 **58** ... KevinGhunowa(5) 10 (P A Blockley) *mid-div: rdn 2f out and n.d after* **20/1**	58
6506	9	hd	**Currency**[3] 4772 9-9-5 **65** ... BarrySavage(7) 7 (J M Bradley) *mid-div: rdn over 2f out: no hdwy after* **16/1**	65
4000	10	1	**Royal Citadel (IRE)**[35] 3793 3-9-3 **64** ...(b[1]) AdamKirby(3) 2 (C G Cox) *racd alone far side: rdn 2f out and no ch after* **20/1**	59+
3355	11	3/4	**Ten Shun**[31] 3898 3-9-2 **60** ...(v) PatDobbs 1 (P D Evans) *prom in centre tl rdn and wknd over 2f out* **14/1**	53
6505	12	1 1/4	**Full Spate**[17] 4324 11-9-4 **57** ... DaneO'Neill 3 (J M Bradley) *slowly away: a bhd* **12/1**	49
00-0	13	4	**Cleveland**[111] 1570 4-9-5 **58** ... LPKeniry 4 (R Hollinshead) *in tch tl rdn and wknd 2f out* **33/1**	40
1415	14	1/2	**Mister Elegant**[2] 4795 4-9-6 **59** ... ChrisCatlin 6 (J L Spearing) *prom tl rdn and wknd qckly wl over 1f out* **15/2**	39
50-0	15	5	**Sharp Duo (IRE)**[182] 531 3-9-4 **62** ... RobbieFitzpatrick 15 (M S Saunders) *a bhd* **50/1**	27
3P00	P		**Storm Centre**[33] 3845 4-9-7 **60** ... GeorgeBaker 5 (Miss J S Davis) *bhd whn p.u and dismntd over 2f out* **33/1**	—

1m 22.19s (-1.11) **Going Correction** -0.15s/f (Firm)
WFA 3 from 4yo+ 5lb **16** Ran SP% **125.0**
Speed ratings (Par 101):100,98,97,96,96 95,95,94,94,93 92,91,86,86,80 —
CSF £47.10 CT £729.10 TOTE £3.10: £1.20, £5.30, £5.40, £2.00; EX 123.30.
Owner Winding Wheel Partnership **Bred** Mrs C J Tribe **Trained** Cropthorne, Worcs

FOCUS
An average but fairly competitive handicap and the form looks solid, despite the fact that high numbers seemed favoured.
Storm Centre Official explanation: jockey said gelding pulled up distressed

4871 THE CROWN AT WHITEBROOK H'CAP 1m 14y

5:25 (5:26) (Class 5) (0-70,71) 3-Y-O+ £5,505 (£1,637; £818; £408) Stalls High

Form				RPR
0-52	1		**Veiled Applause**[9] 4591 3-8-11 **62** ... SebSanders 13 (R M Beckett) *a in tch on ins: rdn to ld ins fnl f: drvn out* **3/1**[1]	72
0004	2	1 3/4	**Elidore**[18] 4288 6-8-13 **58** ... FrancisFerris 3 (B Palling) *led tl rdn and hdd ins fnl f* **10/1**	65+
5350	3	1	**Lockstock (IRE)**[61] 2969 8-8-11 **56** ...(p) RobbieFitzpatrick 8 (M S Saunders) *trckd ldr tl rdn and hdd and no ex ins fnl f* **10/1**	61
2016	4	2 1/2	**Final Tune (IRE)**[23] 4144 3-8-13 **64** ... ChrisCatlin 15 (Miss M E Rowland) *a in tch: drvn and kpt on one pce fnl f* **12/1**	62
2320	5	1 3/4	**Foolish Groom**[45] 3469 5-9-0 **59** ...(v) LPKeniry 16 (R Hollinshead) *in tch: rdn and wknd appr fnl f* **8/1**[3]	54
4155	6	3/4	**Nashaab (USA)**[34] 3812 9-9-6 **65** ...(v) GeorgeBaker 10 (P D Evans) *bhd: rdn 1/2-way: hdwy over 2f out but nvr nr to chal* **17/2**	58
6103	7	3/4	**What-A-Dancer (IRE)**[6] 4674 9-9-4 **63** ...(b) AdrianMcCarthy 2 (R A Harris) *chsd ldrs on outside tl rdn and one pce fr over 1f out* **9/2**[2]	55
0000	8	3/4	**Lord Of Dreams (IRE)**[31] 3918 4-9-3 **62** ... FrankieMcDonald 6 (D W P Arbuthnot) *in tch: rdn over 2f out: one pce after* **12/1**	52
0001	9	1 3/4	**Anduril**[7] 4653 5-9-9 **71** 6ex ...(b) PatrickMathers(3) 11 (Miss M E Rowland) *fly-jmpd leaving stalls: bhd sme hdwy 2f out but nvr on terms* **8/1**[3]	57
-550	10	4	**Mayadeen (IRE)**[23] 4149 4-9-11 **70** ... RobertHavlin 4 (J G M O'Shea) *a towards rr* **33/1**	47
4-40	11	1/2	**Zalzaar (IRE)**[35] 3794 4-9-0 **62** ... AdamKirby(3) 9 (C G Cox) *prom tl wknd wl over 1f out* **14/1**	37

1500 **12** 1/2 **Right Ted (IRE)**[18] 4286 3-8-12 **70**................................ SladeO'Hara(7) 5 43
(T Wall) *chsd ldrs: rdn over 2f out: wknd over 1f out* **28/1**
43-0 **13** *shd* **Bathwick Rox (IRE)**[231] 69 3-8-3 **61** ow3................. TolleyDean(7) 14 34
(P D Evans) *prom to 1/2-way: sn rdn: wknd over 2f out* **33/1**
-064 **14** *11* **Weet For Ever (USA)**[53] 3219 3-8-11 **62**......................... DaneO'Neill 12 10
(P A Blockley) *s.i.s: t.k.h: rdn and wknd wl over 2f out* **25/1**

1m 34.09s (-1.91) **Going Correction** -0.15s/f (Firm)
WFA 3 from 4yo+ 6lb **14** Ran SP% **129.3**
Speed ratings (Par 103):103,101,100,97,96 95,94,93,92,88 87,87,86,75
CSF £35.53 CT £290.03 TOTE £4.10: £2.10, £2.30, £3.80; EX 46.30.
Owner The Wright And Wrong Partnership **Bred** P J McCalmont **Trained** Whitsbury, Hants

FOCUS
Another run-of-the-mill handicap and sound but modest form. The winner is going the right way.
Lord Of Dreams(IRE) Official explanation: jockey said colt hung left-handed
Anduril Official explanation: jockey said gelding turned its head right when blind came off and missed the break

4872 AVONBRIDGE AT WHITSBURY STUD H'CAP 5f 16y
5:55 (5:57) (Class 6) (0-55,58) 3-Y-O+ **£3,238** (£963; £481; £240) **Stalls** High

Form RPR
2332 **1** **Talcen Gwyn (IRE)**[6] 4675 4-9-11 **55**........................(v) DavidKinsella 11 67
(M F Harris) *sn led: racd stands' rail: mde rest: in command fnl f* **4/1**[1]
3400 **2** *1* **Flying Tackle**[7] 4655 8-9-1 **48**..............................(v) AdamKirby(3) 2 56
(I W McInnes) *towards rr tl hdwy 1/2-way: drvn and r.o to go 2nd ins fnl f* **11/1**
0630 **3** *nk* **Seven No Trumps**[20] 4232 9-8-13 **50**........................... BarrySavage(7) 1 57
(J M Bradley) *racd on outside: hdwy 2f out: r.o fnl f* **8/1**[3]
1041 **4** 1/2 **Sir Loin**[8] 4636 5-9-7 **58** 6ex..................................(v) DanielleMcCreery(7) 5 63
(N Tinkler) *broke wl: sn hdd: styd prom: rdn 1/2-way: nt qckn fnl f* **9/2**[2]
0001 **5** *hd* **Great Belief (IRE)**[18] 4306 4-9-9 **53**........................ RobbieFitzpatrick 10 57
(T D McCarthy) *wnt rt s: trckd ldrs: rdn 2f out: nt qckn fnl f* **14/1**
1425 **6** *hd* **King Egbert (FR)**[13] 4462 5-9-4 **55**................................ TolleyDean(7) 14 59+
(A W Carroll) *bhd: rdn 2f out: r.o wl fnl f: nvr nrr* **9/2**[2]
5406 **7** *nk* **Zimbali**[6] 4675 4-9-3 **47**.. JosedeSouza 12 50
(J M Bradley) *towards rr: mde sme late hdwy* **16/1**
0004 **8** 3/4 **Campeon (IRE)**[33] 3833 4-9-5 **49**...............................(b) FrancisNorton 3 49
(J M Bradley) *prom tl rdn and wknd fnl f* **8/1**[3]
0005 **9** 1/2 **Task Complete**[18] 4287 3-9-2 **48**..........................(b) FrankieMcDonald 16 46
(Jean-Rene Auvray) *a towards rr* **66/1**
0360 **10** *shd* **Enjoy The Buzz**[46] 3438 7-9-9 **53**................................. DaneO'Neill 7 51
(J M Bradley) *mid-div: rdn 2f out: one pce after* **8/1**[3]
5546 **11** 3/4 **Snow Wolf**[18] 4278 5-8-12 **49**.................................(p) PietroRomeo(7) 4 44
(J M Bradley) *prom: rdn 1/2-way wknd over 1f out* **25/1**
0005 **12** *2* **Wendals**[12] 4495 3-9-9 **55**...(b[1]) SebSanders 9 43
(Rae Guest) *in tch: rdn 1/2-way: wknd 1f out* **20/1**
0060 **13** *1* **All About Him (USA)**[9] 4587 3-9-2 **48**................................ LPKeniry 13 32
(N I M Rossiter) *a bhd* **50/1**

59.38 secs (-0.22) **Going Correction** -0.15s/f (Firm)
WFA 3 from 4yo+ 2lb **13** Ran SP% **122.6**
Speed ratings (Par 101):95,93,92,92,91 91,91,89,89,88 87,84,82
CSF £48.54 CT £357.21 TOTE £5.30: £1.90, £3.30, £3.20; EX 72.60 Place 6 £1,159.02, Place 5 £27.27..
Owner D K Watkins **Bred** Paul Smyth **Trained** Edgcote, Northants

FOCUS
A moderate sprint and a modest winning time. The stands' side rail seemed the place to be, although the placed horses raced more in the centre, and the form is rated through the runner-up.
T/Plt: £5,320.40 to a £1 stake. Pool: £51,017.90. 7.00 wining tickets. T/Qpdt: £30.00 to a £1 stake. Pool: £2,953.00. 72.65 winning tickets. JS

4073 EPSOM (L-H)
Monday, August 28
OFFICIAL GOING: Good to soft (soft in places on round course)
Wind: Light across Weather: Fine, heavy shower after Race 4 (4.00)

4873 BRITANIACREST RECYCLING EBF MEDIAN AUCTION MAIDEN STKS 7f
2:15 (2:17) (Class 5) 2-Y-O **£4,533** (£1,348; £674; £336) **Stalls** Low

Form RPR
4 **1** **Spirit Of The Mist (IRE)**[12] 4487 2-9-3 .... JohnEgan 2 77
(T J Pitt) *mde all: rdn over 2f out: edgd lft over 1f out: kpt on wl* **15/2**[3]
3 **2** 1 1/4 **Silca Key**[10] 4553 2-8-9 .... EdwardCreighton(3) 1 69
(M R Channon) *trckd ldrs: 3rd st: chsd wnr on inner 2f out: nt clr run over 1f out: hld whn nt clr run last 100yds: kpt on* **3/1**[2]
3 *nk* **Jaasoos (IRE)** 2-9-3 .... PhilipRobinson 3 73+
(M A Jarvis) *s.s: t.k.h and hld up: last st: prog over 2f out: disp 2nd over 1f out: rdn and kpt on same pce* **15/2**[3]
3 **4** *4* **Loch Tay**[29] 3976 2-9-3 .... LDettori 5 63
(M L W Bell) *trckd wnr after 1f: rdn wl over 2f out: lost 2nd 2f out: hanging and btn over 1f out* **1/1**[1]
0 **5** 1 3/4 **Distiller (IRE)**[23] 4161 2-9-3 .... MartinDwyer 6 59
(W R Muir) *t.k.h: hld up: 5th st: effrt 3f out: hanging and nt qckn 2f out: wknd over 1f out* **33/1**
00 **6** 1 3/4 **Dan Tucker**[14] 4428 2-9-3 .... TPQueally 7 55
(B J Meehan) *dwlt: in rr: 6th st: effrt on outer 3f out: nt handling trck and struggling 2f out: wknd* **33/1**
5 **7** 3 1/2 **Oakley Heffert (IRE)**[14] 4428 2-9-3 .... RyanMoore 4 46
(R Hannon) *chsd wnr for 1f: 4th st: lost pl over 2f out: wknd sn after* **11/1**

1m 26.35s (2.40) **Going Correction** +0.30s/f (Good) **7** Ran SP% **112.7**
Speed ratings (Par 94):98,96,96,91,89 87,83
CSF £29.35 TOTE £9.30: £2.80, £2.00; EX 34.30.
Owner Ruth Stuart & Willie McKay **Bred** Newlands House Stud **Trained** Bawtry, S Yorks

FOCUS
This looked a reasonable maiden though inevitably a few did not handle the track. The pace was decent and despite the ground being on the easy side, the field stayed on the inside in the home straight. The race is rated around the runner-up and sixth.

NOTEBOOK
Spirit Of The Mist(IRE) confirmed the promise of his Sandown debut and made every yard under a positive ride. His sire won the Diomed around here, so perhaps it was no surprise that he handled the track as well as he did and he should continue to improve. (op 8-1)
Silca Key ◆, another to show promise on her debut, tried to make her effort between the winner and the inside rail throughout the last couple of furlongs, but never quite had enough room and would have given the winner a lot more to think about otherwise. Her turn is merely delayed. (op 7-2)
Jaasoos(IRE) ◆, a 160,000euros half-brother to three winners including Sonorous and Kirov King, was the only newcomer in the field and it showed early. After missing the break, he collided with the inside rail as he took a fierce grip and then looked very awkward rounding Tattenham Corner, so the fact that he managed to stay on into third shows that he possesses some ability. He should do much better on a more conventional track with this debut under his belt. (op 8-1)
Loch Tay on the face of it was disappointing after holding every chance, especially in view of the promise he showed on his Newmarket debut, but he looked very unhappy on the camber in the home straight and it is not difficult to forgive a horse a below-par effort on this track. (op 4-5 tchd 8-11 and 11-10 and 6-5 in places)
Distiller(IRE) never looked happy on this track and is unlikely to show his true potential until he is handicapped. His pedigree suggests this is about as far as he wants.
Dan Tucker had a real problem handling Tattenham Corner and never offered a threat. His previous efforts suggest he is of limited ability, though nurseries become an option for him now.

4874 CHANTILLY H'CAP 6f
2:50 (2:51) (Class 5) (0-75,74) 3-Y-O **£5,181** (£1,541; £770; £384) **Stalls** High

Form RPR
4612 **1** **Overwing (IRE)**[5] 4691 3-9-3 **70**.. LDettori 4 77
(R M H Cowell) *mde all and led field to nr side in st: drvn over 1f out: styd on wl* **5/1**[3]
0612 **2** 3/4 **Spearit (IRE)**[5] 4703 3-9-7 **74**.. JohnEgan 5 79
(D R C Elsworth) *hld up: 5th and hanging lft st: rdn and effrt 2f out: chsd wnr jst ins fnl f: no imp last 75yds* **3/1**[2]
2363 **3** 1 1/2 **Xaluna Bay (IRE)**[9] 4589 3-9-7 **74**.................................... MartinDwyer 6 74
(W R Muir) *chsd wnr: rdn to chal over 2f out: no ex and btn 1f out* **7/1**
1453 **4** 2 1/2 **Sleeping Storm (IRE)**[10] 4562 3-9-0 **74**................................ KMay(7) 7 67
(B J Meehan) *hld up in tch: 4th st: lost pl over 2f out: sn rdn: nt qckn and no prog after* **15/2**
2442 **5** 1 1/4 **Patavium Prince (IRE)**[10] 4562 3-9-3 **70**.......................... RyanMoore 1 59
(J R Best) *hld up: last but wl in tch st: effrt towards centre 2f out: no prog over 1f out: wknd fnl f* **2/1**[1]
000 **6** 3/4 **Laith (IRE)**[1] 4841 3-8-10 **66**................................... EdwardCreighton(3) 3 53
(Miss V Haigh) *pressed ldng pair: wnt towards centre in st: rdn over 2f out: wknd fnl f* **12/1**
5200 **7** *4* **Danny The Dip**[11] 4532 3-7-12 **56** ow1......................... MarcHalford(5) 2 31
(J J Bridger) *chsd ldrs: 5th st: hung lft towards centre over 2f out: wknd over 1f out* **20/1**

1m 11.58s (0.95) **Going Correction** +0.30s/f (Good) **7** Ran SP% **111.7**
Speed ratings (Par 100):105,104,102,98,97 96,90
CSF £19.39 CT £101.63 TOTE £4.30: £2.60, £2.10; EX 15.80.
Owner Keith Robinson & Ian Robinson **Bred** Noel Finegan And Noel Cogan **Trained** Six Mile Bottom, Cambs

FOCUS
A decent little handicap and the winning time was fair for a race of its type. An interesting pattern to the race as, apart from cutting the corner turning for home, the field stayed against the outside rail throughout and the winner took full advantage. The quartet that came closest to the stands' rail finished in front of the trio that raced more towards the centre. The race is rated negatively through the runner-up.

4875 TOTESPORT.COM SPRINT STKS (H'CAP) 5f
3:25 (3:26) (Class 2) (0-105,105) 3-Y-O+
£18,696 (£5,598; £2,799; £1,401; £699; £175) **Stalls** High

Form RPR
0050 **1** **Bond City (IRE)**[23] 4128 4-9-5 **99**.. LDettori 8 108
(B Smart) *mostly pressed ldr and racd towards nr side: rdn to ld ins fnl f: styd on wl* **9/2**[1]
0504 **2** 1/2 **Cape Royal**[16] 4360 6-8-10 **90**.......................................(bt) RyanMoore 11 97
(J M Bradley) *sn led and grabbed nr side rail: rdn over 1f out: hdd ins fnl f: kpt on but a hld* **5/1**[2]
0050 **3** *nk* **Jayanjay**[2] 4811 7-8-6 **86** oh6....................................... PhilipRobinson 12 92
(Miss B Sanders) *racd against nr side rail: chsd ldrs: rdn 2f out: styd on to take 3rd fnl f: nrst fin* **14/1**
0036 **4** *1* **Night Prospector**[2] 4796 6-8-1 **86** oh5..................... RobynBrisland(5) 10 89+
(G L Moore) *settled in midfield: lost pl and in rr 2f out: pushed along and r.o fnl f: nvr nrr* **12/1**
2003 **5** 3/4 **Texas Gold**[16] 4360 8-9-5 **99**.. MartinDwyer 4 99+
(W R Muir) *racd towards outer and nvr on terms: rdn 1/2-way: styd on fnl f: no ch* **8/1**
4206 **6** 3/4 **Caribbean Coral**[12] 4468 7-8-6 **86** oh3.............................(v) TPQueally 5 83
(J J Quinn) *dwlt: racd towards outer and nvr on terms: rdn 2f out: kpt on fnl f: no ch* **14/1**
0600 **6** *dht* **Glenviews Youngone (IRE)**[24] 4102 3-7-13 **86** oh5... LiamJones(5) 13 83
(Peter Grayson) *hanging lft thrght: chsd ldrs nr side: hung lft to outer fr 1/2-way: fdd fnl f* **20/1**
0000 **8** *nk* **Corridor Creeper (FR)**[25] 4080 9-9-6 **105**..................(p) TravisBlock(5) 7 101
(J M Bradley) *pressed ldng pair: pushed along over 1f out: wknd fnl f* **8/1**
4601 **9** *nk* **Peace Offering (IRE)**[13] 4461 6-8-13 **100**................ VictoriaBehan(7) 3 95
(D Nicholls) *racd on outer and nvr on terms w ldrs: n.d fr over 1f out* **7/1**
2-00 **10** *1* **Musadif (USA)**[23] 4128 8-9-6 **103**..................(t) EdwardCreighton(3) 6 94
(R A Kvisla) *rrd s: nt gng wl in last and nvr a factor: styd on last 100yds* **33/1**
1202 **11** 1 1/4 **Mutamarres**[9] 4601 3-8-4 **93**..(v) PatrickHills(7) 2 80
(Sir Michael Stoute) *racd on outer and nvr on terms: nvr a factor* **6/1**[3]
1600 **12** 1 1/4 **Zowington**[58] 3092 4-8-11 **91**.. OscarUrbina 9 73
(C F Wall) *s.i.s: nvr beyond midfield: hanging lft and wknd over 1f out* **9/1**

55.72 secs (0.04) **Going Correction** +0.25s/f (Good)
WFA 3 from 4yo+ 2lb **12** Ran SP% **122.6**
Speed ratings (Par 109):109,108,107,106,104 103,103,103,102,101 99,97
CSF £27.48 CT £301.37 TOTE £6.50: £2.30, £1.70, £3.10; EX 21.10.
Owner R C Bond **Bred** David Ryan **Trained** Hambleton, N Yorks

FOCUS
A very decent sprint handicap, but not as competitive as it might have been thanks to the bias held by those that were drawn high and who were therefore able to race closest to the stands' rail. The time was decent and the race is rated around the first three.

NOTEBOOK
Bond City(IRE), off the same mark as when third in this last year and well supported in the market following his fine effort in the Stewards' Cup, broke well from his middling draw and was therefore able to edge over to his right and race handily just one off the stands' rail. Once asked for maximum effort, he found enough to edge out the runner-up who had the advantage of the rail which makes this effort a little bit better than it looks. There had been a question mark over him on this easier ground, so the fact that he handled it so well is encouraging for the future. (tchd 5-1)
Cape Royal, runner-up in this last year off a 3lb higher mark, could hardly have done any more without winning. He bounced out from his high draw to bag the stands' rail in front and looked to be in control for most of the way, but found the winner a shade too classy where it mattered. Despite having gone 24 starts since his last win just over a year ago, he remains 3lb above his last winning mark.

Jayanjay, 6lb wrong, finished well against the stands' rail, but it has to be said that he does have a great record here and also had a good draw. (op 16-1)
Night Prospector, another who likes downhill tracks like this and also had a decent draw, ran a fair race from 5lb out of the handicap but he has failed to win since his controversial victory in the Group 2 Temple Stakes here well over two years ago. (tchd 14-1)
Texas Gold, 2lb lower than when winning this last year, has failed to hit the target since but he was always going to find things tough from his draw and probably achieved as much as could be expected. (op 7-1 tchd 9-1)
Caribbean Coral, with the visor back on replacing the cheekpieces, was 3lb wrong and never had the time to get involved in the shake-up from his moderate draw after missing the break as usual. (tchd 12-1)
Glenviews Youngone(IRE), 5lb wrong, had the best draw but threw it all away by hanging down the camber throughout. Official explanation: jockey said filly hung badly left (tchd 12-1)
Peace Offering(IRE) already had it to do from his draw, but after trying to match strides with those closer to the stands' rail he was then carried down the camber by the hanging Glenviews Youngone, exacerbating the distance he was beaten. (op 8-1)
Musadif(USA) blew any remote chance he might have had by completely fluffing the start, but he did make a little late headway, which suggests he retains some ability. He probably needs to drop a bit further in the handicap before he gets truly competitive.
Mutamarres had no chance from his draw the way things turned out and this effort should be ignored. (op 7-1 tchd 15-2)

4876 TOTEPOOL AMATEUR DERBY (A H'CAP FOR GENTLEMAN AMATEUR RIDERS) 1m 4f 10y

4:00 (4:00) (Class 3) (0-90,87) 4-Y-0+

£10,803 (£3,375; £1,686; £844; £421; £212) **Stalls** Centre

Form | | | | RPR
5225 **1** **Nero's Return (IRE)**[16] 4347 5-11-2 **79** .... MrWHogg 11 88
(M Johnston) *prom: led over 5f out: jnd over 3f out: duelled w runner-up after and clr of rest: gained upper hand fnl f* **5/1**[2]
0532 **2** ½ **Incursion**[8] 4626 5-10-5 **68** .... MrJan-ErikNeuroth 1 76
(D Nicholls) *a ldng trio: trckd wnr over 5f out: sustained chal fr over 3f out: no ex ins fnl f* **5/1**[2]
5344 **3** 3½ **Spinning Coin**[11] 4528 4-10-10 **73** ....(p) MrLoekVanDerHam 3 76
(J G Portman) *dwlt: pushed up to chse ldrs: 8th and losing pl st: sn no ch w ldng pair: kpt on to take 3rd over 1f out* **11/1**
1415 **4** 2½ **Great View (IRE)**[30] 3960 7-10-13 **76** ....(p) MrJPO'Farrell 8 75
(Mrs A L M King) *hld up in rr: detached and pushed along bef 1/2-way: 9th st: sme prog to chal for 3rd over 1f out: fdd fnl f* **8/1**
3142 **5** nk **Transvestite (IRE)**[13] 4448 4-11-7 **84** .... MrDiegoSarabia 7 82+
(J W Hills) *hld up: 7th st: c towards nr side and lost grnd: bmpd along and n.d after* **8/1**
4415 **6** nk **Croon**[31] 3890 4-11-3 **80** .... MrSWalker 4 78
(H Morrison) *settled midfield: prog to 3rd st: no imp on clr ldng pair: wknd over 1f out* **10/3**[1]
50 **7** 2½ **Swordsman (GER)**[16] 4346 4-11-10 **87** ....(b) MrSPJones 6 81+
(M L W Bell) *hld up in tch: prog 5f out: 4th and rdn st: c towards centre and lost grnd: wknd over 2f out* **15/2**[3]
1513 **8** 22 **Mr Aitch (IRE)**[18] 4299 4-10-13 **76** ....(t) GerardTumelty 10 34
(R T Phillips) *chsd ldrs: 6th and struggling staight: sn wknd: t.o* **15/2**[3]
0346 **9** ½ **King's Thought**[19] 4244 7-10-11 **74** .... MrMatthewSmith 2 32
(S Gollings) *mde most to over 5f out: 5th and wkng st: t.o* **16/1**
0-00 **10** 15 **Beltane**[64] 2900 8-10-5 **68** oh31 .... MrCVonBallmoos 5 2
(W De Best-Turner) *last after 4f: t.o 1/2-way* **100/1**

2m 43.38s (4.65) **Going Correction** +0.30s/f (Good) **10** Ran SP% **117.4**
Speed ratings (Par 107):96,95,93,91,91 91,89,74,74,64
CSF £30.48 CT £265.12 TOTE £6.30: £2.00, £2.20, £2.30; EX 23.00.
Owner Mrs Christine E Budden **Bred** Philip Brady **Trained** Middleham Moor, N Yorks
■ Stewards' Enquiry : Mr S P Jones three-day ban: careless riding (Sep 10,22 Nov 6)

FOCUS
A rather messy contest in which most of the riders decided to stay on the inside in the home straight whilst a couple ended up in no-man's land down the middle. This turned into something of a war of attrition and the front pair had the race to themselves from a long way out and set the standard for the form.

NOTEBOOK
Nero's Return(IRE), well handicapped at present and with no doubts over his ability to handle the easier ground, was always in a good position and just emerged victorious after a protracted battle with the runner-up. His rider was particularly impressive in never resorting to the whip despite the narrow winning margin. Although the form of these races can be questionable, this effort certainly confirmed his stamina for the trip if nothing else.
Incursion, without a win on the Flat in well over two years but proven on soft ground, was never far away over this shorter trip and never gave in during the course of the dour battle with the winner over the last couple of furlongs. His rider's style was a bit more agricultural than that of the winning pilot, but the gelding kept on running for him. (op 4-1)
Spinning Coin ran a very strange race, holding a good position early but then dropping away rounding the home bend and looking likely to finish tailed off. However, she found her second wind in the home straight and ran on past beaten horses to bag a place in the frame, though she never looked like getting to the front pair. The easier ground was probably not ideal for her. (op 10-1)
Great View(IRE), 7lb higher than when winning over course and distance last month, was always out the back and merely plodded on for fourth without ever looking like getting involved. (op 9-1)
Transvestite(IRE), up another 4lb and trying this trip for the first time, was trying to stay on when carried out into the centre of the track by Swordsman and any chance he may have had disappeared there and then. (op 9-1)
Croon tried to get on terms with the front pair turning for home, but his effort soon petered out. This was his first try on easy ground and it did not appear to suit. (op 7-2 tchd 4-1 in places)
Swordsman(GER) was still in with some sort of chance when his rider seemed set to bring him over to the stands' side turning for home, but he did not go the whole way and ended up in the middle of the track which is where he certainly did not want to be. (op 9-1)
Mr Aitch(IRE) Official explanation: jockey said gelding did not come down hill
King's Thought Official explanation: jockey said horse lost a front shoe and its action

4877 JRA CONDITIONS STKS 1m 2f 18y

4:35 (4:36) (Class 3) 3-Y-0+ **£9,348** (£2,799; £1,399; £700; £349) **Stalls** Low

Form | | | | RPR
14-1 **1** **Ashaawes (USA)**[39] 3681 3-8-11 **102** .... LDettori 1 109+
(Saeed Bin Suroor) *led after 1f: stdd and hdd 6f out: effrt again to ld over 2f out: 2 l clr 1f out: rdn out* **4/1**[3]
-100 **2** 1¼ **Classic Punch (IRE)**[27] 4024 3-8-8 **104** .... JohnEgan 4 104
(D R C Elsworth) *chsd ldng pair: clsd st: rdn and nt qckn over 2f out: styd on to take 2nd last 150yds: gaining but nvr able to chal* **12/1**
0116 **3** 2½ **Road To Love (IRE)**[16] 4358 3-8-8 **110** .... RyanMoore 3 100
(M Johnston) *led for 1f: led again 6f out: led field to nr side: drvn and hdd over 2f out: n.m.r sn after: wknd 1f out* **11/4**[2]
3334 **4** 15 **Enforcer**[30] 3927 4-9-2 **120** .... MartinDwyer 6 73
(W R Muir) *nvr gng wl: a 4th: clsd bef st but sn rdn: wknd over 2f out: sn bhd* **5/6**[1]
3466 **5** 39 **Macho Dancer (IRE)**[3] 4759 3-8-1 **47** ow1 .... EdwardCreighton(3) 2 —
(K J Burke) *dwlt: a last: t.o fr 1/2-way* **150/1**

2m 9.96s (0.92) **Going Correction** +0.30s/f (Good)
WFA 3 from 4yo+ 8lb **5** Ran SP% **109.6**
Speed ratings (Par 107):108,107,105,93,—
CSF £41.12 TOTE £3.80: £1.70, £3.40; EX 24.60.
Owner Godolphin **Bred** Jayeff 'B' Stables **Trained** Newmarket, Suffolk

FOCUS
Not the most competitive of races, made even less so with a 100-1 no-hoper and the odds-on favourite running so poorly, but the pace was good and the winner scored on merit with the runner-up setting the level. On this occasion the runners came over to the stands' side in the home straight.

NOTEBOOK
Ashaawes(USA), on softish ground for the first time, mixed it with Road To Love for the lead at various stages, but once he had emerged victorious from that particular battle the race was his. He still holds some fancy entries, but bearing in mind his inexperience it may be that the best of him will not be seen until next season. (op 7-2 tchd 3-1)
Classic Punch(IRE), back to his winning trip and dropping down from Group company, stayed on to snatch the runner-up spot but was never a threat to the winner. He seems likely to remain a hard horse to place. (op 14-1)
Road To Love(IRE) was given his usual positive ride, but was given no peace by Ashaawes and though he gamely tried to hold on, he eventually had to concede defeat. He is not going to be easy to place off his new inflated mark. (tchd 3-1 and 10-3 in a place)
Enforcer, who had plenty in hand of his rivals on official ratings, was always making hard work of it and he eventually gave up completely. It transpired that a part of one of his feet where he had recently had an abscess removed had burst open. Official explanation: trainer said colt's heel burst open (tchd 10-11 and Evs in places)
Macho Dancer(IRE) had no chance, but did pick up £349.50 for cantering around in a long last. (op 100-1)

4878 TOTE TEXT BETTING 60021 H'CAP 1m 2f 18y

5:10 (5:12) (Class 3) (0-90,88) 3-Y-0+ **£8,096** (£2,408; £1,203; £601) **Stalls** Low

Form | | | | RPR
0026 **1** **Resonate (IRE)**[8] 4626 8-9-1 **74** .... AmirQuinn(3) 10 83
(A G Newcombe) *hed up in last pair: prog on outer 1/2-way: 5th st but led gp of five to nr side: def advantage over 1f out: styd on wl* **10/1**
2511 **2** 3 **Zaafran**[24] 4112 3-9-1 **79** .... PhilipRobinson 9 83+
(M A Jarvis) *led styd far side st and led gp of five: rdn and kpt on wl fnl 2f but no ch w wnr fnl f* **6/1**[3]
1-43 **3** hd **Dynacam (USA)**[11] 4508 3-9-4 **82** .... RyanMoore 7 85
(Sir Michael Stoute) *chsd ldrs: 6th and rdn st: c nr side: chsd wnr 3f out: no imp fnl 2f* **10/3**[1]
105- **4** ¾ **Well Established (IRE)**[313] 5989 4-9-11 **81** .... MartinDwyer 6 83
(M A Jarvis) *hld up: 8th and wl in tch st: c nr side: chsd ldng pair over 2f out: no imp after* **25/1**
416 **5** ¾ **Zaif (IRE)**[25] 4082 3-9-10 **88** .... JohnEgan 11 89
(D R C Elsworth) *in tch: 7th st: c nr side: rdn and no prog over 2f out* **4/1**[2]
1243 **6** shd **Magic Sting**[21] 4203 5-9-12 **82** .... HayleyTurner 1 82
(M L W Bell) *prom: 3rd st: chsd ldr far side after: rdn and one pce over 2f out* **8/1**
3300 **7** ½ **Active Asset (IRE)**[16] 4370 4-9-13 **83** .... LDettori 5 83
(M R Channon) *hld up in rr: 9th st but wl in tch: c nr side: no prog after and fin last of gp of five* **7/1**
4003 **8** 1 **Solo Flight**[24] 4112 9-9-9 **84** .... TravisBlock(5) 3 82
(H Morrison) *s.s: hld up in last: styd far side st: prog to chse ldng pair over 2f out: one pce after* **14/1**
0332 **9** 5 **Star Magnitude (USA)**[23] 4147 5-9-6 **76** .... OscarUrbina 4 65
(S Dow) *mostly chsd ldr tl 4th and losing pl st: styd far side: struggling over 2f out* **8/1**
3200 **10** 1¼ **Awatuki (IRE)**[25] 4082 3-9-2 **80** .... TPQueally 8 67
(A P Jarvis) *t.k.h: prom: chsd ldr briefly ent st: styd far side and sn btn: wknd 2f out* **16/1**

2m 11.39s (2.35) **Going Correction** +0.30s/f (Good)
WFA 3 from 4yo+ 8lb **10** Ran SP% **117.6**
Speed ratings (Par 107):102,99,99,98,98 98,97,96,92,91
CSF £69.45 CT £246.44 TOTE £11.40: £3.60, £2.20, £1.70; EX 97.60.
Owner S Langridge **Bred** D H W Dobson **Trained** Yarnscombe, Devon

FOCUS
A moderate early pace resulted in a modest winning time for a race like this rated through the fourth and fifth to form. There was a marked difference of opinion turning for home with the field splitting in half, five coming stands' side and five staying far side, and it was the nearside group that held sway in providing four of the first five home.

NOTEBOOK
Resonate(IRE), still 2lb higher than for his last turf win which came over course and distance nearly two years ago, was at least proven on soft ground but the key to this victory was his rider making straight for the stands' rail turning for home and he fairly flew home to beat both groups with ease. However, because of the way the race panned out the form may not be totally reliable. (op 9-1)
Zaafran, bidding for a hat-trick off a 3lb higher mark, was given a positive ride but it was strange that her rider, who is one of the best in the business at spotting a track bias, decided to stick on the inside given what had happened earlier in the afternoon. Battling on well, she kept the quartet on her side at bay but could do nothing about the winner on the opposite flank. Given that the next horse home on her side finished sixth, she can be given extra credit for this effort.
Dynacam(USA), who would have appreciated this easier ground, came through to chase the winner home on the nearside but could never get anywhere near him. The Handicapper looks to have hold of her at present. (op 5-2 tchd 7-2 in places)
Well Established(IRE), a stable companion of the runner-up, was another to come nearside and stayed on without offering a threat. This first run in ten months should have put him right.
Zaif(IRE), well backed, never managed to get near the principals. The money suggested he was thought capable of better, but he has now twice been comfortably held off this mark in handicap company since winning his maiden. (op 6-1)
Magic Sting, a course-and-distance winner last month, is now 8lb higher and could never quite get to the leaders though he did finish second best of the far-side group. (tchd 17-2)
Awatuki(IRE) pulled far too hard early to give himself any chance of getting home.

4879 LAND ROVER H'CAP 1m 114y

5:40 (5:44) (Class 4) (0-80,80) 3-Y-0+ **£6,477** (£1,927; £963; £481) **Stalls** Low

Form | | | | RPR
0000 **1** **Rain Stops Play (IRE)**[24] 4108 4-9-4 **77** .... ChrisCavanagh(7) 1 87
(M Quinn) *mde all: rdn 2f out: hrd pressed after: hld on wl nr fin* **10/1**
0002 **2** nk **Border Edge**[10] 4565 8-8-4 **61** oh2 .... MarcHalford(5) 5 71
(J J Bridger) *chsd ldng pair: rdn 3f out: effrt u.p 2f out: pressed wnr fnl f: no ex nr fin* **14/1**
6004 **3** ¾ **Colinca's Lad (IRE)**[5] 4704 4-8-3 **62** .... AshleyHamblett(7) 3 70
(T T Clement) *dwlt: t.k.h and hld up: 7th st: n.m.r briefly wl over 1f out: rdn and styd on fnl f: nrst fin* **16/1**

413 **4** *1 ¼* **Out For A Stroll**[43] 3570 7-8-11 **63** LDettori 9 68
(S C Williams) *hld up in last trio: 8th st: no prog over 2f out: pushed along and r.o fnl f: nvr nr ldrs* **3/1**[1]

2056 **5** *shd* **Night Storm**[11] 4536 5-9-6 **72** TPQueally 11 77
(S Dow) *s.s: hld up in last trio: 9th st: prog on outer to chal 2f out: wknd ins fnl f* **14/1**

-051 **6** *¾* **Ginger Spice (IRE)**[16] 4375 4-9-6 **77** LiamJones(5) 2 81
(W J Haggas) *t.k.h: chsd ldr to over 2f out: fdd over 1f out* **7/2**[2]

3004 **7** *1 ½* **Tajaathub (USA)**[11] 4521 4-9-11 **77** MartinDwyer 6 77
(M Johnston) *chsd ldrs: 4th st: effrt over 2f out: wknd over 1f out* **8/1**

1630 **8** *1 ½* **Dream Rose (IRE)**[26] 4040 3-8-12 **74** EdwardCreighton(3) 7 71
(M R Channon) *chsd ldrs: cl 5th st: rdn over 2f out: steadily wknd* **25/1**

1034 **9** *6* **Aggravation**[10] 4565 4-9-4 **70** JohnEgan 10 55
(D R C Elsworth) *hld up in last trio: last st: rdn and no prog over 2f out: wknd over 1f out* **11/2**[3]

0020 **10** *3* **Quantum Leap**[33] 3854 9-9-4 **70** (v) RyanMoore 8 48
(S Dow) *hld up: 6th st: nudged along and no prog over 2f out: sn eased* **8/1**

1m 47.89s (2.15) **Going Correction** +0.30s/f (Good)
WFA 3 from 4yo+ 7lb **10** Ran SP% **117.0**
Speed ratings (Par 105):102,101,101,99,99 99,97,96,91,88
CSF £140.69 CT £1450.23 TOTE £11.70: £3.20, £3.30, £4.40; EX 181.80 Place 6 £386.67, Place 5£151.56..
Owner Paul Montgomery & Brian Morton **Bred** Lucayan Stud Ltd **Trained** Newmarket, Suffolk

FOCUS
A fair handicap and this time the whole field came across to the stands' side on reaching the home straight. Those that raced up with the pace were at an advantage and the form is not totally convincing.
Aggravation Official explanation: jockey said gelding had no more to give
T/Plt: £264.70 to a £1 stake. Pool: £74,452.25. 205.30 winning tickets. T/Qpdt: £67.30 to a £1 stake. Pool: £3,840.00. 42.20 winning tickets. JN

4566 NEWCASTLE (L-H)
Monday, August 28

OFFICIAL GOING: Good to soft (soft in places)
The track missed much of the overnight rain and the ground was described as 'dead, sticky and hard work'. The stands' side rail enjoyed a big advantage.
Wind: Fresh, half-against Weather: Persistent heavy showers

4880 EBF SALTWELL SIGNS MAIDEN STKS 7f
2:10 (2:10) (Class 5) 2-Y-O **£4,533** (£1,348; £674; £336) **Stalls** High

Form RPR

1 **Wheels In Motion (IRE)** 2-9-3 MickyFenton 17 77
(T P Tate) *mde all stands' rail: kpt on wl fnl f: hld on* **8/1**

4 **2** *shd* **Arena's Dream (USA)**[21] 4196 2-9-3 TonyHamilton 15 77
(R A Fahey) *trckd wnr racing one off stands' side: hdwy to chal 1f out: jst failed* **12/1**

3 *10* **Jardines Bazaar** 2-9-3 DavidAllan 5 52+
(T D Easterby) *s.s: hdwy over 2f out: kpt on to take modest 3rd ins last* **16/1**

4 **4** *5* **Celtic Change (IRE)**[14] 4424 2-9-3 PhillipMakin 9 39
(M Dods) *chsd ldrs: rdn over 2f out: wknd over 1f out* **11/4**[1]

5 *3* **Spirit Of Ecstacy** 2-8-9 GregFairley(3) 14 27
(G M Moore) *dwlt: sme hdwy over 2f out: nvr nr ldrs* **25/1**

4 **6** *3 ½* **The Diamond Bond**[10] 4566 2-9-3 GylesParkin 4 23+
(G R Oldroyd) *bhd and drvn along: kpt on fnl 2f: nvr on terms* **10/1**

7 *1 ¼* **Pegasus Prince (USA)** 2-9-3 TomEaves 1 20+
(Miss J A Camacho) *dwlt: sme hdwy on wd outside 4f out: lost pl 2f out* **16/1**

8 *2 ½* **Macaroni Gin (IRE)** 2-9-3 JimCrowley 13 14
(J Howard Johnson) *sn in rr and drvn along: nvr on terms* **12/1**

9 *9* **Crosby Millie** 2-8-12 DeanMcKeown 3 —
(J R Weymes) *dwlt: a in rr* **20/1**

10 *6* **Philanthropy** 2-9-3 J-PGuillambert 7 —
(M Johnston) *chsd ldrs: drvn and lost pl over 3f out: sn bhd* **5/1**[2]

0 **11** *½* **Littlemadgebob**[64] 2890 2-8-9 AndrewMullen(3) 6 —
(J R Norton) *racd wd: chsd ldrs: edgd lft and lost pl 2f out* **50/1**

33 **12** *2 ½* **Pennyrock (IRE)**[12] 4466 2-9-3 DO'Donohoe 2 —
(K A Ryan) *racd wd: chsd ldrs: lost pl over 2f out* **7/1**[3]

13 *½* **To Hatta (IRE)** 2-9-3 TPO'Shea 8 —
(M R Channon) *dwlt: bhd and drvn along* **10/1**

1m 30.87s (2.87) **Going Correction** +0.375s/f (Good) **13** Ran SP% **122.8**
Speed ratings (Par 94):98,97,86,80,77 73,71,69,58,51 51,48,47
CSF £101.19 TOTE £10.10: £2.70, £3.70, £6.20; EX 109.30.
Owner J Hanson **Bred** Dermot Cantillon And Forenaghts Stud **Trained** Tadcaster, N Yorks

FOCUS
A stiff test for juveniles in the tiring ground and quite a strong headwind. The first two pulled a long way clear and those not racing against the stands'-side rail were at a major disadvantage, making the form difficult to rate.

NOTEBOOK
Wheels In Motion(IRE), an April foal, stands over plenty of ground. He knew his job and raced on much the best ground against the stands' side rail. He had to dig deep in the end but will improve fitness-wise for the outing and looks a fair prospect. (op 9-1)
Arena's Dream(USA), appreciating the step up in trip, shadowed the winner. He threw down the gauntlet but in the end came off just second best. He is surely a ready-made winner. (op 8-1)
Jardines Bazaar, a February foal, is on the leg and narrow. After missing the break he made his way towards the favoured stands' side and in the end finished clear third-best. He looks as though he may need more time yet. (op 12-1)
Celtic Change(IRE), racing away from the favoured stands'-side rail, didn't improve on his initial Thirsk effort but he was racing on much the slowest ground and is well worth another chance. (op 3-1 tchd 7-2 and 5-2)
Spirit Of Ecstacy, nothing to follow, raced wide and edged towards the worst ground towards the far side. (op 33-1 tchd 50-1)
Philanthropy, a narrow type, was well backed but, racing wide, he seemed to hit a very bad patch of ground at the halfway mark and he soon dropped right out. He must be a lot better than he showed here. (op 7-1)

4881 ST JAMES SECURITY CLAIMING STKS 1m 3y(S)
2:45 (2:46) (Class 6) 3-Y-O+ **£2,266** (£674; £337; £168) **Stalls** High

Form RPR

0030 **1** **Hows That**[19] 4266 4-8-12 35 (p) PhillipMakin 14 51
(K R Burke) *trckd ldrs stands' rail: led over 2f out: styd on wl fnl f* **20/1**

0356 **2** *2 ½* **Coronation Flight**[21] 4195 3-8-12 40 DeanMcKeown 12 52
(F P Murtagh) *hld up in midfield stands' rail: hdwy over 2f out: wnt 2nd over 1f out: no imp* **50/1**

2144 **3** *½* **Donna's Double**[10] 4570 11-9-5 51 (p) TonyHamilton 10 52
(Karen McLintock) *sn bhd: hdwy over 2f out: styd on to take 3rd ins last* **8/1**

2300 **4** *1 ¼* **Second Reef**[20] 4233 4-9-13 54 DavidAllan 17 58
(E J Alston) *t.k.h in rr on stands' rail: hdwy and n.m.r 2f out: kpt on fnl f* **12/1**

0400 **5** *8* **Pomfret Lad**[8] 4636 8-9-13 68 GrahamGibbons 8 42
(J J Quinn) *trckd ldrs: wknd over 1f out* **8/1**

3050 **6** *5* **Takanewa (IRE)**[41] 3604 3-9-2 60 TomEaves 15 27
(J Howard Johnson) *led: edgd lft and hdd over 2f out: sn wknd* **20/1**

0400 **7** *1* **Lord Mayor**[10] 4573 5-9-13 74 EddieAhern 7 30
(R M H Cowell) *chsd ldrs on outer: drvn over 3f out: wknd 2f out* **6/1**[3]

0006 **8** *1 ¾* **Top Dirham**[16] 4350 8-9-13 70 DaleGibson 11 26
(M W Easterby) *mid-div: effrt over 2f out: sn btn* **7/1**

6334 **9** *5* **True Night**[2] 4795 9-9-13 67 AdrianTNicholls 3 16
(D Nicholls) *led other 3 far side: no ch w main gp fnl 2f* **5/1**[2]

5131 **10** *9* **Apache Point (IRE)**[12] 4467 9-9-9 60 KimTinkler 5 —
(N Tinkler) *chsd ldrs far side: no ch fnl 2f* **9/2**[1]

4300 **11** *6* **Augustus Livius (IRE)**[49] 3357 3-8-12 43 AndrewMullen(3) 1 —
(W Storey) *chsd ldng pair far side: no ch fnl 2f* **66/1**

2514 **12** *33* **Midge's Girl (IRE)**[116] 1447 3-8-12 48 TPO'Shea 6 —
(Mrs A Duffield) *rrd s: racd towards stands' side: edgd lft over 2f out and ended up far side: sn wl bhd: t.o* **25/1**

-000 **13** *12* **Move On (IRE)**[4] 4726 3-8-6 45 (t) DO'Donohoe 2 —
(B Ellison) *racd far side: bhd and eased over 2f out: t.o* **50/1**

21-0 **14** *5* **Bingo One (IRE)**[102] 1801 3-8-5 67 GregFairley(3) 16 —
(W J H Ratcliffe) *in rr: lost pl and detached 3f out: t.o* **15/2**

000/ **15** *4* **Theme Time (USA)**[1363] 5847 10-8-11 32 (t) J-PGuillambert 9 —
(D Morris) *chsd ldrs: lost pl over 3f out: sn bhd: t.o* **50/1**

1m 43.88s (1.98) **Going Correction** +0.375s/f (Good)
WFA 3 from 4yo+ 6lb **15** Ran SP% **124.1**
Speed ratings (Par 101):105,102,102,100,92 87,86,85,80,71 65,32,20,15,11
CSF £770.17 TOTE £28.90: £8.30, £9.00, £1.70; EX 428.10.True Night was the subject of a friendly claim.
Owner Spigot Lodge Partnership 2 **Bred** Mrs F Denniff **Trained** Middleham Moor, N Yorks
■ Stewards' Enquiry : Adrian T Nicholls two-day ban: used whip in the incorrect place and with excessive frequency (Sep 8,10)

FOCUS
A moderate claimer, the first two had a lot to find on official ratings and overall the form looks decidedly dodgy even though the time was very good. The four who went to the far side were hung out to dry and once again those racing hard against the stands'-side rail enjoyed a big advantage.
True Night Official explanation: jockey said gelding hung right-handed

4882 CHISHOLM BOOKMAKERS BLAYDON RACE (A NURSERY H'CAP) 1m 3y(S)
3:20 (3:21) (Class 3) 2-Y-O
£11,217 (£3,358; £1,679; £840; £419; £210) **Stalls** High

Form RPR

4512 **1** **Rosbay (IRE)**[40] 3633 2-9-0 75 DavidAllan 3 83
(T D Easterby) *hld up: smooth hdwy stands' rail over 2f out: led over 1f out: drvn clr* **14/1**

0130 **2** *3* **Colditz (IRE)**[19] 4250 2-8-6 67 TonyHamilton 9 68
(D W Barker) *trckd ldrs stands' rail: led over 3f out: hdd over 1f out: no ex* **33/1**

3236 **3** *6* **Centenary (IRE)**[11] 4509 2-8-13 74 TomEaves 6 62
(J S Wainwright) *bhd and pushed along: hdwy stands' rail over 2f out: one pce appr fnl f* **16/1**

551 **4** *3* **Sri Pekan Two**[16] 4366 2-9-7 82 EddieAhern 4 64
(P F I Cole) *chsd ldrs: wknd over 1f out* **5/2**[2]

2411 **5** *1 ½* **Fractured Foxy**[10] 4545 2-8-0 61 DaleGibson 10 39
(J J Quinn) *trckd ldrs: wknd over 2f out* **10/1**

5054 **6** *½* **Nota Liberata**[19] 4250 2-8-3 64 NickyMackay 8 41
(G M Moore) *hld up in rr: hdwy on outer over 3f out: lost pl over 1f out* **12/1**

5531 **7** *3* **Lemon Silk (IRE)**[11] 4509 2-8-13 74 MickyFenton 11 45
(T P Tate) *w ldrs: lost pl over 2f out* **5/1**[3]

5240 **8** *8* **Kaladar (IRE)**[11] 4509 2-7-13 63 AndrewMullen(3) 7 16
(K A Ryan) *led tl over 3f out: hung lft: lost pl over 2f out* **66/1**

4445 **9** *30* **Intersky Sports (USA)**[14] 4436 2-8-2 63 (b[1]) DO'Donohoe 2 —
(K A Ryan) *trckd ldrs on outer: t.k.h: lost pl over 3f out: sn bhd: virtually p.u* **20/1**

41 **10** *10* **Mayor Of London (USA)**[10] 4566 2-9-5 80 J-PGuillambert 5 —
(M Johnston) *w ldrs: rdn and lost pl over 4f out: sn wl bhd: virtually p.u* **9/4**[1]

3352 **11** *2 ½* **Global Guest**[12] 4480 2-8-13 74 TPO'Shea 1 —
(M R Channon) *racd on outer: in rr and drvn along: lost tch over 3f out: virtually p.u* **14/1**

1m 45.96s (4.06) **Going Correction** +0.375s/f (Good) **11** Ran SP% **121.2**
Speed ratings (Par 98):94,91,85,82,80 80,77,69,39,29 26
CSF £412.31 CT £7383.84 TOTE £12.40: £3.60, £6.60, £5.20; EX 330.70.
Owner Croft, Taylor, Stone & Hebdon **Bred** Alan Dargan **Trained** Great Habton, N Yorks

FOCUS
A competitive nursery on paper but they went a strong gallop and finished well strung out. Those up there to halfway paid the penalty ultimately and the runner-up looks the best guide to the overall value of the form.

NOTEBOOK
Rosbay(IRE), drawn two from the outside, was dropped in this time and made his way to the favoured stands'-side rail. He came there strongly and revelling in the ground, came clear. (op 10-1)
Colditz(IRE), who has proved a good buy, tracked the leaders and slipped through on the inner to show ahead soon after halfway. In the end the winner proved much too good but even so he seemed to relish the extra yardage.
Centenary(IRE), encountering easy ground for the first time, struggled to go the pace. He kept on in his own time to secure a modest third spot.
Sri Pekan Two, who looked the part beforehand, was always racing away from the favoured stands'-side rail. (op 11-4 tchd 9-4)
Fractured Foxy, stepping up in trip, was tackling much better company than she met in her two selling-race victories. (op 11-1)
Lemon Silk(IRE), 4lb higher, took them along but rolled away from the fence and soon dropped away. Official explanation: jockey said gelding hung left-handed (tchd 11-2)
Mayor Of London(USA), racing wide, seemed to hit a very bad patch of ground just before the halfway mark and he dropped right out in matter of strides. This is best forgotten. (op 3-1 tchd 10-3 in a place)

4883 SPRINGFIELD MOTOR GROUP H'CAP — 2m 19y

3:55 (3:55) (Class 3) (0-95,90) 3-Y-0+

£7,790 (£2,332; £1,166; £583; £291; £146) Stalls Centre

Form — RPR

5403 **1** **Mirjan (IRE)**[31] [3888] 10-10-0 **90**........(b) JimCrowley 2 — 98
(L Lungo) *hld up in rr: drvn over 4f out: styd on to ld 1f out: kpt on wl* **4/1**[1]

2100 **2** 1 ¼ **Numero Due**[69] [2723] 4-9-4 **80**........ NickyMackay 3 — 87
(G M Moore) *chsd ldrs: outpcd over 4f out: hdwy over 2f out: styd on to take 2nd ins last: no real imp* **5/1**[3]

0431 **3** 4 **Dancer's Serenade (IRE)**[23] [4156] 4-8-12 **74** oh3........ MickyFenton 7 — 76
(T P Tate) *rrd s: hdwy to ld after 2f: drvn clr over 5f out: hdd 1f out: wknd ins last* **9/2**[2]

0331 **4** 2 **Indonesia**[19] [4252] 4-8-12 **74**........ TomEaves 6 — 73
(T D Walford) *hld up: hdwy to trck ldrs 10f out: one pce fnl 2f* **7/1**

1505 **5** 1 **Kayf Aramis**[8] [4632] 4-8-12 **74** oh9........ PaulQuinn 5 — 72
(J L Spearing) *t.k.h in rr: reminders 10f out: sn chsng ldrs: lost pl over 1f out* **13/2**

0542 **6** 15 **Mceldowney**[16] [4346] 4-9-11 **87**........ J-PGuillambert 1 — 67
(M Johnston) *led 2f: chsd ldrs: lost pl over 2f out: sn bhd* **4/1**[1]

3-00 **7** 14 **Inchnadamph**[44] [3533] 6-9-6 **82**........(t) DO'Donohoe 4 — 45
(T J Fitzgerald) *sn chsng ldrs: lost pl over 2f out: sn bhd* **10/1**

3m 42.07s (6.87) **Going Correction** +0.475s/f (Yiel) — 7 Ran SP% **109.8**
Speed ratings (Par 107):101,100,98,97,96 89,82
CSF £22.00 TOTE £4.00: £1.70, £3.40; EX 17.30.
Owner Len Lungo Racing Limited **Bred** His Highness The Aga Khan's Studs S C **Trained** Carrutherstown, D'fries & G'way

FOCUS
A very steady pace and they all came across to the stands' side in the home straight. The winner loves the ground and made the most of a good opportunity.

NOTEBOOK
Mirjan(IRE), without a win since his 2004 Northumberland Plate success, looked in trouble turning in and was matched at 95 on the exchanges. However, he stuck on once in line for home, and settled the issue inside the last. He is in line for a third crack at the Cesarewitch in which he has finished seventh in each of the last two runnings. (op 3-1)
Numero Due, just 2lb higher than Thirsk, had the ground to suit and stuck on in game pursuit of the winner. He could have done with a stronger gallop. (op 9-2 tchd 4-1)
Dancer's Serenade(IRE), 3lb out of the handicap, was in effect 5lb higher. Awkward leaving the stalls, as a result of the modest pace he was soon able to take charge. Stepping up the gallop at the halfway mark, he seized the favoured stands' side rail but in the end was readily brushed aside by the first two. (op 11-2)
Indonesia, 4lb higher, was not as effective on this much slower ground. (tchd 15-2)
Kayf Aramis, 9lb out of the handicap, did not have the ground as testing as he likes and in the end he seemed to lose interest. (op 8-1)
Mceldowney, who jumped off in front, set just a modest pace. He ran poorly, dropping right away early in the straight.
Inchnadamph, third behind Sergeant Cecil in last year's Cesarewitch, has looked out of sorts in three starts this time. Official explanation: trainer had no explanation for the poor form shown (op 15-2)

4884 GOSFORTH DECORATING AND BUILDING SERVICES H'CAP — 1m 4f 93y

4:30 (4:32) (Class 6) (0-65,65) 3-Y-0 — £2,914 (£867; £433; £216) Stalls Centre

Form — RPR

50 **1** **Hill Billy Rock (IRE)**[26] [4060] 3-9-4 **62**........ DeanMcKeown 15 — 72+
(G A Swinbank) *hld up in rr: stdy hdwy over 2f out: led 1f out: r.o strly: readily* **11/2**[2]

534 **2** 2 ½ **Sky High Guy (IRE)**[24] [4124] 3-9-7 **65**........ EddieAhern 8 — 71
(S Kirk) *hld up: hdwy outside over 5f out: c stands' rail and led over 1f out: sn hdd and no ex* **8/1**[3]

0332 **3** 2 ½ **Park Lane Princess (IRE)**[10] [4556] 3-8-1 **52**........ KirstyMilczarek(7) 6 — 54
(D M Simcock) *in rr: hdwy centre 3f out: chal appr fnl f: kpt on same pce* **10/1**

3414 **4** nk **Plemont Bay**[9] [4604] 3-8-13 **64**........(v) LukeMorris(7) 13 — 66+
(M L W Bell) *trckd ldrs: led over 3f out: hdd over 1f out: kpt on same pce* **9/2**[1]

0-33 **5** 1 ¾ **Trafalgar Day**[23] [4150] 3-8-13 **60**........ AndrewMullen(3) 2 — 59
(W M Brisbourne) *prom: one pce fnl 2f* **12/1**

2235 **6** ½ **Minthare (IRE)**[5] [4698] 3-9-4 **62**........(p) TonyHamilton 12 — 60
(C Grant) *sn trcking ldrs: effrt over 2f out: kpt on same pce* **14/1**

4623 **7** ¾ **Dubai Around (IRE)**[19] [4255] 3-8-6 **53**........ GregFairley(3) 16 — 50
(Micky Hammond) *sn chsng ldrs: effrt over 2f out: one pce* **9/1**

0665 **8** nk **Silver Mont (IRE)**[4] [4734] 3-8-5 **49**........(b[1]) TPO'Shea 1 — 45
(Mrs A Duffield) *w ldrs: one pce fnl 2f* **10/1**

-000 **9** 1 ¼ **Revolving World (IRE)**[86] [2243] 3-8-11 **55**........(b[1]) DO'Donohoe 5 — 49
(T J Fitzgerald) *sn bhd and drvn along: t.o 4f out: kpt on fnl 2f* **33/1**

0434 **10** 2 **Hunting Haze**[35] [3790] 3-9-2 **60**........ PhillipMakin 11 — 51
(Miss S E Hall) *midfield: hdwy on outside 5f out: c stands' side: chsd ldrs tl wknd appr fnl f* **12/1**

6006 **11** 9 **Tranos (USA)**[19] [4245] 3-9-4 **62**........(v) NickyMackay 10 — 39
(L M Cumani) *hld up in midfield: effrt over 2f out: lost pl over 1f out* **11/1**

6350 **12** shd **Fenners (USA)**[12] [4472] 3-9-2 **60**........(t) DaleGibson 17 — 36
(G P Kelly) *sn bhd: t.o 4f out* **33/1**

2640 **13** 3 ½ **Noble Edge**[16] [4362] 3-8-9 **53**........(p) DavidAllan 14 — 24
(Robert Gray) *chsd ldrs: drvn over 4f out: lost pl over 2f out* **25/1**

0-00 **14** 11 **Celtic Empire (IRE)**[21] [4204] 3-8-8 **52**........ MickyFenton 9 — 5
(Jedd O'Keeffe) *led tl over 3f out: lost pl over 2f out: sn bhd and eased* **20/1**

0-00 **15** 12 **Little Britain (USA)**[19] [4254] 3-8-12 **56**........ TomEaves 4 — —
(J Howard Johnson) *stdd s: hld up: lost pl over 3f out: sn bhd and eased* **50/1**

2m 47.98s (4.43) **Going Correction** +0.475s/f (Yiel) — 15 Ran SP% **119.7**
Speed ratings (Par 98):104,102,100,100,99 98,98,98,97,96 90,90,87,80,72
CSF £43.52 CT £381.12 TOTE £6.00: £2.90, £3.30, £2.40; EX 51.00.
Owner W Powrie And Mrs S Sandbrook **Bred** Darley **Trained** Melsonby, N Yorks
■ Mister Fizzbomb was withdrawn (14/1, ref to ent stalls). R4 applies, deduct 5p in the £.

FOCUS
A low-grade handicap and they possibly went too fast in the conditions. The winner can improve again, the runner-up looks the guide to the overall value of the form and the fourth did best of those who raced in the firing line.
Hill Billy Rock(IRE) Official explanation: trainer said, regarding the improved form shown, gelding was not suited by the ground on its previous start, and had also benefited from the step up in trip
Fenners(USA) Official explanation: jockey said colt had a breathing problem
Celtic Empire(IRE) Official explanation: trainer said gelding was lame following the race and was subsequently found to have an abscess in its foot

4885 CHISHOLM BOOKMAKERS H'CAP — 6f

5:05 (5:05) (Class 4) (0-80,78) 3-Y-0+

£7,478 (£2,239; £1,119; £560; £279; £140) Stalls High

Form — RPR

-000 **1** **Vanadium**[24] [4119] 4-9-4 **70**........ J-PGuillambert 15 — 82
(J G Given) *trckd ldrs: led jst ins last: r.o wl* **20/1**

3404 **2** 2 **Riquewihr**[11] [4507] 6-9-1 **67**........(p) TonyHamilton 7 — 73
(J S Wainwright) *led against stands' side rail: hdd jst ins last: no ex* **16/1**

5444 **3** ½ **Sir Orpen (IRE)**[32] [3879] 3-9-3 **72**........ PhillipMakin 11 — 77
(T D Barron) *hld up in rr: hdwy stands' side 2f out: styd on wl ins last* **13/2**[2]

1421 **4** 1 ½ **Ellens Academy (IRE)**[16] [4357] 11-9-12 **78**........ MickyFenton 10 — 78
(E J Alston) *hld up in rr: hdwy stands' rail over 1f out: styd on towards fin* **8/1**[3]

0-00 **5** 3 **Orphan (IRE)**[43] [3567] 4-9-11 **77**........ EddieAhern 13 — 68
(K R Burke) *hld up towards rr: hdwy 2f out: nvr rchd ldrs* **11/1**

5642 **6** 3 **Titinius (IRE)**[17] [4338] 6-9-1 **70**........ GregFairley(3) 14 — 52
(Micky Hammond) *chsd ldrs: wknd appr fnl f* **9/1**

0105 **7** 1 ½ **Digital**[8] [4629] 9-9-9 **75**........ TPO'Shea 5 — 53
(M R Channon) *s.i.s: sme hdwy 2f out: nvr a factor* **10/1**

0542 **8** nk **Winthorpe (IRE)**[5] [4694] 6-8-10 **62**........ GrahamGibbons 9 — 39
(J J Quinn) *chsd ldrs: wknd appr fnl f* **12/1**

-530 **9** ¾ **Sir Nod**[29] [3986] 4-9-10 **76**........ TomEaves 4 — 50
(Miss J A Camacho) *trckd ldrs: t.k.h: wknd over 1f out* **12/1**

0031 **10** 3 ½ **Petite Mac**[10] [4571] 6-8-4 **63**........ SuzzanneFrance(7) 8 — 27
(N Bycroft) *in rr towards centre: nvr a factor* **12/1**

0052 **11** shd **Countdown**[16] [4357] 4-9-9 **75**........ DavidAllan 3 — 39
(T D Easterby) *chsd ldrs on outer: lost pl over 1f out* **9/1**

4610 **12** 1 ¼ **Aperitif**[23] [4153] 5-9-5 **71**........ AdrianTNicholls 12 — 31
(D Nicholls) *chsd ldrs: lost pl 2f out* **14/1**

0050 **13** ½ **Paris Bell**[9] [4602] 4-9-7 **73**........ PaulQuinn 1 — 31
(T D Easterby) *trckd ldrs on outside: t.k.h: lost pl over 1f out* **10/1**

0000 **14** 5 **Siena Gold**[10] [4573] 4-9-7 **73**........(b[1]) DeanMcKeown 2 — 16
(J G Given) *swtchd lft after s and r alone towards far side: w ldrs: rdn over 2f out: wknd and eased over 1f out* **40/1**

0034 **15** 6 **Balakiref**[2] [4807] 7-9-10 **76**........ DO'Donohoe 6 — 1
(M Dods) *prom: lost pl over 1f out: heavily eased* **5/1**[1]

1m 16.68s (1.59) **Going Correction** +0.375s/f (Good)
WFA 3 from 4yo+ 3lb — 15 Ran SP% **130.5**
Speed ratings (Par 105):104,101,100,98,94 90,88,88,87,82 82,80,80,73,65
CSF £331.74 CT £2388.01 TOTE £28.50: £9.40, £4.40, £3.40; EX 280.70.
Owner Bolton Grange **Bred** Bolton Grange **Trained** Willoughton, Lincs

FOCUS
The first five raced close to the favoured stands'-side rail. It does not look strong form rated through the third.
Vanadium Official explanation: trainer said, regarding the apparent improvement in form, that the gelding appeared to be suited by the ease in ground
Countdown Official explanation: jockey said gelding had no more to give
Balakiref Official explanation: trainer said, regarding the poor form shown, that the gelding needs more cover in his races and raced too close to the pace

4886 JAMES FLETCHER MARQUEE & PAVILION HIRE H'CAP — 5f

5:35 (5:36) (Class 5) (0-75,75) 3-Y-0 — £3,886 (£1,156; £577; £288) Stalls High

Form — RPR

2160 **1** **Sea Salt**[32] [3879] 3-9-7 **75**........ PhillipMakin 5 — 80
(T D Barron) *hld up: hdwy 2f out: led jst ins last: jst hld on* **7/1**[3]

5-50 **2** hd **Mujeak (IRE)**[68] [2763] 3-8-9 **63**........ GrahamGibbons 6 — 72+
(J J Quinn) *s.i.s: sn pushed along: hdwy over 3f out: nt clr run over 1f and jst ins last: swtchd ins: fin wl: jst failed* **10/1**

405 **3** 3 **City For Conquest (IRE)**[14] [4422] 3-9-0 **68**........(v) TomEaves 7 — 61
(K R Burke) *mde most tl hdd jst ins last: fdd* **4/1**[2]

0000 **4** 6 **The Thrifty Bear**[25] [4071] 3-7-11 **58** ow2........(b[1]) KellyHarrison(7) 4 — 30
(C W Fairhurst) *w ldrs on outer: wknd 1f out* **16/1**

2401 **5** 5 **Northern Chorus (IRE)**[36] [3759] 3-9-1 **72**........(v) GregFairley(3) 3 — 26
(A Dickman) *w ldrs on outer: wknd over 1f out* **7/1**[3]

3342 **6** 3 **Queen Cobra (IRE)**[7] [4659] 3-9-6 **74**........(v) EddieAhern 2 — 17
(H Morrison) *w ldrs on outside: lost pl over 2f out* **11/10**[1]

001 **7** 11 **Orpenlina (IRE)**[9] [4613] 3-8-2 **56** oh9........ DaleGibson 1 — —
(R A Fahey) *racd wdst of all: chsd ldrs: rdn and lost pl over 2f out: sn bhd and eased* **8/1**

65.05 secs (3.55) **Going Correction** +0.375s/f (Good) — 7 Ran SP% **118.7**
Speed ratings (Par 100):86,85,80,71,63 58,40
CSF £74.80 TOTE £9.30: £2.50, £6.00; EX 83.00 Place 6 £46,748.51, Place 5 £6,921.05..
Owner J H Tattersall **Bred** D R Tucker **Trained** Maunby, N Yorks

FOCUS
A modest handicap but a very slow winning time for a race like this. No gallop at all and the runner-up looked unlucky.
Queen Cobra(IRE) Official explanation: trainer had no explanation for the poor form shown
T/Jkpt: Not won. T/Plt: Part won. £47,324.70 to a £1 stake. Pool: £64,828.40. 0.15 winning tickets. T/Qpdt: £1,119.90 to a £1 stake. Pool: £3,632.20. 2.40 winning tickets. WG

4607 RIPON (R-H)

Monday, August 28

OFFICIAL GOING: Soft
Wind: Moderate, across

4887 THE BANK HOLIDAY IS FOR RACING (S) STKS — 6f

2:25 (2:26) (Class 6) 2-Y-0 — £2,730 (£806; £403) Stalls Low

Form — RPR

6505 **1** **Burlington Fayr (IRE)**[4] [4724] 2-8-6 48........ MichaelJStainton(5) 4 — 57
(N Tinkler) *mde all stands side: rdn over 1f out: styd on wl* **16/1**

63 **2** 1 ¼ **Birdie Birdie**[16] [4376] 2-8-11........ PaulHanagan 8 — 53
(R A Fahey) *chsde ldrs stands side: rdn along 2f out: kpt on ins last* **5/1**[2]

5040 **3** hd **Poniard (IRE)**[17] [4321] 2-9-2 58........ DanielTudhope 12 — 58
(D W Barker) *trckd ldrs far side: hdwy wl over 1f out: rdn ins last: kpt on* **40/1**

040 **4** 1 ¾ **Straw Boy**[22] [4177] 2-9-2 52........ RobertWinston 11 — 52
(M R Channon) *bhd far side: hdwy 2f out: rdn and kpty on wl f: nrst fin* **12/1**

00 **5** 1 ¼ **Dazzling Olivia (IRE)**[19] [4251] 2-8-11........ DerekMcGaffin 5 — 44
(R A Fahey) *towards rr stands side: rdn along 2f out: kpt on ins last: nrst fin* **40/1**

1230 **6** 1/2 **Tokyo Jo (IRE)**28 [3997] 2-9-2 57............(v) NCallan 17 47
(K R Burke) *cl up far side: bmpd after 1f: hdwy to ld that gp wl over 1f out and ev ch tl drvn and wknd ins last* **7/2**1

6000 **7** 3/4 **Spinning Game**14 [4436] 2-8-13 50............ BenSwarbrick(3) 13 45
(D W Chapman) *in tch far side: hdwy 2f out: rdn ent last and kpt on same pce* **20/1**

420 **8** hd **Dispol Splendid (IRE)**32 [3878] 2-8-11 58............ PaulFessey 1 39
(T D Barron) *cl up stands side: rdn 2f out wknd appr last* **10/1**

3506 **9** 1 3/4 **Flamestone**16 [4376] 2-9-2 57............(b) KerrinMcEvoy 14 39
(J D Bethell) *chsd ldrs far side: rdn along 2f out: sn one pce* **10/1**

0540 **10** 1 **Amelie Brown (IRE)**37 [3720] 2-8-11 56............(b1) MichaelHills 19 31
(N Tinkler) *chsd ldrs far side: rdn along 2f out: sn one pce* **10/1**

0005 **11** shd **Lost Inheritance**8 [4630] 2-8-6............ RoryMoore(5) 20 31
(P T Midgley) *led far side gp: rdn along over 2f out: hdd wl over 1f out and grad wknd* **20/1**

0005 **12** 1 1/4 **Vodkat**37 [3746] 2-8-8............(b1) JasonEdmunds(3) 10 27
(N Tinkler) *swtchd to r far side: a midfield* **50/1**

0340 **13** nk **The Dandy Fox**10 [4547] 2-8-11 52............ RoystonFfrench 9 26
(R Bastiman) *swtchd to r far side: towards rr fr 1/2-way* **16/1**

55 **14** 1 1/2 **Hidden Ace (IRE)**14 [4434] 2-8-11............(b) PaulMulrennan 7 22
(M W Easterby) *chsd ldr stands side: rdn along 2f out: sn wknd* **11/2**3

0600 **15** nk **Ellies Faith**8 [4630] 2-8-4............ SuzzanneFrance(7) 15 21
(N Bycroft) *prom far side: rdn along over 2f out: sn wknd* **25/1**

00 **16** 12 **Josr's Bank**11 [4510] 2-8-11............ LeeEnstone 16 —
(M W Easterby) *chsd ldrs far side: rdn along over 2f out: sn wknd* **50/1**

0 **17** 3 **A Foot In Front**24 [4109] 2-8-11............ NataliaGemelova(5) 6 —
(N Tinkler) *a rr stands side* **66/1**

4366 **18** nk **Dotty's Daughter**20 [4222] 2-8-8 55............(b) SaleemGolam(3) 3 —
(Mrs A Duffield) *chsd ldrs stands side: rdn along over 2f out: sn wknd* **14/1**

00 **19** 16 **Nice One**37 [3746] 2-8-11............ BrianReilly 18 —
(J R Turner) *cl up far side:lost pl and sn bhd* **66/1**

1m 17.9s (4.90) **Going Correction** +0.425s/f (Yiel) **19** Ran SP% **132.8**
Speed ratings (Par 92):84,82,82,79,78 77,76,76,73,72 72,70,70,68,67 51,47,47,26
CSF £92.99 TOTE £29.80: £8.00, £2.40, £14.50; EX 170.90 TRIFECTA Not won..The winner was bought in for 5,500gns.
Owner Dukes Park Racing **Bred** John McEnery **Trained** Langton, N Yorks

FOCUS
Just an ordinary seller. They split into two groups from the start and the first two home raced on the stands' side, although there was not a great deal in it. The winning time was very moderate, even for a race like this and the form is below average for the grade.

NOTEBOOK
Burlington Fayr(IRE), although well held, showed she stays seven furlongs at Musselburgh on her previous start and the testing enough conditions suited her well over this shorter trip. She will carry a penalty in this grade for the rest of the year, and that will make things tougher, although her ability to handle these conditions will stand her in good stead.
Birdie Birdie handled the conditions well enough and basically just found one too good. She ought to find a similar race before the end of the season. Official explanation: jockey said filly hung left (op 6-1)
Poniard(IRE) proved well suited by the return to selling company and fared best of those who raced on the far side of the track.
Straw Boy, dropped into selling company for the first time, ran reasonably and might get seven furlongs.
Dazzling Olivia(IRE), a stablemate of the runner-up, got going too late on this drop into selling company.
Tokyo Jo(IRE) had the ground to suit but was disappointing under her 5lb penalty. (op 5-1)
Hidden Ace(IRE), dropped into a seller for the first time, looked a leading contender judged on the form she had shown in a couple of sand maidens, but proved disappointing on her turf debut. Official explanation: jockey said filly never travelled (op 6-1 tchd 13-2)

4888 BILLY NEVETT MEMORIAL H'CAP 6f
3:00 (3:01) (Class 4) (0-85,84) 3-Y-0 **£6,309** (£1,888; £944; £472; £235) **Stalls** Low

Form RPR

6112 **1** **Al Qasi (IRE)**10 [4573] 3-9-7 **84**............ KerrinMcEvoy 8 109+
(P W Chapple-Hyam) *hld up in tch stands side: hdwy 2f out: rdn and qcknd to ld jst ins last: sn clr* **5/2**2

612 **2** 4 **Greek Renaissance (IRE)**47 [3403] 3-9-4 **81**............ MichaelHills 10 94+
(M P Tregoning) *prom stands side: hdwy 2f out: rdn and ev ch over 1f out tl drvn and one pce ins last* **13/8**1

2121 **3** 2 1/2 **Stonecrabstomorrow (IRE)**17 [4328] 3-9-4 **81**............ NCallan 4 87
(P F I Cole) *prom stands side: hdwy 2f out: rdn to ld over 1f out: drvn and hdd jst ins last: one pce* **6/1**3

3020 **4** 3 1/2 **Charlie Delta**5 [4707] 3-9-4 **81**............ DanielTudhope 5 76
(D Carroll) *hld up towards rr stands side: hdwy wl over 1f out: sn rdn and no imp* **25/1**

0020 **5** hd **The History Man (IRE)**24 [4119] 3-8-8 **71**............(b) PaulMulrennan 1 65
(M W Easterby) *overall ldr stands side: rdn along 2f out: hdd over 1f out and sn wknd* **16/1**

0440 **6** 4 **Rainbow Bay**14 [4422] 3-8-7 **70**............(b1) PaulHanagan 12 52
(R A Fahey) *cl up far side: rdn to ld that gp 2f out: sn drvn and no ch w stands side* **16/1**

0510 **7** nk **Conrad**5 [4707] 3-8-6 **74**............(b1) MichaelJStainton(5) 3 56
(R A Fahey) *a towards rr stands side* **25/1**

4264 **8** 3 **Mulligan's Gold (IRE)**15 [4403] 3-8-6 **69**............ PaulFessey 13 42
(T D Easterby) *led far side gp: rdn along 1/2-way: sn hdd and outpcd* **16/1**

30-0 **9** shd **Island Prince (IRE)**4 [4725] 3-8-6 **72**............ SaleemGolam(3) 7 44
(Mrs A Duffield) *a rr stands side* **33/1**

50-0 **10** 2 1/2 **Double Carpet (IRE)**129 [1109] 3-8-0 **64** oh2 ow3............ RoryMoore(5) 6 33
(G Woodward) *s.i.s: a rr stands side* **100/1**

6005 **11** 3 **Mr Rooney (IRE)**26 [4058] 3-8-9 **72**............ RoystonFfrench 2 28
(M Johnston) *chsd ldrs stands side: rdn along wl over 2f out: sn wknd* **16/1**

0000 **12** 6 **Savernake Blue**13 [4449] 3-9-1 **78**............ RobertWinston 11 16
(M R Channon) *rrd s: prom far side tl rdn along and outpcd fnl 2f* **33/1**

1m 14.48s (1.48) **Going Correction** +0.425s/f (Yiel) **12** Ran SP% **119.0**
Speed ratings (Par 102):107,101,98,93,93 88,87,83,83,80 76,68
CSF £6.55 CT £21.78 TOTE £3.90: £1.50, £1.60, £1.80; EX 6.60 Trifecta £10.30 Pool: £395.50 - 27.17 winning units..
Owner Ziad A Galadari **Bred** T C Butler **Trained** Newmarket, Suffolk

FOCUS
A good three-year-old sprint handicap and the form looks strong. The field again split into two groups, and the much larger bunch on the stands' side dominated.
Rainbow Bay Official explanation: jockey said gelding hung left throughout
Conrad Official explanation: jockey said colt was unsuited by the track
Mulligan's Gold(IRE) Official explanation: jockey said colt hung left
Double Carpet(IRE) Official explanation: jockey said gelding was unsuited by the track
Mr Rooney(IRE) Official explanation: jockey said colt hung left

4889 RIPON ROWELS H'CAP 1m
3:35 (3:36) (Class 2) (0-100,98) 3-Y-0+
£12,464 (£3,732; £1,866; £934; £466; £234) **Stalls** High

Form RPR

06 **1** **Rio Riva**60 [3020] 4-9-8 **93**............ PaulHanagan 3 103
(Miss J A Camacho) *hld up in rr: swtchd outside and stdy hdwy wl over 2f out: rdn to ld and hung rt ent last: sn drvn and kpt on wl* **8/1**

0251 **2** 1/2 **Granston (IRE)**23 [4153] 5-9-4 **89**............ KerrinMcEvoy 10 98
(J D Bethell) *always prom on inner: hdwy to ld 3f out: rdn 2f out: drvn: edgd lft and hdd ent last: kpt on wl u.p* **9/2**2

0215 **3** 1 1/4 **Collateral Damage (IRE)**8 [4634] 3-8-11 **88**............ RobertWinston 11 94
(T D Easterby) *hld up: hdwy on inner over 2f out: swtchd lft and rdn over 1f out ev ch whn hmpd ent last: swtchd lft and kpt on wl* **3/1**1

1460 **4** 3/4 **Sew'N'So Character (IRE)**29 [3973] 5-9-0 **85**............ NCallan 8 90
(M Blanshard) *hld up in tch: hdwy 3f out: rdn to chse ldrs wl over 1f out: kpt on same pce* **8/1**

1540 **5** 1 1/2 **Goodbye Mr Bond**16 [4356] 6-8-12 **88**............ MichaelJStainton(5) 7 90
(E J Alston) *trckd ldrs: effrt and nt clr run 2f out and again over 1f out: kpt on* **13/2**3

3253 **6** 3 **Vicious Warrior**7 [4654] 7-8-9 **80**............ RoystonFfrench 9 76
(R M Whitaker) *prom: effrt to chal over 3f out: rdn along over 2f out and grad wknd* **12/1**

-100 **7** 9 **Fortunate Isle (USA)**61 [2989] 4-9-4 **89**............ MichaelHills 12 67
(B W Hills) *jinked s: sn prom: effrt to dispute ld 3f out: sn rdn and ev ch tl drvn and wknd appr last* **13/2**3

4200 **8** 5 **Little Miss Gracie**8 [4628] 4-9-7 **95**............ SaleemGolam(3) 4 63
(A B Haynes) *sn led: rdn along over 3f out: sn hdd & wknd* **33/1**

2-23 **9** nk **Cross My Mind**16 [4372] 4-8-11 **85**............ BenSwarbrick(3) 2 52
(T Keddy) *a rr* **8/1**

5 **10** shd **Indian's Feather (IRE)**10 [4577] 5-9-0 **85**............(b) PaulMulrennan 1 52
(N Tinkler) *wnt lft s: sn prom on outer: rdn along over 3f out and sn wknd* **50/1**

1m 42.46s (1.36) **Going Correction** +0.425s/f (Yiel)
WFA 3 from 4yo+ 6lb **10** Ran SP% **115.8**
Speed ratings (Par 109):110,109,108,107,106 103,94,89,88,88
CSF £43.59 CT £136.75 TOTE £8.30: £2.40, £2.00, £1.60; EX 60.00 Trifecta £178.20 Pool: £426.91 - 1.70 winning units..
Owner Rio Riva Partnership **Bred** Mrs S Camacho **Trained** Norton, N Yorks
■ Stewards' Enquiry : Paul Hanagan caution: careless riding

FOCUS
A decent handicap run in a good time and the form is sound.

NOTEBOOK
Rio Riva had never previously won in such testing conditions, but he basically handles any ground and posted a fine effort, 93 being the highest mark he has ever won off. He is developing into a very useful handicapper. (op 9-1)
Granston(IRE) had never won on ground worse than good, but he is another who clearly handles most conditions and this was a terrific effort off a career-high mark. (op 5-1 tchd 11-2 and 4-1)
Collateral Damage(IRE) ◆ had the ground to suit, but he was denied a clear run against the rail and was unlucky not to have finished a lot closer. He could pick up a decent handicap this autumn. (op 11-4 tchd 10-3)
Sew'N'So Character(IRE) is very consistent but just hard to win with.
Goodbye Mr Bond did not run enjoy a clear run and was unlucky not to have finished closer. Official explanation: jockey said gelding was unsuited by the track (op 7-1)
Cross My Mind, very easy to back, never went a yard. He probably wants better ground. (op 13-2 tchd 6-1)

4890 RIPON CHAMPION TWO YRS OLD TROPHY, 2006 (LISTED RACE) 6f
4:10 (4:10) (Class 1) 2-Y-0 **£17,115** (£6,537; £3,312; £1,692; £888) **Stalls** Low

Form RPR

0511 **1** **Stevie Gee (IRE)**16 [4377] 2-9-2 92............ RobertWinston 6 101+
(G A Swinbank) *trckd ldrs: hdwy to chse ldr after 2f: rdn to ld wl over 1f out: styd on* **2/1**1

0051 **2** 1 1/2 **Everymanforhimself (IRE)**13 [4460] 2-9-2 96............ KerrinMcEvoy 2 97
(J G Given) *hld up: hdwy on outer 1/2-way: rdn to chal over 1f out: drvn and kpt on fnl f* **5/2**2

511 **3** 2 1/2 **Rainbow Mirage (IRE)**60 [3026] 2-9-2 84............ RoystonFfrench 5 89
(E S McMahon) *trckd ldrs: hdwy 2f out: sn rdn and no imp ent last* **11/2**

100 **4** 3 **Baltimore Jack (IRE)**3 [4766] 2-9-2 83............ MichaelJStainton 3 80
(R M Whitaker) *trckd ldr: effrt over 2f out: sn rdn and wknd wl over 1f out* **14/1**

1230 **5** 1/2 **Amber Valley**66 [2800] 2-8-11 95............ NCallan 1 74
(K A Ryan) *led: rdn along over 2f out: hdd wl over 1f out: sn wknd* **10/3**3

0204 **P** **Dickie Le Davoir**2 [4789] 2-9-2 90............(v) PaulHanagan 4 —
(K R Burke) *a rr: lost tch 1/2-way: t.o and p.u wl over 1f out* **14/1**

1m 15.82s (2.82) **Going Correction** +0.425s/f (Yiel) **6** Ran SP% **113.7**
Speed ratings (Par 102):98,96,92,88,88 —
CSF £7.46 TOTE £2.10: £1.80, £1.90; EX 7.00.
Owner Steve Gray **Bred** Irish National Stud **Trained** Melsonby, N Yorks

FOCUS
A weak renewal of this Listed contest and the form is reasonable but limited.

NOTEBOOK
Stevie Gee(IRE), who landed a gamble in maiden company on the Fibresand at Southwell before defying a mark of 85 on fast ground in a nursery at Redcar, coped with the very different conditions and step up in grade to complete the hat-trick in decisive fashion. This was a very soft race for the grade, but he is improving all the time and should not be underestimated in future. He ought to go well if taking his chance in the Redcar Two-Year-Old Trophy. (op 5-2)
Everymanforhimself(IRE), the winner of a Nottingham nursery off a mark of 92 on his previous start, ran a good race in this higher grade but was well held by the progressive winner. (op 11-4)
Rainbow Mirage(IRE) has progressed well to win his last two starts, but this was a lot tougher and he ran well considering. (op 9-2 tchd 6-1)
Baltimore Jack(IRE) has lost his way since winning a maiden at Ayr on his debut, but acquitted himself creditably this time. (op 33-1)
Amber Valley is not progressing and this was a very disappointing effort. Official explanation: jockey said filly hung right throughout (op 3-1 tchd 7-2)
Dickie Le Davoir Official explanation: jockey said saddle slipped

4891 CHRIS & CHRIS SMITH'S 40TH ANNIVERSARY MAIDEN STKS 1m
4:45 (4:47) (Class 5) 3-4-Y-0 **£3,886** (£1,156; £577; £288) **Stalls** High

Form RPR

344 **1** **Pab Special (IRE)**8 [4634] 3-8-12 70............ AndrewElliott(5) 1 71
(K R Burke) *a cl up: effrt 3f out: rdn to ld 2f out: drvn and styd on wl fnl f* **5/1**3

0-F0 **2** 2 ½ **Zell (IRE)**[8] [4635] 3-8-7 .... MichaelJStainton(5) 9 61
(E J Alston) *keen: a.p: rdn along wl over 1f out: drvn and kpt on ins last* **50/1**

0- **3** *hd* **Abeurbe Condita (IRE)**[338] [5464] 3-9-3 .... RoystonFfrench 4 66
(E S McMahon) *hld up towards rr: hdwy 3f out: rdn along 2f out: styd on to chse wnr ins lst: lost 2nd nr fin* **33/1**

32 **4** *2* **Country Escape**[19] [4247] 3-9-3 .... KerrinMcEvoy 5 62
(C F Wall) *trckd ldrs: pushed along over 2f out: rdn to chse wnr ent last: sn no ex* **7/4**[2]

-332 **5** 2 ½ **Mashaair (IRE)**[18] [4287] 3-9-3 74 .... MichaelHills 8 57
(B W Hills) *led: rdn along 3f out: drvn and hdd 2f out: sn wknd* **6/4**[1]

0U6 **6** 1 ½ **Miss Imperious**[23] [4155] 3-8-12 .... DerekMcGaffin 6 49
(B Smart) *rr tl sme late hdwy* **50/1**

04 **7** *9* **Another Gladiator (USA)**[24] [4117] 3-9-3 .... NCallan 3 36
(K A Ryan) *chsds ldrs: rdn along 3f out: wknd over 2f out* **8/1**

0 **8** *14* **Skodger (IRE)**[8] [4635] 3-9-3 ....(t) PaulFessey 7 8
(G Woodward) *a bhd* **80/1**

1m 44.06s (2.96) **Going Correction** +0.425s/f (Yiel) **8** Ran SP% **112.2**
Speed ratings (Par 103):102,99,99,97,94 93,84,70
CSF £185.65 TOTE £6.70: £1.80, £8.00, £4.60; EX 163.20 Trifecta £439.40 Part won. Pool: £618.90 - 0.10 winning units..
Owner P A Brazier **Bred** Ballyhane Stud **Trained** Middleham Moor, N Yorks

FOCUS
A very weak maiden but the form is sound if modest.
Country Escape Official explanation: jockey said gelding lost a near-fore shoe
Mashaair(IRE) Official explanation: jockey said colt was unsuited by the soft ground
Miss Imperious Official explanation: jockey said filly was unsuited by the undulating track
Skodger(IRE) Official explanation: jockey said colt had a breathing problem

4892 PATELEY BRIDGE H'CAP 1m 1f 170y
5:20 (5:20) (Class 5) (0-70,70) 3-Y-O **£3,886** (£1,156; £577; £288) **Stalls** High

Form RPR

3401 **1** **Lady Disdain**[9] [4610] 3-9-3 69 .... SaleemGolam(3) 7 81
(G M Moore) *hld up: smooth hdwy over 3f out: led over 2f out: sn rdn clr* **7/2**[1]

4033 **2** *8* **Floodlight Fantasy**[22] [4173] 3-9-2 65 ....(p) RoystonFfrench 4 63
(E S McMahon) *chsd ldrs: rdn along over 2f out: drvn over 1f out: kpt on: no ch w wnr* **9/2**[2]

0356 **3** *1* **Can Can Star**[12] [4470] 3-9-1 64 .... KerrinMcEvoy 8 60
(J G Given) *hld up towards rr: hdwy 3f out: rdn over 2f out: kpt on appr last: nrst fin* **10/1**

053 **4** 2 ½ **Lady Lochinver (IRE)**[10] [4567] 3-8-3 52 .... PaulFessey 11 44
(Micky Hammond) *rr: pushed along 3f out: rdn over 2f out: swtchd lft wl over v1f out: styd on ins last* **7/1**

4500 **5** *5* **Rainbow's Classic**[14] [4426] 3-9-0 63 ....(b¹) NCallan 2 47
(K A Ryan) *prom: hdwy to dispute ld over 3f out: rdn and led briefly over 2f out: sn hdd and grad wknd* **10/1**

-266 **6** ¾ **Historic Appeal (USA)**[98] [1881] 3-8-13 69 .... ThomasO'Brien(7) 9 51
(M R Channon) *towards rr: rdn along on inner 3f out: nvr nr ldrs* **11/1**

0436 **7** *1* **Twilight Avenger (IRE)**[19] [4255] 3-7-13 53 oh5 ow2........ RoryMoore(5) 6 34
(W M Brisbourne) *chsd ldrs: rdn along on inner over 3f out: sn wknd* **25/1**

0633 **8** ½ **Sinner Or Saint (IRE)**[19] [4254] 3-9-4 67 .... RobertWinston 5 47
(T D Easterby) *chsd ldng pair: hdwy 4f out: rdn along and hung rt 3f out: wknd and eased 2f out* **6/1**[3]

0230 **9** *nk* **Shaydreambeliever**[22] [4173] 3-9-4 67 .... PaulHanagan 10 46
(R A Fahey) *a rr* **10/1**

5560 **10** 1 ¼ **Linton Dancer (IRE)**[23] [4132] 3-7-13 53 oh3 ow2........ AndrewElliott(5) 1 30
(J R Weymes) *racd wd: sn led: rdn along and jnd over 3f out: hdd & wknd over 2f out* **14/1**

11 *6* **Pistol Dawn**[95] [1971] 3-8-13 62 .... DanielTudhope 13 29
(J J Quinn) *a bhd* **14/1**

2m 8.53s (3.53) **Going Correction** +0.425s/f (Yiel) **11** Ran SP% **120.0**
Speed ratings (Par 100):102,95,94,92,88 88,87,87,86,85 80
CSF £19.15 CT £147.04 TOTE £4.10: £2.30, £1.90, £3.50; EX 30.70 Trifecta £144.10 Pool: £259.89 - 1.28 winning units. Place 6 £132.68, Place 5 £19.01..
Owner Mrs D N B Pearson **Bred** Mrs D N B Pearson **Trained** Middleham Moor, N Yorks
■ Stewards' Enquiry : Paul Fessey one-day ban: careless riding (Sep 8)

FOCUS
Just a modest handicap and not rated positively.
T/Plt: £135.90 to a £1 stake. Pool: £58,735.25. 315.45 winning tickets. T/Qpdt: £32.50 to a £1 stake. Pool: £2,728.20. 62.05 winning tickets. JR

3448 WARWICK (L-H)
Monday, August 28

OFFICIAL GOING: Good (good to soft in places on 5f chute)
Despite the ground not being soft, the jockeys came over towards the stands' side throughout the afternoon.
Wind: Moderate, across Weather: Mainly dry

4893 SEE MORE ON RACING UK NURSERY 5f 110y
2:00 (2:01) (Class 5) 2-Y-O **£3,238** (£963; £481; £240) **Stalls** Centre

Form RPR

1010 **1** **Il Palio (IRE)**[26] [4043] 2-8-12 82 .... JamesMillman(7) 2 85
(B R Millman) *hung rt thrght: mde all: rdn fnl f: r.o* **13/2**[3]

1021 **2** 1 ¼ **Aahayson**[11] [4519] 2-9-4 81 .... PatCosgrave 10 80
(K R Burke) *a.p: rdn and ev ch 1f out: nt qckn* **10/3**[2]

2063 **3** 1 ¾ **Fairfield Princess**[17] [4326] 2-9-4 84 .... StephenDonohoe(3) 3 77
(N A Callaghan) *hld up: rdn and hdwy 2f out: one pce fnl f* **7/1**

013 **4** ¾ **Compton Fields**[44] [3555] 2-9-0 77 .... SteveDrowne 7 68
(R Charlton) *chsd wnr: rdn and edgd lft over 1f out: one pce* **3/1**[1]

630 **5** ½ **Bert's Memory**[19] [4251] 2-8-7 70 .... CatherineGannon 4 59
(K A Ryan) *a.p: one pce fnl 2f* **16/1**

0360 **6** ½ **Copper King**[57] [3117] 2-7-13 62 .... JimmyQuinn 8 49
(A M Balding) *bhd: rdn over 2f out: sme hdwy over 1f out: no imp fnl f* **8/1**

0043 **7** *6* **Rue Soleil**[5] [4693] 2-7-7 61 oh9... DuranFentiman(5) 6 29
(J R Weymes) *hld up: hung rt over 3f out: rdn over 2f out: sn struggling* **10/1**

026 **8** *1* **Nepos**[14] [4434] 2-8-4 67 .... JoeFanning 5 31
(J A Osborne) *s.i.s: short-lived effrt over 1f out: eased whn btn ins fnl f* **11/1**

64.85 secs (-0.65) **Going Correction** -0.25s/f (Firm) **8** Ran SP% **108.3**
Speed ratings (Par 94):94,92,90,89,88 87,79,78
CSF £25.40 CT £137.76 TOTE £9.00: £2.00, £1.40, £2.00; EX 39.90.
Owner Mrs L S Millman **Bred** Blue Bloodstock Limited **Trained** Kentisbeare, Devon

FOCUS
An ordinary nursery and sound enough, with the runner-up setting the level.

NOTEBOOK
Il Palio(IRE) proved a difficult ride for his inexperienced pilot. It must have helped that after this race the jockeys decided that the stands' side was the place to be. (op 8-1)
Aahayson could not defy a 2lb rise in the ratings over this slightly longer trip. (tchd 3-1 and 7-2)
Fairfield Princess was 11lb worse off than when fourth lengths in front of the winner at Windsor in June. (op 6-1)
Compton Fields had no excuses on this occasion on this rather slower ground. (tchd 11-4)
Bert's Memory did not find slight drop back in distance the answer. (op 12-1)
Copper King could never really get competitive over a slightly shorter trip.

4894 TRISH ADUDU MAD SAUSAGE H'CAP 6f 21y
2:35 (2:35) (Class 5) (0-70,71) 3-Y-O+ **£3,238** (£963; £481; £240) **Stalls** Low

Form RPR

0504 **1** **Polish Index**[12] [4496] 4-9-5 65 ....(p) RichardHughes 3 74
(J R Jenkins) *mde all: rdn over 1f out: jst hld on* **14/1**

2364 **2** *shd* **Gilded Cove**[58] [3097] 6-8-13 66 .... RussellKennemore(7) 2 77+
(R Hollinshead) *hld up in mid-div: hdwy 2f out: nt clr run and swtchd lft over 1f out: r.o wl and edgd rt ins fnl f: jst failed* **11/2**[2]

0101 **3** ½ **Tadlil**[16] [4361] 4-9-7 67 .... JamieSpencer 7 74
(J M Bradley) *hld up in mid-div: rdn and hdwy over 1f out: r.o ins fnl f* **11/4**[1]

1655 **4** ¾ **Danetime Lord (IRE)**[58] [3087] 3-9-2 65 ....(p) CatherineGannon 4 70
(K A Ryan) *chsd wnr: swtchd lft 2f out: sn rdn: no ex towards fin* **14/1**

0000 **5** 1 ¼ **The Crooked Ring**[14] [4437] 4-9-3 66 .... StephenDonohoe(3) 6 67
(P D Evans) *hld up and bhd: rdn and hdwy fnl f: nvr nrr* **8/1**

5031 **6** ½ **Summer Recluse (USA)**[8] [4629] 7-9-11 71 6ex.........(t) SteveDrowne 10 71
(J M Bradley) *hld up in mid-div: outpcd 2f out: kpt on ins fnl f* **17/2**

6005 **7** *nk* **Nistaki (USA)**[10] [4573] 5-9-0 63 .... PatrickMathers(3) 5 62
(D Shaw) *t.k.h in rr: rdn over 1f out: kpt on fnl f: nt rch ldrs* **15/2**[3]

0550 **8** *shd* **Nephetriti Way (IRE)**[18] [4294] 5-9-6 66 .... JoeFanning 8 65
(P R Chamings) *hld up and bhd: kpt on fnl f: nt rch ldrs* **20/1**

1010 **9** *nk* **Banjo Bay (IRE)**[10] [4564] 8-9-3 66 ....(t) NeilChalmers(3) 9 64
(Miss Gay Kelleway) *hld up in tch: rdn over 1f out: wknd ins fnl f* **12/1**

3500 **10** *hd* **Bens Georgie (IRE)**[28] [4003] 4-8-12 65 .... JamesMillman(7) 12 62
(D K Ivory) *s.i.s: sn prom: wknd over 1f out* **16/1**

0000 **11** *hd* **Dunn Deal (IRE)**[24] [4119] 6-9-3 63 .... PatCosgrave 1 59
(W M Brisbourne) *prom: rdn over 1f out: wknd ins fnl f* **12/1**

0043 **12** 3 ½ **Parkside Pursuit**[8] [4629] 8-9-2 62 .... PaulFitzsimons 11 48
(J M Bradley) *a bhd* **12/1**

1m 11.47s (-0.63) **Going Correction** -0.075s/f (Good)
WFA 3 from 4yo+ 3lb **12** Ran SP% **122.5**
Speed ratings (Par 103):101,100,100,99,97 96,96,96,95,95 95,90
CSF £92.22 CT £287.56 TOTE £17.80: £4.70, £2.10, £1.60; EX 89.30.
Owner Mrs Stella Peirce **Bred** Michael Ng **Trained** Royston, Herts

FOCUS
A modest, tightly-knit handicap and solid form, with the runner-up to form.
Banjo Bay(IRE) Official explanation: jockey said gelding finished distressed

4895 RACING UK MAIDEN AUCTION STKS (DIV I) 7f 26y
3:10 (3:11) (Class 5) 2-Y-O **£2,590** (£770; £385; £192) **Stalls** Low

Form RPR

0 **1** **Buccellati**[49] [3363] 2-9-1 .... FergusSweeney 12 77
(A M Balding) *a.p: rdn to ld 2f out: edgd lft jst over 1f out: hld on wl ins fnl f* **7/1**[3]

0 **2** *shd* **Shake On It**[53] [3222] 2-8-13 ....(t) StephenCarson 9 75
(R F Johnson Houghton) *hld up: smooth hdwy 2f out: ev ch ins fnl f: r.o* **9/2**[2]

0 **3** 1 ½ **Kalasam**[15] [4388] 2-9-1 .... SteveDrowne 6 73
(W R Muir) *hld up in mid-div: rdn over 2f out: hdwy over 1f out: kpt on ins fnl f* **17/2**

00 **4** *shd* **Hunting Call**[10] [4566] 2-8-11 ....(b¹) CatherineGannon 2 69
(K A Ryan) *led: rdn and hdd 2f out: ev ch whn edgd rt jst over 1f out: nt qckn ins fnl f* **66/1**

4323 **5** 1 ¾ **Angeletta**[14] [4427] 2-8-4 74 .... JimmyQuinn 8 57
(E S McMahon) *a.p: rdn and no hdwy fnl 2f* **2/1**[1]

05 **6** *nk* **Toggle**[18] [4290] 2-9-1 .... RichardHughes 11 68
(R Hannon) *chsd ldr: rdn over 3f out: ev ch over 1f out: hmpd jst ins fnl f: wknd* **16/1**

006 **7** *5* **Princess Zada**[20] [4221] 2-8-4 .... JoeFanning 5 44
(B R Millman) *prom: rdn over 2f out: faltered and lost action over 1f out: eased whn btn ins fnl f* **25/1**

8 *1* **Annia Faustina (IRE)** 2-8-6 .... RichardThomas 4 43
(J L Spearing) *s.i.s: a bhd* **28/1**

24 **9** *shd* **Novista (IRE)**[19] [4264] 2-9-0 .... RHills 10 51
(M H Tompkins) *hld up in mid-div: rdn 3f out: bhd fnl 2f* **9/1**

10 *nk* **Ella Woodcock (IRE)** 2-9-0 .... JamieSpencer 1 50
(J A Osborne) *s.i.s and hmpd: a bhd* **16/1**

11 *1* **Allroundtheoutside** 2-8-11 .... PaulDoe 7 44
(P R Chamings) *s.i.s: hdwy 4f out: wknd 3f out* **25/1**

12 2 ½ **Victor Trumper** 2-8-10 .... StephenDonohoe(3) 3 40
(P W Chapple-Hyam) *s.i.s: a bhd* **7/1**[3]

1m 24.04s (-0.96) **Going Correction** -0.075s/f (Good) **12** Ran SP% **121.4**
Speed ratings (Par 94):102,101,100,100,98 97,92,90,90,90 89,86
CSF £38.19 TOTE £10.40: £2.80, £2.10, £3.50; EX 54.70.
Owner I A Balding **Bred** Burton Agnes Stud Co Ltd **Trained** Kingsclere, Hants
■ Stewards' Enquiry : Catherine Gannon one-day ban: careless riding (Sep 8)
Fergus Sweeney caution: careless riding

FOCUS
A decent winning time for a race like this and 0.29 seconds faster than the other division. The form is rated through the third.

NOTEBOOK
Buccellati is a half-brother to 11-furlong winner Petite Chinoise who went on to be a very useful performer in Denmark. Quietly fancied by his trainer after being too green to do himself justice on his debut, he certainly showed the right attitude and there could be more improvement to come. (op 10-1 tchd 11-1)
Shake On It ◆, who halved in price in the market, was confidently ridden having been fitted with a tongue-tie. He found that the winner would not be denied but his turn is merely delayed. (op 9-1)
Kalasam ◆ is a half-brother to Group 3 winner Torosay Spring and mile and a quarter winner Spring Jim. He seems to be progressing along the right lines and should not be inconvenienced by a longer trip. (op 6-1 tchd 10-1)
Hunting Call was transformed by the fitting of blinkers but it obviously remains to be seen if they can work the oracle again. (op 33-1)
Angeletta could not raise her game in the home straight over an extra furlong. (tchd 11-4 in a place)

Toggle looked held when becoming the meat in the sandwich with 200 yards to go. He seems worth a try back at six furlongs. (op 12-1)
Ella Woodcock(IRE) Official explanation: jockey said gelding was hampered at start

4896 LAW FAMILY CONDITIONS STKS — 7f 26y
3:45 (3:46) (Class 4) 3-Y-O+ — **£6,477** (£1,927; £963; £481) **Stalls** Low

Form — RPR

-010 **1** — **Cesare**^{44} [3534] 5-8-11 102 .... JamieSpencer 1 — 111+
(J R Fanshawe) *trckd ldrs: rdn and edgd lft over 1f out: sn led: readily* **11/10**^{1}

-440 **2** 1 ¾ **Mostashaar (FR)**^{4} [4740] 4-8-11 105 .... RHills 5 — 104
(Sir Michael Stoute) *trckd ldrs: rdn over 1f out: chsd wnr fnl f: no imp* **6/1**

1611 **3** 2 **Dream Theme**^{15} [4391] 3-8-10 100 .... RichardHughes 7 — 100
(B W Hills) *t.k.h in rr: rdn and hdwy over 1f out: one pce fnl f* **9/2**^{3}

0250 **4** 1 **Sir Xaar (IRE)**^{9} [4596] 3-8-9 104 .... FergusSweeney 3 — 97
(B Smart) *sn w ldr: led 2f out: rdn and hdd over 1f out: fdd ins fnl f* **12/1**

0330 **5** 3 **King Marju (IRE)**^{30} [3926] 4-8-11 89 .... (v) PatCosgrave 6 — 88
(K R Burke) *stdd s: plld hrd in rr: rdn over 1f out: no rspnse* **28/1**

323- **6** 6 **Black Charmer (IRE)**^{397} [3836] 3-8-6 110 .... JoeFanning 4 — 78+
(M Johnston) *led: hdd 2f out: sn rdn: wknd over 1f out* **4/1**^{2}

1m 23.27s (-1.73) **Going Correction** -0.075s/f (Good)
WFA 3 from 4yo+ 5lb — **6** Ran SP% **111.2**
Speed ratings (Par 105):106,104,101,100,97 90
CSF £8.12 TOTE £2.00: £1.60, £2.90; EX 11.40.
Owner Cheveley Park Stud **Bred** Cheveley Park Stud Ltd **Trained** Newmarket, Suffolk

FOCUS
A decent turn-out for an event of this grade but the form is notr that solid.

4897 RACING UK MAIDEN AUCTION STKS (DIV II) — 7f 26y
4:20 (4:22) (Class 5) 2-Y-O — **£2,590** (£770; £385; £192) **Stalls** Low

Form — RPR

52 **1** — **Beverly Hill Billy**^{16} [4366] 2-8-11 .... JamieSpencer 3 — 73+
(A King) *hld up in tch: rdn over 1f out: led ins fnl f: r.o* **6/4**^{1}

003 **2** ½ **Bay Of Light**^{32} [3868] 2-8-9 71 .... PaulDoe 7 — 70
(P W Chapple-Hyam) *led: hdd 4f out: rdn to ld 2f out: hdd ins fnl f: kpt on* **6/1**^{3}

3 **3** 1 ¼ **Espejo (IRE)**^{14} [4424] 2-8-13 .... PatCosgrave 1 — 71
(K R Burke) *hld up: hdwy on ins over 3f out: nt clr run and hmpd over 1f out: swtchd lft ins fnl f: nt qckn towards fin* **3/1**^{2}

022 **4** 2 ½ **Anthea**^{15} [4394] 2-8-6 70 .... FergusSweeney 6 — 58
(B R Millman) *chsd ldr: led 4f out to 2f out: sltly hmpd jst over 1f out: btn whn hung rt ins fnl f* **6/1**^{3}

5 3 **Itchycoo Park (IRE)** 2-8-13 .... JoeFanning 10 — 57+
(E J O'Neill) *s.s: t.k.h in rr: hdwy over 1f out: nt rch ldrs* **16/1**

00 **6** ½ **Cheveme (IRE)**^{66} [2800] 2-8-7 ow1 .... DeanCorby$^{(3)}$ 12 — 53
(B W Duke) *prom: rdn over 2f out: wknd over 1f out* **25/1**

0 **7** 5 **Brave Quest (IRE)**^{14} [4434] 2-8-13 .... SteveDrowne 2 — 43
(C J Down) *nvr nr ldrs* **25/1**

00 **8** ½ **Homecroft Boy**^{11} [4525] 2-8-6 .... FrankiePickard$^{(7)}$ 8 — 42
(J A Osborne) *s.i.s: hung rt jst over 1f out: a bhd* **40/1**

5 **9** 2 **Countrywide Style (IRE)**^{11} [4534] 2-8-11 .... JamesDoyle$^{(3)}$ 11 — 38
(N P Littmoden) *a bhd* **33/1**

05 **10** 1 ½ **Hot Cherry**^{12} [4492] 2-8-8 ow1 .... StephenDonohoe$^{(3)}$ 5 — 31
(J M P Eustace) *hld up in mid-div: rdn over 3f out: bhd fnl 2f* **33/1**

0 **11** 5 **Ballyshane Spirit (IRE)**^{10} [4572] 2-9-1 .... PaulEddery 9 — 23
(N A Callaghan) *s.i.s: a bhd* **40/1**

1m 24.33s (-0.67) **Going Correction** -0.075s/f (Good) — **11** Ran SP% **117.9**
Speed ratings (Par 94):100,99,98,95,91 91,85,84,82,80 75
CSF £10.12 TOTE £2.20: £1.30, £2.00, £1.70; EX 13.60.
Owner B Winfield, P Nicholls & A King **Bred** Bearstone Stud **Trained** Barbury Castle, Wilts

FOCUS
A fair time for a race like this despite being 0.29 seconds slower than the first division. The placed horses set a sound but modest standard.

NOTEBOOK
Beverly Hill Billy confirmed the promise of his second at Lingfield and struck oil on this switch to grass. (op 11-8 tchd 6-5, 7-4 in a place and 13-8 in places)
Bay Of Light was again happy to force the pace and there seems no reason why she should not stay a mile. (op 7-1)
Espejo(IRE) ◆ is a half-brother to the six furlong and stretch mile sand winner Union Jack Jackson. Well fancied after his promising Thirsk debut, he did meet trouble in running and probably deserves another chance. (op 4-1)
Anthea had also hung right over course and distance last month and does not appear to be straightforward. (op 11-2 tchd 13-2)
Itchycoo Park(IRE) ◆ showed some promise for the future in the closing stages after missing the break on this debut and is one to keep an eye on. (op 12-1)
Cheveme(IRE) was up in trip and down in class. (op 20-1)

4898 SYD MERCER MEMORIAL H'CAP — 2m 39y
4:55 (4:55) (Class 5) (0-70,64) 3-Y-O+ — **£4,533** (£1,348; £674; £336) **Stalls** Low

Form — RPR

0233 **1** — **Primondo (IRE)**^{14} [4423] 4-9-10 **60** .... (v^{1}) JamieSpencer 6 — 68
(J R Fanshawe) *chsd ldr: rdn to ld over 1f out: edgd rt ins fnl f: r.o* **2/1**^{1}

0642 **2** ¾ **The Grey Man**^{23} [4156] 5-10-0 **64** .... JoeFanning 1 — 71
(E S McMahon) *led: rdn and hdd over 1f out: no ex cl home* **4/1**^{2}

56-0 **3** 1 ½ **Jayer Gilles**^{30} [3952] 6-9-6 **56** .... FergusSweeney 8 — 61
(Dr J R J Naylor) *hld up in mid-div: rdn and hdwy over 2f out: styd on one pce fnl f* **6/1**^{3}

005 **4** 1 ¼ **Blue Away (IRE)**^{3} [4777] 8-9-13 **63** .... RichardHughes 5 — 67
(S Kirk) *hld up in rr: rdn over 3f out: swtchd rt and hdwy over 1f out: one pce fnl f* **7/1**

4006 **5** 1 ¼ **Turner**^{3} [4764] 5-9-2 **52** .... PatCosgrave 4 — 54
(W M Brisbourne) *t.k.h towards rr: hdwy 2f out: rdn over 1f out: wknd ins fnl f* **14/1**

4206 **6** 1 ½ **Trials 'n Tribs**^{14} [4438] 4-8-12 **48** oh5 .... RHills 3 — 48
(C A Cyzer) *hld up towards rr: short-lived effrt over 1f out* **11/1**

60-0 **7** shd **Heart Springs**^{30} [3935] 6-9-4 **54** .... AlanDaly 2 — 54
(Dr J R J Naylor) *hld up in tch: rdn over 1f out: wknd fnl f* **12/1**

3605 **8** 11 **Bukit Fraser (IRE)**^{17} [4331] 5-9-2 **52** .... SteveDrowne 7 — 39
(P F I Cole) *prom: rdn over 2f out: sn wknd* **15/2**

3m 36.25s (3.55) **Going Correction** -0.075s/f (Good) — **8** Ran SP% **114.6**
Speed ratings (Par 103):88,87,86,86,85 84,84,79
CSF £9.93 CT £39.79 TOTE £2.30: £1.20, £1.50, £2.20; EX 8.20.
Owner Mrs Nicolas Kairis **Bred** G And Mrs Middlebrook **Trained** Newmarket, Suffolk

FOCUS
They went no pace in this poor staying handicap won in a very moderate time. The form is ordinary with the runner-up to his best.

4899 WARWICKRACECOURSE.CO.UK MAIDEN STKS — 7f 26y
5:30 (5:32) (Class 5) 3-Y-O+ — **£3,238** (£963; £481; £240) **Stalls** Low

Form — RPR

2206 **1** — **Woodcote Place**^{12} [4488] 3-9-3 72 .... SteveDrowne 7 — 80+
(P R Chamings) *hld up in mid-div: hdwy over 3f out: led ins fnl f: rdn out* **4/1**^{3}

6232 **2** 1 **Uno**^{24} [4113] 3-8-12 77 .... RichardHughes 9 — 72
(B W Hills) *hld up in tch: rdn and ev ch 1f out: nt qckn towards fin* **11/8**^{1}

3220 **3** 1 **Mumaathel (IRE)**^{51} [3317] 3-9-3 79 .... RHills 4 — 74
(M P Tregoning) *w ldr: led over 3f out: rdn and hdd ins fnl f: nt qckn* **5/2**^{2}

0 **4** 3 **Lethal**^{215} [191] 3-9-3 .... JoeFanning 2 — 67
(Ernst Oertel) *t.k.h: led: hdd over 3f out: rdn and hung lft over 1f out: wknd ins fnl f* **66/1**

5 **5** 1 **Brigydon (IRE)**^{46} [3458] 3-9-3 .... JamieSpencer 5 — 64
(J R Fanshawe) *prom tl rdn and wknd 1f out* **9/1**

0 **6** 4 **King's Spear (IRE)**^{131} [1088] 3-9-3 .... PaulDoe 13 — 54+
(P W Chapple-Hyam) *hld up towards rr: rdn over 2f out: nvr nrr* **14/1**

7 6 **Stand By Me** 3-9-3 .... MatthewHenry 14 — 38
(M A Jarvis) *hld up in mid-div: rdn over 3f out: sn struggling* **25/1**

8 hd **Pleasing Gift** 3-8-9 .... StephenDonohoe$^{(3)}$ 8 — 32
(J M P Eustace) *chsd ldrs 4f* **33/1**

0 **9** 2 **Height Of Esteem**^{62} [2948] 3-9-3 .... JimmyQuinn 12 — 32
(M Mullineaux) *plld hrd towards rr: hdwy on ins 3f out: rdn and wknd 2f out* **66/1**

10 3 ½ **Gundula (IRE)** 3-8-12 .... FergusSweeney 6 — 18
(D J S Ffrench Davis) *s.i.s: outpcd: a bhd* **50/1**

11 5 **Raratomba** 3-9-0 .... DeanCorby$^{(3)}$ 10 — 10
(P D Evans) *dwlt: a bhd* **66/1**

12 5 **Just Jasmin** 3-8-12 .... PaulEddery 11 — —
(P D Evans) *dwlt: a bhd* **66/1**

1m 23.43s (-1.57) **Going Correction** -0.075s/f (Good)
WFA 3 from 4yo 5lb — **12** Ran SP% **122.1**
Speed ratings (Par 103):105,103,102,99,98 93,86,86,84,80 74,68
CSF £9.90 TOTE £4.40: £1.30, £1.20, £1.90; EX 11.80.
Owner E D Kessly **Bred** Mrs A M Jenkins **Trained** Baughurst, Hants

FOCUS
Not many seemed to be fancied in this modest maiden and the form is not solid, despite a reasonable time.
Mumaathel(IRE) Official explanation: jockey said gelding ran too free
Height Of Esteem Official explanation: jockey said gelding had a breathing problem

4900 WARWICK RACECOURSE FOR CONFERENCES H'CAP — 1m 4f 134y
6:00 (6:00) (Class 5) (0-75,75) 3-Y-O+ — **£3,238** (£963; £481; £240) **Stalls** Low

Form — RPR

0166 **1** — **Fear To Tread (USA)**^{23} [4159] 3-9-3 **75** .... JimmyQuinn 7 — 83
(J L Dunlop) *a.p: n.m.r on ins 3f out: sustained chal fnl f: hrd rdn to ld cl home* **12/1**

3323 **2** hd **Hawridge King**^{15} [4393] 4-9-5 **66** .... (v^{1}) FergusSweeney 5 — 74
(W S Kittow) *hld up in mid-div: hdwy over 3f out: rdn to ld wl over 1f out: hdd cl home* **6/1**^{2}

6300 **3** 2 ½ **Eastborough (IRE)**^{26} [4036] 7-9-3 **64** .... PatCosgrave 4 — 68
(Stef Liddiard) *hld up and bhd: hdwy over 3f out: sn rdn: one pce fnl f* **8/1**

-031 **4** ½ **Spectral Star**^{15} [4393] 4-9-12 **73** .... JamieSpencer 8 — 77
(J R Fanshawe) *led: rdn and hdd wl over 1f out: wknd ent fnl f* **11/4**^{1}

5454 **5** 3 **Sky Quest (IRE)**^{19} [4244] 8-9-13 **74** .... (tp) StephenCarson 10 — 73
(W R Swinburn) *hld up and bhd: hdwy over 1f out: sn rdn: no imp fnl f* **16/1**

1550 **6** 1 **Olimpo (FR)**^{23} [4160] 5-9-7 **75** .... JamesMillman$^{(7)}$ 3 — 73
(B R Millman) *hld up and bhd: rdn 2f out: sme hdwy over 1f out: nvr trbld ldrs* **12/1**

4461 **7** 4 **Ariodante**^{13} [4448] 4-9-3 **67** .... StephenDonohoe$^{(3)}$ 6 — 59
(J M P Eustace) *prom: rdn 3f out: wknd 2f out* **13/2**^{3}

4302 **8** 10 **Figaro's Quest (IRE)**^{52} [3270] 4-8-12 **59** .... SteveDrowne 2 — 36
(P F I Cole) *hld up: hdwy over 4f out: rdn 3f out: wknd 2f out* **13/2**^{3}

26-0 **9** 3 **Smart John**^{10} [4575] 6-9-8 **69** .... JoeFanning 1 — 41
(D Shaw) *chsd ldr early: lost pl over 8f out: bhd fnl 3f* **7/1**

2m 44.41s (0.81) **Going Correction** -0.075s/f (Good)
WFA 3 from 4yo+ 11lb — **9** Ran SP% **112.5**
Speed ratings (Par 103):94,93,92,92,90 89,87,80,79
CSF £79.54 CT £612.44 TOTE £12.90: £4.40, £1.90, £2.00; EX 121.10 Place 6 £21.93, Place 5 £7.77..
Owner Robin F Scully **Bred** Clovelly Farms **Trained** Arundel, W Sussex
■ Stewards' Enquiry : Fergus Sweeney three-day ban: used whip with excessive frequency (Sep 8,10,11)

FOCUS
A moderate winning time for this modest handicap and rated around the placed horses.
Spectral Star Official explanation: jockey said filly hung left throughout
Figaro's Quest(IRE) Official explanation: jockey said gelding hung right
T/Plt: £92.00 to a £1 stake. Pool: £35,507.05. 281.45 winning tickets. T/Qpdt: £18.00 to a £1 stake. Pool: £1,594.60. 65.50 winning tickets. KH

4787 SARATOGA (R-H)
Saturday, August 26

OFFICIAL GOING: Fast

4908a BERNARD BARUCH H'CAP (GRADE 2) — 1m 1f
10:07 (10:07) 3-Y-O+
£69,767 (£23,255; £11,627; £5,813; £3,488; £775)

RPR

1 — **Ashkal Way (IRE)**^{20} 4-8-3 .... GKGomez 7 — 114
(Saeed Bin Suroor) **7/10**^{1}

2 nk **Dreadnaught (USA)**^{55} 6-8-4 .... (b) CVelasquez 1 — 115
(T Voss, U.S.A) **62/10**

3 ¾ **Interpatation (USA)**^{94} 4-8-1 .... JRVelazquez 5 — 110
(Robert Barbara, U.S.A) **26/1**

4 1 **T. D. Vance (USA)**^{55} 4-8-3 .... RADominguez 8 — 110
(H G Motion, U.S.A) **56/10**^{3}

5 3 ¾ **Leadwithyourchin (USA)**^{42} 4-8-1 .... (b) FJara 6 — 101
(M Hushion, U.S.A) **24/1**

6 ½ **Etesaal (USA)**^{170} [622] 6-8-3 .... ECoa 2 — 102
(Saeed Bin Suroor) **7/10**^{1}

7 *nse* **Quest Star (USA)**[89] 7-8-3 (b) JRLeparoux 4 101
(N J Howard, U.S.A) **53/10**[2]
8 *12* **Terrific Storm (USA)** 5-8-4 (b) KDesormeaux 3 78
(T Pletcher, U.S.A) **123/10**
1m 46.78s **8** Ran SP% **177.8**

Owner Godolphin Racing Inc **Bred** Gainsborough Stud Management Ltd **Trained** Newmarket, Suffolk

NOTEBOOK
Ashkal Way(IRE), a smart handicapper for Brian Ellison in the UK last year, is progressing well in the US for the Godolphin operation and ran out a narrow winner of this Grade 2.
Etesaal(USA), a stablemate of the winner, had conditions to suit but was not at his best.

4887 RIPON (R-H)
Tuesday, August 29

OFFICIAL GOING: Good to soft (soft in places)
Wind: moderate, across

4909 CLARO (S) STKS 1m 1f 170y
2:20 (2:20) (Class 5) 3-4-Y-O **£3,238** (£963; £481; £240) **Stalls** High

Form RPR
1050 **1** **Inside Story (IRE)**[13] 4467 4-9-12 63 (b) RobertWinston 5 58
(M W Easterby) *hld up in rr: hdwy wl over 2f out: rdn to chse ldrs ent last: squeezed through to ld last 50 yds* **7/2**[1]
0025 **2** *3/4* **Carrietau**[20] 4255 3-8-12 43 J-PGuillambert 8 50
(J G Given) *a cl up: rdn 2f out: led over 1f out: drvn and hdd ent last: kpt on wl u.p* **10/1**
6166 **3** *shd* **Ming Vase**[11] 4568 4-9-6 46 JoeFanning 6 50
(P T Midgley) *chsd ldrs: hdwy over 2f out: rdn to chal wl over 1f out: drvn to ld ent last: hdd and no ex last 50 yds* **10/1**
0003 **4** *1 3/4* **Gypsy Royal (IRE)**[15] 4425 4-9-1 40 PaulHanagan 7 42
(G Woodward) *in tch: hdwy wl over 2f out: swtchd lft and rdn over 1f out: kpt on u.p ins last* **11/1**
0000 **5** *1* **Aqua**[17] 4381 4-9-1 36 MickyFenton 12 40
(P T Midgley) *hld up in rr: hdwy on outer 3f out: rdn to chse ldrs wl over 1f out: kpt on same pce ent last* **40/1**
0346 **6** *nk* **Rudaki**[13] 4467 4-9-6 50 TomEaves 3 45
(M E Sowersby) *in tch: hdwy to chse ldrs over 2f out: sn rdn and one pce appr last* **13/2**[2]
500- **7** *shd* **Owners Biscuits**[423] 3114 3-8-4 51 GregFairley(3) 11 39
(M Johnston) *led: rdn along 3f out: drvn wl over 1f out: sn hdd and grad wknd* **20/1**
4420 **8** *3* **Elite Land**[5] 4734 3-8-5 45 SuzzanneFrance(7) 14 39
(N Bycroft) *chsd ldrs: rdn along 3f out: grad wknd fnl 2f* **8/1**[3]
4352 **9** *nk* **Desert Lightning (IRE)**[11] 4568 4-9-5 50 PatrickDonaghy(7) 4 44
(K R Burke) *a.p: effrt on inner 2f out: rdn and ev ch whn n.m.r and hung rt ent last: sn wknd* **7/2**[1]
0251 **10** *5* **Cool Isle**[13] 4491 3-8-10 45 (b) JohnMcAuley(3) 1 30
(P Howling) *wnt rt s and rr: sme hdwy on outer 3f out: sn rdn and nvr a factor* **14/1**
00 **11** *3 1/2* **Northern Promise (IRE)**[91] 2107 3-8-12 PhillipMakin 2 23
(J Parkes) *midfield: rdn along over 3f out: sn wknd* **100/1**
00 **12** *2 1/2* **Gavanello**[73] 2646 3-8-7 NicolPolli(5) 10 19
(M C Chapman) *a rr* **66/1**
000- **13** *3* **Casalese**[274] 6442 4-9-6 32 PaulMulrennan 15 13
(Micky Hammond) *a rr* **100/1**
00-0 **14** *30* **Signor Albertini (IRE)**[44] 2077 3-8-7 35 LeanneKershaw(5) 13 —
(P C Haslam) *in tch: rdn along over 3f out and sn wknd* **100/1**
0000 **15** *4* **Woolfall King (IRE)**[19] 4304 3-8-12 34 NCallan 9 —
(G G Margarson) *chsd ldrs on inner: rdn along over 3f out: sn wknd* **33/1**
2m 8.70s (3.70) **Going Correction** +0.40s/f (Good)
WFA 3 from 4yo 8lb **15** Ran SP% **116.7**
Speed ratings (Par 103):101,100,100,98,98 97,97,95,95,91 88,86,83,59,56
CSF £36.99 TOTE £4.50: £1.80, £3.30, £3.80; EX 54.20 Trifecta £201.00 Part won: Pool £282.23 - 0.20 winning units..The winner was bought in for 5,200gns. Carrietau was claimed by Anthony White for £6,000.
Owner Matthew Green **Bred** Arthur S Phelan **Trained** Sheriff Hutton, N Yorks
■ Stewards' Enquiry : J-P Guillambert one-day ban: started from stall 10 when drawn 8 (Sep 10); one-day ban: used whip with excessive frequency (Sep 11)
Nicol Polli one-day ban: started from stall 8 when drawn 10 (Sep 10)

FOCUS
A pretty moderate affair won by the horse best in at the weights and the form is limited, rated around the placed horses.
Desert Lightning(IRE) Official explanation: jockey said gelding hung right-handed throughout
Woolfall King(IRE) Official explanation: jockey said gelding had no more to give

4910 EAT SLEEP DRINK AT THE NAGS HEAD PICKHILL CONDITIONS STKS 5f
2:50 (2:50) (Class 3) 2-Y-O **£6,855** (£2,052; £1,026; £513; £256) **Stalls** Low

Form RPR
665 **1** **Reebal**[38] 3738 2-9-0 (b) NCallan 1 83
(B J Meehan) *mde all: rdn wl over 1f out: styd on strly u.p ins last* **6/1**
4561 **2** *2* **Sparkling Eyes**[13] 4485 2-8-11 90 MartinDwyer 6 73
(C E Brittain) *chsd wnr: hdwy to chal wl over 1f out: sn rdn and ev ch tl drvn and one pce ins last* **9/4**[2]
1503 **3** *nk* **Ingleby Image**[5] 4727 2-8-11 79 (b[1]) PhillipMakin 7 72
(T D Barron) *chsd ldrs: rdn along and sltly outpcd 2f out: styd on ins last* **11/4**[3]
3014 **4** *5* **Minimum Fuss (IRE)**[25] 4107 2-8-6 52 (b) JohnMcAuley(3) 3 52?
(M C Chapman) *bmpd s: a rr* **100/1**
2310 **5** *6* **Winning Spirit (IRE)**[28] 4026 2-9-4 84 TPQueally 2 39
(J Noseda) *wnt rt s: keen and sn chsng wnr: pushed along 1/2-way: sn rdn and wknd qckly wl over 1f out* **15/8**[1]
62.66 secs (2.46) **Going Correction** +0.40s/f (Good) **5** Ran SP% **107.5**
Speed ratings (Par 98):96,92,92,84,74
CSF £18.81 TOTE £7.40: £2.90, £1.40; EX 16.40.
Owner Nizar Anwar **Bred** Belgrave Bloodstock & Quarry Bstock **Trained** Manton, Wilts

FOCUS
Not a particularly strong conditions event, with few handling the softish ground and the performance of the fourth holding down the level of the form.

NOTEBOOK
Reebal, having shown plenty of speed in his previous starts, proved very much suited by the drop back to the minimum trip on easier ground. He did not go unbacked on this step up in grade and did it well, but he is likely to be saddled with a pretty stiff mark as a result. (op 8-1)
Sparkling Eyes owes her official mark of 90 to her fourth in the Queen Mary, but she took six starts to get off the mark and this daughter of Lujain did not run to that figure on this first start on easy ground. (op 2-1 tchd 5-2)
Ingleby Image, who was wearing blinkers for the first time, was proven in bad ground having won her maiden at Musselburgh in heavy conditions. Official marks suggest that she should have beaten the fourth further than she did, and the form does not look particularly solid. (op 9-4)
Minimum Fuss(IRE), who only has a win in a Fibresand seller to her name, was the most experienced in the line-up. She never got competitive but her proximity still limits the level of the form. (op 66-1)
Winning Spirit(IRE) is a useful performer, albeit he has been expensive to follow, but this sort of ground is not his cup of tea at all and he never looked to be going that well. Official explanation: jockey said colt was unsuited by the soft ground (op 9-4)

4911 CITY OF RIPON STKS (H'CAP) 1m 1f 170y
3:20 (3:21) (Class 3) (0-90,90) 3-Y-0+
£9,348 (£2,799; £1,399; £700; £349; £175) **Stalls** High

Form RPR
2414 **1** **Macorville (USA)**[92] 2081 3-8-7 78 TomEaves 3 89
(G M Moore) *a.p: led 3f out: rdn wl over 1f out: drvn ent last and kpt on wl* **7/2**[2]
-014 **2** *1 3/4* **Moon On A Spoon**[74] 2622 3-8-5 76 JoeFanning 4 84
(J R Fanshawe) *hld up in rr: stdy hdwy on outer wl over 2f out: rdn to chal over 1f out and ev ch tl drvn and one pce ins last* **6/1**[3]
0210 **3** *1 3/4* **Daring Affair**[24] 4160 5-8-11 74 NCallan 11 79
(K R Burke) *trckd ldrs: effrt wl over 2f out: sn rdn and kpt on same pce ent last* **6/1**[3]
360 **4** *nk* **Tsaroxy (IRE)**[24] 4153 4-8-11 74 RobertWinston 8 78
(J Howard Johnson) *hld up in rr: swtchd outside and hdwy over 2f out: sn rdn and kpt on ins last: nrst fin* **20/1**
1306 **5** *1 3/4* **Tidy (IRE)**[5] 4733 6-8-5 71 oh5 GregFairley(3) 9 72
(Micky Hammond) *in tch: effrt on inner 3f out: sn rdn along and no imp fnl 2f* **16/1**
-544 **6** *1/2* **Moohimm (IRE)**[61] 3015 3-8-4 75 MartinDwyer 5 75
(M P Tregoning) *led: rdn along over 3f out: sn hdd and drvn: wknd wl over 1f out* **6/1**[3]
1546 **7** *3* **Snowed Under**[16] 4392 5-9-2 79 EddieAhern 1 74
(J D Bethell) *prom: rdn along 3f out: sn wknd* **14/1**
4552 **8** *3/4* **Torrens (IRE)**[8] 4654 4-9-0 77 PaulHanagan 7 71
(R A Fahey) *trckd ldrs: pushed along over 3f out: sn btn* **11/4**[1]
2010 **9** *9* **Perez (IRE)**[5] 4733 4-8-3 71 oh6 EmmettStack(5) 2 48
(W Storey) *s.i.s: hdwy on outer to join ldrs 1/2-way: rdn along over 3f out: sn wknd* **66/1**
2m 6.83s (1.83) **Going Correction** +0.40s/f (Good)
WFA 3 from 4yo+ 8lb **9** Ran SP% **110.5**
Speed ratings (Par 107):108,106,105,104,103 103,100,100,92
CSF £23.10 CT £113.43 TOTE £4.30: £1.60, £1.90, £1.70; EX 28.50 Trifecta £154.70 Pool £863.27 - 3.96 winning units.
Owner Geoff & Sandra Turnbull **Bred** Brookdale Thoroughbreds Inc **Trained** Middleham Moor, N Yorks

FOCUS
A fair handicap and sound form for the grade best rated through the third.

NOTEBOOK
Macorville(USA) needs to get his toe in, hence his absence over the summer, but he returned in fine fettle and was always travelling well towards the fore. This was only his eighth career start and he remains open to further improvement, ground conditions permitting. (op 3-1)
Moon On A Spoon won over this course and distance on faster ground in June, but she had been subsequently beaten off a 6lb higher mark and had been raised another 2lb since then. Consequently she looked to have a stiff enough task here, but she performed with plenty of credit. The Handicapper is likely to bump her up again for this, though, so she could well remain vulnerable. (op 5-1)
Daring Affair, who goes on most ground and was backed in from double-figure prices, put behind her a disappointing effort at Windsor last time. She too looks high enough in the handicap for the time being, though. (op 10-1)
Tsaroxy(IRE), who is well handicapped on his best form from last year, signalled a return to form, staying on well from off the pace to be closest at the finish over the longest trip he has contested. He likes some ease in the ground and a similar race can be found for him this autumn. (op 16-1)
Tidy(IRE) had his chance but his stamina for this trip was unproven and he did not shape as though seeing it out. He will be happier back over a mile.
Moohimm(IRE) should have appreciated the conditions underfoot but he was disappointing. He has not got home in any of his races this season but is bred to stay, and it looks as though he needs help from the Handicapper. Official explanation: jockey said, regarding appearing to drop hands inside final furlong, colt became unbalanced but he had attempted to maintain 5th place (op 9-2)
Torrens(IRE), who shaped well at Ayr last time, was running off a rating 2lb below his last winning mark. He also had a previous course win to his name and is effective with give in the ground, so he looked to have plenty in his favour. For some reason, though, he failed to shine. Official explanation: jockey said gelding had a breathing problem (op 3-1)

4912 STEVE NESBITT CHALLENGE TROPHY NURSERY 6f
3:50 (3:52) (Class 4) 2-Y-O **£5,829** (£1,734; £866; £432) **Stalls** Low

Form RPR
5321 **1** **Algol**[34] 3830 2-8-6 74 TomEaves 9 84+
(J Howard Johnson) *prom: hdwy to ld over 2f out: qcknd clr over 1f out: kpt on wl fnl f* **7/1**[3]
031 **2** *4* **Lafontaine Bleu**[10] 4608 2-7-12 66 PaulHanagan 1 64
(R A Fahey) *dwlt: hdwy on inner 1/2-way: rdn to chse ldrs over 1f out: drvn and no imp on wnr ins last* **9/4**[1]
3315 **3** *1 1/4* **Ishibee (IRE)**[5] 4727 2-7-8 67 oh2 ow1 (p) DuranFentiman(5) 4 61
(Mrs A Duffield) *trckd ldrs: hdwy to chse wnr 2f out: sn rdn and kpt on same pce* **16/1**
3104 **4** *4* **Ensign's Trick**[4] 4762 2-8-0 73 LiamJones(5) 10 55
(W M Brisbourne) *chsd ldrs: rdn along over 2f out: sn one pce* **22/1**
4521 **5** *1 3/4* **Josr's Magic (IRE)**[22] 4196 2-8-5 73 (b) GrahamGibbons 3 50
(Mrs A Duffield) *led: pushed along and hdd 1/2-way: sn rdn and wknd over 2f out* **8/1**
144 **6** *3* **My Valerina (IRE)**[18] 4326 2-8-6 74 RoystonFfrench 2 42
(Mrs A Duffield) *chsd ldrs: rdn along 1/2-way: sn wknd* **15/2**
2441 **7** *1* **Dolly Coughdrop (IRE)**[11] 4547 2-8-9 77 FrancisNorton 5 42
(K R Burke) *chsd ldrs: rdn along 1/2-way: sn wknd* **9/2**[2]
3231 **8** *1* **Picture Frame**[82] 2382 2-7-13 72 RoryMoore(5) 7 34
(J T Stimpson) *dwlt and swtchd rt s: a towards rr* **16/1**
0365 **9** *1 1/4* **Seaton Snooks**[20] 4251 2-8-0 68 DaleGibson 8 26
(T D Easterby) *a rr* **14/1**

610 **10** *7* **Soviet Palace (IRE)**[25] 4100 2-9-7 **89** NCallan 6 26
(K A Ryan) *cl up: led 1/2-way: rdn and hdd over 2f out: sn wknd* **9/1**

1m 15.52s (2.52) **Going Correction** +0.40s/f (Good) **10** Ran SP% **117.1**

Speed ratings (Par 96):99,93,92,86,84 80,79,77,76,66

CSF £23.18 CT £254.70 TOTE £7.40: £2.30, £1.40, £4.40; EX 26.80 Trifecta £338.40 Pool £686.38 - 1.44 winning units.

Owner Transcend Bloodstock LLP **Bred** W L Caley **Trained** Billy Row, Co Durham

FOCUS

A fair nursery, though a few did not handle the softer ground. However, the winner could hardly have been more impressive and looks destined for better things, while the placed horses set a solid standard.

NOTEBOOK

Algol ◆ had only ever encountered fast ground before this novice debut, but it made no difference and the way he quickened away from his rivals in this wetter ground was especially impressive. This victory strongly suggests he was put in on too lenient a mark and the Handicapper will soon have his revenge, but he may be capable of winning something rather better in any case. (op 5-1)

Lafontaine Bleu, a winner over course and distance in testing ground last time, stayed on against the stands' rail to snatch the runner-up spot, but the winner was in a different league. She will not always bump into one like him. (op 11-4 tchd 3-1 in places)

Ishibee(IRE), whose only previous victory came in a Polytrack seller, was effectively 3lb wrong with her rider's overweight and did not perform at all badly in this company, but she is a lot more exposed than the pair who finished ahead of her.

Ensign's Trick was on easier ground than when bolting up in a course-and-distance seller last month and was firmly put in her place, but it is more likely that she is just too high in the weights at present. (op 20-1)

Josr's Magic(IRE) was given a positive ride as usual, but failed to get home in this ground. (op 9-1)

My Valerina(IRE) Official explanation: jockey said filly was unsuited by the soft ground

Dolly Coughdrop(IRE), raised 7lb for her victory at Catterick when making the most of a track bias, had no such help here and found this much tougher. (op 11-2)

Soviet Palace(IRE) Official explanation: jockey said the colt was unsuited by the soft ground

4913 HAPPY BIRTHDAY VAL BARKER FILLIES' MAIDEN AUCTION STKS 5f

4:20 (4:20) (Class 5) 2-Y-O **£3,886** (£1,156; £577; £288) **Stalls** Low

Form					RPR
00	**1**		**Morinqua (IRE)**[80] 2461 2-8-7 NCallan 2 *(K A Ryan) mde all: rdn over 1f out: styd on strly*	**8/1**	80+
634	**2**	*3 ½*	**Temtation (IRE)**[8] 4657 2-8-5 ow1 EddieAhern 9 *(J R Boyle) a chsng wnr: rdn wl over 1f out: sn drvn and kpt on same pce ent last*	**9/4**[2]	65
2322	**3**	*2 ½*	**Princess Ileana (IRE)**[39] 3693 2-8-7 78 FrancisNorton 11 *(K R Burke) chsd ldrs: rdn along over 2f out: sn no imp*	**13/8**[1]	58
5600	**4**	*1 ½*	**First Valentini**[10] 4608 2-8-4 (t) RoystonFfrench 5 *(N Bycroft) in tch: hdwy over 2f out: sn rdn and no imp appr last*	**25/1**	50
0	**5**	*1 ¾*	**Jenny Geddes (IRE)**[15] 4421 2-8-11 PaulHanagan 8 *(R A Fahey) wnt lft s: outpcd and bhd tl styd on wl appr last*	**7/1**[3]	51
00	**6**	*3*	**By The Edge (IRE)**[20] 4251 2-8-4 DaleGibson 10 *(T D Barron) in tch: rdn along 1/2-way: sn edgd lft and wknd*	**20/1**	33
54	**7**	*5*	**Galaxy Of Stars**[68] 2791 2-8-4 PatrickMathers[(3)] 4 *(D Shaw) a rr*	**25/1**	18
0006	**8**	*3 ½*	**Vizionary**[12] 4510 2-8-11 MickyFenton 1 *(Mrs P Sly) sn outpcd and bhd fr 1/2-way*	**20/1**	9
	9	*6*	**Axis Mundi (IRE)** 2-8-7 PaulMulrennan 7 *(T J Etherington) bmpd s: a outpcd and bhd*	**66/1**	—

62.05 secs (1.85) **Going Correction** +0.40s/f (Good) **9** Ran SP% **111.2**

Speed ratings (Par 91):101,95,91,89,86 81,73,67,58

CSF £23.67 TOTE £9.50: £2.60, £1.40, £1.10; EX 28.50 Trifecta £55.30 Pool £651.37 - 8.36 winning units.

Owner D Mac A'Bhaird **Bred** Corrin Stud **Trained** Hambleton, N Yorks

FOCUS

This was run at a decent pace and the order changed little during the contest. The winning time was very smart for a race like this and 0.61 seconds faster than the earlier juvenile conditions event, but the fourth limits the form.

NOTEBOOK

Morinqua(IRE) ◆ was a revelation on this drop in trip and ran her rivals into the ground. The softer going was obviously not a problem and she can win again in similar conditions. (tchd 7-1)

Temtation(IRE) was always in vain pursuit of the winner and could never get on terms with her. She may be better suited by six now and might be worth switching to nurseries. (op 2-1)

Princess Ileana(IRE), who looked unhappy on the firm ground last time, fared no better on this return to a softer surface and has become extremely expensive to follow. (op 11-8)

First Valentini, by far the most exposed in the field, achieved little in finishing fourth and nothing should be read into her finishing close behind a horse with whom she would have been 17lb better off in a nursery.

Jenny Geddes(IRE), whose breeding suggests she will appreciate further, ran accordingly and is not one to give up on when faced with a greater test, especially once handicapped. (op 10-1)

Galaxy Of Stars Official explanation: jockey said filly was unsuited by the track

4914 WAKEMAN STAYERS H'CAP 2m

4:50 (4:50) (Class 6) (0-65,64) 3-Y-O+ **£3,238** (£963; £481; £240) **Stalls** Low

Form					RPR
-400	**1**		**Fair Spin**[4] 4764 6-8-12 **48** oh1 (p) PaulHanagan 10 *(Micky Hammond) trckd ldrs: hdwy 3f out: rdn top ld over 1f out: drvn ins last: hld on gamely*	**14/1**	57
0400	**2**	*shd*	**Wrenlane**[18] 2286 5-9-3 **53** GrahamGibbons 12 *(J J Quinn) led: pushed along and hdd over 1f out: rdn and rallied ins last: jst hld*	**12/1**	62
6060	**3**	*½*	**Just Waz (USA)**[6] 4698 4-8-8 **49** MichaelJStainton[(5)] 4 *(R M Whitaker) trckd ldrs: effrt and pushed along 3f out: hdwy on inner 2f out: swtchd lft and rdn ins last: styd on wl towards fin*	**9/1**[3]	57
0613	**4**	*6*	**Dance A Daydream**[13] 4472 3-8-10 **60** OscarUrbina 2 *(J R Fanshawe) hld up in rr: n.m.r and checked 4f out: sn pushed along :rdn and hdwy on outer wl over 2f out: kpt on ins last: nt rch ldrs*	**4/1**[1]	61+
2621	**5**	*1*	**Swords**[15] 4438 4-9-7 **57** DeanMcKeown 14 *(Heather Dalton) hld up in rr: swtchd outside and hdwy wl over 2f out: sn rdn and kpt on same pce*	**4/1**[1]	57
0155	**6**	*1 ¾*	**Madiba**[20] 4252 7-9-0 **50** JoeFanning 3 *(P Howling) trckd ldrs: effrt over 3f out: sn rdn along and wknd 2f out*	**4/1**[1]	48
6463	**7**	*shd*	**Mulligan's Pride (IRE)**[12] 4506 5-9-4 **54** (b[1]) RobertWinston 8 *(G A Swinbank) prom: hdwy and cl up 1/2-way: rdn along over 2f out: grad wknd*	**8/1**[2]	52
30-6	**8**	*1 ¼*	**Last Pioneer (IRE)**[93] 2044 4-9-8 **63** TomGreenway[(5)] 9 *(R Ford) hld up in rr: gd hdwy on outer 4f out: rdn to chse ldrs 3f out: wknd over 2f out*	**16/1**	59
2-40	**9**	*1 ¾*	**Singhalongtasveer**[65] 2196 4-8-7 **48** oh4 (vt) EmmettStack[(5)] 5 *(W Storey) midfield: pushed along 4f out: sn wknd*	**25/1**	42
6045	**10**	*7*	**Sandy's Legend (USA)**[179] 570 4-8-13 **54** (p) LiamJones[(5)] 13 *(Mrs L Williamson) a rr*	**20/1**	40
0021	**11**	*¾*	**Dimashq**[12] 4506 4-8-12 **48** oh3 DaleGibson 6 *(Ronald Thompson) chsd ldr: rdn along over 4f out and sn wknd*	**14/1**	33

3m 39.63s (6.63) **Going Correction** +0.40s/f (Good)

WFA 3 from 4yo+ 14lb **11** Ran SP% **116.6**

Speed ratings (Par 101):99,98,98,95,95 94,94,93,92,89 88

CSF £169.69 CT £1600.27 TOTE £17.20: £4.40, £3.70, £3.80; EX 155.60 TRIFECTA Not won. Place 6 £166.79, Place 5 £ 67.12 .

Owner Ms Lynn Thomas **Bred** A S Reid **Trained** Middleham Moor, N Yorks

FOCUS

A modest staying handicap in which the pace was ordinary and those that raced handily were favoured. The front three pulled well clear of the others and the third sets the level.

T/Jkpt: Not won. T/Plt: £437.20 to a £1 stake. Pool: £217,090.98. 362.40 winning tickets. T/Qpdt: £42.20 to a £1 stake. Pool: £6,662.50. 116.60 winning tickets. JR

4915 - 4917a (Foreign Racing) - See Raceform Interactive

[4857] BADEN-BADEN (L-H)

Tuesday, August 29

OFFICIAL GOING: Heavy

4918a DARLEY OETTINGEN-RENNEN (GROUP 2) 1m

4:00 (4:01) 3-Y-O+ **£35,862** (£15,172; £6,897; £4,138)

				RPR
1		**Notability (IRE)**[12] 4529 4-9-1 PhilipRobinson 6 *(M A Jarvis) made all, ridden out final f*	**6/5**[1]	111
2	*1 ½*	**Azarole (IRE)**[5] 4740 5-9-1 JohnEgan 3 *(J S Moore) raced in 3rd, ridden to go 2nd towards stands rail over 1f out, kept on*	**78/10**	108
3	*¾*	**Lateral**[23] 4190 3-9-0 WMongil 1 *(P Schiergen, Germany) held up in last, brought widest of all to stands rail in straight, still last til stayed on well final 100 yards*	**18/10**[2]	112
4	*1 ¾*	**Raptor (GER)**[100] 3-8-7 AStarke 2 *(Mario Hofer, Germany) raced in 4th, ridden over 1f out, unable to quicken*	**41/10**[3]	101
5	*3*	**Starpix (FR)**[173] 622 4-9-1 ASuborics 7 *(H J Brown, South Africa) raced in 2nd, every chance 2f out, hard ridden and weakened over 1f out*	**42/10**	97

1m 44.86s

WFA 3 from 4yo+ 6lb **5** Ran SP% **131.4**

(including 10 Euro stake): WIN 22; PL 18, 28; SF 101.

Owner Sheikh Mohammed **Bred** Darley **Trained** Newmarket, Suffolk

NOTEBOOK

Notability(IRE) enjoys plenty of cut in the ground and, given a good ride from the front by Robinson, kept on pulling out a bit more and never really looked like getting beaten.

[2564] TABY (R-H)

Tuesday, August 29

OFFICIAL GOING: Soft

4919a BREEDERS' TROPHY CLASSIC 1m 1f 165y

8:10 (12:00) 3-Y-O

£40,645 (£20,323; £8,129; £4,877; £3,252; £2,439)

				RPR
1		**Icaros (SWE)**[16] 4419 3-9-2 YvonneDurant 1 *(Wido Neuroth, Norway)*	**11/20**[1]	—
2	*8*	**Elegant Song (SWE)** 3-9-2 DDelgado 4 *(T Gustafsson, Sweden)*	**86/10**[3]	—
3	*nk*	**Nottingham (SWE)** 3-9-2 MMartinez 10 *(L Reuterskiold, Sweden)*	**26/1**	—
4	*3 ½*	**Aura (SWE)**[53] 3326 3-8-12 NCordrey 12 *(T Gustafsson, Sweden)*	**22/1**	—
5	*1 ½*	**Dream Catcher (SWE)**[16] 4420 3-9-2 FJohansson 9 *(R A Kvisla) (53/10)*	**53/10**[2]	—
6	*nk*	**Trym (SWE)** 3-9-2 KAndersen 5 *(B Olsen, Norway)*	**16/1**	—
7	*1*	**Szuma (SWE)** 3-9-2 SaraSlot 2 *(Elisabeth Gautier, Sweden)*	**24/1**	—
8	*1*	**He Magic (DEN)** 3-9-2 JJohansen 6 *(B Olsen, Norway)*	**65/1**	—
9	*hd*	**Happening (SWE)** 3-8-12 MSantos 7 *(T Gustafsson, Sweden)*	**26/1**	—
10	*2 ½*	**Play Truant (SWE)** 3-9-2 ILopez 15 *(J Malmborg)*	**44/1**	—
11	*2*	**Youko (SWE)** 3-9-2 LisaBivemark 11 *(B Bo, Sweden)*	**64/1**	—
12	*9*	**Fairy Chief (SWE)** 3-9-2 (b) FDiaz 8 *(Annike Bye Nunez)*	**76/1**	—
13	*11*	**Lloret De Mar (NOR)** 3-8-12 (b) LHammer-Hansen 14 *(A Lund, Norway)*	**18/1**	—
14	*2*	**Crossoffissio (SWE)**[16] 4419 3-9-2 (b) P-AGraberg 3 *(L Reuterskiold, Sweden)*	**63/1**	—

2m 5.20s **14** Ran SP% **125.8**

(including one SKr stakes): WIN 1.56; PL 1.11, 2.19, 3.23; DF 11.87.

Owner Stall Eos **Bred** Stall Eos **Trained** Norway

[4705] LEICESTER (R-H)

Wednesday, August 30

OFFICIAL GOING: Good (good to firm in places)

Wind: Light, behind Weather: Cloudy with sunny spells

4920 GG.COM MAIDEN AUCTION STKS 5f 218y

2:30 (2:30) (Class 5) 2-Y-O **£4,533** (£1,348; £674; £336) **Stalls** Low

Form					RPR
600	**1**		**Our Ruby**[12] 4552 2-8-8 AdrianMcCarthy 3 *(P W Chapple-Hyam) chsd ldrs: rdn 1/2-way: styd on to ld nr fin*	**8/1**	71

The Form Book, Raceform Ltd, Compton, RG20 6NL

44 **2** *shd* **Shustraya**[12] 4558 2-8-6 .... FergusSweeney 13 69
(P J Makin) *trckd ldr: led on bit over 2f out: rdn over 1f out: edgd rt and hdd nr fin* **4/1**[2]

220 **3** *1 ½* **Beautiful Madness (IRE)**[20] 4295 2-8-1 66.................. DominicFox(3) 2 62
(M G Quinlan) *hld up: hdwy over 2f out: rdn and hung rt fr over 1f out: nt rch ldrs* **15/2**

6634 **4** *2 ½* **Bahamian Love**[48] 3430 2-8-4 70................................ RoystonFfrench 8 55
(B W Hills) *prom: rdn over 2f out: styd on same pce fnl f* **9/2**[3]

44 **5** *hd* **Catlivius (IRE)**[16] 4421 2-8-6 .... NCallan 4 56
(K A Ryan) *led over 3f: rdn over 1f out: edgd rt and no ex fnl f* **7/2**[1]

6 *1* **Aaron's Way** 2-8-4 .... PaulHanagan 6 51
(A W Carroll) *s.s: hdwy over 1f out: nrst fin* **16/1**

4545 **7** *shd* **Nicada (IRE)**[30] 3997 2-8-6 64... GregFairley(3) 14 56
(Miss Gay Kelleway) *chsd ldrs: rdn over 2f out: wknd fnl f* **12/1**

6 **8** *6* **Chant De Guerre (USA)**[13] 4526 2-8-10 .... DaneO'Neill 11 39
(P Mitchell) *hdwy over 4f out: rdn and wknd over 2f out* **11/1**

30 **9** *2 ½* **Lady Saffron (IRE)**[32] 3958 2-8-5 .... JasonEdmunds(3) 7 29
(J Balding) *mid-div: rdn 1/2-way: sn wknd* **80/1**

10 *1 ¾* **Flying Grey (IRE)** 2-8-13 .... TPO'Shea 1 29
(P A Blockley) *s.i.s: sn outpcd* **25/1**

00 **11** *nk* **Bold Adventure**[20] 4295 2-8-13 .... TPQueally 12 28
(W J Musson) *prom to 1/2-way* **50/1**

5 **12** *2 ½* **Julilla**[37] 3799 2-8-6 .... JamieMackay 9 14
(G G Margarson) *mid-div: wknd over 3f out* **66/1**

400 **13** *21* **Fen Dream**[16] 4433 2-8-13 58.. TedDurcan 5 —
(E F Vaughan) *lost pl over 4f out: sn bhd* **25/1**

1m 12.44s (-0.76) **Going Correction** -0.325s/f (Firm) **13** Ran SP% **117.6**
Speed ratings (Par 94):92,91,89,86,86 84,84,76,73,71 70,67,39
CSF £37.96 TOTE £8.90: £3.60, £1.60, £2.50; EX 48.90 Trifecta £215.10 Part won. Pool: £303.08 - 0.34 winning tickets..
Owner Mrs Ruby Williams **Bred** S J Mear **Trained** Newmarket, Suffolk

FOCUS
In all probability a very moderate maiden, unlikely to throw up too many winners.

NOTEBOOK
Our Ruby was off the bridle by halfway but she responded well, showing the right attitude to put her head in front in the last few strides. Suited by this faster ground, she might have needed the run when tackling seven furlongs last time. (op 13-2)
Shustraya, who had shown plenty of ability when fourth in a couple of fillies' maidens, did not do much wrong in this slightly easier grade but after showing in front going well she was just pipped. Her turn should come. (tchd 9-2)
Beautiful Madness(IRE), runner-up in maidens won by useful performers Chin Wag (here) and Harvest Joy before a poor performance last time, was finishing to good effect despite hanging a little. (op 8-1 tchd 9-1)
Bahamian Love lost her action when last of four at Epsom but held an obvious chance on her earlier efforts. She lacked a gear change when one was needed and could be in need of another furlong.
Catlivius(IRE) possessed the pace to claim the lead on the stands' rail but could not counter when headed. She will perhaps be more effective back down at five furlongs. (op 9-2)
Aaron's Way, whose dam was a winning sprinter, shaped with a bit of promise on her debut and should be capable of improvement with this run behind her. (op 18-1)

4921 CLUB ROOM NURSERY — 5f 2y
3:00 (3:00) (Class 5) 2-Y-O — **£4,533** (£1,348; £674) **Stalls** Low

Form — RPR

4315 **1** **Yerevan**[5] 4762 2-8-13 73.. FergusSweeney 2 71+
(R T Phillips) *trckd ldr: led on bit 1/2-way: rdn out* **4/5**[1]

040 **2** *1 ½* **Nou Camp**[16] 4428 2-7-9 58 oh6.................................(b[1]) DominicFox(3) 3 51
(N A Callaghan) *sn led: hdd 1/2-way: rdn over 1f out: styd on same pce* **5/1**[3]

2222 **3** *2 ½* **House Arrest**[14] 4493 2-7-12 58 oh2............................(v[1]) PaulHanagan 5 46+
(A J McCabe) *s.i.s: sn chsng ldrs: rdn 1/2-way: eased whn btn ins fnl f* **15/8**[2]

61.36 secs (0.46) **Going Correction** -0.325s/f (Firm) **3** Ran SP% **107.0**
Speed ratings (Par 94):83,80,76
CSF £4.51 TOTE £1.60; EX 5.70.
Owner Bellflower Racing Ltd **Bred** Jenny Hall Bloodstock Ltd **Trained** Adlestrop, Gloucs

FOCUS
With half the field taken out, leaving just one runner in the handicap proper, this was a decidedly weak nursery. The winner did not need to run to her best to score and the runner-up is the best guide.

NOTEBOOK
Yerevan, a consistent filly, was dropping back from six furlongs. Content to be given a lead, she showed ahead at halfway and completed the job in workmanlike style. She handles easier ground and will be kept on the go. (op 11-10 after 5-4 in a place)
Nou Camp, back down in trip and fitted with blinkers for the first time, kept trying when headed but was always being held. He might be happier back on Polytrack. (op 9-2 tchd 6-1)
House Arrest, claimed out of Ian Wood's yard after finishing runner-up for the fifth successive time in sellers, was her new trainer's first runner. Tried in a visor, she was very awkward leaving the stalls and was always in last place, being eased in the last half-furlong. She looks one to be wary of. (op 6-4)

4922 WEATHERBYS PRINTING H'CAP — 5f 2y
3:30 (3:30) (Class 3) (0-90,88) 3-Y-O
£11,217 (£3,358; £1,679; £840; £419; £210) **Stalls** Low

Form — RPR

6151 **1** **Diane's Choice**[17] 4398 3-8-9 76.. NCallan 1 88
(J Akehurst) *mde all: rdn and hung rt fr over 1f out: r.o* **5/1**[3]

1550 **2** *1 ½* **Grazeon Gold Blend**[8] 4682 3-9-6 87.......................... GrahamGibbons 2 94
(J J Quinn) *a.p: rdn to chse wnr and hung rt fnl f: r.o* **4/1**[2]

1406 **3** *2 ½* **Azygous**[9] 4659 3-9-2 83... TPQueally 6 81
(J Akehurst) *chsd wnr 4f: wknd ins fnl f* **25/1**

6521 **4** *1 ¼* **Tender Process (IRE)**[16] 4422 3-8-5 72........................ RoystonFfrench 7 66
(E S McMahon) *sn pushed along in rr: r.o ins fnl f: nrst fin* **7/4**[1]

0403 **5** *hd* **Supercast (IRE)**[6] 4659 3-8-3 70.......................................(b) PaulHanagan 10 63
(J S Moore) *chsd ldrs: rdn over 1f out: wknd fnl f* **11/1**

-000 **6** *1* **River Thames**[11] 4601 3-9-7 88.. TPO'Shea 11 77
(J A R Toller) *s.i.s: sn chsng ldrs: rdn 1/2-way: wknd fnl f* **14/1**

5063 **7** *1 ¾* **Devine Dancer**[22] 4226 3-8-8 75.. DaneO'Neill 9 58
(H Candy) *s.s: hdwy over 3f out: rdn and wknd over 1f out* **9/1**

6406 **8** *½* **Makabul**[58] 3150 3-8-12 79.. TedDurcan 3 60
(B R Millman) *s.i.s: a in rr* **10/1**

58.92 secs (-1.98) **Going Correction** -0.325s/f (Firm) **8** Ran SP% **111.0**
Speed ratings (Par 104):102,99,95,93,93 91,88,88
CSF £23.73 CT £431.01 TOTE £5.70: £1.30, £1.90, £5.40; EX 36.90 Trifecta £265.30 Part won. Pool: £373.70 - 0.40 winning tickets..
Owner The Grass Is Greener Partnership Ii **Bred** Green Pastures Farm **Trained** Epsom, Surrey

FOCUS
A decent prize and a fair event of its type.

NOTEBOOK
Diane's Choice ◆, who made all at Lingfield last time, repeated the dose off a 4lb higher mark. Grabbing the lead despite stumbling leaving the stalls, she came clear going to the final furlong and was in command when edging away from the fence. A progressive filly, she is well suited by a stiff five furlongs and her trainer will look for something at Sandown for her. (op 6-1 tchd 13-2)
Grazeon Gold Blend, back down to the minimum trip, was keeping on well in the final furlong but the winner had flown. He was clear of the third and, fairly handicapped at present, there could be a race for him back over an easy six. (op 9-2)
Azygous, the winner's stablemate, who has gained all his three victories so far over a turning five furlongs, showed bright pace before the stiff finish found him out. He is due to be dropped a pound but may need to be cut a little more slack by the Handicapper before he scores again. (op 22-1)
Tender Process(IRE) came here in good heart following a win at Thirsk, for which he was raised 6lb. After finding himself at the rear of the field he finished with something of a flourish along the stands' rail, but much too late. This drying ground was not ideal and he is capable of bouncing back on an easier surface. Official explanation: jockey said gelding never travelled (tchd 6-4 and 15-8 in places)
Supercast(IRE), not well drawn, was unable to confirm Windsor form with Azygous despite being 3lb better off. Soft ground suits him better. (op 10-1 tchd 12-1 in a place)
River Thames was a smart two-year-old but he has struggled this term, despite being dropped a total of 12lb. He could never get involved from a wide draw. (op 9-1)
Devine Dancer Official explanation: jockey said filly dwelt in stalls

4923 CHAMPAGNE BAR H'CAP — 1m 60y
4:00 (4:00) (Class 4) (0-85,85) 3-Y-O
£7,790 (£2,332; £1,166; £583; £291; £146) **Stalls** High

Form — RPR

-453 **1** **Demon Docker (IRE)**[11] 4605 3-9-6 84............................... TedDurcan 13 95
(P W Chapple-Hyam) *trckd ldrs: racd keenly: rdn over 2f out: hung rt over 1f out: styd on to ld wl ins fnl f* **9/1**[2]

411 **2** *1 ¼* **Shumookh (IRE)**[10] 4634 3-9-7 85 6ex...................................... RHills 12 93
(M A Jarvis) *led: clr over 1f out: rdn and hdd wl ins fnl f* **1/2**[1]

6230 **3** *1* **Silent Applause**[21] 4249 3-8-6 70...................................... PaulHanagan 5 76
(Dr J D Scargill) *wnt rt s: hld up: hdwy u.p over 1f out: nt rch ldrs* **12/1**[3]

3103 **4** *nk* **Abwaab**[16] 4429 3-9-3 81... DaneO'Neill 8 86
(R F Johnson Houghton) *hld up: swtchd lft over 3f out: rdn and hung rt over 1f out: nt rch ldrs* **12/1**[3]

1025 **5** *¾* **Lyrical Sound (IRE)**[14] 4481 3-9-1 79......................... RoystonFfrench 7 82
(B W Hills) *sn pushed along in rr: r.o u.p ins fnl f: nrst fin* **16/1**

3 **6** *2 ½* **Duke Of Milan (IRE)**[16] 4431 3-8-10 74................................ DavidAllan 9 72
(G C Bravery) *chsd ldrs: rdn over 1f out: wknd ins fnl f* **40/1**

2516 **7** *2* **Imperial Gain (USA)**[25] 4143 3-8-8 75..................(e[1]) SaleemGolam(3) 4 68
(W R Swinburn) *hld up in tch: racd keenly: rdn over 2f out: wknd fnl f* **12/1**[3]

5030 **8** *6* **Ohana**[167] 651 3-8-3 67.. AdrianMcCarthy 6 46
(Miss Gay Kelleway) *s.i.s and hmpd s: hld up: rdn over 3f out: n.d* **100/1**

0006 **9** *1 ½* **Cape Presto (IRE)**[11] 4605 3-8-13 77.................................... TPQueally 2 53
(Mrs C A Dunnett) *trckd ldr: plld hrd: rdn over 3f out: wknd over 1f out* **33/1**

1m 43.59s (-1.71) **Going Correction** -0.175s/f (Firm) **9** Ran SP% **112.0**
Speed ratings (Par 102):101,99,98,98,97 95,93,87,85
CSF £13.34 CT £56.33 TOTE £10.30: £1.70, £1.02, £2.40; EX 21.50 Trifecta £119.40 Pool: £661.32 - 3.93 winning tickets..
Owner Mrs Sue Catt & Partners **Bred** Airlie Stud **Trained** Newmarket, Suffolk

FOCUS
A fair handicap in which the runner-up set just an ordinary pace.
Abwaab Official explanation: jockey said gelding hung right

4924 FREE TIPS @ GG.COM H'CAP — 1m 3f 183y
4:30 (4:30) (Class 5) (0-70,69) 4-Y-O+ — **£5,505** (£1,637; £818; £408) **Stalls** High

Form — RPR

3304 **1** **Leslingtaylor (IRE)**[14] 4472 4-8-7 62.............................. SladeO'Hara(7) 3 72
(J J Quinn) *plld hrd and prom: trckd ldr 10f out: led 3f out: rdn clr over 1f out: styd on* **11/2**[3]

1004 **2** *1 ½* **Love Always**[15] 4448 4-9-6 68.. DaneO'Neill 12 76
(S Dow) *a.p: rdn over 2f out: styd on* **6/1**

3302 **3** *nk* **Red Forest (IRE)**[19] 4320 7-8-6 54...................................(t) DaleGibson 8 61
(J Mackie) *trckd ldr 2f: racd keenly: rdn over 2f out: styd on* **9/2**[1]

4250 **4** *1* **Top Spec (IRE)**[21] 4256 5-9-7 69... TedDurcan 1 75
(J Pearce) *s.s: hld up: hdwy over 2f out: nt clr run over 1f out: sn rdn: styd on same pce ins fnl f* **13/2**

5101 **5** *5* **Bienheureux**[7] 4702 5-8-13 61 6ex..(vt) NCallan 4 59
(Miss Gay Kelleway) *hld up in tch: plld hrd: rdn over 2f out: edgd rt and wknd over 1f out* **5/1**[2]

0426 **6** *1* **Red River Rebel**[14] 4472 8-8-2 50 oh1.............................. RoystonFfrench 2 46
(J R Norton) *led 9f: rdn and wknd over 1f out* **9/1**

1200 **7** *shd* **Padre Nostro (IRE)**[20] 4282 7-8-1 56........................ ChrisGlenister(7) 7 52
(J R Holt) *hld up: effrt and nt clr run over 3f out: n.d* **14/1**

4424 **8** *nk* **Tetragon (IRE)**[7] 4709 6-8-13 61.. DanielTudhope 6 56
(D Carroll) *trckd ldrs: rdn over 2f out: n.m.r and wknd over 1f out* **15/2**

0-00 **9** *6* **Ben Kenobi**[20] 4282 8-8-4 55 oh10 ow5.............................. GregFairley(3) 5 41
(Mrs P Ford) *hld up: effrt over 3f out: wknd 2f out* **66/1**

3003 **10** *14* **Saluscraggie**[18] 4380 4-8-2 50 oh4.................................... PaulHanagan 9 13
(K G Reveley) *hld up: effrt and nt clr run over 2f out: sn wknd* **10/1**

2m 32.84s (-1.66) **Going Correction** -0.175s/f (Firm) **10** Ran SP% **116.9**
Speed ratings (Par 103):98,97,96,96,92 92,92,91,87,78
CSF £38.60 CT £162.05 TOTE £7.20: £2.70, £1.30, £1.90; EX 39.20 Trifecta £345.90 Part won. Pool: £487.23 - 0.34 winning tickets..
Owner Derrick Bloy **Bred** Mrs Peggy Kelly **Trained** Settrington, N Yorks

FOCUS
A moderate handicap in which the pace was not strong.
Red River Rebel Official explanation: trainer said gelding was unsuited by the good to firm ground

4925 LEICESTER RACECOURSE CHRISTMAS PARTY PACKAGES H'CAP — 1m 1f 218y
5:00 (5:01) (Class 6) (0-65,63) 4-Y-O+ — **£3,238** (£963; £481; £240) **Stalls** High

Form — RPR

2323 **1** **Granary Girl**[20] 4289 4-8-7 49... TedDurcan 11 57
(J Pearce) *hld up in tch: rdn to ld over 1f out: r.o* **16/1**

6-44 **2** *1 ½* **Planters Punch (IRE)**[21] 4256 5-9-2 58........................ PaulMulrennan 16 63
(G M Moore) *hld up in tch: rdn over 3f out: r.o* **14/1**

3223 **3** *hd* **Redeye Special**[21] 4248 4-9-2 63...................................... LiamJones(5) 2 68
(M L W Bell) *prom: racd keenly: led over 2f out: hdd over 1f out: no ex ins fnl f* **7/1**[3]

0150 **4** *shd* **Abstract Folly (IRE)**^{14} [4472] 4-9-1 **57**.......................... PaulHanagan 15 62
(J D Bethell) *s.s: hld up: hmpd over 3f out: nt clr run over 1f out: r.o ins fnl f: nrst fin* **12/1**

4236 **5** *½* **Qualitair Wings**^{11} [4606] 7-9-3 **59**.......................... DavidAllan 7 63
(J Hetherton) *s.s: hld up: hdwy over 2f out: r.o* **8/1**

6103 **6** *1 ¼* **Siena Star (IRE)**^{20} [4307] 8-9-5 **61**.......................... HayleyTurner 5 62
(Stef Liddiard) *plld hrd and prom: rdn over 3f out: sn outpcd: styd on ins fnl f* **12/1**

1343 **7** *shd* **Shrine Mountain (USA)**^{68} [2820] 4-8-11 **53**.......................... NCallan 12 54
(J R Holt) *plld hrd and prom: rdn over 2f out: no ex ins fnl f* **8/1**

400- **8** *6* **Musardiere**^{28} [4064] 4-8-9 **54**..........................(p) JasonEdmunds(3) 3 44
(J Balding) *s.i.s: hld up: rdn over 3f out: n.d* **33/1**

0541 **9** *hd* **Oh Danny Boy**^{11} [4606] 5-9-3 **59**.......................... JohnEgan 14 48
(Jane Chapple-Hyam) *hld up in tpouch: rdn over 2f out: wknd over 1f out* **6/1**^{2}

00/0 **10** *½* **Sea Holly (IRE)**^{20} [4307] 6-9-0 **63**.......................... DanielRobinson(7) 8 51
(G G Margarson) *hld up: hmpd over 4f out: rdn over 3f out: n.d* **100/1**

3000 **11** *½* **Itcanbedone Again (IRE)**^{24} [4176] 7-8-4 **49**.......................... GregFairley(3) 13 36
(Ian Williams) *chsd ldr: rdn over 2f out: wknd over 1f out* **28/1**

0044 **12** *2* **Atlantic Story (USA)**^{14} [4467] 4-9-6 **62**..........................(t) DaleGibson 10 46
(M W Easterby) *led over 7f: wknd over 1f out* **25/1**

0265 **13** *6* **Tata Naka**^{11} [4606] 6-8-13 **55**.......................... DaneO'Neill 4 27
(Mrs C A Dunnett) *hld up: rdn over 2f out: sn wknd* **11/1**

1-01 **14** *2 ½* **Le Soleil (GER)**^{141} [972] 5-9-2 **58**.......................... TPQueally 9 25
(B J Curley) *hld up: rdn over 3f out: sn wknd* **9/1**

500/ **15** *23* **Riverweld**^{684} [6195] 4-8-6 **48**.......................... JosedeSouza 1 —
(J R Holt) *plld hrd: prom over 6f* **66/1**

0413 **16** *1 ¾* **Cantarna (IRE)**^{17} [4390] 5-8-12 **59**.......................... AndrewElliott(5) 6 —
(J Mackie) *prom: lost pl 8f out: bhd fnl 4f* **4/1**^{1}

2m 6.63s (-1.67) **Going Correction** -0.175s/f (Firm) **16** Ran SP% **128.0**
Speed ratings (Par 101):99,97,97,97,97 96,96,91,91,90 90,88,83,81,63 62
CSF £226.80 CT £1739.71 TOTE £16.70: £3.40, £5.40, £1.90, £3.70; EX 223.00 TRIFECTA Not won. Place 6 £69.74, Place 5 £29.36.
Owner Jeff Pearce **Bred** Barry Minty **Trained** Newmarket, Suffolk

FOCUS
This routine handicap was run at a fair pace.
Oh Danny Boy Official explanation: jockey said gelding had no more to give
Cantarna(IRE) Official explanation: trainer had no explanation for the poor form shown
T/Jkpt: Not won. T/Plt: £103.00 to a £1 stake. Pool: £78,438.65. 555.45 winning tickets. T/Qpdt: £22.40 to a £1 stake. Pool: £4,471.70. 147.10 winning tickets. CR

4394 LINGFIELD (L-H)
Wednesday, August 30

OFFICIAL GOING: Turf course - good; all-weather - standard
Wind: Mostly across

4926 VALLEY EXPRESS (S) STKS 6f
2:20 (2:22) (Class 6) 2-Y-O **£2,730** (£806; £403) **Stalls** High

Form RPR

026 **1** **Auction Oasis**^{33} [3895] 2-8-6 70.......................... FrancisFerris 2 58
(B Palling) *v fast away: led: crossed to nr side and spreadeagled field: rdn fnl f: jst lasted home* **7/1**

63 **2** *shd* **Tibinta**^{4} [4816] 2-7-13.......................... LukeMorris(7) 5 58
(Rae Guest) *dwlt: wl off the pce tl prog on outer jst over 2f out: drvn to chse wnr ins fnl f: styd on: jst failed* **14/1**

5530 **3** *2 ½* **Mr Mini Scule**^{24} [4178] 2-8-11 59.......................... SteveDrowne 12 55
(A B Haynes) *chsd ldrs but nt on terms: rdn over 2f out: kpt on fr over 1f out to take 3rd nr fin* **10/1**

6614 **4** *hd* **Fair 'n Square (IRE)**^{57} [3160] 2-8-13 63.......................... FrancisNorton 11 57
(J L Spearing) *chsd ldng trio but nt on terms: rdn to try to cl fr 2f out: keeping on but hld whn squeezed out ins fnl f* **7/1**

2000 **5** *nk* **Peppin's Gold (IRE)**^{24} [4178] 2-8-6 62.......................... ChrisCatlin 13 49
(B R Millman) *settled in rr and sn outpcd: effrt over 2f out: kpt on fr over 1f out: n.d* **4/1**^{1}

340 **6** *nk* **Cookies Quiff (IRE)**^{19} [4334] 2-8-11 52.......................... MartinDwyer 7 53
(J S Moore) *free to post: chsd wnr: rdn over 2f out: wknd jst ins fnl f* **12/1**

00 **7** *1 ½* **Peggy's Pearl**^{25} [4138] 2-8-6.......................... LPKeniry 3 43
(J S Moore) *chsd ldng pair: u.p over 2f out: struggling over 1f out: fdd* **50/1**

0066 **8** *1 ¼* **Grimes Glory**^{19} [4334] 2-8-11.......................... RyanMoore 8 45
(R Hannon) *outpcd in rr: n.d: plugged on fnl f* **6/1**^{3}

0423 **9** *1* **Meru Camp (IRE)**^{30} [4007] 2-8-11 60.......................... JimCrowley 4 42
(P Winkworth) *off the pce towards rr: rdn and sme prog 2f out: nvr rchd ldrs: wknd fnl f* **5/1**^{2}

0050 **10** *½* **Tagula Music (IRE)**^{51} [3345] 2-8-6.......................... PaulDoe 9 35
(B Palling) *s.s: outpcd and a wl in rr* **33/1**

5000 **11** *nk* **Fine Leg**^{7} [4688] 2-8-6..........................(t) NickyMackay 6 34
(P J McBride) *outpcd and wl in rr: no prog 2f out: eased fnl f* **25/1**

400 **12** *9* **Equal And Approved**^{19} [4334] 2-8-11 54.......................... RichardHughes 1 12
(R Hannon) *reluctant to enter stalls: outpcd: hrd rdn and no prog over 2f out: sn wknd* **8/1**

1m 12.14s (0.47) **Going Correction** -0.175s/f (Firm) **12** Ran SP% **119.3**
Speed ratings (Par 92):89,88,85,85,84 84,82,80,79,78 78,66
CSF £99.63 TOTE £5.10: £2.00, £4.10, £4.10; EX 93.30.The winner was bought in for 7,200gns. Tibinta was claimed by Andrew Bates for £6,000.
Owner Flying Eight Partnership **Bred** F L Mallaghan **Trained** Tredodridge, Vale Of Glamorgan
■ Stewards' Enquiry : Francis Ferris one-day ban: failed to keep straight from the stalls (Sep 10)
Luke Morris caution: careless riding

FOCUS
Not a bad race for the grade and Auction Oasis blitzed them from the off. The form looks quite solid.

NOTEBOOK
Auction Oasis, who had upwards of 8lb in hand on all her rivals, had shown enough in maidens to suggest she had a race at this level in her and she won the race in the first few strides, shooting out of the stalls and quickly establishing a significant lead, crossing over to the advantageous stands'-side rail. She was clinging on for dear life at the finish, but just did enough to hold on and, although not very big, she can win more races at this sort of level when the emphasis is on speed. (op 4-1)
Tibinta ran well in defeat in this grade last time and she relished the extra furlong here, finishing strongly down the outside away from the favoured rail, and narrowly failing to get up. Clear of the third, she should have little trouble collecting a race at this level.
Mr Mini Scule was more exposed than the front pair and he finished well having, but is likely to continue to find at least one too god, even at this level. (op 16-1 tchd 18-1)
Fair 'n Square(IRE) looked likely to go close on the form of her Brighton maiden win over the progessive Inflight and, although disappointing in a claimer back there last time, the winner of that Just Dust went on to land a decent nursery at Glorious Goodwood. She kept on best she could, but was slipped by the winner and was then squeezed out close home, probably costing her a place. There are races to be won with her at this level. (op 15-2)
Peppin's Gold(IRE), dropping to this grade for the first time, was unable to go the gallop and, although plugging on, she was never in contention. A step back up to seven furlongs should see the filly in a better light. (op 7-2)
Grimes Glory, who was staying on towards the end of his race over seven furlongs last time, struggled on this drop back in trip and remains capable of better over a more suitable distance. (op 7-1)

4927 WEATHERBYS BANK H'CAP 6f
2:50 (2:52) (Class 5) (0-70,69) 3-Y-O **£3,238** (£963; £481; £240) **Stalls** High

Form RPR

063 **1** **Littledodayno (IRE)**^{23} [4199] 3-8-7 **58**.......................... JamesDoyle(3) 11 69
(M Wigham) *racd against nr side rail: trckd ldrs: plld out and effrt to ld over 1f out: shkn up fnl f: a in command* **4/1**^{1}

2224 **2** *¾* **Mr Cellophane**^{9} [4666] 3-9-0 **62**.......................... RichardHughes 16 71
(J R Jenkins) *hld up in midfield: effrt 2f out: swtchd lft and prog over 1f out: chsd wnr last 100yds: r.o but a readily hld* **5/1**^{2}

0000 **3** *1 ½* **Miss Lopez (IRE)**^{13} [4524] 3-8-12 **60**.......................... FrancisNorton 2 65
(K R Burke) *pressed ldr: upsides over 1f out: chsd wnr after but sn hld u.p: lost 2nd last 100yds* **50/1**

3603 **4** *½* **Alwariah**^{7} [4690] 3-8-7 **55**.......................... NickyMackay 7 58
(C E Brittain) *trckd ldrs: effrt 2f out: rdn and kpt on same pce fr over 1f out* **8/1**

0-01 **5** *1* **James Street (IRE)**^{18} [4368] 3-9-7 **69**.......................... MartinDwyer 12 69
(J R Best) *hld up in midfield: pushed along over 2f out: kpt on u.p fnl f: n.d* **5/1**^{2}

0005 **6** *¾* **Jabbara (IRE)**^{8} [4671] 3-8-12 **60**.......................... PatDobbs 6 58
(C E Brittain) *hld up in midfield: rdn on outer 2f out: one pce and no real imp* **16/1**

4400 **7** *hd* **Danish Blues (IRE)**^{28} [4050] 3-8-10 **58**..........................(p) RichardThomas 17 55
(N P Littmoden) *taken down early: t.k.h: hld up in last trio: outpcd 2f out: styd on against nr side rail fnl f: no ch* **33/1**

-500 **8** *1 ½* **Mouchoir**^{61} [3055] 3-9-2 **64**..........................(b) RyanMoore 8 57
(P J Makin) *led and crossed to nr side rail: hdd and sltly hmpd over 1f out: wknd* **15/2**^{3}

0425 **9** *shd* **Discotheque (USA)**^{14} [4494] 3-9-0 **62**.......................... JamieSpencer 10 54
(P Howling) *dwlt: hld up in last trio: swtchd to outer and effrt 2f out: one pce and n.d* **12/1**

-000 **10** *hd* **Milton's Keen**^{11} [4602] 3-8-3 **58**.......................... KirstyMilczarek(7) 9 50
(P S McEntee) *hld up in midfield: pushed along and no prog wl over 1f out: fdd* **33/1**

0000 **11** *½* **Eversden (USA)**^{13} [4532] 3-9-3 **68**..........................(p) AdamKirby(3) 15 58
(C G Cox) *t.k.h: hld up in last trio: outpcd 2f out: no ch after* **14/1**

1006 **12** *¾* **George The Second**^{7} [4703] 3-8-11 **62**.......................... EdwardCreighton(3) 4 50
(Mrs H Sweeting) *pressed ldng pair tl wknd wl over 1f out* **16/1**

5330 **13** *shd* **Thoughtsofstardom**^{34} [3866] 3-8-7 **56** ow1..........................(p) BrianReilly 13 43
(P S McEntee) *hld up in rr: no prog 2f out: no ch after* **25/1**

3350 **14** *10* **Developer (IRE)**^{191} [464] 3-9-5 **67**.......................... IanMongan 3 25
(T G Mills) *stdd s: swtchd fr outside draw and hld up: brief effrt on outer over 2f out: sn wknd: t.o* **16/1**

1m 11.18s (-0.49) **Going Correction** -0.175s/f (Firm) **14** Ran SP% **119.9**
Speed ratings (Par 100):96,95,93,92,91 90,89,87,87,87 86,85,85,72
CSF £22.12 CT £905.85 TOTE £5.60: £1.90, £1.90, £11.30; EX 34.80.
Owner W and L Bamforth **Bred** Lodge Park Stud **Trained** Newmarket, Suffolk
■ Stewards' Enquiry : Richard Hughes caution: careless riding

FOCUS
A modest handicap in which the benefit of racing next to the stands'-side rail was once again highlighted.
Danish Blues(IRE) Official explanation: jockey said gelding ran too free
Eversden(USA) Official explanation: jockey said colt suffered interference in running

4928 LLANERA LIFESTYLE RESORTS NOVICE STKS 7f
3:20 (3:23) (Class 4) 2-Y-O **£4,533** (£1,348; £674; £336) **Stalls** High

Form RPR

05 **1** **My Learned Friend (IRE)**^{25} [4129] 2-8-12.......................... SteveDrowne 2 82
(A M Balding) *mde virtually all and sn crossed to nr side rail: hrd pressed fnl f: styd on wl* **16/1**

21 **2** *shd* **Safe Investment (USA)**^{31} [3976] 2-9-5 90.......................... RichardHughes 8 89
(J H M Gosden) *wl plcd: effrt to chse wnr over 1f out: drvn to chal fnl f: jst hld* **13/8**^{1}

1 **3** *2* **Aqmaar**^{40} [3701] 2-9-5.......................... MartinDwyer 6 87+
(J L Dunlop) *t.k.h: hld up bhd ldrs: nowhere to go fr 1/2-way: effrt and nt clr run over 1f out: swtchd lft and styd on same pce* **10/3**^{3}

0 **4** *1 ½* **Titan Triumph**^{19} [4333] 2-8-12.......................... PaulDoe 9 73
(W J Knight) *plld hrd: hld up in midfield: nohwere to go and lost pl 3f out: effrt over 1f out: kpt on: no ch* **25/1**

55 **5** *1 ¼* **Orange Pekoe (USA)**^{20} [4292] 2-8-12.......................... NickyMackay 3 70
(P Mitchell) *pressed wnr: drvn whn sltly hmpd over 1f out: fdd* **66/1**

0261 **6** *1* **Bright Moon**^{14} [4480] 2-8-11 81.......................... RyanMoore 5 67
(R Hannon) *hld up in tch: effrt on outer over 2f out: nt qckn over 1f out: wknd ins fnl f* **9/1**

7 *nk* **Forefathers (USA)** 2-8-8.......................... JamieSpencer 7 63+
(M L W Bell) *settled in rr: brief effrt over 2f out: wknd fnl f* **11/4**^{2}

8 *nk* **Barbs Pink Diamond (USA)** 2-8-0.......................... JamesDoyle(3) 1 57
(Mrs A J Perrett) *s.s: wl in rr: prog on wd outside 3f out: chsng ldrs 2f out: wknd fnl f* **33/1**

9 *shd* **Alittlebitleft (IRE)** 2-8-8.......................... PatDobbs 10 62
(R Hannon) *dwlt: t.k.h: hld up in last pair: taken to outer and effrt 2f out: wknd fnl f* **50/1**

10 *3* **Amazing King (IRE)** 2-8-1.......................... JackDean(7) 4 54
(W G M Turner) *in tch: pushed along over 2f out: wknd over 1f out* **66/1**

1m 24.1s (-0.11) **Going Correction** -0.175s/f (Firm) **10** Ran SP% **115.5**
Speed ratings (Par 96):93,92,90,88,87 86,85,85,85,82
CSF £41.32 TOTE £18.90: £3.60, £1.10, £1.60; EX 59.80.
Owner N H Harris & Dr E Harris **Bred** B Kennedy **Trained** Kingsclere, Hants
■ Stewards' Enquiry : Martin Dwyer one-day ban: careless riding (Sep 10)

FOCUS
Not a bad little race but the pace was ordinary, resulting in a number racing keenly, and the stands' rail once again proved a big advantage. A much improved effotr from the winner, with the second and third roughly to their marks.

NOTEBOOK

My Learned Friend(IRE) had run with credit in a couple of good maidens on his first two starts, but he beat a couple of previous winners into second and third, and this was a major step up in form on the face of it. However, he did enjoy a perfect trip, setting a steady pace and making every yard next to the hugely favoured stands'-side rail. (op 20-1)

Safe Investment(USA) travelled well three wide of the rail, but when let down he found himself in a battle with a rival who had enjoyed the benefit of racing on a faster strip under the stands' rail and was receiving 7lb from him. He was narrowly denied but finished clear of the rest and was probably the best horse in the race. (op 11-8 tchd 5-4 and 7-4 in places)

Aqmaar raced keenly behind the leader on the rail and had to wait for a gap to deliver his challenge wide of the first two home. He could not pick up when asked, though, no doubt as a result of him wasting his energy early on, and should be happier in a more strongly-run contest. (op 7-2 tchd 4-1 in places)

Titan Triumph, a half-brother to Burning Moon, a ten-furlong winner at three, had the benefit of the stands'-side rail but he pulled hard off the steady early pace and that compromised his chance. It still was not a bad effort, though, and he should be able to find a maiden.

Orange Pekoe(USA) ran a personal best but he did benefit hugely from racing next to the eventual winner, who set a steady pace in front. He might not be able to replicate this in a more truly-run race. (op 100-1)

Bright Moon, who won a nursery off 76 last time out, was disadvantaged by racing on the outside of the pack while the likes of the winner enjoyed the benefit of racing on a faster strip next to the stands'-side rail. (op 12-1)

Forefathers(USA), who cost $680,000, is a half-brother to a juvenile winner in the US out of a mare who was a smart triple winner at around 7f over there. Taken out of a couple of recent engagements due to soft ground, he was well backed for this despite his lack of experience. While he did not threaten in the race itself, it would be a surprise if he was not capable of better in time. (op 3-1 tchd 100-30 in places)

4929 VALLEY VISION H'CAP — 2m (P)

3:50 (3:52) (Class 6) (0-55,55) 3-Y-O+ — **£2,388** (£705; £352) **Stalls** Low

Form	Pos	Dist	Horse / comment	RPR
0025	**1**		**Jadeeron**[18] 4380 7-9-4 **43**....(p) ChrisCatlin 8 (Miss D A McHale) *prom in chsng gp: clsd 5f out: rdn over 2f out: styd on to ld last 150yds: drvn out* **5/1**[2]	55
00-0	**2**	*1 ½*	**Prince Of Medina**[14] 4483 3-9-2 **55**.... MartinDwyer 10 (J R Best) *led: veered rt bnd over 8f out and hdd: chsd ldr: rdn to ld again over 2f out: tired and hdd last 150yds* **20/1**	65
3000	**3**	*2 ½*	**Iamback**[16] 4423 6-9-1 **40**....(t) BrianReilly 12 (Miss D A McHale) *hld up wl in rr: rdn and prog on outer fr 4f out: styd on over 1f out: nrst fin* **16/1**	47
2635	**4**	*1 ¾*	**Ganymede**[7] 4702 5-9-12 **51**.... IanMongan 4 (Mrs L J Mongan) *wl plcd in chsng gp: rdn wl over 3f out: nt qckn and no imp fnl 2f* **11/2**[3]	56
3226	**5**	*½*	**Tip Toes (IRE)**[19] 4330 4-9-4 **46**.... DeanCorby[(3)] 2 (P Howling) *dwlt: hld up in midfield: prog and gng wl enough over 3f out: rdn over 2f out: no rspnse* **16/1**	50
0500	**6**	*2*	**Aristi (IRE)**[16] 4438 5-8-13 **45**....(p) ChrisCavanagh[(7)] 7 (M Quinn) *trckd ldr and sn clr of rest: lft in ld over 8f out: rdn and hdd over 2f out: wknd over 1f out* **10/1**	47
0040	**7**	*nk*	**Chimes At Midnight (USA)**[68] 2822 9-9-3 **42**.... FranciscoDaSilva 5 (Luke Comer, Ire) *hld up and sn last: reminder 7f out: lost tch and rdn over 4f out: poor 12th over 1f out: fin strly* **20/1**	43
6210	**8**	*shd*	**Cemgraft**[7] 4702 5-9-8 **50**....(tp) JamesDoyle[(3)] 6 (A J Lidderdale) *hld up wl in rr: rdn over 3f out: no real imp on ldrs fr over 2f out* **9/2**[1]	51
0100	**9**	*2 ½*	**Galantos (GER)**[28] 4046 5-10-0 **53**....(b[1]) RyanMoore 9 (G L Moore) *wl plcd in chsng gp: rdn over 4f out: struggling 3f out: eased whn btn over 1f out* **6/1**	51
00-0	**10**	*8*	**Fosroc (USA)**[38] 2861 4-9-8 **50**.... AdamKirby[(3)] 11 (B R Johnson) *led chsng gp to 5f out: sn drvn: wknd over 2f out* **25/1**	39
0500	**11**	*9*	**Kaluana Court**[5] 4777 10-9-2 **41**.... FrancisNorton 1 (A W Carroll) *hld up in midfield: rdn and wknd over 3f out* **14/1**	19
4	**12**	*18*	**Belindas Dream (IRE)**[19] 4341 5-9-6 **45**.... RichardHughes 14 (Aidan Anthony Howard, Ire) *dwlt: hld up wl in rr: lost tch over 4f out: t.o over 2f out* **16/1**	—
0340	**13**	*27*	**So Elegant (IRE)**[26] 4104 4-9-8 **47**....(t) DerekMcGaffin 3 (J Jay) *s.v.s: a wl in rr: lost tch 5f out: t.o 3f out* **12/1**	—

3m 26.67s (-2.12) **Going Correction** -0.25s/f (Stan)
WFA 3 from 4yo+ 14lb — **13** Ran SP% **119.0**
Speed ratings (Par 101):95,94,93,92,91 90,90,90,89,85 80,71,58
CSF £104.45 CT £1499.86 TOTE £5.20: £2.50, £4.90, £5.90; EX 133.60.
Owner N Bashir **Bred** Aziz Merza **Trained** Newmarket, Suffolk

FOCUS
A moderate handicap run at an ordinary pace.
Prince Of Medina Official explanation: jockey said gelding hung right
Galantos(GER) Official explanation: jockey said gelding was never travelling
Belindas Dream(IRE) Official explanation: jockey said mare hung badly left

4930 CHARLTON ATHLETIC COMMUNITY TRUST H'CAP — 7f (P)

4:20 (4:22) (Class 6) (0-65,65) 3-Y-O — **£3,238** (£963; £481; £240) **Stalls** Low

Form	Pos	Dist	Horse / comment	RPR
4232	**1**		**Young Bertie**[20] 4291 3-9-4 **62**....(v[1]) SteveDrowne 2 (H Morrison) *a ldng trio: effrt over 2f out: led over 1f out: drvn and drew clr fnl f* **5/2**[1]	74
1052	**2**	*3*	**Whistleupthewind**[21] 4265 3-8-13 **60**....(b) StephenDonohoe[(3)] 1 (J M P Eustace) *a ldng trio: rdn to ld 2f out: hdd over 1f out: kpt on but no ch w wnr* **10/1**[3]	64
5300	**3**	*1 ¼*	**Shunkawakhan (IRE)**[34] 3866 3-9-1 **59**.... NickyMackay 12 (G C H Chung) *chsd ldrs: rdn on outer over 2f out: outpcd wl over 1f out: styd on ins fnl f* **16/1**	60
6665	**4**	*shd*	**Dallma (IRE)**[21] 4243 3-9-4 **62**.... RyanMoore 10 (C E Brittain) *settled in midfield: off the pce 1/2-way: rdn and effrt over 2f out: styd on fr over 1f out: nrst fin* **10/1**[3]	62
0340	**5**	*½*	**Fateful Attraction**[18] 4363 3-9-3 **64**....(b[1]) JamesDoyle[(3)] 5 (I A Wood) *led at decent pce: hdd 2f out: wknd fnl f* **14/1**	63
3445	**6**	*1 ¾*	**Blacktoft (USA)**[21] 4254 3-9-4 **65**.... AdamKirby[(3)] 7 (S C Williams) *taken down early: s.v.s: last and wl off the pce: drvn and styd on fr over 1f out: nvr nrr* **8/1**[2]	60
5-00	**7**	*½*	**Sessile (USA)**[30] 4004 3-9-4 **62**.... IanMongan 8 (J H M Gosden) *hld up towards rr: rdn and wl off the pce over 2f out: n.d after* **12/1**	55
6003	**8**	*nk*	**Doctor David**[17] 4395 3-9-4 **62**.... PatDobbs 3 (Ernst Oertel) *settled in midfield: off the pce 1/2-way: rdn and effrt over 2f out: no imp over 1f out: fdd* **14/1**	55
0320	**9**	*1 ¾*	**Endless Night**[13] 4531 3-8-12 **61**.... TravisBlock[(5)] 9 (H Morrison) *hld up wl in rr: struggling fr 3f out* **8/1**[2]	49
6235	**10**	*nk*	**Some Diva**[49] 3410 3-9-1 **59**.... JamieSpencer 11 (W R Swinburn) *taken down early: hld up wl in rr: struggling 3f out: no ch whn wd bnd 2f out* **8/1**[2]	46
-341	**11**	*½*	**Distant Drums (IRE)**[20] 4277 3-9-4 **62**.... RichardHughes 14 (B W Hills) *hld up wl in rr: gng wl enough 3f out: shkn up and no rspnse over 2f out: eased fnl f* **10/1**[3]	48
5060	**12**	*hd*	**Ockums Razor (IRE)**[40] 3708 3-9-3 **64**.... DeanCorby[(3)] 6 (C A Dwyer) *prom: drvn wl over 2f out: sn wknd* **20/1**	49
-254	**13**	*1 ¼*	**Snow Symphony (IRE)**[21] 4243 3-9-4 **62**.... ChrisCatlin 13 (D M Simcock) *hld up wl in rr: struggling 3f out: no ch whn wd bnd 2f out* **33/1**	44

1m 25.03s (-0.86) **Going Correction** -0.25s/f (Stan) — **13** Ran SP% **123.8**
Speed ratings (Par 98):94,90,89,89,88 86,85,85,83,83 82,82,80
CSF £29.09 CT £360.68 TOTE £3.20: £1.50, £3.10, £5.70; EX 30.20.
Owner M T Bevan **Bred** Red House Stud **Trained** East Ilsley, Berks

FOCUS
A modest handicap, but one that should produce winners.
Dallma(IRE) Official explanation: jockey said saddle slipped
Blacktoft(USA) Official explanation: jockey said gelding was never travelling
Distant Drums(IRE) Official explanation: jockey said filly hung badly left

4931 CHARLTON ATHLETIC £99 SEASON TICKET MAIDEN STKS — 1m 4f (P)

4:50 (4:50) (Class 5) 3-Y-O+ — **£3,238** (£963; £481; £240) **Stalls** Low

Form	Pos	Dist	Horse / comment	RPR
6	**1**		**Crossbow Creek**[27] 3225 8-9-13.... ChrisCatlin 11 (M G Rimell) *t.k.h early: hld up in tch: prog 5f out: chsd ldr wl over 3f out: clsd over 2f out: led over 1f out: sn clr* **14/1**	83
3	**2**	*5*	**Falpiase (IRE)**[20] 4300 4-9-13....(b) NickyMackay 13 (L M Cumani) *racd freely: led: drew clr 4f out: rdn over 2f out: hdd and fnd nil over 1f out* **11/4**[1]	75
3343	**3**	*1 ½*	**Reinstated (IRE)**[13] 4537 3-8-12 **70**.... RichardHughes 12 (B W Hills) *settled in rr: rdn 5f out: prog u.p to chse ldng pair 3f out: kpt on one pce* **7/2**[2]	68
0-2	**4**	*5*	**Land Of Light**[19] 4330 3-9-3.... JimCrowley 6 (G L Moore) *chsd ldr to wl over 3f out: grad wknd* **16/1**	65
	5	*shd*	**Ausone**[143] 4-9-5.... EdwardCreighton[(3)] 4 (Miss J R Gibney) *dwlt: wl in rr: rdn 5f out: plugged on one pce fnl 3f: no ch* **66/1**	59
	6	*4*	**Dangerous Business (IRE)**[88] 2256 5-9-8.... SteveDrowne 9 (H Morrison) *nvr beyond midfield: lost tch and rdn over 4f out: no ch after* **25/1**	53
0353	**7**	*1 ½*	**Gaze**[33] 3911 3-8-12 **69**....(v) PatDobbs 8 (W Jarvis) *prom tl wknd u.p over 3f out* **10/1**	51
	8	*5*	**Theatre Groom (USA)**[28] 7-9-13.... LPKeniry 3 (M R Bosley) *a wl in rr: rdn 5f out: no ch over 3f out* **50/1**	48
23-	**9**	*nk*	**First Slip**[253] 6624 3-9-3.... RyanMoore 5 (Mrs A J Perrett) *hld up in midfield: rdn 5f out: wknd over 3f out* **6/1**	47
0-	**10**	*¾*	**Cockatoo (USA)**[425] 3084 3-9-3.... IanMongan 2 (G L Moore) *drvn in last after 3f: nvr a factor: wl bhd over 3f out* **25/1**	46
	11	*10*	**Shanagolden Juan (IRE)** 3-9-3.... AlanDaly 14 (M R Bosley) *s.s: a wl in rr: wknd 4f out* **100/1**	30
	12	*2*	**Bazil Des Fieffes (FR)** 4-9-13....(b[1]) CDehens 10 (J M Plasschaert, Belgium) *dwlt: rcvrd to chse ldrs after 2f: wknd over 5f out: sn wl bhd* **50/1**	27
00	**13**	*7*	**Persian Warrior (IRE)**[23] 4210 3-9-0.... AdamKirby[(3)] 1 (W R Swinburn) *trckd ldrs: drvn 6f out: wknd 4f out* **40/1**	16
5324	**14**	*dist*	**Avelian (IRE)**[33] 3911 3-9-3 **69**....(v[1]) JamieSpencer 7 (W J Haggas) *trckd ldrs: rdn and wknd 5f out: eased 3f out: virtually p.u fnl 2f* **5/1**[3]	—

2m 31.66s (-2.73) **Going Correction** -0.25s/f (Stan)
WFA 3 from 4yo+ 10lb — **14** Ran SP% **118.0**
Speed ratings (Par 103):99,95,94,91,91 88,87,84,84,83 76,75,70,—
CSF £49.42 TOTE £15.70: £3.90, £1.50, £2.00; EX 57.30 Place 6 £208.27, Place 5 £30.86.
Owner Mark Rimell **Bred** Mrs M R T Rimell **Trained** Leafield, Oxon

FOCUS
Modest maiden form, but very useful hurdler/chaser Crossbow Creek ran out a ready winner.
Persian Warrior(IRE) Official explanation: jockey said gelding hung both ways
Avelian(IRE) Official explanation: jockey said gelding made a noise
T/Plt: £54.40 to a £1 stake. Pool: £57,710.75. 773.55 winning tickets. T/Qpdt: £10.00 to a £1 stake. Pool: £4,136.90. 304.80 winning tickets. JN

4433 WOLVERHAMPTON (A.W) (L-H)

Wednesday, August 30

OFFICIAL GOING: Standard to fast
The going was definitely on the fast side with three track records broken.
Wind: Moderate, behind

4932 WOLVERHAMPTON-RACECOURSE.CO.UK MAIDEN AUCTION STKS — 1m 141y(P)

2:10 (2:10) (Class 4) 2-Y-O — **£6,477** (£1,927; £963; £481) **Stalls** Low

Form	Pos	Dist	Horse / comment	RPR
2	**1**		**Worldly**[13] 4526 2-8-9.... JohnEgan 1 (S Kirk) *w ldr: led over 3f out: clr whn shkn up over 1f out: pushed out* **1/4**[1]	70+
054	**2**	*3 ½*	**Grand Lucre**[17] 4394 2-8-4.... RichardMullen 2 (E J O'Neill) *a.p: rdn 4f out: chsd wnr over 2f out: no imp* **9/1**[3]	58
0	**3**	*6*	**Bret Maverick (IRE)**[12] 4566 2-8-9.... PhillipMakin 4 (J R Weymes) *hld up in tch: rdn 4f out: wknd over 2f out* **66/1**	50
64	**4**	*7*	**Satyricon**[18] 4366 2-8-12.... OscarUrbina 6 (M Botti) *led: hdd over 3f out: sn rdn: wknd 2f out* **15/2**[2]	39
	5	*6*	**Robbie Scott** 2-8-12.... JoeFanning 3 (M Johnston) *rdn over 5f out: a bhd* **16/1**	26
	6	*27*	**Saint Remus (IRE)** 2-8-9.... RobbieFitzpatrick 5 (Peter Grayson) *s.i.s: a bhd: t.o* **66/1**	—

1m 48.08s (-3.68) **Going Correction** -0.425s/f (Stan) — **6** Ran SP% **110.6**
Speed ratings (Par 96):99,95,90,84,79 55
CSF £3.23 TOTE £1.30: £1.10, £3.40; EX 3.60.
Owner The Hon Mrs J M Corbett **Bred** Stratford Place Stud **Trained** Upper Lambourn, Berks

FOCUS
This uncompetitive race went very much as expected with the track record broken. There was little strength in depth and the winner was below form in getting off the mark.

NOTEBOOK
Worldly ◆, runner-up to a subsequent Listed winner on his debut, duly proved far too good for these rivals on this switch to sand. He smashed the still relatively new juvenile course record and looks a fair sort. (op 3-10 tchd 1-3 in a place)
Grand Lucre beat the others easily enough but found that the winner was in a different league. (op 10-1 tchd 11-1)
Bret Maverick(IRE) stepped up on his soft-ground debut at Newcastle earlier in the month but that would not have been difficult. (op 50-1)

4933 HOTEL & CONFERENCING AT DUNSTALL PARK H'CAP 1m 141y(P)
2:40 (2:40) (Class 5) (0-75,74) 3-Y-O **£4,533** (£1,348; £674; £336) **Stalls** Low

Form RPR
3045 **1** **Persian Express (USA)**[11] [4591] 3-9-4 **71** .... MichaelHills 1 79
(B W Hills) *a.p: rdn to ld wl over 1f out: sn edgd rt: r.o wl* **9/1**
1023 **2** 1 ½ **Don Pietro**[14] [4490] 3-9-7 **74** .... EddieAhern 5 79
(D J Coakley) *a.p: rdn 2f out: edgd lft ins fnl f: kpt on to take 2nd post* **11/2**[2]
-242 **3** *shd* **Signal Hill**[22] [4225] 3-8-7 **65** .... LiamJones(5) 6 70
(W J Haggas) *chsd ldr: rdn and ev ch wl over 1f out: nt qckn ins fnl f* **5/1**[1]
4201 **4** ½ **High Class Problem (IRE)**[21] [4243] 3-9-1 **68** .... JoeFanning 3 72
(P F I Cole) *led: rdn and hdd wl over 1f out: sn carried sltly rt: swtchd lft jst ins fnl f: nt qckn* **12/1**
3611 **5** ½ **Night Cru**[33] [3906] 3-9-4 **71** .... GeorgeBaker 9 74
(C F Wall) *hld up in mid-div: rdn over 2f out: styd on fnl f: nt trble ldrs* **6/1**[3]
05-2 **6** *nk* **Birkside**[16] [4431] 3-9-7 **74** .... StephenCarson 11 76
(W R Swinburn) *swtchd lft sn after s: hld up and bhd: rdn and hdwy over 1f out: nt rch ldrs* **5/1**[1]
4050 **7** *hd* **Vodkatini**[28] [4044] 3-8-9 **62** ....(v) OscarUrbina 2 63
(P J Makin) *hld up in mid-div: hdwy on ins over 2f out: no imp fnl f* **9/1**
0603 **8** 4 **Magical Music**[21] [4249] 3-9-6 **73** .... SebSanders 8 66
(J Pearce) *hld up towards rr: sme hdwy whn nt clr run over 2f out: n.d after* **11/2**[2]
0053 **9** *shd* **Chia (IRE)**[20] [4291] 3-8-9 **62** .... FrankieMcDonald 4 55
(D Haydn Jones) *a bhd* **25/1**
-060 **10** 4 **Pommes Frites**[16] [4437] 3-9-6 **73** .... RichardMullen 10 57
(W R Muir) *hld up in mid-div: rdn 3f out: sn bhd* **33/1**
105 **11** 8 **Opera Writer (IRE)**[13] [4533] 3-9-1 **68** ....(v[1]) JimmyFortune 7 36
(J R Boyle) *prom tl wknd over 2f out* **16/1**
1m 47.36s (-4.40) **Going Correction** -0.425s/f (Stan) **11** Ran SP% **118.8**
Speed ratings (Par 100):102,100,100,100,99 99,99,95,95,92 84
CSF £58.50 CT £285.66 TOTE £9.70: £3.00, £2.10, £1.90; EX 66.00.
Owner D M James **Bred** Kingswood Farm **Trained** Lambourn, Berks
FOCUS
A wide-open handicap.

4934 DUNSTALL PARK CENTRE MAIDEN STKS 7f 32y(P)
3:10 (3:11) (Class 3) 2-Y-O **£7,124** (£2,119; £1,059; £529) **Stalls** High

Form RPR
3 **1** **Manchurian**[19] [4323] 2-9-3 .... DO'Donohoe 3 86+
(M J Wallace) *a.p: led wl over 1f out: rdn and r.o wl* **2/1**[2]
2 3 **Thunder Storm Cat (USA)** 2-9-3 .... JoeFanning 5 79
(P F I Cole) *led early: w ldr: led over 3f out: rdn and hdd wl over 1f out: one pce* **12/1**
3 3 **Wolf River (USA)** 2-9-3 .... SebSanders 4 71
(D M Simcock) *s.i.s: hdwy wl over 1f out: sn edgd rt: one pce fnl f* **20/1**
22 **4** 2 **Non Compliant**[65] [2938] 2-9-3 .... EddieAhern 1 66
(J W Hills) *t.k.h in mid-div: hdwy 2f out: sn rdn: wknd ins fnl f* **15/8**[1]
5 2 **Not Another Cat (USA)** 2-9-3 .... PatCosgrave 12 61
(K R Burke) *hld up in tch: rdn 3f out: wknd over 1f out* **25/1**
54 **6** ¾ **Massenzio (IRE)**[82] [2409] 2-9-3 .... JimmyFortune 7 59
(J H M Gosden) *s.i.s: hdwy on outside over 2f out: c wd st: n.d* **7/2**[3]
0 **7** 1 **King's Regiment (IRE)**[31] [3976] 2-9-3 .... PhilipRobinson 6 57
(M A Jarvis) *sn led: hdd over 3f out: rdn and wknd wl over 1f out* **40/1**
0 **8** 5 **Magena Gold**[35] [3844] 2-9-0 .... RichardKingscote(3) 10 44
(R Charlton) *prom tl rdn and wknd over 2f out* **40/1**
9 4 **Sew In Character** 2-9-3 .... DeanMcKeown 2 34
(M Blanshard) *sn mid-div: lost pl over 3f out: sn bhd* **50/1**
6 **10** 1 ½ **Neat 'n Tidy**[10] [4624] 2-8-12 .... MichaelHills 9 25
(C A Cyzer) *hld up towards rr: hdwy over 4f out: wknd wl over 1f out* **66/1**
1m 29.16s (-1.24) **Going Correction** -0.425s/f (Stan) **10** Ran SP% **115.0**
Speed ratings (Par 98):90,86,83,80,78 77,76,70,66,64
CSF £22.49 TOTE £3.40: £1.20, £3.20, £5.90; EX 26.70.
Owner Mrs P Good **Bred** J R And Mrs P Good **Trained** Newmarket, Suffolk
FOCUS
There were plenty available at fancy prices in this potentially decent maiden, a good event for the surface.
NOTEBOOK
Manchurian ◆ built on the promise of his Haydock debut and duly appreciated the extra furlong. There was plenty to like about this performance and connections will consider sending him over to the Curragh for the National Stakes. (op 15-8 tchd 9-4)
Thunder Storm Cat(USA) ◆, a well-bred $350,000 colt, could not cope with the more experienced winner. Normal improvement should soon see him go one better. (op 8-1 tchd 15-2)
Wolf River(USA), another American-bred newcomer with a decent pedigree, was apparently unfancied but ran promisingly enough after an indifferent start and should be better for the experience. (op 25-1)
Non Compliant was narrowly beaten by subsequent York Listed winner Not For Me here last time. He failed to get home after running too freely over the extra furlong. (op 2-1)
Not Another Cat(USA) was yet another decently-bred American newcomer starting his career on sand.
Massenzio(IRE), returning after a break, did not get the run of the race after an indifferent start on this step up from six furlongs. (op 9-2 tchd 5-1)

4935 NAME A RACE TO ENHANCE YOUR BRAND H'CAP 1m 5f 194y(P)
3:40 (3:42) (Class 4) (0-85,85) 3-Y-O+ **£6,477** (£1,927; £963; £481) **Stalls** Low

Form RPR
-204 **1** **Valance (IRE)**[22] [4231] 6-9-12 **80** ....(t) LDettori 4 88
(C R Egerton) *chsd ldr: rdn 4f out: hung lft over 1f out: swtchd rt ins fnl f: styd on to ld last strides* **9/1**[3]
1112 **2** *nk* **Warsaw Pact (IRE)**[31] [3981] 3-9-5 **85** .... SebSanders 5 93
(Sir Mark Prescott) *led: hrd rdn ins fnl f: ct last strides* **8/13**[1]
4121 **3** 3 **Champagne Shadow (IRE)**[12] [4544] 5-9-2 **70** .... CatherineGannon 1 73
(K A Ryan) *hld up in rr: rdn over 2f out: hdwy over 1f out: styd on ins fnl f: nvr nrr* **12/1**
6545 **4** 2 ½ **Wise Owl**[18] [4346] 4-10-0 **82** .... EddieAhern 2 82
(J Pearce) *hld up in tch: rdn over 3f out: wknd over 1f out* **6/1**[2]
4345 **5** 1 ¼ **Cotton Eyed Joe (IRE)**[25] [4156] 5-9-1 **69** .... DeanMcKeown 3 67
(G A Swinbank) *hld up: hdwy over 5f out: hung lft and wknd over 2f out* **6/1**[2]
-042 **6** *dist* **Neutrino**[7] [4698] 4-9-1 **69** .... JimmyFortune 6 —
(P C Haslam) *prom: rdn over 4f out: wknd over 3f out: virtually p.u fnl 2f* **16/1**
2m 59.85s (-7.52) **Going Correction** -0.425s/f (Stan)
WFA 3 from 4yo+ 12lb **6** Ran SP% **114.1**
Speed ratings (Par 105):104,103,102,100,99 —
CSF £15.59 TOTE £7.30: £2.60, £1.10; EX 17.10.
Owner M Haynes, A & J Allison, J Weatherby **Bred** B H Bloodstock **Trained** Chaddleworth, Berks
FOCUS
No hanging about here and the course record for a distance that has not been used that often was smashed by over two seconds.

4936 ENJOY RACING FROM THE ZONGALERO H'CAP 1m 4f 50y(P)
4:10 (4:10) (Class 2) (0-100,97) 3-Y-O **£11,658** (£3,468; £1,733; £865) **Stalls** Low

Form RPR
4013 **1** **Steppe Dancer (IRE)**[18] [4370] 3-9-2 **92** .... EddieAhern 2 99
(D J Coakley) *fly-jmpd leaving stalls: hld up: hdwy on ins and rdn to ld jst over 1f out: hung lft ins fnl f: r.o wl* **4/1**[3]
1603 **2** 3 **Gandor (IRE)**[41] [3681] 3-9-5 **95** .... JimmyFortune 3 97
(J H M Gosden) *chsd ldr: rdn 2f out: ev ch over 1f out: one pce* **12/1**
21 **3** *nk* **Hunters' Glen (USA)**[14] [4471] 3-9-7 **97** ....(t) LDettori 4 99
(Saeed Bin Suroor) *hld up: hdwy over 4f out: rdn over 3f out: ev ch over 1f out: one pce* **7/4**[2]
4343 **4** 3 ½ **King's Head (IRE)**[28] [4039] 3-9-7 **97** ....(p) PhilipRobinson 1 93
(M A Jarvis) *led: rdn and hdd jst over 1f out: wknd ins fnl f* **6/5**[1]
2m 35.71s (-6.71) **Going Correction** -0.425s/f (Stan) **4** Ran SP% **109.5**
Speed ratings (Par 106):105,103,102,100
CSF £33.46 TOTE £6.00; EX 28.00.
Owner Chris Van Hoorn **Bred** Maggiorelli Ice Guarnieri **Trained** West Ilsley, Berks
FOCUS
A competitive decent handicap despite the small field with four in a line on the home straight. A good pace led to the track record being broken for the third time in the afternoon.
NOTEBOOK
Steppe Dancer(IRE) found things opening up on the inside entering the home straight and needed no second invitation. Soon taking command, he did hang into the rails but confirmed his liking for the surface. (op 7-2)
Gandor(IRE), trying a longer trip on his sand debut, appeared to be beaten for speed rather than stamina.
Hunters' Glen(USA) was another upped in distance for this switch from turf. He also appeared to get the trip well enough. (op 11-8)
King's Head(IRE) may have paid the penalty for setting a pace so strong that even he equalled the old course record. (op 6-4 tchd 13-8 in a place)

4937 RINGSIDE SUITE CONFERENCE HALL H'CAP 1m 4f 50y(P)
4:40 (4:41) (Class 4) (0-80,80) 4-Y-O+ **£6,477** (£1,927; £963; £481) **Stalls** Low

Form RPR
4221 **1** **Ardea Brave (IRE)**[19] [4331] 4-8-7 **66** ....(p) OscarUrbina 9 76
(M Botti) *set mod pce: qcknd over 3f out: rdn 2f out: r.o wl* **4/1**[1]
-006 **2** 1 ¼ **Overlord Way (GR)**[56] [3202] 4-8-13 **72** .... SebSanders 5 80
(P R Chamings) *hld up in mid-div: hdwy over 2f out: sn rdn: chsd wnr jst over 1f out: nt qckn* **14/1**
1050 **3** 1 ¾ **Salute (IRE)**[28] [4036] 7-8-7 **67** .... DO'Donohoe 8 72
(P G Murphy) *chsd wnr: rdn over 3f out: lost 2nd jst over 1f out: one pce* **10/1**
6055 **4** 3 ½ **Trifti**[28] [4047] 5-9-7 **80** .... JimmyFortune 3 80
(C A Cyzer) *a.p: rdn 2f out: wknd ins fnl f* **12/1**
2431 **5** *nk* **Finished Article (IRE)**[44] [3594] 9-7-12 **63** oh4 ow1.. KevinGhunowa(5) 4 61
(P A Blockley) *t.k.h in tch: rdn over 2f out: wknd over 1f out* **9/1**
1254 **6** *hd* **Mount Usher**[13] [4508] 4-8-13 **72** .... DeanMcKeown 10 71
(G A Swinbank) *hld up and bhd: hdwy over 2f out: rdn and wknd over 1f out* **4/1**[1]
0505 **7** *shd* **The Violin Player (USA)**[15] [4448] 5-9-1 **74** ....(p) JoeFanning 11 73
(H J Collingridge) *hld up and bhd: rdn over 2f out: no rspnse* **9/2**[2]
2605 **8** 1 ¼ **Dovedon Hero**[21] [4268] 6-8-5 **64** ....(b) RichardMullen 1 61
(P J McBride) *s.i.s: a bhd* **8/1**[3]
2m 38.53s (-3.89) **Going Correction** -0.425s/f (Stan) **8** Ran SP% **102.7**
Speed ratings (Par 105):95,94,93,90,90 90,90,89
CSF £45.35 CT £322.14 TOTE £5.00: £2.50, £4.70, £3.80; EX 56.70 Place 6 £134.11, Place 5 £115.18.
Owner Dioscuri Srl **Bred** Scuderia San Pancrazio Sas **Trained** Newmarket, Suffolk
■ Pass The Port (11/2) was withdrawn on vet's advice. Rule 4 applies, deduct 15p in the £.
FOCUS
A modest pace meant that there was never much danger of a fourth course record being beaten at the meeting.
Dovedon Hero Official explanation: jockey said gelding suffered interference in running
T/Plt: £189.80 to a £1 stake. Pool: £48,582.15. 186.80 winning tickets. T/Qpdt: £69.60 to a £1 stake. Pool: £2,937.00. 31.20 winning tickets. KH

4938 - 4941a (Foreign Racing) - See Raceform Interactive

4918 BADEN-BADEN (L-H)
Wednesday, August 30

OFFICIAL GOING: Heavy

4942a FURSTENBERG-RENNEN (GROUP 3) 1m 2f
4:00 (4:09) 3-Y-O **£24,138** (£10,345; £4,138; £2,759)

RPR
1 **Waleria (GER)** 3-8-7 .... ASuborics 2 106
(H J Groschel, Germany) *held up, 4th straight tracking leaders, brought to stands rail, hard ridden over 1f out, led final 100y, ridden out* **39/10**
2 1 ¾ **Senor Dali (IRE)**[32] [3929] 3-8-11 .... KerrinMcEvoy 7 106
(J L Dunlop) *set steady pace, narrowly headed over 1 1/2f out, led again over 1f out, headed 100y out, one pace* **34/10**[2]
3 *hd* **Dark Dancer (GER)**[38] [3776] 3-8-11 .... ABest 9 106
(W Kelkel, Germany) *prominent on outside pulling hard, led narrowly over 1 1/2f out to over 1f out, one pace* **38/10**[3]
4 2 ½ **Pompeus (GER)** 3-8-9 .... EPedroza 6 100
(T Howart, U.S.A) *disputed 4th early, 6th straight, stayed on at one pace from over 1f out* **228/10**
5 *nk* **Aspectus (IRE)**[38] [3776] 3-9-2 .... ADeVries 1 106
(H Blume, Germany) *tracked leader on inside, 3rd straight, effort over 1 1/2f out, not quicken* **11/10**[1]

6 ½ **Inter Mondo (GER)** 3-8-9 .... TMundry 3 98
(P Rau, Germany) *held up in rear, last straight, never a factor* **126/10**
7 ½ **Dwilano (GER)**[59] [3131] 3-8-9 .... AHelfenbein 8 97
(P Remmert, Germany) *held up, 5th straight, effort on wide outside over 1 1/2f out, soon beaten* **116/10**
2m 10.72s **7** Ran SP% **131.1**
(including 10 Euro stake); WIN 49; PL 15, 16, 16; SF 220.
Owner Frau Dr C Otto **Bred** Frau Dr C Otto **Trained** Germany

NOTEBOOK
Senor Dali(IRE) was given a well-judged front-running ride by McEvoy (who wanted to get to the favoured outside rail in the home straight but was unable to do so with Dark Dancer coming up on his outside). Although just getting the \n\x\x better of a long duel with Dark Dancer, he did not had the finishing speed of the winner, who did manage to make it onto the best ground.

4829 BEVERLEY (R-H)
Thursday, August 31

OFFICIAL GOING: Good to soft (good in places)
Wind: Light, half-against Weather: Overcast

4943 JOHN JENKINS MEMORIAL CLAIMING STKS 7f 100y
5:10 (5:11) (Class 5) 3-Y-O **£3,562** (£1,059; £529; £264) **Stalls** High

Form RPR
4200 **1** **Jaassey**[39] [3762] 3-8-12 57 .... GrahamGibbons 12 65
(T D Walford) *a.p: ride over 1f out: styd on to ld wl ins fnl f* **6/1**[3]
1660 **2** *nk* **Decree Nisi**[22] [4257] 3-9-0 62 .... (v[1]) TPO'Shea 14 66
(Mrs A Duffield) *s.i.s: hld up: plld hrd: hdwy over 2f out: rdn and ev ch ins fnl f: r.o* **16/1**
5452 **3** *1 ¾* **Feelin Irie (IRE)**[7] [4728] 3-9-2 59 .... KimTinkler 6 64
(N Tinkler) *led: rdn over 1f out: hdd wl ins fnl f* **11/2**[2]
0616 **4** *½* **Roman History (IRE)**[16] [4456] 3-8-10 50 .... (p) SilvestreDeSousa 15 57
(Miss Tracy Waggott) *mid-div: hdwy u.p 2f out: styd on* **8/1**
4600 **5** *1 ¼* **What Do You Know**[12] [4591] 3-8-11 68 .... (p) NickyMackay 10 55
(G A Butler) *hld up in tch: rdn over 2f out: styd on same pce ins fnl f* **8/1**
0434 **6** *½* **Carr Hall (IRE)**[20] [3290] 3-8-13 53 .... NCallan 3 55
(T D Easterby) *chsd ldrs: rdn over 2f out: no ex fnl f* **10/1**
2634 **7** *2* **Suhezy (IRE)**[7] [4728] 3-8-5 47 .... AndrewMullen(3) 4 45
(J S Wainwright) *hld up: hdwy over 2f out: sn rdn: no imp fnl f* **14/1**
-003 **8** *7* **Rose Of Inchinor**[14] [4527] 3-8-7 64 .... JosedeSouza 13 27
(M P Tregoning) *chsd ldrs: rdn over 2f out: wknd over 1f out* **7/4**[1]
4040 **9** *3* **No Inkling (IRE)**[8] [4710] 3-8-4 42 .... DO'Donohoe 2 16
(John A Harris) *chsd ldr: rdn over 2f out: wknd over 1f out* **80/1**
4065 **10** *2* **Stanley Bay (IRE)**[24] [4195] 3-8-0 50 .... (v[1]) DuranFentiman(5) 1 12
(T D Easterby) *dwlt: outpcd* **40/1**
5000 **11** *3* **Salisbury World (IRE)**[21] [4304] 3-8-12 39 .... LPKeniry 8 12
(J F Coupland) *s.s: hmpd 1/2-way: a in rr* **66/1**
0000 **12** *nk* **Night Reveller (IRE)**[21] [4304] 3-8-1 28 .... JohnMcAuley(3) 7 —
(M C Chapman) *a in rr* **100/1**
-060 **13** *6* **Royal Song**[17] [4426] 3-8-9 40 .... PatrickMathers(3) 16 —
(D Shaw) *prom over 4f* **100/1**
0100 **14** *3* **Secret Tender (IRE)**[108] [1731] 3-8-7 50 .... AdrianMcCarthy 9 —
(J R Weymes) *mid-div: wknd over 2f out* **80/1**
00-0 **15** *shd* **Poutu (FR)**[10] [4651] 3-7-11 30 .... CharlotteKerton(7) 5 —
(A Berry) *mid-div: wknd 1/2-way* **125/1**
1m 35.87s (1.56) **Going Correction** +0.30s/f (Good) **15** Ran SP% **119.1**
Speed ratings (Par 100):103,102,100,100,98 98,95,87,84,82 78,78,71,68,67
CSF £95.24 TOTE £8.90: £2.20, £4.30, £2.40; EX 130.10.Rose Of Inchinor was claimed by Ron Barr for £8,000.
Owner J Wilcox **Bred** Darley **Trained** Sheriff Hutton, N Yorks

FOCUS
A moderate claimer, but they went a decent enough pace. They all tended to race towards the stands'-side rail in the straight, but a high draw still seemed a big advantage. Sound enough form for the grade.
Rose Of Inchinor Official explanation: trainer's rep said filly was unsuited by the good to soft (soft in places) ground

4944 LAST TURF EVENING MEETING OF YEAR FILLIES' H'CAP 1m 1f 207y
5:40 (5:41) (Class 6) (0-60,60) 3-Y-O+ **£3,238** (£963; £481; £240) **Stalls** High

Form RPR
2401 **1** **Sudden Impulse**[8] [4709] 5-9-8 **53** 6ex .... SilvestreDeSousa 8 62
(A D Brown) *plld hrd and prom: rdn to ld ins fnl f: r.o* **2/1**[1]
2 *shd* **Meadow Soprano (IRE)**[83] [2422] 4-8-9 **40** oh5 .... TPO'Shea 1 49
(M P Sunderland, Ire) *trckd ldrs: rdn to ld 1f out: sn hdd: r.o* **33/1**
3033 **3** *3 ½* **Flashing Floozie**[16] [4455] 3-8-10 **49** .... JamieMackay 3 51
(J G Given) *plld hrd: sn trcking ldr: led over 2f out: rdn and hdd 1f out: no ex* **11/1**
4465 **4** *1 ¾* **Polish Welcome**[21] [4279] 3-8-10 **49** .... GrahamGibbons 10 48
(S C Williams) *hld up: hdwy over 3f out: rdn and nt clr run over 1f out: nvr trbld ldrs* **9/1**[3]
0010 **5** *shd* **Baboosh (IRE)**[21] [4289] 5-10-0 **59** .... DO'Donohoe 12 58
(M Wigham) *prom: rdn and ev ch over 1f out: wknd ins fnl f* **6/1**[2]
1005 **6** *2 ½* **Arsad (IRE)**[8] [4687] 3-9-4 **57** .... NickyMackay 6 51
(C E Brittain) *sn outpcd: hdwy u.p over 1f out: n.d* **12/1**
2020 **7** *2 ½* **Crush On You**[28] [4069] 3-8-4 **50** .... RussellKennemore(7) 5 39
(R Hollinshead) *hld up: n.d* **28/1**
06-0 **8** *1 ¾* **Got To Be Cash**[83] [2407] 7-8-6 **40** oh5 .... PatrickMathers(3) 15 26
(W M Brisbourne) *hld up: hdwy 1/2-way: hmpd over 3f out: rdn and wknd over 1 out* **25/1**
0-05 **9** *¾* **Forest Lodge (IRE)**[74] [2678] 3-8-9 **48** .... LPKeniry 2 32
(D R C Elsworth) *hld up in tch: rdn over 2f out: wknd over 1f out* **10/1**
1145 **10** *½* **Awaken**[16] [4454] 5-9-12 **57** .... MichaelTebbutt 9 40
(Miss Tracy Waggott) *lsowly into stride: hdwy 7f out: wknd wl over 1f out* **11/1**
005/ **11** *2 ½* **Mtilly**[635] [6806] 5-9-2 **50** .... AndrewMullen(3) 4 29
(K G Reveley) *hld up: hdwy over 2f out: wknd over 1f out* **66/1**
350 **12** *shd* **Shardia (IRE)**[26] [4150] 3-8-10 **49** .... DerekMcGaffin 16 28
(J Jay) *hld up: hdwy over 2f out: rdn and wknd over 1f out* **25/1**
0000 **13** *nk* **World At My Feet**[4] [4834] 4-8-9 **47** .... (t) SuzzanneFrance(7) 17 25
(N Bycroft) *plld hrd and prom: lost pl over 8f out: nt clr run over 3f out: hdwy 2f out: wknd over 1f out* **16/1**
-054 **14** *nk* **Whoopee (USA)**[15] [4473] 3-8-8 **47** .... JoeFanning 14 24
(M Johnston) *led over 7f: wknd over 1f out* **16/1**
2m 10.61s (3.31) **Going Correction** +0.30s/f (Good)
WFA 3 from 4yo+ 8lb **14** Ran SP% **118.4**
Speed ratings (Par 98):98,97,95,93,93 91,89,88,87,87 85,85,84,84
CSF £91.65 CT £608.64 TOTE £2.90: £1.60, £7.40, £2.80; EX 89.30.
Owner Mrs S L Salt **Bred** Sagittarius Bloodstock Associates Ltd **Trained** Pickering, York

FOCUS
A weak fillies' handicap in which Sudden Impluse and Meadow Soprano pulled well clear, despite the early pace not appearing that strong, suggesting they are both well handicapped. The form looks sound enough, with the winner back to his best.

4945 ROLLITS SOLICITORS AND PETER STOCKILL LTD MAIDEN STKS 1m 1f 207y
6:10 (6:11) (Class 5) 3-Y-O+ **£3,562** (£1,059; £529; £264) **Stalls** High

Form RPR
4322 **1** **My Arch**[11] [4635] 4-9-11 78 .... NCallan 4 83
(K A Ryan) *chsd ldrs: led over 2f out: drvn out* **10/3**[2]
2-25 **2** *¾* **Piety (IRE)**[49] [3451] 3-8-12 83 .... JoeFanning 8 77
(M Johnston) *chsd ldrs: rdn and ev ch fr over 2f out: styd on* **9/2**[3]
2- **3** *2* **Samurai Way**[316] [5982] 4-9-11 .... NickyMackay 7 78
(L M Cumani) *s.s: hdwy 1/2-way: rdn over 1f out: styd on same pce ins fnl f* **3/1**[1]
0 **4** *2 ½* **Detente**[87] [2304] 3-8-12 .... OscarUrbina 9 68+
(J R Fanshawe) *hld up: hdwy over 2f out: nt clr run over 1f out: nvr nr to chal* **15/2**
0323 **5** *¾* **Muntada**[15] [4489] 3-8-12 74 .... JosedeSouza 6 67
(M P Tregoning) *sn led: hdd over 2f out: wknd fnl f* **7/1**
5046 **6** *8* **Finnegans Rainbow**[5] [3231] 4-9-4 35 .... RussellKennemore(7) 5 56
(M C Chapman) *nvr nrr* **100/1**
3035 **7** *6* **Materialize (USA)**[19] [4375] 3-8-12 71 .... MichaelTebbutt 3 40
(H R A Cecil) *chsd ldrs over 7f* **10/1**
3-65 **8** *1 ¼* **Art Investor**[19] [4374] 3-9-3 77 .... LPKeniry 1 43
(D R C Elsworth) *hld up: rdn and hmpd over 2f out: sn wknd* **11/1**
0 **9** *6* **Dancing Diamonds**[18] [4396] 3-8-12 .... AdrianMcCarthy 10 26
(D M Simcock) *s.i.s: sn mid-div: wknd over 3f out* **66/1**
040- **10** *3* **Robeson**[237] [5838] 4-9-8 67 .... SaleemGolam(3) 2 26
(D M Simcock) *chsd ldrs: rdn over 3f out: sn wknd* **40/1**
50 **11** *9* **Theologicum**[6] [4776] 3-8-12 .... GrahamGibbons 12 3
(Miss J R Gibney) *prom over 6f* **66/1**
6 **12** *35* **Talpour (IRE)**[74] [2682] 6-9-4 .... JamieHamblett(7) 13 —
(M C Chapman) *s.s: outpcd* **150/1**
2m 8.38s (1.08) **Going Correction** +0.30s/f (Good)
WFA 3 from 4yo+ 8lb **12** Ran SP% **115.0**
Speed ratings (Par 103):107,106,104,102,102 95,91,90,85,82 75,47
CSF £17.99 TOTE £4.20: £1.90, £1.80, £1.50; EX 15.30.
Owner J D Spensley & Mrs M A Spensley **Bred** J And A Spensley **Trained** Hambleton, N Yorks

FOCUS
A reasonable maiden for the time of year, and the form is sound among the principals, although the sixth finished closer than expected. They again raced stands' side in the straight.

4946 SAILORS FAMILIES SOCIETY NURSERY 5f
6:40 (6:40) (Class 3) 2-Y-O **£9,715** (£2,890; £1,444; £721) **Stalls** High

Form RPR
5200 **1** **Danum Dancer**[9] [4681] 2-8-10 **73** .... (b[1]) SilvestreDeSousa 1 80
(N Bycroft) *chsd ldrs: led over 1f out: hung rt ins fnl f: rdn out* **6/1**
2051 **2** *3* **Just Joey**[20] [4321] 2-9-7 **84** .... NCallan 8 80
(J R Weymes) *mde most over 3f: no ex ins fnl f* **3/1**[2]
5114 **3** *1 ¾* **Onenightinlisbon (IRE)**[9] [4681] 2-9-6 **83** .... LeeEnstone 7 73
(K R Burke) *sn pushed along and prom: rdn 1/2-way: styd on same pce fnl 2f* **9/4**[1]
51 **4** *3 ½* **Honest Danger**[13] [4550] 2-9-3 **80** .... JoeFanning 4 57
(J R Best) *s.i.s: outpcd: nvr nrr* **7/2**[3]
1566 **5** *6* **Bollin Franny**[19] [4377] 2-8-7 **70** .... (b[1]) DavidAllan 6 26
(T D Easterby) *chsd ldrs to 1/2-way* **7/1**
3041 **6** *3* **Baytown Paikea**[5] [4816] 2-7-11 **65** 6ex .... DuranFentiman(5) 2 10
(P S McEntee) *w ldr tl edgd lft 1/2-way: wkng whn hung lft over 1f out* **16/1**
65.11 secs (1.11) **Going Correction** +0.25s/f (Good) **6** Ran SP% **110.7**
Speed ratings (Par 98):101,96,93,87,78 73
CSF £23.45 CT £49.30 TOTE £8.40: £3.70, £1.80; EX 39.90.
Owner Abbott Gostling McGrane Senior Hart **Bred** Barton Stud **Trained** Brandsby, N Yorks

FOCUS
They finished well strung out and this was a messy race to both watch and analyse. There was a difference of opinion over where to race in the straight and Danum Dancer, who made his effort middle to stands' side, readily saw off both Just Joey and Onenightinlisbon, who stayed far side. Improved form from the winner.

NOTEBOOK
Danum Dancer, fitted with blinkers for the first time off a mark 3lb higher than in future, seemingly raced on the quickest ground centre to stands' side in the straight, whereas the two who followed him home stuck to the far side of the track. It would be unwise to assume this was a total fluke, as he had shown plenty of ability when second at York three starts previously, but there is no doubt he is flattered by the bare result and it remains to be seen whether the headgear will continue to have such a positive effect. (op 17-2)
Just Joey, 3lb higher than when winning on much quicker ground at Haydock on her previous start, seemed to handle the give underfoot just fine but looked at a disadvantage sticking to the far side in the straight, and had no chance with the eventual winner, who raced on the seemingly quicker ground middle to stands' side. (op 5-2)
Onenightinlisbon(IRE) has gained her two wins over this trip, but she struggled to stay in touch from the start and was below form. As it turned out she was racing on the slowest part of the track in the straight, but looked in trouble before that became an issue. (op 5-2 tchd 11-4 in a place)
Honest Danger was beaten by the time he was switched towards the centre of the track and was well below the form he showed when winning a Folkestone maiden on his previous start. (op 10-3)
Bollin Franny failed to perform in first-time blinkers on the softest ground he has encountered. (op 8-1 tchd 13-2)

4947 BP SALTEND H'CAP 1m 4f 16y
7:10 (7:10) (Class 5) (0-75,75) 3-Y-O+ **£5,181** (£1,541; £770; £384) **Stalls** High

Form RPR
1421 **1** **Fossgate**[24] [4205] 5-9-10 **71** .... NCallan 4 81
(J D Bethell) *hld up: hdwy over 3f out: led over 2f out: rdn and hung rt fr over 1f out: r.o* **5/1**[2]
4-00 **2** *½* **Royal Melbourne (IRE)**[122] [1346] 6-8-9 **56** oh1 .... DavidAllan 8 65
(Miss J A Camacho) *s.i.s: hld up: hdwy over 2f out: rdn and hung rt ins fnl f: r.o* **8/1**
06-0 **3** *nk* **Turn Of Phrase (IRE)**[15] [4472] 7-8-9 **56** oh2 .... (b) DO'Donohoe 6 65
(B Ellison) *chsd ldrs: rdn over 1f out: styd on* **16/1**

2025 **4** ½ **Caraman (IRE)**[51] 3388 8-9-3 **64** GrahamGibbons 1 72
(J J Quinn) *a.p: rdn and edgd rt over 1f out: styd on* **8/1**

603 **5** 1 **Aphorism**[15] 4471 3-8-11 **68** OscarUrbina 12 77+
(J R Fanshawe) *mid-div: hdwy u.p over 2f out: nt clr run over 1f out and ins fnl f: styd on* **10/1**

2223 **6** 1½ **Shekan Star**[8] 4698 4-8-6 **56** AndrewMullen(3) 7 60
(K G Reveley) *s.i.s: hld up: hdwy over 2f out: rdn over 1f out: styd on same pce ins fnl f* **6/1**[3]

-531 **7** 1¾ **Baileys Encore**[18] 4402 3-9-2 **73** JoeFanning 9 74
(M Johnston) *led: rdn and hdd over 2f out: wknd fnl f* **9/2**[1]

0606 **8** 1¾ **Tedsdale Mac**[16] 4454 7-8-3 **57** SuzzanneFrance(7) 11 55
(N Bycroft) *s.s: hdwy 1/2-way: wknd over 1f out* **20/1**

12-0 **9** 3½ **Dan's Heir**[128] 1219 4-8-7 **59** LeanneKershaw(5) 13 52
(P C Haslam) *chsd ldr: rdn over 5f out: wknd over 2f out* **16/1**

0304 **10** 11 **Plenty Cried Wolf**[20] 4320 4-8-11 **58** TonyHamilton 3 33
(R A Fahey) *prom: lost pl 1/2-way: wknd 4f out* **7/1**

411/ **11** 12 **Miss Holly**[172] 235 7-8-13 **67** KellyHarrison(7) 5 23
(D Carroll) *s.i.s: hdwy 9f out: wknd 3f out* **16/1**

2m 44.01s (3.80) **Going Correction** +0.30s/f (Good)
WFA 3 from 4yo+ 10lb **11** Ran SP% **115.4**
Speed ratings (Par 103):99,98,98,98,97 96,95,94,91,84 76
CSF £43.87 CT £594.80 TOTE £6.10: £1.80, £3.10, £6.10; EX 47.20.
Owner Mrs James Bethell **Bred** Mrs P A Clark **Trained** Middleham Moor, N Yorks

FOCUS
A modest handicap run at just an ordinary pace. The form looks sound and had been rated at face value, with a personal best from the winner. They all headed towards the stands' side in the straight, but several drifted right under pressure and they were spread out across the track at the line.

4948 WEATHERBYS INSURANCE MAIDEN STKS 5f
7:40 (7:42) (Class 5) 3-Y-0+ **£3,562** (£1,059; £529; £264) **Stalls** High

Form RPR

3-33 **1** **Monashee Brave (IRE)**[113] 1589 3-9-3 78 GrahamGibbons 10 78
(J J Quinn) *mde all: clr over 1f out: rdn out* **5/4**[1]

6520 **2** 7 **Yorke's Folly (USA)**[21] 4306 5-8-9 43 (b) LeanneKershaw(5) 6 48
(C W Fairhurst) *mid-div: hdwy 1/2-way: rdn over 1f out: styd on same pce* **8/1**

6004 **3** shd **Harrington Bates**[12] 4611 5-9-5 45 (v) JosedeSouza 15 52
(R M Whitaker) *outpcd: hdwy and nt clr run over 1f out: nrst fin* **15/2**[3]

305 **4** 1¼ **Signor Whippee**[12] 4611 3-9-0 46 (b) SaleemGolam(3) 9 48
(A Berry) *chsd ldrs: rdn 1/2-way: outpcd appr fnl f* **33/1**

0 **5** hd **Dhurwah (IRE)**[29] 4045 3-8-12 OscarUrbina 16 42
(T Keddy) *prom: rdn 1/2-way: styd on same pce appr fnl f* **11/1**

0-03 **6** shd **Miacarla**[26] 4136 3-8-7 MarkLawson(5) 4 42
(A Berry) *s.i.s: hdwy 1/2-way: sstyd on same pce appr fnl f* **40/1**

050 **7** 2 **Vibrato (USA)**[12] 4613 4-9-2 31 AndrewMullen(3) 17 40
(C J Teague) *chsd ldrs over 3f* **100/1**

050- **8** 1 **Indian Sundance (IRE)**[337] 5547 3-9-3 45 DO'Donohoe 18 36
(R A Fahey) *chsd ldrs over 3f* **33/1**

4060 **9** ¾ **Waggledance (IRE)**[23] 4232 4-8-12 44 KellyHarrison(7) 14 33
(D Carroll) *chsd ldrs over 3f* **14/1**

5-3 **10** shd **Glamaraazi (IRE)**[12] 4611 3-8-12 TonyHamilton 11 28
(R A Fahey) *hld up: rdn over 1f out: nvr nrr* **7/1**[2]

0 **11** 1¾ **Bond Sea Breeze (IRE)**[12] 4611 3-8-12 GylesParkin 13 22
(G R Oldroyd) *chsd ldrs over 3f* **100/1**

-000 **12** 2 **Swallow Senora (IRE)**[14] 4507 4-8-7 38 (b) JamieHamblett(7) 12 15
(M C Chapman) *chsd ldrs 3f* **100/1**

-000 **13** nk **Miss Dixie**[68] 2873 3-8-12 50 JoeFanning 3 13
(T D Easterby) *s.s: outpcd* **20/1**

0-6 **14** 1 **Ponty Carlo (IRE)**[12] 4613 3-9-3 DavidAllan 7 15
(T D Easterby) *chsd ldrs over 3f* **25/1**

0050 **15** 5 **One More Than Ten**[10] 4656 3-9-3 44 (b[1]) NCallan 8 —
(T D Easterby) *outpcd fr 1/2-way* **33/1**

0-00 **16** 1¼ **Hiats**[12] 4611 4-9-0 30 DeclanMcGann(5) 2 —
(J O'Reilly) *dwlt: hdwy over 3f out: wknd 2f out* **100/1**

0 **17** 1¼ **Special Ballot (IRE)**[116] 1503 5-9-0 TPO'Shea 1 —
(G A Swinbank) *s.s: outpcd* **25/1**

P500 **18** 9 **Look Here's May**[21] 4278 4-8-7 37 RussellKennemore(7) 5 —
(R Hollinshead) *s.i.s: outpcd* **66/1**

65.26 secs (1.26) **Going Correction** +0.25s/f (Good)
WFA 3 from 4yo+ 2lb **18** Ran SP% **124.0**
Speed ratings (Par 103):99,87,87,85,85 85,81,80,79,79 76,73,72,70,62 60,58,44
CSF £9.81 TOTE £2.40: £1.20, £2.80, £1.60; EX 16.80 Place 6 £68.91, Place 5 £24.74.
Owner The Mushroom Men **Bred** Golden Vale Stud **Trained** Settrington, N Yorks
■ Stewards' Enquiry : Kelly Harrison caution: careless riding
D O'Donohoe caution: careless riding

FOCUS
The runners were spread out across the track. Take out Monashee Brave, who raced middle to stands' side, and this was basically a banded maiden, but the level looks sound enough around the third, fourth and fifth.
T/Plt: £97.20 to a £1 stake. Pool: £36,970.65. 277.55 winning tickets. T/Qpdt: £17.20 to a £1 stake. Pool: £4,205.60. 180.40 winning tickets. CR

4723 MUSSELBURGH (R-H)
Thursday, August 31
OFFICIAL GOING: Good (good to firm in places)
Wind: Moderate, half across

4949 BANK OF IRELAND BUSINESS AND CORPORATE BANKING MAIDEN AUCTION STKS 1m
2:30 (2:31) (Class 5) 2-Y-0 **£4,210** (£1,252; £625; £312) **Stalls** Low

Form RPR

352 **1** **Dancing Granny**[35] 3878 2-8-2 74 AndrewElliott(5) 6 69
(M L W Bell) *trckd ldrs: pushed along 3f out: gd hdwy on inner to ld wl over 1f out: rdn and styd on wl fnl f* **7/4**[1]

440 **2** 2 **Musical Land (IRE)**[30] 4018 2-8-11 70 SebSanders 4 68
(J R Weymes) *dwelt and sn reminders: hdwy to chse ldr after 3f: chal 3f out and sn rdn: drvn ins last and kpt on* **6/1**[3]

3424 **3** nk **Reem Al Fallah (IRE)**[12] 4608 2-8-6 73 RobertWinston 2 63
(M R Channon) *a.p: effrt over 2f out: sn rdn and hung rt: drvn and kpt on same pce fnl f* **2/1**[2]

502 **4** 1¼ **Keep Your Distance**[29] 4055 2-8-7 68 StephenDonohoe(3) 3 64
(K R Burke) *led: rdn along 3f out: hdd wl over 1f out: drvn and wknd ent last* **8/1**

5 **5** 3½ **Wee Ellie Coburn** 2-8-4 PaulHanagan 5 50
(I Semple) *s.i.s: a rr* **22/1**

305 **6** 15 **Tobago Reef**[42] 3669 2-8-9 63 TomEaves 1 20
(Mrs L Stubbs) *hld up in rr: poushed along 3f out: sn rdn and wknd* **16/1**

1m 43.1s (0.60) **Going Correction** -0.075s/f (Good) **6** Ran SP% **105.3**
Speed ratings (Par 94):94,92,91,90,86 71
CSF £10.90 TOTE £2.70: £1.30, £1.90; EX 12.00.
Owner W J Gredley **Bred** Newsells Park Stud Limited **Trained** Newmarket, Suffolk

FOCUS
A fair juvenile maiden and, while the form is only average, it is still straightforward.

NOTEBOOK
Dancing Granny responded positively for pressure nearing the two-furlong pole and eventually outstayed her rivals to score at the fourth time of asking. The step up to this extra furlong worked the oracle, she looks on a fair official mark at present, and remains open to a little further improvement over this distance. (op 6-4)
Musical Land(IRE) ran in snatches through the early parts after a sluggish start and, while keeping to his task under heavy pressure, he was never a serious threat to the winner. This was a much better effort, and he got the trip well enough, but is clearly not straightforward. (op 8-1)
Reem Al Fallah(IRE) failed to raise her game for this step up to a mile and appeared far from straightforward. She looks flattered by her current official mark. (op 7-4)
Keep Your Distance failed to get home as well as the principals under an aggressive ride on this first attempt at a mile. (tchd 10-1)

4950 BANK OF IRELAND GLOBAL MARKETS (S) STKS 5f
3:00 (3:00) (Class 5) 2-Y-0 **£4,210** (£1,252; £625; £312) **Stalls** High

Form RPR

3065 **1** **Joseph Locke (IRE)**[8] 4693 2-8-11 69 (p) KDarley 5 64
(M Dods) *mde all: rdn wl over 1f out: drvn ins last: styd on* **11/4**[2]

4253 **2** ½ **Caj (IRE)**[15] 4493 2-8-1 55 LiamJones(5) 3 58+
(M Quinn) *trckd ldrs: hdwy 1/2-way: nt clr run and swtchd rt over 1f out: sn rdn and ev ch ins last: kpt on* **6/1**

3660 **3** nk **Dotty's Daughter**[3] 4887 2-8-6 55 (p) RoystonFfrench 6 56
(Mrs A Duffield) *cl up: rdn and hung lft over 1f out: drvn and ev ch ins last: no ex towards fin* **16/1**

3440 **4** 1½ **Sister Etienne (IRE)**[19] 4377 2-8-6 64 TomEaves 2 51
(T D Barron) *hmpd s: sn prom: rdn and ch whn hung rt over 1f out: sn drvn and one pce* **3/1**[3]

000 **5** 10 **Wilde Jasmine (IRE)**[22] 4251 2-8-6 (t) PaulHanagan 1 15
(J R Weymes) *hmpd s: a outpcd and bhd* **40/1**

0522 **6** 14 **Candyland (IRE)**[16] 4444 2-8-6 66 RobertWinston 4 —
(M R Channon) *wnt lft s: slode up: rdn along 1/2-way: wkng whn n.m.r wl over 1f out: sn bhd and heavily eased* **2/1**[1]

61.92 secs (1.42) **Going Correction** +0.125s/f (Good) **6** Ran SP% **107.6**
Speed ratings (Par 94):93,92,91,89,73 50
CSF £17.40 TOTE £3.80: £1.90, £3.20; EX 14.50.The winner was bought in for 6,200gns.
Owner C A Lynch **Bred** Tally-Ho Stud **Trained** Denton, Co Durham

FOCUS
A weak juvenile seller, run at a modest pace, and the form looks typical for the class. The winner stood out at the weights and did not need to match his best to win.

NOTEBOOK
Joseph Locke(IRE), dropped in class, pinged out of the gates and made all to break his duck at the seventh attempt. He should be high on confidence after this, but it must be noted that he was entitled to win at the weights, and did not have to run up to his best to win. (op 5-2)
Caj(IRE) shaped a little better than the bare form and ran another sound enough race in defeat. She again did enough to suggest she may just need another furlong now, however. (op 5-1)
Dotty's Daughter posted an improved effort in defeat and the first-time cheekpieces clearly had a positive effect. She looks best kept to this shorter trip. (tchd 20-1)
Sister Etienne(IRE), down in class, hung her chance away when push came to shove and appears to be going the wrong way at present. (op 7-2 tchd 4-1)
Candyland(IRE), another having her first outing at this lowly level, ran too badly to be true and shaped as though something was amiss. Official explanation: jockey said filly hung left-handed throughout (op 7-4)

4951 BANK OF IRELAND STAYERS H'CAP 1m 6f
3:30 (3:30) (Class 3) (0-90,90) 3-Y-0+ **£11,658** (£3,468; £1,733; £865) **Stalls** High

Form RPR

1113 **1** **Alambic**[19] 4362 3-8-6 **71** SebSanders 2 87+
(Sir Mark Prescott) *trckd ldr: hdwy to ld over 2f out and sn rdn clr: styd on wl fnl f* **4/1**[2]

2214 **2** 3 **Cool Customer (USA)**[26] 4125 3-9-6 **90** LiamJones(5) 6 99
(E A L Dunlop) *hld up in rr: hdwy wl over 2f out: rdn and hung rt over 1f out and ins last: styd on: nt rch wnr* **3/1**[1]

2532 **3** 3 **Reluctant Suitor**[33] 3960 4-8-11 **69** KevinGhunowa(5) 3 74
(J S Goldie) *trckd ldng pair: effrt over 2f out and ev ch: rdn wl over 1f out: drvn and hung lft ent last: one pce* **7/1**[3]

0206 **4** shd **Trance (IRE)**[19] 4346 6-9-10 **80** (p) BenSwarbrick(3) 7 85
(T D Barron) *bhd: rdn along over 3f out: styd on wl appr last: nrst fin* **25/1**

3021 **5** nk **Kristensen**[7] 4723 7-9-1 **68** (v) PaulHanagan 8 72
(Karen McLintock) *hld up: effrt 3f out: sn rdn and kpt on appr last: nrst fin* **9/1**

1150 **6** 1¾ **Silvertown**[23] 4231 11-10-0 **81** TomEaves 1 83
(L Lungo) *led: rdn along 3f out: hdd wl over 2f out: drvn: edgd lft and wknd over 1f out: btn whn hmpd ent last* **14/1**

2106 **7** 3½ **Doctor Scott**[16] 4459 3-9-7 **86** RoystonFfrench 4 83
(M Johnston) *chsd ldrsd: effrt 3f out: sn rdn and wknd fnl 2f* **8/1**

0215 **8** nk **Rayhani (USA)**[13] 4560 3-9-11 **90** (b[1]) KDarley 5 86
(M P Tregoning) *hld up towards rr: hdwy on outer 5f out: rdn along 3f out: drvn and wknd over 2f out* **3/1**[1]

3m 2.32s (-3.38) **Going Correction** -0.075s/f (Good)
WFA 3 from 4yo+ 12lb **8** Ran SP% **114.1**
Speed ratings (Par 107):106,104,102,102,102 101,99,99
CSF £16.36 CT £79.91 TOTE £4.10: £1.70, £1.30, £2.10; EX 17.00.
Owner Lady O'Reilly **Bred** Miss K Rausing And Mrs S M Rogers **Trained** Newmarket, Suffolk
■ Stewards' Enquiry : Liam Jones one-day ban: careless riding (Sep 11)

FOCUS
A decent staying handicap for the track, run at a fair pace, and the form looks solid enough. The front pair are progressive and the winner can rate higher still.

NOTEBOOK
Alambic ◆ got back to winning ways in decisive fashion under a positive ride from Sanders. She was perfectly positioned through the early parts, went to the front with ease when asked for her effort, and had the race in the bag passing two out. This imposing filly is clearly still improving - this was her sixth win from her last seven outings - and strongly appeals as the type to defy an even higher mark in the coming weeks. (op 10-3 tchd 9-2 in a place)
Cool Customer(USA) might have benefited from a stronger early gallop, but he still emerged to have a chance around two out, and still finished nicely clear of the remainder. He is worth another try over this longer distance and helps to give the form a sound look. (op 10-3)

Reluctant Suitor was always handy, and had his chance, but proved no match for the first two when it mattered. He is another who helps to set the standard of this form. (op 8-1)
Trance(IRE) would have been seen to better effect off a stronger early pace, but that is so often the case and he remains one to tread carefully with. (op 18-1)
Kristensen, raised 3lb for winning over course and distance last time, is another who ideally wants a stronger early pace. However, this was a much tougher assignment. (op 10-1)
Silvertown had his chance after dictating the pace and dropped right out when push came to shove in the home straight. (tchd 12-1)
Rayhani(USA), equipped with first-time blinkers, looked tricky under restraint and again ran well below expectations. He may well have peaked now and is one to avoid until showing more signs of enthusiasm. (op 4-1)

4952 BANK OF IRELAND GLOBAL MARKETS H'CAP — 5f
4:00 (4:00) (Class 4) (0-80,80) 3-Y-O+ **£6,477** (£1,927; £963; £481) **Stalls** High

Form RPR
4216 **1** **Smiddy Hill**[8] 4691 4-8-12 **67**........ RoystonFfrench 3 75
(R Bastiman) *in tch: hdwy 2f out: rdn to ld ent last: hld on wl* **6/1**
0462 **2** *shd* **Strawberry Patch (IRE)**[14] 4523 7-8-1 **61** oh6........(p) AndrewElliott[(5)] 5 69
(J S Goldie) *wnt rt s: towards rr tl swtchd outside and hdwy 2f out: rdn and str run ent last: jst failed* **13/2**
2003 **3** *1 ½* **Ptarmigan Ridge**[7] 4725 10-9-3 **72**........ KDarley 6 75
(Miss L A Perratt) *in tch: gd hdwy 2f out: rdn to chal and ev ch over 1f out tl drvn and one pce ins last* **5/1**[3]
3040 **4** *½* **The Leather Wedge (IRE)**[7] 4725 7-8-11 **66**........ TomEaves 1 67
(R Johnson) *cl up: rdn along wl over 1f out: sn one pce* **20/1**
1312 **5** *2 ½* **Aahgowangowan (IRE)**[12] 4589 7-9-4 **78**........(t) LiamJones[(5)] 2 70
(M Dods) *led: rdn along 2f out: drvn and hdd ent last: sn wknd* **7/4**[1]
001 **6** *1 ¾* **Bold Minstrel (IRE)**[24] 4208 4-9-11 **80**........ SebSanders 4 66
(M Quinn) *dwlt: sn outpcd in rr: sme hdwy 2f out: sn rdn and no further prog* **3/1**[2]

60.49 secs (-0.01) **Going Correction** +0.125s/f (Good) **6** Ran SP% **110.4**
Speed ratings (Par 105):105,104,102,101,97 94
CSF £41.12 CT £196.89 TOTE £8.10: £2.50, £3.10; EX 35.50.
Owner I B Barker **Bred** I B Barker **Trained** Cowthorpe, N Yorks

FOCUS
A modest sprint, run at a strong early pace, and the first two came clear. The time was good compared with the seller but this is not strong form, through the runner-up who was 6lb out of the handicap and has been rated up to his best form since his three-year-old season.
Bold Minstrel(IRE) Official explanation: jockey said gelding hit its head on stalls prior to them opening

4953 BANK OF IRELAND H'CAP — 1m
4:30 (4:31) (Class 4) (0-85,82) 3-Y-O+ **£7,772** (£2,312; £1,155; £577) **Stalls** Low

Form RPR
6306 **1** **Royal Dignitary (USA)**[19] 4379 6-9-13 **81**........ RobertWinston 6 91
(D Nicholls) *mde all: pushed clr over 2f out: rdn and styd on wl fnl f* **7/2**[2]
4651 **2** *1 ¼* **Coalpark (IRE)**[16] 4455 3-8-6 **66**........(t) KDarley 1 73
(M Johnston) *chsd wnr: rdn along wl over 2f out: drvn over 1f out: kpt on* **5/1**[3]
452 **3** *nk* **Ballyhurry (USA)**[9] 4518 9-8-7 **66**........ KevinGhunowa[(5)] 4 72
(J S Goldie) *towards rr: hdwy over 2f out: rdn and nt clr run over 1f out: styd on ins last: nrst fin* **10/1**
4114 **4** *1 ½* **Champain Sands (IRE)**[18] 4390 7-8-11 **68**........ StephenDonohoe[(3)] 8 71
(E J Alston) *hld up towards rr: gd hdwy on inner over 2f out: rdn over 1f out: no imp* **8/1**
3214 **5** *¾* **Bolton Hall (IRE)**[14] 4518 4-9-0 **68**........ PaulHanagan 5 69
(R A Fahey) *midfield: hdwy wl over 2f out: rdn wl over 1f out: no imp ins last* **5/2**[1]
20 **6** *nk* **Crosby Vision**[10] 4653 3-8-13 **73**........ SebSanders 2 73
(J R Weymes) *in tch on outer: effrt 3f out: rdn along and one pce fnl 2f* **16/1**
3300 **7** *9* **King Of The Moors (USA)**[12] 4605 3-9-5 **82**........ BenSwarbrick[(3)] 3 61
(T D Barron) *a rr* **10/1**
5110 **8** *2* **Defi (IRE)**[14] 4521 4-9-4 **72**........(b) TomEaves 7 47
(I Semple) *chsd ldrs: hdwy 3f out: rdn over 2f out and sn wknd* **12/1**

1m 40.7s (-1.80) **Going Correction** -0.075s/f (Good)
WFA 3 from 4yo+ 6lb **8** Ran SP% **110.3**
Speed ratings (Par 105):106,104,104,102,102 101,92,90
CSF £19.75 CT £148.23 TOTE £4.60: £1.50, £1.50, £3.10; EX 20.60.
Owner Middleham Park Racing XXXVI **Bred** Bentley Smith, J Michael O'Farrell Jr , Joan Thor **Trained** Sessay, N Yorks

FOCUS
A fair handicap, run at a sound pace, and the form looks fair enough. The winner returned to form, with the third and fourth back to their recent best.

4954 BANK OF IRELAND BUSINESS AND CORPORATE BANKING H'CAP — 1m 6f
5:00 (5:00) (Class 6) (0-65,64) 3-Y-O+ **£3,238** (£963; £481; £240) **Stalls** High

Form RPR
5114 **1** **Danzatrice**[7] 4723 4-9-3 **53**........ TomEaves 3 59
(C W Thornton) *midfield: hdwy 5f out: pushed along 3f out: rdn to ld wl over 1f out: drvn out* **5/1**[3]
5463 **2** *3 ½* **Alisdanza**[18] 4404 4-8-5 **46**........ AndrewElliott[(5)] 4 47
(G A Swinbank) *always prom: effrt to chal 3f out: sn rdn and ev ch tl drvn and one pce ent last* **9/1**
-145 **3** *2 ½* **Crathorne (IRE)**[11] 3220 6-10-0 **64**........ RobertWinston 12 62
(M Todhunter) *hld up in rr: stdy hdwy over 3f out: rdn to chse ldrs over 1f out: sn hung rt and wknd* **10/3**[1]
0341 **4** *shd* **Onyergo (IRE)**[14] 4522 4-9-6 **56**........ SebSanders 7 53
(J R Weymes) *led: rdn along 3f out: drvn and hdd wl over 1f out: wknd ent last* **7/2**[2]
1303 **5** *3 ½* **Hugs Destiny (IRE)**[7] 4723 5-8-10 **53**........ MCGeran[(7)] 10 46
(M A Barnes) *prom: rdn along wl over 2f out: sn wknd* **7/1**
06 **6** *¾* **The Dunion**[15] 4478 3-7-12 **51** oh13 ow5........ LiamJones[(5)] 1 43
(Miss L A Perratt) *prom: rdn along over 3f out and sn wknd* **66/1**
2-00 **7** *½* **Time Marches On**[13] 4568 8-8-10 **46**........ KDarley 5 37
(K G Reveley) *a rr* **20/1**
3030 **8** *shd* **Rouge Et Noir**[30] 3810 8-9-1 **51**........ RoystonFfrench 2 42
(P Monteith) *hld up: a towards rr* **20/1**
3246 **9** *shd* **Nakwa (IRE)**[20] 4320 8-8-7 **46** oh2........ StephenDonohoe[(3)] 8 37
(E J Alston) *trckd ldrs: hdwy 3f out: rdn along over 2f out: drvn and wknd over 1f out* **9/1**

4-00 **10** *47* **Keepers Knight (IRE)**[141] 975 5-8-11 **47**........(p) PaulHanagan 11 —
(Karen McLintock) *in tch: rdn along 1/2-way: sn lost pl and bhd* **16/1**

3m 5.22s (-0.48) **Going Correction** -0.075s/f (Good)
WFA 3 from 4yo+ 12lb **10** Ran SP% **111.4**
Speed ratings (Par 101):98,96,94,94,92 92,91,91,91,64
CSF £45.57 CT £165.22 TOTE £5.60: £1.70, £2.20, £1.30; EX 29.90 Place 6 £203.78, Place 5 £108.10.
Owner 980 Racing **Bred** G G A Gregson **Trained** Middleham Moor, N Yorks

FOCUS
A moderate staying handicap, run at a fair pace. The winner ran to her recent best but the form is limited by the sixth.
T/Plt: £101.10 to a £1 stake. Pool: £43,967.65. 317.45 winning tickets. T/Qpdt: £20.60 to a £1 stake. Pool: £2,708.00. 96.90 winning tickets. JR

4730 REDCAR (L-H)
Thursday, August 31

OFFICIAL GOING: Good to firm (good in places)
After just over 2mm rain overnight the ground was described as 'mainly good'.
Wind: Fresh, half behind Weather: Overcast but dry and warm

4955 WEDDINGS AT REDCAR NURSERY — 7f
2:10 (2:10) (Class 5) 2-Y-O **£3,238** (£963; £481; £240) **Stalls** Centre

Form RPR
61 **1** **So Sweet (IRE)**[26] 4148 2-9-7 **78**........ LDettori 3 87+
(M R Channon) *trckd ldrs: led 4f out: shkn up and qcknd clr over 1f out: easily* **8/13**[1]
0546 **2** *4* **Nota Liberata**[3] 4882 2-8-7 **64**........ PaulMulrennan 7 63
(G M Moore) *chsd ldrs: wnt 2nd over 2f out: no ch w wnr* **5/1**[2]
5300 **3** *3* **Wanchai Night**[24] 4196 2-8-0 **57**........ DaleGibson 6 48
(T D Easterby) *trckd ldrs: t.k.h: effrt over 2f out: kpt on same pce* **16/1**[3]
040 **4** *1 ½* **Devilfishpoker Com**[14] 4509 2-7-7 **55** oh7........(e) DuranFentiman[(5)] 1 42
(R C Guest) *hld up in tch: effrt and chsng ldrs over 3f out: wknd 1f out* **66/1**
6502 **5** *9* **Only A Splash**[13] 4545 2-8-6 **63**........ PaulQuinn 4 27
(D W Chapman) *t.k.h: led eraly: w ldrs: wknd over 2f out* **16/1**[3]
446 **6** *5* **Nufoudh (IRE)**[69] 2827 2-8-8 **65**........ JoeFanning 5 16
(M Johnston) *v free to post: stmbld s: tk fierce hold and sn led: hdd 4f out: edgd lft and wknd over 2f out: eased* **5/1**[2]

1m 24.42s (-0.48) **Going Correction** -0.175s/f (Firm) **6** Ran SP% **108.5**
Speed ratings (Par 94):95,90,87,85,75 69
CSF £3.72 TOTE £1.20: £1.10, £1.90; EX 3.60.
Owner Sheikh Ahmed Al Maktoum **Bred** Patrick Jones **Trained** West Ilsley, Berks

FOCUS
No gallop and a facile winner but a nursery lacking in strength in depth. The winner can better this.

NOTEBOOK
So Sweet(IRE), well named, looked very fit. With no one keen to make it she soon found herself in front, and a shake of the reins was sufficient to see her lengthen and pull well clear. The opposition was weak but she is an awful lot better than a 78-rated filly. (op 4-7 and 4-6 in places)
Nota Liberata, making a quick return to action, finished clear second best but the winner was in a different league. (op 11-2)
Wanchai Night, stepping up to seven furlongs, was once again too keen for his own good, not helped by the lack of any early pace.
Devilfishpoker Com, 7lb 'wrong', was fitted with an eyeshield instead of blinkers. He has an awkward head carriage and is looking fully exposed. (op 80-1)
Only A Splash wanted to go much quicker than his rider would let him and this plater fell in a heap with over two furlongs left to run. (op 33-1)
Nufoudh(IRE), absent since June, is now a gelding. He went a million miles an hour to post then pulled much too hard on the way back. With him it is all in the mind. (op 9-2)

4956 REDCAR CONFERENCE CENTRE MAIDEN AUCTION STKS — 5f
2:40 (2:41) (Class 6) 2-Y-O **£2,388** (£705; £352) **Stalls** Centre

Form RPR
2232 **1** **Durova (IRE)**[16] 4452 2-8-10 73........ DavidAllan 3 67+
(T D Easterby) *mde all: shkn up over 1f out: drew clr ins last: readily* **1/2**[1]
6 **2** *2 ½* **Inspainagain (USA)**[24] 4196 2-8-11........ PhillipMakin 1 59
(T D Barron) *chsd wnr kpt on fnl 2f: no imp* **9/2**[2]
00 **3** *nk* **Strathmore (IRE)**[13] 4545 2-9-1........ TonyHamilton 7 62
(R A Fahey) *chsd ldrs: drvn over 2f out: kpt on fnl f* **16/1**
5 **4** *hd* **Forest Machine**[16] 4452 2-8-11........ PatCosgrave 2 57
(J S Wainwright) *rrd and swvd lft s: sn chsng ldrs: drvn over 2f out: kpt on same pce* **16/1**
0 **5** *1* **John Stanley (IRE)**[20] 4323 2-8-2........ KellyHarrison[(7)] 10 52
(D Carroll) *chsd ldrs: styd on same pce fnl 2f* **40/1**
6 *8* **Hills Place** 2-9-1........ JoeFanning 6 29
(J R Best) *dwlt: in rr: sn bhd: detached 2f out* **6/1**[3]
5 **7** *22* **Neveronamonday (IRE)**[41] 3693 2-8-6........ PaulQuinn 9 —
(A Berry) *sn outpcd and in rr: bhd after 2f: t.o and eased* **80/1**

58.11 secs (-0.59) **Going Correction** -0.175s/f (Firm) **7** Ran SP% **114.6**
Speed ratings (Par 92):97,93,92,92,90 77,42
CSF £3.20 TOTE £1.20: £1.10, £2.40; EX 3.60.
Owner Chris & Antonia Deuters **Bred** Castleton Group **Trained** Great Habton, N Yorks

FOCUS
A very weak event and a golden opportunity for the hitherto luckless winner. Very hard to gauge the merit of this, with the winner exposed as around 10lb better than this level, while none of the others had much form to talk to.

NOTEBOOK
Durova(IRE), runner-up on four of her six starts, was handed a golden opportunity and she made no mistake, value double the official margin. (op 8-11tchd 4-5 in a place)
Inspainagain(USA), very warm beforehand, did just enough to secure second spot but the winner was different gear. What he actually achieved is open to doubt. (op 8-1)
Strathmore(IRE), claimed at Catterick, looked short of pace and a step back up to seven in nursery company looks on the cards. (op 14-1)
Forest Machine, over six lengths behind the winner when making his debut at Carlisle, reared and lost ground at the start. (op 10-1)
John Stanley(IRE), last of eleven on his debut three weeks earlier, moved badly to post. He at least showed a little more this time. (op 33-1 tchd 50-1)
Hills Place, a deep-bodied newcomer, looked to be carrying tons of condition and after missing the break was soon out of contention. (op 9-2 tchd 4-1)
Neveronamonday(IRE) Official explanation: jockey said filly was unsuited by the good to firm (good in places) ground

4957 TEES VALLEY H'CAP 6f

3:10 (3:11) (Class 5) (0-75,76) 3-Y-O+ £3,238 (£963; £481; £240) Stalls Centre

Form RPR

1013 1 Tadlil[3] 4894 4-9-3 67 GregFairley(3) 10 78
(J M Bradley) *chsd ldrs: led 2f out: edgd lft and styd on strly fnl f* 5/1[1]

1323 2 1 ¾ Chairman Bobby[14] 4523 8-8-8 55 (p) TonyHamilton 12 61
(D W Barker) *chsd ldr: led over 2f out: sn hdd: kpt on wl fnl f* 20/1

0205 3 shd High Ridge[19] 4364 7-9-12 73 (p) LDettori 3 79
(J M Bradley) *trckd ldrs: t.k.h: kpt on same pce fnl f* 8/1[3]

0350 4 ¾ Dvinsky (USA)[41] 3718 5-9-9 70 PhillipMakin 13 73
(S R Bowring) *s.i.s: sn chsng ldrs: satyed on same pce fnl f* 18/1

2320 5 ½ Kool Ovation[13] 4569 4-9-11 72 DavidAllan 5 74
(A Dickman) *s.i.s: hday over 2f out: styd on same pce appr fnl f* 9/1

0014 6 shd Compton Plume[23] 4230 6-8-13 60 DaleGibson 14 62
(M W Easterby) *chsd ldrs: kpt on same pce fnl 2f* 11/1

3060 7 hd Tough Love[7] 4733 7-9-10 71 (p) MichaelHills 4 72
(T D Easterby) *sn outpcd and bhd: hdwy over 2f out: styd on wl fnl f* 20/1

5004 8 ½ Figaro Flyer (IRE)[13] 4562 3-9-8 75 DeanCorby(3) 1 75
(P Howling) *sn in rr: hdwy 2f out: styd on ins last* 20/1

0-00 9 ¾ Sparkwell[62] 3041 4-9-9 70 AdrianTNicholls 16 67
(D W Barker) *mid-div: kpt on fnl 2f: nvr rchd ldrs* 22/1

1065 10 shd Paddywack (IRE)[4] 4834 9-8-12 59 (b) PaulQuinn 15 56
(D W Chapman) *s.i.s: in rr tl styd on fnl 2f* 12/1

050 11 ¾ Obe Bold (IRE)[10] 4655 5-8-2 54 oh4 (b) NataliaGemelova(5) 8 49
(A Berry) *led tl over 2f out: wknd over 1f out* 50/1

4425 12 shd Patavium Prince (IRE)[3] 4874 3-9-6 70 JoeFanning 7 64
(J R Best) *sn outpcd and in rr: kpt on fnl 2f: nvr nrr* 11/1

210 13 ½ Frimley's Mattery[8] 4694 6-8-3 55 oh4 ow1 (v) MichaelJStainton(5) 2 48
(R E Barr) *sn bhd: hdwy on wd outside over 1f out: nvr on terms* 22/1

0051 14 1 ¾ Danzig River (IRE)[4] 4834 5-9-8 76 6ex VictoriaBehan(7) 18 64
(D Nicholls) *chsd ldrs on ins: wknd fnl f* 7/1[2]

2204 15 1 ¼ True Magic[16] 4453 5-9-7 68 PatCosgrave 9 52
(J D Bethell) *mid-div: lost pl over 1f out: eased* 16/1

5030 16 2 Whinhill House[11] 4636 6-8-10 62 (p) MarkLawson(5) 17 40
(D W Barker) *chsd ldrs: lost pl over 1f out: eased* 25/1

0333 17 70 The Terrier[18] 4403 3-9-5 69 PaulMulrennan 11 —
(G A Swinbank) *s.v.s: detached in last: virtually p.u over 2f out: t.o: btn 70 l* 10/1

1m 10.3s (-1.40) **Going Correction** -0.175s/f (Firm)
WFA 3 from 4yo+ 3lb 17 Ran SP% 123.7
Speed ratings (Par 103):102,99,99,98,97 97,97,96,95,95 94,94,93,91,89 87,—
CSF £110.36 CT £834.42 TOTE £6.10: £1.70, £5.10, £1.20, £5.90; EX 120.80.
Owner E A Hayward **Bred** Wheelersland Stud **Trained** Sedbury, Gloucs
■ Stewards' Enquiry : L Dettori one-day ban: failed to keep straight from stalls (Sep 11)

FOCUS
They avoided the far side. It looked quite competitive beforehand but it turned into a one-horse sprint. Solid form for the grade, with the winner likely to rate a bit better.
Obe Bold(IRE) Official explanation: trainer said mare had a breathing problem
The Terrier Official explanation: jockey said filly missed the break

4958 JOHN SMITH'S REDCAR STRAIGHT-MILE CHAMPIONSHIP (QUALIFIER) (H'CAP) 1m

3:40 (3:40) (Class 4) (0-85,83) 3-Y-O £6,477 (£1,927; £963; £481) Stalls Centre

Form RPR

2312 1 Daaweitza[13] 4569 3-8-7 72 GregFairley(3) 2 80
(B Ellison) *chsd ldrs: led 1f out: kpt on wl* 11/2

1 2 1 ¼ Very Far (USA)[17] 4431 3-9-7 83 (t) LDettori 1 88+
(Saeed Bin Suroor) *dwlt: sn trcking ldrs on outside: led over 2f out: rdn and swvd lft appr fnl f: sn hdd and no ex* 5/2[1]

0011 3 ¾ Colton[15] 4497 3-8-5 67 DaleGibson 4 70
(J M P Eustace) *trckd ldrs: drvn and outpcd over 3f out: styd on fnl f* 5/1[3]

4511 4 ¾ Choreography[8] 4695 3-8-10 72 6ex AdrianTNicholls 7 74
(D Nicholls) *stdd s: hld up: outpcd over 3f out: kpt on wl appr fnl f* 11/2

0043 5 ¾ Ryedale Ovation (IRE)[19] 4378 3-8-11 73 DavidAllan 6 73
(T D Easterby) *swvd rt s: led tl over 2f out: one pce appr fnl f* 7/2[2]

1465 6 ¾ It's Unbelievable (USA)[21] 4285 3-8-2 69 RoryMoore(5) 9 67
(P T Midgley) *trckd ldrs: drvn over 3f out: one pce fnl 2f* 40/1

041 7 ½ Rigat[34] 3909 3-9-0 76 PhillipMakin 8 73
(T D Barron) *wnt lft s: sn trcking ldrs: one pce fnl 2f* 25/1

-000 8 9 Playtotheaudience[21] 4298 3-9-4 80 TonyHamilton 3 56
(R A Fahey) *in rr: sn drvn along: bhd fnl 3f* 50/1

0603 9 nk River Kintyre[15] 4488 3-8-11 73 MichaelHills 10 49
(B W Hills) *in rr: sn pushed along: lost pl over 2f out: sn bhd and eased* 8/1

1m 36.24s (-1.56) **Going Correction** -0.175s/f (Firm) 9 Ran SP% 117.6
Speed ratings (Par 102):100,98,98,97,96 95,95,86,85
CSF £19.81 CT £74.27 TOTE £9.40: £2.40, £2.00, £1.80; EX 35.20.
Owner Mrs Andrea M Mallinson **Bred** C Mallinson **Trained** Norton, N Yorks

FOCUS
Just a steady gallop. A progressive winner, who ran to his improved sand form, and an unexposed runner-up who is capable of improvement. The form looks sound.
River Kintyre Official explanation: jockey said colt hung badly right under pressure

4959 RACING UK CHANNEL 432 MAIDEN STKS 1m 1f

4:10 (4:11) (Class 5) 3-Y-O+ £3,238 (£963; £481; £240) Stalls Low

Form RPR

4032 1 Alhaitham (USA)[22] 4261 3-9-3 80 (t) TPQueally 7 81+
(J L Dunlop) *mde all: clr over 1f out: pushed out* 4/5[1]

4-5 2 1 ½ Profitable[134] 1081 3-8-12 MichaelHills 3 69
(B W Hills) *chsd ldrs: drvn and outpcd over 5f out: styd on wl to take 2nd ins last* 3/1[2]

-040 3 2 ½ Woolfall Blue (IRE)[12] 3-9-3 79 LDettori 6 69
(G G Margarson) *sn trcking ldrs: wnt 2nd over 3f out: rdn and hung lft over 1f out: wknd ins last* 10/3[3]

0 4 2 ½ Kildare Sun (IRE)[11] 4635 4-9-10 DaleGibson 2 64
(J Mackie) *hld up in rr: kpt on fnl 3f: nvr nr to chal* 66/1

0000 5 5 English Archer[7] 4728 3-9-3 47 PhillipMakin 1 54?
(J R Weymes) *sn trcking ldrs: outpcd and lost pl over 5f out: kpt on fnl 2f* 100/1

00-0 6 16 The Terminator (IRE)[14] 4518 4-9-5 41 DeclanMcGann(5) 5 22
(R Johnson) *sn trcking ldr: wnt 2nd over 6f out: wknd over 3f out* 200/1

0-6 7 ¾ Prinquet (USA)[15] 4495 3-8-5 WilliamCarson(7) 4 16
(C E Brittain) *stdd and lost grnd s: t.k.h: lost pl 4f out: bhd fnl 2f: eased* 33/1

8 8 Fantastic Delight 3-8-12 PaulMulrennan 8 —
(G M Moore) *sn bhd: rn green: t.o 4f out* 50/1

1m 52.61s (-0.79) **Going Correction** -0.175s/f (Firm)
WFA 3 from 4yo 7lb 8 Ran SP% 111.5
Speed ratings (Par 103):96,94,92,90,85 71,70,63
CSF £3.26 TOTE £2.40: £1.10, £1.50, £1.02; EX 4.20.
Owner Hamdan Al Maktoum **Bred** Shadwell Farm LLC **Trained** Arundel, W Sussex

FOCUS
A weakish maiden and basically a three-horse race according to the market. The bare form is less than solid, limited by the fifth, and the winner did not need to be at his best despite being value for a bit extra. Very few ever figured and the winning time was modest for the class.

4960 CHRISTMAS DISCO PARTY NIGHTS H'CAP 1m 6f 19y

4:40 (4:40) (Class 6) (0-65,60) 3-Y-O+ £2,388 (£705; £352) Stalls Low

Form RPR

5220 1 Vice Admiral[19] 4380 3-8-9 53 PaulMulrennan 14 67
(M W Easterby) *trckd ldrs: led over 3f out: clr over 2f out: styd on strly* 11/1

0434 2 4 Lenwade[17] 4423 5-8-7 42 DominicFox(3) 5 50
(G G Margarson) *dwlt: bhd and drvn over 4f out: hdwy over 2f out: fin wl to snatch 2nd nr line* 10/1

2421 3 nk Parchment (IRE)[15] 4472 4-9-6 57 (b) MarkLawson(5) 7 65
(A J Lockwood) *hld up in rr: hdwy on ins 4f out: tk 2nd 1f out: kpt on same pce* 6/1[2]

-054 4 ½ Sun King[19] 4380 9-8-12 51 (t) JamesReveley(7) 1 58
(K G Reveley) *in tch: wnt 2nd over 2f out: kpt on same pce fnl f* 8/1

1463 5 ¾ Let It Be[20] 4320 5-9-7 60 NeilBrown(7) 12 66
(K G Reveley) *hld up in rr: hdwy over 3f out: styd on same pce fnl 2f* 13/2[3]

1342 6 2 York Cliff[6] 4764 8-9-10 56 LDettori 6 59
(W M Brisbourne) *hld up in rr: drvn 4f out: kpt on: nvr nr ldrs* 4/1[1]

4566 7 hd Compton Eclaire (IRE)[11] 4632 6-9-12 58 (v) MichaelHills 13 61
(B Ellison) *bhd: kpt on fnl 3f: nvr trbld ldrs* 12/1

6000 8 1 ½ Rajam[15] 4472 8-9-6 52 (p) TonyHamilton 11 53
(G A Harker) *in tch: effrt over 4f out: hung lft over 2f out: nvr a threat* 6/1[2]

0005 9 5 Step Perfect (USA)[17] 4438 5-8-13 45 (p) PhillipMakin 15 39
(G M Moore) *mid-div: effrt over 4f out: nvr a factor* 25/1

-000 10 shd Michaels Dream (IRE)[19] 4380 7-8-10 42 oh6 (b) CatherineGannon 2 36
(N Wilson) *led after 1f: hdd over 3f out: lost pl over 1f out* 33/1

/000 11 1 ¾ Compton Commander[68] 2871 8-9-6 57 PJMcDonald(5) 4 48
(E W Tuer) *s.i.s: nvr on terms* 33/1

20-2 12 13 Danebank (IRE)[19] 4380 6-9-6 55 GregFairley(3) 3 28
(J Mackie) *led 1f: chsd ldrs: weaakened 3f out: sn bhd and eased* 10/1

-000 13 32 Rockpiler[22] 4252 4-8-11 43 GylesParkin 9 —
(D W Thompson) *mid-div: hdwy 6f out: lost pl over 3f out: sn bhd and eased: t.o* 150/1

3m 2.31s (-2.71) **Going Correction** -0.175s/f (Firm)
WFA 3 from 4yo+ 12lb 13 Ran SP% 117.6
Speed ratings (Par 101):100,97,97,97,96 95,95,94,91,91 90,83,65
CSF £111.63 CT £729.05 TOTE £18.70: £6.80, £4.70, £1.40; EX 134.10.
Owner A C R Stubbs **Bred** Barry Minty **Trained** Sheriff Hutton, N Yorks

FOCUS
A moderate handicap and the early pace was not at all strong, which goes some way to explaining why they finished in a heap behind the runaway winner. The winner was up 10lb on recent efforts but overall the form looks sound enough.
York Cliff Official explanation: jockey said gelding lost its action

4961 GO RACING AT THIRSK ON SATURDAY APPRENTICE H'CAP 7f

5:15 (5:17) (Class 5) (0-75,73) 3-Y-O+ £3,238 (£963; £481; £240) Stalls Centre

Form RPR

1200 1 Pay Time[18] 4405 7-8-7 57 NeilBrown(5) 1 67
(R E Barr) *chsd ldrs: edgd rt fr 1/2-way: led jst ins last: hld on wl* 18/1

015 2 ¾ Kabis Amigos[14] 4518 4-8-6 56 (t) VictoriaBehan(5) 10 65
(D Nicholls) *led: edgd rt fr 1/2-way: hdd jst ins last: no ex towards fin* 13/2[3]

222 3 ½ Sedge (USA)[24] 4198 6-8-12 60 (b[1]) RoryMoore(3) 2 67
(P T Midgley) *chsd ldrs: kpt on same pce ins last* 9/2[2]

0020 4 1 ¼ Curtain Bluff[6] 4772 4-9-11 70 (v) EdwardCreighton 6 74
(M R Channon) *hld up: hdwy over 2f out: kpt on fnl f: nt rch ldrs* 12/1

5303 5 ¾ Pure Imagination (IRE)[33] 3937 5-9-11 73 (b) LiamTreadwell(3) 14 75
(J M Bradley) *hld up: hdwy on ins over 2f out: kpt on same pce fnl f* 17/2

0213 6 2 ½ Neon Blue[22] 4253 5-9-9 71 (p) MichaelJStainton(3) 9 67
(R M Whitaker) *hld up: drvn and lost pl 3f out: styd on fnl f* 4/1[1]

0-60 7 hd Orpen's Astaire (IRE)[86] 2325 3-8-6 59 ow1 MarkLawson(3) 12 52
(Jedd O'Keeffe) *sn bhd: kpt on fnl 2f: nvr nr ldrs* 66/1

0604 8 1 Big Bradford[16] 4456 5-8-4 56 (v) JamesRogers(7) 7 48
(R A Fahey) *rr-div: rdn and hung lft over 1f out: nvr nr ldrs* 15/2

0046 9 2 Stormingmichaelori[18] 4405 3-8-2 59 oh11 ow5 (p) LanceBetts(7) 11 44
(N Wilson) *chsd ldrs: outpcd over 2f out: no ch whn hmpd ins last* 66/1

-056 10 ½ Zarabad (IRE)[91] 2183 4-9-7 73 PatrickDonaghy(7) 5 59
(K R Burke) *chsd ldrs: wknd appr fnl f* 11/1

4551 11 1 ¼ Ayam Jantan[24] 4198 3-8-5 58 GregFairley(3) 3 39
(M Johnston) *chsd ldrs: outpcd fnl 2f* 7/1

5500 12 ½ Eternal Legacy (IRE)[24] 4198 4-8-9 54 oh7 DominicFox 4 35
(J Parkes) *a in rr* 50/1

0350 13 ¾ Final Award (IRE)[22] 4253 3-8-5 55 PaulMulrennan 8 32
(G M Moore) *mid-div: lost pl 3f out: sn bhd* 20/1

-005 14 8 Etijahaat (IRE)[18] 4405 4-8-6 56 DeanWilliams(5) 13 15
(C W Fairhurst) *uns rdr gng to post: sn in rr and pushed along: bhd and eased fnl 2f* 22/1

1m 23.24s (-1.66) **Going Correction** -0.175s/f (Firm)
WFA 3 from 4yo+ 5lb 14 Ran SP% 121.7
Speed ratings (Par 103):102,101,100,99,98 95,95,94,91,91 89,89,88,79
CSF £127.09 CT £649.01 TOTE £28.40: £17.30, £3.70, £1.50; EX 308.60 Place 6 £15.84, Place 5 £12.53.
Owner Mrs R E Barr **Bred** M Paver And M D M Racing Thoroughbreds Ltd **Trained** Seamer, N Yorks
■ Stewards' Enquiry : Rory Moore one-day ban: used whip with excessive frequency and without giving gelding time to respond (Sep 11)

FOCUS
A race run at a fair early pace and the runners raced centre to stands' side. It paid to race handily and the first three home were always up there. The form looks reliable, with a slight personal best from the winner.
Ayam Jantan Official explanation: jockey said gelding had no more to give
Eternal Legacy(IRE) Official explanation: jockey said filly lost its action
Etijahaat(IRE) Official explanation: jockey said gelding bolted to post and never travelled

T/Plt: £12.80 to a £1 stake. Pool: £46,536.30. 2,638.55 winning tickets. T/Qpdt: £12.10 to a £1 stake. Pool: £2,219.00. 135.70 winning tickets. WG

4772 SALISBURY (R-H)

Thursday, August 31

OFFICIAL GOING: Good to firm (good in places)

Wind: Slight, across

4962 SYDENHAMS H'CAP — 5f

2:20 (2:23) (Class 5) (0-70,71) 3-Y-0+ — **£3,886** (£1,156; £577; £288) **Stalls** Centre

Form — RPR

0005 **1** — **Meikle Barfil**[12] [4587] 4-8-11 **55**....(p) RyanMoore 6 — 67
(J M Bradley) *rr early: sn in tch: hdwy to trck ldrs over 1f out: led fnl 110yds: drvn out* — **16/1**

0361 **2** 1 1/2 **Tamino (IRE)**[14] [4532] 3-8-12 **63**.... TravisBlock(5) 12 — 70
(H Morrison) *sn woth ldr: styd chalng tl slt ld jst insdie last: hdd fnl 110yds: one pce* — **6/1**[2]

1533 **3** hd **Blessed Place**[6] [4780] 6-9-11 **69**....(t) JamieSpencer 7 — 75
(D J S Ffrench Davis) *slt ld tl narrowly hdd jst ins fnl f: styd on same pce u.p* — **4/1**[1]

6303 **4** nk **Seven No Trumps**[3] [4872] 9-7-13 **50**.... BarrySavage(7) 11 — 55
(J M Bradley) *in tch:rdn along 1/2-way: styd on fnl f: kpt on cl home* — **15/2**

5521 **5** 1 1/2 **Kennington**[4] [4846] 6-9-13 **71** 6ex....(b) JohnEgan 3 — 71
(Mrs C A Dunnett) *prom: rdn 1/2-way: kpt on fr over 1f out but nvr gng pce to rch ldrs* — **7/1**[3]

0010 **6** shd **Whistler**[6] [4780] 9-9-2 **60**....(b) PaulFitzsimons 2 — 59
(Miss J R Tooth) *s.i.s: bhd: hdwy whn n.m.r 2f out: kpt on ins fnl f: gng on cl home* — **20/1**

3326 **7** hd **Inka Dancer (IRE)**[29] [4054] 4-8-13 **57**.... TedDurcan 8 — 55
(B Palling) *s.i.s: rdn 2f out: kpt on ins fnl f but nt rch ldrs* — **10/1**

3331 **8** 1 **Jucebabe**[6] [4756] 3-9-1 **61** 6ex....(p) FrancisNorton 9 — 56
(J L Spearing) *chsd ldrs: rdn 1/2-way: outpcd fnl f* — **10/1**

6060 **9** 2 **Salviati (USA)**[11] [4636] 9-9-0 **58**....(p) SteveDrowne 5 — 46
(J M Bradley) *slowly away: bhd: kpt on fr over 1f out but nvr in contention* — **20/1**

0236 **10** hd **Whitbarrow (IRE)**[19] [4361] 7-8-10 **61**....(v) JamesMillman(7) 4 — 48
(B R Millman) *outpcd tl sme prog fr over 1f out* — **10/1**

2301 **11** 3/4 **Clearing Sky (IRE)**[12] [4602] 5-8-12 **56**.... MatthewHenry 14 — 40
(J R Boyle) *chsd ldrs: rdn 1/2-way: wknd over 1f out* — **9/1**

0523 **12** 1/2 **Be My Charm**[8] [4710] 3-8-3 **56**.... LauraReynolds(7) 13 — 38
(M Blanshard) *s.i.s: behund: rdn and effrt 1/2-way: nvr gng pce to trble ldrs and sn btn* — **20/1**

5-00 **13** 6 **Turibius**[9] [4675] 7-9-2 **60**....(b) RichardHughes 16 — 21
(T E Powell) *in tch 3f* — **20/1**

60.42 secs (-1.17) **Going Correction** -0.05s/f (Good) — **13** Ran SP% **120.8**
WFA 3 from 4yo+ 2lb
Speed ratings (Par 103):107,104,104,103,101 101,100,99,96,95 94,93,84
CSF £103.72 CT £461.47 TOTE £12.30: £2.70, £2.80, £1.60; EX 133.90.
Owner Terry Warner **Bred** Mrs Henry Keswick **Trained** Sedbury, Gloucs

FOCUS
A modest yet competitive sprint handicap.
Turibius Official explanation: trainer said gelding lost its off-fore shoe

4963 GERRARD INVESTMENT MANAGEMENT E B F NOVICE STKS — 1m

2:50 (2:50) (Class 4) 2-Y-0 — **£5,505** (£1,637; £818) **Stalls** Centre

Form — RPR

1 **1** — **Yazamaan**[13] [4574] 2-9-5 .... RHills 2 — 100+
(J H M Gosden) *tracked ldr: shkn up to ld jst ins fnl 2f: clr ins last: easily* — **4/9**[1]

1442 **2** 6 **Princeton (IRE)**[15] [4474] 2-9-2 83.... TedDurcan 4 — 80
(M R Channon) *racd in cl 3rd: rdn and no imp 2f out: styd on u.p to take 2nd ins last but nvr any ch w easy wnr* — **3/1**[2]

00 **3** 5 **Cry Presto (USA)**[13] [4561] 2-8-12 .... RichardHughes 3 — 65
(R Hannon) *rdn to ld: pusde along over 3f out: rdn dropped whip and hdd jst ins fnl 2f: sn no chnace w wnr: lost 2nd ins last* — **11/2**[3]

1m 42.63s (-0.46) **Going Correction** -0.05s/f (Good) — **3** Ran SP% **109.6**
Speed ratings (Par 96):100,94,89
CSF £2.17 TOTE £1.50; EX 2.00.
Owner Hamdan Al Maktoum **Bred** Shadwell Estate Company Limited **Trained** Newmarket, Suffolk

FOCUS
A poor turnout, but Cry Presto set a good clip and Yazamaan drew right away inside the final furlong. He could turn out to be very good.

NOTEBOOK
Yazamaan, quite an impressive winner on his debut over this trip at Newmarket, had faster conditions to contend with here, but he had been found a great opportunity to supplement that initial win and he readily came clear inside the final furlong. Appreciating the good early pace set by Cry Presto, stamina is clearly the son of Galileo's strong suit, but he will have to raise his game further if he runs in the Racing Post Trophy. (op 1-2 tchd 8-15)
Princeton(IRE) has been generally progressive, running a useful sort close at Hamilton last time on his first try at this distance, but he was no match for the smart winner and could only stay on past the front-running Cry Presto. He stays this trip well and will find life easier back in handicaps. (tchd 10-3)
Cry Presto(USA) has yet to live up to expectations, but he is evidently well thought of by connections and Hughes was keen to lead on the son of Street Cry. He led at a decent clip, but was struggling to hang in with them from two furlongs out and ultimately faded. He is now qualified for a handicap mark and still has some improving to do. (op 6-1 tchd 5-1)

4964 EUROPEAN BREEDERS FUND QUIDHAMPTON MAIDEN FILLIES' STKS — 6f 212y

3:20 (3:22) (Class 2) 2-Y-0 — **£9,715** (£2,890; £1,444; £721) **Stalls** Centre

Form — RPR

1 — **Puggy (IRE)** 2-9-0 ....(t) FJohansson 4 — 79
(R A Kvisla) *s.i.s: sn rcvrd: stdy hdwy on outside fr 3f out to ld ins fnl 2f: pushed out fnl f: readily* — **66/1**

2 **2** 1 1/2 **Fretwork**[19] [4373] 2-9-0 .... RyanMoore 9 — 75
(R Hannon) *trckd ldrs: chal fr over 2f out tl appr fnl f: kpt on but nvr gng pce of wnr ins last* — **5/6**[1]

3 shd **Millisecond** 2-9-0 .... PhilipRobinson 2 — 75+
(M A Jarvis) *chsd ldrs tl led over 2f out: sn pushed along: hdd ins fnl 2f: kpt on same pce ins last* — **9/1**[2]

0 **4** shd **Tarteel (USA)**[26] [4148] 2-9-0 .... RHills 16 — 75+
(J L Dunlop) *hld up in rr: stdy hdwy: swtchd rt and gng wl whn hmpd over 1f out: styd on strly fnl f: nt rcvr* — **9/1**[2]

5 1 1/4 **Satin Braid** 2-9-0 .... MickyFenton 5 — 71+
(B J Meehan) *chsd ldrs: rdn over 2f out: styd on same pce fnl f* — **66/1**

0 **6** 1/2 **Mystery River (USA)**[13] [4558] 2-9-0 .... RichardHughes 10 — 70
(B J Meehan) *chsd ldrs: rdn and edgd rt over 1f out: no ex ins last* — **12/1**

7 1 3/4 **Unreachable Star** 2-9-0 .... KerrinMcEvoy 7 — 65
(Mrs A J Perrett) *s.i.s: rcvrd into mid-div 1/2-way: sn pushed along: kpt on fnl f but nvr gng pce to rch ldrs* — **25/1**

5 **8** hd **Bathwick Fancy (IRE)**[99] [1930] 2-9-0 .... EddieAhern 11 — 65
(J G Portman) *ld tl hdd over 2f out: wknd ins last* — **25/1**

9 1 1/2 **Paradise Walk** 2-9-0 .... SteveDrowne 6 — 61
(R Charlton) *s.i.s: bhd: drvn along over 2f out: styd on fnl f: nvr in contention* — **20/1**

10 nk **Abyla** 2-9-0 .... MartinDwyer 1 — 60
(M P Tregoning) *broke wl: stdd towards rr: drvn and hdwy fr 2f out: nvr gng pce to rch ldrs* — **22/1**

11 1 **Dancing Duo** 2-9-0 .... JohnEgan 8 — 58
(W J Haggas) *bhd tl kpt on fnl 2f* — **20/1**

12 nk **Snow Ballerina** 2-9-0 .... JamieSpencer 3 — 57
(E A L Dunlop) *bhd: sme prog fnl f: nvr in contention* — **10/1**[3]

0 **13** shd **Rumbled**[24] [4207] 2-9-0 .... StephenCarson 13 — 57
(J A Geake) *t.k.h: chsd ldrs to 2f out* — **66/1**

14 4 **Rose Germany** 2-9-0 .... ChrisCatlin 15 — 46
(M R Channon) *outpcd most of way* — **33/1**

15 1/2 **Affiliation (IRE)** 2-9-0 .... DaneO'Neill 12 — 45
(R Hannon) *s.i.s: outpcd* — **33/1**

16 1 **Tarrjoo** 2-9-0 .... TedDurcan 14 — 42
(M R Channon) *mid-div: rdn 1/2-way: sn wknd* — **33/1**

1m 29.93s (0.87) **Going Correction** -0.05s/f (Good) — **16** Ran SP% **126.2**
Speed ratings (Par 97):93,91,91,91,89 89,87,86,85,84 83,83,83,78,78 76
CSF £115.78 TOTE £118.20: £23.30, £1.20, £2.80; EX 626.00.
Owner Investment Ab Rustningen **Bred** Darley **Trained** Upper Lambourn, Berks
■ The first British winner for Lambourn-based Norwegian Roy Kvisla & Fredrik Johansson, both former champions in Sweden.
■ Stewards' Enquiry : Richard Hughes one-day ban: careless riding (Sep 11)

FOCUS
This looked a good maiden on paper that is sure to produce winners, but only one of the 16 that lined up held a Group-race entry and with a 66/1 outsider winning it is questionable how good a race it was.

NOTEBOOK
Puggy(IRE), whose stable had a two-year-old run well first time up at Newmarket earlier in the month, was wearing a tongue tie for this racecourse debut and was dismissed in the betting, but she is from the family of Blue Monday and Lundy's Lane and ran out a ready winner, causing quite an upset in the process. Brought wide with her challenge, she came with a steady run down the outside and was not stopping at the end of her race, suggesting a mile with be no problem in time. She holds no fancy entries, but showed signs of inexperience under pressure and deserves a crack at something better.
Fretwork, who narrowly failed on her debut in soft ground at Newmarket, had faster conditions to contend with here and she looked plenty short enough considering there were so many well-bred fillies in opposition. Moore soon had her in a perfect position, but she could not quicken under pressure and in the end did well to hang on to second, as she was fourth a couple of strides past the line. The combination of a step up in trip back on a slower surface may help the daughter of Galileo, but it remains to be seen which way she goes as many in her ownership do not progress. (op 11-8 tchd 4-5)
Millisecond ◆, out of a top-class miler who was half-sister to another in One So Wonderful, should certainly be effective at this distance and she nosed ahead two furlongs out, but the winner readily went by and she just lost out on second. This was a highly pleasing debut considering the vast majority of her trainer's juveniles needs their first run and winning a maiden should be within her capabilities. (op 6-1)
Tarteel(USA) ran a little better than her finishing position suggested on her racecourse debut at Newmarket, as she hung in there for a long way despite taking a strong hold, and with the experience under her belt it was easy to see her getting involved. However, having been held up early after being squeezed for room, she had an extremely troubled passage and had to wait for gaps and be switched on several occasions. She was finishing strongly and would probably have won had things panned out better, but winning races should not prove to be too much hassle for the daughter of Bahri, who will have the option of nurseries after one more run. Official explanation: jockey said he lost an iron coming out of stalls (op 11-1)
Satin Braid should be effective at around this sort of distance, but she looked the stable's second string if the betting was to be believed. However, she overcame inexperience to claim a staying-on fifth and was not beaten far at all. Improvement should be forthcoming and she will benefit from a mile in time.
Mystery River(USA), the only runner in the field with a Group entry - she is in the Group 1 Fillies' Mile - had the benefit of a previous run when not showing a great deal over six furlongs at Newbury and she was able to step up on that. She did not see out the race as strongly as some, but very much appeals as one to to prosper from a move into handicaps in time. (op 11-1)
Unreachable Star, a half-sister to Grade 1 winner Necklace, looked fit in the paddock beforehand, but she was not the quickest away and ran green before making some good late headway. She will definitely benefit from a step up to a mile, and should come on for the experience, even if there is not that much physical improvement to come.
Bathwick Fancy(IRE) was unable to build on her debut effort, but the best of her is unlikely to be seen until she tackles nurseries.
Paradise Walk, a daughter of Sakhee, never recovered from a slow start and lacked the pace to get in a serious blow. She was going on towards the end of the race though and should relish a mile, with the run also expected to do her the world of good.
Abyla, a half-sister to high-class French performer Sadler's Flag, broke well from her low draw, but was soon settled in rear and was another noted putting in some good late work. She is another whose trainer's juveniles often benefit from a run and there should be significant improvement to come from the daughter of Rock Of Gibraltar. (op 12-1)
Dancing Duo will benefit from a mile in time and she should come on a good deal for the outing. (op 16-1)
Snow Ballerina, who is as well bred as they come, being a half-sister to Derby winner Lammtarra by Sadler's Wells, was always likely to find seven furlongs on fast ground too sharp a test on this racecourse debut and was struggling from quite an early stage. She could be one for a backend maiden when conditions are likely to be much more suitable. (op 12-1)
Rumbled ran well for a long way and is another likely handicap prospect.
Rose Germany is more of a three-year-old prospect and she lacked the knowhow to get involved. (op 50-1)
Affiliation(IRE), a 30,000gns purchase by Danehill Dancer, looked one of the more interesting outsiders, but she was always on the back foot following a slow start and was in need of the experience.
Tarrjoo is another in need of more time and a greater distance.

4965 E B F LOCHSONG FILLIES' STKS (H'CAP) 6f 212y

3:50 (3:53) (Class 2) (0-100,89) 3-Y-0+

£15,580 (£4,665; £2,332; £1,167; £582; £292) **Stalls** Centre

Form				RPR
0202	**1**		**Gaelic Princess**[6] 4782 6-9-1 **78**................................ FergusSweeney 6 (A G Newcombe) *hld up in rr: rapid hdwy on outside over 1f out: str run ins last to ld last strides* **14/1**	88
-452	**2**	*nk*	**Gloved Hand**[62] 3047 4-9-9 **86**.. JamieSpencer 3 (J R Fanshawe) *hld up in rr: rapid hdwy on outside fr 2f out to ld jst ins last: hung bdly rt u.p: ct last strides* **5/2**[1]	95
3433	**3**	*1*	**All Quiet**[10] 4660 5-9-1 **78**.. RichardHughes 5 (R Hannon) *stdd s: hld up in rr: stdy hday fr 2f out:styng on whn carried rt ins last: n.m.r on rails and one pce sn after* **10/1**	85+
5625	**4**	*2½*	**Kindlelight Debut**[5] 4790 6-9-3 **83**............................... JamesDoyle(3) 10 (N P Littmoden) *chsd ldrs: led 2f out: hdd jst ins last: hld on rails whn bdly hmpd sn after* **10/1**	87+
2521	**5**	*½*	**Toffee Vodka (IRE)**[16] 4447 4-8-5 **75**........................... PatrickHills(7) 12 (J W Hills) *mid-div: hdwy whn nt clr run jst ins last: swtchd lft sn after: r.o cl home but nt trble ldrs* **12/1**	74
0421	**6**	*3*	**Puya**[13] 4577 4-9-6 **83**.. DaneO'Neill 2 (H Candy) *chsd ldrs: rdn to chal fr over 2f out tl over 1f out: wkng whn n.m.r jst ins last* **4/1**[2]	74
3064	**7**	*2½*	**Kaveri (USA)**[13] 4577 3-8-13 **81**...................................... MartinDwyer 13 (C E Brittain) *s.i.s: sn mid-div: n.m.r on rails and outpcd 2f out: n.d after* **25/1**	65
1460	**8**	*nk*	**Spinning Ruby**[11] 4628 3-9-6 **88**....................................... RyanMoore 7 (R M Beckett) *chsd ldrs: rdn to chal over 2f out: wknd over 1f out* **20/1**	72
64	**9**	*1¾*	**Meditation**[12] 4593 4-9-0 **80**.. AdamKirby(3) 9 (I A Wood) *led tl hdd 2f out: sn wknd* **8/1**[3]	59
1200	**10**	*1½*	**Pintle**[11] 4628 6-9-10 **87**.. KerrinMcEvoy 11 (J L Spearing) *chsd ldrs over 4f* **20/1**	62
5613	**11**	*nk*	**Stormy Monday**[6] 4772 3-8-4 **72**.. JohnEgan 8 (J W Hills) *chsd ldrs over 4f* **9/1**	46

1m 26.94s (-2.12) **Going Correction** -0.05s/f (Good)
WFA 3 from 4yo+ 5lb **11** Ran SP% **115.6**
Speed ratings (Par 96):110,109,108,105,105 101,98,98,96,94 94
CSF £46.88 CT £323.32 TOTE £14.90: £3.10, £1.30, £2.80; EX 47.80 Trifecta £371.20 Pool: £679.90 - 1.30 winning units..
Owner M K F Seymour **Bred** Mrs N Quinn **Trained** Yarnscombe, Devon
■ Stewards' Enquiry : Jamie Spencer three-day ban: careless riding (Sep 14-16)

FOCUS
A fair fillies' handicap, but Gloved Hand caused plenty of trouble as she hung right inside the final furlong and there were several sufferers, most notably All Quiet and Toffee Vodka. Ordinary form for the grade.

NOTEBOOK
Gaelic Princess, a two-time course-and-distance winner coming into the race, has been running with her usual inconsistency, but she went close at Sandown recently and was able to go one better here, getting up in the final strides to deny the favourite. She takes her racing well and wins in her turn, but will be doing well to score off a higher mark.
Gloved Hand has often shaped as though this would be her ideal distance and it looked as though she had come with a winning run when going on inside the final furlong, but she hung right under pressure, hampering several rivals in the process, and was nabbed close home. She can win off this mark though and this is definitely her trip. (tchd 9-4 and 11-4 in places)
All Quiet may well have joined the front two for a three-way photo had she not been cut off by the runner-up, but this consistent mare should be winning again shortly off what remains a fair mark. (op 11-1)
Kindlelight Debut was beaten at the time of being hampered, but would definitely have been a little closer and this remarkably tough and consistent mare can continue to pay her way. Official explanation: jockey said mare suffered interference in running (op 9-1)
Toffee Vodka(IRE) was unlucky not to challenge for the places, finishing well having been denied a clear run, and she remains progessive. (op 14-1)
Puya got back to winning ways at Newmarket, but was not good enough off a 5lb higher mark and was already on her way back through the field when being squeezed for room. (op 9-2)
Spinning Ruby Official explanation: jockey said filly had been hit in mouth by divot of turf
Meditation has had a cracking season thus far, winning five of her 18 starts, and being placed on numerous occasions, but this was not such a great effort and she dropped away disappointingly having taken them along until a quarter of a mile out. (op 15-2)
Stormy Monday Official explanation: jockey said filly had no more to give

4966 EUROPEAN BREEDERS FUND DICK POOLE FILLIES' STKS (LISTED RACE) 6f

4:20 (4:23) (Class 1) 2-Y-O

£17,034 (£6,456; £3,231; £1,611; £807; £405) **Stalls** Centre

Form				RPR
6412	**1**		**Vital Statistics**[33] 3925 2-8-12 **105**................................. JohnEgan 3 (D R C Elsworth) *hld up rr but in tch: hdwy over 2f out: sn trcking ldr: rdn to ld fnl 110yds: kpt on strly cl home* **10/3**[2]	102
11	**2**	*½*	**Wid (USA)**[20] 4322 2-8-12 .... RHills 1 (J L Dunlop) *sn trcking ldr: led ins fnl 2f: drvn fnl f: hdd and one pce fnl 110yds* **10/11**[1]	101
421	**3**	*5*	**Russian Rosie (IRE)**[13] 4558 2-8-12 **81**........................... EddieAhern 4 (J G Portman) *chsd ldrs: rdn over 2f out: styd on same pce* **5/1**[3]	86
33	**4**	*nk*	**Mimisel**[13] 4559 2-8-12 .... PhilipRobinson 2 (Rae Guest) *bhd: rdn and hdwy fr 2f out: kpt on fr over 1f but nvr in contention* **33/1**	85
1524	**5**	*2*	**Bridge It Jo**[12] 4594 2-8-12 **94**.. JamieSpencer 7 (Miss J Feilden) *sn led: rdn 1/2-way: hdd ins fnl 2f: sn btn* **9/1**	79
	6	*2*	**Sama (IRE)** 2-8-12 .... RyanMoore 8 (C E Brittain) *s.i.s bhd: drvn along and green 3f out: sme prog fnl f but nvr in contention* **40/1**	73
1	**7**	*nk*	**Suki Bear**[24] 4207 2-8-12 .... MartinDwyer 6 (W R Muir) *in tch to 1/2-way* **16/1**	72
3004	**8**	*5*	**Slipasearcher (IRE)**[19] 4344 2-8-12 **88**........................... SteveDrowne 9 (P D Evans) *chsd ldrs over 3f* **28/1**	57
1003	**9**	*2½*	**Christmas Tart (IRE)**[42] 3684 2-8-12 **82**..........................(p) ChrisCatlin 5 (V Smith) *chsd ldrs over 3f* **66/1**	49

1m 13.92s (-1.06) **Going Correction** -0.05s/f (Good) **9** Ran SP% **118.3**
Speed ratings (Par 99):105,104,97,97,94 91,91,84,81
CSF £6.76 TOTE £4.10: £1.40, £1.10, £1.70; EX 9.00.
Owner Setsquare Recruitment **Bred** M P B Bloodstock Ltd **Trained** Newmarket, Suffolk

FOCUS
A fair winning time, even for a race like this, and the front two pulled nicely clear. The form looks quite solid for the grade.

NOTEBOOK
Vital Statistics, a well-experienced and progressive filly whose recent second to Scarlet Runner in the Group 3 Princess Margaret Stakes set the standard, was able to reverse Newmarket form from June with Wid - her saddle slipped that day - finding plenty under pressure and wearing down that rival inside the final half-furlong. She is bred for raw speed, but shapes as though she may get seven furlongs, although the Group 1 Cheveley Park is now her target and she goes there with each-way claims. (op 3-1 tchd 7-2)
Wid(USA) ran out a ready winner of a novice stakes at Haydock and the subsequent impressive win of runner-up La Presse justified her position at the head of the market. She had beaten Vital Statistics at Newmarket earlier in the season, but having gone on racing inside the final quarter mile, she was worn down close home. She remains a smart prospect and may benefit from being ridden with a bit more restraint in future, with a step up to seven furlongs also likely to help. (op 5-4)
Russian Rosie(IRE) won her maiden in good stayle at Newbury latest, but she proved no match for the front pair on this rise in grade and was readily left behind. This earned some valuable black type though and connections will no doubt view this as job done. (op 11-2)
Mimisel had previously finished placed in a couple of reasonable maidens and, although never in the hunt to win the race, she came through late on claim a respectable fourth, reversing earlier Windsor form with Suki Bear in the process. She has yet to win a race, but that should soon be put right on this evidence. (op 25-1)
Bridge It Jo has generally coped well with her forays into Listed company and this was another sound effort considering she was made plenty of use of over a trip probably a shade too far for her. A return to the minimum should see her back winning again. Official explanation: jockey said filly ran too free and hung both ways (op 17-2)
Sama(IRE), whose trainer is not frightened of pitching them in at the deep end on their debuts, was always going to find this an inadequate test, but she shaped remarkably well despite running particularly green and may be worth returning to this level once she has won her maiden, probably over further. (op 33-1)
Suki Bear, a surprise yet quite impressive winner on her debut at Windsor, failed to build on that effort and never threatened to get involved. It was disappointing she could not show more and she now has a bit to prove.

4967 THINK THOROUGHBRED, THINK IRELAND "PERSIAN PUNCH" CONDITIONS STKS 1m 6f 15y

4:50 (4:51) (Class 2) 3-Y-O+

£11,322 (£3,463; £1,784; £945) **Stalls** Far side

Form				RPR
0312	**1**		**Wunderwood (USA)**[30] 4027 7-9-2 104................................. JohnEgan 6 (D R C Elsworth) *trckd ldr: led jst ins fnl 3f: rdn whn strly chal fr 2f out: rdr hit 2nd over hd fnl 110yds: jst hld on* **1/1**[1]	99+
2023	**2**	*nk*	**Collier Hill**[18] 4414 8-9-11 116... DeanMcKeown 4 (G A Swinbank) *3rd tl chsd wnr ins fnl 3f: str chal fr 2f out tl hit over hd fnl 110yds and lost momentum: rallied strly:nt rcvr* **9/4**[2]	108+
50/-	**3**	*20*	**Cave Of The Giant (IRE)**[136] 6149 4-9-2 .... MartinDwyer 1 (T D McCarthy) *led: sn clr: hdd ins fnl 3f: sn lost tch* **50/1**	71?
	4	*17*	**Maraseel (USA)** 3-7-13 .... HayleyTurner 2 (C E Brittain) *hmpd s: v.s.a and bhd: hdwy and rdn 5f out: nvr rchd ldrs: wknd 4f out* **50/1**	42
2451	**U**		**Lightning Strike (GER)**[34] 3888 3-8-6 93......................... SteveDrowne 5 (T G Mills) *whipped rnd and uns rdr s* **10/3**[3]	—

3m 11.32s (5.09) **Going Correction** -0.05s/f (Good)
WFA 3 from 4yo+ 12lb **5** Ran SP% **107.8**
Speed ratings (Par 109):83,82,71,61,—
CSF £3.34 TOTE £2.00: £1.20, £1.40; EX 3.60.
Owner Michael Watt & The Tuesday Syndicate **Bred** Darley Stud Management, L L C **Trained** Newmarket, Suffolk

FOCUS
A controversial contest with third favourite Lightning Strike spooking as the tapes went up and unseating his rider. They did not go very fast in the race and the winning time suffered as a result, with the form not rock solid. Wunderwood just got the better of Collier Hill in the finish, but that may not have been the case had the runner-up not been struck across the nose with the whip.

NOTEBOOK
Wunderwood(USA) has thus far proved to be a good purchase for connections, finishing a gallant second under a big weight at Goodwood and narrowly getting the better of Collier Hill in the finish here, although whether that would have been the case had Egan not accidently struck the runner-up across the nose with his whip is open to serious debate. Nonetheless he showed he is still on the way up at the age of seven and he will now begin his preparation for a crack at the Melbourne Cup, as he is regarded as best fresh. (op 5-4 tchd 11-8 in a place)
Collier Hill is a cracking old performer who has run some good races in defeat this year behind the likes of Heart's Cry and Cherry Mix and he may well have gained a deserved victory had he not been struck across the face with the winning rider's whip. This was a good effort on ground possibly faster than ideal and he may be able to land a similar race later in the season. (op 2-1 tchd 5-2)
Cave Of The Giant(IRE), who is best known as a novice hurdler, was soon in front, but his moment of glory lasted only until around three furlongs out. (op 40-1)
Maraseel(USA), a racecourse debutant, was hampered at the start and it took her a while to get into stride. She never got within touching distance and dropped right away at the end, but this was an impossible ask on her debut and she will face more realistic opportunities in future.
Lightning Strike(GER) looked a lively threat to the 'big two', but he spooked at the start and unshipped his rider. (op 3-1 tchd 11-4)

4968 CHAMPAGNE DUVAL-LEROY H'CAP 1m

5:20 (5:24) (Class 5) (0-70,70) 3-Y-O+

£3,886 (£1,156; £577; £288) **Stalls** Centre

Form				RPR
0022	**1**		**Border Edge**[3] 4879 8-8-13 **59**.. MarcHalford(3) 3 (J J Bridger) *hld up rr but in tch: hdwy on stands side over 2f out: led jst ins last: drvn out* **5/1**[1]	70
0030	**2**	*nk*	**Christmas Truce (IRE)**[13] 4565 7-8-13 **59**................(v) JamesDoyle(3) 8 (Ms J S Doyle) *reminders s: bhd: hday 2f out: n.m.r and swtchd lft to stands side wl over 1f out: str run ins last: a jst hld* **14/1**	69
-005	**3**	*3*	**Dr Thong**[57] 3202 5-9-13 **70**..(t) SteveDrowne 6 (P F I Cole) *rr but in tch: hdwy to chse ldrs 2f out: chal 1f out: outpcd ins last* **10/1**	73
1000	**4**	*nk*	**Luckylover**[29] 4048 3-9-5 **68**... EddieAhern 12 (M G Quinlan) *hld up in rr: rdn and hdwy on far side over 1f out: kpt on but nvr gng pce to rch ldrs* **25/1**	70+
1240	**5**	*¾*	**Deeper In Debt**[26] 4131 8-9-12 **69**...................................... DaneO'Neill 2 (J Akehurst) *chsd ldrs: chal fr 2f out to 1f out: outpcd ins last* **15/2**	70
2210	**6**	*1*	**Carloman**[28] 4076 3-9-2 **65**...(b) MartinDwyer 15 (R M Beckett) *sn led: rdn and hung lft fr centre crse ins fnl 2f: sn narrowly hdd: upsides 1f out: wknd ins last* **13/2**[3]	63
043	**7**	*1¼*	**Treasure House (IRE)**[20] 4325 5-9-9 **66**.......................... TedDurcan 13 (M Blanshard) *s.i.s: sn in tch: chsd ldrs 3f out: slt ld ins fnl 2f tl jst ins last: sn wknd* **7/1**	62
6-06	**8**	*½*	**Wotchalike (IRE)**[18] 4390 4-9-1 **58**.................................... MickyFenton 9 (R J Price) *chsd ldrs: rdn 3f out: one pce fnl 2f* **20/1**	52

00/1 **9** 3/4 **Todlea (IRE)**[21] 4285 6-9-11 **68**....................(t) RichardHughes 7 61
(Jean-Rene Auvray) *hld up in tch: hdwy to chse ldrs whn hmpd ins fnl 2f: stl ev chnace 1f out: sn wknd* **10/1**

0005 **10** 2 **Parnassian**[13] 4575 6-9-10 **67**.................... RichardThomas 16 55
(J A Geake) *bhd: hday to chse ldrs on far side over 2f out: wknd fnl f* **6/1**[2]

0001 **11** shd **Cloud Atlas (IRE)**[8] 4704 3-9-0 **68**.................... NicolPolli(5) 14 56
(S Kirk) *chsd ldrs: chal over 2f out tl over 1f out: wknd qckly* **12/1**

4310 **12** 5 **Life's A Whirl**[31] 4009 4-9-1 **58**....................(p) JohnEgan 11 34
(Mrs C A Dunnett) *chsd ldrs tl wknd over 1f out* **10/1**

1m 42.72s (-0.37) **Going Correction** -0.05s/f (Good)
WFA 3 from 4yo+ 6lb **12** Ran SP% **118.8**
Speed ratings (Par 103):99,98,95,95,94 93,92,91,91,89 89,84
CSF £76.08 CT £681.91 TOTE £4.50: £1.70, £4.70, £3.00; EX 82.00 Place 6 £6.07, Place 5 £2.86.
Owner Allsorts **Bred** R Hutt **Trained** Liphook, Hants

FOCUS
The early pace was ordinary and barely two lengths still covered the whole field passing the two-furlong pole. Those that made their efforts closest to the stands' rail were favoured with the first three home coming widest. Straightforward, modest form.
Christmas Truce(IRE) Official explanation: jockey said gelding missed the break
Carloman Official explanation: jockey said gelding had a breathing problem
T/Jkpt: Not won. T/Plt: £6.40 to a £1 stake. Pool: £65,641.65. 7,389.50 winning tickets. T/Qpdt: £2.40 to a £1 stake. Pool: £2,679.60. 815.70 winning tickets. ST

4932 WOLVERHAMPTON (A.W) (L-H)
Thursday, August 31

OFFICIAL GOING: Standard
Wind: Moderate, behind Weather: Fine

4969 ASDA - BRINGING BETTER VALUE TO WOLVERHAMPTON CLAIMING STKS 5f 216y(P)
7:00 (7:00) (Class 5) 2-Y-O **£3,238** (£963; £481; £240) **Stalls** Low

Form RPR

3300 **1** **Aggbag**[17] 4434 2-8-12 50.................... PaulEddery 10 60
(B P J Baugh) *s.i.s: rdn and hdwy over 1f out: edgd lft and led post* **25/1**

2306 **2** shd **Tokyo Jo (IRE)**[3] 4887 2-8-8 57.................... FrancisNorton 7 56
(K R Burke) *hld up in tch: rdn whn n.m.r jst over 1f out: led nr fin: hdd post* **13/2**

0566 **3** 1/2 **Hephaestus**[16] 4460 2-9-1 72.................... IanMongan 5 61
(M R Channon) *w ldr: rdn 2f out: led over 1f out: sn edgd rt: hdd nr fin* **9/4**[2]

3151 **4** 1/2 **Diamond Hurricane (IRE)**[21] 4284 2-9-6 77.................... DanielTudhope 6 65
(P D Evans) *a.p: rdn over 2f out: kpt on ins fnl f* **15/8**[1]

036 **5** 1 1/4 **Mamora Reef**[52] 3351 2-8-7 74.................... PaulDoe 3 48
(J R Weymes) *led: rdn 2f out: hdd over 1f out: eased whn no ex nr fin* **6/1**[3]

05 **6** 1/2 **Ten Black**[16] 4445 2-9-0.................... JimCrowley 1 53
(J A Osborne) *s.i.s: sn chsng ldrs: rdn over 2f out: one pce fnl f* **16/1**

7 8 **Let's Face It (IRE)** 2-9-6.................... RobbieFitzpatrick 9 35
(Peter Grayson) *s.i.s: rdn 3f out: a bhd* **20/1**

3 **8** 18 **Silver Bolt (IRE)**[10] 4664 2-8-7.................... AshleyHamblett(7) 4 —
(N P Littmoden) *broke wl: sn lost pl and bhd: t.o fnl 2f* **28/1**

1m 15.39s (-0.42) **Going Correction** -0.30s/f (Stan) **8** Ran SP% **111.1**
Speed ratings (Par 94):90,89,89,88,86 86,75,51
CSF £167.55 TOTE £25.00: £4.10, £1.90, £1.90; EX 122.60.
Owner Joe Singh **Bred** D R Tucker **Trained** Audley, Staffs

FOCUS
Probably a moderate claimer, but the standard is hard to assess with career-best form from the winner and some others well below par.

NOTEBOOK
Aggbag has taken time to get over being gelded after joining his current stable in June. Due to run in a maiden at Leicester the previous day when the horsebox broke down, that probably proved a blessing in disguise as he got up to spring a surprise on the line. (op 20-1)
Tokyo Jo(IRE), with the visor left off, got pipped on the post on her first run on Polytrack. (op 11-2 tchd 5-1 and 7-1)
Hephaestus ran his best race since winning when last on this surface on his debut at Lingfield back in March. He appreciated the drop in class and looks quite harshly treated in nurseries. (op 11-4)
Diamond Hurricane(IRE), dropped into a claimer for this sand debut, is giving the impression that he is now ready to tackle seven. (op 5-2)
Mamora Reef eventually had to give best after making the running on this return back up to six. (op 9-2 tchd 13-2)
Ten Black fared better on this drop in grade but his breeding suggests he needs further. (op 14-1)

4970 ASDA - OUR PEOPLE MAKE THE DIFFERENCE H'CAP 5f 216y(P)
7:30 (7:31) (Class 6) (0-60,60) 3-Y-O+ **£2,730** (£806; £403) **Stalls** Low

Form RPR

0234 **1** **Caustic Wit (IRE)**[11] 4629 8-8-13 **58**....................(p) TolleyDean(7) 3 67
(M S Saunders) *chsd ldrs: rdn over 2f out: led wl over 1f out: r.o* **5/1**[1]

6000 **2** 1/2 **Million Percent**[4] 4846 7-9-8 **60**.................... FergusSweeney 9 68
(C R Dore) *hld up in mid-div: hdwy on outside over 3f out: rdn and ev ch over 1f out: r.o* **8/1**

4602 **3** nk **Miskina**[20] 4329 5-9-3 **55**.................... DanielTudhope 4 62
(W M Brisbourne) *prom: hmpd and lost pl sn after s: hdwy on ins over 2f out: rdn over 1f out: nt qckn ins fnl f* **7/1**[3]

0203 **4** nk **Desert Opal**[7] 4735 6-9-8 **60**.................... AlanDaly 7 66
(C R Dore) *chsd ldrs: rdn over 1f out: r.o one pce fnl f* **6/1**[2]

3020 **5** 1 **Val De Maal (IRE)**[18] 4401 6-9-8 **60**....................(b) FrancisNorton 5 63
(Miss J A Camacho) *hld up towards rr: hdwy over 2f out: rdn over 1f out: nt rch ldrs* **9/1**

3504 **6** nk **Gone'N'Dunnett (IRE)**[4] 4846 7-9-1 **60**....................(p) KirstyMilczarek(7) 12 62
(Mrs C A Dunnett) *mde most: hdd wl over 1f out: fdd ins fnl f* **8/1**

000 **7** 1 1/2 **Lifted Way**[22] 4248 7-9-5 **57**.................... JimCrowley 10 54
(P R Chamings) *t.k.h in tch: rdn over 2f out: wknd ins fnl f* **33/1**

3030 **8** nk **Mill By The Stream**[18] 4389 4-9-3 **58**.................... AmirQuinn(3) 6 54
(R Brotherton) *prom: hmpd and lost pl sn after s: nvr nrr* **16/1**

0410 **9** 3/4 **Kahlua Bear**[13] 4564 4-8-13 **54**....................(v) AdamKirby(3) 2 48
(Miss K B Boutflower) *hmpd sn after s: n.d* **14/1**

0121 **10** 2 **Limonia (GER)**[13] 4554 4-8-11 **56**.................... AshleyHamblett(7) 11 44
(N P Littmoden) *prom tl wknd over 2f out* **5/1**[1]

6440 **11** 1 1/4 **Renegade (IRE)**[13] 4564 5-9-3 **55**....................(b) IanMongan 1 39
(Mrs L J Mongan) *sn prom: w ldr over 3f out: rdn over 2f out: wknd over 1f out* **16/1**

4300 **12** 2 **Night Rainbow (IRE)**[8] 4710 3-9-2 **57**.................... PatCosgrave 8 35
(C Tinkler) *prom tl rdn and wknd 2f out* **33/1**

00-0 **13** 5 **Globe Trekker (USA)**[8] 4691 4-9-3 **55**....................(b[1]) RobbieFitzpatrick 13 18
(Peter Grayson) *s.i.s: a in rr: eased whn no ch ins fnl f* **50/1**

1m 14.09s (-1.72) **Going Correction** -0.30s/f (Stan)
WFA 3 from 4yo+ 3lb **13** Ran SP% **118.6**
Speed ratings (Par 101):99,98,97,97,96 95,93,93,92,89 88,85,78
CSF £43.60 CT £292.75 TOTE £5.20: £2.40, £3.40, £2.90; EX 53.90.
Owner Mrs Sandra Jones **Bred** Gainsborough Stud Management Ltd **Trained** Green Ore, Somerset
■ Stewards' Enquiry : Kirsty Milczarek three-day ban: careless riding (Sep 11-13); one-day ban: failed to keep straight from stalls (Sep 14)

FOCUS
A typically competitive low-grade sprint handicap. Ordinary but sound form.
Mill By The Stream Official explanation: jockey said gelding was hampered shortly after start
Renegade(IRE) Official explanation: jockey said gelding hung right-handed

4971 ASDA - SERVING OUR LOCAL COMMUNITY FILLIES' (S) STKS 5f 20y(P)
8:00 (8:01) (Class 6) 2-Y-O **£2,388** (£705; £352) **Stalls** Low

Form RPR

000 **1** **Peggy's Pearl**[1] 4926 2-8-9....................(p) AdamKirby(3) 2 53
(J S Moore) *chsd ldrs: rdn over 1f out: led wl ins fnl f: r.o* **6/1**

1064 **2** nk **Suzieblue (IRE)**[23] 4222 2-9-3 52....................(b) ChrisCatlin 9 57
(J S Moore) *led: rdn over 1f out: hdd wl ins fnl f: kpt on* **10/1**

1220 **3** 3 **Granny Peel (IRE)**[19] 4376 2-9-0 64.................... DNolan(3) 6 46
(M Brittain) *a.p: rdn 2f out: hung lft over 1f out: wknd ins fnl f* **7/4**[1]

6310 **4** 3 1/2 **Diminuto**[8] 4699 2-9-3 57.................... HayleyTurner 3 34
(M D I Usher) *prom tl rdn and wknd over 2f out* **11/4**[2]

5 1 **Weet In Line** 2-8-12.................... FergusSweeney 10 25
(R Hollinshead) *s.i.s: hdwy on outside over 3f out: rdn 2f out: wknd jst over 1f out* **16/1**

53 **6** 4 **Porjenski**[20] 4327 2-8-9.................... AmirQuinn(3) 7 11
(A B Haynes) *nvr nr ldrs* **5/1**[3]

000 **7** 1 3/4 **Rubber Duck (IRE)**[26] 4138 2-8-12....................(b[1]) RobbieFitzpatrick 4 —
(Peter Grayson) *a bhd* **33/1**

0 **8** 2 **Answer Back**[108] 1744 2-8-5.................... JosephWalsh(7) 5 —
(Miss J R Tooth) *s.i.s: a bhd* **100/1**

00 **9** 3 1/2 **Kyoto City**[57] 3188 2-8-12.................... PaulQuinn 1 —
(D W Chapman) *mid-div: nt clr run on ins 3f out: sn bhd* **66/1**

62.39 secs (-0.43) **Going Correction** -0.30s/f (Stan) **9** Ran SP% **114.4**
Speed ratings (Par 89):91,90,85,80,78 72,69,66,60
CSF £62.24 TOTE £8.20: £3.00, £1.80, £1.10; EX 52.00.The winner was sold to Claes Bjorling for 5,000gns.
Owner Michael Hyde **Bred** M Hyde And S Millard **Trained** Upper Lambourn, Berks
■ Stewards' Enquiry : Chris Catlin two-day ban: used whip with excessive force (Sep 11-12)

FOCUS
An ordinary seller. A career-best run from the winner but some of her rivals were well off their best form.

NOTEBOOK
Peggy's Pearl was tried in cheekpieces after apparently failing to stay six furlongs in similar company at Lingfield the previous day. She just got the better of her stable companion and after subsequently changing hands for 5,000gns she now seems destined to race in Sweden. (op 4-1)
Suzieblue(IRE) has alternated between blinkers and cheekpieces in her last few starts. She could not quite hold her stablemate on this All-Weather debut. (op 9-1)
Granny Peel(IRE), claimed when finishing lame at Redcar last time, appeared someway below her best on this first outing for her new stable. (op 11-8 tchd 15-8)
Diminuto had finished three lengths ahead of the runner-up on 5lb better terms when landing a fast-ground Bath seller earlier in the month. (op 9-2)
Weet In Line, a half-sister to six- and seven-furlong winner Weet Watcher, was starting her career in the basement level. (op 25-1)

4972 ASDA - BRITAIN'S LOWEST PRICE RETAILER H'CAP 1m 4f 50y(P)
8:30 (8:30) (Class 5) (0-70,68) 3-Y-O+ **£3,886** (£1,156; £577; £288) **Stalls** Low

Form RPR

0555 **1** **Airbound (USA)**[18] 4402 3-9-4 **66**.................... IanMongan 6 73
(M Johnston) *chsd ldr: rdn over 3f out: led over 2f out: drvn out* **7/1**

3263 **2** 3/4 **Sgt Schultz (IRE)**[7] 4730 3-9-6 **68**.................... FrancisNorton 1 74
(J S Moore) *t.k.h: a.p: rdn to chse wnr 2f out: edgd rt over 1f out: kpt on ins fnl f* **5/1**[3]

6632 **3** 2 1/2 **Will Be (IRE)**[8] 4700 3-9-3 **65**....................(tp) FJohansson 5 67
(R A Kvisla) *hld up and bhd: rdn and hdwy overn 2f out: one pce fnl f* **8/1**

-114 **4** 1 1/4 **Sovereign Spirit (IRE)**[189] 491 4-9-11 **66**....................(t) AdamKirby(3) 4 66
(W R Swinburn) *hld up in mid-div: hdwy over 4f out: rdn over 2f out: btn whn edgd lft 1f out* **7/4**[1]

0250 **5** 1 3/4 **Birthday Star (IRE)**[8] 4702 4-9-9 **61**.................... TPQueally 7 58
(W J Musson) *hld up: rdn and hdwy over 2f out: no further prog* **13/2**

0000 **6** 2 **Western Roots**[19] 4368 5-9-11 **63**.................... AlanDaly 8 57
(M Appleby) *s.s: bhd: rdn 2f out: nvr trbld ldrs* **33/1**

0000 **7** 2 1/2 **Archivist (IRE)**[13] 4556 3-8-2 **50**.................... ChrisCatlin 9 40
(M Blanshard) *hld up in tch: rdn whn n.m.r 3f out: sn wknd* **40/1**

00/0 **8** 7 **Medalla (FR)**[28] 4068 6-9-0 **55**.................... DNolan(3) 2 34
(M Brittain) *led: rdn and hdd over 2f out: sn wknd* **66/1**

3364 **U** **Kinvara Lass (IRE)**[29] 4044 3-8-13 **68**.................... AshleyHamblett(7) 3 —
(L M Cumani) *hld up in mid-div: broke leg and uns rdr 4f out: dead* **9/2**[2]

2m 37.24s (-5.18) **Going Correction** -0.30s/f (Stan)
WFA 3 from 4yo+ 10lb **9** Ran SP% **115.0**
Speed ratings (Par 103):105,104,102,102,100 99,97,93,—
CSF £41.20 CT £287.11 TOTE £8.80: £2.50, £1.10, £2.50; EX 26.60.
Owner Syndicate 2004 **Bred** Dr William O Reed **Trained** Middleham Moor, N Yorks

FOCUS
They did not seem to go any great pace in this modest handicap but the time was decent. The form, rated through the second, does not look that strong.

4973 ASDA - MORE FOR YOU FOR LESS MEDIAN AUCTION MAIDEN STKS 1m 1f 103y(P)
9:00 (9:01) (Class 6) 3-4-Y-O **£3,071** (£906; £453) **Stalls** Low

Form RPR

5652 **1** **Pactolos Way**[19] 4367 3-9-3 64.................... JimCrowley 2 67
(P R Chamings) *hld up in tch: rdn to ld 1f out: r.o wl* **9/1**

4- **2** 1 1/4 **Mantle**[325] 5800 4-9-5.................... IanMongan 5 60
(J R Fanshawe) *hld up in tch: nt clr run and swtchd rt over 1f out: rdn and r.o ins fnl f* **10/1**

463 **3** 1/2 **Casual Affair**[27] 4113 3-9-3 68.................... ChrisCatlin 6 64
(E J O'Neill) *led: rdn and hdd 2f out: ev ch 1f out: nt qckn* **15/2**[3]

2305 **4** 1 1/4 **Great Chieftain (IRE)**[33] 3945 3-9-3 66.................... DaleGibson 8 61
(R A Fahey) *plld hrd in tch: rdn over 2f out: carried rt 1f out: kpt on* **14/1**

6506 **5** *shd* **Semi Detached (IRE)**[15] 4490 3-9-0 70........................ AmirQuinn(3) 12 61
(J R Boyle) *w ldr: rdn to ld 2f out: hdd 1f out: wknd towards fin* **11/1**
6 *½* **Show Winner** 3-9-3 .... TPQueally 3 60+
(J Noseda) *bhd: pushed along early: rdn 3f out: hdwy and hung lft whn nt clr run over 1f out: hung lft ins fnl f: no imp* **6/4**[1]
0-2 **7** *½* **Lucidus**[32] 3987 4-9-10 .... PatCosgrave 10 59
(W J Haggas) *a.p: rdn and ev ch 2f out: edgd rt 1f out: edgd lft ins fnl f: one pce* **6/1**[2]
8 *1¾* **Amron Hill** 3-9-3 .... FergusSweeney 1 56
(R Hollinshead) *hld up in mid-div: rdn and no hdwy fnl 2f* **50/1**
0-5 **9** *1* **Give It Time**[122] 1343 3-8-12 .... JamieMackay 13 49
(J G Given) *swtchd lft sn after s: hld up and bhd: rdn over 2f out: no rspnse* **40/1**
20 **10** *1½* **Medieval Maiden**[10] 4661 3-8-12 .... FrancisNorton 9 46
(W J Musson) *s.i.s: rdn over 2f out: a bhd* **9/1**
0000 **11** *5* **Prima Markova**[15] 4489 3-8-9 45.......................................(t) AdamKirby(3) 11 37
(D J Daly) *swtchd lft sn after s: rdn 3f out: a in rr* **100/1**
0604 **12** *shd* **Lady Duxyana**[21] 4304 3-8-12 42.................................(v[1]) HayleyTurner 4 36
(M D I Usher) *s.s: rdn 3f out: a in rr* **66/1**

1m 59.32s (-3.30) **Going Correction** -0.30s/f (Stan)
WFA 3 from 4yo 7lb 12 Ran SP% **117.0**
Speed ratings (Par 101):102,100,100,99,99 98,98,96,95,94 90,90
CSF £93.27 TOTE £10.90: £3.40, £3.50, £1.10; EX 77.40.
Owner Mrs Alexandra J Chandris **Bred** Mrs J Chandris **Trained** Baughurst, Hants

FOCUS
The track record was broken by 0.29 seconds after three new marks had been set at the course the previous day. Probably a modest maiden, rated around the third.
Show Winner Official explanation: jockey said colt ran green

4974 ASDA - WE'RE ALWAYS HAPPY TO HELP H'CAP 1m 141y(P)
9:30 (9:30) (Class 6) (0-55,55) 3-Y-0+ **£2,730** (£806; £403) **Stalls** Low

Form RPR
3226 **1** **Diamond Dan (IRE)**[13] 4565 4-9-5 53.......................... DanielTudhope 7 61+
(P D Evans) *s.i.s: hld up and bhd: stdy hdwy over 2f out: rdn wl over 1f out: r.o wl to ld last strides* **6/1**[3]
00-0 **2** *hd* **Newcorp Lad**[125] 1276 6-9-5 53..................................... FrancisNorton 13 61
(Mrs G S Rees) *led: rdn wl over 1f out: hdd last strides* **20/1**
0406 **3** *¾* **Gem Bien (USA)**[17] 4439 8-9-5 53....................................(b) PaulQuinn 3 59
(D W Chapman) *t.k.h in tch: rdn 2f out: ev ch ins fnl f: nt qckn* **16/1**
6432 **4** *nk* **Spark Up**[45] 3599 6-9-3 54.....................................(b) StephenDonohoe(3) 5 60
(J W Unett) *hld up in mid-div: hdwy over 2f out: sn rdn: ev ch ins fnl f: nt qckn* **6/1**[3]
66-0 **5** *½* **Danzar**[34] 3909 4-8-13 50.. DNolan(3) 2 55
(M Brittain) *hld up in mid-div: rdn and hdwy on ins wl over 1f out: kpt on same pce fnl f* **40/1**
0560 **6** *2* **Seldemosa**[3] 4869 5-9-6 54.. RobbieFitzpatrick 6 55
(M S Saunders) *a.p: wnt 2nd 4f out: rdn over 2f out: wknd wl ins fnl f* **20/1**
4301 **7** *nk* **Harare**[17] 4439 5-8-9 50..(b) WilliamCarson(7) 4 50
(R J Price) *bhd: hit rails bnd 7f out: rdn over 1f out: kpt on ins fnl f: nvr nrr* **5/1**[2]
P206 **8** *hd* **La Viola**[7] 4726 4-9-7 55...(p) PatCosgrave 1 54
(K R Burke) *broke wl: sn bhd: rdn over 2f out: sme hdwy on ins whn swtchd rt over 1f out: nvr trbld ldrs* **22/1**
1000 **9** *½* **Sonderborg**[18] 4405 5-9-2 50..(p) DaleGibson 9 48
(J Mackie) *hld up towards rr: hdwy on outside 4f out: rdn and wknd over 2f out* **25/1**
1 **10** *¾* **Dannabelle (IRE)**[12] 4585 6-9-4 52 .... TPQueally 12 49
(John A Quinn, Ire) *hld up: hdwy 4f out: rdn over 2f out: wknd over 1f out* **11/4**[1]
0024 **11** *shd* **Balerno**[10] 4667 7-9-7 55 .... PaulEddery 10 52
(Mrs L J Mongan) *t.k.h: prom: rdn over 2f out: wknd fnl f* **14/1**
0330 **12** *1½* **Damburger Xpress**[22] 4266 4-9-3 51.................................. ChrisCatlin 11 45
(D M Simcock) *a towards rr* **9/1**
0250 **13** *dist* **Cavan Gael (FR)**[13] 4575 4-9-2 53 .... DeanCorby(3) 8 —
(P Howling) *chsd ldr tl rdn and wknd rapidly 4f out: t.o: b.b.v* **25/1**

1m 50.05s (-1.71) **Going Correction** -0.30s/f (Stan) 13 Ran SP% **118.5**
Speed ratings (Par 101):95,94,94,93,93 91,91,91,90,90 90,88,—
CSF £126.12 CT £1884.60 TOTE £7.90: £3.30, £5.80, £3.70; EX 327.40 Place 6 £542.86, Place 5 £231.43.
Owner Diamond Racing Ltd **Bred** Golden Vale Stud **Trained** Pandy, Abergavenny

FOCUS
A modest winning time for a slowly-run, low-grade affair. The bare form is modest too, rated through the runner-up and fourth.
Danzar Official explanation: jockey said gelding was short of room final furlong
Cavan Gael(FR) Official explanation: jockey said colt bled from the nose
T/Plt: £188.50 to a £1 stake. Pool: £67,988.35. 263.25 winning tickets. T/Qpdt: £20.10 to a £1 stake. Pool: £5,068.00. 185.80 winning tickets. KH

4975 - 4978a (Foreign Racing) - See Raceform Interactive

3887 CHANTILLY (R-H)
Thursday, August 31
OFFICIAL GOING: Good to soft

4979a PRIX DE TOURELLES (LISTED RACE) (F&M) 1m 4f
2:50 (2:50) 3-Y-0+ **£17,241** (£6,897; £5,172; £3,448; £1,724)

RPR
1 **Acts Of Grace (USA)**[15] 4482 3-8-7 .... DBonilla 7 104
(J L Dunlop) *held up in 5th, switched outside 1 1/2f out, headway to lead 140 yards out, pushed out (19/2)* **19/2**[1]
2 *2* **First Charm (FR)**[137] 6492 4-9-3 .... DBoeuf 5 101
(G Cherel, France)
3 *nk* **Macleya (GER)**[35] 4-9-3 .... JVictoire 4 101
(A Fabre, France)
4 *snk* **Afaf (FR)**[72] 4-9-3 .... FSpanu 3 101
(M Delzangles, France)
5 *4* **Premiere Note**[113] 3-8-7 .... OPeslier 6 95
(A Fabre, France)
6 *6* **Histoire De Moeurs (FR)**[25] 4192 3-8-7 .... TThulliez 2 86
(Y De Nicolay, France)
7 *½* **Zayanida (IRE)**[30] 3-8-7 .... CSoumillon 1 85
(A De Royer-Dupre, France)

2m 30.8s
WFA 3 from 4yo 10lb 7 Ran SP% **9.5**
PARI-MUTUEL: WIN 10.50; PL 5.30, 6.00; SF 181.40.
Owner Prince A A Faisal **Bred** Nawara Stud **Trained** Arundel, W Sussex

NOTEBOOK
Acts Of Grace(USA) made her challenge up the centre of the track and quickened impressively inside the final furlong. Her rivals were made to look rather ordinary and the Princess Royal Stakes at Ascot is now on the cards for this improving filly.

4866 CHEPSTOW (L-H)
Friday, September 1
OFFICIAL GOING: Good
Wind: Moderate, across

4980 32RED.COM MAIDEN AUCTION STKS 1m 14y
2:20 (2:21) (Class 6) 2-Y-O **£2,914** (£867; £433; £216) **Stalls** High

Form RPR
1 **Tembanee (IRE)** 2-9-2 .... PatDobbs 5 74
(R Hannon) *hld up: hdwy 2f out: rdn to ld jst ins fnl f: styd on* **6/1**[3]
4 **2** *1* **Aussie Cricket (FR)**[24] 4221 2-8-8 .... EdwardCreighton(3) 10 67
(D J Coakley) *sn led: t.k.h: hdd 2f out: rallied ins fnl f* **10/3**[2]
6 **3** *1½* **Annual Event (IRE)**[36] 3878 2-8-11 .... RichardMullen 9 64
(E J O'Neill) *a in tch: rdn to ld 2f out: edgd lft and hdd jst ins fnl f: no ex and lost 2nd* **9/4**[1]
556 **4** *5* **Poyle Kiera**[19] 4394 2-8-4 .... FrankieMcDonald 1 46
(M Blanshard) *in tch: rdn over 1f out: no ex* **14/1**
5 *½* **Sosueme Now** 2-8-6 .... LPKeniry 4 46
(A B Haynes) *slowly away: sn mid-div: lost tch w ldrs 2f out* **25/1**
4606 **6** *hd* **Fasuby (IRE)**[4] 4866 2-8-6 54 ow1................... StephenDonohoe(3) 3 49
(P D Evans) *chsd ldrs: rdn over 2f out: sn wknd* **7/1**
56 **7** *¾* **Hocinail (FR)**[32] 4008 2-8-13 .... JimCrowley 11 51
(P Winkworth) *trckd ldr to over 2f out: sn wknd* **25/1**
00 **8** *2½* **Iron Dancer (IRE)**[18] 4433 2-8-11 .... FergusSweeney 7 44
(P A Blockley) *mid-div: rdn 1/2-way: sn bhd* **66/1**
050 **9** *¾* **Pace Telecom Flyer (IRE)**[14] 4566 2-8-11 .... ChrisCatlin 6 42
(J W Hills) *in tch tl rdn and wknd 1/2-way* **12/1**
10 *5* **Grand Officer (IRE)** 2-8-11 .... MickyFenton 8 31
(D J S Ffrench Davis) *a outpcd in rr* **9/1**
0 **11** *hd* **Acosta**[15] 4526 2-8-9 .... RichardThomas 2 29
(Dr J R J Naylor) *outpcd: a bhd* **66/1**

1m 35.99s (-0.01) **Going Correction** -0.175s/f (Firm) 11 Ran SP% **115.7**
Speed ratings (Par 93):93,92,90,85,85 84,84,81,80,75 75
CSF £25.13 TOTE £6.90: £2.80, £1.10, £1.50; EX 26.60 Trifecta £66.50 Pool: £350.69 - 3.74 winning tickets..
Owner A J Ilsley **Bred** Newberry Stud Company **Trained** East Everleigh, Wilts

FOCUS
Just an average juvenile maiden which saw the first three come clear. The second and sixth set the standard.

NOTEBOOK
Tembanee(IRE), a half-brother to Bayeux De Moi, who won over this trip at two, proved green in the preliminaries yet that was not enough to stop him making a winning debut. He took time to find his stride, but picked up nicely as he got the hang of things and had the race in the bag entering the final furlong. (op 8-1)
Aussie Cricket(FR), taken off her feet over five furlongs on debut 24 days previously, deserves credit as she ran very freely in front through the early parts yet was coming back at the winner close home. This proved she stays all of a mile, and she deserves to go one better now. (op 2-1)
Annual Event(IRE), sixth on debut at York 36 days previously, had very much the run of the race yet ultimately failed to see out the extra furlong as well as the first two. She is probably more of a nursery type and will be qualified for that sphere after her next outing. (op 7-2)
Poyle Kiera ran close to her recent level in defeat and helps to set the standard of this form. (op 20-1)
Iron Dancer(IRE) Official explanation: jockey said colt was hampered at start
Grand Officer(IRE) Official explanation: jockey said gelding hung right-handed

4981 VARIETY CLUB CLAIMING STKS 1m 4f 23y
2:50 (2:53) (Class 6) 3-Y-0+ **£2,590** (£770; £385; £192) **Stalls** Low

Form RPR
00-0 **1** **Moonshine Bill**[9] 4709 7-8-12 43.................................... MatthewHenry 1 54
(P W Hiatt) *mde all: rdn over 1f out: drvn out fnl f* **25/1**
0200 **2** *hd* **Yenaled**[4] 4869 9-9-2 50.. SteveDrowne 7 58
(J M Bradley) *mid-div: hdwy to chse wnr over 2f out: kpt on ins fnl f: no imp cl home* **8/1**
0/00 **3** *1* **Zibeline (IRE)**[10] 4676 9-9-10 77.. GeorgeBaker 9 64
(B Ellison) *in rr: hdwy over 3f out: edgd rt and no ex ins fnl f* **7/4**[1]
0553 **4** *3½* **Tuscany Rose**[18] 4435 3-8-2 41 .... HayleyTurner 13 46
(W R Muir) *in rr: swtchd rt over 4f out: styd on one pce after but nvr nr to chal* **25/1**
0000 **5** *1¼* **Lanfredo**[9] 4700 3-8-5 52...(b) ChrisCatlin 4 47
(D W P Arbuthnot) *prom: rdn over 2f out: n.d after* **66/1**
0040 **6** *4* **Ulshaw**[45] 3616 9-9-0 36 .... RoystonFfrench 8 40
(J M Bradley) *hld up: rdn 4f out: no hdwy after* **40/1**
0366 **7** *1* **Is**[22] 4304 3-7-9 36.. DominicFox(3) 10 32
(Rae Guest) *in tch: rdn 4f out: sn btn* **66/1**
0020 **8** *1* **Gateland**[7] 4758 3-8-10 60 .... StephenDonohoe(3) 3 45
(B J Llewellyn) *chsd ldrs tl rdn and wknd 3f out* **16/1**
0336 **9** *½* **Khanjar (USA)**[14] 4544 6-8-13 67.. AndrewElliott(5) 6 40
(K R Burke) *mid-div: wknd wl over 2f out* **2/1**[2]
0045 **10** *1½* **Akritas**[50] 3452 5-9-12 69..(bt) PatDobbs 2 46
(P F I Cole) *trckd wnr tl rdn and wknd qckly over 2f out* **7/1**[3]
0/0- **11** *10* **Batchworth Beau**[472] 1788 5-9-2 39..................................... LPKeniry 12 20
(A M Hales) *hld up: effrt on ins whn short of room over 4f out: sn btn* **150/1**
0 **12** *3½* **Peachy Pear**[65] 2970 3-8-0 ow1........................... EdwardCreighton(3) 11 10
(Mrs L J Young) *a bhd* **50/1**
650- **13** *4* **Dubai Dreams**[10] 6587 6-8-12 48.............................(bt) FergusSweeney 5 4
(M Sheppard) *in rr: rdn 5f out: sn wknd* **33/1**

2m 35.81s (-2.91) **Going Correction** -0.175s/f (Firm)
WFA 3 from 5yo+ 9lb 13 Ran SP% **117.9**
Speed ratings (Par 101):102,101,101,98,98 95,94,94,93,92 86,83,81
CSF £202.45 TOTE £28.90: £5.40, £1.90, £1.10; EX 316.20 TRIFECTA Not won..
Owner Mrs Lucia Stockley & Ken Read **Bred** Lawrence Shepherd **Trained** Hook Norton, Oxon

FOCUS
A very weak affair in which the form horses were not at their best, run at an uneven pace. The first three came clear.

The Form Book, Raceform Ltd, Compton, RG20 6NL

4982 KELLANDS H'CAP 1m 2f 36y
3:25 (3:27) (Class 6) (0-65,65) 3-Y-0+ £3,238 (£963; £481; £240) Stalls Low

Form RPR
0513 1 Jackie Kiely[10] 4673 5-9-10 62 (t) RoystonFfrench 6 70
(R Brotherton) hld up: hdwy over 3f out: led appr fnl f: r.o wl 9/2[1]
0140 2 2 Factual Lad[10] 4673 8-9-8 60 GeorgeBaker 8 65
(B R Millman) a.p: led over 2f out: rdn and hd appr fnl f: nt pce of wnr 14/1
4613 3 2 ½ Greenmeadow[6] 4820 4-9-6 58 LPKeniry 15 59
(S Kirk) mid-div: hdwy 3f out: kpt on one pce fnl 2f 9/2[1]
/000 4 3 ½ Billy Bathwick (IRE)[4] 4869 9-8-4 49 oh3 BarrySavage(7) 10 44
(J M Bradley) mid-div: rdn and hdwy over 2f out: one pce fnl f 33/1
306- 5 nk Gold Guest[313] 5281 7-9-2 57 StephenDonohoe(3) 11 52
(P D Evans) v.s.a: wl in rr: rdn and hdwy over 2f out: nvr nr to chal 12/1
506 6 nk Lady Cree (IRE)[12] 4627 3-9-3 62 (p) RichardMullen 2 56
(W R Muir) in tch: rdn 3f out: wknd over 1f out 20/1
0600 7 ¾ Louise Dupin (IRE)[16] 4483 3-8-9 54 FergusSweeney 14 47
(R M Beckett) in rr: styd on one pce ins fnl 2f 33/1
0302 8 ¾ Double Spectre (IRE)[16] 4483 4-9-11 63 SteveDrowne 5 55
(Jean-Rene Auvray) slowly away: hdwy on ins over 4f out: wknd over 1f out 6/1[2]
0542 9 ½ Roya[15] 4533 3-9-6 65 PatDobbs 7 56
(R Hannon) towards rr: hdwy on ins 4f out: wknd 2f out 8/1
6043 10 6 Henchman[16] 4483 3-8-8 58 (b) AndrewElliott(5) 16 39
(Lady Herries) racd wd: disp ld tl wknd over 2f out 8/1
0604 11 nk Zed Candy (FR)[12] 4635 3-9-5 64 MickyFenton 9 45
(J T Stimpson) a towards rr 25/1
0-50 12 nk Annies Valentine[50] 3451 3-8-1 49 oh9 EdwardCreighton(3) 13 29
(J Gallagher) mid-div tl lost tch 3f out 66/1
0365 13 5 Monte Mayor Junior[11] 4662 3-8-11 56 (v) FrankieMcDonald 12 28
(D Haydn Jones) trckd ldrs: rdn and hung lft fr 2f out: hit rail and nt rcvr 20/1
00 14 nk Generous Lad (IRE)[11] 1738 3-9-2 61 JimCrowley 1 33
(Miss J S Davis) disp ld: dropped out qckly over 2f out 33/1
6055 15 3 Ronsard (IRE)[9] 4709 4-9-3 55 (v[1]) RobbieFitzpatrick 4 22
(T J Pitt) slowly away: sn in tch: wknd wl over 3f out 15/2[3]
50-0 16 24 Indian Dawn (IRE)[21] 4325 3-8-4 49 oh5 ChrisCatlin 3 —
(T H Caldwell) a in rr 100/1

2m 9.16s (-0.74) **Going Correction** -0.175s/f (Firm)
WFA 3 from 4yo+ 7lb 16 Ran SP% 123.7
Speed ratings (Par 101):95,93,91,88,88 88,87,86,86,81 81,81,77,77,74 55
CSF £64.47 CT £308.89 TOTE £5.00: £1.90, £3.40, £2.60, £4.40; EX 49.70 Trifecta £177.10 Part won. Pool: £249.53 - 0.84 winning tickets..
Owner P S J Croft **Bred** Mrs M Chaworth Musters **Trained** Elmley Castle, Worcs

FOCUS
A moderate handicap and the field finished fairly strung out behind the ready winner, who ran to a marginally higher mark than when winning this in 2005. Sound enough form, but ordinary.
Double Spectre(IRE) Official explanation: jockey said gelding missed the break and was tightened up down the straight
Monte Mayor Junior Official explanation: jockey said gelding hung left-handed

4983 JUBORAJ RESTAURANTS SUPPORTS VARIETY CLUB H'CAP 1m 14y
3:55 (3:57) (Class 6) (0-60,60) 3-Y-0+ £3,044 (£905; £452; £226) Stalls High

Form RPR
0460 1 Primeshade Promise[5] 4845 5-8-10 50 StephenDonohoe(3) 1 63
(J M Bradley) trckd ldrs: rdn and hdwy to ld over 1f out: kpt on wl 14/1
3503 2 1 ¾ Lockstock (IRE)[4] 4871 8-9-5 56 (p) JimCrowley 11 65
(M S Saunders) hld up: rdn and hdwy fr 2f out to chse wnr ins fnl f 7/1[3]
6113 3 ¾ Tequila Sheila (IRE)[5] 4844 4-8-10 52 AndrewElliott(5) 9 59
(K R Burke) prom: led over 3f out: rdn and hdd over 1f out: no ex and lost 2nd ins fnl f 9/2[1]
0042 4 hd Elidore[4] 4871 6-9-7 58 FrancisFerris 4 65
(B Palling) a in tch: chsd ldrs 2f out: nt qckn fnl f 5/1[2]
-400 5 1 ¾ Gnillah[23] 4245 3-9-1 57 RoystonFfrench 15 59
(B W Hills) in tch: rdn 1/2-way and sn hung lft: styd on fnl f 20/1
0630 6 1 Chapter (IRE)[15] 4536 4-9-6 60 (b) AmirQuinn(3) 12 60
(Mrs A L M King) in tch: chsd ldrs over 2f out: wknd over 1f out 16/1
455 7 1 My Michelle[4] 4870 5-9-4 55 AdrianMcCarthy 10 53
(B Palling) in rr whn swtchd rt 2f out: mde sme late hdwy 8/1
0006 8 1 ½ Catherines Cafe (IRE)[15] 4531 3-9-1 57 PaulEddery 14 50
(Mrs P N Dutfield) nvr bttr than mid-div 33/1
3205 9 nk Foolish Groom[4] 4871 5-9-8 59 (v) LPKeniry 2 53
(R Hollinshead) racd on outside: hdwy to chse ldrs over 3f out: wknd 2f out 12/1
0000 10 nk Tregarron[4] 4870 5-9-7 58 ChrisCatlin 16 51
(P A Blockley) rdn 3f out: a towards rr 16/1
3100 11 nk Orpen Quest (IRE)[5] 4845 4-9-2 58 (v) KevinGhunowa(5) 6 50
(M J Attwater) prom on outside tl rdn and wknd sn after 1/2-way 22/1
1640 12 shd The Great Delaney[19] 4405 3-9-2 58 RobbieFitzpatrick 7 49
(T J Pitt) chsd ldrs tl wknd 2f out 16/1
0056 13 1 ¾ Danzare[17] 4446 4-9-1 52 SteveDrowne 8 40
(Mrs A J Hamilton-Fairley) in tch tl wknd 3f out 20/1
0145 14 ¾ Dancing Storm[12] 4627 3-9-2 58 FergusSweeney 3 43
(W S Kittow) led tl rdn and hdd over 3f out: sn wknd 9/1
15 12 Lighted Smile (FR)[69] 3-8-10 57 LiamJones(5) 13 15
(C J Gray) in tch tl wknd 3f out 50/1

1m 34.61s (-1.39) **Going Correction** -0.175s/f (Firm)
WFA 3 from 4yo+ 5lb 15 Ran SP% 119.2
Speed ratings (Par 101):99,97,96,96,94 93,92,91,90,90 90,90,88,87,75
CSF £99.83 CT £533.91 TOTE £13.00: £8.90, £3.20, £2.50; EX 220.70 TRIFECTA Not won..
Owner Meelin Racing Syndicate **Bred** Benjamin Collins **Trained** Sedbury, Gloucs

FOCUS
A moderate handicap, but it was run at a fair pace and the form is straightforward enough.

4984 32RED ONLINE CASINO H'CAP 7f 16y
4:30 (4:30) (Class 6) (0-60,60) 3-Y-0+ £3,044 (£905; £452; £226) Stalls High

Form RPR
0500 1 Moon Forest (IRE)[27] 4157 4-8-10 48 (p) StephenDonohoe(3) 9 59
(J M Bradley) mde all: jinked lft u.p jst ins fnl f: r.o wl fnl 100yds 12/1
2652 2 ¾ Only If I Laugh[20] 4363 5-9-4 53 RobbieFitzpatrick 14 62
(M J Attwater) in tch: rdn to chse ldrs over 1f out and sn ev ch: kpt on 7/2[1]
4500 3 2 ½ Zafantage[10] 4671 3-9-7 60 GeorgeBaker 5 61
(S Kirk) in rr hdwy whn nt clr run whn swtchd rt over 2f out: r.o fnl f 12/1
1126 4 shd Baby Barry[5] 4845 9-9-2 56 LiamJones(5) 2 58
(M J Attwater) trckd ldrs: rdn 3f out: nt qckn fnl f 7/1[2]
323 5 ¾ Giverny Spring[20] 4382 3-9-4 57 ChrisCatlin 8 55
(J W Hills) towards rr: rdn 3f out: hdwy over 1f out: nvr nrr 11/1
4360 6 hd Vibe[25] 4211 5-8-12 47 SteveDrowne 10 47
(A W Carroll) towards rr: nt clr run and swtchd lft 2f out: kpt on ins fnl f 8/1[3]
0000 7 3 Arthurs Dream (IRE)[35] 3898 4-8-9 47 JamesDoyle(3) 13 39
(A W Carroll) nvr bttr than mid-div 12/1
000 8 1 Pro Tempore[10] 4675 4-8-12 47 FergusSweeney 16 36
(David Pinder) chsd ldrs tl wknd appr fnl f 50/1
4435 9 ¾ Pink Bay[16] 4484 4-8-9 51 (b) TolleyDean(7) 7 38
(W S Kittow) mid-div: rdn over 3f out: wkng whn carried lft over 1f out 7/1[2]
0-00 10 nk Madam Patti[7] 4756 3-9-0 53 MickyFenton 12 38
(B Palling) prom tl wknd wl over 1f out 40/1
0054 11 1 ½ Buckle And Hyde[21] 4329 3-8-12 51 HayleyTurner 4 32
(Mrs A L M King) a towards rr 25/1
5530 12 ½ Arculinge[9] 4690 3-9-1 54 RoystonFfrench 15 33
(M Blanshard) mid-div: rdn over 3f out: wknd over 1f out 25/1
0006 13 6 Hit's Only Money (IRE)[16] 4496 6-9-6 55 AdrianMcCarthy 11 21
(R A Harris) mid-div: rdn and wknd 2f out 7/1[2]
5050 14 shd Full Spate[4] 4870 11-9-1 57 BarrySavage(7) 3 23
(J M Bradley) mid-div: rdn over 2f out: eased whn btn ins fnl f 25/1
0-00 15 28 Lady Synthia[7] 4756 3-9-7 60 FrancisFerris 6 —
(B Palling) trckd ldrs: rdn 1/2-way: wknd qckly and virtually p.u ins fnl f 80/1

1m 22.32s (-0.98) **Going Correction** -0.175s/f (Firm)
WFA 3 from 4yo+ 4lb 15 Ran SP% 119.4
Speed ratings (Par 101):98,97,94,94,93 93,89,88,87,87 85,85,78,78,46
CSF £49.76 CT £544.40 TOTE £18.40: £4.70, £1.80, £5.00; EX 95.50 Trifecta £188.00 Part won. Pool: £264.84 - 0.30 winning tickets..
Owner Mrs Ann Mooney **Bred** P Conlon And Paul Clarke **Trained** Sedbury, Gloucs

FOCUS
A poor handicap which saw the first two come clear. The winner has slipped a long way and was still way off his old form. The second ran to his all-weather best.

4985 32RED POKER H'CAP 6f 16y
5:00 (5:02) (Class 6) (0-60,60) 3-Y-0+ £3,044 (£905; £452; £226) Stalls High

Form RPR
3550 1 Ten Shun[4] 4870 3-9-1 60 StephenDonohoe(3) 11 71
(P D Evans) mid-div: hdwy over 2f out: rdn to ld wl ins fnl f 14/1
2200 2 1 Cree[20] 4364 4-8-13 53 RichardMullen 8 61
(W R Muir) a.p: rdn to ld over 1f out: hdd wl ins f: no ex 16/1
0334 3 ¾ Stamford Blue[4] 4870 5-8-13 60 (b) TolleyDean(7) 15 66
(R A Harris) outpcd: hdwy 1/2-way: edgd lft over 1f out: kpt on one pce fnl f 9/2[1]
6120 4 2 Peruvian Style (IRE)[14] 4551 5-9-4 58 SteveDrowne 9 58
(J M Bradley) mid-div: rdn and hdwy over 1f out: nt qckn ins fnl f 8/1[3]
006 5 1 ½ Sweetest Revenge (IRE)[17] 4462 5-9-0 54 HayleyTurner 12 49
(M D I Usher) towards rr: rdn and hdwy over 1f out: kpt on one pce ins fnl f 8/1[3]
5560 6 ¾ Cayman Breeze[20] 4365 6-8-11 51 RoystonFfrench 5 44
(J M Bradley) towards rr: mde sme late hdwy 16/1
0050 7 nk Extremely Rare (IRE)[32] 4003 5-9-5 59 MickyFenton 10 51
(M S Saunders) led tl rdn and hdd over 1f out: wknd qckly 12/1
0422 8 ¾ Kitchen Sink (IRE)[12] 4629 4-8-12 52 (e) FergusSweeney 2 42
(P J Makin) chsd ldrs: tl rdn and wknd fnl f 5/1[2]
0203 9 1 ¼ Make My Dream[23] 4242 3-9-4 60 JimCrowley 14 46
(J Gallagher) a towards rr 16/1
0402 10 nk Mostanad[28] 4120 4-8-3 50 BarrySavage(7) 7 35
(J M Bradley) in tch tl rdn 1/2-way: nvr on terms after 25/1
000 11 nk Stokesies Wish[20] 4365 6-8-9 49 ChrisCatlin 16 33
(J L Spearing) in tch tl rdn 1/2-way: sn btn 25/1
1165 12 hd Ballybunion (IRE)[10] 4675 7-9-3 57 AdrianMcCarthy 6 41
(R A Harris) in tch: rdn over 2f out: sn wknd 12/1
0200 13 ½ Gavioli (IRE)[20] 4361 4-8-9 49 LPKeniry 1 31
(J M Bradley) prom on far side tl wknd 2f out 50/1
0015 14 5 Great Belief (IRE)[4] 4872 4-8-13 53 RobbieFitzpatrick 4 20
(T D McCarthy) chsd ldr tl rdn and wknd wl over 1f out 16/1
2000 15 ½ Ruby's Dream[16] 4484 4-8-10 53 (p) AmirQuinn(3) 3 19
(J M Bradley) mid-div: rdn and wknd over 2f out 28/1
6252 16 7 Mannello[65] 2987 3-9-2 58 FrancisFerris 13 3
(B Palling) nvr gng pce: a bhd 16/1

1m 10.52s (-1.88) **Going Correction** -0.175s/f (Firm)
WFA 3 from 4yo+ 2lb 16 Ran SP% 121.6
Speed ratings (Par 101):105,103,102,100,98 97,96,95,93,93 93,92,92,85,84 75
CSF £212.85 CT £1227.91 TOTE £18.70: £4.60, £3.90, £1.80, £2.70; EX 432.20 TRIFECTA Not won. Place 6 £44.10, Place 5 £34.53.
Owner Derek Buckley **Bred** R J Cornelius **Trained** Pandy, Abergavenny

FOCUS
A moderate handicap, but run at a generous early pace. The form looks sound enough.
T/Jkpt: Not won. T/Plt: £27.20 to a £1 stake. Pool: £82,573.60. 2,211.80 winning tickets. T/Qpdt: £13.20 to a £1 stake. Pool: £4,825.50. 270.40 winning tickets. JS

4356 HAYDOCK (L-H)
Friday, September 1

OFFICIAL GOING: Heavy
Race times suggested that the ground was not as bad as the official description might have suggested.
Wind: Light, half-against Weather: Fine

4986 VALE UK E B F MAIDEN STKS 5f
2:30 (2:31) (Class 5) 2-Y-0 £3,886 (£1,156; £577; £288) Stalls Centre

Form RPR
1 Utmost Respect 2-9-3 PaulHanagan 7 79+
(R A Fahey) in tch: led 1f out: edgd lft and sn clr: easily 8/1
2 7 Twitch Hill 2-8-12 DaneO'Neill 3 50
(H Candy) in tch: effrt over 1f out: tk 2nd wl ins fnl f: no ch w wnr 9/2[2]
000 3 nk Vanatina (IRE)[62] 3096 2-8-12 RobertWinston 5 48
(A Bailey) in rr: rdn 1/2-way: sn hung lft: styd on ins fnl f: nt pce to chal 25/1

02U4 **4** *hd* **Princess Ellis**[9] 4693 2-8-12 .... FrancisNorton 6 48
(E J Alston) *racd keenly: led for 1f: remained prom: regained ld under 2f out: hdd 1f out: no ex* **7/1**[3]

5 *1 3/4* **Bungie** 2-9-3 .... EddieAhern 4 47
(Ms Deborah J Evans) *towards rr: rn green: rdn 2f out: kpt on fnl f: nvr able to chal* **8/1**

3 **6** *1/2* **Manhasset Indian (USA)**[18] 4428 2-9-3 .... TPQueally 8 45
(J Noseda) *prom: led after 1f: rdn and hdd under 2f out: sn wknd* **1/1**[1]

00 **7** *1/2* **Misaine (IRE)**[46] 3596 2-9-3 .... PaulMulrennan 2 43
(T J Etherington) *prom: rdn 1/2-way: wknd fnl f* **66/1**

63.82 secs (1.75) **Going Correction** +0.375s/f (Good) 7 Ran SP% **108.2**
Speed ratings (Par 95):101,89,89,89,86 85,84
CSF £38.81 TOTE £10.00: £3.30, £2.20; EX 59.60.
Owner The Rumpole Partnership **Bred** Mrs H B Raw **Trained** Musley Bank, N Yorks

FOCUS
Allowing for the conditions, this was a very smart winning time for a race of its type. It was a case of the winner first, the rest nowhere, but Utmost Respect probably beat little. The ground would have had an effect so it may be unwise to condemn the beaten horses too much. Despite the conditions, previous experience was not an advantage as the first two home were newcomers. The runners came down the centre for much of the journey, but tended to edge over to the far rail in the latter stages.

NOTEBOOK
Utmost Respect ◆, bought by the vendor for just 3,000gns as a foal, is related to useful middle-distance performers Gallery God and St Mawes on the dam's side, so perhaps it was no great surprise that he finished his race so strongly, but what was a surprise was the turn of foot he demonstrated to totally blow this field away and he was even able to ease down in the dying strides. Obviously the testing ground would have counted against some of his rivals, and he might not have had much to beat, but he could hardly have been more impressive and it will be interesting to see if he can perform like this on a sounder surface. (op 12-1 tchd 14-1)
Twitch Hill, a half-sister to High Esteem, Zagala and Make It Happen Now, stayed on against the far rail to win the separate race for second, but the winner was in a different parish. Her pedigree is all speed and she should improve for this initial experience. (op 5-1)
Vanatina(IRE), who has not got within ten lengths of the winner in her three previous outings, on the face of it drags the form right down by making the frame here, but she is bred to be much better than she has shown so far and perhaps she has been waiting for this ground. She would be very interesting in a nursery in similar conditions off a mark of just 50. Official explanation: jockey said filly hung left-handed throughout (op 20-1)
Princess Ellis, the most experienced in the field, mixed it with the favourite for much of the way, but this was the softest ground she has been on and it found her out. (tchd 8-1)
Bungie, a 5,000gns half-brother to four winners including Blue Velvet and Adantino, looked in need of this experience but did show a glimmer of ability. His siblings tended to improve with age so there is hope for him in the longer term. (op 12-1 tchd 15-2 and 14-1 in places)
Manhasset Indian(USA), as on his debut, was given a positive ride and looked to be in control for much of the way, but he suddenly came under pressure entering the last couple of furlongs and fell apart completely. The testing ground may have been the reason for this moderate effort, but he does now have questions to answer. (op 4-6)

4987 GREENE KING IPA E B F MAIDEN STKS 6f
3:00 (3:01) (Class 5) 2-Y-O **£3,886** (£1,156; £577; £288) **Stalls** Centre

Form RPR
23 **1** **Makshoof (IRE)**[31] 4028 2-9-3 .... NCallan 5 77
(M A Jarvis) *mde all: rdn and edgd lft over 1f out: pushed out and kpt on cl home* **1/1**[1]

2 *1 1/4* **Eau Good** 2-9-3 .... KDarley 14 73
(M Johnston) *a.p: rdn and hung lft whn chsd wnr over 1f out: styd on: hld cl home* **8/1**[3]

04 **3** *4* **Tarraburn (USA)**[59] 3173 2-9-3 .... RobertWinston 15 61
(J Howard Johnson) *chsd ldrs: rdn 1/2-way: kpt on ins fnl f: nt pce to trble front pair* **12/1**

0 **4** *hd* **Aquilegia (IRE)**[41] 3721 2-8-12 .... GrahamGibbons 8 55
(E S McMahon) *prom: rdn and edgd lft over 1f out: wknd ins fnl f* **25/1**

000 **5** *1/2* **Rowan Venture**[37] 3844 2-9-3 .... (b) TPQueally 12 59
(M H Tompkins) *chsd ldrs: rdn over 2f out: one pce* **50/1**

0 **6** *5* **Jazzanova**[87] 2321 2-9-3 .... PaulMulrennan 6 44
(M W Easterby) *midfield: rdn 1/2-way: no imp* **100/1**

7 *1/2* **Parisian Dream** 2-9-3 .... MichaelHills 7 42
(B W Hills) *s.v.s: bhd: rdn 1/2-way: sme hdwy over 1f out: n.d* **6/1**[2]

8 *1* **Effigy** 2-9-3 .... DaneO'Neill 10 39
(H Candy) *midfield: rdn 1/2-way: no imp* **8/1**[3]

9 *6* **Milson's Point (IRE)** 2-9-3 .... TomEaves 9 21
(I Semple) *s.s: rn green: a bhd* **33/1**

506 **10** *2* **Avoncreek**[18] 4433 2-9-3 .... DeanMcKeown 1 15
(B P J Baugh) *midfield: wknd over 3f out* **66/1**

11 *7* **Smart Angus** 2-9-3 .... PaulHanagan 3 —
(R A Fahey) *s.s: a bhd* **16/1**

12 *5* **Lady Grey Bear** 2-8-12 .... TonyHamilton 11 —
(R A Fahey) *s.s: a bhd* **16/1**

1m 18.7s (3.80) **Going Correction** +0.425s/f (Yiel) 12 Ran SP% **117.2**
Speed ratings (Par 95):91,89,84,83,83 76,75,74,66,63 54,47
CSF £8.91 TOTE £2.20: £1.20, £2.10, £2.30; EX 13.80.
Owner Hamdan Al Maktoum **Bred** J Egan **Trained** Newmarket, Suffolk

FOCUS
Very few got into this. The principals were all up with the pace throughout, and they appeared to finish pretty tired. As in the first race, the runners raced down the centre before migrating to the far side in the latter stages. Difficult to rate the form highly owing to the proximity of the fifth.

NOTEBOOK
Makshoof(IRE) had the best form and made his experience tell under a positive ride. He did edge left towards the end of the race and finished tired, but always looked to be doing enough to hold off the inexperienced runner-up. His future probably now depends on what nursery mark he gets. (op 11-8 tchd 6-4)
Eau Good ◆, a 32,000gns colt out of a winner at up to nine furlongs, put in a spirited late effort but tended to hang in behind the favourite as he got tired and could never quite get to him. This was a decent debut effort, especially in these conditions, and he should not take long in getting off the mark.
Tarraburn(USA), on much easier ground than in his two previous outings, could not match the front pair in the latter stages, but probably improved again and now qualifies for a mark. (op 16-1)
Aquilegia(IRE), tailed-off last on her debut here in July, performed much better on this very different surface and looks the type to come into her own once handicapped. (op 20-1)
Rowan Venture, who had only beaten a total of four horses in his three previous outings, had been gelded since last seen and was also dropping in trip. He seemed to put up an improved effort, but he raced prominently in a contest that suited those ridden that way and more evidence is needed that the operation has really made that much difference. (op 33-1)
Parisian Dream, a 30,000gns half-brother to Esenin out of the useful Boojum, took an age to leave the stalls and gave his rivals a big start. He was therefore never able to show his true potential and should be given another chance. (op 4-1 tchd 13-2)

4988 VALE UK E B F CLASSIFIED STKS 6f
3:35 (3:35) (Class 3) 3-Y-O+ **£9,715** (£2,890; £1,444; £721) **Stalls** Centre

Form RPR
5152 **1** **Fullandby (IRE)**[13] 4609 4-8-13 87 .... PaulMulrennan 8 98+
(T J Etherington) *dwlt: hld up in tch gng wl: rdn and impr to ld jst over 1f out: edgd rt whn in command ins fnl f: r.o* **4/1**[2]

0215 **2** *1 3/4* **Charles Darwin (IRE)**[13] 4601 3-8-11 89 .... NCallan 6 95+
(M Blanshard) *a.p: led 1/2-way: hdd jst over 1f out: abt a length down and hld whn n.m.r and swtchd lft ins fnl f: nt qckn after* **9/1**

1000 **3** *1* **Commando Scott (IRE)**[69] 2847 5-8-10 90 .... PatrickMathers(3) 3 90
(I W McInnes) *hld up: hdwy 2f out: rdn and edgd rt whn chsd ldrs over 1f out: styd on u.p ins fnl f* **15/2**[3]

1540 **4** *1/2* **Tagula Sunrise (IRE)**[13] 4609 4-8-10 90 .... PaulHanagan 9 86+
(R A Fahey) *in tch: rdn over 2f out: keeping on u.p whn hmpd ins fnl f: no further prog* **4/1**[2]

6006 **5** *1* **Johnston's Diamond (IRE)**[6] 4793 8-8-13 81 .... FrancisNorton 7 86
(E J Alston) *led to 1/2-way: sn rdn: kpt on same pce fnl f* **10/1**

0000 **6** *hd* **Zomerlust**[13] 4609 4-8-13 89 .... GrahamGibbons 5 85
(J J Quinn) *in rr: rdn 1/2-way: kpt on u.p fnl f: nvr able to chal* **7/2**[1]

13/5 **7** *1* **Campo Bueno (FR)**[132] 4-8-13 90 .... KDarley 10 82
(A Berry) *in tch: rdn 2f out: one pce* **20/1**

0-52 **8** *3* **Rainbow Rising (IRE)**[25] 4202 4-8-13 84 .... TomEaves 4 73
(J Howard Johnson) *prom: rdn 2f out: wknd over 1f out* **8/1**

406 **9** *hd* **Art Market (CAN)**[19] 4391 3-8-11 90 .... JoeFanning 2 72
(P F I Cole) *prom: rdn over 2f out: wknd over 1f out* **40/1**

1m 16.59s (1.69) **Going Correction** +0.475s/f (Yiel)
WFA 3 from 4yo+ 2lb 9 Ran SP% **111.4**
Speed ratings (Par 107):107,104,103,102,101 101,99,95,95
CSF £37.55 TOTE £4.00: £1.60, £2.60, £2.70; EX 51.10.
Owner Miss M Greenwood **Bred** Mrs A Haskell Ellis **Trained** Norton, N Yorks
■ Stewards' Enquiry : Paul Mulrennan one-day ban: careless riding (Sep 12)

FOCUS
A decent race of its type, but it would be unwise to go overboard about the form in view of the bad ground. Unlike the two-year-olds in the preceding contests, these older sprinters made straight for the stands' rail after the start and stayed there.

NOTEBOOK
Fullandby(IRE) was by no means best in at these weights, but he does love to get his toe in and he could be spotted travelling supremely well behind the leaders for much of the way. He did not do that much after hitting the front and edged across the runner-up under maximum pressure, but he was definitely the winner on merit. (op 7-2)
Charles Darwin(IRE), one of those most suited by these weights, has only ever won on good or faster ground before now but he has run enough decent races on a softer surface to be sure that he handles it. Up there from the off, he took over at halfway, but after the winner had gone past him a furlong out he firstly had the winning rider's whip flailing in his face and then had to take evasive action when his rival went across him, but in no way did it affect his chances of winning. (op 14-1)
Commando Scott(IRE), on soft ground for the first time since winning at Ayr in May, stayed on in the closing stages, but although he had ideal ground conditions he probably needs a stiffer six or a longer trip in order to show his best. Official explanation: jockey said gelding hung right-handed throughout (tchd 7-1)
Tagula Sunrise(IRE), one of those most favoured by the weights, had suitable ground conditions and was still in there battling when bumped by the runner-up as he took evasive action to avoid the winner. She would not have won, but the interference almost certainly cost her third. (tchd 7-2)
Johnston's Diamond(IRE), who loves this sort of ground, was worst in at these weights, just as he was when winning this race last year. History did not repeat itself though, as despite bagging pole position against the stands' rail early he was just not good enough on this occasion. (op 9-1 tchd 8-1)
Zomerlust, who started favourite after his reasonable effort in the Great St Wilfrid, should have handled the ground but barely went a yard and was nowhere near his best. (tchd 4-1)
Art Market(CAN) was marginally best in at the weights, but that is purely down to the sort of company he kept as a juvenile and this ground would not have done him any favours either. He will remain very hard to place until his official mark drops a lot more. (op 33-1)

4989 KINGS REGIMENT CUP H'CAP 1m 30y
4:05 (4:07) (Class 4) (0-85,83) 3-Y-O+ **£6,477** (£1,927; £963; £481) **Stalls** Low

Form RPR
4202 **1** **Nevada Desert (IRE)**[9] 4696 6-8-10 **68** .... DeanMcKeown 3 79
(R M Whitaker) *a.p: rdn to ld over 1f out: styd on wl* **5/1**[3]

1-00 **2** *3 1/2* **Vanilla Delight (IRE)**[62] 3082 3-8-9 **72** .... RobertWinston 4 75
(J Howard Johnson) *prom: led after 1f: rdn over 2f out: hdd over 1f out: one pce ins fnl f* **33/1**

4010 **3** *1 1/4* **Primo Way**[38] 3812 5-9-9 **81** .... TomEaves 7 83
(I Semple) *hld up: rdn over 2f out: hdwy over 1f out: kpt on ins fnl f: nt rch ldrs* **10/1**

0550 **4** *1 1/2* **Moi Aussi (USA)**[30] 4047 3-9-4 **81** .... JamieMackay 5 79
(Sir Mark Prescott) *midfield: rdn and hdwy over 2f out: no ex ins fnl f* **12/1**

5022 **5** *nk* **Full Victory (IRE)**[9] 4706 4-9-3 **75** .... DaneO'Neill 2 73
(R A Farrant) *racd keenly: in tch: rdn over 2f out: styd on same pce fr over 1f out* **10/3**[2]

0453 **6** *shd* **Merrymadcap (IRE)**[14] 4575 4-9-2 **74** .... FrancisNorton 9 72
(M Blanshard) *in rr: effrt over 2f out: one pce fnl f* **6/1**

2160 **7** *1/2* **Northern Boy (USA)**[45] 3606 3-9-3 **80** .... PhillipMakin 8 77
(T D Barron) *in rr: effrt and swtchd rt over 2f out: nvr able to chal* **8/1**

0256 **8** *5* **Mezuzah**[7] 4760 6-9-3 **75** .... PaulMulrennan 1 62
(M W Easterby) *racd keenly: led for 1f: remained prom: rdn over 2f out: sn wknd* **11/4**[1]

1m 46.49s (0.98) **Going Correction** +0.25s/f (Good)
WFA 3 from 4yo+ 5lb 8 Ran SP% **111.5**
Speed ratings (Par 105):105,101,100,98,98 98,97,92
CSF £132.27 CT £1543.52 TOTE £6.20: £1.60, £4.30, £3.30; EX 82.50.
Owner J Barry Pemberton **Bred** Bryan Ryan **Trained** Scarcroft, W Yorks

FOCUS
The pace was very decent for this handicap, but even so it paid to race handily and nothing could make much impact from off the pace. The winning time was creditable for the grade, given the conditions, and the form looks sound enough.
Full Victory(IRE) Official explanation: trainer said gelding had been struck into
Mezuzah Official explanation: vet said gelding finished distressed

4990 VALE UK H'CAP 1m 3f 200y
4:40 (4:41) (Class 4) (0-85,82) 3-Y-O+ **£6,477** (£1,927; £963; £481) **Stalls** High

Form RPR
4323 **1** **St Savarin (FR)**[12] 4631 5-9-9 **78** .... PaulHanagan 3 95
(R A Fahey) *hld up: hdwy over 2f out: shkn up to ld narrowly 1f out: in command towards fin* **7/2**[2]

2122 **2** *1* **Juniper Girl (IRE)**[7] 4778 3-7-13 **70** LukeMorris(7) 7 86
(M L W Bell) *a.p: rdn to ld over 2f out: edgd lft bef hdd narrowly 1f out: hld towards fin* **11/4**[1]

0131 **3** *10* **Wannabe Posh (IRE)**[55] 3302 3-9-1 **79** EddieAhern 5 81
(J L Dunlop) *hld up: rdn over 3f out: kpt on to take 3rd 1f out: n.d to front pair* **11/4**[1]

1630 **4** *3* **The Composer**[22] 4299 4-9-2 **71** FrancisNorton 1 68
(M Blanshard) *in tch: pushed along 5f out: effrt over 2f out: wknd over 1f out* **8/1**[3]

3403 **5** *2* **Rowan Lodge (IRE)**[17] 4457 4-9-6 **75** (b) TPQueally 6 70
(M H Tompkins) *plld hrd: prom: led over 6f out: rdn and hdd over 2f out: wknd over 1f out* **8/1**[3]

1020 **6** *21* **Aspasias Tizzy (USA)**[12] 4631 3-8-13 **77** KDarley 2 42
(M Johnston) *led: hdd over 6f out: remained prom: rdn over 4f out: wknd over 2f out* **10/1**

15-0 **7** *3 1/2* **Double Deputy (IRE)**[92] 2169 5-9-13 **82** GrahamGibbons 9 42
(J J Quinn) *midfield: pushed along and lost pl 5f out: lft bhd fnl 4f* **25/1**

2m 37.56s (2.57) **Going Correction** +0.30s/f (Good)
WFA 3 from 4yo+ 9lb **7** Ran SP% **110.7**
Speed ratings (Par 105):103,102,95,93,92 78,76
CSF £12.65 CT £27.28 TOTE £4.50: £2.60, £2.10; EX 14.20.
Owner J H Tattersall **Bred** F W Holtkotter **Trained** Musley Bank, N Yorks

FOCUS
The early pace was not at all strong, but things quickened up appreciably in the home straight and the final time was bang on par for a race like this in the conditions. This eventually developed into a duel between the front pair and they pulled miles clear of the others, both recording personal bests.

4991 VALE UK H'CAP (FOR GENTLEMAN AMATEUR RIDERS) 1m 2f 120y
5:10 (5:10) (Class 5) (0-75,73) 3-Y-0+ **£3,123** (£968; £484; £242) **Stalls** High

Form RPR

0104 **1** **Sol Rojo**[15] 4511 4-10-5 **56** oh1 (v) MrSPearce(5) 11 65
(J Pearce) *chsd ldrs: led over 2f out: rdn over 1f out: all out cl home* **7/1**

0500 **2** *3/4* **Scottish River (USA)**[13] 4606 7-11-0 **60** MrLeeNewnes 8 68
(M D I Usher) *dwlt: midfield: hdwy over 4f out: rdn over 2f out: styd on to take 2nd cl home* **9/1**

0545 **3** *1/2* **Gracechurch (IRE)**[16] 4490 3-10-12 **73** MrMDavies(7) 3 80
(M R Channon) *chsd ldrs: lost pl 5f out: rallied to chse wnr over 1f out: no ex and lost 2nd cl home* **7/2**[1]

1133 **4** *nk* **Apsara**[13] 4610 5-11-3 **68** MrSFMagee(5) 5 74
(G M Moore) *led for 1f: remained prom: rdn and ev ch over 2f out: outpcd over 1f out: styd on ins fnl f* **9/2**[2]

4413 **5** *8* **Regal Connection (USA)**[10] 4672 3-11-0 **68** (b) MrSDobson 12 61
(M Johnston) *led after 1f: racd wd on bk st: rdn and hdd over 2f out: wknd fnl f* **8/1**

4020 **6** *3 1/2* **Dower House**[51] 3401 11-11-7 **70** (t) JackMitchell(3) 9 57
(Andrew Turnell) *dwlt: midfield: hdwy on outside over 4f out: rdn and wknd over 1f out* **10/1**

0300 **7** *1 3/4* **Richtee (IRE)**[17] 4451 5-10-11 **62** MrBMcHugh(5) 4 46
(R A Fahey) *chsd ldrs tl rdn and wknd 4f out* **7/1**

2300 **8** *2 1/2* **New England**[14] 4565 4-10-13 **64** MrBenBrisbourne(5) 2 44
(W M Brisbourne) *s.s: in rr: rdn over 2f out: no imp* **25/1**

-256 **9** *5* **Darling Deanie (IRE)**[48] 3547 4-11-8 **68** MrSWalker 7 39
(K A Ryan) *s.s: pushed along over 5f out: a bhd* **11/2**[3]

2m 25.62s (7.89) **Going Correction** +0.35s/f (Good)
WFA 3 from 4yo+ 8lb **9** Ran SP% **114.8**
Speed ratings (Par 103):85,84,84,83,78 75,74,72,68
CSF £67.49 CT £257.72 TOTE £8.50: £2.50, £3.00, £1.70; EX 54.80 Place 6 £226.66, Place 5 £61.11.
Owner sportaracing.com & Lydia Pearce **Bred** Mrs A Yearley **Trained** Newmarket, Suffolk

FOCUS
Rather a messy amateur riders' handicap, with a few getting outpaced at various stages, and the form is probably not that reliable.
T/Plt: £814.00 to a £1 stake. Pool: £66,912.20. 60.00 winning tickets. T/Qpdt: £62.30 to a £1 stake. Pool: £5,536.60. 65.70 winning tickets. DO

4699 KEMPTON (A.W) (R-H)
Friday, September 1

OFFICIAL GOING: Standard
Wind: Light, behind

4992 LONDON WASPS E B F MAIDEN STKS 1m (P)
2:10 (2:11) (Class 4) 2-Y-O **£5,343** (£1,589; £794; £396) **Stalls** High

Form RPR

3 **1** **Monzante (USA)**[42] 3701 2-9-3 RichardHughes 6 86+
(R Charlton) *wl plcd: prog over 2f out: chsd ldr wl over 1f out: pushed into ld 1f out: sn in command* **5/4**[1]

55 **2** *2 1/2* **Maslak (IRE)**[17] 4458 2-9-3 RHills 9 81
(E A L Dunlop) *lw: led: shkn up 2f out: hdd 1f out: kpt on but no ch w wnr* **5/1**[2]

00 **3** *2 1/2* **Furmigadelagiusta**[19] 4388 2-9-3 NickyMackay 5 75
(L M Cumani) *swtg: wl in rr and pushed along 5f out: stdy prog fr 3f out: styd on to take 3rd nr fin* **50/1**

54 **4** *3/4* **Racing Times**[15] 4525 2-9-3 LDettori 3 73
(B J Meehan) *tk fierce hold: hld up tl plld way through to chse ldr over 5f out to wl over 1f out: wknd fnl f* **13/2**[3]

33 **5** *shd* **Fever**[15] 4534 2-9-3 RyanMoore 8 73
(R Hannon) *chsd ldrs: rdn wl over 3f out: outpcd and btn over 2f out: plugged on* **8/1**

6 *2* **Coeur De Lionne (IRE)** 2-9-0 RichardKingscote(3) 1 69
(R Charlton) *str: scope: bkwd: s.s: hld up in last pair: sme prog over 2f out: reminder over 1f out: kpt on: bttr for experience* **33/1**

0 **7** *2* **Spume (IRE)**[19] 4388 2-9-3 JimmyFortune 2 64
(Sir Michael Stoute) *bit bkwd: prom: drvn wl over 2f out: wknd over 1f out* **13/2**[3]

8 *18* **Regal Curtsy** 2-8-12 SebSanders 4 20
(P R Chamings) *lt-f: hld up: struggling fr 3f out: sn wknd: t.o* **33/1**

9 *nk* **Ponte Vecchio (IRE)** 2-8-10 RobbieMills(7) 7 24
(J R Boyle) *w'like: t.k.h early: lost pl and struggling over 5f out: t.o* **50/1**

1m 39.93s (-0.87) **Going Correction** +0.025s/f (Slow) **9** Ran SP% **108.7**
Speed ratings (Par 97):105,102,100,99,99 97,95,77,76
CSF £6.55 TOTE £2.10: £1.30, £2.00, £9.10; EX 6.80.
Owner K Abdulla **Bred** Juddmonte Farms Inc **Trained** Beckhampton, Wilts

FOCUS
A decent maiden for the track, and a very smart winning time for a race like this, 1.37 seconds quicker than the later handicap for older horses. The standard looks solid and the winner can do better.

NOTEBOOK
Monzante(USA) has a decent American pedigree - his sire has fathered a winner of the Kentucky Derby - so his trainer was always confident that he would adapt to the surface. A stylish winner, this leggy, unfurnished type can only improve as he matures, but he has already been gelded to improve his behaviour at home. (op 11-10)
Maslak(IRE) had the run of the race, dictating it from the inside box, and adapted well to the surface. Only beaten by a useful sort in the making, he can win a maiden, but may take the nursery route instead now he is qualified. (op 4-1)
Furmigadelagiusta put in his best effort to date even though he was sweating badly in the parade-ring. He is improving nicely, and capable of winning races, with nurseries now an option. (op 33-1)
Racing Times continues to show promise, and would probably have had more left for the finish had he not pulled so hard. He is now qualified for nurseries, though a maiden win cannot be ruled out on his three runs to date. Official explanation: jockey said gelding pulled hard and hung left
Fever, though showing ability, has been found wanting in maiden company, and will be more at home in nurseries now he is qualified. (tchd 15-2)
Coeur De Lionne(IRE) ◆, whose dam - a half-sister to Sir Percy - has produced three winners from three previous foals, made an eyecatching debut behind his short-priced stable-mate. A 145,000 guinea yearling, he has already been gelded, but looks sure to make significant improvement with this run behind him. His sire was the top-class sprinter Invincible Spirit, but this longer trip seemed to suit him well.
Spume(IRE) looked the part in the paddock but is not up to this standard, and will doubtless be heading for nurseries after one more run. (op 7-1)

4993 E B F TFM SOLUTIONS MAIDEN FILLIES' STKS 6f (P)
2:40 (2:41) (Class 4) 2-Y-O **£5,343** (£1,589; £794; £396) **Stalls** High

Form RPR

4 **1** **Laurentina**[14] 4559 2-9-0 LDettori 11 74
(B J Meehan) *lw: chsd ldrs: rdn and prog 2f out: wnt 2nd 1f out: sustained effrt to ld last strides* **10/11**[1]

00 **2** *hd* **Juncea**[11] 4657 2-9-0 IanMongan 5 73
(H Morrison) *lw: trckd ldr: led wl over 2f out and kicked on: kpt on fnl f: collared last strides* **25/1**

2 **3** *1 1/4* **Herb Paris (FR)**[46] 3591 2-9-0 MartinDwyer 10 70
(M P Tregoning) *s.i.s: sn prom: rdn to chse ldr 2f out to jst over 1f out: hung lft and nt qckn* **7/2**[2]

55 **4** *3/4* **Nicomedia (IRE)**[42] 3707 2-9-0 RyanMoore 2 67
(R Hannon) *prom: rdn over 2f out: kpt on same pce: nvr able to chal* **9/2**[3]

5 *3/4* **Lady Grace (IRE)** 2-9-0 NickyMackay 8 65
(W J Haggas) *neat: scope: lw: pushed along in rr over 4f out: styd on steadily fr over 2f out: nrst fin* **20/1**

0 **6** *3 1/2* **Dee Burgh**[13] 4600 2-9-0 JimmyQuinn 4 55
(J Pearce) *hld up in last pair: pushed along 3f out: kpt on steadily fnl 2f: n.d* **50/1**

7 *1/2* **Kassuta** 2-9-0 SebSanders 7 53
(S C Williams) *cmpt: bkwd: s.s: sn in tch: rdn over 2f out: wknd wl over 1f out* **33/1**

6 **8** *hd* **Inchigeelagh (IRE)**[30] 4049 2-8-9 TravisBlock(5) 1 53
(H Morrison) *prom on wd outside: rdn over 2f out: sn wknd* **40/1**

00 **9** *4* **Morning Song (IRE)**[30] 4053 2-9-0 JimmyFortune 12 41
(N P Littmoden) *snatched up in midfield over 4f out: nvr on terms after: struggling over 2f out* **66/1**

00 **10** *1 3/4* **Swiftly Addicted (IRE)**[29] 4084 2-8-11 AdamKirby(3) 6 35
(A King) *led to wl over 2f out: sn wknd* **20/1**

11 *15* **Dancing Valentine** 2-8-11 StephaneBreux(3) 3 —
(L A Dace) *neat: s.v.s: a detached in last: t.o* **66/1**

1m 13.93s (0.23) **Going Correction** +0.025s/f (Slow) **11** Ran SP% **116.5**
Speed ratings (Par 94):99,98,97,96,95 90,89,89,84,81 61
CSF £34.14 TOTE £1.70: £1.10, £5.40, £1.60; EX 28.00.
Owner John M Carroll **Bred** Glebe Stud And Mrs F Woodd **Trained** Manton, Wilts

FOCUS
A fair race of its type, and the same comment applies for the winning time. The form has been rated through the winner and the third.

NOTEBOOK
Laurentina again looked as if she might not find a run through the pack, but this time it was early enough for the gap to appear, and she stayed on to take it near the finish. Her trainer expects her to be even better over seven furlongs. (op Evens tchd 5-6)
Juncea was a relevation on this surface, and looked the likely winner for much of the final two furlongs. She is now qualified for nurseries, but on this evidence a maiden on Polytrack is well within her capabilities.
Herb Paris(FR) is lightly-made, and unlikely to be a stable star, but she has shown enough in her two races to suggest she can win a maiden on either turf or Polytrack. She will be qualified for nurseries after one more run. (op 4-1tchd 9-2 in a place)
Nicomedia(IRE) ran over seven furlongs on her two previous outings on turf, and again showed promise, suggesting she is at home over both trips. She is now qualified for nurseries, and should do well in that company on either surface. (op 7-2 tchd 5-1 in a place)
Lady Grace(IRE) ◆, a 110,000gns yearling, is related to a number of good winners at around six and seven furlongs. A sturdy sort, she made a pleasing debut and can improve enough to win races, with an extra furlong already within reach.
Dee Burgh is showing signs of improvement, and ran well enough on this surface following a never-dangerous debut on turf. She will come into her own when qualified for nurseries after one more run.
Kassuta is bred to be quick, being by top sprinter Kyllachy and out of a mare related to some speedy types. For a cheap yearling, she acquitted herself well on this debut and looks a nursery type in the making.
Inchigeelagh(IRE) did reasonably well from a poor draw. She will be qualified for nurseries after one more run.
Morning Song(IRE) Official explanation: jockey said filly hung wide on bend

4994 EUROPEAN BREEDERS FUND FILLIES' CONDITIONS STKS 7f (P)
3:15 (3:20) (Class 3) 2-Y-O
£6,855 (£2,052; £1,026; £513; £256; £128) **Stalls** High

Form RPR

1 **Emulate** 2-8-12 RichardHughes 7 80
(B W Hills) *str: scope: bit bkwd: dwlt: hld up in last pair: gd prog over 2f out: shkn up to ld last 150yds: styd on wl* **4/1**[3]

2 *1 1/4* **Maysarah (IRE)** 2-8-12 NickyMackay 5 77
(G A Butler) *tall: scope: lw: t.k.h: hld up in midfield: prog to ld 2f out: drvn fnl f: hdd and outpcd last 150yds* **10/1**

6 **3** ½ **Princess Taylor**[27] 4148 2-8-12 .... OscarUrbina 8 76
(M Botti) *hld up in last: rdn wl over 2f out: prog over 1f out: styd on fnl f: nvr able to chal* **11/4**[2]

1 **4** hd **Ficoma**[24] 4221 2-8-9 .... AdamKirby(3) 3 76
(C G Cox) *led for 2f: styd handy: rdn and nt qckn over 2f out: styd on again fnl f* **9/2**

5 nk **Tinnarinka** 2-8-12 .... RyanMoore 6 75
(R Hannon) *str: bkwd: in tch towards rr: rdn 3f out: no prog tl styd on fr over 1f out: nrst fin* **12/1**

32 **6** 1½ **Silca Key**[4] 4873 2-8-12 .... LDettori 2 71
(M R Channon) *led after 2f: rdn and hdd 2f out: wknd fnl f* **5/2**[1]

7 8 **Proposal** 2-8-12 .... SebSanders 4 51
(C E Brittain) *cmpt: bit bkwd: s.v.s: rcvrd and in tch on outer after 3f: wknd over 2f out* **25/1**

8 3 **Elmasong** 2-8-12 .... JohnEgan 1 44
(J J Bridger) *close-coupled: trckd ldr over 4f out to over 2f out: wknd rapidly* **66/1**

1m 28.04s (1.24) **Going Correction** +0.025s/f (Slow) 8 Ran SP% **115.5**
Speed ratings (Par 96):93,91,91,90,90 88,79,76
CSF £43.37 TOTE £6.00: £2.10, £2.20, £1.50; EX 47.60.
Owner K Abdulla **Bred** Juddmonte Farms Ltd **Trained** Lambourn, Berks

FOCUS
Little form to go on, but probably a smart race for the track and a positive view has been taken of the form.

NOTEBOOK
Emulate, a stocky sort, was carrying plenty of condition, but her appearance was deceptive as she scored a tidy win. This was a decent race in which to make her debut, and this daughter of Alhaarth - half-sister to three other winners - can go on from here, with longer trips likely to suit. (op 5-1)
Maysarah(IRE) ◆, a 175,000 euro yearling from a smart family at up to ten furlongs, made a pleasing debut and is one to note. Beaten only by a potentially useful filly, she should win her maiden before going on to better things herself. (op 16-1)
Princess Taylor was well backed to step up on her Newmarket debut. Though not able to land the money, she handled the surface and can win a routine maiden at least, with continued improvement likely. (op 10-3 tchd 7-2)
Ficoma found this a hotter race than the Bath contest in which she made a successful debut, but she stayed the longer trip and did not let herself down. (op 4-1 tchd 11-2)
Tinnarinka ◆ caught the eye in the paddock, being a nicely-proportioned, strongly-made sort with a summer bloom on her coat. This 27,000 guinea daughter of top miler Observatory will stay at least that far in due course, and is one to keep an eye on. (op 10-1)
Silca Key, a sparely-made sort, was outshone by stronger types in the paddock. This was her first effort on Polytrack, but it was the quality of the opponents, rather than the surface, that defeated her. Official explanation: jockey said filly ran flat (op 2-1 tchd 11-4)

4995 WEATHERBYS INSURANCE APPRENTICE H'CAP (FINAL ROUND) 1m (P)
3:45 (3:45) (Class 4) (0-80,76) 3-Y-0+
£7,790 (£2,332; £1,166; £583; £291; £146) **Stalls** High

Form RPR

6500 **1** **Landucci**[7] 4760 5-9-0 **70** .... PatrickHills(3) 8 78
(J W Hills) *lw: t.k.h: cl up: shkn up to ld 2f out: pushed out and in command fnl f* **7/1**

0230 **2** 1¼ **October Ben**[11] 4660 3-8-3 **66** .... FrankiePickard(5) 5 71
(M D I Usher) *hld up in last: pushed along and prog over 2f out: chsd wnr fnl f: no real imp* **16/1**

4232 **3** 1 **Benandonner (USA)**[19] 4395 3-8-13 **74** .... JamieHamblett(3) 9 77
(E A L Dunlop) *lw: t.k.h: hld up at stdy pce: rdn and hdd 2f out: nt qckn* **3/1**[2]

4522 **4** nk **Jomus**[9] 4704 5-8-9 **62** oh6 .... (b) JamesMillman 4 64
(L Montague Hall) *lw: plld hrd: hld up in tch: poised to chal gng easily 2f out: sn rdn and fnd nil* **5/1**[3]

131- **5** 2 **Stevedore (IRE)**[260] 6586 5-9-0 **70** .... RobbieMills(3) 7 68
(J R Boyle) *t.k.h: trckd ldr: stl gng wl 2f out: bmpd along and fdd over 1f out* **7/1**

134 **6** ½ **Out For A Stroll**[4] 4879 7-8-10 **63** .... AshleyHamblett 2 60
(S C Williams) *lw: t.k.h: racd wd: hld up in tch: last 3f out: c v wd in st and sn struggling* **5/2**[1]

1134 **7** 1¾ **Noble Nova**[39] 3782 3-8-7 **65** .... ThomasO'Brien 3 58
(M R Channon) *cl up: rdn and nt qckn over 2f out: sn n.d* **11/1**

1m 41.3s (0.50) **Going Correction** +0.025s/f (Slow)
WFA 3 from 5yo+ 5lb 7 Ran SP% **109.5**
Speed ratings (Par 105):98,96,95,95,93 92,91
CSF £94.53 CT £373.75 TOTE £8.00: £4.00, £6.00; EX 78.30.
Owner R J Tufft **Bred** D J And Mrs Deer **Trained** Upper Lambourn, Berks

FOCUS
No pace and many hard pullers, so hard to take the form seriously. The winning time was understandably moderate for the grade, 1.37 seconds slower than the earlier two-year-old maiden.
Out For A Stroll Official explanation: jockey said gelding was unsuited by the track

4996 TFM SOLUTIONS H'CAP 2m (P)
4:20 (4:20) (Class 5) (0-70,67) 4-Y-0+ **£3,238** (£963; £481; £240) **Stalls** High

Form RPR

4-01 **1** **French Mannequin (IRE)**[67] 2935 7-8-6 **52** .... (b) JohnEgan 2 62
(P A Blockley) *lw: t.k.h: cl up: effrt to ld 2f out: sn wl clr: easily* **14/1**

4220 **2** 6 **Dark Parade (ARG)**[9] 4702 5-8-12 **65** .... JamieJones(7) 5 68
(G L Moore) *hld up wl in rr: pushed along and prog 4f out: hrd rdn and hung rt over 1f out: wnt 2nd ins fnl f: no ch wnr* **5/1**[1]

0560 **3** nk **Bobsleigh**[15] 4530 7-8-4 **50** .... JimmyQuinn 6 53
(H S Howe) *led: rdn and hdd 2f out: no ch w wnr after: lost 2nd ins fnl f* **10/1**

4006 **4** 1¾ **Moon Emperor**[34] 3935 9-9-7 **67** .... (be) RyanMoore 9 68
(J R Jenkins) *hld up in tch: pushed along over 4f out: cl enough over 2f out: sn outpcd and btn* **8/1**

0400 **5** 4 **Chimes At Midnight (USA)**[2] 4929 9-8-2 **48** oh6 .... NickyMackay 7 44
(Luke Comer, Ire) *ldng trio: lost pl and hrd rdn 7f out: in last pair 3f out: plugged on again fnl f* **16/1**

0040 **6** nk **Papeete (GER)**[15] 4530 5-9-1 **61** .... SebSanders 1 57
(Miss B Sanders) *hld up in last trio: prog 7f out: pressed ldrs 3f out: rdn and wknd rapidly over 1f out: no ch whn n.m.r 1f out* **8/1**

6104 **7** 1¾ **Lefonic**[32] 4011 4-8-13 **59** .... OscarUrbina 4 53
(G C H Chung) *lw: mostly pressed ldr: upsides over 2f out: sn rdn and btn: wkng rapidly whn n.m.r 1f out* **13/2**[3]

5321 **8** 2 **Arch Folly**[35] 3896 4-8-11 **60** .... NeilChalmers(3) 3 51
(Ian Williams) *lw: hld up and sn last: effrt 5f out: wknd u.p over 2f out* **11/1**

1556 **9** shd **Madiba**[3] 4914 7-9-2 **62** .... LDettori 10 53
(P Howling) *wl in tch: rdn 3f out: wknd 2f out* **5/1**[1]

5/30 **10** 14 **Laggan Bay (IRE)**[12] 4626 6-9-6 **66** .... (b) MartinDwyer 8 40
(J S Moore) *hld up in last trio: no prog over 3f out: sn wknd: t.o* **11/2**[2]

3m 28.65s (-2.75) **Going Correction** +0.025s/f (Slow) **10** Ran SP% **114.2**
Speed ratings (Par 103):107,104,103,102,100 100,99,98,98,91
CSF £80.94 CT £739.59 TOTE £11.20: £4.30, £1.60, £4.20; EX 71.10.
Owner J T Billson **Bred** Limestone Stud **Trained** Lambourn, Berks
■ Stewards' Enquiry : Jamie Jones one-day ban: careless riding (Sep12)

FOCUS
An ordinary stayers' race run at a fair pace, but a highly impressive winner, through whom the race has been rated.

4997 SPORTING BOOKMAKERS ANNIVERSARY H'CAP 1m 3f (P)
4:50 (4:51) (Class 3) (0-90,90) 3-Y-0+
£7,790 (£2,332; £1,166; £583; £291; £146) **Stalls** High

Form RPR

5411 **1** **Acrobatic (USA)**[51] 3401 3-9-8 **90** .... RichardHughes 3 104+
(R Charlton) *lw: trckd ldr to 6f out: styd prom: wnt 2nd again 3f out: shkn up to ld wl over 1f out: styd on wl whn pressed fnl f* **9/4**[1]

0520 **2** 1¼ **Royal Jet**[23] 4259 4-9-12 **86** .... JohnEgan 6 96
(M R Channon) *lw: hld up in last: gd prog to trck ldrs over 4f out: effrt over 2f out: chsd wnr jst over 1f out: a hld fnl f* **20/1**

3040 **3** ¾ **High Command**[29] 4082 3-9-5 **87** .... MartinDwyer 5 96
(E A L Dunlop) *dwlt: hld up towards rr and t.k.h: prog 3f out: rdn and styd on to take 3rd ins fnl f* **16/1**

1122 **4** 1¾ **Warsaw Pact (IRE)**[2] 4935 3-9-3 **85** .... SebSanders 1 91
(Sir Mark Prescott) *lw: pushed up to go prom fr wd draw: chsd ldr 6f out: led wl over 3f out: hdd wl over 1f out: one pce* **11/4**[2]

2460 **5** 3 **Nawamees (IRE)**[20] 4347 8-9-11 **85** .... (p) IanMongan 4 86
(G L Moore) *hld up wl in rr: effrt 3f out: kpt on fnl 2f: n.d* **33/1**

1 **6** 3 **Changing Wind (USA)**[23] 4247 3-9-5 **87** .... (t) LDettori 2 83
(Saeed Bin Suroor) *trckd ldrs: rdn over 3f out: steadily wknd fnl 2f* **7/1**[3]

-010 **7** ¾ **Rhinebird**[15] 4508 3-9-4 **86** .... OscarUrbina 11 81
(J R Fanshawe) *hld up wl in rr: rdn 3f out: hanging and no prog over 2f out* **16/1**

6034 **8** 3½ **Punta Galera (IRE)**[7] 4763 3-9-4 **86** .... RyanMoore 7 75
(R Hannon) *nvr beyond midfield: reminders 6f out: rdn and struggling 3f out* **25/1**

-054 **9** ½ **Psychic Star**[14] 4555 3-8-13 **84** .... AdamKirby(3) 8 72
(W R Swinburn) *mde most to wl over 3f out: wknd over 2f out* **50/1**

2313 **10** 5 **Fleeting Memory**[27] 4159 3-8-13 **81** .... (t) JimmyFortune 10 61
(Sir Michael Stoute) *trckd ldrs tl rdn and wknd 3f out* **12/1**

-421 **11** 9 **Swan Queen**[105] 1837 3-8-13 **81** .... JimmyQuinn 9 46
(J L Dunlop) *lw: wl in tch: rdn and wkng whn n.m.r on inner over 2f out: sn bhd* **9/1**

2m 19.08s
WFA 3 from 4yo+ 8lb **11** Ran SP% **112.9**
CSF £52.44 CT £577.23 TOTE £2.90: £1.40, £3.30, £4.20; EX 50.80 Place 6 £288.46, Place 5 £185.69.
Owner K Abdulla **Bred** Juddmonte Farms Inc **Trained** Beckhampton, Wilts

FOCUS
A decent handicap. This was the first time a race had been run over this distance since the Polytrack was laid, and it will not be possible to provide speed figures for races over this trip until more data is available.

NOTEBOOK
Acrobatic(USA) is a progressive type who goes particularly well on this track, notching up a hat-trick with a victory that admittedly took a bit more work than the last one here. There is no reason why he cannot reproduce this form when reverting to turf, and he is a possibility for the Cambridgeshire. (op 15-8)
Royal Jet goes well for John Egan, who has yet to finish out of the first two on him, and he gave the progressive winner a good race. This was a fine All-Weather debut, and he should be able to land a similar race. (op 25-1)
High Command, switched back to Polytrack, came back to form with a creditable effort. He must be worth another go on the surface. (tchd 20-1)
Warsaw Pact(IRE) ran a super race from a bad draw. He has now been beaten twice off his current mark, but he cannot be discarded yet. (tchd 3-1)
Nawamees(IRE), a trusty old warrior, has yet to win on the Flat in Britain, but he continues to do his best and a switch back to jumping is always an option.
Changing Wind(USA) found this a hotter race that the maiden he won here. In addition, though he won that race through his stamina, the extra three furlongs here was stretching him too far. (op 6-1)
Psychic Star Official explanation: jockey said filly hung left
Swan Queen Official explanation: jockey said filly had no more to give
T/Plt: £484.90 to a £1 stake. Pool: £51,911.30. 78.15 winning tickets. T/Qpdt: £372.70 to a £1 stake. Pool: £2,770.10. 5.50 winning tickets. JN

4998 - 5003a (Foreign Racing) - See Raceform Interactive

4975 TRALEE (L-H)
Friday, September 1

OFFICIAL GOING: Good

5004a RUBY STKS (LISTED RACE) 1m
3:15 (3:17) 3-Y-0+ **£24,693** (£7,244; £3,451; £1,175)

RPR

1 **Kalderon (GER)**[5] 4854 6-9-10 102 .... FMBerry 3 107
(T Hogan, Ire) *mde virtually all: rdn and strly pressed ent st: styd on wl u.p ins fnl f* **6/1**

2 1¼ **Arch Rebel (USA)**[12] 4641 5-9-12 110 .... JMurtagh 9 106
(Noel Meade, Ire) *s.i.s: towards rr and outpcd bef 1/2-way: 7th and hdwy over 3f out: 3rd 1f out: kpt on wl: no ex cl home* **11/4**[1]

3 2½ **Cougar Bay (IRE)**[20] 4358 3-9-2 103 .... (b) WMLordan 2 96
(David Wachman, Ire) *chsd ldrs: 7th and drvn along 1/2-way: 5th and prog 3f out: kpt on fnl f* **5/1**[3]

4 nk **Modeeroch (IRE)**[8] 4749 3-9-2 103 .... KJManning 1 95
(J S Bolger, Ire) *prom: 3rd 1/2-way: cl 2nd and chal ent st: ev ch over 1f out: no ex ins fnl f* **9/2**[2]

5 1¾ **Ambika (IRE)**[62] 3102 3-8-13 84 .... JAHeffernan 7 89
(H Rogers, Ire) *chsd ldrs in 6th: kpt on same pce st* **50/1**

6 3 **Bawaader (IRE)**[131] 1171 4-9-7 101 .... (b) PJSmullen 4 86
(D K Weld, Ire) *trckd ldrs: 4th 1/2-way: 3rd 3f out: rdn and one pce st* **5/1**[3]

7 4½ **Rekaab (IRE)**[53] 3371 3-9-2 105 .... DPMcDonogh 6 77
(Kevin Prendergast, Ire) *s.i.s and bhd: no imp st* **7/1**

8 8 **Fit The Cove (IRE)**[131] 1171 6-9-7 100 .... MJKinane 8 61
(H Rogers, Ire) *trckd ldrs: 5th to 1/2-way: wknd bef st* **16/1**

9 4 ½ **Mrs Snaffles (IRE)**[16] 4502 3-8-13 96 .... WSupple 5 49
(Francis Ennis, Ire) *disp ld early: 2nd 1/2-way: wknd qckly 3f out* **20/1**

1m 37.4s
WFA 3 from 4yo+ 5lb **9** Ran SP% **117.6**
CSF £23.33 TOTE £6.60: £2.60, £1.30, £2.50; DF 72.80.
Owner Miss M A Masterson **Bred** Stiftung Gestut Fahrhof **Trained** Nenagh, Co. Tipperary

FOCUS
A race run at a solid pace and it proved an advantage to be up with the pace.

NOTEBOOK
Kalderon(GER) was given a positive ride and prove very game in gaining his first victory since arriving from the continent. A winner seven times on the Flat in Germany and France, he was bought to go hurdling and though he not surprisigly found the Supreme Novices' too tough last season, he showed enough in his only other outing over timber to suggest he can make the grade when returning to that discipline. (op 8/1)
Arch Rebel(USA) gave his rivals a start and then took too long to get into top gear. He was never able to pose a threat to the winner and probably needs a more galloping track than this. (op 9/4 tchd 3/1)
Cougar Bay(IRE) was racing over his shortest trip this year and lacked a turn of speed where it mattered. (op 9/2)

5005 - 5006a (Foreign Racing) - See Raceform Interactive

4942 BADEN-BADEN (L-H)
Friday, September 1

OFFICIAL GOING: Soft

5007a MAURICE LACROIX-TROPHY (GROUP 2) 7f
4:00 (4:13) 2-Y-O
£34,483 (£13,793; £6,897; £3,793; £2,069; £1,034)

RPR
1 **Global Dream (GER)** 2-8-11 .... ABoschert 1 104
(U Ostmann, Germany) *raced in 4th, 5th straight, brought to wide outside and headway over 1 1/2f out, led inside final f, driven out* **36/10**[3]
2 ½ **Sugar Baby Love (GER)**[26] 2-8-9 .... AStarke 3 100
(Mario Hofer, Germany) *held up in last, headway on inside to go 4th straight, led on inside 1 1/2f out, headed inside final f, one pace* **24/10**[1]
3 ½ **Kaleo** 2-8-11 .... EPedroza 4 101
(A Wohler, Germany) *trckd ldr in 3rd, hmpd over 1 1/2f out, not clr run til stayed on wl under pressure fr 1f out, no ex cl home* **24/10**[1]
4 2 ½ **Lucky Millionaire (IRE)** 2-8-7 .... TMundry 7 91
(A Trybuhl, Germany) *raced in 5th, went 4th 3f out, dropped back to last ent str, kept on down outside final 2f but nvr a threat* **9/2**
5 1 ¾ **Oktaj (GER)** 2-8-11 .... FilipMinarik 2 91
(A Savujev, Czech Republic) *led til headed 1 1/2f out, weakened* **16/1**
6 3 **Lunces Lad (IRE)**[13] 4597 2-8-11 .... TedDurcan 6 83
(M R Channon) *raced in 2nd, every chance when hung left over 1 1/2f out, weakened 1f out* **28/10**[2]

1m 27.2s **6** Ran SP% **130.9**
(including 10 Euro stake): WIN 46; PL 13, 11, 12; SF 171.
Owner Gestut Auenquelle **Bred** Gestut Auenquelle **Trained** Germany

NOTEBOOK
Lunces Lad(IRE) was close up on the outside of leader Oktaj and challenged early in the home straight but was soon beaten and may not have handled the ground.

5008a JAPAN RACING ASSOCIATION TROPHY (GONTARD-RENNEN) (LISTED RACE) (FILLIES) 1m 3f
5:15 (5:30) 3-Y-O **£12,414** (£5,172; £2,060; £1,034)

RPR
1 **La Dancia (IRE)** 3-8-7 .... TMundry 8 102
(P Rau, Germany)
2 nk **Soudaine (GER)** 3-8-6 ow1 .... ASuborics 10 101
(P Schiergen, Germany)
3 5 **Ogmore Vale (GER)** 3-8-5 .... ABest 5 92
(P Rau, Germany)
4 1 ¼ **Damascena (GER)**[54] 3-8-9 .... WMongil 2 94
(P Schiergen, Germany)
5 ¾ **Viapervita (IRE)**[63] 3-9-2 .... ADeVries 12 100
(H Blume, Germany)
6 2 ½ **Zakopane (GER)**[110] 1714 3-8-7 .... AStarke 9 87
(P Schiergen, Germany)
7 4 ½ **Ellen Of Doononey (IRE)**[78] 3-8-5 .... DMoffatt 11 78
(G Kussatz, Germany)
8 5 **Flor Y Nata (USA)**[20] 4383 3-9-2 .... FilipMinarik 6 81
(Sir Mark Prescott) *always about same place, ridden & beaten 2f out (57/10)* **57/10**[1]
9 7 **Lalina (GER)**[12] 3-8-5 .... J-PCarvalho 7 58
(Mario Hofer, Germany) **28/1**[2]
10 8 **Sable D'Olonne (IRE)**[44] 3660 3-8-11 .... JVictoire 3 52
(A Savujev, Czech Republic)
11 1 ¼ **Plusvite (SWI)** 3-9-0 .... TCastanheira 1 53
(Karin Suter, Switzerland)
P **Queen Of Saba**[75] 2717 3-9-6 .... MEsposito 4 —
(M Weiss, Switzerland)

2m 28.83s **12** Ran SP% **18.4**
WIN 141; PL 30, 18, 31; SF 561.
Owner Gestut Brummerhof **Bred** Gestut Brummerhof **Trained** Germany

NOTEBOOK
Flor Y Nata(USA) passed her first test by breaking with the field. She settled disputing seventh but her attempt to close up on the outside in the back straight soon came to nothing.

4986 HAYDOCK (L-H)
Saturday, September 2

OFFICIAL GOING: Heavy
Wind: strong, half across Weather: torrential rain before racing

5009 BETFRED BE FRIENDLY H'CAP 5f
1:10 (1:11) (Class 2) (0-100,98) 3-Y-0+
£18,696 (£5,598; £2,799; £1,401; £699; £351) **Stalls** Centre

Form RPR
5042 1 **Cape Royal**[5] 4875 6-8-11 **90** .... (bt) JamieSpencer 5 101
(J M Bradley) *mde all: sn clr: rdn ent fnl f: eased cl home* **13/2**
0050 2 nk **Kenmore**[8] 4760 4-8-6 **85** ow1 .... TomEaves 7 95+
(D Nicholls) *in tch: r.o to take 2nd and hung lft wl ins fnl f: gaining at fin but no ch w wnr* **15/2**
1000 3 2 **Stoneacre Lad (IRE)**[10] 4717 3-8-5 **85** .... (b) RobbieFitzpatrick 2 88
(Peter Grayson) *towards rr: hdwy 1/2-way: chsd wnr and hung lft over 1f out: lost 2nd and no ex wl ins fnl f* **33/1**
0000 4 2 **If Paradise**[28] 4128 5-8-11 **90** .... DaneO'Neill 12 86
(R Hannon) *prom: sn racd alone on stands' rail: rdn over 1f out: hung lft and btn ins fnl f* **16/1**
6000 5 ¾ **Enchantment**[55] 3332 5-8-5 **84** oh1 .... JimmyQuinn 3 78
(J M Bradley) *s.i.s: sn prom: rdn over 1f out: wknd fnl f* **16/1**
5603 6 1 ¾ **Bahamian Pirate (USA)**[6] 4832 11-9-5 **98** .... RobertWinston 9 86
(D Nicholls) *dwlt: sn in midfield: rdn 1/2-way: wl btn over 1f out* **5/1**[1]
3011 7 nk **Cashel Mead**[8] 4771 6-8-5 **89** .... TravisBlock(5) 10 76
(J L Spearing) *broke wl: towards rr over 3f out: effrt whn hung lft over 1f out: sn btn* **6/1**[3]
2321 8 1 ¼ **Smokin Beau**[9] 4725 9-8-5 **84** .... AdrianTNicholls 11 67
(D Nicholls) *prom: rdn 1/2-way: wknd over 1f out* **11/2**[2]
-500 9 2 ½ **Fonthill Road (IRE)**[14] 4609 6-9-4 **97** .... PaulHanagan 6 71
(R A Fahey) *s.s: a bhd* **13/2**
0050 10 5 **Highland Warrior**[35] 3956 7-8-7 **86** ow1 .... JohnEgan 8 43
(J S Goldie) *s.i.s: towards rr: effrt 1/2-way: wknd over 1f out: eased whn btn fnl f* **8/1**

62.36 secs (0.29) **Going Correction** +0.30s/f (Good)
WFA 3 from 4yo+ 1lb **10** Ran SP% **110.6**
Speed ratings (Par 109):109,108,105,102,100 98,97,95,91,83
CSF £51.06 CT £1410.16 TOTE £6.40: £1.80, £2.70, £7.50; EX 73.90 TRIFECTA Not won..
Owner E A Hayward **Bred** D R Brotherton **Trained** Sedbury, Gloucs

FOCUS
With one exception they raced down the centre, and not many got into this. The time was decent but they probably had the best of the conditions. The winner is rated to this year's form.

NOTEBOOK
Cape Royal, who came into this in good heart, made light of the conditions and set a brisk pace down the centre of the track. He held a two-length lead entering the last and won more easily than the margin suggests as he was being eased near the line as the runner-up closed. Ending a lengthy losing run, he might go for the Portland Handicap now, and will have more chance of staying the extra yardage at York than had the race been run at its traditional home of Doncaster. (op 11-2)
Kenmore ◆ was well backed on this drop in trip, having been well beaten from a poor draw over seven at Chester. Staying on well inside the last, he hung in slightly behind the winner as he tried to challenge but was a shade flattered to be beaten only a neck at the end. He is not too consistent, but is well handicapped and will be interesting back at six furlongs. (op 12-1)
Stoneacre Lad(IRE), proven on testing ground, ran a decent race and would have been a bit closer had he not taken himself over to race alone on the far rail, something he has made a habit of doing. (op 25-1)
If Paradise, who has dropped 9lb since the start of the season following some lacklustre efforts, put in a better performance. He raced in isolation on the stands' side, although he was hanging away from the rail from halfway.
Enchantment, a stablemate of the winner, ran respectably on this return from a break and was still disputing second a furlong from home before fading.
Bahamian Pirate(USA) had ground conditions in his favour but was unable to get beyond midfield. (op 11-2)
Cashel Mead, no less than 31lb higher than when winning at Bath in May, could never muster a serious challenge on this bid for a hat-trick. (op 5-1)

5010 BETFREDPOKER.COM OLD BOROUGH CUP (HERITAGE H'CAP) 1m 6f
1:45 (1:47) (Class 2) (0-105,105) 3-Y-0 **£51,816** (£15,416; £7,704; £3,848) **Stalls** Low

Form RPR
5001 1 **Peppertree Lane (IRE)**[14] 4612 3-8-3 **95** .... KDarley 8 106+
(M Johnston) *trckd ldrs: wnt 2nd 5f out: chalng fr over 3f out: led and hung rt over 1f out: edgd lft ins fnl f: drvn out* **9/2**[1]
200 2 ¾ **Quizzene (USA)**[11] 4676 4-8-0 **81** .... (b[1]) AdrianTNicholls 15 90
(M Johnston) *led after 1f: rdn whn pressed over 3f out: hdd over 1f out: swtchd rt ins fnl f: styd on* **16/1**
2046 3 1 ¼ **Solent (IRE)**[10] 4713 4-8-13 **94** .... DaneO'Neill 5 101
(R Hannon) *hld up: hdwy into midfield 6f out: lost pl on bnd 5f out: hung lft over 2f out: clsd over 1f out: r.o ins fnl f* **8/1**
5426 4 shd **Mceldowney**[5] 4883 4-8-6 **87** .... JoeFanning 7 94
(M Johnston) *led for 1f: remained prom: rdn over 3f out: styd on u.p fnl f* **33/1**
2030 5 2 ½ **Lets Roll**[10] 4713 5-8-5 **89** .... SaleemGolam(3) 17 93
(C W Thornton) *prom: rdn over 3f out: no ex ins fnl f* **8/1**
3001 6 shd **Stoop To Conquer**[15] 4560 6-8-1 **82** .... JimmyQuinn 9 85
(J L Dunlop) *midfield: hdwy over 4f out: rdn over 3f out: no ex ins fnl f* **6/1**[3]
3323 7 3 **Ti Adora (IRE)**[11] 4676 4-8-0 **81** .... MatthewHenry 11 81
(P W D'Arcy) *stdd s: hld up: swtchd rt and hdwy over 3f out: rdn over 2f out: no ex ins fnl f* **20/1**
4225 8 12 **River Alhaarth (IRE)**[10] 4713 4-8-10 **91** .... EddieAhern 10 75
(P W Chapple-Hyam) *midfield: rdn over 4f out: wknd over 3f out* **5/1**[2]
1622 9 hd **Frank Sonata**[98] 2010 5-9-10 **105** .... LDettori 4 89
(M G Quinlan) *hld up: effrt over 2f out: no imp: eased whn btn ins fnl f* **6/1**[3]
6361 10 2 **Sweet Indulgence (IRE)**[14] 4604 5-8-3 **84** .... TPO'Shea 1 65
(W J Musson) *hld up: effrt over 2f out: eased whn btn ins fnl f* **40/1**
000- 11 1 ½ **Adopted Hero (IRE)**[169] 568 6-8-9 **90** .... JamieSpencer 3 69
(J Howard Johnson) *midfield: rdn 4f out: sn wknd* **40/1**
-500 12 13 **Red Lancer**[10] 4713 5-8-11 **92** .... PaulHanagan 13 54
(R A Fahey) *in tch: rdn over 4f out: wknd over 3f out* **14/1**

2405 **13** *29* **Castle Howard (IRE)**[13] [4631] 4-8-6 **87**.............................. TPQueally 2 12
(W J Musson) *hld up: rdn over 4f out: nvr on terms: t.o* **20/1**
3m 13.18s (6.89) **Going Correction** +0.65s/f (Yiel)
WFA 3 from 4yo+ 11lb **13** Ran SP% **115.5**
Speed ratings (Par 109):106,105,104,104,103 103,101,94,94,93 92,85,68
CSF £68.95 CT £554.75 TOTE £4.50: £1.90, £5.60, £3.00; EX 55.30 Trifecta £747.90 Part won. Pool: £1,053.46 - 0.70 winning tickets..
Owner P D Savill **Bred** Gestut Wittekindshof **Trained** Middleham Moor, N Yorks

FOCUS
A one-two for Mark Johnston, whose other runner was beaten a short head for third. The pace was only a steady pace and the first two were prominent throughout. A straightforward race to rate.

NOTEBOOK
Peppertree Lane(IRE), 7lb higher than at Ripon, followed up over this longer trip. Never far away, he did not do much once in front, wandering a little and carrying his head a bit high, but won with a bit to spare and should continue on the upgrade granted testing conditions. He could make a quick reappearance in the Mallard Handicap at York, for which he picks up a 6lb penalty. (op 5-1)
Quizzene(USA), soon in front, tried to wind things up in the straight. He was headed by his stablemate with a furlong and a half to run but stuck on well to hold second. The first-time blinkers revitalised him. (op 14-1)
Solent(IRE) ◆, a staying-on sixth in the Ebor last time, was again doing his best work at the end, snatching third on the line. Well at home in soft ground, he looks sure to be suited by a step up to two miles plus and the Cesarewitch looks an interesting target for him. (tchd 9-1)
Mceldowney, brought out quickly after a disappointing effort at Newcastle, ran a solid race and only lost third place on the nod, denying his stable a clean sweep. (op 25-1)
Lets Roll ran another creditable race and deserves a change of luck, but he is too consistent for his own good and the Handicapper has him covered. (tchd 9-1)
Stoop To Conquer, raised 5lb for his win at Newbury, was one of few to become involved from the rear but his promising forward move petered out in the final furlong. (op 13-2 tchd 7-1 in places)
Ti Adora(IRE), having her first run in heavy ground, ran a decent race but does look vulnerable from this career-high mark.
River Alhaarth(IRE), who figured prominently in both the Northumberland Plate and the Ebor, was without the visor he had worn at York. Well held in the straight, he might have found this coming too soon after a hard race last time. Official explanation: vet said colt returned lame on its left-hind (op 11-2 tchd 6-1)
Frank Sonata had conditions to suit, but this was a race in which it proved hard to come from behind. (op 11-2)
Castle Howard(IRE) Official explanation: vet said gelding finished distressed

5011 BETFRED SPRINT CUP (GROUP 1) 6f
2:15 (2:21) (Class 1) 3-Y-O+
£170,340 (£64,560; £32,310; £16,110; £8,070; £4,050) **Stalls** Centre

Form RPR
1051 **1** **Reverence**[9] [4738] 5-9-3 111.............................. KDarley 10 120
(E J Alston) *a.p: led jst over 1f out: drvn out* **11/4**[1]
6010 **2** *nk* **Quito (IRE)**[6] [4832] 9-9-3 112.............................. (b) RobertWinston 3 119
(D W Chapman) *broke wl: sn hld up in rr: rdn over 2f out: hdwy over 1f out: hung rt and wnt 2nd wl ins fnl f: r.o* **9/1**
5432 **3** *1 ¼* **Amadeus Wolf**[9] [4738] 3-9-1 115.............................. NCallan 4 115
(K A Ryan) *racd keenly: prom: rdn over 2f out: edgd rt and nt qckn over 1f out: styd on ins fnl f* **4/1**[2]
5104 **4** *1* **Somnus**[9] [4740] 6-9-3 107.............................. JohnEgan 1 112
(T D Easterby) *towards rr: wnt rt over 2f out: swtchd lft and hdwy over 1f out: styd on ins fnl f* **8/1**[3]
6025 **5** *2* **Red Clubs (IRE)**[9] [4738] 3-9-1 111.............................. MichaelHills 9 106
(B W Hills) *led: rdn and hdd jst over 1f out: no ex ins fnl f* **16/1**
241 **6** *3* **Excusez Moi (USA)**[14] [4609] 4-9-3 99.............................. KerrinMcEvoy 5 97
(C E Brittain) *prom: rdn over 1f out: wknd ins fnl f* **11/1**
4240 **7** *4* **Balthazaar's Gift (IRE)**[27] [4191] 3-9-1 115.............................. JamieSpencer 7 85
(T R George) *s.i.s: in rr: rdn and sme hdwy 2f out: wknd fnl f* **14/1**
1346 **8** *nk* **Miss Sally (IRE)**[20] [4410] 4-9-0.............................. (t) JMurtagh 2 81
(M Halford, Ire) *midfield: rdn 1/2-way: wknd 2f out* **10/1**
0324 **9** *6* **Kodiac**[27] [4191] 5-9-3 109.............................. (b) LDettori 11 66
(J L Dunlop) *in tch: rdn over 2f out: wknd over 1f out* **28/1**
0224 **10** *7* **Philharmonic**[63] [3076] 5-9-3 104.............................. PaulHanagan 6 45
(R A Fahey) *midfield: rdn 1/2-way: wknd 2f out* **25/1**
5510 **11** *7* **Steenberg (IRE)**[9] [4738] 7-9-3 112.............................. TPQueally 8 24
(M H Tompkins) *midfield: pushed along 1/2-way: wknd 2f out* **12/1**
1m 15.78s (0.88) **Going Correction** +0.45s/f (Yiel)
WFA 3 from 4yo+ 2lb **52** Ran SP% **112.7**
Speed ratings (Par 117):112,111,109,108,105 101,96,96,88,78 69
CSF £26.60 TOTE £3.70: £1.60, £3.90, £1.10; EX 30.90 Trifecta £106.40 Pool: £2,952.27 - 19.70 winning tickets..
Owner Mr & Mrs G Middlebrook **Bred** G And Mrs Middlebrook **Trained** Longton, Lancs

FOCUS
Unlike the opening sprint, the field came over to the stands' side. This was not a vintage renewal, the exposed Quito setting the standard, with Reverence 2lb off his Nunthorpe figure and Somnus running his best race of the year in fourth. The winning time was a little below Group 1 standard, even allowing for the deteriorating ground.

NOTEBOOK
Reverence became the first horse since Dayjur in 1990 to complete the Nunthorpe-Sprint Cup double. While the bad ground was never going to pose him any problems, the extra furlong was a concern but, always close up against the stands' rail, he moved past Red Clubs going to the final furlong and was never going to be caught, although his stamina was on the wane at the end as Quito closed him down. With the likelihood of soft ground at Longchamp, he should take a lot of beating back at five furlongs in the Prix de l'Abbaye. (op 5-2)
Quito(IRE), proven over further than this, in contrast to the winner, was having his third run in nine days and put up just about the best performance of his career on his 106th start. Held up in rear as usual, he was still only fifth passing the furlong pole but stayed on strongly and would have got to the flagging favourite with a little further to run. He is a credit to his trainer and should continue to give a good account. (op 8-1)
Amadeus Wolf, always chasing the pace, did not look entirely at home in this bad ground but stayed on for third, finishing a bit closer to Reverence than he had in the Nunthorpe. He has now made the frame at the highest level on his last four starts. (op 7-2)
Somnus ran a creditable race from an unhelpful draw, staying on well in the latter stages once switched to the outer. The winner of this event in 2003, he has now reached the frame in the three subsequent runnings. (op 9-1)
Red Clubs(IRE) showed good pace to lead, but edged to his left when tackled by the eventual winner approaching the final furlong and, his stamina ebbing away, he was relegated three more places inside the last. (tchd 18-1)
Excusez Moi(USA), comfortable winner of the Great St Wilfrid Handicap in soft ground on his latest start, travelled well behind the leaders until coming under pressure going to the furlong pole and weakening out of the places. (op 10-1)
Balthazaar's Gift(IRE) could never get into the hunt after a tardy start. He has not been able to run on fast ground since his excellent second in the Golden Jubilee Stakes at the Royal meeting. (op 12-1)
Miss Sally(IRE) should have had no excuses on account of the ground, but was unable to handle this rise in class. (op 12-1 tchd 14-1)
Steenberg(IRE) Official explanation: vet said gelding finished distressed

5012 BETFRED "TREBLE ODDS ON ALL LUCKYS" SUPERIOR MILE (LISTED RACE) 1m 30y
2:45 (2:46) (Class 1) 3-Y-O+ **£22,712** (£8,608; £4,308; £2,148; £1,076) **Stalls** Low

Form RPR
1500 **1** **Zero Tolerance (IRE)**[9] [4739] 6-9-5 105.............................. JamieSpencer 6 111
(T D Barron) *mde all: rdn over 3f out: r.o ins fnl f* **15/8**[1]
502 **2** *3* **Indian Steppes (FR)**[45] [3648] 7-8-11 89.............................. EddieAhern 3 97
(P S McEntee) *a.p: rdn 2f out: edgd lft ent fnl f: sn wnt 2nd: no imp on wnr towards fin* **16/1**
20-5 **3** *3 ½* **St Petersburg**[9] [4739] 6-9-2 97.............................. TPQueally 4 95
(M H Tompkins) *hld up in rr: rdn over 2f out: tk mod 3rd towards fin: nvr able to chal* **10/3**[3]
3030 **4** *nk* **St Andrews (IRE)**[16] [4529] 6-9-2 105.............................. (p) NCallan 1 94
(M A Jarvis) *chsd wnr: upsides over 2f out: sn rdn: lost 2nd and wknd ins fnl f* **3/1**[2]
1050 **5** *7* **Tanzanite (IRE)**[7] [4808] 4-8-11 93.............................. KerrinMcEvoy 2 75
(D W P Arbuthnot) *hld up: rdn over 1f out: sn btn* **4/1**
1m 48.47s (2.96) **Going Correction** +0.65s/f (Yiel) **5** Ran SP% **108.7**
Speed ratings (Par 111):111,108,104,104,97
CSF £27.00 TOTE £3.20: £1.50, £2.50; EX 20.50.
Owner The Hornsey Warriors Racing Syndicate **Bred** Cliveden Stud Ltd **Trained** Maunby, N Yorks

FOCUS
The winner set a decent pace and led them over to the stands' side in the straight. This was not a strong listed race, with only the first two giving their running.

NOTEBOOK
Zero Tolerance(IRE) was able to get to the front for the first time since winning at York in May and made all the running. Bringing the field across to the stands' side in the straight, he looked in trouble when coming under pressure with over three furlongs to run but eventually responded and was well on top at the line. He picks up a 4lb penalty for the Cambridgeshire, in which he is unlikely to be able to dominate. (op 5-2 tchd 3-1 in a place)
Indian Steppes(FR), who was worst in at the weights, raced in third place before staying on to go second early inside the last. This was one of her best runs to date but she will find things harder in stronger events at this level.
St Petersburg, having only his second run of the year, had a bit to do at the weights. He was never a factor but struggled into third place close home. (op 3-1)
St Andrews(IRE), best in on these terms, tracked the eventual winner and was going the better two furlongs from home, but was unable to quicken when let down and was ultimately disappointing. (op 5-2)
Tanzanite(IRE) had no excuses over the ground this time and failed to run her race. (op 9-2)

5013 BETFREDPOKER.COM NURSERY 1m 30y
3:15 (3:17) (Class 2) 2-Y-O
£12,464 (£3,732; £1,866; £934; £466; £234) **Stalls** Low

Form RPR
0234 **1** **Easy Lover**[8] [4775] 2-9-4 **87**.............................. JamieSpencer 3 91
(J A Osborne) *swtchd rt after s: midfield: hdwy 3f out: led over 1f out: edgd lft wl ins fnl f: styd on* **9/2**[2]
541 **2** *1 ¼* **Guacamole**[45] [3640] 2-8-11 **80**.............................. MichaelHills 8 81
(B W Hills) *a.p: led over 2f out: rdn and hdd over 1f out: nt qckn towards fin* **4/1**[1]
006 **3** *2 ½* **Love Brothers**[34] [3976] 2-8-3 **72**.............................. TPO'Shea 5 68
(M R Channon) *a.p: rdn and ev ch over 2f out: sn hung lft: styd on same pce fnl f* **5/1**[3]
4641 **4** *hd* **Goose Green (IRE)**[16] [4520] 2-7-12 **67** oh2.............................. PaulHanagan 2 63
(M R Channon) *led for 1f: racd in tch after: rdn 2f out: kpt on ins fnl f* **5/1**[3]
002 **5** *1 ¾* **Italian Stallion (IRE)**[15] [4574] 2-8-8 **77**.............................. EddieAhern 1 69
(R Hannon) *in rr: rdn over 3f out: hdwy over 2f out: one pce fr over 1f out* **9/2**[2]
5534 **6** *2 ½* **Fares (IRE)**[16] [4509] 2-8-2 **71**.............................. JimmyQuinn 4 58
(C E Brittain) *in tch: rdn over 2f out: wknd over 1f out* **12/1**
043 **7** *4* **Chookie Hamilton**[17] [4474] 2-7-7 **67** oh3.............................. DuranFentiman(5) 7 45
(I Semple) *rdn 4f out: a bhd* **25/1**
601 **8** *3* **Darfour**[42] [3726] 2-8-6 **75**.............................. JoeFanning 6 47+
(M Johnston) *led after 1f: racd alone on far side in st: hdd over 2f out: wknd over 1f out* **7/1**
1m 50.98s (5.47) **Going Correction** +0.725s/f (Yiel) **8** Ran SP% **113.7**
Speed ratings (Par 101):101,99,97,97,95 92,88,85
CSF £22.58 CT £92.67 TOTE £5.50: £1.80, £1.60, £1.80; EX 21.80.
Owner Mountgrange Stud **Bred** Lordship Stud **Trained** Upper Lambourn, Berks

FOCUS
The runners again came over to the stands' side in the straight. The winner ran to the same mark as at Salisbury and the second to the form of her Kempton win.

NOTEBOOK
Easy Lover ran well on her most recent outing in a listed race but had been held three times in this grade previously. Handling the conditions well, she took the lead against the stands' rail and stayed on dourly. (op 11-2 tchd 6-1and 13-2 in places)
Guacamole, who got off the mark on Polytrack on her latest start, was stepping up to a mile for the first time. Clearly versatile with regards to ground conditions, she ran a sound race but found the winner too strong in the latter stages. (tchd 9-2 tchd 5-1 in a place)
Love Brothers, making his nursery debut, was never far from the pace and stuck on down the outer of the main bunch in the straight. He get the trip well enough. (tchd 11-2)
Goose Green(IRE), successful at 1/4 in a claimer last time, handled the ground well enough but looks held from this sort of mark, although he was 2lb out of the handicap here. (op 8-1)
Italian Stallion(IRE), proven over this trip, but not in testing ground, made his effort on the outside of the group and was making no progress in the final two furlongs. Official explanation: jockey said colt was unsuited by the heavy ground (op 7-2)
Fares(IRE) raced keenly early on and did not get home in this testing ground. (op 14-1)
Darfour, who had previously run only on fast ground, was making his nursery bow. Racing alone in the home straight, his rider electing to stay on the inside rail, he is probably worth another chance. (op 11-2)

5014 BETFREDCASINO.COM MEDIAN AUCTION MAIDEN STKS 1m 30y
3:50 (3:51) (Class 5) 2-Y-O **£3,238** (£963; £481; £240) **Stalls** Low

Form RPR
32 **1** **Striving Storm (USA)**[20] [4415] 2-9-3.............................. EddieAhern 5 70+
(P W Chapple-Hyam) *a.p: led 1/2-way: in command over 1f out: pushed out ins fnl f* **4/11**[1]
0 **2** *1 ¼* **Love On The Rocks**[25] [4228] 2-9-3.............................. NCallan 7 67
(K A Ryan) *a.p: rdn over 2f out: kpt on to take 2nd wl ins fnl f: nt trble wnr* **9/1**[2]
560 **3** *hd* **Obe Royal**[28] [4151] 2-9-3 70.............................. RobertWinston 1 67
(M R Channon) *led to 1/2-way: sn rdn: kpt on same pce fnl 2f* **9/1**[2]
45 **4** *18* **Firestorm (IRE)**[17] [4466] 2-9-3.............................. LeeEnstone 2 29
(C W Fairhurst) *trckd ldrs: rdn 1/2-way: wknd 3f out* **25/1**[3]

5 2 1/2 **Twilight Dawn** 2-8-12 .... JoeFanning 4 19
(M Johnston) *trckd ldrs: pushed along and lost pl 5f out: rallied over 3f out: sn wknd* **9/1**[2]

6 9 **Anewshade** 2-8-5 .... DanielleMcCreery(7) 3 —
(N Tinkler) *upset in stalls: s.s: in rr: effrt over 4f out: wknd over 3f out* **66/1**

1m 54.59s (9.08) **Going Correction** +0.725s/f (Yiel) **6** Ran SP% **108.7**
Speed ratings (Par 95):83,81,81,63,61 52
CSF £4.00 TOTE £1.40: £1.10, £2.70; EX 3.50.
Owner A W Abdo **Bred** Brereton C Jones **Trained** Newmarket, Suffolk
■ Stewards' Enquiry : Danielle McCreery caution: used whip when out of contention.

FOCUS
A slow winning time, even allowing for the conditions. Once again the action took place up the stands' side in the straight. The winner looked different class on his form in France and the first three finished a long way clear.

NOTEBOOK
Striving Storm(USA), runner-up to the highly promising Visionario in a listed race in bad ground at Deauville, faced a simple task. Setting a modest pace and claiming the stands' rail in the home straight, he did the bare minimum required to land this and remains a useful prospect. (op 1-4 tchd 4-9 in places)
Love On The Rocks, unplaced on fast ground on his debut last month, is out of a sister to top-class sprinter Tomba and half-sister to Prix du Jockey-Club winner Holding Court. Not the biggest of individuals, he had little chance with the favourite in the end but showed much improved form in getting the better of a tussle for second. (op 16-1)
Obe Royal, raised in trip after a couple of disappointing runs over five furlongs, narrowly lost out on second, but was suited by the stiffer test and finished a mile clear of the rest. (op 8-1 tchd 15-2)
Firestorm(IRE) plugged on for a remote fourth and is now qualified for nurseries. (op 16-1)
Twilight Dawn, noticeably green, was left well behind in the straight. She is bred to do better with time and over further, being out of a mare who won at up to two miles and who is a half-sister to smart middle-distance performer Fight Your Corner. (op 8-1 tchd 7-1)

5015 BETFRED 600 SHOPS NATIONWIDE H'CAP 1m 2f 120y
4:25 (4:25) (Class 5) (0-70,70) 3-Y-O **£3,886** (£1,156; £577; £288) **Stalls** High

Form				RPR
0040	1		**Mae Cigan (FR)**[14] [4606] 3-8-10 **62** .... NCallan 12	71+
			(M Blanshard) *hld up: hdwy over 3f out: plld out to chal over 1f out: led ins fnl f: r.o* **11/4**[1]	
020	2	3 1/2	**Dik Dik**[24] [4247] 3-8-5 **57** .... (v) KDarley 2	60
			(C N Allen) *trckd ldrs: led over 4f out: rdn and hdd over 2f out: stl ev ch over 1f out: kpt on same pce ins fnl f* **10/1**	
6350	3	nk	**Special Moment (IRE)**[92] [2209] 3-8-12 **64** .... MichaelHills 10	66
			(B W Hills) *a.p: rdn to ld over 2f out: hdd ins fnl f: no ex towards fin* **9/2**[2]	
3440	4	6	**Apache Nation (IRE)**[24] [4255] 3-8-6 **58** .... JimmyQuinn 11	50
			(M Dods) *hld up in tch: effrt over 3f out: wknd over 1f out* **7/1**	
3453	5	5	**Grey Outlook**[6] [4835] 3-8-13 **65** .... PaulHanagan 3	49
			(Miss L A Perratt) *hld up: hdwy 4f out: rdn over 2f out: sn wknd* **13/2**[3]	
0266	6	1 1/4	**Norman Beckett**[27] [4173] 3-9-2 **68** .... TomEaves 8	50
			(I Semple) *led: hdd over 4f out: rdn over 3f out: wknd over 2f out* **9/2**[2]	
624	7	3/4	**Maud's Cat (IRE)**[17] [4489] 3-8-10 **62** .... TPQueally 5	42
			(A P Jarvis) *plld hrd: in tch: rdn over 3f out: wknd over 2f out* **10/1**	
540	8	40	**King Of Rhythm (IRE)**[119] [1483] 3-8-4 **63** .... KellyHarrison(7) 6	—
			(D Carroll) *s.i.s: hld up: hdwy after 3f: wknd over 4f out: t.o* **18/1**	

2m 25.69s (7.96) **Going Correction** +0.80s/f (Soft) **8** Ran SP% **112.3**
Speed ratings (Par 101):103,100,100,95,92 91,90,61
CSF £30.13 CT £117.88 TOTE £3.60: £1.70, £2.50, £1.80; EX 34.40 Place 6 £64.01, Place 5 £9.33.
Owner A D Jones **Bred** J Jay **Trained** Upper Lambourn, Berks

FOCUS
By way of a change they stayed on the far side once into the straight. This was a weakish handicap, although the winner did it well.
T/Plt: £91.60 to a £1 stake. Pool: £114,238.25. 909.90 winning tickets. T/Qpdt: £6.60 to a £1 stake. Pool: £5,678.60. 627.45 winning tickets. DO

4992 KEMPTON (A.W) (R-H)
Saturday, September 2

OFFICIAL GOING: Standard
Race times suggestested that the track was riding fast following the rain, with two older-horse and one juvenile course records being set.
Wind: moderate becoming strong, half behind

5016 TOTESCOOP6 H'CAP 1m 2f (P)
2:05 (2:06) (Class 4) (0-85,85) 3-Y-O+ **£6,477** (£1,927; £963; £481) **Stalls** High

Form				RPR
5113	1		**Stotsfold**[14] [4599] 3-8-11 **81** .... AdamKirby(3) 4	93+
			(W R Swinburn) *lw: stdd s: hld up in rr: prog on outer 3f out: chsd ldr over 1f out: shkn up to ld last 150yds: sn clr* **7/2**[1]	
2134	2	4	**Babcary**[31] [4040] 3-9-1 **82** .... MartinDwyer 10	87
			(M P Tregoning) *led at gd pce: kicked on 2f out: hdd and outpcd last 150yds* **9/2**[2]	
4-15	3	1 1/4	**Vale De Lobo**[16] [4528] 4-8-9 **76** .... JamesMillman(7) 6	78
			(B R Millman) *lw: prom: cl up 2f out: outpcd over 1f out: one pce after* **12/1**	
1006	4	1 1/4	**Royal Amnesty**[24] [4249] 3-8-10 **77** .... OscarUrbina 3	77
			(G C H Chung) *hld up in midfield gng wl: cl up and nt clr run 2f out: rdn and one pce over 1f out* **8/1**	
21-	5	3/4	**Shariki (USA)**[318] [5988] 3-9-1 **82** .... (t) TedDurcan 5	81
			(Saeed Bin Suroor) *lw: s.i.s: sn trckd ldrs: cl up 2f out: rdn and fnd nil over 1f out* **5/1**[3]	
5512	6	1 1/4	**Katchit (IRE)**[24] [4244] 3-9-3 **84** .... RichardHughes 2	82+
			(A King) *wl in rr: rdn over 4f out: prog and cl up 2f out: sn wknd* **9/2**[2]	
1216	7	1 1/4	**Summer Charm**[84] [2457] 4-8-8 **75** .... BRoper(7) 1	69
			(W Jarvis) *wl in rr: rdn and effrt on outer over 2f out: hanging and wknd over 1f out* **20/1**	
6	8	2	**First Friend (IRE)**[22] [4337] 5-9-11 **85** .... JimmyFortune 8	75
			(P Mitchell) *chsd ldr to over 1f out: wknd rapidly* **50/1**	
2130	9	4	**Fyvie**[16] [4528] 3-8-9 **76** .... RichardMullen 9	58
			(E A L Dunlop) *roused along early to go prom: wknd rapidly over 1f out* **16/1**	
-020	10	19	**Brave Fight**[24] [4249] 3-8-10 **77** .... FergusSweeney 12	23
			(A King) *lw: chsd ldrs: rdn 6f out: sn struggling and lost pl: t.o* **16/1**	
6000	11	8	**Shahzan House (IRE)**[93] [2169] 7-8-11 **74** .... (p) AmirQuinn(3) 11	5
			(P G Murphy) *nvr gng wl: a last: t.o over 2f out* **33/1**	

2m 4.44s (-4.56) **Going Correction** -0.10s/f (Stan)
WFA 3 from 4yo+ 7lb **11** Ran SP% **115.5**
Speed ratings (Par 105):114,110,109,108,108 107,106,104,101,86 79
CSF £18.14 CT £168.83 TOTE £4.20: £1.60, £1.70, £2.90; EX 18.40 Trifecta £257.30 Part won. Pool: £362.52 - 0.60 winning tickets..
Owner Mrs P W Harris **Bred** Pendley Farm **Trained** Aldbury, Herts

FOCUS
A decent pace resulted in a new best time for the trip, though this was the only race to use the inner bend into the home straight at the meeting, which raises the possibility that it rode faster. The contest also suggested that those who made their efforts away from the inside rail were at an advantage. Sound form though.
Babcary Official explanation: jockey said filly hung right in straight

5017 TOTEPOOL SIRENIA STKS (GROUP 3) 6f (P)
2:40 (2:41) (Class 1) 2-Y-O
£22,712 (£8,608; £4,308; £2,148; £1,076; £540) **Stalls** High

Form				RPR
0125	1		**Dhanyata (IRE)**[9] [4736] 2-8-11 **95** .... JimmyFortune 7	104
			(B J Meehan) *trckd ldng trio: rdn to chal over 2f out: led over 1f out: sn drvn clr* **6/1**	
4044	2	2	**La Neige**[14] [4607] 2-9-0 **100** .... RichardHughes 1	101
			(M R Channon) *lw: restless stalls: hld up in rr: plld out and effrt over 2f out: r.o fr over 1f out to take 2nd last 75yds: no ch w wnr* **16/1**	
1634	3	3/4	**We'll Confer**[9] [4736] 2-9-0 **100** .... MartinDwyer 5	99
			(K A Ryan) *lw: racd freely: trckd ldr: led wl over 2f out to over 1f out: wknd ins fnl f* **3/1**[1]	
13	4	1 1/2	**Ready For Spring (USA)**[11] [4680] 2-9-0 .... TedDurcan 4	95
			(J Noseda) *lw: sn chsd ldrs: u.p fr 1/2-way: kpt on same pce* **7/2**[2]	
1520	5	1/2	**The Old Fella**[9] [4736] 2-9-0 **97** .... RyanMoore 2	93
			(R Hannon) *pushed along in last pair: effrt u.p over 2f out: plugged on same pce* **10/1**	
0011	6	1 3/4	**Gold Spirit (IRE)**[7] [4789] 2-9-0 **98** .... RichardMullen 9	88
			(E J O'Neill) *chsd ldrs: rdn 1/2-way: wknd wl over 1f out* **7/1**	
1123	7	3	**Bodes Galaxy (IRE)**[10] [4712] 2-9-0 **105** .... MickyFenton 8	79
			(N P Littmoden) *lw: led to wl over 2f out: wknd rapidly over 1f out* **4/1**[3]	
3050	8	5	**Su Doku (USA)**[8] [4767] 2-8-11 **72** .... ChrisCatlin 6	61
			(N P Littmoden) *dwlt: sn struggling in last: a bhd* **100/1**	
10	9	nk	**Arnie's Joint (IRE)**[8] [4766] 2-9-0 .... JamesDoyle 3	63
			(N P Littmoden) *in tch on outer: rdn 1/2-way: wknd tamely 2f out* **50/1**	

1m 12.22s (-1.48) **Going Correction** -0.10s/f (Stan) **9** Ran SP% **111.9**
Speed ratings (Par 105):105,102,101,99,98 96,92,85,85
CSF £91.36 TOTE £6.60: £1.80, £3.20, £1.90; EX 75.60 Trifecta £385.00 Part won. Pool: £542.26 - 0.10 winning tickets..
Owner Mrs Sheila Tucker **Bred** Edmond And Richard Kent **Trained** Manton, Wilts
■ The first running of this race on Polytrack, and indeed the first juvenile Pattern race ever to be run on sand in this country.

FOCUS
With only two of these having run on sand before there were question marks over a few, but the second and third help set a solid standard and the winning time was about as you would expect for a race like this - a new two-year-old best time for the trip.

NOTEBOOK
Dhanyata(IRE) was given a slightly more patient ride than in her recent starts and proved a revelation on this switch to sand. She demonstrated a very decent turn of foot to win her the race and she turned around earlier Pontefract form with Bodes Galaxy in the process, but by a much great margin than a 5lb pull might have suggested. This was a decent effort, though whether the change in surface was the reason, or she is just improving, remains to be seen. (op 7-1)
La Neige stayed on well to snatch the runner-up spot without ever looking like getting to the winner, but this was still a big improvement on his disappointing Ripon effort. He was the most exposed horse in the race, but a repeat of this form should enable him to find another race in slightly lesser company. (tchd 20-1)
We'll Confer, already a winner on Polytrack and just ahead of Dhanyata in the big sales race at York, was weighted to confirm the form but these conditions were very different. He had every chance, but once in front he edged over to the inside rail, which may not have been a help, and was then done for foot. (op 7-2)
Ready For Spring(USA), representing the Acomb Stakes form, had his chance but dropping back a furlong may have done him few favours and he lacked a turn of foot. He was one of the least exposed in the field and can probably do better back over further. (op 11-4 tchd 4-1 in a place)
The Old Fella, well behind both Dhanyata and We'll Confer at York and just behind Gold Spirit at Lingfield prior to that, never looked like getting involved and form lines through the aforementioned trio suggest this is about as good as he is. (op 14-1)
Gold Spirit(IRE), bidding for a hat-trick, failed to transfer his recent turf form on to this different surface.
Bodes Galaxy(IRE), apart from We'll Confer the only other with previous experience of Polytrack, attempted to make all but once in line for home he folded very tamely. He may well have suffered from racing tight against the inside rail in the home straight, but even so this effort and his performance at Lingfield in June do suggest he is much better on turf than he is on sand. (op 7-2)

5018 TOTESPORT.COM SEPTEMBER STKS (GROUP 3) 1m 4f (P)
3:10 (3:11) (Class 1) 3-Y-O+
£28,390 (£10,760; £5,385; £2,685; £1,345; £675) **Stalls** Centre

Form				RPR
6163	1		**Kandidate**[7] [4818] 4-9-4 **114** .... (t) SebSanders 3	115
			(C E Brittain) *lw: hld up in cl tch: gng easily 3f out: effrt 2f out: drvn to ld 1f out: edgd lft but styd on wl* **3/1**[2]	
4110	2	1 1/4	**Crosspeace (IRE)**[20] [4417] 4-9-4 **111** .... RoystonFfrench 2	113
			(M Johnston) *cl up: rdn over 3f out: kpt on wl u.p to chal 1f out: a hld by wnr after* **4/1**[3]	
4564	3	1 1/4	**Self Defense**[14] [4595] 9-9-4 **108** .... MartinDwyer 5	111
			(Miss E C Lavelle) *trckd ldr: led over 2f out and kicked on: hdd and nt qckn 1f out* **9/1**	
0230	4	1 1/2	**Bravo Maestro (USA)**[10] [4713] 5-9-4 **104** .... RyanMoore 1	109
			(N P Littmoden) *dwlt: hld up in last: urged along 3f out: kpt on same pce fnl 2f and no imp ldrs* **8/1**	
-343	5	3 1/2	**Play Me**[14] [4590] 4-9-1 **92** .... TedDurcan 4	100
			(P W Chapple-Hyam) *lw: led: std pce 7f out: rdn and hdd over 2f out: sn btn* **20/1**	
2502	6	3 1/2	**Notable Guest (USA)**[21] [4358] 5-9-7 **111** .... RichardHughes 6	100
			(Sir Michael Stoute) *restless stalls: cl up: rdn 3f out: wknd 2f out* **6/4**[1]	

2m 32.69s (-4.21) **Going Correction** -0.10s/f (Stan) **6** Ran SP% **110.9**
Speed ratings (Par 113):110,109,108,107,105 102
CSF £14.84 TOTE £4.60: £2.70, £1.70; EX 17.20.
Owner A J Richards **Bred** Proton Partnership **Trained** Newmarket, Suffolk
■ The first running of this Group 3 on the track's new Polytrack surface.

FOCUS
The pace appeared to be only modest for much of the way, and despite lowering the course record, the winning time was ordinary for a Group 3 when compared to other races on the day. The form is a bit muddling and has been rated through a best view of the form of the fifth, with the first three all a bit below their best..

NOTEBOOK
Kandidate had a bit of ground to make up with Crosspeace on Goodwood running two starts ago, but he loves this surface and has already landed a big prize here. Given a more patient ride than when beaten at Windsor last time and with the modest pace giving him a better chance of seeing out the trip, he was produced with precision timing and there was only going to be one result once he was unleashed. This was his fifth win on Polytrack in this country. (tchd 10-3)
Crosspeace(IRE) was the first to come off the bridle and although he never gave in, he was unable to confirm Goodwood running with the winner. He still ran a very sound race, however, as he had no previous experience of the surface and the modest gallop was probably not in his favour. (tchd 7-2)
Self Defense, still to win on the Flat in this country, tried to steal the race soon after turning for home but was unable to match the finishing pace of the front pair, who made their efforts wide of him down the centre of the track. He always seems to run his race at this sort of level without being quite good enough to win one. (op 10-1 tchd 12-1)
Bravo Maestro(USA) had a bit to do against most of these on official figures and there were also doubts over his stamina, so the modest pace was something of a help. Switched off last, he stayed on over the last couple of furlongs without looking likely to win and probably achieved as much as could have been expected. (tchd 15-2)
Play Me, who had a mountain to climb on official ratings, set just a modest pace and was merely a sitting duck.
Notable Guest(USA), who did not look totally happy even before the race got under way, was close enough passing the quarter-mile pole but then faded very tamely. Whether the switch to sand was the reason for this dismal effort, or something else, remains to be seen. Official explanation: trainer's rep said horse was unsuited by the surface (op 13-8 tchd 7-4 and 15-8 in places)

5019 MARTIN COLLINS ENTERPRISES H'CAP (LONDON MILE FINAL) 1m (P)
3:40 (3:41) (Class 2) 3-Y-O+
£61,660 (£18,560; £9,280; £4,630; £2,320; £1,170) **Stalls High**

Form RPR
3001 **1** **Killena Boy (IRE)**[8] [4782] 4-8-13 **82** PaulDoe 3 92
(W Jarvis) *racd on outer: hld up in midfield: prog over 3f out: narrow ld fr jst over 2f out: battled on wl fnl f* **20/1**
321 **2** *nk* **Ans Bach**[38] [3852] 3-9-5 **93** (p) PhilipRobinson 15 108+
(M A Jarvis) *hld up in rr: last of main gp whn swtchd to wd outside 2f out: str run fnl f: gaining fast at fin: too much to do* **8/1**[1]
2512 **3** *shd* **Granston (IRE)**[5] [4889] 5-9-6 **89** TedDurcan 5 98
(J D Bethell) *trckd ldrs: effrt 2f out: hanging and nt qckn over 1f out: r.o last 150yds: a jst hld* **8/1**[1]
3002 **4** *½* **Kalankari (IRE)**[31] [4042] 3-9-7 **95** MartinDwyer 1 103
(A M Balding) *pressed ldng pair: chal 3f out: w wnr jst over 2f out tl no ex last 75yds* **10/1**[2]
2012 **5** *½* **Banknote**[21] [4356] 4-9-10 **93** FrancisNorton 13 100
(A M Balding) *hld up towards rr: effrt over 2f out: prog to chse ldrs 1f out: nt qckn fnl f* **8/1**[1]
0162 **6** *hd* **Hits Only Heaven (IRE)**[7] [4796] 4-9-2 **85** (e) SilvestreDeSousa 6 92
(D Nicholls) *w ldr: led over 3f out to jst over 2f out: fdd fnl f* **12/1**[3]
-010 **7** *nk* **Ninth House (USA)**[21] [4379] 4-9-2 **85** (t) RichardMullen 14 91
(D J Daly) *s.i.s: racd on outer in rr: rdn over 2f out: styd on fnl f: nrst fin* **33/1**
2151 **8** *¾* **Waterside (IRE)**[16] [4535] 7-9-7 **90** RyanMoore 9 94
(G L Moore) *lw: trckd ldrs: effrt on inner 2f out: hrd rdn and stl chsng ins fnl f: wknd last 75yds* **10/1**[2]
1240 **9** *nk* **Dancing Guest (IRE)**[7] [4802] 3-8-11 **85** NickyMackay 7 89
(G G Margarson) *hld up towards rr: rdn over 2f out: styd on same pce: nt rch ldrs* **16/1**
1351 **10** *hd* **Bee Stinger**[24] [4241] 4-8-11 **80** ChrisCatlin 4 83
(I A Wood) *lw: hld up towards rr: rdn wl over 2f out: styd on same pce fr over 1f out* **8/1**[1]
6111 **11** *½* **Mcnairobi**[20] [4395] 3-8-10 **84** SebSanders 8 86
(P D Cundell) *lw: hld up in midfield: rdn 2f out: one pce and no imp ldrs* **8/1**[1]
0114 **12** *hd* **Wagtail**[13] [4628] 3-8-13 **87** (t) JimmyFortune 10 89
(E A L Dunlop) *trckd ldrs: gng wl enough 2f out: rdn and nt qckn over 1f out: no imp after* **20/1**
3006 **13** *2* **Namid Reprobate (IRE)**[7] [4802] 3-8-12 **86** (b[1]) SteveDrowne 2 83
(P F I Cole) *trckd ldrs: rdn 2f out: wkng whn squeezed out ins fnl f* **33/1**
0060 **14** *6* **Yarqus**[9] [4739] 3-9-8 **96** RichardHughes 11 79
(C E Brittain) *led to wl over 3f out: wknd rapidly wl over 1f out* **25/1**
0124 **15** *2* **Uhoomagoo**[27] [4187] 8-9-7 **90** (b) CatherineGannon 16 69
(K A Ryan) *sn detached in last and nt gng wl: a struggling* **12/1**[3]
0302 **16** *¾* **Binanti**[16] [4535] 6-9-3 **86** GeorgeBaker 12 63
(P R Chamings) *hld up towards rr: wknd rapidly 2f out* **16/1**

1m 38.43s (-2.37) **Going Correction** -0.10s/f (Stan)
WFA 3 from 4yo+ 5lb **16** Ran SP% **120.1**
Speed ratings (Par 109):107,106,106,106,105 105,105,104,104,103 103,103,101,95,93 92
CSF £160.97 CT £1457.20 TOTE £28.10: £4.60, £2.20, £2.40, £2.40; EX 203.00 Trifecta £2959.10 Pool: £26,673.79 - 6.40 winning tickets..
Owner Capel (CS) Ltd **Bred** John Malone **Trained** Newmarket, Suffolk

FOCUS
The first running of this very valuable contest, which was the culmination of a series of qualifiers throughout the season. The pace was fair, without being breakneck, and not surprisingly for such a competitive race, several had a chance at one stage or another and there was not a lot separating the bulk of the field at the line. Again those that made their efforts away from the inside rail seemed favoured. Rock solid handicap form.

NOTEBOOK
Killena Boy(IRE) was beaten 11 lengths into ninth in his qualifier for this race here in June, but his recent victory over Gaelic Princess at Sandown was handsomely boosted by the runner-up during the week and he was raised just 3lb for that. Racing wide from his low draw, which did appear to be an advantage at this meeting, he hit the front soon after turning in and eventually managed to get the better of a protracted duel with Kalankari. He was fortunate that the runner-up had got into all sorts of bother otherwise the result would have been different, but his connections will not be complaining. (op 16-1)
Ans Bach ◆, another who had hardly covered himself in glory in two previous visits here, has to go down as one of the unluckiest losers of the season. Buried away amongst runners from his inside draw, he had only one behind him turning in and had a great wall of horses immediately in front. Forced to switch to the wide outside in order to get a clear run, he showed a rare burst of finishing speed and passed 12 horses in the last 150 yards, but he was just too late to catch the winner. This must have been heartbreaking for connections and punters, but the Handicapper can hardly raise him too much with the field finishing in such a heap. (op 7-1)
Granston(IRE), who had run very well in his only previous try here, came into this race in good form. He travelled very well, but did not respond immediately when pulled out for his effort and when he did get going, it was always going to be a little bit too late.
Kalankari(IRE), impressive winner of his qualifier back in May, had the outside box but managed to tack across and take a handy position without too much trouble and the result shows that a low draw was no disadvantage. He had every chance, but he came out second best after a dour battle with the winner and was eventually run out of the first three. (tchd 11-1)
Banknote stayed on well down the home straight, but never quite looked like getting there. This was a decent effort in such a competitive race under his big weight.
Hits Only Heaven(IRE), who made all when winning his qualifier in June, was not able to dominate on this own this time so he posted a decent effort under the circumstances off a 7lb higher mark than for that victory.
Ninth House(USA) Official explanation: jockey said colt had a breathing problem
Bee Stinger could never get into the race from off the pace though he was not beaten that far at the line.
Mcnairobi, bidding for a Polytrack four-timer off a 6lb higher mark, never posed a threat and found this much tougher. (op 7-1)

5020 RACING UK AND SETANTA FOR £15 CONDITIONS STKS (C&G) 7f (P)
4:15 (4:15) (Class 3) 2-Y-O **£7,124** (£2,119; £1,059; £529) **Stalls High**

Form RPR
1 **Water Mill (USA)** 2-8-12 MartinDwyer 1 83+
(A M Balding) *rangy: scope: lw: mde all and sn crossed fr outside draw: shkn up 2f out: kpt on wl fnl f: jst hld on* **7/1**[3]
4 **2** *shd* **Black Rock (IRE)**[10] [4716] 2-8-12 PhilipRobinson 2 83
(M A Jarvis) *gd sort: bit bkwd: chsd wnr: rdn over 2f out: styd on ins fnl f: jst failed* **2/1**[2]
1 **3** *½* **Cold Quest (USA)**[10] [4705] 2-9-2 JimmyFortune 5 86
(J H M Gosden) *lw: pressed ldng pair: rdn over 2f out: effrt on inner whn nt clr run and swtchd lft over 1f out: styd on: a hld* **11/8**[1]
4 *3* **Ideally (IRE)** 2-8-12 RyanMoore 6 74
(B W Hills) *leggy: scope: in tch: rdn to chse ldng trio over 1f out: no imp* **14/1**
5 *1 ¾* **Sam Lord** 2-8-12 RobertHavlin 8 69
(J H M Gosden) *w'like: bit bkwd: awkward s: in tch in rr: effrt on inner over 2f out: one pce and no real prog* **20/1**
6 *2 ½* **Majestic Cheer** 2-8-12 TedDurcan 4 63
(M R Channon) *neat: lw: chsd ldrs: rdn over 2f out: no imp: wknd fnl f* **33/1**
7 *1 ¾* **Sir Liam (USA)** 2-8-12 RichardHughes 9 58
(P Mitchell) *neat: dwlt: hld up in tch: pushed along 3f out: sn outpcd: n.d after* **33/1**
5 **8** *1* **Traditionalist (IRE)**[14] [4592] 2-8-12 SebSanders 3 56
(G A Butler) *lw: chsd ldng trio tl wknd rapidly over 1f out* **12/1**
9 *¾* **Da Schadenfreude (USA)** 2-8-9 RichardKingscote[(3)] 7 54
(W G M Turner) *str: scope: bit bkwd: a in rr: last and rdn 3f out: no ch* **25/1**

1m 26.93s (0.13) **Going Correction** -0.10s/f (Stan) **9** Ran SP% **116.8**
Speed ratings (Par 99):95,94,94,90,88 86,84,82,82
CSF £20.85 TOTE £9.20: £1.70, £1.40, £1.30; EX 19.20.
Owner E N Kronfeld **Bred** M L Fiveash And Cheryl Green **Trained** Kingsclere, Hants
■ Stewards' Enquiry : Martin Dwyer caution: careless riding

FOCUS
Some interesting types on show here, including some well-bred newcomers and a previous winner, but the pace was ordinary. Few got into it and the first three home occupied those placings throughout.

NOTEBOOK
Water Mill(USA) ◆, a $330,000 half-brother to three winners in the US, is bred to appreciate this surface and got off to the perfect start. His cause was helped somewhat by being allowed to establish a soft lead despite starting from the outside stall, but he showed the right attitude when the challenges arrived and stayed on to gain a deserved if narrow victory from two horses with previous experience. Indeed given the evidence of the afternoon that the inside rail may have been riding slower than elsewhere, this effort could be considered even better than it already looks, and he is entitled to come on for this initial experience. (op 15-2)
Black Rock(IRE) ◆ looked better suited by this surface than the soft ground at York on his debut and stepped up on that effort. He only just failed to get there and the extra furlong was not a problem. He should be winning before too long. (op 11-8)
Cold Quest(USA), carrying a 4lb penalty for his Leicester win, was never far away but was forced to take evasive action when the winner crossed him just as he was attempting to come up his inside approaching the last furlong. It is hard to say whether he would have won otherwise, but he remains a nice prospect. (op 7-4 tchd 15-8)
Ideally(IRE), a half-brother to three winners, including Bouboulina and All That And More, could never get to the front three but showed that he does possess ability. His breeding suggests he will come into his own over further next season. (op 16-1 tchd 20-1)
Sam Lord, resold for 95,000gns as a two-year-old and a half-brother to four winners, including Yaslin and Crookhaven, looked to need this experience more than most and the best of him may not be seen until he tackles middle-distances. (tchd 25-1)
Traditionalist(IRE) did not build on his promising Newbury debut on this different surface, but should not be written off just yet. (op 16-1)

5021 COLLINGWOOD TEAM SERVICE H'CAP 6f (P)
4:50 (4:50) (Class 4) (0-85,85) 3-Y-O+ **£5,505** (£1,637; £818; £408) **Stalls High**

Form RPR
15-0 **1** **Special Lad**[11] [4682] 4-9-0 **79** RyanMoore 2 91+
(P F I Cole) *lw: t.k.h: hld up in rr: stdy prog over 2f out: drvn to ld 1f out: styd on wl* **5/1**[2]
0-40 **2** *1 ½* **She's My Outsider**[29] [4097] 4-8-7 **72** FrancisNorton 7 79
(I A Wood) *trckd ldng pair: effrt over 2f out: led wl over 1f out to 1f out: one pce* **7/1**
-004 **3** *½* **Cyclical**[35] [3959] 4-9-0 **79** NickyMackay 6 85
(G A Butler) *lw: s.s: pushed along in last pair: effrt 2f out: r.o fnl f to take 3rd nr fin* **8/1**
0425 **4** *¾* **Rezzago (USA)**[44] [3679] 6-8-13 **78** JimmyFortune 3 81
(W R Swinburn) *hld up towards rr: rdn over 2f out: kpt on fr over 1f out: nvr able to chal* **9/2**[1]
20-0 **5** *1 ¼* **Grand Show**[10] [4706] 4-8-13 **78** TedDurcan 9 78
(W R Swinburn) *bit bkwd: hld up wl in rr: rdn and effrt 2f out: kpt on same pce: nvr rchd ldrs* **20/1**
5231 **6** *shd* **Peter Island (FR)**[10] [4703] 3-9-0 **81** (v) JimCrowley 8 80
(J Gallagher) *lw: pressed ldr: led wl over 2f out to wl over 1f out: wknd fnl f* **11/2**[3]
0503 **7** *1* **Jayanjay**[5] [4875] 7-8-8 **74** ow1 SebSanders 1 69
(Miss B Sanders) *racd on outer: chsd ldrs: rdn over 2f out: wknd over 1f out* **9/2**[1]
0600 **8** *1 ¾* **Emilio**[16] [4535] 5-9-6 **85** (t) FJohansson 11 76
(R A Kvisla) *chsd ldrs: u.p and struggling 2f out: wknd over 1f out* **33/1**

044 **9** *1* **Buy On The Red**[18] 4449 5-9-3 **82**.................................(b) MartinDwyer 5 70
(W R Muir) *led to wl over 2f out: wknd u.p over 1f out* **10/1**

0-10 **10** *3 ½* **Little Edward**[17] 4486 8-8-12 **77**................................. RichardHughes 10 54
(R J Hodges) *t.k.h: hld up in tch: wknd rapidly wl over 1f out: eased* **16/1**

1m 12.35s (-1.35) **Going Correction** -0.10s/f (Stan)
WFA 3 from 4yo+ 2lb **10** Ran SP% **114.7**
Speed ratings (Par 105):105,103,102,101,99 99,98,95,94,89
CSF £39.22 CT £275.06 TOTE £6.10: £2.10, £3.00, £3.10; EX 55.10.
Owner Team Havana **Bred** Mrs C F Van Straubeenzee And Miss A G **Trained** Whatcombe, Oxon
■ Jayanjay was Brooke Sanders' last runner before her retirement.

FOCUS
A decent little sprint handicap and the winning time was perfectly acceptable, despite being a little slower than the two-year-olds in the Sirenia. Not for the first time at this meeting, those that made their efforts down the centre of the track held sway. Average form, although the winner remains capable of better.
Jayanjay Official explanation: trainer said gelding was struck into

5022 PANORAMIC BAR & RESTAURANT H'CAP 2m (P)
5:25 (5:25) (Class 4) (0-80,79) 3-Y-O **£5,505** (£1,637; £818; £408) **Stalls** High

Form RPR

0121 **1** **Desert Sea (IRE)**[35] 3935 3-9-5 **77**............................. FergusSweeney 1 90+
(C Tinkler) *lw: dwlt: hld up in last pair: prog 4f out: rdn to chse ldr wl over 1f out: styd on u.p to ld last 100yds* **6/4**[1]

-604 **2** *1* **All The Good (IRE)**[8] 4778 3-9-7 **79**............................. SteveDrowne 4 91
(G A Butler) *lw: hld up in tch: smooth prog over 3f out: led over 2f out: hung lft and rt u.p over 1f out: hdd last 100yds: fnd nil* **11/1**

1362 **3** *3 ½* **El Alamein (IRE)**[35] 3935 3-8-8 **66**............................. SebSanders 5 74
(Sir Mark Prescott) *lw: trckd ldr: rdn to ld briefly wl over 2f out: one pce u.p fnl 2f* **2/1**[2]

4015 **4** *7* **Riff Raff**[7] 4792 3-8-9 **67**............................. RyanMoore 2 66
(W Jarvis) *in tch: drvn 3f out: sn outpcd and btn* **15/2**

6264 **5** *8* **Los Cabos (IRE)**[18] 4459 3-9-5 **77**............................. JimmyFortune 6 67
(J H M Gosden) *b.hind: led: rdn and hdd wl over 2f out: sn wknd* **6/1**[3]

5-03 **6** *3 ½* **Karshaan (FR)**[7] 4800 3-8-10 **68**............................. JimCrowley 7 53
(P Winkworth) *prom tl drvn and wknd wl over 3f out* **20/1**

416 **7** *82* **Bariloche**[7] 805 3-9-3 **75**.............................(v) MartinDwyer 3 —
(J R Boyle) *awkward s: last and losing tch bef 1/2-way: t.o and eased 4f out* **33/1**

3m 27.62s (-3.78) **Going Correction** -0.10s/f (Stan) **7** Ran SP% **115.4**
Speed ratings (Par 103):105,104,102,99,95 93,52
CSF £19.68 TOTE £2.50: £1.40, £4.70; EX 25.20 Place 6 £79.20, Place 5 £46.88.
Owner Bonusprint **Bred** Peter McGlynn **Trained** Compton, Berks

FOCUS
Again the pace was only fair for much of the way, but things quickened up appreciably from the home bend and the winning time was more than acceptable. On this occasion all the runners made sure they stayed out in the middle of the track even after the point where the course widens. A fairly positive view has been taken of the form.
T/Jkpt: £380,240.50 to a £1 stake. Pool: £535,550.00. 1.00 winning ticket. T/Plt: £148.20 to a £1 stake. Pool: £113,141.95. 557.30 winning tickets. T/Qpdt: £24.20 to a £1 stake. Pool: £4,691.90. 142.90 winning tickets. JN

4421 THIRSK (L-H)
Saturday, September 2

OFFICIAL GOING: Heavy (meeting abandoned after race 3 (2.50) due to waterlogging)
After an inch of rain and with ground conditions described as 'like a bog', the meeting was abandoned after three races, before the featured Hambleton Cup.
Wind: Fresh, half-against Weather: Persistent heavy rain

5023 RJF HOMES MAIDEN STKS (DIV I) 6f
1:50 (1:58) (Class 5) 3-Y-O+ **£3,238** (£963; £481; £240) **Stalls** High

Form RPR

04 **1** **Marajel (IRE)**[94] 2146 3-9-3............................. AdrianMcCarthy 10 59
(P W Chapple-Hyam) *dwlt: sn chsng ldrs: led over 1f out: drew clr* **7/2**[2]

20-2 **2** *5* **Turkish Sultan (IRE)**[36] 3909 3-9-3 75............................. DavidAllan 9 44
(T D Easterby) *w ldr: led 3f out: hdd over 1f out: kpt on same pce* **5/2**[1]

3030 **3** *1* **Primarily**[18] 4456 4-9-5 50.............................(v[1]) TonyHamilton 8 41
(A Berry) *led tl 3f out: one pce* **9/1**

0500 **4** *nk* **Vibrato (USA)**[2] 4948 4-9-2 31............................. AndrewMullen[(3)] 13 40
(C J Teague) *dwlt: hdwy over 2f out: hung lft over 1f out: one pce* **100/1**

0036 **5** *1 ½* **Girandola**[8] 4769 3-9-3 60............................. StephenCarson 11 36
(R F Johnson Houghton) *mid-div: kpt on fnl 2f: nvr nr ldrs* **11/2**[3]

0000 **6** *8* **Wolfman**[40] 3781 4-9-0 40.............................(p) MarkLawson[(5)] 4 12
(D W Barker) *chsd ldrs: outpcd over 3f out: no ch after* **33/1**

5040 **7** *7* **Underthemistletoe (IRE)**[38] 3835 4-8-7 38.................(v) NeilBrown[(7)] 5 —
(R E Barr) *w ldrs: lost pl over 2f out* **20/1**

42- **8** *12* **Ribh**[422] 3272 3-8-12............................. DarryllHolland 1 —
(C E Brittain) *w ldrs on outside: lost pl over 2f out: sn bhd: eased* **7/2**[2]

0 **9** *4* **Megavegas**[41] 3759 3-8-7 36............................. RoryMoore[(5)] 2 —
(P T Midgley) *chsd ldrs on outer: hung lft and lost pl over 2f out: sn bhd: eased* **50/1**

00-6 **10** *¾* **Little Trinket**[12] 4663 3-8-5 35............................. SladeO'Hara[(7)] 12 —
(Mrs C A Dunnett) *dwlt: a in rr: bhd over 2f out: eased* **66/1**

03-0 **11** *12* **Nell Tupp**[20] 4403 3-9-3 60............................. PhillipMakin 3 —
(G Woodward) *dwlt: sn chsng ldrs: lost pl 3f out: sn bhd: virtually p.u* **20/1**

12 *89* **Vonnies Night Out** 3-9-3............................. PaulQuinn 6 —
(C J Teague) *s.s: sn detached in rr: t.o after 2f: virtually p.u:* **40/1**

1m 18.98s (6.48) **Going Correction** +1.175s/f (Soft)
WFA 3 from 4yo 2lb **12** Ran SP% **117.7**
Speed ratings (Par 103):103,96,95,94,92 81,72,56,51,50 34,—
CSF £11.76 TOTE £4.80: £1.10, £1.80, £3.00; EX 16.80.
Owner Nagy El Azar **Bred** Mrs Helen Lyons **Trained** Newmarket, Suffolk

FOCUS
A weak sprint maiden run in bad ground. The third is rated just 50, and the fourth 31.
Nell Tupp Official explanation: jockey said gelding was unsuited by the heavy ground

5024 RECTANGLE FILLIES' STKS (H'CAP) 1m
2:20 (2:24) (Class 4) (0-85,83) 3-Y-O+ **£6,477** (£1,927; £963; £481) **Stalls** Low

Form RPR

0-14 **1** **Best Guess (USA)**[45] 3643 3-9-2 **76**............................. AdrianMcCarthy 10 85
(P W Chapple-Hyam) *hld up towards rr: effrt 3f out: hdwy and edgd lft 2f out: sn rdn and styd on wl u.p ins last to ld nr line* **8/1**

1431 **2** *hd* **She's Our Lass (IRE)**[15] 4575 5-9-3 **72**............................. DanielTudhope 9 81
(D Carroll) *hld up in tch: hdwy over 2f out: rdn to ld over 1f out: edgd rt ins last: hdd and no ex nr line* **9/2**[1]

0-06 **3** *½* **Skyelady**[13] 4634 3-9-2 **76**............................. GrahamGibbons 3 83
(Miss J A Camacho) *trckd ldrs: hdwy to ld over 2f out: sn rdn and hdd over 1f out: drvn and kpt on wl fnl f* **16/1**

4334 **4** *2 ½* **Hula Ballew**[12] 4653 6-9-8 **77**............................. PhillipMakin 5 80
(M Dods) *a.p: effrt over 2f out: sn rdn and kpt on same pce appr last* **13/2**[3]

0015 **5** *1* **Typhoon Ginger (IRE)**[9] 4733 11-8-4 **64** oh4............ AndrewElliott[(5)] 6 65
(G Woodward) *dwlt and bhd: swtchd wd and hdwy 2f out: sn rdn and kpt on ins last: nrst fin* **16/1**

4421 **6** *3 ½* **Pearl's Girl**[34] 3975 3-9-0 **79**............................. LiamJones[(5)] 8 72
(W J Haggas) *chsd ldrs: hdwy over 2f out: sn rdn and ev ch tl wknd ent last* **5/1**[2]

3323 **7** *1* **Tour D'Amour (IRE)**[9] 4733 3-8-6 **69** ow1............ StephenDonohoe[(3)] 1 61
(R Craggs) *led: rdn along over 2f out: sn hdd and grad wknd* **9/1**

0446 **8** *2 ½* **Commitment Lecture**[12] 4660 6-8-11 **66**.......................(t) PatCosgrave 2 53
(M Dods) *chsd ldrs: rdn along over 2f out: sn wknd* **8/1**

4150 **9** *17* **Passion Fruit**[30] 4090 5-9-4 **73**............................. DeanMcKeown 13 26
(C W Fairhurst) *hld up: a bhd* **8/1**

3-06 **10** *8* **Startori**[10] 4696 3-9-4 **83**............................. MarkLawson[(5)] 7 20
(B Smart) *cl up: rdn along 1/2-way: wknd 3f out* **20/1**

2322 **11** *hd* **Majestic Halo**[20] 4396 3-9-3 **77**............................. DO'Donohoe 4 14
(E A L Dunlop) *cl up: rdn along 3f out: wknd over 2f out* **9/1**

1m 48.63s (8.93) **Going Correction** +1.25s/f (Soft)
WFA 3 from 5yo+ 5lb **11** Ran SP% **118.0**
Speed ratings (Par 102):105,104,104,101,100 97,96,93,76,68 68
CSF £44.07 CT £580.51 TOTE £7.90: £3.40, £2.10, £5.30; EX 28.10 Trifecta £145.40 Part won. Pool: £204.80 - 0.50 winning tickets..
Owner Fawzi Abdulla Nass **Bred** E P Evans **Trained** Newmarket, Suffolk

FOCUS
A fair handicap in which the testing ground took its toll. The form looks ordinary for the level, though.
Commitment Lecture Official explanation: jockey said mare had no more to give
Passion Fruit Official explanation: jockey said mare lost its action

5025 EUROPEAN BREEDERS FUND CONSTANT SECURITY MAIDEN STKS 1m
2:50 (2:53) (Class 4) 2-Y-O **£6,477** (£1,927; £963; £481) **Stalls** Low

Form RPR

42 **1** **Hadahoo (USA)**[20] 4388 2-9-3............................. DarryllHolland 11 81
(M A Jarvis) *chsd ldrs: led over 6f out: styd on wl fnl 2f: drvn out* **5/4**[1]

0 **2** *1 ¼* **Jeer (IRE)**[21] 4366 2-9-3............................. DO'Donohoe 6 79
(E A L Dunlop) *hld up in mid-field: hdwy over 2f out: wnt 2nd jst ins last: no real imp* **40/1**

3 *5* **Eltanin (IRE)** 2-9-3............................. PaulMulrennan 4 69
(J Howard Johnson) *led over 1f: chsd wnr: wknd fnl f* **16/1**

4 *6* **Swiss Act** 2-9-3............................. DeanMcKeown 13 57
(M Johnston) *sn drvn along: chsd ldrs: wknd over 1f out* **13/2**[3]

0 **5** *4* **Glorious View**[24] 4260 2-9-3............................. DaleGibson 8 49
(M W Easterby) *sn bhd: kpt on fnl 2f: nvr nrr* **66/1**

4 **6** *½* **Brainy Benny (IRE)**[36] 3903 2-9-3............................. JamieMackay 9 48
(N A Callaghan) *t.k.h: trckd ldrs: hung lft and wknd over 1f out* **11/4**[2]

40 **7** *1 ¾* **Admiral Savannah (IRE)**[17] 4466 2-9-3............................. DavidAllan 7 44
(T D Easterby) *s.i.s: kpt on fnl 2f: nvr nr ldrs* **33/1**

8 *6* **Act Sirius (IRE)** 2-9-3............................. TonyHamilton 1 32
(J Howard Johnson) *s.i.s: nvr on terms* **12/1**

9 *10* **Cornell Precedent** 2-9-3............................. GrahamGibbons 10 12
(J J Quinn) *s.i.s: sn in tch: wknd over 2f out* **20/1**

10 *14* **Bollin Fiona** 2-8-12............................. PatCosgrave 12 —
(T D Easterby) *s.i.s: a bhd* **20/1**

00 **11** *32* **Bad Boy Al (IRE)**[12] 4650 2-9-3............................. PhillipMakin 2 —
(D W Barker) *in tch: lost pl after 2f: bhd and eased 3f out: virtually p.u: t.o* **50/1**

1m 50.36s (10.66) **Going Correction** +1.25s/f (Soft) **11** Ran SP% **116.4**
Speed ratings (Par 97):96,94,89,83,79 79,77,71,61,47 15
CSF £76.77 TOTE £2.10: £1.60, £6.00, £3.50; EX 62.70 Place 6 £9.07, Place 5 £5.46.
Owner Sheikh Ahmed Al Maktoum **Bred** Carl Rosen Associates **Trained** Newmarket, Suffolk

FOCUS
A weak maiden lacking any strength in depth and very much a one-horse race run in almost unraceable ground. The first two finished clear and they came home well strung out.

NOTEBOOK
Hadahoo(USA), loaded with the help of a rug, was soon at the head of affairs and in the desperate ground his rider sensibly left nothing to chance. (op 11-8 tchd 13-8)
Jeer(IRE), last of eleven on his debut on the all-weather three weeks earlier, kept on in dour fashion to bustle up the winner. He clearly stays well. (op 33-1)
Eltanin(IRE), a March foal, is up in the air and narrow. He jumped out first but became leg weary in pursuit of the winner. He will not reach full strength until next year.
Swiss Act, a March foal, is long in the back and narrow. From his outside draw he had to be chased along throughout. He will be wiser in future. (op 7-1 tchd 6-1)
Glorious View, home-bred and a half-brother to a couple of winners for this yard, stayed on in his own time and is the type to do better at three. (tchd 80-1)
Brainy Benny(IRE) wouldn't settle and in this bad ground hung violently left. Official explanation: jockey said colt hung left-handed in straight
Admiral Savannah(IRE) showed a fraction more than on his first two starts and is now qualified for a nursery mark. He is bred to make a middle-distance three-year-old. (op 50-1)

5026 SKYBET.COM HAMBLETON CUP (H'CAP) 1m 4f
() (Class 4) (0-80,) 3-Y-O+ £

5027 BAY HORSE AT RAINTON MAIDEN AUCTION STKS 7f
() (Class 5) 2-Y-O £

5028 ERA LOCKS H'CAP 1m
() (Class 5) (0-70,) 3-Y-O+ £

5029 RJF HOMES MAIDEN STKS (DIV II) 6f
() (Class 5) 3-Y-O+ £

5030 END OF SEASON H'CAP 6f
() (Class 5) (0-75,) 3-Y-O+ £

T/Plt: £3.90 to a £1 stake. Pool: £65,763.40. 12,087.30 winning tickets. T/Qpdt: £1.10 to a £1 stake. Pool: £2,980.50. 2,068.60 winning tickets. WG

4969 WOLVERHAMPTON (A.W) (L-H)

Saturday, September 2

OFFICIAL GOING: Standard to fast

Wind: Moderate, behind Weather: Fine

5031 WOLVERHAMPTON-RACECOURSE.CO.UK CLAIMING STKS 7f 32y(P)

7:00 (7:01) (Class 5) 3-Y-O+ **£3,238** (£963; £481; £240) **Stalls** High

Form RPR

3534 **1** **Marmooq**[15] 4573 3-8-11 74 SaleemGolam(3) 1 63
(S C Williams) *mde all: rdn over 1f out: drvn out* **15/8**[1]

4333 **2** ½ **Fulvio (USA)**[64] 3056 6-8-8 55 (v) JPFeatherstone(7) 4 61
(P Howling) *chsd ldr early: prom: wnt 2nd over 2f out: rdn over 1f out: r.o ins fnl f* **14/1**

0036 **3** *hd* **Muscari**[21] 4381 4-8-13 55 TPQueally 7 58
(A P Jarvis) *hld up in mid-div: hdwy on ins over 2f out: rdn wl over 1f out: r.o ins fnl f* **25/1**

/6-0 **4** *1* **Climate (IRE)**[10] 4706 7-9-10 70 NCallan 2 67
(K A Ryan) *hld up and bhd: nt clr run on ins over 2f out: hdwy wl over 1f out: sn rdn and hung lft: nt qckn fnl f* **10/1**

4150 **5** *hd* **Mister Elegant**[5] 4870 4-9-4 59 AdamKirby(3) 6 63
(J L Spearing) *hld up and bhd: gd hdwy on outside and edgd lft fnl f: nrst fin* **10/1**

5020 **6** 2½ **Pitbull**[42] 3725 3-9-9 62 JimmyQuinn 3 61
(Mrs G S Rees) *hld up and bhd: hdwy on ins wl over 1f out: sn rdn: no imp fnl f: saddle slipped* **20/1**

260 **7** ¾ **Dancing Deano (IRE)**[15] 4571 4-9-4 60 (v) HayleyTurner 8 52
(R M Whitaker) *hld up in tch: rdn 3f out: wknd over 1f out* **14/1**

20-6 **8** *hd* **Prince Dayjur (USA)**[117] 1550 7-9-7 75 DeanMcKeown 9 54
(J Pearce) *hmpd and lost pl sn after s: rdn and sme hdwy over 2f out: btn whn sltly hmpd 1f out* **7/1**[3]

0206 **9** *nk* **Franksalot (IRE)**[9] 4729 6-9-13 67 RoystonFfrench 5 60
(I W McInnes) *hld up towards rr: rdn over 2f out: no rspnse* **14/1**

5454 **10** 1¼ **Alfonso**[10] 4692 5-9-4 77 (b) TomEaves 11 47
(I Semple) *s.i.s: hdwy over 5f out: rdn 2f out: wknd over 1f out* **7/2**[2]

5-40 **11** 1½ **White Ladder (IRE)**[8] 4769 3-9-9 64 (b[1]) EddieAhern 10 50
(P F I Cole) *hld up in mid-div: rdn over 2f out: wknd wl over 1f out* **33/1**

0300 **12** *6* **Mill By The Stream**[2] 4970 4-8-9 58 JamesDoyle(3) 12 22
(R Brotherton) *sn chsng wnr: rdn and wknd over 2f out* **33/1**

1m 28.4s (-2.00) **Going Correction** -0.325s/f (Stan)
WFA 3 from 4yo+ 4lb **12** Ran SP% **122.2**
Speed ratings (Par 103):98,97,97,96,95 92,92,91,91,90 88,81
CSF £30.80 TOTE £2.60: £1.40, £2.80, £3.60; EX 36.60.The winner was claimed by A. M. Hales for £8,000.
Owner J W Lovitt & Partners **Bred** Matthews Breeding And Racing Ltd **Trained** Newmarket, Suffolk

FOCUS
This turned out to be a competitive, if average claimer. The winner was a stone plus off his best but the form seems sound enough.
Pitbull Official explanation: jockey said saddle slipped
Prince Dayjur(USA) Official explanation: jockey said gelding suffered interference in running

5032 GET MARRIED AT WOLVERHAMPTON RACECOURSE H'CAP 5f 216y(P)

7:30 (7:30) (Class 6) (0-60,60) 3-Y-O+ **£2,730** (£806; £403) **Stalls** Low

Form RPR

6522 **1** **Only If I Laugh**[1] 4984 5-8-13 53 (v) RobbieFitzpatrick 1 65
(M J Attwater) *mid-div: rdn and hdwy on ins over 2f out: hrd rdn to ld nr fin* **4/1**[1]

2000 **2** *nk* **Tag Team (IRE)**[6] 4846 5-9-3 60 StephenDonohoe(3) 10 71
(John A Harris) *a.p: rdn to ld over 2f out: hdd nr fin* **33/1**

5046 **3** 1¾ **Gone'N'Dunnett (IRE)**[2] 4970 7-9-6 60 (p) JohnEgan 7 66
(Mrs C A Dunnett) *a.p: rdn over 2f out: kpt on same pce fnl f* **10/1**

0002 **4** ½ **Million Percent**[2] 4970 7-9-1 60 LiamJones(5) 8 64
(C R Dore) *mid-div: rdn over 2f out: kpt on u.p ins fnl f* **7/1**[3]

1210 **5** *shd* **Limonia (GER)**[2] 4970 4-8-13 56 JamesDoyle(3) 3 60
(N P Littmoden) *led 1f: a.p: rdn over 1f out: no ex wl ins fnl f* **8/1**

4100 **6** 1¼ **Kahlua Bear**[2] 4970 4-8-11 54 (v) AdamKirby(3) 12 54
(Miss K B Boutflower) *s.i.s: bhd: rdn over 2f out: hdwy wl over 1f out: hld whn n.m.r towards fin* **40/1**

2034 **7** ½ **Desert Opal**[2] 4970 6-9-6 60 EddieAhern 11 59
(C R Dore) *broke wl: sn mid-div: rdn and sme hdwy over 1f out: no further prog fnl f* **17/2**

3-00 **8** 1¾ **King After**[24] 4248 4-9-3 57 GeorgeBaker 2 51+
(J R Best) *in rr: nt clr run over 3f out tl over 2f out: rdn over 1f out: nvr nrr* **20/1**

435 **9** 2½ **Diamond Josh**[28] 4141 4-8-13 53 DeanMcKeown 5 39
(P D Evans) *led after 1f: rdn and hdd over 2f out: wknd jst over 1f out* **4/1**[1]

1000 **10** 1½ **Moon Bird**[33] 4003 4-9-5 59 RoystonFfrench 6 41
(C A Cyzer) *s.i.s: sn mid-div: rdn whn hmpd over 3f out: n.d after* **33/1**

0513 **11** 2½ **Rancho Cucamonga (IRE)**[10] 4694 4-9-2 56 (b) NCallan 4 30
(T D Barron) *s.i.s: towards rr whn bdly hmpd over 3f out: n.d after* **11/2**[2]

400- **12** *5* **Shropshirelass**[324] 5857 3-8-9 54 EdwardCreighton(3) 13 13
(Mrs Norma Pook) *a bhd* **40/1**

4214 **13** *nk* **Fortress**[21] 4354 3-9-4 60 (b) FrancisNorton 9 18
(E J Alston) *chsd ldrs tl rdn and wknd over 2f out* **16/1**

1m 13.95s (-1.86) **Going Correction** -0.325s/f (Stan)
WFA 3 from 4yo+ 2lb **13** Ran SP% **120.0**
Speed ratings (Par 101):99,98,96,95,95 93,93,90,87,85 82,75,75
CSF £154.30 CT £1280.64 TOTE £6.60: £2.20, £12.60, £3.00; EX 212.20.
Owner Phones Direct Partnership **Bred** The Lavington Stud **Trained** Wysall, Notts

FOCUS
Several of these had met in a similar contest here 48 hours earlier. The form looks sound enough for the grade.
King After Official explanation: jockey said gelding was denied a clear run

5033 STAY AT THE WOLVERHAMPTON HOLIDAY INN (S) H'CAP 1m 4f 50y(P)

8:00 (8:00) (Class 6) (0-55,49) 3-5-Y-O **£2,388** (£705; £352) **Stalls** Low

Form RPR

363 **1** **Agilete**[8] 4755 4-9-3 44 EddieAhern 4 58+
(J R Boyle) *hld up towards rr: stdy hdwy over 3f out: led on bit ins fnl f: hrd hld* **7/2**[1]

2510 **2** 1¼ **Cool Isle**[4] 4909 3-8-5 48 ow3 (b) JPFeatherstone(7) 5 54
(P Howling) *a.p: led 3f out: rdn 2f out: hdd ins fnl f: no ch w wnr* **10/1**

2220 **3** *8* **Zaffeu**[88] 2320 5-9-8 49 NCallan 7 42
(A G Juckes) *hld up towards rr: hdwy 4f out: sn rdn: wknd over 1f out* **4/1**[2]

0000 **4** ½ **Shingle Street (IRE)**[19] 4438 4-9-1 45 JamesDoyle(3) 11 37
(I A Wood) *chsd ldr: led 5f out: rdn and hdd 3f out: wknd wl over 1f out* **16/1**

4050 **5** 2½ **Karrnak**[8] 4764 4-9-1 45 (tp) DeanCorby(3) 12 33
(Miss J Feilden) *hld up and bhd: rdn over 3f out: sme hdwy over 1f out: nvr nr ldrs* **25/1**

4403 **6** ½ **King Forever**[25] 4227 4-9-0 41 DaleGibson 10 29
(D E Cantillon) *plld hrd in rr: sme hdwy over 3f out: rdn over 2f out: no further prog* **6/1**[3]

-044 **7** *1* **Beaumont Girl (IRE)**[22] 2935 4-8-10 40 (bt[1]) PatrickMathers(3) 2 26
(Miss M E Rowland) *hld up in mid-div: bhd whn rdn over 3f out* **22/1**

0554 **8** *shd* **Perfectionist**[6] 4848 4-9-5 46 (v[1]) JimmyQuinn 8 32
(Mrs C A Dunnett) *hld up and bhd: hdwy over 5f out: rdn over 3f out: wknd 2f out* **12/1**

0500 **9** *hd* **Helen Wood**[21] 4367 3-8-4 47 FrankiePickard(7) 3 33
(M D I Usher) *s.s: a bhd* **33/1**

0330 **10** *10* **Madam Mac (IRE)**[39] 3824 3-8-7 43 (b[1]) ChrisCatlin 9 13
(B J Meehan) *t.k.h in mid-div: hdwy 5f out: rdn 3f out: sn wknd* **12/1**

614- **11** *11* **Bongoali**[298] 6289 4-9-3 44 TPQueally 6 —
(Mrs C A Dunnett) *led: hdd 5f out: rdn and wknd 4f out* **12/1**

12 *51* **Effect Me Not (IRE)**[99] 2008 4-9-7 48 RobbieFitzpatrick 1 —
(Peter Grayson) *prom: rdn over 5f out: wknd over 4f out: t.o* **8/1**

2m 39.89s (-2.53) **Going Correction** -0.325s/f (Stan)
WFA 3 from 4yo+ 9lb **12** Ran SP% **116.8**
Speed ratings (Par 101):95,94,88,88,86 86,85,85,85,78 71,37
CSF £37.36 CT £146.62 TOTE £4.80: £1.70, £4.20, £1.80; EX 49.90.The winner was sold to Jeff Pearce for 8,000gns.
Owner M Khan X2 **Bred** J W Parker And Lavington Stud **Trained** Epsom, Surrey

FOCUS
A poor event which proved to be a very one-sided contest.

5034 NAME A RACE TO ENHANCE YOUR BRAND NOVICE AUCTION STKS 1m 141y(P)

8:30 (8:30) (Class 5) 2-Y-O **£3,238** (£963; £481; £240) **Stalls** Low

Form RPR

012 **1** **Majuro (IRE)**[9] 4732 2-9-3 86 ChrisCatlin 4 91
(M R Channon) *chsd ldrs: hrd rdn to ld ins fnl f: drvn out* **7/2**[2]

2326 **2** 1½ **Cape Schanck**[21] 4344 2-8-9 76 JohnEgan 1 80
(Jane Chapple-Hyam) *led: rdn over 2f out: hdd and nt qckn ins fnl f* **9/2**[3]

323 **3** 1¼ **Laureldean Express**[30] 4084 2-8-7 80 RichardMullen 3 75
(E J O'Neill) *w ldr: rdn over 2f out: edgd rt ins fnl f: one pce* **5/6**[1]

4253 **4** *7* **Ten Dollars More (IRE)**[24] 4264 2-8-13 74 EddieAhern 5 66
(J A Osborne) *hld up: rdn and hdwy over 2f out: edgd rt and wknd over 1f out* **8/1**

5 *32* **Lady Smock** 2-8-4 JosedeSouza 2 —
(J R Holt) *in rr: rn green and hung rt bnd 7f out: t.o fnl 3f* **80/1**

1m 48.63s (-3.13) **Going Correction** -0.325s/f (Stan) **5** Ran SP% **107.3**
Speed ratings (Par 95):100,98,97,91,62
CSF £17.70 TOTE £3.90: £2.10, £2.30; EX 17.90.
Owner Capital **Bred** Tally-Ho Stud **Trained** West Ilsley, Berks

FOCUS
This was quite competitive despite the small field. Sound form which could be worth a few pounds more.

NOTEBOOK
Majuro(IRE) saw it out well under some strong driving on this step up from seven furlongs. (op 11-4)
Cape Schanck ◆, another previously exclusively campaigned over seven, had been highly tried last time. He did not appear to be beaten for stamina and continues to knock on the door. (op 11-2)
Laureldean Express lacked the required finishing speed over this longer distance. (op Evens tchd 4-5)
Ten Dollars More(IRE) got found out by the longer trip. Official explanation: jockey said colt lost its action (op 13-2)

5035 WOLVERHAMPTON ALWAYS FREE PARKING MAIDEN H'CAP 1m 141y(P)

9:00 (9:01) (Class 6) (0-60,60) 3-Y-O+ **£2,730** (£806; £403) **Stalls** Low

Form RPR

2422 **1** **Starboard Light**[13] 4627 3-9-5 59 SebSanders 5 72
(R M Beckett) *a.p: led over 2f out: rdn and edgd rt over 1f out: drvn out* **11/4**[1]

2024 **2** ¾ **Panic Stations**[21] 4375 3-8-12 59 LukeMorris(7) 9 70
(M L W Bell) *hld up in tch: rdn over 2f out: ev ch whn edgd lft 1f out: nt qckn* **4/1**[2]

0-00 **3** ½ **Keon (IRE)**[23] 4276 4-8-6 47 RussellKennemore(7) 2 57
(R Hollinshead) *a.p: rdn 2f out: ev ch whn n.m.r 1f out: nt qckn* **25/1**

0560 **4** *3* **Postmaster**[12] 4667 4-8-13 47 ChrisCatlin 4 51
(R Ingram) *hld up and bhd: hdwy on ins wl over 1f out: sn rdn: one pce fnl f* **9/1**

506 **5** 3½ **Gattuso**[19] 4426 3-9-5 59 EddieAhern 7 55
(Ms Deborah J Evans) *s.i.s: hld up: hdwy on ins over 3f out: rdn over 2f out: wknd fnl f* **15/2**

0655 **6** ¾ **Peters Delite**[14] 4585 4-9-0 48 PaulHanagan 6 43
(R A Fahey) *prom: rdn 4f out: wknd over 2f out* **7/1**[3]

-565 **7** ¾ **Grand Design**[194] 460 4-9-10 58 RoystonFfrench 12 51
(C A Cyzer) *nvr nr ldrs* **20/1**

6000 **8** 1¼ **Must Be Keen**[6] 4845 7-9-7 55 (t) JohnEgan 10 46
(Ernst Oertel) *mid-div: rdn over 2f out: no rspnse* **40/1**

6406 **9** ½ **Pop Music (IRE)**[29] 4113 3-9-3 60 (b) DeanCorby(3) 13 50
(Miss J Feilden) *a bhd* **25/1**

0404 **10** 1¾ **On Air (USA)**[11] 4671 3-9-6 60 RichardMullen 8 46
(E J O'Neill) *rdn 4f out: a towards rr* **10/1**

5000 **11** ½ **Marcello**[24] 4245 3-9-6 60 (bt[1]) NCallan 3 45
(P F I Cole) *led: rdn and hdd over 2f out: wknd wl over 1f out* **12/1**

4 **12** *30* **Sotanna (IRE)**[18] 4447 4-9-0 48 DaneO'Neill 11 —
(P R Webber) *rdn over 3f out: a in rr: t.o* **16/1**

1m 48.83s (-2.93) **Going Correction** -0.325s/f (Stan)
WFA 3 from 4yo+ 6lb **12** Ran SP% **118.5**
Speed ratings (Par 101):100,99,98,96,93 92,91,90,90,88 88,61
CSF £12.42 CT £232.46 TOTE £3.60: £1.40, £2.10, £8.60; EX 8.50.
Owner Mrs Hugh Maitland-Jones **Bred** Mrs J F Maitland-Jones **Trained** Whitsbury, Hants
■ Stewards' Enquiry : Luke Morris caution: careless riding

FOCUS
A typically modest maiden handicap which did not take much winning, but the time was the pick on the card.

5036 HOLD YOUR CONFERENCE AT WOLVERHAMPTON RACECOURSE H'CAP 7f 32y(P)
9:30 (9:31) (Class 5) (0-70,68) 3-Y-O £3,238 (£963; £481; £240) Stalls High

Form				RPR
0341	1		**Glenbuck (IRE)**[8] [4769] 3-9-4 **68**........(v) FrancisNorton 8 (A Bailey) *led: hdd over 1f out: rdn to ld nr fin* **6/1**[3]	74
0221	2	*nk*	**Hoh Wotanite**[52] [3410] 3-9-4 **68**........ LPKeniry 1 (R Hollinshead) *a.p: led over 1f out: hrd rdn and hdd nr fin* **3/1**[1]	73
0024	3	*hd*	**Flylowflylong (IRE)**[16] [4524] 3-9-1 **65**........ TomEaves 3 (I Semple) *hld up: rdn over 3f out: hdwy on ins 2f out: swtchd rt jst over 1f out: r.o cl home* **13/2**	70
5030	4	*½*	**Valentino Swing (IRE)**[17] [4496] 3-9-1 **68**........ StephenDonohoe(3) 5 (J L Spearing) *hld up: hdwy on outside 2f out: rdn over 1f out: edgd rt ins fnl f: r.o* **16/1**	71
0500	5	*2 ½*	**Hits Only Jude (IRE)**[14] [4602] 3-9-1 **65**........ DeanMcKeown 2 (J Pearce) *hld up: hrd rdn and hdwy over 1f out: one pce fnl f* **6/1**[3]	62
4404	6	*1 ¼*	**Guilded Warrior**[21] [4368] 3-9-3 **67**........ FergusSweeney 9 (W S Kittow) *prom: rdn over 2f out: edgd lft 1f out: sn wknd* **15/2**	61
0203	7	*1 ¼*	**Elegant Times (IRE)**[16] [4524] 3-8-12 **62**........ EddieAhern 7 (T D Easterby) *bhd: late hdwy on outside: nvr nrr* **11/2**[2]	52
3-06	8	*3 ½*	**Dawaleeb (IRE)**[7] [4814] 3-9-1 **65**........ JohnEgan 10 (Jane Chapple-Hyam) *s.i.s: hld up in mid-div: rdn and hdwy over 2f out: wknd wl over 1f out* **16/1**	46
200	9	*hd*	**Rose Lady (IRE)**[85] [2406] 3-8-12 **62**........ ChrisCatlin 6 (M R Channon) *a bhd* **25/1**	43
0004	10	*nk*	**Prettilini**[24] [4265] 3-8-13 **66**........ JamesDoyle(3) 4 (R Brotherton) *hld up in mid-div: rdn 3f out: sn wknd* **12/1**	46
5-23	11	*10*	**Blue Beacon**[185] [551] 3-9-2 **66**........ NCallan 11 (K A Ryan) *sn chsng ldr: rdn and wknd 2f out* **20/1**	20

1m 28.16s (-2.24) **Going Correction** -0.325s/f (Stan) **11** Ran SP% **122.1**
Speed ratings (Par 101):99,98,98,97,95 93,92,88,87,87 76
CSF £25.31 CT £127.56 TOTE £9.40: £3.40, £1.40, £2.60; EX 24.40 Place 6 £68.94, Place 5 £32.26.
Owner Middleham Park Racing XLII **Bred** Mrs Teresa Monaghan **Trained** Cotebrook, Cheshire
FOCUS
A tightly-knit, moderate handicap. The form loks pretty sound and should prove reliable.
T/Plt: £59.60 to a £1 stake. Pool: £66,556.90. 814.75 winning tickets. T/Qpdt: £6.20 to a £1 stake. Pool: £3,150.80. 371.90 winning tickets. KH

5037 - 5040a (Foreign Racing) - See Raceform Interactive

4926 LINGFIELD (L-H)
Sunday, September 3
OFFICIAL GOING: Turf course - good; aw course - standard
Wind: Fresh, behind Weather: Cloudy

5041 HILARY GRAY BIRTHDAY CELEBRATION NURSERY 7f
2:10 (2:16) (Class 4) (0-85,83) 2-Y-O £6,477 (£1,927; £963; £481) Stalls High

Form				RPR
3161	1		**Heywood**[8] [4813] 2-9-7 **83**........ TPO'Shea 7 (M R Channon) *hld up in rr: hdwy wl over 2f out: rdn 2f out: led 1f out: styd on u.p: all out* **7/2**[2]	83
2634	2	*nk*	**Miss Saafend Plaza (IRE)**[37] [3902] 2-9-4 **80**........ RichardHughes 5 (R Hannon) *hld up in rr: hdwy on rail over 2f out: rdn over 1f out: short of room and swtchd lft ins fnl f: r.o wl* **4/1**[3]	79
41	3	*¾*	**Veenwouden**[16] [4553] 2-9-1 **77**........ OscarUrbina 3 (J R Fanshawe) *hld up towards rr: hdwy 2f out: wnt 3rd ins fnl f: kpt on same pce last 100 yds* **2/1**[1]	74
060	4	*1 ¾*	**Maid Of Ale (IRE)**[27] [4207] 2-8-5 **67** ow1........ EddieAhern 13 (B J Meehan) *slowly away: sn prom: ev ch over 2f out: kpt on same pce u.p* **5/1**	60
4560	5	*1*	**Carlitos Spirit (IRE)**[63] [3117] 2-8-4 **66**........ ChrisCatlin 4 (B R Millman) *chsd ldrs: rdn and outpcd over 1f out: kpt on again wl ins fnl f* **25/1**	56
01	6	*½*	**Redcliff (GER)**[19] [4445] 2-9-1 **77**........ JimCrowley 8 (Mrs A J Perrett) *t.k.h: chsd ldr tl led over 2f out: rdn and hdd 1f out: wkng whn short of room ins fnl f* **14/1**	66
006	7	*1 ½*	**Revisionist (IRE)**[45] [3663] 2-8-4 **66**........ RichardSmith 12 (R Hannon) *chsd ldrs: rdn over 2f out: kpt on onepced* **16/1**	51
300	8	*1 ¾*	**Daring You**[70] [2899] 2-7-13 **61** ow1........ FrankieMcDonald 10 (P F I Cole) *racd in midfield: rdn 3f out: sn struggling* **16/1**	41
065	9	*1 ½*	**Global Traffic**[79] [2626] 2-7-12 **60** oh1........ NickyMackay 6 (P F I Cole) *racd in midfield: rdn over 2f out: wknd 2f out* **9/1**	36
050	10	*1*	**Spirited Speedfit (IRE)**[35] [3979] 2-8-2 **67**........ SaleemGolam(3) 2 (G G Margarson) *bhd and rdn after 3f: no ch after* **20/1**	41
1040	11	*¾*	**Hythe Bay**[22] [4344] 2-9-4 **80**........ SteveDrowne 1 (R T Phillips) *led to post: w.w on outer: shkn up wl over 1f out: no rspnse* **25/1**	52
0650	12	*6*	**Chip Leader**[114] [1639] 2-8-5 **67**........ MartinDwyer 11 (R Hannon) *led tl over 2f out: sn wknd: eased last 100 yds* **33/1**	23

1m 22.72s (-1.49) **Going Correction** -0.425s/f (Firm) **12** Ran SP% **136.0**
Speed ratings (Par 97):91,90,89,87,86 86,84,82,80,79 78,71
CSF £20.20 CT £38.94 TOTE £4.90: £1.70, £2.10, £1.20; EX 24.30 Trifecta £80.90 Pool: £352.15 - 3.09 winning units..
Owner Sheikh Mohammed **Bred** R F And S D Knipe **Trained** West Ilsley, Berks
FOCUS
A fair nursery. The first two home raced stands' side and the rail seemed a big advantage. The runner-up anchors the standard.
NOTEBOOK
Heywood was just able to defy an 8lb higher mark than when successful at Sandown on his previous start to make it three wins from his last four starts. He only scraped home, but has progressed into a useful sort and could have more to offer. (op 4-1)
Miss Saafend Plaza(IRE) ◆ was shortened up by the eventual winner when staying on against the near-side rail and might have been a little unlucky. She is still a maiden, but can surely win a nursery or two before the season is out. (op 9-2 tchd 5-1)
Veenwouden ◆ found this tougher than the Folkestone maiden she won last time but emerged with plenty of credit as she raced towards the middle of the track, whereas the front two came up the near-side rail. She looks the type to keep progressing. (op 9-4)
Maid Of Ale(IRE), supported in the market, showed improved form stepped up in trip on her nursery debut. (op 13-2 tchd 7-1)
Carlitos Spirit(IRE), still a maiden, ran okay upped a furlong in trip.
Chip Leader Official explanation: jockey said gelding hung left

5042 DARREN GIBBONS PRE-NUPTIAL H'CAP 7f
2:40 (2:42) (Class 5) (0-75,75) 3-Y-O+ £5,181 (£1,541; £770; £384) Stalls High

Form				RPR
5101	1		**Taranaki**[8] [4795] 8-8-8 **66**........ AshleyHamblett(7) 12 (P D Cundell) *trckd ldrs early: stdd and racd midfield: swtchd onto nr rail and hdwy 2f out: qcknd to ld last 100 yds: pushed out* **10/1**	75
0313	2	*1*	**Trimlestown (IRE)**[11] [4689] 3-9-4 **73**........ DaneO'Neill 11 (H Candy) *prom: ev ch and rdn 2f out: led 1f out: hdd and no ex last 100 yds* **10/1**	78
412	3	*1*	**Secret Assassin (IRE)**[11] [4689] 3-9-6 **75**........ MartinDwyer 13 (W R Muir) *chsd ldr tl led over 2f out: rdn and hdd 1f out: kpt on same pce* **10/1**	77
0450	4	*nk*	**Lizarazu (GER)**[11] [4706] 7-9-1 **73**........(p) TolleyDean(7) 6 (R A Harris) *t.k.h: hld up in tch: rdn and hdwy 2f out: kpt on same pce ins fnl f* **25/1**	76+
2321	5	*nk*	**Young Bertie**[4] [4930] 3-8-8 **68** 6ex........(v) TravisBlock(5) 1 (H Morrison) *in tch on outer: rdn 3f out: ev ch wl over 1f out: onepced ins fnl f* **9/2**[1]	68+
3035	6	*1*	**Pure Imagination (IRE)**[3] [4961] 5-9-8 **73**........ RyanMoore 3 (J M Bradley) *in tch in midfield: rdn over 2f out: kpt on same pce* **7/1**[2]	73+
2055	7	*hd*	**Kings Heir (IRE)**[16] [4562] 3-9-2 **74**........(b[1]) JamesDoyle(3) 17 (R M Beckett) *led tl over 2f out: sn rdn: wknd ins fnl f* **10/1**	71
0114	8	*nk*	**Takitwo**[11] [4689] 3-8-12 **67**........ LPKeniry 10 (P D Cundell) *trckd ldrs: rdn wl over 1f out: kpt on same pce* **12/1**	64
0444	9	*nk*	**Mohawk Star (IRE)**[16] [4575] 5-9-2 **67**........ DavidKinsella 15 (I A Wood) *w.w: rdn 2f out: kpt on ins fnl f: n.d* **8/1**[3]	65
0423	10	*1 ¾*	**Greenwood**[16] [4573] 8-9-7 **72**........ SteveDrowne 8 (P G Murphy) *w.w nin midfield: drvn 2f out: kpt on same pce* **8/1**[3]	65
040	11	*1 ¼*	**Aastral Magic**[16] [4564] 4-9-2 **67**........ RichardHughes 16 (R Hannon) *bhd: drvn 4f out: nvr on terms* **12/1**	57
5060	12	*1 ¼*	**Currency**[6] [4870] 9-8-12 **63**........(p) FrancisNorton 14 (J M Bradley) *chsd ldrs: rdn 1/2-way: wknd over 2f out* **12/1**	50
2140	13	*nk*	**Grand Entrance (IRE)**[18] [4488] 3-9-4 **73**........ EddieAhern 5 (C R Egerton) *wl bhd: swtchd lft 1f out: sme late hdwy: nvr on terms* **12/1**	57
0044	14	*nk*	**Wrighty Almighty (IRE)**[16] [4557] 4-9-7 **72**........(p) JimCrowley 4 (P R Chamings) *in tch on outer: rdn over 2f out: sn struggling* **25/1**	57
-100	15	*2 ½*	**My Obsession (IRE)**[100] [1996] 4-8-9 **63**........ StephenDonohoe(3) 18 (John Berry) *trckd ldrs early: midfield and rdn over 2f out: stuggling whn hmpd 2f out: no ch after* **16/1**	42
0613	16	*5*	**Wheelavit (IRE)**[31] [4078] 3-9-2 **71**........ GeorgeBaker 7 (B G Powell) *hld up bhd: rdn over 2f out: sn no ch* **14/1**	35

1m 21.39s (-2.82) **Going Correction** -0.425s/f (Firm)
WFA 3 from 4yo+ 4lb **16** Ran SP% **140.3**
Speed ratings (Par 103):99,97,96,96,96 94,94,94,93,91 90,89,88,88,85 79
CSF £122.40 CT £1070.46 TOTE £12.50: £2.90, £2.40, £2.30, £8.60; EX 112.50 Trifecta £108.50 Pool: £259.96 - 1.70 winning units..
Owner Miss M C Fraser **Bred** E D Evers **Trained** Compton, Berks
■ Stewards' Enquiry : Ashley Hamblett two-day ban: careless riding (Sept 14-15)
FOCUS
An ordinary handicap run at a good pace from the start. The form looks alright but the near-side rail again looked a big advantage.
Grand Entrance(IRE) Official explanation: jockey said, regarding running and riding, his orders were to drop gelding in and get it settled, as it has run too free on its two previous runs, adding that it appeared to sulk and then failed to get the clearest of runs
Wheelavit(IRE) Official explanation: jockey said gelding never travelled

5043 LINGFIELD PARK 0870 2200022 MAIDEN AUCTION STKS 6f
3:10 (3:12) (Class 4) 2-Y-O £6,477 (£1,927; £963; £481) Stalls High

Form				RPR
2	1		**Diysem (USA)**[15] [4600] 2-9-1........ RyanMoore 12 (B J Meehan) *trckd ldrs: swtchd lft and hdwy over 1f out: sn drvn: hrd rdn to ld ins fnl f* **4/9**[1]	81
3203	2	*¾*	**Baltic Belle (IRE)**[53] [3402] 2-8-8 81 ow1........ RichardHughes 10 (R Hannon) *led against nr side rail: rdn wl over 1f out: hdd and no ex wl ins fnl f* **11/4**[2]	72
	3	*2 ½*	**Support Fund (IRE)** 2-8-4........ StephenCarson 11 (R F Johnson Houghton) *slowly away: wl bhd: swtchd lft and drvn 3f out: gd hdwy on outer over 2f out: chsd ldng pair 1f out: no imp* **20/1**[3]	60
	4	*2*	**Odin Dawn** 2-9-1........ RichardSmith 7 (R Hannon) *racd in midfield: rdn 2f out: kpt on ins fnl f: nt rch ldrs* **33/1**	65
00	5	*nk*	**Golan Way**[9] [4753] 2-8-12........ DavidKinsella 3 (I A Wood) *racd in midfield: rdn and sme hdwy 2f out: kpt on: nt rch ldrs* **25/1**	61
	6	*nk*	**Tokyo Rose** 2-8-7........ PatDobbs 9 (R Hannon) *trckd ldrs: rdn 2f out: wknd fnl f* **20/1**[3]	55
5300	7	*¾*	**Aggresive**[11] [4699] 2-8-9 57........ DarryllHolland 4 (Ernst Oertel) *prom: chsd ldr after 2f tl over 1f out: sn wknd* **50/1**	55
	8	*3*	**Knapton Hill** 2-8-7........ SteveDrowne 2 (H Morrison) *sn outpcd in rr: edgd lft and sme hdwy 2f out: nvr on terms* **20/1**[3]	44
	9	*2*	**Etoile D'Or (IRE)** 2-8-2 ow1........ SaleemGolam(3) 1 (M H Tompkins) *slowly away: a outpcd in rr: sme late hdwy* **33/1**	36
	10	*1 ½*	**Mr Forthright** 2-8-9........ FrancisNorton 5 (J M Bradley) *outpcd in midfield: rdn over 2f out: sn bhd* **25/1**	36
	11	*nk*	**Rotation (IRE)** 2-9-1........ WandersonD'Avila 8 (J W Hills) *outpcd in midfield: nvr on terms* **50/1**	41
0	12	*7*	**Foreland Sands (IRE)**[16] [4550] 2-8-12........ DaneO'Neill 6 (J R Best) *chsd ldr for 2f: sn lost pl: t.o* **50/1**	17
	13	*2*	**Alonso De Guzman (IRE)** 2-8-9........ MartinDwyer 13 (J R Boyle) *v.s.a: a outpcd in rr: t.o* **25/1**	8

69.88 secs (-1.79) **Going Correction** -0.425s/f (Firm) **13** Ran SP% **133.5**
Speed ratings (Par 97):94,93,89,87,86 86,85,81,78,76 76,66,64
CSF £1.75 TOTE £1.50: £1.10, £1.20, £5.50; EX 2.60 Trifecta £14.70 Pool: £352.57 - 16.95 winning units..
Owner Nizar Anwar **Bred** Indian Creek **Trained** Manton, Wilts
FOCUS
A reasonable maiden auction event that should produce some winners, although the seventh limits the form. Once again, the near-side rail looked advantageous.
NOTEBOOK
Diysem(USA), well backed when second on his debut at Newmarket, made hard work of justifying his short price but was conceding 7lb to the runner-up. He might be value for a touch further, as he had to be switched with his effort and the eventual runner-up had the near-side rail to run against, but it remains to be seen how much improvement there is to come. (op 8-13)
Baltic Belle(IRE) was given every chance on the favoured strip of ground on the near-side rail and was just denied. On this evidence, an official mark of 81 is stiff enough.

Support Fund(IRE) ◆, a 13,000gns half-sister to among others, Henri Lebasque, a useful six/eight-furlong winner at two, made a very pleasing introduction. Well off the pace early, she was switched towards the centre of the track at about halfway and stayed on nicely behind two far more experienced rivals, who both have useful form to their name. Open to improvement, she should win a similar race. (tchd 33-1)

Odin Dawn ◆, a 32,000gns half-brother to seven winners, including Desert Kaya, a smart dual mile winner at three, and prolific sprint winner Folga, out of a smart juvenile/sprinter, kept on nicely behind the principals. He can improve with the benefit of this experience and should go close next time.

Golan Way ran a respectable race and will have more options now he is qualified for a handicap mark. (tchd 40-1)

Tokyo Rose, a 25,000gns half-sister to, amongst others, Bandit Queen, a fair dual six-furlong juvenile scorer, out of Ayr Gold Cup winner Wildwood Flower, ran with credit on her racecourse debut.

Aggresive ◆ has had a few chances, but again showed enough to suggest he can make his mark in handicap company.

5044 HOWARD HOLDINGS H'CAP — 6f

3:40 (3:41) (Class 2) (0-100,99) 3-Y-0+

£12,464 (£3,732; £1,866; £934; £466; £234) **Stalls** High

Form — RPR

3002 **1** **Gimasha**[8] [4811] 4-9-0 **93** .... KerrinMcEvoy 7 — 101+
(W Jarvis) *walked to post: t.k.h: hld up in tch: rdn and hdwy 1f out: r.o wl to ld nr fin* **11/4**[2]

2400 **2** *shd* **Obe Brave**[15] [4593] 3-9-2 **97** .... TonyCulhane 5 — 105
(M R Channon) *led against nr side rail: drvn over 1f out: hdd nr fin* **8/1**

0536 **3** ½ **Grantley Adams**[22] [4345] 3-8-13 **94** .... RyanMoore 4 — 101
(M R Channon) *chsd ldrs: wnt 2nd 1/2-way: rdn and ev ch over 1f out: unable qck wl ins fnl f* **10/1**

1210 **4** 1 ¾ **Zidane**[51] [3493] 4-8-11 **90** .... OscarUrbina 1 — 91+
(J R Fanshawe) *swtchd rt and hld up bhd: rdn and hdwy on outer 2f out: chsd ldrs 1f out: no imp ins fnl f* **5/2**[1]

4060 **5** 1 **Loyal Royal (IRE)**[59] [3223] 3-8-9 **90** .... LPKeniry 3 — 88
(D R C Elsworth) *t.k.h: hld up in midfield: rdn wl over 1f out: kpt on same pce* **33/1**

0102 **6** ½ **Lady Livius (IRE)**[22] [4343] 3-8-12 **93** .... DaneO'Neill 8 — 90
(R Hannon) *chsd ldr tl 1/2-way: sn lost pl: n.d after* **16/1**

0053 **7** 1 ¾ **Connect**[12] [4682] 9-8-6 **92** .... (b) PatrickHills(7) 11 — 84
(M H Tompkins) *bhd: rdn and struggling wl over 2f out: sme late hdwy: n.d* **15/2**[3]

0035 **8** *nk* **Texas Gold**[6] [4875] 8-9-6 **99** .... MartinDwyer 2 — 90
(W R Muir) *chsd ldrs on outer: rdn and ev ch 2f out: eased whn btn ins fnl f* **8/1**

2305 **9** *nk* **Blue Tomato**[20] [4430] 5-8-6 **88** .... StephenDonohoe(3) 6 — 78
(J M Bradley) *hld up in rr: effprt u.p over 2f out: nvr on terms* **9/1**

5600 **10** 1 ¼ **Campbeltown (IRE)**[11] [4707] 3-8-9 **90** .... AdrianMcCarthy 10 — 76
(R A Harris) *slowly away: sn in tch: rdn and wknd over wl over 1f out* **25/1**

6044 **11** 1 **Gavarnie Beau (IRE)**[7] [4841] 3-8-4 **85** .... FrancisNorton 9 — 68
(M Blanshard) *bhd: rdn over 2f out: sn no ch* **20/1**

68.81 secs (-2.86) **Going Correction** -0.425s/f (Firm)
WFA 3 from 4yo+ 2lb — **11** Ran SP% **125.7**
Speed ratings (Par 109):102,101,101,98,97 96,94,94,93,92 90
CSF £26.77 CT £204.48 TOTE £3.70: £1.90, £1.80, £3.40; EX 25.70 Trifecta £170.80 Pool: £442.70 - 1.84 winning units..
Owner Ziad A Galadari **Bred** Galadari Sons Stud Company Limited **Trained** Newmarket, Suffolk
■ Stewards' Enquiry : Tony Culhane caution: used whip with excessive frequency and without giving gelding time to respond

FOCUS
A decent sprint handicap, rated through the third, with the winner back to his best. The near-side rail again looked the place to be.

NOTEBOOK
Gimasha, 3lb higher than when second to an unexposed sort over five furlongs at Sandown on her previous start, raced keenly (as she often does), but her rider had conserved just enough energy and she picked up to take a gap between the eventual second and third. The handicapper will make things tougher for her and in the longer term she may be better off trying to pick up some black type in fillies/mares-only company. (op 9-4)

Obe Brave can have no excuses, as he had his optimum conditions and the benefit of the favoured near-side rail to run against. (op 10-1)

Grantley Adams, a stablemate of the runner-up, was never far away and was just held. He is running well, but remains winless so far this season. Official explanation: jockey said gelding hung left

Zidane ◆ never represents value - he has been sent off favourite in eight of his nine starts to date and is just that type of horse - but this was a noteworthy run. Just as he did when riding the favourite in the first race, Oscar Urbina produced his mount with his effort towards the middle of the track, away from the favoured near-side rail, and he had little chance with the front three. He is much better than the bare form suggests, although he might be a false price once again next time. (op 3-1)

Loyal Royal(IRE), returning from a near two-month break, never posed a threat in a race few got involved in from off the pace, but is not without hope.

5045 SURREY MIRROR CLAIMING STKS — 1m 2f (P)

4:10 (4:10) (Class 5) 3-Y-0+

£5,181 (£1,541; £770; £384) **Stalls** Low

Form — RPR

1040 **1** **Impeller (IRE)**[33] [4023] 7-9-10 95 .... MartinDwyer 8 — 98
(W R Muir) *in tch: rdn to chse ldr over 2f out: led ins fnl f: in command after* **4/1**[3]

0224 **2** 1 ¾ **Obrigado (USA)**[35] [3971] 6-9-7 89 .... DarryllHolland 6 — 92
(W J Haggas) *hld up in last: rdn and hdwy on outside over 2f out: chsd wnr ins fnl f: no imp last 100 yds* **11/8**[1]

6-26 **3** 1 ¼ **Zonergem**[170] [661] 8-9-5 89 .... KerrinMcEvoy 1 — 88
(Lady Herries) *trckd ldrs on inner: rdn 3f out: ev ch 1f out: kpt on same pce* **15/2**

0100 **4** 1 ½ **Ninth House (USA)**[1] [5019] 4-9-0 85 .... (t) RichardMullen 9 — 80
(D J Daly) *hld up in tch: rdn wl over 2f out: kpt on same pce fnl f* **7/2**[2]

4565 **5** *nk* **Secretary General (IRE)**[25] [4244] 5-9-5 75 .... EddieAhern 3 — 84
(P F I Cole) *reminders early: in tch in rr: drvn wl over 3f out: kpt on ins fnl f: nt rch ldrs* **8/1**

000/ **6** *nk* **Lunar Sovereign (USA)**[10] [4121] 7-8-11 95 .... (vt) RyanMoore 2 — 76
(D E Pipe) *chsd ldr: led over 4f out: sn rdn and qcknd: hdd ins fnl f: wknd qckly* **16/1**

6000 **7** *hd* **Hayyani (IRE)**[34] [4001] 4-9-0 73 .... (bt) DaneO'Neill 7 — 78
(K McAuliffe) *slowly away: toook t.k.h: hld up in tch: drvn and edgd lft over 2f out: wknd 1f out* **33/1**

0050 **8** 6 **Beckett Hall (IRE)**[7] [4838] 3-8-9 76 .... RichardHughes 10 — 69
(R Hannon) *led tl hdd over 4f out: sn rdn: chsd ldr tl over 2f out: eased whn btn fnl f* **25/1**

-626 **9** 7 **Danehill Dazzler (IRE)**[19] [2892] 4-8-6 74 .... ChrisCatlin 5 — 46
(Ian Williams) *chsd ldrs: rdn 3f out: hmpd bnd over 2f out: no ch after: eased* **14/1**

2m 9.83s (2.04) **Going Correction** +0.025s/f (Slow)
WFA 3 from 4yo+ 7lb — **9** Ran SP% **126.5**
Speed ratings (Par 103):92,90,89,88,88 87,87,82,77
CSF £10.96 TOTE £6.50: £2.10, £1.30, £2.50; EX 12.30 Trifecta £67.90 Pool: £458.41 - 4.79 winning units..Obrigado was claimed by Karen George for £35,000.
Owner D G Clarke & C L A Edginton **Bred** P E Banahan **Trained** Lambourn, Berks

FOCUS
A very good claimer, but the gallop was a little stop-start (as is nearly always the case over this sort of trip on Lingfield's Polytrack) and the winning time was modest. As a result, the form is a little dubious. The front three are better than this grade but were below their best here.

Ninth House(USA) Official explanation: jockey said colt had a breathing problem

5046 BOOK ONLINE FOR A £2 DISCOUNT H'CAP — 1m (P)

4:40 (4:40) (Class 5) (0-70,70) 3-Y-0+

£5,181 (£1,541; £770; £384) **Stalls** High

Form — RPR

0411 **1** **Apres Ski (IRE)**[7] [4845] 3-8-9 **64** 6ex ow2 .... DeanCorby(3) 10 — 71
(J F Coupland) *v.s.a: bhd: rdn and hdwy on outer over 2f out: chsd ldng trio over 1f out: str run to ld on line* **6/1**[3]

0666 **2** *shd* **Titus Lumpus (IRE)**[38] [3869] 3-8-7 **59** .... DarryllHolland 12 — 65
(R M Flower) *chsd ldrs: led over 3f out: drvn wl over 2f out: styd on wl: hdd on line* **14/1**

6300 **3** *nk* **Humility**[50] [3536] 5-8-11 **58** .... EddieAhern 7 — 64
(C A Cyzer) *hld up in midfield: smooth hdwy 3f out: drvn over 1f out: styd on* **12/1**

1423 **4** 1 **Bavarica**[34] [4010] 4-8-6 **60** .... SladeO'Hara(7) 11 — 63
(Miss J Feilden) *hld up in midfield: hdwy over 3f out: chsd ldr over 2f out: rdn wl over 1f out: lost 2nd and wknd ins fnl f* **7/1**

6-44 **5** 2 ½ **Ruse**[30] [4113] 3-8-11 **63** .... OscarUrbina 2 — 61
(J R Fanshawe) *trckd ldrs: rdn 3f out: kpt on same pce fr over 1f out* **11/4**[1]

1042 **6** *nk* **Sovereignty (JPN)**[22] [4368] 4-9-1 **62** .... SteveDrowne 9 — 59
(D K Ivory) *hld up in midfield: hdwy on outer over 3f out: kpt on u.p fnl f: nvr able to chal* **9/2**[2]

0000 **7** 1 **Reaching Out (IRE)**[19] [4454] 4-8-6 **56** .... JamesDoyle(3) 6 — 51
(N P Littmoden) *v.s.a: bhd: hdwy and in tch 4f out: drvn over 2f out: sn struggling* **12/1**

3064 **8** 2 ½ **Keep Bacckinhit (IRE)**[24] [4281] 4-8-9 **56** oh1 .... RyanMoore 3 — 45
(G L Moore) *towards rr: rdn wl over 3f out: no prog* **10/1**

1540 **9** ½ **Missed A Beat**[25] [4241] 4-9-9 **70** .... ChrisCatlin 1 — 58
(M Blanshard) *chsd ldrs tl rdn over 3f out: sn wknd* **8/1**

-000 **10** ½ **King Of Diamonds**[9] [4772] 5-9-0 **61** .... MartinDwyer 4 — 48
(J R Best) *chsd ldr tl rdn wl over 2f out: wknd over 1f out* **12/1**

0300 **11** 3 ½ **True West (USA)**[12] [4673] 3-8-10 **65** .... SaleemGolam(3) 8 — 44
(G C H Chung) *v.s.a: a bhd: nvr on terms* **33/1**

045 **12** 6 **Tiz Timely (USA)**[25] [4247] 3-8-11 **63** .... FergusSweeney 5 — 28
(A M Balding) *racd keenly: led tl over 3f out: sn rdn: wknd over 2f out: eased ins fnl f* **10/1**

1m 38.92s (-0.51) **Going Correction** +0.025s/f (Slow)
WFA 3 from 4yo+ 5lb — **12** Ran SP% **133.6**
Speed ratings (Par 103):103,102,102,101,99 98,97,95,94,94 90,84
CSF £98.82 CT £1031.61 TOTE £8.60: £2.70, £4.50, £3.60; EX 145.00 TRIFECTA Not won..
Owner J F Coupland **Bred** Edward Kelly **Trained** Grimsby, Lincs

FOCUS
A modest handicap run at a good pace. The form does not look all that strong, with the winner up 3lb.

Sovereignty(JPN) Official explanation: jockey said gelding hung right

Reaching Out(IRE) Official explanation: jockey said gelding missed the break

Missed A Beat Official explanation: jockey said filly hung left

Tiz Timely(USA) Official explanation: jockey said filly ran flat

5047 ARENA LEISURE PLC APPRENTICE H'CAP — 1m 2f (P)

5:10 (5:10) (Class 5) (0-75,73) 3-Y-0+

£4,533 (£1,348; £674; £336) **Stalls** Low

Form — RPR

2045 **1** **Cape Diamond (IRE)**[9] [4784] 3-9-4 **73** .... LiamJones 3 — 82
(W R Swinburn) *chsd ldng pair: rdn 2f out: chal 1f out: sn led: r.o wl* **7/1**

0005 **2** 1 ¾ **Northside Lodge (IRE)**[41] [3798] 8-8-12 **65** .... (p) JamieHamblett(5) 4 — 71
(W R Swinburn) *chaased ldr: led over 3f out: rdn wl over 1f out: hdd jst ins fnl f: no ex* **6/1**[3]

3100 **3** 1 **Lisathedaddy**[13] [4660] 4-9-3 **70** .... PatrickHills(5) 7 — 74+
(B G Powell) *slowly away: t.k.h: hld up in rr: hdwy on inner over 2f out: styd on: wnt 3rd nr fin: nt rch ldrs* **6/1**[3]

0-01 **4** *hd* **Al Hazim (IRE)**[18] [4483] 3-9-1 **73** .... AshleyHamblett(3) 5 — 77
(L M Cumani) *led tl hdd over 3f out: ev and rdn wl over 1f out: onepced ins fnl f* **2/1**[1]

0620 **5** 1 **Wester Lodge (IRE)**[12] [4673] 4-9-6 **68** .... (b) MarcHalford 2 — 70
(J M P Eustace) *t.k.h: hld up: rdn and hdwy over 2f out: no imp fnl f* **12/1**

1605 **6** 8 **Bold Diktator**[30] [4108] 4-9-11 **73** .... TravisBlock 6 — 60
(W R Muir) *in tch in midfield: rdn wl over 3f out: wknd over 2f out* **7/1**

0100 **7** 1 ¼ **Terminate (GER)**[15] [4606] 4-8-10 **61** .... (b) VictoriaBehan(3) 1 — 45
(N P Littmoden) *t.k.h: chsd ldrs: rdn wl over 2f out: sn wknd* **6/1**[3]

4205 **8** 7 **Evening**[13] [4660] 3-8-11 **69** .... SladeO'Hara(3) 8 — 40
(B W Hills) *slowly away: hld up in tch: rdn over 3f out: lost tch over 2f out* **11/2**[2]

2m 9.74s (1.95) **Going Correction** +0.025s/f (Slow)
WFA 3 from 4yo+ 7lb — **8** Ran SP% **124.3**
Speed ratings (Par 103):93,91,90,90,89 83,82,76
CSF £52.59 CT £276.26 TOTE £9.90: £2.80, £2.00, £1.90; EX 48.20 Trifecta £275.60 Pool: £524.08 - 1.35 winning units. Place 6 £107.55, Place 5 £77.58.
Owner The Lucky Dozen **Bred** Pat Whyte And Oliver Concannon **Trained** Aldbury, Herts

FOCUS
An ordinary apprentice handicap run in a very modest time for the grade. Weak form at face value.

T/Jkpt: £7,100.00 to a £1 stake. Pool: £10,000.00. 1.00 winning ticket. T/Plt: £42.00 to a £1 stake. Pool: £80,812.50. 1,404.50 winning tickets. T/Qpdt: £7.40 to a £1 stake. Pool: £3,845.60. 383.60 winning tickets. SP

3514 LONGCHAMP (R-H)

Sunday, September 3

OFFICIAL GOING: Good to soft

5048a PRIX LA ROCHETTE (GROUP 3) 7f
2:20 (2:20) 2-Y-O **£27,586** (£11,034; £8,276; £5,517; £2,759)

RPR

1 **Visionario (IRE)**[21] [4415] 2-8-11 CSoumillon 1 110+
(A Fabre, France) *racd in last, wnt 3rd half-way, a gng wl, wnt 2nd over 1 1/2f out, pushed along to ld 50yds out, comf* **2/5**[1]

2 *1* **Holocene (USA)**[20] 2-8-11 C-PLemaire 5 101
(P Bary, France) *raced in 2nd, led 2f out, pushed along & ran on 1 1/2f out, ridden inside final f, headed 50yds out* **14/1**

3 *1* **Cicerole (FR)**[26] 2-8-8 IMendizabal 4 95
(J-C Rouget, France) *raced in 4th, disputing last straight, pushed along to chase leaders 2f out. ridden final f, went 3rd close home* **7/1**[3]

4 *2 1/2* **Lykios (IRE)**[51] [3514] 2-8-11 MBlancpain 3 92
(C Laffon-Parias, France) *led to 2f out, driven 1 1/2f out, no extra final furlong* **5/1**[2]

5 *3/4* **Ascot Family (IRE)**[32] 2-8-8 OPeslier 2 87
(A Lyon, France) *raced in 3rd to half-way, disputing last straight, soon shaken up, never able to challenge* **16/1**

1m 23.8s **Going Correction** +0.35s/f (Good) **5 Ran SP% 113.1**
Speed ratings: 106,104,103,100,100
PARI-MUTUEL: WIN 1.40; PL 1.10, 1.70; SF 4.40.

Owner H H Aga Khan **Bred** Snc Lagardere Elevage **Trained** Chantilly, France

NOTEBOOK
Visionario(IRE), a fine, athletic colt, looks Classic material in the making as he was not extended to win his first Group 3 event. Last early on, he was moved up into a challenging position before the straight and then quickened well to lead with more than a furlong left to run. He was highly impressive and the Prix Jean-Luc Lagardere is his next race.

Holocene(USA) lost very little in defeat. Always well up there, he took the advantage a furlong and a half out but could not quicken in the same manner as the winner. He stayed on like a colt who will make it at this level at least, though. The Prix Thomas Bryon is now a possible target.

Cicerole(FR), given a waiting ride, was fourth for much of the early part of the race but was outpaced when things quickened up. She was putting in her best work at the finish, though, and this was a decent effort on only her second start.

Lykios(IRE) kept up the good work until halfway up the straight and then gradually dropped away on the rail. He does not quite look up to this standard.

5049a PRIX DU MOULIN DE LONGCHAMP (GROUP 1) (C&F) 1m
2:55 (2:57) 3-Y-O+ **£118,221** (£47,297; £23,648; £11,814; £5,917)

RPR

1 **Librettist (USA)**[21] [4416] 4-9-2 LDettori 2 122
(Saeed Bin Suroor) *close up, led after 2f, ridden & ran on 1f out, driven out* **7/4**[1]

2 *1/2* **Stormy River (FR)**[21] [4416] 3-8-12 TThulliez 1 122
(N Clement, France) *in tch, 4th on rail str, pushed along & hdwy to go 2nd 2f out, driven & kpt on fnl f, nrst at fin* **7/1**[3]

3 *1/2* **Manduro (GER)**[21] [4416] 4-9-2 CSoumillon 8 120+
(A Fabre, France) *hld up, last str, hdwy on ins 1 1/2f out, rdn & swtchd out appr fnl f, hrd rdn & fin wl last 150y, nrst fin* **11/4**[2]

4 *2* **Aussie Rules (USA)**[32] [4038] 3-8-12 KFallon 6 117
(A P O'Brien, Ire) *mid-div, disp 5th on rail str, pushed along 2f out, rdn & wnt 3rd 1f out, stayed on til no ex fnl 100y* **9/1**

5 *2* **Irridescence (SAF)**[133] [1180] 5-8-13 FSpanu 7 109
(J E Hammond, France) *led 2f, 2nd straight, pushed along over 2f out, ridden & no extra from 1f out* **10/1**

6 *2* **Kentucky Dynamite (USA)**[56] [3342] 3-8-12 C-PLemaire 3 108
(A De Royer-Dupre, France) *mid-division, disputing 5th straight, pushed along 2f out, stayed on at one pace, never able to challenge* **14/1**

7 *1 1/2* **Quiet Royal (USA)**[28] [4191] 3-8-8 OPeslier 5 101
(C Laffon-Parias, France) *held up, 7th & pushed along straight, ridden 1 1/2f out, no impression* **11/1**

8 *4* **Indesatchel (IRE)**[133] [1171] 4-9-2 NCallan 4 96
(David Wachman, Ire) *towards rear early, headway on outside 3f out, 3rd straight & driven to chase leaders, soon beaten* **25/1**

1m 38.1s **Going Correction** -0.20s/f (Firm)
WFA 3 from 4yo+ 5lb **8 Ran SP% 113.5**
Speed ratings: 113,112,112,110,108 106,104,100
PARI-MUTUEL: WIN 2.00; PL 1.20, 1.60, 1.40; DF 6.30.

Owner Godolphin **Bred** Calumet Farm **Trained** Newmarket, Suffolk

NOTEBOOK
Librettist(USA), who was immediately taken into the lead, set an even pace before injecting even more halfway up the straight. He was tackled by the runner-up at the furlong marker but still had enough in hand to repel the attack. The son of Danzig is unbeaten in four races this season and is now Europe's top miler. The Queen Elizabeth II Stakes at Ascot is his next target before the Breeders' Cup Mile.

Stormy River(FR), despite a hard season, still looked in great shape in the paddock. The grey was settled behind the leaders and looked extremely dangerous when he began his challenge at the furlong marker. He never got to the front but it was still an excellent run, and if he runs again this season it will be in the Prix de la Foret. He remains in training as a four-year-old.

Manduro(GER) did not have the luckiest of runs from his outside draw. Held up early on, he was still towards the tail of the field at the entrance to the straight. Slightly unlucky a furlong and a half out when also outpaced, he made up a lot of late ground and finished best of all. If he runs again it will be in the Champion Stakes at Newmarket.

Aussie Rules(USA) stayed on well through the final stages without ever threatening the first three. His jockey felt that there was not enough pace for the colt to show his best form.

5050 - (Foreign Racing) - See Raceform Interactive

5007 BADEN-BADEN (L-H)

Sunday, September 3

OFFICIAL GOING: Good

5051a GROSSER VOLKSWAGEN PREIS VON BADEN (GROUP 1) 1m 4f
4:00 (4:21) 3-Y-O+
£310,345 (£103,448; £51,724; £13,793; £6,897; £6,207)

RPR

1 **Prince Flori (GER)**[42] [3776] 3-8-9 FilipMinarik 2 118
(S Smrczek, Germany) *always prominent, 3rd straight, led 2f out, driven clear over 1f out, ran on well* **40/1**

2 *3* **Oriental Tiger (GER)**[42] [3776] 3-8-9 ABoschert 3 114
(U Ostmann, Germany) *led after 2f, headed over 3f out, 2nd straight, ran on under pressure to regain 2nd last strides* **14/1**

3 *hd* **Saddex**[42] [3776] 3-8-9 EPedroza 1 113
(P Rau, Germany) *led 2f, led again over 3f out, ridden well over 2f out, headed 2f out, no extra and lost 2nd last strides* **14/1**

4 *1/2* **Egerton (GER)**[21] [4414] 5-9-6 TMundry 5 114
(P Rau, Germany) *mid-division, 5th & ridden straight, kept on one pace under pressure from over 1f out* **97/10**

5 *3 1/2* **Dickens (GER)**[42] [3776] 3-8-9 ASuborics 7 107
(H Blume, Germany) *held up in rear, closed up on inside 5f out, 4th straight, ridden & one pace from well over 1f out* **67/10**[3]

6 *2* **Schiaparelli (GER)**[42] [3776] 3-8-9 AStarke 8 104
(P Schiergen, Germany) *disputed 4th to 3f out, ridden & 6th straight, soon beaten* **7/5**[1]

7 *7* **Norse Dancer (IRE)**[133] [1180] 6-9-6 JohnEgan 6 96
(D R C Elsworth) *held up, 7th straight, went 6th well over 1f out, soon beaten* **84/10**

8 *15* **Fracas (IRE)**[21] [4414] 4-9-6 JamieSpencer 4 73
(David Wachman, Ire) *held up, ridden & close 8th straight, soon beaten, dismounted after line* **26/10**[2]

9 *9* **Donaldson (GER)**[21] [4414] 4-9-6 ADeVries 9 60
(P Rau, Germany) *dwelt start, soon in mid-divison, closed up to 3rd 5f out, weakened quickly 3f out, last straight, tailed off* **22/1**

2m 33.87s
WFA 3 from 4yo+ 9lb **9 Ran SP% 122.5**
(including ten euro stakes): WIN 274; PL 62, 26, 32; SF 2929.
Owner Stall Reni **Bred** H A Wacek **Trained** Germany

NOTEBOOK
Prince Flori(GER) made a lot of the running in the Deutsches Derby but benefited from letting someone else do the work here. Always going well, the prize was his a furlong from home. His trainer, who had favoured the Bosphorus Cup in Turkey over this extremely valuable local prize, attributed Prince Flori's shock success to his having been best able to handle the conditions, which were rough following considerable recent use and heavy rain.
Schiaparelli(GER) beat Dickens, Oriental Tiger and Saddex, with Prince Flori ninth, in the Derby. He finished behind all four this time, looking tall and ungainly when everybody was going for it approaching the straight. Early checks offered no explanation for this disappointing effort.
Norse Dancer(IRE) went past the favourite to reach sixth early in the straight but it was a short-lived effort. His jockey reported that he was never happy on the ground. It was drying on top but in rough condition in places after a lot of rain and six days of racing in the past nine.
Fracas(IRE) was driven along but still well in touch on the outside rail entering the straight. He soon gave way, however, and Spencer dismounted him shortly after passing the post. He was later reported to be sound and it may be that this race came too soon after his fine reappearance at Cologne.

4753 BATH (L-H)

Monday, September 4

OFFICIAL GOING: Good to firm
Wind: mild, across

5052 MITIE ENGINEERING SERVICES MAIDEN AUCTION FILLIES' STKS 5f 11y
2:10 (2:11) (Class 6) 2-Y-O **£2,590** (£770; £385; £192) **Stalls Low**

Form RPR

2302 1 **Foxy Games**[10] [4779] 2-8-3 67 FrancisNorton 2 67
(D J S Ffrench Davis) *chsd ldrs: rdn to ld over 1f out: kpt on: drvn out* **3/1**[1]

2 *nk* **Millachy** 2-8-3 RoystonFfrench 11 66
(B W Hills) *sn pushed along towards rr: hdwy over 2f out: r.o ins fnl f: nrst fin* **4/1**[3]

300 3 *2 1/2* **Clewer**[51] [3545] 2-8-0 61 ow2 KevinGhunowa(5) 12 59
(P A Blockley) *chsd ldrs: rdn over 2f out: ev ch over 1f out: kpt on same pce fnl f* **16/1**

6342 4 *hd* **Temtation (IRE)**[6] [4913] 2-8-5 70 EddieAhern 10 58
(J R Boyle) *led: rdn and hdd over 1f out: kpt on same pce* **7/2**[2]

05 5 *3/4* **Lake Pontchartrain (IRE)**[27] [4221] 2-8-9 RyanMoore 7 60
(S Kirk) *towards rr: hdwy over 2f out: sn rdn: kpt on same pce fnl f* **15/2**

4045 6 *1/2* **Indian Song (IRE)**[20] [4460] 2-8-7 61 KerrinMcEvoy 9 56
(R F Johnson Houghton) *s.i.s: sn mid div: hdwy over 2f out: sn rdn: one pce fnl f* **11/2**

05 7 *4* **Yearning (IRE)**[15] [4624] 2-8-7 FergusSweeney 4 41
(J G Portman) *nvr bttr than mid div* **66/1**

05 8 *1/2* **Dories Dream**[49] [3596] 2-8-3 HayleyTurner 8 36
(Jane Southcombe) *in tch: effrt over 2f out: wknd 1f out* **66/1**

9 *1 3/4* **Desirable Dancer (IRE)** 2-8-9 AdrianMcCarthy 3 35
(R A Harris) *stmbld 4f out: a in rr* **50/1**

050 10 *1 1/4* **Mamalini**[24] [4327] 2-8-3 53 MartinDwyer 5 25
(P D Cundell) *chsd ldrs: rdn 3f out: wknd over 1f out* **25/1**

040 11 *5* **Ella Y Rossa**[97] [2094] 2-8-7 53 ow2 RobertHavlin 1 11
(P D Evans) *mid div for 3f* **50/1**

12 *1 1/4* **Burningfold Babe** 2-8-0 JamesDoyle(3) 6 2
(P Winkworth) *s.i.s: a bhd* **28/1**

62.33 secs (-0.17) **Going Correction** -0.10s/f (Good) **12 Ran SP% 114.5**
Speed ratings (Par 90): 97,96,92,92,91 90,83,83,80,78 70,68
CSF £13.70 TOTE £4.50: £1.10, £1.70, £3.60; EX 20.40.
Owner S J Edwards & Partners **Bred** Bearstone Stud **Trained** Lambourn, Berks

FOCUS
A modest sprint maiden for juvenile fillies, but the time was very creditable. Solid if unspectacular form.

NOTEBOOK
Foxy Games, returned to maiden company, confirmed the promise she showed on her previous starts to get off the mark at the sixth attempt. She is only modest, but is a likeable filly and should continue to give a good account of herself. (op 7-2 tchd 4-1)
Millachy, a 10,500gns half-sister to Millennium Hall, a multiple winner over nine to 13 furlongs, struggled to go the early pace, appearing in need of the experience, but she got the hang of things late on and finished to good effect. This was a promising introduction and she is open to improvement, but it will be worth keeping in mind this was a pretty modest race if she is a short price next time. (op 9-2 tchd 10-3, tchd 5-1 in a place)
Clewer, returning from a 51-day break, ran a respectable race and seems to be going the right way. She might find things easier in nurseries.
Temtation(IRE) showed good early speed but could not sustain her challenge and does not seem to be progressing. Although her running style suggests otherwise, her breeding offers hope that she might do better if given another chance over further. (op 5-2)
Lake Pontchartrain(IRE) should do better over a little further in handicap company. (op 9-1 tchd 10-1 and 7-1)
Indian Song(IRE), dropped in trip and returned to maiden company, ran below her official mark of 61. (op 6-1 tchd 13-2)
Yearning(IRE) Official explanation: jockey said filly hung left-handed

5053 KC EVENTS NURSERY — 1m 5y
2:40 (2:40) (Class 5) (0-75,74) 2-Y-O — **£3,886** (£1,156; £577; £288) **Stalls** Low

Form — RPR
650 **1** **The Illies (IRE)**[35] 4000 2-9-1 **68** RoystonFfrench 14 — 76+
(B W Hills) *mid div: swtchd rt and hdwy over 2f out: led 1f out: sn edgd lft: r.o wl* **11/1**
005 **2** *3* **Red**[52] 3468 2-8-6 **62** JamesDoyle(3) 7 — 63
(R M Beckett) *towards rr: swtchd rt and hdwy over 2f out: sn rdn: styd on wl ins fnl f: wnt 2nd cl home* **25/1**
000 **3** *nk* **Spiderback (IRE)**[40] 3843 2-9-0 **67** RyanMoore 4 — 67
(R Hannon) *s.i.s: towards rr: hdwy over 3f out: sn rdn: kpt on to chse wnr 1f out: lost 2nd cl home* **14/1**
4042 **4** *¾* **Jawaab (IRE)**[9] 4813 2-9-7 **74** MartinDwyer 6 — 73
(E A L Dunlop) *mid div: nt clr run briefly 3f out: hdwy 2f out: sn rdn: styd on fnl f* **5/1**[1]
6414 **5** *3* **Goose Green (IRE)**[2] 5013 2-8-12 **65** RobertHavlin 15 — 57
(M R Channon) *prom: led over 4f out: rdn over 2f out: hdd 1f out: no ex* **8/1**[3]
4040 **6** *2½* **Urban Warrior**[35] 3997 2-8-8 **64** EdwardCreighton(3) 16 — 51
(Mrs Norma Pook) *prom: carried wd on bnd over 4f out: rdn over 2f out: one pce fr over 1f out* **22/1**
1431 **7** *hd* **Sunstroke (IRE)**[11] 4724 2-8-11 **64** FrancisNorton 5 — 50
(M G Quinlan) *chsd ldrs: rdn over 2f out: wknd fnl f* **16/1**
065 **8** *1¼* **Look Who's Dancing**[17] 4572 2-9-4 **71** KerrinMcEvoy 2 — 54
(J L Dunlop) *towards rr: sme hdwy over 2f out: nvr a danger* **9/1**
050 **9** *hd* **Cashcade (IRE)**[83] 2530 2-9-7 **74** FergusSweeney 12 — 57
(A M Balding) *s.i.s: a towards rr* **25/1**
6414 **10** *½* **Silca Soprano**[10] 4767 2-9-2 **69** TonyCulhane 9 — 51
(M R Channon) *a towards rr* **12/1**
600 **11** *½* **Pagan Rules (IRE)**[46] 3663 2-8-13 **66** EddieAhern 8 — 47
(Mrs A J Perrett) *prom: carried wd on bnd over 4f out: rdn 3f out: wknd over 1f out* **16/1**
0210 **12** *½* **Persian Fox (IRE)**[10] 4767 2-9-0 **70** AdamKirby(3) 1 — 50
(G A Huffer) *sn led: rn wd and hdd on bnd over 4f out: chsd ldrs: rdn over 2f out: wknd over 1f out* **13/2**[2]
000 **13** *shd* **Featherlight**[22] 4400 2-8-7 **60** JamieMackay 10 — 39
(N A Callaghan) *a towards rr* **8/1**[3]
0111 **14** *4* **Feisty**[40] 3834 2-8-11 **64** FrancisFerris 11 — 35
(Rae Guest) *chsd ldrs: rdn over 2f out: wknd over 1f out* **16/1**
1 **15** *30* **Slavonic Lake**[62] 3174 2-9-1 **68** IanMongan 3 — —
(I A Wood) *mid div tl wknd over 2f out* **33/1**

1m 40.87s (-0.23) **Going Correction** -0.10s/f (Good) **15** Ran SP% **117.5**
Speed ratings (Par 95):97,94,93,92,89 87,87,86,85,85 84,84,84,80,50
CSF £265.04 CT £3909.00 TOTE £15.80: £4.70, £6.20, £6.40; EX 498.50.
Owner John C Grant **Bred** Glashare House Stud **Trained** Lambourn, Berks

FOCUS
Plenty of runners and they went a good pace from the start, but this was a modest nursery lacking any real strength in depth. The winner looks progressive though, and the form is solid with the placed horses running to their marks.

NOTEBOOK
The Illies(IRE) was well held in a reasonable maiden at Windsor last time, but he had previously shown plenty of ability in a decent race at Newmarket and showed himself on a very favourable mark upped two furlongs in trip on his nursery debut. He will find things tougher off higher marks in more competitive races, but is progressing and will have to be respected, especially if turned out under a penalty. Official explanation: trainer's rep said, regarding the improved form shown, the colts is big and backward and may have benefited from today's step up in trip
Red ◆ was well held in three runs at up to six furlongs in maiden company, but proved suited by the step up to a mile on her nursery debut and ran a promising race behind the well-handicapped winner. This was not a great race, but she looks on a good mark and should be able to find a similar event.
Spiderback(IRE) showed improved form stepped up in trip on his nursery debut and is clearly on a reasonable enough mark. (op 11-1)
Jawaab(IRE) was only 2lb higher than when a slightly unlucky second to Heywood (who has won three of his last four starts) at Sandown last time, but he was below form. He was denied a clear run, but did not seem unlucky and perhaps the track just did not suit. (op 11-2 tchd 6-1 and 9-2)
Goose Green(IRE), making a quick reappearance on very different ground, fared best of those to race handy.
Feisty Official explanation: trainer said filly lost a near-fore shoe
Slavonic Lake Official explanation: jockey said colt never travelled

5054 KC EVENTS (S) STKS — 1m 5y
3:10 (3:11) (Class 6) 3-4-Y-O — **£2,266** (£674; £337; £168) **Stalls** Low

Form — RPR
5240 **1** **Legal Lover (IRE)**[59] 3263 4-9-9 48 KerrinMcEvoy 3 — 64
(R Hollinshead) *mde all: rdn over 2f out: kpt on wl to assert ins fnl f* **15/2**
005 **2** *2* **Rembrandt Quality (USA)**[30] 4142 3-8-13 65 RyanMoore 1 — 54
(N A Callaghan) *trckd ldrs: rdn 3f out:kpt on but a hld ins fnl f* **5/1**[2]
5036 **3** *hd* **Cool Sting (IRE)**[13] 4674 3-9-4 65 LPKeniry 14 — 59
(A M Balding) *mid div: hdwy over 2f out: sn rdn: hung lft jst ins fnl f: no further imp* **13/2**[3]
2620 **4** *1* **Crimson Flame (IRE)**[10] 4757 3-8-13 61 (v) TonyCulhane 13 — 52
(M R Channon) *mid div: stdy prog fr over 2f out: n.m.r jst ins fnl f: one pce after* **3/1**[1]
6020 **5** *2* **Priorina (IRE)**[41] 3817 4-9-4 47 (v) RobertHavlin 6 — 47
(D Haydn Jones) *chsd ldrs: rdn to chal over 2f out: hld whn squeezed up jst ins fnl f* **13/2**[3]
0050 **6** *1* **Waiting For Mary (IRE)**[25] 4286 3-8-8 48 RoystonFfrench 2 — 40
(J G M O'Shea) *mid div: rdn over 2f out: styd on fnl f* **20/1**
4300 **7** *1¼* **Khyber Knight (IRE)**[15] 4627 3-8-8 50 ow3 AdamKirby(3) 16 — 40
(Jane Southcombe) *prom: rdn 3f out: one pce fnl 2f* **20/1**
0056 **8** *2* **Mujelle**[19] 4491 3-8-13 46 (b) JamieMackay 4 — 37
(D K Ivory) *towards rr: sme late prog: nvr a factor* **50/1**
0000 **9** *shd* **Diafa (USA)**[129] 882 4-8-10 49 EdwardCreighton(3) 15 — 32
(J G M O'Shea) *a towards rr* **66/1**
0-00 **10** *2½* **Sharp Duo (IRE)**[7] 4870 3-8-13 62 AdrianMcCarthy 7 — 31
(M S Saunders) *chsd ldrs: rdn 3f out: wknd over 1f out: eased ins fnl f* **33/1**
0006 **11** *10* **Earth Master (IRE)**[33] 4052 3-8-13 48 EddieAhern 5 — 8
(S Kirk) *a towards rr* **9/1**
00-0 **12** *15* **Yeldham Lady**[132] 1224 4-8-10 44 MarcHalford(3) 10 — —
(A J Chamberlain) *a bhd* **100/1**
0-10 **13** *33* **Maid In England**[18] 4533 3-8-13 45 MartinDwyer 12 — —
(G A Ham) *a bhd* **50/1**
0004 **R** **Hawridge Sensation**[25] 4285 4-9-4 49 (v[1]) FergusSweeney 8 — —
(W S Kittow) *ref to r: tk no part* **10/1**

1m 40.79s (-0.31) **Going Correction** -0.10s/f (Good)
WFA 3 from 4yo 5lb **14** Ran SP% **118.1**
Speed ratings (Par 101):97,95,94,93,91 90,89,87,87,84 74,59,26,—
CSF £41.41 TOTE £10.10: £2.70, £2.10, £2.40; EX 64.10.The winner was bought in for 7,200gns.
Owner Tim Leadbeater **Bred** Ballyhane Stud **Trained** Upper Longdon, Staffs

FOCUS
Just an ordinary seller and the winning time was only fractionally quicker than the juvenile nursery. Not strong form, and the winner probably did not need to improve as much as it seems at face value.
Earth Master(IRE) Official explanation: jockey said gelding had no more to give

5055 RICHARDSON GROVES MAIDEN STKS — 5f 161y
3:40 (3:43) (Class 5) 3-Y-O+ — **£3,238** (£963; £481; £240) **Stalls** Low

Form — RPR
0002 **1** **Tilsworth Charlie**[20] 4447 3-8-12 47 (v) RobertHavlin 6 — 50
(J R Jenkins) *chsd ldrs: rdn to chal over 2f out: tk narrow advantage ent fnl f: all out* **50/1**
0464 **2** *shd* **Goodwood March**[9] 4799 3-8-12 60 IanMongan 1 — 50
(J L Dunlop) *chsd ldrs: rdn to ld 2f out: narrowly hdd ent fnl f: rallied gamely: no ex fnl strides* **11/2**[3]
0006 **3** *1¼* **Jessica Wigmo**[30] 4164 3-8-12 45 FrancisNorton 13 — 46
(A W Carroll) *in tch: hdwy to chse ldng pair over 1f out: sn drifted lft: kpt on* **33/1**
0000 **4** *½* **Decider (USA)**[31] 4120 3-9-3 42 LPKeniry 7 — 49+
(J M Bradley) *towards rr: rdn and hdwy fr 2f out: hung lft but styd on ins fnl f* **100/1**
044 **5** *1½* **Royal Senga**[30] 4162 3-8-12 55 FergusSweeney 8 — 40
(C A Horgan) *s.i.s: towards rr: hdwy over 1f out: styng on whn n.m.r wl ins fnl f* **16/1**
3334 **6** *nk* **Balian**[18] 4532 3-9-3 63 (be) RyanMoore 12 — 44
(G L Moore) *mid div: rdn and hdwy 2f out: one pce fnl f* **13/2**
2324 **7** *hd* **Rogue**[19] 4484 4-9-0 62 EddieAhern 5 — 38
(Jane Southcombe) *stmbld leaving stalls: towards rr: stmbld 4f out: r.o ins fnl : nrst fin* **3/1**[2]
0540 **8** *shd* **Flying Dancer**[20] 4450 4-9-0 45 AdrianMcCarthy 16 — 38
(R A Harris) *chsd ldrs: rdn and ev ch 2f out: fdd ins fnl f* **33/1**
5004 **9** *1* **Precautionary**[25] 4305 3-8-5 52 LukeMorris(7) 2 — 35
(Miss J Feilden) *in tch: rdn and effrt over 2f out: wknd fnl f* **20/1**
-300 **10** *½* **Diamond World**[68] 2987 3-8-9 55 AdamKirby(3) 11 — 33
(C A Horgan) *prom: led over 2f out: sn rdn and hdd: wknd fnl f* **20/1**
0- **11** *3½* **Charanne**[497] 1260 3-8-5 BarrySavage(7) 10 — 22
(J M Bradley) *a towards rr* **100/1**
12 *5* **Tatillius (IRE)** 3-9-3 MartinDwyer 14 — 11
(J M Bradley) *s.i.s: towards rr: hdwy 3f out: sn rdn: wknd over 1f out* **22/1**
0040 **13** *5* **Jackie Francis (IRE)**[30] 4164 3-9-3 44 (t) RoystonFfrench 3 — —
(R Brotherton) *led tl over 2f out: grad fdd* **50/1**
5524 **14** *¾* **Cordelia**[39] 3864 3-8-12 63 TonyCulhane 4 — —
(B W Hills) *a towards rr* **11/4**[1]
0- **15** *2½* **King Cugat Kid (USA)**[318] 6009 3-9-3 AntonyProcter 9 — —
(Simon Earle) *s.i.s: a bhd* **66/1**
16 *14* **Votive Daniel (IRE)** 3-9-3 GeorgeBaker 15 — —
(Simon Earle) *s.i.s: a bhd* **50/1**

1m 11.19s (-0.01) **Going Correction** -0.10s/f (Good)
WFA 3 from 4yo 2lb **16** Ran SP% **115.4**
Speed ratings (Par 103):96,95,94,93,91 91,90,90,89,88 84,77,70,69,66 47
CSF £272.41 TOTE £40.60: £7.10, £2.40, £9.10; EX 252.40.
Owner M Ng **Bred** Michael Ng **Trained** Royston, Herts

FOCUS
A very moderate sprint maiden, typical for the time of year, and the winning time was over a second slower than the later handicap won by The Cayterers. The form horses mostly disappointed.
Rogue Official explanation: jockey said filly stumbled
Tatillius(IRE) Official explanation: jockey said saddle slipped

5056 WEATHERBYS PRINTING MAIDEN FILLIES' STKS — 1m 3f 144y
4:10 (4:11) (Class 5) 3-Y-O+ — **£3,238** (£963; £481; £240) **Stalls** Low

Form — RPR
2322 **1** **Kerriemuir Lass (IRE)**[28] 4197 3-8-12 76 PhilipRobinson 2 — 79+
(M A Jarvis) *mde all: drew clr over 1f out: eased last 40yds* **8/11**[1]
534 **2** *6* **Valart**[15] 4625 3-8-9 66 JamesDoyle(3) 5 — 66
(Ms J S Doyle) *trckd ldrs: sltly outpcd and hung lft over 2f out: styd on to go 2nd jst ins fnl f but no ch w wnr* **25/1**
-330 **3** *1¾* **Silken Act (CAN)**[44] 3731 3-8-12 72 KerrinMcEvoy 1 — 63
(Mrs A J Perrett) *s.i.s: bhd: stdy prog over 2f out: hung lft but wnt 3rd ins fnl f: nvr trbld ldrs* **12/1**
602 **4** *1½* **Kalandara (IRE)**[10] 4759 3-8-12 79 RyanMoore 6 — 61
(Sir Michael Stoute) *trckd ldrs: effrt over 2f out: one pce fnl f* **5/2**[2]
-000 **5** *1¼* **Shamsalmaidan (IRE)**[42] 3803 3-8-12 57 MartinDwyer 9 — 58
(C E Brittain) *mid div: effrt 3f out: kpt on same pce fnl 2f* **50/1**
0434 **6** *3* **Izadore (IRE)**[12] 4701 3-8-12 74 EddieAhern 7 — 53
(E A L Dunlop) *chsd wnr: rdn over 2f out: wknd ins fnl f* **17/2**[3]
7 *16* **Jaufrette** 3-8-12 RichardThomas 8 — 27
(Dr J R J Naylor) *s.i.s: a bhd* **150/1**
000- **8** *30* **Filliemou (IRE)**[361] 5062 5-9-7 40 FrancisFerris 4 — —
(A W Carroll) *mid div tl wknd over 2f out* **150/1**

0 9 *11* **Just Jasmin**[7] 4899 3-8-12 RobertHavlin 3 —
(P D Evans) *mid div tl wknd over 2f out* **200/1**

2m 28.03s (-2.27) **Going Correction** -0.10s/f (Good)
WFA 3 from 5yo 9lb **9** Ran SP% **112.3**
Speed ratings (Par 100):103,99,97,96,96 94,83,63,56
CSF £25.63 TOTE £2.10: £1.10, £4.80, £2.20; EX 22.70.
Owner Thurloe Thoroughbreds XV **Bred** P D Savill **Trained** Newmarket, Suffolk

FOCUS
An uncompetitive fillies' maiden which did not take a great deal of winning with the fourth below form. It has been rated through the runner-up and the winner was value for a bit extra.

5057 JOHN SMITH'S EXTRA SMOOTH MAIDEN H'CAP 1m 5f 22y
4:40 (4:40) (Class 5) (0-70,69) 3-Y-0+ **£3,562** (£1,059; £529; £264) **Stalls** High

Form RPR

6-04 **1** **Storm Prospect**[24] 4332 3-8-8 **60** EdwardCreighton(3) 8 75
(C Tinkler) *hld up towards rr: hdwy and nt clr run on rails 3f out: swtchd rt 2f out: str run to ld 1f out: styd on wl* **8/1**[3]

222- **2** *3* **Desert Storm (DEN)**[307] 6215 4-9-9 **62** MartinDwyer 1 72
(Rae Guest) *led: set gd pce: rdn over 2f out: hdd 1f out: no ex* **14/1**

5040 **3** *2* **Hawridge Star (IRE)**[56] 3365 4-9-11 **67** JamesDoyle(3) 11 74
(W S Kittow) *hld up towards rr: rdn and stdy prog fr 3f out: styd on to 3rd ins fnl f* **20/1**

2202 **4** *3* **Phone In**[10] 4758 3-9-2 **65** RyanMoore 2 68
(R Brotherton) *chsd ldr: rdn 3f out: kpt on same pce fnl 2f* **7/2**[2]

3403 **5** *3 ½* **Gouranga**[12] 4687 3-9-3 **66** FergusSweeney 15 63
(H Candy) *chsd ldrs: rdn over 3f out: one pce fnl 2f* **11/1**

34 **6** *7* **Malakiya (IRE)**[16] 4586 3-9-5 **68** KerrinMcEvoy 3 55
(G A Butler) *in tch: rdn 3f out: wknd jst over 1f out* **3/1**[1]

000 **7** *1* **Squiffy**[21] 4431 3-8-11 **60** LPKeniry 13 45
(P D Cundell) *hld up towards rr: rdn 3f out: sme late prog: nvr trbld ldrs* **33/1**

006 **8** *1 ½* **Montana Sky (IRE)**[15] 4625 3-9-2 **65** AdrianMcCarthy 9 48
(R A Harris) *trckd ldrs: rdn over 3f out: wknd over 1f out* **40/1**

0600 **9** *1 ¾* **Adage**[53] 3440 3-8-6 **58** (t) MarcHalford(3) 4 38
(David Pinder) *in tch: rdn 3f out: wknd over 1f out* **25/1**

536 **10** *2* **Noddies Way**[9] 4800 3-8-8 **60** AdamKirby(3) 14 37
(J F Panvert) *mid div: rdn over 3f out: no imp fnl 2f* **14/1**

0-00 **11** *nk* **Beaufort**[24] 4331 4-9-8 **61** GeorgeBaker 7 38
(D K Ivory) *nvr bttr than mid div* **25/1**

4003 **12** *1 ½* **Overlook**[7] 4868 3-8-6 **55** (v) FrancisNorton 12 30
(A M Balding) *a towards rr* **14/1**

2020 **13** *nk* **Fonic Rock (IRE)**[31] 4118 3-8-8 **57** HayleyTurner 10 31
(M L W Bell) *mid div tl 3f out* **14/1**

0-00 **14** *1* **Avicia**[37] 3935 4-9-3 **56** EddieAhern 6 29
(C A Horgan) *sn trcking ldrs: rdn over 3f out: wknd 2f out* **40/1**

-300 **15** *8* **Smart Gal (IRE)**[59] 3256 3-9-6 **69** (t) IanMongan 5 30
(J L Dunlop) *n.m.r sn after s: a bhd* **8/1**[3]

2m 48.91s (-2.59) **Going Correction** -0.10s/f (Good)
WFA 3 from 4yo 10lb **15** Ran SP% **124.7**
Speed ratings (Par 103):103,101,99,98,95 91,91,90,89,87 87,86,86,85,80
CSF £108.80 CT £2178.74 TOTE £9.90: £3.30, £3.00, £9.10; EX 64.30.
Owner Bonusprint **Bred** Mill House Stud **Trained** Compton, Berks

FOCUS
The pace was good and they were soon well strung out. Above-average form for the grade, with the first two less exposed than most. The third ran to this year's form.

5058 FREDDIE PRICE RETIREMENT H'CAP 5f 161y
5:10 (5:12) (Class 5) (0-75,75) 3-Y-0+ **£4,533** (£1,348; £674; £336) **Stalls** Low

Form RPR

110 **1** **The Cayterers**[30] 4157 4-8-1 **63** LukeMorris(7) 13 72
(J M Bradley) *mid div: rdn and hdwy over 2f out: led and hung lft jst ins fnl f: r.o* **12/1**[3]

1354 **2** *½* **Who's Winning (IRE)**[19] 4486 5-9-5 **74** GeorgeBaker 7 82
(B G Powell) *mid div: hdwy over 2f out: sn rdn: led over 1f out: hdd jst ins fnl f: kpt on* **12/1**[3]

2053 **3** *¾* **High Ridge**[4] 4957 7-9-4 **73** (p) RyanMoore 8 78+
(J M Bradley) *mid div: hdwy and nt clr run 1f out: r.o cl home* **9/4**[1]

2010 **4** *1* **Endless Summer**[9] 4793 9-8-10 **65** FrancisNorton 11 71+
(A W Carroll) *mid div: hdwy over 2f out: sn rdn: chalng whn n.m.r and snatched up jst ins fnl f: nt rcvr* **8/1**[2]

2013 **5** *½* **Bahamian Ballet**[31] 4110 4-9-3 **72** IanMongan 9 72
(E S McMahon) *chsd ldrs: rdn wl over 2f out: kpt on same pce fnl f* **14/1**

0000 **6** *shd* **Cornus**[19] 4486 4-9-3 **72** KerrinMcEvoy 4 72+
(J A Osborne) *in tch: nt clr run fr 2f out tl jst ins fnl f: r.o* **16/1**

1240 **7** *hd* **Misaro (GER)**[15] 4629 5-9-3 **72** (b) AdrianMcCarthy 1 71
(R A Harris) *prom: led over 2f out tl over 1f out: kpt on same pce* **25/1**

6310 **8** *1 ¼* **Witchry**[26] 4258 4-9-5 **74** FergusSweeney 6 70
(A G Newcombe) *mid div: hdwy over 2f out: sn rdn: one pce fnl f* **25/1**

0316 **9** *nk* **Summer Recluse (USA)**[7] 4894 7-9-0 **69** (t) RoystonFfrench 12 64
(J M Bradley) *towards rr: sme late prog: n.d* **12/1**[3]

4333 **10** *nk* **Highland Cascade**[19] 4484 4-9-3 **72** JTate 2 66
(J M P Eustace) *chsd ldrs: rdn 3f out: wknd fnl f* **33/1**

3410 **11** *hd* **Atlantic Viking (IRE)**[15] 4629 11-8-8 **63** (v) RobertHavlin 14 56
(P D Evans) *a towards rr* **33/1**

6430 **12** *hd* **Arctic Desert**[37] 3928 6-9-0 **69** EddieAhern 15 61
(A M Balding) *v.s.a: a towards rr* **12/1**[3]

0230 **13** *¾* **Cesar Manrique (IRE)**[9] 4807 4-9-1 **70** MartinDwyer 5 60
(B W Hills) *in tch: rdn over 3f out: wknd fnl f* **8/1**[2]

5333 **14** *1 ¾* **Blessed Place**[4] 4962 6-8-10 **72** (t) AshleyHamblett(7) 10 57
(D J S Ffrench Davis) *led tl over 2f out: grad fdd* **12/1**[3]

0066 **15** *9* **Hornpipe**[62] 3165 4-9-6 **75** FrancisFerris 3 31
(M S Saunders) *s.i.s: a bhd* **50/1**

1m 10.0s (-1.20) **Going Correction** -0.10s/f (Good) **15** Ran SP% **119.5**
Speed ratings (Par 103):104,103,102,101,100 100,99,98,97,97 97,96,95,93,81
CSF £138.88 CT £457.69 TOTE £15.70: £3.80, £3.10, £1.60; EX 199.20.
Owner R D Willis and M C Watts **Bred** Acrum Lodge Stud **Trained** Sedbury, Gloucs
■ Stewards' Enquiry : Luke Morris caution: careless riding

FOCUS
A modest but competitive sprint handicap and the winning time was over a second faster than the earlier maiden won by Tilsworth Charlie. Slight improvement from the winner, with the runner-up to form.
Cornus Official explanation: jockey said gelding was denied a clear run
Arctic Desert Official explanation: jockey said gelding was slowly away
Hornpipe Official explanation: jockey said gelding reared as stalls opened
T/Jkpt: Not won. T/Plt: £3,562.70 to a £1 stake. Pool: £58,321.05. 11.95 winning tickets. T/Qpdt: £113.90 to a £1 stake. Pool: £4,126.00. 26.80 winning tickets. TM

4880 NEWCASTLE (L-H)
Monday, September 4

OFFICIAL GOING: Soft
A total of 24 horses were taken out because of the ground.
Wind: light, across

5059 E B F CLASSIC EXCEL MAIDEN STKS 6f
2:30 (2:30) (Class 5) 2-Y-O **£3,886** (£1,156; £577; £288) **Stalls** High

Form RPR

1 **Sumi Girl (IRE)** 2-8-5 JamesRogers(7) 12 75
(R A Fahey) *towards rr: pushed along after 2f: hdwy and edgd lft over 2f out: styd on to ld appr last: kpt on wl* **50/1**

3 **2** *2 ½* **Love Dubai (USA)**[12] 4716 2-9-3 KDarley 4 73
(M Johnston) *dwlt: sn rdn along to chse ldrs: driven 2f out: kpt on u.p ins last* **2/7**[1]

0 **3** *1* **Miss Percy**[11] 4731 2-8-12 PaulHanagan 7 65
(R A Fahey) *chsd ldrs: rdn along over 2f out: kpt on ins last: nrst fin* **12/1**[3]

4 *¾* **Bollin Fergus** 2-9-3 DavidAllan 6 68
(T D Easterby) *bhd tl styd on fr wl over 1f out: nrst fin* **50/1**

3 **5** *1* **The Grey Berry**[42] 3780 2-9-3 TonyHamilton 11 65
(C Grant) *led: rdn along over 2f out: hdd over 1f out: grad wknd* **50/1**

43 **6** *3 ½* **Captain Jacksparra (IRE)**[14] 4650 2-9-3 DO'Donohoe 8 54
(K A Ryan) *cl up: rdn along 2f out and ev ch tl drvn ent last and sn wknd* **7/1**[2]

7 *2* **Anybody's Guess (IRE)** 2-9-3 TomEaves 5 48
(J S Wainwright) *a rr* **80/1**

66 **8** *3* **Minnow**[21] 4421 2-8-12 PatCosgrave 9 34
(S C Williams) *cl up: rdn along and ev ch 2f out: sn drvn and wknd appr last* **25/1**

0 **9** *3 ½* **Xalted**[36] 3979 2-8-12 PaulQuinn 3 24
(S C Williams) *s.i.s: a bhd* **33/1**

06 **10** *7* **Jazzanova**[3] 4987 2-9-3 PaulMulrennan 2 8
(M W Easterby) *in tch: rdn along 1/2-way: sn wknd* **66/1**

11 *44* **Scottish Spirit (IRE)** 2-9-3 PhillipMakin 1 —
(J S Haldane) *in tch: rdn along 1/2-way: sn wknd* **100/1**

1m 20.3s (5.21) **Going Correction** +0.55s/f (Yiel) **11** Ran SP% **114.3**
Speed ratings (Par 95):87,83,82,81,80 75,72,68,64,54 —
CSF £64.17 TOTE £78.20: £14.00, £1.02, £2.80; EX 279.60 Trifecta £241.40 Part won. Pool £340.00 - 0.70 winning units..
Owner Aidan J Ryan **Bred** R O'Leary **Trained** Musley Bank, N Yorks

FOCUS
A modest juvenile maiden, run at an average pace, and the form is worth treating with a little caution with the runner-up a long way off his debut form.

NOTEBOOK
Sumi Girl(IRE), a half-sister to a ten-furlong winner in Germany, ran green through the early parts before coming through to post a winning debut in ready fashion. She showed a neat turn of foot to settle the issue and, considering she started at odds of 50/1, she was clearly expected to benefit from the experience. Another furlong should also be to her liking before the season's end. (op 33-1)
Love Dubai(USA), a promising third on his debut at York, never looked like justifying his prohibitive odds at any stage and has to rate bitterly disappointing. He may have found this coming a little too soon, and was keeping on at the finish as though he ideally needs a stiffer test, but this effort leaves him with an awful lot to prove now all the same. (op 1-3 tchd 4-11, tchd 2-5 in a place)
Miss Percy, as on her recent Redcar debut, was doing all of her best work towards the finish and never seriously threatened her winning stable companion. She is crying out for another furlong and is going the right way. (tchd 10-1)
Bollin Fergus, whose dam has produced numerous winners at up to a mile, looked clueless through the early stages but stayed on takingly when the penny dropped late on. He will no doubt prove a lot sharper with this debut experience under his belt and looked suited by the easy ground. (op 66-1)
The Grey Berry was aided by racing against the stands' rail through the early parts, but eventually paid for his exertions at the head of affairs. He is well worth another chance when reverting to a less taxing surface.
Captain Jacksparra(IRE) again got warm beforehand and once more found less than looked likely when put under pressure. He now qualifies for nurseries and it would come as a surprise were he not to do a little better in that arena. (op 13-2 tchd 8-1)

5060 CPD DISTRIBUTION MAIDEN STKS 5f
3:00 (3:00) (Class 5) 3-Y-O+ **£3,562** (£1,059; £529; £264) **Stalls** High

Form RPR

054 **1** **Signor Whippee**[4] 4948 3-9-3 46 (b) TonyHamilton 17 54
(A Berry) *trckd ldrs: swtchd lft and hdwy 2f out: led wl over 1f out: sn rdn and kpt on* **25/1**

5252 **2** *1 ½* **Newkeylets**[12] 4695 3-8-12 55 (p) TomEaves 16 44
(I Semple) *cl up: led over 2f out: sn rdn and hdd wl over 1f out: kpt on u.p ins last* **7/1**

-502 **3** *¾* **Mujeak (IRE)**[7] 4886 3-9-3 63 GrahamGibbons 3 47+
(J J Quinn) *s.i.s and bhd: hdwy over 2f out: swtchd rt and rdn over 1f out: kpt on ins last* **5/2**[1]

0564 **4** *1* **Red Chairman**[12] 4697 4-8-13 54 (p) DeclanMcGann(5) 11 43
(R Johnson) *midfield: gd hdwy 2f out: swtchd lft and rdn wl over 1f out: kpt on same pce* **12/1**

4-6 **5** *½* **Targer Place**[135] 1147 3-9-3 DO'Donohoe 9 42
(T T Clement) *in tch: hdwy over 2f out: sn rdn and kpt on same pce ins last* **10/1**

0005 **6** *¾* **Rainbow Prince**[14] 4656 3-9-3 44 PhillipMakin 7 39+
(A Dickman) *s.i.s and bhd: hdwy 2f out: sn rdn and kpt on: nt rch ldrs* **50/1**

0-02 **7** *1* **Choreographic (IRE)**[33] 4059 4-9-4 40 PaulHanagan 15 36
(R A Fahey) *trckd ldrs: pushed along 1/2-way: rdn and n.m.r 2f out: sn btn* **14/1**

4324 **8** *2* **Spinning**[26] 4257 3-8-10 66 DeanHeslop(7) 5 44+
(T D Barron) *s.i.s and bhd: hdwy over 2f out: swtchd outside and styng on whn hmpd over 1f out: nt rcvr* **4/1**[2]

3646 **9** *¾* **Tagula Bay (IRE)**[11] 4735 4-8-13 54 DavidAllan 8 21
(T D Easterby) *chsd ldrs: rdn along 2f out: sn wknd* **5/1**[3]

0600 **10** *8* **Ailsa**[14] 4652 4-8-13 42 DeanMcKeown 1 —f
(C W Thornton) *racd alone far side: outpcd fr 1/2-way* **20/1**

0046 **11** *1* **Martharum**[14] 4656 3-8-10 41 ow1 DNolan(3) 4 —
(J J Quinn) *led: rdn along and hdd over 2f out: wknd wl over 1f out* **33/1**

4/0- **12** *8* **Gifted Lass**[457] 2290 4-8-10 54 JasonEdmunds(3) 2 —
(J Balding) *cl up: rdn along over 2f out: sn wknd* **50/1**

63.85 secs (2.35) **Going Correction** +0.55s/f (Yiel)
WFA 3 from 4yo+ 1lb **12** Ran SP% **116.7**
Speed ratings (Par 103):103,100,99,97,97 95,94,91,89,77 75,62
CSF £181.15 TOTE £17.90: £5.40, £2.80, £1.40; EX 69.40 TRIFECTA Not won..
Owner Alan Berry **Bred** Zubieta Ltd **Trained** Cockerham, Lancs
■ Stewards' Enquiry : Graham Gibbons two-day ban: careless riding (Sep 15-16)

FOCUS
A weak maiden, run at a sound pace in the testing ground, and the field came home fairly strung out. High numbers were favoured, as they were in the first. The winner is pretty exposed.

5061 ARMSTRONG H'CAP 2m 19y
3:30 (3:31) (Class 6) (0-65,59) 3-Y-0+ **£3,238** (£963; £481; £240) **Stalls** Centre

Form RPR
2201 **1** **Vice Admiral**[4] 4960 3-9-1 **59** 6ex PaulMulrennan 3 70
(M W Easterby) *mde all: pushed along 3f out: rdn over 2f out: drvn appr last and styd on wl* **11/2**[3]

55-6 **2** *2* **Rossin Gold (IRE)**[13] 1608 4-9-1 **46** DavidAllan 13 55
(P Monteith) *hld up towards rr: hdwy 4f out: rdn to chse wnr 2f out: sn drvn and kpt on* **10/1**

/064 **3** *2 ½* **Culcabock (IRE)**[7] 4351 6-8-11 **42** oh2 PaulHanagan 7 49
(Miss Lucinda V Russell) *trckd ldrs on inner: hdwy to chse wnr 3f out: rdn over 2f out and kpt on same pce* **7/2**[2]

0000 **4** *3* **Scurra**[21] 4438 7-8-11 **42** oh2 PatCosgrave 4 46
(A C Whillans) *hld up towards rr: swtchd rt and hdwy 3f out: rdn 2f out and sn no imp* **11/1**

0040 **5** *3* **Loaded Gun**[40] 3836 6-8-6 **42** oh2 AndrewElliott(5) 1 43
(W Storey) *keedn: hld up in rr: swtchd wd and hdwy 3f out: rdn 2f out and sn no imp* **16/1**

-400 **6** *¾* **Singhalongtasveer**[6] 4914 4-8-13 **44** (tp) CatherineGannon 9 44
(W Storey) *trckd ldrs: hdwy 4f out: rdn to chse ldrs 3f out: sn btn* **11/1**

0-00 **7** *1* **Channel Crossing**[8] 4845 4-9-0 **48** DNolan(3) 11 47
(W M Brisbourne) *midfield: rdn along over 4f out: sn wknd* **28/1**

3204 **8** *30* **Jolizero**[53] 3454 5-9-11 **56** KDarley 8 25
(John Berry) *keen: trckd ldr: pushed along 7f out: rdn 4f out: drvn and weakened over 3f out: bhd and virtually p.u fnl f* **11/8**[1]

0000 **9** *2* **Sansel**[26] 4263 3-7-5 **42** oh27 CharlotteKerton(7) 12 9
(J Ryan) *chsd leaing pair: rdn along 5f out: sn lost pl and bhd* **100/1**

3m 46.48s (11.28) **Going Correction** +0.65s/f (Yiel)
WFA 3 from 4yo+ 13lb **9** Ran SP% **115.8**
Speed ratings (Par 101):97,96,94,93,91 91,90,75,74
CSF £59.00 CT £219.86 TOTE £5.50: £2.20, £3.40, £1.50; EX 37.30 Trifecta £71.30 Pool £202.06 - 2.01 winning units..
Owner A C R Stubbs **Bred** Barry Minty **Trained** Sheriff Hutton, N Yorks

FOCUS
A modeest staying handicap, run at an uneven pace, which saw the field trail home behind the progressive winner. The second and third are entitled to rate this high on jumps form.
Jolizero Official explanation: trainer said gelding was found to have pulled a muscle in its hindquarters

5062 USG H'CAP 6f
4:00 (4:02) (Class 6) (0-55,55) 3-Y-0+ **£3,238** (£963; £481; £240) **Stalls** High

Form RPR
1500 **1** **Prospect Court**[11] 4729 4-8-8 **51** AndrewMullen(3) 16 63
(A C Whillans) *trckd ldrs: hdwy to ld over 2f out: rdn over 1f out: kpt on wl* **10/1**

0460 **2** *1 ¼* **Outrageous Flirt (IRE)**[28] 4198 4-8-9 **49** PaulHanagan 12 57
(A Dickman) *in tch: hdwy over 2f out: rdn to chse wnr over 1f out: drvn ins last: no imp towards fin* **8/1**[3]

0500 **3** *¾* **Apex**[11] 4735 5-9-0 **54** KimTinkler 15 60
(N Tinkler) *in tch: hdwy over 2f out: rdn to chse wnr wl over 1f out: drvn and nt qckn ent last* **8/1**[3]

0-05 **4** *7* **Nevinstown (IRE)**[42] 3786 6-8-8 **48** TonyHamilton 17 33
(C Grant) *streadied s: hld up and bhd: hdwy on inner 2f out: rdn and kpt on ins last: nrst fin* **17/2**

3564 **5** *¾* **Blue Knight (IRE)**[22] 4401 7-9-0 **54** (vt) GrahamGibbons 5 37
(D Carroll) *towards rr: pushed along over 3f out: rdn 2f out: kpt on appr last: nrst fin* **12/1**

404 **6** *2* **Mandarin Lady**[19] 4494 3-8-11 **53** TomEaves 4 30
(Miss J A Camacho) *midfield: pushed along over 3f out: sn rdn and no hdwy* **12/1**

0402 **7** *7* **Bold Haze**[23] 4361 4-9-1 **55** (v) DeanMcKeown 11 11
(Miss S E Hall) *trckd ldrs: rdn 2f out: sn edgd lft and btn* **7/1**[2]

3101 **8** *nk* **Miss Mujahid Times**[12] 4710 3-8-11 **53** (b) SilvestreDeSousa 7 8
(A D Brown) *led: rdn along and hdd over 2f out: grad wknd* **7/1**[2]

51 **9** *7* **Oeuf A La Neige**[14] 4655 6-8-13 **53** PatCosgrave 1 —
(Miss L A Perratt) *chsd ldrs on outer to 1/2-way: sn rdn: lost pl and bhd* **8/1**[3]

-402 **10** *2* **Guadaloup**[17] 4571 4-8-11 **51** (b) KDarley 8 —
(M Brittain) *dwlt: sn chsng ldrs: rdn along over 2f out: sn wknd* **9/2**[1]

3013 **11** *17* **Markestino**[12] 4695 3-8-8 **50** (t) DavidAllan 3 —
(T D Easterby) *cl up on outer: rdn along 1/2-way: sn wknd: bhd and eased fnl f* **12/1**

1m 17.7s (2.61) **Going Correction** +0.55s/f (Yiel)
WFA 3 from 4yo+ 2lb **11** Ran SP% **119.2**
Speed ratings (Par 101):104,102,101,92,91 88,79,78,69,66 43
CSF £88.86 CT £501.66 TOTE £10.60: £4.00, £2.60, £3.40; EX 62.20 Trifecta £175.10 Pool £246.66 - 1 winning unit..
Owner Mrs L M Whillans **Bred** Mrs G Slater **Trained** Newmill-On-Slitrig, Borders

FOCUS
A moderate sprint which again saw those drawn high at a distinct advantage. Ordinary form, rated through the runner-up.
Mandarin Lady Official explanation: trainer said filly was unsuited by the soft ground
Guadaloup Official explanation: jockey said filly was unsuited by the soft ground
Markestino Official explanation: jockey said gelding moved poorly throughout

5063 SPEEDLINE MAIDEN STKS 1m (R)
4:30 (4:32) (Class 5) 3-Y-0+ **£3,562** (£1,059; £529; £264) **Stalls** High

Form RPR
-256 **1** **Compromiznotension (IRE)**[100] 2016 3-9-3 68 TomEaves 6 68
(I Semple) *mde all: qcknd clr wl over 2f out: rdn ent last and styd on wl* **9/2**[3]

044 **2** *5* **Dechiper (IRE)**[12] 4694 4-9-3 48 DeclanMcGann(5) 4 58
(R Johnson) *hld up: hdwy over 3f out: chsd wnr 2f out: sn rdn and no imp fnl f* **8/1**

0630 **3** *6* **Whittinghamvillage**[11] 4729 5-9-3 51 SilvestreDeSousa 8 41
(D W Whillans) *hld up towards rr: hdwy 3f out: sn rdn: styd on to take poor 3rd pl ins last* **9/2**[3]

0030 **4** *5* **Silver Sail**[14] 4651 3-8-12 40 TonyHamilton 9 31
(J S Wainwright) *cl up: rdn along 3f out: drvn and wknd 2f out* **16/1**

0-2 **5** *shd* **White Lightening (IRE)**[67] 3001 3-9-3 PaulMulrennan 2 36
(J Howard Johnson) *trckd ldrs: effrt on inner to chse wnr 3f out: sn rdn and wknd 2f out* **7/4**[1]

32 **6** *½* **Shiitake**[30] 4155 3-8-12 PatCosgrave 5 30
(Miss L A Perratt) *dwlt: sn in tch: hdwy 4f out: rdn along 3f out: sn outpcd* **7/2**[2]

0005 **7** *32* **Four Kings**[17] 4546 5-9-8 34 CatherineGannon 11 —
(R Allan) *cl up: rdn along over 3f out: sn wknd* **33/1**

1m 47.73s (4.25) **Going Correction** +0.65s/f (Yiel)
WFA 3 from 4yo+ 5lb **7** Ran SP% **114.9**
Speed ratings (Par 103):104,99,93,88,87 87,55
CSF £39.50 TOTE £6.60: £3.10, £3.30; EX 37.20 Trifecta £235.60 Part won. Pool £331.87 - 0.54 winning units..
Owner R Hyndman **Bred** Corduff Stud **Trained** Carluke, S Lanarks

FOCUS
No strength in depth to this moderate maiden and the field finished well strung out on the testing ground. The winner produced a better effort but was still a few pounds off his best. The race has been tentatively rated through the second.
Shiitake Official explanation: jockey said filly had a breathing problem

5064 KNAUF DRYWALL H'CAP 1m 2f 32y
5:00 (5:01) (Class 6) (0-60,60) 3-Y-0+ **£2,590** (£770; £385; £192) **Stalls** Centre

Form RPR
6-03 **1** **Turn Of Phrase (IRE)**[4] 4947 7-9-5 **54** (b) DO'Donohoe 16 64
(B Ellison) *trckd ldrs: hdwy over 2f out: led wl over 1f out: sn rdn and edgd lft: styd on wl fnl f* **6/1**[3]

0511 **2** *3* **Jordans Spark**[23] 4355 5-9-6 **55** PaulMulrennan 4 60
(P Monteith) *hld up towards rr: hdwy over 3f out: rdn to chse ent last: sn drvn edgd lft and kpt on same pce* **10/1**

0003 **3** *nk* **Melodian**[17] 4570 11-9-3 **52** (b) DavidAllan 8 56
(M Brittain) *cl up: rdn along 4f out: led over 2f out: sn drvn and hdd wl over 1f out: grad wknd* **7/1**

2403 **4** *nk* **Royal Flynn**[12] 4709 4-9-8 **57** PhillipMakin 10 61
(M Dods) *hld up and bhd: hdwy over 2f out: rdn and n.m.r over 1f out: kpt on ins last* **9/2**[2]

156U **5** *1 ¾* **Ruby Legend**[17] 4568 8-9-0 **56** (p) JamesReveley(7) 11 57
(K G Reveley) *trckd ldrs: hdwy 3f out: rdn along 2f out and sn one pce* **20/1**

0341 **6** *5* **Wednesdays Boy (IRE)**[14] 4651 3-9-2 **58** (p) TomEaves 1 50
(P D Niven) *in tch on inner: hdwy 3f out: ev ch 2f out: sn rdn and wknd appr last* **7/2**[1]

0150 **7** *1 ¼* **Dispol Peto**[19] 4476 6-8-12 **52** (p) DeclanMcGann(5) 13 42
(R Johnson) *cl up: rdn along 3f out: wknd 2f out* **33/1**

0522 **8** *9* **Woolly Back (IRE)**[21] 4435 5-9-9 **58** PatCosgrave 6 33
(A C Whillans) *keen: in tch tl rdn along over 2f out and sn wknd* **8/1**

363 **9** *2* **Neil's Legacy (IRE)**[12] 4692 4-8-12 **50** AndrewMullen(3) 2 22
(Miss L A Perratt) *dwlt: towards rr: hdwy on inner and ch over 2f out: sn rdn and wknd* **6/1**[3]

3100 **10** *½* **Thornaby Green**[17] 4570 5-8-12 **47** PaulHanagan 3 18
(T D Barron) *led: rdn along 3f out: hdd over 2f out and sn wknd* **9/1**

2m 17.89s (6.09) **Going Correction** +0.65s/f (Yiel)
WFA 3 from 4yo+ 7lb **10** Ran SP% **119.4**
Speed ratings (Par 101):101,98,98,98,96 92,91,84,82,82
CSF £66.10 CT £435.31 TOTE £9.10: £2.00, £3.00, £2.70; EX 87.80 Trifecta £138.70 Part won. Pool £195.43 - 0.10 winning units..
Owner Naughty Diesel Ltd **Bred** Moyglare Stud Farm Ltd **Trained** Norton, N Yorks

FOCUS
A moderate handicap which was run at a sound pace. The form looks straightforward enough.
Neil's Legacy(IRE) Official explanation: jockey said filly was unsuited by the soft ground
T/Plt: £677.40 to a £1 stake. Pool: £58,556.55. 63.10 winning tickets. T/Qpdt: £185.00 to a £1 stake. Pool: £3,825.80. 15.30 winning tickets. JR

4893 WARWICK (L-H)
Monday, September 4

OFFICIAL GOING: Good
Wind: moderate, behind

5065 WBX.COM WORLD BET EXCHANGE NURSERY 5f 110y
1:50 (1:52) (Class 5) (0-75,72) 2-Y-0 **£3,238** (£963; £481; £240) **Stalls** Centre

Form RPR
0420 **1** **Mambo Spirit (IRE)**[10] 4766 2-9-7 **72** J-PGuillambert 3 79
(J G Given) *s.i.s: hld up: hdwy on ins over 2f out: sn rdn: led wl ins fnl f: r.o* **11/2**[2]

01 **2** *½* **Jack Oliver**[30] 4163 2-9-3 **68** SteveDrowne 8 73
(B J Meehan) *chsd ldr: rdn over 1f out: ev ch ins fnl f: r.o* **9/2**[1]

223 **3** *nk* **Brenin Gwalia**[20] 4445 2-8-12 **63** DarryllHolland 6 67
(D M Simcock) *led: rdn 2f out: hdd wl ins fnl f: no ex* **11/2**[2]

6542 **4** *1 ¾* **Mazin Lady**[18] 4519 2-9-0 **65** RobertWinston 11 63
(Miss J A Camacho) *hld up and bhd: hdwy over 2f out: sn rdn: one pce fnl f* **7/1**[3]

600 **5** *1 ¼* **Back In The Red (IRE)**[10] 4753 2-8-5 **56** DaleGibson 4 50
(M Wellings) *hld up in tch: hung lft and lost pl 3f out: rdn and hdwy over 1f out: kpt on* **100/1**

234 **6** *½* **Tipsy Prince**[21] 4433 2-9-2 **67** SebSanders 17 59
(Mrs G S Rees) *swtchd lft sn after s: bhd tl rdn and hdwy on ins 2f out: one pce fnl f* **20/1**

3606 **7** *1 ½* **Copper King**[7] 4893 2-8-11 **62** (v[1]) DaneO'Neill 5 50
(A M Balding) *bhd: rdn over 1f out: hung lft ins fnl f: nvr nrr* **14/1**

4006 **8** *1 ¼* **Queensgate**[10] 4779 2-8-7 **59** ow1 TedDurcan 15 41
(M Blanshard) *t.k.h in tch: rdn and wknd over 1f out* **25/1**

4014 **9** *nk* **Queen Of Narnia**[8] 4857 2-9-0 **65** ChrisCatlin 16 47
(M R Channon) *prom: rdn 2f out: wknd fnl f* **9/1**

0044 **10** *2* **Bertie Swift**[19] 4479 2-9-2 **67** JimCrowley 2 43
(J Gallagher) *n.d* **14/1**

0600 **11** *1 ¼* **Merlins Quest**[66] 3031 2-8-2 **56** SaleemGolam(3) 9 28
(J M Bradley) *nvr bttr than mid-div* **40/1**

0540 **12** *nk* **Mrs Crossy (IRE)**[10] 4779 2-8-9 **60** JoeFanning 1 31
(A W Carroll) *chsd ldrs tl wknd over 1f out* **16/1**

002L **13** *nk* **Linkslade Lad**[20] 4445 2-8-13 64 ......(b) RichardMullen 12 34
(W R Muir) *swvd lft s: a in rr* **16/1**

004 **14** *3/4* **Beat The Bully**[17] 4550 2-8-8 59 ...... TPQueally 7 26
(I A Wood) *chsd ldr 3f* **40/1**

0020 **15** *1 1/2* **Gibsons**[35] 3997 2-7-13 50 ...... JimmyQuinn 10 12
(Mrs P N Dutfield) *bhd fnl 2f* **33/1**

6333 **16** *3 1/2* **Mogok Ruby**[12] 4699 2-9-5 70 ...... MickyFenton 13 21
(L Montague Hall) *s.i.s: short-lived effrt on outside over 2f out: hung lft and wknd over 1f out* **12/1**

64.81 secs (-0.69) **Going Correction** -0.225s/f (Firm) **16** Ran SP% **121.7**
Speed ratings (Par 95):95,94,93,91,89 89,87,85,85,82 80,80,80,79,77 72
CSF £28.24 CT £146.90 TOTE £8.00: £1.90, £1.10, £1.60, £2.00; EX 34.90.
Owner Jones, Jones, Clarke & O'Sullivan **Bred** R Warren **Trained** Willoughton, Lincs

FOCUS
This was the only race of the day to better the standard time and the form of this nursery may well stand up. The winner looked good and the form looks solid through the placed horses.

NOTEBOOK
Mambo Spirit(IRE) ◆ had not got the best of runs when possibly finding the ground too soft over six at Newmarket last time. He needed every yard of this slightly shorter trip to defy top weight and the winning time suggests this was a good performance. (op 7-1 tchd 15-2)
Jack Oliver ◆, who looked fairly treated, gave favourite backers a decent run for their money and lost no caste in defeat. (op 5-1 tchd 4-1)
Brenin Gwalia ◆ adopted his usual tactics over the shortest distance he had encountered so far. He continues to knock on the door. (op 3-1)
Mazin Lady ran a sound enough race off a pound higher mark. (op 6-1)
Back In The Red(IRE) improved considerably on his three starts in maidens but may not be that straightforward. (op 50-1)
Tipsy Prince was not disgraced in a bid to overcome the outside draw. (op 14-1)
Mogok Ruby Official explanation: jockey said colt lost its action in the closing stages

5066 E B F WBX.COM WORLD BET EXCHANGE MAIDEN STKS (C&G) (DIV I) 7f 26y
2:20 (2:22) (Class 5) 2-Y-O **£3,238** (£963; £481; £240) **Stalls** Low

Form RPR

5 **1** **Artimino**[31] 4109 2-9-0 ...... OscarUrbina 8 80+
(J R Fanshawe) *chsd ldrs: led appr fnl f: edgd lft ins last: styd on wl* **7/2**[1]

53 **2** *1 1/4* **Karoo Blue (IRE)**[26] 4260 2-9-0 ...... TedDurcan 3 77
(C E Brittain) *led tl appr fnl f: keeping on same pce whn sltly hmpd last 75yds* **5/1**[2]

3 **3** *1* **Hazzard County (USA)**[24] 4333 2-9-0 ...... DaneO'Neill 13 74
(D M Simcock) *w ldrs: rdn and edgd lft over 1f out: kpt on same pce* **7/2**[1]

24 **4** *1 1/4* **Go On Green (IRE)**[23] 4349 2-9-0 ......(t) RichardMullen 5 71
(E A L Dunlop) *mid-div: effrt over 2f out: styd on wl fnl f* **16/1**

6 **5** *3/4* **Deadline (UAE)**[12] 4716 2-9-0 ...... JoeFanning 7 69
(M Johnston) *chsd ldrs: keeping on same pce whn hmpd over 1f out* **6/1**[3]

0 **6** *1 1/4* **Radical Views**[16] 4600 2-9-0 ...... MickyFenton 14 66+
(B W Hills) *prom: drvn 3f out: kpt on wl fnl f* **10/1**

7 *shd* **Leon Knights** 2-9-0 ...... NickyMackay 10 66+
(G A Butler) *rr-div: reminders over 3f out: kpt on appr fnl f* **50/1**

00 **8** *shd* **Rikochet**[19] 4487 2-9-0 ...... JimCrowley 1 65
(Mrs A J Perrett) *chsd ldrs: one pce fnl 2f* **100/1**

9 *4* **Tetouan** 2-9-0 ...... SteveDrowne 4 55
(R Charlton) *s.i.s: sme hdwy on outside over 2f out: nvr on terms* **12/1**

10 *nk* **Al Shemali** 2-9-0 ...... RobertWinston 6 55
(Sir Michael Stoute) *in rr: sn drvn along: nvr on terms* **14/1**

5U **11** *2* **Munster Mountain (IRE)**[31] 4109 2-9-0 ...... TPO'Shea 9 50
(P A Blockley) *hld up in mid-div: nvr a factor* **125/1**

6 **12** *2* **Master Of Destiny (IRE)**[19] 4485 2-9-0 ...... JimmyQuinn 12 45
(H J Collingridge) *mid-div: nvr a factor* **80/1**

13 *nk* **Ballet Boy (IRE)** 2-9-0 ...... SebSanders 11 44
(Sir Mark Prescott) *s.i.s: in rr and drvn along* **40/1**

14 *11* **Rezeez (USA)** 2-9-0 ...... RHills 2 16
(W J Haggas) *in rr: hmpd and lost pl after 2f: detached over 3f out* **16/1**

1m 23.99s (-1.01) **Going Correction** -0.075s/f (Good) **14** Ran SP% **118.0**
Speed ratings (Par 95):102,100,99,98,97 95,95,95,90,90 88,86,85,73
CSF £19.78 TOTE £5.00: £2.30, £1.90, £1.60; EX 29.80.
Owner Cheveley Park Stud **Bred** Cheveley Park Stud Ltd **Trained** Newmarket, Suffolk
■ Stewards' Enquiry : Oscar Urbina caution: careless riding

FOCUS
A decent winning time for a race of its type and 1.79 seconds faster than the second division. An interesting maiden on paper and one that might well produce a few winners. The form looks quite solid through the first six.

NOTEBOOK
Artimino had disappointed his trainer on his debut over a furlong less but was noticeably green on that occasion. Clearly more clued-up this time, he created a really favourable impression, travelling smoothly just in behind the leaders and then settling the issue quickly once the question was popped. Connections are likely to play a softly, softly approach for the time being but he looks like shaping up into a useful colt but one who, on breeding, is unlikely to stay beyond a mile. (op 4-1)
Karoo Blue(IRE) was thoroughly professional on this his third outing and, although hampered close home, it made no difference to the result. He set a respectable standard for the rest to aim at and, despite being beaten, he should find a maiden without too much difficulty. (op 7-1)
Hazzard County(USA) showed promise when third on his debut and he ran another decent race here despite racing wider than the first two. He should win a maiden. (op 11-4 tchd 4-1)
Go On Green(IRE), upped in trip and tried in a tongue-strap, was a little outpaced early in the straight before finishing strongly through the final furlong. (op 14-1)
Deadline(UAE), stepping up in trip, was quick from the gate but was dropping away when tight for room early in the straight. (op 5-1 tchd 9-2)
Radical Views was not given a hard time and has the profile of a horse who could do considerably better at three. (op 11-1)
Leon Knights, who was coming home to good effect after being a little slow to go, comes from a yard whose juveniles invariably derive much benefit from a first run.
Rikochet ran his best race yet and will win handicaps when he faces a proper stamina test. (op 66-1)
Tetouan, a half-brother to smart middle-distance winners Pongee and Puce, as well as to the dam of Alexandrova, came from the rear and will know more in the future Official explanation: jockey said colt suffered interference in running (tchd 16-1)
Al Shemali, a half-brother to high-class stayer Tungsten Strike, should benefit from this debut experience. (op 12-1)
Ballet Boy(IRE), a half-brother to German 1000 Guineas winner Dahla Oasis and high-class French sprinter Dyhim Diamond, became a bit confused when the stalls opened and then got outpaced. There is more than a good chance that he will turn out to be better than he looked here.
Rezeez(USA), son of an Irish 1000 Guineas winner, was very badly hampered against the fence in the early stages. That hardly represents an ideal debut, but if there are no mental scars he should bounce back. Official explanation: jockey said colt suffered interference in running (op 20-1)

5067 E B F WBX.COM WORLD BET EXCHANGE MAIDEN STKS (C&G) (DIV II) 7f 26y
2:50 (2:58) (Class 5) 2-Y-O **£3,238** (£963; £481; £240) **Stalls** Low

Form RPR

1 **Slate (IRE)** 2-8-11 ...... RichardKingscote(3) 5 69
(J A Osborne) *hld up towards rr: stdy hdwy over 2f out: str run to ld wl ins fnl f* **25/1**

2 **2** *1* **Thabaat**[16] 4592 2-9-0 ...... RHills 11 67
(B W Hills) *a.p: rdn and ev ch over 1f out: nt qckn ins fnl f* **4/11**[1]

6 **3** *nk* **Moorlander (USA)**[19] 4479 2-9-0 ...... JimCrowley 2 66
(Mrs A J Perrett) *a.p: rdn over 2f out: led jst over 1f out: hdd and nt qckn wl ins fnl f* **20/1**

00 **4** *1* **Majestas (IRE)**[30] 4129 2-9-0 ...... DaneO'Neill 8 64
(J G M O'Shea) *led: rdn over 2f out: edgd rt and hdd jst over 1f out: no ex ins fnl f* **50/1**

0 **5** *nk* **Alpes Maritimes**[24] 4333 2-9-0 ...... DarryllHolland 7 63
(G Wragg) *t.k.h in tch: rdn over 2f out: swtchd lft 1f out: kpt on same pce* **50/1**

4 **6** *3/4* **Desert Soul**[82] 2545 2-9-0 ...... JoeFanning 14 61
(M Johnston) *hld up in tch: rdn and ev ch on outside whn rn green over 1f out: fdd ins fnl f* **33/1**

40 **7** *shd* **Bachnagairn**[12] 4705 2-9-0 ...... SteveDrowne 4 61
(R Charlton) *hld up in tch: rdn over 2f out: carried lft 1f out: hld whn swtchd rt wl ins fnl f* **12/1**[3]

8 *1* **Here Comes Buster (IRE)** 2-9-0 ...... PatDobbs 3 58
(R Hannon) *s.i.s: hdwy on ins 3f out: sn rdn: no imp fnl f* **33/1**

6 **9** *1/2* **Downbeat**[72] 2867 2-9-0 ...... JimmyQuinn 6 57
(J L Dunlop) *hld up in mid-div: rdn and no hdwy fnl 2f* **40/1**

10 *1/2* **Arabian Word** 2-9-0 ...... RobertWinston 10 56
(Sir Michael Stoute) *s.s: hdwy over 1f out: nvr nrr* **10/1**[2]

00 **11** *6* **Jafaru**[23] 4366 2-9-0 ...... NickyMackay 12 41
(G A Butler) *a bhd* **100/1**

12 *3* **Me Fein** 2-9-0 ...... TPQueally 13 33
(B J Curley) *s.i.s: a bhd* **66/1**

13 *9* **Mazoran (FR)** 2-9-0 ...... MickyFenton 9 11
(D G Bridgwater) *s.i.s: swtchd lft sn after s: a in rr* **100/1**

1m 25.78s (0.78) **Going Correction** -0.075s/f (Good) **13** Ran SP% **114.4**
Speed ratings (Par 95):92,90,90,89,89 88,88,86,86,85 78,75,65
CSF £30.89 TOTE £34.50: £6.60, £1.02, £3.10; EX 86.10.
Owner Mountgrange Stud **Bred** Swordlestown Stud **Trained** Upper Lambourn, Berks
■ Crossing The Line (12/1) was withdrawn. R4 applies, deduct 5p in the £.

FOCUS
A modest pace led to the winning time being 1.79 seconds slower than the first division. Not easy to rate with the runner-up well off his debut effort.

NOTEBOOK
Slate(IRE) ◆ is a half-brother to triple six-furlong scorer Bohola Flyer and a seven-furlong Irish juvenile winner. This was a highly satisfactory debut and there should be further improvement to come. (tchd 22-1 and 28-1)
Thabaat, who became fractious in the stalls according to his rider, was made a red-hot favourite on the strength of his second at Newbury. He did not do a lot wrong and may have preferred a truer-run contest. Official explanation: jockey said colt became fractious in the stalls (op 2-5, tchd 4-9 in places)
Moorlander(USA) ◆ had learnt from his Salisbury debut and does seem to be progressing along the right lines. (op 28-1)
Majestas(IRE), outpaced in his first two outings, showed significant improvement after making the running and it remains to be seen if he can build on this. (op 66-1)
Alpes Maritimes ◆, who already has the stamp of a three-year-old, is a half-brother to a mile and a half winner. He will do better over further in due course.
Desert Soul ◆ still showed signs of inexperience but ran well for one who is also bred to want a stiffer test of stamina. (op 28-1)

5068 E B F WBX.COM WORLD BET EXCHANGE MAIDEN FILLIES' STKS 7f 26y
3:20 (3:31) (Class 5) 2-Y-O **£3,886** (£1,156; £577; £288) **Stalls** Low

Form RPR

2 **1** **Swift Image**[25] 4302 2-8-11 ...... SaleemGolam(3) 10 75
(S C Williams) *w ldr: led over 1f out: edgd rt and hung lft: styd on wl* **6/1**[3]

5 **2** *2 1/2* **Sophia Gardens**[17] 4558 2-9-0 ...... DaneO'Neill 8 69
(D W P Arbuthnot) *mde most: hdd over 1f out: kpt on same pce* **10/1**

3 *1* **Red Current** 2-9-0 ...... OscarUrbina 6 66
(J R Fanshawe) *trckd ldrs: kpt on wl fnl f* **16/1**

6 **4** *1/2* **Lady Lafitte (USA)**[33] 4041 2-9-0 ...... RHills 11 65
(B W Hills) *chsd ldrs: effrt over 2f out: kpt on wl fnl f* **10/3**[2]

0 **5** *3/4* **Career Girl (USA)**[42] 3796 2-9-0 ...... RichardMullen 4 63
(E A L Dunlop) *mid-div: styd on fnl 2f: nvr rchd ldrs* **33/1**

0 **6** *3/4* **Miss Phuket**[33] 4041 2-9-0 ...... DarryllHolland 3 61
(G Wragg) *trckd ldrs: effrt over 2f out: kpt on same pce* **5/2**[1]

7 *3 1/2* **Ravarino (USA)** 2-9-0 ...... RobertWinston 14 53+
(Sir Michael Stoute) *swtchd lft after s: bhd: r.o fnl 2f: nvr nr ldrs* **13/2**

8 *1 1/2* **Lightning Queen (USA)** 2-9-0 ...... TedDurcan 7 49
(B W Hills) *hld up in rr: hdwy over 2f out: nvr nr ldrs* **20/1**

9 *1/2* **Virginia Reel** 2-9-0 ...... JoeFanning 12 48
(M Johnston) *mid-div: sn drvn along: nvr a threat* **20/1**

05 **10** *1/2* **Musical Affair**[65] 3096 2-9-0 ...... JimmyQuinn 13 46
(F Jordan) *chsd ldrs: lost pl over 1f out* **80/1**

11 *hd* **Hopeful Isabella (IRE)** 2-9-0 ...... SebSanders 1 46
(Sir Mark Prescott) *s.i.s: sme hdwy over 2f out: sn wknd* **20/1**

0 **12** *1/2* **Armillary**[17] 4558 2-9-0 ...... JimCrowley 5 45
(Mrs A J Perrett) *mid-div: drvn over 2f out: nvr a factor* **33/1**

0 **13** *8* **Little Iris**[14] 4657 2-9-0 ...... NickyMackay 9 25
(L M Cumani) *in rr: sn drvn along: detached 2f out* **33/1**

14 *1/2* **Lady Shirley Hunt** 2-9-0 ...... ChrisCatlin 2 23
(A D Smith) *s.s: a wl detached* **66/1**

1m 24.44s (-0.56) **Going Correction** -0.075s/f (Good) **14** Ran SP% **120.1**
Speed ratings (Par 92):100,97,96,95,94 93,89,88,87,86 86,86,76,76
CSF £57.74 TOTE £7.80: £2.40, £2.30, £4.70; EX 65.80.
Owner Wise Move UK Limited **Bred** Old Mill Stud **Trained** Newmarket, Suffolk

FOCUS
A decent winning time for a race like this. A fair maiden but probably no more than that, the principals showing improved form.

NOTEBOOK
Swift Image had shown promise on her introduction but she was a different proposition second time up, winning in grand fashion. Always prominent, she quickly went clear when sent on well over a furlong out, and her very slightly awkward head carriage was surely down to mere greenness. Her dam was a Listed filly and connections hope she can go the same way. She may not run again this year and is not expected to stay more than a mile. (op 11-1)

Sophia Gardens, up a furlong from her debut, made most of the running but had no answer to the winner's turn of foot. She would have been happier had the ground not dried out to the extent that it did, and she will improve on this when there is more cut underfoot. (op 9-1 tchd 12-1)

Red Current, a half-sister to winners, did everything her stable could have hoped on her debut and will step up on this next time. (op 14-1 tchd 12-1)

Lady Lafitte(USA) came here with one fair run to her name and this was another reasonable effort, especially as she lost ground when dwelling at the start. (op 5-2 tchd 7-2)

Career Girl(USA), upped in trip, improved a good deal on her debut effort when she started slowly after the blindfold was removed late.

Miss Phuket finished a little closer to Lady Lafitte than she had at Goodwood. (op 11-4)

Ravarino(USA), a half-sister to useful winners, started slowly and finished with a bit of gusto without having been given a hard time. She should have really enjoyed her first run and is worth remembering for the future. Official explanation: jockey, regarding the running and riding, his orders were to get a nice position, get fairly covered up and do his best, adding that from a wide draw he had no option but to drop in; he got a nice run into the bend but front-runners had quickened away from him and the filly stayed on under hands and heels (op 8-1)

Hopeful Isabella(IRE) is bred to be better than she showed here and there is a good chance she will show that to be the case. (op 16-1)

5069 WBX.COM WORLD BET EXCHANGE H'CAP (PART OF THE WARWICK STAYERS SERIES) 2m 39y

3:50 (3:56) (Class 4) (0-80,77) 3-Y-0+ **£6,477** (£1,927; £963; £481) **Stalls** Low

Form — RPR

2233 **1** **Behlaya (IRE)**[9] 4792 5-9-12 **73** TedDurcan 10 — 81
(T D Easterby) *hld up towards rr: rdn over 6f out: hdwy over 5f out: sustained chal fnl f: led nr fin* **16/1**

5055 **2** *shd* **Kayf Aramis**[7] 4883 4-9-3 **64** (p) SteveDrowne 3 — 72
(J L Spearing) *w ldr: led 7f out: rdn over 2f out: hdd nr fin* **11/1**[3]

1131 **3** *hd* **Alambic**[4] 4951 3-9-3 **77** 6ex SebSanders 6 — 85
(Sir Mark Prescott) *hld up in tch: rdn over 3f out: edgd lft 2f out: ev ch fnl f: r.o* **4/7**[1]

4-01 **4** *2* **Jack Dawson (IRE)**[8] 4848 9-9-12 **76** 6ex StephenDonohoe(3) 8 — 81
(John Berry) *hld up towards rr: rdn and hdwy over 2f out: edgd lft 1f out: nt qckn* **25/1**

1152 **5** *1 3/4* **Rose Bien**[15] 4632 4-9-3 **64** (p) DaneO'Neill 11 — 67
(P J McBride) *hld up and bhd: hdwy ov 4f out: rdn over 3f out: no ex fnl f* **16/1**

5455 **6** *5* **Impostor (IRE)**[18] 4537 3-9-0 **74** OscarUrbina 7 — 71
(J R Fanshawe) *hld up: hdwy over 5f out: rdn over 3f out: wknd fnl f* **20/1**

-011 **7** *1 3/4* **French Mannequin (IRE)**[3] 4996 7-8-11 **58** 6ex (b) TPO'Shea 5 — 53
(P A Blockley) *prom: rdn over 3f out: wknd over 1f out* **7/1**[2]

1220 **8** *13* **Our Monogram**[33] 4036 10-10-0 **75** TPQueally 2 — 54
(R M Beckett) *led: rdn and hdd 7f out: wknd over 5f out* **11/1**[3]

3210 **9** *38* **Arch Folly**[3] 4996 4-8-13 **60** ChrisCatlin 9 — —
(Ian Williams) *bhd fnl 9f: t.o fnl 4f* **40/1**

/300 **P** **Tudor Bell (IRE)**[10] 4764 5-9-7 **68** RobertWinston 4 — —
(J G M O'Shea) *hld up in tch: lost pl over 5f out: bhd whn p.u over 1f out* **100/1**

3m 29.55s (-3.15) **Going Correction** -0.075s/f (Good)
WFA 3 from 4yo+ 13lb — **10** Ran SP% **116.6**
Speed ratings (Par 105):104,103,103,102,101 99,98,92,73,—
CSF £170.41 CT £267.15 TOTE £17.30: £2.30, £2.60, £1.30; EX 128.00.

Owner D Brennan **Bred** His Highness The Aga Khan's Studs S C **Trained** Great Habton, N Yorks

FOCUS
Several of these came into this staying handicap in good hear and the form looks solid.
Tudor Bell(IRE) Official explanation: jockey said gelding pulled up lame

5070 BOTT FOUNDERS H'CAP 7f 26y

4:20 (4:25) (Class 4) (0-85,84) 3-Y-0+ **£6,477** (£1,927; £963; £481) **Stalls** Low

Form — RPR

0015 **1** **Hiccups**[18] 4521 6-8-10 **72** DarryllHolland 12 — 82
(M Dods) *hld up in rr: hdwy over 2f out: swtchd rt 1f out: styd on to ld nr fin* **20/1**

4603 **2** *nk* **Red Romeo**[23] 4379 5-9-4 **80** DaleGibson 3 — 89
(G A Swinbank) *w ldrs: led over 2f out: hung lft and hdd wl ins last* **7/2**[2]

3221 **3** *shd* **Barons Spy (IRE)**[12] 4706 5-8-3 **70** oh1 LiamJones(5) 4 — 79
(R J Price) *trckd ldrs gng wl: upsides over 1f out: no ex towards fin* **11/2**

0031 **4** *1 3/4* **Desert Dreamer (IRE)**[14] 4658 5-9-6 **82** SteveDrowne 14 — 86
(P R Chamings) *s.i.s: hdwy over 2f out: kpt on wl fnl f* **14/1**

3000 **5** *3/4* **Malcheek (IRE)**[13] 4682 4-9-6 **82** RobertWinston 11 — 84
(T D Easterby) *prom: effrt over 2f out: kpt on same pce appr fnl f* **16/1**

0605 **6** *1/2* **Carmenero (GER)**[19] 4488 3-8-10 **76** RichardMullen 7 — 76+
(W R Muir) *hld up in mid-div: hdwy over 2f out: one pce whn n.m.r jst ins last* **14/1**

2360 **7** *1 1/2* **Dry Ice (IRE)**[18] 4535 4-9-4 **80** DaneO'Neill 1 — 77
(H Candy) *sn chsng ldrs: wknd jst ins last* **4/1**[3]

1 **8** *3/4* **Coleridge (AUS)**[31] 4114 7-9-0 **76** JimCrowley 10 — 71
(B G Powell) *hld up in rr: effrt over 2f out: kpt on: nvr trbld ldrs* **25/1**

111 **9** *hd* **Secret Liaison**[12] 4689 3-9-4 **84** SebSanders 2 — 77
(Sir Mark Prescott) *w ldrs: led after 1f: hdd over 2f out: wknd fnl f* **11/4**[1]

1414 **10** *1/2* **Phluke**[18] 4535 5-9-8 **84** StephenCarson 13 — 77
(R F Johnson Houghton) *led 1f: chsd ldrs: lost pl over 1f out* **14/1**

0640 **11** *3/4* **Weet For Ever (USA)**[7] 4871 3-8-4 **70** oh8 (e1) TPO'Shea 9 — 59
(P A Blockley) *dwlt: in rr: sme hdwy 2f out: nvr a factor* **100/1**

60-0 **12** *5* **Sundance (IRE)**[19] 4486 4-9-0 **76** JimmyQuinn 5 — 54
(H J Collingridge) *mid-div: lost pl over 2f out* **33/1**

2006 **13** *1* **Goodenough Mover**[31] 4106 10-9-4 **80** ChrisCatlin 6 — 56
(Andrew Turnell) *chsd ldrs: lost pl over 3f out: sn bhd* **20/1**

1m 23.03s (-1.97) **Going Correction** -0.075s/f (Good)
WFA 3 from 4yo+ 4lb — **13** Ran SP% **127.5**
Speed ratings (Par 105):108,107,107,105,104 104,102,101,101,100 99,94,93
CSF £90.67 CT £477.16 TOTE £33.90: £5.40, £2.00, £2.00; EX 149.70.

Owner J M & Mrs E E Ranson **Bred** Mrs Susan Corbett **Trained** Denton, Co Durham
■ Stewards' Enquiry : Darryll Holland one day ban: careless riding (Sep 15)

FOCUS
Another competitive handicap that featured four last-time-out winners. The form should prove reliable.
Desert Dreamer(IRE) Official explanation: jockey said gelding was slowly away from the stalls
Sundance(IRE) Official explanation: jockey said gelding had no more to give

5071 WBX.COM WORLD BET EXCHANGE MEDIAN AUCTION MAIDEN STKS 1m 22y

4:50 (4:55) (Class 6) 3-4-Y-0 **£2,730** (£806; £403) **Stalls** Low

Form — RPR

6000 **1** **Lady Edge (IRE)**[32] 4070 4-9-3 46 RichardMullen 6 — 60
(A W Carroll) *hld up towards rr: rdn and hdwy over 2f out: edgd lft ins fnl f: r.o to ld last strides* **16/1**

06 **2** *hd* **King's Spear (IRE)**[7] 4899 3-9-3 DarryllHolland 15 — 64
(P W Chapple-Hyam) *w ldr: rdn over 1f out: led wl ins fnl f: hdd last stride* **13/2**

4025 **3** *nk* **Dab Hand (IRE)**[25] 4291 3-9-3 65 ChrisCatlin 9 — 63
(D M Simcock) *led: rdn 2f out: hdd wl ins fnl f* **9/2**[3]

5- **4** *hd* **Bronze Star**[304] 6242 3-8-12 OscarUrbina 14 — 58+
(J R Fanshawe) *hld up: rdn and hdwy over 1f out: r.o wl towards fin* **4/1**[2]

0 **5** *1* **Mill End (IRE)**[55] 3387 4-9-8 RobertWinston 10 — 61
(R M H Cowell) *t.k.h: a.p: rdn and ev ch over 1f out: hld whn n.m.r fin* **66/1**

0 **6** *1/2* **Ektimaal**[12] 4708 3-9-3 RHills 2 — 59+
(E A L Dunlop) *hld up and bhd: rdn and hdwy over 1f out: kpt on ins fnl f* **15/2**

5 **7** *shd* **Fairdonna**[14] 4661 3-8-12 TedDurcan 11 — 54
(D J Coakley) *s.i.s: plld hrd: sn mid-div: hdwy over 4f out: rdn over 2f out: one pce fnl f* **11/4**[1]

0 **8** *1/2* **Pleasing Gift**[7] 4899 3-8-9 StephenDonohoe(3) 13 — 53
(J M P Eustace) *a.p: rdn over 2f out: edgd lft over 1f out: wknd ins fnl f* **33/1**

0 **9** *1 3/4* **Biggin Hill (IRE)**[67] 3029 3-9-3 (t) JoeFanning 1 — 54
(H R A Cecil) *s.i.s: bhd tl hdwy fr over 1f out: nvr trbld ldrs* **12/1**

00 **10** *nk* **Goodenough Prince**[23] 4367 3-9-0 RichardKingscote(3) 8 — 53
(Andrew Turnell) *mid-div: no hdwy fnl 2f* **50/1**

0 **11** *1 3/4* **Stand By Me**[7] 4899 3-9-3 MatthewHenry 5 — 49
(M A Jarvis) *prom: lost pl over 4f out: bhd whn edgd rt over 1f out* **22/1**

-000 **12** *1* **Thomas A Beckett (IRE)**[86] 2466 3-9-3 52 JimCrowley 7 — 47
(P R Chamings) *a towards rr* **50/1**

0 **13** *3* **Pagan Island**[12] 4708 3-9-3 JimmyQuinn 3 — 40
(J A R Toller) *s.i.s: a bhd* **66/1**

00 **14** *8* **Orchard House (FR)**[15] 4635 3-9-0 GregFairley(3) 16 — 21
(J Jay) *mid-div: rdn over 3f out: wknd over 2f out* **100/1**

15 *22* **Ruskin** 3-9-3 (t) DaneO'Neill 12 — —
(K McAuliffe) *s.s: a in rr: t.o* **66/1**

1m 40.59s (0.99) **Going Correction** -0.075s/f (Good)
WFA 3 from 4yo 5lb — **15** Ran SP% **120.2**
Speed ratings (Par 101):92,91,91,91,90 89,89,89,87,87 85,84,81,73,51
CSF £111.37 TOTE £19.10: £4.20, £2.40, £1.90; EX 214.00.

Owner E J Mangan **Bred** E J Mangan **Trained** Cropthorne, Worcs

FOCUS
A moderate winning time for what was a weak maiden. An improved effort from the winner, but unconvincing form.

5072 WBX.COM WORLD BET EXCHANGE APPRENTICE H'CAP 1m 2f 188y

5:20 (5:20) (Class 6) (0-58,57) 3-Y-0+ **£2,388** (£705; £352) **Stalls** Low

Form — RPR

3440 **1** **General Flumpa**[37] 3934 5-9-1 **54** JonjoMilczarek(7) 10 — 61
(C F Wall) *a.p: led 1f out: drvn out* **12/1**

0031 **2** *hd* **Choristar**[8] 4835 5-9-4 **55** 6ex NeilBrown(5) 3 — 67+
(J Mackie) *bdly hmpd and lost pl sn after s: nt clr run on ins over 2f out: rdn and hdwy over 1f out: swtchd rt jst ins fnl f: r.o wl:* **4/1**[1]

4440 **3** *1/2* **Miss Monica (IRE)**[12] 4709 5-8-9 **44** oh2 TolleyDean(3) 13 — 50
(P W Hiatt) *led 1f: prom: rdn over 2f out: ev ch 1f out: nt qckn towards fin* **20/1**

4105 **4** *1 1/2* **Opera Knight**[25] 4282 6-8-7 **44** MarkCoumbe(5) 9 — 47
(A W Carroll) *t.k.h in tch: rdn over 1f out: kpt on ins fnl f* **12/1**

3231 **5** *1 1/4* **Granary Girl**[5] 4925 4-9-2 **55** 6ex StevenCorrigan(7) 8 — 56
(J Pearce) *t.k.h in mid-div: hdwy 6f out: led 2f out: sn edgd lft: hdd 1f out: fdd towards fin* **9/2**[2]

0320 **6** *1 1/2* **Tangarita**[34] 4021 3-8-10 **57** WilliamBuick(7) 6 — 55
(A M Balding) *hld up in mid-div: rdn and no hdwy fnl 2f* **16/1**

0052 **7** *1* **Blue Hedges**[25] 4307 4-9-6 **55** NicolPolli(3) 1 — 52
(H J Collingridge) *bhd tl styd on fnl f: nvr nrr* **6/1**[3]

0040 **8** *3/4* **Pauline's Prince**[22] 4405 4-9-7 **56** RussellKennemore(3) 2 — 51
(R Hollinshead) *stdd s: sn hmpd: rdn and hdwy on ins 2f out: no imp fnl f* **25/1**

3660 **9** *3* **Kernel Dowery (IRE)**[19] 4497 6-8-10 **47** (p) JamieHamblett(5) 15 — 37
(W R Swinburn) *prom: ev ch over 2f out: sn hung lft and n.m.r: wknd over 1f out* **12/1**

4231 **10** *1 3/4* **Guadiana (GER)**[10] 4755 4-8-11 **48** (v) JPFeatherstone(5) 17 — 35
(A W Carroll) *s.i.s: sn mid-div: rdn and c wd st: bhd fnl 2f* **12/1**

60-0 **11** *1* **Trusted Mole (IRE)**[21] 4439 8-9-0 **46** LiamJones 4 — 32
(W M Brisbourne) *rdn over 3f out: a bhd* **9/1**

2452 **12** *nk* **Icannshift (IRE)**[12] 4687 6-9-4 **53** JamesMillman(3) 16 — 38
(T M Jones) *led after 1f: rdn and hdd 2f out: wknd over 1f out* **12/1**

0402 **13** *1* **Cunegonde**[13] 4671 3-8-3 **46** JamieJones(3) 5 — 29
(G L Moore) *hmpd sn after s: a bhd* **14/1**

2m 20.06s (0.66) **Going Correction** -0.075s/f (Good)
WFA 3 from 4yo+ 8lb — **13** Ran SP% **122.1**
Speed ratings: 94,93,93,92,91 90,89,89,86,85 84,84,84
CSF £60.75 CT £984.52 TOTE £16.00: £4.40, £2.20, £7.30; EX 78.80.

Owner Mrs Lucie N Smith **Bred** Chippenham Lodge Stud Ltd **Trained** Newmarket, Suffolk
■ The first winner for Jonjo Milczarek, younger brother of jockey Kirsty Milczarek.
■ Stewards' Enquiry : Steven Corrigan two-day ban: careless riding (Sep 15-16)

FOCUS
A modest winning time for this low-grade handicap. A moderate event, the form anchored by the third.

T/Plt: £36.30 to a £1 stake. Pool: £44,035.40. 884.10 winning tickets. T/Qpdt: £19.20 to a £1 stake. Pool: £2,810.80. 107.90 winning tickets. KH

4544 CATTERICK (L-H)

Tuesday, September 5

OFFICIAL GOING: Good to soft

Wind: Virtually nil

5076 "GEORDIE CHARLTON LIFETIME IN RACING" MEDIAN AUCTION MAIDEN STKS 5f

2:30 (2:31) (Class 6) 2-Y-O £2,730 (£806; £403) Stalls Low

Form RPR

6240 **1** **Lady Lily (IRE)**[17] 4594 2-8-12 75 DanielTudhope 8 75
(H R A Cecil) *chsd ldrs: gd hdwy 2f out: styd on to ld 1f out: pushed out* **11/8**[1]

4 **2** *1* **Final Dynasty**[22] 4434 2-8-12 FrancisNorton 11 71
(Mrs G S Rees) *trckd ldng pair: effrt: n.m.r and rn green wl over 1f out: swtchd lft and hdwy to chse wnr ins last: edgd lft: kpt on* **7/1**

2440 **3** *1 1/4* **Ronnie Howe**[27] 4251 2-9-3 71 PhillipMakin 4 72
(M Dods) *prom: rdn to chal wl over 1f out and ev ch tl drvn and one pce ent last* **5/1**[3]

6052 **4** *1 3/4* **The Nifty Fox**[12] 4727 2-9-3 71 (v[1]) TomEaves 2 66
(T D Easterby) *sn led and clr: rdn 2f out: drvn and hdd 1f out: wknd* **3/1**[2]

5 *2 1/2* **Metal Guru** 2-8-5 RussellKennemore(7) 3 52
(R Hollinshead) *in tch: effrt and hung lft wl over 1f out: kpt on ins last: nrst fin* **25/1**

0 **6** *3* **Forzarzi (IRE)**[12] 4731 2-9-3 TonyHamilton 7 46
(A Berry) *midfield: rdn along wl over 1f out: no hdwy* **100/1**

06 **7** *1 1/4* **Heidi Hi**[12] 4731 2-8-12 PaulMulrennan 6 36
(J R Turner) *cl up: rdn along 1/2-way: sn wknd* **40/1**

8 *3 1/2* **Multitude (IRE)** 2-9-3 DavidAllan 5 29
(T D Easterby) *s.i.s: a rr* **16/1**

00 **9** *2* **Molto Duro (IRE)**[12] 4731 2-8-12 CatherineGannon 10 17
(N Wilson) *dwlt: a rr* **100/1**

10 *7* **Northern Candy** 2-9-3 PaulHanagan 1 —
(A Dickman) *s.i.s: a rr* **25/1**

00 **11** *4* **Semahs Holly**[27] 4251 2-8-12 PaulEddery 9 —
(J O'Reilly) *sn outpcd and bhd fr 1/2-way* **100/1**

61.68 secs (1.08) **Going Correction** +0.075s/f (Good) 11 Ran SP% **115.3**

Speed ratings (Par 93):94,92,90,87,83 78,76,71,68,56 50

CSF £11.07 TOTE £2.30: £1.30, £1.70, £1.70; EX 13.70.

Owner Diamond Racing Ltd **Bred** Owen Bourke **Trained** Newmarket, Suffolk

FOCUS

A modest juvenile maiden, run at a solid early pace, which saw the field track to the stands' side in the straight. Not a strong race but the form is solid.

NOTEBOOK

Lady Lily(IRE), outclassed in Listed company last time, got off the mark at the fifth attempt in workmanlike fashion. She is versatile as regards underfoot conditions, and looks as though she may benefit for a return to a sixth furlong on this evidence, but still looks to be on a high enough handicap mark all the same. (op 6-4 tchd 13-8)

Final Dynasty, fourth on her debut over six furlongs on Wolverhampton's Polytrack, ran green but has to rate better than her finishing position suggests. She would have given the winner more to think about had she been kept by her rider to the stands' side late on and clearly has the ability to go one better in this sort of company. (op 13-2)

Ronnie Howe had every chance on this drop back to the minimum trip and, with an official rating of 71, helps to give the form a fair look. (op 6-1)

The Nifty Fox, sporting a first-time visor, showed up well from the front, but ultimately proved a sitting duck for the principals. He probably wants quicker ground. (op 7-2 tchd 4-1 in places)

Metal Guru, whose dam was a triple winning sprinter, proved distinctly green when push came to shove yet still did enough to suggest she can get closer as she becomes more streetwise. (op 20-1)

5077 OUSE MAIDEN STKS 5f 212y

3:00 (3:01) (Class 5) 3-Y-O+ £3,886 (£1,156; £577; £288) Stalls Low

Form RPR

0520 **1** **The Salwick Flyer (IRE)**[15] 4656 3-9-0 49 StephenDonohoe(3) 2 55
(A Berry) *close up on inner: led after 2f: rdn and hdd 11/2f out: drvn and rallied ins last: led nr fin* **10/1**

0032 **2** *nk* **Knead The Dough**[26] 4306 5-9-0 42 NataliaGemelova(5) 5 54
(A E Price) *trckd ldrs: hdwy to chse winner over 2f out: rdn to ld 11/2f out: drvn ins last: hdd and no ex towards fin* **8/1**

660 **3** *1/2* **Butterfly Bud (IRE)**[9] 4834 3-9-0 65 AndrewMullen(3) 7 53
(J O'Reilly) *chsd ldrs: hdwy wl over 1f out: swtchd lft and rdn to chal ins last: drvn and no ex last 50 yds* **10/3**[2]

2250 **4** *2* **Dulce Sueno**[13] 4695 3-8-12 54 TomEaves 4 42
(I Semple) *chsd ldrs: rdn along over 2f out: kpt on same pce* **11/2**[3]

0-22 **5** *1* **Turkish Sultan (IRE)**[3] 5023 3-9-3 75 DavidAllan 12 44
(T D Easterby) *midfield: rdn along and sme hdwy 2f out: sn drvn and no imp appr last* **2/1**[1]

00 **6** *3/4* **Megavegas**[3] 5023 3-8-12 36 PaulMulrennan 8 36
(P T Midgley) *chsd ldrs: rdn along 2f out: sn one pce* **100/1**

0006 **7** *shd* **Wolfman**[3] 5023 4-9-5 40 (p) PaulHanagan 3 41
(D W Barker) *led 2f: cl up tl rdn along over 2f out and sn wknd* **16/1**

00 **8** *5* **Special Ballot (IRE)**[5] 4948 5-9-0 DeanMcKeown 13 21
(G A Swinbank) *dwlt: a towards rr* **28/1**

0000 **9** *nk* **Swallow Senora (IRE)**[5] 4948 4-8-9 38 (b) AndrewElliott(5) 6 20
(M C Chapman) *s.i.s: a rr* **40/1**

6060 **10** *2 1/2* **Pensata**[24] 4354 3-8-12 39 PatCosgrave 11 13
(Miss L A Perratt) *a towards rr* **66/1**

0 **11** *hd* **City Miss**[17] 4613 3-8-9 GregFairley(3) 1 12
(Miss L A Perratt) *s.i.s: a rr* **100/1**

6640 **12** *nk* **Musette (IRE)**[17] 4613 3-8-7 41 MichaelJStainton(5) 10 11
(R E Barr) *in tch: rdn along over 2f out: sn wknd* **40/1**

0-60 **13** *1 3/4* **Ponty Carlo (IRE)**[5] 4948 3-8-12 (t) DuranFentiman(5) 14 11
(T D Easterby) *rrd s: a rr* **33/1**

000- **14** *4* **Alistair John**[284] 6417 3-9-3 45 FrancisNorton 9 —
(Mrs G S Rees) *s.i.s: a bhd* **25/1**

1m 15.22s (1.22) **Going Correction** +0.075s/f (Good)

WFA 3 from 4yo+ 2lb 14 Ran SP% **116.5**

Speed ratings (Par 103):94,93,92,90,88 87,87,81,80,77 77,76,74,69

CSF £79.86 TOTE £11.60: £2.80, £2.10, £1.10; EX 87.60.

Owner Alan Berry **Bred** Piercetown Stud **Trained** Cockerham, Lancs

FOCUS

A very weak maiden which saw the first three come clear. The level of the form looks pretty sound, if no better than a seller.

5078 DERWENT H'CAP 5f

3:30 (3:30) (Class 6) (0-60,60) 3-Y-O+ £2,730 (£806; £403) Stalls Low

Form RPR

6000 **1** **Dark Champion**[9] 4834 6-8-12 53 (v) DavidAllan 2 67
(R E Barr) *chsd ldr far side: rdn wl over 1f out: styd on to ld last 100 yds* **25/1**

510 **2** *1 3/4* **Oeuf A La Neige**[1] 5062 6-8-12 53 PatCosgrave 1 61
(Miss L A Perratt) *chsd ldr far side: rdn wl over 1f out: kpt on ins last* **14/1**

2134 **3** *1* **Alugat (IRE)**[18] 4546 3-9-3 59 (p) TPO'Shea 10 63
(Mrs A Duffield) *cl up stands side: hdwy to ld that gp and overall ldr 1/2-way: rdn over 1f out: hdd and no ex last 100 yds* **16/1**

3232 **4** *nk* **Chairman Bobby**[5] 4957 8-9-0 55 (p) TonyHamilton 12 58
(D W Barker) *chsd ldrs stands side: rdn along wl over 1f out: kpt on u.p ins last* **15/2**[3]

3230 **5** *nk* **Estoille**[12] 4735 5-8-9 50 PaulHanagan 14 52
(Mrs S Lamyman) *chsd ldrs stands side: rdn along 2f out: kpt on under pressure ins last* **8/1**

0140 **6** *1 1/4* **Compton Classic**[20] 4477 4-8-3 49 (p) KevinGhunowa(5) 8 47
(J S Goldie) *towards rr stands side: rdn 2f out: kpt on u.p ins last: nrst fin* **12/1**

00 **7** *1/2* **Oceanico Dot Com (IRE)**[33] 4091 4-8-7 48 FrancisNorton 3 44
(A Berry) *led far side gp: swtchd rt to join main gp 1/2-way: sn rdn and ev chasnce tl wknd appr last* **22/1**

4622 **8** *nk* **Strawberry Patch (IRE)**[5] 4952 7-9-0 55 (p) DanielTudhope 17 50
(J S Goldie) *cl up stands rail: rdn along 2f out: sn drvn and wknd over 1f out* **7/2**[1]

3260 **9** *1* **Inka Dancer (IRE)**[5] 4962 4-9-2 57 FrancisFerris 15 48
(B Palling) *chsd ldrs: rdn along 2f out: grad wknd appr last* **6/1**[2]

1101 **10** *8* **Bahamian Bay**[19] 4507 4-8-9 53 DNolan(3) 13 15
(M Brittain) *overall ldr stands side: hdd 1/2-way: sn rdn along and wknd wl over 1f out* **8/1**

0535 **11** *1* **She's Our Beauty (IRE)**[19] 4523 3-8-8 50 (v) PhillipMakin 16 9
(D Nicholls) *a towards rr stands side* **12/1**

0450 **12** *1 1/4* **Mystery Pips**[16] 4636 6-9-5 60 (v) KimTinkler 9 14
(N Tinkler) *chsd ldrs stands side: lost pl 1/2-way: sn bhd* **11/1**

-0 **13** *1 1/4* **Capital Lass**[241] 66 3-8-3 50 AndrewElliott(5) 5 —
(D M Simcock) *in tch far side: swtchd rt 1/2-way: sn rdn along and wknd* **25/1**

000- **U** **Harrys House**[270] 6310 4-9-5 60 GrahamGibbons 7 —
(J J Quinn) *uns rdr s* **40/1**

60.61 secs (0.01) **Going Correction** +0.075s/f (Good)

WFA 3 from 4yo+ 1lb 14 Ran SP% **121.2**

Speed ratings (Par 101):102,99,97,97,96 94,93,93,91,78 77,75,73,—

CSF £332.20 CT £5830.63 TOTE £27.90: £6.60, £7.30, £7.80; EX 456.00.

Owner A Suddes **Bred** R G Percival **Trained** Seamer, N Yorks

FOCUS

A moderate sprint. Four of the field stuck to the far side, but two of those came over at halfway leaving the pair who stayed on the far side throughout to finish first and second. The winner and second have been rated to last year's best but the form should be treated with a degree of caution.

Estoille Official explanation: jockey said mare was denied a clear run

Inka Dancer(IRE) Official explanation: jockey said filly was unsuited by the good to soft ground

5079 WEATHERBYS BANK H'CAP 7f

4:00 (4:01) (Class 4) (0-80,78) 3-Y-O £6,477 (£1,927; £963; £481) Stalls Low

Form RPR

3411 **1** **Glenbuck (IRE)**[3] 5036 3-9-0 74 6ex (v) FrancisNorton 13 85
(A Bailey) *cl up: led after 2f: rdn along wl over 1f out: drvn ins last and kpt on wl* **5/1**[2]

2521 **2** *1 1/2* **Chalentina**[42] 3826 3-8-13 73 DanielTudhope 9 81
(H R A Cecil) *trckd ldrs: hdwy to chse wnr 1/2-way: rdn and ev ch 1f out: swtchd lft and drvn and ins last: kpt on same pce* **7/1**[3]

5303 **3** *1 3/4* **Local Fancy**[18] 4577 3-8-12 75 StephenDonohoe(3) 12 78
(J M P Eustace) *in tch: hdwy 3f out: swtchd lft and rdn wl over 1f out: kpt on ins last* **9/1**

4443 **4** *1* **Sir Orpen (IRE)**[8] 4885 3-8-12 72 PhillipMakin 2 72
(T D Barron) *trckd ldrs: effrt 2f out: sn rdn and kpt on same pce* **7/2**[1]

2030 **5** *nk* **Elegant Times (IRE)**[3] 5036 3-8-5 65 oh2 ow1 DavidAllan 6 65
(T D Easterby) *towards rr: swtchd lft and rdn 2f out: styd on appr last: nrst fin* **12/1**

6053 **6** *nk* **La Matanza**[34] 4058 3-8-11 71 TonyHamilton 7 70
(T D Barron) *chsd ldrs: rdn along 2f out: no imp* **25/1**

5500 **7** *1/2* **John Keats**[12] 4725 3-9-3 77 TomEaves 8 75
(I Semple) *led 2f: cl up tl rdn over 2f out and grad wknd* **28/1**

3030 **8** *2* **Night In (IRE)**[26] 4296 3-8-9 69 (t) KimTinkler 3 61
(N Tinkler) *s.i.s: a towards rr* **20/1**

0060 **9** *1* **Colorus (IRE)**[13] 4717 3-9-3 77 (v[1]) PaulHanagan 1 67
(R A Fahey) *chsd ldrs: rdn over 2f out and sn wknd* **12/1**

1631 **10** *nk* **Stonehaugh (IRE)**[49] 3606 3-9-3 77 (t) PaulMulrennan 4 66
(J Howard Johnson) *in tch: rdn along 3f out: sn wknd* **12/1**

0021 **11** *6* **Corrib (IRE)**[50] 3598 3-9-0 74 FrancisFerris 10 47
(B Palling) *s.i.s: a rr* **20/1**

1-03 **12** *1 1/4* **Makfly**[102] 1983 3-9-4 78 GrahamGibbons 11 48
(R Hollinshead) *dwlt: sn outpcd and a rr* **11/1**

3330 **P** **The Terrier**[5] 4957 3-8-4 69 AndrewElliott(5) 5 —
(G A Swinbank) *sn bhd: t.o 1/2-wy: p.u & dismntd ins fnl f* **10/1**

1m 27.27s (-0.09) **Going Correction** +0.075s/f (Good) 13 Ran SP% **118.7**

Speed ratings (Par 103):103,101,99,98,97 97,96,94,93,93 86,84,—

CSF £37.35 CT £248.68 TOTE £5.10: £2.30, £1.60, £8.80; EX 57.00.

Owner Middleham Park Racing XLII **Bred** Mrs Teresa Monaghan **Trained** Cotebrook, Cheshire

FOCUS

A fair handicap and the form looks sound enough. The in-form winner improved again.

Corrib(IRE) Official explanation: jockey said filly was unsuited by the good to soft ground

The Terrier Official explanation: jockey said filly lost its action

5080 SWALE H'CAP 1m 7f 177y

4:30 (4:30) (Class 5) (0-70,69) 3-Y-O+ £4,095 (£1,209; £604) Stalls Low

Form RPR

5322 **1** **Incursion**[8] 4876 5-9-7 69 VictoriaBehan(7) 4 79
(D Nicholls) *trckd ldrs: stdy hdwy over 3f out: rdn to ld appr last: sn clr* **5/2**[1]

3421 **2** *5* **Mister Arjay (USA)**[16] 4632 6-9-9 69 PJMcDonald(5) 12 73
(B Ellison) *chsd ldrs: hdwy over 4f out: led 3f out: rdn 2f out: drvn and hdd appr last: sn one pce* **5/1**[2]

0420 **3** *1* **Thewhirlingdervish (IRE)**[16] 4632 8-9-2 **62**......... NataliaGemelova(5) 9 65
(T D Easterby) *hld up: gd hdwy over 3f out: rdn asnd ev ch 2f out: sn drvn and one pce* **14/1**

0013 **4** *1 1/2* **True (IRE)**[16] 4632 5-8-11 **52** oh2.................................... FrancisNorton 10 53
(Mrs S Lamyman) *hld up in rr: stdy hdwy over 4f out: rdn and ev ch 2f out sn drvn and wknd appr last* **15/2**

3-00 **5** *14* **Oulan Bator (FR)**[13] 4692 6-8-11 **52**............................. PaulHanagan 11 36
(R A Fahey) *midfield: effrt over 4f out: sn rdn along and outpcd: eased fnl 2f* **25/1**

0000 **6** *1/2* **Rajam**[5] 4960 8-8-11 **52**...(v) PaulMulrennan 7 36
(G A Harker) *led: rdn along 4f out: hdd 3f out and sn wknd* **12/1**

0022 **7** *1 1/2* **Jazrawy**[33] 4072 4-8-8 **56**... WilliamCarson(7) 1 38
(P W Hiatt) *chsd ldr: rdn along 4f out: sn wknd* **12/1**

1220 **8** *3 1/2* **Lodgician (IRE)**[27] 4252 4-9-10 **65**........................ GrahamGibbons 3 43
(J J Quinn) *in tch: hdwy to chse ldrs 1/2-way: rdn along over 4f out and sn wknd* **7/1**[3]

2356 **9** *20* **Minthare (IRE)**[8] 4884 3-8-8 **62**......................................(p) TonyHamilton 2 16
(C Grant) *chsd ldrs: rdn along 4f out: sn wknd* **17/2**

06/6 **10** *shd* **Show No Fear**[94] 911 5-9-2 **57**...................................... DanielTudhope 6 10
(G M Moore) *aa bhd: t.o fnl 6f* **33/1**

3060 **11** *9* **Zeydnaa (IRE)**[59] 3284 6-8-11 **52** oh5.............................. TomEaves 8 —
(C R Wilson) *midfield: rdn along 6f out: sn wknd* **28/1**

3m 31.94s (0.54) **Going Correction** +0.075s/f (Good)
WFA 3 from 4yo+ 13lb **11** Ran SP% **112.3**
Speed ratings (Par 103):101,98,98,97,90 90,89,87,77,77 72
CSF £13.08 CT £140.21 TOTE £2.80: £1.10, £1.10, £6.30; EX 9.80.
Owner Mark Russell, Tom Upton **Bred** K J Mercer **Trained** Sessay, N Yorks

FOCUS
A modest staying handicap and the form looks sound with the winner running to this year's best.
Minthare(IRE) Official explanation: jockey said gelding had no more to give

5081 NIDD H'CAP — 5f 212y
5:00 (5:00) (Class 5) (0-70,76) 3-Y-O+ **£3,886** (£1,156; £577; £288) **Stalls** Low

Form RPR

3030 **1** **Trojan Flight**[9] 4831 5-9-6 **70**..(p) PhillipMakin 2 80
(D W Chapman) *towards rr: rdn along on far side 2f out: str run ent last: led last stride* **11/2**[1]

5030 **2** *shd* **Dorn Dancer (IRE)**[18] 4571 4-8-11 **61**.......................... PaulHanagan 3 71
(D W Barker) *chsd ldrs: wd st: rdn and overall ldr stands side over 1f out: drvn ins last: hdd last stride* **15/2**[3]

0505 **3** *1/2* **H Harrison (IRE)**[21] 4449 6-8-13 **66**.......................... PatrickMathers(3) 7 75
(I W McInnes) *chsd ldrs: rdn stands side 2f out: drvn over 1f out: kpt on wl fnl f* **14/1**

0405 **4** *3/4* **Princess Cleo**[19] 4507 3-9-2 **68**.. DavidAllan 8 74
(T D Easterby) *cl up: rdn to ld far side gp 1f out: sn drvn and nt qckn wl ins last* **7/1**[2]

3545 **5** *hd* **Joyeaux**[13] 4694 4-8-12 **62**...(v) SilvestreDeSousa 9 68
(J Hetherton) *towards rr: rdn along on far side 2f out: stayed on wl u.p ins last: nrst fin* **15/2**[3]

0060 **6** *hd* **Divine Spirit**[9] 4834 5-9-0 **64**..(p) DanielTudhope 6 69
(M Dods) *in tch: wd st: hdwy stands side 2f out and ev chance tl rdn and nt qckn ins last* **8/1**

3004 **7** *nk* **Bold Marc (IRE)**[9] 4834 4-9-1 **70**................................(v) AndrewElliott(5) 1 74
(K R Burke) *sn led: styd far side straight: rdn 2f out: drvn and hdd over 1f out: one pce ins last* **8/1**

0510 **8** *1/2* **Danzig River (IRE)**[5] 4957 5-9-5 **76** 6ex....................... VictoriaBehan(7) 4 79
(D Nicholls) *trckd ldrs: hdwy 2f out: swtchd rt and rdn over 1f out: one pce ins last* **7/1**[2]

0350 **9** *1 1/4* **Brut**[27] 4258 4-9-0 **64**.. TonyHamilton 10 63
(D W Barker) *towards rr: hdwy on stands side 2f out: sn rdn and kpt on: nrest fin ish* **25/1**

3330 **10** *1 3/4* **Viewforth**[13] 4694 8-8-12 **62**...(b) TomEaves 11 56
(I Semple) *chsd ldrs: rdn and hdwy stands side 2f out: sn ev ch tl drvn and wknd appr last* **14/1**

060 **11** *1 3/4* **Mint**[45] 3722 3-9-0 **69**... AndrewMullen(3) 12 57
(D W Barker) *chsd ldrs: wd st: rdn along 2f out: grad wknd* **50/1**

0-00 **12** *3 1/2* **Island Prince (IRE)**[8] 4888 3-9-3 **69**............................ TPO'Shea 5 47
(Mrs A Duffield) *sn rdn along: a bhd* **50/1**

644 **13** *1 1/4* **Tetrode (USA)**[15] 4663 4-8-8 **58**..................................... PatCosgrave 13 32
(R M H Cowell) *chsd ldng pair: rdn along over 2f out: sn wknd* **40/1**

0100 **14** *5* **Banjo Bay (IRE)**[8] 4894 8-8-13 **66**....................(t) StephenDonohoe(3) 14 25
(Miss Gay Kelleway) *a towards rr* **14/1**

1m 14.01s (0.01) **Going Correction** +0.075s/f (Good)
WFA 3 from 4yo+ 2lb **14** Ran SP% **116.3**
Speed ratings (Par 103):102,101,101,100,99 99,99,98,96,94 92,87,85,79
CSF £42.62 CT £545.83 TOTE £5.60: £2.40, £2.50, £4.30; EX 44.70.
Owner Timothy O'Gram **Bred** L C And Mrs A E Sigsworth **Trained** Stillington, N Yorks

FOCUS
A modest sprint which saw the first eight closely covered at the finish. Those racing on the far side appeared at a slight advantage. The front pair have been rated to this year's form.
Viewforth Official explanation: jockey said gelding ran too free in early stages

5082 FOSS H'CAP — 1m 3f 214y
5:30 (5:32) (Class 6) (0-60,60) 3-Y-O **£2,730** (£806; £403) **Stalls** Low

Form RPR

2000 **1** **King's Fable (USA)**[12] 4734 3-8-4 **49**........................... GregFairley(3) 13 60
(M Johnston) *midfield: gd hdwy over 5f out: led over 3f out: rdn 2f out: drvn and edgd lft over 1f out: kpt on* **9/1**

5003 **2** *1* **Golden Groom**[12] 4734 3-8-4 **46** oh1.............................. PaulEddery 16 55
(C W Fairhurst) *hld up: hdwy over 5f out: chsd wnr 3f out: rdn 2f out: drvn and kpt on final f* **11/1**

6230 **3** *2* **Dubai Around (IRE)**[8] 4884 3-8-11 **53**.......................... TonyHamilton 7 59
(Micky Hammond) *hld up: hdwy 4f out: rdn to chse ldrs 2f out: sn drvn and kpt on same pce appr last* **8/1**

065 **4** *2* **Light Sentence**[16] 4635 3-9-4 **60**.................................. DeanMcKeown 4 63
(G A Swinbank) *hld up towards rr: pushed along and hdwy 4f out: rdn 3f out: drvn to chse ldrs wl over 1f out: sn no imp* **3/1**[1]

1020 **5** *10* **Three Strings (USA)**[20] 4470 3-9-0 **56**........................(p) PaulHanagan 9 43
(P D Niven) *in tch: effrt over 4f out: sn rdn along wknd over 2f out* **14/1**

6404 **6** *nk* **Peas 'n Beans (IRE)**[12] 4734 3-8-7 **54**......................... AndrewElliott(5) 2 40
(M L W Bell) *tracked ldrs: hdwy to ld over 4f out: rdn along and hdd over 3f out: drvn over 2f out and sn wknd* **4/1**[2]

0050 **7** *1* **Sunny Parkes**[12] 4734 3-8-4 **46** oh4.............................. FrancisNorton 12 31
(M Mullineaux) *chsd ldrs: rdn along over 4f out: outpcd fr over 3f out* **25/1**

-032 **8** *nk* **Knight Valliant**[27] 4255 3-9-0 **56**.................................. TomEaves 8 40
(J Howard Johnson) *a midfield* **13/2**[3]

0006 **9** *3/4* **Madame Constanze (IRE)**[26] 4291 3-8-4 **46** oh1... SilvestreDeSousa 5 29
(Miss Gay Kelleway) *nvr bttr than midfield* **25/1**

-005 **10** *13* **Missouri (USA)**[15] 4651 3-8-5 **47**................................. PaulMulrennan 6 9
(G M Moore) *chsd ldrs: rdn along over 4f out: sn drvn and wknd 3f out* **16/1**

1314 **11** *1 1/4* **Moonlight Fantasy (IRE)**[15] 4651 3-8-9 **51**.................. KimTinkler 1 11
(N Tinkler) *led: rdn along and hdd over 4f out: sn wknd* **10/1**

-506 **12** *2* **Xenia**[24] 4382 3-8-1 **46** oh6..(be) JohnMcAuley(3) 10 —
(T J Etherington) *sn rdn along and a bhd* **100/1**

5000 **13** *17* **Find It Out (USA)**[34] 4060 3-8-11 **53**........................... PatCosgrave 3 —
(T D Barron) *a rr* **33/1**

005- **14** *18* **Francescas Boy (IRE)**[381] 4579 3-8-1 **46** oh1......... AndrewMullen(3) 14 —
(P D Niven) *dwlt: a bhd* **40/1**

4010 **15** *3/4* **Peak Seasons (IRE)**[20] 4470 3-8-7 **56**..........(b) RussellKennemore(7) 11 —
(M C Chapman) *chsd ldr: rn wd bnd after 4f: rdn along 1/2-way and sn wknd* **33/1**

2m 40.51s (1.51) **Going Correction** +0.075s/f (Good) **15** Ran SP% **126.4**
Speed ratings (Par 99):97,96,95,93,87 86,86,85,85,76 75,74,63,51,50
CSF £102.56 CT £846.85 TOTE £12.90: £3.30, £4.50, £2.90; EX 138.00 Place 6 £537.95, Place 5 £377.16.
Owner Mrs S Mason **Bred** Ms K S Farrar **Trained** Middleham Moor, N Yorks

FOCUS
A modest three-year-old handicap which saw the field finish fairly strung out. The front four finished clear and the race has been rated positively.
Peak Seasons(IRE) Official explanation: jockey said gelding was unsuited by the good to soft ground
T/Plt: £589.10 to a £1 stake. Pool: £54,959.85. 68.10 winning tickets. T/Qpdt: £66.00 to a £1 stake. Pool: £3,447.70. 38.60 winning tickets. JR

4920 LEICESTER (R-H)
Tuesday, September 5

OFFICIAL GOING: Good to firm (good in places)
The ground was described as 'near perfect, just on the fast side of good'.
Wind: Moderate, half-behind Weather: Fine and warm

5083 E B F FILBERT MAIDEN FILLIES' STKS — 1m 60y
2:10 (2:11) (Class 4) 2-Y-O **£5,181** (£1,541; £770; £384) **Stalls** High

Form RPR

02 **1** **Millestan (IRE)**[61] 3227 2-9-0 .... EddieAhern 13 74+
(H R A Cecil) *w ldr: led after 2f: set modest pce: qcknd over 3f out: styd on wl: unchal* **15/2**

0 **2** *1 1/2* **Rose Of Petra (IRE)**[24] 4373 2-9-0 .... KerrinMcEvoy 5 71
(Sir Michael Stoute) *led 2f: chsd wnr: kpt on same pce appr fnl f* **6/1**[3]

3 *1 1/2* **Starry Messenger** 2-9-0 .... DaneO'Neill 12 67+
(M P Tregoning) *in rr: hdwy over 2f out: styd on wl fnl f: tk 3rd nr line* **10/1**

0 **4** *1/2* **Fashion Statement**[33] 4084 2-9-0 .... NCallan 7 66
(M A Jarvis) *chsd ldrs: kpt on same pce fnl 2f* **7/1**

0 **5** *nk* **Wateera (IRE)**[24] 4373 2-9-0 .... RHills 2 66
(J L Dunlop) *hld up: hdwy on outside over 3f out: edgd rt and one pce fnl 2f* **20/1**

6 *1* **Gull Wing (IRE)** 2-9-0 .... HayleyTurner 4 63
(M L W Bell) *rr-div: hdwy over 3f out: one pce fnl 2f* **33/1**

5 **7** *1/2* **Inquisitress**[31] 4148 2-9-0 .... MickyFenton 1 62
(J M P Eustace) *trckd ldrs: effrt over 2f out: fdd appr fnl f* **9/2**[2]

8 *4* **Peintre's Wonder (IRE)** 2-9-0 .... RichardMullen 8 54
(E J O'Neill) *in tch: effrt over 3f out: lost pl over 1f out* **22/1**

05 **9** *shd* **Fire In Cairo (IRE)**[15] 4650 2-9-0 .... DaleGibson 14 53
(P C Haslam) *trckd ldrs: t.k.h: wknd over 2f out* **100/1**

10 *2 1/2* **Last Flight (IRE)** 2-9-0 .... JimmyQuinn 6 48
(J L Dunlop) *s.s: nvr on terms* **33/1**

3 **11** *5* **Dansimar**[18] 4574 2-9-0 .... TedDurcan 11 37
(M R Channon) *in tch: t.k.h: drvn over 3f out: sn outpcd* **12/1**

225 **12** *nk* **Baldovina**[58] 3343 2-9-0 .... RyanMoore 3 36
(M Botti) *chsd ldrs: drvn over 3f out: wknd over 1f out* **7/2**[1]

06 **13** *3* **Absent Love**[115] 1675 2-9-0 .... JimmyFortune 9 30
(G G Margarson) *a in rr* **50/1**

00 **14** *1* **Miss Silver Spurs**[48] 3640 2-8-7 .... FrankiePickard(7) 10 27
(M D I Usher) *s.s: a bhd* **150/1**

1m 45.49s (0.19) **Going Correction** -0.075s/f (Good) **14** Ran SP% **114.3**
Speed ratings (Par 94):96,94,93,92,92 91,90,86,86,84 79,78,75,74
CSF £46.35 TOTE £8.20: £2.60, £2.70, £5.10; EX 68.40 Trifecta £345.10 Part won. Pool: £486.17 - 0.34 winning tickets..
Owner Sir Tom Lethbridge **Bred** Nawara Stud Co Ltd **Trained** Newmarket, Suffolk

FOCUS
Just a steady gallop to this ordinary fillies' maiden and the first two were one-two throughout. The bare form cannot be rated much higher but quite a few of these will progress.

NOTEBOOK
Millestan(IRE), bred to be suited by the step up in distance, controlled things from the front and raced with plenty of enthusiasm. She should be able to go on from this. (op 7-1)
Rose Of Petra(IRE), a nice type, looked in tip-top trim. She kept on in gallant pursuit but was never going to pose a real threat. She can surely find an opening. (op 8-1)
Starry Messenger, a March foal, stands over plenty of ground. She sat off the pace before making serious late headway. She is bred to come good over middle distances at three. (op 12-1)
Fashion Statement stepped up on her debut effort, but she looks to lack a gear or two and will need middle distances at three. (op 10-1 tchd 13-2)
Wateera(IRE), who has plenty of size and scope, improved on her debut effort and there ought to be further improvement in her. (tchd 18-1)
Gull Wing(IRE), very noisy in the paddock, will have benefited from this debut outing. (op 16-1)
Inquisitress, who is only small, was friendless in the market and did not run as well as she had done first time. (op 7-2 tchd 5-1)
Last Flight(IRE) Official explanation: jockey said filly missed the break
Dansimar Official explanation: jockey said filly ran too free in early stages
Baldovina, a respectable fifth in a Listed race in Italy on her third start, was in trouble the moment the pace increased and in the end she dropped right away in most disappointing fashion. Official explanation: jockey said filly had no more to give

5084 GGBET.COM BETTING EXCHANGE (S) NURSERY — 7f 9y
2:40 (2:42) (Class 6) (0-65,63) 2-Y-O **£2,590** (£770; £385; £192) **Stalls** Low

Form RPR

040 **1** **Disco Queen (IRE)**[54] 3457 2-9-0 **56**.................................(tp) KDarley 16 62
(P C Haslam) *in tch: led over 2f out: sn rdn: hrd pressed fr over 1f out: r.o gamely towards fin* **16/1**

0404 **2** *nk* **Straw Boy**[8] 4887 2-8-10 **52** RobertWinston 17 57
(M R Channon) *in tch: rdn over 2f out: ev ch fr over 1f out: nt qckn towards fin* **13/2**[1]

0660 **3** *2* **Grimes Glory**[6] 4926 2-8-12 **54** DaneO'Neill 12 54
(R Hannon) *racd keenly: hld up: rdn and hdwy 2f out: r.o ins fnl f: nt rch ldrs* **14/1**

3554 **4** *1* **Denton Hawk**[12] 4724 2-9-1 **57** PhilipRobinson 4 55
(M Dods) *midfield: rdn over 2f out: hdwy over 1f out: styd on wl towards fin* **7/1**[2]

2400 **5** *1* **Kaladar (IRE)**[8] 4882 2-9-7 **63** (p) NCallan 1 58
(K A Ryan) *prom: rdn and ev ch over 2f out: styd on same pce fnl f* **9/1**

0046 **6** *hd* **Mulvany (IRE)**[26] 4284 2-9-6 **62** (b) JimmyFortune 14 57
(B J Meehan) *cl up: rdn and ev ch over 2f out: kpt on same pce fnl f* **9/1**

6066 **7** *1 ¾* **Fasuby (IRE)**[4] 4980 2-8-11 **53** RichardMullen 10 43
(P D Evans) *led: rdn 3f out: hdd over 2f out: wknd fnl f* **12/1**

3265 **8** *¾* **Loch Clutha (IRE)**[24] 4349 2-8-9 **51** LeeEnstone 9 40
(K R Burke) *midfield: rdn over 3f out: one pce fr over 1f out* **40/1**

0520 **9** *1 ½* **Gifted Heir (IRE)**[20] 4480 2-9-2 **58** TedDurcan 2 43
(I A Wood) *racd keenly: midfield: rdn over 3f out: kpt on ins fnl f: nvr able to chal* **8/1**

035 **10** *1* **Autour Du Monde**[63] 3175 2-9-2 **58** (bt[1]) JoeFanning 8 40
(P C Haslam) *wnt lft s: racd keenly in midfield: rdn and hdwy over 2f out: hung rt over 1f out: wknd ins fnl f* **15/2**[3]

4006 **11** *1 ¾* **Pas De Trois**[15] 4665 2-8-8 **50** JimmyQuinn 7 28
(J Pearce) *bmpd s: bhd: rdn 3f out: no imp* **25/1**

062 **12** *3 ½* **Sepia Print (IRE)**[25] 4327 2-9-0 **56** RyanMoore 18 25
(W J Knight) *hld up: rdn over 2f out: no imp* **9/1**

0000 **13** *2* **Spinning Game**[8] 4887 2-8-8 **50** PaulQuinn 13 14
(D W Chapman) *prom: rdn over 3f out: wknd 2f out* **20/1**

0000 **14** *hd* **Nihil Petere (IRE)**[9] 4830 2-8-10 **52** MickyFenton 3 16
(P T Midgley) *s.v.s: a bhd* **66/1**

0000 **15** *nk* **Soundasapound**[32] 4115 2-8-8 **50** HayleyTurner 11 13
(I W McInnes) *rdn 3f out: a bhd* **40/1**

603 **16** *2* **Group Force (IRE)**[15] 4665 2-8-3 **52** (b) PatrickHills[(7)] 15 10
(M H Tompkins) *s.i.s: in rr: hdwy 4f out: rdn 3f out: wknd over 1f out* **14/1**

035 **17** *3 ½* **Marist Madame**[25] 4327 2-8-9 **51** DarryllHolland 6 —
(D K Ivory) *prom: lost pl after 2f: n.d after: eased whn btn over 1f out* **22/1**

0500 **18** *23* **Tagula Music (IRE)**[6] 4926 2-8-4 **46** AdrianTNicholls 5 —
(B Palling) *s.i.s: hld up: hdwy after 2f: sn handy: rdn over 2f out: sn wknd: eased whn btn over 1f out* **33/1**

1m 25.15s (-0.95) **Going Correction** -0.35s/f (Firm) **18** Ran SP% **127.9**
Speed ratings (Par 93):91,90,88,87,86 85,83,83,81,80 78,74,71,71,71 69,65,38
CSF £112.76 CT £1538.22 TOTE £13.90: £5.50, £1.70, £6.60, £2.20; EX 136.40 TRIFECTA Not won.
Winner was bought in for 6,000gns. Straw Boy was claimed by Roy Brotherton for£6,000.
Owner Mrs C Barclay **Bred** B D Burnett **Trained** Middleham Moor, N Yorks

FOCUS
A very modest event in which high numbers were favoured. The time was quite good and a positive view has been taken of the form.

NOTEBOOK
Disco Queen(IRE), tried in a tongue tie and cheekpieces on this nursery debut, appreciated the drop in class to notch her first success. She had run well in a seller at Haydock on her second start and, after going on at halfway, held on well to deny the runner-up. She is only modest but can find further success at this level. (op 14-1)
Straw Boy, back at this trip for the first time since his debut, ran a sound race and came through to chase the winner in the final two furlongs, but could never quite poke his head in front. He tried hard enough and he can soon go one better in this grade. (op 6-1 tchd 7-1)
Grimes Glory, returned to seven, stepped up on his recent efforts as he kept on in the closing stages without reaching the leaders. (op 16-1 tchd 20-1)
Denton Hawk is fully exposed, but he ran with credit from a moderate draw and was keeping on at the end. (op 9-1)
Kaladar(IRE), down in class and with cheekpieces fitted, soon held a prominent position but could find no extra in the closing stages
Mulvany(IRE), in selling grade for the first time, had every chance over two furlongs out but could not find any extra. (op 8-1)
Fasuby(IRE), back down in trip, made the early running and kept on at one pace in the final furlong.
Tagula Music(IRE) Official explanation: jockey said filly lost its action approx 3f out

5085 RACECOURSE VIDEO SERVICES H'CAP 7f 9y
3:10 (3:10) (Class 5) (0-70,70) 3-Y-O+ **£3,238** (£963; £481; £240) **Stalls** Low

Form RPR

1042 **1** **Torquemada (IRE)**[10] 4795 5-9-0 **62** KerrinMcEvoy 1 71+
(W Jarvis) *hld up: hdwy over 2f out: checked over 1f out: r.o wl to ld last 150yds* **10/3**[1]

0556 **2** *1* **Flying Bantam (IRE)**[15] 4655 5-8-11 **66** JamesRogers[(7)] 5 72
(R A Fahey) *trckd ldrs: effrt over 2f out: styd on wl ins last: tk 2nd nr fin* **10/1**

6003 **3** *nk* **Bathwick Emma (IRE)**[8] 4870 3-8-11 **63** RyanMoore 8 66
(P D Evans) *trckd ldr: led over 2f out: edgd rt over 1f out: hdd and no ex ins last* **7/1**[3]

1035 **4** *1* **Vienna's Boy (IRE)**[13] 4706 5-9-8 **70** PhilipRobinson 2 73
(W J Musson) *hld up: effrt 2f out: styd on same pce fnl f* **5/1**[2]

-015 **5** *hd* **James Street (IRE)**[6] 4927 3-9-3 **69** TedDurcan 10 69
(J R Best) *sn chsng ldrs: effrt over 2f out: one pce fnl f* **7/1**[3]

3110 **6** *¾* **Border Artist**[10] 4795 7-9-3 **65** JimmyQuinn 7 65
(J Pearce) *trckd ldrs: effrt over 2f out: hanmpered over 1f out: kpt on same pce* **5/1**[2]

2000 **7** *2* **Danielle's Lad**[8] 4870 10-8-12 **60** (b) DaneO'Neill 6 55
(B Palling) *led tl over 2f out: hung rt and wknd appr fnl f* **28/1**

0401 **8** *3 ½* **Snow Bunting**[12] 4729 8-8-10 **58** MickyFenton 4 44
(Jedd O'Keeffe) *hld up in tch: effrt over 2f out: lost pl over 1f out* **9/1**

0653 **9** *½* **Sea Frolic (IRE)**[23] 4405 5-8-3 **56** oh11 (v) RoryMoore[(5)] 3 40
(Jennie Candlish) *trckd ldrs: wknd over 1f out* **66/1**

0550 **10** *6* **Mystic Man (FR)**[9] 4831 8-9-3 **65** (b) RobertWinston 9 34
(I W McInnes) *hld up: hdwy to chse ldrs over 3f out: wknd over 1f out* **16/1**

1m 23.91s (-2.19) **Going Correction** -0.35s/f (Firm)
WFA 3 from 5yo+ 4lb **10** Ran SP% **111.3**
Speed ratings (Par 103):98,96,96,95,95 94,92,88,87,80
CSF £35.76 CT £215.28 TOTE £4.10: £1.80, £2.70, £1.20; EX 25.40 Trifecta £373.30 Pool: £562.70 - 1.07 winning tickets..
Owner Canisbay Bloodstock **Bred** Oak Lodge Stud/hamford Stud/lileagh Fox **Trained** Newmarket, Suffolk

FOCUS
Just a modest handicap, which did not take too much winning. A slight personal best from the winner.

5086 ROBERT POCHIN LTD PLUMBING & HEATING MAIDEN STKS 1m 1f 218y
3:40 (3:40) (Class 5) 3-Y-O+ **£3,238** (£963; £481; £240) **Stalls** High

Form RPR

463 **1** **Aryaamm (IRE)**[11] 4759 3-8-12 80 PhilipRobinson 9 86+
(M A Jarvis) *mde all: rdn ins fnl f: r.o wl and a in command* **3/1**[1]

043- **2** *3* **Hotel Du Cap**[355] 5253 3-9-3 73 DarryllHolland 11 83
(G Wragg) *a.p: rdn to take 2nd 2f out: no imp on wnr fnl f* **8/1**

3 *½* **Avoriaz (IRE)**[89] 3-9-3 98 NickyMackay 14 82
(L M Cumani) *racd keenly in midfield: hdwy over 3f out: rdn 2f out: kpt on ins fnl f* **7/2**[3]

3344 **4** *2* **Escape Clause (USA)**[15] 4661 3-9-3 82 RyanMoore 13 78
(Sir Michael Stoute) *midfield: rdn and hdwy 2f out: one pce fr over 1f out* **11/2**

4 **5** *2 ½* **Foreigner (IRE)**[11] 4776 3-9-3 NCallan 3 73
(B J Meehan) *racd keenly: prom: rdn over 3f out: wknd fnl f* **10/3**[2]

6 *nk* **The Aldbury Flyer** 3-9-3 EddieAhern 2 72
(W R Swinburn) *midfield: pushed along 5f out: kpt on one pce fnl 2f: no imp on ldrs* **66/1**

6 **7** *3* **Grand Silence (IRE)**[36] 4004 3-9-3 TedDurcan 15 67
(W R Swinburn) *in tch: rdn 3f out: wknd over 1f out* **25/1**

8 *1 ¾* **According To Pete**[63] 5-9-3 PaulPickard[(7)] 12 63
(J M Jefferson) *hld up: kpt on fnl 2f out: nvr trbld ldrs* **50/1**

0 **9** *2 ½* **Nanosecond (USA)**[74] 2825 3-9-3 JimmyFortune 16 59
(J H M Gosden) *midfield: rdn over 3f out: nvr trbld ldrs* **40/1**

5 **10** *nk* **Pearl Of Esteem**[13] 4686 3-8-12 JimmyQuinn 7 53
(J Pearce) *towards rr: rdn 2f out: nvr on terms* **150/1**

11 *shd* **Broughtons Folly** 3-8-12 JDSmith 1 53
(W J Musson) *hld up: rdn over 2f out: nvr on terms* **125/1**

12 *nk* **Generous Jem** 3-8-12 MickyFenton 5 52
(G G Margarson) *s.i.s: in rr: nvr on terms* **100/1**

0- **13** *3 ½* **Memphis Belle**[319] 6013 3-8-12 DaneO'Neill 10 46
(Mrs H Sweeting) *midfield: rdn and wknd 2f out* **100/1**

14 *7* **Accumulus**[141] 6-9-10 RobertWinston 4 37
(Noel T Chance) *prom after 2f: rdn over 3f out: wknd over 2f out: eased whn btn fnl f* **100/1**

5 **15** *½* **Tidal Chorus**[38] 3946 3-8-12 JamieMackay 17 31
(J G Given) *prom tl stmbld and wknd qckly on bnd 5f out* **28/1**

3000 **16** *6* **Bamzooki**[15] 4667 4-9-5 42 RobbieFitzpatrick 6 20
(Mrs C A Dunnett) *s.i.s: hld up: rdn over 3f out: nvr on terms* **150/1**

2m 5.77s (-2.53) **Going Correction** -0.075s/f (Good)
WFA 3 from 4yo+ 7lb **16** Ran SP% **115.1**
Speed ratings (Par 103):107,104,104,102,100 100,97,96,94,94 94,94,91,85,85 80
CSF £24.84 TOTE £6.10: £3.80, £9.80, £4.50; EX 30.90 Trifecta £124.80 Part won. Pool: £175.84 - 0.64 winning tickets..
Owner Sheikh Ahmed Al Maktoum **Bred** Barouche Stud Ireland Ltd **Trained** Newmarket, Suffolk
■ Stewards' Enquiry : Paul Pickard one-day ban: careless riding (Sep 16)

FOCUS
A decent maiden, above average for the time of year and likely to produce winners. The winner was value for a bit extra and the time was good.
Accumulus Official explanation: jockey said gelding ran too free early

5087 PRESTWOLD CONDITIONS STKS 5f 2y
4:10 (4:10) (Class 4) 3-Y-O+
£6,232 (£1,866; £933; £467; £233; £117) **Stalls** Low

Form RPR

3054 **1** **Tax Free (IRE)**[9] 4832 4-8-7 107 AdrianTNicholls 1 109+
(D Nicholls) *w ldr: led eover 2f out: edgd lft 1f out: styd on strly* **8/11**[1]

0256 **2** *3* **Dixie Belle**[21] 4461 3-8-1 90 (t) DaleGibson 7 93
(M G Quinlan) *led tl over 2f out: kpt on: no ch w wnr* **50/1**

0000 **3** *2 ½* **Boogie Street**[46] 3709 5-8-12 102 RyanMoore 2 94
(R Hannon) *chsd ldrs: hung rt and lost pl over 2f out: kpt on to take 3rd insde last* **20/1**

0006 **4** *2 ½* **Dutch Key Card (IRE)**[126] 1393 5-8-7 41 (v[1]) RobbieFitzpatrick 8 80?
(C Smith) *chsd ldrs: outpcd fnl 2f* **300/1**

3344 **5** *¾* **The Trader (IRE)**[12] 4738 8-8-13 108 (b) TedDurcan 6 83
(M Blanshard) *in rr: drvn over 2f out: edgd rt: nvr on terms* **15/8**[2]

-000 **6** *shd* **Maltese Falcon**[21] 4461 6-8-7 103 (t) EddieAhern 4 77
(P F I Cole) *steradied s: drvn over 2f out: nvr a factor* **14/1**[3]

6000 **7** *nk* **Campbeltown (IRE)**[2] 5044 3-8-6 90 AdrianMcCarthy 3 76
(R A Harris) *swvd rt s: chsd ldrs: wknd over 1f out* **100/1**

57.86 secs (-3.04) **Going Correction** -0.35s/f (Firm) course record
WFA 3 from 4yo+ 1lb **7** Ran SP% **107.4**
Speed ratings (Par 105):110,105,101,97,96 95,95
CSF £42.79 TOTE £2.80: £1.20, £3.90; EX 27.70 Trifecta £81.70 Pool: £479.90 - 4.17 winning tickets..
Owner Ian Hewitson **Bred** Denis And Mrs Teresa Bergin **Trained** Sessay, N Yorks

FOCUS
The brisk wind was a factor in the record time. A decent contest, but the proximity of the 41-rated fourth puts a big question mark over the overall value of the form, and the winner did not need to be at his best.
The Trader(IRE) Official explanation: trainer said gelding finished distressed
Maltese Falcon Official explanation: trainer's rep said gelding lost a front shoe

5088 E B F APOLLO MAIDEN STKS (DIV I) 7f 9y
4:40 (4:43) (Class 4) 2-Y-O **£4,533** (£1,348; £674; £336) **Stalls** Low

Form RPR

0 **1** **Celtic Step**[11] 4781 2-9-3 KDarley 7 80
(M Johnston) *led 2f: led over 2f out: wandered: styd on wl towards fin* **11/1**

2 *1* **Western Adventure (USA)** 2-9-3 JimmyFortune 4 78
(E A L Dunlop) *chsd ldrs: drvn over 3f out: outpcd over 2f out: styd on wl fnl f: tk 2nd post* **14/1**

0 **3** *shd* **El Dececy (USA)**[31] 4129 2-9-3 RHills 9 77
(J L Dunlop) *trckd ldrs: effrt over 2f out: kpt on same pce ins last* **10/3**[2]

4042 **4** *¾* **Cadeaux Du Monde**[11] 4766 2-9-3 86 RichardMullen 10 75
(E J O'Neill) *sn trcking ldrs: led after 2f: hdd over 2f out: kpt on same pce fnl f* **7/4**[1]

5 *3* **Ajaan** 2-9-3 EddieAhern 1 68
(H R A Cecil) *trckd ldrs: drvn over 3f out: wknd over 1f out* **7/1**[3]

6 *1* **Apache Dawn** 2-9-3 PhilipRobinson 5 65
(B W Hills) *dwlt: hdwy on outside over 3f out: hung rt: lost pl over 1f out* **7/1**[3]

7 *½* **He's Mine Too** 2-9-3 KerrinMcEvoy 8 64
(J D Bethell) *hld up: effrt over 3f out: lost pl over 1f out* **15/2**

8 *nk* **Anatolian Prince** 2-9-3 .... TedDurcan 3 63
(J M P Eustace) *dwlt: hld up: drvn over 3f out: nvr a threat* **33/1**
9 *3* **King Of The Beers (USA)** 2-9-3 .... AdrianMcCarthy 2 56
(R A Harris) *s.i.s: in rr and sn drvn along: nvr on terms* **66/1**
1m 24.78s (-1.32) **Going Correction** -0.35s/f (Firm) **9** Ran SP% **115.6**
Speed ratings (Par 97):93,91,91,90,87 86,85,85,81
CSF £151.70 TOTE £30.30: £3.10, £3.40, £1.20; EX 147.50 TRIFECTA Not won..
Owner S R Counsell **Bred** Woodcote Stud Ltd **Trained** Middleham Moor, N Yorks
■ Stewards' Enquiry : R Hills seven-day ban: dropped hands and lost 2nd place (Sep 16-22)

FOCUS
The faster of the two divisions and plenty of likely improvers in the line-up. Probably a fair maiden.

NOTEBOOK
Celtic Step, who had clearly learnt plenty first time, regained the lead and stepped up the pace. He went right and then left in front but was firmly in command at the line. He will improve again and will be even better suited by a mile. (op 10-1)
Western Adventure(USA), a May foal, is a round-barrelled type who did not move at all well going to post. He picked up in really good style late in the day and this will have taught him plenty. A stiffer test will see him in an even better light. (tchd 16-1)
El Dececy(USA), who looked in peak condition, improved on his debut effort and looked second best on the day. (op 4-1 tchd 9-2)
Cadeaux Du Monde, having his sixth start, is officially rated 86 after his improved Newmarket effort but that was over six on much easier ground. (op 13-8 tchd 6-4 and 15-8 tchd 2-1 in places)
Ajaan, a half-brother to Epsom Derby runner-up Dragon Dancer, is a lengthy March foal. He was one of the first to come under pressure before dropping away. (op 5-1)
Apache Dawn, a March foal, was the biggest in the line-up. Tricky to load, he hung as if feeling something before dropping right away. He will not come into his own until next year. Official explanation: jockey said colt hung right (op 8-1 tchd 17-2)

5089 E B F APOLLO MAIDEN STKS (DIV II) 7f 9y
5:10 (5:12) (Class 4) 2-Y-O **£4,533** (£1,348; £674; £336) **Stalls** Low

Form RPR
2 **1** **Dijeerr (USA)**[38] [3923] 2-9-3 .... PhilipRobinson 2 89+
(M A Jarvis) *led: qcknd over 3f out: styd on strly fnl f* **1/2**[1]
4 **2** *1 1/4* **Dubai Twilight**[18] [4561] 2-9-3 .... KDarley 7 86
(B W Hills) *trckd ldrs: chal over 2f out: nt qckn fnl f* **5/2**[2]
3 *1 1/2* **Al Tharib (USA)** 2-9-3 .... RHills 5 82
(Sir Michael Stoute) *rrd s: hdwy to chse ldrs over 2f out: no ex fnl f: improve* **14/1**[3]
4 *2* **Kirk Michael** 2-9-3 .... DaneO'Neill 4 77
(H Candy) *trckd ldrs: quite keen: outpcd over 2f out: kpt on fnl f* **33/1**
0 **5** *2 1/2* **Kon Tiki**[17] [4600] 2-8-12 .... JoeFanning 8 66
(M Johnston) *sn chsng ldrs: outpcd over 2f out: wknd over 1f out* **50/1**
0 **6** *2* **Rajeef Ashog**[22] [4428] 2-9-3 .... NickyMackay 1 66
(L M Cumani) *trckd ldrs: effrt over 2f out: wknd over 1f out* **100/1**
7 *4* **Super Cross (IRE)** 2-9-3 .... JimmyFortune 3 56
(E A L Dunlop) *hld up: hdwy on ins over 3f out: lost pl over 2f out* **50/1**
0 **8** *7* **Awe**[26] [4302] 2-9-3 .... RobbieFitzpatrick 6 38
(Mrs C A Dunnett) *w wnr: wknd over 2f out: sn bhd* **200/1**
1m 25.01s (-1.09) **Going Correction** -0.35s/f (Firm) **8** Ran SP% **110.3**
Speed ratings (Par 97):92,90,88,86,83 81,76,68
CSF £1.71 TOTE £1.40: £1.02, £1.10, £2.30; EX 1.90 Trifecta £5.60 Pool: £352.46 - 44.30 winning tickets..
Owner Sheikh Ahmed Al Maktoum **Bred** Monticule **Trained** Newmarket, Suffolk

FOCUS
The slower of the two divisions but probably the stronger half, and it should produce winners. The winner will improve again and the third looks a big improver, but the runner-up was another to let down the Washington Singer form.

NOTEBOOK
Dijeerr(USA), backed to the exclusion of the others, had his own way in front. He stepped up the gallop at the halfway mark and, showing a powerful action, was always in command. He will improve again and looks a good prospect. (op 4-6)
Dubai Twilight, a narrow type, in the end found the winner much too strong. He will be more the finished article next year. (tchd 9-4 and 11-4)
Al Tharib(USA) ◆, a half-brother to two Group 1 winners abroad, is a handsome individual but he is not the most fluent of movers in his slower paces. He moved up on the outside looking a threat only to tire in the closing stages, and looks capable of a fair bit better. (op 10-1)
Kirk Michael, a three-parts brother to the stable's high-class sprinter Gorse, was quite keen to get on with it. After taking time to get organized, he was picking up nicely at the death. He should have learnt from this. (op 25-1 tchd 40-1)
Kon Tiki, a lazy walker, looked fairly paceless but at least she showed a little more than on her debut two weeks earlier. (op 33-1)
Rajeef Ashog, last of fifteen on his debut three weeks earlier, is a medium-sized, powerful individual. He can be made a lot fitter but may not be seen to full advantage until he tries his hand in handicap company at three. (op 66-1)

5090 BETFAIR APPRENTICE H'CAP (PART OF THE BETFAIR "APPRENTICE TRAINING RACE" SERIES) 1m 1f 218y
5:40 (5:40) (Class 5) (0-70,70) 3-Y-0+ **£3,238** (£963; £481; £240) **Stalls** High

Form RPR
4245 **1** **Lysandra (IRE)**[21] [4455] 4-9-6 **68** .... DanielleMcCreery(3) 8 76
(N Tinkler) *s.s: hdwy on ins over 3f out: swtchd lft 2f out: styd on to ld ins last* **9/2**[2]
3004 **2** *1* **Viable**[21] [4457] 4-8-11 **61** .... JosephWalsh(5) 5 67
(Mrs P Sly) *trckd ldrs: led after 3f: hdd and no ex ins last* **8/1**[3]
312 **3** *1 1/2* **Summer Lodge**[20] [4470] 3-9-1 **70** .... (b) PatrickHills(3) 7 74+
(M H Tompkins) *hld up in rr: effrt 4f out: wnt 2nd over 3f out: kpt on same pce fnl f* **9/4**[1]
2303 **4** *1 1/2* **Consonant (IRE)**[18] [4565] 9-9-2 **66** .... MarkCoumbe(5) 4 66
(D G Bridgwater) *sn chsng ldrs: one pce fnl 2f* **8/1**[3]
0/00 **5** *1 3/4* **Sea Holly (IRE)**[6] [4925] 6-8-11 **63** .... DanielRobinson(7) 6 60
(G G Margarson) *hld up in rr: hdwy to chse ldrs over 3f out: one pce* **20/1**
2000 **6** *shd* **Padre Nostro (IRE)**[6] [4924] 7-8-6 **56** .... ChrisGlenister(5) 2 53
(J R Holt) *s.s: effrt 4f out: kpt on fnl f* **8/1**[3]
5114 **7** *hd* **Sforzando**[17] [4606] 5-9-11 **70** .... KristinStubbs 1 67
(Mrs L Stubbs) *s.i.s: drvn 4f out: edgd rt over 2f out: nvr on terms* **9/2**[2]
1000 **8** *19* **Mobane Flyer**[20] [4467] 6-8-6 **56** oh1 .... JamesRogers(5) 3 16
(R A Fahey) *led 3f: lost pl over 3f out: sn bhd* **12/1**
2m 7.07s (-1.23) **Going Correction** -0.075s/f (Good)
WFA 3 from 4yo+ 7lb **8** Ran SP% **112.9**
Speed ratings (Par 103):101,100,99,97,96 96,96,80
CSF £38.79 CT £99.93 TOTE £4.40: £1.30, £2.50, £1.90; EX 31.80 Trifecta £185.60 Part won. Pool: £261.43 - 0.34 winning tickets. Place 6 £165.37, Place 5 £37.96.
Owner Team Fashion Rocks **Bred** Newberry Stud Company **Trained** Langton, N Yorks

FOCUS
A low-grade apprentice handicap and the pace only increased once in line for home. Ordinary form.
Sforzando Official explanation: jockey said mare failed to handle the bend

T/Jkpt: Part won. £7,100.00 to a £1 stake. Pool: £7,872.00. 0.50 winning tickets. T/Plt: £318.10 to a £1 stake. Pool: £61,690.00. 141.55 winning tickets. T/Qpdt: £46.10 to a £1 stake. Pool: £4,042.40. 64.80 winning tickets. WG

5041 LINGFIELD (L-H)
Tuesday, September 5

OFFICIAL GOING: Turf course - good (good to firm in places); all-weather - standard
Turf - the rail had appeared advantageous recently, and in the first two races this time, but the majority of runners avoided the fence in the last two races.
Wind: Light, behind Weather: Mostly fine and warm

5091 EUROPEAN BREEDERS FUND MEDIAN AUCTION MAIDEN STKS 7f
1:50 (1:50) (Class 6) 2-Y-O **£2,730** (£806; £403) **Stalls** High

Form RPR
522 **1** **Farleigh House (USA)**[18] [4572] 2-9-3 87 .... TPQueally 8 80
(M H Tompkins) *trckd ldrs gng easily: led 2f out: shkn up over 1f out: clr and pushed out fnl f* **7/4**[1]
3 **2** *2* **Mount Hermon (IRE)**[19] [4526] 2-9-3 .... SteveDrowne 13 75
(H Morrison) *w ldr gng wl: led 1/2-way to 2f out: sn rdn and no ch w wnr: kpt on* **2/1**[2]
6 **3** *nk* **Edison**[10] [4801] 2-9-0 .... JamesDoyle(3) 15 74
(N P Littmoden) *trckd ldrs: rdn and effrt 2f out: styd on fr over 1f out: n.d to wnr* **17/2**
50 **4** *1* **Oakley Heffert (IRE)**[8] [4873] 2-9-3 .... RichardSmith 4 72+
(R Hannon) *hld up in midfield: rdn and prog 2f out: kpt on fnl f: nvr able to chal* **25/1**
05 **5** *3/4* **Distiller (IRE)**[8] [4873] 2-9-0 .... RichardKingscote(3) 9 70
(W R Muir) *settled in midfield: pushed along 3f out: prog 2f out: kpt on fnl f* **33/1**
6 *shd* **Malt Or Mash (USA)** 2-9-3 .... PatDobbs 11 70
(R Hannon) *dwlt: hld up off the pce in midfield: prog over 2f out: kpt on fr over 1f out: nrst fin* **20/1**
40 **7** *7* **View From The Top**[20] [4487] 2-9-3 .... SebSanders 16 52
(W J Knight) *led to 1/2-way: w ldrs to over 2f out: wkng rapidly whn n.m.r over 1f out* **8/1**[3]
0 **8** *1/2* **Like To Golf (USA)**[17] [4597] 2-9-3 .... JimCrowley 3 51+
(Mrs A J Perrett) *dwlt: a struggling in rr and wl off the pce* **66/1**
55 **9** *nk* **Ireland Dancer (IRE)**[17] [4588] 2-9-3 .... RobertHavlin 1 50+
(W R Muir) *w ldrs to over 2f out: wknd rapidly* **20/1**
00 **10** *1 1/4* **Extractor**[19] [4526] 2-9-3 .... PaulDoe 2 47+
(J L Dunlop) *off the pce in midfield: brief effrt over 2f out: sn shkn up and wknd rapidly* **66/1**
11 *1 1/4* **Pure Velvet (IRE)** 2-8-12 .... FrankieMcDonald 5 39+
(S Kirk) *s.s: a in last trio and struggling* **66/1**
0 **12** *5* **Marlyn Ridge**[91] [2315] 2-9-3 .... TonyCulhane 10 31
(D K Ivory) *sn outpcd and struggling in last trio: nvr a factor* **66/1**
13 *5* **Bring It On Home** 2-9-3 .... GeorgeBaker 12 19
(G L Moore) *s.s: a wl in rr and off the pce: bhd fnl 2f* **50/1**
1m 21.87s (-2.34) **Going Correction** -0.40s/f (Firm) **13** Ran SP% **115.6**
Speed ratings (Par 93):97,94,94,93,92 92,84,83,83,81 80,74,69
CSF £4.50 TOTE £2.40: £1.20, £1.80, £3.30; EX 6.10.
Owner Lordship Stud **Bred** Lordship Stud **Trained** Newmarket, Suffolk
■ Stewards' Enquiry : Pat Dobbs caution: careless riding

FOCUS
Not a bad maiden - the winning time was nearly half a second quicker than the nursery won by 67-rated King Charles - but the first six home came well clear of the remainder and the race lacked strength in depth. They all raced towards the stands'-side rail.

NOTEBOOK
Farleigh House(USA), runner-up to a couple of decent sorts in maiden company at Newmarket on his last two starts, found this easier and ran out a ready winner. He will start finding things a lot harder from now on, but there was plenty to like about this effort and he is progressing nicely. (tchd 13-8 and 15-8, 2-1 in places and 9-4 in a place)
Mount Hermon(IRE), third on his debut at Salisbury in a maiden that is working out, ran his race in second but was basically beaten by a better horse on the day. He should progress and can offer more. (op 7-4)
Edison, a Dewhurst and Racing Post Trophy entry, improved on the form he showed on his debut at Newmarket and gave the impression he will continue to progress. (op 8-1 tchd 9-1)
Oakley Heffert(IRE) failed to build on his debut promise when last of seven at Epsom on his second start, but this was better. He is now qualified for a nursery mark and that will give his connections more options. (tchd 33-1)
Distiller(IRE) was well held in fifth but is now qualified for a handicap mark and might do better.
Malt Or Mash(USA) ◆, a 38,000gns half-brother to winning sprinters in the US, out of a very smart multiple winner on turf at two to four, fared best of the newcomers and should be able to improve quite a bit on this effort. (op 25-1 tchd 33-1 in a place)
View From The Top Official explanation: vet said colt was found to have lost a front shoe
Marlyn Ridge Official explanation: jockey said gelding hung left throughout
Bring It On Home Official explanation: vet said colt was struck into

5092 RACING ALL YEAR ROUND AT LINGFIELD PARK MAIDEN STKS (DIV I) 7f
2:20 (2:22) (Class 5) 3-Y-0+ **£2,590** (£770; £385; £192) **Stalls** High

Form RPR
2250 **1** **Quintrell**[19] [4527] 3-8-12 74 .... FergusSweeney 11 69
(H Candy) *pressed ldr: led 3f out: in command fnl 2f: pushed out* **11/8**[1]
-400 **2** *1 3/4* **Welsh Cake**[84] [2535] 3-8-12 58 .... (t) OscarUrbina 4 64
(Mrs A J Perrett) *in tch: prog 3f out: rdn to chse wnr 2f out: no imp* **8/1**
04 **3** *1 3/4* **Lethal**[8] [4899] 3-9-3 .... PatDobbs 5 64
(Ernst Oertel) *taken steadily to post: led and sn crossed to nr side rail: hdd 3f out: one pce u.p* **11/2**[3]
0005 **4** *5* **Kilmeena Magic**[64] [3149] 4-9-2 40 .... LPKeniry 2 47
(J C Fox) *dwlt: hld up in last pair and wl off the pce: styd on to take modest 4th ins fnl f: nvr a factor* **50/1**
4455 **5** *nk* **Gift Aid**[13] [4690] 3-9-3 50 .... SteveDrowne 9 51
(P J Makin) *chsd ldrs: rdn and edgd lft over 2f out: sn outpcd and btn* **4/1**[2]
0006 **6** *1* **Virginia Plain**[26] [4276] 3-8-7 41 .... (b[1]) EmmettStack(5) 8 43
(Miss Diana Weeden) *rousted along early to chse ldrs: rdn 1/2-way: struggling over 2f out* **66/1**
7 *1/2* **Barney McGrew (IRE)** 3-9-3 .... GeorgeBaker 1 47
(J A R Toller) *racd on outer towards rr: effrt and bmpd over 3f out: no real prog fnl 2f* **12/1**

8 5 **Moving Target (IRE)** 7-9-0 .... LukeMorris(7) 3 35
(Luke Comer, Ire) *dwlt: a struggling and wl off the pce* **33/1**

0-00 9 3 1/2 **Kentavr's Dream**[10] [4806] 3-8-5 40.......... JPFeatherstone(7) 6 20
(P Howling) *chsd ldrs: rdn 1/2-way: wknd u.p wl over 2f out* **66/1**

000- 10 1 3/4 **Simpsons Gamble (IRE)**[330] [5796] 3-9-0 10.......... JamesDoyle(3) 10 20
(R M Flower) *hmpd on inner after 1f: nvr on terms: bhd fnl 2f* **66/1**

0 11 16 **Royal Borough**[10] [4799] 3-9-3 .... SebSanders 7 —
(R M Beckett) *prom: rdn 4f out: wknd rapidly 3f out: eased whn no ch fnl f* **7/1**

1m 21.7s (-2.51) **Going Correction** -0.40s/f (Firm)
WFA 3 from 4yo+ 4lb 11 Ran SP% **118.2**
Speed ratings (Par 103):98,96,94,88,87 86,86,80,76,74 56
CSF £13.35 TOTE £1.20: £1.20, £2.50, £1.40; EX 11.70.
Owner Major M G Wyatt **Bred** Mrs P A Clark **Trained** Kingston Warren, Oxon

FOCUS
Hand-timed. A weak maiden, as the proximity of the 58-rated runner-up and 40-rated fourth suggests.
Moving Target(IRE) Official explanation: jockey said gelding had a breathing problem
Royal Borough Official explanation: jockey said gelding had no more to give

5093 RACING ALL YEAR ROUND AT LINGFIELD PARK MAIDEN STKS (DIV II) 7f
2:50 (2:51) (Class 5) 3-Y-0+ **£2,590** (£770; £385; £192) **Stalls** High

Form RPR

3 1 **Yandina (IRE)**[18] [4563] 3-8-12 .... MichaelHills 4 62
(B W Hills) *racd towards centre: mde virtually all: rdn and hanging lft over 1f out: styd on wl fnl f* **5/4**[1]

0-0 2 1 3/4 **Ebraam (USA)**[116] [1641] 3-9-3 .... DO'Donohoe 5 63
(E A L Dunlop) *hld up bhd ldrs: rdn to chse wnr wl over 1f out: no imp fnl f* **9/2**[3]

05-6 3 1 3/4 **Dream Of Dubai (IRE)**[21] [4455] 5-9-2 40.......... GeorgeBaker 7 53
(P Mitchell) *hld up in last pair: smooth prog 3f out: rdn 2f out: kpt on same pce to take 3rd fnl f* **20/1**

2 4 1 3/4 **Bachelor Party (USA)**[31] [4162] 3-9-3 .... TPQueally 2 53
(J Noseda) *w ldrs: lost pl after 2f: swtchd to wd outside and effrt 1/2-way: rdn over 2f out: nt qckn* **5/2**[2]

060 5 2 **Special Place**[24] [4367] 3-9-3 46.......... SebSanders 10 48
(J A R Toller) *hld up and racd against nr side rail: outpcd and shkn up briefly 2f out: kpt on steadily* **25/1**

00 6 3 **Rowe Park**[48] [3647] 3-9-0 .... EdwardCreighton(3) 1 40
(Mrs L C Jewell) *racd on outer: w ldrs tl wknd rapidly over 1f out* **50/1**

0 7 1 1/2 **Batchworth Blaise**[10] [4799] 3-9-3 .... StephenCarson 3 37
(E A Wheeler) *dwlt and squeezed out s: hld up in last pair: effrt 3f out: wknd over 1f out* **100/1**

05 8 nk **Always A Story**[31] [4162] 4-9-4 .... SaleemGolam(3) 9 36
(Miss D Mountain) *racd towards nr side: cl up to over 2f out: sn wknd* **50/1**

3 9 1 **Tumpuluna (IRE)**[31] [4142] 3-8-12 .... MichaelTebbutt 6 28
(G Prodromou) *hld up bhd ldrs: wl in tch tl wknd 2f out* **12/1**

10 1 1/2 **Efisio Princess** 3-8-12 .... RichardThomas 8 24
(J E Long) *mostly pressed wnr tl wknd u.p 2f out* **50/1**

1m 22.71s (-1.50) **Going Correction** -0.40s/f (Firm)
WFA 3 from 4yo+ 4lb 10 Ran SP% **114.4**
Speed ratings (Par 103):92,90,88,86,83 80,78,78,77,75
CSF £6.62 TOTE £2.10: £1.10, £1.40, £4.90; EX 7.10.
Owner M C & Mrs D A Throsby **Bred** Epona Bloodstock Ltd **Trained** Lambourn, Berks

FOCUS
Like the first division, a very moderate maiden and the form is not worth dwelling on, with the winner a stone off her debut form. It was the slowest of the four seven-furlong races too. Despite the stands' rail looking a big advantage at Lingfield's meeting two days earlier, and the first two races on this card doing little to suggest otherwise, the majority of riders opted to race just off the fence.
Bachelor Party(USA) Official explanation: jockey said colt had lost a shoe

5094 KINGSTON SMITH LLP NURSERY 7f
3:20 (3:20) (Class 5) (0-75,73) 2-Y-0 **£3,886** (£1,156; £577; £288) **Stalls** High

Form RPR

0050 1 **King Charles**[36] [4000] 2-9-1 67.......... DO'Donohoe 13 77+
(E A L Dunlop) *off the pce towards rr and rdn over 4f out: relentless prog fr over 2f out: led last 150yds: won gng away* **9/2**[1]

035 2 1 1/2 **Glorious Prince (IRE)**[26] [4302] 2-8-11 63.......... TPQueally 17 69
(M G Quinlan) *mde most: hrd rdn and hdd wl over 1f out: kpt on to ld again ent fnl f: sn hdd and outpcd* **9/1**

6424 3 5 **Diamond Light (USA)**[20] [4480] 2-9-4 70.......... SebSanders 16 64
(J L Dunlop) *pressed ldr: hrd rdn to ld wl over 1f out: hdd ent fnl f: wknd rapidly* **9/2**[1]

6304 4 1 **Straight Face (IRE)**[26] [4290] 2-9-7 73..........(v[1]) PaulDoe 15 64
(W J Knight) *sn chsd ldrs: outpcd fr over 2f out: no ch after* **7/1**[2]

053 5 1 **Only Hope**[10] [4794] 2-9-1 67.......... TonyCulhane 6 56+
(M R Channon) *hld up in last trio: rdn and effrt over 2f out: styng on whn nt clr run over 1f out: nrst fin* **12/1**

3600 6 1/2 **Regal Ovation**[11] [4773] 2-8-7 59.......... RobertHavlin 14 46
(W R Muir) *chsd ldrs: rdn 3f out: outpcd and struggling 2f out* **16/1**

6510 7 1 1/4 **Babylon Sister (IRE)**[48] [3641] 2-9-3 69.......... RichardSmith 3 53+
(R Hannon) *mostly in last trio: struggling 3f out: kpt on fnl 2f: no ch* **16/1**

0546 8 nk **Mystery World**[106] [1884] 2-8-13 65.......... J-PGuillambert 11 48
(M Johnston) *s.i.s: chsd ldrs after 3f: wknd 2f out* **9/1**

2530 9 1 **Law Of The Land (IRE)**[13] [4688] 2-8-11 66.......... RichardKingscote(3) 8 47
(W R Muir) *hed up towards rr: rdn and no prog wl over 2f out* **14/1**

4303 10 1/2 **Star Strider**[21] [4460] 2-9-4 70.......... SteveDrowne 4 50
(A M Balding) *racd on wd outside: towards rr: effrt u.p 3f out: wknd wl over 1f out* **15/2**[3]

6014 11 1/2 **Shes Millie**[31] [4134] 2-8-3 55.......... FrankieMcDonald 12 33
(J G M O'Shea) *lost pl and rdn after 2f: struggling fnl 4f* **20/1**

0010 12 1 **Inflagranti**[22] [4427] 2-8-11 70.......... AshleyHamblett(7) 9 46
(J G Portman) *chsd ldrs: bmpd along and wknd fr wl over 2f out* **40/1**

000 13 5 **Brierley Lil**[74] [2816] 2-8-4 56.......... RichardThomas 5 19
(J L Spearing) *a wl in rr and struggling over 4f out* **33/1**

405 14 1 3/4 **Fiddlers Spirit (IRE)**[68] [3005] 2-8-1 56 ow1......(v[1]) EdwardCreighton(3) 7 15
(J G M O'Shea) *prom on outer for 3f: sn wknd* **40/1**

1m 22.31s (-1.90) **Going Correction** -0.40s/f (Firm) 14 Ran SP% **119.3**
Speed ratings (Par 95):94,92,86,85,84 83,82,81,80,80 79,78,72,70
CSF £42.66 CT £167.84 TOTE £5.30: £2.10, £3.20, £1.90; EX 56.50.
Owner Khalifa Sultan **Bred** Hunscote House Farm Stud **Trained** Newmarket, Suffolk

FOCUS
A modest nursery - the winning time was nearly half a second slower than the earlier juvenile maiden - and the front two finished well clear. The form looks sound enough and the winner can do better. As in the previous race the majority of the runners avoided the stands' rail, racing towards the middle of the track this time. Even so, those drawn high still dominated.

NOTEBOOK
King Charles improved for the return to seven furlongs on his nursery debut and showed himself on a very favourable mark with a clear-cut success. He would have to be of interest if turned out under a penalty, but should not be totally dismissed once the Handicapper has had his say as he is unexposed and progressive. Official explanation: trainer's rep said, regarding the improved form shown, the gelding had benefited from today's step up in trip (op 11-2)
Glorious Prince(IRE) had a good third in a Yarmouth maiden sandwiched in between a couple of disappointing efforts, but this was a cracking run on his nursery debut. He was unlucky to run into such a well-handicapped rival and the Handicapper will not let him off lightly for finishing so far clear of the remainder, but he should still be up to winning a similar event. (op 8-1 tchd 7-1)
Diamond Light(USA) was no match for the front two when it mattered and is high enough in the weights on this evidence. (op 7-2)
Straight Face(IRE) did not really improve for the first-time visor, although he did not exactly have an easy task off top weight. (op 8-1)
Only Hope, dropped in trip on her nursery debut, fared best of those from a single-figure stall and would have been even closer with a clearer run.

5095 E B F MAIDEN FILLIES' STKS 7f (P)
3:50 (3:51) (Class 5) 2-Y-0 **£4,533** (£1,348; £674; £336) **Stalls** Low

Form RPR

1 **I'm Right (USA)** 2-9-0 .... RobertHavlin 4 76
(M P Tregoning) *hld up bhd ldng gp: effrt and rn green wl over 1f out: prog to chse ldr 1f out: styd on to ld last 100yds* **14/1**

43 2 1/2 **Flying Encore (IRE)**[19] [4525] 2-8-11 .... AdamKirby(3) 3 75
(W R Swinburn) *trckd ldrs: pushed along and outpcd 2f out: effrt again over 1f out: pressed wnr last 100yds: a hld* **3/1**[1]

0 3 1 1/4 **Usk Melody**[24] [4373] 2-9-0 .... SteveDrowne 8 72
(B J Meehan) *sn chsd ldrs: outpcd 2f out: prog on outer over 1f out: hanging and nt qckn ent fnl f: kpt on same pce* **4/1**[2]

22 4 3/4 **Shebang (IRE)**[13] [4688] 2-9-0 .... TPQueally 1 70
(M G Quinlan) *led: kicked at least 2 l clr wl over 1f out: wknd and hdd last 100yds* **3/1**[1]

5 2 1/2 **Gold Hush (USA)** 2-8-7 .... JamieHamblett(7) 11 64+
(Sir Michael Stoute) *settled wl in rr: long way off the pce 1/2-way: shuffled along and styd on steadily fr over 1f out: nvr nr ldrs* **12/1**

6 1/2 **Tonnante** 2-9-0 .... SebSanders 7 63+
(Sir Mark Prescott) *s.i.s: off the pce in midfield: shuffled along fnl 2f: kpt on: nvr nr ldrs* **33/1**

0 7 1/2 **Mid Ocean**[11] [4765] 2-9-0 .... PatDobbs 2 61
(P W D'Arcy) *t.k.h early: prom: rdn to dispute 2nd over 1f out: wknd rapidly ins fnl f* **33/1**

8 1 **Ava's World (IRE)** 2-9-0 .... J-PGuillambert 13 59
(M Johnston) *pressed ldr: rdn and outpcd 2f out: wknd rapidly fnl f* **20/1**

9 3 **Krikket** 2-9-0 .... DO'Donohoe 9 51+
(W J Haggas) *plld hrd: hld up wl in rr: long way adrift 1/2-way: shuffled along and nvr on terms after* **33/1**

10 5 **Miss Marvellous (USA)** 2-9-0 .... OscarUrbina 12 39+
(J R Fanshawe) *pressed ldrs: struggling over 2f out: wknd rapidly and eased over 1f out* **10/1**[3]

05 11 6 **Crystal Plum (IRE)**[13] [4705] 2-9-0 .... MichaelHills 14 24
(B W Hills) *t.k.h: hld up wl in rr: wl adrift 1/2-way: nvr a factor* **14/1**

00 12 14 **Loose Canon**[26] [4302] 2-9-0 .... MichaelTebbutt 10 —
(Mrs C A Dunnett) *racd wd: a wl in rr: t.o over 2f out* **100/1**

13 5 **Darling Belinda** 2-9-0 .... TonyCulhane 5 —
(D K Ivory) *dwlt: v green and sn toiling in rr: t.o* **50/1**

1m 26.06s (0.17) **Going Correction** -0.025s/f (Stan) 13 Ran SP% **116.7**
Speed ratings (Par 92):98,97,96,95,92 91,91,90,86,80 74,58,52
CSF £51.68 TOTE £21.30: £6.30, £2.20, £1.10; EX 72.30.
Owner Gainsborough Stud **Bred** Gainsborough Farm Llc **Trained** Lambourn, Berks
■ Stewards' Enquiry : J-P Guillambert one day ban: failed to keep straight from stalls (Sep 16)

FOCUS
An ordinary fillies' maiden run at a good gallop. With little previous form to go on it has been rated through the second and third.

NOTEBOOK
I'm Right(USA), a half-sister to Faith And Reason, a dual winner over seven furlongs and a mile as a juvenile, was representing the stable successful in this race last year. She overcame greenness and a less than clear run to come home a nice winner on her debut, and she will not have trouble getting another furlong this season. The form may not be that strong but she is open to improvement.
Flying Encore(IRE) took a while to get into top gear but she stayed on well down the outside, albeit always held by the eventual winner. Probably a good guide to the level of the form, she is now eligible to run in nurseries, although a modest maiden still looks within her capabilities. (op 5-2 tchd 7-2)
Usk Melody swung wide into the straight and hung as she tried to make ground. She was closest at the finish, though, and is likely to appreciate another furlong. (op 5-1)
Shebang(IRE), runner-up on her previous two starts, tried to make all from trap one but ended up setting too fast a pace and, hitting the wall with a furlong to run, she could not even hold on to a place. She too is now eligible for a mark but is another with the ability to win a modest maiden when ridden a little more patiently. (op 7-2)
Gold Hush(USA), a half-sister to Meokee, a smart winner over a mile at two and also useful over ten furlongs at three, shaped with modest promise and might do better in time.
Tonnante, whose dam was a high-class performer in Brazil, is the type who will do better over middle distances next season in handicaps.

5096 LINGFIELDPARK.CO.UK H'CAP 7f (P)
4:20 (4:21) (Class 4) (0-80,80) 3-Y-0+ **£5,505** (£1,637; £818; £408) **Stalls** Low

Form RPR

0003 1 **I'm In Love (USA)**[9] [4837] 3-8-12 74..........(p) FJohansson 2 83
(M A Magnusson) *dwlt: sn settled in midfield: effrt and nt clr run over 1f out: r.o ins fnl f: led last 50yds* **13/2**

6202 2 nk **Katiypour (IRE)**[27] [4241] 9-9-8 80.......... GeorgeBaker 9 89
(P Mitchell) *hld up wl in rr: prog on outer fr over 2f out: effrt over 1f out: chal last 100yds: nt qckn and hld by wnr nr fin* **5/1**[1]

3316 3 1 1/4 **Ivory Lace**[17] [4589] 5-9-4 79.......... JamesDoyle(3) 10 85
(S Woodman) *prom: chsd ldr 2f out: drvn to ld ent fnl f: hdd and no ex last 50yds* **14/1**

5001 4 1/2 **Landucci**[4] [4995] 5-8-11 69.......... MichaelHills 12 74
(J W Hills) *hld up: prog to trck ldrs 3f out: wnt 3rd and looked dangerous ent fnl f: nt qckn* **11/2**[2]

6636 **5** ¾ **Mister Benedictine**^{33} [4078] 3-8-11 **76**................. RichardKingscote(3) 8 78
(W R Muir) *a chsng ldrs: rdn and effrt 2f out: kpt on same pce fr over 1f out* **16/1**

0043 **6** ¾ **Cyclical**^{3} [5021] 4-9-4 **79**.......................... AdamKirby(3) 11 80
(G A Butler) *hld up wl in rr: rdn 1/2-way: styd on u.p fr over 1f out: nrst fin* **6/1**^{3}

0526 **7** *shd* **Mandarin Spirit (IRE)**^{16} [4629] 6-8-10 **68**..................(b) OscarUrbina 5 69
(G C H Chung) *t.k.h: led after 1f: hdd & wknd ent fnl f* **16/1**

0104 **8** *shd* **Top Mark**^{34} [4047] 4-9-5 **77**.......................... SteveDrowne 13 77
(H Morrison) *chsd ldr after 2f to 2f out: wknd ins fnl f* **13/2**

200P **9** ½ **Chief Exec**^{39} [3898] 4-9-1 **80**.......................... AshleyHamblett(7) 14 79
(C A Cyzer) *sn rdn in last: a struggling: styd on fnl 2f: no ch* **33/1**

0200 **10** ½ **Quantum Leap**^{8} [4879] 9-8-7 **72**..........................(v) ThomasBubb(7) 7 70
(S Dow) *dwlt: hld up wl in rr: bmpd along fr 3f out: kpt on fnl f: nvr nr ldrs* **33/1**

5105 **11** 1¾ **Adantino**^{24} [4357] 7-9-1 **80**..........................(b) JamesMillman(7) 1 73
(B R Millman) *dwlt: hld up wl in rr: effrt 2f out: no real prog over 1f out* **12/1**

5410 **12** *nk* **Inch By Inch**^{21} [4449] 7-8-13 **74**..........................(b) AmirQuinn(3) 6 66
(P J Makin) *chsd ldrs: rdn 1/2-way: wknd on inner over 2f out* **25/1**

0015 **13** 3 **Indian Sabre (IRE)**^{13} [4703] 3-9-0 **76**.......................... TPQueally 3 59
(J Noseda) *prom: lost pl steadily on inner fr 5f out: pushed along 1/2-way: eased whn no ch fnl f* **33/1**

0440 **14** *shd* **Critic (IRE)**^{25} [4338] 3-9-4 **80**.......................... J-PGuillambert 4 62
(M L W Bell) *prom: drvn and no rspnse 1/2-way: wknd rapidly over 2f out* **20/1**

1m 24.83s (-1.06) **Going Correction** -0.025s/f (Stan)
WFA 3 from 4yo+ 4lb **14** Ran SP% **116.6**
Speed ratings (Par 105):105,104,103,102,101 100,100,100,100,99 97,97,93,93
CSF £35.07 CT £445.57 TOTE £3.10: £1.10, £2.50, £5.70; EX 43.90.
Owner East Wind Racing Ltd **Bred** W Lazy T Ltd **Trained** Upper Lambourn, Berks

FOCUS
An ordinary handicap but the winner is unexposed and open to improvement.
Cyclical Official explanation: jockey said gelding never travelled
Inch By Inch Official explanation: jockey said mare ran flat

5097 CHANGE UK (S) STKS 1m 2f (P)
4:50 (4:50) (Class 6) 3-Y-0+ **£2,730** (£806; £403) **Stalls** Low

Form RPR

0034 **1** **At The Helm (IRE)**^{26} [4276] 4-8-6 47.......................... RichardRowe(7) 8 50+
(W J Knight) *prom: trckd ldr 6f out: led 4f out: sn drew wl clr: 8 l up over 1f out: tired but unchal* **9/2**^{1}

0000 **2** 1¼ **Tiptoeing**^{35} [4016] 3-8-6 42..........................(b^{1}) TPQueally 12 48
(M H Tompkins) *hld up wl in rr: no ch fr 3f out: prog over 2f out: drvn to take 2nd last 150yds: gaining on wnr but hopeless task* **25/1**

5506 **3** 2 **Coda Agency**^{37} [3977] 3-8-11 55.......................... FrankieMcDonald 6 49
(D W P Arbuthnot) *trckd ldr to 6f out: rdn to chse wnr 3f out: sn no imp: lost 2nd last 150yds* **5/1**^{2}

3205 **4** 1 **Milk And Sultana**^{40} [3862] 6-9-4 47.......................... SteveDrowne 7 47
(G A Ham) *hld up towards rr: outpcd and no ch 3f out: styd on fr over 1f out* **6/1**^{3}

6562 **5** *shd* **Sriology (IRE)**^{19} [4511] 5-9-4 48..........................(t) MichaelTebbutt 3 47
(G Prodromou) *ref to go to post unlesss dismntd: hld up in last trio: drvn over 4f out: sn no ch: kpt on u.p fnl 2f* **6/1**^{3}

6660 **6** 2½ **Elms Schoolboy**^{26} [4280] 4-9-2 44..........................(b) JPFeatherstone(7) 13 47
(P Howling) *prom: disp 2nd 3f out: no imp on wnr under str pressure: wknd fnl f* **40/1**

5440 **7** *shd* **Chookie Windsor**^{3} [4282] 3-9-2 47..........................(v) JimCrowley 10 47
(R M Stronge) *nvr beyond midfield: outpcd and no ch fr 3f out* **16/1**

00 **8** 1 **Littleton Aldor (IRE)**^{14} [4670] 6-9-4.......................... AlanDaly 9 40
(W G M Turner) *prom: rdn over 3f out: sn outpcd: wknd fnl 2f* **66/1**

3530 **9** 2 **String Serenade (IRE)**^{43} [3803] 5-8-11 44.......................... TJHowell(7) 11 36
(V Smith) *hld up in midfield: gng wl enough but lost pl bdly over 3f out: in last pair 2f out: kpt on again fnl f* **16/1**

0040 **10** 6 **Ronaldo**^{8} [4869] 3-8-11 49..........................(v^{1}) LPKeniry 14 25
(A M Hales) *led: stdd pce after 3f: hdd 4f out: wknd over 2f out* **33/1**

6304 **11** 3 **Deserted Prince (IRE)**^{9} [4847] 3-8-8 55.......................... DeanCorby(3) 1 19
(M J Wallace) *nvr beyond midfield: outpcd and no ch fr 3f out* **13/2**

0000 **12** *nk* **Bold Cheverak**^{56} [3389] 4-9-1 47.......................... AdamKirby(3) 2 19
(Mrs C A Dunnett) *t.k.h: prom: drvn over 4f out: wknd over 3f out* **25/1**

3500 **13** ¾ **Ballare (IRE)**^{38} [3933] 7-9-9 47..........................(v) FergusSweeney 5 22
(P J Makin) *dwlt: hld up in rr: lost tch fr over 3f out* **10/1**

0P00 **14** 1 **Barton Sands (IRE)**^{45} [3730] 9-9-2 45..........................(t) JamesMillman(7) 4 20
(Ernst Oertel) *hld up in last: nvr a factor: no ch fr 3f out* **12/1**

2m 8.20s (0.41) **Going Correction** -0.025s/f (Stan)
WFA 3 from 4yo+ 7lb **14** Ran SP% **119.9**
Speed ratings (Par 101):97,96,94,93,93 91,91,90,89,84 81,81,81,80
CSF £125.00 TOTE £6.10: £1.80, £5.90, £1.50; EX 228.10.There was no bid for the winner.
Owner The Big Boys **Bred** Mount Coote Stud **Trained** Patching, W Sussex
■ The first winner for Richard Rowe, son of the trainer and former leading jump jockey of the same name.
■ Stewards' Enquiry : J P Featherstone four-day ban: used whip with excessive force when out of contention (Sep 16-19)

FOCUS
A weak seller, run at a steady early gallop, in which the winner received an enterprising ride. Poor form, and shaky too.
Bold Cheverak Official explanation: jockey said gelding ran too free early on
Ballare(IRE) Official explanation: jockey said gelding lost its action in final furlong

5098 BOOK YOUR TICKETS ONLINE MEDIAN AUCTION MAIDEN STKS 1m 4f (P)
5:20 (5:20) (Class 6) 3-4-Y-0 **£2,730** (£806; £403) **Stalls** Low

Form RPR

0 **1** **Jump Ship**^{82} [2578] 3-8-12.......................... SteveDrowne 8 68+
(M P Tregoning) *prom: trckd ldng pair 1/2-way: rdn 2f out: styd on to ld last 150yds: sn clr* **7/2**^{2}

5055 **2** 1¾ **Stumped**^{13} [4708] 3-9-3 66.......................... MichaelHills 1 70
(W J Haggas) *led: rdn over 2f out: hdd and outpcd last 150yds* **4/1**^{3}

3 **3** ½ **Nando's Dream**^{24} [4367] 3-8-12.......................... TPQueally 6 64
(J Noseda) *free to post: hld up: prog to trck ldng trio over 3f out: rdn 2f out: effrt on inner and nt clr run 1f out: one pce after* **6/4**^{1}

23-0 **4** *nk* **First Slip**^{6} [4931] 3-9-3.......................... JimCrowley 5 69
(Mrs A J Perrett) *prom: trckd ldr 7f out: rdn over 2f out: chal 1f out: wknd ins fnl f* **15/2**

00 **5** 10 **Cosmic Messenger (FR)**^{13} [4708] 3-9-0.......................... StephaneBreux(3) 3 53
(L A Dace) *chsd ldr to 7f out: rdn 5f out: sn lost tch w ldrs* **33/1**

0000 **6** *shd* **Camp Attack**^{13} [4700] 3-9-3 57.......................... LPKeniry 9 53
(S Dow) *hld up in rr: sme prog into midfield 4f out: outpcd and shkn up 3f out: n.d after* **20/1**

7 14 **St Fris** 3-9-3.......................... OscarUrbina 2 30
(J A R Toller) *dwlt: a in last trio: wknd over 4f out: t.o* **25/1**

0205 **8** 15 **Croft (IRE)**^{10} [3951] 3-9-3 54..........................(v) GeorgeBaker 7 6
(R M Stronge) *in tch: reminders over 5f out: wknd 4f out: t.o* **33/1**

05 **9** *dist* **Salawat**^{55} [3399] 3-8-12.......................... MichaelTebbutt 4 —
(G Prodromou) *in tch tl wknd rapidly 5f out: sn t.o* **66/1**

2m 33.78s (-0.61) **Going Correction** -0.025s/f (Stan) **9** Ran SP% **110.0**
Speed ratings (Par 101):101,99,99,99,92 92,83,73,—
CSF £15.69 TOTE £5.60: £1.80, £2.20, £1.10; EX 22.30 Place 6 £9.92, Place 5 £8.30.
Owner M H Dixon **Bred** M H Dixon **Trained** Lambourn, Berks

FOCUS
A pretty modest maiden and no more than ordinary form. The favourite did not progress from her debut and the sixth limits the form.
T/Plt: £7.70 to a £1 stake. Pool: £49,754.15. 4,706.90 winning tickets. T/Qpdt: £6.40 to a £1 stake. Pool: £2,703.80. 311.90 winning tickets. JN

5099 - 5104a (Foreign Racing) - See Raceform Interactive

5016 KEMPTON (A.W) (R-H)
Wednesday, September 6

OFFICIAL GOING: Standard
Wind: light, across

5105 EUROPEAN BREEDERS FUND MAIDEN STKS 1m (P)
2:10 (2:11) (Class 4) 2-Y-0 **£4,533** (£1,348; £674; £336) **Stalls** High

Form RPR

6 **1** **Tastahil (IRE)**^{19} [4561] 2-9-3.......................... RHills 1 76
(B W Hills) *led after 2f: mde rest: shkn up and edgd lft fr 2f out: in command fnl f: rdn out* **13/8**^{1}

5 **2** 1¼ **Benny The Bat**^{33} [4103] 2-9-3.......................... SteveDrowne 5 73
(H Morrison) *cl up: chsd wnr over 2f out: edgd lft after: tried to chal over 1f out: nt qckn and hld fnl f* **9/4**^{2}

3 2½ **Dream Lodge (IRE)** 2-9-3.......................... TPQueally 10 68
(J G Given) *wl in rr: rdn 3f out: prog and hung lft over 1f out: styd on to take 3rd ins fnl f* **20/1**

6 **4** 1¾ **Lawyer To World**^{46} [3738] 2-9-3.......................... JimmyFortune 9 64
(N A Callaghan) *led for 2f: cl up: rdn over 2f out: steadily fdd* **14/1**

4 **5** *hd* **Nothing Is Forever (IRE)**^{20} [4534] 2-9-3.......................... JimCrowley 3 63
(Mrs A J Perrett) *hld up in midfield: gng wl enough 3f out: shkn up and hung bdly lft jst over 2f out: hung rt sn after: sn btn* **12/1**

005 **6** 2 **Hemispear**^{25} [4366] 2-8-12 50.......................... PaulFitzsimons 7 54
(Miss J R Tooth) *trckd wnr after 3f to over 2f out: steadily wknd* **50/1**

7 ½ **Dana Music (USA)** 2-9-3.......................... TedDurcan 8 58
(M R Channon) *pushed along early in rr and rn green: hanging 2f out: late prog: nvr nrr* **14/1**

8 3½ **Copernican** 2-9-3.......................... SebSanders 4 50
(Sir Mark Prescott) *chsd ldrs: pushed along over 3f out: steadily lost pl fr over 2f out* **6/1**^{3}

00 **9** 1½ **Speedfit World**^{23} [4424] 2-9-3.......................... RobertWinston 6 47
(G G Margarson) *in tch: rdn over 2f out: wknd rapidly over 1f out* **25/1**

00 **10** ¾ **Converti**^{42} [3851] 2-9-3.......................... PatDobbs 11 45
(P F I Cole) *a wl in rr: rdn 3f out: struggling after* **33/1**

0 **11** 4 **Vietnam**^{58} [3363] 2-9-3.......................... FrankieMcDonald 2 36
(S Kirk) *s.v.s: rcvrd and in tch 1/2-way: wknd rapidly over 2f out* **66/1**

1m 41.14s (0.34) **Going Correction** -0.125s/f (Stan) **11** Ran SP% **119.2**
Speed ratings (Par 97):93,91,89,87,87 85,84,81,79,79 75
CSF £5.03 TOTE £2.30: £1.30, £1.20, £5.40; EX 4.90.
Owner Hamdan Al Maktoum **Bred** Darley **Trained** Lambourn, Berks

FOCUS
An interesting maiden, with a few that have already shown promise up against some potentially interesting newcomers. The winner was well below the form of his debut. It was noticeable that the principals all hung left to varying degrees over the last couple of furlongs.

NOTEBOOK
Tastahil(IRE), who faced a stiff task in a Newbury Listed event on his first outing, found this rather easier and won in workmanlike style under a much more positive ride than on his debut. He is likely to have another run this term, but connections believe he will be a better three-year-old. (op 6-4 tchd 7-4 and 15-8 in a place)
Benny The Bat confirmed the promise of his Newmarket debut with an improved effort, but was never quite able to get to the favourite. He appreciated this extra furlong but shaped as though he will appreciate even further. (op 5-2 tchd 11-4 in places)
Dream Lodge(IRE) ◆ was the real eye-catcher of the race, staying on strongly at the line, and he did much the best of the newcomers. Related to the likes of Sleepytime and Ali-Royal on the dam's side, he should not be long in winning. (op 16-1)
Lawyer To World showed a lot more than on his debut and seems to be going the right way.
Nothing Is Forever(IRE) was staying on when hanging badly to his left entering the last quarter-mile. He already had an outing under his belt which makes greenness less likely, so he does have a small question mark against him now. (op 14-1)
Copernican, a Racing Post Trophy and Derby entry, raced prominently for a long way before gradually dropping away. He is bred to stay further and his sire's progeny usually improve with time, so the best of him is likely to be seen next season. (op 8-1)

5106 EUROPEAN BREEDERS FUND MEDIAN AUCTION MAIDEN STKS 7f (P)
2:40 (2:42) (Class 5) 2-Y-0 **£4,533** (£1,348; £674; £336) **Stalls** High

Form RPR

4 **1** **Benfleet Boy**^{18} [4600] 2-9-3.......................... SteveDrowne 9 80+
(B J Meehan) *dwlt: sn prom: rdn 3f out: edgd lft fr over 2f out: chsd ldr over 1f out: sustained effrt to ld last 150yds: drvn out* **11/4**^{1}

6 **2** ½ **Malyana**^{25} [4373] 2-8-12.......................... PhilipRobinson 12 74
(M A Jarvis) *led: rdn and edgd lft fr over 2f out: hdd last 150yds: kpt on but a hld* **11/4**^{1}

02 **3** ½ **Keidas (FR)**^{39} [3942] 2-8-12.......................... TedDurcan 8 73
(C F Wall) *chsd ldr: edgd lft u.p fr over 2f out: lost 2nd over 1f out: kpt on* **11/2**^{3}

0 **4** 6 **Laddies Poker (USA)**^{12} [4768] 2-9-3.......................... TPQueally 4 63+
(J Noseda) *s.s: wl off the pce in last pair: rdn 1/2-way: prog fr 2f out: styd on to take modest 4th nr fin* **12/1**

0 **5** ¾ **Medici Code**^{34} [4074] 2-9-3.......................... IanMongan 14 61
(H Morrison) *s.i.s: pushed up to midfield: rdn 3f out: outpcd 2f out: plugged on* **50/1**

6 ½ **Grey Rover** 2-9-3.......................... PatDobbs 2 59
(R Hannon) *lost pl and in rr after 2f: brief effrt over 2f out: sn outpcd and btn* **50/1**

60 **7** *1* **Dumas (IRE)**[36] 4028 2-9-3 .... RobertWinston 6 57
(A P Jarvis) *hld up wl in rr: nudged along and sme prog over 2f out: nvr nr ldrs: do bttr* **14/1**

66 **8** *1 1/4* **Sherjawy (IRE)**[32] 4163 2-9-3 .... NickyMackay 5 54
(L M Cumani) *nvr beyond midfield: rdn and no prog over 2f out: wknd fnl f* **50/1**

0 **9** *hd* **Palmiro**[42] 3844 2-9-3 .... MichaelHills 7 53
(W J Haggas) *sn prom: pushed along over 2f out: steadily wknd* **33/1**

10 *8* **Norman Tradition** 2-8-12 .... FergusSweeney 1 28
(A M Balding) *s.s: rcvrd and in tch on outer 4f out: wknd rapidly over 2f out* **33/1**

11 *4* **Spanish Conquest** 2-9-3 .... SebSanders 3 23
(Sir Mark Prescott) *sn drvn and struggling in last pair: v green and nvr a factor* **33/1**

12 *2* **Buxton** 2-9-3 .... RobertHavlin 13 18
(R Ingram) *s.s: drvn and sn struggling in rr: brief effrt 3f out: wknd rapidly 2f out* **20/1**

3264 **13** *18* **Benchmark**[23] 4428 2-9-3 77 .... JimmyFortune 10 —
(R Hannon) *reluctnat to enter stalls: pushed up and prom: wknd rapidly 3f out : eased 2f out: t.o* **4/1[2]**

1m 25.99s (-0.81) **Going Correction** -0.125s/f (Stan) 13 Ran SP% **122.5**
Speed ratings (Par 95):99,98,97,91,90 89,88,87,86,77 73,70,50
CSF £9.57 TOTE £3.20: £1.30, £1.70, £2.20; EX 10.50.
Owner Miss J Semple **Bred** Crandon Park Stud **Trained** Manton, Wilts

FOCUS
Another potentially informative maiden in which the field came over towards the stands' rail on reaching the home straight. The first three home, all of whom had shown ability in their previous outings, pulled well clear of the others and the form looks very solid.

NOTEBOOK
Benfleet Boy, who had shown distinct signs of promise on his Newmarket debut, looked then as though he would appreciate this extra furlong and so it proved as he picked off the runner-up inside the final furlong. He is likely to really come into his own at three. (op 3-1 tchd 5-2, 10-3 in a place)
Malyana ◆ lasted longer in front than on her Newmarket debut and should break her duck before too long, though she does not look up to Fillies' Mile standard at this stage. (op 2-1, tchd 3-1 in places)
Keidas(FR), runner-up at Nottingham last time in a race that has not worked out, nonetheless emerged with plenty of credit in finishing a close third. She now qualifies for a nursery mark. (op 5-1 tchd 6-1)
Laddies Poker(USA) stayed on to finish fourth at a respectful distance, but still improved on his debut effort. However, the best of him may not be seen until he is handicapped. (op 20-1)
Medici Code was another to perform better than on his debut and is also likely to come into his own once handicapped.
Grey Rover, a half-brother to dual ten furlong-winner Strategy, did best of the newcomers but his sire's progeny tend to need time. (op 33-1)
Dumas(IRE) ◆ made some headway soon after turning in, but was basically not given at all a hard time. He now qualifies for a mark and looks capable of better in that sphere. (op 16-1)
Benchmark Official explanation: jockey said colt bled from the nose

5107 TFM NETWORKS H'CAP 7f (P)
3:10 (3:11) (Class 4) (0-85,82) 3-Y-O **£6,477** (£1,927; £963; £481) **Stalls** High

Form RPR

120 **1** **Ceremonial Jade (UAE)**[11] 4802 3-9-3 81 .... OscarUrbina 11 96+
(M Botti) *hld up wl in rr: gd prog over 2f out: led over 1f out: sn clr: comf* **12/1**

3013 **2** *3 1/2* **Sant Elena**[26] 4328 3-9-1 79 .... SteveDrowne 12 85
(G Wragg) *hld up in midfield: prog over 2f out: rdn to chal over 1f out: unavailing chse of wnr after* **7/1[3]**

1616 **3** *hd* **Finsbury**[18] 4602 3-8-13 77 .... TedDurcan 3 82+
(C F Wall) *dropped in fr wd draw and wl in rr: rdn 1/2-way: prog 2f out : styd on to press for 2nd nr fin* **9/2[1]**

4212 **4** *1 3/4* **Press The Button (GER)**[18] 4605 3-9-4 82 .... NickyMackay 8 82
(J R Boyle) *pressed ldrs: rdn over 2f out: outpcd fr over 1f out* **8/1**

2056 **5** *1 3/4* **Tous Les Deux**[19] 4562 3-8-11 75 .... StephenCarson 7 71
(R F Johnson Houghton) *settled in midfield: rdn over 2f out: one pce and no imp on ldrs* **25/1**

1135 **6** *nk* **Cindertrack**[39] 3959 3-8-11 75 .... JimCrowley 10 70
(J A Osborne) *prom: rdn to chal and upsides over 1f out: sn wknd* **25/1**

3065 **7** *1/2* **Grimes Faith**[18] 4593 3-9-2 80 .... PatDobbs 13 74
(R Hannon) *settled wl in rr: shkn up 3f out: no prog tl kpt on fr over 1f out* **16/1**

0600 **8** *1/2* **Trans Sonic**[21] 4488 3-9-4 82 .... TPQueally 6 78+
(A P Jarvis) *led and set gd pce: hdd & wknd over 1f out* **33/1**

1213 **9** *1 1/4* **Stonecrabstomorrow (IRE)**[9] 4888 3-9-3 81 .... MichaelHills 5 70
(P F I Cole) *racd on outer in midfield: rdn and hung lft 2f out: pushed along and no prog after* **5/1[2]**

0006 **10** *1/2* **Genari**[18] 4591 3-9-0 78 .... RobertWinston 4 66
(P F I Cole) *hld up and racd on outer: rdn whn carried lft 2f out: no ch after* **14/1**

0000 **11** *shd* **Calypso King**[18] 4602 3-8-13 77 .... SebSanders 14 65
(J W Hills) *cl up on inner: rdn over 2f out: wknd wl over 1f out* **33/1**

310 **12** *1/2* **Mahrajaan (USA)**[54] 3473 3-9-1 79 .... JimmyFortune 9 65
(J H M Gosden) *trckd ldrs tl wknd 2f out* **14/1**

1400 **13** *shd* **Grand Entrance (IRE)**[3] 5042 3-8-9 73 .... FergusSweeney 2 59
(C R Egerton) *trckd ldr to over 2f out: wknd rapidly* **25/1**

13 **14** *nk* **Nusoor (IRE)**[60] 3296 3-8-13 77 .... RHills 1 62
(W J Haggas) *heavily restrained s: hld up in last and plld hrd: rdn and no rspnse over 2f out* **5/1[2]**

1m 25.17s (-1.63) **Going Correction** -0.125s/f (Stan) 14 Ran SP% **119.5**
Speed ratings (Par 103):104,100,99,97,95 95,94,94,92,92 92,91,91,91
CSF £87.28 CT £451.21 TOTE £12.30: £3.30, £2.90, £2.00; EX 120.40.
Owner Giuliano Manfredini **Bred** Darley **Trained** Newmarket, Suffolk

FOCUS
A very competitive handicap on paper, but ultimately a one-horse race and and the unexposed winner could hardly have been more impressive. The race has been rated around the second.
Nusoor(IRE) Official explanation: jockey said gelding wouldn't face the kickback; vet said gelding was slightly lame

5108 BARRETTSTOWN STUD H'CAP 1m (P)
3:40 (3:40) (Class 4) (0-80,80) 3-Y-O+ **£5,505** (£1,637; £818; £408) **Stalls** High

Form RPR

6512 **1** **Coalpark (IRE)**[6] 4953 3-8-4 66 .... (t) DO'Donohoe 3 76
(M Johnston) *sn trckd ldr: rdn to ld over 2f out: hrd pressed fnl f : kpt on wl nr fin* **4/1[2]**

5120 **2** *nk* **Cross The Line (IRE)**[25] 4378 4-9-7 78 .... SebSanders 6 87
(A P Jarvis) *hld up in rr: prog on inner over 2f out: chsd wnr over 1f out: clsd to chal fnl f: no ex last 50yds* **10/3[1]**

0620 **3** *2 1/2* **Pillars Of Wisdom**[28] 4241 4-9-7 78 .... (t) PaulDoe 8 81
(J L Dunlop) *led: kicked on wl over 2f out: sn hdd: lost 2nd over 1f out: plugged on to hold on for 3rd* **15/2**

4536 **4** *nk* **Merrymadcap (IRE)**[5] 4989 4-9-7 78 .... FrancisNorton 4 81
(M Blanshard) *hld up in tch: rdn and outpcd over 2f out: effrt over 1f out: kpt on but no real imp ldrs* **7/1[3]**

1-20 **5** *1 1/2* **Cursum Perficio**[134] 1207 4-9-3 74 .... SteveDrowne 7 73
(W R Muir) *hld up in tch: rdn 3f out: sn outpcd: one pce u.p after* **8/1**

0565 **6** *1/2* **Night Storm**[9] 4879 5-9-1 72 .... TPQueally 5 70
(S Dow) *s.v.s and lost 6 l: sn in tch in last: rdn and outpcd over 2f out: no imp on outer after* **9/1**

0214 **7** *3 1/2* **Somersault**[18] 4610 3-8-8 70 .... RobertWinston 9 60
(Sir Michael Stoute) *sn pushed along to chse ldrs and nvr gng wl: drvn and struggling over 2f out: wknd over 1f out* **4/1[2]**

-000 **8** *11* **Laugh 'n Cry**[11] 4820 5-8-9 66 oh4 .... NickyMackay 2 31
(C A Cyzer) *hld up: prog to trck ldrs 5f out: wknd rapidly over 2f out* **25/1**

1m 39.91s (-0.89) **Going Correction** -0.125s/f (Stan)
WFA 3 from 4yo+ 5lb 8 Ran SP% **112.3**
Speed ratings (Par 105):99,98,96,95,94 93,90,79
CSF £17.07 CT £94.10 TOTE £5.80: £1.60, £1.50, £2.10; EX 17.80.
Owner Joy And Valentine Feerick **Bred** Rathasker Stud **Trained** Middleham Moor, N Yorks

FOCUS
A fair handicap but it was run at an ordinary pace and the form is probably not that strong. The winner was back to the form he showed last year.
Night Storm Official explanation: jockey said mare missed the break

5109 KEMPTON.CO.UK H'CAP 1m 4f (P)
4:10 (4:11) (Class 4) (0-85,83) 3-Y-O **£6,477** (£1,927; £963; £481) **Stalls** Centre

Form RPR

-131 **1** **Island Odyssey**[85] 2533 3-9-4 83 .... SteveDrowne 2 91
(E A L Dunlop) *dwlt: hld up in 4th: prog to chal 3f out: pressed ldr after: drvn and gained upper hand ins fnl f* **5/1[3]**

-422 **2** *1/2* **Whatizzit**[21] 4490 3-9-0 79 .... JimmyFortune 7 86
(E A L Dunlop) *trckd ldr: led 3f out: sn hrd pressed: edgd lft over 1f out: hdd ins fnl f: kpt on wl but a hld* **3/1[1]**

6600 **3** *5* **Divine River**[10] 4838 3-8-11 76 .... TPQueally 3 75
(A P Jarvis) *dwlt: hld up in last: rapid prog 4f out to chal 3f out: nt qckn 2f out: wknd ins fnl f* **20/1**

-423 **4** *hd* **Dickie's Dream (IRE)**[140] 1077 3-8-5 70 .... FrancisNorton 1 69
(P J McBride) *settled in last trio: rdn over 3f out: outpcd and btn over 2f out: kpt on ins fnl f* **8/1**

104 **5** *4* **Oscillator**[18] 4599 3-8-12 77 .... NickyMackay 4 69
(G A Butler) *dwlt: settled in 5th: hrd rdn and outpcd over 2f out: no ch after* **15/2**

-143 **6** *2 1/2* **Balloura (USA)**[29] 4224 3-8-9 74 .... RHills 6 62
(W J Haggas) *led at stdy pce: hdd 3f out: sn btn: wknd over 1f out* **5/1[3]**

1-50 **7** *14* **Katies Tuitor**[135] 1193 3-8-10 75 .... PatDobbs 5 41
(B W Duke) *settled in last trio: drvn and wknd over 2f out: t.o* **25/1**

-531 **8** *5* **Adelfia (IRE)**[14] 4701 3-9-1 80 .... RobertWinston 8 38
(Sir Michael Stoute) *t.k.h early: trckd ldr to over 3f out: wknd rapidly: t.o* **7/2[2]**

2m 34.55s (-2.35) **Going Correction** -0.125s/f (Stan) 8 Ran SP% **112.0**
Speed ratings (Par 103):102,101,98,98,95 93,84,81
CSF £19.53 CT £269.24 TOTE £6.40: £1.80, £1.20, £6.80; EX 12.10.
Owner Mrs Janice Quy **Bred** Catridge Farm Stud Ltd **Trained** Newmarket, Suffolk

FOCUS
Some progressive middle-distance handicappers on show here and despite the early pace set by Balloura not looking that strong, the winning time was not bad. Pretty ordinary form at face value, rated though the third, but it could turn out better than it looks.
Adelfia(IRE) Official explanation: trainer's representative had no explanation for the poor form shown

5110 PANORAMIC BAR & RESTAURANT H'CAP 1m 2f (P)
4:40 (4:42) (Class 3) (0-90,96) 3-Y-O+
£11,217 (£3,358; £1,679; £840; £419; £210) **Stalls** High

Form RPR

1455 **1** **Great Hawk (USA)**[32] 4147 3-9-3 86 .... (v[1]) RobertWinston 4 103+
(Sir Michael Stoute) *pressed ldr: led 3f out: shkn up and drew clr wl over 1f out: comf* **20/1**

4111 **2** *4* **Acrobatic (USA)**[5] 4997 3-9-13 96 6ex .... JimmyFortune 5 102+
(R Charlton) *towards rr and nt gng that wl: effrt u.p over 2f out: styd on fr over 1f out to take 2nd last 50yds* **4/5[1]**

60-0 **3** *nk* **Babe Maccool (IRE)**[28] 4244 4-9-6 82 .... MichaelHills 10 87
(B W Hills) *led at decent pce: hdd 3f out: sn no ch w wnr: lost 2nd last 50yds* **33/1**

3216 **4** *1* **Let Slip**[18] 4610 4-9-5 81 .... PaulDoe 2 85+
(W Jarvis) *dwlt: settled in last trio: effrt on wd outside over 2f out: kpt on fr over 1f out: n.d* **14/1**

-202 **5** *nk* **Giving**[11] 4810 3-9-7 90 .... SteveDrowne 1 93
(G Wragg) *prom: rdn and nt qckn over 2f out: kpt on same pce after* **6/1[2]**

2335 **6** *nk* **Shogun Prince (IRE)**[18] 4599 3-8-10 79 .... (v) FergusSweeney 8 81
(A King) *hld up in midfield: effrt on inner 3f out: kpt on u.p fnl 2f: nt pce to threaten* **25/1**

62 **7** *hd* **Starnevees (FR)**[46] 3737 5-9-11 87 .... NickyMackay 11 89
(L M Cumani) *fractious bef s: prom: rdn over 2f out: sn outpcd: fdd fnl f* **16/1**

0010 **8** *1 3/4* **Given A Choice (IRE)**[28] 4241 4-9-11 87 .... TPQueally 12 86
(R A Fahey) *prom on inner: rdn over 2f out: wknd over 1f out* **20/1**

0425 **9** *1 1/4* **Della Salute**[20] 4536 4-9-0 76 .... LPKeniry 9 72
(Miss E C Lavelle) *chsd ldrs tl wknd u.p wl over 1f out* **33/1**

5655 **10** *3/4* **Secretary General (IRE)**[3] 5045 5-8-13 75 .... PatDobbs 7 70
(P F I Cole) *dwlt and early reminders: last trio most of way: struggling 3f out: no ch after* **12/1[3]**

1462 **11** *5* **Sonny Parkin**[11] 4805 4-9-2 78 .... (v) DO'Donohoe 13 63
(G A Huffer) *hld up in midfield: effrt on inner whn nt clr run and lost pl over 2f out: wknd over 1f out* **14/1**

3320 **12** *3* **Star Magnitude (USA)**[9] 4878 5-9-6 82 .... SebSanders 6 62
(S Dow) *a towards rr: wknd 2f out* **20/1**

0360 **13** *12* **Herring (IRE)**[18] 4599 3-8-6 75 .... (v) TedDurcan 3 32
(D J Coakley) *in rr: in last pair 1/2-way: sn struggling: t.o* **25/1**

2m 5.18s (-3.82) **Going Correction** -0.125s/f (Stan)
WFA 3 from 4yo+ 7lb 13 Ran SP% **124.6**
Speed ratings (Par 107):110,106,106,105,105 105,105,103,102,102 98,95,86
CSF £35.30 CT £621.56 TOTE £20.80: £4.80, £1.30, £8.40; EX 92.40 Place 6 £12.34, Place 5 £9.05 .

Owner Saeed Suhail **Bred** Clover Iv Llc **Trained** Newmarket, Suffolk

FOCUS

Unusually for the last event on the card, the most valuable contest of the day, and it was certainly run at a true gallop. The winner was very impressive and the form looks sound overall.

NOTEBOOK

Great Hawk(USA) absolutely bolted up. He had become disappointing on turf lately, but a combination of the switch to sand and first-time visor brought about a spectacular transition. It will be fascinating to see where he goes next.

Acrobatic(USA), bidding to make it four on the bounce at this track under a 6lb penalty for last Friday's victory over an extra furlong, was not travelling that well from a long way out and it is testament to his ability that he still managed to run on to finish second, albeit at a respectful distance. He is surely better than he showed here and perhaps this came a bit to soon. He remains a possible for the Cambridgeshire. (op 10-11, tchd evens in places)

Babe Maccool(IRE) had obviously derived some benefit from last month's return from an 11-month absence and performed much better this time after having made much of the running.

Let Slip stayed on down the outside in the home straight and posted another creditable performance on a surface she likes. (op 16-1)

Giving ran with credit having been up with the pace from the off. This is her level, but she is slowly creeping up the handicap despite not winning (op 11-2)

Shogun Prince(IRE) ran a bit better in the visor this time and has already shown that he can win on this surface.

T/Jkpt: Not won. T/Plt: £11.70 to a £1 stake. Pool: £52,870.90. 3,275.75 winning tickets. T/Qpdt: £10.60 to a £1 stake. Pool: £3,207.10. 221.90 winning tickets. JN

[3994] SOUTHWELL (L-H)

Wednesday, September 6

OFFICIAL GOING: Good

Wind: light, half-behind

5111 EUROPEAN BREEDERS FUND MAIDEN STKS (DIV I) 6f

1:50 (1:51) (Class 4) 2-Y-O **£4,857** (£1,445; £722; £360) **Stalls** Low

Form RPR

0 **1** **Smash N'Grab (IRE)**[117] [1647] 2-8-12 NCallan 8 61
(K A Ryan) *sn led: qcknd 2f out: sn rdn and edgd rt ins last: kpt on wl* **11/2**[3]

0 **2** *nk* **Dance Of Dreams**[23] [4428] 2-9-0 JamesDoyle(3) 10 65
(N P Littmoden) *a.p: effrt to chse wnr 2f out: rdn to chal ins last: kpt on* **9/2**[1]

3 *1 3/4* **Baileys Outshine** 2-8-12 JamieMackay 5 55
(J G Given) *a.p: effrt 2f out: sn rdn and ev ch tl drvn and one pce ins last* **11/1**

00 **4** *2 1/2* **Cryptic Clue (USA)**[70] [2967] 2-9-3 PaulQuinn 2 52
(D W Chapman) *keen: chsd ldrs: n.m.r after 2f: hdwy 2f out: sn rdn and kpt on same pce* **12/1**

5 *shd* **Marquee (IRE)** 2-9-3 TPO'Shea 7 52
(P A Blockley) *s.i.s: rapid hdwy to chse ldrs after 2f. rdn over 2f out and sn one pce* **7/1**

0 **6** *3/4* **Amazing King (IRE)**[7] [4928] 2-8-10 JackDean(7) 3 50
(W G M Turner) *towards rr: effrt over 2f out: sn rdn and no imp* **9/1**

7 *1/2* **Didactic** 2-9-3 EddieAhern 4 48
(J A Osborne) *chsd ldrs: rdn along over 2f out: sn wknd* **9/2**[1]

0 **8** *hd* **Crosby Jemma**[13] [4731] 2-8-12 JimmyQuinn 9 43
(J R Weymes) *a towards rr* **33/1**

00 **9** *3/4* **Hits Only Vic (USA)**[13] [4731] 2-9-3 DeanMcKeown 6 45
(J Pearce) *a rr* **33/1**

10 *13* **Swift Cut (IRE)** 2-9-3 AdrianTNicholls 1 6
(A P Jarvis) *dwlt: sn rdn along and n.m.r on inner: swtchd outside halfway: rdn over 2f out: sn wknd and eased fnl f* **5/1**[2]

1m 15.91s (-0.19) **Going Correction** -0.30s/f (Firm) **10** Ran SP% **112.8**

Speed ratings (Par 97):89,88,86,82,82 81,81,80,79,62

CSF £29.39 TOTE £5.90: £2.50, £1.80, £3.60; EX 25.00 TRIFECTA Not won..

Owner The Five K Club **Bred** Paul Kavanagh **Trained** Hambleton, N Yorks

FOCUS

A moderate winning time for the grade and 0.88 seconds faster than the second division. There was next to no worthwhile form on offer beforehand and this was probably very ordinary form, especially with the field finishing in a heap.

NOTEBOOK

Smash N'Grab(IRE), who did not show much on her debut at Nottingham back in May, had clearly learnt a bit from that and she was soon in front. Picking up to extend the lead with quarter of a mile to run, she stuck on valiantly under pressure and saw the sixth furlong out well. There may be more to come from her in nurseries. (op 9-2)

Dance Of Dreams, who played up in the stalls before running down the field on his recent debut at Windsor, had evidently come on a good deal for the experience and ran on to hassle the winner inside the final furlong, but he was always just being held. He will be qualified for nurseries after one more run and looks a likely type for that sphere. (tchd 4-1)

Baileys Outshine, bred to be effective at around this sort of distance, knew her job first time and showed up well early. She held every chance with a furlong to run, but the front pair were a bit too wise for her and she had to make do with third. She can find a small race on this evidence. (op 9-1)

Cryptic Clue(USA), making his debut for connections having been off-loaded by Khalid Abdullah, showed a bit more than on his two previous visits to the course and is now qualified for nurseries.

Marquee(IRE), bred to stay further in time, showed plenty of promise following a slow start and, although flattening out under pressure, he should have learned a good deal from this. (op 15-2)

Didactic, perhaps the most interesting newcomer, has already been gelded and on this evidence he is going to struggle. That said, he did drop away quickly and there may well have been something amiss. (op 4-1)

Swift Cut(IRE) Official explanation: jockey said colt hung right-handed throughout

5112 EUROPEAN BREEDERS FUND MAIDEN STKS (DIV II) 6f

2:20 (2:22) (Class 4) 2-Y-O **£4,857** (£1,445; £722; £360) **Stalls** Low

Form RPR

1 **Trepa (USA)** 2-9-3 KerrinMcEvoy 3 70+
(W Jarvis) *dwlt and in rr: swtchd outside and hdwy over 2f out: rdn to chse ldr over 1f out: styd on wl fnl f to ld nr line* **4/1**[2]

3432 **2** *nk* **Malaaq**[27] [4292] 2-8-12 73 NCallan 9 64+
(M A Jarvis) *cl up: led 2f out: rdn ent last: hdd and no ex nr fin* **4/7**[1]

6 **3** *3 1/2* **Ask Yer Dad**[77] [2759] 2-9-3 MickyFenton 1 59
(Mrs P Sly) *led: pushed along and hdd 2f out: sn rdn and kpt on same pce* **14/1**

00 **4** *hd* **Torver**[19] [4572] 2-8-12 PaulHanagan 10 53
(Dr J D Scargill) *dwlt and towards rr: hdwy 1/2-way: rdn to chse ldrs 2f out: kpt on same pce* **50/1**

0 **5** *1 1/4* **Flying Grey (IRE)**[7] [4920] 2-9-3 TPO'Shea 4 54
(P A Blockley) *chsd ldrs: rdn along wl over 2f out: sn wknd* **50/1**

45 **6** *1/2* **Lady Chastity**[12] [4781] 2-8-9 EdwardCreighton(3) 6 48
(Mrs L J Young) *chsd ldrs: rdn over 2f out: sn wknd* **10/1**[3]

7 *5* **Strobe** 2-8-10 FrankiePickard(7) 8 38
(J A Osborne) *sn outpcd and a bhd* **16/1**

00 **8** *1 1/4* **Hesaguru (IRE)**[18] [4608] 2-9-3 PaulMulrennan 5 34
(J R Norton) *in tch: rdn along 1/2-way: sn wknd* **125/1**

1m 15.03s (-1.07) **Going Correction** -0.30s/f (Firm) 2y crse rec **8** Ran SP% **110.0**

Speed ratings (Par 97):95,94,89,89,88 87,80,79

CSF £6.08 TOTE £4.50: £1.30, £1.02, £2.40; EX 8.70 Trifecta £23.40 Pool: £459.33. 13.93 winning units.

Owner Anthony Foster **Bred** Majestic Farm Llc **Trained** Newmarket, Suffolk

FOCUS

Much the better of the two divisions, a theory backed up by the winning time. It has been rated through the runner-up, while the winner can do better.

NOTEBOOK

Trepa(USA), an expensive purchase, is bred to stay much further in time, but having been slowly away and held up, he produced a tidy burst of speed to cut down the hot favourite and ended up winning with a bit to spare under yet another fine ride from McEvoy. He could be above average on this evidence and, with further improvement highly likely, looks one to keep on the right side of. (op 10-3)

Malaaq, a consistent sort, set a strong standard and she looked the likely winner when going on two out, her jockey looking confident, but she was cut down close home by the colt. She will no doubt find a race eventually, but is hardly one to start backing now. (op 4-6)

Ask Yer Dad had the best of the draw and made full use of it, bursting out in the lead, but he proved no match for the front pair and could only plug on at the one pace. He can do better in nurseries, for which he will be qualified after one more run. (op 12-1 tchd 16-1)

Torver stepped up on previous efforts in what was a weaker maiden and she can now contest handicaps, with a rise in distance also likely to help. (op 40-1)

Flying Grey(IRE) stepped up on his initial effort at Leicester, but is unlikely to be winning until contesting low-grade handicaps. (op 40-1)

Strobe Official explanation: jockey said colt ran green and was outpaced in early stages

5113 READ HUNT INSURANCE BROKERS NURSERY 7f

2:50 (2:55) (Class 4) (0-85,80) 2-Y-O **£5,181** (£1,541; £770; £384) **Stalls** Low

Form RPR

3520 **1** **Hart Of Gold**[12] [4766] 2-9-7 **80** EddieAhern 5 86
(M J Wallace) *cl up: led over 4f out: qcknd clr 2f out: rdn ins last and kpt on* **10/1**

1 **2** *1/2* **Bid For Glory**[38] [3979] 2-9-4 **77** JimmyQuinn 4 81
(H J Collingridge) *slowly into steride: sn pushed along and in tch: hday to trck ldrs 3f out: rdn to chse wnr 2f out: kpt on wl* **6/1**[3]

610 **3** *3* **Charlie Tipple**[54] [3496] 2-9-2 **75** MickyFenton 9 72
(T D Easterby) *bhd: hdwy 2f out: swtchd rt and rdn over 1f out: styd on wl fnl f* **11/2**[2]

2430 **4** *3/4* **Rainbow Fox**[15] [4681] 2-9-5 **78** PaulHanagan 12 73
(R A Fahey) *in tch: hdwy to chse ldrs wl over 2f out: rdn wl over 1f out: kpt on same pce appr last* **17/2**

2534 **5** *1/2* **Ten Dollars More (IRE)**[4] [5034] 2-8-12 **74**......(b[1]) StephenDonohoe(3) 8 68+
(J A Osborne) *in tch whn hmpd and lost pl over 4f out: wd st and hdwy on outer 2f out: sn rdn and kpt on same pce appr last* **14/1**

1004 **6** *3/4* **Baltimore Jack (IRE)**[9] [4890] 2-9-7 **80** KerrinMcEvoy 2 72
(R M Whitaker) *midfield: hdwy to chse ldrs over 2f out: sn rdn and no imp* **8/1**

U010 **7** *2* **Always Best**[28] [4250] 2-8-7 **66** JoeFanning 11 53
(M Johnston) *midfield: hdwy wl over 2f out: sn rdn along and kpt on ins last: nrst fin* **16/1**

064 **8** *1* **Bed Fellow (IRE)**[11] [4794] 2-8-13 **72** AdrianTNicholls 1 56
(A P Jarvis) *chsd ldrs on inner: rdn along 2f out: sn drvn and wknd* **10/1**

055 **9** *3/4* **Having A Ball**[57] [3385] 2-7-12 **57** HayleyTurner 3 40
(P D Cundell) *s.i.s: a rr* **25/1**

3003 **10** *1 3/4* **Wanchai Night**[6] [4955] 2-7-12 **57** DaleGibson 13 35
(T D Easterby) *a rr* **33/1**

2021 **11** *3/4* **Orpen Prince (IRE)**[12] [4761] 2-9-0 **73** NCallan 6 49
(K A Ryan) *keen: cl up: rdn alonhg to chse wnr over 2f out: drvn wl over 1f out: sn wknd* **9/2**[1]

0513 **12** *1 1/4* **Tom Tower (IRE)**[82] [2598] 2-9-3 **76** TonyCulhane 10 49+
(M R Channon) *trcking ldrs whn hmpd over 4f out: sn lost pl and bhd* **12/1**

5025 **13** *17* **Only A Splash**[6] [4955] 2-8-1 **60** PaulQuinn 7 —
(D W Chapman) *led: hung lft and hdd over 4f out: sn rdn along and wknd 3f out* **100/1**

1m 27.56s (-1.64) **Going Correction** -0.30s/f (Firm) 2y crse rec **13** Ran SP% **115.7**

Speed ratings (Par 97):97,96,93,92,91 90,88,87,86,84 83,82,62

CSF £65.82 CT £367.47 TOTE £13.90: £4.50, £2.00, £2.40; EX 71.60 Trifecta £229.00 Pool: £380.62. 1.18 winning units.

Owner Hartshead Mob **Bred** Bearstone Stud **Trained** Newmarket, Suffolk

■ Stewards' Enquiry : Paul Quinn three-day ban: careless riding (Sep 17-19)

FOCUS

A fair nursery, rated through the third and fourth. Improved efforts from the first two.

NOTEBOOK

Hart Of Gold, a winner at Wolverhampton back in June, has been running well in defeat subsequently, but he got loose before the start and looked to have done his winning chances no favours. However, having been up there from the off, he showed a tidy change of pace to go into a clear lead with two furlongs to run and was always doing enough. This was not a particularly good nursery though and he may struggle to defy a higher mark. (tchd 9-1)

Bid For Glory, a winner on his sole previous start at Newmarket in July, missed the break and was unable to obtain a good early position, being ridden along to try and get going. He eventually picked up, running on strongly inside the final furlong to finish clear of the third, but the winner had already flown. He will go up a bit for this, but remains a promising sort and is one to keep on side. (op 7-1 tchd 8-1)

Charlie Tipple showed his Newmarket running to be all wrong and kept on well to finish third, but he will have to improve again to win off of this sort of mark. (op 8-1)

Rainbow Fox bounced back from a moderate effort at York and seemed to see out the trip well enough, but is likely to remain vulnerable off this mark. (tchd 8-1 and 9-1)

Ten Dollars More(IRE) was a little unlucky, although he would never have won. He lost his place before halfway having been hampered, but was going on well close home, and there may yet be another race in him as he seems to be taking his racing well. (op 10-1)

Baltimore Jack(IRE) has not gone on from his debut success and is going to continue to struggle off this mark. Official explanation: jockey said colt was denied a clear run (op 9-1)

Orpen Prince(IRE) failed to last home having raced keenly and was unable to build on his Chester maiden success. Official explanation: trainer's representative had no explanation for the poor form shown (op 7-2)

5114 READ HUNT INSURANCE BROKERS CONDITIONS STKS 7f
3:20 (3:22) (Class 4) 2-Y-O **£6,232** (£1,866; £933; £467; £233) **Stalls** Low

Form RPR
21 **1** **St Philip (USA)**[21] 4479 2-9-2 80 .... GeorgeBaker 5 93
(R M Beckett) *led 1f: cl up: rdn over 1f out: styd on u.p ins last: led last 100 yds* **6/4**[1]
14 **2** *nk* **Codeword (IRE)**[30] 4200 2-9-2 .... JoeFanning 1 92
(M Johnston) *led after 1f: qcknd 2f out: rdn over 1f out: drvn ins last: hdd and no ex last 100 yds* **11/4**[2]
625 **3** *2* **Rabbit Fighter (IRE)**[11] 4809 2-8-12 93 .... TPO'Shea 4 83
(P A Blockley) *trckd ldng pair: effrt 2f out: sn rdn and kpt on same pce appr last* **11/4**[2]
0 **4** *nk* **New Beginning (IRE)**[19] 4572 2-8-12 .... PaulHanagan 2 82
(Mrs S Lamyman) *in tch: hdwy over 2f out: rdn wl over 1f out: kpt on same pce* **100/1**
34 **5** *nk* **Tombi (USA)**[91] 2361 2-8-12 .... TomEaves 3 81
(J Howard Johnson) *hld up in tch: hdwy over 2f out: rdn over 1f out and kpt on same pce* **13/2**[3]

1m 28.31s (-0.89) **Going Correction** -0.30s/f (Firm) 2y crse rec **5** Ran SP% **107.7**
Speed ratings (Par 97):93,92,90,90,89
CSF £5.62 TOTE £2.00: £1.30, £1.60; EX 5.70.
Owner R A Pegum **Bred** Foxfield **Trained** Whitsbury, Hants

FOCUS
A useful-looking juvenile conditions race on paper, fought out by the two previous winners in the race. The early tempo was not strong, and the race turned in to a sprint off the final bend, making the value of the form a bit suspect. The time was slower than the nursery on the card.

NOTEBOOK
St Philip(USA) tracked Codeword, after leading briefly, and came with a strong run inside the final furlong to win with a little bit in hand. Another furlong will hold no fears for him, nor a stronger gallop, and he is progressing the right way, confirming his connections' high opinion of him - he has been entered for the Group 1 Dewhurst Stakes. (op 7-4)
Codeword(IRE) was made favourite to beat subsequent Acomb winner Big Timer last time, and unsurprisingly came up a bit short against that exciting prospect. Awash with sweat down his neck, he tried to steal the race entering the straight, managing to hold off all challengers apart from St Philip. The run was more in keeping with his debut effort and there will be more races to be won with him. (op 3-1 tchd 5-2)
Rabbit Fighter(IRE), not beaten far in the Group 3 Solario Stakes last time, was finding things tough over two furlongs from home and probably did not enjoy the way the race was run. It must still go down as a disappointing effort, however. (op 9-4 tchd 3-1)
New Beginning(IRE) ran unbelievably well in the face of a very difficult task. There did not appear any fluke about the effort, even though the race turned into a sprint, but one must have reservations about the run until it is proven again. (op 66-1)
Tombi(USA), not seen since early June, had some really good form behind him, especially when not beaten far by Coventry Stakes winner Hellvelyn on his debut. However, he was not seen to best effect in a race run to suit pacier types, and may have been more of a threat with a stronger tempo to aim at. With physical scope for improvement, he can be given another chance on a more galloping track. (op 6-1 tchd 7-1)

5115 BETFAIR.COM H'CAP 1m 3f
3:50 (3:51) (Class 3) (0-90,86) 3-Y-O+
£9,348 (£2,799; £1,399; £700; £349; £175) **Stalls** Low

Form RPR
/14- **1** **Sanchi (IRE)**[319] 6018 4-9-12 **86** .... KerrinMcEvoy 9 101+
(Saeed Bin Suroor) *hld up towards rr: swtchd outside 2f out: smooth hdwy to ld over 1f out: pushed clr ent last: easily* **7/1**
3231 **2** *1 ¾* **St Savarin (FR)**[5] 4990 5-9-10 **84** 6ex .... PaulHanagan 5 92
(R A Fahey) *held up in tch: hdwy over 2f out: rdn to chal and ev ch over 1f out: sn drvn and kpt on: no ch w wnr* **10/3**[1]
3311 **3** *1 ½* **Go Solo**[16] 4654 5-9-12 **86** .... DeanMcKeown 8 92
(G A Swinbank) *a.p: effrt 2f out: rdn to ld wl over 1f out: drvn and hdd appr last: kpt on* **9/2**[3]
0261 **4** *2* **Resonate (IRE)**[9] 4878 8-9-3 **80** 6ex .... AmirQuinn(3) 7 83
(A G Newcombe) *hld up gng wl: smooth hdwy on inner 3f out: chsd ldrs 2f out: sn rdn and kpt on same pce* **12/1**
4011 **5** *1* **Lady Disdain**[9] 4892 3-8-2 **75** 6ex .... AndrewElliott(5) 11 76
(G M Moore) *chsd ldrs: effrt 3f out: rdna nd ch 2f out: drvn and grad wknd* **4/1**[2]
3510 **6** *2* **Lucayan Dancer**[20] 4508 6-9-10 **84** .... AdrianTNicholls 3 82
(D Nicholls) *hld up and bhd: hdwy over 3f out: sn rdn and kpt on fnl 2f: nvr nr ldrs* **33/1**
0100 **7** *3 ½* **Go Tech**[20] 4508 6-9-10 **84** .... DavidAllan 4 76
(T D Easterby) *in tch: hdwy on inner 3f out: sn rdn and wknd wl over 1f out* **16/1**
5113 **8** *1* **Prince Picasso**[41] 3871 3-9-0 **82** .... JamieMackay 1 73
(Sir Mark Prescott) *led: rdn along 3f out: drvn 2f out: sn hdd & wknd* **7/1**
4006 **9** *¾* **Sharp Reply (USA)**[22] 4457 4-8-7 **72** .... MichaelJStainton(5) 10 62
(R M Whitaker) *towards rr: hdwy over 4f out: rdn along over 3f out and nvr a factor* **28/1**
-260 **10** *6* **Shape Up (IRE)**[90] 2387 6-9-3 **77** ....(b) MickyFenton 6 57
(R Craggs) *hld up in rr: hdwy on outer 1/2-way: chsd ldrs 4f out: rdn over 3f out and sn wknd* **50/1**
2320 **11** *18* **Nesno (USA)**[30] 4203 3-8-12 **80** .... DarrylHolland 2 31
(J D Bethell) *cl up: rdn along 3f out: wknd over 2f out: eased fnl f* **16/1**

2m 20.13s **Going Correction** -0.30s/f (Firm) course record
WFA 3 from 4yo+ 8lb **11** Ran SP% **114.1**
Speed ratings (Par 107):110,108,107,106,105 104,101,100,100,95 82
CSF £29.13 CT £116.78 TOTE £7.30: £2.00, £2.00, £1.20; EX 30.00 Trifecta £159.40 Pool: £473.88. 2.11 winning units.
Owner Godolphin **Bred** Aylesfield Farms Stud **Trained** Newmarket, Suffolk

FOCUS
A strong race for the grade with plenty of recent winning form. The winner looks smart and there is no reason to believe that the placed horses did not run up to their marks.

NOTEBOOK
Sanchi(IRE) ♦, not seen since finishing fourth in a heavy-ground handicap at Doncaster last October, kept on in really good style to win with plenty in hand. He did not quicken as such, but came with a strong run down the centre of the course that was far too good for his rivals. Open to plenty of improvement, he should be followed for the rest of the season. (op 15-2 tchd 8-1 and 13-2)
St Savarin(FR) had absolutely no chance with the winner but kept on well to beat the rest of his rivals nicely, suggesting he may not have finished winning this season yet. (op 7-2)
Go Solo, who was on a hat-trick, tried his best to go with Sanchi but could not concede the weight in the final stages. He did, however, appear to run up to his recent best. (op 4-1)
Resonate(IRE) could never get on terms but was noted staying on towards the end of the race. (op 14-1)
Lady Disdain, chasing her third win on the bounce, has done really well for a filly that cost only 800gns at the sales. Her two wins, which both came at Ripon and are her total career successes, were on a soft surface, and she failed to land a blow of any kind. (op 3-1 tchd 11-4)
Lucayan Dancer is now a shade high in the handicap after a fair season. (op 25-1)
Prince Picasso, stepping up in trip, was coming back off a break after a slightly disappointing effort at Folkestone, although the form of that race has worked out reasonably well since. He tried to stretch the field up the straight but could not hold on, weakening quickly up the straight. (op 8-1 tchd 9-1)

5116 READ HUNT INSURANCE POLICY CONDITIONS STKS 7f
4:20 (4:22) (Class 3) 3-Y-O
£8,724 (£2,612; £1,306; £653; £326; £163) **Stalls** Low

Form RPR
-140 **1** **Aeroplane**[78] 2721 3-9-0 100 .... EddieAhern 2 110+
(P W Chapple-Hyam) *trckd ldr: effrt 2f out and sn rdn: led 1f out: kpt on* **5/6**[1]
210- **2** *2* **Dickensian (IRE)**[319] 6023 3-8-11 103 ....(vt[1]) KerrinMcEvoy 4 102
(Saeed Bin Suroor) *trckd ldrs: hdwy to chse ldr over 2f out: rdn to chal wl over 1f out: ev ch tl drvn and one pce ins last* **3/1**[2]
2013 **3** *¾* **Come Out Fighting**[18] 4601 3-8-11 95 .... TPO'Shea 5 100
(P A Blockley) *led: rdn along 2f out: drvn and hdd 1f out: one pce ins last* **9/2**[3]
3502 **4** *4* **Pacific Pride**[15] 4682 3-8-11 99 ....(b) TomEaves 6 90
(J Howard Johnson) *hld up: hdwy to chse ldrs over 2f out: rdn wl over 1f out and wknd appr last* **9/1**
1650 **5** *5* **Dingaan (IRE)**[76] 2774 3-8-11 90 .... StephenDonohoe(3) 1 80
(A M Balding) *s.i.s: a rr* **16/1**
4300 **6** *5* **Chief Commander (FR)**[13] 4740 3-9-0 100 .... NCallan 3 67
(Jane Chapple-Hyam) *chsd ldrs: rdn along 3f out: outpcd fr 2f out* **40/1**

1m 25.95s (-3.25) **Going Correction** -0.30s/f (Firm) course record **6** Ran SP% **116.1**
Speed ratings (Par 105):106,103,102,98,92 86
CSF £3.83 TOTE £1.80: £1.20, £1.70; EX 4.50.
Owner Saleh Al Homaizi & Imad Al Sagar **Bred** C R Mason **Trained** Newmarket, Suffolk

FOCUS
A very decent conditions race dominated by two of the classiest horses, and the form seems sound. The first three were nicely clear of the fourth, and should be capable of holding their own next time.

NOTEBOOK
Aeroplane, taking a big step down in class after contesting the Group 1 St James's Palace Stakes last time, has always looked a decent sort and his only modest effort when holding a realistic chance came on soft ground, although he was far from disgraced on it. Tracking Come Out Fighting from the off, he was produced with his effort just over a furlong from home and quickened away from his rivals in useful style. A Group 3 is within his compass. (op 10-11 tchd 4-5, tchd evens in places)
Dickensian(IRE), with a tongue tie and visor fitted for the first time, had not been seen since down the field in last season's Horris Hill Stakes, a race he was made one of the joint favourites for. Not far behind Araafa in that race, he was no match for Aeroplane when that rival quickened, and also looked a touch unwilling after getting a smack with the whip. The winner is smart on his day and he probably had little chance against a race-fit rival, so he can be given a chance to go one better next time if tried in similar company. (op 10-3 tchd 7-2 and 11-4)
Come Out Fighting has taken his racing well during the season, establishing himself as a very useful handicapper in the process. Those efforts had come over five and six furlongs, but the seventh furlong did not appear to be a problem and should give connections more options. (op 6-1)
Pacific Pride returned to form on his latest start after having the blinkers fitted for the first time. With the headgear retained, he was a bit keen early and failed to get home after looking threatening three furlongs from home. (op 7-1)
Dingaan(IRE), rested since a mid-field finish in the Britannia Stakes at Royal Ascot, was slowly away and never got involved at any stage of the race. He certainly did not run like a horse about to win next time, even if returned to an all-weather surface. (op 20-1 tchd 22-1)
Chief Commander(FR) continued his worrying trend of finishing last. He was beaten a long way from home and has lost his form badly. (op 28-1)

5117 STEVE NELLIS H'CAP 6f
4:50 (4:52) (Class 4) (0-85,83) 3-Y-O+ **£5,829** (£1,734; £866; £432) **Stalls** Low

Form RPR
0500 **1** **Paris Bell**[9] 4885 4-8-10 **73** .... PaulQuinn 10 83
(T D Easterby) *towards rr: hdwy on outer wl over 2f out: rdn wl over 1f out: styd on ins last to ld last 100 yds* **20/1**
5300 **2** *½* **Sir Nod**[9] 4885 4-8-12 **75** .... TomEaves 5 83
(Miss J A Camacho) *trckd ldrs: smooth prog wl over 2f out: rdn to ld wl over 1f out: drvn ent last: hdd and no ex last 100 yds* **9/2**[2]
04-0 **3** *¾* **Foreign Edition (IRE)**[15] 4682 4-9-3 **80** .... DavidAllan 6 86
(Miss J A Camacho) *hld up towards rr: hdwy 1/2-way: rdn along and sltly outpcd 2f out: styd on wl u.p ins last* **25/1**
0340 **4** *½* **Balakiref**[9] 4885 7-9-0 **77** .... PhillipMakin 7 81
(M Dods) *dwlt and bhd: hdwy and rdn along over 2f out: styd on u.p ins last: nrst fin* **10/1**
3125 **5** *hd* **Aahgowangowan (IRE)**[6] 4952 7-8-10 **78** ....(t) LiamJones(5) 13 82
(M Dods) *sn led: rdn and qcknd 2f out: drvn and hdd wl over 1f out: wknd ins last* **9/1**
1414 **6** *nk* **River Kirov (IRE)**[23] 4422 3-9-0 **79** .... AdrianMcCarthy 14 82
(P W Chapple-Hyam) *dwlt: sn cl up: chsd ldr 1/2-way: rdn 2f out: drvn and one pce ent last* **11/2**[3]
1050 **7** *½* **Digital**[9] 4885 9-8-12 **75** .... TonyCulhane 3 76+
(M R Channon) *rr: hdwy on inner wl over 1f out: rdn and kpt on ins last* **14/1**
0400 **8** *1 ¾* **Hidden Dragon (USA)**[11] 4807 7-9-3 **80** .... DeanMcKeown 4 76
(J Pearce) *in toucxh: effrt and hdwy over 2f out: sn rdn and wknd over 1f out* **20/1**
403 **9** *1* **Blackheath (IRE)**[10] 4834 10-8-9 **72** .... JoeFanning 11 65
(D Nicholls) *prom: n.m.r bnd after 2f: rdn along 2f out: sn wknd* **14/1**
0233 **10** *hd* **Raymond's Pride**[67] 3069 6-9-6 **83** ....(b) NCallan 8 75
(K A Ryan) *chsd ldrs: n.m.r bnd after 2f: rdn along 2f out and grad wknd* **8/1**
036- **11** *shd* **Anchor Date**[300] 6302 4-8-8 **74** ....(t) PatrickMathers(3) 1 66
(D Shaw) *a towards rr* **40/1**
1025 **12** *1* **Steel Blue**[15] 4682 6-9-5 **82** .... HayleyTurner 2 71+
(R M Whitaker) *chsd ldrs on inner: ridden along wl over 2f out: sn wknd* **7/2**[1]

1m 13.48s (-2.62) **Going Correction** -0.30s/f (Firm)
WFA 3 from 4yo+ 2lb **12** Ran SP% **115.1**
Speed ratings (Par 105):105,104,103,102,102 102,101,99,97,97 97,95
CSF £100.92 CT £2281.87 TOTE £20.60: £5.30, £2.00, £10.10; EX 127.20 TRIFECTA Not won. Place 6 £11.68, Place 5 £4.56.

Owner Ryedale Partners No 8 **Bred** M H Easterby **Trained** Great Habton, N Yorks
FOCUS
A decent sprint handicap run at a good tempo. The form looks sound and should work out.
Anchor Date Official explanation: jockey said colt was denied a clear run
Steel Blue Official explanation: jockey said gelding was denied a clear run
T/Plt: £22.50 to a £1 stake. Pool: £47,709.90. 1,541.90 winning tickets. T/Qpdt: £11.30 to a £1 stake. Pool: £3,158.80. 205.70 winning tickets. JR

5118 - 5121a (Foreign Racing) - See Raceform Interactive

4979 CHANTILLY (R-H)
Wednesday, September 6

OFFICIAL GOING: Good

5122a PRIX D'ARENBERG (GROUP 3) — 5f 110y
1:15 (1:13) 2-Y-O **£27,586** (£11,034; £8,276; £5,517; £2,759)

RPR
1 **Beauty Is Truth**[17] [4644] 2-8-8 ....(b) TThulliez 4 — 108+
(Robert Collet, France) *made virtually all, pulled hard early, quickened clear 2f out, ridden over 1f out, ran on strongly* **81/10[3]**
2 *3* **Iron Lips**[18] [4621] 2-8-8 .... OPeslier 6 — 98
(C Laffon-Parias, France) *held up in rear, headway down outside from 2f out, stayed on to take 2nd close home* **11/1**
3 *nk* **Beta**[24] [4415] 2-8-8 .... TGillet 8 — 97
(J E Pease, France) *prominent on outside, went 2nd well over 1f out, soon ridden and no impression on winner, lost 2nd close home* **18/10[2]**
4 *2 ½* **Numerieus (FR)**[22] [4464] 2-8-8 .... CSoumillon 3 — 89
(Y De Nicolay, France) *held up, switched left and effort 2f out, ridden and stayed on final f to take 4th close home* **6/5[1]**
5 *½* **Jailamigraine (IRE)**[22] [4464] 2-8-8 .... C-PLemaire 1 — 87
(P Bary, France) *prominent on inside, went 2nd briefly over 1 1/2f out, one pace, lost 4th close home* **10/1**
6 *1* **Maka (FR)**[22] [4464] 2-8-8 .... JVictoire 7 — 84
(F Cohen, France) *held up in rear, switched to inside and effort 2f out, no impression* **18/1**
7 *½* **Princess Georgina**[43] [3822] 2-8-8 .... J-PGuillambert 2 — 82
(S C Williams) *tracked leaders til one pace final 2f* **28/1**
8 *6* **Funny World (FR)** 2-8-11 ....(b) DBoeuf 5 — 65
(P Khozian, France) *prominent til weakened 2f out* **14/1**

63.80 secs — 8 Ran SP% **125.0**
PARI-MUTUEL: WIN 9.10; PL 2.40, 3.10, 1.30; DF 30.40.
Owner R C Strauss **Bred** Kilfrush Stud **Trained** Chantilly, France

NOTEBOOK
Beauty Is Truth, smartly into her stride, was quite free early on before settling down. She took control a furlong and a half out and then totally outclassed her rivals, really appreciating the good ground. The Cheveley Park Stakes at Newmarket is next on the agenda.
Iron Lips, held up in the early stages, made her challenge from one and a half out away from the rails. She ran on well but never looked likely to peg back the winner and a longer trip may suit better.
Beta, quickly into her stride, was fifth at the halfway stage before running on at the one pace during the final furlong and a half.
Numerieus(FR) was a disappointing favourite and did not run up to her best. She still had plenty to do at the halfway stage but did run on inside the final furlong and is another who might appreciate a longer distance.
Princess Georgina, settled just behind the leaders, was still there at the halfway stage but was totally outpaced from the two-furlong marker. Her connections felt that the ground was a little tacky.

4980 CHEPSTOW (L-H)
Thursday, September 7

OFFICIAL GOING: Good
Wind: nil

5125 EUROPEAN BREEDERS FUND/WATERAID SILVER CELEBRATION MAIDEN STKS — 7f 16y
2:00 (2:01) (Class 5) 2-Y-O **£3,886** (£1,156; £577; £288) **Stalls** High

Form — RPR
2 — 1 **Amazing Request**[19] [4597] 2-9-3 .... RichardHughes 7 — 84
(R Charlton) *trckd ldrs: rdn over 1f out: styd on u.p to ld fnl 110yds* **8/11[1]**
2 *nk* **Colorado Rapid (IRE)** 2-9-0 .... GregFairley(3) 5 — 83
(M Johnston) *chsd ldrs tl slt ld ins fnl 4f: kpt on u.p over 1f out: hdd and outpcd fnl 110yds* **12/1[3]**
2036 — 3 *2* **Goodbye Cash (IRE)**[12] [4824] 2-8-12 75.... RichardMullen 6 — 73
(P D Evans) *led tl narrowly hdd ins fnl 4f: styd chsng ldrs: one ace fnl f* **16/1**
200 — 4 *½* **Romanov Dynasty (IRE)**[22] [4479] 2-9-3 76....(p) PatDobbs 13 — 77
(R Hannon) *s.i.s: bhd: hdwy 3f out: styd on fr over 1f out but nvr gng pce to rch ldrs* **12/1[3]**
00 — 5 *1 ¼* **Aegis (IRE)**[28] [4295] 2-9-3 .... EddieAhern 8 — 74
(B W Hills) *bhd: drvn along 3f out: hdwy over 1f out: styd on ins last but nvr gng pce to rch ldrs* **66/1**
4 — 6 *1* **Actodos (IRE)**[21] [4526] 2-9-3 .... RobertHavlin 12 — 71
(B R Millman) *bhd: hdwy 1/2-way: rdn over 1f out: hung lft and wknd ins last* **22/1**
0004 — 7 *2* **Venir Rouge**[47] [3726] 2-8-10 71.... JamesMillman(7) 11 — 66
(M Salaman) *chsd ldrs:pushed along over 2f out: wknd whn crossed jst ins last* **66/1**
0024 — 8 *3 ½* **Up In Arms (IRE)**[15] [4688] 2-9-3 75.... JimCrowley 3 — 57
(P Winkworth) *chsd ldrs: rdn over 2f out: wknd over 1f out* **33/1**
9 *nk* **Daweyrr (USA)** 2-9-3 .... MartinDwyer 4 — 57
(M P Tregoning) *bhd: pushed along 1/2-way: styd on cl home* **20/1**
5 — 10 *½* **Leptis Magna**[22] [4479] 2-9-3 .... SebSanders 9 — 55
(W J Knight) *bhd: sme hdwy over 2f out: nvr in contention and wknd fnl f* **16/1**
0 — 11 *1 ½* **Alittlebitleft (IRE)**[8] [4928] 2-9-3 .... FrancisNorton 10 — 52
(R Hannon) *chsd ldrs: wkng whn n.m.r over 2f out* **4/1[2]**
12 *hd* **Arthur's Edge** 2-9-3 .... FergusSweeney 2 — 51
(B Palling) *s.i.s: bhd: hdwy 1/2-way: wknd over 2f out* **100/1**
00 — 13 *1 ½* **Ceris Star (IRE)**[22] [4487] 2-9-3 .... SteveDrowne 1 — 47
(B R Millman) *slowly away: a bhd* **100/1**

1m 22.69s (-0.61) **Going Correction** -0.225s/f (Firm) — 13 Ran SP% **122.1**
Speed ratings (Par 95):94,93,91,90,89 88,85,81,81,81 79,79,77
CSF £10.96 TOTE £1.60: £1.10, £4.10, £3.00; EX 15.30.
Owner K Abdulla **Bred** Juddmonte Farms Ltd **Trained** Beckhampton, Wilts
FOCUS
A fair maiden likely to produce winners. The third ran to her improved Irish form but the proximity of the fifth strikes a note of caution.
NOTEBOOK
Amazing Request, a highly promising second on his debut at Newbury, shaped that day as though in need of a mile, but he just about got away with it at this distance on what is a galloping course and narrowly denied the highly rated runner-up. He is going to improve further for the step up to a mile and deserves a rise in class on the back of this, with middle distances likely to suit next season. (op 10-11)
Colorado Rapid(IRE) holds a host of big-race entries and the fact he was well supported throughout the morning suggested a big run was expected. He drifted back out on course, but knew his job and made them all go, kicking on inside the final quarter mile and nearly holding on. He was a couple of lengths clear of the third and, considering his trainer's juveniles usually benefit a good deal from their first runs, it is reasonable to expect him to win next time before being upped in grade. (op 8-1)
Goodbye Cash(IRE), who ran well in a six-furlong sales race at the Curragh last month, ran above market expectations on this step up in trip and stuck on well to hold on to a place having been on the pace for a long time. (op 14-1)
Romanov Dynasty(IRE) has the look of an exposed sort, but he ran a little better in the first-time cheekpieces and may find easier opportunities at nursery level. (tchd 14-1)
Aegis(IRE) ran his best race to date and the way he was going on at the finish points to him being one to look out for in nurseries. (op 40-1 tchd 80-1 in a place)
Actodos(IRE) travelled well to a point, but in the end was unable to build on his initial effort and the way he hung under pressure was disconcerting. (op 20-1)
Alittlebitleft(IRE), well supported in the market beforehand, was unable to build on a promising start at Lingfield last week and was already struggling when being squeezed for room. This was disappointing, but he will be qualified for handicaps after one more start. Official explanation: jockey said colt was short of room approaching 1f out (op 7-1 tchd 15-2)

5126 INDUSTRIAL PIPEWORK SERVICES SUPPORTING WATERAID MEDIAN AUCTION MAIDEN STKS — 1m 14y
2:30 (2:32) (Class 5) 2-Y-O **£3,238** (£963; £481; £240) **Stalls** High

Form — RPR
1 **Hearthstead Maison (IRE)** 2-9-3 .... MartinDwyer 3 — 81
(M Johnston) *w ldr tl led after 2f: pushed clr fr over 1f out: easily* **9/2[3]**
43 — 2 *2 ½* **Aaim To Prosper (IRE)**[10] [4867] 2-9-3 .... SteveDrowne 1 — 75
(M R Channon) *prom: chsd wnr 2f oit: sn hrd drvn and no imp but r.o wl for clr 2nd* **9/4[1]**
3 *5* **Prince Sabaah (IRE)** 2-9-3 .... RichardHughes 8 — 64
(R Hannon) *s.i.s: bhd: pushed along and hdwy whn n.m.r over 2f out: kpt on fnl f but nvr in contention w ldrs* **14/1**
4 *1 ½* **Horsley Wiz** 2-9-3 .... SebSanders 2 — 60
(E S McMahon) *mid-div: pushed along 1/2-way: hdwy over 2f out: nvr gng pce to rch ldrs and sn one pce* **66/1**
6 — 5 *1 ¼* **Patavian (IRE)**[19] [4592] 2-9-0 .... EdwardCreighton(3) 4 — 57
(M R Channon) *s.i.s: bhd: drvn along over 3f out: styd on fnl f but nvr in contntion* **12/1**
442 — 6 *¾* **Beech Games**[11] [4829] 2-9-3 .... RichardMullen 5 — 56
(E J O'Neill) *sn chsng ldrs: rdn 3f out: wknd ins fnl 2f* **9/2[3]**
0 — 7 *shd* **Allroundtheoutside**[10] [4895] 2-9-3 .... PaulDoe 7 — 55
(P R Chamings) *led 2f: styd pressing wnr tl wknd fr 2f out* **100/1**
8 *7* **Citrus Chief (USA)** 2-9-3 .... AdrianMcCarthy 9 — 39
(R A Harris) *chsd ldrs over 5f* **50/1**
9 *1* **Whaxaar (IRE)** 2-9-3 .... PatDobbs 10 — 37
(S Kirk) *slowly away: a bhd* **50/1**
10 *6* **Petara Bay (IRE)** 2-9-3 .... IanMongan 11 — 23
(T G Mills) *broke wl: sn rdn and wl bhd after 2f* **3/1[2]**
0 — 11 *34* **Almudo (IRE)**[10] [4867] 2-9-3 .... FergusSweeney 6 — —
(B Palling) *chsd ldrs to 1/2-way: virtually p.u fnl f and dismntd after line* **200/1**

1m 33.84s (-2.16) **Going Correction** -0.225s/f (Firm) — 11 Ran SP% **113.4**
Speed ratings (Par 95):101,98,93,92,90 90,89,82,81,75 41
CSF £14.39 TOTE £4.80: £2.00, £1.40, £3.10; EX 20.30.
Owner Hearthstead Homes Ltd **Bred** T Nakata **Trained** Middleham Moor, N Yorks
FOCUS
A decent maiden in which the front two drew clear and the form could rate a bit higher. The likes of the seventh temper enthusiasm, however.
NOTEBOOK
Hearthstead Maison(IRE), a Derby entrant, gained compensation for a stable whose runner was narrowly touched off in the first race and ran out a ready winner from the favourite. Prominent throughout, he picked up well when asked to stretch and had it in the bag well over a furlong out. He will stay further in time, but looks happy at this distance for the moment and is one to keep onside. (op 6-1 tchd 4-1)
Aaim To Prosper(IRE), not beaten far over this course and distance last week, again ran his race but found the newcomer too good on the day. He is now qualified for a handicap mark, but connections may want to get a win into him first, which should not prove too difficult on this evidence. (op 3-1)
Prince Sabaah(IRE) ◆, whose stable introduced two debutants to score over course and distance last week, like that pair showed distinct signs of inexperience early, but he kept on nicely once he grasped what was required of him, albeit not being able to get close to the front pair. This was a most promising start and the son of Spectrum should win his maiden, with progression anticipated. (op 20-1)
Horsley Wiz, who cost just 800gns, ran way above expectations in what was a decent maiden, finishing to quite good effect, and it will be interesting to see if/how he progresses, with easier opportunities likely to come his way. (op 40-1)
Patavian(IRE) failed to build on a promising debut behind a couple of useful sorts at Newbury and does not look blessed with a lot of natural pace. That said, he is likely to be seen to much better effect once handicapping, especially over further. (op 14-1 tchd 20-1)
Beech Games looked certain to be thereabouts, whilst looking highly vulnerable at the same time, but he dropped away tamely and may be regressing. (op 7-2 tchd 6-1)
Petara Bay(IRE), a 340,000gns relation to Percussionist amongst others, was made second favourite on the basis of a strong home reputation and entries in both the Group 2 Royal Lodge and Group 1 Racing Post Trophy this season, but having got away well from the stalls, he soon began to backtrack and was disputing last after a quarter of a mile. He is evidently thought to be a good deal better than this, but has a bit to prove now. Official explanation: jockey said colt ran very green (op 2-1)

5127 WATERAID IN WALES INDIA LINK (S) STKS — 1m 2f 36y
3:05 (3:06) (Class 6) 3-Y-O+ **£2,266** (£674; £337; £168) **Stalls** Low

Form — RPR
640/ — 1 **Alasil (USA)**[206] [5543] 6-9-0 74.... LiamJones(5) 3 — 51
(R J Price) *chsd ldrs: led over 1f out: rdn out* **14/1**
0200 — 2 *1* **Emperor Cat (IRE)**[28] [4285] 5-9-2 45.... EdwardCreighton(3) 7 — 49
(Mrs N S Evans) *bhd: hdwy over 3f out: n.m.r 2f out: styd on u.p to go 2nd fnl f: kpt on but nt rch wnr* **33/1**

25 **3** 2 **No Recollection (IRE)**[15] 4700 3-8-12 63......................(p) EddieAhern 8 45
(M J Wallace) *trckd ldrs: n.m.r on ins fr over 2f out: rdn and kpt on fnl f but no imp cl home* **5/2**[2]

1402 **4** 1 1/4 **Factual Lad**[6] 4982 8-9-3 59.. JamesMillman(7) 5 48
(B R Millman) *mid-div: drvn and hdwy over 2f out: kpt on fnl f but nt rch ldrs* **2/1**[1]

6000 **5** 2 1/2 **Viscount Rossini**[29] 4266 4-9-5 33..........................(v[1]) FrancisNorton 14 38
(A W Carroll) *bhd: hdwy over 5f out: chsd ldrs and rdn 3f out: one pce fnl 2f* **50/1**

00/0 **6** 3/4 **Over Tipsy**[26] 4363 4-9-5 43.. RichardHughes 2 37
(R Hannon) *w ldr 3f: styd cl 2nd tl rdn to ld 2f out: hdd over 1f out: sn btn* **16/1**

0030 **7** 1 1/4 **Weet A Head (IRE)**[10] 4869 5-9-5 54......................(b[1]) FergusSweeney 1 34
(R Hollinshead) *s.i.s: sn in tch: lost pl over 5f out: styng on whn n.m.r 2f out: n.d after* **9/1**

000 **8** nk **Littleton Aldor (IRE)**[2] 5097 6-9-5 .... AlanDaly 4 34
(W G M Turner) *slowly away: bhd: rn wd into st 5f out: kpt on fr over 1f out but nvr in contention* **80/1**

005 **9** 2 1/2 **Primed Up (IRE)**[13] 4755 4-9-10 48..............................(b) SebSanders 12 34
(R M Beckett) *bhd: hdwy on outside fr 5f out: effrt over 3f out: nt rch ldrs and sn wknd* **8/1**[3]

0 **10** 1 **Nahlass**[23] 3647 3-8-4 .... JamesDoyle(3) 16 22
(Ms J S Doyle) *chsd ldrs to 4f out: sn rdn: wknd qckly over 2f out* **50/1**

0000 **11** 1 **King's College (USA)**[10] 4868 3-8-5 47...................(v) JamieJones(7) 15 25
(P D Evans) *led: rdn 3f out: hdd & wknd qckly 2f out* **33/1**

0000 **12** 2 **Smoking Star**[19] 4585 3-8-2 46.. NicolPolli(5) 13 16
(N I M Rossiter) *sn bhd* **100/1**

00-0 **13** 6 **Owners Biscuits**[9] 4909 3-8-7 51...................................... MartinDwyer 6 5
(M Johnston) *sn bhd* **12/1**

5-5U **14** 1 1/4 **Zastra's Pride**[22] 4491 3-8-0 35.............................(t) JackDean(7) 10 3
(W G M Turner) *broke wl: sn bhd* **100/1**

2m 9.95s (0.05) **Going Correction** -0.225s/f (Firm)
WFA 3 from 4yo+ 7lb **14** Ran SP% **116.3**
Speed ratings (Par 101):90,89,87,86,84 84,83,82,80,79 79,77,72,71
CSF £405.67 TOTE £16.90: £3.30, £6.50, £1.70; EX 283.40.There was no bid for the winner. No Recollection (no.11) was claimed by K Goldsworthy for £10,000
Owner Glyn Byard **Bred** Shadwell Farm Inc **Trained** Ullingswick, H'fords

FOCUS
A poor seller, the form anchored by the runner-up and fifth.
Nahlass Official explanation: jockey said filly ran very green

5128 DANIEL MAIDEN STKS 1m 4f 23y
3:35 (3:38) (Class 5) 3-Y-O **£3,238** (£963; £481; £240) **Stalls** Low

Form RPR

4405 **1** **Island Myth (IRE)**[13] 4778 3-9-3 76..............................(b) MartinDwyer 7 72
(M P Tregoning) *trckd ldrs: wnt 2nd 5f out: chal 3f out tl rdn to ld ins fnl 2f: readily* **11/4**[2]

33 **2** 1 1/2 **Moonshadow**[94] 2292 3-8-12 .... EddieAhern 8 65
(H R A Cecil) *led after 1f: rdn 3f out: hdd ins fnl 2f: styd on same pce ins last* **7/4**[1]

3425 **3** 1/2 **Sybella**[54] 3539 3-8-12 78.. IanMongan 4 64
(J L Dunlop) *t.k.h: rr: hdwy 5f out: styd on under prssure fr over 1f out and r.o ins last: nt rch ldrs* **5/1**

-320 **4** 1 1/4 **Montjeu Man**[45] 3794 3-9-3 77.. RichardMullen 1 67
(E A L Dunlop) *in tch: hdwy 4f out: styd on ame pce fnl 2f* **7/2**[3]

-440 **5** 3 **Newport Boy (IRE)**[68] 3075 3-9-3 60.......................... AdrianMcCarthy 2 62
(R A Harris) *chsd ldrs: rdn 4f out: wknd fr 2f out* **25/1**

0 **6** 2 1/2 **Jupiters Moon (IRE)**[18] 4625 3-9-0 .... RichardKingscote(3) 9 58
(R Charlton) *t.k.h: led 1f: styd chsng ldr tl rn wd bnd 5f out: sn rdn: wknd 2f out* **20/1**

00 **7** 15 **Peachy Pear**[6] 4981 3-8-9 .... EdwardCreighton(3) 3 29
(Mrs L J Young) *uns rdr bef s: bhd: hday 5f out: sn wknd* **150/1**

0 **8** 49 **Raratomba**[10] 4899 3-9-3 .... PatDobbs 5 —
(P D Evans) *unruly paddock: mounted on crse: a bhd: lost tch 5f out: t.o* **100/1**

2m 36.1s (-2.62) **Going Correction** -0.225s/f (Firm) **8** Ran SP% **112.2**
Speed ratings (Par 101):99,98,97,96,94 93,83,50
CSF £7.59 TOTE £3.60: £1.20, £1.10, £1.70; EX 9.30.
Owner R C C Villers **Bred** Mrs A M Upsdell **Trained** Lambourn, Berks

FOCUS
As is to be expected for the time of year, a very ordinary maiden. The fifth anchors the form.
Jupiters Moon(IRE) Official explanation: jockey said colt ran too free

5129 WATER FOR LIFE H'CAP 1m 2f 36y
4:10 (4:10) (Class 6) (0-65,68) 3-Y-O **£2,590** (£770; £385; £192) **Stalls** Low

Form RPR

-006 **1** **Royal Premier (IRE)**[100] 2102 3-8-8 54 ow4.............(v) MickyFenton 16 61
(H J Collingridge) *chsd ldrs: chal fr 3f out tl drvn to ld over 1f out: kpet on wl u.p* **25/1**

2546 **2** 1 1/4 **Siakira**[11] 4836 3-9-1 64.. JamesDoyle(3) 6 69
(I A Wood) *bhd: stdy hdwy fr 3f out: styd on to take 2nd nr fin but a hld by wnr* **15/2**

3000 **3** 1 **Khyber Knight (IRE)**[3] 5054 3-8-1 50................... EdwardCreighton(3) 5 53
(Jane Southcombe) *sn led: rdn fr3f out and kpt slt advantage tl hdd over 1f out: styd on same pce and lost 2nd nr fin* **33/1**

1004 **4** 1/2 **Leamington Lad (IRE)**[39] 3977 3-9-2 62...................... SteveDrowne 3 64
(J A Geake) *keen hold: in tch: hdwy whn n.m.r 2f out: styd on again fnl f but nvr gng pce to rch ldrs* **9/2**[2]

2620 **5** 3 **Gigs Magic (USA)**[17] 4651 3-8-7 53............................ MartinDwyer 12 49
(M Johnston) *in tch: hdwy whn n.m.r 2f out: sn shkn up and no imp on ldrs* **7/1**[3]

1142 **6** 6 **River Logic (IRE)**[17] 4651 3-9-2 62................ SilvestreDeSousa 1 47
(A D Brown) *chsd ldrs: rdn fr 3f out: wknd 2f out* **3/1**[1]

614 **7** nk **Pothos Way (GR)**[15] 4700 3-9-4 64................................ JimCrowley 8 48
(P R Chamings) *w ldrs early: rdn to chal 3f out: wknd ins fnl 2f* **8/1**

0400 **8** 2 **Mr Wiseguy**[17] 4662 3-9-4 64.. EddieAhern 9 45
(G C Bravery) *chsd ldrs: rdn and one pce whn n.m.r 2f out: sn btn* **16/1**

300 **9** 2 **Lynford Lady**[135] 1221 3-8-7 53............................... FergusSweeney 15 30
(D J S Ffrench Davis) *s.i.s: a in rr* **20/1**

00-4 **10** 14 **Qik Dip (IRE)**[45] 3798 3-9-1 61.................................. RichardMullen 13 11
(P D Evans) *bhd: brief effrt over 3f out: neever dangerous and sn wknd* **10/1**

0000 **11** 5 **Super Frank (IRE)**[29] 4245 3-8-8 54 ow1.................... RichardHughes 4 —
(G A Butler) *prom early: dropped rr 6f out: n.d after* **10/1**

0000 **12** 1 1/4 **Charles Street Lad (IRE)**[15] 4690 3-8-5 51 oh5 ow1(t) StephenCarson 11 —
(M R Bosley) *bhd: hdwy 5f out: wknd qckly over 3f out* **100/1**

2m 8.83s (-1.07) **Going Correction** -0.225s/f (Firm) **12** Ran SP% **115.2**
Speed ratings (Par 99):95,94,93,92,90 85,85,83,82,70 66,65
CSF £191.84 CT £6093.68 TOTE £29.90: £8.40, £2.30, £6.60; EX 395.50.
Owner Maynard Durrant Partnership I **Bred** Mrs Anne Hughes **Trained** Exning, Suffolk

FOCUS
A moderate handicap in which the winner and third have far-from-solid profiles.
Royal Premier(IRE) Official explanation: trainer said, regarding the improved form shown, the colt had benefited from today's strong riding

5130 DANIEL SUPPORTS WATERAID H'CAP 1m 14y
4:40 (4:42) (Class 6) (0-65,68) 3-Y-0+ **£2,590** (£770; £385; £192) **Stalls** High

Form RPR

5032 **1** **Lockstock (IRE)**[6] 4983 8-9-0 56..................................(p) JimCrowley 3 66
(M S Saunders) *trckd ldrs: chal over 2f out tl led over 1f out: drvn out* **9/1**

1556 **2** 1 1/4 **Nashaab (USA)**[10] 4871 9-9-9 65..............................(v) SteveDrowne 14 72
(P D Evans) *slowly away: bhd: rdn along 3f out: str run on stands rail over 1f out: fin wl: nt rch wnr* **22/1**

0424 **3** nk **Elidore**[6] 4983 6-9-2 58.. FergusSweeney 2 64
(B Palling) *sn led: rdn whn chal fr over 3f out: heded over 1f out: kpt on same pce ins last* **12/1**

-521 **4** 1 **Veiled Applause**[10] 4871 3-9-7 68 6ex............................ SebSanders 13 71+
(R M Beckett) *racd alone stands side tl rdn and edgd to centre crse fr 2f out: kpt on ins last but nvr gng pce to chal* **9/4**[1]

0023 **5** hd **Tiber Tiger (IRE)**[23] 4456 6-9-4 63..........................(b) JamesDoyle(3) 1 66
(N P Littmoden) *bhd: rdn over 2f out: hdwy over 1f out: kpt on ins last but nvr gng pce to rch ldrs* **15/2**[3]

0242 **6** hd **Unlimited**[10] 4870 4-9-3 59.. RobertHavlin 12 62
(R Simpson) *chsd ldrs: rdn over 2f out: wknd ins last* **14/1**

1030 **7** 1/2 **What-A-Dancer (IRE)**[10] 4871 9-9-0 63.....................(b) TolleyDean(7) 5 65
(R A Harris) *chsd ldrs: rdn 3f out: one pce fnl 2f* **33/1**

5421 **8** 3/4 **Tuscarora (IRE)**[18] 4627 7-9-6 62.............................. FrancisNorton 11 62
(A W Carroll) *bhd: hdwy 2f out: styng on whn hmpd ins last: nt rcvr* **14/1**

5015 **9** 1 1/2 **Gallego**[53] 3566 4-9-3 64.. LiamJones(5) 6 60
(R J Price) *s.i.s: bhd: rdn along 1/2-way: styd on fr over 1f out: nvr in contention* **14/1**

-002 **10** nk **Sincerely**[20] 4557 4-9-4 60.. EddieAhern 15 56
(B W Hills) *pressed ldr: rdn over 2f out: wknd ins last* **10/1**

0620 **11** nk **Emotive**[15] 4700 3-9-4 65.. MickyFenton 7 59
(I A Wood) *chsd ldrs: rdn 2f oiut: wkng whn hmpd ins last* **50/1**

5354 **12** 2 1/2 **Blu Manruna**[19] 4591 3-9-0 61..(p) PaulDoe 16 49
(J Akehurst) *rr: neever gng pce to be competitive* **16/1**

0/56 **13** nk **Johannian**[28] 4288 8-9-2 65...................................... BarrySavage(7) 10 54
(J M Bradley) *bhd: effrt 3f out: n.d and sn bhd* **66/1**

1464 **14** 1 **Pleasing**[17] 4660 3-9-3 64.. MartinDwyer 9 49
(J L Dunlop) *chsd ldrs: rdn over 2f out: sn wknd* **7/1**[2]

0-00 **15** 17 **Sakabula (USA)**[39] 3977 3-9-2 63................................ RichardMullen 8 9
(G C Bravery) *early spd: bhd fr 1/2-way* **100/1**

1m 33.2s (-2.80) **Going Correction** -0.225s/f (Firm)
WFA 3 from 4yo+ 5lb **15** Ran SP% **119.4**
Speed ratings (Par 101):105,103,103,102,102 102,101,100,99,99 98,96,95,94,77
CSF £201.14 CT £2425.72 TOTE £13.40: £4.00, £6.40, £4.20; EX 340.00.
Owner Chris Scott **Bred** W H Joyce **Trained** Green Ore, Somerset

FOCUS
A moderate but competitive handicap. Sound form, the first four and the seventh all having run in the same course-and-distance race ten days earlier.
Tiber Tiger(IRE) Official explanation: jockey said gelding hung both ways
Sincerely Official explanation: jockey said filly ran too free
Pleasing Official explanation: jockey said filly lost its action
Sakabula(USA) Official explanation: jockey said filly bled from the nose

5131 WATERAID WELSH PARTNERSHIP H'CAP 5f 16y
5:10 (5:11) (Class 6) (0-65,64) 3-Y-0+ **£2,461** (£732; £365; £182) **Stalls** High

Form RPR

3343 **1** **Stamford Blue**[6] 4985 5-8-8 60..................................(b) TolleyDean(7) 4 69
(R A Harris) *in tch: hdwy fr 2f out: str run to ld ins last: hld on wl* **11/2**[2]

0012 **2** hd **Carcinetto (IRE)**[30] 4223 4-8-5 50 oh4.......................... RichardMullen 3 58
(P D Evans) *pressed ldrs: drvn and slt ld 1f out: sn hdd: styd chalng tl no ex last strides* **9/1**

0051 **3** 1 1/2 **Cerulean Rose**[13] 4780 7-9-1 60.................................. FrancisNorton 5 63
(A W Carroll) *chsd ldrs: rdn over 2f out: kpt on same pce ins last* **5/1**[1]

4256 **4** 1/2 **King Egbert (FR)**[10] 4872 5-8-10 55............................ RichardHughes 1 56
(A W Carroll) *chsd ldrs: rdn and effrt over 1f out: nvr gng pce to rch ldrs* **5/1**[1]

0006 **5** hd **Indian Lady (IRE)**[15] 4690 3-8-8 54 ow1....................(b) MickyFenton 11 54
(Mrs A L M King) *w ldr tl slt advantage fr over 2f tl hdd 1f out: wknd ins last* **40/1**

1650 **6** nk **Ballybunion (IRE)**[6] 4985 7-8-8 56...................... RichardKingscote(3) 13 55
(R A Harris) *w ldrs: chal 1/2-way tl over 1f out: wknd ins last* **12/1**

0051 **7** 1/2 **Meikle Barfil**[7] 4962 4-9-2 61 6ex............................(p) SteveDrowne 10 58
(J M Bradley) *bhd: rdn and hdwy over 1f out: no imp on ldrs ins last* **11/2**[2]

6023 **8** 3/4 **Diamond Katie (IRE)**[17] 4655 4-8-7 52................................ KimTinkler 14 47
(N Tinkler) *in tch: pushed along 1/2-way: nvr gng pce to trble ldrs* **8/1**[3]

0000 **9** nk **Valiant Romeo**[51] 3608 6-8-2 50 oh5.........................(p) SaleemGolam(3) 8 44
(R Bastiman) *slt ld tl narrowly hdd over 2f out: wknd ins last* **25/1**

3056 **10** 1/2 **Convince (USA)**[11] 4846 5-8-12 64................................ BarrySavage(7) 9 56
(J M Bradley) *chsd ldrs: rdn 1/2-way: wknd over 1f out* **16/1**

0106 **11** 1/2 **Whistler**[7] 4962 9-9-1 60..(b) PaulFitzsimons 15 50
(Miss J R Tooth) *slowly inrto stride: bhd: sme hdwy ins last* **16/1**

4020 **12** nk **Mostanad**[6] 4985 4-8-5 50.. EddieAhern 12 39
(J M Bradley) *chsd ldrs over 3f* **14/1**

4060 **13** hd **Zimbali**[10] 4872 4-8-5 50 oh3.. JosedeSouza 16 38
(J M Bradley) *racd along stands side: nvr gng pce to rch ldrs* **33/1**

6040 **14** 7 **Watch Out Jess**[60] 3340 3-8-1 50 oh2.................... EdwardCreighton(3) 7 13
(M Madgwick) *a outpcd* **100/1**

58.05 secs (-1.55) **Going Correction** -0.225s/f (Firm)
WFA 3 from 4yo+ 1lb **14** Ran SP% **121.6**
Speed ratings (Par 101):103,102,100,99,99 98,97,96,96,95 94,94,93,82
CSF £53.62 CT £221.86 TOTE £7.50: £2.40, £3.30, £2.60; EX 108.10 Place 6 £571.15, Place 5 £389.12.
Owner Brian Hicks **Bred** Mrs Wendy Miller **Trained** Earlswood, Monmouths

FOCUS
A moderate sprint handicap. Pretty ordinary form, the winner rated to the mark of his June course win.

T/Jkpt: Not won. T/Plt: £1,110.90 to a £1 stake. Pool: £63,765.85. 41.90 winning tickets. T/Qpdt: £380.00 to a £1 stake. Pool: £4,366.00. 8.50 winning tickets. ST

5009 HAYDOCK (L-H)

Thursday, September 7

OFFICIAL GOING: Heavy

Wind: almost nil

5132 GLASS AGE H'CAP — 1m 3f 200y

2:20 (2:21) (Class 5) (0-75,75) 4-Y-0+ **£5,505** (£1,637; £818; £408) **Stalls** High

Form — RPR

3041 **1** **Leslingtaylor (IRE)**[8] 4924 4-8-4 **68** 6ex.......... SladeO'Hara(7) 4 — 81
(J J Quinn) *chsd ldrs: wnt 2nd over 3f out: led over 2f out: clr over 1f out: styd on wl* **5/2**[2]

1010 **2** *8* **Oddsmaker (IRE)**[23] 4448 5-9-0 **71**..........(t) DeanMcKeown 3 — 73
(M A Barnes) *led: rdn and hdd over 2f out: sn btn* **2/1**[1]

04 **3** *1* **True Companion**[26] 4370 7-9-4 **75**.......... DarryllHolland 2 — 75
(N P Littmoden) *chsd ldr: pushed along 4f out: lost 2nd over 3f out: n.d after* **2/1**[1]

6-00 **4** *58* **Smart John**[10] 4900 6-8-9 **69**.......... PatrickMathers(3) 5 — —
(D Shaw) *s.s: bhd: sn pushed along: rdr dropped whip over 4f out: t.o* **8/1**[3]

2m 37.41s (2.42) **Going Correction** +0.325s/f (Good) 4 Ran SP% **106.3**
Speed ratings (Par 103):104,98,98,59
CSF £7.55 TOTE £3.30; EX 6.60.
Owner Derrick Bloy **Bred** Mrs Peggy Kelly **Trained** Settrington, N Yorks

FOCUS
A weakish handicap which saw the field trail home behind the in-form winner, who was posting a personal best.

5133 CLASSIC DOOR PANELS NURSERY — 6f

2:50 (2:51) (Class 3) (0-90,83) 2-Y-0 **£8,096** (£2,408; £1,203; £601) **Stalls** High

Form — RPR

1050 **1** **Prospect Place**[16] 4681 2-9-1 **77**.......... PhilipRobinson 6 — 84
(M Dods) *hld up: swtchd lft and hdwy wl over 1f out: led ent fnl f: r.o* **5/1**[3]

0453 **2** *1 ½* **Masai Moon**[13] 4774 2-8-12 **74**.......... GrahamGibbons 1 — 77
(B R Millman) *chsd ldrs: rdn over 2f out: ev ch 1f out: sn in 2nd: nt qckn wl ins fnl f* **10/1**

342 **3** *1* **Blithe**[20] 4552 2-9-2 **78**.......... DarryllHolland 7 — 81+
(W J Haggas) *trckd ldrs: nt clr run over 1f out: swtchd rt ins fnl f: styd on towards fin* **2/1**[2]

114 **4** *¾* **Eloquent Rose (IRE)**[99] 2125 2-9-7 **83**.......... TPO'Shea 5 — 80
(Mrs A Duffield) *led: rdn and hdd over 1f out: styd on same pce ins fnl f* **12/1**

413 **5** *hd* **First Mate (IRE)**[16] 4681 2-9-2 **78**.......... J-PGuillambert 3 — 75
(M Johnston) *a.p: rdn to ld over 1f out: hdd ent fnl f: kpt on same pce ins fnl f* **7/4**[1]

1430 **6** *1 ½* **Valley Of The Moon (IRE)**[16] 4681 2-8-13 **75**.......... TonyHamilton 4 — 67
(R A Fahey) *in tch: rdn over 1f out: btn fnl f* **16/1**

1m 16.85s (1.95) **Going Correction** +0.325s/f (Good) 6 Ran SP% **109.0**
Speed ratings (Par 99):100,98,96,95,95 93
CSF £46.67 TOTE £5.90: £2.70, £3.60; EX 60.80.
Owner A Mallen **Bred** Dragon's Stud **Trained** Denton, Co Durham

FOCUS
A fair nursery which was run at a sound pace in the taxing ground. The form may be worth treating with a little caution.

NOTEBOOK
Prospect Place found a trouble-free run on the outside of the pack and showed a neat turn of foot to score readily. He handles a soft surface well and this has to rate a personal-best display. (op 11-2 tchd 6-1)
Masai Moon held every chance and posted another solid effort in defeat. He clearly handles any ground, and does deserve to go one better, but looks weighted to around his best at present nevertheless. (op 14-1)
Blithe, making her handicap debut and dropped back in trip, endured a luckless passage when it mattered and has to rate better than the bare form. She had no trouble with this taxing surface, and clearly has the talent to open her account from this sort of mark, but is proving a little expensive to follow now. (op 7-4)
Eloquent Rose(IRE), fourth in the Hilary Needler last time in late-May from a low draw, had her chance from the front and just lacked the required pace at the business end of the race. This was a respectable effort under top weight on this first attempt over a sixth furlong and she probably needs a slightly quicker surface. (tchd 10-1 and 14-1)
First Mate(IRE) was found wanting nearing the two-furlong pole and has to rate disappointing. He ought to be seen in a better light again when returning to less taxing ground in the future. (tchd 2-1)

5134 RACINGUK.TV EBF MEDIAN AUCTION MAIDEN STKS — 7f 30y

3:25 (3:26) (Class 4) 2-Y-0 **£4,857** (£1,445; £722) **Stalls** Low

Form — RPR

2 **1** **Strobilus**[13] 4768 2-9-3.......... PhilipRobinson 1 — 81+
(M A Jarvis) *mde all: pushed out and r.o ins fnl f* **2/9**[1]

2 *2 ½* **Aureate** 2-9-3.......... KDarley 2 — 75+
(M Johnston) *racd in 2nd pl thrght: rdn and ev ch over 2f out: edgd lft ins fnl f: one pce* **4/1**[2]

3 *8* **Muree Queen** 2-8-5.......... RussellKennemore(7) 3 — 47
(R Hollinshead) *racd in last pl thrght: rdn 4f out: edgd lft and wknd over 2f out* **40/1**[3]

1m 34.72s (2.66) **Going Correction** +0.325s/f (Good) 3 Ran SP% **104.3**
Speed ratings (Par 97):97,94,85
CSF £1.31 TOTE £1.20; EX 1.30.
Owner Sheikh Mohammed **Bred** Darley **Trained** Newmarket, Suffolk

FOCUS
An interesting little juvenile maiden and the first two are both capable of rating better than they showed in this bad ground.

NOTEBOOK
Strobilus, runner-up in a warm maiden at Newmarket, made all to open his account at the second attempt and handled the testing ground without a fuss. He will get further, and looks the type to come into his own next year, but he clearly remains open to improvement this season and it will be interesting to see where he is pitched in next. (tchd 1-4 in places)
Aureate, who has plenty of stamina in his pedigree, proved a little free through the early parts and never looked like getting on terms with the winner. He still did enough to suggest he has talent, however, and should benefit for this debut experience. It may be that he is already in need of a mile. (tchd 7-2 and 9-2)
Muree Queen, a half-sister to a Group 3 winner in Germany, never posed a threat to the first pair and probably found this ground too testing. She can find easier assignments and is entitled to improve for the experience. (op 25-1)

5135 CERVOGLASS FORTUNE STKS (LISTED RACE) — 7f 30y

3:55 (3:56) (Class 1) 3-Y-0+

£17,034 (£6,456; £3,231; £1,611; £807; £405) **Stalls** Low

Form — RPR

0102 **1** **Quito (IRE)**[5] 5011 9-9-5 112..........(b) JimmyFortune 1 — 119
(D W Chapman) *s.i.s: hld up: hdwy over 1f out: sn rdn: edgd lft and led ins fnl f: r.o* **11/8**[1]

0010 **2** *nk* **Mine (IRE)**[40] 3926 8-9-2 108..........(v) DarryllHolland 4 — 115
(J D Bethell) *trckd ldrs: wnt 2nd and gng wl 2f out: rdn to ld jst ins fnl f and edgd lft: sn hdd: r.o* **11/2**

3015 **3** *5* **Dabbers Ridge (IRE)**[14] 4740 4-9-2 102.......... MichaelHills 6 — 102
(B W Hills) *w ldr: led over 3f out: rdn over 1f out: hdd jst ins fnl f: sn wknd* **7/2**[3]

-413 **4** *3* **Polar Ben**[33] 4145 7-9-2 109.......... OscarUrbina 5 — 94
(J R Fanshawe) *hld up: effrt over 2f out: edgd lft over 1f out: wknd fnl f* **3/1**[2]

3/50 **5** *3* **Campo Bueno (FR)**[6] 4988 4-9-2 90.......... TonyHamilton 7 — 87
(A Berry) *trckd ldrs: effrt over 2f out: edgd rt over 1f out: wknd fnl f* **100/1**

23-6 **6** *shd* **Black Charmer (IRE)**[10] 4896 3-8-12 110.......... KDarley 3 — 86
(M Johnston) *led: hdd over 3f out: sn rdn: wknd over 2f out* **25/1**

1m 33.62s (1.56) **Going Correction** +0.325s/f (Good)
WFA 3 from 4yo+ 4lb 6 Ran SP% **109.5**
Speed ratings (Par 111):104,103,97,94,91 90
CSF £9.07 TOTE £2.00: £1.30, £3.00; EX 10.50.
Owner Michael Hill **Bred** Sheikh Mohammed Bin Rashid Al Maktoum **Trained** Stillington, N Yorks

FOCUS
A decent race, rated through the winner, but the time was moderate. The first two came clear.

NOTEBOOK
Quito(IRE), who finished runner-up in the Group 1 Sprint Cup at this track five days previously, just did enough to get up and register a deserved success on this drop in class. He is clearly still very much in love with his racing, enjoys a deep surface, and his versatility as regards trip is a notable plus. This ultra-tough nine-year-old is now likely to turn out quickly in the Group 2 GNER Park Stakes at York. (op 6-4 tchd 13-8 in places)
Mine(IRE) showed his true colours on this return to Listed company and proved most game in defeat. He was clear of the remainder and really does deserve to win in this class. (op 7-1)
Dabbers Ridge(IRE) was found out passing the furlong-marker and was not disgraced at the weights. He acts well with cut, but this ground was probably too taxing for his own liking. (op 9-2)
Polar Ben could not quicken when push came to shove and proved a little disappointing on this return to softer ground. (op 9-4)
Black Charmer(IRE) has yet to convince that he is worthy of his current rating in two outings now as a three-year-old, but he does want better ground than this. (tchd 28-1)

5136 FLOAT GLASS INDUSTRIES H'CAP — 7f 30y

4:30 (4:31) (Class 5) (0-75,76) 3-Y-0+ **£3,886** (£1,156; £577; £288) **Stalls** Low

Form — RPR

6154 **1** **California Laws**[17] 4652 4-8-8 **61**.......... GrahamGibbons 10 — 76+
(T D Barron) *midfield: hdwy 3f out: nt clr run 2f out: swtchd rt and rdn over 1f out: led 1f out: sn edgd lft and r.o wl* **6/1**[2]

320 **2** *3 ½* **Logsdail**[12] 4795 6-9-3 **70**..........(p) OscarUrbina 2 — 75
(G L Moore) *hld up: rdn over 2f out: hdwy over 1f out: styd on to take 2nd post: no ch w wnr* **6/1**[2]

0402 **3** *shd* **Breaking Shadow (IRE)**[11] 4831 4-9-4 **71**.......... PhillipMakin 11 — 76
(T D Barron) *hld up in rr: rdn 3f out: hdwy over 1f out: styd on ins fnl f* **13/2**[3]

0001 **4** *nk* **Vanadium**[10] 4885 4-9-9 **76** 6ex.......... J-PGuillambert 1 — 80
(J G Given) *racd keenly: midfield: hdwy over 2f out: rdn and ev ch 1f out: kpt on same pce ins fnl f* **9/1**

0402 **5** *hd* **High Voltage**[17] 4655 5-8-10 **68**..........(t) AndrewElliott(5) 5 — 72
(K R Burke) *led: rdn 2f out: hdd 1f out: kpt on same pce ins fnl f* **20/1**

-505 **6** *2 ½* **Zhitomir**[17] 4655 8-8-12 **65**.......... DarryllHolland 3 — 62
(M Dods) *swtg: plld hrd: prom: rdn and ev ch over 2f out: wknd ent fnl f* **12/1**

202 **7** *2* **Wizard Of Us**[21] 4511 6-8-8 **61** oh4.......... PaulQuinn 12 — 53
(M Mullineaux) *swtg: trckd ldrs: rdn over 2f out: wkng whn n.m.r and hmpd over 1f out* **14/1**

365 **8** *shd* **Word Perfect**[19] 4610 4-8-9 **62**.......... DaleGibson 6 — 54
(M W Easterby) *prom: rdn over 2f out: wknd over 1f out* **8/1**

5060 **9** *¾* **Looks Could Kill (USA)**[13] 4760 4-9-8 **75**.......... KDarley 7 — 65
(E J Alston) *hld up: effrt whn nt clr run wl over 2f out: no imp* **13/2**[3]

0606 **10** *¾* **Harvest Warrior**[15] 4706 4-8-13 **66**.......... JimmyFortune 8 — 54
(T D Easterby) *towards rr: effrt 2f out: wknd over 1f out* **11/2**[1]

1m 33.44s (1.38) **Going Correction** +0.325s/f (Good) 10 Ran SP% **110.9**
Speed ratings (Par 103):105,101,100,100,100 97,95,95,94,93
CSF £39.38 CT £235.95 TOTE £6.20: £1.90, £2.20, £2.50; EX 57.10.
Owner Rupert Bear Racing **Bred** P Balding **Trained** Maunby, N Yorks

FOCUS
A modest handicap, run at a fair pace, and the winner did the job in great style. Solid form.
Harvest Warrior Official explanation: jockey said gelding hung right-handed throughout

5137 IN YOUR FACE H'CAP — 1m 2f 120y

5:00 (5:01) (Class 4) (0-85,85) 3-Y-0+ **£8,096** (£2,408; £1,203; £601) **Stalls** High

Form — RPR

4141 **1** **Macorville (USA)**[9] 4911 3-9-4 **84** 6ex.......... KDarley 3 — 95+
(G M Moore) *mde virtually all: rdn over 1f out: r.o* **13/8**[1]

6630 **2** *1 ½* **Rawdon (IRE)**[12] 4805 5-9-3 **75**..........(v) HayleyTurner 1 — 83
(M L W Bell) *in tch: rdn to chse wnr and hung lft fr 2f out: nt qckn ins fnl f* **12/1**

6226 **3** *2 ½* **Paparaazi (IRE)**[21] 4508 4-9-0 **72**.......... DaleGibson 2 — 76
(R A Fahey) *hld up: hdwy 3f out: rdn over 2f out: one pce ins fnl f* **14/1**

500 **4** *1 ¼* **Im Spartacus**[15] 4711 4-9-0 **77**.......... MarkLawson(5) 5 — 79
(D W Barker) *racd keenly: prom: rdn over 2f out: wknd fnl f* **20/1**

4125 **5** *¾* **Dark Charm (FR)**[14] 4730 7-9-0 **72**.......... TonyHamilton 4 — 73
(R A Fahey) *hld up: outpcd over 2f out: kpt on ins fnl f: nvr able to chal* **8/1**

0140 **6** *4* **Best Prospect (IRE)**[16] 4676 4-9-12 **84**.......... DarryllHolland 6 — 78
(M Dods) *bmpd s: hld up in rr: hdwy 3f out: rdn over 2f out: wknd over 1f out* **10/3**[2]

3-10 **7** *3 ½* **Conkering (USA)**[59] 3366 3-9-5 **85**.......... OscarUrbina 7 — 73
(J R Fanshawe) *wnt lft s: hld up: rdn over 2f out: sn wknd* **8/1**

3020 **8** *½* **Greenbelt**[98] 2162 5-8-7 **70**.......... AndrewElliott(5) 8 — 57
(G M Moore) *prom: rdn over 3f out: wknd over 2f out: edgd lft wl over 1f out* **13/2**[3]

2m 22.7s (4.97) **Going Correction** +0.325s/f (Good)
WFA 3 from 4yo+ 8lb 8 Ran SP% **115.9**
Speed ratings (Par 105):94,92,91,90,89 86,84,83
CSF £23.54 CT £207.63 TOTE £2.40: £1.40, £3.60, £3.10; EX 27.50.

Owner Geoff & Sandra Turnbull **Bred** Brookdale Thoroughbreds Inc **Trained** Middleham Moor, N Yorks

FOCUS
A fair handicap which saw the field finish fairly strung out on the testing ground. The second and third ran to their recent form behind the progressive winner.

5138 BOHLE MAIDEN STKS 1m 30y
5:30 (5:31) (Class 5) 3-Y-O **£3,886** (£1,156; £577; £288) **Stalls** Low

Form RPR
2322 **1** **Uno**[10] [4899] 3-8-12 77 .... MichaelHills 8 77+
(B W Hills) mde all: clr over 1f out: unchal **1/1**[1]
3 **2** *8* **Brocatello (IRE)**[22] [4471] 3-9-3 .... (b) KDarley 5 66
(M Johnston) dwlt: bhd: rn wd on bnd over 5f out: rdn and carried hd high over 4f out: hdwy over 1f out: tk 2nd wl ins fnl f: no **16/1**
0-3 **3** *3 ½* **Abeurbe Condita (IRE)**[10] [4891] 3-9-3 .... GrahamGibbons 1 59
(E S McMahon) racd keenly: prom: rdn over 3f out: wknd 2f out **12/1**
0 **4** *nk* **Tipsy Me**[17] [4661] 3-8-12 .... HayleyTurner 6 53
(M L W Bell) racd keenly: in tch: rdn to chse wnr over 2f out: hung lft over 1f out: no imp: wknd and lost 2nd wl ins fnl f **10/1**[3]
653 **5** *7* **Rainbow Zest**[12] [4806] 3-9-3 73 .... JimmyFortune 7 44+
(P W Chapple-Hyam) s.i.s: sn prom: rdn over 3f out: wknd 2f out **7/4**[2]
60 **6** *20* **Strong Survivor (USA)**[45] [3794] 3-8-10 .... AshleyHamblett(7) 3 4
(L M Cumani) s.s: sn pushed along: a wl bhd **33/1**
7 *24* **Gary's Indian (IRE)** 3-8-12 .... PaulEddery 2 —
(B P J Baugh) s.s: a wl bhd: t.o **100/1**
0-00 **8** *½* **Kamari Gold**[28] [4301] 3-9-3 40 .... PaulQuinn 9 —
(M Mullineaux) chsd ldrs: rdn over 4f out: wknd over 3f out: t.o **100/1**

1m 47.3s (1.79) **Going Correction** +0.325s/f (Good) **8 Ran SP% 114.0**
Speed ratings (Par 101):104,96,92,92,85 65,41,40
CSF £19.47 TOTE £2.00: £1.10, £2.40, £2.40; EX 11.30 Place 6 £212.31, Place 5 £51.64.
Owner Guy Reed **Bred** Guy Reed **Trained** Lambourn, Berks

FOCUS
No real strength in depth to this maiden and the field came home well strung out. The winner did not have to improve to score, while the second matched his debut form.
Rainbow Zest Official explanation: jockey said colt moved poorly throughout
Gary's Indian(IRE) Official explanation: jockey said filly lost its action leaving stalls
T/Plt: £492.60 to a £1 stake. Pool: £54,122.55. 80.20 winning tickets. T/Qpdt: £7.80 to a £1 stake. Pool: £4,298.90. 402.70 winning tickets. DO

5111 SOUTHWELL (L-H)
Thursday, September 7

OFFICIAL GOING: Good to firm
The ground had dried out overnight and was described as 'genuine good to firm'.
Wind: moderate, half-behind Weather: fine and sunny

5139 SKYBET PRESS RED TO BET ON ATR CONDITIONS STKS 6f
2:10 (2:10) (Class 5) 2-Y-O **£6,232** (£1,866; £933; £467) **Stalls** Low

Form RPR
0343 **1** **Bazroy (IRE)**[12] [4824] 2-8-8 88 .... StephenDonohoe(3) 3 82
(P D Evans) restless in stalls: tracd ldr: t.k.h: effrt over 2f out: led appr fnl f: hld on wl **13/8**[1]
1334 **2** *¾* **Part Timer (IRE)**[13] [4761] 2-9-1 86 .... TedDurcan 1 84
(M R Channon) trckd ldrs: effrt on inner and jinked rt over 2f out: wnt 2nd jst ins last: no ex **15/8**[2]
1 **3** *2 ½* **Pegasus Dancer (FR)**[18] [4630] 2-9-1 .... NCallan 4 76
(K A Ryan) led: hung rt and hdd appr fnl f: one pce **9/4**[3]
00 **4** *11* **Miss Havisham (IRE)**[20] [4566] 2-8-6 .... PaulHanagan 2 34
(J R Weymes) dwlt: sn pushed along in rr: outpcd over 2f out: sn lost tch **50/1**

1m 15.41s (-0.69) **Going Correction** -0.275s/f (Firm) 2y crse rec **4 Ran SP% 105.6**
Speed ratings (Par 95):93,92,88,74
CSF £4.76 TOTE £2.90; EX 4.50.
Owner Barry McCabe **Bred** P D Savill **Trained** Pandy, Abergavenny

FOCUS
No gallop to halfway. The winner had easily the best chance on form but made very hard work of it, pushed hard by the runner-up who had 6lb to find on official ratings. The race could have been rated up to 5lb better.

NOTEBOOK
Bazroy(IRE), with the headgear again dispensed with, look very fit indeed. A problem in the stalls, he was left temporarily short of room leaving the back stretch. He made very hard work of it in the end and this might be as good as he is. (op 15-8 tchd 2-1 in places)
Part Timer(IRE), inclined to get warm in the paddock, jinked away from the running rail once in line for home. He made the winner pull out all the stops and deserves credit for this. (tchd 7-4 and 2-1 in places)
Pegasus Dancer(FR), taken to post early this time, found himself the reluctant leader. He didn't look that happy on the quicker ground and in the end did not see out the extra furlong anywhere near as well as the first two. (op 15-8)
Miss Havisham(IRE), quite a big filly, earned £467 for just turning up. She will not be at her best until next year. (op 40-1 tchd 66-1)

5140 SKYBET.COM NURSERY 6f
2:40 (2:42) (Class 2) 2-Y-O **£12,954** (£3,854; £1,926; £962) **Stalls** Low

Form RPR
6211 **1** **Abunai**[19] [4603] 2-8-8 76 .... JimmyQuinn 12 82+
(R Charlton) trckd ldrs: effrt over 2f out: styd on to ld 1f out: kpt on wl **9/4**[1]
410 **2** *1* **Valdan (IRE)**[20] [4561] 2-9-4 89 .... StephenDonohoe(3) 10 92
(P D Evans) hld up in rr: effrt and edgd rt over 1f out: styd on wl to take 2nd ins last: nt rch wnr **7/1**
002 **3** *1 ¼* **Leonide**[19] [4588] 2-8-7 75 .... NCallan 8 75
(B J Meehan) mde most: hdd 1f out: kpt on same pce **5/1**[2]
2120 **4** *1 ½* **Palo Verde**[16] [4681] 2-9-6 88 .... JoeFanning 3 83
(M Johnston) stmbld s: sn w ldr: kpt on same pce appr fnl f **11/2**[3]
2204 **5** *¾* **Relkida**[13] [4779] 2-8-10 78 .... TedDurcan 1 71
(M R Channon) sn chsng ldrs on ins: effrt over 2f out: one pce **6/1**
0051 **6** *½* **Mac Gille Eoin**[13] [4753] 2-8-2 70 .... FrankieMcDonald 7 61
(J Gallagher) t.k.h: trckd ldrs: lost pl over 4f out: hdwy over 2f out: nvr trbld ldrs **16/1**
5215 **7** *½* **Josr's Magic (IRE)**[9] [4912] 2-8-0 73 .... (b) DuranFentiman(5) 5 63
(Mrs A Duffield) dwlt: effrt over 2f out: nvr trbld ldrs **14/1**
5150 **8** *1 ¾* **Sweet Candy**[13] [4766] 2-8-4 72 .... DO'Donohoe 4 57
(K A Ryan) t.k.h: trckd ldrs: wknd over 1f out **8/1**

1m 15.23s (-0.87) **Going Correction** -0.275s/f (Firm) 2y crse rec **8 Ran SP% 113.3**
Speed ratings (Par 101):94,92,91,89,88 87,86,84
CSF £18.12 CT £70.17 TOTE £2.60: £1.20, £2.20, £1.60; EX 17.90 Trifecta £30.80 Pool £398.40. 9.18 winning units.
Owner A E Oppenheimer **Bred** Hascombe And Valiant Studs **Trained** Beckhampton, Wilts

FOCUS
A £20,000-added nursery but the gallop was not strong. Both the first two deserve credit, the winner progressing again, and the form looks quite sound.

NOTEBOOK
Abunai, 4lb higher and stepping up in trip, did it nicely and always looked to be holding the runner-up's challenge. She is not that big but is all heart. (op 2-1 tchd 11-4)
Valdan(IRE), a keen sort, picked up in good style to get on to the quarters of the winner but, hard as he tried, he was never going to get the better of her. He was conceding her 10lb and deserves plenty of credit for this. (op 4-1)
Leonide set his own pace but in the end was brushed aside by the first two. (op 13-2 tchd 7-1)
Palo Verde, very fit indeed, did not impress going to post. He stumbled leaving the stalls but now looks high enough in the weights. (op 7-1)
Relkida, an excitable type, had the best of the draw but was simply not good enough. (op 13-2 tchd 7-1)
Mac Gille Eoin, raised 9lb after his Bath maiden-race success, would not settle due to the lack of any early pace. (op 14-1 tchd 20-1)

5141 CHARLES LAWRENCE SURFACES LTD H'CAP 1m 4f
3:15 (3:15) (Class 3) (0-95,92) 3-Y-O+ **£9,715** (£2,890; £1,444; £721) **Stalls** Low

Form RPR
0020 **1** **Crime Scene (IRE)**[16] [4676] 3-9-4 92 .... JoeFanning 9 103
(M Johnston) trckd ldrs: led jst ins last: kpt on wl **11/2**
1111 **2** *½* **Trick Or Treat**[14] [4742] 3-9-0 88 .... JamieMackay 1 98+
(J G Given) trckd ldrs: chal over 2f out: led over 1f out: hdd jst ins last: no ex **6/4**[1]
051- **3** *2 ½* **Red Admiral (USA)**[384] [4545] 4-9-13 92 .... KerrinMcEvoy 8 98
(Saeed Bin Suroor) led after 1f: qckd over 4f out: hdd over 1f out: kpt on same pce **4/1**[2]
6502 **4** *1 ½* **Stretton (IRE)**[16] [4676] 8-9-4 83 .... NCallan 2 87
(J D Bethell) hld up in tch: effrt over 3f out: one pce fnl 2f **5/1**[3]
-000 **5** *1 ¾* **Cavallini (USA)**[20] [4560] 4-8-13 78 oh1 .... TomEaves 4 79
(G L Moore) led 1f: chsd ldr: chal over 2f out: one pce **16/1**
1350 **6** *½* **Free To Air**[71] [2986] 3-8-4 78 .... JimmyQuinn 7 78
(A M Balding) stmbld bdly s: hdwy over 4f out: kpt on same pce: nvr a threat **10/1**
10P0 **7** *49* **El Tiger (GER)**[92] [2341] 5-9-5 84 .... TPQueally 6 6
(B J Curley) hld up in tch: drvn over 4f out: sn outpcd: lost pl over 2f out: sn bhd and eased: t.o: btn 49 l **33/1**

2m 34.69s (-5.61) **Going Correction** -0.275s/f (Firm)
WFA 3 from 4yo+ 9lb **7 Ran SP% 110.0**
Speed ratings (Par 107):107,106,105,104,102 102,69
CSF £13.09 CT £32.83 TOTE £6.50: £2.20, £1.30; EX 28.00 Trifecta £58.70 Pool £370.73. 4.48 winning units.
Owner Gainsborough Stud **Bred** Gainsborough Stud Management Ltd **Trained** Middleham Moor, N Yorks

FOCUS
A decent handicap. Just a steady gallop until leaving the back stretch. In the end the first two had it to themselves.

NOTEBOOK
Crime Scene(IRE), loaded with a blanket, appreciated this much quicker ground and in the end seemed to worry the filly out of it. He is not easy to predict however. (op 7-1 tchd 5-1)
Trick Or Treat, 8lb higher on this bid for a six-timer and dropping back in trip, looked nailed on when taking charge still on the steel. She looked unhappy on the quick ground when let down and in the end the colt simply proved too strong. (op 5-4 tchd 13-8)
Red Admiral(USA), absent since making all in a handicap at Salisbury in August from a 10lb lower mark, is a fluent mover. Soon setting his own pace, he quickend it up starting the home turn but in the end the first two were simply too good for him. (op 5-1 tchd 7-2)
Stretton(IRE), who finished over ten lengths ahead of the winner at York on much easier ground, was unsuited by the much slower pace here. (op 9-2 tchd 11-2 in places)
Cavallini(USA), a tall, narrow type, is slipping down the weights but this effort lacked any sparkle whatsoever. (op 20-1)
Free To Air, still 3lb higher than his last win, lost his footing leaving the stalls and could never take a hand. Official explanation: jockey said gelding stumbled leaving stalls (tchd 11-1)
El Tiger(GER) Official explanation: jockey said gelding hung right-handed

5142 RIPPON HOMES CONDITIONS STKS 1m 2f
3:45 (3:45) (Class 2) 3-5-Y-O
£11,217 (£3,358; £1,679; £840; £419; £210) **Stalls** Low

Form RPR
1 **1** **Desert Authority (USA)**[42] [3875] 3-8-11 .... TedDurcan 3 110+
(Saeed Bin Suroor) hld up in tch: hdwy over 4f out: effrt on wd outside over 2f out: wandered: styd on to ld last 50yds **5/2**[2]
4-40 **2** *½* **Blue Ksar (FR)**[76] [2804] 3-8-9 102 .... (t) DO'Donohoe 2 107
(Saeed Bin Suroor) trckd ldr: led 2f out: hdd and no ex wl ins last **16/1**
5323 **3** *2* **Take A Bow**[89] [2431] 5-9-2 100 .... GeorgeBaker 4 103
(P R Chamings) trckd ldrs: chal 1f out: styd on same pce **12/1**
0340 **4** *1 ¼* **Rocamadour**[12] [4828] 4-9-2 104 .... (v[1]) TonyCulhane 6 101
(M R Channon) hld up in last: hdwy over 4f out: n.m.r over 3f out: one pce fnl 2f **7/1**[3]
543- **5** *3* **Into The Dark**[314] [6131] 5-9-2 108 .... (vt) KerrinMcEvoy 5 95
(Saeed Bin Suroor) led: t.k.h: hdd 2f out: hung rt and lost pl over 1f out **1/1**[1]
1400 **6** *2* **Before You Go (IRE)**[12] [4818] 3-9-1 104 .... (v) NCallan 1 97
(T G Mills) trckd ldrs: drvn over 4f out: outpcd and n.m.r on inner over 3f out: lost pl over 1f out **16/1**

2m 7.47s (-7.43) **Going Correction** -0.275s/f (Firm) course record
WFA 3 from 4yo+ 7lb **6 Ran SP% 110.5**
Speed ratings (Par 109):113,112,111,110,107 106
CSF £35.99 TOTE £3.10: £1.50, £4.00; EX 28.40.
Owner Godolphin **Bred** Stoneside Stable **Trained** Newmarket, Suffolk

FOCUS
A one-two for Godolphin, who also had the beaten favourite. A strong pace and a course record but this distance is rarely used here on turf. The winner was still inexperienced and will improve again.

NOTEBOOK
Desert Authority(USA), who looked very fit indeed, rolled about under pressure but was firmly in command at the line. Unbeaten in two starts now, he will improve again. (op 2-1 tchd 11-4)
Blue Ksar(FR), tried over two miles at Royal Ascot, was the neglected of the Godolpin three. He kept tabs on the pacesetter and kicked for home but in the end the winner was the master. (tchd 20-1)
Take A Bow, struggling to hit the target after appearing just twice at four, gave a good acount of himself but this may be as good as he is now.
Rocamadour, in a first-time visor, adopted much more patient tactics. He ran into the back of a horse in front rounding the final turn but never really threatened danger. Third in the French Derby last year, he is a frustrating sort. (op 9-1)

Into The Dark, smart at three, was having his first outing since October. Fit as as a flea and excitable beforehand, he tore along in front but when headed hung and looked reluctant. Official explanation: jockey said gelding ran too free (op 6-5 tchd 5-4 in places)

Before You Go(IRE) had something to prove at this level but just by getting round he picked up £210. (op 12-1)

5143 SKYBET PRESS RED TO BET ON ATR H'CAP — 7f
4:20 (4:20) (Class 3) (0-95,95) 3-Y-0

£9,348 (£2,799; £1,399; £700; £349; £175) **Stalls** Low

Form				RPR
3362	**1**		**Blades Girl**^{22} [4488] 3-8-9 **86** .... (p) NCallan 1 (K A Ryan) *mde all: qcknd 3f out: hung rt and wnt clr over 1f out: readily* **9/2**^{2}	97
2-16	**2**	*4*	**Mobsir**^{103} [2031] 3-8-9 **86** .... RHills 4 (E A L Dunlop) *trckd ldrs: wnt 2nd over 2f out: kpt on same pce* **5/1**^{3}	87
21-	**3**	*1*	**Power Politics (USA)**^{410} [3780] 3-9-4 **95** .... KerrinMcEvoy 2 (Saeed Bin Suroor) *hld up in tch: effrt on ins over 2f out: sn rdn: kpt on same pce* **4/1**^{1}	93
0055	**4**	*hd*	**Red Cape (FR)**^{13} [4782] 3-8-11 **88** .... JimmyQuinn 9 (Jane Chapple-Hyam) *tracxked ldrs on outer: t.k.h: effrt over 2f out: kpt on same pce* **16/1**	85
1-10	**5**	*1 1/4*	**Fast Bowler**^{33} [4144] 3-8-6 **83** .... PaulHanagan 6 (J M P Eustace) *s.i.s: hld up in rr: effrt over 2f out: nvr trbld ldrs* **8/1**	77
1506	**6**	*shd*	**Trafalgar Bay (IRE)**^{19} [4593] 3-9-3 **94** .... GeorgeBaker 3 (S Kirk) *s.i.s: sn trcking ldrs: rdn over 2f out: one pce* **4/1**^{1}	88
5044	**7**	*shd*	**Ingleby Arch (USA)**^{19} [4601] 3-9-4 **95** .... TomEaves 5 (T D Barron) *trckd ldrs: effrt on wd outside over 2f out: one pce* **11/2**	89
060	**8**	*4*	**Art Market (CAN)**^{6} [4988] 3-8-13 **90** .... (b) JoeFanning 7 (P F I Cole) *hld up in rr: effrt over 2f out: sn btn* **28/1**	73
-660	**9**	*2 1/2*	**Dictatrix**^{61} [3316] 3-8-10 **90** .... StephenDonohoe$^{(3)}$ 10 (J M P Eustace) *trckd ldrs on wd outside: rdn over 2f out: sn lost pl* **33/1**	67

1m 26.65s (-2.55) **Going Correction** -0.275s/f (Firm) **9** Ran SP% **113.6**

Speed ratings (Par 105):103,98,97,97,95 95,95,90,87

CSF £26.78 CT £96.06 TOTE £5.00: £1.70, £2.00, £1.90; EX 31.20 Trifecta £86.70 Pool £354.45. 2.90 winning units.

Owner Crown Select **Bred** Crown Select **Trained** Hambleton, N Yorks

FOCUS

The winner found herself in front and, under a fine tactical ride, soon put her stamp on the race when given the office.

NOTEBOOK

Blades Girl capitalised on the best draw. Allowed to set her own pace, she wound it up turning in and and, spurting clear coming to the final furlong, was never in any danger. Her rider deserves full marks. (op 11-2)

Mobsir, absent since flopping in Listed company on soft ground in May, looked to have plenty on his plate on his handicap bow. He kept tabs on the winner but was caught flat-footed. He kept on but she had flown. (op 4-1)

Power Politics(USA), winner of a maiden at Pontefract in July last year on just his second start, is a medium-sized colt. Carrying tons of condition, he stuck to the inner once in line for home. He never looked like picking up sufficiently but to his credit kept going all the way to the line. This will have sharpened him up. (op 7-2 tchd 9-2)

Red Cape(FR), now just 2lb higher than when winning at Newmarket in June, had an outside draw. He was far too keen for his own good but was keeping on in his own time when running out of racing room near the line. (op 12-1 tchd 18-1)

Fast Bowler, 4lb higher than Windsor, missed a beat at the start and could never take a hand.

Trafalgar Bay(IRE), as usual walked to post, could have done with a much stronger gallop. He is the type to pop up in a big-field handicap this backend. (op 11-2)

Ingleby Arch(USA), with the visor left off, struggled once in line for home. (op 15-2)

5144 SKYBET.COM H'CAP — 7f
4:50 (4:51) (Class 4) (0-85,83) 3-Y-0+ **£6,477** (£1,927; £963; £481) **Stalls** Low

Form				RPR
0053	**1**		**Dr Thong**^{7} [4968] 5-8-9 **70** .... (t) TedDurcan 6 (P F I Cole) *chsd ldrs: styd on to lerad last 75yds* **7/1**^{2}	80
1500	**2**	*1/2*	**Passion Fruit**^{5} [5024] 5-8-12 **73** .... DeanMcKeown 1 (C W Fairhurst) *s.i.s: hdwy over 3f out: styd alone far side: upsides ins last: no ex nr fin* **14/1**	82
0000	**3**	*shd*	**Fiefdom (IRE)**^{12} [4790] 4-9-5 **80** .... JimmyQuinn 2 (I W McInnes) *chsd ldrs: kpt on to ld jst ins last: hdd and no ex wl ins fnl f* **14/1**	88
6001	**4**	*1 1/4*	**King Harson**^{21} [4521] 7-8-13 **74** .... PatCosgrave 4 (J D Bethell) *led tl 4f out: led over 2f out: hdd and no ex jst ins last* **15/2**^{3}	79
0245	**5**	*1*	**Byron Bay**^{15} [4696] 4-9-8 **83** .... TomEaves 8 (I Semple) *trckd ldrs: kpt on same pce appr fnl f* **10/1**	86
3122	**6**	*hd*	**Carnivore**^{21} [4521] 4-8-11 **72** .... PaulHanagan 11 (T D Barron) *prom: sn drvn along: outpcd over 4f out: kpt on fnl 2f: nvr a real threat* **2/1**^{1}	74
0314	**7**	*shd*	**Desert Dreamer (IRE)**^{3} [5070] 5-9-7 **82** .... GeorgeBaker 9 (P R Chamings) *hld up in rr: effrt over 2f out: nvr rchd ldrs* **15/2**^{3}	84
-523	**8**	*5*	**Street Warrior (IRE)**^{136} [1185] 3-8-10 **75** .... JoeFanning 10 (M Johnston) *s.i.s: sn pushed laong: lost pl over 4f out: nvr on terms after* **12/1**	64
0005	**9**	*1 1/2*	**Cardinal Venture (IRE)**^{26} [4381] 8-9-1 **76** .... (p) NCallan 3 (K A Ryan) *sn w ldr: led 4f out: hdd over 2f out: lost pl appr fnl f* **9/1**	61
0000	**10**	*1*	**Tanforan**^{13} [4760] 4-9-0 **75** .... TonyCulhane 7 (K G Reveley) *chsd ldrs: outpcd 3f out: sn lost pl* **25/1**	57

1m 26.71s (-2.49) **Going Correction** -0.275s/f (Firm)

WFA 3 from 4yo+ 4lb **10** Ran SP% **113.3**

Speed ratings (Par 105):103,102,102,100,99 99,99,93,91,90

CSF £96.89 CT £1322.90 TOTE £10.00: £2.80, £5.30, £4.60; EX 138.10 Trifecta £228.20 Part won. Pool: £321.53 - 0.10 winning units. Place 6 £147.83, Place 5 £57.61.

Owner Frank Stella **Bred** Mascalls Stud **Trained** Whatcombe, Oxon

FOCUS

A strong pace for this competitive handicap.

Carnivore Official explanation: jockey said gelding hung right

T/Plt: £247.80 to a £1 stake. Pool: £45,997.15. 135.45 winning tickets. T/Qpdt: £42.70 to a £1 stake. Pool: £3,940.10. 68.20 winning tickets. WG

^{5048}LONGCHAMP (R-H)
Thursday, September 7

OFFICIAL GOING: Good

5145a PRIX DE LUTECE (GROUP 3) — 1m 7f
2:00 (2:00) 3-Y-0 **£27,586** (£11,034; £8,276; £5,517; £2,759)

			RPR
1		**Getaway (GER)**^{23} [4465] 3-8-9 .... CSoumillon 3 (A Fabre, France) *held up in 6th, headway on outside to go 4th straight, ridden to lead 1 1/2f out, pushed out final f, easily* **4/5**^{1}	106
2	*2 1/2*	**Vendangeur (IRE)**^{33} [4169] 3-8-9 .... SPasquier 7 (E Lellouche, France) *raced in 3rd on outside, 2nd straight, led narrowly over 2f out to 1 1/2f out, one pace* **34/10**^{2}	103
3	*2*	**Armand**^{26} 3-8-9 .... TThulliez 6 (P Bary, France) *set steady pace, headed over 2f out, still every chance on inside 1 1/2f out, weakened approaching final f* **72/10**	101
4	*1/2*	**Young Poli (FR)**^{68} 3-8-9 .... AClement 1 (A Couetil, France) *held up in last, outpaced entering straight, stayed on well final f to take 4th on line* **48/10**^{3}	101
5	*shd*	**Spectaculaire**^{31} 3-8-9 .... OPeslier 4 (A Fabre, France) *midfield on outside, 3rd straight, one pace final 2f* **16/1**	100
6	*8*	**Antigel (FR)**^{45} 3-8-9 .... TJarnet 2 (W Menuet, France) *raced in 5th, 6th straight, beaten 2f out* **15/1**	92
7	*10*	**Esplendido (FR)**^{41} 3-8-9 .... J-BEyquem 5 (R Chotard, France) *raced in 2nd til weakened 2 1/2f out* **38/1**	82

3m 13.3s **7** Ran SP% **122.4**

PARI-MUTUEL: WIN 1.80; PL 1.20, 1.50; SF 4.40.

Owner Baron G Von Ullmann **Bred** Baron G Von Ullmann **Trained** Chantilly, France

NOTEBOOK

Getaway(GER), held up early on, finally won his first Group race with plenty in hand. The colt was not put into the event until the two-furlong marker and then cruised into the lead with 200 yards left to run. He was never touched with the whip and won with great authority. The Group 2 Prix Hubert de Chaudenay is next on the cards.

Vendangeur(IRE), always up with the pace, was given every possible chance and he ran well, but the favourite had too much in the bag. He just stayed on one-paced at the end.

Armand tried to make every yard of the running and did a good job until halfway up the straight where he became one-paced.

Young Poli(FR) was given an awful lot to do, staying on well to take fourth. The colt quickened well from a furlong and a half out and took fourth place literally on the line. He is better than this performance suggests.

5146a PRIX DU PIN (GROUP 3) — 7f
3:35 (3:35) 3-Y-0+ **£27,586** (£11,034; £8,276; £5,517; £2,759)

			RPR
1		**Price Tag**^{39} [3991] 3-8-8 .... TThulliez 8 (P Bary, France) *held up in mid-division, 8th straight, quickened up well 1 1/2f out to challenge final furlong, led 100yds out, driven out* **11/5**^{1}	110
2	*1*	**Gwenseb (FR)**^{21} [4542] 3-8-8 .... OPeslier 3 (C Laffon-Parias, France) *held up, disputing last straight, pushed along 2f out, finished well down outside final f to take 2nd last strides* **43/10**^{3}	107
3	*nk*	**Helios Quercus (FR)**^{25} [4416] 4-9-1 .... IMendizabal 9 (C Diard, France) *raced in 3rd, headway to press leaders 2f out, every chance inside final furlong, kept on* **39/10**^{2}	109
4	*snk*	**Blue Damask (USA)**^{56} 3-8-11 .... CSoumillon 7 (A Fabre, France) *raced in 2nd, led 1 1/2f out, headed 100yds out, kept on* **15/2**	109
5	*hd*	**Suggestive**^{37} [4025] 8-9-5 .... (b) DBonilla 5 (W J Haggas) *in touch, disputing 4th straight, pushed along to chase leaders 1 1/2f out, ridden 1f out, stayed on to line* **11/1**	113
6	*nk*	**Biniou (IRE)**^{32} [4191] 3-8-11 .... YTake 6 (Robert Collet, France) *mid-division, disputing 6th straight, headway on rail over 1f out, kept on steadily* **27/1**	108
7	*3/4*	**Sendalam (FR)**^{13} 4-9-1 .... THuet 4 (Y Fouin, France) *mid-division, disputing 4th straight, stayed on at one pace til no extra close home* **38/1**	106
8	*hd*	**Nid D'Abeilles (IRE)**^{11} [4862] 4-9-1 .... (b) C-PLemaire 1 (P Bary, France) *raced in last, disputing last straight, effort & ran on from 2f out til no extra final furlong* **10/1**	105
9	*5*	**Starpix (FR)**^{9} [4918] 4-9-1 .... MBlancpain 10 (Diego Lowther, France) *mid-division, disputing 6th straight, pushed along 2f out, never dangerous* **44/1**	92
10	*shd*	**Kendargent (FR)**^{25} [4416] 3-8-11 .... RMarchelli 2 (Y Fouin, France) *led to 1 1/2f out, soon weakened* **13/2**	91

1m 22.7s

WFA 3 from 4yo+ 4lb **10** Ran SP% **121.4**

PARI-MUTUEL: WIN 3.20; PL 1.40, 1.60, 1.60; DF 6.60.

Owner K Abdulla **Bred** Juddmonte Farms Ltd **Trained** Chantilly, France

NOTEBOOK

Price Tag, disqualified from the French Guineas, quickened brilliantly to mow down her rivals from a furlong and a half out and was never really put under pressure. This filly has a lot of speed and she will now be aimed at the Prix de la Foret and, if all goes well, the Breeders' Cup Mile could follow.

Gwenseb(FR) was outpaced in the early part of the contest but she finished well, albeit without threatening the winner.

Helios Quercus(FR) hit the front at the furlong marker and was only run out of second place in the final few strides. He is a very genuine individual and is nearly always involved in the finish of his Group races.

Blue Damask(USA), always in the leading group, led a furlong out but could not quite hang on to the line. He was beaten under half a length for second place and this distance is probably his limit.

Suggestive, smartly away, began to pull and was outpaced early in the straight before running on again at the finish, and his connections regretted that they did not decide to make all the running.

The Form Book, Raceform Ltd, Compton, RG20 6NL

[4808]SANDOWN (R-H)

Friday, September 8

OFFICIAL GOING: Good to firm (firm in places)

Wind: Light, behind Weather: Sunny and warm

5147 SODEXHO PRESTIGE E B F MAIDEN STKS — 5f 6y

1:55 (1:58) (Class 5) 2-Y-O — **£3,886** (£1,156; £577; £288) **Stalls** High

Form — RPR

02 **1** **Oldjoesaid**[25] 4428 2-9-3 KerrinMcEvoy 4 80+
(H Candy) *mde all: stretched away fr 2f out: styd on wl fnl f: readily* **3/1**[1]

32 **2** *1 ½* **Castano**[62] 3308 2-9-3 GrahamGibbons 1 75
(B R Millman) *pressed wnr: rdn and hanging over 1f out: nt qckn and hld fnl f* **11/2**

0 **3** *1 ¼* **Rocker**[91] 2402 2-9-3 TedDurcan 12 70
(P W Chapple-Hyam) *chsd ldrs: plld out and effrt 2f out: kpt on fnl f to take 3rd nr fin* **4/1**[3]

4036 **4** *shd* **Vitznau (IRE)**[17] 4681 2-9-3 73 PatDobbs 9 70
(R Hannon) *chsd ldng pair: rdn and hld whn nt clr run ins fnl f: lost 3rd nr fin* **7/2**[2]

5 *½* **Solid Rock (IRE)** 2-9-3 JimmyFortune 11 68
(T G Mills) *settled in midfield: effrt 2f out: nt clr run over 1f out and again ins fnl f: styd on: nrst fin* **16/1**

6 *¾* **Gower** 2-9-3 SebSanders 8 65
(R Charlton) *chsd ldrs: pushed along 1/2-way: one pce u.p over 1f out* **15/2**

7 *1 ½* **Dualagi** 2-8-12 LPKeniry 7 55
(J S Moore) *prom: rdn over 2f out: wknd fnl f* **33/1**

8 *¾* **Tahafut** 2-8-12 RHills 3 52
(W J Haggas) *hld up in last pair and a off the pce: shuffled along and kpt on steadily: bttr for experience* **12/1**

9 *¾* **Divalini** 2-8-12 JimmyQuinn 2 49
(J Akehurst) *nvr on terms w ldrs: struggling fr 2f out* **33/1**

10 *5* **Miss Autumnal (IRE)** 2-8-12 ChrisCatlin 6 31
(N A Callaghan) *rn green and sn pushed along in rr: nvr a factor* **33/1**

11 *½* **Chart Express** 2-9-0 DeanCorby[(3)] 10 35
(P Howling) *sn rdn and struggling in last pair* **66/1**

61.22 secs (-0.99) **Going Correction** -0.30s/f (Firm) **11** Ran SP% **118.3**

Speed ratings (Par 95):95,92,90,90,89 88,86,84,83,75 74

CSF £19.42 TOTE £3.40: £1.50, £1.60, £1.90; EX 15.60.

Owner J J Byrne **Bred** Mrs R D Peacock **Trained** Kingston Warren, Oxon

FOCUS

A fair sprint maiden that should produce winners. Sound form.

NOTEBOOK

Oldjoesaid, whose recent second in a fair maiden at Windsor entitled him to go close here, handled the drop in distance well and was given yet another superb ride by the ever-impressive McEvoy. Quickly into stride and soon in front, he stayed on strongly under pressure to win with a bit in hand and, although he stays further, this trip looked to suit him well. There may be more to come from the gelding in nurseries. (op 7-2)

Castano had the misfortune of bumping into Conquest at Nottingham last time and this obviosuly represented an easier opportunity, but he lacked the pace of the winner and was again forced to settle for second best. He will find a race eventually.

Rocker failed to take advantage of the rails draw and had to be switched to launch a challenge, but the son of Rock Of Gibraltar was unable to quicken and he just got up for third. He has not had a chance to show his best yet. (op 5-1)

Vitznau(IRE) has an exposed look and was always likely to be vulnerable to the improvers here. He was already in trouble when being blocked and may be ready for a switch to handicaps. (tchd 10-3)

Solid Rock(IRE), another son of brilliant miler Rock Of Gibraltar, made a highly pleasing debut and caught the eye of many, keeping on well having been denied a clear run to just miss out on the places. Natural progression should see him winning his maiden. (op 14-1)

Gower, a speedily-bred relation of the stable's top sprinters Avonbridge and Patavellian, showed a bit of early speed, but his inexperience soon began to tell and he could only plug on. His trainer's juveniles often need a run and improvement can be expected. (op 8-1 tchd 10-1 in a place)

Dualagi, a speedily-bred filly who did well at the Breeze-ups, showed good early speed before dropping away and there were positives to be taken from this.

Tahafut, bred to benefit from a longer distance in future, was in rear throughout and never got into it, but she was not given a hard time and should benefit massively from the experience. Official explanation: jockey said filly hung right-handed throughout

5148 LONDON STOCK EXCHANGE H'CAP — 5f 6y

2:30 (2:31) (Class 4) (0-80,80) 3-Y-O+ — **£5,505** (£1,637; £818; £408) **Stalls** High

Form — RPR

3415 **1** **Forest Dane**[14] 4780 6-8-5 66 RoystonFfrench 2 79
(Mrs N Smith) *hld up in tch: prog 1/2-way: chsd ldng pair over 1f out: rdn to ld jst ins fnl f: sn wl in command* **10/1**

6U20 **2** *1 ¼* **Matsunosuke**[13] 4811 4-9-1 76 MichaelHills 9 85
(A B Coogan) *dwlt: hld up wl in rr: gd prog on outer fr 2f out: r.o to take 2nd last 75yds: no imp on wnr* **5/1**[1]

1113 **3** *½* **Blue Maeve**[14] 4771 6-8-13 74 SilvestreDeSousa 7 81
(A D Brown) *pressed ldr: rdn over 2f out: chal 1f out: one pce fnl f* **13/2**[2]

5455 **4** *1 ½* **Bluebok**[13] 4811 5-9-2 80 (t) StephenDonohoe[(3)] 11 82
(J M Bradley) *led: rdn over 2f out: hdd jst ins fnl f: wknd last 100yds* **8/1**

0006 **5** *1 ¼* **Hoh Hoh Hoh**[13] 4811 4-9-2 80 JamesDoyle[(3)] 6 77
(R J Price) *t.k.h: cl up: pressed ldng pair gng strly 2f out: rdn and no rspnse over 1f out: sn btn* **14/1**

0000 **6** *hd* **Eversden (USA)**[9] 4927 3-8-6 68 (p) PhilipRobinson 1 64
(C G Cox) *wnt lft s: sn detached in last and u.p: no prog tl r.o wl fnl f: nvr nrr* **20/1**

0600 **7** *nk* **One Way Ticket**[13] 4793 6-9-5 80 (p) TedDurcan 3 75
(J M Bradley) *trckd ldrs on outer: rdn 2f out: hanging and wknd over 1f out* **50/1**

0501 **8** *shd* **Blue Aura (IRE)**[18] 4659 3-9-1 77 (b) SebSanders 14 72
(R Charlton) *trckd ldrs: nt qckn wl over 1f out: steadily wknd* **8/1**

3446 **9** *¾* **Seamus Shindig**[14] 4771 4-9-5 80 (p) KerrinMcEvoy 8 72
(H Candy) *trckd ldrs: shkn up and fnd nil wl over 1f out: btn after* **13/2**[2]

3542 **10** *¾* **Who's Winning (IRE)**[4] 5058 5-8-13 74 RobertMiles 13 64+
(B G Powell) *settled in midfield: rdn and outpcd whn nt clr run over 1f out: no ch after* **7/1**[3]

6620 **11** *nk* **Polish Emperor (USA)**[13] 4793 6-9-4 79 (e) JimmyFortune 10 67
(W R Swinburn) *sn wl in rr: rdn 1/2-way: brief effrt over 1f out: sn no prog and btn* **16/1**

0600 **12** *2* **Spanish Ace**[23] 4486 5-8-12 73 TonyCulhane 12 54
(J M Bradley) *dwlt: a wl in rr: shkn up and no prog 2f out* **10/1**

00-0 **13** *5* **Great Fox (IRE)**[33] 4180 5-8-12 73 ChrisCatlin 4 36
(P L Gilligan) *prom tl wknd rapidly 1/2-way* **25/1**

60.01 secs (-2.20) **Going Correction** -0.30s/f (Firm)

WFA 3 from 4yo+ 1lb **13** Ran SP% **119.4**

Speed ratings (Par 105):105,103,102,99,97 97,97,96,95,94 93,90,82

CSF £58.09 CT £371.14 TOTE £14.10: £4.60, £2.00, £2.30; EX 89.20.

Owner The Ember Partnership **Bred** Loan And Development Corporation **Trained** Bury, W Sussex

FOCUS

A routine Sandown sprint. With the far rail moved in three yards there seemed no draw bias. Solid form.

Seamus Shindig Official explanation: jockey said gelding finished distressed

5149 MAIN MARKET H'CAP — 1m 14y

3:05 (3:06) (Class 4) (0-80,77) 3-Y-O+ — **£5,505** (£1,637; £818; £408) **Stalls** High

Form — RPR

0122 **1** **Personify**[22] 4536 4-9-4 72 (p) PhilipRobinson 5 80
(C G Cox) *t.k.h: ldng trio: rdn to ld over 1f out: drvn and hld on wl fnl f* **7/2**[1]

4220 **2** *½* **Fabrian**[13] 4810 8-9-0 73 LiamJones[(5)] 11 79
(R J Price) *led: kicked on 3f out: hdd over 1f out and sltly outpcd: kpt on wl again fnl f* **9/2**[2]

0462 **3** *shd* **Nanton (USA)**[13] 4819 4-9-7 75 JimmyFortune 8 81
(P F I Cole) *sweating: hld up towards rr: prog on outer wl over 2f out: pressed wnr jst over 1f out: kpt on but a hld* **9/2**[2]

6335 **4** *shd* **The Gaikwar (IRE)**[26] 4390 7-9-4 72 (b) TedDurcan 12 78
(R A Harris) *t.k.h: trckd ldrs: stl gng wl 2f out: shkn up over 1f out: drvn and r.o ins fnl f: gaining at fin* **16/1**

-000 **5** *1 ¼* **Liakoura (GER)**[90] 2440 4-9-9 77 KerrinMcEvoy 2 80
(Mrs A J Perrett) *t.k.h: hld up wl in rr: prog on outer over 2f out: looked dangerous jst over 1f out: effrt petered out fnl f* **11/1**

3104 **6** *¾* **Cusoon**[22] 4536 4-9-7 75 (p) GeorgeBaker 3 76
(G L Moore) *hld up wl in rr: prog gng wl over 2f out: nt clr run briefly sn after: rdn and nt qckn over 1f out: one pce* **8/1**[3]

0221 **7** *2* **Border Edge**[8] 4968 8-8-11 65 6ex J-PGuillambert 7 62
(J J Bridger) *chsd ldr to wl over 2f out: steadily fdd* **10/1**

0302 **8** *nk* **Christmas Truce (IRE)**[8] 4968 7-8-6 63 oh4 (p) JamesDoyle[(3)] 6 59
(Ms J S Doyle) *nvr beyond midfield: rdn and nt qckn over 2f out: struggling after* **11/1**

0600 **9** *½* **Sekula Pata (NZ)**[40] 3973 7-9-6 74 RoystonFfrench 4 69
(Christian Wroe, UAE) *hld up wl in rr: rdn wl over 2f out: effrt whn rn into trble wl over 1f out: no ch after* **50/1**

0404 **10** *3* **Farewell Gift**[77] 2819 5-9-1 72 StephaneBreux[(3)] 9 60
(R Hannon) *chsd ldrs: rdn 3f out: wknd 2f out* **20/1**

5266 **11** *1* **Samuel Charles**[30] 4241 8-9-9 77 TPQueally 1 63
(C R Dore) *hld up in last: rdn over 2f out: no prog* **14/1**

5250 **12** *1 ½* **Takes Tutu (USA)**[30] 4241 7-9-0 68 JimmyQuinn 13 50+
(C R Dore) *t.k.h: hld up in midfield: effrt whn hmpd on inner 2f out: nt rcvr* **20/1**

1m 42.99s (-0.96) **Going Correction** +0.025s/f (Good) **12** Ran SP% **119.5**

Speed ratings (Par 105):105,104,104,104,103 102,100,100,99,96 95,94

CSF £18.32 CT £74.53 TOTE £4.50: £1.70, £2.10, £1.60; EX 21.30.

Owner Courtenay Club **Bred** Darley **Trained** Lambourn, Berks

FOCUS

Not a strong handicap by Sandown standards and the form has been rated fairly negatively. The front four, three of whom were closely matched on several strands of recent form, were separated by less than a length.

Sekula Pata(NZ) Official explanation: jockey said gelding was denied a clear run

Takes Tutu(USA) Official explanation: jockey said gelding suffered interference in running

5150 AIM H'CAP — 1m 14y

3:40 (3:41) (Class 3) (0-90,90) 3-Y-O

£7,790 (£2,332; £1,166; £583; £291; £146) **Stalls** High

Form — RPR

231 **1** **Mosharref (IRE)**[19] 4635 3-8-12 82 RHills 7 96+
(B W Hills) *hld up in last trio: effrt whn nt clr run 2f out: gd prog sn after: led jst ins fnl f: r.o wl* **5/1**[2]

4330 **2** *1 ¼* **South Cape**[27] 4379 3-9-4 88 TonyCulhane 11 99
(M R Channon) *trckd ldrs: effrt 2f out: chal and upsides 1f out: r.o but outpcd by wnr last 150yds* **16/1**

1600 **3** *2* **Adventuress**[13] 4808 3-9-1 85 (b) JimmyFortune 13 91
(B J Meehan) *s.i.s and hmpd s: in tch: prog on outer and drvn 2f out: nt qckn over 1f out: styd on again last 150yds* **25/1**

5042 **4** *nk* **Bonnie Prince Blue**[19] 4634 3-8-13 83 MichaelHills 12 89
(B W Hills) *sn trckd ldr: led jst over 2f out: hdd and one pce jst ins fnl f* **9/1**

-115 **5** *shd* **Macedon**[13] 4802 3-8-11 81 LPKeniry 6 86+
(J S Moore) *hld up in midfield on inner: rdn 2f out: nt qckn over 1f out: styd on ins fnl f* **7/1**

6330 **6** *½* **Louie Louie (IRE)**[23] 4488 3-8-11 84 StephenDonohoe[(3)] 1 88+
(N A Callaghan) *hld up in last trio: hrd rdn and no prog wl over 2f out: styd on fr jst over 1f out: n.d* **16/1**

3251 **7** *nk* **Danski**[39] 4004 3-9-1 85 SebSanders 10 89
(P J Makin) *trckd ldng pair: rdn to chal over 2f out: fdd over 1f out* **9/2**[1]

12 **8** *1* **Very Far (USA)**[8] 4958 3-8-13 83 (t) KerrinMcEvoy 3 84
(Saeed Bin Suroor) *s.s: hld up in last: pushed along over 2f out: one pce and nvr nr ldrs* **11/2**[3]

4531 **9** *nk* **Demon Docker (IRE)**[9] 4923 3-9-6 90 6ex TedDurcan 2 91
(P W Chapple-Hyam) *chsd ldrs: rdn 2f out: hld whn n.m.r jst ins fnl f: wknd* **11/1**

4300 **10** *1* **Zabeel House**[20] 4605 3-8-7 77 TPQueally 4 75
(J A R Toller) *hld up in midfield: effrt over 2f out: nt qckn over 1f out: wknd ins fnl f* **33/1**

4100 **11** *1 ¼* **Ocean Pride (IRE)**[64] 3212 3-9-0 84 PatDobbs 5 79
(R Hannon) *hld up in midfield: rdn and lost pl 2f out: n.d after* **66/1**

3114 **12** *1 ¾* **Minister Of State**[40] 3978 3-9-4 88 (p) PhilipRobinson 9 79
(M A Jarvis) *led at gd pce to jst over 2f out: wknd rapidly fnl f* **6/1**

0000 **13** *7* **Grand Jour (IRE)**[119] 1627 3-9-1 85 ChrisCatlin 8 60
(M J Wallace) *lost pl on outer 1/2-way: last and struggling over 2f out: wl bhd after* **25/1**

1m 41.48s (-2.47) **Going Correction** +0.025s/f (Good) **13** Ran SP% **119.2**

Speed ratings (Par 105):113,111,109,109,109 108,108,107,107,106 105,103,96

CSF £78.99 CT £1895.50 TOTE £4.30: £1.90, £5.80, £7.70; EX 142.30.

Owner Hamdan Al Maktoum **Bred** Shadwell Estate Company Limited **Trained** Lambourn, Berks

■ Stewards' Enquiry : R Hills caution: careless riding

FOCUS
A good, competitive three-year-old handicap that is likely to produce its share of winners. The second and third set the standard, and the winner, who travelled well, could well have a three-figure RPR before the end of the season.

NOTEBOOK
Mosharref(IRE) ◆, who looked to have been let in on a decent mark of 82, was ridden with plenty of restraint, but moved smoothly into contention and, although he had to wait for a gap to appear, he picked up nicely once finding his stride. His head carriage was not the most attractive, but this performance suggested he is capable of defying a rise before going on to better things. (op 9-2)
South Cape has generally been running well off a 2lb higher mark, twice finishing third, and he again ran a solid race in defeat, making the winner work for his victory. A return to winning ways may not be far away for the gelding, with the autumn ground unlikely to prove a problem considering he has winning form in heavy.
Adventuress ◆ looked most unlucky. Losing many lengths at the start after being hampered, she made stealthy strides in the straight and finished best of all to just snatch third. Some pieces of her form look good and she remains capable of better. (op 33-1)
Bonnie Prince Blue, a stablemate of the winner, improved to finish second at Pontefract last time behind a useful sort, but he had every chance on this occasion. (op 7-1)
Macedon was slightly disappointing considering the combination of a step up in trip on this better ground was expected to suit, but he was given a bit to do and may benefit from a more positive ride in future. He remains relatively unexposed. (op 13-2)
Louie Louie(IRE) was another making late strides having been given plenty to do, but he has an expsoed look and is unlikely to be winning off this mark. (op 14-1)
Danski, fianlly off the mark in a maiden at Windsor last time, had been raised 7lb for that and a mark of 85 did not make life easy. He held every chance, but dropped away tamely and it emerged he had a problem. Official explanation: jockey said colt had a breathing problem (op 6-1 tchd 11-2 in a place)
Very Far(USA), who ran well off this mark at Redcar last month, was another with obvious claims, but he was in trouble from the word go and ran Flat. His stable's horses are running well in general and he can be given another chance. Official explanation: jockey said colt was slowly away (op 9-2)
Minister Of State, whose early season winning form does not look so good now, disappointed when favourite at Newmarket on his latest start and connections were forced to reach for cheekpieces here. He set a decent clip, but was readily brushed aside and the way he stopped suggests he may have a problem. (op 7-1)

5151 ALPHEUS 10 YEAR ANNIVERSARY MAIDEN STKS — 1m 2f 7y
4:15 (4:18) (Class 5) 3-4-Y-0 — **£3,886** (£1,156; £577; £288) Stalls High

Form — RPR

-252 **1** **Piety (IRE)**[8] 4945 3-8-12 83 RoystonFfrench 3 — 76
(M Johnston) *mde virtually all: rdn over 2f out: kpt on wl u.p: a holding on nr fin* **7/2**[3]

6 **2** *nk* **Show Winner**[8] 4973 3-9-3 TPQueally 2 — 81
(J Noseda) *pushed along in rr 6f out: rdn 3f out: prog over 1f out to chse wnr last 150yds: clsng fin but nvr quite able to chal* **14/1**

3 *1 ½* **Mowazana (IRE)** 3-8-12 RHills 5 — 73
(M P Tregoning) *sn trckd wnr: rdn over 2f out: no imp over 1f out: lost 2nd last 150yds* **14/1**

0222 **4** *1* **Accompanist**[14] 4776 3-9-3 84 JimmyFortune 8 — 76
(J H M Gosden) *trckd ldrs: effrt over 2f out: hanging and fnd nil fr over 1f out* **3/1**[2]

5 *¾* **Red Gala** 3-9-3 KerrinMcEvoy 1 — 75
(Sir Michael Stoute) *settled in rr: pushed along 3f out: rn green and no imp: kpt on fnl f* **8/1**

0 **6** *14* **Desert Joy**[82] 2673 3-8-12 LPKeniry 9 — 43
(D R C Elsworth) *in tch: shkn up 3f out: sn wknd* **33/1**

5-3 **7** *1* **Gravinsky (USA)**[14] 4776 3-9-3 SebSanders 6 — 46
(Mrs A J Perrett) *chsd ldrs: rdn to chal over 2f out: veered wildly and sn gave up: wknd rapidly over 1f out* **12/1**

0-04 **8** *15* **Aeronaut**[45] 3816 3-9-0 38 (t) StephenDonohoe(3) 4 — 18
(J M Bradley) *a in rr: lost tch 4f out: t.o* **100/1**

2- **9** *34* **Scotch Pancake**[353] 5391 3-8-12 TedDurcan 7 — —
(D R C Elsworth) *t.k.h: sddle slipped sn after s and rdr a passenger: w ldrs to 3f out: sn t.o* **9/4**[1]

2m 9.57s (-0.67) **Going Correction** +0.025s/f (Good) — 9 Ran SP% **114.1**
Speed ratings (Par 103):103,102,101,100,100 88,88,76,48
CSF £50.35 TOTE £4.60: £1.60, £3.50, £3.10; EX 63.40.
Owner Highclere Thoroughbred Racing XXXI **Bred** Baronrath And Baroda Studs **Trained** Middleham Moor, N Yorks

FOCUS
This looked a decent three-year-old maiden for the time of year and, despite the favourite not being able to run her race with the slipping saddle, it should produce winners.
Mowazana(IRE) Official explanation: jockey said filly hung right-handed in the closing stages
Desert Joy Official explanation: jockey said filly had a breathing problem
Scotch Pancake Official explanation: jockey said saddle slipped

5152 SUNGARD SECURITIES FINANCE H'CAP — 1m 2f 7y
4:50 (4:51) (Class 4) (0-80,80) 3-Y-0 — **£5,505** (£1,637; £818; £408) Stalls High

Form — RPR

0021 **1** **Altilhar (USA)**[17] 4673 3-8-13 75 (b) SebSanders 2 — 83+
(G L Moore) *trckd ldrs: effrt 2f out: narrow ld jst over 1f out: drvn clr ins fnl f* **7/2**[1]

6325 **2** *2 ½* **Miss Trinidad (USA)**[32] 4204 3-8-13 75 RHills 5 — 79
(B J Meehan) *hld up in last trio: effrt and nt clr run 2f out: prog on outer over 1f out: r.o to take 2nd last strides* **8/1**

4146 **3** *nk* **Bon Viveur**[14] 4784 3-8-10 72 (p) PatDobbs 11 — 75
(R Hannon) *led: drvn over 2f out: narrowly hdd jst over 1f out: one pce: lost 2nd last strides* **11/1**

61 **4** *hd* **Dream Prize (IRE)**[132] 1296 3-9-4 80 KerrinMcEvoy 8 — 83
(Sir Michael Stoute) *nvr gng wl and rdn in last pair: prog u.p over 2f out: chsd ldng pair 1f out: kpt on* **7/2**[1]

5453 **5** *1 ¼* **Gracechurch (IRE)**[7] 4991 3-8-11 73 TonyCulhane 3 — 73+
(M R Channon) *hld up in last pair: effrt whn nt clr run wl over 1f out: styd on ins fnl f: no ch* **9/2**[2]

1552 **6** *hd* **And Again (USA)**[20] 4610 3-8-11 73 ChrisCatlin 1 — 73
(J R Fanshawe) *trckd ldrs: rdn over 2f out: nt qckn and no prog over 1f out: one pce after* **11/2**[3]

000 **7** *2 ½* **Triple Bluff**[77] 2815 3-8-7 69 TedDurcan 12 — 64
(Mrs A J Perrett) *trckd ldrs: rdn over 2f out: no prog over 1f out: wknd ins fnl f* **33/1**

-306 **8** *nk* **Dyanita**[112] 1823 3-8-5 67 RoystonFfrench 9 — 62
(B W Hills) *t.k.h: trckd ldr to 2f out: hanging and wknd over 1f out* **20/1**

2014 **9** *nk* **High Class Problem (IRE)**[9] 4933 3-8-6 68 TPQueally 6 — 62
(P F I Cole) *hld up in midfield: lost pl 2f out: n.m.r over 1f out: no ch after* **12/1**

2m 11.03s (0.79) **Going Correction** +0.025s/f (Good) — **9** Ran SP% **112.9**
Speed ratings (Par 103):97,95,94,94,93 93,91,91,90
CSF £31.24 CT £274.74 TOTE £4.90: £1.90, £2.40, £3.30; EX 36.40 Place 6 £170.24, Place 5 £104.74.
Owner H R Hunt **Bred** Grapestock Llc & Westwood Thoroughbreds Llc **Trained** Woodingdean, E Sussex

FOCUS
Not the strongest of races, but improved form from the first two.
T/Plt: £218.90 to a £1 stake. Pool: £70,479.35. 234.95 winning tickets. T/Qpdt: £48.20 to a £1 stake. Pool: £3,369.00. 51.70 winning tickets. JN

4736 YORK (L-H)
Friday, September 8

OFFICIAL GOING: Good (good to soft in places)
There was a running rail in place on the paddock bend and in the back straight 3m wide. The ground was 'mainly good, good to soft in the back straight'.
Wind: Virtually nil Weather: Fine, warm and sunny

5153 LADBROKES MALLARD STKS (H'CAP) — 1m 5f 197y
1:35 (1:36) (Class 2) (0-110,109) 3-Y-0+ **£19,431** (£5,781; £2,889; £1,443) Stalls Low

Form — RPR

33-2 **1** **Sunday Symphony**[13] 4791 4-9-3 98 LDettori 8 — 114+
(Saeed Bin Suroor) *hld up: hdwy over 5f out: c wd st: led over 3f out: sn clr* **4/1**[2]

512 **2** *5* **Zurbaran (IRE)**[21] 4560 3-7-7 90 oh5 DuranFentiman(5) 3 — 96
(B J Meehan) *chsd ldrs: wnt 2nd over 2f out: no ch w wnr* **9/1**

101 **3** *2 ½* **Mudawin (IRE)**[16] 4713 5-8-12 93 JohnEgan 2 — 96
(Jane Chapple-Hyam) *chsd ldrs: wnt 2nd over 4f out: one pce* **11/2**[3]

0452 **4** *10* **Barolo**[13] 4797 7-10-0 109 (p) JMurtagh 7 — 98
(W R Swinburn) *lw: drvn to join ldr after s: led after 2f: set str pce: hdd over 3f out: sn wknd* **7/1**

3130 **5** *¾* **Greenwich Meantime**[16] 4713 6-8-13 94 PaulHanagan 4 — 81
(R A Fahey) *hld up in rr: effrt over 5f out: nvr on terms* **7/1**

130- **6** *27* **Gold Gun (USA)**[307] 6254 4-9-1 96 NCallan 6 — 46
(K A Ryan) *stdd s: hld up in last: drvn over 3f out: sn bhd* **33/1**

4111 **7** *8* **Strategic Mount**[37] 4039 3-8-4 96 ow2 EddieAhern 1 — 34
(P F I Cole) *restless in stalls: led 2f: w ldr: lost pl over 3f out: sn bhd* **7/4**[1]

2m 58.52s (0.08) **Going Correction** +0.325s/f (Good)
WFA 3 from 4yo+ 11lb — 7 Ran SP% **109.7**
Speed ratings (Par 109):112,109,107,102,101 86,81
CSF £35.26 CT £181.25 TOTE £4.40: £2.20, £4.10; EX 40.20 Trifecta £104.10 Pool: £484.19 - 3.30 winning tickets..
Owner Godolphin **Bred** Darley **Trained** Newmarket, Suffolk
■ The St Leger meeting was switched to York due to redevelopment at Doncaster, and reduced to two days.

FOCUS
This looked a competitive handicap on paper, but at the end of a race in which the fourth and seventh possibly set too strong a pace they were well strung out behind the easy winner, who was much improved and showed Group-class form.

NOTEBOOK
Sunday Symphony, having only his second run of the campaign, gained his first victory since his two-year-old season. He made smooth headway to show ahead early in the home straight and, racing down the centre of the course, soon came clear. He hung a little, something he did more than once last year, but was much too good on the day and was eased down towards the finish with the race in the bag. On the upgrade, he is now a leading fancy for the Cesarewitch, but could go instead for a valuable handicap at the Ascot Festival at the end of this month. (op 9-2)
Zurbaran(IRE), upped in grade, was 5lb out of the weights and in effect 9lb higher than when runner-up at Newbury last time. He ran a sound race, if proving no match for the easy winner, and should continue to progress. (op 11-1)
Mudawin(IRE) was bidding to follow up his shock Ebor success over course and distance off a 5lb higher mark. Always prominent, he tried to go with the winner in the straight but could only plug on at the same pace and was run out of second going to the two pole. (op 5-1)
Barolo was put up 5lb for his narrow second in a Goodwood Listed race. In front after a quarter of a mile, he went faster than was desirable as he was being harried by Strategic Mount, and after being headed early in the home straight he was soon on the retreat. (op 6-1)
Greenwich Meantime was being pushed along leaving the back straight and could never get into the race. He really needs faster ground. (op 9-1)
Gold Gun(USA), sold out of Michael Jarvis's yard and gelded since his last appearance in the November Handicap eleven months ago, was always at the back of the field.
Strategic Mount was bidding for a four-timer, having been raised a total of 20lb. After rearing in the stalls, he grabbed the early lead but was soon headed by Barolo. He tried to match strides with that rival down the back straight, the pair going rather too fast, and it was no surprise that he dropped away once in line for home. The ground was too slow for him aswell and this run can be written off. Official explanation: jockey said colt was unsuited by the good (good to soft places) ground (op 13-8 tchd 15-8 in places)

5154 PERSIMMON HOMES FLYING CHILDERS STKS (GROUP 2) — 5f
2:05 (2:05) (Class 1) 2-Y-0
£39,746 (£15,064; £7,539; £3,759; £1,883; £945) Stalls High

Form — RPR

122 **1** **Wi Dud**[16] 4712 2-9-0 111 NCallan 2 — 112+
(K A Ryan) *lw: mid-div: hdwy over 2f out: led over 1f out: styd on strly* **11/4**[1]

1613 **2** *1 ½* **Bahama Mama (IRE)**[38] 4026 2-8-11 102 DarryllHolland 9 — 104
(J Noseda) *sn outpcd and in rr: hdwy 2f out: n.m.r appr fnl f: squeezed ins last: r.o* **11/2**[3]

1120 **3** *nk* **Hoh Mike (IRE)**[57] 3442 2-9-0 107 LDettori 3 — 106
(M L W Bell) *lw: dwlt: outpcd: hdwy on outside 2f out: edgd rt over 1f out: styd on same pce* **10/3**[2]

2144 **4** *1 ¼* **Siren's Gift**[15] 4737 2-8-11 101 MartinDwyer 8 — 98
(A M Balding) *lw: mid-div: hdwy 2f out: kpt on same pce* **25/1**

6114 **5** *1* **Elhamri**[16] 4712 2-9-0 109 DPMcDonogh 5 — 97
(S Kirk) *chsd ldrs: n.m.r after 1f: kpt on same pce fnl 2f* **11/2**[3]

2411 **6** *shd* **Abby Road (IRE)**[20] 4594 2-8-11 101 KDarley 1 — 94
(B J Meehan) *led: hung lft and hdd over 1f out: sn wknd* **15/2**

1151 **7** *shd* **Not For Me (IRE)**[16] 4715 2-9-0 105 JohnEgan 6 — 97
(T J Pitt) *chsd ldr: ev ch tl wknd 1f out* **8/1**

2001 **8** *¾* **Danum Dancer**[8] 4946 2-9-0 70 (b) DavidAllan 4 — 94?
(N Bycroft) *chsd ldrs: n.m.r whn n.m.r over 1f out* **100/1**

The Form Book, Raceform Ltd, Compton, RG20 6NL

212 **9** *hd* **Fanlight Fanny (USA)**[16] [4715] 2-8-11 95 JimCrowley 7 90
(P Winkworth) *w ldrs: fdd over 1f out* **50/1**

58.39 secs (-0.93) **Going Correction** +0.075s/f (Good) **9** Ran SP% **110.2**
Speed ratings (Par 107):110,107,107,105,103 103,103,102,101
CSF £16.70 TOTE £3.60: £1.40, £2.10, £1.70; EX 22.60 Trifecta £77.00 Pool: £792.10 - 7.30 winning tickets..
Owner J Duddy,L Duddy,P Mcbride,E Duffy **Bred** D R Botterill **Trained** Hambleton, N Yorks

FOCUS
As good a renewal as we have seen of this race in recent years and the winner, who ran to his Gimcrack level, shaped as if he might do a bit better yet. They raced down the centre of the track and the principals all came from off the pace.

NOTEBOOK
Wi Dud, back at the minimum trip, gained his first Group-race success following a brace of seconds. He did it well too, soon in midfield following a slightly slow start before coming through to win cosily. He may go for the Middle Park now, where he could meet Conquest, who beat him in the Gimcrack. (op 3-1 tchd 100-30 in places)
Bahama Mama(IRE) ◆ finished a little further behind Wi Dud than she had in the Molecomb, but that would not have been the case had she enjoyed a clear run. Quickly in rear in a race run at a fast pace, she was soon travelling well, but twice met with trouble when attempting to improve. She ran on to secure second near the finish, but the winner was in command by then. The Cornwallis should provide her with a good opportunity to make amends.
Hoh Mike(IRE), back at five furlongs after a disappointing show in the July Stakes at Newmarket, was slowly away, as he tends to be. Switched left with over two furlongs to run and attempting to challenge on the outer of the group, he kept on quite well if unable to match the pace of the winner. He may step back up to six furlongs in the totepool Two-Year-Old Trophy at Redcar. (op 5-2 tchd 7-2)
Siren's Gift was found out by six furlongs in soft ground in the Lowther here last month. She had her chance, but lacked the pace in the latter stages to turn around Goodwood running with Wi Dud and Bahama Mama.
Elhamri, behind today's winner when fourth in the Gimcrack last time, found himself unable to go the pace at halfway but was running on again at the finish. The stiffer five furlongs of the Cornwallis at Ascot should suit him. (op 13-2 tchd 7-1 in a place)
Abby Road(IRE) was taking on colts for the first time. She showed bright pace to lead but was hanging before being headed and weakened out of the frame inside the last. (op 8-1)
Not For Me(IRE), winner of the Listed Roses Stakes at the Ebor meeting here last month, was still in the firing line with a furlong to run before fading.
Danum Dancer, taking a big step up in class, was not disgraced and would have been a little closer had he not had to check approaching the final furlong.
Fanlight Fanny(USA), runner-up to Not For Me over course and distance last time, was not up to this task but can win more races back at a lower level.

5155 IRISH THOROUGHBRED MARKETING PARK HILL STKS (GROUP 2) (F&M) 1m 5f 197y

2:40 (2:41) (Class 1) 3-Y-O+

£56,780 (£21,520; £10,770; £5,370; £2,690; £1,350) **Stalls** Low

Form RPR
2030 **1** **Rising Cross**[27] [4385] 3-8-7 107 MartinDwyer 4 111
(J R Best) *trckd ldrs: effrt and nt clr run 3f out: hit on hd by rival's whip 1f out: styd on gamely to ld towards fin* **16/1**
61 **2** *3/4* **Anna Pavlova**[15] [4741] 3-8-7 101 PaulHanagan 5 110
(R A Fahey) *hld up: hdwy on wd outside over 3f out: led and hung lft over 1f out: hdd towards fin* **5/1**[3]
6113 **3** *1 1/4* **Allegretto (IRE)**[16] [4714] 3-8-10 107 RyanMoore 7 111
(Sir Michael Stoute) *w ldr: hung lft and no ex ins last* **11/4**[2]
2331 **4** *nk* **Maroussies Wings (IRE)**[22] [4543] 3-8-7 105 KDarley 6 108
(P C Haslam) *hld up: hdwy to chse ldrs 8f out: upsides over 2f out: nt qckn fnl f* **8/1**
1616 **5** *hd* **Quenched**[33] [4192] 3-8-7 102 RichardHughes 2 108
(J H M Gosden) *hld up: hdwy over 3f out: kpt on same pce fnl 2f* **10/1**
-612 **6** *1 3/4* **Guadalajara (GER)**[20] [4595] 5-9-4 110 LDettori 3 105
(Saeed Bin Suroor) *swtg: excitable and skipped parade: led: drvn over 3f out: hdd over 1f out: wknd ins last* **15/8**[1]
2524 **7** *12* **Art Eyes (USA)**[13] [4797] 4-9-4 105 JohnEgan 1 97
(D R C Elsworth) *wnt prom 10f out: wknd over 2f out: eased ins last* **14/1**

2m 58.46s (0.02) **Going Correction** +0.325s/f (Good)
WFA 3 from 4yo+ 11lb **7** Ran SP% **110.9**
Speed ratings (Par 115):112,111,110,110,110 109,102
CSF £86.96 TOTE £17.50: £4.90, £2.10; EX 91.70.
Owner Gary A Tanaka **Bred** J R Wills **Trained** Hucking, Kent
■ A first Group winner for John Best. The Park Hill, and the St Leger, are run over 155 yards further at their Doncaster home.

FOCUS
The pace in the early parts was just ordinary, but it increased with around six furlongs to run. The runners came centre-to-stands' side in the home straight. Rising Cross was suited by the longer trip and improved a few pounds on her Oaks form.

NOTEBOOK
Rising Cross, placed in two Classics earlier in the summer, gained her first Group victory. Tackling her longest trip to date, she looked held going to the final furlong, having failed to get a clear run, but ran on with great bravery when a gap finally appeared to get on top in the last 75 yards. (tchd 20-1)
Anna Pavlova, winner of the Galtres Stakes at the Ebor meeting here, was tackling an extra two furlongs. She came from off the pace to lead with over a furlong to run, racing near the stands' rail and a little way apart from her rivals, but after looking all over the winner she was cut down late on. (op 13-2)
Allegretto(IRE), third in the Yorkshire Oaks, was one of three vying for the lead up the long straight and could pull out no more inside the last, the longer trip just telling. This was a solid effort and she loses nothing in defeat. (op 5-2 tchd 3-1)
Maroussies Wings(IRE), upped in trip, had every chance with a quarter of a mile to run but could not quite hold on in the final furlong. She has made steady improvement this term and this was her best effort to date.
Quenched travelled well enough a little off the pace but was unable to get to the leaders, the longer trip finding her out in the end. She is not quite up to this level. (op 12-1)
Guadalajara(GER), not for the first time, became keyed up before the start. Making the running, she was being pressurised for the lead with half a mile to run and, eventually relinquishing it, she was beaten in the final furlong. (op 7-4 tchd 13-8 and 2-1)

5156 GNER DONCASTER CUP (GROUP 2) 2m 2f

3:15 (3:15) (Class 1) 3-Y-O+

£56,780 (£21,520; £10,770; £5,370; £2,690; £1,350) **Stalls** Low

Form RPR
5241 **1** **Sergeant Cecil**[17] [4677] 7-9-4 111 LDettori 4 118
(B R Millman) *lw: hld up in rr: effrt over 3f out: wnt rt & led over 1f out: styd on wl* **1/1**[1]
21-6 **2** *1* **Alcazar (IRE)**[110] [1875] 11-9-1 114 MickyFenton 7 114
(H Morrison) *lw: trckd ldrs: chal over 2f out: checked and hit by winning rdr's whip over 1f out: swtchd lft: rallied and no ex ins last* **11/2**[2]
1155 **3** *2 1/2* **Baddam**[17] [4677] 4-9-1 103 IanMongan 3 111
(M R Channon) *in tch: drvn over 4f out: one pce fnl 2f* **10/1**
03-0 **4** *1 1/4* **Kasthari (IRE)**[17] [4677] 7-9-1 106 DarryllHolland 1 110
(J Howard Johnson) *led: qcknd 6f out: hdd over 1f out: one pce* **33/1**
3432 **5** *1* **Souvenance**[12] [4863] 3-7-12 102 JamieMackay 5 106
(Sir Mark Prescott) *in tch: effrt over 3f out: one pce fnl 2f* **11/1**
63 **6** *1 1/4* **Clara Allen (IRE)**[13] [4822] 8-8-12 TPO'Shea 2 104
(John E Kiely, Ire) *hld up in last: effrt over 3f out: sn rdn and hung rt: kpt on: nvr nr ldrs* **7/1**[3]
1030 **7** *12* **Tungsten Strike (USA)**[17] [4677] 5-9-4 111 RyanMoore 8 97
(Mrs A J Perrett) *lw: trckd ldr: effrt 4f out: lost pl over 2f out* **15/2**
0300 **8** *8* **Winged D'Argent (IRE)**[17] [4677] 5-9-1 102 (b) JoeFanning 6 85
(M Johnston) *chsd ldrs: drvn over 4f out: sn lost pl* **25/1**

3m 58.37s (10.37)
WFA 3 from 4yo+ 14lb **8** Ran SP% **113.9**
CSF £6.71 TOTE £2.00: £1.10, £1.80, £2.50; EX 6.30 Trifecta £26.80 Pool: £1,294.94 - 34.23 winning tickets..
Owner Terry Cooper **Bred** D E Hazzard **Trained** Kentisbeare, Devon

FOCUS
The pace was reasonable and the runners came towards the stands' side in the straight. A slight personal best under the penalty from Sergeant Cecil, who is just about the pick of the stayers behind Yeats. The form seems sound enough.

NOTEBOOK
Sergeant Cecil, under a 3lb penalty for his Lonsdale Cup win, followed up over this extra two furlongs. Held up before improving leaving the back straight, he went on going to the furlong pole but did the runner-up no favours by edging slightly to his right before staying on well. Runner-up to Millenary in this event at its usual home a year ago, he has now been successful in three of his four visits to York. (op 11-10 tchd 6-5 and 5-4 in places)
Alcazar(IRE), off the track since his seasonal bow in May, ran a cracking race and would have been closer still had he not been tightened up a little by the winner at the furlong pole. This will have put him right for an autumn campaign taking in races like the Prix du Cadran and Prix Royal-Oak at Longchamp. (tchd 6-1)
Baddam has just been found wanting over shorter trips since his Royal Ascot double, but this was his best effort to date. He may return to handicap company in the Cesarewitch now and looks on a fair mark there. (tchd 11-1)
Kasthari(IRE) is without a win on the Flat since dead-heating with Millenary in this event two years ago but this was a decent effort. Setting a fair pace, he was collared by the winner with over a furlong to run and stuck on for fourth prize.
Souvenance was attempting to emulate the same connections' Alleluia, a similar type who won this five years ago. Competing in her sixth different country in as many races this season, she was not disgraced against her elders but was never able to get in a telling challenge. (op 9-1)
Clara Allen(IRE), expected to relish this longer trip, was well supported. After racing in rear, she tried to improve towards the stands' rail in the straight but was not helping her rider and was never really a factor. (op 14-1 tchd 16-1 in places)
Tungsten Strike(USA), who was giving weight away to all his rivals except Sergeant Cecil, has now put in two below-par efforts since his commendable third in the Goodwood Cup. (op 7-1)
Winged D'Argent(IRE) has been mainly disappointing this year and the return of headgear failed to stem the tide.

5157 EUROPEAN BREEDERS FUND CARRIE RED FILLIES' NURSERY 7f

3:50 (3:50) (Class 2) 2-Y-O **£22,669** (£6,744; £3,370; £1,683) **Stalls** Centre

Form RPR
622 **1** **Ronaldsay**[21] [4553] 2-8-0 **74** FrancisNorton 6 79
(R Hannon) *in rr: bmpd and forced wd bnd over 4f out: hdwy on wd outside over 2f out: led jst ins last: hld on towards fin* **12/1**
1323 **2** *nk* **Voodoo Moon**[14] [4761] 2-8-10 **84** JoeFanning 10 88
(M Johnston) *led: kpt on wl fnl 2f: hdd ins last: no ex nr line* **15/2**
2616 **3** *3* **Bright Moon**[9] [4928] 2-8-7 **81** RichardHughes 9 78
(R Hannon) *chsd ldrs: drvn over 2f out: one pce fnl f* **12/1**
2316 **4** *3* **Crystal Gazer (FR)**[14] [4762] 2-8-5 **79** MartinDwyer 8 68
(R Hannon) *w ldrs: effrt over 2f out: wknd last 150yds* **33/1**
2114 **5** *1* **Market Day**[34] [4146] 2-9-7 **95** NCallan 4 82
(L M Cumani) *in rr: wnt rt bnd over 4f out: sn drvn along: kpt on fnl 2f: nvr rchd ldrs* **11/2**[3]
332 **6** *3/4* **Silkie Smooth (IRE)**[33] [4171] 2-8-8 **82** RyanMoore 5 67
(B W Hills) *dwlt: t.k.h in rr: stmbld bnd over 4f out: effrt over 2f out: nvr trbld ldrs* **5/2**[1]
3603 **7** *1* **Cassiara**[37] [4053] 2-8-6 **80** KDarley 2 62
(J Pearce) *sn trcking ldrs: wknd over 1f out* **8/1**
302 **8** *7* **Elizabeth Street (USA)**[51] [3640] 2-8-4 **78** ow1 EddieAhern 3 43
(P F I Cole) *trckd ldrs: effrt over 2f out: wknd over 1f out* **5/1**[2]
0025 **9** *1 1/4* **Security Tiger (IRE)**[22] [4526] 2-7-12 **75** oh1 ow3.. EdwardCreighton(3) 1 37
(M R Channon) *t.k.h: w ldrs: lost pl over 1f out* **16/1**
012 **10** *2 1/2* **Jane Of Arc (FR)**[63] [3265] 2-8-3 **77** PaulHanagan 7 32
(T D Easterby) *mid-div: sn drvn along: lost pl 2f out: sn bhd and eased* **10/1**

1m 25.69s (0.29) **Going Correction** +0.075s/f (Good) **10** Ran SP% **116.8**
Speed ratings (Par 98):101,100,97,93,92 91,90,82,81,78
CSF £99.03 CT £1112.77 TOTE £15.40: £2.80, £1.90, £4.10; EX 117.00 Trifecta £451.50 Part won. Pool: £635.96 - 0.10 winning tickets..
Owner S P Tindall **Bred** Stowell Hill Ltd **Trained** East Everleigh, Wilts

FOCUS
Not a strong nursery considering the prize money on offer, but the first two did well to pull clear They all came across to the stands'-side rail.

NOTEBOOK
Ronaldsay, pushed wide turning in, ended up hard against the stands'-side rail. With the rail to help she did not hang this time but at the line there was nothing at all to spare. She looks a slightly nervous type and her rider was as sympathetic as he could be. (op 11-1)
Voodoo Moon, dictating things from the front, stuck on gamely, only to miss out near the line. This was improved form, but unfortunately her rating will go up again as a result. (op 8-1)
Bright Moon, not seen to best advantage at Lingfield, found this mark, 5lb higher than Salisbury, simply too much. (op 10-1)
Crystal Gazer(FR), an excitable type, seemed to find the seven-furlong trip stretching her stamina to breaking point.
Market Day, 11lb higher than Lingfield, had trouble making the turn. She stuck to her guns in willing fashion and might even be ready for a step up to a mile. (tchd 6-1)
Silkie Smooth(IRE), who looked very fit indeed, took a tug in the rear and her cause was badly dented when she stumbled badly on the turn. (op 11-4 tchd 3-1 in places)

5158 **A1 MEDICAL & GENERAL SCARBROUGH STKS (LISTED RACE)** **5f**
4:25 (4:26) (Class 1) 2-Y-O+ **£16,595** (£6,274; £3,136; £1,568) **Stalls** High

Form RPR
3401 **1** **Celtic Mill**^{34} [4158] 8-9-9 104 ....(p) DarryllHolland 4 114
(D W Barker) *chsd ldrs: styd on to ld ins last: hld on wl* **8/1**
B300 **2** *¾* **Orientor**^{15} [4738] 8-9-9 105 .... DanielTudhope 1 111
(J S Goldie) *lw: mid-div: hdwy 2f out: upsides ins last: no ex* **12/1**
3040 **3** *nk* **Strike Up The Band**^{36} [4080] 3-9-8 103 .... RichardHughes 10 110
(D Nicholls) *lw: w ldr: led over 1f out: hdd and no ex ins last* **7/1^{3}**
1550 **4** *nk* **Fayr Jag (IRE)**^{15} [4738] 7-10-0 110 .... DavidAllan 6 114
(T D Easterby) *chsd ldrs: kpt on same pce appr fnl f* **10/1**
0600 **5** *½* **Mecca's Mate**^{12} [4832] 5-9-4 100 .... PaulHanagan 5 102
(D W Barker) *sn outpcd and in rr: hdwy 2f out: styd on ins last* **12/1**
6646 **6** *¾* **The Tatling (IRE)**^{15} [4738] 9-9-9 110 .... RyanMoore 2 104
(J M Bradley) *sn outpcd and in rr: hdwy over 1f out: styng on fin* **2/1^{1}**
5000 **7** *2* **Gift Horse**^{15} [4738] 6-9-9 105 .... EddieAhern 7 97
(D Nicholls) *s.i.s: kpt on fnl 2f: nvr nr ldrs* **7/2^{2}**
1056 **8** *½* **Mr Wolf**^{12} [4832] 5-9-9 92 ....(p) NCallan 11 95
(D W Barker) *led: edgd lft after 1f: hdd over 1f out: wknd ins last* **20/1**
4000 **9** *2 ½* **Fire Up The Band**^{76} [2847] 7-9-9 100 .... FrancisNorton 9 86
(D Nicholls) *trckd ldrs: wknd over 1f out* **33/1**
0006 **10** *4* **Maltese Falcon**^{3} [5087] 6-9-9 103 ....(t) JoeFanning 3 72
(P F I Cole) *mid-div: drvn over 2f out: sn wknd* **33/1**
0110 **11** *1 ½* **The Lord**^{36} [4080] 6-9-12 102 .... JohnEgan 8 70
(W G M Turner) *mid-div: hung lft and lost pl over 1f out: eased* **25/1**

58.50 secs (-0.82) **Going Correction** +0.075s/f (Good)
WFA 3 from 5yo+ 1lb **11** Ran SP% **118.1**
Speed ratings: 109,107,107,106,106 104,101,100,96,90 88
CSF £94.75 TOTE £7.00: £2.00, £3.30, £2.50; EX 99.20 Trifecta £821.50 Part won. Pool: £1,157.16 - 0.30 winning tickets..
Owner P Asquith **Bred** P Asquith **Trained** Scorton, N Yorks

FOCUS
They went a scorching pace and Strike Up The Band, the only three-year-old in the line-up, deserves plenty of praise, as he was the only one who matched strides with pacesetter Mr Wolf. Straightforward form.

NOTEBOOK
Celtic Mill, winner of this at Doncaster in 2004 and third last year, had his confidence restored after his Windsor success. In the end he did just enough and he now heads for a Group 3 at Newbury next weekend.
Orientor, isolated in stall one, deserves plenty of credit and with a better draw he must be thereabouts in the Gold Cup at Ayr next weekend. (tchd 14-1)
Strike Up The Band ◆, the only three-year-old in the field, looked in peak condition. He was the only one who matched strides with the pacesetter and in the end was just found out. He richly deserves compensation. (op 8-1 tchd 9-1)
Fayr Jag(IRE), with a 5lb penalty for his Group 3 victories, ran right up to his best, especially considering these days he is much happier over six.
Mecca's Mate, taken off her feet, put in some sterling late work and looks back to her best after an indifferent summer.
The Tatling(IRE) had won only once from his most recent 23 starts and age seems to have blunted his speed. He was unable to go the pace, but to his credit never gave up trying all the way to the line. (op 9-4 tchd 5-2 in places)
Gift Horse was well backed but has yet to win over this trip and a tardy start put him on the back foot. He never looked like entering the argument. (tchd 4-1 and 100-30 in a place)
Mr Wolf ◆, bottom on the official rtaings, showed blinding speed to take these along. He will be of real interest returned to handicap company.
Maltese Falcon Official explanation: trainer said gelding lost a near-fore shoe
The Lord Official explanation: jockey said gelding moved poorly throughout

5159 **WEATHERBYS BANK SCEPTRE STKS (LISTED RACE) (F&M)** **7f**
5:00 (5:00) (Class 1) 3-Y-O+ **£17,781** (£6,723; £3,360; £1,680) **Stalls** Centre

Form RPR
102 **1** **Silver Touch (IRE)**^{62} [3316] 3-8-10 99 .... RyanMoore 11 109+
(M R Channon) *lw: hld up: smooth hdwy over 2f out: led 1f out: pushed out* **11/4^{2}**
5202 **2** *1 ¼* **Wake Up Maggie (IRE)**^{62} [3322] 3-8-10 106 .... EddieAhern 4 106
(C F Wall) *sn w ldrs: led over 1f out: sn hdd and no ex* **2/1^{1}**
4-20 **3** *1 ¼* **Highway To Glory (IRE)**^{22} [4542] 3-8-10 100 .... OscarUrbina 6 103
(M Botti) *t.k.h in rr: effrt and edgd rt over 2f out: swtchd lft over 1f out: styd on* **14/1**
-236 **4** *nk* **Cantabria**^{19} [4628] 3-8-10 103 .... RichardHughes 1 102
(Sir Michael Stoute) *led: hung lft and hdd over 1f out: kpt on same pce* **8/1**
4360 **5** *1* **Strut**^{90} [2438] 3-8-10 98 .... SteveDrowne 5 99
(R Charlton) *hld up towards rr: effrt 3f out: kpt on same pce* **20/1**
/626 **6** *nk* **Mamela (GER)**^{52} [3627] 5-9-0 98 .... NCallan 8 99
(L M Cumani) *s.i.s: hdwy 3f out: nvr rchd ldrs* **50/1**
5404 **7** *½* **Tagula Sunrise (IRE)**^{7} [4988] 4-9-0 90 .... PaulHanagan 10 97
(R A Fahey) *hld up on outer: t.k.h: nt clr run over 2f out: no threat after* **16/1**
1213 **8** *nk* **Bosset (USA)**^{20} [4593] 3-8-10 97 .... LDettori 7 97
(J Noseda) *w ldrs: fdd fnl f* **9/2^{3}**
-252 **9** *nk* **Sweet Treat (IRE)**^{19} [4628] 4-9-0 96 .... MartinDwyer 9 96
(J R Fanshawe) *chsd ldrs: drvn 3f out: lost pl over 1f out* **14/1**

1m 24.09s (-1.31) **Going Correction** +0.075s/f (Good)
WFA 3 from 4yo+ 4lb **9** Ran SP% **115.2**
Speed ratings (Par 111):110,108,107,106,105 105,104,104,104
CSF £8.62 TOTE £3.70: £1.60, £1.30, £3.90; EX 9.70 Trifecta £240.10 Pool: £913.12 - 2.70 winning tickets. Place 6 £1,294.66, Place 5 £351.22.
Owner Jaber Abdullah **Bred** Kildaragh Stud **Trained** West Ilsley, Berks

FOCUS
A high-class renewal of this distaff Listed race but the early pace was very steady. The winner has always been well regarded and remains unexposed. She can go on to even better things.

NOTEBOOK
Silver Touch(IRE), quite a big filly, looks to be thriving. Ridden with bags of confidence, she crept there and in the end scored in most decisive fashion, without her rider having to get anywhere near serious with her. She can win better races than this and will make an even better four-year-old. (op 10-3 tchd 7-2 and 5-2)
Wake Up Maggie(IRE) looked to have been found a golden opportunity. She did nothing at all wrong but simply met a better, less-exposed filly. (tchd 9-4)
Highway To Glory(IRE), a very keen type, met traffic problems but stuck on in grim fashion to snatch third spot on the line. A mile suits her even better. (op 16-1 tchd 12-1)
Cantabria, back to seven, set her own pace but she hung under pressure and was readily put in her place. (op 7-1)
Strut, absent since June, had the visor discarded. She had a bit to find and never really threatened.
Mamela(GER) had something to find and this trip looked on the sharp side for her.
Bosset(USA), having just her fifth start, faded disappointingly and her stable is not exactly on fire at the moment. (op 5-1 tchd 11-2 in a place)
T/Jkpt: £30,294.90 to a £1 stake. Pool: £42,669.00. 1.00 winning ticket. T/Plt: £378.20 to a £1 stake. Pool: £143,124.20. 276.25 winning tickets. T/Qpdt: £64.60 to a £1 stake. Pool: £7,578.80. 86.80 winning tickets. WG

4648 BREMEN
Friday, September 8

OFFICIAL GOING: Good

5160a **BREMER STUTEN-MEILE (LISTED RACE) (F&M)** **1m**
5:30 (5:35) 3-Y-O+ **£8,276** (£3,034; £1,655; £828)

RPR
1 **Heat Of The Night**^{19} [4649] 4-9-0 .... THellier 1 99
(P W Chapple-Hyam) *trckd ldr on ins in 3rd or 4th, swtchd off rail and hdwy over 2f out, pushed along to ld over 1f out, pushed clr fnl f (2/1 2/1^{1}*
2 *2* **Tech Engine (GER)**^{131} [1328] 3-8-9 .... EPedroza 2 95
(P Schiergen, Germany)
3 *1 ¼* **Amateis (GER)**^{51} [3661] 3-9-0 .... ABest 5 98
(P Rau, Germany)
4 *½* **A Winning Dream (GER)** 4-9-0 .... FilipMinarik 3 92
(P Schiergen, Germany)
5 *2* **Madura (GER)**^{22} [4542] 3-8-9 .... AStarke 4 88
(Mario Hofer, Germany)
6 *1* **Lasira (GER)**^{27} [4383] 3-9-0 .... WMongil 7 91
(P Schiergen, Germany)
7 **Halabaloo (IRE)**^{748} [4954] 5-9-4 .... ASuborics 6 —
(F Reuterskiold, Sweden)

1m 41.74s
WFA 3 from 4yo+ 5lb **7** Ran SP% **33.3**
(including 10 Euro stake): WIN 20; PL 13, 22, 11; SF 348.
Owner Miss K Rausing **Bred** Miss K Rausing **Trained** Newmarket, Suffolk

NOTEBOOK
Heat Of The Night gained some all-important black type with an easy win that owed much to a fine ride from Hellier. Extricating his mount from the rail just when it looked like she might get boxed in, he took her to the front before the furlong pole and, remembering how she had ducked violently away from the whip at Dusseldorf, never used the stick, pushing her out with hands and heels.

5052 BATH (L-H)
Saturday, September 9

OFFICIAL GOING: Firm
The ground was obviously quick with every race below the standard time.
Wind: Moderate, across. Weather: Fine.

5161 **SAVINGS ASSURED MORTGAGES MEDIAN AUCTION MAIDEN STKS** **5f 11y**
2:15 (2:15) (Class 5) 2-Y-O **£4,210** (£1,252; £625; £312) **Stalls** Low

Form RPR
5422 **1** **Vaunt**^{36} [4109] 2-9-3 81 ....(b) SteveDrowne 10 80
(R Charlton) *s.i.s: sn chsng ldr: led 2f out: rdn out* **10/11^{1}**
4030 **2** *2 ½* **Pernomente (IRE)**^{33} [4196] 2-9-3 71 ....(t) LPKeniry 12 71
(J S Moore) *led: hdd 2f out: sn rdn: no ex ins fnl f* **10/1**
3 *1* **Madrigale** 2-8-9 .... RichardKingscote$^{(3)}$ 5 62
(G L Moore) *s.i.s: sn mid-div: hdwy over 2f out: sn rdn: kpt on ins fnl f* **12/1**
2500 **4** *1 ½* **Benllech**^{85} [2617] 2-8-12 79 .... MichaelJStainton$^{(5)}$ 11 62
(S Kirk) *chsd ldrs on outside: rdn 2f out: edgd lft 1f out: one pce* **6/1^{2}**
6000 **5** *1 ½* **Merlins Quest**^{5} [5065] 2-9-0 56 .... GregFairley$^{(3)}$ 6 57
(J M Bradley) *a.p: rdn over 2f out: no hdwy* **66/1**
0 **6** *nk* **Mr Forthright**^{6} [5043] 2-8-10 .... BarrySavage$^{(7)}$ 8 56
(J M Bradley) *hld up in mid-div: rdn and outpcd wl over 2f out: kpt on fnl f* **80/1**
0 **7** *hd* **Ella Woodcock (IRE)**^{12} [4895] 2-8-10 .... FrankiePickard$^{(7)}$ 1 55+
(J A Osborne) *outpcd: kpt on fnl f: nvr nrr* **80/1**
00 **8** *1* **Time For Change (IRE)**^{26} [4428] 2-8-12 .... AurelioMedeiros$^{(5)}$ 4 51
(B W Hills) *mid-div: rdn over 2f out: hung lft on ins fr over 1f out: no real prog* **33/1**
0 **9** *½* **Georges Pride**^{15} [4753] 2-9-0 .... StephenDonohoe$^{(3)}$ 7 49
(J M Bradley) *rdn over 2f out: wknd over 1f out* **40/1**
10 *½* **Split The Wind (USA)** 2-8-12 .... StephenCarson 9 43
(R F Johnson Houghton) *dwlt: a bhd* **10/1**
11 *7* **Smirfys Gold (IRE)** 2-9-3 .... EddieAhern 2 22
(E S McMahon) *sn bdly outpcd* **13/2^{3}**

60.70 secs (-1.80) **Going Correction** -0.35s/f (Firm) **11** Ran SP% **115.2**
Speed ratings (Par 95):100,96,94,92,89 89,88,87,86,85 74
CSF £10.55 TOTE £1.80: £1.10, £3.10, £2.50; EX 11.30 Trifecta £106.00 Part won. Pool £149.30. - 0.30 winning units..
Owner Lady Rothschild **Bred** Lord Rothschild **Trained** Beckhampton, Wilts

FOCUS
A moderate event, rated through the second, but the time was a stone better than that for the nursery.

NOTEBOOK
Vaunt found a suitable opening on this drop back to the minimum trip. (tchd 5-6)
Pernomente(IRE) was eventually forced to admit defeat after again setting the pace. (op 14-1)
Madrigale ◆ is a half-brother to a Group 3 mile juvenile winner in France and to mile and a half winner Croon. A springer in the market, he will be better for the experience and seems sure to improve over further. (op 25-1)
Benllech, not seen since June, was without the tongue tie he had worn last time after suffering a breathing problem on his previous outing. (op 13-2)
Merlins Quest looks modest on what he has accomplished so far.
Mr Forthright, a half-brother to seven-furlong Fibresand banded winner Tsarbuck, finished closer than had seemed likely at halfway. (tchd 66-1)

5162 **M. J. CHURCH PLANT NURSERY** **5f 11y**
2:45 (2:46) (Class 4) (0-75,74) 2-Y-O **£5,505** (£1,637; £818; £408) **Stalls** Low

Form RPR
4031 **1** **Cuppacocoa**^{20} [4624] 2-8-10 **66** .... AdamKirby$^{(3)}$ 7 69+
(C G Cox) *w ldr: rdn to ld over 1f out: edgd lft ins fnl f: r.o* **9/2^{2}**

0060 **2** *¾* **Queensgate**[5] 5065 2-8-4 **57** FrankieMcDonald 11 57
(M Blanshard) *a.p: rdn over 2f out: hung lft ins fnl f: r.o* **25/1**

5663 **3** *¾* **Hephaestus**[9] 4969 2-8-12 **65** ChrisCatlin 3 62
(M R Channon) *sn outpcd: rdn and hdwy 2f out: kpt on u.p ins fnl f* **10/1**

3003 **4** *¾* **Clewer**[5] 5052 2-8-1 **59** KevinGhunowa(5) 6 54
(P A Blockley) *led: rdn and hdd over 1f out: no ex towards fin* **17/2**

550 **5** *½* **Road To Recovery**[66] 3193 2-9-0 **67** (v[1]) FergusSweeney 5 60
(A M Balding) *chsd ldrs: rdn 2f out: one pce fnl f* **7/2**[1]

0260 **6** *3* **Nepos**[12] 4893 2-8-12 **65** KerrinMcEvoy 2 47
(J A Osborne) *dwlt: rdn and hdwy on outside over 1f out: no further prog fnl f* **16/1**

5133 **7** *2* **Jost Van Dyke**[15] 4779 2-9-0 **67** SteveDrowne 1 42
(B R Millman) *chsd ldrs: rdn over 2f out: wknd over 1f out* **5/1**[3]

144 **8** *3* **Fair 'n Square (IRE)**[10] 4926 2-8-7 **63** StephenDonohoe(3) 12 27
(J L Spearing) *chsd ldrs: rdn over 2f out: wknd wl over 1f out* **12/1**

064 **9** *3 ½* **Avery**[69] 3110 2-9-0 **67** LPKeniry 9 18
(R J Hodges) *hld up in mid-div: rdn over 2f out: sn bhd* **16/1**

5110 **10** *1 ½* **Inflight (IRE)**[15] 4779 2-9-7 **74** EddieAhern 8 20
(R M Beckett) *half-rrd and dwlt: rdn and hdwy over 2f out: wknd over 1f out* **5/1**[3]

61.09 secs (-1.41) **Going Correction** -0.35s/f (Firm) **10** Ran SP% **116.7**
Speed ratings (Par 97):97,95,94,93,92 87,84,79,74,71
CSF £108.18 CT £1098.24 TOTE £4.30: £1.50, £10.10, £3.40; EX 165.70.
Owner John And Anne Soul **Bred** A J Coleing **Trained** Lambourn, Berks

FOCUS
A typically wide-open nursery. The time was a stone slower than that of the opening maiden and with the second and third looking quite limited this is not a race to get to excited about, but the winner is on the upgrade.

NOTEBOOK
Cuppacocoa looked fairly treated and followed up her win in a minor maiden over course and distance last time in decent style. She is no doubt proving popular with mug punters! (op 5-1 tchd 4-1)
Queensgate is certainly at the right end of the handicap and would have made it even closer had she not proved an awkward ride in the closing stages. (op 20-1)
Hephaestus, down 7lb, got taken off his legs on this drop back in distance and appears to need further now. (op 9-1 tchd 11-1)
Clewer had run respectably over course and distance earlier in the week and looked reasonably handicapped on this switch to nurseries. (op 15-2)
Road To Recovery, tried in a visor, had been stepped up to six last time and appeared quite well in based on the form of his first two outings. (op 5-1 tchd 6-1)
Jost Van Dyke Official explanation: jockey said gelding never travelled

5163 LADBROKES CHARITABLE TRUST SUPPORTING JULIAN HOUSE H'CAP 1m 3f 144y
3:20 (3:20) (Class 4) (0-85,84) 3-Y-0- **£7,570** (£2,265; £1,132; £566; £282) **Stalls** Low

Form RPR

0206 **1** **Boot 'n Toot**[25] 4448 5-8-6 **70** oh3 AshleyHamblett(7) 4 79
(C A Cyzer) *s.i.s: plld hrd: swtchd rt and hdwy 2f out: sn rdn: led wl ins fnl f: r.o wl* **10/1**

2542 **2** *1* **Mandatum**[30] 4299 5-9-9 **80** NickyMackay 5 87
(L M Cumani) *led: hrd rdn over 1f out: hdd wl ins fnl f: nt qckn* **4/1**[2]

0042 **3** *1 ½* **Love Always**[10] 4924 4-8-13 **70** oh1 LPKeniry 2 75
(S Dow) *a.p: hrd rdn and ev ch 1f out: one pce* **9/1**

1610 **4** *¾* **Our Teddy (IRE)**[6] 4626 6-9-7 **83** KevinGhunowa(5) 1 86
(P A Blockley) *hld up in tch: rdn over 2f out: swtchd rt ins fnl f: styd on* **7/1**[3]

4545 **5** *2* **Sky Quest (IRE)**[12] 4900 8-9-2 **73** (tp) StephenCarson 12 73
(W R Swinburn) *w ldr: rdn and ev ch over 1f out: wknd ins fnl f* **16/1**

236- **6** *½* **Dahman**[392] 4380 4-9-9 **80** KerrinMcEvoy 7 79
(Saeed Bin Suroor) *prom: rdn over 3f out: wknd wl over 1f out* **7/2**[1]

2102 **7** *1 ¼* **Candle**[23] 4528 3-8-13 **79** FergusSweeney 9 76
(H Candy) *hld up and bhd: rdn over 2f out: nvr trbld ldrs* **7/1**[3]

0-13 **8** *7* **Farringdon**[27] 4392 3-9-3 **83** SteveDrowne 8 69
(M P Tregoning) *hld up in mid-div: rdn over 4f out: wknd over 2f out* **8/1**

0000 **9** *5* **Top Seed (IRE)**[18] 4676 5-9-12 **83** ChrisCatlin 10 61
(M R Channon) *a in rr* **7/1**[3]

/0-0 **10** *5* **Hills Of Aran**[14] 4810 4-9-10 **84** StephenDonohoe(3) 11 54
(W K Goldsworthy) *bhd fnl 4f* **50/1**

2m 26.48s (-3.82) **Going Correction** -0.35s/f (Firm)
WFA 3 from 4yo+ 9lb **10** Ran SP% **117.8**
Speed ratings (Par 105):98,97,96,95,94 94,93,88,85,82
CSF £50.36 CT £381.60 TOTE £16.60: £4.30, £2.60, £2.40; EX 104.70.
Owner Mrs Charles Cyzer **Bred** C A Cyzer **Trained** Maplehurst, W Sussex

FOCUS
They did not appear to go that great a gallop but that was not reflected in the time. Sound form, rated through the runner-up, with the winner to this year's best.
Candle Official explanation: jockey said filly was unsuited by the firm ground

5164 M. J. CHURCH PROPERTIES H'CAP 1m 2f 46y
3:50 (3:51) (Class 3) (0-90,90) 3-Y-0

£11,217 (£3,358; £1,679; £840; £419; £210) **Stalls** Low

Form RPR

2060 **1** **Solva**[24] 4482 3-8-3 **82** KMay(7) 8 91
(B J Meehan) *hld up in tch: wnt 2nd over 1f out: rdn to ld last strides* **12/1**

1342 **2** *nk* **Babcary**[7] 5016 3-8-11 **83** SteveDrowne 5 91
(M P Tregoning) *a.p: led over 6f out: rdn and qcknd clr 2f out: hdd last strides* **5/1**[2]

2122 **3** *2* **Safqa**[13] 4838 3-8-13 **85** PaulEddery 1 90
(B W Hills) *s.i.s: swtchd rt and hdwy 2f out: one pce fnl f* **9/2**[1]

1603 **4** *5* **Billich**[46] 3819 3-8-9 **81** ChrisCatlin 3 76
(E J O'Neill) *t.k.h: t.k.h: rdn over 2f out: styd on fnl f: n.d* **14/1**

4220 **5** *shd* **Robustian**[14] 4810 3-8-9 **81** StephenCarson 7 76
(R F Johnson Houghton) *hld up in tch: rdn over 2f out: wknd over 1f out* **9/1**

2211 **6** *nk* **Early Evening**[22] 4555 3-8-9 **81** FergusSweeney 9 75
(H Candy) *prom: wnt 2nd over 2f out: sn rdn: wknd over 1f out* **9/2**[1]

0363 **7** *4* **Polliwilline (IRE)**[24] 4481 3-8-7 **79** EddieAhern 2 66
(R Hannon) *s.i.s: hld up and bhd: short-lived effrt on outside 3f out* **14/1**

2430 **8** *3 ½* **In Full Cry**[28] 4356 3-8-10 **85** GregFairley(3) 4 65
(M Johnston) *sn prom: rdn over 3f out: wknd over 2f out* **6/1**[3]

-16 **9** *1 ½* **Virtuosity**[42] 3954 3-9-3 **89** KerrinMcEvoy 6 66
(Sir Michael Stoute) *led: hdd over 6f out: rdn 3f out: wknd 2f out* **8/1**

621- **10** *7* **Three Thieves (UAE)**[328] 5919 3-8-7 **79** LPKeniry 11 43
(M S Saunders) *bhd: rdn over 2f out: sn struggling* **16/1**

2m 6.40s (-4.60) **Going Correction** -0.35s/f (Firm) **10** Ran SP% **115.3**
Speed ratings (Par 105):104,103,102,98,98 97,94,91,90,85
CSF £70.24 CT £315.46 TOTE £14.00: £3.40, £2.20, £1.50; EX 81.70.
Owner Usk Valley Stud **Bred** Usk Valley Stud **Trained** Manton, Wilts

FOCUS
Another open-looking handicap. The first three came clear and the form should be sound.

NOTEBOOK
Solva, highly tried last time, was a pound worse off than when a length and a quarter behind Babcary at Glorious Goodwood. She came through to snatch it and turn around the form with the help of her rider's claim.
Babcary burnt off all bar the winner when sent for home at the quarter-mile marker. She was unable to confirm the Glorious Goodwood form with Solva, the 7lb allowance of the winning rider probably making the difference. (tchd 11-2)
Safqa, raised a total of 6lb after a couple of seconds, was not inconvenienced by being back up to the trip she had been beaten a short head over in April.
Billich was not suited by the drop in distance. (tchd 16-1)
Robustian failed to justify some support in the ring. (op 16-1)
Early Evening, back on fast ground, was trying to complete a hat-trick off a 4lb higher mark. (op 11-2)
Virtuosity Official explanation: jockey said filly ran too free

5165 DRAYCOTT WARD LTD H'CAP 1m 5y
4:20 (4:22) (Class 2) (0-100,100) 3-Y-0

£18,696 (£5,598; £2,799; £1,401; £699; £351) **Stalls** Low

Form RPR

3014 **1** **Dark Islander (IRE)**[35] 4126 3-9-4 **100** EddieAhern 5 109+
(J W Hills) *sn chsng ldr: led on bit 2f out: pushed clr fnl f: comf* **11/4**[1]

0325 **2** *2 ½* **Humungous (IRE)**[37] 4082 3-9-1 **97** SteveDrowne 7 100
(C R Egerton) *led: rdn and hdd 2f out: one pce* **4/1**[3]

2102 **3** *3* **Areyoutalkingtome**[15] 4760 3-8-13 **95** FergusSweeney 9 91
(C A Cyzer) *hld up and bhd: hdwy whn swtchd rt over 2f out: sn rdn: one pce* **3/1**[2]

0-00 **4** *¾* **Doctor Dash**[43] 3889 3-8-8 **90** LPKeniry 2 84
(D R C Elsworth) *hld up: rdn and hdwy on ins over 2f out: sn no imp* **16/1**

5050 **5** *nk* **Zato (IRE)**[43] 3889 3-8-12 **94** ChrisCatlin 3 88
(M R Channon) *t.k.h: prom: rdn 3f out: wknd 2f out* **14/1**

3250 **6** *2 ½* **Waterline Twenty (IRE)**[14] 4790 3-8-5 **90** oh5 ow4 StephenDonohoe(3) 6 78
(P D Evans) *sn bhd: rdn over 2f out: no rspnse* **20/1**

2220 **7** *1 ¼* **Desert Realm (IRE)**[17] 4711 3-8-13 **98** GregFairley(3) 8 83
(M Johnston) *rdn over 2f out: sn wknd* **10/1**

221- **8** *shd* **Gramm**[331] 5852 3-8-9 **91** NickyMackay 4 76
(L M Cumani) *mid-div: rdn 3f out: sn bhd* **5/1**

1m 37.39s (-3.71) **Going Correction** -0.35s/f (Firm) **8** Ran SP% **114.7**
Speed ratings (Par 107):104,101,98,97,97 94,93,93
CSF £14.14 CT £34.42 TOTE £3.50: £1.10, £1.40, £1.60; EX 18.80 Trifecta £29.10 Pool £143.56. - 3.50 winning units..
Owner Donald M Kerr **Bred** Addison Racing Ltd Inc **Trained** Upper Lambourn, Berks

FOCUS
This was a pretty hot handicap for this course, although the form is not that solid behind the principals. The winner is progressive.

NOTEBOOK
Dark Islander(IRE) was 8lb higher than when scoring at the Newmarket July meeting prior to performing with credit in Listed company at Glorious Goodwood. There was a lot to like about this performance and he will try to defy the 4lb penalty he picked up here for the Cambridgeshire providing that the ground is good or faster. (op 3-1 tchd 5-2)
Humungous(IRE) ◆ came up against a progressive sort in the winner and should not always meet one so useful. (tchd 9-2)
Areyoutalkingtome, narrowly beaten over seven at Chester last time, showed that the form at Goodwood when he trailed in behind Humungous was all wrong. (op 4-1 tchd 9-2)
Doctor Dash could not take advantage of having been dropped a total of 6lb in the ratings. (tchd 20-1)
Zato(IRE) was 12lb better off than when beaten just over five lengths by the winner at Newmarket in July. (op 11-1)

5166 LADBROKES CHARITABLE TRUST SUPPORTING JULIAN HOUSE H'CAP 1m 2f 46y
4:50 (4:53) (Class 6) (0-60,60) 3-Y-0+ **£3,238** (£963; £481; £240) **Stalls** Low

Form RPR

1411 **1** **Good Article (IRE)**[12] 4869 5-9-9 **57** KerrinMcEvoy 13 67
(D K Ivory) *hld up and bhd: hdwy on outside and hung lft fr 2f out: r.o to ld nr fin* **7/2**[1]

0105 **2** *nk* **Baboosh (IRE)**[9] 4944 5-9-5 **58** StephanieHollinshead(5) 2 67
(M Wigham) *hld up: stdy hdwy on ins over 4f out: hrd rdn and ev ch ins fnl f: r.o* **12/1**

2660 **3** *shd* **Wood Fern (UAE)**[24] 4497 6-8-4 **45** oh5 AshleyHamblett(7) 10 54
(W M Brisbourne) *hld up in mid-div: hdwy over 3f out: rdn over 2f out: led over 1f out: hdd nr fin* **22/1**

3221 **4** *2* **Hurry Up Helen (IRE)**[13] 4847 3-9-0 **55** EddieAhern 4 60
(Mrs L Stubbs) *hld up in mid-div: rdn over 2f out: hdwy wl over 1f out: nt qckn ins fnl f* **9/2**[2]

0340 **5** *shd* **Will The Till**[12] 4869 4-9-0 **51** (b[1]) StephenDonohoe(3) 14 56
(J M Bradley) *sn wl bhd: rdn over 2f out: hdwy over 1f out: r.o ins fnl f* **20/1**

6133 **6** *1 ¾* **Greenmeadow**[8] 4982 4-9-4 **57** MichaelJStainton(5) 12 59
(S Kirk) *prom: rdn to ld wl over 1f out: sn hdd: wknd wl ins fnl f* **15/2**[3]

6000 **7** *hd* **Adobe**[23] 4518 11-9-3 **54** GregFairley(3) 5 55
(W M Brisbourne) *hld up in mid-div: rdn and bmpd over 2f out: no hdwy* **25/1**

0504 **8** *¾* **Oakley Absolute**[12] 4869 4-9-4 **55** StephaneBreux(3) 7 55
(R Hannon) *prom: rdn 3f out: wknd over 1f out* **11/1**

0602 **9** *¾* **Princess Danah (IRE)**[30] 4289 3-9-1 **59** (t) AdamKirby(3) 15 57
(W R Swinburn) *chsd ldr: rdn to ld over 2f out: hdd wl over 1f out: sn wknd* **10/1**

0010 **10** *1* **Wind Chime (IRE)**[15] 4772 9-9-6 **54** FergusSweeney 11 51+
(A G Newcombe) *bhd: rdn and sme hdwy over 2f out: swtchd lft wl over 1f out: sn nt clr run on ins: n.d after* **16/1**

066 **11** *1 ¾* **Lady Cree (IRE)**[8] 4982 3-9-3 **58** (p) SteveDrowne 9 51
(W R Muir) *prom: rdn over 2f out: wkng whn n.m.r on ins jst ins fnl f: eased* **25/1**

6535 **12** *7* **Danish Monarch**[12] 4869 5-8-11 **45** LPKeniry 16 25
(David Pinder) *led: hdd over 2f out: sn rdn: wknd qckly wl over 1f out* **10/1**

5423 **13** *3 ½* **Ruling Reef**[12] 4869 4-8-13 **47** ChrisCatlin 8 20
(M D I Usher) *bhd fnl 3f* **12/1**

000- **14** *67* **Brabinger (IRE)**^{263} [6628] 3-8-4 **45**.............................. StephenCarson 3 —
(B G Powell) *s.i.s: sn wl bhd: t.o fnl 4f* **66/1**

2m 7.89s (-3.11) **Going Correction** -0.35s/f (Firm)
WFA 3 from 4yo+ 7lb **14** Ran SP% **118.2**
Speed ratings (Par 101):98,97,97,96,96 94,94,93,93,92 91,85,82,29
CSF £41.96 CT £813.43 TOTE £3.90: £2.10, £4.20, £8.20; EX 65.80.
Owner T G N Burrage **Bred** T G N Burrage **Trained** Radlett, Herts

FOCUS
A competitive if modest handicap. The form looks sound and should prove reliable.
Wind Chime(IRE) Official explanation: jockey said horse was denied a clear run

5167 CONGRATULATIONS KELLY AND JASON H'CAP — 5f 161y
5:20 (5:23) (Class 5) (0-70,69) 3-Y-0+ **£5,505** (£1,637; £818; £408) **Stalls** Low

Form				RPR
3321	**1**		**Talcen Gwyn (IRE)**^{12} [4872] 4-8-9 **58**.........................(v) DavidKinsella 14 (M F Harris) *mde all: rdn over 1f out: edgd lft wl ins fnl f: r.o* **4/1**^{1}	67
1204	**2**	½	**Peruvian Style (IRE)**^{8} [4985] 5-8-5 **57**.................... StephenDonohoe(3) 9 (J M Bradley) *mid-div: rdn and hdwy over 2f out: sn edgd lft: ev ch ins fnl f: edgd lft: r.o* **9/2**^{2}	64
3500	**3**	1 ¼	**Dance To The Blues (IRE)**^{42} [3936] 5-9-1 **67**..........(p) AdamKirby(3) 11 (B De Haan) *bhd: rdn 3f out: hdwy on outside over 1f out: kpt on ins fnl f* **14/1**	70
3160	**4**	½	**Summer Recluse (USA)**^{5} [5058] 7-9-6 **69**....................(t) SteveDrowne 1 (J M Bradley) *mid-div: hdwy on ins 2f out: rdn over 1f out: running on whn bdly hmpd on ins wl ins fnl f: nt rcvr* **7/1**^{3}	76+
3156	**5**	nk	**Montzando**^{23} [4532] 3-8-5 **56**.. StephenCarson 13 (B R Millman) *a.p: rdn over 2f out: kpt on same pce fnl f* **25/1**	57
0305	**6**	1 ¼	**Matterofact (IRE)**^{15} [4756] 3-8-11 **62**................................. PaulEddery 5 (Mrs P N Dutfield) *a.p: rdn 2f out: eased whn btn towards fin* **25/1**	62+
4240	**7**	hd	**Linda Green**^{30} [4294] 5-9-5 **68**.. ChrisCatlin 10 (M R Channon) *bhd: sme hdwy 2f out: sn rdn: nt clr run on ins wl ins fnl f: nt rcvr* **7/1**^{3}	64+
1504	**8**	shd	**Drumming Party (USA)**^{15} [4780] 4-8-13 **62**.........................(t) LPKeniry 8 (A M Balding) *prom: rdn 2f out: wknd fnl f* **9/1**	58
0430	**9**	shd	**Parkside Pursuit**^{12} [4894] 8-8-4 **60**................................ BarrySavage(7) 12 (J M Bradley) *bhd: rdn and hdwy over 1f out: no imp fnl f* **12/1**	56
0004	**10**	½	**Middleton Grey**^{21} [4602] 8-9-5 **68**............................(b) FergusSweeney 15 (A G Newcombe) *s.i.s: a bhd* **14/1**	62
6030	**11**	7	**Dora's Green**^{22} [4554] 3-8-4 **55** oh7........................ FrankieMcDonald 16 (M Blanshard) *prom: rdn over 2f out: sn n.m.r and wknd* **50/1**	27

69.15 secs (-2.05) **Going Correction** -0.35s/f (Firm)
WFA 3 from 4yo+ 2lb **11** Ran SP% **103.9**
Speed ratings (Par 103):99,98,96,96,95 93,93,93,93,92 83
CSF £16.82 CT £165.04 TOTE £3.50: £1.60, £1.90, £5.20; EX 22.30 Trifecta £64.40 Place 6 £139.25, Place 5 £89.64.
Owner D K Watkins **Bred** Paul Smyth **Trained** Edgcote, Northants
■ Stewards' Enquiry : David Kinsella three-day ban: careless riding (Sep 20-22)

FOCUS
A typically competitive low-grade Bath sprint handicap. It was a bit of a messy race, but the form looks pretty sound with the second and fourth setting the standard.
Linda Green Official explanation: jockey said mare was denied a clear run
T/Plt: £41.60 to a £1 stake. Pool: £53,944.00. 946.10 winning tickets. T/Qpdt: £20.40 to a £1 stake. Pool: £2,867.50. 103.80 winning tickets. KH

4788 CHESTER (L-H)
Saturday, September 9

OFFICIAL GOING: Good to firm (good in places)
Wind: Light, half-behind. Weather: Fine.

5168 HEATHCOTES E B F MAIDEN STKS — 7f 2y
2:30 (2:30) (Class 4) 2-Y-0 **£5,505** (£1,637; £818; £408) **Stalls** Low

Form				RPR
3	**1**		**Plane Painter (IRE)**^{24} [4487] 2-9-3 .... J-PGuillambert 1 (M Johnston) *mde all: rdn over 1f out: r.o ins fnl f* **11/4**^{1}	79
6	**2**	1 ¼	**King's Apostle (IRE)**^{31} [4260] 2-8-12 .... LiamJones(5) 10 (W J Haggas) *chsd wnr: rdn and ev ch over 1f out: edgd lft ins fnl f: edgd rt and nt qckn towards fin* **10/1**	76
03	**3**	1 ¼	**Castara Bay**^{70} [3083] 2-9-3 .... RichardSmith 2 (R Hannon) *s.i.s: sn chsd ldrs: rdn 2f out: styd on ins fnl f* **7/2**^{2}	73
	4	3 ½	**Sandrey (IRE)** 2-9-3 .... RobertHavlin 7 (P W Chapple-Hyam) *chsd ldrs: rdn 2f out: wknd ins fnl f* **6/1**^{3}	64
50	**5**	nk	**Sahara Crystal**^{33} [4207] 2-8-12 .... MichaelTebbutt 4 (H Candy) *in tch: rdn 2f out: one pce fnl f* **16/1**	58
42	**6**	nk	**Fourfoot Bay (IRE)**^{67} [3173] 2-9-3 .... GrahamGibbons 8 (J D Bethell) *slowly into strde: racd keenly: towards rr: hdwy over 2f out: kpt on ins fnl f: nvr able to chal* **6/1**^{3}	63+
	7	2	**Still Calm** 2-9-3 .... DeanMcKeown 6 (B W Hills) *stdd s: bhd: kpt on fnl f: nvr trbld ldrs* **8/1**	58
0	**8**	1 ¾	**Ballet Boy (IRE)**^{5} [5066] 2-9-3 .... SebSanders 11 (Sir Mark Prescott) *a towards rr* **50/1**	53+
5	**9**	1 ½	**Bungie**^{8} [4986] 2-9-3 .... JohnEgan 9 (Ms Deborah J Evans) *midfield: hdwy 3f out: rdn over 2f out: wknd over 1f out* **16/1**	49
	10	5	**Callahan (FR)** 2-9-3 .... PhillipMakin 3 (Ms Deborah J Evans) *dwlt: midfield: rdn and wknd over 2f out* **50/1**	37
	11	3	**Cheery Cat (USA)** 2-8-12 .... MarkLawson(5) 5 (D W Barker) *s.i.s: a bhd* **25/1**	29

1m 28.43s (-0.04) **Going Correction** -0.075s/f (Good) **11** Ran SP% **117.2**
Speed ratings (Par 97):97,95,94,90,89 89,87,85,83,77 74
CSF £30.89 TOTE £3.10: £1.50, £2.80, £1.90; EX 40.70.
Owner Favourites Racing XXIV **Bred** J Cockburn **Trained** Middleham Moor, N Yorks

FOCUS
A fair maiden that should produce winners at two and three, although the level is hard to set with not much previous form to go on. The winner made all from stall one.

NOTEBOOK
Plane Painter(IRE) took full advantage of his good draw to win in fine style. He has loads of scope and is sure to progress further for a stable well capable of improving their horses significantly. (tchd 5-2 and 3-1 in a place)
King's Apostle(IRE) tracked the winner for much of the race but could never get his nose in front. It was a solid effort, however, and he is progressing the right way. A maiden should be won with him before the end of the season. (op 14-1)
Castara Bay, given a break after a couple of fair efforts, spoilt his chance with a slow start. Recovering well to give chase to the winner, he could never quite get on terms and a nursery could be the next step for him. (op 4-1)
Sandrey(IRE), whose price tag at the Sales almost doubled from a foal to a two-year-old, showed more than enough on his debut to suggest he can take a maiden in due course. Moving nicely until the final bend, he could not quicken as well as the more experienced horses, and should improve for his intial effort. It should be noted that he was withdrawn from a race recently due to the heavy ground, so connections clearly feel he needs quick conditions. (op 9-2)
Sahara Crystal had every chance but was not quite good enough against the boys. A return to a fillies' maiden or a nursery would seem the most logical next step. (op 14-1)
Fourfoot Bay(IRE), having his first run since early July, stayed on really well in the final stages to nearly catch the fourth and fifth. He has the talent to win a race at two, possibly a nursery, but may need a bit further. (op 15-2)
Still Calm caught the eye keeping on from the rear of the field and should have learnt plenty for his first run. A well-related sort, he is sure to be better for the run. (op 7-1)
Ballet Boy(IRE) shaped with a bit of promise towards the rear, but is unlikely to be at his best until he is three. He has had two fairly quick runs and a third one is probably not that far off.

5169 HEATHCOTES OUTSIDE H'CAP — 5f 16y
3:00 (3:00) (Class 4) (0-85,83) 3-Y-0+ **£5,829** (£1,734; £866; £432) **Stalls** Low

Form				RPR
2066	**1**		**Caribbean Coral**^{12} [4875] 7-9-5 **83**..........................(v) GrahamGibbons 5 (J J Quinn) *chsd ldrs: qcknd to ld ins fnl f: r.o* **15/2**^{3}	95
0654	**2**	½	**Handsome Cross (IRE)**^{14} [4793] 5-9-4 **82**.............. SilvestreDeSousa 2 (D Nicholls) *led: rdn over 1f out: hdd ins fnl f: nt qckn towards fin* **7/4**^{1}	92
0040	**3**	1 ½	**Mimi Mouse**^{24} [4468] 4-9-0 **78**..................................... J-PGuillambert 3 (T D Easterby) *a.p: rdn over 1f out: styd on same pce ins fnl f* **10/1**	83
010	**4**	½	**Lady Bahia (IRE)**^{28} [4357] 5-8-9 **73**........................(b) RobbieFitzpatrick 4 (Peter Grayson) *s.s: hld up: hdwy 3f out: styd on and edgd lft ins fnl f: nt rch ldrs* **20/1**	76
2503	**5**	hd	**Kings College Boy**^{14} [4793] 6-8-9 **73**..........................(v) TonyHamilton 6 (R A Fahey) *chsd ldrs: rdn over 1f out: kpt on same pce ins fnl f* **6/1**^{2}	75
0242	**6**	1	**Circuit Dancer (IRE)**^{13} [4834] 6-9-0 **78**........................ FrancisNorton 12 (D Nicholls) *hld up: nt clr run 2f out: styng on whn nt clr run and swtchd rt ins fnl f: no imp after* **11/1**	77+
2264	**7**	½	**Blazing Heights**^{17} [4717] 3-9-0 **79**................................ DanielTudhope 8 (J S Goldie) *s.s: sn in midfield: rdn over 1f out: nvr trbld ldrs* **12/1**	76
2001	**8**	nk	**Coconut Moon**^{14} [4793] 4-8-10 **74**...................................... DavidAllan 10 (E J Alston) *in rr: rdn over 1f out: kpt on ins fnl f: nvr trbld ldrs* **9/1**	70
2050	**9**	¾	**Malapropism**^{15} [4771] 6-9-4 **82**... JohnEgan 7 (M R Channon) *midfield: rdn over 1f out: sn edgd lft and outpcd* **14/1**	75
3146	**10**	shd	**Henry Hall (IRE)**^{16} [4725] 10-8-6 **70**................................ KimTinkler 11 (N Tinkler) *racd keenly: chsd ldrs: rdn over 1f out: sn wknd* **33/1**	63
6000	**11**	1	**Kay Two (IRE)**^{14} [4811] 4-9-2 **80**....................................... SebSanders 9 (R J Price) *s.s: n.m.r after 1f: towards rr: outpcd fnl f* **10/1**	69

61.00 secs (-1.05) **Going Correction** -0.075s/f (Good)
WFA 3 from 4yo+ 1lb **11** Ran SP% **121.0**
Speed ratings (Par 105):105,104,101,101,100 99,98,97,96,96 94
CSF £21.54 CT £136.15 TOTE £9.30: £2.60, £1.40, £3.80; EX 26.10.
Owner Dawson, Green, Quinn, Roberts **Bred** P And C Scott **Trained** Settrington, N Yorks

FOCUS
The usual big-field sprint at Chester, that featured a couple of unlucky in-running horses. Average form for the grade, and pretty solid with the second and third rated to their recent best. Those drawn low dominated.

5170 CARLSBERG STAND CUP (LISTED RACE) — 1m 4f 66y
3:35 (3:35) (Class 1) 3-Y-0+ **£16,595** (£6,274; £3,136; £1,568) **Stalls** Low

Form				RPR
-620	**1**		**Foxhaven**^{17} [4713] 4-9-1 105.. FrancisNorton 3 (P R Chamings) *a.p: rdn 2f out: led 1f out: r.o* **3/1**^{2}	106
11	**2**	½	**Soulacroix**^{39} [4027] 5-9-1 103.. JohnEgan 5 (L M Cumani) *hld up in tch: effrt on outside 3f out: rdn and edgd lft whn nt qckn over 1f out: r.o towards fin* **15/8**^{1}	105
2522	**3**	nk	**Camrose**^{22} [4576] 5-9-1 102..(b) SebSanders 2 (J L Dunlop) *trckd ldrs: rdn 2f out: edgd lft ins fnl f: styd on* **11/2**	105
0131	**4**	shd	**Steppe Dancer (IRE)**^{10} [4936] 3-8-7 93 ow1................ J-PGuillambert 1 (D J Coakley) *racd keenly: hld up: rdn over 1f out: r.o ins fnl f* **7/2**^{3}	106
5540	**5**	¾	**Idealistic (IRE)**^{21} [4590] 5-8-10 93................................ RobertHavlin 6 (L M Cumani) *led: rdn and hdd 1f out: no ex ins fnl f* **16/1**	99
2506	**6**	½	**Gavroche (IRE)**^{14} [4791] 5-9-1 98....................................... DavidAllan 4 (J R Boyle) *in rr: rdn 2f out: edgd lft over 1f out: kpt on ins fnl f* **9/1**	103

2m 40.15s (-0.50) **Going Correction** -0.075s/f (Good)
WFA 3 from 4yo+ 9lb **6** Ran SP% **113.3**
Speed ratings (Par 111):98,97,97,97,96 96
CSF £9.23 TOTE £4.20: £2.20, £1.70; EX 10.30.
Owner Mrs Ann Jenkins **Bred** Highclere Stud Ltd **Trained** Baughurst, Hants
■ Stewards' Enquiry : Francis Norton one-day ban: careless riding (Sep 20)

FOCUS
A decent Listed race, where the whole field was covered by about two lengths at the line. The pace was modest and the form is not rock solid, although the third and fifth seem to give a pretty good line to the form. The winner did not need to improve.

NOTEBOOK
Foxhaven, dropping back down in trip after not quite getting home in the Ebor, was ideally positioned throughout to win nicely. He was value for just a bit more than the winning distance and can be expected to maintain his progress over a mile and a half. (op 4-1 tchd 9-2 in a place)
Soulacroix, who was on a hat-trick, had missed a couple of recent engagements due to a foot injury (the Ebor) and heavy ground, but shaped nicely after a short break on his first venture into Listed company. He stays a mile and three-quarters and might be seen to better advantage over further. (op 6-5)
Camrose is a very consistent performer but is always likely to find at least one too good for him in Listed company. His last win was in a handicap off a mark of 89.
Steppe Dancer(IRE), the only three-year-old in the field, performed much better than his official mark and he could easily land a race in Listed company in time. A race such as the Churchill Stakes at Lingfield in November could be the opportunity for him. (op 5-1)
Idealistic(IRE) gave the race its tempo and was not beaten very far, only weakening in the final stages. It was a good effort but one suspects she might be flattered by it. (tchd 20-1)
Gavroche(IRE) failed to pick up from the rear of the field and, although not beaten very far, never quite got involved. He will need to come down the weights quite a bit to have a realistic chance in handicap company, as Listed races seem just beyond him. (op 12-1)

5171 BETDAQ HENRY GEE FILLIES' STKS (LISTED RACE) — 6f 18y
4:10 (4:10) (Class 1) 3-Y-0+
£15,898 (£6,025; £3,015; £1,503; £753; £189) **Stalls** Low

Form				RPR
6453	**1**		**Ripples Maid**^{20} [4633] 3-8-12 92.................................. RichardThomas 3 (J A Geake) *chsd ldrs: swtchd rt over 1f out: rdn to ld ins fnl f: r.o* **6/1**^{3}	79
0310	**2**	1 ½	**Portmeirion**^{20} [4633] 5-9-0 67... SebSanders 9 (S C Williams) *stdd s: hld up: nt clr run 2f out tl hdwy over 1f out: r.o to chse wnr wl ins fnl f: one pce fnl strides* **20/1**	75+

4120 **3** ½ **Daniella**[21] 4589 4-9-0 76....................(p) FrancisFerris 4 73+
(Rae Guest) *towards rr: rdn over 2f out: hdwy whn nt clr run over 1f out: sn swtchd lft: r.o ins fnl f* **25/1**

3011 **4** nk **Indian Maiden (IRE)**[13] 4860 6-9-5 105.................... FrancisNorton 12 77+
(M S Saunders) *midfield: rdn and hdwy over 1f out: styd on ins fnl f* **11/4**[1]

3630 **5** nk **Ooh Aah Camara (IRE)**[34] 4174 3-8-12 97.................... JohnEgan 1 72
(T J Pitt) *midfield: rdn over 2f out: hdwy over 1f out: styd on ins fnl f* **7/1**

-061 **6** ½ **Dizzy Dreamer (IRE)**[17] 4707 3-8-12 97.................... RobertHavlin 5 70
(P W Chapple-Hyam) *in tch: rdn over 1f out: one pce ins fnl f* **9/2**[2]

0604 **6** dht **Moone Cross (IRE)**[34] 4174 3-8-12.................... MichaelTebbutt 6 70
(Mrs John Harrington, Ire) *prom: rdn to ld over 1f out: hdd ins fnl f: fdd* **15/2**

1000 **8** 1 **Angus Newz**[13] 4832 3-9-1 98....................(v) RobbieFitzpatrick 10 70
(M Quinn) *s.s: bhd: rdn and hdwy over 1f out: nvr rchd ldrs* **16/1**

3330 **9** shd **Highland Cascade**[5] 5058 4-9-0 72....................(b[1]) JTate 11 67
(J M P Eustace) *s.i.s: sn in midfield: rdn over 1f out: no imp* **66/1**

0604 **10** 1¼ **Safranine (IRE)**[20] 4636 9-9-0 52.................... AnnStokell 7 63?
(Miss A Stokell) *bhd after 1f* **100/1**

-346 **11** 1¼ **Give Me The Night (IRE)**[184] 623 3-8-12 88.................... J-PGuillambert 2 59
(B Smart) *led: rdn and hdd over 1f out: wknd ins fnl f* **14/1**

3000 **12** 1¼ **Sierra Vista**[28] 4343 6-9-0 98.................... TonyHamilton 8 56
(D W Barker) *chsd ldrs tl rdn and wknd over 1f out* **10/1**

4016 **13** 14 **Elrafa Mujahid**[13] 4844 4-9-0 58....................(t) AdrianMcCarthy 13 14
(Ernst Oertel) *midfield: lost pl after 2f: eased whn btn fnl f* **100/1**

1m 14.3s (-1.35) **Going Correction** -0.075s/f (Good)
WFA 3 from 4yo+ 2lb **13** Ran SP% **117.1**
Speed ratings (Par 108):106,104,103,102,102 101,101,100,100,98 97,95,76
CSF £125.09 TOTE £7.90: £2.60, £5.10, £6.90; EX 163.30.
Owner Rex L Mead **Bred** Compton Down Stud **Trained** Kimpton, Hants
■ Stewards' Enquiry : Michael Tebbutt one-day ban: drop hands and lost 6th place outright (Sep 20)

FOCUS
A mixed bunch for this fillies' and mares' Listed race. The form is held down by the tenth, and the second and third to a lesser extent. The winner is very useful on her day and took full advantage of her good draw, not needing to improve. The beaten favourite was poorly drawn.

NOTEBOOK
Ripples Maid tracked the early pace from her good draw before pouncing in the straight, going away from her rivals once hitting the front. She had finished behind Indian Maiden last time but managed to reverse placings with the aid of a better draw. (op 13-2 tchd 7-1)
Portmeirion was slightly unlucky not to get a bit closer to the winner, but it must be very doubtful that she would have caused Ripples Maid too many problems. However, she can expect a hefty rise in the weights when the Handicapper looks at this effort. (op 25-1)
Daniella, who made the running both times she has won in 2006, did not find a great deal of room when required but, much like the runner-up, she would not have troubled the winner with a clear passage. She can expect her handicap mark to rise considerably after this.
Indian Maiden(IRE), who was carrying a penalty for her recent Group 3 success, had almost the worst of the draw and failed to land a serious blow. One is tempted to forget the run, fair though it was, and give her another chance on a more level playing field. The Rous Stakes at Newmarket, a race she ran in last season, may be her next port of call. (op 3-1 tchd 10-3)
Ooh Aah Camara(IRE) missed the break from her good draw and never really threatened to take a hand in the finish, at a course she usually runs well at. Connections are probably forced to run her in these races as she is fully 17lb higher in the weights than her last success, making it almost impossible for her to have an obvious chance in handicap company.
Dizzy Dreamer(IRE) was probably aiming a bit high after winning a Leicester handicap off a mark of 90 at 16/1. She was not disgraced but was not up to the class. (op 7-1 tchd 8-1)
Moone Cross(IRE) held every chance into the straight but found very little under strong pressure in the final furlong. (op 7-1 tchd 8-1)
Angus Newz had it all to do from a poor draw and was far from disgraced. She ran better than her final position suggests. (op 14-1)

5172 CHESHIRE LIFE NURSERY 7f 2y
4:40 (4:40) (Class 3) (0-95,86) 2-Y-O **£10,094** (£3,020; £1,510; £755; £376) **Stalls** Low

Form RPR

1140 **1** **Grand Prix**[28] 4344 2-9-7 **86**....................(t) RichardSmith 1 90
(R Hannon) *mde all: rdn over 1f out: r.o* **10/1**

5201 **2** 1¾ **Hart Of Gold**[3] 5113 2-9-4 **86** 6ex.................... AndrewMullen(3) 3 85
(M J Wallace) *trckd ldrs: n.m.r and lost pl 2f out: rallied to chse wnr wl ins fnl f: styd on* **11/2**[3]

31 **3** nk **Ravi River (IRE)**[14] 4788 2-9-4 **83**.................... SebSanders 7 82
(B W Hills) *hld up: hdwy 4f out: rdn to take 2nd over 1f out: sn edgd lft: no ex and lost 2nd wl ins fnl f* **11/10**[1]

0655 **4** shd **Cheshire Prince**[15] 4761 2-7-12 **63** oh2.................... PaulQuinn 4 61
(W M Brisbourne) *hld up: rdn and hdwy over 1f out: styd on ins fnl f* **16/1**

433 **5** ½ **King's Causeway (USA)**[27] 4388 2-8-5 **75**.................... LiamJones(5) 2 72
(W J Haggas) *hld up: nt clr run 2f out: rdn and hdwy over 1f out: one pce ins fnl f* **9/2**[2]

2100 **6** 1¾ **Prince Rossi (IRE)**[18] 4681 2-9-4 **83**.................... GrahamGibbons 6 76
(J D Bethell) *in tch: pushed along 3f out: outpcd 2f out: n.d after* **25/1**

522 **7** 1 **Al Raahi**[23] 4509 2-8-11 **76**.................... JohnEgan 5 66
(M R Channon) *prom: rdn and ev ch wl over 2f out: wknd fnl f* **15/2**

1m 27.66s (-0.81) **Going Correction** -0.075s/f (Good) **7** Ran SP% **111.8**
Speed ratings (Par 99):101,99,98,98,97 95,94
CSF £60.06 CT £107.05 TOTE £13.30: £4.50, £2.40; EX 64.20.
Owner Mrs J K Powell **Bred** Plantation Stud **Trained** East Everleigh, Wilts

FOCUS
A useful-looking nursery won by a horse who had the best draw and right racing style for the course, which tempers enthusiasm for the value of the form.

NOTEBOOK
Grand Prix was allowed his own way out in front, which is ideal at this course from stall one, and never looked likely to be caught. It was a fine piece of riding by Smith and the colt would be lucky to repeat this. Official explanation: trainer's rep said, regarding improvement in form, that the colt benefited from the application of a tongue strap for the first time (op 14-1 tchd 9-1)
Hart Of Gold, who was making a quick reappearance after landing a race at Southwell, tracked the leader on the inside rail, but did not quicken when the pace was increased and was slightly left behind on the home bend. He stayed on well for pressure but was not good enough to trouble the winner. (op 7-2)
Ravi River(IRE) was towards the rear and wide early, and failed to put in a serious challenge to the winner, his wide draw not helping his cause. He is almost certainly better than the bare result and can easily be given another chance, considering he holds some big-race entries. (op 11-8)
Cheshire Prince pulled pretty hard towards the back of the field and only got a gap in the home straight. He had plenty to find on official figures, so it was not a bad effort, and he would probably be better suited by a straight course. (op 12-1)
King's Causeway(USA), who did not make best use of his advantageous draw, was slightly unlucky not to have finished a bit closer, as he had to find room off the final bend when making his challenge. He can be given another chance on a more conventional track. (op 5-1)
Al Raahi was up with the leaders early but weakened badly out of the picture once in the home straight. He is becoming difficult to win with. (op 17-2)

5173 HEATHCOTES RESTAURANTS H'CAP 1m 2f 75y
5:15 (5:15) (Class 5) (0-70,67) 3-Y-O+ **£3,562** (£1,059; £529; £264) **Stalls** High

Form RPR

3000 **1** **New England**[8] 4991 4-9-4 **60**.................... RobbieFitzpatrick 4 69
(W M Brisbourne) *s.i.s: racd keenly: hld up: nt clr run over 1f out: hdwy whn swtchd rt ent fnl f: str run to ld fnl strides* **11/1**

0043 **2** hd **Lobengula (IRE)**[21] 4606 4-9-6 **62**.................... SebSanders 3 71
(I W McInnes) *led: rdn and hung rt over 2f out: edgd rt wl ins fnl f: hdd fnl strides* **11/2**[2]

3041 **3** 1½ **Royal Indulgence**[22] 4565 6-8-8 **55**.................... LiamJones(5) 10 61
(W M Brisbourne) *started slowly: racd keenly: hld up: hdwy 7f out: rdn to chal 2f out: hung lft fr over 1f out: hld whn n.m.r cl home* **11/2**[2]

6050 **4** ½ **Wasalat (USA)**[21] 4610 4-9-6 **67**.................... MarkLawson(5) 12 72
(D W Barker) *s.s: in rr: hdwy over 2f out: n.m.r and swtchd rt over 1f out: styd on ins fnl f* **20/1**

0032 **5** 2 **Diktatorship (IRE)**[13] 4847 3-8-4 **53**.................... AdrianMcCarthy 2 54
(Ernst Oertel) *trckd ldrs: rdn over 1f out: one pce ins fnl f* **5/1**[1]

2610 **6** 1¼ **Dream Of Paradise (USA)**[13] 4847 3-8-11 **60**.................... TomEaves 1 59
(Mrs L Williamson) *prom: rdn and ev ch 2f out: wknd ins fnl f* **7/1**[3]

1426 **7** ½ **River Logic (IRE)**[2] 5129 3-8-13 **62**.................... SilvestreDeSousa 9 60
(A D Brown) *midfield: rdn 3f out: wknd ins fnl f* **5/1**[1]

3535 **8** 8 **Stainley (IRE)**[26] 4426 3-9-0 **63**.................... FrancisNorton 8 46
(J D Bethell) *midfield: lost pl 7f out: struggling over 4f out: n.d after* **11/2**[2]

0614 **9** 5 **Topflight Wildbird**[65] 3215 3-8-9 **63**.................... AndrewElliott(5) 6 36
(Mrs G S Rees) *racd keenly: prom: rdn 3f out: wknd over 2f out* **10/1**

2m 11.89s (-1.25) **Going Correction** -0.075s/f (Good)
WFA 3 from 4yo+ 7lb **9** Ran SP% **114.2**
Speed ratings (Par 103):102,101,100,100,98 97,97,90,86
CSF £69.42 CT £371.84 TOTE £15.80: £3.30, £2.10, £2.30; EX 88.30.
Owner Stephen Walker **Bred** Darley **Trained** Great Ness, Shropshire

FOCUS
A modest event. The runner-up set a decent pace and the three who finished around him came from the rear. The winner was gaining his first win on turf, and finished strongly to nick it. The form looks sound, rated around the third, and should prove reliable.

5174 HEATHCOTES CHESTER RACECOURSE H'CAP 1m 7f 195y
5:50 (5:50) (Class 4) (0-80,81) 3-Y-O+ **£5,829** (£1,734; £866; £432) **Stalls** High

Form RPR

1002 **1** **Numero Due**[12] 4883 4-10-1 **81**.................... SebSanders 6 87
(G M Moore) *mde virtually all: rdn over 1f out: all out* **3/1**[1]

0431 **2** hd **Establishment**[14] 4792 9-9-11 **77**.................... J-PGuillambert 1 83
(C A Cyzer) *hld up: rdn over 3f out: hdwy over 1f out: wnt 2nd ins fnl f: r.o: jst failed* **4/1**[3]

0605 **3** 1¾ **Escayola (IRE)**[28] 4369 6-10-0 **80**....................(v) JohnEgan 3 84
(W J Haggas) *in tch: rdn 2f out: sn chsd wnr and hung lft: lost 2nd and styd on same pce ins fnl f* **9/2**

1064 **4** 1¼ **Merrymaker**[14] 4792 6-9-3 **72**.................... PatrickMathers(3) 2 74
(W M Brisbourne) *s.i.s: in rr: rdn over 4f out: styd on ins fnl f: nvr nrr* **6/1**

0213 **5** 1 **Squirtle (IRE)**[15] 4758 3-7-10 **66**.................... LiamJones(5) 5 67
(W M Brisbourne) *s.i.s: in rr and rn in snatches: hdwy over 2f out: no ex ins fnl f* **7/2**[2]

054 **6** 1 **Gallileo Figaro (USA)**[15] 4759 3-7-12 **68** ow1.................... AndrewElliott(5) 7 68
(W M Brisbourne) *w wnr: rdn 5f out: ev ch over 2f out: wknd over 1f out* **18/1**

1654 **7** 3½ **Acuzio**[15] 4764 5-8-9 **61** oh6.................... DavidAllan 4 57
(W M Brisbourne) *chsd ldrs: rdn over 2f out: wkng whn n.m.r over 1f out* **12/1**

030/ **8** 18 **Resonance**[16] 4686 5-8-7 **62**.................... AndrewMullen(3) 9 36
(S Lycett) *slipped and slowly away: sn in tch: rdn over 4f out: wknd 3f out* **40/1**

3m 28.01s (-5.59) **Going Correction** -0.075s/f (Good)
WFA 3 from 4yo+ 13lb **8** Ran SP% **115.1**
Speed ratings (Par 105):110,109,109,108,107 107,105,96
CSF £15.37 CT £52.43 TOTE £4.30: £2.10, £1.80, £1.70; EX 25.60 Place 6 £275.54, Place 5 £158.32.
Owner Trattoria Due/Valueplace Ltd **Bred** London Thoroughbred Services Ltd **Trained** Middleham Moor, N Yorks

FOCUS
Not a great staying race, despite the official ratings, with the sixth and seventh a bit close for comfort. Mark Brisbourne was responsible for half the field. The race has been rated through the first two.
T/Plt: £541.40 to a £1 stake. Pool: £70,790.40. 95.45 winning tickets. T/Qpdt: £470.10 to a £1 stake. Pool: £3,303.90. 5.20 winning tickets. DO

4836 GOODWOOD (R-H)
Saturday, September 9

OFFICIAL GOING: Good (good to firm in places)
The jockeys reported the ground to be fast but not too firm; the fast times were caused by a stiff tail wind throughout the afternoon.
Wind: Fresh, behind Weather: Sunny spells

5175 TURFTRAX.COM STKS (H'CAP) 7f
2:20 (2:21) (Class 2) (0-100,99) 3-Y-O+
£11,217 (£3,358; £1,679; £840; £419; £210) **Stalls** High

Form RPR

4100 **1** **King's Caprice**[14] 4798 5-8-12 **94**....................(t) TravisBlock(5) 3 103
(J A Geake) *mde all: pushed out fnl f: hld on wl* **33/1**

150 **2** nk **Bayeux (USA)**[14] 4790 5-9-7 **98**.................... FJohansson 2 106
(G A Butler) *lw: chsd wnr tl ins fnl 2f: rallied to go 2nd again ins last: kpt on stly: nt quite get up* **12/1**

0031 **3** ¾ **Prince Of Thebes (IRE)**[28] 4348 5-9-8 **99**.................... PaulDoe 6 105
(J Akehurst) *chsd ldrs: wnt 2nd and rdn ins fnl 2f: no imprssion and lost 2nd ins last* **8/1**[3]

0056 **4** 1 **Seulement (USA)**[14] 4790 4-9-0 **91**.................... GeorgeBaker 12 94+
(L M Cumani) *lw: hld up in rr: hdwy over 2f out: chsd ldrs fnl f but no imp* **8/1**[3]

2022 **5** 1 **Compton's Eleven**[14] 4798 5-9-6 **97**.................... TedDurcan 11 98
(M R Channon) *mid-div: hdwy and n.m.r 2f out: styd on fnl f but nvr gng pce to rch ldrs* **6/1**[1]

410 **6** ¾ **Flipando (IRE)**[63] 3313 5-9-0 **91**.................... NCallan 9 90
(T D Barron) *bhd: rdn 3f out: styd on u.p fr over 1f out: nvr in contention* **6/1**[1]

3020 **7** *1 ¼* **Binanti**[7] [5019] 6-8-9 **86** .... JimCrowley 7 82+
(P R Chamings) *in tch early: sn bhd: rdn over 2f out: styd on fnl f but nvr a danger* **16/1**

0335 **8** *nk* **Marching Song**[23] [4529] 4-9-5 **96** .... PatDobbs 5 91+
(R Hannon) *bhd: rdn over 3f out: mod prog fr over 1f out* **8/1**[3]

3-04 **9** *2 ½* **High Bray (GER)**[28] [4372] 5-8-5 **85** oh1 .... MarcHalford(3) 8 73
(D R C Elsworth) *chsd ldrs: rdn 3f out: mod late hdwy u.p* **7/1**[2]

1020 **10** *nk* **Into The Breeze (IRE)**[14] [4790] 6-8-1 **85** .... PatrickHills(7) 10 73
(J W Hills) *bhd: rdn and hdwy on rails over 2f out: nvr gng pce to rch ldrs: wknd fnl f* **8/1**[3]

1000 **11** *½* **Gallantry**[23] [4521] 4-8-8 **85** oh1 .... RoystonFfrench 13 71
(D W Barker) *chsd ldrs: rdn 3f out: wknd ins fnl 2f* **16/1**

1626 **12** *5* **Hits Only Heaven (IRE)**[7] [5019] 4-8-8 **85** ....(e) AdrianTNicholls 1 58
(D Nicholls) *swtg: broke wl: sn in rr on outside and nvr a factor* **14/1**

1m 25.21s (-2.83) **Going Correction** -0.20s/f (Firm) **12** Ran SP% **114.6**
Speed ratings (Par 109):108,107,106,105,104 103,102,101,99,98 98,92
CSF £375.95 CT £3459.72 TOTE £41.00: £8.20, £4.40, £2.70; EX 825.30.
Owner Miss B Swire **Bred** Miss B Swire **Trained** Kimpton, Hants

■ Stewards' Enquiry : Paul Doe caution: used whip down shoulder in forehand position

FOCUS
Competitive, but contested largely by inconsistent types. Horses racing close to the pace were clearly favoured and the form is unconvincing.

NOTEBOOK
King's Caprice, taken to post early, dictated it at just the right tempo under a canny ride - a strategy that suits him perfectly. When the others tried to get past, he had enough in reserve to hold on.
Bayeux(USA)'s four victories have all been over six furlongs, but he gets this trip really well and can be considered at either distance from now on.
Prince Of Thebes(IRE) was raised 6lb for his narrow win last time and, in the circumstances, ran a cracker. (tchd 9-1)
Seulement(USA) did really well in view of the fact that he tried to come from a long way back in a race dominated by the prominent runners. He seems to be finding his form again, and an extra furlong would be in his favour.
Compton's Eleven was short of room at a vital stage and was never quite going to get there, but he is well suited by contests like this and remains in pretty good form. (op 5-1 tchd 9-2)
Flipando(IRE) is probably best suited by a mile, and coming from behind was never going to be easy here because of the way the race was run. (op 13-2)
Hits Only Heaven(IRE) Official explanation: jockey said gelding ran too free

5176 SPORTING INDEX STARDOM STKS (LISTED RACE) 1m
2:50 (2:50) (Class 1) 2-Y-O

£14,195 (£5,380; £2,692; £1,342; £672; £337) **Stalls** High

Form RPR

412 **1** **Caldra (IRE)**[14] [4809] 2-9-0 101 .... GeorgeBaker 6 105+
(S Kirk) *hld up rr but in tch: n.m.r over 2f out and swtchd lft to outside: str run fr over 1f out: to ld fnl 110yds: readily* **5/1**[3]

21 **2** *1 ¼* **Big Robert**[15] [4781] 2-9-0 .... IanMongan 1 102
(W R Muir) *lw: hld up rr but in tch: stdy hdwy on outside to ld ins fnl 2f: hdd and one pce fnl 110yds* **4/1**[2]

1134 **3** *3* **Norisan**[14] [4809] 2-9-0 99 .... OscarUrbina 8 95
(R Hannon) *led after 2f: rdn 3f out: hdd ins fnl 2f: wknd ins last* **9/1**

5312 **4** *shd* **Gweebarra**[18] [4680] 2-9-0 100 .... NCallan 5 95
(K A Ryan) *t.k.h: chsd ldrs: drvn to chal on ins over 2f out: sn no imp: wknd ins fnl f* **4/1**[2]

461 **5** *1 ¼* **Mesbaah (IRE)**[24] [4466] 2-9-0 95 ....(p) TedDurcan 3 92
(M A Jarvis) *led 2f: styd chsng ldr: rdn 3f out: one pce 2f out: wknd fnl f* **11/2**

1032 **6** *9* **Middleham (IRE)**[42] [3962] 2-9-0 104 .... RoystonFfrench 4 71
(M Johnston) *chsd ldrs: rdn along 5f out: hung lft fr over 3f out: sn wknd* **9/4**[1]

0406 **7** *2* **Urban Warrior**[5] [5053] 2-9-0 64 ....(v[1]) EdwardCreighton 7 67
(Mrs Norma Pook) *a bhd* **66/1**

1m 37.21s (-3.06) **Going Correction** -0.20s/f (Firm) 2y crse rec **7** Ran SP% **114.3**
Speed ratings (Par 103):107,105,102,102,101 92,90
CSF £25.14 TOTE £7.20: £3.10, £2.60; EX 27.30.
Owner Norman Ormiston **Bred** S J Macdonald **Trained** Upper Lambourn, Berks

FOCUS
A decent race for staying juveniles, and the principals showed a good level of form for the grade. The first two came clear, and the winner was quite impressive.

NOTEBOOK
Caldra(IRE) has plenty of stamina for a juvenile, and that won him the race, for the extra furlong suited him really well and he won most decisively. With the aid of a stiff tail wind, he smashed the juvenile track record. (op 11-2)
Big Robert travelled well, but his effort materialised earlier than ideal and he appeared to idle in front. This was improved form and, held up a bit longer, he can soon be winning again. (op 9-2)
Norisan was trying a mile for the first time, but seven furlongs looks more suitable at present. (op 10-1)
Gweebarra was trying an extra furlong, but he appeared not to stay it at this stage of his career. (tchd 9-2)
Mesbaah(IRE) found the step up in class beyond him. He may be more of a handicapper in the making. (op 5-1)
Middleham(IRE) ran no race at all, and may have been unsuited by the undulating track. Official explanation: jockey said colt hung left throughout (op 5-2)

5177 MIRROR IMAGE STKS (H'CAP) 1m 1f
3:25 (3:26) (Class 2) (0-100,99) 3-Y-0+

£13,710 (£4,105; £2,052; £1,027; £512; £257) **Stalls** High

Form RPR

1161 **1** **Illustrious Blue**[14] [4798] 3-8-13 **96** .... PaulDoe 12 107+
(W J Knight) *lw: s.i.s: bhd: stdy hdwy on outside fr 2f out: led ins fnl f: styd on strly u.p* **11/4**[1]

0302 **2** *nk* **Tucker**[28] [4348] 4-9-8 **99** ....(p) HayleyTurner 2 108
(W R Swinburn) *lw: led over 6f out: rdn and kpt on wl whn chal fr over 2f out: hdd ins last: kpt on tl no ex cl home* **12/1**

6000 **3** *1 ¼* **Salamanca**[21] [4590] 4-9-2 **93** .... IanMongan 6 100
(S Kirk) *hld up in rr: hdwy on outside over 2f out: kpt on wl u.p fnl f: gng on cl home* **28/1**

022 **4** *nk* **Tabadul (IRE)**[39] [4023] 5-8-13 **90** .... OscarUrbina 1 96
(E A L Dunlop) *trckd ldrs: n.m.r fr 2f out: hdwy over 1f out: styd on same pce ins last* **11/4**[1]

0100 **5** *1 ¼* **Salinja (USA)**[17] [4711] 4-9-4 **95** .... JimCrowley 3 98
(Mrs A J Perrett) *rr: hdwy 4f out: rdn to chal 2f out: one pce whn n.m.r ins last* **33/1**

0604 **6** *hd* **Bustan (IRE)**[13] [4854] 7-9-4 **95** .... GeorgeBaker 8 98+
(G C Bravery) *swtg: hld up in rr: hdwy over 2f out: hung rt over 1f out: n.m.r 1f out and continued to hang rt: nt rcvr* **28/1**

-063 **7** *¾* **Unshakable (IRE)**[15] [4782] 7-8-13 **90** .... JamieMackay 10 92
(Bob Jones) *dropped rr after 2f: rdn over 3f out: kpt on fnl f but nvr gng pce to rch ldrs* **7/1**[2]

-540 **8** *shd* **Activo (FR)**[14] [4805] 5-8-8 **85** oh1 .... TedDurcan 5 86
(S Dow) *rr: hdwy and n.m.r over 2f out: stying on whn hung rt 1f out: nt rch ldrs* **40/1**

0050 **9** *3 ½* **Red Spell (IRE)**[28] [4348] 5-9-0 **91** .... PatDobbs 9 85
(R Hannon) *chsd ldrs:rdn and one pce whn hmpd on rails ins fnl 2f: sn wknd* **9/1**

0035 **10** *½* **Kamanda Laugh**[17] [4711] 5-9-1 **92** .... NCallan 7 85
(K A Ryan) *chsd ldrs: drvn to chal over 2f out: wknd qckly over 1f out* **8/1**[3]

0000 **11** *5* **I'm So Lucky**[16] [4739] 4-9-8 **99** .... RoystonFfrench 4 82
(M Johnston) *led tl hdd over 6f out: wkng whn hmpd over 2f out* **12/1**

1m 54.18s (-2.68) **Going Correction** -0.20s/f (Firm)
WFA 3 from 4yo+ 6lb **11** Ran SP% **114.6**
Speed ratings (Par 109):103,102,101,101,100 100,99,99,96,95 91
CSF £36.91 CT £768.32 TOTE £3.30: £1.70, £2.80, £7.40; EX 36.50.
Owner Mr & Mrs I H Bendelow **Bred** B J And Mrs Crangle **Trained** Patching, W Sussex

FOCUS
A decent enough handicap, but run at a modest pace, which tempers confidence in the form. Few of the participants had been in the best of form lately, the winner being a notable exception.

NOTEBOOK
Illustrious Blue goes well at Goodwood, and his record with Doe on board is impressive, so the combination of the two was right up his street. Effective from seven to nine furlongs, he is still progressing, and has now won at Goodwood four times. He picks up a 4lb penalty for the Cambridgeshire and will be one for the short list there, as the handicapper is struggling to get a hold on him. (tchd 5-2 and 3-1)
Tucker was trying this trip for the first time and looked the likely winner along the inside rail, only to be run out of it by a more progressive sort. His new stable has him back in good form, but he flashed his tail a couple of times under pressure, which was not a good sign. (op 10-1)
Salamanca is on a winning mark after a largely modest season, and on this evidence is running back into form. (op 25-1)
Tabadul(IRE), dropping in trip by a furlong, did not get a perfect passage but remains competitive in races like this. (op 3-1 tchd 10-3, 7-2 in a place)
Salinja(USA) ran much better this time, and looked very dangerous after moving up quickly early in the straight. Brought with a steadier run, he should go even closer. (op 25-1)
Bustan(IRE) still shows flashes of his old form, and did not do badly here except for the fact that he was all over the place on the undulations. Official explanation: jockey said gelding hung badly right from 2f mark (op 25-1 tchd 33-1)
Unshakable(IRE), who won a valuable handicap over a mile here last season, ought not to have found this trip a problem but was not at his best. He has only four career victories to his name, and a horse of his ability should win more often, but it would be dangerous to rule him out in similar contests. (op 6-1)
Red Spell(IRE), though not getting the best of runs, is more effective on Polytrack, with Lingfield his favourite venue. He will be interesting if returning there for valuable events in the coming months. (op 12-1)

5178 EUROPEAN BREEDERS FUND COMMUNITY DAY MAIDEN STKS 1m
4:00 (4:03) (Class 4) 2-Y-O **£5,181** (£1,541; £770; £384) **Stalls** High

Form RPR

52 **1** **Minos (IRE)**[14] [4788] 2-9-3 .... PatDobbs 4 83+
(R Hannon) *mde virtually all: rdn and styd on strly fnl f* **11/10**[1]

2 *1 ¼* **Ajhar (USA)** 2-9-3 .... NCallan 3 80+
(M P Tregoning) *w'like: strong: lw: in tch: drvn and hdwy fr 2f out: qcknd to chse wnr ins last but a hld* **4/1**[2]

03 **3** *1 ¼* **Kalasam**[12] [4895] 2-9-3 .... OscarUrbina 9 78
(W R Muir) *chsd wnr 6f out: drvn along over 2f out and no imp: outpcd and lost 2nd ins last* **10/1**[3]

64 **4** *4* **Fiumicino**[12] [4866] 2-8-9 .... EdwardCreighton(3) 5 64
(M R Channon) *chsd ldrs: rdn 3f out: sn one pce: wknd fnl f* **14/1**

6 **5** *1 ¾* **Murrin (IRE)**[15] [4781] 2-9-3 .... IanMongan 1 65
(T G Mills) *sn chsng ldrs: rdn over 2f out: wknd appr fnl f* **10/1**[3]

0 **6** *hd* **Mystical Moon**[14] [4794] 2-9-3 .... TedDurcan 2 64+
(Lady Herries) *s.i.s: hdwy into mid-div 4f out: sn pushed along and one pce: styd on again ins last* **40/1**

55 **7** *1 ½* **Grand Diamond (IRE)**[14] [4794] 2-9-3 .... JimCrowley 7 61+
(Mrs A J Perrett) *chsd ldrs: rdn over 2f out: wkng whn not much room ins last* **25/1**

00 **8** *½* **Lordship (IRE)**[73] [2979] 2-9-3 .... MatthewHenry 8 60+
(M A Jarvis) *in tch: pushed along over 3f out: kpt on fr over 1f out: nvr in contention* **28/1**

9 *nk* **Mud Monkey** 2-9-3 .... RobertMiles 12 59
(B G Powell) *w'like: leggy: s.i.s: bhd and racd on outside thrght: wd bnd 4f out: sme prog fnl 2f: nvr in contention* **16/1**

10 *½* **Hatton Flight** 2-9-3 .... HayleyTurner 14 58
(A M Balding) *w'like: b.bkwd: bhd: pushed along over 3f out: sme prog fr over 1f out* **25/1**

0 **11** *1 ¼* **Hatherden**[15] [4781] 2-9-3 .... FJohansson 13 56
(Miss E C Lavelle) *a in rr* **66/1**

0 **12** *hd* **Mujahaz (IRE)**[21] [4592] 2-9-3 .... JamieMackay 10 55
(J L Dunlop) *s.i.s: wd bnd over 4f out: a in rr* **20/1**

05 **13** *nk* **Ski For Luck (IRE)**[22] [4574] 2-9-3 .... PaulDoe 11 54+
(J L Dunlop) *a in rr* **25/1**

0 **14** *1 ½* **Grand Officer (IRE)**[8] [4980] 2-9-3 .... RoystonFfrench 6 51
(D J S Ffrench Davis) *w'like: a in rr* **100/1**

1m 39.76s (-0.51) **Going Correction** -0.20s/f (Firm) **14** Ran SP% **123.0**
Speed ratings (Par 97):94,92,91,87,85 85,84,83,83,82 81,81,81,79
CSF £4.59 TOTE £2.10: £1.10, £2.00, £3.40; EX 8.20.
Owner Michael Pescod **Bred** Sean Collins **Trained** East Everleigh, Wilts

FOCUS
A mixed bunch, soon strung out by more than 20 lengths but the pace was not that strong and it was hard to come from behind. The winner only ran to Chester form, but it was a nice start from the second and the standard looks solid, with the first three coming clear.

NOTEBOOK
Minos(IRE) was not as impressive as his odds suggested he ought to have been, but he kept finding a bit more under pressure, having had the run of the race. He got the trip all right, but will step back a furlong now for the Goffs Million at The Curragh. On form that looks to be flying a bit high, but his stable has a fantastic record in races of that nature. (op 6-5 tchd 5-4 in places)
Ajhar(USA) ♦, a Diesis colt from a family with a good record at ten to twelve furlongs, should improve and make a decent three-year-old. However, he showed more than enough on this debut to suggest he can find a maiden this season on the way to later success. (tchd 9-2)

The Form Book, Raceform Ltd, Compton, RG20 6NL

Kalasam is not guaranteed to stay this far on breeding, but he got it reasonably well despite losing second place. He is now qualified for nurseries, and can do well in that sphere, but is capable of winning a routine maiden too. (op 7-1)
Fiumicino is not quite living up to expectations, and looks more of a nursery type - events for which she is now qualified. (tchd 16-1)
Murrin(IRE) again showed a bit of promise, and looks a likely sort for nuseries after one more run. (op 8-1)
Mystical Moon stepped up on his debut effort, and will be interesting in nursery or (next season) handicap company after one more run. (tchd 50-1)
Grand Diamond(IRE) is now qualified for nuseries, and that looks to be his scene. (op 33-1)
Lordship(IRE), who has been gelded since his last run, is now ready to make the step into nursery company. (op 25-1)
Mud Monkey could hardly have gone any wider without going via Chichester. By the high-class ten furlong performer Muhtarram out of a staying mare, he will improve with racing and over longer trips, and is one to keep an eye on. (op 50-1)

5179 SPORTING INDEX STARLIT STKS (LISTED RACE) 6f
4:30 (4:31) (Class 1) 3-Y-0+ **£17,034** (£6,456; £3,231; £1,611; £807) **Stalls** Low

Form				RPR
0541	**1**		**Tax Free (IRE)**[4] 5087 4-9-0 107 ... AdrianTNicholls 2 (D Nicholls) *t.k.h: trckd ldrs: rdn over 2f out: str run on rails fnl f to ld last strides* **5/4**[1]	115
4360	**2**	*nk*	**Ashdown Express (IRE)**[34] 4191 7-9-0 115 ... GeorgeBaker 5 (C F Wall) *lw: hld up in rr: hdwy in centre crse fr 2f out: drvn to take slt ld ins last: ct last strides* **11/4**[2]	114
4200	**3**	*nk*	**Beckermet (IRE)**[13] 4832 4-9-0 105 ... RoystonFfrench 4 (R F Fisher) *t.k.h: trckd ldrs: chal fr over 1f out tl ins last: no ex cl home* **14/1**	113
0130	**4**	*1*	**Paradise Isle**[34] 4174 5-8-13 104 ... TedDurcan 3 (C F Wall) *sn w ldr: rdn and slt ld ins fnl 2f: hdd ins last: kpt on same pce* **11/1**	109
1222	**5**	*2*	**Desert Lord**[13] 4855 6-9-0 107 ... (p) NCallan 6 (K A Ryan) *sn slt ld: hdd ins fnl 2f: wknd ins fnl f* **7/2**[3]	104

69.18 secs (-3.67) **Going Correction** -0.30s/f (Firm) course record
WFA 3 from 4yo+ 2lb **5** Ran SP% **108.3**
Speed ratings (Par 111):112,111,111,109,107
CSF £4.73 TOTE £1.80: £1.40, £1.60; EX 4.40.
Owner Ian Hewitson **Bred** Denis And Mrs Teresa Bergin **Trained** Sessay, N Yorks

FOCUS
Contested by smart sprinters, the first four of whom broke the course record over the Stewards' Cup course. The pace looked ordinary, but they were being carried along by a stiff tail wind, which meant they were going faster than it looked. Straightforward form, rated through the third and fourth.

NOTEBOOK
Tax Free(IRE) went well here in the Stewards' Cup, and confirmed his liking of the track on suitably fast ground, setting his second course record of the week. (op 11-8 tchd 6-4 in places)
Ashdown Express(IRE), who dead-heated in this race last year, was ridden with restraint and came with what looked for a moment to be a winning run in a tactical race. There is no doubting his ability, but he does not win as often as he should. (tchd 3-1)
Beckermet(IRE) goes well at this track, and put in a sterling effort behind two better-fancied rivals. (op 10-1)
Paradise Isle had around half a stone to find at the weights, so ran with credit to finish so close. (tchd 12-1)
Desert Lordis best at five furlongs, and he seemed to confirm that here despite a bold effort. (tchd 3-1)

5180 SPORTING INDEX STKS (H'CAP) 2m
5:05 (5:05) (Class 4) (0-85,80) 3-Y-0+ **£5,505** (£1,637; £818) **Stalls** High

Form				RPR
0200	**1**		**Twill (IRE)**[14] 4792 3-8-11 76 ... TedDurcan 1 (H Morrison) *led 6f: styd disputing 2nd tl chsd ldr over 4f out: led over 3f out: drvn and styd on wl fnl f: readily* **4/1**[3]	83
5432	**2**	*1 ½*	**Theatre (USA)**[38] 4036 7-9-9 75 ... IanMongan 4 (Jamie Poulton) *racd in 3rd: qcknd to ld after 6f: rdn 5f out: hdd over 3f out: hung rt u.p and n.m.r over 1f out: sn no ex* **5/2**[2]	80
1051	**3**	*1 ¾*	**Sir Monty (USA)**[28] 4369 4-9-13 79 ... JimCrowley 3 (Mrs A J Perrett) *swtg: chsd ldr tl disp 2nd fr 10f out: rdn over 3f out: fnd no ex fnl 2f* **8/11**[1]	82

3m 33.96s (3.17) **Going Correction** -0.20s/f (Firm)
WFA 3 from 4yo+ 13lb **3** Ran SP% **106.5**
Speed ratings (Par 105):84,83,82
CSF £11.72 TOTE £5.00; EX 10.40.
Owner de La Warr Racing **Bred** Rathbarry Stud **Trained** East Ilsley, Berks

FOCUS
Sadly lacking in numbers, and run at a stop-start pace which makes the form unreliable.

5181 GOODWOOD RACEHORSE OWNERS GROUP STKS (H'CAP) 5f
5:40 (5:40) (Class 5) (0-75,75) 3-Y-0 **£3,238** (£963; £481; £240) **Stalls** Low

Form				RPR
3022	**1**		**Safari Mischief**[15] 4756 3-8-11 68 ... JimCrowley 3 (P Winkworth) *mde virtually all: hrd drvn and hld on gamely whn chal thrght fnl f* **7/2**[1]	76
0630	**2**	*hd*	**Devine Dancer**[10] 4922 3-9-3 74 ... IanMongan 7 (H Candy) *lw: rr: hdwy 2f out: drvn to chal ins fnl f: kpt on wl but no ex last strides* **11/2**[3]	81
0010	**3**	*1 ¼*	**Highland Song (IRE)**[13] 4834 3-8-12 69 ... RoystonFfrench 8 (R F Fisher) *lw: chsd ldrs: chal 2f out to 1f out: one pce ins fnl f* **7/1**	72
3633	**4**	*hd*	**Xaluna Bay (IRE)**[12] 4874 3-9-2 73 ... TedDurcan 9 (W R Muir) *s.i.s: bhd: hdwy 2f out: pressed ldrs over 1f out: one pce ins last: b.b.v* **9/2**[2]	75
1462	**5**	*½*	**Musical Romance (IRE)**[32] 4226 3-9-2 73 ... (b) OscarUrbina 1 (B J Meehan) *stdd s and slowly away: stl plenty to do ins fnl 2f: r.o ins last: nt rch ldrs* **7/2**[1]	73
0004	**6**	*2*	**Sofinella (IRE)**[21] 4587 3-8-3 67 oh3 ow6 ... MarkCoumbe(7) 2 (A W Carroll) *chsd ldrs to 1/2-way: wknd over 1f out* **8/1**	60
5000	**7**	*3 ½*	**Triskaidekaphobia**[22] 4562 3-8-11 68 ... PaulFitzsimons 4 (Miss J R Tooth) *chsd ldrs: one pce whn hmpd 2f out: sn wknd* **16/1**	48
2000	**8**	*1*	**Danny The Dip**[12] 4874 3-8-1 61 oh7 ... (p) MarcHalford(3) 6 (J J Bridger) *b.hind: pressed ldrs tl hung lft and wknd 2f out* **16/1**	38

57.63 secs (-1.42) **Going Correction** -0.30s/f (Firm) **8** Ran SP% **113.4**
Speed ratings (Par 101):99,98,96,96,95 92,86,85
CSF £22.52 CT £126.19 TOTE £4.80: £1.60, £2.40, £2.10; EX 31.60 Place 6 £441.22, Place 5 £55.88.
Owner P Winkworth **Bred** Bearstone Stud **Trained** Chiddingfold, Surrey

FOCUS
A modest sprint for the course, but sound enough form.
Xaluna Bay(IRE) Official explanation: trainer said filly bled from the nose
Musical Romance(IRE) Official explanation: jockey said filly missed the break
T/Plt: £571.00 to a £1 stake. Pool: £77,007.40. 98.45 winning tickets. T/Qpdt: £39.90 to a £1 stake. Pool: £3,589.20. 66.45 winning tickets. ST

5153 YORK (L-H)
Saturday, September 9

OFFICIAL GOING: Good
The ground had continued to dry out and was described as 'sticky, dead in places but definitely slower than good'.
Wind: Moderate, half-behind Weather: Fine, sunny and warm

5182 LADBROKES PORTLAND (HERITAGE H'CAP) 5f 89y
2:05 (2:05) (Class 2) 3-Y-0+
£31,160 (£9,330; £4,665; £2,335; £1,165; £585) **Stalls** High

Form				RPR
101	**1**		**Fantasy Believer**[14] 4796 8-8-13 93 ... JimmyQuinn 5 (J J Quinn) *midfield: hdwy on outer 2f out: led ent last: sn clr* **20/1**	110
0004	**2**	*3*	**One Putra (IRE)**[14] 4803 4-9-10 104 ... PhilipRobinson 6 (M A Jarvis) *in tch: hdwy 2f out: rdn to disp ld over 1f out and ev ch tl drvn and nt qckn ins last* **20/1**	111
0131	**3**	*½*	**Hogmaneigh (IRE)**[14] 4811 3-9-1 99 ... SaleemGolam(3) 3 (S C Williams) *lw: bmpd s: carried lft and sn in rr: hdwy over 2f out: n.m.r over 1f out: sn rdn and kpt on ins last* **5/1**[1]	104+
0350	**4**	*nk*	**Texas Gold**[6] 5044 8-9-5 99 ... MartinDwyer 8 (W R Muir) *in tch: rdn along 2f out: swtchd rt ins last: kpt on towards fin* **22/1**	103
2204	**5**	*hd*	**Woodcote (IRE)**[14] 4796 4-9-0 94 ... (p) KDarley 10 (C G Cox) *chsd ldrs: hdwy 2f out: sn rdn and edgd rt over 1f out: drvn and one pce ins last* **9/1**[3]	98
0200	**6**	*¾*	**Treasure Cay**[28] 4360 5-9-1 95 ... (t) RobertWinston 2 (P W D'Arcy) *midfield: hdwy 2f out: sn rdn and kpt on ins last: nrst fin* **28/1**	96
0530	**7**	*1*	**Connect**[6] 5044 9-8-12 92 ... (b) TPQueally 13 (M H Tompkins) *midfield: hdwy 2f out: snr idden and kpt on ins last: nrst fin* **14/1**	90
0421	**8**	*1*	**Cape Royal**[7] 5009 6-9-0 94 ... (bt) DarryllHolland 16 (J M Bradley) *led: rdn along wl over 1f out: hdd ent last: wknd* **12/1**	88
4405	**9**	*¾*	**Lafi (IRE)**[13] 4832 7-9-8 102 ... MichaelHills 20 (D Nicholls) *stdd s and bhd tl styd on fnl 2f* **10/1**	94
0022	**10**	*nk*	**Pivotal's Princess (IRE)**[13] 4832 4-9-4 98 ... RichardMullen 4 (E S McMahon) *lw: dwlt: towards rr tl styd on fnl 2f: nvr rch ldrs* **8/1**[2]	89
0215	**11**	*½*	**King Orchisios (IRE)**[28] 4345 3-8-12 96 ... (b[1]) AndrewMullen(3) 12 (K A Ryan) *chsd ldr: rdn along 2f out: drvn and wknd appr last* **14/1**	85
0000	**12**	*nk*	**Corridor Creeper (FR)**[12] 4875 9-9-9 103 ... (p) RHills 14 (J M Bradley) *bhd tl sme late hdwy* **33/1**	91
5056	**13**	*½*	**Masta Plasta (IRE)**[14] 4803 3-9-2 97 ... TomEaves 7 (J Howard Johnson) *in tch: rdn along over 2f out: sn drvn and no imp* **33/1**	83
0120	**14**	*½*	**One More Round (USA)**[35] 4128 8-9-3 100 ... (b) JamesDoyle(3) 9 (N P Littmoden) *a towards rr* **16/1**	85
0501	**15**	*½*	**Bond City (IRE)**[12] 4875 4-9-8 102 ... LDettori 18 (B Smart) *chsd ldrs: rdn along 2f out: sn drvn and wknd over 1f out* **9/1**[3]	85
6160	**16**	*1*	**Indian Trail**[42] 3926 6-9-8 102 ... RichardHughes 1 (D Nicholls) *stdd s: a rr* **25/1**	81
4000	**17**	*2 ½*	**Merlin's Dancer**[35] 4128 6-9-0 94 ... JoeFanning 17 (D Nicholls) *chsd ldr: rdn along 2f out: sn wknd* **33/1**	65
6011	**18**	*2*	**The Jobber (IRE)**[28] 4360 5-9-1 95 ... PaulHanagan 15 (M Blanshard) *a towards rr* **12/1**	59
1306	**19**	*13*	**Qadar (IRE)**[121] 1602 4-9-4 98 ... MickyFenton 11 (N P Littmoden) *prom: rdn along 2f out: sn edgd lft and wkng whn n.m.r and hmpd over 1f out: eased* **50/1**	18

62.44 secs (-2.56)
WFA 3 from 4yo+ 1lb **64** Ran SP% **123.4**
CSF £352.34 CT £1489.27 TOTE £23.80: £4.10, £5.00, £2.30, £5.30; EX 1117.30 Trifecta £1938.00 Part won. Pool £2,729.58. - 0.30 winning units..
Owner The Fantasy Fellowship B **Bred** John Khan **Trained** Settrington, N Yorks
■ A new distance for York, to accommodate the Portland.

FOCUS
Traditionally one of the most competitive sprint handicaps of the season and this year's renewal looked no different on paper, but Fantasy Believer had other ideas and destroyed his field. Surprisingly, this looks a new personal best from Fantasy Believer at the age of 8. The runner-up ran to the blance of his form and it was a good effort after a troubled run from the third.

NOTEBOOK
Fantasy Believer, winner of two of his last three starts, was up another 4lb and found himself racing over this trip for the first time in almost a year. Dismissed in the betting, the in-form gelding destroyed his field in what was a typically competitive renewal and he now heads to the Ayr Gold Cup, with odds of around 10/1 looking reasonable enough for the Scottish showpiece, although he will now have a double penalty.
One Putra(IRE) was always likely to be vulnerable off top weight, but he ran a stormer and battled on well to hold the favourite for second. A highly consistent sort, he is likely to continue to run well in these big sprints without winning. (op 25-1)
Hogmaneigh(IRE) ◆, an unexposed and progressive sprinter, having just the seventh start of his career, was unlucky not to finish at least second as he was bumped at the start and forced to sit well back before meeting trouble when trying to come with his run. This was a good effort off an 8lb higher mark than when winning at Sandown, and he will merit the utmost respect at Ayr, especially as he will be off a 3lb lower mark than this. (op 11-2 tchd 6-1 in a place)
Texas Gold is on a bit of a losing run, but this was a smashing effort from the old boy. Equally effective at five and six furlongs, he was racing here off a 2lb lower mark than when last successful and could sneak a small race somewhere if able to repeat the effort. (op 20-1)
Woodcote(IRE) has run many good races in many good handicaps this year, notably his Stewards Cup seventh when hanging badly under pressure, but he is not a winner and sound placed efforts are all you are likely to get as he lacks a finishing kick. (op 10-1)
Treasure Cay remains a little high in the handicap, but there was nothing wrong with this effort and he was coming home well. Five furlongs is his trip, but he needs some assistance from the Handicapper.
Connect ran his usual race, running on when the race was all over, and he is another who may need some help from the Handicapper.
Cape Royal has been in good form, but he nicked a race at Haydock during the week and was unable to repeat the trick in this much more competitive race on the quicker ground.
Lafi(IRE) came down the stands' side in a race in which most of the action was towards the middle (op 9-1)

Pivotal's Princess(IRE) has returned from a break in good form, twice going down narrowly, and she was rightly one of the leading contenders in the betting here. However, a slow start scuppered her chances here and she could only keep on late through beaten horses. She is better than this effort suggests and can land a decent race off this mark.

Corridor Creeper(FR) made some late ground when switched left towards the outside of the field.

Indian Trail Official explanation: jockey said gelding lost its action

Qadar(IRE) Official explanation: jockey said gelding had a breathing problem

5183 THE SPORTSMAN NEWSPAPER CHAMPAGNE STKS (GROUP 2) (C&G) 7f

2:35 (2:36) (Class 1) 2-Y-0

£56,780 (£21,520; £10,770; £5,370; £2,690; £1,350) **Stalls** Centre

Form				RPR
11	1		**Vital Equine (IRE)**[86] 2586 2-8-12 86 ....(t) RichardMullen 7 (E J O'Neill) *keen: cl up: led 1/2-way: rdn wl over 1f out: drvn ins last: edgd lft and kpt on wl* **16/1**	113
2	2	½	**Eagle Mountain**[14] 4825 2-8-12 .... JAHeffernan 6 (A P O'Brien, Ire) *w'like: cmpt: towards rr: hdwy 2f out: rdn over 1f out: styd on strly ins last* **5/2**[2]	112
12	3	shd	**Cockney Rebel (IRE)**[16] 4736 2-8-12 .... DO'Donohoe 8 (G A Huffer) *lw: trckd ldrs: hdwy over 2f out: rdn to chal over 1f out and ev ch tl drvn and no ex last 75 yds* **13/2**	112
213	4	2	**Kirklees (IRE)**[38] 4037 2-8-12 106 .... JoeFanning 2 (M Johnston) *lw: led: rdn along and hdd 3f out: drvn and wknd wl over 1f out* **10/1**	107
210	5	¾	**Fishforcompliments**[16] 4736 2-8-12 87 ....(b[1]) PaulHanagan 5 (R A Fahey) *towards rr: hdwy over 2f out: sn rdn and kpt on same pce* **50/1**	105
11	6	1	**Thousand Words**[49] 3735 2-8-12 .... RichardHughes 1 (B W Hills) *trckd ldrs: effrt over 2f out: sn rdn and wknd over 1f out* **9/4**[1]	102
213	7	1 ¾	**Celtic Sultan (IRE)**[22] 4561 2-8-12 96 .... TonyCulhane 3 (T P Tate) *in tch: rdn along wl over 2f out: sn btn* **33/1**	98
1	8	5	**Prince Forever (IRE)**[21] 4592 2-8-12 .... PhilipRobinson 4 (M A Jarvis) *keen: chsd ldrs: rdn over 2f out and sn wknd* **9/2**[3]	85

1m 23.29s (-2.11) **Going Correction** -0.125s/f (Firm) **8** Ran SP% **110.7**
Speed ratings (Par 107):107,106,106,104,103 102,100,94
CSF £52.66 TOTE £19.40: £3.60, £1.40, £2.00; EX 71.20 Trifecta £534.60 Part won. Pool £753.04. - 0.60 winning units..
Owner Fasthandle Ltd **Bred** John Costello **Trained** Averham Park, Notts

FOCUS

Not the result many would have wanted from a Classic viewpoint and in all honesty it looked a pretty ordinary renewal, especially with the two potential class acts Thousand Words and Prince Forever fading tamely out of contention. The race is highly unlikely to have a bearing on any of next season's Classics.

NOTEBOOK

Vital Equine(IRE), a winner at Newcastle and Yarmouth earlier in the season on his sole previous appearances, looked to hold place claims at best, with a first-time tongue tie slightly off-putting, but he was ideally positioned throughout and responded well to strong pressure to surge ahead. Although he is by Danetime, there is plenty of stamina on the dam's side and he is now likely to head for the National Stakes at the Curragh on the 17th September, where he will be up against it with the likes of Holy Roman Emperor and Haatef in opposition. (op 25-1)

Eagle Mountain improved on his maiden form when chasing home Teofilio in the Futurity Stakes at the Curragh recently and he again ran well here, staying on strongly close home having been given a fair bit to do by his rider. He may well have won had he been ridden more prominently and the son of Rock Of Gibraltar looks ready for a mile, with something like the Royal Lodge appealing as his type of race. (op 9-4)

Cockney Rebel(IRE), although highly regarded, was only bringing sales-race form into the race and again stepped up on previous efforts.He is clearly smart, but unlikely to find success at this level, although connections think otherwise and he is likely to be put away until reappearing in the Craven, with a view to having a crack at the Guineas. (op 7-1 tchd 15-2)

Kirklees(IRE) has shown himself to be a very useful juvenile and his recent third to Strategic Prince entitled him to go close. His stable had a line on favourite Thousand Words, but he was unable to keep up the gallop having led them until threeout and he faded close home. He probably needs his sights lowering. (op 12-1)

Fishforcompliments, who ran poorly in the sales race behind Cockney Rebel, showed that running to be all wrong in the first-time blinkers, coming home to good effect and showing much improved form. However, he is not up to this level and is another who needs his sights lowered.

Thousand Words, whose stable have won this with the likes of Auction House, Distant Music and Etlaala in recent years, also had subsequent Guineas winner Haafhd turned over at odds-on in it and the fact this unbeaten colt was taking his chance suggsted he is amongst the best at Wetherdown House. He was rightly made favourite, having beaten subsequent Group 3 winner Drumfire at Newbury last time, but having travelled well he failed to pick up under pressure and in the end dropped away somewhat disappointingly. There is plenty of stamina for this distance in the pedigree, so there can be no excuse on that front, and it may just be he had an off day, although when he returns to the track he will have something to prove. (op 2-1, tchd 9-4 in places)

Celtic Sultan(IRE) ran well when third behind Dubai's Touch in a Listed race at Newbury last time, but he was not up to the task here and needs a drop in grade.

Prince Forever(IRE) was another to disappoint. A good winner on his debut at Newbury of a race that worked out just okay, he looked likely to improve, being a son of Giant's Causeway, but he took a grip early on and, like the favourite, found little under pressure. He too has a fair bit to prove now. Official explanation: jockey said colt ran too free early (op 5-1)

5184 GNER PARK STKS (GROUP 2) 7f

3:10 (3:10) (Class 1) 3-Y-0+

£56,780 (£21,520; £10,770; £5,370; £2,690; £1,350) **Stalls** Centre

Form				RPR
-021	1		**Iffraaj**[39] 4025 5-9-6 118 .... LDettori 1 (Saeed Bin Suroor) *lw: trckd ldrs: hdwy over 2f out: rdn to chal wl over 1f out: drvn ent last: kpt on u.p to ld last 100 yds* **4/6**[1]	121
1044	2	¾	**Somnus**[7] 5011 6-9-2 105 .... KDarley 3 (T D Easterby) *trckd ldrs: hdwy over 2f out: rdn over 1f out and ev ch tl drvn and no ex last 100 yds* **20/1**	115
0111	3	nk	**Wasseema (USA)**[14] 4808 3-8-9 112 .... RHills 2 (Sir Michael Stoute) *led: pushed along over 2f out: rdn wl over 1f out: drvn ent last: hdd and no ex last 100 yds* **6/1**[2]	109
5451	4	1 ¼	**King Jock (USA)**[20] 4641 5-9-2 .... PShanahan 5 (R J Osborne, Ire) *in tch: hdwy to chse ldrs over 2f out: sn rdn and kpt on same pce* **20/1**	111
2304	5	2	**Mac Love**[21] 4596 5-9-2 107 .... MartinDwyer 8 (R Charlton) *in tch: hdwy 2f out: sn rdn and no imp appr last* **33/1**	106
1140	6	½	**Speciosa (IRE)**[78] 2802 3-9-1 114 .... MickyFenton 7 (Mrs P Sly) *hdw: chsd ldrs on outer: rdn along 3f out: wknd 2f out* **12/1**	105
1021	7	½	**Quito (IRE)**[2] 5135 9-9-2 112 ....(b) TonyCulhane 4 (D W Chapman) *towards rr: hdwy to chse ldrs over 2f out: sn rdn and btn over 1f out* **15/2**[3]	103
-101	8	nk	**Welsh Emperor (IRE)**[21] 4596 7-9-6 113 .... DarryllHolland 6 (T P Tate) *chsd ldr: rdn along wl over 2f out: grad wknd* **20/1**	106
3104	9	7	**Short Dance (USA)**[36] 4097 3-8-9 107 .... RichardHughes 9 (B W Hills) *in tch: rdn along wl over 2f out: sn wknd* **20/1**	81

1m 21.98s (-3.42) **Going Correction** -0.125s/f (Firm)
WFA 3 from 5yo+ 4lb **9** Ran SP% **115.7**
Speed ratings (Par 115):114,113,112,111,109 108,107,107,99
CSF £21.54 TOTE £1.60: £1.10, £4.80, £1.70; EX 21.90 Trifecta £184.70 Pool £1,275.23. - 4.90 winning units..
Owner Godolphin **Bred** Darley **Trained** Newmarket, Suffolk

FOCUS

An intriguing Group 2 with the established Iffraaj taken on by the highly promising filly Wasseema. It was the Godolphin runner who emerged best, and although less impressive than at Goodwood he wasn't far off his best. The race has been rated to the best of the runner-up's form this year.

NOTEBOOK

Iffraaj, who would have been bidding for a hat-trick had he had a bit more luck in the July Cup, stamped his class over this distance when destroying his field in the Lennox Stakes at Goodwood and, although made to work an awful lot harder here, he was able to defy his penalty. A strong traveller, he failed to pick up immediately, but wore down the front-running Wasseema in the end and was always holding Somnus. This effort suggested he is well worth a try at a mile, and the Breeders' Cup Mile now beckons. He can go close if he is in top shape. (op 8-11 tchd 4-5)

Somnus, fourth in last weekend's Haydock Sprint Cup, has been a grand servant over the years, winning a trio of Group 1s, and he showed here he is still capable of running to a high level, finding only the classy winner too good. Winning opportunities are not easy to come by these days, but there may be a conditions race to be won with him this backend.

Wasseema(USA) ◆, a highly progressive filly who is finally living up to her home reputation, came into this seeking a four-timer, having won her maiden and a brace of Listed races in impressive fashion. This represented a much stiffer task, especially over a furlong shorter, but she ran a cracking race and very nearly made all, only giving way inside the final half a furlong. The return to a mile on quick ground can see further improvement and she looks well up to this level. (op 13-2)

King Jock(USA), a Group 3 winner at Leopardstown last month, held every chance and ran his race, but as expected, he came up a bit shy of the classy winner. He continues to progress quietly. (op 25-1)

Mac Love struggles to make an impact at this sort of level these days and he is another for whom conditions races represent his best chance of winning again. (op 28-1)

Speciosa(IRE), the fairytale 1000 Guineas winner, was not disgraced in either the Oaks or the Coronation Stakes. She could have been expected to need this first run since June and was not disgraced under her Group 1 penalty. (tchd 14-1)

Quito(IRE) is as tough as they come and having been an unlucky runner-up in the Sprint Cup the previous weekend, he dug deep to land a Listed contest back at Haydock during the week. This third run in the space of eight days proved too much however and having taken up his usual position at the back of the field, he was unable to pick up in quite his usual manner. Official explanation: trainer said race may have come too soon (op 7-1 tchd 8-1)

Welsh Emperor(IRE) is a tough and genuine performer whose recent Group 2 win at Newbury entitled him to respect here, especially as the third Caradak went on to win the Celebration Mile. However, he struggled under his penalty and was slightly disappointing, although this was a stronger race for the grade than at Newbury. Official explanation: jockey said gelding was unsuited by the good ground

Short Dance(USA), a rampant winner over a mile here earlier in the season, bounced back to form when fourth at Goodwood behind high-class filly Red Evie, but this proved too hot for her and she dropped right away. (op 16-1)

5185 LADBROKES ST LEGER STKS (GROUP 1) (ENTIRE COLTS & FILLIES) 1m 5f 197y

3:45 (3:48) (Class 1) 3-Y-0

£269,705 (£102,220; £51,157; £25,507; £12,777; £6,412) **Stalls** Low

Form				RPR
1031	1		**Sixties Icon**[39] 4024 3-9-0 115 .... LDettori 11 (J Noseda) *lw: hld up in rr: smooth hdwy 4f out: trckd ldrs on bit 2f out: shkn up to ld ins last: sn clr* **11/8**[1]	123+
2504	2	2 ½	**The Last Drop (IRE)**[18] 4678 3-9-0 100 ....(t) RHills 5 (B W Hills) *in tch: hdwy 4f out: rdn to led over 1f out: drvn: edgd lft and hdd ins last: kpt on one pce* **50/1**	116
1222	3	1	**Red Rocks (IRE)**[18] 4678 3-9-0 114 .... RichardHughes 7 (B J Meehan) *hld up towards rr: hdwy over 3f out: rdn to chse ldrs over 1f out: kpt on same pce* **4/1**[2]	115
2102	4	hd	**Ask**[16] 4742 3-9-0 90 ....(t) RobertWinston 1 (Sir Michael Stoute) *lw: trckd ldrs: hdwy over 3f out: rdn to chal 2f out and ev ch: drvn and edgd rt ent last: kpt on same pce* **16/1**	114
1	5	1	**Tusculum (IRE)**[14] 4822 3-9-0 .... JAHeffernan 12 (A P O'Brien, Ire) *hld up towards rr: pushed along and hdwy over 2f out: sn rdn and styd on ins last: nrst fin* **17/2**	113
5221	6	shd	**Jadalee (IRE)**[14] 4797 3-9-0 110 .... MartinDwyer 6 (M P Tregoning) *midfield: hdwy over 4f out: rdn to chse ldrs over 2f out: sn drvn and kpt on same pce* **15/2**[3]	113
2060	7	½	**Mountain (IRE)**[57] 3517 3-9-0 .... KDarley 9 (A P O'Brien, Ire) *chsd ldrs: hdwy to chal 3f out: sn rdn and ev ch tl drvn and wknd over 1f out* **16/1**	112
1214	8	4	**Mont Etoile (IRE)**[55] 3575 3-8-11 107 .... MichaelHills 4 (W J Haggas) *hld up towards rr: effrt 3f out: sn rdn and no hdwy* **18/1**	103
-100	9	nk	**Championship Point (IRE)**[18] 4678 3-9-0 110 .... TonyCulhane 10 (M R Channon) *chsd ldrs: hdwy to ld over 4f out: rdn over 2f out: drvn and hdd over 1f out: wkng whn hmpd ent last and sn eased* **20/1**	106
1-6	10	1 ½	**Fire And Rain (FR)**[18] 4678 3-9-0 .... CO'Donoghue 2 (A P O'Brien, Ire) *chsd ldrs: rdn along over 3f out: wknd over 2f out* **20/1**	104
1125	11	25	**Galient (IRE)**[21] 4595 3-9-0 96 .... PhilipRobinson 3 (M A Jarvis) *led: rdn along and hdd over 4f out: sn wknd* **18/1**	69

2m 57.29s (-1.15) **Going Correction** +0.15s/f (Good) **11** Ran SP% **118.2**
Speed ratings (Par 115):109,107,107,106,106 106,105,103,103,102 88
CSF £107.46 TOTE £2.50: £1.20, £8.00, £1.40; EX 108.80 Trifecta £868.60 Pool £24,249.47. - 19.82 winning units..
Owner Mrs Susan Roy **Bred** Lordship Stud **Trained** Newmarket, Suffolk

■ This first British Classic for Jeremy Noseda came in a race last run at York in 1945. The first three are all sons of Galileo.

FOCUS

A fairly weak renewal, but further improvement from the winner, who proved different class at the end of a race that had by no means been run at an end-to-end gallop. He will still need to find another 10lb or so to figure at the finish in the Arc, however. The fifth, sixth and seventh give the form a sound base, and the second and fourth were much improved.

NOTEBOOK

Sixties Icon, who looked trained to the minute, travelled supremely well. He showed easily the best turn of foot and a drop back to a mile and a half in the Arc will not be a problem. He will need to find plenty though to trouble the cream of the older horses. (op 13-8 tchd 7-4 in places)

The Last Drop(IRE) improved significantly for the step up in trip and turned the Voltigeur tables on the third. He should make a Cup horse at four.

Red Rocks(IRE), given a much more patient ride, in the end was simply not good enough. He is now likely to drop back in trip, with big prizes in North America tempting opportunities. (tchd 9-2 in places)

Ask, a laid-back individual, looked in peak condition and improved a good deal on his game effort in handicap company here two weeks earlier. This was just his sixth start and there will be even better to come with another year over his head. (op 20-1)

Tusculum(IRE), warm and edgy, was staying on when it was all over and would have preferred a lot more give underfoot. (op 8-1 tchd 9-1)

Jadalee(IRE), very alert in the paddock, could have done with a stronger pace and finished much further behind the winner than he had at Goodwood. It emerged later that he had wrenched his near hind, possibly leaving the stalls, and he is unlikely to run again this year. However, he too should make his presence felt in Group races at four. (op 7-1)

Mountain(IRE) has struggled to make an impact in the top races this year.

Mont Etoile(IRE), the only filly in the race, tried to come from off the pace in a race that was not run at an end-to-end gallop. (op 20-1)

Championship Point(IRE), who kept tabs on the leaders, went on once in line for home but his chance had gone when tightened up. He is simply not up to this level.

Fire And Rain(FR), having just his third career start, is a good-looking colt but clearly all has not been well with him this year.

Galient(IRE) took them along in his own time but he dropped right away when headed and something was clearly amiss. He will bounce back at four. (op 20-1)

5186 GRAHAME STOWE BATESON FAMILY LAW UNIT STRENSALL STKS (GROUP 3) — 1m 208y

4:25 (4:25) (Class 1) 3-Y-0+ — **£29,635** (£11,205; £5,600; £2,800) **Stalls** Low

Form				RPR
0-16	**1**		**Echo Of Light**[38] 4038 4-9-8 114 .... LDettori 9 (Saeed Bin Suroor) *lw: mde all: qcknd over 2f out: pushed clr wl over 1f out: easily* **5/2**[1]	121
1110	**2**	*2 ½*	**Stage Gift (IRE)**[18] 4678 3-8-12 107 .... RobertWinston 2 (Sir Michael Stoute) *lw: hld up in rr: hdwy 3f out and sn pushed along: rdn wl over 1f out: kpt on u.p ins last: no ch w wnr* **10/3**[2]	112+
-230	**3**	*1 ¾*	**Olympian Odyssey**[97] 2278 3-8-12 113 .... RichardHughes 3 (B W Hills) *lw: trckd ldng pair: hdwy to chse wnr 3f out: rdn over 2f out: sn drvn and kpt on same pce* **7/2**[3]	108
2512	**4**	*2 ½*	**Metropolitan Man**[35] 4126 3-8-12 108 .... MartinDwyer 4 (D M Simcock) *chsd wnr: rdn along 3f out: grad wknd* **14/1**	103
11-	**5**	*5*	**Nakheel**[327] 5942 3-8-12 107 .... RHills 6 (M Johnston) *hld up towards rr: hdwy on inner and in tch 3f out: sn rdn and no imp* **13/2**	93
1440	**6**	*1*	**Nayyir**[36] 4098 8-9-8 110 .... KDarley 7 (G A Butler) *trckd ldrs: rdn along 3f out: drvn over 2f out and sn btn* **8/1**	95
6023	**7**	*3*	**Kings Point (IRE)**[23] 4529 5-9-4 105 .... PaulHanagan 1 (R A Fahey) *trckd ldrs: hdwy over 3f out: rdn over 2f out: sn drvn and wknd* **16/1**	85
3200	**8**	*7*	**Sienna Storm (IRE)**[18] 4678 3-8-12 99 .... (b) TPQueally 8 (M H Tompkins) *in tch: rdn along 4f out: sn wknd* **50/1**	71

1m 50.74s (-0.25) **Going Correction** +0.15s/f (Good)
WFA 3 from 4yo+ 6lb — 8 Ran SP% **112.8**
Speed ratings (Par 113):107,104,103,101,96 95,93,86
CSF £10.61 TOTE £3.00: £1.50, £1.50, £1.70; EX 9.10 Trifecta £26.30 Pool £695.20. - 18.70 winning units..
Owner Godolphin **Bred** Kilcarn Stud **Trained** Newmarket, Suffolk
■ Stewards' Enquiry : Robert Winston one-day ban: careless riding (Sep 20)

FOCUS
A new place in the Calendar for this Group 3, with the York September meeting at which it is normally run not being held this year. It lacked in strength and was rather handed on a plate to the winner who was allowed to dictate things from the front and had the ideal rider aboard to execute the tactics.

NOTEBOOK
Echo Of Light, who filled the eye in the paddock, was allowed to dictate his own pace. He quickened up halfway up the straight and was never in any danger. He is not easy to predict but will not be out of place if given a second chance in the Champion Stakes. (op 11-4, tchd 3-1 in places)

Stage Gift(IRE) ◆, dropping right back in trip after finishing out of the numbers in the Great Voltigeur here, looked at his best. He was given a negative ride and did easily best of those held up, but though he kept on well once in clear water the winner had flown. He can surely make his mark at this level, possibly over the intermediate trip at which he has gained all his three wins. (op 3-1, tchd 7-2 in a place)

Olympian Odyssey. absent since suffering a stress fracture in the Prix du Jockey Club in June, looked at his very best. He went down fighting and will be sharper next time. (op 4-1)

Metropolitan Man, quite a keen type, did not truly see out the extra furlong. (op 16-1)

Nakheel, winner of both his starts at two, suffered a pelvic injury in the spring. He was nowhere near at his best on his return but ideally needs further and perhaps softer. Hopefully he will show his true worth at four. (tchd 6-1, tchd 7-1 in a place)

Nayyir is in-and-out these days and this was not one of his better efforts.

5187 KEEPMOAT MAY HILL STKS (GROUP 2) (FILLIES) — 1m

5:00 (5:00) (Class 1) 2-Y-0
£39,746 (£15,064; £7,539; £3,759; £1,883; £945) **Stalls** Low

Form				RPR
2130	**1**		**Simply Perfect**[13] 4853 2-8-12 104 .... DarryllHolland 1 (J Noseda) *t.k.h in rr: drvn and hdwy over 3f out: led last 75yds: styd on wl* **4/1**[3]	106
11	**2**	*1 ¼*	**English Ballet (IRE)**[28] 4371 2-9-1 .... MichaelHills 5 (B W Hills) *sn trcking ldrs: led 2f out: hdd and no ex ins last* **13/8**[1]	106
115	**3**	*¾*	**Sans Reward (IRE)**[28] 4371 2-8-12 90 .... (b[1]) LDettori 4 (B J Meehan) *led: qcknd over 3f out: hdd 2f out: kpt on ins last* **9/1**	101
3111	**4**	*hd*	**Sweet Lilly**[15] 4773 2-8-12 79 .... TonyCulhane 8 (M R Channon) *hld up in rr: effrt 3f out: outpcd 2f out: styd on ins last despite swishing tail* **14/1**	101
11	**5**	*hd*	**Sudoor**[44] 3874 2-8-12 .... RHills 2 (J L Dunlop) *trckd ldrs: chal 2f out: kpt on same pce fnl f* **7/2**[2]	100
1	**6**	*3 ½*	**Baroness Richter (IRE)**[12] 4866 2-8-12 .... RichardHughes 7 (R Hannon) *dwlt: sn chsng ldrs: wknd fnl 2f* **10/1**	92
014	**7**	*3 ½*	**Musical Mirage (USA)**[16] 4732 2-8-12 88 .... DeanMcKeown 6 (G A Swinbank) *trckd ldrs: hung lft and wknd 2f out* **33/1**	84
2341	**8**	*2*	**Easy Lover**[7] 5013 2-8-12 87 .... MartinDwyer 9 (J A Osborne) *chsd ldrs: drvn 3f out: lost pl over 1f out* **12/1**	80
6	**9**	*19*	**Bobansheil (IRE)**[13] 4829 2-8-12 .... KDarley 3 (J S Wainwright) *s.i.s: sn detached in last: sme hdwy 3f out: sn lost pl and bhd* **100/1**	36

1m 39.24s (-0.26) **Going Correction** +0.15s/f (Good) — **9** Ran SP% **117.7**
Speed ratings (Par 104):107,105,105,104,104 101,97,95,76
CSF £11.12 TOTE £5.40: £1.80, £1.30, £2.30; EX 13.70 Trifecta £109.90 Pool £681.54. - 4.40 winning units..
Owner D Smith, M Tabor & Mrs J Magnier **Bred** Trehedyn Stud And Quarry Bloodstock **Trained** Newmarket, Suffolk

FOCUS
This featured some potentially smart staying juveniles, but the winner needed only to reproduce her Curragh form and the second failed to improve again on her Newmarket win. The apparent improvement of the third and fourth is a concern.

NOTEBOOK
Simply Perfect, out of luck in the Moyglare, if anything found the step up in trip in her favour. She really put her head down and battled, but she will need to step up again if she is to make an impression in the Fillies' Mile at Ascot. (op 9-2)

English Ballet(IRE), unbeaten but carrying a Group 3 penalty, is not the biggest. She went on two out but in the end simply could not contain the winner. This might be as good as she is. (tchd 7-4)

Sans Reward(IRE), suited by getting her toe in, had ground to make up on English Ballet on Newmarket running. Fitted with blinkers and allowed to set her own pace, to her credit she fought back when headed.

Sweet Lilly, one of the bigger fillies in the line-up, stuck on after getting tapped for toe and finished best of all despite being very free with the use of her tail. Rated 79 after her nursery win, her proximity puts a big question mark over the exact value of the form. (op 16-1)

Sudoor looked a real threat two furlongs out but in the end she seemed not to truly see out the mile. (op 3-1)

Baroness Richter(IRE) found this altogether much tougher and at this stage of her career was simply not up to the ask. (op 14-1)

Easy Lover Official explanation: trainer's rep said filly lost a front shoe

5188 SYMPHONY GROUP CHAMOSSAIRE STKS (H'CAP) — 1m 2f 88y

5:30 (5:30) (Class 2) (0-110,104) 3-Y-0+**£16,192** (£4,817; £2,407; £1,202) **Stalls** Low

Form				RPR
2000	**1**		**Rohaani (USA)**[16] 4739 4-9-4 97 .... RHills 12 (Sir Michael Stoute) *lw: trckd ldr: led over 3f out: styd on wl ins last* **5/1**[2]	108
4101	**2**	*1*	**Topatoo**[17] 4711 4-8-11 90 .... TPQueally 4 (M H Tompkins) *s.i.s: hld up in last: hdwy on ins over 3f out: chal over 1f out: no ex ins last* **4/1**[1]	99
1146	**3**	*¾*	**Kahlua Kiss**[14] 4818 3-8-9 95 .... MartinDwyer 1 (W R Muir) *trckd ldrs: chal 2f out: no ex ins last* **14/1**	102
0112	**4**	*hd*	**Bolodenka (IRE)**[16] 4739 4-9-5 98 .... PaulHanagan 7 (R A Fahey) *hld up in mid-field: effrt over 3f out: kpt on same pce fnl f* **5/1**[2]	105
2520	**5**	*½*	**Mutawaffer**[17] 4711 5-8-11 90 oh3 .... RobertWinston 9 (R A Fahey) *chsd ldrs: drvn 4f out: one pce fnl 2f* **16/1**	96
436	**6**	*1*	**Capable Guest (IRE)**[36] 4098 4-9-0 93 .... TonyCulhane 5 (M R Channon) *hld up: hdwy to chse ldrs over 3f out: nt clr run over 2f out: wknd towards fin* **11/2**[3]	97
1000	**7**	*2*	**Blue Spinnaker (IRE)**[17] 4711 7-9-3 96 .... PaulMulrennan 11 (M W Easterby) *chsd ldrs: outpcd fnl 2f* **12/1**	97
5405	**8**	*¾*	**Goodbye Mr Bond**[12] 4889 6-8-11 90 oh3 .... JimmyQuinn 2 (E J Alston) *chsd ldrs: hung lft and wknd 1f out* **12/1**	89
/110	**9**	*¾*	**Gentleman's Deal (IRE)**[168] 728 5-8-13 92 .... DaleGibson 13 (M W Easterby) *t.k.h in mid-field: effrt over 3f out: wknd over 1f out* **10/1**	90
3002	**10**	*¾*	**Dunaskin (IRE)**[17] 4711 6-9-2 95 .... MichaelHills 6 (Karen McLintock) *lw: led: qcknd over 4f out: hdd over 3f out: hung rt and lost pl 2f out* **10/1**	92
0350	**11**	*8*	**Boo**[28] 4359 4-8-12 91 .... PatCosgrave 8 (K R Burke) *hld up in rr: pushed along 4f out: lost pl over 2f out: eased* **14/1**	73

2m 12.46s (1.98) **Going Correction** +0.15s/f (Good)
WFA 3 from 4yo+ 7lb — **11** Ran SP% **121.5**
Speed ratings (Par 109):98,97,96,96,96 95,93,93,92,91 85
CSF £26.26 CT £270.81 TOTE £6.80: £2.40, £1.80, £3.40; EX 34.10 Trifecta £652.20 Part won. Pool £918.70. - 0.60 winning units. Place 6 £17.31, Place 5 £4.85.
Owner Hamdan Al Maktoum **Bred** North Wales Llc **Trained** Newmarket, Suffolk
■ This race commemorates Chamossaire, winner of the St Leger when it was last switched to York in 1945.

FOCUS
A competitive handicap, but it was run at a very steady pace and it paid to race up near the lead. The first three are still on the up, the race has been rated through the fourth and fifth.

NOTEBOOK
Rohaani(USA) looked magnificent and went into the stalls like an old sheep with the benefit of a hood. Suited by the much better ground, he travelled comfortably and when called on for a real effort inside the last, he found plenty and was firmly in command at the line. He should continue to give a good account of himself and will be even better at five. (op 6-1, tchd 13-2 in a place)

Topatoo, 7lb higher, was happy to sit last. Making her effort on the inner, she was upisdes coming to the final furlong but the winner had kept something in reserve. (tchd 7-2, tchd 9-2 in a place)

Kahlua Kiss, a stone higher than when successful here in July, became upset leaving the paddock. She ran right up to her best returned to handicap company.

Bolodenka(IRE), set alight leaving the paddock, was racing from a 4lb higher mark and the extra distance was not a problem.

Mutawaffer, 3lb out of the handicap, has not tasted success for over two years and his trainer is clearly experiencing real difficulties determining his optimum trip. He is just the type that might come good over hurdles.

Capable Guest(IRE) needs everything to fall into place but this trip looks to stretch his stamina to the very limit. (op 6-1)

Gentleman's Deal(IRE) has been at stud and has covered 30 mares since he last appeared in the Lincoln at Redcar. (op 9-1)

T/Jkpt: Not won. T/Plt: £17.80 to a £1 stake. Pool: £171,417.16. 7,003.00 winning tickets. T/Qpdt: £2.10 to a £1 stake. Pool: £7,285.90. 2,548.00 winning tickets. JR

5189 - (Foreign Racing) - See Raceform Interactive

4637 LEOPARDSTOWN (L-H)

Saturday, September 9

OFFICIAL GOING: Good to firm

5190a BRUCE BETTING KILTERNAN STKS (GROUP 3) — 1m 2f

2:10 (2:11) 3-Y-0+ — **£44,827** (£13,103; £6,206; £2,068)

			RPR
1		**Frost Giant (USA)**[126] 1486 3-9-1 110 .... KFallon 8 (A P O'Brien, Ire) *trckd ldr in 2nd: led over 1 1/2f out: strly pressed fnl f: kpt on wl u.p: all out* **6/1**	113+

2 *hd* **Cougar Bay (IRE)**[8] 5004 3-9-1 106 WMLordan 2 113
(David Wachman, Ire) *settled 3rd: 4th 3f out: rdn st: 2nd and chal fnl f: kpt on wl u.p* **9/1**
3 *2* **Lord Admiral (USA)**[42] 3964 5-9-8 109 MJKinane 4 109
(Charles O'Brien, Ire) *trckd ldrs: 5th after 1/2-way: hdwy early st: 3rd and chal under 1f out: no ex cl home* **5/1**[3]
4 *1 1/2* **Arch Rebel (USA)**[8] 5004 5-9-8 110 (p) JMurtagh 3 107
(Noel Meade, Ire) *hld up in rr: 7th drvn along and outpcd over 3f out: styd on st* **7/2**[1]
5 *1/2* **Royal Intrigue (IRE)**[61] 3371 3-9-1 103 (b) PJSmullen 1 106
(D K Weld, Ire) *hld up in tch: 6th 3f out: kpt on same pce st* **6/1**
6 *hd* **Heliostatic (IRE)**[20] 4641 3-9-4 112 KJManning 5 108
(J S Bolger, Ire) *led: rdn and strly pressed ent st: hdd over 1 1/2f out: sn no ex* **13/2**
7 *1 1/4* **Cool Touch (IRE)**[20] 4642 3-9-1 107 OCasey 7 103
(Peter Casey, Ire) *5th early: 4th after 1/2-way: cl 3rd and rdn to chal ent st: wknd fr over 1f out* **4/1**[2]
8 *dist* **Jalmira (IRE)**[13] 4854 5-9-5 80 FMBerry 6 —
(C F Swan, Ire) *a towards rr: wknd 4f out: trailing bef st: sn eased: t.o* **40/1**

2m 5.10s **Going Correction** -0.35s/f (Firm)
WFA 3 from 5yo 7lb **8** Ran SP% **113.2**
Speed ratings: 107,106,105,104,103 103,102,—
CSF £56.69 TOTE £5.50: £1.80, £3.40, £1.70; DF 108.50.
Owner Michael Tabor **Bred** J M J Stables Corporation **Trained** Ballydoyle, Co Tipperary

FOCUS
A smart effort off the back of a break from the potentially high-class Frost Giant, and the form looks solid rated around the second to fifth.

NOTEBOOK
Frost Giant(USA), an impressive winner in this grade as a two-year-old, had not been seen since finishing tailed off in the 2000 Guineas at Newmarket, but this represented a much easier task and he also looked certain to be suited by the step up to ten furlongs. Always well placed, he went on inside the final quarter mile and, as was often seen with his sire Giant's Causeway, he stuck his neck out under pressure to repel the runner-up. This was a performance of immense promise and, if as expected he is kept in training, he could develop into high-class racehorse next term. (op 11/2)
Cougar Bay(IRE) is just about up to this level and he ran on well to challenge the winner, but was never getting past. He can find a race at Listed level. (op 8/1)
Lord Admiral(USA), a tough and consistent horse at this sort of level, has now not finished out of the three in his last eight starts, but he has failed to win any of those and this was slightly disappointing. (op 6/1)
Arch Rebel(USA) could only plug on and was disappointing, the first-time cheekpieces failing to do him any good.
Heliostatic(IRE) has not lived up to expectations this season and, although a winner at this level earlier in the year, has not progressed since. (op 6/1)
Jalmira(IRE) Official explanation: vet said mare was found to be clinically abnormal post race

5191a COOLMORE FUSAICHI PEGASUS MATRON STKS (GROUP 1) (F&M) 1m
2:40 (2:40) 3-Y-0+ **£112,068** (£32,758; £15,517; £5,172)

RPR
1 **Red Evie (IRE)**[36] 4097 3-8-12 JamieSpencer 8 114
(M L W Bell) *hld up in tch: 6th 1/2-way: hdwy on outer early st: led 1f out: all out to hold on nr fin* **6/1**[3]
2 *shd* **Peeress**[27] 4416 5-9-3 RyanMoore 2 114+
(Sir Michael Stoute) *trckd ldrs: 5th 1/2-way: 6th early st: sn rdn: r.o strly ins fnl f: jst failed* **7/2**[2]
3 *3/4* **Flashy Wings**[78] 2802 3-8-12 MJKinane 6 112+
(M R Channon) *in rr: pushed along 1/2-way: 7th ent st: r.o wl fr over 1f out: nvr nrr* **7/2**[2]
4 *hd* **Nannina**[35] 4127 3-8-12 JimmyFortune 4 111
(J H M Gosden) *trckd ldrs in 4th: rdn st: 2nd whn edgd lft under 1f out: kpt on same pce* **9/4**[1]
5 *1/2* **Race For The Stars (USA)**[24] 4502 3-8-12 110 KFallon 9 110
(A P O'Brien, Ire) *led: rdn st: hdd 1f out: no ex cl home* **7/1**
6 *1* **Ugo Fire (IRE)**[16] 4749 3-8-12 102 DPMcDonogh 3 108
(Kevin Prendergast, Ire) *prom: 2nd after 1/2-way: rdn st: 4th whn sltly hmpd under 1f out: kpt on same pce* **33/1**
7 *1 1/2* **Bahia Breeze**[14] 4808 4-9-3 FMBerry 1 107+
(Rae Guest) *cl 2nd to 1/2-way: 3rd u.p ent st: 5th whn hmpd and checked under 1f out: no ex* **40/1**
8 *6* **Ardbrae Lady**[13] 4851 3-8-12 105 PJSmullen 5 91
(Joseph G Murphy, Ire) *hld up towards rr: last into st: sn no ex* **50/1**

1m 38.7s **Going Correction** -0.35s/f (Firm)
WFA 3 from 4yo+ 5lb **9** Ran SP% **109.3**
Speed ratings: 114,113,113,112,112 111,109,103
CSF £24.71 TOTE £5.10: £2.30, £1.30, £2.80; DF 31.90.
Owner Terry Neill & Mrs Michael Bell **Bred** Dermot Cantillon And Forenaghts Stud **Trained** Newmarket, Suffolk

FOCUS
A cracking renewal in which Red Evie continued her rapid rise with this crowning glory. She has now won all seven starts this year and could make it eight in the Sun Chariot. Peeress was a little unlucky and is likely to remain a danger in all the top fillies' races at around this distance. A slow time and the performance of the sixth limits the form from a ratings perspective, though.

NOTEBOOK
Red Evie(IRE), who started the year with Yarmouth wins in a maiden and a handicap off a mark of 77, continued her rapid rise through the grades when coming from off a moderate gallop in a Group 3 at Goodwood last month and she took this rise to the top grade in her stride too, quickening well to lead over a furlong out before idling and in the end only just holding the late lunge of Peeress. Although the runner-up was a little unlucky, she could not be begrudged this win and her trainer deserves much credit. This was her seventh straight win of the year and there is no telling how far she can go if continuing to progress. The Sun Chariot looks the natural next step. (op 5/1)
Peeress, cosy winner of the Lockinge on her first try this season, has not been beaten far in several top races since and she was a little unlucky here as, having lost her place before the turn into the straight, she flew home to just miss out on catching the idling winner. This was another cracking effort on ground that would probably have been a shade fast for her and she is likely to remain a threat in all the top mile races, with a repeat bid for the Sun Chariot likely. (op 7/2 tchd 100/30)
Flashy Wings left her Guineas running behind when second in the Coronation Stakes at Ascot and this first run since brought about another cracking effort. She kept on well having looked in trouble and is another likely to take her chance in the Sun Chariot.
Nannina, her Guineas run in soft ground apart, does not know how to run a bad race and she looked one of the likelier winners, having run well when third to the top-class older pair Ouija Board and Alexander Goldrun in the Nassau Stakes. She held every chance, but was unable to quicken under pressure and it is probable that ten furlongs is her best trip now. (op 5/2)
Race For The Stars(USA), a workmanlike winner of a Group 3 at Gowran Park last time, was ridden differently this time but she was always likely to be vulnerable making the running. She was not beaten far at all, but continues to give the impression that she is not proper Group 1 material. (op 6/1)

5193a BAILEYS IRISH CHAMPION STKS (GROUP 1) 1m 2f
3:55 (3:55) 3-Y-0+ **£426,896** (£130,344; £61,379; £20,000; £13,103)

RPR
1 **Dylan Thomas (IRE)**[18] 4679 3-9-0 124 KFallon 2 127
(A P O'Brien, Ire) *trckd ldr in 2nd: led briefly early st: rallied ins fnl f: led again cl home* **13/8**[1]
2 *nk* **Ouija Board**[35] 4127 5-9-4 JamieSpencer 5 124
(E A L Dunlop) *settled 3rd: cl up travelling wl ent st: led 1 1/2f out: strly pressed fnl f: hdd cl home* **11/4**[2]
3 *2 1/2* **Alexander Goldrun (IRE)**[35] 4127 5-9-4 120 KJManning 3 119
(J S Bolger, Ire) *hld up in 4th: 3rd and effrt 1 1/2f out: no imp ins fnl f* **3/1**[3]
4 *1 1/2* **Mustameet (USA)**[27] 4407 5-9-7 117 DPMcDonogh 6 119
(Kevin Prendergast, Ire) *hld up in rr: 4th 1 1/2f out: kpt on same pce* **8/1**
5 *2 1/2* **Ace (IRE)**[28] 4386 5-9-7 114 MJKinane 4 114
(A P O'Brien, Ire) *led: hdd early st: no ex fr over 1f out* **12/1**

2m 2.90s **Going Correction** -0.35s/f (Firm)
WFA 3 from 4yo+ 7lb **6** Ran SP% **108.6**
Speed ratings: 116,115,113,112,110
CSF £6.14 TOTE £2.40: £1.70, £1.20; DF 6.10.
Owner Mrs John Magnier **Bred** Tower Bloodstock **Trained** Ballydoyle, Co Tipperary
■ Stewards' Enquiry : K Fallon caution: used whip down the shoulder in the forehand position

FOCUS
A small field, but three genuinely top-class performers locked horns and the race produced a terrific finish. The strong pace suited both of the first two, and Dylan Thomas achieved an RPR of 129, 2lb higher than George Washington's Guineas mark, which was the previous best for his generation this year, while Ouija Board has been deemed to have run 2lb better than in the Nassau, where she beat Alexander Goldrun so narrowly.

NOTEBOOK
Dylan Thomas(IRE) left his below-par effort on softish ground in the International well behind with a superb effort, the best by any three-year-old colt this year according to RPRs and one good enough to secure a rare win at the top level this term for his generation against their elders. With his stablemate Ace setting a good pace in front, the race was set up for him, but he still had to show plenty of guts to rally after being headed by Ouija Board. His next assignment is likely to be the Breeders' Cup, in which the Classic is currently the favoured option. (op 7/4 tchd 6/4)
Ouija Board enjoyed the strong pace and was travelling best of all as they swung into the straight. She put up a new lifetime best on RPRs, but in hindsight her rider sent her to the front too soon - fully a furlong and a half out - as she was there to be shot at by the rallying favourite. She was possibly unlucky not to win and is another likely to travel over for the Breeders' Cup, in her case for the Filly & Mare Turf. (op 5/2 tchd 3/1)
Alexander Goldrun(IRE), who ran Ouija Board so close in the Nassau, was a little below her best this time and that resulted in her being readily held by the first two. The Prix de l'Opera is likely to be on the cards if she comes out of this race all right. (op 11/4)
Mustameet(USA), a winner of five of his last six starts, including in Group 2 company last time out, deserved to take his chance at this level, but he never really threatened. He should win more races at a slightly lower level, though. (op 7/1)
Ace(IRE), a smart performer in his own right, did his pace-making job well and set a strong gallop to suit his stablemate, the Irish Derby winner Dylan Thomas.

5192 - 5196a (Foreign Racing) - See Raceform Interactive

TOULOUSE
Saturday, September 9
OFFICIAL GOING: Good to soft

5197a PRIX OCCITANIE (LISTED RACE) (FILLIES) 1m 2f 110y
2:05 (2:05) 3-Y-0 **£17,241** (£6,897; £5,172; £3,448; £1,724)

RPR
1 **Epatha (IRE)**[104] 3-9-2 SPasquier 4 100
(J-C Rouget, France)
2 *2* **Penne (FR)**[23] 4543 3-8-12 IMendizabal 3 92
(J-C Rouget, France)
3 *shd* **Dame Hester (IRE)**[21] 4590 3-8-12 J-BEyquem 6 92
(E J O'Neill) *trcked ldr to halfway, pushed along 3f out, 3rd and hrd rdn str, sn outpcd, rallied ins fnl f, jst missed 2nd (20/1)* **20/1**[1]
4 *nk* **Elise**[324] 5995 3-8-12 TThulliez 1 91
(R Gibson, France)
5 *1 1/2* **Perle Noire (IRE)**[20] 3-8-12 F-XBertras 5 89
(F Rohaut, France)
6 *1* **Queenly Bearing**[105] 3-8-12 C-PLemaire 8 87
(H-A Pantall, France)
7 *1 1/2* **Lisselan Rose (USA)** 3-8-12 SMartinMoriano 7 84
(Mme J Bidgood, France)

2m 9.62s **7** Ran SP% **4.8**
PARI-MUTUEL (including 1 Euro stake): WIN 6.00; PL 2.60, 1.70; DF 6.80.
Owner Marquesa De Moratalla **Bred** J G & Mrs Davis **Trained** Pau, France

NOTEBOOK
Dame Hester(IRE), a winner of a Folkestone handicap in the summer off a mark of 79, saw her race out strongly after getting outpaced and gained some valuable black type while only narrowly failing to finish second.

3757 BELMONT PARK (L-H)
Saturday, September 9
OFFICIAL GOING: Turf course - good; dirt course - fast

5198a GARDEN CITY BREEDERS' CUP STKS (GRADE 1) (FILLIES) 1m 1f (T)
9:08 (9:12) 3-Y-0
£87,209 (£29,070; £14,535; £7,267; £4,360; £485)

RPR
1 **Magnificent Song (USA)**[43] 3-8-6 (b) GKGomez 7 111
(T Pletcher, U.S.A) **57/20**[1]
2 *2* **Take The Ribbon (USA)**[20] 3-8-4 JRLeparoux 9 105
(W Dollase, U.S.A) **5/1**[3]
3 *1/2* **Jade Queen (USA)** 3-8-4 JRVelazquez 5 104
(T Pletcher, U.S.A) **68/10**

4 ¾ **Chaibia (IRE)**[39] 4035 3-8-6 .... DBoeuf 1 105
(D Smaga, France) **44/10**[2]
5 ¾ **Maxxi Arte (IRE)** 3-8-4 .... KDesormeaux 6 101
(J Cassidy, U.S.A) **134/10**
6 hd **La Mottie**[14] 4808 3-8-4 .... CDeCarlo 4 101
(J Noseda) *held up in 8th on inside, switched outside over 2f out, stayed on at same pace* **275/10**
7 ¾ **Quite A Bride (USA)**[43] 3-8-6 .... CVelasquez 10 102
(W Mott, U.S.A) **19/2**
8 nk **Carriage Trail (USA)** 3-8-4 .... EPrado 8 99
(C McGaughey III, U.S.A) **105/10**
9 nk **Delmarva (USA)** 3-8-4 .... JCastellano 3 98
(J Kimmel, U.S.A) **162/10**
10 22 **May Night (USA)**[20] 3-8-4 .... MLuzzi 2 57
(Frederick J Seitz, U.S.A) **182/10**
11 16 **In Return (USA)** 3-8-4 .... (b) RMigliore 11 26
(A Goldberg, U.S.A) **202/10**

1m 48.48s 11 Ran SP% **118.4**
PARI-MUTUEL (including $2 stake): WIN 7.70; PL (1-2) 3.70, 5.20;SHOW (1-2-3) 2.70, 3.90, 4.60; SF 34.60.
Owner L And D Farm **Bred** Classicstar **Trained** USA

NOTEBOOK
La Mottie ran much better than her position of outsider of the field suggested was likely on her final start for Jeremy Noseda. She will remain in the US to be trained by Ben Cecil.

5175 GOODWOOD (R-H)
Sunday, September 10

OFFICIAL GOING: Straight course - good (good to firm in places); round course - good to firm
Wind: Light, across Weather: Sunny & warm

5201 UCELLO II AND UBU III TROPHY (H'CAP) (FOR NATIONAL HUNT JOCKEYS) 2m
2:10 (2:10) (Class 5) (0-70,70) 4-Y-0+ **£3,238** (£963; £481; £240) **Stalls** High

Form RPR
05-3 1 **Kanpai (IRE)**[21] 3291 4-10-7 **51** .... (v) PCO'Neill 10 62+
(J G M O'Shea) *mde all: drvn and styd on strly fnl 2f* **6/1**[2]
0552 2 3 ½ **Kayf Aramis**[6] 5069 4-11-8 **66** .... (p) PJBrennan 4 73
(J L Spearing) *chsd wnr fr 1/2-way: hrd drvn over 2f out: kpt on but a hld* **7/2**[1]
5410 3 1 ½ **Linden Lime**[16] 4777 4-11-4 **62** .... SeanCurran 1 67
(Jamie Poulton) *bhd: hday on outside fr 3f out: styd on u.p fnl 2f: kpt on to take 3rd nr fin but nt rch wnr* **11/1**
054 4 shd **Blue Away (IRE)**[13] 4898 8-11-4 **62** .... SEDurack 13 67
(S Kirk) *s.i.s: sn mid-div: hdwy fr 3f out: kpt on u.p ins last but nt rch ldrs15* **9/1**[3]
4-06 5 shd **Top Trees**[21] 2879 8-10-7 **51** oh11 .... RJGreene 8 56
(W S Kittow) *bhd: hrd drvn over 3f out: hdwy fr 2f out: fin wl but nt rch ldrs* **20/1**
3003 6 2 ½ **Eastborough (IRE)**[13] 4900 7-11-5 **63** .... DaveCrosse 2 65
(I A Wood) *hld up towards rr: hdwy on ins whn nt clr run fr over 2f out tl over 1f out: kpt on cl home* **16/1**
5421 7 3 ½ **Equilibria (USA)**[17] 4282 4-10-10 **54** .... PhilipHide 12 52
(G L Moore) *chsd ldrs: disp 2nd to 1/2-way: styd trcking ldrs: rdn over 2f out: wknd ins last* **7/2**[1]
1260 8 6 **Montage (IRE)**[16] 4777 4-10-10 **54** .... JimCrowley 5 45
(J Akehurst) *chsd ldrs: rdn 4f out: wknd 3f out* **14/1**
2066 9 3 **Trials 'n Tribs**[13] 4898 4-10-7 **51** oh10 .... JamieGoldstein 9 38
(C A Cyzer) *chsd ldrs: rdn over 3f out: sn btn* **33/1**
0056 10 6 **Global Challenge (IRE)**[53] 3649 7-11-2 **60** .... LeightonAspell 3 40
(P G Murphy) *rr: bdly hmpd 5f out: nt rcvr* **14/1**
4/0- 11 6 **Critical Stage (IRE)**[22] 1786 7-11-2 **60** .... ChrisHonour 6 33
(J D Frost) *in tch 12f* **20/1**
0000 12 13 **Shakerattleandroll (IRE)**[87] 2577 5-10-11 **55** .... RichardYoung 7 12
(Mrs L Richards) *chsd ldrs 12f* **50/1**
3303 U **Serramanna**[14] 4836 5-10-7 **51** oh3 .... AndrewTinkler 14 —
(Ms J S Doyle) *sddle slipped sn after s: bhd whn rdr uns 5f out* **11/1**

3m 31.3s (0.51) **Going Correction** -0.025s/f (Good) 13 Ran SP% **119.0**
Speed ratings (Par 103):97,95,94,94,94 93,91,88,86,83 80,74,—
CSF £25.87 CT £230.42 TOTE £6.80: £2.40, £1.60, £3.20; EX 36.60.
Owner Samurai Racing Syndicate **Bred** R H Thomas Cox And G William Robinson **Trained** Elton, Gloucs

FOCUS
A novelty handicap for National Hunt jockeys. The time was the pick of those on the round course, and the form is sound rated through the second, third and fifth. The winner was up 7lb on his Flat form.
Global Challenge(IRE) Official explanation: jockey said gelding was badly hampered

5202 HAMMOND AND DESBOROUGH 70TH BIRTHDAY CELEBRATION STKS (H'CAP) 6f
2:40 (2:40) (Class 2) (0-100,99) 3-Y-0+
£12,464 (£3,732; £1,866; £934; £466; £234) **Stalls** Low

Form RPR
5363 1 **Grantley Adams**[7] 5044 3-8-13 **94** .... TonyCulhane 8 103
(M R Channon) *stdd s: bhd: n.m.r ins fnl 3f and 2f out: swtchd lft ins last: str run u.p to ld cl home* **9/2**[2]
0210 2 ½ **Machinist (IRE)**[22] 4609 6-8-13 **92** .... RobertWinston 6 99
(D Nicholls) *s.i.s: sn in tch: hdwy over 1f out: chal ins last: led fnl 50yds: ct cl home* **11/4**[1]
0110 3 hd **Pic Up Sticks**[19] 4682 7-8-8 **90** .... RichardKingscote(3) 7 96
(B G Powell) *chsd ldrs: led over 2f out: rdn and kpt on fr over 1f out: hdd and no ex fnl 50yds* **17/2**
0300 4 ½ **Golden Dixie (USA)**[15] 4811 7-8-12 **91** .... TedDurcan 3 96
(R A Harris) *lw: trckd ldrs: rdn and hdwy over 1f out: str chal ins last: one pce nr fin* **10/1**
3504 5 1 ½ **Texas Gold**[1] 5182 8-9-6 **99** .... RichardMullen 4 99
(W R Muir) *trckd ldrs: drvn to chal 1f out: wkng whn n.m.r wl ins last* **15/2**
0004 6 2 ½ **Pearly Wey**[28] 4391 3-8-8 **89** .... KDarley 5 82
(C G Cox) *sn led: hdd over 2f out: wknd ins fnl f* **5/1**[3]
0364 7 2 ½ **Night Prospector**[13] 4875 6-8-6 **85** oh3 .... LPKeniry 1 70
(G L Moore) *in tch: rdn 1/2-way: sn no ch* **14/1**
4405 8 ¾ **Total Impact**[37] 4102 3-8-8 **89** ow1 .... NCallan 2 72
(C A Cyzer) *w ldr 3f: wknd fr 2f out* **14/1**
0000 9 2 **Godfrey Street**[18] 4717 3-8-9 **90** .... RyanMoore 9 67
(R Hannon) *in tch on outside: wknd ins fnl 2f* **20/1**

69.96 secs (-2.89) **Going Correction** -0.25s/f (Firm)
WFA 3 from 6yo+ 2lb 9 Ran SP% **111.0**
Speed ratings (Par 109):109,108,108,107,105 102,98,97,95
CSF £16.22 CT £95.00 TOTE £5.00: £1.60, £1.50, £2.30; EX 14.40.
Owner Mrs T G Trant **Bred** Miss S N Ralphs **Trained** West Ilsley, Berks

FOCUS
They went a decent enough clip in this good handicap and that suited those held up. Sound form, with the winner slightly improved.

NOTEBOOK
Grantley Adams had run well in defeat on three of his previous four starts, and enjoyed the good pace. A consistent type, chellenging between horses seems to bring out the best in him. (op 5-1)
Machinist(IRE), who had no chance when drawn on the wrong side at Ripon last time, returned to form and was another suited by the good pace. It is a shame that he was mistakenly left out of the Ayr Gold Cup as he would have held a decent chance of following up last year's Silver Cup success.
Pic Up Sticks, who won this race last year, had a 10lb higher rating to contend with this time around. He ran well, but things are likely to continue to be difficult for him off this sort of mark. (op 9-1 tchd 8-1)
Golden Dixie(USA) was probably not helped by being struck by the whip of Texas Gold's rider inside the final furlong, but he is another who looks held off his current mark.
Texas Gold has not won for over a year but his performances have been good enough that the Handicapper has only released his grip slightly. (op 6-1)
Pearly Wey, who lost his form during the summer, used up too much energy in the early stages racing keenly and setting a decent gallop. It would be interesting to see how he would do under a more patient ride as he has the ability to win off this sort of mark. (op 11-2)

5203 ADENSTAR MAIDEN STKS 1m 3f
3:15 (3:16) (Class 5) 3-Y-O **£3,238** (£963; £481; £240) **Stalls** Low

Form RPR
1 **Counterpunch** 3-9-3 .... LDettori 4 79+
(Saeed Bin Suroor) *w'like: lt framed: s.i.s: pushed along to trck ldr after 1f: drvn to ld wl over 1f out: kpt on wl: readily* **5/6**[1]
5 2 ¾ **Pentatonic**[15] 4814 3-8-12 .... RobertWinston 8 73+
(L M Cumani) *hld up rr: hdwy on outside fr 3f out: drvn and qcknd to chse wnr ins last: kpt wl but a hld* **6/1**[2]
5 3 3 ½ **Junior**[21] 4625 3-9-3 .... NCallan 7 72+
(B J Meehan) *unf: scope: chsd ldrs: rdn over 2f out: styd on again ins last but no ch w ldrs* **8/1**[3]
4 1 ¼ **Maraakez** 3-9-3 .... RHills 5 70+
(J H M Gosden) *w'like: sn led: rdn over 2f out: hdd wl over 1f out: wknd fnl f* **6/1**[2]
5 5 3 ½ **Kala Dancer**[16] 4776 3-9-3 .... TedDurcan 3 64
(Lady Herries) *bhd: pushed along: carried hd high and green over 3f out: swtchd to outside and kpt on fnl 2f but n.d* **10/1**
0-0 6 5 **Cockatoo (USA)**[11] 4931 3-9-3 .... JimCrowley 6 56
(G L Moore) *chsd ldrs: rdn 3f out: wknd fr 3f out* **33/1**
05 7 13 **Arabian Tiger**[25] 4471 3-9-3 .... KDarley 9 34+
(P W Chapple-Hyam) *unf: lw: rr: hdwy into mid-div over 4f out: wknd ins fnl 2f: sn eased* **20/1**
0 8 3 ½ **Xeniam (IRE)**[16] 4776 3-9-3 .... LPKeniry 2 28
(A King) *chsd ldrs: rdn 3f out: sn wknd* **100/1**
9 hd **Watchmaker** 3-9-3 .... SteveDrowne 10 28
(W J Knight) *unf: scope: v green fr stalls and drvn in rr: a bhd* **20/1**

2m 31.43s (4.22) **Going Correction** -0.025s/f (Good) 9 Ran SP% **116.8**
Speed ratings (Par 101):83,82,79,79,76 72,63,60,60
CSF £5.97 TOTE £1.90: £1.10, £1.60, £2.50; EX 8.00.
Owner Godolphin **Bred** Darley **Trained** Newmarket, Suffolk

FOCUS
A good three-year-old maide likely to produce a deal of winners, but the pace was slow and the form looks far from solid. The front four could prove better than the bare form.
Arabian Tiger Official explanation: jockey said colt lost its action; vet said colt was lame behind

5204 SELECT RACING UK ON SKY 432 STKS (GROUP 3) 1m 1f 192y
3:45 (3:48) (Class 1) 3-Y-0+
£28,390 (£10,760; £5,385; £2,685; £1,345; £675) **Stalls** High

Form RPR
-131 1 **Pictavia (IRE)**[25] 4482 4-8-11 113 .... LDettori 7 114
(Saeed Bin Suroor) *lw: led tl narrowly hdd 3f out: drvn and dropped 2l 2nd 2f out: rallied gamely u.p fnl f to ld cl home* **1/1**[1]
1102 2 nk **Crosspeace (IRE)**[8] 5018 4-9-0 111 .... RoystonFfrench 2 116
(M Johnston) *bhd: drvn fr 3f out: hdwy 2f out: styng on whn hung rt 1f out: kpt on strly to take 2nd cl home: nt rch wnr* **9/2**[3]
1163 3 nk **Road To Love (IRE)**[13] 4877 3-8-7 110 .... KDarley 6 115
(M Johnston) *trckd ldr: chal 4f out tl led 3f out: rdn 2l clr 2f out: wknd u.p and hdd cl home* **10/3**[2]
1513 4 1 ½ **Primary (USA)**[29] 4387 3-8-10 105 .... TedDurcan 4 116
(W J Haggas) *swtg: chsd ldrs: rdn 3f out: styd on u.p fr over 1f out but nvr a danger* **14/1**
0401 5 5 **Impeller (IRE)**[7] 5045 7-9-0 93 .... RichardMullen 1 103
(W R Muir) *rdn 5f out: a bhd* **33/1**
521- 6 hd **Shahin (USA)**[324] 6013 3-8-7 93 .... RHills 5 103
(M P Tregoning) *rdn 4f out: a bhd* **9/1**

2m 4.03s (-3.72) **Going Correction** -0.025s/f (Good)
WFA 3 from 4yo+ 7lb 6 Ran SP% **110.9**
Speed ratings (Par 113):113,112,112,111,107 107
CSF £5.72 TOTE £2.00: £1.40, £2.20; EX 5.80.
Owner Godolphin **Bred** Gainsborough Stud Management L **Trained** Newmarket, Suffolk

FOCUS
A Group 3 contest run at a good pace and well up to standard. The form looks solid with the first three and the fifth all to form.

NOTEBOOK
Pictavia(IRE) continued Godolphin's fine run of recent form. She may have been the pick at the weights but she had to work very hard for this win, although the way she responded to her rider's urgings to rally and get back to the front in the closing stages was most admirable. She seems very much suited to front-running tactics and will not always have to duel with another smart front-runner like Road To Love in future assignments, especially back against her own sex. (op 11-10 tchd 5-4)
Crosspeace(IRE), successful in two of his previous three starts at the track, had the race run to suit and saw it out strongly, but he was just unable to catch the winner in time. He is clearly up to winning at this level and it would not be a surprise to see him sent abroad in search of Group-race success. (tchd 4-1)

Road To Love(IRE), disappointing on his last two starts, returned to form, but he was denied the outright lead by the favourite and that made things difficult for him. His record on right-handed tracks now reads 110113, while elsewhere his form figures are 7036263. (op 11-4 tchd 5-2)
Primary(USA), third in the Secretariat Stakes in Chicago last time out, had a stone to find with the favourite at these weights, taking weight-for-age into account, and in the circumstances he was far from disgraced. His Group 3 penalty makes things difficult for him in certain types of races. (op 18-1)
Impeller(IRE), who won a claimer last time out, had a mountain to climb at the weights and was predictably outclassed.
Shahin(USA), a promising juvenile last season, was making a belated return to the track after fracturing his off-hind and proved most disappointing. (op 10-1 tchd 12-1)

5205 FEGENTRI WORLD CUP OF NATIONS STKS (AMATEUR RIDERS' H'CAP) (FOR THE RICHMOND BRISSAC TROPHY) 1m 1f

4:20 (4:22) (Class 5) (0-70,68) 3-Y-O+ **£6,246** (£1,937; £968; £484) **Stalls** High

Form — RPR

0/10 **1** **Todlea (IRE)**[10] 4968 6-11-4 **65**.....(t) MlleA-SPacault 8 — 73
(Jean-Rene Auvray) *sn led: mde rest: pushed out fnl f* **14/1**

300 **2** *1 ¼* **Love You Always (USA)**[31] 4307 6-10-7 **54** oh3......(t) MrsMarieKing 11 — 60
(Miss J Feilden) *bhd: hdwy on ins over 3f out: chsd wnr over 1f out: kpt on but a hld* **10/1**[3]

6530 **3** *¾* **Murrumbidgee (IRE)**[16] 4757 3-10-9 **62**..... MissLLammers 3 — 66
(J W Hills) *in tch: racd on outside: wd into st 4f out: rdn and hung rt over 1f out: styd on ins last but nvr gng pce to chal* **16/1**

0043 **4** *¾* **Colinca's Lad (IRE)**[13] 4879 4-11-1 **62**..... MissDGillam 2 — 65
(T T Clement) *chsd ldrs: rdn and one pce whn hmpd over 1f out: wnt rt and one pce ins last* **6/1**[1]

0301 **5** *¾* **Fantasy Crusader**[32] 4240 7-10-9 **56**..... MrFCauthier 1 — 57
(R M H Cowell) *swtg: bhd: hdwy on outside fr 2f out: fin wl but nvr gng pce to rch ldrs* **6/1**[1]

4055 **6** *nk* **They All Laughed**[24] 4511 3-10-1 **54**..... MissCGatta 10 — 54
(P W Hiatt) *bhd: hdwy over 3f out: chsng ldrs and one pce whn hmpd over 1f out* **12/1**

4105 **7** *½* **Alfridini**[15] 4819 5-11-7 **68**..... MrMichaelFigge 6 — 67
(D R C Elsworth) *lw: chsd ldrs: wnt 2nd and rdn 3f out: wknd fnl f* **6/1**[1]

0002 **8** *½* **Height Of Spirits**[22] 4585 4-10-7 **54** oh8..... MrSDobson 5 — 52
(T D McCarthy) *b: b.hind: s.i.s: bhd: hdwy on ins 4f out: chsd ldrs over 2f out: wknd fnl f* **11/1**

6306 **9** *3 ½* **Chapter (IRE)**[9] 4983 4-10-11 **58**.....(p) MissCErni 12 — 49
(Mrs A L M King) *chsd ldrs: pushed along 3f out: wknd ins fnl 2f* **14/1**

6030 **10** *1 ¼* **Underscore (USA)**[27] 4437 4-11-7 **68**.....(p) MrJPMcKeown 7 — 57
(R A Harris) *s.i.s:hdwy to chse ldrs 5f out: pushed along 3f out: wknd 2f out* **10/1**[3]

2034 **11** *10* **Compton Court**[18] 4708 4-11-6 **67**..... MrJThomas 9 — 36
(A M Balding) *chsd ldrs: rdn 3f out: wknd 2f out* **7/1**[2]

3020 **12** *6* **Shosolosa (IRE)**[17] 4730 4-10-12 **59**..... MrDGrilli 4 — 16
(Mrs A L M King) *wd into st: a bhd* **11/1**

1m 58.57s (1.71) **Going Correction** -0.025s/f (Good)
WFA 3 from 4yo+ 6lb — 12 Ran SP% **117.1**
Speed ratings (Par 103):91,89,89,88,87 87,87,86,83,82 73,68
CSF £145.28 CT £2295.54 TOTE £17.80: £4.50, £4.00, £4.10; EX 377.10.
Owner Matt Taylor **Bred** Irish National Stud **Trained** Upper Lambourn, Berks
■ A first winner in Britain for French rider Anne-Sophie Pacault.
■ Stewards' Enquiry : Miss L Lammers caution: careless riding

FOCUS
A modest amateur riders' contest. It did not take much winning and is not form to trust implicitly.

5206 PALLANT HOUSE EUROPEAN BREEDERS FUND MAIDEN STKS 6f

4:55 (4:55) (Class 5) 2-Y-O **£4,533** (£1,348; £674; £336) **Stalls** Low

Form — RPR

42 **1** **Dodge City (USA)**[25] 4492 2-9-3..... LDettori 8 — 94+
(J Noseda) *lw: mde all: racd in centre crse tl hung rt to far rail fr 2f out: sn clr: easily* **11/8**[1]

03 **2** *5* **Nadawat (USA)**[29] 4373 2-8-12..... RHills 2 — 74
(J L Dunlop) *rced stands side: chsd ldrs: r.o to come clr of that gp fnl f but no ch w wnr far side* **3/1**[2]

4 **3** *2 ½* **Danehillsundance (IRE)**[15] 4801 2-9-3..... RyanMoore 4 — 72
(R Hannon) *chsd ldrs: rdn over 2f out: styd on same pce fnl f* **8/1**

06 **4** *nk* **Blue Bamboo**[34] 4207 2-8-12..... JimCrowley 6 — 66
(Mrs A J Perrett) *chsd ldrs: rdn over 2f out: wknd fnl f* **25/1**

24 **5** *1* **To Party (IRE)**[39] 4041 2-8-12..... NCallan 9 — 63
(M P Tregoning) *chsd ldrs: rdn over 2f out: wknd fnl f* **5/1**[3]

6 *2 ½* **Tinted View (USA)** 2-8-12..... KDarley 11 — 55+
(B W Hills) *leggy: s.i.s: sn in rr: hdwy over 1f out: r.o insie last but nvr in contention* **14/1**

6 **7** *nk* **Highland Harvest**[22] 4600 2-9-3..... LPKeniry 7 — 59
(D R C Elsworth) *s.i.s: sn rcvrd to chse ldrs: rdn 1/2-way: wknd over 1f out* **25/1**

0 **8** *nk* **Gilded Youth**[22] 4600 2-9-3..... TedDurcan 5 — 58
(H Candy) *lw: bhd tl styd on fnl f: nvr in contention* **25/1**

6 **9** *5* **Salient**[22] 4597 2-9-3..... SebSanders 3 — 43
(W J Knight) *chsd ldrs to 1/2-way* **25/1**

00 **10** *3* **Lord Orpheus**[15] 4801 2-8-12..... AurelioMedeiros(5) 10 — 34
(B W Hills) *sn outpcd* **100/1**

00 **11** *¾* **Ma Ridge**[18] 4705 2-9-0..... EdwardCreighton(3) 1 — 32
(T D McCarthy) *a bhd* **100/1**

1m 10.64s (-2.21) **Going Correction** -0.25s/f (Firm) — 11 Ran SP% **118.9**
Speed ratings (Par 95):104,97,94,93,92 88,88,88,81,77 76
CSF £5.07 TOTE £2.10: £1.20, £1.60, £2.10; EX 7.00.
Owner Edward, Gregory and Michael Kelly **Bred** Edward J Kelly Jr, George W Kelly & Michael M Kell **Trained** Newmarket, Suffolk

FOCUS
Cracking maiden form from Dodge City who should go on to much better things, and a fairly high standard in behind. The form seems sound and the race should produce winners.

NOTEBOOK
Dodge City(USA) put up a rampant performance on this third start in maidens, putting his experience to good use and drawing right away despite hanging from the centre right the way across to the far rail. He had been disappointing when turned over at short odds at Yarmouth last time, but this more than made up for it and the son of Gone West, who is entered in the Redcar Two-Year-Old Trophy, fully deserves a rise in class, with a longer trip expected to suit in time. (op 13-8 tchd 7-4 in places)
Nadawat(USA), who looked very fit beforehand, like the winner came into this off the back of two runs in maidens and she seemed to appreciate the drop back down to six furlongs, but was no match for the winner. She drew clear of the stands'-side group and is now qualified for nurseries. (op 7-2 tchd 4-1)
Danehillsundance(IRE), who shaped quite well in soft ground on his debut at Newmarket, improved on that under faster conditions and, although no match for the front pair, he can find a small maiden before going handicapping. (op 9-1)
Blue Bamboo seemes to be progressing with racing and this daughter of Green Desert can be expected to improve for the move into handicaps. (op 28-1)
To Party(IRE), edgy and on her toes beforehand, does not look to be progressing, but she can now contest nurseries and may do better in that sphere under a stiffer test of stamina. (op 9-2)
Tinted View(USA), bred to improve for further in time, looked likely to need the experience beforehand and she was unable to lay up early, but got going in the second half of the race and come home nicely into sixth. A scopey type, she should have learned a good deal from this and can find a maiden, probably over further. (op 10-1 tchd 16-1)
Highland Harvest, having his second run, still looked as though he would come on for the outing and he looks the type his trainer will do well with in handicaps at some stage. (tchd 33-1)
Gilded Youth clearly has ability but may not show it until relaxing more in his races.

5207 COUNTRYSIDE ALLIANCE NURSERY STKS (H'CAP) 5f

5:30 (5:30) (Class 4) (0-85,85) 2-Y-O **£4,533** (£1,348; £674; £336) **Stalls** Low

Form — RPR

010 **1** **Another True Story**[22] 4603 2-9-3 **81**..... RyanMoore 2 — 84
(R Hannon) *lw: in tch: pushed along over 2f out: n.m.r over 1f out: swtchd lft and str run u.p to ld fnl 25yds* **7/2**[2]

2233 **2** *½* **Brenin Gwalia**[6] 5065 2-7-13 **63**..... RoystonFfrench 5 — 64
(D M Simcock) *sn led: rdn 2f out: kpt on wl fnl f: ct fnl 25yds* **2/1**[1]

2105 **3** *½* **Alternative**[16] 4779 2-9-7 **85**..... SebSanders 4 — 85+
(R M Beckett) *lw: hld up rr but in tch: no clr run fr 2f out to 1f out: swtchd lft ins last: r.o wl: gng on cl home but nt rch ldrs* **4/1**[3]

0633 **4** *¾* **Fairfield Princess**[13] 4893 2-8-11 **82**..... PatrickHills(7) 1 — 78+
(N A Callaghan) *sldied s: edgd rt and n.m.r over 2f out: drvn to chal over 1f out: one pce ins last* **15/2**

140 **5** *3 ½* **Queen Of Narnia**[6] 5065 2-8-7 **74**..... EdwardCreighton(3) 6 — 58
(M R Channon) *chsd ldrs: ev chnace 2f out: wknd fnl f* **16/1**

3151 **6** *3 ½* **Yerevan**[11] 4921 2-8-11 **75**..... SteveDrowne 3 — 46
(R T Phillips) *chsd ldrs: rdn 1/2-way: wknd 1f out* **9/2**

58.27 secs (-0.78) **Going Correction** -0.25s/f (Firm) — 6 Ran SP% **111.4**
Speed ratings (Par 97):96,95,94,93,87 82
CSF £10.77 TOTE £4.30: £2.40, £1.60; EX 12.50 Place 6 £35.43, Place 5 £17.67.
Owner Fairway Racing **Bred** Miss Alison Wiggins **Trained** East Everleigh, Wilts

FOCUS
Nothing more than a fair nursery, the first three basically running to form.

NOTEBOOK
Another True Story, winner of a modest maiden at Windsor on his second start, flopped on his nursery debut at Newmarket, but this represented an easier opportunity and he responded well to driving to get up close home. This effort very much suggested a sixth furlong will suit, but the son of Piccolo already has a far from reliable look to him and defying a rise may not be easy. (op 4-1)
Brenin Gwalia came into this with a string of solid effort in defeat, but unfortunately for those who followed the favourite, another solid placed effort was all he came away with, being claimed late on by Another True Story. It is surely a matter of time before he finds a small race, especially off what should remain a lowly mark. (op 9-4)
Alternative, not given an overly hard time in defeat at Sandown last time, was entitled to go well whilst looking vulnerable under top weight at the same time and he was going on well close home, but the line came too soon. He looks well worth a try over further.
Fairfield Princess, having her tenth run of the season, again ran well, but she held every chance and did not give the impression she is ready to win off her current mark. (op 8-1)
Queen Of Narnia only has a selling win to her name and she may need to drop a few pounds in the ratings before winning again.
Yerevan, another experienced filly having her 11th start of the term, ran a rare bad race and may be in line for a break. (op 7-2)
T/Plt: £91.10 to a £1 stake. Pool: £72,937.55. 583.95 winning tickets. T/Qpdt: £28.20 to a £1 stake. Pool: £2,826.20. 74.10 winning tickets. ST

5105 KEMPTON (A.W) (R-H)

Sunday, September 10

OFFICIAL GOING: Standard
Wind: Almost nil Weather: Sunny & very warm

5208 WALTERSWINBURNRACING.CO.UK NURSERY 6f (P)

2:20 (2:23) (Class 6) (0-65,65) 2-Y-O **£3,238** (£963; £481; £240) **Stalls** High

Form — RPR

034 **1** **Wachiwi (IRE)**[16] 4753 2-8-13 **60**..... AdamKirby(3) 8 — 63
(A P Jarvis) *sn chsd ldr: rdn to ld 2f out: wandered fr over 1f out: drvn and hld on* **9/1**

005 **2** *½* **Spinning Crystal (IRE)**[41] 4000 2-9-4 **62**..... MichaelHills 4 — 63
(B W Hills) *prom: rdn over 2f out: chsd wnr over 1f out: kpt on but nvr quite able to chal* **5/1**[3]

603 **3** *shd* **Cantique (IRE)**[21] 4624 2-9-2 **60**..... SebSanders 3 — 61
(R M Beckett) *settled in midfield: rdn 2f out: prog jst over 1f out: styd on wl last 150yds: nrst fin* **7/1**

064 **4** *1 ¼* **Tiburon**[25] 4485 2-9-3 **61**..... JimmyFortune 11 — 58
(H Morrison) *s.i.s: hld up towards rr on inner: effrt over 2f out: hrd rdn over 1f out: kpt on same pce* **7/2**[1]

050 **5** *1* **Todwick Owl**[31] 4295 2-9-7 **65**..... JamieMackay 9 — 59
(J G Given) *hld up in last: effrt on inner over 2f out: shkn up over 1f out: styd on: nvr nrr* **9/1**

3413 **6** *1* **La Marmotte (IRE)**[15] 4813 2-9-6 **64**..... EddieAhern 5 — 55
(J W Hills) *racd freely: led to 2f out: wknd rapidly fnl f* **4/1**[2]

0456 **7** *shd* **Indian Song (IRE)**[6] 5052 2-9-3 **61**..... StephenCarson 2 — 52+
(R F Johnson Houghton) *racd wd: chsd ldrs: rdn over 2f out: wknd over 1f out* **10/1**

6030 **8** *2 ½* **Prince Of Charm (USA)**[15] 4813 2-9-2 **63**..... SaleemGolam(3) 7 — 46
(P Mitchell) *lost pl after 2f and sn pushed along in rr: struggling fr over 2f out* **25/1**

3001 **9** *5* **Aggbag**[10] 4969 2-9-5 **63**..... MickyFenton 1 — 31
(B P J Baugh) *a wl in rr: lost tch w main gp 2f out* **20/1**

1664 **10** *¾* **Autumn Storm**[45] 3861 2-9-3 **61**..... IanMongan 10 — 27
(R Ingram) *t.k.h early: trckd ldrs: rdn over 2f out: sn btn: wknd rapidly ins fnl f* **25/1**

6550 **11** *3* **It's No Problem (IRE)**[36] 4163 2-9-4 **62**..... RobertHavlin 12 — 19
(Jean-Rene Auvray) *prom to over 2f out: wknd rapidly* **25/1**

1m 13.84s (0.14) **Going Correction** -0.15s/f (Stan) — 11 Ran SP% **116.8**
Speed ratings (Par 93):93,92,92,90,89 87,87,84,77,76 72
CSF £50.40 CT £332.66 TOTE £10.00: £2.80, £1.70, £1.60; EX 100.30.
Owner Hibiscus And Mrs Ann Jarvis **Bred** Carpet Lady Partnership **Trained** Twyford, Bucks

FOCUS
The first five home were making their debuts in handicap company, so it is hard to be sure of the level of form, but it was probably just a modest nursery.

NOTEBOOK

Wachiwi(IRE) had shown just ordinary form in three runs at up to this trip in maiden company but, making her nursery debut, she put up an improved effort to get off the mark. She looked vulnerable when hitting the front about two furlongs out, but her stuck to her task well, despite wandering a little. She should remain competitive in similar company. (op 10-1)

Spinning Crystal(IRE), making both her handicap and Polytrack debuts, showed improved form in second. She looks on a reasonable mark and might find a similar race. (op 4-1)

Cantique(IRE), back up in trip on her handicap and Polytrack debut, took an age to respond to strong pressure. While this was arguably a career-best effort, she has looked sharper in the past. (op 5-1)

Tiburon, back up in trip and switched to Polytrack for the first time on his handicap debut, did not help his chance with a slow start and could not find the necessary change of pace to pose a threat. (op 9-2)

Todwick Owl, who showed just moderate form in three runs in maiden company, offered some hope on his nursery debut. (tchd 10-1)

La Marmotte(IRE), although displaying sufficient pace to lead, did not appear suited by the drop back in trip and seems better over seven furlongs. (tchd 7-2)

5209 WALTERSWINBURNRACING.CO.UK MEDIAN AUCTION MAIDEN FILLIES' STKS — 7f (P)

2:55 (2:59) (Class 6) 2-Y-O — **£3,238** (£963; £481; £240) **Stalls** High

Form — RPR

5 **1** **Lady Grace (IRE)**[9] 4993 2-9-0 .... MichaelHills 9 — 78+
(W J Haggas) *hld up in midfield: gd prog on inner to ld 2f out: shuffled along over 1f out: in n.d fnl f: pushed out* **5/2**[2]

4 **2** *1 ½* **Elusive Flash (USA)**[44] 3893 2-9-0 .... JosedeSouza 8 — 79+
(P F I Cole) *trckd ldrs: effrt whn bdly bmpd over 2f out: rallied over 1f out: flashed tail and chsd wnr ins fnl f: r.o* **9/4**[1]

6 **3** *2 ½* **Seven Steps (IRE)**[25] 4487 2-9-0 .... EddieAhern 10 — 68
(J W Hills) *trckd ldrs: pushed along 3f out: effrt to chal and w wnr 2f out: outpcd over 1f out: one pce and lost 2nd ins fnl f* **13/2**

0 **4** *3 ½* **Nashharry (IRE)**[20] 4657 2-9-0 .... PatDobbs 1 — 59
(R Hannon) *w ldr: upsides jst over 2f out: steadily fdd fnl 2f* **14/1**

5 *4* **Verbatim** 2-9-0 .... FrancisNorton 4 — 49
(A M Balding) *hld up in rr: wl outpcd fr 2f out: plugged on fnl f* **12/1**

0 **6** *2 ½* **Wanessa Tiger (IRE)**[16] 4765 2-9-0 .... JoeFanning 3 — 43
(M R Channon) *s.s: in tch in rr: wl outpcd fr over 2f out: no ch after* **14/1**

7 *¾* **Sass Cafe (IRE)** 2-9-0 .... JohnEgan 12 — 41
(T J Pitt) *mde most to 2f out: wknd rapidly* **6/1**[3]

30 **8** *1 ¼* **Valeesha**[23] 4552 2-8-7 .... JackDean(7) 7 — 38
(W G M Turner) *chsd ldrs: rdn over 2f out: wknd rapidly wl over 1f out* **66/1**

0 **9** *1* **Barley Moon**[15] 4801 2-9-0 .... JamieMackay 11 — 36
(T Keddy) *a wl in rr: struggling over 2f out: wknd* **66/1**

0 **10** *1 ¼* **Elmasong**[9] 4994 2-8-11 .... MarcHalford(3) 5 — 32
(J J Bridger) *in tch to 2f out: wknd rapidly* **66/1**

11 *2* **Born Dancing** 2-8-11 .... AdamKirby(3) 14 — 27
(J G Portman) *v s.i.s: a in rr: wknd over 2f out* **33/1**

1m 26.7s (-0.10) **Going Correction** -0.15s/f (Stan) — 11 Ran SP% **115.4**

Speed ratings (Par 90):94,92,89,85,80 78,77,75,74,73 70

CSF £8.21 TOTE £3.30: £1.20, £1.10, £1.50; EX 8.50.

Owner F C T Wilson **Bred** Frank Barry **Trained** Newmarket, Suffolk

FOCUS

They finished well-strung out and it is hard to be sure of the level, but it looked a pretty good fillies' maiden. The winner took a step forward and the second, allowed 2l for being hampered, ran to her debut form.

NOTEBOOK

Lady Grace(IRE), a promising fifth in a six-furlong maiden round here on her debut, showed improved form over this longer trip and ran out a clear-cut winner, although she would probably have had to work harder had Elusive Flash not been badly hampered about two furlongs out. She will probably be best off going down the handicap route for now, but there is black type in her pedigree and connections will no doubt hope she will be able to add to that herself at some point. She does, though, have to prove herself just as effective on turf. (op 11-4)

Elusive Flash(USA), fourth in a decent six-furlong maiden at Ascot on her debut, ran a fine race switched to sand and stepped up in trip and can be considered most unlucky not to have finished even closer, as she was badly hampered by Seven Steps around two furlongs out. There was plenty to like about the way she recovered to stay on in the closing stages, but it is worth noting she appeared to have a hard enough race, all things considered. (tchd 5-2)

Seven Steps(IRE), sixth of ten on her debut over this trip at Sandown, seemed to step up a little on that effort and is clearly going the right way. (op 12-1)

Nashharry(IRE) was put in her place when it mattered and looks more of a handicap prospect. (op 16-1)

Verbatim, a half-sister to among others, Double Brandy, a winner at six to eight furlongs, made a satisfactory start and should improve.

Sass Cafe(IRE), a 22,000euros half-sister to top-class miler Ashkalani, out of a three-year-old winner at three in France, offered little but an SP of 6/1 suggests she is thought capable of better. (op 5-1 tchd 7-1)

Born Dancing Official explanation: jockey said filly made a noise

5210 WALTERSWINBURNRACING.CO.UK H'CAP — 1m (P)

3:25 (3:27) (Class 6) (0-60,60) 3-Y-O — **£3,238** (£963; £481; £240) **Stalls** High

Form — RPR

3-34 **1** **Primo Gold**[28] 4405 3-8-13 **58** .... AdamKirby(3) 12 — 68
(W R Swinburn) *hld up towards rr: prog over 2f out: drvn to ld 1f out: hanging lft but styd on wl u.p* **7/2**[1]

0066 **2** *1 ¼* **Possessed**[18] 4700 3-9-2 **58** .... RobertHavlin 10 — 65
(T D McCarthy) *trckd ldrs: effrt over 2f out: hrd rdn and styd on fr over 1f out to take 2nd nr fin* **12/1**

0242 **3** *hd* **Panic Stations**[8] 5035 3-8-11 **60** .... LukeMorris(7) 5 — 67
(M L W Bell) *trckd ldng pair 5f out: rdn to ld over 2f out: hdd 1f out: kpt on same pce* **7/2**[1]

0542 **4** *1 ¾* **Hot Agnes**[18] 4690 3-9-1 **57** .... MichaelTebbutt 6 — 60
(H J Collingridge) *wl in rr: rdn over 3f out: effrt whn nt clr run over 2f out: prog u.p wl over 1f out: no imp last 100yds* **7/1**[2]

0313 **5** *2 ½* **Dark Moon**[19] 4671 3-8-12 **54** .... FrancisNorton 11 — 51
(A M Balding) *trckd ldrs: effrt over 2f out: drvn and stl in tch over 1f out: wknd fnl f* **7/1**[2]

3003 **6** *1* **Shunkawakhan (IRE)**[11] 4930 3-9-0 **59** .... SaleemGolam(3) 2 — 54
(G C H Chung) *racd on outer: in tch: drvn fr 1/2-way: stl chsng ldrs over 1f out: wknd fnl f* **11/1**

000 **7** *1 ¼* **Useful**[42] 3975 3-8-8 **57** .... WilliamCarson(7) 7 — 49
(A W Carroll) *hld up wl in rr: shkn up over 2f out: plugged on one pce: nvr on terms* **66/1**

104P **8** *3 ½* **Nikki Bea (IRE)**[50] 3731 3-9-3 **59** .... JohnEgan 3 — 43
(Jamie Poulton) *sn wl in rr: struggling fr over 2f out* **11/1**

4005 **9** *hd* **Gnillah**[9] 4983 3-9-1 **57** .... MichaelHills 13 — 40
(B W Hills) *wl in rr: effrt and sme prog on inner over 2f out: no hdwy over 1f out: wknd sn after* **14/1**

6200 **10** *nk* **Emotive**[3] 5130 3-9-4 **60** .... EddieAhern 14 — 43
(I A Wood) *hld up in tch on inner: effrt over 2f out: wknd rapidly over 1f out* **16/1**

0525 **11** *5* **Salvestro**[16] 4757 3-9-4 **60** .... (e[1]) JimmyFortune 9 — 31
(Mrs A J Perrett) *mde most to over 2f out: wknd rapidly over 1f out* **10/1**[3]

00-0 **12** *2* **Commander Wish**[71] 3089 3-8-9 **58** .... JPFeatherstone(7) 8 — 25
(P Howling) *pressed ldr to over 2f out: wknd v rapidly over 1f out* **28/1**

006- **13** *10* **Daughters World**[454] 2551 3-8-7 **56** ow1 .... KylieManser(7) 4 — —
(J R Best) *a wl in rr: detached fr 3f out: t.o* **33/1**

0000 **14** *1* **Wally Barge**[165] 797 3-9-2 **58** .... MickyFenton 1 — —
(D K Ivory) *a wl in rr: detached fr 3f out: t.o* **50/1**

1m 40.12s (-0.68) **Going Correction** -0.15s/f (Stan) — **14** Ran SP% **125.3**

Speed ratings (Par 99):97,95,95,93,91 90,89,85,85,85 80,78,68,67

CSF £49.91 CT £168.47 TOTE £5.30: £2.00, £3.60, £2.00; EX 60.20.

Owner Pendley's Dozen **Bred** Bearstone Stud **Trained** Aldbury, Herts

FOCUS

Just a moderate handicap in which the first two home came from double-figure stalls. The form looks sound enough.

5211 OWN A SHARE WITH WALTER SWINBURN H'CAP — 1m (P)

4:00 (4:00) (Class 4) (0-80,80) 3-Y-O

£7,478 (£2,239; £1,119; £560; £279; £140) **Stalls** High

Form — RPR

-120 **1** **Mataram (USA)**[36] 4144 3-8-7 **69** .... KerrinMcEvoy 1 — 81+
(W Jarvis) *hld up wl in rr: stdy prog over 2f out: shkn up to ld jst ins fnl f: sn clr: r.o wl* **3/1**[1]

0650 **2** *1 ¾* **Grimes Faith**[4] 5107 3-9-4 **80** .... PatDobbs 7 — 88
(R Hannon) *trckd ldrs: prog to ld 2f out: drvn and hdd jst ins fnl f: one pce* **16/1**

2302 **3** *¾* **October Ben**[9] 4995 3-7-11 **66** .... FrankiePickard(7) 9 — 72
(M D I Usher) *s.s: hld up wl in rr: brought to outer and stdy prog 3f out: chal wl over 1f out: nt qckn fnl f* **8/1**

0451 **4** *nk* **Persian Express (USA)**[11] 4933 3-9-0 **76** .... MichaelHills 11 — 81
(B W Hills) *trckd ldng pair: poised to chal gng wl 2f out: swtchd to inner and fnd nil over 1f out* **4/1**[2]

0046 **5** *2* **Fratt'n Park (IRE)**[14] 4838 3-8-1 **66** oh2 .... DominicFox(3) 5 — 67
(J J Bridger) *prom: rdn and cl up 2f out: sn nt qckn: one pce after* **22/1**

2415 **6** *¾* **Mujood**[14] 4831 3-9-2 **78** .... StephenCarson 12 — 77
(R F Johnson Houghton) *led for 2f: pressed ldr after: upsides 2f out: wknd jst over 1f out* **7/1**

4650 **7** *1 ¼* **Scroll**[16] 4757 3-8-6 **68** .... (v) EddieAhern 8 — 64
(P Howling) *hld up in tch: swtchd to inner and effrt 2f out: nt qckn over 1f out: wknd ins fnl f* **33/1**

300 **8** *shd* **Wild Academy (IRE)**[23] 4563 3-8-9 **71** ow1 .... MickyFenton 3 — 67
(G C Bravery) *sn last pair and nvr gng wl: rdn and detached 3f out: kpt on fnl 2f: no ch* **33/1**

10-0 **9** *½* **Congressional (IRE)**[20] 4660 3-8-11 **73** .... PhilipRobinson 2 — 68
(M A Jarvis) *racd wd: in tch: drvn over 2f out: wknd u.p over 1f out* **9/1**

3406 **10** *3* **Merchant Bankes**[32] 4243 3-8-3 **68** oh2 ow2 .... SaleemGolam(3) 10 — 56
(W G M Turner) *led after 2f to 2f out: wknd* **33/1**

644 **11** *3* **Regal Sunset (IRE)**[76] 2934 3-8-10 **75** .... AdamKirby(3) 4 — 56
(W R Swinburn) *t.k.h: hld up towards rr: effrt over 2f out: rdn and no rspnse wl over 1f out: wknd* **5/1**[3]

4100 **12** *8* **Debord (FR)**[74] 2990 3-8-6 **68** oh2 ow2 .... JohnEgan 6 — 31
(Jamie Poulton) *a wl in rr: detached in last pair 3f out: t.o* **25/1**

30-0 **13** *5* **Earl Kraul (IRE)**[20] 4662 3-7-13 **66** oh3 .... RobynBrisland(5) 13 — 17
(G L Moore) *chsd ldrs tl wknd rapidly over 3f out: t.o* **50/1**

1m 39.0s (-1.80) **Going Correction** -0.15s/f (Stan) — **13** Ran SP% **120.1**

Speed ratings (Par 103):103,101,100,100,98 97,96,96,95,92 89,81,76

CSF £49.90 CT £369.34 TOTE £4.20: £2.40, £4.70, £1.90; EX 78.70.

Owner Sales Race 2001 Syndicate **Bred** B P Walden Jr And James Anthony **Trained** Newmarket, Suffolk

FOCUS

Just a fair handicap and maybe not that strong for the level, although the form looks sound. The winning time, though, was good, over a second quicker than the mile handicap won by Primo Gold.

Regal Sunset(IRE) Official explanation: jockey said gelding stopped quickly in last half furlong

5212 BECOME PART OF WALTER SWINBURN RACING H'CAP — 6f (P)

4:35 (4:35) (Class 4) (0-85,86) 3-Y-O+

£7,790 (£2,332; £1,166; £583; £291; £146) **Stalls** High

Form — RPR

-402 **1** **She's My Outsider**[8] 5021 4-8-8 **73** .... FrancisNorton 7 — 82
(I A Wood) *trckd ldng pair gng wl: led wl over 1f out: drvn and kpt on wl fnl f* **6/1**[2]

026- **2** *½* **Morse (IRE)**[313] 6216 5-8-10 **75** .... KerrinMcEvoy 10 — 83
(J A Osborne) *prom: rdn to chse wnr over 1f out: tried to chal fnl f: a hld* **10/1**

6031 **3** *¾* **Guest Connections**[14] 4841 3-9-5 **86** .... (v) JohnEgan 8 — 91
(M R Channon) *trckd ldrs: rdn and nt qckn 2f out: kpt on to take 3rd fnl f: nvr able to chal* **9/1**

5-01 **4** *½* **Special Lad**[8] 5021 4-9-6 **85** .... JoeFanning 12 — 89
(P F I Cole) *settled towards rr: rdn and prog over 1f out: looked dangerous ent fnl f: one pce last 150yds* **7/4**[1]

3130 **5** *nk* **Hammer Of The Gods (IRE)**[50] 3728 6-9-1 **80** .... (bt) EddieAhern 3 — 83
(P S McEntee) *pressed ldrs: rdn and cl up wl over 1f out: nt qckn* **6/1**[2]

622 **6** *1 ½* **After The Show**[16] 4771 5-8-13 **78** .... MickyFenton 6 — 76
(Rae Guest) *wl in rr: rdn over 2f out: kpt on fr over 1f out: nrst fin* **10/1**

0356 **7** *shd* **Pure Imagination (IRE)**[7] 5042 5-8-0 **72** .... LukeMorris(7) 9 — 70
(J M Bradley) *sn in last pair: urged along fr 1/2-way: kpt on fnl 2f: n.d* **12/1**

154- **8** *nk* **Belly Dancer (IRE)**[419] 3600 4-9-0 **79** .... JosedeSouza 5 — 76
(P F I Cole) *mostly in last pair tl kpt on fr over 1f out: n.d* **50/1**

3200 **9** *¾* **Zarzu**[14] 4834 7-8-11 **81** .... LiamJones(5) 4 — 76
(C R Dore) *nvr bttr than midfield: in tch 2f out: steadily fdd* **20/1**

0100 **10** *1 ¼* **Anfield Dream**[16] 4771 4-8-11 **76** .... RobertHavlin 2 — 67
(J R Jenkins) *racd wd towards rr: drvn over 2f out: no prog and btn over 1f out* **33/1**

2200 **11** *1* **Millfields Dreams**[23] 4564 7-8-3 **71** oh14 .... DominicFox(3) 1 — 59
(M G Quinlan) *mde most and crossed fr wd draw: hdd & wknd wl over 1f out* **40/1**

3004 **12** 1 3/4 **High Reach**[15] 4811 6-9-6 **85**.. JimmyFortune 11 68
(W R Muir) *trckd ldrs: effrt on inner 2f out: stl chsng ldrs over 1f out: wknd rapidly* **8/1**[3]

1m 12.81s (-0.89) **Going Correction** -0.15s/f (Stan)
WFA 3 from 4yo+ 2lb **12** Ran SP% **124.0**
Speed ratings (Par 105):99,98,97,96,96 94,94,93,92,91 89,87
CSF £65.54 CT £551.51 TOTE £9.00: £2.00, £2.20, £3.30; EX 85.10 Trifecta £359.40 Part won. Pool £506.33. - 0.20 winning units..
Owner Lewis Caterers **Bred** R W K Lewis **Trained** Upper Lambourn, Berks

FOCUS
A decent enough sprint handicap, and the form looks sound.

5213 GO RACING WITH WALTER SWINBURN H'CAP 1m 4f (P)
5:10 (5:11) (Class 6) (0-65,65) 3-Y-0+ **£3,238** (£963; £481; £240) **Stalls** Centre

Form RPR
215 **1** **Swords**[12] 4914 4-9-3 **57**.. JoeFanning 1 66
(Heather Dalton) *dwlt: in tch towards rr: prog to chse ldrs 3f out: rdn to go 2nd 1f out: styd on wl to ld nr fin* **9/2**[2]
1015 **2** *nk* **Bienheureux**[11] 4924 5-9-7 **61**..(vt) JohnEgan 7 70
(Miss Gay Kelleway) *trckd ldrs: effrt 3f out: rdn to ld wl over 1f out: kpt on wl fnl f: hdd nr fin* **11/4**[1]
2505 **3** *3* **Birthday Star (IRE)**[10] 4972 4-8-11 **58**........................ AlanRutter(7) 8 62
(W J Musson) *settled wl in rr: plenty to do over 3f out: stdy prog on inner over 2f out: wnt 3rd ins fnl f: no imp ldng pair* **12/1**
060 **4** *3/4* **Wotchalike (IRE)**[10] 4968 4-9-9 **63**..........................(v) MickyFenton 6 66
(R J Price) *prom: led jst over 4f out: drvn and hdd wl over 1f out: fdd fnl f* **25/1**
0603 **5** *shd* **The Iron Giant (IRE)**[18] 4702 4-9-3 **57**........................ RobertMiles 10 59
(B G Powell) *led to jst over 4f out: styd pressing tl wknd 1f out* **14/1**
2346 **6** *5* **Lady Taverner**[60] 3412 5-9-6 **60**.............................. KerrinMcEvoy 3 54
(J E Long) *settled in midfield: effrt to chse ldrs over 3f out: wknd over 2f out* **12/1**
00 **7** *1 1/4* **Midshipman**[23] 4575 8-9-4 **58**.......................................(tp) TPQueally 11 50
(T Keddy) *rousted along in last pair early: nvr on terms n.d fnl 3f: plugged on* **25/1**
5-00 **8** *4* **Wait For The Will (USA)**[92] 2447 10-9-6 **65**.......... RobynBrisland(5) 12 51
(G L Moore) *settled wl in rr: shkn up and brief effrt 3f out: sn wknd* **25/1**
3002 **9** *2* **Missie Baileys**[18] 4702 4-8-13 **56**..........................(p) AmirQuinn(3) 4 39
(Mrs L J Mongan) *pressed ldr to over 4f out: wknd 3f out* **8/1**
026- **10** *3 1/2* **Desert Image (IRE)**[314] 6195 5-9-10 **64**..................... FrancisNorton 13 41
(C Tinkler) *in tch in midfield tl wknd u.p 3f out* **8/1**
400/ **11** *8* **Priors Dale**[165] 6081 6-9-8 **62**.. PatDobbs 2 26
(Miss E C Lavelle) *pressed ldrs to 5f out: wknd 4f out: t.o* **6/1**[3]
5002 **12** *3 1/2* **Scottish River (USA)**[9] 4991 7-9-0 **61**..................... AshleyMorgan(7) 5 20
(M D I Usher) *s.v.s: wl in rr tl prog into midfield 5f out: wd and wknd bnd over 3f out: t.o* **16/1**
0201 **13** *8* **He's A Star**[27] 4435 4-9-4 **65**............................ RussellKennemore(7) 14 11
(B D Leavy) *chsd ldrs: u.p 1/2-way: sn struggling: t.o* **9/1**

2m 33.4s (-3.50) **Going Correction** -0.15s/f (Stan) **13** Ran SP% **130.8**
Speed ratings (Par 101):105,104,102,102,102 98,98,95,94,91 86,84,78
CSF £18.63 CT £145.22 TOTE £5.90: £2.20, £1.50, £6.40; EX 31.60 Place 6 £90.35, Place 5 £24.71.
Owner Ms Heather Dalton **Bred** Mrs A Yearley **Trained** Norton, Shropshire

FOCUS
Just a modest handicap, but they went a good gallop and probably not bad form for the grade.
Missie Baileys Official explanation: jockey said filly had no more to give
T/Jkpt: Not won. T/Plt: £108.50 to a £1 stake. Pool: £52,585.00. 353.65 winning tickets. T/Qpdt: £29.20 to a £1 stake. Pool: £2,893.30. 73.10 winning tickets. JN

5214 - 5217a (Foreign Racing) - See Raceform Interactive

1176 KREFELD (R-H)
Sunday, September 10

OFFICIAL GOING: Soft

5218a PREIS DER CARGILL DEUTSCHLAND - HERZOG VON RATIBOR-RENNEN (LISTED RACE) 7f
3:15 (3:23) 2-Y-0 **£18,621** (£7,586; £4,138; £2,759; £1,379)

RPR
1 **Lucky It Is (HOL)** 2-8-12 .... AHelfenbein 3 92
(A Trybuhl, Germany)
2 *3/4* **Beltanus (GER)** 2-8-12 .... EPedroza 7 91
(Tim Gibson, Germany)
3 *1* **History Boy**[22] 4592 2-8-12 .... JimmyQuinn 1 88
(D J Coakley) *raced in 3rd on inside, stayed on under pressure final 2f (71/10)*
4 *2 1/2* **Chantra (GER)** 2-8-9 .... MPoirier 8 79
()
5 *1 1/2* **Aleandros (GER)** 2-9-2 .... AStarke 6 82
(Mario Hofer, Germany)
6 *12* **Auenschutze (GER)** 2-9-0 .... ABoschert 9 50
()
7 *2 1/2* **Spejbl (GER)** 2-8-12 .... WPanov 4 42
()
8 *7* **Dosimo (GER)** 2-9-0 .... ASuborics 5 26
()

1m 26.8s **8** Ran
(including 10 Euro stake): WIN 197; PL 33, 20, 21; SF 1491.
Owner Stall Lucky Stables International **Bred** Frau Gerda Kok-Cornet/Niederlande **Trained** Germany

NOTEBOOK
History Boy held a good early position on the inside and, though he allowed the pillar-to-post winner to skip away from him on the home turn, kept going gamely under pressure in the last quarter mile.

5145 LONGCHAMP (R-H)
Sunday, September 10

OFFICIAL GOING: Good

5219a PRIX FOY GRAY D'ALBION BARRIERE (GROUP 2) (C&F) 1m 4f
2:20 (2:23) 4-Y-0+ **£51,103** (£19,724; £9,414; £6,276; £3,138)

RPR
1 **Shirocco (GER)**[100] 2202 5-9-2 .... CSoumillon 4 127
(A Fabre, France) *went 2nd after 2f, led 1 1/2f out, pushed out & ran on well* **13/8**[2]
2 *nk* **Hurricane Run (IRE)**[43] 3927 4-9-2 .... KFallon 2 126
(A Fabre, France) *tracked his leader early, settled in 3rd, pushed along well over 1f out, joined winner 1f out, pushed out & ran on* **10/11**[1]
3 *nk* **Pride (FR)**[77] 2914 6-8-13 .... C-PLemaire 1 123
(A De Royer-Dupre, France) *settled in 4th, about 2 1/2 lengths behind 1 1/2f out, pushed along & qckd ins fnl f, ran on to be nrst at fin* **10/3**[3]
4 *5* **Divine Story (FR)**[14] 5-8-13 .... DBonilla 3 115?
(R Pritchard-Gordon, France) *last to straight, never a factor* **200/1**
5 *8* **Near Honor (GER)**[77] 2914 8-9-2 .... MSautjeau 5 105
(A Fabre, France) *set fair pace til headed 1 1/2f out* **150/1**

2m 32.9s **Going Correction** -0.125s/f (Firm) **5** Ran SP% **114.7**
Speed ratings: 102,101,101,98,92
PARI-MUTUEL: WIN 3.20; PL 1.10, 1.10; SF 5.70.
Owner Baron G Von Ullmann **Bred** Baron G Von Ullmann **Trained** Chantilly, France

FOCUS
A top-quality renewal of this prestigious Arc Trial, but the modest pace and riders' reluctance to give their mounts anything like a hard race means the form is not reliable. That said there is a strong chance they would have finished like they did had there been a fast pace, and the ever-improving Shirocco looks the one to beat come Arc day.

NOTEBOOK
Shirocco(GER) ◆, brilliant winner of last season's Breeders' Cup Turf, has established himself this season as perhaps the leading older horse in Europe and this victory over his only serious rival for that title, stablemate Hurricane Run, further enhanced his reputation. Always well positioned by Soumillon, he looked vulnerable when the favourite drew alongsides, but he willingly stuck out his neck and held on well. With none of the first three being given anything like a hard time the form cannot be treated as cast-iron, but there is no doubting he has improved this year. A running-on fourth behind Hurricane Run in last year's Arc, he had enjoyed a far from ideal preparation in the run up to that race - making his seasonal debut in this event - and then to make matters worse was allotted a dreadful draw on the big day. This time around things have gone much more smoothly and he will surely take all the beating in this year's renewal, provided the ground is on the soft side.

Hurricane Run(IRE), highly impressive winner of last year's Arc, has been unable to match that form this season, with his easy win in a three-runner Tattersalls Gold Cup being followed by defeat by Pride in the Grand Prix de Saint-Cloud and then making mighty hard work of winning the King George from an unsound Electrocutionist. He looked straight enough here and drew alongsides the winner a furlong out, but was unable to go by and had to settle for second. Like the winner, he was not given a hard time and connections will not be bothered by the reverse, but he has yet to suggest he has got any better than last year and should the ground come up on the easy side, he may he hard pressed to confirm last year's placings with his stablemate.

Pride(FR), conqueror of Hurricane Run in the Grand de Saint-Cloud, was having her first start since and really caught the eye in third, running on nicely under another soft ride. This was a good trial for the Arc, but a slowly-run five-runner field was always likely to suit her better than the front pair and a place is the best she can hope for come Arc day.

Divine Story(FR), dropped out last for much of the race, came bowling along at the end to take fourth place, which was the intention of her trainer, who supplemented the mare into the race for that intelligent reason. She now goes for a Listed race in Germany.

5220a PRIX VERMILLE LUCIEN BARRIERE (GROUP 1) (F&M) 1m 4f
2:50 (2:56) 3-Y-0+ **£118,221** (£47,297; £23,648; £11,814; £5,917)

RPR
1 **Mandesha (FR)**[42] 3991 3-8-7 .... CSoumillon 1 119+
(A De Royer-Dupre, France) *hld up in mid-div, 7th str, smooth hdwy on outside from 2f out, led over 1f out, pushed 2 1/2 l clr ins fnl f, eased last 50yds* **7/4**[1]
2 *1 1/2* **Montare (IRE)**[35] 4192 4-9-2 .... OPeslier 4 114
(J E Pease, France) *always close up, 5th straight, ridden 1 1/2f out, chased winner final 150y, ran on one pace* **8/1**
3 *1/2* **Royal Highness (GER)**[35] 4192 4-9-2 .... TThulliez 10 113
(P Bary, France) *always in touch, 6th straight, headway on outside from over 2f out, kept on steadily to end* **10/1**
4 *1 1/2* **Freedonia**[35] 4192 4-9-2 .... TGillet 2 111
(J E Hammond, France) *always close up, 4th straight, not clear run and caught on inside from 2f out to 1f out, ran on final f* **7/2**[2]
5 *nk* **Alix Road (FR)**[21] 4645 3-8-7 .... DBoeuf 9 111
(Mme M Bollack-Badel, France) *9th straight, steady progress on outside final 2f, never near to challenge* **33/1**
6 *3/4* **Fermion (IRE)**[35] 4179 3-8-7 .... KFallon 6 109
(A P O'Brien, Ire) *held up, 10th straight, hdwy on ins over 2f out, moved out wl over 1f out, n.m.r 150yds out, kpt on* **6/1**[3]
7 *1* **Time On**[35] 4192 3-8-7 .... RichardHughes 5 108
(J L Dunlop) *led to over 1f out, gradually faded* **10/1**
8 *3/4* **Ponte Tresa (FR)**[24] 4543 3-8-7 .... C-PLemaire 7 107
(Y De Nicolay, France) *8th straight, never a factor* **25/1**
9 *hd* **Mysterious Lina (FR)**[21] 4645 3-8-7 .... SPasquier 8 107
(P Demercastel, France) *disputed 2nd, 2nd & challenging straight, hard ridden inside final 2f, every chance over 1f out, one pace* **25/1**
10 *3/4* **Mary Louhana**[24] 4543 3-8-7 .... SMaillot 3 105
(M Delzangles, France) *held up in rear, last straight, effort on inside 2f out, disputing 5th when hampered about 140yds out, not recover* **33/1**
11 *6* **Wurfscheibe (GER)**[21] 4648 4-9-2 .... TMundry 11 96
(P Rau, Germany) *disputed 2nd, 3rd straight, weakened 2f out* **14/1**

2m 29.2s **Going Correction** -0.125s/f (Firm)
WFA 3 from 4yo 9lb **11** Ran SP% **122.4**
Speed ratings: 114,113,112,111,111 110,110,109,109,109 105
PARI-MUTUEL: WIN 3.60; PL 1.60, 1.70, 1.90; DF 11.40.
Owner Princess Zahra Aga Khan **Bred** Princes Zahra Aga Khan **Trained** Chantilly, France

FOCUS
A classy performance by top-class filly Mandesha, who was value for around 4l. She may now be supplemented for the Arc.

The Form Book, Raceform Ltd, Compton, RG20 6NL

NOTEBOOK

Mandesha(FR) has quickly developed into a top-class mare and supplemented her Group 1 win over a mile at Deauville with this mightily impressive performance over half a mile further. Having raced on the rail in mid-division for much of the early stages, she was switched to challenge at the beginning of the straight and cruised on over a furlong out. On this fastish ground she definitely stayed the distance, and a supplementary entry into the Arc is not out of the question, but she will do well to give the likes of Shirocco and Hurricane Run a race there and may not even be risked if the ground becomes testing.

Montare(IRE) has had to settle for the runner-up position on four occasions in top-class company this year. She was in mid-division early on and started her run from halfway up the straight, but she could not quicken the same way as the winner. She stayed on bravely to hold second place inside the final furlong and the Prix de Royallieu at the end of the month now looks the perfect race for her.

Royal Highness(GER), second in this race a year ago, put up a much better effort than of late, but has still to really find her 2005 form. She started her run from halfway up the straight and looked likely to be the runner-up three out, but she did not go through with her effort. The Arc still remains a possibility for her.

Freedonia can be considered a little unlucky, although it is unlikely she would have beaten the winner. She had nowhere to go when a fading horse got in her way, as at the same time as the runner-up moved up on her outside. She finished well, but the race was over by the time she was in the clear. A supplementary entry for the Arc is now unlikely, and connections were talking more about an American campaign.

Fermion(IRE) has shown improved form of late, but she was given too much to do here and was unable to quicken. She probably needs her sights lowering slightly for the time being.

Time On set off in front at a good pace and quickened well in the straight, but she was beaten one and a half furlongs out. Softer ground would certainly have helped and her jockey felt she might have been feeling the effects of a long season.

5221a PRIX NIEL CASINO BARRIERE (GROUP 2) (C&F) 1m 4f
3:20 (3:28) 3-Y-0 **£51,103** (£19,724; £9,414; £6,276; £3,138)

RPR

1 **Rail Link**[58] [3517] 3-9-2 .... CSoumillon 2 121
(A Fabre, France) *racd in 3rd, wnt 2nd 5f out, led over 1 1/2f out, hrd rdn & strongly pressed 100yds out, found extra closing stages* **4/7**[1]

2 ½ **Youmzain (IRE)**[19] [4678] 3-9-2 .... RichardHughes 4 120
(M R Channon) *hld up in last, hdwy on ins & 4th str, wnt 2nd 1f out, hrd rdn to press wnr on ins 100yds out, no extra closing stages* **13/2**[3]

3 2 **Sudan (IRE)**[22] [4623] 3-9-2 .... SPasquier 1 117
(E Lellouche, France) *disputed 4th, 5th straight, stayed on at same pace under pressure final 1 1/2f* **20/1**

4 ¾ **Dragon Dancer**[49] [3778] 3-9-2 .... DarryllHolland 6 116
(G Wragg) *led to 1 1/2f out, one pace* **8/1**

5 2 **Papal Bull**[19] [4678] 3-9-2 .... KFallon 5 113
(Sir Michael Stoute) *raced in 2nd to 5f out, 3rd straight on outside, outpaced final 1 1/2f* **9/2**[2]

6 8 **Bremen**[118] [1749] 3-9-2 .... OPeslier 3 101
(A Fabre, France) *disputed 4th, dropped back to last entering straight, soon weakened* **25/1**

2m 31.9s **Going Correction** -0.125s/f (Firm) 6 Ran SP% **114.9**
Speed ratings: 105,104,103,102,101 96
PARI-MUTUEL: WIN 1.50; PL 1.10, 1.30; SF 4.60.
Owner K Abdulla **Bred** Juddmonte Farms Ltd **Trained** Chantilly, France

FOCUS
A decent renewal of the Niel, rated through the third and the fifth.

NOTEBOOK

Rail Link, who adds a high-class third string to the remarkable strength-in-depth Fabre has in the Arc, came through his trial unscathed, but did not win in the fashion many were hoping for, being made to work hard by Youmzain. He did pull out more when required though, and the way he travelled early on suggests he will have place claims in the Arc, although he is unlikely to be risked if the ground comes up soft.

Youmzain(IRE), who ran here rather than take his chance in the St Leger, put up a good performance when winning the Great Voltigeur at York last time and he again travelled impressively. Forced to challenge against the rail, he did not have much room to work with, but quickened really impressively to get to the winner, only for that rival to pull out a bit more. He seems to be getting better with every race and could reach the top if kept in training as a four-year-old.

Sudan(IRE), fifth in the early stages and rounding the final turn, was close to the winner at the start of the straight, but could not match him for pace. In the end he could only stay on at the one pace.

Dragon Dancer, runner-up in the Epsom Derby yet remarkably still a maiden, tried to make all the running and set a pretty decent gallop, but he was outpaced when it mattered. His jockey felt that he was not really suited to the undulating track and it is surely time now to allow the horse to win his maiden.

Papal Bull, a highly progressive colt earlier in the season, ran poorly in the Voltigeur and, although not beaten far here, he gave the impression his improvement has levelled off for the time being.

5222a PRIX DU PETIT COUVERT CASINO BARRIERE DE DINARD (GROUP 3) 5f (S)
3:50 (3:58) 3-Y-O+ **£27,586** (£11,034; £8,276; £5,517; £2,759)

RPR

1 **Majestic Missile (IRE)**[38] [4080] 5-8-12 .... CSoumillon 1 117
(W J Haggas) *soon racing in 4th on rails, led 150yds out, ridden out* **9/2**[2]

2 1 **Peace Offering (IRE)**[13] [4875] 6-8-12 .... KFallon 6 113
(D Nicholls) *led to 150yds out, kept on one pace* **6/1**

3 ¾ **Biniou (IRE)**[3] [5146] 3-8-11 .... TThulliez 2 110
(Robert Collet, France) *headway 2f out, ran on to take 3rd well inside final f* **10/1**

4 1 ½ **Tournedos (IRE)**[14] [4855] 4-8-12 .... RichardHughes 7 105
(R Charlton) *held up, headway 2f out, kept on one pace final f* **5/1**[3]

5 ¾ **Mister Chocolate (IRE)**[18] 3-8-11 .... C-PLemaire 5 102
(Robert Collet, France) *cahsed leader, disputing 2nd 2f out, weakened final f* **25/1**

6 1 **Kourka (FR)**[19] 4-8-9 .... RonanThomas 9 96
(J-M Beguigne, France) *outpaced, last to over 2f out, headway from well over 1f out, one pace inside final f* **16/1**

7 2 **Tycoon's Hill (IRE)**[14] [4860] 7-8-12 .... JAuge 3 91
(Robert Collet, France) *never a factor* **10/1**

8 nse **Latona (FR)**[98] [2276] 4-8-12 .... TGillet 10 91
(J E Pease, France) *mid-division, beaten 2f out* **3/1**[1]

9 2 **Protector (SAF)**[14] [4860] 5-8-12 .... MBlancpain 4 84
(Diego Lowther, France) *disputed 2nd til weakened 2f out* **20/1**

10 2 ½ **Sweet Travel (IRE)**[40] 3-8-8 .... OPeslier 8 72
(A Fabre, France) *mid-division to half-way, last from 2f out* **8/1**

56.00 secs **Going Correction** -0.225s/f (Firm) 10 Ran SP% **117.9**
WFA 3 from 4yo+ 1lb
Speed ratings: 113,111,110,107,106 105,101,101,98,94
PARI-MUTUEL: WIN 5.90; PL 2.80, 4.00, 3.40; DF 24.60.
Owner Flying Tiger Partnership I **Bred** Victor Stud Brendan Cummins And Oliver O'Connor **Trained** Newmarket, Suffolk

FOCUS
A return to form from the winner, in a race rated through the third and fifth.

NOTEBOOK

Majestic Missile(IRE) was given a brilliant ride. Smartly away on the rail and always in the leading group, he took the advantage a furlong and a half out and ran on really strongly on ground which he adores. He will be back for the Abbaye on Arc day before being retired to stud.

Peace Offering(IRE), quickly into his stride on the outside, was in the lead at the halfway stage and tried to dominate the final two furlongs, but he could not quicken like the winner as the race came to an end.

Biniou(IRE), behind on the rails in the early stages, started a run from a furlong and a half out and finished best of all, but he never really got in a blow at the first two.

Tournedos(IRE), well behind early on, made some late progress but never really got into the race.

5223a PRIX GLADIATEUR ROYAL THALASSO BARRIERE (GROUP 3) 1m 7f 110y
4:20 (4:25) 4-Y-O+ **£27,586** (£11,034; £8,276; £5,517; £2,759)

RPR

1 **Le Miracle (GER)**[21] [4647] 5-9-0 .... DBoeuf 2 119
(W Baltromei, Germany) *disputed 3rd, 3rd straight, led distance, soon clear, ran on well* **16/1**

2 5 **Salutino (GER)**[77] [2910] 4-9-0 .... CSoumillon 4 114
(A Fabre, France) *hld up in 6th, wnt 5th str, hdwy over 2f out on outside, rdn & ev ch wl over 1f out, sn one pace* **11/4**[3]

3 1 ½ **Soledad (IRE)**[21] [4647] 6-8-12 .... RonanThomas 1 111
(G Cherel, France) *raced in 2nd to straight, led well over 1f out, headed distance, one pace* **20/1**

4 2 ½ **Gold Magic (FR)**[22] 8-8-12 .... YGourraud 7 108
(J-P Gallorini, France) *last to straight, steady progress to take 4th last strides* **25/1**

5 snk **Policy Maker (IRE)**[21] [4647] 6-9-4 .... SPasquier 3 114
(E Lellouche, France) *raced in 5th, 6th straight, ridden & found nothing over 1f out* **7/4**[1]

6 6 **Petite Speciale (USA)**[86] [2629] 7-8-13 .... C-PLemaire 6 103
(E Lecoiffier, France) *disputed 3rd, 4th straight, weakened well over 1f out* **14/1**

7 ½ **Franklins Gardens**[19] [4677] 6-9-0 .... DarryllHolland 5 103
(M H Tompkins) *led to well over 1f out, soon weakened* **2/1**[2]

3m 15.9s **Going Correction** -0.325s/f (Firm) 7 Ran SP% **117.5**
Speed ratings: 113,110,109,108,108 105,105
PARI-MUTUEL: WIN 9.20; PL 3.40, 2.70; SF 44.10.
Owner Rennstall Gestut Hachtsee **Bred** Comtesse B Von Norman **Trained** Germany

FOCUS
The winner was convincing in turning around soft-ground form with the third and the fifth.

NOTEBOOK

Le Miracle(GER) was running in claimers earlier in his career but totally outclassed his rivals in this Group 3 event. Third early on, he cantered into the straight before drawing clear of his rivals a furlong and a half out. He passed the post alone and may have earned a tilt at the Prix du Cadran.

Salutino(GER) raced in sixth position and was going very well at the entrance to the straight. He came with a very promising run to lead soon after, but had nothing in reserve when tackled by the eventual winner. He appeared not to have a good action in the final furlong and may need softer ground to show his best. The Cadran remains on the cards.

Soledad(IRE) was supplemented into this event and more than recovered the cost. Always prominent, he was one-paced on the rail throughout the final furlong and a half, and is another possible for the Cadran.

Gold Magic(FR), a top-class jumper, was held up in last position and took some time before slipping into top gear. He was putting in his best work at the finish.

Policy Maker(IRE), who seems most effective in soft ground, appeared not to get home.

Franklins Gardens put up a rather disappointing effort. Asked to make all the running, he was still leading at the entrance to the straight but was soon at the end of his tether. He then dropped back to finish a disappointing last, and his jockey was of the opinon that the horse never runs well abroad and that perhaps he had made too much use of him early on.

4919 TABY (R-H)
Sunday, September 10

OFFICIAL GOING: Good

5224a NICKES MINNESLOPNING (LISTED RACE) 1m (D)
1:45 (12:00) 3-Y-O+ **£10,835** (£5,417; £2,600; £1,734; £1,083)

RPR

1 **Maybach**[12] 5-9-4 .... KAndersen 2 94
(B Bo, Sweden)

2 1 **Salt Track (ARG)**[14] [4864] 6-9-4 .... ESki 3 92
(Niels Petersen, Norway)

3 4 **Hartshead**[29] [4348] 7-9-4 .... DeanMcKeown 1 84
(G A Swinbank) *prominent on inside off steady pace, led narrowly halfway til headed over 1 1/2f out, outpaced by first two (28/10)* **28/10**[1]

4 nse **Soy Asturiano (ARG)** 5-9-4 .... GSolis 6 84
()

5 6 **Moltas (SWE)** 4-9-4 .... P-AGraberg 4 72
()

6 17 **Eltizaam (USA)**[103] [2123] 4-9-4 .... LHammer-Hansen 5 38
(B Olsen, Norway)

1m 40.1s 6 Ran SP% **26.3**
(including 1 Euro stake): WIN 2.88; PL 2.01, 2.41; DF 17.02.
Owner Stall Dionysos **Bred** Meridian Stud **Trained** Sweden

NOTEBOOK

Hartshead was firmly put in his place by the first two, but proved that he is effective on dirt, which will open up options when he visits Dubai for the International Festival early next year.

5225a TABY OPEN SPRINT CHAMPIONSHIP (GROUP 3) 5f 165y
3:10 (3:11) 3-Y-O+ **£29,283** (£14,641; £7,028; £4,685; £2,928)

RPR

1 **Bellamont Forest (USA)**[38] 10-9-4 .... DinaDanekilde 11 108
(O Larsen, Sweden) *midfield, headway 2f out, led inside final f, driven out* **277/10**

2 ½ **Solvana (IRE)**[38] 4-9-0 .... NCordrey 12 102
(Wido Neuroth, Norway) *behind early, headway halfway, every chance final f, no extra close home* **53/10**

3 1 ½ **Hide And Seek (SWE)**[322] 10-9-4 .... P-AGraberg 10 101
(H Lundell, Sweden) *raced in 4th, led 2f out to inside final f, one pace* **46/10**[3]

4 ½ **Berri Chis (ARG)** 4-9-4 .... GSolis 6 100
(Vanja Sandrup, Sweden) *midfield, kept on final furlong, never nearer* **153/10**
5 *hd* **Pipoldchap (CHI)**[28] 6-9-4 ....(b) MMartinez 4 99
(F Castro, Sweden) *raced in 3rd to 2f out, one pace* **6/4**[1]
6 *1* **Waquaas**[38] 10-9-4 .... KAndersen 5 96
(B Bo, Sweden) *always midfield* **3/1**[2]
7 *shd* **Cavorting**[121] 4-9-4 .... LHammer-Hansen 7 96
(M Kahn, Sweden) *led to 2f out, one pace* **41/1**
8 *shd* **Soudelor (IRE)**[364] 5163 5-9-4 .... JJohansen 2 95
(Rune Haugen, Norway) *always towards rear* **40/1**
9 *2* **King Nov (ARG)**[12] 4-9-4 .... MLarsen 1 89
(O Stenstrom, Sweden) *always in rear* **25/1**
10 ½ **Senora Thatcher (CHI)**[38] 5-9-0 .... FDiaz 8 84
(M Nygard, Norway) *never a factor* **18/1**
11 *1* **Steve's Champ (CHI)**[38] 6-9-4 ....(b) MSantos 9 85
(Rune Haugen, Norway) *2nd to halfway, weakened quickly under 2f out* **186/10**

1m 10.2s **11** Ran SP% **127.4**
WIN 28.75; PL 3.48, 1.93, 1.88; DF 156.33.
Owner Stall Ole Larsen **Bred** L E Due **Trained** Sweden

5226a STOCKHOLM CUP INTERNATIONAL (GROUP 3) 1m 4f
3:40 (3:38) 3-Y-0+ **£29,283** (£14,641; £7,028; £4,685; £2,928)

RPR
1 **Collier Hill**[10] 4967 8-9-4 .... DeanMcKeown 13 116
(G A Swinbank) *raced in 4th, led 4f out, 2 lengths clear 2f out, pushed out, very easily* **51/100**[1]
2 *9* **Binary File (USA)**[14] 4864 8-9-4 .... MSantos 2 102
(L Kelp, Sweden) *held up towards rear, progress 3f out, went 2nd inside final f, never near winner* **86/10**[3]
3 *2* **Day Walker**[14] 4864 4-9-4 .... KAndersen 12 99
(Rune Haugen, Norway) *midfield, headway to go 3rd 1f out, kept on* **192/10**
4 *1* **Crimson And Gold**[14] 4864 4-9-4 .... FDiaz 1 98
(L Reuterskiold, Sweden) *midfield, one pace final 3f* **21/1**
5 1 ½ **Storm Trooper (GER)**[14] 4864 6-9-4 ....(b) JJohansen 4 95
(Rune Haugen, Norway) *always midfield* **43/1**
6 *hd* **Mick Jerome (IRE)**[35] 4189 5-9-4 .... YvonneDurant 3 95
(Rune Haugen, Norway) *in rear til modest late headway* **25/1**
7 *1* **Alnitak (USA)**[35] 4189 5-9-4 ....(b) MMartinez 11 93
(B Olsen, Norway) *never a factor* **49/1**
8 ½ **Jagodin (IRE)**[346] 6-9-4 .... P-AGraberg 7 93
(B Neuman, Sweden) *raced in 3rd to 4f out, weakened* **51/10**[2]
9 2 ½ **Kingsword (USA)**[38] 5-9-4 .... DinaDanekilde 9 89
(O Larsen, Sweden) *always in rear* **38/1**
10 *2* **Alpino Chileno (ARG)**[35] 4189 7-9-4 ....(b) LHammer-Hansen 8 86
(Rune Haugen, Norway) *raced in 2nd, chased winner 4f out to 2f out, weakened quickly* **107/10**
11 *26* **Sibelius (SWE)**[351] 5-9-4 .... MLarsen 6 47
(Caroline Stromberg) *led to 4f out, weakened, tailed off final 2f* **22/1**

2m 33.5s **11** Ran SP% **126.1**
WIN 1.52; PL 1.29, 2.07, 2.85; DF 8.27.
Owner R H Hall J D Abell R Crowe **Bred** George Strawbridge **Trained** Melsonby, N Yorks

NOTEBOOK
Collier Hill was simply way too good for the best horses Scandinavia could offer and will now head for Cologne, where he is already a course and distance winner, for a 12-furlong Group 1 event on September 24.

VELIEFENDI
Sunday, September 10
OFFICIAL GOING: Firm

5227a TOPKAPI TROPHY (GROUP 2) 1m
2:00 (2:04) 3-Y-0+ **£87,209** (£34,884; £17,442; £8,721)

RPR
1 **Ribella (IRE)**[316] 7-9-4 ow1 .... SKaya 107
(O Isgoren, Turkey) **53/20**[2]
2 *nk* **Kaneko (TUR)**[365] 5142 5-9-6 .... BKurdu 108
(K Saglam, Turkey) **56/10**
3 1 ½ **Kurtiniadis (IRE)** 3-8-12 .... MKaya 102
(Trainer Unknown, Ire) **53/20**[2]
4 *nse* **Sabirli (TUR)**[212] 369 5-9-6 .... HKaratas 105
(C Kurt, Turkey) **1/4**[1]
5 *nk* **Ryono (USA)**[49] 3779 7-9-6 .... TCastanheira 104
(S Smrczek, Germany) **41/10**[3]
6 *1* **Momtic (IRE)**[24] 4529 5-9-6 .... PaulDoe 102
(W Jarvis) *raced in 5th, every chance 2f out, ran on one pace* **11/1**
7 ¾ **Willingly (GER)**[35] 4190 7-9-6 .... FilipMinarik 101
(M Trybuhl, Germany) **13/2**
8 *1* **Lazio (GER)**[84] 2692 5-9-6 .... ADeVries 99
(A Trybuhl, Germany) **96/10**
9 ¾ **Billy Allen (IRE)**[43] 3969 5-9-6 .... FSpanu 97
(F Chappet, France) **59/10**
10 *4* **Mahalle Cocugu (TUR)** 4-9-6 .... SBoyraz 89
() **17/1**

1m 34.6s
WFA 3 from 4yo+ 5lb **10** Ran SP% **220.7**
(including one lira stakes): WIN 3.65 (no place betting).
Owner S Tasbek **Bred** W G McKinley **Trained** Turkey

NOTEBOOK
Momtic(IRE) was unable to sustain his effort in the last two furlongs but still posted a solid effort to finish in front of a trio of French and German horses who all boast decent recent Group or Listed form.

[4686] FOLKESTONE (R-H)
Monday, September 11
OFFICIAL GOING: Good to firm
Wind: almost nil

5231 FOLKESTONE-RACECOURSE.CO.UK MAIDEN AUCTION STKS 6f
2:20 (2:21) (Class 5) 2-Y-0 **£4,210** (£1,252; £625; £312) **Stalls** Low

Form RPR
402 1 **Victory Spirit**[43] 3979 2-8-11 72 .... EddieAhern 5 73
(J L Dunlop) *trckd ldrs: effrt over 1f out: one of five in line ins fnl f: drvn to ld last 50yds* **11/4**[1]
2203 2 *hd* **Beautiful Madness (IRE)**[12] 4920 2-8-4 67 .... TPO'Shea 3 65
(M G Quinlan) *wl in tch: effrt wl over 1f out: rdn to ld jst ins fnl f: hdd last 50yds: kpt on* **5/1**
6344 3 *shd* **Bahamian Love**[12] 4920 2-8-4 68 .... JoeFanning 1 65+
(B W Hills) *hld up in tch: effrt and nt clr run briefly jst over 1f out: rdn to chal ins fnl f: nt qckn last 50yds* **9/2**[3]
4 1 ¾ **House Maiden (IRE)** 2-8-7 ow2 .... AdamKirby[(3)] 2 66+
(D M Simcock) *hld up in last trio: wl off the pce whn shkn up over 1f out: r.o wl last 150yds: fin best of all* **20/1**
5 ½ **Gentle Guru** 2-8-8 .... SteveDrowne 7 62
(R T Phillips) *racd on outer: in tch: prog over 2f out: chal and almost upsides jst over 1f out: fdd* **22/1**
2420 6 *nk* **Dee Jay Wells**[17] 4779 2-9-1 74 .... RyanMoore 9 68
(R Hannon) *led and sn crossed to nr side rail: rdn and hdd over 2f out: kpt on and ch ent fnl f: fdd* **4/1**[2]
60 7 ¾ **Neat 'n Tidy**[12] 4934 2-8-4 .... MatthewHenry 10 55
(C A Cyzer) *t.k.h: trckd ldr after 2f: rdn to ld over 2f out: hdd & wknd jst ins fnl f* **50/1**
8 *4* **Tykie Two** 2-8-4 .... RichardMullen 6 43
(E J O'Neill) *dwlt: sn pushed along: a in last trio and nvr on terms* **14/1**
9 1 ¼ **Siesta (IRE)** 2-8-6 .... MichaelHills 8 41
(J R Fanshawe) *dwlt: wl in rr: prog on wd outside over 2f out: sn shkn up and wknd* **8/1**
00 10 *10* **Foreland Sands (IRE)**[8] 5043 2-8-8 .... KylieManser[(7)] 4 20
(J R Best) *chsd ldr for 2f: wknd over 2f out: t.o* **100/1**

1m 13.62s (0.02) **Going Correction** -0.20s/f (Firm) **10** Ran SP% **111.4**
Speed ratings (Par 95):91,90,90,88,87 87,86,80,79,65
CSF £15.07 TOTE £3.70: £1.10, £1.90, £2.00; EX 12.10 Trifecta £37.10 Pool £243.63 - 4.65 winning units.
Owner Harry Dunlop Racing Partnership **Bred** Nawara Stud Co Ltd **Trained** Arundel, W Sussex

FOCUS
An ordinary maiden and sound but very limited form rated through the first three.

NOTEBOOK
Victory Spirit had already shown enough to be of interest in an ordinary maiden such as this, and he eventually got the job done, albeit narrowly in a three-way photo. He will get another furlong and is likely to go the nursery route now. (op 3-1 tchd 10-3)
Beautiful Madness(IRE), apart from when she was disappointing at Haydock, has performed with a lot of consistency, and her effort is probably a fair guide to the level of the form. She remains vulnerable to improvers. (op 11-2 tchd 13-2)
Bahamian Love is another who is beginning to look exposed, but she is a half-sister to Silver Chariot, a winner over seven furlongs at two, and a step up to that trip may suit her as well. (op 4-1)
House Maiden(IRE), whose dam was a winner over a mile and a half in Germany, is not bred to excel at this distance, so in the circumstances she put up an encouraging effort. Despite showing signs of inexperience, she finished strongest of all, and will benefit greatly from an extra furlong. She has the ability to win a modest contest. (tchd 16-1)
Gentle Guru, whose stable is better known for its jumpers, is a half-sister to Beecroft, a winner over a mile at three in Italy. She did not shape too badly on her debut and is entitled to improve for the run. (op 12-1)
Dee Jay Wells has a rating that suggests he can win a modest race such as this, but he is becoming disappointing. (op 10-3 tchd 9-2 in a place)
Neat 'n Tidy raced too keenly and did not get home. (op 33-1)

5232 NEXT MEETING SEPTEMBER 18TH H'CAP 6f
2:50 (2:52) (Class 6) (0-65,66) 3-Y-0+ **£3,238** (£963; £481; £240) **Stalls** Low

Form RPR
631 1 **Littledodayno (IRE)**[12] 4927 3-8-13 63 .... EdwardCreighton[(3)] 5 74
(M Wigham) *hld up nr side: prog on outer 2f out: led ent fnl f: drvn clr* **7/2**[1]
0155 2 1 ¼ **Hotchpotch (USA)**[24] 4548 3-8-7 54 .... HayleyTurner 12 61+
(J R Best) *racd alone far side: wl on terms w other gp: hrd rdn over 1f out: outpcd by wnr ins fnl f* **14/1**
0320 3 *nk* **Monashee Prince (IRE)**[24] 4564 4-9-4 63 .... SteveDrowne 9 69
(J R Best) *mde most nr side: drvn 2f out: hdd and outpcd ent fnl f* **7/1**
6011 4 *1* **Piddies Pride (IRE)**[32] 4294 4-9-1 60 ....(v) JimmyQuinn 8 63
(Miss Gay Kelleway) *trckd ldrs nr side: rdn 2f out: edgd rt ent fnl f: nt qckn* **8/1**
6000 5 ¾ **Mount Sinai**[35] 4211 3-8-6 60 .... RichardRowe[(7)] 3 61
(W J Knight) *trckd ldrs nr side: urged along over 2f out: fdd fnl f* **50/1**
2124 6 *shd* **Sweet Pickle**[23] 4589 5-9-3 65 ....(e) AmirQuinn[(3)] 1 65+
(J R Boyle) *hld up in rr nr side: gng strly but trapped bhd rivals fr over 1f out: nt rcvr* **7/2**[1]
5603 7 1 ¼ **Danehill Stroller (IRE)**[34] 4223 6-8-12 57 .... DaneO'Neill 13 54
(A M Hales) *w nr side ldr: drvn 2f out: wknd fnl f* **13/2**[3]
2002 8 *shd* **Cree**[10] 4985 4-8-9 54 .... RichardMullen 11 50
(W R Muir) *in tch nr side: u.p and hld whn bmpd ent fnl f: fdd* **9/2**[2]
1000 9 *6* **Banjo Bay (IRE)**[6] 5081 8-9-3 65 ....(t) AdamKirby[(3)] 6 43
(Miss Gay Kelleway) *a in last pair nr side: detached over 2f out* **18/1**

1m 12.21s (-1.39) **Going Correction** -0.20s/f (Firm)
WFA 3 from 4yo+ 2lb **9** Ran SP% **113.5**
Speed ratings (Par 101):101,99,98,97,96 96,94,94,86
CSF £53.00 CT £324.85 TOTE £3.80: £2.20, £4.10, £3.10; EX 67.40 TRIFECTA Not won..
Owner W and L Bamforth **Bred** Lodge Park Stud **Trained** Newmarket, Suffolk
■ Ballybunion (10/1, spread plate at s) was withdrawn. R4, deduct 5p in the £. New market formed.

FOCUS
A modest handicap but the winner looks a progressive type and the form looks solid for the grade rated around the third and fourth.
Sweet Pickle Official explanation: jockey said mare was denied a clear run
Banjo Bay(IRE) Official explanation: jockey said gelding ran flat

5233 BETFAIR.COM H'CAP — 7f (S)

3:20 (3:21) (Class 4) (0-80,80) 4-Y-0+ £7,772 (£2,312; £1,155; £577) Stalls Low

Form RPR

510 1 **Bee Stinger**[9] 5019 4-9-4 80 RyanMoore 1 88
(I A Wood) trckd ldrs: effrt 2f out: drvn to ld narrowly jst over 1f out: hld on u.p nr fin 2/1[1]

0235 2 shd **Silent Storm**[20] 4674 6-8-5 67 JimmyQuinn 4 75
(C A Cyzer) t.k.h: mde most to jst over 1f out: rallied ins fnl f : jst hld 13/2[3]

1011 3 1 1/4 **Taranaki**[8] 5042 8-8-3 72 6ex AshleyHamblett(7) 3 77
(P D Cundell) hld up in rr: prog on outer over 2f out: upsides over 1f out: edgd rt and nt qckn ins fnl f 4/1[2]

4230 4 hd **Greenwood**[8] 5042 8-8-10 72 SteveDrowne 6 76
(P G Murphy) hld up in rr: effrt and nt clr run briefly 2f out: nt qckn over 1f out: kpt on same pce 9/1

5040 5 3/4 **Regal Dream (IRE)**[20] 4674 4-8-6 68 ow1 MichaelHills 2 70
(J W Hills) settled in last: nt clr run wl over 1f out: swtchd to wd outside: rdn and nt qckn 14/1

4504 6 2 **Lizarazu (GER)**[8] 5042 7-8-4 73 (p) TolleyDean(7) 5 70
(R A Harris) trckd ldrs: rdn 2f out: fdd over 1f out 9/1

-400 7 5 **Keyaki (IRE)**[30] 4378 5-8-9 71 EddieAhern 8 55
(C F Wall) racd on outer: wl in tch: effrt over 2f out: wknd over 1f out 11/1

0300 8 9 **Flint River**[16] 4807 8-8-5 72 ow3 TravisBlock(5) 7 33
(H Morrison) t.k.h: mostly trckd ldr to 2f out: sddle slipped and sn no ch 8/1

1m 26.47s (-1.43) **Going Correction** -0.20s/f (Firm) 8 Ran SP% 112.8
Speed ratings (Par 105):100,99,98,98,97 95,89,79
CSF £14.90 CT £46.45 TOTE £3.00: £1.10, £2.30, £1.40; EX 17.20 Trifecta £47.00 Pool £474.64 - 7.16 winning units.
Owner Sporting Occasions No 11 **Bred** Templeton Stud **Trained** Upper Lambourn, Berks

FOCUS
Fair handicap form but the early pace was not particularly strong. The winner did not need to improve to score.
Flint River Official explanation: jockey said saddle slipped

5234 INVICTA MOTORS NURSERY — 5f

3:50 (3:50) (Class 2) 2-Y-0
£12,464 (£3,732; £1,866; £934; £466; £234) Stalls Low

Form RPR

3242 1 **Cosmopolitan Lady**[24] 4550 2-7-13 77 LukeMorris(7) 4 79
(D M Simcock) t.k.h: hld up bhd ldrs: effrt 2f out: rdn to ld against nr side rail 1f out: sn clr 13/2

4121 2 1 1/2 **Black Moma (IRE)**[17] 4779 2-8-5 76 RichardSmith 9 73
(R Hannon) trckd ldrs on outer: rdn 2f out: styd on to chse wnr ins fnl f: no imp 5/2[1]

2026 3 nk **Frisky Talk (IRE)**[17] 4766 2-8-8 79 MichaelHills 5 75
(B W Hills) led: hanging rt fr 2f out: hdd and nt qckn 1f out 11/2[3]

405 4 1/2 **Queen Of Narnia**[1] 5207 2-8-0 74 EdwardCreighton(3) 3 68
(M R Channon) awkward s: hld up: last tl effrt over 1f out: shkn up and styd on: nvr rchd ldrs 25/1

3000 5 shd **Nina Blini**[37] 4146 2-9-7 92 RyanMoore 6 85
(B J Meehan) towards rr and off the pce: prog on outer fr 2f out: one pce and no hdwy fnl f 8/1

1200 6 1 3/4 **Going Straight (IRE)**[23] 4594 2-9-3 88 EddieAhern 2 75
(I A Wood) chsd ldrs: rdn over 2f out: struggling over 1f out: fdd 20/1

3161 7 1 **Danger Alley**[26] 4493 2-7-12 69 oh1 (b) JimmyQuinn 1 52
(E J O'Neill) off the pce in rr: effrt 2f out: shkn up and fond little jst over 1f out 14/1

022 8 1/2 **Pretty Miss**[25] 4510 2-8-3 74 JoeFanning 8 56+
(H Candy) w ldr: carried rt fr 2f out: stl upsides jst over 1f out: wknd and eased ins fnl f 11/4[2]

4235 9 6 **Piccolena Boy**[17] 4753 2-8-0 71 MatthewHenry 7 31
(P Winkworth) a wl in rr: rdn and no prog over 2f out: wknd rapidly fnl f 28/1

59.61 secs (-1.19) **Going Correction** -0.20s/f (Firm) 9 Ran SP% 113.8
Speed ratings (Par 101):101,98,98,97,97 94,92,91,82
CSF £22.19 CT £95.73 TOTE £8.70: £2.10, £1.30, £2.00; EX 29.90 Trifecta £145.00 Pool £425.02 - 2.08 winning units.
Owner The Cosmopolitans **Bred** B H And C F D Simpson **Trained** Newmarket, Suffolk

FOCUS
A decent nursery that was run at a rapid pace. The third governs the form.

NOTEBOOK
Cosmopolitan Lady, finally getting off the mark, was suited by the strong pace. She has tried to make all in her recent runs but was able to sit chasing it here and, when a nice gap opened on the rail, she ran on well to win decisively. (op 7-1)
Black Moma(IRE) could not defy the 6lb rise for her win at Sandown. Unable to get to the front, she kept battling away and went second inside the last, having raced on the outer of the pack down the middle. (op 9-4 tchd 3-1)
Frisky Talk(IRE), back down in trip after a fair run over six in soft ground, showed her customary pace but does look plenty high enough in the handicap. (op 13-2)
Queen Of Narnia was making a quick reappearance. She exited the stalls awkwardly and bumped the eventual winner to leave herself on the back foot, and could only edge closer when it was too late. (op 20-1)
Nina Blini, who has not progressed since finishing third in the Queen Mary Stakes, shaped as if in need of a return to six furlongs. Official explanation: jockey said filly hung left
Danger Alley Official explanation: jockey said colt lost its action
Pretty Miss showed bright pace to dispute the lead until fading in the final furlong. (op 10-3 tchd 7-2)

5235 FOLKESTONE-RACECOURSE.CO.UK H'CAP — 2m 93y

4:20 (4:20) (Class 5) (0-75,74) 3-Y-0+ £4,533 (£1,348; £674; £336) Stalls Low

Form RPR

20 1 **Irish Wolf (FR)**[22] 2723 6-10-0 74 (p) RyanMoore 6 81+
(P Bowen) hld up in 7th: rdn over 4f out: prog on outer u.p 3f out : led over 1f out: drvn out 10/11[1]

6-03 2 2 **Jayer Gilles**[14] 4898 6-8-11 57 oh1 DaneO'Neill 3 62
(Dr J R J Naylor) hld up in tch: prog to press ldrs 3f out: chal and upsides over 1f out: nt qckn and hld by wnr fnl f 5/1[2]

0-02 3 3/4 **Prince Of Medina**[12] 4929 3-7-13 58 HayleyTurner 8 62
(J R Best) t.k.h early: hld up in tch: rdn 3f out: nt qckn and sn outpcd: kpt on to take 3rd nr fin 8/1

5603 4 3/4 **Bobsleigh**[10] 4996 7-8-11 57 oh7 JimmyQuinn 5 60
(H S Howe) trckd ldr: rdn to ld 2f out to over 1f out: wknd ins fnl f 10/1

0210 5 nk **Lysander's Quest (IRE)**[28] 4438 8-8-11 57 oh13 EddieAhern 2 59
(R Ingram) hld up in tch: rdn wl over 2f out: nt qckn and sn outpcd: kpt on again fnl f 14/1

-006 6 13 **Bendarshaan**[15] 4848 6-9-2 62 (v[1]) JoeFanning 7 49
(C A Dwyer) mde most to 2f out: sn wknd 16/1

5304 7 4 **Phoebe Woodstock (IRE)**[15] 4836 4-9-3 66 AdamKirby(3) 4 48
(W R Swinburn) hld up in last: shkn up 4f out: sn lost tch and wl bhd 7/1[3]

0500 8 14 **In On The Act (IRE)**[29] 4395 3-8-5 64 (b[1]) RichardMullen 1 29
(Jamie Poulton) chsd ldrs: rdn over 5f out: lost pl and detached in last pair 3f out: t.o 33/1

3m 36.01s (-4.69) **Going Correction** -0.25s/f (Firm)
WFA 3 from 4yo+ 13lb 8 Ran SP% 117.2
Speed ratings (Par 103):101,100,99,99,99 92,90,83
CSF £5.96 CT £23.44 TOTE £1.80: £1.10, £2.60, £1.40; EX 9.10 Trifecta £44.50 Pool £425.68 - 6.76 winning units.
Owner The Hacking Partnership **Bred** Mrs Magalen Bryant **Trained** Little Newcastle, Pembrokes

FOCUS
This was run at a steady pace before picking up towards the end of the back straight. The winner did not need to improve to take this, with the form held down by the fourth and fifth from out of the weights.

5236 FOLKESTONE RACECOURSE H'CAP — 1m 1f 149y

4:50 (4:51) (Class 5) (0-75,72) 3-Y-0+ £4,533 (£1,348; £674; £336) Stalls Low

Form RPR

4340 1 **Ahmedy (IRE)**[17] 4784 3-9-2 70 JoeFanning 4 77
(M R Channon) hld up in last trio: sme prog 4f out: sustained hdwy fr 2f out: squeezed through ins fnl f to ld last 50yds 12/1

1124 2 nk **Benbrook**[17] 4784 3-9-0 68 DaneO'Neill 9 74
(J L Dunlop) led: drvn over 2f out: styd on wl u.p: hdd fnl 50yds 7/2[1]

-302 3 nk **Peruvian Prince (USA)**[20] 4673 4-9-4 65 TPO'Shea 6 70+
(J A R Toller) hld up towards rr: rdn and nt on terms 3f out: prog over 1f out: r.o ins fnl f: gaining at fin 13/2[3]

2210 4 hd **Billy One Punch**[35] 4209 4-9-6 70 AdamKirby(3) 7 75
(G G Margarson) trckd ldng trio: effrt to press ldr over 1f out: nrly upsides ins fnl f: nt qckn 8/1

2625 5 1 1/2 **Cormorant Wharf (IRE)**[60] 3431 6-9-7 68 RyanMoore 10 70+
(G L Moore) dwlt: hld up in rr: wl outpcd and rdn 3f out: r.o wl fnl f: nrst fin 5/1[2]

3020 6 1 1/2 **Christmas Truce (IRE)**[3] 5149 7-8-8 62 (b) SophieDoyle(7) 1 61
(Ms J S Doyle) sn pressed ldr: rdn over 2f out: wknd over 1f out 16/1

0506 7 1/2 **Press Express (IRE)**[21] 4662 4-9-8 72 StephenDonohoe(3) 5 70
(M L W Bell) hld up in midfield: rdn 3f out: one pce and no imp 2f out: fdd fnl f 7/1

3354 8 hd **The Gaikwar (IRE)**[3] 5149 7-9-8 72 (b) MarcHalford(3) 2 70
(R A Harris) s.s: hld up in last: rdn and no prog 3f out: styd on ins fnl f: no ch 8/1

0000 9 nk **Shahzan House (IRE)**[9] 5016 7-9-6 70 (p) AmirQuinn(3) 8 67
(P G Murphy) trckd ldng pair to 2f out: steadily wknd 40/1

2420 10 1/2 **Alekhine (IRE)**[70] 3151 5-9-11 72 EddieAhern 3 68
(J R Boyle) hld up in last trio: rdn and no prog 3f out: one pce after 8/1

-260 11 shd **Villarosi (IRE)**[22] 4627 4-9-0 68 KylieManser(7) 11 66+
(J R Best) dwlt: sn in tch on inner: bmpd along and lost pl over 3f out: no prog over 1f out 33/1

2m 1.33s (-3.90) **Going Correction** -0.25s/f (Firm)
WFA 3 from 4yo+ 7lb 11 Ran SP% 117.0
Speed ratings (Par 103):105,104,104,104,103 101,101,101,101,100 100
CSF £53.50 CT £304.77 TOTE £15.40: £3.90, £1.90, £2.30; EX 82.30 Trifecta £370.10 Part won. Pool £521.30 - 0.84 winning units. Place 6 £11.17, Place 5 £7.24.
Owner Tareq Al-Mazeedi **Bred** Tareq Al Mazeedi **Trained** West Ilsley, Berks

FOCUS
The runner-up set just a modest pace and the form looks pretty ordinary.
T/Plt: £28.20 to a £1 stake. Pool: £58,681.35. 1,514.35 winning tickets. T/Qpdt: £5.90 to a £1 stake. Pool: £4,113.20. 514.50 winning tickets. JN

4955 REDCAR (L-H)

Monday, September 11

OFFICIAL GOING: Good to firm (firm in places)
Wind: almost nil

5237 EUROPEAN BREEDERS FUND MAIDEN FILLIES' STKS — 6f

2:10 (2:10) (Class 5) 2-Y-0 £3,562 (£1,059; £529; £264) Stalls Centre

Form RPR

22 1 **Carillon (IRE)**[34] 4228 2-9-0 KDarley 5 76
(M Johnston) mde virtually all: rdn over 1f out: edgd rt ins last: styd on 15/2[3]

3 2 1 1/2 **Emaara**[23] 4600 2-9-0 RHills 14 72
(J L Dunlop) keen: sn cl up: ev ch 2f out: sn rdn and one pce appr last 4/5[1]

00 3 1 1/2 **Bluebelle Dancer (IRE)**[24] 4559 2-9-0 MartinDwyer 10 67
(W R Muir) in toch: hdwy to chse ldrs 1/2-way: rdn 2f out and kpt on same pce 9/2[2]

65 4 1 1/2 **Foxxy**[137] 1248 2-8-11 AndrewMullen(3) 16 63
(K A Ryan) towards rr: gd hdwy on outer over 2f out: rdn wl over 1f out: kpt on: nrst fin 50/1

5 5 1 **Solwind (USA)**[37] 4151 2-9-0 MickyFenton 6 60
(B Smart) in tch: hdwy to chse ldrs 1/2-way: rdn along 2f out: edgd lft and one pce appr last 16/1

0006 6 shd **Ruthles Philly**[22] 4630 2-9-0 42 TonyCulhane 3 59
(D W Barker) hld up in rr: stdy hdwy on outer over 2f out: rdn wl over 1f out: kpt on ins last: nrst fin 100/1

5 7 1 1/4 **Bond Casino**[25] 4510 2-9-0 GylesParkin 4 55
(G R Oldroyd) chsd ldrs: rdn along and outpcd 1/2-way: kpt on u.p appr last 66/1

60 8 3 **Olgarena (IRE)**[15] 4830 2-9-0 DavidAllan 7 46
(T D Easterby) prom: rdn along 2f out: grad wknd appr last 66/1

0 9 1 **Cranworth Blaze**[25] 4510 2-9-0 RoystonFfrench 15 43
(T J Etherington) towards rr: hdwy over 2f out: sn rdn and no imp 100/1

10 shd **Lilac Moon (GER)** 2-9-0 PaulHanagan 13 43
(Mrs A Duffield) towards rr: effrt over 2f out: sn rdn: hung lft and no hdwy 50/1

3 11 1/2 **Kilcusnin Queen (IRE)**[22] 4630 2-9-0 DeanMcKeown 8 42
(Adrian Sexton, Ire) prom: rdn along 1/2-way: wknd over 2f out 22/1

12 nk **Two Dreamers** 2-9-0 DarryllHolland 2 41
(A Crook) hmpd after s: a towards rr 100/1

00 13 1 1/4 **Amaretto Venture**[29] 4400 2-9-0 GrahamGibbons 1 37
(J J Quinn) in tch: rdn along 1/2-way: sn wknd 100/1

223 **14** *13* **My Mirasol**[127] 1499 2-9-0 73 .... NCallan 12 —
(K A Ryan) *chsd ldrs: rdn along 1/2-way: sn wknd* **12/1**

P **Lady Rocksam** 2-9-0 .... PaulMulrennan 11 —
(G M Moore) *s.i.s: a bhd: p.u and dismntd over 1f out* **100/1**

1m 11.03s (-0.67) **Going Correction** -0.20s/f (Firm) **15** Ran SP% **115.3**
Speed ratings (Par 92):96,94,92,90,88 88,86,82,81,81 80,80,78,61,—
CSF £12.76 TOTE £6.70: £1.90, £1.10, £1.50; EX 15.50.

Owner Duke Of Roxburghe **Bred** Floors Farming And London Thoroughbred Services Lt **Trained** Middleham Moor, N Yorks

FOCUS

Ordinary maiden form judged by the performance of the sixth, but the race should produce winners.

NOTEBOOK

Carillon(IRE), a staying-on second over seven furlongs at Catterick last time, is bred to appreciate trips upwards of a mile so the drop back in distance did not look a wise move, but she was ridden positively and galloped the opposition into the ground. The step back up in trip can only improve her and she looks one to keep on side with nurseries in mind. (op 7-1)

Emaara, who shaped well in just an average maiden for the course on her debut at Newmarket, is another going to need further in time and she was simply unable to quicken. She has shown more than enough to suggest she can find a maiden, but any success she gains is likely to come at seven furlongs and upwards. (op 4-6)

Bluebelle Dancer(IRE) has got better with each run and this big, tall daughter of Danehill Dancer looks certain to improve for a step up in trip. She can find a maiden before moving into handicaps. (op 13-2)

Foxxy does not do a great deal for the form having finished only fifth in a claimer last time, but it is possible she improved for the extra distance here and she can now contest handicaps. (tchd 66-1)

Solwind(USA) did not improve as much as expected on her initial effort, but she was going on close home and is another likely type for nurseries, once qualified after one more run.

5238 JOHN GARBUTT RACEGOERS CLUB NURSERY 5f

2:40 (2:41) (Class 6) (0-65,65) 2-Y-O **£3,238** (£963; £481; £240) **Stalls** Centre

Form RPR

6005 **1** **Back In The Red (IRE)**[7] 5065 2-8-12 **56** .... NCallan 9 62
(M Wellings) *midfield: hdwy to ld appr fnl f: edgd rt ins last: rdn out* **8/1**

5424 **2** *1 1/4* **Mazin Lady**[7] 5065 2-9-7 **65** .... GrahamGibbons 3 67
(Miss J A Camacho) *s.i.s and swtchd rt s: hld up: hdwy over 1f out: chsd wnr ins fnl f: r.o* **5/1**[1]

5064 **3** *1 1/4* **The Italian Job**[41] 4017 2-9-2 **60** .... DavidAllan 8 57
(T D Easterby) *cl up: drvn over 2f out: kpt on u.p fnl f* **14/1**

6020 **4** *1/2* **Only A Grand**[25] 4509 2-8-13 **57** ....(b) RoystonFfrench 5 52
(R Bastiman) *w ldrs: drvn and wandered over 1f out: no ex ins fnl f* **25/1**

5560 **5** *1 1/2* **The Brat**[24] 4545 2-8-0 **47** ....(v[1]) AndrewMullen[(3)] 7 37
(James Moffatt) *mde most tl hdd and no ex appr fnl f* **50/1**

0532 **6** *hd* **Emefdream**[31] 4321 2-9-4 **62** .... CatherineGannon 15 51
(K A Ryan) *prom: drvn 1/2-way: one pce over 1f out* **15/2**[3]

0144 **7** *shd* **Minimum Fuss (IRE)**[13] 4910 2-8-1 **52** ....(b) JamieHamblett[(7)] 14 41
(M C Chapman) *s.s: bhd tl hdwy over 1f out: hung lft: kpt on fnl f: no imp* **25/1**

2532 **8** *1 3/4* **Caj (IRE)**[11] 4950 2-8-12 **56** .... DarryllHolland 11 38
(M Quinn) *hld up midfield: drvn over 2f out: no imp over 1f out* **7/1**[2]

1500 **9** *1/2* **Emma Told Lies**[42] 3997 2-8-11 **55** .... DaleGibson 6 36
(M W Easterby) *sn outpcd: hdwy and edgd lft over 1f out: nvr rchd ldrs* **14/1**

6004 **10** *hd* **First Valentini**[13] 4913 2-9-0 **58** ....(t) SilvestreDeSousa 16 38
(N Bycroft) *midfield: drvn 1/2-way: outpcd wl over 1f out* **14/1**

040 **11** *1* **Blakeshall Rose**[38] 4109 2-8-8 **52** .... DeanMcKeown 4 28
(A J Chamberlain) *midfield: pushed along over 2f out: sn outpcd* **16/1**

650 **12** *3/4* **My Two Girls (IRE)**[28] 4421 2-9-4 **62** .... MickyFenton 13 36
(P T Midgley) *sn outpcd: hung lft 1/2-way: n.d* **33/1**

550 **13** *3/4* **Hidden Ace (IRE)**[14] 4887 2-8-11 **55** ....(b) PaulMulrennan 2 26
(M W Easterby) *w ldrs tl hung lft and wknd wl over 1f out* **25/1**

2414 **14** *nk* **Bowl Em Over**[53] 3677 2-8-7 **54** ....(p) GregFairley[(3)] 17 24
(M E Sowersby) *prom: drvn 1/2-way: wknd wl over 1f out* **20/1**

320 **15** *1/2* **La Esperanza**[66] 3246 2-8-11 **55** .... PhillipMakin 18 23
(T D Barron) *s.i.s: sn outpcd: no ch fr 1/2-way* **16/1**

5626 **16** *1 1/4* **Almora Guru**[25] 4519 2-9-3 **61** .... MartinDwyer 12 25
(W M Brisbourne) *prom to 1/2-way: sn rdn and wknd* **16/1**

0440 **17** *1* **Suntan Lady (IRE)**[18] 4727 2-8-11 **55** .... TonyCulhane 1 15
(Miss V Haigh) *in tch tl wknd fr 2f out* **33/1**

632 **18** *3/4* **Birdie Birdie**[14] 4887 2-8-11 **55** .... PaulHanagan 10 12
(R A Fahey) *missed break: nvr on terms* **7/1**[2]

58.28 secs (-0.42) **Going Correction** -0.20s/f (Firm) **18** Ran SP% **126.3**
Speed ratings (Par 93):95,93,91,90,87 87,87,84,83,83 81,80,79,78,78 76,74,73
CSF £44.69 CT £574.80 TOTE £6.40: £1.10, £2.30, £3.50, £7.70; EX 61.70.

Owner Mrs Ruth M Serrell **Bred** Mrs Rachanee Butler **Trained** Six Ashes, Shropshire

FOCUS

A modest nursery, but it should produce the occasional winner at a similar level.

NOTEBOOK

Back In The Red(IRE), who shaped well in a fair nursery at Warwick last time, finished one place behind Mazin Lady on that occasion, but she lost ground by hanging that day and it was no surprise to see her reverse the form over this slightly shorter trip. Evidently progressive, she won with a bit to spare and may be capable of defying a rise. Official explanation: trainer had no explanation for the improved form shown other than that the colt had previously run very green (op 9-1)

Mazin Lady has shown more than enough to suggest she can win races, but the drop back to five furlongs did her no favours and she was unable to confirm Warwick form with the winner over this slightly shorter trip, getting going too late. (op 11-2)

The Italian Job has not really progressed and, although running well here, she is likely to remain vulnerable until dropped in grade.

Only A Grand, dropping back from seven furlongs, has generally looked an improved performer in the blinkers, but it was disappointing he failed to see his race out as strongly as the principals. (tchd 28-1)

The Brat, another dropping back two furlongs in trip, showed plenty of zip in the first-time visor, but he was another who was unable to come home as strongly as some, and perhaps a tighter track would suit.

Emefdream went close at Haydock last time, but he was disappointing here off a 2lb higher mark and looks ready for a step up in trip. (op 8-1)

My Two Girls(IRE) Official explanation: jockey said filly lost its action

Birdie Birdie Official explanation: jockey said filly hung left and the bit slipped through its mouth

5239 EUROPEAN BREEDERS FUND - DOUBLE TRIGGER MAIDEN STKS (FOR THE DOUBLE TRIGGER TROPHY) 1m 1f

3:10 (3:10) (Class 5) 2-Y-O **£3,562** (£1,059; £529; £264) **Stalls** Low

Form RPR

5 **1** **Zoom One**[14] 4867 2-9-3 .... MartinDwyer 3 61
(M P Tregoning) *wnt rt s: led 3f: cl up: swtchd rt and pushed along over 2f out: sn rdn and edgd lft: drvn and kpt on to ld ins last* **2/1**[1]

0063 **2** *3/4* **Hair Of The Dog**[18] 4724 2-9-3 55 .... PaulHanagan 7 60
(J G Given) *trckd ldrs: effrt over 2f out: swtchd rt and rdn over 1f out. drvn and ev ch ins last: no ex last 100 yds* **33/1**

03 **3** *1* **Monsieur Dumas (IRE)**[18] 4732 2-9-3 .... MickyFenton 1 58
(T P Tate) *hmpd and switcehd rt sn after s: trckd ldrs: hdwy over 3f out: rdn to ld over 1f out: drvn and hdd ins last: one pce* **14/1**

2363 **4** *3 1/2* **Centenary (IRE)**[14] 4882 2-9-3 72 .... KerrinMcEvoy 8 51
(J S Wainwright) *prom: effrt to ld over 3f out: snr idden along: drvn and hdd over 1f out: sn wknd* **4/1**[3]

5 *nk* **The Quantum Kid** 2-9-3 .... PaulMulrennan 9 50
(T J Etherington) *s.i.s and bhd: pushed along 1/2-way: hdwy 3f out: sn rdn and styd on appr last: nrst fin* **33/1**

6 *nk* **Grand Dream (IRE)** 2-9-3 .... KDarley 6 49
(M Johnston) *cl up: led after 3f: rdn along 2f out: sn drvn and wknd* **9/4**[2]

3 **7** *8* **Jardines Bazaar**[14] 4880 2-9-3 .... DavidAllan 4 33
(T D Easterby) *hmpd s and bhd: hdwy over 4f out: rdn along 3f out: sn btn* **7/1**

U2 **8** *8* **Watch Out**[25] 4520 2-8-10 .... AdeleRothery[(7)] 2 17
(M W Easterby) *a towards rr* **50/1**

1m 54.2s (0.80) **Going Correction** -0.225s/f (Firm) **8** Ran SP% **111.1**
Speed ratings (Par 95):87,86,85,82,82 81,74,67
CSF £65.17 TOTE £3.00: £1.10, £4.20, £3.40; EX 54.90.

Owner Sheikh Ahmed Al Maktoum **Bred** Darley **Trained** Lambourn, Berks

FOCUS

This turned out to be a most disappointing result with the 55-rated runner-up pushing the winner all the way and well-bred newcomer Grand Dream dropping away disappointingly.

NOTEBOOK

Zoom One, who shaped with plenty of promise when third in a decent Chepstow maiden on his debut, looked to hold obvious claims in what was an uncompetitive race and he certainly looked the best of those with experience. Never too far off the gallop, he had to be switched to the outside to come with his run, but picked up well and stayed on too strongly for the 55-rated runner-up. The form does not look good, especially with the Johnston newcomer disappointing, but he remains open to further improvement and should stay ten furlongs this year. (op 5-2)

Hair Of The Dog has been shaping as though this trip would suit, but his form looked nowhere near good enough to trouble the principals, so the fact he went so close underlines the strength of the form. He should have nothing taken away from him, though, and winning races back down in selling level should not prove a problem. (op 40-1)

Monsieur Dumas(IRE) has improved as he has been stepped up in trip and this was another solid effort. He can now contest handicaps and should do well in that sphere. (op 12-1)

Centenary(IRE), who has been running well, again looked set to be close up at the finish, but he failed to run to form and it is possible he failed to stay on this first try beyond a mile. (op 7-2)

The Quantum Kid, who cost 50,000gns, ran a really promising race, keeping on well close home having got behind and run green early. He will find easier opportunities. (op 25-1)

Grand Dream(IRE), whose stable has won this race named after their former top-class stayer Double Trigger twice in recent years, looked a potential cut above his rivals on this racecourse debut, and the son of Grand Lodge appeared certain to see out the trip. In addition, the fact he held an entry in a novice stakes later in the week, and the Derby further down the line, was obviously encouraging. However, having taken it up after three furlongs, he began to look in trouble three furlongs out and in the end faded out of it. Obviously thought capable of better, he deserves another chance to show what he is capable of. (tchd 2-1)

5240 SEE MORE ON RACING UK (S) H'CAP 1m 2f

3:40 (3:41) (Class 6) (0-55,54) 3-5-Y-O **£2,730** (£806; £403) **Stalls** Low

Form RPR

6164 **1** **Roman History (IRE)**[11] 4943 3-8-7 **50** ....(p) SilvestreDeSousa 4 58
(Miss Tracy Waggott) *prom: led over 3f out: hrd pressed 1f out: hld on gamely* **15/2**[3]

3631 **2** *nk* **Agilete**[9] 5033 4-9-1 **51** .... DeanMcKeown 16 58
(J Pearce) *s.i.s: hld up: smooth hdwy 3f out: shkn up to chal 1f out: sn rdn: kpt on towards fin* **11/2**[1]

0005 **3** *2 1/2* **Inchdhuaig (IRE)**[58] 3538 3-8-4 **52** .... LeanneKershaw[(5)] 15 54
(P C Haslam) *keen in midfield: effrt 3f out: kpt on fr over 1f out: nt rch first two* **14/1**

6556 **4** *nk* **Peters Delite**[9] 5035 4-8-10 **46** .... PaulHanagan 9 48
(R A Fahey) *midfield: effrt 3f out: edgd lft over 1f out: kpt on same pce* **8/1**

1663 **5** *nk* **Ming Vase**[13] 4909 4-8-10 **46** .... MickyFenton 11 47
(P T Midgley) *hld up towards rr: effrt 3f out: hung lft: kpt on fnl f: nrst fin* **7/1**[2]

046 **6** *shd* **Sweet Lavinia**[26] 4471 3-8-5 **48** .... KerrinMcEvoy 7 49
(J D Bethell) *bhd: outpcd 4f out: kpt on fr 2f out: nrst fin* **20/1**

6304 **7** *1 1/2* **Boucheen**[15] 4835 3-7-9 **45** oh2 .... WilliamBuick[(7)] 8 43
(Ms Deborah J Evans) *led to over 3f out: rallied: wknd over 1f out* **33/1**

5644 **8** *nk* **Red Chairman**[7] 5060 4-9-4 **54** .... CatherineGannon 12 51
(R Johnson) *stdd s: hld up: effrt outside over 2f out: kpt on fnl f: n.d* **10/1**

0034 **9** *3/4* **Gypsy Royal (IRE)**[13] 4909 4-8-9 **45** oh5 .... DavidAllan 10 41
(G Woodward) *towards rr: rdn 3f out: nvr rchd ldrs* **12/1**

0000 **10** *shd* **World At My Feet**[11] 4944 4-8-2 **45** ....(t) SuzzanneFrance[(7)] 14 41
(N Bycroft) *hld up: pushed along 3f out: n.d* **25/1**

1000 **11** *1 3/4* **Thornaby Green**[7] 5064 5-8-11 **47** .... PhillipMakin 2 39
(T D Barron) *prom tl rdn and wknd over 1f out* **8/1**

3466 **12** *3/4* **Rudaki**[13] 4909 4-9-0 **50** .... RoystonFfrench 1 41
(M E Sowersby) *midfield: drvn over 3f out: sn btn* **11/1**

005 **13** *3/4* **Jiminor Mack**[30] 4382 3-8-4 **50** .... GregFairley[(3)] 3 40
(W J H Ratcliffe) *towards rr: rdn after 4f: nvr on terms* **50/1**

0001 **14** *3 1/2* **Lewis Lloyd (IRE)**[16] 4195 3-8-10 **53** .... NCallan 13 36
(I A Wood) *chsd ldrs tl wknd over 2f out* **11/1**

0-41 **15** *10* **Government (IRE)**[167] 783 5-8-13 **49** .... DarryllHolland 6 13
(M C Chapman) *plld hrd: cl up tl wknd over 3f out* **33/1**

5500 **16** *5* **Chrisjen**[15] 4835 4-8-12 **48** .... PaulMulrennan 17 2
(M W Easterby) *sn cl up: rdn and wknd over 3f out: t.o* **33/1**

2m 4.38s (-2.42) **Going Correction** -0.225s/f (Firm)
WFA 3 from 4yo+ 7lb **16** Ran SP% **121.4**
Speed ratings (Par 101):100,99,97,97,97 97,96,95,95,95 93,93,92,89,81 77
CSF £44.41 CT £579.55 TOTE £11.10: £2.60, £1.40, £5.30, £2.60; EX 60.10.There was no bid for the winner.

Owner B Douglas **Bred** Lodge Park Stud **Trained** Spennymoor, Co Durham

■ Stewards' Enquiry : Dean McKeown one-day ban: used whip with excessive frequency without giving gelding time to respond (Sep 22)

FOCUS
Moderate stuff but sound enough form for the level.
Gypsy Royal(IRE) Official explanation: trainer said filly lost a front shoe
Government(IRE) Official explanation: jockey said gelding ran too free
Chrisjen Official explanation: jockey said filly hung right

5241 REDCAR CONFERENCE CENTRE MAIDEN STKS (DIV I) — 7f

4:10 (4:10) (Class 5) 3-Y-0+ **£2,590** (£770; £385; £192) **Stalls** Centre

Form	Pos	Dist	Horse	Jockey	RPR
3240	**1**		**Spinning**[7] [5060] 3-9-3 66	PhillipMakin 1	65
			(T D Barron) *cl up: led 1/2-way: rdn clr wl over 1f out: styd on*	**2/1**[2]	
3-64	**2**	*3 1/2*	**Miss Thailand**[24] [4563] 3-8-12 80	DarryllHolland 7	51
			(G Wragg) *in tch: pushed along 1/2-way: rdn to chse wnr wl over 1f out: sn drvn and no imp*	**1/2**[1]	
0	**3**	*1 1/2*	**Bella Marie**[23] [4613] 3-8-9	AndrewMullen(3) 10	47
			(L R James) *midfield: hdwy 3f out: rdn to chse ldrs 2f out: sn drvn and one pce*	**100/1**	
6066	**4**	*11*	**Prince Duval (IRE)**[40] [4050] 3-8-10 48	KellyHarrison(7) 4	24
			(D Carroll) *chsd ldrs: rdn along and outpcd 3f out: n.d after*	**20/1**[3]	
-000	**5**	*nk*	**Jabraan (USA)**[21] [4652] 4-9-7 40	PaulQuinn 2	25
			(D W Chapman) *sn chsng ldrs: rdn along 3f out: sn wknd*	**66/1**	
-000	**6**	*3/4*	**Ochil Hills Dancer (IRE)**[21] [4655] 4-9-0 40 ow3(b)	DeclanMcGann(5) 11	21
			(A Crook) *midfield: hdwy on outer to chse ldrs 3f out: sn rdn and wknd over 2f out*	**100/1**	
000/	**7**	*2*	**Distinctlythebest**[734] [5366] 6-9-4 25	GregFairley(3) 8	18
			(F Watson) *led to 1/2-way: sn rdn along and wknd*	**150/1**	
00	**8**	*hd*	**Westcourt Phoenix**[35] [4195] 3-8-12	(b[1]) PaulMulrennan 3	10
			(M W Easterby) *outpcd and bhd fr 1/2-way*	**100/1**	
00-0	**9**	*3*	**Dominello**[23] [4611] 3-9-3 30	PaulHanagan 9	8
			(R A Fahey) *cl up: rdn along 1/2-way: sn wknd*	**50/1**	

1m 23.17s (-1.73) **Going Correction** -0.20s/f (Firm)
WFA 3 from 4yo+ 4lb — **9** Ran SP% **111.8**
Speed ratings (Par 103):101,97,95,82,82 81,79,79,75
CSF £3.12 TOTE £3.30: £1.10, £1.02, £7.90; EX 5.20.
Owner Mrs J Hazell **Bred** Cheveley Park Stud **Trained** Maunby, N Yorks

FOCUS
A weak maiden that saw hot favourite Miss Thailand turned over.

5242 GO RACING AT BEVERLEY THIS WEDNESDAY H'CAP — 1m 6f 19y

4:40 (4:40) (Class 5) (0-70,70) 3-Y-0+ **£3,238** (£963; £481; £240) **Stalls** Low

Form	Pos	Dist	Horse	Jockey	RPR
-000	**1**		**Esprit De Corps**[226] [218] 4-9-1 **57**	SebSanders 14	69
			(Sir Mark Prescott) *cl up: led over 3f out: kpt on strly fnl f*	**15/2**[2]	
0501	**2**	*nk*	**Sa Nau**[18] [4734] 3-7-12 **51** oh2	SilvestreDeSousa 2	63
			(T Keddy) *midfield: pushed along 6f out: hdwy over 2f out: chsd wnr over 1f out: edgd lft: kpt on fnl f*	**10/1**	
5660	**3**	*4*	**Compton Eclaire (IRE)**[11] [4960] 6-8-10 **55**	(b) GregFairley(3) 15	61
			(B Ellison) *dwlt: hld up: hdwy on outside over 2f out: kpt on fnl f: nt rch first two*	**12/1**	
003	**4**	*1*	**Best Of The Lot (USA)**[17] [4764] 4-10-0 **70**	PaulHanagan 8	79+
			(R A Fahey) *hld up: nt clr run over 4f to 3f out: effrt whn nt clr run over 1f out to ent fnl f: kpt on wl: nrst fin*	**16/1**	
-442	**5**	*nk*	**Planters Punch (IRE)**[12] [4925] 5-9-3 **59**	DavidAllan 10	63
			(G M Moore) *midfield: effrt 3f out: no imp over 1f out*	**14/1**	
0544	**6**	*1 1/2*	**Sun King**[11] [4960] 9-8-9 **51** oh1	(t) KerrinMcEvoy 13	53
			(K G Reveley) *hld up: pushed along 3f out: kpt on fnl f: nvr rchd ldrs*	**17/2**	
6250	**7**	*3*	**Jumeirah Scarer**[22] [4632] 5-9-3 **59**	NCallan 12	57
			(K A Ryan) *keen: cl up: effrt and edgd rt 2f out: sn outpcd*	**14/1**	
4635	**8**	*1/2*	**Let It Be**[11] [4960] 5-9-3 **59**	TonyCulhane 1	56
			(K G Reveley) *in tch on ins tl outpcd fr 2f out*	**8/1**[3]	
2011	**9**	*1 3/4*	**Vice Admiral**[7] [5061] 3-8-13 **66** 6ex	PaulMulrennan 3	61
			(M W Easterby) *led to over 3f out: wknd over 1f out*	**4/1**[1]	
4002	**10**	*3*	**Wrenlane**[13] [4914] 5-8-13 **55**	GrahamGibbons 4	46
			(J J Quinn) *keen: prom: effrt over 3f out: outpcd whn n.m.r wl over 1f out*	**10/1**	
2245	**11**	*1*	**Valeureux**[135] [1308] 8-8-10 **52**	RoystonFfrench 7	41
			(J Hetherton) *hld up: rdn over 3f out: outpcd whn blkd 2f out*	**66/1**	
4632	**12**	*1 1/2*	**Alisdanza**[11] [4954] 4-8-9 **51** oh5	DaleGibson 5	38
			(G A Swinbank) *keen: chsd ldrs tl wknd over 3f out*	**16/1**	
0-50	**13**	*2 1/2*	**Give It Time**[11] [4973] 3-8-10 **63**	KDarley 6	47
			(J G Given) *hld up: pushed along over 3f out: sn btn*	**20/1**	
2504	**14**	*5*	**Top Spec (IRE)**[12] [4924] 5-9-12 **68**	DarryllHolland 9	45
			(J Pearce) *dwlt: a bhd*	**9/1**	
0204	**15**	*6*	**Best Port (IRE)**[25] [4506] 10-8-9 **51** oh1	(p) MickyFenton 11	19
			(J Parkes) *hld up: rdn over 4f out: nvr on terms*	**33/1**	

2m 59.81s (-5.21) **Going Correction** -0.225s/f (Firm) course record
WFA 3 from 4yo+ 11lb — **15** Ran SP% **123.6**
Speed ratings (Par 103):105,104,102,101,101 100,99,98,97,96 95,94,93,90,87
CSF £80.84 CT £910.21 TOTE £8.30: £4.40, £4.60, £4.50; EX 132.50.
Owner W E Sturt - Osborne House II **Bred** Miss K Rausing **Trained** Newmarket, Suffolk
■ Stewards' Enquiry : Seb Sanders one-day ban: used whip with excessive frequency (Sep 22)
Silvestre De Sousa seven-day ban: used whip with excessive frequency without giving gelding time to respond (Sep 22-28)

FOCUS
A modest handicap won by unexposed handicap debutant Esprit De Corps.
Esprit De Corps Official explanation: trainer's rep had no explanation for the improved form shown other than that the gelding was having its first run on turf
Valeureux Official explanation: jockey said gelding suffered interference and lost its action

5243 REDCARRACING.CO.UK APPRENTICE H'CAP — 6f

5:10 (5:10) (Class 5) (0-70,67) 3-Y-0+ **£3,238** (£963; £481; £240) **Stalls** Centre

Form	Pos	Dist	Horse	Jockey	RPR
3061	**1**		**Elkhorn**[18] [4735] 4-8-7 **56**	(b) PatrickHills(3) 16	72+
			(Miss J A Camacho) *in tch: hdwy over 2f out: rdn to ld ent last: sn clr*	**11/4**[1]	
5053	**2**	*3 1/2*	**H Harrison (IRE)**[6] [5081] 6-9-6 **66**	PJMcDonald 9	71
			(I W McInnes) *trckd ldrs: hdwy to chse clr ldr 2f out: sn rdn and kpt on same pce ent last*	**5/1**[2]	
2025	**3**	*3/4*	**Favouring (IRE)**[48] [3827] 4-8-2 **55**	(v) WilliamBuick(7) 1	58
			(M C Chapman) *led: clr after 2f: rdn 2f out: hdd ent last: kpt on same pce*	**16/1**	
5130	**4**	*1*	**Rancho Cucamonga (IRE)**[9] [5032] 4-8-7 **56**	(b) NeilBrown(3) 7	56
			(T D Barron) *s.i.s and bhd: hdwy 2f out: sn rdn and kpt on ins last: nrst fin*	**8/1**[3]	
0030	**5**	*shd*	**Quantica (IRE)**[29] [4401] 7-8-7 **53** oh8	StephanieHollinshead 11	52
			(N Tinkler) *in tch: hdwy 2f out: sn rdn and kpty on ins last: nrst fin*	**20/1**	
0000	**6**	*1*	**Amanda's Lad (IRE)**[34] [4232] 6-8-2 **53** oh6	MCGeran(5) 10	49
			(M C Chapman) *chsd ldr: rdn along 1/2-way: wknd wl over 1f out*	**33/1**	
6400	**7**	*1*	**Borodinsky**[27] [4456] 5-8-4 **53** oh7	JamieHamblett(3) 12	46
			(R E Barr) *towards rr: hdwy and rdn alonf wl over 2f out: styd on ins last: nrst fin*	**16/1**	
2600	**8**	*hd*	**Beverley Beau**[25] [4523] 4-8-7 **53** oh7	KristinStubbs 8	46
			(Mrs L Stubbs) *chsd ldrs: rdn 2f out: grad wknd*	**33/1**	
5520	**9**	*1*	**Greek Secret**[19] [4717] 3-9-5 **67**	DeclanMcGann 18	57
			(J O'Reilly) *towards rr: effrt and rdn along over 2f out: kpt on u.p appr last*	**14/1**	
-000	**10**	*shd*	**Sparkwell**[11] [4957] 4-9-7 **67**	VictoriaBehan 3	57
			(D W Barker) *in tch on outer: hdwy to chse ldrs 2f out: sn rdn: edgd lft and wknd over 1f out*	**9/1**	
064	**11**	*nk*	**Bond Free Spirit (IRE)**[37] [4155] 3-8-2 **55**	NSLawes(5) 14	44
			(G R Oldroyd) *dwlt: a towards rr*	**28/1**	
054	**12**	*shd*	**Teyaar**[31] [4324] 10-8-2 **53** oh8	PatrickDonaghy(5) 13	41
			(M Wellings) *chsd ldrs: rdn along over 2f out: sn wknd*	**33/1**	
1300	**13**	*shd*	**Bodden Bay**[35] [4198] 4-8-9 **55**	KellyHarrison 5	43
			(D Carroll) *chsd ldrs: rdn 2f out: sn: drvn: hung lft and wknd over 1f out*	**33/1**	
0650	**14**	*shd*	**Paddywack (IRE)**[11] [4957] 9-8-7 **56**	(b) DanielleMcCreery(3) 17	44
			(D W Chapman) *s.i.s and bhd: hdwy on outer over 2f out: sn rdn and wknd over 1f out*	**12/1**	
0303	**15**	*hd*	**Primarily**[9] [5023] 4-8-2 **53** oh3	(v) WilliamCarson(5) 4	40
			(A Berry) *chsd ldrs: rdn along 1/2-way: sn wknd*	**20/1**	
60-0	**16**	*2*	**High Meadow Girl**[24] [4567] 3-9-3 **65**	KevinGhunowa 6	46
			(J D Bethell) *midfield: rdn along 1/2-way: sn wknd*	**50/1**	
100	**17**	*hd*	**Frimley's Matterry**[11] [4957] 6-8-7 **53** oh3	LeanneKershaw 2	34
			(R E Barr) *midfield: rdn along on outer 1/2-way: sn wknd*	**20/1**	

1m 10.03s (-1.67) **Going Correction** -0.20s/f (Firm)
WFA 3 from 4yo+ 2lb — **17** Ran SP% **122.0**
Speed ratings (Par 103):103,98,97,96,95 94,93,92,91,91 91,90,90,90,90 87,87
CSF £12.54 CT £198.96 TOTE £3.70: £1.10, £2.00, £3.50, £1.90; EX 19.40.
Owner Lee Bolingbroke & Partners VI **Bred** George Strawbridge **Trained** Norton, N Yorks

FOCUS
A moderate handicap won well by the progressive Elkhorn. The form looks sound.

5244 REDCAR CONFERENCE CENTRE MAIDEN STKS (DIV II) — 7f

5:40 (5:40) (Class 5) 3-Y-0+ **£2,590** (£770; £385; £192) **Stalls** Centre

Form	Pos	Dist	Horse	Jockey	RPR
	1		**Green Coast (IRE)** 3-9-3	KerrinMcEvoy 2	81+
			(Saeed Bin Suroor) *chsd ldrs: led on bit over 2f out: sn clr: v easily*	**1/5**[1]	
0-50	**2**	*5*	**Lottie**[26] [4467] 5-9-2 38	(p) DavidAllan 7	44
			(G Woodward) *cl up: drvn 3f out: chsd wnr over 1f out: kpt on: no imp*	**22/1**[3]	
-020	**3**	*1*	**Choreographic (IRE)**[7] [5060] 4-9-7 40	PaulHanagan 10	46
			(R A Fahey) *hld up: effrt over 2f out: no imp over 1f out*	**8/1**[2]	
0066	**4**	*nk*	**Virginia Plain**[6] [5092] 3-8-12 41	(b) DaleGibson 3	39
			(Miss Diana Weeden) *bhd: hdwy 2f out: kpt on fnl f: no imp*	**100/1**	
3562	**5**	*1 1/4*	**Coronation Flight**[14] [4881] 3-8-12 43	DeanMcKeown 9	35
			(F P Murtagh) *hld up: drvn over 2f out: nvr rchd ldrs*	**25/1**	
0	**6**	*hd*	**Boppys Dancer**[23] [4613] 3-9-3	MickyFenton 4	40
			(P T Midgley) *dwlt: bhd: rdn 3f out: sme late hdwy: nt pce to chal*	**100/1**	
-050	**7**	*1 1/4*	**Cabourg (IRE)**[109] [1963] 3-9-3 70	RoystonFfrench 6	37
			(R Bastiman) *prom tl wknd over 2f out*	**8/1**[2]	
-360	**8**	*shd*	**Distant Vision (IRE)**[33] [4255] 3-8-7 38	MarkLawson(5) 1	31
			(A Berry) *w ldrs tl wknd over 2f out*	**100/1**	
0003	**9**	*1 1/2*	**Millbrook Star (IRE)**[45] [3910] 3-8-10 41	(b) JamieHamblett(7) 5	32
			(M C Chapman) *mde most to over 2f out: sn btn*	**100/1**	
	10	*12*	**Slip Star** 3-8-12	PaulMulrennan 8	—
			(T J Etherington) *dwlt: midfield: struggling 3f out: sn btn*	**100/1**	

1m 24.09s (-0.81) **Going Correction** -0.20s/f (Firm)
WFA 3 from 4yo+ 4lb — **10** Ran SP% **118.7**
Speed ratings (Par 103):96,90,89,88,87 87,85,85,83,70
CSF £11.82 TOTE £1.30: £1.10, £3.20, £1.60; EX 9.50 Place 6 51.12, Place 5 £46.07.
Owner Godolphin **Bred** Hadi Al Tajir **Trained** Newmarket, Suffolk

FOCUS
A truly dire maiden that well-bred newcomer Green Coast could not help but win.
T/Jkpt: Not won. T/Plt: £102.10 to a £1 stake. Pool: £52,401.95. 374.45 winning tickets. T/Qpdt: £55.50 to a £1 stake. Pool: £3,563.40. 47.45 winning tickets. RY

[5031] WOLVERHAMPTON (A.W) (L-H)

Monday, September 11

OFFICIAL GOING: Standard
Wind: almost nil

5245 WOLVERHAMPTON RACECOURSE CONFERENCE CENTRE MEDIAN AUCTION MAIDEN STKS — 5f 20y(P)

2:30 (2:31) (Class 5) 2-Y-0 **£3,238** (£963; £481; £240) **Stalls** Low

Form	Pos	Dist	Horse	Jockey	RPR
42	**1**		**Final Dynasty**[6] [5076] 2-8-12	TedDurcan 10	71
			(Mrs G S Rees) *a.p: rdn to ld 1f out: rdn out*	**3/1**[2]	
5303	**2**	*1 1/2*	**Bookiesindex Boy**[42] [3994] 2-9-3 70	(b) RobertHavlin 9	71
			(J R Jenkins) *chsd ldrs: rdn and hung lft fr over 1f out: kpt on ins fnl f*	**9/1**	
32	**3**	*1 1/2*	**Mr Loire**[17] [4753] 2-9-0	RichardKingscote(3) 8	66
			(R Charlton) *w ldr: rdn and ev ch over 1f out: no ex ins fnl f*	**5/2**[1]	
	4	*1/2*	**Gleaming Spirit (IRE)** 2-9-3	JimmyFortune 5	64
			(A P Jarvis) *mde most: rdn and hdd 1f out: no ex ins fnl f*	**10/1**	
63	**5**	*nk*	**Equuleus Pictor**[42] [4002] 2-9-3	FrancisNorton 6	63
			(J L Spearing) *chsd ldrs: rdn over 3f out: outpcd 2f out: kpt on ins fnl f*	**3/1**[2]	
0365	**6**	*3*	**Mamora Reef**[11] [4969] 2-8-12 65	TomEaves 4	47
			(J R Weymes) *chsd ldrs: rdn 3f out: sn wknd*	**16/1**	
3	**7**	*nk*	**Spectacular Joy (IRE)**[80] [2806] 2-9-3	TPQueally 2	51
			(Mrs A Duffield) *outpcd: n.d*	**8/1**[3]	
6056	**8**	*4*	**Breckland Boy**[32] [4302] 2-9-3 58	(v[1]) JohnEgan 7	36
			(Mrs C A Dunnett) *a towards rr*	**50/1**	
	9	*1 1/2*	**High Five Society** 2-8-10	MSemple(7) 1	31
			(S R Bowring) *s.s: a in rr*	**66/1**	
0	**10**	*1/2*	**Let's Face It (IRE)**[11] [4969] 2-9-3	RobbieFitzpatrick 3	29
			(Peter Grayson) *chsd ldrs: rdn 3f out: sn wknd*	**33/1**	

62.58 secs (-0.24) **Going Correction** -0.175s/f (Stan) — **10** Ran SP% **121.1**
Speed ratings (Par 95):94,91,89,88,87 83,82,76,73,73
CSF £31.35 TOTE £4.30: £1.20, £3.70, £1.20; EX 30.90.

Owner TBN Racing **Bred** Capt J H Wilson **Trained** Sollom, Lancs

FOCUS

A moderate maiden in which the winner did not have to improve on her previous effort to score.

NOTEBOOK

Final Dynasty ◆ is learning all the time and built on the promise of her two previous outings. Well regarded, she is likely to take on something rather better from now on. (op 5-2)

Bookiesindex Boy came through to secure the runner-up spot despite proving to be an awkward ride. (op 10-1)

Mr Loire, back to the bare minimum, had no excuses on this switch to sand. (op 11-4 tchd 7-2)

Gleaming Spirit(IRE) is bred to require further so this was quite an encouraging debut. (op 11-1 tchd 12-1)

Equuleus Pictor, trying his luck on sand, gave the impression that he is ready to be stepped up in distance. (op 9-2)

5246 WOLVERHAMPTON-RACECOURSE.CO.UK H'CAP 5f 216y(P)

3:00 (3:01) (Class 5) (0-75,75) 3-Y-0+ **£3,238** (£963; £481; £240) **Stalls** Low

Form / RPR

0550 **1** **Mambazo**[15] 4846 4-8-9 **67**.......................(e) RichardKingscote(3) 13 76
(S C Williams) *stdd and lost pl sn after s: rdn and hdwy on wd outside wl over 1f out: r.o u.p to ld cl home* **25/1**

0040 **2** ½ **Figaro Flyer (IRE)**[11] 4957 3-9-0 **74**.......................DeanCorby(3) 5 82
(P Howling) *s.i.s: hld up towards rr: rdn over 2f out: hdwy whn swtchd rt 1f out: r.o wl u.p* **7/1**[3]

3504 **3** *nk* **Dvinsky (USA)**[11] 4957 5-8-11 **66**.......................RobbieFitzpatrick 7 73
(S R Bowring) *hld up in tch: rdn over 2f out: led wl ins fnl f: sn hdd: nt qckn* **9/1**

5215 **4** *1* **Kennington**[11] 4962 6-8-12 **70**.......................(b) JamesDoyle(3) 11 74
(Mrs C A Dunnett) *a.p: rdn 2f out: ev ch whn edgd lft over 1f out: nt qckn ins fnl f* **20/1**

3642 **5** *hd* **Gilded Cove**[14] 4894 6-8-6 **68**.......................RussellKennemore(7) 2 74+
(R Hollinshead) *bhd: rdn and hdwy whn nt clr run 1f out: n.m.r ins fnl f: r.o* **9/2**[2]

5260 **6** *hd* **Mandarin Spirit (IRE)**[6] 5096 6-8-10 **68**.......................(b) SaleemGolam(3) 6 71
(G C H Chung) *hld up in tch: nt clr run jst over 1f out: n.m.r ins fnl f: r.o* **10/1**

0000 **7** *shd* **Prince Tum Tum (USA)**[35] 4202 6-9-5 **74**.......................JimmyFortune 1 77
(D W Barker) *hld up towards rr: rdn and hdwy whn swtchd lft 1f out: kpt on towards fin* **4/1**[1]

0410 **8** ½ **Norcroft**[30] 4365 4-9-3 **72**.......................(p) JohnEgan 4 73
(Mrs C A Dunnett) *a.p: rdn to ld wl over 1f out: sn edgd rt: edgd lft ins fnl f: sn hdd: no ex* **10/1**

1244 **9** ½ **Ever Cheerful**[212] 376 5-8-13 **75**.......................DeanWilliams(7) 9 75
(G C H Chung) *sn led: rdn and hdd wl over 1f out: sn edgd rt: fdd towards fin* **20/1**

5005 **10** *nk* **Prince Cyrano**[17] 4771 7-9-1 **70**.......................TPQueally 8 71+
(W J Musson) *led early: chsd ldr: rdn 2f out: n.m.r jst over 1f out: eased whn btn cl home* **7/1**[3]

6225 **11** *3* **Rosein**[28] 4437 4-9-1 **70**.......................TedDurcan 3 70+
(Mrs G S Rees) *hld up in tch: rdn whn nt clr run jst over 1f out: eased whn btn ins fnl f* **9/1**

6004 **12** *hd* **Cool Sands (IRE)**[105] 2074 4-8-8 **63**.......................(v) FrancisNorton 12 52
(D Shaw) *swtchd lft sn after s: a bhd* **33/1**

1300 **13** *8* **Desert Light (IRE)**[108] 1981 5-8-5 **63**.......................(v) PatrickMathers(3) 10 28
(D Shaw) *hld up towards rr: rdn over 2f out: sn struggling* **50/1**

1m 14.33s (-1.48) **Going Correction** -0.175s/f (Stan)
WFA 3 from 4yo+ 2lb **13** Ran SP% **119.6**
Speed ratings (Par 103):102,101,100,99,99 99,98,98,97,97 93,92,82
CSF £182.36 CT £1780.82 TOTE £45.60: £12.40, £3.10, £2.60; EX 331.80.
Owner D G Burge **Bred** Barry Taylor **Trained** Newmarket, Suffolk

FOCUS

The pace was not strong and as a result there were plenty of traffic problems in this very competitive sprint.

5247 RINGSIDE SUITE 700 THEATRE STYLE H'CAP 1m 4f 50y(P)

3:30 (3:30) (Class 6) (0-65,65) 3-Y-0 **£2,730** (£806; £403) **Stalls** Low

Form / RPR

0301 **1** **Lolla's Spirit (IRE)**[19] 4697 3-8-6 **58**.......................AndrewElliott(5) 2 65
(M L W Bell) *chsd ldr: led over 3f out: rdn and edgd rt fr over 1f out: drvn out* **9/2**[2]

-000 **2** *nk* **Kick And Prance**[63] 3347 3-8-5 **52**.......................(t) StephenCarson 5 58
(J A Geake) *hld up in mid-div: hdwy over 3f out: rdn over 2f out: r.o ins fnl f: tk 2nd post* **33/1**

0651 **3** *shd* **Wise Choice**[24] 4556 3-8-4 **54**.......................JamesDoyle(3) 3 60
(N P Littmoden) *hld up in tch: rdn 4f out: chsd wnr 2f out: carried sltly rt fr over 1f out: r.o* **7/2**[1]

500 **4** *nk* **Selkirk Lady**[44] 3946 3-8-13 **60**.......................OscarUrbina 10 66
(W R Swinburn) *hld up and bhd: hdwy on outside over 2f out: sn rdn: edgd lft jst ins fnl f: r.o* **8/1**

3041 **5** *7* **Mighty Dancer (IRE)**[32] 4280 3-8-6 **56**.......................StephaneBreux(3) 9 50
(S Kirk) *t.k.h in mid-div: rdn and no real prog fnl 2f* **11/2**[3]

4056 **6** 2½ **Nassar (IRE)**[15] 4847 3-8-5 **55**.......................SaleemGolam(3) 1 45
(G Prodromou) *led: rdn and hdd over 3f out: wknd wl over 1f out* **14/1**

5603 **7** ½ **Princess Of Aeneas (IRE)**[21] 4651 3-8-11 **58**.......................(p) TomEaves 12 48
(I Semple) *hld up towards rr: hdwy over 3f out: sn rdn: wknd over 2f out* **11/1**

00-0 **8** ½ **Arcangela**[131] 1421 3-8-8 **55**.......................JamieMackay 7 44
(J G Given) *hld up in tch: rdn and wknd over 2f out* **20/1**

-000 **9** *shd* **Celtic Empire (IRE)**[14] 4884 3-8-6 **53** ow1.......................TPQueally 6 42
(Jedd O'Keeffe) *a towards rr* **28/1**

1145 **10** 1¼ **Joy In The Guild (IRE)**[17] 4758 3-8-7 **54**.......................LPKeniry 11 41
(W S Kittow) *t.k.h in rr: rdn over 2f out: no rspnse* **10/1**

4050 **11** *5* **Tora Petcha (IRE)**[9] 3303 3-9-4 **65**.......................JimmyFortune 4 44
(R Hollinshead) *sn prom: rdn over 4f out: wknd over 3f out* **13/2**

2m 40.27s (-2.15) **Going Correction** -0.175s/f (Stan) **11** Ran SP% **115.5**
Speed ratings (Par 99):100,99,99,99,94 93,92,92,92,91 88
CSF £146.48 CT £578.10 TOTE £4.30: £2.00, £16.30, £1.70; EX 299.20.
Owner Brett Palos **Bred** Barouche Stud Ireland Ltd **Trained** Newmarket, Suffolk

FOCUS

There was a good finish to this low-grade affair which developed into a four-way go. The race has been rated through the third.

5248 COME EVENING RACING THIS SATURDAY 16TH (S) STKS 1m 141y(P)

4:00 (4:00) (Class 6) 3-Y-0+ **£2,388** (£705; £352) **Stalls** Low

Form / RPR

5010 **1** **Zendaro**[30] 4350 4-9-9 60.......................JohnEgan 5 63
(W M Brisbourne) *hld up towards rr: hdwy over 3f out: rdn over 1f out: led ins fnl f: r.o* **9/2**[1]

3004 **2** ¾ **Second Reef**[14] 4881 4-9-4 54.......................AdrianTNicholls 9 56
(E J Alston) *hld up towards rr: hdwy whn nt clr run and swtchd rt over 1f out: sn rdn: r.o ins fnl f* **7/1**

-003 **3** ½ **Keon (IRE)**[9] 5035 4-8-11 48.......................RussellKennemore(7) 2 55
(R Hollinshead) *hld up in mid-div: hdwy over 3f out: rdn to ld wl over 1f out: hung rt and hdd ins fnl f: nt qckn* **9/1**

2060 **4** 1¼ **La Viola**[11] 4974 4-8-13 53.......................(p) FrancisNorton 13 47
(K R Burke) *hld up in mid-div: rdn and hdwy over 1f out: kpt on same pce fnl f* **6/1**[3]

1050 **5** ¾ **Wodhill Gold**[33] 4266 5-9-9 46.......................(v) DerekMcGaffin 11 56
(D Morris) *bhd: rdn over 3f out: hdwy on outside fnl f: nrst fin* **50/1**

004R **6** 1¾ **Hawridge Sensation**[7] 5054 4-9-4 49.......................(t) LPKeniry 8 47
(W S Kittow) *s.i.s: bhd: rdn and hdwy 2f out: wknd 1f out* **20/1**

1264 **7** *1* **Baby Barry**[10] 4984 9-9-9 54.......................RobbieFitzpatrick 7 50
(M J Attwater) *chsd ldrs: rdn over 2f out: wknd fnl f* **11/2**[2]

0560 **8** ½ **Mujelle**[7] 5054 3-8-5 46.......................(b) JamieJones(7) 3 44
(D K Ivory) *s.i.s and reminder: bhd: rdn 3f out: nvr nr ldrs* **20/1**

0000 **9** 1¼ **Littleton Aldor (IRE)**[4] 5127 6-9-4.......................AlanDaly 10 41
(W G M Turner) *led after 1f: rdn and hdd wl over 1f out: sn wknd* **66/1**

434 **10** *shd* **In Hope**[77] 2937 3-8-4 47.......................JamesDoyle(3) 6 36
(Ernst Oertel) *prom: rdn and cl up whn hmpd on ins 2f out: wknd over 1f out* **14/1**

050 **11** *hd* **Opera Writer (IRE)**[12] 4933 3-8-10 65.......................RobbieMills(7) 1 46
(J R Boyle) *t.k.h in mid-div: short-lived effrt on ins wl over 1f out* **11/2**[2]

-000 **12** 3½ **Turn Around**[18] 4735 6-9-4 50.......................JimmyFortune 4 33
(J Pearce) *s.s: a bhd* **14/1**

03 **13** *5* **Arabian Breeze**[19] 4708 3-8-7.......................TPQueally 12 18
(M Mullineaux) *led 1f: prom: rdn and ev ch over 2f out: wknd over 1f out* **20/1**

1m 50.45s (-1.31) **Going Correction** -0.175s/f (Stan)
WFA 3 from 4yo+ 6lb **13** Ran SP% **116.8**
Speed ratings (Par 101):98,97,96,95,95 93,92,92,91,91 90,87,83
CSF £32.24 TOTE £5.70: £2.10, £3.00, £4.20; EX 48.60.The winner was bought in for 5,000gns. Opera Writer (no.9) was claimed by R Hollinshead for £6,000.
Owner Zen Racing **Bred** Lady Juliet Tadgell **Trained** Great Ness, Shropshire

FOCUS

This may turn out to be a fair seller although the performances of the third and fifth would appear to limit the form.

Arabian Breeze Official explanation: jockey said filly had a breathing problem

5249 THE ZONGALERO RESTAURANT H'CAP 1m 141y(P)

4:30 (4:31) (Class 5) (0-75,75) 3-Y-0+ **£3,238** (£963; £481; £240) **Stalls** Low

Form / RPR

3522 **1** **United Nations**[18] 4733 5-9-8 **72**.......................TonyHamilton 11 81
(N Wilson) *s.i.s: hld up in mid-div: hdwy over 2f out: sn rdn: led wl ins fnl f: r.o* **9/1**

2323 **2** *nk* **Benandonner (USA)**[10] 4995 3-9-3 **73**.......................JimmyFortune 3 82
(E A L Dunlop) *led 1f: a.p: hrd rdn fnl f: r.o wl towards fin* **11/2**[2]

3510 **3** *nk* **Southport Star (IRE)**[19] 4689 3-9-5 **75**.......................OscarUrbina 9 83
(J R Fanshawe) *hld up towards rr: rdn and hdwy whn hung lft fr over 1f out: r.o ins fnl f* **10/1**

4222 **4** *1* **Joshua's Gold (IRE)**[31] 4325 5-9-3 **67**.......................(v) DanielTudhope 13 73
(D Carroll) *hld up in tch: led 2f out: sn rdn: hdd and no ex wl ins fnl f* **6/1**[3]

2440 **5** 1¾ **Bright Sun (IRE)**[35] 4203 5-9-4 **68**.......................(t) KimTinkler 6 70
(N Tinkler) *led after 1f: rdn and hdd 2f out: fdd towards fin* **12/1**

0603 **6** ¾ **Thunderwing (IRE)**[15] 4831 4-9-5 **69**.......................(p) FrancisNorton 1 70
(K R Burke) *hld up in tch: rdn wl over 1f out: no imp fnl f* **9/2**[1]

1023 **7** *nk* **Bijou Dan**[21] 4652 5-9-2 **71**.......................(b) DuranFentiman(5) 10 71
(W G Harrison) *hld up towards rr: hdwy on outside over 3f out: rdn over 2f out: wknd fnl f* **10/1**

0100 **8** *2* **Perez (IRE)**[13] 4911 4-9-3 **72**.......................(v) EmmettStack(5) 2 68
(W Storey) *hld up in mid-div: n.m.r 4f out: rdn over 2f out: wknd 1f out* **33/1**

0000 **9** ½ **Lord Of Dreams (IRE)**[14] 4871 4-9-0 **64**.......................FJohansson 5 59
(D W P Arbuthnot) *s.i.s: nvr nr ldrs* **20/1**

2/00 **10** *shd* **Cadeaux Des Mages**[24] 4575 6-9-6 **70**.......................JamieMackay 4 65
(J G Given) *hld up in mid-div: rdn over 3f out: no rspnse* **40/1**

400- **11** *5* **Benny The Bus**[304] 6315 4-9-3 **67**.......................(p) TedDurcan 7 51
(Mrs G S Rees) *prom: rdn over 2f out: wknd wl over 1f out* **20/1**

0036 **12** ¾ **Crail**[24] 4575 6-9-10 **74**.......................GeorgeBaker 8 57
(C F Wall) *a bhd* **11/2**[2]

1100 **13** 1¾ **Defi (IRE)**[11] 4953 4-9-6 **70**.......................(p) TomEaves 12 49
(I Semple) *a bhd* **16/1**

1m 49.58s (-2.18) **Going Correction** -0.175s/f (Stan)
WFA 3 from 4yo+ 6lb **13** Ran SP% **119.9**
Speed ratings (Par 103):102,101,101,100,99 98,98,96,95,95 91,90,89
CSF £55.48 CT £531.83 TOTE £12.80: £3.60, £1.80, £4.00; EX 49.10.
Owner Mrs Karan Ridley **Bred** Cyril Humphris **Trained** Upper Helmsley, N Yorks

FOCUS

A wide-open handicap and the form looks solid enough rated through the runner-up and fourth.

Thunderwing(IRE) Official explanation: jockey said gelding hung left

Lord Of Dreams(IRE) Official explanation: jockey said colt hung left

5250 STAY AT THE HOLIDAY INN WOLVERHAMPTON H'CAP 5f 20y(P)

5:00 (5:02) (Class 5) (0-70,68) 3-Y-0 **£3,238** (£963; £481; £240) **Stalls** Low

Form / RPR

053 **1** **City For Conquest (IRE)**[14] 4886 3-9-2 **66**.......................(v) FrancisNorton 9 74
(K R Burke) *chsd ldr: edgd sltly lft over 3f out: rdn to ld wl over 1f out: drvn out* **9/2**[2]

0240 **2** ¾ **Even Bolder**[24] 4562 3-8-12 **65**.......................StephaneBreux(3) 5 70
(S Kirk) *hld up and bhd: swtchd rt over 2f out: rdn and hdwy wl over 1f out: r.o ins fnl f: nt rch wnr* **15/2**

1430 **3** 1½ **Hotham**[22] 4636 3-9-4 **68**.......................TonyHamilton 4 68
(N Wilson) *chsd ldrs: n.m.r over 3f out: rdn over 2f out: r.o one pce fnl f* **6/1**[3]

-000 **4** 1½ **Bella Bertolini**[71] 3118 3-8-6 **56**.......................(p) JohnEgan 6 50
(T G Mills) *bhd: rdn over 3f out: hdwy on outside wl over 1f out: edgd lft ins fnl f: one pce* **14/1**

The Form Book, Raceform Ltd, Compton, RG20 6NL

0600 **5** ¾ **Fancy You (IRE)**[26] 4494 3-8-1 **54** oh12.....................(v) JamesDoyle(3) 10 46
(A W Carroll) *sn outpcd: r.o fnl f: nvr nrr* **12/1**

0035 **6** *nk* **Bel Cantor**[16] 4793 3-8-9 **62**.................................... RichardKingscote(3) 1 52
(W J H Ratcliffe) *chsd ldrs: hmpd and lost pl on ins over 3f out: hdwy 2f out: one pce fnl f* **9/4**[1]

3436 **7** ¾ **Crusader's Gold (FR)**[19] 4710 3-8-3 **56** oh5 ow2...(v) SaleemGolam(3) 3 44
(T D Easterby) *outpcd and bhd: sme hdwy on ins over 1f out: edgd lft ins fnl f: n.d* **7/1**

3000 **8** *1* **Ravish**[16] 4799 3-8-4 **54** oh4.......................................(bt) AdrianTNicholls 2 38
(W J Haggas) *s.v.s: wl bhd tl hdwy over 1f out: running on whn n.m.r on ins ins fnl f* **14/1**

0060 **9** *5* **Smart Cassie**[48] 3821 3-8-9 **62**.................................. PatrickMathers(3) 12 28
(D Shaw) *chsd ldrs: hung rt bnd over 2f out: rdn wl over 1f out: wkng whn edgd lft ent fnl f* **40/1**

0300 **10** *2 ½* **Compton Lad**[18] 4725 3-7-13 **54** oh8.......................... DuranFentiman(5) 7 11
(D A Nolan) *led: rdn and hdd wl over 1f out: sn wknd* **40/1**

4440 **11** *2* **Howards Prince**[25] 4523 3-8-6 **56** ow1.............................(p) TomEaves 8 6
(I Semple) *sn chsng ldrs: wkng whn hmpd over 2f out* **16/1**

0004 **12** *2 ½* **The Thrifty Bear**[14] 4886 3-8-4 **54**.................................(b) PaulEddery 11 —
(C W Fairhurst) *chsd ldrs tl rdn and wknd 2f out* **25/1**

61.99 secs (-0.83) **Going Correction** -0.175s/f (Stan) 12 Ran SP% **123.1**
Speed ratings (Par 101):99,97,95,93,91 91,90,88,80,76 73,69
CSF £39.38 CT £211.05 TOTE £4.70: £1.50, £2.50, £2.60; EX 33.60 Place 6 £218.17, Place 5 £134.89.
Owner F D C Partnership **Bred** Ballyhane Stud **Trained** Middleham Moor, N Yorks

FOCUS
A modest handicap rated through the runner-up to his All-Weather best.
T/Plt: £134.30 to a £1 stake. Pool: £49,626.65. 269.70 winning tickets. T/Qpdt: £19.20 to a £1 stake. Pool: £3,004.70. 115.40 winning tickets. KH

5251 - 5256a (Foreign Racing) - See Raceform Interactive

5122 CHANTILLY (R-H)
Monday, September 11

OFFICIAL GOING: Good

5257a PRIX D'AUMALE (GROUP 3) (FILLIES) 1m
1:45 (1:46) 2-Y-O **£27,586** (£11,034; £8,276; £5,517; £2,759)

RPR

1 **Poltava (FR)**[23] 4621 2-8-11 .... DBoeuf 4 104
(D Smaga, France) *made all, pushed along 1 1/2f out, hard ridden 100 yards out, ran on well* **42/10**[3]

2 *1* **Ikat (IRE)**[29] 4415 2-8-11 .... C-PLemaire 1 101
(D Sepulchre, France) *disputed 3rd, headway on inside to chase winner 1 1/2f out, stayed on* **47/10**

3 *2* **Sismix (IRE)**[20] 2-8-11 .... OPeslier 2 97
(C Laffon-Parias, France) *disputed 3rd on outside, 4th and effort 1 1/2f out, kept on at one pace to take 3rd 1f out but no impression on leaders* **13/10**[1]

4 ½ **Alovera (IRE)**[21] 4657 2-8-11 .... CSoumillon 3 96
(M R Channon) *raced in 2nd, pushed along 2f out, one pace* **22/10**[2]

5 *nk* **Mpumalanga**[23] 4621 2-8-11 .... TThulliez 5 95
(R Gibson, France) *sweated up before start, raced keenly in last, always in rear* **17/2**

1m 39.4s (-0.90) 5 Ran SP% **122.0**
PARI-MUTUEL: WIN 5.20; PL 2.10, 2.00; SF 29.20.
Owner M Parrish **Bred** G Cachot & Mlle V Cheron **Trained** Lamorlaye, France

NOTEBOOK
Poltava(FR) was quickly into her stride and bowling along in front at a decent pace. She increased the rhythm early in the straight and then battled on gamely in the final stages and was never really challenged. This claimer has been a terrific investment and she now goes for the Prix Marcel Boussac. She goes well on good ground and is extremely consistent.
Ikat(IRE), in third place rounding the final turn on the rail, made a forward move two out and looked dangerous at the furlong marker, but was held in the final 100 yards.
Sismix(IRE), fourth coming into the straight, looked to be going very easily but could not quicken when things warmed up. She took third place inside the final furlong.
Alovera(IRE) was tucked in behind the leader early on and being pushed along in the straight. A furlong and a half out she had no chance of taking a place in the first two and was caught close home for third place

5091 LINGFIELD (L-H)
Tuesday, September 12

OFFICIAL GOING: Turf course - good; all-weather- standard
Wind: Nil Weather: Hazy Sunshine

5258 LINGFIELD PARK "THE PERFECT WEDDING VENUE" APPRENTICE H'CAP 1m 2f
2:30 (2:30) (Class 6) (0-65,65) 3-Y-O+ **£2,730** (£806; £403) **Stalls** Low

Form RPR

0361 **1** **Air Biscuit (IRE)**[21] 4671 3-9-3 **65**...........................(t) JonjoMilczarek(5) 2 75
(C F Wall) *t.k.h: led for 2f: trckd ldrs tl led 3f out: clr 1f out: pushed out and styd on wl: comf* **5/1**[1]

1520 **2** *3* **Leighton Buzzard**[51] 3762 4-9-5 **62**............................ GaryEdwards(7) 1 66
(N B King) *t.k.h early: settled in midfield: hdwy on inner over 2f out: rdn over 1f out: chsd wnr ins fnl f: no imp* **8/1**

4405 **3** *1* **Newport Boy (IRE)**[5] 5128 3-9-3 **60**..................................... TolleyDean 3 62
(R A Harris) *t.k.h: led after 2f: rdn and hdd 3f out: kpt on same pce u.p fnl f* **10/1**

3563 **4** ½ **Can Can Star**[15] 4892 3-9-6 **63**... JamesMillman 8 64
(J G Given) *slowly away: hld up in rr: rdn over 3f out: hdwy on inner last 2f: kpt on fnl f: nt rch ldrs* **7/1**[3]

0164 **5** *3 ½* **Final Tune (IRE)**[15] 4871 3-9-2 **62**................................ LukeMorris(3) 7 56
(Miss M E Rowland) *t.k.h: chsd ldrs after 2f: rdn wl over 2f out: wknd over 1f out* **13/2**[2]

0052 **6** *1 ½* **Northside Lodge (IRE)**[9] 5047 8-9-4 **57**............(e[1]) JamieHamblett(3) 10 49
(W R Swinburn) *hld up in tch: prog to trck ldrs over 3f out: rdn 3f out: fnd nil and sn btn* **5/1**[1]

0554 **7** *3* **Trifti**[13] 4937 5-9-4 **54**.. NicolPolli 5 40
(C A Cyzer) *t.k.h: settled towards rr after 2f: rdn over 3f out: no prog* **5/1**[1]

1436 **8** *shd* **Blackmail (USA)**[20] 4704 8-9-10 **60**..........................(b) AshleyHamblett 6 46
(P Mitchell) *hld up in rr: rdn over 3f out: no prog* **13/2**[2]

0-00 **9** *1 ¾* **Seejay**[21] 4670 6-8-7 **48** oh10....................................(p) JPFeatherstone(5) 4 30
(B R Johnson) *t.k.h: prom on outer: chsd ldr 1/2-way tl over 3f out: wknd over 2f out* **66/1**

2m 13.83s (4.11) **Going Correction** +0.25s/f (Good)
WFA 3 from 4yo+ 7lb 9 Ran SP% **110.9**
Speed ratings (Par 101):93,90,89,89,86 85,83,82,81
CSF £42.33 CT £366.32 TOTE £5.00: £1.70, £2.50, £4.10; EX 45.40.
Owner M Sinclair **Bred** Farmers Hill Stud **Trained** Newmarket, Suffolk

FOCUS
A modest race restricted to apprentices who had not ridden more than 25 winners. It was run at a steady pace and the form looks weak.
Leighton Buzzard Official explanation: vet said gelding lost an off-fore shoe

5259 NORTHERN MARINE UNDERWRITERS (S) STKS 1m 1f
3:00 (3:00) (Class 6) 3-Y-O+ **£2,730** (£806; £403) **Stalls** Low

Form RPR

5350 **1** **Danish Monarch**[3] 5166 5-9-4 45.............................. AshleyHamblett(7) 5 62
(David Pinder) *in tch: hdwy 3f out: rdn to ld to ld over 1f out: in command ins fnl f: eased nr fin* **12/1**

0056 **2** *1 ½* **Balearic Star (IRE)**[33] 4285 5-8-12 47...................... JamesMillman(7) 3 53
(B R Millman) *bhd: rdn over 3f out: kpt on u.p over 1f out: wnt 2nd last 75 yds: nt rch wnr* **8/1**

0100 **3** *1 ¼* **Bishops Finger**[32] 4332 6-9-11 55.................................(b) RobertHavlin 9 57
(Jamie Poulton) *t.k.h: hld up in midfield: hdwy over 3f out: ev ch wl over 1f out: fdd u.p ins fnl f* **6/1**[3]

5053 **4** *nk* **Salinger (USA)**[21] 4670 4-9-2 44...........................(b) AmirQuinn(3) 11 50
(Mrs L J Mongan) *taken down early: stdd s: plld hrd and hld up in rr: hdwy wl over 2f out: kpt on u.str.p over 1f out: nvr nrr* **7/1**

0630 **5** *1 ½* **Makai**[19] 4728 3-9-5 56.. JoeFanning 2 53
(M Johnston) *chsd ldr tl rdn to ld wl over 2f out: hdd wl over 1f out: wknd ins fnl f* **11/2**[2]

3500 **6** *2 ½* **Comeintothespace (IRE)**[28] 4446 4-9-5 43.......(p) FrankieMcDonald 13 42
(Miss Victoria Roberts) *in tch: hdwy over 3f out: hld hd awkwardly u.p: wknd wl over 1f out* **25/1**

0000 **7** *3* **Flying Penne**[15] 4868 3-8-8 41................................ FrancisNorton 10 31
(R Curtis) *hld up in rr: rdn over 3f out: styd on past btn horses fnl f: n.d* **100/1**

4464 **8** *1 ½* **Didoe**[23] 4627 7-9-0 48.. PaulDoe 12 28
(P W Hiatt) *rrd s: sn chsng ldrs: c wd over 3f out: sn rdn and struggling* **11/2**[2]

0000 **9** *1 ¼* **Romanova (IRE)**[18] 4755 4-9-0 42.............................(b) FergusSweeney 8 26
(Dr J R J Naylor) *chsd ldrs: rdn over 3f out: sn lost pl: no ch after: eased ins fnl f* **50/1**

0/06 **10** *shd* **Over Tipsy**[5] 5127 4-9-5 43.. RichardHughes 1 30
(R Hannon) *led tl rdn and hdd wl over 2f out: sn wknd: eased ins fnl f* **14/1**

6000 **11** *1* **Miss Redactive**[33] 4306 3-8-8 44...................................... HayleyTurner 6 23
(M D I Usher) *bhd: pushed along early: rdn and no rspnse over 3f out* **16/1**

4000 **12** *1 ¼* **Lord Mayor**[15] 4881 5-9-5 70..(p) NCallan 7 26
(R M H Cowell) *v keen to post: plld hrd: hld up in midfield: rdn 3f out: no rspnse: eased ins fnl f* **4/1**[1]

1m 57.27s (1.98) **Going Correction** +0.25s/f (Good)
WFA 3 from 4yo+ 6lb 12 Ran SP% **115.7**
Speed ratings (Par 101):101,99,98,98,96 94,92,90,89,89 88,87
CSF £101.20 TOTE £19.30: £5.90, £2.90, £2.00; EX 119.90.Lord Mayor was claimed by B. Pollock for £6,000. There was no bid for the winner.
Owner Little Farm Partnership II **Bred** The National Stud **Trained** Kingston Lisle, Oxon

FOCUS
A weak seller rated around the fourth.
Balearic Star(IRE) Official explanation: jockey said gelding hung right-handed
Lord Mayor Official explanation: vet said gelding returned lame

5260 SEARCHLIGHT H'CAP 1m 2f
3:35 (3:35) (Class 5) (0-75,81) 3-Y-O **£3,238** (£963; £481; £240) **Stalls** Low

Form RPR

3422 **1** **Regent's Park**[20] 4686 3-9-3 **74**... SteveDrowne 2 81
(R Charlton) *mde all: drvn over 2f out: styd on gamely: edgd lft wl ins fnl f* **13/2**

4535 **2** ¾ **Gracechurch (IRE)**[4] 5152 3-9-2 **73**................................. TonyCulhane 1 79
(M R Channon) *hld up in midfield: lost pl and rdn 4f out: hdwy over 2f out: chsd wnr and swtchd rt 1f out: hld last 100 yds* **6/1**[3]

5232 **3** *3 ½* **Lunar River (FR)**[16] 4836 3-8-9 **66**..............................(t) RichardMullen 4 65
(E A L Dunlop) *trckd ldrs: rdn 3f out: chsd wnr 2f out tl 1f out: fdd ins fnl f* **15/2**

0211 **4** *1* **Altilhar (USA)**[4] 5152 3-9-7 **81** 6ex.....................(b) RichardKingscote(3) 5 78
(G L Moore) *hld up in midfield: rdn over 2f out: fnd little and no prog tl kpt on wl ins fnl f* **9/4**[1]

6-42 **5** *nk* **Dan Buoy (FR)**[20] 4708 3-8-13 **70**................................ FergusSweeney 9 66
(A King) *t.k.h: hld up in midfield: hdwy 6f out: chsd wnr 4f out tl 2f out: wknd* **18/1**

0001 **6** *2* **Lenoir (GER)**[16] 4842 3-8-5 **62**......................................(v) FrancisNorton 7 55
(V Smith) *stdd s: hld up in rr: drvn and effrt 3f out: nvr pce to chal: kpt on ins fnl f* **12/1**

0113 **7** *11* **Colton**[12] 4958 3-8-10 **67**.. NCallan 3 39
(J M P Eustace) *hld up in rr: hrd rdn and effrt over 3f out: no prog: eased fnl f* **9/2**[2]

1022 **8** ¾ **Lester Leaps In (USA)**[41] 4044 3-9-0 **71**..................... RichardHughes 6 41
(R Hannon) *hld up in rr: hdwy over 4f out: rdn over 3f out: sn btn: eased ins fnl f* **10/1**

4020 **9** *8* **Valuta (USA)**[30] 4419 3-8-11 **68**..(vt[1]) FJohansson 8 23
(R A Kvisla) *pressed wnr tl 4f out: sn wknd: eased fnl f: t.o* **50/1**

2m 10.42s (0.70) **Going Correction** +0.25s/f (Good) 9 Ran SP% **112.3**
Speed ratings (Par 101):107,106,103,102,102 100,92,91,85
CSF £43.58 CT £296.28 TOTE £7.80: £2.00, £1.80, £3.00; EX 47.20.
Owner The Queen **Bred** The Queen **Trained** Beckhampton, Wilts

FOCUS
A fair handicap in which the winner dictated the pace throughout.
Altilhar(USA) Official explanation: jockey said gelding ran flat and would be better suited by faster ground
Colton Official explanation: jockey said gelding had no more to give

5261 LINGFIELDPARK.CO.UK MEDIAN AUCTION MAIDEN STKS 6f (P)
4:10 (4:12) (Class 5) 2-Y-O £3,412 (£1,007; £504) Stalls Low

Form RPR

626 1 **Miss Jenny (IRE)**[19] [4737] 2-8-12 87 NCallan 3 80+
(B J Meehan) *cl up: led 3f out: rdn and qcknd clr wl over 2f out: in command fnl f: comf* 4/6[1]

4 2 2 ½ **Obstructive**[76] [2979] 2-9-3 HayleyTurner 9 77+
(Ernst Oertel) *led tl 3f out: kpt on wl but no ch w wnr* 12/1[3]

002 3 1 **Juncea**[11] [4993] 2-8-12 79 SteveDrowne 4 69
(H Morrison) *t.k.h: trckd ldrs: drvn wl over 2f out: kpt on same pce* 3/1[2]

4 1 ½ **Count Ceprano (IRE)** 2-9-3 TedDurcan 11 70+
(W R Swinburn) *slowly away: hld up in rr: hdwy over 1f out: styd on ins fnl f: nvr nrr* 25/1

6020 5 1 **Chingford (IRE)**[20] [4699] 2-8-12 68 FrankieMcDonald 2 62
(D W P Arbuthnot) *racd in midfield: rdn 3f out: outpcd over 2f out: kpt on same pce* 16/1

00 6 shd **Marlyn Ridge**[7] [5091] 2-8-10 JamesMillman(7) 1 66
(D K Ivory) *chsd ldrs on inner: rdn wl over 2f out: kpt on same pce* 80/1

0 7 ½ **Darling Belinda**[7] [5095] 2-8-12 FergusSweeney 8 60
(D K Ivory) *chsd ldrs rdn wl over 2f out: wknd over 1f out* 80/1

6 8 ¾ **Festive Tipple (IRE)**[25] [4550] 2-9-3 JimCrowley 10 62
(P Winkworth) *racd in midfield: rdn and outpcd wl over 2f out* 80/1

600 9 3 **Purple Sands (IRE)**[29] [4428] 2-9-3 54 RichardHughes 7 53
(B J Meehan) *t.k.h: hld up: rdn 3f out: nvr pce to chal* 20/1

10 7 **Jade's Ballet** 2-8-12 PaulFitzsimons 5 27
(E A Wheeler) *dismntd and led to post: t.k.h: chsd ldrs tl rdn 3f out: sn lost pl* 80/1

00 11 1 ¼ **Magena Gold**[13] [4934] 2-9-0 RichardKingscote(3) 6 29
(R Charlton) *a bhd: no ch whn sltly hmpd over 2f out: t.o* 25/1

12 10 **Sangfroid** 2-9-3 JamieMackay 12 —
(Sir Mark Prescott) *rn v green and sn lost tch: t.o fr 1/2-way* 50/1

1m 12.67s (-0.14) **Going Correction** -0.175s/f (Stan) 12 Ran SP% 117.9
Speed ratings (Par 95):93,89,88,86,85 84,84,83,79,69 68,54
CSF £9.69 TOTE £1.90: £1.10, £3.00, £1.30; EX 13.90.
Owner Paul & Jenny Green **Bred** Paul Green **Trained** Manton, Wilts

FOCUS
Not a bad maiden for the track and surface, but the performance of the fifth and ninth limit the form.

NOTEBOOK
Miss Jenny(IRE), who contested the Lowther Stakes at York, was more at home in this company and handled the surface well. Obviously well regarded, she can improve again. (op 8-11 after 4-5 in places)
Obstructive has now run two good races on this surface, the other at Kempton, and is well capable of landing a maiden before going on to better things. (op 14-1)
Juncea has now run well in two successive races and seems well suited by six furlongs on Polytrack. (tchd 11-4 and 7-2)
Count Ceprano(IRE) ◆ caught this eye on this racecourse debut and normal improvement should see him take a similar race. (op 33-1)
Chingford(IRE), stepped up from five furlongs, was beaten by the opposition rather than the trip. (tchd 20-1)
Marlyn Ridge is now eligible for nurseries and ran well enough to have prospects in that company. (op 100-1)

5262 BOOK ONLINE FOR A £2 DISCOUNT NURSERY 7f (P)
4:45 (4:46) (Class 5) (0-75,74) 2-Y-O £3,886 (£1,156; £577; £288) Stalls Low

Form RPR

0501 1 **King Charles**[7] [5094] 2-9-9 74 7ex DO'Donohoe 13 87+
(E A L Dunlop) *chsd ldrs: wnt 2nd over 4f out: rdn to ld over 2f out: clr over 1f out: pushed out: comf* 2/1[1]

2406 2 3 ½ **Ghost Dancer**[20] [4699] 2-9-4 69 NCallan 7 69
(L M Cumani) *in tch: hdwy over 3f out: drvn over 2f out: kpt on: chsd wnr ins fnl f: no imp* 15/2[3]

5562 3 ¾ **Vadinka**[34] [4246] 2-9-4 69 JimCrowley 11 67
(P Winkworth) *chsd ldrs: rdn and chsd wnr over 2f out: btn 1f out: lost 2nd ins fnl f* 10/1

000 4 shd **Diggs Lane (IRE)**[32] [4333] 2-8-4 55 (b[1]) FrancisNorton 4 53
(N A Callaghan) *hld up in midfield: rdn 3f out: n.m.r last 2f: r.o wl ins fnl f* 20/1

0256 5 shd **Our Herbie**[18] [4773] 2-9-3 68 TedDurcan 6 66
(J W Hills) *bhd: rdn over 2f out: r.o wl fnl f: nrst fin* 14/1

0020 6 ½ **Wilmington**[21] [4681] 2-9-7 72 RichardHughes 3 68
(R Hannon) *racd in midfield: hdwy over 3f out: rdn wl over 2f out: kpt on same pce over 1f out* 6/1[2]

046 7 hd **Bertoliver**[29] [4428] 2-9-5 70 SteveDrowne 10 66
(D K Ivory) *hld up in tch: hdwy on outer 3f out: kpt on same pce u.p over 1f out* 16/1

3000 8 5 **Daring You**[9] [5041] 2-8-9 60 (b[1]) JoeFanning 5 43
(P F I Cole) *chsd ldr tl over 4f out: sn drvn along: wknd wl over 2f out* 33/1

555 9 nk **Orange Pekoe (USA)**[13] [4928] 2-9-7 72 GeorgeBaker 2 55
(P Mitchell) *hld up bhd: effrt and rdn wl over 2f out: nvr on terms* 10/1

0542 10 1 **Grand Lucre**[13] [4932] 2-9-7 72 RichardMullen 12 52
(E J O'Neill) *taken down early: led tl over 2f out: wknd rapidly over 1f out* 17/2

3000 11 13 **Aggresive**[9] [5043] 2-8-6 57 HayleyTurner 9 5
(Ernst Oertel) *chsd ldrs tl rdn and wknd qckly 3f out: virtually p.u fnl f: t.o* 50/1

0004 12 6 **Blue Mistral (IRE)**[24] [4588] 2-9-0 65 PaulDoe 8 —
(W J Knight) *sn bhd and pushed along: no ch last 3f: virtually p.u fnl f: t.o* 20/1

252 13 1 **Grange Lili (IRE)**[64] [3351] 2-9-6 71 RobbieFitzpatrick 1 1
(Peter Grayson) *slowly away: a bhd and hanging: no ch last 3f: virtually p.u fnl f: t.o* 16/1

1m 25.27s (-0.62) **Going Correction** -0.175s/f (Stan) 13 Ran SP% 120.9
Speed ratings (Par 95):96,92,91,91,90 90,90,84,84,82 68,61,60
CSF £16.02 CT £131.20 TOTE £1.90: £1.20, £2.70, £2.70; EX 18.00.
Owner Khalifa Sultan **Bred** Hunscote House Farm Stud **Trained** Newmarket, Suffolk

FOCUS
A nursery of reasonable quality for the track, with a progressive winner. The race has been rated through the runner-up.

NOTEBOOK
King Charles, showing he is effective on both sand and turf, made light of a 7lb penalty and is clearly on the upgrade. (op 15-8 tchd 9-4)
Ghost Dancer seemed happy over this extra furlong but the winner was different class. He is running well enough to get off the mark against more routine opponents. Official explanation: trainer's rep said colt lost a front shoe (op 13-2)
Vadinka just about got the extra furlong but, like the runner-up, found the improving winner an impossible opponent to overcome. (op 12-1)
Diggs Lane(IRE), sharpened up by the blinkers, looks capable of winning in nursery company following this promising first attempt, his first outing on sand. He should stay a mile. (op 25-1)
Our Herbie is gradually getting there and will be worth trying back at a mile if he cannot find a race at this trip.
Wilmington ran a fair race but looks a few pounds too high. (op 8-1)
Bertoliver Official explanation: jockey said colt hung right on bend
Grand Lucre Official explanation: jockey said filly had no more to give
Blue Mistral(IRE) Official explanation: jockey said filly did not handle the track

5263 XL INSURANCE H'CAP 6f (P)
5:15 (5:15) (Class 4) (0-80,80) 3-Y-O+ £5,505 (£1,637; £818; £408) Stalls Low

Form RPR

0-05 1 **Grand Show**[10] [5021] 4-9-2 76 TedDurcan 10 85+
(W R Swinburn) *chsd ldr after 1f: rdn to ld over 2f out: sn clr: rdn out* 7/1[3]

5501 2 1 **Mambazo**[1] [5246] 4-8-10 73 6ex (e) JamesDoyle(3) 4 79
(S C Williams) *hld up in midfield on inner: swtchd rt and hdwy over 2f out: r.o u.p: wnt 2nd fnl f: nt rch wnr* 9/2[2]

2022 3 1 ¼ **Katiypour (IRE)**[7] [5096] 9-9-6 80 GeorgeBaker 11 82
(P Mitchell) *hld up in rr: rdn and hdwy over 2f out: swtchd rt 1f out: r.o fnl f: nvr nrr* 2/1[1]

2060 4 1 ½ **Roman Quintet (IRE)**[17] [4807] 6-8-11 71 (b[1]) FJohansson 2 69
(D W P Arbuthnot) *led for 1f: chsd ldrs: rdn and outpcd by wnr over 2f out: wnt 2nd briefly 1f out: fdd fnl f* 8/1

00P0 5 1 ¼ **Chief Exec**[7] [5096] 4-9-6 80 TonyCulhane 6 74
(C A Cyzer) *sn outpcd in last and pushed along: styd on fr over 1f out: nvr nrr* 25/1

0600 6 1 ¾ **Sigismundus (IRE)**[90] [2553] 3-8-7 69 SteveDrowne 3 58
(J R Boyle) *chsd ldrs: rdn over 2f out: wknd wl over 1f out* 33/1

0220 7 3 **Up Tempo (IRE)**[16] [4831] 8-8-6 71 (b) RoryMoore(5) 7 51
(C R Dore) *taken down early: racd wd in midfield: rdn and outpcd wl over 2f out: no ch after* 14/1

0150 8 nk **Russian Rocket (IRE)**[17] [4807] 4-9-6 80 NCallan 1 59
(Mrs C A Dunnett) *chsd ldrs tl rdn wl over 2f out: sn outpcd* 11/1

4160 9 1 **Garstang**[25] [4562] 3-9-2 78 (b) RobbieFitzpatrick 8 54
(Peter Grayson) *led after 1f tl rdn and hdd over 2f out: wknd qckly wl over 1f out* 11/1

02-1 10 19 **Woodsley House (IRE)**[17] [4799] 4-9-1 75 RichardMullen 5 —
(W R Muir) *sn drvn along in midfield: bhd fr 1/2-way: t.o* 9/1

1m 11.69s (-1.12) **Going Correction** -0.175s/f (Stan)
WFA 3 from 4yo+ 2lb 10 Ran SP% 115.2
Speed ratings (Par 105):100,98,97,95,93 91,87,86,85,59
CSF £38.07 CT £88.04 TOTE £8.10: £2.50, £1.70, £1.40; EX 44.40 Place 6 £80.53, Place 5 £25.91.
Owner Mrs P W Harris **Bred** Pendley Farm **Trained** Aldbury, Herts

FOCUS
A competitive sprint featuring eight previous course winners, and it was run at a solid pace.
T/Plt: £52.10 to a £1 stake. Pool: £50,781.40. 710.25 winning tickets. T/Qpdt: £4.70 to a £1 stake. Pool: £3,861.70. 596.20 winning tickets. SP

5147 SANDOWN (R-H)
Tuesday, September 12

OFFICIAL GOING: Good to firm (good in places on round course)
Wind: Nil Weather: Overcast, humid

5264 CONSTRUCTION NEWS MEDIAN AUCTION MAIDEN FILLIES' STKS 5f 6y
2:10 (2:11) (Class 6) 2-Y-O £3,238 (£963; £481; £240) Stalls High

Form RPR

52 1 **Blue Echo**[22] [4657] 2-9-0 PhilipRobinson 7 77+
(M A Jarvis) *lw: mde all and racd against far side rail: drew clr over 1f out: shkn up and styd on fnl f* 2/5[1]

05 2 2 **Ken's Girl**[18] [4754] 2-9-0 IanMongan 6 67
(W S Kittow) *leggy: narrow: in tch: rdn 2f out: prog over 1f out: tk 2nd last 150yds: no ch w wnr* 66/1

6 3 1 ¼ **Tokyo Rose**[9] [5043] 2-9-0 RyanMoore 8 63
(R Hannon) *str: lw: cl up and racd against far side rail: outpcd 2f out: effrt and n.m.r jst over 1f out: kpt on to take 3rd nr fin* 12/1

04 4 nk **Aquilegia (IRE)**[11] [4987] 2-9-0 GrahamGibbons 1 61
(E S McMahon) *dwlt: rcvrd to press wnr after 2f: chal 2f out: hung rt over 1f out: wknd ins fnl f* 25/1

2 5 ½ **Twitch Hill**[11] [4986] 2-9-0 DaneO'Neill 5 60
(H Candy) *str: scope: dwlt: in tch in rr: shkn up 1/2-way: sn outpcd: kpt on ins fnl f* 7/1[2]

56 6 shd **River Tarrant**[45] [3942] 2-9-0 EddieAhern 4 59
(P W Chapple-Hyam) *hld up in last: shkn up 1/2-way: effrt over 1f out: kpt on same pce* 33/1

56 7 9 **Shantina's Dream (USA)**[25] [4558] 2-9-0 (t) SteveDrowne 2 27
(H Morrison) *chsd wnr for 2f: sn wknd: t.o* 15/2[3]

62.31 secs (0.10) **Going Correction** +0.05s/f (Good) 7 Ran SP% 110.6
Speed ratings (Par 90):101,97,95,95,94 94,79
CSF £43.61 TOTE £1.40: £1.10, £8.60; EX 35.50.
Owner Mrs Mary Taylor **Bred** Mrs Mary Taylor And James F Taylor **Trained** Newmarket, Suffolk

FOCUS
A weak fillies' maiden and a straightforward success for Blue Echo.

NOTEBOOK
Blue Echo confirmed the improved form she showed when a close second over six furlongs at Windsor on her previous start with a straightforward success, coping just fine with the drop back in trip. She is likely to find things harder from now on, but is at least going the right way. (op 4-9)
Ken's Girl stepped up on her two previous efforts with a good performance behind the warm favourite. She never looked like winning, but stayed on nicely for second her connections will have more options now that she is eligible for a handicap mark. (tchd 80-1)
Tokyo Rose confirmed the ability she showed on her debut at Lingfield, but she was ultimately well held and may be more of a handicap prospect. (op 12-1)
Aquilegia(IRE) did not help her chance by hanging and this ground may have been faster than she cares for. She might do better now that she is eligible to run in nurseries. (tchd 33-1)
Twitch Hill failed to build on the form that she showed when a moderate second on heavy ground on her debut at Haydock. (op 6-1)

The Form Book, Raceform Ltd, Compton, RG20 6NL

5265 PERI FORMWORK H'CAP — 5f 6y

2:40 (2:42) (Class 4) (0-85,82) 3-Y-O — **£5,505** (£1,637; £818; £408) **Stalls High**

Form — RPR

0510 **1** **Mango Music**[24] [4589] 3-9-4 **82**........ IanMongan 4 — 87
(M R Channon) *t.k.h: trckd ldr: rdn to ld over 1f out: drvn and hld on wl fnl f* **6/1**[1]

1522 **2** *hd* **Libor (IRE)**[16] [4841] 3-9-2 **80**........ EddieAhern 6 — 84
(L M Cumani) *t.k.h: hld up: cruising 2f out: plld out jst over 1f out: chsd wnr ins fnl f: clsng fin: too much to do* **2/1**[1]

4245 **3** *nk* **Scarlet Flyer (USA)**[34] [4242] 3-8-12 **76**........ RyanMoore 2 — 79
(G L Moore) *lw: chsd ldrs: rdn 2f out: nt qckn over 1f out: styd on ins fnl f: a hld* **7/2**[2]

4063 **4** *1* **Azygous**[13] [4922] 3-9-3 **81**........ DaneO'Neill 1 — 80
(J Akehurst) *led at stdy pce: rdn 2f out: hdd and one pce over 1f out* **8/1**

0001 **5** *nk* **Memphis Man**[17] [4812] 3-8-1 **68** oh1........ DominicFox[(3)] 7 — 66
(Miss V Haigh) *dwlt and restrained s: plld hrd: hld up in last: rdn 2f out: styd on ins fnl f: nt rch ldrs* **11/2**

262 **6** *3* **Welcome Approach**[17] [4812] 3-8-10 **74**........ PaulHanagan 5 — 76+
(J R Weymes) *chsd ldrs: rdn 2f out: trying to cl whn bdly hmpd on inner jst ins fnl f: nt rcvr* **5/1**[3]

62.42 secs (0.21) **Going Correction** +0.05s/f (Good) — **6** Ran SP% **113.0**
Speed ratings (Par 103):100,99,99,97,97 92
CSF £18.72 TOTE £8.20: £3.10, £1.70; EX 22.80.
Owner Antoniades Family **Bred** A G Antoniades **Trained** West Ilsley, Berks

FOCUS
It remains to be seen just how strong this form is, as they went a very steady pace early on and the winning time was slower than the opening juvenile maiden.

5266 KPMG EMPLOYMENT TAX IN CONSTRUCTION H'CAP — 1m 2f 7y

3:15 (3:18) (Class 4) (0-85,84) 3-Y-O — **£8,096** (£2,408; £1,203; £601) **Stalls High**

Form — RPR

0340 **1** **Punta Galera (IRE)**[11] [4997] 3-9-4 **84**........ RyanMoore 2 — 91
(R Hannon) *mde all: set stdy pce tl kicked on wl over 2f out: nvr really chal after: drvn out* **6/1**[3]

2326 **2** *3/4* **Midnight Traveller**[66] [3318] 3-8-11 **77**........ PhilipRobinson 1 — 83
(L M Cumani) *lw: hld up in last pair: effrt on outer 3f out: rdn and prog to chse wnr 1f out: clsd but nvr really threatened* **3/1**[1]

2231 **3** *1 1/2* **Pirouetting**[27] [4489] 3-8-10 **76**........ MichaelHills 4 — 79
(B W Hills) *hld up in last pair: stl last whn nt clr run 2f out: plld out and r.o fnl f: hopeless task* **8/1**

3613 **4** *3/4* **Luna Landing**[18] [4784] 3-8-8 **74**........ DaleGibson 7 — 76
(Jedd O'Keeffe) *t.k.h: trckd ldng pair: rdn over 2f out: one pce and no imp on wnr* **7/2**[2]

2240 **5** *1/2* **Black Beauty**[16] [4833] 3-8-13 **79**........ RobertWinston 6 — 80
(M G Quinlan) *hld up in 4th: rdn and nt qckn over 2f out: one pce and n.d after* **7/2**[2]

-650 **6** *2 1/2* **Art Investor**[12] [4945] 3-8-4 **73**........ MarcHalford[(3)] 3 — 69
(D R C Elsworth) *hld up in 5th: rdn and struggling over 2f out: wl btn over 1f out* **16/1**

0321 **7** *3/4* **Alhaitham (USA)**[12] [4959] 3-9-0 **80**........(t) MartinDwyer 8 — 74
(J L Dunlop) *reluctant to go to post: chsd wnr: rdn over 2f out: no imp: wknd 1f out* **6/1**[3]

2m 11.89s (1.65) **Going Correction** +0.05s/f (Good) — **7** Ran SP% **115.0**
Speed ratings (Par 103):95,94,93,92,92 90,89
CSF £24.60 CT £145.24 TOTE £7.90: £3.70, £2.10; EX 30.20.
Owner J A Lazzari **Bred** Bill Dwan **Trained** East Everleigh, Wilts

FOCUS
A fair-looking handicap on paper ruined by the lack of any early pace. The form looks dubious.
Alhaitham(USA) Official explanation: jockey said colt had a respiratory problem

5267 CN PLUS H'CAP — 1m 14y

3:50 (3:52) (Class 6) (0-65,63) 4-Y-O+ — **£3,238** (£963; £481; £240) **Stalls High**

Form — RPR

3020 **1** **Double Spectre (IRE)**[11] [4982] 4-9-4 **63**........ DaneO'Neill 4 — 71
(Jean-Rene Auvray) *hld up in last trio: stdy prog on outer fr over 3f out to ld 2f out: drvn and hld on wl fnl f* **7/1**

3000 **2** *1/2* **Mythical Charm**[17] [4795] 7-8-10 **55**........(t) RobertWinston 10 — 62
(J J Bridger) *hld up in midfield: rdn 2f out: prog and swtchd lft over 1f out: r.o to take 2nd last 75yds: clsd on wnr but a hld* **14/1**

0030 **3** *1/2* **Justcallmehandsome**[76] [2978] 4-7-11 **49**........ FrankiePickard[(7)] 1 — 55
(D J S Ffrench Davis) *hld up and sn detached in last: brought v wd in st: bmpd along and gd prog fr 2f out: tk 3rd nr fin* **20/1**

6005 **4** *3/4* **Simplify**[16] [4842] 4-8-4 **49** oh5........(b) DaleGibson 2 — 53
(T M Jones) *lw: hld up wl in rr: prog 2f out: hrd rdn to chse wnr jst over 1f out: no imp: lost 2 pls last 75yds* **25/1**

3410 **5** *3* **Magic Warrior**[20] [4709] 6-8-12 **57**........ PatDobbs 14 — 54
(J C Fox) *t.k.h: hld up in midfield: rdn over 2f out: nt qckn over 1f out: plugged on* **11/2**[1]

4004 **6** *3/4* **River Gypsy**[27] [4483] 5-8-3 **51**........ MarcHalford[(3)] 11 — 46
(D R C Elsworth) *trckd ldrs: poised to chal gng easily over 2f out: rdn and no rspnse over 1f out* **10/1**

0601 **7** *hd* **Hallings Overture (USA)**[38] [4139] 7-8-10 **55**........ RyanMoore 9 — 50
(C A Horgan) *trckd ldrs: effrt to ld briefly over 2f out: wknd fnl f* **6/1**[2]

0050 **8** *2* **Windy Prospect**[29] [4439] 4-8-4 **49**........(b[1]) PaulHanagan 12 — 39
(P A Blockley) *trckd ldng pair: rdn 2f out: steadily lost grnd fr over 1f out* **16/1**

1225 **9** *hd* **Beau Marche**[16] [4845] 4-8-6 **51**........(b) MartinDwyer 5 — 41
(G G Margarson) *trckd ldrs: rdn over 2f out: wknd over 1f out* **6/1**[2]

-500 **10** *hd* **Dalpe**[41] [4048] 5-8-7 **52**........(p) RichardThomas 13 — 41
(A J Lidderdale) *disp ld at gd pce tl over 2f out: wknd jst over 1f out* **50/1**

2444 **11** *3* **Zafarshah (IRE)**[21] [4670] 7-8-4 **49** oh3........(b) AdrianMcCarthy 6 — 31
(R A Harris) *hld up in midfield: rdn and no prog over 2f out: eased whn no ch fnl f* **13/2**[3]

5650 **12** *21* **Grand Design**[10] [5035] 4-8-10 **55**........ EddieAhern 3 — —
(C A Cyzer) *a wl in rr: wd into st and sn struggling: t.o* **20/1**

0500 **13** *7* **Tuning Fork**[45] [3933] 6-8-6 **51**........ LPKeniry 8 — —
(T M Jones) *disp ld at gd pce to 3f out: wknd rapidly: t.o* **12/1**

1m 44.53s (0.58) **Going Correction** +0.05s/f (Good) — **13** Ran SP% **114.5**
Speed ratings (Par 101):99,98,98,97,94 93,93,91,91,90 87,66,59
CSF £91.28 CT £1919.00 TOTE £8.10: £2.70, £5.60, £5.30; EX 110.00.
Owner The Dragon Partnership **Bred** R Bailey **Trained** Upper Lambourn, Berks

FOCUS
A moderate heat by course standards and, while the form looks sound enough, the race is unlikely to throw up many winners.

5268 GENSET "PEOPLE MAGIC" H'CAP — 7f 16y

4:25 (4:26) (Class 5) (0-75,75) 3-Y-O — **£5,505** (£1,637; £818; £408) **Stalls High**

Form — RPR

0221 **1** **Kasumi**[18] [4772] 3-8-7 **69**........ TravisBlock[(5)] 11 — 79
(H Morrison) *lw: wl plcd on inner: rdn and effrt to chse ldr over 1f out: led last 150yds: pushed out and a holding on* **6/1**[2]

1123 **2** *nk* **Scrummage**[18] [4760] 3-9-3 **74**........(v) RobertWinston 9 — 84
(Sir Michael Stoute) *led at decent pce: drvn over 1f out: hdd last 150yds: kpt on but a hld* **6/4**[1]

5160 **3** *1* **Imperial Gain (USA)**[13] [4923] 3-9-0 **74**........(v) AdamKirby[(3)] 7 — 81
(W R Swinburn) *awkward s and s.i.s: last tl drvn on wd outside and prog over 1f out: r.o fnl f: nrst fin* **12/1**

123 **4** *3* **Secret Assassin (IRE)**[9] [5042] 3-9-4 **75**........ MartinDwyer 14 — 74
(W R Muir) *lw: t.k.h: hld up in midfield: rdn and effrt 2f out: one pce and no imp over 1f out* **9/1**

0002 **5** *nk* **Charlton**[18] [4769] 3-8-13 **70**........(v) IanMongan 12 — 68
(T G Mills) *hld up in last trio: rdn 3f out: kpt on fr over 2f out: nvr on terms* **8/1**[3]

3600 **6** *1/2* **Pigeon Island**[24] [4591] 3-8-13 **70**........ DaneO'Neill 13 — 67
(H Candy) *t.k.h: hld up in last trio: outpcd over 2f out: swtchd to inner wl over 1f out: kpt on: no ch* **16/1**

6121 **7** *nk* **Mocha Java**[22] [4666] 3-8-11 **71**........ AmirQuinn[(3)] 4 — 67
(Mrs L J Mongan) *lw: chsd ldr to 2f out: wknd over 1f out* **8/1**[3]

36 **8** *1 1/2* **Duke Of Milan (IRE)**[13] [4923] 3-9-1 **72**........ DavidAllan 5 — 64
(G C Bravery) *prom: chsd ldr 2f out: hung lft and wknd over 1f out* **25/1**

0565 **9** *1 1/4* **Tous Les Deux**[6] [5107] 3-9-2 **73**........ StephenCarson 3 — 62
(R F Johnson Houghton) *prom: efofrt and cl up over 2f out: sn rdn: wknd over 1f out* **25/1**

4013 **10** *1/2* **Tiber Tilly**[27] [4494] 3-8-11 **68**........ RichardThomas 2 — 56
(N P Littmoden) *prom tl wknd over 2f out* **20/1**

2212 **11** *3/4* **Hoh Wotanite**[10] [5036] 3-8-12 **69**........ LPKeniry 8 — 55
(R Hollinshead) *hld up in rr: rdn over 2f out: hanging lft and no prog* **14/1**

1m 30.55s (-0.54) **Going Correction** +0.05s/f (Good) — **11** Ran SP% **119.2**
Speed ratings (Par 101):105,104,103,100,99 99,98,97,95,95 94
CSF £15.13 CT £105.50 TOTE £6.00: £2.20, £1.10, £3.60; EX 17.80.
Owner Viscountess Trenchard **Bred** Fonthill Stud **Trained** East Ilsley, Berks

FOCUS
Not a bad little handicap for the grade of contest and it was run at a fair pace.

5269 SPEEDY HIRE H'CAP — 7f 16y

4:55 (4:58) (Class 6) (0-65,65) 3-Y-O+ — **£3,238** (£963; £481; £240) **Stalls High**

Form — RPR

046 **1** **Piper's Song (IRE)**[55] [3647] 3-9-2 **63**........ DaneO'Neill 7 — 71+
(H Candy) *tall: str: w'like: scope: hld up in midfield: rdn and prog over 2f out: hanging rt but chsd ldr over 1f out: styd on to ld* **7/1**

0024 **2** *nk* **Million Percent**[10] [5032] 7-8-9 **57**........ LiamJones[(5)] 9 — 64
(C R Dore) *trckd clr ldr: effrt to ld over 2f out: drvn fnl 2f: collared last 50yds* **12/1**

3212 **3** *1* **Motu (IRE)**[19] [4729] 5-9-4 **61**........(v) DanielTudhope 14 — 65
(I W McInnes) *a in ldng trio: drvn to chse ldng pair over 1f out: kpt on but nvr quite able to chal* **4/1**[1]

2426 **4** *shd* **Unlimited**[5] [5130] 4-9-3 **60**........ RobertHavlin 6 — 64
(R Simpson) *t.k.h: hld up towards rr: prog on outer over 2f out: drvn and kpt on fr over 1f out* **5/1**[2]

430 **5** *3/4* **Treasure House (IRE)**[12] [4968] 5-9-8 **65**........ RobertWinston 13 — 68+
(M Blanshard) *hld up in midfield: effrt on inner whn nt clr run wl over 1f out: kpt on fnl f: nvr able to chal* **8/1**

5500 **6** *nk* **Nephetriti Way (IRE)**[15] [4894] 5-9-7 **64**........ IanMongan 8 — 65
(P R Chamings) *sn pushed along towards rr: rdn and effrt on outer over 2f out: hanging rt but kpt on fr over 1f out: nt pce to chal* **16/1**

240 **7** *2* **Balerno**[12] [4974] 7-8-12 **55**........ PaulEddery 10 — 51
(Mrs L J Mongan) *hld up towards rr: effrt and sme prog over 2f out: n.m.r over 1f out: one pce fnl f* **16/1**

4456 **8** *hd* **Blacktoft (USA)**[13] [4930] 3-9-1 **65**........ AdamKirby[(3)] 1 — 64+
(S C Williams) *hld up in last pair fr wd draw: sme prog on inner whn hmpd over 1f out: kpt on fnl f: no ch* **12/1**

006 **9** *2* **Laith (IRE)**[15] [4874] 3-9-1 **62**........ AdrianMcCarthy 3 — 52
(Miss V Haigh) *wl in rr: effrt u.p on outer fr over 2f out: n.d* **40/1**

0620 **10** *2 1/2* **Halfwaytoparadise**[27] [4494] 3-8-8 **62**........(p) JackDean[(7)] 12 — 46
(W G M Turner) *blazed off in front: clr 1/2-way: hdd & wknd over 2f out* **50/1**

4010 **11** *1 1/4* **Snow Bunting**[7] [5085] 8-9-1 **58**........ PaulHanagan 11 — 39
(Jedd O'Keeffe) *a towards rr: struggling u.p over 2f out* **12/1**

3100 **12** *1 1/2* **Blue Empire (IRE)**[16] [4831] 5-9-5 **62**........ RyanMoore 5 — 39
(C R Dore) *chsd ldrs tl wknd over 2f out* **13/2**[3]

-306 **13** *1* **Wainwright (IRE)**[124] [1607] 6-8-9 **57**........ KevinGhunowa[(5)] 4 — 31
(P A Blockley) *hld up in midfield: effrt wl over 2f out: wknd wl over 1f out* **33/1**

0300 **14** *10* **What-A-Dancer (IRE)**[5] [5130] 9-8-13 **63**........(b) TolleyDean[(7)] 2 — 11
(R A Harris) *s.i.s: a last and nvr gng wl: t.o* **14/1**

1m 30.94s (-0.15) **Going Correction** +0.05s/f (Good)
WFA 3 from 4yo+ 4lb — **14** Ran SP% **122.5**
Speed ratings (Par 101):102,101,100,100,99 99,96,96,94,91 90,88,87,75
CSF £89.03 CT £399.74 TOTE £8.50: £2.80, £3.60, £1.90; EX 93.80 Place 6 £97.21, Place 5 £75.15.
Owner Mrs J Graham & Partners **Bred** Patrick M Ryan **Trained** Kingston Warren, Oxon

FOCUS
A competitive, albeit modest handicap run at a decent pace.
Nephetriti Way(IRE) Official explanation: jockey said mare was unsuited by the good to firm (good in places) ground
Blacktoft(USA) Official explanation: jockey said gelding suffered interference in running
What-A-Dancer(IRE) Official explanation: jockey said gelding missed the break

T/Jkpt: £17,145.00 to a £1 stake. Pool: £36,222.00. 1.50 winning tickets. T/Plt: £241.80 to a £1 stake. Pool: £65,925.20. 199.00 winning tickets. T/Qpdt: £75.70 to a £1 stake. Pool: £2,979.70. 29.10 winning tickets. JN

[4843]YARMOUTH (L-H)

Tuesday, September 12

OFFICIAL GOING: Good to firm

Wind: Light, across Weather: Sunny becoming hazy

5270 VAUXHALL HOLIDAY PARK PREMIER CLAIMING STKS 1m 3y

2:20 (2:21) (Class 4) 3-Y-O

£6,232 (£1,866; £933; £467; £233; £117) Stalls High

Form RPR

6210 1 **Ellesappelle**[18] 4769 3-8-0 71 ow7........ AndrewElliott(5) 10 73
(K R Burke) *mde all: drvn out* 7/2[2]

2 2 *nk* **Conservative**[22] 4663 3-8-7 .... RHills 8 74+
(W J Haggas) *hld up: hdwy over 2f out: rdn to chse wnr over 1f out: r.o* 3/1[1]

2450 3 *5* **Malech (IRE)**[25] 4575 3-8-8 68 ow1........ DarrylHolland 9 64
(M L W Bell) *chsd ldrs: rdn over 2f out: no ex fnl f* 5/1[3]

5060 4 *3 1/2* **Renderoc (USA)**[46] 3889 3-8-9 75........(p) JohnEgan 4 57
(J S Moore) *chsd wnr: edgd rt 1/2-way: rdn over 2f out: weakened fnl f* 6/1

2510 5 *1 3/4* **Wee Charlie Castle (IRE)**[20] 4702 3-8-10 69........ OscarUrbina 1 54
(G C H Chung) *hld up: hdwy over 2f out: hung rt over 1f out: sn wknd* 10/1

-130 6 *3* **De La Rue (USA)**[24] 4599 3-9-5 79........ TPQueally 3 56
(M G Quinlan) *hld up in tch: plld hrd: rdn and wknd over 2f out* 12/1

6204 7 *1 1/2* **Crimson Flame (IRE)**[8] 5054 3-8-9 61........ TPO'Shea 6 42
(M R Channon) *chsd ldrs: n.m.r 1/2-way: sn rdn: wknd 2f out* 11/1

006U 8 *shd* **Reflecting (IRE)**[20] 4704 3-8-1 65........ NickyMackay 7 34
(J W Hills) *hld up: rdn over 3f out: n.m.r and wknd over 2f out* 20/1

34- 9 *1 3/4* **Nawayea**[459] 2453 3-8-6 ow1........ StephenDonohoe(3) 5 38
(C N Allen) *rrd s: bhd: rdn and wknd over 2f out* 22/1

1m 39.17s (-0.73) **Going Correction** -0.05s/f (Good) 9 Ran SP% **112.4**

Speed ratings (Par 103):101,100,95,92,90 87,85,85,84

CSF £13.91 TOTE £4.50: £1.40, £1.60, £2.00; EX 12.60 Trifecta £26.70 Pool £206.34, 5.48 winning units..The winner was claimed by G. L. Moore for £9,000. Conservative was claimed by P. G. Murphy for £17,000.

Owner A Rhodes Haulage and P Timmins 2 **Bred** N R Shields **Trained** Middleham Moor, N Yorks

FOCUS

A fair claimer, rated as such, and dominated by the winner, who made all.

Wee Charlie Castle(IRE) Official explanation: jockey said gelding lost a shoe

Nawayea Official explanation: trainer said filly banged its head in the stalls

5271 JACK LEADER CHALLENGE TROPHY FILLIES' NURSERY 7f 3y

2:50 (2:51) (Class 4) (0-85,80) 2-Y-O £5,362 (£1,604; £802; £401; £199) Stalls High

Form RPR

21 1 **Steam Cuisine**[30] 4394 2-9-4 **77**........ TPQueally 4 85+
(M G Quinlan) *trckd ldrs: nt clr run and swtchd lft over 1f out: r.o to ld wl ins fnl f: readily* 7/2[2]

15 2 *nk* **Crumbs Of Comfort (USA)**[32] 4322 2-9-7 **80**........ NickyMackay 2 81
(L M Cumani) *s.i.s: hld up: hdwy and swtchd lft over 2f out: led over 1f out: rdn and hdd wl ins fnl f* 11/2

6342 3 *2* **Miss Saafend Plaza (IRE)**[9] 5041 2-9-7 **80**........ JimmyFortune 1 76
(R Hannon) *trckd ldrs: rdn and ev ch over 1f out: styd on same pce ins fnl f* 7/4[1]

4243 4 *4* **Reem Al Fallah (IRE)**[12] 4949 2-8-11 **70**........ JohnEgan 5 55
(M R Channon) *chsd ldrs: led wl over 1f out: sn rdn and hdd: wknd ins fnl f* 5/1[3]

000 5 *3/4* **Wickedish**[38] 4148 2-7-12 **57** oh4........ JimmyQuinn 3 40
(P Howling) *hld up: effrt over 2f out: nvr trbld ldrs* 33/1

3450 6 *1 1/2* **Cape Dancer (IRE)**[18] 4766 2-8-10 **69**........ TomEaves 7 49
(J S Wainwright) *led 4f: wknd over 1f out* 11/1

5301 7 *1 3/4* **Retaliate**[22] 4665 2-8-11 **70**........ SebSanders 6 45
(M Quinn) *chsd ldr: led 3f out: hdd wl over 1f out: sn wknd* 14/1

1m 26.85s (0.25) **Going Correction** -0.05s/f (Good) 7 Ran SP% **108.6**

Speed ratings (Par 94):96,95,93,88,87 86,84

CSF £20.43 TOTE £4.40: £2.50, £3.10; EX 24.60.

Owner Burns Farm Racing **Bred** Burns Farm Stud **Trained** Newmarket, Suffolk

FOCUS

A fair fillies' nursery won easily by the winner, and the form looks sound.

NOTEBOOK

Steam Cuisine won in good fashion after struggling to find room when making her challenge in the latter stages of the race. Winning with much more in hand than the final result suggests, she is a decent prospect for her stable. (op 4-1)

Crumbs Of Comfort(USA) came with her effort just over a furlong from home and looked for a brief moment like nicking the race from the unlucky-in-running Steam Cuisine. It would have been a very fortunate success had she won, but she was still nicely clear of the third and is holding her form well. (op 4-1)

Miss Saafend Plaza(IRE) had every chance but came up short when under maximum pressure. The Handicapper appears to have her measure now. (tchd 2-1)

Reem Al Fallah(IRE) was another in the race to have every chance but was not good enough. She did tend to hang away to the left under pressure but it made no difference to the final result. A slight drop in grade is required for her to have a chance. (op 6-1)

Wickedish has yet to show enough to make her of any real interest in any company.

5272 THOMAS PRIOR MEMORIAL MAIDEN STKS 6f 3y

3:25 (3:25) (Class 5) 3-Y-0+ £3,886 (£1,156; £577; £288) Stalls High

Form RPR

2242 1 **Mr Cellophane**[13] 4927 3-9-3 62........ JimmyFortune 8 64
(J R Jenkins) *trckd ldrs: led over 1f out: rdn out* 5/1[2]

0 2 *1/2* **Summer Celebrity (IRE)**[26] 4527 3-9-0 ow2........ AntonyProcter 11 59+
(D R C Elsworth) *s.s: hld up: hdwy over 1f out: hung lft ins fnl f: r.o* 50/1

0322 3 *2* **Knead The Dough**[7] 5077 5-9-0 42........ NataliaGemelova(5) 15 56
(A E Price) *chsd ldrs: rdn over 1f out: styd on same pce* 20/1

42-0 4 *hd* **Ribh**[10] 5023 3-8-12 85........ DarrylHolland 14 50
(C E Brittain) *hld up: hdwy over 2f out: chsd wnr over 1f out: no ex ins fnl f* 9/1[3]

0004 5 *2 1/2* **Decider (USA)**[8] 5055 3-9-0 42........ StephenDonohoe(3) 10 48
(J M Bradley) *chsd ldrs: rdn over 2f out: wknd over 1f out* 40/1

0- 6 *2* **Grand Rebecca (IRE)**[363] 5230 3-8-12........ RoystonFfrench 1 37
(G A Huffer) *s.i.s: hld up: nvr nr to chal* 50/1

0600 7 *1 1/4* **Hilltop Fantasy**[77] 2955 5-9-0 37........ MichaelTebbutt 5 33
(V Smith) *w ldr tl led over 3f out: rdn and hdd over 1f out: sn wknd* 100/1

-000 8 *2 1/2* **Sham Ruby**[21] 4670 4-9-0 35........(t) OscarUrbina 4 26
(M R Bosley) *chsd ldrs: rdn and hung lft over 2f out: wknd over 1f out* 66/1

4- 9 *3* **Maraagel (USA)**[404] 4105 3-9-3 .... LDettori 9 22
(Saeed Bin Suroor) *dwlt: sn chsng ldrs: rdn and wknd over 1f out* 4/11[1]

0-0 10 *1 3/4* **Charanne**[8] 5055 3-8-12 .... TomEaves 2 11
(J M Bradley) *a in rr* 100/1

50 11 *1* **Perfect Cover (IRE)**[41] 4045 3-8-12 .... JimmyQuinn 12 8
(J A R Toller) *prom over 4f* 40/1

0-40 12 *5* **Sunny Haze**[91] 2531 3-8-9 33........(v[1]) SaleemGolam(3) 13 —
(Mrs P N Dutfield) *led: hdd over 3f out: sn rdn: wknd over 2f out* 100/1

0-60 13 *1 3/4* **Little Trinket**[10] 5023 3-8-12 30........ JohnEgan 3 —
(Mrs C A Dunnett) *sn outpcd* 80/1

1m 13.29s (-0.41) **Going Correction** -0.05s/f (Good)

WFA 3 from 4yo+ 2lb 13 Ran SP% **119.2**

Speed ratings (Par 103):100,99,96,96,93 90,88,85,81,79 77,71,68

CSF £219.73 TOTE £5.30: £1.10, £12.00, £3.10; EX 283.90 TRIFECTA Not won..

Owner R B Hill **Bred** Buy And Sell Partnership **Trained** Royston, Herts

FOCUS

A very modest maiden judged on official ratings and the winner did not need to improve to score. The form is not likely to amount to very much.

Maraagel(USA) Official explanation: trainer's rep had no explanation for the poor form shown

5273 CONSTITUTION MOTORS HYUNDAI (S) STKS 7f 3y

4:00 (4:00) (Class 6) 3-Y-O £2,331 (£693; £346; £173) Stalls High

Form RPR

0600 1 **Ockums Razor (IRE)**[13] 4930 3-9-3 61........ JohnEgan 1 67
(C A Dwyer) *chsd ldrs: led 3f out: rdn out* 16/1

052 2 *1 1/2* **Rembrandt Quality (USA)**[8] 5054 3-8-12 65........(b[1]) LDettori 14 58
(N A Callaghan) *trckd ldrs: rdn over 1f out: styd on* 15/8[1]

6000 3 *2 1/2* **Franky'N'Jonny**[18] 4769 3-8-7 41........ RoystonFfrench 9 47
(Mrs C A Dunnett) *dwlt: hld up: hdwy over 2f out: rdn over 1f out: styd on same pce* 25/1

0363 4 *nk* **Cool Sting (IRE)**[8] 5054 3-9-3 65........ DarrylHolland 12 56
(A M Balding) *dwlt: outpcd: hdwy over 1f out: nt rch ldrs* 7/2[2]

0036 5 *1* **Shunkawakhan (IRE)**[2] 5210 3-8-12 59........ OscarUrbina 5 48
(G C H Chung) *mid-div: hdwy over 2f out: wknd fnl f* 5/1[3]

5433 6 *3/4* **Sunset Ridge (IRE)**[28] 4450 3-8-7 51........(p) NickyMackay 6 41
(Rae Guest) *chsd ldrs: rdn over 2f out: wknd over 1f out* 6/1

0040 7 *nk* **Precautionary**[8] 5055 3-8-8 52 ow1........ MickyFenton 16 41
(Miss J Feilden) *hld up: hdwy and hung lft fr over 1f out: n.d* 22/1

6003 8 *5* **Marvin Gardens**[33] 4304 3-8-9 40........ StephenDonohoe(3) 4 32
(P S McEntee) *chsd ldrs: rdn over 2f out: wknd over 1f out* 40/1

2200 9 *2* **Lucys Lady**[48] 3839 3-8-2 47........ AndrewElliott(5) 7 22
(K R Burke) *chsd ldrs over 4f* 25/1

10 *1 1/4* **Habanus Livius (IRE)**[55] 3653 3-8-12 47........ JimmyFortune 10 24
(Joseph Quinn, Ire) *s.i.s: outpcd* 14/1

-020 11 *2 1/2* **By Storm**[21] 4671 3-8-4 42........ SaleemGolam(3) 8 13
(John Berry) *chsd ldrs: lost pl over 5f out: n.d after* 40/1

0 12 *1/2* **Lighted Smile (FR)**[11] 4983 3-8-5 52........ WilliamCarson(7) 11 16
(C J Gray) *sn outpcd* 50/1

0-00 13 *2 1/2* **Florida Legend (IRE)**[30] 4396 3-8-7 40 ow3........ DeanCorby(3) 3 8
(Miss J Feilden) *chsd ldrs to 1/2-way* 80/1

1020 14 *nk* **Bekoning (IRE)**[18] 4769 3-8-10 45........ ChrisCavanagh(7) 2 14
(M Quinn) *w ldr 3f: rdn and wknd over 2f out* 66/1

0000 15 *5* **Young Flavio**[20] 4690 3-8-12 42........(b[1]) TomEaves 15 —
(J M Bradley) *mde most 4f: sn wknd* 100/1

1m 26.19s (-0.41) **Going Correction** -0.05s/f (Good) 15 Ran SP% **123.1**

Speed ratings (Par 99):100,98,95,95,93 93,92,87,84,83 80,79,77,76,70

CSF £44.15 TOTE £26.50: £7.40, £1.20, £6.20; EX 165.20 TRIFECTA Not won..There was no bid for the winner. Rembrandt Quality was the subject of a friendly claim

Owner S B Components (international) Ltd **Bred** Minch Bloodstock **Trained** Burrough Green, Cambs

FOCUS

A desperate affair won by a horse who quite recently had been reported as not handling good to firm ground. The form looks a bit dubious.

5274 ATTHERACES.COM FREE VIDEO FORM CONDITIONS STKS 6f 3y

4:35 (4:41) (Class 3) 3-Y-0+

£9,348 (£2,799; £1,399; £700; £349; £175) Stalls High

Form RPR

610- 1 **Riotous Applause**[348] 5571 3-8-2 97........ JimmyQuinn 1 95+
(J R Fanshawe) *racd centre: trckd ldrs: led that gp and overall ldr over 1f out: rdn out* 12/1[2]

2565 2 *2* **Vortex**[47] 3881 7-9-2 105........(t) MickyFenton 6 101
(Miss Gay Kelleway) *racd stands' side chsd ldr tl swtchd centre 4f out: led that gro up and overall ldr over 2f out: hdd over 1f out: styd on s* 14/1[3]

3050 3 *shd* **Blue Tomato**[9] 5044 5-8-6 88........ StephenDonohoe(3) 7 94
(J M Bradley) *racd centre: chsd ldr over 3f: outpcd over 1f out: styd on* 12/1[2]

221- 4 *1* **Goodricke**[374] 4940 4-9-2 117........(vt) LDettori 4 98
(Saeed Bin Suroor) *dwlt: racd centre: hld up: hdwy over 1f out: sn rdn: nt run on* 1/4[1]

0000 5 *1* **Corridor Creeper (FR)**[3] 5182 9-9-7 103........(p) DarrylHolland 2 100
(J M Bradley) *led centre over 3f: wknd ins fnl f* 12/1[2]

0064 6 *4* **Dutch Key Card (IRE)**[7] 5087 5-8-2 41........(v) MarkCoumbe(7) 5 76?
(C Smith) *racd stands' side: overall ldr over 3f: wknd over 1f out* 200/1

1m 12.24s (-1.46) **Going Correction** -0.05s/f (Good)

WFA 3 from 4yo+ 2lb 6 Ran SP% **110.2**

Speed ratings (Par 107):107,104,104,102,101 96

CSF £139.53 TOTE £12.60: £2.60, £2.90; EX 96.10 Trifecta £362.20 Part won. Pool - £510.25, 0.97 winning units..

Owner Car Colston Hall Stud/Hamill **Bred** Car Colston Hall Stud **Trained** Newmarket, Suffolk

■ Turn On The Syle (66/1) was withdrawn (rider Jason Edmunds uns & injured in paddock).

FOCUS

With last year's Haydock Sprint Cup winner Goodricke a major disappointment on his belated reappearance, 88-rated Blue Tomato not beaten far in third, and Dutch Key Card a bit close for comfort, the bare form of this conditions race does not look as strong as one might have expected.

NOTEBOOK

Riotous Applause ◆, the winner of a Redcar maiden before finishing seventh of ten on her final start as a juvenile, took full advantage of the favourite running below par to make a winning return from her 348-day break. She suffered a hairline fracture in the spring, but it was apparently nothing serious. The form may be a little suspect in behind, but this must still rate as a very good effort indeed considering the length of time she had been off. Her trainer said that there is not much left for her this year, but she will stay in training and is an exciting prospect. (op 8-1)

The Form Book, Raceform Ltd, Compton, RG20 6NL

Vortex, without the eye-shield he wore when well down the field over a mile at Yarmouth 47 days previously, ran a respectable race on his return to action, but he had 10lb in hand of Blue Tomato at the weights and was clearly below his best. He looks better over slightly further. (op 16-1 tchd 10-1)

Blue Tomato had plenty to find at the weights and ran as well as could have been expected. (op 16-1)

Goodricke, not seen since winning the Group 1 Haydock Sprint Cup a year previously on his final start for David Loder, had upwards of 8lb in hand of these at the weights but failed to take advantage of what looked a golden opportunity. All off his wins have come on ground good or softer, and it can only be hoped that he returns to his best when getting his favoured conditions. Official explanation: trainer's rep said colt ran flat (op 1-3 tchd 4-11)

Corridor Creeper(FR) was not at his best and seems better suited by five furlongs on easier ground. (op 10-1 tchd 16-1)

5275 BURGH HALL LEISURE COMPLEX SPRINT H'CAP — 5f 43y

5:05 (5:07) (Class 4) (0-85,80) 3-Y-O+

£6,232 (£1,866; £933; £467; £233; £117) **Stalls High**

Form				RPR
4554	**1**		**Bluebok**[4] [5148] 5-9-2 **80**....(t) StephenDonohoe(3) 4 (J M Bradley) *chsd ldrs: rdn over 1f out: r.o to ld wl ins fnl f* **9/2**[3]	88
4032	**2**	*shd*	**Millinsky (USA)**[19] [4725] 5-8-4 **72**.... RobbieMills(7) 9 (Rae Guest) *hld up: hdwy 2f out: hung lft and led ins fnl f: sn hdd: kpt on* **4/1**[2]	80
0016	**3**	*1*	**Bold Minstrel (IRE)**[12] [4952] 4-9-5 **80**.... SebSanders 2 (M Quinn) *chsd ldrs: led 1/2-way: rdn and hdd ins fnl f: styd on same pce* **20/1**	84
3324	**4**	*nk*	**Woodnook**[17] [4812] 3-9-0 **76**.... JimmyFortune 1 (J A R Toller) *dwlt: hld up: hdwy over 1f out: sn rdn: r.o* **6/1**	79
1035	**5**	*¾*	**Holbeck Ghyll (IRE)**[17] [4796] 4-9-3 **78**.... JohnEgan 6 (A M Balding) *s.i.s: sn chsng ldrs: rdn over 1f out: styd on same pce* **10/3**[1]	78
5240	**6**	*1 ¼*	**Conjecture**[27] [4468] 4-8-9 **70**....(b[1]) RoystonFfrench 5 (R Bastiman) *chsd ldr to 1/2-way: sn rdn: wknd ins fnl f* **10/1**	66
6416	**7**	*shd*	**Silver Dane (IRE)**[39] [4110] 4-9-1 **76**....(v) LDettori 3 (Mrs C A Dunnett) *sn outpcd: r.o ins fnl f: nvr nrr* **7/1**	71
5011	**8**	*hd*	**Multahab**[21] [4675] 7-8-2 **66** oh2....(t) SaleemGolam(3) 7 (Miss D A McHale) *prom: rdn over 1f: wknd fnl f* **12/1**	61
6000	**9**	*2 ½*	**One Way Ticket**[4] [5148] 6-9-5 **80**....(p) DarryllHolland 8 (J M Bradley) *led to 1/2-way: wknd over 1f out* **20/1**	66

61.82 secs (-0.98) **Going Correction** -0.05s/f (Good)
WFA 3 from 4yo+ 1lb — 9 Ran SP% **114.4**
Speed ratings (Par 105):105,104,103,102,101 99,99,99,95
CSF £22.62 CT £320.90 TOTE £4.70: £1.40, £2.00, £4.50; EX 30.10 Trifecta £340.50 Pool £498.90 - 1.04 winning units.

Owner E A Hayward **Bred** E Duggan And D Churchman **Trained** Sedbury, Gloucs

FOCUS
A fair sprint handicap and straightforward form to rate.

5276 EDP24.CO.UK H'CAP — 1m 3f 101y

5:35 (5:35) (Class 5) (0-70,70) 3-Y-O+ — **£4,015** (£1,194; £597; £298) **Stalls Low**

Form				RPR
2513	**1**		**High Treason (USA)**[22] [4662] 4-9-11 **69**.... TPQueally 5 (W J Musson) *hld up: hdwy over 2f out: led over 1f out: rdn out* **9/2**[2]	80
6640	**2**	*hd*	**Acknowledgement**[27] [4472] 4-9-5 **63**....(b[1]) JohnEgan 4 (D R C Elsworth) *mid-div: hdwy 4f out: rdn and ev ch ins fnl f: styd on* **33/1**	73
0012	**3**	*1 ¾*	**Mighty Moon**[19] [4723] 3-9-0 **66**....(bt) LDettori 1 (Lady Herries) *chsd ldrs: rdn and nt clr run over 1f out: styd on same pce ins fnl f* **11/4**[1]	73
3305	**4**	*¾*	**Melvino**[19] [4723] 4-9-2 **60**.... MickyFenton 9 (T D Barron) *s.s: hld up: racd keenly: hdwy 2f out: nt clr run and swtchd rt over 1f out: r.o ins fnl f: nrst fin* **9/1**	66
2154	**5**	*nk*	**Taxman (IRE)**[30] [4393] 4-9-11 **69**....(p) DarryllHolland 12 (C E Brittain) *sn chsng ldr: led over 3f out: rdn and hdd over 1f out: no ex ins fnl f* **8/1**	74
4614	**6**	*¾*	**Spaceman**[35] [4224] 3-8-7 **59**....(v) NickyMackay 8 (L M Cumani) *mid-div: hdwy over 2f out: sn rdn: styd on same pce fnl f* **13/2**[3]	63
-150	**7**	*1 ¾*	**Captain General**[24] [4604] 4-9-7 **65**.... JimmyFortune 3 (J A R Toller) *chsd ldrs: rdn over 2f out: wknd fnl f* **12/1**	66
4163	**8**	*1 ¼*	**Darghan (IRE)**[16] [4848] 6-8-11 **62**.... AlanRutter(7) 10 (W J Musson) *hld up: nvr nr to chal* **14/1**	61
0060	**9**	*1 ¾*	**Madame Constanze (IRE)**[7] [5082] 3-8-4 **56** oh11.... JimmyQuinn 13 (Miss Gay Kelleway) *hld up: n.d* **100/1**	52?
0301	**10**	*shd*	**Tayman (IRE)**[20] [4687] 4-9-8 **66**.... SebSanders 11 (G Wragg) *prom: rdn and ev ch over 2f out: wknd over 1f out* **17/2**	62
623	**11**	*5*	**Pochard**[30] [4396] 3-9-1 **70**.... StephenDonohoe(3) 7 (J M P Eustace) *plld hrd and prom: stdd and lost pl over 9f out: bhd fnl 4f* **28/1**	58
2505	**12**	*½*	**Meelup (IRE)**[21] [4673] 6-8-13 **57**....(p) TomEaves 2 (P G Murphy) *led 8f: wknd over 2f out* **25/1**	44

2m 25.42s (-2.08) **Going Correction** -0.10s/f (Good)
WFA 3 from 4yo+ 8lb — 12 Ran SP% **115.4**
Speed ratings (Par 103):103,102,101,101,100 100,99,98,96,96 93,92
CSF £150.20 CT £481.85 TOTE £5.20: £2.10, £7.00, £1.20; EX 174.70 TRIFECTA Not won. Place 6 £905.00, Place 5 £693.41.

Owner S Rudolf **Bred** Helmut Von Finck **Trained** Newmarket, Suffolk

FOCUS
Just an ordinary handicap rated around the third and fourth.

T/Plt: £814.00 to a £1 stake. Pool: £56,650.75. 50.80 winning tickets. T/Qpdt: £101.60 to a £1 stake. Pool: £3,765.10. 27.40 winning tickets. CR

5277 - 5281a (Foreign Racing) - See Raceform Interactive

[4943] BEVERLEY (R-H)

Wednesday, September 13

OFFICIAL GOING: Good to firm
After eight days without any significant rain the ground was described as 'really good, spot on with an excellent cover of grass'.
Wind: light, across Weather: fine, sunny and warm

5282 BEVERLEY-RACECOURSE.CO.UK (S) NURSERY — 5f

2:10 (2:12) (Class 6) (0-65,64) 2-Y-O — **£3,071** (£906; £453) **Stalls High**

Form				RPR
4404	**1**		**Sister Etienne (IRE)**[13] [4950] 2-9-5 **62**.... PhillipMakin 15 (T D Barron) *mde all: rdn over 1f out: styd on* **6/1**[2]	67
6603	**2**	*1 ½*	**Dotty's Daughter**[13] [4950] 2-8-12 **55**....(p) TPO'Shea 8 (Mrs A Duffield) *towards rr: hdwy on outer wl over 1f out: sn rdn and styd on wl fnl f* **16/1**	55
5051	**3**	*¾*	**Burlington Fayr (IRE)**[16] [4887] 2-8-10 **58**.... MichaelJStainton(5) 14 (N Tinkler) *prom: rdn to chse wnr 2f out: drvn and edgd rt over 1f out: kpt on same pce* **8/1**	55
0000	**4**	*2 ½*	**Homes By Woodford**[44] [3994] 2-9-1 **58**.... PaulMulrennan 11 (M W Easterby) *chsd ldrs tl outpcd 1/2-way: styd on ent last: nrst fin* **20/1**	46
2223	**5**	*1 ¾*	**House Arrest**[14] [4921] 2-8-13 **56**.... SebSanders 1 (A J McCabe) *dwlt and swtchd rt s: sn chsng ldrs on inner: rdn along 2f out: sn one pce* **14/1**	38
0350	**6**	*1 ¼*	**Autour Du Monde**[8] [5084] 2-9-1 **58**....(p) JoeFanning 16 (P C Haslam) *cl up: rdn 2f out: sn wknd* **13/2**[3]	35
002	**7**	*½*	**Show Trial (IRE)**[23] [4664] 2-8-9 **52**.... TonyCulhane 4 (M R Channon) *v.s.a and lost 15 l s: bhd tl styd on appr last: nrst fin* **11/1**	27
3056	**8**	*shd*	**Tobago Reef**[13] [4949] 2-9-3 **60**....(b[1]) TomEaves 2 (Mrs L Stubbs) *dwlt and rr tl styd on fnl f: nrst fin* **50/1**	35
3406	**9**	*3*	**Cookies Quiff (IRE)**[14] [4926] 2-8-13 **56**.... LPKeniry 12 (J S Moore) *dwlt: sn chsng ldrs: rdn along over 2f out and grad wknd* **11/1**	20
0030	**10**	*nk*	**Pirner's Brig**[44] [3997] 2-8-12 **55**.... DaleGibson 9 (M W Easterby) *a towards rr* **50/1**	18
53	**11**	*½*	**Ishibee (IRE)**[15] [4912] 2-9-7 **64**....(p) RoystonFfrench 5 (Mrs A Duffield) *a towards rr* **13/2**[3]	25
1054	**12**	*1 ½*	**Top Tier**[28] [4493] 2-8-10 **58**.... LiamJones(5) 13 (Peter Grayson) *bolted to s: chsd ldrs: rdn 1/2-way: sn wknd* **11/2**[1]	14

64.74 secs (0.74) **Going Correction** -0.125s/f (Firm) — 12 Ran SP% **105.3**
Speed ratings (Par 93):89,86,85,81,78 76,75,75,70,70 69,67
CSF £76.79 CT £566.13 TOTE £6.00: £2.30, £3.80, £2.90; EX 100.00.Winner bought in 6,400 gns. Show Trial (no.16) was claimed by D J Ffrench Davis for £6000

Owner Oghill House Stud **Bred** Oghill House Stud **Trained** Maunby, N Yorks

■ Stewards' Enquiry : T P O'Shea caution: careless riding

FOCUS
A moderate event which saw those drawn high at a distinct advantage. The form looks fair for the class.

NOTEBOOK
Sister Etienne(IRE) pinged out, making full use of her decent draw, and belatedly did enough to open her account at the seventh time of asking. She has been disappointing to date and was certainly helped by being drawn high, but is entitled to improve a little now that she has got her head in front.

Dotty's Daughter was doing all of her best work too late in the day and failed to confirm her Musselburgh form with the winner. She was not drawn as well as that rival, however, and still looked to run up to her official mark in defeat. (op 20-1)

Burlington Fayr(IRE), off the mark in this class at Ripon last time, had her chance but was made to look very one-paced when push came to shove.

Homes By Woodford hit a flat spot before running on strongly inside the final furlong. On this evidence he needs another furlong.

House Arrest, with the visor abandoned, did not fare too badly from her low draw, but still appears regressive all the same. (op 12-1)

Pirner's Brig Official explanation: jockey said colt lost its action

Top Tier probably lost her race on the way to post and had nothing in the locker when asked for her effort. She is worth another chance. Official explanation: trainer said filly finished distressed

5283 GEORGE KILBURN MEMORIAL MAIDEN AUCTION STKS (DIV I) — 7f 100y

2:45 (2:46) (Class 5) 2-Y-O — **£2,590** (£770; £385; £192) **Stalls High**

Form				RPR
000	**1**		**Montalembert (USA)**[18] [4824] 2-8-9.... LPKeniry 6 (J S Moore) *trckd ldrs: hung rt over 1f out: led jst ins last: drew clr: readily* **4/1**[2]	81
42	**2**	*4*	**Arch Of Titus (IRE)**[26] [4566] 2-8-13.... MickyFenton 8 (M L W Bell) *t.k.h: trckd ldr: led over 3f out: hdd jst ins last: wknd fnl 75yds* **4/7**[1]	76
3	**3**	*7*	**Muree Queen**[6] [5134] 2-8-4.... PaulQuinn 11 (R Hollinshead) *in tch: drvn over 3f out: kpt ont o take modest 3rd ins last* **20/1**	50
	4	*1 ½*	**One And Gone (IRE)** 2-9-1.... PaulHanagan 5 (R A Fahey) *s.i.s: styd on fnl 2f: nrst fin* **25/1**	58
0	**5**	*¾*	**The Geester**[18] [4815] 2-8-9.... PaulEddery 10 (S R Bowring) *t.k.h: trckd ldrs: one pce fnl 2f* **100/1**	50
03	**6**	*1*	**Woodland Traveller (USA)**[25] [4608] 2-9-1....(t) KimTinkler 7 (N Tinkler) *chsd ldrs: hung rt over 2f out: one pce* **10/1**[3]	54
05	**7**	*shd*	**Juvenescent (USA)**[25] [4608] 2-8-10.... PaulMulrennan 9 (R D E Woodhouse) *led tl over 3f out: wknd over 1f out* **12/1**	48
46	**8**	*shd*	**Milliegait**[41] [4066] 2-8-6.... DavidAllan 4 (T D Easterby) *mid-div: outpcd and lost pl over 4f out: hdwy 2f out: styng on whn bot much room ins last* **12/1**	44
	9	*1 ½*	**Lady Pickpocket** 2-8-0 ow3.... PatrickHills(7) 2 (M H Tompkins) *s.i.s: bhd tl sme hdwy fnl 2f: nvr on terms* **25/1**	42
0	**10**	*6*	**Orotund**[20] [4731] 2-8-4.... DuranFentiman(5) 12 (T D Easterby) *t.k.h in mid-div: lost pl over 2f out: sn bhd* **50/1**	30
	11	*4*	**Moondine (IRE)** 2-8-1.... AndrewMullen(3) 3 (B S Rothwell) *s.i.s: edgd lft over 3f out: sn bhd* **66/1**	15

1m 34.21s (-0.10) **Going Correction** -0.125s/f (Firm) — 11 Ran SP% **125.0**
Speed ratings (Par 95):95,90,82,80,79 78,78,78,76,69 65
CSF £6.73 TOTE £6.10: £1.20, £1.10, £5.00; EX 11.90.

Owner Willie McKay **Bred** Delehanty Stock Farm **Trained** Upper Lambourn, Berks

FOCUS
No strength in depth to this maiden and the first two pulled well clear, the favourite almost certainly below his best on this stiff, uphill finish.

NOTEBOOK

Montalembert(USA), who has been tackling some stiff tasks, carried plenty of market support. He came right away inside the last but he cannot expect a lenient nursery mark. (op 5-1)

Arch Of Titus(IRE), who looked fit and well, would not settle. He took it up turning in but his legs turned to jelly late on. (op 4-6 tchd 1-2 in a place)

Muree Queen, still carrying condition and green to post, improved on her heavy-ground debut effort but she may not be seen to best effect until next year. (op 16-1)

One And Gone(IRE), a March foal, is long in the back. Very green to post, he stayed on after a tardy start and this will have taught him plenty. (op 28-1)

The Geester, very free, at least showed a bit more than he had done on his debut two weeks earlier.

Milliegait, having her third outing, dropped back on the turn for home. She met trouble when staying on from the rear late on and this at least opens up the nursery route for her. Official explanation: jockey said filly lost its action approaching 3f out and was denied a clear run in the closing stages (op 16-1)

Lady Pickpocket Official explanation: jockey said filly hung right throughout

5284 BRECKS SAAB H'CAP — 1m 4f 16y

3:15 (3:15) (Class 4) (0-80,79) 3-Y-O — **£6,477** (£1,927; £963; £481) **Stalls** High

Form — RPR

1342 **1** **Mull Of Dubai**[22] 4672 3-8-4 **65** .... RichardMullen 14 — 71
(J S Moore) *in tch: hdwy 2f out: rdn over 1f out: drvn and styd on ins last to ld on line* **10/1**

-606 **2** *shd* **Charlie Tokyo (IRE)**[17] 4833 3-9-2 **77** .... PaulHanagan 11 — 83
(R A Fahey) *trckd ldrs: hdwy 3f out: rdn to ld over 1f out: drvn ins last: hdd on line* **10/3**[1]

3445 **3** *hd* **Blushing Hilary (IRE)**[65] 3359 3-8-8 **69** ....(p) TomEaves 2 — 75
(Miss J A Camacho) *chsd ldrs: hdwy 3f out: rdn to chal over 1f out and ev ch: drvn ins last: kpt on* **28/1**

501 **4** *1* **Hill Billy Rock (IRE)**[16] 4884 3-8-9 **70** .... DeanMcKeown 1 — 74
(G A Swinbank) *hld up in midfield: hdwy over 4f out: rdn 2f out: drvn and kpt on fnl f* **7/2**[2]

6233 **5** *2 ½* **Bollin Dolly**[31] 4402 3-8-9 **70** .... DavidAllan 10 — 70
(T D Easterby) *led: rdn along 3f out: drvn and hdd over 1f out: wknd ins last* **10/1**

6266 **6** *½* **Pinch Of Salt (IRE)**[95] 2436 3-9-2 **77** .... FrancisNorton 12 — 77
(A M Balding) *chsd ldrs: hdwy on outer 3f out: rdn wl over 1f out: kpt on same pce appr last* **12/1**

521 **7** *1* **Chronomatic**[88] 2646 3-8-5 **73** .... PatrickHills(7) 7 — 71
(M H Tompkins) *hld up in rr: hdwy over 3f out: rdn along 2f out: no imp* **7/1**

6300 **8** *½* **Categorical**[19] 4763 3-8-12 **73** .... PatCosgrave 5 — 70
(K G Reveley) *s.i.s: a towards rr* **40/1**

-434 **9** *nk* **Great Tidings**[89] 2607 3-8-10 **71** .... JoeFanning 4 — 68
(M Johnston) *chsd ldr: rdn along 3f out: wknd fnl 2f* **6/1**[3]

3215 **10** *3* **Markington**[38] 4173 3-8-12 **73** .... DarryllHolland 13 — 65
(J D Bethell) *chsd ldrs: rdn along 3f out: sn wknd* **12/1**

4404 **11** *12* **Cheviot Heights**[18] 4814 3-8-6 **67** .... RoystonFfrench 3 — 40
(S C Williams) *a towards rr* **20/1**

5036 **12** *6* **Calcutta Cup (UAE)**[71] 3177 3-8-12 **73** .... MickyFenton 8 — 36
(Karen McLintock) *keen: chsd ldrs and unbalanced bnd after 1f and sn towards rr: hdwy 5f out: sn rdn along and wknd* **25/1**

2m 38.07s (-2.14) **Going Correction** -0.125s/f (Firm) — **12** Ran SP% **120.1**

Speed ratings (Par 103):102,101,101,101,99 99,98,98,97,95 87,83

CSF £42.13 CT £931.95 TOTE £10.90: £2.70, £1.80, £8.70; EX 75.70.

Owner Mrs Fitri Hay **Bred** B Walters **Trained** Upper Lambourn, Berks

FOCUS

A cracking finish to what was a competitive handicap. The form looks sound based around the performances of the third and fourth.

Pinch Of Salt(IRE) Official explanation: trainer said he'd been unable to refit the tongue strap

5285 MAC AND LENI MEMORIAL H'CAP — 1m 100y

3:50 (3:50) (Class 6) (0-55,55) 3-Y-O+ — **£3,238** (£963; £481; £240) **Stalls** High

Form — RPR

0322 **1** **Able Mind**[37] 4194 6-8-11 **51** .... DNolan(3) 2 — 61
(D W Thompson) *bhd: hdwy on outside over 2f out: hung rt and led 1f out: hld on towards fin* **12/1**

0002 **2** *½* **Flaxby**[28] 4467 4-9-3 **54** ....(bp) DarryllHolland 5 — 63
(J D Bethell) *bhd: hdwy 2f out: fin strly to take 2nd nr fin: nt quite rch wnr* **10/1**

0242 **3** *¾* **Band**[44] 3999 6-9-3 **54** .... SebSanders 8 — 61
(E S McMahon) *chsd ldrs: kpt ont o take 2nd ins last: no ex* **7/1**[2]

0560 **4** *¾* **Splodger Mac (IRE)**[30] 4425 7-8-5 **49** ....(b) SuzzanneFrance(7) 15 — 55
(N Bycroft) *in tch: effrt 2f out: kpt on wl fnl f* **16/1**

3056 **5** *¾* **Bolckow**[34] 4297 3-8-10 **55** .... AndrewMullen(3) 10 — 59
(K A Ryan) *mid-div: edgd rt 2f out: styd on fnl f* **16/1**

0063 **6** *2 ½* **Fairy Monarch (IRE)**[20] 4726 7-8-12 **49** ....(b) MickyFenton 12 — 48
(P T Midgley) *t.k.h in rr: effrt over 2f out: n.m.r over 1f out: nvr nr ldrs* **11/1**

2040 **7** *1* **Hansomelle (IRE)**[21] 4698 4-9-1 **52** .... DaleGibson 13 — 49
(B Mactaggart) *chsd ldrs: one pce whn n.m.r over 1f out* **16/1**

0000 **8** *nk* **Wayward Shot (IRE)**[39] 4154 4-9-1 **52** .... PaulMulrennan 7 — 48
(M W Easterby) *trckd ldrs: led over 3f out: hdd 1f out: sn wknd* **20/1**

0001 **9** *nk* **Jewel Of India**[27] 4511 7-9-2 **53** ....(p) JoeFanning 9 — 49
(Mrs A L M King) *in tch: effrt on outer over 2f out: nvr trbld ldrs* **12/1**

0051 **10** *1* **Enjoy The Magic**[31] 4389 4-8-11 **48** .... DavidAllan 1 — 42
(E J Alston) *trckd ldrs: effrt over 2f out: fdd* **14/1**

0106 **11** *1* **Double Ransom**[21] 4692 7-8-11 **48** ....(b) TonyHamilton 3 — 39
(Mrs L Stubbs) *s.i.s: bhd and drvn along: nvr on terms* **40/1**

002 **12** *hd* **Barry The Brave**[29] 4456 4-9-4 **55** .... DeanMcKeown 11 — 46
(Micky Hammond) *a towards rr* **9/1**[3]

6040 **13** *½* **Big Bradford**[13] 4961 5-9-2 **53** ....(b) PaulHanagan 16 — 43
(R A Fahey) *trckd ldrs: effrt on inner over 2f out: sn wknd* **10/1**

-000 **14** *1 ½* **Barataria**[111] 1947 4-9-4 **55** .... RoystonFfrench 4 — 42
(R Bastiman) *swtchd rt after s: plld hrd in rr: nvr a factor* **40/1**

0-02 **15** *2* **Newcorp Lad**[13] 4974 6-9-4 **55** .... FrancisNorton 14 — 38
(Mrs G S Rees) *trckd ldrs: chal over 3f out: wknd appr fnl f* **5/1**[1]

6303 **16** *¾* **Whittinghamvillage**[9] 5063 5-9-0 **51** .... TomEaves 6 — 32
(D W Whillans) *trckd ldrs: lost pl over 1f out* **25/1**

6-05 **17** *7* **Danzar**[13] 4974 4-8-13 **50** .... DanielTudhope 17 — 16
(M Brittain) *led tl over 3f out: sn lost pl* **12/1**

1m 47.07s (-0.33) **Going Correction** -0.125s/f (Firm)

WFA 3 from 4yo+ 5lb — **17** Ran SP% **126.6**

Speed ratings (Par 101):96,95,94,94,93 90,89,89,89,88 87,86,86,84,82 82,75

CSF £126.07 CT £923.93 TOTE £14.70: £2.80, £2.90, £1.90, £4.10; EX 179.30.

Owner Mrs L Irving **Bred** D H Armitage **Trained** Bolam, Co Durham

FOCUS

A low-grade handicap run at a sound pace. The form looks solid for the level as the principals all came into the race in good form.

Barry The Brave Official explanation: jockey said gelding moved poorly throughout

Danzar Official explanation: jockey said gelding hung left throughout

5286 BRECKS CHEVROLET H'CAP — 5f

4:20 (4:22) (Class 5) (0-75,74) 3-Y-O+ — **£5,181** (£1,541; £770; £384) **Stalls** High

Form — RPR

3002 **1** **Sir Nod**[7] 5117 4-9-5 **74** .... TomEaves 16 — 84
(Miss J A Camacho) *cl up: led 1/2-way: rdn ent last: styd on* **9/4**[1]

6500 **2** *¾* **Paddywack (IRE)**[2] 5243 9-8-5 **60** oh4 ....(b) PaulQuinn 17 — 67
(D W Chapman) *dwlt and bhd: hdwy wl over 1f out: rdn and squeezed through on inner ins last: fin wl* **7/1**[3]

060 **3** *nk* **Middle Eastern**[24] 4629 4-8-5 **60** oh12 .... TPO'Shea 12 — 66
(P A Blockley) *midfield: hdwy 2f out: rdn over 1f out: kpt on u.p ins last: nrst fin* **40/1**

5035 **4** *shd* **Kings College Boy**[4] 5169 6-9-4 **73** ....(b) PaulHanagan 13 — 79
(R A Fahey) *dwlt and towards rr: hdwy after 2f: rdn to chse wnr wl over 1f out: sn drvn and kpt on ins last* **5/1**[2]

0050 **5** *1 ¾* **Nistaki (USA)**[16] 4894 5-8-4 **62** .... PatrickMathers(3) 10 — 62
(D Shaw) *towards rr: effrt on outer 2f out: sn rdn and styd on wl fnl f: nrst fin* **16/1**

0400 **6** *hd* **Never Without Me**[17] 4846 6-8-8 **63** ow2 .... MickyFenton 1 — 62+
(J F Coupland) *wnt lft s and towards rr: hdwy on wd outside wl over 1f out: sn rdn and styd on ins last: nrst fin* **40/1**

0030 **7** *¾* **Bonne De Fleur**[28] 4468 5-8-11 **71** ....(v[1]) MarkLawson(5) 8 — 67
(B Smart) *prom: rdn 2f out: sn drvn and edgd rt over 1f out: sn wknd* **25/1**

6326 **8** *1 ½* **Throw The Dice**[17] 4834 4-8-8 **63** ....(p) DarryllHolland 11 — 54
(D W Barker) *midfield: rdn along 1/2-way: sn no imp* **7/1**[3]

1060 **9** *½* **Whistler**[6] 5131 9-8-5 **60** oh2 ....(p) PaulFitzsimons 9 — 49
(Miss J R Tooth) *dwlt and bhd tl sme late hdwy* **33/1**

0000 **10** *1 ¾* **Triskaidekaphobia**[4] 5181 3-8-12 **68** .... AdrianTNicholls 15 — 51
(Miss J R Tooth) *led: rdn alonga nd hdd 1/2-way: sn drvn and wknd* **20/1**

5214 **11** *¾* **Tender Process (IRE)**[14] 4922 3-9-1 **71** .... SebSanders 4 — 51
(E S McMahon) *in tch: rdn along 2f out: sn wknd* **12/1**

0253 **12** *½* **Favouring (IRE)**[2] 5243 4-8-0 **60** oh5 ....(v) NicolPolli(5) 14 — 38
(M C Chapman) *prom: rdn along over 2f out: sn wknd* **11/1**

0414 **13** *4* **Sir Loin**[16] 4872 5-7-12 **60** oh2 ....(v) DanielleMcCreery(7) 3 — 24
(N Tinkler) *wnt lft s: a towards rr* **28/1**

62.86 secs (-1.14) **Going Correction** -0.125s/f (Firm)

WFA 3 from 4yo+ 1lb — **13** Ran SP% **114.2**

Speed ratings (Par 103):104,102,102,102,99 99,97,95,94,91 90,89,83

CSF £14.49 CT £417.76 TOTE £2.90: £1.80, £2.20, £7.80; EX 16.20.

Owner Brian Nordan **Bred** B Nordan And Mrs S Camacho **Trained** Norton, N Yorks

■ Smiddy Hill (11/2) was withdrawn after proving unruly in the stalls. R4 applies, deduct 5p in the £.

FOCUS

An ordinary sprint handicap in which a high draw proved decisive. The form looks sound enough.

Triskaidekaphobia Official explanation: vet said gelding finished distressed

5287 E B F BILL GRAY LOYAL RACEDAY SERVICE MAIDEN FILLIES' STKS — 7f 100y

4:55 (4:56) (Class 5) 2-Y-O — **£4,210** (£1,252; £625; £312) **Stalls** High

Form — RPR

0 **1** **Practicallyperfect (IRE)**[132] 1442 2-9-0 .... DanielTudhope 5 — 80
(H R A Cecil) *chsd ldr: led over 1f out: hld on wl* **20/1**

42 **2** *1* **La Spezia (IRE)**[17] 4830 2-9-0 .... MickyFenton 2 — 78
(M L W Bell) *hld up in tch: smooth hdwy over 3f out: wnt 2nd appr fnl f: no ex ins last* **6/5**[1]

0 **3** *8* **Nellie Soprano (IRE)**[30] 4428 2-9-0 .... FrancisNorton 11 — 59
(K R Burke) *chsd ldrs: kpt on fnl 2f: tk modest 3rd nr line* **50/1**

05 **4** *½* **Mozayada (USA)**[18] 4788 2-9-0 .... JoeFanning 6 — 58
(M Johnston) *led tl over 1f out: wknd ins last* **16/1**

0 **5** *½* **Proposal**[12] 4994 2-9-0 .... DarryllHolland 10 — 57
(C E Brittain) *rr-div: hdwy over 3f out: kpt on fnl f* **33/1**

0 **6** *1 ¼* **Shanawa (IRE)**[54] 3707 2-9-0 .... TonyCulhane 4 — 54
(M R Channon) *prom: drvn over 3f out: one pce fnl 2f* **14/1**[3]

6 **7** *1 ¼* **Tonnante**[8] 5095 2-9-0 .... SebSanders 9 — 51
(Sir Mark Prescott) *chsd ldrs: outpcd over 2f out: n.d after* **16/1**

4 **8** *8* **Wishing On A Star**[19] 4765 2-9-0 .... RichardMullen 8 — 32
(E J O'Neill) *chsd ldrs: reminders after 2f: hung rt and lost pl over 2f out: no ch whn eased ins last* **13/8**[2]

0 **9** *5* **Miss Taboo (IRE)**[26] 4572 2-9-0 .... AdrianTNicholls 7 — 20
(Miss V Haigh) *s.i.s: a bhd* **100/1**

6 **10** *3 ½* **Anewshade**[11] 5014 2-9-0 .... KimTinkler 3 — 12
(N Tinkler) *s.s: sn detached in rr* **100/1**

0 **11** *3 ½* **Lady Grey Bear**[12] 4987 2-9-0 .... PaulHanagan 1 — 4
(R A Fahey) *swvd lft s: sn bhd and drvn along* **66/1**

1m 34.15s (-0.16) **Going Correction** -0.125s/f (Firm) — **11** Ran SP% **115.1**

Speed ratings (Par 92):95,93,84,84,83 82,80,71,65,61 57

CSF £43.02 TOTE £19.80: £2.90, £1.30, £6.50; EX 79.90.

Owner Diamond Racing Ltd **Bred** Epona Bloodstock Ltd **Trained** Newmarket, Suffolk

FOCUS

A weak maiden in which the first two put plenty of daylight between themselves and the remainder. The race has been rated through the runner-up for the time being.

NOTEBOOK

Practicallyperfect(IRE), who made her debut for Mark Johnston at Redcar in May, is a lazy walker. She had to dig deep to get the better of the favourite but was firmly in command at the line.

La Spezia(IRE), who looked very fit indeed, moved up travelling much the better but at the line she was very much second best. She can find a race but is proving very expensive to follow. (op Evens)

Nellie Soprano(IRE), bred for speed on her dam's side, improved on her debut effort and looks the exception to the rule - she seems to have more stamina than speed. (tchd 66-1)

Mozayada(USA), who looks on the weak side, took them along but she was very leg weary in the closing stages.

Proposal stayed on in her own time and looks the type to do better over middle distances at three.

Tonnante did not shape too badly and no doubt her trainer is already thumbing the 2007 programme book looking for likely opportunities in modest handicaps over much further. (op 14-1)

Wishing On A Star, a good walker, never looked happy, was soon given some sharp reminders and never fired at all. In the end her rider gave up, and this was simply too bad to be true. Official explanation: jockey said filly was never travelling (op 7-4 tchd 6-4)

5288 GO RACING AT PONTEFRACT TOMORROW MAIDEN STKS — 5f

5:25 (5:33) (Class 5) 2-Y-O — £3,886 (£1,156; £577; £288) Stalls High

Form				RPR
3	1		**Deserted Dane (USA)**[18] [4801] 2-9-3 .... DeanMcKeown 4 (G A Swinbank) *qckly away: sn clr: v easily* 7/4[1]	87+
	2	7	**Morristown Music (IRE)** 2-8-12 .... TomEaves 5 (J S Wainwright) *dwlt and in rr: hdwy wl over 1f out: styd on ins last: nrst fin* 50/1	57
3243	3	½	**Isobel Rose (IRE)**[19] [4754] 2-8-12 74 .... RichardMullen 8 (E A L Dunlop) *prom: hdwy to chse wnr 2f out: sn rdn and hung lft: drvn and hung rt: sn one pce* 11/4[2]	55
	4	1	**Staked A Claim (IRE)** 2-9-3 .... PhillipMakin 9 (T D Barron) *chsd wnr: rdn along 1/2-way: drvn and one pce fnl 2f* 6/1[3]	57
00	5	shd	**Le Masque**[20] [4731] 2-9-3 .... RoystonFfrench 14 (B Smart) *chsd ldrs: rdn along over 2f out: sn one pce* 16/1	56
000	6	1 ½	**Misaine (IRE)**[12] [4986] 2-9-3 50 .... DavidAllan 3 (T J Etherington) *chsd ldrs: rdn along 1/2-way: sn wknd* 80/1	51
	7	3	**Bar Humbug** 2-9-3 .... PaulHanagan 11 (R A Fahey) *nvr nr ldrs* 17/2	40
00	8	½	**Xalted**[9] [5059] 2-8-12 .... PaulQuinn 6 (S C Williams) *dwlt: a rr* 40/1	33
	9	3	**Aussie Blue (IRE)** 2-9-3 .... DarryllHolland 1 (R M Whitaker) *v.s.a: a bhd* 16/1	28
0	10	1	**Smart Angus**[12] [4987] 2-9-3 .... TonyHamilton 12 (R A Fahey) *sn outpcd and bhd* 33/1	24
	11	shd	**Beau Petite** 2-8-12 .... JoeFanning 2 (T D Barron) *a towards rr* 33/1	19

63.47 secs (-0.53) **Going Correction** -0.125s/f (Firm) 11 Ran SP% 111.1
Speed ratings (Par 95):99,87,87,85,85 82,78,77,72,70 70
CSF £105.64 TOTE £2.40: £1.40, £11.00, £1.10; EX 92.20.
Owner Arnie Flower **Bred** Skymarc Farm Et Al **Trained** Melsonby, N Yorks
■ Forest Machine (14/1, ref to ent stalls) & West Warning (100/1, broke out of stalls) were withdrawn. R4, deduct 5p in the £.

FOCUS
Not much of a race, but a decent performance from Deserted Dane, who was in a different class.

NOTEBOOK
Deserted Dane(USA) ◆, a promising third on his debut over six furlongs on soft ground at Newmarket, appreciated this quicker surface and ran out a very impressive winner, coping fine with the drop back to the minimum distance. His trainer is of the opinion that he will make a better three-year-old and will give him just one more run this season, possibly in a novice event here. (tchd 13-8)
Morristown Music(IRE), a half-sister to Catcando, a prolific six-furlong/mile winner, and multiple sprint scorer Beyond The Clouds, out of a seven-furlong juvenile scorer, made a pleasing debut behind the clearly above-average winner and should improve. (op 40-1)
Isobel Rose(IRE) again failed to run up to her official mark of 74 and does not seem to be progressing. (op 9-4)
Staked A Claim(IRE), a 44,000euros half-brother to seven winners, including top-class Mount Abu, a multiple winning sprinter, made a respectable introduction and it would be no surprise to see him progress into a decent sort in time. (op 8-1)
Le Masque will have more options now he is eligible for a handicap mark. (op 20-1)
Aussie Blue(IRE) Official explanation: jockey said colt missed the break

5289 GEORGE KILBURN MEMORIAL MAIDEN AUCTION STKS (DIV II) — 7f 100y

5:55 (5:56) (Class 5) 2-Y-O — £2,590 (£770; £385; £192) Stalls High

Form				RPR
5	1		**Oceana Gold**[19] [4774] 2-8-9 .... DarryllHolland 3 (A M Balding) *trckd ldrs: rn wd bnd over 5f out: led over 3f out: styd on strly fnl f: readily* 3/1[1]	72+
0B4	2	2	**Packers Hill (IRE)**[17] [4829] 2-8-11 .... DeanMcKeown 5 (G A Swinbank) *led 1f: trckd ldrs: pulld outside 2f out: wnt 2nd ins last: no real imp* 3/1[1]	69
5	3	¾	**Chasing Memories (IRE)**[31] [4400] 2-8-4 .... RoystonFfrench 11 (B Smart) *w ldrs: kpt on same pce fnl 2f* 11/2[2]	61
0	4	1	**Myfrenchconnection (IRE)**[26] [4566] 2-8-9 .... MickyFenton 9 (P T Midgley) *in rr: hdwy over 2f out: styd on ins last* 66/1	63
0	5	hd	**Harry The Hawk**[96] [2409] 2-8-9 .... GrahamGibbons 2 (T D Walford) *s.i.s: hdwy over 2f out: kpt on fnl f* 50/1	63
3	6	9	**Dilwin (IRE)**[36] [4228] 2-9-1 .... AdrianTNicholls 8 (D Nicholls) *chsd ldrs: drvn over 3f out: n.m.r on inner 2f out: sn lost pl: eased ins last* 3/1[1]	48+
00	7	1 ¼	**Interest (USA)**[25] [4608] 2-8-11 .... PhillipMakin 7 (T D Barron) *in rr: drvn 3f out: nvr a factor* 22/1	41
60	8	nk	**Aitutaki (IRE)**[25] [4608] 2-8-9 .... DavidAllan 10 (T D Easterby) *w ldrs: led after 1f tl over 3f out: lost pl over 1f out* 20/1	38
0	9	1	**Da Schadenfreude (USA)**[11] [5020] 2-8-8 .... JackDean(7) 4 (W G M Turner) *a in rr: bhd fnl 2f* 50/1	42
50	10	10	**Bathwick Fancy (IRE)**[13] [4964] 2-8-7 ow1 .... TomEaves 1 (J G Portman) *s.i.s: sn chsng ldrs: carried wd bnd over 5f out: lost pl 2f out: eased ins last* 9/1[3]	10+

1m 34.26s (-0.05) **Going Correction** -0.125s/f (Firm) 10 Ran SP% 114.9
Speed ratings (Par 95):95,92,91,90,90 80,78,78,77,65
CSF £11.02 TOTE £3.40: £1.50, £1.40, £1.90; EX 16.90 Place 6 £133.91, Place £30.90.
Owner K H Fischer **Bred** The C H F Partnership **Trained** Kingsclere, Hants

FOCUS
Just a modest maiden but the form looks fairly reliable with the second and third running close to their previous figures.

NOTEBOOK
Oceana Gold failed to handle the bend leaving the back straight, but he took it up once in line for home and was right on top at the finish. He looks a likely type for a mile nursery. (op 10-3)
Packers Hill(IRE), pulled out to hunt down the winner, never looked like striking a blow. He basically looks like a one-paced stayer.
Chasing Memories(IRE), best drawn, stepped up on her debut effort, but she still on the weak side and the best of her will not be seen until next year. (op 7-1)
Myfrenchconnection(IRE), tailed off on his debut a month earlier, showed a lot more but he seems to have a lot more stamina than speed. (op 50-1)
Harry The Hawk, beaten out of sight on his first run three months earlier, stayed on nicely under a considerate ride. He looks a likely type for handicaps over further at three. (op 40-1)
Dilwin(IRE), flat out turning in, dropped right away and in the end completed in his own time. This was a bitter disappointment after his sound first run.
T/Plt: £67.00 to a £1 stake. Pool: £50,075.85. 545.05 winning tickets. T/Qpdt: £28.80 to a £1 stake. Pool: £2,799.65. 71.90 winning tickets. JR

5264 SANDOWN (R-H)

Wednesday, September 13

OFFICIAL GOING: Round course - good to soft (soft in places); sprint course - good (good to soft in places)
Wind: almost nil

5290 FLAKT WOODS NURSERY — 5f 6y

2:30 (2:31) (Class 5) (0-75,73) 2-Y-O — £4,533 (£1,348; £674; £336) Stalls High

Form				RPR
3330	1		**Mogok Ruby**[9] [5065] 2-8-11 70 .... JamesMillman(7) 3 (L Montague Hall) *led or disp thrght: def advantage over 1f out: drvn and hld on wl fnl f* 8/1[3]	71
000	2	½	**Swiftly Addicted (IRE)**[12] [4993] 2-8-8 60 .... FergusSweeney 12 (A King) *hld up: in last pair and swtchd lft 2f out: gd prog over 1f out: pressed wnr ins fnl f: nt qckn nr fin* 12/1	59
0050	3	¾	**King Of Tricks**[18] [4816] 2-7-5 50 oh3 .... FrankiePickard(7) 7 (M D I Usher) *disp ld: urged along 2f out: stl w wnr ent fnl f : bmpd along and one pce* 33/1	47
3104	4	¾	**Diminuto**[13] [4971] 2-8-5 57 .... RichardSmith 13 (M D I Usher) *trckd ldrs: pushed along whn nt clr run over 1f out tl ins fnl f: styd on same pce* 12/1	51+
6633	5	1 ½	**Hephaestus**[4] [5162] 2-8-13 65 .... RichardHughes 11 (M R Channon) *racd against far rail: disp ld to jst over 1f out: fdd fnl f* 4/1[1]	53
3150	6	nk	**Tom Paris**[19] [4766] 2-9-6 72 .... (b) MartinDwyer 4 (W R Muir) *s.s: rcvrd and prog to chse ldrs 1/2-way: rdn and no imp over 1f out: fdd* 9/2[2]	59
0324	7	hd	**Silver Hotspur**[44] [4002] 2-9-4 70 .... JimmyFortune 9 (P W Chapple-Hyam) *chsd ldrs: lost pl 1/2-way: hrd rdn over 1f out: nt qckn and no imp* 4/1[1]	57
0100	8	1 ½	**Inflagranti**[8] [5094] 2-9-1 70 .... SaleemGolam(3) 5 (J G Portman) *chsd ldrs: struggling u.p sn after 1/2-way: no ch over 1f out* 12/1	51
055	9	shd	**Red Hot Jazz (IRE)**[60] [3544] 2-8-8 63 .... JamesDoyle(3) 6 (Mrs P N Dutfield) *s.i.s: rcvrd to chse ldrs after 2f: rdn and lost pl wl over 1f out: fdd* 9/1	44
0502	10	2	**Totally Free**[55] [3677] 2-8-5 57 .... (v) FrankieMcDonald 10 (M D I Usher) *last and struggling 1/2-way: no ch after* 12/1	31

64.36 secs (2.15) **Going Correction** +0.20s/f (Good) 10 Ran SP% 113.0
Speed ratings (Par 95):90,89,88,86,84 83,83,81,81,77
CSF £96.23 CT £3019.40 TOTE £13.40: £3.10, £4.20, £8.00; EX 212.80.
Owner The Ruby Partnership **Bred** R Pain **Trained** Epsom, Surrey

FOCUS
This was just a modest sprint nursery for the class, somewhat weakened by withdrawals, and the form may be worth treating with a degree of caution.

NOTEBOOK
Mogok Ruby got off the mark at the seventh time of asking with a ready display on this drop back to the minimum trip. He has often lost his race at the start, but he was smart to break this time and showed a likely attitude under pressure. Whether he can go on from this after a weight rise remains to be seen, but a stiff five looks ideal for him on this evidence. (tchd 9-1)
Swiftly Addicted(IRE) struggled to go the early pace on this first attempt over five furlongs, but she eventually emerged to hold every chance and posted a personal-best in defeat. She is probably better off reverting to six furlongs and has clearly begun handicap life on a fair mark. (tchd 14-1)
King Of Tricks, 3lb out of the handicap, was notably sweating during the race, but that was not enough to stop him from putting up his best performance to date under a positive ride. His proximity at the finish does little for this form, however.
Diminuto was denied a clear passage entering the final furlong, but still held every chance when in the clear and ran close to her recent level on this return to turf. (op 8-1)
Hephaestus was handy from the off and ultimately proved disappointing. He had been running consistently in defeat before this and it may be that he needs a genuinely fast surface. (op 10-3 tchd 9-2)
Tom Paris, back in trip, was always playing catch-up after a sluggish start and again did not look happy on the easy ground. Official explanation: jockey said gelding was unsuited by the good (good to soft in places) ground (op 5-1)
Silver Hotspur, with the blinkers abandoned, failed to raise his game on this nursery bow and again looked far from straightforward. (op 5-1)

5291 ANDREWS AIR CONDITIONING CLAIMING STKS — 5f 6y

3:05 (3:05) (Class 5) 3-Y-O+ — £3,238 (£963; £481; £240) Stalls High

Form				RPR
0104	1		**Endless Summer**[9] [5058] 9-8-8 65 .... JamesDoyle(3) 9 (A W Carroll) *hld up in last: prog 2f out: nt clr run briefly over 1f out: gd hdwy after: rdn and r.o to ld last strides* 3/1[2]	70
3100	2	hd	**Witchry**[9] [5058] 4-9-2 74 .... FergusSweeney 10 (A G Newcombe) *hld up in rr: prog gng strly whn nt clr run twice over 1f out: got through and r.o to ld last 100yds: hdd fnl strides* 8/1	74
-100	3	1	**Little Edward**[11] [5021] 8-8-8 76 .... RichardHughes 12 (R J Hodges) *trckd ldrs: nt clr run wl over 1f out: prog sn after: rdn to chal and upsides 100yds out: nt pce of ldng pair* 9/2[3]	62
0000	4	1 ¼	**Elvina**[49] [3847] 5-8-2 47 .... RichardThomas 7 (A G Newcombe) *prom: drvn to ld wl over 1f out: hdd and outpcd last 100yds* 33/1	52
0500	5	¾	**Plateau**[18] [4793] 7-8-13 78 .... RyanMoore 16 (D Nicholls) *racd against far side rail: w ldrs: lost pl bef 1/2-way and sn drvn: kpt on fnl f: nvr able to chal* 9/4[1]	60
U020	6	hd	**Sounds Simla (IRE)**[19] [4756] 3-8-5 59 .... (p) AdrianMcCarthy 8 (R A Harris) *led to over 3f out: styd pressing ldrs: fdd u.p ins fnl f* 25/1	52
-000	7	½	**Spinetail Rufous (IRE)**[29] [4462] 8-8-5 40 .... SaleemGolam(3) 5 (Miss Z C Davison) *hld up towards rr: effrt on outer 2f out: kpt on same pce: n.d* 66/1	53
3500	8	½	**Developer (IRE)**[14] [4927] 3-8-5 63 .... PaulDoe 1 (T G Mills) *dwlt: last trio tl sme prog on outer over 1f out: nvr pce to rch ldrs* 20/1	49
-043	9	½	**Saintly Place**[26] [4551] 5-8-0 40 .... MarkCoumbe(7) 3 (A W Carroll) *hld up wl in rr: rdn over 1f out: nt qckn and no imp on ldrs* 33/1	48
5400	10	½	**Flying Dancer**[9] [5055] 4-7-8 45 .... LukeMorris(7) 17 (R A Harris) *racd against far rail: nvr beyond midfield: u.p and struggling fr 1/2-way* 50/1	40
4640	11	1	**Bollywood (IRE)**[21] [4690] 3-8-4 49 .... MarcHalford(3) 11 (J J Bridger) *nvr bttr than midfield: rdn and no real prog 2f out* 40/1	44
-550	12	hd	**Straight As A Die**[218] [329] 3-8-0 45 .... JimmyQuinn 2 (R J Hodges) *sn chsd ldrs: rdn and nt qckn 2f out: wknd fnl f* 66/1	36

3346 **13** *1 ¾* **Balian**[9] 5055 3-8-7 63 (p) RichardKingscote(3) 13 40
(G L Moore) *hld up towards rr: rdn and plenty to do whn hmpd wl over 1f out: no ch after* **12/1**

0000 **14** *11* **Galloway Boy (IRE)**[26] 4551 9-8-1 40 ow2 (bt) JamieJones(7) 14 —
(J F Panvert) *prom: led over 3f out to wl over 1f out: wknd rapidly: t.o* **50/1**

00 **15** *5* **Capital Lass**[8] 5078 3-8-0 50 SilvestreDeSousa 15 —
(D M Simcock) *chsd ldrs: wknd 1/2-way: t.o* **25/1**

62.80 secs (0.59) **Going Correction** +0.20s/f (Good)
WFA 3 from 4yo+ 1lb **15** Ran SP% **120.4**
Speed ratings (Par 103):103,102,101,99,97 97,96,95,95,94 92,92,89,72,64
CSF £24.25 TOTE £4.10: £1.20, £2.70, £2.20; EX 38.80.There was no bid for the winner. Plateau was claimed by C R Dore for £12,000.

Owner Seasons Holidays **Bred** Juddmonte Farms **Trained** Cropthorne, Worcs

■ Stewards' Enquiry : Fergus Sweeney caution: used whip without allowing sufficient time to respond

FOCUS
This was a fair race of its type, run at a solid early pace and, rather surprisingly, a high draw if anything proved to be a disadvantage.

Balian Official explanation: jockey said gelding suffered interference in running; vet said gelding was struck into in front

5292 VAILLANT NOVICE STKS 7f 16y
3:35 (3:39) (Class 3) 2-Y-O £7,478 (£2,239; £1,119; £560; £279) Stalls High

Form RPR

021 **1** **Duke Of Tuscany**[18] 4794 2-9-2 83 RyanMoore 3 95
(R Hannon) *mde all: rdn and pressed 2f out: drifted to nr side rail fnl f: styd on wl* **13/8**[1]

2 *nk* **Asperity (USA)** 2-8-9 JimmyFortune 4 87
(J H M Gosden) *hld up bhd ldng trio: chsd wnr 2f out: str chal fnl f: styd on wl but jst hld* **9/4**[2]

0442 **3** *6* **La Neige**[11] 5017 2-9-4 104 RichardHughes 1 81
(M R Channon) *reluctant to enter stalls: trckd ldng pair: cl up 2f out: rdn over 1f out: wknd and eased fnl f* **11/4**[3]

4 *¾* **Contentious (USA)** 2-8-4 KerrinMcEvoy 2 65
(J L Dunlop) *mostly pressed wnr to 2f out: sn wknd* **11/2**

5 *13* **Path To Glory** 2-8-9 AdrianMcCarthy 5 38
(Miss Z C Davison) *unruly bef s: slowly away: a last: lost tch 3f out: t.o* **66/1**

1m 32.39s (1.30) **Going Correction** +0.20s/f (Good) **5** Ran SP% **112.4**
Speed ratings (Par 99):100,99,92,91,77
CSF £5.77 TOTE £2.50: £1.30, £1.50; EX 7.60.

Owner Justin Dowley & Michael Pescod **Bred** Cheveley Park Stud Ltd **Trained** East Everleigh, Wilts

FOCUS
An interesting little novice event, run at no more than a modest early gallop, and the first two came nicely clear. The runners came over to the stands' side in the home straight.

NOTEBOOK
Duke Of Tuscany followed up his Goodwood maiden success with a battling display on this drop back to seven furlongs. He showed a decent attitude when push came to shove, the stiff finish over this trip was to his advantage, and he coped well with the underfoot conditions. While he is clearly just coming good for connections now, he appeals as the type to do much better as a three-year-old, and he will have no trouble getting further next year. (op 7-4 tchd 15-8, 2-1 in places)

Asperity(USA) ◆ represented a stable that had won this event with its only two previous runners Tashkill and Al Jadeed, and he proved very popular in the betting ring beforehand. He ultimately ran a big race in defeat, only just losing out racing down the middle of the track, and clearly has a deal of ability. Considering he ran distinctly green under pressure, he ought to improve a bundle for the experience, and looks a sure-fire winner in the coming weeks. (op 5-2 tchd 11-4 in places)

La Neige, upped in trip, was again fractious at the start, and was taken wide early on by his rider in an attempt to find the better ground. He has to rate a non-stayer at this longer distance on the easy ground and, while he sets a decent standard for the form, he was not at his very best this time. (op 9-4 tchd 3-1)

Contentious(USA), who boasts a choice US pedigree, found just the one pace when it mattered and never looked a serious threat at any stage. She will get further in time and is entitled to improve for the debut experience. (op 8-1)

5293 FUJITSU E B F MAIDEN STKS 1m 14y
4:10 (4:10) (Class 5) 2-Y-O £4,533 (£1,348; £674; £336) Stalls High

Form RPR

45 **1** **Kid Mambo (USA)**[33] 4333 2-9-3 IanMongan 4 84
(T G Mills) *trckd ldr over 5f out: led wl over 2f out and c to nr side rail : drvn clr fnl f* **4/1**[2]

2 *3 ½* **Yossi (IRE)** 2-9-0 SaleemGolam(3) 9 77
(M H Tompkins) *s.i.s: hld up in last pair and rn green: prog over 2f out: chsd wnr over 1f out: no imp fnl f* **25/1**

42 **3** *1* **Emerald Wilderness (IRE)**[28] 4466 2-9-3 RichardHughes 3 74
(M R Channon) *led to wl over 2f out: hung lft sn after: lost 2nd over 1f out: one pce* **2/1**[1]

0 **4** *1 ½* **Private Reason (USA)**[25] 4592 2-9-3 RyanMoore 7 71
(R Hannon) *trckd ldr to over 5f out: styd prom: upsides 3f out: btn 2f out: fdd* **10/1**

0 **5** *½* **Seteem (USA)**[16] 4867 2-9-3 MartinDwyer 2 70
(M P Tregoning) *hld up in tch: shkn up and nt qckn over 2f out: no imp after* **10/1**

05 **6** *½* **Balnagore**[27] 4525 2-9-3 JimmyQuinn 6 69
(J L Dunlop) *in tch: shkn up 3f out: struggling and no prog 2f out: btn after* **6/1**

64 **7** *2 ½* **Altar (IRE)**[19] 4781 2-9-3 KerrinMcEvoy 5 63
(R Hannon) *hld up in tch: pushed along and no prog 3f out: wknd over 1f out* **9/2**[3]

0 **8** *1* **Professor Twinkle**[19] 4781 2-9-3 PaulDoe 1 61
(W J Knight) *dwlt: hld up in rr: prog and cl up 3f out: sn shkn up and wknd* **20/1**

9 *20* **Sadler's Hill (IRE)** 2-9-3 JimmyFortune 8 —
(N A Callaghan) *a in last pair: lost tch over 3f out: t.o* **16/1**

1m 45.09s (1.14) **Going Correction** +0.20s/f (Good) **9** Ran SP% **118.5**
Speed ratings (Par 95):102,98,97,96,95 95,92,91,71
CSF £97.18 TOTE £5.10: £1.40, £5.90, £1.60; EX 150.40.

Owner J Daniels **Bred** R S Evans **Trained** Headley, Surrey

FOCUS
A fair juvenile maiden which again saw the field track over to the stands' side in the home straight. The form appears sound enough.

NOTEBOOK
Kid Mambo(USA) came good at the third time of asking and relished the step up to this extra furlong. He was rightly given a positive ride and, despite not appearing totally happy on the easy surface, still could have been called the winner entering the final furlong. This was a welcome winner for his yard and, with further improvement on the cards, he will now most likely be aimed at the Zetland Stakes at Newmarket over another two furlongs. (op 9-2 tchd 5-1 in a place)

Yossi(IRE) ◆, whose pedigree suggests a mix of stamina and speed, turned in a very pleasing debut effort and looked a brief threat to the winner before his lack of experience ultimately told. Like the majority of debutants from this yard, he ought to improve a deal for the experience, and clearly has a future. (tchd 33-1)

Emerald Wilderness(IRE), as was the case at Beverley 28 days previously, found just the same pace under pressure and his fate was apparent before the furlong marker. He now has the options of nurseries and is a fair benchmark for this form. (op 9-4 tchd 5-2 and 11-4 in places)

Private Reason(USA), up in trip, posted an improved effort and showed the benefit of his recent debut at Newbury. He was still green this time and looks the sort to improve further as he becomes more streetwise. (op 14-1)

Seteem(USA) was ridden handily and simply lacked the required change of gears when it mattered. He probably ran close to his Chepstow debut form and, on the evidence so far, his Group 1 entry looks highly ambitious. (op 9-2)

Balnagore never looked like justifying strong market support at any stage and looks in need of more time. He now qualifies for a handicap mark. (op 12-1)

Altar(IRE) may not have been suited by the easy surface, but still proved disappointing and has not progressed as could have been expected. He may fare a little better now he becomes eligible for a handicap mark, however. (op 4-1 tchd 7-2 and 5-1 in a place)

Sadler's Hill(IRE) Official explanation: jockey said colt hung left

5294 MAIN FILLIES' H'CAP 1m 14y
4:40 (4:40) (Class 4) (0-85,84) 3-Y-O £6,477 (£1,927; £963; £481) Stalls High

Form RPR

0301 **1** **Dansa Queen**[18] 4820 3-8-11 80 AdamKirby(3) 1 89+
(W R Swinburn) *hld up last: prog 3f out to ld over 1f out: drvn out fnl f* **3/1**[1]

4506 **2** *1 ¼* **Oceans Apart**[17] 4837 3-9-4 84 RyanMoore 7 89
(P F I Cole) *hld up in last trio: rdn and prog 2f out: chsd wnr jst ins fnl f: kpt on but no real imp* **7/2**[2]

3004 **3** *½* **Lavenham (IRE)**[17] 4837 3-8-8 74 RichardHughes 9 78
(R Hannon) *t.k.h: hld up in last pair: nt clr run 2f out: prog over 1f out: styd on fnl f: nrst fin* **6/1**

1110 **4** *½* **Mcnairobi**[11] 5019 3-9-3 83 JimmyFortune 5 86
(P D Cundell) *led after 2f: drvn and hdd over 1f out: one pce after* **11/2**[3]

616 **5** *2* **Tawaajud (USA)**[90] 2581 3-8-12 78 MartinDwyer 6 76
(B W Hills) *led for 2f: pressed ldr to 2f out: hrd rdn and nt qckn over 1f out: fdd* **15/2**

341 **6** *½* **Our Faye**[21] 4708 3-8-6 72 FrankieMcDonald 2 71+
(S Kirk) *trckd ldrs: cl up whn nowhere to go 2f out: no prog over 1f out: eased last 100yds* **11/1**

0640 **7** *5* **Wassfa**[45] 3974 3-8-7 73 JimmyQuinn 3 58
(C E Brittain) *chsd ldrs: lost pl over 2f out: struggling after: wknd fnl f* **14/1**

1260 **8** *4* **Gelder**[25] 4610 3-8-2 71 JamesDoyle(3) 8 47
(H Morrison) *trckd ldrs: urged along and nt keen fr 3f out: swished tail and gave up over 1f out* **9/1**

1m 44.27s (0.32) **Going Correction** +0.20s/f (Good) **8** Ran SP% **113.7**
Speed ratings (Par 100):106,104,104,103,101 101,96,92
CSF £13.40 CT £57.85 TOTE £3.30: £1.50, £1.70, £1.40; EX 12.20.

Owner Persistent Partners **Bred** C R Mason **Trained** Aldbury, Herts

■ Stewards' Enquiry : Frankie McDonald one-day ban: careless riding (Sep 24)

FOCUS
This fillies' handicap was run at a sound enough pace and those held up proved at an advantage. The form looks sound but average.

5295 LUCKINS H'CAP 1m 2f 7y
5:15 (5:15) (Class 4) (0-80,79) 3-Y-O+ £5,505 (£1,637; £818; £408) Stalls High

Form RPR

3150 **1** **Fort Churchill (IRE)**[22] 4676 5-9-11 79 (bt) JimmyFortune 6 87
(B Ellison) *hld up in last pair: rdn and prog over 2f out: edgd lft but sustained effrt to ld jst insn fnl f: drvn out* **10/3**[1]

6-55 **2** *¾* **Del Mar Sunset**[18] 4810 7-9-4 75 SaleemGolam(3) 5 84+
(W J Haggas) *hld up in last pair: cruising bhd ldrs 2f out: nt clr run tl ins fnl f: r.o to take 2nd but nt rcvr* **6/1**

2301 **3** *nk* **South O'The Border**[27] 4536 4-9-10 78 IanMongan 2 84
(T G Mills) *trckd ldng pair: wnt 2nd gng easily 2f out: led over 1f out: sn rdn: hdd jst ins fnl f: no ex* **9/2**[3]

4110 **4** *2* **Dove Cottage (IRE)**[69] 3214 4-9-4 72 FergusSweeney 1 74
(W S Kittow) *led to over 1f out: one pce u.p* **14/1**

5162 **5** *1 ½* **William's Way**[23] 4662 4-9-2 70 KerrinMcEvoy 7 69
(I A Wood) *t.k.h: hld up in tch: effrt to chal 2f out: losing pl whn squeezed out over 1f out* **7/1**

-153 **6** *5* **Vale De Lobo**[11] 5016 4-9-0 75 JamesMillman(7) 3 65
(B R Millman) *prog to trck ldrs 1/2-way: rdn over 2f out: wknd over 1f out* **4/1**[2]

043- **7** *13* **Turn 'n Burn**[363] 5254 5-9-3 71 MartinDwyer 4 36
(C A Cyzer) *mostly chsd ldr to 2f out: wknd rapidly over 1f out* **16/1**

06-2 **8** *11* **Art Modern (IRE)**[20] 4336 4-9-9 77 RyanMoore 8 21
(G L Moore) *trckd ldrs to 1/2-way: sn lost pl and last: t.o fnl 2f* **7/1**

2m 12.13s (1.89) **Going Correction** +0.20s/f (Good) **8** Ran SP% **113.1**
Speed ratings (Par 105):100,99,99,97,96 92,81,73
CSF £23.01 CT £88.90 TOTE £4.50: £1.50, £2.60, £1.70; EX 32.00 Place 6 £70.19, Place 5 £6.58.

Owner L D Gamble and Mr & Mrs J H Mathias **Bred** P H Betts **Trained** Norton, N Yorks

■ Stewards' Enquiry : Jimmy Fortune three-day ban: careless riding (Sep 24-26)

FOCUS
A fair handicap, featuring largely exposed handicappers, that was run at an average gallop. The first three came clear and the first and third appear to have run to form.

Art Modern(IRE) Official explanation: jockey said gelding was unsuited by the good to soft (soft in places) ground

T/Plt: £310.40 to a £1 stake. Pool: £63,023.60. 148.20 winning units T/Qpdt: £4.80 to a £1 stake. Pool: £4,610.40. 700.70 winning units. JN

The Form Book, Raceform Ltd, Compton, RG20 6NL

5270 YARMOUTH (L-H)

Wednesday, September 13

OFFICIAL GOING: Good to firm

Wind: Light, against Weather: Sunny

5296 EUROPEAN BREEDERS FUND / AGGBAG MAIDEN FILLIES' STKS 6f 3y

2:20 (2:21) (Class 4) 2-Y-O **£5,362** (£1,604; £802; £401; £199) **Stalls** High

Form RPR

1 **Kaseema (USA)** 2-9-0 .... RHills 6 81+
(Sir Michael Stoute) *s.s: hdwy over 2f out: shkn up to ld over 1f out: edgd rt: r.o* **4/6**[1]

2 1 1/2 **Extravagance (IRE)** 2-9-0 .... NickyMackay 5 77
(L M Cumani) *chsd ldrs: rdn over 1f out: styd on same pce ins fnl f* **14/1**

3 3/4 **Kondakova (IRE)** 2-9-0 .... HayleyTurner 7 74
(M L W Bell) *chsd ldrs: rdn and hung lft fr over 1f out: styd on same pce* **25/1**

4 1/2 **Genuine Call** 2-9-0 .... TPQueally 4 73
(C F Wall) *s.s: hdwy over 1f out: nt trble ldrs* **40/1**

5 1/2 **Red Blooded Woman (USA)** 2-9-0 .... EddieAhern 1 71
(E A L Dunlop) *broke wl: stdd and sn lost pl: r.o ins fnl f: nt trble ldrs* **15/2**[3]

5 6 3/4 **Roca Redonda (IRE)**[26] [4552] 2-9-0 .... DaneO'Neill 3 69
(D J Daly) *led: rdn: edgd rt and hdd over 1f out: wknd ins fnl f* **4/1**[2]

7 nk **Allison's Art (IRE)** 2-9-0 .... ChrisCatlin 8 68
(N A Callaghan) *chsd ldr: rdn and n.m.r over 1f out: son outpcd* **25/1**

06 8 7 **Dee Burgh**[12] [4993] 2-9-0 .... TedDurcan 2 47
(J Pearce) *sn outpcd* **33/1**

1m 15.25s (1.55) **Going Correction** +0.05s/f (Good) 8 Ran SP% **111.5**

Speed ratings (Par 94): 91,89,88,87,86 85,85,75

CSF £10.50 TOTE £1.70: £1.10, £2.30, £3.70; EX 10.20 Trifecta £75.00 Pool £430.10 - 4.07 winning units..

Owner Hamdan Al Maktoum **Bred** Summer Wind Farm **Trained** Newmarket, Suffolk

FOCUS

A nice enough maiden that should produce winners, but the form looks just fair at present.

NOTEBOOK

Kaseema(USA), a $1,100,000 purchase, holds a Cheveley Park entry and she was strong at the head of the market for this racecourse debut. A shade sluggish leaving the stalls, she made her ground up easily enough and picked up when asked to go on, winning with a little bit to spare. This was a satisfactory debut for a horse who cost so much and quotes of 20-1 for the 1000 Guineas look laughable at this stage, but she is bred to improve as she steps up in distance and is undoubtedly capable of better, as she still looked green. (tchd 8-11)

Extravagance(IRE), whose sales price went up to 100,000gns, is bred to appreciate trips in excess of this in time and as a result this was a highly pleasing debut. She kept on well to hold second without being able to match the winner, and can find a maiden on a slower surface. (op 16-1 tchd 12-1)

Kondakova(IRE), a half-sister to several smart performers, holds no notable entries, but she made a pleasing debut nonetheless, and kept on well despite hanging. She is another for whom a rise in distance should bring about improvement. (op 20-1)

Genuine Call did not cost much, but she ran better than her odds entitled her to and kept on nicely into fourth, not being given a hard time. Considering she was slowly away and ran green it should be safe to assume that there is better to come, and this daughter of Tobougg should improve for an extra furlong. (op 33-1)

Red Blooded Woman(USA), who cost 270,000gns, is another with no big-race entries but shaped well on this racecourse debut. Quickly away, she drifted back through the field before running on again and, like with most juveniles from her stable, the experience can be expected to benefit her greatly. (op 8-1)

Roca Redonda(IRE), who shaped well on her recent debut over seven furlongs at Folkestone, was ridden positively on this drop in trip, but she was readily brushed aside over a furlong out and faded disappointingly. She may be more of a nursery prosepct now.

Allison's Art(IRE), a daughter of top-class miler Rock Of Gibraltar, is out of a dam who stayed up to two miles. She was always likely to find the emphasis on speed here against her. (op 28-1)

5297 E.B.F / BENNETTS ELECTRICAL MAIDEN STKS 7f 3y

2:55 (2:55) (Class 4) 2-Y-O **£5,362** (£1,604; £802; £401; £199) **Stalls** High

Form RPR

3 1 **Jaasoos (IRE)**[16] [4873] 2-9-3 .... PhilipRobinson 10 80+
(M A Jarvis) *led over 5f out: rdn clr fnl f* **15/8**[1]

2 3 **Cleide Da Silva (USA)** 2-8-12 .... JohnEgan 7 67
(J Noseda) *a.p: rdn to chsd wnr over 1f out: styd on same pce* **9/2**[2]

3 nk **Monte Alto (IRE)** 2-9-3 .... NickyMackay 4 72
(L M Cumani) *chsd ldrs: rdn over 1f out: styd on same pce* **22/1**

00 4 1 **Habalwatan (IRE)**[42] [4037] 2-9-3 ....(b[1]) NCallan 5 69
(C E Brittain) *s.s: hld up: hdwy over 1f out: nt trble ldrs* **25/1**

5 1 1/4 **Nice To Know (FR)** 2-8-12 .... DO'Donohoe 3 61
(E A L Dunlop) *s.s: hld up: hdwy over 1f out: nt trble ldrs* **40/1**

2 6 2 1/2 **Audit (IRE)**[40] [4107] 2-9-3 ....(v[1]) RobertWinston 1 60
(Sir Michael Stoute) *prom: rdn: hung lft and wknd over 1f out* **6/1**[3]

0 7 3 **Atlantic Light**[17] [4830] 2-8-12 .... J-PGuillambert 6 47
(M Johnston) *led: hdd over 5f out: rdn and wknd over 1f out* **22/1**

3 8 1/2 **Fine Ruler (IRE)**[28] [4479] 2-9-3 .... TedDurcan 11 51
(M R Channon) *dwlt: hld up: rdn over 2f out: n.d* **9/2**[2]

5 9 2 **Itchycoo Park (IRE)**[16] [4897] 2-9-3 .... ChrisCatlin 2 46
(E J O'Neill) *prom: lost pl 1/2-way: sn rdn: wknd and hung lft fr over 2f out* **16/1**

5 10 7 **Royal Rationale (IRE)**[18] [4801] 2-9-3 .... EddieAhern 9 28
(W J Haggas) *hld up: hdwy 1/2-way: wknd 2f out* **9/1**

0 11 9 **Me Fein**[9] [5067] 2-9-3 .... TPQueally 8 6
(B J Curley) *s.s: outpcd* **100/1**

1m 27.02s (0.42) **Going Correction** +0.05s/f (Good) 11 Ran SP% **117.3**

Speed ratings (Par 97): 99,95,95,94,92 89,86,85,83,75 65

CSF £9.41 TOTE £2.90: £1.20, £1.90, £4.10; EX 13.50 Trifecta £147.10 Pool £466.24 - 2.26 winning units..

Owner Sheikh Ahmed Al Maktoum **Bred** Mrs T V Ryan **Trained** Newmarket, Suffolk

FOCUS

A decent performance by Jaasoos, who won what looked a fair maiden in good style.

NOTEBOOK

Jaasoos(IRE), who made a pleasing debut when not beaten far at Epsom, is bred to appreciate this faster surface and his rider did not mess about on the favourite, taking it up after two furlongs and steadily drawing clear when asked to settle the issue. He is going to stay trips in excess of this and it will be interesting to see what mark he gets. (op 7-4 tchd 2-1)

Cleide Da Silva(USA), who cost $250,00 as a two-year-old, knew her job and held every chance on this racecourse debut, but she was no match for the useful-looking winner and could only keep on at the one pace. She may improve physically for this and can probably find a small maiden. (op 3-1 tchd 5-1)

Monte Alto(IRE), who is bred to be effective at around this sort of distance, comes from a stable whose juveniles often benefit a good deal from their first run and as a result this has to go down as a pleasing effort. He should find a maiden. (op 25-1)

Habalwatan(IRE) failed to improve on a mildly promising debut when well-beaten at Goodwood last month, but this was better in the first-time blinkers and he kept on nicely in the closing stages. He is now eligible for nurseries and can do well in that sphere if the headgear works again. (op 33-1)

Nice To Know(FR), another who lost some momentum coming out of the gate, ran better than her odds entitled her to and she was going on well close home. Her stable's juveniles often come on for a run and she should improve for a mile.

Audit(IRE), who made a promising debut at a time when his trainer's juveniles were not running particularly well, shaped very green that day at Newmarket and it was slightly surprising that he was fitted with a visor on this occasion. He was disappointing, but will be eligible for nurseries after one more start and may fare better in that sphere. (op 8-1)

Atlantic Light ran a similar race to when finishing down the field on his debut and is another likely middle-distance handicap type for next season. (op 20-1)

Fine Ruler(IRE), a keeping-on third on his debut at Salisbury, looked certain to improve for this additional furlong, but he never got going after a slow sart and was another to disappoint. Official explanation: jockey said colt ran too free (op 7-1)

5298 DANNY WRIGHT (S) STKS 1m 2f 21y

3:25 (3:25) (Class 6) 3-4-Y-O **£2,331** (£693; £346; £173) **Stalls** Low

Form RPR

3520 1 **Desert Lightning (IRE)**[15] [4909] 4-9-4 50 .... NCallan 5 55
(K R Burke) *hld up: plld hrd: hdwy 1/2-way: chsd ldr over 2f out: led and edgd rt over 1f out: pushed out* **7/2**[1]

0002 2 1 1/4 **Tiptoeing**[8] [5097] 3-8-6 42 ....(b) TPQueally 6 48
(M H Tompkins) *hld up: hdwy 1/2-way: rdn to chse wnr fnl f: styd on* **8/1**[3]

0004 3 1 **Shaika**[50] [3824] 3-8-11 47 .... JamieMackay 14 51
(G Prodromou) *hld up: hdwy 4f out: rdn over 1f out: r.o* **25/1**

2353 4 nk **Simplified**[28] [4491] 3-8-6 41 .... DO'Donohoe 9 45
(J Pearce) *hld up: hdwy over 4f out: rdn over 1f out: no ex ins fnl f* **12/1**

2540 5 3 1/2 **Snow Symphony (IRE)**[14] [4930] 3-8-11 60 .... ChrisCatlin 15 44
(D M Simcock) *hld up: styd on ins fnl f: nrst fin* **8/1**[3]

6600 6 shd **Monmouthshire**[36] [4225] 3-8-11 63 ....(v[1]) EddieAhern 3 44
(M L W Bell) *prom: led over 3f out: rdn and hdd over 1f out: wknd ins fnl f* **8/1**[3]

06 7 2 **City Minx**[21] [4708] 4-8-13 .... DerekMcGaffin 10 35
(D Morris) *hld up: rdn 1/2-way: styd on ins fnl f: nvr nrr* **12/1**

6100 8 nk **Coffin Dodger**[17] [4847] 3-8-8 50 ....(p) StephenDonohoe[(3)] 1 39
(C N Allen) *s.s: hld up: n.d* **15/2**[2]

5102 9 1 1/4 **Cool Isle**[11] [5033] 3-8-5 48 ow1 ....(b) JPFeatherstone[(7)] 13 38
(P Howling) *chsd ldr: rdn over 3f out: wknd over 1f out* **17/2**

0000 10 2 **Archivist (IRE)**[13] [4972] 3-8-11 45 ....(t) TedDurcan 2 33
(M Blanshard) *chsd ldrs: rdn over 4f out: wknd 2f out* **16/1**

11 shd **Constables Art** 3-8-11 .... OscarUrbina 8 33
(N A Callaghan) *s.s: hld up: a in rr* **16/1**

5540 12 5 **Perfectionist**[11] [5033] 4-8-13 43 ....(v) JohnEgan 11 18
(Mrs C A Dunnett) *chsd ldrs: rdn over 3f out: wknd over 2f out* **16/1**

00 13 9 **Lighted Smile (FR)**[1] [5273] 3-8-4 52 .... WilliamCarson[(7)] 12 6
(C J Gray) *led over 6f: sn rdn and wknd* **40/1**

0505 14 1/2 **Karrnak**[11] [5033] 4-9-1 43 ....(tp) DeanCorby[(3)] 16 5
(Miss J Feilden) *chsd ldrs to 1/2-way* **66/1**

5000 15 5 **Aboyne (IRE)**[117] [1829] 3-8-6 55 ....(v[1]) KevinGhunowa[(5)] 7 —
(K F Clutterbuck) *mid-div: hdwy over 4f out: wknd over 2f out* **40/1**

2m 9.06s (0.96) **Going Correction** -0.175s/f (Firm)

WFA 3 from 4yo 7lb 15 Ran SP% **121.1**

Speed ratings (Par 101): 89,88,87,86,84 84,82,82,81,79 79,75,68,67,63

CSF £29.27 TOTE £4.30: £1.90, £3.70, £8.00; EX 35.90 TRIFECTA Not won..There was no bid for the winner.

Owner Spigot Lodge Partnership **Bred** Mrs Eimear Mulhern **Trained** Middleham Moor, N Yorks

FOCUS

Not the greatest of sellers with the runner-up and fourth looking the best guides to the form.

5299 SOUTH PIER LOWESTOFT STKS (H'CAP) (FOR THE GOLDEN JUBILEE TROPHY) 1m 2f 21y

4:00 (4:00) (Class 3) (0-90,89) 3-Y-O+ **£9,715** (£2,890; £1,444; £721) **Stalls** Low

Form RPR

0403 1 **High Command**[12] [4997] 3-9-5 89 .... JohnEgan 6 102+
(E A L Dunlop) *hld up: hdwy over 4f out: led over 1f out: rdn out* **4/1**[1]

1436 2 2 1/2 **Folio (IRE)**[32] [4359] 6-9-4 84 .... StephenDonohoe[(3)] 10 92
(W J Musson) *trckd ldrs: rdn and ev ch over 1f out: styd on same pce ins fnl f* **7/1**

0-00 3 3/4 **Invasian (IRE)**[21] [4711] 5-9-2 82 .... JohnMcAuley[(3)] 11 89
(B J McMath) *s.i.s: sn chsng ldr: led over 7f out: rdn and hdd over 1f out: styd on same pce* **66/1**

3144 4 2 1/2 **Pevensey (IRE)**[32] [4347] 4-9-11 88 .... RobertWinston 7 90
(M A Buckley) *hld up: hdwy over 2f out: rdn over 1f out: wknd ins fnl f* **6/1**[3]

2500 5 3 **Jack Of Trumps (IRE)**[24] [4631] 6-9-5 82 ....(t) EddieAhern 9 79
(G Wragg) *hld up: hdwy over 2f out: wknd fnl f* **12/1**

4604 6 1 1/4 **Sew'N'So Character (IRE)**[16] [4889] 5-9-7 84 .... TedDurcan 12 78
(M Blanshard) *hld up: effrt over 1f out: nvr trbld ldrs* **7/1**

05-4 7 shd **Well Established (IRE)**[16] [4878] 4-9-4 81 .... PhilipRobinson 4 75
(M A Jarvis) *prom: rdn over 2f out: wknd over 1f out* **7/1**

1305 8 3 1/2 **Dragon Slayer (IRE)**[40] [4112] 4-9-2 79 .... ChrisCatlin 8 66
(Ian Williams) *mid-div: hdwy over 4f out: rdn and wknd over 1f out* **20/1**

0-03 9 1 1/2 **Babe Maccool (IRE)**[7] [5110] 4-9-5 82 .... MichaelHills 2 66
(B W Hills) *mid-div: lost pl whn hung lft over 4f out: n.d after* **5/1**[2]

22-0 10 5 **Maggies Farm (USA)**[119] [1781] 3-8-12 82 .... J-PGuillambert 1 57
(M Johnston) *led: hdd over 7f out: rdn and wknd over 1f out* **16/1**

4620 11 17 **Sonny Parkin**[7] [5110] 4-9-1 78 ....(v) DO'Donohoe 3 21
(G A Huffer) *hld up: hmpd over 4f out: n.d* **16/1**

0050 12 2 1/2 **Bahar Shumaal (IRE)**[21] [4711] 4-9-8 85 ....(b) NCallan 5 23
(C E Brittain) *chsd ldrs over 7f* **25/1**

2m 4.56s (-3.54) **Going Correction** -0.175s/f (Firm)

WFA 3 from 4yo+ 7lb 12 Ran SP% **118.0**

Speed ratings (Par 107): 107,105,104,102,100 99,98,96,94,90 77,75

CSF £30.97 CT £1601.96 TOTE £5.80: £2.00, £2.30, £17.20; EX 44.60 TRIFECTA Not won..

Owner Mohammed Jaber **Bred** Whitsbury Manor Stud And Tower Bloodstock **Trained** Newmarket, Suffolk

FOCUS

A good, competitive handicap run at a strong pace. The race has been rated through the third and looks reliable.

NOTEBOOK

High Command, who bounced back to form when a staying-on third at Kempton last time, looked a major player on the best of his efforts from earlier in the season and, under a confident ride from Egan, he ran out quite a comfortable winner. He has yet to be tried at 12 furlongs, but shapes as though he will stay it, despite the dam's side of his pedigree saying otherwise.
Folio(IRE) has really found himself since being upped to ten furlongs, winning at Ripon back in June. However, this was the sixth time this season he has finished runner-up, albeit he appeared to do nothing wrong in defeat. (op 8-1)
Invasian(IRE) ran his best race since his three-year-old days, doing well to claim third following a slow start. He has dropped down to a fair mark now, but it remains to be seen if he can reproduce this.
Pevensey(IRE) has been a model of consistency this season, but he has rarely got his head in front and it was slightly disappointing that he failed to see his race out as well as the others. (tchd 11-2)
Jack Of Trumps(IRE) has been disappointing more often than not this season and he once again failed to find much once asked for maximum effort, the first-time tongue tie appearing to do little to aid him. (op 10-1)
Sew'N'So Character(IRE) had a bit to prove at this distance and was ridden to see it out. He never got involved, and was a shade disappointing. (tchd 17-2 in places)
Babe Maccool(IRE) failed to build on a good effort that saw him finish third behind a useful sort at Kempton last time, and the fact that he hung suggested there may have been something amiss. (op 7-1)

5300 E B F AT THE RACES JOHN MUSKER FILLIES' STKS (LISTED RACE) 1m 2f 21y

4:30 (4:31) (Class 1) 3-Y-0+

£17,034 (£6,456; £3,231; £1,611; £807; £405) **Stalls** Low

Form				RPR
13-0	**1**		**Dance Partner**[18] [4810] 4-9-1 87 PhilipRobinson 8 (J H M Gosden) *mde all: qcknd over 2f out: pushed out* **14/1**	98
1403	**2**	½	**Gower Song**[20] [4741] 3-8-8 95 JohnEgan 5 (D R C Elsworth) *chsd ldrs: hmpd after 1f: rdn over 1f out: r.o* **7/2**[3]	97
6212	**3**	*nk*	**Grain Of Truth**[25] [4590] 3-8-8 94 RobertWinston 6 (Sir Michael Stoute) *trckd ldrs: ev ch over 1f out: sn rdn: fnd nil* **2/1**[1]	96
0601	**4**	1 ¾	**Solva**[4] [5164] 3-8-8 82 EddieAhern 3 (B J Meehan) *hld up: hdwy over 2f out: rdn and hung lft over 1f out: nt rch ldrs* **12/1**	93
0003	**5**	*nk*	**Salamanca**[4] [5177] 4-9-1 93 SteveDrowne 2 (S Kirk) *hld up: hdwy 1/2-way: outpcd over 2f out: styd on u.p* **8/1**	92
1442	**6**	2	**Summer's Eve**[28] [4482] 3-8-8 102 DaneO'Neill 4 (H Candy) *hld up: hdwy over 2f out: rdn and hung lft over 1f out: styd on same pce* **9/4**[2]	89
130-	**7**	5	**Chatila (USA)**[346] [5649] 3-8-8 100 DavidKinsella 1 (J H M Gosden) *hld up: n.d* **40/1**	79
5501	**8**	2	**Spirit Of The Fen (IRE)**[31] [4396] 3-8-8 81 RobertHavlin 10 (J H M Gosden) *chsd ldrs: lost pl over 6f out: rdn and wknd over 2f out* **33/1**	75
2650	**9**	½	**Tata Naka**[14] [4925] 6-9-1 54 HayleyTurner 9 (Mrs C A Dunnett) *chsd wnr 7f: sn rdn and wknd* **100/1**	74?

2m 6.22s (-1.88) **Going Correction** -0.175s/f (Firm)
WFA 3 from 4yo+ 7lb **9** Ran SP% **118.2**
Speed ratings (Par 108):100,99,99,97,97 96,92,90,90
CSF £63.72 TOTE £17.40: £3.00, £1.70, £1.10; EX 95.20 Trifecta £155.90 Pool £816.83 - 3.72 winning units..
Owner Cheveley Park Stud **Bred** Cheveley Park Stud Ltd **Trained** Newmarket, Suffolk

FOCUS

Not a strong Listed race, and something of a tactical affair with the winner able to dicate. The race has been rated around the fourth for the time being.

NOTEBOOK

Dance Partner, a progressive handicapper at three, was well held on her recent belated return to the track. Under a masterful front-running ride from Robinson, she dictated the pace and kept pulling out more when tackled in the last two furlongs. (op 16-1)
Gower Song, never far from the action, really found her stride in the last half-furlong and came through to snatch second close home. The drop in trip was against her, along with the moderate gallop. (op 9-2)
Grain Of Truth travelled well and loomed alongside the eventual winner with over a furlong to run, but she could not get past a more determined rival. A stronger pace would have suited her. (op 15-8 tchd 9-4)
Solva, successful in a Bath handicap four days earlier off a mark of 82, ran well again and did best of those to come from off the pace, although she was not really helping her rider in the latter stages. (op 14-1)
Salamanca, who ran an improved race at Goodwood just four days earlier, was keeping on at the end in an event not run to suit those trying to make ground from off the pace. (op 10-1)
Summer's Eve, runner-up to subsequent Group winner Pictavia last time, tried to improve down the outer in the straight but could never get close enough in what was a steadily-run race. She really needs easier ground. Official explanation: trainer said filly was unsuited by the good to firm ground (op 2-1 tchd 5-2)

5301 SEA-DEER H'CAP 1m 3y

5:05 (5:05) (Class 4) (0-85,85) 3-Y-0+

£7,478 (£2,239; £1,119; £560; £279; £140) **Stalls** High

Form				RPR
0040	**1**		**Glencalvie (IRE)**[18] [4819] 5-8-10 72 (p) DaneO'Neill 5 (J Akehurst) *chsd ldrs: led 2f out: rdn out* **9/2**[2]	80
2311	**2**	*nk*	**Bailieborough (IRE)**[20] [4733] 7-9-6 85 GregFairley(3) 7 (B Ellison) *chsd ldrs: outpcd over 5f out: hdwy over 1f out: r.o* **5/1**[3]	92
3245	**3**	*hd*	**My Princess (IRE)**[29] [4447] 4-8-9 71 oh3 ChrisCatlin 9 (N A Callaghan) *hld up: hdwy u.p over 1f out: r.o* **16/1**	78
5400	**4**	*shd*	**Missed A Beat**[10] [5046] 4-8-9 71 oh1 OscarUrbina 10 (M Blanshard) *hld up in tch: rdn and ev ch over 1f out: unable qck towards fin* **16/1**	78
441	**5**	2	**Pab Special (IRE)**[16] [4891] 3-7-13 71 AndrewElliott(5) 8 (K R Burke) *chsd ldr 6f: styd on same pce fnl f* **8/1**	73
-116	**6**	*nk*	**Baskerville**[109] [2024] 3-9-3 84 EddieAhern 2 (P W Chapple-Hyam) *chsd ldrs: lost pl over 5f out: hdwy u.p over 1f out: no ex ins fnl f* **4/1**[1]	85
-400	**7**	1 ½	**Sam's Secret**[35] [4265] 4-8-9 71 oh3 J-PGuillambert 3 (S Parr) *s.s: hld up: styd on ins fnl f: nvr nrr* **33/1**	69
4603	**8**	½	**Calcutta**[46] [3959] 10-9-9 85 MichaelHills 11 (B W Hills) *hld up: hdwy 1/2-way: effrt over 1f out: no ex* **15/2**	82
1126	**9**	*nk*	**Habshan (USA)**[19] [4782] 6-9-9 85 TedDurcan 1 (C F Wall) *hld up: hdwy over 2f out: wknd ins fnl f* **11/2**	81
0060	**10**	5	**Cape Presto (IRE)**[14] [4923] 3-8-5 72 (v1) RobbieFitzpatrick 6 (Mrs C A Dunnett) *led 6f: sn rdn and wknd* **33/1**	57
2360	**11**	2 ½	**Time For Life (USA)**[89] [2608] 3-8-13 80 (v) RobertWinston 12 (H J Collingridge) *dwlt: hld up: hdwy over 2f out: sn wknd* **33/1**	59
3150	**12**	½	**Diamonds And Dust**[45] [3973] 4-9-8 84 (b) TPQueally 13 (M H Tompkins) *chsd ldrs 5f* **16/1**	62

1m 39.34s (-0.56) **Going Correction** +0.05s/f (Good)
WFA 3 from 4yo+ 5lb **12** Ran SP% **119.6**
Speed ratings (Par 105):104,103,103,103,101 101,99,99,98,93 91,90
CSF £27.12 CT £326.45 TOTE £6.70: £1.80, £2.00, £3.80; EX 40.30 TRIFECTA Not won..
Owner Tattenham Corner Racing **Bred** Top Of The Form Syndicate **Trained** Epsom, Surrey

FOCUS

A fair handicap in which the field raced down the centre of the track. The form makes plenty of sense, with the first four all running within 1lb of their marks.

5302 FISHERMAN'S WHARF FREEHOUSE SOUTH PIER LOWESTOFT H'CAP 7f 3y

5:35 (5:38) (Class 6) (0-60,60) 3-Y-0+ **£3,238** (£963; £481; £240) **Stalls** High

Form				RPR
4401	**1**		**Mountain Pass (USA)**[22] [4670] 4-9-0 52 (p) DaneO'Neill 7 (M J Wallace) *trckd ldrs: rdn to ld ins fnl f: r.o* **8/1**[3]	63
0020	**2**	1	**Sincerely**[6] [5130] 4-9-8 60 OscarUrbina 4 (B W Hills) *trckd ldrs: led over 1f out: rdn and hdd ins fnl f: unable qck* **10/1**	68
5001	**3**	2	**Moon Forest (IRE)**[12] [4984] 4-9-1 53 (p) NCallan 3 (J M Bradley) *led over 5f: no ex ins fnl f* **8/1**[3]	56
001	**4**	*hd*	**Mugeba**[17] [4844] 5-9-6 58 (t) EddieAhern 16 (Miss Gay Kelleway) *hld up: hdwy over 2f out: rdn over 1f out: styd on* **4/1**[1]	60
3061	**5**	1	**Riolo (IRE)**[22] [4674] 4-8-13 56 (b) KevinGhunowa(5) 5 (K F Clutterbuck) *chsd ldrs: rdn over 1f out: styd on same pce* **20/1**	56
4250	**6**	*nk*	**Discotheque (USA)**[14] [4927] 3-9-1 60 DeanCorby(3) 8 (P Howling) *mid-div: rdn over 2f out: nvr trbld ldrs* **33/1**	59
0000	**7**	1	**Go Mo (IRE)**[19] [4772] 4-9-8 60 SteveDrowne 9 (S Kirk) *hld up: hmpd over 2f out: styd on ins fnl f: nvr nrr* **22/1**	56
5221	**8**	¾	**Only If I Laugh**[11] [5032] 5-9-5 57 (b) RobbieFitzpatrick 11 (R A Harris) *hld up: hdwy and edgd lft over 2f out: sn rdn: wknd fnl f* **5/1**[2]	51
4601	**9**	¾	**Primeshade Promise**[12] [4983] 5-9-1 56 StephenDonohoe(3) 10 (J M Bradley) *prom: lost pl 3f out: n.d after* **9/1**	48
3100	**10**	1 ¾	**Life's A Whirl**[13] [4968] 4-9-4 56 (p) JohnEgan 14 (Mrs C A Dunnett) *prom: n.m.r and lost pl over 2f out: n.d after* **12/1**	44
0605	**11**	*nk*	**Kareeb (FR)**[27] [4531] 9-9-5 57 TPQueally 15 (W J Musson) *hld up: hdwy over 2f out: wknd fnl f* **10/1**	44
6-04	**12**	*nk*	**Satisfaction (IRE)**[34] [4300] 3-9-4 60 ChrisCatlin 6 (E J O'Neill) *chsd ldrs over 5f* **9/1**	46
-220	**13**	*hd*	**Tapau (IRE)**[17] [4844] 8-8-6 51 BarrySavage(7) 1 (J M Bradley) *s.s: hdwy 1/2-way: wknd over 1f out* **40/1**	37
2400	**14**	3 ½	**Doctor Dennis (IRE)**[32] [4368] 9-9-7 59 (v) TedDurcan 13 (J Pearce) *hld up: rdn over 2f out: n.d* **16/1**	36
0400	**15**	10	**Wodhill Schnaps**[46] [3931] 5-9-6 58 DerekMcGaffin 2 (D Morris) *sn drvn along: a in rr* **66/1**	9
-000	**16**	5	**Threezedzz**[106] [2098] 8-9-8 60 FrancisFerris 12 (R A Harris) *chsd ldrs: rdn 1/2-way: wkng whn hmpd over 2f out* **25/1**	—

1m 26.12s (-0.48) **Going Correction** +0.05s/f (Good)
WFA 3 from 4yo+ 4lb **16** Ran SP% **130.5**
Speed ratings (Par 101):104,102,100,100,99 98,97,96,96,94 93,93,93,89,77 71
CSF £85.35 CT £686.57 TOTE £11.50: £3.00, £3.60, £2.90, £1.60; EX 144.50 TRIFECTA Not won. Place 6 £42.83, Place 5 £28.66.
Owner B Walsh **Bred** Marablue Farm **Trained** Newmarket, Suffolk
■ Stewards' Enquiry : Robbie Fitzpatrick one-day ban: careless riding (Sep 24)

FOCUS

A low-grade event in which they again raced towards the centre. The winner was well in on his Irish form and ran a personal best on the turf in this country.
Sincerely Official explanation: jockey said filly hung right-handed
T/Jkpt: Not won. T/Plt: £63.60 to a £1 stake. Pool: £66,457.10. 762.35 winning tickets. T/Qpdt: £44.00 to a £1 stake. Pool: £3,809.30. 64.00 winning tickets. CR

5303 - 5306a (Foreign Racing) - See Raceform Interactive

4650 AYR (L-H)

Thursday, September 14

OFFICIAL GOING: Good changing to good to soft after race 2 (2.40)

Wind: light, half behind

5307 SAGA 105.2FM SUTTER'S FLUTTER MAIDEN AUCTION STKS 6f

2:10 (2:10) (Class 5) 2-Y-0 **£3,238** (£963; £481; £240) **Stalls** High

Form				RPR
	1		**Osteopathic Remedy (IRE)** 2-8-13 PaulHanagan 8 (M Dods) *hld up in tch: effrt 2f out: led ins fnl f: hung lft: kpt on strly* **40/1**	79
	2	*nk*	**Doric Charm** 2-8-6 RoystonFfrench 6 (B Smart) *rn green towards rr: outpcd 1/2-way: hdwy over 1f out: ev ch ins fnl f: hld towards fin* **40/1**	71
2	**3**	1 ½	**Eau Good**[13] [4987] 2-8-13 JoeFanning 10 (M Johnston) *led: rdn 2f out: hung lft and hdd ins fnl f: no ex* **1/1**[1]	74
	4	½	**Flores Sea (USA)** 2-8-9 PhillipMakin 1 (T D Barron) *s.i.s: bhd: hdwy whn nt clr run 2f out: swtchd rt and kpt on strly fnl f* **40/1**	68
6	**5**	5	**Para Siempre**[26] [4608] 2-8-8 PaulEddery 2 (B Smart) *cl up tl rdn and wknd fnl f* **20/1**	52
3243	**6**	2	**Perlachy**[40] [4151] 2-8-13 77 DavidAllan 7 (T D Easterby) *w ldrs tl wknd over 1f out* **5/1**[3]	51
0625	**7**	1 ¼	**Eager Igor (USA)**[20] [4766] 2-8-11 73 StephenCarson 4 (R F Johnson Houghton) *hld up: drvn 1/2-way: nvr rchd ldrs* **4/1**[2]	45
46	**8**	1 ½	**Kunte Kinteh**[37] [4228] 2-8-13 AdrianTNicholls 9 (D Nicholls) *w ldrs tl wknd fr 2f out* **20/1**	43
655	**9**	3	**Beaumont Boy**[21] [4731] 2-8-9 67 RobertWinston 11 (G A Swinbank) *midfield: drvn over 2f out: sn btn* **10/1**	30
0	**10**	¾	**Hopeful Isabella (IRE)**[10] [5068] 2-8-8 SebSanders 3 (Sir Mark Prescott) *s.i.s: n.d* **50/1**	27
0	**11**	½	**Milson's Point (IRE)**[13] [4987] 2-8-11 TomEaves 5 (I Semple) *missed break: bhd: lost tch 1/2-way* **50/1**	28

1m 13.51s (-0.16) **Going Correction** -0.15s/f (Firm) **11** Ran SP% **116.5**
Speed ratings (Par 95):95,94,92,91,85 82,80,78,74,73 73
CSF £1057.37 TOTE £53.30: £7.50, £4.50, £1.10; EX 1441.50.
Owner Kevin Kirkup **Bred** Airlie Stud **Trained** Denton, Co Durham
■ Stewards' Enquiry : Paul Hanagan caution: careless riding

The Form Book, Raceform Ltd, Compton, RG20 6NL

FOCUS
A modest juvenile maiden which was run at a sound pace, with a suspicion that the leaders went too hard. The form may be worth treating with a little caution.

NOTEBOOK
Osteopathic Remedy(IRE), the first foal of a ten-furlong three-year-old winner, defied greenness through the early stages and just did enough to register a winning debut in a tight finish. He was clearly suited by the easing ground and, looking at his starting price of 40/1, improvement seems assured for the experience. Another furlong will be will within his compass before long.
Doric Charm, bred to make her mark at around this trip, was doing all of her best work late in the day and only lost out in a tight finish. She ran distinctly green, and looks sure to benefit a deal for the experience, so should really be placed to get off the mark before too long. (op 33-1 tchd 50-1)
Eau Good, runner-up on heavy ground on his debut at Haydock, was given a positive ride and had every chance if good enough. However, he never really looked too happy at any stage and it may be that this came too soon after his debut on the testing ground last time, so he is not one to write off just yet. (op 5-6)
Flores Sea(USA) ◆, who has a deal of stamina on the dam's side of his pedigree, fell out of the gates and was noted finishing his race with purpose. He would have been even closer with a clear passage around two out and looks the one to take from the race with the future in mind. (op 33-1)
Perlachy travelled well up with the early pace until fading tamely at the business end of the race. He is clearly not as effective on this softer ground. (op 13-2)
Eager Igor(USA) never looked a serious threat at any stage and proved very disappointing on this return to maiden company. (op 9-2)

5308 SAGA HEALTH EUROPEAN BREEDERS FUND NOVICE STKS — 1m
2:40 (2:40) (Class 4) 2-Y-O — **£5,829** (£1,734; £866; £432) **Stalls** Low

Form — RPR
1243 **1** **Tencendur (IRE)**[28] 4509 2-9-0 77 ... AdrianTNicholls 1 — 79
(D Nicholls) *mde all: rdn over 2f out: edgd rt ins fnl f: hld on gamely* **16/1**
01 **2** *shd* **Massive (IRE)**[24] 4650 2-9-5 83 ... TonyCulhane 4 — 84
(M R Channon) *chsd ldrs: effrt over 2f out: sn chsng wnr: ev ch fnl f: jst hld* **1/2**[1]
1 **3** *1 1/4* **Wheels In Motion (IRE)**[17] 4880 2-9-5 ... MickyFenton 2 — 81
(T P Tate) *pressed wnr: rdn and outpcd over 1f out: rallied ent fnl f: kpt on ins fnl f* **3/1**[2]
3 **4** *4* **Akiyama (IRE)**[27] 4566 2-8-12 ... TomEaves 5 — 65
(J Howard Johnson) *in tch: shkn up over 2f out: sn outpcd* **11/1**[3]

1m 45.68s (2.19) **Going Correction** +0.20s/f (Good) — **4** Ran SP% **105.9**
Speed ratings (Par 97):97,96,95,91
CSF £24.93 TOTE £8.50; EX 18.60.
Owner Mrs L Scaife, Mrs S Radford **Bred** Michael O'Mahony **Trained** Sessay, N Yorks
■ Stewards' Enquiry : Adrian T Nicholls caution: used whip down shoulder in forehand position
Tony Culhane two-day ban: used whip with excessive frequency (Sep 25-26)

FOCUS
A modest novice event which was run at an uneven pace, the winner making all. The form is not totally convincing.

NOTEBOOK
Tencendur(IRE) got back to winning ways under a tactically astute front-running ride from Nicholls. This would have just about been the softest ground he has raced on to date, and he clearly got all of the extra furlong, but has to rate a little flattered as he was gifted a very easy lead. (op 14-1 tchd 12-1)
Massive(IRE), off the mark over seven furlongs at this venue 24 days previously, took an age to hit his full stride in the home straight and could not get past the winner try as he might. He has the scope to keep improving and will no doubt be seen to better effect off a stronger early gallop in the future. (op 10-11)
Wheels In Motion(IRE), a debut winner at Newcastle on a similar surface, had his chance on this first attempt over a mile and simply lacked the required change of gears when it mattered. He still looked a little green this time and remains open to a little more progression this term. (op 6-4)
Akiyama(IRE) was left behind when the race became serious and looks to need a drop in grade. (op 12-1)

5309 SCOTTISH AUTOTRADER H'CAP — 5f
3:15 (3:16) (Class 5) (0-70,69) 3-Y-O+ — **£4,533** (£1,348; £674; £336) **Stalls** High

Form — RPR
5501 **1** **Ten Shun**[13] 4985 3-8-10 64 ... StephenDonohoe(3) 25 — 76
(P D Evans) *chsd stands side ldrs: effrt 2f out: styd on to ld nr fin: 1st of 14 in gp* **7/1**[2]
3053 **2** *3/4* **Our Little Secret (IRE)**[27] 4546 4-9-1 65 ... SebSanders 19 — 74
(A Berry) *overall ldr stands side: hdd wl ins fnl f: kpt on: 2nd of 14 in gp* **11/1**
2232 **3** *hd* **Hypnosis**[50] 3832 3-8-12 68 ... MarkLawson(5) 14 — 76+
(D W Barker) *chsd stands side ldrs: effrt over 2f out: led briefly wl ins fnl f: jst hld: 3rd of 14 in gp* **16/1**
0302 **4** *shd* **Dorn Dancer (IRE)**[9] 5081 4-8-11 61 ... RobertWinston 23 — 69+
(D W Barker) *hld up stands rail: hdwy over 1f out: kpt on wl fnl f: n.m.r nr fin: 4th of 14 in gp* **5/1**[1]
1406 **5** *4* **Compton Classic**[9] 5078 4-8-5 55 oh6 ...(p) JoeFanning 24 — 49
(J S Goldie) *in tch stands side: effrt over 2f out: no imp fnl f: 5th of 14 in gp* **20/1**
3000 **6** *1/2* **Raccoon (IRE)**[18] 4834 6-8-9 59 ... TonyCulhane 21 — 52
(D W Chapman) *prom stands side: rdn over 2f out: no ex over 1f out: 6th of 14 in gp* **16/1**
3500 **7** *3/4* **Brut**[9] 5081 4-8-7 64 ... VictoriaBehan(7) 13 — 54
(D W Barker) *bhd stands side: hdwy over 1f out: nrst fin: 7th of 14 in gp* **25/1**
0606 **8** *1/2* **Divine Spirit**[9] 5081 5-8-13 63 ...(p) TomEaves 1 — 51+
(M Dods) *hld up in tch far side: hdwy to ld that gp ins fnl f: no ch w stands side: 1st of 7 in gp* **10/1**[3]
3460 **9** *nk* **Colonel Cotton (IRE)**[30] 4453 7-9-4 68 ...(v) PaulHanagan 2 — 55+
(R A Fahey) *hld up far side: hdwy over 1f out: r.o fnl f: 2nd of 7 in gp* **14/1**
0360 **10** *shd* **Ryedane (IRE)**[18] 4834 4-9-4 68 ... DavidAllan 4 — 55+
(T D Easterby) *chsd far side ldrs: led over 1f out to ins fnl f: no ex: 3rd of 7 in gp* **18/1**
5102 **11** *1/2* **Oeuf A La Neige**[9] 5078 6-8-5 55 oh2 ... SilvestreDeSousa 12 — 40
(Miss L A Perratt) *racd on outside of stands side gp: effrt over 2f out: sn no imp: 8th of 14 in gp* **12/1**
0033 **12** *nk* **Ptarmigan Ridge**[14] 4952 10-9-2 69 ... AndrewMullen(3) 9 — 53
(Miss L A Perratt) *midfield on outside of stands side gp: effrt over 2f out: sn no ex: 9th of 14 in gp* **10/1**[3]
0220 **13** *1 1/2* **Obe One**[61] 3524 6-8-5 55 oh1 ... PaulQuinn 10 — 34
(D Nicholls) *bhd stands side: rdn 1/2-way: nvr rchd ldrs: 10th of 14 in gp* **14/1**
1240 **14** *shd* **Rothesay Dancer**[21] 4725 3-9-3 68 ...(p) PhillipMakin 16 — 47
(J S Goldie) *in tch stands side: drvn over 2f out: btn over 1f out: 11th of 14 in gp* **33/1**
0000 **15** *1/2* **Bellanora**[24] 4666 3-8-4 55 oh1 ...(v[1]) StephenCarson 3 — 32+
(R F Johnson Houghton) *racd far side: chsd ldrs: led over 2f to over 2f out: no ex fnl f: 4th of 7 that gp* **50/1**
0350 **16** *shd* **Betsen (IRE)**[30] 4462 4-8-13 63 ...(t) AdrianTNicholls 5 — 40+
(D Nicholls) *chsd far side ldrs tl no ex over 1f out: 5th of 7 in gp* **16/1**
00-0 **17** *3/4* **John O'Groats (IRE)**[28] 4523 8-7-12 55 oh12 ... CharlotteKerton(7) 20 — 29
(W G Harrison) *hld up stands side: rdn over 2f out: nvr on terms: 12th of 14 in gp* **66/1**
1020 **18** *3* **Ashes (IRE)**[66] 3354 4-9-2 66 ... NCallan 8 — 30
(K R Burke) *chsd stands side ldrs tl wknd fr 2f out: 13th of 14 in gp* **18/1**
0005 **19** *2* **Law Maker**[81] 2897 6-8-12 62 ...(v) MickyFenton 11 — 19
(A Bailey) *a bhd stands side: last of 14 in gp* **33/1**
5600 **20** *2* **Millfield (IRE)**[18] 4831 3-9-2 67 ... RoystonFfrench 6 — 18+
(J Howard Johnson) *in tch far side tl wknd over 2f out: 6th of 7 in gp* **50/1**
0600 **21** *3* **Pensata**[9] 5077 3-8-4 55 oh16 ...(b[1]) PaulEddery 7 — —+
(Miss L A Perratt) *led far side to over 2f out: sn wknd: last of 7 that gp* **100/1**

59.42 secs (-1.02) **Going Correction** -0.05s/f (Good)
WFA 3 from 4yo+ 1lb — **21** Ran SP% **125.8**
Speed ratings (Par 103):106,104,104,104,97 97,95,95,94,94 93,93,90,90,89 89,88,83,80,77 72
CSF £76.19 CT £1237.94 TOTE £9.40: £2.60, £2.80, £3.50, £1.90; EX 76.90.
Owner Derek Buckley **Bred** R J Cornelius **Trained** Pandy, Abergavenny

FOCUS
A modest sprint, which saw the seven to race on the far side at a real disadvantage, and high numbers favoured. The first four came clear. Sound form, rated through the second and fourth.

5310 SAGA 105.2FM H'CAP (FOR THE KILKERRAN CUP) — 1m 2f
3:45 (3:45) (Class 2) (0-100,98) 3-Y-O+ — **£11,658** (£3,468; £1,733; £865) **Stalls** Low

Form — RPR
0200 **1** **Krugerrand (USA)**[19] 4810 7-8-13 85 ... StephenDonohoe(3) 4 — 92
(W J Musson) *hld up in tch: effrt over 2f out: kpt on fnl f to ld post* **12/1**
1406 **2** *shd* **Best Prospect (IRE)**[7] 5137 4-9-1 84 ...(t) PhillipMakin 1 — 91
(M Dods) *awkward s: hld up: smooth hdwy 3f out: led over 1f out: kpt on wl u.p: hdd post* **10/1**[2]
220- **3** *3 1/2* **Dream Fantasy (IRE)**[315] 6240 3-9-8 98 ... SebSanders 5 — 99
(Sir Mark Prescott) *led: rdn over 2f out: hdd over 1f out: kpt on same pce* **10/1**[2]
0500 **4** *1/2* **Langford**[41] 4098 6-9-8 94 ... SaleemGolam(3) 8 — 94
(M H Tompkins) *hld up: effrt outside over 2f out: no imp over 1f out* **33/1**
14-1 **5** *nk* **Sanchi (IRE)**[8] 5115 4-9-9 92 6ex ... KerrinMcEvoy 6 — 91
(Saeed Bin Suroor) *trckd ldrs: drvn and outpcd 2f out: no imp after* **4/5**[1]
0000 **6** *3/4* **Artistic Style**[77] 3020 6-9-5 88 ... TomEaves 10 — 86
(B Ellison) *hld up in tch: effrt over 2f out: no imp over 1f out* **11/1**[3]
1000 **7** *hd* **Go Tech**[8] 5115 6-9-1 84 ... DavidAllan 9 — 81
(T D Easterby) *hld up: outpcd over 4f out: kpt on wl fnl f: nrst fin* **33/1**
4003 **8** *2 1/2* **El Coto**[46] 3985 6-9-6 89 ... NCallan 11 — 82
(K A Ryan) *trckd ldrs tl wknd over 2f out* **10/1**[2]
3000 **9** *8* **Baan (USA)**[33] 4359 3-9-6 96 ... JoeFanning 7 — 74
(M Johnston) *cl up tl wknd over 2f out* **14/1**

2m 13.83s (2.11) **Going Correction** +0.35s/f (Good)
WFA 3 from 4yo+ 7lb — **9** Ran SP% **111.4**
Speed ratings (Par 109):105,104,102,101,101 100,100,98,92
CSF £118.72 CT £1217.61 TOTE £13.40: £2.70, £2.50, £2.20; EX 191.50.
Owner The Square Table II **Bred** T Farmer **Trained** Newmarket, Suffolk

FOCUS
A decent handicap, and pretty sound form.

NOTEBOOK
Krugerrand(USA) likes a bit of cut in the ground and, although below his best on his last two starts, his performance at Windsor last month proved he could win off this mark. Together with the runner-up, he finished nicely clear of the rest, and that may spell difficulties when the Handicapper has his say. (op 14-1)
Best Prospect(IRE), who has tended to weaken in the closing stages of his races, had a tongue tie on for the first time, which may explain a few things, and ran well, only getting collared on the line. His stable could not be in better form. (op 12-1)
Dream Fantasy(IRE), who was weak in the market beforehand, was given a positive ride on his belated seasonal reappearance and kept on well after getting headed. This should have done him the world of good and he should be all the sharper for this outing next time. (op 9-1 tchd 12-1)
Langford has run one or two good races this season without convincing that he is handicapped to win off this sort of mark. (op 40-1)
Sanchi(IRE) looked to have plenty going for him under a penalty, but he was in danger of bouncing on this fairly quick return. Under pressure with two furlongs to run, he was soon put in his place, and the ground was clearly not to his liking. A sounder surface will no doubt see him in a better light. Official explanation: jockey said colt was unsuited by the good to soft ground (op 4-6)
Artistic Style, successful in the equivalent of this race for the past two years, had conditions to suit, but he has shown little this season and did not shape much better here. (op 12-1 tchd 10-1)
Go Tech Official explanation: jockey said gelding was unsuited by the good to soft ground

5311 SAGA HOME INSURANCE (S) STKS — 1m 2f
4:20 (4:21) (Class 4) 3-Y-O+ — **£6,477** (£1,927; £963; £481) **Stalls** Low

Form — RPR
6440 **1** **Hawkit (USA)**[22] 4696 5-9-5 69 ... MickyFenton 8 — 74
(A Bailey) *hld up: smooth hdwy 3f out: led over 1f out: sn clr* **4/1**[1]
1310 **2** *6* **Apache Point (IRE)**[17] 4881 9-9-5 60 ... KimTinkler 3 — 63
(N Tinkler) *prom: effrt over 2f out: chsd wnr ins fnl f: no imp* **10/1**
5112 **3** *2* **Jordans Spark**[10] 5064 5-9-0 55 ... MarkLawson(5) 4 — 60
(P Monteith) *keen: hld up: hdwy to ld over 2f out: hdd over 1f out: no ex* **13/2**[3]
100- **4** *2* **Good Investment**[16] 4245 4-9-2 59 ...(p) SilvestreDeSousa 11 — 53
(Miss Tracy Waggott) *led 1f: cl up: ev ch over 2f out: no ex over 1f out* **33/1**
406 **5** *hd* **Scotty's Future (IRE)**[21] 4730 8-9-2 58 ... StephenDonohoe(3) 2 — 56
(A Berry) *s.i.s: hld up: hdwy and in tch over 2f out: sn rdn and no imp* **10/1**
51 **6** *nk* **Son Of Thunder (IRE)**[27] 4568 5-9-5 52 ...(b) PhillipMakin 7 — 55
(M Dods) *hld up: rdn 3f out: kpt on fnl f: nvr rchd ldrs* **14/1**
3360 **7** *5* **Khanjar (USA)**[13] 4981 6-9-2 65 ... NCallan 10 — 43
(K R Burke) *led after 1f to over 2f out: wknd over 1f out* **13/2**[3]
0501 **8** *3 1/2* **Inside Story (IRE)**[16] 4909 4-9-5 63 ...(b) RobertWinston 1 — 40
(M W Easterby) *keen: hld up: rdn over 2f out: sn btn* **11/2**[2]
5505 **9** *1/2* **Insubordinate**[22] 4692 5-9-5 55 ...(e[1]) TonyCulhane 9 — 39
(J S Goldie) *s.i.s: shortlived effrt fr rr over 2f out: wknd* **33/1**

4-00 **10** 2 **Nimrana Fort**[112] [1946] 3-8-9 62 .... PaulHanagan 5 32
(G A Swinbank) *prom: lost pl 1/2-way: n.d after* **15/2**

000- **11** 9 **Circumspect (IRE)**[67] [5324] 4-9-2 62 .... (t) JoeFanning 12 16
(P C Haslam) *prom tl rdn and wknd over 2f out* **50/1**

3340 **12** 1/2 **True Night**[17] [4881] 9-9-5 67 .... AdrianTNicholls 6 18
(D Nicholls) *midfield: losing pl whn hmpd wl over 2f out: eased* **12/1**

4123 **13** 6 **Writ (IRE)**[47] [3934] 4-9-5 55 .... TomEaves 14 7
(I Semple) *chsd ldrs tl wknd fr 3f out* **9/1**

2m 15.78s (4.06) **Going Correction** +0.40s/f (Good)
WFA 3 from 4yo+ 7lb **13** Ran SP% **124.2**
Speed ratings (Par 105):99,94,92,91,90 90,86,83,83,81 74,74,69
CSF £46.17 TOTE £4.70: £1.90, £4.50, £2.80; EX 65.90.The winner was sold to Mr A McLuckie for 16,000gns. Writ was the subject of a friendly claim.
Owner Phil Buchanan **Bred** Hargus Sexton And Sandra Sexton **Trained** Cotebrook, Cheshire

FOCUS
A straightforward seller which has been rated through the second and third-placed horses. The winner is value for further.
True Night Official explanation: jockey said gelding was unsuited by the good to soft ground

5312 EKCO H'CAP 1m
4:50 (4:52) (Class 5) (0-70,74) 3-Y-O **£4,210** (£1,252; £625; £312) **Stalls** Low

Form RPR

4404 **1** **Apache Nation (IRE)**[12] [5015] 3-8-5 **57** .... RoystonFfrench 4 64
(M Dods) *prom: effrt over 2f out: led ent fnl f: kpt on wl* **13/2**[3]

6060 **2** 1 1/2 **Petross**[24] [4655] 3-8-4 **56** oh6 .... PaulQuinn 11 60
(R M Whitaker) *keen: chsd ldrs: led over 2f out to ent fnl f: kpt on* **100/1**

2561 **3** shd **Compromiznotension (IRE)**[10] [5063] 3-9-8 **74** 6ex .... TomEaves 2 78
(I Semple) *led to over 2f out: rallied: kpt on u.p fnl f* **9/2**[2]

4535 **4** 1 **Grey Outlook**[12] [5015] 3-8-12 **64** .... PaulHanagan 5 66+
(Miss L A Perratt) *midfield: effrt over 2f out: r.o fnl f* **16/1**

3230 **5** 1 **Tour D'Amour (IRE)**[12] [5024] 3-8-11 **66** .... StephenDonohoe(3) 13 66
(R Craggs) *s.i.s: hld up: effrt over 2f out: kpt on: nrst fin* **13/2**[3]

3305 **6** hd **Myths And Verses**[21] [4728] 3-8-7 **59** ow1 .... NCallan 14 58
(K A Ryan) *keen: hld up: hdwy over 2f out: no imp fnl f* **20/1**

6330 **7** 5 **Sinner Or Saint (IRE)**[17] [4892] 3-9-1 **67** .... DavidAllan 10 56
(T D Easterby) *cl up tl rdn and wknd 2f out* **20/1**

5-00 **8** 6 **Dream Mountain**[43] [4060] 3-8-8 **60** .... JoeFanning 6 36
(M Johnston) *in tch: drvn 3f out: sn lost pl* **14/1**

2323 **9** 3/4 **Esoterica (IRE)**[33] [4353] 3-9-2 **68** .... (p) PhillipMakin 1 43
(T D Barron) *prom: drvn 3f out: wknd wl over 1f out* **4/1**[1]

0300 **10** 6 **Night In (IRE)**[9] [5079] 3-9-3 **69** .... (t) KimTinkler 9 31
(N Tinkler) *hld up: effrt over 3f out: btn 2f out* **20/1**

0000 **11** 1 3/4 **Considerthelilies (IRE)**[67] [3329] 3-8-1 **56** oh9 .... AndrewMullen(3) 12 14
(Miss L A Perratt) *in tch: drvn over 2f out: sn btn* **100/1**

0205 **12** 1 1/2 **Boy Dancer (IRE)**[24] [4652] 3-8-10 **62** .... TonyCulhane 7 17
(D W Barker) *s.i.s: hld up: rdn 3f out: btn 2f out* **8/1**

422 **13** dist **Penzo (IRE)**[96] [2448] 3-9-4 **70** .... RobertWinston 8 —
(J Howard Johnson) *towards rr: lost tch and eased fr over 2f out* **8/1**

1m 47.39s (3.90) **Going Correction** +0.45s/f (Yiel) **13** Ran SP% **115.9**
Speed ratings (Par 101):98,96,96,95,94 94,89,83,82,76 74,73,—
CSF £563.57 CT £3285.28 TOTE £8.80: £2.60, £14.90, £1.60; EX 677.20.
Owner Doug Graham **Bred** Crone Stud Farms Ltd **Trained** Denton, Co Durham
■ Stewards' Enquiry : Paul Quinn three-day ban: used whip with excessive frequency (Sep 25-27)

FOCUS
A modest handicap in which the field came over and racing next to the stands' rail in the straight proved an advantage. The winner was back to his early three-year-old form, with the second up a stone from out of the handicap.
Penzo(IRE) Official explanation: jockey said gelding lost its action

5313 SAGA MOTOR INSURANCE H'CAP 7f 50y
5:20 (5:21) (Class 5) (0-70,70) 3-Y-O+ **£3,886** (£1,156; £577; £288) **Stalls** Low

Form RPR

5010 **1** **Hypnotic**[21] [4733] 4-9-6 **69** .... (vt[1]) StephenCarson 4 87
(D Nicholls) *keen: mde all: drew clr fr over 2f out* **12/1**

5056 **2** 6 **Zhitomir**[7] [5136] 8-9-2 **65** .... RobertWinston 10 67
(M Dods) *prom: effrt and chsd wnr over 2f out: kpt on fnl f: no imp* **10/1**

6-04 **3** 3/4 **Climate (IRE)**[12] [5031] 7-9-3 **66** .... (b) NCallan 9 66
(K A Ryan) *hld up: rdn 3f out: hdwy wl over 1f out: nrst fin* **12/1**

5562 **4** 1 **Flying Bantam (IRE)**[9] [5085] 5-9-3 **66** .... PaulHanagan 12 63
(R A Fahey) *bhd tl kpt on fr 2f out: nvr nrr* **7/1**[3]

0600 **5** 2 **Tough Love**[14] [4957] 7-9-6 **69** .... (tp) DavidAllan 14 61
(T D Easterby) *bhd: drvn 3f out: hdwy over 1f out: n.d* **16/1**

0532 **6** 3/4 **H Harrison (IRE)**[3] [5243] 6-9-3 **66** .... RoystonFfrench 1 56
(I W McInnes) *cl up tl wknd wl over 1f out* **5/1**[2]

0040 **7** 5 **Dispol Katie**[18] [4831] 5-9-3 **66** .... PhillipMakin 3 43
(T D Barron) *midfield: outpcd over 2f out: n.d after* **10/1**

2136 **8** 1 1/4 **Neon Blue**[14] [4961] 5-9-7 **70** .... (p) DeanMcKeown 6 44
(R M Whitaker) *chsd ldrs tl wknd over 2f out* **10/1**

1326 **9** nk **Sentiero Rosso (USA)**[18] [4831] 4-9-3 **66** .... (t) TomEaves 5 39
(B Ellison) *keen: chsd ldrs: lost pl 3f out: sn n.d* **4/1**[1]

3100 **10** 1 **Charles Parnell (IRE)**[36] [4262] 3-9-3 **70** .... JoeFanning 2 41
(M Dods) *keen: hld up: hdwy 3f out: wknd 2f outt* **20/1**

0204 **11** 3 1/2 **Curtain Bluff**[14] [4961] 4-9-7 **70** .... (v) TonyCulhane 13 32
(M R Channon) *hld up: pushed along 3f out: sn btn* **16/1**

2230 **12** 7 **Sawwaah (IRE)**[22] [4692] 9-9-2 **65** .... (p) AdrianTNicholls 7 8
(D Nicholls) *s.i.s: hld up: rdn 3f out: sn btn: eased whn no ch* **16/1**

1m 35.99s (3.27) **Going Correction** +0.50s/f (Yiel)
WFA 3 from 4yo+ 4lb **12** Ran SP% **114.2**
Speed ratings (Par 103):101,94,93,92,89 89,83,81,81,80 76,68
CSF £122.08 CT £1491.14 TOTE £17.10: £4.60, £4.00, £4.80; EX 128.60 Place 6 £2,390.62, Place 5 £1,232.13.
Owner Bill Wallace/Gary Butters **Bred** Cheveley Park Stud Ltd **Trained** Sessay, N Yorks

FOCUS
An ordinary handicap in which the early pace was not that strong, and the winner made every yard. The form looks sound enough rated around the placed horses, though.
Sawwaah(IRE) Official explanation: jockey said gelding hung badly left-handed in straight
T/Jkpt: Not won. T/Plt: £1,372.30 to a £1 stake. Pool: £67,957.55. 36.15 winning tickets. T/Qpdt: £88.30 to a £1 stake. Pool: £4,929.80. 41.30 winning tickets. RY

[4630] PONTEFRACT (L-H)
Thursday, September 14

OFFICIAL GOING: Good (good to firm in places) changing to good to soft after race 4 (4.00)
After overnight rain the ground was described as 'dead' A heavy storm after race three soon turned it good to soft with the better ground on the outside.
Wind: almost nil Weather: Fine at first but heavy storm after race 3 before faring up again.

5314 BETFAIR.COM APPRENTICE SERIES (ROUND 4) (H'CAP) 1m 2f 6y
2:20 (2:21) (Class 5) (0-70,74) 3-Y-O+ **£3,886** (£1,156; £577; £288) **Stalls** Low

Form RPR

2451 **1** **Lysandra (IRE)**[9] [5090] 4-10-4 **74** 6ex .... DanielleMcCreery 5 81
(N Tinkler) *dwlt: hld up: hdwy and c wd over 2f out: led wl ins fnl f: jst hld on* **8/1**[3]

5131 **2** shd **Jackie Kiely**[13] [4982] 5-9-12 **68** .... (t) TolleyDean 3 75
(R Brotherton) *chsd ldrs: drvn over 4f out: chal ins last: jst failed* **9/2**[1]

5055 **3** 1 **Kylkenny**[44] [4021] 11-9-2 **63** .... (t) NBazeley(5) 4 68
(H Morrison) *trckd ldrs: led over 1f out: hdd wl ins last: no ex* **7/1**[2]

0010 **4** 3 **Orpen Wide (IRE)**[12] [3230] 4-9-11 **67** .... JamieHamblett 8 66
(M C Chapman) *rr-div: drvn over 4f out: hdwy over 1f out: styd on ins last* **8/1**[3]

2365 **5** 1 1/4 **Qualitair Wings**[15] [4925] 7-8-12 **59** .... JamesRogers(5) 10 56
(J Hetherton) *trckd ldrs: chal over 1f out: kpt on same pce* **9/2**[1]

6060 **6** 2 **Tedsdale Mac**[14] [4947] 7-8-13 **55** .... AlanRutter 6 48
(N Bycroft) *rr-div: hdwy over 2f out: nvr trbld ldrs* **10/1**

0-01 **7** 12 **Moonshine Bill**[13] [4981] 7-8-9 **54** oh5 .... WilliamCarson(3) 7 24
(P W Hiatt) *led: hdd over 1f out: wknd and eased fnl f* **9/1**

0002 **8** 1/2 **Kentuckian**[18] [4835] 4-8-7 **54** oh13 .... MCGeran(5) 9 23
(P W Hiatt) *chsd ldrs: lost pl over 1f out* **33/1**

2610 **9** 2 **Tender The Great (IRE)**[76] [3044] 3-9-1 **64** .... ThomasO'Brien 2 30
(V Smith) *mid-div: hdwy to chse ldrs 4f out: lost pl over 1f out* **8/1**[3]

11/0 **10** 25 **Miss Holly**[14] [4947] 7-9-2 **65** .... GaryEdwards(7) 11 —
(D Carroll) *s.s: sn wl ldrs: lost pl over 3f out: t.o 2f out* **33/1**

-060 **11** 12 **Purple Dancer (FR)**[90] [2612] 4-8-12 **54** oh1 .... KevinGhunowa 1 —
(J P L Ewart) *chsd ldrs: drvn over 5f out: lost pl 4f out: t.o 2f out* **16/1**

2m 14.47s (0.39) **Going Correction** +0.225s/f (Good)
WFA 3 from 4yo+ 7lb **11** Ran SP% **113.1**
Speed ratings (Par 103):107,106,106,103,102 101,91,91,89,69 59
CSF £42.09 CT £263.17 TOTE £7.30: £2.10, £2.00, £2.00; EX 23.00.
Owner Team Fashion Rocks **Bred** Newberry Stud Company **Trained** Langton, N Yorks

FOCUS
The winner came widest of all in the home straight and was probably on the quicker ground.
Purple Dancer(FR) Official explanation: jockey said gelding never travelled

5315 LINK 62 MEDIAN AUCTION MAIDEN STKS 5f
2:55 (2:56) (Class 5) 2-Y-O **£3,886** (£1,156; £577; £288) **Stalls** Low

Form RPR

1 **Roheryn (IRE)** 2-9-3 .... DarryllHolland 2 73
(John A Quinn, Ire) *w ldr: led over 2f out: shkn up appr fnl f: sn wnt clr: eased towards fin* **3/1**[2]

63 **2** 1 3/4 **Convivial Spirit**[31] [4434] 2-9-3 .... FergusSweeney 8 67
(E F Vaughan) *trckd ldrs: hung lft and wnt 2nd appr fnl f: kpt on: no ch w wnr* **9/4**[1]

3 3 **Telling** 2-9-3 .... TPO'Shea 7 56
(Mrs A Duffield) *prom: outpcd 2f out: hung lft and styd on fnl f* **12/1**

0500 **4** shd **Silly Gilly (IRE)**[20] [4762] 2-8-12 50 .... FrancisNorton 11 51
(A Berry) *chsd ldrs: one pce fnl 2f* **10/1**

6 **5** 3/4 **Hills Place**[14] [4956] 2-9-3 .... GeorgeBaker 5 53
(J R Best) *outpcd and lost pl after 1f: hdwy over 1f out: kpt on ins last* **9/1**

0050 **6** 1 1/4 **Lost Inheritance**[17] [4887] 2-8-12 50 .... PaulMulrennan 3 44
(P T Midgley) *led tl over 2f out: wknd fnl f* **25/1**

7 1 3/4 **My Maite Mickey** 2-9-3 .... LPKeniry 4 43
(R C Guest) *s.i.s: sn bhd: hdwy over 1f out: styd on ins last* **20/1**

05 **8** shd **John Stanley (IRE)**[14] [4956] 2-8-10 .... KellyHarrison(7) 1 42
(D Carroll) *chsd ldrs: wknd over 1f out* **12/1**

9 6 **Kings Shillings** 2-9-3 .... DanielTudhope 9 21
(D Carroll) *s.i.s: a bhd* **17/2**[3]

10 22 **Dream On Dreamers (IRE)** 2-9-3 .... RichardHughes 10 —
(R C Guest) *s.i.s: sn bhd: t.o 2f out* **14/1**

65.44 secs (1.64) **Going Correction** +0.225s/f (Good) **10** Ran SP% **116.0**
Speed ratings (Par 95):95,92,87,87,86 84,81,81,71,36
CSF £10.09 TOTE £3.90: £1.50, £1.20, £3.50; EX 9.70.
Owner P F Kilmartin **Bred** Special One Partnership **Trained** Blackmiller Hill, Co. Kildare

FOCUS
The fourth and the sixth both have an official rating of just 50 emphasising what a weak event this was but the winner could hardly have done it better. Sound form.

NOTEBOOK
Roheryn(IRE), an April foal, is a close-coupled individual. He thrashed his tail going to post but on the way back was most professional and took this with plenty to spare. (op 4-1)
Convivial Spirit, a negative on the exchanges, hung fire when sent in pursuit of the winner and in the end proved no match. (op 11-4)
Telling, an April foal, was a bargain buy. A good-bodied individual who stands over a fair amount of ground, he made a pleasing debut and will be wiser next time. (op 16-1)
Silly Gilly(IRE), having her seventh start, is officially rated just 50. (op 9-1)
Hills Place improved on his debut effort but he looks to need six or even seven furlongs already. (op 13-2)
Lost Inheritance, having her seventh start, is rated just 50 yet she was good enough to take them along to halfway.
Kings Shillings, a narrow type, is a poor walker and he was always towards the rear after a tardy start. (op 8-1 tchd 7-1 and 9-1)

5316 YORKSHIRE LIGHT INFANTRY VASE H'CAP 1m 4y
3:25 (3:25) (Class 6) (0-60,60) 3-Y-O+ **£3,238** (£963; £481; £240) **Stalls** Low

Form RPR

0363 **1** **Muscari**[12] [5031] 4-9-4 **55** .... DarryllHolland 4 64
(A P Jarvis) *trckd ldrs: wnt 2nd over 2f out: edgd lft and led over 1f out: jst hld* **12/1**

3221 **2** shd **Able Mind**[1] [5285] 6-9-3 **57** 6ex .... DNolan(3) 17 66
(D W Thompson) *mid-div: hdwy on outer over 3f out: wnt 2nd jst ins last: r.o: jst failed* **9/2**[1]

046 **3** *1* **Ali D**^{41} [4108] 8-9-4 **60** AndrewElliott$^{(5)}$ 9 67+
(G Woodward) *s.i.s: bhd: hdwy over 2f out: c v wd: fin wl* **11/1**
0400 **4** *1* **Pauline's Prince**^{10} [5072] 4-9-5 **56** LPKeniry 8 60
(R Hollinshead) *trckd ldrs: kpt on same pce appr fnl f* **25/1**
2401 **5** *nk* **Legal Lover (IRE)**^{10} [5054] 4-8-10 **54** 6ex RussellKennemore$^{(7)}$ 10 58
(R Hollinshead) *led: hdd over 1f out: kpt on same pce* **10/1**^{3}
4550 **6** *½* **Queen's Echo**^{84} [2794] 5-9-6 **57** PaulMulrennan 6 60
(M Dods) *chsd ldrs: styd on same pce fnl 2f* **20/1**
-600 **7** *nk* **Orpen's Astaire (IRE)**^{14} [4961] 3-8-10 **57** TravisBlock$^{(5)}$ 18 59
(Jedd O'Keeffe) *racd wd: bhd: hdwy over 3f out: styd on fnl f* **50/1**
020 **8** *1 ¼* **Wizard Of Us**^{7} [5136] 6-9-6 **57** AdrianMcCarthy 15 56
(M Mullineaux) *mid-div: effrt over 2f out: kpt on: nvr rchd ldrs* **20/1**
0410 **9** *shd* **Burton Ash**^{47} [3947] 4-9-5 **56** LDettori 5 55
(J G Given) *mid-div: effrt 3f out: kpt on: nvr nr ldrs* **9/2**^{1}
4000 **10** *shd* **Dudley Docker (IRE)**^{33} [4378] 4-9-9 **60** DanielTudhope 7 59
(D Carroll) *s.s: stdy hdwy 2f out: nt clr run over 1f out: styng on at fin* **14/1**
2633 **11** *nk* **Ours (IRE)**^{42} [4069] 3-9-4 **60** PatCosgrave 14 58
(J D Bethell) *s.i.s: rr- div: kpt on fnl 2f: nvr on terms* **14/1**
-000 **12** *½* **King After**^{12} [5032] 4-9-4 **55** GeorgeBaker 16 52
(J R Best) *t.k.h: bhd and swtchd lft after s: hdwy on outer over 1f out: nvr on terms* **10/1**^{3}
0050 **13** *13* **Etijahaat (IRE)**^{14} [4961] 4-9-2 **53** J-PGuillambert 3 20
(C W Fairhurst) *chsd ldrs: wknd 2f out* **33/1**
0-02 **14** *1* **Formidable Will (FR)**^{48} [3914] 4-9-4 **55** (tp) DaleGibson 2 19
(M W Easterby) *rr-div: bhd fnl 2f* **7/1**^{2}
-400 **15** *1 ¾* **Alf Tupper**^{70} [3231] 3-8-11 **60** PatrickHills$^{(7)}$ 1 20
(M H Tompkins) *in rr and drvn along: bhd fnl 2f* **14/1**
5000 **16** *9* **Elusive Warrior (USA)**^{27} [4569] 3-9-2 **58** TonyHamilton 13 —
(R A Fahey) *rr-div: lost pl over 2f out: sn wl bhd* **40/1**
0100 **17** *7* **Peak Seasons (IRE)**^{9} [5082] 3-8-7 **56** (b) MCGeran$^{(7)}$ 12 —
(M C Chapman) *chsd ldrs: lost pl 4f out: t.o 2f out* **50/1**

1m 47.31s (1.61) **Going Correction** +0.225s/f (Good)
WFA 3 from 4yo+ 5lb **17** Ran SP% **125.7**
Speed ratings (Par 101):100,99,98,97,97 97,96,95,95,95 95,94,81,80,78 69,62
CSF £62.05 CT £653.89 TOTE £15.70: £2.60, £2.00, £2.50, £5.50; EX 79.60.
Owner Mrs Ann Jarvis **Bred** Gainsborough Stud Management Ltd **Trained** Twyford, Bucks

FOCUS
A low-grade handicap run at a strong pace.
King After Official explanation: jockey said gelding hung left

5317 PONTEFRACT PARK FILLIES' H'CAP 6f
4:00 (4:01) (Class 4) (0-85,79) 3-Y-0+ **£6,477** (£1,927; £963; £481) **Stalls** Low

Form RPR
1363 **1** **Namu**^{18} [4841] 3-8-3 **70** PatrickHills$^{(7)}$ 6 76
(B W Hills) *chsd ldrs: styd on wl fnl f: led last stride* **7/1**^{3}
4042 **2** *shd* **Riquewihr**^{17} [4885] 6-8-10 **68** (p) TonyHamilton 4 74
(J S Wainwright) *chsd ldrs: led jst ins last: hdd post* **7/1**^{3}
2415 **3** *shd* **China Cherub**^{18} [4841] 3-8-13 **73** FergusSweeney 3 78
(H Candy) *chsd ldrs: rdn over 2f out: upsides ins last: r.o* **7/1**^{3}
5002 **4** *hd* **Passion Fruit**^{7} [5144] 5-9-1 **73** RichardHughes 2 78
(C W Fairhurst) *in rr: hdwy and swtchd to wd outside over 1f out: styd on wl towards fin* **7/2**^{2}
2321 **5** *½* **Madame Medusa (IRE)**^{29} [4495] 3-8-12 **72** (v) DarryllHolland 5 75
(J A R Toller) *racd wd: led: hdd jst ins last: no ex nr line* **14/1**
32-1 **6** *nk* **Felicitous**^{24} [4663] 3-9-5 **79** LDettori 1 81
(Saeed Bin Suroor) *hld up: hdwy and c wd 2f out: upides jst ins last: nt qckn last 75yds* **2/1**^{1}
121 **7** *2* **Overwing (IRE)**^{17} [4874] 3-9-1 **75** RHills 7 71
(R M H Cowell) *hld up: hdwy over 2f out: kpt on same pce appr fnl f* **16/1**
1040 **8** *20* **Amy Louise (IRE)**^{18} [4844] 3-8-10 **70** TPO'Shea 9 6
(T D Barron) *racd wd: chsd ldr: lost pl over 2f out: sn bhd: eased* **20/1**
0050 **9** *7* **Malinsa Blue (IRE)**^{36} [4267] 4-8-6 **67** (b) GregFairley$^{(3)}$ 8 —
(S Parr) *s.s: sn prom: lost pl over 2f out: sn bhd: eased* **40/1**

1m 19.46s (2.06) **Going Correction** +0.475s/f (Yiel)
WFA 3 from 4yo+ 2lb **9** Ran SP% **112.8**
Speed ratings (Par 102):105,104,104,104,103 103,100,74,64
CSF £53.63 CT £353.90 TOTE £8.80: £2.00, £2.20, £2.40; EX 60.80.
Owner Philip G Harvey **Bred** Philip Graham Harvey **Trained** Lambourn, Berks

FOCUS
There was a downpour before this race and all but the two trailers came wide off the home turn. It was an ordinary fillies' sprint handicap, but it produced a thrilling finish and the form looks rock solid.

5318 PHIL BULL TROPHY CONDITIONS STKS 2m 1f 216y
4:30 (4:31) (Class 3) 3-Y-0+ **£8,101** (£2,425; £1,212; £607; £302) **Stalls** Low

Form RPR
1441 **1** **Som Tala**^{29} [4469] 3-8-3 83 TPO'Shea 5 91
(M R Channon) *led: drvn over 4f out: kpt on gamely fnl f* **9/4**^{2}
5400 **2** *¾* **Ebtikaar (IRE)**^{23} [4677] 4-9-3 95 RHills 1 90
(J L Dunlop) *hld up: smooth hdwy 6f out: wnt 2nd over 2f out: led briefly appr fnl f: no ex last* **6/4**^{1}
3 *18* **Liberman (IRE)**^{159} [4791] 8-9-3 DaleGibson 6 70
(R Curtis) *s.i.s: sn trcking ldr: drvn 6f out: wknd over 1f out* **16/1**^{3}
5360 **4** *1 ¾* **Matinee Idol**^{21} [4734] 3-7-7 47 DuranFentiman$^{(5)}$ 2 63?
(Mrs S Lamyman) *hld up in last pl: hdwy to chse ldrs 5f out: outpcd over 2f out: sn wknd* **125/1**
52-5 **5** *91* **Corrib Eclipse**^{82} [2849] 7-9-3 99 LDettori 3 —
(Ian Williams) *chsd ldrs: drvn over 5f out: sn lost pl: t.o and virtually p.u 2f out: btn 91 l* **9/4**^{2}

4m 13.48s (10.48) **Going Correction** +0.475s/f (Yiel)
WFA 3 from 4yo+ 14lb **5** Ran SP% **108.2**
Speed ratings (Par 107):95,94,86,85,45
CSF £5.81 TOTE £2.80: £1.80, £1.60; EX 5.90.
Owner Sheikh Ahmed Al Maktoum **Bred** Usk Valley Stud **Trained** West Ilsley, Berks

FOCUS
Just a steady pace but in the end a true test of stamina in the conditions. The winner wanted it more than the runner-up.

NOTEBOOK
Som Tala, who had 12lb to find with the runner-up on official ratings, set his own pace. He wound it up from the front and in the end proved much the more willing. He just seems to stay. (op 5-2 tchd 11-4)
Ebtikaar(IRE), with plenty on his plate on his last two starts, looked to be travelling much the better when taking second spot. Brought to the wide outside in the home straight, he went a neck up for a few strides but in the end was outbattled by the winner who he was meeeting on highly favourable terms. (op 13-8)
Liberman(IRE), who started so brightly under N.H. Rules, was having his first outing for this trainer. In the end the first two ran clean away from him. (op 18-1 tchd 22-1)
Matinee Idol, a maiden after five previous outings, had a mountain to climb over a trip she has yet to show she stays. She picked up £857 for just turning up. (op 100-1)
Corrib Eclipse, who won this in 2004 and was runner-up a year ago, was floundering some way from home and the further they went the further he got behind. He has won in the soft over hurdles so it was a lot more than the ground at fault here. Official explanation: jockey said gelding was unsuited by the good to soft ground (op 7-4)

5319 PONTEFRACT-RACES.CO.UK MAIDEN STKS 1m 2f 6y
5:00 (5:00) (Class 5) 3-Y-0+ **£3,886** (£1,156; £577; £288) **Stalls** Low

Form RPR
2323 **1** **Mobaasher (USA)**^{25} [4625] 3-9-3 83 RHills 13 86
(Sir Michael Stoute) *hld up: hdwy 3f out: hung rt and led appr fnl f: edgd lft: kpt on* **11/2**
2-3 **2** *½* **Samurai Way**^{14} [4945] 4-9-10 GeorgeBaker 16 85
(L M Cumani) *hld up in rr: gd hdwy on ins over 2f out: wnt 2nd jst ins last: no ex nr fin* **9/2**^{3}
24 **3** *3 ½* **Particle (IRE)**^{65} [3376] 3-9-0 GregFairley$^{(3)}$ 1 78
(M Johnston) *led: hdd appr fnl f: one pce* **20/1**
04 **4** *1 ¾* **Detente**^{14} [4945] 3-8-12 FrancisNorton 8 70
(J R Fanshawe) *chsd ldrs: outpcd over 2f out: styng on whn swtchd rt if out: one pce* **12/1**
2423 **5** *3 ½* **Spell Casting (USA)**^{48} [3901] 3-9-3 87 LDettori 2 68
(M H Tompkins) *chsd ldrs: drvn 3f out: one pce whn n.m.r jst ins last* **9/4**^{1}
6 *1 ½* **Smart Cat (IRE)** 3-8-12 DarryllHolland 10 60
(A P Jarvis) *s.i.s: hdwy to chse ldrs over 3f out: wknd over 1f out* **33/1**
6 **7** *nk* **Dangerous Business (IRE)**^{15} [4931] 5-9-5 LPKeniry 11 60+
(H Morrison) *hld up in rr: hdwy and shkn up over 2f out: nvr rchd ldrs* **50/1**
0 **8** *1* **According To Pete**^{9} [5086] 5-9-3 PaulPickard$^{(7)}$ 12 63
(J M Jefferson) *hld up in rr: hdwy on ins over 2f out: nvr nr ldrs* **66/1**
04 **9** *1* **Kildare Sun (IRE)**^{14} [4959] 4-9-10 62 DaleGibson 6 61
(J Mackie) *chsd ldrs: rdn over 2f out: one pce* **100/1**
0 **10** *5* **Intersky High (USA)**^{38} [4204] 4-9-5 PatCosgrave 14 47
(K A Ryan) *s.i.s: hdwy over 5f out: rdn and lost pl over 2f out* **100/1**
22 **11** *¾* **Indication**^{19} [4814] 3-8-12 RichardHughes 15 45
(J H M Gosden) *hld up in rr: smooth hdwy 5f out: effrt over 2f out: wknd and eased over 1f out* **5/2**^{2}
64 **12** *1 ¼* **Lady's Law**^{54} [3750] 3-8-12 PaulMulrennan 4 43
(G G Margarson) *chsd ldrs: lost pl 2f out* **100/1**
6600 **13** *10* **Tip Top Style**^{42} [4069] 3-9-3 48 TonyHamilton 5 29
(J Mackie) *in tch: hrd rdn and lost pl over 2f out: sn bhd* **100/1**
0 **14** *10* **Spiritwind (IRE)**^{115} [1880] 3-9-3 (tp) FergusSweeney 7 10
(W R Swinburn) *in tch: drvn over 4f out: sn lost pl and bhd* **66/1**

2m 17.84s (3.76) **Going Correction** +0.475s/f (Yiel)
WFA 3 from 4yo+ 7lb **14** Ran SP% **117.2**
Speed ratings (Par 103):103,102,99,98,95 94,94,93,92,88 87,86,78,70
CSF £28.39 TOTE £6.30: £1.60, £2.10, £3.60; EX 25.20.
Owner Hamdan Al Maktoum **Bred** Brushwood Stable **Trained** Newmarket, Suffolk
■ Stewards' Enquiry : Greg Fairley caution: careless riding

FOCUS
An average maiden for the time of the year. The first two pulled clear in the end and the winner struck the front hard against the favoured stands'-side rail.
Spiritwind(IRE) Official explanation: jockey said gelding had a breathing problem

5320 GO RACING AT CATTERICK ON SATURDAY H'CAP 1m 4y
5:30 (5:31) (Class 5) (0-75,75) 3-Y-0+ **£3,886** (£1,156; £577; £288) **Stalls** Low

Form RPR
2236 **1** **Major Magpie (IRE)**^{24} [4653] 4-9-3 **69** DarryllHolland 11 81
(M Dods) *hld up in rr: hdwy over 2f out: led ins last: styd on wl* **13/2**^{2}
0155 **2** *2* **James Street (IRE)**^{9} [5085] 3-8-12 **69** LDettori 3 77
(J R Best) *chsd ldrs: led 2f out: hdd and no ex ins last* **15/2**^{3}
0155 **3** *1 ¼* **Typhoon Ginger (IRE)**^{12} [5024] 11-8-4 **61** oh1 AndrewElliott$^{(5)}$ 13 66
(G Woodward) *s.i.s: gd hdwy on ins over 2f out: chal 1f out: kpt on same pce* **12/1**
4312 **4** *½* **She's Our Lass (IRE)**^{12} [5024] 5-9-8 **74** DanielTudhope 16 78
(D Carroll) *hld up in rr: hdwy over 2f out: styd on wl fnl f* **4/1**^{1}
2145 **5** *2 ½* **Bolton Hall (IRE)**^{14} [4953] 4-8-8 **67** JamesRogers$^{(7)}$ 2 66
(R A Fahey) *mid-div: effrt on inner 2f out: kpt on same pce* **11/1**
0560 **6** *¾* **Zarabad (IRE)**^{14} [4961] 4-9-4 **70** PatCosgrave 8 67
(K R Burke) *mid-div: hdwy over 2f out: sn chsng ldrs: wknd fnl f* **28/1**
2040 **7** *½* **Gifted Flame**^{18} [4831] 7-9-1 **67** (p) GrahamGibbons 7 63
(J J Quinn) *s.i.s: sn mid-div: effrt over 2f out: one pce* **17/2**
-030 **8** *6* **Princess Lavinia**^{70} [3224] 3-8-13 **70** RHills 10 54
(G Wragg) *mid-div: effrt 3f out: sn btn* **20/1**
2430 **9** *¾* **Bond Diamond**^{26} [4602] 9-8-6 **63** RoryMoore$^{(5)}$ 4 45
(P T Midgley) *stl had hood on whn stalls opened: s.s: bhd: hdwy on inner over 2f out: wknd over 1f out* **25/1**
0000 **10** *2* **Mineral Star (IRE)**^{22} [4706] 4-9-2 **75** PatrickHills$^{(7)}$ 15 53
(M H Tompkins) *w ldrs on wd outside: wknd over 1f out* **16/1**
130 **11** *2 ½* **Just Lille (IRE)**^{27} [4567] 3-9-1 **72** TPO'Shea 14 45
(Mrs A Duffield) *in tch: effrt on wd outside 2f out: sn wknd* **16/1**
0300 **12** *9* **Boreana**^{41} [4108] 3-8-11 **68** CatherineGannon 6 22
(Jedd O'Keeffe) *chsd ldrs: lost pl 2f out* **33/1**
0020 **13** *5* **Dakota Rain (IRE)**^{36} [4253] 4-9-7 **73** (e) RichardHughes 5 16
(R C Guest) *led tl 2f out: sn wknd* **14/1**
0044 **14** *2 ½* **Kaymich Perfecto**^{21} [4733] 6-9-3 **74** MichaelJStainton$^{(5)}$ 17 12
(R M Whitaker) *sn chsng ldrs on wd outside: lost pl 2f out* **14/1**
014- **15** *2 ½* **Etaar**^{418} [3745] 4-9-8 **74** PaulMulrennan 12 7
(C W Fairhurst) *mid-div: effrt 3f out: sn weakend* **50/1**

1m 47.48s (1.78) **Going Correction** +0.475s/f (Yiel)
WFA 3 from 4yo+ 5lb **15** Ran SP% **113.7**
Speed ratings (Par 103):110,108,106,106,103 103,102,96,95,93 91,82,77,74,72
CSF £43.34 CT £439.01 TOTE £8.70: £3.10, £3.30, £3.90; EX 61.60 Place 6 £84.10, Place 5 £47.16.
Owner Mrs Patsy Monk **Bred** J Hutchinson **Trained** Denton, Co Durham
■ Apres Ski was withdrawn (9/1, unruly in stalls). R4 applies, deduct 10p in the £.

FOCUS
An end-to-end gallop and three of the first four were the backmarkers at halfway. James Street, who was in the thick of the action throughout, deserves plenty of credit.
Bond Diamond Official explanation: jockey said he had problems removing blindfold and was slowly away
Dakota Rain(IRE) Official explanation: jockey said gelding had no more to give
T/Plt: £116.20 to a £1 stake. Pool: £48,447.85. 304.30 winning tickets. T/Qpdt: £39.60 to a £1 stake. Pool: £2,495.70. 46.60 winning tickets. WG

5296 YARMOUTH (L-H)

Thursday, September 14

OFFICIAL GOING: Good

The ground was described as on the easy side following 8mm of rain the night before.

Wind: Light, against Weather: Sunny spells

5321 EUROPEAN BREEDERS FUND MAIDEN STKS — 1m 3y

2:30 (2:30) (Class 4) 2-Y-O — **£5,181** (£1,541; £770; £384) **Stalls** High

Form — RPR

54 **1** **Paceman (USA)**[26] [4597] 2-9-3 .... RyanMoore 9 — 80
(R Hannon) *disp ld tl led over 4f out: rdn and hung lft wl ins fnl f: r.o* **5/2**[2]

2 *nk* **Eco Centrism** 2-9-3 .... (t) JimmyFortune 3 — 79+
(W J Haggas) *dwlt: hld up: hdwy over 2f out: edgd rt over 1f out: ev ch whn bmpd wl ins fnl f: r.o* **16/1**

4 **3** *hd* **Swiss Act**[12] [5025] 2-9-3 .... KDarley 6 — 79
(M Johnston) *chsd ldrs: rdn over 1f out: r.o* **9/1**[3]

3 **4** *1 ¾* **Lion Sands**[20] [4768] 2-9-3 .... NickyMackay 7 — 75
(L M Cumani) *trckd ldrs: racd keenly: rdn over 1f out: styd on same pce* **4/5**[1]

56 **5** *¾* **Polish Red**[17] [4867] 2-9-3 .... EddieAhern 2 — 73
(G G Margarson) *prom: rdn over 2f out: styd on* **28/1**

0 **6** *nk* **Here Comes Buster (IRE)**[10] [5067] 2-9-3 .... SteveDrowne 5 — 73
(R Hannon) *s.i.s: in rr: outpcd 3f out: styd on u.p fr over 1f out* **40/1**

00 **7** *8* **Present**[22] [4705] 2-8-12 .... DerekMcGaffin 10 — 49
(D Morris) *hld up: plld hrd: rdn and wknd over 1f out* **150/1**

00 **8** *3 ½* **Field Sport (FR)**[40] [4140] 2-9-3 .... TedDurcan 1 — 46
(C E Brittain) *sn led: hdd over 4f out: wknd over 1f out* **100/1**

02 **9** *nk* **Kingsmead (USA)**[35] [4303] 2-9-3 .... JohnEgan 4 — 45
(Miss J Feilden) *trckd ldrs: plld hrd: lost pl over 3f out: wknd 2f out* **33/1**

1m 42.17s (2.27) **Going Correction** +0.225s/f (Good) **9** Ran SP% **110.5**

Speed ratings (Par 97):97,96,96,94,94 93,85,82,81

CSF £34.45 TOTE £3.90: £1.30, £2.40, £1.80; EX 40.20 Trifecta £131.00 Pool £428.14 - 2.32 winning units.

Owner Highclere Thoroughbred Racing XLIII **Bred** R D Hubbard **Trained** East Everleigh, Wilts

FOCUS

A decent maiden, but they went no pace at all in the early stages, with the tempo only quickening from halfway. The action took place up the centre of the track. Not easy to enthuse about the bare form, the eighth anchoring it, but some of the principals will rate higher.

NOTEBOOK

Paceman(USA), upped in trip again, was in front before halfway. Challenged on both sides in the latter stages, he stuck his neck out to hold his advantage. He has some big-race entries but is likely to be put away for the season now. (op 9-4)

Eco Centrism, a half-brother to Isidore Bonheur, was settled towards the back off the steady pace before improving on the outer of the bunch with three to run. He threw down a strong challenge to the winner, receiving a nudge from him, and was just held. (op 14-1)

Swiss Act, who is not the biggest, was well beaten on his debut in bad ground, although his half-brother Foxhaven handles testing conditions well. He showed more this time and went down fighting, keeping on to suggest he will stay further. (op 7-1 tchd 10-1 in a place)

Lion Sands was unsuited by the pedestrian early pace, taking a tug, and could not quicken in the latter stages. A truer-run race is what he needs and, given his attractive pedigree, he is worth another chance. (op Evens)

Polish Red, having his third run, was staying on at the end and looks the type for nurseries at around this trip. (op 33-1)

Here Comes Buster(IRE), again slowly away, was never able to enter the argument, but he finished a mile clear of the remainder and looks to have some ability. (op 50-1)

5322 PRESS RED FOR AT THE RACES ACTIVE NURSERY — 1m 3y

3:05 (3:07) (Class 4) (0-85,84) 2-Y-O

£6,855 (£2,052; £1,026; £513; £256; £128) **Stalls** High

Form — RPR

6501 **1** **The Illies (IRE)**[10] [5053] 2-8-11 **74** 6ex .... MichaelHills 6 — 83+
(B W Hills) *dwlt: hld up: hdwy over 1f out: sn chsng ldr: rdn and edgd lft ins fnl f: styd on to ld post* **15/8**[1]

0352 **2** *shd* **Glorious Prince (IRE)**[9] [5094] 2-7-11 **63** .... DominicFox[(3)] 4 — 70
(M G Quinlan) *sn led: rdn over 1f out: hdd post* **9/2**[3]

3520 **3** *1 ¼* **Fongs Gazelle**[28] [4509] 2-8-1 **64** .... NickyMackay 5 — 68
(M Johnston) *chsd ldr: rdn over 1f out: styd on same pce* **22/1**

0025 **4** *3 ½* **Italian Stallion (IRE)**[12] [5013] 2-9-0 **77** .... RyanMoore 2 — 73
(R Hannon) *chsd ldrs: rdn over 2f out: wknd fnl f* **8/1**

1 **5** *1 ½* **Big Player**[22] [4688] 2-9-2 **79** .... OscarUrbina 1 — 72
(W J Haggas) *hld up: hdwy over 2f out: sn rdn: wknd fnl f* **7/2**[2]

6302 **6** *1 ¼* **Colchium (IRE)**[20] [4773] 2-8-6 **69** .... SteveDrowne 7 — 59
(H Morrison) *hld up: racd keenly: hdwy over 2f out: wknd over 1f out* **10/1**

0063 **7** *nk* **Love Brothers**[12] [5013] 2-8-6 **72** .... EdwardCreighton[(3)] 8 — 61
(M R Channon) *hld up in tch: plld hrd: rdn and wknd 2f out* **10/1**

0102 **8** *24* **Dubai Magic (USA)**[52] [3800] 2-9-7 **84** .... JimmyFortune 3 — 18
(C E Brittain) *chsd ldrs over 5f* **11/1**

1m 41.28s (1.38) **Going Correction** +0.225s/f (Good) **8** Ran SP% **117.2**

Speed ratings (Par 97):102,101,100,97,95 94,94,70

CSF £10.85 CT £140.06 TOTE £2.60: £1.30, £2.10, £3.30; EX 18.30 Trifecta £187.70 Pool £647.75 - 2.45 winning units.

Owner John C Grant **Bred** Glashare House Stud **Trained** Lambourn, Berks

FOCUS

The field came up the centre of the track. The runner-up was allowed to dictate the pace and not many got into it. The time was the pick of the three mile races and the form looks solid, based around the second and fourth.

NOTEBOOK

The Illies(IRE) defied the penalty for his win at Bath, but it was a close-run thing. Held up off the moderate pace, he made up his ground well to deliver his challenge inside the last, but the winner proved hard to pass and he only got the verdict on the nod. The step up to this trip has been the making of him. (op 9-4)

Glorious Prince(IRE) seemed to enjoy himself bowling along in front at his own pace. Only let down with over a furlong to run, he picked up well and found plenty but was just unable to fight off the favourite. He saw out the longer trip well and a similar event could come his way, but he is due to race off 5lb higher in future. (op 6-1 tchd 15-2)

Fongs Gazelle, dropped 4lb since her nursery debut and tackling her longest trip so far, was never far from the action, but she could not get by the leader and was also run out of second inside the last. (op 20-1)

Italian Stallion(IRE) ran a better race than he did on heavy ground last time, but in truth he was never a serious factor. (op 9-1 tchd 10-1)

Big Player took a bit of a tug in the early stages which cost him late on as he weakened out of contention over this longer trip. (op 10-3)

Dubai Magic(USA) was beaten before the longer trip became an issue. Official explanation: jockey said gelding ran flat (op 10-1)

5323 AYLSHAM BATHROOM & KITCHEN CENTRE (S) NURSERY — 1m 3y

3:35 (3:38) (Class 6) (0-65,63) 2-Y-O — **£2,331** (£693; £346; £173) **Stalls** High

Form — RPR

6030 **1** **Group Force (IRE)**[9] [5084] 2-9-0 **52** .... TPQueally 16 — 56
(M H Tompkins) *s.i.s: hld up: swtchd rt and hdwy over 1f out: styd on u.p to ld wl ins fnl f* **16/1**

0401 **2** *1* **Disco Queen (IRE)**[9] [5084] 2-9-11 **63** 7ex .... (tp) KDarley 7 — 65
(P C Haslam) *w ldrs: racd keenly: led 2f out: rdn and hdd wl ins fnl f* **7/2**[2]

6603 **3** *1 ½* **Grimes Glory**[9] [5084] 2-9-1 **53** .... RyanMoore 5 — 52
(R Hannon) *mid-div: hdwy 1/2-way: sn rdn: ev ch ins fnl f: no ex* **11/4**[1]

0140 **4** *2 ½* **Shes Millie**[9] [5094] 2-9-3 **55** .... FrankieMcDonald 8 — 48
(J G M O'Shea) *s.i.s: hld up: styd on appr fnl f: nt rch ldrs* **16/1**

0060 **5** *1 ¾* **Pas De Trois**[9] [5084] 2-8-12 **50** .... TedDurcan 2 — 39
(J Pearce) *s.i.s: hld up: plld hrd: hdwy over 2f out: rdn and edgd lft over 1f out: wknd fnl f* **16/1**

050 **6** *½* **Vodka Luge**[32] [4394] 2-9-3 **55** .... EddieAhern 4 — 43
(J W Hills) *trckd ldrs: rdn and ev ch over 1f out: wknd ins fnl f* **9/1**

0000 **7** *nk* **Fine Leg**[15] [4926] 2-8-7 **45** .... (t) RichardMullen 10 — 32
(P J McBride) *hld up: hdwy 1/2-way: rdn and wknd over 1f out* **16/1**

0440 **8** *1 ¼* **Fun Thai**[21] [4724] 2-9-0 **52** .... ChrisCatlin 15 — 36
(M R Channon) *hld up: hdwy over 2f out: rdn: edgd lft and wknd over 1f out* **14/1**

000 **9** *3* **Fath And Furiouth (IRE)**[90] [2626] 2-8-7 **45** .... JamieMackay 9 — 22
(P C Haslam) *hld up: effrt over 2f out: sn hung lft and wknd* **40/1**

544 **10** *2 ½* **Three No Trumps**[45] [4008] 2-9-6 **58** .... DerekMcGaffin 13 — 29
(D Morris) *hld up: rdn over 3f out: sn wknd* **11/1**

4230 **11** *8* **Meru Camp (IRE)**[15] [4926] 2-9-6 **58** .... (b[1]) JimCrowley 3 — 11
(P Winkworth) *w ldr: plld hrd: led over 5f out: hdd 2f out: sn rdn and wknd* **17/2**[3]

000 **12** *2* **Garrya**[26] [4597] 2-9-7 **59** .... SteveDrowne 1 — 7
(R Hannon) *sn led: hdd over 5f out: rdn and wknd 2f out* **14/1**

005 **13** *19* **Sweet Soul Diva**[24] [4665] 2-8-3 **41** .... NickyMackay 14 — —
(Miss V Haigh) *chsd ldrs: rdn over 3f out: n.m.r and wknd over 2f out* **22/1**

1m 43.91s (4.01) **Going Correction** +0.225s/f (Good) **13** Ran SP% **121.4**

Speed ratings (Par 93):88,87,85,83,81 80,80,79,76,73 65,63,44

CSF £72.40 CT £216.36 TOTE £22.00: £4.70, £1.80, £1.70; EX 127.20 Trifecta £178.60 Pool £327.02 - 1.30 winning units.The winner was bought in for 9,000gns. Disco Queen (no. 1) was claimed by M C Pipe for £6,000.

Owner The Force Group **Bred** Bryan Ryan **Trained** Newmarket, Suffolk

FOCUS

An ordinary event of its type. The winner improved to the tune of 9lb. Once more the runners came up the centre of the course.

NOTEBOOK

Group Force(IRE), well beaten behind today's second and third last time, had the blinkers left off here. Dropped in and taken over to the far side of the bunch from her high draw, she came back over towards the stands' side as she picked up the leaders and got to the front in the final 50 yards. Stamina looks her strong suit. Official explanation: trainer said, regarding apparent improvement in form, that the filly had benefited from the blinkers being left off

Disco Queen(IRE), bidding to follow up her Leicester win in this grade under a 7lb penalty, did nothing wrong over this longer trip. She has the right attitude and Martin Pipe obviously liked what he saw. (tchd 4-1)

Grimes Glory, racing over a mile for the first time, ran a solid race but could not reverse Leciester form with today's runner-up despite being 8lb better off. (op 7-2)

Shes Millie picked up her one win so far over five furlongs, but on the evidence of this run she is well suited by a mile.

Pas De Trois, another facing a mile for the first time, ran respectably but was unable to get much closer to today's second and third than he had at Leicester.

Fath And Furiouth(IRE) Official explanation: jockey said gelding hung left

Sweet Soul Diva Official explanation: jockey said filly became very unbalanced and he could not ride her out

5324 GREAT YARMOUTH TOURISM H'CAP — 2m

4:10 (4:11) (Class 5) (0-70,67) 3-Y-O+

£4,674 (£1,399; £699; £350; £174; £87) **Stalls** Low

Form — RPR

22-2 **1** **Desert Storm (DEN)**[10] [5057] 4-9-10 **62** .... RyanMoore 11 — 69+
(Rae Guest) *led after 1f: rdn over 1f out: styd on* **9/2**[1]

1525 **2** *1 ½* **Rose Bien**[10] [5069] 4-9-12 **64** .... (p) JimmyFortune 2 — 69
(P J McBride) *hld up: hdwy over 2f out: sn rdn: r.o: nt rch wnr* **8/1**[3]

4003 **3** *¾* **Delorain (IRE)**[24] [4668] 3-7-12 **49** oh1 .... (v) JimmyQuinn 16 — 53
(J A R Toller) *a.p: rdn to chse wnr over 2f out: no ex wl ins fnl f* **22/1**

2265 **4** *1 ½* **Tip Toes (IRE)**[15] [4929] 4-8-5 **50** oh4 ow1 .... JPFeatherstone[(7)] 3 — 52
(P Howling) *hld up: hdwy and hmpd over 2f out: nt clr run over 1f out: nt rch ldrs* **50/1**

5562 **5** *2* **The Spread**[17] [4868] 3-8-0 **51** .... NickyMackay 5 — 51
(M Blanshard) *chsd ldrs: rdn over 3f out: no ex fnl f* **14/1**

6134 **6** *3 ½* **Dance A Daydream**[16] [4914] 3-8-8 **59** .... OscarUrbina 7 — 55
(J R Fanshawe) *hld up: hdwy over 3f out: rdn and hmpd over 2f out: wknd over 1f out* **6/1**[2]

1144 **7** *1* **Sovereign Spirit (IRE)**[14] [4972] 4-9-11 **66** .... (t) AdamKirby[(3)] 1 — 61
(W R Swinburn) *hld up: hdwy over 4f out: nt clr run and swtchd rt over 2f out: sn rdn: wknd over 1f out* **9/1**

2432 **8** *1 ¼* **Star Rising**[24] [4668] 4-9-0 **52** .... JamieMackay 13 — 45
(N B King) *prom: chsed wnr 1/2-way: rdn over 2f out: wknd ins fnl f* **18/1**

0064 **9** *5* **Moon Emperor**[13] [4996] 9-9-3 **55** .... (b) EddieAhern 4 — 42
(J R Jenkins) *hld up: hdwy over 3f out: bmpd and wknd over 2f out* **16/1**

4342 **10** *1 ¼* **Lenwade**[14] [4960] 5-8-8 **49** oh7 .... DominicFox[(3)] 10 — 35
(G G Margarson) *dwlt: drvn along thrght: sn mid-div: lost pl over 6f out: n.d after* **12/1**

0003 **11** *14* **Iamback**[15] [4929] 6-8-11 **49** oh9 .... (t) TPQueally 14 — 18
(Miss D A McHale) *hld up: hdwy over 4f out: wknd over 3f out* **40/1**

0132 **12** *5* **Rehearsed (IRE)**[20] [4777] 3-8-13 **64** .... SteveDrowne 12 — 27
(H Morrison) *hld up: bhd fnl 5f* **9/2**[1]

0251 **13** *2 ½* **Jadeeron**[15] [4929] 7-8-11 **49** oh1 .... (p) ChrisCatlin 9 — 9
(Miss D A McHale) *hld up: wknd over 4f out* **12/1**

1306 **14** *10* **Whoopsie**[40] [4156] 4-9-1 **53** .... MichaelTebbutt 8 — 1
(S Parr) *rdn to ld 1f: chsd ldrs: wknd over 4f out* **28/1**

1100 **15** *13* **Unique Moment**[41] [4118] 3-8-13 **67** .... (b[1]) JamesDoyle[(3)] 6 — —
(D J S Ffrench Davis) *chsd ldr to 1/2-way: wknd 4f out* **20/1**

224- **16** *80* **Mahmjra**[446] [2906] 4-9-13 **65**.................... KDarley 15 —
(C N Allen) *hld up: bhd fnl 6f* **33/1**

3m 31.81s (0.40) **Going Correction** +0.175s/f (Good)
WFA 3 from 4yo+ 13lb **16** Ran SP% **124.9**
Speed ratings (Par 103):106,105,104,104,103 101,100,100,97,97 90,87,86,81,74 34
CSF £37.54 CT £741.98 TOTE £5.00: £1.60, £2.50, £5.50, £7.00; EX 49.40 Trifecta £265.90 Part won. Pool £374.62 - 0.34 winning units..
Owner A Elsass **Bred** York Stutteri **Trained** Newmarket, Suffolk
■ Stewards' Enquiry : Adam Kirby three-day ban: careless riding (Sep 25-27)

FOCUS
A moderate handicap in which the winner was able to dictate the pace.
Rehearsed(IRE) Official explanation: jockey said filly never travelled
Jadeeron Official explanation: trainer said gelding lost both front shoes
Mahmjra Official explanation: trainer had no explanation for the poor form shown

5325 HALLS GROUP "VICTORY VASE" H'CAP (FOR THE VICTORY VASE) 1m 6f 17y
4:40 (4:41) (Class 2) (0-100,104) 3-Y-0+
£12,464 (£3,732; £1,866; £934; £466; £234) **Stalls** Low

Form RPR
3111 **1** **Rationale (IRE)**[25] [4626] 3-7-12 **79** oh1.................... HayleyTurner 1 91
(S C Williams) *led 5f: chsd ldr: rdn to ld over 1f out: edgd lft ins fnl f: styd on* **3/1**[1]

1442 **2** *½* **Duty (IRE)**[20] [4770] 3-8-8 **89**....................(v[1]) RyanMoore 8 100
(Sir Michael Stoute) *chsd ldr: led 9f out: rdn and hdd over 1f out: ev ch whn n.m.r ins fnl f: kpt on* **4/1**[2]

0630 **3** *3* **Mikao (IRE)**[23] [4676] 5-9-1 **85**.................... TPQueally 4 92
(M H Tompkins) *chsd ldrs: rdn over 2f out: styd on same pce fnl f* **10/1**[3]

2142 **4** *1* **Cool Customer (USA)**[14] [4951] 3-8-11 **92**.................... JimmyFortune 2 98
(E A L Dunlop) *hld up: hdwy u.p over 2f out: hung lft over 1f out: styd on same pce* **4/1**[2]

4264 **5** *1* **Mceldowney**[12] [5010] 4-9-3 **87**.................... KDarley 9 91
(M Johnston) *chsd ldrs: rn in snatches: rdn 1/2-way: styng on same pce whn n.m.r ins fnl f* **11/1**

561/ **6** *2 ½* **Saint Alebe**[1121] [4300] 7-9-8 **92**.................... AntonyProcter 6 93
(D R C Elsworth) *hld up: nvr trbld ldrs* **33/1**

3-21 **7** *1* **Sunday Symphony**[6] [5153] 4-10-6 **104** 6ex.................... TedDurcan 7 103
(Saeed Bin Suroor) *s.i.s: hld up: hdwy over 4f out: hung lft and wknd over 1f out* **3/1**[1]

0400 **8** *18* **Massif Centrale**[20] [4770] 5-9-6 **90**....................(t) JohnEgan 3 64
(D R C Elsworth) *hld up: rdn over 2f out: sn wknd* **28/1**

3m 5.49s (0.19) **Going Correction** +0.175s/f (Good)
WFA 3 from 4yo+ 11lb **8** Ran SP% **113.8**
Speed ratings (Par 109):106,105,104,103,102 101,100,90
CSF £15.04 CT £103.77 TOTE £3.30: £2.10, £1.80, £3.00; EX 14.00 Trifecta £148.20 Pool £428.15 - 2.05 winning units.
Owner Alasdair Simpson **Bred** Middle Park Stud Ltd **Trained** Newmarket, Suffolk
■ Stewards' Enquiry : Jimmy Fortune one-day ban: careless riding (Sep 27)

FOCUS
The first running of this valuable handicap. The pace was only moderate.

NOTEBOOK
Rationale(IRE), stepped up in trip once again, landed the four-timer despite having gone up a stone in all. Getting back in front approaching the final furlong, he won a bit more easily than the half-length margin suggests and might not have stopped winning yet. (op 2-1)
Duty(IRE) raced a little freely in the first-time visor. Showing in front in the back straight, he fought off most of his challengers in the straight but found the progressive winner just too strong. (op 9-2 tchd 5-1)
Mikao(IRE), now 2lb lower than when making a successful reappearance at the Craven meeting in April, ran his race, but two in-form, younger rivals had his measure. (op 14-1)
Cool Customer(USA), proving admirably consistent in recent starts, made his effort towards the outer in the straight but could not find a change of gear. (op 11-2)
Mceldowney, who really needs further, is battling unsuccessfully against a mark currently 11lb higher than for his last victory three months ago.
Saint Alebe had not run since winning the 2003 Ebor at York, having suffered from misplaced vertebrae. He made a satisfactory return to action and will be suited by a greater test of stamina. (op 28-1)
Sunday Symphony, an impressive winner at York last week, was carrying a welter burden. Trying to close in the straight, he was already held when slightly squeezed out with over a furlong to run. He would seem unlikely to go for the Cesarewitch now. (tchd 11-4 and 10-3)

5326 BANHAM POULTRY MAIDEN STKS 6f 3y
5:10 (5:12) (Class 5) 2-Y-0 **£4,210** (£1,252; £625; £312) **Stalls** High

Form RPR
32 **1** **Averticus**[47] [3930] 2-9-3 .... MichaelHills 4 78
(B W Hills) *mde all: qcknd 1/2-way: rdn clr fnl f: eased nr fin* **6/4**[1]

2 *1 ½* **Danny Templeton (IRE)** 2-9-3 .... AntonyProcter 8 73
(D R C Elsworth) *s.s: hdwy over 2f out: hung lft over 1f out: r.o* **20/1**

03 **3** *shd* **L'Oiseau De Feu (USA)**[35] [4292] 2-9-3 .... DO'Donohoe 7 73
(E A L Dunlop) *chsd wnr: rdn over 2f out: styd on same pce fnl f* **10/3**[2]

0 **4** *7* **Lap Of Honour (IRE)**[41] [4105] 2-9-3 .... OscarUrbina 5 52
(N A Callaghan) *chsd ldrs over 4f* **11/2**

5 *1 ¾* **Boschendal (IRE)** 2-8-12 .... EddieAhern 6 42
(J W Hills) *s.s: hld up: wknd over 1f out* **22/1**

6 *1 ¼* **Speedy Suzanne (USA)** 2-8-12 .... JimmyFortune 9 38
(B J Meehan) *dwlt: sn chsng ldrs: rdn and edgd lft over 1f out: sn wknd* **9/2**[3]

7 *5* **The Wily Woodcock** 2-9-3 .... TedDurcan 1 28
(G Wragg) *s.s: hld up: wknd over 2f out* **16/1**

1m 15.92s (2.22) **Going Correction** +0.225s/f (Good) **7** Ran SP% **111.6**
Speed ratings (Par 95):94,92,91,82,80 78,71
CSF £32.53 TOTE £1.80: £1.40, £7.30; EX 32.20 Trifecta £105.10 Pool £447.10 - 3.02 winning units.
Owner D J Deer **Bred** D J And Mrs Deer **Trained** Lambourn, Berks

FOCUS
A modest maiden. There was a big gap back to the fourth and the form should prove sound, the third setting the standard.

NOTEBOOK
Averticus, who had shaped previously as if in need of this extra furlong, put his experience to good use. Smartly away, he quickened things up before the two pole and was never going to be caught. (op 2-1 tchd 9-4 and 5-4)
Danny Templeton(IRE) ◆, a half-brother to four winners out of a mare successful over seven furlongs and a mile, made a promising debut. Very slow to break, he soon recovered to race in midfield but proved green when asked to pick up, edging to his left. He still ran on to snatch second close home and should know a lot more next time. (op 12-1)
L'Oiseau De Feu(USA) ran another decent race, just missing out on second and finishing a long way clear of the others. He is now eligible for handicaps but could win a maiden. (op 2-1 tchd 7-2 in places)
Lap Of Honour(IRE) was outpaced from the halfway point and beaten a fair way in the end. He could need more time. (op 9-1)
Boschendal(IRE), a half-sister to smart miler Mac Love, was green on this debut and never played a serious role. (op 16-1)
Speedy Suzanne(USA), who cost $195,000 earlier this year, looked likely to finish fourth at one stage but ran green and was not persevered with late on. She might do better with the experience behind her. (op 13-2)
The Wily Woodcock is a half-brother to prolific winner The Whistling Teal, but to some very modest performers too. Following a slow start, he was at the rear of the field throughout. (op 8-1)

5327 CONSITUTION MOTORS H'CAP 6f 3y
5:40 (5:40) (Class 6) (0-60,60) 3-Y-0+ **£3,238** (£963; £481; £240) **Stalls** High

Form RPR
0011 **1** **Forces Sweetheart**[22] [4690] 3-9-2 **58**....................(v) HayleyTurner 13 75+
(M L W Bell) *racd centre: chsd ldrs: led over 1f out: hung rt ins fnl f: rdn out* **11/2**[2]

0013 **2** *2 ½* **Moon Forest (IRE)**[1] [5302] 4-8-13 **53**....................(p) RyanMoore 7 62
(J M Bradley) *racd centre: s.i.s: sn chsng ldrs: rdn over 1f out: styd on same pce ins fnl f* **9/2**[1]

2042 **3** *1* **Peruvian Style (IRE)**[5] [5167] 5-9-3 **57**.................... SteveDrowne 8 63
(J M Bradley) *racd centre: hld up: hdwy u.p over 1f out: styd on* **6/1**[3]

2000 **4** *½* **Millfields Dreams**[4] [5212] 7-8-12 **57**....................(p) JerryO'Dwyer[(5)] 5 62
(M G Quinlan) *racd centre: trckd ldrs: rdn over 1f out: no ex ins fnl f* **20/1**

014 **5** *hd* **Mugeba**[1] [5302] 5-9-1 **58**....................(t) AdamKirby[(3)] 12 62
(Miss Gay Kelleway) *racd stands' side: chsd ldr tl led that pair over 1f out: nt rch ldrs* **9/2**[1]

0650 **6** *1 ¾* **Brigadore**[36] [4258] 7-9-6 **60**.................... TPQueally 10 59+
(J G Given) *racd centre: s.s: hld up: r.o ins fnl f: nrst fin* **11/1**

4300 **7** *nk* **Parkside Pursuit**[5] [5167] 8-8-13 **60**.................... BarrySavage[(7)] 6 58
(J M Bradley) *racd centre: hld up: hdwy over 1f out: wknd ins fnl f* **22/1**

0463 **8** *2* **Gone'N'Dunnett (IRE)**[12] [5032] 7-9-5 **59**....................(p) JohnEgan 1 51
(Mrs C A Dunnett) *racd centre: chsd ldrs: rdn over 2f out: wknd fnl f* **8/1**

3500 **9** *¾* **Tiviski (IRE)**[27] [4554] 4-9-0 **54**.................... ChrisCatlin 14 44
(Miss Gay Kelleway) *hung lft: led stands' side over 4f: sn wknd* **50/1**

3404 **10** *¾* **Vindication**[23] [4674] 6-8-10 **57**.................... WilliamBuick[(7)] 11 44
(R M H Cowell) *racd centre: hld up: effrt over 1f out: sn wknd* **18/1**

6034 **11** *1 ¼* **Alwariah**[15] [4927] 3-9-0 **56**.................... TedDurcan 4 40
(C E Brittain) *racd centre: chsd ldrs over 4f* **16/1**

0602 **12** *shd* **Athena's Dream**[35] [4293] 3-9-0 **56**.................... JimmyQuinn 16 39
(C F Wall) *racd centre: hld up: hdwy over 2f out: wknd over 1f out* **25/1**

0150 **13** *¾* **Great Belief (IRE)**[13] [4985] 4-8-12 **52**.................... RobertHavlin 2 33
(T D McCarthy) *led centre over 4f: sn wknd* **40/1**

1m 14.81s (1.11) **Going Correction** +0.225s/f (Good)
WFA 3 from 4yo+ 2lb **13** Ran SP% **114.0**
Speed ratings (Par 101):101,97,96,95,95 93,92,90,89,88 86,86,85
CSF £26.85 CT £152.64 TOTE £5.80: £2.20, £2.20, £2.30; EX 31.60 Trifecta £104.30 Pool £495.52 - 3.37 winning units. Place 6, 54.97, Place 5 £17.05.
Owner Richard I Morris Jr **Bred** Barton Stud Partnership **Trained** Newmarket, Suffolk

FOCUS
A low-grade handicap. Two runners, headed by the eventual fifth, raced down the stands' side, with the remainder towards the centre.
T/Plt: £91.30 to a £1 stake. Pool: £64,306.90. 513.85 winning tickets. T/Qpdt: £16.80 to a £1 stake. Pool: £4,661.90. 204.60 winning tickets. CR

5328 - 5331a (Foreign Racing) - See Raceform Interactive

5307 AYR (L-H)
Friday, September 15

OFFICIAL GOING: Good to soft
Wind: Light, half-against

5332 JAMES BARR EUROPEAN BREEDERS FUND MAIDEN STKS 7f 50y
2:10 (2:12) (Class 4) 2-Y-0 **£5,829** (£1,734; £866; £432) **Stalls** Low

Form RPR
5 **1** **Fushe Jo**[23] [4716] 2-9-3 .... RobertWinston 10 79
(J Howard Johnson) *prom: effrt over 2f out: led 1f out: kpt on strly* **7/1**[3]

42 **2** *3* **Arena's Dream (USA)**[18] [4880] 2-9-3 .... PaulHanagan 5 71
(R A Fahey) *keen early: led: rdn over 2f out: hdd 1f out: kpt on same pce* **7/4**[1]

0 **3** *6* **Cheery Cat (USA)**[6] [5168] 2-9-3 .... TonyHamilton 2 55
(D W Barker) *chsd ldrs: rdn and edgd lft 2f out: sn outpcd* **100/1**

4 *1* **Judge Neptune** 2-9-3 .... DanielTudhope 14 53
(J S Goldie) *s.v.s: bhd tl kpt on wl fnl 2f: bttr for r* **50/1**

0 **5** *1* **Cornell Precedent**[13] [5025] 2-9-3 .... JimmyQuinn 1 50
(J J Quinn) *in tch tl rdn and outpcd fr over 2f out* **50/1**

6 *½* **Amicus Meus (IRE)** 2-9-3 .... MickyFenton 13 49
(A Bailey) *s.i.s: bhd: hdwy and edgd lft over 2f out: kpt on: nvr rchd ldrs* **20/1**

7 *3* **Ice Box (IRE)** 2-8-12 .... RoystonFfrench 8 36
(M Johnston) *prom tl rdn and outpcd over 2f out: n.d after* **8/1**

0 **8** *4* **Spanish Conquest**[9] [5106] 2-9-3 .... JamieMackay 4 31
(Sir Mark Prescott) *hld up: shkn up 3f out: nvr nrr* **100/1**

63 **9** *1 ¾* **Annual Event (IRE)**[14] [4980] 2-8-12 .... RichardMullen 11 21
(E J O'Neill) *prom tl rdn and wknd over 2f out* **7/1**[3]

10 *1* **Mineral Rights (USA)** 2-9-3 .... TomEaves 7 24
(I Semple) *hld up: rdn 3f out: sn btn* **20/1**

0 **11** *4* **Sonara (IRE)**[21] [4768] 2-9-3 .... NCallan 3 13
(M H Tompkins) *hld up: drvn over 3f out: sn btn* **14/1**

65 **12** *1* **Danni Di Guerra (IRE)**[30] [4474] 2-9-3 .... PaulMulrennan 9 11
(P C Haslam) *midfield: pushed along 3f out: sn btn* **100/1**

2 **13** *4* **Starbougg**[33] [4400] 2-8-12 .... PaulEddery 12 —
(B Smart) *hld up: pushed along over 3f out: sn btn* **4/1**[2]

14 *9* **Mandriano (ITY)** 2-8-12 .... MarkLawson[(5)] 6 —
(D W Barker) *cl up tl rdn and wknd 3f out* **66/1**

1m 35.52s (2.80) **Going Correction** +0.375s/f (Good) **14** Ran SP% **117.0**
Speed ratings (Par 97):99,95,88,87,86 85,82,77,75,74 70,69,64,54
CSF £18.06 TOTE £9.40: £2.30, £1.20, £7.00; EX 16.20.
Owner Shearer Fulton and Johnson **Bred** P E Clinton **Trained** Billy Row, Co Durham

FOCUS
An ordinary bunch on looks. Those racing prominently held the edge, and the race has been rated through the winner.

NOTEBOOK

Fushe Jo, who had shown ability on his debut at York, fully confirmed that promise in this lesser event. This half-brother to top hurdler Arcalis will stay a mile and appeals as the type to win more races. (op 5-1)

Arena's Dream(USA) looked the one to beat on his Newcastle second, but failed to settle in the first half of the race and was beloew form. Although vulnerable to the better types in this grade, he should still pick up a small event. (op 2-1 tchd 9-4, 5-2 in places)

Cheery Cat(USA), soundly beaten on his debut, turned in a much better effort this time. He should stay a mile and will be of more interest in ordinary company once handicapped.

Judge Neptune, out of a six-furlong juvenile winner, caught the eye after a very tardy start on this racecourse debut. He is sure to come on for the experience and appeals as the type to win races in due course.

Cornell Precedent fared better than on his debut at Thirsk but left the impression that he will be seen to much better effect in ordinary handicap company in due course.

Spanish Conquest, a brother to smart stayer Vinando, hinted at ability on this turf debut but will be of more interest in middle distance handicaps next term.

Starbougg Official explanation: trainer had no explanation for the poor form shown

5333 HBG PROPERTIES H'CAP 5f

2:45 (2:45) (Class 4) (0-85,85) 3-Y-0+ **£6,477** (£1,927; £963; £481) **Stalls** High

Form RPR

0330 **1** **Ptarmigan Ridge**[1] 5309 10-8-2 **71** oh2 .... AndrewMullen(3) 8 84
(Miss L A Perratt) *in tch: drvn 1/2-way: hdwy and edgd rt over 1f out: kpt on to ld wl ins fnl f* **25/1**

030 **2** *1 1/4* **Blackheath (IRE)**[9] 5117 10-8-6 **72** .... SilvestreDeSousa 22 81
(D Nicholls) *mde most to wl ins fnl f: kpt on* **17/2**[2]

2010 **3** *1* **Oranmore Castle (IRE)**[43] 4085 4-9-0 **80** ....(t) PaulQuinn 20 85
(D Nicholls) *midfield: effrt 2f out: kpt on ins fnl f* **14/1**

6-22 **4** *1 1/4* **Our Fugitive (IRE)**[89] 2674 4-8-11 **77** .... FrancisNorton 2 77
(A W Carroll) *w ldr: rdn over 1f out: kpt on same pce fnl f* **15/2**[1]

040 **5** *shd* **Matty Tun**[21] 4771 7-8-11 **77** .... RobertWinston 15 77+
(J Balding) *hld up stands rail: effrt and hdwy whn no room over 1f out to ins fnl f: r.o* **9/1**[3]

6200 **6** *1* **Chinalea (IRE)**[30] 4486 4-8-7 **76** ow3......................(p) AdamKirby(3) 12 72+
(C G Cox) *bhd: hdwy and swtchd rt over 1f out: kpt on fnl f: nrst fin* **22/1**

0P05 **7** *nk* **Wanchai Lad**[22] 4725 5-8-7 **73** .... DavidAllan 16 68
(T D Easterby) *prom: effrt over 2f out: one pce whn hmpd ins fnl f* **25/1**

1601 **8** *nk* **Sea Salt**[18] 4886 3-8-13 **80** .... PhillipMakin 19 74
(T D Barron) *chsd ldrs tl rdn and no ex over 1f out* **14/1**

3210 **9** *1* **Smokin Beau**[13] 5009 9-8-11 **84** .... VictoriaBehan(7) 1 75
(D Nicholls) *cl up tl rdn and wknd over 1f out* **12/1**

2426 **10** *3/4* **Circuit Dancer (IRE)**[6] 5169 6-8-12 **78** .... AdrianTNicholls 7 66
(D Nicholls) *bhd: drvn along 1/2-way: nvr on terms* **10/1**

0200 **11** *nk* **Ashes (IRE)**[1] 5309 4-8-5 **71** oh5...................... RoystonFfrench 11 58
(K R Burke) *bhd and drvn along: sme hdwy over 1f out: nvr rchd ldrs* **33/1**

6100 **12** *3/4* **Dizzy In The Head**[60] 3584 7-8-9 **75**......................(b) TomEaves 21 59
(I Semple) *cl up tl rdn and wknd fr 2f out* **14/1**

3060 **13** *1 1/2* **Bo McGinty (IRE)**[30] 4468 5-9-2 **82**......................(v) PaulHanagan 3 61
(R A Fahey) *midfield: drvn 1/2-way: sn btn* **12/1**

2400 **14** *1* **Rothesay Dancer**[1] 5309 3-8-4 **71** oh3......................(p) RichardMullen 4 46
(J S Goldie) *midfield: drvn 1/2-way: sn btn* **40/1**

6542 **15** *nk* **Handsome Cross (IRE)**[6] 5169 5-9-2 **82** .... TonyCulhane 10 56
(D Nicholls) *prom: effrt over 2f out: wknd wl over 1f out* **9/1**[3]

2640 **16** *2 1/2* **Blazing Heights**[6] 5169 3-8-12 **79** .... DanielTudhope 5 44+
(J S Goldie) *dwlt and wnt lft s: tacked over to r alone far side: n.d* **25/1**

300- **17** *6* **Trim Image**[413] 3899 4-8-0 **71** .... AndrewElliott(5) 9 15
(K R Burke) *rrd s: nvr on terms* **33/1**

1525 **18** *9* **Harry Up**[42] 4101 5-9-5 **85** .... NCallan 13 —
(K A Ryan) *in tch: wkng whn blkd 2f out: sn btn and eased* **11/1**

60.00 secs (-0.44) **Going Correction** +0.10s/f (Good)
WFA 3 from 4yo+ 1lb **18** Ran SP% **119.3**
Speed ratings (Par 105):107,105,103,101,101 99,99,98,97,95 95,94,91,90,89 85,76,61
CSF £205.48 CT £3187.32 TOTE £25.80: £5.50, £3.00, £4.50, £2.60; EX 217.30.
Owner The Hon Miss Heather Galbraith **Bred** Miss Heather Galbraith **Trained** Ayr, S Ayrshire

FOCUS

An ordinary handicap in which all bar one raced towards the stands side. The pace was sound, but with few progressive types and plenty of the principals below form last time out this is hardly a race to get carried away about.

Ptarmigan Ridge Official explanation: trainer said, regarding apparent improvement in form, the horse was suited by being more covered up

Matty Tun ◆ Official explanation: jockey said gelding was denied a clear run

Chinalea(IRE) Official explanation: jockey said gelding was denied a clear run

Circuit Dancer(IRE) Official explanation: jockey said gelding was denied a clear run

Harry Up Official explanation: jockey said gelding was unsuited by the good to soft ground

5334 KNIGHT FRANK NURSERY 6f

3:20 (3:20) (Class 4) (0-85,83) 2-Y-0 **£6,477** (£1,927; £963; £481) **Stalls** High

Form RPR

1 **1** **Utmost Respect**[14] 4986 2-9-5 **81** .... PaulHanagan 9 88+
(R A Fahey) *trckd ldrs: rdn and hung lft over 1f out: r.o wl to ld ins last* **7/4**[1]

212 **2** *1* **Aahayson**[18] 4893 2-9-7 **83** .... PatCosgrave 11 87
(K R Burke) *led tl ins last: kpt on wl* **9/1**

3211 **3** *4* **Algol**[17] 4912 2-9-7 **83** .... TomEaves 6 75
(J Howard Johnson) *chsd ldrs: effrt over 2f out: kpt on same pce* **9/2**[2]

5221 **4** *1/2* **Dowlleh**[24] 4669 2-9-6 **82** .... RobertWinston 13 73
(M R Channon) *chsd ldrs: edgd rt over 1f out: kpt on ins last* **7/1**

0150 **5** *5* **Mundo's Magic**[28] 4547 2-8-9 **76** .... MarkLawson(5) 12 52
(D W Barker) *hld up: effrt and outpcd over 2f out: hung lft: nvr nr ldrs* **66/1**

5033 **6** *4* **Ingleby Image**[17] 4910 2-9-3 **79** .... PhillipMakin 14 43
(T D Barron) *t.k.h: trckd ldrs: lost pl over 1f out* **12/1**

0651 **7** *2 1/2* **Joseph Locke (IRE)**[15] 4950 2-8-4 **66**......................(p) JimmyQuinn 3 22
(M Dods) *chsd ldrs: wknd 2f out* **14/1**

0604 **8** *1/2* **Alavana (IRE)**[56] 3693 2-7-12 **60** oh5...................... JamieMackay 7 15
(D W Barker) *s.i.s: a in rr* **100/1**

643 **9** *20* **Stay Active (USA)**[34] 4349 2-8-1 **63** .... RoystonFfrench 2 —
(I Semple) *racd wd: sn drvn along of pce: lost pl 3f out: sn bhd: eased* **11/2**[3]

1m 13.62s (-0.05) **Going Correction** +0.10s/f (Good) **9** Ran SP% **109.3**
Speed ratings (Par 97):104,102,97,96,90 84,81,80,54
CSF £16.86 CT £53.95 TOTE £2.30: £1.50, £2.90, £1.60; EX 15.70.
Owner The Rumpole Partnership **Bred** Mrs H B Raw **Trained** Musley Bank, N Yorks

FOCUS

Pretty good form, with the first four all progressive and recent winners. They finished well strung out.

NOTEBOOK

Utmost Respect ◆, given a real chance by the Handicapper after his runaway debut win at Haydock, showed his inexperience when first asked a question but then lengthened in fine style to pull away in the closing stages. He clearly appreciates getting his toe in and will be worthy of serious attention even from his revised mark. (tchd 11-8, 15-8 in places)

Aahayson is all speed and went down fighting. He deserves plenty of credit for this, time may show he was attempting a stiff task conceding the winner weight. (op 14-1)

Algol, 9lb higher, was simply not up to the task. (op 11-4 tchd 5-1 in a place)

Dowlleh, having his eighth start, if anything seemed to appreciate the return to six furlongs. (tchd 15-2, 8-1 in places)

Mundo's Magic wouldn't settle and then started to hang. He is not straightforward and may be best when allowed to jump and run.

Ingleby Image, stepped up in trip and with the headgear dispensed with, wanted to do nothing but pull. This was not the answer. (op 14-1 tchd 12-1 in places)

Stay Active(USA), drawn wide, struggled to get competitive and, after dropping right out at halfway, was virtually pulled up. Something was amiss here. Official explanation: jockey said colt never travelled (op 7-1)

5335 SCOTTISH SUN HARRY ROSEBERY STKS (LISTED RACE) 5f

3:55 (3:56) (Class 1) 2-Y-0

£15,898 (£6,025; £3,015; £1,503; £753; £378) **Stalls** High

Form RPR

1253 **1** **Alzerra (UAE)**[27] 4594 2-8-12 **103** .... TonyCulhane 10 98+
(M R Channon) *chsd ldrs: nt clr run over 2f out to over 1f out: rdn to ld ins fnl f: kpt on wl* **4/1**[2]

1126 **2** *1 1/4* **Holdin Foldin (IRE)**[23] 4715 2-9-3 **95** .... PatCosgrave 1 98
(K R Burke) *swtchd r stands rail sn after s: led to ins fnl f: kpt on same pce* **16/1**

6263 **3** *1 1/2* **Mood Music**[22] 4747 2-9-3 **99** .... RichardMullen 3 93
(E J O'Neill) *chsd ldrs: rdn over 2f out: one pce fnl f* **9/2**[3]

6343 **4** *1 3/4* **We'll Confer**[13] 5017 2-9-3 **102** .... NCallan 9 86
(K A Ryan) *trckd ldrs tl rdn and no ex over 1f out* **6/4**[1]

5245 **5** *1/2* **Bridge It Jo**[15] 4966 2-8-12 **94** .... MickyFenton 5 80
(Miss J Feilden) *bhd: rdn 1/2-way: hdwy over 1f out: nrst fin* **14/1**

0524 **6** *1 1/4* **The Nifty Fox**[10] 5076 2-9-3 **71** .... TomEaves 7 80?
(T D Easterby) *dwlt: rdn in rr 1/2-way: nvr able to chal* **80/1**

5300 **7** *1/2* **Kerry's Dream**[22] 4736 2-8-12 **80** .... DavidAllan 4 73
(T D Easterby) *in tch: drvn 1/2-way: hung lft and wknd over 1f out* **33/1**

1512 **8** *nk* **Southandwest (IRE)**[20] 4824 2-9-3 **92** .... AdamKirby 2 77
(J S Moore) *prom on outside tl wknd wl over 1f out* **5/1**

60.72 secs (0.28) **Going Correction** +0.10s/f (Good) **8** Ran SP% **111.6**
Speed ratings (Par 103):101,99,96,93,93 91,90,89
CSF £60.30 TOTE £4.30: £1.20, £3.30, £1.80; EX 70.40.
Owner Sheikh Ahmed Al Maktoum **Bred** Darley **Trained** West Ilsley, Berks

FOCUS

A fair event in which the pace was sound. The sixth limits the form.

NOTEBOOK

Alzerra(UAE), who had a solid chance at the weights, was surprisingly easy to back but ran right up to her best when the gaps appeared to win with a bit in hand. She falls short of the best of her generation but is a useful sort who will not mind the return to six furlongs and she should continue to give a good account. (op 11-4 tchd 9-2)

Holdin Foldin(IRE), who ran a stinker in Listed company at York on her previous start, returned to something like his best after enjoying the run of the race. A test of speed suits him but he may not be the easiest to place successfully. (op 18-1 tchd 14-1)

Mood Music, a consistent sort, had the run of the race and ran creditably. He looks a good guide to the worth of this form and left the impression that he would be worth another try over six furlongs. (op 5-1)

We'll Confer, who ran creditably in a Group 3 event on Polytrack last time, was well supported but had his limitations exposed in this company. He may be better suited by six furlongs but is another that may not be the easiest to place successfully. (op 7-4 tchd 11-8 and 15-8 in places)

Bridge It Jo ran creditably in the face of a stiffish task and fared the best of those to come from off the pace. The return to six furlongs will be in her favour but she is likely to remain vulnerable in this type of event. (tchd 12-1)

The Nifty Fox, with the visor he wore last time left off here, was not totally disgraced in the face of a very stiff task. The return to modest nursery company will be in his favour but it is a bit of a worry he has not won a race. (op 66-1)

Southandwest(IRE) Official explanation: jockey said gelding was unsuited by the good to soft ground

5336 TOTESPORT.COM AYR SILVER CUP (H'CAP) 6f

4:30 (4:31) (Class 2) 3-Y-0+

£21,812 (£6,531; £3,265; £1,634; £815; £409) **Stalls** High

Form RPR

2153 **1** **Geojimali**[34] 4357 4-8-4 **75** .... SaleemGolam(3) 28 88+
(J S Goldie) *hld up stands rail: n.m.r 1/2-way: gd hdwy appr fnl f: led cl home: 1st of 16 in gp* **20/1**

0006 **2** *hd* **Zomerlust**[14] 4988 4-9-7 **89** .... JimmyQuinn 21 101
(J J Quinn) *in tch stands side: hdwy over 1f out: led that gp ins fnl f: kpt on wl: hdd post: 2nd of 16 in gp* **10/1**[3]

6104 **3** *1/2* **Rising Shadow (IRE)**[24] 4682 5-9-9 **91** .... PhillipMakin 20 102
(T D Barron) *midfield stands side: drvn 1/2-way: kpt on wl fnl f: nrst fin: 3rd of 16 in gp* **10/1**[3]

4214 **4** *1 1/4* **Ellens Academy (IRE)**[18] 4885 11-8-10 **78** .... PaulQuinn 24 85
(E J Alston) *hld up stands side: hdwy over 1f out: kpt on fnl f: nrst fin: 4th of 16 in gp* **28/1**

1431 **5** *shd* **Knot In Wood (IRE)**[24] 4682 4-9-5 **87** 5ex...................... TonyHamilton 6 93+
(R A Fahey) *prom far side: led that gp over 1f out: kpt on fnl f: 1st of 10 in gp* **12/1**

0003 **6** *1/2* **Commando Scott (IRE)**[14] 4988 5-9-5 **90**............ PatrickMathers(3) 23 95
(I W McInnes) *prom stands side: rdn over 2f out: kpt on same pce fnl f: 5th of 16 in gp* **10/1**[3]

2003 **7** *shd* **Nautical**[27] 4602 8-8-9 **77** .... FrancisNorton 27 82+
(A W Carroll) *hld up stands side: repeatedly denied room fr over 2f out to ins fnl f: kpt on: nt rcvr: 6th of 16 in gp* **20/1**

0250 **8** *1/2* **Steel Blue**[9] 5117 6-8-9 **82** .... MichaelJStainton(5) 11 85
(R M Whitaker) *led stands side gp tl hdd and no ex ins fnl f: 7th of 16 in gp* **33/1**

4211 **9** *1 1/4* **Wyatt Earp (IRE)**[48] 3956 5-9-5 **91** .... PaulHanagan 3 90+
(R A Fahey) *chsd far side ldrs: effrt over 2f out: kpt on fnl f: no imp: 2nd of 10 in gp* **8/1**[2]

-520 **10** *shd* **Rainbow Rising (IRE)**[14] 4988 4-9-2 **84** .... TomEaves 18 83
(J Howard Johnson) *prom stands side: rdn over 2f out: no ex over 1f out: 8th of 16 in gp* **40/1**

2000 **11** *hd* **Glencairn Star**[37] [4258] 5-8-7 **78** ow1 AdamKirby(3) 2 77+
(J S Goldie) *chsd far side ldrs: ev ch that gp over 1f out: no ex ins fnl f: 3rd of 10 in gp* **66/1**

3404 **12** *nk* **Balakiref**[3] [5117] 7-8-8 **76** SilvestreDeSousa 4 74+
(M Dods) *hld up far side: hdwy over 1f out: kpt on fnl f: no imp: 4th of 10 in gp* **16/1**

255 **13** *nk* **Aahgowangowan (IRE)**[9] [5117] 7-8-5 **78** (t) LiamJones(5) 22 75
(M Dods) *gd spd stands rail tl wknd fnl f: 9th of 16 in gp* **28/1**

1350 **14** *nk* **Yorkshire Blue**[34] [4378] 7-8-9 **77** RichardMullen 16 73
(J S Goldie) *bhd stands side tl sme late hdwy: nrst fin: 10th of 16 in gp* **50/1**

0600 **15** *hd* **Looks Could Kill (USA)**[8] [5136] 4-8-10 **78** DeanMcKeown 19 73
(E J Alston) *midfield stands side: drvn 1/2-way: no imp fnl 2f; 11th of 16 in gp* **40/1**

4200 **16** *3 1/2* **Beaver Patrol (IRE)**[41] [4128] 4-9-10 **92** MickyFenton 5 77+
(R F Johnson Houghton) *hld up far side: hdwy over 1f out: nvr rchd ldrs: 5th of 10 in gp* **33/1**

0-26 **17** *1/2* **River Falcon**[24] [4682] 6-9-10 **92** DanielTudhope 14 75
(J S Goldie) *midfield stands side: drvn over 2f out: btn over 1f out: 12th of 16 in gp* **12/1**

0300 **18** *1/2* **Gifted Gamble**[104] [2230] 4-9-5 **87** (b) NCallan 15 69
(K A Ryan) *in tch stands side tl wknd wl over 1f out: 13th of 16 in gp* **33/1**

300 **19** *3/4* **Crimson Silk**[27] [4609] 6-9-2 **84** (b) PaulEddery 1 63+
(B Smart) *mde most far side to over 1f out: sn wknd: 6th of 10 in gp* **66/1**

4423 **20** *3/4* **Jimmy The Guesser**[20] [4802] 3-8-9 **79** (p) RoystonFfrench 9 56+
(N P Littmoden) *prom far side: rdn over 2f out: wknd over 1f out: 7th of 10 in gp* **25/1**

3300 **21** *1* **Roman Maze**[20] [4790] 6-9-4 **86** DavidAllan 12 60
(W M Brisbourne) *hld up outside of stands side gp: drvn 1/2-way: btn over 1f out: 14th of 16 in gp* **33/1**

2330 **22** *1 1/4* **Raymond's Pride**[9] [5117] 6-8-12 **83** (b) AndrewMullen(3) 10 53+
(K A Ryan) *w far side ldr tl wknd wl over 1f out: 8th of 10 in gp* **40/1**

1231 **23** *2* **Burning Incense (IRE)**[27] [4601] 3-9-10 **94** (b) RobertWinston 8 58+
(R Charlton) *keen: hld up far side: drvn over 2f out: nvr rchd ldrs: 9th of 10 in gp* **5/1**[1]

0500 **24** *1 1/2* **Highland Warrior**[13] [5009] 7-9-3 **85** TonyCulhane 7 45+
(J S Goldie) *dwlt: hld up far side: rdn over 2f out: nvr rchd ldrs: last of 10 far side* **50/1**

0065 **25** *5* **Johnston's Diamond (IRE)**[14] [4988] 8-8-13 **81** AdrianTNicholls 17 26
(E J Alston) *chsd stands side ldrs tl wknd 2f out: 15th of 16 in gp* **28/1**

6421 **26** *2 1/2* **Stellite**[28] [4569] 6-8-9 **77** ow2 LeeEnstone 13 14
(J S Goldie) *in tch stands side tl wknd over 2f out: last of 16 in gp* **22/1**

1m 13.7s (0.03) **Going Correction** +0.10s/f (Good)
WFA 3 from 4yo+ 2lb **26** Ran SP% **130.4**
Speed ratings (Par 109):103,102,102,100,100 99,99,98,97,97 96,96,95,95,95 90,89,89,88,87 85,84,81,79,72 69
CSF £175.60 CT £2159.09 TOTE £22.20: £3.70, £3.40, £4.00, £5.60; EX 197.30 Trifecta £1722.70 Part won. Pool: £2,426.39 - 0.60 winning tickets..
Owner Fyffees 2 **Bred** Jim Goldie **Trained** Uplawmoor, E Renfrews

FOCUS
A competitive event in which the larger stands'-side group had the edge over those that raced on the far side. The pace was sound throughout and the form should prove reliable.

NOTEBOOK
Geojimali has done nothing but improve this year and he notched his fourth win of 2006 when getting up in the final strides. His style of racing means things need to drop perfectly - as they did here - but he should not be going up too much for this win and he should continue to give a good account.
Zomerlust had conditions to suit and ran his best race since spring from his favourable draw. He has little margin for error from his current mark, though and his inconsistency means he would not really be one for short odds next time. (op 14-1)
Rising Shadow(IRE) has only won once since last summer but had conditions to suit and ran up to his best from his favourable draw. He looks worth another try over seven furlongs. (op 11-1 tchd 12-1 in places)
Ellens Academy(IRE) has been running well for much of the summer and turned in another creditable effort from a favourable draw. He is the type that needs things to drop right but should continue to go well.
Knot In Wood(IRE) ◆, a model of consistency, ran well under his penalty and is almost certainly better than the bare form as he fared best of those that raced on the far side. He is one to keep an eye on in similar company. (tchd 14-1)
Commando Scott(IRE) had conditions to suit and was well drawn but, while running creditably, left the impression that the return to seven furlongs would be in his favour. (op 14-1 tchd 16-1 in a place)
Nautical was the hard luck story of the race as he got no sort of run but, although he is a consistent sort, his modest win record in the last 12 months or so means he would not be one to lump on next time. Official explanation: jockey said gelding was denied a clear run
Burning Incense(IRE)'s record has been one of steady improvement but he failed to settle with the blinkers on again and proved a disappointment. However he has not had much racing, is in good hands, and is well worth another chance. Official explanation: jockey said colt was unsuited by the good to soft ground (tchd 11-2, 6-1 in places)

5337 WEST SOUND H'CAP 1m
5:05 (5:05) (Class 4) (0-85,85) 3-Y-0+ **£6,477** (£1,927; £963; £481) **Stalls** Low

Form RPR

0546 **1** **Wigwam Willie (IRE)**[79] [2974] 4-9-1 **77** (p) NCallan 13 90+
(K A Ryan) *s.i.s: stdy hdwy over 2f out: qcknd to ld ins last: readily* **13/2**[3]

2021 **2** *2* **Nevada Desert (IRE)**[14] [4989] 6-8-12 **74** DeanMcKeown 2 83
(R M Whitaker) *chsd ldrs: led 2f out: hdd and no ex ins last* **6/1**[2]

3344 **3** *1/2* **Hula Ballew**[13] [5024] 6-9-1 **77** RobertWinston 5 85
(M Dods) *rr-div: drvn and hdwy 3f out: chal over 1f out: styd on same pce ins last* **7/1**

1341 **4** *1/2* **Kinsya**[27] [4605] 3-9-0 **84** SaleemGolam(3) 8 91+
(M H Tompkins) *t.k.h: sn in rr: hdwy 3f out: hung bdly rt jst ins last: wandered: kpt on towards fin* **4/1**[1]

5504 **5** *6* **Moi Aussi (USA)**[14] [4989] 3-8-12 **79** (b) JamieMackay 4 74
(Sir Mark Prescott) *s.i.s: hdwy u.p 3f out: nvr nr ldrs* **16/1**

3043 **6** *1* **Zennerman (IRE)**[21] [4769] 3-8-11 **78** DavidAllan 1 71
(W M Brisbourne) *hld up and bhd: drvn 3f out: kpt on: nvr on terms* **25/1**

0021 **7** *3/4* **Baylaw Star**[22] [4726] 5-9-7 **83** RoystonFfrench 6 75
(I W McInnes) *w ldrs: wknd over 1f out* **25/1**

0103 **8** *3/4* **Primo Way**[14] [4989] 5-9-5 **81** (b) TomEaves 10 71
(I Semple) *lost pl after 1f: hdwy to chse ldrs over 2f out: wknd over 1f out* **16/1**

3000 **9** *3/4* **King Of The Moors (USA)**[15] [4953] 3-8-12 **79** PhillipMakin 3 68
(T D Barron) *sn bhd: sme hdwy over 2f out: nvr a factor* **33/1**

0000 **10** *6* **Shot To Fame (USA)**[22] [4739] 7-9-9 **85** (vt[1]) AdrianTNicholls 7 62
(D Nicholls) *led: set mod pce: edgd lft and hdd 2f out: sn wknd: eased* **16/1**

0B41 **11** *hd* **Surwaki (USA)**[33] [4390] 4-9-0 **79** AdamKirby(3) 9 55
(C G Cox) *chsd ldrs: edgd lft and lost pl over 2f out* **12/1**

3030 **12** *1 1/4* **Speed Dial Harry (IRE)**[20] [4790] 4-9-0 **76** (v) RichardMullen 12 50
(K R Burke) *chsd ldrs: lost pl 2f out: eased* **16/1**

1020 **13** *17* **Namroud (USA)**[20] [4790] 7-9-8 **84** PaulHanagan 11 24
(R A Fahey) *chsd ldrs: lost pl over 2f out: sn bhd: heavily eased* **6/1**[2]

1m 45.32s (1.83) **Going Correction** +0.375s/f (Good)
WFA 3 from 4yo+ 5lb **13** Ran SP% **116.3**
Speed ratings (Par 105):105,103,102,102,96 95,94,93,92,86 86,85,68
CSF £42.96 CT £292.64 TOTE £8.00: £2.60, £2.20, £2.20; EX 72.10.
Owner Neil & Anne Dawson Partnership **Bred** Mrs Margaret Christie **Trained** Hambleton, N Yorks

FOCUS
A stop-start gallop but a ready winner, who put up a slight personal best, and they came home well strung out behind him.
King Of The Moors(USA) Official explanation: jockey said gelding had no more to give
Surwaki(USA) Official explanation: jockey said gelding was unsuited by the good to soft ground
Namroud(USA) Official explanation: jockey said gelding lost its action

5338 KPMG H'CAP (FOR THE EGLINTON & WINTON CHALLENGE CUP) 2m 1f 105y
5:35 (5:35) (Class 5) (0-75,77) 4-Y-0+ **£5,505** (£1,637; £818; £408) **Stalls** Low

Form RPR

1 **To Tiger (GER)**[495] 5-8-8 **59** RoystonFfrench 8 69+
(P Monteith) *hld up ins: smooth hdwy to ld 3f out: clr whn hung rt over 1f out: kpt on wl* **33/1**

4203 **2** *6* **Thewhirlingdervish (IRE)**[10] [5080] 8-8-11 **62** DavidAllan 10 67+
(T D Easterby) *hld up: hdwy and brought to stands side over 2f out: chsd wnr over 1f out: no imp fnl f* **15/2**

0456 **3** *3* **Lennel**[29] [4522] 8-8-2 **53** oh8 PaulQuinn 9 54
(A Bailey) *hld up: drvn over 3f out: no imp tl styd on fnl f* **16/1**

1141 **4** *3/4* **Danzatrice**[15] [4954] 4-8-8 **59** TomEaves 7 59
(C W Thornton) *cl up: effrt and drvn 3f out: outpcd wl over 1f out* **7/2**[2]

0340 **5** *shd* **Haatmey**[37] [4268] 4-9-1 **66** (v) TonyCulhane 3 66
(M R Channon) *chsd ldrs: rdn to chal 3f out: wknd over 1f out* **8/1**

134 **6** *1* **Riodan (IRE)**[30] [4469] 4-9-4 **72** DNolan(3) 6 71
(J J Quinn) *led after 2f: set stdy pce to 3f out: wknd 2f out* **5/1**[3]

1651 **7** *5* **Brief Statement (IRE)**[19] [4836] 4-8-6 **62** (p) LiamJones(5) 5 56
(W M Brisbourne) *hld up in tch: effrt over 2f out: btn over 1f out* **5/1**[3]

0/P- **8** *22* **Crackleando**[165] [5789] 5-8-1 **55** AndrewMullen(3) 4 27
(Mrs J C McGregor) *chsd ldrs tl wknd wl over 2f out* **40/1**

3221 **P** **Incursion**[10] [5080] 5-9-12 **77** 6ex AdrianTNicholls 2 —
(D Nicholls) *led after 2f: cl up tl wknd qckly and p.u over 6f out: dead* **3/1**[1]

4m 8.00s (13.23) **Going Correction** +0.375s/f (Good) **9** Ran SP% **114.7**
Speed ratings (Par 103):83,80,78,78,78 77,75,65,—
CSF £259.59 CT £4092.86 TOTE £25.90: £6.40, £1.60, £2.70; EX 248.40 Place 6 £186.65, Place 5 £100.64.
Owner G M Cowan **Bred** Gestut Wittekindshof **Trained** Rosewell, Midlothian

FOCUS
An ordinary event in which the pace was on the steady side in the first half of the contest. The fourth helps set the level.
T/Jkpt: Not won. T/Plt: £131.70 to a £1 stake. Pool: £91,822.95. 508.60 winning tickets. T/Qpdt: £36.40 to a £1 stake. Pool: £5,148.20. 104.50 winning tickets. RY

4592 NEWBURY (L-H)
Friday, September 15

OFFICIAL GOING: Good
Wind: Slight, across

5339 E B F DUBAI TENNIS CHAMPIONSHIPS MAIDEN STKS (DIV I) 7f (S)
2:00 (2:02) (Class 4) 2-Y-0 **£5,829** (£1,734; £866; £432) **Stalls** Centre

Form RPR

2 **1** **Opera Music**[30] [4479] 2-9-3 JohnEgan 1 85
(S Kirk) *h.d.w: trckd ldrs: led over 1f out: drvn and hld on wl thrght fnl f* **11/4**[2]

2 *1/2* **Fifty Cents** 2-9-3 SteveDrowne 4 84+
(R Charlton) *w'like: scope: leggy: trckd ldrs: qcknd to chse wnr fnl f: kpt on wl but nvr quite gng pce to chal* **7/2**[3]

24 **3** *1 1/4* **Putra Square**[24] [4680] 2-9-3 EddieAhern 9 81
(P F I Cole) *lw: chsd ldrs: rdn 2f out: chsd ldrs and edgd lft ins last: styd on same pce* **2/1**[1]

0 **4** *1 1/4* **Rock Anthem (IRE)**[21] [4768] 2-9-3 KDarley 6 77+
(J L Dunlop) *hld up rr: stdy hdwy fr 3f out: chsd ldrs fr 2f out: kpt on same pce ins last* **20/1**

4 **5** *1 1/2* **Odin Dawn**[12] [5043] 2-9-3 DaneO'Neill 13 73
(R Hannon) *chsd ldrs: drvn over 2f out: one pce fr over 1f out* **25/1**

64 **6** *1/2* **Lady Lafitte (USA)**[11] [5068] 2-8-12 MichaelHills 11 67
(B W Hills) *chsd ldr: led 4f out: pushed along and hdd over 1f out: wknd ins last* **16/1**

7 *1* **Sugar Ray (IRE)** 2-9-3 RyanMoore 7 70+
(Sir Michael Stoute) *unf: b.bkwd: chsd ldrs early: outpcd 3f out: drvn and styd on again fr over 1f out: gng on cl home* **10/1**

04 **8** *hd* **Daylami Dreams**[36] [4303] 2-9-3 MartinDwyer 3 69
(J S Moore) *scope: led until hdd 4f out: styd front rank tl outpcd ins fnl f* **66/1**

9 *3* **April Fool** 2-9-3 RichardThomas 10 61
(J A Geake) *cmpt: b.bkwd: bhd: sn pushed along in rr: styd on fr over 1f out: nvr in contention* **10/1**

0 **10** *2* **What Budget**[28] [4558] 2-8-12 LDettori 12 51
(B J Meehan) *outpcd most of way* **33/1**

11 *2* **Potentiale (IRE)** 2-9-3 RHills 8 51
(J W Hills) *w'like: str: b.bkwd: s.i.s: a in rr* **66/1**

12 *5* **Calzaghe (IRE)** 2-9-3 LPKeniry 5 38
(A M Balding) *w;like: str: s.i.s: sn t.k.h and in tch: rdn 3f out: sn btn* **40/1**

1m 26.94s (-0.06) **Going Correction** -0.075s/f (Good) **12** Ran SP% **123.3**
Speed ratings (Par 97):97,96,95,93,91 91,90,89,86,84 81,76
CSF £12.62 TOTE £4.10: £1.80, £1.60, £1.40; EX 14.90.
Owner J C Smith **Bred** Littleton Stud **Trained** Upper Lambourn, Berks

FOCUS
A decent maiden, and probably the stronger of the two divisions. The form has been rated through the time, and the first two could turn out a fair bit better.

NOTEBOOK

Opera Music, second on his debut at Salisbury a month ago, showed the benefit of that experience and duly went one better on this step up to an extra furlong. He picked up nicely when asked for his effort, seeing out the longer trip really well, and looked suited by the easier surface. As a half-brother to his stable's former high-class juvenile Opera Cape it was little surprise that he relished the extra distance and he looks well worth his place at a higher grade now. His trainer indicated that the Horris Hill, back at this track in October, was a likely next step and he clearly holds this colt in high regard. (op 3-1 tchd 10-3)

Fifty Cents ◆, a 120,000gns purchase who is bred to come into his own over longer distances next year, travelled sweetly until running green when push came to shove. He only just lost out and was simply beaten by his lack of experience, so this has to rate a very pleasing debut effort. He holds an entry in the Royal Lodge and, while that will most likely come too soon, it is an indication that this rangy colt is very well thought of. A similar event should be his for the taking. (op 5-1)

Putra Square, fourth in the Group 3 Acomb Stakes on just his second outing last time, failed to really raise his game for this return to maiden company yet still did little wrong in defeat. He already shapes as though he needs a mile, helps to set a decent standard for this form, and should not remain a maiden for too long. Official explanation: jockey said colt hung left-handed (tchd 9-4)

Rock Anthem(IRE), ninth in a good maiden at Newmarket on his debut three weeks ago, turned in an improved effort and kept to his task well under pressure. He appeals as the type to keep improving and may be worth riding more prominently over this trip in the future. (op 16-1)

Odin Dawn improved on his debut at Lingfield 12 days previously and clearly enjoyed racing over the extra furlong. He can find easier opportunities.

Lady Lafitte(USA) eventually paid for her exertions at the head of affairs but ran close to her previous level in defeat. She may prefer a quicker surface and now qualifies for a nursery mark. (op 12-1)

Sugar Ray(IRE), a 290,000gns purchase out of a lightly raced seven furlong juvenile winner, was easy to back ahead of this racecourse debut and shaped as though the experience would be of real benefit. He has scope and can be expected to stay at least ten furlongs next term. (op 8-1 tchd 15-2 and 12-1)

April Fool, the first foal of a very smart mare, was a springer in the betting ring yet never gave his supporters any real hope and ran too green to do himself justice. He is clearly thought capable of better, however, and is one to bear in mind if turning up at one of the smaller tracks in due course. (op 16-1)

5340 E B F DUBAI TENNIS CHAMPIONSHIPS MAIDEN STKS (DIV II) 7f (S)

2:35 (2:37) (Class 4) 2-Y-O **£5,829** (£1,734; £866; £432) **Stalls** Centre

Form	Pos	Dist	Horse / comment	Jockey	RPR
	1		**Proponent (IRE)** 2-9-3 (R Charlton) *gd sort: w'like: scope: trckd ldrs: led ins fnl 2f: styd on strly and in command fnl f: easily* **2/1**[1]	SteveDrowne 12	84+
	2	2	**Opera Crown (IRE)** 2-9-3 (P F I Cole) *cmpt: bkwd: chsd ldrs: rdn 2f out: chsd wnr fr over 1f out but a readily hld* **14/1**	JimmyFortune 7	77
	3	2	**Atraas (IRE)** 2-9-3 (M P Tregoning) *unf: str: chsd ldrs: pushed along and styd on same pce fr over 1f out* **4/1**[3]	RHills 3	72+
4	4	¾	**Ideally (IRE)**[13] 5020 2-9-3 (B W Hills) *chsd ldr tl led over 3f out: pushed along and hdd ins fnl 2f: wknd ins fnl f* **11/4**[2]	MichaelHills 2	70
	5	1 ¼	**Rangali Belle** 2-8-12 (C A Horgan) *w'like: b.bkwd: s.i.s: sn in tch: hdwy over 2f out: kpt on fnl f but nvr gng pce to trble ldrs* **25/1**	JohnEgan 11	62
5	6	shd	**Christalini**[40] 4177 2-9-3 (J C Fox) *rr but in tch: hdwy 3f out: kpt on fnl 2f but nvr gng pce to trble ldrs* **10/1**	RyanMoore 9	66
0	7	2	**Kyllachy Storm**[67] 3344 2-9-3 (R J Hodges) *led tl hdd over 3f out: sn pushed along: wknd ins fnl f* **20/1**	LPKeniry 5	61
	8	½	**Rock 'N' Roller (FR)** 2-9-3 (W R Muir) *leggy: b.bkwd: s.i.s: bhd: sn pushed along: kpt on fnl 2f but nvr in contention* **8/1**	MartinDwyer 4	60
	9	1 ¾	**Polish Star** 2-9-3 (R Hannon) *w'like: scope: b.bkwd: s.i.s: and outpcd in rr: mod prog 2f out* **20/1**	RichardHughes 1	55
00	10	8	**Dancing Reva (IRE)**[20] 4794 2-9-0 (J J Bridger) *early spd* **100/1**	MarcHalford(3) 6	34

1m 27.15s (0.15) **Going Correction** -0.075s/f (Good) **10** Ran SP% **121.2**
Speed ratings (Par 97):96,93,91,90,89 89,86,86,84,75
CSF £32.16 TOTE £3.10: £1.40, £2.80, £1.60; EX 29.10.

Owner B E Nielsen **Bred** Fortbarrington Stud **Trained** Beckhampton, Wilts

FOCUS

This looked the weaker of the two divisions, but it was hard not to be impressed by the debut winner, who looked different class. The form is rated through the fourth horse.

NOTEBOOK

Proponent(IRE) ◆, who cost 160,000gns and is related to numerous winners at around ten and 12 furlongs, justified strong market confidence with an impressive debut display. He travelled kindly just off the pace before quickening when asked to win his race, and he ultimately won with a deal up his sleeve, suggesting he ought to improve plenty for the experience. He holds an entry in next year's Derby, and his pedigree suggests we shall not see the best of him until he steps up in trip as a three-year-old. He is a promising middle-distance prospect and it will be fascinating to see where he is pitched in next. (op 7-2)

Opera Crown(IRE), an 80,000gns purchase out of a 12 furlong three-year-old winner, was handy throughout and kept on to finish a clear second best over trip which looked on the sharp side. He should improve plenty for this experience, and holds entries in the Royal Lodge and Racing Post Trophy, so clearly has a future. (op 12-1)

Atraas(IRE), the first foal of a dam who scored over ten furlongs on her only start at three, proved green when push came top shove and shaped as though he will improve significantly for this debut experience. He is well entered up, and hails from a family his trainer knows very well, so should not be too long in finding a race. (op 9-2 tchd 11-2)

Ideally(IRE), fourth over this trip on Kempton's Polytrack on his debut 13 days previously, was ridden more positively and probably ran right up to that form in defeat. He helps to set the standard for this form and will be eligible for handicaps after his next assignment, but on the evidence so far his Group 2 entry looks ambitious. (op 7-2 tchd 4-1)

Rangali Belle, who cost 24,000gns and is bred to make her mark as a two-year-old, finished her race with a little promise, having been slow to break from the gates. Her stable is not noted for its juvenile runners, so her proximity at the finish may hold down the form, yet she clearly has ability. (tchd 33-1)

Christalini, fifth over six furlongs at this venue on his debut 40 days previously, ran a slightly improved race over this longer trip and still looked distinctly green. He will be eligible for a handicap mark after his next outing. (op 8-1)

5341 DUBAI DUTY FREE CUP (LISTED RACE) 7f (S)

3:10 (3:11) (Class 1) 3-Y-O+

£15,898 (£6,025; £3,015; £1,503; £753; £378) **Stalls** Centre

Form	Pos	Dist	Horse / comment	Jockey	RPR
252-	1		**Sleeping Indian**[335] 5900 5-9-2 113 (J H M Gosden) *lw: in tch: drvn and qcknd to ld 1f out: hld on gamely u.p fnl f* **11/8**[1]	JimmyFortune 13	116
3115	2	nk	**Spinning Queen**[42] 4097 3-8-10 107 (B W Hills) *b.hind: t.k.h: hld up in rr: rapid hdwy over 1f out to chse wnr jst ins last: kpt on wl but no imp cl home* **14/1**	MichaelHills 9	114
0-12	3	hd	**Satchem (IRE)**[62] 3534 4-9-2 112 (Saeed Bin Suroor) *chsd ldrs: drvn to chal over 2f out: stl upsides 1f out: kpt on ins last but nt qckn nr fin* **4/1**[2]	(t) LDettori 7	115
4134	4	nk	**Polar Ben**[8] 5135 7-9-2 109 (J R Fanshawe) *hld up rr: nt clr run fr 2f out: travelling wl whn swtchd rt over 1f out: fin wl: nt rch ldrs* **20/1**	OscarUrbina 5	114+
0101	5	hd	**Cesare**[18] 4896 5-9-2 107 (J R Fanshawe) *s.i.s: sn in tch: drvn along over 2f out: kpt on ins last: gng on cl home but nvr gng pce to rch ldrs* **5/1**[3]	EddieAhern 11	114
1010	6	1 ¼	**Prince Of Light (IRE)**[29] 4529 3-8-12 109 (M Johnston) *w ldr tl led over 4f out: rdn 3f out: kpt slt advantage tl hdd 1f out: wknd ins last* **20/1**	JoeFanning 10	110
40-4	7	1 ¼	**Iceman**[100] 2358 4-9-2 106 (J H M Gosden) *swtg: bhd: pushed along over 2f out and sme hdwy: drvn and kpt on ins last but nvr in contention* **33/1**	RHills 4	107
4302	8	hd	**Assertive**[20] 4803 3-8-12 106 (R Hannon) *lw: chsd ldrs: rdn over 2f out: wknd ins last* **33/1**	RichardHughes 8	107
3045	9	shd	**Mac Love**[6] 5184 5-9-2 107 (R Charlton) *plld hrd: in tch: rdn 2f out: wknd ins last* **20/1**	MartinDwyer 6	106
1612	10	3	**Jedburgh**[45] 4025 5-9-5 106 (J L Dunlop) *lw: s.i.s: bhd: pushed along over 2f out: nvr in contention* **18/1**	(b) TedDurcan 12	102
2504	11	1 ¾	**Sir Xaar (IRE)**[18] 4896 3-8-12 100 (B Smart) *sn pressing ldrs: chal over 2f out:wknd over 1f out: eased whn no ch* **66/1**	KDarley 1	94
1005	12	3 ½	**Royal Power (IRE)**[27] 4596 3-9-4 109 (M R Channon) *chsd ldrs: rdn 3f out: wknd 2f out* **40/1**	RyanMoore 3	91
-000	13	2	**Party Boss**[203] 508 4-9-2 (C E Brittain) *led tl hdd over 4f out: wknd over 2f out* **100/1**	KerrinMcEvoy 2	80

1m 24.71s (-2.29) **Going Correction** -0.075s/f (Good)
WFA 3 from 4yo+ 4lb **13** Ran SP% **115.8**
Speed ratings (Par 111):110,109,109,109,108 107,106,105,105,102 100,96,93
CSF £20.01 TOTE £2.40: £1.30, £2.50, £1.80; EX 25.30.

Owner George Strawbridge **Bred** George Strawbridge **Trained** Newmarket, Suffolk

FOCUS

A strong line-up for the class, and the first five came home in a blanket finish. There were personal bests from the second and fifth.

NOTEBOOK

Sleeping Indian, returning from a 335-day layoff, dug deep when it mattered and has now won first time up in each of his three seasons of racing. He stood out at the weights, and is much better than this grade on his day, but still deserves credit for putting his best foot forward under pressure against some smart rivals. He will be off to stud at the end of the year, but could well take in Prix de la Foret and Challenge Stakes (in which he finished second on his final outing last term) along the way. He ought to benefit from this run and should not be discounted in either. (op 6-4 tchd 7-4)

Spinning Queen, down in class and the sole filly in the line up, tracked the winner from off the pace before making her move inside the final furlong and was only just denied. This was a much-improved effort under her Group 3 penalty and she is a versatile sort as regards underfoot conditions. The Group 1 Sun Chariot next month is a possibility for her, but the extra furlong in that would be of slight concern. (op 12-1)

Satchem(IRE) travelled well under a positive ride and did nothing wrong in defeat over a trip which he probably finds on the sharp side. There are more prizes to be won with this consistent performer. (op 7-2 tchd 3-1)

Polar Ben finished his race with purpose and deserves to be rated better than the bare form, as he was short of room at a crucial stage. This was much more encouraging, and he deserves to find another race this autumn on the softer ground he enjoys so much. (tchd 22-1)

Cesare, upped in class, gave his all in defeat over a trip that now looks on the short side for him. He posted a personal-best in defeat and this versatile performer and can win in Listed company when reverting to a mile. (op 6-1)

Prince Of Light(IRE) ran a brave race from the front on ground he would have found plenty easy enough. He probably also wants a stiffer test nowadays and it is unlikely that we have seen the best of him just yet. (op 25-1 tchd 28-1)

Iceman was never a threat to his winning stable companion, but still did enough to suggest the race would be to his benefit and he is another who ideally wants a quicker surface. He can build on this if remaining sound. (op 40-1)

Assertive probably ran right up to his best in defeat and helps to set the standard of this form. He has had a decent season, and deserves a change of fortune, but is not the easiest to place now.

Mac Love, whose yard had won this with both its two previous runners in the last ten years, spoilt his chances by refusing to settle, yet still appeared to run right up to his recent level in defeat. He is just proving fiendishly hard to actually win with. (op 18-1)

5342 DUBAI DUTY FREE ARC TRIAL (GROUP 3) 1m 3f 5y

3:45 (3:45) (Class 1) 3-Y-O+

£28,390 (£10,760; £5,385; £2,685; £1,345; £675) **Stalls** Low

Form	Pos	Dist	Horse / comment	Jockey	RPR
1403	1		**Blue Monday**[24] 4679 5-9-6 117 (R Charlton) *chsd ldrs: pushed along over 3f out: rdn over 2f out: styd on to ld ins last: kpt on gamely* **2/1**[1]	SteveDrowne 2	119+
1511	2	¾	**Tam Lin**[20] 4818 3-8-12 111 (Sir Michael Stoute) *hld up rr: rapid hdwy on outside over 2f out to ld wl over 1f out: sn rdn: carried hd high: flashed tail and hdd ins last:* **9/4**[2]	RyanMoore 8	118
4131	3	5	**Admiral's Cruise (USA)**[27] 4595 4-9-6 114 (B J Meehan) *hld up rr but in tch: stdy hdwy 4f out: led 2f out: sn rdn: hdd wl over 1f out: sn outpcd by ldung pair* **7/1**[3]	JimmyFortune 5	110
-000	4	2	**Norse Dancer (IRE)**[12] 5051 6-9-3 114 (D R C Elsworth) *rr but in tch: drvn over 3f out: styd on same pce fnl 2f* **14/1**	JohnEgan 3	104
1/31	5	shd	**Crocodile Dundee (IRE)**[20] 4817 5-9-3 107 (L M Cumani) *sn chsng ldr: rdn to chal over 4f out: sn one pce u.p: wknd fnl 2f* **7/1**[3]	LDettori 6	104
0236	6	nk	**Hattan (IRE)**[20] 4817 4-9-3 106 (C E Brittain) *hld up in rr: hdwy on outside over 3f out: chsd ldrs over 2f out: sn btn* **16/1**	KerrinMcEvoy 7	103

4010 **7** *1 ½* **Kaylianni**[44] 4039 3-8-6 87 .... JoeFanning 1 98
(M R Channon) *rr but in tch: hdwy to chse ldrs 4f out: wknd 2f out: no ch whn hmpd on rails over 1f out* **100/1**

20-0 **8** *3* **Phoenix Reach (IRE)**[34] 4386 6-9-3 115 ....(v) MartinDwyer 4 96
(A M Balding) *lw: plld hrd and stl keen hold tl led 4f out: rdn 3f out: hdd 2f out and wknd qckly: edgd lft over 1f out* **12/1**

3222 **9** *1* **Mango Mischief (IRE)**[33] 4417 5-9-0 105 .... DaneO'Neill 9 91
(J L Dunlop) *sn led: hdd 4f out: wknd fr 3f out* **33/1**

2m 17.66s (-4.61) **Going Correction** -0.075s/f (Good)
WFA 3 from 4yo+ 8lb **9** Ran SP% **113.3**
Speed ratings (Par 113):113,112,108,107,107 107,105,103,103
CSF £6.47 TOTE £2.90: £1.20, £1.50, £2.00; EX 8.60.
Owner Mountgrange Stud **Bred** Darley **Trained** Beckhampton, Wilts

FOCUS
An Arc trial in name only. The first two came clear and the form looks solid enough for the level.

NOTEBOOK
Blue Monday, third in Group 1 company the last twice, enjoyed the drop into this class and deservedly got back to winning ways with a resolute display. He has once again proved a most progressive horse, and he clearly stays this trip without much fuss nowadays. His consistency dictates he can seldom be discounted, and he is now likely to have another crack at the top level in the Canadian International at Woodbine. (op 7-4 tchd 9-4)
Tam Lin made good headway from off the pace to nose in front, but his quirks soon came to the fore when he was put under pressure and he was readily held by the winner at the finish. Despite being a very tricky ride, he too has been very progressive this year, and he was nicely clear of the remainder at the finish. (op 11-4)
Admiral's Cruise(USA) held every chance, yet lacked the finishing speed of the first two over a trip that he would have found sharp enough. He remains in good heart and is a decent benchmark for the form. Ther Canadian International is a possible target for him too. (op 15-2)
Norse Dancer(IRE), disappointing at the top level in Germany last time, kept on at just the same pace in the home straight yet still posted an improved effort in defeat. He remains very hard to predict. (op 18-1)
Crocodile Dundee(IRE), off the mark for connections at Windsor last time, failed to convince in this tougher company and ran below his best. His stable is having a slightly quietish spell at present, however, and he may better this in due course. (op 13-2 tchd 11-2)
Hattan(IRE) finished closer to Crocodile Dundee than had been the case in Listed company at Windsor last time, but continues to run below his best all the same. (tchd 20-1)
Kaylianni had a stiff task and ran right up to her best.
Phoenix Reach(IRE) ran much too freely and gave himself little chance of getting home. Official explanation: jockey said horse ran too free (op 11-1 tchd 10-1)

5343 HAYNES, HANSON & CLARK CONDITIONS STKS (C&G) 1m (S)
4:20 (4:21) (Class 2) 2-Y-O

£11,217 (£3,358; £1,679; £840; £419; £210) **Stalls** Centre

Form RPR

22 **1** **Teslin (IRE)**[18] 4867 2-8-12 .... KDarley 4 92
(M Johnston) *trckd ldrs: t.k.h: wnt 2nd 2f out: led over 1f out: pushed out* **15/2**

3 **2** *1 ¼* **Aqaleem**[27] 4597 2-8-12 .... MartinDwyer 6 90
(M P Tregoning) *lw: hld up in rr: pushed along and hdwy over 2f out: rdn over 1f out: edgd lft u.p ins last: tk 2nd last stride: no ch wnr* **7/2**[2]

3 *hd* **Authorized (IRE)** 2-8-12 .... EddieAhern 5 89
(P W Chapple-Hyam) *w'like: tall: s.i.s: sn rcvrd to chse ldrs: led over 2f out: sn rdn: hdd over 1f out: styd on same pce: lost 2nd last strid* **9/2**

003 **4** *2 ½* **Cry Presto (USA)**[15] 4963 2-8-12 79 .... RichardHughes 1 84
(R Hannon) *in tch: drvn along fr over 3f out: kpt on fnl f but nvr in contention* **25/1**

21 **5** *1 ¼* **Diysem (USA)**[12] 5043 2-9-2 .... LDettori 2 86
(B J Meehan) *hld up in rr: shkn up 2f out: kpt on fnl f but nvr gng pce to be competitive* **5/2**[1]

61 **6** *2 ½* **Tastahil (IRE)**[9] 5105 2-9-2 .... RHills 3 81
(B W Hills) *led: rdn 3f out: hdd over 2f out: sn btn* **4/1**[3]

7 *3 ½* **Palamoun** 2-8-12 .... MichaelHills 7 70
(B W Hills) *cmpt: s.i.s: sn chsng ldrs: wknd fr 2f out* **7/1**

1m 40.44s (-0.18) **Going Correction** -0.075s/f (Good) **7** Ran SP% **117.1**
Speed ratings (Par 101):97,95,95,93,91 89,85
CSF £35.08 TOTE £10.10: £3.30, £2.20; EX 40.30.
Owner Joy And Valentine Feerick **Bred** Saud Bin Saad **Trained** Middleham Moor, N Yorks
■ Derby winners Shergar, Shahrastani and Henbit are among a host of top-class middle-distance horses that have won this.

FOCUS
A race that tends to attract backward, backend, future middle-distance types. The bare form is nothing special, but some of these are likely to do much better in time. Much improved form from the winner, and a step up too, as expected, from the second.

NOTEBOOK
Teslin(IRE), whose connections landed this event in 2005 with subsequent Godolphin purchase Winged Cupid, opened his account on this step up in class and looked better the further he went. He proved a little free through the early parts, but showed a good attitude to grind down his rivals when it mattered and is clearly a progressive juvenile. He will need to find a good deal further improvement, however, if he is to figure in any of his current Group entries, but that remains entirely possible and he should make up into nice middle-distance performer next term. (op 9-1 tchd 10-1)
Aqaleem, third on debut at this track 27 days ago and from a stable which has won this with Ethmaar, Nayef and Elshadi, was doing his best work towards the finish, having again proved green through the early parts. He looked to need all of this extra furlong, still has an abundance of scope, and appeals strongly as the type to reach greater heights over longer distances as a three-year-old. (tchd 10-3 and 4-1 in a place)
Authorized(IRE), a 400,000gns purchase as a yearling and the first foal of an unraced half-sister to the high-class Brooklyn's Dance, was given an aggressive ride on this racecourse debut and posted a promising effort in defeat. Connections clearly feel he stays well and it would be a big surprise if he were to remain a maiden for too long. (op 7-2)
Cry Presto(USA), back up in class, ran a more encouraging race in defeat yet his proximity at the finish does hold down this form somewhat. He has faced some stiff tasks and deserves to drop into maiden company for a confidence booster. (op 33-1)
Diysem(USA), who made pretty hard work of landing the odds when off the mark at Lingfield last time, proved very popular in the betting ring yet failed to improve on this step up in class. He may prefer quicker ground and probably needs to be ridden more handily. (op 7-2)
Tastahil(IRE), off the mark over this trip on Kempton's Polytrack nine days previously, proved a little disappointing on this return to turf and may have found this coming too soon. (op 9-2)
Palamoun, whose dam is an unraced half-sister to high-class Supreme Leader, looked much in need of this debut experience. He has a deal of scope, however, and is presumably thought capable of better. (tchd 13-2)

5344 DUBAI DUTY FREE FULL OF SURPRISES E B F FILLIES' CONDITIONS STKS 7f (S)
4:55 (4:56) (Class 2) 2-Y-O

£11,217 (£3,358; £1,679; £840; £419; £210) **Stalls** Centre

Form RPR

6523 **1** **Darrfonah (IRE)**[22] 4737 2-8-12 102 .... KerrinMcEvoy 10 91
(C E Brittain) *sn led and racd alone towards stands side 4f: rdn over 2f out:hdd 1f out: rallied gamely to ld last stride* **11/4**[2]

22 **2** *shd* **Cast In Gold (USA)**[56] 3707 2-8-12 .... LDettori 2 91+
(B J Meehan) *lw: trckd ldrs: drvn to take slt ld 1f out: ct last stride* **8/11**[1]

3 *1 ½* **Basaata (USA)** 2-8-12 .... RHills 7 87
(M P Tregoning) *w'like: scope: rangy: chsd ldrs: drvn to chal 2f out: kpt on same pce ins last* **16/1**[3]

4 *2* **Sues Surprise (IRE)** 2-8-12 .... MichaelHills 6 82+
(B W Hills) *lengthy: unf: s.i.s: bhd: drvn and hdwy fr 2f out: kpt on ins last but nvr gng pce to be competitive* **25/1**

5 *½* **Diamond Diva** 2-8-12 .... EddieAhern 3 81
(J W Hills) *w'like: b.bkwd: chsd ldrs: rdn over 2f out: one pce fr over 1f out* **40/1**

6 *1* **Noojoom (IRE)** 2-8-12 .... MartinDwyer 4 78
(M P Tregoning) *rangy: in tch: rdn and hdwy over 2f out: kpt on same pce ins last* **33/1**

7 *shd* **Mirthful (USA)** 2-8-12 .... RichardHughes 11 78+
(B W Hills) *str: scope: b.bkwd: bhd: drvn over 2f out: styd on fr over 1f out: kpt on cl home but nvr in contention* **16/1**[3]

0 **8** *½* **Peppermint Green**[21] 4765 2-8-12 .... JoeFanning 9 76
(L M Cumani) *chsd ldrs: rdn over 2f out: wknd fnl f* **50/1**

9 *½* **Hi Calypso (IRE)** 2-8-12 .... JimmyFortune 12 75+
(Sir Michael Stoute) *rangy: bhd: pushed along over 2f out: sme prog fnl f but nvr in contention* **20/1**

10 *5* **Muffett's Dream** 2-8-12 .... RichardThomas 1 62
(J A Geake) *w'like: b.bkwd: bhd: rdn over 3f out: nvr in contention* **100/1**

11 *½* **Dangerous Dancer (IRE)** 2-8-12 .... SteveDrowne 8 61
(R Charlton) *w'like: leggy: in tch: rdn over 3f out: sn bhd* **25/1**

12 *7* **Queens Quay** 2-8-12 .... DaneO'Neill 13 43
(R Hannon) *w'like: unf: s.i.s: bhd most of way* **33/1**

2535 **13** *4* **Tumble Jill (IRE)**[59] 3613 2-8-12 52 .... MarcHalford 5 32
(J J Bridger) *pressed ldrs: rdn 3f out: stl ev ch 2f out: wknd rapidly over 1f out* **100/1**

1m 26.25s (-0.75) **Going Correction** -0.075s/f (Good) **13** Ran SP% **121.1**
Speed ratings (Par 98):101,100,99,96,96 95,95,94,93,88 87,79,75
CSF £4.62 TOTE £3.60: £1.30, £1.10, £3.50; EX 7.30.
Owner Saeed Manana **Bred** Darley **Trained** Newmarket, Suffolk

FOCUS
This should work out to be a decent fillies' event and the form looks solid, rated through the runner-up.

NOTEBOOK
Darrfonah(IRE), third in the Lowther Stakes last time, dug deep to reel in the runner-up at the business end of the race and break her duck at the fifth time of asking. The step up to this trip was definitely in her favour and she clearly enjoyed being able to race more prominently, if anything suggesting she is in need of a mile already. No doubt a step back up in class will now be on the agenda and it would not be a surprise to see this game filly take in the Rockfel at Newmarket next month. (tchd 5-2)
Cast In Gold(USA) ◆ again managed to find one too good, but she appeared to do little wrong in defeat and only failed by the smallest of margins. She still has an entry in the Fillies' Mile, and she probably has the ability to run with credit in that event, but it will most likely come too soon for her. A drop into normal maiden company ought to do her confidence the world of good, however, as she would surely go one better in that sort of company. (op 5-6 tchd 10-11 in a place)
Basaata(USA) ◆turned in a very promising debut effort against two above average fillies and was not given a hard time when her chance had gone inside the final furlong. She has a choice pedigree and a maiden should be hers for the taking.
Sues Surprise(IRE) ◆, an 82,000euros purchase who is bred to come into her own over longer distances next year, stayed on nicely having been sluggish from the gates. This was a very pleasing debut. (op 20-1)
Diamond Diva, a cheap purchase and half-sister to smart ten furlong winner Kaylianni among others, showed up well before running green under pressure. She ought to improve a deal for the experience and may need a mile already. (tchd 50-1)

5345 DUBAI DUTY FREE FINEST SURPRISE STKS (H'CAP) 7f (S)
5:25 (5:27) (Class 4) (0-85,85) 3-Y-O+ **£6,477** (£1,445; £1,445; £481) **Stalls** Centre

Form RPR

1226 **1** **Carnivore**[8] 5144 4-8-12 72 .... RyanMoore 14 81+
(T D Barron) *chsd ldrs: drvn to chal ins last: r.o gamely to ld cl home* **9/2**[1]

0000 **2** *nk* **Millennium Force**[23] 4706 8-9-0 74 .... JoeFanning 2 82
(M R Channon) *in tch: rdn and hdwy over 2f out: slt ld over 1f out: hdd and no ex cl home* **25/1**

2530 **2** *dht* **Grizedale (IRE)**[23] 4706 7-9-1 75 ....(t) KerrinMcEvoy 16 83
(J Akehurst) *in tch: rdn and gd hdwy over 1f out: pressed ldrs fnl 110yds: no ex last strides* **11/1**

2503 **4** *1 ¾* **Outer Hebrides**[25] 4658 5-9-1 75 ....(vt) EddieAhern 5 78
(J R Boyle) *lw: in tch: drvn to chal ins fnl 2f: kpt on same pce ins last* **16/1**

3140 **5** *½* **Desert Dreamer (IRE)**[8] 5144 5-9-8 82 .... GeorgeBaker 3 84
(P R Chamings) *bhd: hdwy 2f out: chsd ldrs and edgd lft ins last: kpt on cl home but nt pce to chal* **20/1**

1040 **6** *1 ½* **Orchard Supreme**[43] 4083 3-9-6 84 .... RichardHughes 4 82
(R Hannon) *bhd: hdwy over 2f out: swtchd lft and rdn over 1f out: kpt on same pce ins last* **25/1**

1012 **7** *nk* **Hill Spirit**[20] 4802 3-9-7 85 .... JohnEgan 1 82
(D R C Elsworth) *chsd ldrs: rdn and ev ch 2f out: wknd fnl 110yds* **8/1**[3]

4104 **8** *nk* **Blue Java**[23] 4706 5-8-11 76 .... TravisBlock(5) 17 73
(H Morrison) *chsd ldrs: drvn to chal 2f out: wknd fnl 110yds* **8/1**[3]

0031 **9** *½* **I'm In Love (USA)**[10] 5096 3-9-3 81 6ex ....(p) FJohansson 6 76
(M A Magnusson) *in tch: rdn and effrt 2f out: nvrr gng pce to rch ldrs: styd on one pce* **7/1**[2]

0-53 **10** *hd* **Sling Back (IRE)**[6] 5192 5-9-6 80 .... KDarley 15 75
(Eamon Tyrrell, Ire) *chsd ldrs: wknd and hung rt ins last* **16/1**

0160 **11** *1 ½* **Josie Marcus (USA)**[33] 4395 3-9-1 79 .... LDettori 11 76+
(J Noseda) *in tch: drvn and styng on whn hmpd ins last: nt rcvr* **16/1**

0100 **12** *¾* **Exmoor**[20] 4807 4-9-4 78 .... SteveDrowne 10 67
(R Charlton) *b: chsd ldrs: rdn over 2f out: wknd fnl f* **12/1**

640 **13** *hd* **Meditation**[15] 4965 4-9-3 80 .... JamesDoyle(3) 7 69
(I A Wood) *lw: slt ld tl hdd over 1f out: sn wknd* **25/1**

10 **14** *nk* **Coleridge (AUS)**[11] 5070 7-9-2 76 ....(b[1]) RobertMiles 13 64
(B G Powell) *chsd ldrs: ev ch ins fnl 2f: wknd fnl f* **66/1**

205 **15** *nk* **Cursum Perficio**[9] [5108] 4-8-12 **72**.............................. JimmyFortune 18 59
(W R Muir) *pressed ldrs: rdn 3f out: wknd over 1f out* **50/1**

0531 **16** *2 ½* **Dr Thong**[8] [5144] 5-9-1 **75** 6ex.......................................(t) TedDurcan 12 55
(P F I Cole) *lw: chsd ldrs: rdn over 2f out: btn whn n.m.r over 1f out* **9/1**

33U6 **17** *1 ½* **Alfie Tupper (IRE)**[20] [4819] 3-9-5 **83**................................ DaneO'Neill 8 60+
(S Kirk) *chsd ldrs: wkng whn n.m.r ins fnl 2f* **16/1**

6056 **18** *8* **Bold Diktator**[12] [5047] 4-8-13 **73**......................................(b) MartinDwyer 9 29+
(W R Muir) *chsd ldrs 5f* **66/1**

1m 25.48s (-1.52) **Going Correction** -0.075s/f (Good)
WFA 3 from 4yo+ 4lb **18** Ran SP% **123.7**
Speed ratings (Par 105):105,104,104,102,102 100,100,99,99,98 97,96,96,95,95 92,90,81
WIN: Carnivore £5.10. PL: £1.90, Grizedale £3.20, Millennium Force £5.70, £3.20. EX: C/G £35.40, C/MF £103.10. CSF: C/G £24.70, C/MF £64.03. TRIC: C/G/MF £583.70, C/MF/G £610.92..
Owner The Meat Eaters **Bred** Lord Halifax **Trained** Maunby, N Yorks

FOCUS
This lacked progressive types and the placed runners are on long losing runs, but it was still a fairly competitive handicap for the class and the form looks straightforward enough.
Desert Dreamer(IRE) Official explanation: jockey said gelding hung right-handed final furlong
Exmoor Official explanation: jockey said gelding suffered interference in running
Dr Thong Official explanation: jockey said horse suffered interference in running 1 1/2f out
Bold Diktator Official explanation: jockey said gelding lost a shoe and its action

5346 DUBAI DUTY FREE FOUNDATION H'CAP — 1m 3f 5y
5:55 (5:57) (Class 4) (0-85,85) 3-Y-0+ **£6,477** (£1,927; £963; £481) **Stalls** Low

Form RPR

2113 **1** **Bauer (IRE)**[39] [4197] 3-9-0 **80**.. LDettori 13 97+
(L M Cumani) *lw: hld up in tch: smooth hdwy fr 2f out to ld ins last: sn in command: eased last strides* **11/4**[1]

5003 **2** *¾* **Beau Nash (USA)**[41] [4125] 3-9-3 **83**.................................... EddieAhern 8 94
(P W Chapple-Hyam) *chsd ldr: led over 2f out: sn rdn: hdd ins last: sn one pce but rallied as wnr eased last strides* **6/1**[3]

1425 **3** *4* **Transvestite (IRE)**[18] [4876] 4-9-5 **84**............................. PatrickHills(7) 12 89
(J W Hills) *mid-div: hdwy on outside over 1f out: outpcd by ldrs fnl f but kpt on wl for 3rd* **14/1**

1501 **4** *shd* **Fort Churchill (IRE)**[2] [5295] 5-9-13 **85** 6ex.....................(bt) JoeFanning 2 89
(B Ellison) *chsd ldrs: rdn over 2f out: styd on same pce fr over 1f out* **9/2**[2]

3060 **5** *2 ½* **Coup D'Etat**[20] [4810] 4-9-8 **80**.. TedDurcan 10 80
(J L Dunlop) *lw: bhd: hdwy to chse ldrs whn n.m.r ins fnl 2f: styd on again ins last* **12/1**

6003 **6** *¾* **Divine River**[9] [5109] 3-8-9 **75**... DaneO'Neill 15 74
(A P Jarvis) *bhd: hdwy on outside over 2f out: kpt on but nvr gng pce to rch ldrs* **33/1**

0320 **7** *hd* **Ocean Avenue (IRE)**[28] [4560] 7-9-3 **75**........................ RichardHughes 6 74
(C A Horgan) *led: rdn over 3f out: hdd over 2f out: sn btn* **25/1**

4325 **8** *½* **Eldorado**[35] [4320] 5-8-12 **70** oh1.. RHills 16 68
(S Kirk) *bhd: pushed along 3f out: rdn over 2f out: nvr gng pce to rch ldrs* **16/1**

540 **9** *nk* **Psychic Star**[14] [4997] 3-9-2 **82**... JimmyFortune 1 80
(W R Swinburn) *mid-div: rdn and effrt on rails whn n.m.r ins fnl 2f: kpt on ins last: n.d* **50/1**

4250 **10** *¾* **Della Salute**[9] [5110] 4-9-4 **76**.. MartinDwyer 14 72
(Miss E C Lavelle) *bhd: n.m.r over 2f out: sme hday fnl f: nvr in contention* **50/1**

1500 **11** *nk* **Incidentally (IRE)**[19] [4838] 3-9-2 **82**................................... RyanMoore 7 78
(R Hannon) *bhd: rdn over 4f out: nvr in contention* **25/1**

0203 **12** *1* **Thyolo (IRE)**[26] [4626] 5-9-11 **83**.. KDarley 4 77
(C G Cox) *chsd ldrs: rdn over 2f out: sn btn* **10/1**

4154 **13** *nk* **Great View (IRE)**[18] [4876] 7-9-3 **75**................................(p) HayleyTurner 5 69
(Mrs A L M King) *a in rr* **25/1**

-006 **14** *shd* **Blaise Hollow (USA)**[20] [4805] 4-9-10 **82**.......................... SteveDrowne 3 76
(R Charlton) *lw: bhd most of way* **20/1**

/0-0 **15** *nk* **Deep Purple**[41] [4160] 5-9-7 **79**..(v[1]) LPKeniry 17 72
(A M Balding) *lw: chsd ldrs: rdn over 2f out: sn btn* **33/1**

5460 **16** *¾* **Snowed Under**[17] [4911] 5-9-7 **79**.................................... KerrinMcEvoy 11 71
(J D Bethell) *sn chsng ldrs: rdn 3f out: wknd qckly fr 2f out* **25/1**

0000 **17** *7* **Hayyani (IRE)**[12] [5045] 4-8-12 **70** oh1.................................(bt) JohnEgan 9 51
(K McAuliffe) *chsd ldrs: wkng whn hmpd ins fnl 2f: eased whn no ch fnl f* **40/1**

2m 18.22s (-4.05) **Going Correction** -0.075s/f (Good)
WFA 3 from 4yo+ 8lb **17** Ran SP% **120.9**
Speed ratings (Par 105):111,110,107,107,105 105,104,104,104,103 103,102,102,102,102 101,96
CSF £15.47 CT £200.09 TOTE £2.80: £1.30, £2.00, £2.20, £1.90; EX 21.60 Place 6 £7.12, Place 5 £6.05.
Owner Aston House Stud **Bred** Aston House Stud **Trained** Newmarket, Suffolk

FOCUS
This was run at a sound pace. The winner remains progressive and was value for further. The second and fourth are also going the right way, and so the form of the principals looks solid.
T/Plt: £10.20 to a £1 stake. Pool: £68,255.00. 4,854.20 winning tickets. T/Qpdt: £4.30 to a £1 stake. Pool: £3,678.20. 620.40 winning tickets. ST

4457 NOTTINGHAM (L-H)
Friday, September 15

OFFICIAL GOING: Good
Wind: Light, behind Weather: Fine and sunny

5347 SARREGO MEMORIAL E B F MAIDEN STKS (DIV I) — 6f 15y
2:20 (2:23) (Class 5) 2-Y-0 **£3,238** (£963; £481; £240) **Stalls** High

Form RPR

63 **1** **Selinka**[28] [4558] 2-8-12 .... TPQueally 2 84
(R Hannon) *wnt lft s: racd in centre: trckd ldrs: rdn to ld overall over 1f out: edgd lft ins fnl f: r.o wl* **2/1**[1]

00 **2** *1 ¼* **Golden Desert (IRE)**[30] [4479] 2-9-3 .... IanMongan 6 85
(T G Mills) *qckly swtchd rt s: racd nr side: led overall: rdn and hdd over 1f out: nt qckn and hld towards fin: 1st of 8 in gp* **9/1**

6305 **3** *6* **Bert's Memory**[18] [4893] 2-8-12 66................................. DO'Donohoe 5 62
(K A Ryan) *racd in centre: led gp tl rdn and hdd over 1f out: outpcd by front pair fnl f: 2nd of 5 in gp* **12/1**

0 **4** *1 ¼* **Theoretical**[118] [1853] 2-8-9 .... StephenDonohoe(3) 12 58
(A J McCabe) *s.i.s: racd nr side: sn chsd ldrs: rdn and nt qckn 2f out: kpt on ins fnl f: 2nd of 8 in gp* **66/1**

00 **5** *1 ¾* **Kings Art (IRE)**[23] [4705] 2-9-3 ....(t) DaleGibson 13 58
(B W Hills) *racd nr side: chsd ldrs: rdn over 2f out: sn hung lft: one pce ins fnl f: 3rd of 8 in gp* **9/1**

60 **6** *hd* **Inchigeelagh (IRE)**[14] [4993] 2-8-12 .... RobertHavlin 7 52
(H Morrison) *racd nr side: chsd ldrs: rdn 2f out: one pce fr over 1f out: 4th of 8 in gp* **16/1**

4 **7** *¾* **Rabshih (IRE)**[36] [4302] 2-8-12 .... J-PGuillambert 9 50
(Sir Michael Stoute) *racd nr side: prom: rdn over 2f out: wknd fnl f: 5th of 8 in gp* **10/3**[2]

8 *nk* **Crossing The Line (IRE)** 2-9-3 .... SebSanders 1 54
(Sir Mark Prescott) *wnt lft s: racd in centre: bhd: effrt over 1f out: nvr trbld ldrs: 3rd of 5 in gp* **25/1**

00 **9** *2* **Beaumont (IRE)**[28] [4572] 2-9-3 ....(t) PhilipRobinson 4 48
(M A Jarvis) *racd in centre: w ldr: rdn and wknd over 1f out: 4th of 5 in gp* **16/1**

36 **10** *1 ¼* **Game Lady**[44] [4053] 2-8-12 .... PaulDoe 14 40
(I A Wood) *s.i.s: racd nr side: towards rr: rdn over 1f out: nvr on terms w ldrs: 6th of 8 in gp* **7/1**[3]

0 **11** *11* **Rotation (IRE)**[12] [5043] 2-9-3 .... WandersonD'Avila 10 12
(J W Hills) *racd nr side: hung lft thrght: in tch: rdn and wknd over 2f out: 7th of 8 in gp* **50/1**

0 **12** *1 ¾* **Mazoran (FR)**[11] [5067] 2-9-3 .... RobbieFitzpatrick 3 6
(D G Bridgwater) *wnt lft s: trckd ldrs tl rdn and wknd over 2f out: 5th of 5 in gp* **200/1**

4 **13** *25* **Miss Puffle**[59] [3618] 2-8-12 .... FergusSweeney 11 —
(S Parr) *racd nr side: hung lft thrght: sn pushed along: a bhd: 8th of 8 in gp* **100/1**

1m 13.02s (-1.98) **Going Correction** -0.30s/f (Firm) **13** Ran SP% **117.2**
Speed ratings (Par 95):101,99,91,89,87 87,86,85,83,81 66,64,31
CSF £20.23 TOTE £2.70: £1.10, £2.10, £4.00; EX 24.80.
Owner R Barnett **Bred** W And R Barnett Ltd **Trained** East Everleigh, Wilts

FOCUS
This did not look that strong a maiden and it is unlikely to produce anything anywhere near as good as 2002 winner Oasis Dream. They split into two groups and Selinka, racing down the middle of the track, just got the better of Golden Desert, who raced against the stands' rail. The race has been rated through the fifth and sixth.

NOTEBOOK
Selinka, the first foal of the very useful mare Lady Links, confirmed the promise she showed when third at Newbury on her previous start, coming away from her rivals in good style down the centre of the course. There was plenty to like about this performance and it may be worth upping her in grade. (tchd 9-4 and 5-2 in places)
Golden Desert(IRE) had shown just modest form on his first two runs but shaped much better this time. Showing plenty of pace down the stands' side, he got to the rail early and came well clear of his rivals on his side. He will have more options now he is eligible ro run in nursery company. (op 10-1)
Bert's Memory, on her toes in the paddock, kept on for a remote third but never threatened to get involved (op 8-1 tchd 15-2)
Theoretical, making her debut for her new trainer, did a lot of good late work down the stands' side and might be one to keep an eye on. (op 50-1)
Kings Art(IRE) was well held in the first-time tongue tie but will have more options now he has qualified for a handicap mark. Official explanation: jockey said colt hung left (op 11-1 tchd 12-1)
Rabshih(IRE), a 200,000gns Green Desert filly out of a Sadler's Wells mare, showed ability at Yarmouth but was disappointing this time. (op 9-2)

5348 SARREGO MEMORIAL E B F MAIDEN STKS (DIV II) — 6f 15y
2:55 (2:55) (Class 5) 2-Y-0 **£3,238** (£963; £481; £240) **Stalls** High

Form RPR

1 **Tobermory (IRE)** 2-8-12 .... PhilipRobinson 1 86+
(M A Jarvis) *racd alone far side: mde virtually all: rdn out* **5/4**[1]

0 **2** *2* **Cape Velvet (IRE)**[28] [4559] 2-8-12 .... J-PGuillambert 6 80
(J W Hills) *racd centre: chsd ldrs: led that gp over 2f out: r.o: no ch w wnr: 1st of 9 in gp* **7/1**

3 *7* **Bidable** 2-8-12 .... FergusSweeney 12 59
(B Palling) *racd centre: sn pushed along in rr: styd on fr over 1f out: n.d: 2nd of 9 in gp* **40/1**

6 **4** *2 ½* **One White Sock**[36] [4283] 2-8-9 .... StephenDonohoe(3) 10 52
(J L Spearing) *racd stands' side: led that pair: wknd wl over 1f out: 1st of 2 that side* **33/1**

00 **5** *1* **Style Sunday (IRE)**[21] [4768] 2-9-3 .... SebSanders 3 54
(B W Hills) *led centre to 1/2-way: edgd lft and wknd 2f out: 3rd of 9 in gp* **10/3**[2]

6 *5* **Power Alert** 2-9-0 .... RichardKingscote(3) 13 39
(B R Millman) *chsd ldr stands' side tl hung lft and wknd wl over 1f out: last of 2 in gp* **18/1**

00 **7** *1 ½* **Mujart**[60] [3596] 2-8-5 .... RussellKennemore(7) 4 29
(J A Pickering) *racd centre: chsd ldrs: led that gp 1/2-way: hung lft and hdd over 2f out: wknd over 1f out: 4th of 9 in gp* **100/1**

4 **8** *shd* **Our Blessing (IRE)**[176] [701] 2-9-3 .... TPQueally 7 34
(A P Jarvis) *s.i.s: racd centre: hdwy 4f out: hung lft and wknd over 2f out: 5th of 9 in gp* **13/2**[3]

06 **9** *1* **Ronannis**[19] [4843] 2-9-3 .... DerekMcGaffin 9 31
(J Jay) *racd centre: prom over 3f: 6th of 9 in gp* **100/1**

0 **10** *shd* **Shouldntbethere (IRE)**[29] [4526] 2-9-3 .... RobertHavlin 8 30
(Mrs P N Dutfield) *s.i.s: racd centre: sn outpcd: 7th of 9 in gp* **100/1**

11 *12* **By The River** 2-9-3 .... JimCrowley 2 —
(P Winkworth) *racd centre: sn outpcd: 8th of 9 in gp* **22/1**

0 **12** *2 ½* **Just Lovely**[25] [4657] 2-8-12 ....(bt[1]) DaleGibson 11 —
(M P Tregoning) *slowly in stride: racd centre: sn outpcd: last of 9 in gp* **22/1**

1m 12.81s (-2.19) **Going Correction** -0.30s/f (Firm) **12** Ran SP% **115.7**
Speed ratings (Par 95):102,99,90,86,85 78,76,76,75,75 59,55
CSF £9.71 TOTE £2.20: £1.10, £2.10, £11.60; EX 9.20.
Owner Sheikh Mohammed **Bred** Darley **Trained** Newmarket, Suffolk

FOCUS
Like the first division, not a great maiden. The time was slightly quicker than the first race. Tobermory raced alone on the far side of the track and readily got the better the remainder, who raced middle to stands' side. The race has been rated through the ninth and tenth.

NOTEBOOK
Tobermory(IRE) was clearly suited by racing on her own against the far-side rail, but the chances are that she was basically just the best horse on the day. Out of 1000 Guineas runner-up Kerrera, she was well backed to make a winning debut and duly obliged, never looking in much danger despite racing on her own. She will face much stiffer tasks in future, but is open to plenty of improvement. (op 7-4)
Cape Velvet(IRE), 50-1 and well down the field on her debut at Newbury, showed improved form and was the clear second best. She looks capable of finding a similar race. (op 13-2 tchd 8-1)

Bidable, a half-brother to Oceano Indiano, a multiple mile to ten-furlong winner in Italy, as well as triple hurdles scorer Wayward Melody, kept on reasonably well from off the pace and should have learnt quite a bit. (op 33-1)
One White Sock stepped up on the form she showed on her debut at Chepstow. (op 25-1)
Style Sunday(IRE) was a shade disappointing but has now qualified for a handicap mark. (op 3-1 tchd 11-4)

5349 NOTTINGHAMSHIRE COUNTY CRICKET CLUB NURSERY — 6f 15y
3:30 (3:31) (Class 5) (0-75,75) 2-Y-0 **£3,886** (£1,156; £577; £288) **Stalls** High

Form RPR
010 **1** **Bateleur**^{34} [4377] 2-9-1 **72** .... EdwardCreighton$^{(3)}$ 16 — 74
(M R Channon) *racd nr side: in rr: rdn over 2f out: edgd lft and hdwy fr over 1f out: racd in centre and r.o to ld towards fin* **12/1**
323 **2** ½ **Gap Princess (IRE)**^{29} [4510] 2-8-4 **65** .... JamesRogers$^{(7)}$ 4 — 66
(R A Fahey) *wnt rt s: racd far-side: chsd ldrs: rdn over 1f out: r.o ins fnl f: 1st of 10 in gp* **8/1**^{3}
630 **3** *hd* **Silver Appraisal**^{32} [4424] 2-8-5 **59** .... AdrianMcCarthy 3 — 59
(B Smart) *racd far-side: led overall: rdn over 1f out: hdd towards fin: 2nd of 10 in gp* **33/1**
0516 **4** *3* **Mac Gille Eoin**^{8} [5140] 2-9-2 **70** .... JimCrowley 10 — 61
(J Gallagher) *racd nr side: prom: rdn and hung lft fr over 2f out: one pce whn on far-side towards fin: 3rd of 10 in gp* **11/1**
2346 **5** *shd* **Tipsy Prince**^{11} [5065] 2-8-13 **67** .... J-PGuillambert 15 — 58
(Mrs G S Rees) *racd nr side: chsd ldrs: rdn over 2f out: led gp and kpt on ins fnl f: 1st of 4 in gp* **7/1**^{2}
0224 **6** ¾ **Anthea**^{18} [4897] 2-8-8 **69** .... JamesMillman$^{(7)}$ 17 — 57
(B R Millman) *s.i.s: racd nr side: in tch: rdn 2f out: kpt on ins fnl f: 2nd of 4 in gp* **8/1**^{3}
605 **7** ½ **Luscivious**^{107} [2139] 2-8-11 **68** .... StephenDonohoe$^{(3)}$ 14 — 55
(A J McCabe) *dwlt: racd nr side: led gp: rdn over 2f out: hdd and no ex ins fnl f: 3rd of 4 in gp* **16/1**
0030 **8** 1½ **Blackwater Stream (IRE)**^{34} [4377] 2-9-2 **70** .... RobertHavlin 7 — 52
(Mrs P N Dutfield) *racd far-side: bhd: rdn and hdwy over 1f out: styd on ins fnl f: 4th of 10 in gp* **14/1**
453 **9** ¾ **Madam Gaffer**^{32} [4433] 2-9-1 **69** .... IanMongan 8 — 49
(B J Meehan) *racd far-side: in tch: rdn 2f out: kpt on ins fnl f: nt pce to chal: 5th of 10 in gp* **8/1**^{3}
0134 **10** *1* **Compton Fields**^{18} [4893] 2-9-4 **75** .... (v^{1}) RichardKingscote$^{(3)}$ 13 — 52
(R Charlton) *racd nr side: prom: rdn and hung lft fr over 2f out: wknd ins fnl f: 4th of 4 in gp* **5/1**^{1}
0046 **11** ½ **Wool Mart**^{20} [4804] 2-9-3 **71** .... SebSanders 9 — 47
(M Blanshard) *racd far-side: bhd: rdn 2f out: hdwy over 1f out: wknd ins fnl f: 6th of 10 in gp* **17/2**
000 **12** *3* **Safari Sundowner (IRE)**^{42} [4103] 2-9-1 **69** .... StephenCarson 1 — 36
(P Winkworth) *racd far-side: prom: rdn 2f out: wknd over 1f out: 7th of 10 in gp* **14/1**
000 **13** ¾ **Last Dog Standing (IRE)**^{18} [4867] 2-8-5 **59** .... DaleGibson 5 — 23
(B G Powell) *hmpd s: racd far-side: sn pushed along in midfield: wknd over 1f out: 8th of 10 in gp* **33/1**
0400 **14** 3½ **Kerswell**^{32} [4427] 2-8-11 **65** .... ChrisCatlin 6 — 19
(B R Millman) *racd far-side: chsd ldrs tl rdn and wknd qckly wl over 1f out: 9th of 10 in gp* **33/1**
0040 **15** 1¼ **Beat The Bully**^{11} [5065] 2-8-4 **58** .... (b^{1}) PaulDoe 2 — 8
(I A Wood) *racd far-side: prom: rdn and edgd rt whn wkng over 1f out: 10th of 10 in gp* **50/1**

1m 13.83s (-1.17) **Going Correction** -0.30s/f (Firm) **15** Ran SP% **119.1**
Speed ratings (Par 95):95,94,94,90,89 88,88,86,85,83 83,79,78,73,71
CSF £100.22 CT £3150.91 TOTE £13.40: £3.40, £2.60, £4.40; EX 116.10.
Owner Dave and Gill Hedley **Bred** G Hedley And Mike Channon Bloodstock Limited **Trained** West Ilsley, Berks

FOCUS
Just a modest nursery run in a slower time than both divisions of the juvenile maiden. They split into two groups and Bateleur, who raced in the smaller bunch towards the stands' side, just got the better of Gap Princess, who raced far side, but there was very little in it. The form looks pretty solid rated through the fourth and sixth.

NOTEBOOK
Bateleur finished last when favourite to beat subsequent Listed winner Stevie Gee at Redcar on his previous start, but he has clearly been freshened up by a short break and won in determined style, despite edging to his left. There could be more to come. (op 11-1)
Gap Princess(IRE) was trying a sixth furlong for the first time after showing some modest but promising form in her first three races. She kept on really well down the far-side rail and won the race on that side. (tchd 15-2)
Silver Appraisal, dropped back from seven furlongs, returned to form with a good effort in third. (op 25-1)
Mac Gille Eoin was a lot more exposed than the majority of his rivals, but he had some reasonable form to his name. Racing up with the leaders on the stands' side early on, he threw away any chance he had by hanging over to the far side of the track. (op 9-1 tchd 12-1)
Tipsy Prince travelled well down the stands' side early but could never get on terms. (op 6-1 tchd 15-2)
Compton Fields was well below form upped to his furthest trip to date in a first-time visor. (op 9-2 tchd 4-1 and 11-2)

5350 KONICA MINOLTA EAST FILLIES' H'CAP — 6f 15y
4:05 (4:06) (Class 5) (0-70,70) 3-Y-0+ **£4,533** (£1,348; £674; £336) **Stalls** High

Form RPR
2600 **1** **Inka Dancer (IRE)**^{10} [5078] 4-8-7 **55** .... AdrianMcCarthy 4 — 64
(B Palling) *racd far side: chsd ldrs: rdn over 2f out: led ins fnl f: r.o* **10/1**
311 **2** ¾ **Littledodayno (IRE)**^{4} [5232] 3-9-2 **69** 6ex.......... EdwardCreighton$^{(3)}$ 17 — 76+
(M Wigham) *racd centre: hld up: hdwy and edgd lft over 1f out: r.o: 1st of 5 in gp* **7/4**^{1}
5003 **3** *1* **Dance To The Blues (IRE)**^{6} [5167] 5-9-2 **67** ..(p) RichardKingscote$^{(3)}$ 14 — 71
(B De Haan) *racd centre: mid-div: hdwy and edgd lft over 1f out: r.o: 2nd of 5 in gp* **6/1**^{2}
2105 **4** ½ **Limonia (GER)**^{13} [5032] 4-8-8 **56** ow1.......... RobbieFitzpatrick 8 — 59
(N P Littmoden) *racd far side: chsd ldr: rdn to ld that gp ins fnl f: sn hdd and no ex: 2nd of 9 in gp* **14/1**
0114 **5** ¾ **Piddies Pride (IRE)**^{4} [5232] 4-8-12 **60** .... (v) ChrisCatlin 7 — 60
(Miss Gay Kelleway) *s.i.s: racd far side: hld up: hdwy over 1f out: r.o: 3rd of 9 in gp* **14/1**
-005 **6** *hd* **Suesam**^{20} [4820] 3-9-1 **65** .... RobertHavlin 1 — 65
(B R Millman) *racd far side: led hdd over 4f out: rdn over 1f out: styd on same pce: 4th of 9 in gp* **12/1**
1030 **7** *hd* **Catspraddle (USA)**^{28} [4562] 3-9-6 **70** .... PatDobbs 13 — 69
(R Hannon) *racd far side: led that gp and overall ldr over 4f out: rdn over 1f out: hdd and no ex ins fnl f: 5th of 9 in gp* **25/1**
5230 **8** *nk* **Be My Charm**^{15} [4962] 3-7-11 **54** .... LauraReynolds$^{(7)}$ 11 — 52
(M Blanshard) *racd centre: chsd ldrs: rdn over 1f out: no ex ins fnl f: 3rd of 5 in gp* **40/1**
0300 **9** *nk* **Sprinkle**^{20} [4820] 3-8-9 **59** .... SebSanders 5 — 56
(R M Beckett) *racd far side: hld up: hdwy over 2f out: no ex ins fnl f: 6th of 9 in gp* **14/1**
3010 **10** 1¾ **Clearing Sky (IRE)**^{15} [4962] 5-8-8 **56** .... MatthewHenry 16 — 48
(J R Boyle) *racd alone towards stands' side: chsd ldrs tl hung lft and wknd over 1f out* **20/1**
2340 **11** 1½ **Dasheena**^{125} [1672] 3-8-9 **62** .... StephenDonohoe$^{(3)}$ 15 — 50
(A J McCabe) *s.i.s: racd centre: outpcd: effrt over 2f out: wknd over 1f out: 4th of 5 in gp* **40/1**
6-24 **12** *hd* **Creme Brulee**^{209} [449] 3-8-10 **60** .... TPQueally 3 — 47
(C R Egerton) *racd far side: edgd lft s: chsd ldrs: rdn over 2f out: wknd fnl f: 7th of 9 in gp* **16/1**
0040 **13** *nk* **Prettilini**^{13} [5036] 3-8-6 **63** .... TolleyDean$^{(7)}$ 6 — 49
(R Brotherton) *racd far side: outpcd: 8th of 9 in gp* **40/1**
1304 **14** *1* **Rancho Cucamonga (IRE)**^{4} [5243] 4-8-8 **56** .... (b) JimCrowley 9 — 39
(T D Barron) *racd far side: chsd ldrs over 4f: last of 9 in gp* **15/2**^{3}
2003 **15** *1* **Red Sovereign**^{23} [4691] 5-8-7 **62** .... MarkCoumbe$^{(7)}$ 12 — 42
(D G Bridgwater) *racd centre: chsd ldrs 4f: last of 5 in gp* **28/1**

1m 13.33s (-1.67) **Going Correction** -0.30s/f (Firm)
WFA 3 from 4yo+ 2lb **15** Ran SP% **124.5**
Speed ratings (Par 100):99,98,96,96,95 94,94,94,93,91 89,89,88,87,86
CSF £26.47 CT £123.48 TOTE £14.30: £3.40, £1.50, £2.30; EX 43.60.
Owner Mrs Anita Quinn **Bred** Humphrey Okeke **Trained** Tredodridge, Vale Of Glamorgan

FOCUS
Just a modest fillies' handicap. The majority raced middle to far side and there seemed little bias, although Clearing Sky was well beaten having raced alone against the stands'-side rail. The race has been rated through the winner, third and fourth to the best of this season's form.
Red Sovereign Official explanation: jockey said mare never travelled

5351 LIGHTHOUSE & MERMAID H'CAP — 2m 9y
4:40 (4:40) (Class 3) (0-95,95) 3-Y-0+ **£9,067** (£2,697; £1,348; £673) **Stalls** Low

Form RPR
-005 **1** **Hawridge Prince**^{20} [4817] 6-10-0 **95** .... JimCrowley 2 — 110+
(B R Millman) *hld up in tch: hdwy gng wl 3f out: rdn to ld wl over 1f out: r.o wl to draw clr ins fnl f* **20/1**
2064 **2** *5* **Trance (IRE)**^{15} [4951] 6-8-11 **78** .... (p) ChrisCatlin 5 — 85
(T D Barron) *hld up in rr: struggling 5f out: hdwy over 1f out: styd on to take 2nd wl ins fnl f: nt trble wnr* **6/1**^{3}
1000 **3** *nk* **Ski Jump (USA)**^{24} [4676] 6-8-5 **79** .... (v) JamesRogers$^{(7)}$ 6 — 86
(R A Fahey) *hld up: rdn over 2f out: styd on ins fnl f* **8/1**
0622 **4** *shd* **Velvet Heights (IRE)**^{20} [4792] 4-9-3 **84** .... PhilipRobinson 1 — 91
(J L Dunlop) *prom: rdn to chse wnr over 1f out: no ex and lost 2nd wl ins fnl f* **9/4**^{2}
451U **5** *4* **Lightning Strike (GER)**^{15} [4967] 3-8-13 **93** .... IanMongan 4 — 96
(T G Mills) *led: rdn over 4f out: hdd wl over 1f out: wknd ins fnl f* **6/4**^{1}
0-00 **6** 2½ **Distant Prospect (IRE)**^{44} [4036] 9-8-12 **79** .... FergusSweeney 3 — 79
(A M Balding) *prom: rdn 5f out: wknd 2f out* **12/1**

3m 30.02s (-3.48) **Going Correction** -0.30s/f (Firm)
WFA 3 from 4yo+ 13lb **6** Ran SP% **108.6**
Speed ratings (Par 107):96,93,93,93,91 90
CSF £120.52 CT £947.91 TOTE £21.70: £5.00, £2.10; EX 70.50.
Owner Eric Gadsden **Bred** Downclose Stud **Trained** Kentisbeare, Devon

FOCUS
A decent enough staying handicap, although the early pace seemed just modest. It has been rated through the fourth.

NOTEBOOK
Hawridge Prince, who shaped nicely in a Listed race at Windsor on his previous start, was stepping up to two miles for the first time but saw the trip out well and won impressively. A rise in the weights will make things tougher, but he is unexposed over this sort of distance and there could well be more to come. (op 14-1)
Trance(IRE) was going nowhere for much of the race but finished strongly to grab the runner-up spot in the final furlong. He is probably at his best in a much larger field. (op 9-1)
Ski Jump(USA), like the runner-up, stayed on up the home straight without ever threatening the easy winner (op 15-2 tchd 10-1)
Velvet Heights(IRE) did not have a great deal of room to manoeuvre at one point, but found little when in the clear. (op 15-8)
Lightning Strike(GER), the only three-year-old in the race, led them into the home straight but was readily outpaced when the race really started to take shape. He looks a resolute galloper and is another who might be better in a bigger field where the pace is stronger. (tchd 5-4 and 7-4 in places)

5352 EUROPEAN BREEDERS FUND TRENT MAIDEN FILLIES' STKS — 1m 54y
5:15 (5:15) (Class 5) 2-Y-0 **£3,886** (£1,156; £577; £288) **Stalls** Centre

Form RPR
0 **1** **Treat**^{80} [2958] 2-9-0 .... TPO'Shea 11 — 83
(M R Channon) *hld up: hdwy u.p to ld 3f out: sn edgd lft: hrd rdn and hung lft fr over 1f out: all out* **11/2**^{1}
0 **2** ½ **Latanazul**^{21} [4765] 2-9-0 .... IanMongan 12 — 82
(J L Dunlop) *hld up: hdwy over 2f out: rdn to chse wnr and edgd lft over 1f out: styd on* **11/2**^{1}
0 **3** *5* **Feolin**^{34} [4373] 2-9-0 .... RobertHavlin 7 — 71
(H Morrison) *chsd ldrs: n.m.r and lost pl over 2f out: n.d after* **10/1**
2 **4** ½ **Wild Thyme**^{18} [4866] 2-9-0 .... PatDobbs 6 — 69
(R Hannon) *chsd ldrs: rdn over 2f out: edgd lft and wknd fnl f* **11/2**^{1}
32 **5** *hd* **Quiddity (IRE)**^{24} [4669] 2-9-0 .... ChrisCatlin 13 — 69
(E J O'Neill) *chsd ldrs: rdn over 2f out: wknd fnl f* **7/1**^{2}
6 1½ **Kahara** 2-9-0 .... NickyMackay 1 — 65+
(L M Cumani) *s.i.s: hld up: nt clr run over 2f out: nvr nr to chal* **14/1**
0 **7** *hd* **Neon**^{19} [4830] 2-8-9 .... RoryMoore$^{(5)}$ 3 — 65
(J R Fanshawe) *prom over 6f* **28/1**
00 **8** 1¾ **She's So Pretty (IRE)**^{21} [4765] 2-9-0 .... StephenCarson 9 — 61
(W R Swinburn) *mid-div: rdn over 3f out: no imp* **20/1**
9 *nk* **Monsoon Wedding** 2-9-0 .... PhilipRobinson 2 — 60
(M Johnston) *chsd ldr tl wknd over 1f out* **9/1**^{3}
10 ¾ **Magdalene** 2-9-0 .... AdrianMcCarthy 14 — 59
(Rae Guest) *s.i.s: hld up: racd keenly: a in rr* **40/1**
05 **11** *6* **Career Girl (USA)**^{11} [5068] 2-9-0 .... DO'Donohoe 10 — 45
(E A L Dunlop) *s.i.s: hld up: hdwy over 3f out: hung lft and wknd over 2f out* **16/1**
12 *4* **Dream Again** 2-9-0 .... SebSanders 8 — 36
(Sir Michael Stoute) *chsd ldrs over 5f* **7/1**^{2}
13 1½ **On Watch** 2-9-0 .... FergusSweeney 4 — 32
(H Candy) *s.i.s: hld up: a in rr* **25/1**

14 *15* **Fly The World** 2-9-0 .... TPQueally 5 —
(A P Jarvis) *s.i.s: a in rr: bhd fr 1/2-way* **33/1**

1m 43.54s (-2.86) **Going Correction** -0.30s/f (Firm) **14** Ran SP% **120.2**
Speed ratings (Par 92):102,101,96,96,95 94,94,92,92,91 85,81,79,64
CSF £31.99 TOTE £5.80: £2.20, £2.50, £3.40; EX 39.80.
Owner Highclere Thoroughbred Racing XXXVI **Bred** A J Coleing **Trained** West Ilsley, Berks

FOCUS
This looked like quite a decent fillies' maiden and the third, fourth, fifth and eighth have all been rated as having run to form.

NOTEBOOK
Treat, 20-1 and last of 12 on her debut over seven furlongs at Newbury, showed much improved form over this longer trip and got off the mark under a very strong ride. One hopes the hard ride does not leave its mark, as she is evidently a useful prospect and holds an entry in the Group 1 Fillies' Mile. (op 6-1 tchd 5-1)
Latanazul, far too green to do herself justice on her debut at Newmarket, raced upsides the winner in the early stages towards the rear of the field, but could not quite force herself in front when it mattered. She pulled well clear of the third and should find a similar race before the end of the season. (op 5-1)
Feolin confirmed the promise she showed on her debut at Newmarket and might have been closer had she not lost her place at a crucial stage. (op 14-1)
Wild Thyme, who chased home a stablemate at Chepstow on her debut, was quite keen through the early stages and may have failed to see out the trip. (op 13-2)
Quiddity(IRE) had shown promise on both of her runs, without looking a star, and gives the form some shape. She was never far from the leaders but was unable to quicken when asked. (op 11-2)
Kahara ♦, a brother to St Leger winner Milan, left the impression that there was much better to come and appeals as one to follow. (op 10-1)
Monsoon Wedding ♦, out of a mare who has already produced four individual winners, was another in the field bred to be very effective over middle distances and should be better with time. (op 8-1)
Dream Again, a half-sister to the smart stayer Elusive Dream, does look to have improvement in her. (op 8-1 tchd 9-1)

5353 VISITNOTTINGHAM.COM MAIDEN STKS 1m 54y
5:45 (5:48) (Class 5) 3-4-Y-O **£4,210** (£1,252; £625; £312) **Stalls** Centre

Form RPR
0 **1** **Penryn**[20] 4806 3-9-3 .... AntonyProcter 4 74+
(D R C Elsworth) *midfield: rdn over 3f out: hung lft and hdwy over 2f out: r.o ins fnl f to ld post* **12/1**
43- **2** *hd* **Esthlos (FR)**[277] 6557 3-9-3 .... DerekMcGaffin 6 74
(J Jay) *racd keenly: led for 1f: remained prom: rdn over 2f out: regained ld over 1f out: hdd post* **20/1**
6 **3** *1 ½* **The Aldbury Flyer**[10] 5086 3-9-0 .... StephenDonohoe(3) 16 72+
(W R Swinburn) *midfield: rdn over 2f out: hdwy over 1f out: r.o ins fnl f: nrst fin* **4/1**[2]
06 **4** *1* **Ektimaal**[11] 5071 3-9-3 ....(t) DO'Donohoe 11 69
(E A L Dunlop) *led after 1f: rdn and hdd over 1f out: no ex ins fnl f* **8/1**
42- **5** *2 ½* **Mitanni (USA)**[391] 4572 3-9-3 .... PhilipRobinson 5 64
(Mrs A J Perrett) *in tch: rdn over 2f out: one pce fnl f* **3/1**[1]
6 *1* **Spinning Reel** 3-8-12 .... StephenCarson 12 57+
(W R Swinburn) *hld up: rdn and hdwy 2f out: styd on ins fnl f: nt rch ldrs* **11/1**
40 **7** *5* **Zamhrear**[33] 4396 3-8-12 .... J-PGuillambert 15 47
(C E Brittain) *sn prom: rdn over 2f out: wknd over 1f out* **25/1**
8 *1 ¼* **Desert Island Miss** 3-8-9 .... RichardKingscote(3) 3 45
(W R Swinburn) *midfield: rdn 3f out: sn btn* **15/2**[3]
9 *1* **Natacha Rostow** 3-8-12 .... NickyMackay 2 43
(L M Cumani) *midfield: pushed along 5f out: wknd 2f out* **10/1**
00 **10** *1 ¾* **Pagan Island**[11] 5071 3-9-3 .... TPO'Shea 7 44
(J A R Toller) *prom: rdn 4f out: wknd over 2f out* **33/1**
0 **11** *2 ½* **Mantolini**[37] 4247 3-8-12 .... EmmettStack(5) 13 39
(Pat Eddery) *a bhd* **33/1**
12 *¾* **Crystal Annie** 3-8-12 .... JimCrowley 17 33
(Heather Dalton) *rdn over 3f out: a bhd* **33/1**
13 *8* **Classic Hall (IRE)** 3-8-12 .... PatDobbs 1 17
(S Kirk) *s.v.s: a bhd* **16/1**
0 **14** *40* **Gary's Indian (IRE)**[8] 5138 3-8-12 .... RobbieFitzpatrick 9 —
(B P J Baugh) *midfield: rdn over 4f out: sn wknd: t.o* **80/1**

1m 43.57s (-2.83) **Going Correction** -0.30s/f (Firm)
WFA 3 from 4yo 5lb **14** Ran SP% **117.5**
Speed ratings (Par 103):102,101,100,99,96 95,90,89,88,86 84,83,75,35
CSF £237.10 TOTE £22.20: £4.60, £3.60, £1.90; EX 276.10.
Owner W V & Mrs E S Robins **Bred** Wood Hall Stud Limited **Trained** Newmarket, Suffolk

FOCUS
This looked like an ordinary maiden rated through the third.

5354 MADAME JONES H'CAP 1m 1f 213y
6:15 (6:16) (Class 6) (0-60,60) 3-Y-0+ **£3,238** (£963; £481; £240) **Stalls** Low

Form RPR
56U5 **1** **Ruby Legend**[11] 5064 8-9-5 **56** ....(p) JimCrowley 7 63
(K G Reveley) *a.p: rdn over 1f out: r.o to ld nr fin* **33/1**
53-0 **2** *hd* **Etoile Russe (IRE)**[112] 1996 4-9-9 **60** ....(t) PhilipRobinson 4 67
(P C Haslam) *led: rdn over 1f out: hdd nr fin* **25/1**
1030 **3** *½* **Red Sail**[53] 3803 5-9-0 **54** ....(b) RichardKingscote(3) 9 60
(Dr J D Scargill) *a.p: rdn to chse ldr over 2f out: ev ch fr over 1f out: unable qck towards fin* **16/1**
0520 **4** *nk* **Blue Hedges**[11] 5072 4-9-4 **55** .... MichaelTebbutt 14 61
(H J Collingridge) *hld up: hdwy over 4f out: rdn over 1f out: r.o* **20/1**
0041 **5** *shd* **Uhuru Peak**[39] 4194 5-9-5 **56** ....(bt) DaleGibson 5 61
(M W Easterby) *chsd ldrs: rdn over 3f out: r.o* **12/1**
0413 **6** *½* **Royal Indulgence**[6] 5173 6-9-4 **55** .... RobbieFitzpatrick 10 61+
(W M Brisbourne) *dwlt: hld up: plld hrd: hdwy and nt clr run fr over 1f out: running on whn hmpd wl ins fnl f: nvr able to chal* **6/1**[2]
-010 **7** *½* **Le Soleil (GER)**[16] 4925 5-9-7 **58** .... TPQueally 3 65+
(B J Curley) *trckd ldrs: nt clr run and lost pl over 2f out: hdwy and hmpd over 1f out: styng on whn nt clr run ins fnl f* **14/1**
06-5 **8** *hd* **Gold Guest**[14] 4982 7-9-2 **56** .... StephenDonohoe(3) 6 59
(P D Evans) *hld up in tch: outpcd over 2f out: styd on ins fnl f* **9/2**[1]
1553 **9** *nk* **Typhoon Ginger (IRE)**[1] 5320 11-9-9 **60** .... FergusSweeney 2 63
(G Woodward) *s.i.s: hld up: hdwy over 1f out: nt rch ldrs* **8/1**
5410 **10** *3 ½* **Oh Danny Boy**[16] 4925 5-9-8 **59** .... RobertHavlin 11 55
(Jane Chapple-Hyam) *hld up: effrt over 2f out: n.d* **15/2**[3]
463 **11** *1* **Ali D**[1] 5316 8-9-2 **60** .... JamieJones(7) 1 55
(G Woodward) *hld up: rdn over 2f out: a in rr* **9/1**
0040 **12** *½* **Summer Bounty**[70] 3270 10-9-8 **59** .... ChrisCatlin 12 53
(F Jordan) *s.i.s: hld up: effrt over 2f out: a in rr* **33/1**
56-0 **13** *2 ½* **Oman Gulf (USA)**[137] 1346 5-9-6 **57** .... J-PGuillambert 8 46
(Micky Hammond) *hld up: hld up: hdwy over 2f out: sn rdn and wknd* **33/1**
00-5 **14** *5* **You're My Son**[34] 4367 4-9-8 **59** .... SebSanders 15 39
(A B Haynes) *chsd ldrs: rdn over 3f out: wknd over 1f out* **14/1**
2315 **15** *5* **Granary Girl**[11] 5072 4-9-4 **55** .... DO'Donohoe 13 26
(J Pearce) *hld up: a in rr* **8/1**
0-34 **16** *1* **Mademoiselle**[99] 240 4-9-2 **53** .... TPO'Shea 16 22
(R Curtis) *mid-div: lost pl half way: bhd fnl 3f* **50/1**

2m 9.68s (-0.02) **Going Correction** -0.30s/f (Firm) **16** Ran SP% **122.8**
Speed ratings (Par 101):88,87,87,87,87 86,86,86,85,83 82,81,79,75,71 71
CSF £677.12 CT £12874.92 TOTE £42.20: £6.40, £5.80, £6.30, £5.30; EX 641.10 Place 6 £693.40, Place 5 £243.00.
Owner Mrs J M Grimston **Bred** Huttons Ambo Stud **Trained** Lingdale, Redcar & Cleveland

FOCUS
A moderate handicap and there was not much between the first nine home crossing the winning line. Pretty solid form on balance, though, with the those placed third to eighth all running close to their recent levels.
T/Plt: £693.40 to a £1 stake. Pool: £43,836.45. 46.15 winning tickets. T/Qpdt: £243.00 to a £1 stake. Pool: £2,923.10. 8.90 winning tickets. CR

5332 AYR (L-H)
Saturday, September 16

OFFICIAL GOING: Good to soft
Wind: almost nil

5355 TOTEPLACEPOT H'CAP (FOR THE WEIR MEMORIAL TROPHY) 7f 50y
1:40 (1:42) (Class 3) (0-90,90) 3-Y-O+
£11,217 (£3,358; £1,679; £840; £419; £210) **Stalls** Low

Form RPR
4111 **1** **Glenbuck (IRE)**[11] 5079 3-8-7 **79** ....(v) FrancisNorton 1 91
(A Bailey) *mde all: c to stands side w majority ent st: rdn over 2f out: kpt on gamely fnl f* **7/1**[3]
0000 **2** *1 ½* **Continent**[25] 4682 9-9-4 **87** .... PaulHanagan 8 95
(D Nicholls) *hld up: effrt over 2f out: kpt on fnl f: nt rch wnr* **14/1**
0036 **3** *1 ½* **Commando Scott (IRE)**[1] 5336 5-9-3 **89** .... PatrickMathers(3) 14 93
(I W McInnes) *hld up in tch: hdwy 1/2-way: effrt over 2f out: kpt on same pce fnl f* **13/2**[2]
3500 **4** *2* **Yorkshire Blue**[1] 5336 7-8-8 **77** .... DanielTudhope 11 76+
(J S Goldie) *s.i.s: bhd: styd far side w one other ent st: hdwy 2f out: kpt on fnl f: no imp* **16/1**
3305 **5** *shd* **King Marju (IRE)**[19] 4896 4-9-6 **89** ....(v) NCallan 4 88
(K R Burke) *dwlt: hld up: hdwy and prom 1/2-way: rdn and one pce over 1f out* **14/1**
5243 **6** *1* **Ice Planet**[28] 4609 5-9-7 **90** .... RyanMoore 6 86
(D Nicholls) *hld up: rdn over 2f out: hdwy over 1f out: nvr rchd ldrs* **4/1**[1]
210- **7** *½* **Frank Crow**[330] 6005 3-8-5 **77** .... JimmyQuinn 3 72+
(J S Goldie) *stdd s: hld up: styd far side w one other ent st: no imp fr 2f out* **33/1**
2455 **8** *1* **Byron Bay**[9] 5144 4-8-13 **82** .... TomEaves 9 74
(I Semple) *chsd ldrs tl rdn and wknd over 1f out* **12/1**
0151 **9** *nk* **Hiccups**[12] 5070 6-8-7 **76** .... KDarley 5 67
(M Dods) *prom: drvn over 2f out: wknd fnl f* **8/1**
2000 **10** *nk* **Marshman (IRE)**[22] 4760 7-8-13 **85** .... SaleemGolam(3) 2 76
(M H Tompkins) *prom tl rdn and wknd over 1f out* **8/1**
0106 **11** *nk* **Traytonic**[21] 4798 5-8-10 **86** .... VictoriaBehan(7) 10 76
(D Nicholls) *bhd: rdn 1/2-way: nvr rchd ldrs* **20/1**
0003 **12** *nk* **Fiefdom (IRE)**[9] 5144 4-8-13 **82** .... RoystonFfrench 13 71
(I W McInnes) *bhd: pushed along ent st: n.d* **16/1**
3061 **13** *3* **Royal Dignitary (USA)**[16] 4953 6-9-2 **85** .... AdrianTNicholls 7 66
(D Nicholls) *cl up tl rdn and wknd 2f out* **16/1**

1m 33.49s (0.77) **Going Correction** +0.225s/f (Good)
WFA 3 from 4yo+ 3lb **13** Ran SP% **114.4**
Speed ratings (Par 107):104,102,100,98,98 97,96,95,94,94 94,93,90
CSF £96.80 CT £688.69 TOTE £5.00: £2.10, £4.80, £2.50; EX 259.50.
Owner Middleham Park Racing XLII **Bred** Mrs Teresa Monaghan **Trained** Cotebrook, Cheshire

FOCUS
Mainly exposed performers but a fair handicap in which the pace steadied after a couple of furlongs. The bulk of runners came stands' side entering the straight. Another personal best from the winner, and sound form all told.

NOTEBOOK
Glenbuck(IRE) is thriving at present and turned in a career-best effort to make it four wins in a row with another gutsy display. He goes particularly well with cut in the ground and, although life will be tougher after reassessment, he should continue to give a good account when allowed to dominate. (tchd 13-2 and 15-2 in a place)
Continent, having his first run over this trip for nearly five years, ran creditably. However as he is the type that needs things to drop right and as he is without a win in over two years, he would not be one to lump on at single-figure odds next time.
Commando Scott(IRE), turned out after his exertions in the Silver Cup at this course the previous day, seemed to give it his best shot returned to this longer trip and he looks a good guide to the worth of this form. He likes this ground but has little margin for error from his current mark. (op 6-1)
Yorkshire Blue, who made no show in the previous day's Silver Cup, appreciated the return to this trip and may be a bit better than the bare form as he was one of only two to race on the far side in the straight. However he too will have to improve to win a similar event from his current mark. (tchd 20-1 in a place)
King Marju(IRE) was not totally disgraced back in handicap company but, although he has slipped in the weights, still looks plenty high enough from this mark and the fact that he is without a win for nearly two years has to be a bit of a concern. (op 12-1)
Ice Planet had been running consistently well over sprint distances but failed to improve for the step up to this trip. A stronger overall gallop would have suited but he still has something to prove over seven furlongs. (tchd 7-2 and 9-2 in places)
Frank Crow was not totally disgraced on this first start since last October and this lightly-raced sort is not one to be writing off just yet. (op 25-1)

5356 THE SPORTSMAN NEWSPAPER FIRTH OF CLYDE STKS (GROUP 3) (FILLIES) 6f
2:10 (2:11) (Class 1) 2-Y-O
£28,390 (£10,760; £5,385; £2,685; £1,345; £675) **Stalls** High

Form RPR
106 **1** **Princess Iris (IRE)**[20] 4840 2-8-12 **90** .... FrancisNorton 6 104
(E J O'Neill) *chsd ldrs: led over 1f out: hrd pressed fnl f: hld on wl* **11/1**

10 **2** 1 1/4 **Roxan (IRE)**[87] 2743 2-8-12 .... NCallan 8 102+
(K A Ryan) *s.i.s: sn chsng ldrs: outpcd over 1f out: kpt on wl fnl f: tk 2nd on line* **7/2**[2]

21 **3** *shd* **La Presse (USA)**[24] 4716 2-8-12 .... RyanMoore 2 100
(B W Hills) *dwlt: prom: effrt 2f out: ev ch ins fnl f: no ex last 75yds: lost 2nd post* **5/6**[1]

415 **4** 1/2 **Zanida (IRE)**[24] 4715 2-8-12 85..................... PhillipMakin 3 98
(K R Burke) *led to over 1f out: one pce ins fnl f* **50/1**

1110 **5** 3/4 **Ponty Rossa (IRE)**[25] 4681 2-8-12 87..................... DavidAllan 5 96
(T D Easterby) *hld up in tch: effrt whn nt clr run over 1f out: kpt on fnl f: no imp* **16/1**

1404 **6** 3 1/2 **Hope'N'Charity (USA)**[20] 4840 2-8-12 99..................... AdamKirby 1 86
(C G Cox) *prom tl wknd fr 2f out* **11/2**[3]

2305 **7** 13 **Amber Valley**[19] 4890 2-8-12 93.....................(p) KDarley 7 47
(K A Ryan) *cl up: rdn whn hmpd 1/2-way: sn lost pl and eased* **28/1**

1m 13.28s (-0.39) **Going Correction** +0.075s/f (Good) **7** Ran SP% **111.8**
Speed ratings (Par 102):105,103,103,102,101 96,79
CSF £46.92 TOTE £9.50: £2.80, £2.00; EX 64.60 Trifecta £32.60 Pool: £309.72 - 6.73 winning units..
Owner Team Valor **Bred** Frank Dunne **Trained** Averham Park, Notts
■ Stewards' Enquiry : N Callan one-day ban: careless riding (Sep 27)

FOCUS
Not the most competitive of Group races but run at a decent pace throughout. Mixed messages from the form, but it should stand up at a similar level.

NOTEBOOK
Princess Iris(IRE) appreciated the return to six furlongs and the easy ground and showed a good attitude to record a career-best effort. Although she falls short of the best of her generation, she should continue to give a good account over this trip in this type of event. (tchd 10-1 and 12-1)
Roxan(IRE), disappointing in the Queen Mary at Royal Ascot, showed that run to be all wrong on this first run on easy ground and left the impression that a stiffer test of stamina would be in her favour. She is the sort to win more races. (op 3-1)
La Presse(USA), proven on easy ground, was well supported and ran creditably stepped up to Group company after a fluent win in a traditionally decent York maiden last time. She is worth another chance in similar company. (op 10-11 tchd 11-10)
Zanida(IRE) had the run of the race against the stands' rail and ran creditably but left the impression that she is going to continue to look vulnerable in this type of event. Rated 85, she will be of interest if switched to nursery company.
Ponty Rossa(IRE), well beaten in a York nursery last time, was ridden with a bit more restraint and ran creditably. She looks a bit better than the bare form as she was hampered when asked for an effort and left the impression that a stiffer overall test of stamina would have been in her favour. (op 20-1 tchd 22-1)
Hope'N'Charity(USA) had finished in front of the winner over seven at Goodwood on her previous start but failed to confirm that promise back in trip after racing on the outside of the group. She has now had her limitations exposed on each of her four starts in Group company. (tchd 6-1 in a place)
Amber Valley, sporting first-time cheekpieces, is better than the form indicates but she has been disappointing since her third placing in an Irish Group 3 in June and has plenty to prove at present in this type of event. Official explanation: jockey said filly suffered interference in running (tchd 25-1 in a place)

5357 TOTESCOOP6 AYRSHIRE H'CAP 1m
2:40 (2:42) (Class 2) (0-100,99) 3-Y-0+

£15,580 (£4,665; £2,332; £1,167; £582; £292) **Stalls** Low

Form RPR

2536 **1** **Vicious Warrior**[19] 4889 7-8-8 85 oh6..................... KDarley 10 92
(R M Whitaker) *led to over 1f out: rallied and regained ld ins fnl f: hld on wl* **25/1**

0-53 **2** *hd* **St Petersburg**[14] 5012 6-9-6 97..................... NCallan 3 104
(M H Tompkins) *keen early: prom: effrt over 2f out: led and edgd rt over 1f out: hdd ins fnl f: kpt on u.p: jst hld* **5/1**[3]

3404 **3** 1 **Blythe Knight (IRE)**[23] 4739 6-9-8 99..................... JimmyQuinn 4 103
(J J Quinn) *hld up: smooth hdwy over 2f out: effrt whn hmpd over 1f out: kpt on ins fnl f* **5/1**[3]

061 **4** 2 1/2 **Rio Riva**[19] 4889 4-9-5 96..................... TomEaves 6 94
(Miss J A Camacho) *hld up: rdn over 2f out: hdwy over 1f out: nvr rchd ldrs* **7/2**[2]

1105 **5** 1 1/4 **Fremen (USA)**[23] 4726 6-8-9 86..................... AdrianTNicholls 7 84+
(D Nicholls) *prom: rdn to chal over 2f out: hung lft: one pce whn hmpd over 1f out: no ex* **28/1**

2153 **6** *shd* **Collateral Damage (IRE)**[19] 4889 3-8-7 88..................... DavidAllan 13 83
(T D Easterby) *prom: effrt over 2f out: outpcd wl over 1f out* **11/4**[1]

1510 **7** 3 **Waterside (IRE)**[14] 5019 7-8-13 90..................... RyanMoore 11 78
(G L Moore) *w wnr to over 2f out: sn outpcd* **11/1**

5043 **8** 2 **Dhaular Dhar (IRE)**[21] 4790 4-8-8 85 oh2..................... DanielTudhope 1 69
(J S Goldie) *hld up in tch: drvn over 2f out: btn over 1f out* **8/1**

6254 **9** 1 1/4 **Kindlelight Debut**[16] 4965 6-8-5 85 oh3..................... JamesDoyle(3) 2 66
(N P Littmoden) *chsd ldrs tl wknd fr 2f out* **25/1**

1m 43.72s (0.23) **Going Correction** +0.225s/f (Good)
WFA 3 from 4yo+ 4lb **9** Ran SP% **112.8**
Speed ratings (Par 109):107,106,105,103,102 101,98,96,95
CSF £139.58 CT £742.57 TOTE £24.10: £4.30, £1.80, £2.00; EX 130.80 TRIFECTA Not won..
Owner sportaracing.com **Bred** Hellwood Stud Farm **Trained** Scarcroft, W Yorks
■ Stewards' Enquiry : N Callan 15-day ban (takes into account previous offences; three days deferred): careless riding (Oct 6-17)

FOCUS
Not the most competitive of handicaps for the money and a muddling early gallop means this bare form may be less than reliable. The winner, 6lb out of the weightsm, returned to his form of 2004.

NOTEBOOK
Vicious Warrior has been consistent this year and showed a good attitude to win from 6lb out of the handicap. Things went his way here but he will find life tougher after reassessment, especially against the more progressive sorts. Official explanation: trainer was unable to offer any explanation for the apparent improvement in form
St Petersburg had conditions to suit and returned to his best, despite edging off a true line under pressure, on only this third start of the year. He should continue to give it his best shot when he gets his ground but a further rise in the weights will leave him vulnerable. (op 4-1 tchd 11-2)
Blythe Knight(IRE) ◆ ran really well and advertised his prospects for the totesport Cambridgeshire - in which he ran creditably from a poor draw last year - at the end of this month. He would have gone very close but for being stopped in his tracks at a crucial stage and is well worth an each-way wager for the Newmarket race if the ground is on the easy side.
Rio Riva, who turned in arguably a career-best effort on his previous start, was not disgraced by any means, especially as this race was not really run to suit. A much stronger end-to-end gallop would have suited and he is not one to write off yet. (op 11-4)
Fremen(USA) fared much better than in a Musselburgh claimer last time and is capable of winning again away from progressive sorts when returned to a sound surface. (op 33-1)
Collateral Damage(IRE) was not disgraced in terms of form but was a bit disappointing in view of previous promise on easy ground and he has little room for manouevre from his current mark. (op 9-2)

5358 TOTESPORT AYR GOLD CUP (HERITAGE H'CAP) 6f
3:15 (3:16) (Class 2) 3-Y-0+

£75,214 (£22,520; £11,260; £5,636; £2,812; £1,412) **Stalls** High

Form RPR

5000 **1** **Fonthill Road (IRE)**[14] 5009 6-9-2 97..................... PaulHanagan 6 109
(R A Fahey) *racd w two others far side: cl up: rdn and hdwy to ld 1f out: kpt on strly* **16/1**

1421 **2** 1 **Borderlescott**[42] 4128 4-9-10 105..................... RoystonFfrench 16 114
(R Bastiman) *led main gp stands side: rdn over 1f out: kpt on wl fnl f: jst hld by far side wnr* **11/2**[2]

0-32 **3** *hd* **Advanced**[136] 1404 3-9-7 104..................... NCallan 9 112
(K A Ryan) *chsd stands side ldrs: effrt over 2f out: kpt on wl fnl f* **40/1**

4000 **4** *hd* **Coleorton Dancer**[25] 4682 4-8-10 94.....................(p) AndrewMullen(3) 26 102
(K A Ryan) *towards rr stands side: hdwy over 1f out: kpt on strly: nrst fin* **25/1**

025 **5** *nk* **Andronikos**[21] 4803 4-9-8 103.....................(t) RyanMoore 27 110
(P F I Cole) *bhd stands side: hdwy 2f out: r.o fnl f: nrst fin* **16/1**

3000 **6** *hd* **Out After Dark**[42] 4128 5-9-2 100.....................(p) AdamKirby(3) 22 106
(C G Cox) *prom stands side: effrt over 2f out: kpt on u.p fnl f* **33/1**

0431 **7** 1/2 **Appalachian Trail (IRE)**[21] 4803 5-9-9 104 5ex.....................(b) TomEaves 24 109
(I Semple) *midfield stands side: effrt over 1f out: chsng ldrs ins fnl f: no ex towards fin* **17/2**

6005 **8** 1/2 **Mecca's Mate**[8] 5158 5-9-5 100..................... LDettori 7 103
(D W Barker) *cl up far side trio: led that gp briefly over 1f out: kpt on same pce ins fnl f* **33/1**

3002 **9** *nk* **Orientor**[8] 5158 8-9-10 105..................... DanielTudhope 28 107
(J S Goldie) *hld up stands side: n.m.r over 2f out: kpt on fnl f: no imp* **16/1**

00-5 **10** *hd* **Viking Spirit**[143] 1246 4-8-13 94..................... StephenCarson 25 96
(W R Swinburn) *in tch stands side: rdn over 2f out: kpt on same pce fnl f* **16/1**

621 **11** *shd* **The Kiddykid (IRE)**[41] 4174 6-9-7 105..................... StephenDonohoe(3) 15 107
(P D Evans) *chsd stands side ldrs tl rdn and outpcd ins fnl f* **25/1**

5210 **12** 3/4 **Skhilling Spirit**[28] 4601 3-9-0 97..................... DavidAllan 21 96
(T D Barron) *bhd stands side tl hdwy over 1f out: nrst fin* **33/1**

1313 **13** *shd* **Hogmaneigh (IRE)**[7] 5182 3-8-10 96 5ex..................... SaleemGolam(3) 17 95
(S C Williams) *in tch stands side: n.m.r over 2f out: effrt and cl up over 1f out: wknd wl ins fnl f* **9/2**[1]

1011 **14** 3/4 **Fantasy Believer**[7] 5182 8-9-2 97 8ex..................... JimmyQuinn 23 94
(J J Quinn) *towards rr: drvn 1/2-way: nvr rchd ldrs* **15/2**[3]

3004 **15** 1/2 **Golden Dixie (USA)**[6] 5202 7-8-12 93..................... RobbieFitzpatrick 10 88
(R A Harris) *midfield stands side: drvn over 2f out: btn fnl f* **100/1**

0642 **16** 1/2 **Kostar**[33] 4430 5-8-12 93..................... AdrianTNicholls 1 87
(C G Cox) *led far side trio to over 1f out: sn btn* **40/1**

1000 **17** 4 **Desert Commander (IRE)**[25] 4682 4-9-1 96..................... DO'Donohoe 11 78
(K A Ryan) *chsd stands side ldrs tl wknd over 1f out* **66/1**

0046 **18** 1 1/4 **Obe Gold**[28] 4609 4-9-1 96.....................(v) TonyCulhane 14 74
(M R Channon) *racd on outside of stands side gp: midfield: rdn over 2f out: sn btn* **25/1**

1230 **19** 1 1/4 **Prince Namid**[20] 4832 4-8-12 93..................... MickyFenton 8 67
(Mrs A Duffield) *chsd stands side ldrs tl wknd wl over 1f out* **28/1**

2045 **20** 7 **Woodcote (IRE)**[7] 5182 4-9-0 95..................... KDarley 20 48
(C G Cox) *towards rr: effrt over 2f out: n.d* **20/1**

1010 **21** 1 **Dark Missile**[27] 4633 3-8-12 95..................... FrancisNorton 18 45
(A M Balding) *hld up stands side: rdn over 2f out: wknd over 1f out* **33/1**

1200 **22** 1/2 **One More Round (USA)**[7] 5182 8-9-2 100.....................(b) JamesDoyle(3) 13 49
(N P Littmoden) *hld up outside of stands side gp: shortlived effrt over 2f out: sn btn* **66/1**

0440 **23** 1/2 **Ingleby Arch (USA)**[9] 5143 3-8-12 95.....................(b[1]) PhillipMakin 19 42
(T D Barron) *hld up stands side: rdn over 2f out: sn btn* **50/1**

1m 12.7s (-0.97) **Going Correction** +0.075s/f (Good)
WFA 3 from 4yo+ 2lb **23** Ran SP% **121.7**
Speed ratings (Par 109):109,107,107,107,106 106,105,105,104,104 104,103,103,102,101 100,95,93,92,82 81,80,80
CSF £81.76 CT £3541.34 TOTE £22.50: £4.90, £2.30, £10.10, £6.90; EX 398.80 Trifecta £20475.90 Part won. Pool: £28,839.37 - 0.40 winning units..
Owner Mrs Una Towell **Bred** D N Wallace **Trained** Musley Bank, N Yorks

FOCUS
The events over sprint distances at this course earlier in the week suggested the stands' side was favoured, but the three that raced on the far side showed emphatically there was no bias this time. Of those drawn in the bottom six stalls, four were non-runners due to the ground. With little between the two sides this looks solid form, Fonthill Road running to the figure he posted in this race a year ago.

NOTEBOOK
Fonthill Road(IRE) had been disappointing this year but had reportedly got his back problems sorted out and he returned to the form that saw him finish second in both the Stewards' Cup and this event in 2005, in the process dispelling any notions about the stands' side being the place to be from a draw perspective. On this evidence he is now worth another try in Listed or minor Group company. Official explanation: trainer had no explanation for the apparent improvement in form (op 14-1)
Borderlescott ◆, a most progressive sort, had the run of the race next to the stands' side and ran as well as he had when taking the Stewards' Cup in July. The likelihood is that there is more to come and he appeals strongly as the type to hold his own in Listed and minor Group company. (op 6-1 tchd 13-2 in places)
Advanced ◆, a lightly-raced sort who had been off the track since May, ran a blinder from an ordinary draw on this first run for Kevin Ryan. He will not be inconvenienced by the return to seven furlongs and is the type to win more races.
Coleorton Dancer has not won since April of last year but had conditions to suit, was spot on after two recent starts and returned to something like his best in the first-time cheekpieces. Consistency has not been his strong suit since his last win, though. (op 20-1)
Andronikos is a useful sort who ran creditably from a high draw back in handicap company. Soft ground seems to suit him ideally but he has very little margin for error from this mark in this type of event. (tchd 25-1 in a place)
Out After Dark, a multiple winner last year, has yet to score this term but ran a sound race from his high draw. He is equally effective over a stiff five furlongs but is another that is vulnerable to progressive types in competitive races from his current mark.
Appalachian Trail(IRE) ran creditably under a 5lb penalty. He is unexposed over sprint distances and appeals as the type to win again when there is the prospect of an end-to-end gallop. (op 8-1 tchd 9-1 in a place)
Mecca's Mate has not won since last July but ran creditably, finishing second of the trio who raced on the far side. Whether she is up to winning competitive handicaps from her current mark of 100 is another matter, though.
Orientor Official explanation: jockey said horse was denied a clear run
Hogmaneigh(IRE), one of the few progressive performers on show, was a shade disappointing under his penalty back over this longer trip. However he may be the type to do even better with another winter on his back and is not one to write off just yet. (op 5-1)
Ingleby Arch(USA) Official explanation: jockey said colt never travelled

5359 MCDONALD'S RESTAURANTS NURSERY 1m
3:50 (3:50) (Class 2) (0-95,88) 2-Y-O

£12,464 (£3,732; £1,866; £934; £466; £234) Stalls Low

Form				RPR
3230	1		**Smokey Oakey (IRE)**[21] 4824 2-8-7 77 SaleemGolam(3) 7 (M H Tompkins) *hld up in tch: nt clr run fr 3f out: swtchd rt and qcknd to ld ins fnl f: readily* 9/1	86+
4422	2	3 ½	**Princeton (IRE)**[16] 4963 2-9-2 83 TonyCulhane 4 (M R Channon) *chsd ldrs: led over 1f out to ins last: kpt on: no ch w wnr* 7/1	84
421	3	shd	**White Deer (USA)**[44] 4074 2-9-5 86 KDarley 5 (M Johnston) *keen: disp ld: ev ch tl one pce ins fnl f* 3/1[1]	87
5121	4	1	**Rosbay (IRE)**[19] 4882 2-9-5 86 DavidAllan 6 (T D Easterby) *hld up: effrt 2f out: kpt on fnl f: no imp* 9/2[3]	85
301	5	1	**Kilburn**[42] 4129 2-9-4 88 AdamKirby(3) 1 (C G Cox) *mde most to over 1f out: sn outpcd* 10/3[2]	84
1520	6	hd	**Moonwalking**[30] 4509 2-8-13 80 RyanMoore 2 (Jedd O'Keeffe) *hld up: effrt and prom over 2f out: rdn and keeping on whn hmpd ins fnl f: nt rcvr* 14/1	76
1302	7	nk	**Colditz (IRE)**[19] 4882 2-8-6 73 FrancisNorton 3 (D W Barker) *chsd ldrs tl rdn and wknd over 1f out* 18/1	68
13	8	24	**Tender Moments**[72] 3216 2-9-1 82 NCallan 9 (K A Ryan) *chsd ldrs: rdn 1/2-way: wknd fr over 2f out* 9/1	22

1m 44.93s (1.44) **Going Correction** +0.225s/f (Good) 8 Ran SP% **110.7**
Speed ratings (Par 101):101,97,97,96,95 95,94,70
CSF £65.27 CT £223.71 TOTE £10.80: £2.60, £2.20, £1.60; EX 90.50.
Owner Judi Dench and Bryan Agar **Bred** Hyde Park Stud **Trained** Newmarket, Suffolk
■ Stewards' Enquiry : Tony Culhane caution: careless riding

FOCUS
A fair nursery, run at an ordinary gallop. A much improved performance from Smokey Oakey, who appeals as the type to win more races, and solid form behind him.

NOTEBOOK
Smokey Oakey(IRE) ◆, who never got competitive in a valuable sales race in Ireland last time, appreciated the step up to this much longer trip for this nursery debut and turned in a much improved effort, despite being denied room for much of the straight. On this evidence he is sure to win more races. (op 10-1)
Princeton(IRE) is a consistent sort who ran right up to his best on this first run on easy ground and he looks a good guide to the level of this form. He should continue to give it his best shot but may remain vulnerable to the more progressive sorts. (op 8-1)
White Deer(USA) ran creditably on this handicap debut, despite failing to settle and being taken on for the lead in the early stages. He had no problems with this longer trip and looks the sort to win more races for his current yard. (tchd 11-4)
Rosbay(IRE), raised a stiff-looking 11lb for his Newcastle win, ran creditably. He left the impression that a stronger end-to-end gallop would have been in his favour but may have to come down in the weights again to regain the winning thread. (op 5-1 tchd 11-2)
Kilburn, a Racing Post Trophy and Derby entry who did well to win from a low draw at Goodwood, proved a shade disappointing on this handicap debut but may be better suited by faster ground and is worth another chance. (op 3-1)
Moonwalking shaped better than the bare form as he was playing for a place when getting squeezed out against the far rail in the last half furlong. He looks fairly exposed but is capable of winning away from progressive sorts, granted a decent gallop.

5360 DOONSIDE CUP STKS (SPONSORED BY EASY-BREAKS.COM) (LISTED RACE) 1m 2f
4:25 (4:25) (Class 1) 3-Y-O+

£22,712 (£8,608; £4,308; £2,148; £1,076; £540) Stalls Low

Form				RPR
3315	1		**Mashaahed**[86] 2775 3-8-8 105 RyanMoore 5 (B W Hills) *hld up in tch: hdwy to ld over 2f out: drew clr fr over 1f out* 4/1[2]	107+
2223	2	6	**Ouninpohja (IRE)**[21] 4817 5-9-0 107 (v) TomEaves 7 (I Semple) *trckd ldrs: effrt and ev ch over 2f out: hung lft and carried hd high over 1f out: sn no ex* 9/2[3]	93
4330	3	3	**Profit's Reality (IRE)**[106] 2201 4-9-0 102 RobbieFitzpatrick 3 (P A Blockley) *led after 1f: hdd over 2f out: kpt on same pce* 12/1	87
5354	4	8	**Grey Outlook**[2] 5312 3-8-3 64 RoystonFfrench 2 (Miss L A Perratt) *prom: outpcd 3f out: n.d after* 100/1	67
4-11	5	¾	**Ashaawes (USA)**[19] 4877 3-8-8 110 LDettori 6 (Saeed Bin Suroor) *led 1f: cl up: drvn over 2f out: wknd wl over 1f out: lame* 10/11[1]	71
2300	6	7	**Kew Green (USA)**[21] 4818 8-9-0 109 (t) NCallan 4 (P R Webber) *prom tl rdn and wknd over 2f out* 8/1	57
00-0	7	55	**Howards Dream (IRE)**[117] 1883 8-9-0 20 (t) DavidAllan 1 (D A Nolan) *bhd: lost tch fr 1/2-way* 200/1	—

2m 11.08s (-0.64) **Going Correction** +0.225s/f (Good)
WFA 3 from 4yo+ 6lb 7 Ran SP% **110.9**
Speed ratings (Par 111):111,106,103,97,96 91,47
CSF £20.77 TOTE £4.80: £1.70, £2.10; EX 21.30.
Owner Hamdan Al Maktoum **Bred** Lightbody Celebration Cakes **Trained** Lambourn, Berks

FOCUS
A couple of fair sorts, but with the market leader going lame it did not take anywhere near as much winning as seemed likely. The fourth limits the form.

NOTEBOOK
Mashaahed had no problems with this easier ground and took advantage of the below-par run of the market leader to beat a quirky rival with plenty in hand. He should not be inconvenienced by the return to a mile and a half and may well be capable of a bit better. (op 9-2 tchd 7-2 and 5-1 in a place)
Ouninpohja(IRE), with the visor again fitted, had a decent chance at the weights but once again looked less than straightforward under pressure. Small field scenarios do not appear ideal but his quirks mean he remains one to be wary of at shortish odds. (op 5-1 tchd 11-2 in a place)
Profit's Reality(IRE) had a bit to find at the weights but was not disgraced under suitable conditions. He is best when allowed to dominate and does not look the sort who is going to be easy to place from his current mark or in this type of event. (tchd 14-1)
Grey Outlook, a modest maiden, seemed to excel herself in the face of a stiff task but is almost certainly flattered by her proximity. The return to ordinary handicaps will suit but she is one to watch until getting her head in front. (op 66-1)
Ashaawes(USA), the winner of three of his previous four starts, seemed sure to be involved in what looked a less than competitive event but he proved a major disappointment. He was subsequently found to be lame and, as he is only lightly raced, is well worth another chance in similar company. Official explanation: vet said colt returned lame (op 5-6 tchd Evens and 4-5 in places)
Kew Green(USA) had a decent chance at the weights and is proven in easy ground but continues a long way below his best and is one to watch at present. (op 10-1)

5361 CARRICKS DARLEY HAY ARCHITECTS H'CAP 1m 5f 13y
5:00 (5:00) (Class 3) (0-90,90) 3-Y-O+ £11,658 (£3,468; £1,733; £865) Stalls Low

Form				RPR
0305	1		**Lets Roll**[14] 5010 5-9-6 86 SaleemGolam(3) 7 (C W Thornton) *chsd ldrs: smooth hdwy to ld over 2f out: rdn and edgd lft over 1f out: kpt on strly* 2/1[1]	97
0003	2	3	**Crow Wood**[28] 4259 7-9-9 86 JimmyQuinn 6 (J J Quinn) *in tch: hdwy and ev ch over 2f out: kpt on same pce ins fnl f* 7/1	93
3323	3	3 ½	**Gee Dee Nen**[23] 4742 3-8-10 82 NCallan 5 (M H Tompkins) *hld up in tch: effrt and drvn over 2f out: sn one pce* 3/1[2]	84
4111	4	13	**Alessano**[22] 4770 4-9-11 88 (b) RyanMoore 1 (G L Moore) *led 1f: chsd ldrs tl hung lft and wknd over 2f out* 4/1[3]	72
4664	5	hd	**Rehearsal**[35] 4346 5-9-13 90 (b[1]) TomEaves 3 (L Lungo) *led after 1f: hdd briefly after 3f: hdd over 2f out: wknd* 14/1	73
1060	6	23	**Doctor Scott**[16] 4951 3-8-13 85 RoystonFfrench 4 (M Johnston) *hld up in tch: drvn 3f out: sn wknd* 14/1	36
4433	P		**Flying Clarets (IRE)**[28] 4612 3-8-5 77 PaulHanagan 2 (R A Fahey) *plld hrd and sddle sn slipped: led briefly after 3f: p.u over 5f out* 12/1	—

2m 56.15s (-0.46) **Going Correction** +0.225s/f (Good)
WFA 3 from 4yo+ 9lb 7 Ran SP% **111.9**
Speed ratings (Par 107):110,108,106,98,97 83,—
CSF £15.86 TOTE £2.80: £1.70, £3.10; EX 15.70.
Owner A Crute and Partners **Bred** G G A Gregson **Trained** Middleham Moor, N Yorks

FOCUS
Not a strong handicap, and the pace was just fair. Let's Roll ran to last year's winning figure.

NOTEBOOK
Lets Roll travelled strongly and won an uncompetitive handicap in good fashion to notch his third win over this course and distance. He is suited by cut in the ground, but he have will much more to do if he is to follow up in the competitive Cesarewitch at Newmarket next month, in which he was 14th last year after winning this corresponding race. (tchd 9-4 and 5-2 in a place)
Crow Wood, a versatile sort who ran well over hurdles on his previous start, attracted support and ran creditably. A more strongly run race would have suited but he remains high enough in the weights at present. (op 11-1 tchd 12-1)
Gee Dee Nen, who had conditions to suit, again had his limitations exposed in handicap company but, although vulnerable to progressive or well handicapped sorts, may be worth a try over two miles. (op 4-1 tchd 5-1 in a place)
Alessano had won his three previous starts but was below his recent best from this 9lb higher mark. This sticky ground may not have suited but he may remain vulnerable from his current mark. (op 10-3)
Rehearsal was below his best in the first-time blinkers and, although this ground may not have been in his favour, he will need more leniency from the handicapper if he is to win from his current mark. (op 12-1 tchd 16-1 in a place)
Doctor Scott had not been at his best on his two previous starts and was soundly beaten this time. This was obviously not his form but he is one to have reservations about at present. (tchd 12-1)
Flying Clarets(IRE) is a keen sort who had been running creditably but on this occasion gave his rider some anxious moments before pulling up. Official explanation: jockey said saddle slipped (op 10-1 tchd 9-1)

5362 ANTHEA WE ALL WILL MISS YOU H'CAP 1m 2f
5:30 (5:31) (Class 5) (0-75,75) 3-Y-O+

£5,297 (£1,586; £793; £396; £198; £99) Stalls Low

Form				RPR
0024	1		**Freeloader (IRE)**[24] 4696 6-9-10 75 PaulHanagan 8 (R A Fahey) *led 1f: chsd ldr: smooth hdwy to ld over 2f out: rdn clr* 13/2[3]	89+
0-20	2	4	**Top Jaro (FR)**[129] 1596 3-9-4 75 TonyCulhane 10 (T P Tate) *prom: effrt over 2f out: edgd lft over 1f out: sn chsng wnr: kpt on fnl f* 14/1	81
3065	3	½	**Tidy (IRE)**[18] 4911 6-9-2 67 JimmyQuinn 11 (Micky Hammond) *bhd tl hdwy 2f out: kpt on fnl f: nrst fin* 16/1	72
611-	4	3	**Dispol Foxtrot**[268] 6654 8-9-5 70 AdrianTNicholls 14 (D Nicholls) *s.i.s: hdwy and chsd ldrs over 3f out: ev ch over 2f out: outpcd appr fnl f* 14/1	70
202	5	¾	**Logsdail**[9] 5136 6-9-5 70 (p) RyanMoore 3 (G L Moore) *hld up: effrt over 2f out: kpt on fnl f: no imp* 13/2[3]	68
5323	6	½	**Reluctant Suitor**[16] 4951 4-9-3 68 DanielTudhope 2 (J S Goldie) *hld up in tch: hdwy to ld briefly over 2f out: wknd over 1f out* 4/1[1]	65
4035	7	shd	**Rowan Lodge (IRE)**[15] 4990 4-9-5 73 (b) SaleemGolam(3) 4 (M H Tompkins) *keen: led after 1f: hdd over 2f out: wknd over 1f out* 11/1	70
1265	8	2	**Mistress Twister**[26] 4654 5-9-8 73 PhillipMakin 9 (T D Barron) *hld up: rdn over 2f out: n.d* 10/1	66
420	9	11	**Titian Dancer**[22] 4782 3-8-13 73 (t) AdamKirby(3) 12 (W R Swinburn) *midfield: effrt over 2f out: hung lft and sn btn* 6/1[2]	47
5310	10	¾	**Baileys Encore**[16] 4947 3-9-2 73 KDarley 1 (M Johnston) *chsd ldrs tl wknd over 2f out* 7/1	45
0010	11	9	**Anduril**[19] 4871 5-9-0 68 (b) PatrickMathers(3) 6 (Miss M E Rowland) *plld hrd in midfield: drvn 3f out: sn btn* 20/1	24

2m 12.88s (1.16) **Going Correction** +0.075s/f (Good)
WFA 3 from 4yo+ 6lb 11 Ran SP% **114.9**
Speed ratings (Par 103):98,94,94,92,91 91,90,89,80,79 72
CSF £91.37 CT £1387.49 TOTE £7.50: £2.00, £5.40, £4.60; EX 84.30 Place 6 £509.78, Place 5 £189.24.
Owner Enda Hunston **Bred** David Commins **Trained** Musley Bank, N Yorks

FOCUS
An ordinary handicap in which the pace was fair. Freeloader was at last taking advantage of a good mark and was back to his best.

Titian Dancer Official explanation: jockey said colt hung left from 3f out

T/Jkpt: Not won. T/Plt: £749.00 to a £1 stake. Pool: £135,699.80. 132.25 winning tickets. T/Qpdt: £62.60 to a £1 stake. Pool: £7,993.70. 94.40 winning tickets. RY

[5076]CATTERICK (L-H)

Saturday, September 16

OFFICIAL GOING: Good to firm (good in places)

After 12mm rain two days before the ground was described as 'spot on, almost perfect ground'.

Wind: almost nil Weather: fine but overcast and rather misty

5363 BOOK RACEDAY HOSPITALITY ON 01748 810165 MAIDEN STKS (DIV I) 7f

1:30 (1:31) (Class 5) 3-4-Y-0 **£2,590** (£770; £385; £192) **Stalls** Low

Form RPR

5020 **1** **Cape Sydney (IRE)**[43] 4120 3-8-12 41 CatherineGannon 7 46
(D W Barker) *a.p: hdwy to chse ldr 2f out: rdn to chal over 1f out: styd on to ld last 50 yds* **6/1**[1]

0060 **2** *nk* **Wolfman**[11] 5077 4-9-1 40 (p) MarkLawson(5) 3 50
(D W Barker) *cl up on inner: led over 4f out: rdn 2f out: drvn ent last: hdd and no ex last 50 yds* **10/1**

000- **3** *1 1/4* **Boppys Pride**[286] 6496 3-8-12 40 JamieMoriarty(5) 15 47
(R A Fahey) *midfield: hdwy 3f out: rdn to chse ldrs over 1f out: kpt on same pce ins last* **40/1**

56 **4** *nk* **Tagart**[38] 4261 3-9-0 DNolan(3) 4 46
(J J Quinn) *in tch: hdwy and edgd lft over 2f out: rdn along on inner to chse ldrs over 1f out: kpt on same pce ins last* **20/1**

0005 **5** *1 1/2* **Jabraan (USA)**[5] 5241 4-9-6 40 PaulQuinn 10 42
(D W Chapman) *midfield on outer: hdwy over 2f out: sn rdn and kpt on same pce appr last* **40/1**

6000 **6** *shd* **Ailsa**[12] 5060 4-9-1 42 PaulMulrennan 11 36
(C W Thornton) *stmbld s and bhd: hdwy over 2f out: sn rdn and styd on ins last: nrst fin* **16/1**

0002 **7** *4* **Nautico**[26] 4656 3-8-9 43 GregFairley(3) 9 26
(Miss L A Perratt) *prom: rdn along over 2f out: drvn wl over 1f out and grad wknd* **13/2**[2]

-030 **8** *hd* **Lucky Lil**[75] 3158 4-8-10 48 MichaelJStainton(5) 16 25
(R M Whitaker) *bhd: swtchd outside and hdwy 2f out: sn rdn and kpt on appr last: nrst fin* **7/1**[3]

00- **9** *3* **Deirdre's Dilemma (IRE)**[334] 5952 4-8-10 RoryMoore(5) 13 17
(G C Bravery) *towards rr tl sme late hdwy* **33/1**

4600 **10** *1/2* **Active Audience (IRE)**[23] 4728 3-8-12 42 TonyHamilton 12 16
(A Berry) *in tch: rdn along 3f out: wknd 2f out* **25/1**

00 **11** *hd* **Bond Sea Breeze (IRE)**[16] 4948 3-8-12 GylesParkin 5 15
(G R Oldroyd) *led: hdd over 4f out: rdn along 3f out: wknd fnl 2f* **40/1**

0460 **12** *2 1/2* **Stormingmichaelori**[16] 4961 3-9-3 43 (p) VHalliday 14 13
(N Wilson) *nvr bttr than midfield* **9/1**

0000 **13** *5* **Diamond Heritage**[43] 4113 4-9-3 48 (p) DeanCorby(3) 8 —
(S Parr) *a towards rr* **12/1**

50-6 **14** *1 3/4* **Cumberland Road**[250] 69 3-9-3 58 DaleGibson 1 —
(C A Mulhall) *midfield: hdwy wl over 2f out: rdn and in tch wl over 1f out: sn wknd* **11/1**

000- **15** *2 1/2* **Kincaid**[388] 4670 3-8-12 45 AndrewElliott(5) 6 —
(D W Thompson) *a towards rr* **33/1**

006 **16** *6* **Hippolyte (USA)**[27] 4635 3-8-12 50 JamieMackay 2 —
(J G Given) *chsd ldrs on inner: rdn along and wkng whn n.m.r wl over 2f out: sn in rr* **7/1**[3]

1m 27.04s (-0.32) **Going Correction** -0.125s/f (Firm)
WFA 3 from 4yo 3lb **16** Ran SP% **115.4**
Speed ratings (Par 103):96,95,94,93,92 92,87,87,83,83 83,80,74,72,69 62
CSF £56.11 TOTE £7.60: £2.20, £5.20, £9.70; EX 91.60.
Owner Mark Sumner & Partners **Bred** Larry Ryan **Trained** Scorton, N Yorks

■ The 100th career win for Cathy Gannon, champion apprentice in Ireland in 2004, but only her second since coming to Britain.

FOCUS
A dire maiden which saw the first two (stable companions) come clear. Banded-grade form.
Ailsa Official explanation: jockey said filly stumbled leaving stalls
Active Audience(IRE) Official explanation: jockey said filly suffered interference in running
Hippolyte(USA) Official explanation: trainer had no explanation for the poor form shown

5364 EUROPEAN BREEDERS FUND MAIDEN STKS 5f 212y

2:00 (2:00) (Class 5) 2-Y-O **£3,886** (£1,156; £577; £288) **Stalls** Low

Form RPR

0 **1** **Ava's World (IRE)**[11] 5095 2-8-9 GregFairley(3) 6 76
(M Johnston) *trckd ldng pair: hdwy over 2f out: rdn to ld over 1f out: kpt on wl* **11/2**[3]

0424 **2** *1 3/4* **Cadeaux Du Monde**[11] 5088 2-9-3 83 DeanMcKeown 5 76
(E J O'Neill) *cl up: effrt to chal over 2f out and ev ch tl rdn and one pce ent last* **10/11**[1]

4520 **3** *5* **Fadeyev (IRE)**[21] 4824 2-9-3 73 (p) CatherineGannon 2 61
(K A Ryan) *led: rdn along and jnd over 2f out: drvn and hdd over 1f out: sn wknd* **10/3**[2]

00 **4** *3* **Ballet Boy (IRE)**[7] 5168 2-9-3 SebSanders 1 52+
(Sir Mark Prescott) *dwlt: sn in tch: chsd ldrs and rdn over 2f out: sn one pce* **25/1**

5 *1 1/4* **Mangano** 2-9-3 TonyHamilton 4 48
(A Berry) *keen: chsd ldrs: rdn along 1/2-way: sn wknd* **50/1**

4 **6** *shd* **Bollin Fergus**[12] 5059 2-9-3 PaulMulrennan 9 48
(T D Easterby) *in tch: rdn alonga nd outpcd 1/2-way: bhd after* **10/1**

40 **7** *1 3/4* **Newport Lass (IRE)**[45] 4053 2-8-7 AndrewElliott(5) 8 38
(K R Burke) *a rr* **16/1**

0 **8** *shd* **Anybody's Guess (IRE)**[12] 5059 2-8-12 MarkLawson(5) 7 42
(J S Wainwright) *a bhd* **50/1**

1m 13.63s (-0.37) **Going Correction** -0.125s/f (Firm) **8** Ran SP% **113.6**
Speed ratings (Par 95):97,94,88,84,82 82,79,79
CSF £10.74 TOTE £7.90: £2.70, £1.10, £1.30; EX 13.80.
Owner Atlantic Racing Limited **Bred** Fortbarrington Stud **Trained** Middleham Moor, N Yorks

FOCUS
The winner showed big improvement, but it is doubtful if the second and third ran to their best. There was no strength in depth. With the runner-up having an official rating of 83 the winner's nursery mark could suffer.

NOTEBOOK
Ava's World(IRE), who is only small, was given a more patient ride. She really put her head down and battled and was right on top at the finish. (op 6-1)
Cadeaux Du Monde, rated 83, did nothing wrong but was clearly second best at the line. (op 5-4 tchd 6-4 and 11-8 in a place)
Fadeyev(IRE) took them along but in the end was firmly put in his place. This was his fifth outing and he does not seem to be progressing. (op 3-1)
Ballet Boy(IRE), a son of Sadler's Wells, was having his mandatory third outing. No doubt he will show exactly what he is capable of in handicap company over middle-distances at three. (op 28-1)
Mangano, a March foal, was very keen on his debut.
Bollin Fergus is another bred to come into his own over middle-distances at three. (op 15-2)

5365 RACING AGAIN ON TUESDAY 3RD OCTOBER (S) STKS 1m 5f 175y

2:30 (2:30) (Class 6) 3-Y-O **£2,730** (£806; £403) **Stalls** Low

Form RPR

5534 **1** **Tuscany Rose**[15] 4981 3-8-5 41 TPO'Shea 5 47
(W R Muir) *in tch: hdwy after to trck ldng pair over 5f out: effrt over 2f out: rdn to chal over 1f out: sn drvn: led on post* **7/2**[2]

0330 **2** *shd* **Myrtle Bay (IRE)**[43] 4111 3-8-10 52 SebSanders 6 52
(K R Burke) *led: rn wd bnd after 5f: hung persistently rt after: rdn along and jnd 3f out: drvn wl over 1f out: hdd on line* **6/4**[1]

3 *3 1/2* **Lucky Find (IRE)** 3-8-4 ow2 GregFairley(3) 1 44
(M Mullineaux) *towards rr: hdwy 4f out: rdn along over 2f out: kpt on under pressur appr last* **14/1**

6-06 **4** *3* **Tiltili (IRE)**[54] 3791 3-8-5 50 PaulMulrennan 10 38
(P C Haslam) *trckd ldrs: hdwy to chse ldr 6f out: chal over 3f out: sn ridden and wknd 2f out* **9/2**[3]

-006 **5** *1 1/2* **Plough Maite**[26] 4668 3-8-10 44 DaleGibson 2 41
(D E Cantillon) *prom: rdn along 5f out: sn drvn and wknd over 3f out* **16/1**

0545 **6** *4* **Rockatorri**[19] 4868 3-8-2 40 (b) DominicFox(3) 7 30
(G G Margarson) *chsd ldrs: rdn along over 3f out: wknd over 2f out* **14/1**

-000 **7** *8* **Zahara Joy**[23] 4728 3-8-6 45 ow1 GylesParkin 8 20
(D W Thompson) *a rr* **33/1**

000 **8** *24* **Northern Promise (IRE)**[18] 4909 3-8-7 40 ow2 MarkLawson(5) 3 —
(J Parkes) *a rr: bhd fnl 4f* **66/1**

5530 **9** *2* **Beauchamp Unique**[8] 3637 3-8-6 52 ow1 DeanMcKeown 4 —
(James Moffatt) *a rr: bhd fnl 4f* **8/1**

00-6 **10** *dist* **Renee Lard (IRE)**[21] 3002 3-8-6 35 ow1 TonyHamilton 11 —
(A Berry) *chsd ldr: rdn along 1/2-way: sn wknd and wl bhd fnl 4f* **80/1**

3m 3.30s (-1.20) **Going Correction** -0.125s/f (Firm) **10** Ran SP% **116.4**
Speed ratings (Par 99):98,97,95,94,93 91,86,72,71,—
CSF £9.03 TOTE £4.70: £2.00, £1.50, £2.20; EX 10.10.The winner was bought in for 9,500gns. Myrtle Bay (no.1) was claimed by J C Tuck for £6000
Owner M J Caddy **Bred** M J Caddy **Trained** Lambourn, Berks

FOCUS
A very weak affair which saw the first two come clear in a bobbing finish. It has been rated through the winner.
Beauchamp Unique Official explanation: jockey said filly lost its action

5366 DON'T MISS TOTESPORT SATURDAY 14TH OCTOBER NURSERY 7f

3:05 (3:05) (Class 4) (0-85,88) 2-Y-O **£6,477** (£1,927; £963; £481) **Stalls** Low

Form RPR

4115 **1** **Fractured Foxy**[19] 4882 2-7-7 62 oh4 NataliaGemelova(5) 11 66
(J J Quinn) *hld up: hdwy 1/2-way: chsd ldrs 2f out: rdn over 1f out: kpt on ins last to ld last 50 yds* **14/1**

6360 **2** *nk* **Atheneum (IRE)**[43] 4100 2-8-5 72 GregFairley(3) 9 75
(M Johnston) *in tch: hdwy 3f out: rdn to challeng and carried rt 1f out: led ins last: hdd and no ex last 50 yds* **11/1**

5462 **3** *1 1/4* **Nota Liberata**[16] 4955 2-8-0 64 ow1 DaleGibson 10 64
(G M Moore) *in tch: hdwy on outer wl over 2f out: rdn to chse ldrs over 1f out: kpt on same pce ins last* **17/2**

0046 **4** *hd* **Baltimore Jack (IRE)**[10] 5113 2-8-9 78 MichaelJStainton(5) 4 77
(R M Whitaker) *cl up: rdn and ev ch whn edgd rt 1f out: sn drvn and one pce* **17/2**

2012 **5** *3 1/2* **Hart Of Gold**[7] 5172 2-9-5 88 MarkLawson(5) 2 78
(M J Wallace) *led: rdn along 2f out: drvn and hdd jst ins last: wknd* **7/2**[1]

016 **6** *3* **Terry Molloy (IRE)**[21] 4813 2-8-9 73 PaulMulrennan 6 55
(K R Burke) *cl up: rdn along over 2f out: sn wknd* **20/1**

5131 **7** *nk* **Monkey Glas (IRE)**[38] 4250 2-8-11 75 SebSanders 8 56
(K R Burke) *hld up in tch on inner: pushed along and lost pl 1/2-way: sn in rr: styd on fr over 1f out: nvr a factor* **4/1**[2]

566 **8** *3 1/2* **Namarian (IRE)**[46] 4017 2-7-12 62 oh6 PaulQuinn 7 33
(T D Easterby) *bhd: sme hdwy 3f out: sn rdn and nvr nr ldrs* **66/1**

5603 **9** *4* **Obe Royal**[14] 5014 2-8-6 70 TPO'Shea 5 30
(M R Channon) *s.i.s: a rr* **13/2**[3]

1006 **10** *1/2* **Prince Rossi (IRE)**[7] 5172 2-9-1 79 TonyHamilton 3 38
(J D Bethell) *chsd ldrs: rdn along after 3f: sn wknd* **14/1**

632 **11** *nk* **Tibinta**[17] 4926 2-7-12 62 oh2 CatherineGannon 12 20
(Jedd O'Keeffe) *s.i.s: a rr* **20/1**

044 **12** *11* **Mister Lucky (FR)**[25] 4669 2-8-3 67 JamieMackay 1 —
(Sir Michael Stoute) *chsd ldrs on inner: rdn along 1/2-way: sn wknd* **9/1**

1m 25.86s (-1.50) **Going Correction** -0.125s/f (Firm) **12** Ran SP% **119.3**
Speed ratings (Par 97):103,102,101,101,97 93,93,89,84,84 83,71
CSF £156.70 CT £947.78 TOTE £22.50: £4.70, £4.30, £3.50; EX 325.70.
Owner Mrs E Wright **Bred** Bearstone Stud **Trained** Settrington, N Yorks

FOCUS
The winner was 4lb wrong, but did not need to show big improvement and the form seems sound.

NOTEBOOK
Fractured Foxy, 4lb out of the handicap, is not that big or robust but she is all heart. (op 16-1)
Atheneum(IRE), absent for six week after a poor effort on fast ground at Goodwood, was taken off a straight line as he was about to take charge. In the end he just missed out.
Nota Liberata, always making his effort on the outer, stuck on and will appreciate a mile. He is looking thoroughly exposed though. (op 8-1)
Baltimore Jack(IRE), meeting Hart Of Gold on 10lb better terms, turned round Southwell placings. He came off a straight line and got in the way of the runner-up. (op 10-1)
Hart Of Gold, very keen to get on with it, didn't get home. (op 4-1)
Monkey Glas(IRE), anchored in last place turning in, never left the inside rail. He stayed on all the way to the line but had been set an impossible task.
Obe Royal Official explanation: jockey said colt missed the break

5367 CONSTANT SECURITY SEPTEMBER STKS (H'CAP) 1m 3f 214y

3:40 (3:40) (Class 3) (0-90,87) 3-Y-O+ **£9,715** (£2,890; £1,444; £721) **Stalls** Low

Form RPR

430 **1** **Dzesmin (POL)**[31] 4469 4-8-9 75 (p) RoryMoore(5) 6 83+
(R C Guest) *hld up towards rr: hdwy on outer wl over 2f out: rdn and edgd lft 1f out: sn led and styd on wl* **16/1**

3113 **2** *1 1/2* **Go Solo**[10] 5115 5-9-12 87 DeanMcKeown 5 93
(G A Swinbank) *stmbld s: sn trcking ldrs: effrt on outer over 2f out: rdn to ld over 1f out: drvn and hdd jst ins last: kpt on* **7/2**[1]

0430 **3** 3 **Sporting Gesture**[27] 4626 9-8-12 **73** oh1 .... PaulMulrennan 10 74
(M W Easterby) *hld up in tch: hdwy over 3f out: rdn to chse ldrs wl over 1f out: swtchd lft and styd on ins last: nrest fin* **16/1**

2600 **4** ½ **Shape Up (IRE)**[10] 5115 6-8-7 **73** ....(b) MichaelJStainton(5) 3 73
(R Craggs) *a.p: hdwy to ld 3f out: sn rdn: drvn and hdd over 1f out: kpt on same pce* **33/1**

2251 **5** ¾ **Nero's Return (IRE)**[19] 4876 5-9-5 **83** .... GregFairley(3) 2 82
(M Johnston) *a.p: effrt 4f out and sn disp ld: rdn along over 2f out and ev ch tl drvn over 1f out and sn wknd* **7/2**[1]

5520 **6** hd **Torrens (IRE)**[18] 4911 4-9-0 **80** .... JamieMoriarty(5) 7 78
(R A Fahey) *hld up towards rr: hdwy wl over 2f out: rdn to chse ldrs wl over 1f out: sn wknd* **11/1**

0411 **7** ½ **Leslingtaylor (IRE)**[9] 5132 4-8-7 **75** .... SladeO'Hara(7) 4 73
(J J Quinn) *hld up towards rr: hdwy 3f out: rdn along 2f out: drvn and no imp appr last* **6/1**[2]

6104 **8** 5 **Our Teddy (IRE)**[7] 5163 6-9-8 **83** .... TPO'Shea 8 73
(P A Blockley) *hld up: a rr* **8/1**

614 **9** 11 **Dream Prize (IRE)**[8] 5152 3-8-12 **81** .... JamieMackay 9 53
(Sir Michael Stoute) *s.i.s: a towards rr* **7/1**[3]

0016 **10** 1 **Highest Regard**[38] 4259 4-8-5 **73** oh5 ....(t) AshleyHamblett(7) 11 43
(N P McCormack) *led: rdn along 4f out: hdd 3f out: sn drvn and wknd fnl 2f* **50/1**

0004 **11** 1 **Cool Hunter**[41] 4175 5-9-8 **83** .... SebSanders 1 52
(W R Swinburn) *trckd ldrs: effrt 3f out: rdn over 2f out and sn wknd* **17/2**

2m 34.89s (-4.11) **Going Correction** -0.125s/f (Firm)
WFA 3 from 4yo+ 8lb **11** Ran SP% **117.9**
Speed ratings (Par 107):108,107,105,104,104 104,103,100,93,92 91
CSF £71.60 CT £937.28 TOTE £23.40: £4.40, £2.50, £3.70; EX 148.70.
Owner JAS Partnership **Bred** Marian Pokrywka **Trained** Brancepeth, Co Durham

FOCUS
A very competitive handicap for the track, run at a solid pace. The winner took advantage of a good mark and the second produced another slightly improved effort.

NOTEBOOK
Dzesmin(POL), a triple crown winner in Poland last year, bounced back to form and readily opened his account for current connections at the fourth attempt. The drop back in trip proved to his liking and he has clearly slipped to a decent mark now. He will not mind the return to a slightly stiffer test either. (op 20-1)
Go Solo soon recovered from a tardy start and came through to hold every chance entering the final furlong. He was ultimately outstayed by the winner, but this was a solid effort under top weight and he has developed into a most consistent performer this term. (op 10-3)
Sporting Gesture was doing his best work towards the finish, as can often be the case nowadays, and ran one of his better races. He remains on a lengthy losing run. (op 20-1)
Shape Up(IRE) posted a return to form, despite still looking a little tricky, and may be able to build on this.
Nero's Return(IRE), raised 4lb for scoring at Epsom last time, was given a positive ride and simply looked found out by the higher mark. (tchd 4-1)
Leslingtaylor(IRE), bidding for the hat-trick, simply got found out by a 7lb higher mark on this return to fast ground. Official explanation: jockey said gelding hung right-handed throughout (tchd 13-2)

5368 BOOK RACEDAY HOSPITALITY ON 01748 810165 MAIDEN STKS (DIV II) 7f
4:10 (4:11) (Class 5) 3-4-Y-O £2,590 (£770; £385; £192) **Stalls** Low

Form RPR

0-02 **1** **Ebraam (USA)**[11] 5093 3-9-3 65 .... SebSanders 4 72+
(E A L Dunlop) *trckd ldrs: hdwy to ld wl over 1f out: sn clr: easily* **4/6**[1]

24 **2** 3½ **Contemplation**[113] 1988 3-9-3 .... DeanMcKeown 10 58+
(G A Swinbank) *stdd s: hld up in rr: hdwy 2f out: styd on ins last nrst fin* **11/2**[2]

-000 **3** shd **Little Britain (USA)**[19] 4884 3-8-12 53 .... JamieMoriarty(5) 8 58
(J Howard Johnson) *midfield: hdwy on outer over 2f out: sn rdn and styd on ins last: nrst fin* **33/1**

40 **4** 3½ **Mrs Quince**[42] 4155 4-8-12 .... GregFairley(3) 16 43
(F Watson) *a.p: rdn along over 2f out: kpt on same pce* **33/1**

0500 **5** ½ **Quintin**[23] 4728 3-8-12 43 .... PaulMulrennan 13 42
(T D Easterby) *in tch: hdwy to chse ldrs 2f out: sn rdn and no imp* **12/1**

3030 **6** 3 **Primarily**[5] 5243 4-9-6 50 .... TonyHamilton 1 39
(A Berry) *chsd ldrs on inner: rdn along wl over 2f out: sn btn* **13/2**[3]

00 **7** 1 **City Miss**[11] 5077 3-8-7 .... AndrewElliott(5) 14 31
(Miss L A Perratt) *nvr nr ldrs* **100/1**

-000 **8** nk **Chilsdown**[52] 3835 3-8-10 54 .... AshleyHamblett(7) 6 35
(Ronald Thompson) *a towards rr* **33/1**

6006 **9** 2½ **Born For Diamonds (IRE)**[28] 4611 4-8-10 40(v[1]) MichaelJStainton(5) 15 24
(R E Barr) *keen: cl up: rdn to ld briefly 2f out: sn wknd* **40/1**

500- **10** 1¼ **Regal Lass**[346] 5696 3-8-12 49 .... JamieMackay 11 20
(J G Given) *a towards rr* **16/1**

000P **11** 6 **Madam Moschata**[53] 3814 3-8-7 43 .... MarkLawson(5) 2 4
(D W Barker) *a rr* **50/1**

00 **12** 1¼ **Height Of Esteem**[19] 4899 3-9-0 .... JohnMcAuley(3) 5 6
(M Mullineaux) *led: rdn along and hdd 2f out: sn wknd* **66/1**

13 5 **Sheriff Star** 3-8-5 .... DanielleMcCreery(7) 7 —
(N Tinkler) *v.s.a: a bhd* **50/1**

14 5 **Bond Silver Strand (IRE)** 3-8-12 .... GylesParkin 17 —
(P D Niven) *v.s.a: a bhd* **66/1**

1m 26.55s (-0.81) **Going Correction** -0.125s/f (Firm)
WFA 3 from 4yo 3lb **14** Ran SP% **121.4**
Speed ratings (Par 103):99,95,94,90,90 86,85,85,82,81 74,72,67,61
CSF £4.13 TOTE £1.50: £1.10, £1.60, £7.60; EX 5.30.
Owner Hamdan Al Maktoum **Bred** Shadwell Farm LLC **Trained** Newmarket, Suffolk

FOCUS
A very modest maiden with the third, officially rated just 53, limiting the form. The time was a stone faster than division one of this event.

5369 RICHMOND H'CAP 1m 7f 177y
4:45 (4:45) (Class 6) (0-65,63) 3-Y-0+ £2,730 (£806; £403) **Stalls** Low

Form RPR

6350 **1** **Let It Be**[5] 5242 5-9-10 **59** .... DNolan(3) 17 68
(K G Reveley) *hld up towards rr: stdy hdwy over 4f out: rdn to chse ldr whn lft in ld 1 1/2f out: kpt on ins last* **14/1**

0001 **2** 1 **Esprit De Corps**[5] 5242 4-10-3 **63** 6ex .... SebSanders 12 73+
(Sir Mark Prescott) *trckd ldrs: hdwy to ld 4f out: rdn along whn swvd bdly rt and hdd 1 1/2f out: kpt on u.p ins last* **4/5**[1]

4213 **3** nk **Parchment (IRE)**[16] 4960 4-9-6 **57** ....(b) MarkLawson(5) 15 65
(A J Lockwood) *hld up in rr: hdwy on outer over 3f out: rdn 2f out: styd on wl fnl f: nrst fin* **10/1**[3]

1230 **4** 2 **High Frequency (IRE)**[33] 4423 5-8-6 **45** ....(p) SladeO'Hara(7) 16 50
(A Crook) *in tch: hdwy 6f out: rdn to chse ldr 2f out: sn drvn and one pce* **33/1**

0134 **5** 1¾ **True (IRE)**[11] 5080 5-9-3 **49** .... TonyHamilton 11 52
(Mrs S Lamyman) *hld up in rr: hdwy over 3f out: rdn and styd on fnl 2f: nrst fin* **12/1**

5000 **6** hd **Indian Girl**[19] 4868 3-8-3 **47** .... DaleGibson 14 50
(M R Channon) *hld up in rr: hdwy over 3f out: rdn along on outer 2f out: kpt on ins last: nrst fin* **25/1**

2-00 **7** 5 **Dan's Heir**[16] 4947 4-9-4 **57** ....(p) AshleyHamblett(7) 6 54
(P C Haslam) *hld up towards rr: hdwy over 3f out: rdn and no imp fnl 2f* **40/1**

3414 **8** 2 **Onyergo (IRE)**[16] 4954 4-9-4 **55** .... AndrewElliott(5) 7 49
(J R Weymes) *chsd ldrs: rdn along 4f out: wknd 3f out* **11/1**

0603 **9** 3 **Just Waz (USA)**[18] 4914 4-8-13 **50** ....(p) MichaelJStainton(5) 9 41
(R M Whitaker) *keen: prom: rdn along wl over 3f out: sn wknd* **10/1**[3]

3205 **10** 1¼ **Shamrock Bay**[21] 4393 4-10-0 **60** .... JamieMackay 8 49
(C R Dore) *a towards rr* **40/1**

3035 **11** nk **Hugs Destiny (IRE)**[16] 4954 5-9-0 **53** .... MCGeran(7) 4 42
(M A Barnes) *in tch: rdn along wl over 3f out: sn wknd* **20/1**

0 **12** 2 **Urban Freeway (IRE)**[30] 4511 7-8-13 **52** .... NeilBrown(7) 13 39
(Robert Gray) *chsd ldrs on outer: rdn along 3f out: sn wknd* **50/1**

-005 **13** 9 **Oulan Bator (FR)**[11] 5080 6-8-12 **49** .... JamieMoriarty(5) 2 25
(R A Fahey) *prom: rdn along over 4f out: sn w eakened* **33/1**

0000 **14** 2 **William Tell (IRE)**[19] 4380 4-9-8 **57** .... GregFairley(3) 3 30
(Micky Hammond) *dwlt: a rr* **40/1**

0302 **15** 5 **Irish Ballad**[33] 4438 4-9-9 **55** ....(t) DeanMcKeown 10 22
(W R Swinburn) *led: rdn along and hdd 4f out: wknd qckly* **8/1**[2]

3m 29.92s (-1.48) **Going Correction** -0.125s/f (Firm)
WFA 3 from 4yo+ 12lb **15** Ran SP% **131.3**
Speed ratings (Par 101):98,97,97,96,95 95,92,91,90,89 89,88,84,83,80
CSF £25.91 CT £148.26 TOTE £20.20: £5.00, £1.70, £3.40; EX 58.00.
Owner A Frame **Bred** Sir Eric Parker **Trained** Lingdale, Redcar & Cleveland

FOCUS
A moderate staying handicap which was run at a fair gallop. The overall form seems sound.

5370 CATTERICKBRIDGE.CO.UK FILLIES' H'CAP 7f
5:15 (5:15) (Class 6) (0-60,60) 3-Y-0+ £2,730 (£806; £403) **Stalls** Low

Form RPR

1031 **1** **Sapphire Storm (IRE)**[23] 4728 3-8-7 **54** .... RoryMoore(5) 7 60
(P T Midgley) *trckd ldrs: hdwy over 2f out: rdn to ld and edgd rt over 1f out: drvn: edgd lft and kpt on wl* **8/1**[2]

1303 **2** shd **Walnut Grove**[23] 4728 3-8-9 **54** .... BenSwarbrick(3) 12 60
(T D Barron) *chsd ldrs: hdwy on outer over 2f out: rdn to chal over 1f out and ev ch tl drvn and no ex towards nr fin* **9/1**[3]

4602 **3** 1¼ **Outrageous Flirt (IRE)**[12] 5062 4-8-7 **51** .... MarkLawson(5) 3 53
(A Dickman) *midfield: hdwy 1/2-way: rdn to chse ldrs wl over 1f out: kpt on u.p ins last* **13/2**[1]

2350 **4** ¾ **Some Diva**[17] 4930 3-9-2 **58** .... SebSanders 10 62+
(W R Swinburn) *trckd ldrs: effrt over 2f out and ev ch tl rdn and hld whn squeezed out ent last: kpt on same pce* **8/1**[2]

2506 **5** ½ **Discotheque (USA)**[3] 5302 3-9-1 **60** .... DeanCorby(3) 5 59
(P Howling) *s.i.s and bhd: gd hdwy over 2f out: rdn and chsng ldrs whn n.m.r ent last: kpt on* **14/1**

6040 **6** 1¼ **Safranine (IRE)**[7] 5171 9-8-13 **57** .... AnnStokell(5) 13 53
(Miss A Stokell) *s.i.s and bhd: hdwy on outer 2f out: sn rdn and kpt on ins last: nrst fin* **14/1**

-000 **7** shd **Kudbeme**[23] 4733 4-9-0 **60** .... SuzzanneFrance(7) 14 55+
(N Bycroft) *s.i.s and bhd tl styd on fnlo 2f: nrst fin* **16/1**

-F02 **8** ¾ **Zell (IRE)**[19] 4891 3-8-13 **60** .... MichaelJStainton(5) 16 53
(E J Alston) *midfield: hdwy over 2f out: rdn and in tch over 1f out: sn no imp* **12/1**

6460 **9** ½ **Tagula Bay (IRE)**[12] 5060 4-8-12 **51** .... TonyHamilton 6 43
(T D Easterby) *in tch on inner: hdwy to chse ldrs over 2f out: snm rdn and one pce* **8/1**[2]

4324 **10** 1¾ **Spark Up**[16] 4974 6-8-11 **50** ....(b) JamieMackay 15 37
(J W Unett) *dwlt and bhd: hdwy on outer over 2f out: sn rdn and kpt on: nt rch ldrs* **8/1**[2]

0 **11** 2½ **Pistol Dawn**[19] 4892 3-9-1 **60** .... DNolan(3) 11 40
(J J Quinn) *midfield: rdn along over 2f out and sn lost pl* **25/1**

0506 **12** 1¼ **Takanewa (IRE)**[19] 4881 3-8-13 **55** .... PaulMulrennan 8 32
(J Howard Johnson) *in tch: hdwy to ld 3f out: rdn and hdd wl over 1f out: wknd* **25/1**

0000 **13** 1½ **Rosthwaite (IRE)**[29] 4548 3-8-5 **54** .... AshleyHamblett(7) 4 27
(Ronald Thompson) *a rr* **33/1**

5-30 **14** ½ **Glamaraazi (IRE)**[16] 4948 3-8-9 **56** .... JamieMoriarty(5) 2 28
(R A Fahey) *cl up: rdn along over 2f out: sn wknd* **9/1**[3]

0040 **15** 4 **Bond Angel Eyes**[20] 4835 3-8-12 **54** ....(v[1]) GylesParkin 17 15
(G R Oldroyd) *s.i.s: a bhd* **40/1**

0/30 **16** 5 **Charlottebutterfly**[29] 4554 6-8-8 **50** .... GregFairley(3) 1 —
(P J McBride) *led: rdn along 1/2-way: sn hdd & wknd* **13/2**[1]

1m 26.26s (-1.10) **Going Correction** -0.125s/f (Firm)
WFA 3 from 4yo+ 3lb **16** Ran SP% **131.1**
Speed ratings (Par 98):101,100,99,98,98 96,96,95,95,93 90,88,87,86,81 76
CSF £81.42 CT £535.77 TOTE £5.40: £1.70, £2.70, £1.90, £2.00; EX 41.10 Place 6 £88.81, Place 5 £23.88.
Owner J F Wright **Bred** Dermot Farrington **Trained** Westow, N Yorks

■ Stewards' Enquiry : Rory Moore three-day ban: careless riding (Sep 27-28, Oct 2)

FOCUS
A ragged start to this low-grade fillies' handicap. The level of the form is sound, the winner back to her juvenile best.

T/Plt: £130.90 to a £1 stake. Pool: £40,418.85. 225.30 winning tickets. T/Qpdt: £73.60 to a £1 stake. Pool: £2,079.70. 20.90 winning tickets. JR

5339 NEWBURY (L-H)

Saturday, September 16

OFFICIAL GOING: Good

Wind: Virtually nil

5371 DUBAI DUTY FREE GOLF WORLD CUP MAIDEN STKS 6f 8y

1:50 (1:53) (Class 4) 2-Y-O **£6,477** (£1,927; £963; £481) **Stalls** Centre

Form				RPR
2	1		**Thunder Storm Cat (USA)**[17] 4934 2-9-3 .... JoeFanning 10 (P F I Cole) *swtg: trckd ldrs: led jst ins fnl 2f: drvn and r.o strly fnl f: comf* **6/1**[3]	89
423	2	1 ¼	**Longquan (IRE)**[106] 2185 2-9-3 84 .... JimmyFortune 16 (P J Makin) *pressed ldrs:slt ld over 3f out: hdd jst ins fnl 2f:hrd drvn ins last and kpt on but a hld by wnr* **11/2**[2]	85
	3	¾	**Siamese Cat (IRE)** 2-8-12 .... LPKeniry 6 (B J Meehan) *neat: lw: in tch: rdn halfdway: styd on to chse ldrs over 1f out: kpt on cl home but nvr gng pce to chal* **40/1**	78
44	4	shd	**Endiamo (IRE)**[99] 2402 2-9-3 .... MartinDwyer 11 (M P Tregoning) *sn in tch: drvn 3f out: swtchd rt 2f out: hdwy u.p over 1f out: kpt on ins last but nvr gng pce to chal* **5/4**[1]	83
36	5	3 ½	**Cool Box (USA)**[30] 4525 2-9-3 .... KerrinMcEvoy 13 (Mrs A J Perrett) *slt ld tl hdd over 3f out: styd pressing ldrs and rdn over 2f out: wknd ins last* **16/1**	72
	6	¾	**Cinquante Cinq (IRE)** 2-8-12 .... SteveDrowne 1 (B J Meehan) *cmpt: b.bkwd: slowly away: t.k.h and sn prom: chsd ldrs and rdn 2f out: wknd fnl f* **20/1**	65
	7	nk	**Rasaman (IRE)** 2-9-3 .... PhilipRobinson 14 (M A Jarvis) *chsd ldrs: chal 3f out tl over 2f out: wknd fnl f* **9/1**	69
	8	1 ¼	**Ravinia (USA)** 2-8-12 .... RobertWinston 15 (B J Meehan) *cmpt: str: scope: sn chsng ldrs: rdn over 2f out and styd on one pce* **20/1**	60+
00	9	shd	**Alittlebitleft (IRE)**[9] 5125 2-9-3 .... RichardHughes 7 (R Hannon) *bhd: pushed along over 2f out: kpt on fnl f but nvr in contention* **33/1**	65
	10	nk	**Tivers Jewel (USA)** 2-9-3 .... PaulEddery 17 (Mrs A J Perrett) *tall: str: scope: bwkd: s.i.s: bhd: rdn 1/2-way: kpt on ins last but nvr in contention* **50/1**	64
0	11	hd	**Lordswood (IRE)**[72] 3222 2-9-3 .... JohnEgan 4 (A M Balding) *mid-div: rdn along 1/2-way and sn n.d* **20/1**	63
0	12	3 ½	**Affiliation (IRE)**[16] 4964 2-8-12 .... DaneO'Neill 8 (R Hannon) *outpcd most of way* **100/1**	48
6	13	1 ¾	**Majestic Cheer**[14] 5020 2-9-3 .... TedDurcan 2 (M R Channon) *chsd ldrs: rdn over 2f out: sn btn* **18/1**	48
	14	1	**Cosimo Primo** 2-9-3 .... RichardThomas 3 (J A Geake) *w'like: s.i.s: a outpcd* **50/1**	45
	15	½	**Double Banded (IRE)** 2-9-3 .... MichaelHills 9 (J L Dunlop) *leggy: unf: slowly away: a outpcd* **25/1**	43
0	16	¾	**Arthur's Edge**[9] 5125 2-9-3 .... DarryllHolland 5 (B Palling) *broke wl: sn bhd* **100/1**	41

1m 13.02s (-1.30) **Going Correction** -0.225s/f (Firm) **16** Ran SP% **124.7**

Speed ratings (Par 97):99,97,96,96,91 90,90,88,88,87 87,83,80,79,78 77

CSF £35.95 TOTE £5.80: £2.30, £2.40, £6.40; EX 35.60.

Owner Miss Alfiya Shaykhutdinova **Bred** Gaines-Gentry T/Breds & Overbrook Farm **Trained** Whatcombe, Oxon

FOCUS

Not many of these have fancy entries, but it still looked an above-average maiden and it should produce winners. They appeared to go a decent pace from the start, and the winning time was good, though understandably slightly slower than the following nursery and well over a second slower than the Mill Reef.

NOTEBOOK

Thunder Storm Cat(USA) ◆, a pleasing second to a nice type in a decent seven-furlong maiden at Wolverhampton on his debut, confirmed the promise of that effort with a ready success, proving far from inconvenienced by the drop back in trip and switch to turf. He got himself warm beforehand, but there were never any worries in the race itself and he sustained his challenge in determined style to ultimately win quite nicely. Paul Cole thinks he will be even better on quicker ground and said he will have one more run this season. (tchd 13-2)

Longquan(IRE), second to Strategic Prince at Salisbury before disappointing slightly when favourite for a maiden at Bath, was returning from a 106-day break and ran well. An official mark of 84 is unlikely to make things easy when he switches to handicaps, but he can surely find a maiden before then. (op 6-1 tchd 13-2 in a place)

Siamese Cat(IRE) ◆, a 70,000gns first foal of an unraced half-sister to some high-class performers in the US, was one of three fillies introduced by Brian Meehan in a race contested mainly by colts and was the least fancied of the trio according to the market. However, she acquitted herself with real credit, faring best of the newcomers and offered plenty of promise for the future. She is open to loads of improvement and ought to go close next time, especially if switched to fillies' only company.

Endiamo(IRE), returning from a 99-day break, had to be switched with his effort and never really looked like picking up sufficiently. He races as though in need of a step up in trip, but there is not much stamina in his pedigree and it remains to be seen just what his optimum trip will turn out to be. (op 7-4 tchd 15-8 in places)

Cool Box(USA), dropped back in trip, ran creditably enough but was well held. He will have more options now he is qualified for a handicap mark and might benefit from a step back up in distance.

Cinquante Cinq(IRE) ◆, a sister to Three Secrets, a useful seven furlong/miler, and half-sister to top-class sprinter Carmine Lake, out of a six-furlong juvenile winner, ran with promise against the colts on her racecourse debut. She should be all the better for this experience and is probably worth keeping on side.

Rasaman(IRE), a 72,000gns first foal of a half-sister to the top-class Rakti, made a respectable introduction and is open to improvement. (op 7-1)

Ravinia(USA), a sister to a sprint winner in the US, was the third home of the Meehan trio and is likely to be better for the outing. (op 16-1)

Alittlebitleft(IRE) ◆, dropped a furlong in trip, was a real eye-catcher, staying on nicely in the closing stages without ever posing a threat to the principals. The Stewards looked into his running and noted Richard Hughes' explanation that the colt is lazy at home and a scratchy mover, and that he had to ride him to get home. He will have to be of interest when sent handicapping, although he will have gone into many a notebook off the back of this effort and might be a false price next time. Official explanation: jockey said, regarding the running and riding, his orders were that as colt is lazy at home and a scratchy mover, he had to ride it to get it home, adding that it broke well but, because of its action, he gave it time to warm up; trainer added that colt had been disappointing in its first two runs over 7f (op 40-1)

5372 UPLANDS RACING NURSERY 6f 8y

2:25 (2:26) (Class 2) 2-Y-O

£12,464 (£3,732; £1,866; £934; £466; £234) **Stalls** Centre

Form				RPR
2052	1		**Captain Marvelous (IRE)**[21] 4789 2-9-7 95 .... MichaelHills 13 (B W Hills) *lw: s.i.s: hld up rr but in tch: rapid hdwy over 1f out to ld ins last: kpt on wl* **20/1**	101
3120	2	½	**Oi Vay Joe (IRE)**[22] 4766 2-8-8 82 .... KerrinMcEvoy 1 (W Jarvis) *hld up in tch: hdwy over 1f out: qcknd to chse wnr ins last but nvr quite gng pce to chal* **12/1**	87
21	3	1 ¼	**Leopard King (USA)**[20] 4843 2-9-0 88 .... RobertWinston 4 (Sir Michael Stoute) *pressed ldrs tl slt ld fr 2f out: sn rdn: hdd ins last: sn one pce* **4/1**[1]	89
4100	4	nk	**Okikoki**[22] 4766 2-8-6 80 ....(b[1]) RichardMullen 11 (W R Muir) *pressed ldrs: chal fr 3f out tl jst ins fnl f: kpt on same pce* **50/1**	80
3342	5	½	**Part Timer (IRE)**[9] 5139 2-8-13 87 .... TedDurcan 2 (M R Channon) *chsd ldrs: rdn to chal fr over 2f out tl jst ins last: kpt on same pce* **16/1**	86
224	6	shd	**Non Compliant**[17] 4934 2-8-7 81 .... JohnEgan 15 (J W Hills) *rr but in tch: rdn over 2f out: hdwy over 1f out: styd on ins last but nvr gng pce to rch ldrs* **6/1**	79
3216	7	¾	**Lipocco**[23] 4736 2-9-5 93 .... GeorgeBaker 9 (R M Beckett) *hld up in tch: shkn up 2f out: no imp on ldrs fr over 1f out* **11/2**[3]	89
01	8	shd	**Sylvan (IRE)**[22] 4774 2-7-9 76 .... FrankiePickard[(7)] 6 (S Kirk) *chsd ldrs: rdn 1/2-way: outpcd 2f out: swtchd lft over 1f out: kpt on again ins last* **12/1**	72
214	9	1	**Beauchamp Viceroy**[21] 4804 2-8-5 79 .... JoeFanning 12 (G A Butler) *chsd ldrs: rdn 1/2-way: wknd ins fnl f* **28/1**	72
2411	10	¾	**Cheap Street**[22] 4766 2-8-11 85 .... TPQueally 14 (J G Portman) *hld up rr but in tch: rdn 2f out: styd on ins last but nvr gng pce to rch ldrs* **5/1**[2]	75
1401	11	nk	**El Bosque (IRE)**[21] 4815 2-9-4 92 .... DaneO'Neill 5 (B R Millman) *lw: led 4f out: rdn 3f out: hdd 2f out: wknd over 1f out* **12/1**	82
5320	12	½	**King's Bastion (IRE)**[42] 4146 2-9-0 88 .... HayleyTurner 8 (M L W Bell) *chsd ldrs: rdn and n.m.r 2f out: sn btn* **40/1**	76
4130	13	1 ½	**Fish Called Johnny**[23] 4736 2-9-1 89 .... RichardHughes 10 (B J Meehan) *s.i.s: bhd: rdn and hdwy 1/2-way: nvr gng pce to rch ldrs: wknd ins fnl 2f* **12/1**	73
6030	14	hd	**Ron In Ernest**[31] 4480 2-7-5 72 oh5 .... LukeMorris[(7)] 7 (J A Geake) *led 2f: wknd 2f out* **100/1**	55
3164	15	¾	**Crystal Gazer (FR)**[8] 5157 2-8-3 77 .... MartinDwyer 3 (R Hannon) *chsd ldrs 4f* **33/1**	58

1m 12.87s (-1.45) **Going Correction** -0.225s/f (Firm) **15** Ran SP% **119.5**

Speed ratings (Par 101):100,99,97,97,96 96,95,95,94,93 92,91,89,89,88

CSF £229.75 CT £1191.39 TOTE £19.30: £4.30, £4.70, £2.10; EX 329.70 Trifecta £370.30 Part won. Pool: £521.58 - 0.10 winning units..

Owner R J Arculli **Bred** Duncan A McGregor **Trained** Lambourn, Berks

FOCUS

Traditionally a decent nursery, and this latest renewal was very competitive. The winning time was slightly quicker than the maiden won by Thunder Storm Cat, but over a second slower than the Mill Reef. The fourth and fifth set the standard and the first three all showed improved form.

NOTEBOOK

Captain Marvelous(IRE) had no easy task carrying top weight on his nursery debut, but he made light of that with a very useful performance, showing much improved form. Again slowly away, he travelled like a dream well out the back before displaying a smart change of pace to get to the front. He may now go for the Rockingham Stakes at York. (op 25-1)

Oi Vay Joe(IRE) was very disappointing in a Sales race at Newmarket on his previous start, but he showed that running to be all wrong with a good effort in second. He had to be switched with his challenge, but did not look unlucky.

Leopard King(USA), a Middle Park and Dewhurst entry, could not follow up his Yarmouth maiden success but ran a good race nonetheless off a mark arguably stiff enough considering what he has actually achieved to date. There should be more to come. (op 11-4)

Okikoki returned to form in first-time blinkers and should remain competitive off this sort of mark, providing the headgear continues to have a positive effect.

Part Timer(IRE), a tough sort, ran well on his return to nursery company and looks a typical Channon juvenile, thriving on a busy campaign. (op 50-1)

Non Compliant, a beaten favourite in maiden company at Wolverhampton on his last two starts, including over seven furlongs last time, ran a respectable race dropped back in trip and returned to turf. He has some useful form to his name and could be hard to beat if returned to maiden company against average opposition.

Lipocco, returned to nursery company, could not reproduce the form he showed behind Doctor Brown in a Sales race at York on his previous start. (tchd 6-1)

Cheap Street was making his nursery debut off what looked a fair enough mark, but he was well below the form he showed when winning a Sales race at Newmarket on his previous start and failed in his hat-trick attempt. (op 15-2)

El Bosque(IRE) Official explanation: jockey said colt hung right

5373 DUBAI DUTY FREE MILL REEF STKS (GROUP 2) 6f 8y

2:55 (2:57) (Class 1) 2-Y-O

£39,746 (£15,064; £7,539; £3,759; £1,883; £945) **Stalls** Centre

Form				RPR
1133	1		**Excellent Art**[27] 4644 2-9-1 .... KerrinMcEvoy 4 (N A Callaghan) *trckd ldrs: led gng wl jst ins fnl 2f: hld on gamely whn strly chal ins fnl f: carried rt cl home: all out* **15/8**[2]	113
121	2	shd	**Doctor Brown**[23] 4736 2-9-1 106 .... JimmyFortune 3 (B J Meehan) *chsd ldrs: rdn to chse wnr ins fnl 2f: str chal ins last and edgd rt: styd upsides: no ex last stride* **6/4**[1]	113
0301	3	3 ½	**Dubai Builder**[25] 4681 2-9-1 86 .... JohnEgan 5 (J S Moore) *lw: rr but in tch: rdn 1/2-way: swtchd lft and hdwy appr fnl f: kpt on ins last but nvr gng pce to rch ldrs* **12/1**	102
6132	4	5	**Bahama Mama (IRE)**[8] 5154 2-8-12 102 .... DarryllHolland 6 (J Noseda) *swtg: chsd ldrs: rdn over 2f out: sn btn* **7/2**[3]	84+
1310	5	7	**Chin Wag (IRE)**[20] 4850 2-9-1 93 .... RichardMullen 1 (E S McMahon) *w ldrs over 2f: rdn 1/2-way: wknd qckly 2f out* **40/1**	66
4500	6	10	**Dazed And Amazed**[23] 4736 2-9-1 96 ....(t) RichardHughes 7 (R Hannon) *lw: sn led: headed and wknd jst ins fnl 2f* **20/1**	36

1m 11.68s (-2.64) **Going Correction** -0.225s/f (Firm) **6** Ran SP% **111.9**

Speed ratings (Par 107):108,107,103,96,87 73

CSF £5.03 TOTE £2.70: £1.70, £1.60; EX 4.80 Trifecta £29.50 Pool: £362.50 - 8.70 winning units..

Owner Matthew Green **Bred** Cheveley Park Stud Ltd **Trained** Newmarket, Suffolk

FOCUS

A slightly disappointing turnout numerically, but both Excellent Art and Doctor Brown had some very smart form to their name coming into this and fought out a cracking finish, so this year's Mill Reef looked up to scratch. Dubai Builder had an official rating of just 86, but is clearly much better than that mark suggests and should not be used to hold the form down. They went a really good pace and the winning time was very good, well over a second quicker than both the earlier maiden and nursery.

NOTEBOOK

Excellent Art, third in both the Railway Stakes and the Prix Morny (his trainer is of the opinion he would have been second in France had he not stumbled), gained a deserved first Group-race success, but was made to work very hard indeed. Always travelling strongly off the fast pace, he probably found himself in front much sooner than was ideal and his rider decided to hang on to him, rather than commit for home, which meant he could never get away from Doctor Brown when the race got serious. All things considered, he looks a little bit better than the bare form. Neville Callaghan said that if runs again this season it will be over seven furlongs in the Dewhurst, as he thinks six furlongs is on the sharp side for him now. (op 2-1 tchd 9-4 in a place)

Doctor Brown ◆, whose York Sales race success is working out very well, ran a cracker stepped up to Group company for the first time, just losing out by the narrowest margin. He was well clear of the remainder and looks a fine sprint prospect for next season. (op 13-8)

Dubai Builder, a decisive winner of a York nursery off a mark of 75 on his previous start, left that form well behind with a fine effort behind two very smart performers. Having been well held in three runs in maiden company, this was only really the second time he has had a serious race and there should be more improvement to come. (tchd 11-1)

Bahama Mama(IRE), returned to six furlongs, ran nowhere near the form she showed when second in the Flying Childers at York on her previous start and this might have come too soon. Official explanation: jockey said filly lost its action (op 3-1)

Chin Wag(IRE) was struggling from an early stage and looked out of his depth.

Dazed And Amazed looked to go off too fast in a first-time tongue-tie. He has beaten just one horse home on his last three starts. (op 28-1)

5374 JOHN SMITH'S STKS (HERITAGE H'CAP) 1m 2f 6y

3:30 (3:31) (Class 2) (0-105,104) 3-Y-O+

£62,320 (£18,660; £9,330; £4,670; £2,330; £1,170) **Stalls** Low

Form				RPR
1-46	**1**		**Pinpoint (IRE)**[87] 2742 4-9-3 **94** ... TedDurcan 16 (W R Swinburn) *hld up in rr: hdwy fcrom 3f out: str run u.p fr 2f out: led fnl 110yds: drvn out* **7/1**[2]	104
0-31	**2**	¾	**Charlie Cool**[37] 4298 3-9-2 **99** ... KerrinMcEvoy 20 (W J Haggas) *hld up in rr: rapid hdwy on outside over 3f out: chsd wnr wl ins last but no imp cl home* **9/2**[1]	107+
1114	**3**	½	**Formal Decree (GER)**[20] 4833 3-9-0 **97** ... DarryllHolland 19 (G A Swinbank) *lw: hld up in rr: hdwy on outside over 2f out: nt clr run wl over 1f out: kpt on strly fnl f but no imp on ldrs cl home* **9/1**[3]	105
1011	**4**	*nk*	**Dansili Dancer**[35] 4359 4-9-8 **99** ... DaneO'Neill 6 (C G Cox) *chsd ldrs: rdn over 2f out: led appr fnl f: hdd and no ex fnl 110yds* **9/1**[3]	106
5104	**5**	½	**Great Plains**[35] 4359 4-9-6 **97** ... RichardHughes 18 (Mrs A J Perrett) *led: rdn fr 3f out: kpt slt advantage tl hdd appr fnl f: kpt on same pce* **25/1**	103
1032	**6**	*nk*	**Pearly King (USA)**[20] 4833 3-9-1 **98** ... RobertWinston 15 (Sir Michael Stoute) *mid-div: rdn and hdwy fr 3f out: kpt on fr over 1f out but nvr gng pce to press ldrs* **9/2**[1]	103
1514	**7**	*nk*	**Blue Bajan (IRE)**[21] 4810 4-8-13 **90** ... PaulEddery 12 (Andrew Turnell) *hld up in rr: nt clr run and hmpd 2f out: swtchd rt to outside over 1f out: fin wl: nt rcvr* **20/1**	95+
2304	**8**	¾	**Bravo Maestro (USA)**[14] 5018 5-9-4 **95** ...(b[1]) GeorgeBaker 10 (N P Littmoden) *bhd: hdwy over 2f out: swtchd rt to outside over 1f out: fin wl but nt rch ldrs* **20/1**	98+
1000	**9**	*nk*	**Fortunate Isle (USA)**[19] 4889 4-8-12 **89** ... MichaelHills 3 (B W Hills) *lw: mid-div: hdwy on ins fr 4f out: chsd ldrs 2f out: styd on same pce ins last* **33/1**	92
2200	**10**	*nk*	**Desert Realm (IRE)**[7] 5165 3-8-8 **98** ... WilliamCarson[(7)] 11 (M Johnston) *mid-div 5f out: shkn up over 2f out: kpt on ins last: nt rch ldrs* **50/1**	100
3252	**11**	*shd*	**Humungous (IRE)**[7] 5165 3-9-0 **97** ... JimmyFortune 5 (C R Egerton) *chsd ldr: rdn 3f out: wknd fnl f* **33/1**	99
0400	**12**	1 ¾	**Ofaraby**[24] 4711 6-9-8 **99** ... PhilipRobinson 4 (M A Jarvis) *lw: chsd ldrs: rdn over 2f out: wknd ins fnl f* **22/1**	98
0344	**13**	¾	**Palomar (USA)**[24] 4711 4-9-10 **101** ...(p) SteveDrowne 17 (R Charlton) *hld up in rr: hdwy and nt clr run 2f out: styng on whn bdly hmpd again 1f out: kpt on cl home but nt rcvr* **16/1**	106+
0201	**14**	½	**Crime Scene (IRE)**[9] 5141 3-9-0 **97** 5ex ... JoeFanning 9 (M Johnston) *chsd ldrs: rdn 3f out: wknd fnl f* **16/1**	93
1002	**15**	1 ½	**Classic Punch (IRE)**[19] 4877 3-9-7 **104** ... JohnEgan 14 (D R C Elsworth) *lw: chsd ldrs: rdn over 3f out: wkng whn hmpd 2f out* **16/1**	98
0005	**16**	¾	**Courageous Duke (USA)**[48] 3971 7-9-6 **97** ...(v[1]) TPQueally 2 (J Noseda) *chsd ldrs: rdn 3f out: wknd 2f out* **25/1**	89
0050	**17**	1	**Chantaco (USA)**[35] 4347 4-9-4 **95** ... LPKeniry 8 (A M Balding) *chsd ldrs: rdn 3f out: wknd appr fnl 2f* **16/1**	85
5066	**18**	½	**Gavroche (IRE)**[7] 5170 5-9-9 **100** ... MartinDwyer 13 (J R Boyle) *a in rr* **50/1**	89
-010	**19**	3 ½	**Chancellor (IRE)**[21] 4818 8-9-2 **93** ...(t) HayleyTurner 1 (Ernst Oertel) *chsd ldrs: rdn 3f out: wknd 2f out* **33/1**	76
3500	**20**	3	**Boo**[7] 5188 4-9-0 **91** ...(p) RichardMullen 7 (K R Burke) *rdn and hdwy into mid-div on rails over 3f out: sn wknd* **50/1**	68

2m 4.76s (-3.95) **Going Correction** -0.225s/f (Firm)

WFA 3 from 4yo+ 6lb **20** Ran SP% **128.7**

Speed ratings (Par 109):106,105,105,104,104 104,103,103,103,102 102,101,100,100,99 98,97,97,94,92

CSF £34.08 CT £298.16 TOTE £8.50: £2.40, £1.80, £3.20, £2.70; EX 45.30 Trifecta £532.10 Pool: £1,274.06 - 1.70 winning units..

Owner Full Circle **Bred** Joseph Rogers **Trained** Aldbury, Herts

FOCUS

Blue Monday ran second in this race last year before landing the Cambridgeshire and all bar three of these hold entries in that valuable handicap. This looked a good race beforehand, and although it became a bit messy the result makes plenty of sense, with the finish dominated by progressive horses. Interestingly seven of the first eight were drawn in theoretically disadvantageous double-figure outside stalls.

NOTEBOOK

Pinpoint(IRE) ◆, who has been avoiding fast ground since running good races in both the Victoria Cup and Royal Hunt Cup, was stepping up to his furthest trip to date but got every yard of the distance under a patient ride. This was a cracking effort and he looks a leading contender for the Cambridgeshire, for which he has picked up just a 4lb penalty. (tchd 15-2)

Charlie Cool, like the winner, was stepping up to his furthest trip to date, but he promised to be suited by this sort of distance and ran a fine race from the widest draw off a mark 5lb higher than when winning over a mile at Haydock on his previous start. He will get a 4lb pull at the weights with Pinpoint if taking his chance in the Cambridgeshire, but the drop back in trip is likely to inconvenience him more than it will today's winner. (op 5-1)

Formal Decree(GER), a much-improved handicapper this season, ran a fine race in third and might have finished even closer with a clearer run. Like most of these, he is in the Cambridgeshire. (op 10-1)

Dansili Dancer, the winner of three of his last four starts, ran a huge race off a career-high mark, faring best of those to race handy, and is clearly still improving.

Great Plains looked to have gone off too fast, but he sustained his challenge surprisingly well and his rider must have got a breather into him. A good effort. (tchd 28-1)

Pearly King(USA) ran a respectable race and was not beaten that far. (op 11-2)

Blue Bajan(IRE) endured a terrible run when trying to pick up and was unlucky not to have finished significantly closer.

Palomar(USA) got no luck in-running and is much better than his finishing position suggests. Official explanation: jockey said gelding was denied a clear run

Classic Punch(IRE) Official explanation: jockey said colt suffered interference in running

5375 DUBAI INTERNATIONAL AIRPORT WORLD TROPHY (GROUP 3) 5f 34y

4:05 (4:06) (Class 1) 3-Y-O+

£28,390 (£10,760; £5,385; £2,685; £1,345; £675) **Stalls** Centre

Form				RPR
2562	**1**		**Dixie Belle**[11] 5087 3-8-10 **90** ...(t) TPQueally 7 (M G Quinlan) *mde v all: drvn out fnl f* **50/1**	111
416	**2**	*1*	**Excusez Moi (USA)**[14] 5011 4-9-0 **104** ... KerrinMcEvoy 4 (C E Brittain) *lw: trckd ldrs: rdn 2f out: styd on fnl f and tk 2nd cl home but nvr gng pce to rch wnr* **15/2**[3]	110
1410	**3**	*nk*	**Dandy Man (IRE)**[23] 4738 3-9-2 ... PShanahan 11 (C Collins, Ire) *lw: s.i.s: sn rcvrd to chse ldrs: wnt 2nd over 1f out but nvr gng pce to rch wnr: lost 2nd cl home* **6/4**[1]	112
3033	**4**	1 ¼	**Pivotal Flame**[23] 4738 4-9-0 **109** ...(p) JimmyFortune 2 (E S McMahon) *stdd s: bhd: rdn and hdwy over 1f out: kpt on u.p fnl f but nvr gng pce to rch ldrs* **5/1**[2]	104
6104	**5**	1 ¼	**Green Manalishi**[32] 4461 5-9-0 **103** ... PhilipRobinson 9 (D W P Arbuthnot) *chaed wnr over 3f out: sn rdn: lost 2nd appr fnl f: wknd ins last* **25/1**	100
0216	**6**	1 ¼	**Donna Blini**[44] 4080 3-8-10 **105** ... JohnEgan 5 (B J Meehan) *sn chsng ldrs: rdn 1/2-way: wknd fnl f* **12/1**	92
5002	**7**	*shd*	**Eisteddfod**[20] 4860 5-9-0 **108** ...(b) JoeFanning 10 (P F I Cole) *sn chsng ldrs: drvn and outpcd 1/2-way: kpt on again u.p ins last but nt a danger* **12/1**	95
6466	**8**	2 ½	**The Tatling (IRE)**[8] 5158 9-9-0 **110** ... TedDurcan 8 (J M Bradley) *a outpcd* **8/1**	86
1054	**9**	1 ¾	**Tournedos (IRE)**[6] 5222 4-9-0 **105** ...(p) RichardHughes 3 (R Charlton) *swtg: chsd wnr 2f: sn rdn: wknd qckly over 1f out* **20/1**	80
4011	**10**	*9*	**Celtic Mill**[8] 5158 8-9-0 **104** ...(p) DarryllHolland 6 (D W Barker) *broke wl: sn lost pl and struggling in rr* **15/2**[3]	47

60.16 secs (-2.40) **Going Correction** -0.225s/f (Firm)

WFA 3 from 4yo+ 1lb **10** Ran SP% **117.3**

Speed ratings (Par 113):110,108,107,105,103 101,101,97,94,80

CSF £386.31 TOTE £35.40: £5.60, £2.50, £1.50; EX 320.60 TRIFECTA Not won..

Owner Burns Farm Racing **Bred** Burns Farm Stud **Trained** Newmarket, Suffolk

FOCUS

This looked a reasonable Group 3 beforehand, but Dixie Belle was a shock winner, appearing to show form way out of line with her overall level, and only time will tell what it is worth. It has provisionally been rated through the second, though he had no previous 5f form.

NOTEBOOK

Dixie Belle, although managing to win a Listed race as a juvenile and placing in that grade this year, had not shown any form good enough to win at this level, so this was a bit of a surprise. Quickly into her stride, she soon had a few of these on the stretch and sustained her effort right the way to the line, in the process paying a huge compliment to Tax Free, who gave her 6lb and three-length beating at Leicester last time. This will have significantly boosted her paddock value, but only time will show whether this was a fluke. (op 66-1 tchd 100-1 in places)

Excusez Moi(USA), winner of the Great St Wilfrid before running sixth in the Haydock Sprint Cup, was trying five furlongs for the first time. He travelled well for much of the way, but was just unable to reel in long-time leader Dixie Belle. (tchd 8-1)

Dandy Man(IRE), a disappointment when pulling hard on soft ground in the Nunthorpe on his previous start, failed to take advantage of this drop in grade and was again below his best under his 5lb penalty. Not that quick away, he never looked totally happy chasing the furious pace and basically never looked in a great rhythm. He is much better than he has shown of late. (op 15-8)

Pivotal Flame got going too late to pose a serious threat and was below the form he showed when third in the Nunthorpe on his previous start. He has not won since October 2004 and his confidence needs a boost. (op 11-2 tchd 13-2)

Green Manalishi was well enough placed if he was good enough.

Donna Blini escaped a penalty for last year's Cheveley Park success, but could not take advantage. (op 10-1)

Eisteddfod needs further.

The Tatling(IRE), winner of this race in 2004 and 2005, could not go with them this time. (op 7-1)

Celtic Mill Official explanation: trainer had no explanation for the poor form shown

5376 JOHN SMITH'S EXTRA COLD AND MATTHEW SQUIBB CONDITIONS STKS 1m 1f

4:40 (4:40) (Class 3) 3-Y-O+

£8,724 (£2,612; £1,306; £653; £326; £163) **Stalls** Low

Form				RPR
-402	**1**		**Blue Ksar (FR)**[9] 5142 3-8-6 **102** ...(t) TedDurcan 6 (Saeed Bin Suroor) *lw: trckd ldr tl led appr fnl 3f: drvn along fr 2f out: kpt on strly ins last* **8/1**	107
141-	**2**	1 ½	**Emirates Skyline (USA)**[367] 5226 3-8-6 **101** ... KerrinMcEvoy 7 (Saeed Bin Suroor) *b.bkwd: hld up rr but in tch: hdwy fr 3f out: drvn and styd on to chse wnr 1f out: kpt on but a readily hld* **9/2**[2]	104+
1600	**3**	2 ½	**Snoqualmie Boy**[25] 4679 3-9-1 **111** ... JohnEgan 10 (D R C Elsworth) *lw: chsd ldrs: wnt 2nd and hrd drvn 2f out: no imp on wnr and lost 2nd 1f out: sn no ch* **11/2**[3]	108
0500	**4**	*nk*	**Red Spell (IRE)**[7] 5177 5-8-11 **91** ... JimmyFortune 5 (R Hannon) *lw: bhd: hdwy fr 2f out: hrd rdn and kpt on ins fnl f but nvr gng pce to trble ldrs* **12/1**	98
4402	**5**	½	**Mostashaar (FR)**[19] 4896 4-8-11 **102** ... MartinDwyer 4 (Sir Michael Stoute) *chsd ldrs: rdn over 2f out: no imp: wknd ins last* **13/2**	97
3145	**6**	1 ¼	**Red Somerset (USA)**[21] 4805 3-8-8 **87** ... SteveDrowne 2 (R Hannon) *mid-div: rdn over 2f out: styd on same pce fr over 1f out* **16/1**	97
0304	**7**	*shd*	**St Andrews (IRE)**[14] 5012 6-8-11 **103** ...(p) PhilipRobinson 8 (M A Jarvis) *bhd: shkn up and styd on fnl 2f but nvr in contention* **8/1**	95

0362 **8** ¾ **Azarole (IRE)**[18] 4918 5-8-11 105 .... LPKeniry 9 — 93
(J S Moore) *s.i.s: bhd: rdn 3f out: nvr in contention* **9/1**

2102 **9** 14 **Plum Pudding (IRE)**[66] 3413 3-8-6 92 .... MichaelHills 1 — 65
(R Hannon) *lw: led tl hdd over 3f out: wknd 2f out* **4/1**[1]

6105 **10** 10 **Invention (USA)**[36] 4337 3-8-8 93 .... (v[1]) RichardHughes 3 — 47
(J H M Gosden) *chasded ldrs: wknd qckly ins fnl 3f* **20/1**

1m 50.68s (-3.91) **Going Correction** -0.225s/f (Firm)
WFA 3 from 4yo+ 5lb **10** Ran SP% **117.5**
Speed ratings (Par 107):108,106,104,104,103 102,102,101,89,80
CSF £44.26 TOTE £11.30: £3.00, £1.60, £2.50; EX 26.60.
Owner Godolphin **Bred** Merdian Stud **Trained** Newmarket, Suffolk

FOCUS
A decent, competitive conditions event and useful form for the grade.

NOTEBOOK
Blue Ksar(FR), a promising second to a stablemate in a similar, if slightly weaker, event over on his return from a break at Southwell on his previous start, stepped up on that effort to run out a convincing winner. Always well placed by the in-form Ted Durcan, he found plenty for pressure and was always holding his yard's other runner. He was thought good enough to be sent off odds on for a Group 3 when with Andre Fabre last year (although he was well beaten) and probably deserves a return to that sort of level. His rider thinks he will be even better over ten furlongs on easier ground. (op 13-2)
Emirates Skyline(USA) ◆, too good for a couple of smart sorts in a seven-furlong novice event at Sandown when last seen just over a year previously, looked the more fancied of the Bin Suroor pair, but was always just held by his race-fit stablemate. He is open to improvement and could be one to be with next time. (op 4-1)
Snoqualmie Boy, well held since landing the Listed Hampton Court Stakes at Royal Ascot, including when out of his depth in the International Stakes at York on his previous start, would have appreciated the drop in grade but was readily held under his 6lb penalty. (tchd 6-1)
Red Spell(IRE) is a better horse on the sand, but we know his level on turf - 101 is the highest RPR he has achieved - and he is probably the best guide to the strength of the form. (op 20-1)
Mostashaar(FR), last year's Britannia Stakes winner, failed to prove his stamina upped to his furthest trip to date. (op 11-2 tchd 7-1)
Plum Pudding(IRE) was a good second to the decent Smart Enough in a mile handicap at Newmarket on his previous start, but he had a bit to find at the weights switched to conditions company and it was a little surprising too see him sent off favourite. As it turned out, he failed to give his running. (op 9-2)

5377 JOHN SMITH'S VICTORIA CLUB, AYLESBURY H'CAP — 7f (S)
5:10 (5:13) (Class 4) (0-80,80) 3-Y-O — £6,477 (£1,927; £963; £481) Stalls Centre

Form — RPR

3132 **1** **Trimlestown (IRE)**[13] 5042 3-8-13 75 .... DaneO'Neill 3 — 84
(H Candy) *b.hind: sn chsng ldrs: drvn to ld ins last: hld on all out* **6/1**[2]

0212 **2** shd **Blues In The Night (IRE)**[24] 4707 3-9-2 78 .... JimmyFortune 2 — 87
(P J Makin) *rr but in tch: hdwy over 2f out: str run u.p fnl f: nt quite get up* **4/1**[1]

2453 **3** ¾ **Scarlet Flyer (USA)**[4] 5265 3-9-0 76 .... (b) GeorgeBaker 11 — 83
(G L Moore) *lw: hld up rr but in tch: hdwy whn nt clr run over 1f out: swtchd rt and styd on strly ins last: gng on cl home* **10/1**

1-00 **4** ¾ **Misphire**[28] 4601 3-9-2 78 .... RobertWinston 13 — 83
(M Dods) *chsd ldrs: led 2f out: kpt on u.p tl hdd ins last: one pce* **12/1**

2632 **5** 1¼ **High Octave (IRE)**[22] 4757 3-8-5 67 ow1 .... JohnEgan 12 — 69
(B G Powell) *prom: rdn over 2f out: styd on ins fnl f but nvr gng pce to rch ldrs* **8/1**

0600 **6** nk **Colorus (IRE)**[11] 5079 3-8-12 74 .... LPKeniry 10 — 75
(R A Fahey) *t.k.h: chsd ldrs: rdn 2f out: wknd ins fnl f* **25/1**

6056 **7** ½ **Carmenero (GER)**[12] 5070 3-8-12 74 .... RichardMullen 6 — 74
(W R Muir) *lw: chsd ldrs: pushed along and outpcd 3f out: styd on again u.p ins fnl f but nvr a danger* **12/1**

1034 **8** nk **Abwaab**[17] 4923 3-9-4 80 .... KerrinMcEvoy 17 — 79
(R F Johnson Houghton) *in tch: rdn and hdwy over 1f out: kpt on same pce ins last* **10/1**

0640 **9** nk **Kaveri (USA)**[16] 4965 3-9-3 79 .... JoeFanning 5 — 77
(C E Brittain) *chsd ldr: led 3f out to 2f out: wknd fnl f* **20/1**

5144 **10** 1 **His Master's Voice (IRE)**[21] 4802 3-8-12 74 .... PhilipRobinson 18 — 70
(D W P Arbuthnot) *chsd ldrs: rdn 3f out: wknd fnl f* **15/2**[3]

6365 **11** ½ **Mister Benedictine**[11] 5096 3-8-13 75 .... MartinDwyer 8 — 69
(W R Muir) *chsd ldrs: rdn over 2f out: wknd ins last* **14/1**

6030 **12** hd **River Kintyre**[16] 4958 3-8-9 71 .... MichaelHills 15 — 65
(B W Hills) *bhd: rdn and hung bdly rt fr 2f out: kpt on ins last* **14/1**

0050 **13** hd **Sands Of Barra (IRE)**[22] 4769 3-8-11 73 .... SteveDrowne 16 — 66
(N A Callaghan) *nvr gng pce to be competitive* **20/1**

4534 **14** 3 **Sleeping Storm (IRE)**[19] 4874 3-8-3 72 .... KMay[(7)] 4 — 58
(B J Meehan) *lw: chsd leaders over 4f* **12/1**

0160 **15** nk **Bold Argument (IRE)**[35] 4378 3-8-10 72 .... PaulEddery 7 — 57
(Mrs P N Dutfield) *lw: led tl hd 3f out: wknd 2f out* **25/1**

0010 **16** ½ **Cloud Atlas (IRE)**[16] 4968 3-7-11 66 .... FrankiePickard[(7)] 1 — 50
(S Kirk) *wnt bdly lft s and racd along 4f: joined main gp over 3f out: hung rt and wknd 2f out* **33/1**

1m 25.52s (-1.48) **Going Correction** -0.225s/f (Firm) **16** Ran SP% **131.9**
Speed ratings (Par 103):99,98,98,97,95 95,94,94,94,93 92,92,91,88,88 87
CSF £30.37 CT £262.52 TOTE £6.60: £1.70, £1.50, £2.50, £4.10; EX 17.70 Place 6 £67.76, Place 5 £17.47.
Owner Thurloe Thoroughbreds XVI **Bred** Liam Brennan **Trained** Kingston Warren, Oxon
■ Stewards' Enquiry : Dane O'Neill two-day ban: used whip with excessive frequency without giving gelding time to respond (Sep 27-28)

FOCUS
A fairly competitive handicap, run at a decent pace. Sound form of its type.
Cloud Atlas(IRE) Official explanation: jockey said gelding hung right
T/Plt: £66.20 to a £1 stake. Pool: £116,844.60. 1,287.20 winning tickets. T/Qpdt: £10.10 to a £1 stake. Pool: £5,782.20. 420.30 winning tickets. ST

5065 WARWICK (L-H)
Saturday, September 16

OFFICIAL GOING: Good to soft (soft in places)
Wind: Nil Weather: Overcast

5378 WARWICKRACECOURSE.CO.UK H'CAP — 5f 110y
1:45 (1:46) (Class 6) (0-65,65) 3-Y-O+ — £2,388 (£705; £352) Stalls Centre

Form — RPR

6506 **1** **Brigadore**[2] 5327 7-9-0 60 .... OscarUrbina 12 — 69
(J G Given) *sltly hmpd s: hld up in mid-div: rdn and hdwy over 1f out: led wl ins fnl f: r.o wl* **13/2**[1]

3612 **2** 1 **Tamino (IRE)**[16] 4962 3-8-11 64 .... TravisBlock[(5)] 8 — 70
(H Morrison) *a.p: rdn over 2f out: ev ch ins fnl f: r.o* **15/2**[2]

4/22 **3** hd **Small Stakes (IRE)**[21] 4799 4-9-5 65 .... (t) FergusSweeney 17 — 70
(P J Makin) *hld up: hdwy on outside over 3f out: rdn over 2f out: swtchd rt ins fnl f: r.o wl towards fin* **17/2**

3211 **4** shd **Talcen Gwyn (IRE)**[7] 5167 4-9-2 62 .... (v) DavidKinsella 15 — 67
(M F Harris) *a.p: rdn over 1f out: edgd rt ins fnl f: r.o* **8/1**[3]

1240 **5** shd **Namir (IRE)**[27] 4636 4-9-1 64 .... (vt) AmirQuinn[(3)] 1 — 69
(D Shaw) *a.p: rdn over 1f out: kpt on ins fnl f* **16/1**

0500 **6** nk **Extremely Rare (IRE)**[15] 4985 5-8-11 57 .... PaulDoe 2 — 61
(M S Saunders) *led: rdn 2f out: hdd and no ex wl ins fnl f* **12/1**

2360 **7** ½ **Whitbarrow (IRE)**[16] 4962 7-8-8 61 ow2 .... JamesMillman[(7)] 11 — 63
(B R Millman) *a.p: rdn over 1f out: one pce fnl f* **18/1**

0513 **8** ½ **Cerulean Rose**[9] 5131 7-9-0 60 .... IanMongan 3 — 60
(A W Carroll) *mid-div: rdn 3f out: no real prog fnl f* **8/1**[3]

0510 **9** shd **Meikle Barfil**[9] 5131 4-9-1 61 .... (p) PatDobbs 4 — 61
(J M Bradley) *hld up and bhd: hdwy on ins 2f out: no further prog fnl f* **16/1**

3431 **10** nk **Stamford Blue**[9] 5131 5-8-11 64 .... (b) TolleyDean[(7)] 5 — 63
(R A Harris) *mid-div: rdn over 3f out: no hdwy fnl 2f* **15/2**[2]

0560 **11** hd **Convince (USA)**[9] 5131 5-8-6 59 .... (p) BarrySavage[(7)] 16 — 57
(J M Bradley) *nvr bttr than mid-div* **28/1**

0600 **12** 1¼ **Whistler**[3] 5286 9-8-12 58 .... (b) PaulFitzsimons 9 — 52
(Miss J R Tooth) *outpcd: bhd whn stmbld over 3f out: n.d* **25/1**

5000 **13** ½ **Bens Georgie (IRE)**[19] 4894 4-9-3 63 .... ChrisCatlin 14 — 56
(D K Ivory) *s.i.s: a bhd* **33/1**

3310 **14** 1 **Jucebabe**[16] 4962 3-8-10 58 .... JimCrowley 13 — 47
(J L Spearing) *wnt slty lft s: hld up in mid-div: rdn 2f out: fdd fnl f* **25/1**

0060 **15** nk **George The Second**[17] 4927 3-8-9 60 .... (t) RichardKingscote[(3)] 7 — 48
(Mrs H Sweeting) *prom over 3f* **28/1**

3401 **16** 1¼ **Cosmic Destiny (IRE)**[52] 3847 4-9-2 62 .... EddieAhern 10 — 46
(E F Vaughan) *t.k.h mid-div: wknd 1f out* **10/1**

66.91 secs (1.41) **Going Correction** +0.275s/f (Good)
WFA 3 from 4yo+ 1lb **16** Ran SP% **121.0**
Speed ratings (Par 101):101,99,99,99,99 98,98,97,97,96 96,94,94,92,92 90
CSF £49.22 CT £442.88 TOTE £8.30: £2.50, £2.10, £2.40, £2.80; EX 120.40.
Owner White Rose Poultry Ltd **Bred** Fulling Mill Stud **Trained** Willoughton, Lincs

FOCUS
A blanket finish to this wide-open low grade handicap. Straightforward, sound form.

5379 RACING UK ON SKY 432 MAIDEN STKS (C&G) (DIV I) — 7f 26y
2:15 (2:16) (Class 5) 2-Y-O — £2,590 (£770; £385; £192) Stalls Low

Form — RPR

44 **1** **Don't Panic (IRE)**[21] 4824 2-9-0 .... EddieAhern 10 — 82+
(P W Chapple-Hyam) *mde all: qcknd clr fnl f: eased towards fin* **4/5**[1]

06 **2** 5 **Radical Views**[12] 5066 2-9-0 .... IanMongan 12 — 66
(B W Hills) *chsd wnr: rdn over 1f out: sn outpcd* **14/1**[3]

3 1 **Tenancy (IRE)** 2-8-11 .... RichardKingscote[(3)] 8 — 63
(J A Osborne) *hld up: hdwy over 1f out: nt trble ldrs* **22/1**

32 **4** shd **Love Dubai (USA)**[12] 5059 2-9-0 .... RobertHavlin 2 — 63+
(M Johnston) *s.s: hdwy 1/2-way: styd on ins fnl f: nvr nrr* **7/4**[2]

06 **5** 2 **Amazing King (IRE)**[10] 5111 2-8-7 .... JackDean[(7)] 1 — 58
(W G M Turner) *chsd ldrs: rdn over 2f out: wknd over 1f out* **150/1**

05 **6** 1¾ **Flying Grey (IRE)**[10] 5112 2-8-9 .... KevinGhunowa[(5)] 9 — 53
(P A Blockley) *prom 5f* **100/1**

0 **7** 2½ **Abbotts Account (USA)**[24] 4705 2-9-0 .... JimCrowley 6 — 47
(Mrs A J Perrett) *hld up: rdn over 2f out: n.d* **50/1**

05 **8** 1¾ **Medici Code**[10] 5106 2-8-9 .... TravisBlock[(5)] 3 — 42
(H Morrison) *s.i.s: a in rr* **33/1**

5 **9** 1 **Captain Nemo (USA)**[71] 3247 2-9-0 .... OscarUrbina 11 — 40
(T D Barron) *chsd ldrs 5f* **16/1**

10 7 **Pink Notes** 2-9-0 .... FergusSweeney 5 — 22
(R J Hodges) *sn outpcd* **150/1**

11 33 **Premier Escalon** 2-9-0 .... BrianReilly 7 — —
(F Jordan) *chsd ldrs: lost pl over 5f out: sn bhd* **150/1**

1m 24.95s (-0.05) **Going Correction** +0.075s/f (Good) **11** Ran SP% **116.7**
Speed ratings (Par 95):103,97,96,96,93 91,88,86,85,77 40
CSF £14.59 TOTE £1.80: £1.70, £2.00, £3.30; EX 12.50.
Owner A B S Webb **Bred** Bernard Colclough **Trained** Newmarket, Suffolk

FOCUS
Not many got into a race that was easily the fastest of the four run over the seven-furlong course. The winner was a cut above and did not need to be at his best.

NOTEBOOK
Don't Panic(IRE) had found six furlongs on the short side in a valuable sales race at the Curragh last time. He proved far too good for this opposition and that could be it for the season as his trainer still considers that he has some strengthening to do. (op 8-11 tchd 5-6 and 10-11 in a place)
Radical Views proved no match for the winner having come up against a useful type for this sort of grade. (tchd 12-1)
Tenancy(IRE) ◆ shaped promisingly on this debut and this half-brother to winners over ten and twelve furlongs is likely to do better over further. (op 20-1)
Love Dubai(USA) could never get into it after losing a fair amount of ground at the start but did seem to appreciate the extra furlong. Official explanation: jockey said colt missed the break (op 9-4)
Amazing King(IRE) had plenty to find based on the form of his first two outings. (op 66-1)
Captain Nemo(USA) Official explanation: jockey said colt hung right-handed

5380 SEE MORE ON RACING UK MAIDEN FILLIES' STKS — 7f 26y
2:50 (2:52) (Class 5) 2-Y-O — £3,238 (£963; £481; £240) Stalls Low

Form — RPR

42 **1** **Elusive Flash (USA)**[6] 5209 2-9-0 .... EddieAhern 1 — 80
(P F I Cole) *w ldr: rdn over 2f out: led over 1f out: flashed tail and edgd lft whn hit w whip ins fnl f: r.o wl* **5/6**[1]

052 **2** 2½ **Little Miss Tara (IRE)**[37] 4290 2-9-0 80 .... RichardSmith 12 — 74
(A B Haynes) *led: rdn over 2f out: hdd over 1f out: nt qckn* **13/2**[3]

00 **3** 1¼ **Breezeway (IRE)**[42] 4148 2-9-0 .... RobertHavlin 7 — 70
(B J Meehan) *hld up in tch: rdn and sltly outpcd 2f out: styd on fnl f* **25/1**

4 ½ **Ommadawn (IRE)** 2-9-0 .... OscarUrbina 6 — 69
(J R Fanshawe) *hld up in tch: rdn over 2f out: hung lft over 1f out: one pce* **12/1**

5 ¾ **Run For Ede'S** 2-9-0 .... FergusSweeney 3 — 67
(R M Beckett) *hld up in tch: rdn over 1f out: no ex fnl f* **33/1**

0032 **6** 2½ **Bay Of Light**[19] 4897 2-9-0 75 .... PaulDoe 4 — 61+
(P W Chapple-Hyam) *half-rrd and s.i.s: bhd tl styd on fnl f: nvr trbld ldrs* **3/1**[2]

0 **7** shd **Rose Germany**[16] 4964 2-9-0 .... ChrisCatlin 14 — 60
(M R Channon) *prom: rdn over 2f out: wknd over 1f out* **33/1**

0 **8** *1* **Bellehurst**[26] 4657 2-9-0 .... MichaelTebbutt 9 58
(B J Meehan) *a towards rr* **33/1**
0 **9** *½* **Inimical**[66] 3402 2-9-0 .... FrankieMcDonald 8 56
(W S Kittow) *s.i.s: a bhd* **50/1**
65 **10** *½* **Rowan River**[29] 4553 2-8-7 .... PatrickHills(7) 5 55
(M H Tompkins) *half-rrd and s.s: short-lived effrt on ins over 2f out* **14/1**
11 *15* **Dubai Marina** 2-9-0 .... BrianReilly 13 16
(F Jordan) *s.i.s: sn prom: rdn over 3f out: sn wknd* **100/1**

1m 25.85s (0.85) **Going Correction** +0.075s/f (Good) **11** Ran SP% **122.9**
Speed ratings (Par 92):98,95,93,93,92 89,89,88,87,87 69
CSF £7.04 TOTE £1.80: £1.10, £2.00, £5.90; EX 10.40.
Owner Miss Alfiya Shaykhutdinova **Bred** Thomas-Lakin **Trained** Whatcombe, Oxon

FOCUS
An ordinary maiden. The winner and second ran to form but the overall level might not prove rock solid.

NOTEBOOK
Elusive Flash(USA) made amends for an unlucky defeat at Kempton and ran out a clear-cut winner despite resenting being struck with the whip. (op 15-8 tchd 2-1 in a place)
Little Miss Tara(IRE) turned in another solid front-running performance but had no answer to the winner. (op 11-2)
Breezeway(IRE) seems to be crying out for a mile and is now qualified for nurseries. (op 20-1)
Ommadawn(IRE), a half-sister to a mile juvenile winner, played up in the paddock and proved difficult to mount. She showed definite signs of inexperience under pressure and will hopefully come on for this debut. (op 17-2)
Run For Ede'S is a half-sister to a couple of winners and gave the impression that she should be sharper for the outing. (op 28-1)
Bay Of Light had no chance of making the running this time after fluffing the start. She still seems worth stepping up to a mile. Official explanation: jockey said, regarding running and riding, his orders were to jump out and do his best, adding that filly had been fractious on the way to start and reared as stalls opened and missed the break; trainer added filly had been difficult to saddle and had been standing in the stalls for a long time (op 7-2 tchd 4-1)
Dubai Marina Official explanation: jockey said filly hung right-handed

5381 RACING UK ON SKY 432 MAIDEN STKS (C&G) (DIV II) 7f 26y
3:25 (3:27) (Class 5) 2-Y-O **£2,590** (£770; £385; £192) **Stalls** Low

Form RPR
0 **1** **Victor Trumper**[19] 4895 2-9-0 .... PaulDoe 6 72
(P W Chapple-Hyam) *w ldr: rdn to ld 2f out: sn edgd lft: r.o* **14/1**
6 **2** *hd* **Apache Dawn**[11] 5088 2-9-0 .... IanMongan 4 71
(B W Hills) *chsd ldrs: rdn and ev ch fr over 1f out: r.o* **8/1**
6 **3** *hd* **Malt Or Mash (USA)**[11] 5091 2-9-0 .... PatDobbs 8 71
(R Hannon) *chsd ldrs: rdn and edgd lft fnl f: r.o* **7/1**[3]
4 *2* **Jack Junior (USA)** 2-9-0 .... MichaelTebbutt 7 66+
(B J Meehan) *mid-div: outpcd 1/2-way: hung lft and r.o ins fnl f: nt rch ldrs* **11/1**
0 **5** *½* **Arabian Word**[12] 5067 2-9-0 .... EddieAhern 9 64
(Sir Michael Stoute) *hld up: hdwy 1/2-way: rdn over 1f out: styd on same pce fnl f* **6/1**[2]
055 **6** *1 ¼* **Distiller (IRE)**[11] 5091 2-9-0 73 .... FJohansson 3 61
(W R Muir) *hld up: rdn and hung lft over 1f out: styng on whn hmpd ins fnl f: nt trble ldrs* **16/1**
0 **7** *1 ¼* **Always Sparkle (CAN)**[19] 4867 2-9-0 .... FergusSweeney 1 58
(B Palling) *sn led: rdn and hdd 2f out: wknd fnl f* **66/1**
5U0 **8** *1* **Munster Mountain (IRE)**[12] 5066 2-8-9 .... KevinGhunowa(5) 10 55
(P A Blockley) *prom: rdn over 2f out: wknd over 1f out* **100/1**
46 **9** *2 ½* **Desert Soul**[12] 5067 2-9-0 .... RobertHavlin 2 49
(M Johnston) *s.s: hdwy 1/2-way: wknd over 1f out* **8/1**
0 **10** *6* **Sew In Character**[17] 4934 2-9-0 .... OscarUrbina 11 33
(M Blanshard) *wnt rt s and s.i.s: outpcd* **66/1**
3 **11** *2* **Stanley George (IRE)**[24] 4705 2-9-0 .... MatthewHenry 5 28
(M A Jarvis) *s.s: hld up: rdn 1/2-way: sn wknd* **6/5**[1]

1m 25.79s (0.79) **Going Correction** +0.075s/f (Good) **11** Ran SP% **119.3**
Speed ratings (Par 95):98,97,97,95,94 93,91,90,87,80 78
CSF £122.95 TOTE £18.90: £3.50, £2.60, £2.50; EX 251.60.
Owner Sills Racing & Partner **Bred** P Balding **Trained** Newmarket, Suffolk

FOCUS
This looked the weaker of the two divisions and the time was 0.84 seconds slower. The bare form is probably only ordinary.

NOTEBOOK
Victor Trumper had disappointed connections when missing the break over course and distance on his debut. Showing his true worth here, he held on gamely and his trainer hopes that he will make up into a decent handicapper over longer trips next year. (op 16-1)
Apache Dawn put in a sustained challenge against the far rail and lost nothing in defeat. He does seem to be going the right way. (tchd 17-2)
Malt Or Mash(USA) is another who appears to be progressing along the right lines. (op 15-2 tchd 8-1)
Jack Junior(USA) ♦, friendless in the market on his debut, showed definite signs of ability without being knocked about and seems sure to benefit from the experience. (op 5-1)
Arabian Word, another big drifter in the ring, looks the type to do better when tackling longer distances. (op 11-1)
Distiller(IRE) may be the son of a top-class sprinter but his mother was a dual winning miler so he may well get further.
Desert Soul Official explanation: jockey said colt missed the break
Stanley George(IRE) made a promising debut at Leicester, but things went wrong for him here. Hampered leaving the stalls, he then ran too freely and rather ran into the backs of rivals. Never able to get out of the rear division, he is better than this. Official explanation: jockey said colt got upset in starting stalls and missed the break (op 6-4 tchd 13-8)

5382 CAPITIS VENATUS QUAERO NURSERY 7f 26y
3:55 (3:57) (Class 5) (0-75,75) 2-Y-O **£3,238** (£963; £481; £240) **Stalls** Low

Form RPR
4145 **1** **Goose Green (IRE)**[12] 5053 2-8-8 65 .... EdwardCreighton(3) 10 69
(M R Channon) *hld up in mid-div: hdwy 2f out: sn rdn: led wl ins fnl f: r.o* **11/1**
6554 **2** *shd* **Cheshire Prince**[7] 5172 2-8-4 63 .... LiamJones(5) 7 67
(W M Brisbourne) *hld up in tch: rdn 3f out: ev ch wl ins fnl f: r.o* **5/1**[2]
4060 **3** *1 ¼* **Urban Warrior**[7] 5176 2-8-10 64 .... (v) FrancisFerris 5 64
(Mrs Norma Pook) *hld up and bhd: rdn and hdwy on ins 2f out: plld out wl ins fnl f: r.o wl* **16/1**
5605 **4** *hd* **Carlitos Spirit (IRE)**[13] 5041 2-8-10 64 .... (b[1]) JimCrowley 13 64
(B R Millman) *led: rdn wl over 1f out: hdd wl ins fnl f: no ex* **20/1**
5100 **5** *1 ¼* **Babylon Sister (IRE)**[11] 5094 2-8-11 65 .... PatDobbs 1 62
(R Hannon) *hld up in mid-div: hdwy over 2f out: sn rdn: one pce fnl f* **16/1**
2133 **6** *1 ½* **Stagehand (IRE)**[22] 4773 2-9-0 75 .... JamesMillman(7) 6 68
(B R Millman) *hld up in mid-div: rdn and lost pl over 3f out: rallied over 1f out: styd on and edgd lft fnl f* **9/2**[1]
0424 **7** *3* **Astroangel**[29] 4547 2-8-6 67 .... PatrickHills(7) 4 52+
(M H Tompkins) *s.v.s: hdwy over 2f out: no further prog fnl f* **6/1**[3]
053 **8** *1 ½* **Sunley Sovereign**[69] 3335 2-9-2 70 .... ChrisCatlin 3 51
(M R Channon) *chsd ldr tl over 2f out: rdn and wknd wl over 1f out* **12/1**
040 **9** *7* **Alloro**[92] 2619 2-9-1 69 .... FergusSweeney 12 32
(D J S Ffrench Davis) *a bhd* **33/1**
0604 **10** *1 ¾* **Maid Of Ale (IRE)**[13] 5041 2-8-11 65 .... (b[1]) IanMongan 11 23
(B J Meehan) *s.s: a bhd* **12/1**
5345 **11** *3 ½* **Ten Dollars More (IRE)**[10] 5113 2-9-4 72 .... (b) EddieAhern 2 21
(J A Osborne) *s.i.s: sn in tch: wnt 2nd over 2f out: sn rdn: wknd over 1f out* **9/1**
4243 **12** *½* **Diamond Light (USA)**[11] 5094 2-9-0 68 .... PaulDoe 9 16
(J L Dunlop) *prom: rdn over 3f out: wknd wl over 1f out* **7/1**

1m 26.03s (1.03) **Going Correction** +0.075s/f (Good) **12** Ran SP% **114.8**
Speed ratings (Par 95):97,96,95,95,93 92,88,86,78,76 72,72
CSF £63.08 CT £884.71 TOTE £16.30: £3.90, £1.70, £5.50; EX 78.20.
Owner Box 41 **Bred** Liam Queally **Trained** West Ilsley, Berks

FOCUS
An ordinary nursery, but run at a strong pace. Sound form.

NOTEBOOK
Goose Green(IRE), who gained his only previous win in an uncompetitive claimer, had appeared exposed. Back down at seven furlongs, he forced his head in front well inside the last and just held on. (op 12-1)
Cheshire Prince, who ran a decent race from this mark at Chester, really found his feet in the final furlong and would have got up in a couple more strides. He handled this easy ground well. (op 6-1 tchd 9-2)
Urban Warrior, who proved well at home in easy ground early in the season, was having his third run for this yard. Improving on the inside rail in the straight, he really began to cut down the leaders when he was switched off the fence, but too late.
Carlitos Spirit(IRE), who sweated up in the preliminaries and was keen on the way to the start, set a strong pace in the first-time blinkers. To his credit he battled on in the straight, and he was only worn down well inside the last. (op 22-1 tchd 25-1)
Babylon Sister(IRE) has been held in nurseries since making all in a Polytrack maiden but this was a fair effort.
Stagehand(IRE), back down at seven furlongs, was never in the hunt but did stay on when it was all over. He probably prefers faster ground. (op 7-2)
Maid Of Ale(IRE) Official explanation: jockey said filly did not face the blinkers
Diamond Light(USA) Official explanation: jockey said filly was unsuited by the good to soft (soft in places) ground

5383 CALL INTERCHANGEFX.CO.UK 0800 197 2154 AND SAVE MONEY H'CAP (PART OF THE WARWICK STAYERS SERIES) 2m 39y
4:30 (4:31) (Class 4) (0-85,85) 3-Y-O+
£11,217 (£3,358; £1,679; £840; £419; £210) **Stalls** Low

Form RPR
0021 **1** **Numero Due**[7] 5174 4-9-8 83 .... ChrisCatlin 16 96+
(G M Moore) *chsd ldrs: pushed along 1/2-way: hmpd and outpcd 3f out: rallied over 1f out: hung lft 1f out: styd on to ld wl ins fnl f* **7/1**
5522 **2** *1 ¼* **Kayf Aramis**[6] 5201 4-8-1 65 .... (p) MarcHalford(3) 1 75
(J L Spearing) *w ldr tl led 1/2-way: rdn and hdd over 1f out: ev ch ins fnl f: unable qck* **7/2**[1]
0620 **3** *1 ¾* **Most Definitely (IRE)**[25] 4676 6-9-4 79 .... JimCrowley 11 86
(R M Stronge) *s.i.s: hld up: hdwy over 4f out: led over 1f out: rdn and hdd wl ins fnl f: no ex* **28/1**
0503 **4** *2* **Salute (IRE)**[17] 4937 7-9-2 77 .... RobertHavlin 5 82
(P G Murphy) *chsd ldrs: rdn whn hmpd over 1f out: no ex fnl f* **25/1**
0403 **5** *6* **Hawridge Star (IRE)**[12] 5057 4-8-5 66 .... FrankieMcDonald 7 64
(W S Kittow) *hld up: hdwy over 4f out: wknd over 2f out* **11/1**
4313 **6** *shd* **Dancer's Serenade (IRE)**[19] 4883 4-8-10 71 .... IanMongan 14 69
(T P Tate) *hld up: hdwy 10f out: chsd ldr over 2f out: sn rdn: wknd over 1f out* **10/1**
6422 **7** *nk* **The Grey Man**[19] 4898 5-8-5 66 .... RichardThomas 9 63
(J W Mullins) *s.s: hld up: hdwy 5f out: wknd over 2f out* **20/1**
0201 **8** *5* **High Point (IRE)**[45] 4046 8-8-8 74 .... RobynBrisland(5) 13 65
(G P Enright) *hld up: effrt over 2f out: n.d* **16/1**
2/0- **9** *8* **Mr Ed (IRE)**[392] 2574 8-9-8 83 .... (p) FergusSweeney 4 65
(P Bowen) *hld up: hdwy over 4f out: wknd over 3f out* **14/1**
5226 **10** *5* **Boxhall (IRE)**[21] 4792 4-8-11 72 .... (t) EddieAhern 8 48
(W R Swinburn) *chsd ldrs 13f* **12/1**
3234 **11** *6* **Maystock**[30] 4530 6-8-4 68 .... RichardKingscote(3) 3 37
(B G Powell) *mde most to 1/2-way: wknd over 2f out* **14/1**
-233 **12** *½* **Gandalf**[31] 4469 4-9-2 77 .... OscarUrbina 2 45
(J R Fanshawe) *mid-div: rdn and lost pl over 6f out: wknd 4f out* **9/2**[2]
1563 **13** *15* **Power Of Future (GER)**[32] 4459 3-8-0 76 .... EdwardCreighton(3) 15 26
(H R A Cecil) *chsd ldrs 11f* **6/1**[3]
000- **14** *1 ½* **Zacatecas (GER)**[13] 5164 6-9-3 85 .... MarkCoumbe(7) 6 33
(A J Chamberlain) *sn wl bhd* **100/1**

3m 32.56s (-0.14) **Going Correction** +0.075s/f (Good)
WFA 3 from 4yo+ 12lb **14** Ran SP% **124.6**
Speed ratings (Par 105):103,102,101,100,97 97,97,94,90,88 85,85,77,76
CSF £31.60 CT £675.46 TOTE £8.00: £2.60, £2.00, £7.00; EX 23.80.
Owner J W Andrews **Bred** London Thoroughbred Services Ltd **Trained** Middleham Moor, N Yorks
■ Stewards' Enquiry : Marc Halford two-day ban: careless riding (Sep 27-28)

FOCUS
This was run at a sound pace. The first two are in-form stayers, and the race should prove solid enough.
Mr Ed(IRE) Official explanation: jockey said gelding had no more to give
Maystock Official explanation: jockey said mare was unsuited by the good to soft (soft in places) ground
Gandalf Official explanation: jockey said gelding never travelled
Power Of Future(GER) Official explanation: jockey said filly felt wrong

5384 BEECH-HURST H'CAP 1m 22y
5:05 (5:07) (Class 5) (0-70,70) 3-Y-O+ **£3,238** (£963; £481; £240) **Stalls** Low

Form RPR
324 **1** **Country Escape**[19] 4891 3-9-6 70 .... EddieAhern 16 77+
(C F Wall) *hld up in tch: rdn over 2f out: led 1f out: r.o* **9/2**[2]
0600 **2** *nk* **Pommes Frites**[17] 4933 3-9-6 70 .... PaulDoe 17 77
(W R Muir) *s.i.s: hld up and bhd: rdn and hdwy over 1f out: ev ch wl ins fnl f: nt qckn* **40/1**
2-04 **3** *1 ½* **Royle Dancer**[22] 4757 3-8-4 61 .... RussellKennemore(7) 2 64
(R Hollinshead) *a.p: led over 2f out: sn rdn: hdd 1f out: nt qckn* **20/1**
3452 **4** *shd* **Al Rayanah**[20] 4845 3-8-5 62 .... KirstyMilczarek(7) 3 65
(G Prodromou) *hld up in mid-div: hdwy whn nt clr run briefly 3f out: rdn over 1f out: kpt on one pce fnl f* **12/1**

3221 **5** ½ **Red Rudy**[19] 4870 4-9-8 **68**........ IanMongan 15 70+
(A W Carroll) *hld up and bhd: hdwy 2f out: sn rdn: one pce fnl f* **7/2**[1]
0040 **6** ½ **Bold Marc (IRE)**[11] 5081 4-9-8 **68**........ LeeEnstone 8 69
(K R Burke) *hld up in mid-div: hdwy 2f out: sn rdn: one pce fnl f* **12/1**
0050 **7** 1 ½ **Parnassian**[16] 4968 6-9-5 **65**........ RichardThomas 7 62
(J A Geake) *hld up and bhd: hdwy fr over 1f out: nt rch ldrs* **9/2**[2]
0150 **8** hd **Gallego**[9] 5130 4-8-12 **63**........ LiamJones(5) 10 60+
(R J Price) *s.s: gd late hdwy: nrst fin* **11/1**[3]
2265 **9** 1 ¼ **Musicmaestroplease (IRE)**[36] 4325 3-8-7 **62**........ DuranFentiman(5) 6 56
(S Parr) *hld up towards rr: hdwy over 1f out: no imp fnl f* **20/1**
4243 **10** ½ **Elidore**[9] 5130 6-9-0 **60**........ FrancisFerris 14 53
(B Palling) *led: rdn and hdd over 2f out: wknd over 1f out* **12/1**
0101 **11** ½ **Zendaro**[5] 5248 4-9-6 **66** 6ex........ FergusSweeney 12 58
(W M Brisbourne) *bhd fnl 2f* **14/1**
3504 **12** shd **Society Music (IRE)**[20] 4831 4-9-8 **68**........(p) ChrisCatlin 11 59
(M Dods) *bhd fnl 2f* **11/1**[3]
400 **13** 2 ½ **Aastral Magic**[13] 5042 4-9-5 **65**........ PatDobbs 13 51
(R Hannon) *s.i.s: a bhd* **16/1**
000- **14** 8 **Retirement**[381] 4860 7-9-0 **60**........ JimCrowley 5 27
(R M Stronge) *prom tl rdn and wknd over 1f out* **40/1**
0-00 **15** 5 **Rashida**[19] 505 4-9-5 **65**........(v[1]) RobertHavlin 1 21
(M Appleby) *prom: rdn 3f out: sn wknd* **100/1**

1m 40.99s (1.39) **Going Correction** +0.075s/f (Good)
WFA 3 from 4yo+ 4lb **15** Ran SP% **126.3**
Speed ratings (Par 103):96,95,94,94,93 93,91,91,90,89 89,89,86,78,73
CSF £194.57 CT £3405.89 TOTE £8.90: £2.80, £10.90, £6.50; EX 337.70.
Owner Fighttheban Partnership IV **Bred** Executive Bloodlines **Trained** Newmarket, Suffolk

FOCUS
The runners swung over to the stands' side once into the home straight. The first two home came from the two highest stalls. The form looks pretty modest, rated around the third and fourth.

5385 WARWICK CASTLE H'CAP — 1m 2f 188y
5:35 (5:38) (Class 6) (0-57,58) 3-Y-0+ **£2,388** (£705; £352) **Stalls** Low

Form RPR
4034 **1** **Royal Flynn**[12] 5064 4-9-8 **57**........ JimCrowley 8 64
(M Dods) *hld up: hdwy over 2f out: styd on to ld last strides* **7/1**[3]
2002 **2** shd **Yenaled**[15] 4981 9-9-3 **52**........ OscarUrbina 15 59
(J M Bradley) *hld up: hdwy 4f out: rdn to ld ins fnl f: hdd last strides* **9/1**
0500 **3** 1 **Thebestisyettocome**[93] 2577 4-9-3 **52**........ ChrisCatlin 11 57
(T G Mills) *a.p: rdn and ev ch over 1f out: styd on* **12/1**
4401 **4** hd **General Flumpa**[12] 5072 5-9-2 **58**........ JonjoMilczarek(7) 14 63
(C F Wall) *hld up: hdwy over 1f out: hung lft ins fnl f: r.o* **9/2**[2]
3430 **5** ½ **Shrine Mountain (USA)**[17] 4925 4-9-4 **53**........ FergusSweeney 9 57
(J R Holt) *led 1f: chsd ldr tl led over 2f out: rdn over 1f out: hdd and no ex ins fnl f* **15/2**
0006 **6** ½ **Western Roots**[16] 4972 5-9-3 **52**........ IanMongan 16 55
(M Appleby) *racd wd thrght: prom: rdn and ev ch fr over 1f out tl no ex wl ins fnl f* **20/1**
3405 **7** 2 **Will The Till**[7] 5166 4-8-11 **51**........(b) KevinGhunowa(5) 4 51
(J M Bradley) *s.i.s: hld up: styd on ins fnl f: nrst fin* **9/1**
0061 **8** 1 **Royal Premier (IRE)**[9] 5129 3-9-2 **58**........(v) FJohansson 5 56
(H J Collingridge) *chsd ldrs: rdn 1/2-way: lost pl over 3f out: no imp fnl 2f* **9/1**
6312 **9** 1 ¼ **Agilete**[5] 5240 4-9-2 **51**........ EddieAhern 10 47
(J Pearce) *s.i.s: hld up: hdwy over 3f out: wknd fnl f* **10/3**[1]
000- **10** 2 ½ **Maktu**[462] 2477 4-9-6 **55**........ RobertHavlin 2 46
(P G Murphy) *mid-div: lost pl 1/2-way: n.d after* **66/1**
4506 **11** hd **Khetaab (IRE)**[62] 3570 4-8-12 **50**........(p) EdwardCreighton(3) 1 41
(E J Alston) *led 10f out: rdn and hdd over 2f out: sn wknd* **20/1**
0065 **12** 3 **Turner**[19] 4898 5-8-10 **50**........ LiamJones(5) 13 36
(W M Brisbourne) *s.i.s: hld up: rdn over 3f out: n.d* **11/1**
000- **13** nk **Maguire (GER)**[425] 3602 5-9-1 **50**........ DavidKinsella 12 36
(M F Harris) *chsd ldrs: rdn over 4f out: wknd over 1f out* **33/1**
00 **14** 2 ½ **Midshipman**[6] 5213 8-9-4 **53**........(bt) PaulDoe 6 34
(T Keddy) *dwlt: hdwy 8f out: wknd over 1f out* **16/1**

2m 22.18s (2.78) **Going Correction** +0.075s/f (Good)
WFA 3 from 4yo+ 7lb **14** Ran SP% **131.4**
Speed ratings (Par 101):92,91,91,91,90 90,88,88,87,85 85,83,82,81
CSF £72.57 CT £776.84 TOTE £9.00: £2.90, £3.90, £5.30; EX 93.90 Place 6 £179.36, Place 5 £78.08.
Owner J A Wynn-Williams **Bred** Highclere Stud Ltd **Trained** Denton, Co Durham
■ Stewards' Enquiry : Chris Catlin one-day ban: used whip with excessive frequency (Oct 24)

FOCUS
A low-grade handicap. The field fanned across the track in the home straight. Not a strong race, but the form is sound.
T/Plt: £407.60 to a £1 stake. Pool: £43,859.70. 78.55 winning tickets. T/Qpdt: £71.30 to a £1 stake. Pool: £2,351.40. 24.40 winning tickets. KH

5245 WOLVERHAMPTON (A.W) (L-H)
Saturday, September 16

OFFICIAL GOING: Standard
Wind: Virtually nil

5386 WOLVERHAMPTON-RACECOURSE.CO.UK H'CAP — 7f 32y(P)
7:00 (7:01) (Class 6) (0-65,65) 3-Y-0+ **£2,730** (£806; £403) **Stalls** High

Form RPR
0426 **1** **Sovereignty (JPN)**[13] 5046 4-9-3 **61**........ DarrylHolland 5 70
(D K Ivory) *hld up: hdwy on outside over 2f out: str run to ld ent fnl f: hung rt: all out* **5/1**[2]
223 **2** hd **Sedge (USA)**[16] 4961 6-9-2 **60**........(p) HayleyTurner 10 68
(P T Midgley) *mid-divisision: hdwy whn swtchd lft ent fnl f: r.o: jst failed* **11/2**[3]
1516 **3** ¾ **Captain Darling (IRE)**[35] 4368 6-9-4 **65**........ EdwardCreighton(3) 8 71
(R W Price) *trckd ldr: led briefly over 1f out: nt qckn ins fnl f* **6/1**
5300 **4** ¾ **No Grouse**[32] 4456 6-9-1 **59**........ RobertHavlin 7 63
(E J Alston) *hld up: rdn and hdwy over 1f out: r.o: nvr nrr* **8/1**
0242 **5** hd **Million Percent**[4] 5269 7-8-12 **61**........ LiamJones(5) 3 65
(C R Dore) *in tch: rdn and ev ch ent fnl f: no ex ins* **9/2**[1]
0405 **6** 1 ¼ **Regal Dream (IRE)**[5] 5233 4-9-6 **64**........ EddieAhern 2 64
(J W Hills) *mid-div: hdwy on ins wl over 1f out: fdd ins fnl f* **7/1**
0004 **7** ½ **Kingsmaite**[47] 3995 5-8-13 **64**........(bt) MSemple(7) 6 63
(S R Bowring) *led tl rdn and hdd over 1f out: wknd ins fnl f* **20/1**
4030 **8** nk **Dream Forest (IRE)**[22] 4772 3-8-11 **65**........ JamesMillman(7) 12 63
(Mrs P N Dutfield) *slowly into stgride: effrt on ins over 1f out: nvr on terms* **50/1**
5000 **9** 2 **Right Ted (IRE)**[19] 4871 3-9-4 **65**........ ChrisCatlin 11 58
(T Wall) *a towards rr* **33/1**
0340 **10** ¾ **Desert Opal**[14] 5032 6-9-2 **60**........ TPQueally 1 51
(C R Dore) *trckd ldrs tl rdn and wknd over 1f out* **14/1**
0130 **11** ¾ **Jellytot (USA)**[22] 4769 3-9-3 **64**........ CatherineGannon 9 53
(K A Ryan) *hld up: no hdwy fnl 2f* **25/1**
4-00 **12** 6 **Vlasta Weiner**[29] 4551 6-8-10 **61**........(b) BarrySavage(7) 4 35
(J M Bradley) *prom: rdn over 2f out: wknd wl over 1f out* **25/1**

1m 29.58s (-0.82) **Going Correction** -0.15s/f (Stan)
WFA 3 from 4yo+ 3lb **12** Ran SP% **112.2**
Speed ratings (Par 101):98,97,96,96,95 94,93,93,91,90 89,82
CSF £28.43 CT £168.55 TOTE £8.30: £2.90, £2.20, £2.40; EX 41.40.
Owner Radlett Racing **Bred** Darley Stud Management, L L C **Trained** Radlett, Herts

FOCUS
A competitive heat run at a good pace.

5387 DINE IN THE ZONGALERO RESTAURANT (S) STKS — 7f 32y(P)
7:30 (7:31) (Class 6) 2-Y-O **£2,388** (£705; £352) **Stalls** High

Form RPR
0 **1** **Forced Upon Us**[28] 4600 2-8-8........ EdwardCreighton(3) 7 59
(P J McBride) *hld up on outside: hdwy 1/2-way: sustained run fr over 1f out to ld nr fin* **14/1**
5206 **2** nk **Dansilver**[22] 4767 2-8-4 57........ JosephWalsh(7) 12 58
(D J Wintle) *t.k.h: sn trckd ldr: led 2f out: rdn and kpt on: hdd nr fin* **9/1**
5005 **3** hd **Right Option (IRE)**[37] 4303 2-8-11 66........ DarrylHolland 3 57
(A P Jarvis) *hld up: rdn and hdwy on outside appr fnl f: r.o wl ins: nvr nrr* **6/1**[2]
0535 **4** ¾ **Only Hope**[11] 5094 2-8-6 65........ ChrisCatlin 10 51
(M R Channon) *mid-div: rdn over 2f out: styd on fnl f* **7/4**[1]
056 **5** nk **Ten Black**[16] 4969 2-8-11 58........ TPQueally 5 55
(J A Osborne) *mid-div: rdn 3f out: nt qckn fnl f* **16/1**
0 **6** ¾ **Prima Luna**[36] 4327 2-7-13........ PatrickDonaghy(7) 8 48
(K R Burke) *slowly away: in rr: hdwy ent fnl f but nvr nr to chal* **66/1**
35 **7** 1 **Bridget's Team**[74] 3174 2-8-1........ LeanneKershaw(5) 4 45
(P C Haslam) *a towards rr* **20/1**
5500 **8** ¾ **Hidden Ace (IRE)**[5] 5238 2-8-6 60........(b) TPO'Shea 1 43
(M W Easterby) *in tch: rdn and no hdwy appr fnl f* **17/2**
4005 **9** hd **Kaladar (IRE)**[11] 5084 2-8-11 58........(p) CatherineGannon 9 48
(K A Ryan) *in tch: rdn over 2f out: wknd over 1f out* **8/1**[3]
0005 **10** 6 **Peppin's Gold (IRE)**[17] 4926 2-8-6 58........ JimCrowley 11 27
(B R Millman) *led after 1f: hdd 2f out: sn wknd* **8/1**[3]
00 **11** 5 **Will Doo**[20] 4829 2-8-6........ EmmettStack(5) 2 19
(M E Sowersby) *led for 1f: rdn and wknd over 2f out* **100/1**
0 **12** nk **Maskaraid**[42] 4163 2-8-11........ RobertHavlin 6 18
(B R Millman) *chsd ldrs tl wknd 1/2-way* **66/1**

1m 31.27s (0.87) **Going Correction** -0.15s/f (Stan) **12** Ran SP% **114.7**
Speed ratings (Par 93):89,88,88,87,87 86,85,84,84,77 71,71
CSF £127.33 TOTE £15.10: £4.50, £3.00, £1.80; EX 156.80.The winner was bought in for 6,500gns. Only Hope was claimed by Mr E. Oertel for £6,000. Right Option was claimed by Mr J. Weymes for £6,000.
Owner Mrs Julie King **Bred** Lady Fairhaven **Trained** Newmarket, Suffolk
■ Stewards' Enquiry : Catherine Gannon one-day ban: careless riding (Sep 27)

FOCUS
A number of these were dropping into selling company for the first time and it was one of the least exposed runners in the line-up that came out on top.

NOTEBOOK
Forced Upon Us took advantage of a drop in class to score under a strong ride. This race was very different from his Newmarket introduction, and connections, who went to 6,500gns to retain him, might look at a handicap now. (op 12-1 tchd 16-1)
Dansilver has raised his game since stepping up to this trip and did nothing wrong. This was his All-Weather debut and he is entitled to improve. (op 11-1 tchd 17-2)
Right Option(IRE) had the highest BHB rating and indicated that he appreciated the return to this trip. (op 5-1)
Only Hope looks one to be wary of. Travelling best of all on the top turn, she put her head up under pressure and did not want to know. Some form of headgear could be the order of the day. (op 5-2)
Kaladar(IRE) was much too keen and had nothing left in the straight. (op 9-1)

5388 BOOK YOUR CHRISTMAS PARTY NOW MAIDEN H'CAP — 1m 141y(P)
8:00 (8:00) (Class 5) (0-70,70) 3-Y-0+ **£3,238** (£963; £481; £240) **Stalls** Low

Form RPR
332 **1** **Evident Pride (USA)**[78] 3053 3-9-3 **66**........ SebSanders 10 76
(B R Johnson) *hld up: hdwy on outside to ld 2f out: rdnand edgd lft ent fnl f: jst hld on: all out* **5/1**[3]
2423 **2** shd **Signal Hill**[17] 4933 3-8-12 **66**........(v[1]) LiamJones(5) 3 76
(W J Haggas) *t.k.h: hld up: hdwy 2f out: rdn and ev ch 1f out: pressed wnr to line* **11/4**[1]
4536 **3** shd **Shy Glance (USA)**[24] 4698 4-9-3 **61**........ DaleGibson 2 71
(G A Swinbank) *t.k.h: led for 1f: styd prom: swtchd rt appr fnl f: raliied and pressed ldng pair to line* **8/1**
55 **4** 6 **Another Genepi (USA)**[20] 4844 3-9-5 **68**........ EddieAhern 9 65
(J W Hills) *hld up in rr: styd on past btn horses fr over 1f out but nvr nr to chal* **14/1**
3054 **5** ½ **Great Chieftain (IRE)**[16] 4973 3-9-3 **66**........ PatDobbs 4 62
(R A Fahey) *in tch tl rdn and wknd wl over 1f out* **16/1**
3463 **6** 1 ¼ **Kalatime (IRE)**[20] 4842 3-9-4 **67**........ SteveDrowne 11 61
(A M Balding) *bhd: rdn over 2f out: nvr on terms* **16/1**
4633 **7** hd **Casual Affair**[16] 4973 3-9-5 **68**........ ChrisCatlin 12 61
(E J O'Neill) *prom: rdn 3f out: wknd 2f out* **14/1**
5230 **8** nk **Beldon Hill (USA)**[47] 4010 3-9-5 **68**........ HayleyTurner 13 61
(C E Brittain) *a in rr* **28/1**
00-0 **9** 1 ½ **Benny The Bus**[5] 5249 4-9-9 **67**........(p) DeanMcKeown 6 57
(Mrs G S Rees) *prom: rdn over 2f out: wknd over 1f out* **33/1**
065- **10** 7 **Take It There**[355] 5505 4-9-6 **64**........ RichardThomas 8 39
(A J Lidderdale) *mid-div: rdn over 3f out: sn bhd* **66/1**
0332 **11** ½ **Floodlight Fantasy**[19] 4892 3-9-2 **65**........(v[1]) TedDurcan 1 39
(E S McMahon) *led after 1f: hdd 2f out: wknd rapidly* **4/1**[2]
3402 **12** 5 **Digger Boy**[31] 4491 3-9-2 **65**........ DarrylHolland 5 28
(M A Jarvis) *mid-divisision: bhd fr 1/2-way* **13/2**
04 **13** 3 ½ **Ten To The Dozen**[94] 2542 3-9-7 **70**........ RobertMiles 7 26
(P W Hiatt) *trckd ldrs: rdn and wknd qckly 2f out* **50/1**

1m 49.44s (-2.32) **Going Correction** -0.15s/f (Stan)
WFA 3 from 4yo 5lb **13** Ran SP% **122.7**
Speed ratings (Par 103):104,103,103,98,98 96,96,96,95,88 88,84,80
CSF £19.20 CT £115.94 TOTE £7.00: £2.40, £1.80, £2.50; EX 29.90.

Owner C Lefevre **Bred** Juddmonte Farms Inc **Trained** Ashtead, Surrey
FOCUS
A modest maiden handicap in which the first three came well clear.
Another Genepi(USA) Official explanation: jockey said filly was denied a clear run throughout

5389 EUROPEAN BREEDERS FUND MAIDEN STKS 1m 141y(P)
8:30 (8:31) (Class 5) 2-Y-O **£3,886** (£1,156; £577; £288) **Stalls** Low

Form RPR
432 **1** **Aim To Prosper (IRE)**[9] [5126] 2-9-3 84 TedDurcan 8 76+
(M R Channon) *a.p: led 5f out: rdn clr over 1f out: easily* **4/7**[1]
42 **2** *3 1/2* **Aussie Cricket (FR)**[15] [4980] 2-8-12 TPQueally 6 64
(D J Coakley) *hld up in tch: rdn to chse wnr 2f out: no imp fnl f* **7/2**[2]
3 *3/4* **Robert The Brave** 2-9-3 SteveDrowne 3 67
(A J McCabe) *slowly away: in rr: styd on fr over 1f out to go 3rd nr fin* **66/1**
3060 **4** *1/2* **Tension Point**[22] [4773] 2-9-3 68 EddieAhern 2 66
(J A Osborne) *in tch: rdn 3f out: one pce fnl 2f and lost 3rd nr fin* **14/1**
00 **5** *5* **Vietnam**[10] [5105] 2-9-3 FrankieMcDonald 1 56
(S Kirk) *mid-division: hdwy over 2f out: wknd over 1f out* **100/1**
6 *7* **Ancient Site (USA)** 2-9-3 PaulEddery 5 41
(B P J Baugh) *mid-division: wl bhd fnl 3f* **100/1**
0 **7** *hd* **Lady Shirley Hunt**[12] [5068] 2-8-7 LiamJones[(5)] 10 35
(A D Smith) *prom tl wknd wl over 1f out* **100/1**
0 **8** *1* **Bronzo Di Riace (IRE)**[24] [4705] 2-9-3 CatherineGannon 4 38
(K A Ryan) *led tl hdd 5f out: wknd 2f out* **66/1**
0 **9** *3/4* **Didactic**[10] [5111] 2-9-3 DarryllHolland 9 37
(A J McCabe) *hld up: a in rr* **33/1**
04 **10** *3/4* **Into Action**[19] [4867] 2-9-3 PatDobbs 11 35
(R Hannon) *prom early: stmbld on bnd over 6f out: sn bhd* **11/1**[3]
0 **11** *1/2* **Sangfroid**[4] [5261] 2-9-3 SebSanders 7 34
(Sir Mark Prescott) *racked on outside: hung lft and bhd fr 1/2-way* **40/1**

1m 51.98s (0.22) **Going Correction** -0.15s/f (Stan) **11** Ran SP% **112.2**
Speed ratings (Par 95):93,89,89,88,84 78,77,77,76,75 75
CSF £2.34 TOTE £1.60: £1.10, £1.60, £4.20; EX 3.70.
Owner Aaim To Prosper **Bred** Mrs Stephanie Hanly **Trained** West Ilsley, Berks
FOCUS
An uncompetitive maiden that proved a fine opportunity for Aaim To Prosper to get off the mark.
NOTEBOOK
Aaim To Prosper(IRE) won easily and looks a good staying prospect for next year. This was an easier race than his last two Chepstow assignments and he took full advantage of the opportunity under a positive ride. He is likely to have one more race before being put away for the year. (op 8-11 tchd 4-5 in places)
Aussie Cricket(FR) has displayed an aversion to the stalls and was attended at the start by her trainer. She settled better than had been the case at Chepstow last time but was unable to challenge the impressive winner. She appeared to handle the surface on this All-Weather debut and should be found an opportunity soon. (op 11-4 tchd 4-1)
Robert The Brave, who is closely related to a three-year-old winner in Greece by Primo Dominie, kept on to take minor money but was never a threat to the easy winner. (tchd 80-1)
Tension Point never threatened and has become disappointing.
Lady Shirley Hunt Official explanation: jockey said filly did not handle the bends
Into Action Official explanation: jockey said colt suffered interference on first bend
Sangfroid Official explanation: jockey said colt hung left-handed throughout

5390 GEORGE WALKER MEMORIAL H'CAP 1m 4f 50y(P)
9:00 (9:00) (Class 6) (0-60,60) 3-Y-O+ **£2,730** (£806; £403) **Stalls** Low

Form RPR
1504 **1** **Abstract Folly (IRE)**[17] [4925] 4-9-5 58 DarryllHolland 1 66
(J D Bethell) *hld up in rr: hdwy over 2f out: rdn and styd on to ld post* **11/4**[1]
5053 **2** *shd* **Birthday Star (IRE)**[6] [5213] 4-8-12 58 AlanRutter[(7)] 3 66
(W J Musson) *hld up in rr: hdwy on ins over 2f out: led u.p ins fnl f: edgd rt and hdd post* **11/4**[1]
-031 **3** *1/2* **Turn Of Phrase (IRE)**[12] [5064] 7-9-4 60 (b) GregFairley[(3)] 9 67
(B Ellison) *mid-div: hdwy 3f out: led 2f out: rdn and hdd ins fnl f: no ex cl home* **6/1**[3]
1114 **4** *8* **Zalkani (IRE)**[61] [3594] 6-9-4 57 DeanMcKeown 10 51
(J Pearce) *hld up: sme hdwy 2f out: styd on one pce past btn horses* **5/1**[2]
6160 **5** *2* **I'll Do It Today**[30] [4522] 5-9-6 59 PatDobbs 11 50
(J M Jefferson) *hld up in tch: rdn over 2f out: sn btn* **10/1**
0330 **6** *2 1/2* **Fairlight Express (IRE)**[48] [3983] 6-9-2 55 DaleGibson 5 42
(B G Powell) *trckd ldr: ev ch 2f out: rdn and wknd over 1f out* **16/1**
0050 **7** *2 1/2* **Malibu (IRE)**[24] [4709] 5-9-6 59 HayleyTurner 8 42
(S R Bowring) *mid-div: bhd fnl 3f* **50/1**
0010 **8** *1/2* **Optimum (IRE)**[27] [4632] 4-9-0 58 RoryMoore[(5)] 2 40
(J T Stimpson) *led: rdn 3f out: hdd 2f out: wknd qckly* **14/1**
5000 **9** *2 1/2* **Kathleen Kennet**[91] [2647] 6-9-2 55 SteveDrowne 7 33
(Mrs H Sweeting) *a in rr* **40/1**
0 **10** *1 3/4* **April Attraction (FR)**[22] [4777] 4-9-7 60 PaulEddery 6 35
(C J Down) *trckd ldrs tl rdn and wknd over 3f out* **80/1**
-100 **11** *10* **Explosive Fox (IRE)**[6] [3431] 5-9-5 58 (p) AlanDaly 4 17
(S Curran) *trckd ldrs: rdn 4f out: sn wknd* **14/1**

2m 40.21s (-2.21) **Going Correction** -0.15s/f (Stan) **11** Ran SP% **118.2**
Speed ratings (Par 101):101,100,100,95,93 92,90,90,88,87 80
CSF £9.62 CT £41.84 TOTE £3.50: £1.70, £1.80, £2.20; EX 13.50.
Owner Clarendon Thoroughbred Racing **Bred** John Neary **Trained** Middleham Moor, N Yorks
■ Stewards' Enquiry : Alan Rutter three-day ban: careless riding (Sep 27-28, Oct 2)
FOCUS
A moderate handicap in which the main players all came from off the pace, and the first three finished clear.
Optimum(IRE) Official explanation: jockey said gelding had no more to give
Kathleen Kennet Official explanation: jockey said mare suffered steering problems

5391 BERNASIA AND HENRY'S SILVER WEDDING ANNIVERSARY H'CAP 5f 216y(P)
9:30 (9:30) (Class 5) (0-75,75) 3-Y-O+ **£3,238** (£963; £481; £240) **Stalls** Low

Form RPR
2250 **1** **Rosein**[5] [5246] 4-9-1 70 SebSanders 5 79
(Mrs G S Rees) *prom: rdn to ld over 1f out: kpt on u.p: jst hld on* **8/1**[3]
5012 **2** *hd* **Mambazo**[4] [5263] 4-9-1 73 6ex (e) RichardKingscote[(3)] 6 81
(S C Williams) *t.k.h: a.p: c wd into st: r.o wl fnl f to cl on wnr line* **4/1**[1]
0000 **3** *shd* **Prince Tum Tum (USA)**[5] [5246] 6-9-5 74 DaleGibson 9 82
(D Shaw) *towards rr: rdn over 2f out: hdwy over 1f out: r.o and fin wl fnl f* **7/1**[2]
0006 **4** *1/2* **Cornus**[12] [5058] 4-9-3 72 TPQueally 11 79
(J A Osborne) *hld up: rdn and hdwy whn edgd rt appr fnl f: r.o wl ins* **9/1**
4100 **5** *hd* **Norcroft**[5] [5246] 4-9-3 72 (p) BrianReilly 7 78
(Mrs C A Dunnett) *mid-div: rdn over 1f out: r.o fnl f* **12/1**
0050 **6** *1* **Prince Cyrano**[5] [5246] 7-9-1 70 PatDobbs 1 73
(W J Musson) *mid-div: hdwy on ins to go 2nd 1f out: fdd fnl 100yds* **12/1**
2154 **7** *1 1/4* **Kennington**[5] [5246] 6-8-12 70 (b) GregFairley[(3)] 12 69
(Mrs C A Dunnett) *in tch: rdn over 2f out: wknd ins fnl f* **12/1**
36-0 **8** *2 1/2* **Anchor Date**[10] [5117] 4-9-5 74 (t) HayleyTurner 3 66
(D Shaw) *hld up: rdn wl over 1f out: sn btn* **40/1**
0-30 **9** *1/2* **Smokin Joe**[248] [89] 5-9-3 72 (b) SteveDrowne 8 62
(J R Best) *hld up towards rr: nvr on terms* **25/1**
1041 **10** *shd* **Count Cougar (USA)**[137] [1388] 6-8-11 66 ChrisCatlin 4 56
(S P Griffiths) *led tl rdn and hdd over 1f out: wknd ins fnl f* **11/1**
5323 **11** *1* **Harrison's Flyer (IRE)**[20] [4846] 5-8-12 67 (p) TedDurcan 2 54
(J M Bradley) *mid-divisision: rdn and wknd 2f out* **7/1**[2]
3043 **12** *1 1/2* **Lake Garda**[21] [4807] 5-9-6 75 (b) CatherineGannon 13 57
(K A Ryan) *chsd ldrs: rdn and wknd over 2f out* **8/1**[3]
6440 **13** *16* **Regal Sunset (IRE)**[6] [5211] 3-9-4 75 (v[1]) DarryllHolland 10 9
(W R Swinburn) *slowly away: racd wd: lost tch over 2f out and eased* **20/1**

1m 14.21s (-1.60) **Going Correction** -0.15s/f (Stan)
WFA 3 from 4yo+ 2lb **13** Ran SP% **119.7**
Speed ratings (Par 103):104,103,103,102,102 101,99,96,95,95 94,92,70
CSF £39.11 CT £241.46 TOTE £9.40: £3.60, £2.60, £2.60; EX 63.20 Place 6 £33.82, Place 5 £13.37.
Owner Mrs G S Rees **Bred** J Gittins And Capt J H Wilson **Trained** Sollom, Lancs
■ Stewards' Enquiry : Seb Sanders one-day ban: used whip with excessive frequency (Sep 27)
FOCUS
A fair handicap and, in what proved a handicapper's dream, a blanket covered the first five home.
Regal Sunset(IRE) Official explanation: jockey said gelding fly-leapt as the gates opened and would not face the kick-back
T/Plt: £69.80 to a £1 stake. Pool: £55,474.85. 579.75 winning tickets. T/Qpdt: £5.80 to a £1 stake. Pool: £2,821.20. 358.40 winning tickets. JS

5392 - (Foreign Racing) - See Raceform Interactive

[4849] CURRAGH (R-H)
Saturday, September 16
OFFICIAL GOING: Straight course - good to yielding; round course - good

5393a BALLYGALLON STUD RENAISSANCE STKS (GROUP 3) 6f
2:40 (2:43) 3-Y-O+ **£33,620** (£9,827; £4,655; £1,551)

RPR
1 **Beauty Bright (IRE)**[20] [4855] 3-8-12 97 JAHeffernan 4 109
(A P O'Brien, Ire) *trckd ldrs: 2nd fr 2f out: chal over 1f out: led ins fnl f: styd on wl: comf* **14/1**
2 *1 1/4* **Noelani (IRE)**[23] [4749] 4-9-0 104 MJKinane 2 105
(John M Oxx, Ire) *prom: 2nd early: 3rd 1/2-way: rdn under 2f out: kpt on ins fnl f* **9/2**[2]
3 *shd* **An Tadh (IRE)**[55] [3767] 3-9-4 107 (b[1]) JMurtagh 3 111
(G M Lyons, Ire) *led: rdn and strly pressed over 1f out: hdd ins fnl f: no ex cl home* **10/1**
4 *4* **Indian Maiden (IRE)**[7] [5171] 6-9-3 FMBerry 8 96
(M S Saunders) *trckd ldrs on outer: 5th and prog 2f out: 4th over 1f out: sn no ex* **9/4**[1]
5 *2 1/2* **Beckermet (IRE)**[7] [5179] 4-9-3 DPMcDonogh 7 88
(R F Fisher) *chsd ldrs: 3rd early: 4th u.p 2f out: sn no ex* **9/2**[2]
6 *2 1/2* **Chief Crazy Horse**[23] [4746] 3-9-1 KFallon 6 81
(A P O'Brien, Ire) *hld up: 6th and effrt 2f out: sn no ex* **5/1**[3]
7 *hd* **Absolutelyfabulous (IRE)**[20] [4855] 3-8-12 98 WMLordan 9 77
(David Wachman, Ire) *chsd ldrs: 5th early: 7th and rdn over 2f out: sn no ex* **10/1**
8 *8* **Senor Benny (USA)**[20] [4855] 7-9-3 104 PJSmullen 5 56
(M McDonagh, Ire) *a bhd: trailing fr 2f out* **25/1**

1m 14.2s **Going Correction** +0.125s/f (Good)
WFA 3 from 4yo+ 2lb **8** Ran SP% **112.5**
Speed ratings: 107,105,105,99,96 93,92,82
CSF £73.20 TOTE £24.80: £4.60, £1.70, £2.00; DF 240.90.
Owner Michael Tabor **Bred** Southern Bloodstock **Trained** Ballydoyle, Co Tipperary
FOCUS
Not a particularly strong Group 3 rated through the third.
NOTEBOOK
Beauty Bright(IRE) could have been given a chance on her close second to Indian Maiden at Leopardstown in July, but it was still something of a surprise to see her win her first race at this level. Aidan O'Brien expressed the view that, having been tried over longer trips earlier in the season, it took Beauty Bright a while to get the hang of sprinting when she came back in distance. (op 12/1)
Noelani(IRE), who won this race last year, came here looking to recapture her best form and stayed on quite well under pressure from over a furlong out. Another stakes race success may come her way.
An Tadh(IRE), fitted with blinkers, produced a bold effort from the front and had most of his rivals in serious trouble with over two furlongs to run. This was his best effort since he won a Group 3 over seven furlongs at Leopardstown in June, and he is not short of pace. It would appear that he would not be at all inconvenienced by dropping back to the minimum trip. (op 8/1)
Indian Maiden(IRE), who struck at this level at Deauville last month, raced towards the outside of the field. She picked up a few places heading into the final quarter of a mile but was soon done with. A multiple stakes winner, she was probably not at her best. (op 11/4 tchd 3/1)
Beckermet(IRE) raced prominently but was fighting a losing battle from well over a furlong out. He is a very capable sort at his best but did not seem to match the form that saw him run a close third behind Tax Free and Ashdown Express at Goodwood last weekend. (op 4/1)
Chief Crazy Horse ran respectably in what was a much tougher race than the maiden he won at Tipperary last month. (op 4/1)
Absolutelyfabulous(IRE) probably needs faster ground to be seen at her best.

5394a C.L.WELD PARK STKS (GROUP 3) (FILLIES) 7f
3:10 (3:10) 2-Y-O **£35,917** (£10,537; £5,020; £1,710)

RPR
1 **Arch Swing (USA)**[34] [4406] 2-8-12 MJKinane 4 108+
(John M Oxx, Ire) *trckd ldrs travelling wl: 4th 1/2-way: 3rd 2 1/2f out: led under 2f out: sn rdn clr: easily* **8/1**
2 *4 1/2* **Silk Dress (IRE)**[20] [4853] 2-8-12 97 DMGrant 2 96
(John Joseph Murphy, Ire) *trckd ldrs on outer: 4th 2 1/2f out: 2nd 1 1/2f out: no imp fnl f: kpt on same pce* **33/1**
3 *shd* **Impetious**[15] [5005] 2-8-12 81 WMLordan 5 96
(Eamon Tyrrell, Ire) *hld up in tch: 5th and prog whn edgd rt over 1f out: kpt on u.p ins fnl f* **33/1**

4 *5* **Dimenticata (IRE)**[20] [4853] 2-8-12 104 .... DPMcDonogh 6 83
(Kevin Prendergast, Ire) *hld up in tch: 7th and rdn 2f out: no imp: kpt on same pce* **6/1**[3]
5 *1/2* **Dushinka (IRE)**[20] [4850] 2-8-12 98 .... WSupple 1 81
(Timothy Doyle, Ire) *hld up in tch: rdn and prog on outer under 3f out: 5th over 2f out: no ex fr 1 1/2f out* **14/1**
6 *hd* **Kissinthemoonlight**[29] [4578] 2-8-12 94 ....(b) FMBerry 9 81
(John M Oxx, Ire) *led: rdn and hdd under 2f out: sn wknd* **16/1**
7 *3 1/2* **Nell Gwyn (IRE)**[19] [4904] 2-8-12 .... KFallon 7 72
(A P O'Brien, Ire) *chsd ldrs on far rail: 3rd and drvn along 1/2-way: rdn and no imp 2f out: bdly hmpd and eased over 1f out* **4/1**[2]
8 *shd* **Supposition**[20] [4853] 2-8-12 107 .... PJSmullen 8 72
(D K Weld, Ire) *cl 2nd: rdn to chal under 2 1/2f out: 5th and no imp whn hmpd and checked over 1f out: eased* **4/5**[1]
9 *19* **Asafa (IRE)** 2-8-12 .... KJManning 3 22
(J S Bolger, Ire) *a in rr: wknd fr 2 1/2f out: sn eased* **25/1**

1m 27.1s **Going Correction** +0.125s/f (Good) **9** Ran SP% **123.2**
Speed ratings: 107,101,101,96,95 95,91,91,69
CSF £242.94 TOTE £6.30: £1.50, £8.50, £8.40; DF 402.00.
Owner P Garvey **Bred** T L Folkerth **Trained** Currabeg, Co Kildare
■ Stewards' Enquiry : W M Lordan three-day ban: careless riding (Sep 26,29-30)

FOCUS
A decent renewal on paper, but the performance of the second and third and the disappointing effort of the favourite casts some doubt on the level of the form.

NOTEBOOK
Arch Swing(USA) stepped up on the form of her six-furlong maiden win here last month to record a clear-cut success. Having swept through to lead with well over a furlong to run, she quickly moved clear to put the result beyond doubt. A filly of some potential, she holds an entry in the Prix Marcel Boussac in a fortnight's time but is not sure to take up that engagement. She was introduced at 20-1 for the 1000 Guineas. (op 7/1)
Silk Dress(IRE) ran an excellent race to take second. One of two maidens in the field, she was having her fourth run and had previously shown ability when fourth to Four Sins in a conditions event over this course and distance and when beaten only five lengths in the Moyglare Stakes. She should not have any trouble winning a maiden. (op 25/1)
Impetious, given a patient ride, started a forward move heading into the final quarter of a mile and then edged right near the furlong marker, hampering both Supposition and Nell Gwyn in the process. To her credit she stayed on well in the closing stages to secure third. Already a winner, she had also run quite well to take third behind Four Sins here last month. (op 25/1)
Dimenticata(IRE) could never land a telling blow and was probably not at her best. This run did not match the form of her close second in the Debutante Stakes or her sixth in the Moyglare. (op 5/1)
Dushinka(IRE) started a move with over a quarter of a mile to run but could do no more from over a furlong out and she might do better dropped back in trip. (op 12/1)
Kissinthemoonlight tried to make all and ran respectably. This was much tougher than the Roscommon maiden she won last month.
Nell Gwyn(IRE) was struggling to make an impression when badly hampered by Impetious, after which she was eased. She can do better but the form of her Tralee maiden success left her with something to find at this level. (op 11/4)
Supposition, third in the Moyglare Stud Stakes, was well below her best and something was surely amiss with her. After racing in second, she challenged for the lead with over two furlongs to run but was soon done with and was already well held when hampered. (op 1/1)

5395a IRISH FIELD ST. LEGER (GROUP 1) 1m 6f
3:45 (3:46) 3-Y-0+
£120,413 (£39,724; £19,034; £6,620; £4,551; £2,482)

RPR
1 **Kastoria (IRE)**[27] [4639] 5-9-7 111 ....(t) MJKinane 8 119
(John M Oxx, Ire) *trckd ldrs in 4th: smooth hdwy into 2nd early st: chal over 1f out: rdn to ld 100 yds out: styd on wl* **6/1**[2]
2 *1/2* **Yeats (IRE)**[44] [4081] 5-9-10 121 .... KFallon 5 121
(A P O'Brien, Ire) *settled 2nd: impr to ld over 5f out: rdn st: strly pressed fr over 1f out: hdd 100 yds out: kpt on* **2/7**[1]
3 *10* **The Whistling Teal**[25] [4677] 10-9-10 .... WSupple 2 109
(G Wragg) *hld up in tch: 6th and prog appr st: mod 4th 2f out: kpt on same pce* **20/1**
4 *1 3/4* **Fracas (IRE)**[13] [5051] 4-9-10 111 .... WMLordan 3 107
(David Wachman, Ire) *trckd ldrs in 3rd: 2nd and rdn to chal appr st: 3rd and no imp fr over 2f out: kpt on same pce u.p* **20/1**
5 *shd* **Akarem**[5] [5253] 5-9-10 .... PatCosgrave 1 107
(K R Burke) *trckd ldrs in 5th: 4th 5f out: rdn and no imp st* **33/1**
6 *2* **Frank Sonata**[14] [5010] 5-9-10 .... PJSmullen 7 104
(M G Quinlan) *hld up: 7th 5f out: 6th and rdn st: no imp fr 2f out* **33/1**
7 *1 1/4* **Percussionist (IRE)**[120] [1833] 5-9-10 .... DPMcDonogh 4 103
(J Howard Johnson) *sn led: rdn and hdd over 5f out: wknd bef st* **12/1**[3]
8 *5* **Chimes At Midnight (USA)**[15] [4996] 9-9-10 44....(b) FranciscoDaSilva 6 97?
(Luke Comer, Ire) *a towards rr: drvn along after 1/2-way: no ex fr 5f out* **300/1**

3m 1.00s **Going Correction** -0.10s/f (Good) **8** Ran SP% **115.5**
Speed ratings: 99,98,93,92,91 90,90,87
CSF £8.04 TOTE £5.40: £1.40, £1.10, £2.20; DF 12.80.
Owner H H Aga Khan **Bred** H H Aga Khan's Stud's S C **Trained** Currabeg, Co Kildare

FOCUS
This did not look a particularly competitive renewal on paper and only two mattered from a long way out. The winner is a progressive sort while the runner-up was disappointing in this race for the second year running. The race has been rated through the third.

NOTEBOOK
Kastoria(IRE), a lightly-raced mare having just her 11th career start, has enjoyed a good season and posted a personal best here. Briefly under pressure as Yeats went to the front with over five furlongs to run, she was soon back on an even keel and travelling well in the leader's slipstream off the final bend. When asked for her maximum approaching the final furlong she ran on well to get on top close home and deny the odds-on favourite. Next month's Canadian International at Woodbine is likely to be her next target. (op 5/1 tchd 13/2)
Yeats(IRE), running over this trip for the first time since finishing fourth in last year's renewal, looked likely to take plenty of beating following his successes in the Ascot Gold Cup and Goodwood Cup, but he was again a beaten favourite. While the steady early tempo was not in his favour, he quickly stamped his authority on the race when striking the front with over five furlongs to run, and he answered his rider's every call in the straight. He just could not fend off the winner, though, and it is possible that he is simply a summer horse. He may miss the Melbourne Cup now. (op 1/3)
The Whistling Teal, last year's runner-up, started to improve his position nearing the straight and stayed on under pressure over the final quarter mile without making any inroads on the front pair. Now a ten-year-old, he remains in fine fettle, as his efforts here, in the Lonsdale Stakes and the Group 3 he won at Chester in May indicate. (op 16/1)
Fracas(IRE) ran respectably. After an encouraging return to action in a German Group 1 last month, he was well below his best back at Baden-Baden next time but did show more dash here. He held second approaching the straight but could do no more over the final quarter of a mile. He can do better back over a mile and a half. (op 16/1)
Akarem is a capable performer at Listed level and acquitted himself respectably on this step up in grade. He ran better than when third in a Listed race at Galway five days earlier.
Frank Sonata had plenty to do on official figures and was never able to land a blow.
Percussionist(IRE) was having his first run since winning the Yorkshire Cup in May and would have preferred much softer ground. He set a steady tempo until Yeats went past him and then he weakened out of contention.

5396a CROWN PAINTS H'CAP (PREMIER HANDICAP) 1m 2f
4:15 (4:18) 3-Y-0+ **£24,693** (£7,244; £3,451; £1,175)

RPR
1 **Nurenberg (IRE)**[22] [4785] 4-8-3 72 .... RPCleary(3) 8 84
(M Halford, Ire) *mde all: edgd clr fr over 2f out: styd on wl fnl f: comf* **16/1**
2 *1 3/4* **Kevkat (IRE)**[17] [4941] 5-9-12 92 .... JMurtagh 1 101+
(Eoin Griffin, Ire) *hld up: hdwy over 4f out: 6th early st: mod 2nd under 2f out: kpt on wl* **6/1**[2]
3 *1 1/4* **Karawana (IRE)**[7] [5194] 3-9-8 94 ....(t) MJKinane 2 101+
(John M Oxx, Ire) *hld up in rr: 7th and hdwy over 2f out: 5th 1 1/2f out: 3rd and kpt on ins fnl f* **7/1**[3]
4 *1* **Due Respect (IRE)**[7] [5196] 6-8-9 75 .... FranciscoDaSilva 5 80
(D T Hughes, Ire) *trckd ldrs: 7th bef 1/2-way: 5th and prog ent st: mod 4th 1 1/2f out: kpt on same pce* **20/1**
5 *1/2* **Rockall Blizzard (USA)**[5] [5253] 3-9-6 97 5ex............(p) EMButterly(5) 14 101
(Noel Meade, Ire) *hld up: 6th and hdwy early st: mod 3rd under 2f out: rdn and no imp: no ex ins fnl f* **7/2**[1]
6 *5* **Tsaroxy (IRE)**[18] [4911] 4-8-8 74 .... MCHussey 13 69
(J Howard Johnson) *towards rr: kpt on st* **20/1**
7 *2 1/2* **Our Jaffa (IRE)**[112] [2040] 5-9-2 82 .... WSupple 17 73
(H Rogers, Ire) *hld up: mid-div and rdn early st: kpt on wout threatening fr 2f out* **20/1**
8 *3 1/2* **Davorin (JPN)**[20] [4852] 5-9-7 92 .... PBBeggy(5) 11 76
(R P Burns, Ire) *mid-div: prog into 7th 1/2-way: 4th into st: sn rdn and no imp: no ex whn eased ins fnl f* **9/1**
9 *1 1/2* **Mr Jack Daniells (IRE)**[20] [4852] 5-9-7 87 .... JAHeffernan 10 69
(Anthony Mullins, Ire) *prom: 2nd 1/2-way: rdn bef st: sn wknd* **25/1**
10 *1/2* **Sandie (IRE)**[7] [5192] 3-8-11 88 ....(b[1]) DJMoran(5) 7 69
(J S Bolger, Ire) *nvr a factor* **20/1**
11 *1* **Portant Fella**[11] [5103] 7-9-1 81 ....(p) KJManning 9 60
(Ms Joanna Morgan, Ire) *trckd ldrs: 4th 1/2-way: wknd early st: eased fr over 1f out* **10/1**
12 *3 1/2* **Convincing**[97] [2488] 3-8-4 76 .... DMGrant 4 49
(John Joseph Murphy, Ire) *nvr a factor* **14/1**
13 *12* **Imperial Rose (IRE)**[97] [2488] 4-9-2 85 ....(p) CDHayes(3) 3 36
(H Rogers, Ire) *hld up early: prog into 6th 1/2-way: wknd appr st* **25/1**
14 *1* **High Reef (FR)**[5] [5253] 8-9-7 87 .... FMBerry 16 36
(C F Swan, Ire) *chsd ldrs: stmbld early: wknd fr 4f out* **20/1**
15 *2 1/2* **Monsieur Henri (USA)**[37] [4312] 3-8-13 85 .... KFallon 6 30
(J C Hayden, Ire) *mid-div: prog into 3rd 1/2-way: wknd appr st: eased 1 1/2f out* **14/1**
16 *3 1/2* **Carnbridge (IRE)**[39] [4236] 4-9-2 82 .... NGMcCullagh 12 20
(M J Grassick, Ire) *trckd ldrs: 6th early: wknd over 4f out: trailing st* **12/1**
17 *1 1/2* **Caheerloch (IRE)**[74] [3183] 4-9-6 86 ....(b) PJSmullen 15 22
(D K Weld, Ire) *trckd ldrs on inner: 4th 1/2-way: 3rd early st: sn wknd: eased over 1f out* **12/1**

2m 7.50s **Going Correction** -0.10s/f (Good)
WFA 3 from 4yo+ 6lb **17** Ran SP% **134.2**
Speed ratings: 103,101,100,99,99 95,93,90,89,89 88,85,75,75,73 70,69
CSF £107.06 CT £765.52 TOTE £22.20: £4.10, £1.90, £1.40, £4.20; DF 325.40.
Owner Barouche Stud Ireland Ltd **Bred** Barouche Stud Ireland Ltd **Trained** the Curragh, Co Kildare

NOTEBOOK
Tsaroxy(IRE) was under strong pressure towards the rear of the field early in the straight and kept on in the closing stages.
Caheerloch(IRE) Official explanation: vet said gelding broke a blood vessel

5219 LONGCHAMP (R-H)
Saturday, September 16

OFFICIAL GOING: Soft

5399a PRIX DES CHENES (GROUP 3) (C&G) 1m
2:20 (2:21) 2-Y-0 **£27,586** (£11,034; £8,276; £5,517; £2,759)

RPR
1 **Spirit One (FR)**[28] [4622] 2-9-2 .... DBoeuf 2 109+
(P Demercastel, France) *made all, ran green when asked to quicken well over 1f out, stretched clear approaching final f, easily* **1/2**[1]
2 *6* **San Domenico**[38] 2-9-2 .... C-PLemaire 1 97
(P Bary, France) *raced in 3rd, went 2nd well over 1f out, soon ridden and one pace* **86/10**
3 *2 1/2* **Cervinio (USA)**[46] 2-9-2 .... IMendizabal 3 92
(J-C Rouget, France) *raced in 5th, pushed along straight, hard ridden well over 1f out, took 3rd last strides* **51/10**[3]
4 *shd* **Prince De Conde (USA)**[18] 2-9-2 .... CSoumillon 4 92
(Robert Collet, France) *tracked winner, ridden and beaten when hung sharply left 1f out, lost 3rd last strides* **10/1**
5 *5* **Mezzolino (FR)** 2-9-2 .... TJarnet 6 82
(D Fechner, Germany) *raced in 4th, ridden and beaten 2f out* **22/1**
6 *10* **Grand Vista**[55] [3777] 2-9-2 .... SPasquier 5 62
(A Fabre, France) *held up, last straight, soon beaten* **48/10**[2]

1m 45.1s **Going Correction** +0.50s/f (Yiel) **6** Ran SP% **124.2**
Speed ratings: 106,100,97,97,92 82
PARI-MUTUEL: WIN 1.50; PL 1.20, 2.30; SF 6.00.
Owner B Chehboub **Bred** Kamel & Boualem Chehboub **Trained** France

NOTEBOOK
Spirit One(FR), stepped up to Group company for the first time, was in command soon after the start and never looked in any danger, quickening well when asked at the furlong marker. However, he did not beat a great deal and will face stronger opposition when he turns out for the Criterium International next month.
San Domenico was going well coming into the straight but was left behind by the winner.
Cervinio(USA), given a waiting ride, made some late progress to take third place literally on the line.
Prince De Conde(USA), always well placed, could not quicken and lost third place by hanging left inside the final furlong.

5400a PRIX DU PRINCE D'ORANGE (GROUP 3) 1m 2f
2:55 (2:55) 3-Y-O £27,586 (£11,034; £8,276; £5,517; £2,759)

RPR
1 **Best Name**[76] 3127 3-8-12 .... C-PLemaire 1 113
(Robert Collet, France) *held up in rear, last straight, still last 1f out, strong run on outside to lead 50 yards out, ran on well* **24/10**[2]
2 ½ **Champs Elysees**[82] 2942 3-8-12 .... SPasquier 6 112
(A Fabre, France) *held up in midfield, went 3rd over 3f out, ridden and every chance inside final f, ran on to take 2nd close home* **6/1**[3]
3 1 ½ **Daramsar (FR)**[21] 3-8-12 .... CSoumillon 3 109
(A De Royer-Dupre, France) *tracked leader after 2f, 2nd straight, led 1f out to 50 yards out, no extra* **Evs**[1]
4 2 **Senor Dali (IRE)**[17] 4942 3-8-12 .... DBonilla 4 106
(J L Dunlop) *with leaders, led briefly after 2f, soon settled in 3rd on rails, 4th straight, kept on at one pace final 1 1/2f* **10/1**
5 snk **Major Grace (FR)**[34] 3-8-12 ....(b) TThulliez 7 105
(Y De Nicolay, France) *slowly into stride, 7th straight, kept on but never near to challenge* **32/1**
6 ½ **Markovitch**[35] 4358 3-8-12 .... OPeslier 8 105
(P W Chapple-Hyam) *led over 7f out, headed 1f out, one pace* **26/1**
7 1 ½ **Daltaya (FR)**[97] 2491 3-8-11 .... MPoirier 5 101
(A De Royer-Dupre, France) *midfield, 5th straight, weakened over 1f out* **Evs**[1]
8 1 ½ **Barastraight**[28] 4623 3-9-0 .... IMendizabal 2 101
(J-C Rouget, France) *led 2f, 6th straight, brief effort on inside 2f out, beaten approaching final f* **67/10**

2m 14.1s **Going Correction** +0.50s/f (Yiel) **8 Ran SP% 172.5**
Speed ratings: 95,94,93,91,91 91,90,88
PARI-MUTUEL: WIN 3.40; PL 1.10, 1.30, 1.10; DF 12.10.
Owner P Vidal **Bred** Newsells Park Stud Ltd **Trained** Chantilly, France

NOTEBOOK
Best Name, the French Derby runner-up having his first run since July, produced a superb turn of foot to get up and win having been dropped right out the back early on. This trip looks to suit him best and he might now be aimed at the Prix Dollar.
Champs Elysees, always in the leading group but towards the outside, took the lead running into the final furlong but could not hold Best Name's late challenge.
Daramsar(FR) hit the front halfway up the straight but conceded the advantage at the furlong marker. He gives the impression that a return to a mile and a half will suit better.
Senor Dali(IRE), smartly into his stride, was hampered slightly in the straight before running on without posing a threat.
Markovitch took the lead soon after the start and stayed in that position until a furlong and a half out. He looked a little bit out of his depth and has been marked down for a career in a Dubai next year.

4692 HAMILTON (R-H)
Sunday, September 17
OFFICIAL GOING: Good to soft (good in places)
Wind: Almost nil.

5401 TOTEPLACEPOT H'CAP 6f 5y
2:30 (2:30) (Class 5) (0-75,75) 3-Y-O £4,533 (£1,348; £674; £336) Stalls Centre

Form RPR
0536 1 **La Matanza**[12] 5079 3-8-12 **69** .... PhillipMakin 13 77
(T D Barron) *chsd ldrs: led centre over 2f out: hld on wl fnl f* **10/1**
0015 2 1 **Memphis Man**[5] 5265 3-8-10 **67** .... J-PGuillambert 3 72
(Miss V Haigh) *dwlt: hld up centre: hdwy over 1f out: kpt on fnl f: wnt 2nd cl home: nt rch wnr* **10/1**
0003 3 hd **Miss Lopez (IRE)**[18] 4927 3-8-4 **61** oh2 .... FrancisNorton 10 65
(K R Burke) *hld up towards rr far side: hdwy and prom over 1f out: kpt on fnl f: hld towards fin* **11/1**
3314 4 hd **Soto**[39] 4262 3-9-1 **72** .... PaulMulrennan 7 75
(M W Easterby) *chsd centre ldrs: rdn 1/2-way: effrt over 1f out: kpt on fnl f: no ex nr fin* **7/1**[2]
0243 5 1 **Flylowflylong (IRE)**[15] 5036 3-8-9 **66** .... TomEaves 8 66
(I Semple) *in tch centre: drvn 1/2-way: kpt on same pce fnl f* **6/1**[1]
0503 6 ¾ **Lambency (IRE)**[30] 4568 3-7-13 **61** oh19 .... AndrewElliott(5) 6 59
(J S Goldie) *towards rr towards far side: effrt over 2f out: no imp fnl f* **66/1**
4406 7 2 **Rainbow Bay**[20] 4888 3-8-12 **69** ....(v[1]) PaulHanagan 15 61
(R A Fahey) *in tch far side: effrt over 2f out: sn one pce* **8/1**[3]
1056 8 nk **Westport**[25] 4707 3-9-4 **75** .... NCallan 4 66
(K A Ryan) *midfield centre: drvn over 2f out: sn no ex* **12/1**
5201 9 ½ **The Salwick Flyer (IRE)**[12] 5077 3-7-13 **61** oh9 .... NataliaGemelova(5) 2 51
(A Berry) *in tch centre: drvn 1/2-way: no ex whn n.m.r 1f out* **20/1**
2640 10 2 **Mulligan's Gold (IRE)**[20] 4888 3-8-10 **67** .... RyanMoore 5 51
(T D Easterby) *s.i.s: bhd centre: rdn and no imp whn carried rt 2f out: nvr on terms* **12/1**
0205 11 nk **The History Man (IRE)**[20] 4888 3-8-12 **69** ....(b) RobertWinston 12 52
(M W Easterby) *overall ldr far side to over 2f out: wknd over 1f out* **9/1**
5023 12 shd **Mujeak (IRE)**[13] 5060 3-8-10 **67** .... GrahamGibbons 1 50
(J J Quinn) *towards rr centre: drvn and hung bdly rt fr 2f out: n.d* **10/1**
6333 13 9 **Woodwee**[164] 893 3-7-11 **61** oh4 .... PatrickDonaghy(7) 9 17
(J R Weymes) *spd centre to over 2f out: sn btn* **33/1**
2005 14 1 ¼ **Maison Dieu**[38] 4296 3-8-4 **61** oh1 .... JimmyQuinn 14 13
(E J Alston) *towards rr far side: rdn and struggling fr 1/2-way* **10/1**
450- 15 3 **Miss Sure Bond (IRE)**[296] 6423 3-8-8 **65** .... KDarley 11 8
(B Smart) *s.i.s: a bhd towards far side* **33/1**

1m 12.51s (-0.59) **Going Correction** +0.025s/f (Good) **15 Ran SP% 120.1**
Speed ratings (Par 101): 104,102,102,102,100 99,97,96,96,93 93,92,80,79,75
CSF £101.92 CT £1156.44 TOTE £13.50: £4.40, £3.10, £5.50; EX 200.80.
Owner J G Brown **Bred** A C M Spalding **Trained** Maunby, N Yorks
■ Stewards' Enquiry : Graham Gibbons one-day ban: careless riding (Sep 28)

FOCUS
Just a modest sprint handicap. They split into two groups early on, with some going far side and the others down the middle, but they came together in the closing stages and there seemed to be no major bias.

5402 EUROPEAN BREEDERS FUND RACINGUK.TV MAIDEN STKS 1m 65y
3:00 (3:01) (Class 5) 2-Y-O £3,886 (£1,156; £577; £288) Stalls High

Form RPR
0 1 **Clarricien (IRE)**[20] 4867 2-9-3 .... RyanMoore 8 76
(E J O'Neill) *unruly in stalls: missed break: rdn and plenty to do 1/2-way: gd hdwy over 1f out: led ins fnl f: sn clr* **11/4**[1]
2 3 **Ashn Thunder** 2-9-3 .... KDarley 4 69
(M Johnston) *chsd ldrs: led 3f out: rdn over 1f out: hdd ins fnl f: nt pce of wnr* **3/1**[2]
6 3 1 **Lets Get Cracking (FR)**[34] 4424 2-9-3 .... NCallan 1 67
(K A Ryan) *chsd ldrs: effrt and ev ch 3f out: one pce over 1f out* **13/2**[3]
5 4 2 **Robbie Scott**[18] 4932 2-9-3 .... JoeFanning 3 62
(M Johnston) *towards rr: rdn 1/2-way: hdwy over 1f out: kpt on: no impresssion* **20/1**
004 5 1 ¾ **Majestas (IRE)**[13] 5067 2-9-3 70 .... RobertWinston 6 58
(J G M O'Shea) *hld up in tch: effrt over 3f out: no ex over 1f out* **7/1**
04 6 8 **Sonar Sound (GER)**[33] 4458 2-9-3 .... MickyFenton 2 40
(T P Tate) *keen: cl up: led over 4f to 3f out: wknd wl over 1f out* **11/4**[1]
46 7 1 ¼ **Rockfonic**[27] 4650 2-9-3 ....(b[1]) PaulHanagan 5 37
(J R Weymes) *s.i.s: plld hrd bhd ldng gp: wknd fr 3f out* **33/1**
000 8 39 **Eldon Endeavour**[75] 3173 2-9-3 48 .... TomEaves 7 —
(B Storey) *led to over 4f out: wknd over 3f out* **100/1**

1m 50.43s (1.13) **Going Correction** +0.025s/f (Good) **8 Ran SP% 112.9**
Speed ratings (Par 95): 95,92,91,89,87 79,78,39
CSF £10.92 TOTE £3.40: £1.60, £1.60, £2.30; EX 12.90.
Owner P Scholes **Bred** Newtownbarry House Stud **Trained** Averham Park, Notts

FOCUS
This was probably a better maiden than it might have looked at first glance, and it is likely to throw up a few winners.

NOTEBOOK
Clarricien(IRE) ◆, 33-1 and seventh of 13 on his debut over this trip at Chepstow, left that form well behind to get off the mark at the second attempt, but it was by no means a straightforward victory. Unruly in the stalls, he was very slowly into his stride and, although the steady early pace allowed him to make up some of the lost ground without expending too much energy, he still looked in trouble when the race began to get serious. However, the stiff finish was to his advantage and he really found his stride late on, finishing his race very strongly to pull well clear and not crossing the line like a horse who had been on the back foot from the off. It remains to be seen what this form is worth, but this has to be considered a good effort and he looks open to any amount of improvement when he grows up and gets the hang of things. He is a nice middle-distance prospect for next year. (op 4-1)
Ashn Thunder, a 75,000gns half-brother to Aspasias Tizzy, a 12-furlong winner at three, out of a useful turf miler in the US, made a pleasing debut but was probably just found out by his inexperience. He looked to have the race won when hitting the front, but could not hold off the strong-finishing Clarricien, who had the benefit of a previous run. He looks well up to finding a similar race. (op 5-2 tchd 10-3)
Lets Get Cracking(FR) did not improve that much on the form he showed on his debut over seven furlongs at Thirsk, but he looks a nice prospect for middle-distance handicaps next year. (op 15-2)
Robbie Scott, like the third home, will surely show his best form in middle-distance handicaps from next year onwards. (op 16-1)
Majestas(IRE) did not improve for the step up to a mile and was below his official mark of 70. (op 8-1)
Sonar Sound(GER) failed to confirm the promise he showed in a decent race at Nottingham on his previous start and was a major disappointment. Official explanation: trainer had no explanation for the poor form shown (op 9-4 tchd 3-1 in places)

5403 TOTEQUADPOT "PREMIER" CLAIMING STKS 1m 1f 36y
3:35 (3:36) (Class 5) 3-5-Y-O £5,181 (£1,541; £770; £384) Stalls High

Form RPR
630 1 **Neil's Legacy (IRE)**[13] 5064 4-8-8 49 .... RoystonFfrench 2 61
(Miss L A Perratt) *hld up: hdwy over 2f out: led appr fnl f: kpt on wl* **25/1**
2436 2 5 **Magic Sting**[20] 4878 5-9-4 81 .... HayleyTurner 4 61
(M L W Bell) *keen: prom: led gng wl over 3f out: rdn and hdd appr fnl f: kpt on same pce* **4/5**[1]
30 3 3 **Hill Of Almhuim (IRE)**[30] 4570 3-8-8 67 ....(v) FrancisNorton 5 50
(K R Burke) *hld up in tch: drvn 3f out: kpt on fnl f: nt rch first two* **10/1**[3]
2666 4 3 **Norman Beckett**[15] 5015 3-8-8 66 ....(b[1]) TomEaves 7 44
(I Semple) *prom: rdn and outpcd over 3f out: rallied over 1f out: nvr rchd ldrs* **14/1**
1312 5 ½ **Burnley Al (IRE)**[24] 4726 4-8-8 64 ....(b) MarkLawson(5) 8 43
(A Berry) *prom: ev ch 3f out: wknd wl over 1f out* **6/1**[2]
1000 6 2 **Perez (IRE)**[6] 5249 4-8-8 60 ....(v) AndrewElliott(5) 9 39
(W Storey) *cl up tl rdn and wknd fr 2f out* **33/1**
2006 7 1 ¾ **Bessemer (JPN)**[34] 4437 5-9-1 70 ....(p) DanielTudhope 3 38
(D Carroll) *hld up: hdwy to chse ldrs 3f out: wknd over 1f out* **10/1**[3]
1450 8 5 **Awaken**[17] 4944 5-8-11 59 ow3 .... MickyFenton 10 24
(Miss Tracy Waggott) *hld up: rdn over 3f out: hung rt and sn btn* **14/1**
0230 9 nk **Bijou Dan**[6] 5249 5-9-5 56 ....(b) DerekMcGaffin 1 31
(W G Harrison) *hld up: drvn over 3f out: nvr on terms* **16/1**
10 25 **Domesday (UAE)**[224] 5-8-12 ....(v[1]) JohnMcAuley(3) 6 —
(W G Harrison) *led to over 3f out: sn wknd* **100/1**

1m 58.35s (-1.31) **Going Correction** +0.025s/f (Good)
WFA 3 from 4yo+ 5lb **10 Ran SP% 115.0**
Speed ratings (Par 103): 106,101,98,96,95 94,92,88,87,65
CSF £44.67 TOTE £20.30: £3.20, £1.10, £2.50; EX 60.40.Magic Sting was claimed by Brian Rothwell for £25,000.
Owner Terry & Mrs Linda Pardoe **Bred** Patrick M Ryan **Trained** Ayr, S Ayrshire
■ Stewards' Enquiry : Francis Norton three-day ban: used whip with excessive frequency without giving gelding time to respond (Sep 28, Oct 2-3)

FOCUS
This looked a fair claimer beforehand, but they probably went too fast in front and 49-rated Neil's Legacy took advantage having been held up well off the pace.
Burnley Al(IRE) Official explanation: jockey said gelding was unsuited by the good to soft (good in places) ground
Awaken Official explanation: jockey said mare had a breathing problem

5404 TOTESPORT.COM 2-Y-O FINAL (NURSERY H'CAP) 6f 5y
4:10 (4:10) (Class 2) 2-Y-O
£12,464 (£3,732; £1,866; £934; £466; £234) Stalls Centre

Form RPR
16 1 **Hinton Admiral**[65] 3492 2-9-4 **90** .... JoeFanning 5 99+
(M Johnston) *mde all: pushed along over 1f out: styd on strly to go clr fnl f* **2/1**[1]
1141 2 3 **Ingleby Princess**[43] 4134 2-8-6 **78** .... RyanMoore 6 78
(T D Barron) *chsd ldrs: outpcd over 2f out: rallied to chse wnr ins fnl f: no imp* **9/2**[2]
2026 3 1 ¼ **Fathom Five (IRE)**[30] 4547 2-8-12 **84** .... PaulEddery 8 80
(B Smart) *in tch: effrt over 1f out: rdn and nt qckn fnl f* **14/1**
446 4 ½ **My Valerina (IRE)**[19] 4912 2-8-1 **73** .... RoystonFfrench 1 68
(Mrs A Duffield) *racd wd in midfield: drvn 1/2-way: edgd lft: kpt on fnl f: no imp* **16/1**
4410 5 hd **Dolly Coughdrop (IRE)**[19] 4912 2-8-5 **77** .... FrancisNorton 3 71
(K R Burke) *keen: cl up tl rdn and nt qckn appr fnl f* **10/1**

 The Form Book, Raceform Ltd, Compton, RG20 6NL

0430 **6** *shd* **Rue Soleil**[20] 4893 2-7-12 **70** oh9 .... PaulHanagan 4 64
(J R Weymes) *keen towards rr: effrt over 1f out: nvr rchd ldrs* **66/1**
01 **7** *6* **Triple Shadow**[25] 4693 2-8-2 **74** .... MartinDwyer 7 50
(T D Barron) *bhd: drvn 1/2-way: nvr on terms* **13/2**
1603 **8** *7* **Narrjoo (USA)**[22] 4789 2-9-7 **93** .... TonyCulhane 2 48
(M R Channon) *prom: effrt over 2f out: wknd over 1f out* **5/1**[3]
1300 **9** *4* **As One Does**[26] 4681 2-9-1 **87** .... NCallan 9 30
(K A Ryan) *w ldr: rdn over 2f out: wknd wl over 1f out* **16/1**

1m 13.53s (0.43) **Going Correction** +0.025s/f (Good) 9 Ran SP% **110.5**
Speed ratings (Par 101):98,94,92,91,91 91,83,73,68
CSF £9.93 CT £88.69 TOTE £2.60: £1.40, £1.70, £3.40; EX 11.30 Trifecta £66.30 Pool: £364.40 - 3.90 winning units.
Owner Gainsborough Stud **Bred** Gainsborough Stud Management Ltd **Trained** Middleham Moor, N Yorks

FOCUS
This looked a decent enough nursery beforehand, but Hinton Admiral was basically too good for this lot.

NOTEBOOK
Hinton Admiral, the winner of a course-and-distance maiden before running below expectations over seven furlongs in the Superlative Stakes at Newmarket, benefited from both the drop in trip and grade on his return from over two months off and ran out a pretty impressive winner. A Royal Lodge and Dewhurst entry, he is clearly held in high regard and deserves another chance back in Pattern company. (tchd 15-8 and 9-4)
Ingleby Princess, 4lb higher than when winning over the course and distance on her previous start, ran a good race but was basically no match whatsoever for Hinton Admiral. (op 4-1 tchd 5-1 and 11-2 in places)
Fathom Five(IRE) probably does not have much in hand of the Handicapper, but this was a decent effort. (op 12-1 tchd 16-1)
My Valerina(IRE), who unseated her rider beforehand, is pretty exposed but ran a fair race. (op 20-1)
Dolly Coughdrop(IRE) looks high enough in the weights. (op 12-1 tchd 9-1)
Rue Soleil, racing from 9lb out of the handicap, lets the form down somewhat but he has run the odd decent race. (op 50-1)
Triple Shadow, off the mark over five furlongs here on his previous start, did not help his chance by racing keenly. (op 4-1 tchd 7-1 in places)
Narrjoo(USA) might have been unsuited by the easy ground, but he is in danger of becoming disappointing. (op 7-1)

5405 EUROPEAN BREEDERS FUND FLOWER OF SCOTLAND STKS (LISTED RACE) (F&M) 5f 4y

4:45 (4:45) (Class 1) 3-Y-0+
£17,034 (£6,456; £2,421; £2,421; £807; £405) **Stalls** Centre

Form RPR
0000 **1** **Angus Newz**[8] 5171 3-9-2 **96** ....(v) RobertWinston 1 98
(M Quinn) *chsd one other towards stands side: effrt 2f out: led ins fnl f: drvn out* **22/1**
-200 **2** *½* **Nidhaal (IRE)**[44] 4097 3-8-12 **98** .... MartinDwyer 10 92
(E A L Dunlop) *towards rr on outside of centre gp: hdwy and hung to stands side over 1f out: kpt on wl fnl f: nt rch wnr* **7/1**
0220 **3** *1* **Pivotal's Princess (IRE)**[8] 5182 4-8-13 **98** .... GrahamGibbons 16 89
(E S McMahon) *cl up centre gp: effrt and led that gp ins fnl f: kpt on but hld by stands side pair wl ins last* **4/1**[2]
3460 **3** *dht* **Give Me The Night (IRE)**[8] 5171 3-8-12 **88** .... RoystonFfrench 2 89
(B Smart) *racd w one other stands side: led to ins fnl f: kpt on same pce* **50/1**
-066 **5** *nk* **Waterways (IRE)**[64] 3561 3-8-12 .... NGMcCullagh 15 88
(P J Prendergast, Ire) *cl up centre: led that gp over 1f out to ins fnl f: nt qckn* **10/1**
3102 **6** *shd* **Portmeirion**[8] 5171 5-8-13 **67** .... J-PGuillambert 3 87
(S C Williams) *hld up centre: hdwy over 1f out: kpt on fnl f: nrst fin* **25/1**
1512 **7** *½* **Terentia**[25] 4717 3-8-12 **98** .... SebSanders 13 85
(E S McMahon) *cl up centre: effrt and rdn whn checked appr fnl f: kpt on same pce* **9/2**[3]
0000 **8** *hd* **Sierra Vista**[8] 5171 6-8-13 **98** .... PaulHanagan 7 85
(D W Barker) *in tch centre: effrt over 2f out: one pce over 1f out* **12/1**
0021 **9** *¾* **Gimasha**[14] 5044 4-8-13 **96** .... KerrinMcEvoy 12 82+
(W Jarvis) *in tch: effrt whn n.m.r over 1f out: sn no imp* **5/2**[1]
0554 **10** *3* **Clare Hills (IRE)**[70] 3332 3-8-12 **92** ....(p) PatCosgrave 8 71
(K R Burke) *w centre ldr tl wknd over 1f out* **50/1**
0010 **11** *½* **Coconut Moon**[8] 5169 4-8-13 **74** .... DavidAllan 14 69
(E J Alston) *bhd centre: drvn 1/2-way: nvr rchd ldrs* **50/1**
-100 **12** *1 ¾* **Free Roses (IRE)**[21] 4855 3-9-2 .... JimmyQuinn 5 67
(Edward Lynam, Ire) *s.i.s: a bhd centre* **25/1**
0605 **13** *5* **Hello Roberto**[40] 4226 5-8-13 **70** ....(p) NCallan 11 45
(R A Harris) *led centre gp to over 1f out: sn wknd* **100/1**
0-00 **14** *2 ½* **Gilt Linked**[79] 3049 3-8-12 **80** .... TomEaves 9 36
(J S Wainwright) *s.i.s: plld hrd in rr: rdn and wknd over 2f out* **100/1**

59.85 secs (-1.35) **Going Correction** +0.025s/f (Good)
WFA 3 from 4yo+ 1lb 14 Ran SP% **115.9**
Speed ratings (Par 111):111,110,108,108,108 107,107,106,105,100 100,97,89,85
CSF £156.73 TOTE £24.10: £4.70, £2.30; EX 201.30 TRIFECTA PL. Pivotal's Princess £1.20 Give Me The Night £6.30.
Owner J G Dooley **Bred** Henry And Mrs Rosemary Moszkowicz **Trained** Newmarket, Suffolk

FOCUS
A typical Listed sprint for fillies and mares. The field split into two groups early on and the bare result suggests Angus Newz and Give Me The Night were at an advantage racing together, away from the rest, towards the near side.

NOTEBOOK
Angus Newz had been well below her best in recent starts but bounced right back to form with a determined success, displaying a fine attitude when strongly challenged. She probably raced on the best ground - the running of Give Me The Night, the only other horse to race with her on the near side, suggests that is the case - but she is smart at her best and deserves to keep taking her chance at this level. (op 20-1)
Nidhaal(IRE), below form over seven at Goodwood on her previous start, proved better suited by this stiff five furlongs on easy ground and was just held having drifted across to the near side. Six furlongs may just prove to be her optimum distance. (op 9-1 tchd 13-2)
Pivotal's Princess(IRE), without a win since July 2005, ran a fine race to fare second best of those who raced up the centre from the start. (op 3-1)
Give Me The Night(IRE), rated just 88, ran a big race to pick up some all important black type. However, she is probably flattered, considering she raced away from the main group of runners towards the near side, and the only other horse to stay with her was the winner. (op 3-1)
Waterways(IRE), trained in Ireland, did not run badly back in fifth but was probably just a little below her best. (op 9-1 tchd 11-1)
Portmeirion confirmed her second in a Listed race at Chester was no fluke and she is clearly much better than her current rating of 67 suggests. (op 20-1)
Terentia has progressed into a very useful sort in handicaps and looked well worth a try in this grade, but she was a little bit below her best. (op 5-1 tchd 11-2 and 6-1 in a place)
Gimasha was well below the form she showed to win a handicap off a mark of 93 at Lingfield on her previous start and was done no favours when squeezed up over a furlong out. Official explanation: jockey said filly was denied a clear run (tchd 11-4 in places)
Free Roses(IRE) Official explanation: jockey said filly reared as the stalls opened

5406 TOTESPORT 0800 221 221 H'CAP 1m 65y

5:15 (5:15) (Class 4) (0-85,83) 3-Y-0+ **£6,477** (£1,927; £963; £481) **Stalls** High

Form RPR
4650 **1** **King's Revenge**[21] 4833 3-8-5 **70** ....(b) DavidAllan 5 79
(T D Easterby) *chsd ldrs: led over 2f out: sn rdn: hung lft appr fnl f: kpt on strly* **20/1**
2660 **2** *3* **Regent's Secret (USA)**[25] 4696 6-9-4 **79** .... DanielTudhope 6 81+
(J S Goldie) *hld up: rdn 1/2-way: hdwy whn nt clr run over 1f out: kpt on fnl f: nt rch wnr* **18/1**
2531 **3** *nk* **Middlemarch (IRE)**[25] 4696 6-8-10 **71** .... DaleGibson 7 72
(J S Goldie) *hld up: rdn 1/2-way: hdwy over 1f out: kpt on fnl f: no imp* **11/2**[3]
1600 **4** *4* **Northern Boy (USA)**[16] 4989 3-8-12 **77** .... PhillipMakin 9 69
(T D Barron) *hld up: effrt over 2f out: edgd rt: sn no imp* **10/1**
1541 **5** *1 ½* **California Laws**[10] 5136 4-8-8 **69** oh1 .... GrahamGibbons 2 58
(T D Barron) *in tch: drvn over 3f out: outpcd fr 2f out* **5/2**[1]
0210 **6** *¾* **Baylaw Star**[2] 5337 5-9-8 **83** .... RoystonFfrench 1 70
(I W McInnes) *chsd ldrs tl wknd over 2f out* **16/1**
0004 **7** *nk* **Toshi (USA)**[24] 4726 4-8-12 **73** ....(p) TomEaves 8 59
(I Semple) *hld up: effrt 3f out: btn over 1f out* **8/1**
0302 **8** *15* **Wahoo Sam (USA)**[43] 4153 6-9-0 **75** .... NCallan 10 27
(K A Ryan) *led to over 2f out: sn wknd* **9/2**[2]
0001 **9** *24* **Rain Stops Play (IRE)**[20] 4879 4-9-5 **80** .... SebSanders 4 —
(M Quinn) *cl up tl wknd 3f out: eased whn btn* **11/2**[3]

1m 49.24s (-0.06) **Going Correction** +0.025s/f (Good)
WFA 3 from 4yo+ 4lb 9 Ran SP% **113.6**
Speed ratings (Par 105):101,98,97,93,92 91,91,76,52
CSF £321.10 CT £2243.18 TOTE £24.00: £4.80, £4.10, £1.30; EX 246.00 Place 6 £ 218.20 Place 5 £ 47.05 ,.
Owner W H Ponsonby **Bred** Helshaw Grange Farm And C J Whiston **Trained** Great Habton, N Yorks

FOCUS
A fair handicap run at a strong pace.
King's Revenge Official explanation: trainer said, regarding apparent improvement in form, that the gelding benefited from reapplication of blinkers and the better ground
Wahoo Sam(USA) Official explanation: jockey said gelding had no more to give
Rain Stops Play(IRE) Official explanation: jockey said gelding lost its action
T/Jkpt: Not won. T/Plt: £156.60 to a £1 stake. Pool: £69,675.30. 324.60 winning tickets. T/Qpdt: £14.60 to a £1 stake. Pool: £3,913.90. 197.60 winning tickets. RY

5407 - (Foreign Racing) - See Raceform Interactive

5392 CURRAGH (R-H)

Sunday, September 17

OFFICIAL GOING: Straight course - good to yielding; round course - good

5408a LAING O'ROURKE BLENHEIM STKS (LISTED RACE) 6f

2:10 (2:12) 2-Y-0 **£24,693** (£7,244; £3,451; £1,175)

RPR
1 **Brave Tin Soldier (USA)**[25] 4716 2-9-1 .... KFallon 6 105+
(A P O'Brien, Ire) *broke wl: settled 3rd: rdn to chal 2f out: led 1f out: sn drew clr: comf* **15/8**[1]
2 *2 ½* **Invincible Force (IRE)**[22] 4824 2-9-1 .... EddieAhern 4 98
(Ms Deborah J Evans) *cl up: 2nd 1/2-way: led under 2f out: hdd 1f out: nt pce of wnr* **7/2**[2]
3 *1* **Bazroy (IRE)**[10] 5139 2-9-1 .... StephenDonohoe 10 95
(P D Evans) *rrd up and uns rdr in stalls: broke wl: sn led: hdd under 2f out: 3rd and kpt on fnl f* **14/1**
4 *nk* **Flash McGahon (IRE)**[24] 4747 2-9-4 **101** .... MJKinane 3 97
(John M Oxx, Ire) *trckd ldrs: 4th 1/2-way: rdn and kpt on fr 1 1/2f out* **5/1**[3]
5 *1 ¼* **City Of Tribes (IRE)**[24] 4747 2-9-1 **99** .... JMurtagh 2 90
(G M Lyons, Ire) *hld up towards rr: prog 2f out: 5th over 1f out: kpt on same pce* **13/2**
6 *nk* **Dianella (IRE)**[21] 4856 2-8-12 .... WSupple 7 86
(David P Myerscough, Ire) *chsd ldrs on outer: 5th 2f out: rdn and one pce* **25/1**
7 *shd* **El Soprano (IRE)**[32] 4499 2-8-12 **85** ....(b[1]) DPMcDonogh 8 86
(Kevin Prendergast, Ire) *sn trckd ldrs: 5th 1 1/2f out: no ex fr over 1f out* **16/1**
8 *6* **Plato's Republic (USA)** 2-9-1 .... PShanahan 1 71
(C Collins, Ire) *chsd ldrs on stand's rail: rdn and dropped towards rr after 1/2-way: kpt on same pce fr over 1f out* **33/1**
9 *3* **Mythical Echo (USA)**[21] 4853 2-8-12 **92** .... WMLordan 5 59
(David Wachman, Ire) *towards rr: no imp fr 2f out* **8/1**
10 *hd* **Saint Andrew (IRE)**[21] 4850 2-9-1 **95** .... PJSmullen 9 61
(Peter Casey, Ire) *chsd ldrs to 1/2-way: no ex fr 2f out* **16/1**

1m 13.2s **Going Correction** +0.075s/f (Good) 10 Ran SP% **123.3**
Speed ratings: 111,107,106,105,104 103,103,95,91,91
CSF £8.88 TOTE £2.80: £1.50, £1.40, £5.90; DF 11.00.
Owner Michael Tabor **Bred** Classicstar **Trained** Ballydoyle, Co Tipperary

FOCUS
A fair Listed contest rated through the runner-up. The winner won cosily enough and is improving.

NOTEBOOK
Brave Tin Soldier(USA) looks to be progressing with each run and there should be better to come from him. His trainer won this race with Ad Valorem two years ago before he went on to win the Middle Park, and Aidan O'Brien put forward that race as a possible target for this colt. He looks quite capable of holding his own in better company. (op 2/1 tchd 9/4)
Invincible Force(IRE), already a four-time winner this season, was appearing for the first time since winning a valuable sales race last month. He made much of the running and fought back well when briefly headed by Bazroy but he could not match the winner over the final furlong. He is a decent sort and could be able to make his mark at this level. (op 4/1)
Bazroy(IRE) produced a fine effort in third and ran to a similar level with the runner-up as when third in a big sales race last month. This looked much tougher than the conditions event he won at Southwell last time but he has been holding his form well in an industrious campaign.
Flash McGahon(IRE) travelled well for much of the race and ran creditably in his bid to follow up a Listed-race success at Tipperary last month. He stayed on from over a furlong out and only just failed to secure third. (op 4/1)
City Of Tribes(IRE) was staying on towards the finish and produced a similar effort to the one he posted when fourth behind Flash McGahon at Tipperary. (op 7/1)
Dianella(IRE) came here with two good maiden runs to her name and ran respectably. She should not have too much trouble picking up a maiden.

5410a LAING O'ROURKE NATIONAL STKS (GROUP 1) (ENTIRE COLTS & FILLIES) 7f

3:10 (3:11) 2-Y-O

£124,413 (£39,586; £18,896; £6,482; £4,413; £2,344)

RPR

1 **Teofilo (IRE)**[22] 4825 2-9-1 113 ... KJManning 5 117+
(J S Bolger, Ire) *settled 2nd: rdn to ld under 2f out: qcknd clr 1f out: styd on wl: impressive* **2/1**[2]

2 1 1/4 **Holy Roman Emperor (IRE)**[35] 4409 2-9-1 119 ... KFallon 6 114+
(A P O'Brien, Ire) *trckd ldrs in 3rd: 2nd and rdn to chal 1 1/2f out: outpcd whn edgd sltly lft 1f out: kpt on wl* **4/9**[1]

3 4 1/2 **Eyshal (IRE)**[24] 4750 2-9-1 89 ... (t) MJKinane 1 96?
(John M Oxx, Ire) *trckd ldrs in 4th: rdn 2f out: mod 3rd and no imp ins fnl f* **25/1**[3]

4 1 **Slaney Time (IRE)**[28] 4638 2-9-1 82 ... (b[1]) DJMoran 2 94?
(J S Bolger, Ire) *led: rdn 2 1/2f out: hdd under 2f out: kpt on same pce* **100/1**

5 2 1/2 **Davidii (IRE)**[8] 5195 2-9-1 ... JMurtagh 3 87
(K J Condon, Ire) *trckd ldrs in 5th: effrt 2f out: sn no ex* **33/1**

6 13 **Flash Harry**[65] 3505 2-9-1 ... DMGrant 4 52
(John Joseph Murphy, Ire) *a in rr: lost tch fr 1/2-way* **100/1**

1m 26.4s **Going Correction** +0.075s/f (Good) **6** Ran SP% **111.4**
Speed ratings: 109,107,102,101,98 83
CSF £3.22 TOTE £2.30: £1.30, £1.10; DF 3.30.
Owner Mrs J S Bolger **Bred** J S Bolger **Trained** Coolcullen, Co Carlow

FOCUS
A match on paper, and both the front two quickened well to pull clear of the rest in a race in which the first four furlongs were run in a slower time than the opening maiden, though the overall time was quicker. The winner's provisional RPR of 119 is lower than that recorded by recent winners Dubawi (122) and Hawk Wing (121) but on a par with One Cool Cat in what looks an above average renewal. What's more, he was impressive and could be anything.

NOTEBOOK
Teofilo(IRE) made if four from four with an impeccable display that consolidated his reputation as an exceptional juvenile and also confirmed him an outstanding three-year-old prospect. He never looked in danger of defeat from the moment that he took over from his pacemaker under two furlongs down, but perhaps the most impressive aspect of his victory was that it was achieved with a turn of foot that took him clear of a six-furlong Group 1 winner. For a horse who had been generally hailed as a middle-distance prospect for next year after his victory in the Futurity Stakes, it was quite something to witness his acceleration this time. In the short term Jim Bolger has to decide whether to call a halt to the season now or take in another race. Longer term it may not be ludicrously extravagant to describe Teofilo as a potential Triple Crown candidate, for on this evidence he has the pace for the Guineas, while his stamina for the Derby trip is not in question and he is by Galileo, who sired the first three home in this year's St Leger. His temperament is ideal and, crucially, he appears to be a very sound horse, so the sky is the limit. (op 13/8)
Holy Roman Emperor(IRE), who had carved such a strong reputation with his triumph in the Phoenix Stakes, did very little wrong. He was ideally positioned when Teofilo quickened the tempo of the race but seemed to hit a slightly flat patch and was quite simply beaten for toe. The positive is that he showed no lack of stamina, and his ranking as one of the season's top performers is assuredly not in question. To judge from his trainer's post-race remarks it will be no surprise to see him in action again this term. (op 4/7)
Eyshal(IRE) faced a very stiff task against two such classy rivals and showed improved form in third, doing more than enough to suggest that he will win his maiden when dropped back in class. (op 20/1)
Slaney Time(IRE) did his job of pace-making to perfection.
Davidii(IRE) is still a maiden but has improved with every race. (op 40/1)

5411a LAING O'ROURKE SOLONAWAY STKS (LISTED RACE) 1m

3:40 (3:40) 3-Y-O+ **£24,693** (£7,244; £3,451; £1,175)

RPR

1 **Ivan Denisovich (IRE)**[36] 4387 3-9-1 113 ... KFallon 7 112
(A P O'Brien, Ire) *trckd ldrs: 5th 1/2-way: 4th and drvn along early st: 3rd and chal 1f out: styd on wl to ld cl home* **11/10**[1]

2 nk **Latino Magic (IRE)**[7] 5216 6-9-5 106 ... RMBurke 3 111
(R J Osborne, Ire) *hld up towards rr: 8th 2f out: hdwy on outer fr over 1f out: r.o wl to go 2nd cl home* **14/1**

3 shd **Dunelight (IRE)**[44] 4098 3-9-1 ... (b[1]) MJKinane 5 111
(C G Cox) *settled 2nd: chal 2f out: slt advantage fr over 1f out: kpt on u.p: hdd cl home* **6/1**[3]

4 1/2 **Quinmaster (USA)**[21] 4854 4-9-5 112 ... JMurtagh 6 110
(M Halford, Ire) *led: rdn and strly pressed 2f out: narrowly hdd over 1f out: kpt on* **3/1**[2]

5 shd **Anna Karenina (IRE)**[21] 4851 3-8-12 92 ... DMGrant 8 107
(David Wachman, Ire) *mid-div: 6th 1/2-way: prog early st: 4th whn nt clr run 1f out: kpt on* **20/1**

6 1/2 **Ugo Fire (IRE)**[8] 5191 3-8-12 106 ... DPMcDonogh 1 106
(Kevin Prendergast, Ire) *hld up in tch: 7th 2f out: kpt on fr over 1f out* **8/1**

7 1 1/4 **Duff (IRE)**[41] 4213 3-9-1 107 ... FMBerry 10 107
(Edward Lynam, Ire) *trckd ldrs in 3rd: rdn and nt clr run under 2f out: no ex fnl f* **14/1**

8 3 **Tolpuddle (IRE)**[126] 1711 6-9-5 107 ... (t) WMLordan 2 101
(T Stack, Ire) *hld up in rr: no imp fr 2f out* **14/1**

9 3 **Common World (USA)**[21] 4864 7-9-10 110 ... JAHeffernan 9 100
(T Hogan, Ire) *s.i.s and hld up: 8th 1/2-way: no ex fr 2f out* **16/1**

10 1 1/2 **Home Sweet Home (IRE)**[21] 4837 3-8-12 ... PJSmullen 4 89
(P D Evans) *chsd ldrs on outer: 4th 1/2-way: wknd early st* **40/1**

1m 36.2s **Going Correction** -0.40s/f (Firm)
WFA 3 from 4yo+ 4lb **10** Ran SP% **131.1**
Speed ratings: 113,112,112,112,112 111,110,107,104,102
CSF £23.96 TOTE £1.90: £1.20, £3.80, £2.20; DF 59.20.
Owner Mrs John Magnier **Bred** Irving Cowan **Trained** Ballydoyle, Co Tipperary

FOCUS
Solid Listed-grade form rated through the third.

NOTEBOOK
Ivan Denisovich(IRE) was the clear pick on form but he only got there by the skin of his teeth, and with the help of an immensely persuasive ride by Kieren Fallon. This was not a performance up to the level he had shown when third in the St James's Palace or second in the Secretariat Stakes at Arlington last month, but it should at least serve as a confidence-booster when he returns to Group level. (op 6/4)
Latino Magic(IRE), essentially a high-class handicapper, ran his best race of the season so far, reversing Irish Cambridgeshire form with Quinmaster.
Dunelight(IRE) has some smart handicap form in Britain to his name and his performance is probably a fair guide to the level of the form. (op 6/1 tchd 13/2)
Quinmaster(USA), who has been terrifically progressive in handicaps, made a determined bid from the front and kept on when headed. He is certainly worth another shot at a race like this. (op 3/1 tchd 5/2)
Anna Karenina(IRE) had plenty to find on the book and did not shape at all badly in the circumstances. (op 16/1)
Ugo Fire(IRE) did not run one of her better races.

5412 - 5413a (Foreign Racing) - See Raceform Interactive

1974 FRANKFURT (L-H)

Sunday, September 17

OFFICIAL GOING: Good

5414a MERRILL LYNCH EURO-CUP (GROUP 2) 1m 2f

4:00 (4:04) 3-Y-O+ **£27,586** (£10,345; £4,138; £2,759)

RPR

1 **Nordtanzerin (GER)**[28] 4648 3-8-2 ... FilipMinarik 6 105
(P Schiergen, Germany) *raced in 2nd behind clear leader, led 1 1/2f out, driven clear final f* **9/10**[1]

2 2 1/2 **Bailamos (GER)**[22] 4828 6-9-0 ... WMongil 7 106
(H Hesse, Germany) *raced in 4th, ridden 1 1/2f out, took 2nd inside final f, no impression on winner* **72/10**

3 3/4 **Sommertag (GER)**[77] 3131 3-8-6 ... ASuborics 3 103
(P Schiergen, Germany) *last early, headway halfway, 3rd straight, went 2nd approaching final f, lost 2nd inside final f, one pace* **24/10**[2]

4 1 3/4 **Alpacco (IRE)**[205] 513 4-9-0 ... AGoritz 5 102
(Mario Hofer, Germany) *raced in 5th, last and slightly detached entering straight, stayed on closing stages to take 4th close home* **86/10**

5 1/2 **Pandim (GER)** 3-8-7 ow1 ... (b) JPalik 1 100
(W Hickst, Germany) *soon led, 10 lengths clear halfway, headed 1 1/2f out, one pace* **182/10**

6 1/2 **White Lightning (GER)**[22] 4828 4-9-0 ... RJuracek 4 100
(U Stech, Norway) *3rd early, 5th straight, hard ridden 1 1/2f out, weakened inside final f* **7/2**[3]

2m 10.55s
WFA 3 from 4yo+ 6lb **6** Ran SP% **132.1**
(including 10 Euro stake): WIN 19; PL 14, 26; SF 161.
Owner Gestut Wittekindshof **Bred** Gestut Wittekindshof **Trained** Germany

WOODBINE (L-H)

Sunday, September 17

OFFICIAL GOING: Firm

5415a SUMMER STKS (GRADE 3) 1m (T)

8:29 (8:34) 2-Y-O

£75,000 (£25,000; £13,750; £7,500; £3,750; £200)

RPR

1 **Dreaming Of Anna (USA)**[50] 2-8-7 ... RDouglas 9 115
(W Catalano, U.S.A) **43/20**[2]

2 3 1/4 **Marcavelly (USA)** 2-8-10 ... EPrado 4 111
(W Mott, U.S.A) **27/20**[1]

3 4 3/4 **Orna (USA)** 2-8-10 ... SCallaghan 2 100
(Michael J Doyle, U.S.A) **55/1**

4 1/2 **Streets Ahead**[23] 4775 2-8-10 ... RichardHughes 5 98
(A M Balding) *held up in 6th, 7th straight, stayed on at same pace under strong pressure final 2f* **5/1**[3]

5 3/4 **Seaside Links (CAN)** 2-8-10 ... (b) ERamsammy 8 97
(M Casse, Canada) **40/1**

6 1 1/4 **Walk With Kings (CAN)** 2-8-10 ... TKabel 7 94
(M Frostad, Canada) **171/10**

7 2 1/4 **L A Boy (USA)** 2-8-10 ... KDesormeaux 3 89
(R McAnally, U.S.A) **17/1**

8 1 1/4 **Samurai Prince (USA)** 2-8-10 ... JStein 1 86
(G Aimonetti, Canada) **69/1**

9 nk **Approval Rating (USA)** 2-8-10 ... PHusbands 6 85
(M Casse, Canada) **62/10**

1m 35.03s **9** Ran SP% **121.6**
PARI-MUTUEL (including $2 stake): WIN 6.30; PL (1-2) 4.10, 2.70;SHOW (1-2-3) 3.70, 2.60, 11.00; SF 11.20.
Owner Frank C Calabrese **Bred** Frank C Calabrese **Trained** USA

NOTEBOOK
Dreaming Of Anna(USA), racing against the colts, won in fine style and her rider said afterwards that he thinks she is the best filly he has ever ridden. She will now be aimed the Breeders' Cup Juvenile Fillies.
Streets Ahead has progressed into a smart sort in recent starts, winning his maiden at Salisbury and following up in a Listed race at the same venue. Judged on that form he looked to have an outstanding chance at this level on his first run abroad, but he failed to produce his very best. It might be that this ground was a little faster than he cares for.

5416a WOODBINE MILE (GRADE 1) 1m (T)

10:06 (10:09) 3-Y-O+

£300,000 (£100,000; £55,000; £30,000; £15,000; £200)

RPR

1 **Becrux (ITY)**[22] 4-8-5 ... PValenzuela 10 113
(N Drysdale, U.S.A) **167/20**

2 nk **Rebel Rebel (IRE)**[42] 4-8-7 ... (b) EPrado 11 115
(R Dutrow Jr, U.S.A) **123/20**

3 1 1/4 **Ad Valorem (USA)**[35] 4416 4-8-12 ... PHusbands 5 117
(A P O'Brien, Ire) *held up in 10th, headway over 1f out, stayed on gamely under pressure final f* **103/20**[3]

4 hd **Sweet Return**[22] 6-8-9 ... KDesormeaux 2 114
(R McAnally, U.S.A) **99/10**

5 3/4 **Remarkable News (VEN)**[42] 4-8-9 ... JCastellano 7 112
(A Penna Jr, U.S.A) **47/10**[2]

6 1 **Therecomesatiger (USA)**[78] 4-8-5 ... (b) MGuidry 3 106
(T Proctor, U.S.A) **143/10**

7 hd **Three Valleys (USA)**[42] 5-8-7 ... RADominguez 8 108
(R J Frankel, U.S.A) **59/20**[1]

8 1 **Diamond Green (FR)**[42] 5-8-5 ... JSantos 6 104
(R J Frankel, U.S.A) **244/10**

9 1 **Captain Kurt (NZ)**[309] 4-8-5 ... (b) EmmaJayneWilson 13 102
(Melody Conlon, U.S.A) **125/10**

10 *1 1/2* **Dalavin (USA)**^{22} 5-8-5 ....(b) CMontpellier 12 99
(Audre Cappuccitti, Canada) **82/1**
11 *nk* **Shoal Water (CAN)**^{21} 6-8-5 .... RLandry 4 98
(M Frostad, Canada) **48/1**
12 *4 3/4* **Vanderlin**^{46} [4038] 7-8-7 .... RichardHughes 1 90
(A M Balding) *close up on inside early, 9th halfway, weakened over 2f out* **226/10**
13 *14* **Ballast (IRE)**^{395} [4513] 5-8-5 .... TKabel 9 60
(H G Motion, U.S.A) **37/1**

1m 33.99s **13** Ran SP% **121.0**
PARI-MUTUEL (including $2 stake): WIN 18.70; PL (1-2) 8.00, 7.50;SHOW (1-2-3) 5.90, 6.10, 5.10; SF 145.20.
Owner Team Valor & Gary Barber **Bred** Scuderia Siba Spa **Trained** USA

FOCUS
The tenth running of the Grade 1 $1 million Woodbine Mile, previously run as the Atto Mile. The second and fourth set the standard.

NOTEBOOK
Becrux(ITY) appears to have improved since being gelded and gave trainer Neil Drysdale his third win in the Woodbine Mile. It would be no surprise to see him turn up in the Breeders' Cup Mile.
Rebel Rebel(IRE), second in the 2000 Guineas in 2005 when trained by Neville Callaghan, has taken well to racing in North America and reversed recent form with Three Valleys to claim second.
Ad Valorem(USA), winner of the Queen Anne at Royal Ascot but unsuited by soft ground when below form in the Jacques le Marois, ran a respectable race back in third.
Sweet Return, runner-up in the 2002 Solario Stakes when trained by Ian Wood, has developed into a very smart sort in the US and appears to set the standard.
Three Valleys(USA), the 2003 Coventry winner when trained by Roger Charlton, has been in good form in the US this year but was not at his best this time.
Vanderlin did well in a couple of races at Woodbine this time last year, but he offered little on this occasion.

5231 FOLKESTONE (R-H)

Monday, September 18

OFFICIAL GOING: Good to firm
Wind: Blustery, behind Weather: Sunny and bright

5417 TTL EQUIPMENT MANAGEMENT MAIDEN AUCTION STKS 7f (S)
2:20 (2:22) (Class 5) 2-Y-O £3,238 (£963; £481; £240) Stalls Low

Form RPR
1 **Roodolph** 2-8-9 .... StephenCarson 10 74+
(R F Johnson Houghton) *a gng wl: trckd ldrs: led wl over 1f out: pushed clr: easily* **25/1**
0 **2** *2 1/2* **Sir Liam (USA)**^{16} [5020] 2-8-12 .... SaleemGolam$^{(3)}$ 8 73
(P Mitchell) *t.k.h early: hld up midfield: swtchd rt and hdwy 2f out: kpt on to chse wnr jst ins fnl f: no imp* **14/1**
3 *2 1/2* **Aegean Prince** 2-9-1 .... DaneO'Neill 6 67+
(R Hannon) *rrd s: bhd: rdn and hdwy over 3f out: kpt on same pce fnl f* **4/1**^{2}
4 *2* **Charlotte Grey**^{37} 2-8-4 .... JimmyQuinn 9 50
(C N Allen) *chsd ldrs: rdn 2f out: n.m.r over 1f out: kpt on same pce* **22/1**
6 **5** *1* **Aaron's Way**^{19} [4920] 2-8-1 .... LiamJones$^{(5)}$ 2 49
(A W Carroll) *t.k.h: led tl rdn and hdd wl over 1f out: wknd fnl f* **5/1**^{3}
6 *1* **Coyote Creek** 2-9-3 .... KerrinMcEvoy 13 67+
(E F Vaughan) *racd in midfield tl stmbld and lost pl over 4f out: rdn 3f out: swtchd rt over 1f out: kpt on: n.d* **7/2**^{1}
7 *hd* **Dansil In Distress** 2-8-8 .... PatDobbs 1 48
(S Kirk) *chsd ldrs tl rdn over 2f out: sn wknd* **12/1**
46 **8** *shd* **The Skerret**^{23} [4794] 2-8-9 .... PhillipMakin 14 49
(P Winkworth) *chsd ldr tl wl over 1f out: sn wknd* **7/1**
9 *nk* **Le Singe Noir** 2-8-7 ow1 .... AdamKirby$^{(3)}$ 12 49+
(D M Simcock) *rn green: hld up in midfield: effrt over 2f out: no imp over 1f out* **12/1**
10 *3* **Isabella's Best (IRE)** 2-8-3 .... SeanYourston$^{(7)}$ 4 41
(E J O'Neill) *sn pushed along: midfield tl 1/2-way: sn wl bhd* **25/1**
11 *2* **Classic Blue (IRE)** 2-8-4 .... MartinDwyer 5 30
(E J O'Neill) *slowly away: a bhd* **9/1**
12 *10* **Iamtheone (IRE)** 2-9-3 .... LPKeniry 3 16
(Bob Jones) *sn outpcd in last: t.o* **40/1**

1m 25.67s (-2.23) **Going Correction** -0.55s/f (Hard) **12** Ran SP% **117.9**
Speed ratings (Par 95):90,87,84,82,80 79,79,79,79,75 73,61
CSF £325.16 TOTE £37.50: £13.70, £6.00, £1.50; EX 400.20 Trifecta £109.80 Part won. Pool: £154.72 - 0.50 winning units..
Owner Eden Racing (II) **Bred** Mrs H Johnson Houghton And Mrs R F Johnson Houg **Trained** Blewbury, Oxon

FOCUS
A modest winning time for the type of race, and the form is only modest, but the debut winner impressed all the same.

NOTEBOOK
Roodolph, a gelded half-brother to his stable's former smart juvenile Roodeye, ran out an impressive debut winner and is value for a bit further than his winning margin. While he is bred for speed, this trip was clearly to his liking and he looked well suited by the underfoot conditions. This may not have been a strong maiden, but there was a lot to like about the manner of his victory and he is obviously entitled to improve for the experience. (op 33-1)
Sir Liam(USA) ultimately paid for refusing to settle early on, but still managed to step up on his recent All-Weather debut and is going the right way. He will be of more interest when eligible for nurseries after his next outing. (op 12-1 tchd 16-1)
Aegean Prince, related to winners from five to 12 furlongs, proved popular in the betting ring yet his supporters knew their fate after he reared as the stalls opened. In the circumstances he did well to finish as close as he did and should be much sharper next time. Official explanation: jockey said colt missed the break (op 11-2)
Charlotte Grey, a sister to Blue Patrick, was making her British debut after having shown just moderate form in four previous starts on the All-Weather at Mijas in Spain. Her previous experience told on this turf bow and she looked to need all of this distance. (op 25-1)
Aaron's Way, sixth on her debut at Leicester 19 days previously, pulled her way to the front early on and had no more to offer when pressed before the final furlong. She is capable of a little better and will be qualified for nurseries after her next assignment. (op 4-1)
Coyote Creek, a 20,000gns purchase bred to make his mark over a longer trip in due course, lost momentum when stumbling early on and not that surprisingly hit a flat spot at halfway. He kept on without threatening and, considering he was popular in the betting ring, is presumably thought capable of a deal better. Official explanation: jockey said colt stumbled mid-race (op 5-1)
Le Singe Noir Official explanation: jockey said gelding hung badly left

5418 DAWSONRENTALS MACMILLAN H'CAP 7f (S)
2:55 (2:58) (Class 6) (0-65,68) 3-Y-O £3,238 (£963; £481; £240) Stalls Low

Form RPR
4002 **1** **Welsh Cake**^{13} [5092] 3-8-11 **58** ....(bt) MartinDwyer 10 68
(Mrs A J Perrett) *mde all on far side: clr wl over 1f out: rdn out* **12/1**
2421 **2** *3 1/2* **Mr Cellophane**^{6} [5272] 3-9-7 **68** 6ex .... MickyFenton 12 69
(J R Jenkins) *racd far side: chsd ldrs: wnt 2nd and drvn 2f out: no ch w wnr after* **7/1**^{2}
5003 **3** *1 1/4* **Zafantage**^{17} [4984] 3-8-11 **58** .... PatDobbs 13 56
(S Kirk) *chsd ldrs far side: rdn over 2f out: kpt on same pce u.p* **16/1**
5500 **4** *shd* **Antigoni (IRE)**^{22} [4837] 3-9-4 **65** ....(v^{1}) LPKeniry 9 62
(A M Balding) *v.s.a: hld up on far side: rdn over 2f out: styd on ins fnl f: n.d* **8/1**^{3}
1552 **5** *3/4* **Hotchpotch (USA)**^{7} [5232] 3-8-7 **54** .... RichardThomas 11 49
(J R Best) *chsd wnr on far side tl over 2f out: wknd over 1f out* **4/1**^{1}
0004 **6** *1* **Rondo**^{26} [4695] 3-8-10 **57** .... PhillipMakin 6 50
(T D Barron) *taken down early: racd stands side: rdn wl over 2f out: no ch w far side: 1st of 4 in gp* **12/1**
0000 **7** *3/4* **Royal Citadel (IRE)**^{21} [4870] 3-8-13 **63** ....(b) AdamKirby$^{(3)}$ 5 54
(C G Cox) *led stands side gp: rdn 1/2-way: no ch w far side: 2nd of 4 in gp* **14/1**
3410 **8** *shd* **Distant Drums (IRE)**^{19} [4930] 3-8-12 **59** .... JamieSpencer 8 50
(B W Hills) *racd far side: rdn over 2f out: sn outpcd* **11/1**
-405 **9** *3/4* **Waddon (IRE)**^{26} [4689] 3-9-4 **65** ....(b^{1}) PhilipRobinson 3 54
(C G Cox) *swtchd rt s: racd alone in centre: nvr trbld ldrs* **7/1**^{2}
-060 **10** *3/4* **Dawaleeb (IRE)**^{16} [5036] 3-9-1 **62** .... StephenCarson 2 49
(Jane Chapple-Hyam) *chsd ldr on stands side: rdn 3f out: no ch w far side: 3rd of 4 in gp* **40/1**
0056 **11** *1/2* **Jabbara (IRE)**^{19} [4927] 3-8-11 **58** .... KerrinMcEvoy 7 43
(C E Brittain) *swtchd rt s: hld up in rr on far side: rdn and wknd over 2f out* **12/1**
4146 **12** *1* **Dado Mush**^{24} [4757] 3-8-11 **61** ....(v^{1}) SaleemGolam$^{(3)}$ 14 44
(T T Clement) *t.k.h: hld up midfield far side: rdn wl over 2f out: sn bhd* **20/1**
500 **13** *3* **Cool Tiger**^{28} [4663] 3-8-10 **60** .... StephenDonohoe$^{(3)}$ 1 35
(P Howling) *sn outpcd in rr on stands side: no ch: 4th of 4 in gp* **33/1**

1m 23.76s (-4.14) **Going Correction** -0.55s/f (Hard) **13** Ran SP% **110.2**
Speed ratings (Par 99):101,97,95,95,94 93,92,92,91,90 90,89,85
CSF £76.68 CT £701.24 TOTE £11.00: £3.80, £2.10, £3.40; EX 41.90 TRIFECTA Not won..
Owner Usk Valley Stud **Bred** Usk Valley Stud **Trained** Pulborough, W Sussex
■ Light Dreams was withdrawn (9/1, vet's advice.) R4 applies, deduct 10p in the £.
■ Stewards' Enquiry : Adam Kirby caution: improper riding - used whip down the shoulder in the forehand position

FOCUS
A modest handicap which saw those that raced far side at an advantage and it may be best not to take the form too literally.
Royal Citadel(IRE) Official explanation: jockey said filly hung right from 4f out

5419 MC GROUP NURSERY 6f
3:25 (3:26) (Class 6) (0-65,65) 2-Y-O £3,238 (£963; £481; £240) Stalls Low

Form RPR
0052 **1** **Spinning Crystal (IRE)**^{8} [5208] 2-9-4 **62** .... JamieSpencer 8 65
(B W Hills) *chsd ldrs on far side: rdn wl over 1f out: styd on wl u.p to ld last 50 yds: readily* **9/2**^{1}
0602 **2** *1 1/4* **Queensgate**^{9} [5162] 2-9-1 **59** .... FrankieMcDonald 13 58
(M Blanshard) *led on far side: rdn 2f out: kpt on gamely tl hdd and outpcd last 50 yds* **11/1**
0636 **3** *nk* **My Tiger Lilly**^{33} [4480] 2-8-12 **56** .... MartinDwyer 9 54
(W J Knight) *pressed ldr on far side: ev ch u.p last 2f: no ex ins fnl f* **12/1**
0040 **4** *hd* **Blue Mistral (IRE)**^{6} [5262] 2-9-7 **65** .... PaulDoe 14 64+
(W J Knight) *chsd ldrs on far side: rdn 2f out: unable qckn u.p ins fnl f* **28/1**
6335 **5** *1/2* **Hephaestus**^{5} [5290] 2-9-7 **65** .... TPO'Shea 12 61
(M R Channon) *hld up in tch on far side: rdn and effrt wl over 1f out: no imp ins fnl f: 5th of 8 in gp* **6/1**^{2}
055 **6** *shd* **Lake Pontchartrain (IRE)**^{14} [5052] 2-9-4 **62** .... LPKeniry 4 58
(S Kirk) *hld up on stands side: rdn and hdwy wl over 2f out: kpt on but no ch w far side: 1st of 6 in gp* **16/1**
6033 **7** *3/4* **Cantique (IRE)**^{8} [5208] 2-8-13 **60** .... AdamKirby$^{(3)}$ 3 54
(R M Beckett) *chsd ldrs on stands side: kpt on same pce u.p last 2f: no ch w far side: 2nd of 6 in gp* **9/1**
6400 **8** *shd* **Eastern Princess**^{24} [4773] 2-9-0 **58** .... RichardThomas 11 51
(J A Geake) *bmpd s: racd in midfield on far side: rdn and no prog wl over 1f out: 6th of 8 in gp* **16/1**
004 **9** *nk* **Torver**^{12} [5112] 2-9-2 **60** .... KerrinMcEvoy 10 53
(Dr J D Scargill) *hld up rr on far side: rdn and effrt wl over 1f out: kpt on same pce: 7th of 8 in gp* **12/1**
3235 **10** *hd* **Shreddy Shrimpster**^{60} [3678] 2-8-12 **56** .... PatDobbs 1 48
(A B Haynes) *hld up on stands side: hdwy 1/2-way: kpt on same pce fnl f: no ch w far side: 3rd of 6 in gp* **22/1**
51 **11** *nk* **Distant Flash**^{49} [4007] 2-9-0 **58** .... JimmyQuinn 7 49
(G L Moore) *hld up in rr on far side: rdn and effrt over 2f out: no prog: 8th of 8 in gp* **12/1**
053 **12** *1* **Oh So Saucy**^{31} [4550] 2-9-2 **60** .... GeorgeBaker 2 48
(C F Wall) *prom on stands side: rdn 1/2-way: no ch w far side: 4th of 6 in gp* **8/1**^{3}
0042 **13** *3 1/2* **Whipchord (IRE)**^{35} [4427] 2-9-5 **63** .... DaneO'Neill 6 41
(R Hannon) *chsd ldrs on stands side: led that gp 1/2-way: no ch w far side: wknd fnl f: 5th of 6 in gp* **6/1**^{2}
0640 **14** *5* **Avery**^{9} [5162] 2-9-0 **65** .... JamesMillman$^{(7)}$ 5 28
(R J Hodges) *led stands side tl 1/2-way: sn lost pl and no ch: 6th of 6 in gp* **50/1**

1m 11.67s (-1.93) **Going Correction** -0.55s/f (Hard) **14** Ran SP% **120.8**
Speed ratings (Par 93):90,88,87,87,87 86,85,85,85,85 84,83,78,72
CSF £53.39 CT £567.47 TOTE £4.80: £1.90, £4.50, £3.30; EX 62.60 Trifecta £117.30 Part won. Pool: £165.33 - 0.34 winning units..
Owner Triermore Stud **Bred** C O P Hanbury **Trained** Lambourn, Berks

FOCUS
A modest nursery which again saw those on the far side at an advantage. The form looks fair and sound enough rated around the fourth and fifth.

NOTEBOOK
Spinning Crystal(IRE), who finished second on her nursery debut at Kempton eight days previously, duly went one better in good style and broke her duck at the fifth attempt on this return to turf. Her yard remains in decent form at present and, with an extra furlong sure to be within her compass, she ought to have more to offer. (op 4-1)

Queensgate showed up well from the front and simply lacked the finishing speed of the winner late on. She is edging closer to a career-first success and had no trouble with the extra furlong.
My Tiger Lilly, dropped 6lb after her nursery debut 33 days previously, enjoyed the drop back to this trip and ran a solid race. She can find easier opportunities to get off the mark. (op 11-1)
Blue Mistral(IRE), dropping in trip, was aided by her high draw and ran an improved race in defeat. She looks to be in the Handicapper's grip, however. (op 33-1)
Hephaestus failed to improve as expected for this return to quicker ground and is in danger of going the wrong way. (op 7-1 tchd 8-1)
Cantique(IRE), just behind the winner at Kempton last time, failed to raise her game on this return to turf and looked very one paced. (op 10-1)
Shreddy Shrimpster Official explanation: jockey said filly was denied a clear run
Avery Official explanation: jockey said colt had no more to give

5420 COBELFRET MACMILLAN CANCER SUPPORT H'CAP 6f
4:00 (4:00) (Class 3) (0-95,95) 3-Y-0+ **£11,658** (£3,468; £1,733; £865) **Stalls** Low

Form RPR
0000 **1** **Munaddam (USA)**[27] 4682 4-9-6 **95** MartinDwyer 9 104
(E A L Dunlop) *slowly away: sn rcvrd and racd in midfield: swtchd lft over 2f out: str run u.p fnl f to ld nr fin* **13/2**[3]
1511 **2** ¾ **Diane's Choice**[19] 4922 3-8-7 **84** ow1 DaneO'Neill 4 91
(J Akehurst) *chsd ldrs: rdn over 1f out: ev ch ins fnl f: kpt on same pce wl ins fnl f* **12/1**
465 **3** ½ **My Gacho (IRE)**[51] 3956 4-8-8 **83** (b) PhillipMakin 12 89
(T D Barron) *led: rdn over 1f out: hdd and no ex wl ins fnl f* **9/2**[1]
0640 **4** ¾ **Swinbrook (USA)**[45] 4106 5-8-12 **87** (v) KerrinMcEvoy 11 90
(J A R Toller) *chsd ldrs: rdn jst over 1f out: n.m.r briefly 1f out: kpt on ins fnl f* **5/1**[2]
0503 **5** nk **Blue Tomato**[6] 5274 5-8-9 **87** StephenDonohoe(3) 10 89
(J M Bradley) *slowly away: bhd: hdwy and swtchd lft over 1f out: r.o ins fnl f: nt rch ldrs* **7/1**
3000 **6** shd **Judd Street**[65] 3535 4-9-4 **93** StephenCarson 6 95
(R F Johnson Houghton) *t.k.h: trckd ldrs: ev ch and shkn up over 1f out: fdd last 100 yds* **14/1**
000/ **7** nk **Avening**[27] 6-8-7 **82** ow1 (bt) PatDobbs 5 83
(J E Hammond, France) *hld up in rr: rdn and effrt wl over 1f out: kpt on but nvr pce to rch ldrs* **8/1**
1016 **8** 2 **Guildenstern (IRE)**[31] 4573 4-8-6 **81** (t) LPKeniry 7 76
(H Morrison) *chsd ldr tl wl over 2f out: wknd u.p wl over 1f out* **14/1**
5300 **9** ½ **Connect**[9] 5182 9-8-9 **91** (b) PatrickHills(7) 3 85
(M H Tompkins) *sn bhd and pushed along: nvr on terms* **12/1**
0000 **10** 1¾ **Godfrey Street**[8] 5202 3-8-13 **90** JamieSpencer 8 78
(R Hannon) *chsd ldrs: rdn wl over 2f out: wknd 2f out: eased ins fnl f* **25/1**
0550 **11** 1¼ **Tony The Tap**[27] 4682 5-8-8 **83** PhilipRobinson 2 68
(B Palling) *racd in midfield: in tch tl 1/2-way: sn bhd: eased fnl f* **11/1**
2402 **12** nk **Romany Nights (IRE)**[45] 4106 6-8-10 **85** (b) JimmyQuinn 1 69
(Miss Gay Kelleway) *a bhd: no ch last 2f* **14/1**

69.38 secs (-4.22) **Going Correction** -0.55s/f (Hard) course record
WFA 3 from 4yo+ 2lb **12 Ran SP% 119.4**
Speed ratings (Par 107):106,105,104,103,102 102,102,99,99,96 95,94
CSF £82.76 CT £396.35 TOTE £7.90: £3.40, £3.40, £2.50; EX 61.10 Trifecta £248.40 Part won. Pool: £349.86 - 0.20 winning units..
Owner Hamdan Al Maktoum **Bred** Shadwell Farm LLC **Trained** Newmarket, Suffolk

FOCUS
A decent sprint handicap for the track. The early pace was strong and the first seven were fairly closely covered at the finish, but the form looks solid.

NOTEBOOK
Munaddam(USA) overcame a sluggish start and eventually motored home inside the final furlong to defy top weight and score. He has been running with credit in some of the top sprint handicaps this term, so success was deserved, and it should have done his confidence the world of good for an impending return to a higher level. (op 9-2)
Diane's Choice, bidding for a hat-trick, held every chance and was only mugged by the winner late on. This was another improved effort in defeat and her latest 7lb rise in the weights was clearly fair. (op 11-1 tchd 10-1)
My Gacho(IRE) put in a brave effort from the front and was helped by his high draw. He is a consistent sort, who helps to set the level of this form, and deserves to taste success again now. (op 13-2)
Swinbrook(USA) ran one of his better races on this return from a 45-day break and was tight for room at a crucial stage, so can be rated a little better than the bare form. However, he continues to look tricky. Official explanation: jockey said gelding was denied a clear run (op 7-1)
Blue Tomato, as if often the case, was doing his best work towards the finish and posted another solid effort in defeat. He has been running consistently well for most of the season and is another who helps to set the level of this form. (tchd 15-2)
Judd Street eventually paid for refusing to settle through the early parts, but still ran a much-improved race and looks to have benefited for his recent break. He is one to bear in mind next time.
Avening, having his first run in Britain since 2004, failed to really quicken when it mattered and was never a serious threat from off the pace. He probably requires easier ground now. (op 15-2 tchd 7-1)

5421 FORD BILL GURMIN MEMORIAL H'CAP 1m 4f
4:30 (4:38) (Class 3) (0-90,90) 3-Y-0 **£11,658** (£3,468; £1,733; £865) **Stalls** Low

Form RPR
2140 **1** **Dream Champion**[30] 4612 3-8-7 **79** TPO'Shea 5 86+
(M R Channon) *hld up in tch: pushed along wl over 3f out: swtchd lft and hdwy 2f out: rdn to ld jst ins fnl f: hld on wl* **10/1**
6213 **2** hd **My Petra**[32] 4528 3-8-4 **76** JimmyQuinn 7 83
(A King) *t.k.h: led for 1f: chsd ldrs: hugged inner bnd over 2f out: led u.p over 1f out: hdd jst ins fnl f: kpt on* **5/1**[3]
1311 **3** 2½ **Island Odyssey**[12] 5109 3-9-1 **87** DO'Donohoe 4 90
(E A L Dunlop) *w.w in tch: hdwy over 3f out: rdn 2f out: kpt on one pce fnl f* **9/2**[2]
3460 **4** 1 **Lake Poet (IRE)**[47] 4039 3-9-4 **90** KerrinMcEvoy 8 91+
(C E Brittain) *hld up in rr on inner: rdn 2f out: swtchd lft over 1f out: kpt on: no ch w ldrs* **11/8**[1]
4316 **5** 1 **Belanak (IRE)**[29] 4631 3-8-11 **83** DaneO'Neill 1 83
(Sir Michael Stoute) *chsd ldr after 2f tl over 1f out: wknd u.p fnl f* **9/2**[2]
1436 **6** 2 **Balloura (USA)**[12] 5109 3-7-13 **76** oh4 LiamJones(5) 3 73
(W J Haggas) *led after 1f: rdn and hdd wl over 1f out: wknd 1f out* **16/1**
6034 **7** nk **Billich**[9] 5164 3-8-6 **78** MartinDwyer 2 74
(E J O'Neill) *t.k.h: hld up in rr: rdn and c wd bnd over 2f out: no imp* **10/1**

2m 33.55s (-6.95) **Going Correction** -0.35s/f (Firm) **7 Ran SP% 119.2**
Speed ratings (Par 105):109,108,107,106,105 104,104
CSF £61.67 CT £262.60 TOTE £10.60: £4.30, £2.10; EX 45.60 Trifecta £154.30 Pool: £315.31 - 1.45 winning units..
Owner Jaber Abdullah **Bred** G W Turner And Miss S J Turner **Trained** West Ilsley, Berks
■ Peppertree (9/4, bolted bef start) was withdrawn. R4 applies, deduct 30p in the £. New market formed.

FOCUS
Another decent handicap for the track, despite the late withdrawal of Peppertree, which was run at a solid pace. The form looks solid enough, rated through the second.

NOTEBOOK
Dream Champion responded strongly for pressure passing the three-furlong pole and eventually just did enough to repel the runner-up at the line. The return to faster ground was clearly much to his liking and this does appear to be his optimum trip now. The Handicapper will raise him again for this, but he appeals as the type who could have more to offer, especially as a four-year-old. (new market op 22-1)
My Petra gave her all under a strong ride from Quinn, but ultimately paid for running freely early on and was just pipped. She has developed into a consistent filly at around this trip and was nicely clear of the remainder at the finish. (new market op 11-2 tchd 15-2 and 4-1)
Island Odyssey, raised another 4lb for scoring at Kempton last time, did little wrong in defeat and was simply found out by her new mark on this return to turf. She has done well this season, being success three times from her five outings to date, and is a decent benchmark for the form. (new market op 6-1 tchd 7-1 and 4-1)
Lake Poet(IRE) may have been better served by a slightly more positive ride, but still was not disgraced under top weight and enjoyed the drop to this lower class. (new market op 11-4 tchd 3-1)
Belanak(IRE) had his chance and looks too high in the weights on recent evidence. (new market op 8-1 tchd 10-1)

5422 ESSEX TRAILERS H'CAP 1m 1f 149y
5:00 (5:04) (Class 6) (0-65,63) 4-Y-0+ **£3,238** (£963; £481; £240) **Stalls** Low

Form RPR
4111 **1** **Good Article (IRE)**[9] 5166 5-9-2 **61** KerrinMcEvoy 12 67+
(D K Ivory) *t.k.h: hld up in midfield: plld out and hdwy wl over 1f out: str run fnl f to ld nr fin* **11/4**[1]
1036 **2** hd **Siena Star (IRE)**[19] 4925 8-9-2 **61** MickyFenton 7 67
(J R Boyle) *hld up in midfield: hdwy 4f out: chsd ldr 2f out: styd on u.p to ld last 100 yds: hdd nr fin* **12/1**
0434 **3** 1½ **Colinca's Lad (IRE)**[8] 5205 4-9-3 **62** PhilipRobinson 2 65
(T T Clement) *led: rdn and qcknd over 2f out: kpt on wl tl hdd and no ex last 100 yds* **9/2**[2]
-036 **4** 3 **Take A Mile (IRE)**[16] 4240 4-8-6 **58** PatrickHills(7) 3 55+
(B G Powell) *hld up in midfield: outpcd wl over 2f out: kpt on fnl f: nt trble ldrs* **14/1**
5202 **5** 1¼ **Leighton Buzzard**[6] 5258 4-9-0 **62** StephenDonohoe(3) 1 57
(N B King) *chsd ldrs tl lost pl wl over 3f out: kpt on again u.p fnl f* **13/2**
2210 **6** nk **Border Edge**[10] 5149 8-9-1 **63** MarcHalford(3) 6 58
(J J Bridger) *chsd ldr tl 5f out: ldr rdn wl over 2f out: wknd over 1f out* **11/1**
3015 **7** 2 **Fantasy Crusader**[8] 5205 7-8-8 **56** AdamKirby(3) 11 47
(R M H Cowell) *chsd ldrs: hdwy to chse ldr 5f out tl 2f out: wknd qckly over 1f out* **8/1**
2133 **8** hd **Looks The Business (IRE)**[25] 4432 5-8-13 **63** LiamJones(5) 10 53
(W G M Turner) *hld up towards rr: effrt u.p over 2f out: no hdwy* **6/1**[3]
/0-0 **9** 1 **Noble Calling (FR)**[15] 4332 9-8-7 **52** LPKeniry 8 40
(R J Hodges) *slowly away: a bhd* **40/1**
S4-0 **10** 2½ **Persona (IRE)**[236] 186 4-9-0 **62** JohnMcAuley(3) 9 46
(B J McMath) *hld up towards rr: rdn and no hdwy wl over 2f out* **66/1**
3130 **11** 7 **Competitor**[138] 1400 5-8-13 **58** (v) DaneO'Neill 4 28
(J Akehurst) *hld up in rr: rdn over 3f out: sn no ch* **12/1**

2m 2.48s (-2.75) **Going Correction** -0.35s/f (Firm) **11 Ran SP% 117.9**
Speed ratings (Par 101):97,96,95,93,92 92,90,90,89,87 81
CSF £38.13 CT £146.94 TOTE £3.10: £1.20, £2.60, £2.20; EX 42.90 Trifecta £144.60 Part won. Pool: £203.73 - 0.87 winning units. Place 6 £1,312.35, Place 5 £313.56.
Owner T G N Burrage **Bred** T G N Burrage **Trained** Radlett, Herts

FOCUS
A moderate handicap, run at an uneven pace, and the first two came clear. The winner remains most progressive and the form looks sound rated around the placed horses.
Fantasy Crusader Official explanation: jockey said gelding did not feel right
T/Jkpt: Not won. T/Plt: £1,529.00 to a £1 stake. Pool: £65,247.75. 31.15 winning tickets. T/Qpdt: £124.40 to a £1 stake. Pool: £5,047.00. 30.00 winning tickets. SP

5208 KEMPTON (A.W) (R-H)
Monday, September 18

OFFICIAL GOING: Standard
Wind: Light, half-behind Weather: Fine and warm

5423 E B F OPTICHROME PRINTERS MAIDEN STKS 1m (P)
2:10 (2:13) (Class 4) 2-Y-0 **£5,505** (£1,637; £818; £408) **Stalls** High

Form RPR
46 **1** **Brainy Benny (IRE)**[16] 5025 2-9-3 JimmyFortune 8 81
(N A Callaghan) *trckd ldr: led 3f out: rdn and hung lft across crse fnl 2f and ended on nr side rail: styd on wl* **11/2**[3]
6 **2** 2 **Coeur De Lionne (IRE)**[17] 4992 2-9-3 SteveDrowne 9 76
(R Charlton) *cl up: chsd wnr over 2f out: sn rdn: hung lft over 1f out: no imp* **6/5**[1]
3 hd **Filios (IRE)** 2-9-3 NickyMackay 3 76
(L M Cumani) *hld up bhd ldrs: pushed along and effrt 2f out: styd on fr over 1f out: jst hld for 2nd* **14/1**
0634 **4** 2½ **Recruit**[24] 4773 2-9-3 **76** RyanMoore 6 70
(R Hannon) *drvn to go prom: hrd rdn and nt qckn over 2f out: one pce after* **2/1**[2]
0 **5** 5 **Mud Monkey**[9] 5178 2-9-3 MichaelHills 5 59
(B G Powell) *hld up bhd ldrs: pushed along 3f out: sn outpcd: no imp after* **12/1**
0 **6** 2½ **Copernican**[12] 5105 2-9-3 SebSanders 7 53+
(Sir Mark Prescott) *led to 3f out: wknd 2f out* **16/1**
000 **7** 5 **Miss Silver Spurs**[13] 5083 2-8-12 **45** JimCrowley 2 36
(M D I Usher) *taken down early: t.k.h: hld up in tch: rdn 3f out: sn struggling* **66/1**
8 24 **Break 'N' Dish** 2-9-0 NeilChalmers(3) 4 —
(B R Johnson) *s.s: a last: wknd over 3f out: t.o* **50/1**

1m 41.37s (0.57) **Going Correction** 0.0s/f (Stan) **8 Ran SP% 117.9**
Speed ratings (Par 97):97,95,94,92,87 84,79,55
CSF £12.94 TOTE £5.70: £1.70, £1.10, £3.00; EX 13.20.
Owner Zayat Stables Ltd **Bred** Paul And Eilidh Hyland **Trained** Newmarket, Suffolk

FOCUS
Not the strongest of maidens in terms of depth, but the pace was sound enough and the winning time was about par for the type of race, suggesting the form is solid.

The Form Book, Raceform Ltd, Compton, RG20 6NL

NOTEBOOK

Brainy Benny(IRE) seemed to appreciate this surface rather better than the soft ground he has been encountering. The only worry was that he again hung left, which is becoming something of a trait, but it did not cost him this time. He may be best going the other way round. (op 9-2 tchd 6-1)

Coeur De Lionne(IRE) improved on his debut effort here, but despite holding every chance was unable to take advantage of the winner's wayward path in the latter stages. He should be up to winning an ordinary maiden on this surface. (op 5-4 tchd 11-10 and 11-8 in places)

Filios(IRE) ◆, a 33,000gns half-brother to three winners, kept on well in the home straight and did best of the newcomers. There is a mixture of speed and stamina in his pedigree and he should have learnt plenty from this. (op 12-1)

Recruit, the most experienced in the line-up, had his chance but was just not good enough. He will remain vulnerable to more progressive sorts in races like this, but has already been beaten off his current mark in a nursery so is not going to be easy to place. (tchd 9-4)

Mud Monkey did not have the speed to play an active role this time, but it should be a different story when he contests middle-distance handicaps next year. (op 16-1)

Copernican made much of the running before dropping away. He needs more time and should do better in handicaps next season, though a longer trip may not be necessary.

5424 E B F TFM NETWORKS MAIDEN FILLIES' STKS (DIV I) 7f (P)

2:45 (2:46) (Class 4) 2-Y-O £4,857 (£1,445; £722; £360) **Stalls** High

Form RPR

0 **1** **Folly Lodge**[44] [4148] 2-9-0 MichaelHills 5 80
(B W Hills) *trckd ldrs gng wl: led over 2f out: shkn up over 1f out: hung lft and pressed fnl f: pushed out and won shade comf* **3/1**[1]

5 **2** *1* **Tinnarinka**[17] [4994] 2-9-0 RyanMoore 2 77
(R Hannon) *in tch: pushed along and prog over 2f out: drvn to chal 1f out: edgd lft: styd on but a hld* **10/3**[2]

3 *nk* **Elhareer (IRE)** 2-9-0 SteveDrowne 1 76
(B J Meehan) *hld up in rr but wl in tch: prog 2f out: rdn to try to chal 1f out: hanging lft and kpt on same pce* **4/1**[3]

63 **4** *½* **Princess Taylor**[17] [4994] 2-9-0 OscarUrbina 8 75
(M Botti) *trckd ldrs gng wl: chal and upsides over 2f out: pressed wnr after: edgd lft and one pce fnl f* **4/1**[3]

5 *2 ½* **Asturias** 2-9-0 EddieAhern 4 68
(J W Hills) *hld up in last pair: outpcd over 2f out: reminder and prog over 1f out: styd on: nrst fin* **20/1**

05 **6** *1 ¼* **Kon Tiki**[13] [5089] 2-9-0 JoeFanning 6 65
(M Johnston) *pressed ldr: upsides over 2f out: sn shkn up and outpcd: fdd* **14/1**

7 *1* **Juzilla (IRE)** 2-9-0 SebSanders 11 63
(W R Swinburn) *trckd ldrs: outpcd over 2f out: grad fdd* **20/1**

8 *8* **Red Spinel** 2-9-0 (t) JimmyFortune 10 42
(E A L Dunlop) *in tch in rr: rdn 3f out: wl btn over 2f out: wknd* **12/1**

9 *6* **Ishismart** 2-9-0 TonyCulhane 9 26
(R Hollinshead) *led to over 2f out: wknd rapidly* **33/1**

10 *3 ½* **Tizzydore (IRE)** 2-9-0 FJohansson 7 17
(A M Balding) *s.i.s: a in last pair and nvr gng wl: bhd over 2f out* **25/1**

1m 28.1s (1.30) **Going Correction** 0.0s/f (Stan) **10** Ran SP% **118.7**

Speed ratings (Par 94):92,90,90,89,87 85,84,75,68,64

CSF £12.67 TOTE £4.50: £1.80, £1.30, £1.70; EX 18.00.

Owner O F Waller & T D Rootes **Bred** Shutford Stud **Trained** Lambourn, Berks

FOCUS

An ordinary fillies' maiden, but several of these are likely to improve with time and the form appears sound enough despite a modest winning time for a race of its type despite being 0.82 seconds faster than the second division. Whether by accident or design, the principals all hung over to the stands' rail in the closing stages.

NOTEBOOK

Folly Lodge, seventh in a Newmarket maiden on her debut that has produced a couple of winners, had obviously learnt from that and she showed the right sort of attitude to keep her rivals at bay late on. There should be other races to be won with her and her pedigree suggests this sort of trip will suit her best. (tchd 7-2)

Tinnarinka put in a spirited late effort again the stands' rail and improved from her debut effort on this track, but she looks in need of an extra furlong now. (op 4-1 tchd 3-1 in places)

Elhareer(IRE) ◆, a half-sister to Figaro Flyer, came through to hold every chance but then tended to run a little green. She still did best of the newcomers and should come on for this debut, whilst her breeding suggests she will not get much further than this. (op 7-2)

Princess Taylor had every chance starting up the home straight, but lacked the pace to take advantage. She was unable to confirm recent course form with Tinnarinka and as she now qualifies for a nursery mark. That may be a better option. (op 7-2 tchd 9-2)

Asturias, a 25,000gns debutante, never got involved but did offer some encouragement late on. Although by a sprinter, there is plenty of stamina on the dam's side and this performance suggests she is going to need further.

Kon Tiki again failed to see out the trip, but does at least now qualify for a nursery mark. (op 12-1)

Ishismart Official explanation: jockey said filly hung left-handed

5425 E B F TFM NETWORKS MAIDEN FILLIES' STKS (DIV II) 7f (P)

3:15 (3:15) (Class 4) 2-Y-O £4,857 (£1,445; £722; £360) **Stalls** High

Form RPR

60 **1** **Regal Quest (IRE)**[46] [4084] 2-9-0 JohnEgan 4 75
(S Kirk) *prom: chsd ldr over 2f out: led over 1f out: sn rdn clr* **10/3**[2]

2 **2** *4* **Dragon Flower (USA)**[31] [4558] 2-9-0 MichaelHills 10 64
(B W Hills) *hld up in midfield: lost pl on inner over 3f out: effrt over 2f out: rdn and styd on to take 2nd nr fin: no ch* **8/13**[1]

3 *½* **Guarantia** 2-9-0 TPQueally 2 63
(C E Brittain) *trckd ldr: led 3f out: kicked on over 2f out: hdd over 1f out and no ch w wnr: lost 2nd nr fin* **25/1**

4 *1* **Vallemeldee (IRE)** 2-9-0 RyanMoore 1 60
(P W D'Arcy) *dwlt: sn in tch on outer: pressed ldrs over 2f out: rdn and sn outpcd* **33/1**

0 **5** *1 ½* **Joyful Tears (IRE)**[26] [4705] 2-9-0 JimmyFortune 8 57+
(E A L Dunlop) *trckd ldrs: outpcd over 2f out: pushed along and kpt on steadily* **14/1**[3]

6 *nk* **Sweet Request** 2-9-0 SebSanders 9 56
(R M Beckett) *hld up in last: pushed along 3f out: effrt on inner 2f out but wl outpcd: n.d* **25/1**

7 *1* **Toccata (IRE)** 2-9-0 NickyMackay 7 53
(D M Simcock) *t.k.h: hld up in tch: pushed along over 2f out: sn outpcd and btn* **20/1**

0 **8** *½* **Fly The World**[3] [5352] 2-9-0 DarryllHolland 3 52
(A P Jarvis) *led to 3f out: wknd rapidly* **66/1**

9 *¾* **Windbeneathmywings (IRE)** 2-9-0 EddieAhern 5 50
(J W Hills) *in tch in rr tl wknd over 2f out* **33/1**

0 **10** *¾* **Krikket**[13] [5095] 2-9-0 TonyCulhane 6 48
(W J Haggas) *plld hrd early: hld up: wknd over 2f out* **25/1**

1m 28.92s (2.12) **Going Correction** 0.0s/f (Stan) **10** Ran SP% **115.3**

Speed ratings (Par 94):87,82,81,80,79 78,77,76,76,75

CSF £5.17 TOTE £3.80: £1.10, £1.10, £5.80; EX 7.50.

Owner J C Smith **Bred** Barnane Stud **Trained** Upper Lambourn, Berks

FOCUS

A modest winning time for a race like this, 0.82 seconds slower than the first division. An ordinary early pace resulted in a few pulling for their heads, but despite a much more clear-cut winner than in the other division, the modest time must raise questions over the true strength of the form.

NOTEBOOK

Regal Quest(IRE) had the edge in experience on all of her rivals and made no mistake, sprinting right away towards the end after having raced keenly early on. Though impressive to the eye, the winning time does put a dampener on the true merit of the form, but she is obviously going the right way and both her style of running and her pedigree suggests she could develop into a nice middle-distance handicapper next season. (op 3-1 tchd 7-2)

Dragon Flower(USA), so promising on her Newbury debut, again did not get going until it was far too late despite the extra furlong, which was surprising given her speed-laden pedigree. It remains to be seen what sort of trip is going to suit her best. (op 4-7)

Guarantia was given a positive ride and made a bold bid for glory soon after turning for home, but was then swamped for speed by the winner. She still performed best of the newcomers and, as her dam is a half-sister to the likes of Luso, Warrsan and Needle Gun, it is reasonable to assume she is going to need more time and a longer trip. (op 20-1 tchd 33-1)

Vallemeldee(IRE) had every chance and posted a very creditable debut effort despite the apparent weakness of the form due to the winning time. She is related to some decent French sprinters on the dam's side, but this performance suggests she may have inherited more of her sire's stamina. (op 20-1)

Joyful Tears(IRE) improved a little from her Leicester debut, but will need to improve again in order to start repaying her 150,000gns price tag. (tchd 16-1)

Sweet Request, a half-sister to a couple of winners, including Sweet Return, made a little bit of progress in the home straight and should come on for the experience. (op 20-1)

5426 NORMAN HILL MEMORIAL MAIDEN STKS (DIV I) 1m 4f (P)

3:50 (3:51) (Class 4) 3-4-Y-O £4,857 (£1,445; £722; £360) **Stalls** Centre

Form RPR

4-52 **1** **Profitable**[18] [4959] 3-8-12 73 MichaelHills 5 79
(B W Hills) *hld up: prog fr 7f out: effrt to dispute ld over 2f out: edgd lft in sustained battle fnl 2f: narrow ld 1f out: jst hld on* **9/2**[2]

5 **2** *shd* **Red Gala**[10] [5151] 3-9-3 RyanMoore 2 84
(Sir Michael Stoute) *dwlt: sn rcvrd and prom: prog to dispute ld over 2f out: carried lft fr over 1f out: jst hld* **15/8**[1]

4-2 **3** *2* **Mantle**[18] [4973] 4-9-6 OscarUrbina 10 76
(J R Fanshawe) *trckd ldrs: chsd ldng pair over 2f out: clr of rest over 1f out: nt qckn and no imp fnl f* **9/2**[2]

0 **4** *6* **Broughtons Folly**[13] [5086] 3-8-12 TPQueally 3 66
(W J Musson) *hld up wl in rr: stdy prog 4f out: reminder to chse clr ldng trio over 1f out: no ch but kpt on wl* **50/1**

36 **5** *4* **Primitive Academy**[69] [3376] 4-9-11 EddieAhern 12 65
(H R A Cecil) *led to over 2f out: sn outpcd and btn* **8/1**

45 **6** *2* **Foreigner (IRE)**[13] [5086] 3-9-3 JimmyFortune 7 61
(B J Meehan) *trckd ldrs and throwing hd around several times: easily outpcd fr over 2f out* **6/1**[3]

00 **7** *5* **Janaah**[54] [3849] 3-8-12 SebSanders 13 48
(C E Brittain) *prom: chsd ldr briefly over 3f out: sn rdn: wknd over 2f out* **25/1**

0000 **8** *7* **Cativo Cavallino**[23] [4800] 3-9-3 50 IanMongan 4 42
(Jamie Poulton) *t.k.h: hld up wl in rr: effrt on wd outside over 3f out: wknd rapidly over 2f out* **33/1**

0 **9** *3* **Amron Hill**[18] [4973] 3-9-3 SteveDrowne 9 37
(R Hollinshead) *dwlt: t.k.h: hld up in last trio: sme prog over 4f out: wknd over 2f out* **20/1**

6 **10** *2 ½* **Aberlady Bay (IRE)**[26] [4701] 3-8-12 DarryllHolland 1 28
(T T Clement) *in tch in midfield: wknd rapidly over 2f out* **25/1**

06 **11** *7* **Jupiters Moon (IRE)**[11] [5128] 3-9-0 RichardKingscote(3) 14 22
(R Charlton) *in tch in midfield tl lost pl rapidly 5f out: t.o 3f out* **20/1**

040- **12** *9* **Son Of Bathwick (IRE)**[214] [4991] 4-9-11 48 (vt[1]) FJohansson 11 8
(Mrs Norma Pook) *chsd ldr to over 3f out: wknd rapidly: t.o* **66/1**

0- **13** *3 ½* **Monte Carrio**[277] [6585] 3-8-13 ow1 JerryO'Dwyer(5) 8 3
(C Drew) *rdn and struggling towards rr 7f out: last and wkng 5f out: t.o* **66/1**

0 **14** *18* **Sky Walk**[37] [4367] 3-9-3 JohnEgan 6 —
(Jamie Poulton) *a wl in rr: t.o over 3f out* **66/1**

2m 34.54s (-2.36) **Going Correction** 0.0s/f (Stan)

WFA 3 from 4yo 8lb **14** Ran SP% **123.1**

Speed ratings (Par 105):107,106,105,101,98 97,94,89,87,85 81,75,72,60

CSF £12.30 TOTE £5.80: £1.90, £1.30, £1.50; EX 12.60.

Owner Gainsborough Stud **Bred** Gainsborough Stud Management Ltd **Trained** Lambourn, Berks

■ Stewards' Enquiry : Michael Hills caution: careless riding

FOCUS

Still a fair time for a race like this despite being 0.61 seconds slower than the second division. The front three pulled clear of the rest and in fact there were some decent margins throughout the whole field, which suggests the form is very solid.

Foreigner(IRE) Official explanation: jockey said gelding hung left-handed

Janaah Official explanation: jockey said filly had no more to give

5427 SCOTTISH & NEWCASTLE UK H'CAP 6f (P)

4:20 (4:20) (Class 4) (0-85,81) 3-Y-O £5,505 (£1,637; £818; £408) **Stalls** High

Form RPR

0543 **1** **Violet Ballerina (IRE)**[26] [4703] 3-8-2 72 (b) KMay(7) 8 82
(B J Meehan) *trckd ldng pair: led 2f out: urged along and in command fnl f* **13/2**[2]

0000 **2** *1 ½* **Calypso King**[12] [5107] 3-8-10 73 RyanMoore 6 78
(J W Hills) *hld up in last trio: prog on inner fr over 1f out: styd on wl to take 2nd last strides: no ch* **11/1**

1254 **3** *shd* **Gwilym (GER)**[24] [4756] 3-8-5 68 ow1 EddieAhern 5 73
(D Haydn Jones) *stdd s: hld up in last trio: prog on inner over 2f out: chsd wnr jst ins fnl f: no imp: lost 2nd nr fin* **7/1**[3]

6000 **4** *1 ¼* **Trans Sonic**[12] [5107] 3-9-3 80 DarryllHolland 11 81
(A P Jarvis) *led: drvn and hdd 2f out: lost 2nd jst ins fnl f: fdd* **9/1**

3631 **5** *2* **Namu**[4] [5317] 3-8-6 76 6ex SladeO'Hara(7) 7 71
(B W Hills) *nvr bttr than midfield: rdn and no prog over 2f out: one pce after* **13/2**[2]

0440 **6** *shd* **Gavarnie Beau (IRE)**[15] [5044] 3-8-12 75 SteveDrowne 9 70
(M Blanshard) *chsd ldrs: rdn and no prog over 2f out: grad fdd* **7/1**[3]

0402 **7** ½ **Figaro Flyer (IRE)**[7] 5246 3-8-11 **74**.................. TonyCulhane 3 67
(P Howling) *chsd ldrs: rdn wl over 2f out: no imp over 1f out: wknd ins fnl f* **4/1**[1]

0000 **8** 1¼ **Savernake Blue**[21] 4888 3-8-12 **75**.................. JohnEgan 2 65
(M R Channon) *nvr bttr than midfield: rdn and no prog over 2f out: wknd fnl f* **16/1**

3426 **9** *nk* **Queen Cobra (IRE)**[21] 4886 3-9-0 **77**.................. RobertHavlin 4 66
(H Morrison) *racd wd: a in rr: struggling over 2f out* **16/1**

2316 **10** *nk* **Peter Island (FR)**[16] 5021 3-9-4 **81**..................(v) JimCrowley 1 69
(J Gallagher) *pressed ldr to over 2f out: sn wknd* **7/1**[3]

00-0 **11** *8* **Simpsons Gamble (IRE)**[13] 5092 3-8-4 **67** oh40.... AdrianMcCarthy 10 31
(R M Flower) *chsd ldrs to 1/2-way: wknd over 2f out: sn bhd* **50/1**

1m 13.27s (-0.43) **Going Correction** 0.0s/f (Stan) 11 Ran SP% **116.2**
Speed ratings (Par 103):102,100,99,98,95 95,94,93,92,92 81
CSF £74.99 CT £517.48 TOTE £7.10: £2.00, £3.30, £2.80; EX 102.60.
Owner Racegoers Club Owners Group **Bred** James F Hanly **Trained** Manton, Wilts

FOCUS
A fair little sprint handicap of its type and the pace was generous enough. Those that raced closest to the inside rail seemed to hold an advantage.
Gavarnie Beau(IRE) Official explanation: jockey said gelding lost its action

5428 TFM NETWORKS H'CAP 1m (P)
4:50 (4:53) (Class 4) (0-85,85) 3-Y-0+ **£5,505** (£1,637; £818; £408) **Stalls** High

Form RPR

1202 **1** **Cross The Line (IRE)**[12] 5108 4-9-3 **80**.................. DarrylHolland 3 91+
(A P Jarvis) *trckd ldrs: gng easily 3f out: wnt 3rd over 1f out: drvn to ld jst ins fnl f: r.o wl* **4/1**[1]

0504 **2** 1¾ **Norton (IRE)**[23] 4819 9-9-5 **82**.................. IanMongan 1 89
(T G Mills) *w ldr: led 1/2-way: drvn over 2f out: hdd jst ins fnl f: kpt on u.p* **12/1**

2140 **3** ½ **Optimus (USA)**[50] 3973 4-9-0 **77**.................. NickyMackay 4 83
(G A Butler) *s.i.s: sn rcvrd to trck ldrs: rdn to chal 2f out: ev ch 1f out: one pce fnl f* **4/1**[1]

0-12 **4** 1¾ **Tommy Toogood (IRE)**[147] 1190 3-9-1 **82**.................. MichaelHills 11 84+
(B W Hills) *hld up in rr: prog over 2f out: rdn and kpt on fr over 1f out: nt rch ldrs* **11/2**[2]

1110 **5** *3* **Fajr (IRE)**[117] 1938 4-9-5 **82**.................. RyanMoore 10 77+
(Miss Gay Kelleway) *hld up in midfield: rdn 3f out: sme prog over 1f out: nvr gng pce to rch ldrs* **7/1**[3]

100 **6** 1½ **Coleridge (AUS)**[3] 5345 7-8-13 **76**..................(e[1]) RobertMiles 7 68
(B G Powell) *hld up in midfield: lost pl sltly over 3f out: hrd rdn on inner 2f out: no imp* **33/1**

1004 **7** ¾ **Ninth House (USA)**[15] 5045 4-9-8 **85**..................(t) JimmyFortune 14 75
(D J Daly) *hld up wl in rr: rdn and struggling over 2f out: n.d after* **9/1**

3356 **8** 2½ **Shogun Prince (IRE)**[12] 5110 3-8-11 **78**.................. SteveDrowne 9 62
(A King) *led to 1/2-way: wknd u.p 2f out* **11/1**

-100 **9** ½ **Royal Reservation**[139] 1384 3-8-13 **80**.................. EddieAhern 12 63
(P W Chapple-Hyam) *a towards rr: rdn and struggling wl over 2f out* **10/1**

-000 **10** *2* **Love Thirty**[31] 4577 4-9-3 **80**.................. TonyCulhane 8 58
(M R Channon) *nvr bttr than midfield: rdn and wknd over 2f out* **40/1**

5215 **11** 2½ **Toffee Vodka (IRE)**[18] 4965 4-9-3 **80**.................. JohnEgan 5 53
(J W Hills) *trckd ldrs tl wknd rapidly over 2f out* **10/1**

60 **12** *hd* **First Friend (IRE)**[16] 5016 5-9-5 **82**.................. TPQueally 13 54
(P Mitchell) *t.k.h: hld up in last: nvr a factor: wl btn over 2f out* **40/1**

-330 **U** **Celebration Song (IRE)**[104] 2330 3-9-2 **83**.................. SebSanders 2 —
(W R Swinburn) *stmbld and uns rdr sn after s* **10/1**

1m 39.98s (-0.82) **Going Correction** 0.0s/f (Stan)
WFA 3 from 4yo+ 4lb 13 Ran SP% **129.0**
Speed ratings (Par 105):104,102,101,100,97 95,94,92,91,89 87,87,—
CSF £58.35 CT £188.35 TOTE £5.00: £1.60, £2.40, £2.40; EX 47.40.
Owner Eurostrait Ltd **Bred** Genesis Green Stud Ltd **Trained** Twyford, Bucks

FOCUS
A decent handicap in which the pace was solid without being breakneck. The form appears solid rated around the placed horses.

5429 NORMAN HILL MEMORIAL MAIDEN STKS (DIV II) 1m 4f (P)
5:20 (5:22) (Class 4) 3-4-Y-0 **£4,857** (£1,445; £722; £360) **Stalls** Centre

Form RPR

43-2 **1** **Hotel Du Cap**[13] 5086 3-9-3 85.................. DarrylHolland 3 95+
(G Wragg) *sn prom: led wl over 3f out: forged wl clr fr over 2f out* **3/1**[2]

54 **2** *9* **His Honour (IRE)**[122] 1822 3-9-3.................. SteveDrowne 4 79
(R Charlton) *prom: pushed along 5f out: effrt over 2f out: chsd clr wnr wl over 1f out: no imp* **13/2**

3253 **3** *nk* **Altenburg (FR)**[31] 4560 4-9-11 80.................. RyanMoore 13 78
(Mrs N Smith) *hld up wl in rr: prog to trck ldrs 4f out: rdn to dispute 2nd over 1f out: carried hd high and fnd little* **2/1**[1]

3530 **4** *5* **Gaze**[19] 4931 3-8-5 67.................. BRoper(7) 10 65
(W Jarvis) *hld up towards rr: in tch 4f out: bdly outpcd wl over 2f out: styd on again fnl f* **11/1**

6 **5** *nk* **Sunset Boulevard (IRE)**[37] 4374 3-9-3.................. TPQueally 8 70
(J Noseda) *rn green in rr early: stdy prog fr 1/2-way: cl up over 3f out : sn rdn: wknd 2f out* **16/1**

4-0 **6** *1* **Battalion (IRE)**[68] 3419 3-9-3.................. JimmyFortune 1 68
(Sir Michael Stoute) *led to wl over 3f out: wknd 2f out* **14/1**

332 **7** *7* **Moonshadow**[11] 5128 3-8-12 80.................. EddieAhern 14 52
(H R A Cecil) *mostly trckd ldr to 5f out: hrd rdn and struggling over 3f out: sn wknd* **9/2**[3]

000 **8** 1¼ **Beaufort**[14] 5057 4-9-11 57.................. OscarUrbina 7 55
(D K Ivory) *v restless stalls: in tch in midfield tl wknd over 3f out* **50/1**

00-6 **9** *11* **Telegonus**[168] 850 3-9-3 76.................. RobertHavlin 2 37
(C E Longsdon) *in tch in midfield tl wknd rapidly over 3f out* **25/1**

0 **10** *shd* **Well Versed**[24] 4776 3-8-12.................. SebSanders 6 32
(C F Wall) *trckd ldrs: rdn and wl in tch 3f out: wknd rapidly over 2f out* **20/1**

11 *11* **Inveraray**[77] 3-8-12.................. JimCrowley 9 15
(P S Felgate) *stdd s: hld up in rr: lost tch over 4f out: t.o* **33/1**

5 **12** *10* **Ausone**[19] 4931 4-9-6.................. IanMongan 5 —
(Miss J R Gibney) *chsd ldrs for 5f: sn wknd u.p: t.o* **25/1**

00 **13** *36* **Ath Tiomain (IRE)**[28] 4661 3-9-3.................. TonyCulhane 12 —
(D J S Ffrench Davis) *a in last pair: t.o 4f out* **40/1**

2m 33.93s (-2.97) **Going Correction** 0.0s/f (Stan)
WFA 3 from 4yo 8lb 13 Ran SP% **130.5**
Speed ratings (Par 105):109,103,102,99,99 98,93,93,85,85 78,71,47
CSF £23.55 TOTE £5.00: £1.90, £3.00, £1.30; EX 22.40.
Owner J L C Pearce **Bred** J L C Pearce **Trained** Newmarket, Suffolk

FOCUS
A decent winning time for a race like this and 0.61 seconds faster than the first division. The winner was extremely impressive and with the field finishing spread out, the form looks sound.

5430 JOHN SMITH'S BACKING WINNERS H'CAP 1m 4f (P)
5:50 (5:51) (Class 3) (0-95,94) 3-Y-0+
£7,790 (£2,332; £1,166; £583; £291; £146) **Stalls** Centre

Form RPR

6035 **1** **Balanced Budget**[37] 4370 3-9-0 **90**.................. TPQueally 1 103+
(J Noseda) *trckd ldrs: prog to ld wl over 2f out: drvn and styd on wl fnl 2f* **9/1**

5202 **2** 1¾ **Royal Jet**[17] 4997 4-9-7 **89**.................. JohnEgan 10 98
(M R Channon) *trckd ldrs: effrt to chse wnr over 2f out: clr of rest fnl 2f : nt qckn and readily hld* **7/2**[1]

-140 **3** *4* **Kyoto Summit**[46] 4082 3-9-0 **90**.................. NickyMackay 8 93+
(L M Cumani) *hld up towards rr: lost pl and last 3f out: prog over 2f out: wnt 3rd 1f out: styd on but no ch* **11/2**[2]

4605 **4** 2½ **Nawamees (IRE)**[17] 4997 8-9-1 **83**..................(p) JimmyFortune 4 82
(G L Moore) *hld up in last pair: prog on outer over 3f out: n.m.r over 2f out: chsd clr ldng pair over 1f out to 1f out: fdd* **10/1**

2242 **5** *5* **Obrigado (USA)**[15] 5045 6-9-7 **89**.................. DarryllHolland 3 80
(Karen George) *stdd s: hld up in detached last: sweeping run on outer over 3f out : hrd rdn 2f out: fnd nil* **8/1**

-016 **6** *5* **Pass The Port**[212] 454 5-8-12 **80** oh2.................. EddieAhern 6 63
(D Haydn Jones) *hld up towards rr: rdn and wl outpcd over 2f out: wknd* **16/1**

-433 **7** 1¼ **Dynacam (USA)**[21] 4878 3-8-6 **82**.................. RyanMoore 9 63
(Sir Michael Stoute) *hld up towards rr: effrt on inner but wl outpcd over 2f out: wknd over 1f out* **6/1**[3]

3100 **8** *nk* **I Have Dreamed (IRE)**[23] 4810 4-9-2 **84**.................. IanMongan 5 64
(T G Mills) *led to over 7f out: led 5f out to wl over 2f out: wknd rapidly* **8/1**

61 **9** *8* **Crossbow Creek**[10] 4931 8-9-3 **85**.................. JimCrowley 7 52
(M G Rimell) *plld hrd: led over 7f out to 5f out: wknd rapidly 3f out* **13/2**

-000 **10** 2½ **Gig Harbor**[65] 3534 7-9-12 **94**.................. OscarUrbina 2 57
(Miss E C Lavelle) *chsd ldr for 4f: wknd rapidly over 3f out* **20/1**

2m 32.94s (-3.96) **Going Correction** 0.0s/f (Stan)
WFA 3 from 4yo+ 8lb 10 Ran SP% **117.2**
Speed ratings (Par 107):113,111,109,107,104 100,100,99,94,92
CSF £40.79 CT £193.84 TOTE £12.70: £3.80, £1.50, £1.90; EX 63.70 Place 6 £13.07, Place 5 £8.09.
Owner Hesmonds Stud **Bred** Hesmonds Stud Ltd **Trained** Newmarket, Suffolk
■ Stewards' Enquiry : Jimmy Fortune two-day ban: careless riding (Oct 2-3)
Darryll Holland three-day ban (reduced from five days on appeal): improper riding (Sep 29, Oct 2-3)

FOCUS
A decent pace resulted in a smart winning time for the grade and significantly faster than both divisions of the maiden. The front pair pulled well clear and the whole field finished well spread out, so the form looks solid.

NOTEBOOK
Balanced Budget ◆, on sand for the first time, seemed to relish this surface and, once hitting the front soon after turning in, the race was his. He stayed the trip so much better this time and there are more races to be won with him on this surface. (tchd 8-1)
Royal Jet, for the second time at this track, did nothing wrong and pulled right away from the others, but was just unfortunate to come up against a decent performer. If there is any justice he will go one better here before too long. (op 11-4)
Kyoto Summit, trying sand for the first time, did not enjoy the clearest of passages and by the time he got into top gear the front pair had already skipped clear. He is well worth another try on Polytrack. (op 5-1 tchd 6-1)
Nawamees(IRE) has run plenty of decent races on Polytrack and did so again, but he really should have won a Flat race in this country by now and the fact that he has not done so after numerous attempts makes him an obvious lay. (tchd 11-1)
Obrigado(USA), making his debut for the yard having been claimed after finishing runner-up at Epsom last time, was switched right off out the back as the front-runners got on with it. He looked likely to take a hand in the finish when moving into contention turning for home, but found nothing like as much off the bridle as had looked likely.
Pass The Port, an experienced Polytrack performer though making his debut here, should come on for this first outing since February. (op 14-1)
Dynacam(USA) never landed a blow and as yet her sand form does not match her turf efforts. (op 9-2)
I Have Dreamed(IRE), in and out of the lead for much of the way, was again disappointing and ran like a non-stayer on this occasion. (tchd 15-2)
Crossbow Creek pulled his way to the front before halfway and gave himself little chance of seeing it out. (op 6-1)
T/Plt: £30.50 to a £1 stake. Pool: £46,086.40. 1,102.90 winning tickets. T/Qpdt: £13.30 to a £1 stake. Pool: £3,090.70. 171.40 winning tickets. JN

5083 LEICESTER (R-H)
Monday, September 18

OFFICIAL GOING: Good to firm (firm in places)
Wind: Light, behind Weather: Fine

5431 E B F LADBROKES.COM NOVICE STKS 7f 9y
2:00 (2:15) (Class 4) 2-Y-0 **£4,416** (£1,321; £660; £330; £164) **Stalls** Low

Form RPR

134 **1** **Ready For Spring (USA)**[16] 5017 2-9-5 100.................. TedDurcan 4 85+
(J Noseda) *chsd ldr: rdn to ld over 1f out: r.o* **4/7**[1]

222 **2** 1½ **Gazboolou**[28] 4650 2-8-12 79.................. PatCosgrave 1 74
(K R Burke) *led: rdn and hdd over 1f out: styd on same pce* **6/1**[3]

0556 **3** 1½ **Distiller (IRE)**[2] 5381 2-8-12 73.................. RichardMullen 3 70
(W R Muir) *pld hrd and prom: outpcd over 1f out: styd on ins fnl f* **25/1**

4 *1* **Hanbrin Bhoy (IRE)** 2-8-8.................. RoystonFfrench 5 63
(R Dickin) *chsd ldrs: hung rt 1/2-way: rdn over 1f out: no ex ins fnl f* **66/1**

1 **5** *5* **Greek Envoy**[25] 4732 2-8-11 86.................. MichaelJStainton(5) 2 58
(T P Tate) *s.i.s: in rr: hung rt over 4f out: wknd over 2f out* **3/1**[2]

1m 26.28s (0.18) **Going Correction** -0.30s/f (Firm) 5 Ran SP% **108.3**
Speed ratings (Par 97):86,84,82,81,75
CSF £4.42 TOTE £1.40: £1.20, £1.60; EX 3.60.
Owner B J McElroy **Bred** J J Pletcher **Trained** Newmarket, Suffolk

FOCUS
A decent contest but a very moderate winning time for the grade, although the form looks fair enough rated around the placed horses.

The Form Book, Raceform Ltd, Compton, RG20 6NL

NOTEBOOK

Ready For Spring(USA), unsuited by the drop back to six furlongs when a slightly disappointing fourth in a Group 3 at Kempton earlier in the month, faced a much simpler task and with his main market rival disappointing he should have run out a cosy winner. The runner-up made him work hard though and in the end it was just a workmanlike win, but he was shouldering a penalty and a mile should be within his compass. (op 4-6 tchd 1-2)

Gazboolou had shown fair form when runner-up on all three previous starts and he was again forced to settle for the runner-up spot, albeit he gave the favourite a race. He will find a race eventually, but is hardly one to start following now. (op 13-2)

Distiller(IRE) again showed enough to suggest he will be winning once contesting handicaps, running on again inside the final furlong having pulled hard early. (op 16-1)

Hanbrin Bhoy(IRE), who looked to hold little chance on this racecourse debut in what looked a decent affair, shaped surprisingly well and, although probably flattered, he did himself no favours in hanging and deserves a chance to show this to be no fluke.

Greek Envoy, who did it so well on his debut at Redcar last month, was sluggish to get going and he was never travelling, making no ground and looking awkward under pressure. He is clearly better than this, but the way he ran his race was off-putting with the future in mind. Official explanation: jockey said colt was unsuited by the track (op 10-3 tchd 4-1)

5432 LADBROKES.COM (S) STKS — 7f 9y

2:35 (2:38) (Class 6) 3-Y-O £2,590 (£770; £385; £192) Stalls Low

Form RPR

0200 **1** **Crush On You**[18] 4944 3-8-6 48 .... GrahamGibbons 16 — 51
(R Hollinshead) *hld up: hdwy and nt clr run over 1f out: r.o to ld wl ins fnl f* **5/1**[2]

3040 **2** 1 1/4 **Boucheen**[7] 5240 3-8-11 43 .... DanielTudhope 4 — 53
(Ms Deborah J Evans) *led: rdn and hdd 2f out: ev ch ins fnl f: styd on same pce* **16/1**

6040 **3** nk **Lady Duxyana**[18] 4973 3-8-6 42 .... (v) RichardSmith 5 — 47
(M D I Usher) *s.s: hdwy over 2f out: sn rdn and hung rt: led 1f out: hdd and no ex wl ins fnl f* **25/1**

5066 **4** 1 3/4 **Pontefract Glory**[26] 4695 3-8-11 39 .... (b) RobertWinston 7 — 47
(M Dods) *hld up: hdwy u.p over 1f out: styd on* **8/1**

0000 **5** hd **Quote Unquote**[36] 4401 3-8-1 50 .... RoryMoore(5) 11 — 42
(J Parkes) *chsd ldrs: led 2f out: rdn and hdd 1f out: styd on same pce* **40/1**

000 **6** 1/2 **Bournonville**[111] 2101 3-8-8 42 .... DominicFox(3) 9 — 46
(M Wigham) *mid-div: hdwy over 2f out: sn rdn: styd on same pce ins fnl f* **25/1**

3354 **7** 1/2 **She Whispers (IRE)**[149] 1149 3-8-6 51 .... RichardMullen 12 — 39
(W M Brisbourne) *hld up: hdwy over 2f out: rdn over 1f out: styd on same pce* **11/1**

00-0 **8** 3/4 **Alistair John**[13] 5077 3-8-11 40 .... J-PGuillambert 6 — 42
(Mrs G S Rees) *prom: jnd ldr 1/2-way: rdn and ev ch over 1f out: wknd ins fnl f* **50/1**

6602 **9** 1/2 **Decree Nisi**[18] 4943 3-9-2 60 .... (v) RoystonFfrench 17 — 46
(Mrs A Duffield) *s.i.s: hdwy 1/2-way: rdn and ev ch over 1f out: wknd ins fnl f* **11/4**[1]

0050 **10** 2 1/2 **Canary Girl**[39] 4304 3-8-1 37 .... AndrewElliott(5) 8 — 30
(Mrs C A Dunnett) *chsd ldrs: rdn over 2f out: hung rt and wknd over 1f out* **50/1**

4640 **11** nk **Royal Bandit**[86] 2864 3-8-11 63 .... (b1) ChrisCatlin 3 — 34
(N A Callaghan) *mid-div: rdn 1/2-way: wknd over 1f out* **11/2**[3]

0000 **12** 5 **Salisbury World (IRE)**[18] 4943 3-8-11 39 .... FrancisNorton 14 — 21
(J F Coupland) *s.s: outpcd: effrt over 2f out: sn wknd* **28/1**

0400 **13** 1 1/4 **No Inkling (IRE)**[18] 4943 3-8-3 39 .... AndrewMullen(3) 10 — 13
(John A Harris) *prom over 4f* **40/1**

3000 **14** 2 **Bertie Bear**[24] 4769 3-8-11 37 .... (v) JamieMackay 1 — 12
(G G Margarson) *s.i.s: outpcd* **33/1**

5000 **15** nk **Helen Wood**[16] 5033 3-7-13 45 .... FrankiePickard(7) 15 — 7
(M D I Usher) *dwlt: outpcd* **40/1**

-000 **16** 3 **Distant Mind (IRE)**[132] 1576 3-7-13 40 .... KirstyMilczarek(7) 18 — —
(Mrs C A Dunnett) *hld up: wknd 1/2-way* **100/1**

0-00 **17** 12 **Earl Kraul (IRE)**[8] 5211 3-8-11 70 .... NCallan 13 — —
(G L Moore) *chsd ldrs over 4f* **8/1**

1m 24.92s (-1.18) **Going Correction** -0.30s/f (Firm) **17** Ran SP% **121.5**
Speed ratings (Par 99):94,92,92,90,90 89,88,88,87,84 84,78,77,74,74 71,57
CSF £73.95 TOTE £8.50: £2.50, £3.60, £11.00; EX 95.10.There was no bid for the winner. Decree Nisi was claimed by Mr G. Doel for £6,000.
Owner D Coppenhall **Bred** Tweenhills Stud And Stuart McPhee **Trained** Upper Longdon, Staffs

FOCUS
Poor selling form rated at face value.
Bournonville Official explanation: jockey said gelding had no more to give
Decree Nisi Official explanation: jockey said gelding ran too freely
Earl Kraul(IRE) Official explanation: jockey said gelding was unsuited by the firm ground

5433 LADBROKESCASINO.COM H'CAP — 5f 2y

3:05 (3:05) (Class 3) (0-95,95) 3-Y-O+
£7,790 (£2,332; £1,166; £583; £291; £146) Stalls Low

Form RPR

0110 **1** **The Jobber (IRE)**[9] 5182 5-9-5 95 .... NCallan 1 — 107
(M Blanshard) *chsd ldrs: rdn to ld ins fnl f: r.o* **9/1**

4210 **2** 1 1/4 **Cape Royal**[9] 5182 6-9-4 94 .... (bt) FrancisNorton 4 — 101
(J M Bradley) *w ldr: rdn to ld and hung rt over 1f out: hdd and unable qckn ins fnl f* **9/1**

0004 **3** nk **If Paradise**[16] 5009 5-8-12 88 .... RichardHughes 3 — 94
(R Hannon) *led over 3f: styd on same pce ins fnl f* **9/2**[2]

0065 **4** 1 1/4 **Hoh Hoh Hoh**[10] 5148 4-8-2 81 oh3 .... JamesDoyle(3) 10 — 82
(R J Price) *dwlt: hdwy over 1f out: nt rch ldrs* **12/1**

0-20 **5** 4 **Fictional**[22] 4855 5-9-4 94 .... RichardMullen 12 — 81
(E J O'Neill) *outpcd: sme hdwy over 1f out: nvr trbld ldrs* **9/2**[2]

1000 **6** 1 **Peopleton Brook**[83] 2946 4-8-10 86 .... TedDurcan 7 — 69
(J M Bradley) *prom: rdn 1/2-way: wknd over 1f out* **33/1**

1103 **7** nk **Pic Up Sticks**[8] 5202 7-9-0 90 .... KDarley 8 — 72
(B G Powell) *chsd ldrs: rdn 1/2-way: wknd over 1f out* **8/1**[3]

0005 **8** nk **Enchantment**[16] 5009 5-8-5 81 .... ChrisCatlin 6 — 62
(J M Bradley) *chsd ldrs 3f* **16/1**

0661 **9** 2 1/2 **Caribbean Coral**[9] 5169 7-8-13 89 .... (v) GrahamGibbons 9 — 61
(J J Quinn) *sn outpcd* **8/1**[3]

2006 **10** 3 **Treasure Cay**[9] 5182 5-9-4 94 .... (t) RobertWinston 5 — 55
(P W D'Arcy) *dwlt: outpcd: in rr whn hung rt 1/2-way* **4/1**[1]

57.85 secs (-3.05) **Going Correction** -0.30s/f (Firm) course record
WFA 3 from 4yo+ 1lb **10** Ran SP% **115.1**
Speed ratings (Par 107):112,110,109,107,101 99,99,98,94,89
CSF £86.00 CT £332.94 TOTE £8.80: £3.00, £3.80, £2.30; EX 38.30.
Owner Mrs Rosemary Wilkerson & Partners **Bred** Dr T J Molony **Trained** Upper Lambourn, Berks

FOCUS
A decent sprint handicap and they went a good gallop with Cape Royal and If Paradise sharing the duties, and as a result the winning time was decent and the form looks solid.

NOTEBOOK

The Jobber(IRE), on a hat-trick going into a competitive sprint handicap at York, was unable to produce his best there, but he bounced back to form on this faster surface and he ran on too strongly for Cape Royal. A tough and progressive sprinter, he took 0.01 seconds off the course record and he may reappear under a penalty at Haydock at the weekend. Fast ground is imperative. (tchd 10-1)

Cape Royal loves to go at it hard from the gate and those tactics worked a treat when he bolted up in heavy ground at Haydock earlier this month. He looked to hold good claims again, having finished ahead of The Jobber at York last time, but having been forced to share pace-setting duties, he did not have much left in the tank. He can continue to pay his way whilst in this sort of form. (op 17-2)

If Paradise, who is ideally served by some cut in the ground, helped set a searching gallop with Cape Royal. In the end however, he was unable to quicken on the ground and it was a decent effort taking the fast conditions into account. He continues to fall in the handicap and he should be getting plenty of give underfoot at this time of the year. (op 4-1)

Hoh Hoh Hoh has been creeping back to form, but he did himself no favours with a sluggish start and could only run on when it was too late. He is handicapped to win and should be doing so sooner rather than later. (tchd 14-1)

Fictional, who was most recently tried in Group 3 company at the Curragh, failed to go the early clip and could only plug on at the one pace, ending up well held. (op 6-1)

Peopleton Brook ran well on this first start since June and is entitled to come on appreciably for the outing. (op 28-1)

Treasure Cay was reported to have slipped leaving the stalls and never felt right thereafter. Official explanation: jockey said horse slipped on leaving stalls and felt wrong thereafter (op 7-2 tchd 9-2)

5434 LADBROKES.COM FILLIES' NURSERY — 5f 218y

3:40 (3:40) (Class 4) (0-85,85) 2-Y-O £4,416 (£1,321; £660; £330; £164) Stalls Low

Form RPR

2401 **1** **Lady Lily (IRE)**[13] 5076 2-8-11 75 .... TedDurcan 13 — 78
(H R A Cecil) *trckd ldrs: racd keenly: led over 1f out: rdn out* **9/2**[2]

3021 **2** 1 **Foxy Games**[14] 5052 2-8-4 68 .... FrancisNorton 5 — 68+
(D J S Ffrench Davis) *hld up: racd keenly: hdwy over 1f out: r.o wl* **14/1**

1440 **3** 1 **Minimum Fuss (IRE)**[7] 5238 2-7-7 62 oh12 .... AurelioMedeiros(5) 11 — 59
(M C Chapman) *chsd ldrs: led over 4f out: rdn and hdd over 1f out: styd on same pce ins fnl f* **100/1**

0335 **4** 1 **Popolo (IRE)**[23] 4804 2-8-2 66 .... HayleyTurner 4 — 60+
(M L W Bell) *hld up: hmpd and lost pl over 3f out: hdwy over 1f out: nt rch ldrs* **11/1**

4054 **5** 3/4 **Queen Of Narnia**[7] 5234 2-8-3 70 .... EdwardCreighton(3) 12 — 62
(M R Channon) *hld up: hdwy over 2f out: styd on same pce fnl f* **12/1**

31 **6** 3 1/2 **Golden Dagger (IRE)**[24] 4765 2-9-7 85 .... NCallan 14 — 66
(K A Ryan) *hld up: hdwy 1/2-way: sn rdn: wknd fnl f* **6/1**[3]

530 **7** 3/4 **Tee Off (IRE)**[52] 3893 2-8-12 76 .... (t) RobertWinston 8 — 55
(B W Hills) *hld up: nt clr run over 2f out: swtchd rt and hdwy over 1f out: wknd ins fnl f* **11/1**

422 **8** hd **Early Promise (IRE)**[68] 3408 2-8-2 66 .... RoystonFfrench 3 — 44
(P L Gilligan) *prom: outpcd 2f out: swtchd rt and styd on ins fnl f* **33/1**

2102 **9** hd **Top Royelle**[23] 4804 2-9-2 80 .... RichardHughes 9 — 58
(R Hannon) *chsd ldrs: rdn over 2f out: wknd fnl f* **7/1**

1 **10** 3/4 **Mystery Ocean**[24] 4754 2-9-4 82 .... FergusSweeney 6 — 58
(R M Beckett) *hld up in tch: rdn over 2f out: wkng whn hmpd ins fnl f* **10/1**

10 **11** 3/4 **Sunley Gift**[89] 2743 2-8-13 77 .... ChrisCatlin 2 — 50
(M R Channon) *led: hdd over 4f out: rdn over 2f out: wknd fnl f* **20/1**

2352 **12** 2 1/2 **Fly Time**[23] 4816 2-7-5 62 oh10 .... MCGeran(7) 10 — 28
(H J Manners) *chsd ldrs: rdn over 2f out: wkng whn hmpd ins fnl f* **66/1**

2342 **13** 8 **Hester Brook (IRE)**[38] 4334 2-7-9 62 oh1 .... DominicFox(3) 7 — 4
(J G M O'Shea) *chsd ldrs over 4f* **50/1**

4115 **14** 9 **Frontline In Focus (IRE)**[27] 4681 2-9-5 83 .... PatCosgrave 1 — —
(K R Burke) *prom: lost pl 1/2-way: wknd 2f out* **4/1**[1]

1m 11.18s (-2.02) **Going Correction** -0.30s/f (Firm) **14** Ran SP% **117.2**
Speed ratings (Par 94):101,99,98,97,96 91,90,90,89,88 87,84,73,61
CSF £61.61 CT £5548.92 TOTE £4.60: £2.00, £4.60, £16.50; EX 59.10.
Owner Diamond Racing Ltd **Bred** Owen Bourke **Trained** Newmarket, Suffolk

FOCUS
This looked an alright fillies' nursery beforehand - over half the field had finished in the first two on their previous start - but Minimum Fuss running third from 12lb out of the handicap casts doubt over the strength of the form, which is best rated through the runner-up. The winning time, though, was decent for the grade.

NOTEBOOK

Lady Lily(IRE), off the mark in an ordinary five-furlong maiden at Catterick on her previous start, appeared to put up a slightly improved effort to follow up over this extra furlong on the switch to nursery company, continuing the good run of the Henry Cecil yard. She is progressing nicely and might be able to defy a higher mark. (tchd 4-1, 5-1 in places)

Foxy Games, off the mark in a five-furlong maiden at Bath on her previous start, ran well on her return to nursery company and continues in good form. She is clearly suited by either five or six furlongs. (op 20-1)

Minimum Fuss(IRE), whose best previous effort came when winning a five-furlong seller on the Fibresand for Mick Easterby, appeared to produce a much-improved performance with the blinkers left off this time, taking third from 12lb out of the handicap. It is hard to see where this effort came from - her highest RPR previously was 55 - and it remains to be seen whether she will reproduce this sort of form.

Popolo(IRE) ◆, who has been shaping as though in need of further, looked unlucky as she lost her place when hampered at halfway before staying on again. She will have to be of interest off this sort of mark when stepped up in trip. (tchd 9-1)

Queen Of Narnia, who has been kept very busy lately, did not really improve for the return to six furlongs. (op 33-1)

Golden Dagger(IRE) was well below the form she showed when winning a seven-furlong nursery on easy ground at Newmarket on her previous start, and appeared unsuited by the drop in distance and switch to a much faster surface. (op 5-1 tchd 9-2)

Tee Off(IRE) Official explanation: jockey said filly hung left on the good to firm ground

Top Royelle Official explanation: jockey said filly was unsuited by the firm ground

Mystery Ocean Official explanation: jockey said filly was unsuited by the firm ground

Frontline In Focus(IRE) had shown a useful level of form on her last three starts, but ran no sort of race this time. Official explanation: jockey said filly finished distressed; vet said filly bled from the nose (op 7-2)

5435 LADBROKES.COM CLAIMING STKS — 1m 1f 218y

4:10 (4:10) (Class 6) 3-4-Y-O £2,590 (£770; £385; £192) Stalls High

Form RPR

5010 **1** **Inside Story (IRE)**[4] 5311 4-9-1 63 .... (b) RobertWinston 4 — 73+
(M W Easterby) *hld up: hdwy 3f out: led 1f out: sn clr* **3/1**[2]

123 **2** *3* **Summer Lodge**[13] 5090 3-9-5 70 ....(b) NCallan 7 — 74
(M H Tompkins) *dwlt: sn chsng ldrs: led over 2f out: rdn and edgd rt over 1f out: sn hdd and outpcd* **1/1**[1]

2000 **3** *5* **Emotive**[8] 5210 3-8-2 64 ....(p) AshleyHamblett(7) 11 — 57+
(I A Wood) *chsd ldrs: led 6f out: hdd over 2f out: nt clr run and wknd fnl f* **6/1**[3]

050 **4** *6* **Always Turn Left (IRE)**[77] 3152 3-8-4 51 .... FrancisNorton 8 — 38
(H S Howe) *led 4f: rdn over 2f out: wkng whn hung rt over 1f out* **11/1**

40-0 **5** *½* **Robeson**[18] 4945 4-9-0 65 .... ChrisCatlin 2 — 41
(D M Simcock) *chsd ldrs: rdn over 3f out: wknd over 2f out* **12/1**

5006 **6** *nk* **Bint Il Sultan (IRE)**[24] 4755 4-8-6 39 .... RichardMullen 10 — 33
(W M Brisbourne) *hld up: hdwy over 4f out: rdn and wknd over 2f out* **28/1**

0000 **7** *nk* **Diafa (USA)**[14] 5054 4-8-5 42 .... EdwardCreighton(3) 5 — 34
(J G M O'Shea) *hld up: rdn over 3f out: sn wknd* **28/1**

0000 **8** *12* **Prima Markova**[18] 4973 3-8-6 45 ....(b[1]) RoystonFfrench 6 — 16
(D J Daly) *chsd ldrs 7f* **33/1**

050- **9** *19* **Ahaz**[271] 6649 4-8-9 35 .... JamesDoyle(3) 1 — —
(J F Coupland) *prom: lost pl over 7f out: bhd fr 1/2-way* **100/1**

0-0 **10** *6* **Flaming Shot (IRE)**[260] 8 4-8-6 50 .... RoryMoore(5) 3 — —
(Jennie Candlish) *plld hrd and prom: wknd over 3f out* **66/1**

2m 5.27s (-3.03) **Going Correction** -0.30s/f (Firm)
WFA 3 from 4yo 6lb — **10** Ran SP% **117.6**
Speed ratings (Par 101):100,97,93,88,88 88,87,78,63,58
CSF £6.19 TOTE £4.40: £1.10, £1.20, £1.90; EX 8.70.The winner was claimed by Neville Callaghan for £10,000.
Owner Matthew Green **Bred** Arthur S Phelan **Trained** Sheriff Hutton, N Yorks
■ Stewards' Enquiry : N Callan one-day ban: careless riding (Oct 2)

FOCUS
The bare form of this claimer looks reasonable for the grade, rated through the second, but there was not that much strength in depth and they finished well strung out.
Flaming Shot(IRE) Official explanation: jockey said colt was unsuited by the firm ground

5436 LADBROKES.COM HIGHFIELDS H'CAP — 1m 60y
4:40 (4:41) (Class 5) (0-75,75) 3-Y-0+ — **£3,238** (£963; £481; £240) **Stalls High**

Form — RPR

5230 **1** **Street Warrior (IRE)**[11] 5144 3-9-2 **73** .... KDarley 11 — 85
(M Johnston) *chsd ldrs: outpcd over 2f out: rallied over 1f out: edgd rt and r.o to ld wl ins fnl f* **7/1**

050 **2** *1 ½* **Cursum Perficio**[3] 5345 4-9-4 **71** ....(p) RichardMullen 5 — 79
(W R Muir) *chsd ldr: rdn over 1f out: ev ch ins fnl f: styd on same pce* **14/1**

2213 **3** *½* **Barons Spy (IRE)**[14] 5070 5-9-2 **72** .... JamesDoyle(3) 3 — 79+
(R J Price) *hld up: hdwy over 1f out: nt rch ldrs* **4/1**[1]

3011 **4** *shd* **Rakata (USA)**[28] 4660 4-9-8 **75** .... RichardHughes 10 — 82
(P F I Cole) *led: rdn over 1f out: hdd wl ins fnl f* **11/2**[2]

3034 **5** *1 ¼* **Consonant (IRE)**[13] 5090 9-8-5 **65** .... MarkCoumbe(7) 13 — 69
(D G Bridgwater) *hld up: hdwy 1/2-way: rdn over 1f out: styd on same pce fnl f* **25/1**

/101 **6** *2* **Todlea (IRE)**[8] 5205 6-9-4 **71** 6ex ....(t) HayleyTurner 7 — 70
(Jean-Rene Auvray) *prom: rdn over 2f out: wknd fnl f* **14/1**

0261 **7** *¾* **Saxon Lil (IRE)**[22] 4831 4-9-5 **72** .... FrancisNorton 12 — 70
(J L Spearing) *trckd ldrs: racd keenly: rdn over 2f out: wknd fnl f* **10/1**

5656 **8** *¾* **Night Storm**[12] 5108 5-9-4 **71** .... ChrisCatlin 4 — 67
(S Dow) *hld up: rdn over 3f: styd on ins fnl f: nvr nrr* **12/1**

2224 **9** *1 ¼* **Joshua's Gold (IRE)**[7] 5249 5-9-0 **67** ....(v) DanielTudhope 6 — 60
(D Carroll) *hld up: n.d* **13/2**[3]

2500 **10** *3 ½* **Takes Tutu (USA)**[10] 5149 7-9-1 **68** .... RobertWinston 8 — 53
(C R Dore) *dwlt: hld up: rdn over 3f out: n.d* **14/1**

050 **11** *3* **Monsignor Fred**[70] 3346 4-8-12 **65** .... FergusSweeney 2 — 43
(H Candy) *hld up: a in rr* **28/1**

5212 **12** *2 ½* **Chalentina**[13] 5079 3-9-3 **74** .... TedDurcan 9 — 46
(H R A Cecil) *stmbld s: sn prom: rdn and wknd over 2f out* **7/1**

1m 42.49s (-2.81) **Going Correction** -0.30s/f (Firm)
WFA 3 from 4yo+ 4lb — **12** Ran SP% **117.8**
Speed ratings (Par 103):102,100,100,99,98 96,95,95,93,90 87,84
CSF £100.32 CT £454.39 TOTE £8.20: £2.80, £4.90, £2.10; EX 139.30 Place 6 £176.48, Place 5 £129.91.
Owner Luk King Tin **Bred** Monsieur Laurent Cottrell **Trained** Middleham Moor, N Yorks

FOCUS
A modest but competitive handicap in which Street Warrior broke the course record. The fourth represents the best guide to the form.
Chalentina Official explanation: jockey said filly slipped on leaving stalls
T/Plt: £355.00 to a £1 stake. Pool: £50,585.85. 104.00 winning tickets. T/Qpdt: £37.00 to a £1 stake. Pool: £3,455.60. 69.10 winning tickets. CR

5437 - 5440a (Foreign Racing) - See Raceform Interactive

5282 BEVERLEY (R-H)
Tuesday, September 19

OFFICIAL GOING: Good to firm (firm in places)
After just 7mm rain over the previous two weeks the ground was described as 'fast'.
Wind: Fresh, half-against Weather: Fine and sunny but breezy

5441 RACING UK ON SKY 432 (S) STKS — 1m 4f 16y
2:10 (2:10) (Class 5) 3-Y-0 — **£3,238** (£963; £481; £240) **Stalls High**

Form — RPR

1020 **1** **Cool Isle**[6] 5298 3-8-8 48 ....(b) DeanCorby(3) 1 — 45
(P Howling) *chsd ldrs: led 1f out: kpt on* **9/4**[1]

0 **2** *1 ¼* **Constables Art**[6] 5298 3-8-11 ....(b[1]) MickyFenton 5 — 43
(N A Callaghan) *led: pushed along over 7f out: hung rt and hdd 1f out: kpt on same pce* **9/2**[3]

5456 **3** *¾* **Rockatorri**[3] 5365 3-8-3 40 ....(b) DominicFox(3) 3 — 37
(G G Margarson) *chsd ldr: nt clr run over 2f out: styd on fnl f* **6/1**

3660 **4** *shd* **Is**[18] 4981 3-8-6 35 .... JamieMackay 4 — 37
(Rae Guest) *hld up in tch: effrt over 3f out: kpt on fnl 2f: nvr able chal* **5/1**

0003 **5** *2 ½* **The Preacher**[11] 4016 3-8-11 47 ....(p) TomEaves 2 — 38
(J S Wainwright) *sn chsng ldrs: drvn 4f out: one pce* **5/2**[2]

2m 41.05s (0.84) **Going Correction** -0.10s/f (Good) — **5** Ran SP% **108.5**
Speed ratings (Par 101):93,92,91,91,89
CSF £12.00 TOTE £2.60: £1.30, £3.00; EX 15.00.There was no bid for the winner.
Owner Rory Murphy **Bred** The C H F Partnership **Trained** Newmarket, Suffolk

FOCUS
A rock bottom seller. The number of runners suffered through it not being a handicap.

5442 BOOK YOUR JINGLE JIVE PLACE NOW NOVICE STKS — 5f
2:40 (2:42) (Class 4) 2-Y-O — **£5,181** (£1,541; £770; £384) **Stalls High**

Form — RPR

1 **Handsome Falcon** 2-8-8 .... TonyHamilton 9 — 77+
(R A Fahey) *rangy: tall: scope: sn outpcd: hdwy over 2f out: edgd lft over 1f out: kpt on wl ins last: led nr fin* **14/1**

2100 **2** *nk* **Ice Mountain**[45] 4152 2-9-0 86 .... MarkLawson(5) 4 — 87
(B Smart) *chsd ldr: led appr fnl f: hdd nr fin* **7/2**[2]

1 **3** *¾* **Russian Silk**[106] 2281 2-8-9 .... TomEaves 5 — 74
(Jedd O'Keeffe) *swvd lft s: sn chsng ldrs: upsides 1f out: no ex wl ins last* **11/2**[3]

5365 **4** *6* **Mr Klick (IRE)**[35] 4464 2-9-2 86 .... PaulMulrennan 7 — 59
(N Wilson) *chsd ldrs: edgd lft over 1f out: sn wknd* **11/2**[3]

1300 **5** *3* **Chjimes (IRE)**[79] 3126 2-9-5 93 .... PatCosgrave 3 — 52
(K R Burke) *sn chsng ldrs on outside: wknd over 1f out* **7/2**[2]

5612 **6** *1 ½* **Sparkling Eyes**[21] 4910 2-8-11 85 .... MickyFenton 1 — 38
(C E Brittain) *chsd ldrs on wd outside: wknd over 1f out* **3/1**[1]

5543 **7** *¾* **Mind The Style**[35] 4444 2-9-5 80 ....(t) DaleGibson 8 — 44
(W G M Turner) *led tl hdd & wknd appr fnl f* **14/1**

0 **8** *2 ½* **Axis Mundi (IRE)**[21] 4913 2-8-2 .... AndrewElliott(5) 6 — 23
(T J Etherington) *sn outpcd in last: nvr on terms* **100/1**

65.20 secs (1.20) **Going Correction** +0.05s/f (Good) — **8** Ran SP% **114.5**
Speed ratings (Par 97):92,91,90,80,75 73,72,68
CSF £62.72 TOTE £16.40: £3.00, £1.50, £2.10; EX 56.20.
Owner B Shaw **Bred** Miss D Fleming **Trained** Musley Bank, N Yorks

FOCUS
A decent contest although the winner was the only newcomer in the field. The winning time was modest and the well-supported runner-up, along with the third, are the best guides to the form.

NOTEBOOK
Handsome Falcon, a big newcomer, showed his inexperience but under a good ride put his head in front near the line. He looks to have bags of scope for improvement and should make a good-class sprint handicapper at three. (op 18-1)
Ice Mountain, fresh after a five-week break, did not totally impress going to post. He went on but just missed out in the end. (op 11-2 tchd 6-1)
Russian Silk, back after 106 days, ran a stormer in the end just being found lacking. He deserves credit for this. (op 6-1)
Mr Klick(IRE), who won a claimer here in May, has plenty of toe but is struggling to make his mark raised in class. (op 9-2)
Chjimes(IRE), absent for almost three months, looked to be carrying tons of condition and raced wide. He ran as if needing the outing and his best form has come on easy ground.
Sparkling Eyes, who looked very fit indeed, raced wide and never looked like posing a threat. This was her eighth start and it may be catching up on her. Official explanation: jockey said filly ran flat (op 11-4 tchd 7-2, 4-1 in a place)

5443 VIOLET AND EDDIE SMITH MEMORIAL CONDITIONS STKS — 5f
3:15 (3:15) (Class 3) 3-Y-0+
£8,724 (£2,612; £1,306; £653; £326; £163) **Stalls High**

Form — RPR

2240 **1** **Philharmonic**[17] 5011 5-8-9 103 .... PaulHanagan 8 — 96+
(R A Fahey) *chsd ldrs on inner: n.m.r and outpcd after 1f: hdwy and nt clr run 2f out: swtchd lft: r.o wl to ld nr fin* **7/2**[2]

0403 **2** *nk* **Strike Up The Band**[11] 5158 3-8-8 104 .... AdrianTNicholls 7 — 95+
(D Nicholls) *chsd ldrs: nt clr run on inner 2f out: swtchd lft over 1f out: r.o wl: no ex nr fin* **7/4**[1]

4050 **3** *hd* **Lafi (IRE)**[10] 5182 7-8-9 100 .... TomEaves 1 — 94
(D Nicholls) *racd on outer: hd 2f out: led 1f out: hdd and no ex towards fin* **6/1**

5010 **4** *3* **Bond City (IRE)**[10] 5182 4-8-9 102 .... MickyFenton 4 — 83
(B Smart) *chsd ldrs: chal 1f out: kpt on same pce* **5/1**[3]

0150 **5** *shd* **Pawan (IRE)**[23] 4832 6-8-4 76 ....(b) AnnStokell(5) 2 — 83?
(Miss A Stokell) *chsd ldrs: edgd lft and outpcd over 1f out: styd on ins last* **40/1**

0560 **6** *hd* **Mr Wolf**[11] 5158 5-8-9 95 .... TonyHamilton 9 — 82
(D W Barker) *led tl hdd 1f out: no ex* **11/2**

0300 **7** *3 ½* **Black Oval**[41] 4267 5-8-1 44 ow4 .... MarkCoumbe(7) 5 — 69?
(S Parr) *sn outpcd: nvr on terms* **300/1**

0060 **8** *3 ½* **Maltese Falcon**[11] 5158 6-8-9 100 ....(b[1]) GrahamGibbons 6 — 57
(P F I Cole) *w ldrs: wkng whn hmpd appr fnl f* **14/1**

2305 **9** *2 ½* **Estoille**[14] 5078 5-8-4 50 .... MichaelJStainton(5) 3 — 48
(Mrs S Lamyman) *chsd ldrs on outer: lost pl over 1f out* **200/1**

62.73 secs (-1.27) **Going Correction** +0.05s/f (Good)
WFA 3 from 4yo+ 1lb — **9** Ran SP% **114.9**
Speed ratings (Par 107):112,111,111,106,106 105,100,94,90
CSF £9.99 TOTE £3.80: £1.40, £1.10, £2.40; EX 8.20.
Owner R Cowie **Bred** Raymond Cowie **Trained** Musley Bank, N Yorks
■ Stewards' Enquiry : Adrian T Nicholls one-day ban: careless riding (Oct 2)

FOCUS
A smart renewal of this Class 3 event. The pace was not strong, the complexion of the race changed late on and the first three came clear. The proximity of the lowly-rated Pawan and Black Opal emphasise the lack of any real pace.

NOTEBOOK
Philharmonic, sharper for his Haydock outing, found the ground plenty lively enough. Like the runner-up he had to seek an opening but showed real courage to get up near the line. He thoroughly deserved this. (op 4-1 tchd 3-1)
Strike Up The Band looked at his very best. He had the leader covered but with those on the outside pressing, he found himself very short of room. He stayed on in game fashion when switched but the winner proved fractionally too strong near the line. He richly deserves compensation. (op 15-8 tchd 2-1)
Lafi(IRE), well backed on the morning line, looked in fine trim. He moved up on the outer to take charge a furlong out at which point he touched 1.1 on the exchanges. In the end he just missed out and has not tasted success since the 2004 Wokingham. (op 11-2)
Bond City(IRE) could not dominate and in the end the first three ran right away from him. (op 11-2 tchd 6-1)
Pawan(IRE), who had two stone to find, picked up a total of £576 on his 83rd career start.
Mr Wolf, who had a bit to find, took them along but did not go flat out until halfway. He seems better on left-handed tracks and five of his last six wins have been at Pontefract. (op 13-2)
Black Oval had almost four stone to find yet was not disgraced. Her reward was £250 appearance money, cash simply thrown down the drain surely. (op 250-1)
Maltese Falcon, in first-time blinkers, was on the retreat when tightened up. His rider reported that he had a breathing problem. Official explanation: jockey said gelding had a breathing problem (op 12-1 tchd 16-1)

5444 GO RACING AT REDCAR TOMORROW H'CAP 7f 100y
3:50 (3:51) (Class 5) (0-70,69) 3-Y-0+ £3,238 (£963; £481; £240) Stalls High

Form RPR

305 1 **Treasure House (IRE)**^{7} [5269] 5-9-3 **65**............................ DaleGibson 5 74
(M Blanshard) *rr-div: hrd drvn over 3f out: styd on strly ins last: led nr fin* **10/1**

0104 2 ¾ **Orpen Wide (IRE)**^{5} [5314] 4-9-2 **67**.............................(b) GregFairley$^{(3)}$ 2 74
(M C Chapman) *rr-div: hdwy on outside over 2f out: edgd rt and styd on ins last: no ex towards fin* **12/1**

600 3 *nk* **Dancing Deano (IRE)**^{17} [5031] 4-8-6 **59**..........(v) MichaelJStainton$^{(5)}$ 10 65
(R M Whitaker) *t.k.h: trckd ldr: led over 1f out: no ex and hdd nr fin* **16/1**

0002 4 ¾ **Redwood Rocks (IRE)**^{34} [4475] 5-8-12 **65**................ MarkLawson$^{(5)}$ 16 69
(B Smart) *led tl over 1f out: no ex ins last* **11/1**

0000 5 ½ **Kudbeme**^{3} [5370] 4-8-5 **60**.. SuzzanneFrance$^{(7)}$ 9 63
(N Bycroft) *chsd ldrs: edgd lft over 1f out: styd on same pce ins last* **16/1**

6005 6 *shd* **Tough Love**^{5} [5313] 7-9-7 **69**...................................(tp) DavidAllan 15 72
(T D Easterby) *chsd ldrs: n.m.r 2f out: styd on same pce fnl f* **7/1**^{2}

522 7 *hd* **Rembrandt Quality (USA)**^{7} [5273] 3-8-8 **59**................(b) PatCosgrave 1 61
(N A Callaghan) *t.k.h in rr: hdwy on ins and nt clr run over 1f out: swtchd lft: styd on ins last* **12/1**

5450 8 ¾ **Moonstreaker**^{65} [3569] 3-8-10 **61**.. VHalliday 13 62
(R M Whitaker) *mid-div: drvn over 3f out: kpt on same pce appr fnl f* **40/1**

2123 9 ½ **Motu (IRE)**^{7} [5269] 5-8-10 **61**................................(v) PatrickMathers$^{(3)}$ 11 60
(I W McInnes) *chsd ldrs: effrt on outside over 2f out: one pce* **15/2**^{3}

0340 10 *1* **Aggravation**^{22} [4879] 4-9-2 **69**......................... StephanieHollinshead$^{(5)}$ 7 66
(D R C Elsworth) *hld up towards rr: hdwy on ins over 2f out: n.m.r: one pce* **9/1**

0421 11 *1* **Torquemada (IRE)**^{14} [5085] 5-9-4 **66**................................ TomEaves 14 60
(W Jarvis) *s.i.s: sn prom: effrt over 2f out: wknd fnl f* **9/4**^{1}

4000 12 1½ **Sam's Secret**^{6} [5301] 4-9-6 **68**.................................(p) MickyFenton 4 59
(S Parr) *s.i.s: sn mid-div: effrt 3f out: nvr a factor* **25/1**

1320 13 *23* **Linda's Colin (IRE)**^{27} [4706] 4-9-6 **68**.........................(p) PaulMulrennan 8 1
(R A Harris) *prom: rn wd bnd over 4f out: lost pl over 2f out: sn bhd: eased* **22/1**

1m 32.8s (-1.51) **Going Correction** -0.10s/f (Good)
WFA 3 from 4yo+ 3lb **13 Ran SP% 120.2**
Speed ratings (Par 103):104,103,102,101,101 101,101,100,99,98 97,95,69
CSF £122.63 CT £1969.43 TOTE £12.40: £3.50, £3.00, £5.30; EX 144.60.
Owner J M Beever **Bred** Lisieux Stud **Trained** Upper Lambourn, Berks
■ Stewards' Enquiry : Tom Eaves caution: careless riding

FOCUS
A modest handicap and the first two both came from off the pace which stepped up markedly from the halfway mark. The form is straightforward and sound, rated around the first two.
Motu(IRE) Official explanation: jockey said gelding hung left going round bend
Linda's Colin(IRE) Official explanation: jockey said gelding finished distressed

5445 BRIAN AND JASON MERRINGTON MEMORIAL STKS (H'CAP) 1m 1f 207y
4:25 (4:25) (Class 6) (0-60,60) 3-Y-0+ £2,590 (£770; £385; £192) Stalls High

Form RPR

6054 1 **Bridegroom**^{27} [4702] 4-8-10 **49**.. MarcHalford$^{(3)}$ 8 60
(D R C Elsworth) *hld up towards rr: hdwy on ins over 2f out: squeezed between horses to ld last 75yds: r.o* **6/1**^{2}

0056 2 *1* **Arsad (IRE)**^{19} [4944] 3-8-11 **53**.............................. SilvestreDeSousa 1 63
(C E Brittain) *mid-div: hdwy over 2f out: styd on wl ins last* **25/1**

0636 3 *nk* **Fairy Monarch (IRE)**^{6} [5285] 7-8-13 **49**.........................(b) MickyFenton 6 58
(P T Midgley) *s.i.s: sn detached in last: hdwy on outer over 2f out: hrd rdn and edgd rt: styd on wl ins last* **16/1**

0312 4 *nk* **Choristar**^{15} [5072] 5-9-9 **59**.. TomEaves 17 67
(J Mackie) *chsd ldrs: wnt cl 2nd over 1f out: no ex ins last* **11/4**^{1}

0440 5 1¼ **Atlantic Story (USA)**^{20} [4925] 4-9-7 **57**.............................(t) DaleGibson 16 63
(M W Easterby) *led tl hdd ins last: wknd towards fin* **11/1**

4021 6 1¾ **Rotuma (IRE)**^{32} [4570] 7-9-4 **54**.................................(b) PatCosgrave 5 57
(M Dods) *in tch: drvn over 4f out: kpt on same pce fnl 2f* **6/1**^{2}

4654 7 *1* **Polish Welcome**^{19} [4944] 3-8-0 **47**............................ AndrewElliott$^{(5)}$ 12 48
(S C Williams) *chsd ldrs: one pce fnl 2f* **10/1**^{3}

2066 8 ½ **Virginia Rose (IRE)**^{26} [4734] 3-8-7 **49**.............................. JamieMackay 3 49
(J G Given) *prom on outer: lost pl over 4f out: edgd rt and kpt on fnl 2f* **20/1**

3000 9 *hd* **Richtee (IRE)**^{18} [4991] 5-9-5 **60**................................ JamieMoriarty$^{(5)}$ 9 60
(R A Fahey) *in tch: lost pl over 3f out: kpt on fnl 2f* **16/1**

0606 10 *nk* **Tedsdale Mac**^{5} [5314] 7-8-12 **55**............................ SuzzanneFrance$^{(7)}$ 4 54
(N Bycroft) *bhd: effrt on outside 3f out: kpt on: nvr rchd ldrs* **20/1**

0010 11 *8* **Lewis Lloyd (IRE)**^{8} [5240] 3-8-11 **53**............................. GrahamGibbons 13 37
(I A Wood) *w ldrs: lost pl 2f out* **33/1**

0036 12 *shd* **Zarova (IRE)**^{38} [4353] 4-9-1 **51**.. PaulMulrennan 10 35
(M W Easterby) *sn in tch: chsd ldrs over 2f out: lost pl over 1f out* **22/1**

0-40 13 ¾ **Wolds Dancer**^{109} [2193] 4-8-12 **48**...................................... DavidAllan 19 30
(T D Easterby) *sn bhd: sme hdwy over 2f out: sn wknd* **25/1**

4316 14 *5* **Star Sign**^{33} [4518] 4-9-10 **60**.. PaulHanagan 14 33
(D W Barker) *a in rr* **20/1**

6400 15 3½ **Noble Edge**^{22} [4884] 3-8-5 **50**.. GregFairley$^{(3)}$ 15 16
(Robert Gray) *chsd ldrs: lost pl over 2f out* **33/1**

0603 16 *10* **Tom Forest**^{38} [4350] 4-9-7 **60**..............................(p) AndrewMullen$^{(3)}$ 7 7
(K A Ryan) *in rr: lost pl 3f out: sn bhd* **22/1**

2m 4.76s (-2.54) **Going Correction** -0.10s/f (Good)
WFA 3 from 4yo+ 6lb **16 Ran SP% 121.0**
Speed ratings (Par 101):106,105,104,104,103 102,101,101,100,100 94,94,93,89,86 78
CSF £152.48 CT £2277.18 TOTE £7.60: £2.10, £4.80, £3.20, £1.10; EX 275.30.
Owner Charles Green **Bred** Cheveley Park Stud Ltd **Trained** Newmarket, Suffolk
■ Stewards' Enquiry : Micky Fenton one-day ban: used whip with excessive frequency (Oct 2)

FOCUS
Fast and furious stuff and the first three came from off the pace. The winning time was decent for the grade and the form looks reliable.
Virginia Rose(IRE) Official explanation: jockey said filly hung right

5446 SEE YOU AGAIN IN 2007 H'CAP 1m 100y
5:00 (5:00) (Class 5) (0-75,75) 3-Y-0 £3,238 (£963; £481; £240) Stalls High

Form RPR

0113 1 **Prince Evelith (GER)**^{73} [3298] 3-9-0 **71**............................ PaulHanagan 8 87+
(G A Swinbank) *mid-div: effrt over 3f out: styd on to ld ins last: drvn out* **9/4**^{1}

5400 2 *1* **King Of Rhythm (IRE)**^{17} [5015] 3-7-12 **62** ow1......... KellyHarrison$^{(7)}$ 11 62
(D Carroll) *prom: effrt over 2f out: edgd lft jst ins last: styd on* **40/1**

2236 3 *shd* **Jenny Soba**^{32} [4567] 3-7-13 **61** oh11........................ NataliaGemelova$^{(5)}$ 4 61
(R M Whitaker) *hld up in rr: hdwy over 2f out: sn chsng ldrs: styd on ins last* **28/1**

4656 4 ¾ **It's Unbelievable (USA)**^{19} [4958] 3-8-5 **67**.................... RoryMoore$^{(5)}$ 12 65
(P T Midgley) *t.k.h: w ldr: led over 3f out: hdd and no ex ins last* **16/1**

5005 5 *hd* **Rainbow's Classic**^{22} [4892] 3-8-1 **61**.......................(p) AndrewMullen$^{(3)}$ 1 59
(K A Ryan) *led tl over 3f out: kpt on same pce fnl f* **20/1**

3230 6 1½ **Esoterica (IRE)**^{5} [5312] 3-8-11 **68**..............................(b) TonyHamilton 14 63
(T D Barron) *chsd ldrs: effrt on ins over 2f out: hung rt: one pce fnl f* **7/1**^{2}

2040 7 ¾ **Dimelight**^{34} [4470] 3-8-4 **64**......................................(b^{1}) MarcHalford$^{(3)}$ 9 57
(D R C Elsworth) *hld up in rr: effrt 2f out: styd on ins last* **12/1**

-166 8 1¼ **Jordan's Light (USA)**^{45} [4154] 3-8-3 **63**.......................... GregFairley$^{(3)}$ 6 54
(T J Pitt) *chsd ldrs: drvn over 2f out: fdd appr fnl f* **7/1**^{2}

5300 9 1¼ **Royal Composer (IRE)**^{41} [4257] 3-8-6 **63**............................ DavidAllan 7 51
(T D Easterby) *prom: effrt on outer over 2f out: sn outpcd* **14/1**

0060 10 1½ **George's Flyer (IRE)**^{63} [3621] 3-8-4 **61** oh3.................(b) DaleGibson 15 46
(R A Fahey) *bhd and drvn along: kpt on fnl 2f: nvr on terms* **25/1**

1416 11 *shd* **Punjabi**^{73} [3301] 3-9-4 **75**.. MickyFenton 5 60+
(Mrs G S Rees) *s.i.s: effrt on outside over 2f out: nvr a factor* **7/1**^{2}

6365 12 *2* **Damelza (IRE)**^{32} [4567] 3-8-13 **70**..............................(t) PaulMulrennan 10 50
(T D Easterby) *mid-div: hdwy in ins over 2f out: n.m.r: lost pl over 1f out* **9/1**^{3}

543- 13 *6* **Ivans Ride (IRE)**^{274} [6617] 3-8-6 **63**........................ GrahamGibbons 13 31
(J J Quinn) *t.k.h in rr: bhd fnl 2f* **25/1**

1m 46.63s (-0.77) **Going Correction** -0.10s/f (Good) **13 Ran SP% 116.9**
Speed ratings (Par 101):99,98,97,97,96 95,94,93,92,90 90,88,82
CSF £127.02 CT £2099.37 TOTE £3.00: £1.30, £14.20, £6.10; EX 142.20 Place 6 £225.90, Place 5 £129.49.
Owner Allan Stennett **Bred** Gestut Etzean **Trained** Melsonby, N Yorks
■ Stewards' Enquiry : Kelly Harrison caution: careless riding

FOCUS
Just a steady gallop and the winner can progress further. The proximity of the third, 11lb out of the handicap, puts a question mark over the value of the form.
Esoterica(IRE) Official explanation: jockey said gelding hung right in straight
Dimelight Official explanation: jockey said filly ran too free early stages
Damelza(IRE) Official explanation: jockey said filly ran too free early stages
T/Plt: £225.70 to a £1 stake. Pool: £48,300.50. 156.20 winning tickets. T/Qpdt: £39.20 to a £1 stake. Pool: £3,529.30. 66.60 winning tickets. WG

4669 BRIGHTON (L-H)
Tuesday, September 19

OFFICIAL GOING: Good to firm
Wind: Fresh, across Weather: Sunny

5447 H.B.L.B. NURSERY 5f 213y
2:00 (2:01) (Class 4) (0-85,84) 2-Y-0 £4,857 (£1,445; £722; £360) Stalls Low

Form RPR

6136 1 **Disco Dan**^{46} [4100] 2-9-0 **77**.. SebSanders 4 80+
(D M Simcock) *s.s: hld up in rr: hdwy 2f out: rdn to ld ins fnl f: styd on wl* **5/2**^{1}

5004 2 1½ **Stir Crazy (IRE)**^{29} [4665] 2-8-3 **66**.. ChrisCatlin 3 65
(M R Channon) *led tl ins fnl f: nt pce of wnr* **12/1**

1506 3 *nk* **Tom Paris**^{6} [5290] 2-8-6 **72**...(b) SaleemGolam$^{(3)}$ 9 70
(W R Muir) *in tch: rdn to press ldrs 2f out: one pce fnl f* **11/1**

5004 4 ½ **Benllech**^{10} [5161] 2-8-9 **72**... PatDobbs 2 68
(S Kirk) *prom: wnt 2nd wl over 1f out: no ex fnl f* **13/2**^{2}

005 5 1½ **Golan Way**^{16} [5043] 2-8-3 **69**.. JamesDoyle$^{(3)}$ 1 61
(I A Wood) *hld up in rr: rdn and styd on fnl 2f: nvr nrr* **11/1**

0040 6 1½ **Beckenham's Secret**^{24} [4813] 2-8-10 **73**................................ DaneO'Neill 6 60
(B R Millman) *chsd ldr tl ins fnl 2f: sn wknd* **12/1**

0040 7 2½ **Slipasearcher (IRE)**^{19} [4966] 2-9-4 **84**................ StephenDonohoe$^{(3)}$ 10 64
(P D Evans) *chsd ldrs: rdn 3f out: wknd over 1f out* **10/1**

21 8 *nk* **Cherri Fosfate**^{119} [1912] 2-8-8 **78**..................................(p) JackDean$^{(7)}$ 5 57
(W G M Turner) *sn towards rr: rdn and hung lft 2f out: n.d* **15/2**^{3}

1514 9 *2* **Diamond Hurricane (IRE)**^{19} [4969] 2-8-13 **76**............ DanielTudhope 8 49
(P D Evans) *wd: hld up towards rr: mod effrt 3f out: wknd 2f out* **10/1**

314 10 *5* **Chervil**^{39} [4322] 2-9-6 **83**.. OscarUrbina 7 41
(Mrs A J Perrett) *dwlt: hld up in midfield: rdn 2f out: hung rt and lft: no rspnse* **13/2**^{2}

1m 10.44s (0.34) **Going Correction** -0.025s/f (Good) **10 Ran SP% 117.2**
Speed ratings (Par 97):96,94,93,92,90 88,85,85,82,75
CSF £34.94 CT £290.89 TOTE £2.90: £1.70, £3.20, £4.80; EX 28.10 Trifecta £183.20 Part won. Pool: £258.16 - 0.20 winning tickets..
Owner David Cohen **Bred** T G And B B Mills **Trained** Newmarket, Suffolk

FOCUS
A routine nursery in which the paddock pick outclassed the opposition. The form is rated around the runner-up and fifth.

NOTEBOOK
Disco Dan, who had more scope than his rivals, was given a patient ride, and the fact that he missed the break was probably intentional. He goes well on this track, having already won over course and distance, and won a shade cosily in the end having been brought with a well-timed run. (op 11-4 tchd 3-1 in places)
Stir Crazy(IRE) ran a sound race from the front, dictating at a pace which was not too strong, and ran better than of late. However, the winner was much too strong in the end. (op 14-1)
Tom Paris put in a solid performance, but the winner was a cut above his rivals. (op 10-1)
Benllech ran a fair first race in nursery company, and looks at home in this company, but is probably a couple of pounds too high. (op 11-2)
Golan Way, making his nursery debut, ran as if seven furlongs would suit. (op 14-1)
Beckenham's Secret's form has tailed off a bit, and once again he did not get home. It might be worth dropping him back to five furlongs. (op 16-1 tchd 20-1)
Cherri Fosfate soon lost a good early position, and began to get unbalanced on the camber when the race hotted up. A more conventional track may suit better. (op 8-1)
Chervil looked unhappy on the track in the home straight, and folded up tamely. Official explanation: jockey said filly stopped very quickly (op 6-1)

5448 ENTREMETTIER (S) STKS 5f 59y
2:30 (2:30) (Class 6) 2-Y-0 £2,266 (£674; £337; £168) Stalls Low

Form RPR

6032 1 **Dotty's Daughter**^{6} [5282] 2-8-3 55..............................(p) SaleemGolam$^{(3)}$ 6 59
(Mrs A Duffield) *prom: led over 1f out: rdn out* **4/1**^{1}

4560 2 *1* **Indian Song (IRE)**^{9} [5208] 2-8-6 60..................................(b^{1}) StephenCarson 3 55
(R F Johnson Houghton) *prom: rdn to press wnr over 1f out: nt qckn fnl f* **9/2**^{2}

1044 **3** ¾ **Diminuto**[6] [5290] 2-8-11 57 RichardSmith 13 57
(M D I Usher) *wd: hld up in midfield: hdwy and hung lft fr 2f out: one pce fnl f* **10/1**

5303 **4** 1 ¼ **Mr Mini Scule**[20] [4926] 2-8-11 60 DaneO'Neill 2 53
(A B Haynes) *hld up in midfield gng wl: rdn and hung lft 2f out: styd on same pce* **9/1**

0344 **5** 2 **Ten For Tosca (IRE)**[24] [4816] 2-8-11 57 SebSanders 11 46
(J A Osborne) *hld up towards rr: drvn along and styd on fnl 2f: nt pce to chal* **7/1**

6640 **6** ½ **Autumn Storm**[9] [5208] 2-8-11 61 ChrisCatlin 10 44
(R Ingram) *chsd ldr: led over 3f out tl over 1f out: sn wknd* **14/1**

536 **7** ¾ **Porjenski**[19] [4971] 2-8-6 50 FergusSweeney 8 36
(A B Haynes) *towards rr: rdn 2f out: nt rch ldrs* **50/1**

5320 **8** 2 ½ **Caj (IRE)**[8] [5238] 2-8-1 56 LiamJones(5) 9 27
(M Quinn) *sn pushed along: chsd ldrs 3f* **6/1**[3]

00 **9** shd **Answer Back**[19] [4971] 2-8-3 JamesDoyle(3) 1 27
(Miss J R Tooth) *outpcd and bhd: nvr nr ldrs* **100/1**

0255 **10** hd **Peggys Flower**[34] [4493] 2-8-8 64 StephenDonohoe(3) 7 31
(N A Callaghan) *hld up in tch: rdn and hung lft 2f out: sn btn* **13/2**

6530 **11** 5 **Lord Blue Boy**[61] [3677] 2-8-8 54 AmirQuinn(3) 4 13
(W G M Turner) *dwlt: outpcd: sn wl bhd* **20/1**

400 **12** 4 **Suntan Lady (IRE)**[8] [5238] 2-8-6 55 AdrianMcCarthy 5 —
(Miss V Haigh) *led over 1f: hrd rdn 2f out: sn wknd* **33/1**

62.85 secs (0.55) **Going Correction** -0.025s/f (Good) 12 Ran SP% **114.7**
Speed ratings (Par 93):94,92,91,89,86 85,84,80,79,79 71,65
CSF £20.22 TOTE £3.10: £1.20, £2.30, £4.30; EX 18.20 Trifecta £107.40 Part won. Pool: £151.36 - 0.30 winning tickets..The winner was bought in for 5,600gns. Peggys Flower was claimed by Michael Wigham for £6,000.
Owner Middleham Park Racing Ix **Bred** Peter Baldwin **Trained** Constable Burton, N Yorks

FOCUS
A modest seller, but run at a decent pace and the form is average.

NOTEBOOK
Dotty's Daughter gained her reward after some good recent efforts over this trip. It was not a great race, but she did it convincingly, and handled the track conspicuously better than many of her rivals. (op 9-2)
Indian Song(IRE), blinkered for the first time, did well on this first venture into selling company, having found a nice gap on the inside rail. This looks to be her level nowadays. (op 7-2)
Diminuto put in a sound effort under her winner's 5lb penalty depite drifting down the camber. She holds her form well.
Mr Mini Scule travelled remarkably well over this shorter trip, but failed to pick up when coming off the bridle. He could win at this level given an extra furlong again. (op 10-1)
Ten For Tosca(IRE) ran as if he might be better suited by a six furlong seller, particularly on a track as sharp as this. (op 15-2)
Autumn Storm looks at home in races like this, but she was taken on for the lead and did too much too soon. (tchd 12-1)
Caj(IRE) found the track too sharp, and was never travelling. (tchd 13-2)
Answer Back Official explanation: jockey said filly was unsuited by the track
Lord Blue Boy Official explanation: jockey said gelding never travelled

5449 EUROPEAN BREEDERS FUND MAIDEN STKS 6f 209y
3:05 (3:05) (Class 5) 2-Y-O **£3,886** (£1,156; £577; £288) **Stalls** Low

Form RPR

02 **1** **Rose Of Petra (IRE)**[14] [5083] 2-8-12 SebSanders 2 81
(Sir Michael Stoute) *mde virtually all: pushed clr fnl f: comf* **9/4**[2]

33 **2** 4 **Hazzard County (USA)**[15] [5066] 2-9-3 DaneO'Neill 5 76
(D M Simcock) *stdd s: hld up in tch: eased rt and chsd wnr wl over 1f out: rdn and nt qckn: hung lft whn btn* **2/1**[1]

546 **3** 2 ½ **Massenzio (IRE)**[20] [4934] 2-9-3 77 DavidKinsella 4 69
(J H M Gosden) *chsd ldng pair: wnt 2nd over 2f out tl wl over 1f out: hung lft: no ex* **11/1**

2200 **4** 3 ½ **Folio (USA)**[28] [4681] 2-9-3 79 OscarUrbina 6 60
(B W Hills) *in tch: rdn over 2f out: no rspnse* **5/2**[3]

0 **5** 1 ½ **Gutter Press (IRE)**[37] [4394] 2-8-12 (b[1]) LPKeniry 7 51
(J S Moore) *sn outpcd and bhd* **66/1**

02 **6** 5 **Dance Of Dreams**[13] [5111] 2-9-0 JamesDoyle(3) 3 43
(N P Littmoden) *chsd wnr tl wknd over 2f out* **16/1**

1m 22.26s (-0.44) **Going Correction** -0.025s/f (Good) 6 Ran SP% **108.4**
Speed ratings (Par 95):101,96,93,89,87 82
CSF £6.61 TOTE £3.20: £1.80, £1.30; EX 7.50.
Owner Ballymacoll Stud **Bred** Ballymacoll Stud Farm Ltd **Trained** Newmarket, Suffolk

FOCUS
An above-average maiden for the track, run at a fair pace in a decent time. The runner-up sets the standard.

NOTEBOOK
Rose Of Petra(IRE), from a stable which has few runners here, handled the track well and outclassed her rivals. (op 13-8)
Hazzard County(USA) can win a race at this level, but on this occasion he ran into an above-average sort for the track. Official explanation: jockey said colt ran too free (op 11-4)
Massenzio(IRE) is struggling to win a maiden and may be more at home in nurseries, but she did not look happy on this difficult track as she began to tire. (op 16-1)
Folio(USA) is failing to live up to the promise of his first two starts, and this was downright disappointing. (tchd 11-4)
Gutter Press(IRE), blinkered her on only his second start, was soon left a long way behind and looks to be heading for handicaps after one more run, though he has shown little to date.
Dance Of Dreams will be more at home in more run-of-the-mill company, and probably back at six furlongs. (op 12-1 tchd 9-1)

5450 WALLY COOMES MEMORIAL H'CAP 7f 214y
3:40 (3:40) (Class 6) (0-60,59) 3-Y-0+ **£2,730** (£806; £403) **Stalls** Low

Form RPR

4000 **1** **Trevian**[38] [4363] 5-8-13 50 DaneO'Neill 10 59+
(J M Bradley) *hld up towards rr: hdwy and nt clr run over 2f out: styd on wl to ld fnl strides* **9/1**

0202 **2** nk **Sincerely**[6] [5302] 4-9-8 59 OscarUrbina 13 68
(B W Hills) *hld up in midfield: hdwy 2f out: drvn to ld fnl 75 yds: jst ct* **4/1**[2]

0560 **3** 1 ¼ **Danzare**[18] [4983] 4-8-10 50 NeilChalmers(3) 11 56
(Mrs A J Hamilton-Fairley) *t.k.h in midfield: rdn and styd on fnl 2f: nrst fin* **25/1**

0512 **4** nk **Hadath (IRE)**[28] [4674] 9-8-10 54 (b) PatrickHills(7) 14 59
(B G Powell) *prom: hung lft and led 1f out: hdd and no ex fnl 75 yds* **9/1**

5-63 **5** nk **Dream Of Dubai (IRE)**[14] [5093] 5-9-5 56 GeorgeBaker 2 60
(P Mitchell) *bhd: swtchd rt and hmpd over 2f out: gd late hdwy* **20/1**

4006 **6** 1 ¼ **Kew The Music**[133] [1570] 6-9-4 55 ChrisCatlin 7 56+
(M R Channon) *bhd: rdn over 2f out: styd on wl fnl f* **14/1**

0153 **7** ¾ **Start Of Authority**[29] [4667] 5-8-10 47 JimCrowley 6 49+
(J Gallagher) *t.k.h: chsd ldrs: led 2f out tl 1f out: n.m.r on rail fnl f: hmpd and eased fnl 50 yds* **7/1**[3]

2121 **8** nk **Prince Valentine**[35] [4446] 5-9-3 54 (p) SebSanders 3 62+
(G L Moore) *hld up towards rr: hdwy and nt clr run fr over 2f out tl ins fnl f: nt rcvr* **7/2**[1]

0000 **9** shd **Adobe**[10] [5166] 11-8-9 53 AshleyHamblett(7) 12 52
(W M Brisbourne) *midfield and wd: rdn 3f out: nt pce to chal* **16/1**

2600 **10** 1 ¼ **Almowj**[78] [3138] 3-8-4 52 WilliamCarson(7) 4 48
(C E Brittain) *prom tl wknd ins fnl 2f* **25/1**

6010 **11** ½ **Primeshade Promise**[6] [5302] 5-9-2 56 StephenDonohoe(3) 15 51
(J M Bradley) *prom tl sltly hmpd and wknd over 1f out* **12/1**

0000 **12** nk **Reaching Out (IRE)**[16] [5046] 4-9-0 54 (b[1]) JamesDoyle(3) 5 48
(N P Littmoden) *s.s: t.k.h towards rr: rdn over 2f out: n.d* **16/1**

0000 **13** 1 ¼ **Laugh 'n Cry**[13] [5108] 5-9-7 58 FergusSweeney 9 49
(C A Cyzer) *mid-div: hung bdly lft fnl 2f: no imp* **50/1**

5100 **14** ½ **Fantasy Defender (IRE)**[31] [4585] 4-8-9 49 (v) AdamKirby(3) 1 39
(Ernst Oertel) *mid-div: hrd rdn and btn 2f out* **16/1**

-000 **15** 4 **Mayden Dawn**[25] [4757] 3-8-11 52 AdrianMcCarthy 8 33
(Miss E C Lavelle) *led tl 2f out: sn wknd: eased whn no ch fnl f* **50/1**

1m 36.12s (1.08) **Going Correction** -0.025s/f (Good)
WFA 3 from 4yo+ 4lb 15 Ran SP% **123.1**
Speed ratings (Par 101):93,92,91,91,90 89,88,88,88,87 86,86,85,84,80
CSF £43.02 CT £893.83 TOTE £10.80: £3.40, £1.90, £6.80; EX 70.30 TRIFECTA Not won..
Owner Folly Road Racing Partners (1996) **Bred** L A C Ashby **Trained** Sedbury, Gloucs
■ Stewards' Enquiry : Oscar Urbina one-day ban: used whip with excessive frequency (Oct 2)
Patrick Hills one-day ban: careless riding (Oct 2)

FOCUS
A moderate handicap with a comparatively slow winning time, and several hard-luck stories in this typical Brighton handicap. The form looks reasonably sound, rated through the runner-up.
Fantasy Defender(IRE) Official explanation: jockey said gelding was denied a clear run

5451 MEUC/MERLIN RACING TO SAVE LIVES H'CAP 1m 3f 196y
4:15 (4:16) (Class 6) (0-60,60) 3-Y-0+ **£2,730** (£806; £403) **Stalls** High

Form RPR

5-00 **1** **Liberty Run (IRE)**[106] [2305] 4-9-0 51 NeilChalmers(3) 10 61
(Mrs A J Hamilton-Fairley) *mid-div: rdn and hdwy over 1f out: styd on to ld ins fnl f* **33/1**

2233 **2** 2 ½ **Regency Red (IRE)**[35] [4451] 8-8-11 50 LiamJones(5) 15 56
(W M Brisbourne) *s.s: towards rr: hdwy and hung lft 2f out: styd on to take 2nd ins fnl f* **14/1**

6035 **3** 1 **The Iron Giant (IRE)**[9] [5213] 4-9-9 57 RobertMiles 12 61
(B G Powell) *prom: led 4f out: hdd and no ex ins fnl f* **16/1**

3054 **4** 1 ¾ **Melvino**[7] [5276] 4-9-12 60 PhillipMakin 6 62
(T D Barron) *s.s: towards rr: rdn and styd on fnl 3f: nvr nrr* **7/2**[1]

0005 **5** ½ **Shamsalmaidan (IRE)**[15] [5056] 3-9-0 59 AdamKirby(3) 7 62+
(C E Brittain) *towards rr: rdn and hdwy whn n.m.r 2f out: styng on whn hmpd over 1f out: nrst fin* **33/1**

6354 **6** 2 ½ **Ganymede**[20] [4929] 5-9-0 51 (p) AmirQuinn(3) 16 48
(Mrs L J Mongan) *prom tl wknd 1f out* **14/1**

0200 **7** ½ **Fonic Rock (IRE)**[15] [5057] 3-8-10 55 StephenDonohoe(3) 2 51
(M L W Bell) *in tch: outpcd and lost pl 4f out: kpt on again fnl f* **14/1**

030- **8** nk **Krasivi's Boy (USA)**[178] [5760] 4-9-4 52 GeorgeBaker 11 48
(G L Moore) *chsd ldrs tl wknd ins fnl 2f* **25/1**

4360 **9** 1 ¼ **Blackmail (USA)**[7] [5258] 8-9-12 60 (b) SebSanders 3 57+
(P Mitchell) *towards rr: rdn 3f out: sme hdwy over 1f out: no imp: eased whn wl hld ins fnl f* **8/1**[3]

0006 **10** 4 **Suzuki (IRE)**[22] [4868] 3-8-8 50 DavidKinsella 13 37
(H Morrison) *bhd: gd hdwy 5f out: hung lft and wknd ins fnl 2f* **50/1**

050 **11** shd **You Live And Learn**[36] [4431] 3-8-13 60 TravisBlock(5) 5 47+
(H Morrison) *bhd: rdn over 2f out: sme hdwy whn n.m.r over 1f out: nt rch ldrs* **10/1**

1052 **12** 3 **Baboosh (IRE)**[10] [5166] 5-9-12 60 (p) DaneO'Neill 4 42
(M Wigham) *mid-div: hrd rdn over 2f out: wknd wl over 1f out* **9/2**[2]

0220 **13** 1 ¼ **Jazrawy**[14] [5080] 4-9-7 55 ChrisCatlin 9 35
(P W Hiatt) *prom tl wknd over 4f out* **25/1**

6200 **14** ½ **Plain Champagne (IRE)**[46] [4104] 4-9-4 52 RichardThomas 8 31
(Dr J R J Naylor) *rdn 3f out: a bhd* **33/1**

0645 **15** 3 **Garston Star**[44] [4176] 5-8-12 46 LPKeniry 1 21
(J S Moore) *prom tl wknd over 2f out* **10/1**

4520 **16** 9 **Icannshift (IRE)**[15] [5072] 6-9-3 51 FergusSweeney 14 11
(T M Jones) *led tl 4f out: sn wknd: wl bhd and eased over 1f out* **16/1**

2m 31.1s (-1.10) **Going Correction** -0.025s/f (Good)
WFA 3 from 4yo+ 8lb 16 Ran SP% **119.9**
Speed ratings (Par 101):102,100,99,98,98 96,96,95,95,92 92,90,89,89,87 81
CSF £416.04 CT £7476.14 TOTE £51.50: £8.30, £2.80, £3.40, £1.50; EX 1270.50 TRIFECTA Not won..
Owner Fairley Risky **Bred** Mrs Amanda Brudenell And Mr & Mrs R A Simmons **Trained** Bramshill, Hants

FOCUS
A modest race, but run at a decent pace, with most of the principals coming from behind and the form appears sound and should prove reliable.
Icannshift(IRE) Official explanation: jockey said gelding had no more to give

5452 WEATHERBYS INSURANCE H'CAP 1m 1f 209y
4:50 (4:52) (Class 6) (0-60,60) 3-Y-0 **£3,238** (£963; £481; £240) **Stalls** High

Form RPR

2214 **1** **Hurry Up Helen (IRE)**[10] [5166] 3-8-13 55 RobbieFitzpatrick 2 63
(Mrs L Stubbs) *chsd ldrs: led 3f out: hrd rdn over 1f out: pushed out nr fin* **9/2**[1]

4363 **2** nk **Lady Georgette (IRE)**[32] [4556] 3-9-0 56 ChrisCatlin 16 63
(E J O'Neill) *hld up in midfield: hdwy to chse wnr fnl 2f: kpt on wl nr fin: jst hld* **11/2**[2]

0060 **3** 2 ½ **Tranos (USA)**[22] [4884] 3-8-11 60 AshleyHamblett(7) 7 63
(L M Cumani) *rrd s: hld up in rr: hdwy and hmpd on rail over 2f out: hung lft over 1f out: styd on* **8/1**

0006 **4** nk **Camp Attack**[14] [5098] 3-8-13 55 LPKeniry 5 57
(S Dow) *towards rr: hdwy 2f out: hung lft over 1f out: no imp* **25/1**

0556 **5** 5 **They All Laughed**[9] [5205] 3-8-12 54 RobertMiles 6 47
(P W Hiatt) *bhd and wd: hrd rdn and styd on fnl 2f: nvr nrr* **14/1**

0604 **6** shd **Sasetti (IRE)**[32] [4556] 3-9-1 57 (t) OscarUrbina 9 49
(J R Fanshawe) *mid-div: effrt over 2f out: no imp* **6/1**[3]

0-40 **7** 2 **Bowl Of Cherries**[25] [4757] 3-8-1 46 JamesDoyle(3) 15 35
(I A Wood) *dwlt: sn chsng ldrs: rdn over 4f out: wknd over 2f out* **12/1**

The Form Book, Raceform Ltd, Compton, RG20 6NL

604- **8** *hd* **Chelsey Jayne (IRE)**[319] [6246] 3-8-11 **60**................ ThomasO'Brien(7) 8 48
(M R Channon) *dwlt: towards rr: rdn and drifted bdly lft over 2f out: nt trble ldrs* **20/1**
0003 **9** *shd* **Khyber Knight (IRE)**[12] [5129] 3-8-5 **50**..................... SaleemGolam(3) 12 38
(Jane Southcombe) *sn led: hdd 3f out: wknd over 1f out* **14/1**
5-00 **10** *shd* **Zafarilla (IRE)**[43] [4198] 3-7-13 **46** oh1........................... EmmettStack(5) 3 34
(Pat Eddery) *towards rr: drvn along over 2f out: n.d* **28/1**
0603 **11** *shd* **Salonga (IRE)**[27] [4700] 3-9-4 **60**.................................... GeorgeBaker 14 48
(C F Wall) *in tch on outside tl wknd 3f out* **7/1**
5500 **12** *2 1/2* **Machhapuchhare**[45] [4150] 3-7-13 **46** oh1..................... LiamJones(5) 13 29
(W M Brisbourne) *dwlt: sn prom: wknd over 2f out* **16/1**
000 **13** *shd* **Persian Warrior (IRE)**[20] [4931] 3-8-12 **57**.................(p) AdamKirby(3) 10 40
(W R Swinburn) *prom tl wknd over 2f out* **18/1**

2m 2.96s (0.36) **Going Correction** -0.025s/f (Good) **13** Ran SP% **115.7**
Speed ratings (Par 99):97,96,94,94,90 90,88,88,88,88 88,86,86
CSF £26.29 CT £192.37 TOTE £3.40: £1.50, £2.10, £2.80; EX 17.30 Trifecta £23.50 Pool: £143.76 - 4.34 winning tickets..
Owner Des Thurlby **Bred** G Callanan **Trained** Norton, N. Yorks

FOCUS
A modest handicap rated through the fourth.
They All Laughed Official explanation: jockey said gelding struck into itself
Salonga(IRE) Official explanation: jockey said filly was unsuited by the track
Persian Warrior(IRE) Official explanation: jockey said gelding hung both ways

5453 BET365.COM H'CAP 5f 213y
5:25 (5:25) (Class 5) (0-70,69) 3-Y-0+ **£3,238** (£963; £481; £240) **Stalls** Low

Form RPR
1101 **1** **The Cayterers**[15] [5058] 4-8-11 **67**............................. LukeMorris(7) 15 78+
(J M Bradley) *towards rr nr outside: swtchd lft and hdwy 2f out: swtchd lft again and led over 1f out: pushed clr fnl f: comf* **9/2**[1]
6001 **2** *2* **Inka Dancer (IRE)**[4] [5350] 4-8-11 **60** 6ex.................... AdrianMcCarthy 3 65
(B Palling) *prom: chal over 1f out: nt pce of wnr fnl f* **7/1**[3]
6030 **3** *1/2* **Danehill Stroller (IRE)**[8] [5232] 6-8-8 **57**............................. LPKeniry 16 61
(A M Hales) *bhd: hrd rdn and gd hdwy fnl 2f: nrst fin* **16/1**
5606 **4** *nk* **Cayman Breeze**[18] [4985] 6-8-6 **55** oh6..................... FergusSweeney 6 58
(J M Bradley) *in tch: rdn to press ldrs 2f out: one pce fnl f* **10/1**
440 **5** *1 1/2* **Buy On The Red**[17] [5021] 5-9-6 **69**.............................. SebSanders 13 67
(W R Muir) *chsd ldrs on outside: kpt on same pce fnl 2f* **7/1**[3]
/000 **6** *1/2* **Smirfys Systems**[26] [4735] 7-8-2 **56**............................. LiamJones(5) 4 53
(W M Brisbourne) *prom tl wknd over 1f out* **20/1**
1246 **7** *3/4* **Sweet Pickle**[8] [5232] 5-8-13 **65**...............................(e) AmirQuinn(3) 14 59
(J R Boyle) *wnt rt s: towards rr: rdn over 2f out: nt rch ldrs* **5/1**[2]
0440 **8** *1* **Wrighty Almighty (IRE)**[16] [5042] 4-9-6 **69**...................(b[1]) GeorgeBaker 8 60
(P R Chamings) *s.s: bhd: rdn and styd on fnl 2f: n.d* **16/1**
1400 **9** *1/2* **Piccostar**[62] [3646] 3-9-4 **69**.................................... DaneO'Neill 2 59
(A B Haynes) *chsd ldrs tl no ex over 1f out* **20/1**
2030 **10** *1 1/2* **Make My Dream**[18] [4985] 3-8-7 **58**.............................. JimCrowley 12 43
(J Gallagher) *chsd ldrs over 4f* **20/1**
4000 **11** *shd* **Pachello (IRE)**[34] [4486] 4-9-0 **66**.............................(t) StephenDonohoe(3) 5 51
(J M Bradley) *led at str pce tl wknd over 1f out* **20/1**
350 **12** *2 1/2* **Diamond Josh**[17] [5032] 4-7-13 **55** oh3........................ JamieHamblett(7) 1 33
(P D Evans) *chsd ldrs 4f: eased whn btn 1f out* **12/1**
3000 **13** *nk* **Parkside Pursuit**[5] [5327] 8-8-2 **58**........................ BarrySavage(7) 11 35
(J M Bradley) *outpcd: a towards rr* **20/1**
4600 **14** *1 1/2* **Whisper Inthe Wind (IRE)**[34] [4494] 3-8-3 **57** oh5 ow2 SaleemGolam(3) 10 29
(Miss J Feilden) *mid-div: rdn and btn 2f out* **66/1**
0410 **15** *1 1/4* **Shinko (IRE)**[28] [4671] 3-8-3 **57**................................ JamesDoyle(3) 9 25
(Miss J Feilden) *outpcd: a bhd* **20/1**
2005 **16** *3* **The Grey One (IRE)**[91] [2727] 3-8-4 **55** oh3.....................(p) ChrisCatlin 7 14
(J M Bradley) *chsd ldrs to 1/2-way* **20/1**

69.26 secs (-0.84) **Going Correction** -0.025s/f (Good) **16** Ran SP% **123.2**
WFA 3 from 4yo+ 2lb
Speed ratings (Par 103):104,101,100,100,98 97,96,95,94,92 92,89,88,86,85 81
CSF £30.10 CT £494.58 TOTE £4.80: £1.30, £2.40, £5.20, £2.90; EX 29.00 Trifecta £154.80 Part won. Pool: £218.14 - 0.20 winning tickets. Place 6 £60.36, Place 5 £24.44.
Owner R D Willis and M C Watts **Bred** Acrum Lodge Stud **Trained** Sedbury, Gloucs

FOCUS
A competitive sprint that looks sound enough rated around the runner-up and fourth.
T/Jkpt: Not won. T/Plt: £70.80 to a £1 stake. Pool: £69,793.80. 718.95 winning tickets. T/Qpdt: £19.20 to a £1 stake. Pool: £3,984.30. 152.80 winning tickets. LM

4801 NEWMARKET (ROWLEY) (R-H)
Tuesday, September 19

OFFICIAL GOING: Good to firm
A card made up solely of races for two-year-olds.
Wind: Light, behind Weather: Sunny

5454 "WINTER WONDERLAND AT NEWMARKET RACECOURSES" MEDIAN AUCTION MAIDEN STKS 6f
1:15 (1:19) (Class 4) 2-Y-0 **£4,533** (£1,348; £674; £336) **Stalls** Low

Form RPR
0460 **1** **Bertoliver**[7] [5262] 2-9-3 70.. PhilipRobinson 12 75
(D K Ivory) *mde all: rdn out* **14/1**
0 **2** *shd* **Swift Cut (IRE)**[13] [5111] 2-9-3 .... DarryllHolland 2 75
(A P Jarvis) *w'like: chsd ldrs: rdn over 1f out: r.o* **40/1**
3 *1/2* **Heroes** 2-9-3 .... BrianReilly 11 73
(G A Huffer) *w'like: chsd ldrs: rdn over 1f out: r.o* **33/1**
4040 **4** *2 1/2* **Billy Red**[59] [3734] 2-9-3 66.. TonyCulhane 13 67
(J R Jenkins) *chsd wnr: rdn over 1f out: sn edgd lft: no ex ins fnl f* **25/1**
5 *nk* **Minnis Bay (CAN)** 2-9-3 .... KerrinMcEvoy 10 66+
(E F Vaughan) *leggy: dwlt: hld up: hdwy over 1f out: nrst fin* **16/1**
5 **6** *1/2* **Sam Lord**[17] [5020] 2-9-3 .... JimmyFortune 4 65
(J H M Gosden) *str: lw: s.i.s: plld hrd and sn prom: rdn over 2f out: styd on same pce appr fnl f* **3/1**[2]
4 **7** *nk* **Sandrey (IRE)**[10] [5168] 2-9-3 .... EddieAhern 1 66+
(P W Chapple-Hyam) *w'like: trckd ldrs: plld hrd: rdn whn hmpd 1f out: eased whn btn* **5/2**[1]
8 *3/4* **Marvo** 2-9-3 .... JimmyQuinn 9 62+
(M H Tompkins) *w'like: s.s: hdwy over 1f out: nvr nrr* **50/1**
9 *nk* **Silaah** 2-9-3 .... MartinDwyer 3 61
(E A L Dunlop) *leggy: s.s: n.d* **9/1**[3]
0 **10** *1 1/2* **Tahafut**[11] [5147] 2-8-12 .... NickyMackay 5 52
(W J Haggas) *chsd ldrs: rdn over 2f out: hung rt and wknd over 1f out* **14/1**
11 *1* **Metropolitan Chief** 2-9-3 .... RyanMoore 15 55
(D M Simcock) *str: scope: dwlt: sn prom: wknd over 2f out* **16/1**
12 *1 1/4* **Sonning Star (IRE)** 2-9-3 .... AntonyProcter 16 52
(D R C Elsworth) *w'like: scope: bit bkwd: s.i.s: hung rt: outpcd* **33/1**
13 *1 1/4* **Scantlebury** 2-9-3 .... SteveDrowne 14 48
(S Kirk) *w'like: cl cpld: s.i.s: outpcd* **10/1**
14 *2 1/2* **Welsh Auction** 2-9-0 .... EdwardCreighton(3) 7 42
(G A Huffer) *w'like: bit bkwd: chsd ldrs over 4f* **33/1**
00 **15** *shd* **Armillary**[15] [5068] 2-8-12 .... TedDurcan 17 37
(Mrs A J Perrett) *hld up: wknd over 2f out* **40/1**

1m 12.43s (-0.67) **Going Correction** -0.25s/f (Firm) **15** Ran SP% **117.3**
Speed ratings (Par 97):94,93,93,89,89 88,88,87,87,85 83,82,80,77,76
CSF £489.26 TOTE £18.50: £6.30, £9.90, £9.70; EX 677.70.
Owner Mrs A Shone **Bred** Pillar To Post Racing **Trained** Radlett, Herts

FOCUS
This looked a relatively weak maiden by course standards although the first three came clear. The form is best rated around the exposed winner and fourth.

NOTEBOOK
Bertoliver, held from a mark of 70 in a nursery a week previously, pinged out to bag the favoured stands'-side rail and eventually just did enough to repel the runner-up at the line. Considering that he came into this looking exposed after four outings, it is surprising he was able to win such an event, and it dictates that the race was merely modest. He did enjoy the drop back in trip, however, and may have a little more to offer in nurseries now. (op 16-1)
Swift Cut(IRE), well backed prior to disappointing on his recent debut at Southwell, showed the clear benefit of that experience and only failed by the smallest of margins. He looked suited by this straight track and may benefit for a step up to seven furlongs now. (tchd 50-1)
Heroes, a 30,000gns half-brother to seven furlong three-year-old winner Usk Poppy, posted a pleasing debut effort and deserves extra credit as he was forced to race wide without cover throughout. He looks sure to improve a deal for the experience and has a future.
Billy Red, who has had a gelding operation since his last outing 59 days previously, probably ran close to his official mark in defeat and helps put this form into perspective. (tchd 28-1)
Minnis Bay(CAN) ◆, a $40,000 half-brother to four sprint winners in the US, was not given a hard time after making a sluggish start and never threatened. However, he still fared the best of those to come from behind and looks the one to take out of the race with the future in mind.
Sam Lord, fifth at Kempton over this trip on debut 17 days previously, proved disappointing and spoilt his chances by refusing to settle through the early parts. He has it to prove now, and while it would be a surprise were he not to prove better in time, his Group 1 Middle Park entry does look very ambitious. (op 5-2)
Sandrey(IRE), whose stable had taken the last two renewals of this maiden, was tight for room against the stands'-side rail at a crucial stage and shaped slightly better than the bare form. He will become eligible for nurseries after his next outing. (op 9-4)

5455 NEWMARKETRACECOURSES.CO.UK NOVICE STKS 6f
1:45 (1:47) (Class 3) 2-Y-0 **£7,124** (£2,119; £1,059; £529) **Stalls** Low

Form RPR
1 **1** **Traffic Guard (USA)**[75] [3222] 2-9-5 94.............................. MartinDwyer 6 98+
(J S Moore) *lw: chsd ldr over 4f out: led 1/2-way: drvn out* **7/4**[1]
1004 **2** *nk* **Resignation (IRE)**[27] [4715] 2-9-5 94................................ RyanMoore 3 97
(R Hannon) *racd keenly: led 1f: rdn and n.m.r over 1f out: r.o* **7/2**[3]
15 **3** *5* **He's A Humbug (IRE)**[27] [4712] 2-9-5 .... DO'Donohoe 4 82
(K A Ryan) *lw: chsd ldrs: rdn over 1f out: wknd ins fnl f* **5/2**[2]
12 **4** *1* **Resplendent Alpha**[24] [4815] 2-9-5 90................................ SteveDrowne 5 79
(P Howling) *led 5f out: hdd 1/2-way: rdn and wknd over 1f out* **6/1**
04 **5** *nk* **Lap Of Honour (IRE)**[5] [5326] 2-8-12 .... KerrinMcEvoy 1 71
(N A Callaghan) *lw: dwlt: outpcd* **20/1**

1m 10.67s (-2.43) **Going Correction** -0.25s/f (Firm) **5** Ran SP% **106.2**
Speed ratings (Par 99):106,105,98,97,97
CSF £7.50 TOTE £2.60: £1.30, £1.50; EX 8.60.
Owner Uplands Acquisitions Limited **Bred** F Penn And John R Penn **Trained** Upper Lambourn, Berks

FOCUS
The fastest of the three races over the trip on the day and a decent winning time for a race like this. The first two came clearand this looks sound form.

NOTEBOOK
Traffic Guard(USA), off the mark on debut at Newbury 75 days previously, followed up in tenacious fashion and is clearly an improving juvenile. He showed a willing attitude to repel the runner-up late on and did enough to suggest he will have no trouble with an extra furlong in due course. It will be interesting to see where he is pitched in next and he does hold an entry in the Group 1 Dewhurst Stakes. (op 13-8)
Resignation(IRE), who had two handlers and was on his toes in the paddock, was coming back at the winner near the finish and showed improved form for this return to a quicker surface. He was well clear of the remainder, and there are more prizes to be won with him, but his tendency to race freely will always be of slight concern. (op 9-2)
He's A Humbug(IRE), a disappointing favourite in the Gimcrack last time, failed to raise his game as expected on this return to faster ground and was well held by the first two. He has it to prove now. (op 15-8 tchd 11-4 in places)
Resplendent Alpha, who looked fit, did not have any excuses and ultimately his limitations were exposed. He is not going to prove that easy to place from his current rating. (tchd 13-2)
Lap Of Honour(IRE) was never a factor and still looked much in need of the experience. He now has the option of nurseries, however, and this expensive colt ought to really fare better in that arena.

5456 RACING UK ON SKY 432 E B F MAIDEN FILLIES' STKS 1m
2:20 (2:26) (Class 4) 2-Y-0 **£6,477** (£1,927; £963; £481) **Stalls** Low

Form RPR
23 **1** **Light Shift (USA)**[60] [3707] 2-9-0 .... TedDurcan 2 86
(H R A Cecil) *lw: chsd ldrs: rdn and hung rt over 1f out: led ins fnl f: r.o* **15/8**[1]
2 *1/2* **Sunlight (IRE)** 2-9-0 .... PhilipRobinson 3 85
(M A Jarvis) *w'like: leggy: led: rdn over 1f out: hdd ins fnl f: styd on* **9/1**
3 **3** *2* **Circle Of Love**[84] [2958] 2-9-0 .... KerrinMcEvoy 13 80
(J L Dunlop) *lw: chsd ldrs: rdn over 1f out: styd on same pce* **5/2**[2]
4 *3 1/2* **Thinking Positive** 2-9-0 .... RyanMoore 12 72+
(J H M Gosden) *leggy: scope: tall: hld up: hdwy over 2f out: nt trble ldrs* **7/1**[3]
5 **5** *1 3/4* **Satin Braid**[19] [4964] 2-9-0 .... SteveDrowne 4 68
(B J Meehan) *chsd ldrs: rdn over 2f out: wknd over 1f out* **10/1**
6 *4* **Four Miracles** 2-9-0 .... JimmyQuinn 15 59
(M H Tompkins) *w'like: bit bkwd: outpcd: sme hdwy over 1f out: n.d* **50/1**
7 *2 1/2* **Maid To Believe** 2-9-0 .... EddieAhern 10 53
(J L Dunlop) *cmpt: chsd ldrs: rdn over 3f out: wknd 2f out* **16/1**
8 *1/2* **Shimoni** 2-9-0 .... PaulDoe 1 52
(W J Knight) *w'like: scope: s.s: outpcd: styd on ins fnl f: nrst fin* **66/1**

0 **9** *½* **Lightning Queen (USA)**[15] 5068 2-9-0 .... TonyCulhane 5 51
(B W Hills) *lw: hld up: rdn over 2f out: sn wknd* **25/1**

0 **10** *hd* **Cushat Law (IRE)**[66] 3537 2-9-0 .... DarryllHolland 14 50
(W Jarvis) *w'like: prom over 5f* **50/1**

11 *1* **Aphrodisia** 2-9-0 .... HayleyTurner 7 48
(S C Williams) *w'like: bit bkwd: s.i.s: a in rr* **33/1**

12 *¾* **Milla's Rocket (IRE)** 2-9-0 .... DO'Donohoe 11 46
(D J Daly) *w'like: lw: s.i.s: rdn 1/2-way: sme hdwy over 2f out: sn wknd* **33/1**

0 **13** *3* **Dancing Duo**[19] 4964 2-9-0 .... NickyMackay 8 39
(W J Haggas) *leggy: scope: hld up in tch: rdn over 3f out: sn wknd* **40/1**

14 *9* **Above And Below (IRE)** 2-9-0 .... JimmyFortune 6 19
(M Quinn) *leggy: unf: bit bkwd: dwlt: in rr: rdn over 2f out: sn wknd* **50/1**

1m 36.9s (-2.47) **Going Correction** -0.25s/f (Firm) **14** Ran SP% **120.4**
Speed ratings (Par 94):102,101,99,96,94 90,87,87,86,86 85,84,81,72
CSF £18.56 TOTE £2.90: £1.40, £2.90, £1.40; EX 24.40.
Owner Niarchos Family **Bred** Flaxman Holdings Ltd **Trained** Newmarket, Suffolk

FOCUS
An above-average fillies' maiden rated around the winner and third. This was the fastest of the three races over the trip at the meeting and a decent time for a contest of its type.

NOTEBOOK
Light Shift(USA) ◆, who had two handlers in the paddock and looked very fit, got off the mark at the third attempt despite not looking too happy on the quick ground. She rates a promising filly for connections, with the promise of better to come as she steps up in trip next year, and she will no doubt be happier on an easier surface. (op 7-4 tchd 2-1)
Sunlight(IRE) ◆, bred to be suited by longer distances as a three-year-old, had very much the run of the race against the stands' side rail and finished a clear second-best. This was a pleasing debut effort and she will no doubt win races for her connections. (op 12-1)
Circle Of Love, third on debut at Newbury 84 days previously, was not disgraced considering she was forced to race without cover from her high draw and was in turn clear of the remainder at the finish. She appeared to stay the extra furlong well enough and can be placed to strike on one of the smaller tracks before the season's end. (tchd 3-1)
Thinking Positive, representing a stable with a very good record in this event, was doing her best work towards the finish and did more than enough to suggest she can get a lot closer with this experience under her belt. A longer trip will be much to her liking next season. (op 10-1)
Satin Braid, a good walker, was just found wanting near the final furlong marker and failed to see out the extra furlong. She will get this trip in time without fuss, but looks best kept to a sharper test in the short term and can soon find a race.
Shimoni, bred to make her mark over this sort of trip, was always playing catch up after a sluggish start yet was still noted as finishing her race with a degree of promise.

5457 SNAP ON EQUIPMENT SOLUTIONS E B F MAIDEN STKS (C&G) (DIV I) 7f

2:55 (2:56) (Class 4) 2-Y-O **£5,829** (£1,734; £866; £432) **Stalls** Low

Form RPR

1 **Broghill** 2-9-0 .... JimmyFortune 8 77+
(J H M Gosden) *leggy: scope: w ldr: led over 5f out: rdn and hung rt over 1f out: styd on wl: eased nr fin* **12/1**

2 *1¾* **Broomielaw** 2-9-0 .... DO'Donohoe 4 72+
(E A L Dunlop) *leggy: scope: tall; s.i.s: hld up: hdwy 1/2-way: rdn and nt clr run over 2f out: hdwy over 1f out: r.o wl* **6/1**[3]

3 *1¾* **Shevchenko (IRE)** 2-9-0 .... DarryllHolland 7 67+
(J Noseda) *unf: scope: lw: hld up in tch: rdn to chse wnr over 1f out: styd on same pce ins fnl f* **2/1**[1]

00 **4** *1¼* **Fairly Honest**[80] 3083 2-9-0 .... AntonyProcter 12 64
(D R C Elsworth) *hld up: hdwy and hung lft over 1f out: styd on same pce ins fnl f* **66/1**

0 **5** *1½* **Morning Farewell**[51] 3976 2-9-0 .... EddieAhern 9 60
(P W Chapple-Hyam) *lw: chsd ldrs: rdn over 3f out: wknd fnl f* **10/1**

6 *1¾* **Desert Dew (IRE)** 2-9-0 .... TonyCulhane 1 70+
(B W Hills) *unf: lw: chsd ldrs: nt clr run and lost pl over 2f out: rallying whn hmpd over 1f out: nt rcvr* **7/1**

0 **7** *¾* **Oscarshall (IRE)**[93] 2680 2-9-0 .... JimmyQuinn 5 53
(M H Tompkins) *hld up: hdwy whn hmpd over 1f out: wknd ins fnl f* **66/1**

8 *¾* **Chord** 2-9-0 .... RyanMoore 3 51
(Sir Michael Stoute) *unf: scope: led: hdd over 5f out: rdn over 2f out: wknd over 1f out* **12/1**

9 *13* **Mountain Call (IRE)** 2-9-0 .... NickyMackay 2 16
(Mrs A J Perrett) *w'like: scope: bit bkwd: s.i.s: hld up: wknd over 3f out* **66/1**

10 *nk* **Crimson Monarch (USA)** 2-9-0 .... KerrinMcEvoy 11 15
(Mrs A J Perrett) *w'like: bit bkwd: s.s: outpcd* **25/1**

26 **11** *½* **Sahrati**[45] 4129 2-9-0 .... TedDurcan 6 14+
(C E Brittain) *chsd ldrs: rdn over 2f out: wkng whn hmpd over 1f out* **7/2**[2]

1m 25.8s (-0.70) **Going Correction** -0.25s/f (Firm) **11** Ran SP% **115.1**
Speed ratings (Par 97):94,92,90,88,86 84,84,83,68,67 67
CSF £79.23 TOTE £15.70: £4.30, £2.10, £1.60; EX 85.90.
Owner Duke Of Devonshire **Bred** The Duke Of Devonshire **Trained** Newmarket, Suffolk

FOCUS
A decent maiden which should produce a deal of future winners although the winning time was 1.53 seconds slower than the second division. The form is rated to the best view of the fourth's previous efforts for now.

NOTEBOOK
Broghill ◆, the first foal of a well-related seven furlong three-year-old winner, ran out a decisive winner and got his career off to a perfect start. She showed a neat turn of foot to settle the issue nearing the final furlong, despite looking green, and is value for further than the winning margin. He holds an entry in next year's Derby, and appeals as the sort to do better as a three-year-old, but this attractive colt would not look out of place at a higher level should connections find a suitable opportunity before the season's end. (op 9-1)
Broomielaw ◆, an attractive colt who cost 190,000gns as a foal and is a half-brother to smart middle-distance performer Unfurled, motored home inside the final furlong and turned in a very promising debut effort. He would have given the winner more to think about with a clearer passage around two out and ultimately looked better the further he went. A similar race should be his for the taking in due course and he rates a smart prospect for next season. (op 8-1)
Shevchenko(IRE), a 250,000euros colt whose parents were both Guineas winners, had his chance and simply failed to see out the trip as well as the front pair. This should serve as a beneficial education and, like the first pair, he rates a decent future prospect. (op 7-4)
Fairly Honest ◆, returning from an 80-day break, posted by far his best effort to date and deserves a little extra credit as he was drawn widest of all. He now qualifies for a handicap mark and is one to be with in that sphere when stepping up to a mile. (tchd 80-1)
Morning Farewell was put in his place at the business end of the race, but still improved on the level of his debut on the July course 51 days previously. He can find easier opportunities. (op 8-1)
Desert Dew(IRE), a 250,00gns half-brother to high-class middle-distance performer Indian Creek, was given a horrible introduction and should have been allowed his head through the early parts against the favoured stands'-side rail. He is much better than the bare form.
Oscarshall(IRE) looked very fit following his absence since his debut, but he failed to find anything for pressure and looks in need of more time.
Chord, a half-bother to high-class filly Chorist, was extremely green in the preliminaries and this debut experience was clearly much-needed. (op 14-1)
Mountain Call(IRE) is a good-bodied colt but never figured after a slow start.
Crimson Monarch(USA) Official explanation: jockey said colt bronked leaving stalls
Sahrati, well backed, failed to run his race on this return from a 42-day break and clearly something was amiss. (op 9-2)

5458 SNAP ON EQUIPMENT SOLUTIONS E B F MAIDEN STKS (C&G) (DIV II) 7f

3:30 (3:31) (Class 4) 2-Y-O **£5,829** (£1,734; £866; £432) **Stalls** Low

Form RPR

1 **Adagio** 2-9-0 .... KerrinMcEvoy 8 89
(Sir Michael Stoute) *w'like: scope: chsd ldrs: ev ch fr over 1f out: r.o to ld post* **11/2**[3]

2 *shd* **Tybalt (USA)** 2-9-0 .... JimmyFortune 1 89
(J H M Gosden) *w'like: lengthy: lw: chsd ldrs: nt clr run over 2f out: swtchd rt over 1f out: sn rdn to ld and hung rt: hdd post* **15/2**

2 **3** *5* **Aureate**[12] 5134 2-9-0 .... DarryllHolland 4 75
(M Johnston) *unf: scope: lw: led over 5f: wknd ins fnl f* **5/2**[2]

5 **4** *1¼* **Solid Rock (IRE)**[11] 5147 2-9-0 .... IanMongan 6 72
(T G Mills) *hld up in tch: rdn over 2f out: edgd lft and wknd fnl f* **14/1**

0 **5** *1¼* **Camps Bay (USA)**[25] 4781 2-9-0 .... PhilipRobinson 11 68
(Mrs A J Perrett) *chsd ldrs: rdn whn hmpd over 1f out: sn wknd* **33/1**

6 *hd* **Mia's Boy** 2-9-0 .... EddieAhern 2 68
(P W Chapple-Hyam) *chsd ldrs: rdn over 2f out: wknd over 1f out* **6/4**[1]

7 *6* **Summer Dancer (IRE)** 2-9-0 .... AntonyProcter 3 52
(D R C Elsworth) *w'like: bit bkwd: s.i.s: swtchd rt over 5f out: hdwy 1/2-way: hung rt and wknd over 2f out* **20/1**

8 *2* **Zell Am See** 2-9-0 .... JimmyQuinn 10 46
(M H Tompkins) *neat: s.i.s: hld up: wknd over 2f out* **100/1**

9 *3½* **Nordic Affair** 2-9-0 .... RyanMoore 7 37
(D R C Elsworth) *w'like: scope: lw: s.s: outpcd* **33/1**

10 *½* **Musheed (IRE)** 2-9-0 .... MartinDwyer 12 36
(E A L Dunlop) *w'like: lw: dwlt: hld up: wknd over 2f out* **33/1**

000 **11** *3* **Hits Only Vic (USA)**[13] 5111 2-9-0 52 .... DO'Donohoe 9 27
(J Pearce) *sn outpcd* **100/1**

1m 24.27s (-2.23) **Going Correction** -0.25s/f (Firm) **11** Ran SP% **118.0**
Speed ratings (Par 97):102,101,96,94,93 93,86,83,79,79 75
CSF £43.12 TOTE £6.90: £2.10, £2.00, £1.40; EX 37.70.
Owner D Smith, M Tabor & Mrs J Magnier **Bred** New England Stud, Myriad And Elite Bloodstock **Trained** Newmarket, Suffolk
■ Stewards' Enquiry : Jimmy Fortune two-day ban: careless riding (Oct 4-5)

FOCUS
A decent maiden, nothing more, in which the front two drew five lengths clear of Aureate. The form looks more sound than the first division.

NOTEBOOK
Adagio, a nice, attractive 200,000gns purchase who boasts a Racing Post Trophy entry, was never more than a length off the pace set by Aureate and it was clear from two furlongs out the race lay between himself and the runner-up, the pair easily travelling better than anything else. He took his time to find top stride, Tybalt nosing ahead of him at one point, but he rallied well under McEvoy and got there in the last strides. There was plenty to like about this performance and the son of Grand Lodge, who showed distinct signs of greeness, is likely to have one more run this season, although connections would not be drawn on whether it would be in the Racing Post Trophy. (op 5-1 tchd 6-1)
Tybalt(USA), a son of Storm Cat whose dam was placed in the Breeders' Cup Mile, holds a Derby entry and he had to wait to get his run, but was in the clear in plenty of time and held every chance, being nailed close home by Adagio. Clear of the third, he should win his maiden, but had a hard enough race in defeat and it remains to be seen which way he goes from this. (op 10-1 tchd 11-1)
Aureate, who made a pleasing debut behind a fair sort in a three-runner heavy ground maiden at Haydock, put his experience to good use and attempted to make all on the rail, but was readily left trailing by the front pair when it mattered. He has shown enough to win an ordinary maiden and in the longer term, looks a decent handicap prospect. (op 10-3)
Solid Rock(IRE), who made a pleasing debut over five furlongs on his debut at Sandown, was expected to be suited by the extra distance, but having made some headway he faded close home and may have found the quarter of a mile leap up too much at once. He appeals as more of a handicap prospect for next season. (op 16-1)
Camps Bay(USA) stepped up on his debut effort and, although lacking the speed of some of the principals, he is not going to be seen at his best until tackling handicaps at three.
Mia's Boy, an expensive purchase who came into this with a tall reputation, appeared to know his job, but he found little for pressure and flopped badly. Surely capable of better, he did not have any obvious excuse for the poor showing, but probably deserves to be given another chance, with his stable housing plenty of good juveniles. (op 6-5)
Summer Dancer(IRE), bred to appreciate trips upwards of a mile, shaped reasonably well and briefly threatened to get involved, but he dropped away inside the final quarter of a mile and plainly needed the experience. (tchd 25-1)
Nordic Affair, who is bred to be relatively speedy, cost 50,000gns and the booking of the champion jockey elect caught the eye. He was negative in the betting however and really struggled in the race itself, soon getting behind and running particularly green. He should come on appreciably for the outing and a significantly imrpoved effort can be expected next time.
Musheed(IRE) holds no entries of note and he really showed very little on this racecourse debut. He may improve with experience, but is unlikely to do much this season. Official explanation: jockey said colt had a breathing problem

5459 UAE EQUESTRIAN AND RACING FEDERATION NURSERY 1m

4:00 (4:02) (Class 2) 2-Y-O **£12,954** (£3,854; £1,926; £962) **Stalls** Low

Form RPR

5011 **1** **King Charles**[7] 5262 2-8-13 **82** 6ex .... DO'Donohoe 5 84
(E A L Dunlop) *racd stands' side: chsd ldr tl rdn to ld that gp over 1f out: r.o u.p to ld post* **7/2**[1]

0050 **2** *shd* **Zafonical Storm (USA)**[38] 4344 2-8-9 **78** .... DarryllHolland 4 79
(B W Duke) *led centre: rdn and hung lft fr over 2f out: hdd over 1f out: rallied u.p to ld ins fnl f: hdd post* **40/1**

12 **3** *hd* **Bid For Glory**[13] 5113 2-8-12 **81** .... JimmyQuinn 1 82
(H J Collingridge) *b: racd stands' side: chsd ldrs: nt clr run over 1f out: sn swtchd rt: r.o u.p* **11/2**[3]

5412 **4** *shd* **Guacamole**[17] 5013 2-8-13 **82** .... TonyCulhane 7 83
(B W Hills) *racd centre: hmpd 6f out: hdwy to chse ldr over 3f out: carried rt fr over 2f out: led over 1f out: hdd ins fnl f: r.o* **10/1**

5514 **5** *3* **Sri Pekan Two**[22] 4882 2-8-10 **79** .... EddieAhern 6 73
(P F I Cole) *racd centre: hld up: hdwy over 3f out: rdn over 1f out: styd on same pce* **9/2**[2]

1611 **6** *1* **Heywood**[16] 5041 2-9-4 **87** .... TedDurcan 2 79
(M R Channon) *lw: racd stands' side: chsd ldrs: rdn and hung rt over 2f out: no ex fnl f* **9/1**

410 **7** *1¾* **Mayor Of London (USA)**[22] 4882 2-8-11 **80** .... MartinDwyer 3 68
(M Johnston) *led stands' side over 6f: wknd fnl f* **12/1**

5156 **8** *15* **Dora Explora**[38] [4371] 2-9-7 **90**.. JimmyFortune 9 43
(P W Chapple-Hyam) *wnt rt s: racd centre: chsd ldrs over 5f* **16/1**

21 **9** *24* **Worldly**[20] [4932] 2-9-2 **85**.. RyanMoore 8 —
(S Kirk) *lw: racd centre: hmpd 6f out: chsd ldr over 4f: wknd 2f out: eased* **7/2**[1]

1m 37.56s (-1.81) **Going Correction** -0.25s/f (Firm) **9** Ran SP% **113.1**
Speed ratings (Par 101):99,98,98,98,95 94,92,77,53
CSF £135.64 CT £756.55 TOTE £3.70: £1.50, £7.10, £2.30; EX 174.60.

Owner Khalifa Sultan **Bred** Hunscote House Farm Stud **Trained** Newmarket, Suffolk

■ Stewards' Enquiry : Darryll Holland one-day ban: careless riding (Oct 5)

FOCUS

This developed into a highly-competitive nursery with the front four being separated by two short heads and a head at the line. Although not rated too positively due to a 40/1 shot finishing second, the form looks pretty good and the race should produce winners.

NOTEBOOK

King Charles, who caught the eye on more than one occasion in maidens, has flourished since going handicapping, following up his Lingfield Turf win with a smooth display back there on the Polytrack - 7lb higher mark - and although leaving it late here, he was driven to snatch it on the line under a penalty. Kept to the stands' side throughout, the step up to a mile brought about further improvement and the son of King's Best still looks to be on the up, suggesting a four-timer is not beyond the realms of possibility. (op 5-2)

Zafonical Storm(USA), who was not the only horse to run below par at the Shergar Cup meeting on 'funny' ground, had previously run well on his only start in nursery company - third to Eddie Jock at Newmarket - and he was allowed to go off at large odds taking that form into account. Opting to race down the centre of the track, he ended up edging across towards the stands' side and very nearly caused an upset, being nailed in the dying stride. The mile clearly helped and he can find a similar race off this mark.

Bid For Glory, a winner at the July course on his debut, got going all to late when second on his nursery debut over seven furlongs, and he was again slightly unfortunate, not getting the split when he wanted it. It could be argued he is unlucky not to be unbeaten and he still has more to offer. (op 7-1)

Guacamole, runner-up to a fair sort on her nursery debut at Haydock, had previously won her maiden and this was another sound effort considering nothing really went her way in the race. She is another with claims of being unlucky and her ability to handle heavy ground will help at this time of year.

Sri Pekan Two has in all honesty been disappointing since moving into nurseries, flopping badly at Newcastle last month and failing to pick up as anticipated on this occasion. He was comfortably held at the line and the son of Montjeu may already be in need of ten furlongs. (op 5-1)

Heywood, winner of three of his last four races, including his last two starts in nurseries off marks of 75 and 83, was up another 4lb and did not look certain to be suited by the extra furlong. He held a good early position, but started to hang under pressure and failed to see out his race. He may be in the Handicapper's grip now. (op 10-1)

Mayor Of London(USA) won his maiden in soft ground at Newcastle back in August, but he has failed to build on it in two nurseries outings, being virtually pulled up last time and dropping away without much of a fight on this occasion. He is going to need some help from the Handicapper.

Dora Explora, who has been contesting some fair races, had two handlers in the paddock and should have fared much better on this drop in grade, but she ran too bad to be true and fell away tamely. This mark is going to make life impossible for her. (op 20-1)

Worldly, who confirmed the promise of his debut second to the useful Streets Ahead by winning a nine furlong Wolverhampton maiden, looked one of the likelier winners on this nursery debut, but he dropped away very quickly and it transpired he had broken a blood-vessel. Official explanation: jockey said gelding bled from the nose (op 4-1)

5460 NGK SPARK PLUGS MEDIAN AUCTION MAIDEN STKS 1m

4:35 (4:37) (Class 4) 2-Y-O **£4,533** (£1,348; £674; £336) **Stalls** Low

Form RPR

1 **Empire Day (UAE)** 2-9-3 .... DO'Donohoe 16 84+
(M Johnston) *leggy: scope: mid-div: hdwy 1/2-way: led 2f out: hung lft over 1f out: rdn out* **12/1**

2 *1* **Sunshine Kid (USA)** 2-9-3 .... JimmyFortune 11 82+
(J H M Gosden) *leggy: lw: a.p: rdn over 1f out: r.o* **8/1**

0 **3** *½* **Rosie's Glory (USA)**[38] [4373] 2-8-12 .... TonyCulhane 1 76
(B J Meehan) *prom: rdn over 2f out: r.o* **4/1**[2]

63 **4** *1¼* **Edison**[14] [5091] 2-9-3 .... RyanMoore 2 78
(N P Littmoden) *led stands' side 6f: sn rdn: no ex ins fnl f* **7/1**

5 **5** *3* **Vanquisher (IRE)**[25] [4768] 2-9-3 .... TedDurcan 9 71
(W J Haggas) *chsd ldrs: rdn over 2f out: wknd fnl f* **5/1**[3]

6 *½* **Ekhtiaar** 2-9-3 .... MartinDwyer 4 70
(J H M Gosden) *w'like: bit bkwd: chsd ldrs: rdn and ev ch over 1f out: wknd fnl f* **7/2**[1]

7 *1¾* **Sunley Peace** 2-9-3 .... AntonyProcter 5 66
(D R C Elsworth) *w'like: bit bkwd: s.s: hld up: swtchd rt over 2f out: nvr nr to chal* **50/1**

8 *3* **Force Group (IRE)** 2-9-3 .... DarryllHolland 6 59
(M H Tompkins) *w'like: chsd ldrs: rdn over 2f out: sn wknd* **25/1**

9 *½* **Brouhaha** 2-9-3 .... BrianReilly 3 58
(Miss Diana Weeden) *w'like: scope: dwlt: hld up: rdn over 2f out: sn hung rt and wknd* **66/1**

10 *¾* **Francesco** 2-9-3 .... HayleyTurner 10 56
(M L W Bell) *str: bit bkwd: hld up: hdwy 1/2-way: wknd 2f out* **40/1**

00 **11** *shd* **Like To Golf (USA)**[14] [5091] 2-9-3 .... PhilipRobinson 14 56
(Mrs A J Perrett) *racd alone centre tl edgd lft over 3f out: overall ldr tl hdd 2f out: sn wknd* **50/1**

12 *1¼* **El Dottore** 2-9-3 .... EddieAhern 12 53
(M L W Bell) *b.hind: leggy: hld up: hdwy 1/2-way: wknd 2f out* **20/1**

13 *shd* **Fighting Mood** 2-9-3 .... JimmyQuinn 7 52
(A M Balding) *w'like: s.i.s: hld up: wknd over 2f out* **33/1**

14 *3* **Cordwain** 2-9-3 .... PaulDoe 15 46
(J H M Gosden) *w'like: dwlt: a in rr: wknd 3f out* **20/1**

15 *hd* **Credit Slip** 2-9-3 .... KerrinMcEvoy 8 45
(J L Dunlop) *w'like: scope: hld up: wknd 3f out* **25/1**

16 *65* **The Flying Cowboy (IRE)** 2-9-3 .... IanMongan 13 —
(N P Littmoden) *leggy: bit bkwd: chsd ldrs over 4f* **50/1**

1m 38.88s (-0.49) **Going Correction** -0.25s/f (Firm) **16** Ran SP% **120.2**
Speed ratings (Par 97):92,91,90,89,86 85,84,81,80,79 79,78,78,75,75 10
CSF £92.80 TOTE £14.60: £3.90, £2.30, £2.10; EX 87.50.

Owner Sheikh Maktoum Bin Mohammed Al Maktoum **Bred** Darley **Trained** Middleham Moor, N Yorks

FOCUS

The slowest of the three races over the trip on the day and a modest time for the grade. That said, the race should still produce winners, with the form rated around the third, fourth and fifth.

NOTEBOOK

Empire Day(UAE), a Derby entrant whose dam is a half-sister to the smart German-trained El Tiger, has the looks a of a typical two-year-old from his stable - tall, scopey and unfurnished - so it was most pleasing he was able to make a winning debut from what looked a decent field. Despite running around under pressure and showing distinct signs of greeness, he was able to win with a bit in hand and he most definitely looks one to keep on side for the remainder of the season, with middle distances likely to help him progress further at three. (op 14-1)

Sunshine Kid(USA), a Racing Post Trophy entrant, is American bred through and through and he also looks a three-year-old in the making. That did not stop him making a highly promising debut though and, although not able to get the winner, he should learn a great deal for the experience. Winning a maiden should prove a formality before going on to better things. (tchd 10-1)

Rosie's Glory(USA), never in the hunt in soft ground on her debut at the July course, appreciated the combination of a step up to a mile on this faster ground and ran well, but the two colts proved her superior. She has shown enough to suggest a maiden should come her way. (op 9-2)

Edison, a bit edgy beforehand, attempted to put his experience to good use and make all, but he was outclassed in the end and could not quicken. He is now qualified for nurseries and should do better in that sphere. (op 6-1)

Vanquisher(IRE), a little bit on edge beforehand, confirmed the promise of his July course debut and, although dropping away towards the finish, the best of him is unlikely to be seen until tackling handicaps next season. (op 4-1)

Ekhtiaar, a Derby entrant, cost 85,000gns and looked one of the likelier winners, but having held a good early position, he failed to pick up an faded inside the final furlong. He should come on for the experience. (op 9-2)

Sunley Peace, who looked as though the experience would do him good in the paddock, shaped with promise and kept on without being given too hard a time. Improvement should be forthcoming and he looks one to be interested in in future.

Brouhaha was very green in the preliminaries.

Like To Golf(USA) showed up well to a point and, although dropping away in the end, he will soon be qualified for nurseries. (op 40-1)

Cordwain, a 72,000gns Derby entrant, has already been gelded, but still looked one of the more interesting outsiders. However, he was always struggling in rear and on this evidence is not going to be up to much. (op 25-1)

The Flying Cowboy(IRE) Official explanation: trainer said colt lost its action

5461 NATWEST DIFFERENT VIEW OF YOUR BUSINESS NURSERY 6f

5:10 (5:10) (Class 3) 2-Y-O **£8,420** (£2,505; £1,251; £625) **Stalls** Low

Form RPR

0101 **1** **Bateleur**[4] [5349] 2-7-13 **77** 6ex ow1.. EdwardCreighton[(3)] 2 84+
(M R Channon) *trckd ldrs: rdn over 1f out: r.o to ld wl ins fnl f* **3/1**[1]

1230 **2** *1¾* **Just Dust**[24] [4804] 2-8-7 **82**.. MartinDwyer 5 80
(D R C Elsworth) *led over 4f: rallied to ld 1f out: hdd wl ins fnl f* **13/2**[3]

0512 **3** *shd* **Everymanforhimself (IRE)**[22] [4890] 2-9-7 **96**................ KerrinMcEvoy 4 94
(J G Given) *chsd ldrs: rdn over 2f out: ev ch ins fnl f: unable qckn* **3/1**[1]

013 **4** *½* **Ede's Dot Com (IRE)**[53] [3917] 2-8-8 **83**.. PaulDoe 8 80
(W J Knight) *w ldrs: rdn and ev ch fr over 1f out: no ex wl ins fnl f* **16/1**

0100 **5** *hd* **See In The Dark (IRE)**[25] [4766] 2-7-11 **79**.. KMay[(7)] 1 75
(B J Meehan) *trckd ldrs: outpcd 2f out: r.o ins fnl f* **9/1**

3030 **6** *¾* **Star Strider**[14] [5094] 2-7-12 **73** oh4.. HayleyTurner 7 67
(A M Balding) *w ldrs: led over 1f out: sn rdn and hdd: no ex* **20/1**

4240 **7** *¾* **Astroangel**[3] [5382] 2-7-12 **73** oh6..(b[1]) JimmyQuinn 6 64
(M H Tompkins) *s.s: hld up: racd keenly: rdn over 1f out: no imp* **12/1**

2100 **8** *2* **Persian Fox (IRE)**[15] [5053] 2-7-12 **73** oh7....................(p) NickyMackay 3 58
(G A Huffer) *dwlt: hld up: hdwy over 2f out: wknd fnl f* **18/1**

4212 **9** *12* **High Style**[32] [4547] 2-8-13 **88**.. RyanMoore 9 37
(R Hannon) *hld up: hdwy over 2f out: wknd over 1f out* **5/1**[2]

1m 12.7s (-0.40) **Going Correction** -0.25s/f (Firm) **9** Ran SP% **113.6**
Speed ratings (Par 99):92,89,89,88,88 87,86,83,67
CSF £22.48 CT £62.00 TOTE £3.30: £1.20, £2.60, £1.30; EX 18.90 Place 6 £241.27, Place 5 £11.10.

Owner Dave and Gill Hedley **Bred** G Hedley And Mike Channon Bloodstock Limited **Trained** West Ilsley, Berks

FOCUS

The slowest of the three races over the trip at the meeting and a moderate time for a race like this. The form looks dubious and is limited by the fourth.

NOTEBOOK

Bateleur, cosy winner of his maiden at Bath back in July, has left behind a disappointing nursery debut effort, winning at Nottingham off a mark of 72, and defying the penalty here in the style of a useful sort. His dam was placed at up to ten furlongs so there is reason to believe he will stay further and the son of Fraam may not have done improving yet. (tchd 5-2)

Just Dust, having his 11th start of the season, has been holding his form well and, although still 9lb higher than when last winning, he ran a good race in second. (op 5-1)

Everymanforhimself(IRE), runner-up to Stevie Gee in the Ripon Two-Year-Old Trophy, has looked at his best over six furlongs and he ran another fine race on this return to handicap company. (op 7-2 tchd 9-2)

Ede's Dot Com(IRE), third on his nursery debut at Wolverhampton, ran his race and had every chance, but failed to see it out as well as some and may come on for this first start since July. (op 14-1)

See In The Dark(IRE) left a couple of disappointing efforts behind with a running-on fifth, but winning off this mark is not going to be easy for the exposed gelding. (op 12-1)

Star Strider has been disappointing since going handicapping and, having gone on over a furlong out, he soon dropped away. (op 16-1)

T/Plt: £706.70 to a £1 stake. Pool: £47,049.20. 48.60 winning tickets. T/Qpdt: £7.40 to a £1 stake. Pool: £4,890.90. 482.95 winning tickets. CR

5462 - 5463a (Foreign Racing) - See Raceform Interactive

5407 CURRAGH (R-H)

Tuesday, September 19

OFFICIAL GOING: Yielding changing to yielding to soft after race 1 (1.30)

5464a SHELBOURNE HOTEL GOFFS FILLIES FIVE HUNDRED 7f

2:40 (2:54) 2-Y-O

£337,241 (£95,862; £44,137; £20,000; £8,275; £689)

RPR

1 **Silk Blossom (IRE)**[26] [4737] 2-9-0 .... MichaelHills 2 95+
(B W Hills) *chsd ldrs: 7th 1/2-way: sn rdn: chal in 2nd and bdly hmpd ins fnl f: no imp after: kpt on same pce: fin 2nd, awrdd r* **9/4**[1]

2 *1¼* **Wait Watcher (IRE)**[31] [4600] 2-9-0 .... TPO'Shea 18 96
(P A Blockley) *chsd ldrs: rdn to chal and ld fr 1f out: drifted to lft ins fnl f: kpt on wl: fin 1st, 1¼l: plcd 2nd* **20/1**

3 *nk* **Cliche (IRE)**[25] [4765] 2-9-0 .... JamieSpencer 8 92
(Sir Michael Stoute) *towards rr: rdn and r.o wl without rching ldrs fr over 1f out* **11/1**

4 1 3/4 **In Safe Hands (IRE)**[37] 4412 2-9-0 .... FMBerry 13 87
(Declan Gillespie, Ire) *chsd ldrs: 10th 2f out: kpt on wout threatening u.p fr over 1f out* **20/1**

5 shd **Theann**[37] 4406 2-9-0 .... KFallon 26 87
(A P O'Brien, Ire) *chsd ldrs: travelling wl and led 1 1/2f out: hdd 1f out: sn no imp u.p and kpt on same pce* **13/2**[2]

6 1/2 **Anna's Rock (IRE)**[77] 3178 2-9-0 78................................ KJManning 11 86
(J S Bolger, Ire) *prom: no imp u.p and kpt on same pce fr over 1f out* **25/1**

7 1 3/4 **Drifting Snow**[114] 2052 2-9-0 .... PJSmullen 3 81
(D K Weld, Ire) *chsd ldrs: 8th 1/2-way: no imp u.p and kpt on same pce fr over 1f out* **8/1**[3]

8 3/4 **Amusing (IRE)**[66] 3556 2-9-0 .... DMGrant 15 79
(John Joseph Murphy, Ire) *mid-div: kpt on without threatening fr over 1f out* **66/1**

9 1 3/4 **Gee Kel (IRE)**[62] 3658 2-9-0 101.. WSupple 23 74
(Francis Ennis, Ire) *prom: 5th 1/2-way: no ex and kpt on same pce u.p fr over 1f out* **10/1**

10 1 3/4 **Petite Cherie (IRE)**[52] 3963 2-9-0 99........................(t) RichardHughes 6 69
(G M Lyons, Ire) *towards rr: rdn and kpt on without threatening fr 2f out* **25/1**

11 1/2 **Musthav (IRE)**[23] 4850 2-9-0 93...(p) WJLee 19 68
(T Stack, Ire) *towards rr: kpt on wout threatening fr 1/2-way* **33/1**

12 1 3/4 **Onida (IRE)**[25] 4765 2-9-0 .... MJKinane 16 63
(C G Cox) *mid-div: kpt on same pce u.p fr under 2f out* **14/1**

13 1 **St Anna Arresi (IRE)**[37] 4406 2-9-0 .... JMurtagh 10 61
(M Halford, Ire) *mid-div: kpt on same pce u.p fr under 2f out* **25/1**

14 hd **Tralanza (IRE)**[18] 4999 2-9-0 .... CO'Donoghue 14 60
(P J Prendergast, Ire) *chsd ldrs: no imp u.p fr under 2f out* **50/1**

15 1/2 **Unlock (IRE)**[8] 5251 2-9-0 85.. WMLordan 22 59
(D K Weld, Ire) *chsd ldrs: 4th 1/2-way: no ex u.p and kpt on same pce fr wl over 1f out* **20/1**

16 shd **Pelican Waters (IRE)**[32] 4578 2-9-0 87............................ JohnEgan 27 59
(Mrs John Harrington, Ire) *nvr bttr than mid-div* **20/1**

17 1 1/4 **Isola Star (IRE)**[23] 4850 2-9-0 .... DPMcDonogh 12 55
(David P Myerscough, Ire) *prom: led 1/2-way: hdd 1 1/2f out: sn no ex* **20/1**

18 1 **So Sweet (IRE)**[19] 4955 2-9-0 .... JoeFanning 24 52
(M R Channon) *prom: rdn and on terms briefly 2f out: sn no imp u.p* **10/1**

19 3/4 **Nicomedia (IRE)**[18] 4993 2-9-0 .... CDHayes 7 50
(R Hannon) *nvr bttr than mid-div* **33/1**

20 1/2 **Maysarah (IRE)**[18] 4994 2-9-0 .... FJohansson 5 49
(G A Butler) *mid-div best: kpt on same pce u.p fr under 2f out* **25/1**

21 2 **Spritza (IRE)**[62] 3640 2-9-0 .... KDarley 21 44
(M L W Bell) *nvr bttr than mid-div* **25/1**

22 shd **Delphia (IRE)**[32] 4578 2-9-0 76....................................... JAHeffernan 20 43
(T Hogan, Ire) *mid-div: no imp u.p fr under 2f out* **50/1**

23 2 **Queen Noverre (IRE)**[32] 4552 2-9-0 .... RichardMullen 17 38
(E J O'Neill) *nvr bttr than mid-div* **20/1**

24 nk **There's A Light (IRE)**[18] 4999 2-9-0 .... PShanahan 4 37
(C Collins, Ire) *chsd ldrs: lost pl and no ex u.p fr under 2f out* **33/1**

25 2 **Braydeen (IRE)**[41] 4271 2-9-0 .... RobertWinston 1 32
(D K Weld, Ire) *sn led: hdd 1/2-way: sn wknd* **20/1**

26 5 1/2 **Tribiani (IRE)**[28] 4683 2-9-0 .... DJCondon 25 17
(Gerard Cully, Ire) *a towards rr* **100/1**

27 9 **Moverra (IRE)**[32] 4578 2-9-0 77.................................(b1) NGMcCullagh 9 —
(M J Grassick, Ire) *chsd ldrs: rdn and wknd fr 2f out* **50/1**

1m 29.7s **Going Correction** +0.425s/f (Yiel) **27** Ran SP% **158.1**
Speed ratings: 102,104,102,100,100 99,97,96,94,92 92,90,88,88,88 88,86,85,84,84 81,81,79,79,76 70,60
CSF £64.05 TOTE £3.70: £1.80, £5.10, £2.80, £9.50; DF 339.70.
Owner E D Kessly **Bred** Richard F Barnes **Trained** Lambourn, Berks
■ Stewards' Enquiry : T P O'Shea four-day ban: careless riding (Sep 29,30, Oct 1,2)

FOCUS
A dramatic inaugural running of this race, as the first home Wait Watcher was disqualified in favour of the runner-up Silk Blossom. The form of this type of race rarely works out and it has been rated conservatively as a result.

NOTEBOOK
Silk Blossom(IRE), who won what looked a below-par Lowther Stakes last time, was on and off the bridle early and was not finding a great deal of room from her rails position during the early part of the race. However, she responded in good style to her jockey's urgings and would have been a most unfortunate loser had she not got the race in the Stewards' room. Clearly a filly with plenty of class, she now heads for the Rockfel Stakes, a race that holds particular significance for next season's fillies' Classics. (op 2/1 tchd 11/4)
Wait Watcher(IRE), who only landed a maiden on her last start, drifted left under a right-handed drive inside the final furlong and hampered Silk Blossom, who was coming with what her jockey described as a strong run. In what looked a decision that could go either way, Silk Blossom got the race as the Stewards deemed that Wait Watcher had improved her position in relation to the runner-up. Connections of the runner-up intend to appeal against the decision, but the run represented a big improvement in form and she is going the right way. One hopes that connections take on the 'winner' again in the Rockfel to determine which is the better filly. (op 16/1 tchd 20/1)
Cliche(IRE) stayed on well over the final quarter of a mile without reaching the leaders. Still a maiden, she has obvious scope for improvement, and connections should not have to wait long before she registers her first success. (op 12/1 tchd 14/1)
In Safe Hands(IRE) ran a good race and stayed on well over the final furlong and a half. She had previously shown plenty of promise when second to Alexander Tango in a maiden here in July before a slightly disappointing effort last time after rearing leaving the stalls, and seemed to appreciate the ease in the ground.
Theann, who is impeccably bred, was travelling strongly heading into the final stages of the race but did not find a great deal off the bridle inside the final furlong. She should not have any trouble winning a maiden but her ideal trip is yet to be determined. She still holds an entry in the Group 1 Cheveley Park Stakes over six furlongs, so she clearly shows connections plenty of pace. (op 6/1 tchd 7/1)
Onida(IRE) was unable to make any impression on the leaders from off the pace. This did not look up to the standard of her earlier efforts, so she is entitled to another chance. (op 12/1)
So Sweet(IRE), who was subject to a late jockey change after Dettori could not get to the course, ran well below her recent efforts. The ground may have been the reason.
Nicomedia(IRE) had not really shown enough in her previous races to have a serious chance, and she came up short of the required class needed for such a valuable race, although she was fully entitled to take her chance due to the conditions of the race.
Maysarah(IRE) possibly found the race too much after a promising debut. She will be better judged on her effort next time.
Spritza(IRE) did not seem to stay seven furlongs last time and never got involved at any stage.
Queen Noverre(IRE) ran nowhere near the form she showed in her previous three races and can be excused one poor effort in a different country.

5465a IRISH NATIONAL STUD BLANDFORD STKS (GROUP 2) (F&M) 1m 2f
3:15 (3:29) 3-Y-0+ **£56,034** (£16,379; £7,758; £2,586)

RPR

1 **Red Bloom**[30] 4646 5-9-4 110.. JamieSpencer 2 114+
(Sir Michael Stoute) *trckd ldrs: mainly 3rd: rdn to chal and ld under 2f out: clr and styd on wl fnl f: comf* **11/8**[1]

2 1 3/4 **Sina Cova (IRE)**[27] 4714 4-9-4 107................................ DPMcDonogh 3 110
(Peter Casey, Ire) *prom: mainly 2nd: rdn to chal and ld briefly over 2f out: sn hdd and no imp: kpt on same pce* **20/1**

3 1 1/4 **Paris Winds (IRE)**[24] 4826 3-8-12 .... WMLordan 11 108
(David Wachman, Ire) *chsd ldrs in 5th: 4th and no imp u.p fr under 2f out: 3rd and kpt on same pce fr over 1f out* **25/1**

4 3 **Be My Queen (IRE)**[8] 5253 3-8-12 102............................ JAHeffernan 5 102
(A P O'Brien, Ire) *mid-div: mainly 8th: no imp u.p fr over 2f out: kpt on into 4th without threatening fr over 1f out* **14/1**

5 3/4 **Blessyourpinksox (IRE)**[23] 4851 5-9-4 101.......................... FMBerry 7 101
(Peter Casey, Ire) *towards rr: 10th 1/2-way: no imp u.p and kpt on without threatening fr over 2f out* **10/1**

6 3/4 **Kushnarenkovo**[8] 5253 3-8-12 97...................................... MJKinane 10 100
(A P O'Brien, Ire) *sn led: rdn bef st: strly pressed and hdd over 2f out: sn no ex: kpt on same pce* **25/1**

7 4 **Race For The Stars (USA)**[10] 5191 3-8-12 110...................... KFallon 9 92
(A P O'Brien, Ire) *mid-div: mainly 7th: 6th bef st: no imp u.p and kpt on same pce fr over 2f out* **5/2**[2]

8 1 1/2 **Sacrosanct (IRE)**[8] 5253 3-8-12 94................................ CO'Donoghue 6 90
(A P O'Brien, Ire) *towards rr: niggled along bef st: sn no imp: kpt on same pce* **33/1**

9 4 **Strawberry Dale (IRE)**[30] 4646 4-9-4 .... RichardHughes 1 82
(J D Bethell) *trckd ldrs in 4th: 5th bef st: no ex u.p fr 2f out* **9/1**[3]

10 5 1/2 **Chenchikova (IRE)**[177] 753 3-8-12 .... PJSmullen 8 73
(A P O'Brien, Ire) *rr of mid-div: 9th bef st: no ex u.p fr over 2f out* **12/1**

11 3 **Sakkara Star (IRE)**[23] 4851 3-8-12 96..............................(b1) JMurtagh 4 67
(M Halford, Ire) *chsd ldrs in 6th: 7th bef st: no ex u.p fr over 2f out* **25/1**

2m 5.70s **Going Correction** -0.05s/f (Good)
WFA 3 from 4yo+ 6lb **11** Ran SP% **123.4**
Speed ratings: 112,110,109,107,106 106,102,101,98,94 91
CSF £39.84 TOTE £2.10: £1.40, £4.80, £2.30; DF 40.10.
Owner Cheveley Park Stud **Bred** Cheveley Park Stud Ltd **Trained** Newmarket, Suffolk

FOCUS
A pretty weak Group 2. The winner scored for the second year running with lots in hand and the race has been rated through the fourth.

NOTEBOOK
Red Bloom, who had to prove her effectiveness on ground with ease in it, won with a ton in hand and was going like a winner from some way out. It is difficult to believe that she has improved again, so the more likely senario is that she only had to reproduce her previous best to land this Group 2 prize again. (op 5/4 tchd 6/4)
Sina Cova(IRE), a Group 3 winner over a mile and a half this season, failed to make any impact in the Yorkshire Oaks on her previous start but shaped much better after racing prominently in the early stages. She kept on all the way to the line but was well held by the winner from over a furlong out.
Paris Winds(IRE), who cost a lot at the sales and is the daughter of a very useful mare, won her maiden over a mile at the course only last month and gave a good account of herself. She can only progress for the experience.
Be My Queen(IRE), only touched off in a Listed race when stepped up to a mile and a half at Galway on her previous start, made headway early in the straight but never threatened to get to the leaders.
Blessyourpinksox(IRE), a Listed winner and suited by easy ground, kept on steadily over the last two furlongs without ever posing a threat. (op 12/1)
Race For The Stars(USA) has failed to live up to the promise of last season, and while she has run some good races this year, she is not one to count on. (op 9/4)
Strawberry Dale(IRE) ran her second disappointing race in a row and seems to have lost her form. It might be that she does not travel very well, as she always seems to run badly when sent abroad. (op 8/1)

5466a SHELBOURNE HOTEL GOFFS MILLION 7f
3:55 (4:07) 2-Y-0
£679,310 (£196,551; £93,103; £44,827; £21,379; £6,206)

RPR

1 **Miss Beatrix (IRE)**[23] 4853 2-8-9 110.......................... DPMcDonogh 29 100+
(Kevin Prendergast, Ire) *dwlt: towards rr on far side: impr travelling wl 2f out: rdn to ld over 1f out: sn clr: comf* **6/1**[2]

2 1 1/4 **Regime (IRE)**[23] 4829 2-9-0 .... JamieSpencer 11 105+
(M L W Bell) *towards rr: rdn and styd on wl to ld stands side gp ins fnl f: nt trble wnr* **16/1**

3 3/4 **Drumfire (IRE)**[24] 4809 2-9-0 .... JoeFanning 19 100
(M Johnston) *trckd ldrs on far side: no imp u.p and kpt on same pce fr over 1f out* **7/1**

4 hd **Emerald Hill (IRE)**[79] 3126 2-9-0 .... JMurtagh 20 99
(M Halford, Ire) *sn led on far side: hdd and no imp u.p fr over 1f out: kpt on same pce* **14/1**

5 nk **Laddies Poker (USA)**[13] 5106 2-9-0 .... TPQueally 23 98
(J Noseda) *chsd ldrs on far side: no imp u.p and kpt on same pce fr over 1f out* **100/1**

6 1 1/4 **Finsceal Beo (IRE)**[18] 5005 2-8-9 .... KJManning 10 93+
(J S Bolger, Ire) *chsd ldrs on stands side: led gp 2f out: sn no imp u.p: kpt on same pce* **8/1**

7 1 **Karayel (IRE)**[82] 3026 2-9-0 .... CDHayes 28 92
(R Hannon) *prom on far side: no imp u.p and kpt on same pce fr over 1f out* **50/1**

8 2 1/2 **New World Order (IRE)**[30] 4638 2-9-0 .... FMBerry 24 85
(Declan Gillespie, Ire) *chsd ldrs on far side: no imp u.p and kpt on same pce fr over 1f out* **20/1**

9 1 3/4 **Nazdaq (IRE)** 2-9-0 .... RPCleary 26 81
(M Halford, Ire) *chsd ldrs on far side: no imp u.p and kpt on same pce fr 1 1/2f out* **33/1**

10 2 1/2 **Armigerent (IRE)**[27] 4712 2-9-0 .... KDarley 15 77+
(M Johnston) *mid-div on stands side: kpt on without threatening fr over 1f out* **33/1**

11 1/2 **He's A Decoy (IRE)**[67] 3492 2-9-0 106............................... WMLordan 8 76+
(David Wachman, Ire) *chsd ldrs on stands side: no imp u.p and kpt on same pce fr under 2f out* **13/2**[3]

12 1 3/4 **The Real Thing (IRE)**[52] 3962 2-8-9 89........................... PShanahan 18 63
(C Collins, Ire) *chsd ldrs on far side: no imp u.p and kpt on same pce fr wl over 1f out* **20/1**

13 *nk* **Fly Free**[10] [5189] 2-8-9 .... PJSmullen 3 65+
(D K Weld, Ire) *prom on stands side: no imp u.p and kpt on same pce fr 2f out* **9/2**[1]

14 *1 ½* **Codeword (IRE)**[13] [5114] 2-9-0 .... J-PGuillambert 5 66+
(M Johnston) *prom on stands side: no imp fr 2f out* **33/1**

15 *hd* **Blue Coral (IRE)**[45] [4167] 2-9-0 .... RobertWinston 17 65+
(D K Weld, Ire) *sn prom on stands side: no imp fr under 2f out* **14/1**

16 *nk* **Frosty Night (IRE)**[25] [4783] 2-9-0 .... RoystonFfrench 22 62
(M Johnston) *chsd ldrs on far side: no imp u.p fr under 2f out* **20/1**

17 *4* **Lios Tulcha (IRE)** 2-9-0 .... NGMcCullagh 9 54+
(D T Hughes, Ire) *mid-div best on stands side* **100/1**

18 *shd* **Four Sins (GER)**[37] [4412] 2-8-9 .... MJKinane 14 49+
(John M Oxx, Ire) *chsd ldrs on stands side: no imp u.p fr 2f out* **6/1**[2]

19 *2 ½* **C'Est Ca**[24] [4821] 2-9-0 .... DJCondon 2 47+
(W P Mullins, Ire) *mid-div on stands side: no imp fr 2f out* **100/1**

20 *1 ¼* **Romanov Dynasty (IRE)**[12] [5125] 2-9-0 .... WSupple 1 43+
(R Hannon) *n.d fr after 1/2-way on stands side* **100/1**

21 *nk* **Minos (IRE)**[10] [5178] 2-9-0 .... RichardHughes 7 43+
(R Hannon) *chsd ldrs to 2f out on stands side* **16/1**

22 *1 ¾* **Johannesburg Jack (IRE)**[25] [4775] 2-9-0 .... MCHussey 25 38+
(H Morrison) *chsd ldrs on stands side: no imp u.p fr under 2f out* **50/1**

23 *2 ½* **Basalt (IRE)** 2-9-0 .... JAHeffernan 6 31+
(A P O'Brien, Ire) *mid-div best on stands side* **25/1**

24 *1 ¼* **Charlie Farnsbarns (IRE)**[67] [3492] 2-9-0 ....(b[1]) LDettori 4 28+
(B J Meehan) *prom on stands side: no ex fr 2f out* **20/1**

25 *nk* **Deadshot Keen (IRE)**[66] [3531] 2-9-0 ....(b[1]) MichaelHills 16 24
(B J Meehan) *chsd ldrs on far side: no ex u.p fr under 2f out* **66/1**

26 *1 ½* **Lannleire (IRE)**[5] [5330] 2-9-0 65........ RMBurke 13 23+
(H Rogers, Ire) *nvr a factor on stands side* **100/1**

27 *¾* **Frederick Ozanam (IRE)**[52] [3961] 2-9-0 .... KFallon 12 21+
(A P O'Brien, Ire) *nvr a factor on stands side* **14/1**

28 *5* **Spirit Of The Mist (IRE)**[22] [4873] 2-9-0 .... JohnEgan 27 7+
(T J Pitt) *n.d fr after 1/2-way on stands side* **16/1**

1m 29.4s **Going Correction** +0.425s/f (Yiel) **28** Ran SP% **163.4**
Speed ratings: 106,104,103,103,103 101,100,97,95,92 92,90,89,88,88 87,83,82,80,78 78,76,73,72,71 70,69,63
CSF £112.41 TOTE £6.80: £2.30, £4.10, £2.20, £5.30; DF 269.80.
Owner William Durkan **Bred** Bill Durkan **Trained** Friarstown, Co Kildare
■ The first running of this event, Europe's richest race for two-year-olds.

FOCUS
A very well-contested race for such a valuable prize. The winner has won a Group 1, so the race should work out, despite the slight nagging doubt about the form as a result of the field splitting into two groups and the far side appearing to have a distinct advantage. It has been rated through the third, fourth, sixth and seventh.

NOTEBOOK
Miss Beatrix(IRE), the Moyglare Stakes winner, led over a furlong from home and came away for a decisive success on her side of the track. The Danehill Dancer filly has not stopped improving since she contested the opening juvenile maiden of the season, but is now finished for the year. She will be aimed at either the English or Irish 1000 Guineas and must be considered one of the best juvenile fillies around. (op 5/1)
Regime(IRE) came up the stands' side, which was the opposite side to the winner, and stayed on strongly to establish a clear lead over his group with a furlong to run, but could not get on terms with the winner. A promising colt, he has evidently progressed a lot since landing a Beverley maiden and could now come under consideration for the Racing Post Trophy. (op 14/1)
Drumfire(IRE), who won a seemingly modest renewal of the Group 3 Solario Stakes at Sandown last month, could never get on terms with Miss Beatrix but acquitted himself well. His trainer is adept at bringing tough horses through the ranks and he looks sure to go close in some valuable races next season. (op 6/1)
Emerald Hill(IRE) made much of the running on the far side before giving way to the winner with over a furlong to run. He was having his first outing since finishing a creditable fifth in the Railway Stakes here in July and lost little in defeat. He could be capable of landing a good prize.
Laddies Poker(USA), who raced on the far side, ran a terrific race and stepped up markedly on the form of his fourth in a Kempton maiden earlier this month. A maiden should prove a formality if running anywhere near this form next time.
Fly Free, who was an impressive winner of a maiden on his only previous start, was somehow made favourite over proven Group-class animals and unsurprisingly came up well short of the required class. He can, however, be given another chance as he is clearly highly rated by the stable. (op 5/1)

5468 - 5470a (Foreign Racing) - See Raceform Interactive

2913 SAINT-CLOUD (L-H)
Tuesday, September 19

OFFICIAL GOING: Good

5471a PRIX SARACA (LISTED RACE) 6f
1:30 (1:30) 2-Y-0 **£17,241** (£6,897; £5,172; £3,448; £1,724)

RPR

1 **Law Lord**[19] 2-9-0 .... CSoumillon 6 91
(A Fabre, France)

2 *nse* **Finikas**[21] 2-9-0 .... YBarberot 3 91
(S Wattel, France)

3 *3* **Testama (FR)**[31] 2-8-11 .... TJarnet 7 79
(J De Roualle, France)

4 *hd* **Afra Tsitsi (FR)**[31] [4621] 2-8-11 .... YLerner 1 78
(C Lerner, France)

5 *hd* **Gold Spirit (IRE)**[17] [5017] 2-9-0 .... FrancisNorton 5 81
(E J O'Neill) *cl up on outside, disp 2nd str, effrt whn slightly hmpd 1f out, one pace, lost 3rd cle hme (44/10)* **44/10**[1]

6 *2* **Right Place (FR)**[8] 2-9-0 ....(b) JGrosjean 2 75
(Robert Collet, France)

7 *4* **Ripping**[57] [3796] 2-8-11 .... C-PLemaire 4 60
(P Bary, France)

1m 12.5s **Going Correction** -0.775s/f (Hard) **7** Ran SP% **18.5**
Speed ratings: 97,96,92,92,92 89,84
PARI-MUTUEL: WIN 2.00; PL 1.50, 3.70; SF 14.60.
Owner Sheikh Mohammed **Bred** Bloomsbury Stud **Trained** Chantilly, France

NOTEBOOK
Gold Spirit(IRE) was slightly hampered a furlong out and that probably cost him third place. He appreciated the return to turf.

5472a PRIX JOUBERT (LISTED RACE) (FILLIES) 1m 4f
2:30 (2:30) 3-Y-0 **£17,241** (£6,897; £5,172; £3,448; £1,724)

RPR

1 **Princesse Dansante (IRE)**[24] 3-8-12 .... TThulliez 5 98
(F Doumen, France) **214/10**[2]

2 *nk* **Ivory Gala (FR)**[67] [3515] 3-8-12 .... IMendizabal 11 98
(B J Meehan) *pressed ldr off slow pce, niggled along 3f out, rdn to ld narrowly 1 1/2f out, joined 1f out, hdd 100y out, kpt on (25/1)* **25/1**[3]

3 *2 ½* **Baldoria (IRE)**[114] 3-9-2 .... JHorcajada 4 98
(M Delcher-Sanchez, Spain) **12/1**[1]

4 *½* **Rouge (FR)** 3-8-12 .... OPeslier 1 93
(C Laffon-Parias, France)

5 *snk* **Varevees**[35] [4465] 3-8-12 .... GAvranche 9 93
(J Boisnard, France)

6 *hd* **Shamarkanda (FR)**[49] [4035] 3-8-12 .... C-PLemaire 2 93
(Y De Nicolay, France)

7 *snk* **Summer Shower**[145] 3-8-12 .... JVictoire 6 92
(A Fabre, France)

8 *2* **Bayria (IRE)**[43] 3-8-12 .... CSoumillon 10 89
(A De Royer-Dupre, France)

9 *½* **Oriental Lady (IRE)**[120] 3-8-12 .... SPasquier 7 89
(E Lellouche, France)

10 *½* **Ardies**[83] 3-8-12 .... MBlancpain 8 88
(C Laffon-Parias, France)

11 **Fantastic Santanyi**[104] [2374] 3-8-12 ....(b) ASuborics 3 88
(Mario Hofer, Germany)

2m 33.7s **Going Correction** -0.45s/f (Firm) **11** Ran SP% **16.0**
Speed ratings: 104,103,102,101,101 101,101,100,99,99 99
PARI-MUTUEL: WIN 22.40; PL 5.40, 6.60, 4.60; DF 183.00.
Owner A Smurfit **Bred** Dermot Cantillon & Forenaughts Stud **Trained** Bouce, France

NOTEBOOK
Ivory Gala(FR), unlucky in running on her previous visit to France, was always prominent in a race run at a steady early pace, and that proved a distinct tactical advantage. She finished clear of the third and connections will be pleased to have secured her some valuable black type.

2062 CAPANNELLE (R-H)
Tuesday, September 19

OFFICIAL GOING: Standard

5473a PREMIO SIBERIAN EXPRESS-TROFEO ASTE SGA (DIRT) 1m
3:40 (3:55) 3-Y-0 **£8,621** (£3,793; £2,069; £1,034)

RPR

1 **Rumsfeld (ITY)**[24] [4805] 3-8-6 ....(t) MPasquale 1 104
(M Botti) *tongue tie, sn pressing ldr, 2nd str on inside, led wl over 2f out, pushed clr over 1f out, driven out (97/100F)* **97/100**[1]

2 *5* **Lift Cape (IRE)**[121] [1871] 3-8-6 .... MEsposito 7 94
(V Caruso, Italy) *5.96/1* **596/100**[2]

3 *1 ½* **Mr Kings Best (IRE)** 3-8-6 .... PAragoni 12 91
(G Colella, Italy) *34/1* **34/1**[3]

4 *1 ¼* **Villa Sciarra (IRE)**[177] [758] 3-8-6 .... MDemuro 6 88
(A Peraino, Italy)

5 *½* **Golden Knife (IRE)**[322] [6222] 3-8-3 .... MVargiu 10 84
(M Fratini, Italy)

6 *nk* **Samantha Queen (IRE)** 3-8-6 .... GGentilesca 2 86
(S Postiglione, Italy)

7 *2* **Fairy Inchinor** 3-8-6 .... DVargiu 8 82
(E Borromeo, Italy)

8 *4* **San Langfuhr (ITY)** 3-8-9 .... SBasile 3 77
(M Massimi Jr, Italy)

9 *2 ½* **Modern Tate (IRE)** 3-8-6 .... FBranca 11 69
(R Brogi, Italy)

10 *4* **Wild Groove (USA)**[303] 3-8-9 .... GBietolini 6 64
(Gianluigi Bietolini, Italy)

11 *1 ½* **Gautami** 3-8-9 ....(b) ASanna 9 61
(L Baldi, Italy)

12 *nse* **Stuck Of Caffeina (ITY)**[331] [6052] 3-8-6 .... GTemperini 4 58
(R Brogi, Italy)

1m 41.4s **12** Ran SP% **68.0**
(including one euro stakes): WIN 1.97; PL 1.30, 2.05, 4.08; DF 6.62.
Owner E Bulgheroni **Bred** Az Ag Beluschi Fabeni Fausto **Trained** Newmarket, Suffolk

NOTEBOOK
Rumsfeld(ITY), trying an All-Weather surface for the first time, broke well. Indeed his rider could have made all if he had wanted to as the race soon resolved itself into a contest between the first two. There was only one in it in the straight.

5201 GOODWOOD (R-H)
Wednesday, September 20

OFFICIAL GOING: Good
Wind: moderate, across

5474 IBETX.COM CLAIMING STKS (H'CAP) 1m
2:10 (2:10) (Class 6) (0-60,61) 3-Y-0+ **£3,238** (£963; £481; £240) **Stalls** High

Form RPR

3244 **1** **Gracie's Gift (IRE)**[34] [4531] 4-9-7 **56**........ DaneO'Neill 8 64
(A G Newcombe) *lw: mid-div: rdn and hdwy over 2f out: led and edgd rt jst ins fnl f: jst hld on* **7/1**[2]

3010 **2** *nk* **Harare**[20] [4974] 5-8-12 **50**........(b) JamesDoyle[(3)] 11 57+
(R J Price) *s.i.s: bhd: swtchd lft 2f out: sn rdn and hdwy: styd on strly but hung rt ins fnl f: jst failed* **12/1**

5040 **3** *shd* **Oakley Absolute**[11] [5166] 4-9-4 **53**........(v) RichardHughes 18 60
(R Hannon) *in tch: rdn over 2f out: styd on strly ins fnl f: wnt 3rd fnl strides* **10/1**[3]

3631 **4** *1* **Muscari**[6] [5316] 4-9-12 **61** 6ex........ DarryllHolland 3 66
(A P Jarvis) *chsd ldr: rdn over 2f out: ev ch 1f out: kpt on same pce* **12/1**

640 **5** *½* **Keep Backkinhit (IRE)**[17] [5046] 4-9-6 **55**........(b[1]) RyanMoore 7 59
(G L Moore) *mid-div: rdn 3f out: no imp tl styd on ins fnl f* **14/1**

4350 **6** 1 **Pink Bay**[19] 4984 4-9-0 **49** .... FergusSweeney 20 50+
(W S Kittow) *mid-div: nt clr run 3f out: sn swtchd lft: rdn over 1f out: styd on* **16/1**

2065 **7** ½ **Mucho Loco (IRE)**[26] 4769 3-9-0 **53** .... (b) EddieAhern 17 53
(J G Portman) *b: in tch: rdn over 2f out: kpt on same pce fnl f* **10/1**[3]

5250 **8** nk **Salvestro**[10] 5210 3-9-7 **60** .... KerrinMcEvoy 4 59
(Mrs A J Perrett) *hld up towards bk half of mid-div: rdn 3f out: styd on fnl f* **25/1**

0006 **9** ½ **Blue Line**[25] 4795 4-9-0 **49** .... ChrisCatlin 12 47
(M Madgwick) *hld up towards rr: rdn over 2f out: styd on fnl f: nrst fin* **25/1**

406 **10** ½ **Future Deal**[35] 4483 5-9-7 **56** .... GeorgeBaker 14 53
(C A Horgan) *s.i.s: towards rr: sme late prog: nvr a danger* **12/1**

0000 **11** ½ **Marcello**[18] 5035 3-9-4 **57** .... (t) JimmyFortune 16 58+
(P F I Cole) *lw: chsd ldr: rdn to ld over 1f out: hdd jst ins fnl f: sn hmpd on rails and snatched up* **33/1**

1040 **12** ½ **Aberdeen Park**[23] 4869 4-8-12 **50** .... (b) RichardKingscote(3) 1 45
(Mrs H Sweeting) *s.i.s: towards rr: hdwy over 2f out: wknd fnl f* **40/1**

10 **13** ½ **Dannabelle (IRE)**[20] 4974 6-9-3 **52** .... JamieSpencer 10 46
(John A Quinn, Ire) *led: rdn and hdd over 1f out: wknd ins fnl f* **7/2**[1]

2040 **14** 1 **Crimson Flame (IRE)**[8] 5270 3-9-6 **59** .... TonyCulhane 5 50
(M R Channon) *s.i.s: sn rcvrd to chse ldrs: rdn 3f out: wknd over 1f out* **33/1**

3135 **15** nk **Dark Moon**[10] 5210 3-8-12 **54** .... NeilChalmers(3) 19 45
(A M Balding) *chsd ldrs: rdn over 2f out: wknd fnl f* **10/1**[3]

5400 **16** nk **Aristofilia**[47] 4113 3-9-6 **59** .... JoeFanning 6 49
(P F I Cole) *chsd ldrs: rdn over 2f out: nt clr run over 1f out and again ins fnl f: no ch after* **33/1**

0300 **17** 2½ **Rowan Warning**[79] 3153 4-9-8 **57** .... NickyMackay 13 41
(J R Boyle) *lw: mid-div: effrt over 2f out: wknd over 1f out* **22/1**

0000 **18** 1¾ **Moon Bird**[18] 5032 4-9-7 **56** .... J-PGuillambert 15 36
(C A Cyzer) *s.i.s: a towards rr* **40/1**

3200 **19** nk **Endless Night**[21] 4930 3-9-7 **60** .... (t) SteveDrowne 2 40
(H Morrison) *a towards rr* **25/1**

0060 **20** 9 **Hit's Only Money (IRE)**[19] 4984 6-9-6 **55** .... (p) PatDobbs 9 14
(R A Harris) *mid-div tl wknd over 2f out* **28/1**

1m 40.66s (0.39) **Going Correction** -0.10s/f (Good)
WFA 3 from 4yo+ 4lb **20** Ran SP% **130.7**
Speed ratings (Par 101):94,93,93,92,92 91,90,90,89,89 88,88,87,86,86 86,83,81,81,72
CSF £82.08 CT £884.08 TOTE £8.90: £2.10, £4.30, £2.30, £2.40; EX 136.70.
Owner Samuel Jefford **Bred** Richard O'Hara **Trained** Yarnscombe, Devon

FOCUS
Quite a competitive claimer, run at a sound pace. The form is ordinary but solid enough.
Future Deal Official explanation: jockey said mare stumbled on leaving stalls
Marcello Official explanation: jockey said colt was hampered inside final furlong
Dannabelle(IRE) Official explanation: jockey said mare ran too free
Moon Bird Official explanation: jockey said filly missed the break

5475 IBETX MONEY MAN EBF MAIDEN STKS 1m 1f

2:45 (2:46) (Class 4) 2-Y-O **£4,533** (£1,348; £674; £336) **Stalls** High

Form RPR

0 **1** **Philanthropy**[23] 4880 2-9-3 .... JoeFanning 4 84
(M Johnston) *w'like: led for 1f: trckd ldng pair: rn sltly wd ent st: rdn over 2f out: led jst ins fnl f: kpt on wl* **7/1**

523 **2** 2 **Eglevski (IRE)**[36] 4458 2-9-3 81 .... JimmyFortune 3 80
(J L Dunlop) *led after 1f: rdn and hrd pressed fr 3f out: hdd jst ins fnl f: no ex* **9/4**[2]

3 **3** 1¼ **Prince Sabaah (IRE)**[13] 5126 2-9-3 .... (t) RichardHughes 1 78
(R Hannon) *w'like: trckd ldr after 1f: rdn to chal 3f out: kpt on same pce fr over 1f out* **5/1**[3]

3 **4** hd **Starry Messenger**[15] 5083 2-8-12 .... MartinDwyer 7 72
(M P Tregoning) *unf: swtg: chsd ldrs in 4th: carried sltly wd ent st: sn rdn: hung rt fr over 1f out: kpt on to regain 4th cl home* **5/4**[1]

30 **5** ½ **Dansimar**[15] 5083 2-8-12 .... TonyCulhane 6 71
(M R Channon) *restrained s: in last pair: rdn and hdwy into 4th 3f out: one pce fnl f* **25/1**

0 **6** 6 **Disintegration (IRE)**[34] 4525 2-9-3 .... DaneO'Neill 5 64
(A King) *s.i.s: in last pair: effrt 3f out: wknd 1f out* **33/1**

0 **7** 5 **Bring It On Home**[15] 5091 2-9-3 .... RyanMoore 2 54
(G L Moore) *in tch: drvn fr over 4f out: wknd over 2f out* **50/1**

1m 57.11s (0.25) **Going Correction** -0.10s/f (Good) 7 Ran SP% **113.1**
Speed ratings (Par 97):94,92,91,90,90 85,80
CSF £22.63 TOTE £8.60: £3.30, £1.70; EX 23.70.
Owner Jumeirah Racing **Bred** Darley **Trained** Middleham Moor, N Yorks

FOCUS
Juvenile maidens over further than a mile are not always the strongest of races, but this looked a reasonable enough contest and is rated around the runner-up.

NOTEBOOK
Philanthropy ran well below expectations on his debut over seven furlongs at Newcastle, but the step up in trip suited ideally and he basically just outstayed this lot. He took a while to get on top, giving the impression he is very much still learning, and should be able to improve again next time. The Listed Zetland Stakes over ten furlongs at Newmarket could be a suitable target. (op 9-2)
Eglevski(IRE), third to the smart Sesmen in a novice event over a mile at Nottingham on his previous start, had every chance but Philanthropy was just too strong in the closing stages. He should stay further than this nine-furlong trip next year, but it might just have stretched him at this stage of his career. (tchd 5-2 in places)
Prince Sabaah(IRE), a promising third on his debut at Chepstow, could find only the one pace upped a furlong in trip and fitted with a tongue-tie for the first time. (op 7-1)
Starry Messenger, who was a pleasing third on her debut over a mile at Leicester, failed to build on that and did not appear at home the track, hanging to her right under pressure. A more galloping track should suit better and she can yet confirm that initial promise. (op 6-4 tchd 13-8 in a place)
Dansimar came with a promising-looking effort but was unable to sustain her challenge to the line. She is probably more of a handicap prospect. (op 33-1)
Disintegration(IRE) got warm before the race and failed to take a hand at any stage.

5476 IBETX MONEY MAN STKS (H'CAP) 6f

3:20 (3:20) (Class 4) (0-85,85) 3-Y-O+ **£5,505** (£1,637; £818; £408) **Stalls** Low

Form RPR

6122 **1** **Greek Renaissance (IRE)**[23] 4888 3-9-1 **82** .... DarryllHolland 8 111+
(M P Tregoning) *lw: mde virtually all: shkn up to qckn clr 1f out: readily* **7/2**[1]

4151 **2** 5 **Forest Dane**[12] 5148 6-8-3 **71** .... JamesDoyle(3) 7 76
(Mrs N Smith) *hld up towards rr: nt clr run over 2f out: rdn and hdwy over 1f out: wnt 2nd jst ins fnl f: no ch w wnr* **8/1**[3]

0152 **3** nk **Memphis Man**[3] 5401 3-8-4 **71** oh4 .... JoeFanning 9 75
(Miss V Haigh) *t.k.h towards rr: hdwy over 2f out: sn rdn: wnt 3rd 1f out: kpt on same pce* **12/1**

3006 **4** nk **Kingscross**[25] 4807 8-8-13 **78** .... FergusSweeney 16 81+
(M Blanshard) *s.i.s: towards rr: grad swtchd rt and hdwy fr 2f out: styd on ins fnl f* **10/1**

0000 **5** 1 **Kay Two (IRE)**[11] 5169 4-8-12 **77** .... TPQueally 5 77
(R J Price) *prom: rdn over 2f out: one pce fnl f* **25/1**

2341 **6** shd **Caustic Wit (IRE)**[20] 4970 8-8-0 **72** .... TolleyDean(7) 6 72
(M S Saunders) *chsd ldrs: rdn over 2f out: kpt on same pce fnl f* **20/1**

130 **7** shd **Nusoor (IRE)**[14] 5107 3-8-10 **77** .... MartinDwyer 3 77
(W J Haggas) *hld up mid-div: rdn over 1f out: no imp* **14/1**

1204 **8** hd **Saviours Spirit**[147] 1246 5-8-12 **77** .... IanMongan 13 76
(T G Mills) *hung rt thrght: chsd ldrs: rdn over 2f out: one pce fnl f* **33/1**

4040 **9** 1½ **Balakiref**[5] 5336 7-8-12 **77** .... JamieSpencer 14 67
(M Dods) *towards rr: rdn 3f out: styd on past btn horses ins fnl f: n.d* **12/1**

-034 **9** dht **Calabaza**[33] 4564 4-8-6 **71** oh4 .... KerrinMcEvoy 12 61
(W Jarvis) *in tch: rdn over 2f out: one pce fnl f* **8/1**[3]

-400 **11** ½ **Angel Sprints**[25] 4811 4-9-1 **83** .... SaleemGolam(3) 17 71
(C J Down) *w wnr: rdn over 2f out: wknd fnl f* **25/1**

0134 **12** ¾ **Roman Quest**[68] 3487 3-8-8 **75** .... SteveDrowne 11 61
(H Morrison) *lw: mid-div: rdn 2f out: no imp whn n.m.r ins fnl f* **5/1**[2]

0533 **13** 1 **High Ridge**[16] 5058 7-8-8 **73** .... (p) RyanMoore 2 56
(J M Bradley) *a towards rr* **10/1**

0060 **14** ½ **Goodenough Mover**[16] 5070 10-8-12 **77** .... HayleyTurner 10 59
(Andrew Turnell) *mid-div tl hung rt and outpcd 2f out* **33/1**

3640 **15** 1½ **Night Prospector**[10] 5202 6-9-3 **82** .... RichardHughes 1 59
(G L Moore) *a bhd* **16/1**

000- **16** 1¾ **Dramaticus**[419] 3883 4-9-6 **85** .... TonyCulhane 4 57
(B Palling) *t: bit bkwd: swtg: in tch tl wknd over 1f out* **66/1**

1m 10.04s (-2.81) **Going Correction** -0.10s/f (Good)
WFA 3 from 4yo+ 2lb **16** Ran SP% **127.1**
Speed ratings (Par 105):114,107,106,106,105 105,104,104,102,102 102,101,99,99,97 94
CSF £29.85 CT £320.00 TOTE £4.20: £1.80, £2.50, £3.70, £2.70; EX 29.30 Trifecta £463.00 Pool: £932.54 - 1.43 winning units..
Owner Ballymacoll Stud **Bred** Ballymacoll Stud Farm Ltd **Trained** Lambourn, Berks

FOCUS
A fair sprint handicap in which Greek Renaissance marked himself down as a smart sort in the making, taking apart a competitive field and recording a hugely impressive winning time.

5477 CHARLES JAMES HOMES FOUNDATION STKS (LISTED RACE) 1m 1f 192y

3:55 (3:55) (Class 1) 3-Y-O+

£17,034 (£6,456; £3,231; £1,611; £807; £405) **Stalls** High

Form RPR

111- **1** **Imperial Stride**[382] 4948 5-9-0 120 .... KerrinMcEvoy 1 105+
(Saeed Bin Suroor) *hld up: stdy prog u.p fr 2f out: hrd rdn and hung rt 1f out whn chalng: led line* **10/11**[1]

1463 **2** shd **Kahlua Kiss**[11] 5188 3-8-3 95 .... PaulDoe 9 100
(W R Muir) *hld up: hdwy to trck ldrs and nt clr run 2f out tl ins fnl f: r.o to ld fnl strides: ct line* **16/1**

1000 **3** nk **Championship Point (IRE)**[11] 5185 3-8-8 109 .... RyanMoore 6 104
(M R Channon) *lw: hld up: swtchd lft over 3f out: sn rdn and hdwy: pressed ldr and ev ch thrght fnl f: no ex fnl strides* **10/3**[2]

3233 **4** shd **Take A Bow**[13] 5142 5-9-0 100 .... GeorgeBaker 5 104
(P R Chamings) *led for 1f: trckd ldrs: rdn to ld over 2f out: hrd pressed after: no ex whn hdd fnl strides* **14/1**

11-5 **5** shd **Nakheel**[11] 5186 3-8-8 107 .... MartinDwyer 10 106+
(M Johnston) *lw: trckd ldrs: nt clr run and dropped rr bhd wkng horse over 1f out: swtchd lft and r.o stongly fnl f: unlucky* **11/2**[3]

4015 **6** 1½ **Impeller (IRE)**[10] 5204 7-9-0 93 .... EddieAhern 7 101
(W R Muir) *lw: in tch: smooth hdwy to ld on rails 3f out: rdn and hdd over 2f out: kpt on same pce ins fnl f* **20/1**

5255 **7** 5 **Desert Cristal (IRE)**[68] 3490 5-8-9 81 .... DarryllHolland 2 87
(J R Boyle) *pushed into ld after 1f: rdn and hdd 3f out: grad fdd fr 2f out* **66/1**

2200 **8** 2½ **Local Spirit (USA)**[25] 4808 3-8-3 102 .... JoeFanning 8 82
(C E Brittain) *racd keenly: w ldr: rdn over 2f out: wknd over 1f out: hung lft ins fnl f* **25/1**

2m 5.91s (-1.84) **Going Correction** -0.10s/f (Good)
WFA 3 from 4yo+ 6lb **8** Ran SP% **113.5**
Speed ratings (Par 111):103,102,102,102,102 101,97,95
CSF £17.70 TOTE £1.90: £1.10, £3.40, £1.30; EX 20.60.
Owner Godolphin **Bred** Cliveden Stud Ltd **Trained** Newmarket, Suffolk

FOCUS
This looked a decent Listed race on paper, but the first five finished in a heap and the form should be treated with a bit of caution, with the proximity of the fifth suggesting the form is far from solid.

NOTEBOOK
Imperial Stride, a progressive performer for Sir Michael Stoute last season, needed an operation to remove bone flakes from a fetlock and this was his first outing for over a year. Understandably rusty but looking fit enough, he was well below the form he showed last term and only scrambled home, but he showed the right attitude to go through with his effort after taking a smack on the nose from a rival jockey's whip and is sure to improve with the outing under his belt. Connections are mulling over sending him down under for a tilt at the Melbourne Cup, or alternatively he could stay in Britain for the Dubai Champion Stakes. (tchd 5-6 and evens in places)
Kahlua Kiss, successful in a handicap off only 73 less than three months ago, came agonisingly close to a first Listed victory. Had she enjoyed a clear passage, she would have won, but as it was she was just denied by the favourite's late thrust. (op 14-1)
Championship Point(IRE), well held in top company since winning the Predominate Stakes here in May, ran better on this drop in both class and trip. He looked the likeliest winner at one stage but could not quite get there. (op 4-1 tchd 9-2 in places)
Take A Bow took a narrow lead against the rail and battled on, but could not quite last out. He is a smart and consistent individual but a little difficult to place. (op 10-1)
Nakheel, who became rather warm in the preliminaries, was sharper for his return to action at York. Going well when getting shuffled to the back off the field below the distance, he ran on strongly when switched wide but need a few more strides. He could go for the Champion Stakes now. (op 6-1)
Impeller(IRE) faced a stiff task at the weights and ran a commendable race in the circumstances, only fading out of the picture inside the final furlong. (op 25-1)
Desert Cristal(IRE) Official explanation: jockey said mare was unsuited by the good ground
Local Spirit(USA) failed to settle as she disputed the lead with the rank outsider and eventually dropped away.

The Form Book, Raceform Ltd, Compton, RG20 6NL

5478 **SOUTH DOWNS STKS (H'CAP)** **1m 3f**
4:30 (4:30) (Class 4) (0-85,82) 3-Y-O £5,505 (£1,637; £818; £408) Stalls Low

Form RPR
2205 **1** **Robustian**[11] 5164 3-9-0 **78**........ StephenCarson 6 84
(R F Johnson Houghton) *in tch: wnt 3rd 6f out: rdn to chal over 2f out: kpt on gamely u.p to ld fnl strides: drvn out* **15/2**[3]
4051 **2** *nk* **Island Myth (IRE)**[13] 5128 3-9-3 **81**........(b) MartinDwyer 1 86
(M P Tregoning) *trckd ldr: led over 3f out: sn rdn and hrd pressed: no ex whn hdd fnl strides* **9/1**
-431 **3** *1* **Quantum (IRE)**[52] 3977 3-9-1 **79**........ JimmyFortune 5 83+
(J H M Gosden) *swtg: trckd ldrs: niggled along over 4f out: effrt 3f out: bmpd over 2f out: kpt on ins fnl f* **13/8**[1]
6062 **4** *nk* **Charlie Tokyo (IRE)**[7] 5284 3-8-8 **77**........ JamieMoriarty(5) 7 80
(R A Fahey) *hld up: smooth hdwy fr 4f out to join ldrs on bit wl over 2f out: rdn wl over 1f out: nt qckn* **4/1**[2]
1-00 **5** *½* **Astrobella**[94] 2679 3-9-0 **78**........ TPQueally 8 80
(M H Tompkins) *b.hind: s.i.s: bhd: rdn and hdwy fr over 3f out: nt clr run briefly over 2f out: kpt on same pce fnl f* **50/1**
-440 **6** *4* **Always Baileys (IRE)**[30] 4654 3-8-8 **72**........ JoeFanning 4 68
(M Johnston) *hld up: tk clsr order 5f out: effrt and hung rt over 2f out: one pce after* **14/1**
21-0 **7** *19* **Three Thieves (UAE)**[11] 5164 3-8-12 **76**........ SteveDrowne 2 40
(M S Saunders) *sn led: rdn and hdd over 3f out: grad fdd* **25/1**
3-04 **8** *5* **First Slip**[15] 5098 3-8-6 **70**........(b[1]) JimCrowley 10 26
(Mrs A J Perrett) *swtg: trckd ldrs tl lost pl after 3f: rdn over 3f out: wknd 2f out* **25/1**
4051 **9** *dist* **Villa Sonata**[30] 4662 3-8-10 **74**........ JamieSpencer 9 —
(J R Fanshawe) *trckd ldrs tl lost pl 6f out: lost action 5f out: virtually p.u after* **4/1**[2]

2m 26.31s (-0.90) **Going Correction** -0.10s/f (Good) **9** Ran SP% **116.2**
Speed ratings (Par 103):99,98,98,97,97 94,80,77,—
CSF £70.98 CT £162.89 TOTE £8.50: £1.90, £2.50, £1.30; EX 72.90.
Owner Michael Doran & R F Johnson Houghton **Bred** T J Cooper **Trained** Blewbury, Oxon
■ Stewards' Enquiry : Martin Dwyer one-day ban: used whip with excessive frequency (Oct 2)

FOCUS
Not the strongest event of its type and limited by the proximity of the third and fifth.
Always Baileys(IRE) Official explanation: jockey said gelding hung right
Villa Sonata Official explanation: vet said filly had been struck into

5479 **JOIN THE RACING UK CLUB STKS (H'CAP)** **1m 4f**
5:05 (5:05) (Class 4) (0-80,80) 3-Y-O+ £5,505 (£1,637; £818; £408) Stalls Low

Form RPR
-514 **1** **Halla San**[33] 4544 4-8-12 **71**........ JamieMoriarty(5) 11 88
(R A Fahey) *hld up towards rr: hdwy over 3f out: sn rdn: chal over 1f out: kpt on gamely u.str.p to ld fnl strides* **10/1**
1313 **2** *hd* **Wannabe Posh (IRE)**[19] 4990 3-9-2 **78**........ EddieAhern 4 94
(J L Dunlop) *mid-div: hdwy over 3f out: led over 2f out: sn rdn and hrd pressed: kpt on gamely but no ex whn hdd fnl strides* **5/1**[2]
0-30 **3** *4* **Balance Of Power**[148] 1206 4-9-11 **79**........(t) RichardHughes 6 89
(R Charlton) *mid-div: hdwy over 3f out: rdn to chse ldng pair over 2f out: no further imp* **6/1**[3]
0000 **4** *6* **Top Seed (IRE)**[11] 5163 5-9-12 **80**........ TonyCulhane 2 80
(M R Channon) *lw: hld up bhd: rdn and stdy prog fr over 3f out: swtchd lft over 2f out: styd on* **20/1**
4315 **5** *4* **Finished Article (IRE)**[21] 4937 9-8-12 **66** oh1........ J-PGuillambert 10 63+
(P A Blockley) *hld up towards rr: rdn and weaved way through field fr 3f out: styd on* **33/1**
3023 **6** *2* **Peruvian Prince (USA)**[9] 5236 4-8-12 **66** oh1........ DarryllHolland 14 57
(J A R Toller) *mid-div: nt clr run 4f out: sn rdn: kpt on same pce fnl 2f* **16/1**
0423 **7** *2 ½* **Love Always**[11] 5163 4-9-1 **69**........ PatDobbs 1 56
(S Dow) *trckd ldrs: effrt 3f out: one pce fnl 2f* **14/1**
2202 **8** *1 ¼* **Fabrian**[12] 5149 8-9-2 **73**........ JamesDoyle(3) 5 58
(R J Price) *led for 1f: trckd ldr: led 4f out: sn rdn and hdd: sn one pce* **14/1**
2332 **9** *1 ¾* **Shore Thing (IRE)**[34] 4530 3-8-9 **71**........ TPQueally 15 53
(M H Tompkins) *mid-div: smooth hdwy to join ldrs over 3f out: rdn and ev over 2f out: one pce after* **5/1**[2]
0005 **10** *5* **Cavallini (USA)**[13] 5141 4-9-6 **74**........ RyanMoore 16 48
(G L Moore) *in tch tl lost over 6f out: nvr threatened after* **10/1**
6421 **11** *3 ½* **Buster Hyvonen (IRE)**[32] 4586 4-9-7 **75**........ JamieSpencer 9 43
(J R Fanshawe) *trckd ldrs: led over 3f out: rdn and hdd over 2f out: grad fdd: eased ins fnl f* **4/1**[1]
0-00 **12** *7* **Hills Of Aran**[11] 5163 4-9-6 **77**........ AdamKirby(3) 8 34
(W K Goldsworthy) *in tch: drvn along over 5f out: sn bhd* **66/1**
2160 **13** *hd* **Summer Charm**[18] 5016 4-9-6 **74**........ KerrinMcEvoy 7 31
(W Jarvis) *a towards rr* **16/1**
0000 **14** *9* **Triple Bluff**[12] 5152 3-8-4 **66** oh1........ MartinDwyer 3 8
(Mrs A J Perrett) *led after 1f: rdn and hdd 4f out: sn wknd* **33/1**

2m 33.95s (-4.97) **Going Correction** -0.10s/f (Good)
WFA 3 from 4yo+ 8lb **14** Ran SP% **123.0**
Speed ratings (Par 105):112,111,109,105,102 101,99,98,97,94 91,87,87,81
CSF £58.83 CT £337.82 TOTE £13.70: £3.70, £1.80, £2.80; EX 97.00.
Owner Mrs Catherine Reynard **Bred** Hascombe And Valiant Studs **Trained** Musley Bank, N Yorks
■ A first winner in England for Jamie Moriarty.

FOCUS
This looked a fair enough handicap beforehand, the pace was strong throughout, the time was very smart, and they finished well strung out behind the front pair, making the form looked solid.
Hills Of Aran Official explanation: jockey said colt never travelled
Summer Charm Official explanation: jockey said filly never picked up

5480 **RACING UK ON SKY 432 APPRENTICE STKS (H'CAP)** **5f**
5:40 (5:40) (Class 5) (0-70,69) 3-Y-O+ £3,238 (£963; £481; £240) Stalls Low

Form RPR
0002 **1** **Dancing Mystery**[32] 4587 12-8-11 **63**........(b) LiamJones(3) 4 73
(E A Wheeler) *mde all: kpt on wl: edgd rt fnl 50yds: rdn out* **8/1**[2]
0122 **2** *1 ¼* **Carcinetto (IRE)**[13] 5131 4-8-1 **55** oh3........ JamieJones(5) 8 64+
(P D Evans) *chsd ldrs: rdn over 2f out: sddle slipped whn holding ev ch over 1f out: nt rcvr* **10/1**[3]
3230 **3** *hd* **Harrison's Flyer (IRE)**[4] 5391 5-9-4 **67**........(p) NeilChalmers 16 72
(J M Bradley) *b: lw: mid-div: hdwy 2f out: rdn and ev ch 1f out: kpt on* **10/1**[3]
0201 **4** *¾* **Zazous**[33] 4564 5-8-11 **60**........ MarcHalford 9 62
(J J Bridger) *lw: towards rr: rdn over 2f out: running on whn stopped briefly ins fnl f: wnt 4th cl home* **10/1**[3]
4010 **5** *¾* **Cosmic Destiny (IRE)**[4] 5378 4-8-6 **62**........ JPFeatherstone(7) 3 61+
(E F Vaughan) *rrd leaving stalls: bhd: nt clr run whn swtchd rt and mde rapid prog to chal over 1f out: no ex ins fnl f* **20/1**
0600 **6** *½* **Salviati (USA)**[20] 4962 9-7-13 **55**........(p) PietroRomeo(7) 10 53
(J M Bradley) *b: towards rr: hdwy and nt clr run 2f out: styd on ins fnl f: nrst fin* **20/1**
564 **7** *½* **King Egbert (FR)**[13] 5131 5-8-6 **55** oh1........ JamesDoyle 15 51+
(A W Carroll) *s.i.s: bhd: styd on fnl f: nrst fin* **6/1**[1]
000 **8** *hd* **Succeed (IRE)**[46] 4164 3-8-5 **55** oh3........ RichardKingscote 11 50
(Mrs H Sweeting) *prom: rdn and ev ch over 1f out: one pce fnl f* **66/1**
2322 **9** *hd* **Light Mozart**[112] 2134 3-8-9 **66**........ WilliamCarson(7) 12 60
(C E Brittain) *chsd ldrs: rdn over 2f out: one pce fnl f* **10/1**[3]
1604 **10** *nk* **Summer Recluse (USA)**[11] 5167 7-9-6 **69**........(t) AdamKirby 20 62
(J M Bradley) *swtg: sn restrained rr: sme late prog: nvr a danger* **8/1**[2]
00 **11** *nk* **Borzoi Maestro**[74] 3297 5-8-1 **55** oh5........(p) KevinGhunowa(5) 7 47
(M Wellings) *prom tl wknd over 1f out* **33/1**
065 **12** *1* **Sweetest Revenge (IRE)**[19] 4985 5-7-13 **55** oh3... AshleyMorgan(7) 13 44
(M D I Usher) *b: nvr bttr than mid-div* **33/1**
2300 **13** *shd* **Be My Charm**[5] 5350 3-7-12 **55** oh1........ LauraReynolds(7) 18 43
(M Blanshard) *s.i.s: towards rr: making sme late prog whn nt clr run 1f out* **33/1**
3203 **14** *nk* **Monashee Prince (IRE)**[9] 5232 4-8-9 **63**........ KylieManser(5) 2 50
(J R Best) *in tch tl wknd over 1f out* **12/1**
0206 **15** *1 ½* **Sounds Simla (IRE)**[7] 5291 3-8-9 **59**........(p) AmirQuinn 6 41
(R A Harris) *chsd ldrs: rdn over 2f out: wknd over 1f out* **25/1**
4310 **16** *shd* **Stamford Blue**[4] 5378 5-8-10 **64**........(b) TolleyDean(5) 19 45
(R A Harris) *s.i.s: sn drvn to chse ldrs: wknd over 1f out* **8/1**[2]
4642 **17** *5* **Goodwood March**[16] 5055 3-8-8 **58**........ SaleemGolam 1 21
(J L Dunlop) *lw: hung bdly rt thrght and bit slipped through mouth: a towards rr* **8/1**[2]

57.67 secs (-1.38) **Going Correction** -0.10s/f (Good)
WFA 3 from 4yo+ 1lb **17** Ran SP% **126.5**
Speed ratings (Par 103):107,105,104,103,102 101,100,100,100,99 99,97,97,96,94 94,86
CSF £81.50 CT £856.97 TOTE £8.60: £2.70, £2.50, £2.90, £2.70; EX 147.90 Place 6 85.52, Place 5 30.63.
Owner Astrod TA Austin Stroud & Co **Bred** Mrs D Price **Trained** Whitchurch-on-Thames, Oxon

FOCUS
A modest but typically competitive sprint handicap and sound enough form rated around the third and fourth.
Zazous Official explanation: jockey said gelding was struck into
King Egbert(FR) Official explanation: vet said gelding finished lame
Goodwood March Official explanation: jockey said that the bit slipped
T/Jkpt: Part won. £84,777.10 to a £1 stake. Pool: £119,404.50. 0.50 winning tickets. T/Plt: £71.40 to a £1 stake. Pool: £85,416.45. 873.05 winning tickets. T/Qpdt: £11.50 to a £1 stake. Pool: £5,245.60. 335.10 winning tickets. TM

5237 REDCAR (L-H)
Wednesday, September 20

OFFICIAL GOING: Firm
The ground was 'lightning fast' and with a strong wind half-behind in all four track records were broken on the day.
Wind: strong, half-behind Weather: fine but windy

5481 **E B F CONSTANT SECURITY MAIDEN STKS** **7f**
2:00 (2:00) (Class 5) 2-Y-O £3,886 (£1,156; £577; £288) Stalls Centre

Form RPR
532 **1** **Karoo Blue (IRE)**[16] 5066 2-9-3 79........ SebSanders 16 77
(C E Brittain) *chsd ldrs: styd on wl fnl f: led nr fin* **5/2**[2]
62 **2** *hd* **King's Apostle (IRE)**[11] 5168 2-9-3........ PaulHanagan 6 76
(W J Haggas) *w ldrs: led after 2f: rdn and hung lft over 1f out: hdd towards fin* **9/2**[3]
04 **3** *1 ¼* **Until When (USA)**[24] 4843 2-9-3........ PhilipRobinson 12 73
(B Smart) *led 2f: chsd ldrs: styd on same pce fnl f* **7/1**
22 **4** *5* **Cavalry Guard (USA)**[27] 4731 2-9-3........ TedDurcan 3 60
(H R A Cecil) *swvd bdly lft s: hdwy to chse ldrs after 2f: hrd drvn over 2f out: hung rt and wknd appr fnl f* **6/4**[1]
0 **5** *1 ½* **Macaroni Gin (IRE)**[23] 4880 2-9-3........ PaulMulrennan 13 56
(J Howard Johnson) *dwlt: hdwy 3f out: kpt on: nvr nr ldrs* **40/1**
0 **6** *7* **Pegasus Prince (USA)**[23] 4880 2-9-3........ TomEaves 5 37
(Miss J A Camacho) *hdwy to chse ldrs after 2f: wknd over 2f out* **25/1**
4200 **7** *5* **Dispol Splendid (IRE)**[23] 4887 2-8-12 50........ RobbieFitzpatrick 9 18
(P T Midgley) *chsd ldrs: lost pl over 2f out* **100/1**
8 *½* **Sheriff's Silk** 2-9-3........ PaulEddery 14 22
(B Smart) *s.i.s: a outpcd and bhd* **80/1**
9 *1 ¾* **Graceful Steps (IRE)** 2-8-12........ RichardMullen 10 12
(E J O'Neill) *dwlt: outpcd and bhd: rdn and hung lft 3f out* **14/1**
00 **10** *5* **A Foot In Front**[23] 4887 2-9-3........ KimTinkler 11 4
(N Tinkler) *in tch: lost pl 3f out: sn bhd* **200/1**

1m 21.28s (-3.62) **Going Correction** -0.475s/f (Firm) 2y crse rec **10** Ran SP% **114.9**
Speed ratings (Par 95):101,100,99,93,91 83,78,77,75,69
CSF £13.71 TOTE £4.10: £1.40, £1.60, £2.60; EX 12.90.
Owner Sheikh Marwan Al Maktoum **Bred** Darley **Trained** Newmarket, Suffolk

FOCUS
Probably a fair maiden, even with favourite Cavalry Guard again disappointing, run on lightning-quick ground. The form looks reasonable, rated around the principals.

NOTEBOOK
Karoo Blue(IRE) has been progressing with racing and his recent second at Warwick behind the useful Artimino entitled him to go close once more. The below-par performance of the favourite obviously made his task easier and he dug deep under a strong ride from Sanders to narrowly edge out King's Apostle. Provisionally rated 79, he looks the sort to progress further in nurseries and is one to keep on side. (op 3-1)
King's Apostle(IRE), on his toes in the paddock and keen to post, ran well to finish second to a useful sort in Plain Painter at Chester last time and this was another good effort on ground that would probably have been a shade fast for the son of King's Best. He is now qualified for nurseries and it should not be too long before he is winning. (op 4-1)
Until When(USA) has improved with each run and he appreciated the step back up to seven furlong, but was just unable to quicken on with the front pair. He is another who is now eligible to contest handicaps and he should stay a mile in time. (op 8-1)
Cavalry Guard(USA), who showed a very poor action going to post, failed to build on a promising debut when turned over at odds of 1/4 here last time and he again failed to deliver, the step up to seven furlongs failing to bring about any improvement. The fact he moved poorly beforehand and hung during the race suggests he found the ground, which did ride very fast, too quick and a slower surface may aid him in future. (tchd 13-8)

Macaroni Gin(IRE), who showed very little on his debut at Newcastle, stepped up massively on that effort in what was a better race and was putting in some good late work. He will stay further in time and is another likely sort for handicaps next season. (op 50-1)

5482 PMPS ALWAYS ACHIEVING NURSERY 1m
2:35 (2:36) (Class 6) (0-65,71) 2-Y-O £3,238 (£963; £481; £240) Stalls Centre

Form RPR

5500 **1** **Mastership (IRE)**[24] 4829 2-9-0 **58** .... SebSanders 3 66
(C E Brittain) *dwlt and rr: hdwy 1/2-way: rdn to ld over 1f out: carried bdly lft ins last: hld on wl* **14/1**

0100 **2** *shd* **Always Best**[14] 5113 2-9-3 **61** .... KDarley 7 69
(M Johnston) *a.p: cl up 1/2-way: rdn and ev ch over 1f out: hung bdly lft ins last: kpt on* **11/1**

5200 **3** *5* **Gifted Heir (IRE)**[15] 5084 2-8-11 **55** .... RichardMullen 18 52
(I A Wood) *in tch: hdwy to chse ldrs over 2f out: sn rdn and kpt on same pce appr last* **25/1**

1451 **4** *hd* **Goose Green (IRE)**[4] 5382 2-9-10 **71** 6ex........ EdwardCreighton(3) 5 67
(M R Channon) *hld up in tch: hdwy over 2f out: rdn to chse ldrs over 1f out: sn drvn and one pce* **11/2**[2]

4310 **5** *1 1/2* **Sunstroke (IRE)**[16] 5053 2-9-1 **62** .... DominicFox(3) 1 55
(M G Quinlan) *cl up: led 3f out: rdn 2f out: drvn and hdd over 1f out: grad wknd* **14/1**

000 **6** *1* **Distant Sunset (IRE)**[46] 4163 2-9-1 **59** .... MichaelHills 13 49
(B W Hills) *dwlt and bhd tl styd on fnl 2f: nrst fin* **8/1**

0050 **7** *2* **Go Red**[35] 4466 2-9-0 **58** .... PaulMulrennan 12 44
(M W Easterby) *keen: led 2f: cl up tl rdn along wl over 2f out and sn wknd* **50/1**

0632 **8** *shd* **Hair Of The Dog**[9] 5239 2-8-11 **55** .... PaulHanagan 8 40
(J G Given) *in tch: rdn along 3f out: btn over 2f out* **3/1**[1]

004 **9** *3/4* **Cryptic Clue (USA)**[14] 5111 2-8-13 **57** .... PaulQuinn 2 41
(D W Chapman) *chsd ldrs: rdn along 3f out: drvn over 2f out and sn wknd* **40/1**

546 **10** *1 1/2* **Arabellas Homer**[35] 4466 2-8-11 **55** .... TomEaves 4 35
(Miss J A Camacho) *cl up: led after 2f: pushed along and hdd 3f out: sn wknd* **16/1**

060 **11** *hd* **Salto Chico**[45] 4171 2-9-2 **60** .... DavidAllan 10 40
(W M Brisbourne) *towards rr: rdn along and sme hdwy 3f out: no imp fnl 2f* **66/1**

0040 **12** *9* **First Valentini**[9] 5238 2-9-0 **58** ....(t) JimmyQuinn 11 17
(N Bycroft) *a towards rr* **50/1**

0650 **13** *1 1/4* **Global Traffic**[17] 5041 2-9-0 **58** .... DaleGibson 16 14
(P F I Cole) *a towards rr* **16/1**

405 **14** *9* **Spence's Choice (IRE)**[56] 3834 2-8-7 **58** .... AdeleRothery(7) 9 —
(M W Easterby) *s.i.s: a rr* **66/1**

10 **15** *1* **Slavonic Lake**[16] 5053 2-9-5 **63** .... MickyFenton 17 —
(I A Wood) *in tch on outer: rdn along 1/2-way: sn wknd and bhd* **50/1**

1110 **16** *3 1/2* **Feisty**[16] 5053 2-9-6 **64** .... FrancisFerris 15 —
(Rae Guest) *midfield: hdwy on outer 1/2-way: rdn to chse ldrs whn lost action and eased over 1f out: virtually p.u fnl f* **14/1**

004 **17** *24* **Greek God**[35] 4474 2-9-0 **58** ....(b[1]) TedDurcan 14 —
(W Jarvis) *s.i.s: rr whn stmbld bdly after 1f: sn bhd and eased* **7/1**[3]

1m 34.37s (-3.43) **Going Correction** -0.475s/f (Firm) 2y crse rec **17** Ran SP% **119.2**
Speed ratings (Par 93):98,97,92,92,91 90,88,88,87,85 85,76,75,66,65 61,37
CSF £149.97 CT £3901.86 TOTE £21.00: £3.50, £2.50, £6.20, £1.60; EX 158.60.
Owner Sheikh Marwan Al Maktoum **Bred** Darley **Trained** Newmarket, Suffolk

FOCUS
A modest but competitive nursery in which the front two drew clear and set the standard for the form.

NOTEBOOK
Mastership(IRE) looked a promising nursery prospect on his first couple of starts, but poor efforts at Lingfield and most recently Beverley - first-time in blinkers - resulted in him being hard to fancy. However, with the headgear left off he overcame a slow start and, as with his stablemate in the first, he battled on doggedly to just edge out the determined runner-up. Winning here off a mark of 58, he saw the mile out well and there could be more to come from the son of Best Of the Bests, off what should remain a lowly mark. Official explanation: trainer's rep said, regarding the improved form shown, the colt had run too free in blinkers last time and had benefited from today's better ground
Always Best, winner of a bad race at Leicester back in July, has since disappointed in nurseries, looking in desperate need of a mile, and having dropped down to a decent mark it was no surprise to see him go close. A strong traveller throughout, he battled back determinely to nearly thwart the winner and would probably have won had he not hung on the firm ground under pressure. He should find a race off this mark, with a slower surface likely to improve him further.
Gifted Heir(IRE), who finished second to Always Best at Leicester back in July, has since been disappointing, but this was a lot better and, although unable to bridge the gap on the runner-up, it was a most encouraging effort. He can be found a race off this sort of mark.
Goose Green(IRE), shouldering a 6lb penalty for last week's narrow Warwick victory, looked vulnerable under top weight, but he ran well and may have benefited from a slightly more positive ride. (op 5-1)
Sunstroke(IRE) failed to improve for a mile at Bath last time and she again gave the impression this trip stretched her. (op 16-1)
Distant Sunset(IRE) looked one of the more interesting contenders on this nursery debut, stepping up in trip after three runs, but he got going too late having slightly missed the break and could only run on through beaten horses. He should be able to find a race off this sort of mark.
Go Red ran his best race to date and travelled well for a long way, but did not appear to see out the trip as well as some. He could be of interest down in trip.
Hair Of The Dog has shown improved form the last twice which led to him being favourite for this nursery debut, but he found little under pressure and was most disappointing. (op 7-2)
Arabellas Homer Official explanation: jockey said filly stumbled 1f out and was unsuited by the firm ground
Spence's Choice(IRE) Official explanation: jockey said gelding lost its action
Feisty Official explanation: jockey said filly lost its action
Greek God Official explanation: jockey said colt stumbled at 7f mark

5483 JOHN SMITH'S REDCAR STRAIGHT-MILE CHAMPIONSHIP (QUALIFIER) (PREMIER CLAIMING STKS) 1m
3:10 (3:10) (Class 4) 3-Y-0+ £5,505 (£1,637; £818; £408) Stalls Centre

Form RPR

4623 **1** **Nanton (USA)**[12] 5149 4-10-0 75 .... JimmyQuinn 1 86
(P F I Cole) *hld up: stdy hdwy 3f out: led over 1f out: styd on strly* **11/4**[2]

1055 **2** *2* **Fremen (USA)**[4] 5357 6-9-11 86 .... AdrianTNicholls 2 79
(D Nicholls) *hld up in rr: hdwy over 2f out: hung lft and wnt 2nd 1f out: no imp* **9/4**[1]

6040 **3** *5* **Efidium**[27] 4733 8-8-10 60 ....(b) DNolan(3) 15 55
(N Bycroft) *mid-div: effrt to chse ldrs 3f out: styd on same pce fnl f* **11/1**

0500 **4** *hd* **Dispol Isle (IRE)**[27] 4729 4-8-10 64 .... TedDurcan 9 52
(T D Barron) *prom: one pce fnl 2f* **9/1**

6440 **5** *1* **Red Chairman**[9] 5240 4-8-12 50 .... DeclanMcGann(5) 12 57
(R Johnson) *trckd ldrs: wknd over 1f out* **33/1**

554 **6** *1* **Methusaleh (IRE)**[53] 3945 3-9-10 76 .... DavidAllan 14 65
(T D Easterby) *hld up in rr: sme hdwy on ins over 2f out: nvr nr ldrs* **13/2**[3]

-502 **7** *4* **Lottie**[9] 5244 5-8-6 38 .... PaulHanagan 18 34
(G Woodward) *w ldrs: led over 3f out: hdd over 1f out: sn wknd* **22/1**

2001 **8** *3* **Jaassey**[20] 4943 3-8-11 58 .... GrahamGibbons 5 36
(T D Walford) *a in rr* **10/1**

4000 **9** *nk* **Pepper Road**[27] 4729 7-8-13 45 .... RoystonFfrench 3 33
(R Bastiman) *bhd: effrt 3f out: sn btn* **50/1**

5000 **10** *1 1/2* **Zap Attack**[50] 4019 6-8-8 36 .... EdwardCreighton(3) 4 28
(J Parkes) *dwlt: t.k.h: sn trcking ldrs: wknd over 1f out* **100/1**

0500 **11** *4* **Filey Buoy**[35] 4467 4-8-8 42 .... MichaelJStainton(5) 7 21
(R M Whitaker) *mid-div: effrt 3f out: sn wknd* **66/1**

0060 **12** *6* **Young Mr Grace (IRE)**[27] 4729 6-8-13 52 .... MickyFenton 16 7
(B S Rothwell) *led tl over 3f out: sn lost pl: eased* **20/1**

-000 **13** *1* **Make Us Flush**[48] 4070 4-8-8 40 .... TonyHamilton 11 —
(A Berry) *prom: lost pl over 2f out* **125/1**

-000 **14** *2 1/2* **Lazzoom (IRE)**[107] 2282 3-8-10 45 .... StephenDonohoe(3) 8 3
(Miss Tracy Waggott) *chsd ldrs: lost pl over 2f out* **66/1**

1m 32.42s (-5.38) **Going Correction** -0.475s/f (Firm) course record
WFA 3 from 4yo+ 4lb **14** Ran SP% **117.0**
Speed ratings (Par 105):107,105,100,99,98 97,93,90,90,89 85,79,78,75
CSF £8.38 TOTE £4.20: £1.80, £1.20, £3.70; EX 11.50.The winner was claimed by N Wilson for £23,000. Jaasey (no 11) was claimed by J. Calderbank for £10,000.
Owner Sir George Meyrick **Bred** Samuel H And Mrs Rogers, Jr **Trained** Whatcombe, Oxon

FOCUS
A fair claimer in which the two at the head of the market drew nicely clear. The form is rated around the winner and the fifth.
Methusaleh(IRE) Official explanation: trainer said gelding lost its action
Jaassey Official explanation: jockey said gelding was unsuited by the firm ground
Zap Attack Official explanation: jockey said gelding had no more to give
Young Mr Grace(IRE) Official explanation: jockey said gelding lost its action
Lazzoom(IRE) Official explanation: jockey said gelding was unsuited by the firm ground

5484 PERTEMPS H'CAP 1m 2f
3:45 (3:45) (Class 5) (0-70,70) 3-Y-0+ £3,238 (£963; £481; £240) Stalls Low

Form RPR

4405 **1** **Bright Sun (IRE)**[9] 5249 5-9-8 **68** ....(t) KimTinkler 11 75
(N Tinkler) *chsd ldr: hdwy to ld 2 1/2f out: rdn wl over 1f out: drvn ins last and styd on wl* **10/1**

0313 **2** *1 1/4* **Turn Of Phrase (IRE)**[4] 5390 7-9-0 **60** ....(b) DO'Donohoe 3 65
(B Ellison) *hld up in rr: hdwy on inner 3f out: rdn over 1f out: chsd wnr ins last: kpt on* **9/2**[2]

1334 **3** *shd* **Apsara**[19] 4991 5-9-8 **68** .... TomEaves 5 73
(G M Moore) *chsd ldrs: rdn along 3f out and sn outpcd: swtchd outside and drvn over 1f out: styd on wl fnl f* **8/1**

0504 **4** *shd* **Wasalat (USA)**[11] 5173 4-9-2 **67** .... MarkLawson(5) 10 72
(D W Barker) *s.i.s and bhd: hdwy 1/2-way: effrt to chse ldrs on wd outside 2f out and sn rdn: drvn and no ex ent last* **10/1**

3240 **5** *3/4* **Avelian (IRE)**[21] 4931 3-9-2 **68** ....(tp) PaulHanagan 8 71
(W J Haggas) *in tch: rdn along and outpcd 3f out: styd on u.p appr last: nrst fin* **20/1**

2104 **6** *2 1/2* **Billy One Punch**[9] 5236 4-9-10 **70** .... SebSanders 7 68
(G G Margarson) *in tch: hdwy 4f out: rdn to chal 2f out and ev ch tl drvn and wknd ent last* **6/1**[3]

630 **7** *3* **Ali D**[5] 5354 8-8-9 **60** .... AndrewElliott(5) 16 53
(G Woodward) *bhd tl sme late hdwy* **14/1**

5121 **8** *nk* **Coalpark (IRE)**[14] 5108 3-9-3 **69** ....(t) KDarley 1 64+
(M Johnston) *prom: rdn along over 3f out: drvn and wknd 2f out* **7/2**[1]

0-00 **9** *3/4* **Razed**[106] 2324 3-9-0 **69** .... GregFairley(3) 2 60
(M Johnston) *dwlt: sn trcking ldrs: rdn along over 3f out: sn wknd* **40/1**

0202 **10** *1 1/2* **Emperor's Well**[27] 4730 7-8-11 **57** ....(b) PaulMulrennan 17 45
(M W Easterby) *led: rdn along 3f out: sn hdd & wknd* **16/1**

0344 **11** *1/2* **Westering Home (IRE)**[35] 4470 3-8-11 **63** .... MickyFenton 12 50
(J Mackie) *a rr* **14/1**

2305 **12** *2* **Tour D'Amour (IRE)**[6] 5312 3-8-11 **66** .... StephenDonohoe(3) 14 49
(R Craggs) *chsd ldrs: rdn along over 3f out: sn wknd* **14/1**

2m 4.95s (-1.85) **Going Correction** -0.125s/f (Firm)
WFA 3 from 4yo+ 6lb **12** Ran SP% **117.1**
Speed ratings (Par 103):102,101,100,100,100 98,95,95,95,93 93,91
CSF £53.85 CT £384.63 TOTE £14.00: £3.40, £1.70, £3.00; EX 95.40.
Owner Leeds Plywood And Doors Ltd **Bred** Terence McDonald **Trained** Langton, N Yorks

FOCUS
A modest handicap but they went a good pace and the form looks solid enough.
Ali D Official explanation: jockey said gelding never travelled
Coalpark(IRE) Official explanation: trainer's rep had no explanation for the poor form shown

5485 TRANSMORE VAN HIRE (S) STKS 1m 2f
4:20 (4:20) (Class 6) 3-5-Y-0 £2,730 (£806; £403) Stalls Low

Form RPR

0042 **1** **Second Reef**[9] 5248 4-9-1 54 .... DavidAllan 16 57
(E J Alston) *swtchd lft sn after s: hld up in rr: stdy hdwy on ins over 3f out: swtchd rt 2f out: styd on to ld ins last* **7/1**[2]

0000 **2** *3/4* **Thornaby Green**[9] 5240 5-8-8 46 .... DeanHeslop(7) 7 56
(T D Barron) *led tl hdd and no ex ins last* **16/1**

4625 **3** *nk* **Keisha Kayleigh (IRE)**[35] 4467 3-8-7 54........(v) StephenDonohoe(3) 3 56
(B Ellison) *chsd ldrs: chal 1f out: no ex towards fin* **9/2**[1]

0565 **4** *1 1/4* **Bolckow**[7] 5285 3-8-6 55 .... AndrewMullen(3) 4 53
(K A Ryan) *sn prom: kpt on same pce fnl 2f* **8/1**[3]

0610 **5** *7* **Rock Haven (IRE)**[28] 4709 4-9-7 52 ....(p) MickyFenton 15 46
(J Mackie) *chsd ldrs: hung lft and wknd over 1f out* **14/1**

0000 **6** *nk* **World At My Feet**[9] 5240 4-8-10 45 ....(t) JimmyQuinn 8 34
(N Bycroft) *mid-div: hdwy over 3f out: sn chsng ldrs: wknd 2f out* **25/1**

3013 **7** *nk* **Seattle Robber**[25] 4137 4-9-7 63 ....(b) TPO'Shea 1 45
(P A Blockley) *prom: rdn over 2f out: sn btn* **9/2**[1]

0-32 **8** *nk* **Frenchgate**[37] 4425 5-9-1 40 .... RoystonFfrench 12 38
(I W McInnes) *prom on outer: effrt over 3f out: wknd over 2f out* **8/1**[3]

0500 **9** *hd* **Etijahaat (IRE)**[6] 5316 4-9-1 53 .... PaulMulrennan 10 38
(C W Fairhurst) *swtchd lft s: hld up in rr: sme hdwy 3f out: nvr on terms* **33/1**

2250 **10** *1 3/4* **Beau Marche**[8] 5267 4-9-7 51 ....(b) SebSanders 2 40
(G G Margarson) *chsd ldrs: wknd over 2f out* **10/1**

2300 **11** *3/4* **Airedale Lad (IRE)**[34] 4511 5-9-1 45 .... VHalliday 11 33
(R M Whitaker) *in rr: sme hdwy 3f out: nvr a factor* **22/1**

5564 **12** *2* **Peters Delite**^{9} [5240] 4-9-1 46 .... PaulHanagan 13 — 29
(R A Fahey) *mid-div: effrt over 3f out: sn lost pl* **7/1**^{2}

0005 **13** *4* **Aqua**^{22} [4909] 4-8-10 36 .... RobbieFitzpatrick 5 — 17
(P T Midgley) *mid-div: hdwy u.p 3f out: sn wknd* **50/1**

000 **14** *3 1/2* **Gavanello**^{22} [4909] 3-8-2 39 .... JamieHamblett$^{(7)}$ 17 — 15
(M C Chapman) *in rr: sme hdwy 5f out: nvr on terms* **100/1**

046/ **15** *5* **Delfinia**^{528} [3138] 5-8-10 38 .... SilvestreDeSousa 14 — —
(Miss Tracy Waggott) *bhd: reminders 6f out* **50/1**

0- **16** *1* **Welcome Spirit**^{341} [5878] 3-8-3 ow1 .... RussellKennemore$^{(7)}$ 6 — 4
(J S Haldane) *bhd: sme hdwy over 3f out: sn lost pl* **100/1**

000- **17** *33* **Apple Annie**^{470} [2364] 3-8-4 40 .... CatherineGannon 9 — —
(M E Sowersby) *in tch: lost pl over 3f out: sn bhd: t.o* **66/1**

2m 5.04s (-1.76) **Going Correction** -0.125s/f (Firm)
WFA 3 from 4yo+ 6lb **17** Ran SP% **123.8**
Speed ratings (Par 101):102,101,101,100,94 94,94,93,93,92 91,90,86,84,80 79,52
CSF £108.56 TOTE £7.70: £2.10, £6.00, £1.90; EX 166.30.There was no bid for the winner
Owner Valley Paddocks Racing Limited **Bred** A Brazier **Trained** Longton, Lancs

FOCUS
An ordinary seller in which the first four pulled well clear. The race has been rated around the third.
Frenchgate Official explanation: jockey said gelding was unsuited by the firm ground

5486 PERTEMPS EMPLOYMENT ALLIANCE H'CAP — 5f
4:55 (4:55) (Class 5) (0-70,70) 3-Y-0+ **£3,238** (£963; £481; £240) **Stalls** Centre

Form — RPR

1460 **1** **Henry Hall (IRE)**^{11} [5169] 10-9-3 **68** .... KimTinkler 18 — 77
(N Tinkler) *stdd and swtchd lft s: sn in tch: pushed along and hdwy 2f out: rdn to chse ldr ins last: styd on to ld nr line* **11/1**

0404 **2** *hd* **The Leather Wedge (IRE)**^{20} [4952] 7-8-11 **62** .... SebSanders 10 — 70
(R Johnson) *dwlt: sn led: clr 2f out: rdn ent last: hdd and no ex nr line* **6/1**^{2}

1604 **3** *1* **Strensall**^{27} [4725] 9-9-2 **67** .... PaulHanagan 12 — 71
(R E Barr) *prom: rdn to chse ldr 2f out: drvn and nt qckn ent last* **12/1**

3600 **4** *shd* **Ryedane (IRE)**^{6} [5309] 4-9-3 **68** .... DavidAllan 15 — 72
(T D Easterby) *chsd ldrs: rdn along wl over 1f out: kpt on u.p ins last* **7/1**^{3}

2114 **5** *hd* **Talcen Gwyn (IRE)**^{4} [5378] 4-8-11 **62** .... (v) TedDurcan 17 — 65
(M F Harris) *chsd ldrs on wd outside: rdn wl over 1f out: kpt on ins last* **11/4**^{1}

2406 **6** *nk* **Conjecture**^{8} [5275] 4-9-5 **70** .... RoystonFfrench 8 — 72
(R Bastiman) *chsd ldr: rdn 2f out: kpt on same pce appr last* **6/1**^{2}

0230 **7** *hd* **Diamond Katie (IRE)**^{13} [5131] 4-8-2 **56** oh5 .... AndrewMullen$^{(3)}$ 6 — 57
(N Tinkler) *chsd ldrs: rdn along and outpcd 1/2-way: kpt on u.p appr last* **16/1**

0001 **8** *1* **Dark Champion**^{15} [5078] 6-8-2 **58** .... (v) MichaelJStainton$^{(5)}$ 9 — 55
(R E Barr) *midfield: rdn along 2f out: sn drvn and no imp* **6/1**^{2}

5335 **9** *1* **Trombone Tom**^{43} [4232] 3-8-6 **58** oh3 ow2 .... PaulMulrennan 3 — 51
(J R Norton) *prom: rdn along 2f out: sn wknd* **20/1**

600 **10** *nk* **Mint**^{15} [5081] 3-8-13 **65** .... TonyHamilton 1 — 57
(D W Barker) *a towards rr* **33/1**

6020 **11** *1 3/4* **Slipperfoot**^{32} [4611] 3-8-4 **56** oh1 .... (p) GrahamGibbons 2 — 41
(J J Quinn) *a towards rr* **25/1**

0000 **12** *hd* **Soviet Legend (IRE)**^{49} [4056] 3-8-1 **56** oh9 .... (b) EdwardCreighton$^{(3)}$ 5 — 40
(T J Etherington) *midfield: rdn along 1/2-way: sn wknd* **100/1**

6220 **13** *nk* **Weakest Link**^{31} [4636] 5-8-5 **56** oh9 .... (p) PaulQuinn 16 — 39
(E J Alston) *a towards rr* **28/1**

500 **14** *2* **Obe Bold (IRE)**^{20} [4957] 5-8-0 **56** oh8 .... (v) NataliaGemelova$^{(5)}$ 7 — 31
(A Berry) *in tch: rdn along and outpcd after 2f: sn bhd* **33/1**

56.01 secs (-2.69) **Going Correction** -0.475s/f (Firm) course record
WFA 3 from 4yo+ 1lb **14** Ran SP% **122.9**
Speed ratings (Par 103):102,101,100,99,99 99,98,97,95,95 92,92,91,88
CSF £72.07 CT £827.35 TOTE £14.00: £4.40, £1.90, £4.50; EX 67.40.
Owner James Marshall & Mrs Susan Marshall **Bred** Newberry Stud Company **Trained** Langton, N Yorks

FOCUS
A modest sprint handicap, with quite a few horses out of the handicap, dominated by those drawn in double digits. The course record was lowered by the winner and the form looks sound.

5487 TRANSMORE VAN HIRE H'CAP — 6f
5:30 (5:31) (Class 6) (0-65,69) 3-Y-0+ **£2,388** (£705; £352) **Stalls** Centre

Form — RPR

0611 **1** **Elkhorn**^{9} [5243] 4-8-13 **56** .... (b) TomEaves 13 — 66
(Miss J A Camacho) *sn trcking ldrs: led ins last: rdn out* **4/5**^{1}

0310 **2** *3/4* **Petite Mac**^{23} [4885] 6-8-13 **63** .... SuzzanneFrance$^{(7)}$ 17 — 71
(N Bycroft) *in rr: hdwy over 1f out: styd on wl towards fin* **18/1**

3112 **3** *1/2* **Littledodayno (IRE)**^{5} [5350] 3-9-7 **69** 6ex .... EdwardCreighton$^{(3)}$ 7 — 76
(M Wigham) *mid-div: hdwy 2f out: styd on to take 2nd ins last: no ex* **5/1**^{2}

0146 **4** *1/2* **Compton Plume**^{20} [4957] 6-9-2 **59** .... DaleGibson 2 — 64
(M W Easterby) *sn chsng ldrs: outpcd over 2f out: styd on fnl f* **16/1**

0505 **5** *hd* **Nistaki (USA)**^{7} [5286] 5-9-2 **62** .... PatrickMathers$^{(3)}$ 18 — 66
(D Shaw) *chsd ldrs: styd on fnl f* **11/1**

0000 **6** *nk* **Observatory Star (IRE)**^{27} [4735] 3-9-1 **60** .... TedDurcan 3 — 64
(T D Easterby) *hld up: hdwy 2f out: styd on fnl f* **25/1**

3004 **7** *1/2* **No Grouse**^{4} [5386] 6-9-2 **59** .... DavidAllan 9 — 61
(E J Alston) *sn outpcd and in rr: hdwy 2f out: styd on ins last* **10/1**^{3}

0300 **8** *nk* **Whinhill House**^{20} [4957] 6-8-11 **59** .... (p) MarkLawson$^{(5)}$ 14 — 63+
(D W Barker) *chsd ldrs: led over 2f out: hdd & wknd ins last* **25/1**

4000 **9** *1 3/4* **Flur Na H Alba**^{27} [4735] 7-9-0 **57** .... (v) GrahamGibbons 4 — 53
(J J Quinn) *chsd ldrs: wknd over 1f out* **28/1**

5000 **10** *nk* **Brut**^{6} [5309] 4-9-5 **62** .... PaulHanagan 16 — 57
(D W Barker) *s.i.s: kpt on fnl 2f: nvr nr ldrs* **22/1**

0406 **11** *1 1/2* **Safranine (IRE)**^{4} [5370] 9-8-9 **57** .... AnnStokell$^{(5)}$ 8 — 47
(Miss A Stokell) *mid-div: drvn over 2f out: sn outpcd* **33/1**

-000 **12** *3/4* **Golband**^{34} [4507] 4-8-10 **60** .... AshleyHamblett$^{(7)}$ 10 — 48
(R F Marvin) *led tl over 2f out: sn wknd* **100/1**

060 **13** *5* **Laith (IRE)**^{8} [5269] 3-9-3 **62** .... MickyFenton 5 — 35
(Miss V Haigh) *s.i.s: hung lft and bhd fnl 2f* **50/1**

68.68 secs (-3.02) **Going Correction** -0.475s/f (Firm)
WFA 3 from 4yo+ 2lb **13** Ran SP% **122.2**
Speed ratings (Par 101):101,100,99,98,98 98,97,96,94,94 92,91,84
CSF £17.50 CT £57.79 TOTE £1.80: £1.10, £4.60, £1.60; EX 20.90 Place 6 £215.82, Place 5 £132.34.
Owner Lee Bolingbroke & Partners VI **Bred** George Strawbridge **Trained** Norton, N Yorks

FOCUS
An ordinary handicap and straightforward form to rate based on the performances of the third and fourth.
No Grouse Official explanation: jockey said gelding was unsuited by the firm ground
Whinhill House Official explanation: jockey said saddle slipped
Safranine(IRE) Official explanation: jockey said mare was unsuited by the firm ground

T/Plt: £314.60 to a £1 stake. Pool: £54,123.05. 125.55 winning tickets. T/Qpdt: £38.90 to a £1 stake. Pool: £3,695.80. 70.20 winning tickets. JR

5488 - 5490a (Foreign Racing) - See Raceform Interactive

5314 PONTEFRACT (L-H)
Thursday, September 21

OFFICIAL GOING: Good to firm
Wind: Slight behind

5491 EUROPEAN BREEDERS FUND POPPIN LANE MAIDEN STKS (DIV I) — 6f
2:30 (2:31) (Class 4) 2-Y-0 **£4,533** (£1,348; £674; £336) **Stalls** Low

Form — RPR

1 **Passified** 2-8-12 .... JohnEgan 9 — 68
(D R C Elsworth) *in tch: hdwy over 2f out: chsd ldrs over 1f out: sn rdn and styd on to ld last 75 yds* **7/2**^{2}

43 **2** *hd* **Danehillsundance (IRE)**^{11} [5206] 2-9-3 .... RyanMoore 11 — 72
(R Hannon) *a.p: rdn along wl over 1f out: led jst ins last: sn drvn: hdd and no ex last 75 yds* **13/8**^{1}

0 **3** *2 1/2* **Multitude (IRE)**^{16} [5076] 2-9-3 .... DavidAllan 7 — 65
(T D Easterby) *led: rdn along 2f out: drvn and hdd jst ins last: kpt on same pce* **33/1**

4 *3/4* **My Super Bird (USA)** 2-9-3 .... JoeFanning 3 — 62+
(M Johnston) *chsd ldres: rdn along and sltly outpcd 2f out: styd on wl fnl f* **11/2**

0 **5** *2* **Yungaburra (IRE)**^{85} [2973] 2-9-3 .... RobertWinston 4 — 56
(G A Swinbank) *trckd ldrs: pushed along 2f out: eased ins last* **5/1**^{3}

004 **6** *1* **Miss Havisham (IRE)**^{14} [5139] 2-8-12 45 .... DarryllHolland 1 — 48
(J R Weymes) *prom: rdn along over 2f out: grad wknd* **25/1**

0 **7** *3/4* **Surprise Pension (IRE)**^{33} [4608] 2-9-3 .... GrahamGibbons 5 — 51
(J J Quinn) *a towards rr* **33/1**

8 *7* **Run Free** 2-9-3 .... TomEaves 10 — 30
(N Wilson) *a towards rr* **16/1**

0 **9** *1 1/2* **Kings Shillings**^{7} [5315] 2-9-3 .... DanielTudhope 6 — 26
(D Carroll) *s.i.s: a rr* **25/1**

10 *6* **Soylent Green** 2-8-5 .... CharlotteKerton$^{(7)}$ 2 — 3
(S Parr) *s.i.s: a rr* **66/1**

11 *68* **Good Etiquette** 2-9-3 .... TonyHamilton 8 — —
(Mrs S Lamyman) *dwlt: a rr* **33/1**

1m 18.61s (1.21) **Going Correction** +0.05s/f (Good) **11** Ran SP% **116.3**
Speed ratings (Par 97):93,92,89,88,85 84,83,74,72,64 —
CSF £8.77 TOTE £5.00: £1.60, £1.20, £6.40; EX 11.60.
Owner D R C Elsworth **Bred** The Lavington Stud **Trained** Newmarket, Suffolk

FOCUS
Probably a fair maiden and the front two drew clear, but the winning time was 0.35 seconds slower than the second division, suggesting the form is ordinary.

NOTEBOOK
Passified, related to several very speedy sorts, comes from a stable whose juveniles tend to need their first run, but she knew her job sufficiently and really picked up well in the final furlong to mow down the favourite. There was plenty to like about this effort and the daughter of Compton Place looks worthy of a rise in class, possibly the £250000 Tattersalls Auction Stakes at Newmarket, a race his trainer won with Cape Columbine. (op 4-1 tchd 10-3)
Danehillsundance(IRE), who ran to a similar level as on his debut when third behind Dodge City at Goodwood last time, looked to have been found a good opportunity and he was given every chance to win, but he may have bumped into a useful filly and had no answer to her inside the final half a furlong. A reproduction of this effort should see him winning sooner rather than later. (tchd 6-4 and 7-4)
Multitude(IRE) stepped up massively on his debut effort and improved for the rise to six furlongs. He will be qualified for nurseries after one more run and should do well in that sphere.
My Super Bird(USA), who should be suited by this distance at this stage of his career, has already been gelded but he showed ability and actually shaped as though a rise in distance would help. His stable's juveniles often improve for a run and there should be more to come. (op 6-1 tchd 13-2 and 5-1)
Yungaburra(IRE) was another to show significantly improved form on his debut effort, not being beaten far despite being eased late on as a result of feeling the fast ground. He is another likely type for nurseries, once qualified. Official explanation: trainer said colt was unsuited by the good to firm ground (op 6-1)
Good Etiquette Official explanation: trainer said gelding was unsuited by the good to firm ground

5492 RACING UK ON CHANNEL 432 FILLIES' NURSERY — 1m 4y
3:00 (3:00) (Class 4) (0-85,74) 2-Y-0 **£5,181** (£1,541; £770; £384) **Stalls** Low

Form — RPR

644 **1** **Fiumicino**^{12} [5178] 2-9-1 **68** .... RobertWinston 9 — 76
(M R Channon) *towards rr: hdwy on outer after 3f and sn trcking ldrs: effrt 2f out: rdn to ld ent fnl f and sn drvn: kpt on* **5/1**^{2}

5203 **2** *1/2* **Fongs Gazelle**^{7} [5322] 2-8-11 **64** .... JoeFanning 12 — 71
(M Johnston) *a.p: led 3f out: rdn wl over 1f out: drvn and hdd ent last: kpt on wl u.p* **4/1**^{1}

030 **3** *1/2* **Doubly Guest**^{56} [3868] 2-8-9 **62** .... EddieAhern 5 — 68+
(G G Margarson) *hld up in tch: rival's cap tangled in bridle after 2f: hdwy 3f out: rdn to chse ldng pair over 1f out: drvn and kpt on ins* **20/1**

0000 **4** *5* **Featherlight**^{17} [5053] 2-8-3 **56** .... (b^{1}) ChrisCatlin 10 — 50
(N A Callaghan) *cl up: rdn along 3f out: kpt on same pce fnl 2f* **18/1**

605 **5** *5* **Dee Cee Elle**^{87} [2924] 2-8-7 **60** .... KDarley 7 — 43
(M Johnston) *bhd tl styd on fnl 2f: nrst fin* **20/1**

0301 **6** *1/2* **Group Force (IRE)**^{7} [5323] 2-8-3 **56** 6ex .... JimmyQuinn 11 — 38
(M H Tompkins) *stdd and swtchd lft s: hld up and bhd tl swtchd wd and hdwy ent st: sn rdn and no imp* **10/1**

4316 **7** *5* **Coconut Queen (IRE)**^{27} [4761] 2-9-4 **71** .... RoystonFfrench 6 — 41
(Mrs A Duffield) *chsd ldrs: rdr lost cap after 2f: rdn along over 3f out and sn wknd* **8/1**

3143 **8** *1 3/4* **Capannina**^{41} [4335] 2-9-6 **73** .... TPQueally 8 — 39
(J Noseda) *a rr* **4/1**^{1}

5000 **9** *3/4* **Splendored Love (USA)**^{34} [4558] 2-8-11 **64** .... RyanMoore 3 — 28
(R Hannon) *trckd ldrs on inner: rdn along over 2f out: wknd over 2f out* **18/1**

200 **10** *5* **Lady Best (IRE)**^{25} [4829] 2-8-9 **62** .... (b^{1}) PaulHanagan 1 — 15
(J R Weymes) *a towards rr* **50/1**

3521 **11** *nk* **Dancing Granny**^{21} [4949] 2-9-2 **74** .... AndrewElliott$^{(5)}$ 13 — 26
(M L W Bell) *sn led: rdn along and hdd 3f out: sn wknd* **6/1**^{3}

1m 46.09s (0.39) **Going Correction** +0.05s/f (Good) **11** Ran SP% **113.2**
Speed ratings (Par 94):100,99,99,94,89 88,83,81,81,76 75
CSF £23.59 CT £370.10 TOTE £6.90: £2.00, £1.70, £6.80; EX 25.00.
Owner Mrs T G Trant **Bred** Eurostrait Ltd **Trained** West Ilsley, Berks

FOCUS
The front trio drew clear in what was a modest nursery and the form looks sound.

NOTEBOOK

Fiumicino has shown improved form since being upped to this distance and the move into handicap company brought about the necessary improvement for her to get her head in front. She is bred to appreciate further in time, being related to several stayers, and there should be more to come from her. (op 7-1 tchd 9-2)

Fongs Gazelle has raised her game since being upped to this distance and, having finished a good third to The Illies at Yarmouth last time, she again ran a good race in defeat. She may stay a bit further and seems to be progressing with racing. (op 7-2)

Doubly Guest ◆ was probably unlucky. Having qualified for this with the standard three runs, she moved up menacingly, but a rival jockey's cap got caught up in her bridle and distracted her by flapping around in front of her nose. Still only beaten a length, she may have won without the distraction, but will remain on a lowly mark and can gain compensation sooner rather than later.

Featherlight was a bit adrift of the front trio, but she showed improved form in the first-time blinkers and very much shaped as though ten furlongs will help. (op 20-1)

Dee Cee Elle was struggling from an early stage on this nursery debut, but she put in some good late work and will be of definite interest in ten-furlong nurseries. (op 25-1)

Group Force(IRE), a cosy winner in first-time blinkers at Yarmouth, was entitled to respect under a 6lb penalty, but this was a better race and she was unable to make any impression having been held up.

Capannina has twice run well in defeat since winning at Wolverhampton in July, but she was well below form on this step up to a mile and was beaten far too early for it to be put down to the distance. Official explanation: trainer had no explanation for the poor form shown (op 3-1)

5493 S B HONDA H'CAP — 5f

3:30 (3:31) (Class 5) (0-75,75) 3-Y-0+ — **£4,533** (£1,348; £674; £336) **Stalls** Low

Form — RPR

2405 **1** **Namir (IRE)**[5] [5378] 4-8-5 **64**.....(vt) PatrickMathers(3) 5 — 70
(D Shaw) *trckd ldrs: hdwy 2f out: rdn to ld ins last: drvn and kpt on wl towards fin* **10/1**

0135 **2** *hd* **Bahamian Ballet**[17] [5058] 4-9-1 **71**..... RichardMullen 14 — 76
(E S McMahon) *rr: hdwy 2f out: swtchd outside and rdn ent last: fin wl* **11/1**

1353 **3** *shd* **Bahamian Duke**[26] [4812] 3-8-0 **62**..... AndrewElliott(5) 4 — 67
(K R Burke) *a.p: effrt 2f out: rdn and edgd lft ent last: sn drvn and kpt on* **10/1**

5420 **4** *1* **Winthorpe (IRE)**[24] [4885] 6-8-7 **63**..... GrahamGibbons 9 — 65
(J J Quinn) *in tch: hdwy to chse ldrs wl over 1f out: sn rdn and nt qckn ins last* **14/1**

0354 **5** *½* **Kings College Boy**[8] [5286] 6-9-3 **73**.....(b) PaulHanagan 16 — 73
(R A Fahey) *midfield: hdwy opn outer 2f out: rdn and edgd lft over 1f out: sn drvn and kpt on same pce ins last* **8/1**[3]

0006 **6** *hd* **Amanda's Lad (IRE)**[10] [5243] 6-8-0 **61** oh14..... AurelioMedeiros(5) 3 — 60
(M C Chapman) *chsd ldrs on inner: rdn wl over 1f out: kpt on same pce ins last* **80/1**

5002 **7** *nk* **Paddywack (IRE)**[8] [5286] 9-8-5 **61** oh5.....(b) PaulQuinn 7 — 64+
(D W Chapman) *sn outpcd and bhd: hdwy wl over 1f out: swtchd rt 1f out: swtchd lft and nt clr run ins last: kpt on* **10/1**

0302 **8** *1 ½* **Blackheath (IRE)**[6] [5333] 10-9-2 **72**..... JoeFanning 12 — 65+
(D Nicholls) *midfield: hdwy to chse ldrs wl over 1f out: sn rdn and nt clr run ent last: swtchd lft and n.m.r: no imp* **13/2**[2]

4054 **9** *¾* **Princess Cleo**[16] [5081] 3-8-11 **68**..... DavidAllan 10 — 58
(T D Easterby) *chsd ldrs: rdn wl over 1f out: edgd lft: n.m.r and wknd ent last* **8/1**[3]

3350 **10** *1* **Almaty Express**[135] [1563] 4-8-8 **64**.....(b) DarryllHolland 1 — 50
(J R Weymes) *led: clr 1/2-way: rdn wl over 1f out: hdd & wknd ins last* **20/1**

1133 **11** *shd* **Blue Maeve**[13] [5148] 6-9-4 **74**..... SilvestreDeSousa 8 — 60+
(A D Brown) *stmbld s: rr tl styd on fnl 2f* **11/4**[1]

6000 **12** *1 ½* **Whistler**[5] [5378] 9-8-5 **61** oh3.....(b) PaulFitzsimons 13 — 41
(Miss J R Tooth) *a towards rr* **40/1**

6030 **13** *1 ¼* **Straffan (IRE)**[28] [4729] 4-8-5 **61** oh20.....(b) DaleGibson 11 — 37
(J Hetherton) *a towards rr* **100/1**

00 **14** *½* **Alexia Rose (IRE)**[25] [4834] 4-8-5 **61** oh7..... FrancisNorton 2 — 35
(A Berry) *midfield: rdn along on inner over 2f out: wknd over 1f out* **50/1**

3500 **15** *41* **Betsen (IRE)**[7] [5309] 4-8-7 **63**.....(t) AdrianTNicholls 15 — —+
(D Nicholls) *chsd ldrs: pushed along whn n.m.r and lost pl wl over 1f out: sn heavily eased* **22/1**

63.75 secs (-0.05) **Going Correction** +0.05s/f (Good)
WFA 3 from 4yo+ 1lb — **15** Ran SP% **120.2**
Speed ratings (Par 103):102,101,101,99,99 98,98,95,94,93 92,90,88,87,22
CSF £108.31 CT £1168.21 TOTE £13.20: £4.20, £4.20, £3.80; EX 173.60.
Owner ownaracehorsecouk (S A Mapletoft) **Bred** B Kennedy **Trained** Danethorpe, Notts
■ Stewards' Enquiry : Andrew Elliott two-day ban; careless riding (Oct 2-3)

FOCUS

An ordinary handicap run that produced a tight finish. The form, rated around the third, is limited by the proximity of the sixth from out of the handicap.

Paddywack(IRE) Official explanation: jockey said gelding was denied a clear run
Blackheath(IRE) Official explanation: jockey said gelding was denied a clear run
Princess Cleo Official explanation: jockey said filly suffered interference in running

5494 DALBY SCREW-DRIVER H'CAP — 1m 2f 6y

4:00 (4:01) (Class 2) (0-100,98) 3-Y-0+
£12,464 (£3,732; £1,866; £934; £466; £234) **Stalls** Low

Form — RPR

4/11 **1** **Corran Ard (IRE)**[97] [2621] 5-9-0 **85**..... RyanMoore 5 — 93+
(Evan Williams) *hld up in tch: hdwy 3f out: rdn to chal over 1f out: drvn to ld ins last: hld on wl* **5/2**[1]

0020 **2** *hd* **Along The Nile**[26] [4810] 4-8-12 **83**.....(t) TonyCulhane 4 — 91
(K G Reveley) *hld up in rr: hdwy on outer wl over 1f out: rdn and ev ch ins last: drvn and no ex towards fin* **12/1**

-420 **3** *1 ½* **Book Of Music (IRE)**[26] [4791] 3-9-7 **98**..... RobertWinston 8 — 104+
(Sir Michael Stoute) *trckd ldrs on inner: effrt and n.m.r wl over 1f out: swtchd rt and rdn whn nt clr run ins last: kpt on* **4/1**[2]

0000 **4** *nk* **Go Tech**[7] [5310] 6-8-12 **83**..... DavidAllan 3 — 88
(T D Easterby) *set stdy pce: qcknd 3f out: rdn over 1f out: drvn and hdd ins last: kpt on same pce* **4/1**[2]

5000 **5** *¾* **Red Lancer**[19] [5010] 5-9-4 **89**..... PaulHanagan 2 — 92
(R A Fahey) *towards rr and hmpd after 1f: hdwy on outer wl over 1f out: sn rdn along: edgd lft and kpt on ins last: nrst fin* **11/2**[3]

0035 **6** *½* **Salamanca**[8] [5300] 4-9-9 **94**..... SteveDrowne 1 — 96
(S Kirk) *in tch: rdn along over 3f out: drvn and one pce fr wl over 1f out* **10/1**

0413 **7** *1 ¾* **Day To Remember**[81] [3128] 5-9-7 **92**.....(t) EddieAhern 9 — 91
(E F Vaughan) *cl up: rdn along 2f out: wknd appr last* **8/1**

2m 11.67s (-2.41) **Going Correction** +0.05s/f (Good)
WFA 3 from 4yo+ 6lb — **7** Ran SP% **111.9**
Speed ratings (Par 109):111,110,109,109,108 108,107
CSF £31.71 CT £113.97 TOTE £3.00: £1.70, £4.20; EX 40.70 Trifecta £78.30 Pool £540.75, 4 w/u.
Owner E Salmon **Bred** Eamon Salmon **Trained** Cowbridge, Vale Of Glamorgan

FOCUS

A decent handicap run at a fair pace and another good performance by the tough and progressive Corran Ard.

NOTEBOOK

Corran Ard(IRE) ◆, who overcame a long absence to score at Sandown back in April, defied a 4lb rise back there over ten furlongs next time and he looked to hold every chance of completing the hat-trick on this first start since. As was the case with both his previous wins, he showed a determined attitude and willingly stuck his neck out to hold the challenge of Along The Nile. He seems to only do enough and as a result should not go up too much in the weights, giving him every chance of making it four. (op 10-3 tchd 7-2)

Along The Nile, who ran so poorly at Sandown last month, left all memories of that effort behind with a storming run in second, running on strongly but being unable to get by the determined winner. He should find a race of this nature if able to repeat the form. (op 9-1)

Book Of Music(IRE), who blatantly failed to stay a mile and five at Chester, was aided by the drop back in trip and would have been involved in the finish had he received a bit more luck in running, not getting the breaks when he needed them. He has yet to realise his potential and is not one to give up on just yet. (op 7-2)

Go Tech is capable of decent form on his day and he gave it a bold go from the front, but was brushed aside racing into the final furlong and was run out of the placings. (tchd 9-2)

Red Lancer ran an improved race on this drop in distance and was unlucky not to get closer, being hampered early and never really able to get in a blow. He has been threatening to win again and is one to keep a close eye on in the coming weeks. (op 6-1)

Salamanca was struggling some way out and remains winless in over a year. (op 11-1)

Day To Remember has been in decent form, but the way he dropped away was disappointing. (tchd 15-2)

5495 EUROPEAN BREEDERS FUND FRIER WOOD MAIDEN STKS — 1m 4y

4:30 (4:31) (Class 4) 2-Y-O — **£5,181** (£1,541; £770; £384) **Stalls** Low

Form — RPR

1 **Ommraan (IRE)** 2-9-3..... PhilipRobinson 10 — 77
(M A Jarvis) *hld up in tch: carried wd bnd after 1f: hdwy 3f out: rdn to ld ent last: edgd lft and styd on wl* **10/11**[1]

05 **2** *nk* **Alpes Maritimes**[17] [5067] 2-9-3..... DarryllHolland 5 — 76
(G Wragg) *trckd ldrs: hdwy 2f out: swtchd rt and rdn over 1f out: styd on strly ins last: jst hld* **9/1**[3]

3 **3** *shd* **Tempelstern (GER)**[25] [4829] 2-9-3..... TedDurcan 7 — 76
(H R A Cecil) *prom: rn wd bnd after 1f: hdwy 3f out: led 2f out and sn rdn: drvn and hdd ent last: edgd rt and kpt on* **13/8**[2]

0 **4** *10* **Cadwell**[51] [4018] 2-9-3..... AdrianTNicholls 1 — 53
(D Nicholls) *led: rdn along 3f out: hdd 2f out: wknd over 1f out* **66/1**

5 *1 ¼* **Bayonyx (IRE)** 2-9-3..... TomEaves 2 — 50
(J Howard Johnson) *hld up: hdwy over 3f out: rdn along 2f out: kpt on ins last: nrst fin* **20/1**

00 **6** *nk* **Crosby Jemma**[15] [5111] 2-8-12..... JimmyQuinn 6 — 45
(J R Weymes) *chsd ldrs: rdn along over 2f out: grad wknd* **100/1**

0 **7** *½* **Amanda Carter**[38] [4424] 2-8-12..... PaulHanagan 12 — 43
(R A Fahey) *s.i.s: a rr* **50/1**

0 **8** *2 ½* **Fairy Slipper**[25] [4830] 2-8-12..... TonyHamilton 8 — 38
(Jedd O'Keeffe) *dwlt: a towards rr* **100/1**

0 **9** *7* **Sadler's Hill (IRE)**[8] [5293] 2-9-3..... ChrisCatlin 11 — 27
(N A Callaghan) *keen: cl up tl rdn along over 3f out and sn wknd* **50/1**

05 **10** *2* **Glorious View**[19] [5025] 2-9-3..... DaleGibson 13 — 22
(M W Easterby) *a rr* **100/1**

000 **11** *14* **Hesaguru (IRE)**[15] [5112] 2-9-3 45..... PaulMulrennan 4 — —
(J R Norton) *a rr* **400/1**

1m 47.28s (1.58) **Going Correction** +0.05s/f (Good) — **11** Ran SP% **113.9**
Speed ratings (Par 97):94,93,93,83,82 82,81,79,72,70 56
CSF £9.86 TOTE £2.00: £1.30, £1.50, £1.10; EX 10.80.
Owner Sheikh Ahmed Al Maktoum **Bred** Tony Doyle **Trained** Newmarket, Suffolk

FOCUS

Not many could be fancied in this ordinary maiden, and it was not a surprise to see the principals finish well clear. The form looks sound enough.

NOTEBOOK

Ommraan(IRE), who cost 175,000gns, is a half-brother to Coney Kitty, a Listed-race winner in Ireland and Grade 3 winner in the US. He was a bit keen in the early stages and was carried wide on the bend, but he always looked likely to overhaul the Cecil-trained colt and found the line coming just in time to hold on from the fast-finishing runner-up. There should be better to come from him and he is a nice middle-distance prospect for next season. (op Evens)

Alpes Maritimes has improved with each start and the step up to a mile was always going to suit him. Staying on strongly in the closing stages, he might well have got there in a few more strides, and stamina certainly seems to be his strong suit. (op 8-1)

Tempelstern(GER), whose debut form had been given a boost when the winner went on to finish runner-up in the Goffs Million, ran another good race in defeat, but he ran wide on the first bend and his rider looked down on more than one occasion, and the impression left was that he was not at home on the fast ground. He can win his maiden on an easier surface. (op 15-8)

Cadwell showed the benefit of his debut run and knew a lot more about what was required this time. Making the running from his inside draw position, he could not live with the first three in the final two furlongs, but he shaped with a modicum of promise.

Bayonyx(IRE), who has a good middle-distance pedigree, kept on late without getting seriously involved and shaped as though there might be better to come in time. (op 25-1)

5496 EUROPEAN BREEDERS FUND POPPIN LANE MAIDEN STKS (DIV II) — 6f

5:00 (5:01) (Class 4) 2-Y-O — **£4,533** (£1,348; £674; £336) **Stalls** Low

Form — RPR

45 **1** **Odin Dawn**[6] [5339] 2-9-3..... RyanMoore 3 — 78
(R Hannon) *trckd ldrs: hdwy 2f out: swtchd rt and rdn over 1f out: styd on ins last to ld last 100 yds* **11/4**[2]

65 **2** *1 ¼* **Deadline (UAE)**[17] [5066] 2-9-3..... JoeFanning 4 — 74
(M Johnston) *led: rdn along wl over 1f out: drvn ent last: hdd and one pce last 100 yds* **5/2**[1]

03 **3** *3* **Rocker**[13] [5147] 2-9-3..... EddieAhern 9 — 65
(P W Chapple-Hyam) *chsd ldrs: hdwy on outer 2f out: sn rdn and ev ch tl one pce ins last* **9/2**[3]

50 **4** *nk* **Leptis Magna**[14] [5125] 2-9-3..... PaulDoe 8 — 65+
(W J Knight) *towards rr: hdwy 2f out: swtchd rt and rdn over 1f out: kpt on ins last: nrst fin* **14/1**

6050 **5** ½ **Luscivious**[6] 5349 2-9-0 68..............................(b[1]) StephenDonohoe(3) 6 63
(A J McCabe) *cl up: rdn 2f out: wknd over 1f out* **33/1**

46 **6** 1 **Venetian Dancer (IRE)**[29] 4705 2-9-3 .... TedDurcan 5 60
(M J Wallace) *chsd ldrs: rdn along 2f out: bmpd and wknd over 1f out* **6/1**

7 3½ **Scene Three** 2-8-12 .... GrahamGibbons 1 45
(J J Quinn) *s.i.s: bhd tl sme late hdwy* **66/1**

63 **8** nk **Ask Yer Dad**[15] 5112 2-9-3 .... MickyFenton 7 49
(Mrs P Sly) *midfield: rdn along on outer over 2f out: no hdwy* **20/1**

05 **9** 2½ **Jenny Geddes (IRE)**[23] 4913 2-8-12 .... PaulHanagan 2 36
(R A Fahey) *chsd ldrs on inner: rdn along 3f out: sn wknd* **14/1**

5 **10** ¾ **Onatopp (IRE)**[56] 3878 2-8-12 .... DavidAllan 10 34
(T D Easterby) *prom on outer: rdn along over 2f out: sn wknd* **20/1**

11 34 **Hillside Smoki (IRE)** 2-8-12 .... TonyHamilton 11 —
(A Berry) *slowly away: a outpcd and wl bhd* **100/1**

1m 18.26s (0.86) **Going Correction** +0.05s/f (Good) **11 Ran SP% 116.0**
Speed ratings (Par 97):96,94,90,89,89 87,83,82,79,78 33
CSF £9.31 TOTE £3.70: £1.40, £1.20, £1.90; EX 11.20.
Owner D J Walker **Bred** I Wilson **Trained** East Everleigh, Wilts

FOCUS
Just an ordinary maiden, but the winning time was 0.35 seconds faster than the first division and looks more solid.

NOTEBOOK
Odin Dawn has run well in defeat behind a couple of useful sorts in maidens and this lesser affair presented him with a great opportunity to break his maiden. He took his time to get on top, but won going away in the end and should prove as effective at seven furlongs, with him also having the option on nurseries now. (op 3-1 tchd 9-4)
Deadline(UAE) looked the one to beat, but he was not particularly well suited by the drop back to six furlongs and found himself readily outpaced by the winner. He is qualified for nurseries now though and should do better in that sphere, back up in trip. (op 3-1 tchd 9-4 in a place)
Rocker failed to improve as anticipated for this step back up to six furlongs, but he is another who can now contest nurseries. (op 4-1)
Leptis Magna ran a nice race on this third maiden start, keeping on into fourth without being given an overly hard time. The move into handicaps is going to make him interesting and he looks one to keep on side for his rookie trainer, who has made a really encouraging start.
Luscivious ran a little better in the first-time blinkers, but he failed to see his race out and remains exposed.
Venetian Dancer(IRE) is another who can now concentrate on nurseries, with a step back up in trip likely to suit. (op 7-1 tchd 15-2)

5497 BETFAIR.COM APPRENTICE SERIES H'CAP (FINAL ROUND) 1m 2f 6y
5:30 (5:31) (Class 6) (0-65,71) 3-Y-O+ **£3,238** (£963; £481; £240) **Stalls Low**

Form RPR

3611 **1** **Air Biscuit (IRE)**[9] 5258 3-9-8 71 6ex..............................(t) JonjoMilczarek(5) 9 79+
(C F Wall) *hld up: stdy hdwy on outer over 3f out: led 1f out: edgd lft ins last: comf* **9/4**[1]

2-P0 **2** 1¾ **Royal Master**[114] 2108 4-9-3 55.............................. AshleyHamblett 10 60
(P C Haslam) *prom: hdwy over 3f out: rdn to chal over 1f out and ev ch tl one pce ins last* **14/1**

6U51 **3** 1½ **Ruby Legend**[6] 5354 8-9-9 61 6ex..............................(p) JamesReveley 13 63
(K G Reveley) *chsd ldrs: hdwy over 2f out: rdn wl overr 1f out: kpt on same pce ins last* **8/1**

0000 **4** 1 **Captivate**[131] 1661 3-8-0 49 oh9..............................(p) MCGeran(5) 6 49
(A J McCabe) *dwlt and bhd: hdwy on inner wl over 1f out: kpt on ins last: nrst fin* **50/1**

0016 **5** 2 **Lenoir (GER)**[9] 5260 3-9-4 62..............................(v) ThomasO'Brien 11 58
(V Smith) *in tch: hdwy to chse ldrs over 2f out: sn rdn and kpt on same pce appr last* **7/1**

6363 **6** 2 **Fairy Monarch (IRE)**[2] 5445 7-8-11 49..............................(b) DanielleMcCreery 5 41
(P T Midgley) *hld up and bhd: hdwy on outer wl over 1f out: nt rch ldrs* **9/2**[2]

0000 **7** shd **Galloping Gertie**[91] 2789 4-8-6 49 oh19.............................. JPFeatherstone(5) 15 41
(J Hetherton) *midfield: rdn along over 3f out: sn btn* **100/1**

0042 **8** ½ **Viable**[16] 5090 4-9-6 63.............................. JosephWalsh(5) 17 54
(Mrs P Sly) *led and sn clr: rdn along over 2f out: hdd 1f out and wknd qckly* **8/1**

5126 **9** nk **Kirkhammerton (IRE)**[61] 2137 4-8-4 49 oh7..............................(v) AdamCarter(7) 16 40
(A J McCabe) *chsd clr ldr: rdn over 2f out: wknd over 1f out* **22/1**

0600 **10** 4 **Parisian Playboy**[135] 1573 6-8-11 49 oh8..............................(t) CharlotteKerton 14 32
(A D Brown) *chsd ldrs: rdn along over 3f out: sn wknd* **66/1**

4260 **11** 32 **River Logic (IRE)**[12] 5173 3-9-2 60.............................. TolleyDean 7 —
(A D Brown) *chsd ldrs: rdn along over 3f out: sn wknd* **6/1**[3]

2m 14.24s (0.16) **Going Correction** +0.05s/f (Good)
WFA 3 from 4yo+ 6lb **11 Ran SP% 113.4**
Speed ratings (Par 101):101,99,98,97,96 94,94,93,93,90 64
CSF £34.79 CT £214.04 TOTE £2.80: £1.40, £3.70, £2.80; EX 40.50 Place 6 £37.13, Place 5 £24.71.
Owner M Sinclair **Bred** Farmers Hill Stud **Trained** Newmarket, Suffolk
■ Tolley Dean won this series for the second year running, despite finishing last here.
■ Stewards' Enquiry : Ashley Hamblett one-day ban: used whip down the horse's shoulder in forehand position (Oct 2)

FOCUS
Modest form, anchored by the performance of the fourth from out of the handicap.
River Logic(IRE) Official explanation: jockey said gelding never travelled
T/Jkpt: £10,243.90 to a £1 stake. Pool: £115,425.25. 8.00 winning tickets. T/Plt: £98.30 to a £1 stake. Pool: £82,821.85. 614.50 winning tickets. T/Qpdt: £18.70 to a £1 stake. Pool: £3,687.80. 145.80 winning tickets. JR

5498 - 5500a (Foreign Racing) - See Raceform Interactive

4343
ASCOT (R-H)
Friday, September 22
OFFICIAL GOING: Good to soft changing to soft after race 1 (2.00)
Wind: almost nil

5501 JEAN BRYANT MEMORIAL H'CAP 6f
2:00 (2:02) (Class 2) (0-100,100) 3-Y-O
£15,580 (£4,665; £2,332; £1,167; £582; £292) **Stalls Centre**

Form RPR

1121 **1** **Al Qasi (IRE)**[25] 4888 3-8-13 95.............................. KerrinMcEvoy 17 112+
(P W Chapple-Hyam) *lw: a travelling wl trcking ldrs: led over 2f out: r.o wl to assert ins fnl f: readily* **9/4**[1]

2310 **2** 2 **Burning Incense (IRE)**[7] 5336 3-8-12 94..............................(b) SteveDrowne 18 105
(R Charlton) *lw: hld up towards rr: hdwy over 2f out: sn rdn: wnt 2nd ent fnl f: kpt on but a hld by wnr* **10/1**

2152 **3** 1¾ **Charles Darwin (IRE)**[21] 4988 3-8-7 89.............................. PaulHanagan 3 95
(M Blanshard) *lw: trckd ldrs: rdn and ev ch over 1f out: kpt on same pce* **14/1**

4531 **4** ¾ **Ripples Maid**[13] 5171 3-8-10 92.............................. RichardThomas 11 96
(J A Geake) *in tch: rdn 2f out: kpt on to go 4th ins fnl f* **10/1**

5066 **5** ½ **Trafalgar Bay (IRE)**[15] 5143 3-8-11 93.............................. JamieSpencer 5 95+
(S Kirk) *lw: squeezed out s: towards rr: rdn over 2f out: styd on wl fr over 1f out: nt rch ldrs* **12/1**

1121 **6** 2 **Buachaill Dona (IRE)**[30] 4717 3-9-2 98.............................. AdrianTNicholls 15 94+
(D Nicholls) *racd freely: hld up mid-div: hdwy over 2f out: ev ch wl over 1f out: sn rdn: one pce fnl f* **6/1**[2]

2150 **7** ¾ **King Orchisios (IRE)**[13] 5182 3-9-0 96..............................(p) NCallan 6 90
(K A Ryan) *wnt lft s: led tl over 2f out: sn one pce* **20/1**

2031 **8** shd **Damika (IRE)**[40] 4403 3-8-8 90.............................. MichaelHills 13 84
(R M Whitaker) *s.i.s: towards rr: hdwy 2f out: sn rdn: no further imp* **14/1**

4002 **9** nk **Obe Brave**[19] 5044 3-9-3 99.............................. LDettori 2 92
(M R Channon) *a mid-div* **17/2**[3]

1003 **10** 2½ **Phantom Whisper**[41] 4345 3-8-6 88.............................. JimCrowley 9 73
(B R Millman) *mid-div for 4f: hung rt fnl 2f* **33/1**

0420 **11** 4 **Gallery Girl (IRE)**[30] 4717 3-8-7 89.............................. DavidAllan 10 62
(T D Easterby) *trckd ldrs: rdn over 2f out: grad fdd* **25/1**

6505 **12** 1¾ **Dingaan (IRE)**[16] 5116 3-8-6 88..............................(b[1]) MartinDwyer 7 56
(A M Balding) *lw: s.i.s: a towards rr* **50/1**

0313 **13** ½ **Guest Connections**[12] 5212 3-8-5 87 ow1..............................(v) JohnEgan 16 54
(M R Channon) *s.i.s: towards rr: hdwy 3f out: wknd 2f out* **20/1**

6153 **14** 1¾ **The Snatcher (IRE)**[30] 4707 3-8-12 94.............................. RichardHughes 12 55
(R Hannon) *mid-div: rdn 3f out: wknd 2f out* **33/1**

0133 **15** nk **Come Out Fighting**[16] 5116 3-8-13 95.............................. TPO'Shea 14 55
(P A Blockley) *mid-div tl wknd 2f out* **16/1**

1026 **16** 1½ **Lady Livius (IRE)**[19] 5044 3-8-11 93.............................. RyanMoore 8 49
(R Hannon) *chsd ldrs tl wknd over 2f out* **28/1**

1m 13.23s (-1.67) **Going Correction** -0.10s/f (Good) **16 Ran SP% 125.3**
Speed ratings (Par 107):107,104,102,101,100 97,96,96,96,92 87,85,84,82,81 79
CSF £23.14 CT £285.25 TOTE £3.30: £1.40, £2.70, £3.00, £2.40; EX 35.60 Trifecta £678.90 Part won. Pool £956.28, 0.10 winning units..
Owner Ziad A Galadari **Bred** T C Butler **Trained** Newmarket, Suffolk

FOCUS
A decent and competitive sprint handicap. Despite the stalls being placed against the stands' rail, the field all bunched towards the centre of the track and the front pair came from the two highest berths. Surprisingly, given the rain that had fallen and the ground being described as soft by the jockeys, the winning time was just 0.11 seconds slower than the best time recorded since the redevelopment, set by Les Arcs in the Golden Jubilee at the Royal Meeting. The form looks strong and solid.

NOTEBOOK
Al Qasi(IRE) ◆, proven in soft ground and whose defeat of Greek Renaissance at Ripon last time now looks very smart form indeed, continued his rise up the ladder with a very smooth victory off an 11lb higher mark. He was always travelling very well and only needed to be nudged out to see off the runner-up. At his current rate of improvement, he looks a potential Pattern-class sprinter. (op 3-1)
Burning Incense(IRE), switched off out the back as usual, put his Ayr Silver Cup flop firmly behind him with a very solid effort. He briefly looked a threat to the favourite when brought with his effort wide entering the last furlong, but could do little when that rival found extra. He almost certainly ran into a high-class sprinting prospect here so there was no disgrace in this defeat. (op 9-1)
Charles Darwin(IRE) ◆, a winner on his last visit here, was racing off a 5lb higher mark but posted a fine effort in defeat and did much the best of those drawn low. He seems to handle all ground and there will be other days for him.
Ripples Maid, left alone by the Handicapper following her victory in a Chester Listed event last time, showed that he was right to do so and she was not disgraced in finishing a staying-on fourth back against the boys. She looks capable of winning off this sort of mark, but that may not be so important with her value as a broodmare assured. (op 9-1)
Trafalgar Bay(IRE) ◆, despite having gained his last two victories over this trip, gives the impression that he needs the extra furlong these days and was noted finishing well from off the pace after getting pinched out by the pair drawn either side of him at the start. He is gradually creeping back down the handicap and there could be another race in him before the turf season ends.
Buachaill Dona(IRE), raised 7lb for his York success, had every chance but did not help his cause by racing too freely back over this extra furlong and that eventually look its toll. (op 9-2)
King Orchisios(IRE) made much of the early running before finding the demands too great. The Handicapper seems to have his measure at present.

5502 PRINCESS ROYAL PRICEWATERHOUSECOOPERS STKS (GROUP 3) (F&M) 1m 4f
2:35 (2:37) (Class 1) 3-Y-O+
£28,390 (£10,760; £5,385; £2,685; £1,345; £675) **Stalls High**

Form RPR

2161 **1** **Acts Of Grace (USA)**[22] 4979 3-8-6 93.............................. KerrinMcEvoy 1 108
(J L Dunlop) *hld up in midfield: hdwy over 3f out: led over 2f out: styd on wl: rdn out* **14/1**

4032 **2** 1¼ **Gower Song**[9] 5300 3-8-6 95.............................. JohnEgan 5 107
(D R C Elsworth) *hld up towards rr: hdwy 4f out: chsd wnr over 1f out: kpt on wl: a hld* **12/1**

-202 **3** 3 **Bunood (IRE)**[29] 4741 3-8-6 96.............................. MartinDwyer 12 102
(J L Dunlop) *t.k.h: hld up in tch: effrt 3f out: kpt on to take 3rd ins fnl f* **17/2**

-341 **4** 1¾ **Reform Act (USA)**[46] 4212 3-8-6 .... PJSmullen 8 100
(D K Weld, Ire) *in tch: jnd ldrs over 2f out: one pce appr fnl f* **9/2**[2]

11-6 **5** 5 **Under The Rainbow**[138] 1509 3-8-6 88.............................. EddieAhern 4 93
(P W Chapple-Hyam) *stdd in rr s: hdwy on outside 3f out: wknd 2f out* **50/1**

4631 **6** 19 **Aryaamm (IRE)**[17] 5086 3-8-7 87 ow1.............................. LDettori 15 67
(M A Jarvis) *lw: w ldrs: led over 3f out tl over 2f out: wknd qckly* **16/1**

0-62 **7** 2 **Aunt Julia**[118] 2023 4-9-0 100.............................. SteveDrowne 2 64
(R Hannon) *bhd: rdn over 2f out: passed btn horses* **25/1**

1225 **8** 5 **Scottish Stage (IRE)**[50] 4079 3-8-6 109.............................. RyanMoore 13 57+
(Sir Michael Stoute) *lw: towards rr and nvr gng wl: rdn and hdwy 3f out: wknd 2f out* **5/2**[1]

6165 **9** 28 **Quenched**[14] 5155 3-8-6 105.............................. RichardHughes 9 17
(J H M Gosden) *chsd ldrs tl wknd over 2f out: eased whn no ch over 1f out* **6/1**[3]

1665 **10** 7 **Power Girl (GER)**[29] 4741 4-9-0 98.............................. JamieSpencer 11 8
(P F I Cole) *led tl over 3f out: sn wknd: eased whn no ch over 1f out* **20/1**

4220 **11** 56 **Teide Lady**[35] 4565 3-8-6 66.............................. FrancisFerris 10 —
(Rae Guest) *w ldrs tl sddle slipped and p.u over 5f out: sn wl bhd and eased* **100/1**

-256 **12** 10 **Guilia**[76] 3293 3-8-6 100.............................. NCallan 14 —
(Rae Guest) *in tch tl wknd 4f out: eased whn no ch fnl 2f* **9/1**

10-1 **13** *5* **Soft Centre**[139] 1472 3-8-6 102 DaneO'Neill 7 —
(Mrs A J Perrett) *lw: in tch: rdn 7f out: struggling to hold pl whn hmpd over 5f out: sn wl bhd and eased* **12/1**

2m 35.64s (2.64) **Going Correction** +0.45s/f (Yiel)
WFA 3 from 4yo 8lb **13** Ran SP% **121.1**
Speed ratings (Par 113):109,108,106,105,101 89,87,84,65,61 23,17,13
CSF £168.72 TOTE £16.30: £4.40, £3.10, £2.50; EX 154.70 Trifecta £411.50 Pool £985.49, 1.70 winning units.
Owner Prince A A Faisal **Bred** Nawara Stud **Trained** Arundel, W Sussex
■ This event was previously run at Ascot's October meeting.

FOCUS
Not the most competitive of Group races despite the size of the field, but the pace was decent The winning time confirms the ground on the round course was more testing than the straight - the runners made for the outside of the track under the trees racing up from Swinley Bottom - and the conditions seemed to take their toll on several of these fillies, particularly those that forced the pace, for the field finished spread out all over Berkshire. The level of the form looks fairly sound, rated through the third.

NOTEBOOK
Acts Of Grace(USA) ◆ had landed a Listed race over this trip on easy ground at Chantilly last time, so she was never going to be bothered by the softening ground here. Given a patient ride, she stayed on well after taking it up soon after turning for home and looks a filly very much on the up. (op 16-1)
Gower Song, a most consistent filly but facing her stiffest task to date, was suited by the return to this trip and by the decent pace which enabled her to be switched off early and produced late. Her finishing effort was not quite enough to get her on terms with the winner, but this was still a career-best effort. (tchd 11-1)
Bunood(IRE), a stable-companion of the winner and, like her, suited by the softening ground, plugged on to take third but never looked like winning and failed to confirm York running with Gower Song on identical terms. (op 14-1)
Reform Act(USA) has shown her best form in Ireland on good or faster ground, so may not have been helped by the rain, especially as she was trying her longest trip to date. Under the circumstances she ran well, especially as she did best of those that raced closer to the pace. (tchd 4-1)
Under The Rainbow, racing for the first time since her dismal effort in the Pretty Polly on her reappearance back in May, looked a brief threat on the wide outside soon after turning in but her effort soon flattened out. This was still not a bad effort at this level and she was entitled to have needed it.
Aryaamm(IRE), taking a massive step up in class, raced up with the pace for a long way but, like most of those that were at the sharp end early, she failed to get home. (op 14-1)
Scottish Stage(IRE), already proven in top company and the best horse in the race on official ratings, never looked happy. It was only her class that saw her emerge with a very brief chance soon after straightening up for home before the wheels came off. This was far too bad to be true. Official explanation: jockey said filly lost its action (op 9-4 tchd 3-1)
Quenched should have performed better on this drop in class yet in the event she ran a stinker. The ground may have been one reason, though she did run well enough on soft ground on her racecourse debut. Official explanation: jockey said filly had no more to give (op 8-1)
Teide Lady Official explanation: jockey said saddle slipped

5503 WATERSHIP DOWN STUD SALES STKS 6f 110y
3:10 (3:15) (Class 2) 2-Y-O
£136,570 (£54,628; £27,314; £13,643; £6,821; £6,821) **Stalls** Centre

Form RPR
0142 **1** **Indian Ink (IRE)**[29] 4737 2-8-9 RichardHughes 22 105+
(R Hannon) *lw: a travelling wl: mid div: smooth hdwy to ld on bit 2f out: sn cruised clr: impressive* **9/4**[1]
3 **2** *3* **Siamese Cat (IRE)**[6] 5371 2-8-12 PJSmullen 24 100
(B J Meehan) *n.m.r s: bhd: hdwy over 2f out: rdn to go 2nd over 1f out: no ch w wnr* **20/1**
5 **3** *3* **Diamond Diva**[7] 5344 2-8-0 ChrisCatlin 12 80
(J W Hills) *mid-div: rdn and hdwy 2f out: styd on but edgd lft ins fnl f* **25/1**
3 **4** *3 ½* **Whazzis**[28] 4762 2-8-10 JamieSpencer 2 81
(W J Haggas) *s.i.s: towards rr: rdn and hdwy 2f out: chsd ldrs over 1f out: kpt on same pce* **8/1**
032 **5** *1 ½* **Baltic Belle (IRE)**[19] 5043 2-8-6 85 RyanMoore 16 73
(R Hannon) *towards rr: styd on fr over 1f out: nvr trbld ldrs* **25/1**
30 **6** *¾* **Naughty Thoughts (IRE)**[32] 4657 2-8-2 CatherineGannon 4 67
(K A Ryan) *in tch: rdn whn short of room briefly 2f out: styd on fnl f* **66/1**
4213 **7** *1 ¾* **Russian Rosie (IRE)**[22] 4966 2-8-4 ow1 EddieAhern 3 64
(J G Portman) *prom: rdn to ld over 2f out: sn hdd: one pce after* **8/1**
0100 **8** *2* **Addictive**[28] 4761 2-8-0 PaulHanagan 19 55
(S C Williams) *mid-div: rdn over 2f out: one pce after* **80/1**
0000 **9** *nk* **Riverside Dancer (USA)**[29] 4736 2-8-6 87 (p) NCallan 13 60
(K A Ryan) *in tch: effrt 3f out: wknd fnl f* **33/1**
4131 **10** *2 ½* **Pretty Majestic (IRE)**[28] 4762 2-8-11 88 LDettori 28 59
(M R Channon) *lw: mid-div: rdn and hdwy over 2f out: chsd wnr wl over 1f out: wknd fnl f* **4/1**[2]
1145 **11** *1 ¾* **Market Day**[14] 5157 2-8-9 85 KerrinMcEvoy 8 52
(L M Cumani) *in tch: nt clr run 3f out: sn rdn: no imp after* **14/1**
0205 **12** *2* **Chingford (IRE)**[10] 5261 2-8-2 FrankieMcDonald 15 40
(D W P Arbuthnot) *in tch: rdn over 2f out: grad fdd* **100/1**
6040 **13** *hd* **Maid Of Ale (IRE)**[6] 5382 2-8-8 TPO'Shea 20 45
(B J Meehan) *towards rr: sme hdwy over 2f out: wknd over 1f out* **100/1**
63 **14** *½* **Seven Steps (IRE)**[12] 5209 2-8-5 ow1 JohnEgan 9 41
(J W Hills) *chsd ldrs: rdn 3f out: wknd over 1f out* **66/1**
3232 **15** *½* **Voodoo Moon**[14] 5157 2-8-0 74 AdrianTNicholls 1 34
(M Johnston) *nvr bttr than mid-div* **13/2**[3]
1500 **16** *1 ½* **Sweet Candy**[15] 5140 2-8-4 (p) AndrewMullen 17 34
(K A Ryan) *led tl over 2f out: sn wknd* **100/1**
3454 **17** *½* **Buddies Girl (IRE)**[27] 4813 2-8-4 75 RichardSmith 6 33
(R Hannon) *mid-div until wknd 2f out* **50/1**
10 **18** *½* **Suki Bear**[22] 4966 2-8-9 MartinDwyer 27 37
(W R Muir) *towards rr: hdwy over 2f out: sn hung lft: wknd over 1f out* **50/1**
136 **19** *3* **Eliza May**[83] 3084 2-8-9 88 DO'Donohoe 21 29
(K A Ryan) *chasd ldrs tl wknd over 1f out* **40/1**
1054 **20** *7* **Naayla (IRE)**[38] 4460 2-8-12 JimmyFortune 5 13
(B J Meehan) *s.i.s: a in rr* **66/1**
0400 **21** *hd* **Ella Y Rossa**[18] 5052 2-8-2 52 ow4 SaleemGolam 7 —
(P D Evans) *bhd fnl 2f* **100/1**
04 **22** *3* **Theoretical**[7] 5347 2-8-4 AdrianMcCarthy 26 —
(A J McCabe) *a towards rr* **100/1**

1m 22.29s (0.79) **Going Correction** +0.20s/f (Good) **22** Ran SP% **125.4**
Speed ratings (Par 101):103,99,96,92,90 89,87,85,84,82 80,77,77,77,76 74,74,73,70,62 61,58
CSF £54.40 TOTE £3.20: £2.00, £5.50, £7.30; EX 51.80 Trifecta £794.40 Pool £1,230.80, 1.10 winning units.
Owner Raymond Tooth **Bred** Killeen Castle Stud **Trained** East Everleigh, Wilts

FOCUS
A wide range of abilities in this valuable sales race, and it was not as competitive as the size of the field might suggest. They raced centre to stands' side until those drawn low migrated towards the middle as the race progressed, and at the finish the high drawn horses who had raced there throughout were at an advantage. The fourth and sixth look the best guides to the form.

NOTEBOOK
Indian Ink(IRE) had the best form, and her second in the Lowther last time had already been handsomely advertised several times since. She was always cruising just behind the leaders and, once given her head, she fairly powered clear, winning impressively without needing to reproduce her York form. She was favourably drawn, but would probably have won wherever she had been berthed. The Group 1 Cheveley Park Stakes could be next on the agenda. (tchd 5-2 and 11-4 in places)
Siamese Cat(IRE) ◆ emerged from the pack to chase home the classy favourite and put daylight between herself and the rest, but the winner was much too good for her on this occasion. She did have a decent draw as things turned out, but this was still a cracking effort just six days after making her racecourse debut, especially under joint top weight, and it should not be long before she gets off the mark.
Diamond Diva ◆, another to perform very well having only recently made her racecourse debut, in her case seven days earlier, had a low weight thanks to her modest purchase price and ran a blinder to stay on and make the frame. She should be able to get off the mark before too long and she should appreciate a mile at least judging by her breeding.
Whazzis ◆ was 2lb better off with Pretty Majestic for a three-length beating at Chester last month, but she was making her debut then and she comprehensively turned the form around here. Her performance was even better considering those drawn very low seemed to be at quite a disadvantage and she looks a winner waiting to happen. (op 11-1)
Baltic Belle(IRE) did not get going until it was too late and found that the principals had gone beyond recall. She is much more exposed than the trio that finished immediately ahead of her, but does have the ability to win a race. Things will fall right for her one day.
Naughty Thoughts(IRE) ◆ showed her Windsor running to be all wrong and this effort was much more in line with her promising Haydock debut. Her talented trainer should find the right opportunity for her.
Russian Rosie(IRE), probably not helped by her low draw, nonetheless had every chance and may have found this slightly longer trip in the softening ground a little bit too much.
Addictive ◆, who had excuses for both defeats since winning her maiden, ran with plenty of credit at a monster price and will find easier opportunities than this. (op 100-1)
Pretty Majestic(IRE) should have been helped by the widest draw, but after holding every chance she failed to get home. This was the softest ground she had encountered and it may have sapped her stamina. (op 5-1)
Voodoo Moon had a bit to find on adjusted official ratings, but the number one stall was probably at least as big a negative. (tchd 7-1)

5504 DJP INTERNATIONAL H'CAP 1m (S)
3:45 (3:50) (Class 4) (0-85,85) 3-Y-O
£6,477 (£1,927; £963; £481) **Stalls** Centre

Form RPR
21-2 **1** **Queen's Best**[108] 2330 3-8-12 79 RyanMoore 4 92+
(Sir Michael Stoute) *lw: t.k.h: hld up in tch: led wl over 1f out: rdn and r.o wl: readily* **3/1**[1]
0232 **2** *1 ¾* **Don Pietro**[23] 4933 3-8-8 75 EddieAhern 6 85
(D J Coakley) *chsd ldrs: wnt 2nd 1f out: kpt on: nt pce of wnr* **22/1**
-312 **3** *1 ¼* **Prince Ary**[34] 4599 3-8-13 80 JamieSpencer 7 87
(B W Hills) *hld up in rr: gd hdwy 2f out: drvn and no imp fnl f* **10/1**
0255 **4** *1* **Lyrical Sound (IRE)**[23] 4923 3-8-11 78 OscarUrbina 19 83
(B W Hills) *hld up in midfield: rdn to chse ldrs 2f out: styd on same pce* **25/1**
6502 **5** *½* **Grimes Faith**[12] 5211 3-8-11 78 RichardHughes 8 82
(R Hannon) *hld up towards rr: hdwy over 2f out: one pce fnl f* **20/1**
2550 **6** *1 ½* **Rubenstar (IRE)**[56] 3889 3-8-12 79 NCallan 5 80
(M H Tompkins) *hld up in rr: rdn and styd on fnl 2f: nvr nrr* **20/1**
0424 **7** *½* **Bonnie Prince Blue**[14] 5150 3-9-2 83 MichaelHills 2 83
(B W Hills) *towards rr: rdn over 2f out: nrst fin* **10/1**
4112 **8** *1 ¼* **Cool Ebony**[39] 4426 3-8-13 80 JimmyQuinn 14 78
(M Dods) *w ldrs tl wknd fnl 2f* **18/1**
2303 **9** *½* **Silent Applause**[23] 4923 3-8-4 71 oh1 PaulHanagan 11 68
(Dr J D Scargill) *lw: bhd: rdn 3f out: sme late hdwy* **25/1**
6115 **10** *½* **Night Cru**[23] 4933 3-8-5 72 ow1 JohnEgan 15 67
(C F Wall) *lw: w ldrs tl wknd 2f out* **14/1**
2211 **11** *shd* **Kasumi**[10] 5268 3-8-7 74 5ex SteveDrowne 17 69
(H Morrison) *lw: chsd ldrs: effrt over 2f out: wknd over 1f out* **9/1**[3]
-350 **12** *1 ¾* **Bomber Command (USA)**[113] 2177 3-8-9 76 KerrinMcEvoy 10 68
(J W Hills) *mde most tl wknd wl over 1f out* **22/1**
24-0 **13** *¾* **Amwaal (USA)**[105] 2404 3-8-12 79 MartinDwyer 18 69
(J L Dunlop) *chsd ldrs: rdn 3f out: wknd 2f out* **33/1**
0-21 **14** *¾* **Highland Blaze (USA)**[27] 4806 3-9-3 84 LDettori 1 73
(Saeed Bin Suroor) *lw: t.k.h: in tch 5f* **9/2**[2]
0261 **15** *6* **Glenmuir (IRE)**[70] 3473 3-8-8 82 JamesMillman(7) 12 59
(B R Millman) *lw: in tch: squeezed for room and dropped into midfield over 6f out: wknd over 2f out* **20/1**
0060 **16** *3* **Genari**[16] 5107 3-8-9 76 PJSmullen 9 47
(P F I Cole) *prom 5f* **20/1**

1m 42.65s (0.85) **Going Correction** +0.20s/f (Good) **16** Ran SP% **121.7**
Speed ratings (Par 103):103,101,100,99,98 97,96,95,94,94 94,92,91,90,84 81
CSF £77.42 CT £474.73 TOTE £3.70: £1.40, £3.30, £1.80, £8.50; EX 85.80 Trifecta £676.10 Part won. Pool £952.28, 0.40 winning units..
Owner Cheveley Park Stud **Bred** Darley **Trained** Newmarket, Suffolk

FOCUS
A decent handicap, though the pace was ordinary and the whole field were still within a couple of lengths of each other passing the two-furlong pole. The runners came down the centre of the track for most of the way, but they all edged over towards the far rail inside the last couple of furlongs. The form, rated around the third and fourth, looks solid.
Prince Ary Official explanation: jockey said gelding lost its action and both front shoes 6f out
Glenmuir(IRE) Official explanation: jockey said gelding hung right

5505 E B F RATCLIFFES SYNDICATION CLASSIFIED STKS 1m 2f
4:20 (4:23) (Class 3) 3-Y-O+
£11,217 (£3,358; £1,679; £840; £419; £210) **Stalls** High

Form RPR
5140 **1** **Blue Bajan (IRE)**[6] 5374 4-9-2 90 MichaelHills 12 96+
(Andrew Turnell) *swtg: restrained s: hld up last: stdy prog fr over 2f out: shkn up to ld jst ins fnl f: r.o wl: readily* **11/2**[3]
165 **2** *1 ¼* **Zaif (IRE)**[25] 4878 3-8-7 87 MarcHalford(3) 5 94
(D R C Elsworth) *in tch: rdn and hdwy over 2f out: nt clr run briefly over 1f out : kpt on to go 2nd ins fnl f* **25/1**
31 **3** *½* **Speedy Sam**[26] 4838 3-8-10 86 NCallan 7 93
(K R Burke) *lw: led for 1f: trckd ldr: led again over 2f out: sn rdn: edgd lft over 1f out: hdd ins fnl f: no ex* **13/2**

11- **4** *nk* **Dubai On**[353] [5691] 3-8-7 89 .... LDettori 10 89
(Saeed Bin Suroor) *lw: hld up: hdwy 2f out: rdn and ev ch 1f out: wandered u.p: no ex* **2/1**[1]

0100 **5** *nk* **Kaylianni**[7] [5342] 3-8-7 87 .... JoeFanning 4 89
(M R Channon) *trckd ldrs: rdn to chal over 2f out: ev ch 1f out: no ex* **9/1**

0005 **6** *5* **Red Lancer**[1] [5494] 5-9-2 89 .... PaulHanagan 9 83
(R A Fahey) *in tch: rdn over 2f out: kpt on same pce* **12/1**

224 **7** *2* **Tabadul (IRE)**[13] [5177] 5-9-2 90 .... MartinDwyer 2 84+
(E A L Dunlop) *lw: led after 1f: rdn and narrowly hdd over 2f out: wknd jst over 1f out: eased ins fnl f* **4/1**[2]

/30- **8** *3/4* **Eva Soneva So Fast (IRE)**[366] [5404] 4-9-2 82 .... JimmyQuinn 1 78
(J L Dunlop) *hld up: short lived effrt over 2f out* **66/1**

416 **9** *5* **Inchloch**[31] [4676] 4-9-2 86 .... RichardHughes 13 69
(B G Powell) *hld up: rdn over 2f out: wknd over 1f out* **12/1**

2m 11.86s (3.86) **Going Correction** +0.575s/f (Yiel)
WFA 3 from 4yo+ 6lb **9** Ran SP% **112.8**
Speed ratings (Par 107):107,106,105,105,105 101,99,98,94
CSF £124.03 TOTE £7.40: £2.00, £5.40, £1.70; EX 162.50 Trifecta £697.10 Part won. Pool £981.95, 0,44 winning units..
Owner Dr John Hollowood **Bred** Dr J Hollowood **Trained** Broad Hinton, Wilts
■ Stewards' Enquiry : N Callan one-day ban: used whip with excessive frequency without giving colt time to respond and down the shoulder in forehand position (Oct 3)

FOCUS
A race run at just a fair pace, though unlike in the earlier race on the round course, the field stayed against the inside rail on the run up from Swinley Bottom rather than heading for the trees. The front five finished in a bit of a heap, but they pulled well clear of the rest and the form looks solid, rated through the third.

NOTEBOOK
Blue Bajan(IRE), so unlucky in the very valuable handicap at Newbury six days earlier, was happy to sit out the back for much of the way but when asked to get into contention turning for home he always looked as though he could pick up his rivals any time he wanted. Making his effort widest of all, he duly found more than enough with his rider never needing to resort to the whip. Despite incurring a 4lb penalty for this, he is still not sure to get into the Cambridgeshire but would probably have each-way possibilities if he does. (tchd 6-1, 13-2 in a place)
Zaif(IRE) showed why there was money for him in a messy race at Epsom last time and did not go unbacked at big prices here. With this contest proving much more straightforward, he was able to show his true potential but even though he had to briefly wait to see some daylight in the home straight, the winner proved too good in the run to the line. He is still not completely exposed and looks capable of winning off this sort of mark. (op 33-1)
Speedy Sam was given a positive ride over this extra furlong and had every chance, but did not see his race out as well as the front pair. He is yet to finish out of the frame in seven outings and should find other opportunities. (tchd 7-1)
Dubai On, unbeaten in two outings at two and racing for the first time in nearly a year, was buried in the pack before moving into a challenging position on the outside soon after turning in. She failed to find as much as expected however, and what was especially worrying was how high she carried her head, which suggested she was not enjoying it at all. She has questions to answer now. (op 15-8 tchd 7-4 and 9-4)
Kaylianni has spent the majority of her career facing impossible tasks, including in the Oaks and the Newbury Arc Trial. This was more realistic, but she was not quite up to it, though in fairness she was not beaten that far and finished well clear of the rest. (op 10-1)
Red Lancer, making a quick reappearnce after finishing unplaced at Pontefract the previous day, had every chance but was just not good enough and needs even more help from the Handicapper.
Tabadul(IRE) made much of the running, but patently failed to see out his race in the conditions. A less forceful ride would appear to suit him better. Official explanation: jockey said gelding was unsuited by the soft ground (op 5-1 tchd 11-2 in a place)
Inchloch Official explanation: jockey said gelding had no more to give

5506 BOLLINGER CHAMPAGNE CHALLENGE SERIES FINAL H'CAP (FOR GENTLEMAN AMATEURS) 1m 4f

4:55 (4:55) (Class 4) (0-80,80) 4-Y-0+
£6,002 (£1,875; £937; £469; £234; £118) **Stalls** High

Form RPR

03/1 **1** **Altay**[36] [4508] 9-11-2 77 .... MrBMcHugh(5) 4 76
(R A Fahey) *lw: plld hrd: w ldrs: outpcd by ldr over 2f out: 3 length 2nd and hld whn lft in narrow ld 1/2f out: hld on nr fin* **5/1**[1]

5000 **2** *nk* **Wellington Hall (GER)**[48] [4149] 8-11-3 76 .... MrJOwen(3) 3 74
(P W Chapple-Hyam) *hld up towards rr: rdn and r.o fnl 2f: catching wnr nr fin* **14/1**

1521 **3** *3/4* **Forthright**[62] [3748] 5-11-5 80 .... MrMJJSmith(5) 18 77
(A W Carroll) *lw: plld hrd: prom: hld whn lft level w wnr 1/2f out: nt qckn fnl 50 yds* **11/2**[2]

5454 **4** *nk* **Wise Owl**[23] [4935] 4-11-7 80 .... MrSPearce(3) 10 77
(J Pearce) *lw: hld up in midfield: eased outside and hdwy 2f out: hld whn lft disputing cl 2nd 1/2f out: nt qckn* **8/1**

303U **5** *1 1/4* **Serramanna**[12] [5201] 5-10-9 68 oh13 ow7 .... MrMatthewSmith(3) 2 63
(Ms J S Doyle) *hld up in rr: rdn and hdwy over 2f out: styd on* **66/1**

4211 **6** *nk* **Fossgate**[22] [4947] 5-11-3 76 .... JackMitchell(3) 16 71
(J D Bethell) *chsd ldrs: outpcd 3f out: styd on again fnl f* **6/1**[3]

2106 **7** *1/2* **Border Edge**[4] [5422] 8-10-0 63 .... RyanBird(7) 15 57
(J J Bridger) *led and t.k.h under restraint: hdd over 2f out: sn outpcd* **33/1**

516- **8** *hd* **Dovedale**[350] [5714] 6-10-0 61 oh6 .... MrCRNelson(5) 1 55
(H S Howe) *lw: wd: t.k.h in midfield: hdwy 7f out: rdn and btn over 2f out* **25/1**

3232 **9** *2* **Hawridge King**[25] [4900] 4-10-12 68 .... (v) MrSDobson 17 59
(W S Kittow) *in tch tl rdn and btn over 2f out* **6/1**[3]

3621 **10** *6* **Undeterred**[46] [4206] 10-10-12 73 .... MrPCollington(5) 5 55
(K J Burke) *towards rr: rdn and struggling 4f out: n.d after* **16/1**

0-25 **11** *7* **Bay Hawk**[19] [4432] 4-11-0 70 .... MrSWalker 14 43
(B G Powell) *towards rr: rdn and n.d fnl 3f* **16/1**

1500 **12** *nk* **Gallego**[6] [5384] 4-10-0 63 .... MrMPrice(7) 12 35
(R J Price) *lw: s.i.s: bhd: hdwy into midfield 7f out: wknd over 2f out* **25/1**

0020 **13** *5* **Scottish River (USA)**[12] [5213] 7-10-5 61 .... MrLeeNewnes 7 26
(M D I Usher) *a bhd* **11/1**

002 **B** **Love You Always (USA)**[12] [5205] 6-9-12 61 oh10 .... (t) MrRBirkett(7) 13 —
(Miss J Feilden) *t.k.h in rr: n.d fnl 4f: bhd whn rn into stricken horse and b.d 1/2 f out* **33/1**

6510 **P** **Brief Statement (IRE)**[7] [5338] 4-10-1 62 .... (v) MrBenBrisbourne(5) 9 65
(W M Brisbourne) *in tch: wnt prom 7f out: led and qcknd clr over 2f out: 3l up whn broke leg 1/2f out: p.u: dead* **11/1**

2m 43.64s (10.64) **Going Correction** +0.575s/f (Yiel) **15** Ran SP% **121.9**
Speed ratings (Par 105):87,86,86,86,85 85,84,84,83,79 74,74,71,—,—
CSF £71.78 CT £407.66 TOTE £5.00: £2.20, £5.10, £2.30; EX 85.20 TRIFECTA Not won. Place 6 £513.25, Place 5 £255.59.
Owner R M Jeffs & J Potter **Bred** Exors Of The Late J T Robson **Trained** Musley Bank, N Yorks

FOCUS
A pedestrian early gallop resulted in several pulling hard early, and the race developed into something of a sprint from the home bend, allowing horses out of the handcap to finish close-up and rendering the form suspect. Brief Statement had the race won when tragically breaking down well inside the last furlong and handing the race to the favourite.
Scottish River(USA) Official explanation: jockey said gelding stumbled rounding Swinley Bottom
T/Jkpt: £7,100.00 to a £1 stake. Pool: £10,000.00. 0.50 winning tickets. T/Plt: £400.10 to a £1 stake. Pool: £144,509.95. 263.65 winning tickets. T/Qpdt: £23.60 to a £1 stake. Pool: £8,099.00. 253.00 winning tickets. TM

5132 HAYDOCK (L-H)

Friday, September 22

OFFICIAL GOING: Good (good to soft in places)
Wind: light, behind

5507 HAYDOCK PARK ANNUAL BADGEHOLDERS MAIDEN FILLIES' STKS 6f

2:15 (2:17) (Class 5) 2-Y-0 **£3,238** (£963; £481; £240) **Stalls** High

Form RPR

1 **Fantasy Parkes** 2-8-10 .... RobertWinston 9 74+
(K A Ryan) *s.i.s: midfield: n.m.r over 3f out: sn swtchd rt: hdwy over 2f out: r.o to ld towards fin* **4/1**[2]

334 **2** *1/2* **Mimisel**[22] [4966] 2-9-0 92 .... PhilipRobinson 8 77
(Rae Guest) *chsd ldrs: rdn to ld over 1f out: hdd towards fin* **6/5**[1]

3 **3** *2 1/2* **Baileys Outshine**[16] [5111] 2-9-0 .... J-PGuillambert 3 69
(J G Given) *a.p: led over 3f out: rdn and hdd over 1f out: edgd rt ins fnl f: one pce after* **16/1**

56 **4** *1 3/4* **Distant Stars (IRE)**[32] [4657] 2-9-0 .... GrahamGibbons 15 64
(E S McMahon) *bmpd s: a.p: rdn and edgd lft over 1f out: one pce ins fnl f* **8/1**[3]

6 **5** *1* **Hansomis (IRE)**[60] [3780] 2-9-0 .... DaleGibson 14 61
(B Mactaggart) *wnt rt s: chsd ldrs: rdn 2f out: kpt on same pce* **100/1**

0 **6** *1 1/2* **Knapton Hill**[19] [5043] 2-9-0 .... TonyCulhane 11 57
(H Morrison) *prom: rdn over 2f out: wknd ins fnl f* **16/1**

7 *1/2* **Dressed To Dance (IRE)** 2-8-10 .... TedDurcan 17 51
(B J Meehan) *s.i.s: towards rr: hdwy over 2f out: rdn over 1f out: kpt on ins fnl f: nt rch ldrs* **16/1**

03 **8** *3* **Miss Percy**[18] [5059] 2-9-0 .... TonyHamilton 10 46
(R A Fahey) *midfield: rdn 4f out: bmpd 3f out: nvr trbld ldrs* **10/1**

00 **9** *2* **Sagassa**[115] [2106] 2-8-9 .... LiamJones(5) 13 40
(W De Best-Turner) *chsd ldrs tl rdn and wknd over 2f out* **100/1**

10 *1 3/4* **Grethel (IRE)** 2-8-10 .... FrancisNorton 1 31
(A Berry) *s.s: sn hung lft: towards rr: hung rt over 2f out: kpt on fnl f: nvr trbld ldrs* **50/1**

26 **11** *1/2* **Waiheke Island**[90] [2854] 2-9-0 .... PaulMulrennan 6 33
(B Mactaggart) *led: hdd over 3f out: rdn and wknd over 1f out* **33/1**

12 *1* **Danum Diva (IRE)** 2-8-10 .... RobbieFitzpatrick 12 26
(T J Pitt) *s.s: bhd: sme hdwy fnl f: nvr trbld ldrs* **14/1**

00 **13** *nk* **Hopeful Isabella (IRE)**[8] [5307] 2-9-0 .... JamieMackay 16 29
(Sir Mark Prescott) *s.i.s: a in rr* **100/1**

14 *1 1/2* **Chicamia** 2-8-10 .... TPQueally 5 21
(M Mullineaux) *s.s: a bhd* **50/1**

0 **15** *hd* **Cape Jasmine (IRE)**[105] [2409] 2-9-0 .... TomEaves 4 24
(J Howard Johnson) *midfield: rdn and hung rt over 3f out: wknd over 2f out* **40/1**

16 *nk* **Miss Daawe** 2-8-10 .... MickyFenton 2 19
(S Parr) *a towards rr* **50/1**

0 **17** *nk* **Lady Toyah (IRE)**[102] [2500] 2-9-0 .... RoystonFfrench 7 22
(Mrs L Williamson) *midfield: bmpd 3f out: wknd 2f out* **100/1**

1m 13.7s (-1.20) **Going Correction** -0.35s/f (Firm) **17** Ran SP% **125.2**
Speed ratings (Par 92):94,93,90,87,86 84,83,79,77,74 74,72,72,70,70 69,69
CSF £8.97 TOTE £4.90: £1.50, £1.30, £3.50; EX 10.10.
Owner Joseph Heler **Bred** Joseph Heler **Trained** Hambleton, N Yorks

FOCUS
A fair fillies' maiden in which the first two came clear. The winner looks a useful prospect but the form is held down somewhat by the performance of the fifth.

NOTEBOOK
Fantasy Parkes, whose dam was a very smart performer at two, is herself a half-sister to Bajan Parkes, a winner over six furlongs as a juvenile, but there is stamina on her sire side courtesy of Fantastic Light. Well regarded and supported in the market, she was making a belated racecourse debut but showed she is a smart performer in the making by getting the better of a rival rated 92. It took her a while to get the hang of things but she stayed on well in the closing stages and is going to do better when she steps up in trip next year. Her trainer thinks she will be effective over a mile at three. (op 13-2)
Mimisel, fourth in a Listed race on her previous start, looked to hold strong claims back in maiden company, and she was unlucky to run into a well-regarded newcomer. She finished clear of the rest and a regular maiden should come her way. (op 11-8 tchd 6-4 in places)
Baileys Outshine, third behind a Kevin Ryan-trained filly on her debut, found herself repeating the feat. This was a slight improvement on her previous form and nurseries become an option after one more run. Official explanation: jockey said filly hung right (tchd 20-1)
Distant Stars(IRE), who has now had the required three runs for a mark, might do better in nursery company.
Hansomis(IRE) was beaten a long way on her debut but did a lot better this time. She is unlikely to win a maiden, though, and should do better once handicapped.
Knapton Hill showed the benefit of her debut outing and knew her job better this time, racing prominently for a long way. (op 12-1)
Dressed To Dance(IRE), a half-sister to Widely Accepted, a winner over a mile at two, was given a nice introduction and should do better in time over further.

5508 JMC IT 25TH ANNIVERSARY MAIDEN STKS (C&G) 6f

2:45 (2:45) (Class 5) 2-Y-0 **£3,238** (£963; £481; £240) **Stalls** High

Form RPR

4232 **1** **Longquan (IRE)**[6] [5371] 2-9-0 84 .... FergusSweeney 5 81+
(P J Makin) *trckd ldrs: smooth hdwy to ld 2f out: sn clr: easily* **6/4**[1]

3044 **2** *4* **Straight Face (IRE)**[17] [5094] 2-8-11 72 .... (v) StephenDonohoe(3) 11 66
(W J Knight) *a.p: rdn to chse wnr fr wl over 1f out: sn no imp* **8/1**

0 **3** *nk* **Woqoodd**[39] [4428] 2-9-0 .... PhilipRobinson 9 65
(M A Jarvis) *led: rdn along and hdd 2f out: grad wknd* **11/1**

4 *shd* **Binocular** 2-9-0 .... RobertWinston 3 65
(B W Hills) *towards rr: hdwy over 2f out: rdn over 1f out: kpt on ins last: nrst fin* **7/1**

06 **5** *4* **Rajeef Ashog**[17] [5089] 2-9-0 .... NickyMackay 14 53
(L M Cumani) *midfield whn stmbld after 1f: hdwy 1/2-way: rdn to chse ldrs 2f out: sn no imp* **33/1**

3 **6** *4* **The King And I (IRE)**[113] [2172] 2-9-0 .... PatDobbs 10 41
(Miss E C Lavelle) *chsd ldrs: rdn along over 2f out: sn wknd* **13/2**[3]

7 *3/4* **Royal Guest** 2-9-0 .... TonyCulhane 13 39
(M R Channon) *dwlt and towards rr tl sme late hdwy* **11/2**[2]

8 *nk* **Shavoulin (USA)** 2-9-0 .... TedDurcan 2 38
(Christian Wroe, UAE) *outpcd and towards rr fr 1/2-way* **33/1**

0 **9** *nk* **Smirfys Gold (IRE)**[13] [5161] 2-9-0 .... GrahamGibbons 1 37
(E S McMahon) *chsd ldrs: rdn wl over 2f out: sn wknd* **80/1**

50 **10** *3/4* **Bungie**[13] [5168] 2-9-0 .... J-PGuillambert 7 35
(Ms Deborah J Evans) *chsd ldrs: rdn along and wknd 1/2-way* **66/1**

11 *6* **Currahee** 2-9-0 .... TomEaves 8 17
(Miss J A Camacho) *dwlt: a rr* **33/1**

0 **12** *7* **Woodland Symphony**[130] [1730] 2-9-0 .... FrancisNorton 4 —
(N Tinkler) *in tch: rdn along 1/2-way: sn wknd* **50/1**

13 *nk* **Stay Quiet (USA)** 2-9-0 .... PhillipMakin 12 —
(T D Barron) *a towards rr* **25/1**

1m 13.31s (-1.59) **Going Correction** -0.35s/f (Firm) **13** Ran SP% **118.0**
Speed ratings (Par 95):96,90,90,90,84 79,78,78,77,76 68,59,58
CSF £13.01 TOTE £2.10: £1.30, £2.40, £2.90; EX 19.80.

Owner R & G Marchant D M Ahier J P Carrington **Bred** J F Tuthill **Trained** Ogbourne Maisey, Wilts

FOCUS
Run in a slightly faster time than the fillies took in the preceding race, the winner did not need to improve to win this maiden easily. The form looks sound enough, rated around the first two.

NOTEBOOK
Longquan(IRE) already had a number of efforts in the book which pointed to him being plenty good enough to win a maiden such as this, and he finally got off the mark at the fifth attempt. He did not need to improve to win this but it should have done his confidence some good and he could be interesting in nursery company. (op 7-4 tchd 15-8, 2-1 in a place)
Straight Face(IRE), exposed as a fair performer at best, had 12lb to find with the winner on official ratings and that proved beyond him. He is always likely to run into one or two too strong in maiden company and probably needs a little help from the assessor before he is in a position to win a handicap. (op 10-1)
Woqoodd, whose dam was unraced but is a half-sister to Cheyenne Dream, a dual winner at two and later a very smart performer over trips around a mile in France, again showed speed before weakening in the closing stages. He may need more time. (op 9-1)
Binocular, a half-brother to a number of winners including useful juvenile Well Warned, stayed on late in the day and is likely to derive plenty from the experience. (op 9-1)
Rajeef Ashog, whose dam won the German 1000 Guineas, stumbled early on in the race, which could not have helped his confidence. He has shown some ability in maiden company so far but looks one for handicaps next year.
The King And I(IRE), a 50-1 shot when third on his debut back in June, failed to build on that promise on his second start. (op 9-2)
Smirfys Gold(IRE) Official explanation: jockey said colt hung left-handed throughout
Woodland Symphony Official explanation: trainer said gelding struck into itself

5509 ADELE CARR FINANCIAL RECRUITMENT NURSERY 6f
3:20 (3:21) (Class 4) (0-85,76) 2-Y-O **£5,181** (£1,541; £770; £384) **Stalls** High

Form RPR

0023 **1** **Leonide**[15] [5140] 2-9-7 **75** .... RobertWinston 4 81
(B J Meehan) *mde all: rdn over 1f out: edgd lft and hld on wl towards fin* **10/3**[2]

2264 **2** *hd* **Impromptu**[28] [4774] 2-9-7 **75** .... GeorgeBaker 1 80
(R M Beckett) *hld up: hdwy over 2f out: swtchd lft over 1f out: sn rdn: r.o ins fnl f* **13/2**[3]

0454 **3** *1* **Bid For Gold**[38] [4452] 2-9-7 **75** .... PaulMulrennan 3 77
(Jedd O'Keeffe) *chsd ldrs: rdn to take 2nd 2f out and ev ch: edgd lft over 1f out: lost 2nd and nt qckn ins fnl f* **11/1**

3232 **4** *shd* **Gap Princess (IRE)**[7] [5349] 2-8-2 **63** .... JamesRogers(7) 6 65+
(R A Fahey) *hld up: rdn 2f out: edgd lft and hdwy over 1f out: edgd rt ins fnl f: r.o towards fin* **9/4**[1]

2034 **5** *4* **No Worries Yet (IRE)**[70] [3468] 2-9-1 **69** .... FrancisNorton 10 59
(J L Spearing) *hld up: rdn and hdwy over 1f out: kpt on ins fnl f: nvr able to chal* **9/1**

100 **6** *9* **Arnie's Joint (IRE)**[20] [5017] 2-9-4 **75** .... JamesDoyle(3) 7 38
(N P Littmoden) *prom: rdn over 2f out: wknd over 1f out* **12/1**

1044 **7** *5* **Ensign's Trick**[24] [4912] 2-8-11 **70** .... LiamJones(5) 2 18
(W M Brisbourne) *chsd ldrs: rdn whn rdr dropped whip 2f out: sn wknd* **16/1**

5130 **8** *2* **Tom Tower (IRE)**[16] [5113] 2-9-7 **75** .... TedDurcan 9 17
(M R Channon) *prom: rdn over 2f out: sn wknd* **15/2**

066 **9** *3/4* **Bentley**[144] [1333] 2-8-2 **59** ow2 .... PatrickMathers(3) 8 —
(D Shaw) *chsd ldrs: rdn 3f out: sn wknd* **25/1**

1m 13.21s (-1.69) **Going Correction** -0.35s/f (Firm) **9** Ran SP% **114.7**
Speed ratings (Par 97):97,96,95,95,89 77,71,68,67
CSF £25.16 CT £212.48 TOTE £4.10: £1.60, £2.00, £3.10; EX 23.60.

Owner Ed McCormack **Bred** P D And Mrs Player **Trained** Manton, Wilts

■ Stewards' Enquiry : Robert Winston two-day ban: used whip with excessive frequency and without giving mount time to respond (Oct 3-4)

FOCUS
An ordinary nursery but the first four pulled nicely clear and the form looks solid enough, rated through the third.

NOTEBOOK
Leonide, third in a higher grade of nursery at Southwell last time, appreciated the drop in class and battled on well for his rider. He should get seven furlongs. (op 7-2)
Impromptu, running in a handicap for the first time, was given a waiting ride and ran on well once switched out to challenge inside the last two furlongs. He has the ability to win a similar race off this sort of mark. (op 8-1)
Bid For Gold, another running in a nursery for the first time, was stepping back up to six furlongs for the first time since his racecourse debut, and he did not quite see it out as well as the first two. (op 10-1 tchd 12-1)
Gap Princess(IRE) ◆, who won her race on the wrong side at Nottingham last time, finished to some effect from off the pace and only narrowly missed out on third place. Her stable is flying at present and she looks sure to win a nursery like this in the coming weeks. (op 2-1 tchd 5-2, 11-4 in a place)
No Worries Yet(IRE) struggled to get into it from off the pace and the first four finished comfortably clear of her in the end. It was her first outing for 70 days, though, so she might improve a bit for the run. (op 8-1)
Arnie's Joint(IRE) has gone backwards since his debut win at Warwick.

5510 RACINGUK.TV (S) STKS 1m 2f 120y
3:55 (3:56) (Class 5) 3-4-Y-O **£5,505** (£1,637; £818; £408) **Stalls** High

Form RPR

0635 **1** **Evolution Ex (USA)**[43] [4301] 4-9-4 65 .... PhillipMakin 3 61
(K R Burke) *trckd ldrs: hdwy 3f out: led 2f out: rdn over 1f out: drvn ins last and hld on wl* **8/1**

3120 **2** *shd* **Agilete**[6] [5385] 4-9-10 51 .... J-PGuillambert 10 67
(J Pearce) *hld up in midfield: hdwy 3f out: rdn to chal over 1f out and ev ch tl no ex nr fin* **25/1**

1232 **3** *4* **Summer Lodge**[4] [5435] 3-8-11 70 .... (v[1]) TPQueally 12 54
(M H Tompkins) *hld up and bhd: hdwy on outer over 3f out: rdn and n.m.r wl over 1f out: swtchd rt and styd on: nrst fin* **7/2**[2]

5004 **4** *shd* **Dancing Flame**[43] [4297] 3-8-6 52 .... PaulQuinn 5 49
(E J Alston) *a prom: effrt 3f out and ch tl rdn and kpt on same pce fnl 2f* **33/1**

4453 **5** *hd* **Blushing Hilary (IRE)**[9] [5284] 3-8-6 69 .... (p) TomEaves 9 49
(Miss J A Camacho) *in tch: hdwy to chse ldrs 4f out: rdn along 3f out: drvn and one pce fr wl over 1f out* **10/3**[1]

6000 **6** *1/2* **Adage**[18] [5057] 3-8-6 55 .... (t) FergusSweeney 4 48
(David Pinder) *hld up: hdwy 3f out: rdn 2f out: styd on appr last: nrst fin* **50/1**

3065 **7** *2 1/2* **Riverhill (IRE)**[26] [4835] 3-8-11 51 .... RobertWinston 6 49
(J Howard Johnson) *led: rdn along 3f out: hdd 2f out: sn drvn and wknd appr last* **16/1**

3125 **8** *3/4* **Burnley Al (IRE)**[5] [5403] 4-9-10 64 .... (b) FrancisNorton 1 53
(A Berry) *in tch on inner: rdn along 3f out: wknd over 2f out* **9/1**

0645 **9** *3/4* **Naini Tal**[30] [4701] 3-8-6 70 .... LPKeniry 11 41
(D R C Elsworth) *a towards rr* **12/1**

0330 **10** *shd* **Holiday Cocktail**[56] [3914] 4-9-4 62 .... MickyFenton 13 46
(Miss J Feilden) *chsd ldrs: rdn along over 3f out: wknd over 2f out* **7/1**[3]

0006 **11** *2* **Perez (IRE)**[5] [5403] 4-9-7 60 .... (v) DNolan(3) 14 48
(W Storey) *nvr bttr than midfield* **33/1**

0400 **12** *2 1/2* **Hansomelle (IRE)**[9] [5285] 4-8-13 52 .... DaleGibson 16 33
(B Mactaggart) *chsd ldrs on outer: rdn along 3f out: sn drvn and wknd* **33/1**

00 **13** *12* **Biggin Hill (IRE)**[18] [5071] 3-8-11 .... (t) TedDurcan 15 18
(H R A Cecil) *hld up: a rr* **12/1**

00 **14** *nk* **Nahlass**[15] [5127] 3-8-3 .... JamesDoyle(3) 8 12
(Ms J S Doyle) *a rr* **100/1**

06 **15** *4* **Dark Emotion**[64] [3681] 3-8-6 .... LiamJones(5) 17 10
(W De Best-Turner) *cl up: rdn along over 3f out: sn wknd* **100/1**

0-20 **16** *1 1/2* **Lucidus**[22] [4973] 4-9-4 65 .... TonyCulhane 7 8
(W J Haggas) *a rr* **8/1**

2m 17.01s (-0.72) **Going Correction** +0.10s/f (Good)
WFA 3 from 4yo 7lb **16** Ran SP% **127.9**
Speed ratings (Par 103):106,105,103,102,102 102,100,100,99,99 98,96,87,87,84 83
CSF £207.10 TOTE £14.60: £3.80, £7.20, £1.60; EX 305.20.There was no bid for the winner. Summer Lodge (no 11) was clamed by Paul J Dixon for £30,000

Owner Hit The Beach Partnership **Bred** James Ryan **Trained** Middleham Moor, N Yorks

FOCUS
Modest plating-class form and not solid.

5511 BANK OF IRELAND H'CAP 1m 2f 120y
4:30 (4:30) (Class 4) (0-85,85) 3-Y-O+ **£6,477** (£1,927; £722; £722) **Stalls** High

Form RPR

1366 **1** **Brief Goodbye**[27] [4810] 6-9-5 **79** .... MickyFenton 2 86
(John Berry) *hld up: hdwy over 3f out: rdn over 1f out: r.o to ld fnl strides* **10/1**

3000 **2** *hd* **Active Asset (IRE)**[25] [4878] 4-9-8 **82** .... TonyCulhane 16 89
(M R Channon) *in tch: hdwy over 3f out: rdn over 2f out: led ins fnl f: hdd fnl strides* **16/1**

21-0 **3** *1/2* **Sacranun**[98] [2621] 4-9-11 **85** .... (v[1]) NickyMackay 15 91
(L M Cumani) *trckd ldrs: rdn to ld over 1f out: hdd ins fnl f: hld fnl strides* **20/1**

6121 **3** *dht* **Celtic Spirit (IRE)**[28] [4784] 3-9-0 **81** .... GeorgeBaker 4 89+
(R M Beckett) *hld up: hdwy over 3f out: nt clr run over 2f out: sn swtchd rt: r.o ins fnl f* **7/4**[1]

5-26 **5** *1/2* **Birkside**[23] [4933] 3-8-7 **74** .... StephenCarson 13 79
(W R Swinburn) *a.p: led over 2f out: hdd over 1f out: edgd lft ent fnl f: stl ev ch tl no ex fnl strides* **8/1**[2]

6252 **6** *1/2* **Quince (IRE)**[109] [2290] 3-9-4 **85** .... FrancisNorton 10 89+
(J Pearce) *midfield: rdn over 3f out: hdwy over 1f out: r.o ins fnl f* **12/1**

6302 **7** *1/2* **Rawdon (IRE)**[15] [5137] 5-9-4 **78** .... (v) HayleyTurner 5 81
(M L W Bell) *prom: rdn over 3f out: kpt on same pce fnl f* **8/1**[2]

320- **8** *nk* **Supreme Charter**[367] [5393] 3-8-13 **80** .... RoystonFfrench 14 83
(M Johnston) *led: hdd 7f out: regained ld 5f out: rdn over 3f out: hdd over 2f out: no ex ins fnl f* **33/1**

4511 **9** *3/4* **Lysandra (IRE)**[8] [5314] 4-8-5 **72** .... DanielleMcCreery(7) 7 74
(N Tinkler) *hld up in rr: swtchd rt over 2f out: hdwy over 1f out: styd on ins fnl f: nt rch ldrs* **9/1**[3]

1-0 **10** *shd* **It's A Dream (FR)**[155] [1092] 3-9-2 **83** .... LPKeniry 8 84
(D R C Elsworth) *midfield: lost pl 4f out: hdwy over 1f out: kpt on ins fnl f* **16/1**

5400 **11** *1/2* **Activo (FR)**[13] [5177] 5-9-10 **84** .... TedDurcan 3 84
(S Dow) *in tch: rdn over 2f out: fdd ins fnl f* **25/1**

0030 **12** *2* **Solo Flight**[25] [4878] 9-9-4 **83** .... TravisBlock(5) 1 80
(H Morrison) *hld up: hdwy over 3f out: rdn 2f out: no imp fnl f* **25/1**

023 **13** *4* **Yeoman Spirit (IRE)**[153] [1139] 3-8-8 **75** .... FergusSweeney 12 65
(A M Balding) *midfield: rdn 3f out: wknd 2f out* **25/1**

004 **14** *2 1/2* **Im Spartacus**[15] [5137] 4-9-1 **75** .... RobertWinston 9 60
(D W Barker) *s.i.s: in rr: hdwy to ld 7f out: hdd 5f out: rdn over 3f out: wknd over 2f out* **20/1**

0224 **15** *7* **Cripsey Brook**[40] [4392] 8-8-10 **77** .... (t) JamesReveley(7) 11 50
(K G Reveley) *midfield: wknd over 2f out* **28/1**

0P00 **16** *8* **El Tiger (GER)**[15] [5141] 5-9-6 **80** .... (b[1]) TPQueally 17 38
(B J Curley) *midfield: rdn and wknd over 2f out* **66/1**

2m 19.6s (1.87) **Going Correction** +0.10s/f (Good)
WFA 3 from 4yo+ 7lb **16** Ran SP% **126.1**
Speed ratings (Par 105):97,96,96,96,96 95,95,95,94,94 94,92,89,88,82 77
PL: Sacranun £5.30, Celtic Spirit £1.50 Tricast: Sacranun £1,578.59, Celtic Spirit £202.92 CSF £147.37 TOTE £16.90: £3.00, £4.40; EX 190.50.

Owner J McCarthy **Bred** Chippenham Lodge Stud Ltd **Trained** Newmarket, Suffolk

■ Stewards' Enquiry : T P Queally caution: used whip down the shoulder in forehand position
Tony Culhane one-day ban: used whip with excessive frequency (Oct 3)

FOCUS
A fair handicap but they went a steady pace early and the winning time was moderate for the grade, 2.59 seconds slower than the seller. The form does not look solid.
El Tiger(GER) Official explanation: jockey said gelding hung right-handed

5512 GRIFFITHS & ARMOUR H'CAP 1m 30y
5:05 (5:06) (Class 3) (0-90,90) 3-Y-0+
£9,348 (£2,799; £1,399; £700; £349; £175) **Stalls** Low

Form RPR
1305 **1** **Abbey Cat (IRE)**[76] [3282] 3-8-5 **77** RobbieFitzpatrick 11 86
(G A Swinbank) *a cl up: rdn 2f out: led 1f out: drvn and hdd ins last: styd on to ld nr line* **25/1**
2250 **2** *shd* **Skidrow**[29] [4739] 4-9-1 **88** AndrewElliott(5) 2 97
(M L W Bell) *led: rdn along 2f out: hdd 1f out: drvn and rallied to ld wl ins last: hdd and no ex nr line* **9/2**[1]
0120 **3** *1 3/4* **Ingratitude (IRE)**[78] [3224] 3-8-10 **85** JamesDoyle(3) 7 90
(R M Beckett) *in tch: hdwy to chse ldrs over 2f out: sn rdn and styd on same pce ins last* **16/1**
1100 **4** *1* **Gentleman's Deal (IRE)**[13] [5188] 5-9-8 **90** DaleGibson 6 93+
(M W Easterby) *midfield: hdwy 3f out: rdn wl over 1f out: styd on ins last: nrst fin* **14/1**
3221 **5** *1 1/2* **Uno**[15] [5138] 3-8-8 **80** TonyCulhane 4 79
(B W Hills) *chsd ldrs on inner: hdwy 3f out and ch tl rdn and wknd appr last* **5/1**[2]
2002 **6** *nk* **Arm Candy (IRE)**[35] [4577] 3-9-2 **88** RoystonFfrench 14 87
(J A R Toller) *in tch: hdwy on outer 3f out: rdn to chse ldrs 2f out: drvn and wknd appr last* **14/1**
1550 **7** *3/4* **Dancing Lyra**[52] [4023] 5-8-8 **81** JamieMoriarty(5) 3 78
(R A Fahey) *midfield: hdwy on inner 3f out: in tch and rdn 2f out: sn drvn and wknd* **6/1**[3]
1030 **8** *3 1/2* **Primo Way**[7] [5337] 5-8-13 **81** (b) TomEaves 1 70
(I Semple) *midfield: effrt and sme hdwy over 2f out: sn rdn and no imp* **16/1**
4210 **9** *2* **Jihaaz (IRE)**[78] [3224] 3-8-12 **84** RobertWinston 12 68
(B W Hills) *towards rr tl sme late hdwy* **15/2**
2213 **10** *1/2* **O'Tara (IRE)**[28] [4763] 3-8-8 **80** TPQueally 5 63
(M H Tompkins) *towards rr tl sme late hdwy* **10/1**
1200 **11** *1 1/4* **Our Putra**[39] [4429] 3-8-9 **81** PhilipRobinson 13 61
(M A Jarvis) *prom: rdn along 3f out: drvn over 2f out and sn wknd* **8/1**
120 **12** *3* **Future's Dream**[26] [4833] 3-8-8 **80** PatCosgrave 10 53
(K R Burke) *prom: rdn along over 4f out: sn wknd* **11/1**
1010 **13** *3* **Danelor (IRE)**[173] [843] 8-8-5 **76** PatrickMathers(3) 15 42
(D Shaw) *nvr a factor* **66/1**
16-0 **14** *1* **Celticello (IRE)**[179] [763] 4-8-12 **83** StephenDonohoe(3) 8 47
(Heather Dalton) *midfield: hdwy on outer and in tch 3f out: sn rdn and wknd over 2f out* **33/1**
15 *1 1/2* **Stolen Summer (IRE)**[114] [2153] 3-8-12 **84** MickyFenton 9 45
(B S Rothwell) *a bhd* **50/1**
50 **16** *2* **Indian's Feather (IRE)**[25] [4889] 5-8-12 **80** (b) KimTinkler 17 36
(N Tinkler) *midfield: hdwy on outer to chse ldrs over 3f out: sn rdn and wknd over 2f out* **66/1**

1m 45.37s (-0.14) **Going Correction** +0.10s/f (Good)
WFA 3 from 4yo+ 4lb **16** Ran SP% **126.3**
Speed ratings (Par 107):104,103,102,101,99 99,98,95,93,92 91,88,85,84,82 80
CSF £136.12 CT £1988.84 TOTE £42.70: £5.20, £1.70, £4.40, £4.20; EX 246.50.
Owner Abbadis Racing Club **Bred** Mrs Marion Daly **Trained** Melsonby, N Yorks

FOCUS
A decent handicap in which they went fairly steady in the early stages and those that raced towards the fore were at an advantage. The form is not rock solid but is rated at face value for now.

NOTEBOOK
Abbey Cat(IRE), up there throughout in a race that favoured those who raced with the pace, responded well to pressure, rallied after being headed and got her head in front where it mattered. She clearly benefited from a mid-season break and got the mile well.
Skidrow, another who was prominent all the way in a race run at a steady gallop early on, went head-to-head with the eventual winner for the best part of the final three furlongs and only just lost out. He has now finished in the frame six times since his last win and has been a model of consistency this term. (op 4-1 tchd 7-2)
Ingratitude(IRE) had enough cut in the ground to show his best form and ran well on his return from a 78-day break. He had looked on a pretty stiff mark beforehand but could well be up to defying it this autumn when he can get his toe in. (tchd 14-1 and 18-1)
Gentleman's Deal(IRE) showed the benefit of his York outing and ran quite well in a race which was not run to suit him. He did best of the hold-up horses and is worth bearing in mind for a similar contest.
Uno, who was raised 3lb for her win in an uncompetitive maiden last time out, is probably more effective in truly testing conditions. (op 15-2)
Arm Candy(IRE), another who did not race far off the pace, had every chance.
Dancing Lyra, who has done all his winning on turf in soft and heavy ground, was returning from a little break and did not have the race run to suit. There could be another race in him this autumn when conditions allow. (op 13-2 tchd 7-1)

5513 RACING UK FOR £15 PER MONTH H'CAP 1m 3f 200y
5:35 (5:37) (Class 5) (0-70,70) 3-Y-0+ **£3,238** (£963; £481; £240) **Stalls** High

Form RPR
1140 **1** **Sforzando**[17] [5090] 5-9-4 **69** KristinStubbs(7) 2 78
(Mrs L Stubbs) *s.i.s: hld up: hdwy 4f out: led ins fnl f: r.o* **20/1**
0102 **2** *1 1/2* **Oddsmaker (IRE)**[15] [5132] 5-9-9 **70** (t) StephenDonohoe(3) 5 77
(M A Barnes) *plld hrd: midfield: hdwy after 4f: led over 3f out: rdn over 2f out: hdd ins fnl f: no ex cl home* **7/1**[3]
0401 **3** *3/4* **Mae Cigan (FR)**[20] [5015] 3-9-2 **68** FrancisNorton 10 74+
(M Blanshard) *in rr: hdwy 3f out: rdn over 1f out: r.o ins fnl f* **7/1**[3]
5040 **4** *3/4* **Top Spec (IRE)**[11] [5242] 5-9-10 **68** J-PGuillambert 7 73
(J Pearce) *midfield: rdn and hdwy 3f out: edgd lft over 1f out: styd on ins fnl f* **16/1**
6062 **5** *1 1/2* **Duroob**[26] [4848] 4-8-13 **64** PatrickDonaghy(7) 1 66
(K R Burke) *midfield: hdwy 4f out: rdn over 3f out: no ex ins fnl f* **10/1**
0044 **6** *1 3/4* **Cleaver**[30] [4698] 5-9-4 **62** TedDurcan 14 61
(Lady Herries) *hld up: rdn and hdwy over 2f out: carried hd high u.p: kpt on ins fnl f* **7/1**[3]
3023 **7** *1 1/4* **Karlani (IRE)**[77] [3249] 3-9-2 **68** RobertWinston 17 65
(G A Swinbank) *prom: rdn 3f out: carried hd awkwardly u.p: wknd over 1f out* **4/1**[1]
0034 **8** *2 1/2* **Best Of The Lot (USA)**[11] [5242] 4-9-7 **70** JamieMoriarty(5) 12 63
(R A Fahey) *led for 3f: remained prom: rdn and wknd over 2f out* **5/1**[2]
0254 **9** *2 1/2* **Caraman (IRE)**[22] [4947] 8-9-8 **66** GrahamGibbons 13 55
(J J Quinn) *racd keenly: prom: led after 3f: hdd over 3f out: rdn over 2f out: sn wknd* **10/1**
-100 **10** *3/4* **Epicurean**[81] [3141] 4-9-7 **65** MickyFenton 9 53
(Mrs K Walton) *hld up: rdn over 3f out: no imp* **25/1**
-020 **11** *1 1/4* **Zaville**[91] [2822] 4-9-0 **65** JamesO'Reilly(7) 4 51
(J O'Reilly) *midfield: lost pl over 3f out: n.d after* **33/1**
0550 **12** *2 1/2* **Magnum Opus (IRE)**[97] [2656] 4-9-12 **70** RobbieFitzpatrick 6 52
(T J Pitt) *prom: rdn over 3f out: sn wknd* **25/1**
0000 **13** *3 1/2* **Shahzan House (IRE)**[11] [5236] 7-9-12 **70** (p) LPKeniry 8 47
(P G Murphy) *prom tl rdn and wknd over 3f out* **50/1**
14 *9* **Adios (GER)**[572] 7-9-7 **65** RoystonFfrench 16 27
(P D Niven) *midfield tl wknd over 4f out* **66/1**
03-0 **15** *5* **Escoffier**[237] [218] 4-8-11 **60** EmmettStack(5) 11 14
(Pat Eddery) *midfield: rdn over 4f out: wknd over 2f out* **50/1**
2666 **16** *18* **Historic Appeal (USA)**[25] [4892] 3-9-1 **67** TonyCulhane 15 —
(M R Channon) *a bhd* **16/1**

2m 39.28s (4.29) **Going Correction** +0.10s/f (Good)
WFA 3 from 4yo+ 8lb **16** Ran SP% **124.9**
Speed ratings (Par 103):89,88,87,87,86 84,84,82,80,80 79,77,75,69,66 54
CSF £150.76 CT £1108.26 TOTE £27.20: £4.60, £2.00, £2.20, £3.20; EX 138.80 Place 6 £77.82, Place 5 £57.06.
Owner Mrs L Stubbs **Bred** M E Wates **Trained** Norton, N. Yorks
■ Stewards' Enquiry : J-P Guillambert one-day ban: careless riding (Oct 3)

FOCUS
A modest contest run at a steady early pace and in a very moderate winnng time for the class of race. The form is not strong, but is rated at face value.
Shahzan House(IRE) Official explanation: jockey said gelding had a breathing problem
T/Plt: £122.30 to a £1 stake. Pool: £57,516.30. 343.25 winning tickets. T/Qpdt: £86.50 to a £1 stake. Pool: £2,796.40. 23.90 winning tickets. DO

5514 - 5518a (Foreign Racing) - See Raceform Interactive

3777 MAISONS-LAFFITTE (R-H)
Friday, September 22

OFFICIAL GOING: Good to soft

5519a LA COUPE DE MAISONS-LAFFITTE (GROUP 3) (STRAIGHT) 1m 2f (S)
3:00 (2:59) 3-Y-0+ **£27,586** (£11,034; £8,276; £5,517; £2,759)

RPR
1 **Musical Way (FR)**[12] 4-8-10 RonanThomas 4 105
(P Van De Poele, France) *settled in mid-div, hdwy to trck ldr fr wl over 1f out, ran on to ld wl ins fnl f, rdn out* **128/10**
2 *hd* **Advice**[65] [3662] 5-9-0 CSoumillon 1 109
(A Fabre, France) *mid-div on rails, led 2f out til caught wl ins fnl f, ran on* **49/10**[2]
3 *2* **Corre Caminos (FR)**[93] [2741] 4-9-7 TJarnet 9 112
(M Delzangles, France) *hld up in rr, 8th 4f out, moved to outside 2f out, ran on fnl f but too late to worry first two* **4/5**[1]
4 *nk* **Blip**[16] [5124] 4-9-0 DBoeuf 8 105
(D Smaga, France) *mid-div, hdwy on ins wl over 1f out, 3rd ins fnl f, no extra closing stages* **12/1**
5 *1* **Musketier (GER)**[40] [4417] 4-9-0 C-PLemaire 6 103
(P Bary, France) *always prom, ev ch 2f out, wknd fnl f* **79/10**
6 *2* **Kachgai (IRE)**[34] [4623] 3-8-8 OPeslier 2 99
(E Libaud, France) *disp 2nd til wknd fr wl over 1f out* **72/10**[3]
7 *3* **Mohandas (FR)**[27] [4828] 5-9-0 JVictoire 3 94
(W Hefter, Germany) *disp 2nd tl wknd fr wl over 1f out* **10/1**
8 *2 1/2* **Sister Trouble (FR)**[111] [2257] 3-8-5 DBonilla 5 87
(F Head, France) *a in rear* **28/1**
9 *20* **Thistle Suite**[124] [1873] 8-9-8 TGillet 7 62
(M Delzangles, France) *led, clr first 4f, hdd and wknd 2f out* **4/5**[1]

1m 59.7s
WFA 3 from 4yo+ 6lb **9** Ran SP% **179.0**
PARI-MUTUEL: WIN 13.80; PL 2.00, 1.60, 1.30; DF 29.30.
Owner S Constantinidis **Bred** Sarl Haras Du Tallis **Trained** France

NOTEBOOK
Musical Way(FR) caused a surprise as she was being upped in class quite considerably. Quickening inside the final furlong, she took the race in the final two strides, securing a first Group-race success for her trainer. She will now be aimed at the Group 1 Premio Lydia Tesio in Rome next month.
Advice, given every possible chance, looked like the winner a furlong and a half out when he took the lead, but he was outpaced by the winner in the dying moments of the race.
Corre Caminos(FR), carrying top weight, was towards the tail of the field early on but ran on well at the finish and was not given a hard time by his jockey. This outing will have put him spot on for the Champion Stakes, and this Group 1 winner should go well at Newmarket, particularly if there is cut in the ground.
Blip, who made her run up the stands' rail, ran on well from a furlong and a half out but lost third place in the final 50 yards.

5501 ASCOT (R-H)
Saturday, September 23

OFFICIAL GOING: Good to soft (soft in places on round course)
Wind: Virtually nil.

5520 SPACE PROPERTY H'CAP 1m (S)
2:00 (2:02) (Class 2) (0-100,99) 3-Y-0+
£18,696 (£5,598; £2,799; £1,401; £699; £351) **Stalls** Centre

Form RPR
-100 **1** **Supaseus**[71] [3491] 3-8-5 **86** JohnEgan 16 99
(H Morrison) *lw: trckd ldrs: rdn to ld jst over 2f out: edgd sltly rt ins fnl f: kpt on wl* **11/2**[2]
302 **2** *2* **South Cape**[15] [5150] 3-8-9 **90** TonyCulhane 4 98
(M R Channon) *in tch: rdn over 2f out: edgd rt fr over 1f out: chsd wnr but a ins fnl f* **14/1**
1111 **3** *1 1/2* **Envision**[28] [4819] 3-8-8 **89** RyanMoore 18 94
(R Hannon) *trckd ldrs: rdn to chal 2f out: kpt on but edgd rt ins fnl f* **7/1**
0040 **4** *3/4* **Wise Dennis**[30] [4739] 4-9-5 **96** DarryllHolland 20 99
(A P Jarvis) *lw: mid-div: rdn and hdwy 2f out: kpt on fnl f* **15/2**
2150 **5** *1/2* **Kelucia (IRE)**[50] [4098] 5-8-12 **89** SebSanders 15 91
(R M Beckett) *lw: hld up towards rr: rdn over 2f out: no imp tl styd on ins fnl f: nrst fin* **16/1**

Form	Pos	Dist	Horse	RPR
0506	6	1	**Pentecost**[42] 4348 7-9-8 **99**.......... MartinDwyer 17 (A M Balding) *stdd s: racd freely towards rr: rdn and sme hdwy 2f out: kpt on same pce fnl f* **14/1**	98
0630	7	shd	**Unshakable (IRE)**[14] 5177 7-8-13 **90**.......... OscarUrbina 19 (Bob Jones) *b: b.hind: in tch: outpcd 2f out: styd on again wl ins fnl f* **8/1**	89
5123	8	¾	**Granston (IRE)**[21] 5019 5-9-0 **91**..........(v[1]) KerrinMcEvoy 13 (J D Bethell) *led: rdn and hdd jst over 2f out: sn one pce* **5/1**[1]	88
040/	9	3 ½	**Barathea Blazer**[294] 4862 7-9-4 **95**.......... RichardMullen 21 (K McAuliffe) *bkwd: b: hld up towards rr: rdn and sme hdwy 2f out: no imp after* **66/1**	84
-303	10	nk	**Arminius (IRE)**[30] 4740 3-9-3 **98**.......... RichardHughes 11 (R Hannon) *mid-div: rdn 3f out: one pce fnl 2f* **12/1**	87
5300	11	1 ½	**My Paris**[50] 4098 5-9-7 **98**.......... NCallan 8 (K A Ryan) *trckd ldr: rdn over 2f out: wknd over 1f out* **6/1**[3]	83
3210	12	nk	**Audience**[30] 4739 6-9-1 **92**.......... PaulDoe 22 (J Akehurst) *lw: a towards rr* **14/1**	77
35-0	13	2 ½	**Cape Greko**[87] 2988 4-9-4 **95**.......... FJohansson 10 (A M Balding) *hld up towards rr: tk clsr order over 3f out: rdn over 2f out: wknd over 1f out* **50/1**	74

1m 39.89s (-1.91) **Going Correction** -0.025s/f (Good)
WFA 3 from 4yo+ 4lb **13** Ran SP% **118.7**
Speed ratings (Par 109):108,106,104,103,103 102,102,101,97,97 96,95,93
CSF £79.90 CT £569.27 TOTE £7.10: £2.40, £3.70, £2.40; EX 130.70 Trifecta £321.60 Pool £1,404.29 - 3.10 winning units..
Owner Ben & Sir Martyn Arbib **Bred** Arbib Bloodstock Partnership **Trained** East Ilsley, Berks

FOCUS
Nine non-runners on account of the going reduced the competitiveness of this decent handicap, although the winning time suggests that the ground was not that soft at all. A high draw proved an advantage. The runner-up is a pretty good guide to the form, and the unexposed winner can go on to better things.

NOTEBOOK
Supaseus, who ran well from a poor draw over the course and distance in the Britannia earlier in the season, appreciated the easier ground having struggled somewhat on a sound surface at Newmarket on his last start back in July. Gelded since that run, he came home a good winner, and it would not be a surprise to see him develop into a Pattern-class performer next year. (6-1 in places)
South Cape has been running well on fast ground recently, but he is just as effective with a little give. Drawn low in a race that favoured those housed in the high numbers, his performance is probably worth rating a bit better than the bare form suggests, and he will not always run into a rival so well handicapped.
Envision was tackling tougher opposition than has been the case recently but he continued his run of good form with a solid effort in third, completing a one-two-three for the three-year-olds. (op 13-2)
Wise Dennis has had excuses of late and is on a mark he should be able to win off, but he was a bit disappointing here from a good draw and remains one of those horses that finds winning difficult. (op 7-1 tchd 8-1)
Kelucia(IRE), who tends to finish her races strongly, did so again. Her style of racing means that several things have to fall into place for her to win, though, not least luck in running. (op 20-1)
Pentecost has a good record here - his course and distance record now reads 141041566 - but he raced too freely in rear this time and a stronger all-round pace would have suited him better.
Unshakable(IRE) has a pretty poor strike-rate and has not been at his best this season.
Granston(IRE), backed into favouritism, wore a visor for the first time and tried to make every yard. He was running off a career-high mark, though, and his recent run of consistent efforts came to an end. (op 7-1)
Barathea Blazer, not seen on the Flat for over a year, was entitled to need this first outing since being pulled up over hurdles in December, and the trip would have been far too sharp for him nowadays anyway - he is entered for the Cesarewitch.

5521 JUDDMONTE ROYAL LODGE STKS (GROUP 2) (C&G) 1m (R)
2:35 (2:37) (Class 1) 2-Y-O

£70,975 (£26,900; £13,462; £6,712; £3,362; £1,687) **Stalls** High

Form	Pos	Dist	Horse	RPR
3	1		**Admiralofthefleet (USA)**[71] 3492 2-8-12.......... MJKinane 7 (A P O'Brien, Ire) *rangy: lw: trckd ldrs: nt clr run and swtchd lft 3f out: nt clr run over 2f out: sn shkn up: led ins fnl f: r.o wl* **11/2**	115+
15	2	2 ½	**Medicine Path**[52] 4037 2-8-12.......... RichardMullen 5 (E J O'Neill) *hld up bhd ldrs: rdn and hdwy fr 3f out: led over 1f out: sn edgd rt: no ex whn hdd ins fnl f* **4/1**[2]	110
2134	3	2	**Kirklees (IRE)**[14] 5183 2-8-12 106.......... JoeFanning 1 (M Johnston) *lw: prom: led over 3f out: rdn over 2f out: hdd over 1f out: kpt on same pce* **4/1**[2]	106
310	4	hd	**Champlain**[71] 3492 2-8-12 99.......... PhilipRobinson 4 (M A Jarvis) *trckd ldrs: effrt over 2f out: kpt on same pce fr over 1f out* **5/1**[3]	106
011	5	9	**Gold Option**[29] 4783 2-8-12 90.......... RichardHughes 6 (J H M Gosden) *lw: stdd s: hld up bhd ldrs: chal over 2f out: sn btn* **7/2**[1]	87
0	6	2	**Abide With Me (USA)**[9] 5328 2-8-12.......... JAHeffernan 3 (A P O'Brien, Ire) *cmpt: sn led at decent pce: narrowly hdd over 3f out: sn rdn: wknd over 1f out* **12/1**	82
3124	7	63	**Gweebarra**[14] 5176 2-8-12 100.......... NCallan 8 (K A Ryan) *chsd ldrs tl lost action over 3f out: sn eased* **17/2**	—

1m 41.06s (-1.04) **Going Correction** +0.125s/f (Good) **7** Ran SP% **112.5**
Speed ratings (Par 107):110,107,105,105,96 94,31
CSF £26.66 TOTE £5.90: £2.70, £2.90; EX 43.30 Trifecta £200.80 Pool £1,307.07 - 4.62 winning units..
Owner M Tabor,Mrs J Magnier, Niarchos Family **Bred** Quaybloodstock Niarchos Family **Trained** Ballydoyle, Co Tipperary

FOCUS
Not a strong renewal on paper but they went fast from the gate and the winning time was fair for a race of its type and 0.83 seconds quicker than the Fillies' Mile. The form has been rated around the third and fourth, and Admiralofthefleet, who looked a strong stayer, is among the race's better winners.

NOTEBOOK
Admiralofthefleet(USA) wore down Medicine Path in the final furlong and on this evidence he looks sure to improve for a step up in distance next season. A mile and a half might not be what his pedigree says he wants but it would not be a surprise to see him get it, although ten furlongs may turn out to be his best trip. He was given quotes of 33-1 for the 2000 Guineas and 40-1 for the Derby after this and, while he has plenty of scope and should progress over the winter, it will be a surprise if his stable does not have stronger candidates for those races. (op 5-1 tchd 6-1)
Medicine Path, fifth in the Vintage Stakes on his last start, was the first off the bridle, but the leaders went too fast early and in the straight he came through to have every chance. The O'Brien-trained colt outstayed him in the end, but he showed his Goodwood form to be all wrong and looks to be going the right way. (op 9-2 tchd 5-1)
Kirklees(IRE) helped force a strong early pace, and he paid the price in the latter stages, failing to confirm Vintage Stakes form with Medicine Path. Held at Group 2 level three times now, he might appreciate dropping down in grade slightly, and the Autumn Stakes back here next month might fit the bill. (tchd 7-2)
Champlain, disappointing in the Superlative Stakes last time out, had his chance in the straight but could only plug on at the one pace. He has not lived up to the promise of his Chesham Stakes win and looks likely to prove difficult to place. (op 4-1)
Gold Option looked a threat turning into the straight but he just could not pick up on this easier surface. It would be harsh to judge him on this performance and he should be given another chance to prove his Group-race credentials on quicker ground. Official explanation: trainer said colt was unsuited by the good to soft (soft in places) ground (op 4-1)
Abide With Me(USA) set a good gallop which eventually played into the hands of his stablemate. (op 14-1)
Gweebarra Official explanation: trainer had no explanation for the poor form shown

5522 MEON VALLEY STUD FILLIES' MILE (GROUP 1) 1m (R)
3:10 (3:14) (Class 1) 2-Y-O

£134,324 (£50,909; £25,478; £12,703; £6,363; £3,193) **Stalls** High

Form	Pos	Dist	Horse	RPR
1301	1		**Simply Perfect**[14] 5187 2-8-12 106.......... DarryllHolland 5 (J Noseda) *swtg: trckd ldrs: rdn to chal over 2f out: led over 1f out: sn wandered u.p: wnt rt cl home: drvn out* **11/4**[2]	111
01	2	1 ½	**Treat**[8] 5352 2-8-12.......... JamieSpencer 2 (M R Channon) *lw: prom: rdn to ld 2f out: sn drifted rt: hdd over 1f out: rallied: ¾ l down whn n.m.r and snatched up cl home* **16/1**	110+
112	3	¾	**English Ballet (IRE)**[14] 5187 2-8-12.......... MichaelHills 8 (B W Hills) *lw: trckd ldrs: rdn over 2f out: wnt 3rd over 1f out: kpt on* **5/2**[1]	106
2013	4	2 ½	**Satulagi (USA)**[42] 4371 2-8-12 97.......... JohnEgan 6 (J S Moore) *hld up: tk clsr order over 2f out: sn rdn: styd on to go 4th ins fnl f* **25/1**	100
1410	5	1 ¾	**Gaudeamus (USA)**[27] 4853 2-8-12.......... KJManning 4 (J S Bolger, Ire) *lt-f: hld up: hdwy over 2f out: sn rdn: kpt on same pce fnl f* **12/1**	96
111	6	2	**Sesmen**[27] 4840 2-8-12 105.......... OscarUrbina 7 (M Botti) *led: t.k.h: rdn and narrowly hdd 2f out: wknd fnl f* **3/1**[3]	91
35	7	nk	**Alexander Tango (IRE)**[27] 4853 2-8-12.......... WMLordan 3 (T Stack, Ire) *hld up: rdn and effrt 2f out: one pce after* **9/1**	91
01	8	2 ½	**Lost In Wonder (USA)**[27] 4830 2-8-12 82.......... RyanMoore 1 (Sir Michael Stoute) *trckd ldrs: rdn over 3f out: sn one pce* **8/1**	85

1m 41.89s (-0.21) **Going Correction** +0.125s/f (Good) **8** Ran SP% **118.8**
Speed ratings (Par 106):106,104,103,101,99 97,97,94
CSF £46.80 TOTE £3.50: £1.70, £2.50, £1.40; EX 52.40 Trifecta £176.80 Pool £2,224.02 - 8.93 winning units..
Owner D Smith, M Tabor & Mrs J Magnier **Bred** Trehedyn Stud And Quarry Bloodstock **Trained** Newmarket, Suffolk

FOCUS
This featured the first two from the May Hill and the Prestige Stakes winner, but it lacked an outstanding prospect and Simply Perfect, assessed through the third and fourth, has been rated a little below the recent norm for winners of this race, despite improving on her May Hill form. The early pace was not that strong, resulting in a winning time just acceptable for a race of its stature, 0.83 seconds slower than the Royal Lodge.

NOTEBOOK
Simply Perfect became the fourth winner of the May Hill Stakes to follow up here in the last 11 years. She had the runner-up's measure when she tightened that one up a little in the closing stages, and while that manoeuvre exaggerated the winning distance slightly, she was a deserved winner. Tough and steadily progressive, she is versatile with regard to ground conditions and looks an excellent second-string for her stable for the 1000 Guineas, for which she is now a 16-1 shot. (op 10-3 tchd 5-2 in places)
Treat only won her maiden at Nottingham eight days earlier, and had a hard race in the process, so in the circumstances she ran a storming race in this Group 1 contest, determinedly rallying after being headed inside the final two furlongs. The Rockfel looks a suitable short-term target and her trainer reckons she will get as far as a mile and a half next year, although her pedigree suggests that is doubtful. (tchd 20-1)
English Ballet(IRE) had prospects of reversing May Hill form with Simply Perfect on 3lb better terms, but she was not up to it. She is another who could bid to return to winning ways in the Rockfel. (op 3-1 tchd 10-3)
Satulagi(USA), the most exposed filly in the line-up, ran close to her Sweet Solera form with English Ballet but is simply not quite up to this class. She could prove difficult to place next season. (op 33-1)
Gaudeamus(USA), not far behind Simply Perfect in the Moyglare last time out, was disappointing considering that she was, apart from the winner, the only other previous Group 2 winner in the line-up. It would appear that she has her limitations. (op 14-1)
Sesmen, a bit too keen for her own good, led them into the straight but she was soon headed and one-paced under pressure. Connections had expressed reservations about her ability to handle the easier ground beforehand and she may well show this form to be all wrong granted a lead back on a sounder surface. (op 11-4 tchd 7-2)
Alexander Tango(IRE) trapped wide throughout, could not make any impression on the leaders in the straight and failed to confirm her Moyglare form with Simply Perfect or Gaudeamus. She may need quicker gound to be seen at her best. (op 8-1 tchd 10-1)
Lost In Wonder(USA), whose Beverley maiden win left her with plenty to find at this level, got warm beforehand and was never really a threat once the race got serious. Perhaps a stronger pace would have suited her, as she will get a mile and a half next year. (tchd 9-1 and 10-1 in a place)

5523 TOTESPORT.COM STKS (HERITAGE H'CAP) 7f
3:45 (3:48) (Class 2) 3-Y-O+

£62,320 (£18,660; £9,330; £4,670; £2,330; £1,170) **Stalls** Centre

Form	Pos	Dist	Horse	RPR
1-50	1		**All Ivory**[133] 1667 4-8-10 **94**.......... JimmyFortune 14 (R Charlton) *lw: racd in 6th: rdn and hdwy 2f out: led ins fnl f: r.o wl: rdn out* **16/1**	105
1521	2	1 ¼	**Fullandby (IRE)**[22] 4988 4-8-6 **93**.......... SaleemGolam[(3)] 18 (T J Etherington) *racd in 7th on far side: mid-div: nt clr run and swtchd lft over 1f out: r.o strly: wnt 2nd cl home* **12/1**	103+
1001	3	shd	**King's Caprice**[14] 5175 5-8-8 **97**..........(t) TravisBlock[(5)] 13 (J A Geake) *trckd ldr on far side: rdn to ld 2f out: no ex whn hdd ins fnl f* **20/1**	104
1462	4	¾	**Polar Magic**[35] 4593 5-9-2 **100**.......... JamieSpencer 17 (J R Fanshawe) *lw: s.i.s: raced in last on far side: swtchd lft over 1f out: r.o strly: nrst fin* **9/2**[1]	105
2110	5	¾	**Wyatt Earp (IRE)**[8] 5336 5-8-7 **91**.......... PaulHanagan 15 (R A Fahey) *racd in 4th on far side: rdn over 2f out: kpt on fnl f* **12/1**	94
-230	6	hd	**Cross My Mind**[26] 4889 4-7-13 **86** ow1.......... EdwardCreighton[(3)] 2 (T Keddy) *s.i.s: bhd on stand side: rdn and hdwy 2f out: styd on: nrst fin: 1st of 6 in grp* **14/1**	89+

0225 **7** 1 ¼ **Compton's Eleven**[14] [5175] 5-8-12 **96**................................ JohnEgan 11 95
(M R Channon) *racd in 5th on far side: rdn over 2f out: kpt on same pce fnl f* **14/1**

3350 **8** *shd* **Marching Song**[14] [5175] 4-8-10 **94**................................ RyanMoore 22 93+
(R Hannon) *lw: bhd on far side: nt clr run on rails over 1f out: r.o ins fnl f: nrst fin* **14/1**

0101 **9** *shd* **Paper Talk (USA)**[42] [4372] 4-8-13 **97**................................ MichaelHills 3 96+
(B W Hills) *bhd on stands side: rdn over 2f out: styd on but drifted rt ins fnl f: 2nd of 6 in grp* **14/1**

0000 **10** *nk* **Bahiano (IRE)**[35] [4593] 5-8-11 **95**................................ DarryllHolland 8 93+
(C E Brittain) *chsd ldrs in 4th on stand side: effrt 2f out: one pce fnl f: 3rd of 6 in grp* **25/1**

2021 **11** *nk* **Gaelic Princess**[23] [4965] 6-7-9 **82** oh1................................ CDHayes(3) 12 79
(A G Newcombe) *racd in 8th on far side: nvr bttr than mid div* **33/1**

0102 **12** ¾ **Mine (IRE)**[16] [5135] 8-9-10 **108**................................(v) MJKinane 20 103
(J D Bethell) *lw: bhd on far side until swtchd lft over 1f out: styd on: nvr a factor* **8/1**[3]

1210 **13** 1 ¼ **Mr Lambros**[149] [1262] 5-8-1 **85** ow3................................ MartinDwyer 24 77
(A M Balding) *led far side gp: rdn and hdd 2f out: wknd fnl f* **25/1**

6113 **14** *shd* **Dream Theme**[26] [4896] 3-8-13 **100**................................ RichardHughes 21 92
(B W Hills) *towards rr on far side: rdn and sme hdwy 2f out: wknd fnl f* **16/1**

0313 **15** ¾ **Prince Of Thebes (IRE)**[14] [5175] 5-9-1 **99**................................ SebSanders 6 89+
(J Akehurst) *lw: led stands side gp tl wknd over 1f out: 4th of 6 in grp* **16/1**

6100 **16** ½ **Trafalgar Square**[93] [2776] 4-8-2 **86**................................ DavidKinsella 23 75
(J Akehurst) *lw: chsd ldrs in 3rd on far side tl wknd over 1f out* **8/1**[3]

00-4 **17** *shd* **Esquire**[29] [4782] 4-8-5 **89**................................ KerrinMcEvoy 5 77+
(Saeed Bin Suroor) *chsd ldr on stands side: effrt 2f out: sn wknd: 5th of 6 in grp* **7/1**[2]

0223 **18** 1 ¼ **Katiypour (IRE)**[11] [5263] 9-7-12 **82** oh2................................ FrankieMcDonald 9 67+
(P Mitchell) *chsd ldrs in 3rd on stands side tl wknd and edgd rt fr over 1f out: last of 6 in grp* **50/1**

1m 26.26s (-1.84) **Going Correction** -0.025s/f (Good)
WFA 3 from 4yo+ 3lb **18** Ran SP% **130.0**
Speed ratings (Par 109):109,107,107,106,105 105,104,103,103,103 103,102,100,100,99 99,99,97
CSF £195.00 CT £3882.13 TOTE £26.20: £5.60, £2.60, £8.00, £1.70; EX 304.30 Trifecta £6655.40 Pool £79,678.35 - 8.50 winning units..
Owner K Abdulla **Bred** Juddmonte Farms **Trained** Beckhampton, Wilts
■ Stewards' Enquiry : Saleem Golam one-day ban: careless riding (Oct 4)

FOCUS
Six non-runners and not quite up to the usual standard. The field split into two groups and those drawn middle to far side had a clear edge at the finish, with the sextet coming up the stands' side perhaps at a disadvantage equating to as much as 7lb to 9lb.

NOTEBOOK
All Ivory, who won this race last year when it was staged at Newmarket, was 4lb higher in the handicap this time around and had not raced since May, but he was brought here fit and well. He benefited from racing off the pace on the favoured far side and came through to win well when the leaders tired. Although something of a seven-furlong specialist so far, he is likely to be just as effective over a mile, and the key to him seems to be a strong pace.
Fullandby(IRE), an improved performer since dropping back to sprinting, was having his first outing over seven furlongs since July 2005. Held up off the pace on the far side like the winner, he ran on well to claim second late on and proved without doubt that he is just as effective over this distance as he is over six. He is at his best in strongly-run races with cut in the ground, and there are further races to be won with him when conditions allow. (op 10-1)
King's Caprice had conditions to suit and was only 3lb higher than for his Goodwood win, but making all was always going to be difficult for him here and in the end he had to settle for tracking the pace. He got to the front two furlongs out, but went for home too soon and was pulled back inside the last. It was a good effort, considering.
Polar Magic has started favourite or joint-favourite for eight of his last 11 starts but has won only once, at 6-4. A bookies horse for the past two years, he ran his usual race, staying on strongly from off the pace but all too late. He has the ability to win a race of this sort but he is on a stiff mark now and is just too expensive to follow. (op 5-1)
Wyatt Earp(IRE), whose stable remains in good form, has done most of his winning over six furlongs, but he does have a victory over seven to his name, albeit on the tight track at Catterick. He seemed to get the trip alright, but the Handicapper might just have his measure for the time being.
Cross My Mind ◆ ran poorly last time but he had run well earlier in the summer and returned to form here, winning his race on the stands' side. He is probably even more effective on fast ground and is worth bearing in mind for a good handicap this backend. In fact, he could well be one who will be kept on the go over the winter on the All-Weather.
Compton's Eleven finds winning difficult and the Handicapper has been slow to loosen his grip.
Marching Song has run well without winning this year off marks in the mid-90s, and he ran well enough again despite not getting the best of luck in running.
Paper Talk(USA), only 2lb higher for his Newmarket win, finished a creditable second on the stands' side.
Bahiano(IRE) remains in the Handicapper's grip.
Mine(IRE) is now on a 6lb higher mark than when successful in the Bunbury Cup earlier in the season, and he never really got competitive, despite being drawn on the right side and having the race run to suit. (op 9-1)
Mr Lambros went too fast in front on the far side and set it up for the closers. (op 33-1)
Trafalgar Square, who is arguably at his best over seven furlongs with some cut in the ground, and was well drawn on the far side, appeared to have plenty in his favour despite this being his first outing since the Royal meeting, and he was well backed as a result. He was disappointing, though.
Esquire reportedly works well at home but his performances on the track have not matched up to that so far. (op 10-1)

5524 QUEEN ELIZABETH II STKS (GROUP 1) 1m (R)
4:20 (4:27) (Class 1) 3-Y-O+

£141,950 (£53,800; £26,925; £13,425; £6,725; £3,375) **Stalls** High

Form RPR

-123 **1** **George Washington (IRE)**[27] [4839] 3-8-13 .... MJKinane 7 131+
(A P O'Brien, Ire) *lw: hld up bhd ldrs: travelling wl and switced lft jst over 1f out: sn qckn d into ld: readily* **13/8**[1]

4115 **2** 1 ¼ **Araafa (IRE)**[52] [4038] 3-8-13 **120**................................ CSoumillon 3 126
(J Noseda) *trckd ldrs: rdn to ld over 1f out: hdd ins fnl f: nt pce of wnr* **7/1**

6321 **3** 2 **Court Masterpiece**[52] [4038] 6-9-3 **119**................................ JamieSpencer 8 122
(E A L Dunlop) *lw: hld up: smooth hdwy 2f out: swtchd lft over 1f out: sn rdn: kpt on* **13/2**

0402 **4** 1 ¼ **Killybegs (IRE)**[27] [4839] 3-8-13 **113**................................ MichaelHills 6 119
(B W Hills) *prom: led wl over 2f out: sn rdn: hdd over 1f out: kpt on same pce* **33/1**

10-3 **5** 3 ½ **Proclamation (IRE)**[95] [2722] 4-9-3 **122**................................ KerrinMcEvoy 2 111
(Saeed Bin Suroor) *hld up: short-lived effrt 2f out* **5/1**[3]

1111 **6** 2 **Librettist (USA)**[20] [5049] 4-9-3 **122**................................ LDettori 1 106
(Saeed Bin Suroor) *lw: in tch: hdwy to join ldrs on outer 5f out: bmpd on bnd ent st: ev ch 2f out: sn wknd* **3/1**[2]

04 **7** 10 **River Tiber**[27] [4839] 3-8-13 .... DavidMcCabe 5 83
(A P O'Brien, Ire) *led after 1f: rdn and hdd wl over 2f out: grad fdd* **100/1**

3021 **8** ¾ **Ivan Denisovich (IRE)**[6] [5411] 3-8-13 ....(v[1]) JAHeffernan 4 82
(A P O'Brien, Ire) *lw: prom tl over 2f out* **28/1**

1m 40.06s (-2.04) **Going Correction** +0.125s/f (Good)
WFA 3 from 4yo+ 4lb **8** Ran SP% **113.0**
Speed ratings (Par 117):115,113,111,110,107 105,95,94
CSF £13.43 TOTE £3.20: £1.50, £1.70, £1.80; EX 17.30 Trifecta £80.10 Pool £4,166.83 - 36.91 winning units..
Owner Mrs John Magnier, M Tabor & D Smith **Bred** Lael Stables **Trained** Ballydoyle, Co Tipperary
■ Stewards' Enquiry : J A Heffernan six-day ban (reduced from 14 days on appeal): careless riding (Oct 5-10)

FOCUS
A championship mile race, featuring five individual Group 1 winners, and George Washington, who put up the performance of a true champion, has been rated the race's best winner since Dubai Millennium. The winning time was close to par for such a prestigious contest when compared to the other three races over the same course and distance on the day. George Washington was impressive again and has been rated value for another length. Araafa and Killybegs both showed improved form too.

NOTEBOOK
George Washington(IRE), brilliant in the Guineas and excused his defeat in the Irish equivalent when the ground came up bottomless and he reportedly suffered a serious muscle injury, nevertheless had questions to answer here following a messy prep at Goodwood last time. The ground was nowhere near as soft as some had feared it would be, and that was the cue for the money to come for him pre-race. Doubts about how he would handle the occasion were soon quashed, as he behaved impeccably in the preliminaries, and in the race itself things could not have gone any better. Held up off a decent gallop set by his pacemaker, he travelled well throughout and, once the gap came and he was asked to quicken approaching the final furlong, he soon put the race to bed, with Kinane only having to push him out to score readily. It was a majestic performance, and in beating a quality field in such a manner he confirmed himself Europe's champion miler. He will now bid to enhance his reputation further in the Breeders' Cup Mile, where he will surely take the world of beating. (op 2-1)
Araafa(IRE), who paid the penalty for chasing a fast pace in the Sussex Stakes, redeemed his reputation. He put up a great effort in second - a clear personal best - and was just unlucky to be beaten by one of the best milers of recent years. He finished nicely clear of Sussex Stakes winner Court Masterpiece in third and the chances are that this level of performance would have been good enough to win many renewals of this race.
Court Masterpiece had the race run to suit but on this stiffer course and easier ground he could not quite reproduce the level of form he showed at his favourite track last time in the Sussex Stakes. He remains a high-class performer, though, and the Prix de la Foret on Arc weekend should present him with a great chance of winning another Group 1. (tchd 7-1)
Killybegs(IRE) might not have helped himself by racing prominently throughout in a race run at a good clip, but he did show that his close second in the Celebration Mile was no fluke. Although vulnerable in the best races, he is finishing the year off strongly and could be another worth considering for the Prix de la Foret, although the Challenge Stakes at Newmarket would perhaps be a better option.
Proclamation(IRE) has gone backwards since joining Godolphin and, despite appearing to have conditions to suit, he failed to run up to his Queen Anne form, let alone the level of his Sussex Stakes win last season. However, like his stable companion, he was reported as lame in front after the race. (tchd 6-1)
Librettist(USA) was chasing a six-timer and a hat-trick of Group 1 wins following narrow successes in the Prix Jacques Le Marois and Prix du Moulin, but he was disappointing. Dettori was unhappy with the riding of Seamus Heffernan on Ivan Denisovich, whom he claimed kept him wide on the bend, but the interference, such as it was, was no excuse for this tame effort. He was subsequently reported to have finished lame in front. (op 11-4)
River Tiber did his pacemaking job well.
Ivan Denisovich(IRE) helped his stablemate set a true gallop, but his rider was initially found guilty of improper riding and 'team tactics' and stood down 14 days for forcing Librettist wide on the bend. The ban was later reduced to six days for careless riding, but not until after a war of words which widened further the rift between Godolphin and Ballydoyle. (op 25-1 tchd 33-1)

5525 INDEPENDENT NEWSPAPER ROSEMARY STKS (H'CAP) (LISTED RACE) 1m (R)
4:50 (5:02) (Class 1) (0-110,103) 3-Y-O+

£17,034 (£6,456; £3,231; £1,611; £807; £405) **Stalls** High

Form RPR

1140 **1** **Wagtail**[21] [5019] 3-8-3 **89**................................(t) MartinDwyer 4 98+
(E A L Dunlop) *hld up bhd: nt clr run and swtchd lft over 1f out: r.o strly: led fnl 50yds: rdn out* **14/1**

2123 **2** 1 **Grain Of Truth**[10] [5300] 3-8-8 **94**................................(v[1]) RyanMoore 1 101
(Sir Michael Stoute) *lw: wnt lft s: towards rr: hdwy and nt clr run jst over 2f out: sn rdn: r.o to ld jst ins fnl f: ct fnl 50yds* **9/4**[1]

6266 **3** ¾ **Mamela (GER)**[15] [5159] 5-9-1 **97**................................ NCallan 2 102
(L M Cumani) *hld up towards rr: c wd and hdwy ent st 3f out: led wl over 1f out: sn edgd rt: hdd ins fnl f: no ex* **14/1**

1043 **4** 2 ½ **Song Of Passion (IRE)**[52] [4042] 3-8-5 **91**................................ RichardHughes 5 90
(R Hannon) *trckd ldrs: rdn to ld briefly 2f out: kpt on same pce fnl f* **13/2**

13-5 **5** 2 **Tiana**[28] [4808] 3-8-12 **98**................................ JimmyFortune 6 93+
(J H M Gosden) *mid-div: hdwy on rails 3f out: nt clr run over 2f out: sn rdn: kpt on same pce fnl f* **9/2**[2]

022 **6** ¾ **Indian Steppes (FR)**[21] [5012] 7-8-9 **91**................................ LDettori 12 84
(P S McEntee) *trckd ldrs: effrt whn n.m.r 2f out: one pce fr over 1f out* **5/1**[3]

-120 **7** 3 **Dash To The Front**[35] [4590] 3-8-3 **89** oh5................................ JoeFanning 9 75+
(J R Fanshawe) *in tch: nt clr run and snatched up 2f out: nt a danger after* **11/1**

2520 **8** 3 **Sweet Treat (IRE)**[15] [5159] 4-8-13 **95**................................ JamieSpencer 3 74+
(J R Fanshawe) *mid-div: hdwy and nt clr run on rails over 2f out: swtchd lft: hmpd and snatched up over 1f out: no ch after* **9/1**

5100 **9** 1 ½ **After You**[28] [4808] 3-8-9 **95**................................ MichaelHills 10 71
(B W Hills) *lw: led: rdn and hdd 2f out: grad fdd* **20/1**

060- **10** *shd* **Parisette**[430] [3635] 4-8-7 **89** oh17................................(t) SaleemGolam 8 64
(A J Lidderdale) *bkwd: trckd ldrs: rdn wl over 2f out: n.m.r 2f out: wknd fnl f* **100/1**

2200 **11** 3 **Teide Lady**[1] [5502] 3-8-3 **89** oh23................................ FrancisFerris 7 58
(Rae Guest) *plld hrd: trckd ldrs: rdn wl over 2f out: sn wknd* **100/1**

1m 40.97s (-1.13) **Going Correction** +0.125s/f (Good)
WFA 3 from 4yo+ 4lb **11** Ran SP% **117.4**
Speed ratings (Par 111):110,109,108,105,103 103,100,97,95,95 92
CSF £45.24 CT £398.53 TOTE £19.00: £3.60, £1.60, £4.80; EX 77.70 Trifecta £1214.70 Part won. Pool £1,710.88 - 0.97 winning units..
Owner Hesmonds Stud **Bred** Jeremy Gompertz **Trained** Newmarket, Suffolk
■ Stewards' Enquiry : N Callan two-day ban: careless riding (Oct 4-5)

FOCUS

Not a particularly strong Listed handicap but they went a decent pace in the early stages, and when the leaders weakened in the straight the result was bunching at the two-furlong marker, with many getting in each other's way.

NOTEBOOK

Wagtail got caught up in the general bunching two furlongs out but, to her credit, found a great turn of foot once in line for home and came with a strong late run to deny the favourite and claim her third win from five starts on turf. She is progressive and could well score off level weights in Listed company before long if maintaining this improvement. (op 16-1 tchd 20-1)

Grain Of Truth, who was stepping back from ten furlongs, was suited by the decent early pace and did nothing wrong in defeat. She was just unlucky to find the winner in possession of a smarter turn of foot over this mile trip. (op 2-1 tchd 5-2 in places)

Mamela(GER) is difficult to place off her current mark but this race gave her a better chance than of late and she ran well, avoiding the trouble on her inside two furlongs out and getting first run on a number of her rivals.

Song Of Passion(IRE) did best of those who raced up with the pace in a race which was run at a decent early gallop and suited those held up for a late run. (tchd 7-1)

Tiana, having only her second run of the campaign, was stuck on the rail when the field bunched up two furlongs out and there was no way through. She ran on when in the clear but it was all too late. Official explanation: jockey said filly was denied a clear run (op 11-2 tchd 6-1)

Indian Steppes(FR) was another denied a clear run, but she had more time to make up the deficit conceded than the filly who finished in front of her. (tchd 9-2)

Dash To The Front, who looks high in the handicap for what she has achieved, was also caught up in the bunching a quarter mile out, but she made little progress once in the clear. (op 8-1)

Sweet Treat(IRE) can be forgiven this as she followed Tiana through and never got any daylight at all in the straight, including after being switched left off the rail. (op 10-1 tchd 11-1)

After You went a decent clip in front and when she tired in the straight she caused much of the bunching in behind. (op 16-1)

5526 CAPLAN GORDON CARTER STKS (H'CAP) — 2m

5:25 (5:31) (Class 2) (0-100,96) 3-Y-O+ **£11,658** (£3,468; £1,733; £865) **Stalls** High

Form — RPR

4322 **1** **Theatre (USA)**[14] [5180] 7-8-10 **78** oh3 .... JohnEgan 12 — 88
(Jamie Poulton) *hld up bhd: rdn and stdy hdwy fr over 3f out: led appr fnl f: styd on wl* **8/1**

51U5 **2** *3* **Lightning Strike (GER)**[8] [5351] 3-8-12 **92** .... IanMongan 11 — 98+
(T G Mills) *lw: trckd ldr's strong pace: led 1/2-way: rdn 3f out: hdd ent fnl f: no ex* **10/1**

3000 **3** *5* **Winged D'Argent (IRE)**[15] [5156] 5-9-13 **95** .... (b) JoeFanning 2 — 95
(M Johnston) *hld up towards rr: pushed along 1/2-way: stdy prog fr 4f out: chsd ldng pair over 2f out: no further imp* **7/1**

-411 **4** *10* **Fair Along (GER)**[29] [4777] 4-9-4 **86** .... JamieSpencer 8 — 74+
(P J Hobbs) *led at strong pce: hdd 1/2-way: chsd ldr: rdn 3f out: wknd 2f out* **6/4**[1]

4312 **5** *3* **Establishment**[14] [5174] 9-8-11 **79** .... LDettori 10 — 64
(C A Cyzer) *hld up bhd: rdn along and lot to do 6f out: styd on past btn horses fr 3f out* **6/1**[3]

0016 **6** *3 1/2* **Stoop To Conquer**[21] [5010] 6-8-13 **81** .... RyanMoore 6 — 62
(J L Dunlop) *in tch: rdn 3f out: wknd 2f out* **7/2**[2]

1B0- **7** *49* **Garden Society (IRE)**[281] [6592] 9-9-2 **87** .... SaleemGolam(3) 5 — 9
(T T Clement) *bit bkwd: chsd ldrs tl wknd 4f out* **50/1**

0 **8** *hd* **Honduras (SWI)**[20] [4096] 5-9-12 **94** .... GeorgeBaker 4 — 16
(G L Moore) *swtg: a towards rr* **33/1**

30-6 **9** *58* **Gold Gun (USA)**[15] [5153] 4-9-10 **92** .... (p) NCallan 9 — —
(K A Ryan) *lw: chsd ldrs tl 5f out: t.o* **40/1**

3m 27.94s (-8.56) **Going Correction** +0.125s/f (Good)
WFA 3 from 4yo+ 12lb — **9** Ran SP% **116.6**
Speed ratings (Par 109):110,108,106,101,99 97,73,73,44
CSF £83.19 CT £590.84 TOTE £10.30: £2.30, £2.30, £2.10; EX 60.40 Trifecta £175.80 Pool £1,572.89 - 6.35 winning units. Place 6 £196.23, Place 5 £46.65.
Owner Chris Steward **Bred** A E Paulson **Trained** Telscombe, E Sussex

FOCUS

A decent staying handicap in which the leaders took each other on at the head of affairs at too strong a pace and set it up for the closers. As such, the form is not rock solid.

NOTEBOOK

Theatre(USA) was 3lb out of the handicap but the key to him is a strong pace, and that is what he got here. The beneficiary of a suicidal pace up front, he came through in the closing stages to run out a clear winner. Everything dropped right this time and he would not be an obvious candidate to follow up. (op 12-1 tchd 14-1)

Lightning Strike(GER), denied an uncontested lead, went too fast in the early stages in his battle with Fair Along, and the result was that he had less in the locker at the finish than his rider would have liked. It was a good effort in the circumstances for him to hang on for second. (op 11-1)

Winged D'Argent(IRE) looked to be having the race run to suit and, as they turned into the straight, he had his chance, but he could not match the winner's finishing effort. He is on a 15-race losing run but has faced some stiff tasks in amongst those efforts and is finally dropping back to a more feasible mark now. (op 6-1 tchd 8-1)

Fair Along(GER), racing off a 15lb higher mark than when successful at Salisbury last time, was taken on for the lead by Lightning Strike. He eventually lost that battle and they both just ended up setting it up for the winner, who was held up well off the pace. (op 13-8 tchd 15-8)

Establishment has been in good form recently and the strong pace should have suited his come-from-behind style of racing, but disappointingly he made little headway in the closing stages. (tchd 11-2)

Stoop To Conquer was another who proved a bit disappointing considering that the race was run to suit him. (op 10-3)

T/Jkpt: Not won. T/Plt: £205.80 to a £1 stake. Pool: £180,907.84. 641.55 winning tickets. T/Qpdt: £16.20 to a £1 stake. Pool: £8,244.70. 376.50 winning tickets. TM

[5168] CHESTER (L-H)

Saturday, September 23

OFFICIAL GOING: Good to firm

Wind: Nil Weather: Sunny and warm

5527 GERRARD SEEL CHAMPAGNE BOIZEL MAIDEN AUCTION STKS — 7f 122y

2:20 (2:21) (Class 4) 2-Y-O **£4,533** (£1,348; £674; £336) **Stalls** Low

Form — RPR

4 **1** **Porcelain (IRE)**[57] [3908] 2-8-10 .... RobertWinston 9 — 74
(A Dickman) *a.p: led over 3f out: rdn 2f out: r.o gamely whn pressed ins fnl f* **13/2**[3]

02 **2** *shd* **Shake On It**[26] [4895] 2-8-11 .... (t) StephenCarson 1 — 75
(R F Johnson Houghton) *swtg: racd keenly: a.p: wnt 2nd 2f out: sn rdn: ev ch ins fnl f: r.o* **11/10**[1]

3235 **3** *1 3/4* **Angeletta**[26] [4895] 2-8-2 **74** .... ChrisCatlin 7 — 62
(E S McMahon) *led: hdd over 3f out: rdn over 1f out: styd on ins fnl f and nt pce of front pair* **9/2**[2]

0250 **4** *4* **Security Tiger (IRE)**[15] [5157] 2-8-8 **71** .... TPO'Shea 2 — 58
(M R Channon) *midfield: hdwy over 3f out: rdn over 2f out: one pce fr over 1f out* **9/2**[2]

0 **5** *hd* **Crosby Millie**[26] [4880] 2-8-8 .... PhillipMakin 12 — 57
(J R Weymes) *hld up: hdwy on outside over 1f out: styd on ins fnl f: nt rch ldrs* **66/1**

0500 **6** *2* **Pace Telecom Flyer (IRE)**[22] [4980] 2-8-9 **55** .... EddieAhern 6 — 53
(J W Hills) *trckd ldrs: rdn and lost pl over 3f out: n.d after* **25/1**

0 **7** *shd* **Citrus Chief (USA)**[16] [5126] 2-9-3 .... PatDobbs 4 — 61
(R A Harris) *s.s: sn in midfield: effrt 2f out: no imp fr over 1f out* **40/1**

00 **8** *shd* **Da Schadenfreude (USA)**[10] [5289] 2-9-3 .... DaleGibson 10 — 61
(W G M Turner) *midfield: rdn over 2f out: no imp fr over 1f out* **100/1**

0 **9** *5* **King Of The Beers (USA)**[18] [5088] 2-9-1 .... FrancisNorton 5 — 46
(R A Harris) *towards rr: pushed along over 5f out: nvr on terms* **20/1**

00 **10** *5* **Spin Dancer**[57] [3915] 2-8-2 .... PaulQuinn 3 — 21
(W M Brisbourne) *stdd s: hld up: pushed along 4f out: nvr on terms* **100/1**

11 *hd* **Berbatov** 2-8-9 .... J-PGuillambert 8 — 27
(Ms Deborah J Evans) *s.i.s: rdn over 4f out: a bhd* **25/1**

00 **12** *8* **Best Warning**[29] [4765] 2-8-2 .... MatthewHenry 11 — —
(J Ryan) *trckd ldrs: rdn over 3f out: wknd over 2f out: eased fnl f* **66/1**

1m 34.03s (-0.72) **Going Correction** -0.275s/f (Firm) — **12** Ran SP% **117.2**
Speed ratings (Par 97):92,91,90,86,85 83,83,83,78,73 73,65
CSF £13.15 TOTE £6.50: £1.80, £1.20, £1.70; EX 12.70.
Owner The Maroon Stud **Bred** T Hirschfeld **Trained** Sandhutton, N Yorks

FOCUS

Not a great maiden and a modest winning time for the type of race, with the form limited by the proximity of the sixth. Very few ever got into this and the front trio, who were up at the sharp end throughout, pulled well clear of the others.

NOTEBOOK

Porcelain(IRE) confirmed the promise of her Thirsk debut over this slightly longer trip and showed the right attitude to keep the favourite at bay after she looked sure to be swallowed up. The form may not add up to much, but she is entitled to improve again and the influence of her sire and the evidence of this performance suggests she will get a bit further. (tchd 11-2)

Shake On It, awash with sweat, raced handily from the inside draw but was inclined to take a fierce hold. He was brought through to hold every chance off the final bend, but as at Warwick he came up against a rival who simply refused to give in and went down by the narrowest margin. He has the ability to win a small maiden like this and nurseries also become an option for him now. (tchd 6-5 and 5-4 in places)

Angeletta, given a positive ride, stuck on pretty well after being headed and managed to finish a little closer to the runner-up than she had at Warwick, but she is much more exposed than both the front pair and will remain vulnerable to an improver in races like this. (op 5-1 tchd 11-2)

Security Tiger(IRE) did best of those that were held up in a contest dominated by those that raced up with the pace, but she has had a few chances now and is not progressing. (op 11-2)

Crosby Millie never got into the race, but still improved a fair amount on her debut effort on this quicker ground. She is bred to stay further and may not be totally without hope once handicapped. (op 80-1)

King Of The Beers(USA) Official explanation: jockey said colt ran green

5528 LEGAT OWEN NURSERY — 5f 16y

2:50 (2:50) (Class 4) (0-85,77) 2-Y-O **£6,477** (£1,927; £722; £722) **Stalls** Low

Form — RPR

4201 **1** **Mambo Spirit (IRE)**[19] [5065] 2-9-7 **77** .... J-PGuillambert 1 — 84+
(J G Given) *mde virtually all: rdn over 1f out: r.o wl: eased cl home* **7/2**[1]

2321 **2** *1 1/4* **Durova (IRE)**[23] [4956] 2-9-3 **73** .... DavidAllan 5 — 75
(T D Easterby) *trckd ldrs: n.m.r wl over 2f out: rdn to chse wnr over 1f out: no ch towards fin* **7/1**

2U44 **3** *nk* **Princess Ellis**[22] [4986] 2-8-4 **60** .... PaulQuinn 11 — 60+
(E J Alston) *midfield: hdwy on outside 3f out: edgd lft over 1f out: styd on ins fnl f* **50/1**

1 **3** *dht* **Roheryn (IRE)**[9] [5315] 2-9-5 **75** .... TPQueally 6 — 75+
(John A Quinn, Ire) *s.i.s: bhd: rdn and hdwy over 1f out: swtchd rt ins fnl f: fin wl* **4/1**[2]

31 **5** *nk* **Lucky Bee (IRE)**[37] [4510] 2-9-5 **75** .... RobertWinston 7 — 74
(G A Swinbank) *midfield: n.m.r wl over 2f out: sn hdwy: styd on ins fnl f* **7/2**[1]

421 **6** *nk* **Final Dynasty**[12] [5245] 2-9-0 **73** .... StephenDonohoe(3) 4 — 71
(Mrs G S Rees) *trckd ldrs: lost pl 2f out: r.o ins fnl f* **5/1**[3]

5004 **7** *4* **Silly Gilly (IRE)**[9] [5315] 2-7-7 **54** oh1 .... (p) NicolPolli(5) 8 — 38
(A Berry) *towards rr: effrt over 1f out: no imp fnl f* **50/1**

3223 **8** *1 1/2* **Princess Ileana (IRE)**[25] [4913] 2-9-2 **72** .... FrancisNorton 10 — 50
(K R Burke) *in tch: n.m.r wl over 1f out: sn rdn and wknd* **14/1**

0416 **9** *1* **Baytown Paikea**[23] [4946] 2-8-4 **60** .... CatherineGannon 2 — 35
(P S McEntee) *w wnr: rdn over 2f out: wknd over 1f out* **20/1**

440 **10** *1 1/4* **Miss Kool Kat (USA)**[136] [1587] 2-8-10 **69** .... AndrewMullen(3) 12 — 39
(K A Ryan) *rdn over 2f out: a bhd* **33/1**

60.86 secs (-1.19) **Going Correction** -0.275s/f (Firm) — **10** Ran SP% **111.9**
Speed ratings (Par 97):98,96,95,95,95 94,88,85,84,82
3rd Pl: Roheryn £1.00; Princess Erris £3.50; T/C MS-D-R £49.60; MS-D-PE £519.54 CSF £26.10 TOTE £4.20: £1.70, £2.90; EX 38.50.
Owner Jones, Jones, Clarke & O'Sullivan **Bred** R Warren **Trained** Willoughton, Lincs

FOCUS

A fair nursery of its type, run at a solid pace, and the draw once again played its part at least as far as the winner is concerned. The form looks sound though, and has been rated fairly positively. The four non-runners included the pair who would have started from the two widest stalls.

NOTEBOOK

Mambo Spirit(IRE), raised 5lb for his Warwick victory where he was held up, had the plum draw this time so his rider made sure there was no messing about and soon had him at the head of affairs. Railing like a greyhound, he never looked like getting caught but he had everything in his favour here and will need to improve again in order to land the hat-trick off a higher mark. (op 3-1)

Durova(IRE), making her nursery debut on her eighth outing, had the winner in her sights throughout but, although staying on, she could make no impression. She is extremely consistent and should find another opportunity based on that alone. (op 8-1)

Roheryn(IRE) ◆ was conceding experience to his rivals, having only raced once before, and that probably cost him. After missing the break - a cardinal sin here - he found himself stone last rounding the final bend and though he stayed on to dead heat for the minor berth the damage had already been done. He can be rated better than the bare result and there are more races to be won with him. Official explanation: jockey said gelding reared as stalls opened (tchd 40-1)

Princess Ellis ◆, another making her nursery debut, appreciated this return to a quicker surface and ran with a lot of credit from her wide draw. She is yet to win, but looks capable of winning a nursery from this sort of mark when more favourably berthed. (tchd 40-1)

Lucky Bee(IRE), having only her third outing, stayed on without managing to land a blow and this sharper track probably did not play to her strengths. The dam's side of her pedigree suggests she needs a stiffer test. (op 3-1)
Final Dynasty, having only her second outing on turf, may not have been suited by this quicker ground, but was not disgraced and there will be other days. (tchd 11-2)

5529 INNOSPEC H'CAP — 7f 2y

3:20 (3:21) (Class 3) (0-95,93) 3-Y-O+ **£11,658** (£3,468; £1,733; £865) **Stalls** Low

Form / RPR

4140 **1** **Phluke**[19] 5070 5-8-11 **83** StephenCarson 3 — 91
(R F Johnson Houghton) *mde all: rdn over 1f out: hld on wl towards fin* **8/1**

0430 **2** *nk* **Dhaular Dhar (IRE)**[7] 5357 4-8-11 **83** PhillipMakin 10 — 90
(J S Goldie) *midfield: hdwy 2f out: sn rdn: wnt 2nd ins fnl f: r.o strly* **8/1**

0363 **3** *1* **Commando Scott (IRE)**[7] 5355 5-9-0 **89** PatrickMathers(3) 1 — 94
(I W McInnes) *trckd ldrs: rdn over 1f out: nt qckn towards fin* **5/1**[1]

441 **4** *1 1/4* **Inter Vision (USA)**[29] 4760 6-9-2 **88** RobertWinston 8 — 89
(A Dickman) *prom: rdn and ev ch over 1f out: no ex wl ins fnl f* **11/2**[2]

0436 **5** *shd* **Zennerman (IRE)**[8] 5337 3-7-13 **79** oh3 LiamJones(5) 4 — 80
(W M Brisbourne) *trckd ldrs: rdn over 2f out: styd on same pce ins fnl f* **25/1**

0501 **6** *1/2* **Silver Dip**[27] 4837 3-8-10 **85** FrancisNorton 6 — 85
(B W Hills) *trckd ldrs: rdn over 2f out: one pce ins fnl f* **7/1**[3]

3000 **7** *nk* **Roman Maze**[8] 5336 6-8-10 **82** EddieAhern 11 — 81
(W M Brisbourne) *racd keenly: hld up: hdwy 4f out: rdn over 1f out: kpt on ins fnl f* **12/1**

0604 **8** *shd* **Josh**[28] 4790 4-8-8 **83** (p) AndrewMullen(3) 12 — 82
(K A Ryan) *hld up: rdn over 2f out: styd on towards fin* **12/1**

0062 **9** *nk* **Zomerlust**[8] 5336 4-9-7 **93** GrahamGibbons 7 — 91
(J J Quinn) *midfield: effrt over 2f out: one pce ins fnl f* **8/1**

0005 **10** *nk* **Malcheek (IRE)**[19] 5070 4-8-9 **81** DavidAllan 2 — 81+
(T D Easterby) *s.i.s: plld hrd: bhd: rdn over 1f out: styng on whn nt clr run ins fnl f: sn eased* **8/1**

005 **11** *3/4* **Orphan (IRE)**[26] 4885 4-8-7 **79** oh4 ChrisCatlin 5 — 74
(K R Burke) *midfield: rdn over 1f out: outpcd ins fnl f* **25/1**

0000 **12** *12* **Shot To Fame (USA)**[8] 5337 7-8-10 **82** (t) PaulQuinn 9 — 46
(D Nicholls) *midfield: wknd 2f out: eased whn btn over 1f out* **14/1**

1m 25.68s (-2.79) **Going Correction** -0.275s/f (Firm)
WFA 3 from 4yo+ 3lb **12 Ran SP% 118.7**
Speed ratings (Par 107):104,103,102,101,100 100,100,99,99,99 98,84
CSF £70.77 CT £358.61 TOTE £8.90: £2.40, £3.00, £2.30; EX 110.10.
Owner Mrs R F Johnson Houghton **Bred** Mrs R F Johnson Houghton **Trained** Blewbury, Oxon

FOCUS
A decent handicap, but one that was spoiled to an extent. Firstly, the two inside stalls - which were within a separate bank to the other ten - opened late and the pair who started from those gates conceded at least a length to their rivals, which is a significant amount around here. Then once under way, the early pace was modest and like the opening contest this turned into a sprint from the final bend. Very few ever got into the race as a result though, and the true value of the form is questionable, and has been rated fairly negatively through the winner.

NOTEBOOK
Phluke, who has a good record on turning tracks like this, especially left-handed ones, had everything go his way. Thanks to the two stalls on his inside opening late, he was soon able to bag the inside rail in front and set his own pace. Then by kicking clear off the final bend, he was able to just about gain enough of a lead to see him last home. (op 9-1)
Dhaular Dhar(IRE), who has a fine record here, posted another decent effort and did best of those that tried to come from off the pace, only just failing to get there. He will always be one to watch out for on this track.
Commando Scott(IRE) ◆ ran an excellent race considering he had plenty going against him on this occasion. Firstly the ground was probably faster than ideal, but even more significant was that his stall opened later than the vast majority of his rivals which cost him at least a length. He was able to take a handy position thanks to the modest early pace and did have every chance against the inside rail in the home straight, but given how far he was beaten he may conceivably have done even better with a level break. (op 13-2)
Inter Vision(USA), raised 4lb for his course-and-distance victory last month, was always in a handy position and seemed to run his race with no excuses. (tchd 5-1and 6-1 in places)
Zennerman(IRE), without a win in 14 months, is gradually dropping to a more feasible mark and was not disgraced here from 3lb out of the handicap. (op 20-1)
Silver Dip, raised 3lb for her Goodwood victory, could never land a blow and would almost certainly have preferred a stronger early gallop.
Roman Maze, gradually slipping down the weights, was not suited by the way the race was run which was compounded by his wide draw. (op 16-1)
Josh is not easy to predict, but the way the race was run and the outside stall give him valid excuses.
Zomerlust, runner-up in the Ayr Silver Cup and now 4lb higher, does stay this far despite never having won beyond six, but he would not have been suited by this quicker ground. (op 13-2)
Malcheek(IRE) ◆ can be excused this as his was the other stall that opened late and nothing went right for him even after that. Better handicapped now, he remains one to keep an eye on. Official explanation: jockey said gelding hit the gate as stalls opened and was slowly away (op 7-1)
Shot To Fame(USA) Official explanation: jockey said gelding clipped heels

5530 THE SPORTSMAN H'CAP — 1m 2f 75y

3:55 (3:55) (Class 2) (0-100,98) 3-Y-O
£20,565 (£6,157; £3,078; £1,541; £768; £386) **Stalls** High

Form / RPR

1131 **1** **Stotsfold**[21] 5016 3-8-8 **91** AdamKirby(3) 7 — 105+
(W R Swinburn) *s.i.s: hld up: hdwy over 3f out: led over 1f out: pushed out and in command ins fnl f* **4/1**[2]

2001 **2** *2 1/2* **Salute Him (IRE)**[28] 4810 3-8-11 **91** TPO'Shea 3 — 97
(M R Channon) *led: rdn 3f out: hdd over 1f out: no ex ins fnl f* **10/1**

1200 **3** *1* **Purple Moon (IRE)**[32] 4676 3-9-3 **97** RobertWinston 6 — 102
(Sir Michael Stoute) *midfield: rdn over 2f out: hdwy over 1f out: sn edgd lft: styd on ins fnl f* **5/1**[3]

1223 **4** *1 1/4* **Safqa**[14] 5164 3-8-5 **85** EddieAhern 9 — 87
(B W Hills) *s.i.s: hld up: rdn over 2f out: hdwy over 1f out: kpt on ins fnl f* **9/1**

4301 **5** *shd* **Thumpers Dream**[29] 4759 3-8-4 **84** oh2 FrancisNorton 5 — 86
(H R A Cecil) *trckd ldrs: rdn 3f out: no ex ins fnl f* **12/1**

0315 **6** *1* **Numeric (GER)**[30] 4742 3-8-9 **89** (b) RobertHavlin 1 — 89+
(J H M Gosden) *s.i.s: midfield: lost pl 4f out: nt clr run over 1f out: sn swtchd rt: kpt on ins fnl f* **6/1**

3401 **7** *1* **Punta Galera (IRE)**[11] 5266 3-8-8 **88** (b[1]) PatDobbs 4 — 86
(R Hannon) *prom: rdn whn n.m.r under 2f out: sn wknd* **25/1**

2213 **8** *6* **Noble Gent (IRE)**[27] 4833 3-9-4 **98** DO'Donohoe 2 — 85
(Saeed Bin Suroor) *in tch: rdn over 2f out: hung lft and wknd over 1f out* **10/3**[1]

3422 **9** *7* **Babcary**[14] 5164 3-8-6 **86** DaleGibson 8 — 60
(M P Tregoning) *midfield: rdn over 2f out: sn wknd* **10/1**

2m 7.15s (-5.99) **Going Correction** -0.275s/f (Firm) course record **9 Ran SP% 113.8**
Speed ratings (Par 107):112,110,109,108,108 107,106,101,96
CSF £42.67 CT £202.28 TOTE £3.30: £1.80, £3.00, £1.60; EX 40.90.
Owner Mrs P W Harris **Bred** Pendley Farm **Trained** Aldbury, Herts

FOCUS
A competitive handicap run at a true gallop and the winning time was decent for the type of race. The form looks rock solid rated around the placed horses.

NOTEBOOK
Stotsfold ◆, a winner over course and distance on his only previous visit here, had been raised a hefty 10lb for his decisive victory on the Kempton Polytrack last time, but he made light of it with another impressive display. Patiently ridden early, he eventually won going away and the Handicapper is having a real problem keeping up with him. He is obviously a versatile sort and with another year on his back he could eventually become very decent indeed. (op 3-1)
Salute Him(IRE), raised 4lb for his Sandown victory, again tried to make all the running and made a good fist of it, but he came up against a rival who may eventually end up in even better company than this, so there was no disgrace in this. (op 12-1)
Purple Moon(IRE) stayed on without ever really looking like winning and may be worth another try at 12 furlongs. This looks to be more his level.
Safqa was given a very negative ride, never looked like getting to the principals at any stage, and her final position was as close as she got. (op 10-1)
Thumpers Dream, winner of a course-and-distance maiden on her last visit, found this company a bit too hot on her handicap debut.
Numeric(GER), a course-and-distance winner at the big May Meeting, has done most of his racing since over further. Kept towards the inside of the field for most of the way, he met trouble in running on more than one occasion and can be rated a bit better than the bare result. (op 7-1)
Noble Gent(IRE) never looked happy and probably needs to get his toe in to show his best. (op 7-2)

5531 MONDI PACKAGING H'CAP — 1m 5f 89y

4:30 (4:31) (Class 4) (0-80,82) 3-Y-O+ **£7,772** (£2,312; £1,155; £577) **Stalls** Low

Form / RPR

4103 **1** **Linden Lime**[13] 5201 4-9-0 **62** FrancisNorton 2 — 69+
(Jamie Poulton) *racd keenly: a.p: nt clr run over 2f out: rdn to ld over 1f out: r.o* **8/1**

0005 **2** *1* **Jeepstar**[45] 4259 6-9-7 **72** AdamKirby(3) 11 — 78
(S C Williams) *led: rdn over 3f out: hdd over 1f out: styd on: hld cl home* **7/1**[3]

6540 **3** *1/2* **Acuzio**[14] 5174 5-8-9 **57** oh2 DavidAllan 1 — 62
(W M Brisbourne) *racd keenly: in tch: rdn over 2f out: swtchd rt over 1f out: styd on towards fin* **33/1**

3236 **4** *3/4* **Reluctant Suitor**[7] 5362 4-9-4 **66** PhillipMakin 13 — 70+
(J S Goldie) *hld up: rdn over 2f out: hdwy over 1f out: r.o ins fnl f: nrst fin* **7/1**[3]

2332 **5** *hd* **Regency Red (IRE)**[4] 5451 8-8-4 **57** oh7 EmmettStack(5) 5 — 61
(W M Brisbourne) *midfield: rdn over 1f out: styd on ins fnl f* **22/1**

4303 **6** *shd* **Sporting Gesture**[7] 5367 9-9-10 **72** PaulMulrennan 12 — 75
(M W Easterby) *prom: rdn and ev ch over 2f out: no ex ins fnl f* **12/1**

2135 **7** *nk* **Squirtle (IRE)**[14] 5174 3-8-8 **65** ChrisCatlin 3 — 68
(W M Brisbourne) *in tch: rdn over 2f out: one pce ins fnl f* **12/1**

3426 **8** *1 1/2* **York Cliff**[23] 4960 8-8-4 **57** LiamJones(5) 10 — 58
(W M Brisbourne) *hld up: rdn and hdwy 2f out: one pce ins fnl f* **20/1**

0644 **9** *2 1/2* **Merrymaker**[14] 5174 6-9-6 **71** PatrickMathers(3) 6 — 68
(W M Brisbourne) *s.i.s: in rr: rdn over 2f out: no imp* **11/1**

-014 **10** *12* **Jack Dawson (IRE)**[19] 5069 9-9-11 **76** StephenDonohoe(3) 16 — 55
(John Berry) *hld up: rdn over 4f out: nvr on terms* **10/1**

-015 **11** *1 1/4* **Sendinpost**[35] 4604 3-8-5 **62** GrahamGibbons 9 — 39
(S C Williams) *midfield: rdn 4f out: wknd over 2f out* **5/1**[2]

3313 **12** *6* **Meadow Mischief (FR)**[29] 4770 3-9-11 **82** (b) RobertWinston 15 — 50
(E A L Dunlop) *s.i.s: in rr: hdwy 8f out: chalng 3f out: sn rdn: wknd 2f out* **9/2**[1]

2m 51.44s (-3.98) **Going Correction** -0.275s/f (Firm)
WFA 3 from 4yo+ 9lb **12 Ran SP% 115.8**
Speed ratings (Par 105):101,100,100,99,99 99,99,98,96,89 88,84
CSF £59.90 CT £1748.23 TOTE £10.50: £3.10, £2.50, £8.60; EX 73.90.
Owner R C Moules **Bred** R C Moules **Trained** Telscombe, E Sussex

FOCUS
Quite a competitive staying handicap, but another race on the card to be run at a modest pace and, as with the earlier contests, that very much suited those that raced handily. There are doubts over the form raised by the proximity of the third and fifth.
Sendinpost Official explanation: trainer said filly became unbalanced and did not handle the bends
Meadow Mischief(FR) Official explanation: trainer's rep said, regarding poor form shown, that the race was not run to suit the colt as the rider had to make too much use of him from a wide draw

5532 UK HYGIENE H'CAP — 5f 16y

5:05 (5:07) (Class 4) (0-85,85) 3-Y-O+ **£7,772** (£2,312; £1,155; £577) **Stalls** Low

Form / RPR

4260 **1** **Circuit Dancer (IRE)**[8] 5333 6-8-12 **78** AdrianTNicholls 1 — 88
(D Nicholls) *mde virtually all: rdn over 1f out: r.o wl* **3/1**[1]

3301 **2** *1 3/4* **Ptarmigan Ridge**[8] 5333 10-8-7 **76** GregFairley(3) 13 — 82+
(Miss L A Perratt) *midfield: hdwy whn nt clr run 2f out: nt clr run again over 1f out: r.o strly ins fnl f: nt rch wnr* **14/1**

5420 **3** *shd* **Handsome Cross (IRE)**[8] 5333 5-9-5 **85** PaulQuinn 7 — 88+
(D Nicholls) *broke wl: in tch: nt clr run 2f out: rdn and swtchd rt over 1f out: styd on ins fnl f* **10/1**

0600 **4** *1 3/4* **Bo McGinty (IRE)**[8] 5333 5-8-8 **81** (b) JamesRogers(7) 4 — 81+
(R A Fahey) *midfield: n.m.r and hmpd 2f out: rdn over 1f out: styd on ins fnl f: edgd lft towards fin* **7/1**[2]

-331 **5** *1 3/4* **Monashee Brave (IRE)**[23] 4948 3-8-11 **78** GrahamGibbons 16 — 68+
(J J Quinn) *in rr: nt clr run 2f out: hdwy over 1f out: r.o ins fnl f: nrst fin* **20/1**

0403 **6** *3/4* **Mimi Mouse**[14] 5169 4-8-11 **77** PaulMulrennan 8 — 65
(T D Easterby) *chsd ldrs: rdn 2f out: hung rt and one pce ins fnl f* **20/1**

2405 **7** *1 1/4* **Toy Top (USA)**[33] 4659 3-8-13 **80** (b) PhillipMakin 3 — 63
(M Dods) *hmpd jst after s: towards rr: hdwy 2f out: swtchd rt over 1f out: styd on ins fnl f: nt rch ldrs* **14/1**

2124 **8** *nk* **Shes Minnie**[33] 4659 3-8-10 **77** (p) RobertWinston 15 — 59
(J G M O'Shea) *towards rr: rdn over 1f out: styd on ins fnl f: nvr nrr* **20/1**

0163 **9** *hd* **Bold Minstrel (IRE)**[11] 5275 4-9-0 **80** ChrisCatlin 5 — 61
(M Quinn) *prom: rdn over 1f out: wknd fnl f* **9/1**[3]

0000 **10** *1 1/2* **Campbeltown (IRE)**[18] 5087 3-9-4 **85** (p) EddieAhern 14 — 61
(R A Harris) *outpcd: kpt on fnl f: nt pce to chal* **40/1**

5602 **11** *hd* **Spiritual Peace (IRE)**[40] 4422 3-8-9 **79** (p) AndrewMullen(3) 9 — 54
(K A Ryan) *midfield: rdn over 2f out: wknd over 1f out* **25/1**

-224 **12** ½ **Our Fugitive (IRE)**[8] 5333 4-8-11 77 .... FrancisNorton 2 50
(A W Carroll) *prom: rdn over 1f out: wknd qckly* **3/1**[1]

0500 **13** 3 ½ **Malapropism**[14] 5169 6-9-0 80 .... TPO'Shea 12 41
(M R Channon) *midfield on outside: rdn over 2f out: wknd over 1f out* **25/1**

-000 **14** 8 **Gilt Linked**[6] 5405 3-8-13 80 .... CatherineGannon 10 12
(J S Wainwright) *midfield: wknd 2f out* **66/1**

60.07 secs (-1.98) **Going Correction** -0.275s/f (Firm)
WFA 3 from 4yo+ 1lb **14** Ran SP% **120.8**
Speed ratings (Par 105):104,101,101,98,95 94,92,91,91,89 88,87,82,69
CSF £43.88 CT £345.89 TOTE £2.80: £1.40, £4.20, £3.20; EX 78.20 Place 6 £97.21, Place 5 £75.88.
Owner David Fish **Bred** Michael Staunton **Trained** Sessay, N Yorks
■ Magic Glade was withdrawn (14/1, inj on way to start). R4 applies, deduct 5p in the £.

FOCUS
A decent sprint handicap run at a true pace and but not rated as high as it could have been. Circuit Dancer's victory meant that both five-furlong races on the card were won by stall one, but a couple of those drawn out in the River Dee did perform well in this race.
Spiritual Peace(IRE) Official explanation: jockey said gelding hung right
Our Fugitive(IRE) Official explanation: jockey said gelding was not striding out in home straight
T/Plt: £172.60 to a £1 stake. Pool: £64,945.85. 274.55 winning tickets. T/Qpdt: £205.30 to a £1 stake. Pool: £2,164.20. 7.80 winning tickets. DO

5507 HAYDOCK (L-H)

Saturday, September 23

OFFICIAL GOING: Good (good to soft in places)
Wind: Virtually nil

5533 BRIAN CHADWICK 40TH BIRTHDAY CELEBRATION H'CAP 1m 6f
2:25 (2:25) (Class 3) (0-90,90) 3-Y-0+
£11,217 (£3,358; £1,679; £840; £419; £210) **Stalls** Low

Form RPR

003- **1** **Tees Components**[270] 5744 11-10-0 88 .... (t) TomEaves 7 98
(K G Reveley) *hld up and bhd: hdwy on inner over 3f out: rdn wl over 1f out: styd on strly ins last to ld last 100 yds* **50/1**

1020 **2** ¾ **Candle**[14] 5163 3-8-9 79 .... DaneO'Neill 16 87
(H Candy) *in tch: hdwy over 3f out: swtchd lft and effrt to ld wl over2f out: sn rdn: drvn ins last: hdd and no ex last 100 yds* **16/1**

1122 **3** ¾ **Bollin Derek**[35] 4612 3-8-1 71 .... JimmyQuinn 12 78
(T D Easterby) *a.p: rdn along and outpcd over 2f out: drvn over 1f out kpt on ins last* **7/2**[1]

500 **4** nk **Swordsman (GER)**[26] 4876 4-9-6 85 .... (b) AndrewElliott(5) 1 92
(M L W Bell) *trckd ldrs: hdwy 4f out: rdn and outpaced over 2f out: kpt on u.p ins last* **20/1**

363 **5** 2 ½ **Madroos**[35] 4604 3-8-11 81 .... RHills 8 85
(J L Dunlop) *towards rr: hdwy over 3f out: rdn over 2f out: styd on appr last: nrst fin* **12/1**

0060 **6** 1 **Sharp Reply (USA)**[17] 5115 4-8-9 69 .... HayleyTurner 6 71
(R M Whitaker) *towards rr: hdwy on outer 3f out: rdn along 2f out: kpt on appr last: nrst fin* **66/1**

002 **7** nk **Quizzene (USA)**[21] 5010 4-9-8 82 .... (b) RoystonFfrench 15 84
(M Johnston) *cl up: led over 5f out: rdn clr over 4f out: hdd wl over 2f out: sn drvn and wknd wl over 1f out* **17/2**

2312 **8** ½ **St Savarin (FR)**[17] 5115 5-9-8 87 .... JamieMoriarty(5) 9 88
(R A Fahey) *hld up towards rr: hdwy over 2f out: sn rdn and kpt on: nt rch ldrs* **8/1**[3]

-162 **9** 2 ½ **Corum (IRE)**[35] 4604 3-9-4 88 .... KDarley 10 85
(J H M Gosden) *trckd ldrs: hdwy 5f out: chal on outer 3f out and ev ch tl rdn 2f out and grad wknd* **5/1**[2]

0040 **10** ½ **Karlu (GER)**[52] 4046 4-8-12 72 .... PaulEddery 3 69
(Pat Eddery) *towards rr. hdwy on outer 3f out: sn rdn:edgd lft and no imp fnl 2f* **25/1**

1022 **11** 12 **Oddsmaker (IRE)**[1] 5513 5-8-3 70 .... (t) MCGeran(7) 14 50
(M A Barnes) *midfield: rdn along over 3f out: nvr a factor* **14/1**

3134 **12** nk **Salesin**[30] 4742 3-9-6 90 .... TedDurcan 5 70
(L M Cumani) *midfield: hdwy on outer 3f out: sn rdn along and wknd 2f out* **17/2**

5-31 **13** 7 **Monolith**[90] 2894 8-9-6 83 .... GregFairley(3) 11 53
(L Lungo) *towards rr: bhd fnl 4f* **16/1**

6-16 **14** 13 **Into The Shadows**[140] 991 6-9-7 88 .... JamesReveley(7) 13 40
(K G Reveley) *a rr* **25/1**

-000 **15** 33 **Dr Sharp (IRE)**[128] 1809 6-9-8 82 .... MickyFenton 4 —
(T P Tate) *led: rdn along over 6f out: hdd over 5f out: wknd wl over 3f out* **16/1**

00-6 **16** 2 ½ **Gold Ring**[29] 4770 6-10-0 88 .... RobertHavlin 2 —
(J A Geake) *trckd ldrs: pushed along on inner over 6f out: rdn along whn n.m.r and hit rail over 5f out: sn lost pl and bhd* **50/1**

3m 4.31s (-1.98) **Going Correction** 0.0s/f (Good)
WFA 3 from 4yo+ 10lb **16** Ran SP% **120.9**
Speed ratings (Par 107):105,104,104,103,102 101,101,101,100,99 92,92,88,81,62 61
CSF £681.42 CT £3531.70 TOTE £78.60: £13.60, £2.70, £1.60, £5.60; EX 1649.50 Trifecta £248.50 Part won. Pool £350.10 - 0.10 winning units..
Owner Tees Components Ltd **Bred** P Young **Trained** Lingdale, Redcar & Cleveland

FOCUS
A decent staying handicap that was run at a solid pace. The first four came clear and the race has been rated positively.

NOTEBOOK
Tees Components, having his first outing since injuring himself when unseating on his chase debut last year, picked up strongly from off the pace and eventually scored with a little to spare. He has slipped to a decent mark, and is clearly still as good as ever, with a likely return to hurdling now on the cards for this veteran. (op 66-1)
Candle proved well suited by the stiffer test and showed much-improved form. The easier surface also appeared to her liking and there ought to be more to come now connections can be confident she stays. (tchd 20-1)
Bollin Derek fared the best of those to race up with the early pace and got the longer trip well. He is a consistent performer, despite proving a little expensive to follow, but will no doubt go up a few pounds for this. Official explanation: jockey said colt slipped on the bend (op 4-1)
Swordsman(GER) ran an improved race on ground he would have found plenty soft enough and certainly proved suited by the step back up to this longer distance. He is perhaps still a touch high in the weights at present, however. (op 25-1)
Madroos, ridden to get the longer trip, was staying on all too late and is slightly better than the bare form. He will surely be ridden more handily in the future now connections know he stays.
Sharp Reply(USA), up in trip, was another doing his best work towards the finish and ran his best race for some time. He too can be ridden more prominently over this sort of trip in the future and can find easier assignments. Official explanation: jockey said gelding slipped on bend
Quizzene(USA), back to form in first-time blinkers over course and distance last time, eventually paid for his early exertions and the blinkers clearly failed to have the same effect on this drop in class. (op 7-1)
Corum(IRE), whose stable won this event in 2005, did little to convince that he stays this longer trip and is probably at his best when able to dominate over 12 furlongs. (op 11-2)
Salesin has to rate disappointing on this, the first time he has taken on older horses. (op 9-1)
Dr Sharp(IRE) Official explanation: jockey said gelding lost its action
Gold Ring Official explanation: jockey said gelding slipped on the bend

5534 AKZO NOBEL PREMIER H'CAP 6f
2:55 (2:57) (Class 2) (0-100,98) 3-Y-0+ **£12,954** (£3,854; £1,926; £962) **Stalls** High

Form RPR

0412 **1** **Stanley Goodspeed**[28] 4807 3-8-1 84 oh2 .... (t) JamesDoyle(3) 7 93
(J W Hills) *hld up: hdwy over 2f out: rdn to ld ins last: sn drvn and jst hld on* **10/1**

4315 **2** shd **Knot In Wood (IRE)**[8] 5336 4-8-9 87 .... TonyHamilton 12 95
(R A Fahey) *dwlt: hdwy on outer over 2f out: rdn and str run ins last: jst failed* **3/1**[1]

6000 **3** shd **Zowington**[26] 4875 4-8-10 88 .... TedDurcan 5 96
(C F Wall) *cl up: led 2f out: rdn over 1f out: hdd ins last: sn drvn and rallied: jst hld* **25/1**

1043 **4** 1 ¼ **Rising Shadow (IRE)**[8] 5336 5-9-2 94 .... JimmyQuinn 3 98+
(T D Barron) *towards rr. hdwy 2f out: rdn and nt clr run ins last: kpt on towards fin* **13/2**[3]

3040 **5** 1 **Pieter Brueghel (USA)**[28] 4796 7-8-3 88 .... VictoriaBehan(7) 8 89
(D Nicholls) *prom: rdn over 1f out: wknd ins last* **12/1**

0050 **6** 1 ¼ **Mecca's Mate**[7] 5358 5-9-6 98 .... RoystonFfrench 1 96
(D W Barker) *in tch: hdwy to chse ldrs 2f out: sn rdn and no imp ent last* **12/1**

/505 **7** ¾ **Campo Bueno (FR)**[16] 5135 4-8-9 87 .... KDarley 6 82
(A Berry) *led: rdn along and hdd 2f out: drvn appr last and grad wknd* **33/1**

2144 **8** 2 **Ellens Academy (IRE)**[8] 5336 11-8-1 84 oh6 .... MichaelJStainton(5) 2 73
(E J Alston) *s.i.s: a towards rr* **20/1**

2102 **9** nk **Machinist (IRE)**[13] 5202 6-9-0 92 .... AdrianTNicholls 4 80
(D Nicholls) *in tch: rdn along over 2f out: sn outpcd* **8/1**

0002 **10** ¾ **Continent**[7] 5355 9-8-11 89 .... DaneO'Neill 10 75
(D Nicholls) *s.i.s: a rr* **12/1**

0502 **11** ½ **Kenmore**[21] 5009 4-8-10 88 .... TomEaves 11 73
(D Nicholls) *trckd ldrs: rdn along over 2f out: sn wknd* **5/1**[2]

1600 **12** 1 ¾ **Dazzling Bay**[47] 4202 6-8-10 88 .... MickyFenton 9 67
(T D Easterby) *chsd ldrs: rdn along over 2f out: sn wknd* **33/1**

1m 11.7s (-3.20) **Going Correction** -0.375s/f (Firm)
WFA 3 from 4yo+ 2lb **12** Ran SP% **112.8**
Speed ratings (Par 109):106,105,105,104,102 101,100,97,97,96 95,93
CSF £36.30 CT £737.88 TOTE £10.30: £2.80, £1.70, £6.20; EX 40.50 Trifecta £460.20 Pool £648.20 - 1.00 winning unit..
Owner R J Tufft **Bred** Burton Agnes Stud Co Ltd **Trained** Upper Lambourn, Berks

FOCUS
A competitive sprint for the class which saw a close finish between the first three. Solid form, rated around the placed horses.

NOTEBOOK
Stanley Goodspeed, 2lb out of the handicap, narrowly got back to winning ways under a well-judged ride from Doyle. This has to rate a personal-best effort, he has been improved for the recent application of a tongue tie, and is versatile as regards underfoot conditions. He should have more to offer despite a higher future mark. (op 12-1)
Knot In Wood(IRE) was only beaten by the smallest of margins and turned in another solid effort. He remains progressive and this likeable sprinter can find compensation before the season's end. (op 7-2)
Zowington has to rate a little unlucky, as he fared the best of those to force the strong early pace and was ultimately beaten in a bobbing finish. This was much his best effort since scoring from this mark on his seasonal reappearance and he looks to be back in decent heart now. However, he will now go up a few pounds for this no doubt.
Rising Shadow(IRE) endured a troubled passage entering the final furlong and can be rated better than the bare form suggests. He is in good heart at present, but does find it hard to get his head in front all the same. Official explanation: jockey said gelding was denied a clear run (tchd 7-1)
Pieter Brueghel(USA) ran his usual race under a positive ride and helps to set the level of this form. (op 14-1)
Kenmore, back to form when flying home to finish second over five furlongs at this venue 21 days previously, had his chance over this extra furlong and proved a little disappointing. He proved very easy to back, however, and it may be that he wants genuinely soft ground now. Official explanation: trainer had no explanation for the poor form shown (op 7-2)

5535 LESTER PIGGOTT "START TO FINISH" H'CAP 5f
3:30 (3:31) (Class 2) (0-100,99) 3-Y-0+ **£19,431** (£5,781; £2,889; £1,443) **Stalls** High

Form RPR

0000 **1** **Sierra Vista**[6] 5405 6-9-3 97 .... TomEaves 3 109
(D W Barker) *mde all: rdn clr wl over 1f out: styd on* **16/1**

0043 **2** 1 ½ **If Paradise**[5] 5433 5-8-8 88 .... DaneO'Neill 11 95
(R Hannon) *a.p: rdn wl over 1f out: kpt on u.p ins last* **15/2**

2100 **3** ¾ **Smokin Beau**[8] 5333 9-8-2 85 oh1 .... JamesDoyle(3) 10 89
(D Nicholls) *chsd ldrs: hdwy 2f out: sn rdn and kpt on appr last* **14/1**

-260 **4** hd **River Falcon**[8] 5336 6-8-12 92 .... DanielTudhope 15 95
(J S Goldie) *dwlt: hdwy 2f out: sn rdn and styd on wl fnl f* **7/1**[3]

5100 **5** hd **Sir Edwin Landseer (USA)**[91] 2847 6-9-0 97 .... (p) NeilChalmers(3) 12 99
(Christian Wroe, UAE) *wnt rt s: towards rr: hdwy 2f out: sn rdn and styd on ins last: nrst fin* **33/1**

2102 **6** nk **Cape Royal**[5] 5433 6-9-0 94 .... (bt) TedDurcan 17 95
(J M Bradley) *prom: rdn along wl over 1f out: wknd ent last* **11/2**[2]

0110 **7** 1 ½ **Cashel Mead**[21] 5009 6-8-9 89 .... KDarley 7 85
(J L Spearing) *midfield: effrt and sme hdwy over 2f out: sn rdn and no imp appr last* **14/1**

2500 **8** ½ **Steel Blue**[8] 5336 6-8-5 85 oh4 .... HayleyTurner 6 79
(R M Whitaker) *chsd ldrs: rdn along 2f out: sn one pce* **16/1**

1113 **9** shd **Fantasy Explorer**[31] 4717 3-8-9 90 .... JimmyQuinn 16 84
(J J Quinn) *chsd ldrs: rdn along 2f out: sn one pce* **9/2**[1]

0006 **10** shd **Green Park (IRE)**[35] 4601 3-8-8 89 .... TonyHamilton 5 82
(R A Fahey) *chsd ldrs: rdn along over 2f out: sn wknd* **20/1**

5000 **11** ¾ **Highland Warrior**[8] 5336 7-8-5 85 oh5 .... RoystonFfrench 9 76
(J S Goldie) *s.i.s and bhd: hdwy wl over 1f out: rdn ent last and sn no imp* **33/1**

6006 **12** 1 **Glenviews Youngone (IRE)**[26] 4875 3-8-5 86 oh4 ow1 RobbieFitzpatrick 13 73
(Peter Grayson) *a towards rr* **33/1**

405 **13** 2 **Matty Tun**[8] 5333 7-8-5 85 oh8 .... DeanMcKeown 8 65
(J Balding) *a towards rr* **12/1**

5045 **14** 3 ½ **Texas Gold**[13] [5202] 8-9-5 **99** .... RHills 4 66
(W R Muir) *chsd ldrs: rdn along 2f out: sn wknd* **14/1**

0 **15** 1 ¼ **Ascot Lady (IRE)**[40] [4422] 3-7-13 **85** oh8 .... AndrewElliott(5) 14 48
(J Balding) *s.i.s: a rr* **66/1**

0304 **16** 6 **Johannes (IRE)**[62] [3761] 3-8-10 **91** .... (t) AdrianTNicholls 2 32
(D Nicholls) *chsd ldrs on outer: rdn along over 2f out: sn wknd* **14/1**

58.61 secs (-3.46) **Going Correction** -0.375s/f (Firm)
WFA 3 from 5yo+ 1lb **16** Ran SP% **119.0**
Speed ratings (Par 109):112,109,108,108,107 107,104,104,103,103 102,100,97,92,90 80
CSF £122.09 CT £1808.75 TOTE £18.80: £4.60, £2.20, £3.60, £2.40; EX 120.10 Trifecta £384.10 Part won. Pool £541.04 - 0.30 winning units..
Owner David T J Metcalfe **Bred** Mrs M Beddis **Trained** Scorton, N Yorks

FOCUS
A typically competitive handicap for the class and the form looks solid enough. The winner returned to her best and posted a very decent winning time in the process.

NOTEBOOK
Sierra Vista, down in class, bounced back to her best by making all for a convincing success. She has been helped by a slight drop in the weights, taking her back down to her last winning mark, and this does look to be her optimum trip. She would have to be of interest if turning out again quickly. (op 14-1)
If Paradise ran another solid race in defeat and reversed his recent Leicester form with Cape Royal in the process. He is on a decent mark no doubt, but has become fiendishly hard to actually win with. (op 8-1)
Smokin Beau posted a return to form and is clearly not handicapped out of winning just yet. (op 18-1)
River Falcon was always playing catch-up after a slow start and is a little better than his finishing position suggests. He could yet find a race this term as he ideally wants softer ground. (op 8-1)
Sir Edwin Landseer(USA) caught the eye staying on all too late and has clearly benefited for his recent break.
Cape Royal had his chance and failed to confirm his recent Leicester form with the runner-up. He is just back in the Handicapper's grip now. (op 5-1 tchd 6-1)
Fantasy Explorer ran below his best, but ideally wants faster ground and may just be feeling the effects of a recent busy period. (op 5-1 tchd 11-2)
Matty Tun Official explanation: jockey said gelding bled from the nose
Texas Gold Official explanation: jockey said gelding was unsuited by the good (good to soft places) ground
Johannes(IRE) Official explanation: jockey said colt never travelled and felt wrong

5536 TOMMY KEARNS 75TH BIRTHDAY E B F MAIDEN FILLIES' STKS 1m 30y
4:05 (4:10) (Class 5) 2-Y-O **£4,533** (£1,348; £674; £336) **Stalls** Low

Form RPR

04 **1** **Tarteel (USA)**[23] [4964] 2-9-0 .... RHills 9 88+
(J L Dunlop) *hld up in rr: stdy hdwy 3f out: rdn to ld over 1f out: clr ins last* **13/8**[1]

62 **2** 6 **Malyana**[17] [5106] 2-9-0 .... MatthewHenry 6 74
(M A Jarvis) *led: rdn along over 2f out: drvn and hdd over 1f out: kpt on same pce* **9/4**[2]

0 **3** 1 ¼ **Monsoon Wedding**[8] [5352] 2-9-0 .... KDarley 8 71
(M Johnston) *chsd ldng pair: rdn along and outpcd over 2f out: kpt on ins last* **9/1**

34 **4** nk **Princess Palatine (IRE)**[92] [2807] 2-9-0 .... PatCosgrave 7 71
(K R Burke) *cl up: rdn and ev ch 2f out tl drvn over 1f out and grad wknd* **14/1**

24 **5** 2 **Wild Thyme**[8] [5352] 2-9-0 .... DaneO'Neill 10 66
(R Hannon) *in tch: hdwy to chse ldrs 3f out: sn rdn and kpt on same pce fnl 2f* **9/2**[3]

6 7 **Karmest** 2-9-0 .... TedDurcan 2 50
(E S McMahon) *a bhd* **33/1**

5 **7** 5 **Spirit Of Ecstacy**[26] [4880] 2-9-0 .... DanielTudhope 4 38
(G M Moore) *chsd ldrs: rdn along 4f out: sn wknd* **25/1**

0 **8** 5 **Two Dreamers**[12] [5237] 2-9-0 .... TomEaves 5 27
(A Crook) *in tch: rdn along and lost pl over 4f out: sn bhd* **66/1**

0 **9** ½ **Bollin Fiona**[21] [5025] 2-8-9 .... DuranFentiman(5) 3 26
(T D Easterby) *in tch: rdn along over 4f out: sn wknd* **66/1**

1m 45.57s (0.06) **Going Correction** 0.0s/f (Good) **9** Ran SP% **113.5**
Speed ratings (Par 92):99,93,91,91,89 82,77,72,71
CSF £5.12 TOTE £2.50: £1.10, £1.60, £2.10; EX 5.30.
Owner Hamdan Al Maktoum **Bred** Shadwell Farm LLC **Trained** Arundel, W Sussex

FOCUS
A fair fillies' maiden in which the winner proved in a different league and the form looks sound rated through the runner-up, fourth and fifth.

NOTEBOOK
Tarteel(USA) ◆, very unlucky under today's rider at Salisbury last time, made amends with an easy success on this first attempt at a mile. She may not be that straightforward, but her ability to handle different ground is going to prove an advantage and she certainly has the scope to improve further. A longer trip will also play to her strengths next season. (tchd 9-4)
Malyana, a runner-up at Kempton last time, again had her chance from the front yet was eventually put firmly in her place by the winner. She is a decent benchmark for the form, and now has the options of nurseries, where she should be allotted a mark around 80. (tchd 2-1 and 5-2)
Monsoon Wedding, ninth over this trip on debut at Nottingham eight days previously, stepped up on that effort and did more than enough to suggest she is already in need of a stiffer test. She can improve again for this experience. (op 7-1 tchd 10-1)
Princess Palatine(IRE), returning from a 92-day break, showed up well until nearing the final furlong and has to rate a non-stayer of this longer trip. She may have needed the run, however, and should be the type to fare better now she is eligible for nurseries. (op 16-1)
Wild Thyme was made to look very one paced and failed to confirm Nottingham form with Monsoon Wedding. She may have found this coming a touch too soon and does now qualify for a handicap mark, so is not one to write off just yet. (op 6-1)
Spirit Of Ecstacy Official explanation: jockey said filly bolted to start

5537 CASINO 36 STOCKPORT E B F MAIDEN STKS (C&G) 1m 30y
4:40 (4:40) (Class 5) 2-Y-O **£4,533** (£1,348; £674; £336) **Stalls** Low

Form RPR

0 **1** **Petara Bay (IRE)**[16] [5126] 2-9-0 .... DaneO'Neill 10 85+
(T G Mills) *a.p: hdwy to ld 3f out: rdn 2f out: styd on strly appr last* **11/2**[2]

2 **2** 2 ½ **Ajhar (USA)**[14] [5178] 2-9-0 .... RHills 12 79
(M P Tregoning) *hld up in tch: hdwy on outer 3f out: chal and edgd rt 2f out: sn rdn and hung lft ent last: one pce* **4/5**[1]

0 **3** 3 **Super Cross (IRE)**[18] [5089] 2-9-0 .... JTate 9 72
(E A L Dunlop) *a.p: effrt and ev ch 3f out: sn rdn and kpt on same pce fnl 2f* **66/1**

3 **4** 3 ½ **Dream Lodge (IRE)**[17] [5105] 2-9-0 .... J-PGuillambert 2 64
(J G Given) *chsd ldrs on inner: rdn along 3f out: kpt on same pce fnl 2f* **17/2**

5 1 **Inchnacardoch (IRE)** 2-9-0 .... FergusSweeney 3 62
(A King) *towards rr: hdwy over 4f out: rdn along wl over 2f out: styd on ins last: nrst fin* **33/1**

60 **6** 1 **Downbeat**[19] [5067] 2-9-0 .... JimmyQuinn 1 59
(J L Dunlop) *midfield: pushed along and hdwy 3f out: rdn over 2f out and sn no imp* **33/1**

7 2 ½ **Wraith** 2-9-0 .... TedDurcan 6 54
(H R A Cecil) *bmpd s and bhd tl styd on fnl 2f: nrst fin* **10/1**

8 2 ½ **Danehill Silver** 2-9-0 .... MickyFenton 11 48
(R Hollinshead) *midfield: hdwy on wd outside 3f out: rdn over 2f out: edgd lft and sn btn* **80/1**

9 nk **Find Me (USA)** 2-9-0 .... KDarley 7 47
(M Johnston) *wnt lft s: towards rr: rdn along and hdwy on inner 3f out: drvn wl over 1f out and sn btn* **7/1**[3]

10 2 **Butlers Best** 2-9-0 .... HayleyTurner 14 43
(E J O'Neill) *in tch: rdn along over 3f out: grad wknd* **33/1**

4 **11** 2 ½ **Horsley Wiz**[16] [5126] 2-9-0 .... RobbieFitzpatrick 15 37
(E S McMahon) *nvr nr ldrs* **33/1**

12 2 **Cinaman (IRE)** 2-9-0 .... RoystonFfrench 5 32
(R F Fisher) *chsd ldrs: rdn along 3f out: wknd over 2f out* **33/1**

060 **13** 10 **Joella's Lad**[115] [2139] 2-9-0 **35** .... (p) DanielTudhope 4 9
(Ms Deborah J Evans) *led: rdn along and hdd 3f out: sn wknd* **100/1**

00 **14** 74 **Swan Of Raunds**[36] [4566] 2-9-0 .... (v) TomEaves 13 —
(J R Norton) *s.i.s: a bhd* **100/1**

1m 46.22s (0.71) **Going Correction** 0.0s/f (Good) **14** Ran SP% **122.5**
Speed ratings (Par 95):96,93,90,87,86 85,82,80,79,77 75,73,63,—
CSF £9.91 TOTE £7.40: £2.10, £1.10, £10.60; EX 21.60.
Owner Mrs B Ecclestone **Bred** Swettenham Stud **Trained** Headley, Surrey

FOCUS
A fair juvenile maiden that saw the field finish fairly strung out behind the comfortable winner. The form looks solid enough with the runner-up, fourth and sixth close to form.

NOTEBOOK
Petara Bay(IRE), clueless when a beaten on his debut at Chepstow 16 days previously, showed that effort to be all wrong and ran out a convincing winner. He clearly enjoyed the chance to race handily, looked suited by the good ground, and shaped as though he will have no trouble in staying further - something his pedigree strongly suggests. It will be very interesting to see where connections put him in next and he does hold an entry in the Racing Post Trophy. (op 5-1)
Ajhar(USA), second on his debut at Goodwood a fortnight previously, failed to find that much off the bridle and hung when put under maximum pressure. He still probably ran close to his debut form, and finished nicely clear of the rest, plus time may tell there was no disgrace in this defeat. (tchd Evens and 11-10 in places)
Super Cross(IRE) showed improved form over this extra furlong and has clearly come on since his debut 18 days previously. His future lies with the Handicapper and this 100,000euros purchase should do better as he becomes more streetwise. (op 50-1)
Dream Lodge(IRE) failed to really improve on his recent Kempton debut and looks to need more time. He may also do better when ridden with more patience in the future. (op 8-1)
Inchnacardoch(IRE), the first foal of an unraced half-sister to high-class miler Inchinor among others, caught the eye finishing his race with a degree of promise and looks certain to improve for the experience. (op 50-1)
Find Me(USA), a half-brother to US champion turf mare Fiji, looked greatly in need of this debut experience and proved disappointing. He holds two Group 1 entries and is presumably thought capable of an awful lot better. (op 12-1)

5538 EUROPEAN BREEDERS FUND "REPROCOLOR" FILLIES' H'CAP 1m 2f 120y
5:15 (5:15) (Class 3) (0-90,84) 3-Y-O+ **£11,658** (£3,468; £1,733; £865) **Stalls** High

Form RPR

-221 **1** **Dayrose**[31] [4686] 3-9-2 **84** .... JamieHamblett(7) 5 90
(Sir Michael Stoute) *hld up: pushed along and hdwy 3f out: swtchd lft and rdn over 1f out: styd on ins last to ld last strides* **7/1**[3]

3221 **2** shd **Kerriemuir Lass (IRE)**[19] [5056] 3-9-6 **81** .... KDarley 10 87
(M A Jarvis) *led: rdn along 3f out: hdd wl over 1f out: sn drvn and rallied to ld last 50yds: hdd on line* **5/1**[2]

0-31 **3** nk **Mabadi (USA)**[84] [3066] 3-9-3 **78** .... RHills 8 83
(B W Hills) *keen: hld up towards rr: gd hdwy 3f out: led wl over 1f out: rdn ins last: hdd and no ex last 50yds* **12/1**

3400 **4** 5 **Tcherina (IRE)**[49] [4149] 4-9-2 **75** .... DuranFentiman(5) 2 72
(T D Easterby) *trckd ldrs: rdn along wl over 2f out: kpt on same pce appr last* **20/1**

2103 **5** 2 **Daring Affair**[25] [4911] 5-9-6 **74** .... PatCosgrave 3 68
(K R Burke) *chsd ldrs: rdn along 3f out: wknd over 2f out* **14/1**

0115 **6** 1 **Lady Disdain**[17] [5115] 3-9-4 **79** .... DanielTudhope 9 71
(G M Moore) *hld up: gd hdwy on wd outside 3f out: rdn to chse ldrs over 2f out: sn drvn and wknd* **9/1**

433P **7** 3 **Flying Clarets (IRE)**[7] [5361] 3-8-11 **77** .... JamieMoriarty(5) 4 64
(R A Fahey) *towards rr: gd hdwy on inner 1/2-way: cl up 4f out: rdn 3f out wknd fnl 2f* **14/1**

142 **8** 5 **Lake Shabla (USA)**[29] [4784] 3-9-7 **82** .... DO'Donohoe 6 60
(E A L Dunlop) *hmpd shortly after s and bhd: gd hdwy 3f out: rdn over 2f out and sn btn* **11/8**[1]

2116 **9** 1 ½ **Early Evening**[14] [5164] 3-9-6 **81** .... DaneO'Neill 7 57
(H Candy) *trckd ldrs: hdwy on outer over 3f out and sn ev ch tl rdn 2f out and sn wknd* **11/1**

-060 **10** 7 **Startori**[21] [5024] 3-9-5 **80** .... PaulEddery 1 44
(B Smart) *prom: rdn along over 3f out: sn wknd* **33/1**

2m 17.66s (-0.07) **Going Correction** 0.0s/f (Good)
WFA 3 from 4yo+ 7lb **10** Ran SP% **118.3**
Speed ratings (Par 104):100,99,99,96,94 93,91,88,86,81
CSF £42.61 CT £419.81 TOTE £9.30: £3.00, £1.80, £2.90; EX 51.00 Place 6 £92.66, Place 5 £31.13.
Owner Sir Evelyn De Rothschild **Bred** Southcourt Stud **Trained** Newmarket, Suffolk

FOCUS
A decent fillies' handicap for the class and the form looks solid enough with the first three coming clear.

NOTEBOOK
Dayrose, off the mark at Folkestone a month previously, responded to her rider's urgings and eventually just did enough to reel in the leaders close home and follow up on this handicap debut. Her rider's allowance proved an advantage, but she is clearly still going the right way and remains relatively unexposed. (op 8-1)
Kerriemuir Lass(IRE), belatedly off the mark at Bath 19 days previously, proved game in defeat on this return to handicap company and her confidence had clearly been boosted. This consistent filly remains capable of success in this division. (op 9-2)
Mabadi(USA) ◆, last seen breaking her duck at Chester 84 days previously, ultimately paid for running too freely on this return to action yet was still only just denied. She is entitled to come on for the run and should be placed to strike again before too long. (op 16-1)
Tcherina(IRE) ran close to her official mark in defeat, improving in the process, and helps to set the level of this form. (op 25-1)

Lake Shabla(USA), well backed, probably lost her race at the start and never gave her supporters any real hope. She is better than this. Official explanation: jockey said filly was struck into (op 15-8)

T/Plt: £110.70 to a £1 stake. Pool: £84,882.40. 559.60 winning tickets. T/Qpdt: £10.30 to a £1 stake. Pool: £3,342.00. 239.30 winning tickets. JR

5539 - 5542a (Foreign Racing) - See Raceform Interactive

4414 COLOGNE (R-H)

Saturday, September 23

OFFICIAL GOING: Good

5543a GROSSE EUROPA-MEILE (GROUP 2) — 1m

4:00 (4:13) 3-Y-O+ — **£27,586** (£10,690; £4,138; £2,759)

RPR

1 — **Lateral**[25] 4918 3-8-9 .... WMongil 4 — 118
(P Schiergen, Germany) *prominent, 2nd straight, led over 1f out, went clear inside last, pushed out* — **18/10**[2]

2 6 **Vega's Lord (GER)**[62] 3-8-9 .... TMundry 3 — 106
(P Rau, Germany) *raced in 4th, disputing 3rd straight, ridden 2f out, went 2nd just inside final furlong* — **144/10**

3 hd **Arcadio (GER)**[55] 3993 4-9-4 .... ASuborics 2 — 111
(P Schiergen, Germany) *raced in last, ran on on outside straight, ridden over 1f out, went 3rd inside final furlong* — **6/4**[1]

4 1 ¼ **Raptor (GER)**[25] 4918 3-8-9 .... AStarke 6 — 104
(Mario Hofer, Germany) *mid-division, effort 1 1/2f out, ran on at one pace* — **76/10**

5 ¾ **Willingly (GER)**[13] 5227 7-9-1 .... ADeVries 1 — 104
(M Trybuhl, Germany) *led to over 1f out, no extra inside final furlong* — **131/10**

6 2 ½ **Bebe Vettori (GER)** 4-9-1 .... EPedroza 8 — 99
(A Wohler, Germany) *always mid-division* — **37/10**[3]

7 3 **Mannico (GER)**[139] 1526 3-8-9 .... AHelfenbein 5 — 91
(Mario Hofer, Germany) *held up, disputing 3rd straight, ridden 2f out, never in contention* — **30/1**

8 26 **Aurea (GER)**[17] 5123 3-8-5 .... JBojko 7 — 35
(A Trybuhl, Germany) *held up in last, 7th straight, never in contention* — **157/10**

1m 35.08s
WFA 3 from 4yo+ 4lb — 8 Ran SP% **131.4**
(Including 10 Euro stake): WIN 28; PL 15, 27, 13; SF 408.
Owner Stiftung Gestut Fahrhof **Bred** Stiftung Gestut Fahrhof **Trained** Germany

5520 ASCOT (R-H)

Sunday, September 24

OFFICIAL GOING: Good to soft (soft in places on round course)

Wind: Virtually nil

5546 SECURITY COMPANY NURSERY — 7f

2:15 (2:16) (Class 3) 2-Y-O
£9,348 (£2,799; £1,399; £700; £349; £175) **Stalls** Centre

Form — RPR

2302 1 — **Just Dust**[5] 5461 2-8-8 **82** .... MarcHalford(3) 17 — 87
(D R C Elsworth) *wnt rt s: mde virtually all: rdn over 2f out: hrd pressed thrght fnl f: jst hld on* — **25/1**

51 2 hd **Artimino**[20] 5066 2-8-11 **82** .... JamieSpencer 11 — 86
(J R Fanshawe) *lengthy: lw: hmpd sn after s: towards rr: hdwy over 2f out: sn rdn to chse ldrs over 1f out: r.o ins fnl f: jst failed* — **3/1**[1]

051 3 hd **My Learned Friend (IRE)**[25] 4928 2-8-9 **80** .... FrancisNorton 18 — 84
(A M Balding) *bmpd s: sn in tch: rdn to chal wl over 1f out: ev ch ins fnl f: no ex fnl strides* — **7/1**

4532 4 shd **Masai Moon**[17] 5133 2-8-4 **75** .... RoystonFfrench 4 — 79
(B R Millman) *towards rr: rdn and stdy prog fr 2f out: ev ch ins fnl f: no ex cl home* — **20/1**

6310 5 1 ¼ **Golden Balls (IRE)**[31] 4736 2-9-1 **86** .... RyanMoore 16 — 86
(R Hannon) *mid div: rdn and hdwy over 1f out: nt clr run bhd ldrs ent fnl f: kpt on* — **14/1**

31 6 2 **Farley Star**[37] 4552 2-8-8 **79** .... SteveDrowne 6 — 74
(R Charlton) *bdly hmpd sn after s: mid div: swtchd rt over 1f out: styd on ins fnl f* — **13/2**[3]

5346 7 1 ¼ **Fares (IRE)**[22] 5013 2-7-13 **70** .... NickyMackay 2 — 62
(C E Brittain) *in tch: rdn over 2f out: kpt on same pce* — **66/1**

31 8 1 ¼ **Jaasoos (IRE)**[11] 5297 2-9-1 **86** .... PhilipRobinson 8 — 75
(M A Jarvis) *chsd ldrs: rdn 2f out: one pce fnl f* — **9/2**[2]

310 9 3 ½ **Simba Sun (IRE)**[29] 4824 2-9-2 **87** .... SebSanders 14 — 67
(R M Beckett) *prom: rdn and ev ch wl over 1f out: grad fdd* — **14/1**

514 10 3 **Honest Danger**[24] 4946 2-8-7 **78** .... HayleyTurner 1 — 50
(J R Best) *chsd ldrs: rdn over 2f out: wknd over 1f out* — **66/1**

3520 11 2 **Global Guest**[27] 4882 2-8-2 **73** .... ChrisCatlin 10 — 40
(M R Channon) *squeezed out sn after s: a towards rr* — **66/1**

016 12 1 ½ **Lunces Lad (IRE)**[23] 5007 2-9-2 **87** .... TedDurcan 7 — 50
(M R Channon) *lw: hld up towards rr: hdwy over 2f out: sn rdn: wknd over 1f out* — **16/1**

1 13 hd **Slate (IRE)**[20] 5067 2-8-6 **77** .... JohnEgan 9 — 39
(J A Osborne) *leggy: racd keenly: sn mid-div: rdn and nt clr run over 1f out: wknd fnl f* — **14/1**

1202 14 7 **Oi Vay Joe (IRE)**[8] 5372 2-9-0 **85** .... KerrinMcEvoy 13 — 29
(W Jarvis) *in tch: rdn over 2f out: wknd over 1f out* — **8/1**

1m 28.22s (0.12) **Going Correction** +0.10s/f (Good) — 14 Ran SP% **119.1**
Speed ratings (Par 99):103,102,102,102,101 98,97,95,91,88 86,84,84,76
CSF £95.51 CT £603.22 TOTE £18.30: £4.60, £2.00, £2.50; EX 121.80 Trifecta £432.00 Pool £754.64 - 1.24 winning units..
Owner Matthew Green **Bred** T O C S Ltd And W G M Turner **Trained** Newmarket, Suffolk
■ Stewards' Enquiry : Hayley Turner four-day ban: careless riding (Oct 5-8)

FOCUS
This looked like a good, competitive nursery beforehand, but it was quite a rough race, with several hampered in some major bunching soon after the start. They tended to race towards the far side, but off the rail.

NOTEBOOK
Just Dust, returned to seven furlongs, displayed a tremendously game attitude to make pretty much every yard and gain his fourth success of the year. He could be considered a little fortunate, as he avoided all the trouble in behind, but he still had to hold off numerous challengers and there was no fluke about this success. (op 20-1)

Artimino ◆, off the mark in a maiden at Warwick on his previous start, was probably unlucky not to follow up as he was one of the chief sufferers of the bunching soon after the start. He did well to get up for second in the circumstances, and he will have to be of interest off this sort of mark in future. (op 7-2)

My Learned Friend(IRE), off the mark in a novice event at Lingfield on his previous start, ran a fine race in third, especially considering he was bumped soon after the start. He should have more to offer. (op 9-1 tchd 10-1)

Masai Moon ◆, trying seven furlongs for the first time, stayed on nicely from well off the pace and this must rate as a decent effort. He is still a maiden but can surely find a race before this season is out.

Golden Balls(IRE), returned to seven furlongs and switched to nursery company for the first time, ran well. He was denied a clear run late on, but was held at the time. (op 16-1)

Farley Star ◆ was badly hampered in the early bunching and is better than she was able to show. (op 8-1)

Jaasoos(IRE) ran below the form he showed when winning a Yarmouth maiden on fast ground on his previous start and may have been unsuited by these easier conditions. (op 7-2)

Oi Vay Joe(IRE), upped to seven furlongs for the first time, was on his toes in the paddock and got warm beforehand. He could not build on his recent Newbury second and was not helped by the bunching soon after the start. Official explanation: jockey said colt was hampered shortly after start

5547 GROSVENOR CASINOS CUMBERLAND LODGE STKS (GROUP 3) — 1m 4f

2:45 (2:47) (Class 1) 3-Y-O+
£28,390 (£10,760; £5,385; £2,685; £1,345; £675) **Stalls** High

Form — RPR

6113 1 — **Young Mick**[32] 4713 4-9-0 104 .... (v) RobertWinston 3 — 116+
(G G Margarson) *hld up: hdwy on rails 3f out: led over 1f out: kpt on wl: pushed out* — **7/2**[2]

2203 2 1 ¾ **Munsef**[36] 4595 4-9-0 112 .... RHills 6 — 112
(J L Dunlop) *hld up: swtchd lft over 2f out: sn rdn and hdwy: wnt 2nd and edgd rt fr 1f out: kpt on but a hld by wnr* — **11/4**[1]

6232 3 1 ¾ **Glistening**[32] 4713 4-9-0 102 .... JamieSpencer 1 — 110
(L M Cumani) *lw: led after 1f: rdn 2f out: hdd over 1f out: kpt on same pce* — **7/2**[2]

6201 4 1 ½ **Foxhaven**[15] 5170 4-9-0 105 .... FrancisNorton 5 — 108
(P R Chamings) *lw: trckd ldrs: rdn over 3f out: n.m.r briefly 1f out: kpt on same pce* — **9/1**

3303 5 2 **Profit's Reality (IRE)**[8] 5360 4-9-0 102 .... RyanMoore 4 — 105
(P A Blockley) *hld up: swtchd rt and hdwy 2f out: sn rdn: no further imp* — **22/1**

1631 6 5 **Kandidate**[22] 5018 4-9-3 113 .... (t) SebSanders 2 — 101
(C E Brittain) *trckd ldrs: rdn over 2f out: wknd jst over 1f out* — **12/1**

1022 7 ½ **Crosspeace (IRE)**[14] 5204 4-9-0 110 .... RoystonFfrench 7 — 97
(M Johnston) *keen early: in tch: tk clsr order 5f out: rdn and ev ch 2f out: wknd ent fnl f* — **5/1**[3]

-130 8 51 **Birkspiel (GER)**[120] 2010 5-9-3 107 .... DarrylIHolland 9 — 29
(S Dow) *led for 1f: trckd ldr: rdn 4f out: sn btn: t.o fnl 2f* — **33/1**

2m 34.56s (1.56) **Going Correction** +0.50s/f (Yiel) — 8 Ran SP% **112.8**
Speed ratings (Par 113):114,112,111,110,109 106,105,71
CSF £13.16 TOTE £4.10: £1.50, £1.20, £1.60; EX 12.50 Trifecta £41.40 Pool £1,931.37 - 33.09 winning units..
Owner M F Kentish **Bred** M F Kentish **Trained** Newmarket, Suffolk

FOCUS
Not a strong Group 3 but a first Group win and tenth of the season for Young Mick.

NOTEBOOK
Young Mick took the step into Group company in his stride and recorded a remarkable tenth win from 19 starts this year. Remaining on the inside in the home straight, he took advantage of a nice gap as the field shunned the rail and scored decisively, idling once in front. Unbeaten in four trips to Ascot now, he has a range of options for the rest of the year, among them Hong Kong in December. (op 4-1)

Munsef was settled in rear before being switched to the outer once in line for home. He kept on well, but could never seriously trouble the winner. He has had a decent season and deserves to collect a Group race. (op 9-4)

Glistening was a whisker in the front of Young Mick in the Ebor and was 2lb worse off here. This was a creditable effort, especially considering that he had to make his own running on this drop in trip and that the ground was not ideal. (op 4-1)

Foxhaven, upped in class after landing a Listed event at Chester, ran creditably but was already held when slightly chopped for room at the furlong pole. (op 8-1)

Profit's Reality(IRE) kept on up the inside without being able to land a blow. He is a consistent individual but is proving hard to place. (op 20-1)

Kandidate, under a penalty for his win at this level at Kempton, was well held on this very different surface but did confirm the Polytrack form with Crosspeace. (op 10-1)

Crosspeace(IRE), runner-up in this grade on his last two starts, was one of half a dozen battling it out with two furlongs to run but could not sustain his effort. (op 11-2 tchd 6-1)

Birkspiel(GER), appearing for the first time since finishing lame here in May, faced a stiff task under the penalty he acquired when winning at Bremen the previous month and was the first beaten. (op 50-1 tchd 25-1)

5548 TOTESPORT 0800 221 221 STKS (HERITAGE H'CAP) — 1m 4f

3:15 (3:17) (Class 2) 3-Y-O+
£43,624 (£13,062; £6,531; £3,269; £1,631; £819) **Stalls** High

Form — RPR

1444 1 — **Pevensey (IRE)**[11] 5299 4-8-8 **87** .... DavidAllan 4 — 96
(M A Buckley) *t.k.h: stdd towards rr after 3f: rdn and hdwy fr 2f out: led narrowly jst ins fnl f: drvn out* — **16/1**

0013 2 nk **Group Captain**[32] 4711 4-9-4 **97** .... RichardHughes 7 — 106
(R Charlton) *in tch: tk clsr order 7f out: rdn to chal 2f out: sn hung rt: ev ch thrght fnl f: no ex fnl strides* — **8/1**

0011 3 shd **Peppertree Lane (IRE)**[22] 5010 3-8-10 **97** .... KDarley 5 — 106
(M Johnston) *lw: trckd ldrs: led narrowly over 2f out: sn hrd pressed and rdn: hdd jst ins fnl f: kpt on but n.m.r after* — **15/8**[1]

3506 4 2 **Thunder Rock (IRE)**[32] 4711 4-8-9 **88** .... RyanMoore 11 — 94
(Sir Michael Stoute) *trckd ldrs: rdn over 2f out: kpt on same pce* — **8/1**

-130 5 ¾ **Millville**[33] 4676 6-9-3 **96** .... PhilipRobinson 10 — 100
(M A Jarvis) *lw: t.k.h in mid-div: hdwy over 3f out: rdn over 2f out: kpt on same pce* — **20/1**

2614 6 1 ¼ **Resonate (IRE)**[18] 5115 8-7-12 **80** .... CDHayes(3) 3 — 82
(A G Newcombe) *lw: hld up towards rr: swtchd lft and hdwy 3f out: swtchd rt 2f out: styd on* — **33/1**

12 7 shd **Soulacroix**[15] 5170 5-9-10 **103** .... KerrinMcEvoy 16 — 105
(L M Cumani) *sn stdd into mid-div: dropped rr 5f out: styd on again fr 2f out* — **6/1**[2]

3610 8 3 **Sweet Indulgence (IRE)**[22] 5010 5-8-4 **83** .... NickyMackay 12 — 80
(W J Musson) *mid-div: rdn over 2f out: sn one pce* — **33/1**

3440 **9** 3/4 **Palomar (USA)**[8] [5374] 4-9-7 **100**................................(p) SteveDrowne 14 96
(R Charlton) *lw: hld up towards rr: hdwy into mid-div 4f out: nt clr run 3f out: sn rdn: no imp* **7/1**[3]
1300 **10** 1/2 **Hearthstead Wings**[32] [4713] 4-9-7 **100**..........................(v) JoeFanning 13 95
(M Johnston) *led tl over 2f out: grad fdd* **25/1**
3040 **11** 1 1/2 **Odiham**[32] [4713] 5-9-1 **94**..(v) EddieAhern 1 87
(H Morrison) *a towards rr* **16/1**
4604 **12** 3 1/2 **Lake Poet (IRE)**[6] [5421] 3-8-3 **90**................................. FrancisNorton 17 77
(C E Brittain) *in tch: rdn over 2f out: sn wknd* **16/1**
5200 **13** 29 **Counsel's Opinion (IRE)**[29] [4818] 9-9-9 **102**.................. GeorgeBaker 9 43
(C F Wall) *a bhd: t.o fnl 2f* **33/1**

2m 36.67s (3.67) **Going Correction** +0.50s/f (Yiel)
WFA 3 from 4yo+ 8lb **13** Ran SP% **118.9**
Speed ratings (Par 109):107,106,106,105,104 104,104,102,101,101 100,97,78
CSF £129.49 CT £353.88 TOTE £20.20: £4.90, £2.50, £1.60; EX 173.10 Trifecta £1008.70 Part won. Pool £1,420.77 - 0.20 winning units..
Owner C C Buckley **Bred** Barronstown Stud And Orpendale **Trained** Castle Bytham, Lincs

FOCUS
A good and competitive handicap run at a decent pace and producing a close finish.

NOTEBOOK
Pevensey(IRE), who is admirably consistent, belied his trainer's misgivings about the ground to land this big prize. Coming with a strong run from out of the pack before getting the best of a three-way struggle, he is probably still progressing. (op 25-1)
Group Captain, back up in trip, was racing from a career-high mark. He had every chance in the final furlong, but was always wanting to hang right, not helping his rider, and was just held. (op 6-1)
Peppertree Lane(IRE) was just 2lb higher than when scoring over two furlongs further at Haydock. Showing in front once into the straight, he was narrowlly headed by the winner with a furlong left but battled on despite being tight for room against the rail. (op 2-1tchd 9-4 in places)
Thunder Rock(IRE) has been well supported for several decent races this year but it has not happened for him, and he is yet to land a handicap. Back up in trip, he was keeping on at the end but lacked the pace to play a serious role. (op 10-1 tchd 11-1)
Millville is usually most consistent and this sound effort proved his poor run at York last time was an aberration. He does like this ground and should have his conditions for the remainder of the season.
Resonate(IRE), returning to a higher grade, kept on in the latter stages and saw out this longer trip well enough.
Soulacroix, who could have done without the rain, lost his pitch at around halfway but was keeping on again in the last two furlongs. He will appreciate the return to further but the Melbourne Cup is out now, as he needed to win this to qualify for Flemington. (op 11-2)

5549 JOHN GUEST DIADEM STKS (GROUP 2) 6f
3:50 (3:53) (Class 1) 3-Y-O+

£51,102 (£19,368; £9,693; £4,833; £2,421; £1,215) **Stalls** Centre

Form RPR
0255 **1** **Red Clubs (IRE)**[22] [5011] 3-8-12 110.............................. MichaelHills 17 118
(B W Hills) *racd keenly: trckd ldr: rdn to ld over 1f out: in command whn veered bdly lft fnl 50yds* **6/1**[3]
1501 **2** 1 1/4 **Baltic King**[28] [4832] 6-9-0 112......................................(t) SteveDrowne 13 114+
(H Morrison) *mid-div: hdwy over 2f out: chalng whn n.m.r on rails 1f out: kpt on to go 2nd fnl strides* **4/1**[1]
5504 **3** nk **Fayr Jag (IRE)**[16] [5158] 7-9-0 110.. DavidAllan 14 113
(T D Easterby) *led: rdn and hdd over 1f out: kpt on ins fnl f: lost 2nd fnl strides* **16/1**
3020 **4** 1 **Assertive**[9] [5341] 3-8-12 106... RyanMoore 16 110
(R Hannon) *towards rr: rdn and hdwy over 1f out: styd on to go 4th jst ins fnl f* **33/1**
5-03 **5** 1 1/4 **Ratio**[28] [4860] 8-9-0 ....(bt) PhilipRobinson 12 106
(J E Hammond, France) *lw: hld up bhd: rdn and stdy prog fr 2f out: styd on: nvr trbld ldrs* **12/1**
0442 **6** nk **Somnus**[15] [5184] 6-9-0 109.. KDarley 8 105
(T D Easterby) *chsd ldrs: rdn over 2f out: kpt on same pce* **4/1**[1]
0010 **7** nk **La Chunga (USA)**[49] [4191] 3-8-9 107..........................(v[1]) DarryllHolland 1 101
(J Noseda) *lw: a mid-div* **20/1**
3123 **8** nk **Firenze**[50] [4128] 5-8-11 99.. JamieSpencer 9 101
(J R Fanshawe) *mid-div: rdn 2f out: one pce fnl f* **11/2**[2]
5100 **9** 2 **Steenberg (IRE)**[22] [5011] 7-9-4 111...................................... JoeFanning 6 102
(M H Tompkins) *chsd ldrs: rdn 2f out: wknd fnl f* **20/1**
2410 **10** 3/4 **Presto Shinko (IRE)**[49] [4191] 5-9-0 108......................... RichardHughes 2 95
(R Hannon) *towards rr: nt clr run over 1f out: no imp after* **9/1**

1m 13.71s (-1.19) **Going Correction** +0.10s/f (Good)
WFA 3 from 4yo+ 2lb **10** Ran SP% **105.7**
Speed ratings (Par 115):111,109,108,107,105 105,105,104,102,101
CSF £24.14 TOTE £7.20: £2.30, £1.70, £3.50; EX 44.60 Trifecta £322.40 Pool £1,090.10 - 2.40 winning units..
Owner R J Arculli **Bred** J Fike **Trained** Lambourn, Berks
■ There were seven non-runners including Excusez Moi (8/1, withdrawn on vet's advice at s.) Rule 4 applies, deduction 10p in £.

FOCUS
With so many withdrawals not a strong race for the grade but a decisive winner who is value for further.

NOTEBOOK
Red Clubs(IRE) has been running with credit in some of the top sprints since winning the Greenham over seven furlongs in the spring. After striking the front and edging right to take the far rail, he suddenly veered badly across the course in the last half-furlong, possibly shying at the grandstand's shadow, but was already well in command by then. He will stay in training next year and can challenge for top sprint honours, although his Group 2 penalty will count aginst him in lesser grade. (op 8-1 tchd 9-1)
Baltic King, who ran his best race of the season when landing the Wokingham over this course and distance, has generally been found wanting in this grade but this was a decene effort. After the winner went across him slightly when he was attempting to challenge at the furlong pole, he kept on to secure second near the line. (op 9-2)
Fayr Jag(IRE), back over six, pinged the gates and set the pace until the winner past him. It was only in the last few strides that he was caught for second place, a position he filled in this race a year ago when it was run at Newmarket.
Assertive, a consistent sort at six or seven furlongs, was staying on well when it was all too late.
Ratio, equipped with blinkers and a tongue tie, was keeping on past beaten rivals at the end and could have done with a stronger all-round pace. (op 9-1)
Somnus had no excuses on account of the ground and was a little below par. (tchd 9-2)
La Chunga(USA), who was visored for the first time, could never get involved from her wide draw. She is a better filly on fast ground.
Firenze, slightly jarred up when third in the Stewards' Cup, was unable to handle this rise in grade on easier ground. Official explanation: trainer said mare was unsuited by the good to soft ground (op 6-1)
Presto Shinko(IRE) Official explanation: jockey said gelding lost its action

5550 MILES & MORRISON OCTOBER STKS (LISTED RACE) (F&M) 7f
4:25 (4:26) (Class 1) 3-Y-O+

£17,034 (£6,456; £3,231; £1,611; £807; £405) **Stalls** Centre

Form RPR
1332 **1** **Makderah (IRE)**[51] [4097] 3-8-10 104... RHills 2 104+
(M P Tregoning) *lw: led after 1f: 3l clr 1f out: kpt on: rdn out* **6/5**[1]
-203 **2** 1 3/4 **Highway To Glory (IRE)**[16] [5159] 3-8-10 100................. OscarUrbina 10 100
(M Botti) *hld up bhd: nt clr run and swtchd lft over 2f out: styd on wl to go 2nd ins fnl f: nt rch wnr* **11/2**[3]
4522 **3** 1 3/4 **Gloved Hand**[24] [4965] 4-8-13 88.. JamieSpencer 6 95
(J R Fanshawe) *hld up towards rr: rdn over 2f out: no imp tl styd on ins fnl f: wnt 3rd fnl strides* **9/1**
2250 **4** shd **Home Sweet Home (IRE)**[7] [5411] 3-8-10 92..........(p) RobertWinston 16 95
(P D Evans) *chsd ldrs: rdn over 2f out: kpt on same pce* **16/1**
3621 **5** nk **Blades Girl**[17] [5143] 3-8-10 94...(p) NCallan 15 94
(K A Ryan) *prom: rdn over 2f out: kpt on same pce* **14/1**
4501 **6** 1 3/4 **Three Wrens (IRE)**[35] [4628] 4-9-2 97......................... NickyMackay 13 92
(D J Daly) *mid-div: rdn over 2f out: sn one pce* **14/1**
4235 **7** 2 1/2 **Antica (IRE)**[32] [4707] 3-8-10 89.. JoeFanning 7 83
(M H Tompkins) *mid-div: hdwy over 2f out: sn rdn: wknd fnl f* **16/1**
010 **8** hd **Tara Too (IRE)**[28] [4841] 3-8-10 87.............................. PhilipRobinson 14 82
(D W P Arbuthnot) *led for 1f: chsd ldrs tl wknd 1f out* **33/1**
504 **9** 4 **Kalaforte (SAF)**[24] 4-8-13 85..(b) TedDurcan 9 72
(R Simpson) *chsd ldrs: rdn 3f out: wknd over 1f out* **80/1**
0421 **10** 3 **Imperial Ice (SAF)**[57] [3969] 4-9-2 100............................... RyanMoore 5 67
(R Simpson) *racd keenly in tch: rdn over 2f out: wknd fnl f* **40/1**
2364 **11** 22 **Cantabria**[16] [5159] 3-8-10 100....................................... RichardHughes 3 7
(Sir Michael Stoute) *lw: wnt rt s and bmpd: sn cl up: effrt over 2f out: sn btn: eased fnl f* **9/2**[2]
0664 **12** 14 **Virginia Plain**[13] [5244] 3-8-10 41.......................................(b) JimCrowley 4 —
(Miss Diana Weeden) *wnt lft and bmpd s: sn pushed along: a towards rr: t.o fnl 2f* **100/1**

1m 27.42s (-0.68) **Going Correction** +0.10s/f (Good)
WFA 3 from 4yo 3lb **12** Ran SP% **121.7**
Speed ratings (Par 111):107,105,103,102,102 100,97,97,92,89 64,48
CSF £8.03 TOTE £2.20: £1.30, £1.90, £2.60; EX 9.90 Trifecta £67.90 Pool £1.054.29 - 11.01 winning units..
Owner Hamdan Al Maktoum **Bred** Shadwell Estate Company Limited **Trained** Lambourn, Berks

FOCUS
A reasonable fillies' Listed event in which Makderah had the best form and looked value for more than the winning margin.

NOTEBOOK
Makderah(IRE) ◆, who had run very creditably behind subsequent Group 1 winner Red Evie on her last two starts, had nothing of that one's calibre to contend with this time and took advantage. She appeared to idle in front and is probably value for more like double the winning margin. She looks ready for a return to Group company. (op 6-4 tchd 13-8 in a place)
Highway To Glory(IRE) was denied a clear run when trying to stay on, but was not unlucky as Makderah was idling in front. This was a good effort and she will not always run into a horse of Makderah's class in Listed company. (op 7-1)
Gloved Hand, just denied in a handicap off a mark of 86 at Salisbury on her previous start, acquitted herself with credit returned to Listed company to pick up some valuable black type. (op 8-1)
Home Sweet Home(IRE), fitted with cheekpieces for the first time, ran better than when last in a mile Listed race at the Curragh on her previous start. There could be more to come and she looks worth persevering with in this sort of company. (tchd 20-1)
Blades Girl, the ready winner of handicap at Southwell off a mark of 86 on her previous start, was just run out of the places in the last furlong on this step up in grade. (op 12-1)
Cantabria was badly bumped at the start and that probably knocked the stuffing out of her.

5551 SIS FENWOLF STKS (LISTED RACE) 2m
5:00 (5:00) (Class 1) 3-Y-O+

£17,034 (£6,456; £3,231; £1,611; £807; £405) **Stalls** High

Form RPR
0051 **1** **Hawridge Prince**[9] [5351] 6-9-3 95....................................... JimCrowley 4 115+
(B R Millman) *hld up: tk clsr order 6f out: wnt 2nd on bit over 2f out: led wl over 1f out: styd on strly: eased nr fin* **6/1**[3]
2206 **2** 5 **Frank Sonata**[8] [5395] 5-9-6 104... RyanMoore 8 111
(M G Quinlan) *hld up: rdn and stdy prog fr 2f out: styd on ins fnl f to snatch 2nd fnl stride: no ch w wnr* **7/1**
-335 **3** nk **Lost Soldier Three (IRE)**[29] [4791] 5-9-3 106................. NickyMackay 9 108
(L M Cumani) *hld up in tch: tk clsr order 3f out: sn rdn: chsd wnr jst ins fnl f: lost 2nd fnl stride* **7/1**
0304 **4** 1 1/4 **Bulwark (IRE)**[33] [4677] 4-9-3 103..............................(be) KerrinMcEvoy 2 106
(Mrs A J Perrett) *trckd ldr: led wl over 2f out: sn rdn: hdd wl over 1f out: wknd ins fnl f* **11/2**[2]
61/6 **5** nk **Saint Alebe**[10] [5325] 7-9-3 92.. AntonyProcter 7 106
(D R C Elsworth) *swtg: b.bkwd: hld up last: swtchd lft over 2f out: sn rdn: styd on ins fnl f: nvr trbld ldrs* **20/1**
560- **6** 2 **Midas Way**[183] [5087] 6-9-3 100.. SebSanders 1 103
(P R Chamings) *hld up in tch: rdn over 2f out: sn one pce* **25/1**
31-0 **7** 2 **Kindling**[147] [1332] 4-8-12 96... KDarley 5 96
(M Johnston) *trckd ldrs: rdn 3f out: one pce fnl 2f* **8/1**
0-20 **8** 45 **Franklins Gardens**[14] [5223] 6-9-3 110.................................... NCallan 3 47
(M H Tompkins) *swtg: led tl wl over 2f out: wknd qckly* **13/8**[1]
0000 **9** 7 **Hippodrome (IRE)**[29] [4817] 4-9-3 90................................ EddieAhern 6 39
(R Simpson) *lw: chsd ldrs: rdn 4f out: wknd over 2f out* **66/1**

3m 36.85s (0.35) **Going Correction** +0.50s/f (Yiel) **9** Ran SP% **114.0**
Speed ratings (Par 111):103,100,100,99,99 98,97,75,71
CSF £45.53 TOTE £6.80: £2.20, £2.50, £1.90; EX 71.30 Trifecta £682.20 Pool £1,681.52 - 1.75 winning units. Place 6 £39.37, Place 5 £16.12..
Owner Eric Gadsden **Bred** Downclose Stud **Trained** Kentisbeare, Devon

FOCUS
This looked a reasonable Listed event beforehand, but nothing could live with Hawridge Prince, who was value for a little more than the five-length winning margin. They went just a steady pace early on.

NOTEBOOK
Hawridge Prince ◆, an impressive winner of a handicap off a mark of 95 when upped to two miles for the first time at Nottingham on his previous start, followed up in this tougher company in tremendous style, absolutely thrashing some smart sorts. Rod Millman, trainer of Sergeant Cecil, looks to have another potentially high-class stayer on his hands and the Jockey Club Cup at Newmarket in October could be a suitable target. In the longer term he appeals as one to keep in mind for some of next season's Cup races. (op 5-1)
Frank Sonata, sixth of eight in the Irish St Leger on his previous start, ran a respectable race in second but was no match whatsoever for the impressive winner. (op 8-1)

Lost Soldier Three(IRE), given another chance over two miles, did not really build on the promise he showed at Chester on his previous start and was beaten a fair way into third. He remains unproven over a trip this far. (op 6-1 tchd 11-2)
Bulwark(IRE) has struggled a touch since being forced up in grade and his improvement has very much levelled out. He was unable to sustain his challenge and has to be considered a little disappointing. (op 6-1 tchd 13-2)
Saint Alebe, having just his second start since winning the 2003 Ebor, stayed on far too late and never posed a threat. (tchd 22-1)
Franklins Gardens failed to take advantage of the drop in grade and was a major disappointment. He stayed towards the inside rail for much of the way, despite all of his rivals opting to race further out, but he was beaten too far for that to be used as the main excuse. (op 7-4)
T/Jkpt: Not won. T/Plt: £52.00 to a £1 stake. Pool: £141,821.34. 1,990.80 winning tickets. T/Qpdt: £13.60 to a £1 stake. Pool: £6,175.55. 335.10 winning tickets. TM

4949 MUSSELBURGH (R-H)

Sunday, September 24

OFFICIAL GOING: Soft (meeting abandoned after race 3 (3.30pm) due to unsafe ground conditions)
Wind: Virtually nil

5552 EBF ROYAL SCOTS MAIDEN STKS — 1m 1f
2:25 (2:25) (Class 4) 2-Y-O — £5,181 (£1,541; £770; £384) Stalls High

Form	Pos	Dist	Horse / Details	RPR
0	1		**Act Sirius (IRE)**[22] 5025 2-9-3 ... PaulMulrennan 3 (J Howard Johnson) *set stdy pace: qckngd over 3f out: rdn over 2f out: kpt on wl* **8/1**	77
4402	2	2 1/2	**Musical Land (IRE)**[24] 4949 2-9-3 73 ... PaulHanagan 5 (J R Weymes) *trckd ldrs: hdwy to chse wnr over 2f out: sn rdn and no imp ins last* **2/1**[1]	72
54	3	5	**Robbie Scott**[7] 5402 2-9-3 ... J-PGuillambert 2 (M Johnston) *trckd wnr: rdn along wl over 2f out: sn one pce* **9/4**[2]	62
0430	4	1 3/4	**Chookie Hamilton**[22] 5013 2-9-3 63 ... TomEaves 6 (I Semple) *keen: hld up in tch: hdwy 3f out: rdn along over 2f out: sn btn* **10/1**	59
0	5	3	**Irish Poet (IRE)**[27] 4867 2-9-3 ... RichardMullen 4 (E J O'Neill) *trckd ldrs: pushed along 4f out: rdn along 3f out: sn wknd* **5/1**[3]	53
60	6	1 3/4	**Bobansheil (IRE)**[15] 5187 2-8-12 ... TonyHamilton 1 (J S Wainwright) *a rr* **12/1**	44

2m 2.52s (8.66) **Going Correction** +0.75s/f (Yiel) **6** Ran SP% **108.7**
Speed ratings (Par 97):91,88,84,82,80 78
CSF £22.89 TOTE £9.60: £4.20, £1.20; EX 23.30.
Owner Transcend Bloodstock LLP **Bred** Allevamento Annarosa Di Schirone Vitantonio **Trained** Billy Row, Co Durham

FOCUS
Modest maiden form and, despite the steady early pace, quite a test for these juveniles in the ground.

NOTEBOOK
Act Sirius(IRE), who cost 150,000gns as a yearling, is a half-brother to Excelsius, a useful winner over a mile. He stepped up considerably on his debut effort, setting a steady pace in the testing conditions before bringing the field over to the stands' side in the straight and seeing the trip out best of all. Stamina is clearly his forte. (op 10-1)
Musical Land(IRE) looked the one to beat, having already shown fair form in maiden company, but he had not tackled ground as soft as this before and the winner outstayed him.
Robbie Scott has plenty of stamina in his pedigree, being a half-brother to Scott's View and Doctor Scott, and might have been expected to do a bit better than this, but he is one for next year really, and will be interesting once he moves into handicaps. (op 7-4 tchd 5-2)
Chookie Hamilton, officially rated 10lb lower than the runner-up, did not settle in the early stages and that counted against her chances of getting home in the ground. (op 9-1 tchd 7-1)
Irish Poet(IRE), whose dam was placed over six furlongs at two and is a half-sister to Silveris, a dual nine-furlong winner at two and later a winner over hurdles, might be seen to better effect on a faster surface. (op 7-1)

5553 RSP CONSULTING ENGINEERS (S) STKS — 1m 1f
2:55 (2:55) (Class 5) 3-Y-O+ — £3,238 (£963; £481; £240) Stalls High

Form	Pos	Dist	Horse / Details	RPR
0050	1		**Aqua**[4] 5485 4-8-8 36 ... RoryMoore(5) 14 (P T Midgley) *trckd ldrs on inner: hdwy to ld wl over 2f out: rdn wl over 1f out: kpt on u.p ins last* **50/1**	49
5201	2	1 1/4	**Desert Lightning (IRE)**[11] 5298 4-9-10 52 ... PatCosgrave 7 (K R Burke) *trckd ldrs: hdwy 3f out: rdn to chal over 1f out and ev ch tl drvn and one pce ins last* **7/1**[3]	58
6465	3	2 1/2	**Ulysees (IRE)**[39] 4475 7-9-10 64 ... PaulHanagan 1 (I Semple) *hld up and bhd: hdwy over 2f out: swtchd rt and rdn over 1f out: styd on ins last: nrst fin* **8/1**	53+
2300	4	hd	**Sawwaah (IRE)**[10] 5313 9-9-10 64 ... (v) AdrianTNicholls 16 (D Nicholls) *hld up and bhd: hdwy over 2f out: rdn over 1f out: styd on ins last: nrst fin* **9/1**	52+
523	5	1/2	**Ballyhurry (USA)**[24] 4953 9-9-4 66 ... DanielTudhope 8 (J S Goldie) *hld up in midfield: hdwy to chse ldrs 2f out: sn rdn and one pce ent last* **7/2**[1]	45
0500	5	dht	**Cabourg (IRE)**[13] 5244 3-8-13 65 ... DO'Donohoe 5 (R Bastiman) *chsd ldrs: rdn along over 2f out: sn drvn and kpt on same pce ent last* **14/1**	45
6030	7	1	**Princess Of Aeneas (IRE)**[13] 5247 3-8-8 57 ... (p) TomEaves 3 (I Semple) *towards rr: hdwy 4f out: rdn along 3f out: kpt on same pce fnl 2f* **12/1**	38
5220	8	shd	**Woolly Back (IRE)**[20] 5064 5-9-1 55 ... (p) AndrewMullen(3) 6 (A C Whillans) *midfield: hdwy 3f out rdn along 2f out: sn drvn and kpt on same pce* **16/1**	43
3102	9	1	**Apache Point (IRE)**[10] 5311 9-9-10 60 ... KimTinkler 11 (N Tinkler) *chsd ldrs: rdn along wl over 2f out: grad wknd* **11/2**[2]	47
0	10	1 1/4	**Domesday (UAE)**[7] 5403 5-8-13 ... DuranFentiman(5) 2 (W G Harrison) *dwlt and bhd tl sme late hdwy* **100/1**	38
5060	11	3/4	**Khetaab (IRE)**[8] 5385 4-9-4 47 ... PaulQuinn 4 (E J Alston) *a towards rr* **22/1**	37
/000	12	28	**Cadeaux Des Mages**[13] 5249 6-9-4 67 ... J-PGuillambert 9 (J G Given) *led 2f: cl up tl rdn along 3f out and sn wknd* **8/1**	—
030-	13	nk	**Supershot (IRE)**[86] 2484 8-9-4 57 ... TonyCulhane 13 (O Brennan) *s.i.s: a bhd* **40/1**	—
000/	14	3/4	**Down To The Woods (USA)**[346] 2053 8-9-4 ... (t) PaulMulrennan 10 (N Wilson) *cl up: led after 2f: rdn along and hdd wl over 2f out: sn wknd* **100/1**	—
0000	15	18	**Lazzoom (IRE)**[4] 5483 3-8-13 45 ... (p) MickyFenton 12 (Miss Tracy Waggott) *midfield: bhd fr 1/2-way* **50/1**	—

2m 1.14s (7.28) **Going Correction** +0.75s/f (Yiel)
WFA 3 from 4yo+ 5lb **15** Ran SP% **115.3**
Speed ratings (Par 103):97,95,93,93,93 93,92,92,91,90 89,64,64,63,47
CSF £350.44 TOTE £49.70: £12.50, £3.10, £2.70; EX 257.20.There was no bid for the winner.
Owner Mrs M Hills **Bred** Mrs M J Hills **Trained** Westow, N Yorks

FOCUS
Moderate plating form and a shock result.
Aqua Official explanation: trainer said, regarding apparent improvement in form, that the filly was better suited by the soft ground

5554 CHILDREN FIRST H'CAP — 7f 30y
3:30 (3:30) (Class 4) (0-80,80) 3-Y-O+ — £3,571 (£3,571; £818; £408) Stalls High

Form	Pos	Dist	Horse / Details	RPR
0014	1		**King Harson**[17] 5144 7-9-1 74 ... PatCosgrave 6 (J D Bethell) *led: rdn over 2f out: drvn and hdd ins last: rallied gamely nr line* **8/1**[3]	83
2560	1	dht	**Mezuzah**[23] 4989 6-9-1 74 ... PaulMulrennan 11 (M W Easterby) *prom: hdwy to chal over 2f out: sn rdn: drvn to ld ins last: jnd on line* **9/1**	83
0520	3	1 3/4	**Countdown**[27] 4885 4-9-2 75 ... TonyHamilton 8 (T D Easterby) *bhd: hdwy and rdn over 2f out: swtchd rt and drvn over 1f out: styd on ins last: nrst fin* **8/1**[3]	80
4210	4	shd	**Stellite**[9] 5336 6-9-2 75 ... DanielTudhope 4 (J S Goldie) *hld up towards rr: hdwy 3f out: rdn to chse ldrs wl over 1f out: drvn and one pce ins last* **11/2**[2]	79
0101	5	2 1/2	**Hypnotic**[10] 5313 4-9-5 78 ... (vt) AdrianTNicholls 13 (D Nicholls) *trckd ldrs on inner: hdwy 1/2-way: rdn along over 2f out: sn one pce* **7/2**[1]	76
1-30	6	1 1/2	**Just Intersky (USA)**[80] 3224 3-9-3 79 ... DeanMcKeown 10 (K A Ryan) *in tch: hdwy to chse ldrs over 3f out: rdn over 2f out and kpt on same pce* **14/1**	73
0000	7	nk	**King Of The Moors (USA)**[9] 5337 3-9-0 76 ... PhillipMakin 9 (T D Barron) *dwlt and bhd tl styd on fnl 2f* **16/1**	70
3020	8	2 1/2	**Wahoo Sam (USA)**[7] 5406 6-9-2 75 ... DO'Donohoe 1 (K A Ryan) *cl up: rdn along over 2f out: sn drvn and wknd* **16/1**	62
0040	9	3 1/2	**Tajaathub (USA)**[27] 4879 4-9-3 76 ... J-PGuillambert 2 (M Johnston) *midfield: hdwy 3f out: rdn and wknd 2f out* **11/1**	55
6413	10	hd	**Stoic Leader (IRE)**[38] 4521 6-9-7 80 ... PaulHanagan 14 (R F Fisher) *towards rr: sme hdwy on outer over 2f out: sn rdn and btn* **10/1**	58
0000	11	5	**Tanforan**[17] 5144 4-8-13 72 ... MickyFenton 3 (K G Reveley) *a rr* **16/1**	38
644P	12	nk	**Heureux (USA)**[35] 4634 3-9-1 77 ... (v[1]) TomEaves 7 (J Howard Johnson) *midfield: rdn along 3f out: sn wknd* **20/1**	42
5000	13	3	**John Keats**[19] 5079 3-8-12 74 ... (p) TonyCulhane 12 (I Semple) *prom: rdn along 1/2-way: sn wknd* **20/1**	31

1m 34.22s (4.28) **Going Correction** +0.75s/f (Yiel)
WFA 3 from 4yo+ 3lb **13** Ran SP% **121.1**
Speed ratings (Par 105):105,105,103,102,100 98,97,95,91,90 85,84,81
WIN: King Harson £4.90, Mezuzah £4.50. PL: KH £3.40, M £2.80, Countdown £3.40. EX: KH/M £31.00, M/KH £29.60. CSF: KH/M £39.66, M/KH £40.18. TRIC: KH/M/C £299.08, M/KH/C £302.23. Place 6 £23.31, Place 5 £11.20..
Owner C J Burley **Bred** Mrs Anne Bell **Trained** Middleham Moor, N Yorks
■

Owner Woodford Group Plc **Bred** Mrs Rebecca Philipps **Trained** Sheriff Hutton, N Yorks
■ There was controversy over the dead heat, for they were close together near the stands' rail and no mirror image was available.

FOCUS
A fair handicap in which the dead-heaters for first place raced prominently throughout.

5555 ROYAL SCOTS CLUB CUP NURSERY — 1m
() (Class 4) (0-85,) 2-Y-O £

5556 MUSSELBURGH NEWS CLAIMING STKS — 1m 4f
() (Class 5) 3-Y-O+ £

5557 EDINBURGH AUDI H'CAP — 2m
() (Class 4) (0-80,) 3-Y-O+ £

5558 EAST LOTHIAN NEWS H'CAP — 5f
() (Class 6) (0-60,) 3-Y-O+ £

T/Plt: £31.80 to a £1 stake. Pool £43,675.60 - 1,000.10 winning units. T/Qpdt: £2.40 to a £1 stake. Pool £2,948.80 - 886.30 winning units. JR

5559 - (Foreign Racing) - See Raceform Interactive

5543 COLOGNE (R-H)

Sunday, September 24

OFFICIAL GOING: Good

5560a IVG-EUROSELECT-PREIS (LISTED RACE) (F&M) — 1m 4f
2:05 (2:05) 3-Y-O+ — £8,966 (£2,757; £1,379; £690)

Pos	Dist	Horse / Details	RPR
1		**Anatola (GER)**[316] 4-9-5 ... ASuborics 1 (P Schiergen, Germany)	105
2	1 1/4	**Penelope Star (GER)** 3-8-9 ... AStarke 3 (H Blume, Germany)	101
3	1 3/4	**Kiswahili**[29] 4791 4-9-5 ... WMongil 2 (Sir Mark Prescott) *raced in 4th, switched outside 1 1/2f out, ran on same pace but never threatened first two (2/1)*	100
4	3/4	**Daytona (GER)**[65] 3719 5-9-5 ... TMundry 5 (P Rau, Germany)	99
5	1/2	**Rave Reviews (IRE)**[336] 6053 5-9-5 ... EPedroza 4 (A Wohler, Germany)	98

2m 31.06s
WFA 3 from 4yo+ 8lb **5** Ran
(including 10 Euro stake): WIN 67; PL 18, 14; SF 133.
Owner Gestut Schlenderhan **Bred** Gestut Schlenderhan **Trained** Germany

NOTEBOOK
Kiswahili kept going well enough to secure the minor place berth but never looked like getting to the front two.

5561a IVG - PREIS VON EUROPA (GROUP 1) 1m 4f
4:15 (4:21) 3-Y-O+ **£68,966** (£24,138; £11,724; £5,517)

RPR

1 **Youmzain (IRE)**[14] 5221 3-8-10 .... KFallon 5 118
(M R Channon) *held up, 6th straight, strong run on inside to lead last 100 yards* **4/5**[1]

2 ½ **Egerton (GER)**[21] 5051 5-9-6 .... TMundry 2 119
(P Rau, Germany) *a close up, 4th straight, led narrowly on outside 2f out, drifted right 150 yards out, hdd 100 yards out, no ex* **61/10**

3 1 ¾ **Enforcer**[27] 4877 4-9-6 .... MartinDwyer 1 116
(W R Muir) *prom, 3rd straight, pressed ldr and ev ch 1 ¼f , slightly hmpd and switched left 150 yards out, kpt on* **34/10**[2]

4 ½ **Oriental Tiger (GER)**[21] 5051 3-8-10 .... ABoschert 7 114
(U Ostmann, Germany) *led after 1f, tried to run out and 5 lengths detached first bend, still last but in tch str, stayed on strongly last 2f* **38/10**[3]

5 5 **Brisant (GER)**[29] 4828 4-9-6 .... AHelfenbein 3 108
(M Trybuhl, Germany) *left in lead after 3f, headed 2f out, soon weakened* **21/1**

6 ½ **Quelle Amore (GER)**[35] 4648 3-8-6 .... ASuborics 4 101
(A Wohler, Germany) *prominent early, 2nd straight, soon weakened* **119/10**

7 5 **All Spirit (GER)**[42] 4414 4-9-6 .... EPedroza 6 100
(N Sauer, Germany) *always in rear* **20/1**

2m 28.51s (-4.39) 7 Ran SP% **130.3**
WFA 3 from 4yo+ 8lb
WIN 18; PL 12, 14, 16; SF 108.
Owner Jaber Abdullah **Bred** Frank Dunne **Trained** West Ilsley, Berks

NOTEBOOK
Youmzain(IRE) squeezed through a narrow gap up the inside rail to hit the front with 100 yards to run and did it nicely, while clearly benefiting from a superb ride in an incident-packed race. The Gran Premio del Jockey Club in Milan on October 15 and the Hong Kong Vase at Sha Tin in December are possible future targets.
Egerton(GER) enjoyed this faster ground. Hitting the front with over two furlongs to run, he seemed to be holding Enforcer at bay when he hung across that rival inside the final furlong. Headed by Youmzain shortly afterwards, he was a little fortunate to keep second place given the severity of the German rules.
Enforcer was pressing Egerton for the lead, but had come under strong pressure, when Dwyer was forced to stop riding and switch outside around 100 yards from home. The Canadian International in Toronto on October 22nd is now on his agenda.
Oriental Tiger(GER) has a volatile temperament and threw away his chance when almost running off the course on the first bend. Back in touch but still in last on the home turn, he stayed on stoutly and looked a danger to all for a moment passing the furlong pole before his effort petered out. He still did remarkably well to finish so close given the ground he had forfeited.

LE CROISE-LAROCHE
Saturday, September 23
OFFICIAL GOING: Good

5562a PRIX ASSOCIATION NOEL HEUREUX AVEC EUX (H'CAP) 1m 1f
3:00 (12:00) 4-Y-0+ **£4,828** (£1,931; £1,448; £966; £483)

RPR

1 **Eckleberry (IRE)**[37] 4-9-0 .... (b) FSpanu 14 79
(M Delzangles, France)

2 nk **Alqaayid**[17] 5-8-12 .... SColas 3 76?
(P W Hiatt)

3 ½ **Go For Success (USA)**[12] 6-9-0 .... (b) THuet 6 77
(E Hautin, France)

4 4 **Hunaudieres (FR)**[51] 5-9-1 .... FSanchez 2 70
(Mlle C Cardenne, France)

5 nse **Quelle Beaute (FR)**[12] 6-8-11 .... DBonilla 4 66
(H Hosselet, France)

6 ½ **Lost Music (FR)**[288] 4-9-6 .... JCabre 10 74
(J-V Toux, France)

7 1 **Cote Soleil (FR)**[126] 4-9-1 .... FGeroux 9 68
(R Laplanche, France)

8 2 **The Jewel (FR)**[12] 4-9-1 .... (b) C-PLemaire 1 64
(H Vanderdussen, Belgium)

9 nk **Miss Tocqueville (FR)**[12] 5-8-10 .... JCrocquevieille 13 58
(P Van De Poele, France)

10 1 ½ **Togambo (FR)**[183] 4-9-2 .... FPanicucci 5 61
(P Chatelain, France)

0 **Arel's Day (FR)**[330] 4-9-2 .... FDiFede 15 —
(N Branchu, France)

0 **Makena (FR)**[134] 4-8-11 .... Jgaultier 11 —
(B Dutruel, France)

0 **Nord (FR)**[115] 6-8-9 .... RonanThomas 8 —
(Stall Passy, France)

0 **Lester Quercus (FR)**[17] 7-9-0 .... (b) DBoeuf 7 —
(J Van Handenhove, France)

0 **Version Originale (FR)**[27] 5-8-5 .... RCampos 12 —
(Mme N Rossio, France)

1m 51.7s 15 Ran
PARI-MUTUEL (Including 1 Euro stake): WIN 15.40; PL 4.30, 3.00, 4.00;DF 121.10.
Owner Mme A Bernheim **Bred** Skymarc Farm Inc **Trained** France

5161 BATH (L-H)
Monday, September 25
OFFICIAL GOING: Good to firm
Wind: light, against

5563 EUROPEAN BREEDERS FUND MAIDEN STKS 5f 161y
2:20 (2:22) (Class 5) 2-Y-0 **£3,368** (£1,002; £500; £250) **Stalls** Low

Form RPR

322 1 **Maker's Mark (IRE)**[31] 4774 2-9-3 81 .... DaneO'Neill 5 71+
(H Candy) *t.k.h in mid-div: swtchd rt and hdwy 2f out: sn rdn: edgd lft and led ins fnl f: rdn out* **8/13**[1]

0 2 1 ¼ **Izabela Hannah**[35] 4657 2-8-12 .... MartinDwyer 11 62
(R M Beckett) *s.i.s: rdn over 2f out: hdwy over 1f out: r.o wl towards fin* **12/1**[3]

3 3 ½ **Support Fund (IRE)**[22] 5043 2-8-12 .... StephenCarson 2 60
(R F Johnson Houghton) *hld up in tch: outpcd and rdn over 2f out: rallied over 1f out: swtchd rt ins fnl f: r.o* **4/1**[2]

5 4 ½ **Metal Guru**[20] 5076 2-8-5 .... RussellKennemore(7) 15 58
(R Hollinshead) *a.p: rdn to ld 2f out: hdd ins fnl f: no ex towards fin* **50/1**

00 5 1 **Kyllachy Storm**[10] 5340 2-9-3 .... RichardHughes 9 60
(R J Hodges) *chsd ldrs: rdn over 2f out: one pce fnl f* **12/1**[3]

00 6 ½ **Gib (IRE)**[94] 2816 2-8-12 .... MichaelHills 7 53
(B W Hills) *s.i.s: bhd: hdwy over 1f out: nt rch ldrs* **33/1**

3 7 shd **Bidable**[10] 5348 2-8-12 .... FergusSweeney 6 53
(B Palling) *prom: rdn over 2f out: wknd ins fnl f* **20/1**

0 8 1 **Crossing The Line (IRE)**[10] 5347 2-9-3 .... JamieMackay 1 54
(Sir Mark Prescott) *sltly hmpd sn after s: bhd: kpt on fnl f: n.d* **50/1**

00 9 1 **Ella Woodcock (IRE)**[16] 5161 2-8-10 .... FrankiePickard(7) 4 51
(J A Osborne) *bhd tl hdwy on ins over 1f out: n.d* **100/1**

0034 10 nk **Clewer**[16] 5162 2-8-12 59 .... TPO'Shea 8 45
(P A Blockley) *led: rdn and hdd 2f out: wknd ins fnl f* **25/1**

11 nk **Launch It Lily** 2-8-5 .... JackDean(7) 3 44
(W G M Turner) *s.i.s: stmbld sn after s: nvr trbld ldrs* **100/1**

0 12 nk **Strobe**[19] 5112 2-9-0 .... RichardKingscote(3) 12 48
(J A Osborne) *s.i.s: outpcd* **50/1**

13 2 ½ **Croeso Bach** 2-8-12 .... SteveDrowne 14 35
(J L Spearing) *rrd and wnt rt s: a bhd* **33/1**

600 14 1 **Neat 'n Tidy**[14] 5231 2-8-12 58 .... NCallan 13 31
(C A Cyzer) *hld up in tch: rdn over 2f out: wknd over 1f out* **66/1**

00 15 2 ½ **Georges Pride**[16] 5161 2-9-3 .... LPKeniry 10 28
(J M Bradley) *w ldr: rdn over 2f out: sn wknd* **100/1**

1m 12.08s (0.88) **Going Correction** +0.025s/f (Good) **15** Ran SP% **122.1**
Speed ratings (Par 95):95,93,92,92,90 90,89,88,87,86 86,86,82,81,78
CSF £8.67 TOTE £1.70: £1.10, £2.80, £1.50; EX 12.80 TRIFECTA Pool £294.63 - 6.56 winning units.
Owner First Of Many Partnership **Bred** Chris McHale And Oghill House Stud **Trained** Kingston Warren, Oxon

FOCUS
A moderate affair with plenty available at fancy prices. The bare form is limited but the winner travelled quite well and could be capable of better.

NOTEBOOK
Maker's Mark(IRE) was hardly winning out of turn and found a change to more patient tactics enabling him to justify being a heavily-backed favourite. (op 10-11 tchd Evens in a place)
Izabela Hannah ◆ did not go unsupported but again lost ground at the start. She came home in a style that suggests she can soon go one better. (op 20-1)
Support Fund(IRE) ◆ appears to be going the right way and looks capable of picking up a similar event over at least a full six furlongs. (op 7-2)
Metal Guru showed the benefit of her debut over the bare minimum at Catterick at the beginning of the month. (op 66-1)
Kyllachy Storm had failed to get home in better company over seven furlongs at Newbury last time. (op 10-1 tchd 14-1)
Gib(IRE) ◆, who did not have things go her way in a couple of outings over six in June, took a long time to warm up. Now qualified for nurseries, she is one to keep an eye on when given a stiffer test of stamina. (op 28-1)
Strobe Official explanation: jockey said colt ran green

5564 BRISTOL UNIVERSITY AND LITERARY CLUB H'CAP 2m 1f 34y
2:50 (2:52) (Class 5) (0-75,75) 3-Y-O+ **£3,886** (£1,156; £577; £288) **Stalls** Low

Form RPR

2340 1 **Maystock**[9] 5383 6-9-6 **67** .... MichaelHills 11 75
(B G Powell) *hld up in mid-div: stdy hdwy over 4f out: rdn to ld over 1f out: drvn out* **12/1**

0344 2 ¾ **Synonymy**[30] 4800 3-7-12 **57** .... NickyMackay 7 64
(M Blanshard) *hld up in mid-div: hdwy over 4f out: nt clr run and swtchd rt over 1f out: sn rdn: styd on ins fnl f* **10/1**

2146 3 2 **Takafu (USA)**[44] 4369 4-9-7 **75** .... JamesMillman(7) 2 80
(W S Kittow) *hld up in tch: rdn 4f out: ev ch over 2f out: no ex ins fnl f* **10/1**

/300 4 2 ½ **Laggan Bay (IRE)**[24] 4996 6-9-3 **64** .... (b) LPKeniry 9 66
(J S Moore) *hld up and bhd: hdwy over 2f out: rdn over 1f out: wknd ins fnl f* **20/1**

6034 5 1 ¼ **Bobsleigh**[14] 5235 7-8-11 **58** oh6 .... JimmyQuinn 3 58
(H S Howe) *prom: rdn to ld over 2f out: hdd over 1f out: wknd fnl f* **20/1**

-032 6 3 ½ **Jayer Gilles**[14] 5235 6-8-11 **58** oh1 .... FergusSweeney 6 54
(Dr J R J Naylor) *hld up and bhd: stdy hdwy over 4f out: rdn 3f out: swtchd rt wl over 1f out: sn wknd* **6/1**[2]

2200 7 5 **Our Monogram**[21] 5069 10-9-12 **73** .... MartinDwyer 12 63
(R M Beckett) *chsd ldr: reminders after 2f: rdn and ev ch 2f out: wknd 1f out* **8/1**[3]

6-30 8 6 **Dundry**[110] 2357 5-9-13 **74** .... (p) RyanMoore 8 57
(G L Moore) *hld up and bhd: hdwy on ins over 3f out: rdn over 2f out: eased whn btn fnl f* **8/1**[3]

/00- 9 31 **Penalty Clause (IRE)**[22] 5518 6-8-8 **62** oh19 ow4 JPFeatherstone(7) 10 8
(P Howling) *hld up in mid-div: dropped rr 8f out: t.o* **50/1**

2-21 10 7 **Desert Storm (DEN)**[11] 5324 4-9-4 **65** .... NCallan 5 2
(Rae Guest) *led: rdn and hdd over 2f out: wknd qckly: t.o* **7/4**[1]

0000 11 27 **Smoking Star**[18] 5127 3-7-7 **57** oh13 .... NicolPolli(5) 4 —
(N I M Rossiter) *prom tl wknd over 4f out: t.o* **100/1**

300 **12** *36* **Rebelling (IRE)**[8] [3347] 3-8-2 **61** ow1 (b) RichardThomas 1 —
(M F Harris) *a bhd: t.o* **66/1**

3m 47.09s (-2.51) **Going Correction** -0.05s/f (Good)
WFA 3 from 4yo+ 12lb 12 Ran SP% **112.7**
Speed ratings (Par 103):103,102,101,100,99 98,95,93,78,75 62,45
CSF £113.79 CT £1240.69 TOTE £13.70: £3.60, £2.80, £2.10; EX 169.50 TRIFECTA Not won. Pool £459.46.
Owner Stock Hill Racing **Bred** Stock Hill Stud **Trained** Morestead, Hants

FOCUS
This modest handicap took even less winning with the favourite a flop. The winner was 2lb off her turf best, with the second back to his early form.
Desert Storm(DEN) Official explanation: trainer had no explanation for the poor form shown

5565 EUROPEAN BREEDERS FUND MAIDEN STKS 1m 2f 46y
3:20 (3:22) (Class 4) 2-Y-O **£6,477** (£1,927; £963; £481) **Stalls** Low

Form RPR
2 **1** **Opera Crown (IRE)**[10] [5340] 2-9-3 RyanMoore 3 73+
(P F I Cole) *mde all: rdn over 2f out: hung lft ins fnl f: r.o* **2/5**[1]
06 **2** *hd* **Here Comes Buster (IRE)**[11] [5321] 2-9-3 DaneO'Neill 5 73
(R Hannon) *a.p: rdn over 2f out: ev ch ins fnl f: r.o* **9/2**[2]
0604 **3** *4* **Tension Point**[9] [5389] 2-9-3 **73** MartinDwyer 8 65
(J A Osborne) *hld up: rdn over 2f out: hdwy over 1f out: one pce fnl f* **14/1**
4 *1 1/2* **Flamed Amazement** 2-9-3 KDarley 1 63
(M Johnston) *chsd wnr: ev ch over 2f out: sn rdn: wknd over 1f out* **10/1**[3]
5 **5** *6* **Sosueme Now**[24] [4980] 2-8-12 LPKeniry 2 46
(A B Haynes) *hld up in tch: rdn and wknd over 2f out* **100/1**
6 *1/2* **Haut La Vie** 2-9-3 StephenCarson 6 50
(R F Johnson Houghton) *s.s: rdn over 4f out: a bhd* **33/1**
7 *9* **Bish Basher (IRE)** 2-9-3 TPO'Shea 7 33
(P A Blockley) *hld up: rdn over 3f out: sn struggling* **66/1**

2m 12.33s (1.33) **Going Correction** -0.05s/f (Good) 7 Ran SP% **110.8**
Speed ratings (Par 97):92,91,88,87,82 82,75
CSF £2.30 TOTE £1.50: £1.10, £1.70; EX 2.80 Trifecta £12.90 Pool £631.48 - 34.60 winning units.
Owner Axom (I) **Bred** Paget Bloodstock **Trained** Whatcombe, Oxon

FOCUS
A slow pace led to a time over two and a half seconds slower than the subsequent two divisions of the three-year-old fillies' maiden. The form is not solid.

NOTEBOOK
Opera Crown(IRE) might have been better off setting a stronger pace and he did well to hold on after not helping his rider in the closing stages. (op 1-2)
Here Comes Buster(IRE) was supported to turn over the favourite on this step up in distance but he could not quite take advantage of the hotpot hanging. (op 7-1)
Tension Point, ridden to get the trip, was probably beaten for speed rather than stamina. (op 16-1 tchd 20-1)
Flamed Amazement is stoutly bred and from a winning family. (op 7-1)

5566 BRISTOL UNIVERSITY AND LITERARY CLUB MAIDEN FILLIES' STKS (DIV I) 1m 2f 46y
3:50 (3:53) (Class 5) 3-Y-0+ **£2,720** (£809; £404; £202) **Stalls** Low

Form RPR
-362 **1** **Regal Velvet**[40] [4489] 3-8-12 **75** RichardHughes 1 87+
(J H M Gosden) *hld up in mid-div: hdwy over 2f out: rdn to ld jst over 1f out: qcknd clr ins fnl f: comf* **7/2**[2]
3 **2** *3 1/2* **Mowazana (IRE)**[17] [5151] 3-8-12 RHills 9 77
(M P Tregoning) *w ldr: led 3f out: sn rdn: hdd jst over 1f out: one pce* **7/4**[1]
40 **3** *2* **Shout (IRE)**[138] [1583] 3-8-12 SteveDrowne 3 74
(R Charlton) *a.p: rdn 3f out: one pce fnl 2f* **7/4**[1]
-025 **4** *5* **Golden Sprite**[60] [3865] 3-8-12 **60** DaneO'Neill 12 64
(B R Millman) *a.p: rdn and ev ch over 1f out: wknd fnl f* **25/1**
5342 **5** *3/4* **Valart**[21] [5056] 3-8-9 **66** JamesDoyle(3) 11 63
(Ms J S Doyle) *s.i.s: hld up in mid-div: hdwy on outside over 3f out: rdn over 2f out: wknd fnl f* **12/1**[3]
50 **6** *7* **Pearl Of Esteem**[20] [5086] 3-8-12 JimmyQuinn 7 49
(J Pearce) *s.i.s: bhd: rdn and sme hdwy over 2f out: wknd over 1f out* **100/1**
3060 **7** *1 1/4* **Dyanita**[17] [5152] 3-8-12 **63** MichaelHills 8 47
(B W Hills) *hld up in tch: ev ch 3f out: rdn 2f out: wknd over 1f out* **20/1**
0 **8** *6* **Gundula (IRE)**[28] [4899] 3-8-12 FergusSweeney 2 36
(D J S Ffrench Davis) *s.i.s: rdn over 2f out: a bhd* **150/1**
9 *1 3/4* **La Grande Zoa (IRE)** 3-8-12 NCallan 10 32
(R M Beckett) *s.i.s: a bhd* **50/1**
6 **10** *14* **Bonnie Belle**[31] [4776] 3-8-12 MartinDwyer 13 6
(J R Boyle) *a bhd: eased whn no ch over 1f out* **50/1**
00-0 **11** *16* **Filliemou (IRE)**[21] [5056] 5-9-4 **35** FrancisFerris 5 —
(A W Carroll) *led: rdn and hdd 3f out: wknd rapidly: t.o* **200/1**
12 *4* **Bisaat (USA)** 3-8-9 RichardKingscote(3) 6 —
(M S Saunders) *s.i.s: a bhd: rdn and t.o 3f out* **66/1**

2m 9.72s (-1.28) **Going Correction** -0.05s/f (Good)
WFA 3 from 5yo 6lb 12 Ran SP% **118.8**
Speed ratings (Par 100):103,100,98,94,94 88,87,82,81,70 57,54
CSF £9.69 TOTE £4.40: £1.60, £1.10, £1.10; EX 9.40 Trifecta £21.40 Pool £453.12 - 15.02 winning units.
Owner Cheveley Park Stud **Bred** Cheveley Park Stud Ltd **Trained** Newmarket, Suffolk

FOCUS
An ordinary maiden. The form seems to make sense, with the winner showing improvement, the second and third close to their debut form and the fourth setting the standard.
Valart Official explanation: jockey said filly was hanging badly left-handed
Pearl Of Esteem Official explanation: jockey said filly left stalls awkwardly
Dyanita Official explanation: jockey said filly lost its action a furlong out
Bisaat(USA) Official explanation: jockey said filly never travelled

5567 BRISTOL UNIVERSITY AND LITERARY CLUB MAIDEN FILLIES' STKS (DIV II) 1m 2f 46y
4:20 (4:24) (Class 5) 3-Y-0+ **£2,720** (£809; £404; £202) **Stalls** Low

Form RPR
52 **1** **Pentatonic**[15] [5203] 3-8-12 NickyMackay 11 72+
(L M Cumani) *a.p: led wl over 1f out: rdn out* **2/1**[2]
33 **2** *2 1/2* **Moon Valley**[30] [4814] 3-8-12 MartinDwyer 8 67
(M P Tregoning) *a.p: rdn over 3f out: ev ch over 1f out: nt qckn fnl f* **3/1**[3]
4605 **3** *hd* **Over Ice**[46] [4286] 3-8-9 **62** RichardKingscote(3) 13 67
(Karen George) *bhd: rdn over 3f out: hdwy on outside 2f out: r.o one pce fnl f* **40/1**
3-36 **4** *1 1/4* **Best Lady (IRE)**[35] [4661] 3-8-12 **73** MichaelHills 10 65
(B W Hills) *hld up in mid-div: hdwy 3f out: rdn and one pce whn n.m.r wl ins fnl f* **11/2**
04 **5** *shd* **Seeking Kali (IRE)**[43] [4396] 3-8-12 (v[1]) RyanMoore 2 64
(Sir Michael Stoute) *led: rdn over 2f out: hdd wl over 1f out: no ex fnl f* **15/8**[1]
0 **6** *2* **Mamonta**[137] [1613] 3-8-12 DaneO'Neill 12 61
(D M Simcock) *s.i.s: hld up in mid-div: sme hdwy over 2f out: sn rdn: no further prog* **100/1**
00-0 **7** *5* **Shropshirelass**[23] [5032] 3-8-12 **50** FJohansson 4 51
(Mrs Norma Pook) *chsd ldr: rdn over 2f out: wknd over 1f out* **100/1**
005 **8** *5* **Maria Antonia (IRE)**[107] [2465] 3-8-12 **60** TPO'Shea 9 42
(P A Blockley) *t.k.h in mid-div: hdwy over 3f out: wknd over 2f out* **100/1**
0 **9** *1 1/2* **Jaufrette**[21] [5056] 3-8-12 RichardThomas 1 39
(Dr J R J Naylor) *s.s: rdn over 3f out: a bhd* **100/1**
00- **10** *9* **Sahara Sun (IRE)**[336] [6072] 3-8-12 FergusSweeney 5 22
(A King) *hld up and plld hrd: rdn over 3f out: a bhd* **100/1**
0- **11** *1 1/4* **Hot Baby (IRE)**[370] [5391] 3-8-12 JamieMackay 7 19
(M L W Bell) *s.s: a bhd* **66/1**
0-6 **12** *6* **Highband**[90] [2951] 3-8-12 LPKeniry 3 8
(M Madgwick) *prom: rdn 4f out: wknd 3f out* **250/1**

2m 9.65s (-1.35) **Going Correction** -0.05s/f (Good) 12 Ran SP% **117.8**
Speed ratings (Par 100):103,101,100,99,99 98,94,90,88,81 80,75
CSF £8.45 TOTE £3.60: £1.20, £1.10, £6.80; EX 9.00 Trifecta £53.90 Pool £360.69 - 4.75 winning units.
Owner Helena Springfield Ltd **Bred** Meon Valley Stud **Trained** Newmarket, Suffolk

FOCUS
There was rather more strength in depth here in a race won in a similar time to the first division, but the third and seventh limit the form. The winner did not need to improve.

5568 MEA PROJECT MANAGEMENT H'CAP 1m 5y
4:50 (4:55) (Class 5) (0-70,69) 3-Y-0 **£3,886** (£1,156; £577; £288) **Stalls** Low

Form RPR
0544 **1** **Hassaad**[47] [4254] 3-9-2 **67** (t) RHills 1 78
(W J Haggas) *hld up in rr: hdwy on outside 2f out: rdn over 1f out: r.o to ld wl ins fnl f* **20/1**
0021 **2** *1 1/4* **Welsh Cake**[7] [5418] 3-8-13 **64** 6ex (bt) RyanMoore 3 72
(Mrs A J Perrett) *led over 1f: a.p: led 2f out: sn rdn: hdd wl ins fnl f: nt qckn* **5/1**[2]
000 **3** *nk* **Reeling N' Rocking (IRE)**[30] [4814] 3-8-13 **64** MichaelHills 14 71
(B W Hills) *hld up in mid-div: rn wd bnd over 4f out: rdn and hdwy 2f out: kpt on ins fnl f* **25/1**
4221 **4** *1* **Starboard Light**[23] [5035] 3-8-8 **62** JamesDoyle(3) 4 67
(R M Beckett) *hld up in tch: rdn 2f out: nt qckn ins fnl f* **8/1**
0304 **5** *hd* **Valentino Swing (IRE)**[23] [5036] 3-9-3 **68** SteveDrowne 10 73
(J L Spearing) *hld up towards rr: hdwy over 3f out: rdn 2f out: one pce fnl f* **33/1**
6325 **6** *shd* **High Octave (IRE)**[9] [5377] 3-9-1 **66** MartinDwyer 12 70+
(B G Powell) *sltly hmpd sn after s: hld up and bhd: rdn and hdwy over 1f out: one pce fnl f* **11/2**[3]
1242 **7** *nk* **Benbrook**[14] [5236] 3-9-4 **69** RichardHughes 7 73
(J L Dunlop) *led over 6f out: rdn and hdd 2f out: no ex fnl f* **7/2**[1]
050 **8** *3/4* **Drawback (IRE)**[88] [3030] 3-8-11 **62** RichardThomas 15 64
(R A Harris) *bhd: hdwy fnl f: nrst fin* **100/1**
6006 **9** *2* **Pigeon Island**[13] [5268] 3-9-2 **67** DaneO'Neill 9 64
(H Candy) *prom: ev ch over 3f out: sn rdn: wknd wl over 1f out* **11/1**
1140 **10** *2 1/2* **Takitwo**[22] [5042] 3-9-2 **67** LPKeniry 6 59
(P D Cundell) *hld up in mid-div: hdwy over 3f out: rdn over 2f out: wknd wl over 1f out* **16/1**
0056 **11** *1 3/4* **Suesam**[10] [5350] 3-8-12 **63** FergusSweeney 16 51
(B R Millman) *prom: rdn over 2f out: wknd wl over 1f out* **20/1**
3011 **12** *nk* **Emily's Place (IRE)**[39] [4533] 3-9-3 **68** JimmyQuinn 13 55
(J Pearce) *hld up and bhd: hdwy on ins over 3f out: rdn 2f out: sn wknd* **10/1**
4503 **13** *3* **Malech (IRE)**[13] [5270] 3-9-1 **66** NCallan 8 46
(M L W Bell) *prom: rdn over 2f out: sn wknd* **20/1**
5020 **14** *8* **Boldinor**[67] [3682] 3-8-13 **64** AlanDaly 2 26
(N E Berry) *hld up in tch: rdn and wknd over 2f out* **50/1**
1340 **15** *1* **Noble Nova**[24] [4995] 3-8-13 **64** TPO'Shea 11 23
(M R Channon) *hld up towards rr: hdwy on outside over 3f out: rdn and wknd over 2f out: eased whn no ch over 1f out* **25/1**

1m 40.64s (-0.46) **Going Correction** -0.05s/f (Good) 15 Ran SP% **116.6**
Speed ratings (Par 101):100,98,98,97,97 97,96,96,94,91 89,89,86,78,77
CSF £104.42 CT £2590.18 TOTE £24.50: £7.40, £2.50, £8.90; EX 143.30 Trifecta £219.40 Part won. Pool £309.12 - 0.50 winning units. Pool £154.56.
Owner Hamdan Al Maktoum **Bred** Shadwell Estate Company Limited **Trained** Newmarket, Suffolk

FOCUS
A tightly-knit low-grade contest. The level of the form looks sound enough.

5569 TELETEXT RACING "HANDS AND HEELS" APPRENTICE H'CAP 5f 161y
5:20 (5:23) (Class 6) (0-58,58) 3-Y-0+ **£2,396** (£712; £356; £177) **Stalls** Low

Form RPR
5000 **1** **Chatshow (USA)**[92] [2897] 5-9-0 **58** MarkCoumbe(5) 12 71+
(A W Carroll) *hld up towards rr: hdwy over 2f out: rdn to ld over 1f out: r.o wl* **9/2**[1]
6105 **2** *1 1/2* **Davids Mark**[29] [4846] 6-8-4 **48** FrankiePickard(5) 8 56
(J R Jenkins) *hld up in mid-div: hdwy 2f out: chsd wnr fnl f: kpt on* **9/1**
2300 **3** *1 3/4* **Diamond Katie (IRE)**[5] [5486] 4-8-9 **51** DanielleMcCreery(3) 15 53
(N Tinkler) *hld up in mid-div: hdwy over 2f out: one pce fnl f* **7/1**[3]
0500 **4** *1 1/4* **Full Spate**[24] [4984] 11-8-7 **53** BarrySavage(7) 11 51
(J M Bradley) *stdd s: swtchd rt and hdwy over 1f out: sn rdn: kpt on same pce fnl f* **25/1**
403 **5** *nk* **Supreme Kiss**[31] [4756] 3-8-8 **54** JemmaMarshall(5) 3 51
(Mrs N Smith) *dwlt: t.k.h: swtchd rt and hdwy whn nt clr run over 1f out: no imp fnl f* **12/1**
2200 **6** *1 1/4* **Tapau (IRE)**[12] [5302] 8-8-2 **48** PietroRomeo(7) 5 41
(J M Bradley) *s.i.s: hld up and bhd: hdwy on outside whn hung rt wl over 1f out: no further prog* **33/1**
3223 **7** *hd* **Knead The Dough**[13] [5272] 5-8-13 **55** JamieHamblett(3) 1 47
(A E Price) *hld up in mid-div: swtchd rt over 2f out: nt clr run over 1f out: no real prog fnl f* **10/1**
1565 **8** *1/2* **Montzando**[16] [5167] 3-9-0 **55** (p) JamesMillman 14 45
(B R Millman) *chsd ldr: led briefly wl over 1f out: wknd ins fnl f* **10/1**
0-55 **9** *3/4* **Chilly Cracker**[33] [4691] 4-8-8 **50** AlanRutter(3) 10 38
(John Berry) *chsd ldrs: rdn over 1f out: sn wknd* **14/1**

0000 **10** 1 1/2 **Danielle's Lad**[20] 5085 10-9-4 **57**.............................(b) KirstyMilczarek 16 40
(B Palling) *bhd: rdn 3f out: hdwy on outside whn carried rt over 1f out: n.d after* **25/1**
0523 **11** 3/4 **Princely Vale (IRE)**[43] 4389 4-8-6 **50**.............................(b) JackDean(5) 7 30
(W G M Turner) *led: rdn and hdd wl over 1f out: sn wknd* **14/1**
3063 **12** 11 **Cabriole**[37] 4613 3-8-9 **55**... JonjoMilczarek(5) 4 —
(H R A Cecil) *hld up in tch: rdn 2f out: sn wknd: no ch whn hmpd on ins ent fnl f: eased* **6/1[2]**
000- **13** 1/2 **Young Valentino**[279] 6625 4-8-4 **50**............................. WilliamBuick(7) 9 —
(A W Carroll) *prom tl wknd over 2f out* **50/1**
0000 **14** 14 **Ravish**[14] 5250 3-8-4 **50**...(bt) BRoper(5) 2 —
(W J Haggas) *s.v.s: a t.o* **25/1**

1m 11.18s (-0.02) **Going Correction** +0.025s/f (Good)
WFA 3 from 4yo+ 2lb **14** Ran SP% **110.6**
Speed ratings (Par 101):101,99,96,95,94 92,92,92,91,89 88,73,72,54
CSF £37.82 CT £279.42 TOTE £4.50: £1.90, £3.10, £2.80; EX 50.10 TRIFECTA Not won. Pool £128.16. Place 6 £63.16, Place 5 £56.65.
Owner One Under Par Racing **Bred** Juddmonte Farms Inc **Trained** Cropthorne, Worcs

FOCUS
A weak handicap and the bare form is ordinary, rated through the runner-up. The winner had slipped to a good mark.
Montzando Official explanation: jockey said gelding jinked left on leaving stalls
Cabriole Official explanation: jockey said filly stumbled 1 1/2f out
T/Plt: £96.20 to a £1 stake. Pool: £55,916.70. 423.90 winning tickets. T/Qpdt: £6.30 to a £1 stake. Pool: £3,957.70. 460.80 winning tickets. KH

5447 BRIGHTON (L-H)

Monday, September 25

OFFICIAL GOING: Good changing to good to soft after race 2 (3.00)
Wind: moderate, against

5570 EUROPEAN BREEDERS FUND MEDIAN AUCTION MAIDEN STKS 5f 213y
2:30 (2:30) (Class 6) 2-Y-O **£3,238** (£963; £481; £240) **Stalls** Low

Form RPR
224 **1** **Shebang (IRE)**[20] 5095 2-8-12 70.. TPQueally 9 69
(M G Quinlan) *mde all: clr whn flashed tail ins fnl f but unchal* **15/8[1]**
0442 **2** 2 1/2 **Straight Face (IRE)**[3] 5508 2-9-3 72.................................(v) PaulDoe 10 66
(W J Knight) *chsd wnr thrght: no imp fr over 1f out* **4/1[3]**
04 **3** 1 1/4 **Nashharry (IRE)**[15] 5209 2-8-12 .... PatDobbs 11 58
(R Hannon) *s.i.s: sn in tch on outside: kpt on one pce fnl f* **9/1**
0044 **4** shd **Benllech**[6] 5447 2-9-3 72.. GeorgeBaker 7 62
(S Kirk) *s.i.s: sed to come over to stands' side but sn racd centre on outside: hung lft over 1f out: one pce* **3/1[2]**
02L0 **5** 1 **Linkslade Lad**[21] 5065 2-9-3 64...................................(p) RichardMullen 4 59
(W R Muir) *towards rr: sme hdwy over 1f out but nvr on terms* **16/1**
06 **6** 1 **Mr Forthright**[16] 5161 2-9-0 .... StephenDonohoe(3) 2 56
(J M Bradley) *chsd ldrs tl rdn and one pce fr over 1f out* **16/1**
0 **7** 1 1/4 **Desirable Dancer (IRE)**[21] 5052 2-8-12 .... MickyFenton 6 48
(R A Harris) *chsd ldrs tl wknd 2f out* **66/1**
500 **8** hd **Eastern Playboy (IRE)**[45] 4334 2-9-3 40..................... DerekMcGaffin 5 52
(J Jay) *trckd ldrs: rdn 2f out: sn wknd* **33/1**
00 **9** 1 **Elmasong**[15] 5209 2-8-9 .... DominicFox(3) 1 44
(J J Bridger) *hld up in rr: nvr on terms* **66/1**
06 **10** 9 **Fistral**[33] 4688 2-9-3 .... ChrisCatlin 3 22
(M R Channon) *s.i.s: a bhd* **11/1**
00 **11** 3/4 **Sangfroid**[9] 5389 2-9-3 .... SebSanders 12 20
(Sir Mark Prescott) *uns rdr on way to s: sn in rr and nvr on terms* **66/1**

1m 11.41s (1.31) **Going Correction** +0.225s/f (Good) **11** Ran SP% **117.3**
Speed ratings (Par 93):100,96,95,94,93 92,90,90,88,76 75
CSF £9.30 TOTE £3.00: £1.10, £2.00, £2.50; EX 10.50.
Owner Liam Mulryan **Bred** Farmers Hill Stud **Trained** Newmarket, Suffolk

FOCUS
A modest maiden. The form looks straightforward enough rated through the second and third.

NOTEBOOK
Shebang(IRE) found the drop back to this trip in her favour and she readily made all to open her account at the fourth time of asking. She has not done a great deal wrong in her career to date, and it may prove that a stiff six furlongs is her optimum trip this year, although she can be expected to get a mile without fuss as a three-year-old. (tchd 7-4 and 2-1 in a place)
Straight Face(IRE) again managed to find one too good. He is a sound enough benchmark for the form, and it should be noted he was giving weight to the winner, plus he probably found this coming a little too soon. Whether he is quite up to his current official mark is in doubt, however, and he may be more one for the impending All-Weather season. (op 5-1)
Nashharry(IRE), back down in trip, never figured after a sluggish start yet was noted as finishing her race with a degree of promise. She needed this run to qualify for a handicap mark and really should fare better in that sphere. (op 8-1)
Benllech proved at a disadvantage in being brought down the centre of the track in an attempt to tack stands' side and can be rated a little better than the bare form. However, he has nevertheless become frustrating to follow. (op 5-2)

5571 HBLB MAIDEN STKS 6f 209y
3:00 (3:00) (Class 5) 3-Y-0+ **£3,238** (£963; £481; £240) **Stalls** Low

Form RPR
24 **1** **Bachelor Party (USA)**[20] 5093 3-9-3 .... TPQueally 5 65
(J Noseda) *hld up in tch: pushed along to ld over 1f out: hung rt: r.o wl ins fnl f* **15/8[1]**
4320 **2** 1 3/4 **Never Say Deya**[34] 4671 3-8-12 50...................................... ChrisCatlin 2 55
(M R Channon) *led after 2f: rdn and hdd over 1f out: kpt on but nt qckn ins fnl f* **6/1**
064 **3** nk **Ektimaal**[10] 5353 3-9-3 64...(t) RichardMullen 7 59
(E A L Dunlop) *trckd ldrs: rdn and kpt on one pce fnl f* **5/2[2]**
5405 **4** 2 **Snow Symphony (IRE)**[12] 5298 3-9-3 58........................... DarryllHolland 3 54
(D M Simcock) *led for 2f: rdn wl over 1f out: no hdwy after* **5/1[3]**
400 **5** 3/4 **Zamhrear**[10] 5353 3-8-12 48... SebSanders 6 47
(C E Brittain) *slowly away: effrt over 1f out but nvr nr to chal* **9/1**
4000 **6** 6 **Wodhill Schnaps**[12] 5302 5-9-6 52...........................(p) DerekMcGaffin 1 36
(D Morris) *a towards rr* **33/1**
00 **7** 1 1/4 **Batchworth Blaise**[20] 5093 3-9-3 ....(b[1]) PaulFitzsimons 8 33
(E A Wheeler) *t.k.h: chsd ldrs but rdn and bhd fnl 2f* **50/1**
0-00 **8** 4 **Command Respect**[90] 2951 3-8-12 35........................(v[1]) JimCrowley 4 18
(E F Vaughan) *hld up in mid-div: rdn and wknd over 2f out* **33/1**

1m 24.08s (1.38) **Going Correction** +0.225s/f (Good)
WFA 3 from 5yo 3lb **8** Ran SP% **112.1**
Speed ratings (Par 103):101,99,98,96,95 88,87,82
CSF £13.08 TOTE £2.90: £1.10, £1.90, £2.00; EX 12.80.
Owner B J McElroy **Bred** John J Greely Iii **Trained** Newmarket, Suffolk

FOCUS
They all came near side in the straight. The runner-up had an official rating of 50 and this looked a very moderate maiden. The winner did not need to be at his best.
Ektimaal Official explanation: trainer's rep said gelding had a breathing problem

5572 IAN CARNABY APPRENTICE H'CAP 7f 214y
3:30 (3:30) (Class 5) (0-75,75) 3-Y-O+ **£3,238** (£963; £481; £240) **Stalls** Low

Form RPR
2453 **1** **My Princess (IRE)**[12] 5301 4-9-5 **71**............................. JerryO'Dwyer 4 81
(N A Callaghan) *hld up in rr: hdwy and swtchd lft over 2f out: rdn and r.o fnl f to ld cl home* **6/1[3]**
0014 **2** nk **Landucci**[20] 5096 5-9-6 **75**... PatrickHills(3) 2 84
(J W Hills) *hld up: hdwy to ld over 1f out: rdn and hdd cl home* **9/4[1]**
3000 **3** 1 3/4 **Flint River**[14] 5233 8-9-3 **69**... TravisBlock 6 74
(H Morrison) *t.k.h: led tl hdd over 1f out: rdn and kpt on one pce fnl f* **15/2**
5046 **4** 3 1/2 **Lizarazu (GER)**[14] 5233 7-9-3 **72**.................................(p) TolleyDean(3) 3 69
(R A Harris) *hdwy 1/2-way to trck ldrs: ev ch fr over 2f out to over 1f out: sn btn* **8/1**
0-00 **5** 3/4 **Congressional (IRE)**[15] 5211 3-8-7 **70**................... DanielRobinson(7) 7 65
(M A Jarvis) *hld up in tch: rdn over 2f out: hung lft over 1f out and sn no ch* **11/1**
3540 **6** 2 1/2 **The Gaikwar (IRE)**[14] 5236 7-9-3 **72**.....................(b) KevinGhunowa(3) 5 61
(R A Harris) *s.i.s: hld up: rdn over 3f out: wknd 2f out* **13/2**
4210 **7** 4 **Tuscarora (IRE)**[18] 5130 7-8-7 **62**........................... AshleyHamblett(3) 8 42
(A W Carroll) *trckd ldr to 1/2-way: sn rdn wknd 2f out* **5/1[2]**
8 7 **Princely Ted (IRE)**[197] 5-8-6 **61** oh1.....................(t) ThomasO'Brien(3) 1 25
(E J Creighton) *prom tl rdn 1/2-way: sn bhd* **20/1**

1m 37.32s (2.28) **Going Correction** +0.225s/f (Good)
WFA 3 from 4yo+ 4lb **8** Ran SP% **111.0**
Speed ratings (Par 103):97,96,94,91,90 88,84,77
CSF £18.72 CT £98.27 TOTE £3.70: £1.80, £1.30, £2.50; EX 14.10.
Owner T Mohan & Allan McNamee **Bred** J Sheehan **Trained** Newmarket, Suffolk
■ Stewards' Enquiry : Jerry O'Dwyer caution: used whip in incorrect place

FOCUS
Just a fair handicap restricted to apprentice riders who had not ridden more than 50 winners. They tended to race centre to near side in the straight. The winner was up 3lb on her form this year, with the second running to this year's form.

5573 BRAKES FOOD SERVICE SOLUTIONS CLAIMING STKS 6f 209y
4:00 (4:02) (Class 6) 4-Y-O+ **£2,590** (£770; £385; £192) **Stalls** Low

Form RPR
0004 **1** **Megalala (IRE)**[41] 4450 5-8-6 43.................................... MarcHalford(3) 4 59
(J J Bridger) *a int tch: drvn to ld wl ins fnl f: kpt on* **40/1**
5600 **2** 1 **Convince (USA)**[9] 5378 5-8-10 57......................(p) StephenDonohoe(3) 9 60
(J M Bradley) *trckd ldrs: led over 3f out tl hdd over 1f out: kpt on* **8/1**
4011 **3** shd **Mountain Pass (USA)**[12] 5302 4-9-3 58.........................(p) DO'Donohoe 5 64
(M J Wallace) *in tch: led over 1f out: rdn and hdd wl ins fnl f: lost 2nd cl home* **7/2[1]**
405 **4** 1 **Keep Backckinhit (IRE)**[5] 5474 4-8-6 55........................(b) JimCrowley 10 51
(G L Moore) *in tch towards stands' side: rdn over 1f out: tan on wl ins fnl f* **13/2[3]**
5124 **5** 1 **Hadath (IRE)**[6] 5450 9-8-4 54...(b) PatrickHills(7) 6 53
(B G Powell) *racd far side fnl 3f: ev ch tl no hdwy appr fnl f* **9/2[2]**
4040 **6** 1 **Vindication**[11] 5327 6-9-3 53...(t) GeorgeBaker 1 56
(R M H Cowell) *hld up: hdwy 1/2-way: sn chsng ldrs: one pce fnl f* **16/1**
0000 **7** 2 1/2 **Go Mo (IRE)**[12] 5302 4-9-7 58.. PatDobbs 11 54
(S Kirk) *in tch: rdn 3f out: no hdwy appr fnl f* **9/1**
60-4 **8** shd **Phlaunt**[38] 4554 4-8-1 44 ow2................................... ThomasO'Brien(7) 3 41
(R F Johnson Houghton) *hld up towards rr: nvr nr to chal* **14/1**
0600 **9** hd **Warden Warren**[40] 4496 8-9-7 44.....................................(p) TPQueally 8 53
(Mrs C A Dunnett) *hld up: rdn and hdwy 2f out: wknd appr fnl f* **25/1**
4056 **10** 1 1/2 **Regal Dream (IRE)**[9] 5386 4-9-7 67........................(v[1]) DarryllHolland 13 49
(J W Hills) *hld up: a towards rr* **13/2[3]**
5500 **11** nk **Mystic Man (FR)**[20] 5085 8-9-7 63................................(b) SebSanders 15 48
(I W McInnes) *mid-divisision: wknd wl over 1f out* **14/1**
0504 **12** 6 **Wodhill Be**[29] 4844 6-8-8 45.. DerekMcGaffin 16 20
(D Morris) *a towards rr* **50/1**
13 1/2 **Johnnie Black (IRE)**[337] 4-8-8 45...................... EdwardCreighton(3) 7 21
(E J Creighton) *t.k.h: trckd ldrs: wknd wl over 1f out* **40/1**
0000 **14** 1 1/4 **Pyramid**[76] 3386 4-8-5 45...(p) RichardMullen 14 12
(A J Lidderdale) *led tl hdd over 3f out: sn wknd* **50/1**
0000 **15** 1 1/2 **Bamzooki**[20] 5086 4-8-0 42... AdrianMcCarthy 12 3
(Mrs C A Dunnett) *hld up in mid-div: bhd fnl 3f* **33/1**

1m 23.61s (0.91) **Going Correction** +0.225s/f (Good) **15** Ran SP% **123.0**
Speed ratings (Par 101):103,101,101,100,99 98,95,95,95,93 93,86,85,84,82
CSF £329.90 TOTE £56.80: £11.00, £3.20, £1.20; EX 424.20.There was no bid for the winner.
Owner Tommy Ware **Bred** J E Gallagher **Trained** Liphook, Hants

FOCUS
A moderate claimer in which it proved difficult to make up ground from off the pace. The majority of these raced middle to near side in the straight, although they were strung out across the course at the line. An improved run from the winner, with the third running to his recent form.
Mystic Man(FR) Official explanation: jockey said gelding had no more to give

5574 SUSSEX CRIMESTOPPERS 0800 555 111 H'CAP 1m 1f 209y
4:30 (4:31) (Class 6) (0-65,65) 3-Y-O **£3,108** (£924; £462; £230) **Stalls** High

Form RPR
2141 **1** **Hurry Up Helen (IRE)**[6] 5452 3-9-0 **61** 6ex.............. RobbieFitzpatrick 4 69
(Mrs L Stubbs) *mde virtually all: rdn over 1f out: r.o wl* **13/2[3]**
0615 **2** 3/4 **Kavachi (IRE)**[29] 4838 3-9-4 **65**....................................... GeorgeBaker 15 72+
(G L Moore) *hld up: racd wd: chsd other runner on stands' side over 3f out tl hdd it 2f out: chsd wnr fnl frlong* **13/2[3]**
0465 **3** 1 3/4 **Fratt'n Park (IRE)**[15] 5211 3-9-0 **64**........................... DominicFox(3) 12 68
(J J Bridger) *hld up: hdwy 4f out: kpt on fnl f* **22/1**
5462 **4** hd **Siakira**[18] 5129 3-9-4 **65**.. TPQueally 11 68
(I A Wood) *chsd ldrs: rdn and ev ch over 1f out: no hdwy fnl f* **20/1**
0044 **5** 3/4 **Leamington Lad (IRE)**[18] 5129 3-9-1 **62**......................... RobertHavlin 3 64
(J A Geake) *mid-div: rdn over 3f out: styd on fnl f* **10/1**
2323 **6** 2 1/2 **Lunar River (FR)**[13] 5260 3-9-4 **65**.......................(vt[1]) RichardMullen 9 62
(E A L Dunlop) *hld up: hdwy 3f out: styd on fnl f* **11/2[2]**
4053 **7** nk **Newport Boy (IRE)**[13] 5258 3-8-13 **60**......................... DarryllHolland 10 57
(R A Harris) *w wnr to over 3f out: rdn and wknd appr fnl f* **9/1**
006 **8** 2 1/2 **Star Berry**[49] 4210 3-8-0 **54**... KMay(7) 13 46
(B J Meehan) *s.i.s: hld up: nvr on terms* **33/1**

0660 **9** 3/4 **Lady Cree (IRE)**[16] 5166 3-8-7 **54**........................(p) PaulDoe 16 44+
(W R Muir) *cme stands'side and led other horse that side fr over 3f out to 2f out: sn wknd* **25/1**
0000 **10** *hd* **Squiffy**[21] 5057 3-8-10 **57**........................ ChrisCatlin 5 47
(P D Cundell) *hld up in rr: nvr on terms* **33/1**
6000 **11** 3 1/2 **Dancing Melody**[31] 4757 3-8-4 **51**........................ DavidKinsella 8 34
(J A Geake) *mid-div: rdn and wknd 2f out* **33/1**
0202 **12** 3/4 **Dik Dik**[23] 5015 3-8-10 **57**........................(v) OscarUrbina 2 39
(C N Allen) *prom: wkng whn short of room over 1f out* **14/1**
0325 **13** 8 **Diktatorship (IRE)**[16] 5173 3-8-5 **52**........................ AdrianMcCarthy 14 19
(Ernst Oertel) *in tch: wkng whn hung lft over 1f out* **10/1**
000- **14** 5 **Accent (IRE)**[384] 5016 3-8-10 **57**........................ SebSanders 6 14
(Sir Mark Prescott) *t.k.h: prom tl wknd over 2f out* **5/2**[1]

2m 5.67s (3.07) **Going Correction** +0.225s/f (Good) **14** Ran SP% **127.3**
Speed ratings (Par 99):96,95,94,93,93 91,91,89,88,88 85,84,78,74
CSF £47.01 CT £894.96 TOTE £6.40: £2.80, £3.60, £4.80; EX 48.60.
Owner Des Thurlby **Bred** G Callanan **Trained** Norton, N. Yorks

FOCUS
A moderate handicap. The majority of these raced middle to far side in the straight, but Kavachi took second having raced with just one other horse (Lady Cree) on the near side. Another improved run from the winner, with the overall form pretty sound.
Diktatorship(IRE) Official explanation: jockey said gelding hung badly left-handed
Accent(IRE) Official explanation: trainer's rep had no explanation for the poor form shown

5575 BET365 CALL 08000 322 365 H'CAP 5f 59y
5:00 (5:00) (Class 5) (0-75,75) 3-Y-0+ **£3,238** (£963; £361; £361) **Stalls** Low

Form RPR
2303 **1** **Harrison's Flyer (IRE)**[5] 5480 5-8-7 **66**........................(p) NeilChalmers(3) 11 73
(J M Bradley) *hld up: hdwy whn hung lft over 1f out: r.o to ld ins fnl f: jst hld on* **6/1**[2]
6040 **2** *shd* **Summer Recluse (USA)**[5] 5480 7-8-13 **69**........................(t) DarryllHolland 2 76
(J M Bradley) *in tch: rdn 1/2-way: r.o strly ins fnl f: jst failed* **9/1**
5420 **3** *shd* **Who's Winning (IRE)**[17] 5148 5-9-5 **75**........................ GeorgeBaker 8 82
(B G Powell) *hld up in rr: rdn 1/2-way: hung lft over 1f out: rn wl ins fnl f* **6/1**[2]
2006 **3** *dht* **Chinalea (IRE)**[10] 5333 4-9-3 **73**........................(p) SebSanders 4 80+
(C G Cox) *in tch: rdn to ld over 1f out: hdd ins fnl f: nt n btn by much* **7/2**[1]
0105 **5** 2 **Cosmic Destiny (IRE)**[5] 5480 4-8-5 **61**........................ ChrisCatlin 13 60
(E F Vaughan) *hld up in rr: hdwy 1/2-way: effrt over 1f out: sn btn* **9/1**
0221 **6** 1/2 **Safari Mischief**[16] 5181 3-8-13 **70**........................ JimCrowley 9 68
(P Winkworth) *led tl rdn and hde over 1f out: wknd ins fnl f* **9/1**
-666 **7** 1 **Semenovskii**[31] 4780 6-8-10 **66**........................ HayleyTurner 5 60
(Mrs N Smith) *mid-div: rdn and wknd 1f out* **10/1**
6050 **8** 1 1/2 **Hello Roberto**[8] 5405 5-8-11 **70**........................(p) AmirQuinn(3) 3 59
(R A Harris) *trckd ldr: rdn and wknd over 1f out* **14/1**
2400 **9** 3/4 **Misaro (GER)**[21] 5058 5-9-1 **71**........................(b) MickyFenton 10 57
(R A Harris) *chsd ldrs: bhd fr 1/2-way* **12/1**
1145 **10** 2 1/2 **Talcen Gwyn (IRE)**[5] 5486 4-8-6 **62**........................(v) DavidKinsella 12 39
(M F Harris) *chsd ldr: hung bdly lft and wknd over 1f out* **7/1**[3]

62.72 secs (0.42) **Going Correction** +0.225s/f (Good)
WFA 3 from 4yo+ 1lb **10** Ran SP% **116.7**
Speed ratings (Par 103):105,104,104,104,101 100,99,96,95,91
CSF £58.99 TOTE £4.30: £1.80, £3.20; EX 34.90 TRIFECTA PL: Who's Winning £1.20, Chinalea £1.00. TRICAST: HF/SR/WW £173.94, HF/SR/C £111.88.
Owner racingsharescouk **Bred** Geoff Mulcahy **Trained** Sedbury, Gloucs

FOCUS
A modest but very competitive sprint handicap in which they raced middle to near side in the straight. Straightforward to rate, the winner not needing to improve and the next three pretty much to form.
Talcen Gwyn(IRE) Official explanation: jockey said gelding hung badly left-handed

5576 JIM HICKS MEMORIAL H'CAP 5f 213y
5:30 (5:31) (Class 6) (0-60,60) 3-Y-0+ **£3,207** (£947; £473) **Stalls** Low

Form RPR
-000 **1** **Turibius**[25] 4962 7-9-1 **55**........................ JimCrowley 7 64
(G L Moore) *hld up: hdwy and swtchd rt over 1f out: led wl ins fnl f* **14/1**
0065 **2** *nk* **Indian Lady (IRE)**[18] 5131 3-8-11 **53**........................(b) SebSanders 2 61
(Mrs A L M King) *chsd ldrs: led 2f out: rdn and hdd ins fnl f: kpt on* **9/1**
0020 **3** 1 1/4 **Cree**[14] 5232 4-9-0 **54**........................ RichardMullen 1 58
(W R Muir) *trckd ldrs rdn over 2f out: nt qckn ins fnl f* **11/2**[3]
0004 **4** 1 1/4 **Millfields Dreams**[11] 5327 7-8-11 **56**........................(p) JerryO'Dwyer(5) 4 57
(M G Quinlan) *a.p: ev ch 2f out tl one pce ins fnl f* **10/1**
0021 **5** 1 **Tilsworth Charlie**[21] 5055 3-8-13 **55**........................(v) RobertHavlin 9 53
(J R Jenkins) *chsd ldrs: rdn over 1f out: one pce ins fnl f* **20/1**
1054 **6** *hd* **Limonia (GER)**[10] 5350 4-9-1 **55**........................ MickyFenton 3 52
(N P Littmoden) *led tl hdd 2f out: nt qckn fnl f* **8/1**
-240 **7** *nk* **Creme Brulee**[10] 5350 3-9-1 **57**........................ ChrisCatlin 5 53
(C R Egerton) *s.i.s: hdwy over 1f out: fdd ins fnl f* **14/1**
0132 **8** 2 **Moon Forest (IRE)**[11] 5327 4-9-1 **55**........................(p) DarryllHolland 8 45
(J M Bradley) *nvr bttr than mid-div* **3/1**[1]
0615 **9** *shd* **Riolo (IRE)**[12] 5302 4-8-11 **56**........................(b) KevinGhunowa(5) 6 46
(K F Clutterbuck) *s.i.s: nvr on terms* **12/1**
0423 **10** 1 **Peruvian Style (IRE)**[11] 5327 5-9-2 **59**........................ StephenDonohoe(3) 14 46
(J M Bradley) *mid-div: no hdwy fnl 2f* **5/1**[2]
0000 **11** 3/4 **Mayden Dawn**[6] 5450 3-8-10 **52**........................(v[1]) AdrianMcCarthy 11 36
(Miss E C Lavelle) *s.i.s: a bhd* **25/1**
1006 **12** 2 **Kahlua Bear**[23] 5032 4-8-10 **53**........................(v) NeilChalmers(3) 16 31
(Miss K B Boutflower) *a in rr* **14/1**
6440 **13** *hd* **Tetrode (USA)**[20] 5081 4-8-12 **52**........................ HayleyTurner 13 30
(R M H Cowell) *in tch to 1/2-way* **50/1**
14 3 **Broadfield Lady (IRE)**[197] 6-9-1 **58**........................ EdwardCreighton(3) 10 27
(E J Creighton) *prom to 1/2-way* **50/1**
0000 **15** *nk* **Danny The Dip**[16] 5181 3-8-9 **54**........................ MarcHalford(3) 12 22
(J J Bridger) *mid-division: lost tch over 2f out* **33/1**

1m 11.08s (0.98) **Going Correction** +0.225s/f (Good)
WFA 3 from 4yo+ 2lb **15** Ran SP% **130.4**
Speed ratings (Par 101):102,101,99,98,96 96,96,93,93,92 91,88,88,84,83
CSF £138.39 CT £817.47 TOTE £18.90: £4.20, £5.00, £3.10; EX 163.30 Place 6 £25.81, Place 5 £17.48.
Owner Vogue Development Company (kent) Ltd **Bred** Bearstone Stud **Trained** Woodingdean, E Sussex

FOCUS
A modest yet competitive sprint handicap. Sound form, with the winner having slipped to a nice mark and capable of better still.
T/Jkpt: Not won. T/Plt: £13.10 to a £1 stake. Pool: £65,172.75. 3,615.80 winning tickets. T/Qpdt: £12.50 to a £1 stake. Pool: £2,644.40. 155.80 winning tickets. JS

5401 HAMILTON (R-H)
Monday, September 25

OFFICIAL GOING: Good to soft (soft in places)
Wind: virtually nil

5577 HAMILTON PARK H'CAP 5f 4y
2:10 (2:10) (Class 5) (0-70,69) 3-Y-0+ **£3,238** (£963; £481; £240) **Stalls** Centre

Form RPR
6050 **1** **George The Best (IRE)**[32] 4735 5-8-5 **55** oh2........................ PaulHanagan 13 63
(Micky Hammond) *a.p: swtchd lft after 1f: rdn and hung lft over 1f out. drvn ins last: styd on to ld last 50 yds* **7/1**[3]
5455 **2** *nk* **Joyeaux**[20] 5081 4-8-12 **62**........................(v) DavidAllan 2 69
(J Hetherton) *cl up: led wl over 1f out: rdn ent last: hdd and nt qckn last 50 yds* **8/1**
2522 **3** *nk* **Newkeylets**[21] 5060 3-8-1 **55** oh1........................(p) AndrewMullen(3) 4 61
(I Semple) *dwlt and towards rr stands side: hdwy 2f out: rdn over 1f out: kpt on ins last: nrst fin* **18/1**
0020 **4** *hd* **Paddywack (IRE)**[4] 5493 9-8-10 **60**........................(b) PhillipMakin 7 65+
(D W Chapman) *trckd ldrs: hdwy whn bdly hmpd over 1f out: swtchd lft and rdn ent last: styd on wl towards fin* **5/1**[2]
6060 **5** 1/2 **Divine Spirit**[11] 5309 5-8-13 **63**........................(p) JamieSpencer 11 66
(M Dods) *towards rr: hdwy on outer 2f out: sn rdn and kpt on ins last: nrst fin* **5/1**[2]
5061 **6** 3/4 **Brigadore**[9] 5378 7-9-2 **66**........................ LDettori 8 67
(J G Given) *hld up hdwy 2f out: swtchd rta nd rdn over 1f out: kpt on same pce ins last* **9/2**[1]
1020 **7** 1 3/4 **Oeuf A La Neige**[11] 5309 6-8-5 **55** oh2........................ JoeFanning 5 49
(Miss L A Perratt) *chsd ldrs: rdn along 2f out: n.m.r over 1f out: sn wknd* **12/1**
0-00 **8** *hd* **John O'Groats (IRE)**[11] 5309 8-7-12 **55** oh12......(p) CharlotteKerton(7) 6 49
(W G Harrison) *cl up: rdn along whn hmpd over 1f out: sn wknd* **100/1**
4600 **9** 1 3/4 **Colonel Cotton (IRE)**[11] 5309 7-8-10 **65**........................(v) JamieMoriarty(5) 3 52
(R A Fahey) *chsd ldrs: rdn over 1f out: wknd ent last* **12/1**
0-56 **10** 2 **Sokoke**[129] 1816 5-8-4 **57** oh10 ow2........................ SaleemGolam(3) 1 37
(D A Nolan) *sn led and overall elader stands side: rdn along over 2f out: hdd wl over 1f out and sn wknd* **200/1**
6220 **11** 4 **Strawberry Patch (IRE)**[20] 5078 7-8-11 **61**........................(p) DanielTudhope 16 27
(J S Goldie) *chsd ldr far side: hdwy to ld that gp 1f out: no ch w stands side* **10/1**
0000 **12** 1 1/2 **Titian Saga (IRE)**[33] 4703 3-8-7 **58**........................ AdrianTNicholls 12 18
(D Nicholls) *chsd ldrs on outer: rdn along over 2f out: sn w eakened* **33/1**
-003 **13** *hd* **Briery Blaze**[53] 4071 3-8-4 **55** oh1........................ RoystonFfrench 9 15
(Mrs K Walton) *a rr* **25/1**
0500 **14** 1/2 **Legal Set (IRE)**[125] 1914 10-8-3 **58** oh15 ow3........................(t) AnnStokell(5) 14 16
(Miss A Stokell) *led far side gp: rdn along 2f out: hdd & wknd 1f out* **100/1**
0006 **15** 7 **Ochil Hills Dancer (IRE)**[14] 5241 4-8-0 **55** oh18..(b) AndrewElliott(5) 15 —
(A Crook) *a rr far side* **250/1**

61.72 secs (0.52) **Going Correction** +0.225s/f (Good)
WFA 3 from 4yo+ 1lb **15** Ran SP% **114.5**
Speed ratings (Par 103):104,103,103,102,101 100,97,97,94,91 85,82,82,81,70
CSF £57.29 CT £987.22 TOTE £8.60: £2.50, £3.20, £2.90; EX 66.00.
Owner M D Hammond **Bred** E R Breeding **Trained** Middleham Moor, N Yorks

FOCUS
An ordinary event in which the bulk of the field raced centre to stands side. The trio that stayed far side never got competitive. Straightforward form based around the second to the sixth.
Titian Saga(IRE) Official explanation: jockey said filly hung right-handed final 3f

5578 TOTESPORT 0800 221 221 CONDITIONS STKS 6f 5y
2:40 (2:40) (Class 2) 3-Y-0+
£12,464 (£3,732; £1,866; £934; £466; £234) **Stalls** Centre

Form RPR
3202 **1** **Bygone Days**[200] 619 5-8-9 107........................ LDettori 11 113+
(Saeed Bin Suroor) *trckd ldrs gng wl: smooth hdwy 2f out: qckd to ld ins last: comf* **3/1**[3]
0001 **2** 3/4 **Fonthill Road (IRE)**[9] 5358 6-8-9 102........................ PaulHanagan 1 109
(R A Fahey) *trckd ldrs: hdwy 2f out: effrt and ev ch ent last: sn rdn and nt qckn* **2/1**[1]
0020 **3** 2 **Eisteddfod**[9] 5375 5-9-2 108........................ JamieSpencer 5 110
(P F I Cole) *hld up: hdwy 2f out: rdn ent last: kpt on* **5/2**[2]
1505 **4** 1/2 **Pawan (IRE)**[6] 5443 6-8-9 76........................(b) AnnStokell 2 102?
(Miss A Stokell) *cl up: led 1/2-way: rdn wl over 1f out: hdd & wknd ins last* **66/1**
6036 **5** 2 **Bahamian Pirate (USA)**[23] 5009 11-8-9 100........................ AdrianTNicholls 4 96
(D Nicholls) *towards rr and outpcd 1/2-way: styd on appr last: nt rch ldrs* **12/1**
5024 **6** 1 1/4 **Pacific Pride**[19] 5116 3-8-7 99........................(v[1]) TomEaves 3 92
(J Howard Johnson) *chsd ldrs: rdn along 2f out: wknd appr last* **12/1**
0650 **7** 5 **Johnston's Diamond (IRE)**[10] 5336 8-8-9 78........................(p) DavidAllan 6 77
(E J Alston) *sn led: rdn along and hdd 1/2-way: sn drvn and wknd 2f out* **50/1**
3-66 **8** 3/4 **Black Charmer (IRE)**[18] 5135 3-8-7 105........................ JoeFanning 7 75
(M Johnston) *prom: rdn along 1/2-way: sn outpcd* **20/1**
00 **9** 25 **Deer Park Countess**[51] 4136 5-8-4........................(t) FrancisNorton 10 —
(D A Nolan) *s.i.s: a bhd* **500/1**

1m 13.2s (0.10) **Going Correction** +0.225s/f (Good)
WFA 3 from 4yo+ 2lb **9** Ran SP% **110.7**
Speed ratings (Par 109):108,107,104,103,101 99,92,91,58
CSF £8.70 TOTE £3.80: £1.40, £1.30, £1.50; EX 11.40.
Owner Godolphin **Bred** J A E Hobby **Trained** Newmarket, Suffolk

FOCUS
A few no-hopers but otherwise a decent event for the track and one in which the pace was sound. The winner impressed in travelling well and looks improved. The race has been rated through the runner-up, with the fourth holding down the form.

NOTEBOOK
Bygone Days ◆, a smart handicapper, ran as well as he ever has done on this first run for Godolphin and first run since early March to win a fair event with more in hand than the official margin suggests. He goes particularly well with cut in the ground and appeals as the type to win more races for this yard when he gets suitable conditions. (tchd 7-2, 4-1 in places)
Fonthill Road(IRE), who returned to form with a vengeance when winning the Ayr Gold Cup earlier this month, had conditions to suit and gave it his best shot. He is more than capable of winning a similar event given a bit of cut in the ground. (op 7-4 tchd 9-4)

The Form Book, Raceform Ltd, Compton, RG20 6NL

Eisteddfod, back over a more suitable trip and with the blinkers left off this time, ran creditably attempting to concede 7lb to his two main market rivals. He would have been closer had he not been checked in the closing stages but the inteference did not affect the result and his Group 3 penalty may continue to be his undoing at this level. (op 10-3)
Pawan(IRE), who ran well in the face of a very stiff task at Beverley on his previous start, again ran out of his skin on most unfavourable terms. However his modest strike-rate and the fact he is fully exposed suggests he would not be one to lump on at short odds from his current mark of 76 back in a handicap.
Bahamian Pirate(USA) retains plenty of ability and ran a typical race. However he is the type that needs things to fall right and, given he has not won for over two years, is one for the layers rather than the backers in this type of event.
Pacific Pride was not totally disgraced in the first-time visor but he has mainly been disappointing since winning his maiden and a current rating of 99 means he is not going to be the easiest to place successfully. (op 14-1)

5579 TOTEPOOL SERIES FINAL (HANDICAP STKS) 1m 1f 36y
3:10 (3:10) (Class 3) 3-Y-0+ **£9,715** (£2,890; £1,444; £721) **Stalls** High

Form RPR

4254 **1** **Barbirolli**[29] 4842 4-7-8 **59** LukeMorris(7) 9 — 71
(W M Brisbourne) *midfield: hdwy over 4f out: led 2f out: rdn clr ent last: kpt on wl* **12/1**

2263 **2** *3 1/2* **Paparaazi (IRE)**[18] 5137 4-9-0 **72** PaulHanagan 14 — 77
(R A Fahey) *midfield: hdwy over 4f out: rdn to chse ldrs wl over 1f out: kpt on u.p ins last* **13/2**[3]

2110 **3** *nk* **Wind Star**[46] 4298 3-9-5 **87** AndrewElliott(5) 12 — 91
(G A Swinbank) *trckd ldrs: hdwy over 4f out: chal over 3f out and ev ch tl rdn and one pce fr wl over 1f out* **8/1**

4653 **4** *3/4* **Ulysees (IRE)**[1] 5553 7-8-6 **64** RoystonFfrench 1 — 67
(I Semple) *towards rr: hdwy 3f out: rdn along over 2f out: kpt on u.p ins last: nrst fin* **12/1**

3655 **5** *1/2* **Qualitair Wings**[11] 5314 7-8-0 **58** FrancisNorton 2 — 60
(J Hetherton) *dwlt and towards rr: hdwy over 3f out: rdn along over 2f out: kpt on ins last: nrst fin* **7/1**

4000 **6** *1 1/4* **Hansomelle (IRE)**[3] 5510 4-8-1 **62** oh6 ow6 AndrewMullen(3) 3 — 61
(B Mactaggart) *prom: rdn along over 3f out: wknd over 2f out* **40/1**

5363 **7** *2* **Shy Glance (USA)**[9] 5388 4-8-5 **63** DaleGibson 13 — 58
(G A Swinbank) *led: rdn along over 3f out: hdd 2f out and sn wknd* **4/1**[1]

4136 **8** *1 3/4* **Royal Indulgence**[10] 5354 6-7-12 **61** oh1 ow5 LiamJones(5) 7 — 53
(W M Brisbourne) *dwlt: a towards rr* **11/1**

5050 **9** *3/4* **Insubordinate**[11] 5311 5-7-7 **56** oh3 (e) DuranFentiman(5) 8 — 46
(J S Goldie) *dwlt: a towards rr* **25/1**

4164 **10** *nk* **Chief Scout**[35] 4654 4-9-4 **76** TomEaves 4 — 66
(I Semple) *chsd ldrs: rdn along over 3f out: sn wknd* **5/1**[2]

3560 **11** *1 3/4* **Inch High**[35] 4652 8-7-11 **62** oh11 ow6 KellyHarrison(7) 11 — 48
(J S Goldie) *chsd ldr: rdn along over 3f out: wknd over 2f out* **40/1**

065 **12** *hd* **Scotty's Future (IRE)**[11] 5311 8-7-6 **57** oh1 ow1 CharlotteKerton(7) 5 — 43
(A Berry) *a rr* **25/1**

1144 **13** *1* **Champain Sands (IRE)**[25] 4953 7-8-4 **67** MichaelJStainton(5) 6 — 51
(E J Alston) *hld up: effrt over 3f out: sn wknd* **16/1**

2m 1.01s (1.35) **Going Correction** +0.45s/f (Yiel)
WFA 3 from 4yo+ 5lb **13** Ran SP% **115.8**
Speed ratings (Par 107):107,103,103,102,102 101,99,98,97,97 95,95,94
CSF £82.26 CT £664.42 TOTE £13.30: £3.60, £2.90, £2.90; EX 94.40.
Owner P Wright-Bevans **Bred** Gainsborough Stud Management Ltd **Trained** Great Ness, Shropshire
■ Stewards' Enquiry : Charlotte Kerton two-day ban: used whip when out of contention (Oct 6-7)

FOCUS
An ordinary handicap but one in which the pace was sound throughout and the field came centre to stands' side in the straight. The runner-up is an obvious guide to the form, but the sixth strikes a note of caution.

NOTEBOOK
Barbirolli had only won once in 23 previous starts but appreciated the cut in the ground and the decent gallop and won with plenty to spare. Unless the handicapper goes crazy, there is every reason to think he can win again before the season is out. (op 11-1)
Paparaazi(IRE) has not won for over a year but extended his run of creditable efforts this season. The return to a mile and a quarter will suit and he should continue to give it his best shot but he has little margin for error from this mark.
Wind Star ◆, a dual fast-ground winner this summer, ran well after a short break on this first run on easy ground. He fared the best of those that were up with the strong pace and looks the sort to win again back on a sound surface. (op 6-1)
Ulysees(IRE) had slipped to a fair mark, had the race run to suit and ran creditably. He goes well at this course but is the type that needs things to fall just right and, as such, is not really one to be lumping on at short odds next time.
Qualitair Wings does not win as often as his ability suggests he ought to and he ran a typical race after getting the strong pace that suits him best. He is the type that needs things to drop right and remains one to be wary of at single-figure odds. (tchd 8-1)
Hansomelle(IRE) has struggled for any consistency this year but was not totally disgraced from 6lb out of the handicap and carrying the same amount of overweight. She has not won for nearly two years and would not be an obvious one to rectify matters from her proper mark next time. (op 33-1)
Shy Glance(USA) has had a few chances but can be forgiven this as he failed to settle at the head of a truly-run race and not surprisingly did not get home in the conditions. He is capable of picking up a small event on either turf or sand. (op 11-2 tchd 6-1)

5580 EUROPEAN BREEDERS FUND MEDIAN AUCTION MAIDEN STKS 1m 65y
3:40 (3:40) (Class 5) 2-Y-0 **£3,886** (£1,156; £577; £288) **Stalls** High

Form RPR

43 **1** **Swiss Act**[11] 5321 2-9-3 JoeFanning 5 — 81+
(M Johnston) *mde virtually all: rdn over 2f out: styd on* **4/9**[1]

2 *1 1/4* **Hohlethelonely** 2-9-3 JamieSpencer 3 — 79
(M L W Bell) *cl up: effrt over 2f out and sn rdn: ev ch tiull drvn and kpt on same pce fnl f* **7/2**[2]

06 **3** *8* **Wanessa Tiger (IRE)**[15] 5209 2-8-12 RobertWinston 1 — 57
(M R Channon) *hld up: hdwy 3f out: rdn to chse ldng pair 2f out: sn outpcd* **10/1**[3]

60 **4** *1 3/4* **Tonnante**[12] 5287 2-8-12 J-PGuillambert 2 — 53
(Sir Mark Prescott) *trckd ldng pair: effrt 3f out: sn rdn along and wknd fnl 2f* **14/1**

03 **5** *3/4* **Bret Maverick (IRE)**[26] 4932 2-9-3 PhillipMakin 4 — 57
(J R Weymes) *trckd ldrs: rdn along over 3f out: sn wknd* **40/1**

1m 53.22s (3.92) **Going Correction** +0.45s/f (Yiel) **5** Ran SP% **109.7**
Speed ratings (Par 95):98,96,88,87,86
CSF £2.27 TOTE £1.40: £1.10, £1.50; EX 2.50.
Owner Markus Graff **Bred** Highclere Stud Ltd **Trained** Middleham Moor, N Yorks

FOCUS
An ordinary gallop in which the two market leaders pulled clear in the last quarter mile in this uncompetitive event. A fair maiden, the first two finishing clear. The form seems to make sense.

NOTEBOOK
Swiss Act, who had run creditably at Yarmouth on his previous start, put his experience to good use and showed a good attitude to beat a potentially fair newcomer. He will stay at least a mile and a quarter and is the sort to win more races for his current stable. (tchd 1-2)
Hohlethelonely, related to winners at up to middle distances, showed a fair level of ability on this racecourse debut, despite appearing unsuited by the muddling gallop. He should stay further and is the type to win in ordinary company granted a suitable test. (op 4-1)
Wanessa Tiger(IRE) had not shown much on her first two starts and, although not totally disgraced in terms of form this time, was readily left behind once the tempo picked up. She should do better in ordinary handicap company. (op 11-1)
Tonnante, easy to back, was not totally disgraced and left the impression that the step up to middle distances and the switch to ordinary handicap company would see her in a much better light next year. (tchd 16-1)
Bret Maverick(IRE), who was not totally disgraced on sand on his previous start, had his limitaions exposed and is likely to remain vulnerable in this type of event. (op 28-1)

5581 TOTEEXACTA APPRENTICE SERIES H'CAP (FINAL OF HAMILTON PARK APPRENTICE SERIES) 1m 3f 16y
4:10 (4:10) (Class 6) (0-65,63) 3-Y-0+ **£3,238** (£963; £481; £240) **Stalls** High

Form RPR

0446 **1** **Cleaver**[3] 5513 5-9-11 **62** AndrewElliott 5 — 73
(Lady Herries) *hld up and bhd: hdwy 3f out: rdn over 1f out: styd on ins last to ld last 100 yds* **6/1**[2]

4046 **2** *1 1/2* **Peas 'n Beans (IRE)**[20] 5082 3-8-1 **51** LukeMorris(6) 6 — 60
(M L W Bell) *hld up and bhd: hdwy 3f out: rdn to ld wl over 1f out and sn hung bdly lft: drvn: hdd andno ex last 100 yds* **12/1**

6205 **3** *2 1/2* **Gigs Magic (USA)**[18] 5129 3-8-3 **52** WilliamCarson(5) 7 — 57
(M Johnston) *a.p: led 3f out: sn rdn and hdd wl over 1f out: edgd lft and kpt on same pce* **14/1**

4425 **4** *2 1/2* **Planters Punch (IRE)**[14] 5242 5-9-7 **58** (v) LiamJones 1 — 59
(G M Moore) *trckd ldrs: hdwy on outer over 3f out and sn ev ch: rdn and hung lft over 2f out: sn drvn and one pce* **8/1**[3]

0553 **5** *1/2* **Kylkenny**[11] 5314 11-9-4 **63** (t) NBazeley(8) 13 — 63
(H Morrison) *hld up: stdy hdwy over 4f out: rdn to chse ldrs 3f out: kpt on same pce fnl 2f* **7/2**[1]

643F **6** *1* **Impeccable Guest (IRE)**[114] 2246 3-8-9 **56** LeanneKershaw(3) 14 — 55
(P C Haslam) *chsd ldr: hdwy to ld over 4f out: rdn along and hdd 3f out: grad wknd fnl 2f* **25/1**

-000 **7** *2* **Channel Crossing**[21] 5061 4-8-7 **49** oh7 PatrickDonaghy(5) 16 — 44
(W M Brisbourne) *led: rdn along and hdd over 4f out: grad wknd* **66/1**

250 **8** *2 1/2* **Archie Babe (IRE)**[119] 2075 10-9-0 **51** MichaelJStainton 11 — 42
(J J Quinn) *trckd ldrs: rdn along over 3f out: sn wknd* **10/1**

1123 **9** *shd* **Jordans Spark**[11] 5311 5-9-1 **55** NeilBrown(3) 2 — 46
(P Monteith) *a towards rr* **12/1**

443 **10** *2* **Donna's Double**[28] 4881 11-9-0 **51** (p) PJMcDonald 8 — 39
(Karen McLintock) *hld up: hdwy to chse ldrs over 3f out: sn rdn: drvn and wknd over 2f out* **10/1**

2236 **11** *2 1/2* **Shekan Star**[25] 4947 4-8-12 **55** JamesReveley(6) 4 — 39
(K G Reveley) *nvr nr ldrs* **8/1**[3]

4460 **12** *1* **Balwearie (IRE)**[33] 4698 5-9-0 **56** (p) MCGeran(5) 12 — 38
(Miss L A Perratt) *midfield: hdwy over 4f out: cl up 3f out: sn rdn and wknd 2f out* **12/1**

0534 **13** *12* **Lady Lochinver (IRE)**[28] 4892 3-8-2 **51** JamesRogers(5) 15 — 14
(Micky Hammond) *chsd ldrs: rdn along over 4f out: sn wknd* **20/1**

0500 **14** *10* **Taili**[44] 4351 5-8-9 **49** oh39 (v) CharlotteKerton(3) 3 — —
(D A Nolan) *in tch: rdn along over 3f out: sn wknd* **500/1**

2m 30.71s (4.45) **Going Correction** +0.45s/f (Yiel)
WFA 3 from 4yo+ 7lb **14** Ran SP% **117.0**
Speed ratings (Par 101):101,99,98,96,95 95,93,91,91,90 88,87,79,71
CSF £71.78 CT £968.93 TOTE £7.80: £2.20, £5.30, £4.60; EX 84.30.
Owner Seymour Bloodstock (uk) Ltd **Bred** J M Greetham **Trained** Patching, W Sussex

FOCUS
A strongly-run race which enabled those held up to come through in the closing stages. The winner and third both ran close to form.

5582 TOTESPORT.COM BUTTONHOOK H'CAP 1m 5f 9y
4:40 (4:40) (Class 3) (0-95,93) 3-Y-0+
£11,217 (£3,358; £1,679; £840; £419; £210) **Stalls** High

Form RPR

1411 **1** **Macorville (USA)**[18] 5137 3-9-1 **90** TomEaves 4 — 98
(G M Moore) *trckd ldrs: hdwy to chse wnr over 3f out and sn pushed along: rdn to ld 2f out: drvn ent last and hld on gamely* **5/1**[3]

1424 **2** *nk* **Cool Customer (USA)**[11] 5325 3-9-2 **91** JamieSpencer 6 — 99
(E A L Dunlop) *dwlt: hld up in rr: hdwy 3f out: swtchd lft and rdn 2f out: drvna nd styd on to chal ent last: no ex nr fin* **7/2**[1]

1330 **3** *shd* **Tilt**[86] 3078 4-9-5 **85** FrancisNorton 7 — 93+
(B Ellison) *hld up in rr: hdwy 2f out: sn rdn and styd on strly ins last: jst failed* **11/2**

2001 **4** *3 1/2* **Twill (IRE)**[16] 5180 3-8-4 **79** PaulHanagan 1 — 82
(H Morrison) *led 2f: chsd ldr tl rdn along over 2f out and grad wknd* **7/1**

3051 **5** *1/2* **Lets Roll**[9] 5361 5-9-10 **93** SaleemGolam(3) 2 — 95
(C W Thornton) *trckd ldrs: hdwy on outer over 3f out: rdn over 2f out and grad wknd* **4/1**[2]

00-0 **6** *nk* **Contact Dancer (IRE)**[138] 1584 7-9-9 **89** RoystonFfrench 3 — 91
(M Johnston) *trckd ldrs: hdwy over 4f out: rdn along 3f out: drvn and one pce fnl 2f* **20/1**

51-3 **7** *1/2* **Red Admiral (USA)**[18] 5141 4-9-12 **92** LDettori 5 — 93
(Saeed Bin Suroor) *cl up: led after 2f: rdn along 3f out: hdd 2f out: sn drvn and wknd* **11/2**

2m 57.02s (3.62) **Going Correction** +0.45s/f (Yiel)
WFA 3 from 4yo+ 9lb **7** Ran SP% **106.9**
Speed ratings (Par 107):106,105,105,103,103 103,102
CSF £19.76 TOTE £5.60: £2.50, £2.40; EX 16.00.
Owner Geoff & Sandra Turnbull **Bred** Brookdale Thoroughbreds Inc **Trained** Middleham Moor, N Yorks
■ Stewards' Enquiry : Jamie Spencer one-day ban: used whip with excessive force (Oct 6)

FOCUS
A decent handicap but a muddling gallop and a most gritty display from the progressive winner. The first three are on the upgrade and the form should work out.

NOTEBOOK
Macorville(USA), up in trip, had conditions to suit and showed a tremendously gutsy attitude to notch his fourth win in his last five starts. The November Handicap (run at Windsor this year) will be an obvious option if the ground is sufficiently testing and, judging by his improvement this year, he would have fair claims if lining up for that race. (op 7-2)
Cool Customer(USA), already a winner three times over middle distances this year, ran right up to his best back on easy ground. A more end-to-end gallop would have suited and he can win again away from progressive sorts.

Tilt ◆, not disgraced in the Northumberland Plate in early July, showed more than enough on this first run since to suggest he can win a decent handicap around middle distances granted give in the ground and a more end-to-end gallop. (op 6-1)
Twill(IRE), who beat two rivals over two miles at Goodwood on his previous start, had the run of the race but had his limitations exposed in this company back over this shorter trip. He is likely to remain vulnerable from this mark. (op 8-1 tchd 17-2)
Lets Roll, who returned to winning ways in an uncompetitive event at Ayr last time, had his limitations exposed from this 7lb higher mark. A stronger gallop would have suited but he is likely to remain vulnerable from this mark in handicaps. (op 9-2)
Red Admiral(USA) had the run of the race but folded tamely and this race could have come too quickly after his recent reappearance run at Southwell. He is worth another chance when allowed his own way in front. (tchd 6-1)

5583 HAMILTON PARK MAIDEN STKS — 1m 1f 36y
5:10 (5:10) (Class 5) 3-4-Y-O — **£3,238** (£963; £481; £240) **Stalls** High

Form — RPR
3302 **1** **Montpellier (IRE)**[56] [4004] 3-9-3 80 .... JamieSpencer 8 — 81+
(E A L Dunlop) *trckd ldrs: smooth hdwy 3f out: led on bit ins last: easily* **4/6**[1]
0-2 **2** 2½ **Melpomene**[38] [4549] 3-8-12 .... JoeFanning 2 — 60
(M Johnston) *sn led: rdn along over 2f out: drvn over 1f out: hdd ins last: kpt on: but no ch w wnr* **15/8**[2]
3 5 **Cross Of Lorraine (IRE)** 3-9-3 .... (b[1]) TomEaves 5 — 55
(I Semple) *towards rr: rdn along and hdwy over 2f out: kpt on appr last: nvr nr ldrs* **40/1**
4 3½ **Dandys Hurricane** 3-9-3 .... AdrianTNicholls 7 — 48
(D Nicholls) *towards rr: rdn along over 3f out: stgayed on appr last: nvr nr ldrs* **25/1**
F020 **5** 4 **Zell (IRE)**[9] [5370] 3-8-7 60 .... MichaelJStainton[(5)] 3 — 35
(E J Alston) *in tch: hdwy on outer over 3f out: rdn along over 2f out and sn btn* **12/1**[3]
0304 **6** nk **Silver Sail**[21] [5063] 3-8-12 40 .... (p) TonyHamilton 4 — 34
(J S Wainwright) *chsd ldrs: rdn along 3f out: wknd fnl 2f* **50/1**
6/0- **7** 6 **Lerida**[106] [5790] 4-9-8 .... PaulMulrennan 1 — 27
(Miss Lucinda V Russell) *a bhd* **100/1**
0500 **8** 9 **Heads Turn (IRE)**[33] [4697] 3-8-12 40 .... (b[1]) DavidAllan 6 — 4
(E J Alston) *prom: rdn along over 4f out: sn wknd* **100/1**

2m 5.99s (6.33) **Going Correction** +0.45s/f (Yiel)
WFA 3 from 4yo 5lb — **8** Ran SP% **112.7**
Speed ratings (Par 103):89,86,82,79,75 75,70,62
CSF £1.98 TOTE £1.80: £1.10, £1.10, £3.50; EX 2.40 Place 6 £136.64, Place 5 £30.15.
Owner Gainsborough Stud **Bred** M H Ings **Trained** Newmarket, Suffolk

FOCUS
An uncompetitive maiden in which the winner won with a good deal more in hand than the official margin suggested. The time was slow though and the form is dubious, rated through the poor sixth.
T/Plt: £150.00 to a £1 stake. Pool: £63,226.10. 307.55 winning tickets. T/Qpdt: £39.60 to a £1 stake. Pool: £3,052.10. 57.00 winning tickets. JR

5474 GOODWOOD (R-H)
Tuesday, September 26

OFFICIAL GOING: Good (good to soft in places on straight course)
Wind: Light, across. Weather: Fine.

5585 ELECTROLUX PROFESSIONAL NURSERY STKS (H'CAP) — 1m
2:00 (2:01) (Class 4) (0-85,82) 2-Y-O — **£4,533** (£1,348; £674; £336) **Stalls** High

Form — RPR
51 **1** **Zoom One**[15] [5239] 2-9-2 77 .... DaneO'Neill 10 — 80+
(M P Tregoning) *lw: mde virtually all: drvn 2 l clr over 1f out: tired fnl f: hld on* **7/1**[2]
005 **2** ½ **Aegis (IRE)**[19] [5125] 2-9-0 75 .... JamieSpencer 14 — 77
(B W Hills) *swtg: dwlt: nt keen in last pair: hrd rdn 3f out: no prog tl r.o strly fr over 1f out: wnt 2nd last 75yds: nt rch wnr* **8/1**
0003 **3** ½ **Spiderback (IRE)**[22] [5053] 2-8-7 68 .... RichardHughes 12 — 69
(R Hannon) *settled in midfield: hrd rdn 3f out: hanging 2f out: prog over 1f out: styd on to take 3rd nr fin* **10/1**
400 **4** nk **Bachnagairn**[22] [5067] 2-8-7 68 .... SteveDrowne 13 — 68+
(R Charlton) *prom: rdn and nt qckn wl over 2f out: kpt on to dispute 2nd 1f out: one pce* **15/2**[3]
0300 **5** nk **Prince Of Charm (USA)**[16] [5208] 2-7-12 59 oh1 .... JimmyQuinn 8 — 58
(P Mitchell) *settled in rr: stdy prog wl over 2f out: rdn to chse wnr over 1f out: one pce and lost 3 pls ins fnl f* **50/1**
0424 **6** 1¼ **Jawaab (IRE)**[22] [5053] 2-8-13 74 .... MartinDwyer 5 — 70
(E A L Dunlop) *lw: w ldrs: chsd wnr over 2f out to over 1f out: fdd fnl f* **10/1**
421 **7** 5 **Hadahoo (USA)**[24] [5025] 2-9-7 82 .... PhilipRobinson 2 — 67
(M A Jarvis) *lw: w wnr to 3f out: sn rdn: wknd over 1f out* **7/4**[1]
003 **8** 2 **Grand Heights (IRE)**[35] [4669] 2-9-2 77 .... LDettori 4 — 57
(J L Dunlop) *wl in tch: rdn and effrt wl over 2f out: hanging and wknd over 1f out* **7/1**[2]
0240 **9** 5 **Up In Arms (IRE)**[19] [5125] 2-8-13 74 .... StephenCarson 1 — 43
(P Winkworth) *chsd ldrs early: lost pl bdly bef 1/2-way: toiling and wl in rr over 2f out: plodded on* **33/1**
0603 **10** 1 **Urban Warrior**[10] [5382] 2-8-5 66 .... (v) FrancisFerris 9 — 33
(Mrs Norma Pook) *chsd ldrs: rdn over 3f out: nt qckn over 2f out: sn wknd rapidly* **12/1**
2160 **11** shd **Cavort (IRE)**[74] [3496] 2-9-1 81 .... EmmettStack[(5)] 11 — 47
(Pat Eddery) *s.s: a wl in rr: rdn and struggling 1/2-way* **25/1**
500 **12** 5 **Lay The Cash (USA)**[32] [4774] 2-7-12 59 oh9 .... AdrianMcCarthy 7 — 14
(J S Moore) *chsd ldrs: rdn over 3f out: wknd over 2f out* **20/1**
0500 **13** 1¾ **Cashcade (IRE)**[22] [5053] 2-8-7 68 .... (b[1]) JoeFanning 3 — 19
(A M Balding) *a wl in rr: struggling bef 1/2-way: bhd fnl 3f* **25/1**
4266 **14** 5 **Callisto Moon**[90] [2979] 2-8-12 73 .... TPO'Shea 6 — 12
(P A Blockley) *lw: dwlt: nvr gng wl: rdn and struggling bef 1/2-way* **25/1**

1m 41.22s (0.95) **Going Correction** +0.175s/f (Good) — **14** Ran SP% **131.3**
Speed ratings (Par 97):102,101,101,100,100 99,94,92,87,86 86,81,79,74
CSF £62.67 CT £429.28 TOTE £8.30: £2.70, £2.80, £3.60; EX 91.80.
Owner Sheikh Ahmed Al Maktoum **Bred** Darley **Trained** Lambourn, Berks
■ Stewards' Enquiry : Richard Hughes one-day ban: used whip with excessive frequency (Oct 7)

FOCUS
A competitive nursery and a fair winning time for a race of its type. It has been rated through the sixth, with the first four all improving. The runners decided to come wide once into the home straight, but that did not affect the usual advantage held by those drawn on the inside with the first four home starting from the five highest stalls.

NOTEBOOK
Zoom One, who stamina was never going to be in doubt having won over nine furlongs at Redcar, was wisely given a positive ride and made just about all to win in game style. He was the least exposed in the field so there is every reason to believe he could progress into a nice middle-distance handicapper next year. (op 15-2)
Aegis(IRE) gave himself an enormous amount to do and was being niggled at and carrying his head at a funny angle during the first part of the contest, but he made up a huge amount of ground over the last couple of furlongs and nearly pulled it off. He has the ability and obviously stamina is not a problem, but his earlier reluctance might be. Official explanation: jockey said colt hung right-handed
Spiderback(IRE) ran another decent race over this trip and was staying on well at the end. His breeding does not suggest he will get much further than this, but a similar race should be within his compass. (op 9-1)
Bachnagairn, making his nursery debut over an extra furlong, had every chance but could never quite get the better of the winner and merely stayed on at one pace. He is bred to stay further and his family tend to improve at three. (op 7-1)
Prince Of Charm(USA), a pound wrong, was brought through to hold every chance and was unfortunate to get run out of the money. He had looked pretty modest before this and this was a big improvement. (tchd 66-1)
Jawaab(IRE), up there from the start, had every chance but did not see the mile out so well this time and finished further behind Spiderback than he had at Bath despite meeting him on 1lb better terms. He does not seem to be progressing.
Hadahoo(USA), winner of a Thirsk maiden in bottomless ground which has already produced three winners, raced prominently for much of the way but eventually folded very tamely on this less-taxing surface. (op 5-2 tchd 11-4 in a place)
Grand Heights(IRE), making his nursery debut, is bred to relish this trip but failed to pick up and was disappointing. Official explanation: jockey said colt hung right-handed (op 6-1 tchd 15-2)
Urban Warrior Official explanation: jockey said gelding was unsuited by the good (good to soft places) ground

5586 SHARP COMMERCIAL MICROWAVE OVEN EUROPEAN BREEDERS FUND MEDIAN AUCTION MAIDEN FILLIES' STKS — 6f
2:30 (2:31) (Class 5) 2-Y-O — **£3,562** (£1,059; £529; £264) **Stalls** Low

Form — RPR
43 **1** **Lorena Wood (USA)**[111] [2355] 2-9-0 .... LDettori 5 — 71
(B J Meehan) *pressed ldr: rdn to chal over 1f out: styd on wl fnl f to ld nr fin* **6/4**[1]
5 **2** hd **Gentle Guru**[15] [5231] 2-9-0 .... SteveDrowne 12 — 70
(R T Phillips) *w'like: lw: racd on outer: mde most: hrd pressed fr over 1f out: kpt on wl: hdd nr fin* **7/1**
63 **3** nk **Tokyo Rose**[14] [5264] 2-9-0 .... RichardHughes 6 — 70
(R Hannon) *lw: trckd ldng trio: rdn to chal over 1f out: nrly upsides ins fnl f: a jst hld* **4/1**[2]
6 **4** 3 **Baby Dordan (IRE)**[109] [2402] 2-9-0 .... JamieSpencer 10 — 61
(D J Daly) *carried rt s: hld up towards rr: prog 2f out: swtchd rt and rdn ent fnl f: kpt on but nt pce to rch ldrs* **5/1**[3]
3 **5** 4 **Madrigale**[17] [5161] 2-8-11 .... RichardKingscote[(3)] 1 — 49
(G L Moore) *cmpt: str: racd alone against nr side rail: wl in tch tl wknd u.p 2f out* **17/2**
50 **6** 1¼ **Ranavalona**[52] [4161] 2-9-0 .... MartinDwyer 9 — 45
(A M Balding) *wnt rt s: racd on outer: sn in tch: effrt and cl up 2f out : wknd rapidly over 1f out* **22/1**
7 ½ **Ishimagic** 2-8-11 .... DominicFox[(3)] 11 — 43
(J J Bridger) *leggy: dwlt and carried rt s: detached last and struggling bef 1/2-way: kpt on to pass wkng rivals* **50/1**
8 ¾ **La Cuvee** 2-9-0 .... TPQueally 8 — 41
(R M Beckett) *leggy: chsd ldrs: rdn 2f out: wknd rapidly* **16/1**
0 **9** nk **Born Dancing**[16] [5209] 2-8-11 .... (t) NeilChalmers[(3)] 13 — 40
(J G Portman) *unf: b.hind: wnt rt s: sn w ldrs on outer: upsides wl over 1f out: wknd v rapidly* **80/1**
5 **10** 2 **Boschendal (IRE)**[12] [5326] 2-9-0 .... JoeFanning 7 — 34
(J W Hills) *lw: dwlt: hld up in rr: effrt over 2f out: sn shkn up and wknd rapidly* **25/1**
11 1¼ **Iolanthe** 2-8-7 .... KMay[(7)] 3 — 30
(B J Meehan) *unf: scope: b.hind: bit bkwd: nvr on terms: rdn and struggling 1/2-way: wknd* **25/1**
000 **12** 1¾ **Sagassa**[4] [5507] 2-9-0 .... AdrianMcCarthy 4 — 25
(W De Best-Turner) *wl in tch tl wknd rapidly 2f out* **100/1**
040 **13** 1 **The Light Fandango**[36] [4657] 2-8-7 58 .... TolleyDean[(7)] 2 — 22
(R A Harris) *rdn and struggling in rr bef 1/2-way: sn no ch* **40/1**

1m 13.9s (1.05) **Going Correction** +0.05s/f (Good) — **13** Ran SP% **124.2**
Speed ratings (Par 92):95,94,94,90,85 83,82,81,81,78 76,74,73
CSF £12.57 TOTE £2.30: £1.20, £2.50, £1.50; EX 21.80.
Owner Andy J Smith **Bred** High Creek Farm **Trained** Manton, Wilts
■ Stewards' Enquiry : L Dettori one-day ban: used whip with excessive frequency and without giving filly time to respond (Oct 7)

FOCUS
An ordinary fillies' maiden dominated by the market principals and rated around the winner, the form not looking that strong. Only one horse raced against the stands' rail, whilst the majority raced more towards the centre. With a decent margin between the third and fifth home, those that finished out of the frame will need to improve a lot in order to win a race.

NOTEBOOK
Lorena Wood(USA) appreciated the extra furlong and showed the right attitude in the three-way battle to the line. She may not have needed to improve much in order to win this and her immediate future lies in the hands of the Handicapper. (tchd 11-8 and 13-8, 7-4 in places)
Gentle Guru, stepped up from her Folkestone debut and, having been up at the sharp end from the off, she was only just denied. There should be a small race in her. (op 8-1)
Tokyo Rose ran as though this return to six was in her favour, but she did not have much room to play with between the front pair in the latter stages and the winning jockey's whip flailing in her face probably did her few favours either. She can now be handicapped and that is probably where her future lies. (op 6-1)
Baby Dordan(IRE), done few favours at the start, could never got on terms with the front trio though she did pull a long way clear of the rest. This was probably not much of an improvement on her debut effort here. (op 9-2 tchd 11-2)
Madrigale, up a furlong, ran a solo tight against the stands' rail and it is impossible to say whether that helped or hindered her performance. This was certainly no improvement on her debut effort though and, as she is bred to stay further, she may be the type that will come to herself next season. Official explanation: jockey said filly was unsuited by the good (good to soft places) ground (op 11-1 tchd 8-1)
Ranavalona was awkward leaving the stalls and then failed to get home. However, she can now be handicapped and her pedigree suggests she may be a better filly at three.
Ishimagic was green in the paddock and during the race. (op 33-1)

5587 WESTLER FOODS STKS (H'CAP) 2m

3:05 (3:05) (Class 5) (0-70,68) 3-Y-0+ £3,562 (£1,059; £529; £264) Stalls High

Form				RPR
03U5	1		**Serramanna**[4] 5506 5-8-9 **48** JamesDoyle(3) 14 (Ms J S Doyle) *hld up wl in rr: plenty to do 5f out: stdy prog 4f out: rdn to ld 2f out: hld on wl fnl f* 9/1	61
0-	2	3/4	**Jockser (IRE)**[123] 5972 5-9-10 **60** JoeFanning 4 (J W Mullins) *lw: hld up in midfield: prog to trck ldrs 3f out: rdn to chal 2f out: kpt on wl but jst hld fnl f* 10/1	72
05-4	3	5	**Cava Bien**[61] 1219 4-8-13 **49** RobertHavlin 15 (B J Llewellyn) *lw: trckd ldrs: rdn 3f out: chsd ldng pair over 1f out: one pce and sn no ch* 12/1	55
2331	4	2	**Primondo (IRE)**[29] 4898 4-10-0 **64** (v) JamieSpencer 12 (J R Fanshawe) *swtg: pushed along early: in tch: prog and cl up 3f out: rdn and nt qckn over 2f out: hanging sn after: one pce* 11/2[3]	68
-036	5	shd	**Karshaan (FR)**[24] 5022 3-9-3 **65** StephenCarson 9 (P Winkworth) *led for 2f: styd cl up: effrt to join ldr wl over 3f out: upsides over 2f out: wknd over 1f out* 25/1	69
2202	6	4	**Dark Parade (ARG)**[25] 4996 5-8-12 **55** JamieJones(7) 2 (G L Moore) *t.k.h: hld up in midfield: rdn 4f out: stl cl up over 2f out: sn wknd* 5/1[2]	54
4035	7	3 1/2	**Gouranga**[22] 5057 3-9-2 **64** DaneO'Neill 8 (H Candy) *hld up in midfield: effrt 4f out: chsng ldrs over 2f out: sn wknd* 12/1	59
2105	8	5	**Lysander's Quest (IRE)**[15] 5235 8-9-0 **50** TPQueally 13 (R Ingram) *wl in tch: lost pl 6f out: stl in tch at rr of main gp 3f out: hanging and wknd rapidly over 2f out: eased* 14/1	39
0631	9	nk	**Wings Of Dawn**[32] 4758 3-8-5 **53** MartinDwyer 11 (M P Tregoning) *pressed ldrs: rdn to ld over 2f out: hdd 2f out and sltly hmpd: wknd rapidly* 4/1[1]	42
4003	10	shd	**Kalantera (IRE)**[31] 3399 3-9-0 **62** (b[1]) AdrianMcCarthy 16 (C L Popham) *t.k.h: prom: effrt to ld 5f out and tried to kick on: hdd & wknd rapidly over 2f out* 50/1	50
0560	11	16	**Global Challenge (IRE)**[16] 5201 7-9-10 **60** (e[1]) SteveDrowne 6 (P G Murphy) *a wl in rr: t.o last over 4f out* 25/1	29
3600	12	8	**Blackmail (USA)**[7] 5451 8-9-9 **59** (b) LDettori 1 (P Mitchell) *lw: hld up tl rapid prog to ld after 2f: pushed along 6f out: hdd 5f out: sn wknd: t.o* 14/1	19
055	13	5	**Dipped Wings (IRE)**[130] 1826 3-8-7 **55** PaulDoe 10 (J L Dunlop) *hld up in detached last: struggling over 5f out: t.o* 20/1	9
441-	14	35	**Grasp**[178] 5973 4-9-11 **61** GeorgeBaker 7 (G L Moore) *a wl in rr: struggling 6f out: t.o 4f out* 12/1	—
005	P		**Cosmic Messenger (FR)**[21] 5098 3-8-12 **60** PatDobbs 5 (L A Dace) *hld up in rr: no prog and btn 5f out: sn wknd: t.o whn p.u ins fnl f: dismntd* 40/1	—

3m 33.21s (2.42) **Going Correction** +0.175s/f (Good)
WFA 3 from 4yo+ 12lb 15 Ran SP% **124.4**
Speed ratings (Par 103):100,99,97,96,96 94,92,89,89,89 81,77,75,57,—
CSF £93.00 CT £1107.23 TOTE £13.80: £4.30, £3.90, £4.80; EX 225.80.
Owner W Wood **Bred** Plantation Stud **Trained** Upper Lambourn, Berks

FOCUS
A moderate staying handicap and the pace was ordinary. The form looks very sound through the fourth and fifth, with the winner well in on her Ascot effort, the second and third on fair marks on their hurdles form. As in the first race on the round course, the field came stands' side on reaching the straight.
Cava Bien Official explanation: jockey said gelding hung left-handed
Wings Of Dawn Official explanation: jockey said filly had no more to give
Blackmail(USA) Official explanation: jockey said gelding ran too free
Cosmic Messenger(FR) Official explanation: jockey said gelding pulled up lame

5588 MERBURY CATERING CONSULTANTS SUPREME STKS (GROUP 3) 7f

3:40 (3:40) (Class 1) 3-Y-0+
£28,390 (£10,760; £5,385; £2,685; £1,345; £675) Stalls High

Form				RPR
0224	1		**Stronghold**[73] 3534 4-8-12 115 RichardHughes 8 (J H M Gosden) *lw: swtg: trckd clr ldr to over 2f out: sn shkn up: effrt to chal over 1f out: led ins fnl f: rdn out* 2/1[1]	117
/26-	2	1	**Byron**[465] 2722 5-8-12 111 (t) LDettori 1 (Saeed Bin Suroor) *trckd clr ldng pair tl wnt 2nd over 2f out: rdn to ld 1f out: hdd ins fnl f: outpcd nr fin* 5/1[3]	114
4514	3	1 3/4	**King Jock (USA)**[17] 5184 5-9-2 PShanahan 6 (R J Osborne, Ire) *hld up off the pce: rdn 2f out: kpt on fr over 1f out to take 3rd nr fin* 8/1	113
1344	4	hd	**Polar Ben**[11] 5341 7-8-12 109 JamieSpencer 7 (J R Fanshawe) *hld up off the pce: sme prog over 2f out: rdn and nt qckn over 1f out: kpt on same pce after* 7/2[2]	109
203	5	1/2	**Daniella**[17] 5171 4-8-9 76 (p) FrancisFerris 5 (Rae Guest) *led and sn clr: drvn over 2f out: hdd & wknd 1f out* 50/1	105?
0000	6	2	**Babodana**[30] 4864 6-8-12 109 TPQueally 4 (M H Tompkins) *hld up off the pce: rdn over 2f out: sn no prog and btn* 16/1	102
6120	7	1/2	**Jedburgh**[11] 5341 5-9-2 106 (b) PhilipRobinson 3 (J L Dunlop) *lw: hld up off the pce: shkn up 2f out: swtchd rt over 1f out: nt qckn and no prog* 12/1	105
0210	8	14	**Quito (IRE)**[17] 5184 9-8-12 114 (b) RobertWinston 2 (D W Chapman) *b.hind: stdd s: hld up in last: shkn up over 2f out: sn btn: eased fnl f* 7/1	65

1m 27.22s (-0.82) **Going Correction** +0.175s/f (Good) 8 Ran SP% **111.4**
Speed ratings (Par 113):111,109,107,107,107 104,104,88
CSF £11.53 TOTE £2.90: £1.20, £1.90, £2.30; EX 14.90.
Owner K Abdulla **Bred** Juddmonte Farms **Trained** Newmarket, Suffolk

FOCUS
A fair Group 3 on paper, but the pace was not strong and the form is not solid, with the final time ordinary for a race of its type and the proximity of the 76-rated Daniella lending doubts. Again the field came wide into the straight and not many got into it.

NOTEBOOK
Stronghold, not seen since disappointing slightly on Polytrack in July, was racing over the shortest trip of his career. Leading the bulk of the field whilst the pacemaker got on with it for most of the way, he came off the bridle a fair way out and did not respond immediately, but it was always likely that he would get stronger as the race progressed and so it proved. He may now go for the Challenge Stakes over this trip at Newmarket next and the likely strong pace there will suit him. (tchd 9-4 in a place and 15-8 in places)
Byron, returning from a break of 15 months, looked fit enough. He had every chance and it would be harsh to say that his absence made the difference between victory and defeat. He can only have benefited from this though, and it would be no surprise to see him reverse the form with the winner should they meet again at Newmarket next month. (tchd 11-2)
King Jock(USA) ran his race without ever looking like winning, but faced a stiff task against the front pair under his penalty. He looks better suited by a bit further these days. (op 10-1)
Polar Ben tried his usual come-from-behind tactics, but never looked like getting on terms with the leaders in a race dominated by those that raced handily. (op 11-4)
Daniella was soon able to establish a clear lead and it took a while for the others to get to her. She was probably flattered as those that raced prominently seemed favoured in this contest, whilst this performance will not help her handicap mark either. (op 66-1)
Babodana never got involved and continues to perform well below his best. (tchd 20-1)
Jedburgh would have preferred faster ground and was another of those that failed to make any impact from off the pace. Official explanation: jockey said horse was unsuited by the good (good to soft places) ground (op 18-1 tchd 20-1)
Quito(IRE) has had a cracking season, but ran poorly again and looks to have had enough for the year. Official explanation: jockey said rig ran flat (op 6-1)

5589 SUPPORT FAIRTRADE WITH FFI THE COFFEE PEOPLE MAIDEN STKS 1m 1f 192y

4:15 (4:17) (Class 5) 3-Y-0 £3,562 (£1,059; £529; £264) Stalls High

Form				RPR
	1		**Moonlit Skies** 3-9-3 LDettori 6 (Saeed Bin Suroor) *w'like: trckd ldr: shkn up over 2f out: led wl over 1f out: in command fnl f: pushed out* 5/2[2]	83+
3235	2	1 3/4	**Muntada**[26] 4945 3-8-12 72 MartinDwyer 8 (M P Tregoning) *led: rdn and hdd wl over 1f out: kpt on same pce* 7/2[3]	73
62	3	nk	**Show Winner**[18] 5151 3-9-3 TPQueally 4 (J Noseda) *swtg: trckd ldr: rdn over 2f out: nt qckn and hld fr over 1f out: one pce* 11/8[1]	77
0-	4	10	**Montchara (IRE)**[418] 4105 3-9-3 SteveDrowne 1 (G Wragg) *w'like: scope: hld up in last pair: wd bnd 1/2-way and detached in last: plugged on fnl 3f to take modest 4th ins fnl f* 16/1	58+
	5	3	**Corviglia** 3-8-12 JamieSpencer 9 (J R Fanshawe) *w'like: lengthy: bit bkwd: in tch: pushed along to chse ldng trio over 4f out: sn lft bhd: wknd fnl f* 9/1	48+
0	6	2	**Sterling Moll**[51] 4179 3-8-12 AdrianMcCarthy 5 (W De Best-Turner) *s.i.s: hld up in last pair: lost tch over 4f out: no ch* 66/1	44
0060	7	4	**Montana Sky (IRE)**[22] 5057 3-9-3 61 GeorgeBaker 3 (R A Harris) *chsd ldng trio to over 4f out: sn wknd* 50/1	41
00	P		**Well Versed**[8] 5429 3-8-12 JimmyQuinn 2 (C F Wall) *hld up in tch: lost action over 3f out: p.u 2f out* 25/1	—

2m 10.35s (2.60) **Going Correction** +0.175s/f (Good) 8 Ran SP% **116.1**
Speed ratings (Par 101):96,94,94,86,83 82,79,—
CSF £11.82 TOTE £3.20: £1.30, £1.40, £1.10; EX 15.00.
Owner Godolphin **Bred** Darley **Trained** Newmarket, Suffolk

FOCUS
An uncompetititive maiden and a three-horse race according to the market, which is how it proved as the main trio pulled miles clear of the others. With the third below par the form does not look straightforward, although the winner was value for a bit extra. Also a modest winning time for a race of its type.
Well Versed Official explanation: jockey said filly lost its action; vet said filly returned slightly lame

5590 PREMIER FOODS STKS (H'CAP) 1m

4:50 (4:50) (Class 4) (0-80,80) 3-Y-0+ £5,829 (£1,734; £866; £432) Stalls High

Form				RPR
5645	1		**Kingsholm**[34] 4704 4-9-4 **73** MartinDwyer 13 (A M Balding) *b.hind: prom: trckd ldng pair 1/2-way: led over 2f out and gng wl: rdn over 1f out: jst hld on* 11/1	85
5025	2	nk	**Grimes Faith**[4] 5504 3-9-6 **79** RichardHughes 7 (R Hannon) *hld up towards rr: prog gng easily 3f out: chsd wnr over 1f out: sn rdn: clsd last 100yds: too much to do* 9/1	90
2501	3	2 1/2	**Quintrell**[21] 5092 3-9-0 **73** DaneO'Neill 14 (H Candy) *lw: dwlt: sn in tch on inner: styd far side in st and nrly on terms w wnr 2f out: rdn and kpt on same pce after* 15/2[3]	79
2405	4	3 1/2	**Black Beauty**[14] 5266 3-9-5 **78** RobertWinston 10 (M G Quinlan) *in tch in midfield: rdn and effrt over 2f out: kpt on same pce and no ch w ldrs* 8/1	76+
0225	5	1	**Full Victory (IRE)**[25] 4989 4-9-7 **76** SteveDrowne 4 (R A Farrant) *towards rr: rdn over 2f out: sme prog over 1f out: no ch w ldrs* 14/1	71
6100	6	1	**Tender The Great (IRE)**[12] 5314 3-8-4 **63** AdrianMcCarthy 5 (V Smith) *hld up in last trio: sme prog over 2f out: shkn up over 1f out: one pce and nvr nr ldrs* 50/1	56
4440	7	3/4	**Mohawk Star (IRE)**[23] 5042 5-8-11 **66** JoeFanning 6 (I A Wood) *wl in rr: pushed along bef 1/2-way: swtchd rt and prog over 2f out: hanging u.p and no hdwy fnl f* 20/1	57
3U60	8	2	**Alfie Tupper (IRE)**[11] 5345 3-9-7 **80** GeorgeBaker 9 (S Kirk) *sn last: styd far side in st: struggling over 2f out: plugged on* 16/1	67
0401	9	1/2	**Glencalvie (IRE)**[13] 5301 5-9-5 **74** (p) LDettori 3 (J Akehurst) *prom on outer: lost pl 3f out: sn shkn up and btn* 11/2[1]	59
6000	10	1 3/4	**Sekula Pata (NZ)**[18] 5149 7-9-1 **70** TPO'Shea 16 (Christian Wroe, UAE) *trckd ldrs: rdn 3f out: wknd rapidly 2f out* 40/1	51
3540	11	hd	**Blu Manruna**[19] 5130 3-8-4 **63** oh3 PaulDoe 1 (J Akehurst) *prom on outer: rdn wl over 3f out: sn struggling and btn* 33/1	44
025	12	hd	**Logsdail**[10] 5362 6-9-0 **69** (p) TPQueally 15 (G L Moore) *b: lw: mde most to over 2f out: wknd rapidly* 7/1[2]	49
-063	13	hd	**Skyelady**[24] 5024 3-9-4 **77** TomEaves 11 (Miss J A Camacho) *chsd ldrs: lost pl and struggling in rr 3f out: no ch after* 7/1[2]	57
1130	14	1/2	**Celtic Spa (IRE)**[38] 4602 4-8-13 **71** SaleemGolam(3) 2 (P D Evans) *a wl in rr: rdn and btn 3f out* 25/1	50
0516	15	6	**Ginger Spice (IRE)**[29] 4879 4-9-3 **77** LiamJones(5) 12 (W J Haggas) *pressed ldr to 3f out: wknd rapidly* 11/1	42
0005	16	1	**Liakoura (GER)**[18] 5149 4-9-7 **76** PatDobbs 17 (Mrs A J Perrett) *lw: chsd ldrs: wknd rapidly wl over 2f out* 8/1	39

1m 40.19s (-0.08) **Going Correction** +0.175s/f (Good)
WFA 3 from 4yo+ 4lb 16 Ran SP% **129.5**
Speed ratings (Par 105):107,106,104,100,99 98,97,95,95,93 93,93,93,92,86 85
CSF £107.72 CT £815.98 TOTE £14.50: £3.20, £2.50, £2.10, £2.40; EX 146.00 Trifecta £544.40 Pool £766.90. - 1 winning unit..
Owner J C, J R And S R Hitchins **Bred** J C , J R And S R Hitchins **Trained** Kingsclere, Hants

FOCUS
An ordinary but competitive handicap run at a good pace and whilst the bulk of the field made for the stands' side on reaching the home straight, a couple stayed closer to the inside rail including the eventual third. The winner had slipped to a winning mark while the second is pretty exposed.

Glencalvie(IRE) Official explanation: trainer said gelding was unsuited by the good (good to soft places) ground

5591 CROSSE & BLACKWELL STKS (H'CAP) 7f
5:25 (5:28) (Class 4) (0-85,83) 3-Y-0+ £5,505 (£1,637; £818; £408) Stalls High

Form RPR

2061 **1** **Woodcote Place**[29] 4899 3-9-1 **80** .... SteveDrowne 7 93+
(P R Chamings) *lw: t.k.h: hld up wl in rr: prog and nt clr run over 2f out: hdwy to ld over 1f out: rdn and styd on wl* **7/1**[3]

3600 **2** *1 ½* **Dry Ice (IRE)**[22] 5070 4-9-2 **78** .... DaneO'Neill 8 87
(H Candy) *hld up towards rr: stdy prog over 2f out: rdn to chal over 1f out: chsd wnr after: no imp fnl f* **6/1**[2]

0113 **3** *1 ½* **Taranaki**[15] 5233 8-8-3 **72** .... AshleyHamblett[(7)] 4 77
(P D Cundell) *hld up wl in rr: stdy prog over 2f out: hanging rt and urged along over 1f out: kpt on to take 3rd last strides* **10/1**

0002 **4** *shd* **Millennium Force**[11] 5345 8-9-1 **77** .... JoeFanning 9 82
(M R Channon) *lw: hld up wl in rr: prog in centre and pushed along 3f out: rdn to chal over 1f out: fdd ins fnl f* **7/1**[3]

0030 **5** *1 ¾* **Fiefdom (IRE)**[10] 5355 4-9-6 **82** .... RobertWinston 12 82+
(I W McInnes) *prom: pushed along 3f out: stl cl up u.p over 1f out: fdd* **14/1**

2315 **6** *½* **Magic Rush**[31] 4807 4-8-13 **78** .... EdwardCreighton[(3)] 15 77+
(Mrs Norma Pook) *mde most to over 1f out: wknd fnl f* **5/1**[1]

1040 **7** *shd* **Blue Java**[11] 5345 5-8-9 **76** .... TravisBlock[(5)] 2 75
(H Morrison) *prom: u.p 3f out: hanging 2f out: fdd over 1f out* **8/1**

2004 **8** *hd* **Material Witness (IRE)**[31] 4798 9-9-7 **83** .... MartinDwyer 1 81
(W R Muir) *lw: pressed ldr: upsides and rdn over 1f out: wknd fnl f* **9/1**

2200 **9** *½* **Dr Synn**[32] 4772 5-8-7 **69** oh4 .... PaulDoe 10 66
(J Akehurst) *towards rr: rdn 1/2-way: prog u.p and cl up over 1f out: sn wknd* **16/1**

3630 **10** *nk* **Polliwilline (IRE)**[17] 5164 3-8-12 **77** .... RichardHughes 11 73
(R Hannon) *settled in midfield: nt clr run briefly over 2f out: sn rdn and one pce: fdd fnl f* **16/1**

2304 **11** *¾* **Greenwood**[15] 5233 8-8-10 **72** .... RobertHavlin 6 66
(P G Murphy) *hld up wl in rr: gng wl enough 3f out: shkn up over 1f out: no ch and nvr nr ldrs* **25/1**

1000 **12** *3* **Ocean Pride (IRE)**[18] 5150 3-9-2 **81** ....(b) PatDobbs 16 67
(R Hannon) *lw: prom tl wknd u.p wl over 1f out* **33/1**

6130 **13** *nk* **Stormy Monday**[26] 4965 3-8-2 **74** .... PatrickHills[(7)] 13 60
(J W Hills) *dwlt: sn w ldrs: wknd u.p over 2f out* **16/1**

4533 **14** *3* **Scarlet Flyer (USA)**[10] 5377 3-8-12 **77** ....(b) TPQueally 3 55
(G L Moore) *hld up towards rr: gng wl enough 3f out: rdn and wknd 2f out* **16/1**

5302 **15** *2 ½* **Grizedale (IRE)**[11] 5345 7-9-2 **78** ....(t) JimmyQuinn 5 49
(J Akehurst) *hld up in rr: shkn up over 2f out: no prog and btn whn n.m.r wl over 1f out: wknd* **14/1**

1m 28.03s (-0.01) **Going Correction** +0.175s/f (Good)
WFA 3 from 4yo+ 3lb **15** Ran SP% **129.8**
Speed ratings (Par 105):107,105,103,103,101 100,100,100,99,99 98,95,95,91,88
CSF £52.22 CT £440.89 TOTE £9.40: £2.90, £3.00, £3.70; EX 96.90 Place 6 £105.92, Place 5 £29.40..
Owner E D Kessly **Bred** Mrs A M Jenkins **Trained** Baughurst, Hants
■ Stewards' Enquiry : Ashley Hamblett one-day ban: used whip with excessive frequency, down the shoulder in the forehand position and without giving gelding time to respond (Nov 16)

FOCUS
A fair handicap, run at a solid pace, and the form looks sound rated through the third and fourth horses. The first four all came from the rear.
Magic Rush Official explanation: jockey said gelding was unsuited by the good (good to soft places) ground
Material Witness(IRE) Official explanation: jockey said gelding had no more to give
T/Jkpt: Not won. T/Plt: £144.40 to a £1 stake. Pool: £77,696.90. 392.65 winning tickets. T/Qpdt: £31.70 to a £1 stake. Pool: £4,414.60. 102.80 winning tickets. JN

5347 NOTTINGHAM (L-H)
Tuesday, September 26
OFFICIAL GOING: Good (good to soft in places)
Wind: Light, against Weather: Sunny

5592 EUROPEAN BREEDERS FUND TRENT BRIDGE MAIDEN FILLIES' STKS 6f 15y
2:10 (2:11) (Class 5) 2-Y-0 £3,886 (£1,156; £577; £288) Stalls High

Form RPR

4550 **1** **Miss Ippolita**[33] 4737 2-9-0 75 .... KerrinMcEvoy 4 69
(J R Jenkins) *mde all far side: rdn out* **12/1**

3624 **2** *½* **Party (IRE)**[54] 4084 2-9-0 81 .... RyanMoore 16 67
(R Hannon) *wnt rt s: racd stands' side: chsd ldrs: rdn to ld that gp ins fnl f: r.o: 1st of 9 in gp* **2/1**[1]

00 **3** *3* **Rumbled**[26] 4964 2-9-0 .... RichardThomas 15 58
(J A Geake) *sn led stands' side gp: rdn over 1f out: hdd and no ex ins fnl f: 2nd of 9 in gp* **28/1**

4 *shd* **Rhuepunzel** 2-9-0 .... NCallan 17 58
(P F I Cole) *racd stands' side: hmpd s: sn chsng ldrs: rdn and ev ch over 1f out: wknd ins fnl f: 3rd of 9 in gp* **7/1**[2]

5 *1 ¾* **Cherie's Dream** 2-9-0 .... LPKeniry 13 52
(D R C Elsworth) *racd stands' side: wnt rt s: outpcd: hdwy over 1f out: nrst fin: 4th of 9 in gp* **11/1**

000 **6** *½* **Mujart**[11] 5348 2-8-7 42 .... RussellKennemore[(7)] 6 51
(J A Pickering) *racd far side: prom: rdn to chse wnr 2f out: no ex fnl f: 2nd of 6 in gp* **66/1**

00 **7** *nk* **Krikket**[8] 5425 2-9-0 .... DO'Donohoe 11 50+
(W J Haggas) *racd stands' side: wnt rt s: outpcd: styd on ins fnl f: nrst fin: 5th of 9 in gp* **40/1**

8 *hd* **Cat Six (USA)** 2-9-0 .... KDarley 14 49
(B J Meehan) *racd stands' side: w ldr: rdn and ev ch over 1f out: sn edgd lft and wknd: 6th of 9 in gp* **11/1**

00 **9** *1 ¼* **Little Iris**[22] 5068 2-9-0 .... NickyMackay 12 46+
(L M Cumani) *racd stands' side: sn pushed along and prom: wknd over 1f out: 7th of 9 in gp* **33/1**

10 *1 ¼* **Sangreal** 2-9-0 .... PatCosgrave 3 42
(K R Burke) *racd far side: chsd ldrs over 4f: 3rd of 6 in gp* **20/1**

002 **11** *shd* **Grazie Mille**[45] 4376 2-9-0 60 .... RoystonFfrench 10 42
(R Brotherton) *racd stands' side: hmpd s: hld up: wknd over 1f out: 8th of 9 in gp* **20/1**

12 *1* **Tumbelini** 2-9-0 .... SebSanders 1 39
(C F Wall) *racd far side: in rr: rdn over 2f out: sn wknd: 4th of 6 in gp* **14/1**

13 *3* **Edgefour (IRE)** 2-9-0 .... JimCrowley 5 30
(B I Case) *racd far side: chsd wnr: rdn over 2f out: sn wknd: 5th of 6 in gp* **100/1**

05 **14** *2 ½* **Ocean Blaze**[39] 4559 2-8-7 .... JamesMillman[(7)] 8 22
(B R Millman) *racd far side: chsd ldrs: hung rt and wknd 2f out: fin last on stands' side* **8/1**[3]

15 *2* **Apple Blossom (IRE)** 2-9-0 .... TedDurcan 2 16
(G Wragg) *racd far side: s.s: outpcd: last of 6 in gp* **14/1**

1m 15.38s (0.38) **Going Correction** -0.10s/f (Good) **15** Ran SP% **115.5**
Speed ratings (Par 92):93,92,88,88,85 85,84,84,82,81 81,79,75,72,69
CSF £32.03 TOTE £14.20: £3.10, £1.30, £11.70; EX 45.00.
Owner R M Ellis **Bred** Michael Ng **Trained** Royston, Herts
■ Stewards' Enquiry : D O'DonohoeM 28-day ban: in breach of Rule 157 (Oct 7-21, Oct 23-Nov 4)

FOCUS
A fair fillies' maiden, which saw the six who raced on the far side apparently at a disadvantage, therefore the winner deserves extra credit. The form is only modest but the race should produce its share of future winners.

NOTEBOOK
Miss Ippolita, outclassed in the Lowther last time, relished the drop back into maiden company and ran out a convincing winner. She deserves extra credit as she was probably at a disadvantage in racing on the far rail and eventually came right away from her rivals on that side. Her connections indicated she is now likely to be put away for the season and she can be expected to improve further as she steps up in trip next term. (op 14-1)
Party(IRE), returning from a 54-day break, emerged on top of those to race on the stands' side yet may not have been all that suited by this return to six furlongs. She does deserve a change of fortune, but has become expensive to follow and may be more of one for the upcoming All-Weather season. (tchd 9-4)
Rumbled showed up well for a long way and posted her best effort to date. She now has the option of nurseries and can be expected to stay further in that sphere. (op 25-1)
Rhuepunzel, a half-sister to the useful miler Zietory - who won over this trip at two, knew her job and only tired out of contention in the final stages. She is entitled to come on for this debut experience and has a race of this nature within her compass before the year is out. (op 6-1)
Cherie's Dream, whose dam scored over 12 furlongs as a three-year-old, was doing her best work towards the finish and looks sure to benefit for the experience. (op 10-1 tchd 12-1)
Krikket, making her turf debut after showing just moderate form in two previous starts on Polytrack, needed this run for a handicap mark and was another who was doing her best work towards the finish under a fairly considerate ride. The stewards later inquired into her running and found her rider in breach of Rule 157 and suspended him for 28 days. Trainer William Haggas was also hit with a £5,000 fine and the filly suspended from racing for 40 days. Official explanation: 40-day suspension: (Sep 29-Nov 7); jockey said, regarding running and riding, his orders were to get the filly settled and do his best, adding that having jumped awkwardly from the stalls and lost ground he tried to ease her into the race but was hanging left-handed throughout; trainer's rep added that the filly is a buzzy sort and is light mouthed, having had a history of mouth problems
Cat Six(USA), who has a nice US pedigree and cost $140,000 as a foal, ran well until appearing to blow-up nearing the final furlong and should be sharper with this debut experience under her belt. (op 10-1)
Ocean Blaze Official explanation: jockey said filly hung right-handed

5593 UNITED PALLET NETWORK H'CAP 6f 15y
2:45 (2:45) (Class 5) (0-75,75) 3-Y-0+ £3,238 (£963; £481; £240) Stalls High

Form RPR

P050 **1** **Wanchai Lad**[11] 5333 5-9-1 **70** ....(t) DavidAllan 14 81
(T D Easterby) *trckd ldrs stands side: hdwy to ld wl over 1f out: sn rdn and kpt on wl* **20/1**

1000 **2** *1 ½* **Charles Parnell (IRE)**[12] 5313 3-8-10 **67** .... DanielTudhope 15 73
(M Dods) *hld up towards rr stands side: haedway over 2f out: rdn to chse wnr ent last: kpt on* **25/1**

0500 **3** *1 ½* **Digital**[20] 5117 9-9-4 **73** .... ChrisCatlin 11 75
(M R Channon) *rr stand side: hdwy wl over 2f out: swtchd lft and rdn wl over 1f out: kpt on ins last: nrst fin* **11/1**

0064 **4** *2* **Cornus**[10] 5391 4-9-3 **72** .... KDarley 4 68
(J A Osborne) *trckd ldrs far side: effrt over 2f out and sn rdn: swtchd rt over 1f out: styd on ins last* **10/1**

2501 **5** *shd* **Rosein**[10] 5391 4-9-1 **70** .... J-PGuillambert 2 65
(Mrs G S Rees) *cl up far side: rdn along over 2f out: drvn and one pce appr last* **8/1**[3]

6425 **6** *½* **Gilded Cove**[15] 5246 6-8-6 **68** .... RussellKennemore[(7)] 3 62
(R Hollinshead) *rr far side: hdwy over 2f oyt: sn rdn and kpt on ins last: nrst fin* **8/1**[3]

0411 **7** *1 ½* **Scuba (IRE)**[34] 4694 4-8-12 **67** ....(b) MickyFenton 1 56
(H Morrison) *led far side gp: rdn along wl over 2f out: drvn and wknd over 1f out* **7/1**[2]

000 **8** *hd* **Danjet (IRE)**[143] 1482 3-8-12 **72** .... StephenDonohoe[(3)] 17 61
(J M Bradley) *cl up stands side: rdn along and ch 2f out: sn drvn and wknd* **33/1**

626 **9** *nk* **Welcome Approach**[14] 5265 3-9-3 **74** .... PhillipMakin 7 62
(J R Weymes) *chsd ldrs far side: rdn along over 2f out: sn wknd* **33/1**

5100 **10** *1* **Danzig River (IRE)**[21] 5081 5-9-6 **75** .... AdrianTNicholls 13 60
(D Nicholls) *hld up stands side: effrt and sme hdwy wl over 2f out: sn rdn and btn* **16/1**

2005 **11** *hd* **Canadian Danehill (IRE)**[68] 3692 4-8-6 **68** .... WilliamBuick[(7)] 16 52
(R M H Cowell) *overall ldr stands side: rdn along over 2f out: sn hdd & wknd* **16/1**

0050 **12** *5* **Pearly Poll**[78] 3349 3-8-12 **69** .... SebSanders 6 38
(R M Beckett) *a rr far side* **25/1**

6200 **13** *hd* **Polish Emperor (USA)**[18] 5148 6-9-6 **75** ....(p) TedDurcan 5 51+
(W R Swinburn) *cl up far side: rdn along over 2f out: sn drvn and wknd wl over 1f out* **12/1**

5041 **14** *1 ¼* **Polish Index**[29] 4894 4-8-13 **68** ....(p) RyanMoore 10 33
(J R Jenkins) *cl up stands side: rdn along wl over 2f out: sn wknd* **7/1**[2]

0340 **15** *3* **Calabaza**[6] 5476 4-8-12 **67** ....(b) KerrinMcEvoy 9 23
(W Jarvis) *in tchstands side: rdn along wl over 2f out: sn wknd* **6/1**[1]

6-00 **16** *4* **Anchor Date**[10] 5391 4-8-12 **70** ....(t) PatrickMathers[(3)] 8 14
(D Shaw) *a bhd stands side* **40/1**

1m 13.69s (-1.31) **Going Correction** -0.10s/f (Good)
WFA 3 from 4yo+ 2lb **16** Ran SP% **119.2**
Speed ratings (Par 103):104,102,100,97,97 96,94,94,93,92 92,85,85,83,79 74
CSF £418.65 CT £3177.93 TOTE £25.30: £4.70, £4.70, £2.60, £2.50; EX 403.40.
Owner Ambrose Turnbull **Bred** G T Lucas **Trained** Great Habton, N Yorks

FOCUS
A modest sprint handicap, where anything drawn low had no chance. Arguably, you could treat it as two separate races, as both sides of the track produced promising displays for the future. The winner had slipped to a nice mark.
Polish Index Official explanation: jockey said gelding had no more to give

The Form Book, Raceform Ltd, Compton, RG20 6NL

Calabaza Official explanation: jockey said gelding never travelled

5594 HALIFAX ESTATE AGENTS H'CAP — 2m 9y

3:20 (3:20) (Class 4) (0-85,80) 3-Y-O — **£6,477** (£1,927; £963; £481) **Stalls** Low

Form	Pos	Dist	Horse	Jockey	RPR
1222	1		**Juniper Girl (IRE)**[25] 4990 3-8-11 77 (M L W Bell) *chsd ldrs: led 3f out: rdn over 1f out: clr fnl f: eased nr fin* **4/1**[2]	LukeMorris(7) 6	86+
3433	2	3/4	**Reinstated (IRE)**[27] 4931 3-8-11 70 (B W Hills) *s.i.s: hld up: nt clr run over 3f out: hdwy 2f out: sn rdn: styd on: nt rch wnr* **7/1**[3]	MichaelHills 4	75+
31	3	1/2	**Rainbow's Edge**[123] 1988 3-9-4 77 (R Charlton) *hld up in tch: chsd wnr 3f out: sn rdn: hung lft over 1f out: styd on same pce* **5/4**[1]	RyanMoore 5	81
4253	4	hd	**Sybella**[19] 5128 3-9-3 76 (J L Dunlop) *prom: outpcd over 2f out: rallied over 1f out: styd on same pce ins fnl f* **17/2**	IanMongan 2	80
4340	5	2 1/2	**Great Tidings**[13] 5284 3-8-11 70 (M Johnston) *led: rdn and hdd 4f out: wknd fnl f* **10/1**	KDarley 1	71
3506	6	3/4	**Free To Air**[19] 5141 3-8-11 77 (A M Balding) *hld up: hdwy 3f out: rdn and rdr dropped reins over 1f out: no ex* **14/1**	WilliamBuick(7) 7	77
210	7	5	**Chronomatic**[13] 5284 3-8-13 72 (M H Tompkins) *hld up: rdn over 2f out: wknd over 1f out* **16/1**	NCallan 8	66
3320	8	2	**Moonshadow**[8] 5429 3-9-7 80 (H R A Cecil) *chsd ldr tl led 4f out: rdn and hdd 3f out: wknd 2f out* **25/1**	TedDurcan 3	72

3m 33.91s (0.41) **Going Correction** -0.325s/f (Firm) — **8** Ran SP% **113.0**

Speed ratings (Par 103):85,84,84,84,83 82,80,79

CSF £31.05 CT £52.75 TOTE £6.00: £1.70, £2.10, £1.10; EX 31.00.

Owner M B Hawtin **Bred** Mrs E Kent **Trained** Newmarket, Suffolk

FOCUS

A pedestrian winning time for the type of race and, while the winner is value for further than her winning margin, the form is not strong, rated through the second.

5595 EUROPEAN BREEDERS FUND MAIDEN FILLIES' STKS (DIV I) — 1m 54y

3:55 (3:55) (Class 5) 2-Y-O — **£3,886** (£1,156; £577; £288) **Stalls** Centre

Form	Pos	Dist	Horse	Jockey	RPR
	1		**Shorthand** 2-9-0 (Sir Michael Stoute) *hld up in tch on inner: hdwy 3f out: swtchd rt and qcknd to ld over 1f out: styd on* **13/2**[3]	KerrinMcEvoy 6	88+
6	2	1 1/4	**Gull Wing (IRE)**[21] 5083 2-9-0 (M L W Bell) *a.p: rdn along and outpcd over 2f out: styd on ins last* **11/1**	HayleyTurner 1	82
22	3	nk	**Fretwork**[26] 4964 2-9-0 (R Hannon) *led: pushed along and qcknd 3f out: rdn 2f out: hdd and drvn over 1f out: one pce ins last* **4/5**[1]	RyanMoore 9	81
6	4	5	**Pairumani Princess (IRE)**[52] 4140 2-9-0 (E A L Dunlop) *towards rr tl styd on fnl 2f* **40/1**	DO'Donohoe 2	70
03	5	4	**Nellie Soprano (IRE)**[13] 5287 2-9-0 (K R Burke) *chsd ldr: rdn along 3f out: wknd fnl 2f* **50/1**	PhillipMakin 11	61
	6	1 3/4	**Handset (USA)** 2-9-0 (H R A Cecil) *prom: rdn along 3f out: sn outpcd* **14/1**	TedDurcan 3	57
	7	1 3/4	**Puissant Princess (IRE)** 2-9-0 (E J O'Neill) *chsd ldrs: rdn along 3f out: drvn and wknd 2f out* **6/1**[2]	RichardMullen 5	53
0	8	2	**Last Flight (IRE)**[21] 5083 2-9-0 (J L Dunlop) *a rr* **66/1**	IanMongan 7	48
	9	nk	**Legend House (FR)** 2-9-0 (M Johnston) *s.i.s: a rr* **20/1**	KDarley 4	47
05	10	hd	**Proposal**[13] 5287 2-9-0 (C E Brittain) *chsd ldrs: rdn along over 3f out: sn wknd* **50/1**	SebSanders 10	47
	11	12	**Pastel Rose (USA)** 2-9-0 (M R Channon) *s.i.s: a bhd* **33/1**	ChrisCatlin 8	19

1m 42.84s (-3.56) **Going Correction** -0.325s/f (Firm) — **11** Ran SP% **113.7**

Speed ratings (Par 92):104,102,102,97,93 91,89,87,87,87 75

CSF £66.19 TOTE £6.80: £2.10, £2.00, £1.10; EX 56.70.

Owner J M Greetham **Bred** J M Greetham **Trained** Newmarket, Suffolk

FOCUS

A very decent winning time for a race like this and 0.8 seconds faster than the second division. The first three finished clear. The race will produce winners both this season and next.

NOTEBOOK

Shorthand ◆, a sister to the 2006 Musidora winner Short Skirt, who was also placed in the Oaks, made a highly satisfactory racecourse debut despite being a bit weak in the market before the off. Under only hands and heels riding, she won with a bit in hand and could follow in the footsteps of her sister and run in the Rockfel Stakes at Newmarket in October. (op 7-2)

Gull Wing(IRE) ◆ improved from her first run and showed plenty of determination under pressure to snatch the runners'-up position. Bred to stay well, she is a filly to follow. (op 9-1)

Fretwork cut out a lot of the early running and ended up a target for the eventual winner to aim at. She has slightly disappointed since her highly encouraging first effort, but she will win a race and might be a nice sort for middle-distance handicaps next season. (op 11-10 tchd 8-11 and 6-5 in places and 5-4 in places)

Pairumani Princess(IRE) is the sort of horse that appeals as one to be with when making her handicap debut. She is bred to stay well and middle distances next season will probably be her niche. (op 33-1)

Nellie Soprano(IRE) ran right up to her best but was easily dismissed by the leaders.

Handset(USA) looked too green on her debut to do herself justice and is entitled to improve considerably for the run. She is nicely bred and can do better. (op 12-1)

Puissant Princess(IRE), a very well bred filly, is on the big side and may require more time. It would be a surprise if she did not prove to be better than the final position suggests. (op 8-1 tchd 9-1)

5596 EUROPEAN BREEDERS FUND MAIDEN FILLIES' STKS (DIV II) — 1m 54y

4:30 (4:30) (Class 5) 2-Y-O — **£3,886** (£1,156; £577; £288) **Stalls** Centre

Form	Pos	Dist	Horse	Jockey	RPR
	1		**Kayah** 2-9-0 (R M Beckett) *hld up: hdwy over 3f out: led 2f out: pushed out* **11/2**	SebSanders 7	73+
05	2	1 1/2	**Wateera (IRE)**[21] 5083 2-9-0 (J L Dunlop) *chsd ldrs: n.m.r and lost pl over 3f out: swtchd rt and hdwy over 1f out: sn rdn to chse wnr: styd on* **9/4**[1]	RHills 2	70
0056	3	2 1/2	**Hemispear**[20] 5105 2-9-0 56 (Miss J R Tooth) *prom: rdn over 2f out: styd on same pce appr fnl f* **33/1**	PaulFitzsimons 4	64
0	4	1/2	**Allison's Art (IRE)**[13] 5296 2-9-0 (N A Callaghan) *led 1f: led again over 4f out: hdd 2f out: wknd ins fnl f* **9/2**[3]	ChrisCatlin 6	63
0	5	hd	**Galingale (IRE)**[30] 4830 2-9-0 (Mrs P Sly) *prom: chsd ldr 3f out: sn ev ch: wknd ins fnl f* **10/1**	MickyFenton 9	63
	6	4	**Comma (USA)** 2-9-0 (Sir Michael Stoute) *hld up: hdwy over 2f out: wknd and eased fnl f* **3/1**[2]	RyanMoore 8	53
	7	1	**Grangehurst** 2-9-0 (Miss J R Gibney) *s.i.s: hld up: n.d* **33/1**	IanMongan 1	51
	8	2	**Guilty Pleasure** 2-9-0 (G C Bravery) *s.i.s: hld up: n.d* **25/1**	DavidAllan 5	47
006	9	4	**Elle's Angel (IRE)**[62] 3838 2-9-0 45 (B R Millman) *led 7f out: hdd over 4f out: wknd over 2f out* **33/1**	JimCrowley 3	37
5	10	1 1/2	**Twilight Dawn**[24] 5014 2-9-0 (M Johnston) *s.i.s: hdwy over 6f out: wknd 2f out* **12/1**	KDarley 10	34

1m 43.64s (-2.76) **Going Correction** -0.325s/f (Firm) — **43** Ran SP% **118.8**

Speed ratings (Par 92):100,98,96,95,95 91,90,88,84,82

CSF £18.04 TOTE £7.20: £2.50, £1.10, £11.20; EX 25.00.

Owner J H Richmond-Watson **Bred** Lawn Stud **Trained** Whitsbury, Hants

FOCUS

This looked much the weaker of the two divisions and the form is held down by the proximity of the 56-rated third horse. The winning time was 0.8 seconds slower than the first division, but still very creditable for a race of its type.

NOTEBOOK

Kayah, who has a deal of stamina in her pedigree and is out of a dam who won over this trip as a juvenile, got her career off to a perfect start and justified strong market support in the process. She was not fully extended to win, and is entitled to improve for the experience so it will be interesting to see where she is pitched in next. However, she will most likely not come into her own until next season. (op 10-1)

Wateera(IRE) took an age to hit her full stride from off the pace and was never a serious threat to the winner. This was still her best effort to date, however, and she is probably in need of a stiffer test. She now has the option of nurseries. (op 11-4 tchd 2-1, 3-1 in places)

Hemispear, having only her second outing on turf, had her chance and posted a personal-best effort. She stays this trip well, but her proximity at the finish does hold down this form, and she will have most likely now blown what may have been a decent handicap mark.

Allison's Art(IRE) just failed to see out the longer trip as well as the principals under an aggressive ride. She will have no trouble staying this trip and beyond next year, but looks worth riding more patiently over this distance in the short term. (tchd 5-1)

Galingale(IRE) stepped up on the level of her debut at Beverley 30 days previously and held every chance. She is going the right way and will become eligible for nurseries after her nest assignment. (op 11-1)

Comma(USA), whose dam was top-class at around ten furlongs in the US, looked much in need of this debut experience and never threatened from off the pace. She should have learnt plenty from this and her breeding suggests she may prefer faster ground in the future. (op 11-4 tchd 7-2)

5597 COLWICK PARK NURSERY — 1m 1f 213y

5:05 (5:07) (Class 5) (0-70,70) 2-Y-O — **£3,238** (£963; £481; £240) **Stalls** Low

Form	Pos	Dist	Horse	Jockey	RPR
0630	1		**Love Brothers**[12] 5322 2-9-7 70 (M R Channon) *hld up and bhd: swtchd to wd outside and hdwy 3f out: rdn over 1f out: styd on to ld ins last: edgd lft and kpt on* **12/1**	ChrisCatlin 11	77+
6006	2	1	**Regal Ovation**[21] 5094 2-8-7 56 (W R Muir) *led: rdn 3f out: drvn over 1f out: hdd ins last: kpt on wl u.p* **16/1**	DarryllHolland 7	61
1002	3	1 1/2	**Always Best**[6] 5482 2-8-12 61 (M Johnston) *a.p. rdn along wl over 2f out: drvn wl over 1f out and kpt on same pce* **5/2**[1]	KDarley 6	63
0060	4	1/2	**Revisionist (IRE)**[23] 5041 2-9-1 64 (R Hannon) *hld up towards rr: hdwy 3f out: swtchd lft and rdn wl over 1f out: styd on ins last* **14/1**	RyanMoore 12	65+
030	5	nk	**Abounding**[75] 3435 2-8-6 55 (R M Beckett) *dwlt and towards rr: hdwy 1/2-way: rdn to chse ldrs over 2f out: kpt on same pce* **33/1**	NickyMackay 4	56
0052	6	1 1/4	**Red**[22] 5053 2-9-1 64 (R M Beckett) *hld up: hdwy on outer over 3f out:swtchd lft wl over 2f out: effrt and n.m.r wl over 1f out: sn rdn and kpt on* **7/2**[2]	SebSanders 15	62
6305	7	1 3/4	**Down The Brick (IRE)**[41] 4480 2-9-0 70 (B R Millman) *midfield: hdwy and in tch over 4f out: rdn along 3f out: kpt on same pce fnl 2f* **16/1**	JamesMillman(7) 5	65
033	8	shd	**Monsieur Dumas (IRE)**[15] 5239 2-9-2 70 (T P Tate) *midfield: hdwy on outer over 3f out: rdn along and edgd lft over 2f out: sn drvn and no imp* **18/1**	MichaelJStainton(5) 9	65
666	9	1/2	**Bollin Felix**[39] 4566 2-8-8 57 (T D Easterby) *bhd tl styd on fnl 2f* **16/1**	DavidAllan 16	51
005	10	shd	**Vietnam**[10] 5389 2-8-13 62 (S Kirk) *in tch: hdwy on inner 3f out: rdn to chse ldrs 2f out: wknd appr last* **50/1**	LPKeniry 2	56
0040	11	3	**Greek God**[6] 5482 2-8-9 58 (W Jarvis) *chsd ldrs: rdn along 3f out: grad wknd* **12/1**	KerrinMcEvoy 1	46
000	12	1/2	**Rikochet**[22] 5066 2-9-3 66 (Mrs A J Perrett) *chsd ldrs: hdwy 3f out: rdn along 2f out and sn wknd* **14/1**	JimCrowley 10	53
005	13	2 1/2	**Musical Award (IRE)**[30] 4829 2-9-3 66 (M G Quinlan) *chsd ldrs on outer: rdn along over 3f out: sn wknd* **9/1**[3]	RichardMullen 14	48
060	14	1 1/2	**Killer Heels**[39] 4552 2-8-9 58 (S Kirk) *promienntt: rdn along over 3f out and sn wknd* **33/1**	FrankieMcDonald 8	37
136	15	7	**Beau Sancy**[43] 4436 2-9-7 70 (R A Harris) *s.i.s: a rr* **40/1**	(b[1]) TedDurcan 13	36
0603	16	3/4	**Little Tiny Tom**[39] 4545 2-7-13 55 (C N Kellett) *chsd ldrs: rdn along over 3f out: sn wknd* **66/1**	(p) PaulPickard(7) 3	20

2m 8.82s (-0.88) **Going Correction** -0.325s/f (Firm) — **16** Ran SP% **124.2**

Speed ratings (Par 95):90,89,88,87,87 86,84,84,84,84 82,81,79,78,72 72

CSF £188.41 CT £644.58 TOTE £12.10: £2.20, £4.80, £1.60, £3.50; EX 325.70.

Owner Graeme Love **Bred** The Kingwood Partnership **Trained** West Ilsley, Berks

FOCUS

A modest winning time. The runner-up ties the form down a bit, but it would be a surprise if the race does not produce winners.

NOTEBOOK

Love Brothers is bred to stay well and found the trip ideal for him. His future lies in staying handicaps next season, but he handles ease in the ground well and could easily be seen again before the end of the season. He is a real strong-galloping sort and it would not be a surprise to see him take his chance in the Zetland Stakes at Newmarket in October. (op 10-1)

Regal Ovation had every chance but could not hold the winner in the final stages. He is fully exposed and could hold the form down, but his dam stayed well and the extreme distance for juveniles may have bought the best out in him. (op 14-1)

Always Best was another in the race to have every chance inside the final furlong, although it is possible to argue that he may have finished a little bit closer had he not been squeezed for room in the final half-furlong. He appeared to run somewhere near to his best and seemed to see the trip out well. (tchd 11-4)

Revisionist(IRE) ◆ did not have the clearest of passages and looks a real galloper. The trip suited him well and he would be of interest next time if tried over the same distance. He will probably make up into a middle-distance handicapper next season. (tchd 16-1)

Abounding, as antisipated, improved for the step up in trip and stayed on nicely inside the last furlong. A similar race is within her scope. (op 28-1)

Red did not have the clearest of runs but kept on nicely when finding room. She is bred to stay well and is better than her finishing position suggests. (op 4-1 tchd 9-2 in places)
Down The Brick(IRE) caught the eye, staying on nicely just behind the leaders. It was a big step up in trip and he will be of some interest next time. Official explanation: jockey said gelding was denied a clear run (op 14-1)

5598 RACING UK ON CHANNEL 432 MAIDEN STKS 1m 54y
5:35 (5:38) (Class 5) 3-Y-O+ £3,238 (£963; £481; £240) Stalls Centre

Form RPR
1 **Shotfire Ridge** 3-9-3 .... RyanMoore 16 78
(E F Vaughan) *hld up: hdwy to ld 2f out: rdn out* **28/1**
6- 2 1 ¼ **Seabow (USA)**[361] 5592 3-9-3 .... (t) KerrinMcEvoy 2 75+
(Saeed Bin Suroor) *trckd ldrs: n.m.r over 2f out: rdn to chse wnr over 1f out: styd on* **5/4**[1]
04 3 1 ¾ **Tipsy Me**[19] 5138 3-8-12 .... HayleyTurner 5 66+
(M L W Bell) *slowly into stride: hld up: nt clr run over 3f out tl hdwy over 1f out: styd on* **20/1**
05 4 hd **Wizards Dream**[99] 2712 3-9-3 .... LPKeniry 4 71
(D R C Elsworth) *prom: outpcd over 2f out: rallied over 1f out: styd on* **12/1**
0 5 6 **Crystal Annie**[11] 5353 3-8-9 .... StephenDonohoe(3) 9 52
(Heather Dalton) *hld up: rdn over 3f out: styd on ins fnl f: nrst fin* **100/1**
6 shd **Sound Of Nature (USA)** 3-9-3 .... TedDurcan 3 64+
(H R A Cecil) *hld up in tch: nt clr run over 2f out: hmpd and lost pl over 1f out: n.d after* **15/8**[2]
05 7 1 **Mill End (IRE)**[22] 5071 4-9-7 .... SebSanders 10 55
(R M H Cowell) *prom: ev ch over 2f out: sn rdn: hung lft and wknd over 1f out* **50/1**
03 8 7 **Bordello**[92] 2934 3-9-3 .... MichaelHills 7 39
(B W Hills) *w ldr tl led over 3f out: rdn and hdd 2f out: wknd fnl f* **8/1**[3]
0 9 1 ½ **Dream Master (IRE)**[31] 4806 3-9-3 .... MickyFenton 17 35
(J Ryan) *mid-div: rdn over 3f out: sn wknd* **100/1**
0- 10 2 **Alkhabar (USA)**[423] 3935 3-9-3 .... RHills 11 31
(J L Dunlop) *hld up: hdwy over 3f out: hung lft and wknd over 1f out* **14/1**
0 11 5 **Bond Silver Strand (IRE)**[10] 5368 3-8-12 .... DavidAllan 15 14
(P D Niven) *chsd ldrs: rdn over 2f out: wknd over 1f out* **100/1**
12 3 **Thou Shalt Not** 3-9-3 .... JimCrowley 13 12
(P S Felgate) *s.s: a in rr* **100/1**
0 13 shd **Definitely Blue**[32] 4776 3-8-12 .... DarryllHolland 6 7
(C F Wall) *dwlt: outpcd: effrt over 3f out: sn wknd* **100/1**
14 1 **Lucky Tern** 3-8-10 .... BarrySavage(7) 8 10
(J M Bradley) *led over 4f: sn wknd* **100/1**
15 5 **Little Wishes** 3-8-5 .... CharlotteKerton(7) 12 —
(S Parr) *a in rr* **100/1**
16 32 **Hi Perry** 4-9-2 .... KevinGhunowa(5) 1 —
(M Wellings) *s.s: outpcd* **100/1**

1m 42.38s (-4.02) **Going Correction** -0.325s/f (Firm)
WFA 3 from 4yo 4lb 16 Ran SP% **122.8**
Speed ratings (Par 103):107,105,104,103,97 97,96,89,88,86 81,78,78,77,72 40
CSF £63.69 TOTE £43.80: £6.50, £1.20, £3.60; EX 114.80.
Owner Wood Hall Stud Limited **Bred** Wood Hall Stud **Trained** Newmarket, Suffolk

FOCUS
A fair three-year-old maiden which saw the first four come clear. The form seems sounder than most late-season maidens and should work out.
Hi Perry Official explanation: vet said colt returned lame

5599 TRENT BRIDGE H'CAP 1m 1f 213y
6:05 (6:08) (Class 5) (0-75,75) 3-Y-O+ £3,238 (£963; £481; £240) Stalls Low

Form RPR
3232 1 **Benandonner (USA)**[15] 5249 3-9-4 **74** .... DO'Donohoe 10 83
(E A L Dunlop) *mde all: pushed along over 2f out: rdn wl over 1f out: drvn and edgd rt ins last: kpt on gamely* **13/2**[2]
4250 2 ½ **Risk Runner (IRE)**[78] 3365 3-9-5 **75** .... (v) JDSmith 7 83
(A King) *hld up and bhd: swtchd outside and hdwy 3f out: rdn and str run fr wl over 1f out: edgd lft ins last: kpt on* **9/1**
0350 3 1 ¼ **Rowan Lodge (IRE)**[10] 5362 4-9-6 **70** .... NCallan 1 75
(M H Tompkins) *trckd ldrs. effrt over 2f out: rdn over 1f out: drvn ent last: kpt on same pce towards fin* **15/2**[3]
1401 4 shd **Silverhay**[33] 4730 5-9-10 **74** .... (p) RyanMoore 9 79
(T D Barron) *hld up in tch: hdwy wl over 2f out: rdn over 1f out: styd on ins last: n.m.r towards fin* **11/2**[1]
1430 5 1 ¼ **Truly Fruitful (IRE)**[32] 4784 3-9-2 **72** .... PatCosgrave 14 75
(K R Burke) *a.p: effrt 3f out: rdn 2f out and ev ch tl drvn and one pce ent last* **16/1**
0206 6 1 ¼ **Dower House**[25] 4991 11-9-4 **68** .... (t) ChrisCatlin 6 68
(Andrew Turnell) *hld up and behind: stdy hdwy on outer 3f out: rdn to chse ldrs whn carried lft ent last: kpt on same pce* **20/1**
1625 7 hd **William's Way**[13] 5295 4-9-6 **70** .... DarryllHolland 8 70
(I A Wood) *towards rr: hdwy wl over 2f out: rdn wl over 1f out: no imp ins last* **14/1**
3401 8 1 **Ahmedy (IRE)**[15] 5236 3-9-3 **73** .... TedDurcan 13 71
(M R Channon) *hld up: hdwy wl over 2f out: rdn and n.m.r wl over 1f out: no imp* **8/1**
5060 9 ½ **Press Express (IRE)**[15] 5236 4-9-6 **70** .... (v[1]) SebSanders 5 67
(M L W Bell) *trckd ldrs: hdwy 3f out: effrt 2f out: sn rdn and wknd appr last* **10/1**
2600 10 2 **Villarosi (IRE)**[15] 5236 4-9-2 **66** .... HayleyTurner 4 59
(J R Best) *in tch: rdn along wl over 2f out: no hdwy* **40/1**
-014 11 nk **Al Hazim (IRE)**[23] 5047 3-9-3 **73** .... NickyMackay 12 66
(L M Cumani) *chsd wnr: rdn along 3f out: drvn 2f out and sn wknd* **8/1**
0 12 nk **Ma'Am (USA)**[36] 4662 4-9-8 **72** .... RichardMullen 2 64
(I A Wood) *s.i.s: sn in tch on inner: rdn along over 3f out and grad wknd* **33/1**
6304 13 ½ **The Composer**[25] 4990 4-9-6 **70** .... FrancisNorton 15 61
(M Blanshard) *hld up: hdwy on outer 3f out: rdn along 2f out: drvn and wkng whn n.m.r wl over 1f out* **12/1**
1000 14 6 **Jakarmi**[96] 2794 5-9-5 **69** .... MickyFenton 16 49
(B Palling) *chsd ldrs: hdwy 3f out: rdn along over 2f: sn drvn and wknd* **16/1**

2m 7.12s (-2.58) **Going Correction** -0.325s/f (Firm)
WFA 3 from 4yo+ 6lb 14 Ran SP% **118.1**
Speed ratings (Par 103):97,96,95,95,94 93,93,92,92,90 90,90,89,84
CSF £61.36 CT £452.89 TOTE £6.50: £2.30, £4.70, £2.80; EX 87.70 Place 6 £43.07, Place 5 £19.82..
Owner Gainsborough Stud **Bred** Gainsborough Farm Llc **Trained** Newmarket, Suffolk
■ Stewards' Enquiry : J D Smith two-day ban: careless riding (Oct 7-8)

FOCUS
A modest winning time for the grade. The winner probably nicked it from the front, but quite a few of the runners seemed to have every chance, and the form looks reliable enough for the grade.
Risk Runner(IRE) Official explanation: jockey said gelding hung right home straight
William's Way ◆ Official explanation: jockey said gelding was denied a clear run
T/Plt: £60.10 to a £1 stake. Pool: £43,346.45. 526.10 winning tickets. T/Qpdt: £5.20 to a £1 stake. Pool: £2,856.70. 403.50 winning tickets. JR

5602 - 5604a (Foreign Racing) - See Raceform Interactive

5258 LINGFIELD (L-H)
Wednesday, September 27

OFFICIAL GOING: Standard
Wind: moderate, behind

5605 SCOTS GROUP APPRENTICE H'CAP 6f (P)
1:20 (1:22) (Class 5) (0-70,70) 3-Y-O £3,238 (£963; £481; £240) Stalls Low

Form RPR
360 1 **Duke Of Milan (IRE)**[15] 5268 3-8-12 **68** .... JonjoMilczarek(5) 3 74
(G C Bravery) *hmpd on inner after 1f: hld up wl in rr: prog 2f out: r.o wl u.str.p to ld last strides: jst hld on* **10/1**
3405 2 shd **Fateful Attraction**[28] 4930 3-8-11 **62** .... (b) JamieMoriarty 10 68
(I A Wood) *dwlt: hld up wl in rr on outer: wd bnd 2f out: gd prog over 1f out: r.o wl fnl f: jst failed* **11/1**
3215 3 nk **Young Bertie**[24] 5042 3-9-3 **68** .... (v) AndrewElliott 12 73
(H Morrison) *pressed ldr: rdn to ld over 1f out: collared last strides* **9/4**[1]
3400 4 hd **Dasheena**[12] 5350 3-8-4 **60** .... MCGeran(5) 4 64
(A J McCabe) *rrd s: hld up towards rr: gng wl 1/2-way: prog 2f out: chsd ldng pair over 1f out: styd on but outpcd nr fin* **33/1**
4303 5 2 ½ **Hotham**[16] 5250 3-9-3 **68** .... LiamJones 7 65
(N Wilson) *led: rdn and hdd over 1f out: wknd ins fnl f* **15/2**[3]
3220 6 1 ½ **Light Mozart**[7] 5480 3-8-10 **66** .... WilliamCarson(5) 6 58
(C E Brittain) *trckd ldng trio: rdn and no imp 2f out: wknd fnl f* **8/1**
5650 7 shd **Tous Les Deux**[15] 5268 3-9-2 **70** .... ThomasO'Brien(3) 9 62
(R F Johnson Houghton) *struggling in rr over 3f out: plugged on fnl f: nvr on terms* **5/1**[2]
0630 8 2 ½ **Egyptian Lord**[56] 4056 3-8-9 **63** .... (b) KevinGhunowa(3) 11 47
(Peter Grayson) *pressed ldng pair: rn wd bnd 2f out: sn btn* **25/1**
4000 9 ¾ **Piccostar**[8] 5453 3-8-13 **67** .... JamesMillman(3) 2 49
(A B Haynes) *n.m.r on inner after 1f: struggling bef 1/2-way: nvr a factor* **12/1**
005 10 1 ¾ **Mount Sinai**[16] 5232 3-8-3 **59** .... RichardRowe(5) 5 36
(W J Knight) *chsd ldrs: rdn bef 1/2-way: wknd 2f out* **12/1**
-400 11 6 **White Ladder (IRE)**[25] 5031 3-8-8 **59** .... AurelioMedeiros 8 18
(P F I Cole) *chsd ldrs: wknd over 2f out* **33/1**
4445 12 43 **Dragon Flame (IRE)**[112] 2356 3-8-8 **62** .... DeanWilliams(3) 1 —
(M Quinn) *bdly hmpd on inner after 1f: nt rcvr: t.o 1/2-way: virtually p.u* **50/1**

1m 11.74s (-1.07) **Going Correction** -0.20s/f (Stan) 12 Ran SP% **114.8**
Speed ratings (Par 101):99,98,98,98,94 92,92,89,88,86 78,20
CSF £107.37 CT £339.13 TOTE £15.30: £4.10, £3.70, £1.60; EX 211.60.
Owner Broken Reign Racing **Bred** Irish National Stud **Trained** Newmarket, Suffolk

FOCUS
A modest handicap which was run at a sound pace. The first four came clear. Ordinary form, with the second and fourth exposed.
Egyptian Lord Official explanation: jockey said gelding hung right
Piccostar Official explanation: jockey said filly suffered interference in running
Dragon Flame(IRE) Official explanation: jockey said colt suffered interference in running

5606 GPLONDON.COM NURSERY 6f (P)
1:50 (1:51) (Class 5) (0-75,74) 2-Y-O £4,533 (£1,348; £674; £336) Stalls Low

Form RPR
10 1 **Fabuleux Millie (IRE)**[39] 4594 2-9-6 **73** .... JosedeSouza 7 78
(R M Beckett) *hld up: prog to trck ldng trio 1/2-way: shkn up over 1f out: pushed along and r.o to ld last 50yds: cleverly* **15/2**[2]
5623 2 nk **Vadinka**[5] 5262 2-9-2 **69** .... MatthewHenry 9 73
(P Winkworth) *a ldng trio: rdn to ld over 1f out: hdd and hld last 50yds* **12/1**
012 3 1 ¼ **Jack Oliver**[23] 5065 2-9-4 **71** .... JamieSpencer 10 71
(B J Meehan) *settled towards rr: nt clr run over 2f out and plenty to do after: effrt over 1f out: r.o fnl f: no ch to rch ldng pair* **5/4**[1]
10 4 nk **Danetime Music (IRE)**[39] 4594 2-9-5 **72** .... DO'Donohoe 6 71
(M J Wallace) *dwlt and bdly hmpd s: wl off the pce in last pair: prog on outer over 2f out: styd on wl fnl f: nrst fin* **12/1**
3301 5 1 ¾ **Mogok Ruby**[14] 5290 2-8-10 **70** .... JamesMillman(7) 11 64
(L Montague Hall) *jnd ldr after 2f: led 1/2-way: hdd over 1f out: fdd* **12/1**
0306 6 1 **Star Strider**[8] 5461 2-9-2 **69** .... DarryllHolland 1 60
(A M Balding) *led to 1/2-way: sn rdn: wknd over 1f out* **10/1**
6253 7 1 **Pango's Legacy**[39] 4603 2-9-7 **74** .... TedDurcan 2 62
(H Morrison) *trckd ldrs: rdn 2f out: sn lost pl: wknd fnl f* **9/1**[3]
046 8 ¾ **What A Treasure (IRE)**[33] 4754 2-9-2 **69** .... NickyMackay 3 55
(L M Cumani) *a wl in rr: pushed along and no prog 2f out* **10/1**
0636 9 nk **Hucking Hill (IRE)**[49] 4246 2-9-4 **71** .... HayleyTurner 8 56
(J R Best) *chsd ldrs: rdn over 2f out: sn struggling* **16/1**
2520 10 ½ **Grange Lili (IRE)**[15] 5262 2-9-2 **69** .... RobbieFitzpatrick 12 52
(Peter Grayson) *s.s: a struggling in last pair: wll bhd 2f out: nrst fin* **33/1**

1m 12.21s (-0.60) **Going Correction** -0.20s/f (Stan) 10 Ran SP% **116.3**
Speed ratings (Par 95):96,95,93,93,91 89,88,87,87,86
CSF £93.13 CT £185.99 TOTE £8.20: £2.30, £3.20, £1.30; EX 78.10.
Owner Mrs Ralph Beckett **Bred** Ashley Guest And Mrs John Guest **Trained** Whitsbury, Hants

FOCUS
A fair nursery and the form looks solid for the class.

NOTEBOOK
Fabuleux Millie(IRE) ◆, all at sea on taxing ground in Listed company when last seen, relished the drop in class and return to a sound surface and ran out a cosy winner. She is clearly a useful filly in the making, stayed the longer trip without fuss and is value for further than her winning margin. (op 13-2)
Vadinka, back down in trip, has to rate a little flattered by his proximity to the cosy winner at the finish yet still posted a personal-best effort in defeat. He was nicely clear of the remainder and, while he will go up a few pounds for this, it would be a surprise were he not placed to go one better on this surface in due course.
Jack Oliver, making his All-Weather debut, was given a fair bit to do from off the pace and never threatened to hit the front at any stage. However, he was not helped by his wide draw and still ran close to his official mark in defeat, so there will be other days for him no doubt. (op 11-8 tchd 6-4 in places)

Danetime Music(IRE) ◆, behind today's winner in Listed company at Newbury last time, ran better than her finishing position suggests as she was beaten by as much ground as he lost when getting badly hampered at the start. She clearly enjoyed the return to a sound surface and can win again before too long on this evidence. Official explanation: jockey said filly was hampered at the start (op 10-1)
Mogok Ruby, off the mark at Sandown a fortnight previously, had been left alone by the Handicapper for that success and did enough to suggest he can get closer again when reverting to a stiff five furlongs from this mark.
Star Strider
What A Treasure(IRE) failed to raise her game on this nursery debut and looked far from straightforward. (op 9-1)

5607 P & M ELECTRICAL SERVICES E.B.F. MAIDEN STKS (DIV I) 7f (P)

2:20 (2:20) (Class 5) 2-Y-O £3,238 (£963; £481; £240) **Stalls** Low

Form RPR
60 **1** **Salient**[17] [5206] 2-9-3 ... PaulDoe 12 80
(W J Knight) *chsd ldrs: pushed along 1/2-way: prog on outer over 2f out: rdn to ld wl over 1f out: styd on wl* **100/1**
5 **2** *1 1/4* **Tredegar**[47] [4323] 2-9-3 ... TedDurcan 10 77
(P F I Cole) *pressed ldng pair: effrt 2f out: rdn and nt qckn over 1f out: styd on to take 2nd nr fin* **11/2**
2 **3** *1/2* **Cleide Da Silva (USA)**[14] [5297] 2-8-12 ... DarryllHolland 4 70
(J Noseda) *trckd ldrs: rdn 2f out: n.m.r sn after: kpt on same pce fnl f* **7/4**[1]
23 **4** *shd* **Herb Paris (FR)**[26] [4993] 2-8-12 ... JosedeSouza 3 70
(M P Tregoning) *t.k.h: pressed ldr: led briefly 2f out: one pce u.p after* **9/2**[3]
34 **5** *2* **Loch Tay**[30] [4873] 2-9-3 ... JamieSpencer 7 70+
(M L W Bell) *s.i.s: wl in rr tl prog to chse ldng gp 3f out: outpcd wl over 1f out: pushed along and kpt on steadily* **3/1**[2]
64 **6** *3* **Lawyer To World**[21] [5105] 2-9-0 ... StephenDonohoe(3) 1 62
(N A Callaghan) *chsd ldrs: rdn 2f out: n.m.r sn after: wknd fnl f* **33/1**
3 **7** *1 3/4* **Wolf River (USA)**[28] [4934] 2-9-3 ... NickyMackay 8 58
(D M Simcock) *wl in rr: rdn 3f out: nvr on terms after* **12/1**
0 **8** *shd* **Potentiale (IRE)**[12] [5339] 2-9-3 ... MichaelHills 6 57
(J W Hills) *hld up in rr: outpcd fr 3f out: no ch* **66/1**
06 **9** *1 1/4* **Copernican**[9] [5423] 2-9-3 ... JamieMackay 11 54+
(Sir Mark Prescott) *stdd s: settled in last: wl off the pce 3f out: shkn up over 1f out: nvr a factor* **100/1**
42 **10** *2* **Obstructive**[15] [5261] 2-9-3 ... HayleyTurner 2 49
(D K Ivory) *sn led: rdn and hdd 2f out: wknd rapidly fnl f* **16/1**
11 *1* **Water Margin (IRE)** 2-9-3 ... RobertHavlin 9 46
(T G Mills) *pushed along towards rr whn stmbld over 4f out: a in rr after* **50/1**
0 **12** *17* **Inside Straight (IRE)**[103] [2604] 2-9-3 ... RichardSmith 5 2
(R Hannon) *prom 1f: sn lost pl: wkng whn squeezed out 1/2-way: eased fnl f: t.o* **33/1**

1m 25.03s (-0.86) **Going Correction** -0.20s/f (Stan) 12 Ran SP% **119.8**
Speed ratings (Par 95):96,94,94,93,91 88,86,86,84,82 81,61
CSF £591.25 TOTE £110.00: £18.50, £1.50, £1.70; EX 903.60.
Owner Hesmonds Stud **Bred** Hesmonds Stud Ltd **Trained** Patching, W Sussex

FOCUS
This was probably just an average maiden, run at a sound pace. The winner sprung a big surprise but the form of the next four seems to make sense. The winning time was 0.53 seconds faster than the second division.

NOTEBOOK
Salient ran out a ready winner to get off the mark at the third attempt and defy his unbelievably huge starting price. He had run with promise on his debut at Newbury, and may not have handled Goodwood on his previous outing, but still stepped up and showed his true colours on this All-Weather bow. He also clearly stays this trip very well, despite his sprinting pedigree, and should have more to offer now he has got his head in front. (op 66-1)
Tredegar, fifth on his debut at Haydock last month, was doing his best work at the finish and looks in need of a mile now. He is going the right way and will be eligible for nurseries after his next assignment. (op 4-1)
Cleide Da Silva(USA), second on her debut at Yarmouth a fortnight previously, failed to improve for this switch to the Polytrack and ran a very similar race. She already looks a handicapper in the making. (op 2-1 tchd 9-4 in places)
Herb Paris(FR), up in trip, ultimately paid for running freely through the early parts and was just run out of the placings close home. She now qualifies for a handicap mark and should not be overburdened in that sphere. (tchd 4-1)
Loch Tay, a disappointing favourite at Epsom last time, was always playing catch-up after a sluggish start and again performed below expectations. He would benefit for the switch to a more galloping track in the short term and, while he is proving expensive to follow, should not be underestimated now he is qualified for a handicap rating. (op 7-2)

5608 P & M ELECTRICAL SERVICES E.B.F. MAIDEN STKS (DIV II) 7f (P)

2:50 (2:50) (Class 5) 2-Y-O £3,238 (£963; £481; £240) **Stalls** Low

Form RPR
65 **1** **Murrin (IRE)**[18] [5178] 2-9-3 ... RobertHavlin 12 74
(T G Mills) *t.k.h: hld up in rr: gd prog gng strly over 2f out: led 1f out: edgd rt but sn clr* **10/3**[3]
0 **2** *2 1/2* **Henry The Seventh**[110] [2402] 2-9-3 ... MichaelHills 11 67
(J W Hills) *settled in tch: prog 1/2-way: rdn to ld over 1f out: hdd 1f out: styd on and clr of rest but no ch w wnr* **25/1**
3 *3* **Gunner's View** 2-9-3 ... JamieSpencer 1 66+
(B J Meehan) *sn cl up on inner: lost pl 4f out: effrt whn nt clr run 2f out : no ch after: kpt on to take modest 3rd fnl f* **5/2**[1]
0 **4** *1/2* **Lapina (IRE)**[96] [2816] 2-8-12 ... DavidKinsella 6 53
(Pat Eddery) *rdn thrght: chsd ldrs: outpcd 2f out: plugged on* **33/1**
0 **5** *shd* **Divine Love (IRE)**[30] [4866] 2-8-12 ... RobbieFitzpatrick 7 53
(E J O'Neill) *chsd ldr to 4f out: sn rdn: towards rr and struggling over 1f out: kpt on fnl f* **14/1**
60 **6** *1* **Master Of Destiny (IRE)**[23] [5066] 2-9-3 ... TedDurcan 2 55
(H J Collingridge) *in tch in rr: rdn and effrt over 2f out: outpcd over 1f out: no ch after* **66/1**
244 **7** *hd* **Go On Green (IRE)**[23] [5066] 2-9-3 76 ...(t) DO'Donohoe 4 55
(E A L Dunlop) *wl in tch: prog on inner gng wl 3f out: nt clr run 2f out: no hdwy whn n.m.r 1f out: wknd* **3/1**[2]
60 **8** *5* **Festive Tipple (IRE)**[15] [5261] 2-9-3 ... MatthewHenry 8 42
(P Winkworth) *prominemt: led 1/2-way: rdn and hdd over 1f out: wknd rapidly* **25/1**
004 **9** *nk* **Habalwatan (IRE)**[14] [5297] 2-9-3 75 ...(b) DarryllHolland 5 41
(C E Brittain) *led to 1/2-way: styd chsng ldrs: wl outpcd over 1f out: swtchd rt and wknd* **11/2**
10 *2* **Beshairt** 2-8-6 ow1 ... JamesMillman(7) 10 32
(D K Ivory) *a in last pair and struggling off the pce* **33/1**
00 **11** *16* **Spanish Conquest**[12] [5332] 2-9-3 ... JamieMackay 9 —
(Sir Mark Prescott) *a last: rdn and t.o bef 1/2-way* **40/1**

1m 25.6s (-0.29) **Going Correction** -0.20s/f (Stan) 11 Ran SP% **116.2**
Speed ratings (Par 95):93,90,86,86,86 84,84,78,78,76 58
CSF £89.06 TOTE £3.80: £1.10, £5.20, £2.00; EX 100.20.
Owner London & Surrey Finance Ltd **Bred** E Campion **Trained** Headley, Surrey

FOCUS
This maiden looked the weaker of the two divisions and the field came home fairly strung out. Little form to go on. The winning time was 0.53 seconds slower than the first division.

NOTEBOOK
Murrin(IRE), despite taking a keen hold through the early parts, made a winning All-Weather debut in good fashion and lost his maiden tag at the third attempt in the process. The drop back to this trip played to his strengths and, while this may not have taken a great deal of winning, he looks the type to improve again now his confidence will have been boosted. (op 3-1)
Henry The Seventh, last of 14 on his debut at Haydock in June, showed vastly-improved form on this switch to the All-Weather and has clearly benefited for the break. He only tired late on and, as he was nicely clear of the remainder at the finish, can be placed to strike on this surface in due course. (op 33-1)
Gunner's View, related to winners in the US, ran green when push came to shove yet still posted a fair debut effort. He should come on plenty for the experience and, considering he was sent off as favourite, is presumably thought capable of better. (op 3-1 tchd 10-3 in a place)
Lapina(IRE), ninth on her debut at Goodwood in June, shaped as though this return to action was needed and looks more of a handicap prospect. She ought to get further in time.
Go On Green(IRE) proved disappointing on this All-Weather bow and was treading water prior to being short of room before the final furlong. He has it to prove now. (op 11-4 tchd 7-2)
Habalwatan(IRE) ran out of gas in the home straight and performed well below his recent level. Official explanation: jockey said colt had no more to give (tchd 6-1)

5609 PREMIER SHOWFREIGHT (S) STKS 1m 2f (P)

3:20 (3:20) (Class 6) 3-Y-O+ £2,388 (£705; £352) **Stalls** Low

Form RPR
0-00 **1** **Cetshwayo**[37] [4668] 4-9-0 68 ... TedDurcan 8 61
(J M P Eustace) *trckd ldrs: prog 4f out: led wl over 2f out: drvn and hdd jst over 1f out: kpt on wl to ld again post* **14/1**
1003 **2** *shd* **Bishops Finger**[15] [5259] 6-9-5 51 ...(b) RobertHavlin 9 66
(Jamie Poulton) *settled towards rr: prog 4f out: chsd ldr over 2f out: rdn to ld jst over 1f out: hdd last stride* **5/1**[2]
0550 **3** *2* **Ronsard (IRE)**[26] [4982] 4-8-11 56 ... StephenDonohoe(3) 7 57
(P D Evans) *settled in rr: pushed along over 4f out: sn lost tch w ldrs: prog over 2f out: wnt 3rd over 1f out: clsng grad fin* **6/1**
0500 **4** *7* **Malibu (IRE)**[11] [5390] 5-8-9 55 ... LiamJones(5) 4 44
(M Appleby) *chsd ldr to 6f out: styd prom: rdn and outpcd fr 3f out: sn no ch* **20/1**
0000 **5** *3 1/2* **Soubriquet (IRE)**[24] [4537] 3-8-8 65 ...(b[1]) DO'Donohoe 2 37
(T G Mills) *hld up wl in rr: pushed along 5f out: sn lost tch and wl bhd: styd on fr over 1f out: no ch* **11/2**[3]
0562 **6** *3/4* **Balearic Star (IRE)**[15] [5259] 5-8-7 46 ... JamesMillman(7) 5 36
(B R Millman) *t.k.h: hld up wl in rr: sme prog over 3f out: nvr rchd ldrs: wknd over 1f out* **11/2**[3]
040/ **7** *3 1/2* **City Affair**[66] [2061] 5-9-0 ... LPKeniry 6 29
(J G M O'Shea) *taken down early and mounted on crse: chsd ldrs: u.p fr 1/2-way: sn struggling* **33/1**
0341 **8** *1/2* **At The Helm (IRE)**[22] [5097] 4-8-7 50 ... RichardRowe(7) 11 28
(W J Knight) *hld up: prog fr 7f out to ld over 4f out and kicked 3 l clr: hdd wl over 2f out: wknd rapidly over 1f out* **9/2**[1]
5000 **9** *11* **Cool Tiger**[9] [5418] 3-8-5 60 ... JohnMcAuley(3) 3 7
(P Howling) *led to over 4f out: sn wknd* **40/1**
00-0 **10** *5* **Retirement**[11] [5384] 7-8-11 50 ... EdwardCreighton(3) 1 —
(R M Stronge) *in tch to over 4f out: sn wknd* **33/1**
2500 **11** *6* **Cavan Gael (FR)**[27] [4974] 4-8-7 53 ... JPFeatherstone(7) 10 —
(P Howling) *prom: drvn over 5f out: sn wknd and wl bhd* **16/1**

2m 4.94s (-2.85) **Going Correction** -0.20s/f (Stan)
WFA 3 from 4yo+ 6lb 11 Ran SP% **105.5**
Speed ratings (Par 101):103,102,101,95,92 92,89,89,80,76 71
CSF £64.46 TOTE £15.40: £3.10, £2.10, £1.60; EX 118.50.There was no bid for the winner. Ronsard was claimed by J C Tuck for £5,500
Owner Mrs Jan Wootton **Bred** White Horse Bloodstock Ltd **Trained** Newmarket, Suffolk
■ Coda Agency was withdrawn (15/2, vet's advice). R4 applies, deduct 10p in the £.

FOCUS
Not the worst seller of all time and the front three drew well clear. The runner-up is the best guide.
At The Helm(IRE) Official explanation: jockey said filly had no more to give

5610 JOHN SMITH'S H'CAP 1m 4f (P)

3:50 (3:51) (Class 5) (0-75,74) 3-Y-O+ £3,238 (£963; £481; £240) **Stalls** Low

Form RPR
1500 **1** **Captain General**[15] [5276] 4-9-1 63 ... MartinDwyer 12 75+
(J A R Toller) *chsd ldrs: n.m.r and lost pl over 3f out: renewed effrt 2f out: drvn and r.o wl fnl f to ld last strides* **16/1**
0142 **2** *nk* **Moon On A Spoon**[29] [4911] 3-9-0 70 ... JamieSpencer 9 77
(J R Fanshawe) *confidently rdn: hld up in rr: smooth prog fr 3f out: urged into ld ins fnl f: hdd and nt qckn last strides* **2/1**[1]
1031 **3** *3/4* **Linden Lime**[4] [5531] 4-9-6 68 6ex ... AdrianMcCarthy 10 74
(Jamie Poulton) *hld up towards rr: prog over 3f out: drvn to ld jst over 1f out : hdd ins fnl f: styd on* **15/2**[2]
0526 **4** *1 1/2* **Northside Lodge (IRE)**[15] [5258] 8-9-0 65 ...(p) StephenDonohoe(3) 14 69
(W R Swinburn) *hld up towards rr: prog over 3f out: chsd ldrs over 2f out: nt qckn over 1f out: styd on* **33/1**
1545 **5** *1/2* **Taxman (IRE)**[15] [5276] 4-9-10 72 ...(p) DarryllHolland 13 75
(C E Brittain) *prog to go prom 6f out: led over 3f out: drvn and hdd jst over 1f out: wkng nr fin* **8/1**[3]
604 **6** *1 3/4* **Wotchalike (IRE)**[17] [5213] 4-8-9 62 ...(v) LiamJones(5) 7 62
(R J Price) *settled in midfield: outpcd fr 3f out: rdn and styd on fr over 1f out: n.d* **20/1**
0062 **7** *2 1/2* **Overlord Way (GR)**[28] [4937] 4-9-12 74 ... PaulDoe 8 70
(P R Chamings) *unruly preliminaries: s.s: hld up: prog 6f out: pressed ldr 3f out: sn rdn: wknd over 1f out* **12/1**
5050 **8** *1/2* **The Violin Player (USA)**[28] [4937] 5-9-8 70 ...(p) RobbieFitzpatrick 15 65
(H J Collingridge) *dwlt: hld up in last pair: effrt over 3f out but sn outpcd and no ch: plugged on* **12/1**
3000 **9** *2* **Fen Game (IRE)**[47] [4336] 4-9-6 68 ... RobertHavlin 11 60
(J H M Gosden) *wl in tch: effrt and gng wl over 3f out: drvn over 2f out: stl chsng ldrs over 1f out: wknd rapidly fnl f* **14/1**
6205 **10** *hd* **Wester Lodge (IRE)**[24] [5047] 4-9-4 66 ...(b) JTate 16 58
(J M P Eustace) *racd freely: sn led and clr: hdd over 3f out: wknd over 2f out* **50/1**

3024 **11** *5* **Bowled Out (GER)**[35] [4687] 4-9-2 64 .... MichaelHills 6 48
(P J McBride) *settled in rr: outpcd and struggling over 3f out: bhd over 2f out* **14/1**

2225 **12** *3/4* **Tranquilizer**[179] [832] 4-9-10 72 ....(t) TPO'Shea 1 54
(D J Coakley) *prom tl wknd 3f out* **14/1**

100- **13** *3* **Coustou (IRE)**[295] [6029] 6-8-13 64 ....(p) EdwardCreighton(3) 4 42
(R M Stronge) *a towards rr: rdn over 4f out: sn wknd and bhd* **66/1**

5551 **14** *24* **Airbound (USA)**[27] [4972] 3-9-0 70 .... J-PGuillambert 5 9
(M Johnston) *chsd ldr to 5f out: wknd rapidly: t.o* **17/2**

24-0 **15** *6* **Mahmjra**[13] [5324] 4-9-0 62 ....(v) PFredericks 3 —
(C N Allen) *prom 4f: sn wknd: t.o last over 4f out* **66/1**

2m 30.43s (-3.96) **Going Correction** -0.20s/f (Stan)
WFA 3 from 4yo+ 8lb **15** Ran SP% **120.7**
Speed ratings (Par 103):105,104,104,103,102 101,100,99,98,98 95,94,92,76,72
CSF £46.19 CT £276.22 TOTE £26.80: £6.00, £1.60, £2.50; EX 121.90.
Owner M E Wates **Bred** M E Wates **Trained** Newmarket, Suffolk

FOCUS
A modest yet competitive handicap. Sound form, rated around the third and the fifth. The first two are less exposed than most in the field.
Airbound(USA) Official explanation: jockey said colt lost its action

5611 PLATFORM BUILDING MATERIALS MAIDEN STKS (DIV I) 1m (P)
4:20 (4:20) (Class 5) 3-Y-O+ **£2,590** (£770; £385; £192) **Stalls** High

Form RPR

33 **1** **Dorelia (IRE)**[32] [4799] 3-8-12 .... JamieSpencer 5 71+
(J H M Gosden) *trckd ldrs: prog over 2f out: led over 1f out: shkn up and kpt on wl fnl f* **4/1**[2]

0 **2** *1 1/4* **Calming Waters**[49] [4247] 3-9-3 .... RobertHavlin 4 73
(D W P Arbuthnot) *t.k.h: snatched up after 1f: prog fr rr over 2f out: n.m.r wl over 1f out: styd on to take 2nd ins fnl f* **20/1**

2240 **3** *1 1/4* **Just Logic (IRE)**[37] [4661] 3-9-3 76 .... DarryllHolland 7 70
(J Noseda) *led: drvn and hdd over 1f out: one pce* **7/2**[1]

455 **4** *nk* **Marbaa (IRE)**[93] [2919] 3-9-3 70 .... LPKeniry 11 70
(S Dow) *s.i.s: settled in rr: prog over 2f out: bmpd twice wl over 1f out: styd on ins fnl f* **20/1**

6400 **5** *nk* **Wassfa**[14] [5294] 3-8-12 70 .... HayleyTurner 2 64
(C E Brittain) *t.k.h early: prom: effrt and cl up on inner 2f out: hrd rdn and fdd fnl f* **10/1**

00 **6** *4* **Pleasing Gift**[23] [5071] 3-8-9 .... StephenDonohoe(3) 6 55
(J M P Eustace) *wl in rr: pushed along and struggling over 3f out: nvr on terms: plugged on u.p fr over 1f out* **25/1**

0 **7** *nk* **Desert Island Miss**[12] [5353] 3-8-12 .... TedDurcan 1 54
(W R Swinburn) *dwlt: wl in tch: shkn up over 2f out: no prog and btn wl over 1f out* **20/1**

3325 **8** *1* **Mashaair (IRE)**[30] [4891] 3-9-3 70 .... MartinDwyer 12 57
(B W Hills) *plld hrd: hld up towards rr: shkn up and no rspnse over 2f out* **7/2**[1]

-0 **9** *nk* **Opus Magnus (IRE)**[146] [1430] 3-9-0 .... AmirQuinn(3) 9 56
(P J Makin) *pressed ldr: rdn over 3f out: wknd wl over 1f out* **25/1**

10 *nk* **Ifatfirst (IRE)** 3-9-3 .... JosedeSouza 8 55
(M P Tregoning) *trckd ldrs: pushed along whn bmpd sltly over 2f out: sn wknd* **9/2**[3]

06 **11** *4* **Kindallachan**[42] [4489] 3-8-12 .... MichaelHills 10 41
(G C Bravery) *a in rr: struggling wl over 2f out* **50/1**

12 *18* **Kia Ora** 3-9-3 .... MichaelTebbutt 3 5
(J Akehurst) *rn green: in tch to 1/2-way: sn wknd: t.o* **50/1**

1m 39.0s (-0.43) **Going Correction** -0.20s/f (Stan) **12** Ran SP% **117.6**
Speed ratings (Par 103):94,92,91,91,90 86,86,85,85,85 81,63
CSF £83.66 TOTE £4.60: £1.80, £4.20, £1.70; EX 104.40.
Owner Faisal Salman **Bred** Park Place International Ltd **Trained** Newmarket, Suffolk
■ Stewards' Enquiry : Jamie Spencer caution: careless riding

FOCUS
A moderate winning time for the grade and just over a second slower than the second division. The form is dubious and far from solid.

5612 PLATFORM BUILDING MATERIALS MAIDEN STKS (DIV II) 1m (P)
4:50 (4:52) (Class 5) 3-Y-O+ **£2,590** (£770; £385; £192) **Stalls** High

Form RPR

32-4 **1** **Sotik Star (IRE)**[39] [4605] 3-9-3 72 .... JamieSpencer 3 84+
(P J Makin) *trckd ldr: led wl over 3f out: kicked 2 l clr over 2f out: hung rt fnl 2f: jst hld on* **5/2**[1]

46-6 **2** *shd* **Nawaadi**[158] [1135] 3-9-3 80 .... MartinDwyer 8 81
(M P Tregoning) *prom: shkn up to chse wnr over 3f out: looked hld fr 2f out: edgd rt but styd on fnl f: jst failed* **4/1**[3]

3-00 **3** *3* **Chasing A Dream**[117] [2188] 3-8-12 70 .... MichaelHills 9 69
(B W Hills) *prom: disp 2nd fr over 3f out to wl over 1f out: pushed along and nt qckn* **12/1**

4 *nk* **Khun John (IRE)** 3-9-3 .... LPKeniry 4 73
(B J Meehan) *chsd ldrs: hrd rdn fr 2f out: one pce over 1f out* **50/1**

00- **5** *2 1/2* **Chelsea Chelsea**[363] [5574] 3-9-3 ....(t) JosedeSouza 11 68
(P F I Cole) *sn wl in rr: outpcd and pushed along over 3f out: no ch after: rdn and r.o fnl f: nrst fin* **25/1**

0- **6** *2 1/2* **Wonderful One (IRE)**[349] [5850] 3-8-12 .... RobertHavlin 12 57
(J H M Gosden) *hld up and racd wd: sme prog 3f out: sn outpcd and btn* **14/1**

4 **7** *3/4* **Reload (IRE)**[49] [4247] 3-9-3 .... DarryllHolland 6 60
(J Noseda) *nvr beyond midfield: n.m.r and urged along 5f out: outpcd over 3f out: no ch after* **11/4**[2]

50 **8** *5* **Fairdonna**[23] [5071] 3-8-12 .... TPO'Shea 7 44
(D J Coakley) *plld hrd: hld up: effrt 3f out: wknd rapidly wl over 1f out* **10/1**

60 **9** *shd* **Grand Silence (IRE)**[22] [5086] 3-9-3 ....(t) TedDurcan 10 48
(W R Swinburn) *settled in last pair: outpcd and bhd fr 3f out* **14/1**

0 **10** *13* **Cut To (USA)**[44] [4431] 3-9-0 .... DeanCorby(3) 2 18
(J Akehurst) *dwlt: a in rr: wknd 3f out: t.o* **50/1**

55 **11** *2 1/2* **Fantastic Promise (USA)**[224] [419] 3-8-12 .... DavidKinsella 1 8
(J H M Gosden) *dwlt: sn led: drvn and hdd wl over 3f out: wknd rapidly: t.o* **25/1**

1m 37.97s (-1.46) **Going Correction** -0.20s/f (Stan) **11** Ran SP% **117.0**
Speed ratings (Par 103):99,98,95,95,93 90,89,84,84,71 69
CSF £12.19 TOTE £3.50: £1.50, £1.80, £2.90; EX 17.10 Place 6 £31.88, Place 5 £16.06.
Owner D Ladhams M Holland J Ritchie G Marchant **Bred** Holborn Trust Co **Trained** Ogbourne Maisey, Wilts

FOCUS
An ordinary winning time for the grade, but the time was a second quicker than the first division. The second and third offer a fairly sound level and the race should produce winners.
Wonderful One(IRE) Official explanation: jockey said filly hung right
Fairdonna Official explanation: jockey said filly ran too freely in the early stages
T/Plt: £66.10 to a £1 stake. Pool: £48,299.95. 532.95 winning tickets. T/Qpdt: £51.00 to a £1 stake. Pool: £3,129.10. 45.40 winning tickets. JN

5059 NEWCASTLE (L-H)
Wednesday, September 27
OFFICIAL GOING: Good (good to soft in places)
Wind: breezy, half behind

5613 GOSFORTH DECORATING AND BUILDING SERVICES MAIDEN AUCTION STKS (DIV I) 7f
1:40 (1:42) (Class 6) 2-Y-O **£1,943** (£578; £288; £144) **Stalls** High

Form RPR

460 **1** **Milliegait**[14] [5283] 2-8-7 65 .... DavidAllan 13 74
(T D Easterby) *mde all stands side: qcknd clr wl over 1f out: rdn ins last amd kpt on wl* **15/2**[3]

0 **2** *2* **World Spirit**[32] [4801] 2-8-4 .... FrancisNorton 6 66
(Rae Guest) *trckd ldrs far side: hdwy to ld that gp over 1f out: sn rdn and kpt on* **10/1**

0 **3** *3 1/2* **Delta Shuttle (IRE)**[35] [4716] 2-8-9 .... PatCosgrave 16 62
(K R Burke) *chsd ldrs stands side: pushed along 1/2-way: rdn wl over 2f out: kpt on u.p ins last* **4/1**[2]

40 **4** *4* **Our Blessing (IRE)**[12] [5348] 2-9-1 .... RobertWinston 7 57
(A P Jarvis) *hld up far side: hdwy over 2f out: rdn wl over 1f out: sn one pce* **15/2**[3]

0 **5** *2* **Isabella's Best (IRE)**[9] [5417] 2-8-10 .... RichardMullen 10 47
(E J O'Neill) *prom stands side: rdn along wl over 2f out: sn outpcd* **20/1**

04 **6** *1/2* **Myfrenchconnection (IRE)**[14] [5289] 2-8-12 .... MickyFenton 9 48
(P T Midgley) *in tch stands side: rdn along wl over 2f out: sn no hdwy* **8/1**

43 **7** *3* **Lusolly**[76] [3448] 2-8-12 .... TPQueally 3 40
(M G Quinlan) *led far side: gp: rdn along and ev ch over 2f out: drvn and hdd that side over 1f out: wknd* **3/1**[1]

0 **8** *nk* **Mineral Rights (USA)**[12] [5332] 2-8-12 .... TomEaves 11 39
(I Semple) *cl up stands side: rdn along over 2f out: sn drvn and wknd* **33/1**

03 **9** *3/4* **Cheery Cat (USA)**[12] [5332] 2-9-1 .... TonyHamilton 8 40
(D W Barker) *chsd ldrs far side: rdn along over 2f out: sn btn* **16/1**

10 *1/2* **Culroy** 2-8-9 .... TonyCulhane 5 33
(N Tinkler) *dwlt and towards rr far side tl sme late hdwy* **50/1**

565 **11** *1 3/4* **Ishetoo**[60] [3940] 2-8-12 58 .... DanielTudhope 1 31
(A Dickman) *a rr far side* **20/1**

50 **12** *hd* **Julilla**[28] [4920] 2-8-4 .... JimmyQuinn 14 23
(G G Margarson) *in tch stands side: rdn along 1/2-way: sn wknd* **50/1**

05 **13** *3/4* **The Geester**[14] [5283] 2-8-9 .... PaulEddery 4 26
(S R Bowring) *racd far side: bhd fr 1/2-way* **40/1**

0060 **14** *3* **Focus Star**[81] [3286] 2-8-9 55 .... PaulHanagan 2 18
(J M Jefferson) *chsd ldrs far side: rdn along 3f out: sn wknd* **50/1**

15 *13* **Culachy Forest** 2-8-12 .... KDarley 15 —
(N Tinkler) *racd wout tongue strap - s.i.s: a bhd stands side* **33/1**

460 **16** *8* **Rockfonic**[10] [5402] 2-9-1 .... JoeFanning 12 —
(J R Weymes) *dwlt: a rr stands side: bhd and eased wl over 1f out* **50/1**

1m 28.74s (0.74) **Going Correction** +0.10s/f (Good) **16** Ran SP% **120.3**
Speed ratings (Par 93):99,96,92,88,85 85,81,81,80,80 78,77,77,73,58 49
CSF £71.30 TOTE £7.80: £2.60, £3.80, £1.70; EX 112.00 Trifecta £84.20 Part won. Pool: £118.65 - 0.10 winning units..
Owner Mrs E J Wills **Bred** Ian H Wills **Trained** Great Habton, N Yorks

FOCUS
An ordinary event in which the field split evenly and there was little material difference between the two sides. The winning time was 0.6 seconds faster than the second division. Little to go on, but the winner showed improved form.

NOTEBOOK
Milliegait had not built on a promising debut run on faster ground on her next two starts, but appreciated these easier conditions and turned in her best effort yet. She will stay a mile and may do even better in ordinary nursery company granted suitable underfoot conditions. (op 8-1)
World Spirit, who had hinted at ability on her debut over six furlongs on soft ground, turned in a much-improved effort to pull clear of the group that raced on the far side. She looks more than capable of picking up a similar event.
Delta Shuttle(IRE) did not show much in a much better race than this on his debut at York, but fared better this time. He kept responding for pressure and will be seen to better effect over further in modest nursery company in due course. (op 7-2)
Our Blessing(IRE), well beaten on his turf debut after showing ability on Polytrack on his racecourse debut, was not disgraced after a sluggish start. Although likely to remain vulnerable in this grade, he may do better in modest nursery company. (op 8-1)
Isabella's Best(IRE) fared better than on her debut at Folkestone, but is another that will not be seen to best effect until tackling modest handicaps.
Myfrenchconnection(IRE) showed improved form in a modest maiden at Beverley last time, but failed to build on that effort on this slower ground. His future lies in low-grade handicaps.
Lusolly looked to have strong claims in this company on his form on a sound surface in the summer, but ran as though this race was needed on this first run for two-and-a-half months. Faster ground should help his cause and he is not one to write off yet. (op 7-2)
Culachy Forest Official explanation: trainer said he was unable to fit the declared tongue-strap

5614 GOSFORTH DECORATING AND BUILDING SERVICES MAIDEN AUCTION STKS (DIV II) 7f
2:10 (2:10) (Class 6) 2-Y-O **£1,943** (£578; £288; £144) **Stalls** High

Form RPR

0 **1** **Ben Chorley**[39] [4600] 2-8-12 .... DanielTudhope 1 77
(P W Chapple-Hyam) *prom: led over 1fout: pushed out fnl f* **10/3**[2]

0 **2** *2* **High Five Society**[16] [5245] 2-8-9 .... PaulEddery 2 69
(S R Bowring) *bhd: drvn and struggling after 2f: gd hdwy 2f out: chsd wnr ins fnl f: no imp* **100/1**

004 **3** *1* **Hunting Call**[30] [4895] 2-8-12 70 ....(b) FrancisNorton 16 69
(K A Ryan) *led tl hdd over 1f out: one pce and lost 2nd ins fnl f* **20/1**

422 **4** *1 3/4* **Arena's Dream (USA)**[12] [5332] 2-8-12 80 .... PaulHanagan 5 65
(R A Fahey) *keen in midfield: nt clr run over 3f to over 2f out: hdwy over 1f out: r.o fnl f: no imp* **11/4**[1]

3522 **5** *shd* **Glorious Prince (IRE)**[13] [5322] 2-9-1 68 .... RobertWinston 12 67
(M G Quinlan) *dwlt: hld up: effrt over 2f out: no imp fnl f* **4/1**[3]

33 **6** *6* **Muree Queen**[14] [5283] 2-8-8 ow1 .... GrahamGibbons 11 45
(R Hollinshead) *prom: outpcd over 2f out: n.d after* **33/1**

0B42 **7** *1/2* **Packers Hill (IRE)**[14] [5289] 2-8-12 73 .... DeanMcKeown 9 47
(G A Swinbank) *w ldr to over 2f out: wknd over 1f out* **11/2**

8 *nk* **Northern Dare (IRE)** 2-9-1 .... AdrianTNicholls 8 50
(D Nicholls) *bhd: effrt outside over 3f out: sn n.d* **100/1**

The Form Book, Raceform Ltd, Compton, RG20 6NL

9 *1* **Bold Nevison (IRE)** 2-9-1 .... RoystonFfrench 3 47
(B Smart) *s.i.s: effrt whn n.m.r over 2f out: n.d* **66/1**

10 *3 1/2* **Kentucky Boy (IRE)** 2-8-12 .... PaulMulrennan 15 35
(Jedd O'Keeffe) *s.i.s: bhd: rdn 1/2-way: nvr on terms* **100/1**

000 11 *2* **A Foot In Front**[7] 5481 2-8-9 ....(v[1]) KimTinkler 14 27
(N Tinkler) *chsd ldrs tl wknd over 2f out* **100/1**

33 12 *4* **Espejo (IRE)**[30] 4897 2-9-1 .... PatCosgrave 4 22
(K R Burke) *racd wd in midfield: rdn over 2f out: sn btn* **11/2**

2000 13 *5* **Dispol Splendid (IRE)**[7] 5481 2-8-4 50........................ JoeFanning 13 —
(P T Midgley) *chsd ldrs tl wknd over 2f out* **50/1**

04 14 *3* **Prince Noel**[34] 4731 2-8-9 .... TonyHamilton 10 —
(N Wilson) *prom to 1/2-way: sn rdn and btn* **33/1**

00 15 *nk* **Anybody's Guess (IRE)**[11] 5364 2-8-9 .... AndrewMullen(3) 6 —
(J S Wainwright) *sn rdn in rr: lost tch fr 1/2-way* **100/1**

1m 29.34s (1.34) **Going Correction** +0.10s/f (Good) **15** Ran SP% **119.6**
Speed ratings (Par 93):96,93,92,90,90 83,83,82,81,77 75,70,64,61,61
CSF £323.27 TOTE £4.20: £1.60, £32.10, £5.50; EX 507.30 TRIFECTA Not won..
Owner Diamond Racing Ltd **Bred** Mrs A Yearley **Trained** Newmarket, Suffolk

FOCUS
Another ordinary event but, unlike the first race, the whole field raced stands' side. The winning time was 0.6 seconds slower than the first division. The third sets the standard.

NOTEBOOK
Ben Chorley, who showed ability in a race that worked out well at Newmarket, proved well suited by this extra furlong and easier ground and won an ordinary event in comfortable fashion. He appeals as the type to progress in nurseries. (op 4-1 tchd 3-1)
High Five Society, well beaten over five furlongs on Polytrack on his debut, proved well suited by this much stiffer test of stamina on this turf bow. Although he is likely to remain vulnerable in this grade, he may do better once handicapped.
Hunting Call, who showed improved form tried in blinkers on his previous start, had the run of the race and ran to a similar level. However, he was beaten on merit and is always likely to struggle against the better types in this grade.
Arena's Dream(USA) is starting to look exposed and did not entirely impress with his head-carriage, but shaped better than the bare form as he was denied room as the leaders were quickening away. He looks capable of picking up an uncompetitive race. (op 5-2 tchd 3-1)
Glorious Prince(IRE) was not disgraced on this first run on easy ground and back in maiden company. He has had a few chances, but is capable of winning a small nursery back on a sound surface. (op 9-2 tchd 5-1)
Muree Queen again had his limitations exposed in this type of event, but left the impression that he may do better in modest handicaps over further next year.
Bold Nevison(IRE) Official explanation: jockey said colt was denied a clear run
Anybody's Guess(IRE) Official explanation: jockey said gelding finished sore

5615 EBF/NORTHGATE VEHICLE HIRE LTD MAIDEN STKS 6f
2:40 (2:43) (Class 5) 2-Y-O **£3,886** (£1,156; £577; £288) **Stalls** High

Form RPR

1 **Chief Operator (USA)** 2-9-3 .... LDettori 8 87+
(Saeed Bin Suroor) *trckd ldrs: hdwy to ld wl over 2f out: shkn up ent last: satyed on wl* **6/5**[1]

02 2 *2* **Swift Cut (IRE)**[8] 5454 2-9-3 .... PaulHanagan 12 75
(A P Jarvis) *trckd ldrs: hdwy 2f out: rdn and ch ent last: sn drvn and nt qckn* **4/1**[2]

06 3 *6* **Forzarzi (IRE)**[22] 5076 2-9-3 .... FrancisNorton 15 57
(A Berry) *chsd ldrs: rdn along over 2f out: drvn and wknd ent last* **100/1**

0 4 *3/4* **Tomorrow's Dancer**[35] 4716 2-9-3 .... RobertWinston 13 55+
(K A Ryan) *s.i.s and bhd: stdy hdwy on inner 3f out: in tch whn hmpd 2f out: swtchd lft and kpt on ins last: nrst fin* **9/1**[3]

000 5 *1/2* **Umpa Loompa (IRE)**[53] 4129 2-9-3 56........................(v[1]) AdrianTNicholls 1 53
(D Nicholls) *chsd ldrs: hdwy and cl up over 2f out: sn rdn and wknd over 1f out* **33/1**

00 6 *2 1/2* **Shandelight (IRE)**[34] 4731 2-8-12 .... VHalliday 17 41
(Mrs A Duffield) *in tch: rdn along and hung rt 2f out: kpt on ins last* **50/1**

00 7 *1 1/2* **Littlemadgebob**[30] 4880 2-8-12 .... PaulMulrennan 6 36
(J R Norton) *in tch: hdwy to chse ldrs 1/2-way: rdn along and cl up 2f out: sn wknd* **100/1**

46 8 *6* **Bollin Fergus**[11] 5364 2-9-3 .... GrahamGibbons 10 23
(T D Easterby) *bhd fr 1/2-way* **14/1**

30 9 *1 1/4* **Jardines Bazaar**[16] 5239 2-9-3 .... DavidAllan 11 20
(T D Easterby) *bhd fr 1/2-way* **10/1**

10 *1 3/4* **Moral Fibre (IRE)** 2-9-3 .... JoeFanning 5 14
(M Johnston) *a towards rr* **11/1**

0 11 *1 1/4* **Dream On Dreamers (IRE)**[13] 5315 2-9-3 .... PaulEddery 7 11
(R C Guest) *bhd fr 1/2-way* **100/1**

12 *8* **Presque Perdre** 2-9-3 .... TonyCulhane 3 —
(K G Reveley) *dwlt: a rr* **25/1**

13 *9* **Fara's Kingdom** 2-9-3 .... TomEaves 16 —
(Miss J A Camacho) *a bhd* **20/1**

0 14 *hd* **Mandriano (ITY)**[12] 5332 2-9-3 .... TonyHamilton 4 —
(D W Barker) *chsd ldrs: rdn wl over 2f out: sn wknd* **100/1**

0 15 *24* **Scottish Spirit (IRE)**[23] 5059 2-9-3 .... DaleGibson 14 —
(J S Haldane) *led: rdn along 1/2-way: sn hdd & wknd* **100/1**

1m 16.87s (1.78) **Going Correction** +0.10s/f (Good) **15** Ran SP% **118.0**
Speed ratings (Par 95):92,89,81,80,79 76,74,66,64,62 60,50,38,37,5
CSF £4.93 TOTE £1.90: £1.10, £1.20, £16.50; EX 4.93 Trifecta £92.10 Pool: £196.08 - 1.51 winning units..
Owner Godolphin **Bred** Darley **Trained** Newmarket, Suffolk
■ Remarkably, Chief Operator was only the second Godolphin juvenile to reach the track this year. He was their first winner.

FOCUS
Another race lacking strength but a fluent winner and the field again came stands' side. Not much previous form to go on but the winner is probably capable of better.

NOTEBOOK
Chief Operator(USA) ◆, a half brother to the top-class Crimplene and smart Dutch Gold, had his sights set at a modest level and ran out a fluent winner on this racecourse debut. Always travelling well, he only needed to be shaken up to assert in the closing stages and he looks the sort to hold his own in slightly stronger company. (op 5-4 tchd 11-8 and 11-10, 6-4 in a place)
Swift Cut(IRE), just touched off on fast ground in an ordinary Newmarket maiden last time, again did nothing wrong against a potentially fair sort and pulled clear of the remainder. He should stay seven furlongs and is capable of winning a similar event.
Forzarzi(IRE) ran his best race to date but, while firmly put in his place in the closing stages, left the impression that the step up to seven furlongs and into modest handicaps would offer his best chance of success.
Tomorrow's Dancer bettered the form of his debut in a better race than this at York despite meeting trouble. He too should be seen to better effect over further once qualified for a handicap mark. (op 12-1)
Umpa Loompa(IRE), tried in a visor back over this shorter trip, ran well for a long way but is invariably going to look vulnerable in this type of event.
Shandelight(IRE) hinted at ability after being off the bridle some way out and she will benefit from the switch into modest handicap company and a step up in distance.

5616 EBF/NOBLE SELF DRIVE LTD MAIDEN STKS 1m (R)
3:10 (3:11) (Class 5) 2-Y-O **£3,886** (£1,156; £577; £288) **Stalls** Centre

Form RPR

3634 1 **Centenary (IRE)**[16] 5239 2-9-3 70........................ RobertWinston 9 70
(J S Wainwright) *hld up in tch: drvn 3f out: no imp tl hdwy over 1f out: led and edgd lft wl ins fnl f: r.o* **9/1**[3]

05 2 *1* **Macaroni Gin (IRE)**[7] 5481 2-9-3 .... PaulMulrennan 2 68
(J Howard Johnson) *led at ordinary gallop: rdn over 2f out: hdd and no ex wl ins fnl f* **25/1**

3 *nk* **Sivota (IRE)** 2-9-3 .... TonyCulhane 4 69+
(T P Tate) *hld up: pushed along 1/2-way: hdwy whn nt clr run over 1f out: hmpd ins fnl f: r.o* **33/1**

6 4 *3/4* **Coyote Creek**[9] 5417 2-9-3 .... RichardMullen 5 65
(E F Vaughan) *cl up: rdn over 2f out: one pce fnl f* **10/1**

5 *shd* **Provost** 2-9-3 .... KDarley 8 65
(M Johnston) *chsd ldrs: rdn over 2f out: kpt on same pce fnl f* **1/1**[1]

54 6 *1* **Sendali (FR)**[32] 4788 2-9-3 .... PatCosgrave 1 63
(J D Bethell) *chsd ldrs: rdn over 2f out: one pce fnl f* **16/1**

4 7 *nk* **One And Gone (IRE)**[14] 5283 2-9-3 .... PaulHanagan 6 62
(R A Fahey) *in tch: effrt over 2f out: one pce whn n.m.r ins fnl f* **20/1**

5 8 *1 1/4* **Wee Ellie Coburn**[27] 4949 2-8-12 .... TomEaves 3 54
(I Semple) *s.i.s: hld up: rdn over 2f out: no imp fnl f* **50/1**

9 *6* **Overrule (USA)** 2-9-3 .... TPQueally 7 45
(J Noseda) *hld up: rdn over 3f out: btn 2f out* **5/2**[2]

1m 45.4s (1.92) **Going Correction** +0.10s/f (Good) **9** Ran SP% **117.1**
Speed ratings (Par 95):94,93,92,91,91 90,90,89,83
CSF £202.93 TOTE £11.00: £3.00, £6.80, £7.50; EX 150.60 TRIFECTA Not won..
Owner T H Heckingbottom **Bred** Miss Carol O'Brien **Trained** Kennythorpe, N Yorks

FOCUS
With the two market leaders disappointing and only a couple of lengths covering the majority, this looked a very ordinary event, rated around the winner. The pace was only fair.

NOTEBOOK
Centenary(IRE) has had a few chances but, in a race where the market leaders were disappointing, did not have to improve too much to get off the mark. A stiffer test of stamina would have been in his favour, but he is likely to remain vulnerable to more progressive sorts.
Macaroni Gin(IRE) had shown improved form at Redcar on his previous start and put up his best effort yet after enjoying the run of the race. He had things in his favour here though, and is likely to remain vulnerable in this type of event.
Sivota(IRE), a half-brother to several winners up to a mile and a quarter, shaped better than the bare form on this racecourse debut and he is likely to leave this bare form behind in due course granted a stiffer test of stamina. (op 25-1 tchd 50-1 in a place)
Coyote Creek, who hinted at ability on his debut, had the run of the race and was not disgraced. However he left the impression that a stiffer test of stamina and a step into modest handicap company would suit. (op 9-1)
Provost, a half brother to a couple of winners over sprint distances, started at a fairly short price for this racecourse debut but proved a big disappointment. He would not be one to write off just yet, but his engagements in the Group 1 Dewhurst and Racing Post Trophy look optimistic to say the least. (op 10-11 tchd 11-10 in places)
Sendali(FR) had the run of the race and was not disgraced, but looks the type to do better in ordinary handicap company over middle distances next year. (op 11-1)
Overrule(USA), who cost $190,000 and is from a stable that has a strong hand in the juvenile department, attracted support but proved a big disappointment on this racecourse debut. He is not one to write off just yet though. Official explanation: jockey said colt hung right-handed throughout (op 4-1 tchd 9-2 in a place)

5617 TRANSMORE VAN HIRE LTD H'CAP 1m 3y(S)
3:40 (3:41) (Class 5) (0-70,70) 3-Y-O+ **£3,562** (£1,059; £529; £264) **Stalls** High

Form RPR

1042 1 **Orpen Wide (IRE)**[8] 5444 4-9-2 67........................(b) GregFairley(3) 16 81
(M C Chapman) *mde all stands side: rdn 2f out: styd on strly* **5/1**[1]

1106 2 *3* **Border Artist**[22] 5085 7-9-2 64........................ DeanMcKeown 9 71
(J Pearce) *hld up stands side: hdwy 3f out: rdn to chse wnr wl over 1f out: drvn and no imp ins last* **14/1**

0004 3 *4* **Luckylover**[27] 4968 3-9-1 67........................ TPQueally 15 65
(M G Quinlan) *cl up stands side: rdn along 3f out: drvn 2f out and kpt on same pce* **7/1**[3]

0400 4 *1/2* **Gifted Flame**[13] 5320 7-9-3 65........................ GrahamGibbons 17 62
(J J Quinn) *dwlt: hld up in tch stands side: hdwy 3f out: rdn to chse ldrs over 2f out: sn drvn and kpt on same pce* **7/1**[3]

4460 5 *1/2* **Commitment Lecture**[25] 5024 6-9-2 64........................(t) PhillipMakin 11 60
(M Dods) *trckd ldrs stands side: rdn alonga nd outpce over 2f out: kpt on u.p ins last* **9/1**

0004 6 *8* **Trans Sonic**[9] 5427 3-9-4 70........................(v[1]) RobertWinston 6 47
(A P Jarvis) *hld up in rr far side: hdwy over 2f out: sn rdn and kpt on ins last: no ch w stands side* **8/1**

5415 7 *nk* **California Laws**[10] 5406 4-9-3 68........................ SaleemGolam(3) 8 44+
(T D Barron) *cl up far side: hdwy to ld that gp wl over 2f out: sn rdn and wknd wl over 1f out* **11/2**[2]

0060 8 *1 1/2* **Top Dirham**[30] 4881 8-9-3 65........................ DaleGibson 10 38
(M W Easterby) *hld up stands side: a towards rr* **16/1**

0200 9 *7* **Greenbelt**[20] 5137 5-9-5 67........................ DanielTudhope 7 24+
(G M Moore) *hld up in rr far side: hdwy 3f out: rdn 2f out and sn btn* **12/1**

1154 10 *2* **Xpres Maite**[60] 3943 3-8-11 70........................(p) MSemple(7) 14 22
(S R Bowring) *cl up stands side: rdn along over 3f out and sn wknd* **20/1**

0004 11 *2* **Buddy Brown**[68] 3694 4-9-3 65........................ TomEaves 13 13
(J Howard Johnson) *chsd ldrs stands side: rdn along after 3f: sn wknd* **33/1**

6100 12 *29* **Aperitif**[30] 4885 5-9-8 70........................ AdrianTNicholls 1 —
(D Nicholls) *led far side gp: rdn along and hdd wl over 2f out: sn wknd* **14/1**

14-0 13 *3* **Etaar**[13] 5320 4-9-8 70........................ PaulMulrennan 4 —
(C W Fairhurst) *a rr far side* **66/1**

0360 14 *12* **Calcutta Cup (UAE)**[14] 5284 3-9-4 70........................ MickyFenton 3 —
(Karen McLintock) *chsd ldrs far side: rdn along 1/2-way: sn wknd* **33/1**

1m 42.01s (0.11) **Going Correction** +0.10s/f (Good)
WFA 3 from 4yo+ 4lb **14** Ran SP% **117.2**
Speed ratings (Par 103):103,100,96,95,95 87,86,85,78,76 74,45,42,30
CSF £70.27 CT £506.94 TOTE £5.70: £1.30, £8.40, £2.50; EX 81.40 Trifecta £105.60 Part won. Pool: £148.84 - 0.10 winning units..
Owner Andy & Bev Wright **Bred** Mrs Marian Maguire **Trained** Market Rasen, Lincs

FOCUS
The field divided into two groups and those racing on the far side were at a considerable disadvantage. Sound form, the winner back to his early three-year-old level.

5618 CARTRUX RENTAL LTD H'CAP 2m 19y

4:10 (4:10) (Class 5) (0-70,66) 3-Y-O £3,238 (£963; £481; £240) Stalls Centre

Form RPR

5012 **1** **Sa Nau**[16] [5242] 3-8-10 **55** ..... FrancisNorton 15 64
(T Keddy) *hld up midfield: effrt 3f out: rallied over 1f out: led ins fnl f: hld on wl* **9/4**[1]

1144 **2** ¾ **Leo McGarry (IRE)**[38] [4632] 3-8-12 **60** ..... SaleemGolam(3) 6 68
(S C Williams) *trckd ldrs: effrt over 2f out: led briefly ins fnl f: kpt on towards fin* **7/2**[2]

0032 **3** 1 ½ **Golden Groom**[22] [5082] 3-8-4 **49** ..... DeanMcKeown 1 55
(C W Fairhurst) *keen in midfield: rdn and outpcd over 2f out: rallied over 1f out: styd on fnl f* **11/2**[3]

-500 **4** hd **Give It Time**[16] [5242] 3-9-1 **60** ..... JoeFanning 7 66
(J G Given) *set stdy pce: rdn over 1f out: hdd and no ex ins fnl f* **33/1**

0466 **5** 2 ½ **Sweet Lavinia**[16] [5240] 3-8-3 **48** ..... JimmyQuinn 16 51
(J D Bethell) *hld up: drvn over 3f out: no imp tl kpt on fnl f: nrst fin* **20/1**

0546 **6** 4 **Galileo Figaro (USA)**[18] [5174] 3-9-4 **66** ..... PatrickMathers(3) 11 64
(W M Brisbourne) *keen: hld up: effrt over 3f out: no imp fr 2f out* **14/1**

0640 **7** 1 ¼ **Gettysburg (IRE)**[54] [4111] 3-8-2 **47** oh2 ..... RoystonFfrench 2 43
(J Howard Johnson) *midfield: rdn over 2f out: sn no imp* **16/1**

5341 **8** 1 ½ **Tuscany Rose**[11] [5365] 3-8-2 **47** oh2 ..... RichardMullen 12 42
(W R Muir) *trckd ldrs: ev ch over 2f out: wknd over 1f out* **12/1**

6650 **9** 3 ½ **Silver Mont (IRE)**[30] [4884] 3-8-2 **47** oh2 ..... (bt) PaulEddery 3 37
(S R Bowring) *cl up: rdn and ev ch 3f out: wknd 2f out* **16/1**

0-00 **10** 3 **Arcangela**[16] [5247] 3-8-6 **51** ..... PaulHanagan 8 38
(J G Given) *chsd ldrs to over 4f out: sn btn* **25/1**

0000 **11** 2 ½ **Gavanello**[7] [5485] 3-7-9 **47** oh8 ..... PaulPickard(7) 4 31
(M C Chapman) *bhd: rdn 4f out: sn btn* **100/1**

0500 **12** ¾ **Sunny Parkes**[22] [5082] 3-7-11 **47** oh7 ..... DuranFentiman(5) 14 30
(M Mullineaux) *hld up outside: rdn over 4f out: sn btn* **50/1**

-546 **13** 2 **Pukka Tique**[117] [2209] 3-9-6 **65** ..... GrahamGibbons 9 46
(R Hollinshead) *towards rr: drvn over 4f out: sn btn* **25/1**

04-0 **14** 8 **Chelsey Jayne (IRE)**[8] [5452] 3-9-1 **60** ..... TonyCulhane 13 31
(M R Channon) *bhd: drvn 1/2-way: nvr on terms* **33/1**

0-00 **15** 32 **Mr Bilbo Baggins**[33] [4776] 3-8-2 **47** ..... AdrianTNicholls 10 —
(J S Moore) *midfield: drvn 5f out: sn btn* **40/1**

3m 41.14s (5.94) **Going Correction** +0.10s/f (Good) **15** Ran SP% **118.2**
Speed ratings (Par 101):89,88,87,87,86 84,83,83,81,79 78,78,77,73,57
CSF £8.18 CT £38.80 TOTE £3.30: £1.10, £1.90, £2.30; EX 12.80 Trifecta £38.10 Pool: £263.35 - 4.90 winning units..
Owner Howard Fielding **Bred** Juddmonte Farms Ltd **Trained** Newmarket, Suffolk

FOCUS
An ordinary handicap in which the pace was steady and the winning time was very moderate. Although the winner remains one to keep on the right side, this bare form may not prove entirely reliable.

5619 EBF/VANMONSTER.CO.UK FILLIES' H'CAP 7f

4:40 (4:41) (Class 5) (0-75,75) 3-Y-0+ £3,562 (£1,059; £529; £264) Stalls High

Form RPR

0024 **1** **Passion Fruit**[13] [5317] 5-9-7 **75** ..... DeanMcKeown 17 86
(C W Fairhurst) *trckd ldrs gng wl: swtchd lft and smooth hdwy to ld wl over 1f out: readily* **5/1**[1]

0002 **2** 2 **Smart Ass (IRE)**[31] [4844] 3-8-8 **65** ..... KDarley 14 71
(J S Moore) *midfield: hdwy 3f out: rdn to chse wnr ent last: sn drvn and no imp* **7/1**[3]

3242 **3** ¾ **Neardown Beauty (IRE)**[48] [4305] 3-9-3 **74** ..... FrancisNorton 16 78
(I A Wood) *hld up towards rr on inner: nt clr run and swtchd wd to outside 3f out: rdn to chse ldrs wl over 1f out: kpt on ins last* **6/1**[2]

50-0 **4** 1 ¾ **Miss Sure Bond (IRE)**[10] [5401] 3-8-8 **65** ..... (b) RobertWinston 10 65
(B Smart) *led: rdn along over 2f out: hdd wl over 1f out and kpt on same pce* **50/1**

023 **5** ½ **Light Dreams**[33] [4757] 3-8-7 **64** ..... (v) PaulHanagan 7 62
(W J Knight) *trckd ldrs: effrt over 2f out: sn rdn and no imp* **9/1**

11-4 **6** ½ **Dispol Foxtrot**[11] [5362] 8-9-2 **70** ..... AdrianTNicholls 9 67
(D Nicholls) *dwlt: sn outpcd and bhd: rdn along 1/2-way: styd on u.p fnl 2f: nrst fin* **7/1**[3]

3400 **7** 7 **Noble Nova**[2] [5568] 3-8-8 **65** ow1 ..... TonyCulhane 6 44
(M R Channon) *cl up: rdn along 3f out: grad wknd* **20/1**

5400 **8** 1 ½ **Choysia**[40] [4567] 3-9-2 **73** ..... TomEaves 3 48
(D W Barker) *cl up: rdn along wl over 2f out: drvn and wknd wl over 1f out* **25/1**

0305 **9** nk **Elegant Times (IRE)**[22] [5079] 3-8-4 **61** oh1 ..... DavidAllan 11 35
(T D Easterby) *chsd ldrs: rdn along 1/2-way: sn wknd* **14/1**

3416 **10** nk **Our Faye**[14] [5294] 3-8-9 **71** ..... MichaelJStainton(5) 13 44
(S Kirk) *hld up: effrt and sme hdwy 1/2-way: sn rdn along and wknd* **9/1**

3300 **11** 1 ¾ **Highland Cascade**[18] [5171] 4-9-3 **71** ..... MickyFenton 8 40
(J M P Eustace) *a rr* **20/1**

5004 **12** shd **Dispol Isle (IRE)**[7] [5483] 4-8-10 **64** ..... JoeFanning 2 32
(T D Barron) *keen: in tch on outer: rdn al0ong halfway and sn wknd* **16/1**

0-56 **13** 15 **Sea Of Calm (USA)**[149] [1351] 3-8-5 **62** ..... RichardMullen 1 —
(E A L Dunlop) *towards rr: rdn along on outer 1/2-way: sn wknd and bhd* **7/1**[3]

0-00 **14** 7 **High Meadow Girl**[16] [5243] 3-8-4 **61** oh1 ..... JimmyQuinn 4 —
(J D Bethell) *chsd ldrs: rdn along 1/2-way: sn wknd* **40/1**

1m 28.7s (0.70) **Going Correction** +0.10s/f (Good)
WFA 3 from 4yo+ 3lb **14** Ran SP% **118.8**
Speed ratings (Par 100):100,97,96,94,94 93,85,84,83,83 81,81,64,56
CSF £35.84 CT £182.43 TOTE £5.00: £1.30, £3.00, £1.90; EX 42.70 Trifecta £80.40 Pool: £237.92 - 2.10 winning units..
Owner G H & S Leggott **Bred** G H And Simon Leggott **Trained** Middleham Moor, N Yorks

FOCUS
A run-of-the-mill event in which the field raced stands' side but the gallop was less than frenetic and those held up were at a disadvantage. High numbers came out on top. Sound form among the stands'-side group.
Sea Of Calm(USA) Official explanation: jockey said filly was never travelling

5620 NORTHGATE PLC H'CAP 5f

5:10 (5:10) (Class 6) (0-65,70) 3-Y-0+ £2,590 (£770; £385; £192) Stalls High

Form RPR

2003 **1** **Special Gold**[38] [4636] 4-8-7 **52** ..... (b) DavidAllan 2 62
(T D Easterby) *racd w one other far side: pressed ldr that side: rdn over 2f out: led wl ins fnl f: hld on wl* **16/1**

00-U **2** ½ **Harrys House**[22] [5078] 4-9-1 **60** ..... (p) GrahamGibbons 1 68
(J J Quinn) *racd w one other far side: led tl wl ins fnl f: kpt on* **33/1**

6000 **3** 1 **Trick Cyclist**[41] [4523] 5-8-10 **55** ..... (b) DaleGibson 12 59
(M W Easterby) *dwlt: hld up stands side: hdwy to ld that gp ins fnl f: kpt on wl: nt rch far side pair* **16/1**

3102 **4** 1 ¼ **Petite Mac**[7] [5487] 6-8-11 **63** ..... SuzzanneFrance(7) 16 63
(N Bycroft) *dwlt: bhd: swtchd centre 1/2-way: kpt on wl fnl f: nrst fin* **8/1**[2]

0000 **5** nk **Brut**[7] [5487] 4-9-1 **60** ..... PaulHanagan 6 59
(D W Barker) *prom chsng gp stands side: effrt over 2f out: edgd to stands rail over 1f out: one pce fnl f* **16/1**

0204 **6** ½ **Paddywack (IRE)**[2] [5577] 9-9-1 **60** ..... (b) TonyCulhane 7 57
(D W Chapman) *sn bhd and outpcd stands side gp: hdwy over 1f out: nrst fin* **9/2**[1]

4042 **7** ½ **The Leather Wedge (IRE)**[7] [5486] 7-8-12 **62** ..... DeclanMcGann(5) 11 57
(R Johnson) *led and clr stands side gp: hung lft and hdd that gp ins fnl f: no ex* **9/1**[3]

3000 **8** ¾ **Whinhill House**[7] [5487] 6-8-7 **59** ..... (p) VictoriaBehan(7) 17 52
(D W Barker) *hld up stands rail: n.m.r over 2f out: kpt on fnl f: no imp* **8/1**[2]

4600 **9** nk **Tagula Bay (IRE)**[11] [5370] 4-8-0 **50** ..... DuranFentiman(5) 15 41
(T D Easterby) *prom stands side gp tl rdn and no ex over 1f out* **14/1**

5645 **10** ½ **Blue Knight (IRE)**[23] [5062] 7-8-7 **52** ..... (vt) DanielTudhope 5 42
(D Carroll) *racd centre: bhd and outpcd: rdn whn hung bdly lft fr 2f out: nvr on terms* **11/1**

4051 **11** ½ **Namir (IRE)**[6] [5493] 4-9-8 **70** 6ex ..... (vt) PatrickMathers(3) 3 58
(D Shaw) *racd on outside of stands side gp: pushed along 1/2-way: nvr rchd ldrs* **10/1**

000 **12** hd **Mint**[7] [5486] 3-9-2 **65** ..... AndrewMullen(3) 10 52
(D W Barker) *prom chsng gp stands side: rdn 1/2-way: btn over 1f out* **50/1**

2324 **13** 4 **Chairman Bobby**[22] [5078] 8-8-10 **55** ..... (p) TonyHamilton 13 28
(D W Barker) *prom stands side gp: rdn 1/2-way: sn lost pl* **9/1**[3]

2020 **14** 1 ¾ **Howards Princess**[53] [4135] 4-9-1 **60** ..... (p) TomEaves 9 26
(I Semple) *prom stands side gp to 1/2-way: sn rdn and btn* **25/1**

3350 **15** 15 **Trombone Tom**[7] [5486] 3-8-7 **53** ..... PaulMulrennan 14 —
(J R Norton) *hld up stands side gp: n.m.r 1/2-way: nvr rchd ldrs* **16/1**

2452 **16** 1 ½ **Mystic Queen (IRE)**[82] [3257] 3-8-8 **54** ..... RobertWinston 8 —
(A P Jarvis) *in tch stands side gp to 1/2-way: sn rdn and wknd* **14/1**

61.78 secs (0.28) **Going Correction** +0.10s/f (Good)
WFA 3 from 4yo+ 1lb **16** Ran SP% **123.4**
Speed ratings (Par 101):101,100,98,96,96 95,94,93,92,92 91,90,84,81,57 55
CSF £479.90 CT £8598.62 TOTE £17.30: £3.70, £8.80, £4.10, £2.80; EX 316.90 TRIFECTA Not won. Place 6 £261.56, Place 5 £113.53.
Owner Frickley Holdings Ltd **Bred** Barry Minty **Trained** Great Habton, N Yorks

FOCUS
A modest handicap run at a good pace, but this time the two that raced on the far side filled the first two placings.
Mystic Queen(IRE) Official explanation: jockey said filly moved poorly throughout
T/Jkpt: £50,929.50 to a £1 stake. Pool: £71,731.75. 1.00 winning ticket. T/Plt: £675.70 to a £1 stake. Pool: £61,142.95. 66.05 winning tickets. T/Qpdt: £17.00 to a £1 stake. Pool: £4,566.20. 198.00 winning tickets. RY

4962 SALISBURY (R-H)

Wednesday, September 27

OFFICIAL GOING: Good changing to good to soft after race 2 (2.30)
Wind: moderate, across

5621 AXMINSTER CARPETS APPRENTICE H'CAP 1m

2:00 (2:01) (Class 6) (0-65,65) 3-Y-0+ £3,238 (£963; £481; £240) Stalls Centre

Form RPR

3-04 **1** **Bank On Benny**[31] [4845] 4-8-8 **58** ..... WilliamBuick(7) 13 68
(P W D'Arcy) *hld up rr: hdwy 3f out: chsd ldr 1f out: styd on to ld fnl 110yds: pushed out* **8/1**

544 **2** 1 ½ **Dixieland Boy (IRE)**[41] [4527] 3-9-1 **65** ..... KirstyMilczarek(3) 5 71
(P J Makin) *led: rdn 3l clr ins fnl 2f: hdd and no ex fnl 110yds* **10/1**

000 **3** 1 **Aastral Magic**[11] [5384] 4-9-5 **62** ..... (p) TravisBlock 14 66
(R Hannon) *chsd ldrs: wnt 2nd ins fnl 3f: no imp on ldr:one pce fnl f* **18/1**

0630 **4** 2 **Scutch Mill (IRE)**[35] [4704] 4-9-2 **62** ..... (t) JamieJones(3) 8 61
(Karen George) *slowly away: bhd: hrd drvn and hdwy fr 2f out: styd on fnl f but nt rch ldrs* **33/1**

4525 **5** 1 ½ **Ermine Grey**[58] [4001] 5-8-8 **59** ..... MarkCoumbe(8) 16 55
(A W Carroll) *bhd: rdn 3f out: hdwy fr 2f out: kpt on fnl f but nt rch ldrs* **6/1**[2]

5303 **6** nk **Murrumbidgee (IRE)**[17] [5205] 3-8-12 **62** ..... PatrickHills(3) 15 57
(J W Hills) *in tch: rdn over 2f out: styd on same pce appr fnl f* **5/1**[1]

0003 **7** ¾ **Emotive**[9] [5435] 3-9-0 **64** ..... (p) AshleyHamblett(3) 9 58
(I A Wood) *bhd: sn pushed along: styd on fr over 1f out: nt rch ldrs* **20/1**

-635 **8** 6 **Dream Of Dubai (IRE)**[8] [5450] 5-8-13 **56** ..... JerryO'Dwyer 10 36
(P Mitchell) *chsd ldrs: rdn over 2f out: wknd fnl f* **14/1**

0000 **9** 3 **Threezedzz**[14] [5302] 8-8-9 **58** ..... (t) TolleyDean(6) 4 31
(R A Harris) *chsd ldrs: rdn 3f out: wknd over 1f out* **25/1**

0000 **10** 2 **Harcourt (USA)**[114] [2305] 6-9-6 **63** ..... LiamTreadwell 7 31
(M Madgwick) *bhd: rdn 3f out: nvr in contention* **33/1**

0321 **11** nk **Lockstock (IRE)**[20] [5130] 8-8-8 **61** ..... (p) BenjaminWishart(10) 2 29
(M S Saunders) *racd wd and w ldrs: edgd rt 3f out: rdn and hung rt over 2f out: sn btn* **6/1**[2]

56-0 **12** 2 **Blandford Flyer**[147] [1416] 3-8-8 **60** ..... JamieHamblett(5) 1 23
(W R Swinburn) *chsd ldrs: rdn over 3f out: wknd over 2f out* **33/1**

0206 **13** 1 ¼ **Christmas Truce (IRE)**[16] [5236] 7-8-10 **61** ..... (b) SophieDoyle(8) 3 21
(Ms J S Doyle) *slowly away: a in rr* **12/1**

3146 **14** 2 **Charlie Bear**[30] [4870] 5-8-10 **58** ..... JemmaMarshall(5) 6 13
(Miss Z C Davison) *bhd: rdn and hdwy over 2f out: sn wknd* **7/1**[3]

0000 **15** 1 ¾ **Admiral Compton**[10] [2752] 5-8-10 **58** ..... KMay(5) 11 9
(J R Boyle) *chsd ldrs 5f* **14/1**

050/ **16** 4 **One Good Thing (USA)**[272] 4-9-3 **65** ..... (v[1]) JosephWalsh(5) 12 7
(Christian Wroe, UAE) *chsd ldrs to 1/2-way: sn btn* **50/1**

1m 44.53s (1.44) **Going Correction** +0.20s/f (Good)
WFA 3 from 4yo+ 4lb **16** Ran SP% **123.6**
Speed ratings (Par 101):100,98,97,95,94 93,92,86,83,81 81,79,78,76,74 70
CSF £80.39 CT £1471.90 TOTE £9.00: £2.00, £3.00, £2.60, £7.70; EX 116.90.
Owner Paul D'Arcy **Bred** Gilridge Bloodstock Ltd **Trained** Newmarket, Suffolk

■ A first winner for 18-year-old William Buick, son of Walter, himself eight-times champion jockey in Scandinavia.
■ Stewards' Enquiry : Kirsty Milczarek one-day ban: failed to keep straight from stalls (Oct 8)

FOCUS
Just a modest handicap restricted to apprentice riders who had not ridden more than 50 winners. The pace appeared decent enough throughout and all bar unplaced Lockstock raced towards the far side throughout. Sound form.

Ermine Grey Official explanation: jockey said gelding hung left-handed

5622 ALLIED IRISH BANK SOUTHAMPTON EBF MAIDEN STKS (DIV I) 1m
2:30 (2:31) (Class 4) 2-Y-O **£4,210** (£1,252; £625; £312) **Stalls** Centre

Form RPR
00 1 **Spume (IRE)**[26] 4992 2-9-3 KerrinMcEvoy 7 79+
(Sir Michael Stoute) *chsd ldrs: wnt 2nd 2f out: drvn and styd on strly fnl f: led cl home* **9/2**[2]
62 2 ¾ **Coeur De Lionne (IRE)**[9] 5423 2-9-3 SteveDrowne 5 77
(R Charlton) *sn led: pushed along over 1f out: hdd and outpcd cl home* **6/5**[1]
0 3 3 **Bajan Pride**[32] 4794 2-9-3 RyanMoore 9 70
(R Hannon) *bhd: hdwy 1/2-way: chsd ldrs 2f out: kpt on same pce fnl f* **9/2**[2]
4 ¾ **Strikeen (IRE)** 2-9-3 IanMongan 2 69
(T G Mills) *chsd ldrs: rdn over 2f out: wknd ins fnl f* **25/1**
06 5 1 ¼ **Mystical Moon**[18] 5178 2-9-3 JohnEgan 10 66+
(Lady Herries) *bhd: pushed along over 2f out: kpt on fnl f but nvr gng pce to be competitive* **7/1**[3]
00 6 2 ½ **Mujahaz (IRE)**[18] 5178 2-9-3 RHills 11 60
(J L Dunlop) *bhd: stl 2l last over 2f out: styd on fr over 1f out: gng on ins last but nvr in contention* **14/1**
05 7 hd **Mud Monkey**[9] 5423 2-9-3 GeorgeBaker 8 60
(B G Powell) *t.k.h: sn in tch: rdn over 2f out: wknd fnl f* **20/1**
8 1 **New Light** 2-8-12 StephenCarson 1 52
(R F Johnson Houghton) *t.k.h: chsd ldrs: rdn over 1f out: sn wknd* **33/1**
00 9 1 ½ **Franchoek (IRE)**[30] 4867 2-9-3 FergusSweeney 6 54
(A King) *bhd: hdwy on outside 3f out: wknd ins fnl 2f* **40/1**
00 10 ¾ **Acosta**[26] 4980 2-9-3 (b[1]) RichardThomas 4 52
(Dr J R J Naylor) *in tch: rdn 3f out: wknd 2f out* **100/1**
00 11 4 **Shouldntbethere (IRE)**[12] 5348 2-9-3 AntonyProcter 3 43
(Mrs P N Dutfield) *s.i.s: sn in tch and t.k.h: wknd 2f out* **100/1**

1m 45.63s (2.54) **Going Correction** +0.20s/f (Good) 11 Ran SP% **117.0**
Speed ratings (Par 97):95,94,91,90,89 86,86,85,84,83 79
CSF £9.69 TOTE £5.60: £1.80, £1.20, £1.80; EX 14.60.
Owner Ballymacoll Stud **Bred** Ballymacoll Stud Farm Ltd **Trained** Newmarket, Suffolk
■ Stewards' Enquiry : Ian Mongan one-day ban: failed to keep straight from stalls (Oct 8)

FOCUS
Probably just an ordinary maiden and they again stayed far side. They finished quite tired, despite the pace appearing far from frantic early on, and the ground was duly changed from 'good' to 'good to soft'. The winning time was 0.13 seconds slower than the second division, but the form looks slightly stronger.

NOTEBOOK
Spume(IRE) finished down the field on his debut at Leicester and was again well held when behind Coeur De Lionne at Kempton last time, but he has clearly benefited from those outings and showed improved form under a good ride from Kerrin McEvoy. The form does not look anything special, but he is open to further improvement and should not be too harshly treated by the Handicapper. (op 4-1 tchd 5-1)
Coeur De Lionne(IRE) looked to have an easy enough time of things up front, but the ground was probably riding a little more testing than it had first appeared and he could not sustain his challenge near the line. He has shown enough to suggest he can win a race and will have more options now he is qualified for a handicap mark, but things are unlikely to get any easier. (tchd 11-8, 6-4 in places)
Bajan Pride kept on well enough at the one pace and, being a half-brother to recent two-mile winner Serramanna, he is likely to come into his own over further when handicapped. (op 11-2 tchd 4-1)
Strikeen(IRE), a 57,000gns half-brother to amongst others multiple 7-9f winner Provosky, made a satisfactory debut and should improve.
Mystical Moon ◆ is now qualified for a handicap mark and is open to plenty of improvement. (op 9-1)
Mujahaz(IRE) ◆ is another now eligible for an official mark and he should do better. (op 11-1)
New Light, a half-sister to smart sprinter Bygone Days, gave the impression the run would do her good.

5623 ALLIED IRISH BANK SOUTHAMPTON EBF MAIDEN STKS (DIV II) 1m
3:00 (3:02) (Class 4) 2-Y-O **£4,210** (£1,252; £625; £312) **Stalls** Centre

Form RPR
0 1 **Ladies Best**[35] 4705 2-9-3 KerrinMcEvoy 7 79+
(Sir Michael Stoute) *hld up in rr:swtchd lft to outside 3f out: str run fr 2f out to chal 1f out: sn led: c clr cl home: readily* **11/2**
46 2 2 ½ **Actodos (IRE)**[20] 5125 2-9-3 GeorgeBaker 9 73
(B R Millman) *led 2f: styd chsng ldrs: wnt 2nd 2f out and no imp styd on same pce to chse wnr fnl 110yds* **8/1**
3 1 ¾ **Composing (IRE)** 2-8-12 SteveDrowne 3 64
(H Morrison) *s.i.s: chsd ldrs: pushed along over 2f out: kpt on fnl f but nvr gng pce to be competitive* **25/1**
0 4 ½ **Rock 'N' Roller (FR)**[12] 5340 2-9-3 RyanMoore 4 68
(W R Muir) *bhd:pushed along over 3f out: kpt on fr over 1f out: styd on cl home but nvr in contention* **10/3**[2]
0034 5 ½ **Cry Presto (USA)**[12] 5343 2-9-3 85 (b[1]) RichardHughes 2 67
(R Hannon) *led after 2f: rdn over 1f out: hdd & wknd qckly jst ins last* **7/2**[3]
0 6 ½ **Crimson Monarch (USA)**[8] 5457 2-9-3 JimCrowley 8 66
(Mrs A J Perrett) *chsd ldrs: rdn over 2f out: wknd fnl f* **25/1**
03 7 5 **El Dececy (USA)**[22] 5088 2-9-3 RHills 5 54
(J L Dunlop) *chsd ldr 5f out: rdn 3f out: wknd ins fnl 2f* **5/2**[1]
00 8 2 **Brave Quest (IRE)**[30] 4897 2-9-3 IanMongan 10 49
(C J Down) *t.k.h: chsd ldrs early: dropped rr 1/2-way: nvr in contention after* **66/1**
9 9 **Encircled** 2-8-12 FergusSweeney 6 24
(D Haydn Jones) *slowly away: a bhd* **40/1**
10 8 **Golden Prospect** 2-9-3 EddieAhern 1 10
(J W Hills) *s.i.s: sme prog into mid-div 1/2-way: sn bhd* **40/1**
11 17 **Cuban Night** 2-9-3 ChrisCatlin 11 —
(D J S Ffrench Davis) *slowly away: sn wl bhd* **50/1**

1m 45.5s (2.41) **Going Correction** +0.20s/f (Good) 11 Ran SP% **116.4**
Speed ratings (Par 97):95,92,90,90,89 89,84,82,73,65 48
CSF £44.58 TOTE £8.10: £2.50, £2.80, £6.30; EX 51.00.
Owner Saeed Suhail **Bred** The Lavington Stud **Trained** Newmarket, Suffolk

FOCUS
Like the first division, by no means a great maiden. Not much form to go on, and it has been rated through the runner-up. They appeared to go fast enough considering the ease in the ground and most of these again finished quite tired. Once again, they stayed far side. The winning time was 0.13 seconds faster than the first division.

NOTEBOOK
Ladies Best clipped heels when down the field on his debut at Leicester, but he has clearly gone the right way from that initial experience and ran out a clear-cut winner. He was last of the main group at about halfway, but his jockey is a fine judge of pace and he picked up well when switched wide for his sustained effort. Like his stablemate who won the first division, he might not have achieved a great deal strictly on form, but there should be plenty more to come. (op 5-1 tchd 6-1)
Actodos(IRE), although well held on his first two starts, had shown ability and this was another respectable effort. He is coming along nicely and will have more options now he is qualified for a handicap mark. (op 12-1)
Composing(IRE) ◆, the first foal of a half-sister to top-class French juvenile Lady Of Chad, was one of only two fillies in the field and fared best of the newcomers. Her connections will surely have been delighted with this introduction and she looks well up to finding a race. (op 20-1)
Rock 'N' Roller(FR), not without promise on his debut at Newbury, again showed ability and should make a nice handicapper next season. (op 4-1 tchd 9-2 and 3-1)
Cry Presto(USA) has been highly tried to date and is presumably held in some regard by his connections, but he failed to take advantage of the switch to maiden company. Fitted with blinkers for the first time, he probably just did a bit too much towards the front end and could not sustain his challenge. He is better than he showed. (op 9-2)
Crimson Monarch(USA) showed some ability and should find his level once handicapped. (op 22-1)
El Dececy(USA), upped to a mile for the first time and switched to an easy surface, failed to show his best. Official explanation: jockey said colt was unsuited by the good to soft ground (op 15-8)
Golden Prospect, a half-brother to smart Violet Park, travelled quite well early on and offered some promise. (tchd 50-1)

5624 PORTWAY EBF NOVICE STKS 6f 212y
3:30 (3:31) (Class 4) 2-Y-O **£4,857** (£1,445; £722; £360) **Stalls** Centre

Form RPR
1 1 **Tembanee (IRE)**[26] 4980 2-9-0 RichardHughes 5 90
(R Hannon) *trckd ldrs: led appr fnl f: drvn out* **11/2**[3]
13 2 1 ¼ **Aqmaar**[28] 4928 2-9-5 RHills 1 92
(J L Dunlop) *w ldr tl led appr fnl 3f: rdn 2f out: hdd appr fnl f: styd on same pce* **11/8**[1]
10 3 nk **Furnace (IRE)**[32] 4809 2-9-5 92 EddieAhern 4 91
(M L W Bell) *chsd ldrs: rdn 2f out: styd on same pce ins fnl f* **7/4**[2]
56 4 ½ **Christalini**[12] 5340 2-8-12 PatDobbs 6 83
(J C Fox) *hld up rr but in tch: drvn and hdwy fr 2f out: chsng ldrs but one pce whn edgd rt fnl 110yds: kpt on* **33/1**
522 5 4 **Little Miss Tara (IRE)**[11] 5380 2-8-7 80 SteveDrowne 2 67
(A B Haynes) *slt ld tl hdd over 3f out: sn rdn: wknd appr fnl f* **9/1**
100 6 1 ¼ **Carson's Spirit (USA)**[70] 3641 2-9-5 84 (b[1]) FergusSweeney 3 76
(W S Kittow) *t.k.h: chsd ldrs: rdn 2f out: wknd appr fnl f* **18/1**

1m 29.89s (0.83) **Going Correction** +0.20s/f (Good) 6 Ran SP% **112.1**
Speed ratings (Par 97):103,101,101,100,96 94
CSF £13.54 TOTE £5.30: £2.40, £1.70; EX 11.70.
Owner A J Ilsley **Bred** Newberry Stud Company **Trained** East Everleigh, Wilts

FOCUS
Just the six runners, but a reasonable enough novice event. They opted to race down the centre of the track this time, having stayed far side in the previous three races. A decent winning time for a race of its type. The race has been rated through the third.

NOTEBOOK
Tembanee(IRE) landed just an ordinary maiden on his debut at Chepstow, but he picked up a lighter penalty than his main market rivals as a result and followed up in determined style, showing much improved form in the process. His trainer thinks he still has some filling out to do and expects him to make a nice three-year-old. He is in the sales. (op 7-1)
Aqmaar ran a creditable enough race in defeat, but looks the type who will benefit from a bigger field and a more strongly-run race. (op 7-4 tchd 5-4)
Furnace(IRE) was thought good enough to contest the Solario Stakes at Sandown on his previous start, but he was well beaten that day and again failed to build on the promise he showed when winning on his debut at Newmarket. (op 11-8 tchd 2-1)
Christalini ◆ ran a cracking race, building on the form he showed in a couple of maidens at Newbury. There was no fluke about this effort and he must not be underestimated in future.
Little Miss Tara(IRE), the only filly in the field, was getting plenty of weight from her rivals but was still well held. She should find things easier in either maiden or nursery company. (op 10-1)

5625 POSHCHATEAUX.COM CLAIMING STKS 1m 1f 198y
4:00 (4:00) (Class 5) 3-4-Y-O **£3,562** (£1,059; £529; £264) **Stalls** High

Form RPR
-300 1 **Looker**[91] 2990 3-8-0 67 JamesDoyle(3) 13 66
(R M Beckett) *led 1f: styd chsng ldrs: led jst ins fnl 2f: hrd rdn whn strly chal thrght fnl f: hld on all out* **6/1**[3]
3013 2 shd **South O'The Border**[14] 5295 4-9-10 78 IanMongan 10 81
(T G Mills) *chsd ldrs: rdn and styd on fr 2f out: str chal ins fnl f: fin strly: jst failed* **13/8**[1]
5000 3 nk **Incidentally (IRE)**[12] 5346 3-9-4 78 (b[1]) RyanMoore 7 80
(R Hannon) *led after 1f:hdd 1m out:styd chsng ldrs: slt ld over 3f out: narrowly hdd ins fnl 2f:str chal ins last:jst failed* **13/2**
1403 4 6 **Optimus (USA)**[9] 5428 4-9-7 77 (t) FJohansson 5 66
(G A Butler) *bhd: rdn and hdwy over 1f out: styd on u.p ins last but nvr in contention* **4/1**[2]
0541 5 2 **Bridegroom**[8] 5445 4-9-5 49 AntonyProcter 9 60
(D R C Elsworth) *bhd: styd on fr 3f out: sn rdn: kpt on same pce fr over 1f out* **9/1**
-400 6 ¾ **Bamboo Banks (IRE)**[120] 2102 3-8-8 72 RichardHughes 3 54+
(J L Dunlop) *bhd: styd on fnl 2f: nvr in contention* **16/1**
0005 7 1 **Lanfredo**[26] 4981 3-8-7 44 ow1 (b) SteveDrowne 8 51
(D W P Arbuthnot) *chsd ldrs: rdn and hung rt 2f out: sn btn* **66/1**
1030 8 1 ¾ **Nefski Alexander (USA)**[42] 4490 3-9-4 72 (b[1]) EddieAhern 12 58
(P F I Cole) *chsd ldrs: rdn 3f out: wknd 2f out* **20/1**
2- 9 nk **Noah Jameel**[548] 764 4-9-1 FergusSweeney 1 49
(A G Newcombe) *a bhd: nvr in contention* **25/1**
-000 10 ½ **Expression Echo (IRE)**[71] 3610 4-8-7 39 ChrisCatlin 11 40
(A G Newcombe) *bhd: sme hdwy over 3f out: nvr in contention* **66/1**
066- 11 6 **Impulsive Madam**[338] 6077 3-8-1 44 FrankieMcDonald 4 28
(S Kirk) *bhd: rdn and sme hdwy 4f out: sn wknd* **80/1**
0000 12 22 **Grandos (IRE)**[33] 4755 4-8-9 43 (p) RichardKingscote(3) 2 —
(Karen George) *bhd most of way* **100/1**
2400 13 hd **Colonel Bilko (IRE)**[148] 1387 4-8-12 41 JohnEgan 6 —
(J J Bridger) *plld hrd: led after 2f: wnt wd bnd 7f out: hdd over 3f out: wknd qckly* **50/1**

2m 10.34s (1.88) **Going Correction** +0.20s/f (Good)
WFA 3 from 4yo 6lb 13 Ran SP% **117.4**
Speed ratings (Par 103):100,99,99,94,93 92,91,90,90,89 85,67,67
CSF £15.16 TOTE £7.80: £2.40, £1.40, £2.80; EX 22.30.The winner was claimed by J Gallagher for £10,000

Owner J H Richmond-Watson **Bred** Lawn Stud **Trained** Whitsbury, Hants

FOCUS

Not a bad claimer dominated by horses with the highest official marks. The fifth and seventh hold down the form. They all came down the centre of the track.

Lanfredo Official explanation: jockey said gelding hung right-handed

Grandos(IRE) Official explanation: jockey said gelding finished distressed

Colonel Bilko(IRE) Official explanation: jockey said gelding ran too free

5626 AVONBRIDGE AT WHITSBURY CONDITIONS STKS 6f

4:30 (4:31) (Class 2) 2-Y-O £10,282 (£3,078; £1,539; £770) **Stalls** Centre

Form RPR

3013 **1** **Dubai Builder**[11] 5373 2-8-12 104 JohnEgan 2 92
(J S Moore) *chsd ldrs tl rdn and outpcd 2f out: rallied u.p fr over 1f out: str run ins last to ld last stride* **10/11**[1]

0042 **2** *shd* **Resignation (IRE)**[8] 5455 2-9-1 94 RyanMoore 4 95
(R Hannon) *t.k.h: trckd ldrs: drvn to ld ins fnl f: kpt on: ct last stride* **3/1**[2]

521 **3** *½* **Blue Echo**[15] 5264 2-8-7 80 PhilipRobinson 1 85
(M A Jarvis) *led: rdn 2f out: hdd ins last: styd chalng tl no ex cl home* **9/2**[3]

3106 **4** *7* **Scented Present**[57] 4026 2-9-1 98 RichardHughes 5 72
(B J Meehan) *trckd ldrs: rdn over 2f out: wknd 1f out: eased whn no ch* **7/1**

1m 17.0s (2.02) **Going Correction** +0.20s/f (Good) 4 Ran SP% **108.1**

Speed ratings (Par 101):94,93,93,83

CSF £3.86 TOTE £1.90; EX 3.90.

Owner Uplands Acquisitions Limited **Bred** Theakston Stud **Trained** Upper Lambourn, Berks

FOCUS

Perhaps a slightly disappointing turnout numerically, but still a fascinating conditions event. The winner was 9lb of his Mill Reef Stakes run. They did not appear to go much of a pace until about halfway. The action took place more towards the near side this time, but not against the rail.

NOTEBOOK

Dubai Builder just prevailed in what was a cracking finish and is probably a little bit better than the bare form. Turned out 11 days after having a tough enough race when third in the Mill Reef Stakes, he was held up in a race run at just a steady early pace and was caught out when the sprint to the line began. He did well to recover and get up literally on the line and is progressing into a smart sort. He is entered in the Dewhurst, but is not sure to run as his connections feel he has had quite a hard race and they might put him away for next year. (op 8-11 tchd Evens)

Resignation(IRE), second to the winner's stablemate, Traffic Guard, in a similar event at Newmarket on his previous start, ran another fine race in defeat. His effort is all the more creditable considering he was conceding 3lb to Dubai Builder, although he was better placed than the winner given how the race was run. (op 7-2)

Blue Echo will have found this tougher than the maiden she won at Sandown last time, but acquitted herself with credit against two nice types. (tchd 4-1)

Scented Present, whose trainer won this race in 1996 with Tomba, has some decent form to his name but was well held this time. (op 10-1)

5627 WOOD BMW H'CAP 6f

5:00 (5:00) (Class 4) (0-85,88) 3-Y-O+ £6,477 (£1,927; £963; £481) **Stalls** Centre

Form RPR

0654 **1** **Hoh Hoh Hoh**[9] 5433 4-8-13 78 KerrinMcEvoy 14 93
(R J Price) *sn led: rdn and hdd ins fnl f: rallied u.p to ld again last stride* **14/1**

1221 **2** *shd* **Greek Renaissance (IRE)**[7] 5476 3-9-7 88 6ex RHills 13 103
(M P Tregoning) *wnt lft s: trckd ldrs: rdn to ld ins fnl f: hdd last stride* **4/7**[1]

3000 **3** *3½* **Gifted Gamble**[12] 5336 4-9-6 85 (b) RichardHughes 3 89+
(K A Ryan) *hld up in rr: hdwy over 1f out: fin wl but nt rch ldrs* **25/1**

0000 **4** *½* **Godfrey Street**[9] 5420 3-9-4 85 RyanMoore 7 88
(R Hannon) *chsd ldrs: rdn over 2f out: wknd ins last* **25/1**

0064 **5** *1¾* **Kingscross**[7] 5476 8-8-13 78 FergusSweeney 6 75
(M Blanshard) *bhd: hdwy over 1f out: kpt on ins last but n.d* **12/1**[3]

2040 **6** *shd* **Saviours Spirit**[7] 5476 5-8-12 77 IanMongan 15 74
(T G Mills) *chsd ldrs: rdn over 2f out: wknd ins last* **33/1**

5010 **7** *¾* **Blue Aura (IRE)**[19] 5148 3-8-7 77 (b) RichardKingscote(3) 5 72
(R Charlton) *in tch: rdn over 2f out: styd on same pce fr over 1f out* **25/1**

6300 **8** *½* **Fast Heart**[41] 4521 5-9-4 83 (t) StephenCarson 8 76
(D Nicholls) *rr: rdn 1/2-way: nvr gng pce to rch ldrs* **33/1**

0132 **9** *½* **Sant Elena**[21] 5107 3-8-13 80 SteveDrowne 12 72
(G Wragg) *bmpd s: in tch: rdn 1/2-way: wknd over 1f out* **7/1**[2]

3006 **10** *nk* **Auwitesweetheart**[39] 4598 4-8-9 77 JamesDoyle(3) 4 68
(B R Millman) *sn outpcd: rdn and sme prog fnl f* **50/1**

0600 **11** *¾* **Goodenough Mover**[7] 5476 10-8-12 77 ChrisCatlin 11 66
(Andrew Turnell) *chsd ldrs: rdn over 2f out: wknd over 1f out* **33/1**

1444 **12** *1¼* **Mimiteh (USA)**[49] 4242 3-8-9 76 EddieAhern 9 61
(R M Beckett) *in tch 4f* **50/1**

1405 **13** *¾* **Desert Dreamer (IRE)**[12] 5345 5-9-2 81 GeorgeBaker 1 64
(P R Chamings) *a towards rr* **16/1**

-200 **14** *¾* **Fisberry**[75] 3471 4-9-1 80 JimCrowley 2 61
(M S Saunders) *a outpcd* **50/1**

3023 **15** *11* **Jaad**[80] 3331 3-8-13 80 PatDobbs 16 28
(Christian Wroe, UAE) *chsd ldrs over 3f* **33/1**

1m 14.64s (-0.34) **Going Correction** +0.20s/f (Good)

WFA 3 from 4yo+ 2lb 15 Ran SP% **125.6**

Speed ratings (Par 105):110,109,105,104,102 102,101,100,99,99 98,96,95,94,80

CSF £21.33 CT £249.01 TOTE £19.40: £3.30, £1.20, £5.20; EX 49.20.

Owner Multi Lines 2 **Bred** D R Botterill **Trained** Ullingswick, H'fords

FOCUS

This looked a one-horse race beforehand, but it did not unfold as many might have expected. They tended to race down the middle. The winning time was decent. The winner was back to his three-year-old best and the second is worth another chance, with the third doing best of those from the rear.

5628 PLAY FREE & WIN MONEY AT 123RACING.COM H'CAP 1m 6f 15y

5:30 (5:30) (Class 5) (0-75,72) 3-Y-O+ £3,886 (£1,156; £577; £288) **Stalls** Far side

Form RPR

3443 **1** **Spinning Coin**[30] 4876 4-10-0 72 (p) RyanMoore 1 83
(J G Portman) *mde all: rdn and styd on gamely fnl 2f* **6/1**[2]

6402 **2** *3* **Acknowledgement**[15] 5276 4-9-8 66 (b) JohnEgan 2 73
(D R C Elsworth) *hld up in rr: hdwy on outside fr 3f out: styd on to chse wnr over 1f out: no imp* **6/1**[2]

4230 **3** *1½* **Love Always**[7] 5479 4-9-11 69 PatDobbs 7 74
(S Dow) *t.k.h: chsd ldrs: travelling wl 3f out: chsd wnr 2f out: sn rdn: wknd fnl f* **14/1**

3214 **4** *1¼* **La Via Ferrata (IRE)**[41] 4537 3-8-8 62 FergusSweeney 3 65
(A G Newcombe) *chsd ldrs tl outpcd 5f out: rdn over 3f out: styd on fnl 2f but nt rch ldrs* **11/1**

61-0 **5** *hd* **Gifted Musician**[158] 1132 4-9-12 70 EddieAhern 8 73
(J L Dunlop) *in tch: rdn 3f out: styd on same pce fnl 2f* **14/1**

3405 **6** *nk* **Haatmey**[12] 5338 4-9-6 64 (v) ChrisCatlin 11 66
(M R Channon) *bhd: hrd drvn 5f out: styd on fr over 1f out: gng on cl home but nvr in contention* **10/1**

4556 **7** *nk* **Impostor (IRE)**[23] 5069 3-9-4 72 (v[1]) OscarUrbina 6 74
(J R Fanshawe) *chsd ldrs: rdn over 3f out: sn one pce* **17/2**[3]

0/-3 **8** *1* **Cave Of The Giant (IRE)**[27] 4967 4-9-12 70 RobertMiles 14 71
(T D McCarthy) *chsd ldrs tl stdd rr 9f out: drvn and styd on again fnl 2f* **40/1**

4020 **9** *3* **Bob's Your Uncle**[35] 4702 3-8-9 66 NeilChalmers(3) 5 62
(J G Portman) *bhd: hdwy 5f out: sn rdn: wknd 2f out* **22/1**

0044 **10** *5* **Stolen Hours (USA)**[47] 4331 6-9-7 65 KerrinMcEvoy 4 54
(J Akehurst) *sn chsng wnr: rdn 4f out: wknd over 2f out* **9/2**[1]

30/0 **11** *9* **Resonance**[18] 5174 5-8-7 58 (b[1]) JosephWalsh(7) 13 35
(S Lycett) *bhd: hdwy 5f out: sn wknd* **66/1**

0420 **12** *8* **Himba**[32] 4800 3-8-6 60 JimCrowley 9 26
(Mrs A J Perrett) *in tch: rdn over 4f out: sn wknd* **18/1**

4361 **13** *1¾* **Kentucky Warbler (IRE)**[35] 4698 3-8-12 71 TravisBlock(5) 10 34
(H Morrison) *t.k.h: in tch tl rdn and wknd qckly over 3f out* **9/2**[1]

3m 8.38s (2.15) **Going Correction** +0.20s/f (Good)

WFA 3 from 4yo+ 10lb 13 Ran SP% **119.8**

Speed ratings (Par 103):101,99,98,97,97 97,97,96,94,92 86,82,81

CSF £41.40 CT £491.87 TOTE £7.60: £2.10, £1.80, £3.60; EX 37.90 Place 6 £100.92, Place 5 £18.18.

Owner Hockham Racing **Bred** Freedom Farm Stud **Trained** Compton, Berks

FOCUS

Just a modest staying handicap - as usual for this course and distance, started with a flip start - and they tended to stay far side in the straight. Quite straightforward to rate, the winner to this year's best.

Kentucky Warbler(IRE) Official explanation: jockey said filly ran too free

T/Plt: £234.20 to a £1 stake. Pool: £69,776.95. 217.45 winning tickets. T/Qpdt: £28.60 to a £1 stake. Pool: £3,615.60. 93.50 winning tickets. ST

5629 - 5630a (Foreign Racing) - See Raceform Interactive

5355 AYR (L-H)

Thursday, September 28

OFFICIAL GOING: Soft (heavy in places)

Wind: Breezy, half-across Weather: Overcast

5631 SOUTH WEST SOUND H'CAP 5f

2:35 (2:35) (Class 6) (0-58,58) 3-Y-O+ £2,866 (£846; £423) **Stalls** Low

Form RPR

4065 **1** **Compton Classic**[14] 5309 4-8-8 49 (p) LeeEnstone 7 59
(J S Goldie) *prom far side: effrt over 1f out: kpt on to ld cl home* **16/1**

401 **2** *hd* **How's She Cuttin' (IRE)**[40] 4611 3-8-7 49 PhillipMakin 3 58
(T D Barron) *led: hung rt u.p ins fnl f: hdd cl home* **5/1**[1]

5000 **3** *1* **Sharp Hat**[42] 4523 12-8-6 47 PaulQuinn 6 53
(D W Chapman) *towards rr far side: hdwy over 1f out: kpt on fnl f* **33/1**

5223 **4** *½* **Newkeylets**[3] 5577 3-8-12 54 (p) TomEaves 4 58
(I Semple) *trckd far side ldrs: effrt 2f out: one pce fnl f* **17/2**[3]

0001 **5** *½* **Trumpita**[38] 4656 3-8-4 46 DavidAllan 8 48
(T D Easterby) *trckd far side ldrs: rdn 1/2-way: one pce fnl f* **12/1**

0043 **6** *½* **Harrington Bates**[28] 4948 5-8-2 48 (v) MichaelJStainton(5) 18 49+
(R M Whitaker) *racd w one other stands side: rdn 1/2-way: kpt on fnl f: nt rch far side* **14/1**

4002 **7** *hd* **Flying Tackle**[31] 4872 8-8-7 48 (v) RoystonFfrench 15 48
(I W McInnes) *outpcd centre: hdwy 2f out: edgd lft and kpt on fnl f: no imp* **12/1**

1222 **8** *1¼* **Carcinetto (IRE)**[8] 5480 4-8-11 52 J-PGuillambert 1 48
(P D Evans) *prom far side: rdn 1/2-way: one pce over 1f out* **6/1**[2]

3000 **9** *hd* **Bodden Bay**[17] 5243 4-8-11 52 DanielTudhope 17 47+
(D Carroll) *racd w one other stands side: prom: drvn 1/2-way: one pce over 1f out* **25/1**

4000 **10** *1* **Hout Bay**[32] 4834 9-8-9 50 (b) JoeFanning 5 41
(D W Chapman) *outpcd far side: sme hdwy over 1f out: nvr rchd ldrs* **17/2**[3]

0200 **11** *3* **Oeuf A La Neige**[3] 5577 6-8-12 53 PatCosgrave 14 34
(Miss L A Perratt) *racd on outside of far side gp: hld up: rdn over 2f out: sn btn* **11/1**

304 **12** *shd* **Drum Dance (IRE)**[35] 4735 4-8-9 50 (p) KimTinkler 9 31
(N Tinkler) *racd on outside of far side gp: struggling fr over 2f out: sn btn* **16/1**

4120 **13** *1½* **Bond Becks (IRE)**[42] 4523 6-9-2 57 RobertWinston 12 33
(B Smart) *dwlt: sn prom towards far side: rdn and wknd fr 2f out* **14/1**

3000 **14** *1* **Desert Light (IRE)**[17] 5246 5-9-0 58 (v) PatrickMathers(3) 2 30
(D Shaw) *chsd ldrs 2f: sn lost pl* **66/1**

0423 **15** *3½* **Mister Incredible**[152] 1304 3-8-9 58 (p) TJHowell(7) 16 19
(V Smith) *prom centre tl wknd fr 2f out: eased whn no ch* **33/1**

000 **16** *6* **Oceanico Dot Com (IRE)**[23] 5078 4-8-5 46 DeanMcKeown 11 —
(A Berry) *racd centre: sn outpcd: nvr on terms* **33/1**

0010 **17** *10* **Orpenlina (IRE)**[31] 4886 3-8-5 47 TonyHamilton 13 —
(R A Fahey) *a bhd centre* **33/1**

63.22 secs (2.78) **Going Correction** +0.425s/f (Yiel)

WFA 3 from 4yo+ 1lb 17 Ran SP% **117.9**

Speed ratings (Par 101):94,93,92,91,90 89,89,87,87,85 80,80,78,76,70 61,45

CSF £84.88 CT £2632.53 TOTE £20.80: £4.80, £1.90, £8.30, £2.00; EX 160.40.

Owner J S Goldie **Bred** James Thom And Sons And Peter Orr **Trained** Uplawmoor, E Renfrews

FOCUS

A weak sprint, yet still fairly competitive for the class, and all bar two of the field raced towards the far side. The form looks straightforward and sound.

Carcinetto(IRE) Official explanation: jockey said filly was unsuited by the soft (heavy in places) ground

5632 WEST SOUND MANAGING DIRECTOR'S MEDIAN AUCTION MAIDEN STKS 6f

3:10 (3:10) (Class 5) 2-Y-O £3,368 (£1,002; £500; £250) **Stalls** Low

Form RPR

2 **1** **Doric Charm**[14] 5307 2-8-12 RoystonFfrench 3 75+
(B Smart) *mde all: pushed along 2f out: kpt on strly* **6/4**[1]

2 **2** *3* **Morristown Music (IRE)**[15] 5288 2-8-12 TomEaves 8 66
(J S Wainwright) *wnt rt s: trckd ldrs: effrt and chsd wnr over 1f out: kpt on fnl f: no imp* **7/1**[3]

3 *5* **Snow Dancer (IRE)** 2-8-12 PaulQuinn 4 51
(A Berry) *towards rr: hdwy 2f out: no imp fnl f* **50/1**

4 **4** 3/4 **Judge Neptune**[13] 5332 2-9-3 .... DanielTudhope 9 54
(J S Goldie) *wnt rt s: bhd tl hdwy fnl f: nvr nr to chal* **9/2**[2]
35 **5** 1 1/2 **The Grey Berry**[24] 5059 2-9-3 .... TonyHamilton 5 49
(C Grant) *pressed wnr to over 1f out: sn wknd* **14/1**
260 **6** 1 **Waiheke Island**[6] 5507 2-8-12 .... DaleGibson 7 41
(B Mactaggart) *in tch: rdn 1/2-way: btn over 1f out* **17/2**
7 16 **Caviar Heights (IRE)** 2-9-3 .... PatCosgrave 1 —
(Miss L A Perratt) *s.i.s: a bhd* **25/1**
0403 **8** 16 **Poniard (IRE)**[31] 4887 2-9-3 59........ RobertWinston 2 —
(D W Barker) *chsd ldrs to 1/2-way: sn wknd: eased whn no ch fnl f* **11/1**

1m 16.35s (2.68) **Going Correction** +0.425s/f (Yiel) 8 Ran SP% **102.0**
Speed ratings (Par 95):99,95,88,87,85 84,62,41
CSF £9.39 TOTE £1.90: £1.10, £1.60, £7.20; EX 6.40.
Owner Doric Charm Partnership **Bred** P A Mason **Trained** Hambleton, N Yorks
■ Inflagrantedelicto was withdrawn (10/1, vet's advice). R4 applies, deduct 5p in the £.

FOCUS
A modest maiden which saw the field trail home behind the ready winner. The form is difficult to assess but the runner-up is the best guide.

NOTEBOOK
Doric Charm, second on debut over course and distance a fortnight previously, duly went one better with a decisive success from the front and justified strong market support in the process. She is clearly going the right way, appreciates cut in the ground and is entitled to improve a little again for this outing. (op 7-4)
Morristown Music(IRE), runner-up on her debut at Beverley 15 days previously, stuck to her task without threatening the winner and ran another sound enough race. She saw out the extra furlong well enough, seemed to act on the much softer ground, and was well clear of the rest at the finish. (op 11-2)
Snow Dancer(IRE), bred to maker her mark at around this trip, ran green through the early parts and did enough to suggest she ought to be sharper with this experience under her belt. (op 33-1 tchd 66-1)
Judge Neptune struggled to go the early pace on this drop to six furlongs and, on this evidence, he really needs to return to a stiffer test. He will have to option of nurseries after his next outing. (op 4-1 tchd 5-1 in places)
Poniard(IRE) Official explanation: jockey said gelding lost its action

5633 WEST FM BREAKFAST SHOW NURSERY 1m
3:45 (3:45) (Class 4) (0-85,83) 2-Y-0 **£5,181** (£1,541; £770; £384) **Stalls** Low

Form RPR
654 **1** **Foxxy**[17] 5237 2-8-7 69 ow1........ NCallan 1 69
(K A Ryan) *prom: drvn and outpcd over 2f out: rallied over 1f out: styd on u.p to ld towards fin* **16/1**
5310 **2** shd **Lemon Silk (IRE)**[31] 4882 2-8-12 74........ DavidAllan 3 74
(T P Tate) *keen: hld up: effrt and rdn over 2f out: hdwy to ld 1f out: kpt on u.p: hdd towards fin* **15/2**
01 **3** 1 1/4 **Celtic Step**[23] 5088 2-9-3 79........ JoeFanning 4 76
(M Johnston) *led: rdn 2f out: hdd 1f out: kpt on same pce* **5/2**[2]
422 **4** 4 **Arch Of Titus (IRE)**[15] 5283 2-9-2 78........ SebSanders 2 66
(M L W Bell) *keen in rr: hdwy over 2f out: ch ent fnl f: sn no ex* **3/1**[3]
4222 **5** 8 **Princeton (IRE)**[12] 5359 2-9-7 83........ RobertWinston 7 54
(M R Channon) *prom: rdn over 2f out: hung lft: wknd over 1f out* **2/1**[1]
5024 **6** 2 1/2 **Keep Your Distance**[28] 4949 2-8-6 68........(t) PaulMulrennan 6 33
(K R Burke) *w ldr: rdn over 2f out: wkng whn n.m.r over 1f out* **25/1**
0660 **7** 41 **Bentley**[6] 5509 2-7-12 60 oh3........ DaleGibson 5 —
(D Shaw) *in tch 2f: sn wknd* **50/1**

1m 50.83s (7.34) **Going Correction** +0.90s/f (Soft) 7 Ran SP% **110.4**
Speed ratings (Par 97):99,98,97,93,85 83,42
CSF £117.72 TOTE £12.90: £4.50, £3.30; EX 116.00.
Owner The C H F Partnership **Bred** The C H F Partnership **Trained** Hambleton, N Yorks

FOCUS
A fair little nursery which was run at a solid pace. The first three came clear and the form is rated positively through the runner-up.

NOTEBOOK
Foxxy proved game under maximum pressure and narrowly got off the mark on this nursery bow. The step up to this longer trip was clearly much to her liking, and the soft ground played to her strengths, but she will have to improve again in order to defy a likely future weight rise. (op 11-1)
Lemon Silk(IRE) proved his effectiveness for an easy surface, and was only just denied, yet ultimately paid for refusing to settle through the early stages. He was still nicely clear of the remainder at the finish. (op 8-1)
Celtic Step, off the mark at the second attempt at Leicester 23 days previously, failed to see out the extra furlong under an aggressive ride on the softer ground. He is not one to write off on the back of this display and will do better when encountering a sound surface again in due course. (op 9-4 tchd 11-4 in places)
Arch Of Titus(IRE), making his nursery debut, spoilt his chances by pulling too hard early on and never figured. He is in danger of going the wrong way. (tchd 10-3)
Princeton(IRE) dropped out disappointingly when push came to shove and ran well below his recent level. He has it to prove now, but probably needs slightly better ground in any case. Official explanation: jockey said colt was unsuited by the soft (heavy in places) ground (op 11-4)

5634 WEST SOUND 25TH BIRTHDAY STKS (H'CAP) 1m 5f 13y
4:20 (4:20) (Class 3) (0-90,85) 3-Y-0+ **£9,715** (£2,890; £1,444; £721) **Stalls** Low

Form RPR
1 **Heart Of Svetlana (IRE)**[89] 3106 3-8-11 82........ JoeFanning 3 88+
(M Johnston) *mde all: hrd pressed over 2f out: hld on gamely fnl f* **5/2**[2]
2364 **2** hd **Reluctant Suitor**[5] 5531 4-8-9 71 oh5........(p) DanielTudhope 5 77
(J S Goldie) *trckd ldrs: chal over 2f out: rdn and edgd lft over 1f out: kpt on fnl f: jst hld* **7/2**[3]
5240 **3** 7 **Charlotte Vale**[96] 2850 5-8-10 72........ PaulMulrennan 1 68
(Micky Hammond) *hld up in tch: stdy hdwy over 3f out: rdn and outpcd over 2f out* **4/1**
6224 **4** 9 **Velvet Heights (IRE)**[13] 5351 4-9-8 84........ NCallan 2 68
(J L Dunlop) *cl up tl rdn and wknd over 2f out* **7/4**[1]

3m 12.14s (15.53) **Going Correction** +0.90s/f (Soft)
WFA 3 from 4yo+ 9lb 4 Ran SP% **107.2**
Speed ratings (Par 107):88,87,83,78
CSF £10.70 TOTE £3.80; EX 8.60.
Owner Steve Macdonald **Bred** Mrs Karen Daley **Trained** Middleham Moor, N Yorks

FOCUS
A fair handicap, but a slightly disappointing turn out for the prizemoney. The first two came well clear with the second the best guide to the level.

NOTEBOOK
Heart Of Svetlana(IRE) ◆ showed a decent attitude to repel the runner-up and record a winning British debut for her new stable. She loves this sort of ground, and saw out the longer trip really well, so it ought to give her connections plenty of further options now they can be confident she stays. (tchd 11-4 in places)
Reluctant Suitor, equpiied with first-time cheekpieces and 5lb out of the handicap, held every chance yet was just worried out of it inside the final 100 yards. This was a respectable effort at the weights, and he ideally needs better ground, but he still does not really convince when put under maximum pressure. (op 4-1 tchd 9-2)
Charlotte Vale was left behind when the race became serious and shaped as though this return from a 96-day break was needed. She can be expected to get a little closer next time out. (op 9-2 tchd 5-1 in places)
Velvet Heights(IRE) proved very disappointing and is now becoming very expensive to follow. He has shown form on a similar surface in the past, so can have no excuses on that front. Official explanation: jockey said colt was unsuited by the soft (heavy in places) ground (op 6-4)

5635 WEST SOUND CASH FOR KIDS H'CAP 6f
4:55 (4:55) (Class 5) (0-70,70) 3-Y-0+ **£3,238** (£963; £481; £240) **Stalls** Low

Form RPR
3650 **1** **Word Perfect**[21] 5136 4-8-12 60........(b[1]) DaleGibson 17 74
(M W Easterby) *racd w two others on stands side: mde all: rdn 2f out: styd on strly to go clr ins fnl f* **16/1**
3300 **2** 2 1/2 **Viewforth**[23] 5081 8-8-13 61........(b) TomEaves 11 67
(I Semple) *cl up far side: led that gp over 1f out: kpt on fnl f: nt rch stands side wnr* **25/1**
0400 **3** nk **Dispol Katie**[14] 5313 5-9-1 63........ PhillipMakin 5 68
(T D Barron) *cl up far side: ev ch that gp over 1f out: kpt on ins fnl f* **20/1**
0616 **4** 1 1/4 **Brigadore**[3] 5577 7-9-4 66........ SebSanders 9 67
(J G Given) *dwlt: hld up far side: hdwy over 1f out: kpt on fnl f: nrst fin* **17/2**
0160 **5** nk **The London Gang**[56] 4067 3-8-13 63........(v) NCallan 1 63
(P D Evans) *towards rr far side: drvn 1/2-way: no imp tl styd on wl fnl f: nrst fin* **16/1**
3024 **6** hd **Dorn Dancer (IRE)**[14] 5309 4-9-2 64........ RobertWinston 2 64
(D W Barker) *hld up far side: stdy hdwy over 2f out: rdn over 1f out: kpt on same pce fnl f* **6/1**[1]
4032 **7** 2 **Briery Lane (IRE)**[35] 4735 5-8-8 61........(p) AndrewElliott[(5)] 18 55
(Mrs K Walton) *racd w two others stands side: cl up tl outpcd over 1f out* **8/1**[3]
5003 **8** 3/4 **Apex**[24] 5062 5-8-6 54........ KimTinkler 16 46
(N Tinkler) *racd w two others stands side: cl up tl rdn and no ex over 1f out* **8/1**[3]
025 **9** hd **High Voltage**[21] 5136 5-9-6 68........(t) PatCosgrave 3 59
(K R Burke) *led far side to over 1f out: wknd ins fnl f* **12/1**
0562 **10** shd **Zhitomir**[14] 5313 8-9-2 64........ PaulMulrennan 12 55
(M Dods) *w far side ldr tl wknd over 1f out* **14/1**
0040 **11** 1 1/2 **Cool Sands (IRE)**[17] 5246 4-8-4 55........(v) PatrickMathers[(3)] 4 41
(D Shaw) *hld up far side: effrt over 2f out: no imp whn hmpd 1f out* **50/1**
2000 **12** 1/2 **Hits Only Cash**[34] 4771 4-9-2 64........ DeanMcKeown 7 49
(J Pearce) *bhd and sn rdn along far side: nvr on terms* **14/1**
0320 **13** 1/2 **Bond Playboy**[77] 3459 6-8-13 61........(p) GylesParkin 10 44
(G R Oldroyd) *in tch far side: drvn 1/2-way: btn over 1f out* **50/1**
6003 **14** 6 **Dancing Deano (IRE)**[9] 5444 4-8-6 59........(v) MichaelJStainton[(5)] 14 24
(R M Whitaker) *chsd ldrs: drvn 1/2-way: wknd over 1f out* **12/1**
2400 **15** 1 1/4 **Linda Green**[19] 5167 5-9-6 68........ JoeFanning 13 29
(M R Channon) *racd on outside of far side gp: hld up: pushed along 1/2-way: nvr on terms* **14/1**
4060 **16** 1 **Rainbow Bay**[11] 5401 3-9-0 69........(v) JamieMoriarty[(5)] 8 27
(R A Fahey) *bhd far side: rdn 1/2-way: nvr on terms* **33/1**
0501 **17** 1 **George The Best (IRE)**[3] 5577 5-8-8 59 6ex........ GregFairley[(3)] 15 14
(Micky Hammond) *prom on outside of far side gp tl wknd fr 2f out* **7/1**[2]

1m 15.65s (1.98) **Going Correction** +0.425s/f (Yiel)
WFA 3 from 4yo+ 2lb 17 Ran SP% **122.2**
Speed ratings (Par 103):103,99,99,97,97 96,94,93,93,92 90,90,89,81,79 78,77
CSF £383.33 CT £8014.65 TOTE £21.40: £3.40, £5.20, £4.10, £3.80; EX 494.50.
Owner Mrs Jean Turpin **Bred** Mrs Jean Turpin **Trained** Sheriff Hutton, N Yorks
■ Stewards' Enquiry : Paul Mulrennan caution: careless riding
Andrew Elliott one-day ban: failed to keep straight from the stalls (Oct 11)

FOCUS
A modest sprint that saw the main bulk of the field go to the far side, but the winner made all on the stands'-side rail. The race is rated around the second and fourth.

5636 WEST SOUND SUPERSCOREBOARD H'CAP 7f 50y
5:25 (5:26) (Class 6) (0-60,60) 3-Y-0+ **£2,866** (£846; £423) **Stalls** Low

Form RPR
400 **1** **Scotland The Brave**[32] 4831 6-9-7 60........(v) SebSanders 6 73
(J D Bethell) *pressed ldr: led 3f out: drvn out fnl f* **11/2**[2]
0006 **2** 2 **Hansomelle (IRE)**[3] 5579 4-8-8 50........ GregFairley[(3)] 7 58
(B Mactaggart) *towards rr: hdwy over 2f out: chsd wnr over 1f out: kpt on fnl f: no imp* **6/1**[3]
5506 **3** 3 1/2 **Queen's Echo**[14] 5316 5-9-2 55........(t) PhillipMakin 10 54
(M Dods) *hld up in tch: effrt over 2f out: kpt on fnl f: no imp* **6/1**[3]
1133 **4** 3 **Tequila Sheila (IRE)**[27] 4983 4-8-8 52........ AndrewElliott[(5)] 11 44
(K R Burke) *cl up: effrt over 2f out: edgd lft and no ex over 1f out* **11/2**[2]
6404 **5** 3 **Attacca**[35] 4729 5-8-13 52........ NCallan 5 36
(J R Weymes) *prom: effrt over 2f out: no ex whn hmpd over 1f out* **14/1**
1230 **6** 5 **Writ (IRE)**[14] 5311 4-9-0 53........ TomEaves 1 25
(I Semple) *in tch: rdn 3f out: btn over 1f out* **20/1**
-022 **7** 9 **Mystical Ayr (IRE)**[119] 2165 4-9-0 58........ JamieMoriarty[(5)] 13 7
(Miss L A Perratt) *bhd: rdn 1/2-way: kpt on fnl f: n.d* **5/1**[1]
-000 **8** 3 1/2 **Penny Whisper (IRE)**[121] 2109 3-9-0 56........ RoystonFfrench 4 —
(I W McInnes) *keen: led to 3f out: sn rdn and wknd* **33/1**
0650 **9** shd **The City Kid (IRE)**[26] 3995 3-9-4 60........(v) J-PGuillambert 3 —
(P D Evans) *chsd ldrs: lost pl over 3f out: n.d after* **50/1**
0305 **10** 1 **Quantica (IRE)**[17] 5243 7-8-11 50........ KimTinkler 9 —
(N Tinkler) *plld hrd in midfield on outside: rdn over 2f out: sn btn* **15/2**
0066 **11** nk **Kew The Music**[9] 5450 6-9-2 55........ JoeFanning 8 —
(M R Channon) *missed break: nvr on terms* **14/1**
0004 **12** 3/4 **Quadrophenia**[36] 4710 3-8-11 53........ JamieMackay 14 —
(J G Given) *bhd: rdn 1/2-way: nvr on terms* **33/1**
0630 **13** 1 1/2 **Red Vixen (IRE)**[48] 4329 3-8-2 51........ KirstyMilczarek[(7)] 2 —
(C N Allen) *towards rr on ins: rdn over 3f out: sn btn* **25/1**
0356 **14** 4 **Silk Merchant (IRE)**[73] 3582 3-9-4 60........ RobertWinston 12 —
(J Howard Johnson) *bhd: rdn 1/2-way: sn struggling* **50/1**

1m 37.97s (5.25) **Going Correction** +0.90s/f (Soft)
WFA 3 from 4yo+ 3lb 14 Ran SP% **119.5**
Speed ratings (Par 101):106,103,99,96,92 87,76,72,72,71 71,70,68,64
CSF £35.38 CT £206.79 TOTE £6.90: £2.50, £2.90, £2.40; EX 53.70.
Owner Robert Gibbons **Bred** R F Gibbons **Trained** Middleham Moor, N Yorks
■ Stewards' Enquiry : Andrew Elliott two-day ban: careless riding (Oct 9-10)

FOCUS
A moderate handicap and the field came home fairly strung out, so the form is best assessed around the principals.
Quantica(IRE) Official explanation: jockey said gelding hung right-handed into straight

5637 WORLD FAMOUS WEST SOUND BURNS SUPPER H'CAP — 1m
5:55 (5:55) (Class 6) (0-60,60) 3-Y-O — **£2,866** (£846; £423) **Stalls** Low

Form — RPR
4041 **1** **Apache Nation (IRE)**[14] 5312 3-9-4 **60** .... RoystonFfrench 2 — 69
(M Dods) *in tch on ins: hdwy to ld over 2f out: hrd pressed ins fnl f: hld on wl* **9/2**[1]
0602 **2** ¾ **Petross**[14] 5312 3-8-9 **56** .... MichaelJStainton(5) 5 — 63
(R M Whitaker) *plld hrd: chsd ldrs: effrt over 1f out: chal ins fnl f: hld towards fin* **7/1**[3]
0400 **3** 2½ **Beautiful Summer (IRE)**[43] 4470 3-8-10 **57** .... JamieMoriarty(5) 4 — 59
(R A Fahey) *keen in midfield: effrt over 2f out: hung lft: rallied over 1f out: kpt on fnl f: nt rch first two* **33/1**
0520 **4** 5 **Taranis**[35] 4728 3-8-10 **52** .... SebSanders 13 — 44
(Sir Mark Prescott) *midfield: outpcd 1/2-way: rallied u.p over 1f out: nrst fin* **9/2**[1]
0333 **5** 2½ **Flashing Floozie**[28] 4944 3-8-7 **49** .... JamieMackay 1 — 36
(J G Given) *cl up: effrt and ev ch over 2f out: wknd over 1f out* **9/1**
U100 **6** nk **Wizby**[76] 3472 3-8-12 **54** .... PatCosgrave 8 — 40
(P D Evans) *midfield: outpcd over 2f out: rallied appr fnl f: nvr rchd ldrs* **14/1**
3056 **7** 5 **Myths And Verses**[14] 5312 3-9-1 **57** .... NCallan 3 — 33
(K A Ryan) *keen: hld up ins: hdwy and prom over 2f out: wknd over 1f out* **12/1**
0046 **8** hd **Rondo**[10] 5418 3-9-1 **57** .... PhillipMakin 12 — 33
(T D Barron) *racd wd: hld up: rdn over 2f out: sn btn* **12/1**
0026 **9** 22 **Fadansil**[36] 4697 3-8-10 **52** .... TonyHamilton 7 — —
(J Wade) *bhd: struggling over 3f out: sn btn* **80/1**
0400 **10** 1½ **Bond Angel Eyes**[12] 5370 3-8-8 **50** .... GylesParkin 9 — —
(G R Oldroyd) *led to over 2f out: sn btn* **100/1**
0600 **11** 3½ **Baileys Polka**[32] 4847 3-8-8 **50** ....(b) J-PGuillambert 14 — —
(J G Given) *racd wd: bhd: rdn and wd st: sn btn* **20/1**
0516 **12** 1½ **Grand Palace (IRE)**[110] 2466 3-8-9 **54** .... PatrickMathers(3) 11 — —
(D Shaw) *stdd s: rdn in rr 1/2-way: nvr on terms* **20/1**
426 **13** 38 **Our Mary (IRE)**[35] 4728 3-8-7 **49** ....(t) TomEaves 6 — —
(Robert Gray) *chsd ldrs to 3f out: sn wknd* **20/1**
3202 **14** 54 **Never Say Deya**[3] 5571 3-8-8 **50** .... RobertWinston 10 — —
(M R Channon) *prom tl wknd 3f out* **11/2**[2]

1m 51.1s (7.61) **Going Correction** +0.90s/f (Soft) — **14** Ran SP% **115.8**
Speed ratings (Par 99):97,96,93,88,86 85,80,80,58,57 53,52,14,—
CSF £31.06 CT £684.59 TOTE £4.10: £2.00, £2.70, £14.50; EX 42.70 Place 6 £1,989.59, Place 5 £644.74.
Owner Doug Graham **Bred** Crone Stud Farms Ltd **Trained** Denton, Co Durham

FOCUS
A moderate handicap that was run at an average pace. The form looks straightforward but has not been rated positively.
Myths And Verses Official explanation: jockey said filly hung right-handed in straight
Never Say Deya Official explanation: jockey said filly lost its action in straight
T/Plt: £4,011.20 to a £1 stake. Pool: £60,992.50. 11.10 winning tickets. T/Qpdt: £566.40 to a £1 stake. Pool: £3,138.40. 4.10 winning tickets. RY

5454 NEWMARKET (ROWLEY) (R-H)
Thursday, September 28

OFFICIAL GOING: Good
Wind: Light, half-behind Weather: Overcast

5638 PRESTIGE E B F MAIDEN FILLIES' STKS — 6f
2:20 (2:22) (Class 4) 2-Y-O — **£6,477** (£1,927; £963; £481) **Stalls** Low

Form — RPR
1 **Dream Scheme** 2-9-0 .... JamieSpencer 4 — 85+
(E A L Dunlop) *w'like: scope: hld up in tch: led on bit 1f out: nt extended* **3/1**[1]
2 3½ **Awwal Malika (USA)** 2-9-0 .... KerrinMcEvoy 10 — 66
(C E Brittain) *gd sort: leggy: hld up: hdwy over 1f out: r.o: no ch w wnr* **15/2**
00 **3** 1 **Barley Moon**[18] 5209 2-9-0 .... MickyFenton 2 — 63
(T Keddy) *led: rdn and hdd 1f out: no ex* **50/1**
4 1 **Arabian Treasure (USA)** 2-9-0 .... RyanMoore 9 — 60+
(Sir Michael Stoute) *gd sort: bit bkwd: b.hind: trckd ldrs: outpcd 1/2-way: hdwy over 1f out: styd on same pce ins fnl f* **3/1**[1]
0 **5** ½ **Etoile D'Or (IRE)**[25] 5043 2-9-0 .... TPQueally 11 — 64+
(M H Tompkins) *s.i.s: hld up: nt clr run over 1f out: r.o: nrst fin* **14/1**
6 1¼ **Tasleem (IRE)** 2-9-0 .... RHills 7 — 54
(B W Hills) *small: lt-f: s.i.s: hld up: plld hrd: hung rt thrght: effrt over 1f out: nt run on* **7/1**[3]
7 ¾ **Danehill Kikin (IRE)** 2-9-0 .... MichaelHills 1 — 52
(B W Hills) *gd sort: chsd ldr: rdn and ev ch over 1f out: sn wknd* **6/1**[2]
8 3½ **Noddledoddle (IRE)** 2-9-0 ....(t) OscarUrbina 5 — 42
(J Ryan) *leggy: scope: hld up: n.d* **33/1**
9 ¾ **Go Dancing** 2-9-0 .... AdrianMcCarthy 3 — 39
(P W Chapple-Hyam) *neat: chsd ldrs: rdn over 2f out: wknd over 1f out* **9/1**
0 **10** ½ **Meerlust**[34] 4753 2-9-0 ....(v[1]) ChrisCatlin 8 — 38
(E F Vaughan) *hld up: rdn over 2f out: sn wknd* **66/1**

1m 14.69s (1.59) **Going Correction** +0.15s/f (Good) — **10** Ran SP% **111.6**
Speed ratings (Par 94):95,90,89,87,87 85,84,79,78,78
CSF £24.87 TOTE £4.00: £1.40, £3.50, £6.30; EX 33.80.
Owner Gainsborough Stud **Bred** Gainsborough Stud Management Ltd **Trained** Newmarket, Suffolk

FOCUS
The proximity of Barley Moon and Etoile D'Or, who had both previously shown just moderate form, suggests this was a weak maiden by Newmarket's standards. They all stayed towards the near-side rail.

NOTEBOOK
Dream Scheme, a sister to Magic Mission, a high-class, prolific winner at around a mile, out of a winner at the same trip, made an impressive racecourse debut. Settled just off the leaders, she moved into contention going easily and did not have to be seriously asked to draw clear. It is hard to knock such a performance, but it would be probably be unwise to get carried away at this stage, as the likes of Barley Moon and Etoile D'Or, who had previously shown just moderate form, finished a bit close for comfort. Judging by the ease of her victory, it also looked as though she had done plenty of work and a few of those in behind may be open to more improvement. Still, she did everything that was asked of her and deserves to be tested in a higher grade; that should tell us more. (op 11-4)
Awwal Malika(USA), a $125,000 purchase, out of a smart French/US miler, never threatened the winner but kept on nicely without being given an unnecessarily hard time. It remains to be seen what this form is worth, but she is open to plenty of improvement. (op 9-1)
Barley Moon had shown very limited ability on her two previous starts, but her half-sister Meditation is at her best when forcing the pace and the change to much more positive tactics brought about an improved effort. She was surrounded by newcomers, so it is difficult at this stage to get a handle on exactly what she achieved, but she is now qualified for a handicap and could do reasonably in that sphere.
Arabian Treasure(USA), a $270,000 sister to Barcardero, a dual winner at up to 12 furlongs, came under pressure a little way out and looked in need of this experience. She should be a lot sharper next time. (op 11-4 tchd 7-2)
Etoile D'Or(IRE), well beaten on her debut over this trip on the turf at Lingfield, stepped up on that effort and would have been slightly closer with a clearer run. She looks a fair handicap prospect and needs one more run for an official mark. (op 16-1)
Tasleem(IRE), a sister to Judhoor, a useful dual six-furlong winner at two and three, gave her rider a torrid time, pulling incredibly hard early and carrying her head on one side in the direction of the stands'-side rail for pretty much the entire race. She must have a fair amount of ability to manage to finish so close, but cannot be backed until she proves she can settle and behave better in a race.
Official explanation: jockey said filly hung right-handed throughout (op 9-2)
Danehill Kikin(IRE), out of a nine-furlong juvenile winner who was later high-class over middle-distances, struggled when the pace was increased and looks in need of further. (op 9-1)

5639 "WINTER WONDERLAND AT NEWMARKET RACECOURSES" H'CAP — 1m
2:55 (2:55) (Class 3) (0-95,94) 3-Y-O+
£8,724 (£2,612; £1,306; £653; £326; £163) **Stalls** Low

Form — RPR
1020 **1** **Plum Pudding (IRE)**[12] 5376 3-9-2 **92** .... RyanMoore 6 — 102
(R Hannon) *lw: racd stands' side: chsd ldr tl led over 2f out: drvn out* **8/1**[3]
0010 **2** ¾ **Rain Stops Play (IRE)**[11] 5406 4-8-8 **80** .... ChrisCatlin 15 — 88+
(M Quinn) *racd alone far side: w ldrs: rdn over 1f out: r.o* **33/1**
1105 **3** ¾ **Fajr (IRE)**[10] 5428 4-8-10 **82** .... JimmyQuinn 11 — 88+
(Miss Gay Kelleway) *b: b.hind: racd stands' side: hld up: nt clr run over 1f out: r.o* **16/1**
1200 **4** shd **Motaraqeb**[92] 2988 3-8-9 **85** .... RHills 17 — 91
(Sir Michael Stoute) *lw: s.i.s: hld up: hdwy over 1f out: sn rdn and hung lft: styd on* **16/1**
-124 **5** 2 **Tommy Toogood (IRE)**[10] 5428 3-8-6 **82** .... MichaelHills 9 — 83
(B W Hills) *racd stands' side: chsd ldrs: rdn over 2f out: no ex fnl f* **10/1**
0023 **6** 1 **Leningrad (IRE)**[49] 4298 3-9-4 **94** .... JamieSpencer 13 — 93
(M L W Bell) *racd stands' side: hld up: hdwy over 1f out: styd on same pce fnl f* **11/2**[1]
022 **7** ½ **South Cape**[5] 5520 3-9-0 **90** .... TonyCulhane 4 — 88
(M R Channon) *racd stands' side: trckd ldrs: rdn over 1f out: wknd ins fnl f* **13/2**[2]
0011 **8** shd **Killena Boy (IRE)**[26] 5019 4-8-13 **85** .... PaulDoe 16 — 83
(W Jarvis) *racd stands' side: trckd ldrs: plld hrd: rdn over 2f out: wknd fnl f* **10/1**
1260 **9** ½ **Habshan (USA)**[15] 5301 6-8-12 **84** .... TedDurcan 10 — 81
(C F Wall) *racd stands' side: chsd ldrs: rdn over 2f out: wknd fnl f* **40/1**
-000 **10** ¾ **Johnny Jumpup (IRE)**[118] 2200 4-9-8 **94** .... GeorgeBaker 7 — 89
(R M Beckett) *racd stands' side: hld up: nt clr run over 1f out: nvr trbld ldrs* **33/1**
0-60 **11** shd **Ettrick Water**[110] 2435 7-9-1 **87** ....(v) NickyMackay 12 — 82
(L M Cumani) *led stands' side over 5f: sn rdn: wknd fnl f* **25/1**
5461 **12** hd **Wigwam Willie (IRE)**[13] 5337 4-8-8 **83** ....(p) AndrewMullen(3) 3 — 77
(K A Ryan) *racd stands' side: hld up in tch: rdn over 3f out: wknd over 1f out* **10/1**
1124 **13** nk **Moody Tunes**[97] 2809 3-8-4 **80** .... RichardMullen 8 — 74
(K R Burke) *lw: racd stands' side: prom: rdn over 2f out: wknd over 1f out* **25/1**
610- **14** ½ **Able Baker Charlie (IRE)**[306] 4476 7-9-7 **93** .... OscarUrbina 1 — 85
(J R Fanshawe) *racd stands' side: chsd ldrs: rdn over 2f out: sn wknd* **33/1**
2103 **15** nk **Davenport (IRE)**[92] 2983 4-8-4 **83** ow1 .... JamesMillman(7) 2 — 75
(B R Millman) *s.i.s: racd stands' side: a in rr* **12/1**
2021 **16** 1¼ **Cross The Line (IRE)**[10] 5428 4-8-9 **81** 6ex .... RichardHughes 18 — 70
(A P Jarvis) *racd stands' side: mid-div: rdn over 3f out: wknd wl over 1f out* **11/1**
-300 **17** 9 **Giganticus (USA)**[76] 3491 3-9-2 **92** .... MartinDwyer 5 — 60
(B W Hills) *racd stands' side: hld up in tch: lost pl 1/2-way: wknd over 2f out* **16/1**

1m 39.07s (-0.30) **Going Correction** +0.15s/f (Good)
WFA 3 from 4yo+ 4lb — **17** Ran SP% **119.7**
Speed ratings (Par 107):107,106,105,105,103 102,101,101,101,100 100,100,99,99,99 97,88
CSF £263.95 CT £4204.40 TOTE £9.20: £2.20, £7.00, £4.40, £4.20; EX 233.50.
Owner Hyde Sporting Promotions Limited **Bred** Tom Deane **Trained** East Everleigh, Wilts

FOCUS
Quite a decent handicap rated around the third and fourth. Rain Stops Play tried his luck racing alone on the far side of the track and ran a terrific race to take second. The remainder stayed towards the near side.

NOTEBOOK
Plum Pudding(IRE) failed to give his running when favourite for a decent conditions event over nine furlongs at Newbury on his previous start but, returned to handicap company and dropped back a furlong in trip, he came right back to his best. Given a really positive ride, he sustained his challenge in likeable fashion to hold off all the challengers on the near side, as well as Rain Stops Play's gallant effort on the far side, defying 12lb higher mark than when winning here earlier in the season in the process. A tough sort, he should have plenty more to offer and looks a particularly nice prospect for some of the big handicaps at around a mile next season.
Rain Stops Play(IRE) attempted to repeat the trick of his course and distance success back in May, when he raced alone far side of the track, and was just denied. The stalls were on the near side, so this was a terrific effort considering the ground he would have lost going far side.
Fajr(IRE), switched from the sand for just his fourth start on turf, was only 2lb higher than when winning over course and distance earlier in the season and ran another fine race. He might have been even closer with a clearer run and, clearly versatile regards conditions, he is one to respect in this sort of company.

The Form Book, Raceform Ltd, Compton, RG20 6NL

Motaraqeb ◆, returned to form off the back of a three-month break and showed enough to suggest he could be ready to fulfil earlier potential. He might benefit from a step up to ten furlongs. (op 14-1)
Tommy Toogood(IRE) ran well but finished just a little way off the front four. He is lightly raced and could be open to some improvement. (op 9-1)
Leningrad(IRE), at one time considered a Derby horse, stayed on without ever really looking likely to get there. He might be capable of better when returned to further, but has never really appealed as a horse to be following. Official explanation: jockey said colt ran too free (tchd 5-1)
South Cape, 2lb lower than in future, could not match the form of his recent Ascot second. (op 6-1 tchd 7-1 and 8-1 in a place)
Killena Boy(IRE), chasing the hat-trick off a mark 3lb higher than when winning a valuable handicap at Kempton on his previous start, raced keenly and was not at his best. (op 11-1)
Johnny Jumpup(IRE) ◆, returning from a 118-day break, would have been closer with a better run and could be one to keep in mind for a similar race when there is a bit of cut in the ground this autumn. Official explanation: jockey said gelding was denied a clear run
Able Baker Charlie(IRE) Official explanation: jockey said gelding was denied a clear run
Giganticus(USA) Official explanation: jockey said colt had a breathing problem

5640 NGK SPARK PLUGS MAIDEN STKS (C&G) 1m
3:30 (3:39) (Class 4) 2-Y-O **£6,477** (£1,927; £963; £481) **Stalls** Low

Form RPR
2 **1** **Asperity (USA)**[15] 5292 2-9-0 ...... JimmyFortune 14 96+
(J H M Gosden) *lw: racd alone: mde all: styd on wl* **8/11**[1]
2 5 **Life (IRE)** 2-9-0 ...... LDettori 1 81+
(J Noseda) *cmpt: scope: a.p: chsd wnr 2f out: styd on same pce fnl f* **9/2**[2]
0 **3** 1 **Palamoun**[13] 5343 2-9-0 ...... MichaelHills 11 79
(B W Hills) *lw: hld up: hdwy over 2f out: rdn over 1f out: styd on same pce* **8/1**[3]
4 3 **Salaasa (USA)** 2-9-0 ...... RHills 9 73
(M Johnston) *chsd ldrs: rdn over 2f out: wknd over 1f out* **16/1**
0 **5** ¾ **Sunley Peace**[9] 5460 2-9-0 ...... AntonyProcter 15 71
(D R C Elsworth) *s.i.s: sn mid-div: outpcd 3f out: n.d after* **33/1**
0 **6** 3 **Anatolian Prince**[23] 5088 2-9-0 ...... TedDurcan 10 64
(J M P Eustace) *bkwd: chsd wnr over 5f: wknd over 1f out* **50/1**
7 ½ **Hurricane Thomas (IRE)** 2-9-0 ...... KDarley 2 63
(M Johnston) *leggy: scope: trckd ldrs: racd keenly: wknd over 1f out* **25/1**
00 **8** 2 **Sonara (IRE)**[13] 5332 2-9-0 ...... TPQueally 3 59
(M H Tompkins) *hld up: hdwy 3f out: sn rdn and wknd* **100/1**
9 ½ **Arctic Wings (IRE)** 2-9-0 ...... MartinDwyer 6 58
(W R Muir) *w'like: s.s: nvr nrr* **50/1**
0 **10** 1 **River Deuce**[41] 4572 2-8-11 ...... SaleemGolam(3) 5 56
(M H Tompkins) *chsd ldrs: rdn over 3f out: wknd over 2f out* **66/1**
00 **11** nk **Abbotts Account (USA)**[12] 5379 2-9-0 ...... JimCrowley 7 55
(Mrs A J Perrett) *hld up: effrt over 3f out: wknd over 2f out* **40/1**
0 **12** 3 **Apache Chant (USA)**[36] 4705 2-9-0 ......(b[1]) JTate 13 48
(E A L Dunlop) *lw: hld up: n.d* **100/1**
13 3½ **Nassmaan (IRE)** 2-9-0 ...... AdrianMcCarthy 16 41
(P W Chapple-Hyam) *w'like: scope: hld up: a in rr* **50/1**
14 5 **Calculating (IRE)** 2-9-0 ......(t) RobertHavlin 8 30
(J H M Gosden) *w'like: scope bit bkwd: s.s: a in rr: wknd over 3f out* **33/1**
15 13 **Sir Duke (IRE)** 2-9-0 ...... RyanMoore 4 —
(P W D'Arcy) *w'like: bkwd: s.s: sn pushed along in rr: bhd fr 1/2-way* **33/1**

1m 40.22s (0.85) **Going Correction** +0.15s/f (Good) **15** Ran SP% **117.5**
Speed ratings (Par 97):101,96,95,92,91 88,87,85,85,84 83,80,77,72,59
CSF £3.19 TOTE £1.80: £1.10, £1.70, £2.40; EX 5.00.
Owner George Strawbridge **Bred** Equine Stable Ltd **Trained** Newmarket, Suffolk

FOCUS
This looked like a decent maiden, even though they finished well strung out and the form looks solid rated around the third, fifth and sixth. The winner opted to race on his own, roughly halfway between the centre of the track and the near-side rail; the others stayed near side.

NOTEBOOK
Asperity(USA) ◆, a very pleasing second on his debut in a seven-furlong novice event at Sandown, built on that promise to run out a mightily impressive winner on this switch to maiden company. Kept away from his rivals more towards the centre of the track, he was soon in a good rhythm and nothing ever looked like going with him once he was asked to lengthen. Understandably held in very high regard by his connections, he could now be put away for the winter and aimed at next year's Craven Stakes back over this course and distance. Providing he winters without any major problems, he certainly looks capable of developing into a Group horse and it is by no means out of the question that he could be a Guineas candidate. (op 4-5 tchd 5-6 in places)
Life(IRE) ◆, a 260,000gns brother to smart Inchiri, a middle-distance winner, out of a useful mile to 12-furlong three-year-old, holds a Racing Post Trophy entry and made a pleasing introduction behind the potentially smart winner. He should win next time before stepping up in grade. (op 4-1 tchd 5-1 and 11-2 in a place)
Palamoun, last of seven in a good conditions event on his debut at Newbury, was left behind by Asperity when it mattered having travelled well, but this still represents improved form. He probably ran into two very nice horses and should not be too long in winning. (tchd 9-1)
Salaasa(USA), the first foal of a triple seven-furlong/mile winner, made a pleasing introduction and is open to loads of improvement.
Sunley Peace shaped well in a similar event over course and distance on his debut and this was another pleasing effort. He should continue to progress and might make a useful handicapper in time.
Calculating(IRE), a $225,000 first foal of a quite smart miler, lost his chance with a very slow start but should be much better for the experience.

5641 UNICOIN HOMES NOEL MURLESS STKS (LISTED RACE) 1m 6f
4:05 (4:10) (Class 1) 3-Y-O
£15,898 (£6,025; £3,015; £1,503; £753; £378) **Stalls** High

Form RPR
100 **1** **Novellara**[56] 4079 3-8-9 98 ...... RichardHughes 1 102
(H R A Cecil) *wnt lft s: plld hrd and sn trcking ldrs: rdn 2f out: hmpd ins fnl f: styd on u.p to ld post* **11/2**
122 **2** shd **Zurbaran (IRE)**[20] 5153 3-9-0 90 ...... MickyFenton 4 107
(B J Meehan) *lw: led over 9f: rdn and hung lft fr over 1f out: led ins fnl f: hdd post* **4/1**[2]
4244 **3** 1½ **Cresta Gold**[35] 4741 3-8-9 101 ...... PaulHanagan 7 100
(A Bailey) *chsd ldr 5f: led over 4f out: rdn over 1f out: hdd and unable qckn ins fnl f* **10/3**[1]
5000 **4** 6 **Kassiopeia (IRE)**[56] 4079 3-8-9 88 ...... TonyCulhane 6 92
(M R Channon) *hld up: rdn over 3f out: wknd over 2f out* **16/1**
1326 **5** 5 **Bandama (IRE)**[35] 4742 3-9-0 98 ...... RyanMoore 2 90
(Mrs A J Perrett) *hld up in tch: rdn over 3f out: wknd over 2f out* **9/2**[3]
2000 **6** 2½ **Sienna Storm (IRE)**[19] 5186 3-9-0 99 ...... RHills 3 86
(M H Tompkins) *hld up in tch: rdn and wknd over 2f out* **25/1**
0020 **7** 2 **Classic Punch (IRE)**[12] 5374 3-9-0 103 ...... JohnEgan 5 83
(D R C Elsworth) *hld up: hdwy 5f out: rdn and wknd over 2f out* **10/3**[1]

3m 0.40s (0.27) **Going Correction** +0.15s/f (Good) **7** Ran SP% **109.5**
Speed ratings (Par 109):105,104,104,100,97 96,95
CSF £25.17 TOTE £6.10: £2.60, £2.00; EX 19.10.
Owner K Abdulla **Bred** Juddmonte Farms Ltd **Trained** Newmarket, Suffolk

FOCUS
A pretty ordinary Listed event and the form, rated around the placed horses, is not strong for the grade. The front two ended up making their challenges well away from the far side rail, more towards the centre of the track.

NOTEBOOK
Novellara, highly tried this season, had not quite progressed as one might have hoped after winning on her debut at Salisbury earlier in the campaign but, dropped into Listed company, she got back on track with a game success. She looks value for more than the short-head winning margin, as she was hampered and no doubt intimidated when the runner-up continually hung to his left in the closing stages. On this evidence, she looks up to winning a fillies/mares' Group race, but she has picked up some valuable black type and her connections may be tempted to retire her to the paddocks. (op 9-2)
Zurbaran(IRE), stepped up to Listed company for the first time, ran a fine race but continually hung to his left in the closing stages and that might well have cost him the race. If connections can iron out that problem, he could do better again. (op 9-2 tchd 5-1 in a place)
Cresta Gold stuck to the far-side rail, whereas the front two drifted out more towards the centre of the track, and she was ultimately just run out of it. This was a decent effort and she has picked up some more black type. (op 9-4)
Kassiopeia(IRE) looked a threat when moving into contention, but was quickly found out when her main rivals began their challenges.
Bandama(IRE) was again below form and might need better ground if he is going to see out this sort of trip. (op 11-2)
Classic Punch(IRE) was totally unsuited by the step up in trip and ran no sort of race. It is not easy to work out both his optimum conditions, and the grade he should be running in. Official explanation: vet said colt was distressed (op 9-2 tchd 5-1)

5642 ROUS STKS (LISTED RACE) 5f
4:40 (4:41) (Class 1) 3-Y-O+
£15,898 (£6,025; £3,015; £1,503; £753; £378) **Stalls** Low

Form RPR
0110 **1** **Fantasy Believer**[12] 5358 8-8-12 104 ...... JimmyQuinn 9 113+
(J J Quinn) *hld up: nt clr run and swtchd lft over 1f out: r.o wl to ld post* **12/1**
4113 **2** shd **Prince Tamino**[78] 3414 3-8-11 103 ...... SteveDrowne 2 113
(H Morrison) *trckd ldrs: rdn to ld ins fnl f: hdd post* **4/1**[1]
2203 **3** 1 **Pivotal's Princess (IRE)**[11] 5405 4-8-7 97 ...... WSupple 11 104
(E S McMahon) *lw: chsd ldrs: led over 1f out: hdd and unable qckn ins fnl f* **8/1**[3]
0005 **4** ¾ **Corridor Creeper (FR)**[16] 5274 9-8-12 102 ......(p) RyanMoore 6 106
(J M Bradley) *w ldrs: rdn over 1f out: styd on* **16/1**
0110 **5** ½ **Celtic Mill**[12] 5375 8-9-1 107 ......(p) JohnEgan 5 108
(D W Barker) *chsd ldrs: outpcd over 1f out: styd on ins fnl f* **14/1**
4660 **6** shd **The Tatling (IRE)**[12] 5375 9-8-12 108 ...... JamieSpencer 14 104
(J M Bradley) *lw: dwlt: hld up: hdwy over 1f out: styd on* **8/1**[3]
0210 **7** nk **Gimasha**[11] 5405 4-8-7 96 ...... KerrinMcEvoy 13 98
(W Jarvis) *chsd ldrs: rdn over 1f out: styd on same pce* **11/1**
1045 **8** 1½ **Green Manalishi**[12] 5375 5-8-12 102 ...... LDettori 10 98
(D W P Arbuthnot) *disp ld over 3f: wknd ins fnl f* **10/1**
2401 **9** ½ **Philharmonic**[9] 5443 5-8-12 103 ...... PaulHanagan 12 96
(R A Fahey) *hld up: hdwy 1/2-way: sn rdn: wknd ins fnl f* **6/1**[2]
1060 **10** nk **Empress Jain**[56] 4080 3-8-6 99 ...... PhilipRobinson 4 90
(M A Jarvis) *disp ld over 3f: wknd ins fnl f* **33/1**
2166 **11** 1¾ **Donna Blini**[12] 5375 3-8-6 103 ...... EddieAhern 3 83
(B J Meehan) *lw: s.i.s: hdwy 1/2-way: wknd fnl f* **8/1**[3]
-020 **12** ½ **Murfreesboro**[76] 3494 3-8-11 97 ......(v[1]) JimmyFortune 7 87
(J H M Gosden) *s.i.s: racd alone fnl 4f: outpcd* **20/1**
4603 **13** 1¼ **Give Me The Night (IRE)**[11] 5405 3-8-6 83 ...... KDarley 8 77
(B Smart) *hmpd s: sn prom: rdn 1/2-way: wknd 2f out* **50/1**

59.04 secs (-1.43) **Going Correction** +0.15s/f (Good)
WFA 3 from 4yo+ 1lb **13** Ran SP% **114.9**
Speed ratings (Par 111):117,116,115,114,113 113,112,110,109,108 106,105,103
CSF £56.11 TOTE £14.00: £4.20, £1.60, £3.10; EX 91.20.
Owner The Fantasy Fellowship B **Bred** John Khan **Trained** Settrington, N Yorks
■ Stewards' Enquiry : Steve Drowne one-day ban: used whip with excessive frequency and without allowing sufficient time for response (Oct 9)

FOCUS
A reasonable enough Listed sprint and the form appears sound, rated around the placed horses. They raced near side, but off the rail.

NOTEBOOK
Fantasy Believer ran below expectations in the Ayr Gold Cup last time, but he had previously looked most progressive and coped with the step up in class to gain his fifth success of the year, picking up in fine style when switched inside with his effort about a furlong out. It is rather bizarre that he seems to be peaking at the age of eight, but it is possible there could be even more to come. (op 10-1)
Prince Tamino ◆, returned to the minimum trip on his first venture into Listed company, did everything right and was just collared on the line. Only three, he still has loads more to offer and looks capable of making up into a Group-class sprinter next season. (tchd 7-2)
Pivotal's Princess(IRE) probably just travelled too well for own good, as she found herself in front a touch sooner than was ideal. Ridden with slightly more restraint, she could do better again. Official explanation: vet said filly was distressed (op 9-1)
Corridor Creeper(FR) had conditions to suit and returned to form with a solid effort in fourth.
Celtic Mill had no easy task conceding weight all round and ran well considering.
The Tatling(IRE) looks just short of this level these days. (op 15-2)
Philharmonic would have found this tougher than the Beverley conditions race he won on his previous start, but was not at his best in any case. (op 13-2 tchd 15-2 in a place)
Empress Jain Official explanation: jockey said filly hung right

5643 EUROPEAN BREEDERS FUND FILLIES' H'CAP 6f
5:15 (5:16) (Class 2) (0-100,99) 3-Y-O+
£11,217 (£3,358; £1,679; £840; £419; £210) **Stalls** Low

Form RPR
311 **1** **Cape**[33] 4807 3-8-8 81 ...... JamieSpencer 3 90+
(J R Fanshawe) *s.i.s: racd centre: hld up: swtchd rt and hdwy over 1f out: shkn up to ld ins fnl f: r.o* **1/1**[1]
-004 **2** ¾ **Misphire**[12] 5377 3-8-4 77 ...... MartinDwyer 9 84
(M Dods) *racd centre: chsd ldrs: rdn to ld over 1f out: sn hung lft: hdd ins fnl f: kpt on* **15/2**[2]

1404 **3** *nk* **Leopoldine**[55] 4102 3-9-2 **89** .... SteveDrowne 4 95
(H Morrison) *lw: racd centre: sn led: rdn and hdd over 1f out: edgd lft ins fnl f: styd on* **12/1**

-634 **4** *1 3/4* **Perfect Story (IRE)**[195] 657 4-8-9 **80** .... JohnEgan 6 81
(J A R Toller) *racd centre: a.p: rdn over 1f out: styd on same pce* **14/1**

6400 **5** *shd* **Kaveri (USA)**[12] 5377 3-8-4 **77** .... KerrinMcEvoy 2 78
(C E Brittain) *racd stands' side: swtchd centre 4f out: hld up: rdn over 2f out: edgd lft over 1f out: nt trble ldrs* **16/1**

6300 **6** *1/2* **Gamble In Gold (IRE)**[47] 4345 3-9-0 **87** .... RyanMoore 5 86
(R Hannon) *lw: racd centre: hld up: rdn over 2f out: n.d* **20/1**

5101 **7** *nk* **Mango Music**[16] 5265 3-8-11 **84** .... ChrisCatlin 7 82
(M R Channon) *racd centre: chsd ldrs: rdn over 1f out: styd on same pce* **14/1**

0260 **8** *3/4* **Lady Livius (IRE)**[6] 5501 3-9-6 **93** .... RichardHughes 1 89
(R Hannon) *racd stands' side: lft alone fnl 4f: chsd ldrs: rdn over 1f out: no ex fnl f* **16/1**

00 **9** *6* **Ascot Lady (IRE)**[5] 5535 3-8-4 **77** .... PaulHanagan 10 55
(J Balding) *lw: racd centre: plld hrd and prom: wknd over 1f out* **50/1**

0001 **10** *4* **Angus Newz**[11] 5405 3-9-5 **99** 6ex .... (v) ChrisCavanagh(7) 8 65
(M Quinn) *dwlt: racd centre: hdwy to join ldr 5f out: rdr dropped whip 2f out: sn wknd* **8/1**[3]

1m 12.85s (-0.25) **Going Correction** +0.15s/f (Good)
WFA 3 from 4yo 2lb **10** Ran SP% **112.4**
Speed ratings (Par 96):107,106,105,103,103 102,102,101,93,87
CSF £8.22 CT £56.41 TOTE £1.80: £1.20, £2.00, £3.90; EX 7.90 Trifecta £114.90 Pool: £1,117.30 - 6.90 winning units..
Owner Wyck Hall Stud **Bred** Wyck Hall Stud Ltd **Trained** Newmarket, Suffolk

FOCUS
A good fillies' handicap rated around the placed horses. The majority of these race towards the middle of the track.

NOTEBOOK
Cape ◆ readily defied a 6lb higher mark than when winning on the July course on her previous start to complete the hat-trick. Her trainer does very well with his older fillies and she is open to further improvement next year. (op 5-6 tchd 4-5 and 11-10 in a place)
Misphire ◆ ran a good race behind the potentially well-handicapped winner and looks to be nearing top form. She should be placed to effect before the turf season is out. (op 17-2 tchd 9-1)
Leopoldine ran a good race but six furlongs on easy ground just found her out. She might prove best over five furlongs.
Perfect Story(IRE) ran with credit off the back of a 195-day break and could be one to watch for in the forthcoming All-Weather season - she won twice on the Polytrack last winter.
Kaveri(USA) might have appreciated the drop back in trip, but she was still well held.
Angus Newz ran nowhere near the form she showed when winning a five-furlong Listed race at Hamilton on her previous start. (op 9-1)

5644 REG DAY MEMORIAL H'CAP 1m 6f
5:45 (5:50) (Class 4) (0-85,83) 3-Y-O **£6,477** (£1,927; £963; £481) **Stalls** High

Form RPR

6042 **1** **All The Good (IRE)**[26] 5022 3-9-7 **83** .... FJohansson 8 93
(G A Butler) *chsd ldrs: rdn to ld over 1f out: sn hung lft: styd on* **11/1**

4313 **2** *2* **Quantum (IRE)**[8] 5478 3-9-3 **79** .... (v1) JimmyFortune 4 86
(J H M Gosden) *hld up: hdwy over 3f out: rdn over 1f out: edgd rt ins fnl f: kpt on* **3/1**[1]

6035 **3** *1 1/4* **Aphorism**[28] 4947 3-8-6 **68** .... MartinDwyer 7 73
(J R Fanshawe) *chsd ldrs: rdn and ev ch 2f out: styd on same pce fnl f* **12/1**

3233 **4** *nk* **Gee Dee Nen**[12] 5361 3-9-4 **80** .... RHills 6 86+
(M H Tompkins) *lw: stmbld s: sn prom: nt clr run and lost pl over 3f out: hdwy over 1f out: nvr able to chal* **3/1**[1]

2315 **5** *shd* **Hernando Royal**[40] 4612 3-9-2 **78** .... SteveDrowne 5 82
(H Morrison) *chsd ldr: led over 2f out: rdn and hdd over 1f out: styd on same pce* **8/1**[3]

0036 **6** *2 1/2* **Divine River**[13] 5346 3-8-10 **72** .... JamieSpencer 2 73
(A P Jarvis) *hld up: hdwy over 3f out: rdn over 1f out: wknd ins fnl f* **14/1**

3421 **7** *2 1/2* **Mull Of Dubai**[15] 5284 3-8-5 **67** .... JohnEgan 1 64
(J S Moore) *lw: hld up: plld hrd: hdwy over 3f out: hung lft over 2f out: wknd over 1f out* **7/1**[2]

4234 **8** *2 1/2* **Dickie's Dream (IRE)**[22] 5109 3-8-8 **70** .... RichardMullen 9 64
(P J McBride) *lw: led: rdn and hdd over 2f out: wknd fnl f* **10/1**

-521 **9** *2* **Profitable**[10] 5426 3-9-3 **79** 6ex .... MichaelHills 3 70
(B W Hills) *hld up: hdwy over 3f out: rdn and wknd over 1f out* **17/2**

3m 5.43s (5.30) **Going Correction** +0.15s/f (Good) **9** Ran SP% **115.9**
Speed ratings (Par 103):90,88,88,87,87 86,85,83,82
CSF £44.30 CT £411.97 TOTE £12.40: £3.70, £1.50, £3.60; EX 55.60 Place 6 £120.80, Place 5 £46.02.
Owner Future In Mind Partnership **Bred** Mount Coote Partnership **Trained** Blewbury, Oxon

FOCUS
A fair staying handicap run at a steady early gallop and the overall time was moderate, being over 5.03sec slower than the earlier Listed race. The form is rated at face value around those in the frame behind the winner.
T/Jkpt: Not won. T/Plt: £147.80 to a £1 stake. Pool: £77,010.30. 380.15 winning tickets. T/Qpdt: £7.90 to a £1 stake. Pool: £4,684.90. 433.90 winning tickets. CR

5605 LINGFIELD (L-H)
Friday, September 29

OFFICIAL GOING: Turf course - soft (good to soft in places); all-weather - standard
Wind: Moderate, behind Weather: Overcast with frequent heavy showers

5645 EUROPEAN BREEDERS FUND TURF MAIDEN STKS 5f
1:50 (1:50) (Class 5) 2-Y-O **£3,886** (£1,156; £577; £288) **Stalls** High

Form RPR

33 **1** **Baileys Outshine**[7] 5507 2-8-12 .... J-PGuillambert 16 65
(J G Given) *racd against nr side rail: mde virtually all: clr w runner-up over 1f out: hld on gamely nr fin* **7/2**[2]

6 **2** *shd* **Gower**[21] 5147 2-9-3 .... SebSanders 12 70
(R Charlton) *racd towards nr side: pressed wnr thrght: sustained battle and clr of rest over 1f out: jst pipped* **9/2**

3 *2 1/2* **Excessive** 2-8-12 .... PaulDoe 4 56+
(W Jarvis) *s.i.s: wl adrift in last trio: rdn and r.o wl on outer fr over 1f out: nrst fin* **20/1**

500 **4** *1/2* **Bungie**[7] 5508 2-9-3 .... GeorgeBaker 10 59
(Ms Deborah J Evans) *racd towards centre: prom: shkn up over 1f out: one pce* **100/1**

0503 **5** *1 1/4* **King Of Tricks**[16] 5290 2-9-3 **50** .... HayleyTurner 14 54
(M D I Usher) *trckd ldrs on nr side: nt clr run briefly over 2f out: sn swtchd lft and outpcd: kpt on* **66/1**

0400 **6** *nk* **Beat The Bully**[14] 5349 2-8-10 **50** .... (b) SophieDoyle(7) 8 53
(I A Wood) *racd towards centre: wl on terms for 3f: steadily fdd* **100/1**

322 **7** *1* **Castano**[21] 5147 2-9-3 **77** .... JimCrowley 1 50
(B R Millman) *racd centre: w ldrs for 3f: fdd* **4/1**[3]

32 **8** *1/2* **All You Need (IRE)**[62] 3958 2-9-3 .... LPKeniry 7 48
(R Hollinshead) *racd centre: w ldrs for 3f: wknd over 1f out* **3/1**[1]

5 **8** *dht* **Earl Compton (IRE)**[34] 4815 2-9-3 .... PatDobbs 17 48
(P F I Cole) *dwlt: hld up against nr side rail: shkn up and no prog 2f out* **12/1**

10 *shd* **Come What May** 2-8-12 .... ChrisCatlin 2 43+
(Rae Guest) *racd centre: off the pce tl trckd ldrs gng wl 2f out: trapped bhd them after and eased fnl f: do bttr* **20/1**

65 **11** *1 1/4* **Hills Place**[15] 5315 2-9-3 .... MickyFenton 5 43
(J R Best) *a struggling and wl in rr* **33/1**

0 **12** *3/4* **Welsh Auction**[10] 5454 2-9-3 .... BrianReilly 11 40
(G A Huffer) *prom 2f: sn lost pl and struggling* **25/1**

13 *shd* **Hereford Boy** 2-9-3 .... RoystonFfrench 6 40
(D K Ivory) *v s.i.s: rn green and a wl in rr* **33/1**

00 **14** *5* **Strobe**[4] 5563 2-9-0 .... RichardKingscote(3) 9 22
(J A Osborne) *sn rdn and outpcd: nvr a factor* **33/1**

60.66 secs (1.72) **Going Correction** +0.25s/f (Good) **14** Ran SP% **118.8**
Speed ratings (Par 95):96,95,91,91,89 88,86,86,86,86 84,82,82,74
CSF £17.25 TOTE £5.50: £2.10, £1.90, £7.00; EX 19.70 TRIFECTA Not won..
Owner G R Bailey Ltd (baileys Horse Feeds) **Bred** P And Mrs A G Venner **Trained** Willoughton, Lincs

FOCUS
The jockeys reported that the ground was on the soft side. A fairly average maiden for the track, rated around the fifth and sixth and, as is usually the case on the straight track here, the draw played an important part in the outcome.

NOTEBOOK
Baileys Outshine, dropping in trip, was quick to bag the position next to the stands' rail in front, and eventually got the better of the runner-up on the nod. She had shown enough in two previous outings to suggest she could win a race like this and the drop to the minimum trip proved no problem at all. (op 3-1)
Gower ◆, whose dam is a half-sister to the stable's star sprinters Avonbridge and Patavellian, stepped up on his debut effort and showed good speed throughout. He only just missed out and it should not be long before he goes one better. (op 11-2)
Excessive ◆ was the real eye-catcher of the race, coming from a mile back to grab third after having to be switched out into the centre of the track. A half-sister to two winners, she is bred for speed and looks a sure-fire future winner. (op 16-1)
Bungie improved on previous efforts but does tend to limit the form.
King Of Tricks stayed on late but is more exposed than most and will surely be better off back in handicaps.
Beat The Bully seems best with some cut in the ground and along with the two in front of him helps set the level for the form.
Castano was disappointing and the ground could not be offered as an excuse, but he did race up the centre of the track which did not appear the place to be. (op 10-3)
All You Need(IRE) was a bit disappointing considering his previous form, but had never previously encountered soft ground and it appeared not to suit. (op 4-1 tchd 9-2)
Come What May ◆ can be rated rather better than her finishing position would suggest as she was locked away behind a couple of rivals and failed to see daylight when she needed it. A 50,000gns sister to Etlaala, she can be expected to improve a good deal on this. Official explanation: jockey said filly was denied a clear run (op 16-1)

5646 BRISTOL STREET MOTORS ALL COMMERCIAL & RENTAL NEEDS COVERED CLAIMING STKS 6f
2:20 (2:20) (Class 6) 2-Y-O **£2,590** (£770; £385; £192) **Stalls** High

Form RPR

3010 **1** **Retaliate**[17] 5271 2-8-12 **68** .... SebSanders 16 71
(M Quinn) *led after 2f and sn racd against nr side rail: mde rest: rdn clr fr jst over 1f out: in n.d after* **9/2**[1]

1330 **2** *1 3/4* **Jost Van Dyke**[20] 5162 2-8-11 **67** .... JimCrowley 3 65+
(B R Millman) *prom: chsd wnr 1/2-way: rdn 2f out: kpt on same pce and nvr able to chal* **12/1**

00 **3** *1 1/4* **Ballyshane Spirit (IRE)**[32] 4897 2-8-11 .... RoystonFfrench 17 61
(N A Callaghan) *dwlt: wl in rr and wl off the pce: pushed along and prog fr 1/2-way: swtchd lft over 1f out: styd on to take 3rd nr fin* **20/1**

4136 **4** *1/2* **La Marmotte (IRE)**[19] 5208 2-8-11 **64** .... J-PGuillambert 18 60
(J W Hills) *racd against nr side rail: led for 2f: rdn bef 1/2-way: one pce u.p fnl 2f* **5/1**[2]

3450 **5** *shd* **Ten Dollars More (IRE)**[13] 5382 2-8-10 **70** .... (b) RichardKingscote(3) 14 61
(J A Osborne) *off the pce in midfield: prog over 2f out: disp 3rd ent fnl f: wknd nr fin* **11/2**[3]

6 *1 3/4* **Raquel White** 2-8-3 .... FrankieMcDonald 2 46+
(S Kirk) *s.s: wl adrift in last pair: prog and shkn up 2f out: styd on wl fnl f: nrst fin* **33/1**

7 *1/2* **Go Dude** 2-8-11 .... FrancisNorton 15 52
(J Ryan) *s.i.s: outpcd and sn pushed along: kpt on fr over 2f out: n.d* **40/1**

0042 **8** *1 1/2* **Stir Crazy (IRE)**[10] 5447 2-9-1 **66** .... ChrisCatlin 10 52
(M R Channon) *sn pressed ldrs: rdn and wknd wl over 1f out* **15/2**

4530 **9** *5* **Madam Gaffer**[14] 5349 2-8-1 **66** .... KMay(7) 8 30
(B J Meehan) *nvr beyond midfield and a off the pce: no ch over 2f out* **8/1**

10 *1* **Benayoun** 2-8-6 .... PatrickHills(7) 11 32
(M H Tompkins) *rn green and sn wl outpcd in last: nvr a factor* **20/1**

0005 **11** *1 1/4* **Rowan Venture**[28] 4987 2-8-11 **64** .... PaulDoe 13 26
(M H Tompkins) *chsd ldrs: rdn over 2f out: wknd rapidly over 1f out: eased whn no ch* **12/1**

5203 **12** *1 1/2* **Fadeyev (IRE)**[13] 5364 2-8-13 **72** .... (p) CatherineGannon 1 24
(K A Ryan) *racd centre: on terms w ldrs to 1/2-way: sn wknd* **9/1**

00 **13** *nk* **Maskaraid**[13] 5387 2-8-6 .... RobertHavlin 12 16
(B R Millman) *nvr beyond midfield and a off the pce: wknd over 1f out* **100/1**

0 **14** *shd* **Jade's Ballet**[17] 5261 2-7-11 ow1 .... LiamJones(5) 5 12
(E A Wheeler) *dwlt: a wl in rr and wl off the pce* **66/1**

06 **15** *1 1/2* **Colonel Klink (IRE)**[97] 2857 2-8-11 .... LPKeniry 9 16
(J S Moore) *s.s: outpcd and a wl bhd* **40/1**

30 **16** *5* **Silver Bolt (IRE)**[29] 4969 2-8-4 .... (b1) JamesDoyle(3) 4 —
(N P Littmoden) *racd alone towards far side most of way: a bhd* **66/1**

1m 14.59s (2.92) **Going Correction** +0.25s/f (Good) **16** Ran SP% **119.8**
Speed ratings (Par 93):90,87,86,85,85 82,82,80,73,72 70,68,68,68,66 59
CSF £53.30 TOTE £4.40: £1.80, £5.90, £5.00; EX 98.60 TRIFECTA Not won..

Owner M J Quinn **Bred** Helshaw Grange Farm And C J Whiston **Trained** Newmarket, Suffolk

FOCUS

This was a modest juvenile claimer and very few ever got into it. Again the draw played its part with the highest three stalls finishing in the first four.

NOTEBOOK

Retaliate, whose previous win was in similar conditions, soon took over in pole position against the rail and made full use of it. The return to six furlongs and the easy ground were both very much in her favour. (op 11-2 tchd 6-1 and13-2 in places)

Jost Van Dyke, whose win came in a seller, ran a fine race considering he was drawn in stall three, even though he broke well and was able to angle across to take a handy position without too much bother. He had never raced on easy ground before so this was encouraging.

Ballyshane Spirit(IRE) improved on his two previous efforts down in class and trip. He now qualifies for a nursery mark and may find an opportunity there. (op 16-1)

La Marmotte(IRE) made the early running from the stands' rail draw, but she could not maintain the advantage for long and just kept on in her own time. (op 4-1 tchd 11-2)

Ten Dollars More(IRE), back over his winning distance, ran with a some credit but his current rating looks on the high side. (op 6-1)

Raquel White was unfancied and missed the break but did offer a little promise, coming from a long way off the pace.

Go Dude was another to show signs of ability on this debut but will probably need further. (op 33-1)

5647 CLOSE PROPERTY FINANCE NURSERY 7f

2:55 (2:55) (Class 5) (0-75,75) 2-Y-O **£3,238** (£963; £481; £240) **Stalls** High

Form				RPR
2565	**1**		**Our Herbie**[17] 5262 2-9-0 **68** ... J-PGuillambert 15 (J W Hills) *settled at bk of main gp: stdy prog on wd outside fr 3f out: rdn to ld jst over 1f out: sn in command: pushed out nr fin* **15/2**[3]	74
0055	**2**	1 1/4	**Golan Way**[10] 5447 2-9-1 **69** ... FrancisNorton 3 (I A Wood) *in tch: prog 3f out: rdn to chal over 1f out: chsd wnr fnl f: kpt on but a readily hld* **16/1**	72
0505	**3**	4	**Todwick Owl**[19] 5208 2-8-8 **62** ... JamieMackay 12 (J G Given) *trckd ldng pair: effrt to ld 2f out: hdd jst over 1f out: fdd* **16/1**	55
5563	**4**	3/4	**Distiller (IRE)**[11] 5431 2-9-2 **70** ... RichardMullen 13 (W R Muir) *reluctant to go to post: chsd ldrs: hrd rdn fr 2f out: kpt on same pce* **12/1**	61
0500	**5**	2 1/2	**Spirited Speedfit (IRE)**[26] 5041 2-8-8 **62** ... MickyFenton 11 (G G Margarson) *prom towards centre: rdn and lost pl over 2f out: no real imp after* **20/1**	47
504	**6**	shd	**Oakley Heffert (IRE)**[24] 5091 2-9-6 **74** ... PatDobbs 8 (R Hannon) *chsd ldrs: bdly outpcd and pushed along 1/2-way: styd on u.p again fr over 1f out* **16/1**	59+
4206	**7**	3/4	**Dee Jay Wells**[18] 5231 2-9-5 **73** ... FJohansson 17 (R Hannon) *chsd ldrs but nvr on terms: hrd rdn over 2f out: no real prog* **12/1**	56
4514	**8**	nk	**Goose Green (IRE)**[9] 5482 2-8-12 **69** ... EdwardCreighton(3) 2 (M R Channon) *racd on outer: in tch: effrt over 2f out: no prog over 1f out: wknd* **11/1**	51
646	**9**	nk	**Lady Lafitte (USA)**[14] 5339 2-8-9 **70** ... PatrickHills(7) 6 (B W Hills) *racd towards centre: w ldr: stl upsides over 1f out: wknd rapidly* **10/1**	51
600	**10**	1	**Buckie Massa**[35] 4766 2-9-5 **73** ... GeorgeBaker 1 (S Kirk) *stdd s and swtchd to nr side: hld up in detached last: effrt against rail over 2f out: no prog over 1f out* **16/1**	52
4021	**11**	1	**Victory Spirit**[18] 5231 2-9-7 **75** ... SebSanders 5 (J L Dunlop) *bmpd s: nvr on terms towards rr: rdn and struggling 3f out* **11/1**	51
360	**12**	1	**Raffaas**[55] 4129 2-9-4 **72** ... (b[1]) DaleGibson 4 (M P Tregoning) *bmpd s: a wl in rr and nvr gng wl* **12/1**	46
6612	**13**	1 1/4	**Suhayl Star (IRE)**[35] 4761 2-9-5 **73** ... JDSmith 10 (W J Musson) *led at str pce against nr side rail: edgd lft and hdd 2f out: wknd rapidly* **13/2**[2]	44
040	**14**	32	**Avoid The Cat**[55] 4138 2-8-9 **63** ... JimCrowley 7 (Mrs A J Perrett) *dwlt: sn struggling and u.p: t.o over 2f out* **33/1**	—
323	**15**	17	**Mr Loire**[18] 5245 2-8-13 **70** ... RichardKingscote(3) 18 (R Charlton) *n.m.r after 1f against nr side rail: nvr gng after: t.o 3f out* **5/1**[1]	—

1m 26.8s (2.59) **Going Correction** +0.25s/f (Good) **15** Ran SP% **121.8**

Speed ratings (Par 95):95,93,89,88,85 85,84,83,83,82 81,80,78,42,22

CSF £122.78 CT £1917.63 TOTE £10.70: £4.00, £10.30, £5.20; EX 263.30 TRIFECTA Not won..

Owner Amity Finance,Tom Kelly,Miss Wendy Hall **Bred** Itchen Valley Stud **Trained** Upper Lambourn, Berks

FOCUS

A fair nursery and in view of what had happened in the first two races, it was perhaps no surprise that several of the jockeys wanted to bag the position against the stands' rail and there wasn't much room between those that tried as they bunched together. The action eventually unfolded down the centre of the track.

NOTEBOOK

Our Herbie, despite starting from stall 15, made his sustained effort widest of all and won with a degree of comfort. He shapes as though he will stay a bit further. (op 17-2 tchd 9-1)

Golan Way, encountering soft ground for the first time, like the winner came down the middle from his low draw and improved on previous efforts. He appeared to get the longer trip well enough. (tchd 20-1)

Todwick Owl was always close to the pace and seems to have improved since moving into nurseries.

Distiller(IRE) stayed on to snatch fourth and again showed ability, but he is due to go up another 4lb which will make things a bit harder in this sort of company.

Spirited Speedfit(IRE), having his first try on soft ground, ran a bit better than on his nursery debut here last time. (op 16-1)

Oakley Heffert(IRE) ran as though he needs a mile at least, but may prefer a sounder surface.

Victory Spirit Official explanation: jockey said colt had no more to give

Suhayl Star(IRE) eventually won the battle for the early lead against the rail, but may have done too much too early in the conditions and failed to get home on ground probably softer than he likes. (tchd 6-1 and 7-1)

Mr Loire, starting from the rails draw, was slightly messed about at the start as his rivals moved across him towards the rail, but not enough to explain this poor effort. It is possible the ground may have been against him. Official explanation: jockey said gelding was unsuited by the soft (good to soft places) ground (op 6-1)

5648 EUROPEAN BREEDERS FUND AWT MAIDEN STKS 6f (P)

3:30 (3:30) (Class 5) 2-Y-O **£3,886** (£1,156; £577; £288) **Stalls** Low

Form				RPR
4	**1**		**Count Ceprano (IRE)**[17] 5261 2-9-3 ... StephenCarson 7 (W R Swinburn) *hld up in tch and a gng wl: prog over 1f out: shkn up to ld ins fnl f: sn in command* **2/1**[1]	76+
0	**2**	1 1/4	**Kassuta**[28] 4993 2-8-12 ... HayleyTurner 3 (S C Williams) *trckd ldng pair: wnt 2nd over 1f out: rdn to ld last 150yds: sn hdd and outpcd* **20/1**	65
0404	**3**	1 1/2	**Billy Red**[10] 5454 2-9-3 66 ... RobertHavlin 4 (J R Jenkins) *mde most: drvn and hanging over 1f out: hdd and wl outpcd last 150yds* **14/1**[3]	65
06	**4**	1 1/4	**Napoleon Dynamite (IRE)**[121] 2130 2-9-3 ... J-PGuillambert 8 (J W Hills) *trckd ldrs: pushed along over 2f out: rdn and nt qckn over 1f out: one pce after* **14/1**[3]	61
035	**5**	shd	**King Joshua (IRE)**[41] 4597 2-9-3 86 ... FJohansson 1 (G A Butler) *trckd ldrs: pushed along over 2f out: hanging lft and nt qckn over 1f out: one pce after* **2/1**[1]	61
50	**6**	shd	**Royal Rationale (IRE)**[16] 5297 2-8-12 ... LiamJones(5) 10 (W J Haggas) *racd wd thrght: in tch: pushed along and prog over 2f out: wd bnd sn after: nudged along and nvr nr ldrs after: do bttr* **20/1**	67+
00	**7**	1 1/2	**Samdaniya**[33] 4840 2-8-12 ... RichardMullen 2 (C E Brittain) *pressed ldr to over 1f out: wknd* **9/2**[2]	51
00	**8**	2	**Crossing The Line (IRE)**[4] 5563 2-9-3 ... SebSanders 9 (Sir Mark Prescott) *pushed along in rr 4f out: struggling and nvr on terms after* **20/1**	50+
0	**9**	nk	**Divalini**[21] 5147 2-8-12 ... PatDobbs 12 (J Akehurst) *dwlt: in rr whn bmpd 4f out: in tch tl wknd over 1f out* **50/1**	44
0	**10**	3/4	**Alonso De Guzman (IRE)**[26] 5043 2-9-0 ... AmirQuinn(3) 5 (J R Boyle) *dwlt: bmpd and hmpd 4f out: last and struggling after* **66/1**	47+
	11	2	**Putra Laju (IRE)** 2-9-3 ... FrankieMcDonald 6 (J W Hills) *a in rr: wknd 2f out* **66/1**	41

1m 12.54s (-0.27) **Going Correction** -0.20s/f (Stan) **11** Ran SP% **117.4**

Speed ratings (Par 95):93,91,89,87,87 87,85,82,82,81 78

CSF £51.59 TOTE £2.90: £1.30, £5.50, £2.40; EX 70.00 Trifecta £402.00 Part won. Pool: £566.33 - 0.68 winning tickets..

Owner Mrs P W Harris **Bred** Pendley Farm **Trained** Aldbury, Herts

■ Stewards' Enquiry : Liam Jones ten-day ban: failed to take all reasonable and permissible measures (Oct 10-19)

FOCUS

Not the strongest of maidens and the early pace was modest, but the form appears solid enough and the first two home were only having their second outings, so may well continue to progress.

NOTEBOOK

Count Ceprano(IRE) had made an eye-catching debut over course and distance earlier this month and progressed from that, showing a nice turn of foot to see off his rivals. He looks a nice sort for next season. (op 9-4 tchd 5-2 in places)

Kassuta ◆, a speedily-bred filly who was always close to the pace, also improved from her debut effort and she should find an opportunity in a race like this.

Billy Red tried to steal the race from the front, but was done for finishing speed. He has shown ability in maidens, but was the most experienced in the field and lacks the scope of the pair that finished in front of him. (tchd 16-1)

Napoleon Dynamite(IRE) did not perform at all badly on this first start since May. He is entitled to come on for the run and can now be handicapped.

King Joshua(IRE), having his first encounter with Polytrack, seemed to have every chance back over a shorter trip, but has not built on the promise of his second outing at Ascot and his current rating looks harsh. Official explanation: jockey said colt stumbled 3f out (op 5-2)

Royal Rationale(IRE) ◆ had every chance turning for home despite racing a little wide, but was by no means knocked about in the straight and his jockey received a ten-day ban. He now qualifies for a mark and looks capable of better. Official explanation: jockey said, regarding running and riding, that his orders were to take a handy position and keep wide as the colt does not like to be amongst other horses, adding that he was hampered in the straight and became unbalanced, which is why he did not ride more vigorously; trainer's rep confirmed, but felt the jockey could have ridden more positively up home straight

Alonso De Guzman(IRE) Official explanation: jockey said gelding was hampered 2f out

Putra Laju(IRE) Official explanation: jockey said colt was hampered 2f after start

5649 WESTMINSTER CONSULTANTS 20TH ANNIVERSARY H'CAP 7f (P)

4:05 (4:05) (Class 4) (0-85,85) 3-Y-O **£5,505** (£1,637; £818; £204; £204) **Stalls** Low

Form				RPR
2-16	**1**		**Felicitous**[15] 5317 3-8-12 **79** ... SebSanders 6 (Saeed Bin Suroor) *hld up wl in rr: prog on outer wl over 1f out: str run to ld last 75yds: readily* **13/2**[2]	88+
0560	**2**	hd	**Carmenero (GER)**[13] 5377 3-8-6 **73** ... RichardMullen 12 (W R Muir) *hld up wl in rr: prog on outer 2f out: drvn to ld ins fnl f: r.o but hdd and hld last 75yds* **11/1**	81
3000	**3**	1 1/4	**Zabeel House**[21] 5150 3-8-7 **74** ... MickyFenton 2 (J A R Toller) *hld up in last: stl last wl over 1f out: rapid prog on wd outside fnl f: snatched 3rd nr fin: too much to do* **16/1**	79+
2-04	**4**	hd	**Ribh**[17] 5272 3-8-8 **75** ... SilvestreDeSousa 3 (C E Brittain) *trckd ldng pair: rdn to ld jst over 1f out: hdd and outpcd last 150yds* **33/1**	79
2130	**4**	dht	**Stonecrabstomorrow (IRE)**[23] 5107 3-9-0 **81** ... PatDobbs 14 (P F I Cole) *trckd ldrs on outer: effrt 2f out: drvn to join ldr jst ins fnl f: outpcd last 100yds* **8/1**[3]	85
4230	**6**	nk	**Jimmy The Guesser**[14] 5336 3-8-13 **83** ... JamesDoyle(3) 7 (N P Littmoden) *trckd ldrs: rdn and nt qckn whn short of room over 1f out: kpt on fnl f: nvr able to chal* **8/1**[3]	86
2430	**7**	1 1/2	**North Walk (IRE)**[34] 4802 3-8-12 **79** ... CatherineGannon 8 (K A Ryan) *chsd ldrs: rdn whn n.m.r 2f out and lost pl: n.d after: kpt on* **16/1**	79
0120	**8**	nk	**Hill Spirit**[14] 5345 3-9-1 **85** ... MarcHalford(3) 10 (D R C Elsworth) *hld up in rr: effrt 2f out: rdn and one pce over 1f out: no imp* **11/2**[1]	84
0000	**9**	nk	**Savernake Blue**[11] 5427 3-8-8 **75** ... RobertHavlin 13 (M R Channon) *t.k.h: sn w ldr: stl upsides over 1f out: wknd fnl f* **40/1**	73
1356	**10**	nk	**Cindertrack**[23] 5107 3-8-6 **73** ... JimCrowley 4 (J A Osborne) *mde most: tried to kick on over 1f out: sn hdd and fdd* **16/1**	70
2120	**11**	hd	**Hoh Wotanite**[17] 5268 3-8-4 **71** oh2 ... ChrisCatlin 11 (R Hollinshead) *hld up in midfield: rdn and no prog over 1f out: one pce* **8/1**[3]	68
1440	**12**	nk	**His Master's Voice (IRE)**[13] 5377 3-8-7 **74** ... FergusSweeney 1 (D W P Arbuthnot) *settled towards rr: effrt 2f out: rdn and btn whn nt clr run briefly over 1f out* **10/1**	70
302	**13**	1/2	**Perfect Treasure (IRE)**[51] 4242 3-8-4 **71** oh1 ... (t) RoystonFfrench 9 (J A R Toller) *rdn towards rr fr 4f out: one pce and nvr on terms after* **20/1**	66
31	**14**	3/4	**Yandina (IRE)**[24] 5093 3-8-1 **75** ... PatrickHills(7) 5 (B W Hills) *hld up in midfield on inner: cl up and pushed along over 1f out: nowhere to go and lost all ch after* **8/1**[3]	68+

1m 24.36s (-1.53) **Going Correction** -0.20s/f (Stan) **14** Ran SP% **118.4**

Speed ratings (Par 103):100,99,98,98,98 97,96,95,95,95 94,94,93,93

CSF £73.36 CT £1132.30 TOTE £6.90: £2.70, £3.80, £7.40; EX 107.90 TRIFECTA Not won..

Owner Godolphin **Bred** Darley **Trained** Newmarket, Suffolk
FOCUS
A typically competitive Lingfield Polytrack handicap and several were still in with a chance a furlong out.
His Master's Voice(IRE) Official explanation: jockey said colt was denied a clear run
Yandina(IRE) Official explanation: jockey said filly was denied a clear run

5650 ROTO-ZIP RELAUNCH MAIDEN STKS (DIV I) 1m 5f (P)
4:40 (4:40) (Class 5) 3-Y-0+ **£2,590** (£770; £385; £192) **Stalls** Low

Form RPR
040 **1** **Florimund**[67] [3794] 3-9-3 .... RoystonFfrench 11 83+
(Sir Michael Stoute) *trckd ldrs: prog to go 2nd over 2f out: shkn up to ld over 1f out: drew rt away* **4/1**[2]
433 **2** *7* **Shahmina (IRE)**[37] [4701] 3-8-12 75 .... RobertHavlin 10 67
(J H M Gosden) *trckd ldrs gng easily: led wl over 2f out: rdn and hdd over 1f out: no ch w wnr* **5/2**[1]
0-06 **3** *7* **Cockatoo (USA)**[19] [5203] 3-9-3 .... (p) GeorgeBaker 8 62
(G L Moore) *hld up towards rr: drvn and prog over 3f out: wnt 3rd 2f out but no ch w clr ldng pair* **16/1**
6230 **4** *2* **Pochard**[17] [5276] 3-8-9 70 .... StephenDonohoe(3) 1 54
(J M P Eustace) *prom: rdn fr 5f out: outpcd over 3f out: plugged on* **9/1**
5 **5** *4* **Always Stylish (IRE)**[85] [3231] 3-9-0 .... GregFairley(3) 5 53
(M Johnston) *pressed ldr: led over 3f out to wl over 2f out: sn wl outpcd* **8/1**[3]
0000 **6** *1 3/4* **Snowberry Hill (USA)**[37] [4700] 3-8-10 55 .... JPFeatherstone(7) 7 50
(P Howling) *hld up in last pair: lost tch over 4f out: sn wl adrift: plugged on steadily fr over 2f out* **33/1**
2322 **7** *3* **Nimra (USA)**[37] [4701] 3-8-12 79 .... FJohansson 4 40
(G A Butler) *led: hrd rdn and hdd over 3f out: sn btn* **5/2**[1]
8 *27* **Brief Passing (IRE)** 7-9-9 .... EdwardCreighton(3) 9 5
(Luke Comer, Ire) *a wl in rr: rdn 7f out: t.o over 4f out: passed three wkng rivals nr fin* **66/1**
9 *hd* **Kai Kuri (IRE)**[27] 5-9-7 .... RobertMiles 6 —
(P W Hiatt) *s.s: in tch in rr to 5f out: sn wknd: t.o over 2f out* **33/1**
-005 **10** *hd* **War Feather**[144] [1540] 4-9-7 40 .... LiamJones(5) 2 4
(T D McCarthy) *t.k.h: prom: rdn over 6f out: wknd over 4f out: t.o* **40/1**
4036 **11** *1 1/4* **King Forever**[27] [5033] 4-9-12 37 .... (e) DaleGibson 3 2
(D E Cantillon) *t.k.h: hld up: wknd 5f out: t.o 3f out* **33/1**

2m 43.53s (-4.77) **Going Correction** -0.20s/f (Stan)
WFA 3 from 4yo+ 9lb **11** Ran SP% **116.9**
Speed ratings (Par 103):106,101,97,96,93 92,90,74,74,73 73
CSF £13.77 TOTE £5.30: £1.90, £1.40, £3.20; EX 12.60 Trifecta £97.20 Pool: £540.86 - 3.95 winning tickets..
Owner K Abdulla **Bred** Juddmonte Farms Ltd **Trained** Newmarket, Suffolk
FOCUS
A very moderate staying maiden in which only a few could be given any real chance but they went a decent pace, the time was 1.95sec faster than the second division, and they duly finished well spread out.

5651 ROTO-ZIP RELAUNCH MAIDEN STKS (DIV II) 1m 5f (P)
5:15 (5:15) (Class 5) 3-Y-0+ **£2,590** (£770; £385; £192) **Stalls** Low

Form RPR
243 **1** **Particle (IRE)**[15] [5319] 3-9-0 80 .... GregFairley(3) 7 69
(M Johnston) *trckd ldr after 3f: led over 4f out and kicked on: styd on stoutly and clr fr over 2f out* **6/4**[1]
0465 **2** *3 1/2* **Dream Shared**[56] [4118] 3-8-12 70 .... RichardMullen 11 58
(E A L Dunlop) *cl up: chsd wnr wl over 3f out: sn drvn and nt qckn: no imp after* **4/1**[2]
5360 **3** *1 1/2* **Noddies Way**[25] [5057] 3-9-3 56 .... JimCrowley 2 61
(J F Panvert) *rn in snatches in last trio: prog 5f out: kpt on fr 3f out: tk 3rd fnl f* **16/1**
365 **4** *2* **Primitive Academy**[11] [5426] 4-9-12 .... ChrisCatlin 5 58
(H R A Cecil) *prom: pushed along over 5f out: chsd ldng pair over 3f out but sn outpcd: one pce after* **10/1**
0055 **5** *3 1/2* **Shamsalmaidan (IRE)**[10] [5451] 3-8-12 59 .... SebSanders 1 48
(C E Brittain) *in tch in rr: wl outpcd 4f out and no ch: plugged on fr over 2f out* **15/2**
0600 **6** *2 1/2* **Madame Constanze (IRE)**[17] [5276] 3-8-9 45 .... JamesDoyle(3) 4 44
(Miss Gay Kelleway) *hld up in tch: gng wl enough over 4f out: rdn and outpcd over 3f out: wknd 2f out* **25/1**
00 **7** *4* **Versatile**[35] [4784] 3-9-3 68 .... FrancisNorton 9 43
(G A Ham) *settled in last trio: wl outpcd fr 4f out: no ch after* **33/1**
6500 **8** *7* **Grand Design**[17] [5267] 4-9-0 50 .... AshleyHamblett(7) 3 28
(C A Cyzer) *t.k.h: hld up in last trio: rdn and struggling 5f out: sn bhd* **20/1**
0 **9** *hd* **Jeu D'Esprit (IRE)**[34] [4814] 3-8-12 .... J-PGuillambert 10 27
(J G Given) *led for 2f: prom tl rdn and wknd over 4f out* **25/1**
456 **10** *17* **Foreigner (IRE)**[11] [5426] 3-9-3 .... RobertHavlin 8 7
(B J Meehan) *led after 2f to over 4f out: wknd rapidly: t.o* **5/1**[3]
0/ **11** *dist* **High Bounce (USA)**[659] [5601] 6-9-12 .... LPKeniry 6 —
(R J Hodges) *stdd s: plld hrd and pressed ldrs after 3f: wknd 7f out: sn hopelessly t.o* **100/1**

2m 45.48s (-2.82) **Going Correction** -0.20s/f (Stan)
WFA 3 from 4yo+ 9lb **11** Ran SP% **119.8**
Speed ratings (Par 103):100,97,96,95,93 92,89,85,85,74 —
CSF £6.94 TOTE £2.30: £1.50, £1.70, £3.20; EX 9.00 Trifecta £67.10 Pool: £233.67 - 2.47 winning tickets..
Owner Michael H Watt **Bred** M Lagardere **Trained** Middleham Moor, N Yorks
FOCUS
This looked the weaker of the two divisions, as can be gleaned from the winning time which was slower by nearly two seconds.
Madame Constanze(IRE) Official explanation: jockey said filly ran too free
High Bounce(USA) Official explanation: jockey said gelding ran too free

5652 BETFAIR APPRENTICE H'CAP (PART OF THE BETFAIR "APPRENTICE TRAINING RACE" SERIES) 1m 4f (P)
5:45 (5:45) (Class 6) (0-60,60) 3-Y-0+ **£2,730** (£806; £403) **Stalls** Low

Form RPR
3020 **1** **Treetops Hotel (IRE)**[62] [3928] 7-9-5 53 .... LiamJones 7 66
(B R Johnson) *hld up midfield: sweeping run on outer to ld 2f out: sn wl clr: unchal* **8/1**
0660 **2** *3* **Mutamaasek (USA)**[37] [4702] 4-9-6 59 .... (p) WilliamCarson(5) 8 67
(Lady Herries) *wl plcd: effrt but outpcd 2f out: chsd wnr 1f out: styd on but no ch* **16/1**
3011 **3** *2 1/2* **Lolla's Spirit (IRE)**[18] [5247] 3-9-0 59 .... JamieHamblett(3) 9 63
(M L W Bell) *hld up towards rr: pushed along and effrt over 2f out: sn outpcd: urged along and styd on to take 3rd ins fnl f: no ch* **4/1**[1]
5003 **4** *3 1/2* **Thebestisyettocome**[13] [5385] 4-9-4 52 .... KevinGhunowa 14 50
(T G Mills) *prom: rdn and outpcd 2f out: one pce after* **13/2**[3]
100/ **5** *1/2* **Habitual (IRE)**[19] [4207] 5-9-4 52 .... AshleyHamblett 13 50
(John A Quinn, Ire) *hld up wl in rr: sme prog 3f out: sn outpcd: kpt on fr over 1f out* **20/1**
5100 **6** *shd* **Mister Completely (IRE)**[36] [3454] 5-9-0 55 .... MJMurphy(7) 4 52
(Ms J S Doyle) *dwlt: hld up in last pair: no ch whn wnr wnt clr 2f out: styd on steadily: nrst fin* **25/1**
5050 **7** *shd* **Meelup (IRE)**[17] [5276] 6-9-4 52 .... (p) TolleyDean 11 49
(P G Murphy) *pressed ldr: rdn 3f out: lost pl jst over 2f out: fdd* **16/1**
0020 **8** *shd* **Missie Baileys**[19] [5213] 4-9-7 55 .... JamieJones 16 52
(Mrs L J Mongan) *trckd ldrs: rdn and outpcd over 2f out: kpt on fnl f* **14/1**
1005 **9** *1 3/4* **Raise The Heights (IRE)**[51] [4245] 3-9-4 60 .... PatrickHills 12 54
(C Tinkler) *s.s: wl in rr: no ch fnl 2f: plugged on* **6/1**[2]
2200 **10** *hd* **Jazrawy**[10] [5451] 4-9-7 55 .... JamesMillman 1 49
(P W Hiatt) *led: rdn 3f out: hdd & wknd 2f out* **25/1**
1144 **11** *1/2* **Zalkani (IRE)**[13] [5390] 6-9-0 55 .... StevenCorrigan(7) 2 48
(J Pearce) *hld up wl in rr: effrt over 2f out: sn outpcd and btn* **8/1**
4014 **12** *hd* **General Flumpa**[13] [5385] 5-9-5 58 .... JonjoMilczarek(5) 3 51
(C F Wall) *trckd ldng pair and racd on inner: rdn and cl up 2f out: hld whn bdly hmpd jst over 1f out: nt rcvr* **8/1**
0225 **13** *3 1/2* **Opera Comica**[191] [695] 3-9-4 60 .... MichaelJStainton 6 47
(J H M Gosden) *hld up wl in rr: struggling fr over 2f out* **12/1**
0/0- **14** *1/2* **Montecristo**[528] [1129] 13-9-5 60 .... LukeMcJannet(7) 10 46
(Rae Guest) *racd wd: in tch tl wknd over 2f out* **33/1**
3205 **15** *3* **Bramcote Lorne**[56] [4111] 3-8-11 58 .... MarkCoumbe(5) 5 40
(S Parr) *racd on inner in midfield: n.m.r 2f out: wknd* **9/1**

2m 32.0s (-2.39) **Going Correction** -0.20s/f (Stan)
WFA 3 from 4yo+ 8lb **15** Ran SP% **132.5**
Speed ratings (Par 101):99,97,95,93,92 92,92,92,91,91 90,90,88,88,86
CSF £135.78 CT £609.16 TOTE £9.10: £2.10, £8.60, £2.40; EX 136.40 TRIFECTA Not won. Place 6 £721.67, Place 5 £271.82.
Owner Tann Racing **Bred** Miss Jill Finegan **Trained** Ashtead, Surrey
■ Stewards' Enquiry : Kevin Ghunowa two-day ban: careless riding (Oct 10, Nov 16)
FOCUS
This looked a competitive if modest affair and the early pace was by no means strong.
Bramcote Lorne Official explanation: jockey said gelding lost its action 2f out
T/Plt: £1,308.50 to a £1 stake. Pool: £52,612.70. 29.35 winning tickets. T/Qpdt: £91.70 to a £1 stake. Pool: £3,880.80. 31.30 winning tickets. JN

5638
NEWMARKET (ROWLEY) (R-H)
Friday, September 29

OFFICIAL GOING: Soft
Wind: Fresh, across Weather: Cloudy with sunny spells

5653 SOMERVILLE TATTERSALL STKS (GROUP 3) (C&G) 7f
1:30 (1:31) (Class 1) 2-Y-O
£34,068 (£12,912; £6,462; £3,222; £1,614; £810) **Stalls** High

Form RPR
116 **1** **Thousand Words**[20] [5183] 2-8-12 104 .... RichardHughes 12 110+
(B W Hills) *lw: swtg: trckd ldrs: led over 1f out: sn edgd lft: drvn out* **15/2**
21 **2** *2 1/2* **Dijeerr (USA)**[24] [5089] 2-8-12 92 .... PhilipRobinson 7 103
(M A Jarvis) *lw: chsd ldr: led over 2f out: rdn and hdd over 1f out: styd on same pce ins fnl f* **9/1**
3 **3** *nk* **Ferneley (IRE)**[34] [4825] 2-8-12 .... WSupple 3 103
(Francis Ennis, Ire) *chsd ldrs: rdn over 1f out: styd on same pce fnl f* **5/1**[2]
110 **4** *hd* **Baby Strange**[101] [2719] 2-8-12 102 .... PaulHanagan 5 105+
(P A Blockley) *prom: outpcd over 2f out: r.o ins fnl f* **9/1**
212 **5** *hd* **Big Robert**[20] [5176] 2-8-12 105 .... MartinDwyer 9 102+
(W R Muir) *hld up: rdn over 1f out: r.o ins fnl f: nrst fin* **4/1**[1]
4 **6** *nk* **Jack Junior (USA)**[13] [5381] 2-8-12 .... RHills 8 101+
(B J Meehan) *dwlt: hdwy 2f out: sn rdn: styd on same pce fnl f* **33/1**
211 **7** *1 3/4* **St Philip (USA)**[23] [5114] 2-8-12 94 .... KerrinMcEvoy 11 96
(R M Beckett) *led over 4f: wknd ins fnl f* **9/1**
441 **8** *3/4* **Don't Panic (IRE)**[13] [5379] 2-8-12 87 .... EddieAhern 4 95
(P W Chapple-Hyam) *b.hind: prom: rdn over 2f out: wknd over 1f out* **13/2**[3]
1020 **9** *1 3/4* **Sadeek**[36] [4736] 2-8-12 104 .... NCallan 1 90
(K A Ryan) *lw: hld up: hdwy over 2f out: sn rdn: wknd fnl f* **16/1**
1553 **10** *12* **Danebury Hill**[34] [4809] 2-8-12 100 .... (t) LDettori 10 60
(B J Meehan) *hld up: rdn over 2f out: wknd over 1f out* **8/1**

1m 28.42s (1.92) **Going Correction** +0.475s/f (Yiel) **10** Ran SP% **111.7**
Speed ratings (Par 105):108,105,104,104,104 104,102,101,99,85
CSF £69.85 TOTE £7.10: £2.20, £3.50, £2.30; EX 53.20.
Owner K Abdulla **Bred** Juddmonte Farms Ltd **Trained** Lambourn, Berks
FOCUS
A fair renewal won in impressive fashion by Thousand Words, who bounced back from his Champagne disappointment to beat a decent-looking field, with Ferneley giving the form a solid look.
NOTEBOOK
Thousand Words, who looked a live 2000 Guineas candidate until bombing out in the Champagne Stakes, capitalised on the drop in grade and ran out a ready winner, handling the ground better than he had done at York. He is now likely to contest the Dewhurst, bidding to emulate former stable companion Haafhd who had also met with defeat in the Champagne, before a potential crack at the Guineas in May. (op 11-2 tchd 8-1in places)
Dijeerr(USA), cosy winner of just a fair race at Leicester, stepped up on that maiden success and kept on without threatening the winner, but with the soft ground he was unable to display the change of pace he showed last time. He too holds the Dewhurst entry, but could only have prospects of reversing form with the winner if it were to ride fast. (tchd 10-1 in a place)
Ferneley(IRE) has developed into a very useful juvenile, finishing third behind Teofilo in the Futurity Stakes latest, and he ran another sound race in defeat without proving a match for the smart winner. It is possible the soft ground was against him, but he gives the form a solid look and should be capable of winning more races at Listed/Group 3 level. (op 11-2 tchd 6-1, 13-2 in a place)
Baby Strange, not seen since finishing in mid-division in the Coventry Stakes, looked to appreciate the seventh furlong and kept on again close home to just miss out on third. Despite seeing it out so well, connections are now likely to aim him at the Cornwallis Stakes back over the minimum distance. (op 11-1)
Big Robert, runner-up to Caldra in a Listed contest at Goodwood earlier in the month, failed to cope with the drop back in trip and only found his stride after the race was beyond him. A mile looks his trip and he remains capable of better back on a sound surface. (tchd 7-2)

Jack Junior(USA), a pleasing fourth on his debut at Warwick, was taking a massive jump in class, but it was interesting Richard Hills was in the saddle, having struck up a good relationship with the owners' David Junior the previous season, and he displayed plenty of ability in keeping on to stake his claim for a place. Not beaten far at all, winning a maiden should prove a formality before stepping back up in grade. (op 25-1)

St Philip(USA) has been progressive, running out a hard-fought winner at Southwell last time, but he dropped away inside the final furlong and was probably not up to this grade. (op 8-1)

5654 SKY BET CHEVELEY PARK STKS (GROUP 1) (FILLIES) 6f

2:00 (2:02) (Class 1) 2-Y-O

£96,526 (£36,584; £18,309; £9,129; £4,573; £2,295) **Stalls** High

Form				RPR
1421	**1**		**Indian Ink (IRE)**[7] 5503 2-8-12 108 .... RichardHughes 7 (R Hannon) *chsd ldrs: rdn over 1f out: r.o to ld wl ins fnl f* **3/1**[1]	111
1251	**2**	*nk*	**Dhanyata (IRE)**[27] 5017 2-8-12 106 .... JimmyFortune 1 (B J Meehan) *lw: chsd ldrs: rdn to ld 1f out: hdd wl ins fnl f* **16/1**	110
312	**3**	*1 ¼*	**Silca Chiave**[33] 4853 2-8-12 109 .... TedDurcan 4 (M R Channon) *lw: hld up: hdwy over 2f out: rdn over 1f out: edgd rt: r.o* **11/2**[2]	106
213	**4**	*hd*	**La Presse (USA)**[13] 5356 2-8-12 .... MichaelHills 8 (B W Hills) *disp ld tl led over 2f out: rdn and hdd 1f out: no ex wl ins fnl f* **18/1**	106
5	**5**	*1 ¼*	**Theann**[10] 5464 2-8-12 .... MJKinane 12 (A P O'Brien, Ire) *a.p: rdn over 1f out: styd on same pce* **12/1**[3]	102
632	**6**	*hd*	**Magic America (USA)**[40] 4644 2-8-12 .... C-PLemaire 10 (Mme C Head-Maarek, France) *lw: gd sort: hld up in tch: outpcd over 2f out: styd on ins fnl f* **3/1**[1]	101
4661	**7**	*hd*	**Beauty Is Truth**[23] 5122 2-8-12 ....(b) TThulliez 5 (Robert Collet, France) *prom: rdn over 2f out: styd on same pce fnl f* **14/1**	101
1315	**8**	*2*	**Scarlet Runner**[36] 4737 2-8-12 109 .... KerrinMcEvoy 3 (J L Dunlop) *disp ld over 3f: wknd ins fnl f* **20/1**	95
12	**9**	*¾*	**Blue Rocket (IRE)**[35] 4762 2-8-12 87 .... NCallan 2 (T J Pitt) *s.i.s: hld up: rdn over 2f out: n.d* **33/1**	93
4121	**10**	*shd*	**Vital Statistics**[29] 4966 2-8-12 107 .... JohnEgan 6 (D R C Elsworth) *hld up: rdn over 2f out: n.d* **12/1**[3]	92
112	**11**	*3*	**Wid (USA)**[29] 4966 2-8-12 105 .... RHills 11 (J L Dunlop) *s.i.s: hld up: hdwy over 2f out: sn rdn: wknd fnl f* **16/1**	83

1m 14.81s (1.71) **Going Correction** +0.475s/f (Yiel) **11** Ran SP% **112.2**

Speed ratings (Par 106):107,106,104,104,103 102,102,99,98,98 94

CSF £53.06 TOTE £3.60: £1.50, £4.60, £2.10; EX 69.40.

Owner Raymond Tooth **Bred** Killeen Castle Stud **Trained** East Everleigh, Wilts

FOCUS

The withdrawal of ante-post Guineas favourite Sander Camillo, due to the ground, took much of the gloss away and this was by no means a great renewal of what is traditionally one of most significant juvenile filly events. The first seven were covered by little more than three lengths, and three of the first five went to post with sales-race form. Sander Camillo would have won by a good couple of lengths on her Cherry Hinton form, so it will be surprising if it has much bearing on the opening fillies classic of 2007

NOTEBOOK

Indian Ink(IRE), who capitalised on the drop in grade when running out an impressive winner of the Watership Down Stud Stakes at Ascot a week earlier, had previously run a good race in defeat behind Silk Blossom in the Lowther Stakes at York and her extra stamina came into play as she ground it out from the resolute Dhantaya to record a first Group 1 success. This was not a vintage renewal, but the daughter of Indian Ridge relishes a soft surface and it enabled her to reverse Royal Ascot form with both Scarlet Runner and Vital Statistics. There is enough stamina in her pedigree to suggest she will stay a mile, but the Guineas is unlikely to be run on the soft ground she prefers. (op 11-4)

Dhanyata(IRE), another bringing sales race form into the contest, having finished fifth behind Doctor Brown at York, confirmed she is on the up when winning a modest Group 3 on the Polytrack at Kempton earlier in the month and this was another huge step forward. Under pressure fully three furlongs out, she appeared to handle the soft ground better than she had done at York and it was only in the final strides Indian Ink began to gain the upper edge. Six furlongs is as far she wants to go though and, like so many good sprinting juveniles, finding races for her next season is going to be tough. (op 18-1 tchd 20-1)

Silca Chiave, a half-sister to Silcas Sister and Golden Silca, stepped up massively on her Newbury maiden win when losing out by just a short head to Miss Beatrix in the Group 1 Moyglare Stud Stakes at the Curragh, and looked one of the likelier winners following the withdrawal of Sander Camillo. She threatened to come through and dispute the lead over two furlongs out, but soon became outpaced and hit a flat spot, only to stay on again to claim third close home. As she showed at the Curragh, seven furlongs is not a problem and she is a likely sort for the Rockfel back here on Champions Day. (op 9-2 tchd 6-1)

La Presse(USA) created a strong impression when destroying a useful-looking field of colts in a York maiden last month, but failed to live up to expectations when only third in a Group 3 at Ayr latest. This was better, and she was able to reverse debut form with Wid, showing plenty of pace and making most of the running until a furlong out, but unless improving for a fast surface next season, she is going to continue to fall a fair way short at this level. (op 20-1)

Theann, by Rock Of Gibraltar out of high-class sprinting mare Cassandra Go, left a disappointing debut effort behind when running the very smart Arch Swing close and again ran well in defeat when fifth behind Silk Blossom in a valuable sales race at the Curragh. This drop back to six furlongs was not in her favour however and, as was to be expected, she found herself outclassed. She can make her mark at Group level but the plan now is surely to lose her maiden tag. (op 14-1)

Magic America(USA), whose trainer took this three times in the 80s and 90s, was racing without blinkers for the first time when runner-up to Dutch Art in the Group 1 Prix Morny last time and on that evidence she was the one to beat. However, she failed to reproduce the effort on this first venture outside her homeland and it is possible the return of headgear is required as she was outpaced a long way from home and failed to perform with any sparkle, getting going only when the race was beyond her. (op 11-4)

Beauty Is Truth, a Group 3 winner at Chantilly earlier in the month, looked to have a fair bit to find with most of these and she was unable to reverse Morny form with her compatriot. (op 16-1)

Scarlet Runner was a most progressive sort in the summer, placing behind Sander Camillo at Royal Ascot and winning the Princess Margaret, but she came unstuck on soft ground in the Lowther and again floundered in the ground. Her two most recent runs are best ignored, but she has lost the progressive edge and is probably best put away until next season now.

Blue Rocket(IRE) held nothing more than place claims following a defeat in a minor event at Chester and she failed to get involved. She needs returning to a more realistic level.

Vital Statistics was perhaps one of the most disappointing as she has been running well all season and confirmed her improvement with victory over Wid, who had beaten her earlier in the season, at Salisbury last month. Restrained from an early stage, she never picked up and it is possible, although by Indian Ridge, she failed to fire in the ground – her two most recent previous victories both came on good to firm. (op 10-1)

Wid(USA) was nibbled at in the market, but she was another who could not get her feet out of the ground. She deserves another chance. (op 20-1)

5655 £250000 TATTERSALLS OCTOBER AUCTION STKS 6f

2:35 (2:38) (Class 2) 2-Y-O

£123,125 (£49,250; £24,600; £14,775; £9,825; £4,925) **Stalls** High

Form				RPR
121	**1**		**Caldra (IRE)**[20] 5176 2-9-1 .... RyanMoore 4 (S Kirk) *racd nr side: trckd ldrs: rdn 2f out: r.o to ld wl ins fnl f: drvn out: 1st of 13 in gp* **9/2**[1]	107
0111	**2**	*½*	**Tobosa**[49] 4335 2-9-1 77 .... KerrinMcEvoy 12 (W Jarvis) *lw: racd nr side: in tch: effrt over 2f out: led over 1f out: hdd wl ins fnl f: hld fnl strides: 2nd of 13 in gp* **10/1**[3]	106
2122	**3**	*5*	**Aahayson**[14] 5334 2-8-13 78 .... PatCosgrave 2 (K R Burke) *racd nr side: led overall: rdn and hdd over 1f out: kpt on same pce fnl f: 3rd of 13 in gp* **25/1**	89
1	**4**	*½*	**Passified**[8] 5491 2-8-6 .... JohnEgan 19 (D R C Elsworth) *racd far side: midfield: hdwy 2f out: swtchd rt whn nt clr run over 1f out: r.o to ld gp wl ins fnl f: nt rch overall ldrs:* **14/1**	80+
31	**5**	*¾*	**Chataway**[59] 4028 2-8-13 .... LDettori 23 (B J Meehan) *racd far side: in tch: effrt 2f out: led gp briefly ins fnl f: one pce towards fin: 2nd of 14 in gp* **6/1**[2]	85
2221	**6**	*1 ¼*	**Tudor Prince (IRE)**[34] 4801 2-8-11 88 .... JimmyFortune 3 (B J Meehan) *lw: racd nr side: in tch: rdn 2f out: ev ch wl over 1f out: edgd rt and no ex ins fnl f: 4th of 13 in gp* **6/1**[2]	79
2	**7**	*hd*	**We'll Come**[34] 4801 2-8-13 .... PhilipRobinson 6 (M A Jarvis) *racd nr side: midfield: rdn and hdwy over 2f out: edgd rt over 1f out: styd on u.p ins fnl f: 5th of 13 in gp* **14/1**	80
4601	**8**	*½*	**Bertoliver**[10] 5454 2-8-9 .... DaneO'Neill 30 (D K Ivory) *racd far side: led gp: rdn 2f out: hdd ins fnl f: no ex towards fin: 3rd of 14 in gp* **66/1**	75
32	**9**	*hd*	**Expensive Detour (IRE)**[33] 4843 2-8-7 .... TomEaves 22 (Mrs L Stubbs) *racd far side: trckd ldrs: rdn 2f out: styd on same pce fnl f: 4th of 14 in gp* **33/1**	72
0311	**10**	*1*	**Cuppacocoa**[20] 5162 2-8-5 66 ow1 .... KDarley 20 (C G Cox) *racd far side: midfield: hdwy 1/2-way: sn rdn: no ex inisde fnl f: 5th of 14 in gp* **50/1**	67
1060	**11**	*nk*	**Major Third (IRE)**[49] 4321 2-8-7 70 .... DavidAllan 8 (T D Easterby) *racd nr side: hld up: rdn and sme hdwy 1/2-way: kpt on ins fnl f: nt pce to chal: 6th of 13 in gp* **100/1**	68
3	**12**	*hd*	**Den's Gift (IRE)**[111] 2432 2-8-11 .... AdamKirby 17 (C G Cox) *racd far side: midfield: rdn and outpcd over 2f out: kpt on ins fnl f: 6th of 14 in gp* **50/1**	72
0356	**13**	*shd*	**Marmaida (IRE)**[34] 4815 2-8-2 84 .... NickyMackay 24 (W J Knight) *racd far side: w ldrs tl rdn over 2f out: one pce ins fnl f: eased towards fin: 7th of 14 in gp* **50/1**	63
4010	**14**	*¾*	**El Bosque (IRE)**[13] 5372 2-8-9 96 .... GrahamGibbons 29 (B R Millman) *racd far side: midfield: rdn over 2f out: one pce ins fnl f: 8th of 14 in gp* **33/1**	67
002	**15**	*½*	**Golden Desert (IRE)**[14] 5347 2-8-13 .... IanMongan 5 (T G Mills) *b. racd nr side: prom: rdn over 2f out: wknd fnl f: 7th of 13 in gp* **50/1**	70
0050	**16**	*nk*	**Musical Award (IRE)**[3] 5597 2-8-11 .... TPQueally 15 (M G Quinlan) *swtchd to r far side after 1f: in rr: rdn over 2f out: kpt on fnl f: nt trble ldrs: 9th of 14 in gp* **100/1**	67
413	**17**	*1 ¼*	**Veenwouden**[26] 5041 2-8-10 .... JamieSpencer 16 (J R Fanshawe) *lw: racd far side: hld up: rdn over 2f out: sme hdwy over 1f out: no imp fnl f: 10th of 14 in gp* **16/1**	62
32	**18**	*1 ½*	**Mount Hermon (IRE)**[24] 5091 2-8-9 .... SteveDrowne 11 (H Morrison) *lw: racd nr side: towards rr: kpt on fnl f: nvr trbld ldrs: 8th of 13 in gp* **25/1**	57
445	**19**	*¾*	**Marine Parade**[41] 4600 2-8-13 78 .... MJKinane 14 (R Hannon) *racd nr side: hld up: rdn over 2f out: nvr on terms: 9th of 13 in gp* **50/1**	58
3424	**20**	*shd*	**Temtation (IRE)**[25] 5052 2-8-0 .... PaulHanagan 13 (J R Boyle) *racd nr side: in tch: rdn and wknd over 2f out: 10th of 13 in gp* **100/1**	45
3	**21**	*1*	**Aegean Prince**[11] 5417 2-8-7 .... RichardHughes 10 (R Hannon) *dwlt: swtchd rt s: racd nr side: hld up: rdn 2f out: nvr on terms: 11th of 13 in gp* **33/1**	49
1100	**22**	*½*	**Espartano**[89] 3126 2-8-9 91 .... NCallan 18 (M J Wallace) *racd far side: towards rr: rdn and sme hdwy over 2f out: wknd ins fnl f: 11th of 14 in gp* **12/1**	50
632	**23**	*shd*	**Convivial Spirit**[15] 5315 2-8-5 .... JoeFanning 21 (E F Vaughan) *racd far side: a bhd: 12th of 14 in gp* **100/1**	45
006	**24**	*1 ½*	**Marlyn Ridge**[17] 5261 2-8-5 .... SaleemGolam 26 (D K Ivory) *racd far side: a bhd: 13th of 14 in gp* **100/1**	41
2433	**25**	*1 ½*	**Isobel Rose (IRE)**[16] 5288 2-8-6 76 ....(v[1]) EddieAhern 9 (E A L Dunlop) *b.hind: racd nr side: rdn 1/2-way: a towards rr: 12th of 13 in gp* **40/1**	37
433	**26**	*hd*	**Greyt Big Stuff (USA)**[101] 2733 2-8-9 81 ....(b[1]) RobertWinston 28 (B J Meehan) *racd far side: w ldrs: rdn 1/2-way: u.p whn n.m.r and hmpd over 1f out: sn wknd: 14th of 14 in gp* **50/1**	40
033	**27**	*¾*	**Kalasam**[20] 5178 2-8-9 .... MartinDwyer 7 (W R Muir) *lw: racd nr side: prom: rdn 1/2-way: wknd 2f out: 13th of 13 in gp* **66/1**	37
4423	**U**		**La Neige**[16] 5292 2-8-13 98 .... TonyCulhane 27 (M R Channon) *rrd and uns rdr s* **18/1**	—

1m 14.67s (1.57) **Going Correction** +0.475s/f (Yiel) **28** Ran SP% **126.7**

Speed ratings (Par 101):108,107,100,100,99 97,97,96,96,94 94,94,94,93,92 91,90,88,87,87 85,85,85,83,81 80,79,—

CSF £40.52 TOTE £5.70: £2.50, £4.40, £8.00; EX 47.40.

Owner Norman Ormiston **Bred** S J Macdonald **Trained** Upper Lambourn, Berks

FOCUS

A valuable sales race run only 0.6 sec slower than the Middle Park, and fractionally faster than the Cheveley Park. It was dominated by the highest-weighted pair, who came clear. The form looks solid, although the field split into two groups, with those in the stands'-side group holding an advantage.

NOTEBOOK

Caldra(IRE), who has looked an improved performer since being stepped up to seven furlongs and a mile recently, got a good tow on this drop back in distance and proved too strong for the runner-up on the climb to the line. He is clearly improving and may attempt to secure his first Group win in the Autumn Stakes at Ascot next month. (tchd 5-1 in a place)

Tobosa, another who has been improving with racing, was on a four-timer and although the drop in trip proved no problem he came up against a rival who is a little ahead of him at present. This was his first run on soft ground and he seemed to handle it, but he was well clear of the rest and is fully entitled to take his chance in the Group 3 Horris Hill Stakes next.

Aahayson is a consistent performer and again ran his race. The fact that he was beaten so far by the first two gives an indication of the progress they have made.

Passified ◆, a good winner on fast ground on her debut the previous week, ran a race full of promise on this much softer surface. She was drawn on the wrong side as the race worked out, but again showed a turn of foot to pass her rivals and looks capable of better again with this experience under her belt. (op 12-1)
Chataway, whose Goodwood success had been franked by the subsequent wins of the next three home, ran well having been drawn on the less-favoured side of the track and lost little in defeat. As a gelding he has no fancy entries, but he looks to have more good races in him at this sort of trip, although he may prefer faster ground. (op 5-1)
Tudor Prince(IRE), who appreciated the return to an easier surface when winning on the July course last month, showed up throughout on the nearside and appeared to do little wrong behind some useful rivals. (op 7-1)
We'll Come finished much closer to Tudor Prince than he had on their meeting last month and should be capable of winning his maiden before developing into a useful handicapper.
Bertoliver, a course and distance winner on much faster ground the previous week, was another to perform well from his high draw and helps give the form substance. (op 50-1)
Expensive Detour(IRE), placed in ordinary maidens on a sound surface and nibbled at at long prices, ran well and now qualifies for a handicap mark. He should be up to winning races.
Cuppacocoa, bidding for a hat-trick in this much higher grade, was also facing a longer trip and softer ground. He fared quite well, having raced with the far-side group, and still looks reasonably handicapped. (op 33-1)
Espartano Official explanation: jockey said gelding was never travelling
Kalasam Official explanation: jockey said colt was unsuited by the soft ground

5656 SHADWELL MIDDLE PARK STKS (GROUP 1) (ENTIRE COLTS) 6f
3:10 (3:12) (Class 1) 2-Y-O
£96,526 (£36,584; £18,309; £9,129; £4,573; £2,295) **Stalls** High

Form RPR
111 **1** **Dutch Art**[40] 4644 2-8-12 .... LDettori 2 121+
(P W Chapple-Hyam) *h.d.w: w ldr tl led over 2f out: shkn up and r.o wl* **6/5**[1]
1221 **2** *2* **Wi Dud**[21] 5154 2-8-12 111 .... NCallan 1 114
(K A Ryan) *trckd ldrs: rdn and ev ch over 1f out: edgd rt ins fnl f: styd on same pce* **10/1**
0521 **3** *1 1/4* **Captain Marvelous (IRE)**[13] 5372 2-8-12 95 .... MichaelHills 6 110
(B W Hills) *lw: w ldr: rdn and ev ch over 1f out: edgd lft and no ex ins fnl f* **33/1**
1112 **4** *1 1/4* **Hellvelyn**[47] 4409 2-8-12 112 .... TedDurcan 5 107
(B Smart) *trckd ldrs: rdn and ev ch over 1f out: wkng whn n.m.r wl ins fnl f* **11/2**
221 **5** *1 1/4* **Brave Tin Soldier (USA)**[12] 5408 2-8-12 .... MJKinane 4 103
(A P O'Brien, Ire) *lw: gd sort: sn led: hdd over 2f out: rdn and wknd over 1f out* **9/2**[2]
5211 **6** *16* **Conquest (IRE)**[37] 4712 2-8-12 113 .... (b) JimmyFortune 3 55
(W J Haggas) *trckd ldrs tl wknd over 1f out* **5/1**[3]
1m 14.07s (0.97) **Going Correction** +0.475s/f (Yiel) **6** Ran SP% **107.7**
Speed ratings (Par 109):112,109,107,106,104 83
CSF £12.89 TOTE £1.90: £1.40, £3.90; EX 10.80.
Owner Mrs Susan Roy **Bred** Cromlech Bloodstock **Trained** Newmarket, Suffolk
■ Stewards' Enquiry : N Callan caution: careless riding

FOCUS
A good winner, who has been rated value for a shade more than the bare margin, but not the strength in depth one would like to see. The second ran his usual solid race and the third continues improving, so sound enough form.

NOTEBOOK
Dutch Art's credentials looked cast iron coming into this, having won over five and six furlongs, on fast and heavy ground, and already proven himself at Group 1 level. His recent Morny success meant he was the one to beat and having settled nicely on the pace, he went on over two out before drawing away quite impressively. Undoubtedly the best sprinting two-year-old this season, his ability to stay the mile of the Guineas looks suspect as his pedigree suggests he is all speed, but his trainer is of a different opinion and believes we have still to see the best of him. (op Evens tchd 5-4 in places and 10-11 in a place)
Wi Dud is a tough sprinting juvenile who never goes down without a fight, and having finished second to Conquest in the Gimcrack he gained a deserved first Group success in the Flying Childers. It would have been slightly disappointing had he won this, but in being comfortably held in second he provides a good guide to the level of the form and connections will no doubt be keen to get him out again. (op 17-2)
Captain Marvelous(IRE), a nursery winner off 95 at Newbury last time out, had previously fallen short in two tries at Pattern level so it was something of a surprise to see him finish so close up. There is no denying he has progressed, but he looks the type who is going to find winning very tough indeed next season. (op 40-1)
Hellvelyn, winner of the Coventry Stakes, lost little in defeat when runner-up to Holy Roman Emperor in the Pheonix Stakes, but this was not such a good effort and he was already beaten when squeezed for room. It is possible the very soft ground was no good for him and he could be worth another chance, but any future success is most unlikely to come at Group 1 level. (op 6-1)
Brave Tin Soldier(USA) had bumped into a couple of useful sorts when second to Chataway and La Presse in maidens at Goodwood and York respectively, but got it right when winning a Listed race at the Curragh. He had a bit to find on this rise in grade and having led to over two furlongs out he was soon brushed aside. He is another who needs to have his sights lowered. (op 5-1)
Conquest(IRE), a highly talented colt who would have been coming into this in search of a four-timer had he put it all in at Royal Ascot, proved himself to be a class act when cutting down Wi Dud in the Gimcrack, but unfortunately slipped his tongue over the bit and was unable to run his race. He would have been bang there if reproducing his York effort and he deserves another chance, with the possibility of him maturing from two to three. Official explanation: jockey said colt lost its action (op 6-1)

5657 PEARL SMITH GODOLPHIN STKS (LISTED RACE) 1m 4f
3:45 (3:47) (Class 1) 3-Y-O+
£15,898 (£6,025; £3,015; £1,503; £753; £378) **Stalls** High

Form RPR
2434 **1** **Degas Art (IRE)**[49] 4337 3-8-6 105 .... KerrinMcEvoy 11 112
(D R C Elsworth) *lw: swtg: mde all: lft alone far side over 5f out: styd on wl* **10/1**
43-5 **2** *1 3/4* **Into The Dark**[22] 5142 5-9-0 105 .... (t) LDettori 4 109
(Saeed Bin Suroor) *hld up: hdwy 1/2-way: sn swtchd centre: led main gp over 1f out: sn rdn and edgd lft: styd on: nt reach wnr, who raced alone* **10/1**
3151 **3** *3/4* **Mashaahed**[13] 5360 3-8-10 110 .... RHills 3 112+
(B W Hills) *hld up: swtchd centre over 5f out: hdwy over 2f out: styd on same pce ins fnl f* **3/1**[2]
-322 **4** *5* **Khyber Kim**[34] 4817 4-9-0 106 .... DaneO'Neill 5 101
(H Candy) *prom: swtchd centre over 5f out: led that gp 4f out: rdn and hdd over 1f out: sn wknd* **11/4**[1]
0435 **5** *1 1/4* **Akarem**[13] 5395 5-9-4 110 .... PatCosgrave 8 103
(K R Burke) *lw: chsd ldrs: swtchd centre over 5f out: rdn and wknd over 1f out* **12/1**
4006 **6** *8* **Before You Go (IRE)**[22] 5142 3-8-7 100 ow1 .... RyanMoore 1 88
(T G Mills) *lw: hld up: swtchd centre over 5f out: hdwy over 2f out: wknd over 1f out* **33/1**
5223 **7** *11* **Camrose**[20] 5170 5-9-0 102 .... (b) JimmyFortune 7 70
(J L Dunlop) *hld up: hdwy and swtchd centre over 5f out: wknd over 2f out* **16/1**
-063 **8** *4* **Day Walker**[19] 5226 4-9-0 .... EddieAhern 2 64
(Rune Haugen, Norway) *s.i.s: hld up: swtchd centre over 5f out: n.d* **50/1**
1-60 **9** *1* **Fire And Rain (FR)**[20] 5185 3-8-6 .... MJKinane 9 63
(A P O'Brien, Ire) *chsd ldrs: swtchd centre over 5f out: wknd over 2f out* **6/1**[3]
0-05 **10** *shd* **Storm Trooper (GER)**[19] 5226 6-9-0 .... (b) ASuborics 6 62
(Rune Haugen, Norway) *hld up: hdwy and swtchd centre over 5f out: wknd 3f out* **100/1**
66 **11** *3/4* **Savannah**[34] 4822 3-8-6 .... KDarley 13 61
(A P O'Brien, Ire) *chsd wnr 10f out tl swtchd to ld centre gp over 5f out: hdd that gp 4f out: rdn and wknd over 2f out* **50/1**
3035 **12** *1 1/4* **Profit's Reality (IRE)**[5] 5547 4-9-0 102 .... RobbieFitzpatrick 10 59
(P A Blockley) *lw: hld up: swtchd centre over 5f out: rdn and wknd over 2f out* **20/1**
0040 **13** *1 1/2* **Tiger Tiger (FR)**[38] 4676 5-9-0 93 .... IanMongan 12 57
(Jamie Poulton) *hld up: swtchd centre over 5f out: wknd over 3f out* **20/1**
152/ **14** *51* **Fantasy Ride**[699] 6472 4-9-0 .... JimmyQuinn 14 —
(J Pearce) *b: h.d.w: hld up: wkng whn swtchd centre over 5f out* **66/1**
2m 35.66s (2.16) **Going Correction** +0.475s/f (Yiel)
WFA 3 from 4yo+ 8lb **14** Ran SP% **116.6**
Speed ratings (Par 111):111,109,109,106,105 99,92,89,89,89 88,87,86,52
CSF £96.60 TOTE £12.10: £3.60, £2.90, £1.70; EX 130.20.
Owner Matthew Green **Bred** Millsec Limited **Trained** Newmarket, Suffolk

FOCUS
A good race for the grade rated through the runner-up. The field began racing towards the far rail, but soon moved towards the centre, leaving only McEvoy on Degas Art to race there alone.

NOTEBOOK
Degas Art(IRE) had started to lose his progressive look and a disappointing effort over ten furlongs at the course last time did little to alter that view. However, the return to a softer surface enabled him to improve and under a fine tactical ride from McEvoy, who elected to stay far side on his own, he ran out a ready winner. This is clearly his trip and he ground it out determinedly, fully deserving the victory having had to give best to the likes of Red Rocks, Papal Bull and Youmzain earlier in the season. A fine physical specimen, he should progress further from three to four and looks capable of winning at Group level.
Into The Dark looked a potential top-notcher at three, but he failed to progress last season and his reappearance effort at Southwell suggested he had regressed. This though altered that view as he seemed refreshed by the change of tactics, keeping on dourly into second.. He can score at this level if able to build on this. (op 17-2 tchd 8-1)
Mashaahed made a pleasing return from a break when winning impressively from Ouninpohja at Ayr and the return to 12 furlongs did not look set to pose a problem having finished third to Papal Bull over it at Chester back in May. Ridden with restraint, he made steady progress through the field to reach a challenging position, but could not quicken out of the ground. This was a good effort under his 4lb Listed penalty from a horse who has yet to run a bad race, and he should develop further over the winter. (tchd 11-4)
Khyber Kim looked to improve for the step up to this distance when just losing out to Crocodile Dundee at Windsor and, with his ability to handle cut in the ground unquestionable, he was rightly made favourite. However, on a more testing course, he appeared to fail to see it out and ended up being comfortably held. (tchd 100-30 in a place and 3-1 in places)
Akarem has had a good season of it, winning at this level and running several good races in defeat. Having faced an impossible task in the Irish St Leger latest he was expected to bounce back, but was unable to do so and may have found the ground too testing. (op 14-1)
Fire And Rain(FR), a winner from Mashaahed on his sole outing at two, made his belated reappearance in the Great Voltigeur and things only got harder when being asked to contest the St Leger. This looked a sensible opportunity for him to get back on track, but he dropped right away having held a good early position and is one to leave well alone at present. (op 13-2 tchd 7-1)

5658 MACMILLAN CANCER SUPPORT E B F MAIDEN STKS (DIV I) 7f
4:20 (4:22) (Class 4) 2-Y-O **£5,829** (£1,734; £866; £432) **Stalls** High

Form RPR
6 **1** **Desert Dew (IRE)**[10] 5457 2-9-3 .... MichaelHills 9 93+
(B W Hills) *lw: led 3f: led again over 2f out: rdn out* **7/2**[2]
2 *1 3/4* **Urban Spirit** 2-9-3 .... RichardHughes 8 89
(B W Hills) *w'like: leggy: trckd ldrs: outpcd over 1f out: r.o ins fnl f* **33/1**
3 **3** *1 1/4* **Al Tharib (USA)**[24] 5089 2-9-3 .... RHills 13 86
(Sir Michael Stoute) *a.p: rdn over 1f out: styd on* **3/1**[1]
2 **4** *1 3/4* **Murbek (IRE)**[44] 4487 2-9-3 .... MartinDwyer 5 81
(M A Jarvis) *w'like: trckd ldr: led 4f out: hdd over 2f out: rdn and hung lft over 1f out: no ex* **5/1**[3]
5 *3/4* **Cat De Mille (USA)** 2-9-3 .... AdrianMcCarthy 7 79+
(P W Chapple-Hyam) *cmpt: scope: s.i.s: hld up: racd keenly: hdwy over 2f out: nt trble ldrs* **33/1**
6 *1/2* **Mount Parnassus**[12] 5407 2-9-3 .... MJKinane 14 78
(A P O'Brien, Ire) *lw: gd sort: chsd ldrs: rdn over 2f out: wknd fnl f* **7/1**
7 *nk* **Lazy Darren** 2-9-3 .... DaneO'Neill 4 77+
(M Wigham) *w'like: hld up: styd on appr fnl f: nrst fin* **100/1**
6 **8** *2* **Rudry Dragon (IRE)**[56] 4105 2-9-3 .... RobbieFitzpatrick 2 72
(P A Blockley) *hld up: hdwy over 4f out: rdn over 1f out: wknd fnl f* **25/1**
9 *hd* **Mount Hadley (USA)** 2-9-3 .... RyanMoore 15 71
(E A L Dunlop) *gd sort: hld up: rdn over 2f out: n.d* **25/1**
10 *1* **Guiseppe Verdi (USA)** 2-9-3 .... JimmyFortune 1 69
(J H M Gosden) *gd sort: b.bkwd: s.s: hdwy over 5f out: rdn and wknd over 1f out* **14/1**
11 *3* **Express Wish** 2-9-3 .... LDettori 12 61
(J Noseda) *gd sort: scope: s.i.s: plld hrd and sn prom: rdn over 2f out: wknd over 1f out* **13/2**
12 *1* **Just Two Numbers** 2-9-3 .... KerrinMcEvoy 11 58
(W Jarvis) *w'like: hld up: a in rr* **22/1**
13 *1 3/4* **Giovanni D'Oro (IRE)** 2-9-3 .... OscarUrbina 16 54
(N A Callaghan) *lw: leggy: scope: s.s: a bhd* **33/1**
0 **14** *59* **Zell Am See**[10] 5458 2-9-3 .... TPQueally 6 —
(M H Tompkins) *plld hrd and prom: lost pl 5f out: wknd 3f out* **100/1**
1m 30.09s (3.59) **Going Correction** +0.475s/f (Yiel) **14** Ran SP% **119.2**
Speed ratings (Par 97):98,96,94,92,91 91,90,88,88,87 83,82,80,13
CSF £123.59 TOTE £4.50: £1.60, £5.90, £1.80; EX 137.60.
Owner Gainsborough Stud **Bred** Mrs Rebecca Philipps **Trained** Lambourn, Berks

FOCUS
A pretty strong maiden that could be rated higher and looks sure to produce winners, although the proximity of a very cheap purchase in seventh tempers confidence a little.

NOTEBOOK

Desert Dew(IRE), who received a poor ride when getting an horrific run through on his debut over course and distance, was a costly purchase at 250,000gns and the softer ground looked likely to suit the son of Indian Ridge. Ridden prominently on this occasion, he still showed signs of inexperience, but picked up well to regain the lead before running on strongly to win with something in hand. The Horris Hill at Newbury in October now looks a likely target and it is not hard to see him going close if the ground turns up soft. (op 4-1)

Urban Spirit ◆, a stablemate of the winner, is bred to appreciate trips in excess of this and was dismissed in the betting, but he appeared to know his job well enough and held a prominent position throughout. Although proving no match for his stable companion, he shaped with immense promise and should be winning once tackling a mile, possibly on a better surface. (tchd 28-1)

Al Tharib(USA), a huge son of Silver Hawk who holds a trio of Group 1 entries, was given anything but a hard time when third in a decent maiden on his debut at Leicester, and looked a worthy favourite with that run under his belt. However, the softer ground was not necessarily to his liking and he was unable to pick up out of it, just staying on at the one pace. He looks certain to improve for a mile though and deserves another chance back on a faster surface, the colt looking certain to progress from two to three. (op 10-3 tchd 4-1)

Murbek(IRE), runner-up to a useful-looking sort on his debut at Sandown last month, holds Dewhurst and Racing Post entries and he was expected to build on that debut effort, but the softer ground looked to hold him back and he hung under pressure. He is probably better than this, but not up to Group level on the evidence so far. (op 9-2)

Cat De Mille(USA) ◆ fared best of the debutants, running on for fifth after a slow start. He should be capable of a fair bit better, especially on a sounder surface (op 40-1)

Mount Parnassus, who shaped well on his recent debut at the Curragh, holds all the remaining big-race entries as one would expect from the operation, but having held a prominent early position he soon came under the pump and ultimately dropped away. He may need more time and deserves another chance on faster ground. (tchd 15-2, 8-1 in a place)

Lazy Darren, who cost just 1,700gns, ran better than his odds entitled him to and was going on quite nicely close home. He should come into his own at three and can win races on this evidence.

Express Wish, who as a son of Danehill Dancer should have handled the ground, recovered from a slow start, but pulled too hard and so it was no surprise to see him drop right away in the end. There was enough in this effort to suggest he can win races, but he will obviously need to improve. (op 7-1)

Zell Am See Official explanation: trainer said colt finished distressed

5659 MACMILLAN CANCER SUPPORT E B F MAIDEN STKS (DIV II) 7f

4:55 (4:57) (Class 4) 2-Y-O £5,829 (£1,734; £866; £432) Stalls High

Form					RPR
	1		**Supersonic Dave (USA)** 2-9-3	JamieSpencer 14	84+
			(B J Meehan) *neat: trckd ldrs: led over 1f out: shkn up and r.o*	**8/1**	
4	2	3/4	**Kirk Michael**[24] 5089 2-9-3	DaneO'Neill 13	82
			(H Candy) *chsd ldr: led over 4f out: hdd over 1f out: r.o*	**7/2**[2]	
	3	3/4	**Glen Nevis (USA)** 2-9-3	LDettori 3	80+
			(J Noseda) *w'like: scope: hld up: hdwy 2f out: r.o*	**13/2**[3]	
	4	4	**Rhaam** 2-9-3	RHills 5	70+
			(B W Hills) *lw: w'like: scope: hld up: hdwy over 1f out: nt rch ldrs*	**12/1**	
	5	hd	**Mystic Dancer** 2-9-3	RyanMoore 4	69+
			(Sir Michael Stoute) *gd sort: hld up in tch: outpcd over 2f out: hdwy over 1f out: no imp ins fnl f*	**10/3**[1]	
	6	1/2	**Cape Hawk (IRE)** 2-9-3	RichardHughes 2	68
			(R Hannon) *gd sort: s.i.s: hdwy over 4f out: rdn over 1f out: wknd fnl f*	**14/1**	
	7	3 1/2	**Inchlaggan (IRE)** 2-9-3	MichaelHills 8	59
			(B W Hills) *gd sort: hld up: nvr nr to chal*	**16/1**	
0	8	1 1/4	**Tetouan**[25] 5066 2-9-3	SteveDrowne 1	56+
			(R Charlton) *prom over 4f*	**9/1**	
	9	nk	**Tasweet (IRE)** 2-9-3	MartinDwyer 7	55
			(J H M Gosden) *w'like: prom: rdn over 1f out: sn hung lft and wknd*	**9/1**	
	10	1/2	**Sumner (IRE)** 2-9-3	TPQueally 12	53
			(M H Tompkins) *leggy: scope: hld up: hdwy 1/2-way: wknd over 1f out*	**40/1**	
	11	2 1/2	**Bold Bobby Be (IRE)** 2-9-3	IanMongan 10	52+
			(J L Dunlop) *cmpt: b.bkwd: hld up: a in rr*	**25/1**	
0	12	3	**Ponte Vecchio (IRE)**[28] 4992 2-9-3	PatCosgrave 9	39
			(J R Boyle) *lw: hld up: rdn over 2f out: a in rr*	**50/1**	
	13	2 1/2	**Hamilton House** 2-9-3	JimmyQuinn 15	33
			(M H Tompkins) *cmpt: bkwd: chsd ldrs over 4f*	**66/1**	
0	14	18	**Chart Express**[21] 5147 2-9-0	DeanCorby(3) 6	—
			(P Howling) *sn led: hdd over 4f out: wknd over 2f out*	**100/1**	

1m 31.38s (4.88) **Going Correction** +0.475s/f (Yiel) **14 Ran SP% 120.7**

Speed ratings (Par 97):91,90,89,84,84 83,79,78,78,77 74,71,68,47

CSF £35.28 TOTE £9.60: £2.70, £1.80, £2.10; EX 40.40.

Owner Roldvale Limited **Bred** A B Hancock III **Trained** Manton, Wilts

FOCUS

Although run 1.31 sec slower, there is not much between this and the first division on a line through Kirk Michael, who had finished one place behind Al Tharib on his debut at Leicester, the latter named finishing third in the first division.

NOTEBOOK

Supersonic Dave(USA), a son of Swain, comes from a stable whose juveniles tend to improve for their debut run, but he overcame visible signs of greenness and ran on strongly to win with a bit in hand. This was a decent maiden and, with significant improvement anticipated, he may well make his mark at a higher level this season, if asked to race again at two. He will stay a mile in time and is definitely one to keep on side. (op 10-1)

Kirk Michael, whose debut fourth behind Dijeerr at Leicester received a boost when that one finished second in the opening Group 3 event, looked set to go close on ground he is bred to handle, being by Selkirk, and he ran his race, but looked to bump into a smart sort. He should find a race before long. (op 4-1)

Glen Nevis(USA), a son of Gulch, comes from a stable that is more than capable of producing one to win first time up, but he got a bit too far back early and, although making some notable late gains, the winner had flown. He is another who should have little trouble winning a maiden if this effort is anything to go by. (op 6-1 tchd 7-1)

Rhaam ◆, a half-brother to the smart Alfie Flits, holds a Derby entry and being by top-class middle-distance performer Fantastic Light it was no surprise to see him putting in his best work late. He should improve in time and will relish a mile. (tchd 11-1)

Mystic Dancer, a brother to Medicean who holds a Racing Post Trophy entry, was rightly towards the head of the market, but he did not look overly happy in the ground and as a result it was a pleasing debut. He should progress from two to three and is one to be with in future. (op 7-2 tchd 4-1)

Cape Hawk(IRE) overcame a slow start to reach a challenging position, but the mid-race move told in the end and he faded out of it. He should learn from the experience. (op 11-1)

Inchlaggan(IRE), another expected to need further in time, never really threatened to get involved on this racecourse debut, but he should come on for the run and is likely to make a better three-year-old. (op 20-1)

Tetouan failed to step up on a mildly promising debut and is probably one for handicaps next season. (op 10-1)

Tasweet(IRE), a close relation of Mutamarres, appeared to know his job, but he hung under pressure and looked far from happy in the ground. He is likely to be capable of better next season on a faster surface. (op 7-1)

Bold Bobby Be(IRE) Official explanation: jockey said colt hung left from 2f out

5660 GREENE KING IPA H'CAP 1m 2f

5:30 (5:32) (Class 2) (0-100,98) 3-Y-O

£11,217 (£3,358; £1,679; £840; £419; £210) Stalls High

Form					RPR
1-	1		**Rampallion**[350] 5870 3-8-11 91	LDettori 4	105+
			(Saeed Bin Suroor) *s.i.s: hld up: hdwy and hung lft over 1f out: sn rdn : r.o to ld nr fin*	**15/8**[1]	
13-	2	nk	**Priors Hill (IRE)**[378] 5271 3-8-13 93	(t) KerrinMcEvoy 1	103+
			(Saeed Bin Suroor) *chsd ldrs: rdn and hung lft over 1f out: r.o*	**12/1**	
1112	3	1	**Acrobatic (USA)**[23] 5110 3-9-4 98	RichardHughes 2	106
			(R Charlton) *lw: trckd ldrs: led over 2f out: rdn over 1f out: hdd nr fin*	**6/1**	
4031	4	1 1/4	**High Command**[16] 5299 3-9-2 96	RyanMoore 6	102
			(E A L Dunlop) *hld up: hdwy over 2f out: rdn over 1f out: styd on same pce ins fnl f*	**11/2**[3]	
2100	5	3/4	**Layazaal (IRE)**[33] 4833 3-9-0 94	MartinDwyer 10	99
			(J L Dunlop) *hld up: hdwy over 3f out: ev ch over 2f out: no ex ins fnl f*	**16/1**	
2526	6	1 3/4	**Quince (IRE)**[7] 5511 3-8-5 85	(v) JimmyQuinn 8	87
			(J Pearce) *hld up in tch: rdn over 1f out: styd on same pce*	**16/1**	
-004	7	hd	**Doctor Dash**[20] 5165 3-8-7 87	PaulHanagan 11	88
			(D R C Elsworth) *led and racd alone over 6f: rdn over 1f out: styd on same pce*	**10/1**	
2311	8	2	**Mosharref (IRE)**[21] 5150 3-8-9 89	(t) RHills 3	87+
			(B W Hills) *lw: s.i.s: hld up: hdwy over 1f out: wknd ins fnl f*	**4/1**[2]	
1356	9	15	**Barodine**[89] 3119 3-8-4 84	EddieAhern 7	55
			(H R A Cecil) *lw: chsd ldr: led over 3f out: rdn and hdd over 2f out: sn wknd*	**20/1**	
1456	10	1 3/4	**Red Somerset (USA)**[13] 5376 3-8-10 90	JimmyFortune 9	57
			(R Hannon) *prom over 7f*	**20/1**	

2m 11.77s (6.06) **Going Correction** +0.475s/f (Yiel) **10 Ran SP% 122.5**

Speed ratings (Par 107):94,93,92,91,91 89,89,88,76,74

CSF £28.78 CT £117.82 TOTE £3.10: £1.40, £3.20, £2.20; EX 21.70 Place 6 £65.06, Place 5 £18.10.

Owner Godolphin **Bred** Side Hill Stud **Trained** Newmarket, Suffolk

FOCUS

A good, competitive handicap in which the two who ended up stands' side came out on top, making it a one-two for Godolphin. The form should work out, for the first four all look progressive.

NOTEBOOK

Rampallion ◆, winner of what has turned out to be a very useful maiden on his sole outing at two - the likes of Classic Punch, Smart Enough, Cool Customer and Ermine Sea behind - was having his first outing for Godolphin and he looked the one to beat if straight for this reappearance, with his ability to handle cut in the ground already proven. Held up early, he and the runner-up ended up nearer the stands' side, but they emerged on top and he just edged out his stable companion. Although he looked fit in the paddock, the outing should bring him on and he remains open to further improvement. (op 10-3)

Priors Hill(IRE), seemingly the Godolphin second string, boasted smart form at two, having finished third to Winged Cupid in the Haynes, Hanson and Clarke, and he made quite a bit of appeal on this reappearance, although the application of a first-time tongue tie was a slight negative. He too looked straight enough to run a race though and raced towards the centre having every chance, but he began to edge left well over a furlong out, in the end just lost out to the favourite. He is bred to get 12 furlongs and there could be more to come from him.

Acrobatic(USA) has been most progressive this season, winning four times, although only once on turf, before Great Hawk ended his run by routing him at Kempton. He showed here his improvement may not simply have been down to switching to Polytrack, as he went on over two furlongs out and ran on strongly, only to find the unexposed Godolphin pair too good up the stands' side. Although 8lb higher than when last winning, he still looks on a feasible mark. (op 13-2)

High Command has hardly run a bad race all season and got back to winning ways off a 7lb lower mark at Yarmouth last time. This represented a much stiffer task though and he ran as well as could have been expected, keeping on well having been held up. Although there is plenty of speed in his pedigree, he shapes for all the world as though he is ready for 12 furlongs, appearing to take after his Derby-winning sire. (op 9-2 tchd 11-2 in a place)

Layazaal(IRE) ran too bad to be true at Beverley last time and this was a lot better, but he is not shaping like a horse ready to win and he may need some further assistance from the Handicapper.

Quince(IRE) is still 7lb higher than when last successful and this was as good a run as he could have hoped for. (op 14-1)

Doctor Dash has been threatening to return to form, but the idea of racing alone towards the far rail did not pay off. He kept plugging away though and fully deserves another chance.

Mosharref(IRE), quite impressive off a 7lb lower mark at Sandown but wearing a first-time tongue tie here, found the combination of ten furlongs and this ground too much for him. This can be ignored as he had looked a horse going places on fast ground. (tchd 9-2)

T/Jkpt: Not won. T/Plt: £64.50 to a £1 stake. Pool: £117,786.25. 1,332.70 winning tickets. T/Qpdt: £20.20 to a £1 stake. Pool: £6,575.30. 240.00 winning tickets. CR

5661 - (Foreign Racing) - See Raceform Interactive

5214 CORK (R-H)

Friday, September 29

OFFICIAL GOING: Yielding to soft

5662a MITCHELSTOWN (C & G) MAIDEN 1m

3:45 (3:47) 2-Y-O £7,148 (£1,665; £734; £424)

				RPR
1		**Consul General** 2-9-0	PJSmullen 13	101+
		(D K Weld, Ire) *chsd ldrs: travelling wl to dispute ld 2 1/2f out: led over 2f out: sn qcknd clr: impressive*	**7/1**[3]	
2	7	**Eyshal (IRE)**[12] 5410 2-9-0 102	(t) FMBerry 5	86+
		(John M Oxx, Ire) *trckd ldrs: 6th 1/2-way: prog to mod 3rd 2f out: kpt on wout threatening*	**1/1**[1]	
3	1/2	**Anton Chekhov** 2-9-0	CO'Donoghue 8	87+
		(A P O'Brien, Ire) *chsd ldrs: rdn in 2nd and racd wd ent st: 4th 2 1/2f out: kpt on wout threatening fnl f*	**9/1**	
4	2 1/2	**Salazaar (IRE)** 2-9-0	DMGrant 15	79+
		(David Wachman, Ire) *chsd ldrs early: checked and lost pl after 3f: rdn in 6th 2 1/2f out: kpt on*	**20/1**	
5	1/2	**Mootamaress (IRE)**[9] 5489 2-9-0	(b[1]) DPMcDonogh 7	78
		(Kevin Prendergast, Ire) *sn led: jnd 2 1/2f out: rdn and hdd over 2f out: sn no imp*	**8/1**	
6	5 1/2	**Hernando Cortes** 2-8-7	SMLevey(7) 14	66
		(A P O'Brien, Ire) *mid div: rdn 1/2-way: kpt on wout threatening st*	**20/1**	

7 5 **Alpine Eagle (IRE)** 2-8-9 .... DJMoran(5) 10 55
(Mrs John Harrington, Ire) *chsd ldrs: rdn in 3rd 4f out: 7th 2 1/2f out: sn no imp* **33/1**
8 shd **Valerius (IRE)**[31] 4915 2-9-0 .... RMBurke 18 55
(David P Myerscough, Ire) *towards rr: no imp st* **16/1**
9 1 3/4 **Itsabeautifulday (IRE)**[31] 4915 2-8-11 .... RPCleary(3) 17 51
(M Halford, Ire) *towards rr: no imp st* **25/1**
10 1/2 **Colonial Cross (IRE)**[15] 5328 2-9-0 .... JMurtagh 12 50
(M Halford, Ire) *chsd ldrs: 4th 1/2-way: rdn fr 3f out: no ex fr 2f out* **6/1**[2]
11 4 1/2 **Dorset Square (IRE)** 2-8-9 .... PBBeggy(5) 6 40
(John Joseph Murphy, Ire) *a towards rr* **33/1**
12 2 **Sonnium (IRE)**[16] 5303 2-9-0 .... DJCondon 3 36
(W P Mullins, Ire) *a towards rr* **33/1**
13 hd **Colour Me Blue (IRE)**[8] 5499 2-9-0 ....(b[1]) KJManning 4 35
(J S Bolger, Ire) *mid div: 7th 1/2-way: no imp st* **14/1**
14 1 1/4 **Hard Gossip (IRE)** 2-8-11 .... CDHayes(3) 16 33
(T G McCourt, Ire) *nvr bttr than mid div* **33/1**
15 1/2 **Castle Caw (IRE)**[31] 4915 2-8-11 .... WJLee(3) 1 31
(Miss G Lee, Ire) *nvr a factor* **50/1**
16 1 1/2 **Luzdeluna (IRE)**[53] 4215 2-8-7 .... KTMaher(7) 9 28
(Patrick J Flynn, Ire) *nvr a factor* **25/1**
17 23 **Hawk Gold (IRE)** 2-9-0 .... NGMcCullagh 11 —
(M P Sunderland, Ire) *a bhd* **33/1**
18 9 **Drombeg Pride (IRE)** 2-9-0 .... MCHussey 2 —
(Augustine Leahy, Ire) *s.i.s and a bhd* **50/1**

1m 40.7s **18 Ran SP% 146.3**
CSF £15.24 TOTE £7.60: £2.50, £1.10, £4.70, £16.20; DF 10.80.
Owner K Abdulla **Bred** Juddmonte Farms Ltd **Trained** The Curragh, Co Kildare

NOTEBOOK
Consul General ◆ made a most impressive debut, running out a clear winner from the colt who finished third in the National Stakes on his previous outing. He put up the sort of RPR his top-class stablemate Grey Swallow achieved in his maiden and looks well capable of winning a Listed race next time before going on to even better things. He could be 2000 Guineas material. (op 6/1)
Eyshal(IRE) Official explanation: trainer's representative said colt did not act on the ground

5584 CHANTILLY (R-H)
Friday, September 29

OFFICIAL GOING: Good to soft

5664a PRIX ECLIPSE (GROUP 3) 6f
2:00 (2:00) 2-Y-O **£27,586** (£11,034; £8,276; £5,517; £2,759)

RPR
1 **Iron Lips**[23] 5122 2-8-8 .... OPeslier 2 103
(C Laffon-Parias, France) *tracked leader in 3rd on inside, switched right 1 1/2f out, ridden to lead inside final f, ran on well, comfortably* **43/10**[3]
2 1 1/2 **Invincible Force (IRE)**[12] 5408 2-8-11 .... CSoumillon 5 101
(Ms Deborah J Evans) *raced in 2nd, pushed along over 1 1/2f out, led over 1f out, headed inside final f, one pace* **23/10**[1]
3 2 **Adamantinos**[33] 4857 2-8-11 .... JVictoire 4 95
(Frau E Mader, Germany) *raced in 4th, pushe along over 2f out, stayed on at one pace under pressure final f to take 3rd close home* **13/2**
4 nk **Out Of Time (FR)**[61] 3990 2-8-12 .... IMendizabal 3 95
(J-C Rouget, France) *led to over 1f out, one pace* **28/10**[2]
5 2 **Ascot Family (IRE)**[26] 5048 2-8-8 .... SPasquier 7 85
(A Lyon, France) *held up in last, ridden to go 5th over 1 1/2f out but never near leaders* **11/1**
6 1 **Mpumalanga**[18] 5257 2-8-8 .... FSpanu 6 82
(R Gibson, France) *held up towards rear, ridden 2f out, no response* **13/1**
7 4 **Right Place (FR)**[4] 2-8-11 ....(b) JAuge 1 73
(Robert Collet, France) *always towards rear, ridden & weakened over 1 1/2f out* **22/1**

1m 12.6s **7 Ran SP% 108.6**
PARI-MUTUEL: WIN 5.30; PL 2.20, 1.70; SF 20.40.
Owner Wertheimer Et Frere **Bred** Wertheimer Et Frere **Trained** Chantilly, France

NOTEBOOK
Iron Lips, who played up and was nervous in the paddock before the start, eventually won with authority. Close up behind the leader, she made a forward move a furlong and a half out and was never really troubled from then onwards, having taken the lead inside the final furlong. She will now run over the same distance in the Criterium de Maisons-Laffitte.
Invincible Force(IRE), slowly into his stride, soon made up ground and settled just behind the pace. He had the advantage a furlong out but had nothing in hand to hold off the winner. There are no plans for him at the moment.
Adamantinos made a forward move in front of the stands but was one-paced in the final stages. He took third place close home.
Out Of Time(FR), smartly away, was going well until the furlong marker and then gradually dropped out of contention. He lost third place in the final few strides.

5423 KEMPTON (A.W) (R-H)
Saturday, September 30

OFFICIAL GOING: Standard
Meeting transferred from Epsom.
Wind: Almost nil Weather: Sunshine and showers

5665 OCEAN TRAILERS DISTRIBUTION CONDITIONS STKS 1m (P)
2:10 (2:10) (Class 2) 2-Y-O **£12,464** (£3,732; £1,866; £934; £466) **Stalls** High

Form RPR
14 1 **Rallying Cry (USA)**[78] 3492 2-9-0 .... RobertHavlin 4 98
(J H M Gosden) *mde all: rdn and hung lft 2f out: hanging lft after and strly pressed fnl f: hld on wl* **4/5**[1]
31 2 hd **Monzante (USA)**[29] 4992 2-9-0 87 .... MartinDwyer 1 97
(R Charlton) *settled in 4th: prog to press wnr over 2f out: carried lft 2f out: edgd lft but str chal fnl f: jst hld* **5/2**[2]
0121 3 3 1/2 **Majuro (IRE)**[28] 5034 2-8-11 91 .... IanMongan 5 86
(M R Channon) *trckd ldng pair: disp 2nd over 2f out: sn rdn: cl up over 1f out: wknd fnl f* **7/1**[3]
215 4 9 **Diysem (USA)**[15] 5343 2-9-0 89 .... DaneO'Neill 2 68
(B J Meehan) *chsd wnr to over 2f out: wknd v tamely* **7/1**[3]
5 1 1/2 **Charming Escort** 2-8-8 .... HayleyTurner 3 59?
(T T Clement) *s.s: a last: rdn 3f out: sn btn* **66/1**

1m 38.56s (-2.24) **Going Correction** -0.125s/f (Stan) **5 Ran SP% 110.6**
Speed ratings (Par 101): 106,105,102,93,91
CSF £3.06 TOTE £1.60: £1.10, £1.70; EX 2.60.
Owner H R H Princess Haya Of Jordan **Bred** Flaxman Holdings Ltd **Trained** Newmarket, Suffolk

FOCUS
The winner set a reasonable pace. The race has been rated at face value for now, the winner running up to his Newmarket mark and the second improving.

NOTEBOOK
Rallying Cry(USA) was fourth in the Group 2 Superlative Stakes at Newmarket on his previous start, a length behind recent Royal Lodge winner Admiralofthefleet. Setting his own pace, he hung left up the straight but held off the challenge of the runner-up in gritty fashion. He looks a smart colt and middle-distances will suit him next year. (op 6-5)
Monzante(USA) was up in class after winning a maiden over course and distance a month ago. He took a little time to knuckle down when asked for his effort in the straight, but ran on well in the latter stages while being carried across the track. This was an improved effort. (op 15-8)
Majuro(IRE), proven on this surface, put up a decent effort in this stronger company. He looks a likely type for nurseries. (op 5-1 tchd 8-1)
Diysem(USA), making his All-Weather bow, was ridden more handily this time but faded disappointingly in the straight. (op 9-1 tchd 6-1)
Charming Escort is out of an unraced half-sister to a couple of high-class performers in South Africa. After a tardy start, he was in last place throughout and was left well behind in the straight. (op 33-1)

5666 DIGIBET.COM H'CAP 1m (P)
2:40 (2:40) (Class 3) (0-90,90) 3-Y-O
£11,217 (£3,358; £1,679; £840; £419; £210) **Stalls** High

Form RPR
4514 1 **Persian Express (USA)**[20] 5211 3-7-13 76 .... AurelioMedeiros(5) 11 89
(B W Hills) *hld up in rr: prog towards inner 3f out: led 2f out: shuffled along and clr fnl f* **14/1**
003 2 2 1/2 **Adventuress**[22] 5150 3-8-6 85 ....(b) KMay(7) 4 92
(B J Meehan) *prog on outer to chse ldrs 1/2-way: wd bnd 3f out: bmpd along and kpt on to take 2nd fnl f: no ch w wnr* **9/1**
1113 3 1 **Envision**[7] 5520 3-9-3 89 .... DaneO'Neill 13 94
(R Hannon) *hld up on inner: prog 3f out: pressed ldrs 2f out: one pce fr over 1f out* **4/1**[1]
-162 4 nk **Mobsir**[23] 5143 3-9-0 86 .... MartinDwyer 14 90
(E A L Dunlop) *trckd ldrs: narrow ld wl over 2f: hdd and hung lft 2f out: chsd wnr tl fdd fnl f* **4/1**[1]
4542 5 1 **Penfection (IRE)**[43] 4555 3-9-0 86 .... LPKeniry 10 88
(M Botti) *trckd ldrs gng wl: shkn up and nt qckn wl over 1f out: one pce after* **14/1**
505 6 1 **Zato (IRE)**[21] 5165 3-9-4 90 .... IanMongan 8 89
(M R Channon) *pressed ldr after 1f: upsides wl over 2f out: fdd over 1f out* **10/1**
-105 7 hd **Fast Bowler**[23] 5143 3-8-10 82 .... JTate 1 81
(J M P Eustace) *hld up: sme prog 1/2-way: drvn over 2f out: sn outpcd: one pce after* **16/1**
0400 8 nk **My Amalie (IRE)**[64] 3891 3-9-4 90 .... HayleyTurner 9 88
(C E Brittain) *hld up in last pair: effrt on inner over 2f out: one pce and no imp on ldrs* **33/1**
6150 9 3/4 **Tempsford Flyer (IRE)**[60] 4029 3-8-4 83 .... PatrickHills(7) 2 80
(J W Hills) *t.k.h: trckd ldrs: rdn over 2f out: wknd over 1f out* **8/1**[3]
2400 10 1 1/2 **Dancing Guest (IRE)**[28] 5019 3-8-10 85 .... GregFairley(3) 6 78
(G G Margarson) *t.k.h: hld up wl in rr: rdn and no prog over 2f out* **14/1**
1104 11 2 1/2 **Mcnairobi**[17] 5294 3-8-3 82 .... AshleyHamblett(7) 7 69+
(P D Cundell) *s.s: hld up in last pair: c wdst of all bnd 3f out: no prog fnl 2f* **15/2**[2]
0340 12 6 **Abwaab**[14] 5377 3-8-8 80 .... StephenCarson 5 54
(R F Johnson Houghton) *nvr on terms w ldrs: wd bnd 3f out: wknd 2f out* **20/1**
0000 13 1 1/2 **Grand Jour (IRE)**[22] 5150 3-8-13 85 ....(t) RobertHavlin 12 55
(M J Wallace) *led to wl over 2f out: wkng rapidly whn n.m.r sn after* **25/1**
1100 14 1 **Ludovico**[134] 1836 3-9-1 87 .... PatDobbs 3 55
(K A Ryan) *nvr bttr than midfield: rdn and struggling 3f out: sn bhd* **33/1**

1m 38.45s (-2.35) **Going Correction** -0.125s/f (Stan) **14 Ran SP% 122.3**
Speed ratings (Par 105): 106,103,102,102,101 100,100,99,98,97 94,88,87,86
CSF £131.22 CT £622.38 TOTE £19.50: £5.90, £3.40, £2.40; EX 259.00.
Owner D M James **Bred** Kingswood Farm **Trained** Lambourn, Berks

FOCUS
A fair handicap, run at a reasonable pace. It has been rated around the second and the fourth.

NOTEBOOK
Persian Express(USA) was beaten off this mark here last time when she saw daylight far too soon according to connections. Ridden more patiently here, she struck the front with two furlongs to go and came clear in decent style. Her three best runs to date have been on this surface and there could be more to come.
Adventuress, unlucky on her latest start, ran another good race particularly considering she was trapped wide all the way. She was staying on to good effect late in the day and is due a change of fortune. (op 8-1)
Envision has enjoyed an excellent season and this solid Polytrack debut opens up more opportunities for him. He still looks on a fair mark. (tchd 9-2)
Mobsir, thought good enough to contest a Listed race earlier in the season, was upped in trip for this sand bow. He was never far away but, after showing narrowly ahead, could not sustain his effort. A return to seven furlongs should suit him. (op 7-2 tchd 10-3)
Penfection(IRE), making her debut on an artificial surface, travelled well just behind the leaders but when let down she found less than she had promised to. The drop in trip was not ideal.
Zato(IRE), back on sand, had his chance and ran up to recent form in defeat. (op 16-1)

5667 SPORTS BETTING WITH DIGIBET.COM H'CAP 6f (P)
3:15 (3:15) (Class 2) (0-100,100) 3-Y-O+
£24,928 (£7,464; £3,732; £1,868; £932; £468) **Stalls** High

Form RPR
02 1 **Mutamared (USA)**[56] 4128 6-9-4 98 .... PatDobbs 11 110+
(K A Ryan) *hld up in midfield: prog on inner 2f out: rdn to ld last 150yds: styd on wl* **5/2**[1]
000 2 3/4 **Intrepid Jack**[42] 4593 4-8-9 94 .... TravisBlock(5) 2 104
(H Morrison) *trckd ldrs: led jst over 2f out: rdn over 1f out: hdd last 150yds: styd on* **9/2**[2]
0-50 3 3/4 **Viking Spirit**[14] 5358 4-9-0 94 .... StephenCarson 4 102
(W R Swinburn) *hld up in last pair: prog on inner over 2f out: styd on fr over 1f out to take 3rd nr fin: nvr able to chal* **11/2**[3]

1005 **4** *shd* **Sir Edwin Landseer (USA)**[7] 5535 6-8-4 **87**..........(p) NeilChalmers(3) 5 95
(Christian Wroe, UAE) *hld up: prog on wd outside over 2f out: coaxed along to cl on ldrs over 1f out: rdn and no rspnse fnl f* **7/1**
0450 **5** *shd* **Texas Gold**[7] 5535 8-9-2 **96**.............................. MartinDwyer 10 103
(W R Muir) *chsd ldrs: rdn and prog 2f out: looked dangerous jst over 1f out: fnd nil fnl f* **12/1**
2000 **6** *shd* **Beaver Patrol (IRE)**[15] 5336 4-8-10 **90**.......................... RobertHavlin 6 97+
(R F Johnson Houghton) *hld up towards rr: pushed along whn nt clr run over 2f out: nt clr run briefly over 1f out: r.o fnl f: nt rch ldrs* **16/1**
1422 **7** *2* **Didn't We (IRE)**[49] 4345 3-8-1 **88**.........................(b) KevinGhunowa(5) 12 89
(T G Mills) *drvn to ld: hdd over 2f out: grad wknd u.p* **10/1**
1030 **8** *nk* **Pic Up Sticks**[12] 5433 7-8-6 **89**.............................. RichardKingscote(3) 9 89
(B G Powell) *pressed ldr: upsides over 2f out: sn rdn and nt qckn: fdd* **20/1**
0040 **9** *½* **Saabiq (USA)**[69] 3761 3-8-10 **92**....................................... HayleyTurner 8 91
(C E Brittain) *a in rr: rdn and no real prog over 2f out: one pce after* **33/1**
3060 **10** *6* **Qadar (IRE)**[21] 5182 4-9-6 **100**.. IanMongan 3 81
(N P Littmoden) *a struggling in rr: u.p and losing tch over 2f out* **22/1**
035 **11** *1 ½* **Blue Tomato**[12] 5420 5-8-6 **89**.. GregFairley(3) 7 65
(J M Bradley) *trckd ldrs: wkng rapidly whn n.m.r wl over 1f out* **20/1**

1m 12.05s (-1.65) **Going Correction** -0.125s/f (Stan)
WFA 3 from 4yo+ 2lb **11** Ran SP% **114.1**
Speed ratings (Par 109):106,105,104,103,103 103,100,100,99,91 89
CSF £11.83 CT £56.12 TOTE £2.80: £1.40, £2.50, £1.90; EX 18.40.
Owner Errigal Racing **Bred** E J Hudson Jr, Irrevocable Trust & Kilroy T'Bred **Trained** Hambleton, N Yorks
■ Stewards' Enquiry : Travis Block one-day ban: failed to keep straight from the stalls (Oct 11)

FOCUS
A high-class and valuable handicap, and solid form. The winner did not need to improve on his Stewards' Cup effort.

NOTEBOOK
Mutamared(USA), runner-up in the Stewards' Cup last time, has been scratched from his last three assignments due to unsuitably soft ground, most recently in a Group 2 contest. Successful on his only previous start on this surface, he ran on strongly to show ahead inside the last and scored comfortably. He should be capable of better still. (op 2-1 tchd 15-8)
Intrepid Jack won a juvenile maiden on his only previous experience of Polytrack. Back sprinting after a couple of runs over seven, he took a narrow lead but could not repel the winner, although he finished nearer that rival than he had in the Stewards' Cup on 4lb better terms. (tchd 5-1)
Viking Spirit, sharper for his run in the Ayr Gold Cup, straightened up with only one behind him but finished strongly on the inside to snatch third. He is fresher than most at this stage of the year. (op 13-2)
Sir Edwin Landseer(USA), a winner on sand in Dubai, looked a big threat when switched out for his run but did not pick up as well as he might have.
Texas Gold, an infrequent runner on sand, ran a decent race until it came to being asked for his effort, when he found nothing. He is best over the minimum trip. (tchd 14-1)
Beaver Patrol(IRE) came home strongly and would have been a fair bit closer with an uninterrupted passage.

5668 KEMPTON.CO.UK NURSERY 5f (P)
3:50 (3:50) (Class 5) (0-85,84) 2-Y-O **£4,533** (£1,348; £674; £336) **Stalls** High

Form RPR
0263 **1** **Frisky Talk (IRE)**[19] 5234 2-8-10 **78**..................... AurelioMedeiros(5) 12 81
(B W Hills) *mde all and set str pce: hrd pressed fnl f: hld on wl* **5/1**[2]
2332 **2** *nk* **Brenin Gwalia**[20] 5207 2-7-12 **68** ow2...................... KirstyMilczarek(7) 8 70
(D M Simcock) *trckd ldng pair: chsd wnr 2f out: urged along to chal fnl f: nt qckn and hld nr fin* **7/2**[1]
0540 **3** *2 ½* **Naayla (IRE)**[8] 5503 2-8-10 **80**...................................(b[1]) KMay(7) 1 73
(B J Meehan) *outpcd in rr: struggling and hanging 2f out: r.o fnl f to snatch 3rd last stride* **8/1**[3]
610 **4** *shd* **Danger Alley**[19] 5234 2-8-5 **68**......................................(b) JamieMackay 5 61
(E J O'Neill) *chsd ldng trio: rdn 1/2-way but clr of rest: no imp: one pce after* **16/1**
0302 **5** *nk* **Pernomente (IRE)**[21] 5161 2-8-8 **71**..................................(t) LPKeniry 6 63
(J S Moore) *chsd wnr to 2f out: wknd fnl f* **12/1**
4322 **6** *½* **Malaaq**[24] 5112 2-8-10 **73**.. MartinDwyer 4 63
(M A Jarvis) *s.i.s: outpcd and wd in last trio: styd on fr over 1f out: no ch* **5/1**[2]
1042 **7** *shd* **Hucking Hope (IRE)**[38] 4699 2-8-7 **70**............................ RobertMiles 7 59
(J R Best) *outpcd towards rr and wd: styd on u.p fnl f: no ch* **10/1**
0002 **8** *½* **Swiftly Addicted (IRE)**[17] 5290 2-7-13 **62**................... DavidKinsella 10 50
(A King) *outpcd in last pair: prog on inner over 1f out: styng on and ch of 3rd whn rn out of room nr fin* **8/1**[3]
2006 **9** *½* **Going Straight (IRE)**[19] 5234 2-9-7 **84**........................... DaneO'Neill 2 70
(I A Wood) *chsd clr ldrs: no imp 2f out: wknd fnl f* **12/1**
0545 **10** *3* **Queen Of Narnia**[12] 5434 2-8-9 **72**.............................. RobertHavlin 9 47
(M R Channon) *outpcd and a struggling towards rr* **14/1**
3300 **11** *2* **Bush Breakfast**[51] 4284 2-8-6 **69**................................. HayleyTurner 11 37
(P Winkworth) *chsd clr ldrs: rdn and no imp 2f out: wknd* **50/1**
2350 **12** *½* **Piccolena Boy**[19] 5234 2-8-5 **68**................................ StephenCarson 3 34
(P Winkworth) *chsd clr ldrs tl wknd u.p 2f out* **33/1**

60.43 secs (0.03) **Going Correction** -0.125s/f (Stan) **12** Ran SP% **119.7**
Speed ratings (Par 95):94,93,89,89,88 88,87,87,86,81 78,77
CSF £23.04 CT £143.16 TOTE £6.90: £1.80, £1.90, £3.00; EX 24.50.
Owner Paul McNamara **Bred** Yeomanstown Stud **Trained** Lambourn, Berks
■ A double for Aurelio Medeiros, only his second and third winners in Britain.

FOCUS
Solid enough nursery form, the winner making all at a good pace. Not many were able to get involved.

NOTEBOOK
Frisky Talk(IRE) made a winning Polytrack debut under a good ride. Bustled along to secure the lead from her inside draw, she set a strong pace which soon had them strung out behind and kept on well to repel the favourite's challenge. She has bags of pace and should add to her gains on this surface.
Brenin Gwalia, never far from the action, had to be switched to come with his challenge and could never quite get past the all-the-way winner. He is well capable of getting off the mark but has now been a beaten favourite on four of his last five starts, which suggests caution is advisable. (op 4-1)
Naayla(IRE) was fitted with blinkers for the first time. Drawn low and forced to race wide throughout, she finished well to get the best of a blanket finish for third and will be suited by a return to six furlongs. (op 17-2)
Danger Alley, whose two wins thus far came in selling company at Yarmouth, was always chasing the leaders and stayed on at the same pace. This was a solid effort and he obviously handles this surface. (tchd 18-1)
Pernomente(IRE) was returning to Polytrack for the first time since the spring on this nursery debut. Never far from the pace, he was still in third place entering the final furlong but was beginning to tire at that stage and was run out of the places. (op 14-1)
Malaaq, dropped back to five furlongs for this sand debut, found everything happening too quickly and did not handle the bends too well, but made up a deal of ground when it was all over. She is proving costly to follow. Official explanation: jockey said filly would not face the kickback (tchd 9-2)
Hucking Hope(IRE) could not go the strong pace, and although she was finishing strongly it was much too late. (op 8-1)
Swiftly Addicted(IRE) ◆, outpaced in rear until really finding her feet in the straight, would probably have been third had she not run into a cul-de-sac late on. She will be of interest back over six furlongs. Official explanation: jockey said filly was denied a clear run (op 9-1)

5669 OCEAN TRAILERS DISTRIBUTION MAIDEN STKS 1m 2f (P)
4:25 (4:27) (Class 5) 3-Y-O **£5,505** (£1,637; £818; £408) **Stalls** High

Form RPR
0403 **1** **Woolfall Blue (IRE)**[30] 4959 3-9-3 79.................................. IanMongan 8 77
(G G Margarson) *mde all: set stdy pce tl kicked on 3f out: rdn and hung lft jst over 1f out: styd on wl* **8/1**
2-0 **2** *1 ¼* **Scotch Pancake**[22] 5151 3-8-12 .... AntonyProcter 12 70
(D R C Elsworth) *dwlt: t.k.h: hld up in midfield: prog to go 4th 3f out: rdn to chse wnr last 100yds: no imp nr fin* **2/1**[1]
3 *1 ¾* **Glamis Castle (USA)** 3-9-3 .... MartinDwyer 14 72+
(Sir Michael Stoute) *settled in midfield: pushed along over 3f out: r.o fnl f to take 3rd nr fin* **14/1**
5-30 **4** *nk* **Gravinsky (USA)**[22] 5151 3-9-3 79.................................(b[1]) PatDobbs 2 71
(Mrs A J Perrett) *chsd wnr after 1f: drvn and no imp 2f out: fdd fnl f* **20/1**
5 *½* **Lunar Landscape (USA)** 3-9-3 .... DaneO'Neill 4 70+
(Saeed Bin Suroor) *s.s: hld up: last pair tl prog over 3f out: shkn up and styd on: nvr rchd ldrs* **4/1**[3]
0 **6** *¾* **Debutante**[47] 4431 3-8-5 .... AshleyHamblett(7) 7 64+
(L M Cumani) *hld up wl in rr: nt clr run 4f out and hmpd sn after: prog over 2f out: styd on: nrst fin* **50/1**
7 *½* **Right To Play (USA)** 3-9-3 .... RobertHavlin 5 68+
(J H M Gosden) *dwlt: hld up: last pair tl prog 4f out: nt clr run over 3f out: sn shkn up: kpt on fnl f: no ch* **7/2**[2]
60 **8** *2* **Aberlady Bay (IRE)**[12] 5426 3-8-12 .... HayleyTurner 10 59
(T T Clement) *wl plcd: effrt to dispute 2nd 3f out: wknd wl over 1f out* **66/1**
53 **9** *1 ½* **Junior**[20] 5203 3-8-10 .... KMay(7) 9 61
(B J Meehan) *nvr beyond midfield: rdn and no real prog over 3f out: fdd fnl 2f* **9/1**
0 **10** *3 ½* **St Fris**[25] 5098 3-9-3 .... JTate 6 54
(J A R Toller) *nvr on terms: rdn and struggling in rr over 2f out* **50/1**
00 **11** *1* **Spiritwind (IRE)**[16] 5319 3-9-3 ....(tp) StephenCarson 11 52
(W R Swinburn) *chsd wnr for 1f: prom tl wknd rapidly over 3f out* **66/1**
0-0 **12** *5* **King Cugat Kid (USA)**[26] 5055 3-9-0 .... RichardKingscote(3) 1 43
(Simon Earle) *settled in midfield: prog on outer 4f out: rdn and wknd wl over 2f out* **100/1**
13 *nk* **Alujawill (IRE)** 3-9-3 .... LPKeniry 13 42
(J G M O'Shea) *a wl in rr: struggling 4f out* **100/1**

2m 8.34s (-0.66) **Going Correction** -0.125s/f (Stan) **13** Ran SP% **117.0**
Speed ratings (Par 101):97,96,94,94,93 93,92,91,90,87 86,82,82
CSF £23.19 TOTE £10.90: £2.10, £1.50, £3.60; EX 36.30.
Owner J F Bower **Bred** Calley House Syndicate **Trained** Newmarket, Suffolk

FOCUS
The form looks a little suspect despite seeming to make sense based around the winner and fourth. There were some eyecatching performances, with the third, fifth, sixth and seventh all shaping better than the bare form.

5670 ABACUS LIGHTING H'CAP 7f (P)
5:00 (5:00) (Class 4) (0-80,80) 3-Y-O+ **£5,505** (£1,637; £818; £408) **Stalls** High

Form RPR
0142 **1** **Landucci**[5] 5572 5-8-7 **73**.. PatrickHills(7) 13 82
(J W Hills) *hld up in midfield on inner: prog over 2f out: effrt to ld 1f out: pushed out and jst hld on* **11/2**[2]
5034 **2** *hd* **Outer Hebrides**[15] 5345 5-9-4 **80**.............................(vt) AmirQuinn(3) 11 88
(J R Boyle) *hld up towards rr: prog on inner over 2f out: nt clr run and swtchd lft over 1f out: r.o and gaining fast at fin* **9/1**
4156 **3** *½* **Mujood**[20] 5211 3-9-1 **77**.. StephenCarson 1 84
(R F Johnson Houghton) *racd on outer: prom: rdn to chal 2f out: nt qckn over 1f out: styd on ins fnl f* **20/1**
1040 **4** *nk* **Top Mark**[25] 5096 4-8-12 **76**... TravisBlock(5) 10 82
(H Morrison) *cl up: effrt to ld 2f out: rdn and hdd 1f out: one pce nr fin* **11/1**
4254 **5** *1* **Rezzago (USA)**[28] 5021 6-9-4 **77**... DaneO'Neill 3 80+
(W R Swinburn) *s.i.s: hld up wl in rr: effrt 2f out: styd on fr over 1f out: nrst fin* **7/1**[3]
6163 **6** *nk* **Finsbury**[24] 5107 3-8-9 **78**... JonjoMilczarek(7) 4 81+
(C F Wall) *racd wd: hld up in last trio: plenty to do 2f out: gd prog over 1f out: no imp last 100yds* **5/1**[1]
26-2 **7** *nk* **Morse (IRE)**[20] 5212 5-9-1 **77**................................ RichardKingscote(3) 2 79
(J A Osborne) *pressed ldr: rdn to chal 2f out: fdd fnl f* **12/1**
1000 **8** *hd* **Exmoor**[15] 5345 4-9-3 **76**.. MartinDwyer 14 77
(R Charlton) *pushed along in last pair 1/2-way: prog on inner 2f out: styd on: nt rch ldrs* **9/1**
6203 **9** *2* **Pillars Of Wisdom**[24] 5108 4-9-4 **77**..................................(t) IanMongan 6 73
(J L Dunlop) *led to 2f out: wknd fnl f* **12/1**
54-0 **10** *¾* **Belly Dancer (IRE)**[20] 5212 4-9-4 **77**................................... PatDobbs 9 71
(P F I Cole) *hld up in last trio: rdn and struggling over 2f out: kpt on fnl f: no ch* **11/1**
21 **11** *5* **She's My Outsider**[20] 5212 4-9-4 **77**............................... RobertHavlin 5 58
(I A Wood) *racd on outer: chsd ldrs tl wknd rapidly 2f out* **15/2**
1006 **12** *1* **Coleridge (AUS)**[12] 5428 7-9-1 **74**................................(b) RobertMiles 8 53
(B G Powell) *t.k.h: hld up bhd ldrs: wkng whn n.m.r 2f out* **50/1**
5310 **13** *hd* **Dr Thong**[15] 5345 5-9-2 **75**..(tp) JosedeSouza 7 53
(P F I Cole) *t.k.h: hld up in midfield: rdn and wknd over 2f out* **16/1**

1m 25.86s (-0.94) **Going Correction** -0.125s/f (Stan)
WFA 3 from 4yo+ 3lb **13** Ran SP% **121.0**
Speed ratings (Par 105):100,99,99,98,97 97,97,96,94,93 87,86,86
CSF £55.22 CT £963.45 TOTE £5.60: £2.20, £3.70, £7.40; EX 56.30.
Owner R J Tufft **Bred** D J And Mrs Deer **Trained** Upper Lambourn, Berks

FOCUS
A fair handicap for the grade and the form looks sound, with the second and fourth to form.
Coleridge(AUS) Official explanation: trainer's rep said gelding bled from the nose

5671 THANK YOU JULIAN THICK APPRENTICE DERBY H'CAP 1m 4f (P)
5:35 (5:35) (Class 4) (0-80,80) 3-Y-O+ **£5,505** (£1,637; £818; £408) **Stalls** Centre

Form RPR

2211 **1** **Ardea Brave (IRE)**[31] 4937 4-8-13 **71**.....(p) NicolPolli(5) 3 78
(M Botti) *mde all: hrd pressed fnl 2f: rdn and hld on wl* **7/2**[1]

0004 **2** ½ **Top Seed (IRE)**[10] 5479 5-9-7 **77**..... TravisBlock(3) 7 83
(M R Channon) *hld up towards rr: effrt over 2f out: r.o to chal fnl f: nt qckn last 100yds* **11/2**[3]

1540 **3** ¾ **Great View (IRE)**[15] 5346 7-8-13 **66** oh4.....(v) AmirQuinn 8 71
(Mrs A L M King) *trckd ldng pair: rdn on inner over 2f out: styd on but a hld* **8/1**

2061 **4** *nk* **Boot 'n Toot**[21] 5163 5-9-3 **75**..... AshleyHamblett(5) 5 80
(C A Cyzer) *s.s: hld up in 7th: rdn and prog on outer 2f out: tried to chal fnl f: nt qckn* **6/1**

5-40 **5** ½ **Well Established (IRE)**[17] 5299 4-9-6 **80**..... DanielRobinson(7) 6 84
(M A Jarvis) *trckd wnr: bmpd along fr 2f out: one pce and lost pls fnl f* **8/1**

5400 **6** 1½ **Wingman (IRE)**[49] 4347 4-9-8 **80**..... PatrickHills(5) 1 82
(J W Hills) *hld up in tch: effrt over 2f out: rdn and no rspnse over 1f out* **5/1**[2]

20-0 **7** *10* **Supreme Charter**[8] 5511 3-9-4 **79**..... GregFairley 4 65
(M Johnston) *chsd ldng pair: rdn 4f out: starting to weaken whn stmbld bdly over 1f out* **11/2**[3]

6210 **8** *22* **Undeterred**[6] 5506 10-8-10 **70**..... WilliamBuick(7) 2 20
(K J Burke) *rel to r and lft 20 l: ct up and in tch 1/2-way: wknd 4f out: eased fnl 2f* **10/1**

2m 33.0s (-3.90) **Going Correction** -0.125s/f (Stan)
WFA 3 from 4yo+ 8lb 8 Ran SP% **115.3**
Speed ratings (Par 105):108,107,107,106,106 105,98,84
CSF £23.01 CT £143.09 TOTE £3.80: £1.50, £3.20, £2.10; EX 24.60 Place 6 £32.06, Place 5 £27.94.
Owner Dioscuri Srl **Bred** Scuderia San Pancrazio Sas **Trained** Newmarket, Suffolk
■ Stewards' Enquiry : Ashley Hamblett one-day ban: used whip down the shoulder in the forehand position (Oct 11)

FOCUS
A fair handicap. The winner dictated a moderate pace and it turned into a bit of a sprint up the straight.
T/Plt: £42.40 to a £1 stake. Pool: £54,003.95. 929.40 winning tickets. T/Qpdt: £12.70 to a £1 stake. Pool: £3,041.20. 176.30 winning tickets. JN

5653 NEWMARKET (ROWLEY) (R-H)
Saturday, September 30

OFFICIAL GOING: Good to soft
Wind: Light, across Weather: Fine

5672 FINNFOREST E B F OH SO SHARP STKS (LISTED RACE) (FILLIES) 7f
2:05 (2:06) (Class 1) 2-Y-O
£17,034 (£6,456; £3,231; £1,611; £807; £405) **Stalls** High

Form RPR

631 **1** **Selinka**[15] 5347 2-8-12 84..... RyanMoore 9 95
(R Hannon) *s.i.s: outpcd: swtchd lft and hdwy over 1f out: r.o to ld post* **10/1**

1 **2** *shd* **Puggy (IRE)**[30] 4964 2-8-12.....(t) FJohansson 3 95
(R A Kvisla) *lw: hld up: nt clr run over 2f out tl hdwy over 1f out: rdn to ld wl ins fnl f: hdd post* **10/1**

3 **3** *2* **Guarantia**[12] 5425 2-8-12.....(t) SebSanders 10 90
(C E Brittain) *led: rdn over 1f out: hdd wl ins fnl f* **18/1**

15 **4** *nk* **Italian Girl**[34] 4840 2-8-12 96..... JamieSpencer 7 89
(A P Jarvis) *lw: hld up: hdwy over 2f out: rdn over 1f out: styd on* **5/1**[2]

021 **5** ½ **Millestan (IRE)**[25] 5083 2-8-12 78..... EddieAhern 6 88
(H R A Cecil) *a.p: chsd ldr 1/2-way: rdn over 1f out: styd on same pce ins fnl f* **16/1**

316 **6** *1* **Golden Dagger (IRE)**[12] 5434 2-8-12 83..... NCallan 11 85
(K A Ryan) *chsd ldrs: rdn over 2f out: styd on same pce fnl f* **11/1**

15 **7** 3½ **Alderney (USA)**[80] 3415 2-8-12..... PhilipRobinson 8 77
(M A Jarvis) *lw: racd keenly: trckd ldr to 1/2-way: rdn over 1f out: wknd fnl f* **7/2**[1]

13 **8** ½ **Boreal Applause**[50] 4322 2-8-12 91..... PaulHanagan 15 75
(E A L Dunlop) *hld up: rdn over 2f out: wknd over 1f out* **25/1**

14 **9** *shd* **Alovera (IRE)**[19] 5257 2-8-12 100..... TedDurcan 5 75
(M R Channon) *hld up: hdwy 1/2-way: rdn and edgd lft over 2f out: hung rt and wknd over 1f out* **15/2**

01 **10** 1¾ **Folly Lodge**[12] 5424 2-8-12..... MichaelHills 2 71
(B W Hills) *lw: hld up: hdwy 1/2-way: wknd over 2f out* **16/1**

1 **11** *1* **Emulate**[29] 4994 2-8-12..... RichardHughes 12 68
(B W Hills) *hld up: rdn over 2f out: wknd over 1f out* **11/2**[3]

1m 28.28s (1.78) **Going Correction** +0.35s/f (Good) 11 Ran SP% **113.4**
Speed ratings (Par 100):103,102,100,100,99 98,94,93,93,91 90
CSF £102.15 TOTE £11.40: £3.10, £2.80, £5.80; EX 113.50 TRIFECTA Not won..
Owner R Barnett **Bred** W And R Barnett Ltd **Trained** East Everleigh, Wilts
■ Stewards' Enquiry : F Johansson one-day ban: careless riding (Oct 11)

FOCUS
An ordinary renewal of this fillies' Listed contest, but it was run at a sound pace and produced a decent time for the grade. The principals came from the rear but the form is limited by the fifth.

NOTEBOOK
Selinka, from a family of sprinters, handled the longer trip well and, after being held up at the back, swooped late to steal the prize on the line. She is clearly progressive and her paddock value is assured, but it remains to be seen if she can hold her own in Group company. (op 11-1)
Puggy(IRE) ◆, a surprise winner of a Salisbury maiden, proved that no fluke and, after going on and looking sure to win, was collared only on the line. She is out of a half-sister to Blue Monday and Lundy's Lane, so should get a mile, and she deserves compensation at a similar level. (op 11-1)
Guarantia, making her turf debut, made the running and stuck to her task when headed. She should have no trouble picking up a maiden before no doubt returning to this grade. (op 20-1 tchd 16-1)
Italian Girl, who had today's winner well behind when scoring on her debut, put a somewhat disappointing effort at Goodwood behind her, but has still to prove she is up to this level. (op 4-1)
Millestan(IRE) has been progressive of late, but this step up in grade and drop in trip found her out. She will be more at home in handicaps.
Golden Dagger(IRE) , a soft-ground winner over this trip, was one of the first in trouble but responded to pressure and did well to finish as close as she did. (op 12-1)
Alderney(USA), encountering soft going for the first time, faded quickly after running a bit free up with the pace early. Official explanation: vet said filly lost a near-fore shoe (tchd 4-1 in places)
Alovera(IRE) could have been expected to handle the ground but was struggling soon after halfway. (op 8-1)
Emulate, who won her maiden on Polytrack, never got into contention on this turf debut.

5673 COUNTRYWIDE STEEL AND TUBES JOEL STKS (GROUP 3) 1m
2:35 (2:35) (Class 1) 3-Y-O+
£28,390 (£10,760; £5,385; £2,685; £1,345; £675) **Stalls** High

Form RPR

-123 **1** **Satchem (IRE)**[15] 5341 4-9-0 112.....(t) KerrinMcEvoy 6 118
(Saeed Bin Suroor) *lw: racd centre: prom: rdn and outpcd wl over 1f out: rallied to ld ins fnl f: styd on strly* **10/3**[2]

110- **2** 1¼ **Pinson (IRE)**[350] 5902 4-9-0 118..... TedDurcan 4 115
(Saeed Bin Suroor) *lw: hld up centre: hdwy over 2f out: ev ch ins fnl f: nt pce of wnr* **5/1**[3]

1633 **3** 1½ **Road To Love (IRE)**[20] 5204 3-8-10 110..... RHills 1 112
(M Johnston) *b. off fore: led centre gp: overall ldr and rdn over 1f out: edgd rt and hdd ins fnl f: one pce* **6/1**

0006 **4** *2* **Babodana**[4] 5588 6-9-0 109..... SebSanders 5 108
(M H Tompkins) *sn cl up towards far side: rdn and outpcd over 1f out: kpt on ins fnl f* **16/1**

2303 **5** ¾ **Olympian Odyssey**[21] 5186 3-8-10 113..... RichardHughes 9 106
(B W Hills) *overall ldr towards far side: hdd over 1f out: no ex* **9/4**[1]

0230 **6** ¾ **Kings Point (IRE)**[21] 5186 5-9-0 105..... PaulHanagan 7 105
(R A Fahey) *cl up towards far side: outpcd over 2f out: n.d after* **28/1**

0004 **7** 2½ **Norse Dancer (IRE)**[15] 5342 6-9-0 108..... JohnEgan 2 99
(D R C Elsworth) *hld up centre: rdn over 3f out: wknd over 2f out* **10/1**

0-40 **8** *2* **Iceman**[15] 5341 4-9-0 105..... RyanMoore 3 95
(J H M Gosden) *chsd centre ldrs tl wknd over 2f out* **11/1**

1m 39.95s (0.58) **Going Correction** +0.35s/f (Good)
WFA 3 from 4yo+ 4lb 8 Ran SP% **111.6**
Speed ratings (Par 113):111,109,108,106,105 104,102,100
CSF £19.30 TOTE £4.10: £1.60, £1.60, £1.80; EX 15.20 Trifecta £52.90 Pool: £947.20 - 12.70 winning tickets..
Owner Godolphin **Bred** K Molloy **Trained** Newmarket, Suffolk

FOCUS
A fair Group 3 in which the field split into two groups early, but ended up racing together in the middle of the track. The time was 1.12sec slower than the following fillies' Group 1. A one-two for Godolphin.

NOTEBOOK
Satchem(IRE) ◆, who has returned in decent form following a year off, scored in determined style and recorded his first Group win since his juvenile days. He has the right attitude and can be placed to win more races at this level. (op 3-1 tchd 7-2)
Pinson(IRE) ◆, making his first appearance since flopping in the Dubai Champion Stakes here just under a year ago, put up a fine performance on this return and looked likely to score before finding his stable companion too strong. He should be winning again before long on this evidence, with soft ground and another couple of furlongs no problem. (op 11-2)
Road To Love(IRE) has done well in handicaps but had been held in two previous attempts at this level and was again found out, despite doing little wrong. He may prove to be a twilight horse, but it is not beyond the bounds of possibility that he will improve with age, much as his sire did. (tchd 7-1 in a place)
Babodana, a regular at this sort of level at around a mile, ran his race and continues to pay his way, but has not scored since taking the Lincoln back in 2004. (tchd 18-1 in a place)
Olympian Odyssey set the pace on the far side and eventually came across to join the others, but he was in trouble going into the dip. In three subsequent efforts he has not lived up to the promise of his third in the 2,000 Guineas, but he has time on his side. Official explanation: jockey said colt was never travelling (tchd 5-2 in places)
Kings Point(IRE) has always struggled at this level and in any case his best form has been on fast ground.
Norse Dancer(IRE), who in recent runs has not looked the same horse who regularly performed well in Group 1 company and it is to be hoped he can be found a place at stud for next season. (op 12-1)
Iceman was struggling from an early stage and has yet to recapture his juvenile form following a long absence. (tchd 14-1 in a place)

5674 KINGDOM OF BAHRAIN SUN CHARIOT STKS (GROUP 1) (F&M) 1m
3:10 (3:11) (Class 1) 3-Y-O-**£113,560** (£43,040; £21,540; £10,740; £5,380) **Stalls** High

Form RPR

1152 **1** **Spinning Queen**[15] 5341 3-8-12 107..... MichaelHills 9 119
(B W Hills) *b. hind: mde all: rdn clr over 1f out: r.o wl* **12/1**

1625 **2** *9* **Soviet Song (IRE)**[34] 4839 6-9-2 113..... OscarUrbina 6 100
(J R Fanshawe) *hld up in tch: rdn over 2f out: sn outpcd: wnt 2nd wl ins fnl f* **9/2**[3]

2123 **3** *nk* **Alexander Goldrun (IRE)**[21] 5193 5-9-2..... KJManning 7 99
(J S Bolger, Ire) *lw: chsd wnr: rdn over 2f out: sn outpcd: lost 2nd wl ins fnl f* **6/4**[1]

-023 **4** 2½ **Musicanna**[80] 3416 5-9-2 109.....(t) RichardHughes 1 94
(J R Fanshawe) *lw: trckd ldrs: rdn over 2f out: hung rt and wknd over 1f out* **8/1**

1111 **5** *34* **Red Evie (IRE)**[21] 5191 3-8-12 108..... JamieSpencer 3 23
(M L W Bell) *b. hind: hld up: pushed along 6f out: rdn over 2f out: wknd and eased over 1f out* **9/4**[2]

1m 38.83s (-0.54) **Going Correction** +0.35s/f (Good)
WFA 3 from 5yo+ 4lb 5 Ran SP% **107.8**
Speed ratings (Par 117):116,107,106,104,70
CSF £58.45 TOTE £10.80: £3.10, £2.20; EX 53.90 Trifecta £80.50 Pool: £646.84 - 5.70 winning tickets..
Owner Marston Stud & Cavendish Investing Ltd **Bred** R A Bonnycastle And Marston Stud **Trained** Lambourn, Berks

FOCUS
A quality field but a race weakened by four withdrawals, including Speciosa and Peeress, and in the end a surprise result. The time was well up to par for the grade, being 1.12sec faster than the preceding Group 3 contested by colts, but the form is impossible to rate with confidence, with nothing solid to base it on and the winner seemingly stepping up significantly on previous form.

NOTEBOOK
Spinning Queen, returning to this trip for the first time since the 1000 Guineas, looked to have improved in recent runs but seemed a Group 3 filly at best and was held by Red Evie on Goodwood form. However, she set off in front at a decent clip and had her rivals in trouble at the bushes, eventually drawing right awayto show seemingly much improved form. The Breeders' Cup Mile is being considered but she is due to go to the sales at the end of the year. (op 14-1)
Soviet Song(IRE), who has not fired as often as in the past this season, was struggling from some way out and merely battled on past her old rival Alexander Goldrun to claim the runner-up spot. She may take her chance in the Champion Stakes, but retirement is looming. (tchd 5-1)

Alexander Goldrun(IRE), who was dropping back to this trip for the first time since finishing second to Soviet Song in the 2005 Falmouth Stakes, was ridden positively but could not respond when the winner quickened away from her on ground that possibly did not suit. A credit to connections, she was contesting her 20th successive Group 1 and is now likely to go for the Hong Kong Cup in December back over ten furlongs, a race she won in 2004. (op 7-4 tchd 15-8 and 2-1 in places)
Musicanna, third in this race in 2005, looked to have conditions to suit but has yet to score at Group level and had her limitations exposed once again. Official explanation: trainer said mare was in season (tchd 7-1)
Red Evie(IRE), who came into this off the back of seven successive wins, culminating in the Group 1 Matron Stakes, ran no sort of race, being in trouble at an early stage. Her trainer reported she may have had enough for the time being, but the ground could have been another factor. She could well be back next year and should prove this running all wrong. Official explanation: trainer said filly was probably feeling the effects of a long season (op 15-8 tchd 7-4)

5675 TOTESPORT CAMBRIDGESHIRE (HERITAGE H'CAP) 1m 1f

3:45 (3:47) (Class 2) 3-Y-O+

£93,480 (£27,990; £13,995; £7,005; £3,495; £1,755) **Stalls** High

Form	Pos	Dist	Horse	RPR
1143	**1**		**Formal Decree (GER)**[14] [5374] 3-8-9 **97**...................... JamieSpencer 17 (G A Swinbank) *hld up: hdwy over 2f out: rdn to ld overall and hung lft over 1f out: r.o* **9/1**[3]	116+
1401	**2**	*4*	**Blue Bajan (IRE)**[8] [5505] 4-8-11 **94** 4ex...................... AdrianTNicholls 10 (Andrew Turnell) *lw: hld up: hdwy over 3f out: rdn over 1f out: styd on* **25/1**	105
-461	**3**	*1*	**Pinpoint (IRE)**[14] [5374] 4-9-1 **98** 4ex.................................. TedDurcan 16 (W R Swinburn) *hld up: hdwy over 3f out: rdn and edgd lft over 1f out: styd on same pce* **10/1**	107
2334	**4**	*shd*	**Take A Bow**[10] [5477] 5-9-3 **100**.. JimCrowley 9 (P R Chamings) *hld up in tch: rdn over 2f out: nt clr run over 1f out: styd on* **40/1**	109
1411	**5**	*5*	**Smart Enough**[37] [4739] 3-9-3 **105**.................................... KerrinMcEvoy 8 (M A Magnusson) *lw: led main gp over 7f: wknd ins fnl f* **9/2**[1]	104+
0564	**6**	*½*	**Seulement (USA)**[21] [5175] 4-8-8 **91**.............................. NickyMackay 1 (L M Cumani) *hld up: hdwy over 2f out: sn rdn: edgd rt and wknd over 1f out* **50/1**	89
0350	**7**	*½*	**Kamanda Laugh**[21] [5177] 5-8-6 **92**............................ AndrewMullen(3) 5 (K A Ryan) *chsd ldrs: rdn over 3f out: wknd fnl f* **100/1**	89
-312	**8**	*1 ¼*	**Charlie Cool**[14] [5374] 3-8-11 **99**................................... RichardHughes 4 (W J Haggas) *hld up: hdwy over 3f out: wknd over 1f out* **12/1**	93
1611	**9**	*hd*	**Illustrious Blue**[21] [5177] 3-8-12 **100** 4ex........................... PaulDoe 29 (W J Knight) *hld up: effrt when nt clr run over 2f out: swtchd left and ran on strongly* **20/1**	94+
5004	**10**	*nk*	**Red Spell (IRE)**[14] [5376] 5-8-8 **91**....................................... RyanMoore 7 (R Hannon) *hld up: hdwy over 2f out: rdn and wknd over 1f out* **50/1**	84
4000	**11**	*nk*	**Ofaraby**[14] [5374] 6-9-1 **98**.. MatthewHenry 3 (M A Jarvis) *hld up: hdwy over 3f out: rdn and wknd over 1f out* **100/1**	91
4043	**12**	*nk*	**Blythe Knight (IRE)**[14] [5357] 6-9-2 **99**.................. GrahamGibbons 30 (J J Quinn) *prom: rdn over 2f out: wknd over 1f out* **25/1**	91
0000	**13**	*1*	**Blue Spinnaker (IRE)**[21] [5188] 7-8-10 **96**................ SaleemGolam(3) 18 (M W Easterby) *prom 7f* **50/1**	86
3300	**14**	*3*	**Royal Alchemist**[77] [3534] 4-9-8 **105**................................... MJKinane 11 (B J Meehan) *lw: prom: rdn over 2f out: wknd over 1f out* **50/1**	89
6046	**15**	*1 ¼*	**Bustan (IRE)**[21] [5177] 7-8-13 **96**.................................... MickyFenton 24 (G C Bravery) *hld up: n.d* **100/1**	78
1251	**16**	*hd*	**Spectait**[57] [4098] 4-9-8 **105**.. SebSanders 33 (Sir Mark Prescott) *racd alone far side: overall ldr tl hung lft and hdd over 1f out: wknd ins fnl f* **10/1**	86+
3000	**17**	*1*	**My Paris**[7] [5520] 5-9-1 **98**..(p) NCallan 15 (K A Ryan) *chsd ldrs: rdn over 2f out: wkng whn hmpd over 1f out* **40/1**	77
1212	**18**	*shd*	**Fairmile**[49] [4359] 4-8-13 **99**.................................... AdamKirby(3) 32 (W R Swinburn) *hld up: nvr trbld ldrs* **8/1**[2]	78+
0326	**19**	*1 ½*	**Pearly King (USA)**[14] [5374] 3-8-3 **98**......................(t) JamieHamblett(7) 14 (Sir Michael Stoute) *lw: hld up: n.d* **25/1**	74
1005	**20**	*nk*	**Salinja (USA)**[21] [5177] 4-8-12 **95**.................................... OscarUrbina 13 (Mrs A J Perrett) *mid-div: rdn over 3f out: sn wknd* **100/1**	70
366	**21**	*nk*	**Capable Guest (IRE)**[21] [5188] 4-8-10 **93**............................. JohnEgan 21 (M R Channon) *hld up: hdwy over 3f out: wknd wl over 1f out* **33/1**	68
0000	**22**	*2 ½*	**Royal Island (IRE)**[37] [4739] 4-8-13 **96**.............................. JoeFanning 20 (M Johnston) *chsd ldrs: lost pl 6f out: n.d after* **50/1**	66
2620	**23**	*1 ¾*	**Ace Of Hearts**[37] [4739] 7-9-3 **100**..................................... GeorgeBaker 23 (C F Wall) *hld up in tch: wknd over 2f out* **50/1**	66
1124	**24**	*1 ½*	**Bolodenka (IRE)**[21] [5188] 4-9-1 **98**.................................. PaulHanagan 25 (R A Fahey) *hld up: wknd over 2f out* **20/1**	61
0001	**25**	*3*	**Rohaani (USA)**[21] [5188] 4-9-4 **101** 4ex.................................... RHills 12 (Sir Michael Stoute) *s.i.s: hdwy over 7f out: wknd over 2f out* **25/1**	58
1-06	**26**	*1 ¾*	**Stagelight (IRE)**[84] [3313] 4-9-7 **104**..................................... TPQueally 6 (J Noseda) *chsd ldrs over 6f* **18/1**	58
400	**27**	*6*	**Another Bottle (IRE)**[78] [3493] 5-9-0 **97**......................... SteveDrowne 22 (R Charlton) *hld up: wknd over 2f out* **33/1**	39
4105	**28**	*6*	**Hinterland (IRE)**[49] [4358] 4-9-8 **105**............................ PhilipRobinson 35 (M A Jarvis) *prom 6f* **20/1**	35
0505	**29**	*7*	**Tanzanite (IRE)**[28] [5012] 4-8-10 **93**................................. FJohansson 31 (D W P Arbuthnot) *lw: chsd ldrs: rdn over 3f out: wknd over 2f out* **66/1**	9
4130	**30**	*2 ½*	**Day To Remember**[9] [5494] 5-8-9 **92**..............................(t) EddieAhern 27 (E F Vaughan) *s.i.s: rdn over 3f out: a in rr* **40/1**	—
3404	**31**	*1 ¾*	**Rocamadour**[23] [5142] 4-9-7 **104**..(v) KJManning 2 (M R Channon) *lw: chsd ldrs over 5f* **66/1**	11
0404	**32**	*1 ¼*	**Wise Dennis**[7] [5520] 4-8-13 **96**..................................... DarryllHolland 34 (A P Jarvis) *hld up: plld hrd: wknd wl over 2f out* **33/1**	—
2123	**33**	*7*	**Dunelight (IRE)**[13] [5411] 3-9-3 **105**...................................(v) KDarley 19 (C G Cox) *s.i.s: sn chsng ldrs: wknd over 2f out* **33/1**	—

1m 52.79s (0.84) **Going Correction** +0.35s/f (Good)
WFA 3 from 4yo+ 5lb **33** Ran SP% **137.9**
Speed ratings (Par 109):110,106,105,105,101 100,100,99,98,98 98,98,97,94,93 93,92,92,90,90 90,88,86,85,82 81,75,70,64
CSF £222.06 CT £2354.38 TOTE £11.90: £3.40, £6.80, £3.60, £9.60; EX 381.10 Trifecta £2680.30 Pool: £22,650.51 - 6.00 winning tickets..
Owner Mrs K Pratt & S P racing Investments S A **Bred** Gestut Olympia **Trained** Melsonby, N Yorks
■ Jamie Spencer, who became available after Cesare was taken out, replaced declared rider Dean McKeown.

FOCUS
What looked a typically competitive renewal of this top handicap was turned into a procession by the winner. With the exception of Spectait the field raced in one group down the centre of the track. The leaders may well have gone too quick, but there were few hard-luck stories and the form looks solid, with the first four finishing clear.

NOTEBOOK
Formal Decree(GER) ◆ has progressed really well this season and had alreadt risen 27lb in the handicap. Although just 3lb better off with Pinpoint for a length and a quarter defeat at Newbury, he turned around that result in no uncertain terms and was tremendously impressive. Out the back early, he needed to be niggled to pick up, but once into full stride he swept past his rivals and settled the issue in a matter of strides. He will be forced into Pattern races before long but shapes as though he is well up to winning one, with further improvement very much on the cards and every chance he will be even more effective when steped up to a mile and a half. (op 15-2)
Blue Bajan(IRE), unlucky in running when a length and a half behind the winner at Newbury, was 3lb worse off. He had established his credentials with a good win at Ascot on soft ground and did his best, but the winner was far too strong.
Pinpoint(IRE), carrying a penalty for beating the first two at Newbury, ran well and gave the winner a tow through the field, but he could not respond when that rival swept past, although he kept on well enough. (op 11-1)
Take A Bow, who was beaten a neck in this race in 2004, has continued to run well since although he has been comparatively lightly raced, having had 11 months off at one stage. He performed well again, but is going to get little respite from the Handicapper as a result. (tchd 50-1)
Smart Enough, a rapidly-improving colt whose front-running wins at the Newmarket July and York Ebor meetings resulted in him being a strong favourite for this, again tried to make the running but was possibly forced to do too much too soon and paid the penalty in the closing stages. He still did best of the pace horses, and as this was only his seventh outing he can be expected to bounce back next season. He looks a Group performer in the making. (op 11-2)
Seulement(USA), who was a reserve and only took part following the withdrawal of the top-weight, ran a fine race. He has not won since coming to Britain, but has slipped in the handicap as a result and looks to have a race in him on this evidence. (tchd 66-1)
Kamanda Laugh likes this track and ran another good race, but he may have found the trip stretching him on this ground.
Charlie Cool, one of the least experienced in the line-up, had finished ahead of the first two when runner-up at Newbury so should have finished closer. However, this was his first encounter with soft ground and it may not have suited. (op 14-1)
Illustrious Blue ◆, who has been in such great form for new connections, was unlucky not to finish considerably closer. He was just starting to pick up when he ran up the back of rivals approaching the two-furlong marker, and that left him with too much to do. Switched left to come up the stands' side of the pack, he ran on so strongly that he might even have been placed had he enjoyed better luck.
Red Spell(IRE) performed with credit, but despite some decent efforts on turf this season seems to be at his best on Polytrack. Official explanation: jockey said gelding had had no more to give (tchd 66-1)
Ofaraby ran another decent race but is still paying handicap-wise for his fine season in 2005.
Blythe Knight(IRE), winner of the Lincoln in the spring, put up another creditable performance but could not improve on his fourth and seventh in the two previous runnings.
Spectait raced by himself down the far rail and was in front going into the dip, but he weakened pretty quickly from that point.
Fairmile, whose form this year gave him a major chance in this, never figured and, although he has won on soft ground, it may be that he is more effective on a sound surface.

5676 EUROPEAN BREEDERS FUND JERSEY LILY FILLIES' NURSERY 7f

4:20 (4:21) (Class 2) 2-Y-O

£18,696 (£5,598; £2,799; £1,401; £699; £351) **Stalls** High

Form	Pos	Dist	Horse	RPR
3423	**1**		**Blithe**[23] [5133] 2-8-12 **78**.. MichaelHills 17 (W J Haggas) *prom: effrt over 2f out: led ins fnl f: pushed out* **7/2**[1]	85+
1151	**2**	*1 ½*	**Fractured Foxy**[14] [5366] 2-7-8 **65**........................... NataliaGemelova(5) 16 (J J Quinn) *a cl up: led 2f out to ins fnl f: kpt on: nt pce of wnr* **14/1**	68
326	**3**	*¾*	**Silca Key**[29] [4994] 2-8-3 **72**.................................. EdwardCreighton(3) 2 (M R Channon) *keen: prom: effrt 2f out: kpt on ins fnl f* **16/1**	73
211	**4**	*1 ¼*	**Steam Cuisine**[18] [5271] 2-9-3 **83**.. TPQueally 14 (M G Quinlan) *hld up midfield: effrt whn n.m.r briefly appr 2f out: rdn and r.o fnl f: nrst fin* **11/2**[2]	81+
325	**5**	*hd*	**Baltic Belle (IRE)**[8] [5503] 2-9-0 **80**................................ KerrinMcEvoy 1 (R Hannon) *hld up: hdwy outside of gp over 1f out: kpt on fnl f: nrst fin* **12/1**	78
601	**6**	*hd*	**Regal Quest (IRE)**[12] [5425] 2-9-2 **82**..................................... JohnEgan 4 (S Kirk) *trckd ldrs: effrt and ev ch 2f out: no ex ins fnl f* **7/1**[3]	79
041	**7**	*¾*	**World's Heroine (IRE)**[65] [3878] 2-9-2 **82**........................... FJohansson 3 (G A Butler) *hld up: hdwy over 1f out: no imp fnl f* **25/1**	77
3105	**8**	*¾*	**La Roca (IRE)**[36] [4775] 2-9-7 **87**..(t) SebSanders 8 (R M Beckett) *bhd: drvn 1/2-way: hdwy over 1f out: nvr rchd ldrs* **25/1**	81
3423	**9**	*hd*	**Miss Saafend Plaza (IRE)**[18] [5271] 2-9-3 **83**................... RyanMoore 9 (R Hannon) *bhd: rdn 1/2-way: hdwy outside over 1f out: nt pce to chal* **22/1**	76
5354	**10**	*¾*	**Only Hope**[14] [5387] 2-8-1 **64** oh1 ow6.......................(v[1]) JamesDoyle(3) 10 (Ernst Oertel) *hld up: hdwy over 2f out: no ex fnl f* **33/1**	61
152	**11**	*3*	**Crumbs Of Comfort (USA)**[18] [5271] 2-9-4 **84**............... NickyMackay 5 (L M Cumani) *hld up towards rr: shortlived effrt over 2f out: sn btn* **20/1**	68
326	**12**	*6*	**Silkie Smooth (IRE)**[22] [5157] 2-9-2 **82**........................ JamieSpencer 15 (B W Hills) *led to over 2f out: wknd over 1f out* **10/1**	51
6163	**13**	*1 ¼*	**Bright Moon**[22] [5157] 2-9-0 **80**.. RichardHughes 7 (R Hannon) *bhd: drvn 1/2-way: nvr on terms* **16/1**	46
500	**14**	*6*	**Bathwick Fancy (IRE)**[17] [5289] 2-8-3 **69**......................(t) PaulHanagan 6 (J G Portman) *midfield: drvn 1/2-way: btn over 1f out* **66/1**	20
261	**15**	*5*	**Miss Jenny (IRE)**[18] [5261] 2-9-7 **87**..................................... MJKinane 11 (B J Meehan) *lw: midfield: outpcd 3f out: sn btn* **10/1**	25
0003	**16**	*1 ¾*	**Boogie Dancer**[33] [4866] 2-8-3 **69**.............................. AdrianTNicholls 13 (H S Howe) *chsd ldrs to 1/2-way: sn lost pl* **66/1**	3
001	**17**	*13*	**Morinqua (IRE)**[32] [4913] 2-9-2 **82**... NCallan 12 (K A Ryan) *plld hrd: cl up: led briefly over 2f out: wknd over 1f out* **25/1**	—

1m 28.62s (2.12) **Going Correction** +0.35s/f (Good) **17** Ran SP% **121.0**
Speed ratings (Par 98):101,99,98,97,96 96,95,94,94,93 90,83,82,75,69 67,52
CSF £47.25 CT £727.68 TOTE £5.00: £1.70, £3.40, £3.80, £2.00; EX 76.90.
Owner Cheveley Park Stud **Bred** Cheveley Park Stud Ltd **Trained** Newmarket, Suffolk

FOCUS
A decent fillies' nursery run only 0.34 sec slower than the opening juvenile fillies' Listed race. The form looks solid, rated around the first two.

NOTEBOOK
Blithe ◆, who had already showed that she could handle the trip and ground, was unlucky in running last time but had everything fall right on this occasion and duly got off the mark. She looks the sort who could improve with this under her belt and may well follow up. (tchd 4-1 and 9-2 in a place)
Fractured Foxy ◆ has progressed really well since winning a couple of sellers last month and ran her race again. She briefly looked set to score but the winner picked up past her and she could not respond. She remains reasonably handicapped and can win again before the season is out.
Silca Key, back on her favoured easy ground for her handicap debut after disappointing on the All-Weather last time, ran her race but did not help her cause by taking a hold early on. She has races in her, possibly at a slightly lower level.
Steam Cuisine, bidding for a hat-trick, possibly found the ground easier than she would have liked and briefly failed to get a run. She looks capable of better. (op 9-2)

Baltic Belle(IRE) has a fair amount of experience and handled the easy ground and longer trip. Although she was doing her best work late on, she may prefer a sharper track. (op 14-1)
Regal Quest(IRE), who got off the mark in a Polytrack maiden, coped with her first experience of easy ground but did not seem to get up the hill. (op 8-1)
World's Heroine(IRE) seemed to have every chance, but may not have been as well suited by the easy ground as the fast surface she won on last time. (op 33-1)
Silkie Smooth(IRE) Official explanation: jockey said filly had run too freely
Morinqua(IRE) Official explanation: jockey said filly had had no more to give

5677 TOTEEXACTA H'CAP — 7f

4:55 (4:55) (Class 2) (0-100,98) 3-Y-0+

£12,464 (£3,732; £1,866; £934; £466; £234) **Stalls** High

Form — RPR

/20- **1** — **Army Of Angels (IRE)**[441] [3543] 4-9-7 **97**.................... KerrinMcEvoy 15 — 111+
(Saeed Bin Suroor) *lw: trckd ldrs gng wl: led over 1f out: pushed clr ins fnl f: readily* **12/1**

2100 **2** *5* **Skhilling Spirit**[14] [5358] 3-9-3 **96**.. RyanMoore 3 — 97
(T D Barron) *missed break: bhd: hdwy 3f out: chsd wnr ins fnl f: no imp* **7/1**[3]

2250 **3** *1 1/2* **Compton's Eleven**[7] [5523] 5-9-5 **95**.................................... TedDurcan 8 — 92
(M R Channon) *lw: hld up in tch: hdwy over 2f out: kpt on fnl f: nrst fin* **10/1**

4101 **4** *1* **Muzher (IRE)**[35] [4802] 3-8-9 **88**..(p) RHills 7 — 83
(B W Hills) *trckd ldrs: effrt over 2f out: one pce fnl f* **7/1**[3]

5020 **5** *1 1/4* **Kenmore**[7] [5534] 4-8-12 **88**.. JamieSpencer 2 — 79
(D Nicholls) *bhd: pushed along 1/2-way: hdwy appr fnl f: nvr rchd ldrs* **6/1**[2]

0201 **6** *3/4* **Plum Pudding (IRE)**[2] [5639] 3-9-5 **98** 6ex.................. RichardHughes 11 — 87
(R Hannon) *led to over 1f out: wknd ins fnl f* **4/1**[1]

1013 **7** *3/4* **Minority Report**[35] [4798] 6-9-6 **96**............................ NickyMackay 16 — 83
(L M Cumani) *hld up in tch: effrt 2f out: no imp fnl f* **8/1**

3633 **8** *3/4* **Commando Scott (IRE)**[7] [5529] 5-8-10 **89**............ PatrickMathers(3) 19 — 74
(I W McInnes) *prom: effrt over 2f out: edgd rt and outpcd over 1f out* **7/1**[3]

4410 **9** *3* **Jamieson Gold (IRE)**[35] [4790] 3-8-12 **91**......................... MichaelHills 9 — 69
(B W Hills) *hld up: rdn over 2f out: n.d* **10/1**

-040 **10** *6* **High Bray (GER)**[21] [5175] 5-8-4 **83**................................ MarcHalford(3) 1 — 45
(D R C Elsworth) *hld up: hdwy 3f out: wknd over 1f out* **14/1**

00-0 **11** *1 3/4* **Dramaticus**[10] [5476] 4-8-7 **83** oh5.................................... FrancisFerris 12 — 40
(B Palling) *w ldrs tl wknd appr 2f out* **100/1**

0060 **12** *14* **Jalamid (IRE)**[33] [4348] 4-9-0 **90**..(t) MickyFenton 6 — 11
(G C Bravery) *bhd: rdn and hung rt 3f out: nvr on terms* **50/1**

1m 27.66s (1.16) **Going Correction** +0.35s/f (Good)
WFA 3 from 4yo+ 3lb — 12 Ran SP% **118.4**
Speed ratings (Par 109):107,101,99,98,97 96,95,94,91,84 82,66
CSF £93.51 CT £897.42 TOTE £13.90: £3.90, £2.50, £2.80; EX 141.30.
Owner Godolphin **Bred** Gerard Callanan **Trained** Newmarket, Suffolk

FOCUS

A good handicap run at a decent pace and resulting in a clear-cut winner. However, the form does not look that solid behind.

NOTEBOOK

Army Of Angels(IRE) ◆, who had been absent since the 2005 July meeting, came back with a terrific performance to complete a fine day for a stable that had picked up three Group races earlier in the afternoon. He looks improved for the break and on this evidence will be contesting Pattern races sooner rather than later. (op 14-1)
Skhilling Spirit, who handles soft ground and appeared to stay this trip earlier in the season, was slowly away but then came through to deliver his challenge meeting the rising ground. Although he ran on well the winner easily drew away from him. He still looks progressive and a flatter track over this trip may well suit him. (op 8-1)
Compton's Eleven is pretty reliable in this sort of contest and kept on at the end without ever looking like winning. He has not won in Britain for over two years, so is likely to be back off to Dubai again in the winter, having picked up a race there in each of the last two seasons. (tchd 11-1 in a place)
Muzher(IRE), who had won his last two turf races under similar conditions, had looked a reluctant hero last time and had cheekpieces fitted on this occasion. He appeared to have every chance but could only stick on at the one pace. (op 8-1)
Kenmore ◆, whose last win was over course and distance just under a year ago, has struggled for form for his new stable apart from one surprising effort over the minimum trip. He did not look an easy ride on this occasion, but he has slipped back close to his last winning mark and may be one to bear in mind for a similar contest before the end of the season. (op 11-2)
Plum Pudding(IRE), a winner here just two days previously, was dropping back a furlong and carrying a 6lb penalty. He was unable to dominate his rivals and a return to a mile on good ground will see him to better effect. (op 9-2 tchd 5-1 in a place)
Minority Report had raced solely on a sound surface prior to this, and in the circumstances ran quite well. However, he did not look as effective on it and may have to wait until next year to get his ground again. (op 9-1)
Commando Scott(IRE), who ran a couple of decent races over course and distance last backend, did so again but his wins have come on flatter tracks.

5678 SUFFOLK INSULATION AND RENOVATION SERVICES H'CAP — 1m 4f

5:30 (5:30) (Class 3) (0-95,96) 3-Y-0+

£8,724 (£2,612; £1,306; £653; £326; £163) **Stalls** High

Form — RPR

6303 **1** — **Mikao (IRE)**[16] [5325] 5-8-12 **84**.................................... SaleemGolam(3) 17 — 94
(M H Tompkins) *a.p: styd far side ent st: chsd ldr over 3f out: rdn to ld that grp and overall ldr over 1f out: r.o: fin long way clr of h* **10/1**

3230 **2** *3/4* **Ti Adora (IRE)**[28] [5010] 4-8-12 **81** oh1.................................. JohnEgan 4 — 90
(P W D'Arcy) *lw: chsd ldrs: c centre ent st: rdn to ld that gp over 1f out: r.o: 1st of 10 in gp* **10/1**

-300 **3** *3* **Spear Thistle**[126] [2013] 4-8-9 **81** oh1............................. JamesDoyle(3) 5 — 85
(Mrs N Smith) *b. nr hind: hld up: wnt centre ent st: hdwy over 2f out: rdn over 1f out: styd on same pce fnl f: 2nd of 10 in gp* **33/1**

5110 **4** *3/4* **Cold Turkey**[143] [1584] 6-9-12 **95**.. RyanMoore 2 — 98
(G L Moore) *hld up: c centre ent st: hdwy over 2f out: sn rdn: no ex fnl f: 3rd of 10 in gp* **9/1**[3]

0463 **5** *hd* **Solent (IRE)**[28] [5010] 4-9-11 **94**.................................. RichardHughes 7 — 97+
(R Hannon) *chsd ldrs: c centre ent st: rdn over 2f out: no ex fnl f: 4th of 10 in gp* **7/2**[1]

4301 **6** *5* **Dzesmin (POL)**[14] [5367] 4-8-13 **82**..............................(p) PhilipRobinson 10 — 77
(R C Guest) *lw: swtg: hld up: c centre ent st: hdwy over 2f out: wknd over 1f out: 5th of 10 in gp* **12/1**

3310 **7** *3* **Nobelix (IRE)**[60] [4027] 4-9-3 **86**.. JamieSpencer 3 — 76
(J R Fanshawe) *chsd ldr tl c centre and led that gp ent s: rdn and hdd over 1f out: sn wknd: 6th of 10 in gp* **14/1**

0032 **8** *2 1/2* **Crow Wood**[14] [5361] 7-9-5 **88**..................................... GrahamGibbons 8 — 74
(J J Quinn) *chsd ldrs: c centre ent s: rdn and wknd over 2f out: 7th of 10 in gp* **12/1**

3221 **9** *2 1/2* **My Arch**[30] [4945] 4-9-2 **85**.. NCallan 6 — 67
(K A Ryan) *chsd ldrs: c centre ent st: rdn and wknd 2f out: 8th of 10 in gp* **11/2**[2]

0000 **10** *5* **Fortunate Isle (USA)**[14] [5374] 4-9-4 **87**.......................... MichaelHills 15 — 61
(B W Hills) *led: styd far side enetering st: rdn and hdd over 1f out: wknd qckly: remote 2nd of 5 in gp* **11/1**

1214 **11** *2* **Whispering Death**[36] [4770] 4-9-0 **83**..........................(v) KerrinMcEvoy 13 — 54
(W J Haggas) *hld up: wnt centre ent st: effrt over 2f out: sn wknd: 9th of 10 in gp* **12/1**

0060 **12** *nk* **Blaise Hollow (USA)**[15] [5346] 4-8-12 **81** oh3............... SteveDrowne 16 — 51
(R Charlton) *hld up: styd far side ent st: rdn and wknd over 2f out : remote 3rd of 5 in gp* **33/1**

4544 **13** *3/4* **Wise Owl**[8] [5506] 4-8-12 **81** oh1... MJKinane 14 — 50
(J Pearce) *hld up: styd far side ent st: rdn and wknd over 2f out : remote 4th of 5 in gp* **11/1**

/0-0 **14** *4* **Mr Ed (IRE)**[14] [5383] 8-8-12 **81** oh1..................................(p) PaulHanagan 12 — 44
(P Bowen) *hld up: wnt centre over 8f out: wknd over 3f out: last of 10 in gp* **25/1**

5100 **15** *29* **Nihal (IRE)**[34] [4833] 3-8-8 **85**.. JoeFanning 11 — —
(M Johnston) *b. hind: chsd ldrs: styd far side ent st: wknd 3f out: poor last of 5 in gp* **20/1**

2m 35.29s (1.79) **Going Correction** +0.35s/f (Good)
WFA 3 from 4yo+ 8lb — **15** Ran SP% **126.7**
Speed ratings (Par 107):108,107,105,105,104 101,99,97,96,92 91,91,90,88,68
CSF £106.78 CT £3198.36 TOTE £13.50: £4.70, £3.60, £11.70; EX 125.90 Place 6 £3,138.80, Place 5 £222.00.
Owner Ben Allen **Bred** Kildaragh Stud **Trained** Newmarket, Suffolk

FOCUS

A decent handicap run at a solid gallop in which the field split into two groups once in the straight, with the winner coming down the far-side rail. There were not many progressive types in the field and the form is not all that strong.

NOTEBOOK

Mikao(IRE), a course and distance winner here in the spring, got a good lead in the group that stayed far side and taking over in the dip, ran on strongly to hold the filly who came up the centre. This was his highest winning mark to date, but he was a long way clear of the rest of his group and it would be no surprise to see him win again if returning here before the end of the season.
Ti Adora(IRE) is a tough mare and all ground comes alike to her. She won the race in the main group but the winner on the far rail had gone beyond recall. She deserves another success as she has been running consistently well since the spring. (op 9-1)
Spear Thistle has not won for the best part of two years, during which time his handicap mark has remained steady. He could do with some help from the assessor, but in the meantime is one to keep in mind for when the ground is really testing.
Cold Turkey ◆, returning from a five-month break, ran really well on this return to action and this will have set him up nicely for a winter campaign that will probably mix hurdling and racing on Polytrack. (op 12-1)
Solent(IRE) handles all sorts of ground, but recent efforts suggest a longer trip and even softer going suits best. (op 5-1)
Dzesmin(POL), whose win last time came on much faster ground, did not look as comfortable on this softer surface and faded late on. (op 14-1 tchd 16-1)
Nobelix(IRE), who beat today's runner-up on fast ground at Haydock when stealing the race from the front, was 8lb worse off with that rival but has performed nowhere near as well since and failed again despite having previous form on the surface.
My Arch found this a different kettle of fish from the class 5 handicap he won at Beverley. (op 5-1)
Fortunate Isle(USA) Official explanation: jockey said colt had had no more to give
T/Jkpt: Not won. T/Plt: £1,827.90 to a £1 stake. Pool: £179,540.75. 71.70 winning tickets.
T/Qpdt: £170.60 to a £1 stake. Pool: £11,185.60. 48.50 winning tickets. CR

5481 REDCAR (L-H)

Saturday, September 30

OFFICIAL GOING: Good

The ground was described as 'just on the slow side of good, slower than that down the stands' side rail'.
Wind: light, half behind Weather: fine, sunny and warm

5679 EUROPEAN BREEDERS FUND MAIDEN FILLIES' STKS — 7f

1:45 (1:46) (Class 4) 2-Y-0 — **£5,181** (£1,541; £770; £384) **Stalls** Centre

Form — RPR

1 — **Ransom Captive (USA)** 2-9-0 .... FrancisNorton 15 — 84+
(M A Magnusson) *wnt lft s and towards rr: swtchd lft 1/2-way: gd hdwy over 2f out: rdn over 1f out: styd on to ld last 100yds* **13/2**[3]

2 *1* **Thunderousapplause** 2-9-0 .... PaulMulrennan 13 — 82+
(K A Ryan) *trckd ldrs: smooth hdwy 2f out: rdn to ld over 1f out: hdd and no ex last 100yds* **14/1**

032 **3** *nk* **Nadawat (USA)**[20] [5206] 2-9-0 74...................................... JimmyQuinn 9 — 81
(J L Dunlop) *led: rdn along and hdd over 1f out: kpt on same pce ins last* **7/2**[2]

422 **4** *3* **La Spezia (IRE)**[17] [5287] 2-9-0 80.................................. TonyCulhane 11 — 73
(M L W Bell) *chsd ldrs: hdwy over 2f out: rdn wl over 1f out: sn drvn and no imp* **15/8**[1]

06 **5** *1 1/4* **Miss Phuket**[26] [5068] 2-9-0 .... RobertWinston 16 — 70
(G Wragg) *hld up in midfield: hdwy 2f out: styd on ins last: nrst fin* **14/1**

50 **6** *nk* **Inquisitress**[25] [5083] 2-8-11 .... StephenDonohoe(3) 14 — 69
(J M P Eustace) *in tch: pushed along and sltly outpcd 3f out: sn rdn and kpt on fnl 2f* **15/2**

0 **7** *1* **Ice Box (IRE)**[15] [5332] 2-9-0 .... RoystonFfrench 10 — 67
(M Johnston) *cl up: rdn along 3f out: grad wknd* **25/1**

55 **8** *6* **Solwind (USA)**[19] [5237] 2-9-0 .... TomEaves 7 — 52
(B Smart) *cl up: rdn along wl over 2f out: grad wknd* **33/1**

5 **9** *5* **Asturias**[12] [5424] 2-9-0 .... J-PGuillambert 2 — 39
(J W Hills) *cl up on outer: rdn along 1/2-way: sn wknd* **16/1**

10 *1 1/4* **Forsters Plantin** 2-9-0 .... PatCosgrave 8 — 36
(J J Quinn) *a rr* **50/1**

11 *nk* **Zarnitza (USA)** 2-9-0 .... RichardMullen 5 — 36
(E A L Dunlop) *a rr* **20/1**

0 **12** *hd* **Lady Pickpocket**[17] [5283] 2-9-0 .... DaleGibson 12 — 35
(M H Tompkins) *a bhd* **66/1**

0000 **13** *3* **Rose Court**[49] [4376] 2-9-0 42... DavidAllan 3 — 28
(K G Reveley) *hmpd s: a rr* **100/1**

0 **14** *1/2* **Danum Diva (IRE)**[8] [5507] 2-9-0 .... RobbieFitzpatrick 1 — 26
(T J Pitt) *chsd ldrs on outer: rdn along 1/2-way: sn wknd* **50/1**

15 *17* **Bunderos (IRE)** 2-9-0 .... ChrisCatlin 6 — —
(Mrs A Duffield) *a bhd* **50/1**

1m 24.95s (0.05) **Going Correction** -0.025s/f (Good) — **15** Ran SP% **121.2**
Speed ratings (Par 94):98,96,96,93,91 91,90,83,77,76 75,75,72,71,52
CSF £87.49 TOTE £7.20: £2.20, £6.90, £2.10; EX 95.00.

Owner Eastwind Racing Ltd and Martha Trussell **Bred** T F Van Meter Ii **Trained** Upper Lambourn, Berks

FOCUS

A good maiden for the course likely to produce its share of winners and rated positively.

NOTEBOOK

Ransom Captive(USA), a half-sister to a useful US winner, was soon well off the pace and looked to be struggling, but she realised what was required of her at just past halfway and began to make headway. Even with a furlong to run she looked booked for a place at best, but hit overdrive close home and got up to win going away. This was a highly pleasing introduction and given her stable is capable of housing a useful sort, it would not surprise to see her progress further. (op 9-1)

Thunderousapplause, whose stable has had a good year with their juveniles, travelled best of all and looked all over the winner when going on a furlong out, but she soon began to paddle under pressure and was eclipsed by her fellow debutant. Speedily bred, it was quite surprising she was making her debut at this distance and the drop to six furlongs should see her winning, as long as she can find some good ground before the season is out. (op 16-1)

Nadawat(USA), who seemed to appreciate the drop back to six furlongs when finding only the useful Dodge City too good at Goodwood last time, was made plenty of use of and kept on surprisingly well to nearly reclaim second. She may be capable of better in nurseries. (op 11-4)

La Spezia(IRE) has been holding her form well without suggesting she is progressing, but this was a step in the wrong direction as she found little for pressure having held a good position. She is becoming slightly frustrating. (op 5-2)

Miss Phuket comes from a stable who have had a poor season, but his was her third start in maiden company and it was an eyecatching one. She really picked up well inside the final quarter mile and ran on nicely despite not being given a hard time. She will soon have the option of handicaps and she looks certain to improve for a mile. (op 16-1)

Inquisitress has not really built on a promising debut, but she is another who can now improve once handicapping. (op 6-1 tchd 8-1)

5680 JOHN SMITH'S REDCAR STRAIGHT-MILE CHAMPIONSHIP FINAL (H'CAP) 1m

2:20 (2:20) (Class 2) 3-Y-O+

£18,696 (£5,598; £2,799; £1,401; £699; £351) **Stalls** Centre

Form				RPR
6231	**1**		**Nanton (USA)**[10] 5483 4-8-11 **82** ... JimmyQuinn 14 (N Wilson) *hld up towards rr: hdwy over 2f out: led jst ins last: hld on towards fin* **8/1**	89
614	**2**	*3/4*	**Rio Riva**[14] 5357 4-9-5 **95** ... JamieMoriarty(5) 16 (Miss J A Camacho) *s.s: hdwy extreme stands' side over 2f out: styd on ins last: jst hld* **6/1**[1]	100
0403	**3**	*1/2*	**Efidium**[10] 5483 8-7-5 **69** oh10 ... (b) LukeMorris(7) 2 (N Bycroft) *sn chsng ldrs: kpt on same pce ins last* **40/1**	73
1130	**4**	*1/2*	**Colton**[18] 5260 3-7-12 **73** oh6 ... DaleGibson 7 (J M P Eustace) *dwlt: sn mid-div: drvn over 3f out: kpt on wl fnl 2f* **25/1**	76
6	**5**	*hd*	**Flipando (IRE)**[21] 5175 5-9-5 **90** ... PhillipMakin 12 (T D Barron) *t.k.h towards rr: hdwy over 2f out: kpt on wl fnl f* **8/1**	93
5313	**6**	*1/2*	**Middlemarch (IRE)**[13] 5406 6-8-0 **71** ... (b) AdrianMcCarthy 3 (J S Goldie) *led: hung rt and hdd jst ins last: no ex* **10/1**	72
3121	**7**	*1 1/2*	**Daaweitza**[30] 4958 3-8-2 **77** ... RichardMullen 6 (B Ellison) *w ldrs: styd on same pce fnl 2f* **12/1**	75
0552	**8**	*1/2*	**Fremen (USA)**[10] 5483 6-8-8 **79** ... SilvestreDeSousa 1 (D Nicholls) *w ldrs on wd outside: fdd appr fnl f* **7/1**[2]	76
3560	**9**	*shd*	**Spring Goddess (IRE)**[49] 4379 5-8-5 **76** ... ChrisCatlin 15 (A P Jarvis) *hld up in rr: rdn over 2f out: styd on: nt rch ldrs* **16/1**	73
0212	**10**	*5*	**Nevada Desert (IRE)**[15] 5337 6-8-4 **75** ... DavidAllan 11 (R M Whitaker) *w ldrs: lost pl 2f out* **12/1**	60
0010	**11**	*1/2*	**Jaassey**[10] 5483 3-7-7 **73** oh15 ... DuranFentiman(5) 4 (A Crook) *chsd ldrs on outer: wknd over 1f out* **66/1**	57
5601	**12**	*1*	**Mezuzah**[6] 5554 6-8-9 **80** 6ex ... PaulMulrennan 9 (M W Easterby) *chsd ldrs: lost pl 2f out* **12/1**	62
3441	**13**	*3/4*	**Jubilee Street (IRE)**[62] 3985 7-8-13 **84** ... RoystonFfrench 8 (Mrs A Duffield) *hld up in mid-div: rdn over 2f out: sn wknd* **10/1**	64
4130	**14**	*2 1/2*	**Stoic Leader (IRE)**[6] 5554 6-8-9 **80** ... RobertWinston 5 (R F Fisher) *trckd ldrs: t.k.h: wknd over 1f out* **25/1**	54
3112	**15**	*1 1/4*	**Bailieborough (IRE)**[17] 5301 7-8-12 **86** ... StephenDonohoe(3) 17 (B Ellison) *chsd ldrs stands' side: rdn and lost pl over 2f out* **15/2**[3]	57

1m 36.2s (-1.60) **Going Correction** -0.025s/f (Good)

WFA 3 from 4yo+ 4lb **15** Ran SP% **119.5**

Speed ratings (Par 109):107,106,105,105,105 104,103,102,102,97 96,95,95,92,91

CSF £52.82 CT £1866.72 TOTE £8.70: £3.20, £3.20, £8.10; EX 64.40 Trifecta £238.60 Part won. Pool: £336.06 - 0.50 winning tickets..

Owner Themackemracers **Bred** Samuel H And Mrs Rogers, Jr **Trained** Upper Helmsley, N Yorks

FOCUS

A competitive handicap, although with two of the front three having run in claiming company last time and the third and fourth racing from out of the handicap, it is debatable how good a race it was.

NOTEBOOK

Nanton(USA), back to winning ways in claiming company over course and distance latest, gave his connections an immediate return on their investment and defied a mark of 82 in workmanlike fashion. The change in scenery has clearly done him good, but whether he can defy a further rise is debatable. (op 17-2 tchd 9-1 in a place)

Rio Riva, bidding for his third win of the season, did himself no favours with a slow start and then decided to stick against the stands' side. He came through with his challenge, but was never quite getting to the winner. He is capable of winning off this mark. (tchd 13-2 and 7-1 in a place)

Efidium, third behind Nanton at the course last time, had a 2lb pull at the weights but it was not enough to see him close the gap and really it was as good a run as connections could have hoped for. (op 50-1)

Colton, a dual winner in August, looked to have lost his form when finishing well beaten at Lingfield earlier in the month, but he bounced back to something like his best. Racing here off a 12lb higher mark than when last winning, he may need some assistance from the Handicapper before scoring again. (op 22-1)

Flipando(IRE), a tough and consistent sort who rarely runs a bad race, got going all too late having been held up and was never getting there in time.

Fremen(USA), runner-up to Nanton at the course last time, should not have been far away off the same terms, but he failed to run his race and is not running up to the level of form which saw him win twice back in the summer.

Jubilee Street(IRE) Official explanation: jockey said gelding was unsuited by the good ground

Stoic Leader(IRE) Official explanation: jockey said gelding ran too free in the early stages

Bailieborough(IRE) Official explanation: jockey said gelding was never travelling and lost its action latterly

5681 TOTEPOOL TWO-YEAR-OLD TROPHY (LISTED RACE) 6f

2:50 (2:52) (Class 1) 2-Y-O

£113,560 (£43,040; £21,540; £10,740; £5,380; £2,700) **Stalls** Centre

Form				RPR
0010	**1**		**Danum Dancer**[22] 5154 2-8-3 82 ... (b) SilvestreDeSousa 17 (N Bycroft) *a.p centre: hdwy to ld 2f out: sn rdn and styd on strly ins last* **16/1**	88
5113	**2**	*1 3/4*	**Rainbow Mirage (IRE)**[33] 4890 2-8-12 89 ... RobbieFitzpatrick 6 (E S McMahon) *chsd ldrs towards far side: hdwy over 2f out: rdn and ev ch over 1f out: kpt on same pce ins last* **33/1**	92
4313	**3**	*1*	**Bazroy (IRE)**[13] 5408 2-8-9 88 ... StephenDonohoe 16 (P D Evans) *a.p centre: rdn and ch 2f out: drvn and one pce ent last* **28/1**	86
610	**4**	*3/4*	**Evens And Odds (IRE)**[69] 3777 2-9-2 85 ... PaulMulrennan 5 (K A Ryan) *towards rr: hdwy towards far side 1/2-way: rdn over 2f out: styd on wl fnl f: nrst fin* **33/1**	91
411	**5**	*1*	**College Scholar (GER)**[35] 4804 2-9-0 85 ... ChrisCatlin 15 (M R Channon) *prom centre: hdwy and overall ldr 1/2-way: rdn and hddf 2f out: sn drvn and grad wknd* **25/1**	86
1203	**6**	*nk*	**Hoh Mike (IRE)**[22] 5154 2-8-12 107 ... TonyCulhane 8 (M L W Bell) *dwlt: midfield and rdn along 1/2-way: drvn 2f out: kpt on fnl f* **7/4**[1]	83
345	**7**	*1/2*	**Tombi (USA)**[24] 5114 2-9-2 ... (t) TomEaves 2 (J Howard Johnson) *dwlt: chsd ldrs towards far side: hdwy and ch 2f out: sn rdn and one pce appr last* **100/1**	85
0464	**8**	*nk*	**Baltimore Jack (IRE)**[14] 5366 2-8-12 80 ... J-PGuillambert 11 (R M Whitaker) *chsd ldrs towards far side: rdn along wl over 2f out: sn edgd rt and kpt on same pce* **100/1**	80
1144	**9**	*3/4*	**Eloquent Rose (IRE)**[23] 5133 2-8-4 83 ... FrancisNorton 10 (Mrs A Duffield) *prom towards far side: rdn along 1/2-way: grad wknd fnl 2f* **33/1**	70
3	**10**	*1*	**Kompete**[166] 1053 2-7-12 ... AdrianMcCarthy 14 (V Smith) *in tch centre: hdwy to chse ldrs 1/2-way: rdn along over 2f out sn drvn: edgd rt and wknd* **33/1**	61
2321	**11**	*1 1/2*	**Longquan (IRE)**[8] 5508 2-8-12 84 ... FergusSweeney 26 (P J Makin) *hld up towards stands side: hdwy over 2f out: sn rdn and no imp* **9/1**	70
5111	**12**	*1/2*	**Stevie Gee (IRE)**[33] 4890 2-9-1 100 ... RobertWinston 3 (G A Swinbank) *towards rr: pushed along 1/2-way: sn rdn and no imp* **7/2**[2]	72
0263	**13**	*1 1/2*	**Fathom Five (IRE)**[13] 5404 2-8-9 84 ... PaulEddery 21 (B Smart) *chsd ldrs towards stands side: rdn along 1/2-way: sn wknd* **150/1**	61
1165	**14**	*1 1/4*	**Gold Spirit (IRE)**[11] 5471 2-8-12 104 ... RichardMullen 18 (E J O'Neill) *prom towards stands side: rdn along wl over 2f out: gradully sn wknd* **25/1**	61
1400	**15**	*1/2*	**Mubaashir (IRE)**[79] 3442 2-9-2 100 ... JimmyQuinn 23 (E A L Dunlop) *a towards rr stands side* **33/1**	63
1300	**16**	*1/2*	**Fish Called Johnny**[14] 5372 2-9-0 89 ... MichaelTebbutt 22 (B J Meehan) *hld up towards stands side: effrt and sme hdwy 1/2-way: sn rdn and wknd* **66/1**	60
3005	**17**	*3/4*	**Chjimes (IRE)**[11] 5442 2-8-9 93 ... (v[1]) PatCosgrave 25 (K R Burke) *chsd ldrs towards stands side: rdn along 1/2-way: sn wknd* **50/1**	52
404	**18**	*1/2*	**Our Blessing (IRE)**[3] 5613 2-8-6 ... DaleGibson 20 (A P Jarvis) *a towards rr stands side* **200/1**	48
010	**19**	*1 1/2*	**Triple Shadow**[13] 5404 2-8-12 74 ... PhillipMakin 1 (T D Barron) *overall ldr towards far side: rdn along and hdd 1/2-way: wknd 2f out* **80/1**	49
2230	**20**	*2 1/2*	**My Mirasol**[19] 5237 2-7-12 73 ... CatherineGannon 4 (K A Ryan) *s.i.s: a bhd towards far side* **200/1**	28
1002	**21**	*2 1/2*	**Ice Mountain**[11] 5442 2-9-0 86 ... DavidAllan 13 (B Smart) *chsd ldrs centre: rdn along over 2f out: sn wknd* **66/1**	36
421	**22**	*1*	**Dodge City (USA)**[20] 5206 2-9-2 ... RoystonFfrench 24 (J Noseda) *prom on stands rail: rdn along halwfayt: sn wknd* **11/2**[3]	35
600	**23**	*3/4*	**Dumas (IRE)**[24] 5106 2-8-9 ... GylesParkin 19 (A P Jarvis) *chsd ldrs towards stands side: rdn along 1/2-way and sn wknd* **150/1**	26
053	**24**	*7*	**Mandy's Maestro (USA)**[42] 4607 2-8-9 68 ... MichaelJStainton 12 (R M Whitaker) *in tch towards far side: rdn along over 3f out: sn wknd* **200/1**	5

1m 11.15s (-0.55) **Going Correction** -0.025s/f (Good) **24** Ran SP% **126.7**

Speed ratings (Par 103):102,99,98,97,96 95,94,94,93,92 90,89,87,85,85 84,83,82,80,77 74,72,71,62

CSF £479.56 TOTE £24.40: £4.70, £9.30, £4.60; EX 910.10 TRIFECTA Not won..

Owner Abbott Gostling McGrane Senior Hart **Bred** Barton Stud **Trained** Brandsby, N Yorks

FOCUS

The usual big field for what is traditionally one of the most competitive two-year-old races of the season, but it looked to be lacking a little in the class department and the result did little to alter the view. The form, such as it is, looks pretty solid, but usually at least a handful run to levels in the high 90s or low 100s, and that was not the case on this occasion.

NOTEBOOK

Danum Dancer, rated some 18lb inferior to market leader Hoh Mike, finished over three lengths behind that rival when 100/1 at York latest, but the 9lb swing in the weights was obviously in his favour. Despite the difference, it was hard to envisage him winning such a valuable contest, but he was the last one to come off the bridle and galloped on strongly when asked to score with a bit in hand. It is difficult to know where he will go from here, but he is clearly progressive and even if he never does another thing, his owners have not had a bad return on their 1,000gns purchase. (op 12-1)

Rainbow Mirage(IRE), who had a bit to find with Stevie Gee on recent Ripon form, was able to comprehensively turn it around and, having looked in deep trouble with well over two furlongs to go, he picked up really strongly to come through for second. He is most progressive and the son of Spectrum looks well worth stepping up to seven furlongs now.

Bazroy(IRE) has progressed with racing this season, and having finished a highly-creditable third behind Brave Tin Soldier and subsequent scorer Invincible Force in a Listed race at the Curragh latest it was no surprise to see him run so well. He stayed on dourly for pressure, having been up there from the off, and connections will no doubt be keen to keep him on the go. (tchd 33-1)

Evens And Odds(IRE) found the rise into Group company beyond him when last of eight at Maisons-Lafitte when last seen back in July, but he showed himself to be a useful juvenile nonetheless with a spirited effort in fourth, doing well considering he was being vigorously scrubbed along at just past halfway. He is bred to stay a mile in time and remains capable of better. (op 50-1)

College Scholar(GER) has been progressive in winning his maiden and defying a mark of 79 in a Newmarket nursery. This represented a step up, but he coped well and stuck on gamely for fifth, just holding the favourite. He is bred to appreciate at least seven furlongs and is another likely to be capable of better. (tchd 20-1)

Hoh Mike(IRE), a smart early-season juvenile, has had his limitations exposed the last twice and this was further evidence his best days are behind him. Ridden along after just a couple of furlongs, he kept on well enough under strong pressure, but never threatened to play a part in the finish. Official explanation: jockey said colt was never travelling (tchd 2-1)
Tombi(USA) is still a maiden, but this represented a big step forward and he should really have little trouble finding an ordinary maiden, That said, he had a hard race and was treading water as the crossed they line, so it will be interesting to see if he progresses.
Baltimore Jack(IRE) ran an improved race on this drop back in trip and was noted putting in some good late work. He is nothing special, but gives the impression he can be found another race.
Stevie Gee(IRE) looked the main danger to the favourite, having progressed from maiden to nursery to Listed company in completing a hat-trick, but he failed to run his race and looked Flat. On a line through Rainbow Mirage he should have been bang there and probably deserves another chance. Official explanation: jockey said colt ran flat (op 4-1 tchd 9-2 in a place)
Gold Spirit(IRE) Official explanation: jockey said colt was unsuited by the good ground
Dodge City(USA) looked one of the more interesting contenders having got it right at the third time of asking when routing his field at Goodwood, but he was at a disadvantage in racing against the stands' side rail and it was soon apparent he was down on the main group and in the end he dropped right out, being allowed to come home in his own time. Official explanation: jockey said colt was unsuited by the good ground (op 6-1)
Dumas(IRE) Official explanation: jockey said colt was unsuited by the good ground

5682 GUISBOROUGH STKS (LISTED RACE) 7f

3:25 (3:25) (Class 1) 3-Y-0+

£15,898 (£6,025; £3,015; £1,503; £753; £378) **Stalls** Centre

Form RPR

0230 **1** **New Seeker**[63] 3926 6-9-0 108 (b) TomEaves 6 115
(P F I Cole) *led: qcknd clr 3f out: hung lft over 1f out: kpt on wl* **5/1**[2]

1605 **2** *2 ½* **Suggestive**[23] 5146 8-9-5 108 (b) TonyCulhane 2 113
(W J Haggas) *swvd rt s: hld up: hdwy over 2f out: carried lft jst ins last: styd on to take 2nd towards fin* **15/2**

44-0 **3** *½* **Duff (IRE)**[13] 5411 3-8-11 PatCosgrave 9 107
(Edward Lynam, Ire) *chsd wnr: rdn and edgd lft 1f out: kpt on same pce* **14/1**

130- **4** *1 ¾* **Stepping Up (IRE)**[343] 6023 3-8-11 108 RobertWinston 8 102+
(Saeed Bin Suroor) *hld up towards rr: effrt 3f out: sn outpcd: styd on wl fnl f* **6/1**[3]

1000 **5** *½* **Steenberg (IRE)**[6] 5549 7-9-7 111 DaleGibson 1 108
(M H Tompkins) *rr-div: effrt over 2f out: kpt on: nvr nr ldrs* **16/1**

14- **6** *½* **Great Britain**[379] 5269 4-9-0 102 ChrisCatlin 11 100
(Saeed Bin Suroor) *hld up: hdwy over 2f out: sn chsng ldrs: wknd fnl f* **8/1**

035 **7** *1* **Beckermet (IRE)**[14] 5393 4-9-0 105 RoystonFfrench 3 97
(R F Fisher) *chsd ldrs: wknd over 1f out* **16/1**

0106 **8** *3 ½* **Prince Of Light (IRE)**[15] 5341 3-9-0 108 J-PGuillambert 5 91
(M Johnston) *chsd ldrs: one pce fnl 2f: eased ins last* **7/1**

21-4 **9** *7* **Goodricke**[18] 5274 4-9-0 117 (bt[1]) RichardMullen 7 70
(Saeed Bin Suroor) *swvd lft s: sn drvn in rr: lost pl over 2f out: eased fnl f* **4/1**[1]

0030 **10** *3 ½* **Nautical**[15] 5336 8-9-0 77 FrancisNorton 4 61
(A W Carroll) *trckd ldrs: drvn 3f out: sn lost pl* **66/1**

652 **11** *1 ¾* **Vortex**[18] 5274 7-9-0 103 (vt) JimmyQuinn 10 56
(Miss Gay Kelleway) *chsd ldrs: outpcd over 3f out: sn lost pl: bhd whn eased fnl f* **12/1**

1m 22.87s (-2.03) **Going Correction** -0.025s/f (Good)
WFA 3 from 4yo+ 3lb **11** Ran SP% **113.9**
Speed ratings (Par 111):110,107,106,104,104 103,102,98,90,86 84
CSF £40.94 TOTE £7.10: £2.30, £3.60, £4.10; EX 55.40.
Owner Elite Racing Club **Bred** Shadwell Estate Company Limited **Trained** Whatcombe, Oxon
■ Stewards' Enquiry : Pat Cosgrave caution: careless riding

FOCUS
A fair race for the grade that saw a welcome return to winning ways for New Seeker, on his first start for Paul Cole. The time was reasonable and the form appears sound, with the placed horses and the sixth close to their marks.

NOTEBOOK
New Seeker, having his first start for the Cole yard, was below par when bidding to win the valuable Totesport International Handicap for a third time back in July, but he had been off since and was clearly all the better for the break. He went about his business in his usual fashion, blazing the trail, and it was clear from some way out he was going to take some pegging back. This was his first win of the season and it is quite possible he could add to it as long as he finds some reasonable ground. (op 9-2 tchd 11-2)
Suggestive, shouldering a Group 3 penalty, ran a good race considering the ground would not have been ideal and he was being intimidated by Duff in the final furlong. Unfortunately he is likely to remain hard to place. (op 8-1)
Duff(IRE), an Irish raider, had shown enough in two starts this season to suggest he is up to winning at this level and this was a fair effort. He may find an easier opportunity back home.
Stepping Up(IRE), a useful juvenile for Mark Johnston, was making his belated reappearance and he looked rusty, getting going far too late. He should improve for a mile and is another with better still expected of him. (op 8-1)
Steenberg(IRE) has been in fair form, but was always likely to be vulnerable under his Group 2 penalty and this was as good a run as connections could have hoped for. (op 14-1)
Great Britain, one of three representing last year's winning connections, interestingly had last year's winning jockey on and he was nibbled at in the market. Having only the third start of his career, he travelled strongly for a long way, but as was the case on his second and final start at three, he failed to see his race out. He remains capable of a good deal better and looks well worth a try at six furlongs. (op 11-1)
Beckermet(IRE) has been heavily campaigned this season and as yet has failed to get his head in front. This trip seems to stretch him and he faded from over a furlong out. Official explanation: jockey said gelding was unsuited by the good ground (op 12-1)
Prince Of Light(IRE) has not really gone on as expected having won a conditions event and Listed race at Chester and Goodwood respectively in July and August, this now the third consecutive occasion in which he has dropped away disappointingly. (tchd 8-1)
Goodricke looks to have completely lost the plot and, as yet, has failed to display any sign that he has trained on from three to four. A huge disappointment when only fourth at odds of 1/4 on his reappearance at Yarmouth, connections were quick to reach for the blinkers and they backfired spectacularly. He is one to avoid. Official explanation: jockey said colt had a breathing problem (op 10-3)
Vortex Official explanation: jockey said gelding was unsuited by the good ground

5683 REDCARRACING.CO.UK SUPER (S) STKS 1m 3f

4:00 (4:00) (Class 5) 3-5-Y-0 **£5,505** (£1,637; £818; £408) **Stalls** Low

Form RPR

0654 **1** **Light Sentence**[25] 5082 3-8-9 58 RobertWinston 12 58+
(G A Swinbank) *hld up in rr: gd hdwy on outer 3f out: rdn: edgd lft and led 2f out: hdd wl over 1f out: drvn ins last: led last 50 yds* **7/2**[1]

6253 **2** *nk* **Keisha Kayleigh (IRE)**[10] 5485 3-8-7 54 (b[1]) StephenDonohoe[(3)] 14 58
(B Ellison) *hld up in rr: gd hdwy on outer 3f out: led wl over 1f out: rdn ins last: hdd and no ex last 50yds* **8/1**

516 **3** *4* **Son Of Thunder (IRE)**[16] 5311 5-9-8 52 (b) PhillipMakin 13 56
(M Dods) *stdd s: hld up and bhd: stdy hdwy 3f out: rdn to chse ldrs wl over 1f out: drvn and one pce ent last* **12/1**

0022 **4** *shd* **Flaxby**[17] 5285 4-9-2 55 PatCosgrave 4 50+
(J D Bethell) *hld up in rr: hdwy and nt clr run over 2f out: swtchd ins and rdn wl over 1f out: kpt on u.p ins last* **15/2**

1202 **5** *3* **Agilete**[8] 5510 4-9-8 63 J-PGuillambert 3 51
(J Pearce) *hld up: hdwy 5f out: chsd ldrs 3f out: rdn over 2f out and sn no imp* **5/1**[2]

5654 **6** *1* **Bolckow**[10] 5485 3-8-9 52 PaulMulrennan 5 43
(K A Ryan) *trckd ldrs: hdwy on inner to ld over 3f out: rdn and hdd 2f out: grad wknd* **20/1**

303 **7** *7* **Hill Of Almhuim (IRE)**[13] 5403 3-8-9 65 (v) FrancisNorton 10 31
(K R Burke) *chsd ldrs: rdn along wl over 3f out: sn wknd* **11/2**[3]

-001 **8** *nk* **Cetshwayo**[3] 5609 4-9-8 68 TomEaves 15 37
(J M P Eustace) *midfield: hdwy on outer 5f out: rdn to chse ldrs over 3f out: sn drvn and wknd* **12/1**

03 **9** *5* **Princess Toto**[42] 3717 3-7-13 LeanneKershaw[(5)] 2 17
(P C Haslam) *chsd ldrs on inner: rdn along 4f out: sn wknd* **18/1**

00-4 **10** *shd* **Good Investment**[16] 5311 4-9-2 58 (p) AdrianMcCarthy 1 22
(Miss Tracy Waggott) *cl up: rdn along over 3f out: sn wknd* **20/1**

0002 **11** *nk* **Thornaby Green**[10] 5485 5-8-9 53 DeanHeslop[(7)] 7 21
(T D Barron) *led: rdn along and hdd over 3f out: sn wknd* **16/1**

0200 **12** *3* **Zaville**[8] 5513 4-8-7 62 ow3 JamesO'Reilly[(7)] 9 14
(J O'Reilly) *chsd ldrs: rdn along over 4f out and sn wknd* **12/1**

500/ **13** *17* **Royal Approach**[743] 5622 5-8-6 52 JamieMoriarty[(5)] 6 —
(J R Norton) *in tch: rdn along 4f out: sn wknd* **100/1**

2m 22.34s (1.34) **Going Correction** +0.175s/f (Good)
WFA 3 from 4yo+ 7lb **13** Ran SP% **121.9**
Speed ratings (Par 103):102,101,98,98,96 95,90,90,86,86 86,84,72
CSF £31.47 TOTE £4.70: £2.00, £2.00, £4.50; EX 47.10.There was no bid for the winner.
Owner Mrs J Porter **Bred** Brook Stud Bloodstock Ltd **Trained** Melsonby, N Yorks
■ Stewards' Enquiry : Robert Winston two-day ban: used whip with excessive frequency (Oct 11-12)

FOCUS
An above-average seller run in a reasonable time with the first two clear.

5684 SHEPHERD CONSTRUCTION H'CAP 5f

4:35 (4:37) (Class 5) (0-70,70) 3-Y-0+ **£5,181** (£1,541; £770; £384) **Stalls** Centre

Form RPR

6111 **1** **Elkhorn**[10] 5487 4-9-1 66 (b) TomEaves 19 78+
(Miss J A Camacho) *hld up: hdwy stands' side over 2f out: led ins last: r.o wl* **5/2**[1]

323 **2** *1 ½* **Hypnosis**[16] 5309 3-8-13 70 MarkLawson[(5)] 12 77
(D W Barker) *unruly s: chsd ldr: led 1f out: hdd and no ex ins last* **14/1**

0532 **3** *shd* **Our Little Secret (IRE)**[16] 5309 4-8-13 67 StephenDonohoe[(3)] 4 74
(A Berry) *swvd rt s: sn prom: kpt on same pce fnl f* **12/1**

6004 **4** *2* **Ryedane (IRE)**[10] 5486 4-9-2 67 DavidAllan 14 66
(T D Easterby) *chsd ldrs: edgd lft and kpt on same pce appr fnl f* **12/1**

1523 **5** *nk* **Memphis Man**[10] 5476 3-9-4 70 (p) J-PGuillambert 7 68
(Miss V Haigh) *bhd: hdwy 2f out: styd on ins last* **16/1**

0-U2 **6** *shd* **Harrys House**[3] 5620 4-8-9 60 (p) PaulMulrennan 5 58
(J J Quinn) *chsd ldrs far side: one pce fnl 2f* **10/1**[3]

0420 **7** *¾* **The Leather Wedge (IRE)**[3] 5620 7-8-12 63 PaulEddery 23 58
(R Johnson) *led: edgd lft and hdd 1f out: fdd* **9/1**[2]

4000 **8** *hd* **Rothesay Dancer**[15] 5333 3-8-10 65 (p) DNolan[(3)] 22 60
(J S Goldie) *chsd ldrs: one pce fnl 2f* **40/1**

603 **9** *shd* **Middle Eastern**[17] 5286 4-8-9 60 ow1 TonyCulhane 15 54
(P A Blockley) *mid-div: kpt on fnl 2f: nvr rchd ldrs* **14/1**

6043 **10** *½* **Strensall**[10] 5486 9-8-10 66 RoryMoore[(5)] 16 58
(R E Barr) *mid-div: kpt on fnl 2f: nvr nr ldrs* **20/1**

0000 **11** *hd* **Hout Bay**[2] 5631 9-8-5 56 oh6 (b) PaulQuinn 13 48
(D W Chapman) *bhd: kpt on fnl 2f: nvr on terms* **28/1**

6600 **12** *½* **Vegas Boys**[50] 4324 3-9-0 66 DaleGibson 1 56
(M Wigham) *in rr whn sltly hmpd after 2f: sme hdwy fnl 2f* **25/1**

4066 **13** *nk* **Conjecture**[10] 5486 4-9-2 67 RoystonFfrench 18 56
(R Bastiman) *sn in rr and drvn along: nvr on terms* **11/1**

0010 **14** *nk* **Dark Champion**[10] 5486 6-8-2 58 (v) DuranFentiman[(5)] 9 46
(R E Barr) *a towards rr* **33/1**

4601 **15** *1* **Henry Hall (IRE)**[10] 5486 10-9-5 70 KimTinkler 17 54
(N Tinkler) *chsd ldrs: fdd appr fnl f* **10/1**[3]

0130 **16** *shd* **Muara**[68] 3781 4-8-5 56 oh2 FrancisNorton 3 40
(D W Barker) *prom on outside: outpcd over 2f out: no threat after* **33/1**

0066 **17** *1 ¼* **Amanda's Lad (IRE)**[9] 5493 6-8-0 56 oh1 MichaelJStainton[(5)] 10 35
(M C Chapman) *mid-div: swtchd lft after 2f: nvr a factor* **33/1**

0560 **18** *1 ½* **Brunelleschi**[80] 3403 3-9-1 67 (e[1]) FergusSweeney 11 41
(P L Gilligan) *in rr whn hmpd after 2f* **50/1**

6000 **19** *2 ½* **Millfield (IRE)**[16] 5309 3-8-5 62 (b[1]) JamieMoriarty[(5)] 6 27
(J Howard Johnson) *s.s and hmpd sn after s: a bhd* **25/1**

00-0 **20** *¾* **Trim Image**[15] 5333 4-9-2 67 PhillipMakin 21 29
(K R Burke) *unruly in stalls: sn bhd* **40/1**

3000 **21** *½* **Black Oval**[11] 5443 5-8-5 56 oh6 RichardMullen 2 16
(S Parr) *mid-div: sltly hmpd after 2f: sn bhd* **50/1**

58.20 secs (-0.50) **Going Correction** -0.025s/f (Good)
WFA 3 from 4yo+ 1lb **21** Ran SP% **133.2**
Speed ratings (Par 103):103,100,100,97,96 96,95,95,94,94 93,93,92,92,90 90,88,85,81,80 79
CSF £35.90 CT £395.61 TOTE £3.30: £1.50, £2.60, £3.00, £3.50; EX 59.30.
Owner Lee Bolingbroke & Partners VI **Bred** George Strawbridge **Trained** Norton, N Yorks
■ Stewards' Enquiry : Michael J Stainton two-day ban: careless riding (Oct 11,12)

FOCUS
A modest handicap sprint, but Elkhorn has progressed out of all recognition and recorded his fourth course win. The form looks sound rated around the placed horses. This race was hand-timed.
The Leather Wedge(IRE) Official explanation: jockey said gelding lost its action
Hout Bay Official explanation: jockey said gelding was denied a clear run in the closing stages

5685 THANKS & SEE YOU NEXT SEASON H'CAP 1m 2f

5:10 (5:10) (Class 5) (0-75,75) 3-Y-0+ **£5,181** (£1,541; £770; £384) **Stalls** Low

Form RPR

3645 **1** **Trouble Mountain (USA)**[43] 4570 9-9-4 68 (t) DaleGibson 10 77
(M W Easterby) *in rr: drvn over 4f out: hdwy 3f out: styd on wl to ld last 75yds* **16/1**

1401 **2** *1* **Sforzando**[8] 5513 5-9-1 72 KristinStubbs(7) 14 79
(Mrs L Stubbs) *s.i.s: hdwy on wd outside over 3f out: kpt on to take 2nd nr line* **11/1**

1662 **3** *½* **Dium Mac**[43] 4570 5-8-13 70 SuzzanneFrance(7) 4 76
(N Bycroft) *hld up in mid-div: hdwy on ins and hung rt 3f out: wnt 2nd over 1f out: kpt on same pce* **8/1**

2010 **4** *½* **Exit Smiling**[85] 3262 4-9-1 70 RoryMoore(5) 3 75
(P T Midgley) *trckd ldrs: led over 3f out: hdd and no ex ins last* **20/1**

0000 **5** *6* **Tanforan**[6] 5554 4-9-8 72 DavidAllan 1 66
(K G Reveley) *hld up in rr: hdwy over 3f out: sn chsng ldrs: wknd over 1f out* **33/1**

5044 **6** *½* **Wasalat (USA)**[10] 5484 4-8-12 67 MarkLawson(5) 16 60
(D W Barker) *in rr: hdwy over 3f out: hung lft and wknd appr fnl f* **25/1**

5352 **7** *½* **Gracechurch (IRE)**[18] 5260 3-9-5 75 TonyCulhane 7 67
(M R Channon) *hld up in mid-div: effrt 3f out: lost pl over 1f out* **4/1**[1]

3343 **8** *1* **Apsara**[10] 5484 5-9-4 68 PaulMulrennan 2 58
(G M Moore) *dwlt: drvn along and sn chsng ldrs: outpcd whn hmpd 3f out: no threat after* **12/1**

4051 **9** *hd* **Bright Sun (IRE)**[10] 5484 5-9-7 71 (t) KimTinkler 15 61
(N Tinkler) *trckd ldrs: wknd over 1f out* **14/1**

6004 **10** *nk* **Shape Up (IRE)**[14] 5367 6-9-2 71 (b) MichaelJStainton(5) 5 60
(R Craggs) *in tch: effrt over 3f out: wkng whn n.m.r 1f out* **14/1**

505/ **11** *7* **West Highland Way (IRE)**[700] 6480 5-9-1 68 StephenDonohoe(3) 6 44
(Mrs H O Graham) *in rr: lost pl over 3f out* **100/1**

0114 **12** *shd* **Gala Sunday (USA)**[37] 4730 6-8-11 68 (bt) AdeleRothery(7) 17 44
(M W Easterby) *led tl over 3f out: lost pl over 2f out* **25/1**

-202 **13** *1 ¾* **Top Jaro (FR)**[14] 5362 3-9-5 75 RobertWinston 8 47
(T P Tate) *trckd ldrs: lost pl and eased 2f out* **11/2**[2]

341- **14** *¾* **Stargazer Jim (FR)**[322] 6325 4-9-0 69 LiamJones(5) 12 40
(W J Haggas) *in rr: effrt over 3f out: sn btn* **6/1**[3]

0000 **15** *2* **Playtotheaudience**[30] 4958 3-9-0 75 JamieMoriarty(5) 9 42
(R A Fahey) *mid-div: effrt over 3f out: sn btn* **33/1**

011- **16** *1* **Prince Of Love (IRE)**[348] 5939 3-9-2 72 TomEaves 13 37
(Jedd O'Keeffe) *rr-div: effrt on outside over 5f out: lost pl over 3f out* **12/1**

2m 7.65s (0.85) **Going Correction** +0.175s/f (Good)
WFA 3 from 4yo+ 6lb **16** Ran SP% **123.0**
Speed ratings (Par 103):103,102,101,101,96 96,95,95,94,94 89,88,87,86,85 84
CSF £170.73 CT £1534.65 TOTE £20.40: £3.70, £3.00, £2.10, £5.00; EX 324.30 Place 6 £2,851.79, Place 5 £1,161.86.
Owner Mrs Jean Turpin **Bred** Robert B Berger **Trained** Sheriff Hutton, N Yorks
■ Stewards' Enquiry : Suzzanne France three-day ban: careless riding (Oct 11-13)

FOCUS
They went a decent gallop in what was a modest handicap and the form looks sound, with the first three close to their marks.
T/Plt: £6,386.40 to a £1 stake. Pool: £69,988.20. 8.00 winning tickets. T/Qpdt: £355.80 to a £1 stake. Pool: £4,231.50. 8.80 winning tickets. JR

5386 WOLVERHAMPTON (A.W) (L-H)
Saturday, September 30

OFFICIAL GOING: Standard
Wind: Almost nil Weather: Shower during Race 1 (7.00)

5686 GED AND CLARE TIE THE KNOT MEDIAN AUCTION MAIDEN STKS 5f 216y(P)
7:00 (7:00) (Class 5) 2-Y-O £3,886 (£1,156; £577; £288) Stalls Low

Form RPR

2246 **1** **Non Compliant**[14] 5372 2-9-3 80 EddieAhern 5 84+
(J W Hills) *sn prom: rdn to ld wl over 1f out: sn clr: eased considerably ins fnl f* **2/5**[1]

220 **2** *5* **Early Promise (IRE)**[12] 5434 2-8-12 64 BrianReilly 4 60+
(P L Gilligan) *chsd ldrs: rdn over 3f out: kpt on to take 2nd ins fnl f: no ch w wnr* **14/1**

05 **3** *2* **Yungaburra (IRE)**[9] 5491 2-9-3 DeanMcKeown 12 56
(G A Swinbank) *led: rdn and hdd wl over 1f out: wknd fnl f* **9/1**[3]

6 **4** *1 ½* **Money For Fun**[36] 4774 2-8-9 AdamKirby(3) 6 46
(J S Moore) *sn chsng ldr: rdn and lost 2nd over 2f out: wknd 1f out* **18/1**

5 *nk* **Superjain** 2-8-5 PaulPickard(7) 9 45
(J M Jefferson) *s.i.s: hld up and bhd: stdy hdwy on outside over 3f out: hung lft over 1f out: no further prog* **66/1**

0530 **6** *2 ½* **Sunley Sovereign**[14] 5382 2-9-3 68 AdrianTNicholls 8 42
(M R Channon) *broke wl: chsd ldrs: rdn and wknd over 2f out* **12/1**

5200 **7** *2* **Global Guest**[6] 5546 2-8-10 73 ThomasO'Brien(7) 1 36
(M R Channon) *a bhd* **8/1**[2]

00 **8** *shd* **Desirable Dancer (IRE)**[5] 5570 2-8-5 TolleyDean(7) 7 31
(R A Harris) *s.i.s: sn pushed along in mid-div: hdwy over 2f out: edgd lft wl over 1f out: sn wknd* **66/1**

5060 **9** *hd* **Avoncreek**[29] 4987 2-8-10 55 (p) SoniaEaton(7) 11 35
(B P J Baugh) *sn bhd* **66/1**

10 *8* **Kilvickeon (IRE)** 2-9-3 RobbieFitzpatrick 2 11
(Peter Grayson) *s.i.s: a bhd* **33/1**

5000 **11** *12* **Delta Queen**[43] 4545 2-8-12 40 JimCrowley 3 —
(C N Kellett) *sn bhd* **66/1**

1m 15.13s (-0.68) **Going Correction** -0.20s/f (Stan) **11** Ran SP% **121.1**
Speed ratings (Par 95):96,89,86,84,84 80,78,78,77,67 51
CSF £8.20 TOTE £1.60: £1.02, £2.60, £2.30; EX 6.60.
Owner Nigel Howlett Partnership **Bred** Wyck Hall Stud Ltd **Trained** Upper Lambourn, Berks

FOCUS
A modest maiden in which the winner was a different class to the rest.

NOTEBOOK
Non Compliant had given a good account of himself at Newbury last time and proved to be in a different league to this opposition. He now seems set to return to nurseries. (op 4-6)
Early Promise(IRE) did nothing more than finish best of the rest but continues to shape as though an extra furlong will help. (op 10-1)
Yungaburra(IRE) seemed to pay the penalty for having too much use made of him. (op 7-1)
Money For Fun did not really progress on this switch to sand. Official explanation: jockey said filly hung right-handed (op 12-1)
Superjain, a half-sister to several winners, should be better for the experience and may benefit from stronger handling. (op 33-1)
Sunley Sovereign did not find the combination of a switch to the All-Weather and coming back to six the answer. (op 11-1 tchd 14-1)

5687 WOLVERHAMPTON-RACECOURSE.CO.UK (S) STKS 5f 20y(P)
7:30 (7:30) (Class 6) 2-Y-O £2,388 (£705; £352) Stalls Low

Form RPR

0321 **1** **Dotty's Daughter**[11] 5448 2-8-11 60 (p) JimCrowley 11 59
(Mrs A Duffield) *towards rr: rdn and hdwy over 2f out: edgd lft and led ins fnl f: drvn out* **3/1**[1]

0 **2** *nk* **Bar Humbug**[17] 5288 2-8-11 TonyHamilton 13 58
(R A Fahey) *hld up in mid-div: rdn and hdwy on outside over 2f out: hung lft fr over 1f out: r.o* **9/1**

3520 **3** *nk* **Fly Time**[12] 5434 2-7-13 52 MCGeran(7) 4 52
(H J Manners) *a.p: rdn to ld and edgd lft over 1f out: hdd ins fnl f: nt qckn* **12/1**

5 **4** *nk* **Weet In Line**[30] 4971 2-8-6 AdrianTNicholls 8 51
(R Hollinshead) *s.i.s: rdn over 3f out: hdwy and swtchd rt over 1f out: r.o wl towards fin* **20/1**

4506 **5** *hd* **Ask Don't Tell (IRE)**[47] 4427 2-8-8 60 EdwardCreighton(3) 10 55
(Tom Dascombe) *s.i.s: sn swtchd lft: n.m.r on ins over 3f out: rdn and hdwy wl over 1f out: kpt on same pce fnl f* **6/1**[3]

103 **6** *1 ¾* **Sunken Rags**[112] 2451 2-8-11 67 PatCosgrave 5 49
(K R Burke) *hld up in tch: edgd lft over 3f out: rdn and hung lft over 1f out: one pce fnl f* **4/1**[2]

3400 **7** *1 ¼* **The Dandy Fox**[33] 4887 2-8-6 49 (b1) JimmyQuinn 12 39
(R Bastiman) *t.k.h: sn mid-div: rdn and no hdwy fnl 2f* **22/1**

5300 **8** *4* **Lord Blue Boy**[11] 5448 2-8-11 54 (b1) EddieAhern 6 30
(W G M Turner) *s.v.s: nvr nrr* **50/1**

0540 **9** *nk* **Top Tier**[17] 5282 2-8-11 58 (b1) RobbieFitzpatrick 2 29
(Peter Grayson) *led: hdd over 2f out: sn rdn: led briefly wl over 1f out: wknd fnl f* **9/1**

00 **10** *½* **Lady Toyah (IRE)**[8] 5507 2-8-0 ow1 TolleyDean(7) 1 23
(Mrs L Williamson) *prom: rdn 3f out: wknd wl over 1f out* **40/1**

0 **11** *1* **Temple Air (IRE)**[82] 3345 2-8-4 JackDean(7) 9 23
(W G M Turner) *outpcd* **66/1**

0642 **12** *5* **Suzieblue (IRE)**[30] 4971 2-8-11 60 (b) LPKeniry 3 5
(J S Moore) *w ldr: led over 2f out: rdn and hdd wl over 1f out: sn wknd* **6/1**[3]

63.34 secs (0.52) **Going Correction** -0.20s/f (Stan) **12** Ran SP% **116.3**
Speed ratings (Par 93):87,86,86,85,85 82,80,74,73,72 71,63
CSF £28.37 TOTE £3.70: £2.10, £4.00, £6.10; EX 39.10.The winner was bought in for 6,600gns. Fly Time was claimed by Anthony Bithell for £6,000. Weet In Line was claimed by K. Burke for £6,000.
Owner Middleham Park Racing Ix **Bred** Peter Baldwin **Trained** Constable Burton, N Yorks

FOCUS
A very competitive if ordinary seller producing a close finish and rated through the winner.

NOTEBOOK
Dotty's Daughter has certainly benefitted since swapping blinkers for cheekpieces and followed up her win in a similar contest at Brighton. (op 7-2)
Bar Humbug ◆ was dropped in class after presumably disappointing when a springer in the market on his debut at Beverley earlier in the month. He may have made it an even closer-run thing had he not hung left and seems capable of taking a similar contest. Official explanation: jockey said colt hung left in straight (op 10-1 tchd 11-1)
Fly Time, back in the right sort of company, was subsequently claimed for £6,000.
Weet In Line again made a sluggish start but finished as well as any after being forced to switch and was another one claimed. (op 22-1)
Ask Don't Tell(IRE) has struggled in better company since making a winning debut over course and distance in April. Dropped into a seller, she may need a return to six. (op 13-2 tchd 15-2)
Sunken Rags, another course and distance winner in the spring, had not been seen since finishing third of four in a Musselburgh seller in June. (op 7-2 tchd 3-1)

5688 THE ZONGALERO RESTAURANT OVERLOOKS THE TRACK CLAIMING STKS 7f 32y(P)
8:00 (8:00) (Class 5) 3-Y-O+ £3,238 (£963; £481; £240) Stalls High

Form RPR

0040 **1** **Ninth House (USA)**[12] 5428 4-9-12 84 (t) EddieAhern 6 91+
(D J Daly) *hld up and bhd: hdwy over 1f out: led ins fnl f: readily* **3/1**[1]

0-60 **2** *3* **Prince Dayjur (USA)**[28] 5031 7-9-0 70 DeanMcKeown 3 71
(J Pearce) *a.p: rdn over 2f out: r.o one pce fnl f* **12/1**

2040 **3** *hd* **Curtain Bluff**[16] 5313 4-9-8 75 (v) ChrisCatlin 2 78
(M R Channon) *hld up in mid-div: hdwy over 2f out: rdn over 1f out: kpt on same pce fnl f* **10/1**

0100 **4** *1 ¼* **Cloud Atlas (IRE)**[14] 5377 3-9-5 70 LPKeniry 9 75
(S Kirk) *hld up in mid-div: hdwy on outside 2f out: sn rdn: one pce fnl f* **33/1**

3560 **5** *½* **Pure Imagination (IRE)**[20] 5212 5-9-1 70 GregFairley(3) 11 70
(J M Bradley) *mid-div: rdn whn swtchd lft and hdwy over 1f out: one pce fnl f* **12/1**

5341 **6** *nk* **Marmooq**[28] 5031 3-9-2 74 AdamKirby(3) 10 73
(A M Hales) *sn led: rdn wl over 1f out: hdd & wknd ins fnl f* **6/1**[2]

5645 **7** *nk* **Serieux**[53] 4230 7-9-8 71 HayleyTurner 12 72
(D Nicholls) *t.k.h in mid-div: rdn and lost pl over 2f out: sme late hdwy* **17/2**

0060 **8** *hd* **Bessemer (JPN)**[13] 5403 5-9-12 73 (p) DanielTudhope 7 76
(D Carroll) *hld up and bhd: rdn wl over 1f out: nvr nrr* **10/1**

2440 **9** *¾* **Ever Cheerful**[19] 5246 5-9-5 74 DeanWilliams(7) 5 74
(G C H Chung) *plld hrd: chsd ldr over 5f out: rdn and ev ch over 2f out: wknd ins fnl f* **25/1**

4002 **10** *hd* **Just James**[40] 4658 7-9-8 85 AdrianTNicholls 8 69
(D Nicholls) *outpcd in rr: sme hdwy over 1f out: n.d* **6/1**[2]

040U **11** *2 ½* **Funfair Wane**[40] 4658 7-9-8 82 SilvestreDeSousa 1 63
(D Nicholls) *led early: prom: rdn and hung lft over 1f out: wknd fnl f* **8/1**[3]

5000 **12** *16* **Mystic Man (FR)**[5] 5573 8-9-8 77 JimmyQuinn 4 21
(I W McInnes) *a bhd: eased whn no ch fnl f* **22/1**

1m 28.41s (-1.99) **Going Correction** -0.20s/f (Stan)
WFA 3 from 4yo+ 3lb **12** Ran SP% **119.9**
Speed ratings (Par 103):103,99,99,97,97 97,96,96,95,95 92,74
CSF £40.75 TOTE £4.90: £1.70, £3.70, £3.10; EX 74.10.The winner was claimed by Nick Littmoden for £14,000. Curtain Bluff was claimed by Claes Bjorling for £12,000. Ever Cheerful was claimed by D. G. Bridgwater for £14,000.
Owner Ms S Hamilton **Bred** Juddmonte Farms Inc **Trained** Newmarket, Suffolk

FOCUS
A fair claimer run at a sound pace and the form looks solid.
Mystic Man(FR) Official explanation: jockey said gelding moved badly

5689 WBX.COM WORLD BET EXCHANGE H'CAP 1m 141y(P)
8:30 (8:30) (Class 5) (0-75,75) 3-Y-O+ **£3,238** (£963; £481; £240) **Stalls** Low

Form RPR

1110 **1** **Luis Melendez (USA)**[46] 4457 4-9-4 **73**............(t) EdwardCreighton(3) 10 82
(Tom Dascombe) *mde all: rdn over 2f out: hld on wl u.p ins fnl f* **9/1**

0345 **2** *shd* **Consonant (IRE)**[12] 5436 9-9-2 **75**.................. MarkCoumbe(7) 8 84
(D G Bridgwater) *a.p: rdn over 2f out: ev ch fnl f: r.o* **16/1**

6030 **3** *½* **Magical Music**[31] 4933 3-9-1 **72**.................................. JimmyQuinn 1 80
(J Pearce) *hld up in mid-div: swtchd rt and hdwy over 2f out: sn rdn: r.o ins fnl f* **11/1**

502 **4** *nk* **Cursum Perficio**[12] 5436 4-9-5 **74**..........................(p) AdamKirby(3) 2 81
(W R Muir) *a.p: rdn over 2f out: r.o one pce fnl f* **9/2**[2]

2300 **5** *½* **Bijou Dan**[13] 5403 5-8-13 **70**..........................(v[1]) DuranFentiman(5) 12 76
(W G Harrison) *s.i.s: bhd: rdn over 2f out: hdwy on outside over 1f out: r.o wl ins fnl f: nrst fin* **16/1**

5221 **6** *hd* **United Nations**[19] 5249 5-9-8 **74**................................ TonyHamilton 7 80+
(N Wilson) *mid-div: pushed along over 6f out: n.m.r over 3f out: rdn and hdwy over 1f out: kpt on ins fnl f* **9/4**[1]

4160 **7** *1 ¼* **Punjabi**[11] 5446 3-9-4 **75**.. J-PGuillambert 4 78+
(Mrs G S Rees) *hld up and bhd: n.m.r on ins over 6f out: smooth hdwy over 3f out: rdn and edgd rt over 1f out: wknd wl ins fnl* **16/1**

2352 **8** *3* **Silent Storm**[19] 5233 6-9-8 **74**.................................... EddieAhern 3 71
(C A Cyzer) *sltly hmpd s: rdn and hdwy on ins over 2f out: wknd over 1f out* **7/1**[3]

6036 **9** *shd* **Thunderwing (IRE)**[19] 5249 4-9-2 **68**........................(p) PatCosgrave 13 64
(K R Burke) *prom: rdn over 3f out: wknd over 2f out* **10/1**

0160 **10** *1* **Empire Dancer (IRE)**[48] 4395 3-8-10 **74**............ KirstyMilczarek(7) 5 68
(C N Allen) *a bhd* **33/1**

-414 **11** *1 ½* **Donna Giovanna**[232] 364 3-9-3 **74**................................. JimCrowley 6 65
(J A Osborne) *mid-div: rdn over 2f out: sn lost pl* **18/1**

1535 **12** *6* **Golden Applause (FR)**[47] 4429 4-9-4 **73**..................... AmirQuinn(3) 11 52
(Mrs A L M King) *hld up in mid-div: rdn over 3f out: sn wknd* **14/1**

1m 48.62s (-3.14) **Going Correction** -0.20s/f (Stan)
WFA 3 from 4yo+ 5lb **12** Ran SP% **121.4**
Speed ratings (Par 103):105,104,104,104,103 103,102,99,99,98 97,92
CSF £147.71 CT £1636.89 TOTE £11.50: £3.00, £3.00, £2.90; EX 246.00.
Owner Oneway **Bred** Bloomsbury Stud **Trained** Lambourn, Berks

FOCUS
A good finish to this competitive low-grade affair and the form looks reliable with the fourth and fifth to form.
Golden Applause(FR) Official explanation: jockey said filly was unsuited by the surface

5690 RINGSIDE SUITE 700 THEATRE STYLE CONFERENCE H'CAP 1m 1f 103y(P)
9:00 (9:04) (Class 6) (0-58,58) 3-Y-O **£2,730** (£806; £403) **Stalls** Low

Form RPR

6020 **1** **Princess Danah (IRE)**[21] 5166 3-8-12 **57**..................(tp) AdamKirby(3) 3 68
(W R Swinburn) *hld up in tch: rdn over 2f out: led over 1f out: r.o* **4/1**[1]

3002 **2** *½* **Tabulate**[81] 3379 3-8-13 **55**... ChrisCatlin 13 65
(P L Gilligan) *hld up and bhd: hdwy wl over 1f out: sn rdn and edgd lft: r.o ins fnl f: nt rch wnr* **8/1**

0000 **3** *1 ½* **Picture Show (USA)**[34] 4845 3-8-13 **55**......................... HayleyTurner 2 62
(C E Brittain) *hld up in tch: lost pl over 4f out: nt clr run over 3f out: hdwy over 2f out: rdn and edgd lft ins fnl f: nt qckn* **11/1**

0-40 **4** *3 ½* **Qik Dip (IRE)**[23] 5129 3-9-2 **58**............................... DanielTudhope 10 58
(P D Evans) *hld up towards rr: rdn and hdwy on outside wl over 1f out: one pce fnl f* **20/1**

6000 **5** *¾* **Louise Dupin (IRE)**[29] 4982 3-9-0 **56**............................. MickyFenton 4 55
(R M Beckett) *s.i.s: rdn over 5f out: hdwy over 3f out: wknd fnl f* **6/1**[2]

0050 **6** *shd* **Gnillah**[20] 5210 3-8-6 **55** ow1.. SladeO'Hara(7) 11 54
(B W Hills) *w ldrs: led over 3f out: rdn over 2f out: hdd over 1f out: wknd ins fnl f* **8/1**

2250 **7** *1 ¼* **Royal Tavira Girl (IRE)**[59] 4052 3-8-10 **57**................ JerryO'Dwyer(5) 8 53
(M G Quinlan) *hld up towards rr: hdwy on ins whn nt clr run 2f out: sn swtchd rt and rdn: wknd fnl f* **16/1**

000 **8** *¾* **Lynford Lady**[23] 5129 3-9-2 **58**..................................(b[1]) JimmyQuinn 1 53
(D J S Ffrench Davis) *hld up in mid-div: n.m.r and lost pl 3f out: sn rdn: n.d after* **40/1**

1450 **9** *2 ½* **Dancing Storm**[29] 4983 3-9-0 **56**..................................(p) LPKeniry 12 46
(W S Kittow) *hld up in tch: rdn 3f out: wknd over 1f out* **14/1**

6006 **10** *5* **Monmouthshire**[17] 5298 3-9-2 **58**................................(v) EddieAhern 9 39+
(M L W Bell) *n.m.r s: hld up and bhd: hdwy over 2f out: rdn whn n.m.r and stmbld bdly ent st: rdr nrly uns* **7/1**[3]

6106 **11** *¾* **Dream Of Paradise (USA)**[21] 5173 3-8-7 **54**................ LiamJones(5) 5 33
(Mrs L Williamson) *led: hdd over 5f out: rdn 4f out: wknd 3f out* **8/1**

0600 **12** *6* **Blanc Visage**[100] 2795 3-8-13 **58**......................... EdwardCreighton(3) 7 26
(Mrs H Sweeting) *hld up towards rr: rdn over 5f out: no rspnse* **25/1**

0040 **13** *4* **Orange Stravinsky**[38] 4697 3-9-1 **57**........................(p) J-PGuillambert 6 17
(P C Haslam) *chsd ldr: led over 5f out: hdd over 3f out: wknd wl over 1f out* **14/1**

2m 0.89s (-1.73) **Going Correction** -0.20s/f (Stan) **13** Ran SP% **118.7**
Speed ratings (Par 99):99,98,97,94,93 93,92,91,89,84 84,78,75
CSF £34.23 CT £330.92 TOTE £5.70: £2.50, £2.00, £4.60; EX 43.60.
Owner The Great Danes **Bred** King Bloodstock **Trained** Aldbury, Herts

FOCUS
There were only two previous winners in this tightly-knit low-grade affair but the pace was reasonable and the race, which looks sound, is rated fairly positively.
Blanc Visage Official explanation: jockey said gelding was very reluctant race

5691 WORLD BET EXCHANGE WBX.COM H'CAP 1m 4f 50y(P)
9:30 (9:30) (Class 5) (0-70,68) 3-Y-O+ **£3,238** (£963; £481; £240) **Stalls** Low

Form RPR

2450 **1** **Inch Lodge**[80] 3413 4-9-11 **66**.. PaulEddery 9 72
(Miss D Mountain) *led after 1f: rdn over 2f out: edgd lft ins fnl f: r.o* **20/1**

665 **2** *nk* **Edas**[43] 4544 4-9-11 **66**... GrahamGibbons 1 71
(J J Quinn) *hld up in mid-div: rdn and hdwy on ins 2f out: swtchd rt 1f out: r.o towards fin: nt rch wnr* **8/1**[3]

3/0- **3** *shd* **Baranook (IRE)**[119] 299 5-8-12 **60**......................... JosephWalsh(7) 7 65
(D J Wintle) *a.p: rdn over 2f out: sltly outpcd over 1f out: rallied ins fnl f: r.o* **50/1**

151 **4** *hd* **Swords**[20] 5213 4-9-6 **61**.. DeanMcKeown 8 66
(Heather Dalton) *hld up towards rr: hdwy over 2f out: rdn wl over 1f out: r.o ins fnl f* **9/4**[1]

3010 **5** *½* **Tayman (IRE)**[18] 5276 4-9-9 **64**...................................... EddieAhern 2 69+
(G Wragg) *hld up in tch: wnt 2nd 2f out: sn rdn: n.m.r ins fnl f: eased cl home* **7/2**[2]

046 **6** *hd* **Wotchalike (IRE)**[3] 5610 4-9-2 **62**........................(v) LiamJones(5) 11 66
(R J Price) *hld up towards rr: rdn and hdwy over 2f out: styd on fnl f* **8/1**[3]

0030 **7** *½* **Russian Dream (IRE)**[72] 3686 3-9-2 **68**......................... AdamKirby(3) 12 71
(W R Swinburn) *hld up and bhd: nt clr run over 2f out tl swtchd rt wl over 1f out: late hdwy: nrst fin* **14/1**

8 *¾* **Milton Star (IRE)**[491] 6376 7-9-7 **65**........................ PatrickMathers(3) 4 67
(John A Harris) *hld up in mid-div: no hdwy fnl 3f* **40/1**

0362 **9** *1 ¾* **Siena Star (IRE)**[12] 5422 8-8-9 **63**.............................. MickyFenton 10 62
(J R Boyle) *swtchd lft sn after s: n.d* **9/1**

0545 **10** *nk* **Great Chieftain (IRE)**[14] 5388 3-9-2 **65**..................... TonyHamilton 6 64
(R A Fahey) *t.k.h: led 1f: chsd ldr tl rdn 2f out: sn wknd* **16/1**

0640 **11** *2 ½* **Keshya**[49] 4351 5-9-2 **57**.. ChrisCatlin 3 52
(N P Littmoden) *a bhd* **16/1**

3000 **12** *½* **Dinner Date**[38] 4702 4-8-12 **58**...................... StephanieHollinshead(5) 5 52
(T Keddy) *hld up in mid-div: hdwy 3f out: sn rdn: wknd over 1f out* **22/1**

2m 40.45s (-1.97) **Going Correction** -0.20s/f (Stan)
WFA 3 from 4yo+ 8lb **12** Ran SP% **117.2**
Speed ratings (Par 103):98,97,97,97,97 97,96,96,95,94 93,92
CSF £164.96 CT £7689.06 TOTE £19.60: £4.00, £2.70, £18.40; EX 323.20 Place 6 £792.13, Place 5 £653.05.
Owner David Fremel **Bred** Gainsborough Stud Management Ltd **Trained** Newmarket, Suffolk

FOCUS
There was a bunch finish to this modest contest after they went no pace. The form looks somewhat dubious and is best rated through the fourth and sixth to previous form.
T/Plt: £1,269.30 to a £1 stake. Pool: £61,120.95. 35.15 winning tickets. T/Qpdt: £449.90 to a £1 stake. Pool: £2,675.20. 4.40 winning tickets. KH

3764 FAIRYHOUSE (R-H)
Saturday, September 30

OFFICIAL GOING: Soft

5692a IRISH STALLION FARMS EUROPEAN BREEDERS FUND MAIDEN 6f
2:15 (2:18) 2-Y-O **£8,101** (£1,887; £832; £480)

RPR

1 **Evening Time (IRE)** 2-8-12 .... DPMcDonogh 8 98+
(Kevin Prendergast, Ire) *trckd ldrs: 6th 1/2-way: 5th and hdwy early st: led 1 1/2f out: sn drew clr: styd on strly: impressive* **3/1**[1]

2 *9* **Crown Colony**[37] 4750 2-9-3 .... DMGrant 16 76
(David Wachman, Ire) *a.p: 3rd 1/2-way: 2nd and chal st: led briefly under 2f out: sn hdd and outpcd* **7/2**[2]

3 *1 ½* **Slaney Time (IRE)**[13] 5410 2-8-12 **96**...........................(b) DJMoran(5) 15 72
(J S Bolger, Ire) *sn led: rdn and hdd under 2f out: 3rd and no ex fr over 1f out* **8/1**

4 *2 ½* **Facchetti (USA)**[14] 5392 2-9-3 .... JAHeffernan 17 64+
(A P O'Brien, Ire) *drvn along to chsd ldrs: 5th 1/2-way: 4th into st: sn rdn and no imp* **4/1**[3]

5 *½* **Albert Einstein (IRE)** 2-9-3 .... CO'Donoghue 7 63+
(A P O'Brien, Ire) *hld up: 9th early st: kpt on fnl f* **10/1**

6 *1 ¼* **White Gables (IRE)**[14] 5392 2-9-3 **75**.................................... JMurtagh 9 59
(M Halford, Ire) *prom: 4th 1/2-way: 5th and rdn early st: no imp fr 1 1/2f out* **12/1**

7 *8* **Love To Boogie (IRE)**[12] 5437 2-8-12 .... KFallon 10 30
(David Wachman, Ire) *hld up: kpt on fr 1 1/2f out* **8/1**

8 *nk* **Meancog (IRE)**[37] 4743 2-8-12 **70**... MCHussey 6 29
(Peter Henley, Ire) *trckd ldrs in 6th: rdn early st: drifted rt over 1f out: sn no ex* **25/1**

9 *¾* **Headford View (IRE)** 2-8-12 .... NGMcCullagh 4 27
(James Halpin, Ire) *nvr a factor: kpt on one pced st* **25/1**

10 *½* **Silver Snipe** 2-8-12 .... PBBeggy(5) 14 30
(John Joseph Murphy, Ire) *towards rr: no imp st* **25/1**

11 *nk* **Laragh Hill (IRE)**[26] 5073 2-9-0 .... CDHayes(3) 13 29
(G M Lyons, Ire) *nvr bttr than mid-div* **25/1**

12 *nk* **Doorock (IRE)** 2-9-0 .... RPCleary(3) 3 28
(M Halford, Ire) *a bhd* **25/1**

13 *½* **Mulligans Pursuit (IRE)** 2-9-3 .... FMBerry 1 27
(M P Sunderland, Ire) *nvr a factor* **25/1**

14 *3 ½* **Lucky Elle (IRE)** 2-8-7 .... HelenKeohane(5) 2 11
(Irene J Monaghan, Ire) *s.i.s and a bhd* **25/1**

15 *½* **Miss Gorica (IRE)**[17] 5303 2-8-12 .... DavidMcCabe 11 10
(Ms Joanna Morgan, Ire) *chsd ldrs: 8th 1/2-way: no imp st: hmpd and stmbld over 1f out: eased* **25/1**

16 *1* **Seminole Sun (IRE)**[14] 5392 2-8-12 ....(b[1]) RMBurke 12 7
(Martin Browne, Ire) *prom: 2nd 1/2-way: 3rd into st: sn wknd qckly* **14/1**

17 *2 ½* **Singalullaby (IRE)** 2-9-3 .... PJSmullen 18 4
(D K Weld, Ire) *chsd ldrs early: wknd bef st* **10/1**

18 *28* **Strokestown Percy (IRE)** 2-9-3 .... WSupple 5 —
(Niall Moran, Ire) *bhd fr 1/2-way: t.o st* **16/1**

1m 17.7s **18** Ran SP% **158.6**
CSF £15.96 TOTE £2.90: £1.30, £1.80, £1.50, £2.80; DF 22.40.
Owner Mrs W Whitehead **Bred** J F Tuthill **Trained** Friarstown, Co Kildare
■ Stewards' Enquiry : David McCabe one-day ban: careless riding (Oct 11)

NOTEBOOK
Evening Time(IRE) ◆, a half sister to the useful soft-ground 7f handicapper Lake Andre, clearly appreciated the underfoot conditions and ran out a highly impressive first-time-out winner from some fair yardsticks. She is unlikely to be seen again until next season, when a mile should be within her compass and she may well prove a contender for the Irish 1000 Guineas. (op 2/1)

5693 - 5699a (Foreign Racing) - See Raceform Interactive

5399 LONGCHAMP (R-H)
Saturday, September 30

OFFICIAL GOING: Good

5700a PRIX CHAUDENAY CASINO BARRIERE DE MENTON (GROUP 2) 1m 7f
1:15 (1:17) 3-Y-O **£51,103** (£19,724; £9,414; £6,276; £3,138)

RPR

1 **Vendangeur (IRE)**[23] 5145 3-9-2 .... SPasquier 3 110
(E Lellouche, France) *mid-div, 5th hlf-way, took closer order 4f out, 3rd straight, pushed along to ld 1 1/2f out, rdn fnl f, just held on* **8/1**

2 *shd* **Ponte Tresa (FR)**[20] [5220] 3-8-13 .... OPeslier 4 107
(Y De Nicolay, France) *mid-div, 4th hlf-way, rdn & hdwy 1 1/2f out, challenged fnl f, every chance 100yds out, just failed* **25/1**

3 *1/2* **Getaway (GER)**[23] [5145] 3-9-2 .... CSoumillon 1 110
(A Fabre, France) *hld up, 7th hlf-way, disp 5th straight, pushed along 2f out, rdn to chs leader 1 1/2f out, stayed on at one pace to line* **4/6**[1]

4 *1* **Mary Louhana**[20] [5220] 3-8-13 .... SMaillot 5 106
(M Delzangles, France) *held up, 8th straight, ridden & stayed on in centre from 1 1/2f out, took 4th close home* **33/1**

5 *1/2* **Grey Mystique (IRE)**[46] [4465] 3-8-13 .... IMendizabal 8 105
(J-C Rouget, France) *held up, last straight, stayed on steadily but never dangerous* **7/1**[3]

6 *nk* **Aigle D'Or**[72] 3-9-2 .... C-PLemaire 7 108
(H-A Pantall, France) *mid-division, 6th half-way, disputing 5th straight, ridden 1 1/2f out, never in contention* **20/1**

7 *8* **Gravitas**[21] 3-9-2 .... LDettori 2 100
(A Fabre, France) *led, pushed along straight, headed 1 1/2f out, no extra* **6/1**[2]

8 *4* **Ermine Sea**[46] [4465] 3-9-2 .... JimmyFortune 9 96
(J H M Gosden) *prominent, 2nd half-way, driven straight, ridden & weakened over 1 1/2f out* **14/1**

9 *3* **Young Poli (FR)**[23] [5145] 3-9-2 .... AClement 6 93
(A Couetil, France) *prominent, 3rd half-way, disputing 5th straight, soon one pace* **33/1**

3m 9.90s **Going Correction** -0.20s/f (Firm) **9** Ran SP% **119.0**
Speed ratings: 114,113,113,113,112 112,108,106,104
PARI-MUTUEL: WIN 8.10; PL 1.10, 1.70, 1.10; DF 107.60.
Owner Ecurie Wildenstein **Bred** Dayton Investments Ltd **Trained** Lamorlaye, France

FOCUS
This looked just an ordinary Group 2.

NOTEBOOK
Vendangeur(IRE) has been thereabouts in decent company all season and thoroughly deserved a victory at Group level. Fifth early on, he challenged the leaders halfway up the straight and battled on gamely to hold the runner-up's desperate late challenge. He may now take in the Prix Royal-Oak and he could turn into a good Cup horse next year.
Ponte Tresa(FR), stepped up to her furthest trip to date, was flying at the end, having had to wait for a gap. She looked unlucky.
Getaway(GER) was a disappointing odds on favourite. Given a waiting ride, he made his effort on the outside in the straight but could find only the one pace. The ground was probably quicker than he cares for.
Mary Louhana, given a waiting ride, made up plenty of ground up the centre of the track during the final furlong and pinched fourth place with 50 yards left to run.
Ermine Sea, a British raider, could not reverse recent Deauville placings with Getaway and Grey Mistique and was not at his best.

5701a PRIX DE LA FORET CASINO BARRIERE DE BIARRITZ (GROUP 1) 7f
2:20 (2:24) 3-Y-0+ **£98,517** (£29,560; £29,560; £9,845; £4,931)

RPR

1 **Caradak (IRE)**[34] [4839] 5-9-3 .... LDettori 11 117
(Saeed Bin Suroor) *prom, disp close 4th straight, ran on to challenge 1 1/2f out, rdn to ld 1f out, found extra close home, driven out* **4/1**[2]

2 *snk* **Welsh Emperor (IRE)**[21] [5184] 7-9-3 .... IMendizabal 3 117
(T P Tate) *led, ridden & ran on 2f out, joined 1 1/2f out, headed 1f out, stayed on gamely under pressure to line* **50/1**

2 *dht* **Linngari (IRE)**[34] [4858] 4-9-3 .... (t) YTake 9 117
(Diego Lowther, France) *raced in close 2nd, driven to challenge 1 1/2f out, led briefly in final furlong, pressed winner to line* **25/1**

4 *3/4* **Stormy River (FR)**[27] [5049] 3-9-0 .... TThulliez 5 115+
(N Clement, France) *always in touch, 6th straight, pushed along to chs ldrs 1 1/2f out, rdn over 1f out, stayed on to take 4th close home* **3/1**[1]

5 *snk* **New Girlfriend (IRE)**[48] [4416] 3-8-10 .... JAuge 1 111
(Robert Collet, France) *prominent, 3rd on rail straight, pushed along 2f out, ridden over 1f out, one pace final 150yds* **66/1**

6 *1/2* **Gwenseb (FR)**[23] [5146] 3-8-10 .... MBlancpain 2 109
(C Laffon-Parias, France) *held up, disputing last straight, good headway on rail from 2f out, ridden over 1f out, nearest at finish* **25/1**

7 *snk* **Marchand D'Or (FR)**[55] [4191] 3-9-0 .... DBonilla 8 113
(F Head, France) *held up, 11th straight, effort on outside 2f out, never threatened leaders* **5/1**[3]

8 *snk* **Impressionnante**[62] [3991] 3-8-10 .... OPeslier 12 108
(C Laffon-Parias, France) *held up, 10th straight, pushed along 2f out, ran on til ridden & no extra from 1f out* **11/1**

9 *shd* **Silver Touch (IRE)**[22] [5159] 3-8-10 .... SPasquier 10 108
(M R Channon) *mid-division, 9th straight, driven 1 1/2f out, never nearer* **8/1**

10 *1 1/2* **Sabasha (FR)**[24] [5123] 3-8-10 .... RMarchelli 7 104
(F Rohaut, France) *mid-division, 7th straight, ridden to chase leaders 2f out, no extra from 1f out* **66/1**

11 *nk* **Sleeping Indian**[15] [5341] 5-9-3 .... JimmyFortune 6 107
(J H M Gosden) *mid-division, 8th straight, pushed along 2f out, never in challenging position* **11/2**

12 *snk* **Price Tag**[23] [5146] 3-8-10 .... C-PLemaire 13 103
(P Bary, France) *held up, 12th straight, never dangerous* **10/1**

13 *shd* **Phantom Rose (USA)**[24] [5123] 3-8-10 .... CSoumillon 14 103
(A Fabre, France) *held up, disputing last straight, never a factor* **20/1**

14 *1 1/2* **Indian Maiden (IRE)**[14] [5393] 6-9-0 .... DBoeuf 4 100
(M S Saunders) *prominent, disputing 4th straight, pushed along 2f out, one pace from 1 1/2f out* **50/1**

1m 20.9s **Going Correction** -0.10s/f (Good)
WFA 3 from 4yo+ 3lb **14** Ran SP% **124.9**
Speed ratings: 104,103,103,102,102 102,102,101,101,100 99,99,99,97
PARI-MUTUEL: WIN 5.00; PL 2.40, 5.50 (Linngari), 9.80 (Welsh Emperor);DF 28.60 (with Linngari), 52.30 (with Welsh Emperor).
Owner Godolphin **Bred** His Highness The Aga Khan's Studs S C **Trained** Newmarket, Suffolk

FOCUS
On paper this was a strong renewal of the Prix de la Foret, with by far the biggest field in recent years. 13 of the 16 runners were already Group winners - three of the three-year-olds at this level, if one includes the disqualified Pouliches winner Price Tag. Unfortunately the early pace was far from strong and those racing prominently were at such an advantage that none of the first five were ever worse than sixth, and the first nine home were covered by only around two lengths. As a result it is impossible to rate the form that highly by Group 1 standards.

NOTEBOOK
Caradak(IRE), the narrow winner of the Celebration Mile on his previous start when he had a below-par George Washington back in third, gained a thoroughly deserved first Group 1 success under a superb ride, and improved on last year's second in this very race in the process. Always well placed, he made his way to the front running into the final furlong and stuck on most gamely under pressure. He may now be aimed at the Breeders' Cup Mile, but his main target is apparently the Hong Kong Mile.
Linngari(IRE) looked incredibly dangerous on the rail running into the final furlong but he couldn't quite find enough to catch the winner. Quickly into his stride, he fought all the way up the straight but finally had to share second. He is clearly a horse who goes well on good ground
Welsh Emperor(IRE), who beat Caradak in the Hungerford Stakes before running down the field in the Park Stakes, soon led after breaking smartly and kept on most gamely when headed. A fine effort considering he is arguably even better with more give underfoot.
Stormy River(FR) ♦, a half-length second to Librettist in the Prix du Moulin on his previous start, was probably just found out by the drop back to seven furlongs, especially considering the steady pace. He is likely to be given a rest now but will remain in training next year, when he could be seen to even better advantage.
New Girlfriend(IRE) was top-class at two but she has been running too keen all this season and did so again this time. She kept on reasonably well in the circumstances, but again gave the impression that she might have done better if she had been campaigned as a sprinter.
Gwenseb(FR) did best of those coming from off the pace. She did well to finish as close as she did, having had only one behind her into the straight.
Marchand D'Or(FR), so impressive in the Maurice de Gheest, was too keen under restraint here and was one of several who could have done with a stronger gallop. He was also short of room at a crucial stage.
Silver Touch(IRE) looked a little unlucky as she was short of room at the furlong marker.
Sleeping Indian ♦, a Listed winner at Newbury on his return from an absence, was short of room in the straight and looked as unlucky as any, as he was held in by Impressionnante until it was all too late. He will merit respect if going once more for the Challenge Stakes, in which he was second last year.
Indian Maiden(IRE), prominent early on, was a beaten force by the furlong marker before dropping out quickly to finish last. She is better over shorter on easier ground, but has had a hard season in any case.

5702a PRIX DE ROYALLIEU HOTEL HERMITAGE BARRIERE (GROUP 2) (FILLIES) 1m 4f 110y
2:50 (2:56) 3-Y-0+ **£51,103** (£19,724; £9,414; £6,276; £3,138)

RPR

1 **Montare (IRE)**[20] [5220] 4-9-2 .... (p) OPeslier 5 110
(J E Pease, France) *held up in rear, 7th straight, headway on outside well over 1f out, ridden 1f out, ran on to lead last strides* **11/4**[1]

2 *hd* **Lahudood**[27] [5050] 3-8-8 ow1 .... FSpanu 2 111
(J E Hammond, France) *led 2f, close 4th straight on inside, led well over 1f out til caught last strides* **8/1**

3 *1* **Alix Road (FR)**[20] [5220] 3-8-7 .... TThulliez 1 109
(Mme M Bollack-Badel, France) *prominent early, settled in 6th to straight, headway over 1f out, ran on one pace final f* **20/1**

4 *1* **Princesse Dansante (IRE)**[11] [5472] 3-8-7 .... SPasquier 3 107
(F Doumen, France) *broke well, soon restrained in rear, last straight, headway on outside from 2f out, ran on to take 4th ins fnl f* **33/1**

5 *1/2* **Rising Cross**[22] [5155] 3-9-0 .... LDettori 7 113
(J R Best) *led after 2f, headed well over 1f out, kept on one pace* **11/2**[3]

6 *2* **Short Skirt**[38] [4714] 3-8-7 .... TJarnet 8 103
(Sir Michael Stoute) *dwelt, soon close up, disputed 2nd after 4f, 2nd straight, ridden & beaten approaching final f* **3/1**[2]

7 *shd* **Chelsea Rose (IRE)**[48] [4407] 4-9-2 .... PShanahan 4 103
(C Collins, Ire) *always in touch, 3rd straight, ridden & disputed 2nd 2f out, weakened approaching final f* **3/1**[2]

8 *1 1/2* **Celebre Vadala (FR)**[55] [4192] 3-8-7 .... CSoumillon 6 101
(A Fabre, France) *mid-division, 5th straight, last from 1 1/2f out* **12/1**

2m 39.5s **Going Correction** -0.20s/f (Firm)
WFA 3 from 4yo 8lb **8** Ran SP% **118.6**
Speed ratings: 107,106,106,105,105 104,104,103
PARI-MUTUEL: WIN 3.10; PL 1.30, 1.70, 2.60; DF 7.20.
Owner George Strawbridge **Bred** George Strawbridge **Trained** Chantilly, France

FOCUS
Nobody wanted to go on and in the end Frankie Dettori decided to take it up on the penalised Rising Cross. The winner had finished runner-up at this level on her last four starts and deserved a change of luck.

NOTEBOOK
Montare(IRE), who had cheekpieces back on, thoroughly deserved her first victory of the season. She came with a progressive run to lead inside the final half-furlong and, although she did not enjoy receiving the one tap she had when challenging, she got up to lead in the final moments. The Prix Royal-Oak is now on the cards and she will be one of the leading contenders for that race.
Lahudood, running at this level for the first time, looked unlikely to be beaten with a furlong to run, having burst into the lead 300 yards out. There are no plans at the moment but she deserves to win a Group race before being retired to stud.
Alix Road(FR), considering she was a rank outsider, put up a decent effort. Towards the tail of the field early on, she quickened from a furlong out but could never quite get to the first two.
Princesse Dansante(IRE), who put up a reasonable effort, followed the winner for much of the race but was unable to accelerate in the same way when it mattered.
Rising Cross, carrying a penalty for a previous win, made the running as nothing else wanted to, and she was in front until halfway up the straight. She battled on in game fashion, but was found out and probably deserves a rest now.
Short Skirt did not reproduce her excellent form from earlier in the year. Taken into second place soon after the start, she was going nowhere from halfway up the straight and looks a little past her best. Softer ground might have suited her better.
Chelsea Rose(IRE) has shown her best form over shorter.

5703a PRIX DANIEL WILDENSTEIN CASTEL MARIE-LOUISE DE LA BAULE (GROUP 2) 1m
3:25 (3:28) 3-Y-0+ **£51,103** (£19,724; £9,414; £6,276; £3,138)

RPR

1 **Echo Of Light**[21] [5186] 4-9-2 .... LDettori 2 120+
(Saeed Bin Suroor) *a in touch, 3rd str, soon pushed along, chal 1 1/2f out, rdn to ld appr fnl f, drifted left last 150yds, driven out* **5/6**[1]

2 *2* **Picaresque Coat (JPN)**[70] 4-9-2 .... YTake 1 113
(Y Ikee, Japan) *frist to show, led at half-way, ridden and ran on 2f out, headed approaching final f, stayed on* **16/1**

3 *3/4* **Hello Sunday (FR)**[34] [4862] 3-8-11 .... C-PLemaire 3 111
(Mme C Head-Maarek, France) *mid-division, disputing 4th straight, ridden & stayed on from 1f out, took 3rd on line* **7/1**[3]

4 *snk* **Notability (IRE)**[32] [4918] 4-9-4 .... CSoumillon 4 113
(M A Jarvis) *led to half-way, 2nd straight, ridden 1 1/2f out, stayed on at one pace under pressure, lost 3rd on line* **5/1**[2]

5 *snk* **Svedov (FR)**[34] 4862 5-9-2 .... SPasquier 8 111
(E Lellouche, France) *held up, disputing 4th straight, ridden & headway to dispute 3rd final f, no extra under pressure last 100yds* **12/1**

6 *2 1/2* **Special Kaldoun (IRE)**[48] 4416 7-9-2 .... DBoeuf 6 105
(D Smaga, France) *held up, 7th & pushed along straight, never a factor* **10/1**

7 *8* **Only Him**[186] 3-8-11 .... OPeslier 7 86
(A Fabre, France) *held up in last, pushed along approaching straight, never a factor* **7/1**[3]

8 *1 1/2* **Sendalam (FR)**[23] 5146 4-9-2 .... FSpanu 5 83
(Y Fouin, France) *held up, 6th straight, driven 2f out, one pace from well over 1f out* **40/1**

1m 37.0s **Going Correction** -0.30s/f (Firm)
WFA 3 from 4yo+ 4lb 8 Ran SP% **121.3**
Speed ratings: 115,113,112,112,111 109,101,99
PARI-MUTUEL: WIN 1.80; PL 1.30, 2.20, 1.60; DF 14.20.
Owner Godolphin **Bred** Kilcarn Stud **Trained** Newmarket, Suffolk

FOCUS
With the third, fourth and fifth all running to their best, this Group 2 race looks well up to par, and the winner looks likely to make up into a Group 1 performer next term.

NOTEBOOK
Echo Of Light ◆, although wandering when taking the advantage in the straight, outclassed his field in this Group 2 event. He was always well up and took the advantage halfway up the straight and, although he hung left in the final stages, he still won with plenty in hand. There are no immediate plans for him but it is confirmed that he remains in training next year.
Picaresque Coat(JPN), a Japanese trained four-year-old and stable companion of Deep Impact, attempted to lead from pillar to post and had built up a lead of several lengths entering the straight. He stayed on in a genuine manner throughout the final stages, and put up a good performance considering this was his first race outside of Japan. Considering how he ran here and the fact that he has won over nine furlongs in the past, it was a surprise that he was not supplemented into the Arc as a pacemaker for his more illustrious stablemate.
Hello Sunday(FR) ran a very sound race and certainly seems to be on the upgrade. He was settled in fourth place towards the outside and battled on gamely to take third place by a narrow margin. He now goes for the Prix Perth at Saint Cloud.
Notability(IRE) was not disgraced considering the weight he had to carry. He was tucked in second place early on then battled on gamely to only lose third place with fifty yards left to run.

5704a PRIX DOLLAR CASINO BARRIERE DE MONTREUX (GROUP 2) 1m 1f 165y
3:55 (3:55) 3-Y-O+ **£51,103** (£19,724; £9,414; £6,276; £3,138)

RPR

1 **Soldier Hollow**[49] 4386 6-9-0 .... OPeslier 2 118
(P Schiergen, Germany) *raced in 2nd, pushed along to lead 2f out, ridden over 1 1/2f out, ran on well to line* **3/1**[2]

2 *nk* **Manduro (GER)**[27] 5049 4-9-4 .... CSoumillon 1 121
(A Fabre, France) *disputing 3rd half-way, 5th straight, pushed along to chase leaders over 2f out, rdn over 1f out, nrst at fin* **4/5**[1]

3 *2 1/2* **Boris De Deauville (IRE)**[42] 4623 3-8-9 .... YBarberot 3 113
(S Wattel, France) *led to 2f out, kept on under pressure* **20/1**

4 *1 1/2* **Sudan (IRE)**[20] 5221 3-8-9 .... SPasquier 5 110
(E Lellouche, France) *held up, disputing last straight, driven to chase leaders over 1 1/2f out, stayed on, just missed 3rd* **11/1**

5 *3* **Atlantic Air (FR)**[48] 4417 4-9-0 .... TThulliez 6 103
(Y De Nicolay, France) *held up, disputing last straight, ridden 2f out, not quicken* **16/1**

6 *2* **Touch Of Land (FR)**[49] 4386 6-9-4 .... C-PLemaire 4 103
(H-A Pantall, France) *in touch, disputing 3rd at half-way, 3rd straight, pushed along 1 1/2f out, no impression* **6/1**[3]

1m 59.4s **Going Correction** -0.20s/f (Firm)
WFA 3 from 4yo+ 6lb 6 Ran SP% **113.8**
Speed ratings: 112,111,109,108,106 104
PARI-MUTUEL: WIN 4.30; PL 1.60, 1.30; SF 8.80.
Owner Gestut Park Wiedingen **Bred** Car Colston Hall Stud **Trained** Germany

FOCUS
Solid Group 2 form rated around the winner and runner-up performing to their best.

NOTEBOOK
Soldier Hollow, who had form in the book to hold solid claims in this company, was given a brilliant ride by his jockey, who realised there could be a lack of early pace and got the six-year-old tucked in just behind the leader. He quickened impressively just over a furlong out, held on gamely to the line, and the Champion Stakes is now on the cards, as is the Premio Roma.
Manduro(GER), an incredibly consistent colt, was once again unlucky as he had absolutely nowhere to go halfway up the straight. His jockey had to be patient but by the time he was in the clear the winner had built up a lead of three lengths. He quickened well inside the final furlong but the winning post came a few strides too soon. He is another possible for the Champion Stakes.
Boris De Deauville(IRE), who was bought as a jumper but is already a Group 3 winner on the Flat, was soon in the lead. The winner tackled him halfway up the straight, though, and he could only stay on one-paced afterwards.
Sudan(IRE) did not really take part in the race until halfway up the straight, having been dropped out early on.

3427 SAN SIRO (R-H)
Saturday, September 30

OFFICIAL GOING: Good

5705a PREMIO CASCINA SFORZINI (MAIDEN) (FILLIES) 1m
2:15 (2:27) 2-Y-O **£6,897** (£3,034; £1,655; £828)

RPR

1 **Sopran Slam (IRE)**[83] 3343 2-9-0 .... DVargiu 15 —
(B Grizzetti, Italy)

2 *2 1/4* **Marahute (ITY)** 2-9-0 .... SLandi 7 —
(L Camici, Italy)

3 *1 3/4* **Lonesome Tonight**[112] 2475 2-9-0 .... MDemuro 8 —
(L D'Auria, Italy)

4 *3/4* **Tirzia (IRE)**[112] 2475 2-9-0 .... DPorcu 9 —
(R Feligioni, Italy)

5 *3/4* **Money Penny (ITY)** 2-8-10 .... SMulas 4 —
(B Grizzetti, Italy)

6 *1 3/4* **Mardus Di San Jore** 2-9-0 .... PConvertino 2 —
(M Marcialis, Italy)

7 *2 1/4* **Mimita (IRE)**[112] 2475 2-9-0 .... WGambarota 13 —
(M Cicarelli, Italy)

8 *snk* **Widow Blach** 2-9-0 .... CColombi 5 —
(Nicola De Chirico, Italy)

9 *hd* **Matispingo (IRE)** 2-9-0 .... MTellini 14 —
(Laura Grizzetti, Italy)

10 *3/4* **Inchinora** 2-9-0 .... IRossi 6 —
(M Ciciarelli, Italy)

11 *13* **Toga (ITY)** 2-9-0 .... MEsposito 3 —
(M Bebbu, Italy)

12 *9* **Fantastic Mist** 2-8-10 .... MMonteriso 12 —
(M Guarnieri, Italy)

13 *dist* **Teorea (ITY)** 2-9-0 .... LManiezzi 11 —
(R Menichetti, Italy)

14 *dist* **Desert Cactus (IRE)** 2-8-10 .... EBotti 10 —
(M Botti) *in touch to straight, lost position over 3f out, tailed off SP 1.52-1F* **152/100**[1]

1m 41.7s 14 Ran SP% **39.7**
(Including 1 Euro stake): WIN 2.63; PL 1.40, 2.58, 2.67; DF 14.55.
Owner Azienda Agricola San Uberto **Bred** Azienda Agricola San Uberto In Cerrecchia Srl **Trained** Italy

5328 TIPPERARY
Sunday, October 1

OFFICIAL GOING: Flat course - heavy; hurdle course - soft (heavy in places); chase course - yielding to soft

5706a ABERGWAUN STKS (LISTED RACE) 5f
2:15 (2:19) 3-Y-O+ **£22,448** (£6,586; £3,137; £1,068)

RPR

1 **Peace Offering (IRE)**[21] 5222 6-9-1 .... AdrianTNicholls 10 113
(D Nicholls) *prom on stands' side: 3rd after 1/2-way: rdn to ld 1f out: kpt on wl* **5/2**[1]

2 *1* **Osterhase (IRE)**[70] 3767 7-9-4 114 .... (b) FMBerry 9 112
(J E Mulhern, Ire) *broke wl and led: racd on stands' rail: strly pressed 2f out: hdd 1f out: kpt on* **5/1**

3 *2* **Miss Donovan**[42] 4637 3-8-12 79 .... MCHussey 8 99
(Declan Gillespie, Ire) *hld up in tch: prog into 4th and rdn to chal 1 1/2f out: 3rd and kpt on ins fnl f* **25/1**

4 *1 1/4* **Sister Sox (IRE)**[12] 5463 6-8-12 88 .... (p) JMurtagh 12 95
(M Halford, Ire) *chsd ldrs on stands' side: kpt on same pce fr over 1f out* **12/1**

5 *3/4* **Waterways (IRE)**[14] 5405 3-8-12 97 .... NGMcCullagh 7 92
(P J Prendergast, Ire) *cl up on stands' side: 2nd and chal 2f out: no ex fr over 1f out* **9/2**[3]

6 *3/4* **Senor Benny (USA)**[12] 5463 7-9-1 104 .... DPMcDonogh 4 92
(M McDonagh, Ire) *prom on far side: rdn and one pce fr 1 1/2f out* **4/1**[2]

7 *nk* **Benwilt Breeze (IRE)**[12] 5463 4-9-1 96 .... (t) WSupple 1 91
(G M Lyons, Ire) *racd on far rail: rdn 2f out: 4th over 1f out: sn no ex* **12/1**

8 *1* **Gist (IRE)**[12] 5462 3-8-12 75 .... (b) SMGorey 5 85
(W J Martin, Ire) *chsd ldrs on stands' side: no imp fr 2f out* **25/1**

9 *2 1/2* **Shinko Dancer (IRE)**[12] 5463 3-8-12 79 .... (bt) PShanahan 3 76
(H Rogers, Ire) *prom on far side: rdn and wknd fr under 2f out* **16/1**

10 *5* **Cliffs Of Duneen**[12] 5463 3-8-12 78 .... CDHayes 6 58
(T G McCourt, Ire) *chsd ldrs on stands' side: wknd fr 2f out: trailing fnl f* **25/1**

11 *1/2* **Final Contest (USA)**[26] 5102 6-8-12 42 .... RMBurke 11 56
(Patrick Morris, Ire) *a bhd: trailing fr 2f out* **100/1**

58.80 secs 12 Ran SP% **117.2**
CSF £14.33 TOTE £3.90: £1.70, £1.70, £9.20; DF 9.10.
Owner Lady O'Reilly **Bred** Chevington Stud **Trained** Sessay, N Yorks

FOCUS
The proximity of 79-rated Miss Donovan in third suggests this was a pretty ordinary Listed race. They did, though, go a good pace considering the heavy ground

NOTEBOOK
Peace Offering(IRE), second in a Group 3 at Longchamp on his previous start, appreciated the drop in grade and ran out a clear-cut winner. All four of his previous wins were achieved on ground good or faster, but he handled the testing conditions well. His trainer said that might be it for the year now. (op 3/1)
Osterhase(IRE), chasing the hat-trick off the back of a 70-day break, ran reasonably but only had two lengths to spare over a rival rated 79, so he was clearly not at his best. He would not have been suited by the testing ground. (op 3/1)
Miss Donovan, fourth in a Leopardstown handicap off a mark of 80 after winning her maiden, produced easily her best effort to date, chasing the leaders all the way and keeping on inside the final furlong. Her proximity does little for the form, but full credit to connections for finding her some valuable black type. (op 20/1)
Sister Sox(IRE) goes well over this course and distance and kept on without posing a real threat. (op 10/1)
Waterways(IRE), whose only win this season came on fast ground at Cork, handles easy ground well. She ran fast but was under pressure almost two furlongs out and faded in the closing stages. (op 4/1)
Senor Benny(USA) another with plenty of soft ground form, raced on the far side and was well held by those nearer the stands.

5707a EL GRAN SENOR STKS (LISTED RACE) 7f 100y
2:45 (2:48) 2-Y-O **£22,448** (£6,586; £3,137; £1,068)

RPR

1 **Zafonical Storm (USA)**[12] 5459 2-9-1 .... DJMoran 2 102+
(B W Duke) *mde all: qcknd clr under 2f out: styd on strly fnl f* **20/1**

2 *4 1/2* **Chinese Whisper (IRE)**[19] 5278 2-9-1 .... JAHeffernan 1 91
(A P O'Brien, Ire) *trckd ldr in 2nd: rdn and outpcd under 2f out: no imp fnl f* **1/2**[1]

3 *1/2* **Warriors Key (IRE)**[36] 4821 2-9-1 .... DPMcDonogh 5 90
(Kevin Prendergast, Ire) *hld up in tch: last and pushed along 1/2-way: impr into cl 4th on outer appr st: mod 3rd and no imp fr under 2f out* **4/1**[2]

4 *hd* **Essexford (IRE)**[14] 5407 2-8-12 .... FMBerry 4 87
(John M Oxx, Ire) *trckd ldrs in 3rd: rdn ent st: 4th under 2f out: kpt on u.p fnl f* **7/1**[3]

5 *21* **Jopau**[35] 4850 2-9-1 92 .... JMurtagh 6 40
(G M Lyons, Ire) *hld up in rr: prog into 4th bef 1/2-way: rdn and wknd ent st* **12/1**

1m 40.4s 6 Ran SP% **111.6**
CSF £30.93 TOTE £11.50: £4.80, £1.10; DF 26.90.
Owner Briton International **Bred** Millsec, Ltd **Trained** Lambourn, Berks

FOCUS
This looked a reasonable Listed event beforehand, but there was something of a shock result.

The Form Book, Raceform Ltd, Compton, RG20 6NL

NOTEBOOK

Zafonical Storm(USA), a close second off a mark of 78 in a Newmarket nursery over a mile on his previous start, improved significantly on that effort to run out a most convincing winner stepped up to Listed company. Having led pretty much from the start at a decent pace, it appeared as though the challengers were queueing up behind him early in the straight but he kept on well from over a furlong out. This might be it for the season. (op 20/1 tchd 25/1)

Chinese Whisper(IRE), the easy winner of a Galway maiden on his previous start, was produced with every chance but was unable to reel in the long-time leader. More will be needed if he is to make his mark at this level. (op 1/2 tchd 4/9)

Warriors Key(IRE), who was being bustled along before the straight, improved to deliver a challenge on the outside but could do no more from over a furlong out. This was a respectable effort. (op 3/1)

Essexford(IRE) was looking to build on her Curragh maiden win last month. She may prefer better ground but will have to improve if she is to make an impact at Listed level. (op 5/1)

Jopau was fighting a losing battle from a quarter of a mile out. A useful two- time winner, he probably wants better ground to be seen at his best.

5708a COOLMORE STUD HOME OF CHAMPIONS CONCORDE STKS (GROUP 3) — 7f 100y

3:45 (3:45) 3-Y-O+ **£35,862** (£10,482; £4,965; £1,655)

RPR

1 — **Noelani (IRE)**[15] 5393 4-9-0 104 .... FMBerry 2 — 109
(John M Oxx, Ire) *prom: 4th 1/2-way: 3rd into st: rdn to ld over 1f out: strly pressed wl ins fnl f: styd on u.p* **7/1**

2 nk **Ugo Fire (IRE)**[14] 5411 3-8-12 106 .... DPMcDonogh 9 — 108
(Kevin Prendergast, Ire) *hld up towards rr: 7th after 1/2-way: 4th and hdwy 1 1/2f out: 2nd and chal wl ins fnl f: styd on u.p* **13/2**[3]

3 1 **Hurricane Cat (USA)**[78] 3559 3-9-1 109 .... JAHeffernan 4 — 109
(A P O'Brien, Ire) *6th early: dropped towards rr 1/2-way: 7th early st: hdwy on outer 1 1/2f out: 3rd and kpt on wl fnl f* **6/1**[2]

4 3 **Latino Magic (IRE)**[14] 5411 6-9-3 107 .... RMBurke 8 — 103
(R J Osborne, Ire) *hld up: 8th 1/2-way: nt clr run early st: kpt on ins fnl f* **10/1**

5 ½ **Modeeroch (IRE)**[30] 5004 3-8-12 103 .... (t) DJMoran 5 — 99
(J S Bolger, Ire) *prom: 2nd 1/2-way: chal ent st: led 1 1/2f out: hdd over 1f out: sn no ex* **10/1**

6 1 ¾ **Short Dance (USA)**[22] 5184 3-8-12 .... PShanahan 6 — 96
(B W Hills) *led: strly pressed ent st: hdd 1 1/2f out: no ex fnl f* **4/1**[1]

7 2 ½ **Common World (USA)**[14] 5411 7-9-6 110 .... (p) WSupple 10 — 97
(T Hogan, Ire) *s.i.s and drvn along: hdwy into 5th 1/2-way: rdn appr st: wknd fr over 1f out* **9/1**

8 1 ¾ **Jazz Princess (IRE)**[127] 2041 4-9-3 106 .... JMurtagh 1 — 90
(M Halford, Ire) *settled 4th: 6th 1/2-way: rdn st: no ex whn eased fnl f* **4/1**[1]

9 7 **Altius (IRE)**[140] 1708 3-9-1 103 .... DavidMcCabe 11 — 76
(A P O'Brien, Ire) *chsd ldrs: 3rd 1/2-way: wknd ent st: eased fnl f* **20/1**

10 hd **Yellow Ridge (IRE)**[22] 5192 3-9-1 75 .... FranciscoDaSilva 7 — 76
(Luke Comer, Ire) *sn towards rr: rdn and wknd fr 1/2-way* **33/1**

1m 39.3s
WFA 3 from 4yo+ 2lb — **11** Ran SP% **116.0**
CSF £51.70 TOTE £5.80: £1.90, £1.60, £3.20; DF 82.10.
Owner Lady Clague **Bred** Newberry Stud Company **Trained** Currabeg, Co Kildare
■ Stewards' Enquiry : F M Berry two-day ban: used whip with excessive frequency (Oct 12,14)

FOCUS

A competitive renewal of this Group 3 contest rated through the runner-up.

NOTEBOOK

Noelani(IRE) returned to her very best to land her second victory at this level on what was the final start of her career. (op 6/1)

Ugo Fire(IRE), who has run some good races in defeat this term, seemed to enjoy this ground and showed enough to suggest that she might be able to strike again at stakes level before the end of the season. She stuck to her task well under pressure from the turn in to secure the runner-up spot. (op 7/1)

Hurricane Cat(USA), who has run a couple of solid races in defeat this term, had only one rival behind him turning in but was putting in some good work in the closing stages and looks as though he could be worth trying over further. (op 5/1)

Latino Magic(IRE) has been running well this season without winning and posted a solid effort without ever being able to land a telling blow. He would have preferred quicker ground.

Modeeroch(IRE), a previous course and distance winner, raced in second and had a spell in lead before the winner took over. She could do no more from over a furlong out and would probably prefer better ground. (op 8/1)

Short Dance(USA) has not been at her best lately. She set out to make all and looked as if she might still fight it out for the placings when headed, but had no more to give from over a furlong out. (op 7/2 tchd 9/2)

2492 DORTMUND (R-H)

Sunday, October 1

OFFICIAL GOING: Good

5709a GROSSER PREIS VON DSW21 - 122ND DEUTSCHES ST LEGER (GROUP 3) (ENTIRE COLTS & FILLIES) — 1m 6f

3:40 (3:51) 3-Y-O **£27,586** (£10,345; £4,138; £2,759)

RPR

1 — **Schiaparelli (GER)**[28] 5051 3-9-2 .... AStarke 2 — 102
(P Schiergen, Germany) *racd in 3rd, rdn and hdwy on ins to ld 2 1/2f out, wl in control fr over 1f out, eased closing stages* **1/5**[1]

2 1 ½ **N'Oubliez Jamais (GER)**[108] 3-9-2 .... ADeVries 4 — 100
(H Blume, Germany) *led to 2 1/2f out, strongly pressed for 2nd throughout final 2f, stayed on gamely but no chance with wnr* **11/2**[2]

3 nk **Elcanos (GER)**[70] 3776 3-9-2 .... ASuborics 6 — 100
(Mario Hofer, Germany) *went 2nd after 3f, ridden and disputing 2nd 2f out, stayed on at one pace* **69/10**[3]

4 1 ¾ **Damascena (GER)**[30] 5008 3-8-12 .... WMongil 5 — 94
(P Schiergen, Germany) *went 4th after 4f, ridden over 2f out, stayed on same pace* **94/10**

5 nse **Atamane (GER)**[92] 3-9-2 .... J-PCarvalho 3 — 98
(Mario Hofer, Germany) *raced in 5th, kept on under pressure final 2f but never threatened leaders* **117/10**

6 10 **Diskretion (GER)**[129] 3-8-12 .... (b) AHelfenbein 1 — 82
(W Hickst, Germany) *last throughout, tailed off from over 1f out* **166/10**

3m 3.43s — **6** Ran SP% **134.5**
(Including 10 Euros stake): WIN 12; PL 11, 14; SF 43.
Owner Stall Blankenese **Bred** Gestut Karlshof **Trained** Germany

4418 HANOVER (L-H)

Sunday, October 1

OFFICIAL GOING: Good

5710a GROSSER PREIS DER DR DUVE INKASSO (LISTED RACE) (F&M) — 6f 110y

3:25 (3:35) 3-Y-O+ **£8,276** (£3,034; £1,655; £828)

RPR

1 — **Deauville (GER)**[45] 4542 3-8-12 .... (b) VSchulepov 15 — 97
(Frau E Mader, Germany)

2 1 ¼ **Creative Mind (IRE)**[35] 4837 3-9-0 .... CarolinLippert 12 — 95
(E J O'Neill) *led narrowly til headed inside final furlong, just held on for 2nd SP 51-10* **51/10**[1]

3 nse **Jalta (GER)**[74] 3661 3-8-7 .... AGoritz 9 — 88
(H Steinmetz, Germany)

4 ½ **Priere**[42] 4649 4-9-4 .... J-MBreux 1 — 96
(N Clement, France)

5 1 ¼ **Slade (GER)**[147] 4-9-2 .... FilipMinarik 2 — 90
(Andreas Lowe, Germany)

6 ½ **Timbalada (GER)** 3-8-12 .... ABoschert 7 — 86
(U Ostmann, Germany)

7 ¾ **Birthday Art (GER)**[74] 3661 4-9-0 .... RJuracek 14 — 84
(P Vovcenko, Germany)

8 nk **Zuccarella (GER)** 3-8-7 .... PJWerning 3 — 78
(J Warren, Germany)

9 1 ¼ **Zoom (GER)** 3-8-7 .... JBojko 6 — 75
(Tim Gibson, Germany)

10 ½ **Zita (GER)**[35] 4858 4-9-0 .... AWhelan 8 — 78
(P Bradik, Germany)

11 nk **Best Dancing (GER)** 4-9-0 .... ABest 11 — 77
(C Von Der Recke, Germany)

12 1 ¼ **Ninifee (GER)** 5-9-2 .... EFrank 5 — 76
(W Hickst, Germany)

13 nk **Lirope (GER)**[767] 5-9-4 .... HGrewe 13 — 77
(Frau A Glodde, Germany)

14 5 **Zackmunde (GER)**[57] 3-8-7 .... APietsch 4 — 53
(Frau A Glodde, Germany)

15 dist **Annatira (GER)**[42] 4649 5-9-4 .... (b) MTimpelan 10 — —
(E Kurdu, Germany)

1m 19.82s
WFA 3 from 4yo+ 1lb — **15** Ran SP% **16.4**
(Including 10 Euros stake): WIN 66; PL 20, 18, 36, 15; SF 463.
Owner Mme E Hilger **Bred** Dr Klaus Schulte **Trained** Germany

NOTEBOOK

Creative Mind(IRE) did not seem affected by a late change of jockey (Dane O'Neill having been held up at Heathrow) and, having made most of the running, just held on for second place to accomplish her mission of gaining black type.

5700 LONGCHAMP (R-H)

Sunday, October 1

OFFICIAL GOING: Good

5711a PRIX DU CADRAN CASINO LES PRINCES BARRIERE DE CANNES (GROUP 1) — 2m 4f

1:05 (1:04) 4-Y-O+ **£98,517** (£39,414; £19,707; £9,845; £4,931)

RPR

1 — **Sergeant Cecil**[23] 5156 7-9-2 .... LDettori 5 — 120
(B R Millman) *held up in rear, 6th straight, headway well over 1f out, strong run to lead well inside final f* **2/1**[1]

2 ¾ **Shamdala (IRE)**[39] 4714 4-8-13 .... CSoumillon 2 — 116
(A De Royer-Dupre, France) *tracked leader, led over 2f out, hard ridden 1f out, caught well inside final f* **9/1**

3 ½ **Le Miracle (GER)**[21] 5223 5-9-2 .... DBoeuf 1 — 119
(W Baltromei, Germany) *led to over 2f out, hard ridden and every chance well inside final f, ran on* **11/4**[2]

4 1 ½ **Reefscape**[42] 4647 5-9-2 .... KFallon 3 — 117
(A Fabre, France) *raced in 3rd til inside final f, hard ridden and ran on at one pace* **10/3**[3]

5 5 **Petite Speciale (USA)**[21] 5223 7-8-13 .... C-PLemaire 4 — 109
(E Lecoiffier, France) *disputed 4th, 5th straight, never able to challenge* **50/1**

6 ¾ **Alcazar (IRE)**[23] 5156 11-9-2 .... MickyFenton 7 — 111
(H Morrison) *disputed 4th, 4th straight, soon beaten* **7/1**

7 1 ½ **Baddam**[23] 5156 4-9-2 .... IanMongan 6 — 110
(M R Channon) *always in rear, last straight, ridden and beaten 2f out* **20/1**

4m 20.9s **Going Correction** -0.45s/f (Firm) — **7** Ran SP% **112.3**
Speed ratings: 87,86,86,85,83 83,83
PARI-MUTUEL (including 1 Euro stake): WIN 2.20; PL 1.40, 2.00;SF 10.50.
Owner Terry Cooper **Bred** D E Hazzard **Trained** Kentisbeare, Devon

FOCUS

Despite the absence of Gold Cup winner Yeats, this looked like a good renewal of the Group 1 Prix du Cadran, with a case to be made for several of these beforehand. However, it was not quite the test one might expect for such an extreme trip, as the early pace was just steady.

NOTEBOOK

Sergeant Cecil, chasing the hat-trick on his return to Group 1 company after winning both the Lonsdale Cup and Doncaster Cup, looked in trouble early in the straight but suddenly found another gear and took the lead running into the last 50 yards. He may bid to gain back-to-back Group 1 wins in the Prix Royal-Oak back at Longchamp later in October, and another crack at the Ascot Gold is his main aim next year.

Shamdala(IRE), well below her best in the Yorkshire Oaks on her previous start, was trying this trip for the first time and returned to form with a fine effort in defeat. Always up with the pace, she looked to have the event in her grasp running into the final furlong before the winner mowed her down close home. She may now go for the Prix Royal-Oak provided she comes out of this race in good order.

Le Miracle(GER), a German challenger who was bidding to follow up his recent success in an extended mile seven Group 3 round here, was rather strangely asked to make the running which is difficult to understand as he usually comes with a devastating late run. He set an even pace and kicked for home early in the straight, but surrendered his lead running into the final furlong and could only run on at the one pace. He is another possible for the Royal-Oak.

Reefscape, last year's winner, has not quite had the season many expected, despite finishing second to Yeats in the Ascot Gold Cup. Never far away, he was caught for speed early in the straight when things warmed up and could only stay on at the one pace.
Alcazar(IRE), runner-up to Sergeant Cecil in the Doncaster Cup on his previous start, lost a bandage during the race. He was fourth for a long time, but failed to quicken early in the straight and this ground may have been a little lively for him.
Baddam, third to Sergeant Cecil and Alcazar in the Doncaster Cup on his previous start, was never really seen with a chance and might not be quite up to this class.

5712a PRIX DE L'ABBAYE DE LONGCHAMP MAJESTIC BARRIERE (GROUP 1) 5f (S)

2:15 (2:16) 2-Y-0+ **£98,517** (£39,414; £19,707; £9,845; £4,931)

RPR

1 **Desert Lord**[22] 5179 6-9-11 (b) JamieSpencer 12 119
(K A Ryan) *made all, ridden 1 1/2f out, driven out* **25/1**

2 *nk* **Reverence**[29] 5011 5-9-11 KDarley 13 118
(E J Alston) *prominent, disputing 3rd and pushed along halfway, went 3rd approaching final f, took 2nd final stride* **9/4**[1]

3 *snk* **Moss Vale (IRE)**[38] 4738 5-9-11 KFallon 11 118
(D Nicholls) *close up, 2nd halfway, effort 2f out, kept on but lost 2nd final stride* **4/1**[2]

4 *1 ½* **Biniou (IRE)**[21] 5222 3-9-11 TThulliez 5 112
(Robert Collet, France) *towards rear, ridden and ran on through field from halfway, took 4th 1f out, nearest finish* **33/1**

5 *nk* **Amadeus Wolf**[29] 5011 3-9-11 NCallan 9 111
(K A Ryan) *in touch, 6th and ridden halfway, headway 1 1/2f out, stayed on* **6/1**[3]

6 *nk* **Beauty Bright (IRE)**[15] 5393 3-9-8 PJSmullen 2 107
(A P O'Brien, Ire) *midfield on rails, pushed along halfway, kept on at one pace* **18/1**

7 *1 ½* **Majestic Missile (IRE)**[21] 5222 5-9-11 (t) CSoumillon 14 105
(W J Haggas) *in touch on outside, driven 2f out, unable to quicken* **10/1**

8 *snk* **Pivotal Flame**[15] 5375 4-9-11 (p) SebSanders 4 104
(E S McMahon) *prominent, disputing 2nd halfway, ridden and kept on til no extra final f* **14/1**

9 *2* **Red Clubs (IRE)**[7] 5549 3-9-11 MichaelHills 3 97
(B W Hills) *in touch, 5th halfway, weakened 1 1/2f out* **7/1**

10 *½* **Gift Horse**[23] 5158 6-9-11 JohnEgan 10 95
(D Nicholls) *midfield, ridden and one pace from over 2f out* **25/1**

11 *1 ½* **Meliksah (IRE)**[17] 12-9-11 TRicher 6 90
(Mrs D Smith, Germany) *in touch to halfway* **200/1**

12 *hd* **Excusez Moi (USA)**[15] 5375 4-9-11 KerrinMcEvoy 7 89
(C E Brittain) *towards rear on outside, never a factor* **16/1**

13 *¾* **Mister Chocolate (IRE)**[17] 3-9-11 OPeslier 8 86
(Robert Collet, France) *always behind* **100/1**

14 *hd* **Kodiac**[29] 5011 5-9-11 (b) MJKinane 1 86
(J L Dunlop) *always behind* **40/1**

54.80 secs **Going Correction** -0.45s/f (Firm) **14** Ran SP% **119.0**
Speed ratings: 114,113,113,110,110 109,107,107,104,103 100,100,99,99
PARI-MUTUEL: WIN 24.10; PL 3.90, 1.50, 2.70; DF 21.00.
Owner Bull & Bell Partnership **Bred** Cheveley Park Stud Ltd **Trained** Hambleton, N Yorks

FOCUS
As usual the British raiders completely dominated France's premier sprint - there were only two home-based runners. The result provided further evidence that there is very little between the top European sprinters, and just how weak a division it remains. The first three home were drawn in double-figure stalls.

NOTEBOOK
Desert Lord made both his debut for Kevin Ryan and his first start of the season in a handicap at Kempton off a mark of 83, but he has fairly thrived for his new trainer and developed into a very smart sprinter indeed. His last run was a shade disappointing, and he had not run in Group 1 company since finishing down the field in the 2002 Dewhurst when with Sir Michael Stoute, but the fast ground was very much in his favour and he flew out of the stalls. With blinkers back on he was never headed, and he ran on very bravely in the final stages to hold the favourite and post a considerably improved effort in a time bettered only once before in this famous five-furlong dash. Connections now have their eyes on the Hong Kong Sprint in December.
Reverence is probably the best sprinter in Britain judged on his wins in the Nunthorpe and Haydock Sprint Cup, but unfortunately for him the ground had come up much faster than ideal for what should have been his ideal race. He was in fourth position at the halfway stage, and his final charge took him into second place on the line, but at the end of the day the ground beat him. He has now been retired for the season.
Moss Vale(IRE), unlucky in running in the Nunthorpe on his previous start, was smartly into his stride. He got close to the winner at halfway but was being held throughout the final furlong and lost second place as the race came to a close. A tilt at the Hong Kong Sprint is also on the cards for this five-year-old.
Biniou(IRE), successful only in a Listed race at Deauville from 14 starts, but third behind Majestic Missile and Peace Offering in a Group 3 over the course and distance on his previous start, fared easily best of the usual weak home challenge. He had plenty to do at the halfway stage but put in his best work up the rail inside the final furlong to show much improved form in fourth. He had changed hands for 180,000 euros at the previous evening's sale and now joins Robert Cowell in Newmarket.
Amadeus Wolf, who has been running well in defeat in most of the top sprints this season, was settled behind the leading group and ran on from a furlong and a half out up the centre of the track, but he was never a real threat as the race came to a close.
Beauty Bright(IRE), successful in a Group 3 at the Curragh on her previous start, did not have the stable jockey on board and found the competition tougher at this level.
Majestic Missile(IRE), in front of Biniou when winning a course and distance Group 3 on his previous start, was not well away and had to race in mid-division early on. His challenge started a furlong and a half out but he could only stay on at the same pace in the latter stages.
Pivotal Flame, smartly out of the stalls, raced up the centre of the track. He tried to follow the pace from two out, but found nothing under pressure during the closing stages.
Red Clubs(IRE), succesful in the Group 2 Diadem Stakes at Ascot on his previous start, made a good start and was close to the leaders during the early part of the race, but he was short of room next to the rail at the two-furlong marker and gradually dropped away thereafter.
Gift Horse was always in mid-division and never a danger from two out.
Excusez Moi(USA), in good form in Group company since winning the Great St Wilfrid, was never seen with a real chance and was nearly always towards the tail of the field.
Kodiac made no show and was always behind.

5713a PRIX DE L'OPERA CASINO BARRIERE D'ENGHIEN (GROUP 1) (FILLIES) 1m 2f

2:50 (2:50) 3-Y-0+ **£98,517** (£39,414; £19,707; £9,845; £4,931)

RPR

1 **Mandesha (FR)**[21] 5220 3-8-12 CSoumillon 6 122+
(A De Royer-Dupre, France) *hld up in 5th, hdwy on ins over 2f out whn* **hard rdn and n.m.r appr fnl f and 150 yds out, led 120 yds out, rdn out** **2/1**[2]

2 *¾* **Satwa Queen (FR)**[42] 4646 4-9-2 TThulliez 5 120
(J De Roualle, France) *raced in 4th, led 2f out, edged right under pressure appr fnl f and 150 yards out, headed 120 yards out, ran on* **20/1**

3 *2 ½* **Alexandrova (IRE)**[39] 4714 3-8-12 KFallon 3 117
(A P O'Brien, Ire) *hld up, last and pushed along ent str, hdwy on outside fr 2f out, 5th and hard rdn 1f out, kpt on to take 3rd 70 yds out* **8/11**[1]

4 *1 ½* **Irridescence (SAF)**[28] 5049 5-9-2 WCMarwing 2 113
(J E Hammond, France) *led to 2f out, kept on one pace, lost 3rd 70 yards out* **9/1**[3]

5 *½* **Nannina**[22] 5191 3-8-12 JimmyFortune 1 113
(J H M Gosden) *disputed 2nd, 2nd straight, every chance well over 1f out, one pace* **20/1**

6 *10* **Dionisia (USA)**[105] 2694 3-8-12 C-PLemaire 4 95
(L M Cumani) *tracked leader, 3rd straight, soon beaten* **28/1**

2m 0.90s **Going Correction** -0.45s/f (Firm)
WFA 3 from 4yo+ 5lb **6** Ran SP% **114.2**
Speed ratings: 110,109,107,106,105 97
PARI-MUTUEL: WIN 2.20; PL 1.40, 3.00; SF 12.20.
Owner Princess Zahra Aga Khan **Bred** Princes Zahra Aga Khan **Trained** Chantilly, France
■ Mandesha broke the course record.

FOCUS
Much the smallest field since the race attained Group 1 status in 2000, but there has surely never been one of such quality. While it was a shame that Ouija Board did not take up her engagement, and that the clash with the Sun Chariot removed Soviet Song and this race's 2004 winner Alexander Goldrun from calculations, nobody could quibble with a line-up that featured five winners of 11 Group 1s, among them a dual Classic winner and a highly impressive French filly who some would have fancied for the Arc, plus a lightly raced filly who looked well worth another chance at this level when impressive in a Group 2 last time.

NOTEBOOK
Mandesha(FR) ◆, a Group 1 winner over a mile earlier in the season before following up impressively in the Prix Vermeille, was considered a possible for the Arc, but connections opted to keep her to her own sex, presumably with the knowledge she stays in training and there is always next year. The decision was justified when she squeezed up the inside to lead well inside the final furlong and win convincingly, having travelled smoothly. She will be put away for the year and return in next season's Prix Ganay.
Satwa Queen(FR), the winner of a ten-furlong Group 2 at Deauville on her previous start, ran her heart out and looked the probable winner half way up the straight before being reeled in. Races such as the EP Taylor and the Breeders Cup Fillies & Mares are possible targets.
Alexandrova(IRE), an impressive winner of both the English and Irish Oaks before effortlessly landing the Yorkshire Oaks last time, did not show her best form on this drop in trip. Given a waiting ride, she was always just being niggled and became badly outpaced early in the straight. She ran on quite well again at the finish, but had too much ground to make up and never looked like getting there. Her trainer felt she ran a little lazily, but the outing will have sharpened her up well if she is to go for the Breeders' Cup Filly & Mare Turf.
Irridescence(SAF), having just her second start since landing the Group 1 Queen Elizabeth II Cup at Sha Tin much earlier in the year, ran well. Asked to make all the running, she did so at a respectable pace and was just run out of it in the last couple of furlongs. She might just prove better over slightly shorter.
Nannina, this year's Coronation Stakes winner, had her ground and was being stepped back up to ten furlongs off the back of her fourth in the Matron Stakes at the Curragh. She was below form and may well be past her best after a long and hard season. She stays in training at four, when there will be no shortage of opportunities.
Dionisia(USA), making her debut for Luca Cumani and having her first start since landing the Italian Oaks 105 days previously, started the race well and settled in second position, but she was soon completely outpaced. This was certainly not her best form.

5714a PRIX MARCEL BOUSSAC ROYAL BARRIERE DE DEAUVILLE (GROUP 1) (FILLIES) 1m

3:20 (3:25) 2-Y-0 **£118,221** (£47,297; £23,648; £11,814; £5,917)

RPR

1 **Finsceal Beo (IRE)**[12] 5466 2-8-11 KJManning 9 117
(J S Bolger, Ire) *hld up, 7th and shaken up on rail str, went 2nd and chal 1 1/2f out, led appr fnl f, sn rdn and qcknd clr, easily* **20/1**

2 *5* **Darrfonah (IRE)**[16] 5344 2-8-11 KerrinMcEvoy 10 106
(C E Brittain) *midfield, 6th straight, ridden and stayed on from 1 1/2f out, went 2nd 150 yards out* **14/1**

3 *nk* **Legerete (USA)**[24] 2-8-11 OPeslier 11 105+
(A Fabre, France) *hld up, 11th on ins str, ran on through field fr 2f out, rdn and stayed on wl fnl f, tk 3rd 150 yds out, jst missed 2nd* **3/1**[1]

4 *1* **Poltava (FR)**[20] 5257 2-8-11 DBoeuf 8 103+
(D Smaga, France) *led, shaken up 2f out, headed approaching final f, no extra* **11/2**[2]

5 *nk* **Bicoastal (USA)**[35] 4840 2-8-11 (b) LDettori 12 102
(B J Meehan) *in touch, 4th straight, ridden 2f out, disputing 2nd 1 1/2f out, kept on til no extra final 150 yards* **11/2**[2]

6 *snk* **Ikat (IRE)**[20] 5257 2-8-11 C-PLemaire 13 101
(D Sepulchre, France) *midfield, ridden and ran on 1 1/2f out on rail to no extra final 150 yards* **14/1**

7 *½* **Bal De La Rose (IRE)**[36] 2-8-11 CSoumillon 5 100
(F Rohaut, France) *towards rear, 8th straight, ridden 1 1/2f out, never in challenging position* **8/1**[3]

8 *nk* **Impetious**[15] 5394 2-8-11 NCallan 3 100
(Eamon Tyrrell, Ire) *prominent, 2nd straight, driven 2f out, weakened final f* **66/1**

9 *3* **Cumin (USA)**[35] 4840 2-8-11 MichaelHills 2 93
(B W Hills) *in touch, 6th on outside straight, ridden 1 1/2f out, soon one pace* **8/1**[3]

10 *5* **Sismix (IRE)**[20] 5257 2-8-11 SPasquier 7 81
(C Laffon-Parias, France) *never dangerous* **14/1**

11 *1 ½* **Sugar Baby Love (GER)**[30] 5007 2-8-11 WCMarwing 6 78
(Mario Hofer, Germany) *held up, never a factor* **8/1**[3]

12 *6* **Nell Gwyn (IRE)**[15] 5394 2-8-11 KFallon 1 64
(A P O'Brien, Ire) *prominent, 3rd straight, pushed along over 2f out, one pace* **25/1**

13 *5* **Princess Taise (USA)**[35] 4840 2-8-11 JoeFanning 4 52
(M Johnston) *midfield, pushed along halfway, 12th straight, never dangerous* **16/1**

1m 34.9s **Going Correction** -0.55s/f (Hard) **13** Ran SP% **125.1**
Speed ratings: 115,110,109,108,108 108,107,107,104,99 97,91,86
PARI-MUTUEL: WIN 20.20; PL 4.30, 6.20, 2.90; DF 185.90.
Owner M A Ryan **Bred** Rathbarry Stud **Trained** Coolcullen, Co Carlow

FOCUS
This year's renewal of the Prix Marcel Boussac looked a pretty ordinary one by Group 1 standards, but there was no fluke about the wide-margin win of Finsceal Beo, who set a new time record for the race and was made second favourite for the 1,000 Guineas behind Sander Camillo, whom she is now rated the equal of.

NOTEBOOK

Finsceal Beo(IRE), a winner on her debut at Leopardstown back in April, but off the track with a hairline fracture for over four months before running second off a mark of 94 in a Tralee nursery, and then running well from a poor draw in the Goffs Million at the Curragh, put up probably the most impressive victory of the meeting. Seventh into the straight, she made her run up the far rail, led a furlong out and drew clear in scintillating fashion. She is unlikely to race again this year and her main targets in 2007 will be the 1000 Guineas followed by the Irish equivalent.

Darrfonah(IRE), off the mark in a seven-furlong conditions event at Newbury on her previous start, put up a very honourable performance in second. In mid-division for much of the time, she came with a progressive run from two out and the further she went the better she looked. She will no doubt be tried over longer distances next year.

Legerete(USA), successful in a minor race over the course and distance on her previous start, put up a fine effort considering her inexperience. Second last entering the straight, she quickened well from a furlong and a half out and was really flying inside the final furlong. She is certainly a very promising filly in the making.

Poltava(FR), the winner of a Group 3 over this trip on her previous start, never runs a bad race and would have probably taken second place but for hanging left halfway up the straight. She was asked to make all and was still travelling well within herself at the entrance to the straight, but for some unknown reason she started to veer left. It was only when she was straightened inside the final furlong that she began to run on again.

Bicoastal(USA), second in the Prestige Stakes on her previous start, has been rated as having run 3lb off that effort over this extra furlong.

Cumin(USA), third in the Prestige Stakes on her previous start, was quickly into her stride and well up with the leading group, but she could not go the pace from a furlong and a half out.

Princess Taise(USA), last of ten in the Prestige Stakes on her previous start, was never going that well. In mid-division soon after the start, she was 12th into the straight and was not dangerous afterwards.

5715a PRIX JEAN-LUC LAGARDERE (GRAND CRITERIUM) (GROUP 1) (C&F) 7f

3:55 (3:58) 2-Y-O **£137,924** (£55,179; £27,590; £13,783; £6,903)

RPR

1 **Holy Roman Emperor (IRE)**[14] [5410] 2-9-0 .... KFallon 5 120+
(A P O'Brien, Ire) *held up, disputing close 6th straight, pushed along and quickened over 2f out, driven to lead 1 1/2f out, driven out* **7/4**[2]

2 2 **Battle Paint (USA)**[24] 2-9-0 .... IMendizabal 2 115
(J-C Rouget, France) *tracked leaders on rail, disp 3rd straight, pushed along 3f out, led 2 1/2f out, headed 1 1/2f out, kept on, just hld 2nd* **10/1**

3 3/4 **Vital Equine (IRE)**[22] [5183] 2-9-0 .... RichardMullen 8 113
(E J O'Neill) *prom, disp 3rd str, rdn and ev ch over 1 1/2f out, ran on under pressure final stages, just missed 2nd* **8/1**[3]

4 nk **He's A Decoy (IRE)**[12] [5466] 2-9-0 .... MJKinane 7 112
(David Wachman, Ire) *held up, last straight, ridden and ran on from 2 1/2f out, took 4th final furlong* **50/1**

5 1 1/2 **Fleeting Shadow (IRE)**[62] [4012] 2-9-0 .... PJSmullen 1 108
(D K Weld, Ire) *led, pushed along and ran on straight, ridden over 2f out, headed 2 1/2f out, no extra from over 1f out* **20/1**

6 1 1/2 **Visionario (IRE)**[28] [5048] 2-9-0 .... CSoumillon 4 104+
(A Fabre, France) *last towards outside, 8th straight, effort and ran on from over 2f out til no extra 1f out* **13/8**[1]

7 5 **Trinity College (USA)**[36] [4825] 2-9-0 .... JamieSpencer 10 91
(A P O'Brien, Ire) *midfield, 5th straight, never able to challenge* **16/1**

8 3 **Sandwaki (USA)**[42] [4644] 2-9-0 .... OPeslier 9 83
(C Laffon-Parias, France) *held up, disputing close 6th straight, ridden 2f out, unable to quicken* **25/1**

9 2 1/2 **To The Max (IRE)**[64] [3923] 2-9-0 .... C-PLemaire 6 77
(R Hannon) *raced in 2nd, weakened 2 1/2f out* **28/1**

1m 18.6s **Going Correction** -0.35s/f (Firm) **9** Ran SP% **114.6**
Speed ratings: 107,104,103,103,101 100,94,90,88
PARI-MUTUEL: WIN 2.80 (coupled with Trinity College); PL 1.90, 2.00,2.50; DF 15.90.
Owner Mrs John Magnier **Bred** Tower Bloodstock **Trained** Ballydoyle, Co Tipperary

FOCUS

The largest field in many years lined up for France's top juvenile race, but while it was quite a good renewal, it was a little short of some of the very best recent runnings. The form has been rated through the third, and the winner put in a performance more in keeping with his Phoenix Stakes win than his National Stakes defeat.

NOTEBOOK

Holy Roman Emperor(IRE), winner of both the Group 2 Railway Stakes and the Group 1 Phoenix Stakes before running second to a potential star in Teofilo in the National Stakes, provided Aidan O'Brien with his seventh winner in this race. Not hurried along early on, he was towards the tail of the field and still had some ground to make up on the entrance to the straight, but he picked up smartly when asked for his effort two out. He could well now re-oppose Teofilo in the Dewhurst Stakes.

Battle Paint(USA) ◆, the winner of his first two starts in minor company, including over course and distance on his previous start, posted a fine effort for one so inexperienced on this step up to the highest level. Never far from the lead, he took the advantage on the far rail half way up the straight but could not resist Holy Roman Emperor's challenge. The Criterium International is apparently now on the cards.

Vital Equine(IRE), the winner of his first three starts, including the Group 2 Champagne Stakes at York on his previous outing, was given every possible chance and ran very creditably. He is clearly going the right way and he may well be allowed to take his chance in the Dewhurst.

He's A Decoy(IRE), unsuited by easy ground in the Goffs Million at the Curragh on his previous start, was behind in the early part of this race as waiting tactics were employed. Under pressure early in the straight, he took fourth in the last few strides and looks as though he will appreciate a longer trip.

Fleeting Shadow(IRE), off the mark in a Galway maiden on his previous start, did not run badly, upped significantly in class.

Visionario(IRE), the winner of his first three starts, including in Listed and Group 3 company, is highly regarded but was never in a good position and made his effort widest of all. While he may simply have found this cmpany too tough, there is a good chance he is a lot better than this.

Trinity College(USA), the winner of a Cork maiden before running fourth to Teofilo in the Futurity Stakes at the Curragh, was well held upped in class.

To The Max(IRE), not seen since successful in a six-furlong Ascot newcomers' race in July, faced a stiff task and was a spent force early in the straight.

5716a PRIX DE L'ARC DE TRIOMPHE LUCIEN BARRIERE (GROUP 1) (C&F) 1m 4f

4:35 (4:34) 3-Y-0+ **£788,138** (£315,310; £157,655; £78,759; £39,448)

RPR

1 **Rail Link**[21] [5221] 3-8-11 .... SPasquier 4 129
(A Fabre, France) *midfield, 5th straight, switched out and headway 2f out, driven to lead 1f out, ran on well* **8/1**

2 nk **Pride (FR)**[21] [5219] 6-9-2 .... C-PLemaire 5 126
(A De Royer-Dupre, France) *held up in rear, last straight, headway 2f out, not clear run 1f out, switched out and finished well* **11/1**

3 1/2 **Hurricane Run (IRE)**[21] [5219] 4-9-5 .... KFallon 1 127+
(A Fabre, France) *raced in 4th, close 4th when not clear run towards inside well over 1f out, ran on final f* **5/2**[2]

4 2½ **Best Name**[15] [5400] 3-8-11 .... OPeslier 3 120+
(Robert Collet, France) *held up, 6th straight, effort on inside, not much room appr final f, ran on to take 5th cl hme: fin 5th ½l & 2l: plcd 4th* **100/1**

5 snk **Irish Wells (FR)**[35] [4861] 3-8-11 .... DBoeuf 7 120
(F Rohaut, France) *soon led, hdd 2f out, one pce : fin 6th, plcd 5th* **125/1**

6 4 **Sixties Icon**[22] [5185] 3-8-11 .... LDettori 8 114
(J Noseda) *held up, 7th straight, never a factor: fin 7th, plcd 6th* **10/1**

7 1 1/2 **Shirocco (GER)**[21] [5219] 5-9-5 .... CSoumillon 6 112
(A Fabre, France) *prominent, pressed leader halfway, 2nd straight, every ch wl over 1f out, hrd rdn and wknd over 1f out: fin 8th, plcd 7th* **11/4**[3]

D 1/2 **Deep Impact (JPN)**[98] [2911] 4-9-5 .... YTake 2 128
(Y Ikee, Japan) *with ldr early, settled disp 2nd, 3rd straight, led 2f out, sn u.p, hdd 1f out, no ex last 100 yds: fin 3rd, nk & ½l: disq* **9/4**[1]

2m 26.3s **Going Correction** -0.45s/f (Firm)
WFA 3 from 4yo+ 7lb **8** Ran SP% **116.3**
Speed ratings: 111,110,108,107,107 104,103,110
PARI-MUTUEL: WIN 24.60; PL 2.20, 2.10, 1.40; DF 53.10.
Owner K Abdulla **Bred** Juddmonte Farms Ltd **Trained** Chantilly, France

■ The time was officially recorded as 2min 31.7, but repeated hand times confirm it was 2 min 26.3, a difference of 27 lengths. Deep Impact subsequently disq (banned substance in sample)

FOCUS

The smallest field assembled for the Arc since 1941, but there was no doubting the quality. Among the eight-strong field was the 2005 hero Hurricane Run, returning to defend his crown off the back of winning the King George, Shirocco, who had been unbeaten since finishing fourth in last year's Arc, and Deep Impact, the 2005 Japanese Triple Crown winner who was backed by his countrymen as if defeat was an impossibility. Add to that Grand Prix de Saint-Cloud winner Pride, St Leger hero Sixties Icon and Prix Niel winner Rail Link and it was certainly one of the most eagerly anticipated Arc's in recent years. Predictably though, the early pace was not strong, with hat-trick seeking Group 2 winner Irish Wells not in the business of making things easier for rivals known to appreciate a strong gallop, and none of the older horses was seen to full advantage. Rail Link established himself the season's best middle-distance three-year-old, but in Arc terms it was the performance of a Bago or a Lammtarra, rather than a Peintre Celebre or a Montjeu.

NOTEBOOK

Rail Link, successful in the Group 1 Grand Prix de Paris before returning from a break to take the Prix Niel, a race that had produced the winner of the Arc no fewer than nine times in the last 12 years, continued that incredible trend. Given an excellent ride by his talented jockey, the colt did not pull during the early stages when the pace was moderate and, when switched to challenge two furlongs out, he lengthened his stride to lead at the furlong marker. He stayed on well to the finish and this beautifully bred individual still has further scope for improvement. He will not race again this season and will be campaigned in the best middle-distance races next year.

Pride(FR), tenderly handled when just behind Shirocco and Hurricane Run in the Prix Foy last time, having previously beaten last year's winner in the Grand Prix de Saint-Cloud, did not have her favoured soft ground but still acquitted herself with honour. She seemed to switch off in the early part of the race due to the lack of pace and only really began to concentrate after entering the straight, but then produced her usual late burst from a furlong and a half out and was still running on at the finish, improving significantly on her two previous efforts in the race and failing only narrowly. She goes to stud at the end of the year, but in the meantime has options in the Champion Stakes, the EP Taylor at Woodbine, the Japan Cup and the Hong Kong Vase. As a six-year-old, she has been a great advertisement for keeping fillies in training.

Hurricane Run(IRE) ◆, last year's brilliant winner, was bidding to become the first horse to land back-to-back Arc wins since Alleged 28 years previously. He was already a dual winner at the top level this season, landing the Tattersalls Gold Cup at the Curragh and the King George at Ascot, but had also been beaten twice, by Pride when below form in Grand Prix de Saint-Cloud and by Shirocco in a muddling Prix Foy on his latest start. Racing on ground that was quicker than he would ideally have liked, he found the leaders were never going fast enough for him and he was far too short of room from an early stage had Fallon wanted to move him into a more prominent position. He was still boxed in by the time they straightened up and got into the clear far too late for a horse who is at his best coming from off a strong pace, as he takes a furlong or two to hit top stride. He was unlucky and is much better than his finishing position suggests. He may now be aimed at the Champion Stakes at Newmarket and, if there is a bit of ease in the ground and they go a good gallop, it will take a very special horse to stop him gaining compensation. The Breeders' Cup Turf is another possible target.

Best Name, the fast-finishing Prix du Jockey Club second, was checked when trying for a run up the inside halfway up the straight, but for which he would have been a bit closer. He stays in training and remains capable of better. His trainer reckons ten furlongs is his best trip.

Irish Wells(FR), less than a length behind Best Name in the Prix du Jockey Club too, set just a steady pace, racing wide off the rail down the back straight.

Sixties Icon, a very easy winner of the St Leger on his previous start and supplemented into this race at a cost of 60,000euros, was bidding to become the first horse to follow up in the Arc in the same year. He ran like a horse a little over the top, though, and this was certainly not his true form. He will no doubt be given a nice rest now, before a campaign at the top level in 2007.

Shirocco(GER) was unbeaten since running fourth to Hurricane Run in this race last year, his wins including last year's Breeders' Cup Turf, this year's Coronation Cup and, most recently, a muddling Prix Foy (from Hurricane Run and Pride). He completely failed to run his race, probably largely due to the unsuitably fast ground, but he must not be dismissed if returning to the States for the Breeders' Cup.

Deep Impact(JPN), a Japanese superstar and beaten only once in his previous 11 starts, came into his first race in Europe considered by many the best middle-distance horse in the world and was backed by his travelling supporters as though defeat was out of the question, incredibly being sent off at 1-2 on the PMU. No-one wanted to take on the pacemaking roll early on, though, and when someone did it was only a very moderate gallop for the first six furlongs, and this led to the colt pulling. He moved smoothly into the lead two furlongs out but found no extra under pressure inside the final furlong. It was still great performance considering he had not been out since late June, and if this Arc had been run at a true pace he might well have gone even closer. He has now gone back to Japan and there are no immediate plans, but connections are reportedly keen on another tilt at the race, and if that materialises he might well have a different preparation.

NAKAYAMA

Sunday, October 1

OFFICIAL GOING: Firm

5717a SPRINTERS STKS (GROUP 1) 6f (T)

7:40 (12:00) 3-Y-0+ **£486,039** (£192,449; £120,900; £69,091; £46,883)

RPR

1 **Takeover Target (AUS)**[79] [3494] 7-8-13 .... JayFord 13 126
(J Janiak, Australia) *pressed leader til led over 2f out, ran on strongly* **32/10**[1]

2 2 1/2 **Meisho Bowler (JPN)**[119] 5-8-13 .... YFukunaga 4 118
(T Shirai, Japan) **196/10**

3 *nk* **Tagano Bastille (JPN)**[147] 3-8-9 .... MKatsuura 2 114
(Kaneo Ikezoe, Japan) **168/1**
4 *hd* **Silent Witness (AUS)**[147] [1527] 7-8-13 .... FCoetzee 14 117
(A S Cruz, Hong Kong) *led to over 2f out, one pace* **53/10**[2]
5 *nk* **Benbaun (IRE)**[35] [4855] 5-8-13 .... DO'Donohoe 9 116
(M J Wallace) *raced in 5th, stayed on final 2f* **271/10**
6 ½ **Cheerful Smile (JPN)**[140] 6-8-9 .... YIwata 16 110
(Y Ikee, Japan) **86/10**
7 *hd* **Les Arcs (USA)**[79] [3494] 6-8-13 .... ESaint-Martin 3 114
(T J Pitt) *raced in 7th, switched outside and ridden 2f out, stayed on at one pace* **6/1**[3]
8 *nk* **She Is Tosho (JPN)**[189] 6-8-9 .... KenichiIkezoe 5 109
(A Tsurudome, Japan) **53/10**[2]
9 *hd* **Orewa Matteruze (JPN)**[119] 6-8-13 .... YShibata 7 112
(H Otonashi, Japan) **64/10**
10 *hd* **Blue Shotgun (JPN)**[189] 7-8-13 .... YFujioka 10 111
(K Take, Japan) **43/1**
11 *nk* **Venus Line (JPN)** 5-8-9 .... NAkiyama 1 107
(N Hori, Japan) **161/10**
12 *nse* **Golden Cast (JPN)**[189] 6-8-13 .... FKomaki 6 110
(K Hashiguchi, Japan) **97/1**
13 1¼ **Symboli Escape (JPN)** 5-8-13 .... MEbina 12 107
(T Kubota, Japan) **153/10**
14 *nk* **Keeneland Swan (USA)**[189] 7-8-13 .... LInnes 8 106
(Hideyuki Mori, Japan) **137/1**
15 2½ **Tamamo Hot Play (JPN)**[189] 5-8-13 .... KWatanabe 11 98
(K Minai, Japan) **48/1**
16 1½ **Suteki Shinsukekun (USA)**[147] 3-8-9 .... HGoto 15 91
(Hideyuki Mori, Japan) **189/10**

68.10 secs
WFA 3 from 5yo+ 1lb 16 Ran SP% **125.8**
(including Y100 stake): WIN 420; PL 180, 570, 3680; DF 5920.
Owner J & B Janiak **Bred** Meringo Stud Farm **Trained** Australia

NOTEBOOK
Takeover Target(AUS) had apparently come on a ton since being beaten on his Japanese debut three weeks ago and scooted clear in the last quarter mile. He now heads for the Hong Kong Sprint at Sha Tin on December 10 with the Global Sprint Challenge already in the bag, and a US$1 million bonus up for grabs if he wins that race.
Benbaun(IRE) was never far off the pace and kept going well depite his jockey feeling that rain during the afternoon had got into the ground enough to adversely affect his chance. He will renew rivalry with the winner in Hong Kong.
Les Arcs(USA) ran creditably enough, but this was not one of his best efforts and connections will now mull over the prospect of keeping him going for Hong Kong.

5705 SAN SIRO (R-H)
Sunday, October 1

OFFICIAL GOING: Soft

5718a PREMIO FEDERICO TESIO (GROUP 3) 1m 3f
2:50 (3:05) 3-Y-0+ £29,900 (£13,383; £7,681; £3,840)

RPR
1 **Fair Nashwan**[470] [2734] 4-8-7 .... DVargiu 5 110
(B Grizzetti, Italy) *held up, last straight, headway in centre from 2f out, challenged inside final f, ran on well to lead 100yds out* **109/20**[3]
2 ½ **Groom Tesse**[35] [4861] 5-9-0 .... (b) SLandi 3 116
(L Camici, Italy) *soon led, headed 3f out, led again 2 1/2f out, ridden 1 1/2f out, caught 100yds out, ran on* **7/10**[1]
3 3 **Miles Gloriosus (USA)**[106] [2671] 3-8-5 .... LManiezzi 4 108
(R Menichetti, Italy) *mid-division, 5th straight, effort 2 1/2f out, ran on at one pace, never near leader* **18/1**
4 1¾ **Inter Mondo (GER)**[32] [4942] 3-8-5 .... IRossi 8 105
(P Rau, Germany) *held up, stayed on from 1 1/2f out to take 4th, never dangerous* **46/1**
5 *hd* **El Tango (GER)**[49] [4414] 4-8-10 .... THellier 7 104
(P Schiergen, Germany) *tracked leaders, 4th straight, ridden 2f out, unable to quicken* **11/5**[2]
6 ¾ **Simonas (IRE)**[36] [4828] 7-8-10 .... (b) EPedroza 2 103
(A Wohler, Germany) *in touch, took closer order 5f out, 3rd straight, under pressure over 2f out, soon one pace* **64/10**
7 1½ **Seamount (GER)**[350] 5-8-10 .... BClos 6 100
(W Figge, Germany) *mid-division, ridden 2 1/2f out to chase leaders, one pace* **21/1**
8 13 **El Biba D'Or (IRE)**[66] [3887] 7-8-10 .... (b) PConvertino 1 80
(P Giannotti, Italy) *prominent, 2nd straight, led 3f out to 2 1/2f out, soon weakened* **29/1**

2m 22.3s
WFA 3 from 4yo+ 6lb 8 Ran SP% **134.4**
(including one euro stakes): WIN 6.46; PL 1.64, 1.17, 2.82; DF 4.03.
Owner Scuderia Blueberry **Bred** Scuderia Blueberry S R L **Trained** Italy

5228 BELMONT PARK (L-H)
Sunday, October 1

OFFICIAL GOING: Standard

5719a JEROME BREEDERS' CUP H'CAP (GRADE 2) 1m
10:12 (10:15) 3-Y-0 £55,395 (£18,465; £9,283; £4,667; £2,769)

RPR
1 **Discreet Cat (USA)**[37] [4787] 3-8-12 .... GKGomez 2 128+
(Saeed Bin Suroor) *close up, led entering straight, soon clear, unchallenged* **1/20**[1]
2 10¼ **Valid Notebook (USA)** 3-8-2 .... JCastellano 5 98
(Patrick L Reynolds, U.S.A) **9/1**[3]
3 7½ **Nar (USA)** 3-8-1 .... CVelasquez 3 82
(N Zito, U.S.A) **53/20**[2]
4 10¼ **Quietly Go (USA)**[36] 3-8-2 .... (b) EPrado 1 62
(B Baffert, U.S.A) **221/10**
5 2½ **Noonmark (USA)**[62] 3-8-3 .... JRVelazquez 5 58
(S Blasi, U.S.A) **137/10**

1m 36.46s 5 Ran SP% **143.8**
PARI-MUTUEL (Including $2 stake): WIN 2.10; PL (1-2) 2.10, 3.10; SF 6.00.
Owner Godolphin Racing Inc **Bred** E Paul Robsham **Trained** Newmarket, Suffolk

NOTEBOOK
Discreet Cat(USA) ◆, stepped back up a furlong in trip and returned to Graded/Group company, followed up his win in a Saratoga allowance race with another effortless victory. Making just his second start in more than six months, he stretched his unbeaten record to five in a time almost four seconds quicker than the earlier juvenile maiden. Under a tight grip from Garrett Gomez, he soon pulled his way to the front and, with none of his four rivals able to get anywhere near him when it mattered, he came home alone with rider little more than a passenger. A fine effort considering he was conceding between 9lb-11lb to the rest of the field. His trainer said afterwards that he will either be aimed at the Breeders' Cup Classic or the Cigar Mile, but the Breeders' Cup Sprint also later emerged as a possible target.

5491 PONTEFRACT (L-H)
Monday, October 2

OFFICIAL GOING: Good to soft
The going was described as 'genuine soft' and as usual in such conditions they tended to race wide with the best ground in the straight on the stands' side.
Wind: fresh, half behind Weather: fine and sunny but breezy

5720 E B F SATURDAY RACING AT SANTA ROSA MAIDEN STKS 1m 2f 6y
2:10 (2:10) (Class 4) 2-Y-0 £5,181 (£1,541; £770; £384) Stalls Low

Form RPR
5232 1 **Eglevski (IRE)**[12] [5475] 2-9-3 80 .... TedDurcan 8 79
(J L Dunlop) *trckd ldr: led 1/2-way: wd st and rdn 2f out: drvn ins last and styd on wl* **11/4**[1]
33 2 ¾ **Prince Sabaah (IRE)**[12] [5475] 2-9-3 .... (t) PatDobbs 7 78
(R Hannon) *in tch: hdwy to trck ldrs 4f out: rdn along over 2f out: swtchd lft and drvn ent last: styd on wl* **15/2**[3]
2 3 *nk* **Yossi (IRE)**[19] [5293] 2-9-0 .... SaleemGolam(3) 12 77
(M H Tompkins) *stdd s and keen: in tch on outer: hdwy to trck ldrs 4f out rdn along 2f out: swtchd lft and rdn ent last: styd on wl* **4/1**[2]
052 4 2 **Alpes Maritimes**[11] [5495] 2-9-3 75 .... RobertWinston 2 74
(G Wragg) *trckd ldrs: hdwy to chse wnr 3f out: rdn to chal wl over 1f out and ev ch tl drvn and wknd wl ins last* **11/4**[1]
5 5 2½ **Bayonyx (IRE)**[11] [5495] 2-9-3 .... TomEaves 6 69
(J Howard Johnson) *hld up: n.m.r and bhd wl over 2f out: swtchd lft and gd hdwy over 1f out: styd on ins last: nrst fin* **25/1**
04 6 *hd* **New Beginning (IRE)**[26] [5114] 2-9-3 .... PaulHanagan 5 69
(Mrs S Lamyman) *midfield: hdwy and in tch 4f out: rdn along over 2f out: kpt on u.p appr last* **25/1**
606 7 1½ **Bobansheil (IRE)**[8] [5552] 2-8-12 .... TonyHamilton 4 61
(J S Wainwright) *towards rr: hdwy over 3f out: sn rdn along and kpt on same pce fr over 1f out* **200/1**
8 1½ **Shady Green (IRE)** 2-9-3 .... PaulMulrennan 9 63
(K A Ryan) *dwlt and bhd: hdwy over 3f out: edgd lft wl over 2f out: sn rdn and no imp* **40/1**
02 9 1 **Love On The Rocks**[30] [5014] 2-9-0 .... AndrewMullen(3) 1 61
(K A Ryan) *midfield: hdwy and in tch 4f out: sn rdn along and nvr a factor* **12/1**
6320 10 12 **Hair Of The Dog**[12] [5482] 2-9-3 66 .... JamieMackay 3 38
(J G Given) *led to 1/2-way: sn rdn along: wknd 3f out* **66/1**
11 16 **Atlantic Coast (IRE)** 2-9-3 .... JoeFanning 11 8
(M Johnston) *dwlt: hdwy and in tch after 4f: rdn along 4f out and sn wknd* **20/1**
0060 12 28 **Taran Tregarth**[57] [4171] 2-8-12 35 .... FergusSweeney 10 —
(A Bailey) *a rr* **200/1**

2m 19.92s (5.84) **Going Correction** +0.50s/f (Yiel) 12 Ran SP% **110.2**
Speed ratings (Par 97): 96,95,95,93,91 91,90,89,88,78 65,43
CSF £20.97 TOTE £3.70: £1.50, £2.10, £1.90; EX 21.60.
Owner Windflower Overseas Holdings Inc **Bred** Windflower Overseas Holdings Inc **Trained** Arundel, W Sussex
■ Stewards' Enquiry : Ted Durcan one-day ban: used whip with excessive frequency (Oct 13)
Pat Dobbs one-day ban: careless riding (Oct 13)

FOCUS
A fair juvenile maiden full of future middle-distance prospects. The form looks straightforward and pretty solid with the first three coming clear.

NOTEBOOK
Eglevski(IRE) relished the step up to this longer trip and gamely broke his duck at the fifth time of asking. He has not done a great deal wrong in his career to date, seems versatile as regards underfoot conditions, and has the makings of a nice middle-distance handicapper for next year. (op 9-4)
Prince Sabaah(IRE) managed to finish a little closer to the winner than had been the case at Goodwood 12 days previously and posted another sound effort. He got all of this extra distance and now qualifies for a handicap mark. (op 9-1 tchd 7-1)
Yossi(IRE), a promising second on debut at Sandown last time, ultimately paid for running a little freely early on. This was still another solid effort, however, and he was clear of the remainder at the finish. He is another who rates as a nice middle-distance handicapper in the making. (op 7-2)
Alpes Maritimes failed to build on the promise of his narrow defeat at this venue 11 days previously and simply failed to see out the longer trip as well as the principals. He is an imposing gelding and the best of him will not be seen until he fills out next year. (op 3-1 tchd 10-3 in places)
Bayonyx(IRE), behind Alpes Martines on debut at this track 11 days previously, ran better than his finishing position suggests and looked well suited by the step up to this longer trip. He will be qualified for nurseries after his next assignment and is well worth riding more positively over this trip in the future. (op 33-1)
Love On The Rocks was never really put into the race on this step up in trip and is one to become more interested in now he becomes eligible for a handicap rating. (op 11-1)

5721 SOCA WARRIORS NURSERY 6f
2:40 (2:41) (Class 5) (0-75,75) 2-Y-0 £3,886 (£1,156; £577; £288) Stalls Low

Form RPR
043 1 **Tarraburn (USA)**[31] [4987] 2-9-1 69 .... TomEaves 17 73
(J Howard Johnson) *chsd ldrs: styd on to ld ins last: hld on towards fin* **16/1**
4623 2 *nk* **Nota Liberata**[16] [5366] 2-8-9 63 .... JoeFanning 16 66
(G M Moore) *w ldrs: led over 2f out: hdd ins last: kpt on towards fin* **13/2**[3]
2400 3 1¾ **Astroangel**[13] [5461] 2-9-0 68 .... (b) RHills 2 66
(M H Tompkins) *s.i.s: hdwy on ins over 2f out: sn chsng ldrs: styd on same pce fnl f* **16/1**

4306 **4** *5* **Rue Soleil**[15] 5404 2-8-11 **65** PhillipMakin 3 48
(J R Weymes) *chsd ldrs: chal over 2f out: fdd fnl f* **33/1**
5326 **5** *1 3/4* **Emefdream**[21] 5238 2-8-8 **62** CatherineGannon 14 40
(K A Ryan) *chsd ldrs: one pce fnl 2f* **25/1**
005 **6** *1 1/2* **Le Masque**[19] 5288 2-8-11 **65** TedDurcan 15 38
(B Smart) *mid-div: hdwy on wd outside over 2f out: nvr nr ldrs* **25/1**
050 **7** *2 1/2* **Fire In Cairo (IRE)**[27] 5083 2-8-5 **59** DeanMcKeown 5 25
(P C Haslam) *prom: effrt on inner over 2f out: nvr a threat* **16/1**
315 **8** *hd* **Lucky Bee (IRE)**[9] 5528 2-9-7 **75** RobertWinston 6 40
(G A Swinbank) *in tch: effrt over 2f out: hung rt fnl f: nvr a threat* **3/1**[1]
0521 **9** *nk* **Spinning Crystal (IRE)**[14] 5419 2-8-11 **65** TonyCulhane 8 29
(B W Hills) *in tch: effrt 2f out: fdd fnl f* **7/2**[2]
4422 **10** *1* **Straight Face (IRE)**[7] 5570 2-9-7 **75** (v) PaulDoe 7 36
(W J Knight) *prom: rdn over 2f out: sn btn* **12/1**
000 **11** *nk* **Speedfit World**[26] 5105 2-8-6 **60** DavidAllan 13 20
(G G Margarson) *s.i.s: sn rdn along: nvr on terms* **11/1**
4403 **12** *nk* **Minimum Fuss (IRE)**[14] 5434 2-8-0 **61** PaulPickard(7) 1 20
(M C Chapman) *w ldrs on inner: chal over 2f out: wknd appr fnl f* **40/1**
6500 **13** *1* **Chip Leader**[29] 5041 2-8-10 **64** ow1 PatDobbs 12 20
(R Hannon) *a in rr* **50/1**
050 **14** *1 3/4* **Jenny Geddes (IRE)**[11] 5496 2-8-5 **59** PaulHanagan 9 10
(R A Fahey) *s.i.s: sn rdn along: nvr a factor* **12/1**
150 **15** *8* **Josr's Magic (IRE)**[25] 5140 2-9-0 **71** (v1) SaleemGolam(3) 11 —
(Mrs A Duffield) *led tl over 2f out: sn lost pl: eased* **16/1**
0130 **16** *5* **Movethegoalposts**[45] 4547 2-9-0 **68** (b1) RoystonFfrench 4 —
(M Johnston) *in tch: lost pl over 2f out: eased* **25/1**

1m 20.9s (3.50) **Going Correction** +0.50s/f (Yiel) **16** Ran SP% **126.7**
Speed ratings (Par 95):96,95,93,86,84 82,78,78,78,76 76,76,74,72,61 55
CSF £113.49 CT £1809.14 TOTE £17.60: £3.00, £2.00, £4.30, £5.00; EX 142.00.
Owner Transcend Bloodstock LLP **Bred** Bayer, Cantrell & Cantrell **Trained** Billy Row, Co Durham
■ Stewards' Enquiry : Robert Winston one-day ban: careless riding (Oct 13)

FOCUS
A modest nursery that was rather messy but looks fairly solid rated around the placed horses with the field finishing fairly strung out on the easy ground.

NOTEBOOK
Tarraburn(USA), making his nursery debut, showed a willing attitude under pressure and just did enough to open his account at the fourth time of asking. He is clearly suited by an easy surface and has the scope to build on this.
Nota Liberata held every chance, and stuck to his task when headed by the winner, but could not get back on top of that rival try as he might. While he may prove happier back over another furlong, he just lacks a finishing kick when it matters, and will always look vulnerable to anything progressive. He still rates a decent benchmark for the form.
Astroangel was never a serious factor after missing the break, but this still represents a big step up on her most recent effort and she does enjoy an easy surface. Further respite from the Handicapper is probably required, however.
Rue Soleil dropped out when put under maximum pressure and failed to raise her game on this drop in class. She is on danger of going the wrong way. (op 40-1)
Lucky Bee(IRE) did not look at all suited by this softer ground and found the burden of top weight all too much. She is certainly not one to write off on the back of this effort. Official explanation: jockey said filly was unsuited by the good to soft ground (op 10-3)
Spinning Crystal(IRE) was another who failed to run her race on this, the softest ground she has encountered to date. (op 9-2)
Movethegoalposts Official explanation: jockey said colt never travelled

5722 TRINIDAD & TOBAGO H'CAP 1m 4y
3:10 (3:10) (Class 3) (0-95,95) 3-Y-O
£9,348 (£2,799; £1,399; £700; £349; £175) **Stalls** Low

Form RPR
4112 **1** **Shumookh (IRE)**[33] 4923 3-8-11 **88** RHills 2 109+
(M A Jarvis) *sn led: pushed clr over 2f out: styd on strly* **7/2**[2]
1536 **2** *6* **Collateral Damage (IRE)**[16] 5357 3-8-10 **87** DavidAllan 5 93
(T D Easterby) *in tch: hdwy 2f out: rdn to chse wnr ent last: sn no imp* **8/1**
2100 **3** *3* **Jihaaz (IRE)**[10] 5512 3-8-5 **82** JoeFanning 8 82
(B W Hills) *chsd ldrs: rdn along 2f out: kpt on same pce* **12/1**
1365 **4** *4* **Electric Warrior (IRE)**[53] 4298 3-8-4 **81** oh2 PaulHanagan 10 72
(K R Burke) *in tch: hdwy 2f out: sn rdn and kpt on ins last* **33/1**
1001 **5** *2 1/2* **Supaseus**[9] 5520 3-9-3 **94** JohnEgan 6 80
(H Morrison) *keen: hld up in rr: swtchd towards outer and hdwy 3f out: pushed along over 2f out: sn rdn and kpt on fnl f* **11/8**[1]
21-3 **6** *1 1/2* **Power Politics (USA)**[25] 5143 3-9-4 **95** LDettori 9 78
(Saeed Bin Suroor) *cl up: rdn along 3f out: sn wknd: eased fnl f* **8/1**
3414 **7** *2* **Kinsya**[17] 5337 3-8-7 **84** NickyMackay 11 63
(M H Tompkins) *hld up: hdwy and in tch 1/2-way: rdn along 3f out and sn wknd* **15/2**[3]
6600 **8** *15* **Dictatrix**[25] 5143 3-8-7 **84** RoystonFfrench 7 31
(J M P Eustace) *chsd ldrs: rdn along 1/2-way: sn wknd* **33/1**
610- **9** *34* **Capricorn Run (USA)**[368] 5572 3-9-0 **91** TedDurcan 1 —
(Saeed Bin Suroor) *prom: rdn along over 3f out: sn wknd* **20/1**
0 **10** *1 1/4* **Stolen Summer (IRE)**[10] 5512 3-8-1 **81** oh1 AndrewMullen(3) 4 —
(B S Rothwell) *a bhd* **66/1**

1m 47.51s (1.81) **Going Correction** +0.50s/f (Yiel) **10** Ran SP% **118.1**
Speed ratings (Par 105):110,104,101,97,94 93,91,76,42,40
CSF £30.75 CT £315.49 TOTE £4.40: £1.90, £2.10, £3.50; EX 35.80.
Owner Hamdan Al Maktoum **Bred** Shadwell Estate Company Limited **Trained** Newmarket, Suffolk

FOCUS
A decent winning time for the type of race and the form, rated through the runner-up and third, looks fair enough for the class. The field finished fairly strung out.

NOTEBOOK
Shumookh(IRE) made amends for a disappointing effort at Leicester 33 days previously and made all for a most convincing success. He could have been called the winner before the two-furlong marker, was not fully extended to score, and clearly appreciated the easier surface. This will boost his confidence no end and he could work his way up to Listed class as a four-year-old. (op 4-1)
Collateral Damage(IRE) emerged to finish a clear second-best without being able to seriously threaten the winner at any stage. The easing of the ground was much to his liking, he is a fair benchmark for the form, and may just pick up another race on this sort of ground before the season's end. (op 7-1)
Jihaaz(IRE) showed his true colours with an improved display, enjoying the softer surface, yet appeals as the type to do even better when ridden more prominently over this trip. (op 9-1)
Electric Warrior(IRE) ran a sound race from 2lb out of the handicap and looks to have benefited from his recent break. He can find easier opportunties. (op 28-1)
Supaseus, who came good in style at Ascot nine days previously under today's rider, proved tricky and tended to run in snatches through the early stages. He was eventually keeping on all too late and, while he clearly has the talent to progress further, his attitude will rightly now come under scrutiny. (op 15-8 tchd 2-1 in places)
Power Politics(USA) had his chance, yet ultimately found the burden of top weight beyond him. This was the softest ground he would have encountered to date and he is not one to write off when reverting to a quicker surface in due course. (op 6-1)
Kinsya met support in the betting ring, and looked a player before the turn for home, yet he looked to down tools under pressure and has a little to prove after this. (op 11-1)
Capricorn Run(USA) Official explanation: jockey said colt was unsuited by the good to soft ground
Stolen Summer(IRE) Official explanation: jockey said gelding lost its action

5723 MALBERN DIRECT H'CAP 2m 1f 22y
3:40 (3:40) (Class 5) (0-75,70) 3-Y-O+ **£3,886** (£1,156; £577; £288) **Stalls** Low

Form RPR
2032 **1** **Thewhirlingdervish (IRE)**[17] 5338 8-8-13 **60** DuranFentiman(5) 6 71
(T D Easterby) *hld up: hdwy 6f out: led 1f out: styd on wl* **10/1**
3004 **2** *5* **Laggan Bay (IRE)**[7] 5564 6-9-8 **64** (b) JohnEgan 1 70
(J S Moore) *hld up in rr: hdwy to trck ldrs 10f out: led over 2f out: hung lft over 1f out: sn hdd and no ex* **6/1**[3]
4212 **3** *1 3/4* **Mister Arjay (USA)**[27] 5080 6-9-8 **69** PJMcDonald(5) 2 73
(B Ellison) *chsd ldrs: kpt on same pce fnl f* **6/1**[3]
530/ **4** *3* **Hirvine (FR)**[96] 5435 8-8-10 **52** oh7 RoystonFfrench 10 53
(D McCain Jnr) *sn chsng ldrs: outpcd 3f out: hung rt and styd on fnl f* **11/1**
4320 **5** *7* **Accordello (IRE)**[95] 3019 5-9-4 **60** TonyCulhane 3 53
(K G Reveley) *hld up in rr: hdwy 7f out: chsng ldrs and pushed along over 4f out: wknd over 1f out* **3/1**[1]
0134 **6** *1* **Great As Gold (IRE)**[137] 1808 7-9-8 **64** (p) TomEaves 7 56
(B Ellison) *prom: effrt over 3f out: wknd over 1f out* **4/1**[2]
-000 **7** *6* **Hills Of Aran**[12] 5479 4-10-0 **70** (b1) FergusSweeney 11 55
(W K Goldsworthy) *w ldrs: led over 4f out: hdd over 2f out: sn wknd* **66/1**
0110 **8** *3 1/2* **Vice Admiral**[21] 5242 3-8-11 **64** PaulMulrennan 4 45
(M W Easterby) *led after 2f: hdd over 4f out: lost pl over 1f out* **9/1**
4001 **9** *12* **Fair Spin**[34] 4914 6-8-10 **52** oh2 (p) PaulHanagan 8 20
(Micky Hammond) *hld up in rr: hdwy 6f out: sn chsng ldrs and drvn: lost pl over 1f out: eased ins last* **9/1**
00-0 **10** *29* **Jidiya (IRE)**[142] 1666 7-8-13 **55** PaulEddery 5 —
(Mrs H O Graham) *led 2f: lost pl 7f out: sn bhd: t.o 3f out* **100/1**
00-5 **11** *33* **Tioga Gold (IRE)**[34] 490 7-8-7 **52** oh22 (t) AndrewMullen(3) 9 —
(L R James) *rel to r: hdwy and in tch 8f out: lost pl over 5f out: sn bhd: t.o 3f out: virtually p.u* **200/1**

3m 58.09s (7.59) **Going Correction** +0.50s/f (Yiel)
WFA 3 from 4yo+ 11lb **11** Ran SP% **114.0**
Speed ratings (Par 103):102,99,98,97,94 93,90,89,83,69 54
CSF £66.86 CT £393.68 TOTE £9.90: £2.70, £2.00, £2.30; EX 63.40.
Owner Mrs M H Easterby **Bred** Yeomanstown Stud **Trained** Great Habton, N Yorks
■ Stewards' Enquiry : Duran Fentiman caution: careless riding

FOCUS
A modest marathon handicap and the form is quite straightforward rated around the winner and third. The winner was full value for his winning margin.

5724 BUCCOO REEF "PREMIER" CLAIMING STKS 1m 4y
4:10 (4:11) (Class 4) 3-Y-O **£6,477** (£1,927; £963; £481) **Stalls** Low

Form RPR
5613 **1** **Compromiznotension (IRE)**[18] 5312 3-8-6 74 ow1 TomEaves 4 81
(I Semple) *a.p: led wl over 1f out: sn rdn: drvn ins last and kpt on gamely* **7/1**
3226 **2** *1 1/2* **Go Figure (IRE)**[133] 1898 3-9-0 76 (t) LDettori 11 86
(B J Meehan) *hld up: gd hdwy 3f out: rdn to chal wl over 1f out and ev ch tl drvn and no ex wl ins last* **9/2**[2]
5100 **3** *5* **Conrad**[35] 4888 3-8-4 73 PaulHanagan 3 66
(R A Fahey) *chsd ldrs: rdn along 2f out: drvn and edgd lft over 1f out: sn one pce* **14/1**
-030 **4** *2* **Makfly**[27] 5079 3-9-0 77 (p) TedDurcan 1 71
(R Hollinshead) *towards rr: gd hdwy 2f out: sn rdn and kpt on ins last: nrst fin* **33/1**
0250 **5** *3/4* **Porters (USA)**[60] 4082 3-9-3 87 PatDobbs 5 73
(R Hannon) *chsd ldrs: rdn 2f out: drvn and hung lft over 1f out: sn btn* **6/1**[3]
6501 **6** *3* **King's Revenge**[15] 5406 3-9-0 76 (b) DavidAllan 14 63
(T D Easterby) *prom: effrt and ev ch over 2f out: sn rdn and wknd over 1f out* **8/1**
0142 **7** *3/4* **Munaa (IRE)**[37] 4820 3-8-2 72 ow2 SaleemGolam(3) 12 53
(K R Burke) *prom: rdn along 3f out: sn wknd* **7/1**
4000 **8** *8* **Mister Becks (IRE)**[79] 3538 3-7-11 46 PaulPickard(7) 9 35
(M C Chapman) *led: racd on own on inner rail: rdn 3f out: hdd wl over 1f out: wknd* **200/1**
-005 **9** *5* **Divisive**[47] 4489 3-7-13 52 RoystonFfrench 10 20
(G Wragg) *a towards rr* **100/1**
515 **10** *14* **Final Esteem**[47] 4478 3-8-6 69 TonyHamilton 15 —
(I Semple) *s.i.s: a rr* **40/1**
6002 **11** *1 1/4* **Pommes Frites**[16] 5384 3-8-4 73 PaulDoe 16 —
(W R Muir) *s.i.s: hdwy to chse ldrs on outer 1/2-way: rdn along over 3f out: sn drvn and wknd* **14/1**
1000 **12** *26* **Peak Seasons (IRE)**[18] 5316 3-8-4 51 (b) JTate 8 —
(M C Chapman) *chsd ldrs: lost pl 1/2-way and sn bhd* **200/1**
3051 **U** **Abbey Cat (IRE)**[10] 5512 3-8-4 81 PaulQuinn 13 —
(G A Swinbank) *chsd ldrs: rdn along over 2f out: hld whn stmbld bdly and uns rdr over 1f out* **10/3**[1]

1m 49.46s (3.76) **Going Correction** +0.50s/f (Yiel) **13** Ran SP% **112.4**
Speed ratings (Par 103):101,99,94,92,91 88,88,80,75,61 59,33,—
CSF £35.75 TOTE £5.20: £1.50, £2.20, £4.70; EX 37.70.There were no claims for the winner
Owner R Hyndman **Bred** Corduff Stud **Trained** Carluke, S Lanarks

FOCUS
A good, competitive claimer likely to produce winners, although the time was ordinary.

5725 DEM WINDOW SOLUTIONS H'CAP 1m 4f 8y
4:40 (4:40) (Class 6) (0-60,60) 3-Y-O+ **£3,238** (£963; £481; £240) **Stalls** Low

Form RPR
654 **1** **Pee Jay's Dream**[63] 3998 4-9-2 **53** PaulMulrennan 11 63
(M W Easterby) *trckd ldrs: led 4f out tl 1f out: kpt on wl to regain ld nr fin* **11/1**
4011 **2** *nk* **Sudden Impulse**[32] 4944 5-9-8 **59** SilvestreDeSousa 7 69
(A D Brown) *hld up in mid-div: hdwy 3f out: led 1f out: hdd and no ex towards fin* **6/1**
5403 **3** *2 1/2* **Acuzio**[9] 5531 5-9-6 **57** DavidAllan 12 63
(W M Brisbourne) *chsd ldrs: chal 2f out: edgd lft ins last: styd on same pce* **12/1**
5004 **4** *nk* **Selkirk Lady**[21] 5247 3-9-2 **60** TedDurcan 4 65
(W R Swinburn) *hld up in mid-field: hdwy 3f out: swtchd lft over 1f out: kpt on same pce* **11/2**[3]

0532 **5** 1/2 **Birthday Star (IRE)**[16] 5390 4-9-1 **52**.................................... JohnEgan 2 58+
(W J Musson) *hld up in rr: nt much on ins on bnd 8f out: gd hdwy 3f out: swtchd lft ins last: nt rch ldrs* **4/1**[1]

0006 **6** 3 1/2 **Padre Nostro (IRE)**[27] 5090 7-8-11 **55**.................... ChrisGlenister(7) 3 54
(J R Holt) *in rr: hdwy on ins over 3f out: one pce fnl 2f* **66/1**

6555 **7** 7 **Qualitair Wings**[7] 5579 7-9-7 **58**.................... DerekMcGaffin 17 45
(J Hetherton) *s.i.s: sme hdwy over 3f out: nvr on terms* **14/1**

0050 **8** 1/2 **Celtic Carisma**[95] 3019 4-9-2 **53**.................................... TonyCulhane 16 40
(K G Reveley) *hld up in rr: sme hewady 3f out: nvr a factor* **16/1**

5204 **9** 1 1/4 **Blue Hedges**[17] 5354 4-9-4 **55**.................................... MichaelTebbutt 9 40
(H J Collingridge) *hld up in rr: smooth hdwy on outside over 3f out: shkn up and wknd 2f out* **28/1**

4000 **10** 2 1/2 **Mr Wiseguy**[25] 5129 3-9-2 **60**.................................... PhillipMakin 14 41
(G C Bravery) *s.i.s: nvr a factor* **66/1**

0066 **11** 3/4 **Bendarshaan**[21] 5235 6-9-9 **60**....................................(b) JoeFanning 6 39
(C A Dwyer) *prom: effrt 3f out: lost pl wl over 1f out* **40/1**

-001 **12** 2 1/2 **Liberty Run (IRE)**[13] 5451 4-9-2 **56**.................... NeilChalmers(3) 5 31
(Mrs A J Hamilton-Fairley) *mid-div: effrt over 3f out: sn btn* **14/1**

0000 **13** nk **Richtee (IRE)**[13] 5445 5-9-2 **58**.................................... JamieMoriarty(5) 18 33
(R A Fahey) *chsd ldrs: lost pl 3f out* **20/1**

0022 **14** 20 **Yenaled**[16] 5385 9-9-3 **54**.................................... LDettori 15 —
(J M Bradley) *led after 2f: hdd 4f out: sn lost pl: bhd whn eased over 1f out: t.o* **5/1**[2]

006/ **15** 9 **Gagarin (FR)**[1449] 5235 6-9-4 **55**.................................... DeanMcKeown 10 —
(Miss L C Siddall) *mid-div: lost pl over 4f out: sn wl bhd: t.o 3f out* **100/1**

-020 **16** 21 **Newcorp Lad**[19] 5285 6-9-2 **53**....................................(p) PaulHanagan 13 —
(Mrs G S Rees) *mid-div: drvn 4f out: sn wknd: t.o 2f out: virtually p.u* **28/1**

0555 **17** 3 **Shamsalmaidan (IRE)**[3] 5651 3-8-12 **59**.................... SaleemGolam(3) 8 —
(C E Brittain) *led 2f: lost pl 4f out: t.o 2f out: virtually p.u* **40/1**

2m 48.0s (7.70) **Going Correction** +0.50s/f (Yiel)
WFA 3 from 4yo+ 7lb **17 Ran SP% 122.1**
Speed ratings (Par 101):94,93,92,91,91 89,84,84,83,81 81,79,79,66,60 46,44
CSF £70.52 CT £825.82 TOTE £16.90: £2.80, £2.20, £2.50, £1.80; EX 135.10.
Owner P Bown & R Edmonds **Bred** Downfield Cottage Stud **Trained** Sheriff Hutton, N Yorks

FOCUS
A moderate winning time for the grade but the form looks fairly sound on paper.
Blue Hedges Official explanation: jockey said colt had no more to give
Yenaled Official explanation: jockey said gelding ran too free

5726 CARONI MAIDEN STKS (DIV I) 1m 4y
5:10 (5:11) (Class 5) 3-Y-O **£3,238** (£963; £481; £240) **Stalls** Low

Form RPR

6-22 **1** **Woolly Bully**[156] 1291 3-9-3 69.................................... LDettori 4 71+
(G A Huffer) *hld up: hdwy to trck ldrs 1/2-way: rdn to ld ent last: sn clr and eased* **15/8**[2]

3 **2** 2 1/2 **Avoriaz (IRE)**[27] 5086 3-9-3 92.................................... NickyMackay 7 63
(L M Cumani) *hld up towards rr: hdwy on outer over 3f out: chsd ldrs 2f out: rdn over 1f out: tk 2nd wl ins last: no ch w wnr* **4/5**[1]

5625 **3** 2 **Coronation Flight**[21] 5244 3-8-12 45.................... DeanMcKeown 1 54
(F P Murtagh) *racd on inner rail: prom: rdn along 2f out: kpt on same pce ent last* **50/1**

3 **4** 2 1/2 **Cross Of Lorraine (IRE)**[7] 5583 3-9-3 ....(b) TomEaves 3 54
(I Semple) *cl up: rdn to ld 2f out: drvn and hdd ent last: grad wknd* **33/1**

3046 **5** 6 **Silver Sail**[7] 5583 3-8-12 40....................................(p) PaulHanagan 10 36
(J S Wainwright) *chsd ldrs: rdn along 3f out: sn outpcd* **66/1**

06 **6** 3 **Boppys Dancer**[21] 5244 3-8-12 .... JamieMoriarty(5) 8 35
(P T Midgley) *chsd ldrs: pushed along 1/2-way: sn rdn and wknd* **200/1**

0400 **7** nk **Shangazi (USA)**[38] 4759 3-8-12 63.................................... TonyCulhane 9 29
(B W Hills) *led: rdn along 3f out: hdd 2f out and sn wknd* **18/1**

0 **8** 10 **Sheriff Star**[16] 5368 3-8-5 .... DanielleMcCreery(7) 5 8
(N Tinkler) *s.i.s: a bhd* **200/1**

205 **9** 3/4 **Vampyrus**[37] 4806 3-9-3 70.................................... FergusSweeney 6 12
(H Candy) *a rr* **11/1**[3]

10 5 **Dodaa (USA)** 3-9-3 .... TonyHamilton 2 —
(N Wilson) *chsd ldrs: rdn along over 3f out: sn wknd* **100/1**

1m 49.63s (3.93) **Going Correction** +0.50s/f (Yiel) **10 Ran SP% 112.3**
Speed ratings (Par 101):100,97,95,93,87 84,83,73,72,67
CSF £3.48 TOTE £3.30: £1.10, £1.10, £5.10; EX 4.90.
Owner Six Star Racing **Bred** Kirtlington Stud Ltd **Trained** Newmarket, Suffolk

FOCUS
Modest maiden form.
Vampyrus Official explanation: jockey said gelding had no more to give

5727 CARONI MAIDEN STKS (DIV II) 1m 4y
5:40 (5:40) (Class 5) 3-Y-O **£3,238** (£963; £481; £240) **Stalls** Low

Form RPR

4-00 **1** **Amwaal (USA)**[10] 5504 3-9-3 75.................................... RHills 2 76
(J L Dunlop) *chsd ldrs: led over 2f out: drvn clr appr fnl f: eased towards fin* **11/4**[2]

3 **2** 7 **Cooperstown**[43] 4635 3-9-3 .... TomEaves 9 61
(J Howard Johnson) *s.i.s: sn in tch: effrt 3f out: styd on to go 2nd ins last: no ch w wnr* **6/4**[1]

2335 **3** 1 **Bollin Dolly**[19] 5284 3-8-12 69.................................... DavidAllan 5 54
(T D Easterby) *racd wd: chsd ldr: led over 3f out: hdd over 2f out: hung rt: kpt on same pce* **11/2**[3]

5000 **4** 6 **Laheen (IRE)**[129] 1997 3-8-12 51.................................... NickyMackay 8 42
(M H Tompkins) *s.i.s: sn pushed along: hdwy over 2f out: snatched modest 4th on line* **33/1**

004 **5** shd **Samarinda (USA)**[93] 3100 3-9-3 67.................................... TonyCulhane 1 46
(Mrs P Sly) *hld up in rr: hdwy 4f out: sn chsng ldrs: wknd appr fnl f* **15/2**

03 **6** 5 **Bella Marie**[21] 5241 3-8-12 .... PaulMulrennan 4 31
(L R James) *in rr: sme hdwy 3f out: nvr a factor* **50/1**

7 6 **Miss Provence** 3-8-12 .... RobertWinston 10 18
(G Wragg) *mid-div: hdwy on outside over 4f out: rdn and wknd over 2f out* **8/1**

4 **8** 6 **Dandys Hurricane**[7] 5583 3-8-12 .... HMuya(5) 7 11
(D Nicholls) *hld up in rr: bhd fnl 3f* **33/1**

0030 **9** 14 **Millbrook Star (IRE)**[9] 5244 3-9-3 45....................................(b) JTate 3 —
(M C Chapman) *set str pce: hdd over 3f out: lost pl over 2f out: sn bhd* **100/1**

00 **10** 29 **Bond Silver Strand (IRE)**[6] 5598 3-8-12 .... PaulHanagan 6 —
(P D Niven) *bhd: t.o 2f out* **100/1**

1m 49.61s (3.91) **Going Correction** +0.50s/f (Yiel) **10 Ran SP% 114.8**
Speed ratings (Par 101):100,93,92,86,85 80,74,68,54,25
CSF £6.97 TOTE £3.80: £1.80, £1.30, £1.50; EX 10.40 Place 6 £296.96, Place 5 £186.50.

Owner Hamdan Al Maktoum **Bred** Shadwell Farm LLC **Trained** Arundel, W Sussex

FOCUS
A modest maiden that was probably the weaker of the two divisions and the form is not straightforward.
T/Jkpt: Not won. T/Plt: £398.30 to a £1 stake. Pool: £67,548.50. 123.80 winning tickets. T/Qpdt: £34.30 to a £1 stake. Pool: £3,540.00. 76.35 winning tickets. JR

4815 WINDSOR (R-H)
Monday, October 2

OFFICIAL GOING: Good to soft (good in places) changing to soft after race 2 (3.00)
Wind: almost nil

5728 BISHOP METAL RECYCLING MAIDEN STKS (DIV I) 6f
2:30 (2:32) (Class 5) 3-Y-O+ **£2,590** (£770; £385; £192) **Stalls** High

Form RPR

000 **1** **North Fleet**[40] 4690 3-9-3 50.................................... SteveDrowne 4 63
(J M Bradley) *uns rdr and bolted bef s: mde virtually all: hrd pressed fnl 2f: styd on wl* **16/1**

2 1 **La Colline (GER)** 3-8-12 .... EddieAhern 3 55
(W J Haggas) *s.s: sn trckd ldrs: effrt to join wnr 2f out: kpt on fnl f but hld last 100yds* **8/1**

02 **3** 2 1/2 **Summer Celebrity (IRE)**[20] 5272 3-8-12 .... AntonyProcter 10 48
(D R C Elsworth) *dwlt: hld up but sn in tch: effrt 2f out: rdn to chse ldng pair over 1f out: kpt on but no imp* **9/4**[1]

6535 **4** 1 1/2 **Danawi (IRE)**[37] 4799 3-9-3 60.................................... RichardHughes 14 48
(R Hannon) *in tch in midfield: outpcd wl over 1f out: kpt on same pce u.p* **7/2**[2]

240 **5** 1 1/4 **Cordelia**[28] 5055 3-8-12 63.................................... RyanMoore 8 39
(B W Hills) *squeezed out s and sn in last pair: prog over 2f out: hanging over 1f out: one pce fnl f* **4/1**[3]

500 **6** 2 1/2 **Hello Deauville (FR)**[37] 4814 3-8-12 40.................... DaneO'Neill 1 32
(J Akehurst) *w wnr to 2f out: grad wknd* **33/1**

7 shd **Palmistry** 3-9-3 .... LPKeniry 9 36
(A M Balding) *dwlt: sn rcvrd to trck ldrs: shkn up and rn green 2f out: stmbld over 1f out: no ch after* **6/1**

8 3 **Champion's Way (IRE)** 4-9-4 .... JimCrowley 5 27
(B R Millman) *dwlt: in tch in midfield tl wknd u.p fr 2f out* **16/1**

6660 **9** 2 1/2 **Silvanella (IRE)**[108] 2602 3-8-5 45.................... BenjaminWishart(7) 12 15
(M S Saunders) *prom: chsng ldng pair wl over 1f out: sn rdn and hanging bdly: wknd rapidly* **40/1**

6000 **10** 5 **Tantien**[79] 3541 4-8-8 35.................... StephanieHollinshead(5) 11 —
(T Keddy) *wnt lft s and bmpd: wl in rr: nt clr run wl over 2f out: no ch* **66/1**

0030 **11** 1/2 **Marvin Gardens**[20] 5273 3-9-3 40.................................... BrianReilly 13 3
(P S McEntee) *rrd s: nvr on terms: brief effrt on outer 2f out: sn wknd* **33/1**

000 **12** 2 1/2 **Stokesies Luck (IRE)**[50] 4401 3-9-3 45....................(p) RichardThomas 7 —
(J L Spearing) *wnt bdly rt s: w ldrs to 1/2-way: wknd rapidly* **50/1**

-400 **13** 15 **Sunny Haze**[20] 5272 3-8-7 35.................................... TravisBlock(5) 6 —
(Mrs P N Dutfield) *w ldrs to 1/2-way: wknd rapidly: t.o* **66/1**

1m 13.9s (0.23) **Going Correction** +0.15s/f (Good)
WFA 3 from 4yo 1lb **13 Ran SP% 123.4**
Speed ratings (Par 103):104,102,99,97,95 92,92,88,84,78 77,74,54
CSF £137.63 TOTE £25.00: £7.80, £3.60, £1.10; EX 348.10 TRIFECTA Not won..
Owner G & L Johnson **Bred** Miss T Armstrong **Trained** Sedbury, Gloucs

FOCUS
The winning time was 1.79 seconds faster than the second division, but the runners in this race probably had the best of the ground. This looked a very ordinary maiden with the winner rated just 50 and also a messy start, caused by Stokesies Luck diving right from stall 7 and colliding with Tantien, who swerved left from stall 11 and the incident did few favours to the trio drawn between the pair. As it usually the case when there is a bit of cut in the ground here, the runners made for the far side of the track.
Cordelia Official explanation: jockey said filly suffered interference shortly after start

5729 BISHOP METAL RECYCLING MAIDEN STKS (DIV II) 6f
3:00 (3:03) (Class 5) 3-Y-O+ **£2,590** (£770; £385; £192) **Stalls** High

Form RPR

6420 **1** **Goodwood March**[12] 5480 3-8-12 58.................................... IanMongan 8 55
(J L Dunlop) *dwlt: hld up towards rr: prog against far side rail to ld 2f out: sn clr: styd on wl* **8/1**[3]

000 **2** 2 **Milton's Keen**[33] 4927 3-9-3 55.................................... BrianReilly 3 54
(P S McEntee) *w ldr: led 4f out to 2f out: no ch w wnr after* **25/1**

0 **3** nk **Efisio Princess**[27] 5093 3-8-12 .... RichardThomas 11 48
(J E Long) *bmpd s: towards rr: rdn over 2f out: prog on outer over 1f out: styd on: nrst fin* **66/1**

/223 **4** 2 1/2 **Small Stakes (IRE)**[16] 5378 4-9-4 65....................................(t) RyanMoore 4 46
(P J Makin) *hld up in midfield: effrt 2f out: sn rdn and no rspnse: btn after* **8/15**[1]

0365 **5** 1 1/4 **Girandola**[30] 5023 3-9-3 55.................................... DaneO'Neill 6 42
(R F Johnson Houghton) *dwlt: wl in rr: shkn up 2f out: plugged on same pce: n.d* **12/1**

000 **6** hd **Batchworth Blaise**[7] 5571 3-9-3 ....(b) PaulFitzsimons 2 41
(E A Wheeler) *pressed ldrs tl wknd over 1f out* **100/1**

2230 **7** 1 **Knead The Dough**[7] 5569 5-9-1 55.................... MarcHalford(3) 10 38
(A E Price) *pressed ldrs: rdn 2f out: wknd jst over 1f out* **14/1**

-000 **8** 2 1/2 **Millsy**[46] 4507 4-8-13 49.................................... LPKeniry 9 26
(J L Spearing) *led for 2f: styd prom tl wknd over 1f out* **33/1**

05 **9** 7 **Dhurwah (IRE)**[32] 4948 3-8-12 .... SteveDrowne 7 5
(T Keddy) *chsd ldrs: rdn over 2f out: sn wknd* **20/1**

0063 **10** 2 **Jessica Wigmo**[28] 5055 3-8-5 50.................... MarkCoumbe(7) 13 —
(A W Carroll) *bmpd s: racd alone nr side and sn wl off the pce: hung lft towards far side fnl 2f* **33/1**

26 **11** 13 **Jodrell Bank (IRE)**[37] 4799 3-8-12 60.................... KerrinMcEvoy 12 —
(W Jarvis) *wnt rt and bmpd twice s: a in rr: wknd over 2f out: t.o* **15/2**[2]

0 **12** 6 **Votive Daniel (IRE)**[28] 5055 3-9-3 .... AntonyProcter 1 —
(Simon Earle) *dwlt: a in rr: wknd over 2f out: t.o* **100/1**

0 **13** 30 **Tatillius (IRE)**[28] 5055 3-9-3 .... KDarley 5 —
(J M Bradley) *w ldrs for 2f: wknd rapidly and sn wl t.o* **25/1**

1m 15.69s (2.02) **Going Correction** +0.275s/f (Good)
WFA 3 from 4yo+ 1lb **13 Ran SP% 124.3**
Speed ratings (Par 103):97,94,93,90,88 88,87,84,74,72 54,46,6
CSF £195.16 TOTE £8.50: £1.60, £7.70, £19.40; EX 415.30 TRIFECTA Not won..

Owner Goodwood Racehorse Owners Group (Eleven) **Bred** Bricklow Ltd **Trained** Arundel, W Sussex

FOCUS

Another relatively weak maiden rated around the runner-up, and the winning time was 1.79 seconds slower than the first division, though the ground had probably deteriorated in the meantime. All but one of the runners raced towards the far side of the track.

Jodrell Bank(IRE) Official explanation: jockey said filly was unsuited by the soft ground

Tatillius(IRE) Official explanation: jockey said gelding lost its action

5730 EUROPEAN BREEDERS FUND MAIDEN STKS — 1m 67y

3:30 (3:32) (Class 5) 2-Y-O £4,533 (£1,348; £674; £336) Stalls High

Form / RPR

5 **1** **Ajaan**[27] 5088 2-9-3 EddieAhern 13 — 76
(H R A Cecil) *settled in midfield: plenty to do 3f out: stdy prog after: rdn to ld jst over 1f out: edgd lft but styd on wl* **4/1**[2]

55 **2** 1 1/4 **Vanquisher (IRE)**[13] 5460 2-9-3 KerrinMcEvoy 1 — 73
(W J Haggas) *trckd ldrs: shkn up and outpcd 2f out: styd on wl again ins fnl f to take 2nd nr fin* **4/1**[2]

06 **3** 1/2 **Mystery River (USA)**[32] 4964 2-8-12 IanMongan 2 — 67
(B J Meehan) *led: grabbed far side rail in st: hdd over 2f out: rallied and upsides over 1f out: pressed wnr tl no ex last 100yds* **8/1**

52 **4** 5 **Benny The Bat**[26] 5105 2-9-3 SteveDrowne 11 — 61
(H Morrison) *unruly in stalls: trckd ldng pair: led over 2f out to jst over 1f out : wknd* **3/1**[1]

00 **5** 1/2 **Professor Twinkle**[19] 5293 2-9-3 DaneO'Neill 8 — 60
(W J Knight) *t.k.h early: hld up in midfield: outpcd 3f out: shuffled along and kpt on steadily* **16/1**

0 **6** 1 **Windbeneathmywings (IRE)**[14] 5425 2-8-12 RichardHughes 4 — 53
(J W Hills) *trckd ldr to over 2f out: wknd over 1f out* **20/1**

7 1/2 **Veracity** 2-9-3 PhilipRobinson 5 — 57
(M A Jarvis) *settled in midfield: outpcd 3f out: n.d after: plugged on* **8/1**

0 **8** 3 **Find Me (USA)**[9] 5537 2-9-3 KDarley 12 — 50
(M Johnston) *mostly in last trio: pushed along 4f out: sme prog 2f out: no hdwy fnl f* **6/1**[3]

0 **9** 3/4 **Fighting Mood**[13] 5460 2-9-3 FJohansson 3 — 48
(A M Balding) *pushed up to press ldrs: wknd over 2f out* **33/1**

00 **10** 5 **Dawson Creek (IRE)**[68] 3843 2-9-3 LPKeniry 9 — 37
(B Gubby) *lost pl after 2f: n.m.r bnd over 5f out: struggling 4f out* **50/1**

4042 **11** 2 **Straw Boy**[27] 5084 2-9-0 56 EdwardCreighton(3) 10 — 33
(R Brotherton) *dwlt: hld up in last trio: sme prog over 3f out: wknd 2f out* **16/1**

5350 **12** 16 **Tumble Jill (IRE)**[17] 5344 2-8-9 52 MarcHalford(3) 14 — —
(J J Bridger) *a in last trio: wknd over 3f out: t.o* **33/1**

1m 50.03s (4.43) **Going Correction** +0.475s/f (Yiel) 12 Ran SP% **125.9**

Speed ratings (Par 95):96,94,94,89,88 87,87,84,83,78 76,60

CSF £21.11 TOTE £5.40: £1.90, £1.90, £2.50; EX 21.30 Trifecta £89.30 Part won. Pool £125.80 - 0.54 winning units..

Owner Niarchos Family **Bred** Miss K Rausing And Course Investment Limited **Trained** Newmarket, Suffolk

FOCUS

An ordinary juvenile maiden in which the front three eventually pulled clear of the rest and the form, rated around the placed horses, could be better than rated. Once again the whole field came up the far side in the straight.

NOTEBOOK

Ajaan ◆, all the better for his debut effort, needed every yard of this longer trip to get on top of his rivals, just as his breeding suggested he might. The form is probably nothing special, but he is likely to make an even better three-year-old and should continue to improve as she goes up in trip. (op 5-1)

Vanquisher(IRE) ◆, like the winner, appreciated the greater test of stamina created by the softening ground and may have finished even closer had he not run out of room when the winner edged across him entering the last furlong. He now qualifies for a mark and certainly has a race in him. (op 5-1)

Mystery River(USA) set the pace and managed to get the position next to the far rail once in line for home. Although she was unable to hold on to the advantage, she kept on battling right to the line and has more options now that she can be handicapped. (op 15-2)

Benny The Bat was never far away and held every chance, but appeared to get very tired inside the last furlong in the conditions. His behaviour at the start gives him a possible excuse for this effort, but he did carry his head rather high in the closing stages, which is more of a worry. (tchd 7-2 and 4-1 in a place)

Professor Twinkle ◆ was staying on late without being given a hard time and is one to watch out for now that he can be handicapped. There is plenty of stamina on the dam's side of his pedigree and he shaped here as though he will appreciate further. (op 20-1)

Windbeneathmywings(IRE) ran better than on her debut, but did not appear to see out the trip in the conditions.

5731 PETER AND CORAL'S 25TH WEDDING ANNIVERSARY NURSERY — 5f 10y

4:00 (4:01) (Class 4) (0-95,89) 2-Y-O £5,181 (£1,541; £770; £384) Stalls High

Form / RPR

021 **1** **Oldjoesaid**[24] 5147 2-9-2 84 DaneO'Neill 9 — 95+
(H Candy) *w ldr: led 2f out: rdn clr jst over 1f out: in n.d after* **5/2**[2]

6334 **2** 3 1/2 **Fairfield Princess**[22] 5207 2-8-8 81 TravisBlock(5) 6 — 78+
(N A Callaghan) *trckd ldrs: rdn to chse wnr over 1f out: no imp: eased whn btn last 75yds* **11/1**

6651 **3** 1 1/4 **Reebal**[34] 4910 2-9-7 89 (b) RyanMoore 5 — 79
(B J Meehan) *pressed ldrs: rdn and nt qckn over 2f out: lost pl: kpt on again to take 3rd ins fnl f* **6/1**[3]

4105 **4** 2 1/2 **Dolly Coughdrop (IRE)**[15] 5404 2-8-7 75 LPKeniry 8 — 56
(K R Burke) *chsd ldrs: u.p 2f out: sn outpcd and btn* **16/1**

1 **5** 3/4 **Tobermory (IRE)**[17] 5348 2-9-7 89 PhilipRobinson 2 — 67
(M A Jarvis) *led to 2f out: wknd jst over 1f out* **9/4**[1]

5450 **6** 1/2 **Queen Of Narnia**[2] 5668 2-8-1 72 EdwardCreighton(3) 1 — 48
(M R Channon) *dwlt: hld up in last pair: hrd rdn 2f out: brief effrt over 1f out: sn wknd* **20/1**

4260 **7** 2 **Lord Charles**[104] 2724 2-9-2 87 AmirQuinn(3) 7 — 56
(W G M Turner) *hld up: racd away fr rest of field in centre: no prog wl over 1f out: sn wknd* **14/1**

2421 **8** 3 **Cosmopolitan Lady**[21] 5234 2-8-7 82 LukeMorris(7) 4 — 40+
(D M Simcock) *awkward s: hld up in last pair: hrd rdn and floundering whn bmpd over 1f out: wknd* **13/2**

62.21 secs (1.11) **Going Correction** +0.275s/f (Good) 8 Ran SP% **112.6**

Speed ratings (Par 97):102,96,94,90,89 88,85,80

CSF £28.86 CT £148.38 TOTE £2.90: £1.10, £3.50, £2.40; EX 31.10 Trifecta £185.50 Pool £355.33 - 1.36 winning units.

Owner J J Byrne **Bred** Mrs R D Peacock **Trained** Kingston Warren, Oxon

FOCUS

A fair winning time for the type of race given the conditions. This looked a decent nursery and the form looks strong and very solid. Again most of the field went straight over to the far side soon after the start.

NOTEBOOK

Oldjoesaid, making his nursery debut, was always up with the pace and, with the easy ground bringing his stamina into play, he forged right away from his rivals in the last furlong. Under the right conditions the hat-trick looks a distinct possibility. (op 10-3 tchd 2-1)

Fairfield Princess, encountering her softest surface to date, did not appear to be inconvenienced by it and just ran into a more progressive rival on the day. Her consistency should mean she will find another race, and as she is already a winner on sand she could be kept on the go for some time yet. (op 10-1 tchd 12-1)

Reebal, making his nursery debut, could not gain the early lead this time but still emerged with credit under joint top weight. (op 8-1)

Dolly Coughdrop(IRE), who has plenty of experience and likes testing ground, has shown her best form over an extra furlong but still looks a few pounds too high in the weights. (op 20-1)

Tobermory(IRE) was making her nursery debut after winning her only previous start and the Handicapper appeared not to have taken any chances. Quickly bagging the favoured far rail in front, she failed to get home and the easier ground was probably not in her favour. (op 11-8)

Queen Of Narnia never got involved and looks totally exposed now.

Lord Charles raced wide of his rivals more towards the centre of the track and it did not do him any favours.

Cosmopolitan Lady, raised 5lb for his Folkestone victory, never got into the race and seemed to be found out by this sticky ground. Official explanation: jockey said filly was unsuited by the soft ground (op 15-2)

5732 GOLDRING SECURITY H'CAP — 1m 3f 135y

4:30 (4:30) (Class 4) (0-85,85) 3-Y-O £6,477 (£1,927; £963; £481) Stalls Low

Form / RPR

1 **1** **Counterpunch**[22] 5203 3-9-4 85 KerrinMcEvoy 4 — 106+
(Saeed Bin Suroor) *s.i.s: hld up in last pair: stdy prog 4f out: shkn up to ld wl over 1f out: drew clr fnl f* **9/2**[3]

3132 **2** 5 **Wannabe Posh (IRE)**[12] 5479 3-9-3 84 EddieAhern 3 — 91
(J L Dunlop) *hld up in rr: pushed along and prog over 3f out: rdn and hung lft over 2f out: chsd wnr jst over 1f out: no imp* **11/4**[1]

2042 **3** 2 **Conservation (FR)**[44] 4586 3-8-6 73 PhilipRobinson 10 — 77
(P W Chapple-Hyam) *led at decent pce: rdn and hdd wl over 1f out: one pce after* **9/2**[3]

0510 **4** 1 3/4 **Villa Sonata**[12] 5478 3-8-7 74 SteveDrowne 8 — 76
(J R Fanshawe) *trckd ldng pair: effrt 3f out: cl up 2f out: sn outpcd and btn* **14/1**

2132 **5** 12 **My Petra**[14] 5421 3-8-13 80 DaneO'Neill 6 — 65
(A King) *chsd ldr: pushed along over 3f out: wknd over 2f out* **4/1**[2]

400 **6** 13 **Psychic Star**[17] 5346 3-8-11 78 IanMongan 5 — 45
(W R Swinburn) *chsd ldrs: rdn over 4f out: wknd 3f out: t.o* **14/1**

1-00 **7** 3 1/2 **It's A Dream (FR)**[10] 5511 3-9-1 82 LPKeniry 2 — 44
(D R C Elsworth) *t.k.h early: trckd ldrs: stl wl in tch 3f out: sn wknd rapidly: eased: t.o* **9/1**

-005 **8** 2 1/2 **Astrobella**[12] 5478 3-8-11 78 KDarley 7 — 36
(M H Tompkins) *in tch in midfield: rdn 5f out: hung lft and wknd over 3f out: t.o* **16/1**

6434 **9** 1 1/2 **Zilcash**[56] 4206 3-8-4 71 oh1 DavidKinsella 1 — 27
(A King) *hld up in last pair: rdn 1/2-way: sn wknd: t.o over 3f out* **20/1**

2m 34.11s (4.01) **Going Correction** +0.475s/f (Yiel) 9 Ran SP% **117.0**

Speed ratings (Par 103):105,101,100,99,91 82,80,78,77

CSF £17.55 CT £59.08 TOTE £4.30: £2.10, £1.20, £2.10; EX 13.60 Trifecta £68.60 Pool £546.60 - 5.65 winning units.

Owner Godolphin **Bred** Darley **Trained** Newmarket, Suffolk

FOCUS

This looked a decent handicap beforehand, but few of them were seen at their best and they finished well strung out. The third sets the standard.

It's A Dream(FR) Official explanation: jockey said colt had no more to give

Zilcash Official explanation: jockey said gelding had no more to give

5733 AT THE RACES (S) STKS — 1m 2f 7y

5:00 (5:00) (Class 5) 3-Y-O £3,238 (£963; £481; £240) Stalls Low

Form / RPR

0000 **1** **Helen Wood**[14] 5432 3-8-2 40 FrankiePickard(7) 14 — 65
(M D I Usher) *dwlt: hld up in last pair: gd prog fr 4f out: led over 2f out: shkn up and steadily drew clr* **66/1**

4636 **2** 7 **Kalatime (IRE)**[16] 5388 3-8-9 62 SteveDrowne 7 — 53
(A M Balding) *trckd ldrs: effrt to chal wl over 2f out: sn nt qckn and outpcd by wnr: vain pursuit after* **7/4**[1]

0403 **3** 8 **Lady Duxyana**[14] 5432 3-8-9 40 (v) RichardSmith 6 — 40
(M D I Usher) *hld up in midfield: prog to chse ldrs over 3f out: sn outpcd by ldng pair: plugged on* **25/1**

-000 **4** 2 **Earl Kraul (IRE)**[14] 5432 3-9-0 60 (b[1]) RyanMoore 10 — 41
(G L Moore) *prom: chsd ldr over 4f out to 3f out: sn wl btn* **10/1**

0022 **5** 5 **Tiptoeing**[19] 5298 3-8-9 45 (b) KDarley 15 — 28
(M H Tompkins) *led after 3f and maintained str pce: clr 4f out: hdd & wknd over 2f out* **9/2**[2]

340 **6** 1 1/2 **In Hope**[21] 5248 3-8-6 45 MarcHalford(3) 9 — 25
(D K Ivory) *nvr beyond midfield: lost tch w ldrs 4f out: hrd rdn and effrt over 3f ot: no ch* **20/1**

4400 **7** 3/4 **Chookie Windsor**[27] 5097 3-9-6 47 (v) JimCrowley 8 — 35
(R M Stronge) *hld up wl in rr and racd wd: lost tch w ldrs 4f out: hrd rdn and brief effrt over 3f out: no ch* **16/1**

0000 **8** 3 1/2 **Flying Penne**[20] 5259 3-8-9 45 DaneO'Neill 13 — 18
(R Curtis) *hld up wl in rr: nvr a factor: u.p in brief effrt over 3f out* **33/1**

0300 **9** 1 1/4 **Dream Forest (IRE)**[16] 5386 3-8-7 57 JamesMillman(7) 11 — 21
(Mrs P N Dutfield) *hld up wl in rr: struggling and wl bhd over 4f out: no ch* **9/1**

-000 **10** 10 **Hahns Peak**[107] 2644 3-8-11 45 AmirQuinn(3) 12 — 4
(Mrs A L M King) *t.k.h early: hld up in last pair: wl bhd 4f out: t.o* **33/1**

6000 **11** 10 **Lady Becks (IRE)**[100] 2877 3-8-2 47 (p) LukeMorris(7) 3 — —
(C Roberts) *dwlt: hld up wl in rr: lost tch over 4f out: t.o* **66/1**

3-00 **12** 18 **Bathwick Rox (IRE)**[35] 4871 3-9-0 56 (b) KerrinMcEvoy 4 — —
(P D Evans) *led for 3f: chsd ldr to over 4f out: wknd rapidly: t.o* **7/1**[3]

02 **13** 42 **Constables Art**[13] 5441 3-8-9 (b) TravisBlock(5) 1 — —
(N A Callaghan) *t.k.h early: prom 4f: sn rdn and struggling: t.o* **5/1**

0000 **14** 19 **Bertie Bear**[14] 5432 3-9-0 40 (v) EddieAhern 2 — —
(G G Margarson) *chsd ldrs tl wknd 5f out: t.o* **25/1**

2m 14.97s (6.67) **Going Correction** +0.475s/f (Yiel) 14 Ran SP% **124.5**

Speed ratings (Par 101):92,86,80,78,74 73,72,69,68,60 52,38,4,—

CSF £179.71 TOTE £98.60: £13.60, £1.60, £5.70; EX 291.10 TRIFECTA Not won..The winner was sold to Martin Pipe for 12,000gns. Kalatime was claimed by R C Tozer for £6,000

Owner Ron Goddard and Partners **Bred** Mrs J A Gawthorpe **Trained** Upper Lambourn, Berks

FOCUS

A weak seller in which they finished well strung out in a moderate time and not a race to dwell on.

Tiptoeing Official explanation: vet said filly was struck into on near fore-leg

Dream Forest(IRE) Official explanation: jockey said gelding never travelled

Hahns Peak Official explanation: jockey said gelding was hampered on bend

Bathwick Rox(IRE) Official explanation: jockey said gelding had no more to give final half of race

5734 ROYAL WINDSOR FIREWORKS EXTRAVAGANZA 28TH OCTOBER H'CAP — 1m 67y

5:30 (5:30) (Class 5) (0-70,70) 3-Y-0+ **£3,238** (£963; £481; £240) **Stalls** High

Form RPR

0500 **1** **Parnassian**[16] 5384 6-8-11 **63** ... RichardThomas 12 — 76
(J A Geake) *wl in tch: trckd ldrs 4f out: rdn to ld in centre 2f out: sn clr: styd on wl* **7/2**[1]

-425 **2** *3 ½* **Dan Buoy (FR)**[20] 5260 3-9-0 **69** ... EddieAhern 8 — 75
(A King) *led to over 3f out: styd towards nr side: kpt on again u.p to take 2nd fnl f: no ch w wnr* **9/1**

101- **3** *1 ½* **Robinzal**[22] 5981 4-9-1 **67** ...(t) SteveDrowne 9 — 70
(C J Mann) *t.k.h early: hld up in tch: effrt and rdn over 3f out: c centre after: kpt on u.p fr over 1f out* **10/1**

3400 **4** *nk* **Aggravation**[13] 5444 4-9-1 **67** ... AntonyProcter 2 — 69
(D R C Elsworth) *stdd s: hld up in last trio: effrt 3f out: plugged on in centre fnl 2f: n.d* **12/1**

0461 **5** *1 ¾* **Piper's Song (IRE)**[20] 5269 3-8-12 **67** ... DaneO'Neill 14 — 65
(H Candy) *trckd ldng pair: wnt towards far side 3f out: stl in tch 2f out: fdd* **7/1**[3]

3503 **6** *¾* **Rowan Lodge (IRE)**[6] 5599 4-9-4 **70** ... KDarley 7 — 67
(M H Tompkins) *hld up: effrt and wnt to far side rail 3f out: in tch over 2f out: wknd over 1f out* **7/2**[1]

31-5 **7** *½* **Stevedore (IRE)**[31] 4995 5-9-4 **70** ... KerrinMcEvoy 3 — 66
(J R Boyle) *pressed ldr: led over 3f out: styd towards nr side: hdd 2f out: wknd over 1f out* **7/1**[3]

6030 **8** *2 ½* **Dispol Veleta**[90] 3168 5-9-1 **67** ... JimCrowley 5 — 57
(Miss T Spearing) *dwlt: hld up in last trio: prog and pushed along 4f out: no hdwy 2f out: wknd* **25/1**

3000 **9** *½* **Wild Academy (IRE)**[22] 5211 3-8-13 **68** ... PhilipRobinson 1 — 57
(G C Bravery) *hld up towards rr: struggling and rdn over 3f out: no real prog* **20/1**

0021 **10** *9* **Asaateel (IRE)**[124] 2132 4-8-13 **65** ... RyanMoore 6 — 35
(G L Moore) *a in rr: last and losing tch 3f out* **11/2**[2]

11 *5* **Inwaan (IRE)**[86] 3-9-1 **70** ...(t) LPKeniry 4 — 30
(P R Webber) *chsd ldrs tl wknd 3f out: sn bhd* **20/1**

1m 48.85s (3.25) **Going Correction** +0.475s/f (Yiel)
WFA 3 from 4yo+ 3lb — 11 Ran SP% **125.0**
Speed ratings (Par 103):102,98,97,96,94 94,93,91,90,81 76
CSF £37.72 CT £249.81 TOTE £4.70: £2.60, £3.40, £2.40; EX 56.00 Trifecta £242.90 Pool £376.41 - 1.10 winning units. Place 6 £217.69, Place 5 £99.44.
Owner Miss B Swire **Bred** Miss B Swire **Trained** Kimpton, Hants

FOCUS

Just a modest handicap in which they were spread out across the track in the straight and the form is messy and not solid.

Inwaan(IRE) Official explanation: jockey said gelding was unsuited by the soft ground

T/Plt: £290.50 to a £1 stake. Pool: £63,093.60. 158.50 winning tickets. T/Qpdt: £29.30 to a £1 stake. Pool: £5,829.80. 147.15 winning tickets. JN

5686 WOLVERHAMPTON (A.W) (L-H)

Monday, October 2

OFFICIAL GOING: Standard to fast

Wind: light, half behind

5735 RINGSIDE SUITE 700 THEATRE STYLE MEDIAN AUCTION MAIDEN STKS — 5f 216y(P)

1:50 (1:50) (Class 5) 2-Y-0 **£4,210** (£1,252; £625; £312) **Stalls** Low

Form RPR

3 **1** **Kondakova (IRE)**[19] 5296 2-8-12 ... JamieSpencer 10 — 74
(M L W Bell) *hld up and bhd: hdwy on outside 3f out: rdn and edgd lft fr over 1f out: led wl ins fnl f: r.o* **4/1**[2]

2 *1* **Herotozero (IRE)**[18] 5328 2-9-0 ... AdamKirby(3) 1 — 76
(Gerard O'Leary, Ire) *led: rdn wl over 1f out: hdd and nt qckn wl ins fnl f* **20/1**

0 **3** *1 ¼* **Le Singe Noir**[14] 5417 2-9-3 ... J-PGuillambert 12 — 72
(D M Simcock) *sn outpcd and bhd: rdn and hdwy on outside over 1f out: r.o ins fnl f* **40/1**

02 **4** *½* **Call Me Rosy (IRE)**[49] 4433 2-8-12 ... JimmyQuinn 3 — 66
(C F Wall) *hld up in mid-div: rdn and hdwy over 1f out: kpt on same pce fnl f* **7/1**[3]

3032 **5** *3 ½* **Bookiesindex Boy**[21] 5245 2-9-3 73 ...(b) RobertHavlin 11 — 60
(J R Jenkins) *hld up in mid-div: hdwy on outside 3f out: rdn and hung lft over 1f out: wknd ins fnl f* **8/1**

052 **6** *1* **Ken's Girl**[20] 5264 2-8-12 72 ... ChrisCatlin 6 — 52
(W S Kittow) *w ldr tl rdn 2f out: wknd over 1f out* **8/1**

0363 **7** *nk* **Goodbye Cash (IRE)**[15] 5407 2-8-9 75 ... StephenDonohoe(3) 4 — 51
(P D Evans) *prom: rdn over 2f out: btn whn nt clr run on ins ins fnl f* **3/1**[1]

032 **8** *½* **Beautiful Madness (IRE)**[21] 5231 2-8-12 67 ... TPQueally 7 — 49
(M G Quinlan) *hld up in mid-div: rdn over 2f out: wknd over 1f out* **7/1**[3]

4 **9** *2 ½* **Gleaming Spirit (IRE)**[21] 5245 2-9-0 ... JamesDoyle(3) 8 — 47
(A P Jarvis) *prom: ev ch over 2f out: rdn and wknd over 2f out* **8/1**

000 **10** *1 ¼* **Iron Dancer (IRE)**[31] 4980 2-8-12 51 ... KevinGhunowa(5) 5 — 43
(P A Blockley) *a bhd* **100/1**

6 **11** *nk* **Saint Remus (IRE)**[33] 4932 2-9-3 ... RobbieFitzpatrick 9 — 42
(Peter Grayson) *a bhd* **100/1**

0200 **12** *hd* **Gibsons**[28] 5065 2-9-3 53 ... GrahamGibbons 2 — 41
(Mrs P N Dutfield) *chsd ldrs tl rdn and wknd over 2f out* **66/1**

13 *¾* **Jete (IRE)** 2-9-0 ...(v[1]) PatrickMathers(3) 13 — 39
(D Shaw) *sn wl bhd* **66/1**

1m 14.57s (-1.24) **Going Correction** -0.225s/f (Stan) — 13 Ran SP% **115.5**
Speed ratings (Par 95):99,97,96,95,90 89,88,88,84,83 82,82,81
CSF £87.23 TOTE £5.00: £1.70, £4.60, £14.10; EX 90.70.
Owner Luke Lillingston **Bred** Mount Coote Stud And Partners **Trained** Newmarket, Suffolk

FOCUS

An ordinary maiden that looks pretty reliable with the fourth to form.

NOTEBOOK

Kondakova(IRE) confirmed the promise of her Yarmouth debut despite being inclined to go left. She again gave the impression that she will get further. (op 7-2)

Herotozero(IRE) ◆ forced the pace over this shorter trip having shown ability in two runs over seven in Ireland. He can find a suitable opportunity. (op 16-1)

Le Singe Noir ◆ had run green on his debut at Folkestone a fortnight earlier. He did well to finish so close after getting taken off his legs early on from a wide draw and a return to a longer distance can pay dividends. (op 33-1)

Call Me Rosy(IRE) finished second over course and distance in August and produced another sound effort in what looked a bit stronger contest. (tchd 15-2)

Bookiesindex Boy had also given the impression he was better suited to five furlongs on his previous attempt at this trip. (op 9-1)

Ken's Girl was having his first run at beyond the minimum trip on this switch to sand. (op 7-1)

5736 BOOK NOW FOR CHRISTMAS H'CAP — 1m 5f 194y(P)

2:20 (2:21) (Class 6) (0-60,60) 3-Y-0+ **£3,412** (£1,007; £504) **Stalls** Low

Form RPR

3020 **1** **Irish Ballad**[16] 5369 4-9-0 **52** ...(t) AdamKirby(3) 11 — 64
(W R Swinburn) *a.p: rdn to ld wl over 1f out: carried rt ins fnl f: drvn out* **8/1**

2600 **2** *hd* **Montage (IRE)**[22] 5201 4-9-3 **52** ...(p) TPQueally 4 — 64
(J Akehurst) *w ldr: led over 5f out: rdn over 2f out: led wl over 1f out: ev ch whn edgd rt ins fnl f: r.o* **10/3**[1]

3155 **3** *6* **Finished Article (IRE)**[12] 5479 9-9-6 **55** ... J-PGuillambert 13 — 58
(P A Blockley) *stdd s: hld up in rr: hdwy over 3f out: rdn over 2f out: one pce* **16/1**

6146 **4** *nk* **Spaceman**[20] 5276 3-9-0 **58** ...(v) JamieSpencer 5 — 61
(L M Cumani) *hld up in mid-div: lost pl 4f out: rdn and hdwy over 2f out: c wd st: one pce fnl f* **4/1**[2]

1040 **5** *1 ½* **Lefonic**[31] 4996 4-9-8 **57** ... ChrisCatlin 6 — 58
(G C H Chung) *hld up in tch: rdn over 2f out: wknd fnl f* **14/1**

0110 **6** *3* **French Mannequin (IRE)**[28] 5069 7-9-6 **60** ...(b) KevinGhunowa(5) 8 — 57
(P A Blockley) *t.k.h in tch: rdn over 5f out: sn lost pl and bhd: n.d after* **13/2**[3]

4320 **7** *2 ½* **Star Rising**[18] 5324 4-9-1 **50** ... RobertHavlin 10 — 43
(N B King) *hld up towards rr: hdwy 6f out: rdn over 2f out: sn wknd* **9/1**

05/ **8** *shd* **Trouville (IRE)**[52] 4340 7-9-2 **51** ... JimmyQuinn 7 — 44
(Gerard O'Leary, Ire) *hld up towards rr: rdn over 3f out: no rspnse* **12/1**

0050 **9** *1* **Lady Pilot**[140] 1745 4-9-7 **59** ... JamesDoyle(3) 9 — 51
(Ms J S Doyle) *hld up in mid-div: hdwy on ins over 3f out: wknd over 2f out* **20/1**

0150 **10** *1 ¾* **Boulevin (IRE)**[87] 3270 6-8-10 **48** ... StephenDonohoe(3) 1 — 37
(R J Price) *s.i.s: hld up and bhd: hdwy over 4f out: rdn and wknd over 2f out* **20/1**

0125 **11** *9* **Rare Coincidence**[15] 4522 5-9-8 **60** ...(p) DNolan(3) 2 — 37
(R F Fisher) *led: hdd over 5f out: rdn over 4f out: sn wknd* **15/2**

2050 **12** *6* **Shamrock Bay**[11] 5369 4-9-0 **56** ... JamieJones(7) 12 — 24
(C R Dore) *hld up towards rr: rdn over 5f out: no rspnse* **33/1**

3m 2.68s (-4.69) **Going Correction** -0.225s/f (Stan)
WFA 3 from 4yo+ 9lb — 12 Ran SP% **122.0**
Speed ratings (Par 101):104,103,100,100,99 97,96,96,95,94 89,86
CSF £34.93 CT £432.96 TOTE £10.50: £2.40, £1.30, £4.60; EX 42.40.
Owner Chua, White, Moore & Jurd **Bred** The Kingwood Partnership **Trained** Aldbury, Herts

FOCUS

A moderate contest run at a modest pace until the runner-up went on just after halfway. The over all time was decent and with the front pair clear, the form may prove reasonable.

5737 MOORCROFT RACEHORSE WELFARE CENTRE H'CAP — 5f 216y(P)

2:50 (2:50) (Class 6) (0-65,65) 3-Y-0+ **£3,412** (£1,007; £504) **Stalls** Low

Form RPR

0002 **1** **Tag Team (IRE)**[30] 5032 5-9-2 **63** ... JamieSpencer 10 — 72
(John A Harris) *led 1f: w ldr: rdn wl over 1f out: led wl ins fnl f: r.o* **10/3**[1]

0-00 **2** *nk* **Benny The Bus**[16] 5388 4-9-2 **63** ... GrahamGibbons 3 — 71
(Mrs G S Rees) *hld up towards rr: rdn and hdwy over 2f out: r.o ins fnl f* **12/1**

650 **3** *1 ¼* **Sweetest Revenge (IRE)**[12] 5480 5-9-4 **65** ... HayleyTurner 8 — 69
(M D I Usher) *prom: lost pl 4f out: rdn over 2f out: gd hdwy on outside fnl f: r.o* **12/1**

3060 **4** *nk* **Wainwright (IRE)**[20] 5269 6-8-11 **63** ...(b) KevinGhunowa(5) 11 — 66
(P A Blockley) *s.i.s: hdwy on outside 3f out: sn rdn: hung lft over 1f out: r.o ins fnl f* **16/1**

3416 **5** *nk* **Caustic Wit (IRE)**[12] 5476 8-8-7 **61** ...(p) TolleyDean(7) 9 — 64
(M S Saunders) *a.p: rdn over 2f out: nt clr run on ins and swtchd rt over 1f out: nt qckn ins fnl f* **9/2**[2]

0005 **6** *hd* **The Crooked Ring**[35] 4894 4-9-0 **64** ...(b[1]) StephenDonohoe(3) 4 — 66
(P D Evans) *led after 1f: rdn wl over 1f out: hdd and no ex wl ins fnl f* **15/2**

0400 **7** *¾* **Cool Sands (IRE)**[4] 5635 4-8-12 **62** ...(v) PatrickMathers(3) 5 — 62
(D Shaw) *bhd: rdn over 2f out: nvr nrr* **9/1**

1150 **8** *1 ½* **Further Outlook (USA)**[38] 4780 12-9-0 **64** ... AdamKirby(3) 1 — 59
(Miss Gay Kelleway) *prom: rdn over 2f out: wknd wl over 1f out* **7/1**[3]

3000 **9** *¾* **Polar Force**[81] 3447 6-9-2 **63** ... RobbieFitzpatrick 13 — 56
(Mrs C A Dunnett) *prom: rdn 2f out: wknd fnl f* **16/1**

0000 **10** *1 ¼* **Desert Light (IRE)**[4] 5631 5-9-0 **61** ...(v) DanielTudhope 6 — 50
(D Shaw) *a bhd* **12/1**

1130 **11** *1* **Hillbilly Cat (USA)**[40] 4703 3-9-1 **63** ... ChrisCatlin 7 — 49
(R Ingram) *hld up in mid-div: rdn and wknd wl over 1f out* **16/1**

304- **12** *5* **Global Guardian**[325] 6316 3-9-1 **63** ... J-PGuillambert 2 — 34
(Mrs G S Rees) *a bhd* **20/1**

1m 13.99s (-1.82) **Going Correction** -0.225s/f (Stan)
WFA 3 from 4yo+ 1lb — 12 Ran SP% **121.0**
Speed ratings (Par 101):103,102,100,100,100 99,98,96,95,94 92,86
CSF £45.79 CT £446.37 TOTE £2.80: £1.30, £4.30, £4.50; EX 59.50.
Owner Cleartherm Glass Sealed Units Ltd **Bred** Miss Sally Hodgins **Trained** Eastwell, Leics

FOCUS

They went a decent pace in this closely-knit low-grade event and the form, rated around the placed horses, looks solid.

5738 WOLVERHAMPTON-RACECOURSE.CO.UK NURSERY — 7f 32y(P)

3:20 (3:20) (Class 6) (0-65,65) 2-Y-0 **£3,238** (£963; £481; £240) **Stalls** High

Form RPR

5450 **1** **Nicada (IRE)**[33] 4920 2-9-2 **61** ... JimmyQuinn 4 — 67
(Miss Gay Kelleway) *a.p: rdn over 3f out: led 1f out: rdn out* **8/1**[3]

420 **2** *1 ½* **Jord (IRE)**[108] 2626 2-8-11 **61** ... NataliaGemelova(5) 2 — 63
(A J McCabe) *led: hdd over 4f out: led 2f out: sn rdn: hdd 1f out: nt qckn* **16/1**

5300 **3** *3* **Law Of The Land (IRE)**[27] [5094] 2-9-5 **64**........................ RobertHavlin 9 59
(W R Muir) *t.k.h: sn prom: rdn over 2f out: swtchd lft wl over 1f out: one pce* **16/1**

056 **4** *½* **Flying Grey (IRE)**[16] [5379] 2-9-4 **63**.............................. J-PGuillambert 1 57
(P A Blockley) *hld up towards rr: rdn and hdwy on ins over 2f out: kpt on same pce fnl f* **8/1**[3]

6506 **5** *½* **Ambrosiano**[38] [4753] 2-9-6 **65**.. GeorgeBaker 6 58
(Miss E C Lavelle) *hld up and bhd: stdy hdwy on outside over 2f out: c wd st: rdn over 1f out: hung lft ins fnl f: nvr nrr* **11/1**

0556 **6** *shd* **Lake Pontchartrain (IRE)**[14] [5419] 2-9-0 **62**................ AdamKirby(3) 11 54
(S Kirk) *sn prom: rdn wl over 1f out: wknd over 1f out* **6/1**[2]

0010 **7** *shd* **Aggbag**[22] [5208] 2-9-4 **63**.. RobbieFitzpatrick 8 55
(B P J Baugh) *bhd: rdn and hdwy on ins wl over 1f out: nvr trbld ldrs* **25/1**

2606 **8** *¾* **Nepos**[23] [5162] 2-8-13 **61**.................................... StephenDonohoe(3) 5 51
(A J McCabe) *chsd ldr: led over 4f out: rdn and hdd 2f out: wknd 1f out* **10/1**

005 **9** *3* **Kings Art (IRE)**[17] [5347] 2-9-6 **65**..................................(t) JamieSpencer 7 48
(B W Hills) *hld up in mid-div: rdn over 3f out: wknd over 2f out: eased whn no ch ins fnl f* **2/1**[1]

4600 **10** *2* **Rosie Cross (IRE)**[49] [4427] 2-9-3 **62**.......................... StephenCarson 10 40
(R F Johnson Houghton) *hld up in mid-div: rdn over 3f out: wknd over 2f out* **12/1**

0050 **11** *3 ½* **Rowan Venture**[3] [5646] 2-9-5 **64**.......................................(b) TPQueally 12 33
(M H Tompkins) *a bhd* **16/1**

000 **12** *5* **Alnwick**[60] [4074] 2-9-2 **61**.. ChrisCatlin 3 18
(P D Cundell) *s.i.s: wl bhd fnl 3f* **14/1**

1m 30.09s (-0.31) **Going Correction** -0.225s/f (Stan) 12 Ran SP% **123.1**
Speed ratings (Par 93):92,90,86,86,85 85,85,84,81,78 74,69
CSF £133.97 CT £2050.02 TOTE £8.30: £2.70, £5.20, £3.30; EX 103.80.
Owner S P Cook **Bred** Peadar Kelly **Trained** Exning, Suffolk
■ Gay Kelleway's first winner from her new base at Exning outside Newmarket.

FOCUS
A tightly-knit, modest nursery that looks sound and could rate slightly higher.

NOTEBOOK
Nicada(IRE) found the combination of a 4lb drop in the weights and being back up to seven furlongs doing the trick. (op 10-1)
Jord(IRE) ◆ had not been seen since disappointing when favourite in a York seller in June on her final run for Jamie Osborne. Supported in the ring, she was always keen to force the pace over this extra furlong and can take a similar low-grade contest off this sort of mark. (op 9-1)
Law Of The Land(IRE) can be a free-going sort and may have been a bit too keen for his own good on this Polytrack debut.
Flying Grey(IRE), far more patiently ridden, was another to handle the surface well enough on his first try on sand.
Ambrosiano, back up to seven, had also been inclined to go left in the closing stages at Bath on his previous outing. Official explanation: jockey said, regarding running and riding, his orders were to ride the colt with restraint because previously it has failed to get home, adding that it is green and weak and he was told not to race with others in order to teach it to relax; trainer's rep confirmed, expressed his satisfaction with the ride, adding that it had been given confidence to pass horses, where it had failed before (op 10-1)
Lake Pontchartrain(IRE) had been shaping as though she would be suited by a step up to seven. (op 9-2)
Kings Art(IRE) Official explanation: jockey said colt hung badly left-handed

5739 THE ZONGALERO RESTAURANT H'CAP 1m 141y(P)
3:50 (3:52) (Class 4) (0-85,85) 3-Y-O+ **£7,124** (£2,119; £1,059; £529) **Stalls** Low

Form RPR
3241 **1** **Country Escape**[16] [5384] 3-8-10 **79**.................................. JimmyQuinn 2 92
(C F Wall) *hld up in tch: rdn wl over 1f out: edgd rt and led ins fnl f: drvn out* **13/2**

11- **2** *½* **Alpine Reel (IRE)**[469] [2780] 5-8-10 **78**............................. AdamKirby(3) 7 90
(W R Swinburn) *chsd ldr: rdn 2f out: ev ch ins fnl f: nt qckn* **4/1**[1]

2215 **3** *2* **Uno**[10] [5512] 3-8-9 **78**.. RobertHavlin 6 86
(B W Hills) *led: rdn over 1f out: hdd ins fnl f: no ex* **11/2**[3]

4111 **4** *3 ½* **Apres Ski (IRE)**[29] [5046] 3-7-11 **71** oh4........................... LiamJones(5) 3 71
(J F Coupland) *hld up in mid-div: rdn and hdwy on ins over 2f out: no further prog* **8/1**

5364 **5** *½* **Merrymadcap (IRE)**[26] [5108] 4-8-12 **77**............................. DaleGibson 9 76
(M Blanshard) *hld up in mid-div: rdn and hdwy on outside wl over 1f out: sn edgd lft: no imp* **10/1**

3500 **6** *1 ¼* **Bomber Command (USA)**[10] [5504] 3-8-12 **81**............. J-PGuillambert 4 78
(J W Hills) *hld up and bhd: rdn and sme hdwy wl over 1f out: n.d* **8/1**

1/ **7** *½* **Ballinteni**[710] [6330] 4-9-6 **85**.. ChrisCatlin 10 81
(Saeed Bin Suroor) *hld up in mid-div: lost pl on outside over 3f out: sn rdn: edgd lft over 1f out: n.d after* **5/1**[2]

3620 **8** *1 ¼* **Resplendent Nova**[119] [2302] 4-8-13 **81**........................ DeanCorby(3) 11 74
(P Howling) *prom: rdn over 2f out: wknd wl over 1f out* **22/1**

0-00 **9** *2 ½* **Arry Dash**[156] [1302] 6-8-12 **77**... JamieSpencer 8 65
(M J Wallace) *a bhd* **14/1**

0100 **10** *2* **Danelor (IRE)**[10] [5512] 8-8-5 **73**................................. PatrickMathers(3) 5 57
(D Shaw) *hld up towards rr: rdn 3f out: no rspnse* **40/1**

5540 **11** *5* **Trifti**[20] [5258] 5-8-12 **77**.. FrancisFerris 12 50
(C A Cyzer) *hld up in tch: rdn over 2f out: wknd wl over 1f out* **9/1**

1m 47.56s (-4.20) **Going Correction** -0.225s/f (Stan)
WFA 3 from 4yo+ 4lb 11 Ran SP% **120.2**
Speed ratings (Par 105):109,108,106,103,103 102,101,100,98,96 92
CSF £33.43 CT £159.47 TOTE £9.60: £2.60, £1.60, £1.70; EX 44.10.
Owner Fighttheban Partnership IV **Bred** Executive Bloodlines **Trained** Newmarket, Suffolk

FOCUS
A fair handicap run at a strong pace that led to a good time and the form looks solid and reliable.

5740 SPONSOR A RACE BY CALLING 0870 220 2442 H'CAP 1m 1f 103y(P)
4:20 (4:20) (Class 6) (0-65,64) 3-Y-O+ **£3,238** (£963; £481; £240) **Stalls** Low

Form RPR
040 **1** **Kildare Sun (IRE)**[18] [5319] 4-9-4 **62**................................. DaleGibson 12 72
(J Mackie) *a.p: led over 2f out: rdn over 1f out: r.o* **33/1**

0201 **2** *¾* **Sanctity**[47] [4470] 3-9-0 **62**...(v[1]) JamieSpencer 10 73+
(J R Fanshawe) *set slow pce: hdd over 6f out: remained prom: rdn whn nt clr run in ins and swtchd rt over 1f out: r.o ins fnl* **6/1**[3]

0066 **3** *nk* **Western Roots**[16] [5385] 5-9-3 **61**...................................... GeorgeBaker 4 69
(M Appleby) *hld up and bhd: hdwy over 3f out: rdn and nt qckn ins fnl f* **15/2**

4560 **4** *1* **Blacktoft (USA)**[20] [5269] 3-8-12 **63**................................. AdamKirby(3) 6 69
(S C Williams) *hld up and bhd: hdwy over 2f out: sn rdn: one pce fnl f* **8/1**

0000 **5** *hd* **Lord Of Dreams (IRE)**[21] [5249] 4-9-1 **62**..................... JamesDoyle(3) 7 68
(D W P Arbuthnot) *hld up in mid-div: hdwy over 2f out: sn rdn: rdr lost whip 1f out: one pce* **9/1**

0001 **6** *½* **New England**[23] [5173] 4-9-6 **64**.................................. RobbieFitzpatrick 2 69
(W M Brisbourne) *hld up and bhd: rdn over 2f out: c wd st: hdwy over 1f out: r.o* **5/1**[1]

0300 **7** *2* **Ohana**[33] [4923] 3-9-0 **62**... AdrianMcCarthy 5 63
(Miss Gay Kelleway) *prom: lost pl on ins over 3f out: rdn and swtchd rt over 1f out: no hdwy* **33/1**

4004 **8** *nk* **Pauline's Prince**[18] [5316] 4-8-12 **63**.................... RussellKennemore(7) 8 63
(R Hollinshead) *t.k.h in mid-div: hdwy over 3f out: rdn over 2f out: edgd lft over 1f out: wknd fnl f* **16/1**

3416 **9** *hd* **Lauro**[45] [4570] 6-8-11 **62**.. DawnRankin(7) 3 62
(Miss J A Camacho) *s.i.s: a bhd* **8/1**

4234 **10** *1 ¾* **Bavarica**[29] [5046] 4-8-9 **60**.. SladeO'Hara(7) 9 57
(Miss J Feilden) *hld up: hdwy over 6f out: ev ch over 2f out: sn rdn: wknd over 1f out* **9/1**

5105 **11** *5* **Wee Charlie Castle (IRE)**[20] [5270] 3-9-1 **63**.................. ChrisCatlin 11 50
(G C H Chung) *s.i.s: a bhd* **16/1**

0331 **12** *5* **Risk Free**[238] [313] 9-8-13 **60**...............................(v) StephenDonohoe(3) 13 38
(P D Evans) *t.k.h: prom: led over 6f out: hdd over 2f out: sn wknd* **20/1**

-211 **13** *nk* **Bold Phoenix (IRE)**[175] [940] 5-9-2 **60**...............................(b) TPQueally 1 37
(B J Curley) *hld up in mid-div: lost pl 6f out: bhd whn rdn over 3f out* **11/2**[2]

2m 3.10s (0.48) **Going Correction** -0.225s/f (Stan)
WFA 3 from 4yo+ 4lb 13 Ran SP% **122.7**
Speed ratings (Par 101):88,87,87,86,86 85,83,83,83,81 77,72,72
CSF £223.67 CT £1676.69 TOTE £55.30: £11.20, £2.30, £2.50; EX 352.20.
Owner Mrs Barbara Woodworth **Bred** Gordan Woodworth **Trained** Church Broughton , Derbys

FOCUS
A modest contest and the fact they went no gallop for the first three furlongs resulted in a very slow winning time. The form does not look that solid.
Blacktoft(USA) Official explanation: jockey said gelding raced too keen early

5741 TWILIGHT RACING AND SUPPER MEDIAN AUCTION MAIDEN STKS 1m 4f 50y(P)
4:50 (4:50) (Class 5) 3-4-Y-O **£3,238** (£963; £481; £240) **Stalls** Low

Form RPR
33 **1** **Nando's Dream**[27] [5098] 3-8-12 .... TPQueally 4 60+
(J Noseda) *a.p: hrd rdn over 1f out: led and edgd rt wl ins fnl f: r.o* **7/2**[2]

4-23 **2** *nk* **Mantle**[14] [5426] 4-9-5 74.. JamieSpencer 9 60+
(J R Fanshawe) *hld up in tch: ev ch ins fnl f: rdn and nt qckn whn carried rt towards fin* **4/7**[1]

2323 **3** *1 ¾* **Summer Lodge**[10] [5510] 3-9-0 69.........................(b) StephenDonohoe(3) 7 62
(A J McCabe) *hld up in mid-div: hdwy over 5f out: led 2f out: sn rdn: hdd and no ex wl ins fnl f* **13/2**[3]

32 **4** *1 ¾* **Ha'Penny Beacon**[87] [3258] 3-8-12 .... DanielTudhope 6 54
(D Carroll) *hld up in mid-div: rdn and hdwy on ins over 2f out: one pce fnl f* **12/1**

0500 **5** *2* **Go Amwell**[51] [4367] 3-9-3 46.. RobertHavlin 5 56
(J R Jenkins) *hld up in tch: rdn over 2f out: wknd wl over 1f out* **100/1**

4060 **6** *2* **Merchant Bankes**[22] [5211] 3-9-3 64...................................... DaleGibson 1 53
(W G M Turner) *led: rdn and hdd 2f out: wknd over 1f out* **25/1**

0660 **7** *8* **Kirstys Lad**[57] [4172] 4-9-5 40.. LiamJones(5) 2 40
(M Mullineaux) *rdn over 3f out: a bhd* **100/1**

2606 **8** *nk* **Kokila**[153] [1387] 3-8-12 52.. JimmyQuinn 10 34
(M H Tompkins) *a bhd* **40/1**

0-0 **9** *9* **Royalties**[87] [3261] 4-9-5 .... GeorgeBaker 8 20
(M A Allen) *a bhd* **150/1**

6/50 **10** *1 ¼* **Glads Image**[139] [1765] 4-9-2 35...................................... JohnMcAuley(3) 3 18
(S W Hall) *a bhd* **150/1**

0000 **11** *19* **Distant Mind (IRE)**[14] [5432] 3-8-9 35............................ AdamKirby(3) 11 —
(Mrs C A Dunnett) *sn chsng ldr: rdn and wknd qckly wl over 2f out: eased over 1f out* **150/1**

2m 42.38s (-0.04) **Going Correction** -0.225s/f (Stan)
WFA 3 from 4yo 7lb 11 Ran SP% **117.2**
Speed ratings (Par 103):91,90,89,88,87 85,80,80,74,73 60
CSF £5.76 TOTE £4.80: £1.10, £1.10, £1.90; EX 9.90 Place 6 £1,042.04, Place 5 £224.78.
Owner Hesmonds Stud **Bred** Hesmonds Stud Ltd **Trained** Newmarket, Suffolk

FOCUS
A weak maiden run at a slow pace resulting in a very moderate winning time. The form is very moderate and limited by the fifth.
T/Plt: £972.00 to a £1 stake. Pool: £47,138.75. 35.40 winning tickets. T/Qpdt: £48.00 to a £1 stake. Pool: £3,529.30. 54.30 winning tickets. KH

5742 - 5745a (Foreign Racing) - See Raceform Interactive

5363 CATTERICK (L-H)
Tuesday, October 3

OFFICIAL GOING: Good (good to soft in places)
The ground was described as 'genuine good to soft'.
Wind: Light, half across Weather: Fine but overcast

5746 14TH OCTOBER IS TOTESPORT SATURDAY MAIDEN STKS (DIV I) 5f
2:20 (2:20) (Class 5) 2-Y-O **£3,238** (£963; £481; £240) **Stalls** Low

Form RPR
5246 **1** **The Nifty Fox**[18] [5335] 2-9-3 77.. DavidAllan 3 77
(T D Easterby) *trckd ldng pair: swtchd rt and hdwy wl over 1f out: rdn to chal ins last: drvn: edgd lft and kpt on to ld last 75 yds* **3/1**[2]

32 **2** *½* **Emaara**[22] [5237] 2-8-12 .... JimmyQuinn 1 71
(J L Dunlop) *cl up: rdn along over 1f out: ev ch ins last: sn drvn: n.m.r and no ex last 50 yds* **10/11**[1]

4403 **3** *1 ¼* **Ronnie Howe**[28] [5076] 2-9-3 73... PhillipMakin 8 71
(M Dods) *sn led: rdn along over 1f out: hmpd ins last: hdd & wknd last 75 yds* **9/2**[3]

4 *1 ¼* **Warm Tribute (USA)** 2-8-12 .... DuranFentiman(5) 4 67
(W G Harrison) *s.i.s and bhd tl styd on appr last: nrst fin* **66/1**

06 **5** *hd* **Billy Ruffian**[78] [3596] 2-9-3 .... GrahamGibbons 6 66
(T D Easterby) *chsd ldrs: rdn along 2f out: sn one pce* **25/1**

00 **6** *3* **Darcy's Pride (IRE)**[69] [3830] 2-8-12 .... PaulHanagan 9 50
(D W Barker) *chsd ldrs: rdn along 2f out: grad wknd* **66/1**

7 *½* **O'Dwyer (IRE)**[54] [4309] 2-9-3 .... SilvestreDeSousa 7 53
(A D Brown) *a rr* **16/1**

00 **8** *nk* **Cranworth Blaze**[22] [5237] 2-8-12 .... RoystonFfrench 10 47
(T J Etherington) *dwlt: racd alone towards stands' side: sn outpcd and wl bhd tl styd on appr last* **50/1**

00 **9** *5* **West Warning**[71] 3787 2-9-3 ....(b) PaulMulrennan 5 34
(M W Easterby) *sn rdn along and a rr* **100/1**
63.25 secs (2.65) **Going Correction** +0.30s/f (Good) 9 Ran SP% **111.2**
Speed ratings (Par 95):90,89,87,85,84 80,79,78,70
CSF £5.69 TOTE £3.80: £1.10, £1.10, £1.10; EX 7.40.
Owner Roy Peebles **Bred** Mrs Norma Peebles **Trained** Great Habton, N Yorks

FOCUS
A modest maiden that only concerned three horses in the market, and in the race itself. The race is rated around the placed horses.

NOTEBOOK
The Nifty Fox had done too much too soon in a visor when last seen over this course and distance, but he chased the pace this time and was able to reverse form with Ronnie Howe. The form is not strong and he might struggle off his current mark in handicap company. (op 5-2)
Emaara, beaten at odds-on last time out, was well backed to get off the mark at the third time of asking but again failed to justify short odds. The drop back to five furlongs did not seem to bother her and she clearly has her limitations. (op Evens tchd 11-10)
Ronnie Howe had finished in front of The Nifty Fox over this course and distance on his last start, but could not confirm the form with the more patiently ridden winner this time. He had every chance, though, and his performance is probably a fair guide to the level of the form. (op 5-1)
Warm Tribute(USA), whose dam is a half-sister to two minor winners in the US, is bred to need a longer trip than this in time, so he shaped with a bit of promise, staying on well late in the day for fourth place. (op 50-1)
Billy Ruffian, a half-brother to five-furlong juvenile winners Zaragossa, Antonia's Dilemma, Bond Domingo and Coranglais, is now eligible for a mark and will be of more interest in modest handicap company. (op 28-1 tchd 33-1)

5747 RACING UK FOR £15 PER MONTH NURSERY 5f 212y
2:50 (2:55) (Class 6) (0-65,65) 2-Y-O **£2,730** (£806; £403) **Stalls** Low

Form RPR
3465 **1** **Tipsy Prince**[18] 5349 2-9-4 **62** .... JimmyQuinn 9 67
(Mrs G S Rees) *hld up in rr: hdwy outside over 2f out: led 1f out: hld on wl* **5/1**[1]
0005 **2** *¾* **Merlins Quest**[24] 5161 2-8-11 **58** .... GregFairley(3) 11 61
(J M Bradley) *chsd ldrs: chal 1f out: no ex ins last* **25/1**
3053 **3** *shd* **Bert's Memory**[18] 5347 2-9-4 **65** .... AndrewMullen(3) 6 67
(K A Ryan) *s.i.s: hdwy on ins over 2f out: edgd rt and styd on wl ins last* **9/1**
0004 **4** *nk* **Susanna's Prospect (IRE)**[38] 4815 2-9-5 **63** .... ChrisCatlin 2 64+
(B J Meehan) *bhd: hdwy over 1f out: fin strly* **6/1**[2]
0051 **5** *¾* **Back In The Red (IRE)**[22] 5238 2-9-4 **62** .... DeanMcKeown 12 62+
(M Wellings) *prom: hmpd over 2f out: nt clr run over 1f out and ins last: styd on wl towards fin* **8/1**
0260 **6** *nk* **La Vecchia Scuola (IRE)**[80] 3555 2-9-7 **65** .... AdrianTNicholls 7 63
(D Nicholls) *mde most: hdd 1f out: no ex* **16/1**
0160 **7** *nk* **Merry Moon (IRE)**[47] 4509 2-9-0 **58** .... PhillipMakin 1 55+
(M Dods) *chsd ldrs: n.m.r over 1f out: kpt on same pce* **8/1**
0513 **8** *½* **Burlington Fayr (IRE)**[20] 5282 2-9-1 **59** .... KimTinkler 10 55
(N Tinkler) *w ldrs: one pce fnl f* **14/1**
0404 **9** *1 ¼* **Blue Mistral (IRE)**[15] 5419 2-9-6 **64** .... PaulDoe 4 56
(W J Knight) *s.i.s: bhd and hung lft over 2f out: hdwy on outside over 1f out: nt rch ldrs* **8/1**
530 **10** *nk* **Ishibee (IRE)**[20] 5282 2-9-6 **64** ....(p) RoystonFfrench 14 55
(Mrs A Duffield) *chsd ldrs on outer: rdn over 2f out: fdd over 1f out* **25/1**
01 **11** *hd* **Smash N'Grab (IRE)**[27] 5111 2-9-3 **61** .... DO'Donohoe 8 52+
(K A Ryan) *hld up in mid-div: hdwy on inner 2f out: one pce whn n.m.r ins last* **15/2**[3]
050 **12** *3 ½* **Juvenescent (USA)**[20] 5283 2-9-4 **62** .... PaulMulrennan 3 42+
(R D E Woodhouse) *w ldrs: wkng whn n.m.r on inner 1f out: sn eased* **14/1**
6303 **13** *2* **Silver Appraisal**[18] 5349 2-9-3 **61** .... PaulEddery 13 35
(B Smart) *mid-div: lost pl over 4f out: sn bhd* **14/1**
40 **14** *½* **Fair 'n Square (IRE)**[24] 5162 2-8-13 **60** .... StephenDonohoe(3) 5 32
(J L Spearing) *sn bhd and drvn along* **25/1**
1m 17.78s (3.78) **Going Correction** +0.425s/f (Yiel) 14 Ran SP% **123.5**
Speed ratings (Par 93):91,90,89,89,88 88,87,87,85,84 84,80,77,76
CSF £140.02 CT £1093.71 TOTE £7.10: £1.90, £11.20, £3.20; EX 228.40.
Owner Mrs G S Rees **Bred** Capt J H Wilson **Trained** Sollom, Lancs

FOCUS
A competitive nursery run at a good pace and looks sound enough rated around the third and fourth.

NOTEBOOK
Tipsy Prince, who won his race on the wrong side at Nottingham last time and was dropping back to the minimum trip, appreciated the good gallop and stayed on well from the rear down the centre of the track to record his first success. He will not mind a return to six furlongs on this evidence. (op 15-2)
Merlins Quest did not run badly in a Bath maiden last time against higher-rated rivals and built on that effort here. It was a creditable run, expecially as he was towards the fore throughout in a race run at a good gallop, and there should be a minor race in him. (tchd 20-1)
Bert's Memory looked vulnerable under top weight but was not at all disgraced. She is fairly consistent and is probably a reasonable guide to the level of the form. (op 12-1)
Susanna's Prospect(IRE), who faced a stiff task at Windsor last time and looked likely to do better on this handicap debut, struggled with the early pace but finished well. Her pedigree suggests that she will handle softer ground and it will not be a surprise to see her off the mark before the season is out. (op 8-1)
Back In The Red(IRE), hampered and short of room in the straight, would have been placed at least with a clear run. He remains progressive. Official explanation: jockey said colt was denied a clear run (op 6-1)
La Vecchia Scuola(IRE), dropped 6lb since her handicap debut, set a strong gallop and paid for her effort late on.
Merry Moon(IRE) was denied racing room approaching the final furlong and shaped a bit better than her finishing position would suggest. (op 12-1)

5748 WILLIAM HILL LONG SERVICE FILLIES' NURSERY STKS (H'CAP) 7f
3:20 (3:21) (Class 4) (0-85,83) 2-Y-O **£6,477** (£1,927; £963; £481) **Stalls** Low

Form RPR
41 **1** **Laurentina**[32] 4993 2-9-1 **80** .... StephenDonohoe(3) 1 83+
(B J Meehan) *hld up: stdy hdwy on inner 1/2-way: chsd ldrs and n.m.r over 1f out: rdn ins last: led nr fin* **3/1**[1]
3160 **2** *hd* **Coconut Queen (IRE)**[12] 5492 2-8-5 **70** .... SaleemGolam(3) 4 72
(Mrs A Duffield) *chsd ldrs: rdn along wl over 1f out: styd on u.p ins last to ld last 75 yds: hdd and no ex nr fin* **20/1**
14 **3** *nk* **Ficoma**[32] 4994 2-8-11 **76** .... AdamKirby(3) 15 78+
(C G Cox) *chsd ldrs on outer: hdwy wl over 1f out: sn rdn and edgd lft ent last: styd on and ev ch tl no ex last 50 yds* **16/1**
01 **4** *1* **Ava's World (IRE)**[17] 5364 2-9-4 **83** .... GregFairley(3) 6 82
(M Johnston) *led: rdn along 2f out: drvn over 1f out: hdd and no ex wl ins last* **7/1**
4322 **5** *¾* **Cassie's Choice (IRE)**[50] 4424 2-8-9 **71** .... DavidAllan 2 68
(B Smart) *midfield: hdwy to chse ldrs over 2f out: sn rdn and kpt on u.p ins last: nrst fin* **11/1**
1412 **6** *1 ½* **Ingleby Princess**[16] 5404 2-9-3 **79** .... PhillipMakin 13 72
(T D Barron) *cl up: rdn along 2f out: drvn over 1f out and grad wknd* **13/2**[3]
2324 **7** *nk* **Gap Princess (IRE)**[11] 5509 2-8-5 **67** .... PaulHanagan 10 59
(R A Fahey) *keen: in tch: effrt over 2f out: sn rdn and no imp* **4/1**[2]
046 **8** *3* **Pret A Porter (UAE)**[37] 4830 2-8-6 **68** .... ChrisCatlin 7 53
(M R Channon) *bhd tl styd on fnl 2f* **16/1**
0650 **9** *1 ¾* **Look Who's Dancing**[29] 5053 2-8-7 **69** .... PaulDoe 12 49
(J L Dunlop) *cl up: rdn along 3f out: sn wknd* **14/1**
003 **10** *1 ½* **Xaar Too Busy**[40] 4731 2-8-3 **65** ....(v) RoystonFfrench 8 41
(Mrs A Duffield) *chsd ldrs: rdn along 3f out: sn wknd* **33/1**
640 **11** *½* **The Mighty Ogmore**[46] 4547 2-8-0 **67** ow2....................(p) RoryMoore(5) 14 42
(R C Guest) *a rr* **33/1**
050 **12** *7* **Career Girl (USA)**[18] 5352 2-8-5 **67** .... DO'Donohoe 9 24
(E A L Dunlop) *s.i.s: a bhd* **14/1**
1m 30.17s (2.81) **Going Correction** +0.425s/f (Yiel) 12 Ran SP% **114.9**
Speed ratings (Par 94):100,99,99,98,97 95,95,91,89,88 87,79
CSF £67.16 CT £822.95 TOTE £3.70: £1.70, £4.70, £5.00; EX 85.90.
Owner John M Carroll **Bred** Glebe Stud And Mrs F Woodd **Trained** Manton, Wilts

FOCUS
Not a bad fillies' nursery, the form looks solid rated through the runner-up to course form, and the race could well throw up a few future winners.

NOTEBOOK
Laurentina got a good run round on the inside rail and stuck her neck out in a close finish to justify favouritism. She got the extra furlong well and looks the type to improve again. (op 11-4 tchd 100-30 in a place)
Coconut Queen(IRE) appreciated returning to the scene of her maiden success, which came over this course and distance in August and ran well off what had looked a fairly stiff mark beforehand. (op 16-1)
Ficoma ran well from her poor stall out wide, and saw the trip out well. She will be one to be interested in when faring better with the draw.
Ava's World(IRE), who won her maiden over six furlongs here last time, did not look to have been given a particularly favourable mark for her handicap debut, but she again had plenty of use made of her, and ran a solid race in defeat. (op 17-2)
Cassie's Choice(IRE), who has solid maiden form to her name, ran a decent race from her good, low draw on her handicap debut. Her performance is probably a fair guide to the level of the form. (op 12-1)
Ingleby Princess ran a fair race from her wide draw. She has some solid nursery form to her name and is another who helps set the level of the form. (op 7-1)
Gap Princess(IRE) was a bit too keen for her own good on this step up in trip and did not see it out as strongly as one or two of her rivals. (op 7-2)

5749 SUBSCRIBE TO RACING UK 08700 506957 H'CAP 5f 212y
3:50 (3:50) (Class 4) (0-85,85) 3-Y-O+ **£5,505** (£1,637; £818; £408) **Stalls** Low

Form RPR
4302 **1** **Dhaular Dhar (IRE)**[10] 5529 4-9-4 85 .... DanielTudhope 7 96
(J S Goldie) *in tch: effrt and n.m.r over 1f out: r.o wl to ld post* **5/1**[1]
0003 **2** *shd* **Gifted Gamble**[6] 5627 4-9-4 85 ....(b) PaulMulrennan 6 96
(K A Ryan) *chsd ldrs: edgd rt and led 1f out: hdd last stride* **9/1**
5001 **3** *2* **Paris Bell**[27] 5117 4-8-10 77 .... DavidAllan 1 82+
(T D Easterby) *s.i.s: bhd tl styd on wl fnl 2f* **8/1**
5050 **4** *hd* **Campo Bueno (FR)**[10] 5534 4-9-0 84 ....(b[1]) StephenDonohoe(3) 10 88
(A Berry) *prom on outer: kpt on same pce appr fnl f* **25/1**
0014 **5** *nk* **Vanadium**[26] 5136 4-8-9 76 .... PaulHanagan 9 80+
(J G Given) *prom: edgd lft 1f out: kpt on same pce* **7/1**[2]
0301 **6** *nk* **Trojan Flight**[28] 5081 5-8-7 74 ....(p) DeanMcKeown 14 77
(D W Chapman) *hld up in last: swtchd to wd outside over 2f out: styd on wl: nt rch ldrs* **15/2**[3]
4050 **7** *shd* **Toy Top (USA)**[10] 5532 3-8-10 78 ....(b) PhillipMakin 5 80
(M Dods) *sn chsng ldrs: kpt on same pce fnl f* **20/1**
403 **8** *1 ¼* **First Order**[38] 4811 5-9-4 85 .... TomEaves 11 84
(I Semple) *unruly in stalls: bhd: keeping on same pce whn nt clr run jst ins last* **8/1**
1000 **9** *1 ½* **Dizzy In The Head**[18] 5333 7-8-3 73 ....(b) AndrewMullen(3) 2 67
(I Semple) *chsd ldrs: wknd fnl f: eased towards fin* **20/1**
5250 **10** *nk* **Harry Up**[18] 5333 5-9-4 85 .... DO'Donohoe 3 78
(K A Ryan) *led tl hdd & wknd 1f out* **14/1**
1510 **11** *1 ½* **Hiccups**[17] 5355 6-8-9 76 .... RoystonFfrench 13 65
(M Dods) *restless in stalls: hld up in rr: kpt on fnl 2f: nvr on terms* **11/1**
5054 **12** *7* **Pawan (IRE)**[8] 5578 6-8-5 77 ow1....................(b) AnnStokell(5) 4 45
(Miss A Stokell) *s.i.s: effrt on ins over 2f out: wknd and eased fnl f* **10/1**
1330 **13** *3 ½* **Blue Maeve**[12] 5493 6-8-7 74 .... SilvestreDeSousa 12 31
(A D Brown) *chsd ldrs: lost pl over 2f out: sn bhd* **8/1**
1m 15.16s (1.16) **Going Correction** +0.425s/f (Yiel)
WFA 3 from 4yo+ 1lb 13 Ran SP% **121.7**
Speed ratings (Par 105):109,108,106,105,105 105,105,103,101,100 98,89,84
CSF £48.93 CT £375.95 TOTE £6.60: £1.90, £3.20, £3.70; EX 60.50.
Owner J S Goldie **Bred** Gainsborough Stud Management Ltd **Trained** Uplawmoor, E Renfrews

FOCUS
A fair sprint handicap run at a decent pace and the form looks solid and reliable, rated around the runner-up and fourth.
Pawan(IRE) Official explanation: jockey said gelding was unsuited by the good (good to soft places) ground

5750 SKYRAM H'CAP 1m 7f 177y
4:20 (4:20) (Class 6) (0-60,59) 3-Y-O+ **£2,730** (£806; £403) **Stalls** Low

Form RPR
-000 **1** **Dan's Heir**[17] 5369 4-8-13 **52** ....(p) AshleyHamblett(7) 7 63
(P C Haslam) *hld up in rr: stdy hdwy over 4f out: chsd ldrs 2f out: swtchd rt and rdn over 1f out: styd on to ld ins last* **11/1**
4140 **2** *1* **Onyergo (IRE)**[17] 5369 4-9-6 **52** .... PhillipMakin 15 62
(J R Weymes) *hld up: hdwy 6f out: led 3f out amd rdn clr: drvn over 1f out: edgd rt and hdd ins last* **18/1**
0450 **3** *5* **Three Boars**[52] 4380 4-9-3 **49** ....(b) SilvestreDeSousa 8 53
(S Gollings) *hld up in midfield: hdwy over 6f out: rdn to chse ldrs 2f out: drvn and kpt on same pce ent last* **11/1**
1345 **4** *2 ½* **True (IRE)**[17] 5369 5-9-2 **48** .... TonyHamilton 3 49
(Mrs S Lamyman) *midfield: stdy hdwy 1/2-way: led 4f out: rdn and hdd 3f out: sn drvn and kpt on same pce appr last* **8/1**

-002 **5** *2 ½* **Royal Melbourne (IRE)**[33] 4947 6-9-13 **59**........................ TomEaves 13 57
(Miss J A Camacho) *hld up and bhd: gd hdwy over 4f out: rdn to chse ldrs 2f out: sn drvn and no imp appr last* **7/1**[3]

2500 **6** *1* **Jumeirah Scarer**[22] 5242 5-9-8 **57**.............................. AndrewMullen(3) 1 54
(K A Ryan) *trckd ldrs on inner: pushed along and outpcd 4f out: kpt on u.p appr last* **8/1**

4254 **7** *¾* **Planters Punch (IRE)**[8] 5581 5-9-12 **58**..................(v) GrahamGibbons 6 54
(G M Moore) *prom: rdn along 4f out: wknd 3f out* **6/1**[2]

10-5 **8** *½* **Next Flight (IRE)**[233] 389 7-9-3 **49**.. DavidAllan 4 44
(R E Barr) *chsd ldrs: rdn along over 4f out: sn wknd* **33/1**

2133 **9** *hd* **Parchment (IRE)**[17] 5369 4-9-8 **59**..........................(b) MarkLawson(5) 2 54
(A J Lockwood) *midfield: effrt over 4f out: sn rdn along and no hdwy* **4/1**[1]

3060 **10** *9* **Whoopsie**[19] 5324 4-9-4 **50**.. DanielTudhope 11 34
(S Parr) *led: rdn along and hdd 4f out: sn wknd* **20/1**

1315 **11** *5* **Lake Wakatipu**[80] 3522 4-9-13 **59**.................................. JimmyQuinn 10 37
(M Mullineaux) *hld up and bhd: rapid hdwy on outer 31/2f out: rdn to chse ldrs 2f out: sn drvn and wknd* **9/1**

0210 **12** *1 ¾* **Dimashq**[35] 4914 4-8-13 **45**.. ChrisCatlin 14 21
(Ronald Thompson) *hld up in rr: hdwy 4f out: rdn along and in tch 3f out: sn drvn and wknd* **25/1**

00 **13** *7* **Urban Freeway (IRE)**[17] 5369 7-8-12 **47**........................ GregFairley(3) 9 15
(Robert Gray) *chsd ldr: rdn along over 4f out: sn wknd* **50/1**

2450 **14** *½* **Valeureux**[22] 5242 8-9-4 **50**..(t) MichaelTebbutt 12 17
(J Hetherton) *midfield: rdn along 1/2-way: sn outpcd and bhd* **25/1**

0600 **15** *2 ½* **Zeydnaa (IRE)**[28] 5080 6-9-0 **46**.................................. RoystonFfrench 5 10
(C R Wilson) *a towards rr: bhd fr 1/2-way* **16/1**

3m 39.32s (7.92) **Going Correction** +0.425s/f (Yiel) **15 Ran SP% 124.2**
Speed ratings (Par 101):97,96,94,92,91 91,90,90,90,85 83,82,78,78,77
CSF £186.99 CT £2246.81 TOTE £12.30: £3.50, £8.50, £5.50; EX 556.40.
Owner Peter W Tomlinson **Bred** R P Williams **Trained** Middleham Moor, N Yorks
■ Stewards' Enquiry : Ashley Hamblett one-day ban: used whip down the shoulder in the forehand position (Oct 15)

FOCUS
They went a fair gallop in this staying handicap and the principals all came from off the pace. The form looks sound enough rated around the first three.
Zeydnaa(IRE) Official explanation: jockey said gelding was unsuited by the good (good to soft places) ground

5751 BOOK ON-LINE AT CATTERICKBRIDGE.CO.UK H'CAP 1m 3f 214y
4:50 (4:50) (Class 5) (0-75,74) 3-Y-0+ **£3,886** (£1,156; £577; £288) **Stalls Low**

Form RPR
6134 **1** **Luna Landing**[21] 5266 3-9-8 **74**.................................... DanielTudhope 10 87
(Jedd O'Keeffe) *trckd ldrs: qcknd to ld over 2f out: sn clr: readily* **7/2**[1]

4406 **2** *6* **Always Baileys (IRE)**[13] 5478 3-8-13 **68**........................ GregFairley(3) 1 71
(M Johnston) *chsd ldrs: outpcd over 2f out: styd on to take modest 2nd ins last* **6/1**[3]

3544 **3** *1* **Grey Outlook**[17] 5360 3-8-12 **64**.. TomEaves 12 66
(Miss L A Perratt) *hld up: hdwy 4f out: hung lft over 1f out: styd on ins last* **10/1**

3250 **4** *¾* **San Deng**[57] 4205 4-9-4 **63**.. PaulMulrennan 4 64
(Micky Hammond) *chsd ldrs: one pce fnl 2f* **10/1**

3430 **5** *1* **Apsara**[3] 5685 5-9-9 **68**.. PhillipMakin 6 67
(G M Moore) *led tl over 2f out: one pce* **9/2**[2]

-000 **6** *2 ½* **Razed**[13] 5484 3-8-12 **64**.. RoystonFfrench 13 59
(M Johnston) *s.s: in rr: drvn over 5f out: sme hdwy on ins over 2f out: nvr nr ldrs* **18/1**

2-10 **7** *shd* **Millagros (IRE)**[211] 603 6-9-8 **67**.................................... PaulHanagan 7 62
(I Semple) *hld up towards rr: hdwy 4f out: fdd fnl f* **9/1**

005 **8** *3 ½* **Dunlin**[131] 1955 3-8-10 **62**.. JimmyQuinn 9 51
(H Morrison) *trckd ldrs: rdn and hung lft over 2f out: sn btn* **13/2**

0236 **9** *¾* **Platinum Charmer (IRE)**[61] 4086 6-8-9 **54** oh1.............(p) LeeEnstone 5 42
(K R Burke) *trckd ldrs: outpcd over 3f out: wknd over 1f out: eased ins last* **15/2**

1/00 **10** *26* **Miss Holly**[19] 5314 7-8-10 **62**.................................... KellyHarrison(7) 11 8
(D Carroll) *s.i.s: drvn 5f out: t.o 3f out* **50/1**

0000 **11** *24* **Kalush**[36] 4668 5-8-6 **56** oh19 ow2................................ AnnStokell(5) 8 —
(Miss A Stokell) *s.s: a last: t.o 3f out* **100/1**

2m 43.28s (4.28) **Going Correction** +0.425s/f (Yiel)
WFA 3 from 4yo+ 7lb **11 Ran SP% 116.2**
Speed ratings (Par 103):102,98,97,96,96 94,94,92,91,74 58
CSF £24.05 CT £192.04 TOTE £4.00: £1.50, £2.50, £3.00; EX 30.70.
Owner W R B Racing 47 (wrbracing.com) **Bred** Chippenham Lodge Stud Ltd **Trained** Middleham Moor, N Yorks

FOCUS
A modest handicap and, although the winner was impressive, the form is probably just ordinary although sound enough, rated around the placed horses.

5752 GO RACING AT YORK THIS FRIDAY APPRENTICE H'CAP 5f
5:20 (5:21) (Class 6) (0-58,58) 3-Y-0+ **£3,412** (£1,007; £504) **Stalls Low**

Form RPR
1343 **1** **Alugat (IRE)**[28] 5078 3-9-3 **58**....................................(p) SaleemGolam 13 72
(Mrs A Duffield) *racd towards centre: chsd ldr: rdn to ld entering last: edgd lft and kpt on* **10/1**

0003 **2** *1* **Trick Cyclist**[6] 5620 5-9-0 **55**....................................(b) PaulMulrennan 6 65
(M W Easterby) *led on far rail: rdn over 1f out: drvn and hdd ent last: kpt on same pce* **9/2**[1]

0005 **3** *2* **Brut**[6] 5620 4-9-0 **58**.. MarkLawson(3) 15 61
(D W Barker) *in tch towards centre: hdwy to chse ldng pair over 1f out: sn rdn and kpt on: nrst fin* **8/1**[2]

0100 **4** *1 ¼* **Dark Champion**[3] 5684 6-9-3 **58**...............................(b) PatrickMathers 2 57
(R E Barr) *midfield: hdwy wl over 1f out: sn rdn and kpt on ins last: nrst fin* **9/1**

0000 **5** *2 ½* **Titian Saga (IRE)**[8] 5577 3-8-12 **58**............................ VictoriaBehan(5) 9 48
(D Nicholls) *racd towards centre: chsd ldrs: rdn along and hung lft 2f out: sn one pce* **33/1**

1010 **6** *½* **Miss Mujahid Times**[29] 5062 3-8-12 **53**.................(b) SilvestreDeSousa 4 41
(A D Brown) *racd towards far rail: chsd ldrs: rdn 2f out and grad wknd* **8/1**[2]

0660 **7** *shd* **Amanda's Lad (IRE)**[3] 5684 6-8-7 **55**............................ DawnRankin(7) 5 43
(M C Chapman) *chsd ldrs towards far side: rdn along 2f out: sn wknd* **18/1**

0546 **8** *1* **Limonia (GER)**[8] 5576 4-9-0 **55**.. JamesDoyle 10 39
(N P Littmoden) *in tch: rdn along wl over 1f out: sn no imp* **8/1**[2]

4500 **9** *¾* **Mystery Pips**[28] 5078 6-8-12 **58**........................(v) DanielleMcCreery(5) 3 39
(N Tinkler) *racd towards far side: a rr* **16/1**

2010 **10** *shd* **The Salwick Flyer (IRE)**[16] 5401 3-8-11 **52**............ StephenDonohoe 7 33
(A Berry) *prom towards centre: rdn along 1/2-way: sn wknd* **25/1**

0200 **11** *¾* **Slipperfoot**[13] 5486 3-8-13 **54**...(p) DNolan 1 32
(J J Quinn) *a towards rr far side* **25/1**

1200 **12** *2 ½* **Bond Becks (IRE)**[5] 5631 6-9-2 **57**.................................. GregFairley 8 26
(B Smart) *chsd ldrs towards far side: rdn 2f out: sn wknd* **17/2**[3]

6006 **13** *3* **Salviati (USA)**[13] 5480 9-8-5 **53**.................................. BarrySavage(7) 12 11
(J M Bradley) *s.i.s: a rr* **12/1**

0006 **14** *1 ¼* **Smirfys Systems**[14] 5453 7-8-9 **53**................................ LiamJones(3) 11 7
(W M Brisbourne) *a towards rr* **14/1**

030- **15** *1 ½* **Tancred Times**[409] 4577 11-8-13 **54**............................ AndrewMullen 14 —
(D W Barker) *a towards rr* **66/1**

61.94 secs (1.34) **Going Correction** +0.30s/f (Good) **15 Ran SP% 118.8**
Speed ratings (Par 101):101,99,96,94,90 89,89,87,86,86 85,81,76,74,71
CSF £51.52 CT £395.35 TOTE £7.20: £2.30, £2.20, £3.00; EX 30.60.
Owner Ian West & Partners **Bred** Rathbarry Stud **Trained** Constable Burton, N Yorks
■ Stewards' Enquiry : Dawn Rankin caution: careless riding

FOCUS
A moderate sprint handicap in which it paid to race prominently. The form looks sound for the level, though, with the runner-up the best guide.

5753 14TH OCTOBER IS TOTESPORT SATURDAY MAIDEN STKS (DIV II) 5f
5:50 (5:51) (Class 5) 2-Y-O **£3,238** (£963; £481; £240) **Stalls Low**

Form RPR
0505 **1** **Luscivious**[12] 5496 2-9-0 67................................(b) StephenDonohoe(3) 6 82+
(A J McCabe) *mde all: clr over 2f out: rdn out: unchal* **16/1**

4242 **2** *4* **Mazin Lady**[22] 5238 2-8-12 68.. TomEaves 4 63
(Miss J A Camacho) *trckd ldrs: wnt 2nd over 1f out: no imp* **9/4**[2]

3 *1 ½* **Bond Platinum Club** 2-8-12.. PhillipMakin 2 57
(B Smart) *sn outpcd: hdwy over 1f out: kpt on* **14/1**

033 **4** *nk* **Rocker**[12] 5496 2-9-3 73.. ChrisCatlin 8 61
(P W Chapple-Hyam) *chsd ldrs: kpt on same pce fnl 2f* **13/8**[1]

044 **5** *nk* **Aquilegia (IRE)**[21] 5264 2-8-12 67.............................. GrahamGibbons 5 55
(E S McMahon) *chsd ldrs: one pce fnl 2f* **9/2**[3]

4 **6** *3* **Glen Avon Girl (IRE)**[47] 4510 2-8-12................................ DavidAllan 1 44
(T D Easterby) *chsd ldrs: wknd appr fnl f* **9/1**

5 **7** *1 ¾* **Mangano**[17] 5364 2-9-3.. TonyHamilton 3 43
(A Berry) *chsd ldrs: lost pl over 1f out* **100/1**

00 **8** *8* **Orotund**[20] 5283 2-8-12.. DuranFentiman(5) 10 14
(T D Easterby) *s.i.s: a outpcd and bhd* **100/1**

9 *1 ½* **Inverted** 2-9-3.. RoystonFfrench 7 —
(Mrs A Duffield) *s.i.s: sn outpcd: bhd fnl 2f* **33/1**

10 *13* **Bayshambles (IRE)** 2-9-0.................................. PatrickMathers(3) 9 —
(R E Barr) *s.v.s: a detached in last* **100/1**

62.33 secs (1.73) **Going Correction** +0.30s/f (Good) **10 Ran SP% 115.5**
Speed ratings (Par 95):98,91,89,88,88 83,80,67,65,44
CSF £51.86 TOTE £16.80: £3.10, £1.20, £5.30; EX 72.30 Place 6 £221.39, Place 5 £211.60.
Owner Paul J Dixon And Keith Barratt **Bred** R J Turner **Trained** Babworth, Notts
■ The first training success for former jump jockey Alan McCabe.

FOCUS
A modest maiden that could be rated higher, in which it again paid to race prominently. Kyllachy sired the first two home.

NOTEBOOK
Luscivious had shown plenty of speed on his last three starts, all over six furlongs and, despite his price, it was not a huge surprise to see him far more effective over the minimum trip on this sharp track. The ease of his victory was unexpected though, and on this performance he would certainly be of interest in a five-furlong nursery, especially under a penalty.
Mazin Lady had to settle for the runner-up spot for the third time in her last four starts. She beat the rest well enough but clearly has her limitations. Perhaps a slightly stiffer test will suit her, but her pedigree is all speed. (op 5-2 tchd 3-1, 10-3 in a place)
Bond Platinum Club, a half-sister to high-class juvenile Lord Kintyre, is bred for the job, but she struggled with the early pace and took a while to get the hang of things. Her best work was being put in at the finish, though, and with this run under her belt it would not be a surprise to see her go in next time in similar company. (op 12-1)
Rocker was outpaced on this drop back to five furlongs and never really threatened. (op 15-8 tchd 11-8, 2-1 in a place)
Aquilegia(IRE) should have been happier on this easier surface having hung on good to firm ground at Sandown last time, but she proved a bit disappointing. (op 4-1)
Glen Avon Girl(IRE), who is a half-sister to five-furlong winners Sighting and Tatweer, might do better once handicapped. (op 8-1 tchd 10-1)
Inverted Official explanation: jockey said saddle slipped
T/Jkpt: Not won. T/Plt: £939.90 to a £1 stake. Pool: £71,394.65. 55.45 winning tickets. T/Qpdt: £347.70 to a £1 stake. Pool: £3,430.90. 7.30 winning tickets. JR

5431 LEICESTER (R-H)
Tuesday, October 3

OFFICIAL GOING: Soft (good to soft in places; heavy in dip)
Wind: Light, behind Weather: Cloudy with sunny spells

5754 E B F HARE MAIDEN FILLIES' STKS (DIV I) 7f 9y
2:10 (2:11) (Class 5) 2-Y-O **£3,886** (£1,156; £577; £288) **Stalls Low**

Form RPR
0 **1** **Hi Calypso (IRE)**[18] 5344 2-9-0 .... RyanMoore 3 76+
(Sir Michael Stoute) *s.i.s: hdwy 1/2-way: swtchd rt over 1f out: styd on to ld wl ins fnl f* **11/4**[1]

2 *nk* **Beautiful Reward (FR)** 2-9-0 .... JamieSpencer 7 75+
(J R Fanshawe) *dwlt: hld up: hdwy over 2f out: edgd rt fnl f: r.o* **9/1**

3 *hd* **Fashion Model** 2-9-0 .... PhilipRobinson 6 75+
(M A Jarvis) *chsd ldr: led over 1f out: hdd wl ins fnl f: kpt on* **12/1**

05 **4** *1 ½* **Joyful Tears (IRE)**[15] 5425 2-9-0 .... JoeFanning 14 71
(E A L Dunlop) *hld up: hdwy over 2f out: ev ch ins fnl f: no ex towards fin* **20/1**

6 **5** *1* **Kashmir Lady (FR)**[46] 4553 2-9-0 .... DaneO'Neill 4 69
(H Candy) *hld up: plld hrd: hdwy over 1f out: styd on same pce ins fnl f* **12/1**

52 **6** *1* **Sophia Gardens**[29] 5068 2-9-0 .... SteveDrowne 12 66
(D W P Arbuthnot) *chsd ldrs: rdn over 1f out: no ex fnl f* **11/2**[3]

7 *5* **Kanonkop** 2-8-11 .... EdwardCreighton(3) 9 54
(Miss J R Gibney) *s.i.s: nvr trbld ldrs* **80/1**

8 *shd* **Step To The Stars (IRE)** 2-9-0 .... KDarley 5 53
(M Johnston) *s.i.s: hdwy to ld 6f out: hdd over 1f out: wknd fnl f* **10/1**

00 **9** *½* **Zoorina**[61] 4084 2-9-0 ....(t) MartinDwyer 13 52
(M P Tregoning) *mid-div: rdn 1/2-way: wknd 2f out* **20/1**

22 **10** ¾ **Dragon Flower (USA)**[15] 5425 2-9-0 .... MichaelHills 2 50
(B W Hills) *led 1f: chsd ldrs: wkng whn n.m.r over 1f out* 7/2[2]

11 6 **Chiff Chaff** 2-9-0 .... HayleyTurner 8 35
(M L W Bell) *sn outpcd* 33/1

12 3½ **Snugfit** 2-9-0 .... MickyFenton 10 26
(G G Margarson) *s.s: outpcd* 40/1

1m 28.51s (2.41) **Going Correction** +0.175s/f (Good) **12** Ran SP% **114.9**
Speed ratings (Par 92):93,92,92,90,89 88,82,82,82,81 74,70
CSF £25.34 TOTE £3.80: £1.60, £2.90, £2.80; EX 31.30 TRIFECTA Not won..
Owner Philip Newton **Bred** Philip Newton **Trained** Newmarket, Suffolk

FOCUS
There were a few fillies that appealed as potentially nice types beforehand and in the race itself, so it is a maiden that should work out. The time, though, was a little less encouraging; it was by far the slowest of the four seven-furlong races on the card and nearly a second slower than the second division of this race, and difficult to rate with confidence.

NOTEBOOK
Hi Calypso(IRE), well held but not without promise on her debut over this trip at Newbury, has clearly gone the right way since and showed improved form to get off the mark at the second attempt. The winning time is not very encouraging, but this looked a reasonable maiden and she deserves her chance in better company. She should make a nice three-year-old. (tchd 5-2)
Beautiful Reward(FR) ◆, a 90,000euros half-sister to Horse Man, a ten-furlong winner in France, smart Italian performer Toto Le Heros and two staying types, made a pleasing debut. She was well off the pace early and basically looked to be running a little green, but she stayed on very nicely when getting the hang of things in the latter stages. It will be disappointing if she does not progress and go one better. (op 12-1)
Fashion Model ◆, a half-sister to several winners, including mile-winner Gracious Dancer, and dual middle-distance scorer Jazil, was another to shape with plenty of promise on her racecourse introduction. She was just run out of it in the closing stages and should be well up to finding a similar race with the benefit of this experience. (op 10-1)
Joyful Tears(IRE) ◆ stepped up on two moderate efforts and gave the impression she can do better still. Finishing so close will not have done her handicap mark any favours, but she still looks capable of improving further in that sphere. (op 16-1)
Kashmir Lady(FR), despite racing keenly, improved on the form she showed on her debut at Folkestone. (op 16-1)
Sophia Gardens promised to be suited by the switch to soft ground but she was well held and failed to build on her two previous efforts. (op 7-1)
Dragon Flower(USA), so promising on her debut at Newbury but beaten at odds on at Kempton last time, was a major disappointment this time and may not have been suited by the soft ground. (op 10-3 tchd 4-1)

5755 TELETEXT RACING "HANDS AND HEELS" APPRENTICE SERIES H'CAP 7f 9y
2:40 (2:42) (Class 5) (0-70,70) 3-Y-0+ **£3,238** (£963; £481; £240) **Stalls** Low

Form RPR

0040 **1** **Middleton Grey**[24] 5167 8-9-6 **67** ....(b) LukeMorris 10 76
(A G Newcombe) *dwlt: hdwy 1/2-way: led over 2f out: edgd lft over 1f out: styd on* 11/1

2540 **2** 1 **Way To The Stars**[45] 4591 3-9-1 **67** .... WilliamBuick(3) 6 74+
(A M Balding) *sn outpcd: hdwy over 1f out: nt rch wnr* 16/1

4524 **3** hd **Al Rayanah**[17] 5384 3-8-13 **62** .... KirstyMilczarek 11 68
(G Prodromou) *plld hrd and prom: ev ch over 2f out: styd on* 9/1

0000 **4** 2 **Danielle's Lad**[8] 5569 10-8-7 **57** ....(b) RichardRowe(3) 13 58
(B Palling) *chsd ldrs: led over 4f out: hdd over 2f out: styd on same pce appr fnl f* 20/1

3600 **5** 1½ **Whitbarrow (IRE)**[17] 5378 7-8-12 **59** .... JamesMillman 5 56
(B R Millman) *led: hdd over 4f out: styd on same pce appr fnl f* 12/1

0303 **6** 1 **Danehill Stroller (IRE)**[14] 5453 6-8-8 **55** .... JamieHamblett 1 49
(A M Hales) *s.i.s: hld up: plld hrd: hdwy over 2f out: nt trble ldrs* 8/1[3]

5600 **7** shd **Broken Spur (FR)**[59] 4143 3-9-3 **66** ....(t) PatrickHills 7 60
(B W Hills) *hld up: hdwy over 1f out: nvr nrr* 12/1

0033 **8** 1¼ **Bathwick Emma (IRE)**[5] 5085 3-9-0 **63** .... ThomasO'Brien 15 54
(P D Evans) *prom: rdn over 2f out: styd on same pce* 9/1

3100 **9** ½ **Stamford Blue**[13] 5480 5-9-2 **63** ....(b) TolleyDean 14 52
(R A Harris) *mid-div: outpcd fnl 3f* 7/1[2]

041 **10** 2 **Marajel (IRE)**[31] 5023 3-9-4 **70** .... MCGeran(3) 2 54
(P W Chapple-Hyam) *chsd ldrs over 4f* 3/1[1]

6000 **11** 2½ **Villarosi (IRE)**[7] 5599 4-9-5 **66** ....(v[1]) KylieManser 9 44
(J R Best) *chsd ldrs over 4f: eased fnl f* 25/1

000/ **12** ½ **Rifleman (IRE)**[53] 3563 6-8-12 **62** ....(t) JamesRogers(3) 4 38
(B Ellison) *sn outpcd* 16/1

-000 **13** ½ **Mystic Roll**[119] 2318 3-8-13 **65** .... MarkWaite(3) 8 40
(Jane Chapple-Hyam) *outpcd* 50/1

6006 **14** 5 **Sigismundus (IRE)**[21] 5263 3-8-10 **59** .... KMay 16 21
(J R Boyle) *prom over 4f* 25/1

0000 **15** 1¾ **Threezedzz**[6] 5621 8-8-8 **58** ....(b) JackDean(3) 17 16
(R A Harris) *chsd ldrs over 4f* 33/1

1m 27.81s (1.71) **Going Correction** +0.175s/f (Good)
WFA 3 from 4yo+ 2lb **15** Ran SP% **121.4**
Speed ratings (Par 103):97,95,95,93,91 90,90,88,88,86 83,82,82,76,74
CSF £164.94 CT £1664.05 TOTE £11.40: £3.30, £6.30, £3.10; EX 276.90 TRIFECTA Not won..
Owner B P Ryan **Bred** Mount Coote Stud **Trained** Yarnscombe, Devon

FOCUS
A modest handicap restricted to apprentice riders who had not ridden more than ten winners at the start of the current turf season. The winning time was slower than both the second division of the juvenile maiden and the three-year-old maiden. The third sets and ordinary standard.

5756 RAYMOND EDWARDS BIRTHDAY FILLIES' H'CAP 5f 218y
3:10 (3:11) (Class 5) (0-70,70) 3-Y-0+ **£3,238** (£963; £481; £240) **Stalls** Low

Form RPR

0111 **1** **Forces Sweetheart**[19] 5327 3-9-1 **66** ....(v) HayleyTurner 5 82
(M L W Bell) *hld up: hdwy over 2f out: styd on to ld nr fin* 11/1

6501 **2** hd **Word Perfect**[5] 5635 4-9-2 **66** 6ex ....(b) DaleGibson 13 81
(M W Easterby) *chsd ldrs: led over 2f out: rdn over 1f out: hdd nr fin* 9/2[1]

0145 **3** 2½ **Mugeba**[19] 5327 5-8-7 **57** ....(t) MartinDwyer 6 65
(Miss Gay Kelleway) *hld up: rdn 2f out: r.o ins fnl f: nt rch ldrs* 11/1

4552 **4** 1½ **Joyeaux**[8] 5577 4-8-12 **62** ....(v) RyanMoore 17 65
(J Hetherton) *dwlt: swtchd lft 1/2-way: swtchd rt and hdwy over 1f out: nt rch ldrs* 12/1

422 **5** 1 **Riquewihr**[19] 5317 6-9-0 **69** ....(p) JamieMoriarty(5) 1 69
(J S Wainwright) *led: hdd over 4f out: rdn over 2f out: styd on same pce fnl f* 10/1[3]

5130 **6** 1 **Cerulean Rose**[17] 5378 7-8-9 **59** .... JoeFanning 4 56
(A W Carroll) *hld up: rdn 1/2-way: styd on ins fnl f: nt trble ldrs* 12/1

0050 **7** hd **Sabrina Brown**[38] 4807 5-9-2 **66** ....(t) StephenCarson 12 62
(J A Geake) *chsd ldrs: led over 4f out: rdn and hdd over 2f out: wknd ins fnl f* 7/1[2]

0033 **8** 1½ **Dance To The Blues (IRE)**[18] 5350 5-8-13 **66**(p) RichardKingscote(3) 7 58
(B De Haan) *chsd ldrs: rdn over 2f out: wknd fnl f* 16/1

5006 **9** hd **Extremely Rare (IRE)**[17] 5378 5-8-8 **58** ow2 .... MickyFenton 14 49
(M S Saunders) *chsd ldrs: rdn and ev ch over 1f out: wknd fnl f* 12/1

0652 **10** ¾ **Indian Lady (IRE)**[8] 5576 3-8-4 **55** oh2 ....(b) TPO'Shea 11 44
(Mrs A L M King) *s.i.s: sn chsng ldrs: rdn and wknd over 1f out* 16/1

65-0 **11** 1¾ **Take It There**[17] 5388 4-8-13 **63** .... RichardThomas 3 47
(A J Lidderdale) *prom: lost pl over 4f out: n.d after* 50/1

0040 **12** shd **Quadrophenia**[5] 5636 3-8-4 **55** oh2 .... JamieMackay 8 39
(J G Given) *chsd ldrs: rdn over 2f out: sn wknd* 50/1

20-0 **13** 2 **Bernie's Beau (IRE)**[157] 1279 3-9-0 **65** .... TedDurcan 18 43
(R Hollinshead) *hld up: effrt and nt clr run over 1f out: n.d* 100/1

6150 **14** 1 **Nightstrike (IRE)**[37] 4837 3-9-0 **65** .... DaneO'Neill 9 40
(H Candy) *hld up in tch: rdn 1/2-way: wknd over 1f out* 33/1

0000 **15** ½ **Marriage Value (IRE)**[104] 2756 3-9-5 **70** .... TPQueally 16 43
(J A Osborne) *hld up: hdwy 1/2-way: rdn and wknd over 1f out* 33/1

4003 **16** 1¾ **Dispol Katie**[5] 5635 5-8-13 **63** .... JamieSpencer 10 31
(T D Barron) *mid-div: rdn 1/2-way: wknd over 1f out* 9/2[1]

0520 **17** 2½ **Disco Ball**[89] 3226 3-9-5 **70** .... SteveDrowne 15 30
(G Wragg) *prom over 3f* 25/1

1m 13.55s (0.35) **Going Correction** +0.175s/f (Good)
WFA 3 from 4yo+ 1lb **17** Ran SP% **124.1**
Speed ratings (Par 100):104,103,100,98,97 95,95,93,93,92 89,89,87,85,85 82,79
CSF £57.82 CT £598.62 TOTE £8.90: £1.80, £1.50, £2.90, £3.00; EX 58.50 Trifecta £186.30 Part won. Pool: £262.52 - 0.20 winning units..
Owner Richard I Morris Jr **Bred** Barton Stud Partnership **Trained** Newmarket, Suffolk

FOCUS
A modest fillies' sprint handicap run in a fair time and the form rated positively around the first two.
Dispol Katie Official explanation: jockey said mare became upset in stalls
Disco Ball Official explanation: jockey said filly hung right-handed

5757 STOAT (S) STKS 1m 1f 218y
3:40 (3:41) (Class 6) 3-Y-0 **£2,590** (£770; £385; £96; £96) **Stalls** High

Form RPR

0050 **1** **Maria Antonia (IRE)**[8] 5567 3-8-6 60 .... TPO'Shea 4 51+
(P A Blockley) *plld hrd and prom: led over 2f out: rdn clr fnl f: eased nr fin* 7/1

0050 **2** 2½ **Lanfredo**[6] 5625 3-8-11 45 ....(p) SteveDrowne 9 51
(D W P Arbuthnot) *chsd ldrs: outpcd over 2f out: rallied over 1f out: styd on* 7/2[2]

000 **3** shd **Pickwick Miss (USA)**[60] 4113 3-8-7 47 ow1 .... FergusSweeney 8 47
(D M Simcock) *sn led: rdn and hdd over 2f out: styd on same pce fnl f* 11/1

0000 **4** ½ **Queen Of Diamonds (IRE)**[36] 4868 3-8-6 45 .... RobertHavlin 6 45
(Mrs P N Dutfield) *hld up: hdwy over 3f out: rdn over 1f out: styd on same pce fnl f* 14/1

00 **4** dht **Lady Suffragette (IRE)**[55] 4263 3-8-6 .... CatherineGannon 5 45
(John Berry) *chsd ldrs: rdn over 2f out: styd on same pce fnl f* 22/1

1000 **6** 3½ **Coffin Dodger**[20] 5298 3-8-4 49 .... KirstyMilczarek(7) 7 44
(C N Allen) *s.i.s: hld up: rdn over 2f out: no imp* 4/1[3]

5124 **7** ¾ **Mister Maq**[13] 4533 3-9-2 60 ....(b) JimCrowley 1 47
(M Dods) *s.i.s: hld up: hdwy over 2f out: wknd fnl f* 5/2[1]

4563 **8** 13 **Rockatorri**[14] 5441 3-8-6 35 ....(b) HayleyTurner 2 14
(G G Margarson) *prom: jnd ldr over 6f out tl rdn over 3f out: wknd wl over 1f out* 9/1

0000 **9** dist **Northern Promise (IRE)**[17] 5365 3-8-11 40 ....(b[1]) MickyFenton 10 —
(J Parkes) *sn pushed along in rr: wknd over 4f out* 66/1

2m 11.07s (2.77) **Going Correction** +0.35s/f (Good) **9** Ran SP% **114.1**
Speed ratings (Par 99):102,100,99,99,99 96,96,85,—
CSF £31.34 TOTE £7.70: £1.70, £1.70, £3.20; EX 34.70 Trifecta £166.80 Pool: £411.25 - 1.75 winning units..The winner was bought in for 4,000gns.
Owner Pedro Rosas **Bred** J McElroy **Trained** Lambourn, Berks

FOCUS
A very moderate race and not that solid, as is to be expected in selling company, rated through the runner-up.

5758 QUORN H'CAP 1m 3f 183y
4:10 (4:11) (Class 2) (0-100,97) 3-Y-0 **£11,217** (£3,358; £1,679; £840; £419; £210) **Stalls** High

Form RPR

1301 **1** **Green Room (FR)**[39] 4778 3-8-11 **90** .... RyanMoore 8 100+
(J L Dunlop) *chsd ldrs: led 2f out: rdn and hung rt over 1f out: hung lft ins fnl f: styd on* 9/2[2]

1112 **2** 2 **Trick Or Treat**[26] 5141 3-8-13 **92** .... JamieMackay 2 98
(J G Given) *prom: rdn over 1f out: styd on same pce* 15/8[1]

2010 **3** nk **Crime Scene (IRE)**[17] 5374 3-9-4 **97** .... KDarley 7 103
(M Johnston) *chsd ldr: rdn to ld over 2f out: sn hdd: styd on same pce ins fnl f* 11/2

1105 **4** 1½ **Nelsons Column (IRE)**[37] 4833 3-8-9 **88** .... NickyMackay 5 92
(G M Moore) *led: rdn and hdd over 2f out: no ex fnl f* 8/1

3231 **5** hd **Mobaasher (USA)**[19] 5319 3-8-4 **83** .... MartinDwyer 1 86
(Sir Michael Stoute) *hld up: rdn over 2f out: nt trble ldrs* 5/1[3]

-313 **6** 3 **Mabadi (USA)**[10] 5538 3-8-4 **83** oh2 .... RHills 4 81
(B W Hills) *hld up: rdn over 2f out: n.d* 6/1

2m 37.49s (2.99) **Going Correction** +0.35s/f (Good) **6** Ran SP% **110.4**
Speed ratings (Par 107):104,102,102,101,101 99
CSF £12.94 CT £42.79 TOTE £6.50: £3.40, £1.10; EX 18.00 Trifecta £51.00 Pool: £530.27 - 7.37 winning units..
Owner Nigel & Carolyn Elwes **Bred** Aylesfield Farms Stud Ltd **Trained** Arundel, W Sussex

FOCUS
Quite a good handicap despite the size of the field, and the pace seemed fair. The form appears sound rated around the placed horses.

NOTEBOOK
Green Room(FR) defied an 8lb higher mark than when winning at Salisbury on her previous start with a convincing success, despite wandering around under pressure. She is progressing into a very useful filly and is one to keep on-side when there is ease in the ground. (op 5-1 tchd 11-2)
Trick Or Treat, 4lb higher than when second at Southwell on her previous start, ran another honest race to gain her seventh straight top two placing. The Handicapper will continue to have his say, but she remains progressive. (op 13-8 tchd 2-1)
Crime Scene(IRE) could not confirm recent Southwell form with Trick Or Treat and this ground may have been a little softer than he cares for. (op 7-1)
Nelsons Column(IRE) stuck on surprisingly well when headed, but this ground was still softer than he likes. (op 9-1 tchd 10-1)
Mobaasher(USA) found this tougher than the Pontefract maiden he won on his previous start and it remains to be seen whether he is progressing. (op 13-2)
Mabadi(USA), effectively 5lb higher than when winning at Haydock on her previous start, was beaten some way out and may not have been suited by the testing ground. (op 9-2)

The Form Book, Raceform Ltd, Compton, RG20 6NL

5759 SQUIRREL CONDITIONS STKS 1m 1f 218y
4:40 (4:40) (Class 3) 2-Y-O **£6,855** (£2,052; £1,026; £513) **Stalls** High

Form RPR
01 **1** **Philanthropy**[13] 5475 2-9-1 83 .... JoeFanning 4 84
(M Johnston) *sn led: rdn and hdd over 1f out: rallied to ld wl ins fnl f: r.o* **1/1**[1]
012 **2** *hd* **Massive (IRE)**[19] 5308 2-9-1 83 .... TedDurcan 1 84
(M R Channon) *chsd wnr: rdn to ld over 1f out: sn edgd rt: hdd wl ins fnl f* **11/10**[2]
0 **3** *22* **Storm Path (IRE)**[53] 4333 2-8-11 .... RyanMoore 2 40
(C E Brittain) *prom over 6f* **12/1**[3]
040 **4** *21* **Oedipuss (IRE)**[59] 4161 2-8-6 46 .... EmmettStack(5) 3 2
(K J Burke) *prom: racd keenly: rdn and wknd over 2f out* **100/1**

2m 11.94s (3.64) **Going Correction** +0.35s/f (Good) 4 Ran SP% **106.3**
Speed ratings (Par 99):99,98,81,64
CSF £2.30 TOTE £2.00; EX 2.50.
Owner Jumeirah Racing **Bred** Darley **Trained** Middleham Moor, N Yorks

FOCUS
This conditions event only concerned two horses and they fought out a terrific finish and were close to their marks.

NOTEBOOK
Philanthropy put up a much-improved effort to get off the mark over nine furlongs at Goodwood on his previous start and probably stepped up again to follow up, coping with both the longer trip and switch to soft ground. He again gave the impression a race like the Zetland Stakes could be a suitable target. (op 10-11 tchd 11-10)
Massive(IRE), upped two furlongs in trip and racing on the softest ground he has ever tried, ran a fine in defeat and is the first horse to lose out to Johnston runner in a battle. He has more to offer. (op 5-4 tchd Evens)
Storm Path(IRE), last in a seven-furlong Newmarket maiden on his debut, was beaten some way out and this ground may have been softer than he wants.

5760 E B F HARE MAIDEN FILLIES' STKS (DIV II) 7f 9y
5:10 (5:14) (Class 5) 2-Y-O **£3,886** (£1,156; £577; £288) **Stalls** Low

Form RPR
5420 **1** **Onida (IRE)**[14] 5464 2-9-0 87 .... KerrinMcEvoy 4 90
(C G Cox) *mde all: rdn out* **2/1**[2]
02 **2** *1 1/4* **Latanazul**[18] 5352 2-9-0 .... RHills 1 87
(J L Dunlop) *a.p: rdn to chse wnr fnl f: styd on* **13/8**[1]
3 **3** *7* **Millisecond**[33] 4964 2-9-0 .... PhilipRobinson 3 72+
(M A Jarvis) *chsd wnr tl rdn and edgd rt over 1f out: sn wknd and eased* **7/2**[3]
0 **4** *4* **Virginia Reel**[29] 5068 2-9-0 .... KDarley 13 59
(M Johnston) *in rr: hdwy 1/2-way: wknd 2f out* **20/1**
00 **5** *1 1/4* **Inimical**[17] 5380 2-9-0 .... FergusSweeney 14 56
(W S Kittow) *prom: rdn over 2f out: sn wknd* **50/1**
6 *nk* **News Of The Day (IRE)** 2-9-0 .... JoeFanning 9 56
(M Johnston) *chsd ldrs over 4f* **20/1**
0 **7** *3 1/2* **Dressed To Dance (IRE)**[11] 5507 2-9-0 .... TedDurcan 2 47
(B J Meehan) *s.i.s: hld up: hdwy u.p over 2f out: sn wknd* **16/1**
8 *7* **Orange Lady (IRE)** 2-9-0 .... JamieSpencer 8 29+
(M L W Bell) *hld up: wknd over 2f out* **20/1**
0 **9** *1 1/2* **Tizzydore (IRE)**[15] 5424 2-9-0 .... SteveDrowne 7 26+
(A M Balding) *prom over 4f* **66/1**
00 **10** *16* **Queen Of Fools (IRE)**[46] 4559 2-9-0 .... MartinDwyer 5 —
(R Hannon) *sn outpcd* **33/1**

1m 27.56s (1.46) **Going Correction** +0.175s/f (Good) 10 Ran SP% **120.2**
Speed ratings (Par 92):98,96,88,84,82 82,78,70,68,50
CSF £5.32 TOTE £3.20: £1.20, £1.10, £1.50; EX 6.10 Trifecta £14.00 Pool: £283.17 - 14.35 winning units..
Owner Oh Five Partnership **Bred** Barouche Stud Ireland Ltd **Trained** Lambourn, Berks
■ Ravarino (10/1) was withdrawn on vet's advice. R4 applies, deduct 5p in the £.

FOCUS
The principals offered some useful form, but this fillies' maiden appeared to lack the strength in depth of the first division. The winning time was nearly a full second quicker than the first division and the form looks pretty solid.

NOTEBOOK
Onida(IRE) was not at her best in a valuable sales race in Ireland last time, but she had previously shown useful form in reasonable company and confirmed that to get off the mark in pretty straightforward fashion. She deserves her chance back in a higher grade. (old market op 5-2 tchd 11-4 in places)
Latanazul, dropped a furlong in trip and returned to soft ground, did not run badly but failed to build on her second to subsequent Fillies' Mile runner-up Treat. On this evidence, a return to further is likely to suit. (old market op 9-4 tchd 11-4 new market op 6-4)
Millisecond failed to build on the form she showed when third to subsequent Oh So Sharp Stakes runner-up Puggy in a fast-ground maiden at Salisbury on her debut and this soft surface did not appear to suit. (old market tchd 3-1 and 4-1)
Virginia Reel was beaten a fair way but this represents an improvement on her debut effort at Warwick. (old market op 25-1 tchd 28-1)
Inimical ran well enough and will have more options now she is qualified for a handicap mark. (old market op 100-1)

5761 DORMOUSE MAIDEN STKS 7f 9y
5:40 (5:44) (Class 5) 3-Y-O **£3,238** (£963; £481; £240) **Stalls** Low

Form RPR
2-24 **1** **Edaara (IRE)**[110] 2580 3-8-12 85 .... RHills 15 73+
(W J Haggas) *trckd ldrs: led on bit over 2f out: pushed clr fnl f* **11/8**[1]
0-00 **2** *6* **Double Carpet (IRE)**[36] 4888 3-9-3 55 .... JoeFanning 1 62
(G Woodward) *chsd ldrs: rdn over 2f out: outpcd over 1f out* **66/1**
225 **3** *nk* **Turkish Sultan (IRE)**[28] 5077 3-9-3 70 .... RyanMoore 10 61
(T D Easterby) *hld up: hdwy over 2f out: sn rdn: nrst fin* **12/1**
5-2 **4** *6* **Wind Shuffle (GER)**[60] 1564 3-9-3 .... MickyFenton 4 46
(T P Tate) *chsd ldrs: rdn over 2f out: sn wknd* **5/1**[2]
550 **5** *2 1/2* **Vacation (IRE)**[38] 4802 3-9-3 75 .... AdrianMcCarthy 9 39+
(V Smith) *hld up: hmpd wl over 1f out: n.d* **8/1**[3]
00 **6** *shd* **Ashford Castle (IRE)**[164] 1134 3-9-3 .... JamieSpencer 6 39
(B J Meehan) *chsd ldrs: led over 4f out: hdd over 2f out: wknd over 1f out* **14/1**
56 **7** *1 3/4* **Dixie Storm (USA)**[118] 2343 3-9-3 .... (t) SteveDrowne 14 34+
(A M Balding) *hld up: hmpd wl over 1f out: n.d* **12/1**
00 **8** *3/4* **Amron Hill**[15] 5426 3-8-10 .... RussellKennemore(7) 5 32
(R Hollinshead) *led: hdd over 4f out: wknd over 1f out* **66/1**
3- **9** *3* **Iannis (IRE)**[361] 5718 3-9-3 .... TPQueally 17 25
(J Noseda) *trckd ldrs: racd keenly: rdn over 2f out: sn wknd* **5/1**[2]
0-0 **10** *1 1/4* **Glitterati**[188] 795 3-8-12 .... LPKeniry 2 16
(J S Moore) *prom: rdn whn hmpd wl over 1f out: sn wknd* **66/1**
00 **11** *2 1/2* **Haughton Hope**[70] 3826 3-9-3 .... RobertHavlin 18 15
(T J Pitt) *in rr fr 1/2-way* **100/1**
506 **12** *4* **Footstepsinthesnow (IRE)**[80] 3554 3-8-12 50 .... MartinDwyer 8 —
(M A Buckley) *prom over 4f: in rr whn hmpd wl over 1f out* **28/1**
0-6 **13** *30* **Grand Rebecca (IRE)**[21] 5272 3-8-12 .... TPO'Shea 7 —
(G A Huffer) *mid-div: rdn 1/2-way: sn wknd: bhd whn hmpd wl over 1f out* **66/1**
00- **14** *16* **Caspian Rose**[479] 2490 3-8-12 .... RobbieFitzpatrick 12 —
(M J Attwater) *plld hrd and prom: lost pl over 4f out: sn bhd* **100/1**
30 **U** **Tumpuluna (IRE)**[28] 5093 3-8-5 .... KirstyMilczarek(7) 13 —
(G Prodromou) *hld up: plld hrd: hdwy over 4f out: cl up whn broke leg and uns rdr wl over 1f out: dead* **50/1**

1m 27.03s (0.93) **Going Correction** +0.175s/f (Good) 15 Ran SP% **122.0**
Speed ratings (Par 101):101,94,93,86,84 83,81,81,77,76 73,68,34,16,—
CSF £148.66 TOTE £2.10: £1.10, £16.70, £3.40; EX 151.60 Trifecta £240.30 Part won. Pool: £338.54 - 0.10 winning units. Place 6 £204.95, Place 5 £98.53.
Owner Hamdan Al Maktoum **Bred** Tarworth Bloodstock Investments Ltd **Trained** Newmarket, Suffolk

FOCUS
The proximity of the 55-rated Double Carpet suggests this maiden did not take a lot of winning and sets the standard, but the time was the fastest of the four races run over seven furlongs on this card, albeit two of those were for juveniles.
Footstepsinthesnow(IRE) Official explanation: jockey said filly lost its action
T/Plt: £448.00 to a £1 stake. Pool: £63,928.25. 104.15 winning tickets. T/Qpdt: £24.10 to a £1 stake. Pool: £4,045.50. 124.10 winning tickets. CR

HOPPEGARTEN (R-H)
Tuesday, October 3

OFFICIAL GOING: Good

5762a PREIS DER DEUTSCHEN EINHEIT (GROUP 3) 1m 2f
3:35 (3:41) 3-Y-O+ **£22,069** (£6,897; £3,448; £2,069)

RPR
1 **Karavel (GER)**[93] 3133 3-8-7 .... KFallon 5 109
(P Schiergen, Germany) *held up in 7th, headway on outside from 2f out, went 2nd over 1f out, hard ridden to lead post* **42/10**[3]
2 *shd* **Saddex**[30] 5051 3-8-11 .... TMundry 1 113
(P Rau, Germany) *led, set slow pace, headed post* **3/5**[1]
3 *1 3/4* **Waleria (GER)**[34] 4942 3-8-7 .... VSchulepov 6 106
(H J Groschel, Germany) *held up in rear, headway on inside from over 1 1/2f out, n.m.r and switched left ins fnl f, kpt on* **26/10**[2]
4 *nk* **White Lightning (GER)**[16] 5414 4-9-4 .... RJuracek 4 111
(U Stech, Norway) *pressed leader in 2nd, hard ridden and one pace from over 1f out* **117/10**
5 *1 1/2* **Dwilano (GER)**[34] 4942 3-8-11 .... AHelfenbein 3 107
(P Remmert, Germany) *raced in 4th, one pace final 2f* **30/1**
6 *3 1/2* **Obrigado (GER)** 5-9-4 .... WPanov 7 102
(M Sowa, Germany) *held up in last, always in rear* **29/1**
7 *nk* **Arpino (GER)**[108] 2671 3-8-11 .... WMongil 2 100
(P Schiergen, Germany) *raced in 3rd, weakened over 1f out* **28/1**
8 *2 1/2* **Mentik (RUS)** 4-9-4 .... IPerishkov 8 97
(W Hickst, Germany) *held up, 5th straight, never a factor* **25/1**

2m 8.00s
WFA 3 from 4yo+ 5lb 8 Ran SP% **131.2**
(including 10 Euro stake): WIN 52; PL 14, 11, 12; SF 99.
Owner Gestut Schlenderhan **Bred** Gestut Schlenderhan **Trained** Germany

MULHEIM (R-H)
Tuesday, October 3

OFFICIAL GOING: Good

5763a BERBERIS-RENNEN (LISTED RACE) 7f
3:55 (4:06) 2-Y-O **£10,345** (£4,138; £3,103; £2,069; £1,034)

RPR
1 **Rolling Home (GER)** 2-8-9 .... EPedroza 6 94+
(A Wohler, Germany)
2 *1* **Kick Back (GER)** 2-8-5 .... ABest 1 88+
(P Schiergen, Germany)
3 *1 3/4* **Pakama (GER)** 2-8-5 .... AStarke 5 83
(Mario Hofer, Germany)
4 *1 1/4* **Montalembert (USA)**[20] 5283 2-8-11 .... JohnEgan 3 86
(J S Moore) *held up disputing 3rd, 3rd on inside straight, ridden well over 1f out, kept on at one pace (5/2)* **5/2**[1]
5 *hd* **Syllable** 2-8-5 .... AGoritz 2 79
(Mario Hofer, Germany)
6 *2* **Andorn (GER)** 2-8-9 .... JPalik 4 78
(P Schiergen, Germany)

1m 27.76s
(including 10 Euro stake): WIN 31; PL 17, 29; SF 337. 6 Ran SP% **28.6**
Owner Stall Express **Bred** Hannes K Gutschow **Trained** Germany

NOTEBOOK
Montalembert(USA), a clear winner of a Beverley maiden last time out, had a lot more on his plate in this company and was not disgraced.

5592 NOTTINGHAM (L-H)
Wednesday, October 4

OFFICIAL GOING: Soft (good to soft in places)
Wind: light, across

5764 WBX.COM WORLD BET EXCHANGE FILLIES' NOVICE AUCTION STKS 6f 15y
2:20 (2:21) (Class 5) 2-Y-O **£3,238** (£963; £481; £240) **Stalls** High

Form RPR
21 **1** **Doric Charm**[6] 5632 2-8-13 .... RoystonFfrench 5 78+
(B Smart) *chsd ldr: led over 4f out: rdn over 1f out: r.o* **4/6**[1]

65 **2** *3* **Aaron's Way**[16] 5417 2-8-5 PaulHanagan 8 61
(A W Carroll) *s.i.s: hld up: plld hrd: hdwy 1/2-way: chsd wnr fnl f: no imp* **11/1**[3]

0060 **3** *3/4* **Princess Zada**[37] 4895 2-8-4 53 AdrianMcCarthy 3 58
(B R Millman) *hld up: hdwy over 1f out: edgd rt: nt trble ldrs* **50/1**

5000 **4** *3 1/2* **Bathwick Fancy (IRE)**[4] 5676 2-8-6 69 (t) TomEaves 4 49
(J G Portman) *hld up: sme hdwy over 1f out: n.d* **33/1**

0006 **5** *shd* **Mujart**[8] 5592 2-8-5 45 ChrisCatlin 11 48
(J A Pickering) *prom: chsd wnr over 2f out: rdn over 1f out: edgd lft and wknd fnl f* **50/1**

5556 **6** *1* **Dancing Daisy (IRE)**[54] 4327 2-8-6 55 ow2 RobertHavlin 9 46
(Mrs P N Dutfield) *sn outpcd: styd on fnl f: nt trble ldrs* **100/1**

1020 **7** *5* **Top Royelle**[16] 5434 2-9-2 80 RyanMoore 2 41
(R Hannon) *chsd ldrs: rdn over 2f out: wknd over 1f out* **5/2**[2]

8 *1 3/4* **Swift Princess (IRE)** 2-8-9 PatCosgrave 6 29
(K R Burke) *s.i.s: sn chsng ldrs: hung lft thrght: wknd wl over 1f out* **14/1**

1000 **9** *12* **Inflagranti**[21] 5290 2-9-0 63 TPQueally 10 —
(J G Portman) *led: hdd over 4f out: rdn and wknd over 1f out* **50/1**

06 **10** *1 3/4* **Blissfully**[78] 3605 2-8-8 MickyFenton 1 —
(S Parr) *unruly in stalls: chsd ldrs over 3f* **100/1**

0 **11** *5* **Miss Daawe**[12] 5507 2-8-4 RichardMullen 7 —
(S Parr) *prom: rdn over 3f out: wknd over 2f out* **100/1**

1m 16.86s (1.86) **Going Correction** +0.325s/f (Good) 11 Ran SP% **115.4**
Speed ratings (Par 92):100,96,95,90,90 88,82,79,63,61 54
CSF £9.59 TOTE £1.70: £1.10, £2.60, £9.40; EX 10.40.
Owner Doric Charm Partnership **Bred** P A Mason **Trained** Hambleton, N Yorks

FOCUS
The far rail had been moved in by four yards, making the straight narrower than at the previous meeting. The runners all came down the nearside of the track and the first three pulled clear. A moderate juvenile contest and although the winner scored easily the form does not look solid.

NOTEBOOK
Doric Charm only needed to repeat her Ayr running to follow up in this and, on the sharp end throughout, her supporters never had a moment's worry. She should make up into a nice sprint handicapper next season though fast ground remains an unknown. (op 8-11 tchd 4-5 in places)
Aaron's Way ◆ travelled well off the pace and stayed on well over the last couple of furlongs without causing the winner a problem. She is going the right way and can now be handicapped, so is one to note. (op 12-1)
Princess Zada, unplaced in her four previous starts, stayed on well over the last two furlongs having made her effort wider than most. She has looked no great shakes before now, so the easier ground was probably the reason behind this improved effort and it will be interesting to see if connections try to exploit her current mark in handicap company under similar conditions.
Bathwick Fancy(IRE), another unplaced in all four of her previous attempts, plodded on late over this shorter trip without landing a blow. She finished amongst some much lower-rated rivals, which suggests her current handicap mark is too high and is therefore likely to remain hard to place for the time being.
Mujart, another yet to make the frame after four outings, performed better than her official mark entitled her to just as she did here the previous week, but it would be dangerous to get carried away. She needs a drop in grade.
Top Royelle may need a longer trip now, but she is proven on an easy surface so this has to go down as very disappointing. (tchd 11-4)

5765 GASKET CUTTERS' ASSOCIATION H'CAP 6f 15y
2:50 (2:52) (Class 5) (0-75,76) 3-Y-0+ **£3,238** (£963; £481; £240) **Stalls** High

Form RPR

0501 **1** **Wanchai Lad**[8] 5593 5-9-5 76 6ex (t) DavidAllan 14 86
(T D Easterby) *racd stands' side: a.p: led overall over 1f out: rdn out* **7/1**[2]

0464 **2** *3/4* **Lizarazu (GER)**[9] 5572 7-8-8 72 (p) TolleyDean(7) 15 80
(R A Harris) *racd stands' side: hld up: swtchd lft and hdwy 1/2-way: rdn over 1f out: styd on: 2nd of 10 in gp* **33/1**

0-06 **3** *2 1/2* **My Only Sunshine**[128] 2074 7-8-7 64 ChrisCatlin 17 65
(M J Wallace) *racd stands' side: hld up: hdwy over 2f out: rdn over 1f out: edgd lft: styd on same pce: 3rd of 10 in gp* **28/1**

0400 **4** *3/4* **Balakiref**[14] 5476 7-9-4 75 JamieSpencer 2 73+
(M Dods) *racd far side: hld up: hdwy over 1f out: rdn to ld that gp ins fnl f: r.o: no ch w stands' side: 1st of 7 in gp* **6/1**[1]

0050 **5** *hd* **Marker**[47] 4564 6-8-8 65 RichardThomas 12 63
(J A Geake) *racd stands' side: chsd ldrs: outpcd 2f out: styd on ins fnl f: 4th of 10 in gp* **8/1**[3]

0246 **6** *hd* **Dorn Dancer (IRE)**[6] 5635 4-8-7 64 (p) TomEaves 16 61
(D W Barker) *racd stands' side: hld up: hdwy over 1f out: r.o: 5th of 10 in gp* **10/1**

4434 **7** *1/2* **Sir Orpen (IRE)**[29] 5079 3-8-13 71 (b[1]) PhillipMakin 11 67
(T D Barron) *led stands' side over 4f: no ex: 6th of 10 in gp* **8/1**[3]

1540 **8** *1 1/2* **Kennington**[18] 5391 6-8-12 69 (b) JohnEgan 3 60+
(Mrs C A Dunnett) *racd far side: chsd ldrs: rdn and ev ch that side ins fnl f: no ex: 2nd of 7 in gp* **20/1**

0644 **9** *nk* **Cornus**[8] 5593 4-8-12 72 StephenDonohoe(3) 5 62+
(A J McCabe) *racd far side: chsd ldrs: rdn to ld that gp over 1f out: hdd and no ex ins fnl f: 3rd of 7 in gp* **9/1**

1210 **10** *3* **Mocha Java**[22] 5268 3-8-13 71 IanMongan 9 52
(Mrs L J Mongan) *racd stands' side: chsd ldrs over 4f: 7th of 10 in gp* **12/1**

0630 **11** *1 1/4* **Capricho (IRE)**[84] 3413 9-8-11 68 JimmyQuinn 6 45+
(J Akehurst) *racd far side: hld up: effrt over 1f out: sn wknd: 4th of 7 in gp* **20/1**

3605 **12** *2* **Cheney Hill**[39] 4812 3-8-7 65 DaneO'Neill 7 36+
(H Candy) *racd far side: led that gp over 4f: sn wknd: 5th of 7 in gp* **25/1**

0506 **13** *shd* **Prince Cyrano**[18] 5391 7-8-12 69 TPQueally 13 40
(W J Musson) *racd stands' side: hld up: effrt over 2f out: wknd over 1f out: 8th of 10 in gp* **20/1**

4256 **14** *3/4* **Gilded Cove**[8] 5593 6-8-4 68 RussellKennemore(7) 4 37+
(R Hollinshead) *racd far side: chsd ldrs: outpcd: 6th of 7 in gp* **12/1**

1140 **15** *nk* **Joy And Pain**[95] 3089 5-8-8 70 (b[1]) KevinGhunowa(5) 8 38
(R A Harris) *racd stands' side: chsd ldrs: rdn whn rdr dropped reins 2f out wknd fnl f: 9th of 10 in gp* **50/1**

250 **16** *nk* **High Voltage**[6] 5635 5-8-6 68 (t) AndrewElliott(5) 1 35+
(K R Burke) *w ldr far side: over 4f: wknd qckly: last of 7 in gp* **14/1**

0-60 **17** *9* **Musical Guest (IRE)**[156] 1349 3-9-0 72 TonyCulhane 10 12
(G G Margarson) *racd stands' side: sn outpcd: last of 10 in gp* **50/1**

1m 16.22s (45.00) **Going Correction** +0.325s/f (Good)
WFA 3 from 4yo+ 1lb 17 Ran SP% **118.6**
Speed ratings (Par 103):104,103,99,98,98 98,97,95,95,91 89,86,86,85,85 84,72
CSF £226.27 CT £3396.38 TOTE £7.60: £1.80, £5.40, £6.20, £2.10; EX 129.20.
Owner Ambrose Turnbull **Bred** G T Lucas **Trained** Great Habton, N Yorks

FOCUS
A fair handicap won by a sprinter that has found his form again and the runner-up sets the standard. The stands' side dominated again.

Cheney Hill Official explanation: jockey said gelding hung to the right

5766 EUROPEAN BREEDERS FUND MAIDEN STKS 5f 13y
3:20 (3:21) (Class 4) 2-Y-0 **£4,533** (£1,348; £674; £336) **Stalls** High

Form RPR

1 **Now Look Out** 2-9-3 GrahamGibbons 6 74+
(E S McMahon) *s.i.s: sn chsng ldrs: hung rt over 1f out: rdn to ld ins fnl f: r.o* **7/1**[3]

22 **2** *1/2* **Hurricane Flyer**[45] 4630 2-9-3 RichardMullen 7 72
(E J O'Neill) *led: racd keenly: hmpd over 1f out: hdd and unable qckn ins fnl f* **7/4**[1]

03 **3** *4* **Multitude (IRE)**[13] 5491 2-9-3 DavidAllan 1 58
(T D Easterby) *chsd ldrs: hung lft over 3f out: sn rdn: styd on same pce appr fnl f* **5/1**[2]

03 **4** *1* **Woqoodd**[12] 5508 2-9-3 PhilipRobinson 4 54
(M A Jarvis) *chsd ldrs: rdn 1/2-way: styd on same pce fnl 2f* **7/4**[1]

00 **5** *1/2* **Smirfys Gold (IRE)**[12] 5508 2-9-3 RobbieFitzpatrick 3 52
(E S McMahon) *chsd ldrs: outpcd 1/2-way: n.d after* **33/1**

000 **6** *1/2* **Answer Back**[15] 5448 2-8-9 40 RichardKingscote(3) 8 46
(Miss J R Tooth) *chsd ldr to 1/2-way: sn outpcd* **100/1**

7 *3/4* **Shrewd Dude** 2-9-3 GeorgeBaker 2 48
(Carl Llewellyn) *s.s: outpcd: running on whn nt clr run ins fnl f: n.d* **20/1**

00 **8** *16* **Frill A Minute**[41] 4731 2-8-5 DawnRankin(7) 5 —
(Miss L C Siddall) *sn outpcd* **100/1**

63.07 secs (1.27) **Going Correction** +0.325s/f (Good) 8 Ran SP% **111.6**
Speed ratings (Par 97):102,101,94,93,92 91,90,64
CSF £18.77 TOTE £8.30: £2.00, £1.10, £1.80; EX 20.50.
Owner S L Edwards **Bred** S L Edwards **Trained** Hopwas, Staffs

FOCUS
A maiden lacking strength in depth and not easy to rate, but the front pair pulled right away and are the ones to focus on. The winning time was very fair for a race like this.

NOTEBOOK
Now Look Out ◆, a half-brother to three winners including Look Here Now, is bred for speed and was soon able to take a handy position. Once it came down to a battle between him and the runner-up over the last furlong, he showed just the right attitude despite wandering slightly and giving his rival a bump. His winning siblings all improved as three-year-olds, which makes the future look very bright for him indeed. (op 9-1)
Hurricane Flyer bounced out from his high draw and tried to make every yard. He tried his best to hold off the newcomer, but was just unable to do so and getting a bump from his rival made no difference. He has now finished runner-up in all three of his starts, but there is nothing wrong with his attitude and this performance should be rated through the distance back to the third. He now qualifies for nurseries and his turn is merely delayed. (op 15-8 tchd 2-1, 85-40 in a place)
Multitude(IRE), who raced wider than most from the lowest stall, found this drop back to five no help and was found wanting for a turn of foot. He is another that now qualifies for nurseries and a return to a stiffer test should see him in a better light. (op 11-2)
Woqoodd, who has not been getting home when ridden positively over six, was always struggling to go the pace on this first attempt over the minimum trip. He also qualifies for nurseries, but does have a question mark against him now. Official explanation: jockey said colt was unsuited by soft ground (op 11-8 tchd 2-1 in places)
Smirfys Gold(IRE) ran a bit better than in his two previous outings, but probably achieved little.
Shrewd Dude, who fetched 20,000gns as a two-year-old, was absolutely clueless for the early part of this debut, but there was a hint in the latter stages that he does possess some ability. His pedigree suggested that he was always going to find this far too short, but there is probably better to come from him some way down the line. Official explanation: jockey said colt was denied a clear run

5767 WBX.COM WORLD BET EXCHANGE (S) H'CAP 1m 1f 213y
3:50 (3:51) (Class 6) (0-55,53) 3-Y-0 **£2,388** (£705; £352) **Stalls** Low

Form RPR

0200 **1** **By Storm**[22] 5273 3-8-1 47 oh4 ow3 KirstyMilczarek(7) 8 53
(John Berry) *chsd ldrs: led 2f out: edgd lft ins fnl f: rdn out* **22/1**

3323 **2** *nk* **Park Lane Princess (IRE)**[37] 4884 3-8-13 52 RyanMoore 2 57
(D M Simcock) *hld up in tch: nt clr run over 1f out: sn rdn to chse wnr: styd on* **11/4**[1]

6440 **3** *1/2* **Snake Skin**[71] 3828 3-8-13 52 JimCrowley 3 56
(J Gallagher) *a.p: nt clr run over 1f out: sn rdn: styd on* **15/2**[3]

0050 **4** *1 1/2* **Jiminor Mack**[23] 5240 3-8-5 47 RichardKingscote(3) 10 48
(W J H Ratcliffe) *hld up: hdwy u.p over 2f out: styd on same pce ins fnl f* **40/1**

006- **5** *1* **Josh You Are**[408] 4629 3-8-11 50 JamieSpencer 7 50
(M J Wallace) *s.s: hdwy over 2f out: rdn over 1f out: no imp* **8/1**

0043 **6** *nk* **Shaika**[21] 5298 3-8-8 47 JamieMackay 5 46
(G Prodromou) *hld up: plld hrd: hdwy over 3f out: rdn over 1f out: no ex ins fnl f* **8/1**

0305 **7** *3* **Top Level (IRE)**[49] 4491 3-8-6 45 TPQueally 12 39
(M G Quinlan) *hld up: hdwy over 2f out: nt clr run and wknd over 1f out* **14/1**

6305 **8** *3/4* **Makai**[22] 5259 3-9-0 53 (b[1]) JoeFanning 13 45
(M Johnston) *led 1f: chsd ldrs: led over 2f out: sn hdd: wknd fnl f* **7/1**[2]

-000 **9** *2 1/2* **Sirbrit**[93] 3145 3-8-8 50 (v[1]) StephenDonohoe(3) 14 38
(W J Musson) *hld up: n.d* **11/1**

-400 **10** *1/2* **Bowl Of Cherries**[15] 5452 3-8-6 45 FrancisNorton 9 32
(I A Wood) *chsd ldrs: rdn over 2f out: wknd over 1f out* **9/1**

4000 **11** *12* **No Inkling (IRE)**[16] 5432 3-8-5 44 oh9 (p) DO'Donohoe 15 9
(John A Harris) *led 9f out: hdd over 2f out: wknd over 1f out* **80/1**

0003 **12** *9* **Franky'N'Jonny**[22] 5273 3-8-8 47 JohnEgan 16 —
(Mrs C A Dunnett) *hld up: rdn over 2f out: a in rr* **12/1**

0500 **13** *1/2* **Canary Girl**[16] 5432 3-8-5 44 oh9 HayleyTurner 6 —
(Mrs C A Dunnett) *plld hrd: prom over 7f* **80/1**

00-0 **14** *33* **Apple Annie**[14] 5485 3-8-0 44 oh4 EmmettStack(5) 11 —
(M E Sowersby) *s.i.s: a in rr: bhd fr 1/2-way* **66/1**

2m 15.42s (5.72) **Going Correction** +0.45s/f (Yiel) 14 Ran SP% **116.6**
Speed ratings (Par 99):95,94,94,93,92 92,89,89,87,86 77,69,69,—
CSF £78.20 CT £514.86 TOTE £22.00: £5.40, £1.70, £2.80; EX 112.90.There was no bid for the winner. Park Lane Princess was claimed by D Pipe for £6,000
Owner H R Moszkowicz **Bred** Henry And Mrs Rosemary Moszkowicz **Trained** Newmarket, Suffolk

FOCUS
A very average seller unlikely to produce many winners, and not surprisingly the slowest of the four races over the trip. The form is weak and rated around the placed horses.
Josh You Are ◆ Official explanation: jockey said gelding was unruly in stalls
Franky'N'Jonny Official explanation: jockey said filly had no more to give

The Form Book, Raceform Ltd, Compton, RG20 6NL

5768 WBX.COM WORLD BET EXCHANGE MAIDEN STKS (DIV I) 1m 1f 213y

4:20 (4:22) (Class 5) 3-Y-0+ £2,590 (£770; £385; £192) Stalls Low

Form RPR

6-2 **1** **Seabow (USA)**[8] 5598 3-9-3 ....(t) LDettori 2 80+
(Saeed Bin Suroor) *hld up in tch: led 2f out: sn rdn clr: eased nr fin* **9/4**[2]

5- **2** 2½ **Galactic Star**[348] 6001 3-9-3 .... RyanMoore 4 72+
(Sir Michael Stoute) *hld up: hdwy over 2f out: edgd lft over 1f out: styd on same pce* **9/2**[3]

5-2 **3** ½ **Font**[167] 1101 3-9-3 .... JamieSpencer 6 71+
(J R Fanshawe) *s.i.s: hld up: hdwy 3f out: styd on same pce appr fnl f* **13/8**[1]

500 **4** 8 **Shardia (IRE)**[34] 4944 3-8-12 47 .... ChrisCatlin 5 52
(J Jay) *hld up: hdwy over 2f out: n.d* **150/1**

26 **5** ½ **Longhill Tiger**[70] 3849 3-9-3 .... MickyFenton 1 56
(G G Margarson) *chsd ldrs: led 3f out: hdd & wknd 2f out* **33/1**

32 **6** 1 **Falpiase (IRE)**[35] 4931 4-9-8 .... NickyMackay 10 54
(L M Cumani) *prom over 7f* **15/2**

-642 **7** shd **Miss Thailand**[23] 5241 3-8-12 70 .... DarryllHolland 8 49
(G Wragg) *prom: hmpd and lost pl after 1f: swtchd rt and hdwy over 3f out: hung lft and wknd over 1f out* **16/1**

0020 **8** 12 **Credential**[109] 2641 4-9-8 56 .... DO'Donohoe 14 33
(John A Harris) *racd keenly: prom 8f* **80/1**

060- **9** 2½ **Lady Lucinda**[393] 5025 5-8-10 35 .... ChrisGlenister(7) 9 23
(J R Holt) *hld up: hdwy 1/2-way: wknd over 2f out* **200/1**

50- **10** ½ **Georgie's Lass (IRE)**[439] 3681 7-9-0 .... JamesDoyle(3) 3 22
(R J Price) *mid-div: wknd over 3f out* **200/1**

-050 **11** 1½ **Wolf Pack**[65] 3999 4-9-5 46 .... EdwardCreighton(3) 13 24
(R W Price) *led 7f: wknd 2f out* **200/1**

0-00 **12** 1 **Indian Dawn (IRE)**[33] 4982 3-8-12 40 .... DuranFentiman(5) 15 23
(T H Caldwell) *hld up: effrt over 3f out: sn wknd* **200/1**

0 **13** 3 **Thou Shalt Not**[8] 5598 3-9-3 .... JimCrowley 11 17
(P S Felgate) *s.i.s: hld up: a in rr* **150/1**

00 **14** 31 **Gigi Glamor**[40] 4759 4-9-3 .... PaulMulrennan 12 —
(W M Brisbourne) *racd keenly: prom 7f* **200/1**

0 **15** 2½ **Little Wishes**[8] 5598 3-8-12 .... DanielTudhope 7 —
(S Parr) *w ldr to 1/2-way: wknd over 3f out* **200/1**

2m 13.34s (3.64) **Going Correction** +0.45s/f (Yiel)
WFA 3 from 4yo+ 5lb **15** Ran SP% **113.2**
Speed ratings (Par 103):103,101,100,94,93 93,92,83,81,80 79,78,76,—,—
CSF £12.03 TOTE £3.50: £1.30, £1.70, £1.30; EX 16.80.
Owner Godolphin **Bred** Gainsborough Farm Llc **Trained** Newmarket, Suffolk

FOCUS
A reasonable maiden, where the first three drew well clear and the fourth is the best guide but also limits the form. Two or three caught the eye for the future for various reasons.
Galactic Star Official explanation: jockey said colt hung to the left

5769 WBX.COM WORLD BET EXCHANGE H'CAP 1m 1f 213y

4:50 (4:51) (Class 4) (0-85,85) 3-Y-0+ £6,477 (£1,927; £963; £481) Stalls Low

Form RPR

-003 **1** **Invasian (IRE)**[21] 5299 5-9-6 **82** .... TPQueally 2 92
(B J McMath) *mde all: hrd rdn fnl f: edgd rt: all out* **8/1**

0624 **2** nk **Charlie Tokyo (IRE)**[14] 5478 3-8-12 **79** ....(b[1]) PaulHanagan 16 89
(R A Fahey) *hld up: hdwy over 3f out: rdn and hung lft over 1f out: ev ch ins fnl f: nt qckn* **10/1**

5014 **3** 2½ **Fort Churchill (IRE)**[19] 5346 5-9-7 **83** ....(bt) TomEaves 12 88
(B Ellison) *hld up in tch: rdn whn hmpd over 1f out: swtchd lft: styd on same pce* **8/1**

-100 **4** ¾ **Conkering (USA)**[27] 5137 3-9-1 **82** .... JamieSpencer 15 86
(J R Fanshawe) *hld up in tch: chsd wnr over 3f out: rdn and ev ch 2f out: no ex fnl f* **14/1**

-510 **5** 1½ **Sunisa (IRE)**[131] 1991 5-9-1 **77** .... MickyFenton 5 78
(J Mackie) *hld up: styd on ins fnl f: nt trble ldrs* **25/1**

40/1 **6** 1½ **Alasil (USA)**[27] 5127 6-8-7 **74** .... LiamJones(5) 4 72
(R J Price) *chsd ldrs: rdn over 2f out: hung lft and wknd over 1f out* **33/1**

2521 **7** 1¼ **Piety (IRE)**[26] 5151 3-9-2 **83** .... JoeFanning 13 79
(M Johnston) *chsd ldrs: rdn over 2f out: wknd over 1f out* **7/1**[3]

1156 **8** 1½ **Lady Disdain**[11] 5538 3-8-10 **77** .... JohnEgan 9 70
(G M Moore) *hld up: rdn over 2f out: n.d* **11/1**

4013 **9** hd **Mae Cigan (FR)**[12] 5513 3-8-2 **69** oh1 .... FrancisNorton 14 62
(M Blanshard) *hld up: sme hdwy over 2f out: sn edgd lft and wknd* **5/1**[2]

1660 **10** 3½ **Indian Edge**[84] 3404 5-8-10 **72** .... FrancisFerris 7 59
(B Palling) *chsd wnr over 6f: wknd over 2f out* **40/1**

36-6 **11** ½ **Dahman**[25] 5163 4-9-2 **78** .... LDettori 3 64
(Saeed Bin Suroor) *hld up: nt clr run over 4f out: sn rdn: n.d* **4/1**[1]

-160 **12** 2 **Virtuosity**[25] 5164 3-9-4 **85** .... RyanMoore 10 67
(Sir Michael Stoute) *hld up: shkn up over 3f out: no rspnse* **14/1**

05-0 **13** 3½ **Unsuited**[137] 1850 7-8-2 **69** oh10 .... NataliaGemelova(5) 6 45
(J E Long) *sn pushed along in rr: bhd fr 1/2-way* **100/1**

3020 **14** nk **Rawdon (IRE)**[12] 5511 5-9-1 **77** ....(v) HayleyTurner 1 52
(M L W Bell) *s.s: a in rr* **14/1**

0000 **15** 25 **Fortunes Favourite**[46] 4586 6-8-1 **70** oh24 ow1 .... KristinStubbs(7) 8 —
(J E Long) *dwlt: in rr: effrt over 3f out: sn hung lft and wknd* **150/1**

2m 11.54s (1.84) **Going Correction** +0.45s/f (Yiel)
WFA 3 from 4yo+ 5lb **15** Ran SP% **119.7**
Speed ratings (Par 105):110,109,107,107,105 104,103,102,102,99 99,97,94,94,74
CSF £82.19 CT £669.87 TOTE £8.10: £3.50, £4.10, £2.30; EX 133.10 TRIFECTA Not won..
Owner Dr K Sanderson **Bred** Dr Karen Monica Sanderson **Trained** Newmarket, Suffolk
■ Brian McMath's first winner for nine years, although he did not hold a licence for five years during that period.

FOCUS
A fair winning time for the grade and the fastest of the four races over the trip at this meeting. The form looks solid and reliable.
Dahman Official explanation: trainer had no explanation for the poor form shown

5770 WBX.COM WORLD BET EXCHANGE MAIDEN STKS (DIV II) 1m 1f 213y

5:20 (5:21) (Class 5) 3-Y-0+ £2,590 (£770; £385; £192) Stalls Low

Form RPR

3 **1** **Clear Sailing**[42] 4686 3-9-3 .... DarryllHolland 14 83+
(Mrs A J Perrett) *hld up: hdwy 4f out: rdn to ld and edgd lft over 1f out: styd on* **7/2**[2]

52 **2** ½ **Red Gala**[16] 5426 3-9-3 .... RyanMoore 8 82+
(Sir Michael Stoute) *hld up in tch: rdn 4f out: hmpd and outpcd over 3f out: rallied over 1f out: styd on* **2/1**[1]

00 **3** 5 **According To Pete**[20] 5319 5-9-1 .... PaulPickard(7) 1 73
(J M Jefferson) *hld up in tch: racd keenly: outpcd over 2f out: rallied over 1f out: nt trble ldrs* **50/1**

2 **4** hd **Sculastic**[39] 4806 3-9-3 .... NickyMackay 3 73
(L M Cumani) *chsd ldrs: outpcd and hung lft over 2f out: rallied over 1f out: styd on* **5/1**[3]

63 **5** 1 **The Aldbury Flyer**[19] 5353 3-9-3 .... AdamKirby 4 71
(W R Swinburn) *s.i.s: hld up: hdwy over 3f out: no ex fnl f* **16/1**

3-45 **6** ½ **Tennis Star (IRE)**[56] 4249 3-9-3 78 .... SteveDrowne 9 70
(R Charlton) *mid-div: hdwy 1/2-way: rdn and ev ch over 1f out: wknd ins fnl f* **16/1**

2224 **7** nk **Accompanist**[26] 5151 3-9-3 84 ....(v[1]) RobertHavlin 5 69
(J H M Gosden) *s.i.s: sn prom: rdn over 1f out: wknd ins fnl f* **9/1**

8 5 **Balashi (USA)** 3-9-3 .... LDettori 10 60
(Saeed Bin Suroor) *sn chsng ldr: led over 3f out: rdn and hdd over 1f out: wknd fnl f* **7/1**

-040 **9** 3½ **Asbury Park**[142] 1740 3-9-3 62 .... FergusSweeney 13 54
(M R Bosley) *chsd ldrs: hmpd over 3f out: sn wknd* **80/1**

0-0 **10** ½ **Memphis Belle**[29] 5086 3-8-12 .... ChrisCatlin 2 48
(Mrs H Sweeting) *hld up: rdn over 3f out: a in rr* **100/1**

640 **11** 10 **Zirkel (IRE)**[68] 3901 3-9-3 75 .... DO'Donohoe 12 35
(Mrs A L M King) *hld up: rdn over 3f out: sn wknd* **50/1**

0006 **12** 1½ **Meantime (USA)**[56] 4268 3-8-10 62 .... KirstyMilczarek(7) 7 33
(G Prodromou) *chsd ldrs over 7f* **100/1**

505 **13** 1¾ **Inchmarlow (IRE)**[75] 3698 3-8-12 48 .... DuranFentiman(5) 6 29
(T H Caldwell) *led over 6f: wknd over 2f out* **125/1**

5 **14** 13 **Corviglia**[8] 5589 3-8-12 .... JamieSpencer 11 1
(J R Fanshawe) *hld up: bhd fnl 4f* **33/1**

2m 13.32s (3.62) **Going Correction** +0.45s/f (Yiel)
WFA 3 from 5yo 5lb **14** Ran SP% **117.4**
Speed ratings (Par 103):103,102,98,98,97 97,97,93,90,89 81,80,79,68
CSF £10.35 TOTE £4.10: £1.60, £1.20, £13.10; EX 12.30 Place 6 £47.13, Place 5 £31.79.
Owner K Abdulla **Bred** Juddmonte Farms Ltd **Trained** Pulborough, W Sussex

FOCUS
An interesting maiden with some promising sorts in it and the form looks a little stronger than the first division.
The Aldbury Flyer Official explanation: jockey said gelding became unbalanced 2f out
T/Jkpt: Not won. T/Plt: £50.60 to a £1 stake. Pool: £78,007.30. 1,123.65 winning tickets. T/Qpdt: £14.90 to a £1 stake. Pool: £4,284.20. 211.60 winning tickets. CR

5718 SAN SIRO (R-H)

Wednesday, October 4

OFFICIAL GOING: Good

5771a PREMIO CASTELLETTO TICINO (UNRACED COLTS & GELDINGS) 1m 1f

4:50 (5:00) 2-Y-0 £6,897 (£3,034; £1,655; £828)

RPR

1 **Perdono (USA)** 2-9-0 .... EPedroza 6 —
(A Wohler, Germany)

2 3 **Sopran Promo (IRE)** 2-9-0 .... DVargiu 12 —
(B Grizzetti, Italy)

3 3½ **Socrepes (ITY)** 2-9-0 .... MEsposito 1 —
(F Contu, Italy)

4 ½ **Purple Night** 2-9-0 .... MMonteriso 7 —
(Doris Schonherr)

5 4 **Amjad (GER)** 2-9-0 .... SUrru 11 —
(A Aiello, Italy)

6 3½ **Armus (IRE)** 2-9-0 .... WGambarota 2 —
(M Ciciarelli, Italy)

7 2 **Montjeu Boy (IRE)** 2-9-0 .... EBotti 13 —
(M Botti) *midfield, 6th straight, 5th on inside 2f out, one pace (4/1)*

8 ¾ **Vesozchi (IRE)** 2-9-0 .... PSirigu 5 —
(B Grizzetti, Italy)

9 2¾ **Princekris** 2-9-0 .... IRossi 9 —
(M Ciciarelli, Italy)

10 16 **Black Horse (ITY)** 2-9-0 .... SMulas 8 —
(L Batzella, Italy)

12 4 **Surangi** 2-9-0 .... PConvertino 10 —
(Gianfranco Verricelli, Italy)

13 **Taking The Gold (ITY)** 2-9-0 .... LManiezzi 4 —
(M Innocenti, Italy)

1m 55.8s **13** Ran
(including 1 Euro stake): WIN 2.75; PL 1.39, 1.29, 2.29; DF 3.08.
Owner Turfsyndikat Stall Wohler **Bred** Mineola Farm II Limited Partnership **Trained** Germany

NOTEBOOK
Montjeu Boy(IRE), a half-brother to a couple of juvenile winners, is out of a mare who finished second in a Listed race over seven furlongs at two.

5645 LINGFIELD (L-H)

Thursday, October 5

OFFICIAL GOING: Standard
Wind: Fresh, behind Weather: Steady rain

5772 LINGFIELDPARK.CO.UK NURSERY 5f (P)

1:50 (1:51) (Class 6) (0-65,65) 2-Y-0 £3,238 (£963; £481; £240) Stalls High

Form RPR

3355 **1** **Hephaestus**[17] 5419 2-9-6 **64** .... TedDurcan 5 69
(M R Channon) *mid-div: pushed along after 2f: hdwy over 1f out: rdn to ld fnl 100 yds* **7/2**[1]

5164 **2** nk **Mac Gille Eoin**[20] 5349 2-9-6 **64** .... JimCrowley 10 68
(J Gallagher) *b.hind: t.k.h: in tch on outside: wd st: r.o fr over 1f out: jst hld* **5/1**[2]

6540 **3** 1 **La Quinta (IRE)**[85] 3409 2-9-7 **65** .... LDettori 8 65
(B J Meehan) *lw: hld up in rr: rdn and hdwy over 1f out: clsd on ldrs fnl f* **11/2**[3]

6022 **4** ½ **Queensgate**[17] 5419 2-9-1 **59** .... FrankieMcDonald 2 58
(M Blanshard) *prom: hrd rdn over 1f out: kpt on same pce* **11/2**[3]

4160 **5** nk **Baytown Paikea**[12] 5528 2-9-0 **58** .... BrianReilly 4 55
(P S McEntee) *led: hrd rdn over 1f out: hdd and no ex fnl 100 yds* **20/1**

5065 **6** hd **Ask Don't Tell (IRE)**[5] 5687 2-8-13 **60**.................. EdwardCreighton(3) 7 57
(Tom Dascombe) *s.i.s: t.k.h: hld up and bhd: rdn and r.o fnl 2f: nrst fin* **10/1**

202 **7** ¾ **Early Promise (IRE)**[5] 5686 2-9-6 **64**................................. ChrisCatlin 3 58+
(P L Gilligan) *towards rr: rdn and unable to chal fnl 2f* **5/1**[2]

5400 **8** ½ **Mrs Crossy (IRE)**[31] 5065 2-9-0 **58**................................ FrancisNorton 9 50
(A W Carroll) *chsd ldrs tl wknd over 1f out* **14/1**

5000 **9** ½ **Chip Leader**[3] 5721 2-9-5 **63**... RyanMoore 1 53
(R Hannon) *chsd ldr most of way: 3rd and btn whn n.m.r and snatched up ins fnl f* **14/1**

59.45 secs (-0.33) **Going Correction** -0.25s/f (Stan) **9** Ran SP% **113.5**
Speed ratings (Par 93):92,91,89,89,88 88,87,86,85
CSF £20.40 CT £93.30 TOTE £3.90: £1.60, £2.00, £2.40; EX 26.30 Trifecta £208.20 Pool: £372.47 - 1.27 winning tickets..
Owner Box 41 **Bred** M F Kentish **Trained** West Ilsley, Berks

FOCUS
A modest nursery, and with little covering the whole field at the line the form looks nothing special, though the winner was back to form and the level looks sound enough through the placed horses.

NOTEBOOK
Hephaestus, who made a winning racecourse debut over course and distance back in March, has rather struggled since but the return to this surface did the trick. He was not travelling as well as a few of his rivals for most of the contest, but hit the front in plenty of time and showed a good attitude at the finish. Given his record at this track it seems likely he will be kept on the go here throughout the winter. (tchd 4-1)
Mac Gille Eoin, who has been showing improved form since being stepped up to beyond the minimum trip in his recent starts, was forced to race widest from his outside draw which was probably not ideal on this return to five and he could never quite get there. This was a solid effort under the circumstances. (op 6-1)
La Quinta(IRE), reappearing from a three-month break, was given a patient ride and although she had to wait for a clear passage through the field, she was not inconvenienced to any great degree and her finishing position is a true reflection of her performance. (tchd 6-1)
Queensgate, without a win in nine attempts and making her sand debut, had every chance but lacked a turn of foot in the straight. She may need an extra furlong on this surface. (op 9-2)
Baytown Paikea blasted off in front as usual, but could not see it out against these rivals and probably needs to drop back down in class. (op 16-1)
Ask Don't Tell(IRE) was again doing her best work late and needs the extra furlong. (op 9-1 tchd 11-1)

5773 BOOK YOUR CHRISTMAS PARTY HERE MAIDEN FILLIES' STKS 6f (P)
2:20 (2:24) (Class 4) 2-Y-O **£5,505** (£1,637; £818; £408) **Stalls** Low

Form RPR

1 **Rainbow Promises (USA)** 2-9-0 .... LDettori 3 96+
(B J Meehan) *w'like: scope: leggy: chsd clr ldr: led over 2f out: pushed clr over 1f out: easily* **10/11**[1]

2 5 **Laura's Best (IRE)** 2-9-0 .... KerrinMcEvoy 4 78
(W J Haggas) *leggy: hld up in tch: effrt 2f out: r.o to take 2nd ins fnl f: no ch w wnr* **7/1**[3]

4 **3** 2 **Genuine Call**[22] 5296 2-9-0 .... SebSanders 8 72
(C F Wall) *unf: prom in chsng gp: chsd easy wnr over 2f out tl ins fnl f* **4/1**[2]

4 1 **Londolozi (USA)** 2-9-0 .... MatthewHenry 7 69
(M A Jarvis) *w'like: scope: bit bkwd: hld up in mid: shkn up & hmpd over 2f out: running on whn squeezed out over 1f out: nrst fin: impr* **20/1**

0 **5** nk **Miss Autumnal (IRE)**[27] 5147 2-9-0 ....(b[1]) ChrisCatlin 10 68
(N A Callaghan) *chsd ldrs: rdn over 2f out: wknd over 1f out* **66/1**

0 **6** 1 ¼ **Barbs Pink Diamond (USA)**[36] 4928 2-9-0 .... RyanMoore 12 64
(Mrs A J Perrett) *wd: towards rr: pushed along fnl 2f: nvr rchd chalng position* **7/1**[3]

7 1 ¼ **Gwyllion (USA)** 2-9-0 .... RobertHavlin 2 61
(J H M Gosden) *w'like: bit bkwd: trckd ldrs: effrt 2f out: wknd 1f out* **8/1**

00 **8** 5 **Lady Firecracker (IRE)**[41] 4774 2-9-0 .... GeorgeBaker 11 46
(J R Best) *s.i.s: rdn over 3f out: a bhd* **16/1**

9 ½ **Savanagh Forest (IRE)** 2-8-9 ow2....................... ChrisCavanagh(7) 9 46
(M Quinn) *leggy: s.s: a bhd* **50/1**

10 3 **Classic Siren (IRE)** 2-9-0 .... RHills 5 35
(J W Hills) *w'like: bit bkwd: s.i.s: towards rr: rdn and n.d fr 1/2-way* **33/1**

11 5 **My Silver Monarch (IRE)** 2-9-0 .... SteveDrowne 6 20
(H S Howe) *w'like: bit bkwd: s.s: a wl bhd* **66/1**

60 **12** 10 **Damhsoir (IRE)**[94] 3148 2-9-0 .... FrancisNorton 1 —
(H S Howe) *temperamental to post: led and racd freely: sn 5 l clr: hdd & wknd rapidly over 2f out: saddle slipped* **66/1**

1m 11.03s (-1.78) **Going Correction** -0.25s/f (Stan) 2y crse rec **12** Ran SP% **128.5**
Speed ratings (Par 94):101,94,91,90,89 88,86,79,79,75 68,55
CSF £8.77 TOTE £2.00: £1.10, £2.30, £1.70; EX 11.40 Trifecta £27.90 Pool: £410.43 - 10.43 winning tickets..
Owner Andrew Rosen **Bred** Edward J Kelly Jr & Michael M Kelly **Trained** Manton, Wilts

FOCUS
This looked quite a good fillies' maiden beforehand - a few of these took the eye in the paddock - but nothing could live with the highly-regarded Rainbow Promises, who showed a level of form seldom seen in two-year-old maidens on the all-weather. The winning time was decent for the type of race, and this looks a race that is sure to work out.

NOTEBOOK
Rainbow Promises(USA) ◆, a 95,000gns half-sister to Universal Power, a triple winner in Hong Kong, and to two winners in the US, out of a quite useful triple winner over a mile in Italy, is held in high regard and made a very impressive racecourse debut, breaking the juvenile course record by almost half a second and putting up a level of performance that would make her a ready-made winner of a Listed race. Quite an attractive filly, she knew her job well enough and nothing could live with her when she was asked for her effort. "She's definitely a Group filly, and she might be a Guineas filly", was Brian Meehan's reaction. (op 11-8 tchd 6-4 in places)
Laura's Best(IRE) ◆, a half-sister to mile winner Who Could Tell, and to a triple winner in the US, is another quite attractive sort and justified some market support with a pleasing debut behind the potentially smart winner. She is open to improvement and should win a maiden, either this year or next, before stepping up in grade. (op 8-1)
Genuine Call, a promising fourth in a reasonable Yarmouth maiden on her debut, ran another encouraging race against some potentially nice types. An ordinary maiden may come her way, but she will have more options once qualified for a handicap mark. (op 7-2)
Londolozi(USA) ◆, closely related to True Cause, a smart dual mile winner at two, out of a smart performer over seven to ten furlongs, looked a nice type in the paddock and was unlucky not to finish closer. Short of room before the turn into the straight, she again met with trouble when trying to stay on just over a furlong from the finish and can improve a fair bit next time. Official explanation: jockey said filly was denied a clear run
Miss Autumnal(IRE) beat only one on her debut at Sandown, but she is bred to be pretty useful and showed improved form in the first-time blinkers. She is going the right way now and could do better again.
Barbs Pink Diamond(USA) seems to be going the right way and should find her level when handicapped. Official explanation: jockey said filly didn't face the kick-back (tchd 13-2 and 15-2)
Gwyllion(USA), a 260,000euros first foal of a dual six to seven-furlong winner at two, later a triple middle-distance scorer, finished up well held but should be able to improve. (op 15-2)
Lady Firecracker(IRE) Official explanation: jockey said filly didn't face the kick-back
Savanagh Forest(IRE) Official explanation: jockey said filly missed the break
My Silver Monarch(IRE) Official explanation: jockey said filly missed the break
Damhsoir(IRE) Official explanation: jockey said saddle slipped

5774 JUMPING HERE ON NOVEMBER 8TH MEDIAN AUCTION MAIDEN STKS 1m (P)
2:50 (2:53) (Class 5) 3-4-Y-O **£3,238** (£963; £481; £240) **Stalls** High

Form RPR

0253 **1** **Dab Hand (IRE)**[31] 5071 3-9-3 64...................................... RyanMoore 4 61
(D M Simcock) *lw: set modest pce: mde all: steadily qcknd fr 3f out: hrd rdn over 1f out: hld on wl fnl f* **9/4**[2]

6000 **2** ¾ **Simpsons Ross (IRE)**[61] 4143 3-9-3 53.......................... JimmyQuinn 3 61+
(R M Flower) *trckd ldrs: effrt ent st: styd on to take 2nd fnl 75 yds: a hld* **14/1**

0605 **3** ½ **Special Place**[30] 5093 3-9-3 54.. SebSanders 7 58
(J A R Toller) *plld hrd: in tch: jnd ldrs 3f out: nt qckn fnl f* **33/1**

4 2 **Khyberie** 3-8-12 .... SteveDrowne 6 49+
(G Wragg) *leggy: dwlt: hld up in midfield: wd st: r.o fr over 1f out: improve* **20/1**

300 **5** ¾ **Fire Of Love**[201] 669 3-8-9 62....................................... JamesDoyle(3) 8 47
(N P Littmoden) *pressed wnr tl no ex fnl f* **16/1**

6 nk **Depraux (IRE)** 3-9-3 .... KerrinMcEvoy 9 51+
(W J Haggas) *w'like: lw: in tch on outside: outpcd and wd st: styd on fnl f* **11/2**[3]

0 **7** 1 ½ **Natacha Rostow**[20] 5353 3-8-12 .... NickyMackay 2 43
(L M Cumani) *w'like: bit bkwd: dwlt: towards rr: pushed along over 4f out: nvr rchd ldrs* **33/1**

00 **8** nk **Votive Daniel (IRE)**[3] 5729 3-9-3 .... AntonyProcter 11 47
(Simon Earle) *w'like: bhd: pushed along over 2f out: styd on fnl f* **100/1**

5-4 **9** 3 **Bronze Star**[31] 5071 3-8-12 .... JamieSpencer 1 35+
(J R Fanshawe) *trckd ldrs: 4th and hld whn hmpd on rail ent st: nt rcvr: disputing 5th whn eased ins fnl f* **15/8**[1]

00 **10** 1 **Mantolini**[20] 5353 3-8-12 .... EmmettStack(5) 5 38
(Pat Eddery) *lw: a bhd* **66/1**

3655 **11** 2 **Girandola**[3] 5729 3-9-3 55.. DaneO'Neill 10 33
(R F Johnson Houghton) *wd: t.k.h towards rr: rdn and n.d fnl 2f* **11/1**

1m 39.73s (0.30) **Going Correction** -0.25s/f (Stan) **11** Ran SP% **114.9**
Speed ratings (Par 103):88,87,86,84,84 83,82,81,78,77 75
CSF £30.79 TOTE £3.10: £1.40, £4.30, £6.40; EX 46.00 TRIFECTA Not won..
Owner Byculla Thoroughbreds **Bred** Philip Brady **Trained** Newmarket, Suffolk

FOCUS
This looked a moderate maiden and there was no early pace on. A very moderate winning time for the grade, 2.21 seconds slower than the following 60-65 handicap.
Depraux(IRE) Official explanation: jockey said gelding hung right on home bend
Bronze Star Official explanation: jockey said filly was hampered on home bend

5775 FURLONGS & FAIRWAYS H'CAP 1m (P)
3:20 (3:20) (Class 6) (0-65,65) 3-Y-O+ **£3,238** (£963; £481; £240) **Stalls** High

Form RPR

0465 **1** **Molem**[56] 4288 4-9-5 **65**...(tp) JamieSpencer 8 77
(Lady Herries) *mde virtually all: jnd by runner-up fnl f: rallied wl: jst prevailed* **10/3**[1]

2425 **2** shd **Million Percent**[19] 5386 7-8-9 **60**................................ LiamJones(5) 9 72
(C R Dore) *lw: chsd ldrs: rdn to join wnr fnl f: kpt on wl: jst tched off* **9/1**

2022 **3** 4 **Sincerely**[16] 5450 4-9-2 **62**.. OscarUrbina 11 64
(B W Hills) *hld up in midfield: effrt over 2f out: styd on to take 3rd ins fnl f* **9/2**[2]

4261 **4** ½ **Sovereignty (JPN)**[19] 5386 4-8-10 **63**...................... JamesMillman(7) 12 64
(D K Ivory) *wd: towards rr: rdn and r.o fnl 2f: nrst fin* **7/1**

6500 **5** 1 ½ **Scroll**[25] 5211 3-9-2 **65**..(v) J-PGuillambert 1 63
(P Howling) *in tch: rdn over 2f out: one pce* **12/1**

1062 **6** ½ **Border Artist**[8] 5617 7-9-4 **64**.. JimmyQuinn 10 61
(J Pearce) *towards rr: rdn over 2f out: styd on fnl f* **6/1**[3]

1010 **7** 1 **Zendaro**[19] 5384 4-9-0 **60**.. JohnEgan 6 54
(W M Brisbourne) *dwlt: plld hrd and sn prom: wknd ent st* **15/2**

2106 **8** 2 ½ **Carloman**[35] 4968 3-9-1 **64**..(bt) SebSanders 5 52
(R M Beckett) *prom tl wknd over 1f out* **6/1**[3]

000/ **9** 1 ¼ **Electrique (IRE)**[52] 6395 6-8-13 **62**..................(v[1]) StephenDonohoe(3) 3 47
(A J McCabe) *dwlt: a bhd* **33/1**

-000 **10** 1 ½ **Elgin Marbles**[101] 2920 4-9-0 **60**.................................... DaneO'Neill 2 42
(A B Haynes) *in tch: outpcd over 3f out: n.d after* **40/1**

1m 37.52s (-1.91) **Going Correction** -0.25s/f (Stan)
WFA 3 from 4yo+ 3lb **10** Ran SP% **117.2**
Speed ratings (Par 101):99,98,94,94,92 92,91,88,87,86
CSF £34.41 CT £137.30 TOTE £3.40: £1.20, £3.20, £1.80; EX 38.60 Trifecta £93.80 Pool: £177.10 - 1.34 winning tickets..
Owner Seymour Racing Partnership **Bred** Shadwell Estate Company Limited **Trained** Patching, W Sussex

FOCUS
As in the previous maiden, the early pace was modest but they were sprinting at the end and the race produced a cracking finish. Very few ever got into this and the front pair were up there from the start.

5776 NCP SPACE PROVING H'CAP 1m 4f (P)
3:50 (3:50) (Class 3) (0-95,90) 3-Y-O+ **£11,658** (£3,468; £1,733; £865) **Stalls** Low

Form RPR

1/ **1** **Descartes**[712] 6352 4-9-5 **86**.. LDettori 11 102+
(Saeed Bin Suroor) *lw: scope: stdd s: hld up in rr: hdwy 1/2-way and a gng wl: led over 1f out: rdn out* **9/4**[1]

4253 **2** 1 **Transvestite (IRE)**[20] 5346 4-8-8 **82**.............................. PatrickHills(7) 4 93
(J W Hills) *hld up towards rr: wd and hdwy ent st: r.o to take 2nd ins fnl f* **8/1**

2022 **3** 2 **Royal Jet**[17] 5430 4-9-9 **90**.. JohnEgan 2 98
(M R Channon) *lw: in tch: swtchd rt and effrt over 2f out: chsd wnr over 1f out tl ins fnl f: no ex* **10/3**[2]

-263 **4** 1 ½ **Zonergem**[32] 5045 8-9-8 **89**.. RyanMoore 9 95
(Lady Herries) *hld up and bhd: shkn up and hdwy over 1f out: no imp fnl f* **16/1**

0100 **5** 1 ½ **Given A Choice (IRE)**[29] 5110 4-9-5 **86**......................... PaulHanagan 7 89
(R A Fahey) *chsd ldrs: outpcd fnl 2f* **16/1**

2550 **6** 2 **Desert Cristal (IRE)**[15] 5477 5-9-0 **81**........................... JamieSpencer 5 81
(J R Boyle) *prom tl wknd 3f out* **14/1**

3113 **7** *1* **Island Odyssey**[17] 5421 3-8-13 **87** .... SteveDrowne 8 85
(E A L Dunlop) *prom: led 3f out tl over 1f out: wknd fnl f* **7/1**[3]
4000 **8** *5* **Activo (FR)**[13] 5511 5-9-1 **82** .... TedDurcan 10 72
(S Dow) *cl up: jnd ldrs 3f out: wknd over 1f out* **20/1**
-552 **9** *3/4* **Del Mar Sunset**[22] 5295 7-8-13 **83** .... SaleemGolam(3) 1 72
(W J Haggas) *a bhd* **20/1**
11-0 **10** *nk* **Zabeel Palace**[245] 279 4-9-6 **87** ....(t) KerrinMcEvoy 6 76
(Saeed Bin Suroor) *led tl 3f out: sn wknd* **17/2**

2m 28.22s (-6.17) **Going Correction** -0.25s/f (Stan) course record
WFA 3 from 4yo+ 7lb **10** Ran SP% **115.9**
Speed ratings (Par 107):110,109,108,107,106 104,104,100,100,99
CSF £20.82 CT £57.55 TOTE £3.00: £1.40, £2.80, £1.10; EX 19.90 Trifecta £51.60 Pool: £447.54 - 6.15 winning tickets..
Owner Godolphin **Bred** Darley **Trained** Newmarket, Suffolk

FOCUS
A decent middle-distance handicap and, with the winner's stablemate setting a fair pace, even if he did slow it a touch at about halfway, the course record was lowered by almost a second. The winner looks Listed class at least, and the second and third also recorded personal bests.

NOTEBOOK
Descartes ◆, not seen since winning a heavy-ground juvenile maiden over a mile at Newbury almost two years previously, made a most pleasing return to action, coping just fine with both the significant step up in trip and switch to Polytrack. He only had a length to spare at the line, but appeared to get tired in the straight having travelled very strongly and is open to a deal of improvement. Considering he was just treading water a touch close home, it is to his credit that he still managed to break the track record by almost a second. He should still look reasonably treated for handicaps once reassessed, but his connections will no doubt be keen to test him in pattern company at some stage and, provided he goes the right way from this, he could well prove up to that sort of level in time. (op 7-4)
Transvestite(IRE) ran another good race in defeat and is holding his form well, but time is likely to show he faced an impossible task against Descartes. (tchd 7-1)
Royal Jet, in great form on Kempton's Polytrack in recent starts, showed himself just as effective at Lingfield with a fine effort off top weight. (op 4-1)
Zonergem ran surprisingly well returned to handicap company but is just a hard horse to win with on the Flat.
Given A Choice(IRE) was only 1lb higher than when last winning and did not seem to have any excuses.
Zabeel Palace looked very fit on this return from a break, but failed to see his race out, having raced quite freely. Official explanation: jockey said gelding ran too free in early stages (op 8-1 tchd 9-1)

5777 HALLOWEEN FAMILY FUN DAY OCTOBER 26TH H'CAP — 6f (P)
4:20 (4:20) (Class 4) (0-85,85) 3-Y-0+ **£7,124** (£2,119; £1,059; £529) **Stalls** Low

Form RPR
-051 **1** **Grand Show**[23] 5263 4-9-1 **82** .... TedDurcan 3 92+
(W R Swinburn) *lw: t.k.h: trckd ldrs: rdr dropped whip and led jst ins fnl f: rdn out: jst hld on* **7/4**[1]
-014 **2** *shd* **Special Lad**[25] 5212 4-9-4 **85** ....(t) LDettori 12 95+
(P F I Cole) *lw: stdd s: t.k.h in rr: effrt and wd st: fin strly: jst failed* **9/2**[2]
405 **3** *1 1/4* **Buy On The Red**[16] 5453 5-8-12 **79** .... KerrinMcEvoy 9 85
(W R Muir) *lw: mid-div: effrt 2f out: styd on fnl f* **12/1**
6206 **4** *shd* **Brandywell Boy (IRE)**[67] 3970 3-8-10 **78** .... SebSanders 5 84
(D J S Ffrench Davis) *prom: rdn to chal over 1f out: one pce fnl f* **16/1**
1305 **5** *nk* **Hammer Of The Gods (IRE)**[25] 5212 6-8-12 **79**.....(bt) JamieSpencer 8 84
(P S McEntee) *lw: wd: chsd ldrs: rdn to chal over 1f out: one pce fnl f* **6/1**[3]
3163 **6** *hd* **Ivory Lace**[30] 5096 5-8-9 **79** .... JamesDoyle(3) 10 83
(S Woodman) *bhd: rdn 1/2-way: styd on wl fnl f* **14/1**
0004 **7** *1 1/4* **Godfrey Street**[8] 5627 3-9-3 **85** .... RyanMoore 7 85
(R Hannon) *towards rr: effrt over 1f out: no imp* **8/1**
2000 **8** *hd* **Zarzu**[25] 5212 7-8-11 **78** .... JohnEgan 6 78
(C R Dore) *mid-div: effrt 2f out: no imp whn n.m.r ins fnl f* **33/1**
0006 **9** *1/2* **River Thames**[36] 4922 3-9-3 **85** .... MartinDwyer 4 83
(J A R Toller) *chsd ldrs: led over 2f out tl wknd jst ins fnl f* **12/1**
0040 **10** *1 3/4* **High Reach**[25] 5212 6-9-4 **85** ....(p) RichardMullen 1 78
(W R Muir) *chsd ldrs over 3f* **33/1**
0150 **11** *5* **Purus (IRE)**[82] 3532 4-8-13 **80** .... DaneO'Neill 2 58
(P Mitchell) *led tl over 2f out: wknd wl over 1f out* **14/1**

1m 10.82s (-1.99) **Going Correction** -0.25s/f (Stan)
WFA 3 from 4yo+ 1lb **11** Ran SP% **120.4**
Speed ratings (Par 105):103,102,101,101,100 100,98,98,97,95 88
CSF £9.35 CT £73.72 TOTE £2.50: £1.40, £1.70, £3.30; EX 9.60 Trifecta £100.00 Pool: £339.55 - 2.41 winning tickets..
Owner Mrs P W Harris **Bred** Pendley Farm **Trained** Aldbury, Herts

FOCUS
A fair sprint handicap for the grade. The first two are both likely to do better.

5778 RACING HERE AGAIN TOMORROW H'CAP — 7f (P)
4:50 (4:51) (Class 5) (0-75,79) 3-Y-0+ **£3,238** (£963; £481; £240) **Stalls** Low

Form RPR
4000 **1** **Keyaki (IRE)**[24] 5233 5-8-11 **68** .... SebSanders 14 76
(C F Wall) *chsd ldrs: led 1f out: drvn out: jst hld on* **25/1**
2423 **2** *shd* **Neardown Beauty (IRE)**[8] 5619 3-9-1 **74** .... RyanMoore 13 82+
(I A Wood) *s.i.s: bhd: plld outside over 1f out: rapid hdwy fnl f: jst failed* **9/2**[1]
1421 **3** *nk* **Landucci**[5] 5670 5-9-1 **79** 6ex .... PatrickHills(7) 6 86
(J W Hills) *lw: hld up bhd ldrs: rdn over 1f out: kpt on* **6/1**[2]
0000 **4** *1/2* **Hayyani (IRE)**[20] 5346 4-8-13 **70** ....(bt) RichardMullen 9 76
(K McAuliffe) *mid-div: effrt and wd st: styd on fnl f* **12/1**
2000 **5** *1* **Quantum Leap**[30] 5096 9-9-0 **71** ....(v) JimmyQuinn 11 74
(S Dow) *mid-div: effrt over 2f out: kpt on fnl f* **20/1**
234 **6** *shd* **Secret Assassin (IRE)**[23] 5268 3-9-1 **74** .... MartinDwyer 7 77
(W R Muir) *trckd ldr: led briefly over 1f out: no ex fnl f* **11/1**
3166 **7** *shd* **First Approval**[71] 3841 3-8-12 **71** .... RHills 10 74
(B W Hills) *rr of midfield: rdn and outpcd 2f out: kpt on fnl f* **33/1**
-300 **8** *hd* **Smokin Joe**[19] 5391 5-9-0 **71** ow1 .... GeorgeBaker 8 73
(J R Best) *hld up and bhd: wd st: gd late hdwy* **16/1**
0500 **9** *1* **Sands Of Barra (IRE)**[19] 5377 3-8-11 **70** .... KerrinMcEvoy 12 70
(N A Callaghan) *led 2f: prom tl wknd 1f out* **12/1**
5043 **10** *hd* **Dvinsky (USA)**[24] 5246 5-8-10 **67** .... PaulDoe 4 66
(M A Allen) *dwlt: towards rr: effrt into midfield whn nt clr run and swtchd lft ins fnl f: unable to chal* **12/1**
0560 **11** *2* **Bold Diktator**[20] 5345 4-8-11 **68** ....(b) SteveDrowne 5 62
(W R Muir) *chsd ldrs tl wknd over 1f out* **33/1**
0122 **12** *1/2* **Mambazo**[19] 5391 4-9-4 **75** ....(e) AdamKirby 3 68
(S C Williams) *mid-div: effrt 2f out: nt pce to chal* **9/1**
0604 **13** *1 1/4* **Roman Quintet (IRE)**[23] 5263 6-8-13 **70** .... LDettori 2 59
(D W P Arbuthnot) *led after 2f tl wknd over 1f out* **7/1**[3]
5103 **14** *1* **Southport Star (IRE)**[24] 5249 3-9-2 **75** .... JamieSpencer 1 62
(J R Fanshawe) *s.i.s: hld up in rr: effrt on rail early st: unable to chal: eased fnl f* **6/1**[2]

1m 23.8s (-2.09) **Going Correction** -0.25s/f (Stan)
WFA 3 from 4yo+ 2lb **14** Ran SP% **121.0**
Speed ratings (Par 103):101,100,100,99,98 98,98,98,97,97 94,94,92,91
CSF £130.76 CT £805.38 TOTE £40.70: £12.60, £2.20, £2.20; EX 337.60 TRIFECTA Not won. Place 6 £14.01, Place 5 £8.30.
Owner S Oldroyd **Bred** Rathbarry Stud **Trained** Newmarket, Suffolk

FOCUS
An all right handicap for the grade, but the first eight were covered by only around two lengths or so. Interestingly, the first two home were drawn in double-figure stalls.
Mambazo Official explanation: jockey said gelding ran too free in early stages
Southport Star(IRE) Official explanation: trainer's representative said gelding failed to quicken turning into straight and had no more to give
T/Jkpt: £1,451.90 to a £1 stake. Pool: £282,214.50. 138.00 winning tickets. T/Plt: £23.00 to a £1 stake. Pool: £87,643.85. 2,777.45 winning tickets. T/Qpdt: £8.00 to a £1 stake. Pool: £4,358.45. 401.10 winning tickets. LM

5664 CHANTILLY (R-H)
Thursday, October 5

OFFICIAL GOING: Soft

5779a PRIX DE BONNEVAL (LISTED RACE) — 5f 110y
2:30 (2:37) 3-Y-0+ **£17,241** (£6,897; £5,172; £3,448; £1,724)

RPR
1 **Strike Up The Band**[16] 5443 3-8-11 .... AdrianTNicholls 3 114
(D Nicholls) *made all, ridden final f, driven out* **268/10**
2 *2* **One Putra (IRE)**[26] 5182 4-9-2 .... PhilipRobinson 4 111
(M A Jarvis) *raced in 2nd on stands side, ridden over 1f out, stayed on but not pace of winner* **23/1**
3 *1/2* **Tycoon's Hill (IRE)**[25] 5222 7-9-2 .... OPeslier 5 109
(Robert Collet, France) **12/1**
4 *snk* **Ratio**[11] 5549 8-9-2 .... FSpanu 7 109
(J E Hammond, France) **53/10**[3]
5 *3/4* **Kourka (FR)**[25] 5222 4-8-8 .... RonanThomas 8 98
(J-M Beguigne, France) **12/1**
6 *nk* **Borderlescott**[19] 5358 4-8-11 .... RoystonFfrench 11 100
(R Bastiman) *led far side, drifted into centre 1 1/2f out, no extra close home* **24/10**[1]
7 *shd* **Jet Express (SAF)**[210] 620 4-8-11 .... MBlancpain 6 100
(Diego Lowther, France) **72/1**
8 *1 1/2* **Abundance (USA)**[39] 4860 4-8-8 .... C-PLemaire 1 92
(Mme C Head-Maarek, France) **67/10**
9 *4* **Matrix (GER)**[39] 4858 5-9-2 .... DBoeuf 12 87
(W Baltromei, Germany) **11/1**
10 *nk* **Poseidon's Bride (USA)**[21] 3-8-8 .... SPasquier 10 79
(A Fabre, France) **47/10**[2]
11 **Gauguin (IRE)**[10] 3-8-11 ....(b) JAuge 2 82
(Robert Collet, France) **12/1**
12 **Blue Damask (USA)**[28] 5146 3-8-11 .... CSoumillon 9 82
(A Fabre, France) **63/10**

66.10 secs **12** Ran SP% **130.1**
PARI-MUTUEL: WIN 27.80; PL 7.70, 6.80, 6.70; DF 76.80.
Owner The Oak Apple Syndicate **Bred** Miss A J Rawding And P M Crane **Trained** Sessay, N Yorks

NOTEBOOK
Strike Up The Band, who loves to get his toe in, put up a really good effort to win this Listed prize. Smartly away, he led from soon after the start and was never really seriously challenged. He was going away at the post and looks to have a bright future in front of him in next year's top sprints.
One Putra(IRE) was always in second position behind the winner on the stands' side. Pushed along from two out, he just stayed on one-paced, and probably did not really appreciate the soft ground.
Borderlescott was unfortunately taken across to the far side of the track with three others. At the halfway stage his group was five lengths adrift of the runners on the stands' side and, although his jockey tacked him across to the centre of the track to make his challenge, the race was over when he arrived on the scene. This outing is best forgotten.

5772 LINGFIELD (L-H)
Friday, October 6

OFFICIAL GOING: Standard
Wind: fresh behind

5780 HALLOWEEN FAMILY FUN DAY OCTOBER 26TH MEDIAN AUCTION MAIDEN STKS (DIV I) — 7f (P)
2:00 (2:00) (Class 5) 2-Y-O **£3,886** (£1,156; £577; £288) **Stalls** Low

Form RPR
022 **1** **Swift Cut (IRE)**[9] 5615 2-9-3 .... DarryllHolland 8 76+
(A P Jarvis) *trckd ldrs: hdwy to ld over 2f out: clr and in command over 1f out: eased nr fin* **7/4**[1]
66 **2** *3/4* **Priory Bay (USA)**[76] 3726 2-9-3 .... JimmyFortune 4 72
(E A L Dunlop) *in tch: hdwy 3f out: rdn over 2f out: chsd wnr over 1f out: kpt on* **9/2**[3]
0020 **3** *6* **Show Trial (IRE)**[23] 5282 2-8-12 **52** .... AdamKirby 10 51
(D J S Ffrench Davis) *w.w in midfield: hdwy 3f out: chsd ldng pair wl over 1f out: no imp u.p fnl f* **33/1**
4 *hd* **Sweet World** 2-9-3 .... DaneO'Neill 2 56
(A P Jarvis) *slowly away: bhd: shkn up and hdwy 2f out: rdn and kpt on fnl f: nvr nrr* **20/1**
5 *hd* **Ardmaddy (IRE)** 2-9-3 .... TPO'Shea 7 55
(J A R Toller) *slowly away: bhd: pushed along 3f out: sn struggling: kpt on wl ins fnl f: n.d* **16/1**
6 *nk* **Genki (IRE)** 2-9-3 .... SteveDrowne 9 55
(R Charlton) *slowly away: rn green in rr: sme hdwy and rn v wd bnd over 2f out: kpt on fnl f: n.d* **8/1**
00 **7** *1/2* **Allroundtheoutside**[29] 5126 2-9-3 .... PaulDoe 1 53
(P R Chamings) *slowly away: sn rcvrd and in midfield: drvn over 2f out: kpt on same pce* **14/1**

056 **8** *nk* **Toggle**[39] 4895 2-9-3 71 .... RyanMoore 5 53
(R Hannon) *led tl over 2f out: sn drvn: wknd over 1f out* **11/4**[2]
3500 **9** *1* **Tumble Jill (IRE)**[4] 5730 2-8-9 52 .... AmirQuinn(3) 11 45
(J J Bridger) *chsd ldr tl wl over 2f out: sn rdn: wknd wl over 1f out* **66/1**
0 **10** *3* **Split The Wind (USA)**[27] 5161 2-8-12 .... StephenCarson 3 37
(R F Johnson Houghton) *trckd ldrs: rdn 3f out: lost pl over 2f out: sn no ch* **25/1**
11 *25* **Wise Decision (IRE)** 2-8-12 .... ChrisCatlin 6 —
(E J O'Neill) *slowly away: sn pushed along and struggling: t.o fr 1/2-way* **10/1**

1m 26.01s (0.12) **Going Correction** -0.125s/f (Stan) **11** Ran SP% **127.0**
Speed ratings (Par 95):94,93,86,86,85 85,84,84,83,80 51
CSF £10.54 TOTE £1.80: £1.60, £1.20, £4.40; EX 8.30 Trifecta £56.10 Pool: £414.30 - 5.24 winning tickets..
Owner Geoffrey Bishop and Ann Jarvis **Bred** P A Mason **Trained** Twyford, Bucks

FOCUS
A weak maiden, as the proximity of the 52-rated Show Trial suggests, but the front two pulled clear and the winner is rated as having run close to previous form. The winning time was 0.19 seconds slower than the second division.

NOTEBOOK
Swift Cut(IRE), upped a furlong in trip and switched to Polytrack for the first time, confirmed the ability he showed when second on his last two starts, winning eased down and probably value for another couple of lengths. This was not much of a race, but the front two were clear and he should not be underestimated in future.
Priory Bay(USA), who shaped well on his debut at Newmarket but was beaten at odds on next time on Lingfield's turf track, returned to form off the back of a 76-day break and finished well clear of the remainder. He might be able to find a similar race, but his connections will have more options now he is qualified for a handicap mark. (op 4-1)
Show Trial(IRE), upped in trip and switched to Polytrack for the first time on her first start since leaving Mick Channon's yard, ran a good race. She might be a touch better than her official rating of 52, but still looks a reasonable guide to the form.
Sweet World ◆, a 10,000gns half-brother to among others the smart Montestefano, a dual mile winner at three in Italy, out of an eight-furlong scorer, was the eye-catcher of the race, keeping on nicely late in the day without ever threatening his stablemate.
Ardmaddy(IRE), a 60,000gns half-brother to the smart Ibiscus, a triple sprint winner at two in Italy, out of a six-furlong juvenile scorer, began to get the hang of things late on and should improve next time.
Genki(IRE), a 55,000gns purchase, out of a mile-winner in Italy, was badly in need of this first racecourse experience, running green early after starting slowly and then hanging badly to his right on the final bend. It is to his credit he still managed to finish so close and he will have learnt plenty from this. (tchd 9-1)
Toggle, switched to Polytrack for the first time, ran below his official mark of 71 and again gave the impression he might be worth a try over shorter. (op 3-1)

5781 LINGFIELDPARK.CO.UK (S) STKS 6f (P)
2:30 (2:30) (Class 5) 3-4-Y-0 **£3,238** (£963; £481; £240) **Stalls** Low

Form RPR
4100 **1** **Came Back (IRE)**[124] 2263 3-9-2 65 .... EddieAhern 10 68
(J A Osborne) *trckd ldrs tl led over 2f out: edgd rt briefly u.p over 1f out: styd on* **12/1**
6001 **2** *1* **Ockums Razor (IRE)**[24] 5273 3-9-2 65 .... DarryllHolland 6 65
(C A Dwyer) *bhd: hdwy wl over 2f out: chsd wnr ins fnl f: no imp u.p* **3/1**[1]
0000 **3** *¾* **Solicitude**[50] 4533 3-8-6 60 .... RobertHavlin 12 53
(D Haydn Jones) *sn outpcd in last and drvn: styd on wl over 1f out: nvr nrr* **20/1**
4000 **4** *nk* **Danish Blues (IRE)**[37] 4927 3-8-11 55 .... (p) ChrisCatlin 2 57
(N P Littmoden) *slowly away and wnt rt s: bhd: hdwy 2f out: hrd drvn and no ex ins fnl f* **12/1**
4000 **5** *½* **Aristofilia**[16] 5474 3-8-6 57 .... TedDurcan 4 50
(P F I Cole) *racd in midfield: rdn 1/2-way: kpt on but nvr pce to rch ldrs* **6/1**[3]
0365 **6** *shd* **Shunkawakhan (IRE)**[24] 5273 3-8-11 55 .... OscarUrbina 11 55
(G C H Chung) *chsd ldrs: hdwy over 2f out: ev ch and drvn 2f out: wknd ins fnl f* **8/1**
5354 **7** *1* **Danawi (IRE)**[4] 5728 3-8-11 60 .... RyanMoore 9 52
(R Hannon) *sn outpcd in last pair: kpt on u.p fnl f: n.d* **7/2**[2]
6000 **8** *nk* **African Concerto (IRE)**[62] 4164 3-8-11 52 .... FrankieMcDonald 5 51
(S Kirk) *hld up in rr: rdn and effrt 2f out: kpt on fnl f: nt rch ldrs* **16/1**
0000 **9** *4* **Danny The Dip**[11] 5576 3-8-8 54 .... (b[1]) MarcHalford(3) 3 39
(J J Bridger) *racd in midfield on inner: nt clr run over 2f out: swtchd rt wl over 1f out: no prog u.p* **33/1**
0500 **10** *1½* **Burhaan (IRE)**[106] 2793 4-8-9 52 .... AmirQuinn(3) 8 35
(J R Boyle) *led tl 2f out: wknd qckly over 1f out* **16/1**
5000 **11** *6* **Developer (IRE)**[23] 5291 3-8-11 55 .... IanMongan 7 17
(T G Mills) *pressed ldr tl wl over 2f out: sn wknd* **9/1**
12 *½* **Same Old Scene (IRE)** 3-8-11 .... MickyFenton 1 15
(J R Best) *t.k.h: racd in midfield: in tch util wknd wl over 2f out* **33/1**

1m 12.27s (-0.54) **Going Correction** -0.125s/f (Stan)
WFA 3 from 4yo 1lb **12** Ran SP% **120.4**
Speed ratings (Par 103):98,96,95,95,94 94,93,92,87,85 77,76
CSF £47.76 TOTE £11.00: £3.20, £1.50, £10.00; EX 39.70 TRIFECTA Not won..There was no bid for the winner. Danawi was claimed by M R Hoad for £6,000
Owner J A Osborne **Bred** Yeomanstown Stud **Trained** Upper Lambourn, Berks
■ Stewards' Enquiry : Ian Mongan two-day ban: careless riding (Oct 17-18)

FOCUS
As is to be expected in a seller, weak form rated through the runner-up. The winning time was almost a second slower than the following handicap.
Ockums Razor(IRE) Official explanation: jockey said gelding hung left
Same Old Scene(IRE) Official explanation: jockey said gelding had a breathing problem

5782 LINGFIELD PARK GOLF COURSE H'CAP 6f (P)
3:05 (3:05) (Class 5) (0-75,75) 3-Y-0+ **£4,533** (£1,348; £674; £336) **Stalls** Low

Form RPR
3244 **1** **Woodnook**[24] 5275 3-9-3 75 .... JimmyFortune 7 87
(J A R Toller) *w.w in midfield: hdwy over 2f out: rdn to chse ldr over 1f out: styd on wl to ld nr fin* **11/2**[2]
1512 **2** *nk* **Forest Dane**[16] 5476 6-8-11 71 .... JamesDoyle(3) 8 82
(Mrs N Smith) *t.k.h: trckd ldrs tl led 2f out: pressed and rdn wl ins fnl f: hdd nr fin* **11/2**[2]
330 **3** *2* **High Ridge**[16] 5476 7-9-2 73 .... (p) DaneO'Neill 10 78
(J M Bradley) *bhd: rdn and hdwy 2f out: styd on ins fnl f: wnt 3rd on line: nvr nrr* **12/1**
6334 **4** *hd* **Xaluna Bay (IRE)**[27] 5181 3-9-1 73 .... MartinDwyer 12 78
(W R Muir) *chsd ldrs: effrt and rdn over 2f out: kpt on one pced fnl f* **16/1**
1220 **5** *hd* **Mambazo**[1] 5778 4-9-4 75 .... (e) AdamKirby 6 79
(S C Williams) *t.k.h: hld up in rr: rdn and hdwy on outer over 2f out: kpt on: nt rch ldrs* **5/1**[1]
5003 **6** *1* **Digital**[10] 5593 9-9-2 73 .... ChrisCatlin 4 74
(M R Channon) *s.i.s: bhd: styd on ins fnl f: nvr nrr* **12/1**
5030 **7** *½* **Jayanjay**[34] 5021 7-9-1 72 .... SebSanders 1 71
(P Mitchell) *hld up in midfield on inner: rdn 2f out: kpt on same pce fnl f* **9/1**[3]
0002 **8** *1¼* **Calypso King**[18] 5427 3-9-1 73 .... RyanMoore 11 69
(J W Hills) *hld up in rr: rdn over 2f out: nvr on terms* **5/1**[1]
1005 **9** *hd* **Norcroft**[20] 5391 4-9-1 72 .... (p) AdrianMcCarthy 2 67
(Mrs C A Dunnett) *chsd ldrs: rdn over 2f out: wknd wl over 1f out* **25/1**
4160 **10** *1¼* **Silver Dane (IRE)**[24] 5275 4-9-3 74 .... (v) TedDurcan 5 65
(Mrs C A Dunnett) *t.k.h: chsd ldr after 2f: rdn over 2f out: wknd wl over 1f out* **16/1**
430 **11** *¾* **No Time (IRE)**[50] 4531 6-8-13 70 .... EddieAhern 9 59
(J A Osborne) *led after 1f tl rdn and hdd 2f out: sn wknd* **14/1**
6315 **12** *½* **Namu**[18] 5427 3-8-9 72 .... AurelioMedeiros(5) 3 60
(B W Hills) *led for 1f: chsd ldrs tl rdn over 2f out: wknd qckly* **14/1**

1m 11.32s (-1.49) **Going Correction** -0.125s/f (Stan)
WFA 3 from 4yo+ 1lb **12** Ran SP% **118.4**
Speed ratings (Par 103):104,103,100,100,100 99,98,96,96,94 93,93
CSF £35.80 CT £353.24 TOTE £6.50: £2.50, £2.70, £2.50; EX 37.10 Trifecta £288.50 Part won. Pool: £406.42 - 0.34 winning tickets..
Owner Mrs Julia Scott **Bred** Glebe Stud **Trained** Newmarket, Suffolk

FOCUS
A fair sprint handicap run in a time almost a full second quicker than the earlier seller. Straightforward form and sound.

5783 LINGFIELDPARK.CO.UK NURSERY 1m (P)
3:35 (3:35) (Class 4) (0-85,85) 2-Y-O **£6,477** (£1,927; £963; £481) **Stalls** High

Form RPR
21 **1** **Strobilus**[29] 5134 2-9-7 85 .... PhilipRobinson 6 97+
(M A Jarvis) *slowly away: t.k.h and sn chsng ldrs: chsd ldr over 2f out: rdn to ld ent fnl f: r.o strly* **11/2**[3]
461 **2** *3* **Brainy Benny (IRE)**[18] 5423 2-9-1 79 .... JimmyFortune 10 84
(N A Callaghan) *t.k.h: chsd ldrs: led and qcknd over 2f out: hdd ent fnl f: outpcd by wnr last 100 yds* **7/1**
0052 **3** *2½* **Aegis (IRE)**[10] 5585 2-8-11 75 .... (b[1]) MichaelHills 9 74
(B W Hills) *chsd ldrs: rdn over 2f out: sn chsng ldng pair: no imp* **7/1**
521 **4** *shd* **Beverly Hill Billy**[39] 4897 2-9-0 78 .... DaneO'Neill 5 77
(A King) *hld up bhd: rdn 3f out: hdwy over 2f out: kpt on: nvr pce to rch ldrs* **10/1**
1 **5** *1* **I'm Right (USA)**[31] 5095 2-9-1 79 .... MartinDwyer 12 76
(M P Tregoning) *t.k.h: hld up in midfield on outer: hdwy over 3f out: rdn over 2f out: kpt on one pced* **5/1**[2]
421 **6** *nk* **Elusive Flash (USA)**[20] 5380 2-9-7 85 .... EddieAhern 8 81
(P F I Cole) *w.w in tch: rdn and effrt whn edgd lft bnd over 2f out: kpt on but nt pce to rch ldrs* **9/1**
6312 **7** *hd* **Cesc**[53] 4436 2-9-1 79 .... JimmyQuinn 4 75+
(P J Makin) *slowly away: hld up wl bhd: rdn and hdwy whn hmpd bnd over 2f out: kpt on u.p: nvr nrr* **5/2**[1]
220 **8** *1¾* **Al Raahi**[27] 5172 2-8-12 76 .... TedDurcan 3 68
(M R Channon) *hld up bhd: plld wd and effrt 3f out: racd awkwardly 2f out: nvr trbld ldrs* **33/1**
4335 **9** *3* **King's Causeway (USA)**[27] 5172 2-8-10 74 .... DarryllHolland 2 59
(W J Haggas) *t.k.h: hld up in midfield: rdn over 3f out: wkng whn hmpd twice bnd over 2f out* **12/1**
6344 **10** *6* **Recruit**[18] 5423 2-8-8 72 .... (b[1]) RyanMoore 1 43
(R Hannon) *slowly away: sn pushed up and chsng ldrs: rdn 3f out: sn wknd* **25/1**
1336 **11** *hd* **Stagehand (IRE)**[20] 5382 2-8-11 75 .... AdrianMcCarthy 11 45
(B R Millman) *led tl over 2f out: sn wknd: eased ins fnl f* **20/1**
2250 **12** *nk* **Baldovina**[31] 5083 2-8-13 77 .... OscarUrbina 7 47
(M Botti) *hld up bhd: rdn 3f out: no real prog* **16/1**

1m 37.16s (-2.27) **Going Correction** -0.125s/f (Stan) **12** Ran SP% **129.8**
Speed ratings (Par 97):106,103,100,100,99 99,98,97,94,88 87,87
CSF £47.37 CT £287.58 TOTE £8.40: £2.60, £1.90, £2.10; EX 63.50 Trifecta £271.00 Part won. Pool: £381.78 - 0.68 winning tickets..
Owner Sheikh Mohammed **Bred** Darley **Trained** Newmarket, Suffolk

FOCUS
The winning time was very smart and this is strong nursery form, the winner impressing.

NOTEBOOK
Strobilus ◆ followed up his win in a three-runner seven-furlong maiden on heavy ground at Haydock with a pretty impressive success under joint-top weight. He is progressing into a very useful sort and deserves his chance in better company. (op 9-2)
Brainy Benny(IRE), off the mark over this trip in a maiden on Kempton's Polytrack on his previous start, ran well switched to nursery company for the first time. He was no match for the impressive winner late on, but did well to finish clear of the remainder considering how keenly he raced early on and he could have more to offer if settling better in future. (tchd 8-1)
Aegis(IRE), who did not totally convince with his attitude when second off this mark at Goodwood on his previous start, ran okay in first-time blinkers without finding the required improvement. Having travelled well just off the pace, he did not find as much as had looked likely and only stayed on at the one pace. (op 8-1)
Beverly Hill Billy, the winner of a seven-furlong Warwick maiden on his previous start, ran respectably stepped back up in trip and returned to Polytrack on his nursery debut, but never really threatened having had to come from well back. (op 8-1)
I'm Right(USA), successful on her debut in an ordinary seven-furlong maiden round here, is a little bit better than she was able to show, as she was caught wide from her unfavourable draw and raced keenly. She was due to be raised 3lb.
Elusive Flash(USA), off the mark in a seven-furlong Warwick maiden on her previous start, ran with credit but will probably be more at home in fillies' only company. (op 8-1 tchd 10-1)
Cesc ◆, 5lb higher than when second over seven furlongs at Wolverhampton on his previous start, was given a poor ride by Jimmy Quinn and should have finished an awful lot closer. After starting slowly, he was soon buried away towards the inside rail and lost what was already a bad position on the turn into the straight, dropping back to last at one point. He then met with all sorts of trouble when trying to make up some of the lost ground and the race was all over by the time he finally got in the clear. He is much better than his finishing position suggests. (op 6-1)
King's Causeway(USA) ◆ did not enjoy a clear run and is better than he was able to show. (op 8-1)
Stagehand(IRE) Official explanation: jockey said colt ran flat

5784 HALLOWEEN FAMILY FUN DAY OCTOBER 26TH MEDIAN AUCTION MAIDEN STKS (DIV II) 7f (P)

4:10 (4:11) (Class 5) 2-Y-0 £3,886 (£1,156; £577; £288) Stalls Low

Form RPR

6 **1** **Ekhtiaar**[17] 5460 2-9-3 .... RHills 7 86+
(J H M Gosden) *trckd ldrs: hmpd after 2f: chsd ldr wl over 2f out: led 1f out: pushed clr: readily* **15/8**[2]

34 **2** 2 ½ **Whazzis**[14] 5503 2-8-12 .... JimmyFortune 9 74
(W J Haggas) *prom: led after 2f: rdn over 2f out: hdd 1f out: no ch w wnr after* **4/5**[1]

3 2 **Subadar** 2-9-3 .... SteveDrowne 6 74
(R Charlton) *slowly away: sn chsng ldrs: rdn over 2f out: chsd ldng pair 2f out: kpt on same pce* **11/1**

30 **4** 1 ¼ **Blue Monkey (IRE)**[127] 2178 2-9-3 .... MartinDwyer 10 71+
(M L W Bell) *t.k.h: hld up: hdwy 2f out: kpt on fnl f: n.d* **10/1**[3]

0 **5** ¾ **Putra Laju (IRE)**[7] 5648 2-9-3 .... MichaelHills 8 69
(J W Hills) *chsd ldrs: rdn over 2f out: outpcd wl over 1f out* **50/1**

6 1 ½ **Give Evidence** 2-9-3 .... DarryllHolland 11 65
(A P Jarvis) *slowly away: sn prom on outer: rdn over 3f out: kpt on same last 2f* **33/1**

7 2 ½ **Baba Ganouge (IRE)** 2-8-12 .... RyanMoore 5 53
(B J Meehan) *sn pushed along: bhd fr 1/2-way* **25/1**

04 **8** shd **Lapina (IRE)**[9] 5608 2-8-12 .... DavidKinsella 4 53
(Pat Eddery) *sn rdn: a bhd: no ch fr 1/2-way* **40/1**

9 ¾ **Atlantic Dame (USA)** 2-8-12 .... EddieAhern 2 51
(Mrs A J Perrett) *hld up bhd: n.d* **25/1**

50 **10** 1 ½ **Earl Compton (IRE)**[7] 5645 2-9-3 ....(t) TedDurcan 3 52
(P F I Cole) *racd in midfield: rdn wl over 2f out: sn struggling* **40/1**

4 **11** 1 ¾ **Charlotte Grey**[18] 5417 2-8-12 .... JimmyQuinn 1 43
(C N Allen) *led for 2f: chsd ldrs tl wl over 2f out: sn wknd* **33/1**

1m 25.82s (-0.07) **Going Correction** -0.125s/f (Stan) **39** Ran SP% **128.2**
Speed ratings (Par 95):95,92,89,88,87 85,83,82,82,80 78
CSF £3.84 TOTE £3.50: £1.40, £1.10, £2.70; EX 5.40 Trifecta £24.40 Pool: £636.13 - 18.47 winning tickets..
Owner Hamdan Al Maktoum **Bred** Mrs M L Parry And P M Steele-Mortimer **Trained** Newmarket, Suffolk

■ Stewards' Enquiry : Jimmy Fortune 16-day ban (takes into account previous offences; three days deferred): careless riding (Oct 27-Nov 8)

FOCUS

A reasonable maiden and the winning time was 0.19 seconds quicker than the first division. The form is not easy to rate and could be too low.

NOTEBOOK

Ekhtiaar, a beaten favourite when sixth of 16 on his debut over a mile at Newmarket, put up an improved effort over this shorter trip on his Polytrack debut. He looks a nice three-year-old prospect. (op 2-1)

Whazzis, a pleasing third on her debut in a conditions event at Chester before running fourth to subsequent Cheveley Park winner Indian Ink in a Sales race at Ascot, failed to take advantage of the drop into maiden company. The slightly longer trip and new surface should not have been a problem and she has to be considered disappointing, even if she did run into a nice type. (op 5-4 tchd 11-8)

Subadar, a half-brother to some decent sprint types, including the high-class Deportivo, made a respectable debut. If his breeding his anything to go by, he could well prove best over shorter in time. (op 8-1)

Blue Monkey(IRE), a beaten favourite when last seen 127 days previously, ran with credit and should be sharper next time. His connections will have more options now he is qualified for a handicap mark. (op 9-1)

Putra Laju(IRE) improved on his debut effort, showing up well for a long way before getting tired. He might be one to keep in mind for handicaps and needs one more run for a mark.

Give Evidence, a 25,000gns first foal of a dual seven-furlong winner, showed ability and should be better for the experience.

5785 DINE IN THE TRACKSIDE CARVERY H'CAP 7f (P)

4:45 (4:45) (Class 3) (0-90,90) 3-Y-0+

£10,594 (£3,172; £1,586; £793; £396; £198) Stalls Low

Form RPR

1201 **1** **Ceremonial Jade (UAE)**[30] 5107 3-9-2 **90**..........(t) OscarUrbina 3 106+
(M Botti) *b: confidently rdn: hld up bhd: smooth hdwy over 2f out: swtchd rt over 1f out: sn chalng: led ins fnl f: r.o wl* **7/4**[1]

016 **2** hd **Rochdale**[55] 4357 3-9-2 **90**.......... PhilipRobinson 8 106
(M A Jarvis) *chsd ldrs: wnt 2nd 3f out: led u.p wl over 1f out: hdd ins fnl f: kpt on gamely* **10/1**

5200 **3** ¾ **Bouboulina**[55] 4343 3-9-2 **90**.......... RyanMoore 4 104
(E A L Dunlop) *racd in midfield: rdn over 2f out: hdwy 2f out: ev ch 1f out: one pced ins fnl f* **14/1**

6404 **4** 3 ½ **Swinbrook (USA)**[18] 5420 5-9-0 **86**..........(v) JimmyFortune 7 91
(J A R Toller) *hld up in midfield: rdn and effrt over 2f out: kpt on ins fnl f* **7/1**[3]

6260 **5** 1 **Hits Only Heaven (IRE)**[27] 5175 4-8-13 **85**..........(e) SilvestreDeSousa 9 87
(D Nicholls) *chsd ldrs: rdn wl over 2f out: wknd 1f out* **6/1**[2]

2540 **6** 1 ¼ **Kindlelight Debut**[20] 5357 6-9-1 **90**.......... JamesDoyle(3) 6 89
(N P Littmoden) *nvr gng wl in rr: sme late prog: nvr on terms* **12/1**

6600 **7** nk **San Antonio**[41] 4819 6-8-12 **84**..........(b) MickyFenton 10 82
(Mrs P Sly) *sn led: rdn over 2f out: hdd wl over 1f out: fdd fnl f* **20/1**

0554 **8** 1 **Red Cape (FR)**[29] 5143 3-8-13 **87**.......... RobertHavlin 5 83
(Jane Chapple-Hyam) *chsd ldrs: rdn wl over 2f out: wknd over 1f out* **14/1**

5500 **9** 1 ¾ **Northern Desert (IRE)**[160] 1302 7-8-12 **84**.......... ChrisCatlin 14 75
(P W Hiatt) *hld up wl bhd: hdwy 3f out: no prog wl over 1f out* **33/1**

3156 **10** nk **Magic Rush**[10] 5591 4-8-8 **83**.......... EdwardCreighton(3) 2 73
(Mrs Norma Pook) *chsd ldr tl 3f out: wknd u.p 2f out* **12/1**

1401 **11** 7 **Phluke**[13] 5529 5-9-0 **86**.......... StephenCarson 12 58
(R F Johnson Houghton) *chsd ldrs: rdn and wknd over 2f out* **16/1**

3130 **12** 2 **Guest Connections**[14] 5501 3-8-12 **86**..........(v) TedDurcan 1 53
(M R Channon) *slowly away: towards rr: rdn 3f out: sn wl bhd: eased over 1f out* **25/1**

0611 **13** 10 **Woodcote Place**[10] 5591 3-8-12 **86** 6ex.......... SteveDrowne 13 27
(P R Chamings) *hld up bhd: lost tch 3f out: wnt lame over 2f out: eased: t.o* **6/1**[2]

1m 22.85s (-3.04) **Going Correction** -0.125s/f (Stan) course record
WFA 3 from 4yo+ 2lb **13** Ran SP% **132.7**
Speed ratings (Par 107):112,111,110,106,105 104,104,102,100,100 92,90,78
CSF £22.99 CT £216.35 TOTE £3.40: £1.60, £2.90, £4.10; EX 30.50 Trifecta £203.40 Pool: £346.80 - 1.21 winning tickets..
Owner Giuliano Manfredini **Bred** Darley **Trained** Newmarket, Suffolk

FOCUS

A good, competitive handicap and the winning time was decent for the grade. The first three are all unexposed and progressive, and they finished clear of a well-handicapped fourth, so the form should work out.

NOTEBOOK

Ceremonial Jade(UAE) ◆, an impressive winner over this trip on Kempton's Polytrack on his previous start, was just able to defy a 9lb higher mark, with the first-time tongue-tie seemingly not an issue. He only won by a head, but always looked like doing enough and this was a pretty decent handicap for the grade. His connections are hopeful he could develop into a Listed/Group horse. (op 5-2)

Rochdale, racing over his furthest trip to date and switched to Polytrack for the first time, ran a blinder off the back of a 55-day break, just going down to a very useful sort in the making. (op 8-1)

Bouboulina, highly tried on turf since winning her maiden over course and distance on her sole start as a juvenile, was given every chance and ran well, again showing her liking for Polytrack. (op 9-1)

Swinbrook(USA), having his first run over seven furlongs since finishing fourth in the Bunbury Cup, was no match for the front three and was not quite at his best. (op 13-2)

Hits Only Heaven(IRE) appreciated the return to Polytrack, but the Handicapper appears to be in charge. (op 7-1 tchd 15-2)

Kindlelight Debut, returned to her favoured Polytrack surface, had no easy task off a career-high mark but ran well. She might do even better back over a mile. (tchd 14-1)

Magic Rush Official explanation: jockey said gelding hung left

Phluke Official explanation: jockey said gelding ran flat

Guest Connections Official explanation: jockey said gelding suffered interference on final bend

Woodcote Place was chasing the hat-trick following a couple of wins on turf, but he went lame during the race. Official explanation: jockey said colt suffered interference on final bend (op 15-2)

5786 JUMPING HERE ON NOVEMBER 8TH H'CAP 1m 2f (P)

5:15 (5:15) (Class 5) (0-75,75) 3-Y-0+ £5,505 (£1,637; £818; £408) Stalls Low

Form RPR

1046 **1** **Cusoon**[28] 5149 4-9-7 **75**.......... RyanMoore 5 83+
(G L Moore) *t.k.h: in tch: rdn and prog 2f out: swtchd lft over 1f out: led ins fnl f: hld on wl* **9/2**[1]

2265 **2** shd **Red Birr (IRE)**[157] 1380 5-9-5 **73**.......... DaneO'Neill 9 80
(P R Webber) *hld up in midfield: hdwy on outer over 3f out: styd on u.p to ld ins fnl f: sn hdd: jst hld* **9/2**[1]

1000 **3** ¾ **Winners Delight**[65] 4051 5-9-6 **74**.......... GeorgeBaker 8 80
(C F Wall) *hld up towards rr: hdwy 3f out: rdn and effrt 2f out: ev ch 1f out: no ex last 100 yds* **10/1**

6250 **4** 1 ¾ **William's Way**[10] 5599 4-9-2 **70**.......... DarryllHolland 11 73
(I A Wood) *t.k.h: hld up in midfield: hdwy to ld 3f out: sn drvn: hdd ins fnl f: fdd last 100 yds* **11/1**

43-0 **5** ¾ **Turn 'n Burn**[23] 5295 5-9-0 **68**.......... TedDurcan 3 69
(C A Cyzer) *hld up towards rr: drvn over 2f out: r.o fnl f: nt rch ldrs* **25/1**

400 **6** ¾ **Smooth Jazz**[62] 4149 4-9-4 **72**.......... SebSanders 10 72
(R M Beckett) *racd wd in midfield: hdwy 3f out: hrd rdn over 2f out: hung lft over 1f out: wknd* **9/1**

1116 **7** shd **Newnham (IRE)**[218] 556 5-9-7 **75**.......... EddieAhern 14 75
(J R Boyle) *hld up in rr: rdn and hdwy over 2f out: styd on fnl f: nt rch ldrs* **15/2**[2]

43 **8** ½ **True Companion**[29] 5132 7-9-3 **74**.......... JamesDoyle(3) 7 73
(N P Littmoden) *chsd ldr tl 3f out: sn rdn: wknd wl over 1f out* **9/1**

4200 **9** 1 **Alekhine (IRE)**[25] 5236 5-8-13 **67**.......... MartinDwyer 13 64
(J R Boyle) *hld up wl in rr: prog over 2f out: kpt on: nvr able to chal* **25/1**

6521 **10** 1 ½ **Pactolos Way**[36] 4973 3-8-13 **72**.......... JimCrowley 12 66
(P R Chamings) *t.k.h: chsd ldrs: wnt 2nd over 2f out tl 2f out: sn wknd* **16/1**

0000 **11** nk **Barry Island**[98] 3048 7-9-3 **74**.......... MarcHalford(3) 6 67
(D R C Elsworth) *slowly away: sn racing in midfield: rdn and wknd over 2f out* **10/1**

40/5 **12** 5 **Unicorn Reward (IRE)**[31] 5101 6-9-4 **72**.......... RobertHavlin 4 56
(Mrs L C Jewell) *hld up in midfield: rdn wl over 2f out: sn struggling* **50/1**

1-00 **13** 1 ½ **Three Thieves (UAE)**[16] 5478 3-8-13 **72**.......... SteveDrowne 2 53
(M S Saunders) *chsd ldrs tl rdn and wknd over 3f out: sn no ch* **20/1**

1332 **14** 1 ¼ **Captain Margaret**[156] 1419 4-9-5 **73**.......... JimmyQuinn 1 52
(J Pearce) *led at stdy pce tl 3f out: wknd over 2f out* **8/1**[3]

2m 7.89s (0.10) **Going Correction** -0.125s/f (Stan)
WFA 3 from 4yo+ 5lb **14** Ran SP% **126.1**
Speed ratings (Par 103):94,93,93,91,91 90,90,90,89,88 88,84,82,81
CSF £22.72 CT £202.44 TOTE £6.20: £1.90, £1.80, £5.50; EX 29.10 Trifecta £202.60 Part won. Pool: £285.49 - 0.80 winning tickets..
Owner The Winning Hand **Bred** Mrs Dare Wigan And Dominic Wigan **Trained** Woodingdean, E Sussex

FOCUS

This looked a reasonable handicap for the grade but, as is so often case over this sort of trip at Lingfield, the pace was steady, resulting in a very moderate time. The form overall should perhaps be treated with a bit of caution, although the winner didn't look flattered and can do better again.
T/Plt: £37.30 to a £1 stake. Pool: £60,251.00. 1,177.40 winning tickets. T/Qpdt: £12.60 to a £1 stake. Pool: £3,970.80. 232.20 winning tickets. SP

5182 YORK (L-H)

Friday, October 6

OFFICIAL GOING: Soft (good to soft in places)

The ground was described as 'very soft, heavy in places and very hard work'.
Wind: Fresh, half-behind Weather: Overcast and blustery

5787 GARBUTT & ELLIOTT STKS (H'CAP) 1m 2f 88y

2:20 (2:20) (Class 3) (0-95,95) 3-Y-0+ £8,096 (£2,408; £1,203; £601) Stalls Low

Form RPR

/11- **1** **Scriptwriter (IRE)**[452] 3395 4-9-3 **91**.......... KerrinMcEvoy 1 108+
(Saeed Bin Suroor) *trckd ldrs: hdwy to ld 3f out: rdn over 1f out: hung bdly lft ins last: drvn and styd on* **8/1**[3]

1012 **2** 1 ½ **Topatoo**[27] 5188 4-8-10 **91**.......... PatrickHills(7) 5 105
(M H Tompkins) *hld up in tch: smooth hdwy on inner 4f out: chal on bit wl over 1f out and ev ch tl edgd lft and no ex last 100 yds* **9/2**[2]

-160 **3** 7 **Into The Shadows**[13] 5533 6-8-12 **86**.......... PaulHanagan 9 87
(K G Reveley) *hld up towards rr: stdy hdwy on inner over 3f out: rdn to chse ldrs wl over 1f out: kpt on same pce ins last* **40/1**

205 **4** 6 **Mutawaffer**[27] 5188 5-8-9 **88**.......... JamieMoriarty(5) 18 79
(R A Fahey) *a.p: rdn along over 2f out: drvn and kept on appr last* **33/1**

2001 **5** 3 ½ **Krugerrand (USA)**[22] 5310 7-8-12 **89**.......... StephenDonohoe(3) 13 81+
(W J Musson) *hld up in rr: hdwy 3f out: rdn along 2f out: sn no imp* **14/1**

13-2 **6** 1 **Priors Hill (IRE)**[7] 5660 3-9-0 **93**..........(t) LDettori 4 76
(Saeed Bin Suroor) *trckd ldrs: effrt 3f out: sn rdn along: drvn and wknd 2f out* **9/4**[1]

4062 **7** 2 **Best Prospect (IRE)**[22] 5310 4-8-13 **87**..........(t) PhillipMakin 20 66
(M Dods) *hld up towards rr: gd hdwy on outer 3f out: rdn to chse ldrs 2f out: sn drvn and btn* **12/1**

0202 **8** 3/4 **Along The Nile**[15] 5494 4-8-11 **85**..........(t) FrancisNorton 16 63
(K G Reveley) *hld up and bhd: hdwy 3f out: rdn over 2f out and sn no imp* **40/1**

4300 **9** 1 **In Full Cry**[27] 5164 3-8-4 **83**.......... JoeFanning 10 59
(M Johnston) *in tch: rdn along over 3f out: sn wknd* **28/1**

0143 **10** 1/2 **Fort Churchill (IRE)**[2] 5769 5-8-6 **83**..........(bt) GregFairley(3) 12 58
(B Ellison) *in tch: rdn along over 2f out: sn wknd* **10/1**

4362 **11** 5 **Folio (IRE)**[23] 5299 6-8-11 **85**.......... TPQueally 14 51
(W J Musson) *nvr nr ldrs* **25/1**

0020 **12** 6 **Dunaskin (IRE)**[27] 5188 6-9-7 **95**.......... KDarley 6 50
(Karen McLintock) *cl up: rdn along 4f out: grad wknd* **20/1**

0002 **13** 1 1/2 **Active Asset (IRE)**[14] 5511 4-8-9 **83**.......... TonyCulhane 7 35
(M R Channon) *a towards rr* **33/1**

104- **14** 2 1/2 **Pugilist**[394] 5048 4-8-10 **84**.......... DanielTudhope 3 32
(B J Meehan) *led: rdn along and hdd 3f out: sn wknd* **33/1**

006 **15** 10 **Artistic Style**[22] 5310 6-8-12 **86**.......... TomEaves 8 16
(B Ellison) *chsd ldrs: rdn along wl over 2f out: sn wknd* **16/1**

0004 **16** 8 **Go Tech**[15] 5494 6-8-8 **82**.......... DavidAllan 11 —
(T D Easterby) *chsd ldrs: rdn along over 3f out: sn wknd* **40/1**

6046 **17** *dist* **Sew'N'So Character (IRE)**[23] 5299 5-8-9 **83**.......... RobertWinston 15 —
(M Blanshard) *a rr* **25/1**

2m 15.5s (5.02) **Going Correction** +0.70s/f (Yiel)
WFA 3 from 4yo+ 5lb **17** Ran SP% **121.4**
Speed ratings (Par 107):107,105,100,95,92 91,90,89,88,88 84,79,78,76,68 62,—
CSF £38.27 CT £1366.65 TOTE £8.50: £2.10, £1.60, £6.40, £6.10; EX 46.80.
Owner Godolphin **Bred** Newgate Stud Co **Trained** Newmarket, Suffolk

FOCUS
A big field of handicappers but they went a sensible pace in the conditions; not that many got into it and the front pair pulled well clear and the form has been rated positively. The field came centre to stands' side on reaching the home straight.

NOTEBOOK
Scriptwriter(IRE), having only his fifth outing and his first in 15 months, travelled well just behind the leaders but looked sure to be swallowed up by the runner-up when the race became a match between the pair over the last furlong or so. However, despite zig-zagging all over the track on the run to the line, he still had enough forward momentum to eventually win a shade cosily. Obviously still green, how far he would have won by had he kept straight is anyone's guess and he could prove a nice sort for connections if brought back as a five-year-old.
Topatoo, who has an outstanding record on this track, travelled like a dream and it looked a question of how far when she ranged alongside the eventual winner over a furlong out, but a combination of her rival's gameness, and possibly strength from the saddle, caused her to lose out. She was rather unfortunate to bump into such a progressive sort, especially considering how far she pulled clear of the others, and if returning next season she will always have to be considered at this venue. (tchd 5-1 in a place)
Into The Shadows ◆, all the better for her recent reappearance from a four-month break, had her ground and ran a fine race at a huge price. She could never get to the front pair, but pulled clear of the others and with the ground likely to remain in her favour, there should be a race in her on the Flat before returning to hurdles. (op 50-1)
Mutawaffer ran well after having been up with the pace throughout, but finished behind Topatoo for the third race running. Despite having not won for over three years, he is not getting any help from the Handicapper.
Krugerrand(USA) ◆, a winner on the second day of this meeting and raised 4lb for his Ayr victory, was held up as usual but got into traffic difficulties when trying to get closer in the home straight and stayed on late without being knocked about. He can be rated a bit better than his finishing position might suggest. Official explanation: jockey said gelding was denied a clear run (tchd 12-1)
Priors Hill(IRE), presumably the Godolphin first string on jockey bookings, was in a good position throughout but did not find a lot when put under pressure. Unlike his stable companion the winner, he did have a recent outing under his belt but that does raise the possibility that he bounced. Official explanation: jockey said colt ran flat (op 2-1 tchd 5-2 in a place)
Best Prospect(IRE), closely matched with Kruggerand on recent Ayr running, looked like getting involved when moving up stylishly against the stands' rail halfway up the home straight but his effort soon flattened out.
Go Tech Official explanation: jockey said gelding was unsuited by the soft (good to soft places) ground

5788 ACORN WEB OFFSET STKS (NURSERY H'CAP) 6f
2:50 (2:53) (Class 3) 2-Y-O **£7,124** (£2,119; £1,059; £529) **Stalls** Centre

Form RPR

2113 **1** **Algol**[21] 5334 2-9-3 **83**.......... TomEaves 4 89
(J Howard Johnson) *led tl over 3f out: led over 2f out: hrd rdn and hld on towards fin* **10/1**

5324 **2** 3/4 **Masai Moon**[12] 5546 2-8-9 **75**.......... GrahamGibbons 2 79
(B R Millman) *chsd ldrs: wnt 2nd appr fnl f: no ex towards fin* **8/1**[3]

204P **3** 1 **Dickie Le Davoir**[39] 4890 2-9-6 **86**.......... PhillipMakin 7 87
(K R Burke) *in rr: hdwy over 2f out: edgd lft snd styd on fnl f* **50/1**

1 **4** *nk* **Osteopathic Remedy (IRE)**[22] 5307 2-9-6 **86**.......... DanielTudhope 20 86
(M Dods) *bhd: edgd lft and hdwy over 2f out: kpt on same pce fnl f* **11/1**

01 **5** 2 1/2 **Al Khaleej (IRE)**[85] 3457 2-9-2 **82**.......... LDettori 17 74
(E A L Dunlop) *in rr stands' side: hdwy over 2f out: kpt on fnl f* **3/1**[1]

1530 **6** 1 1/4 **Opal Noir**[45] 4681 2-9-2 **87**.......... JamieMoriarty(5) 3 76
(J Howard Johnson) *chsd ldrs: effrt over 2f out: edgd lft and kpt on same pce* **33/1**

6232 **7** 1 **Nota Liberata**[4] 5721 2-7-12 **64** oh1.......... NickyMackay 15 50
(G M Moore) *mid-div: kpt on fnl 2f: nvr nr ldrs* **12/1**

045 **8** 1 **Lap Of Honour (IRE)**[17] 5455 2-8-10 **76**.......... KerrinMcEvoy 6 59
(N A Callaghan) *in rr: sme hdwy far side over 2f out: nvr nr ldrs* **16/1**

0030 **9** 1/2 **Christmas Tart (IRE)**[36] 4966 2-8-13 **79**..........(v[1]) FrancisNorton 8 60
(V Smith) *s.i.s: kpt on towards far side fnl 2f: nvr on terms* **50/1**

1204 **10** 2 **Palo Verde**[29] 5140 2-9-5 **85**.......... J-PGuillambert 14 60
(M Johnston) *chsd ldrs: drvn over 2f out: sn outpcd* **20/1**

13 **11** 2 **Roheryn (IRE)**[13] 5528 2-8-10 **76**.......... PatCosgrave 11 45
(John A Quinn, Ire) *bmpd s: sn chsng ldrs: wknd over 1f out* **7/1**[2]

13 **12** 1 1/4 **Pegasus Dancer (FR)**[29] 5139 2-9-0 **80**.......... DO'Donohoe 1 45
(K A Ryan) *chsd ldrs: wknd over 1f out* **20/1**

4543 **13** 2 1/2 **Bid For Gold**[14] 5509 2-8-9 **75**.......... PaulMulrennan 5 33
(Jedd O'Keeffe) *mid-div: drvn over 2f out: sn wknd* **33/1**

652 **14** 6 **Deadline (UAE)**[15] 5496 2-8-11 **77**.......... JoeFanning 13 17
(M Johnston) *swvd lft s: mid-div: sn drvn along: lost pl 3f out* **14/1**

3200 **15** 2 **King's Bastion (IRE)**[20] 5372 2-9-5 **85**.......... TPQueally 18 19
(M L W Bell) *a in rr* **66/1**

1620 **16** *nk* **Kyshanty**[41] 4813 2-9-1 **81**.......... RichardHughes 16 14
(R Hannon) *prom: rdn over 2f out: sn btn* **50/1**

0312 **17** 19 **Lafontaine Bleu**[38] 4912 2-8-0 **66**.......... PaulHanagan 9 —
(R A Fahey) *sn towards rr: virtually p.u* **10/1**

3654 **18** 2 1/2 **Mr Klick (IRE)**[17] 5442 2-9-1 **81**.......... RobertWinston 10 —
(N Wilson) *chsd ldrs: lost pl over 2f out: virtually p.u* **25/1**

1m 15.99s (3.43) **Going Correction** +0.65s/f (Yiel) **18** Ran SP% **122.0**
Speed ratings (Par 99):103,102,100,100,96 95,93,92,91,89 86,84,81,73,70 70,45,41
CSF £78.00 CT £3824.53 TOTE £10.70: £2.40, £2.30, £7.10, £2.80; EX 71.30.
Owner Transcend Bloodstock LLP **Bred** W L Caley **Trained** Billy Row, Co Durham

FOCUS
A very competitive nursery on paper, but again few ever got into it and the race is best rated through the fourth. As in the opening contest, the field raced centre to stands' side but the draw did not appear to play much part in the outcome.

NOTEBOOK
Algol was always vying for the lead and ultimately ground out a very game and determined victory. He seems to go on any ground and the fact that this win was gained off a 9lb higher mark than for his last success suggests he remains on the up.
Masai Moon, back down in trip, was always within striking distance and was produced with his effort in plenty of time, but found the determined winner was not for passing. He is very consistent and if there is any justice he will record that elusive first win sooner rather than later.
Dickie Le Davoir, pulled up with a slipping saddle last time, had his ideal ground and stayed on well over the last couple of furlongs to perform best of those that were held up. There will be other days. (op 66-1)
Osteopathic Remedy(IRE) ◆, having only his second start and whose debut victory has been well advertised by the runner-up scoring twice since, was drawn closest to the stands' rail but was switched left and tucked in behind his rivals after leaving the stalls. Staying on well in the closing stages, considering his inexperience he performed with plenty of credit off what had looked a stiff mark and there are more races to be won with him. (op 12-1)
Al Khaleej(IRE), racing closest to the stands' rail, never looked like getting involved. He may just have needed this after three months off, but this also looked to be an inadequate test. (op 4-1)
Opal Noir ran a bit better than on his nursery debut here last time, but still looks to be on a stiff enough mark.
Nota Liberata, 1lb wrong, was probably not helped by the shorter trip as he was doing his best work late, but he is still a maiden after 11 attempts.
Christmas Tart(IRE) Official explanation: jockey said filly was denied a clear run
Palo Verde was unable to dominate thanks to the winner and his efforts to keep tabs on him eventually took their toll.
Roheryn(IRE) was messed around at the start, but was still close enough if good enough and this modest effort may have been due to the softer ground rather than the extra furlong. (op 6-1)
Kyshanty Official explanation: jockey said colt was unsuited by the soft (good to soft places) ground
Lafontaine Bleu Official explanation: jockey said filly had lost its action

5789 TSG STKS (H'CAP) 1m
3:25 (3:26) (Class 2) (0-100,103) 3-Y-O+ **£11,658** (£3,468; £1,733; £865) **Stalls** Low

Form RPR

20-1 **1** **Army Of Angels (IRE)**[6] 5677 4-9-9 **103** 6ex.......... LDettori 7 116
(Saeed Bin Suroor) *hld up in rr: smooth hdwy 3f out: led on bit ent last: edgd lft and pushed out* **5/2**[1]

1610 **2** 1 1/2 **Wavertree Warrior (IRE)**[84] 3493 4-8-9 **89**.......... JoeFanning 1 98
(N P Littmoden) *dwlt: sn cl up: rdn to ld 2f out: drvn and jnd over 1f out: hdd ent last: one pce* **33/1**

5362 **3** 1 3/4 **Collateral Damage (IRE)**[4] 5722 3-8-4 **87**.......... DavidAllan 5 92
(T D Easterby) *hld up in rr: hdwy whn n.m.r over 2f out and again wl over 1f out: sn rdn and kpt on ins last: nrst fin* **12/1**[3]

1111 **4** 1 1/2 **Glenbuck (IRE)**[20] 5355 3-8-3 **86**..........(v) FrancisNorton 9 88
(A Bailey) *led: rdn along 3f out: hdd 2f out: sn drvn and grad wknd appr last* **16/1**

1004 **5** 1 **Gentleman's Deal (IRE)**[14] 5512 5-8-10 **90**.......... RobertWinston 12 90
(M W Easterby) *stdd s and bhd: hdwy 3f out: rdn 2f out: styd on appr last: nrst fin* **20/1**

6300 **6** 1/2 **Unshakable (IRE)**[13] 5520 7-8-8 **88**.......... TonyCulhane 3 87
(Bob Jones) *in tch whn hmpd on inner over 6f out: hdwy 3f out: rdn to chse ldrs whn carried sltly lft over 1f out: sn no imp* **12/1**[3]

5361 **7** *nk* **Vicious Warrior**[20] 5357 7-8-7 **87**.......... DeanMcKeown 8 85
(R M Whitaker) *cl up: rdn along 3f out: drvn 2f out and grad wknd* **33/1**

-501 **8** *nk* **All Ivory**[13] 5523 4-9-5 **99**.......... RichardHughes 2 96
(R Charlton) *s.i.s: sn trcking ldrs: pushed along over 3f out: sn rdn: edgd lft and wknd wl over 1f out* **7/1**[2]

2502 **9** 4 **Skidrow**[14] 5512 4-8-5 **90**.......... AndrewElliott(5) 11 78
(M L W Bell) *chsd ldrs: rdn along 3f out: drvn and wknd fnl 2f* **18/1**

200 **10** *nk* **Namroud (USA)**[21] 5337 7-8-5 **85** oh1.......... PaulHanagan 4 72
(R A Fahey) *chsd ldrs: rdn along 1/2-way: sn wknd* **66/1**

1-21 **11** 21 **Queen's Best**[14] 5504 3-8-4 **87**.......... KerrinMcEvoy 10 26
(Sir Michael Stoute) *midfield: pushed along 5f out: rdn 3f out and sn btn* **5/2**[1]

-532 **12** 2 1/2 **St Petersburg**[20] 5357 6-9-4 **98**.......... TPQueally 13 31
(M H Tompkins) *a rr* **12/1**[3]

1m 42.59s (3.09) **Going Correction** +0.70s/f (Yiel)
WFA 3 from 4yo+ 3lb **12** Ran SP% **116.0**
Speed ratings (Par 109):112,110,108,107,106 105,105,105,101,100 79,77
CSF £109.72 CT £859.13 TOTE £3.50: £1.60, £6.60, £2.70; EX 103.30.
Owner Godolphin **Bred** Gerard Callanan **Trained** Newmarket, Suffolk

FOCUS
A decent handicap run at a good pace and the field came down more towards the centre of the track in the straight than in the first two races. The form looks strong rated around the placed horses, despite the demise of one of the joint-favourites.

NOTEBOOK
Army Of Angels(IRE) ◆, carrying a 6lb penalty for his Newmarket success on his return from a long lay-off just six days earlier, was a candidate to bounce but dispelled any worries on that score and only needed to be nudged out to prevail after hitting the front on the bridle. He proved that this trip in testing conditions hold no terrors for him, but he will not find many opportunities in handicaps off his new mark and, being a gelding, it will be interesting to see what Godolphin do with him now. (op 9-4 tchd 11-4 in places)
Wavertree Warrior(IRE) ◆, returning from a three-month break, ran a blinder after having been up with the pace throughout and can count himself a bit unfortunate to have come up against such an unexposed and progressive sort like the winner. He acts well on Polytrack as well as turf, so there should be plenty of opportunities for him in the coming months. (op 25-1)
Collateral Damage(IRE) ◆ had his ideal ground, but rather found himself trapped in a pocket when trying to get closer halfway up the home straight, and by the time he got through the front pair had got away from him. This was still a creditable effort and, with the ground likely to remain favourable, there could be another opportunity waiting for him before the turf season ends. (op 14-1)
Glenbuck(IRE), up another 7lb in his bid for a five-timer, had the ground in his favour but he had not performed very well in two previous tries at this trip and, having been given his usual positive ride, he failed to see it out.

Gentleman's Deal(IRE) stayed on from off the pace in the latter stages, but could never really get on terms. He is unbeaten in three previous outings on sand and it will be interesting to see if he seeks out another opportunity there in the coming weeks. Official explanation: jockey said, regarding running and riding, his orders were to drop the horse in in the early stages and it did not get the clearest of runs in the straight, adding that it stayed on one paced closing stages, tending to hang to its left (tchd 22-1)
Unshakable(IRE) got into a spot of bother early on which left him with more ground to make up than would otherwise have been the case and he was not up to it. He is talented on his day, but has only managed to win twice in well over four years which hardly makes him an attractive betting proposition. (op 11-1)
Vicious Warrior Official explanation: jockey said gelding hung left
All Ivory, raised 5lb for his Ascot victory, failed to see out the trip in the ground. (op 8-1)
Queen's Best should have relished this ground, so this was too bad to be true. Official explanation: jockey said filly never travelled (tchd 11-4)

5790 SAWFISH SOFTWARE EBF MAIDEN STKS 6f
4:00 (4:01) (Class 4) 2-Y-0 **£6,541** (£1,946; £972; £485) **Stalls** Centre

Form RPR
1 **Kafuu (IRE)** 2-9-3 LDettori 3 77+
(J Noseda) *trckd ldrs gng wl: led on bit over 1f out: smoothly* **5/2[1]**
0 2 2 1/2 **Run Free**[15] [5491] 2-9-3 RobertWinston 5 67
(N Wilson) *in tch: drvn over 2f out: styd on to take 2nd nr fin* **50/1**
23 3 hd **Eau Good**[22] [5307] 2-9-0 (b[1]) GregFairley(3) 9 66
(M Johnston) *bmpd s: sn trcking ldrs: kpt on same pce fnl f* **3/1[2]**
4 2 1/2 **Drawn Gold** 2-9-3 GrahamGibbons 10 58+
(R Hollinshead) *dwlt: sn chsng ldrs: one pce fnl 2f* **11/1**
0 5 1 **Grethel (IRE)**[14] [5507] 2-8-9 StephenDonohoe(3) 6 50
(A Berry) *chsd ldrs: outpcd over 2f out: kpt on fnl f* **100/1**
3 6 3/4 **Eltanin (IRE)**[34] [5025] 2-9-3 TomEaves 4 53
(J Howard Johnson) *led: hdd over 2f out: edgd lft over 1f out: sn wknd* **9/2[3]**
324 7 1/2 **Love Dubai (USA)**[20] [5379] 2-9-3 80 JoeFanning 8 52
(M Johnston) *swvd rt s: chsd ldrs: hrd drvn over 2f out: wknd over 1f out* **3/1[2]**
0400 8 1/2 **First Valentini**[16] [5482] 2-8-12 54 (b) RoystonFfrench 7 45
(N Bycroft) *w ldrs: led over 2f out: hdd over 1f out: sn wknd* **100/1**
0 9 3 **Aussie Blue (IRE)**[23] [5288] 2-9-3 DeanMcKeown 2 41
(R M Whitaker) *unruly in stalls: a outpcd and in rr* **20/1**
060 10 29 **Jazzanova**[32] [5059] 2-9-3 50 PaulMulrennan 1 —
(M W Easterby) *chsd ldrs on outer: hung lft and lost pl over 2f out: sn bhd: eased* **100/1**

1m 17.0s (4.44) **Going Correction** +0.65s/f (Yiel) 10 Ran SP% **114.8**
Speed ratings (Par 97):96,92,92,89,87 86,86,85,81,42
CSF £135.07 TOTE £2.90: £1.40, £6.10, £1.50; EX 115.60.
Owner Saleh Al Homaizi & Imad Al Sagar **Bred** J Hanly **Trained** Newmarket, Suffolk

FOCUS
Probably an ordinary maiden for the track and an unexceptional time, but a taking performance by the winner.

NOTEBOOK
Kafuu(IRE), a 220,000gns yearling whose dam was quite a useful miler in France and the US, certainly knew his job at the first time of asking. Having travelled supremely well, he quickened up nicely without his rider having to get serious with him and, even though he might not have beaten much, he does look to be a colt of some potential. (op 9-4 tchd 11-4)
Run Free stepped up considerably from his debut effort and battled on to eventually win the separate race for second. Although by a sprinter, there is plenty of stamina on the dam's side and the more testing ground here compared with his first outing seemed to suit him. (tchd 40-1)
Eau Good, tried in blinkers, was never far away and kept on to make the frame for the third time in as many starts. He does not seem to be improving, but does now qualify for nurseries which widens his options. (op 4-1)
Drawn Gold, a half-brother to five winners including Goldeva and Royal Cavalier, both of whom did the Hollinshead yard proud, showed enough on this debut to suggest that he will not let the side down given a bit more time. (op 10-1)
Grethel(IRE) was a lot less green than when well beaten on her debut and showed a bit more here at a huge price, but handicaps are likely to bring out the best in her in due course.
Eltanin(IRE), who made his debut over a mile, was given a positive ride on this marked drop in trip but still did not get home. His breeding suggests that middle-distances will suit him next season. (op 5-1 tchd 11-2)
Love Dubai(USA) was not suited by this return to six, but does not seem to be progressing all the same. (tchd 11-4)

5791 PARSONAGE COUNTRY HOUSE HOTEL STKS (H'CAP) 5f
4:35 (4:35) (Class 5) (0-75,76) 3-Y-0+ **£5,505** (£1,637; £818; £408) **Stalls** Centre

Form RPR
0005 1 **Kay Two (IRE)**[16] [5476] 4-9-4 75 TPQueally 16 84
(R J Price) *cl up: led over 1f out: rdn: edgd rt and hdd ins last: drvn and styd on to ld last strides* **9/1**
000 2 nk **Danjet (IRE)**[10] [5593] 3-8-12 72 StephenDonohoe(3) 1 80
(J M Bradley) *led: rdn along and hdd over 1f out: drvn and rallied to ld ins last: hdd last strides* **33/1**
0063 3 nk **Chinalea (IRE)**[11] [5575] 4-9-2 73 (p) LDettori 15 80
(C G Cox) *midfield: hdwy on outer 2f out: rdn and styd on ent last: ev ch tl drvn and nt qckn towards fin* **13/2[3]**
6400 4 1/2 **Blazing Heights**[21] [5333] 3-9-4 75 DanielTudhope 4 80
(J S Goldie) *s.i.s and bhd: gd hdwy 1/2-way: rdn to chal over 1f out and ev ch tl drvn and nt qckn towards fin* **25/1**
5011 5 nk **Wanchai Lad**[2] [5765] 5-9-5 76 6ex (t) DavidAllan 11 80
(T D Easterby) *in tch: pushed along 1/2-way: rdn and styng on whn n.m.r and swtchd lft ent last: kpt on: nrst fin* **7/2[1]**
3545 6 1 **Kings College Boy**[15] [5493] 6-9-1 72 (v) PaulHanagan 6 73
(R A Fahey) *in tch: pushed along whn bmpd and outpcd 2f out: styd on u.p ins last: nrst fin* **14/1**
1111 7 2 **Elkhorn**[6] [5684] 4-9-1 72 6ex (b) TomEaves 17 66
(Miss J A Camacho) *in tch: hdwy on outer to chse ldrs wl over 1f out: sn rdn and one pce ins last* **9/2[2]**
050 8 hd **Orphan (IRE)**[13] [5529] 4-9-2 73 PatCosgrave 2 66
(K R Burke) *outpcd and rdn along in rr 1/2-way: hdwy wl over 1f out: kpt on ins last: nrst fin* **25/1**
0-00 9 1 **Sundance (IRE)**[32] [5070] 4-9-1 72 RichardHughes 3 62
(H J Collingridge) *chsd ldrs: rdn along 2f out: sn drvn and one pce* **20/1**
2240 10 1 1/2 **Our Fugitive (IRE)**[13] [5532] 4-9-4 75 FrancisNorton 13 60
(A W Carroll) *prom: rdn along over 2f out: sn n.m.r and wknd* **10/1**
6006 11 hd **Colorus (IRE)**[20] [5377] 3-8-10 72 (b) JamieMoriarty(5) 7 56
(R A Fahey) *chsd ldrs: hung lft over 2f out: sn rdn and btn* **33/1**
4260 12 nk **Queen Cobra (IRE)**[18] [5427] 3-9-4 75 (v) JoeFanning 12 58
(H Morrison) *dwlt: a towards rr* **33/1**
6040 13 1 3/4 **Quality Street**[42] [4780] 4-8-8 72 JosephWalsh(7) 19 49
(P Butler) *nvr nr ldrs* **66/1**
3031 14 shd **Harrison's Flyer (IRE)**[11] [5575] 5-8-13 73 6ex (p) NeilChalmers(3) 14 50
(J M Bradley) *nvr bttr than midfield* **11/1**
3300 15 3/4 **Blue Maeve**[3] [5749] 6-9-3 74 KerrinMcEvoy 8 48
(A D Brown) *chsd ldrs: rdn along over 2f out: sn wknd* **33/1**
-100 16 1 1/4 **Violent Velocity (IRE)**[140] [1812] 3-9-3 74 GrahamGibbons 5 44
(J J Quinn) *a towards rr* **66/1**
1000 17 nk **Maktavish**[41] [4793] 7-9-1 72 (p) RoystonFfrench 9 41
(R Brotherton) *cl up: rdn along 2f out: sn wknd* **33/1**
0000 18 1 1/2 **Glencairn Star**[21] [5336] 5-9-4 75 TonyCulhane 20 39
(J S Goldie) *a towards rr* **33/1**
0000 19 3/4 **One Way Ticket**[24] [5275] 6-8-10 74 (p) BarrySavage(7) 10 35
(J M Bradley) *chsd ldrs: pushed along whn bmpd over 2f out and sn wknd* **66/1**
04 20 16 **Lady Bahia (IRE)**[27] [5169] 5-9-1 72 (b) RobbieFitzpatrick 18 —
(Peter Grayson) *v.s.a: a bhd* **50/1**

62.30 secs (2.98) **Going Correction** +0.65s/f (Yiel) 20 Ran SP% **124.4**
Speed ratings (Par 103):102,101,101,100,99 98,94,94,93,90 90,89,87,86,85 83,83,80,79,54
CSF £283.87 CT £2110.51 TOTE £12.70: £2.70, £9.00, £1.80, £5.70; EX 585.90.
Owner H McGahon, D McCarthy & B Llewellyn **Bred** Roger A Ryan **Trained** Ullingswick, H'fords
■ Stewards' Enquiry : Stephen Donohoe one-day ban: not riding to draw (Oct 17)

FOCUS
A typically competitive sprint handicap with not much covering the first six home and the form looks solid with the third the best guide. The field all raced centre to stands' side but, as in the earlier nursery, there was no advantage in the draw.
Lady Bahia(IRE) Official explanation: jockey said mare missed the break

5792 BETFAIR APPRENTICE TRAINING SERIES FINALE STKS (H'CAP) 1m 4f
5:05 (5:06) (Class 4) (60-92,82) 3-Y-0+ **£5,829** (£1,734; £866; £432) **Stalls** Centre

Form RPR
4110 1 **Leslingtaylor (IRE)**[20] [5367] 4-9-4 74 SladeO'Hara 1 85
(J J Quinn) *chsd ldrs: styd on wl to ld ins last* **12/1**
33P0 2 1 3/4 **Flying Clarets (IRE)**[13] [5538] 3-8-7 75 JamesRogers(5) 7 83
(R A Fahey) *t.k.h: led: clr over 7f out: edgd rt 3f out: edgd lft over 1f out: hdd and no ex ins last* **33/1**
6100 3 2 1/2 **Sweet Indulgence (IRE)**[12] [5548] 5-9-9 82 AlanRutter(3) 5 86+
(W J Musson) *hld up in rr: stdy hdwy over 3f out: styd on wl fnl f* **20/1**
2334 4 3 **Gee Dee Nen**[8] [5644] 3-9-3 80 PatrickHills 2 80
(M H Tompkins) *prom: edgd lft and one pce fnl f* **5/1[1]**
5024 5 1 1/4 **Stretton (IRE)**[29] [5141] 8-9-5 82 DanielRobinson(7) 4 80
(J D Bethell) *hld up in rr: smooth hdwy over 3f out: kpt on: nvr rchd ldrs* **12/1**
2-32 6 5 **Samurai Way**[22] [5319] 4-9-12 82 AshleyHamblett 12 72
(L M Cumani) *chsd ldrs: wknd over 1f out* **6/1[2]**
4004 7 1 **Tcherina (IRE)**[13] [5538] 4-9-4 74 MichaelJStainton 20 63
(T D Easterby) *hld up in rr div: hdwy on wd outside over 3f out: nvr rchd ldrs* **7/1**
3036 8 hd **Sporting Gesture**[13] [5531] 9-8-10 71 AdeleRothery(5) 11 60
(M W Easterby) *chsd ldrs: wknd over 1f out* **40/1**
1341 9 3/4 **Luna Landing**[3] [5751] 3-9-3 80 6ex JamesMillman 6 67
(Jedd O'Keeffe) *mid-div: effrt over 4f out: sn rdn: wknd 2f out* **8/1**
5141 10 1 **Halla San**[16] [5479] 4-9-5 78 JamesReveley(3) 17 64
(R A Fahey) *rr-div: effrt on outer 3f out: nvr a factor* **13/2[3]**
2403 11 1 1/4 **Charlotte Vale**[8] [5634] 5-9-2 72 LiamJones 9 56
(Micky Hammond) *hld up in rr: hdwy over 3f out: nvr on terms* **20/1**
5110 12 2 **Lysandra (IRE)**[14] [5511] 4-9-4 77 DanielleMcCreery(3) 3 58
(N Tinkler) *s.i.s: bhd: sme hdwy on wd outside 3f out: nvr on terms* **50/1**
0656 13 3/4 **Bentley Brook (IRE)**[52] [3639] 4-8-13 69 (b[1]) KevinGhunowa 10 49
(P A Blockley) *t.k.h: trckd ldrs: lost pl over 1f out* **100/1**
14 5 **Amour Multiple (IRE)**[169] 7-9-3 78 JosephWalsh(5) 15 50
(S Lycett) *trckd ldrs: hung lft and lost pl over 3f out* **100/1**
4012 15 3 **Sforzando**[6] [5685] 5-9-2 72 KristinStubbs 16 40
(Mrs L Stubbs) *s.i.s: nvr on terms* **16/1**
6140 16 nk **Dream Prize (IRE)**[20] [5367] 3-9-0 80 (v[1]) JamieHamblett(3) 14 48
(Sir Michael Stoute) *rr-div: sme hdwy 4f out: sn wknd* **18/1**
5206 17 18 **Torrens (IRE)**[20] [5367] 4-9-8 78 RussellKennemore 18 19
(R A Fahey) *mid-div: effrt 4f out: lost pl over 2f out: sn bhd and eased* **40/1**
0166 18 16 **Pass The Port**[18] [5430] 5-9-7 77 DeanWilliams 19 —
(D Haydn Jones) *hld up in rr: brief effrt on outer 4f out: sn wknd: virtually p.u* **33/1**
100- 19 40 **Rosecliff**[163] [5972] 4-9-0 75 JonjoMilczarek(5) 13 —
(Heather Dalton) *chsd ldrs: lost pl over 2f out: bhd whn heavily eased over 1f out: virtually p.u: t.o* **40/1**

2m 42.4s (10.00) **Going Correction** +0.70s/f (Yiel)
WFA 3 from 4yo+ 7lb 19 Ran SP% **121.1**
Speed ratings (Par 105):94,92,91,89,88 85,84,84,83,83 82,80,80,77,75 74,62,52,25
CSF £368.51 CT £7603.14 TOTE £17.50: £3.30, £6.30, £6.40, £1.60; EX 452.40 Place 6 £427.31, Place 5 £152.02.
Owner Derrick Bloy **Bred** Mrs Peggy Kelly **Trained** Settrington, N Yorks
■ Dean Williams is the winner of this series for apprentice riders.

FOCUS
A big field and a very competitive handicap on paper, but a very moderate early gallop spoilt it to a degree and it proved very hard for horses to make up ground from off the pace. The winning time was unsurprisingly very moderate for the grade and the form is rated at face value, but does not look strong.
Samurai Way Official explanation: jockey said colt was unsuited by the soft (good to soft places) ground
Luna Landing Official explanation: jockey said gelding had no more to give
Pass The Port Official explanation: jockey said gelding lost its action
T/Jkpt: Not won. T/Plt: £569.50 to a £1 stake. Pool: £131,422.16. 168.45 winning tickets. T/Qpdt: £67.30 to a £1 stake. Pool: £6,561.40. 72.10 winning tickets. JR

5793 - 5800a (Foreign Racing) - See Raceform Interactive

5604 SAINT-CLOUD (L-H)
Friday, October 6

OFFICIAL GOING: Good

5801a PRIX THOMAS BRYON (GROUP 3) 1m
1:45 (1:44) 2-Y-0 **£27,586** (£11,034; £8,276; £5,517; £2,759)

RPR
1 **Makaan (USA)**[26] 2-8-12 DBonilla 1 107
(F Head, France) *tracked leader til led over 1f out, driven out* **46/10**

2 ¾ **Holocene (USA)**33 5048 2-8-12 .... C-PLemaire 4 105
(P Bary, France) *disp 3rd, wnt 3rd halfway, caught on ins fr over 2f out til edged out 1 1/2f out, ran on fnl f, nvr rchd wnr* **23/10**2

3 ¾ **Russian Desert (IRE)**22 2-8-12 .... CSoumillon 5 104
(A Fabre, France) *held up in rear, last from half-way til headway on outside from over 1f out, stayed on* **17/10**1

4 1 ½ **Slickly Royal (FR)**17 2-8-12 .... RonanThomas 3 100
(P Demercastel, France) *led to over 1f out, weakened final f* **13/1**

5 snk **Troque (FR)**20 2-8-12 .... TJarnet 6 100
(F Doumen, France) *held up in rear, went 5th at half-way, 4th & hard ridden 1 1/2f out, one pace* **10/1**

6 8 **Sanvic (IRE)**59 2-8-12 .... SPasquier 2 82
(J-C Rouget, France) *disputed 3rd to half-way, 4th straight, ridden & beaten well over 1f out, eased* **43/10**3

1m 41.5s **6** Ran SP% **120.3**

PARI-MUTUEL: WIN 5.60; PL 2.30, 1.90; SF 17.60.

Owner Hamdan Al Maktoum **Bred** Shadwell Farm Inc **Trained** France

FOCUS

A poor time, and it is difficult to rate this race any higher.

NOTEBOOK

Makaan(USA) settled behind the leader and was going well in the straight. Asked to quicken a furlong and a half out, he stayed on well and looks sure to stay further than a mile. There is plenty of scope for further improvement and he will now head for the Criterium International back over this course and distance.

Holocene(USA) did not have the best of luck as he could not challenge exactly when his jockey wished. Third early on and rounding the final turn, he had to wait behind the fading pacemaker before getting a clear run to the line. He quickened but never really looked like catching the winner.

Russian Desert(IRE) was only having his second ever career start, but he was a heavily-backed favourite and proved a little disappointing. Not hassled early on, he was brought with his run up the centre of the track, but he never looked a serious danger to the first two. A longer trip will certainly suit him.

Slickly Royal(FR) ran an honest race but is not quite up to this class. He was asked to try and make all, and he did a good job until halfway up the straight, when he began to gradually drop out of contention.

5546 ASCOT (R-H)

Saturday, October 7

OFFICIAL GOING: Straight course - good to soft; round course - soft

Wind: Virtually nil

5802 WILLMOTT DIXON CORNWALLIS STKS (GROUP 3) 5f

1:10 (1:10) (Class 1) 2-Y-O

£22,712 (£8,608; £4,308; £2,148; £1,076; £540) **Stalls** Low

Form RPR

2531 1 **Alzerra (UAE)**22 5335 2-8-11 103 .... MartinDwyer 9 109
(M R Channon) *lw: hld up towards rr: hdwy over 2f out: shkn up to ld over 1f out: r.o wl* **4/1**1

2036 2 1 ¾ **Hoh Mike (IRE)**7 5681 2-9-0 108 .... JamieSpencer 7 106
(M L W Bell) *lw: settled in rr: smooth hdwy wl over 1f out: rdn to go 2nd jst ins fnl f: kpt on but no further imp on wnr* **11/2**3

1110 3 2 **Enticing (IRE)**44 4738 2-9-0 106 .... MichaelHills 3 99
(W J Haggas) *chsd ldrs: rdn and ev ch over 1f out: edgd sltly rt ins fnl f: kpt on same pce* **5/1**2

1324 4 2 **Bahama Mama (IRE)**21 5373 2-8-11 105 .... DarryllHolland 8 88
(J Noseda) *mid div: rdn and hdwy 2f out: kpt on same pce fnl f* **5/1**2

1145 5 3 **Elhamri**29 5154 2-9-0 109 .... DPMcDonogh 1 81
(S Kirk) *lw: hung rt virtually thrght: led: rdn and hdd over 1f out: wknd ins fnl f* **6/1**

1053 6 hd **Alternative**27 5207 2-9-0 86 .... SebSanders 4 80
(R M Beckett) *lw: chsd ldrs: rdn and ev ch over 1f out: one pce fnl f* **66/1**

1230 7 3 **Bodes Galaxy (IRE)**35 5017 2-9-0 105 .... JohnEgan 6 69
(N P Littmoden) *prom: rdn over 2f out: wknd 1f out* **16/1**

4116 8 shd **Abby Road (IRE)**29 5154 2-8-11 101 .... KDarley 2 66
(B J Meehan) *rrd s: sn mid-div: rdn over 2f out: wknd over 1f out* **10/1**

5205 9 1 **The Old Fella**35 5017 2-9-0 95 .... RyanMoore 11 65
(R Hannon) *mid-div for over 2f* **33/1**

1122 10 hd **Invincible Force (IRE)**8 5664 2-9-0 100 .... EddieAhern 10 64
(Ms Deborah J Evans) *rrd s: nvr bttr than mid-div* **7/1**

61.94 secs (0.54) **Going Correction** +0.30s/f (Good) **10** Ran SP% **114.9**

Speed ratings (Par 105):107,104,101,97,93 92,87,87,86,85

CSF £25.48 TOTE £6.20: £2.10, £2.30, £2.30; EX 44.90 Trifecta £296.40 Pool £1,716.29 - 4.11 winning units..

Owner Sheikh Ahmed Al Maktoum **Bred** Darley **Trained** West Ilsley, Berks

FOCUS

The stalls were against the stands' rail and the runners stayed there throughout. The early pace was strong, but those that helped set it may have gone off too quick and ultimately paid the penalty. The winning time was perfectly creditable for a race like this, 0.66 seconds quicker than the later Class 2 handicap for older sprinters, despite that the form has been rated negatively, with several below their earlier form.

NOTEBOOK

Alzerra(UAE) seems to really have come to herself now as the ground has eased. She stays further than this so the rapid pace played right into her hands, and when the gap appeared between Alternative and Bodes Galaxy she was quickly through it and away. She was quoted for the 1,000 Guineas afterwards and is likely to run in a trial in the spring, but she looks more of a sprinting prospect. (op 6-1)

Hoh Mike(IRE), given a patient ride, followed the winner through the same gap but could never make any serious inroads into her advantage. This was a better effort back on an easy surface and he does appear best over this trip, but he may not be the easiest horse to place next season. (op 13-2 tchd 7-1)

Enticing(IRE), faced with a more realistic task following her run in the Nunthorpe, did not have much room to play with between Elhamri and the stands' rail when making her effort over a furlong out, but her momentum was never significantly affected and the front two were pulling away from her in the closing stages. She may prefer better ground, but looks another that is going to be hard to place next term. (op 7-2)

Bahama Mama(IRE), unproven on an easy surface, had her chance but lacked a turn of foot where it mattered on this return to five. (op 7-2)

Elhamri helped set a decent pace along with Bodes Galaxy, but the pair merely succeeded in running themselves into the ground. It appears that he needs a faster surface. (op 10-1)

Alternative showed up for a long way and certainly ran with credit on this significant rise in class, but may have put his handicap mark in jeopardy in doing so.

Bodes Galaxy(IRE) could never dominate on his own thanks to Elhamri and they merely cut each others' throats.

Abby Road(IRE) never figured and has been disappointing since winning at Newbury. (op 8-1)

Invincible Force(IRE) raced wide of his field on this return to the minimum trip, but how much of an effect that had on this modest effort is difficult to say. It transpired he had cut his mouth, and than can't have helped. Official explanation: vet said gelding returned with a cut mouth (op 15-2)

5803 E B F WILLMOTT DIXON HARVEST STKS (LISTED RACE) (F&M) 1m 4f

1:40 (1:42) (Class 1) 3-Y-O+

£17,034 (£6,456; £3,231; £1,611; £807; £405) **Stalls** High

Form RPR

12 1 **Anna Pavlova**29 5155 3-8-12 106 .... PaulHanagan 3 109+
(R A Fahey) *lw: towards rr: swtchd to outside rail over 6f out and stdy prog: swtchd lft over 1f out: sn led: veered lft: rdn out* **15/8**1

1122 2 5 **Trick Or Treat**4 5758 3-8-9 92 .... JamieMackay 8 99
(J G Given) *led for 2f: trckd ldrs: swtchd to outside rail 6f out tl 3f out: rdn to ld 2f out: hdd 1f out: no ex* **12/1**

2302 3 nk **Ti Adora (IRE)**7 5678 4-9-2 80 .... DarryllHolland 4 99
(P W D'Arcy) *trckd ldrs: swtchd to outside rail 6f out tl 3f out: sn rdn: styd on to go 3rd ins fnl f* **11/1**

1410 4 ¾ **Tartouche**41 4861 5-9-7 103 .... SebSanders 13 103
(Lady Herries) *lw: trckd ldrs: led over 6f out and styd on inside rail: rdn and hdd 2f out: kpt on same pce* **7/2**2

1-65 5 5 **Under The Rainbow**15 5502 3-8-9 88 .... EddieAhern 14 91
(P W Chapple-Hyam) *trckd ldrs: styd on inside rail over 6f out: rdn over 3f out: one pce fnl 2f* **20/1**

-620 6 8 **Aunt Julia**15 5502 4-9-2 100 .... RyanMoore 6 79
(R Hannon) *towards rr: swtchd to outside rail over 6f out tl 3f out: rdn and hdwy over 2f out: no further imp fr over 1f out* **25/1**

2023 7 nk **Bunood (IRE)**15 5502 3-8-9 96 .... RHills 5 79
(J L Dunlop) *led tl tk main gp to outside rail over 6f out: remained cl up: rdn over 3f out: wknd 2f out* **9/2**3

1005 8 ¾ **Kaylianni**15 5505 3-8-9 87 .... JoeFanning 9 78
(M R Channon) *hld up towards rr: swtchd to outside rail 6f out tl 3f out: sme prog over 2f out: n.d* **66/1**

1440 9 29 **Pine Cone (IRE)**65 4079 4-9-2 92 .... FergusSweeney 10 37
(A King) *mid-div tl wknd 3f out* **66/1**

3-00 10 hd **Desert Move (IRE)**45 4713 4-9-2 95 .... MartinDwyer 2 37
(M R Channon) *swtchd to outside rail over 6f out tl 3f out: a bhd* **66/1**

2202 11 3 **Fusili (IRE)**147 1669 3-8-9 90 .... ChrisCatlin 1 33
(N P Littmoden) *mid-div tl swtchd to outside rail over 6f* **40/1**

613 12 shd **Peppertree**69 3974 3-8-9 85 .... JamieSpencer 12 33
(J R Fanshawe) *lw: s.i.s: bhd: swtchd to outside rail over 6f out tl 3f out: hdwy wl over 2f out: wknd wl over 1f out* **14/1**

5405 13 1 **Idealistic (IRE)**28 5170 5-9-2 93 .... JimmyFortune 7 31
(L M Cumani) *lw: in tch: swtchd to outside rail over 6f out tl 3f out: sn wknd* **28/1**

2m 37.76s (4.76) **Going Correction** +0.675s/f (Yiel)

WFA 3 from 4yo+ 7lb **13** Ran SP% **116.9**

Speed ratings (Par 111):111,107,107,106,103 98,98,97,78,78 76,76,75

CSF £24.37 TOTE £2.50: £1.20, £2.40, £3.60; EX 22.60 Trifecta £194.20 Pool £1,247.64 - 4.56 winning units..

Owner Galaxy Racing **Bred** Raymond Cowie **Trained** Musley Bank, N Yorks

FOCUS

As at the last meeting here, the ground looked much slower on the round course than the straight and it proved too much for a few of these. All bar two of the runners made for the outside of the track on the run up from Swinley Bottom, but as that pair eventually finished in the first five, the advantage, if any, was marginal. The winning time was creditable for a race like this given the conditions, 0.38 seconds faster than the following 83-103 handicap and the first two were close to their marks.

NOTEBOOK

Anna Pavlova ◆, whose ability to handle testing conditions was never in doubt, was off the bridle some way out but once she caught up with the leaders after turning in, she was back on the bridle. Despite heading straight for the members' enclosure once hitting the front, she was striding out to such purpose that she was still able to pull right away from her rivals. She is a filly on the up and appears to have the ability to win a middle-distance Group race next season, especially given similar conditions to these. (op 7-4 tchd 2-1)

Trick Or Treat, who has been in such cracking form in the second half of this season, is now rated 36lb higher than when winning the first of her five races in July, but was still 11lb badly in with the winner on adjusted official ratings. With neither her stamina or her ability to handle the ground in doubt, she was rightly given a positive ride and although she could not match the finishing pace of the favourite, she still emerges with plenty of credit. (op 14-1)

Ti Adora(IRE), a most consistent filly, has gained her last two victories over 14 furlongs and it was her stamina that enabled her to stay on and make the frame and earn valuable black type. This was a smashing effort considering she was worst in at the weights and had shown her very best previous form on faster ground. (op 12-1)

Tartouche had no problem with the ground, but faced a stiff task with her penalty. Up there from the start, she stayed against the inside rail whilst all but one of her rivals went for a stroll under the trees on the run up from Swinley Bottom and was still in front when the field merged. She never stopped trying, but could not match the finishing pace of the front three where it mattered and it later transpired that she had finished lame. Official explanation: vet said mare returned lame (op 4-1 tchd 10-3)

Under The Rainbow, never far away, also stayed against the inside rail on the run up from Swinley Bottom. She was close enough turning in, but lacked the pace to get involved and the fact that she reversed recent course form with Bunood may not mean much. She has won on soft ground, but looks worth another try on a faster surface, though that may have to wait until next season. (op 16-1)

Aunt Julia finished a lot closer to Under The Rainbow than she did here two weeks earlier and reversed the form with Bunood, but was still well beaten.

Bunood(IRE), who had a couple of these behind her when third in a Group race over course and distance two weeks earlier, had not been beaten far by Anna Pavlova at York before that. However, being given a much more positive ride this time merely resulted in a below-par performance as she failed to get home. (op 11-2)

Kaylianni Official explanation: vet said filly returned lame

Pine Cone(IRE) Official explanation: jockey said filly had no more to give

Desert Move(IRE) Official explanation: jockey said filly was unsuited by the soft ground

Peppertree Official explanation: trainer said filly was unsuited by the soft ground

5804 LADBROKES.COM STKS (HERITAGE H'CAP) 1m 4f

2:10 (2:12) (Class 2) (0-105,103) 3-Y-O+

£46,740 (£13,995; £6,997; £3,502; £1,747; £877) **Stalls** High

Form RPR

0113 1 **Peppertree Lane (IRE)**13 5548 3-8-13 **99** .... KDarley 9 112+
(M Johnston) *lw: mid-div: hdwy over 3f out: led 2f out: styd on wl: jinked lft nr fin: rdn out* **7/2**1

3120 2 1 ¼ **St Savarin (FR)**14 5533 5-8-8 **87** .... PaulHanagan 15 95
(R A Fahey) *mid-div: nt clr run briefly over 3f out: hdwy over 2f out: sn rdn: styd on: wnt 2nd fnl stride* **16/1**

1114 **3** *shd* **Alessano**[21] 5361 4-8-7 **86**..(b) JimCrowley 12 94
(G L Moore) *chsd ldrs: rdn to ld briefly jst over 2f out: styd on but a hld by wnr: lost 2nd fnl stride* **33/1**

2003 **4** *2* **Purple Moon (IRE)**[14] 5530 3-8-11 **97**.............................. RyanMoore 10 102
(Sir Michael Stoute) *hld up towards rr: hdwy over 3f out: rdn to chse ldrs over 2f out: kpt on same pce* **8/1**[3]

3000 **5** *1* **Hearthstead Wings**[13] 5548 4-9-4 **97**..............................(v) JoeFanning 6 100
(M Johnston) *mid-div: rdn over 3f out: kpt on same pce fnl 2f* **33/1**

4441 **6** *nk* **Pevensey (IRE)**[13] 5548 4-8-11 **90**................................ MartinDwyer 16 93
(M A Buckley) *hld up towards rr: rdn and hdwy over 2f out: kpt on same pce fnl f* **14/1**

1652 **7** *2 ½* **Zaif (IRE)**[15] 5505 3-8-0 **89**... MarcHalford(3) 5 88
(D R C Elsworth) *lw: hld up towards rr: effrt on outer 3f out: one pce fnl 2f* **14/1**

1311 **8** *1 ¾* **Stotsfold**[14] 5530 3-9-0 **100**.. AdamKirby 13 97+
(W R Swinburn) *hld up towards rr: hdwy and nt clr run over 2f out: sn rdn: no further imp* **9/1**

P-65 **9** *1 ½* **Diego Cao (IRE)**[136] 1933 5-8-1 **83**.............................. JamesDoyle(3) 18 77
(Mrs N Smith) *bit bkwd: towards rr: sme late prog: nvr a factor* **50/1**

4111 **10** *hd* **Macorville (USA)**[12] 5582 3-8-8 **94** ow1......................... JamieSpencer 4 88
(G M Moore) *in tch: rdn 3f out: effrt 2f out: wknd fnl f* **8/1**[3]

0400 **11** *3* **Tiger Tiger (FR)**[8] 5657 5-9-0 **93**.. JohnEgan 7 83
(Jamie Poulton) *a towards rr* **33/1**

201- **12** *1 ¼* **Come On Jonny (IRE)**[336] 6254 4-9-10 **103**................... SebSanders 3 91+
(R M Beckett) *led tl jst over 2f out: grad fdd* **16/1**

0056 **13** *7* **Red Lancer**[15] 5505 5-8-9 **88**... EddieAhern 2 65
(R A Fahey) *mid-div tl 3f out* **25/1**

1111 **14** *9* **Rationale (IRE)**[23] 5325 3-7-13 **85**................................ JamieMackay 11 49
(S C Williams) *racd alone in mid-div towards outside tl wknd over 3f out* **8/1**[3]

0032 **15** *shd* **Beau Nash (USA)**[22] 5346 3-8-1 **87**........................... AdrianMcCarthy 17 51
(P W Chapple-Hyam) *lw: chsd ldrs tl wknd over 3f out: lame* **6/1**[2]

2m 38.14s (5.14) **Going Correction** +0.675s/f (Yiel)
WFA 3 from 4yo+ 7lb **15** Ran SP% **119.6**
Speed ratings (Par 109):109,108,108,106,106 105,104,103,102,101 99,99,94,88,88
CSF £59.07 CT £1608.33 TOTE £4.10: £1.70, £6.90, £12.50; EX 88.50 Trifecta £4652.20 Pool £14,218.92 - 2.17 winning units..
Owner P D Savill **Bred** Gestut Wittekindshof **Trained** Middleham Moor, N Yorks

FOCUS
A very competitive handicap run at a decent pace in the conditions, and on this occasion the field stayed on the inside on the run up from Swinley Bottom, though one was kept wider than the others. The winning time was right on par for the grade in the conditions, just 0.38 seconds slower than the preceding fillies' Listed event. Solid form rated through those in the frame behind the winner.

NOTEBOOK
Peppertree Lane(IRE) ◆, 1lb better off with Pevensey for a half-length beating over course and distance two week earlier, loves this ground and stays further than this so the fast early pace proved absolutely ideal and, as a result, he was able to comprehensively turn the form around. He was idling at the finish as well, which suggests he had a bit more in hand than the official margin and there is probably even better to come from him next season, though it appears that soft ground is a prerequisite. (op 9-2)
St Savarin(FR), back over his best trip and with the ground in his favour, stayed on very well down the home straight but the winner was different class. He remains 9lb above his last winning mark and is unlikely to be lowered after this. (op 20-1)
Alessano, like the winner, stays further than this and goes in the ground, so he also found the rapid pace bringing his stamina into play. Although dropped 2lb since his last run, he remains 7lb above his last winning mark so will need to find improvement from somewhere.
Purple Moon(IRE) had questions to answer on this ground, but he appreciated the return to this longer trip and although he could never quite get on terms with the leaders, he still comprehensively turned around last month's Chester form with Stotsfold on 9lb better terms. (op 11-1 tchd 12-1)
Hearthstead Wings is steadily sliding back down the weights and ran better than of late, but he was never able to get anywhere near his stable companion. (tchd 40-1)
Pevensey(IRE) could not confirm recent course-and-distance form with the winner on just 1lb worse terms, but although there was cut in the ground then his very best form prior to that had been on a faster surface. Official explanation: jockey said gelding was unsuited by the soft ground
Stotsfold, up another 9lb in his bid for a hat-trick, was held up for a late run as usual and did not see much daylight when first attempting to get closer, though to be honest when he did his final effort was rather limited. The softer ground was almost certainly a bigger handicap for him than his inflated mark. Official explanation: jockey said gelding had no more to give (op 6-1)
Macorville(USA), bidding for a four-timer off a 4lb higher mark, loves this ground but he failed to get home this time in this better contest.
Rationale(IRE), bidding for a five-timer off a 6lb higher mark, took a very strange route. He was taken to the outside of the track on the run down to Swinley Bottom and around the far bend, before coming up the centre of the track racing away from it. Suffice to say the tactic did not work, though to be fair his wins have all come on faster ground. (op 13-2)
Beau Nash(USA) can be excused this, as he was lame on a foreleg afterwards. Official explanation: vet said gelding returned lame right-fore (tchd 13-2)

5805 LES AMBASSADEURS CLUB AUTUMN STKS (GROUP 3) 1m (R)
2:45 (2:47) (Class 1) 2-Y-O

£22,712 (£8,608; £4,308; £2,148; £1,076; £540) **Stalls** High

Form RPR

1211 **1** **Caldra (IRE)**[8] 5655 2-9-0 107.. DPMcDonogh 1 109+
(S Kirk) *lw: trckd ldrs: qcknd up wl to ld wl over 1f out: r.o wl: readily* **6/4**[1]

451 **2** *5* **Kid Mambo (USA)**[24] 5293 2-9-0 89.................................... IanMongan 4 98
(T G Mills) *lw: s.i.s: in tch: rdn wl over 3f out: wnt 2nd wl over 1f out: kpt on but nt pce of wnr* **25/1**

1 **3** *3* **Moudez (IRE)**[43] 4768 2-9-0 .... JamieSpencer 8 91
(D M Simcock) *lw: hld up: swtchd lft over 2f out: sn shkn up and hdwy: wnt 3rd over 1f out: no further imp on ldng pair* **4/1**[3]

51 **4** *7* **Overturn (IRE)**[52] 4487 2-9-0 ....(t) AdamKirby 3 76
(W R Swinburn) *lw: trckd ldrs: rdn over 2f out: wknd over 1f out* **8/1**

1 **5** *2* **Hearthstead Maison (IRE)**[30] 5126 2-9-0 .... JoeFanning 5 72
(M Johnston) *prom: led 4f out: rdn and hdd wl over 1f out: sn edgd lft: wknd* **7/2**[2]

31 **6** *2 ½* **Manchurian**[38] 4934 2-9-0 98.. JimmyFortune 7 66
(M J Wallace) *s.i.s: in last trio: swtchd lft over 2f out: sn rdn: no imp* **20/1**

1343 **7** *1 ¼* **Norisan**[28] 5176 2-9-0 99.. RyanMoore 6 63
(R Hannon) *a towards rr* **20/1**

2311 **8** *4* **Spanish Hidalgo (IRE)**[43] 4767 2-9-0 92.......................... EddieAhern 2 55
(J L Dunlop) *led tl 4f out: sn rdn: wknd 2f out* **10/1**

1m 43.56s (1.46) **Going Correction** +0.40s/f (Good) **8** Ran SP% **115.8**
Speed ratings (Par 105):108,103,100,93,91 88,87,83
CSF £48.71 TOTE £2.40: £1.20, £4.80, £1.70; EX 53.70 Trifecta £244.50 Pool £1,553.22 - 4.51 winning units..
Owner Norman Ormiston **Bred** S J Macdonald **Trained** Upper Lambourn, Berks
■ A race won by the likes of Nayef, Dr Fong and Nashwan in the past and this year's winner looks well up to scratch.

FOCUS
This looked a decent juvenile Group contest and a solid pace throughout makes the form look smart. The winning time suggests that the ground was a bit softer than on the straight course, but not as slow as the stretch away from the stands down to Swinley Bottom encountered by the runners in the two previous races. Taking that into account, the time was still most creditable for a race like this and the winner could rate higher.

NOTEBOOK
Caldra(IRE) ◆, back up to a mile after his win in the big sales race over six furlongs at Newmarket, relished the easy ground and the strong pace and the further they went the better he was going. He was pulling right away from his rivals at the line and although it is a shame that being a gelding he will not be able to attempt Classic glory, he remains an exciting prospect for other big prizes next season. (op 7-4 tchd 2-1)
Kid Mambo(USA) ◆ continued his progress even though he was not in the same league as the winner, as he beat the rest fair and square. He will not always run into one so smart and shapes as though he will appreciate even further.
Moudez(IRE), proven in soft ground but trying an extra furlong and upped in class on only his second start, was switched right off out the back and although he stayed on down the outside in the home straight to make the frame, he never looked like landing a blow. He still has scope and will appreciate middle-distances next season. (tchd 7-2 and 9-2 in a place)
Overturn(IRE), tried in a tongue tie, found this step up in class too much and may not have handled the softer ground either. The best of him is likely to be seen next season and he is bred to appreciate a much stiffer test. (op 11-1)
Hearthstead Maison(IRE) faced a stiffer task than when winning a Chepstow maiden on his debut and, having been given a positive ride, was just not up to it. Official explanation: vet said gelding returned slightly lame (op 3-1 tchd 11-4)
Manchurian found the step up in class to much on this return to turf and the ground may not have suited either. Official explanation: jockey said colt was unsuited by the soft ground (op 25-1)
Norisan, along with the winner, had much more experience under his belt than the others, but he is nothing like as progressive and finished much further behind him than he did at Goodwood last time on this softer ground. (tchd 16-1 and 25-1 in a place)
Spanish Hidalgo(IRE) showed that he could handle soft ground when winning a Newmarket nursery under top weight last time, but was unable to dominate these rivals in this much classier contest. (tchd 9-1)

5806 TOUCH BRIEFINGS HYPERION CONDITIONS STKS 7f
3:20 (3:21) (Class 2) 2-Y-O

£9,348 (£2,799; £1,399; £700; £349; £175) **Stalls** Low

Form RPR

2150 **1** **Charlie Farnsbarns (IRE)**[18] 5466 2-9-0 95.......................... KDarley 2 104
(B J Meehan) *lw: chsd ldr: led 2f out: sn hung rt: r.o: rdn out* **20/1**

1212 **2** *2* **Eddie Jock (IRE)**[43] 4775 2-9-4 103............................... JamieSpencer 4 103
(M L W Bell) *hld up: tk clsr order over 2f out: rdn and ev ch wl over 1f out: sn edgd rt: wnt 2nd ins fnl f but a hld* **9/2**[3]

1 **3** *1 ¾* **Broghill**[18] 5457 2-9-0 .... JimmyFortune 1 95
(J H M Gosden) *hld up: rdn and stdy hdwy fr 2f out: hung rt fr over 1f out: styd on to go 3rd ins fnl f* **10/3**[2]

31 **4** *2* **Sakhee's Secret**[54] 4428 2-9-0 .... SteveDrowne 7 90
(H Morrison) *lw: bmpd s: t.k.h: hld up: hdwy over 2f out: rdn and ev ch over 1f out: wknd ins fnl f* **4/5**[1]

1420 **5** *½* **Codeword (IRE)**[18] 5466 2-9-0 93....................................... JoeFanning 6 88
(M Johnston) *wnt rt start: prom: led after 4f: edgd rt and hdd 2f out: sn hmpd: kpt on same pce* **25/1**

3 **6** *nk* **Northern Jem**[58] 4302 2-9-0 .... EddieAhern 3 88
(G G Margarson) *s.i.s: sn chsng ldrs: rdn 2f out: sn one pce* **40/1**

5123 **7** *8* **Everymanforhimself (IRE)**[18] 5461 2-9-4 96.................. SebSanders 8 72
(J G Given) *chsd ldrs: rdn over 2f out: ev ch and short of room over 1f out: sn wknd* **16/1**

1401 **8** *4* **Grand Prix**[28] 5172 2-9-0 92..(t) RyanMoore 5 58
(R Hannon) *led for over 4f: sn wknd* **16/1**

1m 29.89s (1.79) **Going Correction** +0.30s/f (Good) **8** Ran SP% **119.6**
Speed ratings (Par 101):101,98,96,94,93 93,84,79
CSF £110.05 TOTE £19.00: £3.20, £1.70, £1.50; EX 76.30 Trifecta £333.20 Pool £1,225.20 - 2.61 winning units..
Owner The English Girls **Bred** Tinnakill Partnership I **Trained** Manton, Wilts

FOCUS
A fair two-year-old contest and the winning time was about par for the grade in the conditions with the runner-up rated a length below previous winning form. Unlike in the first race on the straight track, the runners quickly made for the centre of the course and raced there for most of the way, but then they all hung to such a degree that they ended up against the far rail.

NOTEBOOK
Charlie Farnsbarns(IRE), beaten out of sight in the Goffs Million last time, showed that the soft ground there could not have been the only reason for his moderate effort as he handled these conditions well enough, though admittedly this was his easiest task since winning his maiden. Making his effort towards the nearside of the group, he did hang right in the latter stages, taking the whole field with him, but was the best horse on the day. This looks to be more his level, though he may not be an easy horse to place next season.
Eddie Jock(IRE) is a consistent sort at this level and stayed on well late on if unable to match the winner for finishing pace. His best form has been on faster ground, which makes this effort all the more creditable, but he is another that may prove hard to place next season. (op 7-2 tchd 5-1)
Broghill was taking on some battle-hardened rivals on only his second start and the ground was also very different to when he made his winning debut at Newmarket, but being by Selkirk he was bred to appreciate it. He did stay on without quite being able to get involved, but the experience should have done him good and he will probably appreciate a bit further in time. (op 7-2)
Sakhee's Secret, whose Windsor maiden victory has worked out well, was given a patient ride but performed as though not seeing out the extra furlong in the ground. (op 5-4 tchd 11-8 in places)
Codeword(IRE), who finished a long way in front of Charlie Farnsbarns in the Goffs Million though still well beaten himself, had every chance but looked to have run his race when the winner went across him entering the last couple of furlongs.
Northern Jem, beaten in a maiden on his debut, though offering some promise, found this too much of an ask at this stage of his career. (op 33-1)

5807 MITSUBISHI ELECTRIC H'CAP 5f
3:55 (3:55) (Class 2) (0-105,100) 3-Y-O+

£12,464 (£3,732; £1,866; £934; £466; £234) **Stalls** Low

Form RPR

0450 **1** **Woodcote (IRE)**[21] 5358 4-9-0 **94**....................................(p) AdamKirby 1 103
(C G Cox) *mde all: hung rt thrght: racd alone on stands' rails: kpt on gamely: drvn out* **11/1**

0040 **2** *nk* **Godfrey Street**[2] 5777 3-8-6 **86** oh3................................. MartinDwyer 7 94
(R Hannon) *hld up: rdn 2f out: r.o strly ins fnl f: wnt 2nd cl home: nt rch wnr* **11/1**

1523 **3** ½ **Charles Darwin (IRE)**[15] 5501 3-8-9 **89**........................ PaulHanagan 11 95
(M Blanshard) *lw: prom: rdn 2f out: ev ch 1f out: no ex* **5/1**[2]

0060 **4** *hd* **Green Park (IRE)**[14] 5535 3-8-6 **86**.................................... JoeFanning 2 91
(R A Fahey) *rrd leaving stalls: towards rr: hdwy 2f out: sn rdn: kpt on ins fnl f* **20/1**

3000 **5** *nk* **Connect**[19] 5420 9-8-7 **90**..(b) SaleemGolam(3) 5 94
(M H Tompkins) *hld up: swtchd rt over 2f out and hdwy: chalng whn struck on hd by rdrs whip 1f out: kpt on* **16/1**

2300 **6** 1 ½ **Prince Namid**[21] 5358 4-8-11 **91**...................................... SebSanders 12 90
(Mrs A Duffield) *rrd bdly stalls: bhd: hdwy or 2f out: rdn to chal and hung lft 1f out: kpt on same pce* **8/1**

0503 **7** ½ **Lafi (IRE)**[18] 5443 7-9-6 **100**... JohnEgan 3 97+
(D Nicholls) *hld up: hdwy over 1f out: styng on whn nt clr run jst ins fnl f: kpt on cl home* **8/1**

0054 **8** *shd* **Corridor Creeper (FR)**[9] 5642 9-9-6 **100**.......................(p) RyanMoore 6 97
(J M Bradley) *lw: prom: rdn over 2f out: wknd fnl f* **4/1**[1]

5210 **9** 2 ½ **Idle Power (IRE)**[42] 4796 8-8-9 **92**................................ AmirQuinn(3) 10 80
(J R Boyle) *lw: prom: rdn over 2f out: grad fdd* **16/1**

0450 **10** ½ **Green Manalishi**[9] 5642 5-9-6 **100**.. EddieAhern 9 86
(D W P Arbuthnot) *chsd ldrs: rdn 2f out: sn wknd* **14/1**

1026 **11** *shd* **Cape Royal**[14] 5535 6-9-0 **94**.......................................(bt) JamieSpencer 8 80
(J M Bradley) *chsd ldrs: rdn over 2f out: wknd fnl f* **15/2**[3]

0040 **12** 3 ½ **Golden Dixie (USA)**[21] 5358 7-8-10 **90**.......................... SteveDrowne 4 63
(R A Harris) *b: mid-div for 3f* **12/1**

62.60 secs (1.20) **Going Correction** +0.30s/f (Good) **12** Ran SP% **118.2**
Speed ratings (Par 109):102,101,100,100,99 97,96,96,92,91 91,86
CSF £126.03 CT £697.98 TOTE £15.20: £4.20, £3.70, £2.00; EX 298.10 Trifecta £971.40 Part won. Pool £1,368.24 - 0.50 winning units..
Owner Dennis Shaw **Bred** Liscannor Stud Ltd **Trained** Lambourn, Berks

FOCUS
Amazingly for a decent sprint handicap like this, the field sauntered through the first couple of furlongs, perhaps mindful of getting home in the ground, and the race became a three-furlong sprint. The majority came down the centre of the track, but the eventual winner raced apart from the others much closer to the stands' rail. The winning time was not surprisingly moderate for a race like this, 0.66 seconds slower than the two-year-olds in the Cornwallis and the form is rated around the placed horses, although not positively.

NOTEBOOK
Woodcote(IRE) was given a shrewd ride in that his jockey did not take him across to race with the others from the lowest stall, but kept him apart from them closer to the rail, if not tight against it. Finding plenty when asked, he did hang towards his rivals in the closing stages, but was always just doing enough and considering how well he has run in some red-hot sprints this season, it seems incredible that this was his first win since his racecourse debut. Official explanation: trainer said, regarding apparent improvement in form, the gelding was better suited by the track (op 10-1)
Godfrey Street ◆, unplaced on the Lingfield Polytrack two days earlier and 3lb wrong here, has nonetheless dropped a very long way in the weights during the course of the season and put up a much better effort on ground he likes. There is still time for him to find an opportunity in similar conditions on turf, but he does act on sand as well. (op 14-1)
Charles Darwin(IRE), who does most of his racing over an extra furlong these days, was always thereabouts and kept on battling away to post another decent effort at a track he likes. (op 13-2)
Green Park(IRE) ◆ handles easy ground, but soon found himself at the back of the field and in a sprint unusually run at a modest early pace, that was probably not ideal. Under the circumstances he did well to finish as close as he did and as he is now 4lb lower than for his last win, is worth keeping an eye on. Official explanation: jockey said gelding was hampered close home
Connect is on a winning mark just now and stayed on well down the middle of the track despite getting a crack across the face with a whip passing the furlong pole. He has not won for 15 months, however, which is a bit of a worry.
Prince Namid had trip and ground in his favour, but he was another that found himself in the wrong position in a steadily run sprint after fluffing the start. His finishing effort on the far side of the field was never going to be enough.
Corridor Creeper(FR) should have relished these conditions, but after showing to the fore to past halfway he dropped away very disappointingly. A fast-run race probably suits him better, but that could be said of plenty in this field. (tchd 7-2 and 9-2 in places)
Golden Dixie(USA) Official explanation: jockey said gelding had no more to give

5808 GOODING GROUP H'CAP 1m 2f
4:30 (4:30) (Class 2) (0-105,104) 3-Y-0+
£12,464 (£2,799; £2,799; £934; £466; £234) **Stalls** High

Form RPR

4203 **1** **Book Of Music (IRE)**[16] 5494 3-8-10 **98**.......................... RyanMoore 11 107
(Sir Michael Stoute) *lw: trckd ldrs: rdn over 2f out: swtchd rt to rails ins fnl f: r.o: led fnl strides* **9/2**[3]

1045 **2** *nk* **Great Plains**[21] 5374 4-9-0 **97**.. JimmyFortune 7 105
(Mrs A J Perrett) *trckd ldr: rdn over 2f out: chal 1f out: disp wl ins fnl f: hdd fnl strides* **5/1**

6110 **2** *dht* **Illustrious Blue**[7] 5675 3-8-13 **101**... PaulDoe 10 109
(W J Knight) *hld up towards rr: stdy prog fr 4f out: rdn to chse ldrs over 1f out: disp wl ins fnl f: hdd fnl strides* **4/1**[2]

5001 **4** ¾ **Zero Tolerance (IRE)**[35] 5012 6-9-7 **104**...................... JamieSpencer 3 111
(T D Barron) *lw: led: hrd rdn over 2f out: drifted off rails over 1f out: battled on gamely but no ex whn hdd wl ins fnl f* **3/1**[1]

0066 **5** *shd* **Before You Go (IRE)**[8] 5657 3-8-12 **100**............................ IanMongan 9 107
(T G Mills) *lw: in tch: drvn along fr over 5f out: styd on u.str.p fr over 1f out* **25/1**

2000 **6** ½ **Desert Realm (IRE)**[21] 5374 3-8-8 **96**................................ JoeFanning 2 104+
(M Johnston) *mid-div: rdn and hdwy over 2f out: cl 6th whn n.m.r and snatched up on rails ins fnl f* **14/1**

2000 **7** 9 **Counsel's Opinion (IRE)**[13] 5548 9-9-1 **98**.................... GeorgeBaker 6 87
(C F Wall) *lw: hld up bhd: hdwy over 3f out: rdn over 2f out: sn wknd* **20/1**

3022 **8** 5 **Tucker**[28] 5177 4-9-5 **102**..(p) AdamKirby 12 81
(W R Swinburn) *lw: t.k.h trcking ldrs: rdn 3f out: wknd 2f out* **10/1**

40/0 **9** 12 **Barathea Blazer**[14] 5520 7-8-12 **95**.................................. PaulHanagan 5 51
(K McAuliffe) *bit bkwd: b: a towards rr* **50/1**

1300 **10** 1 ½ **Day To Remember**[7] 5675 5-8-7 **90**..............................(t) MartinDwyer 4 44
(E F Vaughan) *a towards rr* **9/1**

2m 12.5s (4.50) **Going Correction** +0.675s/f (Yiel)
WFA 3 from 4yo+ 5lb **10** Ran SP% **116.2**
Speed ratings (Par 109):109,108,108,108,108 107,100,96,86,85
2nd Pl GP 2.10, IB 1.80. Ex BM-GP 15.70. BM-IB 11.00. CSF BM-GP 13.29, BM-IB 11.14. Place 6 £119.08, Place 5 £68.56 TOTE £4.60: £1.80.
Owner Gainsborough **Bred** Wentworth Racing Pty Ltd **Trained** Newmarket, Suffolk
■ Stewards' Enquiry : Ryan Moore one-day ban: careless riding (Oct 18)

FOCUS
There were five almost in a line just 50 yards from the post, but this was a decent handicap and run at a true pace in the conditions, so the form has been rated positively.

NOTEBOOK
Book Of Music(IRE), who travelled well and relished the return to a softer surface, made full use of the gap that appeared when the leader hung off the inside rail a furlong from home and forced his way to the front in the shadow of the post. He is still relatively unexposed and could be even better as a four-year-old, so could be a nice prospect for top middle-distance handicaps or even Listed races next term. (op 10-3)
Illustrious Blue, whose trainer voiced concerns over his ability to see out this longer trip in the testing ground, came to win his race down the outside a furlong from home but his effort just flattened out in the last few strides. This trip on a sounder surface would not hold any fears for him. (op 6-1 tchd 13-2)
Great Plains, still 8lb above his last winning mark, was always close to the pace but had to work very hard to get on terms with the leader in the home straight. When he did finally manage it, he found himself surrounded on both sides and just lost out. (op 6-1 tchd 13-2)
Zero Tolerance(IRE), whose last three wins have been over a mile, has won over this trip in soft ground and was well backed beforehand. Adopting his customary front-running role, he tried to kick clear of his rivals once in line for home and for a while it looked like he might succeed, but he started to hang as he got tired and was run right out of the placings inside the last half-furlong. (op 5-1)
Before You Go(IRE) came off the bridle a very long way out, but to his great credit he kept on finding a bit more and was one of five in line well inside the last furlong, but could not quite quicken enough. He still looks to be on a stiff mark, but this was his best effort for a little while.
Desert Realm(IRE), whose best efforts have mainly been achieved on faster ground, may well have finished even closer had the door not been shut in his face against the inside rail by the winner entering the last furlong. However, with one win from 17 starts he is no certainty to gain compensation. (op 16-1)
Tucker Official explanation: jockey said colt had no more to give
Day To Remember Official explanation: jockey said gelding lost its action
T/Jkpt: Not won. T/Plt: £124.90 to a £1 stake. Pool: £128,039.70. 747.95 winning tickets. T/Qpdt: £45.20 to a £1 stake. Pool: £5,183.40. 84.80 winning tickets. TM

5787 YORK (L-H)
Saturday, October 7

OFFICIAL GOING: Soft (good to soft in places)
The ground had become 'very tacky' overnight according to the jockeys. The stands' side was at a disadvantage.
Wind: Fresh, half-against. Weather: Overcast, very breezy and very cool.

5809 NEWTON INVESTMENT MANAGEMENT ROCKINGHAM STKS (LISTED RACE) 6f
2:05 (2:05) (Class 1) 2-Y-O **£14,817** (£5,602; £2,800; £1,400) **Stalls** Centre

Form RPR

1104 **1** **Baby Strange**[8] 5653 2-9-0 102... TPO'Shea 4 108+
(P A Blockley) *trckd ldrs centre: hdwy to ld over 1f out: rdn clr ins last: styd on wl* **10/3**[2]

161 **2** 6 **Hinton Admiral**[20] 5404 2-9-0 99.................................... J-PGuillambert 3 90
(M Johnston) *trckd ldr centre: hdwy to ld over 2f out: rdn and hdd over 1f out: kpt on same pce* **7/4**[1]

4216 **3** 2 ½ **Final Dynasty**[14] 5528 2-8-9 72.. KerrinMcEvoy 6 77
(Mrs G S Rees) *chsd ldrs towards stands rail: pushed along over 2f out: edgd lft to centre over 1f out: kpt on same pce* **50/1**

4154 **4** 1 **Zanida (IRE)**[21] 5356 2-8-9 94.. PatCosgrave 2 74
(K R Burke) *overall ldr centre: rdn along and hdd over 2f out: sn one pce* **12/1**

2111 **5** 3 **Abunai**[30] 5140 2-8-9 83... JimmyQuinn 11 65
(R Charlton) *racd stands side: a towards rr* **15/2**[3]

0101 **6** *nk* **Danum Dancer**[7] 5681 2-9-3 90................................(b) SilvestreDeSousa 5 72
(N Bycroft) *led stands side gp: rdn along over 2f out: sn wknd* **9/1**

2130 **7** 5 **Celtic Sultan (IRE)**[28] 5183 2-9-0 96................................ TonyCulhane 7 54
(T P Tate) *chsd ldrs stands side: rdn along ½-way: sn wknd* **11/1**

1132 **8** 3 ½ **Rainbow Mirage (IRE)**[7] 5681 2-9-0 89................. RobbieFitzpatrick 10 44
(E S McMahon) *chsd ldrs stands' side: rdn along over 2f out: sn wknd* **9/1**

3425 **9** 1 ¾ **Part Timer (IRE)**[21] 5372 2-9-0 86.. TedDurcan 9 38
(M R Channon) *a bhd stands side* **25/1**

1m 14.87s (2.31) **Going Correction** +0.45s/f (Yiel) **9** Ran SP% **113.0**
Speed ratings (Par 103):102,94,90,89,85 84,78,73,71
CSF £9.29 TOTE £3.90: £1.70, £1.40, £6.00; EX 8.90 Trifecta £179.00 Pool £302.60 - 1.20 winning units..
Owner Market Avenue Racing Club Ltd **Bred** Michael John Williamson **Trained** Lambourn, Berks

FOCUS
The form looks a bit messy as the three who raced up the centre of the track enjoyed an advantage. Only Final Dynasty stopped them from finishing one-two-three.

NOTEBOOK
Baby Strange, fourth in a Group 3 at Newmarket last time, had proven ability to handle soft ground and did not find the drop back to six furlongs in this class hurting him one bit. He did enjoy the benefit of racing up the centre of the track, where the ground appeared to be best, but he won in such an authoritative manner that he would have won wherever he had raced. He looks well up to returning to Group company now, and the Killavullan Stakes at Leopardstown at the end of this month could be on the agenda. (op 11-4 tchd 7-2)
Hinton Admiral, a winner of a nursery off 90 last time, also raced up the centre of the track, where the ground appeared to be fastest. He could not live with the winner in the final furlong but stayed on to retain second place, and both his breeding and style of racing suggest he will appreciate a return to seven furlongs. Indeed, next year he should make up into a smart middle-distance performer. (op 15-8 tchd 2-1 in places)
Final Dynasty ran a much better race on this soft surface, leaving her fast-ground defeat at Chester well behind. She will go up a bit in the handicap for this, but black type will be compensation enough for connections.
Zanida(IRE), who made the running on the better ground up the centre of the track, is likely to be difficult to place for the rest of the season and next year as a three-year-old.
Abunai should not have had too many problems with this softer ground, being a daughter of Pivotal, but she had a bit to find with the principals on her previous form and ended up racing bang up on the stands'-side rail, which was not the place to be. (op 13-2)
Danum Dancer made the running on the unfavoured stands' side and could not repeat his Two-Year-Old Trophy form. (op 10-1 tchd 11-1)
Rainbow Mirage(IRE) Official explanation: jockey said colt was unsuited by the soft (good to soft in places) ground

5810 WOODFORD RESERVE BOURBON STKS (H'CAP) 1m 208y
2:35 (2:35) (Class 4) (0-85,88) 3-Y-O+ **£8,096** (£2,408; £1,203; £601) **Stalls** Low

Form RPR

4140 **1** **Kinsya**[5] 5722 3-9-2 **84**.. TPQueally 11 94
(M H Tompkins) *midfield: gd hdwy 3f out: cl up and ev ch over 1f out: rdn ins last: styd on to ld nr fin* **14/1**

2213 **2** *nk* **Bold Act (IRE)**[42] 4810 4-9-4 **82**........................ DaneO'Neill 10 91+
(H Candy) *in tch: hdwy wl over 2f out: rdn to ld 1f out: drvn ins last: hdd and nt qckn nr fin* **11/2**[1]

5520 **3** *shd* **Fremen (USA)**[7] 5680 6-9-0 **78**........................ AdrianTNicholls 15 87
(D Nicholls) *hld up in rr: gd hdwy on outer wl over 2f out: rdn over 1f out: str run ins last and ev ch tl no ex nr fin* **25/1**

4023 **4** *3/4* **Breaking Shadow (IRE)**[30] 5136 4-8-9 **73**........................ JimmyQuinn 4 81
(T D Barron) *hld up: hdwy 3f out: rdn to chse ldrs and n.m.r over 1f out: swtchd rt and drvn ins last: nrst fin* **12/1**

5213 **5** *1* **Forthright**[15] 5506 5-9-2 **80**........................ FrancisNorton 8 86
(A W Carroll) *in tch: hdwy to trck ldrs 1/2-way: effrt and ev ch 2f out tl rdn and nt qckn ins last* **17/2**

1210 **6** *1* **Daaweitza**[7] 5680 3-8-6 **77**........................ GregFairley(3) 1 81
(B Ellison) *trckd ldrs: hdwy to ld 3f out: rdn over 2f out: drvn and hdd 1f out: wknd ins last* **14/1**

2632 **7** *3/4* **Paparaazi (IRE)**[12] 5579 4-8-8 **72**........................ TonyHamilton 18 74
(R A Fahey) *hld up: hdwy on outer 3f out: rdn to chse ldrs wl over 1f out kpt on same pce* **12/1**

2361 **8** *1 3/4* **Major Magpie (IRE)**[23] 5320 4-8-11 **75**........................ TomEaves 6 74
(M Dods) *hld up: hdwy 3f out: rdn 2f out and kpt on: nrst fin* **8/1**[3]

5016 **9** *1 1/2* **King's Revenge**[5] 5724 3-8-8 **76**........................(b) DavidAllan 3 72
(T D Easterby) *midfield: hdwy on inenr 3f out: rdn to chse ldrs wl over 1f out: sn drvn and wknd ent last* **16/1**

3124 **10** *9* **She's Our Lass (IRE)**[23] 5320 5-8-10 **74**........................ KerrinMcEvoy 17 52
(D Carroll) *midfield: effrt over 3f out: sn rdn along and nvr a factor* **11/2**[1]

3530 **11** *5* **European Dream (IRE)**[29] 4298 3-8-11 **79**........................(p) PaulEddery 12 47
(R C Guest) *hld up: hdwy 4f out: rdn along wl over 2f out and sn btn* **20/1**

0130 **12** *6* **Instructor**[71] 3890 5-8-11 **80**........................ JamieMoriarty(5) 13 36
(R A Fahey) *chsd ldrs: rdn along 4f out: sn wknd* **33/1**

1200 **13** *5* **Future's Dream**[15] 5512 3-8-9 **77**........................(p) PatCosgrave 2 23
(K R Burke) *chsd ldr: led 1/2-way: rdn along and hdd 3f out: sn wknd* **25/1**

0031 **14** *7* **Invasian (IRE)**[3] 5769 5-9-10 **88** 6ex........................ MickyFenton 7 20
(B J McMath) *led to 1/2-way: sn rdn along and wknd over 3f out* **7/1**[2]

10-0 **15** *2* **Frank Crow**[21] 5355 3-8-9 **77**........................ DanielTudhope 5 5
(J S Goldie) *a towards rr* **25/1**

0/0- **16** *nk* **Never Will**[85] 3504 5-9-6 **84**........................ RobertWinston 14 11
(K A Ryan) *prom: rdn along over 4f out: sn wknd* **33/1**

2216 **17** *6* **United Nations**[7] 5689 5-8-9 **76** ow2........................ DNolan(3) 20 —
(N Wilson) *a towards rr* **33/1**

1m 55.69s (4.70) **Going Correction** +0.80s/f (Soft)
WFA 3 from 4yo+ 4lb **17** Ran SP% **124.6**
Speed ratings (Par 105):111,110,110,109,109 108,107,105,104,96 92,86,82,76,74 74,68
CSF £83.04 CT £1930.90 TOTE £24.00: £5.30, £1.90, £4.90, £3.20; EX 131.10 TRIFECTA Not won..
Owner Roalco Limited **Bred** Whitsbury Manor Stud And Clarendon Farms **Trained** Newmarket, Suffolk

FOCUS
A fair handicap and a decent winning time for the grade and solid form to boot, rated through the fourth, fifth and sixth.
Kinsya Official explanation: trainer was unable to offer any explanation for the apparent improvement in form
She's Our Lass(IRE) Official explanation: jockey said mare never travelled
United Nations Official explanation: jockey said gelding was unsuited by the soft (good to soft places) ground

5811 SHEPHERD BUILDING GROUP STKS (H'CAP) 2m 2f

3:10 (3:10) (Class 3) (0-95,91) 3-Y-0+ **£8,096** (£2,408; £1,203; £601) **Stalls** Low

Form RPR

2221 **1** **Juniper Girl (IRE)**[11] 5594 3-8-2 **84**........................ LukeMorris(7) 1 101+
(M L W Bell) *hld up: hmpd and hit rail after 3f: hdwy 6f out: chal 3f out: sn led and rdn clr wl over 1f out: wandered ins last: styd on* **4/1**[1]

03-1 **2** *6* **Tees Components**[14] 5533 11-10-0 **91**........................(t) TomEaves 10 101
(K G Reveley) *hld up in rr: hdwy 5f out: rdn to chse ldrs over 2f out: styd on u.p fnl f* **11/1**[3]

0642 **3** *4* **Trance (IRE)**[22] 5351 6-9-1 **78**........................(p) PhillipMakin 3 84
(T D Barron) *sn rdn along in rr: rn in snatches: hdwy on outer 3f out: rdn to chse wnr wl over 1f out: sn drvn and no imp* **12/1**

0003 **4** *1/2* **Ski Jump (USA)**[22] 5351 6-8-11 **79**........................(v) JamieMoriarty(5) 2 84
(R A Fahey) *trckd ldrs: hdwy 5f out: effrt and ev ch 3f out: sn rdn and same pce fnl 2f* **10/1**[2]

5222 **5** *4* **Kayf Aramis**[21] 5383 4-8-10 **73** oh5........................(p) KerrinMcEvoy 6 74
(J L Spearing) *a prom: smooth hdwy 4f out: disp ld 3f out: sn rdn and wknd 2f out* **4/1**[1]

4411 **6** *8* **Som Tala**[23] 5318 3-8-13 **88**........................ TPO'Shea 11 80
(M R Channon) *hld up: hdwy 1/2-way: cl up 4f out: rdn along 3f out and sn wknd* **4/1**[1]

2645 **7** *1* **Mceldowney**[23] 5325 4-9-8 **85**........................ J-PGuillambert 7 76
(M Johnston) *chsd ldrs: rdn along over 5f out: sn btn* **12/1**

0000 **8** *10* **Dr Sharp (IRE)**[14] 5533 6-9-3 **80**........................ TonyCulhane 4 60
(T P Tate) *led: rdn along over 4f out: hdd 3f out and sn wknd* **11/1**[3]

0014 **9** *51* **Twill (IRE)**[12] 5582 3-8-3 **78**........................ NickyMackay 5 —
(H Morrison) *hld up in tch: hdwy over 6f pout: rdn to chse ldrs 4f out: sn drvn and wknd* **12/1**

4030 **10** *49* **Ten Carat**[66] 4036 6-8-12 **75**........................ RobertWinston 8 —
(M Todhunter) *prom tl rdn along and wknd over 6f out* **25/1**

4m 6.51s (18.51)
WFA 3 from 4yo+ 12lb **10** Ran SP% **112.7**
CSF £48.90 CT £479.36 TOTE £5.30: £1.90, £2.50, £4.00; EX 47.10 Trifecta £556.10 Part won. Pool £783.30 - 0.80 winning units..
Owner M B Hawtin **Bred** Mrs E Kent **Trained** Newmarket, Suffolk

FOCUS
Despite the testing conditions this staying contest was run at a good pace and produced a proper test at the trip. The form looks sound, rated around the placed horses.

NOTEBOOK
Juniper Girl(IRE) did well to overcome trouble in running early in the race to eventually run out an impressive winner. Only out of the first two in two of her 11 career starts to date, she has improved since being stepped up to staying distances, and clearly handles soft ground well. She can progress again, but will have to as the Handicapper is likely to put up a fair amount for this clear-cut success. (tchd 9-2)
Tees Components was a shock winner at Haydock last time but there was no fluke about the result, and he proved that here, running on under pressure from the back of the field to post an effort right up there with his best. He was unlucky in a way to run into an improving three-year-old as he beat the rest clearly. (op 8-1 tchd 12-1 in a place)
Trance(IRE) is a pretty consistent performer, which means he does not get much relief from the Handicapper. He remains 3lb above his last winning mark. (op 16-1)
Ski Jump(USA), back over the course and distance he last won over, would have found this ground plenty soft enough and in the circumstances he ran a decent race.
Kayf Aramis, running from 5lb out of the handicap, travelled stronger than anything into the straight but found little off the bridle. Despite his apparent stiff task at the weights this was a touch disappointing. (op 9-2 tchd 5-1)
Som Tala, who had never before run in ground as soft as this, was running off a mark 10lb higher than for his last handicap win. He looks as though he might now be in the grip of the assessor. (op 9-2)

5812 CORAL SPRINT TROPHY (H'CAP) 6f

3:45 (3:45) (Class 2) (0-105,105) 3-Y-0+**£22,669** (£6,744; £3,370; £1,683) **Stalls** Centre

Form RPR

0434 **1** **Rising Shadow (IRE)**[14] 5534 5-8-7 **94**........................ FrancisNorton 6 108
(T D Barron) *s.i.s: hdwy over 2f out: edgd rt and styd on to ld nr fin* **12/1**

3152 **2** *nk* **Knot In Wood (IRE)**[14] 5534 4-8-4 **91** oh2........................ DaleGibson 15 104
(R A Fahey) *hld up in rr: hdwy over 2f out: led jst ins last: hdd towards fin* **13/2**[1]

0006 **3** *1 3/4* **Out After Dark**[21] 5358 5-8-13 **100**........................(p) PhilipRobinson 11 108
(C G Cox) *chsd ldrs: kpt on sme pce ins last* **10/1**

2604 **4** *hd* **River Falcon**[14] 5535 6-8-4 **91** oh1........................ NickyMackay 18 98
(J S Goldie) *hld up in rr: hdwy 2f out: styd on: nt rch ldrs* **11/1**

0506 **5** *1 3/4* **Mecca's Mate**[14] 5534 5-8-10 **97**........................ TomEaves 8 99
(D W Barker) *chsd ldrs: chal appr fnl f: keeping on same pce whn crowded last 75yds* **20/1**

3021 **6** *hd* **Dhaular Dhar (IRE)**[4] 5749 4-7-13 **91** 6ex........................ DuranFentiman(5) 17 92
(J S Goldie) *in rr: hdwy over 2f out: kpt on same pce fnl f* **20/1**

414 **7** *3/4* **Inter Vision (USA)**[14] 5529 6-8-1 **91** oh3........................ EdwardCreighton(3) 9 90
(A Dickman) *led after 1f: hdd jst ins last: wknd towards fin* **50/1**

4400 **8** *1/2* **Ingleby Arch (USA)**[21] 5358 3-8-3 **91**........................ SilvestreDeSousa 12 89
(T D Barron) *mid-div: drvn 3f out: kpt on: nvr able chal* **50/1**

1105 **9** *1/2* **Wyatt Earp (IRE)**[14] 5523 5-8-4 **91**........................ RoystonFfrench 4 87
(R A Fahey) *chsd ldrs: one pce fnl 2f* **10/1**

1002 **10** *nk* **Skhilling Spirit**[7] 5677 3-8-9 **97**........................ PhillipMakin 10 92
(T D Barron) *s.i.s: hdwy over 2f out: no imp whn sltly hmpd over 1f out* **11/1**

255 **11** *1 3/4* **Andronikos**[21] 5358 4-9-2 **103**........................(t) JimmyQuinn 14 93
(P F I Cole) *t.k.h in rr: kpt on fnl 2f: nvr nr ldrs* **9/1**[3]

0020 **12** *2 1/2* **Obe Brave**[15] 5501 3-8-11 **99**........................ TonyCulhane 13 82
(M R Channon) *chsd ldrs: wknd fnl f* **20/1**

3130 **13** *2 1/2* **Hogmaneigh (IRE)**[21] 5358 3-8-12 **100**........................ J-PGuillambert 2 75
(S C Williams) *hld up in mid-div: effrt 2f out: wknd appr fnl f* **13/2**[1]

210 **14** *4* **The Kiddykid (IRE)**[21] 5358 6-9-1 **105**........................ StephenDonohoe(3) 5 68
(P D Evans) *led 1f: chsd ldrs: wknd 2f out* **16/1**

-205 **15** *1/2* **Fictional**[19] 5433 5-8-6 **93**........................ RichardMullen 20 55
(E J O'Neill) *s.i.s: a in rr* **33/1**

0004 **16** *3/4* **Coleorton Dancer**[21] 5358 4-8-5 **95**........................(p) AndrewMullen(3) 7 54
(K A Ryan) *chsd ldrs: wknd appr fnl f* **8/1**[2]

0246 **17** *8* **Pacific Pride**[12] 5578 3-8-9 **97**........................ RobertWinston 3 32
(J Howard Johnson) *mid-div: lost pl over 2f out* **28/1**

1600 **18** *4* **Indian Trail**[28] 5182 6-9-1 **102**........................ AdrianTNicholls 1 25
(D Nicholls) *chsd ldrs: edgd lft and lost pl over 1f out: eased* **40/1**

1m 13.7s (1.14) **Going Correction** +0.45s/f (Yiel)
WFA 3 from 4yo+ 1lb **18** Ran SP% **123.2**
Speed ratings (Par 109):110,109,107,107,104 104,103,102,102,101 99,96,92,87,86 85,75,69
CSF £79.08 CT £849.11 TOTE £13.70: £3.30, £2.00, £2.40, £3.30; EX 112.60 Trifecta £1753.30 Part won. Pool £2,469.50 - 0.40 winning units..
Owner G Morrill **Bred** 6c Stallions Ltd **Trained** Maunby, N Yorks
■ Stewards' Enquiry : Francis Norton one-day ban: careless riding (Oct 18)

FOCUS
A highly-competitive sprint handicap with the action all taking place towards the centre of the track. The form has a rock solid look about it.

NOTEBOOK
Rising Shadow(IRE), an habitual slow starter, made up for his Haydock misfortune. Pushing his stablemate Skhilling Spirit out of the way, he showed real heart for a battle to put his head in front where it really matters. (op 11-1)
Knot In Wood(IRE), 4lb higher, came from way off the pace to take charge but in the end the winner proved fractionally too strong. He looks better than ever and may make an even better sprinter at five. (op 7-1)
Out After Dark, back on the same mark as when he won last year's Portland, confirmed he is back to form. This seems to be his time of the year. (op 11-1)
River Falcon, happy to sit at the back, made ground towards the slower part of the track and deserves full credit for this. He can surely end his drought this backend. (op 10-1)
Mecca's Mate keeps running with credit but she is still 11lb higher than her last handicap success.
Dhaular Dhar(IRE), under his penalty, was running from a career-high mark. He ran with credit in this much stronger handicap but seems better suited by seven furlongs. (tchd 25-1)
Inter Vision(USA) adopted totally different tactics and ran really well on ground a good deal more testing than he prefers. (tchd 66-1)
Hogmaneigh(IRE) has started to go in his coat and, racing towards the far side, never really threatened. He will bounce back at four. (tchd 6-1 and 7-1)

5813 CORAL "BOOKMAKER OF THE YEAR" STKS (CONDITIONS RACE) 1m 2f 88y

4:20 (4:21) (Class 3) 3-Y-0+
£9,348 (£2,799; £1,399; £700; £349; £175) **Stalls** Low

Form RPR

0000 **1** **Ofaraby**[7] 5675 6-9-2 97........................ PhilipRobinson 2 106+
(M A Jarvis) *hld up in rr: hdwy on outside over 3f out: led 1f out: edgd lft: drvn rt out* **3/1**[2]

311/ **2** *3/4* **Northern Splendour (USA)**[782] 4807 4-9-2 102........................ RichardMullen 3 104
(Saeed Bin Suroor) *led: qckd over 3f out: hdd 1f out: kpt on wl towards fin* **8/1**[3]

41-2 **3** *3 1/2* **Emirates Skyline (USA)**[21] 5376 3-8-11 101........................ KerrinMcEvoy 7 97
(Saeed Bin Suroor) *trckd ldr: chal over 2f out: kpt on same pce appr fnl f* **10/11**[1]

213 **4** *1 1/4* **Hunters' Glen (USA)**[38] 4936 3-8-13 97........................(t) TedDurcan 6 97
(Saeed Bin Suroor) *trckd ldrs: effrt 3f out: styd on same pce* **10/1**

5060 **5** *3* **Grand Passion (IRE)**[42] 4818 6-9-9 100........................ NickyMackay 5 97
(G Wragg) *trckd ldrs: drvn over 3f out: wknd over 1f out* **22/1**

10-2 **6** *15* **Dickensian (IRE)**[31] 5116 3-8-11 103........................(vt) TPQueally 1 63
(Saeed Bin Suroor) *hld up in rr: drvn over 3f out: wknd over 1f out: heavily eased* **9/1**

2m 18.38s (7.90) **Going Correction** +0.80s/f (Soft)
WFA 3 from 4yo+ 5lb **6** Ran SP% **111.9**
Speed ratings (Par 107):100,99,96,95,93 81
CSF £25.69 TOTE £4.20: £2.20, £2.80; EX 33.10.

Owner T G Warner **Bred** Red House Stud **Trained** Newmarket, Suffolk

FOCUS

No gallop until the final half mile resulting in a moderate winning time for a race of its class. Godolphin had four of the six runners but Ofaraby was a thoroughly deserving winner. However the form is paper thin.

NOTEBOOK

Ofaraby put his disappointing Cambridgeshire effort behind him, quickening up in good style in a race run at a modest pace. Once in front he edged towards the far rail and, seeming to idle, had to be kept right up to his work. (op 7-2)

Northern Splendour(USA), absent since winning his last two start at two, looked to be carrying plenty of condition. He stepped up the gallop from the front and was coming back for more at the line. (op 13-2)

Emirates Skyline(USA), seemingly the Godolphin number one this time, had the pacesetter covered but after moving almost upsides, when asked a serious question he could do no more than keep on at the same pace. (op 11-10)

Hunters' Glen(USA), who had a bit to find, had no excuse apart from the ground was softer than he has encountered before.

Grand Passion(IRE), who was up against it, was having his first outing for six weeks and again did not shine. (op 18-1)

Dickensian(IRE), very edgy in the paddock, was in a bad frame of mind and after leaving the paddock was taken straight to post rather than parade in front of the stands. He seems to be going the wrong way. (op 8-1 tchd 10-1)

5814 SHIRLEY HEIGHTS E B F MAIDEN STKS — 1m

4:55 (4:55) (Class 4) 2-Y-O — **£7,124** (£2,119; £1,059; £529) **Stalls** Low

Form				RPR
	1		**Victorian Prince (IRE)** 2-9-3 .... RichardMullen 11 (E J O'Neill) *rangy: scope: trckd ldrs: led over 1f out: r.o wl* **12/1**	81+
	2	*3*	**Cut The Cake (USA)** 2-8-12 .... TPQueally 7 (J Noseda) *tall: unf: hld up in rr: gd hdwy over 3f out: upsides over 1f out: kpt on to take 2nd nr line* **9/2**[2]	70
23	**3**	*shd*	**Aureate**[18] 5458 2-9-3 .... J-PGuillambert 9 (M Johnston) *trckd ldr: led over 4f out: hdd over 1f out: kpt on same pce* **11/8**[1]	75
	4	*1*	**Top Tiger** 2-8-10 .... PatrickHills(7) 1 (M H Tompkins) *neat: sn bhd: hdwy over 2f out: styd on strly fnl f* **20/1**	73+
63	**5**	*1 ½*	**Lets Get Cracking (FR)**[20] 5402 2-9-3 .... CatherineGannon 15 (K A Ryan) *led: hdd over 4f out: hung lft and one pce fnl 2f* **10/1**	70
	6	*1 ½*	**Topazleo (IRE)** 2-9-3 .... TomEaves 8 (J Howard Johnson) *rangy: unf: dwlt: sn trcking ldrs: outpcd 3f out: kpt on fnl f* **20/1**	67
3	**7**	*½*	**Tenancy (IRE)**[21] 5379 2-9-3 .... TedDurcan 6 (J A Osborne) *prom: one pce fnl 2f* **13/2**[3]	66
00	**8**	*7*	**Oscarshall (IRE)**[18] 5457 2-9-3 .... JimmyQuinn 2 (M H Tompkins) *in tch: effrt and prom 3f out: wknd over 1f out* **20/1**	52
	9	*1*	**Attila's Peintre** 2-9-3 .... DeanMcKeown 10 (P C Haslam) *rangy: scope: s.i.s: in rr: sme hdwy over 2f out: nvr on terms* **40/1**	50
	10	*5*	**Crystal Prince** 2-9-3 .... TonyCulhane 5 (T P Tate) *w'like: leggy: scope: s.i.s: nvr a factor* **16/1**	40
	11	*1*	**Blue Jet (USA)** 2-8-12 .... MichaelJStainton(5) 13 (R M Whitaker) *leggy: sn in rr* **33/1**	38
05	**12**	*19*	**Harry The Hawk**[24] 5289 2-9-3 .... GrahamGibbons 3 (T D Walford) *s.s: t.k.h in rr: rn v wd bnd over 5f out: sn wl bhd* **25/1**	—
	13	*2*	**Steel Silk (IRE)** 2-9-3 .... KerrinMcEvoy 14 (G Woodward) *cmpt: bkwd: s.i.s: a bhd: t.o* **20/1**	—

1m 46.19s (6.69) **Going Correction** +0.80s/f (Soft) — 13 Ran SP% **124.6**

Speed ratings (Par 97):98,95,94,93,92 90,90,83,82,77 76,57,55

CSF £61.73 TOTE £17.10: £4.10, £1.90, £1.30; EX 86.00.

Owner Victory Racing **Bred** London Thoroughbred Services Ltd **Trained** Averham Park, Notts

FOCUS

Just an ordinary maiden with the third setting the standard for the time being.

NOTEBOOK

Victorian Prince(IRE), who is well developed and stands over plenty of ground, certainly knew his job. In the end he won going away and looks a fair prospect. (op 10-1)

Cut The Cake(USA), a late-May foal, is up in the air. She went down fighting and will be much more the finished article next year. (op 13-2)

Aureate, who has plenty of size, went on and stepped up the gallop but in the end he had no excuse. (op 7-4 tchd 15-8 in a place)

Top Tiger, a half-brother to three winners including Topatoo, is a smallish April foal. He picked up in really good style late on under a sympathetic ride and this should have taught him plenty. (op 25-1)

Lets Get Cracking(FR) took them along but was simply not good enough. At least this opens up the handicap route for him. (op 14-1 after 33-1 in a place)

Topazleo(IRE), a January foal, has size and scope but he looks the type who will not come into his own until next year. (op 12-1)

Tenancy(IRE) gave a problem or two in the stalls and did not improve on his initial effort. Official explanation: jockey said colt had no more to give (op 11-2)

Harry The Hawk Official explanation: jockey said gelding hung violently right

Steel Silk(IRE) Official explanation: jockey said colt ran green

5815 COLDSTREAM GUARDS ASSOCIATION STKS (H'CAP) — 1m 5f 197y

5:25 (5:27) (Class 5) (0-75,75) 3-Y-O+ — **£5,505** (£1,637; £818; £408) **Stalls** Low

Form				RPR
1223	**1**		**Bollin Derek**[14] 5533 3-9-1 **71** .... DavidAllan 7 (T D Easterby) *trckd ldrs: led over 2f out: styd on wl* **7/4**[1]	84+
0606	**2**	*1 ¾*	**Sharp Reply (USA)**[14] 5533 4-9-5 **66** .... DeanMcKeown 5 (R M Whitaker) *mid-div: hdwy on outside over 5f out: hung lft and c stands' side: styd on to chse wnr ins last: no real imp* **16/1**	77
0055	**3**	*4*	**Halland**[86] 3454 8-9-1 **62** .... MickyFenton 3 (T J Fitzgerald) *gave problems gng to s: s.i.s: hdwy over 4f out: kpt on same pce appr fnl f* **40/1**	67
1414	**4**	*1*	**Danzatrice**[22] 5338 4-8-10 **57** .... TomEaves 4 (C W Thornton) *mid-div: hdwy over 4f out: kpt on same pce fnl 2f* **9/1**[3]	61
0625	**5**	*6*	**Duroob**[15] 5513 4-8-11 **63** .... AndrewElliott(5) 15 (K R Burke) *mde most: hdd over 2f out: wknd over 1f out* **14/1**	59
100	**6**	*5*	**Chronomatic**[11] 5594 3-9-0 **70** .... TPQueally 17 (M H Tompkins) *in rr: hdwy on outside whn hmpd over 4f out: sn prom: wknd over 1f out* **33/1**	59
0035	**7**	*3 ½*	**Ransom Strip (USA)**[59] 4256 3-8-10 **66** .... DanielTudhope 2 (M Brittain) *mid-div: hdwy 4f out: wknd 2f out* **66/1**	50
5060	**8**	*32*	**Bill Bennett (FR)**[130] 2104 5-9-2 **63** .... RobertWinston 1 (J Jay) *prom: lost pl 3f out: sn bhd: t.o* **20/1**	2
0340	**9**	*16*	**Best Of The Lot (USA)**[15] 5513 4-8-12 **64** .... JamieMoriarty(5) 6 (R A Fahey) *sn w ldr: lost pl over 2f out: eased: t.o* **9/1**[3]	—
0426	**10**	*4*	**Neutrino**[8] 4935 4-9-5 **73** .... AshleyHamblett(7) 13 (P C Haslam) *hld up in rr: effrt 4f out: hung lft and lost pl 3f out: sn bhd: t.o* **22/1**	—
3501	**11**	*10*	**Let It Be**[21] 5369 5-9-1 **62** .... TonyCulhane 14 (K G Reveley) *prom: lost pl 6f out: sn bhd: t.o* **12/1**	—
5460	**12**	*5*	**Pukka Tique**[10] 5618 3-8-6 **62** .... DaleGibson 9 (R Hollinshead) *lost tch 4f out: sn wl bhd: t.o* **66/1**	—
0056	**13**	*48*	**Berkhamsted (IRE)**[119] 2447 4-9-8 **72** .... EdwardCreighton(3) 12 (Tom Dascombe) *rrd s: t.o 4f out: virtually p.u: hopelessly t.o* **25/1**	—
2330	**14**	*5*	**Gandalf**[21] 5383 4-10-0 **75** .... JimmyQuinn 20 (J R Fanshawe) *sn trcking ldrs: lost pl over 4f out: sn bhd: virtually p.u: hopelessly t.o* **14/1**	—
1-05	**15**	*13*	**Gifted Musician**[10] 5628 4-9-8 **69** .... KerrinMcEvoy 11 (J L Dunlop) *hld up towards rr: hdwy and hung bdly rt bnd over 5f out: sn lost pl: c stands' side: virtually p.u: hopelessly t.o* **4/1**[2]	—

3m 9.04s (10.60) **Going Correction** +0.80s/f (Soft)

WFA 3 from 4yo+ 9lb — **15** Ran SP% **124.6**

Speed ratings (Par 103):101,100,97,97,93 90,88,70,61,59 53,50,23,20,12

CSF £32.38 CT £883.99 TOTE £2.60: £1.50, £5.60, £11.80; EX 42.10 Place 6 £88.71, Place 5 £59.34.

Owner Sir Neil Westbrook **Bred** Sir Neil And Lady Westbrook **Trained** Great Habton, N Yorks

■ Stewards' Enquiry : Jimmy Quinn two-day ban: careless riding (Oct 18-19)

FOCUS

A true test in the ground and they finished strung out like washing but the form is not that strong. The winner will make a decent stayer at four.

Berkhamsted(IRE) Official explanation: jockey said gelding reared in stalls as gates opened

Gandalf Official explanation: jockey said gelding lost its action in straight

Gifted Musician Official explanation: jockey said gelding hung right and lost a front shoe

T/Plt: £168.70 to a £1 stake. Pool: £132,072.05. 571.25 winning tickets. T/Qpdt: £43.00 to a £1 stake. Pool: £5,369.20. 92.25 winning tickets. JR

FLEMINGTON (L-H)

Saturday, October 7

OFFICIAL GOING: Good

5817a BART CUMMINGS STKS — 1m 4f 143y

4:35 (4:35) 4-Y-O+ — **£28,632** (£8,547; £3,846; £1,709; £855)

			RPR
1		**Irazu (AUS)**[153] 3-8-5 .... DMoor 9 (S J Richards, Australia)	108
2	*hd*	**Aznavour (NZ)** 4-8-5 .... SBaster 13 (Danny O'Brien, Australia)	99
3	*1*	**Bay Story (USA)**[377] 5496 4-8-6 .... DNikolic 5 (B Ellison) *broke wl and trvlng easily in 4th 3l off ld, came 3 wd 4f out & wnt 3rd, dropped to 7th early str, but rallied to retake 3r* **10/1**[1]	99
4	*snk*	**Cefalu (CHI)** 5-9-0 .... JimCassidy 6 (Lee Freedman, Australia)	107
5	*snk*	**On A Jeune (AUS)**[168] 6-9-8 .... DGauci 10 (P Montgomerie, Australia)	115
6	*hd*	**Genebel (AUS)**[213] 5-8-5 .... BShinn 4 (M Moroney & A Scott, New Zealand)	97
7	*1 ½*	**Lions Gate (AUS)**[511] 5-8-7 .... CraigAWilliams 8 (T McEvoy, Australia)	97
8	*½*	**Sentire (NZ)** 5-8-7 .... MZahra 12 (R Laing, Australia)	97
9	*2 ½*	**Uma King (AUS)** 6-8-5 .... StevenKing 3 (Mick Price, Australia)	91
10	*1*	**Tommifrancs (AUS)** 5-8-11 .... (b) BMelham 7 (Lee Freedman, Australia)	96
11	*5*	**Brindabella (AUS)**[231] 5-8-5 .... ClareLindop 1 (L Macdonald, Australia)	83
12	*6*	**Count Ricardo (AUS)**[693] 6652 5-9-0 .... (b) MAllen 11 (S Theodore, Australia)	83

2m 38.22s

WFA 3 from 4yo+ 8lb — **12** Ran SP% **9.1**

SP's: 12-1, 11-1, 10-1, 25-1 Tommifrancs 9-2F.

Owner Mrs M Richards et al **Bred** M & Mrs C Marodis **Trained** Australia

NOTEBOOK

Bay Story(USA), who has travelled to Australia as a galloping companion for Melbourne Cup hope Carte Diamond, ran well on his first start since September 2005 and debut for the Ellison stable. He should come on for this and is now to be aimed at the Sandown Classic on November 18.

5719 BELMONT PARK (L-H)

Saturday, October 7

OFFICIAL GOING: Dirt - fast; turf - firm

5818a BELDAME STKS (GRADE 1) (F&M) — 1m 1f (D)

8:36 (8:36) 3-Y-O+

£209,302 (£69,797; £34,884; £17,442; £10,465; £6,976)

			RPR
1		**Fleet Indian (USA)**[43] 5-8-11 .... JSantos 2 (T Pletcher, U.S.A) **9/10**[1]	118
2	*hd*	**Balletto (UAE)**[43] 4-8-11 .... JCastellano 6 (T Albertrani, U.S.A) **63/20**[2]	118
3	*7*	**Round Pond (USA)**[41] 4-8-11 .... EPrado 5 (M Matz, U.S.A) **41/10**[3]	104
4	*4 ¼*	**Teammate (USA)**[28] 3-8-8 .... CVelasquez 4 (H A Jerkens, U.S.A) **99/10**	97
5	*1 ½*	**Sweet Symphony (USA)**[155] 4-8-11 .... FJara 3 (W Mott, U.S.A) **178/10**	93
6	*1*	**Take D'Tour (USA)**[27] 5228 5-8-11 .... ECoa 1 (D Fawkes, U.S.A) **109/10**	91

1m 48.69s

WFA 3 from 4yo+ 4lb — **6** Ran SP% **119.2**

PARI-MUTUEL (including $2 stakes): WIN 3.80; PL (1-2) 2.40, 2.90; SHOW (1-2-3) 2.20, 2.40, 2.50; SF 13.20.

Owner Paul H Saylor **Bred** Thomas & Lakin **Trained** USA

FOCUS

A key trial for the Breeders' Cup Distaff.

NOTEBOOK
Fleet Indian(USA) gained her eighth straight success and her sixth of the year with a game effort, keeping on well to hold off a late challenge from Balletto. She is now 13 from 18 and is likely to be aimed at the Breeders' Cup Distaff.
Balletto(UAE) was just held and will also be aimed at the Breeders' Cup Distaff.

5819a FLOWER BOWL INVITATIONAL STKS (GRADE 1) (F&M) (INNER TURF) 1m 2f (T)
9:08 (9:08) 3-Y-O+ **£209,302** (£69,767; £34,884; £17,442; £10,465)

				RPR
1		**Honey Ryder (USA)**^{56} 4385 5-8-9 (T Pletcher, U.S.A)	(b) JRVelazquez 4 **47/20^{2}**	119
2	*nse*	**Film Maker (USA)**^{56} 4385 6-8-7 (H G Motion, U.S.A)	(b) RADominguez 5 **6/4^{1}**	117
3	½	**Jade Queen (USA)**^{28} 5198 3-8-3 (T Pletcher, U.S.A)	MLuzzi 2 **17/1**	117
4	3 ¾	**Angara**^{70} 5-8-11 (W Mott, U.S.A)	FJara 3 **54/10**	113
5	1 ¼	**Argentina (IRE)**^{70} 4-8-7 (R J Frankel, U.S.A)	EPrado 1 **53/20^{3}**	107

2m 2.47s
WFA 3 from 4yo+ 5lb 5 Ran SP% **118.4**
PARI-MUTUEL: WIN 6.70; PL (1-2) 3.10, 2.70; SHOW (1-2-3) 2.80, 2.20, 3.90; SF 13.20.
Owner Glencrest Farm **Bred** Wimborne Farm Inc **Trained** USA

FOCUS
Some key pointers for the Breeders' Cup Filly & Mare Turf.
NOTEBOOK
Honey Ryder(USA) gained her fourth victory from her last five starts and will now head for the Breeders' Cup Filly & Mare Turf.
Film Maker(USA) ran a game race in second and is likely to re-oppose the winner in the Breeders' Cup Filly & Mare Turf, where she will bid to improve on her second in 2004 and her third in 2005.

5820a VOSBURGH STKS (GRADE 1) 6f (D)
9:43 (9:43) 3-Y-O+ **£139,535** (£46,512; £23,256; £11,628; £6,977)

				RPR
1		**Henny Hughes (USA)**^{42} 3-8-10 (K McLaughlin, U.S.A)	JRVelazquez 1 **19/20^{1}**	121
2	2 ¾	**War Front (USA)**^{35} 4-8-12 (H A Jerkens, U.S.A)	JSantos 2 **66/10^{3}**	114
3	½	**Attila's Storm (USA)**^{259} 4-8-12 (R Schosberg, U.S.A)	(b) CVelasquez 4 **198/10**	113
4	3 ¼	**Who's The Cowboy (USA)**^{322} 4-8-12 (K Sleeter, U.S.A)	(b) ELKingJr 3 **121/10**	103
5	¾	**Silver Train (USA)**^{83} 4-8-12 (R Dutrow Jr, U.S.A)	EPrado 5 **7/5^{2}**	101

68.13 secs
WFA 3 from 4yo 1lb 5 Ran SP% **118.5**
PARI-MUTUEL: WIN 3.90; PL (1-2) 2.80, 5.20; SHOW (1-2-3) 2.30, 3.90,4.70; SF 19.40.
Owner Zabeel Racing International **Bred** Liberation Farm, Trackside Farm & Cho Llc **Trained** USA

FOCUS
A valuable piece of form with regards to the Breeders' Cup Sprint.
NOTEBOOK
Henny Hughes(USA), facing older horses for the first time, easily landed his third straight race and put himself firmly at the head of the sprint division. He could be hard to beat in the Breeders' Cup Sprint.

5821a JOE HIRSCH TURF CLASSIC INVITATIONAL (GRADE 1) (TURF) 1m 4f
10:20 (10:23) 3-Y-O+
£209,302 (£69,767; £34,884; £17,442; £10,465; £3,488)

				RPR
1		**English Channel (USA)**^{56} 4386 4-9-0 (T Pletcher, U.S.A)	JRVelazquez 5 **13/20^{1}**	121
2	4 ½	**Freedonia**^{27} 5220 4-8-11 (J E Hammond, France)	TGillet 3 **61/20^{2}**	111
3	*nk*	**Royal Highness (GER)**^{27} 5220 4-8-11 (P Bary, France)	TThulliez 7 **10/1**	111
4	*hd*	**Interpatation (USA)**^{14} 4-9-0 (Robert Barbara, U.S.A)	TGTurner 6 **28/1**	114
5	*1*	**Frost Giant (USA)**^{28} 5190 3-8-9 (A P O'Brien, Ire)	EPrado 1 **58/10^{3}**	114
6	1 ½	**Dreadnaught (USA)**^{42} 4908 6-9-0 (T Voss, U.S.A)	(b) CVelasquez 4 **129/10**	110
7	*11*	**Icy Atlantic (USA)**^{14} 5-9-0 (T Pletcher, U.S.A)	MLuzzi 2 **13/20^{1}**	93

2m 28.69s
WFA 3 from 4yo+ 7lb 7 Ran SP% **180.3**
PARI-MUTUEL: WIN 3.30 (coupled with Icy Atlantic in all pools); PL (1-2) 2.10, 3.40; SHOW (1-2-3) 2.10, 2.50, 3.00; SF 9.40.
Owner J T Scatuorchio **Bred** Keene Ridge Farm **Trained** USA

FOCUS
An important race with the Breeders' Cup Turf in mind and English Channel won well, despite the early pace appearing steady.
NOTEBOOK
English Channel(USA) gained his ninth win from 15 career starts in pretty straightforward fashion and will head to the Breeders' Cup Turf as one of the leading home contenders.
Frost Giant(USA), the winner of a ten-furlong Group 3 at the Curragh on his previous start, ran well upped in class on ground faster than he cares for and would have been closer with a clearer run.

5822a JOCKEY CLUB GOLD CUP (GRADE 1) 1m 2f (D)
11:00 (11:00) 3-Y-O+ **£261,628** (£87,209; £43,605; £21,802)

				RPR
1		**Bernardini (USA)**^{42} 3-8-10 (T Albertrani, U.S.A)	JCastellano 1 **3/20^{1}**	128+
2	6 ¾	**Wanderin Boy (USA)**^{21} 5-9-0 (N Zito, U.S.A)	EPrado 3 **9/1^{3}**	115
3	*6*	**Andromeda's Hero (USA)**^{35} 4-9-0 (N Zito, U.S.A)	CVelasquez 4 **176/10**	104
4	19 ½	**Dylan Thomas (IRE)**^{28} 5193 3-8-10 (A P O'Brien, Ire)	JRVelazquez 2 **44/10^{2}**	70

2m 1.02s
WFA 3 from 4yo+ 5lb 4 Ran SP% **120.9**
PARI-MUTUEL: WIN 2.30; PL (1-2) 2.10, 3.50; SF 5.80.
Owner Darley Stable **Bred** Darley **Trained** USA

FOCUS
A poor turnout for a famous race and, with Dylan Thomas failing to act on the dirt, Bernardini did not need to be at his best to cement his position at the head of the market for the Breeders' Cup Classic, winning in the manner that was expected.
NOTEBOOK
Bernardini(USA) had next to nothing to beat, with his only serious rival, Dylan Thomas, failing to handle the dirt, and won as expected. This did not tell us anything we did not already know, but his earlier form entitled him to favouritism in the Breeders' Cup Classic and he will be hard to beat at Churchill Downs.
Dylan Thomas(IRE), the Irish Derby and Irish Champion Stakes winner, was trying dirt for the first time and was in trouble soon after the start. He will appreciate a return to turf and may now be aimed at the Breeders' Cup Turf.

KEENELAND (L-H)
Saturday, October 7
OFFICIAL GOING: Dirt - fast; turf - firm

5823a LANE'S END BREEDERS' FUTURITY (GRADE 1) 1m 110y
10:00 (10:01) 2-Y-O **£180,233** (£58,140; £29,070; £14,535; £8,721)

				RPR
1		**Great Hunter (USA)**^{31} 2-8-9 (Doug O'Neill, U.S.A)	(b) VEspinoza 2 **58/10^{2}**	117
2	1 ¾	**Circular Quay (USA)**^{33} 2-8-9 (T Pletcher, U.S.A)	GKGomez 1 **2/5^{1}**	114
3	*nse*	**Street Sense (USA)**^{27} 5230 2-8-9 (C Nafzger, U.S.A)	CHBorel 7 **119/10**	113
4	*3*	**Birdbirdistheword (USA)** 2-8-9 (K McPeek, U.S.A)	RAlbarado 5 **178/10**	107
5	1 ¾	**Passport (USA)** 2-8-9 (F Brothers, U.S.A)	CLanerie 6 **93/10^{3}**	104
6	3 ¼	**Bold Start (USA)** 2-8-9 (K McPeek, U.S.A)	LMelancon 8 **38/1**	97
7	11 ½	**Teuflesberg (USA)**^{51} 2-8-9 (Jamie Sanders, U.S.A)	(b) WillieMartinez 4 **188/10**	74
8	12 ¾	**French Transition (USA)** 2-8-9 (P L Biancone, U.S.A)	(b) JRLeparoux 3 **114/10**	49

1m 44.09s 8 Ran SP% **124.8**
PARI-MUTUEL (including $2 stake): WIN 13.60; PL (1-2) 4.00, 2.40; SHOW (1-2-3) 3.40, 2.20, 4.40; SF 26.00.
Owner J Paul Reddam **Bred** Ivy Dell Stud **Trained** USA

FOCUS
A key form race with the Breeders' Cup Juvenile in mind.
NOTEBOOK
Great Hunter(USA) had won only one of five career starts coming into this, but improved that record in decisive fashion, turning over the previously unbeaten Circular Quay. He is likely to take his chance in the Breeders' Cup Juvenile.
Circular Quay(USA) lost his unbeaten record but is likely to re-oppose the winner in the Breeders' Cup Juvenile.

5824a SHADWELL TURF MILE (GRADE 1) 1m
10:40 (10:43) 3-Y-O+ **£216,279** (£69,767; £34,884; £13,953; £13,953)

				RPR
1		**Aussie Rules (USA)**^{34} 5049 3-8-11 (A P O'Brien, Ire) *started slowly, raced in 7th, headway 5-wide entering straight, finished fast to lead well inside final f, driven clear*	(v^{1}) GKGomez 3 **49/10^{3}**	117
2	1 ¾	**Remarkable News (VEN)**^{20} 5416 4-9-0 (A Penna Jr, U.S.A)	RDouglas 4 **53/10**	113
3	*nse*	**Old Dodge (BRZ)**^{28} 5200 5-9-0 (R Horgan, Canada)	RAlbarado 7 **50/1**	113
4	*hd*	**Cosmonaut (USA)**^{28} 5199 4-9-0 (P L Biancone, U.S.A)	JRLeparoux 6 **83/10**	113
4	*dht*	**Miesque's Approval (USA)**^{28} 5200 7-9-0 (M D Wolfson, U.S.A)	ECastro 2 **29/10^{2}**	113
6	*nse*	**Three Valleys (USA)**^{20} 5416 5-9-0 (R J Frankel, U.S.A)	RBejarano 9 **58/10**	112
7	¾	**Silent Name (JPN)**^{76} 4-9-0 (G Mandella, U.S.A)	VEspinoza 1 **26/10^{1}**	111
8	3 ½	**Hendrix (USA)**^{42} 5-9-0 (Craig Dollase, U.S.A)	DFlores 5 **19/1**	104
9	*nk*	**British Blue (USA)**^{541} 6-9-0 (J Ruvalcaba, U.S.A)	COMejia 8 **72/1**	103

1m 34.23s
WFA 3 from 4yo+ 3lb 9 Ran SP% **120.0**
PARI-MUTUEL: WIN 11.80; PL (1-2) 6.60, 7.60; SHOW (1-2-3) 5.60, 8.00,15.60; SF 99.60.
Owner Mrs J Magnier,M Tabor,F Salman **Bred** Belgrave Bloodstock Ltd **Trained** Ballydoyle, Co Tipperary

NOTEBOOK
Aussie Rules(USA), the French Guineas winner, was fitted with blinkers and raced on Lasix for the first time. He was last away from the stalls, but was always travelling well and found plenty to run out a clear-cut winner on his US debut. The Breeders' Cup Mile is the obvious next step, but his powerful yard also have George Washington and Ad Valorem as possibles for that race at Churchill Downs.

SANTA ANITA (R-H)
Saturday, October 7
OFFICIAL GOING: Dirt - fast; turf - firm

5825a OAK TREE BREEDERS' CUP MILE (GRADE 2) (TURF) 1m (T)
9:36 (9:37) 3-Y-O+ **£87,209** (£29,070; £17,442; £8,721; £2,326)

				RPR
1		**Aragorn (IRE)**^{42} 4-8-11 (N Drysdale, U.S.A)	CNakatani 3 **1/5^{1}**	120+
2	*1*	**Courtnall (USA)**^{40} 5-8-7 (Craig Dollase, U.S.A)	(b) PValenzuela 1 **127/10**	112
3	½	**Lord Admiral (USA)**^{28} 5190 5-8-7 (Charles O'Brien, Ire) *held up in last, headway on inside over 2f out, swicthed outside 1 1/2f out, stayed on, nearest finish*	ASolis 7 **108/10^{3}**	111

4 1 **Buckland Manor (USA)**[217] 6-8-7 .... JValdivia 5 109
(J Paco Gonzalez, U.S.A) **93/10**[2]
5 3 ½ **Wild Buddy (USA)**[42] 7-8-7 .... (b) JKCourt 2 102
(Steve Knapp, U.S.A) **93/10**[2]
6 ½ **Salty Humor (USA)**[69] 4-8-7 .... (b) AGryder 8 101
(S McCarthy, U.S.A) **44/1**
7 1 ¾ **That's An Outrage (USA)**[112] 5-8-7 .... TBaze 6 98
(M Puhich, U.S.A) **62/1**

1m 32.87s **7** Ran SP% **122.3**
PARI-MUTUEL (including $2 stake): WIN 2.40; PL (1-2) 2.20, 4.60; SHOW (1-2-3) 2.10, 2.10, 2.10; SF 11.20.
Owner Ballygallon Stud Ltd **Bred** Ballygallon Stud **Trained** USA

FOCUS
A trial for the Breeders' Cup Mile.

NOTEBOOK
Aragorn(IRE), previously trained by John Oxx and David Loder, has developed into a high-class performer in the US and did what was required in his prep for the Breeders' Cup Mile. He looks to be the leading home contender for the mile event at Churchill Downs.
Lord Admiral(USA) ran a stormer for his Irish connections.

5826a GOODWOOD BREEDERS' CUP H'CAP (GRADE 2) 1m 1f (D)
11:17 (11:19) 3-Y-0+ **£174,419** (£58,140; £34,884; £17,442; £5,814)

RPR
1 **Lava Man (USA)**[47] 5-9-0 .... (b) CNakatani 4 127+
(Doug O'Neill, U.S.A) **3/5**[1]
2 2 ¼ **Brother Derek (USA)**[35] 3-8-3 .... ASolis 7 116
(Dan L Hendricks, U.S.A) **44/10**[2]
3 1 **Giacomo (USA)**[47] 4-8-6 .... MESmith 2 113
(J Shirreffs, U.S.A) **86/10**
4 ½ **Preachinatthebar (USA)**[47] 5-8-5 .... (b) JKCourt 5 111
(B Baffert, U.S.A) **207/10**
5 ¾ **Super Frolic (USA)**[47] 6-8-5 .... DCohen 3 110
(V Cerin, U.S.A) **62/10**[3]
6 6 ½ **Magnum (ARG)**[47] 5-8-5 .... MPedroza 6 97
(Darrell Vienna, U.S.A) **98/10**
7 12 **Romeo Plus (ARG)**[161] 6-8-0 ow1 .... NArroyoJr 1 70
(P Gallagher, U.S.A) **77/1**

1m 48.15s
WFA 3 from 4yo+ 4lb **7** Ran SP% **120.5**
PARI-MUTUEL: WIN 3.20; PL (1-2) 2.20, 3.40; SHOW (1-2-3) 2.10, 2.40, 2.40; SF 13.20.
Owner STD Racing Stable and Jason Wood **Bred** Lonnie Arterburn & Eve & Kim Kuhlmann **Trained** USA

FOCUS
Some key form lines for the Breeders' Cup Classic.

NOTEBOOK
Lava Man(USA) defied top weight to land his seventh straight race of the year in good style and now heads for the Breeders' Cup Classic, having already been supplemented at a cost of $150,000.

5827a ANCIENT TITLE BREEDERS' CUP STKS (GRADE 1) 6f (D)
12:47 (12:52) 3-Y-0+ **£69,767** (£29,070; £17,442; £8,721; £2,907)

RPR
1 **Bordonaro (USA)**[68] 5-8-12 .... PValenzuela 6 120
(B Spawr, U.S.A) **2/5**[1]
2 1 **Thor's Echo (USA)**[52] 4-8-12 .... (b) DCohen 4 117
(Doug O'Neill, U.S.A) **101/10**
3 5 ¾ **Jungle Prince (USA)**[278] 5-8-12 .... (b) ADelgadillo 1 100
(J Garcia, U.S.A) **10/1**
4 1 ¾ **Pure As Gold (USA)**[48] 4-8-12 .... (b) JKCourt 3 95
(J Carava, U.S.A) **49/10**[2]
5 ¾ **Spellbinder (USA)**[33] 5-8-12 .... (b) CNakatani 2 92
(Richard E Mandella, U.S.A) **92/10**[3]
6 3 ½ **Zanzibar (ARG)**[364] 5-8-12 .... (b) JValdivia 5 82
(J W Sadler, U.S.A) **15/1**

67.93 secs **6** Ran SP% **122.5**
PARI-MUTUEL: WIN 2.80; PL (1-2) 2.20, 4.40; SHOW (1-2-3) 2.10, 2.20, 2.10; SF 17.20.
Owner Fred Carrillo & Daniel Cassella **Bred** Fred Carrillo & Daniel A Cassella **Trained** North America

FOCUS
A race that could provide some Breeders' Cup Sprint formlines.

NOTEBOOK
Bordonaro(USA) won nicely and set his connections a real poser as they will have to pay a supplementary fee of $180,000 if they want to run him in the Breeders' Cup Sprint.

5563 BATH (L-H)
Sunday, October 8

OFFICIAL GOING: Good
Wind: Moderate, half-behind.

5828 TOTEPLACEPOT NOVICE STKS 1m 5y
2:30 (2:31) (Class 4) 2-Y-0 **£6,153** (£1,830; £914; £456) **Stalls** Low

Form RPR
3105 1 **Golden Balls (IRE)**[14] 5546 2-9-7 85 .... JimmyFortune 7 93
(R Hannon) *trckd ldrs: led 2f out: rdn clr* **5/2**[2]
4321 2 3 **Aaim To Prosper (IRE)**[22] 5389 2-9-7 84 .... DaneO'Neill 1 86
(M R Channon) *in tch: rdn over 2f out: styd on to chse wnr appr fnl f* **5/1**[3]
01 3 4 **Practicallyperfect (IRE)**[25] 5287 2-9-2 80 .... EddieAhern 11 72
(H R A Cecil) *trckd ldr: led briefly over 2f out: sn one pce* **8/1**
21 4 1 ¼ **Amazing Request**[31] 5125 2-9-7 87 .... RichardHughes 6 74
(R Charlton) *sn led: rdn over 3f out: hdd over 2f out: one pce after* **9/4**[1]
5 1 **Duty Free (IRE)** 2-8-11 .... SteveDrowne 3 62
(H Morrison) *slowly away: in rr: rdn 3f out: styd on one pce ins fnl 2f* **25/1**
03 6 nk **Rosie's Glory (USA)**[19] 5460 2-8-9 .... ChrisCatlin 9 59
(B J Meehan) *in tch: rdn 1/2-way: wknd over 1f out* **6/1**
7 2 ½ **Towy Girl (IRE)** 2-8-3 .... JamesDoyle(3) 8 50
(I A Wood) *middiv: rdn over 3f out: wknd wl over 1f out* **25/1**
210 8 2 **Cherri Fosfate**[19] 5447 2-8-7 75 .... (p) JackDean(7) 5 54
(W G M Turner) *mid-div: hdwy over 4f out: rdn 3f out: wknd 2f out* **50/1**
0045 9 12 **Majestas (IRE)**[21] 5402 2-9-0 68 .... FergusSweeney 4 26
(J G M O'Shea) *trckd ldrs: rdn over 3f out: wknd 2f out* **100/1**
0 10 11 **Calzaghe (IRE)**[23] 5339 2-9-0 .... FrancisNorton 2 —
(A M Balding) *in tch: rdn over 4f out: sn wknd* **66/1**

1m 41.09s (-0.01) **Going Correction** +0.05s/f (Good) **10** Ran SP% **113.5**
Speed ratings (Par 97):102,99,95,93,92 92,89,87,75,64
CSF £14.31 TOTE £3.60: £1.30, £2.00, £2.40; EX 17.60 Trifecta £107.20 Pool £450.17. - 2.98 winning units..
Owner M Sines **Bred** Mrs Noelle Walsh **Trained** East Everleigh, Wilts

FOCUS
A good novice event, but they finished well strung out. The winning time was fair for the grade and the form looks pretty solid.

NOTEBOOK
Golden Balls(IRE) ◆ already had some useful form to his name but, upped to a mile for the first time, he appeared to put up an improved effort and was pretty impressive. This trip suited, but he apparently may be dropped back in distance for the Horris Hill before going to the sales. (tchd 11-4)
Aaim To Prosper(IRE), the easy winner of an extended-mile maiden at Wolverhampton on his previous start, would have found this tougher but ran a good race to take a clear second. (op 8-1)
Practicallyperfect(IRE), off the mark on her debut for the Henry Cecil yard in an extended seven-furlong maiden at Beverley on her previous start, ran well in this much more competitive contest and is going the right way. She could do even better in fillies-only company. (op 11-2)
Amazing Request looked in need of this trip when winning his maiden over seven furlongs at Chepstow, but he proved a little disappointing. He might just need more time and should come back a better three-year-old if looked after now. (op 11-4)
Duty Free(IRE) ◆, a 60,000gns half-brother to triple winner over hurdles winners Downing Street, faced a stiff task on his debut but ran well. He is a nice three-year-old prospect.
Rosie's Glory(USA) shaped well when third in a maiden at Newmarket on her previous start, but she was seemingly not ready for this step up in class. (op 5-1)

5829 TOTESPORT 0800 221 221 NURSERY 5f 11y
3:00 (3:03) (Class 4) (0-85,86) 2-Y-0 **£7,124** (£2,119; £1,059; £529) **Stalls** Low

Form RPR
4221 1 **Vaunt**[29] 5161 2-9-2 80 .... (b) SteveDrowne 10 85
(R Charlton) *mid-div: hdwy 2f out: led 1f out: drvn out* **13/2**[3]
01 2 ½ **Another True Story**[28] 5207 2-9-8 86 .... RichardHughes 11 89
(R Hannon) *towards rr: rdn 1/2-way: r.o to chse wnr ins fnl f* **10/1**
3066 3 nk **Star Strider**[11] 5606 2-8-4 68 .... FrancisNorton 8 70
(A M Balding) *outpcd in rr: hdwy over 1f out: r.o wl fnl f: nvr nrr* **40/1**
3110 4 1 ¾ **Cuppacocoa**[9] 5655 2-8-7 71 .... AdamKirby 7 67
(C G Cox) *chsd ldrs: rdn 1/2-way: kpt on one pce fnl f* **9/1**
2214 5 ¾ **Dowlleh**[23] 5334 2-9-2 80 .... ChrisCatlin 6 73
(M R Channon) *trckd ldr: led over 1f out: led 1f out: fdd ins fnl f* **16/1**
615 6 shd **Nobilissima (IRE)**[50] 4603 2-8-5 69 .... EddieAhern 12 62
(J L Spearing) *prom on outside: rdn over 2f out: rdn over 2f out: one pce ins fnl f* **14/1**
2011 7 hd **Mambo Spirit (IRE)**[15] 5528 2-9-7 85 .... J-PGuillambert 5 77
(J G Given) *mid-div: rdn over 2ff out: swtchd rt over 1f out: nvr nr to chal* **13/2**[3]
5403 8 ½ **Naayla (IRE)**[8] 5668 2-8-8 79 .... (b) KMay(7) 3 69
(B J Meehan) *chsd ldrs: rdn over 2f out: fdd fnl f* **16/1**
3221 9 ½ **Maker's Mark (IRE)**[13] 5563 2-9-3 81 .... DaneO'Neill 1 69
(H Candy) *sn pushed along in mid-div: wknd over 1f out* **3/1**[1]
0420 10 ¾ **Stir Crazy (IRE)**[9] 5646 2-8-0 67 .... EdwardCreighton(3) 9 53
(M R Channon) *a outpcd in rr* **50/1**
231 11 ½ **Makshoof (IRE)**[37] 4987 2-9-3 81 .... RHills 2 65
(M A Jarvis) *led tl rdn and hdd over 1f out: wknd qckly* **10/3**[2]
4605 12 17 **Princely Royal**[78] 3727 2-7-6 63 oh6 ow1 .... LukeMorris(7) 4 —
(J J Bridger) *a bhd: struggling wl in rr fr 1/2-way* **100/1**

61.93 secs (-0.57) **Going Correction** -0.20s/f (Firm) **12** Ran SP% **117.7**
Speed ratings (Par 97):96,95,94,91,90 90,90,89,88,87 86,59
CSF £68.98 CT £2400.52 TOTE £8.60: £2.70, £3.30, £8.70; EX 72.40 TRIFECTA Not won..
Owner Lady Rothschild **Bred** Lord Rothschild **Trained** Beckhampton, Wilts

FOCUS
A good, competitive sprint nursery and the form looks strong.

NOTEBOOK
Vaunt ◆ posted his best performance yet to follow up his course and distance maiden success. He looked set to win in style when sent to the front, but may just have idled a touch. He appeals as a sprinter to keep on the right side of. (op 17-2)
Another True Story, 5lb higher than when winning at Goodwood on his previous start, just got going too late. On this evidence, he might be worth a try over six furlongs. (op 9-1 tchd 11-1)
Star Strider, dropped back in trip and returned to turf, flew home having struggled to go early. He has dropped to a fair mark and would have to be of interest in similar company back over another furlong.
Cuppacocoa, the winner of a maiden and nursery over course and distance over course and distance before running a creditable tenth of 28 in a sales race at Newmarket, seemed to have her chance and gives the form a solid look. (op 8-1 tchd 10-1)
Dowlleh ran well but may not have been ideally suited by the drop back in trip.
Mambo Spirit(IRE), chasing the hat-trick, was seemingly found out by an 8lb higher mark than when winning at Chester on his previous start. Official explanation: jockey said colt never travelled (op 6-1)
Maker's Mark(IRE) could not build on his recent success in a course maiden and was beaten some way out. (op 4-1)
Makshoof(IRE), the winner of a six-furlong maiden on heavy ground at Haydock on his previous start, would have found this a very different test and was well beaten. (op 3-1 tchd 11-4)
Princely Royal Official explanation: jockey said gelding never travelled

5830 TOTEQUADPOT MEDIAN AUCTION MAIDEN STKS 1m 2f 46y
3:30 (3:32) (Class 6) 3-4-Y-0 **£3,238** (£963; £481; £240) **Stalls** Low

Form RPR
3236 1 **Lunar River (FR)**[13] 5574 3-8-12 63 .... (t) JimmyFortune 9 66+
(E A L Dunlop) *chsd ldrs: led on bit over 2f out: kpt up to work: comf* **5/4**[1]
-445 2 5 **Ruse**[35] 5046 3-8-12 63 .... SteveDrowne 7 55
(J R Fanshawe) *mid-div: rdn and styd on fr over 2f out to chse easy wnr ins fnl f* **9/4**[2]
340 3 1 ½ **Moves Goodenough**[104] 2919 3-9-3 73 .... ChrisCatlin 10 57
(Andrew Turnell) *hld up: stdy hdwy 1/2-way: chsd wnr over 1f out tl no ex ins fnl f* **11/1**
0-40 4 1 ½ **Phlaunt**[13] 5573 4-9-3 45 .... StephenCarson 8 49
(R F Johnson Houghton) *towardsa rr: rdn over 4f out and lost pce: styd on one pce ins fnl 2f* **25/1**
005 5 hd **Mrs Solese (IRE)**[99] 3073 3-8-12 67 .... EddieAhern 13 49
(J R Boyle) *led tl hdd over 2f out: wknd qckly* **10/1**
000 6 8 **Orchard House (FR)**[34] 5071 3-8-12 35 .... LiamJones(5) 4 38
(J Jay) *mid-div: rdn 3f out: sn btn* **100/1**
7 2 ½ **Coppington Melody (IRE)** 3-8-12 .... AdamKirby 11 29
(B W Duke) *in rr: rdn 3f out: nvr on terms* **25/1**

0 **8** *3* **Alujawill (IRE)**[8] 5669 3-9-3 .... FergusSweeney 6 28
(J G M O'Shea) *a bhd* **100/1**

9 *shd* **Party Boy (IRE)**[106] 2884 4-9-5 .... (bt[1]) JamesDoyle(3) 3 28
(Edgar Byrne, Ire) *in tch tl rdn and wknd 4f out* **40/1**

0-00 **10** *8* **King Cugat Kid (USA)**[8] 5669 3-9-0 45........ RichardKingscote(3) 5 13
(Simon Earle) *trckd ldrs: rdn 4f out: sn wknd* **100/1**

0- **11** *3 ½* **Poliama**[510] 1761 4-9-3 .... DaneO'Neill 2 1
(Evan Williams) *trckd ldr tl riden 3f out: sn wknd* **8/1**[3]

00 **12** *dist* **Hensting House**[76] 3794 3-9-3 .... AlanDaly 1 —
(Dr J R J Naylor) *slowly away: wl bhd whn virtually p.u over 2f out: t.o* **100/1**

2m 11.44s (0.44) **Going Correction** +0.05s/f (Good)
WFA 3 from 4yo 5lb 12 Ran SP% **117.8**
Speed ratings (Par 101):100,96,94,93,93 87,85,82,82,76 73,—
CSF £3.81 TOTE £2.40: £1.10, £1.30, £2.90; EX 5.70 Trifecta £28.20 Pool £286.38. - 7.20 winning units..
Owner The Moonlight Partnership **Bred** M Daguzan-Garros & Rolling Hills Farm **Trained** Newmarket, Suffolk

FOCUS
A very weak maiden and the form is worth little. The first three were not at their best in finishing not far clear of the poor fourth and sixth.
Coppington Melody(IRE) Official explanation: jockey said filly hung left-handed throughout
Poliama Official explanation: jockey said filly's stride shortened in closing stages
Hensting House Official explanation: vet said gelding was found to have a heart irregularity

5831 TOTE TEXT BETTING 60021 H'CAP 1m 2f 46y
4:00 (4:01) (Class 6) (0-60,60) 3-Y-0+ **£3,238** (£963; £481; £240) **Stalls** Low

Form RPR

0254 **1** **Golden Sprite**[13] 5566 3-9-2 **60**........ JimCrowley 15 68
(B R Millman) *hld up in rr: smooth hdwy on outside 3f out: led 1f out: rdn: all out* **18/1**

5000 **2** *shd* **Gallego**[16] 5506 4-9-2 **60**........ LiamJones(5) 7 68
(R J Price) *hld up wl in rr: making hdwy whn swtchd rt over 1f out: str run fnl f: jst failed* **11/1**

163 **3** *2* **Son Of Thunder (IRE)**[8] 5683 5-9-2 **55**........ (b) JimmyQuinn 2 59
(M Dods) *mid-division: hdwy on ins over 2f out: ev ch 1f out: no ex ins fnl f* **5/1**[3]

6030 **4** *1* **Salonga (IRE)**[19] 5452 3-9-2 **60**........ GeorgeBaker 10 62
(C F Wall) *led 6f out: hdd 1f out: no ex fnl f* **16/1**

0/0 **5** *½* **Armanatta (IRE)**[21] 5412 5-9-3 **56**........ EddieAhern 11 57
(Mrs A M O'Shea, Ire) *in tch: hdwy over 2f out: rdn and ev ch appr fnl f: no ex ins* **10/1**

5415 **6** *½* **Bridegroom**[11] 5625 4-8-13 **55**........ MarcHalford(3) 5 55+
(D R C Elsworth) *towards rr: hdway over 2f out: rdn and one pce fnl f* **4/1**[1]

-500 **7** *¾* **Smoothly Does It**[48] 2862 5-9-6 **59**........ ChrisCatlin 16 58
(Mrs A J Bowlby) *bhd tl hdwy over 2f out: one pce fnl f* **22/1**

0520 **8** *nk* **Baboosh (IRE)**[19] 5451 5-9-6 **59**........ DaneO'Neill 13 57
(M Wigham) *towards rr: hdwy over 3f out: sn rdn: fdd fnl f* **10/1**

0353 **9** *1* **The Iron Giant (IRE)**[8] 5451 4-9-2 **55**........ RobertMiles 8 52
(B G Powell) *prom: rdn to chsd ldrs 2f out: wknd fnl f* **17/2**

0403 **10** *5* **Oakley Absolute**[18] 5474 4-9-2 **55**........ RichardHughes 3 42
(R Hannon) *trckd ldrs: rdn over 2f out: sn btn* **9/2**[2]

0000 **11** *3* **Wilderness Bay (IRE)**[69] 4005 4-9-3 **56**........ FergusSweeney 12 37
(M R Bosley) *mid-div: rdn 3f out: sn wknd* **50/1**

006- **12** *nk* **Beautiful Mover (USA)**[415] 4551 4-9-0 **58**........ NataliaGemelova(5) 14 39
(J E Long) *in tch: rdn 4f out: wknd qckly over 1f out* **40/1**

0200 **13** *3* **Shosolosa (IRE)**[28] 5205 4-9-2 **58**........ (p) AmirQuinn(3) 9 33
(Mrs A L M King) *chsd ldr 6f out tl wknd 2f out* **16/1**

00-0 **14** *5* **Sheriff's Deputy**[46] 4709 6-8-13 **55**........ NeilChalmers(3) 1 21
(C N Kellett) *trckd ldrs tl rdn and wknd 3f out* **50/1**

-400 **15** *2 ½* **Zalzaar (IRE)**[41] 4871 4-9-4 **57**........ AdamKirby 6 18
(C G Cox) *led to 6f out: hmpd on ins over 4f out: rdn and sn btn* **16/1**

1300 **16** *16* **Competitor**[20] 5422 5-9-2 **55**........ (v) PatDobbs 4 —
(J Akehurst) *mid-div: rdn and wknd over 3f out: eased wl over 1f out* **33/1**

2m 11.26s (0.26) **Going Correction** +0.05s/f (Good)
WFA 3 from 4yo+ 5lb 16 Ran SP% **128.4**
Speed ratings (Par 101):100,99,98,97,97 96,96,95,95,91 88,88,86,82,80 67
CSF £206.59 CT £1163.60 TOTE £19.30: £3.70, £2.40, £1.80, £4.40; EX 246.00 TRIFECTA Not won..
Owner G J & Mrs M Palmer **Bred** G J And Mrs Palmer **Trained** Kentisbeare, Devon

FOCUS
A moderate handicap run at just an ordinary pace. The winner improved by 4lb, with the runner-up running to form and the fourth to her All-Weather best.
Beautiful Mover(USA) Official explanation: jockey said filly had no more to give
Shosolosa(IRE) Official explanation: jockey said filly had no more to give

5832 TOTESPORT.COM H'CAP 5f 11y
4:30 (4:32) (Class 3) (0-95,100) 3-Y-0+
£11,217 (£3,358; £1,679; £840; £419; £210) **Stalls** Low

Form RPR

002 **1** **Intrepid Jack**[8] 5667 4-9-4 **95**........ SteveDrowne 16 107
(H Morrison) *hld up on outside: hdwy 2f out: str run to ld wl ins fnl f* **4/1**[2]

0006 **2** *1* **Judd Street**[20] 5420 4-9-2 **93**........ StephenCarson 9 101
(R F Johnson Houghton) *a in tch: rdn to ld 1f out: hdd wl ins fnl f* **9/1**

0260 **3** *shd* **Cape Royal**[1] 5807 6-9-3 **94**........ (bt) FrancisNorton 15 102
(J M Bradley) *prom on on outside: rdn and r.o wl fnl f* **11/1**

0600 **4** *¾* **Maltese Falcon**[19] 5443 6-9-2 **93**........ (t) JosedeSouza 3 98
(P F I Cole) *slowly away: in rr tl hdwy over 1f out: r.o: nvr nrr* **40/1**

5541 **5** *nk* **Bluebok**[26] 5275 5-8-7 **84**........ (t) JimmyQuinn 14 88
(J M Bradley) *in tch: rdn to chse ldrs 1/2-way: nt qckn ins fnl f* **16/1**

6541 **6** *¾* **Hoh Hoh Hoh**[11] 5627 4-8-8 **85** ow1........ DaneO'Neill 7 87
(R J Price) *chsd ldrs: rdn and one pce fr over 1f out* **7/2**[1]

4220 **7** *¾* **Didn't We (IRE)**[8] 5667 3-8-10 **87**........ (b) JimmyFortune 6 86
(T G Mills) *mid-div: rdn 2f out: nt qckn after* **20/1**

0610 **8** *shd* **Magic Glade**[101] 3027 7-7-13 **81**........ LiamJones(5) 12 79
(R Brotherton) *led tl rdn and hdd 1f out: wknd ins fnl f* **50/1**

0400 **9** *½* **Golden Dixie (USA)**[1] 5807 7-8-13 **90**........ JimCrowley 5 87
(R A Harris) *towards rr: nvr on terms* **20/1**

0432 **10** *hd* **If Paradise**[15] 5535 5-8-11 **88**........ RichardHughes 11 84
(R Hannon) *mid-div: rdn 1/2-way: nvr nr to chal* **9/2**[3]

0300 **11** *1 ¾* **Pic Up Sticks**[8] 5667 7-8-9 **89**........ RichardKingscote(3) 10 79
(B G Powell) *towards rr: effrt 1/2-way: one pce after* **20/1**

0006 **12** *¾* **Peopleton Brook**[20] 5433 4-8-7 **84**........ ChrisCatlin 8 71
(J M Bradley) *trckd ldrs tl wknd 2f out* **33/1**

6610 **13** *1* **Caribbean Coral**[20] 5433 7-8-12 **89**........ (v) GrahamGibbons 2 72
(J J Quinn) *bhd whn rdn 1/2-way: nvr got into r* **14/1**

1100 **14** *½* **Cashel Mead**[15] 5535 6-8-10 **87**........ EddieAhern 1 69
(J L Spearing) *always bhd* **18/1**

0000 **15** *13* **Campbeltown (IRE)**[15] 5532 3-7-12 **82**........ (p) TolleyDean(7) 4 17
(R A Harris) *a bhd: lost tch 1/2-way* **66/1**

60.45 secs (-2.05) **Going Correction** -0.20s/f (Firm) 15 Ran SP% **119.7**
Speed ratings (Par 107):108,106,106,105,104 103,102,102,101,100 98,96,95,94,73
CSF £35.95 CT £382.01 TOTE £5.00: £2.20, £3.00, £4.50; EX 67.10 Trifecta £303.70 Part won. Pool £427.75. - 0.40 winning units..
Owner Michael T Lynch **Bred** Fonthill Stud **Trained** East Ilsley, Berks

FOCUS
They raced up the centre of the track. Quite a good sprint handicap, and the form looks solid through the placed horses.

NOTEBOOK
Intrepid Jack, racing over five furlongs for the first time, understandably took a while to pick up but was well on top at the finish. This was a good effort, but six furlongs is probably his best trip. (op 11-2 tchd 6-1)
Judd Street, 10lb higher than when winning at Windsor earlier in the season, was given every chance and was just denied. (op 17-2)
Cape Royal beat only one home at Ascot the previous day, but this was much better. (op 10-1 tchd 12-1)
Maltese Falcon has been well beaten in the face of some stiff tasks lately, but the Handicapper had given him a bit of a chance and he ran well, especially considering he lost ground at the start. He might be able to do even better back over six furlongs.
Bluebok could not defy a 4lb higher mark than when winning at Yarmouth on his previous start.
Hoh Hoh Hoh could not defy a 7lb higher mark than when winning over six furlongs at Salisbury on his previous start and, on this evidence, will be suited by a return to further one easier ground. (op 4-1)
If Paradise had been running well in defeat lately, but was disappointing this time. (tchd 4-1)
Pic Up Sticks Official explanation: jockey said gelding was unsuited by the good ground

5833 TOTEEXACTA H'CAP 1m 5y
5:00 (5:01) (Class 4) (0-85,83) 3-Y-0+ **£8,096** (£2,408; £1,203; £601) **Stalls** Low

Form RPR

6451 **1** **Kingsholm**[12] 5590 4-8-13 **77**........ FrancisNorton 15 89+
(A M Balding) *mid-div: hdwy on outside 1/2-way: led over 1f out: kpt up to work fnl f* **5/1**[1]

2322 **2** *1 ½* **Don Pietro**[16] 5504 3-8-11 **78**........ EddieAhern 5 86
(D J Coakley) *mid-div: hdwy on outside over 2f out: chsd wnr fr over 1f out: but no imp ins fnl f* **6/1**[3]

4333 **3** *½* **All Quiet**[38] 4965 5-8-13 **77**........ RichardHughes 3 84
(R Hannon) *mid-div: hdwy over 2f out: rdn over 1f out: nt qckn ins fnl f* **9/1**

244- **4** *hd* **Master Mahogany**[218] 4760 5-8-11 **75**........ JimCrowley 8 82+
(R J Hodges) *stmbld leaving stalls: in rr tl hdwy over 2f out: styd on: nvr nrr* **33/1**

5506 **5** *2* **Rubenstar (IRE)**[16] 5504 3-8-3 **77**........ PatrickHills(7) 7 79
(M H Tompkins) *in rr tl hdwy on ins over 2f out: ev ch appr fnl f: fdd ins* **10/1**

2610 **6** *nk* **Glenmuir (IRE)**[16] 5504 3-9-1 **82**........ GeorgeBaker 6 83
(B R Millman) *hld up: hdwy 2f out: sn rdn and one pce* **33/1**

5350 **7** *½* **Golden Applause (FR)**[8] 5689 4-8-9 **73**........ (p) FergusSweeney 16 73
(Mrs A L M King) *in tch: led over 2f out: hdd over 1f out: sn btn* **66/1**

6002 **8** *nk* **Dry Ice (IRE)**[12] 5591 4-9-2 **80**........ (b[1]) DaneO'Neill 9 79
(H Candy) *mid-div: effor over 2f out: sn rdn and wknd* **11/2**[2]

1120 **9** *shd* **Cool Ebony**[16] 5504 3-8-12 **79**........ JimmyQuinn 11 78
(M Dods) *hld up in tch: rdn 3f out: wknd appr fnl f* **14/1**

4240 **10** *½* **Bonnie Prince Blue**[16] 5504 3-9-1 **82**........ SteveDrowne 1 80
(B W Hills) *chsd ldrs: rdn 3f out: wknd fnl f* **11/1**

1221 **11** *5* **Personify**[30] 5149 4-8-10 **74**........ (p) AdamKirby 12 61
(C G Cox) *prom tl wknd over 2f out* **6/1**[3]

5042 **12** *1 ¼* **Norton (IRE)**[20] 5428 9-9-5 **83**........ JimmyFortune 13 67
(T G Mills) *trckd ldrs: rdn over 2f out: sn wknd* **10/1**

2106 **13** *1 ½* **Baylaw Star**[21] 5406 5-8-11 **80**........ LiamJones(5) 10 60
(I W McInnes) *led tl hdd over 2f out: wknd qckly* **50/1**

1030 **14** *5* **Davenport (IRE)**[10] 5639 4-8-9 **80**........ JamesMillman(7) 4 49
(B R Millman) *a bhd* **16/1**

1m 40.23s (-0.87) **Going Correction** +0.05s/f (Good)
WFA 3 from 4yo+ 3lb 14 Ran SP% **119.0**
Speed ratings (Par 105):106,104,104,103,101 101,101,100,100,100 95,93,92,87
CSF £33.09 CT £273.54 TOTE £6.20: £3.00, £1.80, £3.00; EX 48.80 Trifecta £314.40 Part won. Pool £442.93. - 0.80 winning units. Place 6 £178.14, Place 5 £100.33..
Owner J C, J R And S R Hitchins **Bred** J C , J R And S R Hitchins **Trained** Kingsclere, Hants

FOCUS
A fair handicap and, just as in the previous sprint, they majority of these tended to come up the centre of the track. The form looks sound, rated through the second and third.
Davenport(IRE) Official explanation: jockey said gelding was never travelling
T/Jkpt: Not won. T/Plt: £277.80 to a £1 stake. Pool: £86,409.40. 227.00 winning tickets. T/Qpdt: £18.80 to a £1 stake. Pool: £5,256.90. 206.20 winning tickets. JS

5552 MUSSELBURGH (R-H)
Sunday, October 8

OFFICIAL GOING: Good to soft (good in places)
After four dry days the ground was described as 'on the soft side of good'.
Wind: Moderate, half-behind. Weather: Overcast, cool and breezy.

5834 SUBSCRIBE ONLINE@RACINGUK.TV BANDED STKS 5f
2:20 (2:20) (Class 7) 3-Y-0+ **£2,218** (£654; £327) **Stalls** Low

Form RPR

4012 **1** **How's She Cuttin' (IRE)**[10] 5631 3-9-3 50........ PhillipMakin 5 61
(T D Barron) *chsd ldrs: led over 2f out: hung rt: hld on towards fin* **3/1**[1]

0003 **2** *nk* **Sharp Hat**[10] 5631 12-9-0 47........ TonyCulhane 4 57
(D W Chapman) *mid-div: hdwy 2f out: wnt 2nd ins last: no ex towards fin* **7/1**[2]

0651 **3** *¾* **Compton Classic**[10] 5631 4-9-5 52........ (p) LeeEnstone 10 59
(J S Goldie) *werved lft s: mid-div: hdwy 2f out: nt qckn ins last* **8/1**[3]

0000 **4** *1 ¾* **Black Oval**[8] 5684 5-8-7 47........ MarkCoumbe(7) 6 48
(S Parr) *sn outpcd and bhd: hdwy 2f out: styd on wl ins last* **33/1**

0- **5** *2* **Without A Paddle**[45] 4744 3-8-10 46........ (b) StephenDonohoe(3) 7 40
(Daniel Mark Loughnane, Ire) *bhd: hdwy on outer 2f out: nvr trbld ldrs* **33/1**

340- **6** *nk* **Molotov**[330] 6326 6-9-1 48........ DanielTudhope 13 40
(M Dods) *in rr: hdwy on outer 2f out: nvr nr to chal* **7/1**[2]

000- **7** *½* **Bond Puccini**[437] 3866 4-8-10 48........ DuranFentiman(5) 11 39
(G R Oldroyd) *w ldrs: wknd over 1f out* **100/1**

5100 **8** *nk* **Grand View**[64] [4157] 10-9-0 47....................(p) PaulMulrennan 15 37
(J R Weymes) *in rr: sme hdwy 2f out: nvr a factor* **50/1**

0004 **9** *shd* **Elvina**[25] [5291] 5-9-2 49.................................... LPKeniry 14 38
(A G Newcombe) *chsd ldrs: wknd over 1f out* **14/1**

4000 **10** *shd* **Angelofthenorth**[45] [4735] 4-8-12 50..................... AndrewElliott(5) 17 39
(C J Teague) *s.v.s: sme hdwy on outer 2f out: nvr on terms* **10/1**

0015 **10** *dht* **Trumpita**[10] [5631] 3-8-13 46.................................... DavidAllan 1 35
(T D Easterby) *mid-div: drvn over 2f out: nvr a factor* **8/1**[3]

0050 **12** *shd* **Sundried Tomato**[64] [4157] 7-8-12 45..................(p) MichaelTebbutt 12 33
(D W Chapman) *chsd ldrs: lost pl over 1f out* **25/1**

3000 **13** *6* **Compton Lad**[27] [5250] 3-8-13 46............................(t) MickyFenton 16 13
(D A Nolan) *chsd ldrs: lost pl 2f out* **66/1**

0002 **14** *1* **Desert Dust**[46] [4710] 3-8-12 45............................(b) RobertWinston 3 8
(R M H Cowell) *led over 2f: sn lost pl* **10/1**

5350 **15** *18* **She's Our Beauty (IRE)**[33] [5078] 3-9-1 48...............(v) AdrianTNicholls 8 —
(D Nicholls) *bmpd s: in rr: hrd rdn 1f out: threw hd in air: nt keen: virtually p.u* **12/1**

62.51 secs (2.01) **Going Correction** +0.25s/f (Good) 15 Ran SP% **118.9**
Speed ratings (Par 97):93,92,91,88,85 84,84,83,83,83 83,83,73,71,43
CSF £21.24 TOTE £3.70: £1.60, £2.80, £2.40; EX 22.00.
Owner Christopher McHale **Bred** A M Burke **Trained** Maunby, N Yorks
■ A banded meeting, and with £250 appearance money per runner just one horse was withdrawn on account of the ground.

FOCUS
It was an advantage to race as close as possible to the stands' side rail. Very modest Banded stuff with the entire field having the same chance beforehand on official ratings. The first three filled the same three places, in a different order, in an Ayr handicap ten days earlier.
Angelofthenorth Official explanation: jockey said filly missed the break
Compton Lad Official explanation: jockey said gelding hung left
She's Our Beauty(IRE) Official explanation: jockey said filly lost its action

5835 SCOTTISH RACING MAIDEN AUCTION STKS 5f
2:50 (2:50) (Class 7) 2-Y-O **£2,047** (£604; £302) **Stalls** Low

Form RPR

0204 **1** **Only A Grand**[27] [5238] 2-8-4 55..............................(b) RoystonFfrench 3 60
(R Bastiman) *chsd ldrs: str run on ins to ld ins last: drvn clr* **10/1**

0420 **2** *4* **Violet's Pride**[58] [4321] 2-8-0 67.............................. DuranFentiman(5) 12 47
(S Parr) *w ldrs on outside: led over 1f out: hdd and no ex ins last* **17/2**

322 **3** *1* **Brenin Gwalia**[8] [5668] 2-8-12 71.............................. AdrianTNicholls 2 50
(D M Simcock) *led: hung rt and hdd over 1f out: kpt on same pce* **1/1**[1]

006 **4** *1 ¼* **Darcy's Pride (IRE)**[5] [5746] 2-8-8 .... PaulHanagan 5 42
(D W Barker) *mid-div: hdwy on outside over 1f out: styd on ins last* **20/1**

2235 **5** *½* **House Arrest**[25] [5282] 2-8-2 55.............................. DominicFox(3) 9 37
(A J McCabe) *chsd ldrs on outside: one pce fnl 2f* **10/1**

5004 **6** *3* **Bungie**[9] [5645] 2-8-6 65.............................. JohnCavanagh(7) 1 34
(Ms Deborah J Evans) *chsd ldrs: wknd over 1f out* **7/1**[3]

0 **7** *shd* **My Maite Mickey**[24] [5315] 2-8-11 .... LPKeniry 4 32
(R C Guest) *mid-div: outpcd over 2f out: no threat after* **33/1**

3 **8** *3 ½* **Telling**[24] [5315] 2-8-11 .... TonyCulhane 11 19
(Mrs A Duffield) *gave problems leaving paddock: sn outpcd: hung lft over 2f out: nvr a threat* **6/1**[2]

000 **9** *5* **Kyoto City**[38] [4971] 2-7-13 30.............................. AndrewElliott(5) 10 —
(D W Chapman) *dwlt: outpcd* **125/1**

0 **10** *4* **Northern Candy**[33] [5076] 2-8-10 .... SilvestreDeSousa 7 —
(A Dickman) *restless in stalls: s.s: a bhd* **50/1**

11 *5* **Senora Lenorah** 2-8-8 .... DavidAllan 13 —
(D A Nolan) *s.v.s: a last* **100/1**

62.51 secs (2.01) **Going Correction** +0.25s/f (Good) 11 Ran SP% **116.9**
Speed ratings (Par 89):93,86,85,83,82 77,77,71,63,57 49
CSF £87.68 TOTE £11.10: £1.90, £2.80, £1.10; EX 93.00.
Owner S Lorimer **Bred** Shade Oak Stud **Trained** Cowthorpe, N Yorks

FOCUS
A very modest maiden auction event but a seemingly much improved effort from the winner, up 16lb. With the time poor and the third beaten once again, this does not look form to put much faith in.

NOTEBOOK
Only A Grand, who cost just that, was dropping back to five after four times failing to make the cut in nursery company. With plenty to find with the favourite and the runner-up, she burst clear inside the last for a well-deserved first victory. (op 17-2)
Violet's Pride, absent for two months, showed bags of toe down the unfavoured outside but in the end she was left for dead by the winner. (op 8-1)
Brenin Gwalia, ideally drawn, took them along but he hung away from the fence and in the end was simply not good enough. It was however his first encounter with easy ground. (op 11-10 tchd 6-5 and 5-4 in places)
Darcy's Pride(IRE) is gradually getting the hang of things and is ready for a step back up to six furlongs. (op 25-1)
House Arrest, who usually plies her trade in selling company, did well from an unfavourable outside draw. (op 8-1)
Bungie had the plum draw but he came up well short on ground he is proven on.
Telling, a bit of a handful leaving the paddock, never fired and this may be best overlooked. (op 13-2 tchd 7-1)

5836 DRUMMOND MILLER LLP SUPPORTING ST COLUMBA'S BANDED STKS 1m 6f
3:20 (3:20) (Class 7) 3-Y-O+ **£2,388** (£705; £352) **Stalls** High

Form RPR

0660 **1** **Virginia Rose (IRE)**[19] [5445] 3-9-1 48.............................. PaulHanagan 6 61+
(J G Given) *trckd ldrs: wnt 2nd over 3f out: shkn up to ld over 1f out: sn pushed clr: eased towards fin* **7/2**[1]

0055 **2** *6* **Mystified (IRE)**[87] [3456] 3-9-0 50..............................(b) DNolan(3) 14 54
(R F Fisher) *led 2f: chsd ldrs: led over 5f out: hdd over 1f out: no ch w wnr* **18/1**

5445 **3** *2* **Totally Scottish**[92] [3291] 10-9-3 48.............................. JamesReveley(7) 13 49
(K G Reveley) *mid-div: effrt 4f out: one pce fnl 2f* **5/1**[2]

0650 **4** *hd* **Turner**[22] [5385] 5-9-5 48.............................. MarkFlynn(5) 10 49
(W M Brisbourne) *hld up in mid-div: hdwy over 3f out: hung rt: one pce fnl 2f* **10/1**

4034 **5** *1* **My Legal Eagle (IRE)**[121] [2408] 12-9-10 48.............................. TonyCulhane 11 48
(E G Bevan) *hld up in rr: hdwy on inner and nt clr run 4f out: kpt on same pce fnl 2f* **11/2**[3]

0-50 **6** *2 ½* **Next Flight (IRE)**[5] [5750] 7-9-11 49.............................. DavidAllan 9 45
(R E Barr) *hld up in mid-div: effrt over 3f out: kpt on: nvr nr to chal* **7/1**

-005 **7** *¾* **Sovereign State (IRE)**[12] [3637] 9-9-9 47..............................(p) TonyHamilton 8 42
(D W Thompson) *chsd ldrs: one pce fnl 3f* **25/1**

0000 **8** *1 ¼* **Sparkbridge (IRE)**[75] [3815] 3-9-3 50.............................. DanielTudhope 2 43
(R F Fisher) *swtchd rt s: in rr and pushed along 7f out: sme hdwy on outer over 2f out: nvr nr ldrs* **33/1**

0300 **9** *20* **Rouge Et Noir**[12] [4954] 8-9-11 49.............................. RoystonFfrench 7 14
(P Monteith) *s.i.s: sn mid-div: lost pl over 2f out: sn bhd and eased* **8/1**

4500 **10** *5* **Valeureux**[5] [5750] 8-9-5 50.............................. PaulPickard(7) 3 8
(J Hetherton) *racd wd: sn w ldrs: led after 2f: hdd over 5f out: sn lost pl and bhd: eased* **16/1**

000 **11** *12* **Urban Freeway (IRE)**[5] [5750] 7-9-6 47..............................(bt[1]) GregFairley(3) 5 —
(Robert Gray) *w ldrs: lost pl over 4f out: sn bhd and eased* **40/1**

0360 **12** *21* **Zarova (IRE)**[19] [5445] 4-9-10 48.............................. RobertWinston 4 —
(M W Easterby) *hld up in rr: sme hdwy 4f out: sn lost pl and bhd: virtually p.u* **15/2**

3m 9.20s (3.50) **Going Correction** +0.175s/f (Good)
WFA 3 from 4yo+ 9lb 12 Ran SP% **119.1**
Speed ratings (Par 97):97,93,92,92,91 90,89,89,77,74 68,56
CSF £70.18 TOTE £4.40: £1.90, £4.50, £1.80; EX 71.10.
Owner The Living Legend Racing Partnership II **Bred** Abbeville & Meadow Court Studs & Tower Bloodstock **Trained** Willoughton, Lincs

FOCUS
A rock bottom Banded event with all twelve runners having the same chance on official ratings, but it turned out to be a one-sided contest. Not solid form, rated through the runner-up.

5837 RACING UK FOR £15 PER MONTH MAIDEN CLAIMING STKS 1m 4f
3:50 (3:50) (Class 7) 3-Y-O+ **£2,047** (£604; £302) **Stalls** High

Form RPR

0300 **1** **Princess Of Aeneas (IRE)**[14] [5553] 3-8-0 57........(p) RoystonFfrench 10 50
(I Semple) *trckd ldrs: effrt over 3f out: led over 1f out: edgd lft: drvn clr ins last* **10/3**[2]

0000 **2** *5* **Channel Crossing**[13] [5581] 4-9-3 45..............................(p) DNolan(3) 4 55
(W M Brisbourne) *led: hdd over 1f out: kpt on same pce* **12/1**

6320 **3** *2* **Alisdanza**[27] [5242] 4-8-10 45.............................. AndrewElliott(5) 11 47
(G A Swinbank) *trckd ldrs: effrt over 3f out: one pce fnl 2f* **2/1**[1]

0-05 **4** *3* **Robeson**[20] [5435] 4-9-6 55.............................. AdrianTNicholls 2 48
(D M Simcock) *hld up: hdwy 7f out: one pce fnl 3f* **20/1**

305- **5** *4* **Manhattan Jack**[459] [3234] 5-9-6 55.............................. DeanMcKeown 9 42
(G A Swinbank) *hld up in rr: hdwy 4f out: one pce fnl 2f* **5/1**[3]

0000 **6** *2 ½* **Expression Echo (IRE)**[11] [5625] 4-9-1 40.............................. LPKeniry 13 33
(A G Newcombe) *bhd: sme hdwy 4f out: nvr nr ldrs* **18/1**

025- **7** *½* **Cream Of Esteem**[427] [4195] 4-9-6 45.............................. RobertWinston 14 37
(M Todhunter) *bhd: kpt on fnl 3f: nvr a factor* **11/2**

0000 **8** *17* **Galloping Gertie**[17] [5497] 4-8-4 40.............................. PaulPickard(7) 5 3
(J Hetherton) *racd wd: mid-div: lost pl over 5f out: bhd fnl 3f* **66/1**

00-0 **9** *12* **Procrastinate (IRE)**[32] [4723] 4-9-6 45.............................. DanielTudhope 8 —
(R F Fisher) *s.i.s: hld up in rr: lost pl over 3f out: sn bhd* **33/1**

500- **10** *13* **The Loose Screw (IRE)**[418] [4445] 8-9-6 40.............................. PaulHanagan 3 —
(C W Thornton) *sn w ldrs: lost pl over 2f out: sn bhd* **33/1**

0-0 **11** *1 ½* **Welcome Spirit**[18] [5485] 3-8-6 .... RussellKennemore(7) 6 —
(J S Haldane) *chsd ldrs: lost pl over 3f out: sn bhd: t.o 2f out* **100/1**

5 **12** *nk* **Hialeah**[12] [4227] 5-9-1 ....(b[1]) GregFairley(3) 1 —
(Robert Gray) *rrd s: sn chsng ldrs: lost pl over 3f out: sn bhd* **40/1**

2m 39.87s (2.97) **Going Correction** +0.175s/f (Good)
WFA 3 from 4yo+ 7lb 12 Ran SP% **117.0**
Speed ratings (Par 97):97,93,92,90,87 86,85,74,66,57 56,56
CSF £39.10 TOTE £4.10: £1.40, £3.20, £1.30; EX 39.50.The winner was claimed by D McCain Jnr for £2,000.
Owner The Mathieson Partnership **Bred** Mrs J A Dene **Trained** Carluke, S Lanarks

FOCUS
A poor maiden claimer in which they finished well strung out. The winner was the clear pick at the weights and the form looks a little suspect.

5838 SCOTTISH RACING "YOUR BEST BET" BANDED STKS 1m 1f
4:20 (4:20) (Class 7) 3-Y-O+ **£2,047** (£604; £302) **Stalls** High

Form RPR

0000 **1** **Komreyev Star**[45] [4730] 4-9-2 45.............................. SilvestreDeSousa 5 52
(M Mullineaux) *chsd ldrs: led over 2f out: hdd 1f out: styd on to ld nr fin* **14/1**

0006 **2** *nk* **Ailsa**[22] [5363] 4-9-2 45.............................. PaulMulrennan 3 51
(C W Thornton) *hld up: hdwy over 3f out: led 1f out: no ex and hdd nr fin* **16/1**

6253 **3** *2* **Coronation Flight**[6] [5726] 3-8-12 45.............................. DeanMcKeown 8 47
(F P Murtagh) *in rr: hdwy on outside over 2f out: hung rt: kpt on fnl f* **4/1**[1]

0006 **4** *1* **Huxley (IRE)**[160] [1353] 7-9-2 45..............................(t) AdrianTNicholls 12 45
(D J Wintle) *s.s: hdwy 3f out: kpt on: nvr rchd ldrs* **7/1**

2050 **5** *nk* **Majehar**[127] [2221] 4-8-13 45.............................. StephenDonohoe(3) 10 44
(A G Newcombe) *sn bhd: hdwy on outside over 2f out: kpt on wl fnl f* **10/1**

0000 **6** *¾* **Mycenean Prince (USA)**[30] [3785] 3-8-12 45.............................. LPKeniry 15 43
(R C Guest) *in rr: hdwy over 3f out: kpt on: nvr a threat* **33/1**

0402 **7** *1* **Boucheen**[20] [5432] 3-8-5 45.............................. JohnCavanagh(7) 4 41
(Ms Deborah J Evans) *led: edgd lft and hdd over 2f out: sn wknd* **5/1**[2]

6065 **8** *1 ¾* **Ever Special (IRE)**[65] [1501] 3-8-12 45.............................. RoystonFfrench 13 37
(P C Haslam) *trckd ldrs: wknd over 1f out* **12/1**

1060 **9** *shd* **Double Ransom**[25] [5285] 7-9-2 45..............................(b) TonyHamilton 6 37
(Mrs L Stubbs) *dwlt: sn mid-div: hdwy over 3f out: wknd over 1f out* **9/1**

5600 **10** *2 ½* **Inch High**[13] [5579] 8-9-4 47.............................. DanielTudhope 11 34
(J S Goldie) *chsd ldrs: lost pl over 1f out* **8/1**

0501 **11** *2 ½* **Aqua**[14] [5553] 4-8-11 45.............................. RoryMoore(5) 14 27
(P T Midgley) *chsd ldrs: lost pl over 2f out* **6/1**[3]

4-00 **12** *¾* **Red River Rock (IRE)**[129] [2165] 4-9-2 45.............................. PaulHanagan 1 26
(T J Fitzgerald) *mid-div: hdwy over 3f out: wknd 2f out* **20/1**

000 **13** *1 ¼* **Explode**[46] [4709] 9-8-9 45..............................(b) DawnRankin(7) 16 23
(Miss L C Siddall) *in rr: hdwy on inner over 3f out: wknd 2f out* **66/1**

1m 57.42s (3.56) **Going Correction** +0.175s/f (Good)
WFA 3 from 4yo+ 4lb 13 Ran SP% **123.1**
Speed ratings (Par 97):91,90,88,88,87 87,86,84,84,82 80,79,78
CSF £222.69 TOTE £15.50: £3.60, £6.40, £1.80; EX 331.90.
Owner Garry Whittaker **Bred** G And Mrs Whittaker **Trained** Alpraham, Cheshire
■ Stewards' Enquiry : Silvestre De Sousa two-day ban: used whip with excessive frequency (Oct 19-20)
Paul Mulrennan five-day ban: using whip with excessive frequency, without giving mount time to respond and down the shoulder in the forehand position (Oct 19-21, 23-24)

FOCUS
An ordinary race run in a moderate winning time, even for a banded race. Just average form for the grade, rated through the second and fourth.
Aqua Official explanation: trainer said filly had not been suited by the going which was good to soft

5839 RACING UK AND SETANTA FOR £15 BANDED STKS 1m
4:50 (4:50) (Class 7) 3-Y-O+ **£2,218** (£654; £327) **Stalls** High

Form RPR

3636 **1** **Fairy Monarch (IRE)**[17] 5497 7-9-5 50..........................(b) MickyFenton 1 58
(P T Midgley) *dwlt: in rr: hdwy over 3f out: plld wd 1f out: styd on wl to ld last 75yds* **6/1**[3]

0000 **2** *1 ¼* **Barataria**[25] 5285 4-9-5 50.. RoystonFfrench 12 55
(R Bastiman) *chsd ldrs: styd on to ld ins last: sn hdd and no ex* **11/2**[2]

3030 **3** *1* **Whittinghamvillage**[25] 5285 5-9-0 48........................... GregFairley(3) 13 51
(D W Whillans) *chsd ldrs: upsides 1f out: unable qckn* **9/1**

4 *1 ¼* **Cameo Story**[45] 4745 3-9-2 50.................................. AdrianTNicholls 9 50
(Andrew Oliver, Ire) *chsd ldr: led over 2f out: hdd ins last: wknd towards fin* **12/1**

0203 **5** *hd* **Choreographic (IRE)**[27] 5244 4-9-2 47........................... PaulHanagan 8 52+
(R A Fahey) *mid-div: hdwy over 3f out: nt clr run over 1f out: no run and eased ins last: nt rcvr* **4/1**[1]

3540 **6** *3 ½* **She Whispers (IRE)**[20] 5432 3-8-11 48.............. StephenDonohoe(3) 11 39
(W M Brisbourne) *mid-div: hdwy on ins over 2f out: nvr trbld ldrs* **9/1**

0040 **7** *nk* **The Thrifty Bear**[27] 5250 3-8-9 50......................... KellyHarrison(7) 6 41
(C W Fairhurst) *trckd ldrs: t.k.h: hung rt and wknd fnl f* **20/1**

-000 **8** *2 ½* **Fuel Cell (IRE)**[129] 2181 5-8-10 48........................(bt) JamesO'Reilly(7) 14 33
(J O'Reilly) *s.i.s: nvr on terms* **16/1**

000 **9** *2 ½* **Frimley's Matterry**[27] 5243 6-8-13 49................... MichaelJStainton(5) 2 28
(R E Barr) *mid-div: effrt on outer 3f out: sn btn* **14/1**

0000 **10** *½* **Halcyon Magic**[51] 4575 8-9-0 48..................................(b) DominicFox(3) 5 26
(M Wigham) *a towards rr* **16/1**

6650 **11** *nk* **Capitalise (IRE)**[75] 3823 3-9-1 49.............................. MichaelTebbutt 10 26
(V Smith) *a towards rr* **12/1**

-054 **12** *6* **Nevinstown (IRE)**[34] 5062 6-9-3 48.............................. TonyHamilton 7 11
(C Grant) *set str pce: hdd over 2f out: lost pl over 1f out* **9/1**

1m 43.82s (1.32) **Going Correction** +0.175s/f (Good)
WFA 3 from 4yo+ 3lb 12 Ran SP% **118.2**
Speed ratings (Par 97):100,98,97,96,96 92,92,90,87,87 86,80
CSF £38.88 TOTE £7.40: £2.40, £2.50, £2.90; EX 39.60.
Owner M E Elsworthy **Bred** Charlie Moore **Trained** Westow, N Yorks

FOCUS
Solid form for the grade, with the winner running up to his recent best and fourth running to his Irish form.
Choreographic(IRE) Official explanation: jockey said gelding was denied a clear run

5840 SUBSCRIBE TO RACING UK ON 08700 506949 BANDED STKS 7f 30y
5:20 (5:20) (Class 7) 3-Y-O+ **£2,047** (£604; £302) **Stalls** High

Form RPR

4350 **1** **Cut Ridge (IRE)**[45] 4729 7-9-0 45...................................(p) TonyHamilton 8 55
(J S Wainwright) *led: qcknd over 3f out: kpt on wl: unchal* **6/1**

5004 **2** *2 ½* **Vibrato (USA)**[36] 5023 4-9-0 45.......................................(p) PaulHanagan 9 49
(C J Teague) *prom: kpt on to take 2nd ins last: no imp* **12/1**

-000 **3** *1 ¼* **John O'Groats (IRE)**[13] 5577 8-8-7 45...............(p) CharlotteKerton(7) 14 45
(W G Harrison) *chsd ldrs: wnt 2nd over 2f out: kpt on same pce* **20/1**

0301 **4** *2 ½* **Hows That**[41] 4881 4-9-0 45..(p) PhillipMakin 1 39
(K R Burke) *chsd ldrs: outpcd over 3f out: kpt on one pce fnl 2f* **7/2**[2]

0201 **5** *3* **Cape Sydney (IRE)**[22] 5363 3-8-12 45............................ CatherineGannon 4 31
(D W Barker) *chsd ldrs: outpcd over 3f out: kpt on one pce fnl 2f* **5/1**[3]

0040 **6** *½* **Song Huntress**[59] 4278 3-8-12 45.. LPKeniry 13 30+
(A G Newcombe) *mid-div: hmpd and lost pl bnd over 5f out: hdwy and hung rt over 2f out: nvr a threat* **40/1**

6030 **7** *1* **Nilsatisoptimum (USA)**[46] 4710 3-8-12 45...........(t) SilvestreDeSousa 5 27
(M Mullineaux) *chsd ldrs: outpcd over 3f out: no threat after* **11/1**

1260 **8** *hd* **Kirkhammerton (IRE)**[17] 5497 4-8-11 45..........(b) StephenDonohoe(3) 6 27+
(A J McCabe) *sn in rr: sme hdwy over 2f out: nvr on terms* **9/1**

0/40 **9** *shd* **Ho Pang Yau**[48] 4652 8-9-0 45.. LeeEnstone 7 26
(J S Goldie) *sn bhd: sme hdwy on outer over 2f out: nvr on terms* **14/1**

0000 **10** *1* **Diamond Heritage**[22] 5363 4-9-0 45........................(p) DanielTudhope 10 24
(S Parr) *mid-div: edgd rt over 1f out: nvr a factor* **33/1**

6023 **11** *4* **Miskina**[38] 4970 5-8-11 45.. GregFairley(3) 11 13
(W M Brisbourne) *trckd ldrs: t.k.h: edgd lft and lost pl over 2f out* **3/1**[1]

5140 **12** *5* **Midge's Girl (IRE)**[41] 4881 3-8-12 45........................(v) RoystonFfrench 2 —
(Mrs A Duffield) *s.i.s: a in rr* **20/1**

0000 **13** *12* **Tilen (IRE)**[98] 3115 3-8-12 45..(b) MickyFenton 3 —
(S Parr) *hld up in rr: lost tch 3f out* **50/1**

1m 31.82s (1.88) **Going Correction** +0.175s/f (Good)
WFA 3 from 4yo+ 2lb 13 Ran SP% **127.7**
Speed ratings (Par 97):96,93,91,88,85 84,83,83,83,82 77,71,58
CSF £76.53 TOTE £9.20: £3.60, £2.70, £5.40; EX 82.90 Place 6 £37.25, Place 5 £21.20..
Owner Hurn Racing Club **Bred** Mrs Chris Harrington **Trained** Kennythorpe, N Yorks

FOCUS
Modest form and not totally reliable based on the performances of the placed horses.
Kirkhammerton(IRE) Official explanation: jockey said gelding got carried wide on bend leaving back straight
Midge's Girl(IRE) Official explanation: jockey said filly ran wide on bend leaving back straight
T/Plt: £43.70 to a £1 stake. Pool: £52,447.10. 874.65 winning tickets. T/Qpdt: £25.10 to a £1 stake. Pool: £2,164.50. 63.70 winning tickets. WG

5735 WOLVERHAMPTON (A.W) (L-H)
Sunday, October 8

OFFICIAL GOING: Standard
Wind: Fresh, behind Weather: Cloudy with sunny spells

5841 DICKY & GINGER MAIDEN STKS 7f 32y(P)
2:10 (2:11) (Class 4) 2-Y-O **£4,731** (£1,416; £708; £354; £176) **Stalls** High

Form RPR

34 **1** **Dream Lodge (IRE)**[15] 5537 2-9-3 .... JamieMackay 11 79
(J G Given) *a.p: led and hung lft fr over 1f out: drvn out* **20/1**

5 **2** *nk* **Minnis Bay (CAN)**[19] 5454 2-9-3 .... RyanMoore 4 78
(E F Vaughan) *mid-div: hdwy 1/2-way: rdn and hung lft fnl f: r.o* **7/2**[2]

62 **3** *1 ¼* **Apache Dawn**[22] 5381 2-9-3 .... MichaelHills 8 75
(B W Hills) *led: hung rt over 2f out: hdd and hmpd over 1f out: styd on same pce ins fnl f* **3/1**[1]

4 *½* **Sagredo (USA)** 2-9-3 .... SebSanders 5 74
(Sir Mark Prescott) *mid-div: outpcd 4f out: hdwy and nt clr run over 1f out: r.o* **66/1**

30 **5** *1* **Stanley George (IRE)**[22] 5381 2-9-3 .... DarryllHolland 3 71
(M A Jarvis) *chsd ldrs: rdn over 1f out: styd on same pce* **15/2**[3]

54 **6** *2* **Solid Rock (IRE)**[19] 5458 2-9-3 .... KerrinMcEvoy 9 66
(T G Mills) *chsd ldrs: rdn over 2f out: styd on same pce appr fnl f* **3/1**[1]

4 **7** *5* **Fujisan**[93] 3242 2-9-3 .... KDarley 10 54
(M Johnston) *w ldr tl rdn over 2f out: wknd over 1f out* **8/1**

02 **8** *2 ½* **Henry The Seventh**[11] 5608 2-9-3 .... TedDurcan 6 48
(J W Hills) *hdwy over 5f out: rdn over 2f out: sn wknd* **14/1**

0 **9** *6* **Kilvickeon (IRE)**[8] 5686 2-9-3 .... TomEaves 2 33
(Peter Grayson) *hld up: outpcd 4f out: sn bhd* **100/1**

10 *½* **Super Nebula** 2-9-3 .... BrianReilly 12 31
(P L Gilligan) *sn outpcd* **100/1**

60 **11** *1 ¾* **Rudry Dragon (IRE)**[9] 5658 2-9-3 .... TPO'Shea 1 27
(P A Blockley) *s.i.s: sme hdwy 1/2-way: wknd over 2f out* **10/1**

12 *34* **Follow The Buzz** 2-9-0 .... SaleemGolam(3) 7 —
(J M Bradley) *s.s: outpcd* **100/1**

1m 29.12s (-1.28) **Going Correction** -0.125s/f (Stan) 12 Ran SP% **120.1**
Speed ratings (Par 97):102,101,100,99,98 96,90,87,80,80 78,39
CSF £89.53 TOTE £19.50: £2.10, £2.60, £1.70; EX 72.60.
Owner The G-Guck Group **Bred** C H Wacker Iii **Trained** Willoughton, Lincs

FOCUS
A modest juvenile maiden, run at a fair pace, which saw the first two fight out a tight finish. The level seems sound through the time and the fifth and sixth but could prove a little high.

NOTEBOOK
Dream Lodge(IRE) defied his wide draw and got off the mark at the third attempt on this return to Polytrack. The drop to this trip proved to his liking, as did the return to a sound surface, and he has the scope to do well in handicaps next year at around a mile. (op 22-1)
Minnis Bay(CAN), popular in the betting ring, appreciated the step up to the extra furlong yet still looked green when push came to shove. He is well up to getting off the mark in something similar before the season's end. (op 4-1 tchd 5-1)
Apache Dawn, making his All-Weather debut, again showed a tendency to hang right under pressure and was beaten before the final furlong marker. He now qualifies for nurseries and appeals as the type to do better as a three-year-old. (op 10-3 tchd 7-2)
Sagredo(USA), an already gelded half-brother to 12-16 furlong winner Etching, was putting in all of his best work towards the finish and not that surprisingly already looks to require a stiffer test. He should come on a fair bit for the experience. (op 50-1)
Stanley George(IRE) finished a lot closer to the runner-up than had been the case at Warwick last time and posted a much more encouraging effort in defeat. He now has the option of nurseries. (op 9-1)
Solid Rock(IRE), making his All-Weather bow, found just the same pace when it mattered and ran disappointingly. He probably wants a mile now and should find his feet in handicaps. Official explanation: jockey said colt ran too free (op 7-2)

5842 NIEL JACKSON MID-MORNING H'CAP 5f 216y(P)
2:40 (2:40) (Class 4) (0-80,80) 3-Y-O+ **£5,362** (£1,604; £802; £401; £199) **Stalls** Low

Form RPR

5015 **1** **Rosein**[12] 5593 4-8-11 **73**.. TedDurcan 13 82
(Mrs G S Rees) *chsd ldrs: rdn over 1f out: styd on u.p to ld nr fin* **14/1**

3344 **2** *hd* **Xaluna Bay (IRE)**[2] 5782 3-8-10 **73**...................................... KerrinMcEvoy 3 81
(W R Muir) *a.p: chsd ldr over 2f out: rdn to ld 1f out: hdd nr fin* **6/1**[3]

0204 **3** *½* **Charlie Delta**[41] 4888 3-8-13 **76**.. RyanMoore 6 83
(D Carroll) *prom: lost pl over 4f out: hdwy u.p over 1f out: r.o* **12/1**

4020 **4** *½* **Figaro Flyer (IRE)**[20] 5427 3-8-10 **76**.............................. DeanCorby(3) 5 81
(P Howling) *hld up: rdn over 1f out: r.o ins fnl f: nrst fin* **20/1**

4-03 **5** *hd* **Foreign Edition (IRE)**[32] 5117 4-9-4 **80**................................. TomEaves 4 84
(Miss J A Camacho) *chsd ldrs: outpcd over 3f out: hdwy over 1f out: r.o* **3/1**[1]

20- **6** *3* **Turn On The Style**[243] 4915 4-9-3 **79**...............................(b) BrianReilly 1 74
(J Balding) *s.i.s: sn rcvrd to ld: clr over 2f out: rdn and hdd 1f out: sn wknd* **25/1**

2064 **7** *nk* **Brandywell Boy (IRE)**[3] 5777 3-9-1 **78**............................ SebSanders 10 73
(D J S Ffrench Davis) *mid-div: hdwy over 2f out: sn rdn and edgd lft: styd on same pce appr fnl f* **7/1**

0003 **8** *1* **Prince Tum Tum (USA)**[22] 5391 6-9-0 **76**.......................... DaleGibson 7 68
(D Shaw) *in rr whn hmpd 4f out: styd on ins fnl f: nvr nrr* **9/1**

0402 **9** *2* **Summer Recluse (USA)**[13] 5575 7-8-8 **70**..................(t) DarryllHolland 8 56
(J M Bradley) *in rr: rdn over 2f out: n.d* **10/1**

2205 **10** *shd* **Mambazo**[2] 5782 4-8-10 **75**...(e) SaleemGolam(3) 2 60
(S C Williams) *hld up: rdn over 2f out: n.d* **7/2**[2]

000- **11** *1 ¾* **Skip Of Colour**[330] 6336 6-8-4 **66** oh11.................. AdrianMcCarthy 11 46
(P A Blockley) *chsd ldr over 3f: wknd over 1f out* **66/1**

5600 **12** *4* **Brunelleschi**[8] 5684 3-8-3 **66** oh2.................................. FrancisFerris 12 34
(P L Gilligan) *chsd ldrs over 3f* **50/1**

0000 **U** **Savernake Blue**[9] 5649 3-8-7 **70**... TPO'Shea 9 —
(M R Channon) *rrd and uns rdr s* **25/1**

1m 14.51s (-1.30) **Going Correction** -0.125s/f (Stan)
WFA 3 from 4yo+ 1lb 13 Ran SP% **123.4**
Speed ratings (Par 105):103,102,102,101,101 97,96,95,92,92 90,84,—
CSF £94.11 CT £1099.01 TOTE £13.50: £3.30, £2.30, £3.10; EX 181.50.
Owner Mrs G S Rees **Bred** J Gittins And Capt J H Wilson **Trained** Sollom, Lancs

FOCUS
A fair sprint and the form looks sound enough for the class, rated through the fourth. The first five were fairly closely covered at the finish.
Summer Recluse(USA) Official explanation: jockey said gelding would not face kickback

5843 NO.1 FOR WOLVERHAMPTON 107.7 THE WOLF NURSERY 7f 32y(P)
3:10 (3:12) (Class 2) 2-Y-O
£9,348 (£2,799; £1,399; £700; £349; £175) **Stalls** High

Form RPR

4062 **1** **Ghost Dancer**[26] 5262 2-8-4 **71**.. NickyMackay 9 72
(L M Cumani) *hld up: hdwy over 2f out: rdn to ld 1f out: r.o* **10/1**

6116 **2** *½* **Heywood**[19] 5459 2-9-5 **86**... TPO'Shea 12 86+
(M R Channon) *hld up: nt clr run over 2f out: swtchd rt and hdwy over 1f out: r.o* **12/1**

1310 **3** *¾* **Monkey Glas (IRE)**[22] 5366 2-8-8 **75**.............................. PatCosgrave 10 73
(K R Burke) *chsd ldrs: led and edgd lft over 2f out: rdn and hung lft over 1f out: sn hdd: styd on same pce* **25/1**

2210 **4** *nk* **Billy Dane (IRE)**[45] 4736 2-9-6 **87**.. LDettori 1 84+
(B J Meehan) *trckd ldrs: effrt and hmpd over 1f out: swtchd rt ins fnl f: nt rcvr* **3/1**[2]

51 **5** *nk* **Lady Grace (IRE)**[28] 5209 2-9-2 **83**................................. KerrinMcEvoy 3 79+
(W J Haggas) *slowly in to stride: hld up: hdwy over 2f out: hmpd over 1f out: r.o ins fnl f: nvr able to chal* **7/1**

426 **6** *6* **Fourfoot Bay (IRE)**[29] 5168 2-8-10 **77**............................ DarryllHolland 6 58
(J D Bethell) *free to post: s.i.s: hld up and bhd: nvr nrr* **25/1**

321 **7** *hd* **Averticus**[24] 5326 2-8-12 **79**... MichaelHills 5 60
(B W Hills) *chsd ldrs: hmpd over 2f out: wknd over 1f out* **6/1**[3]

1020 **8** 2 **Dubai Magic (USA)**[24] 5322 2-9-3 **84**................................ SebSanders 4 60+
(C E Brittain) *chsd ldrs: rdn and hung lft over 1f out: hld whn hmpd sn after* **20/1**

0210 **9** ½ **Orpen Prince (IRE)**[32] 5113 2-8-3 **73**....................(p) AndrewMullen(3) 7 48
(K A Ryan) *chsd ldrs: rdn over 2f out: wknd over 1f out* **33/1**

213 **10** 4 **Leopard King (USA)**[22] 5372 2-9-7 **88**.........................(v1) RyanMoore 2 53+
(Sir Michael Stoute) *led over 4f: wkng whn hmpd over 1f out* **15/8**[1]

0250 **11** 7 **Only A Splash**[32] 5113 2-7-5 **65** oh15.................... DanielleMcCreery(7) 8 12
(D W Chapman) *hld up: a in rr: wknd over 2f out* **100/1**

1m 29.09s (-1.31) **Going Correction** -0.125s/f (Stan) 11 Ran SP% **119.7**
Speed ratings (Par 101):102,101,100,100,99 93,92,90,89,85 77
CSF £115.90 CT £1856.94 TOTE £10.40: £2.40, £3.40, £3.40; EX 53.00.
Owner Kevin Bailey & Philip Booth **Bred** Floors Farming **Trained** Newmarket, Suffolk
■ Stewards' Enquiry : Pat Cosgrave three-day ban: careless riding (Oct 19,20,23)

FOCUS
A decent nursery for the track. The first four came clear and the form seems solid.

NOTEBOOK
Ghost Dancer, whose previous effort at Lingfield has worked out well, came through to belatedly open his account under a well-judged ride from Mackay. He has improved since stepping up to his trip and should have more to offer now he has got his head in front. (op 9-1)
Heywood picked up well once switched to the outside in the straight and ran another sound race in defeat. He has done well this term, winning four times to date, and is clearly best suited by this shorter trip. (op 20-1)
Monkey Glas(IRE) hung markedly left when asked for maximum effort, doing a number of his rivals little favours in the process, yet still turned in a much better effort in defeat. He is tricky, but has the talent to score from this mark during the winter. (op 33-1)
Billy Dane(IRE) ◆ lost his chance when hampered by Monkey Glas nearing the final furlong and can be considered a little unlucky. He evidently likes this venue and well up to winning from his current mark when things go his way. (op 4-1 tchd 9-2)
Lady Grace(IRE), making her handicap debut, was always playing catch-up after a sluggish start and was another not done any favours when Monkey Glas hung left in the home straight. She is capable of better. (op 5-1)
Fourfoot Bay(IRE), having his first run in a nursery, lost any chance at the start and is clearly not straightforward. He still left the impression he can do better with further experience, however. Official explanation: jockey said colt ran too free (op 33-1)
Leopard King(USA), equipped with a first-time visor for the All-Weather bow, was starting to tread water prior to being hampered and has to rate as disappointing. He has it to prove now. (op 2-1 tchd 9-4)

5844 TIM HAYCOCK DRIVE MAIDEN STKS (DIV I) 1m 141y(P)
3:40 (3:40) (Class 5) 3-4-Y-O **£2,590** (£770; £385; £192) **Stalls** Low

Form RPR

3444 **1** **Escape Clause (USA)**[33] 5086 3-9-3 80........................... RyanMoore 6 68+
(Sir Michael Stoute) *hld up: hdwy 1/2-way: led 2f out: hung rt over 1f out: styd on wl* **7/4**[1]

34 **2** 3 **Red Countess**[115] 2578 3-8-12 .... KerrinMcEvoy 11 57+
(Mrs A J Perrett) *chsd ldrs: lost pl 4f out: hdwy over 2f out: hung lft over 1f out: styd on* **9/4**[2]

0056 **3** nk **Networker**[67] 4056 3-9-0 45.. SaleemGolam(3) 12 61
(P J McBride) *hld up in tch: jnd ldrs over 3f out: rdn over 1f out: styd on same pce* **50/1**

6400 **4** 2½ **Weet For Ever (USA)**[34] 5070 3-9-3 57................................ TPO'Shea 3 56
(P A Blockley) *chsd ldr tl led over 3f out: hdd 2f out: wknd fnl f* **25/1**

-003 **5** 8 **Chasing A Dream**[11] 5612 3-8-12 68.............................. MichaelHills 10 34
(B W Hills) *led: hdd over 7f out: rdn and wknd over 2f out* **4/1**[3]

06- **6** 1¾ **Greytown**[398] 5005 3-8-12 .... PhilipRobinson 1 31
(M A Jarvis) *led over 7f out: hdd over 3f out: wknd 2f out* **7/1**

-000 **7** 1½ **Ruby Sunrise (IRE)**[98] 1225 4-8-9 40........................... SoniaEaton(7) 2 27
(B P J Baugh) *hld up: a in rr* **100/1**

05 **8** 2½ **Crystal Annie**[12] 5598 3-8-12 .... NickyMackay 5 22
(Heather Dalton) *mid-div: sn pushed along: wknd 3f out* **20/1**

00-0 **9** 1 **Red Pride (IRE)**[193] 797 3-9-0 52.................................. DeanCorby(3) 4 25
(Miss J Feilden) *mid-div: wknd 3f out* **66/1**

053- **10** hd **Zagreus (GER)**[155] 3816 4-9-0 45....................................(p) MCGeran(7) 8 25
(H J Manners) *outpcd: sme hdwy over 2f out: sn wknd* **66/1**

1m 50.03s (-1.73) **Going Correction** -0.125s/f (Stan)
WFA 3 from 4yo 4lb 10 Ran SP% **114.2**
Speed ratings (Par 103):102,99,99,96,89 88,86,84,83,83
CSF £5.39 TOTE £2.30: £1.20, £1.50, £10.50; EX 9.40.
Owner James Wigan **Bred** George Strawbridge And London Thoroughbred Service **Trained** Newmarket, Suffolk

FOCUS
The winning time was about par for a race like this, despite being 1.2 seconds faster than the second division. A weak maiden, the form held down by the proximity of a 45-rated performer in third.

5845 ALAN NICKLIN EVENING CONDITIONS STKS 1m 141y(P)
4:10 (4:10) (Class 3) 3-Y-0+ **£7,790** (£2,332; £1,166; £583; £291; £146) **Stalls** Low

Form RPR

0-65 **1** **Kilworth (IRE)**[220] 561 3-8-11 107... LDettori 2 99+
(Saeed Bin Suroor) *chsd ldrs: shkn up to ld 1f out: r.o* **5/2**[1]

0000 **2** 1½ **Party Boss**[23] 5341 4-9-1 102... RyanMoore 3 96
(C E Brittain) *led: rdn and hdd 1f out: styd on same pce* **8/1**

3040 **3** ¾ **St Andrews (IRE)**[22] 5376 6-9-1 100..........................(p) PhilipRobinson 9 94
(M A Jarvis) *hld up: hdwy over 1f out: r.o* **6/1**

6-20 **4** 4 **Desert Destiny**[240] 369 6-9-1 101..............................(v) KerrinMcEvoy 5 86
(Saeed Bin Suroor) *chsd ldr: rdn over 2f out: hung lft and wknd over 1f out* **9/2**[3]

23 **5** 2½ **Areyoutalkingtome**[29] 5165 3-9-1 94............................... MichaelHills 6 84
(C A Cyzer) *hld up: hdwy and nt clr run over 2f out: wknd over 1f out* **12/1**

1- **6** 1¼ **Shelhom**[352] 6001 3-8-11 95... TedDurcan 4 78
(Saeed Bin Suroor) *prom: stmbld over 7f out: rdn and hung rt over 2f out: sn wknd* **9/1**

1546 **7** hd **Momtic (IRE)**[28] 5227 5-9-7 104.. PaulDoe 7 83
(W Jarvis) *hld up: hdwy over 2f out: sn rdn and wknd* **4/1**[2]

3- **8** 3½ **Da Bookie (IRE)**[27] 5255 6-9-1 67.. TPO'Shea 1 70
(P A Blockley) *hld up: a in rr* **80/1**

5-00 **9** 12 **Cape Greko**[15] 5520 4-9-1 90....................................(v1) DarryllHolland 8 45
(A M Balding) *chsd ldrs 6f* **40/1**

1m 48.37s (-3.39) **Going Correction** -0.125s/f (Stan)
WFA 3 from 4yo+ 4lb 9 Ran SP% **113.5**
Speed ratings (Par 107):110,108,108,104,102 101,100,97,87
CSF £23.00 TOTE £3.50: £1.10, £2.80, £3.30; EX 35.80.
Owner Godolphin **Bred** John Bernard O'Connor **Trained** Newmarket, Suffolk

FOCUS
A decent event for the track which saw the first three come clear. The early pace was just fair. Fair form, rated through the first two, although there are doubts over several of the field.

NOTEBOOK
Kilworth(IRE), who disappointed on dirt in Dubai ealier this year, ran out a ready winner on this belated debut for connections and was value for a little further than the winning margin. He looks best kept to this trip for the short term, should improve a deal for the outing, and is reportedly due to step back up into Group company now. (tchd 2-1)
Party Boss showed the benefit of his recent return from a break at Newbury 23 days previously and posted by far his best effort of the year. All of his six previous wins have been on this surface and, despite the fact he had the run of the race out in front, he is clearly a different proposition on Polytrack. Placing him successfully again will not be easy, however.
St Andrews(IRE), having his first outing on the All-Weather, showed a bit more enthusiasm than of late and was nicely clear of the remainder at the finish. This experience may well help to get him back on track. (op 13-2 tchd 7-1)
Desert Destiny, last seen disappointing in Dubai back in February, found little when asked for maximum effort and again did little to convince with his attitude. He is entitled to improve for the run, but is likely to remain hard to place from his current rating. (op 5-1 tchd 11-2)
Areyoutalkingtome was not disgraced at the weights and has developed into a likeable performer. He is likely to go up a few pounds for this, however. (tchd 14-1)
Shelhom, winner of his sole start at two when with Michael Jarvis and gelded since then, is probably worth forgiving this form as he stumbled early on and looked much in need of the outing. He is now with top connections and can do better in time. (op 15-2 tchd 10-1)
Momtic(IRE), another having his first taste of the All-Weather, was giving weight away all round yet still turned in a below-par display. He ideally needs a stronger early pace. (op 9-2)
Cape Greko Official explanation: jockey said gelding stopped very quickly

5846 107.7 THE WOLF STAYERS H'CAP 2m 119y(P)
4:40 (4:40) (Class 5) (0-75,75) 3-Y-0+ **£3,238** (£963; £481; £240) **Stalls** Low

Form RPR

3442 **1** **Synonymy**[13] 5564 3-8-1 59.. NickyMackay 8 67
(M Blanshard) *chsd ldrs: rdn over 2f out: styd on to ld wl ins fnl f* **5/1**[3]

5034 **2** nk **Salute (IRE)**[22] 5383 7-9-5 66... SebSanders 9 74
(P G Murphy) *chsd ldr tl led over 3f out: rdn over 1f out: hdd wl ins fnl f* **7/1**

5455 **3** 2½ **Taxman (IRE)**[11] 5610 4-9-10 71......................................(p) RyanMoore 4 76
(C E Brittain) *hld up in tch: rdn and hung lft over 1f out: styd on same pce ins fnl f* **11/4**[1]

2340 **4** 1 **Dickie's Dream (IRE)**[10] 5644 3-8-7 65.......................... DarryllHolland 2 69
(P J McBride) *chsd ldrs: rdn over 2f out: no ex fnl f* **5/1**[3]

466 **5** 2 **Wotchalike (IRE)**[8] 5691 4-9-0 61...............................(v) KerrinMcEvoy 5 62
(R J Price) *hld up: hdwy over 2f out: sn rdn: hung lft over 1f out: styd on same pce* **12/1**

4332 **6** 3 **Reinstated (IRE)**[12] 5594 3-9-0 72.................................. MichaelHills 6 70
(B W Hills) *dwlt: hld up: hmpd 3f out: hdwy and nt clr run over 2f out: sn rdn: eased whn btn fnl f* **4/1**[2]

16-0 **7** 5 **Dovedale**[16] 5506 6-8-9 56.. TedDurcan 1 48
(H S Howe) *hld up: riddden and wknd over 2f out* **16/1**

1106 **8** 7 **French Mannequin (IRE)**[6] 5736 7-8-13 60.................(v) TPO'Shea 10 43
(P A Blockley) *prom tl wknd over 2f out* **16/1**

0406 **9** 15 **Ulshaw**[37] 4981 9-8-2 56 oh16.. BarrySavage(7) 7 21
(J M Bradley) *hld up: rdn 1/2-way: wknd over 3f out* **66/1**

3 **10** 4 **Liberman (IRE)**[24] 5318 8-10-0 75.................................. DaleGibson 3 36
(R Curtis) *led: hdd over 3f out: wknd over 2f out* **25/1**

3m 41.25s (-1.88) **Going Correction** -0.125s/f (Stan)
WFA 3 from 4yo+ 11lb 10 Ran SP% **117.3**
Speed ratings (Par 103):99,98,97,97,96 94,92,89,82,80
CSF £40.20 CT £115.98 TOTE £9.20: £3.10, £3.60, £2.00; EX 50.20.
Owner G H Phillips,J M Beever & D G Chambers **Bred** Biddestone Stud **Trained** Upper Lambourn, Berks

FOCUS
A modest staying handicap which was run at just an average pace. Pretty ordinary form, but it does appear to make sense.
French Mannequin(IRE) Official explanation: jockey said mare hung badly left

5847 TIM HAYCOCK DRIVE MAIDEN STKS (DIV II) 1m 141y(P)
5:10 (5:10) (Class 5) 3-4-Y-0 **£2,590** (£770; £385; £192) **Stalls** Low

Form RPR

4 **1** **Khun John (IRE)**[11] 5612 3-9-3 .... LDettori 8 67+
(B J Meehan) *chsd ldrs: carried wd 7f out: sn led: rdn over 1f out: r.o* **5/6**[1]

6 **2** ¾ **Spinning Reel**[23] 5353 3-8-12 .... TedDurcan 6 60+
(W R Swinburn) *hld up: hdwy over 5f out: rdn to chse wnr fnl f: r.o* **9/2**[2]

5 **3** 1¾ **Kilgary (USA)**[98] 3112 3-8-12 .... DarryllHolland 9 56+
(J Noseda) *a.p: chsd wnr over 3f out: rdn and hung lft over 1f out: styd on same pce* **5/1**[3]

6330 **4** 3½ **Ours (IRE)**[24] 5316 3-9-3 58.. SebSanders 11 54
(J D Bethell) *s.i.s: hld up: hdwy and hung lft over 1f out: no imp fnl f* **10/1**

0660 **5** 1 **Trials 'n Tribs**[28] 5201 4-9-2 40... MichaelHills 4 47
(C A Cyzer) *hld up: rapid hdwy 4f out: son w ldrs: rdn and wknd over 1 f out* **14/1**

4060 **6** nk **Pop Music (IRE)**[36] 5035 3-9-0 58................................ SaleemGolam(3) 1 51
(Miss J Feilden) *chsd ldr: lft in ld 7f out: sn hdd: rdn over 2f out: sn outpcd* **25/1**

0 **7** 1¾ **Ifatfirst (IRE)**[11] 5611 3-9-3 .... KerrinMcEvoy 3 48
(M P Tregoning) *sn led: hung rt and hdd 7f out: remained handy tl rdn and wknd 2f out* **12/1**

0 **8** ¾ **Inveraray**[20] 5429 3-8-12 .... DaleGibson 5 41
(P S Felgate) *chsd ldrs: lost pl over 3f out: n.d after* **66/1**

-000 **9** 9 **Kentavr's Dream**[33] 5092 3-8-5 35.......................... JPFeatherstone(7) 2 22
(P Howling) *hld up: wknd over 3f out* **100/1**

0000 **10** ¾ **Galaxy Bound (IRE)**[164] 1263 3-9-0 45...............(v) PatrickMathers(3) 10 26
(D Shaw) *hld up: plld hrd: rdn over 3f out: sn wknd* **66/1**

0 **11** 12 **Lucky Tern**[12] 5598 3-8-10 .... BarrySavage(7) 7 —
(J M Bradley) *plld hrd and prom: wknd 3f out* **100/1**

1m 51.23s (-0.53) **Going Correction** -0.125s/f (Stan)
WFA 3 from 4yo 4lb 11 Ran SP% **121.7**
Speed ratings (Par 103):97,96,94,91,90 90,88,88,80,79 68
CSF £4.97 TOTE £1.90: £1.10, £1.90, £1.40; EX 8.70 Place 6 £369.20, Place 5 £195.62..
Owner The Strawberries To A Donkey Partnership **Bred** Sti Engineering Srl **Trained** Manton, Wilts

FOCUS
A modest winning time for the grade, 1.2 seconds slower than the first division and the form is very ordinary. The front three are all likely to prove better than the bare form.
Ifatfirst(IRE) Official explanation: jockey said gelding hung badly right
T/Plt: £149.90 to a £1 stake. Pool: £66,482.00. 323.70 winning tickets. T/Qpdt: £14.50 to a £1 stake. Pool: £3,683.50. 186.80 winning tickets. CR

5848 - (Foreign Racing) - See Raceform Interactive

5462 CURRAGH (R-H)

Sunday, October 8

OFFICIAL GOING: Soft to heavy

5849a HACKETT'S WATERFORD TESTIMONIAL STKS (LISTED RACE) 6f

2:35 (2:36) 3-Y-O+ **£24,693** (£7,244; £3,451; £1,175)

RPR

1 **Ugo Fire (IRE)**[7] 5708 3-8-12 104 DPMcDonogh 1 110
(Kevin Prendergast, Ire) *trckd ldrs: 4th 1/2-way: impr to ld over 2f out: clr over 1f out: easily* **3/1**[1]

2 3 ½ **Senor Benny (USA)**[7] 5706 7-9-2 103 KFallon 4 102
(M McDonagh, Ire) *hld up: 7th and hdwy 2f out: mod 3rd over 1f out: kpt on* **8/1**

3 2 **Cheyenne Star (IRE)**[45] 4749 3-8-12 101 PJSmullen 5 93
(Ms F M Crowley, Ire) *trckd ldrs: 6th 1/2-way: 3rd and hdwy 2f out: 2nd 1 1/2f out: sn no ex* **5/1**[3]

4 1 ¼ **Miss Sally (IRE)**[36] 5011 4-9-2 107 JMurtagh 3 92
(M Halford, Ire) *chsd ldrs in 3rd: 4th and rdn under 2f out: kpt on same pce* **7/2**[2]

5 1 ½ **Abigail Pett**[98] 3129 3-8-12 106 KJManning 8 85
(J S Bolger, Ire) *hld up: 8th 2f out: kpt on wout threatening fr over 1f out* **8/1**

6 3 ½ **Fit The Cove (IRE)**[15] 5542 6-9-2 96 (b) WSupple 11 77
(H Rogers, Ire) *chsd ldrs: 6th u.p 2f out: one pce* **16/1**

7 3 ½ **Sanfrancullinan (IRE)**[88] 3422 4-8-13 74 RPCleary 10 64
(M Halford, Ire) *towards rr: rdn after 1/2-way: no imp* **50/1**

8 4 **Gist (IRE)**[7] 5706 3-8-12 78 (b) NGMcCullagh 6 52
(W J Martin, Ire) *chsd ldrs to 1/2-way: wknd over 2f out* **25/1**

9 3 **Osterhase (IRE)**[7] 5706 7-9-5 114 (b) FMBerry 2 49
(J E Mulhern, Ire) *led: hdd over 2f out: sn wknd: virtually p.u fnl f* **5/1**[3]

10 2 ½ **Lahiba (IRE)**[19] 5463 5-8-13 80 (b) JohnEgan 9 35
(M Halford, Ire) *cl up: 2nd 1/2-way: wknd over 1 1/2f out: eased ins fnl f* **25/1**

11 dist **Fay Mayr**[8] 5693 3-8-12 CDHayes 7 —
(Edward Lynam, Ire) *s.i.s: trailing 1/2-way: eased under 2f out: completely t.o* **66/1**

1m 20.3s **Going Correction** +1.25s/f (Soft)
WFA 3 from 4yo+ 1lb **11** Ran SP% **119.8**
Speed ratings: 111,106,103,102,100 95,90,85,81,78 —
CSF £27.48 TOTE £3.90: £1.50, £2.20, £2.40; DF 38.20.
Owner Norman Ormiston **Bred** Sweetman Bloodstock **Trained** Friarstown, Co Kildare

FOCUS
The winner was the only one to fire and the form is limited by the seventh, while the second and fourth also came here out of form.

NOTEBOOK
Ugo Fire(IRE), who was dropping back in trip after losing out narrowly in a Group 3 event over an extended seven furlongs at Tipperary a week previously, belatedly got off the mark for the season, winning decisively on ground she handles well. Soon tracking the leaders, she found herself in front when Osterhase weakened rapidly with under a quarter of a mile to run and she stuck to her task well to win driven out. It has yet to be decided whether she will remain in training next year. (op 11/4)
Senor Benny(USA), another tried and trusted performer on testing ground, ran his best race for some time. He made steady headway over the last quarter-mile and stayed on quite well to claim second spot inside the last without troubling the winner.
Cheyenne Star(IRE), a three-time winner from this trip up to a mile on ground never softer than yielding, had been only touched off at this level of competition on good ground over an extended seven at Tipperary at August when today's winner finished third. Held up, she improved after halfway and went second a furlong and a half out before weakening inside the final furlong.
Miss Sally(IRE), winner of this race a year ago, has failed to score since making a successful start to the season over this trip at Cork in May. She had made little impact when tried at Group 1 level at Haydock on her previous start and she could make little impression here having tracked the leaders to beyond halfway.
Abigail Pett, a triple winner on fast ground last year, had performed creditably when fifth on ground even more testing than this in the Irish 1,000 Guineas in May. Off the track since early July and without the blinkers, she never counted, although she did keep on from behind over the last couple of furlongs.
Osterhase(IRE) again found the ground completely against him and, after leading for about half a mile, he was done with pretty quickly and was eased when all hope of running in the money had gone. (op 3/1)
Fay Mayr Official explanation: jockey said filly lost her action and was eased 2f out; trainer said filly sustained a serious injury behind

5850a FLAME OF TARA EUROPEAN BREEDERS FUND STKS (LISTED RACE) (FILLIES) 6f

3:05 (3:07) 2-Y-O **£33,672** (£9,879; £4,706; £1,603)

RPR

1 **Evening Time (IRE)**[8] 5692 2-8-12 DPMcDonogh 11 110+
(Kevin Prendergast, Ire) *in tch on outer: smooth hdwy into 3rd 1/2-way: led over 2f out: sn qcknd clr: rdn and styd on wl: impressive* **5/4**[1]

2 5 **Theann**[9] 5654 2-8-12 106 KFallon 8 96
(A P O'Brien, Ire) *hld up in tch: prog after 1/2-way: 2nd and chsd ldr under 2f out: no imp: kpt on same pce* **2/1**[2]

3 shd **Newgate Lodge (IRE)**[19] 5467 2-8-12 JMurtagh 3 96
(M Halford, Ire) *hld up: sme prog whn checked 2 1/2f out: 7th 1 1/2f out: mod 3rd over 1f out: kpt on* **10/1**[3]

4 9 **Bon News (IRE)**[27] 5251 2-8-12 KJManning 7 71
(J S Bolger, Ire) *towards rr: kpt on to go remote 4th ins fnl f* **33/1**

5 3 **Wildwish (IRE)**[56] 4406 2-8-12 (b[1]) NGMcCullagh 10 62
(Enda Kelly, Ire) *s.i.s and hld up: hdwy 2f out: mod 3rd 1 1/2f out: sn no ex* **50/1**

6 1 ½ **Divine Night (IRE)**[20] 5437 2-8-12 WMLordan 1 58
(David Wachman, Ire) *trckd ldrs on stand's rail: 4th 1/2-way: sn rdn and no imp* **10/1**[3]

7 4 **Fly By Magic (IRE)**[20] 5437 2-8-12 FMBerry 5 47
(Patrick Carey, Ire) *trckd ldrs: 6th after 1/2-way: no ex fr 2f out* **20/1**

8 4 **Sweet Peak (IRE)**[18] 5489 2-8-12 80 (b) WSupple 9 36
(Eamon Tyrrell, Ire) *chsd ldrs to 1/2-way: no ex fr 2f out* **25/1**

9 9 **Zadalla**[22] 5392 2-8-12 PShanahan 6 10
(Andrew Oliver, Ire) *prom early: wkng whn bmpd 2 1/2f out: no ex* **50/1**

10 12 **Siobhans Pearl (IRE)**[24] 5330 2-8-12 77 RPCleary 13 —
(Miss Martina Anne Doran, Ire) *prom: rdn and wknd fr 1/2-way: trailing fr over 1f out* **33/1**

11 5 **Kissinthemoonlight**[22] 5394 2-8-12 91 (b) MJKinane 2 —
(John M Oxx, Ire) *led: rdn and hdd over 2f out: sn wknd: eased fnl f* **11/1**

12 13 **Mythical Echo (USA)**[21] 5408 2-8-12 90 (b[1]) DMGrant 4 —
(David Wachman, Ire) *chsd ldr in 2nd: rdn after 1/2-way: wknd fr over 2f out: trailing fnl f* **16/1**

1m 20.76s **Going Correction** +1.25s/f (Soft) **13** Ran SP% **128.6**
Speed ratings: 108,101,101,89,85 83,77,72,60,44 37,20
CSF £3.87 TOTE £2.20: £1.30, £1.50, £1.60; DF 3.80.
Owner Mrs W Whitehead **Bred** J F Tuthill **Trained** Friarstown, Co Kildare

FOCUS
The winner confirmed her recent impressive debut and looks a very bright prospect, although soft ground is thought important to her.

NOTEBOOK
Evening Time(IRE), who won by nine lengths on her debut at Fairyhouse last month, handled this tougher assignment in much the same manner and again trounced her rivals. Held up, she arrived full of running with her effort soon after halfway and was in front with over two to run. Soon ridden clear, she stayed on well and confirmed her ability to handle this type of testing ground. She is likely to be aimed at next year's Irish 1,000 Guineas. (op 5/4 tchd 6/4)
Theanna smart sort of maiden, had been beaten less than three lengths when fifth on soft ground in the Cheveley Park Stakes on her previous start. She was beaten further, which could be interpreted as a compliment to the winner of this race. She began her effort over 2f out and was soon second, but she was unable to make any impression on the winner from over 1f out. (op 7/4 tchd 9/4)
Newgate Lodge(IRE)dropping down in trip after her head win over 7f here last month, looked a bit unlucky not to have finished second. Held up, she ran into trouble as a couple of rivals weakened in front of her over 2f out. She kept plugging away and only just missed out on the runner-up spot.
Bon News(IRE), sixth over 7f on her debut at Galway last month, stayed on from behind over the last 2f without being in serious contention. She will appreciate going back up in distance. (op 25/1)

5851a JUDDMONTE BERESFORD STKS (GROUP 2) 1m

3:35 (3:35) 2-Y-O **£56,034** (£16,379; £7,758; £2,586)

RPR

1 **Eagle Mountain**[29] 5183 2-9-1 112 KFallon 3 117+
(A P O'Brien, Ire) *hld up: 5th 1/2-way: 4th and hdwy ent st: led under 2f out: sn rdn clr: eased cl home: v easily* **4/7**[1]

2 7 **Capital Exposure (USA)**[49] 4638 2-9-1 PJSmullen 5 103
(D K Weld, Ire) *trckd ldrs: 3rd 1/2-way: cl 4th and rdn 2f out: mod 3rd over 1f out: kpt on* **5/1**[2]

3 ¾ **Silent Waves (USA)**[67] 4037 2-9-1 JoeFanning 6 102
(M Johnston) *sn led: strly pressed st: hdd under 2f out: sn rdn and outpcd: no ex ins fnl f* **5/1**[2]

4 4 ½ **Malacara**[108] 2796 2-9-1 CO'Donoghue 1 93
(A P O'Brien, Ire) *prom: cl 2nd 1/2-way: chal ent st: wknd fr under 2f out* **14/1**[3]

5 10 **Right Or Wrong (IRE)**[17] 5499 2-9-1 DPMcDonogh 4 73
(Kevin Prendergast, Ire) *hld up: 6th 1/2-way: no imp st* **14/1**[3]

6 4 ½ **Mica's Island (IRE)**[20] 5439 2-9-1 87 WSupple 7 64
(Andrew Oliver, Ire) *2nd early: 4th 1/2-way: wknd ent st* **25/1**

7 12 **New World Order (IRE)**[19] 5466 2-9-1 FMBerry 2 40
(Declan Gillespie, Ire) *a in rr: trailing st: eased fnl f* **25/1**

1m 43.4s **Going Correction** +0.45s/f (Yiel) **7** Ran SP% **118.0**
Speed ratings: 111,104,103,98,88 84,72
CSF £4.24 TOTE £1.70: £1.20, £3.00; DF 4.90.
Owner Derrick Smith **Bred** London Thoroughbred Services L **Trained** Ballydoyle, Co Tipperary
■ A ninth victory in this event for Aidan O'Brien.

FOCUS
The winner was very impressive and could have been rated higher, but given the ground conditions a more prudent view has been taken.

NOTEBOOK
Eagle Mountain overpowered his rivals in the final quarter of a mile, and the manner of this performance suggests that he is well worth his place at the highest level. A maiden winner here in May, he had since gone on to underline his potential with second places in the Group 2 events won by Teofilo here and Vital Equine at York. This looked a gilt-edged opportunity for him to record his first Group success and he proved much too strong for the opposition. Stepping up to a mile for the first time, he was settled in fifth before creeping closer as the runners neared the straight. Approaching the two-furlong marker he was almost on terms with the pacesetting Silent Waves and he soon moved to the front. He wasted little time in opening up an unassailable lead and seemed to relish every yard of the trip. Aidan O'Brien pointed the way towards the Racing Post Trophy, run this year at Newbury, and Eagle Mountain should take plenty of beating. (op 4/7 tchd 4/6)
Capital Exposure(USA) was taking a marked step up in class from the Leopardstown maiden that he won in August and was also encountering very different ground conditions. He was unable to match the winner when that rival surged clear, but he stuck to his task well to win the battle for second. Quicker ground will show him off to best effect and he can be expected to improve from what was only his second run. He remains an interesting sort for next season.
Silent Waves(USA), a good winner of his first two starts, was having his first run since finishing a creditable fourth to Strategic Prince in the Vintage Stakes at Glorious Goodwood. He made the running and still looked to be going well enough turning in, but he was soon fighting a losing battle as Eagle Mountain moved past. (op 9/2)
Malacara was running for the first time since making a winning debut in a Tipperary maiden in June. He raced prominently but was unable to make any further impression from two furlongs out. He may well need quicker ground, but will have to improve if he is to make his presence felt at Stakes level.
Right Or Wrong(IRE) was taking a big step up in class from the Listowel maiden he won last month and was unable to land a telling blow.

5853a HACKETTS.IE IRISH CESAREWITCH (PREMIER H'CAP) 2m

4:35 (4:37) 3-Y-O+ **£22,448** (£6,586; £3,137; £1,068) **Stalls** Far side

RPR

1 **Iktitaf (IRE)**[166] 6332 5-8-8 80 (t) PJSmullen 1 87+
(Noel Meade, Ire) *hld up in tch: hdwy on inner appr st: 2nd under 2f out: led under 1f out: kpt on wl u.p: all out* **10/3**[1]

2 ½ **Majestic Concorde (IRE)**[59] 4313 3-7-13 87 SMGorey(5) 13 93+
(D K Weld, Ire) *trckd ldrs: 5th 1/2-way: 3rd into st: chal fr over 1f out: ev ch: no ex nr fin* **8/1**[3]

3 shd **Clara Allen (IRE)**[30] 5156 8-9-7 100 TMolloy(7) 11 106+
(John E Kiely, Ire) *hld up towards rr: hdwy on stand's side early st: cl 4th and chal over 1f out: ev ch: no ex cl home* **12/1**

4 2 ½ **Man On The Nile (IRE)**[21] 5413 6-8-10 82 DPMcDonogh 14 85+
(W P Mullins, Ire) *trckd ldrs in 6th: lost pl over 4f out: prog 2f out: 5th over 1f out: kpt on* **9/2**[2]

5 ¾ **Mrs Gillow (IRE)**[21] 5413 5-9-1 92 (b) DJMoran(5) 16 95
(J S Bolger, Ire) *settled 2nd: led ent st: rdn and strly pressed fr 2f out: hdd under 1f out: no ex* **16/1**

6 *3* **Antigua Bay (IRE)**[220] 1770 5-7-13 76 .... HelenKeohane(5) 4 — 76
(William Coleman O'Brien, Ire) *hld up: 7th and prog 4f out: 4th early st: no imp fr over 1f out: kpt on same pce* **100/1**

7 *4 ½* **Mudawin (IRE)**[30] 5153 5-9-9 95 .... JohnEgan 5 — 90
(Jane Chapple-Hyam) *led after 3f: hdd u.p ent st: no ex fr 1 1/2f out* **12/1**

8 *5* **Rhythm 'N' Blues (IRE)**[22] 5398 3-8-4 87 .... NGMcCullagh 8 — 77
(John M Oxx, Ire) *reluctant ldr: hdd after 3f: 5th 6f out: no ex early st* **12/1**

9 *5 ½* **Grand Revival (IRE)**[21] 5413 4-8-4 76 .... (b) WMLordan 10 — 61
(David P Myerscough, Ire) *hld up: 9th 4f out: no imp st* **14/1**

10 *nk* **Clearing The Water (IRE)**[21] 5413 4-9-2 88 .... KFallon 6 — 72
(W P Mullins, Ire) *mid-div on inner: no ex st* **10/1**

11 *nk* **Athlumney Lad (IRE)**[39] 4941 7-8-8 80 .... (b) MJKinane 9 — 64
(Noel Meade, Ire) *settled 3rd: 4th into st: wknd fr 2f out* **12/1**

12 *7* **Menwaal (FR)**[27] 5253 4-9-7 98 .... CPGeoghegan(5) 12 — 75
(Kevin Prendergast, Ire) *mid-div: 8th 1/2-way: 5th 4f out: wknd st* **20/1**

13 *3* **Pacolet (IRE)**[7] 5470 7-8-4 76 .... DMGrant 3 — 50
(Patrick J Flynn, Ire) *hld up: rdn 4f out: no ex st* **14/1**

14 *23* **Charlies First (IRE)**[19] 5470 6-8-3 80 .... OCasey(5) 2 — 31
(Peter Casey, Ire) *towards rr: prog on outer after 1/2-way: 6th appr st: no ex fr 2f out: virtually p.u fr over 1f out: t.o* **8/1**[3]

15 *nk* **Chimes At Midnight (USA)**[8] 5697 9-8-4 76 ....(b) FranciscoDaSilva 7 — 27
(Luke Comer, Ire) *hld up in rr: rdn and wknd over 4f out: t.o st* **100/1**

16 *dist* **Wilman (IRE)**[27] 5253 3-9-3 100 .... JMurtagh 15 — —
(M Halford, Ire) *mid-div: 7th 1/2-way: wknd and eased 4f out: completely t.o* **16/1**

3m 46.7s **Going Correction** +0.75s/f (Yiel)
WFA 3 from 4yo+ 11lb — **16** Ran SP% **135.2**
Speed ratings: 81,80,80,79,79 77,75,72,70,69 69,66,64,53,53 —
CSF £33.13 CT £312.40 TOTE £4.00: £1.70, £2.30, £4.40, £2.00; DF 119.10.
Owner Mrs P Sloan **Bred** Shadwell Estate Company Limited **Trained** Castletown, Co Meath

FOCUS
The form looks sound, the winner running to the level he showed in 2004, while the second and fourth are the types to rate higher.

NOTEBOOK
Iktitaf(IRE), on his first Flat start for nearly two years, produced a cracking effort to land this prize on his first run since winning a Grade 1 novice hurdle at Punchestown last April. Given a patient ride, he was still nearly last as the field approached the turn in, but he picked up well on the inner when asked to raise his effort. He scythed his way through the field to dispute the lead nearing the final furlong and kept on well in the closing stages to make sure of victory. He may run next in a conditions hurdle at Down Royal next month and will be aimed at the Champion Hurdle. (op 3/1)
Majestic Concorde(IRE) ran a superb race for a relatively inexperienced three-year-old. He was having only his fourth run of the season - he had already won twice this term - and was running from 6lb out of the handicap. He pushed the winner all the way and is a horse to look forward to for next year. He is certainly good enough to land a decent prize. (op 7/1)
Clara Allen(IRE), who had been performing creditably at Stakes level, was running off a 21lb higher mark than when winning this race last year and gave a good account of herself. She coped well with the testing ground, which probably wasn't in her favour, and launched a determined bid for the lead on the outside with over a furlong to run before being unable to do any more close home. (op 8/1)
Man On The Nile(IRE) did not enjoy the best of passages and lost a few places before the straight. He stayed on well from the rear from the turn in but could never quite reach the leaders. This represented a sound effort off a 22lb higher mark than when gaining his first Flat win in August. (op 4/1)
Mrs Gillow(IRE) ran second in this last year and posted another creditable effort. She had a brief spell in the lead at one stage in the straight before having to give best. A tough and consistent mare, she is a thorough credit to her connections.
Antigua Bay(IRE), who moved into the reckoning with over half a mile to run, didn't run at all badly and could be of interest at a lower level of competition next time.
Mudawin(IRE) set out to make all but he was fighting a losing battle from two furlongs out. He may need better ground.

5854a RATHBARRY STUD'S BARATHEA FINALE STKS (LISTED RACE) — 1m 4f
5:05 (5:11) 3-Y-O+ — **£24,693** (£7,244; £3,451; £1,175)

RPR

1 **Frank Sonata**[14] 5551 5-9-10 .... TPQueally 5 — 115
(M G Quinlan) *settled 3rd: led 5f out: rdn clr early st: strly pressed ins fnl f: kpt on wl u.p* **12/1**

2 *1* **Scorpion (IRE)**[371] 5651 4-9-7 120 .... KFallon 15 — 111+
(A P O'Brien, Ire) *hld up: 6th and hdwy appr st: 2nd over 1f out: chal and ev ch ins fnl f: drifted lft: kpt on u.p* **15/8**[1]

3 *7* **Kushnarenkovo**[19] 5465 3-8-11 97 .... PJSmullen 4 — 97
(A P O'Brien, Ire) *trckd ldrs in 4th: impr into cl 2nd appr st: rdn and outpcd 2f out: mod 3rd 1f out: kpt on* **20/1**

4 *¾* **Sacrosanct (IRE)**[19] 5465 3-8-11 94 .... CO'Donoghue 2 — 96
(A P O'Brien, Ire) *mid-div: prog into 6th 4f out: kpt on u.p st* **20/1**

5 *shd* **Nick's Nikita (IRE)**[29] 5194 3-8-11 100 .... JMurtagh 3 — 96
(M Halford, Ire) *hld up towards rr: prog into 8th appr st: 4th over 1f out: kpt on same pce* **12/1**

6 *1 ½* **Galatee (FR)**[144] 1785 3-9-2 111 .... KJManning 10 — 98
(J S Bolger, Ire) *trckd ldrs in 5th: 4th 4f out: rdn early st: kpt on same pce u.p fr over 1f out* **9/4**[2]

7 *½* **Kerdem (IRE)**[8] 5699 3-9-0 101 .... (b) MJKinane 1 — 96
(John M Oxx, Ire) *trckd ldrs: 5th 1/2-way: 3rd appr st: no imp fr 1 1/2f out: no ex fnl f* **7/1**[3]

8 *nk* **Rockall Blizzard (USA)**[22] 5396 3-9-3 106 .... (p) FMBerry 8 — 98
(Noel Meade, Ire) *mid-div: prog into 5th appr st: rdn 2f out: no ex fnl f* **12/1**

9 *21* **Arosa (IRE)**[27] 5253 3-8-11 95 .... NGMcCullagh 9 — 61
(David Wachman, Ire) *nvr a factor: trailing 2f out: eased fnl f* **25/1**

10 *11* **Zulu Queen (IRE)**[40] 4917 3-8-11 90 .... (t) DMGrant 12 — 44
(David Wachman, Ire) *settled 6th: wknd over 4f out: trailing st: eased over 1f out* **20/1**

11 *6* **Magicalmysterytour (IRE)**[67] 4039 3-9-0 90 .... DavidMcCabe 6 — 38
(A P O'Brien, Ire) *led: hdd 5f out: wknd bef st: trailing whn eased over 1f out* **20/1**

12 *1 ½* **Yellow Ridge (IRE)**[7] 5708 3-9-0 75 .... FranciscoDaSilva 13 — 36
(Luke Comer, Ire) *a bhd: rdn and lost tch over 4f out: trailing st* **100/1**

13 *½* **Talwin (IRE)**[16] 5517 3-8-11 96 .... DPMcDonogh 11 — 32
(Kevin Prendergast, Ire) *nvr a factor: trailing st: eased over 1f out* **14/1**

14 *7* **Still Going On**[32] 5121 9-9-7 57 .... (b) CPGeoghegan 14 — 25
(Miss Martina Anne Doran, Ire) *nvr a factor: trailing st: eased over 1f out* **100/1**

15 *8* **Changeable**[350] 6056 4-9-4 95 .... WMLordan 7 — 10
(T Stack, Ire) *cl 2nd: wknd under 5f out: trailing st: eased* **20/1**

2m 44.2s **Going Correction** +0.75s/f (Yiel)
WFA 3 from 4yo+ 7lb — **15** Ran SP% **137.4**
Speed ratings: 112,111,106,106,106 105,104,104,90,83 79,78,77,73,67
CSF £35.92 TOTE £12.40: £2.00, £1.60, £12.90; DF 41.80.
Owner W P Flynn **Bred** Bishop Wilton Stud **Trained** Newmarket, Suffolk

FOCUS
A decent Listed race, rated through the fourth, with the winner running up to his best.

NOTEBOOK
Frank Sonata produced a career best to defeat this useful field. He had failed to make an impression in the Irish St Leger here last month but benefited from being ridden much handier. Making his bid for the lead nearing the entrance to the straight, he soon opened up a useful lead. He was strongly pressed by Scorpion in the closing stages, but ran on well to hang on for the third Listed victory of his career. He now has the option of going for either the Prix Royal-Oak or the St Simon Stakes at Newbury later this month. (op 10/1)
Scorpion(IRE), returning to action after fracturing a hind pastern, thrilled connections with his first run since last year's Arc on ground that would not show him to best effect. Settled towards the rear, he made good progress inside the final half mile and ran on well under pressure to challenge Frank Sonata, but his lack of a recent outing probably told against him in the closing stages. He can be expected to improve considerably for this and will be a very interesting contender wherever he goes next. (op 11/8 tchd 9/4)
Kushnarenkovo coped well with conditions and ran a good race. She already has a Group 3 placing to her name but this was probably a more meritorious effort. She will be of interest at Listed level over the remainder of the season.
Sacrosanct(IRE) didn't run at all badly. She has struggled to make her presence felt at Stakes level, but this run suggested that she might gain a valuable black type placing before the end of the year.
Nick's Nikita(IRE) was stepping up from handicap company and turned in a creditable effort but could be worth trying back over ten furlongs.
Galatee(FR) was beaten for the first time in her career. She started off this season in terrific style with three consecutive victories but was running here for the first time since May, having been suffering from an abnormal white blood cell count which kept her out of the Oaks. She can be expected to improve significantly for this run and will be of considerable interest if running again this season. (op 9/4 tchd 7/4)
Kerdem(IRE) was taking a big step up in class from the handicap he won at Fairyhouse recently and he wasn't disgraced, gradually fading over the final couple of furlongs. (op 8/1)

5855 - (Foreign Racing) - See Raceform Interactive

4649 DUSSELDORF (R-H)
Sunday, October 8

OFFICIAL GOING: Soft

5856a GROSSER PREIS DER LANDESHAUPTSTADT DUSSELDORF (GROUP 3) — 1m 100y
3:40 (3:48) 3-Y-O+ — **£22,069** (£8,966; £4,483; £2,414)

RPR

1 **Wiesenpfad (FR)** 3-8-8 .... ASuborics 1 — 105
(W Hickst, Germany) *held up, headway towards inside to lead inside final f, ran on well, easily* **19/10**[1]

2 *4 ½* **Mharadono (GER)**[64] 3-8-8 .... WPanov 2 — 96
(P Hirschberger, Germany) *raced in 2nd, brought widest of all to race against stands rail in straight, stayed on to take 2nd close home* **43/1**

3 *¾* **Apollo Star (GER)**[21] 4-9-0 .... J-PCarvalho 5 — 98
(Mario Hofer, Germany) *led and soon clear, 5 length clear entering straight, headed inside final f, lost 2nd close home* **98/10**

4 *½* **Lucidor (GER)**[85] 3563 3-8-8 .... VSchulepov 8 — 94
(Frau E Mader, Germany) *held up, stayed on steadily final 2f to take 4th on line* **96/10**

5 *shd* **Blueberry Forest (IRE)**[217] 8-9-0 .... EFrank 3 — 96
(P Hirschberger, Germany) *held up, stayed on at one pace final 2f* **32/1**

6 *4* **Mannico (GER)**[15] 5543 3-8-8 .... PHeugl 4 — 85
(Mario Hofer, Germany) *raced in 4th, ridden and beaten 2f out* **82/10**

7 *1 ½* **Austriaco (GER)**[56] 4418 4-9-0 .... WMongil 7 — 85
(R Suerland, Germany) *raced in 3rd, taken to outside and ridden entering straight, little response* **7/2**[3]

8 *¾* **Santiago (GER)**[63] 4190 4-9-0 .... ABoschert 6 — 84
(U Ostmann, Germany) *midfield, 6th straight, some headway 1 1/2f out, weakened inside final f* **23/10**[2]

9 *4 ½* **Glad To Be Fast (IRE)**[220] 563 6-9-0 .... (b) JPalik 10 — 75
(Mario Hofer, Germany) *never a factor* **15/1**

10 *2 ½* **Genios (GER)**[43] 4828 5-9-0 .... ABest 9 — 70
(Dr A Bolte, Germany) *never a factor* **25/1**

1m 47.41s
WFA 3 from 4yo+ 3lb — **10** Ran SP% **132.0**
(including 10 Euro stake): WIN 29; PL 19, 70, 28; SF 851.
Owner Frau Heide Harzheim **Bred** Gestut Ravensberg **Trained** Germany

5414 FRANKFURT (L-H)
Sunday, October 8

OFFICIAL GOING: Soft

5857a STUTENPREIS DER MEHL-MULHENS-STIFTUNG (GROUP 3) (F&M) — 1m 2f 165y
3:55 (3:59) 3-Y-O+ — **£22,069** (£8,966; £4,483; £2,414)

RPR

1 **La Dancia (IRE)**[37] 5008 3-8-10 .... TMundry 2 — 108
(P Rau, Germany) *raced in 2nd, led narrowly 2f out, ridden clear inside final f* **19/10**[2]

2 *1 ¾* **Nordtanzerin (GER)**[21] 5414 3-8-10 .... FilipMinarik 6 — 105
(P Schiergen, Germany) *led til headed narrowly 2f out, still every chance til no extra inside final f* **7/10**[1]

3 *2 ½* **Wellola (IRE)**[110] 4-9-4 .... THellier 3 — 103
(H Blume, Germany) *held up in rear, stayed on at one pace to take 3rd over 1f out* **19/2**

4 *3 ½* **Spatzolita (GER)**[43] 4828 7-9-4 .... (b) AHelfenbein 5 — 96
(D K Richardson, Germany) *held up, ridden and beaten over 1 1/2f out* **98/10**

5 *3* **Smart Move (GER)**[49] 4648 4-9-4 .... JVictoire 4 — 91
(H Blume, Germany) *held up, dropped to last and lost touch 4f out, modest late headway to take 5th close home* **135/10**

The Form Book, Raceform Ltd, Compton, RG20 6NL

6 *nk* **Dame Hester (IRE)**[29] 5197 3-8-10 .... RichardMullen 1 88
(E J O'Neill) *raced in 3rd, ridden over 2f out, soon weakened* **68/10**[3]

2m 24.95s
WFA 3 from 4yo+ 6lb **6** Ran SP% **131.8**
(including 10 Euro stake): WIN 29; PL 12, 11; SF 50.
Owner Gestut Brummerhof **Bred** Gestut Brummerhof **Trained** Germany

NOTEBOOK
Dame Hester(IRE) was ill at ease on the testing ground and dropped away quickly in the final quarter mile.

5771 SAN SIRO (R-H)
Sunday, October 8

OFFICIAL GOING: Good to soft

5858a PREMIO DORMELLO (GROUP 3) (FILLIES) 1m
4:00 (4:02) 2-Y-O **£51,703** (£25,148; £14,421; £7,210)

RPR

1 **Scoubidou (GER)** 2-8-11 .... ADeVries 2 100
(H Blume, Germany) *first to show, settled in 3rd, headway on inside 2f out, led approaching final f, ridden out* **15/2**

2 *¾* **Donoma (IRE)** 2-8-11 .... EBotti 11 99
(A Botti, Italy) *soon led, headed approaching final f, ran on* **56/10**

3 *snk* **Carolines Secret** 2-8-11 .... AStarke 3 98
(Mario Hofer, Germany) *in rear to straight, headway on inside over 3f out, 4th 2f out, stayed on steadily* **49/10**[2]

4 *6 ½* **Big Bertha (GER)**[63] 2-8-11 .... IMendizabal 12 83
(A Wohler, Germany) *behind til headway 2f out on outside, stayed on, nearest finish* **5/1**[3]

5 *1* **Love Profusion (USA)**[133] 2062 2-8-11 .... GMarcelli 7 81
(L Riccardi, Italy) *always in touch, 5th straight, 4th over 2f out, one pace* **77/1**

6 *¾* **Paint In Green (IRE)** 2-8-11 .... MMonteriso 6 79
(A Botti, Italy) *played up in stalls, never nearer than midfield* **59/10**

7 *1* **Troppo Bello (IRE)** 2-8-11 .... CFiocchi 14 77
(L Polito, Italy) *midfield, effort on outside 3f out, soon one pace* **107/10**

8 *2 ¼* **Loa Loa (GER)** 2-8-11 .... EPedroza 8 72
(A Wohler, Germany) *close up on outside til weakened over 2f out* **31/10**[1]

9 *nse* **Muccia (IRE)**[88] 3428 2-8-11 .... OPeslier 1 72
(G Miliani, Italy) *prominent, 6th straight, weakened 2f out* **51/10**

10 *1* **Iuturna (USA)**[91] 3343 2-8-11 .... LManiezzi 13 69
(R Menichetti, Italy) *2nd straight, weakened 2f out* **22/1**

11 *11* **Mimetico (IRE)** 2-8-11 .... PConvertino 5 44
(B Grizzetti, Italy) *always in rear* **27/1**

12 *½* **Sweet Wind Music**[91] 3343 2-8-11 .... DVargiu 10 43
(B Grizzetti, Italy) *prominent, 4th straight, soon beaten* **51/10**

13 *¾* **She Cat (IRE)** 2-8-11 .... MEsposito 15 41
(V Caruso, Italy) *always behind* **28/1**

14 *9* **Susi Applause** 2-8-11 .... SMulas 4 21
(B Grizzetti, Italy) *started slowly, always behind, tailed off final 2f* **27/1**

1m 42.8s **14** Ran SP% **157.0**
(including 1 Euro stake): WIN 8.50; PL 2.82, 2.46, 2.29; DF 47.54.
Owner Stall Schwindelfrei **Bred** Thomas Schaffer **Trained** Germany

5631 AYR (L-H)
Monday, October 9

OFFICIAL GOING: Heavy
After two wet nights the ground was described as 'very heavy especially on the round course'.
Wind: moderate, half against Weather: Fine

5859 NORTH AYRSHIRE SCHOOLS BUILD PROJECT E B F MAIDEN FILLIES' STKS 1m
2:10 (2:10) (Class 4) 2-Y-O **£5,181** (£1,541; £770; £384) **Stalls** Low

Form RPR

04 1 **Fashion Statement**[34] 5083 2-9-0 .... RobertWinston 7 81+
(M A Jarvis) *trckd ldr: led 2f out: drew wl clr fnl f* **15/8**[1]

0 2 *8* **Peintre's Wonder (IRE)**[34] 5083 2-9-0 .... PaulHanagan 3 65
(E J O'Neill) *trckd ldrs: hung lft and kpt on to take modest 2nd last 100yds* **16/1**

306 3 *2* **Naughty Thoughts (IRE)**[17] 5503 2-9-0 73............ CatherineGannon 1 61
(K A Ryan) *hld up in tch: effrt over 3f out: wnt 2nd appr fnl f: one pce* **9/2**[2]

03 4 *7* **Feolin**[24] 5352 2-9-0 .... MickyFenton 4 47
(H Morrison) *led: hdd 2f out: wknd appr fnl f* **15/8**[1]

05 5 *1* **Crosby Millie**[16] 5527 2-9-0 .... PhillipMakin 5 45
(J R Weymes) *sn trcking ldrs: drvn over 3f out: lost pl over 1f out* **33/1**

6 *12* **Voss** 2-9-0 .... J-PGuillambert 6 21
(M Johnston) *sn trcking ldrs: pushed along over 3f out: wknd 2f out: eased* **17/2**[3]

7 *65* **Never Cross (IRE)** 2-9-0 .... TomEaves 2 —
(B Storey) *s.i.s: sn pushed along and in rr: t.o 3f out: btn 65 l* **66/1**

1m 53.03s (9.54) **Going Correction** +1.125s/f (Soft) **7** Ran SP% **108.6**
Speed ratings (Par 94):97,89,87,80,79 67,2
CSF £31.74 TOTE £2.60: £2.00, £7.60; EX 27.00.
Owner P D Savill **Bred** P D Savill **Trained** Newmarket, Suffolk

FOCUS
A weak maiden fillies' race and in the end the winner saw it out much the best in the desperate ground.

NOTEBOOK
Fashion Statement, easily the strongest filly in the paddock, made light of the desperate ground and her stamina saw her pull a long way clear. She should make an even better three-year-old. (op 13-8 tchd 2-1)
Peintre's Wonder(IRE), loaded with the help of a blanket, is on the leg and narrow. She had finished half-a-dozen lengths behind the winner when she made her debut at Leicester five weeks earlier and hopefully she will strengthen over the winter.
Naughty Thoughts(IRE), having her fourth outing, did not see out the mile anywhere near as well as the first two. (op 5-1 tchd 11-2)
Feolin, nothing to look at, took them along but she fell in a heap coming to the final furlong. (tchd 2-1, 9-4 in places)
Crosby Millie, loaded with a blanket, is a very weak looking type who should be seen to better advantage in handicap company next year.

5860 JOE CARR MEMORIAL NURSERY 6f
2:40 (2:41) (Class 5) (0-75,74) 2-Y-O **£3,886** (£1,156; £577; £288) **Stalls** Centre

Form RPR

4651 1 **Tipsy Prince**[6] 5747 2-9-1 68 6ex............................ J-PGuillambert 10 72
(Mrs G S Rees) *hld up: hdwy over 2f out: swtchd lft over 1f out: led ins last: r.o wl* **7/2**[1]

550 2 *1 ¾* **Ocean Of Champagne**[80] 3713 2-8-3 56............(v[1]) SilvestreDeSousa 8 55
(A Dickman) *chsd ldrs towards stands' side: kpt on to take 2nd nr fin* **20/1**

5000 3 *hd* **Sweet Candy**[17] 5503 2-8-12 65............................ CatherineGannon 7 63
(K A Ryan) *led towards centre: hdd and no ex ins last* **8/1**

531 4 *2 ½* **Davaye**[46] 4727 2-9-1 68............................ LeeEnstone 11 59
(K R Burke) *swtchd rt after s: chsd ldrs: kpt on wl ins last* **8/1**

000 5 *2 ½* **Soviet Sound (IRE)**[56] 4421 2-8-0 53............................ PaulHanagan 9 36
(Jedd O'Keeffe) *chsd ldrs: hung rt over 1f out: kpt on same pce* **11/1**

0040 6 *6* **Cryptic Clue (USA)**[19] 5482 2-8-3 56 ow1............... AdrianTNicholls 4 21
(D W Chapman) *in rr: kpt on fnl 2f: nvr a threat* **25/1**

1600 7 *1* **Merry Moon (IRE)**[6] 5747 2-8-5 58............................ DaleGibson 12 20
(M Dods) *swtchd rt after s: racd stands' side: w ldrs: wknd fnl f* **15/2**[3]

5552 8 *2* **Muncaster Castle (IRE)**[46] 4724 2-7-12 56............ DuranFentiman[(5)] 6 12
(R F Fisher) *in tch: rdn over 2f out: wknd over 1f out* **8/1**

6333 9 *½* **Howards Tipple**[55] 4452 2-9-7 74............................ TomEaves 2 29
(I Semple) *swtchd lft after s: prom on outside: wknd over 1f out* **6/1**[2]

0004 10 *½* **Homes By Woodford**[26] 5282 2-7-9 55............................ AdeleRothery[(7)] 13 8
(M W Easterby) *hld up in rr: hdwy over 2f out: nvr a factor* **25/1**

0540 11 *15* **Perilore (IRE)**[46] 4724 2-7-5 51 oh16............................ CharlotteKerton[(7)] 3 —
(A Berry) *dwlt: racd on outer: hung lft and bhd fnl 2f: eased* **200/1**

3564 12 *14* **Lovers Kiss**[90] 3380 2-7-8 54 oh4 ow3............................ LanceBetts[(7)] 5 —
(N Wilson) *chsd ldrs: lost pl over 2f out: sn bhd: eased* **40/1**

0643 13 *¾* **The Italian Job**[28] 5238 2-8-6 59............................ PaulMulrennan 1 —
(T D Easterby) *swtchd lft after s: prom on outer: lost pl over 2f out: sn bhd and eased* **11/1**

1m 22.06s (8.39) **Going Correction** +1.05s/f (Soft) **13** Ran SP% **113.7**
Speed ratings (Par 95):86,83,83,80,76 68,67,64,64,63 43,24,23
CSF £79.66 CT £520.76 TOTE £4.00: £1.60, £5.70, £3.70; EX 60.40.
Owner Mrs G S Rees **Bred** Capt J H Wilson **Trained** Sollom, Lancs

FOCUS
A moderate winning time for a race like this, but the winner proved tough under pressure and the form seems sound enough for the grade.

NOTEBOOK
Tipsy Prince was again fitted with ear plugs but one came out during the race. In no hurry to join issue, in the end he made light of his penalty. Now he has learnt to settle he is progressing at a rate of knots. (op 9-4)
Ocean Of Champagne, sporting a visor for the first time, seemed unfazed by the testing conditions and claimed second spot almost on the line. (op 16-1)
Sweet Candy, 3lb below her Wolverhampton winning mark, showed bags of toe to take them along. She was swept aside by the winner then lost second spot near the line. All toe, Polytrack might prove the answer again. (op 10-1)
Davaye, back after a six weeks off, went to race down the stands' side rail. It was a disadvantage and she deserves credit for the way she stuck to her task.
Soviet Sound(IRE), easily the biggest and strongest in the line-up, was a lively order on the morning line on his handicap debut. The lack of a recent outing may not have been in his favour. (op 9-1)
Merry Moon(IRE) was switched to race hard against the stands' side rail and that was almost certainly a disadvantage. (op 8-1 tchd 9-1)

5861 BETTY BURNS H'CAP 7f 50y
3:15 (3:15) (Class 5) (0-70,70) 3-Y-O+ **£3,238** (£963; £481; £240) **Stalls** Far side

Form RPR

0400 1 **Amy Louise (IRE)**[25] 5317 3-8-13 65............................ RobertWinston 7 75
(T D Barron) *mid-divsion: hdwy over 2f out: styd on to ld towards fin* **25/1**

4001 2 *¾* **Scotland The Brave**[11] 5636 6-9-2 66....................(v) GrahamGibbons 13 74
(J D Bethell) *led: hdd and no ex wl ins last* **4/1**[1]

6022 3 *3* **Petross**[11] 5637 3-8-3 60............................ MichaelJStainton[(5)] 4 60
(R M Whitaker) *trckd ldrs: t.k.h: stmbld over 3f out: styd on ins last: tk 3rd nr line* **5/1**[3]

0406 4 *shd* **Bold Marc (IRE)**[23] 5384 4-9-3 67............................ LeeEnstone 5 67
(K R Burke) *chsd ldrs: kpt on same pce appr fnl f* **16/1**

0000 5 *¾* **Bellsbank (IRE)**[60] 4296 3-8-7 59............................ SilvestreDeSousa 3 57
(A Bailey) *chsd ldrs: kpt on same pce fnl 2f* **16/1**

4150 6 *1 ½* **California Laws**[12] 5617 4-9-3 67............................ PaulHanagan 12 61
(T D Barron) *prom: effrt over 2f out: kpt on same pce* **9/2**[2]

0220 7 *7* **Mystical Ayr (IRE)**[11] 5636 4-8-5 58............................ AndrewMullen[(3)] 2 34
(Miss L A Perratt) *in rr: hdwy over 3f out: lost pl over 1f out* **10/1**

2435 8 *4* **Flylowflylong (IRE)**[22] 5401 3-8-13 65............................ TomEaves 6 30
(I Semple) *chsd ldrs: drvn over 2f out: wknd over 1f out* **16/1**

0600 9 *1* **Top Dirham**[12] 5617 8-8-12 62............................ DaleGibson 9 25
(M W Easterby) *hld up in rr: nvr a factor* **33/1**

5620 10 *hd* **Zhitomir**[11] 5635 8-8-13 63............................ PhillipMakin 14 25
(M Dods) *trckd ldrs: c stands' side over 3f out: sn btn* **12/1**

11 *9* **Richelieu**[9] 5693 4-9-6 70............................ RMBurke 10 9
(J J Lambe, Ire) *mid-divsion: effrt over 2f out: sn wknd* **33/1**

5606 12 *1* **Zarabad (IRE)**[25] 5320 4-9-4 68............................ PaulMulrennan 1 4
(K R Burke) *chsd ldrs: lost pl over 1f out* **18/1**

4110 13 *1 ¼* **Scuba (IRE)**[13] 5593 4-9-3 67............................(b) MickyFenton 11 —
(H Morrison) *rr-div: hdwy and c wd over 2f: hung bdly lft and sn lost pl* **14/1**

0120 14 *18* **Onlytime Will Tell**[135] 2020 8-9-5 69............................ AdrianTNicholls 8 —
(D Nicholls) *hld up in rr: detached 3f out: sn t.o* **16/1**

1m 40.1s (8.28) **Going Correction** +1.125s/f (Soft) **14** Ran SP% **116.8**
WFA 3 from 4yo+ 2lb
Speed ratings (Par 103):102,101,97,97,96 95,87,82,81,81 70,69,68,47
CSF £117.44 CT £608.01 TOTE £27.30: £6.30, £2.00, £1.70; EX 160.60.
Owner P D Savill **Bred** P D Savill **Trained** Maunby, N Yorks

FOCUS
The stalls could not be used and this was a flip start resulting in a hand time. The form is modest rated through the runner-up.

5862 RACING UK AND SETANTA FOR £15 CLAIMING STKS 1m 1f 20y
3:45 (3:46) (Class 5) 3-Y-O **£3,238** (£963; £481; £240) **Stalls** Low

Form RPR

6664 1 **Norman Beckett**[22] 5403 3-9-0 64............................(v[1]) TomEaves 8 71
(I Semple) *hdwy to ld after 1f: edgd lft and clr over 1f out: drvn rt out* **4/1**[3]

006 **2** *5* **Stolen Glance**[63] 4197 3-8-12 66.................................. PaulMulrennan 6 59
(M W Easterby) *in rr: drvn along 6f out: rdn to go 2nd 3f out: kpt on: no real imp* **5/2**[1]

0-33 **3** *12* **Abeurbe Condita (IRE)**[32] 5138 3-9-0 63................. GrahamGibbons 4 37
(E S McMahon) *trckd ldrs: effrt 3f out: one pce* **11/4**[2]

030 **4** *1 ½* **Hill Of Almhuim (IRE)**[9] 5683 3-9-0 57.......................(v) PaulHanagan 7 34
(K R Burke) *chsd ldrs: one pce fnl 2f* **11/2**

6546 **5** *6* **Bolckow**[9] 5683 3-8-9 52... AndrewMullen(3) 2 20
(K A Ryan) *hld up in rr: hdwy over 4f out: one pce fnl 3f* **15/2**

0044 **6** *1 ¼* **Dancing Flame**[17] 5510 3-8-9 52................................ AdrianTNicholls 5 15
(E J Alston) *led 1f: chsd ldrs: wknd over 1f out* **12/1**

6-00 **7** *21* **Seallarain**[65] 4136 3-8-1 35 ow3............................... KevinGhunowa(5) 10 —
(A Berry) *mid-div: lost pl over 4f out: sn bhd* **150/1**

0-00 **8** *12* **Crystal Bay (IRE)**[144] 1791 3-7-11 30.......................... DuranFentiman(5) 9 —
(A Berry) *in rr: sn pushed along: detached over 3f out: sn t.o* **200/1**

-500 **9** *21* **Lord Adonis (IRE)**[143] 1826 3-9-3 50...........................(t) MickyFenton 3 —
(K J Burke) *in rr: sn drvn along: detached over 3f out: sn t.o: virtually p.u* **40/1**

2m 8.97s (8.97) **Going Correction** +1.125s/f (Soft) **9** Ran SP% **113.7**
Speed ratings (Par 101):105,100,89,88,83 82,63,52,34
CSF £14.20 TOTE £5.50: £1.90, £1.40, £1.40; EX 15.40.The winner was claimed by Michael Mullineaux for £12,000
Owner Robert Reid **Bred** Mike Channon Bloodstock Ltd **Trained** Carluke, S Lanarks
FOCUS
Poor fare and a race in which few figured with a chance. It is probable that only the winner showed his form.

5863 DAILY RECORD H'CAP 1m 1f 20y
4:20 (4:20) (Class 4) (0-85,76) 3-Y-0+ **£6,477** (£1,927; £963; £481) **Stalls** Low

Form RPR

1640 **1** **Chief Scout**[14] 5579 4-9-7 75.. TomEaves 4 84
(I Semple) *sn drvn along: sn in rr: hdwy over 3f out: led over 1f out: kpt on wl* **15/2**

4 **2** *5* **Auenmoon (GER)**[141] 1864 5-9-6 74........................... RobertWinston 9 73
(P Monteith) *trckd ldrs: led after 2f: hdd over 1f out: no ex* **6/1**[2]

00 **3** *5* **Little Bob**[136] 1987 5-8-11 65......................................(b) GrahamGibbons 6 54
(J D Bethell) *chsd ldrs: chal over 1f out: one pce* **17/2**

0 **4** *1 ¾* **King's Jester (IRE)**[47] 3062 4-9-8 76................................... RMBurke 2 62
(J J Lambe, Ire) *hld up in rr: stdy hdwy 3f out: rdn over 1f out: one pce* **33/1**

6004 **5** *1* **Northern Boy (USA)**[22] 5406 3-9-3 75............................ PhillipMakin 1 59
(T D Barron) *led 1f: t.k.h: trckd ldrs: wknd appr fnl f* **8/1**

415 **6** *shd* **Pab Special (IRE)**[26] 5301 3-8-12 70........................... PaulMulrennan 8 53
(K R Burke) *led after 1f: hdd after 2f: chsd ldrs: one pce appr fnl f* **12/1**

630- **7** *½* **Ace Baby**[497] 2127 3-8-12 70.................................... CatherineGannon 10 52
(K J Burke) *w ldrs on outer: wknd over 1f out* **125/1**

650 **8** *1* **The Osteopath (IRE)**[44] 4802 3-9-2 74.......................(p) PaulHanagan 7 54
(M Dods) *trckd ldrs: effrt 3f out: wknd fnl f* **4/1**[1]

1-46 **9** *3* **Dispol Foxtrot**[12] 5619 8-9-1 69.................................. AdrianTNicholls 3 43
(D Nicholls) *s.i.s: hdwy on outer 7f out: sn chsng ldrs: c wd over 3f out: lost pl over 2f out* **7/1**[3]

4401 **10** *8* **Hawkit (USA)**[25] 5311 5-9-2 70... MickyFenton 5 28
(P Monteith) *t.k.h in rr: c v wd over 3f out: wknd over 2f out: eased* **4/1**[1]

2m 10.59s (10.59) **Going Correction** +1.125s/f (Soft)
WFA 3 from 4yo+ 4lb **10** Ran SP% **111.6**
Speed ratings (Par 105):97,92,88,86,85 85,85,84,81,74
CSF £49.67 CT £383.11 TOTE £9.70: £3.50, £2.20, £2.60; EX 70.00.
Owner Black & White Communication (Scotland) L **Bred** J R And Mrs P Good **Trained** Carluke, S Lanarks
FOCUS
The field fanned out across the track in the last couple of furlongs. The race has been rated through the winner and the second in line with his jumps form, but it is doubtful whether the form will prove reliable.
Hawkit(USA) Official explanation: jockey said gelding had a breathing problem

5864 SUBSCRIBE TO RACING UK ON 08700 506949 H'CAP 5f
4:50 (4:53) (Class 5) (0-70,70) 3-Y-0 **£3,238** (£963; £481; £240) **Stalls** Centre

Form RPR

2140 **1** **Tender Process (IRE)**[26] 5286 3-9-4 70......................... PaulHanagan 6 84+
(E S McMahon) *hld up: hdwy over 2f out: edgd lft ins last: led towards fin* **7/2**[2]

0121 **2** *½* **How's She Cuttin' (IRE)**[1] 5834 3-8-4 56......................... DaleGibson 5 69
(T D Barron) *led: rdn and edgd rt ins last: hdd and no ex last 50yds* **11/4**[1]

2050 **3** *4* **The History Man (IRE)**[22] 5401 3-9-1 67..................(b) PaulMulrennan 1 66
(M W Easterby) *w ldr: kpt on same pce appr fnl f* **7/1**[3]

0103 **4** *3* **Highland Song (IRE)**[30] 5181 3-8-11 68.............. KevinGhunowa(5) 7 57
(R F Fisher) *w ldrs: kpt on same pce appr fnl f* **10/1**

2234 **5** *hd* **Newkeylets**[11] 5631 3-8-1 56 oh1...........................(p) AndrewMullen(3) 4 44
(I Semple) *dwlt: sn chsng ldrs: one pce fnl 2f* **7/1**[3]

5350 **6** *3 ½* **Amber Glory**[163] 1279 3-8-10 62................................ CatherineGannon 8 38
(K A Ryan) *w ldrs: wknd over 1f out* **28/1**

541 **7** *hd* **Signor Whippee**[35] 5060 3-8-6 58 oh1 ow2..............(b) TonyHamilton 10 34
(A Berry) *w ldrs: lost pl over 1f out* **16/1**

5036 **8** *1 ¼* **Lambency (IRE)**[22] 5401 3-7-13 56 oh1................. DuranFentiman(5) 13 27
(J S Goldie) *s.i.s: outpcd and in rr: kpt on fnl 2f: nvr a factor* **16/1**

0300 **9** *1 ¾* **Sweetly Sharp (IRE)**[59] 4324 3-7-11 56 oh16....... CharlotteKerton(7) 11 21
(A Berry) *mid-div: hung lft over 2f out: sn lost pl* **100/1**

6000 **10** *5* **Pensata**[25] 5309 3-8-4 56 oh21.................................(b) SilvestreDeSousa 3 4
(Miss L A Perratt) *sn outpcd and in rr* **100/1**

64.93 secs (4.49) **Going Correction** +1.05s/f (Soft) **10** Ran SP% **100.2**
Speed ratings (Par 101):106,105,98,94,93 88,87,85,82,74
CSF £10.02 CT £36.84 TOTE £4.20: £1.60, £1.50, £2.00; EX 13.50.
Owner J J Staunton **Bred** Timothy Coughlan **Trained** Hopwas, Staffs
■ Hotham was withdrawn (5/1, refused to enter stalls). R4 applies, deduct 15p in the £.
FOCUS
Little solid form to go on on in this race, but the first two have been rated positively, with the winner unexposed and runner-up progressing.

5865 DAWN HOMES H'CAP 6f
5:20 (5:24) (Class 6) (0-62,62) 3-Y-0+ **£2,590** (£770; £385; £192) **Stalls** Centre

Form RPR

5010 **1** **George The Best (IRE)**[11] 5635 5-8-12 58.................. PaulHanagan 4 69
(Micky Hammond) *racd far side: w ldrs: led over 1f out: edgd rt ins last: hld on* **12/1**

6513 **2** *hd* **Compton Classic**[1] 5834 4-8-6 52............................. DanielTudhope 9 62
(J S Goldie) *hld up: hdwy over 2f out: chal ins last: no ex nr fin* **6/1**[1]

0040 **3** *1 ½* **Dispol Isle (IRE)**[12] 5619 4-8-7 60.................................. NeilBrown(7) 23 66
(T D Barron) *mid-div: hdwy over 2f out: kpt on same pce ins last* **10/1**

4 *2 ½* **Controvento (IRE)**[39] 4976 4-8-5 51 oh5..............(b) CatherineGannon 3 49
(Eamon Tyrrell, Ire) *w ldrs far side: led after 2f: hung bdly rt 2f out: sn hdd: ended up alone stands' side: kpt on fnl f* **20/1**

-U26 **5** *2* **Harrys House**[9] 5684 4-9-2 62.................................(p) GrahamGibbons 12 54
(J J Quinn) *racd far side: chal over 1f out: fdd jst ins last* **9/1**[3]

0066 **6** *1 ¾* **Champagne Cracker**[96] 3190 5-9-0 60........................ TonyHamilton 15 47
(I Semple) *t.k.h: hdwy over 2f out: kpt on fnl f* **25/1**

/0-0 **7** *shd* **Toberogan (IRE)**[44] 4823 5-8-8 54.................................. MickyFenton 10 41
(W A Murphy, Ire) *sn in rr: hdwy 2f out: styd on ins last* **9/1**[3]

436 **8** *¾* **Harrington Bates**[11] 5631 5-8-0 51 oh4............(v) NataliaGemelova(5) 18 36
(R M Whitaker) *chsd ldrs: one pce fnl 2f* **14/1**

0546 **9** *hd* **Piccolo Prince**[47] 4694 5-8-9 55................................ AdrianTNicholls 13 39
(E J Alston) *in rr: hdwy 2f out: kpt on ins last* **9/1**[3]

2000 **10** *2 ½* **Oeuf A La Neige**[11] 5631 6-8-5 51 oh1.................. SilvestreDeSousa 11 28
(Miss L A Perratt) *chsd ldrs: one pce fnl 2f* **12/1**

3260 **11** *1 ½* **Throw The Dice**[26] 5286 4-8-11 62...........................(p) MarkLawson(5) 21 34
(D W Barker) *chsd ldrs towards stands' side: edgd lft 2f out: one pce* **8/1**[2]

0300 **12** *nk* **Straffan (IRE)**[18] 5493 4-8-5 51 oh6................................(p) DaleGibson 1 22
(J Hetherton) *racd far side: led 2f: wknd over 1f out* **66/1**

0000 **13** *1* **Hout Bay**[9] 5684 9-8-0 51 oh4.................................(b) DuranFentiman(5) 19 19
(D W Chapman) *mid-div: effrt over 2f out: nvr able chal* **12/1**

60-0 **14** *1 ½* **Blissphilly**[98] 3141 4-8-2 51 oh21..................................... DominicFox(3) 2 15
(M Mullineaux) *chsd ldrs: edgd lft 2f out: sn wknd* **200/1**

0460 **15** *¾* **Rondo**[11] 5637 3-8-8 55...(b[1]) PhillipMakin 16 16
(T D Barron) *chsd ldrs 4f: sn lost pl* **16/1**

000 **16** *2 ½* **Height Of Esteem**[23] 5368 3-8-1 51 oh6..................... JohnMcAuley(3) 6 5
(M Mullineaux) *in rr: sn drvn along: nvr a factor* **125/1**

00-0 **17** *6* **Hebenus**[92] 3334 7-8-1 52 oh11 ow1......................... KevinGhunowa(5) 5 —
(T A K Cuthbert) *mid-div: drvn over 2f out: nvr a factor* **150/1**

-550 **18** *½* **Stylistic (IRE)**[63] 4216 5-8-10 56... RMBurke 20 —
(J J Lambe, Ire) *s.i.s: nvr on terms* **80/1**

0000 **19** *¾* **Loaderfun (IRE)**[43] 4831 4-9-0 60................................(t) RobertWinston 7 —
(N Wilson) *chsd ldrs: lost pl over 1f out* **16/1**

0306 **20** *¾* **Primarily**[23] 5368 4-8-7 53 oh4 ow2....................................(p) TomEaves 8 —
(A Berry) *prom: lost pl over 2f out* **25/1**

3330 **21** *1 ¾* **Woodwee**[22] 5401 3-8-10 57.. PaulMulrennan 14 —
(J R Weymes) *trckd ldrs: t.k.h: lost pl 2f out* **50/1**

0000 **22** *15* **Zap Attack**[19] 5483 6-8-2 51 oh11.............................. AndrewMullen(3) 17 —
(J Parkes) *sn bhd: detached and eased over 1f out* **100/1**

1m 19.79s (6.12) **Going Correction** +1.05s/f (Soft)
WFA 3 from 4yo+ 1lb **22** Ran SP% **126.1**
Speed ratings (Par 101):101,100,98,95,92 90,90,89,89,85 83,83,81,79,78 75,67,66,65,64 62,42
CSF £78.04 CT £785.23 TOTE £15.90: £3.20, £2.10, £3.30, £3.40; EX 130.70 Place 6 £42.69, Place 5 £19.00.
Owner M D Hammond **Bred** E R Breeding **Trained** Middleham Moor, N Yorks
FOCUS
A big field for this run-of-the-mill handicap, in which the runners tended to concentrate centre-track once they had sorted themsleves out. Run-of-the-mill form, the winner rated to his best.
George The Best(IRE) Official explanation: trainer's rep said, regarding apparent improvement in form, that the gelding's previous run may have come too soon, two runs in three days
T/Plt: £66.90 to a £1 stake. Pool: £50,533.80. 550.85 winning tickets. T/Qpdt: £18.50 to a £1 stake. Pool: £4,186.90. 166.60 winning tickets. WG

5728 WINDSOR (R-H)
Monday, October 9

OFFICIAL GOING: Soft (good to soft in places)
Wind: light, behind

5866 READING POST PINE RIVERS KINDERGARTEN NURSERY 1m 67y
2:30 (2:30) (Class 5) (0-75,75) 2-Y-0 **£3,238** (£963; £481; £240) **Stalls** High

Form RPR

0640 **1** **Bed Fellow (IRE)**[33] 5113 2-9-2 70.................................. SebSanders 8 72
(A P Jarvis) *led at str pce: hdd halfway: led again 2f out: hung lft after: jst hld on* **25/1**

0254 **2** *nk* **Italian Stallion (IRE)**[25] 5322 2-9-7 75............................ RyanMoore 10 76
(R Hannon) *settled in midfield and wl off the pce: pushed along 1/2-way: prog u.p over 2f out: r.o fnl f: gaining at fin* **12/1**

0033 **3** *nk* **Spiderback (IRE)**[13] 5585 2-9-1 69........................(b[1]) RichardHughes 11 69
(R Hannon) *dwlt: off the pce in midfield: pushed along over 3f out: modest prog u.p tl r.o wl fnl f: gaining at fin* **6/1**[2]

2353 **4** *nk* **Angeletta**[16] 5527 2-9-1 69.. JimmyFortune 13 69
(E S McMahon) *chsd clr ldng pair and clr of rest 1/2-way: wnt 2nd over 1f out: hanging lft and n.m.r ins fnl f: eased nr fin* **14/1**

5210 **5** *nk* **Dancing Granny**[18] 5492 2-9-6 74.................................. JamieSpencer 5 73
(M L W Bell) *hld up in midfield and wl off the pce: prog over 2f out: drvn and styd on wl fnl f: too much to do* **25/1**

5225 **6** *2* **Glorious Prince (IRE)**[12] 5614 2-9-2 70............................... TPQueally 2 65
(M G Quinlan) *pressed ldr: led 1/2-way and kicked on: hdd 2f out: hanging and wknd fnl f* **16/1**

422 **7** *¾* **Aussie Cricket (FR)**[23] 5389 2-9-3 71.............................. TedDurcan 6 64
(D J Coakley) *off the pce in midfield: sme prog u.p over 2f out: no imp over 1f out* **12/1**

51 **8** *½* **Oceana Gold**[26] 5289 2-9-4 72.. LDettori 7 64
(A M Balding) *chsd clr ldrs: rdn 3f out: no imp over 1f out: fdd* **7/4**[1]

1000 **9** *¾* **Addictive**[17] 5503 2-8-12 69...................................... SaleemGolam(3) 12 59
(S C Williams) *chsd clr ldng trio over 5f out: wknd fr 2f out* **16/1**

3050 **10** *1 ¾* **Down The Brick (IRE)**[13] 5597 2-9-0 68........................... JimCrowley 3 54
(B R Millman) *a wl in rr: drvn and wd over 3f out: no prog* **50/1**

6010 **11** *hd* **Darfour**[37] 5013 2-9-7 75... RoystonFfrench 1 61
(M Johnston) *pushed along in midfield 5f out: struggling u.p fr over 2f out* **25/1**

6030 **12** *1 ½* **Obe Royal**[23] 5366 2-8-13 67.. JohnEgan 9 50
(M R Channon) *dwlt: a wl in rr: struggling and wl off the pce 1/2-way* **28/1**

6301 **13** *1 ¾* **Love Brothers**[13] 5597 2-9-7 75.................................... ChrisCatlin 4 54
(M R Channon) *v s.i.s: nvr a factor: last and rdn 1/2-way* **7/1**[3]

5542 **14** *nk* **Cheshire Prince**[23] 5382 2-8-9 66.......................... StephenDonohoe(3) 14 44
(W M Brisbourne) *nvr on terms: drvn and struggling in rr over 3f out* **11/1**

1m 45.85s (0.25) **Going Correction** -0.075s/f (Good) **14** Ran SP% **122.2**
Speed ratings (Par 95):95,94,94,94,93 91,91,90,89,88 87,86,84,84
CSF £290.67 CT £2054.71 TOTE £40.10: £13.10, £4.20, £2.70; EX 380.90 TRIFECTA Not won..
Owner Geoffrey Bishop and Ann Jarvis **Bred** Rathasker Stud **Trained** Twyford, Bucks
■ Stewards' Enquiry : Seb Sanders caution: careless riding

FOCUS
They went a good pace, especially considering the ease in the ground, but they still finished in a bunch and this was a clearly a very competitive nursery. The level of form looks fair. They raced far side in the straight.

NOTEBOOK
Bed Fellow(IRE) was well held on his nursery debut over seven furlongs on the turf at Southwell, but proved suited by the step back up in trip on soft ground and got off the mark at the fifth attempt under a forceful ride. He was hanging to his left close home, but his connections felt he was just idling and there are more races to be won with him on soft ground.
Italian Stallion(IRE) was just held under joint-top weight and this represents his best effort yet. He is a fair middle-distance/staying prospect. (op 11-1)
Spiderback(IRE), a stablemate of the runner-up, did not help his chance with a slow start and was doing his best work late on. He seemed to take well to the fitting of first-time blinkers and saw his race out well. (op 11-2 tchd 5-1)
Angeletta, stepped up to her furthest trip to date on her return to nursery company, had to be eased close home after being hampered and might have finished second with an uninterrupted run.
Dancing Granny finished last on her nursery debut at Pontefract, but this was much better and she would arguably have been in the shake up had her rider not given her so much to do.
Oceana Gold could not build on his recent Beverley maiden success and may not have been suited by the soft ground. (op 15-8 tchd 2-1)
Love Brothers Official explanation: jockey said colt was hampered at the start

5867 EUROPEAN BREEDERS FUND MAIDEN STKS (DIV I) — 6f
3:00 (3:01) (Class 5) 2-Y-O — **£3,886** (£1,156; £577; £288) **Stalls** High

Form	Pos	Dist	Horse / details	RPR
3	1		**Heroes**[20] 5454 2-9-3 ... BrianReilly 4 (G A Huffer) *cl up: sltly outpcd over 2f out: prog wl over 1f out: led jst ins fnl f: forged clr* **11/2**[3]	84+
33	2	2 ½	**Kyle (IRE)**[152] 1587 2-9-3 ... RichardHughes 14 (R Hannon) *cl up: trckd ldng pair over 2f out: effrt gng wl to ld over 1f out: hdd and nt qckn jst ins fnl f* **5/2**[2]	76+
4242	3	2	**Cadeaux Du Monde**[23] 5364 2-9-3 83 ... (b[1]) ChrisCatlin 2 (E J O'Neill) *pressed ldr to wl over 1f out: n.m.r against rail sn after: kpt on same pce* **2/1**[1]	70
0	4	nk	**Doyles Lodge**[70] 4000 2-9-3 ... FergusSweeney 6 (H Candy) *in tch in midfield: shkn up to try to cl 2f out: kpt on fnl f: nvr able to chal* **20/1**	69
00	5	hd	**Darling Belinda**[27] 5261 2-8-12 ... TPQueally 7 (D K Ivory) *led: rdn and hanging lft fr over 2f out: hdd over 1f out: wknd ins fnl f* **50/1**	64
00	6	2	**Dancing Duo**[20] 5456 2-8-12 ... NickyMackay 15 (W J Haggas) *settled in midfield and nvr on terms: shkn up briefly over 1f out: one pce* **66/1**	58
	7	2 ½	**Incony** 2-8-12 ... TedDurcan 8 (W R Swinburn) *dwlt: off the pce towards rr: kpt on fnl f: n.d* **28/1**	50
0	8	2 ½	**Kyloe Belle (USA)**[52] 4559 2-8-12 ... LDettori 9 (Mrs A J Perrett) *off the pce towards rr: pushed along and no real imp fnl 2f* **11/1**	43
0	9	2	**April Fool**[24] 5339 2-9-3 ... RichardThomas 12 (J A Geake) *s.s: wl in rr: nvr a factor* **10/1**	42
	10	shd	**Mountain Cat (IRE)** 2-9-3 ... PhilipRobinson 13 (W J Musson) *wl in rr: pushed along briefly 2f out: nt clr run over 1f out: nvr a factor* **25/1**	41
0	11	2 ½	**Hereford Boy**[10] 5645 2-9-3 ... RobertHavlin 3 (D K Ivory) *chsd ldrs tl wknd rapidly wl over 1f out* **100/1**	34
	12	2	**Little Carmela** 2-8-12 ... JamieMackay 5 (S C Williams) *s.s: rn green in last: a bhd* **40/1**	23
	13	¾	**High Lite** 2-8-12 ... JamieSpencer 11 (M L W Bell) *dwlt: a in last trio and wl off the pce* **12/1**	20

1m 13.83s (0.16) **Going Correction** -0.075s/f (Good) — 13 Ran SP% 121.3
Speed ratings (Par 95):95,91,89,88,88 85,82,79,76,76 72,70,69
CSF £18.85 TOTE £8.10: £2.60, £1.30, £1.30; EX 22.00 Trifecta £66.40 Pool £301.22 - 3.22 winning units.
Owner Six Star Racing **Bred** Usk Valley Stud **Trained** Newmarket, Suffolk
■ Stewards' Enquiry : T P Queally three-day ban: dropped hands and lost fourth place (Oct 20, 21-23)

FOCUS
A reasonable sprint maiden, but the winning time was 0.44 seconds slower than the second division. They again raced far side in the straight. Nice efforts from the first two, who can improve again.

NOTEBOOK
Heroes shaped well on his debut over this trip on fast ground at Newmarket and built on that effort to run out an emphatic winner, coping just fine with the much easier conditions. On this evidence, he will be suited by a little further, and he may have one more run this year. (op 5-1 tchd 9-2 and 6-1)
Kyle(IRE), upped in trip and racing on soft ground for the first time on his return from five months off the track, travelled strongly but found little off the bridle and was basically outstayed by the winner. (tchd 2-1)
Cadeaux Du Monde did not seem to take well to the first-time blinkers and was below his official mark of 83. He is not progressing. (op 5-2 tchd 3-1)
Doyles Lodge ◆ offered some promise on his debut over course and distance just over two months previously and this was another encouraging effort, keeping on well late on having always just been a little further back than was maybe ideal. He is going the right way. (tchd 25-1)
Darling Belinda ran a good race, faring best of the fillies, and will have more options now she is qualified for a handicap mark. Official explanation: jockey said filly hung right in straight (tchd 40-1)

5868 SILVER ALTMAN H'CAP — 1m 3f 135y
3:35 (3:36) (Class 5) (0-70,70) 3-Y-O — **£3,886** (£1,156; £577; £288) **Stalls** Low

Form	Pos	Dist	Horse / details	RPR
4210	1		**Mull Of Dubai**[11] 5644 3-9-0 **66** ... JohnEgan 15 (J S Moore) *hld up wl in rr: stdy prog over 3f out: nt clr run briefly over 2f out: effrt to ld over 1f out: hung lft but r.o strly* **15/2**	74
3503	2	1 ½	**Special Moment (IRE)**[37] 5015 3-8-12 **64** ... MichaelHills 5 (B W Hills) *trckd ldrs: prog to ld wl over 2f out: hdd over 1f out: r.o but hld whn n.m.r ins fnl f* **10/1**	70
0445	3	3 ½	**Leamington Lad (IRE)**[14] 5574 3-8-9 **61** ... RichardThomas 6 (J A Geake) *prominent: lost pl over 4f out: sn rdn in rr: styd on again fr over 1f out: tk 3rd nr fin* **11/2**[2]	62
6323	4	nk	**Will Be (IRE)**[39] 4972 3-9-1 **67** ... (tp) FJohansson 11 (R A Kvisla) *dwlt: towards rr: pushed along over 3f out: prog against far rail 2f out: kpt on same pce fnl f* **25/1**	67
3303	5	¾	**Silken Act (CAN)**[35] 5056 3-9-4 **70** ... (b[1]) RyanMoore 4 (Mrs A J Perrett) *t.k.h: hld up in rr: prog over 3f out: rdn to chse ldng pair over 1f out: no imp and lost 2 pls nr fin* **12/1**	69
054	6	1 ¼	**Wizards Dream**[13] 5598 3-9-4 **70** ... LPKeniry 8 (D R C Elsworth) *settled in midfield: lost pl 5f out: pushed along towards rr 3f out: renewed effrt 2f out: hanging lft and plugged on* **6/1**[3]	67
6000	7	1 ¼	**Your Amount (IRE)**[51] 4606 3-8-13 **65** ... JDSmith 14 (W J Musson) *trckd ldrs: lost pl on inner bnd over 5f out: rdn and prog over 3f out: nt qckn over 2f out: edgd lft and fdd over 1f out* **25/1**	60
0200	8	shd	**Bob's Your Uncle**[12] 5628 3-8-9 **61** ... NickyMackay 10 (J G Portman) *prom: chsd ldr over 2f out to wl over 1f out: wknd* **15/2**	56
2300	9	½	**Shaydreambeliever**[42] 4892 3-8-9 **66** ... JamieMoriarty(5) 16 (R A Fahey) *towards rr: rdn and struggling over 3f out: brief effrt 2f out: sn no prog* **28/1**	61
0316	10	7	**Sarwin (USA)**[112] 2713 3-8-9 **61** ... PhilipRobinson 1 (W J Musson) *awkward s: mostly in last pair: nvr a factor: passed eased rivals last 2f* **25/1**	45
1411	11	6	**Hurry Up Helen (IRE)**[14] 5574 3-9-1 **67** ... JamieSpencer 12 (Mrs L Stubbs) *mostly chsd ldr tl rdn and wknd over 3f out: eased over 1f out* **9/2**[1]	42
4135	12	14	**Regal Connection (USA)**[38] 4991 3-9-1 **67** ... (b) RoystonFfrench 9 (M Johnston) *mde most to wl over 2f out: wknd rapidly: eased: t.o* **12/1**	21
6033	13	½	**El Capitan (FR)**[43] 4847 3-8-7 **59** ... RichardHughes 2 (Miss Gay Kelleway) *hld up: stdy prog and wl in tch 3f out: sn wknd: eased: t.o* **16/1**	12
2405	14	1 ¾	**Avelian (IRE)**[19] 5484 3-9-0 **66** ... (tp) TedDurcan 13 (W J Haggas) *dwlt: a wl in rr: rdn and no prog over 3f out: eased fnl 2f: t.o* **22/1**	17
050	15	19	**Arabian Tiger**[29] 5203 3-9-4 **70** ... JimmyFortune 7 (P W Chapple-Hyam) *prom tl wknd rapidly 3f out: eased: t.o* **50/1**	—

2m 32.28s (2.18) **Going Correction** +0.30s/f (Good) — 15 Ran SP% 123.0
Speed ratings (Par 101):104,103,100,100,99 99,98,98,97,93 89,79,79,78,65
CSF £74.60 CT £455.56 TOTE £10.50: £2.80, £2.90, £2.50; EX 86.20 TRIFECTA Not won..
Owner Mrs Fitri Hay **Bred** B Walters **Trained** Upper Lambourn, Berks

FOCUS
Just a modest handicap in which they raced far side in the straight. Average form, rated through the second, fourth and fifth.
Wizards Dream Official explanation: jockey said colt hung left
Hurry Up Helen(IRE) Official explanation: jockey said filly was unsuited by the soft (good to soft places) ground

5869 PITMAN COHEN H'CAP — 1m 2f 7y
4:05 (4:05) (Class 4) (0-85,84) 3-Y-O — **£6,477** (£1,927; £963; £481) **Stalls** Low

Form	Pos	Dist	Horse / details	RPR
6242	1		**Charlie Tokyo (IRE)**[5] 5769 3-8-8 **79** ... (b) JamieMoriarty(5) 3 (R A Fahey) *hld up in last trio: stdy prog gng wl fr 3f out: coaxed into ld ins fnl f: edgd rt u.p: hld on* **11/2**[3]	89
2321	2	nk	**Benandonner (USA)**[13] 5599 3-8-12 **78** ... JimmyFortune 8 (E A L Dunlop) *led: hrd rdn and pressed fr over 2f out: hdd ins fnl f: battled on wl* **12/1**	88
1213	3	1 ½	**Celtic Spirit (IRE)**[17] 5511 3-9-3 **83** ... SebSanders 1 (R M Beckett) *prom: pressed ldr over 3f out to over 1f out: one pce* **2/1**[1]	90
3123	4	hd	**Prince Ary**[17] 5504 3-9-0 **80** ... MichaelHills 7 (B W Hills) *dwlt: t.k.h: hld up in tch: rdn and effrt 2f out: nt qckn over 1f out: kpt on same pce after* **6/1**	87
3262	5	¾	**Midnight Traveller**[27] 5266 3-8-13 **79** ... NickyMackay 10 (L M Cumani) *trckd ldrs: rdn and nt qckn over 2f out: lost pl: kpt on again ins fnl f* **12/1**	84
4041	6	½	**Forroger (CAN)**[44] 4805 3-8-11 **77** ... PhilipRobinson 4 (M A Jarvis) *hld up in last: stl last 2f out: swtchd to wd outside over 1f out: r.o fnl f: hopeless task* **4/1**[2]	81
2502	7	3	**Risk Runner (IRE)**[13] 5599 3-8-11 **77** ... (v) JDSmith 2 (A King) *hld up: prog 1/2-way: cl up over 2f out: sn drvn: wknd jst over 1f out* **16/1**	76
0000	8	2	**Silver Blue (IRE)**[45] 4782 3-9-4 **84** ... RyanMoore 9 (R Hannon) *in tch: rdn over 4f out: sn struggling in rr* **33/1**	79
2262	9	nk	**Go Figure (IRE)**[7] 5724 3-8-10 **76** ... (t) LDettori 5 (B J Meehan) *sn hld up in last pair: hrd rdn over 2f out: no prog* **12/1**	71
0-00	10	3	**Supreme Charter**[9] 5671 3-8-12 **78** ... RoystonFfrench 6 (M Johnston) *prom: rdn over 2f out: nt look keen and grad lost pl* **33/1**	67
-100	11	2	**Cortesia (IRE)**[46] 4741 3-9-3 **83** ... GeorgeBaker 11 (P W Chapple-Hyam) *s.i.s: sn rcvrd and trckd ldr to over 3f out: wknd over 2f out* **66/1**	69

2m 10.4s (2.10) **Going Correction** +0.30s/f (Good) — 11 Ran SP% 119.3
Speed ratings (Par 103):103,102,101,101,100 100,98,96,96,93 92
CSF £69.71 CT £178.02 TOTE £7.30: £1.50, £4.00, £1.40; EX 75.50 Trifecta £349.80 Pool £561.69 - 1.14 winning units.
Owner S L Tse **Bred** J Donnelly **Trained** Musley Bank, N Yorks

FOCUS
A fair handicap, but they went just an ordinary gallop for much of the way. The winning time was almost identical to the following maiden, a race also run a steady pace early on. They again went far side in the straight. The form seems to make sense.
Supreme Charter Official explanation: jockey said gelding hung right in straight

5870 WINDSOR FIREWORKS EXTRAVAGANZA SATURDAY 28TH OCTOBER MAIDEN STKS — 1m 2f 7y
4:40 (4:41) (Class 5) 3-Y-O+ — **£4,533** (£1,348; £674; £336) **Stalls** Low

Form	Pos	Dist	Horse / details	RPR
3-3	1		**Nosferatu (IRE)**[130] 2175 3-9-3 ... JamieSpencer 11 (Mrs A J Perrett) *a ldng trio: pushed along 1/2-way: chsd ldr 4f out: urged into narrow ld over 1f out: rdn to assert last 100yds* **5/2**[1]	80+
0423	2	1 ¼	**Conservation (FR)**[7] 5732 3-9-3 73 ... PhilipRobinson 1 (P W Chapple-Hyam) *led: hrd pressed 2f out: hdd over 1f out: pressed wnr and clr of rest tl no ex last 100yds* **3/1**[2]	78
623	3	3 ½	**Show Winner**[13] 5589 3-9-3 85 ... TPQueally 10 (J Noseda) *hld up in rr: pushed along and prog fr 3f out: trckd ldng pair 2f out and ch: hanging lft and one pce after* **5/1**[3]	72
3	4	3	**Glamis Castle (USA)**[9] 5669 3-9-3 ... RyanMoore 7 (Sir Michael Stoute) *settled in midfield: pushed along 4f out: prog 2f out: kpt on steadily but nvr on terms* **8/1**	66
	5	½	**Blend** 3-8-12 ... RichardHughes 14 (J H M Gosden) *dwlt: sn wl in tch: shkn up 4f out: effrt over 2f out: sn outpcd and btn* **7/1**	60+
65	6	shd	**Sunset Boulevard (IRE)**[21] 5429 3-9-3 ... (v[1]) JohnEgan 6 (J Noseda) *settled in rr: prog 3f out: nt onb terms w ldrs 2f out: pushed along and kpt on steadily* **20/1**	65
0	7	5	**La Grande Zoa (IRE)**[14] 5566 3-8-12 ... SebSanders 8 (R M Beckett) *chsd ldrs: cl enough 3f out: steadily wkng whn shkn up over 1f out* **33/1**	51

8 1 ½ **Queens Destiny** 3-8-12 .... StephenCarson 12 49
(P W Hiatt) *unruly bef s: v.s.a and detached last: rdn and styd on fr 3f out: nvr nrr* **100/1**

0-4 9 1 ¾ **Montchara (IRE)**[13] 5589 3-9-3 .... TedDurcan 13 50
(G Wragg) *trckd ldrs: wnt 3rd 4f out and gng bttr than most: shkn up and wknd tamely over 2f out* **33/1**

000 10 6 **Goodenough Prince**[35] 5071 3-9-0 54............ RichardKingscote(3) 9 40
(Andrew Turnell) *prom tl wknd u.p wl over 2f out* **100/1**

11 2 **Moonlight Safari (IRE)** 3-8-12 .... JimCrowley 5 31
(P Winkworth) *s.s: a wl in rr: struggling 4f out* **66/1**

12 1 ¼ **Earth And Sky (USA)** 3-9-3 .... LDettori 4 34
(Saeed Bin Suroor) *dwlt: in tch in midfield: shkn up over 4f out: sme prog 3f out: nvr on terms: wknd and eased 2f out* **6/1**

-500 13 3 **Annies Valentine**[38] 4982 3-8-12 40............ ChrisCatlin 2 23
(J Gallagher) *mostly chsd ldr to 4f out: sn wknd* **100/1**

00 14 18 **Cut To (USA)**[12] 5612 3-9-0 .... DeanCorby(3) 15 —
(J Akehurst) *a towards rr: u.p and wknd 3f out: t.o* **100/1**

00 15 20 **Forever Thine**[45] 4776 3-8-7 .... TravisBlock(5) 3 —
(J A Geake) *dwlt: a struggling in last trio: t.o* **100/1**

2m 10.38s (2.08) **Going Correction** +0.30s/f (Good) **15** Ran SP% **125.2**
Speed ratings (Par 103):103,102,99,96,96 96,92,91,89,84 83,82,79,65,49
CSF £9.92 TOTE £3.40: £1.60, £1.50, £2.60; EX 16.60 Trifecta £99.90 Pool £523.81 - 3.72 winning units.
Owner Lady Clague **Bred** Newberry Stud Company **Trained** Pulborough, W Sussex

FOCUS
This looked like a reasonable maiden for the time of year, but it was a slightly bizarre race to watch and the form may want treating with some caution. Nosferatu came under pressure a long way out and quickly got into a duel with Conservation, but nothing could make any impression from behind, suggesting the early pace was just ordinary and the front pair were suited by committing so far from the finish. The winning time was almost identical to the previous handicap, a race also run at a steady gallop early on. They raced far side in the straight.

5871 EUROPEAN BREEDERS FUND MAIDEN STKS (DIV II) 6f
5:10 (5:10) (Class 5) 2-Y-O £3,886 (£1,156; £577; £288) Stalls High

Form RPR

00 1 **Apache Dream (IRE)**[80] 3700 2-8-12 .... LDettori 2 75+
(B J Meehan) *trckd ldrs: led over 2f out: 3 l clr over 1f out: eased nr fin* **9/4**[1]

2 ½ **Princess Valerina** 2-8-12 .... MichaelHills 6 74
(B W Hills) *s.s: hld up in last trio: gd prog 2f out: chsd clr wnr last 150yds: clsng wl fin* **8/1**[3]

6232 3 2 **Vadinka**[12] 5606 2-9-3 73............ JimCrowley 3 73
(P Winkworth) *led to over 2f out: sn outpcd by wnr: one pce and lost 2nd last 150yds* **9/2**[2]

0000 4 ¾ **Aggresive**[27] 5262 2-9-3 61............ OscarUrbina 14 70
(D K Ivory) *chsd ldrs: rdn wl over 2f out: outpcd over 1f out: one pce after* **33/1**

5 2 ½ **Rhyming Slang (USA)** 2-9-3 .... TPQueally 10 63
(J Noseda) *nvr on terms w ldrs: pushed along in rr over 2f out: kpt on fnl f* **9/2**[2]

6 shd **Caught You Looking** 2-8-12 .... TedDurcan 8 57
(W R Swinburn) *sn in midfield: pushed along and outpcd wl over 1f out: one pce after* **14/1**

2530 7 1 ½ **Pango's Legacy**[12] 5606 2-8-12 74............ TravisBlock(5) 7 58
(H Morrison) *w ldr to over 2f out: wknd wl over 1f out* **9/2**[2]

8 5 **Stars Above** 2-8-12 .... SebSanders 5 38
(Sir Mark Prescott) *dwlt: sn in tch: cl enough 1/2-way: wknd 2f out: eased* **33/1**

00 9 3 **Inside Straight (IRE)**[12] 5607 2-9-3 .... RichardHughes 13 34
(R Hannon) *w ldr to over 2f out: wknd rapidly* **50/1**

00 10 1 **Rotation (IRE)**[24] 5347 2-9-3 .... WandersonD'Avila 4 31
(J W Hills) *sn struggling in last pair: nvr a factor* **100/1**

11 hd **Compton Charlie** 2-9-3 .... RyanMoore 9 30
(J G Portman) *veered s: rn green in last and a bhd* **20/1**

06 12 1 ½ **Yve Sam La Champ**[133] 2072 2-9-3 .... FrancisNorton 1 26
(A W Carroll) *nvr on terms w ldrs: wknd over 2f out* **100/1**

1m 13.39s (-0.28) **Going Correction** -0.075s/f (Good) **12** Ran SP% **117.7**
Speed ratings (Par 95):98,97,94,93,90 90,88,81,77,76 75,73
CSF £20.21 TOTE £2.50: £1.60, £2.60, £1.50; EX 17.90 Trifecta £100.20 Pool £218.89 - 1.55 winning units.
Owner Sangster Family **Bred** Swettenham Stud **Trained** Manton, Wilts

FOCUS
A fair sprint maiden run in a time 0.44 seconds faster than the first division, and 0.17 seconds quicker than the following older-horse handicap. The third and fourth temper enthusiasm for the form, however.

NOTEBOOK
Apache Dream(IRE) ◆ had finished down the field on her two previous starts, but they were in very hot maidens at Newbury and she found this a suitable opportunity on her return from nearly three months off the track. Always going best, she was eased close home and was probably value for more like two lengths. (op 11-4)
Princess Valerina ◆, a half-sister to Bonnie Prince Blue, a dual six-furlong winning juvenile, made a most pleasing debut. She is flattered to get so close to the winner, as that one was eased close home, but did finish her race very nicely indeed and, with normal improvement, will be hard to beat next time. (tchd 15-2)
Vadinka seemed to run his race under a positive ride and, officially rated 73, he gives the form some substance. (op 6-1 tchd 13-2)
Aggresive is an inconsistent type and only rated 61, but he has shown glimpses of fair form and should not be used to hold the form down too much. (tchd 40-1)
Rhyming Slang(USA), a $90,000 half-brother to useful Bad Kitty, a triple sprint winner at two in the US, out of a multiple winner in the States, was in trouble soon after the start. He is unlikely to have appreciated the soft ground and can leave this behind in due course. (op 5-2)
Pango's Legacy ran well below his official mark of 74 and may not have been suited by the soft ground. Official explanation: jockey said colt was unsuited by the soft (good to soft places) ground (tchd 5-1)

5872 ARENA LEISURE H'CAP 6f
5:40 (5:42) (Class 5) (0-70,70) 3-Y-O+ £3,886 (£1,156; £577; £288) Stalls High

Form RPR

0630 1 **Pamir (IRE)**[122] 2417 4-8-12 63............(b) JimCrowley 10 74
(P R Chamings) *mde all: hrd rdn over 1f out: jnd ins fnl f: hld on wl* **18/1**

5011 2 shd **Ten Shun**[25] 5309 3-9-0 69............ StephenDonohoe(3) 3 80
(P D Evans) *wl plcd: drvn and effrt 2f out: jnd wnr ins fnl f: jst hld last strides* **10/3**[1]

4212 3 1 **Mr Cellophane**[21] 5418 3-9-2 68............ RichardHughes 15 76
(J R Jenkins) *rrd s: t.k.h and hld up in rr: stdy prog and swtchd to far side 2f out: chal fnl f: no ex last 100yds* **10/1**

4000 4 1 ½ **Linda Green**[11] 5635 5-9-0 65............ ChrisCatlin 7 69
(M R Channon) *chsd ldrs: drvn and nt qckn wl over 1f out: styd on again ins fnl f* **12/1**

6164 5 ½ **Brigadore**[11] 5635 7-9-0 65............ OscarUrbina 8 67
(J G Given) *broke out of stalls bef s: dwlt: in tch in rr: prog fr 1/2-way: rdn and kpt on fr over 1f out* **10/1**

2300 6 ½ **Cesar Manrique (IRE)**[35] 5058 4-9-4 69............ MichaelHills 16 70
(B W Hills) *trckd ldrs on outer: shkn up and nt qckn over 1f out: one pce after* **11/1**

035 7 shd **Supercast (IRE)**[40] 4922 3-9-4 70............ JohnEgan 2 70
(J S Moore) *in tch: effrt against far rail whn n.m.r over 1f out: kpt on fnl f: n.d* **33/1**

0500 8 ½ **Sabrina Brown**[6] 5756 5-9-1 66............(t) RichardThomas 5 65
(J A Geake) *mostly pressed wnr to over 1f out: fdd* **9/1**

4250 9 1 ½ **Patavium Prince (IRE)**[39] 4957 3-9-3 69............ GeorgeBaker 11 63
(J R Best) *dwlt: wl off the pce in last pair: styd on fnl 2f out: nvr nrr* **16/1**

1041 10 ½ **Endless Summer**[26] 5291 9-9-0 65............ FrancisNorton 14 58+
(A W Carroll) *t.k.h: hld up in rr: taken towards far side fr 1/2-way: nt clr run over 1f out: nvr nr ldrs* **8/1**[3]

6500 11 1 ½ **Tous Les Deux**[12] 5605 3-9-1 67............ StephenCarson 12 55
(R F Johnson Houghton) *chsd ldrs tl rdn and wknd over 1f out* **20/1**

-063 12 5 **My Only Sunshine**[5] 5765 7-8-13 64............ JamieSpencer 1 37+
(M J Wallace) *in tch: effrt towards far side and cl enough 2f out: wknd and eased over 1f out* **5/1**[2]

2402 13 1 **Even Bolder**[28] 5250 3-8-12 67............ StephaneBreux(3) 4 37
(S Kirk) *chsd ldrs tl wknd u.p over 2f out* **33/1**

0410 14 ¾ **Marajel (IRE)**[6] 5755 3-9-4 70............ JimmyFortune 9 38
(P W Chapple-Hyam) *chsd ldrs tl wknd 2f out: no ch whn hmpd ins fnl f* **11/1**

1600 15 1 **Bold Argument (IRE)**[23] 5377 3-9-4 70............ RobertHavlin 6 35
(Mrs P N Dutfield) *drvn in last after 2f: nvr a factor* **40/1**

0500 16 9 **Pearly Poll**[13] 5593 3-8-13 65............(p) SebSanders 13 3
(R M Beckett) *struggling on outer and nt looking keen 1/2-way: t.o* **33/1**

1m 13.56s (-0.11) **Going Correction** -0.075s/f (Good)
WFA 3 from 4yo+ 1lb **16** Ran SP% **130.6**
Speed ratings (Par 103):97,96,95,93,92 92,92,91,89,88 86,80,78,77,76 64
CSF £78.79 CT £703.16 TOTE £22.40: £4.60, £1.30, £2.50, £2.40; EX 132.10 Trifecta £351.80 Part won. Pool £495.50 - 0.74 winning units. Place 6 £48.67, Place 5 £7.58.
Owner Patrick Chamings Sprint Club **Bred** James Kavanagh **Trained** Baughurst, Hants

FOCUS
A modest sprint handicap run in a slower time than the second division of the two-year-old maiden, but typically competitive. They tended to race middle to far side. Just average form.
Patavium Prince(IRE) Official explanation: jockey said gelding hung right
T/Jkpt: Not won. T/Plt: £76.70 to a £1 stake. Pool: £79,057.25. 751.95 winning tickets. T/Qpdt: £10.10 to a £1 stake. Pool: £5,473.90. 397.20 winning tickets. JN

5841 WOLVERHAMPTON (A.W) (L-H)
Monday, October 9

OFFICIAL GOING: Standard to fast
Wind: light, across

5873 FRANK CONLON LIFETIME IN RACING MEDIAN AUCTION MAIDEN STKS (DIV I) 5f 216y(P)
1:50 (1:50) (Class 6) 3-Y-O £2,047 (£604; £302) Stalls Low

Form RPR

0-00 1 **Alistair John**[21] 5432 3-9-3 40............ DeanMcKeown 10 58
(Mrs G S Rees) *led early: led again over 4f out: rdn out* **40/1**

4555 2 1 ¼ **Gift Aid**[34] 5092 3-9-3 49............ DarryllHolland 4 54
(P J Makin) *sn led: hdd over 4f out: outpcd over 2f out: rallied over 1f out: r.o* **11/8**[1]

5 3 shd **Tembladora (IRE)**[130] 2167 3-8-12 .... EddieAhern 1 49
(J W Hills) *a.p: chsd wnr 4f out: rdn over 1f out: styd on same pce* **2/1**[2]

5000 4 3 **Canary Girl**[5] 5767 3-8-12 35............ HayleyTurner 6 40
(Mrs C A Dunnett) *prom: outpcd over 2f out: styd on ins fnl f* **66/1**

5060 5 nk **Kissi Kissi**[66] 4113 3-8-12 50............ RobbieFitzpatrick 3 39
(M J Attwater) *s.i.s: hdwy over 3f out: sn rdn: wknd ins fnl f* **11/1**

6-00 6 ½ **Pertemps Heroine**[52] 4563 3-8-12 47............ JimmyQuinn 7 38
(A D Smith) *sn outpcd: styd on ins fnl f: nvr nrr* **22/1**

006 7 1 ½ **Megavegas**[34] 5077 3-8-7 40............ RoryMoore(5) 2 33
(P T Midgley) *prom over 3f* **33/1**

4360 8 shd **Crusader's Gold (FR)**[28] 5250 3-9-3 49............(b[1]) KDarley 9 38
(T D Easterby) *chsd ldrs: rdn over 2f out: wknd over 1f out* **9/2**[3]

0-00 9 2 ½ **Dominello**[28] 5241 3-8-10 30............ JamesRogers(7) 8 30
(R A Fahey) *sn outpcd: bhd whn hung lft over 1f out* **100/1**

0300 10 2 ½ **Millbrook Star (IRE)**[7] 5727 3-8-10 45............(b) JamieHamblett(7) 5 23
(M C Chapman) *s.i.s: outpcd* **80/1**

1m 14.72s (-1.09) **Going Correction** -0.30s/f (Stan) **10** Ran SP% **115.4**
Speed ratings (Par 99):95,93,93,89,88 88,86,86,82,79
CSF £94.01 TOTE £33.50: £7.30, £1.40, £1.02; EX 117.80.
Owner Mrs G S Rees **Bred** J Gittins And Capt J H Wilson **Trained** Sollom, Lancs

FOCUS
A dire maiden and the form is put into perspective by the 35-rated fourth. It has been rated through the second and fourth.

5874 FRANK CONLON LIFETIME IN RACING MEDIAN AUCTION MAIDEN STKS (DIV II) 5f 216y(P)
2:20 (2:22) (Class 6) 3-Y-O £2,047 (£604; £302) Stalls Low

Form RPR

0 1 **Hello Man (IRE)**[21] 5438 3-9-3 .... KDarley 4 73+
(Eamon Tyrrell, Ire) *a.p: chsd ldr over 2f out: led over 1f out: rdn clr* **9/1**

53-0 2 3 **One Night In Paris (IRE)**[181] 969 3-8-12 65............ EddieAhern 5 59
(M J Wallace) *hld up in tch: rdn over 2f out: styd on same pce fnl f* **9/4**[1]

0002 3 shd **Ceredig**[75] 3842 3-9-3 60............(t) DarryllHolland 10 64
(W R Muir) *chsd ldr tl led over 3f out: rdn and hdd over 1f out: edgd rt and no ex fnl f* **11/2**

0030 4 1 ¼ **Crafty Fox**[90] 3381 3-9-3 59............ DaneO'Neill 1 60
(A P Jarvis) *sn led: hdd over 3f out: rdn over 1f out: no ex* **7/2**[3]

5050 5 7 **Optical Seclusion (IRE)**[67] 4071 3-9-3 50............(b) DavidAllan 8 39
(T J Etherington) *broke wl: lost pl over 4f out: n.d after* **40/1**

0-00 6 3 **Charanne**[27] 5272 3-8-5 35............ BarrySavage(7) 6 25
(J M Bradley) *s.i.s: hdwy over 2f out: sn hung rt and wknd* **80/1**

0000 7 ½ **Night Reveller (IRE)**[39] 4943 3-8-5 30............ RussellKennemore(7) 7 24
(M C Chapman) *s.i.s: outpcd* **80/1**

6600 **8** *3* **Silvanella (IRE)**[7] 5728 3-8-12 45 FrancisFerris 3 15
(M S Saunders) *chsd ldrs 4f* **40/1**

0000 **9** *1 ½* **Royal Citadel (IRE)**[21] 5418 3-8-12 61 (p) AdamKirby 2 10
(C G Cox) *chsd ldrs over 3f* **5/2**[2]

0505 **10** *7* **Master Malarkey**[49] 4663 3-9-3 45 (b) AdrianMcCarthy 9 —
(Mrs C A Dunnett) *prom: rdn over 3f out: wknd over 2f out* **40/1**

1m 13.79s (-2.02) **Going Correction** -0.30s/f (Stan) **10** Ran SP% **116.7**
Speed ratings (Par 99):101,97,96,95,85 81,81,77,75,65
CSF £29.31 TOTE £9.60: £2.30, £1.10, £1.90; EX 28.80.
Owner Tailor Made Syndicate **Bred** William Moloney **Trained** The Curragh, Co Kildare

FOCUS
A moderate maiden which was run at a fair pace. The winner was full value for his winning margin and the form looks pretty solid. The stronger of the two divisions.

5875 SPONSOR A RACE BY CALLING 0870 220 2442 H'CAP 1m 5f 194y(P)
2:50 (2:50) (Class 5) (0-70,69) 3-Y-0+ **£3,238** (£963; £481; £240) **Stalls** Low

Form RPR

2505 **1** **Santando**[55] 4457 6-9-10 **64** (b) EddieAhern 6 78+
(C E Brittain) *hld up: hdwy over 3f out: edgd lft over 2f out: led wl over 1f out: rdn clr and hung lft fnl f: eased nr fin* **10/1**

0500 **2** *1 ¼* **The Violin Player (USA)**[12] 5610 5-9-11 **68** (p) JamesDoyle(3) 4 79
(H J Collingridge) *hld up: hdwy over 3f out: rdn and ev ch whn hmpd over 2f out: styd on* **11/1**

0152 **3** *4* **Bienheureux**[29] 5213 5-9-10 **64** DarryllHolland 9 69+
(Miss Gay Kelleway) *hld up: hdwy and nt clr run over 3f out: hmpd over 2f out: sn rdn: styd on same pce appr fnl f* **7/2**[1]

4535 **4** *1* **Blushing Hilary (IRE)**[17] 5510 3-9-6 **69** (p) DaneO'Neill 3 73
(Miss J A Camacho) *hld up in tch: ev ch whn edgd rt and hmpd over 2f out: wknd over 1f out* **25/1**

5304 **5** *1 ½* **Gaze**[21] 5429 3-9-4 **67** PaulDoe 10 69
(W Jarvis) *mid-div: hdwy 1/2-way: led over 3f out: rdn and hdd wl over 1f out: wknd fnl f* **20/1**

2024 **6** *1* **Phone In**[35] 5057 3-9-3 **66** DavidAllan 13 66
(R Brotherton) *led: rdn and hdd over 6f out: rdr dropped whip 4f out: wknd wl over 1f out* **8/1**[3]

7 *3* **Phoenix Hill (IRE)**[383] 5414 4-9-6 **63** NeilChalmers(3) 1 59
(D R Gandolfo) *s.i.s: hld up: hdwy over 2f out: sn rdn and wknd* **33/1**

0 **8** *6* **Milton Star (IRE)**[9] 5691 7-9-6 **63** PatrickMathers(3) 7 51
(John A Harris) *chsd ldrs: rdn over 4f out: wknd 3f out* **25/1**

5252 **9** *1 ¾* **Rose Bien**[25] 5324 4-9-10 **64** (b[1]) TonyCulhane 5 49
(P J McBride) *s.i.s: hld up: rdn 6f out: hmpd and wknd over 3f out* **7/2**[1]

0530 **10** *1* **Newport Boy (IRE)**[14] 5574 3-8-9 **58** AdrianMcCarthy 8 42
(R A Harris) *chsd ldrs: rdn over 3f out: hmpd and wknd over 2f out* **25/1**

0433 **11** *42* **Musical Magic**[47] 4697 3-8-8 **57** (v[1]) JimmyQuinn 11 —
(J Noseda) *chsd ldrs: rdn over 4f out: wkng whn hmpd over 3f out: eased* **12/1**

01 **12** *33* **Jump Ship**[34] 5098 3-9-5 **68** KDarley 2 —
(M P Tregoning) *chsd ldr tl led over 6f: wknd and eased over 3f out* **4/1**[2]

3m 1.98s (-5.39) **Going Correction** -0.30s/f (Stan)
WFA 3 from 4yo+ 9lb **12** Ran SP% **119.9**
Speed ratings (Par 103):103,102,100,99,98 98,96,92,91,91 67,48
CSF £107.02 CT £468.32 TOTE £11.70: £3.10, £3.90, £1.70; EX 76.20.
Owner Mrs J M Khan **Bred** R N And Mrs Khan **Trained** Newmarket, Suffolk

FOCUS
A modest handicap and the winner is value for further than his winning margin. The first two had slipped to good marks and finished clear of the third.
The Violin Player(USA) Official explanation: jockey said gelding suffered interference on bend
Bienheureux Official explanation: jockey said gelding was hampered on final bend
Blushing Hilary(IRE) Official explanation: jockey said filly suffered interference on final bend
Jump Ship Official explanation: jockey said filly lost its action; vet said filly had a high heart rate

5876 WOLVERHAMPTON-RACECOURSE.CO.UK (S) STKS 7f 32y(P)
3:25 (3:26) (Class 6) 2-Y-O **£2,388** (£705; £352) **Stalls** High

Form RPR

5300 **1** **Madam Gaffer**[10] 5646 2-8-6 68 EddieAhern 10 62
(B J Meehan) *sn outpcd: hdwy over 2f out: rdn to ld over 1f out: r.o* **4/1**[2]

0330 **2** *1 ¼* **Cantique (IRE)**[21] 5419 2-8-6 62 NelsonDeSouza 12 59
(R M Beckett) *s.i.s: sn outpcd: hdwy over 1f out: rdn to chse wnr and hung lft ins fnl f: styd on* **4/1**[2]

0560 **3** *2* **Tobago Reef**[26] 5282 2-8-11 60 DarryllHolland 2 59
(Mrs L Stubbs) *led: hung rt fr over 2f out: rdn and hdd over 1f out: styd on same pce* **9/1**

3302 **4** *½* **Jost Van Dyke**[10] 5646 2-9-3 68 DaneO'Neill 6 64
(B R Millman) *s.i.s: hdwy over 4f out: rdn and ev ch over 1f out: sn hung rt and no ex* **7/2**[1]

0100 **5** *3* **Aggbag**[7] 5738 2-9-3 63 RobbieFitzpatrick 5 57
(B P J Baugh) *prom: outpcd over 2f out: hdwy over 1f out: wknd ins fnl f* **14/1**

0466 **6** *1* **Mulvany (IRE)**[34] 5084 2-8-11 60 (b) KDarley 7 48
(B J Meehan) *chsd ldr: rdn and ev ch 2f out: hmpd and wknd over 1f out* **5/1**[3]

00 **7** *3* **Meerlust**[11] 5638 2-8-3 (b[1]) JamesDoyle(3) 9 36
(E F Vaughan) *prom: rdn 1/2-way: wknd over 2f out* **33/1**

456 **8** *2 ½* **Lady Chastity**[33] 5112 2-8-3 65 EdwardCreighton(3) 8 30
(Mrs L J Young) *w ldr tl rdn and hmpd over 2f out: sn wknd* **12/1**

00 **9** *1 ¾* **Byanita (IRE)**[49] 4657 2-8-6 FrancisFerris 3 25
(B Palling) *chsd ldrs: rdn over 2f out: wknd over 1f out* **40/1**

06 **10** *12* **Prima Luna**[23] 5387 2-8-6 TPO'Shea 1 —
(K R Burke) *s.i.s: outpcd* **12/1**

00 **11** *9* **Alevic (IRE)**[93] 3279 2-8-11 (v[1]) MichaelTebbutt 4 —
(J R Norton) *sn outpcd* **80/1**

1m 29.7s (-0.70) **Going Correction** -0.30s/f (Stan) **11** Ran SP% **117.6**
Speed ratings (Par 93):92,90,88,87,84 83,79,76,74,61 50
CSF £20.21 TOTE £5.90: £1.60, £1.80, £2.80; EX 20.60.The winner was bought in for 8,500gns. Cantique was claimed by A G Newcombe for £6,000
Owner Miss J Semple **Bred** T R Lock **Trained** Manton, Wilts

FOCUS
A fairly competitive event for the class and the form looks fair enough.

NOTEBOOK
Madam Gaffer found the further drop in grade right up her street and mowed down her rivals to win going away on this step back up to a seventh furlong. She was entitled to win at the weights, however, and has clearly now found her sort of level. (op 9-2)
Cantique(IRE), down in class, did not help her cause with a slow start and eventually took too long to find her full stride. She is capable of winning at this level and seemed to stay all of the extra furlong. (op 3-1)
Tobago Reef had his chance from the front and was not disgraced. He could find a race of this nature when ridden with greater patience in the future. Official explanation: jockey said gelding hung right throughout (tchd 10-1)
Jost Van Dyke, making his All-Weather debut, did not look to stay this longer trip and is worth another chance when reverting to six furlongs in this class. (tchd 10-3 and 4-1)
Aggbag tended to run in snatches and does look flattered by his current official mark.
Mulvany(IRE) failed to raise his game on this All-Weather bow and is another who has to rate flattered by his official mark. (op 11-2 tchd 9-2)

5877 HOTEL & CONFERENCING AT DUNSTALL PARK H'CAP 7f 32y(P)
3:55 (3:56) (Class 4) (0-85,84) 3-Y-0+ **£5,505** (£1,637; £818; £408) **Stalls** High

Form RPR

0050 **1** **Malcheek (IRE)**[16] 5529 4-9-3 **81** DavidAllan 2 92+
(T D Easterby) *led 2f: led again over 2f out: edgd rt over 1f out: rdn out* **10/1**

1304 **2** *1 ½* **Stonecrabstomorrow (IRE)**[10] 5649 3-9-1 **81** NelsonDeSouza 1 88
(P F I Cole) *chsd ldrs: hmpd and outpcd 1/2-way: rallied over 2f out: chsd wnr over 1f out: styd on same pce ins fnl f* **6/1**[3]

0024 **3** *½* **Millennium Force**[13] 5591 8-8-12 **76** (v) TonyCulhane 9 82
(M R Channon) *mid-div: rdn 4f out: hdwy over 1f out: styd on* **7/1**

2545 **4** *½* **Rezzago (USA)**[9] 5670 6-8-12 **76** AdamKirby 11 80
(W R Swinburn) *mid-div: hdwy over 2f out: rdn and hung lft over 1f out: styd on same pce* **4/1**[1]

4050 **5** *shd* **Desert Dreamer (IRE)**[12] 5627 5-9-2 **80** PaulDoe 4 84+
(P R Chamings) *hld up: hdwy over 1f out: nt rch ldrs* **14/1**

1636 **6** *1 ¾* **Finsbury**[9] 5670 3-8-12 **78** KDarley 8 78
(C F Wall) *hld up: hdwy over 1f out: nrst fin* **11/2**[2]

0000 **7** *shd* **Roman Maze**[16] 5529 6-9-2 **80** EddieAhern 3 79
(W M Brisbourne) *s.i.s: hld up: hdwy over 2f out: rdn and edgd rt over 1f out: no ex* **7/1**

0305 **8** *1 ½* **Fiefdom (IRE)**[13] 5591 4-9-4 **82** JimmyQuinn 6 77
(I W McInnes) *mid-div: lost pl over 4f out: n.d after* **28/1**

060 **9** *1* **Marajaa (IRE)**[149] 1667 4-9-6 **84** DeanMcKeown 7 77
(W J Musson) *chsd ldrs: edgd lft 1/2-way: wknd over 1f out* **16/1**

0141 **10** *1 ¾* **King Harson**[15] 5554 7-9-0 **78** DarryllHolland 12 66
(J D Bethell) *chsd ldrs: rdn over 2f out: wknd over 1f out* **7/1**

2100 **11** *3* **Chicken Soup**[45] 4760 4-9-1 **79** (v[1]) TPO'Shea 10 59
(T J Pitt) *chsd ldr: led 5f out: rdn and hdd over 2f out: hmpd and wknd over 1f out* **12/1**

600 **12** *1 ½* **First Friend (IRE)**[21] 5428 5-8-13 **77** DaneO'Neill 5 54
(P Mitchell) *a in rr: bhd fnl 3f* **25/1**

1m 27.59s (-2.81) **Going Correction** -0.30s/f (Stan)
WFA 3 from 4yo+ 2lb **12** Ran SP% **123.8**
Speed ratings (Par 105):104,102,101,101,101 99,98,97,96,94 90,88
CSF £72.07 CT £467.07 TOTE £10.80: £2.80, £2.60, £3.30; EX 99.40.
Owner Mrs Susie Dicker **Bred** Carrigbeg Stud **Trained** Great Habton, N Yorks

FOCUS
A fair handicap which was run at a sound pace. It paid to be drawn low. The form looks solid.
Fiefdom(IRE) Official explanation: jockey said gelding hung right-handed throughout

5878 HOLIDAY INN DUNSTALL PARK H'CAP 5f 20y(P)
4:30 (4:30) (Class 6) (0-62,62) 3-Y-0+ **£2,730** (£806; £403) **Stalls** Low

Form RPR

2046 **1** **Paddywack (IRE)**[12] 5620 9-8-13 **60** (b) TonyCulhane 3 69
(D W Chapman) *chsd ldrs: rdn to ld ins fnl f: r.o* **15/2**

3400 **2** *shd* **Desert Opal**[23] 5386 6-8-6 **58** (p) LiamJones(5) 10 66
(C R Dore) *hld up: hdwy over 1f out: r.o* **9/1**

0000 **3** *¾* **Sparkwell**[28] 5243 4-9-1 **62** DeanMcKeown 6 68+
(D Shaw) *hld up: hdwy and nt clr run over 1f out: swtchd rt ins fnl f: r.o wl* **20/1**

5000 **4** *¾* **Mystery Pips**[6] 5752 6-8-11 **58** (v) KimTinkler 5 62
(N Tinkler) *w ldrs: led 1/2-way: hdd over 1f out: ev ch ins fnl f: unable qck* **14/1**

0000 **5** *½* **Desert Light (IRE)**[7] 5737 5-8-9 **59** (v) PatrickMathers(3) 1 61
(D Shaw) *chsd ldrs: rdn over 3f out: styd on* **33/1**

4230 **6** *1* **Peruvian Style (IRE)**[14] 5576 5-8-10 **57** JimmyQuinn 9 56+
(J M Bradley) *hld up: hdwy and hmpd 1f out: nvr able to chal* **15/2**

1055 **7** *shd* **Cosmic Destiny (IRE)**[14] 5575 4-8-12 **59** DaneO'Neill 2 58
(E F Vaughan) *w ldrs: led 4f out: hdd 1/2-way: rdn to ld over 1f out: hdd and no ex ins fnl f* **5/2**[1]

6450 **8** *nk* **Blue Knight (IRE)**[12] 5620 7-8-13 **60** (vt) EddieAhern 4 58
(D Carroll) *sn outpcd: nvr nrr* **13/2**[3]

6300 **9** *½* **Egyptian Lord**[12] 5605 3-8-13 **60** (b) RobbieFitzpatrick 8 57
(Peter Grayson) *chsd ldrs: rdn over 1f out: wknd ins fnl f* **25/1**

500 **10** *2 ½* **Almaty Express**[18] 5493 4-9-1 **62** (b) DarryllHolland 12 51
(J R Weymes) *led 1f: rdn 1/2-way: wknd over 1f out* **5/1**[2]

5100 **11** *1 ¼* **Meikle Barfil**[23] 5378 4-8-13 **60** (p) KDarley 11 45
(J M Bradley) *hld up: a in rr* **12/1**

301 **12** *hd* **Mynd**[132] 2096 6-8-13 **60** FrancisFerris 13 45
(B Palling) *mid-div: rdn 1/2-way: sn wknd* **14/1**

61.90 secs (-0.92) **Going Correction** -0.30s/f (Stan) **12** Ran SP% **124.7**
Speed ratings (Par 101):95,94,93,92,91 90,89,89,88,84 82,82
CSF £75.56 CT £1339.56 TOTE £5.70: £3.10, £2.10, £10.80; EX 43.70.
Owner David W Chapman **Bred** Colm McEvoy **Trained** Stillington, N Yorks
■ Stewards' Enquiry : Liam Jones one-day ban: used whip without giving gelding time to respond (Oct 20)

FOCUS
An ordinary sprint, run at a strong pace, and the form looks sound enough for the grade.
Almaty Express Official explanation: jockey said gelding ran wide off first turn
Mynd Official explanation: jockey said gelding stumbled leaving stalls

5879 RINGSIDE SUITE 700 THEATRE STYLE CONFERENCE H'CAP 1m 1f 103y(P)
5:00 (5:00) (Class 5) (0-70,70) 3-Y-O **£3,238** (£963; £481; £240) **Stalls** Low

Form RPR

1450 **1** **Cantabilly (IRE)**[43] 4838 3-9-2 **68** TonyCulhane 2 75
(M R Channon) *a.p: led over 1f out: rdn out* **14/1**

43-2 **2** *1 ¼* **Esthlos (FR)**[24] 5353 3-9-4 **70** EddieAhern 6 74
(J Jay) *hld up: hdwy over 2f out: hung lft over 1f out: styd on* **14/1**

2000 **3** *hd* **Teide Lady**[16] 5525 3-9-0 **66** FrancisFerris 13 70
(Rae Guest) *s.i.s: in rr: hdwy over 1f out: r.o* **33/1**

214 **4** *¾* **Veiled Applause**[32] 5130 3-9-2 **68** NelsonDeSouza 3 71
(R M Beckett) *chsd ldrs: hmpd over 2f out: rdn and hung lft over 1f out: swtchd rt: kpt on* **9/2**[2]

242 **5** *½* **Contemplation**[23] 5368 3-8-13 **65** DeanMcKeown 11 67+
(G A Swinbank) *hld up: nt clr run fr over 2f out tl r.o ins fnl f: nvr nr to chal* **10/1**

5440 **6** *5* **Star Of The Desert (IRE)**[43] [4838] 3-9-4 **70** .... AdamKirby 4 62
(C G Cox) *disp ld tl rdn 2f out: wknd over 1f out* **9/1**
4232 **7** *shd* **Signal Hill**[23] [5388] 3-8-11 **68** ....(b[1]) LiamJones(5) 9 60
(W J Haggas) *hld up in tch: plld hrd: led wl over 1f out: sn rdn: hdd & wknd* **4/1**[1]
6564 **8** *nk* **It's Unbelievable (USA)**[20] [5446] 3-8-10 **67** .... RoryMoore(5) 7 58
(P T Midgley) *s.i.s: hld up: hdwy over 3f out: rdn and wknd over 1f out* **25/1**
063- **9** *3/4* **Hilltop Destiny**[304] [6532] 3-9-2 **68** .... MichaelTebbutt 8 58
(V Smith) *hld up: hdwy over 2f out: sn wknd* **66/1**
0060 **10** *1 1/2* **Pigeon Island**[14] [5568] 3-8-13 **65** .... DaneO'Neill 10 52
(H Candy) *w ldrs tl rdn over 2f out: sn wknd* **5/1**[3]
4005 **11** *2 1/2* **Wassfa**[12] [5611] 3-8-13 **65** .... HayleyTurner 5 47
(C E Brittain) *chsd ldrs: rdn over 3f out: wknd 2f out* **22/1**
210 **12** *1 3/4* **Coalpark (IRE)**[19] [5484] 3-9-3 **69** ....(t) KDarley 1 48
(M Johnston) *mde most tl wl over 1f out: wkng whn hmpd sn after* **8/1**
062 **13** *43* **King's Spear (IRE)**[35] [5071] 3-8-12 **64** .... DarrylHolland 12 —
(P W Chapple-Hyam) *hdwy over 5f out: wknd 3f out* **6/1**

1m 59.91s (-2.71) **Going Correction** -0.30s/f (Stan) **13** Ran SP% **125.3**
Speed ratings (Par 101):100,98,98,98,97 93,93,92,92,90 88,87,48
CSF £198.08 CT £6251.65 TOTE £17.20: £3.60, £4.60, £9.00; EX 227.00 Place 6 £214.32, Place 5 £159.72.
Owner A R Parrish **Bred** W P Iceton **Trained** West Ilsley, Berks

FOCUS
A modest three-year-old handicap which was run at a decent early pace. The form looks just fair.
T/Plt: £178.30 to a £1 stake. Pool: £50,272.75. 205.75 winning tickets. T/Qpdt: £103.90 to a £1 stake. Pool: £3,007.00. 21.40 winning tickets. CR

5779 CHANTILLY (R-H)
Monday, October 9

OFFICIAL GOING: Soft

5880a CRITERIUM DE VITESSE (LISTED RACE) 5f
1:15 (1:14) 2-Y-O **£17,241** (£6,897; £5,172; £3,448; £1,724)

RPR
1 **Beta**[33] [5122] 2-8-12 .... TGillet 6 101
(J E Pease, France)
2 *nk* **Mood Music**[24] [5335] 2-8-11 .... RichardMullen 7 99
(E J O'Neill) *close up til led 2f out, ridden over 1f out, headed and no extra last strides SP 78-10* **78/10**[2]
3 *3* **Numerieus (FR)**[33] [5122] 2-8-12 .... CSoumillon 3 89
(Y De Nicolay, France)
4 *3/4* **Jailamigraine (IRE)**[33] [5122] 2-8-8 .... C-PLemaire 1 82
(P Bary, France)
5 *nk* **Hitra (USA)**[55] [4464] 2-8-8 .... DBoeuf 4 81
(Mme C Head-Maarek, France)
6 *nk* **Holdin Foldin (IRE)**[24] [5335] 2-8-11 .... PatCosgrave 2 83
(K R Burke) *led to 2f out, one pace, weakened and lost 4th close home SP 42-10* **42/10**[1]
7 *3* **Selam (GER)**[79] 2-8-8 .... TJarnet 8 69
(U Suter, France)
8 *6* **Prianca (GER)** 2-8-8 ....(b) OPeslier 9 48
(Mario Hofer, Germany)

60.60 secs **8** Ran SP% **30.6**
PARI-MUTUEL: WIN 3.70; PL 1.40, 2.10, 1.50; DF 13.80.
Owner Niarchos Family **Bred** The Niarchos Family **Trained** Chantilly, France

NOTEBOOK
Mood Music was only thwarted well inside the final furlong and this was a decent effort in defeat. Second early on, he took the lead about one and a half furlongs out but could not hold the eventual winner's well-timed late challenge.
Holdin Foldin(IRE) was the fastest away in this five-furlong dash but was passed before the final furlong and then gradually dropped out of contention

5881a PRIX SCARAMOUCHE (LISTED RACE) 1m 7f
1:45 (1:44) 3-Y-0+ **£17,241** (£6,897; £5,172; £3,448; £1,724)

RPR
1 **Macleya (GER)**[39] [4979] 4-9-1 .... JVictoire 8 106
(A Fabre, France)
2 *3* **Caprice Meill (FR)**[20] 6-9-1 .... TJarnet 5 103
(E Leenders, France)
3 *2 1/2* **Atlantique Nord (FR)**[189] 6-9-4 .... TThulliez 6 103
(D De Watrigant, France)
4 *shd* **Sentry Duty (FR)**[42] 4-9-4 .... CSoumillon 10 103
(E Libaud, France)
5 *1/2* **The French (FR)**[13] 4-9-4 .... DBonilla 1 102
(F Legros, France)
6 *shd* **Milongo (FR)**[61] 4-9-4 .... BrigitteRenk 11 102
(Brigitte Renk, Switzerland)
7 *3/4* **Soterio (GER)**[78] [3775] 6-9-4 .... DBoeuf 4 102
(W Baltromei, Germany)
8 *8* **Kindling**[15] [5551] 4-9-1 .... JoeFanning 7 91
(M Johnston) *midfield on outside, disp 5th str, slightly hmpd and dropped back to last over 2f out, no danger after SP 8-1* **8/1**[1]
9 *3/4* **Cloudor (FR)**[13] 4-9-4 ....(b) RonanThomas 9 93
(P Demercastel, France)
10 *6* **High Fidelity (GER)**[58] 3-8-5 .... SPasquier 3 84
(A Fabre, France)
11 **Benta Berri (FR)**[351] 4-9-9 ....(b) IMendizabal 2 92
(R Martin-Sanchez, Spain)

3m 24.2s
WFA 3 from 4yo+ 10lb **11** Ran SP% **11.1**
PARI-MUTUEL: WIN 6.10 (coupled with High Fidelity); PL 3.90, 12.50,3.30; DF 42.70.
Owner Mme A Fabre **Bred** Gestut Schlenderhan **Trained** Chantilly, France

NOTEBOOK
Kindling did not have the best of trips and is better than she showed. Well placed rounding the final turn, she was hampered with over two furlongs to run and dropped right out.

5754 LEICESTER (R-H)
Tuesday, October 10

OFFICIAL GOING: Good to soft (good in places)
Wind: Light, across Weather: Hazy sunshine

5882 EBF LADBROKES.COM SOAR MAIDEN STKS (DIV I) 1m 60y
1:50 (1:51) (Class 5) 2-Y-0 **£3,886** (£1,156; £577; £288) **Stalls** Low

Form RPR
0 **1** **Maid To Believe**[21] [5456] 2-8-12 .... JimmyQuinn 8 68
(J L Dunlop) *prom: outpcd over 2f out: rallied over 1f out: r.o to ld wl ins fnl f: comf* **25/1**
2 *3/4* **Waymark (IRE)** 2-9-3 .... PhilipRobinson 10 72
(M A Jarvis) *chsd ldrs: rdn to ld over 1f out: hdd wl ins fnl f* **9/1**[2]
3 *1/2* **Eulogize** 2-8-12 .... MartinDwyer 5 65
(E A L Dunlop) *hld up: hdwy over 2f out: r.o* **16/1**[3]
06 **4** *hd* **Crimson Monarch (USA)**[13] [5623] 2-9-3 .... JimCrowley 3 70
(Mrs A J Perrett) *hld up: rdn over 3f out: hdwy over 1f out: r.o* **33/1**
2 **5** *2* **Life (IRE)**[12] [5640] 2-9-3 .... LDettori 2 65
(J Noseda) *hld up in tch: led over 2f out: rdn: edgd rt and hdd over 1f out: no ex ins fnl f* **2/7**[1]
4 **6** *shd* **My Super Bird (USA)**[19] [5491] 2-9-3 .... KDarley 1 65
(M Johnston) *prom: racd keenly: effrt and hmpd over 1f out: styd on same pce* **16/1**[3]
0 **7** *1 1/4* **Grangehurst**[14] [5596] 2-8-12 .... ChrisCatlin 9 57
(Miss J R Gibney) *led: rdn and hdd over 2f out: wknd fnl f* **100/1**
8 *3* **Lindhoven (USA)** 2-9-3 .... BrettDoyle 7 55
(C E Brittain) *chsd ldr over 5f out to over 2f out: hmpd and wknd over 1f out* **100/1**
9 *9* **Spellbinding (IRE)** 2-8-12 .... DeanMcKeown 4 30
(J M P Eustace) *hld up: rdn 1/2-way: wknd 3f out* **100/1**
10 *9* **Highland Legacy** 2-9-3 .... DarrylHolland 6 14
(M L W Bell) *s.s: rdn 1/2-way: wknd over 3f out* **28/1**

1m 49.36s (4.06) **Going Correction** +0.35s/f (Good) **10** Ran SP% **112.7**
Speed ratings (Par 95):93,92,91,91,89 89,88,85,76,67
CSF £213.36 TOTE £27.20: £5.30, £2.20, £3.40; EX 530.10 TRIFECTA Not won..
Owner Normandie Stud Ltd **Bred** Normandie Stud Ltd **Trained** Arundel, W Sussex
■ Stewards' Enquiry : L Dettori caution: careless riding

FOCUS
With the odds-on favourite disappointing this race took less winning, and it was run in an ordinary winning time, despite being 0.6 seconds faster than the second division. It is doubtful if the bare form is worth much more than it has been rated.

NOTEBOOK
Maid To Believe, a half-sister to three juvenile winners, and also to King's Kama, a ten-furlong winner at three, improved for her debut at Newmarket three weeks earlier, settling better and running out a comfortable winner on this easier ground. She should make up into a nice middle-distance filly next season.
Waymark(IRE), who cost 260,000euros, is out of a mare who won over a mile at two in France and was later a high-class triple winner in the US. There was plenty to like about this debut and he too is likely to be seen to best effect next year when stepped up to middle distances. (op 8-1)
Eulogize, whose dam is a half-sister to a number of winners, including top-class juvenile Dazzle, is bred to appreciate a bit of give in the ground and was running on well at the end of the race. She could well get off the mark in a similar contest before the season is out. (op 14-1)
Crimson Monarch(USA), a half-brother to two winners in the US, including a multiple sprint winner, has improved with every outing and is now eligible for a handicap mark. He should do better in that sphere. (op 28-1)
Life(IRE) was backed as though defeat was out of the question, but he disappointed badly. Not knocked about once it was clear he was going to play no part in the finish, it is to be hoped that something comes to light, as his Newmarket debut suggested he had a bright future. Official explanation: jockey said colt had a breathing problem (op 4-11 after early 2-5)
My Super Bird(USA), whose stable's two-year-olds usually improve for their debut outings, had an extra two furlongs to cover this time, but he raced too keenly in the early stages. Although held when hampered approaching the final furlong, he would have finished closer with a clearer run. (op 18-1)

5883 EBF LADBROKES.COM REFERENCE POINT MAIDEN STKS (C&G) 7f 9y
2:20 (2:21) (Class 5) 2-Y-0 **£4,533** (£1,348; £674; £336) **Stalls** Low

Form RPR
0 **1** **Mount Hadley (USA)**[11] [5658] 2-9-0 .... BrettDoyle 10 88
(E A L Dunlop) *chsd ldr: led over 2f out: rdn and hung lft over 1f out: r.o* **40/1**
2 *1 1/4* **Cabinet (IRE)** 2-9-0 .... JimmyQuinn 12 85
(Sir Michael Stoute) *mid-div: hdwy over 2f out: rdn to chse wnr over 1f out: styd on same pce ins fnl f* **16/1**
3 **3** *2 1/2* **Monte Alto (IRE)**[27] [5297] 2-9-0 .... NickyMackay 1 79
(L M Cumani) *chsd ldrs: rdn over 2f out: no ex fnl f* **13/2**
32 **4** *3/4* **Hurlingham**[95] [3253] 2-9-0 .... KDarley 5 77
(M Johnston) *chsd ldrs: rdn over 2f out: no ex fnl f* **4/1**[1]
5 *nk* **Harland** 2-9-0 .... PhilipRobinson 16 76
(M A Jarvis) *racd alone to 1/2-way: chsd ldrs: rdn over 1f out: no ex fnl f* **14/1**
6 *1* **The Carlton Cannes** 2-9-0 .... DarrylHolland 13 74
(G Wragg) *outpcd: hdwy over 1f out: wknd ins fnl f* **25/1**
7 *1* **Hope Road** 2-9-0 .... OscarUrbina 7 71
(J R Fanshawe) *hld up: hdwy over 1f out: nvr trbld ldrs* **20/1**
8 *shd* **Optical Illusion (USA)** 2-9-0 .... LDettori 4 71
(E A L Dunlop) *hld up: hdwy over 2f out: wknd fnl f* **11/2**[3]
9 *3 1/2* **Mujma** 2-9-0 .... MartinDwyer 6 62
(Sir Michael Stoute) *prom: rdn over 2f out: wknd over 1f out* **9/2**[2]
224 **10** *1/2* **Cavalry Guard (USA)**[20] [5481] 2-9-0 80 ....(v[1]) ChrisCatlin 9 61
(H R A Cecil) *chsd ldrs: rdn over 2f out: wknd over 1f out* **7/1**
5 **11** *11* **Marquee (IRE)**[34] [5111] 2-9-0 .... TPO'Shea 8 33
(P A Blockley) *led over 4f: wknd over 1f out* **33/1**
12 *1 3/4* **Bergonzi (IRE)** 2-9-0 .... RobertHavlin 3 29
(J H M Gosden) *sn outpcd* **10/1**
13 *1 3/4* **Vital Tryst** 2-9-0 .... JamieMackay 11 25
(J G Given) *s.i.s: outpcd* **40/1**

1m 27.34s (1.24) **Going Correction** +0.15s/f (Good) **13** Ran SP% **117.5**
Speed ratings (Par 95):98,96,93,92,92 91,90,90,86,85 72,70,68
CSF £549.55 TOTE £59.10: £9.10, £3.50, £1.70; EX 2137.80 TRIFECTA Not won..
Owner Saeed Maktoum Al Maktoum **Bred** Gainsborough Farm Llc **Trained** Newmarket, Suffolk

FOCUS
This looked a decent maiden on paper and, despite the shock result, the form should work out. The third and fourth, plus the time, set the standard for now.

NOTEBOOK

Mount Hadley(USA), a half-brother to juvenile winners Sky Galaxy and Moonshine Girl, ran out a shock winner on his second ever start. Prominent throughout, he showed the benefit of his introduction at Newmarket 11 days earlier and, despite running green and hanging to the left, eventually ran out a clear winner. He could well make his mark in better grade before being put away for the winter.

Cabinet(IRE), whose stable won this race last year with Papal Bull and in total had been successful in this race in five of the previous nine seasons, is a half-brother to Ryedale Ovation, a five-furlong winner at two, and to Magic Instinct, a dual winner over middle distances at three. He finished nicely clear of the rest and normal improvement should see him go one better next time.

Monte Alto(IRE), who had easier ground to deal with than on his debut, did best of those drawn in single figures and ran a solid race in third. (op 9-1 tchd 10-1)

Hurlingham did not run quite as well on this easier ground, although he was perhaps handicapped by a low draw. (op 5-2)

Harland, whose dam was a dual winner at three in France and Group 2-placed over middle distances, shaped with promise on his debut. He will get a lot further in time but should improve enough for this outing to win over seven furlongs or a mile this year. (tchd 16-1)

The Carlton Cannes, a brother to Hotel Du Cap, a 12-furlong winner at three, showed his inexperience with a slow start but did not shape too badly once he got himself involved. He is likely to be brought along slowly and should be seen to better effect next year. (tchd 28-1)

Mujma, a half-brother to Under The Rainbow, who won the Zetland Stakes at two, cost 210,000gns as a yearling. He was the preferred representative from the stable according to the betting, but dropped out after racing prominently for a long way. He should improve for the outing. (op 5-1 tchd 11-2)

5884 LADBROKES.COM CONDITIONS STKS 7f 9y

2:50 (2:50) (Class 4) 2-Y-O £4,533 (£1,348; £674) Stalls Low

Form				RPR
1213	1		**Majuro (IRE)**[10] 5665 2-8-13 91 ... ChrisCatlin 1 (M R Channon) *mde all: racd keenly: drvn clr fnl f* **4/11**[1]	87+
1	2	7	**Carwell (IRE)**[74] 3908 2-8-11 ... KDarley 4 (M Johnston) *chsd wnr: rdn over 1f out: eased whn btn fnl f* **5/2**[2]	70+
404	3	11	**Oedipuss (IRE)**[7] 5759 2-8-8 46 ... EmmettStack(5) 2 (K J Burke) *chsd ldrs: rdn 1/2-way: wknd over 2f out* **50/1**[3]	42

1m 27.56s (1.46) **Going Correction** +0.15s/f (Good) 3 Ran SP% **103.8**

Speed ratings (Par 97):97,89,76

CSF £1.43 TOTE £1.40; EX 1.20.

Owner Capital **Bred** Tally-Ho Stud **Trained** West Ilsley, Berks

FOCUS

A poor turnout for this conditions event, and effectively a match. The winner was just below his mark.

NOTEBOOK

Majuro(IRE) took a while to assert himself but he drew clear in the closing stages and on this evidence he will not at all mind a return to a mile. He seems pretty versatile with regard to ground conditions. (op 2-5)

Carwell(IRE), a winner of a firm-ground maiden on her debut in July, had a fairly stiff task on her plate in receipt of only 2lb from a colt rated 91. She ran well for a long way, though, and briefly looked a threat approaching the final furlong, but she was unable to get past the favourite and was eased right down once her chance of victory had gone. She deserves rating better than the seven-length beaten distance suggests. (op 9-4)

Oedipuss(IRE) is only plating class and was out of his depth in this company, but credit must go to his connections, as he managed to pick up £674.10 for finishing third in a three-runner race. (op 33-1)

5885 LADBROKESCASINO.COM (S) H'CAP 7f 9y

3:25 (3:25) (Class 6) (0-60,60) 3-4-Y-O £2,590 (£770; £385; £192) Stalls Low

Form				RPR
0000	1		**Bodden Bay**[12] 5631 4-8-10 **50** ... DarryllHolland 18 (D Carroll) *mde all far side: rdn clr over 1f out: unchal* **12/1**	61
4020	2	1 1/4	**Bold Haze**[36] 5062 4-8-9 **54** ...(v) MichaelJStainton(5) 14 (Miss S E Hall) *racd centre: s.i.s: plld hrd and sn prom: chsd wnr and edgd rt 1/2-way: sn rdn: styd on* **12/1**	62
0650	3	1 1/2	**Mucho Loco (IRE)**[20] 5474 3-8-10 **52** ...(b) JimCrowley 10 (J G Portman) *racd centre: hld up in tch: rdn over 1f out: styd on: nt rch ldrs* **5/1**[1]	56
1254	4	1 3/4	**Mon Petite Amour**[88] 3488 3-8-7 **49** ...(p) PhilipRobinson 9 (D W P Arbuthnot) *racd centre: chsd ldrs: rdn over 2f out: styd on* **11/1**	48
040	5	1/2	**Drum Dance (IRE)**[12] 5631 4-8-9 **49** ... ChrisCatlin 1 (N Tinkler) *racd centre: prom: lost pl over 4f out: hdwy over 1f out: nt rch ldrs* **9/1**	47
0000	6	1	**Marcello**[20] 5474 3-8-13 **55** ...(t) NelsonDeSouza 11 (P F I Cole) *racd centre: chsd ldr of that gp tl rdn over 2f out: styd on same pce appr fnl f* **10/1**	50
0060	7	hd	**Catherines Cafe (IRE)**[39] 4983 3-8-10 **52** ...(v1) RobertHavlin 13 (Mrs P N Dutfield) *racd centre: chsd ldrs: rdn over 2f out: styd on same pce appr fnl f* **16/1**	47
6300	8	2 1/2	**Red Vixen (IRE)**[12] 5636 3-8-0 **49** ... KirstyMilczarek(7) 2 (C N Allen) *racd centre: chsd ldrs: rdn over 2f out: wknd over 1f out* **25/1**	37
1660	9	3/4	**Taras Tornado**[127] 2284 3-8-8 **50** ... JimmyQuinn 5 (J J Quinn) *racd centre: hmpd s: hld up: racd keenly: nvr trbld ldrs* **10/1**	36
-000	10	2 1/2	**Sharp Duo (IRE)**[36] 5054 3-8-8 **50** ... PaulDoe 6 (M S Saunders) *racd centre: wnt lft s: sn prom: lost pl 5f out: swtchd rt and hdwy over 2f out: wknd over 1f out* **33/1**	30
3000	11	5	**Rowan Warning**[20] 5474 4-9-1 **55** ... LDettori 8 (J R Boyle) *racd centre: hld up: swtchd rt and hdwy over 2f out: sn rdn and wknd* **7/1**[3]	22
3000	12	4	**Sprinkle**[25] 5350 3-8-13 **55** ...(b1) MartinDwyer 17 (R M Beckett) *s.i.s: racd centre: hld up: swtchd rt and hdwy over 2f out: rdn and hung rt over 1f out: sn wknd* **14/1**	12
2020	13	1	**Wiltshire (IRE)**[112] 2728 4-9-1 **55** ...(b) RobbieFitzpatrick 4 (P T Midgley) *racd centre: dwlt: a in rr* **18/1**	9
2001	14	2	**Crush On You**[22] 5432 3-8-6 **48** ... KDarley 3 (R Hollinshead) *racd centre: prom 5f* **6/1**[2]	—
260	15	24	**Our Mary (IRE)**[12] 5637 3-8-2 **49** ...(t) EmmettStack(5) 12 (Robert Gray) *led centre to 1/2-way: sn wknd: eased fnl f* **50/1**	—
062-	16	1	**Rambling Socks**[310] 6496 3-8-11 **53** ...(b) PaulEddery 16 (S R Bowring) *racd far side: chsd wnr to 1/2-way: sn bhd* **28/1**	—

1m 27.87s (1.77) **Going Correction** +0.15s/f (Good)

WFA 3 from 4yo 2lb 16 Ran SP% 125.4

Speed ratings (Par 101):95,93,91,89,89 88,87,85,84,81 75,71,69,67,40 39

CSF £148.06 CT £866.81 TOTE £15.50: £3.30, £3.40, £1.70, £2.90; EX 239.50 TRIFECTA Not won..There was no bid for the winner.

Owner Andy Franks & Steve Franks **Bred** Gary Middlemiss **Trained** Warthill, N Yorks

FOCUS

An ordinary selling handicap in which once again a double-figure draw appeared to help. The form seems sound enough.

5886 EBF LADBROKES.COM SOAR MAIDEN STKS (DIV II) 1m 60y

4:00 (4:01) (Class 5) 2-Y-O £3,886 (£1,156; £577; £288) Stalls Low

Form				RPR
3	1		**Glen Nevis (USA)**[11] 5659 2-9-3 ... LDettori 1 (J Noseda) *chsd ldr tl led over 2f out: clr over 1f out: eased ins fnl f* **4/9**[1]	75+
26	2	1	**Audit (IRE)**[27] 5297 2-9-3 ... MartinDwyer 8 (Sir Michael Stoute) *trckd ldrs: rdn over 1f out: nt run on* **7/1**[2]	73
05	3	3	**Camps Bay (USA)**[21] 5458 2-9-3 ... JimCrowley 6 (Mrs A J Perrett) *prom: rdn over 2f out: styd on same pce fnl f* **9/1**[3]	66
00	4	3	**Last Flight (IRE)**[14] 5595 2-8-12 ... ChrisCatlin 10 (J L Dunlop) *hld up: hdwy over 3f out: rdn over 2f out: wknd over 1f out* **16/1**	54
06	5	2 1/2	**Disintegration (IRE)**[20] 5475 2-9-3 ... RobertHavlin 9 (A King) *hld up: hdwy over 2f out: wknd over 1f out* **28/1**	53
	6	shd	**Wait For The Light** 2-9-3 ... BrettDoyle 7 (E A L Dunlop) *s.i.s: hld up: hdwy over 2f out: wknd over 1f out* **33/1**	53
6	7	7	**Grand Dream (IRE)**[29] 5239 2-9-3 ... KDarley 4 (M Johnston) *led over 5f: rdn and wknd over 1f out* **16/1**	37
00	8	6	**Sky Beam (USA)**[43] 4866 2-8-12 ... PaulDoe 3 (J L Dunlop) *hld up: hdwy over 3f out: rdn and wknd over 2f out* **50/1**	18
	9	hd	**Solo City** 2-9-3 ... TPO'Shea 5 (P A Blockley) *s.i.s: outpcd: wknd 3f out* **100/1**	23

1m 49.96s (4.66) **Going Correction** +0.35s/f (Good) 72 Ran SP% **112.9**

Speed ratings (Par 95):90,89,86,83,80 80,73,67,67

CSF £3.65 TOTE £1.30: £1.02, £1.50, £1.50; EX 4.30 Trifecta £10.90 Pool: £495.95 - 32.07 winning tickets..

Owner Sheikh Marwan Al Maktoum **Bred** Nutbush Farm **Trained** Newmarket, Suffolk

FOCUS

An uncompetitive maiden in which they almost finished in perfect market order. The winning time was modest for the type of race as well, 0.6 seconds slower than the first division. The third helps set the standard.

NOTEBOOK

Glen Nevis(USA) did not need to improve on his Newmarket debut effort to win this and he could have won by a lot further had his rider wished. Despite his speedy pedigree, the extra furlong was not a problem. (op 4-7 tchd 4-6)

Audit(IRE) had the visor dispensed with this time, but again did not look to be putting it all in and is hugely flattered by his proximity to the winner.

Camps Bay(USA) plugged on to record his best placing on his third start, but probably did not improve on his last effort. The most important thing, however, is that he now qualifies for nurseries and that is surely going to be his best avenue to get off the mark. (op 10-1)

Last Flight(IRE) looks slow, but she is bred for stamina and is likely to improve for the switch to modest middle-distance handicaps next term. (op 18-1)

Disintegration(IRE) had only beaten a total of three horses in two previous outings and did not achieve much here. His only hope is that he improves for middle-distances next season, as his pedigree suggests he should, and he is another that now qualifies for handicaps. (tchd 25-1)

Sky Beam(USA) Official explanation: jockey said filly lost its action

5887 LADBROKES.COM CLAIMING STKS 1m 3f 183y

4:35 (4:35) (Class 5) 3-4-Y-O £3,238 (£963; £481; £240) Stalls High

Form				RPR
400-	1		**War At Sea (IRE)**[16] 5669 4-9-9 77 ... ChrisCatlin 8 (P J Hobbs) *chsd ldrs: rdn over 3f out: led over 2f out: edgd lft: over 1f out: styd on* **6/1**[3]	64
0502	2	1 3/4	**Lanfredo**[7] 5757 3-8-9 45 ...(p) PhilipRobinson 2 (D W P Arbuthnot) *w ldr tl led 8f out: rdn and hdd over 2f out: ev ch over 1f out: styd on same pce ins fnl f* **7/1**	55
2000	3	1	**Jazrawy**[11] 5652 4-8-11 52 ... WilliamCarson(7) 6 (P W Hiatt) *hld up: hdwy over 4f out: rdn and ev whn hung lft over 2f out: styd on* **16/1**	55
4062	4	1	**Always Baileys (IRE)**[7] 5751 3-9-0 68 ... KDarley 4 (M Johnston) *prom: rdn over 4f out: sn hung rt: styd on same pce fnl f* **1/1**[1]	56
0006	5	4	**Adage**[18] 5510 3-8-11 52 ...(t) NeilChalmers(3) 1 (David Pinder) *hld up: rdn over 3f out: nvr trbld ldrs* **12/1**	50
4006	6	2	**Bamboo Banks (IRE)**[13] 5625 3-9-0 67 ... JimmyQuinn 7 (J L Dunlop) *hld up: hdwy over 2f out: rdn and ev ch over 1f out: wknd ins fnl f* **4/1**[2]	47
0065	7	7	**Plough Maite**[10] 5365 3-8-12 45 ... DaleGibson 5 (D E Cantillon) *led 4f: rdn and wknd over 2f out* **40/1**	34
0000	8	25	**Flying Penne**[8] 5733 3-8-2 45 ... FrankieMcDonald 3 (R Curtis) *s.s: hdwy over 9f out: wknd 3f out* **100/1**	—

2m 38.04s (3.54) **Going Correction** +0.35s/f (Good)

WFA 3 from 4yo 7lb 8 Ran SP% **113.8**

Speed ratings (Par 103):102,100,100,99,96 95,90,74

CSF £46.58 TOTE £8.20: £2.00, £1.20, £4.40; EX 28.60 Trifecta £281.20 Pool: £534.73 - 1.35 winning tickets..Wnr clmd A Carroll £12,000, Always Baileys T Wall £10,000, Lanfredo P. Martin £5,000.

Owner Whistlejacket Partnership **Bred** Ballymacoll Stud Farm Ltd **Trained** Withycombe, Somerset

■ Stewards' Enquiry : Chris Catlin one-day ban; careless riding (Oct 23)

FOCUS

A weak claimer in which the field spread themselves right across the track in the home straight. The form looks modest and the winner was miles off last season's Flat form.

5888 LADBROKESCASINO.COM FILLIES' CONDITIONS STKS 1m 60y

5:05 (5:13) (Class 4) 3-Y-O £5,678 (£1,699; £849) Stalls Low

Form				RPR
315-	1		**Pure Illusion (IRE)**[397] 5066 3-8-12 96 ... MartinDwyer 3 (Saeed Bin Suroor) *mde all: rdn over 1f out: styd on* **4/5**[1]	86+
6111	2	1 1/2	**Air Biscuit (IRE)**[19] 5497 3-8-12 76 ...(t) KDarley 5 (C F Wall) *chsd ldrs: rdn over 1f out: styd on same pce ins fnl f* **9/2**[3]	83
5425	3	3/4	**Penfection (IRE)**[10] 5666 3-8-12 85 ...(t) OscarUrbina 4 (M Botti) *chsd wnr tl rdn over 1f out: no ex ins fnl f* **9/4**[2]	81

1m 46.87s (1.57) **Going Correction** +0.35s/f (Good) 3 Ran SP% **104.5**

Speed ratings (Par 100):106,104,103

CSF £4.10 TOTE £1.50; EX 3.40.

Owner Godolphin **Bred** Swettenham Stud **Trained** Newmarket, Suffolk

FOCUS

A raced marred by the fatal injury to the 4-6 favourite Royal Proposal (due to make her debut for Godolphin) going to the start. (R4 applies, deduct 55p in the £, new market formed.) Despite there only being three runners, the pace was decent and the race still went to Godolphin. The form is not solid.

5889 **LADBROKES.COM H'CAP** **1m 1f 218y**
5:35 (5:37) (Class 5) (0-75,75) 3-Y-O+ **£3,238** (£963; £481; £240) **Stalls** High

Form RPR

2020 **1** **Fabrian**[20] 5479 8-9-6 **73** ... JamesDoyle(3) 5 84
(R J Price) *a.p: led 3f out: rdn out* **7/1**[3]

6451 **2** *1* **Trouble Mountain (USA)**[10] 5685 9-9-7 **71** ... (t) DaleGibson 4 80
(M W Easterby) *hld up: hdwy u.p over 1f out: styd on wl* **11/2**[1]

0201 **3** *1* **Double Spectre (IRE)**[28] 5267 4-9-1 **65** ... RobertHavlin 2 72
(Jean-Rene Auvray) *hld up: hdwy over 4f out: rdn to chse wnr over 1f out: styd on same pce ins fnl f* **9/1**

2066 **4** *nk* **Dower House**[14] 5599 11-9-2 **66** ... (t) ChrisCatlin 3 73
(Andrew Turnell) *hld up: hdwy over 2f out: sn rdn: styd on same pce ins fnl f* **20/1**

0300 **5** *5* **Dispol Veleta**[8] 5734 5-9-3 **67** ... JamieMackay 1 64
(Miss T Spearing) *hld up: hdwy u.p over 2f out: nt rch ldrs* **50/1**

3040 **6** *¾* **The Composer**[14] 5599 4-9-2 **66** ... OscarUrbina 15 62
(M Blanshard) *hld up: nt clr run over 3f out: styd on aproaching fnl f: nvr nrr* **8/1**

2504 **7** *2 ½* **William's Way**[4] 5786 4-9-6 **70** ... DarryllHolland 13 61
(I A Wood) *hld up: rdn over 2f out: nvr nrr* **11/1**

0104 **8** *¾* **Exit Smiling**[10] 5685 4-9-6 **70** ... RobbieFitzpatrick 16 59
(P T Midgley) *chsd ldrs: rdn over 2f out: wknd over 1f out* **11/1**

4303 **9** *1* **Libre**[94] 3311 6-8-13 **63** ... BrianReilly 17 51
(F Jordan) *s.i.s: hld up: rdn over 3f out: wknd over 1f out* **16/1**

0350 **10** *1* **Materialize (USA)**[40] 4945 3-9-0 **69** ... JimmyQuinn 9 55
(H R A Cecil) *hld up: hdwy u.p 3f out: wknd 2f out* **14/1**

0354 **11** *shd* **Snark (IRE)**[87] 3547 3-9-4 **73** ... MartinDwyer 7 58
(P J Makin) *chsd ldrs: rdn over 2f out: wknd over 1f out* **6/1**[2]

11-0 **12** *1* **Prince Of Love (IRE)**[10] 5685 3-9-1 **70** ... FrankieMcDonald 11 54
(Jedd O'Keeffe) *hld up in tch: plld hrd: rdn over 4f out: wknd 3f out* **22/1**

0000 **13** *9* **Jakarmi**[14] 5599 5-9-3 **67** ... KDarley 6 33
(B Palling) *chsd ldrs: led 4f out: hdd 3f out: wknd and eased over 1f out* **20/1**

3001 **14** *3* **Looker**[13] 5625 3-8-12 **67** ... JimCrowley 10 28
(J Gallagher) *chsd ldrs over 7f* **8/1**

1140 **15** *5* **Gala Sunday (USA)**[10] 5685 6-8-10 **67** ... (bt) AdeleRothery(7) 14 18
(M W Easterby) *led 6f: wknd 3f out* **33/1**

-615 **16** *dist* **Capistrano**[141] 1881 3-9-3 **72** ... TPO'Shea 12 —
(Mrs P Sly) *chsd ldrs over 5f* **33/1**

2m 9.93s (1.63) **Going Correction** +0.35s/f (Good)
WFA 3 from 4yo+ 5lb **16** Ran SP% **125.3**
Speed ratings (Par 103):107,106,105,105,101 100,98,97,97,96 96,95,88,85,81 —
CSF £42.46 CT £363.40 TOTE £10.00: £1.70, £2.40, £4.80, £4.90; EX 58.20 TRIFECTA Not won. Place 6 £592.58, Place 5 £96.61.
Owner Glyn Byard **Bred** Juddmonte Farms **Trained** Ullingswick, H'fords

FOCUS
An ordinary handicap, but the big field made it a competitive one and the pace was decent, with the time the pick of those on the round course. Those that set it paid for it late on though, and the winner was the only one to race prominently and still be there at the end. The form looks pretty solid and should prove reliable.
Snark(IRE) Official explanation: jockey said colt had no more to give
Jakarmi Official explanation: jockey said gelding had a breathing problem
Capistrano Official explanation: jockey said gelding swallowed its tongue
T/Plt: £774.20 to a £1 stake. Pool: £47,993.00. 45.25 winning tickets. T/Qpdt: £11.80 to a £1 stake. Pool: £4,332.10. 270.90 winning tickets. CR

5371 NEWBURY (L-H)
Tuesday, October 10

OFFICIAL GOING: Soft
Wind: Mild, behind

5890 **NEWVOICEMEDIA MAIDEN STKS (DIV I)** **7f (S)**
1:30 (1:32) (Class 4) 2-Y-O **£4,533** (£1,348; £674; £336) **Stalls** High

Form RPR

1 **Hollow Ridge** 2-8-12 ... RichardHughes 18 76
(B W Hills) *t.k.h: hld up towards rr: prog into mid-div over 2f out:swtchd lft over 1f out: r.o wl: led and edgd rt cl home* **10/1**

2 *hd* **Mr Napper Tandy** 2-9-0 ... EdwardCreighton(3) 16 80
(M R Channon) *mid-div: tk clsr order 2f out: sn rdn: r.o strly ins fnl f: wnt cl 2nd whn bmpd fnl strides* **8/1**

3 *shd* **Athar (IRE)** 2-9-3 ... RyanMoore 12 80
(R Hannon) *in tch: hdwy 2f out: rdn to ld 1f out: kpt on but no ex whn narrowly hdd and bmpd cl home* **8/1**

0 **4** *1 ½* **Shavoulin (USA)**[18] 5508 2-9-0 ... SaleemGolam(3) 3 76
(Christian Wroe, UAE) *wnt rt s: led: rdn and hrd pressed fr 2f out: narrowly hdd 1f out: cl 4th but hld whn n.m.r and snatched up cl home* **50/1**

00 **5** *½* **Gilded Youth**[30] 5206 2-9-3 ... DaneO'Neill 10 75
(H Candy) *chsd ldr: rdn and ev ch 2f out: kpt on same pce fnl f* **16/1**

0 **6** *2* **Paradise Walk**[40] 4964 2-8-9 ... RichardKingscote(3) 5 65
(R Charlton) *mid-div: rdn over 2f out: hung lft over 1f out: styd on fnl f* **7/1**[3]

7 *2 ½* **Bold Saxon (IRE)** 2-9-3 ... RichardSmith 6 64
(M D I Usher) *chsd ldrs: rdn and ev ch appr fnl f: kpt on same pce* **100/1**

8 *4* **Montrose Man** 2-9-3 ... KerrinMcEvoy 4 54
(B J Meehan) *sltly hmpd s: sn in tch: effrt 2f out: wknd fnl f* **7/1**[3]

9 *1 ½* **Polish World (USA)** 2-9-3 ... JamieSpencer 7 50
(E A L Dunlop) *wnt rt s: t.k.h towards rr: rdn over 2f out: no imp* **6/1**[2]

0 **10** *1 ¼* **Guiseppe Verdi (USA)**[11] 5658 2-9-3 ... JimmyFortune 13 47
(J H M Gosden) *chsd ldrs: rdn and effrt 2f out: sn btn* **10/3**[1]

0 **11** *nk* **Ishimagic**[14] 5586 2-8-9 ... DominicFox(3) 2 41
(J J Bridger) *chsd ldrs tl wknd 2f out* **50/1**

0 **12** *5* **Nordic Affair**[21] 5458 2-9-3 ... JohnEgan 9 34
(D R C Elsworth) *s.i.s: a towards rr* **20/1**

13 *1 ¼* **Tivers Song (USA)** 2-9-3 ... EddieAhern 11 31
(Mrs A J Perrett) *a towards rr* **33/1**

14 *4* **Palmetto Point** 2-9-3 ... SteveDrowne 1 21
(H Morrison) *s.i.s: a towards rr* **50/1**

15 *9* **Adversane** 2-9-3 ... IanMongan 15 —
(J L Dunlop) *s.i.s: a towards rr* **40/1**

16 *3* **Art Of Poker (IRE)** 2-9-3 ... MichaelHills 17 —
(B W Hills) *short of room sn after s: a bhd* **20/1**

17 *1* **Philandering** 2-9-3 ... (t) StephenCarson 8 —
(R F Johnson Houghton) *s.i.s: a bhd* **50/1**

1m 30.36s (3.36) **Going Correction** +0.425s/f (Yiel) **17** Ran SP% **123.3**
Speed ratings (Par 97):97,96,96,94,94 92,89,84,82,81 81,75,74,69,59 55,54
CSF £81.15 TOTE £8.90: £2.90, £3.40, £3.10; EX 105.00.
Owner K Abdulla **Bred** Juddmonte Farms Ltd **Trained** Lambourn, Berks

FOCUS
This was an interesting first division of the maiden and several of these are likely to progress from the experience, although the form is nothing special on paper. The winning time was 0.44 seconds faster than the second division.

NOTEBOOK
Hollow Ridge ◆ needed every yard of this trip and just got up to make a winning debut despite hanging right in the closing stages and hampering a couple of her rivals. Out of the Irish Oaks and Ribblesdale winner Bolas, she is a half-sister to a winner at up to two miles so it was no surprise that connections afterwards suggested she will appreciate further next season. (op 6-1)
Mr Napper Tandy ◆ may have been unlucky not to make a winning debut as he was coming with a promising run between the winner and third-home Athar when squeezed for room as Hollow Ridge hung into him right at the death. He is less stoutly bred than than the winner and his future probably lies at around a mile. He looks sure to win races. (op 10-1)
Athar(IRE) ◆ was another to make a very encouraging debut and only just lost out having been close to the pace throughout. Out of a two-year-old winner in Belgium, he should not be hard to place. (op 16-1)
Shavoulin(USA) had the edge in experience on the front trio and tried to make it count under a positive ride. He had already run his race when receiving a bump from the winner, but this was still a step up from his debut effort and he seems to be going the right way.
Gilded Youth, who had shown signs of ability in his first two outings, had every chance and ran his best race to date. He now qualifies for a mark. (tchd 20-1)
Paradise Walk still looked green, just as she did on her debut, and tended to hang in the latter stages. She does not seem to be without ability, but may need more time. (op 8-1 tchd 9-1)
Montrose Man, a half-brother to two winners, is bred to appreciate this sort of trip but raced wider than the majority of the field and can be expected to improve. (op 9-1)
Polish World(USA) ◆, a $550,000 colt whose winning dam is related to some smart performers including Orpen, did not help his chances by pulling very hard in the early stages, but still gave the impression that he is capable of a lot better. The Stewards enquired into his performance and noted the connections' explanations that he jumped badly right on leaving the stalls and raced very keen before getting tired. Official explanation: jockey said, regarding running and riding, his orders were to settle colt in mid-division, bring him along and make an effort from halfway, adding that he was unable to carry orders out as colt jumped badly right on leaving stalls, was very keen, and got very tired closing stages (tchd 13-2)
Guiseppe Verdi(USA) was expected to improve from his Newmarket debut, but ultimately he proved disappointing after showing up early. Perhaps he needs better ground. (op 4-1)

5891 **NEWVOICEMEDIA MAIDEN STKS (DIV II)** **7f (S)**
2:00 (2:06) (Class 4) 2-Y-O **£4,533** (£1,348; £674; £336) **Stalls** High

Form RPR

1 **Mythical Kid (USA)** 2-9-3 ... KerrinMcEvoy 1 84+
(Sir Michael Stoute) *trckd ldrs: led 1f out: pushed clr ins last: comf* **9/2**[1]

4 **2** *3* **Contentious (USA)**[27] 5292 2-8-12 ... IanMongan 10 71
(J L Dunlop) *trckd ldrs: led 2f out: rdn and hdd 1f out: kpt on ins last but no ch w wnr* **9/2**[1]

3 *2 ½* **Limbo King** 2-9-3 ... RHills 5 70
(J W Hills) *bhd: hdwy 3f out: drvn and kpt on fr over 1f out to take 3rd ins last but no ch w ldrs* **25/1**

52 **4** *2 ½* **Tinnarinka**[22] 5424 2-8-12 ... RyanMoore 8 59
(R Hannon) *chsd ldrs: chal ins fnl 3f: wknd ins last* **11/2**[2]

5 *1 ½* **Balliasta (IRE)** 2-8-12 ... MichaelHills 2 55
(B W Hills) *s.i.s: bhd: hdwy 1/2-way: outpcd over 2f out: kpt on again ins last* **20/1**

60 **6** *hd* **Majestic Cheer**[24] 5371 2-9-3 ... JohnEgan 4 59
(M R Channon) *chsd ldrs: rdn over 2f out: wknd fnl f* **12/1**

64 **7** *¾* **Mo (USA)**[46] 4768 2-9-3 ... (t) FJohansson 17 57
(R A Kvisla) *plld hrd: sn led: hdd 2f out: wknd over 1f out* **8/1**[3]

8 *shd* **Halkerston** 2-9-3 ... AdamKirby 13 57
(C G Cox) *in tch: hdwy to chse ldrs 3f out: sn drvn: wknd over 1f out* **25/1**

8 *dht* **First Buddy** 2-9-3 ... JamieSpencer 11 57
(W J Haggas) *s.i.s: bhd: hdwy whn nt clr run and swtchd lft over 2f out: styd on ins last but nvr in contention* **11/2**[2]

0 **10** *nk* **Alfresco**[85] 3591 2-9-3 ... JimmyFortune 14 56
(Pat Eddery) *bhd: sme prog fnl f but nvr in contention* **25/1**

0 **11** *2 ½* **Perfect Reward**[95] 3253 2-9-3 ... EddieAhern 15 50
(Mrs A J Perrett) *nvr bttr than mid-div:* **20/1**

6 **12** *8* **Power Alert**[25] 5348 2-9-3 ... GeorgeBaker 7 30
(B R Millman) *chsd ldrs: rdn over 2f out: sn btn* **66/1**

13 *2 ½* **Night Falcon** 2-8-12 ... SteveDrowne 6 19
(H Morrison) *s.i.s: pushed along 1/2-way: a bhd* **20/1**

0 **14** *nk* **Tivers Jewel (USA)**[24] 5371 2-9-3 ... PatDobbs 9 23
(Mrs A J Perrett) *mid-div to 1/2-way: sn bhd* **16/1**

2062 **15** *2* **Dansilver**[24] 5387 2-8-10 **60** ... JosephWalsh(7) 16 18
(D J Wintle) *prssed ldrs to 1/2-way* **66/1**

0 **16** *3 ½* **Cosimo Primo**[24] 5371 2-9-3 ... RichardThomas 12 9
(J A Geake) *bhd most of way* **100/1**

1m 30.8s (3.80) **Going Correction** +0.425s/f (Yiel) **82** Ran SP% **121.6**
Speed ratings (Par 97):95,91,88,85,84 83,83,82,82,82 79,70,67,67,65 61
CSF £20.67 TOTE £5.20: £2.10, £2.20, £9.40; EX 32.80.
Owner Gainsborough **Bred** And Mrs G Middlebrook **Trained** Newmarket, Suffolk

FOCUS
The official ground was changed to soft before this second division and it was run slightly slower than the first leg, but this could prove a decent maiden with the field finishing well strung out and should be at least this good.

NOTEBOOK
Mythical Kid(USA) ◆, a $1.4m colt, half-brother to Divine Proportions and Whipper, was an easy-to-back joint-favourite, but he always travelled well from his outside stall and picked up when asked to win in cosy fashion. He has no fancy entries and there are no plans, despite him being priced up for the first two colts' Classics by the leading bookmakers, but he looks sure to improve for the experience and can win good races next season. (op 7-2 tchd 11-2)
Contentious(USA) ◆ was the only one to make a race of it in the last quarter-mile and this Irish 1000 Guineas entry, showing the benefit of her debut last month, drew well clear of the rest and should be winning her maiden before long. (op 7-1)
Limbo King, a half-brother to Carnivore, made an encouraging debut, keeping on past beaten rivals and, although having less physical scope than some of those that finished around him, clearly has a fair amount of ability.
Tinnarinka making her turf debut after two decent efforts on Polytrack, showed up well until fading in the closing stages. She now qualifies for a handicap mark. (op 9-2 tchd 4-1)
Balliasta(IRE), a half-sister to the useful Panama City, made an encouraging debut and should come on for the experience. (op 11-1)
Majestic Cheer, another having his third outing, still looks as though he has some developing to do and he could be interesting in handicaps next season. (op 25-1)

Mo(USA) again made the running but was too keen for his own good and gradually faded out of contention. He is another who is now qualified for a handicap mark. (op 9-1)
First Buddy, from a family that improves with age, was well backed on this debut but missed the break and never got involved. He is likely to have learnt a fair amount and should be seen to better effect next season. (op 13-2 tchd 7-1)
Halkerston, from the family of Stagecraft and Opera House, showed definite signs of ability and is another who can be expected to benefit from the run. (op 13-2 tchd 7-1)
Alfresco ◆, encountering much softer ground than on his debut, proved difficult to load and then missed the break. However, he was noted making steady late headway under considerate handling and could be one to look out for once plying his trade in handicaps. (op 33-1)

5892 JOHN HUTCHINGS BIRTHDAY MAIDEN STKS (C&G) (DIV I) 1m (S)
2:30 (2:38) (Class 4) 2-Y-O **£4,533** (£1,348; £674; £336) **Stalls** High

Form RPR
1 **Go On Be A Tiger (USA)** 2-9-0 .... JohnEgan 5 82
(M R Channon) *mid-div: rdn and hdwy over 2f out: r.o strly to ld ins fnl f: readily* **5/1**[2]
2 1 ½ **Yeaman's Hall** 2-9-0 .... FergusSweeney 2 79
(A M Balding) *trckd ldrs: led 2f out: sn rdn: kpt on whn hdd ins fnl f but nt pce of wnr* **28/1**
05 3 4 **Sunley Peace**[12] [5640] 2-9-0 .... AntonyProcter 3 70
(D R C Elsworth) *mid-div: tk clsr order 3f out: effrt 2f out: kpt on to go 3rd ins fnl f but no ch w ldng pair* **10/1**
3 4 1 ½ **Atraas (IRE)**[25] [5340] 2-9-0 .... RHills 4 67
(M P Tregoning) *racd freely: prom: led briefly over 2f out: sn rdn: one pce fnl f* **13/8**[1]
5 3 **Mardi** 2-9-0 .... KerrinMcEvoy 9 60
(W J Haggas) *towards rr: tk clsr order over 4f out: rdn over 2f out: kpt on same pce* **9/1**[3]
6 ½ **Heights Of Golan** 2-9-0 .... AdamKirby 7 59
(I A Wood) *led tl over 2f out: sn rdn: wknd fnl f* **66/1**
7 shd **I Predict A Riot (IRE)** 2-9-0 .... MichaelHills 1 59
(J W Hills) *s.i.s: towards rr: rdn over 2f out: sme late prog: nvr a danger* **33/1**
8 ¾ **Make Haste (IRE)** 2-9-0 .... SteveDrowne 6 57
(R Charlton) *s.i.s: towards rr: racd green over 3f out: sme late hdwy: nvr a threat* **12/1**
20 9 3 ½ **Colonel Flay**[46] [4766] 2-9-0 .... RichardHughes 8 49
(Mrs P N Dutfield) *a towards rr* **14/1**
10 9 **Sularno** 2-9-0 .... DaneO'Neill 10 30
(H Morrison) *in tch: rdn over 2f out: sn wknd* **33/1**
0345 11 2 ½ **Cry Presto (USA)**[13] [5623] 2-9-0 80 .... (b) RyanMoore 11 24
(R Hannon) *trckd ldrs: ev ch 2f out: wknd qckly: eased fnl f* **5/1**[2]

1m 46.45s (5.83) **Going Correction** +0.425s/f (Yiel) 11 Ran SP% **115.7**
Speed ratings (Par 97):87,85,81,80,77 76,76,75,72,63 60
CSF £139.33 TOTE £5.70: £2.20, £7.70, £3.70; EX 235.70.
Owner Jaber Abdullah **Bred** Gainsborough Farm Llc **Trained** West Ilsley, Berks

FOCUS
A decent-looking maiden featuring some nicely-bred juveniles including the winner, but enthusiasm for the strength of the form is tempered slightly by a very moderate winning time for the type of race, just over four seconds slower than the second division, but it has been given a chance ratings-wise.

NOTEBOOK
Go On Be A Tiger(USA) ◆, first foal of that top-class filly Queen's Logic, took time to find full stride but he really got the hang of things late on and was well on top at the line. He will not be seen again this season, but despite the slow winning time he is still one to look out for next term and ought to stay further than this. (op 4-1 tchd 11-2)
Yeaman's Hall ◆ ran a debut full of promise and pulled nicely clear of the rest. Although a half-brother to the multiple-winning sprint handicapper Elkhorn, there is stamina in his pedigree and this performance suggests he will get further than a mile. (op 33-1)
Sunley Peace is progressing with each run and though firmly put in his place by the two newcomers, probably recorded his best effort yet and now qualifies for a nursery mark. (op 12-1 tchd 14-1)
Atraas(IRE) was a bit disappointing in view of his promising debut here last month, but he was plenty keen enough in the early stages and perhaps this softer ground was not to his liking. Official explanation: jockey said colt was unsuited by soft ground (op 7-4 tchd 15-8)
Mardi, whose dam won over nine furlongs, ran a perfectly creditable debut and will appreciate further in time. (op 14-1)
Heights Of Golan, a half-brother to eight winners, showed plenty of ability having made a good deal of the running and will appreciate middle-distances next season. (op 50-1)
I Predict A Riot(IRE), a 50,000gns colt out of a half-sister to Regal Archive, showed some ability on this debut and can be expected to progress in time.
Make Haste(IRE), a 240,000gns full-brother to three winners including Subtle Power, looked to need this initial experience and should come into his own over middle-distances next year. (op 14-1)
Cry Presto(USA), by far the most experienced in the field, ended up well beaten and seems to be going the wrong way. Official explanation: jockey said colt had no more to give (op 11-2 tchd 4-1)

5893 JOHN HUTCHINGS BIRTHDAY MAIDEN STKS (C&G) (DIV II) 1m (S)
3:00 (3:07) (Class 4) 2-Y-O **£4,533** (£1,348; £674; £336) **Stalls** High

Form RPR
2 1 **Sunshine Kid (USA)**[21] [5460] 2-9-0 .... JimmyFortune 11 93
(J H M Gosden) *trckd ldrs: led wl over 1f out: pushed clr ins last* **7/4**[1]
22 2 3 ½ **Ajhar (USA)**[17] [5537] 2-9-0 .... RHills 8 85
(M P Tregoning) *t.k.h early: hdwy 1/2-way: drvn to chse wnr jst ins last: kpt on same pce* **7/2**[3]
63 3 2 **Malt Or Mash (USA)**[24] [5381] 2-9-0 .... RyanMoore 2 81
(R Hannon) *chsd ldr: chal and rdn 2f out: kpt on same pce ins last* **11/1**
243 4 hd **Putra Square**[25] [5339] 2-9-0 87 .... EddieAhern 5 80
(P F I Cole) *led: rdn 2f out: hdd wl over 1f out: wknd ins last* **9/4**[2]
5 ½ **Seal Point (USA)** 2-8-11 .... SaleemGolam(3) 1 79
(Christian Wroe, UAE) *s.i.s: bhd: hdwy 3f out: styd on ins fnl f but nvr gng pce to rch ldrs* **66/1**
6 2 ½ **Tranquil Tiger** 2-9-0 .... RichardHughes 6 74
(H R A Cecil) *rrd s: sn pushed along to chse ldrs: styd prom tl wknd fnl f* **16/1**
03 7 ¾ **Bajan Pride**[13] [5622] 2-9-0 .... DaneO'Neill 4 72
(R Hannon) *chsd ldrs: rdn over 2f out: wknd appr fnl f* **33/1**
0 8 2 ½ **Dana Music (USA)**[34] [5105] 2-9-0 .... JohnEgan 10 67
(M R Channon) *bhd: rdn and effrt over 2f out: sn rch ldrs and nvr in contention after* **40/1**
0 9 5 **Credit Slip**[21] [5460] 2-9-0 .... IanMongan 9 56
(J L Dunlop) *s.i.s: a in rr* **100/1**
6 10 5 **Haut La Vie**[15] [5565] 2-9-0 .... StephenCarson 7 45
(R F Johnson Houghton) *bmpd s: a in rr* **100/1**
02 11 nk **Sir Liam (USA)**[22] [5417] 2-9-0 .... JamieSpencer 12 44
(P Mitchell) *hld up in rr: hdwy to trck ldrs fr 3f out: sn wknd* **16/1**
12 ½ **Mon Tour** 2-8-7 .... SophieDoyle(7) 3 43
(I A Wood) *s.i.s: a bhd* **66/1**

1m 42.44s (1.82) **Going Correction** +0.425s/f (Yiel) **64** Ran SP% **119.8**
Speed ratings (Par 97):107,103,101,101,100 98,97,95,90,85 84,84
CSF £8.12 TOTE £3.00: £1.40, £1.90, £2.40; EX 11.90.
Owner Stonerside Stable Llc **Bred** Stonerside Stable **Trained** Newmarket, Suffolk

FOCUS
The second division of this maiden for colts and geldings was run just over four seconds faster than the first, but nothing really came from off the pace. The form has been rated positively and should work out well.

NOTEBOOK
Sunshine Kid(USA) ◆ showed the benefit of his previous outing in a race that is starting to work out well. This Derby entry ran on strongly after hitting the front and, scoring in a very good time, should get further. He is still in the Racing Post Trophy, but a lot depends on how he comes out of this. Wherever he goes, he will take a deal of beating next time. (tchd 2-1 and 9-4 in a place)
Ajhar(USA) has now been runner-up on all three starts and help sets the level for the form, but he does not appear to do much wrong and his turn should come eventually. (op 4-1)
Malt Or Mash(USA) ◆ looks to be improving with experience and ran well for a long way without being able to trouble the principals. He now qualifies for a handicap mark and looks up to winning good races, especially when there is cut in the ground. (op 14-1)
Putra Square helps set the standard for the form, having been in the frame in three previous outings. He set a decent gallop but was brushed aside inside the last quarter-mile, and a confidence booster at one of the minor tracks may now be in order. He may also prefer a sounder surface. (op 11-4)
Seal Point(USA) ◆ caught the eye, staying on steadily after being slowly away. This half-brother to Notjustaprettyface will know much more next time. (op 50-1)
Tranquil Tiger, bred to be suited by middle distances, looked to be in need of the experience but showed ability and better will be seen of him next time.
Bajan Pride, who had shown promise in two previous outings on good ground; showed up for a good way but may not have handled the soft ground ans he faded late on.
Sir Liam(USA) Official explanation: jockey said colt was unsuited by soft ground

5894 MJ RECRUITMENT EBF MAIDEN FILLIES' STKS 6f 8y
3:35 (3:40) (Class 4) 2-Y-O **£5,181** (£1,541; £770; £384) **Stalls** High

Form RPR
6242 1 **Party (IRE)**[14] [5592] 2-9-0 80 .... RyanMoore 8 82
(R Hannon) *sn pumped along in mid div: hrd rdn and stdy prog fr over 1f out: grad swtchd lft: styd on strly: led cl home* **11/8**[1]
36 2 shd **Lady Alize (USA)**[46] [4765] 2-9-0 .... (t) FJohansson 9 82
(R A Kvisla) *in tch: sltly outpcd 2f out: styd on strly ins fnl f to go 2nd cl home: jst denied* **6/1**[2]
3 shd **Miss Lucifer (FR)** 2-9-0 .... MichaelHills 3 81
(B W Hills) *s.i.s: sn in tch: led 2f out: sn rdn: kpt on u.p: ct cl home* **7/1**[3]
4 1 **Salsa Steps (USA)** 2-9-0 .... SteveDrowne 4 78
(H Morrison) *mid-div: hdwy over 2f out: sn rdn: wnt 2nd briefly ins fnl f: no ex* **7/1**[3]
5 nk **Galipette** 2-9-0 .... RichardHughes 7 78
(H R A Cecil) *prom: rdn to chse ldr over 1f out: kpt on* **7/1**[3]
6 1 **Dramatic Turn** 2-9-0 .... EddieAhern 12 75
(Mrs A J Perrett) *led: rdn and hdd 2f out: remained cl up: no ex ins fnl f* **16/1**
0 7 3 **Regal Curtsy**[39] [4992] 2-9-0 .... IanMongan 1 66
(P R Chamings) *prom: rdn and ev ch 2f out: wknd fnl f* **50/1**
00 8 5 **Rose Germany**[24] [5380] 2-9-0 .... JohnEgan 14 51
(M R Channon) *trckd ldrs: effrt 2f out: wknd jst over 1f out* **20/1**
9 ¾ **Hayley's Flower (IRE)** 2-9-0 .... PatDobbs 6 48
(J C Fox) *s.i.s: a towards rr* **50/1**
10 9 **Fruits D'Amour (IRE)** 2-9-0 .... JimmyFortune 15 21
(S Kirk) *dwlt: a bhd* **25/1**
11 shd **Hippodrome Corner** 2-9-0 .... RichardSmith 11 21
(R Hannon) *s.i.s: a towards rr* **40/1**
12 1 ¼ **Pajada** 2-8-7 .... FrankiePickard(7) 10 17
(M D I Usher) *s.i.s: towards rr: hdwy 3f out: wknd 2f out* **50/1**

1m 16.53s (2.21) **Going Correction** +0.425s/f (Yiel) **12** Ran SP% **116.7**
Speed ratings (Par 94):102,101,101,100,100 98,94,88,87,75 74,73
CSF £8.62 TOTE £2.10: £1.10, £2.20, £2.20; EX 10.70.
Owner Highclere Thoroughbred Racing XXXV **Bred** Al Ca Torre Di Canicarao **Trained** East Everleigh, Wilts

FOCUS
With six fillies virtually in a line half a furlong from home, this may not have been the strongest of maidens but still a very decent winning time for a race of its type. The form is rated around the front pair and the form is fair.

NOTEBOOK
Party(IRE), by far the most experienced in the field, gained an overdue first win after several near misses, but it looked long odds against her winning for a long time as she was off the bridle a fair way from home and only got up in the shadow of the post. The softer ground probably helped as she ideally needs further and was only running over this trip due to limited opportunities elsewhere. She is currently rated 80, which looks an exploitable mark under the right conditions. (op 7-4 tchd 15-8,2-1 in a place)
Lady Alize(USA) did nothing wrong and having caught the leader just yards from the post, the winner's even later effort snatched the race from her. Her two previous outings had been over seven furlongs and she looks to need a return to that trip now that she qualifies for nurseries. (op 13-2)
Miss Lucifer(FR), a half-sister to a winner over similar trips to this, looked like making a winning debut as she was still in front yards from the line before getting swamped on both sides. There should be a race like this in her. (op 9-1)
Salsa Steps(USA) ◆, a half-sister to two middle-distance winners out of the Irish Oaks winner Dance Design, made a very encouraging debut to finish so close as she is bred to need much further than this, so she should really come into her own next season when faced with a stiffer test. (op 10-1)
Galipette, a half-sister to Camacho, ran with credit on this debut. (op 9-2)
Dramatic Turn, speedily bred being by Pivotal out of Eveningperformance, showed up prominently for a long way and seems sure to improve. (op 11-1 tchd 10-1 and 18-1)
Fruits D'Amour(IRE) Official explanation: jockey said filly missed the break

5895 BETDAQ.CO.UK FILLIES' H'CAP 1m 2f 6y
4:10 (4:10) (Class 4) (0-85,85) 3-Y-O+ **£5,829** (£1,734; £866; £432) **Stalls** Low

Form RPR
6-15 1 **Abhisheka (IRE)**[114] [2679] 3-9-3 85 .... KerrinMcEvoy 4 107+
(Saeed Bin Suroor) *sn trcking ldr: led ins fnl 4f: pushed clr fr 2f out: easily* **5/1**[1]
416 2 6 **Adraaj (USA)**[53] [4555] 3-8-13 81 .... (v1) JimmyFortune 11 87
(E A L Dunlop) *chsd ldrs: wnt 2nd over 2f out: sn no ch w wnr and carried hd high: styd on for clr 2nd* **25/1**

2234 **3** *3* **Safqa**[17] [5530] 3-9-3 **85** .... RHills 13 — 85
(B W Hills) *in tch: hdwy fr 3f out: one pce fnl 2f* **6/1**[3]

-141 **4** *½* **Best Guess (USA)**[38] [5024] 3-8-11 **79** .... AdrianMcCarthy 3 — 78
(P W Chapple-Hyam) *chsd ldrs: rdn 3f out: one pce fr over 2f out* **11/2**[2]

420 **5** *4* **Lake Shabla (USA)**[17] [5538] 3-9-0 **82** .... RyanMoore 8 — 73
(E A L Dunlop) *bhd: rdn and hdwy on outside fr 3f out but nvr in contention* **5/1**[1]

3015 **6** *1¾* **Thumpers Dream**[17] [5530] 3-9-0 **82** .... RichardHughes 10 — 70
(H R A Cecil) *chsd ldrs: rdn over 3f out: sn btn* **15/2**

4653 **7** *nk* **Fratt'n Park (IRE)**[15] [5574] 3-7-13 **70** oh6 .... DominicFox(3) 2 — 57
(J J Bridger) *rr: hdwy on ins 4f out: nvr gng pce to rch ldrs: wknd over 2f out* **33/1**

5506 **8** *2½* **Desert Cristal (IRE)**[5] [5776] 5-9-4 **81** .... IanMongan 1 — 64
(J R Boyle) *sn led: hdd ins fnl 4f: sn rdn: wknd fr 3f out* **10/1**

3252 **9** *2* **Miss Trinidad (USA)**[32] [5152] 3-8-9 **77** .... SteveDrowne 5 — 56
(B J Meehan) *a in rr* **12/1**

2101 **10** *¾* **Ellesappelle**[28] [5270] 3-8-2 **73** ow2 .... RichardKingscote(3) 6 — 50
(G L Moore) *bhd most of way* **16/1**

5040 **11** *12* **Kalaforte (SAF)**[16] [5550] 4-9-7 **84** .... EddieAhern 12 — 39
(R Simpson) *chsd ldrs: rdn 3f out: sn wknd: eased whn no ch last* **40/1**

2520 **12** *23* **Noora (IRE)**[53] [4555] 5-9-1 **78** .... (v) AdamKirby 9 — —
(C G Cox) *bhd: rdn and hdwy 5f out: wknd over 3f out* **16/1**

2m 11.0s (2.29) **Going Correction** +0.425s/f (Yiel)
WFA 3 from 4yo+ 5lb — 12 Ran SP% **112.5**
Speed ratings (Par 102):107,102,99,99,96 94,94,92,90,90 80,62
CSF £126.95 CT £758.48 TOTE £5.70: £2.10, £5.30, £2.00; EX 93.40.
Owner Godolphin **Bred** Gainsborough Stud Management Ltd **Trained** Newmarket, Suffolk

FOCUS
A fair fillies' handicap, with a number of relatively unexposed types and dominated by one of them. A fairly positive view has been taken of the race, with the winner much too good for these.
Kalaforte(SAF) Official explanation: jockey said filly lost its action
Noora(IRE) Official explanation: jockey said mare was unsuited by soft ground

5896 ELECTROLUX PROFESSIONAL H'CAP — 7f (S)
4:45 (4:47) (Class 5) (0-75,75) 3-Y-0+ — **£5,181** (£1,541; £770; £384) **Stalls** High

Form — RPR

5013 **1** **Quintrell**[14] [5590] 3-9-0 **73** .... FergusSweeney 1 — 90
(H Candy) *chsd ldr in centre: led wl over 1f out: sn rdn clr: r.o wl* **12/1**

6600 **2** *5* **Indian Edge**[6] [5769] 5-9-1 **72** .... FrancisFerris 2 — 76
(B Palling) *chsd ldng pair in centre: rdn to ld over 2f out: hdd wl over 1f out: kpt on but a hld by wnr* **40/1**

4232 **3** *1¾* **Neardown Beauty (IRE)**[5] [5778] 3-9-1 **74** .... RyanMoore 10 — 73
(I A Wood) *s.i.s: racd in 6th on stand side: swtchd lft 2f out: sn rdn and hdwy: styd on to go 3rd ins fnl f* **4/1**[1]

1300 **4** *1¾* **Nusoor (IRE)**[20] [5476] 3-9-2 **75** .... RHills 3 — 70
(W J Haggas) *led in centre: rdn and hdd over 2f out: sn one pce: lost 3rd ins fnl f* **16/1**

1133 **5** *½* **Taranaki**[14] [5591] 8-8-8 **72** .... JamieHamblett(7) 12 — 66+
(P D Cundell) *towards rr on stand side: racd in 12th:hdwy and nt clr run briefly over 1f out: styd on: nt rch ldrs* **14/1**

0000 **6** *1½* **Exmoor**[10] [5670] 4-9-4 **75** .... SteveDrowne 7 — 65
(R Charlton) *racd in mid div (8th) on stand side: rdn over 3f out: kpt on same pce fnl 2f* **8/1**[3]

3040 **7** *½* **Greenwood**[14] [5591] 8-9-0 **71** .... IanMongan 6 — 59
(P G Murphy) *chsd ldrs in 4th on stand side: rdn over 2f out: wknd ins fnl f* **33/1**

2110 **8** *1½* **Kasumi**[18] [5504] 3-8-10 **74** .... TravisBlock(5) 5 — 59
(H Morrison) *chsd ldrs in 3rd on stand side: rdn over 2f out: sn one pce* **12/1**

4153 **9** *5* **China Cherub**[26] [5317] 3-9-1 **74** .... DaneO'Neill 14 — 46
(H Candy) *mid div (7th) on stand side: effrt 2f out: wknd over 1f out* **9/1**

2255 **10** *5* **Full Victory (IRE)**[14] [5590] 4-9-4 **75** .... RichardHughes 16 — 34
(R A Farrant) *led stand side gp but overall prom: rdn over 2f out: grad fdd* **15/2**[2]

2610 **11** *4* **Saxon Lil (IRE)**[22] [5436] 4-9-0 **71** .... KerrinMcEvoy 8 — 19
(J L Spearing) *towards rr (10th) on stand side: hdwy over 2f out: sn rdn: wknd over 1f out* **16/1**

0400 **12** *4* **Blue Java**[14] [5591] 5-9-4 **75** .... LPKeniry 9 — 13
(H Morrison) *mid div (9th) on stand side tl wknd over 2f out* **14/1**

1603 **13** *7* **Imperial Gain (USA)**[28] [5268] 3-9-2 **75** .... (v) JamieSpencer 15 — —
(W R Swinburn) *hld up last on stand side: making hdwy whn bdly hmpd 2f out: nt rcvr and sn eased* **8/1**[3]

0-00 **14** *6* **Dramaticus**[10] [5677] 4-8-13 **70** .... AdrianMcCarthy 11 — —
(B Palling) *chsd ldrs in 5th on stand side tl wknd 2f out* **66/1**

500 **15** *6* **Indian's Feather (IRE)**[18] [5512] 5-9-4 **75** .... JohnEgan 17 — —
(N Tinkler) *a in last trio on stand side* **25/1**

3033 **16** *¾* **Local Fancy**[35] [5079] 3-9-1 **74** .... EddieAhern 4 — —
(J M P Eustace) *chsd ldr on stand side: edgd lft 3f out: sn wknd* **16/1**

1m 29.45s (2.45) **Going Correction** +0.425s/f (Yiel)
WFA 3 from 4yo+ 2lb — 16 Ran SP% **121.1**
Speed ratings (Par 103):103,97,95,93,92 91,90,88,83,77 72,68,60,53,46 45
CSF £440.88 CT £2359.55 TOTE £16.90: £3.70, £10.40, £1.10, £3.80; EX 798.20.
Owner Major M G Wyatt **Bred** Mrs P A Clark **Trained** Kingston Warren, Oxon

FOCUS
A competitive handicap in which the jockeys had a difference of opinion as to where the best ground was. While the bulk of the field raced towards the stands' side, three decided to stay far side from their low draws and as they finished in the first four, that suggests they were on the quicker ground. The form may therefore not prove entirely reliable.
Full Victory(IRE) Official explanation: jockey said gelding had no more to give
Saxon Lil(IRE) Official explanation: jockey said filly had no more to give

5897 MAR-KEY GROUP APPRENTICE H'CAP — 1m 3f 5y
5:20 (5:21) (Class 5) (0-75,73) 3-Y-0+ — **£3,238** (£963; £481; £240) **Stalls** Low

Form — RPR

5131 **1** **High Treason (USA)**[28] [5276] 4-9-6 **73** .... AlanRutter(5) 15 — 81+
(W J Musson) *hld up rr: stdy hdwy 3f out to ld over 2f out: drvn out fnl f* **7/2**[1]

1060 **2** *1½* **Border Edge**[18] [5506] 8-8-11 **62** .... JamesMillman(3) 5 — 68
(J J Bridger) *sn led: hdd over 2f out: styd on u.p but nvr gng pce of wnr fnl f* **20/1**

2541 **3** *½* **Barbirolli**[15] [5579] 4-9-2 **67** .... LukeMorris(3) 11 — 72
(W M Brisbourne) *in tch: hdwy over 3f out: hrd drvn to chse ldrs fr 2f out: no ex ins last* **5/1**[2]

3U51 **4** *1* **Serramanna**[14] [5587] 5-8-11 **59** oh4 .... JamieMoriarty 3 — 63
(Ms J S Doyle) *bhd: hrd drvn over 3f out: styd on fnl f but nvr gng pce to rch ldrs* **8/1**

1-00 **5** *1* **Kyles Prince (IRE)**[52] [4604] 4-9-8 **73** .... PatrickHills(3) 10 — 75
(P J Makin) *bhd: hdwy 3f out: chsd ldrs over 2f out: one pce fr over 1f out* **10/1**

0200 **6** *½* **Scottish River (USA)**[18] [5506] 7-8-4 **59** .... AshleyMorgan(7) 6 — 60+
(M D I Usher) *s.i.s: bhd: kpt on fr over 2f out: styd on ins last but nvr in contention* **20/1**

1630 **7** *1¼* **Darghan (IRE)**[28] [5276] 6-8-6 **61** .... DebraEngland(7) 16 — 60
(W J Musson) *bhd: styd on fnl 2f: nt rch ldrs* **12/1**

1006 **8** *hd* **Mister Completely (IRE)**[11] [5652] 5-8-6 **59** oh9 .... SophieDoyle(5) 14 — 58
(Ms J S Doyle) *bhd: sme hdwy fr 3f out: nvr rchd ldrs* **40/1**

1600 **9** *3* **Summer Charm**[20] [5479] 4-9-3 **70** .... BRoper(5) 4 — 64
(W Jarvis) *bhd: rdn over 3f out: nvr rchd ldrs* **11/1**

0000 **10** *2* **Harcourt (USA)**[13] [5621] 6-8-9 **62** .... JackDean(5) 9 — 53
(M Madgwick) *chsd ldrs: rdn 3f out: wknd 2f out* **50/1**

0120 **11** *2½* **Sforzando**[4] [5792] 5-9-8 **73** .... KristinStubbs(3) 1 — 60
(Mrs L Stubbs) *s.i.s: bhd: sme prog fnl 2f* **12/1**

0314 **12** *6* **Spectral Star**[43] [4900] 4-9-11 **73** .... RoryMoore 13 — 50
(J R Fanshawe) *chsd ldrs: led 3f out: hdd over 2f out: sn wknd* **7/1**[3]

0000 **13** *1¼* **Dancing Melody**[15] [5574] 3-8-2 **59** oh13 .... JamieJones(3) 17 — 34
(J A Geake) *in tch: rdn over 3f out: sn wknd* **50/1**

60 **14** *8* **Dangerous Business (IRE)**[26] [5319] 5-9-0 **62** .... TravisBlock 12 — 24
(H Morrison) *chsd ldrs 1m* **14/1**

15 *3½* **Willy (SWE)**[257] 4-9-6 **73** .... (t) WilliamBuick(5) 2 — 30
(R A Kvisla) *chsd ldrs tl wknd 3f out* **50/1**

16 *¾* **Captain Oats (IRE)**[368] [5725] 3-8-12 **69** .... NicolPolli(3) 7 — 25
(Mrs P Ford) *mid-div 1m* **66/1**

-000 **17** *12* **Pocket Too**[169] [1193] 3-8-0 **59** oh4 .... (p) JosephWalsh(5) 8 — —
(M Salaman) *chsd ldrs 7f* **50/1**

2m 29.62s (7.35) **Going Correction** +0.425s/f (Yiel)
WFA 3 from 4yo+ 6lb — 17 Ran SP% **123.3**
Speed ratings (Par 103):90,88,88,87,87 86,85,85,83,82 80,75,74,69,66 66,57
CSF £80.88 CT £362.52 TOTE £4.70: £1.50, £3.70, £1.80, £2.20; EX 111.40 Place 6 £197.32, Place 5 £41.32.
Owner S Rudolf **Bred** Helmut Von Finck **Trained** Newmarket, Suffolk

FOCUS
This modest apprentices' handicap was run at a good early gallop but they eased up before halfway resulting in a very moderate winning time for the grade. The form looks sound enough, although the fourth does limit it.
Summer Charm Official explanation: jockey said filly was unsuited by soft ground
Spectral Star Official explanation: jockey said filly hung left-handed
T/Jkpt: £7,206.80 to a £1 stake. Pool: £45,677.50. 4.50 winning tickets. T/Plt: £196.10 to a £1 stake. Pool: £56,262.55. 209.35 winning tickets. T/Qpdt: £23.20 to a £1 stake. Pool: £4,452.80. 141.65 winning tickets. ST

5613 NEWCASTLE (L-H)
Tuesday, October 10

OFFICIAL GOING: Soft (good to soft in places)
Wind: Light, half-behind

5898 E.B.F./GOSFORTH DECORATING & BUILDING SERVICES MAIDEN FILLIES' STKS (DIV I) — 7f
1:40 (1:41) (Class 5) 2-Y-0 — **£3,238** (£963; £481; £240) **Stalls** Centre

Form — RPR

1 **Magic Echo** 2-9-0 .... PhillipMakin 3 — 69
(M Dods) *chsd far side ldrs: outpcd over 2f out: rallied to ld wl ins fnl f: styd on: 1st of 5 in gp* **66/1**

6 **2** *1½* **Comma (USA)**[14] [5596] 2-9-0 .... RobertWinston 5 — 65
(Sir Michael Stoute) *led far side: qcknd clr and overall ldr over 2f out: tied up and hdd wl ins fnl f: 2nd of 5 in gp* **5/1**[2]

05 **3** *1* **Etoile D'Or (IRE)**[12] [5638] 2-9-0 .... GrahamGibbons 2 — 63
(M H Tompkins) *chsd far side ldrs: drvn over 2f out: kpt on fnl f: 3rd of 5 in gp* **12/1**

65 **4** *¾* **Hansomis (IRE)**[18] [5507] 2-9-0 .... PaulHanagan 9 — 61
(B Mactaggart) *led stands side: rdn over 2f out: kpt on fnl f: nt rch far side: 1st of 5 in gp* **25/1**

5 *3* **Cornflower (USA)** 2-9-0 .... WSupple 10 — 54
(Saeed Bin Suroor) *missed break: sn chsng stands side ldrs: effrt and ev ch that gp over 2f out: outpcd fnl f: 2nd of 5 in gp* **4/5**[1]

0 **6** *3½* **Isola Madre**[43] [4866] 2-9-0 .... RoystonFfrench 6 — 46
(M Johnston) *prom stands side: outpcd 3f out: rallied over 1f out: no imp: 3rd of 5 in gp* **14/1**

0 **7** *1¼* **Galway Girl (IRE)**[54] [4510] 2-9-0 .... DavidAllan 7 — 43
(T D Easterby) *chsd ldrs stands side: rdn and hung lft 3f out: outpcd fr 2f out: 4th of 5 in gp* **33/1**

8 *3½* **Kimono My House** 2-9-0 .... J-PGuillambert 8 — 34
(J G Given) *sn outpcd stands side: sme hdwy 3f out: btn over 1f out: last of 5 in gp* **33/1**

64 **9** *10* **Baby Dordan (IRE)**[14] [5586] 2-9-0 .... MickyFenton 1 — 10
(D J Daly) *chsd far side ldrs to over 2f out: wknd: 4th of 5 in gp* **13/2**[3]

0 **10** *6* **Snugfit**[7] [5754] 2-9-0 .... TonyCulhane 4 — —
(G G Margarson) *bhd far side: wknd 3f out: last of five in gp* **100/1**

1m 31.95s (3.95) **Going Correction** +0.35s/f (Good) — 10 Ran SP% **112.1**
Speed ratings (Par 92):91,89,88,87,83 79,78,74,63,56
CSF £350.88 TOTE £64.10: £15.60, £1.70, £2.50; EX 663.60.
Owner D C Batey **Bred** D C Batey **Trained** Denton, Co Durham

FOCUS
A modest fillies' maiden which saw those racing on the far side at an advantage. The form is worth treating with caution.

NOTEBOOK
Magic Echo, a sister to the yard's modest miler Queen's Echo, picked up strongly under pressure late on and ultimately won going away. She proved well suited by the deep surface, was clearly expected by connections to have needed the run, and shaped as though she may already need a mile.
Comma(USA), whose yard have a good record in this event, looked the most likely winner when clear on the far side nearing the final furlong, but she failed to sustain her effort in the final 100 yards and finished a tired horse. This was still an improved effort, however, and she ought to come into her own over a longer trip next year. A faster surface will also likely play more to her strengths. (op 9-2 tchd 6-1)
Etoile D'Or(IRE), who had yet to encounter ground this soft, found just the same pace under pressure and seemed to stay the extra furlong well enough. She ought to fare better now she is eligible for a handicap rating. (op 10-1)
Hansomis(IRE) showed up well enough under a positive ride and emerged a clear winner on the unfavoured stands' side. She enjoyed this easier ground and now has the option of nurseries.

The Form Book, Raceform Ltd, Compton, RG20 6NL

Cornflower(USA), whose dam was a useful winner over this trip at two and also scored over 12 furlongs as a three-year-old, was backed almost as if defeat was out of the question ahead of this racecourse debut. However, having proved fractious at the start, she found nothing when put under pressure and ultimately proved bitterly disappointing. She is presumably thought capable of a lot better, but looks one to tread carefully with. (op 10-11 tchd 8-11 and evens in a place)

Baby Dordan(IRE) failed to raise her game over this longer trip and looked all at sea on the deep surface. She is not one to write off just yet and she now becomes eligible for a nursery mark. (op 15-2 tchd 8-1)

5899 E.B.F./GOSFORTH DECORATING & BUILDING SERVICES MAIDEN FILLIES' STKS (DIV II) 7f

2:10 (2:11) (Class 5) 2-Y-O **£3,238** (£963; £481; £240) **Stalls** Centre

Form	Pos	Dist	Horse	RPR
3342	1		**Mimisel**18 [5507] 2-9-0 88 ... SebSanders 2 (Rae Guest) *cl up: led 2f out: rdn clr appr fnl f* **4/5**1	65
50	2	3	**Onatopp (IRE)**19 [5496] 2-9-0 ... DavidAllan 6 (T D Easterby) *led: rdn and hdd 2f out: kpt on: nt pce of wnr* **25/1**	58
6	3	1 ½	**Four Miracles**21 [5456] 2-9-0 ... TPQueally 7 (M H Tompkins) *dwlt: hld up: hdwy 1/2-way: outpcd over 2f out: rallied over 1f out: nt rch first two* **13/2**3	54
0000	4	3 ½	**Sagassa**14 [5586] 2-9-0 45 ... MickyFenton 4 (W De Best-Turner) *keen: chsd ldrs tl rdn and one pce fr 2f out* **80/1**	46
	5	nk	**Final Curtain** 2-9-0 ... FrancisNorton 3 (M A Magnusson) *prom: effrt over 2f out: wknd ins fnl f* **17/2**	45
6000	6	2	**Ellies Faith**43 [4887] 2-8-7 40 ... SuzzanneFrance(7) 5 (N Bycroft) *keen: chsd ldrs to 3f out: sn wknd* **80/1**	40
0	7	½	**Scene Three**19 [5496] 2-9-0 ... GrahamGibbons 10 (J J Quinn) *prom: rdn 3f out: sn wknd* **28/1**	39
	8	3 ½	**Mosquera's Rock (IRE)** 2-9-0 ... RoystonFfrench 8 (M Johnston) *hld up in tch: outpcd 1/2-way: sn n.d* **6/1**2	31
	9	1 ¾	**Silent Beauty (IRE)** 2-9-0 ... PaulHanagan 1 (S C Williams) *missed break: bhd: struggling fr 1/2-way* **20/1**	27
	10	20	**La Nuage** 2-9-0 ... PaulMulrennan 9 (T J Etherington) *bhd: lost tch fr 1/2-way* **33/1**	—

1m 32.43s (4.43) **Going Correction** +0.35s/f (Good) **46** Ran SP% **111.2**

Speed ratings (Par 92):88,84,82,78,78 76,75,71,69,46

CSF £30.74 TOTE £1.50: £1.10, £3.70, £1.50; EX 14.50.

Owner Bradmill Ltd **Bred** C J Mills **Trained** Newmarket, Suffolk

FOCUS

The second division of this fillies' maiden was run at just an ordinary pace. The winner did not need to be at her best to score and the form looks weak.

NOTEBOOK

Mimisel belatedly lost her maiden tag and has to rate full value for her winning margin. She has not done a great deal wrong in her career to date, enjoyed this step up to seven furlongs, and evidently relishes soft underfoot conditions. It is unlikely that she had to be at her best to take this, however. (op Evens tchd 11-10)

Onatopp(IRE) seemed to enjoy being ridden from the front and posted her best effort to date. The softer ground also looked to suit and she can find easier opportunities now that she is qualified for a handicap rating. (op 33-1)

Four Miracles took too long to hit full stride and is better than his finishing position suggests,. This was a definite step in the right direction, she will probably enjoy the return to a sounder surface in the future, and she will be qualified for a handicap rating after her next assignment. (op 7-1)

Sagassa paid for running too freely, but enjoyed the softer ground and still posted her best effort to date over the extra furlong. Her proximity at the finish does hold down the form, however. (op 66-1)

Final Curtain, a 45,000gns half-sister to useful three-year-old Familiar Territory, looked in need of this debut experience and probably wants less taxing ground. (op 11-2)

Mosquera's Rock(IRE), an 80,000euros purchase whose dam was a Listed winner in Germany on heavy ground, never threatened from off the pace and this debut experience was badly needed. She can be expected to leave this form behind in due course. (op 5-1)

5900 WEATHERBYS INSURANCE MAIDEN STKS (C&G) (DIV I) 7f

2:40 (2:42) (Class 5) 2-Y-O **£2,914** (£867; £433; £216) **Stalls** Centre

Form	Pos	Dist	Horse	RPR
0	1		**Marvo**21 [5454] 2-9-0 ... TPQueally 11 (M H Tompkins) *in tch: smooth hdwy 3f out: rdn to ld appr last: edgd lft and styd on wl* **13/2**3	76
34	2	3	**Akiyama (IRE)**26 [5308] 2-9-0 ... RobertWinston 10 (J Howard Johnson) *prom: effrt over 2f out: rdn to dispute ld over 1f out and ev ch tl kpt on same pce ins last* **13/2**3	68
3	3	nk	**Sivota (IRE)**13 [5616] 2-9-0 ... TonyCulhane 9 (T P Tate) *sn led: rdn along wl over 1f out: hdd appr last: sn drvn and kpt on same pce* **6/1**2	67
043	4	6	**Until When (USA)**20 [5481] 2-9-0 77 ... RoystonFfrench 2 (B Smart) *cl up on inner: effrt over 2f out: sn rdn and ev ch tl wknd over 1f out* **4/1**1	52
40	5	3 ½	**One And Gone (IRE)**13 [5616] 2-9-0 ... PaulHanagan 4 (R A Fahey) *bhd tl styd on fnl 2f: nrst fin* **9/1**	44
05	6	2 ½	**Cornell Precedent**25 [5332] 2-9-0 ... GrahamGibbons 5 (J J Quinn) *in tch: rdn along over 3f out: sn btn* **16/1**	37
	7	3 ½	**Majestic Chief** 2-9-0 ... PatCosgrave 7 (K A Ryan) *bhd tl styd on fnl 2f* **8/1**	29
3	8	¾	**Robert The Brave**24 [5389] 2-8-11 ... StephenDonohoe(3) 14 (A J McCabe) *dwlt: sn prom on wd outside: pushed along 1/2-way: rdn 3f out and sn wknd* **10/1**	27
	9	1	**Spanish Affair** 2-9-0 ... PaulMulrennan 6 (Jedd O'Keeffe) *bhd fr 1/2-way* **50/1**	24
	10	1 ½	**Bishop Auckland (IRE)** 2-9-0 ... WSupple 3 (Mrs A Duffield) *chsd ldrs: rdn along wl over 2f out: sn wknd* **28/1**	20
00	11	nk	**Mandriano (ITY)**13 [5615] 2-8-9 ... MarkLawson(5) 8 (D W Barker) *a rr* **100/1**	20
	12	1	**Jazz Festival (USA)** 2-9-0 ... PhillipMakin 1 (T D Barron) *s.i.s: a bhd* **20/1**	17
	13	2 ½	**Red Fama** 2-8-7 ... SuzzanneFrance(7) 13 (N Bycroft) *midfield: rdn along 1/2-way: sn wknd* **28/1**	11
44	14	1 ½	**Judge Neptune**12 [5632] 2-9-0 ... DanielTudhope 12 (J S Goldie) *a bhd* **10/1**	7

1m 31.7s (3.70) **Going Correction** +0.35s/f (Good) **14** Ran SP% **120.7**

Speed ratings (Par 95):92,88,88,81,77 74,70,69,68,66 66,65,62,60

CSF £46.23 TOTE £8.50: £2.50, £2.00, £2.30; EX 56.80.

Owner The Marvo Partnership **Bred** Mystic Meg Limited **Trained** Newmarket, Suffolk

FOCUS

A modest juvenile maiden, run at an average pace, and the field came home fairly strung out. The winner was full value for his winning margin.

NOTEBOOK

Marvo ◆, supported in the betting ring, got off the mark at the second attempt under a no-nonsense ride from Queally. There was a fair amount to like about the manner in which he settled the issue nearing the final furlong, he clearly relished the softer ground, and had no trouble with the extra furlong. He is an improving colt and has the making of a nice handicapper for next year. (op 9-1)

Akiyama(IRE) ran his race on this return to seven furlongs, but was made to look ordinary by the winner when that rival asserted for home. He may just need all of a mile on this evidence and is now qualified for nurseries. (op 7-1)

Sivota(IRE), third on his debut over a mile at this track 13 days previously, ran to a similar level and did not prove all that suited by the drop in trip. He should do much better in handicaps next year when faced with a suitably stiffer test. (op 5-1)

Until When(USA) had his chance and again was found wanting at the business end of the race. He probably needs a less taxing surface, and does look a little flattered by his current official mark, but still helps to set the level of this form all the same. (op 10-3 tchd 5-1)

One And Gone(IRE) was doing his best work towards the finish, without ever threatening, and should find life easier now he is qualified for nurseries. Official explanation: jockey said, regarding the running and riding, his orders were to drop colt in and ride it to get home on the soft (good to soft) ground, adding that colt was still weak mentally and physically and became tired towards the end (op 10-1)

5901 WEATHERBYS INSURANCE MAIDEN STKS (C&G) (DIV II) 7f

3:15 (3:15) (Class 5) 2-Y-O **£2,914** (£867; £433; £216) **Stalls** Centre

Form	Pos	Dist	Horse	RPR
0	1		**Al Shemali**36 [5066] 2-9-0 ... RobertWinston 2 (Sir Michael Stoute) *in tch: hdwy to ld over 1f out: pushed out ins fnl f: comf* **11/8**1	89
	2	¾	**Gemology (USA)** 2-9-0 ... WSupple 5 (Saeed Bin Suroor) *hld up: hdwy over 2f out: chsd wnr and rdn over 1f out: kpt on ins fnl f* **5/2**2	87
	3	11	**Marriaj (USA)** 2-9-0 ... MickyFenton 1 (B Smart) *in tch: rdn and outpcd over 2f out: rallied appr fnl f: kpt on: no ch w first two* **16/1**	61
60	4	3 ½	**Pietersen (IRE)**153 [1588] 2-9-0 ... (b1) PhillipMakin 13 (T D Barron) *plld hrd: cl up: ev ch 2f out: no ex fnl f* **14/1**	52
0	5	2	**Moral Fibre (IRE)**13 [5615] 2-9-0 ... RoystonFfrench 8 (M Johnston) *towards rr: drvn 1/2-way: no imp fr over 2f out* **20/1**	48
0	6	2 ½	**Currahee**18 [5508] 2-9-0 ... DavidAllan 12 (Miss J A Camacho) *bhd: rdn 1/2-way: hdwy 2f out: nvr rchd ldrs* **33/1**	42
04	7	2 ½	**Cadwell**19 [5495] 2-9-0 ... AdrianTNicholls 7 (D Nicholls) *w ldr: led 1/2-way to over 1f out: sn wknd* **14/1**	36
00	8	1 ½	**Surprise Pension (IRE)**19 [5491] 2-9-0 ... GrahamGibbons 4 (J J Quinn) *midfield: drvn 1/2-way: wknd 2f out* **50/1**	32
0	9	2	**Culachy Forest**13 [5613] 2-8-7 ... DanielleMcCreery(7) 11 (N Tinkler) *missed break: nvr on terms* **66/1**	27
U20	10	8	**Watch Out**29 [5239] 2-9-0 ... PaulMulrennan 9 (M W Easterby) *in tch to 3f out: sn rdn and btn* **50/1**	8
4	11	5	**Warm Tribute (USA)**7 [5746] 2-8-9 ... DuranFentiman(5) 3 (W G Harrison) *led to 1/2-way: wknd 2f out* **11/1**3	—
	12	6	**Gyration (IRE)** 2-9-0 ... J-PGuillambert 10 (J G Given) *hld up: rdn 1/2-way: btn 2f out* **16/1**	—

1m 30.45s (2.45) **Going Correction** +0.35s/f (Good) **55** Ran SP% **117.2**

Speed ratings (Par 95):100,99,86,82,80 77,74,72,70,61 55,48

CSF £4.26 TOTE £2.00: £1.10, £1.30, £4.80; EX 4.50.

Owner Saeed Suhail **Bred** Minster Stud **Trained** Newmarket, Suffolk

FOCUS

No real strength in depth to this second division of this maiden, but the first two came well clear, and both look capable of rating higher in due course. The form should prove sound.

NOTEBOOK

Al Shemali ◆, very well backed, showed the clear benefit of his debut at Warwick 36 days previously - a race that has worked out well - and got off the mark with a cosy win. He was always holding the runner-up, is value for a little further than the winning margin, and evidently relished the deep surface. It would be no surprise to see this Derby entry rate a deal higher as a three-year-old and he should have no trouble in staying further in due course. (op 15-8 tchd 2-1 in a place)

Gemology(USA) ◆, a 115,000euros purchase bred to make his mark at around a mile, posted a very pleasing debut effort and was the only one to give the winner any sort of race. He should benefit for the experience, handled the easy ground well, and winning a maiden should really prove a formality in the coming weeks. (op 9-4 tchd 11-4, 3-1 in places)

Marriaj(USA), a half-bother to numerous winners, most notably the smart Inamorato, had refused to go into the stalls on his intended debut in September and had been withdrawn three days prior to this due to the testing ground at York. In the circumstances he did not shape without promise on the soft ground and left the impression he will be better served by the step up to a mile before too long.

Pietersen(IRE) eventually paid the price for refusing to settle in the first-time blinkers and was well beaten. He probably needed this return from a five-month break, however, and may fare better now he has the option of nurseries. (op 18-1)

Warm Tribute(USA) Official explanation: jockey said colt hung right-handed

Gyration(IRE) Official explanation: jockey said colt lost its action

5902 WEATHERBYS BANK H'CAP 6f

3:50 (3:50) (Class 5) (0-70,72) 3-Y-O **£4,112** (£1,223; £611; £305) **Stalls** Centre

Form	Pos	Dist	Horse	RPR
1111	1		**Forces Sweetheart**7 [5756] 3-9-6 **72** 6ex ... (v) HayleyTurner 17 (M L W Bell) *racd alone stands side:a.p: rdn over 1f out: led ins last and styd on strly* **9/2**1	86
5200	2	2 ½	**Greek Secret**29 [5243] 3-8-7 **66** ... JamesO'Reilly(7) 16 (J O'Reilly) *swtchd to far side and in tch: gd hdwy over 2f out: rdn over 1f out: styd on u.p to ld that gp wl ins last* **18/1**	72
0000	3	nk	**John Keats**16 [5554] 3-9-4 **70** ... PaulHanagan 14 (I Semple) *in tch far side: gd hdwy 2f out: rdn to chal over 1f out and ev ch tl drvn and one pce ins last* **12/1**	75
0002	4	¾	**Charles Parnell (IRE)**14 [5593] 3-9-2 **68** ... DanielTudhope 7 (M Dods) *trckd ldrs far side: gd hdwy to ld that gp over 1f out: drvn and hddins last: one pce* **6/1**2	71
0-04	5	6	**Miss Sure Bond (IRE)**13 [5619] 3-8-8 **60** ... (b) RobertWinston 13 (B Smart) *prom far side: rdn and ev ch 2f out tl drvn and wknd over 1f out* **12/1**	45
1	6	1 ¾	**Methaaly (IRE)**124 [2383] 3-9-3 **69** ... TonyCulhane 1 (W J Haggas) *trckd ldrs on far rail: swtchd rt and hdwy wl over 1f out: sn rdn and no imp* **9/2**1	49
3666	7	3 ½	**Making Music**54 [4507] 3-8-11 **63** ... (p) DavidAllan 10 (T D Easterby) *chsd ldrs far side: rdn al0ong over 2f out: sn drvn and wknd wl over 1f out* **10/1**	32
-230	8	shd	**Blue Beacon**38 [5036] 3-8-11 **63** ... CatherineGannon 11 (K A Ryan) *a towards rr* **66/1**	32

6554 **9** *1 3/4* **Danetime Lord (IRE)**[43] 4894 3-8-9 **64**................(p) AndrewMullen(3) 12 28
(K A Ryan) *cl up far side: rdn over 2f out: sn wknd* **7/1**[3]

3000 **10** *shd* **Night In (IRE)**[26] 5312 3-8-13 **65**.. KimTinkler 3 28
(N Tinkler) *overall ldr far side: rdn along 2f out: drvn and hdd over 1f out: sn wknd* **16/1**

4004 **11** *shd* **Dasheena**[13] 5605 3-8-7 **62** ow2............................ StephenDonohoe(3) 9 25
(A J McCabe) *chsd ldrs far side: rdn along wl over 2f out: sn wknd* **14/1**

-460 **12** *nk* **Hang Loose**[145] 1801 3-8-12 **67**.................................. JohnMcAuley(3) 8 29
(S W Hall) *a rr far side* **50/1**

0 **13** *10* **Alocin (IRE)**[146] 1783 3-9-0 **66**.................................. SilvestreDeSousa 6 —
(A D Brown) *a rr far side* **18/1**

0030 **14** *3* **Rose Of Inchinor**[40] 4943 3-8-7 **62**......................... PatrickMathers(3) 15 —
(R E Barr) *chsd ldrs far side: rdn along 1/2-way: sn wknd* **33/1**

1m 16.25s (1.16) **Going Correction** +0.35s/f (Good) **14** Ran SP% **117.1**
Speed ratings (Par 101):106,102,102,101,93 90,86,86,83,83 83,83,69,65
CSF £86.15 CT £655.60 TOTE £2.60: £2.10, £4.90, £2.60; EX 68.70.
Owner Richard I Morris Jr **Bred** Barton Stud Partnership **Trained** Newmarket, Suffolk
FOCUS
A modest sprint which saw the bang in-form winner prevail despite racing alone on the stands' side. His performance has been rated at face value, with the placed form sound on the far side.
Methaaly(IRE) Official explanation: jockey said gelding hung right-handed

5903 ST JAMES SECURITY MEDIAN AUCTION MAIDEN STKS 1m 4f 93y
4:25 (4:25) (Class 6) 3-4-Y-0 **£2,590** (£770; £385; £192) **Stalls** Low

Form RPR

5443 **1** **Grey Outlook**[7] 5751 3-8-12 64...................................... RoystonFfrench 4 68+
(Miss L A Perratt) *hld up in tch: smooth hdwy to ld 2f out: rdn clr appr fnl f* **4/1**[3]

5340 **2** *7* **Moonlight Music (IRE)**[61] 4279 3-8-12 66.................. RichardMullen 8 58
(E J O'Neill) *trckd ldrs: effrt and ev ch 2f out: sn chsng wnr: no imp fnl f* **10/3**[2]

3233 **3** *1/2* **Summer Lodge**[8] 5741 3-9-0 69..........................(b) StephenDonohoe(3) 2 62
(A J McCabe) *sn chsng ldrs: led briefly over 2f out: sn one pce* **11/4**[1]

0 **4** *1/2* **Generous Jem**[35] 5086 3-8-12 .... SebSanders 1 57
(G G Margarson) *hld up: hdwy and prom 3f out: rdn and hung lft: no imp fr over 1f out* **6/1**

0030 **5** *1/2* **Saluscraggie**[41] 4924 4-9-5 46... DavidAllan 9 56
(K G Reveley) *hld up: effrt over 2f out: flashed tail u.p: no imp over 1f out* **12/1**

0004 **6** *7* **Laheen (IRE)**[8] 5727 3-8-12 51.. TPQueally 3 46
(M H Tompkins) *in tch: lost pl 1/2-way: n.d after* **14/1**

2050 **7** *11* **Bramcote Lorne**[11] 5652 3-9-3 56................................ DanielTudhope 6 36
(S Parr) *in tch: drvn 3f out: wknd 2f out* **8/1**

06 **8** *3 1/2* **Sterling Moll**[14] 5589 3-8-12 .... MickyFenton 7 26
(W De Best-Turner) *chsd ldrs tl wknd over 2f out* **50/1**

-000 **9** *8* **Hiats**[40] 4948 4-9-3 30.. JamesO'Reilly(7) 5 20
(J O'Reilly) *plld hrd: led to over 2f out: wknd* **100/1**

2m 48.87s (5.32) **Going Correction** +0.50s/f (Yiel)
WFA 3 from 4yo 7lb **9** Ran SP% **112.5**
Speed ratings (Par 101):102,97,97,96,96 91,84,82,76
CSF £17.14 TOTE £4.50: £1.80, £1.30, £1.50; EX 12.80.
Owner Ken McGarrity **Bred** Elsdon Farms **Trained** Ayr, S Ayrshire
FOCUS
A weak maiden and the form can be rated around the third. The winner probably did not have to improve.

5904 BET365 H'CAP 1m 2f 32y
4:55 (4:55) (Class 5) (0-70,70) 3-Y-0+ **£3,562** (£1,059; £529; £264) **Stalls** Centre

Form RPR

6623 **1** **Dium Mac**[10] 5685 5-9-1 **70**...................................... SuzzanneFrance(7) 15 82
(N Bycroft) *hld up: gd hdwy on outer over 2f out: rdn to chal over 1f out: led wl ins last: kpt on strly* **8/1**[2]

0112 **2** *1 1/4* **Sudden Impulse**[8] 5725 5-8-11 **59**........................... SilvestreDeSousa 5 69
(A D Brown) *in tch: hdwy to chse ldrs wl over 2f out: rdn to ld 1f out: sn drvn: hdd and no ex wl ins last* **5/2**[1]

2200 **3** *3* **Mystical Ayr (IRE)**[1] 5861 4-8-7 **58**......................... AndrewMullen(3) 10 63
(Miss L A Perratt) *bhd: gd hdwy on outer over 2f out: sn rdn and styd on fnl f: nrst fin* **14/1**

6534 **4** *1/2* **Ulysees (IRE)**[15] 5579 7-9-1 **63**... PaulHanagan 3 67+
(I Semple) *hld up in rr: hdwy and nt clr run on inner over 2f out: swtchd rt and rdn wl over 1f out: styd on ins last: nrst fin* **14/1**

1000 **5** *nk* **Epicurean**[18] 5513 4-9-0 **62**... MickyFenton 8 65
(Mrs K Walton) *bhd: hdwy on outer wl over 2f out: sn rdn and kpt on same pce appr last* **33/1**

2000 **6** *3/4* **Greenbelt**[13] 5617 5-9-3 **65**... WSupple 12 67
(G M Moore) *trckd ldrs: pushed along: n.m.r and sltly outpcd over 2f out: sn rdn and kpt on ins last* **25/1**

3132 **7** *1 1/4* **Turn Of Phrase (IRE)**[20] 5484 7-8-13 **61**.................(b) TonyHamilton 14 61
(B Ellison) *trckd ldrs on inner: efgfort 3f out: sn rdn along and outpcd over 2f out: kpt on appr last* **9/1**[3]

0341 **8** *1/2* **Royal Flynn**[24] 5385 4-8-11 **59**.. RobertWinston 9 58
(M Dods) *midfield: gd hdwy on outer 3f out: edgd lft and rdn to ld over 2f out: drvn and hdd over 1f out: wknd* **9/1**[3]

5036 **9** *3* **Rowan Lodge (IRE)**[8] 5734 4-9-8 **70**................................... TPQueally 7 63
(M H Tompkins) *towards rr: hdwy over 2f out: sn rdn and no imp* **14/1**

0653 **10** *1* **Tidy (IRE)**[24] 5362 6-9-2 **67**... GregFairley(3) 1 58
(Micky Hammond) *in tch on inner: rdn along wl over 2f out: plugged on at same pce* **11/1**

1046 **11** *8* **Billy One Punch**[20] 5484 4-9-8 **70**................................. TonyCulhane 13 47
(G G Margarson) *hld up: gd hdwy 3f out: rdn and ev ch 2f out: sn drvn and wknd* **20/1**

1111 **12** *1 3/4* **Good Article (IRE)**[22] 5422 5-9-3 **65**................................. SebSanders 2 39
(D K Ivory) *trckd leaders on inner: hdwy 3f out: rdn and ev ch 2f out: sn drvn and wknd* **9/1**[3]

1020 **13** *5* **Apache Point (IRE)**[16] 5553 9-8-12 **60**.............................. KimTinkler 16 25
(N Tinkler) *midfield: effrt and in tch 3f out: sn rdn and btn* **28/1**

5040 **14** *14* **Garibaldi (GER)**[103] 3024 4-8-11 **66**............................. JamesO'Reilly(7) 6 6
(J O'Reilly) *cl up: rdn along over 3fr out and sn wknd* **50/1**

05/0 **15** *5* **West Highland Way (IRE)**[10] 5685 5-9-1 **66**...... StephenDonohoe(3) 11 —
(Mrs H O Graham) *a towards rr* **100/1**

0432 **16** *2* **Lobengula (IRE)**[31] 5173 4-9-2 **64**.................................. RoystonFfrench 4 —
(I W McInnes) *led: rdn along 3f out: sn hdd & wknd* **16/1**

160 **17** *dist* **Highest Regard**[24] 5367 4-9-6 **68**............................(t) J-PGuillambert 17 —
(N P McCormack) *prom: rdn along over 3f out and sn wknd* **33/1**

2m 16.15s (4.35) **Going Correction** +0.50s/f (Yiel) **17** Ran SP% **124.8**
Speed ratings (Par 103):102,101,98,98,97 97,96,95,93,92 86,84,80,69,65 64,—
CSF £26.66 CT £293.21 TOTE £9.00: £2.50, £1.60, £4.30, £2.60; EX 34.30.
Owner J A Swinburne **Bred** T Umpleby **Trained** Brandsby, N Yorks
FOCUS
A modest handicap, run at a strong early pace, and the form looks sound enough for the grade. A clear personal best from the generally progressive winner.
Lobengula(IRE) Official explanation: jockey said gelding ran too freely

5905 JOHN SMITH'S H'CAP 1m 4f 93y
5:25 (5:26) (Class 5) (0-70,69) 3-Y-0+ **£3,238** (£963; £481; £240) **Stalls** Low

Form RPR

4461 **1** **Cleaver**[15] 5581 5-9-7 **65**.. SebSanders 4 72+
(Lady Herries) *hld up and bhd: smooth hdwy on outside over 2f out: rdn to ld 1f out: kpt on strly* **7/4**[1]

541 **2** *2* **Pee Jay's Dream**[8] 5725 4-9-1 **59** 6ex.......................... PaulMulrennan 5 63
(M W Easterby) *prom: rdn to ld briefly over 1f out: kpt on fnl f: nt pce of wnr* **4/1**[2]

00 **3** *shd* **Milton Star (IRE)**[1] 5875 7-9-2 **63**.......................... PatrickMathers(3) 13 67
(John A Harris) *midfield: hdwy to chse ldr 5f out: led over 3f to over 1f out: kpt on u.p fnl f* **22/1**

4600 **4** *6* **Balwearie (IRE)**[15] 5581 5-8-11 **55** oh1....................(p) RoystonFfrench 2 51
(Miss L A Perratt) *midfield: lost pl over 4f out: rallied over 2f out: sn no imp* **8/1**

600 **5** *2 1/2* **Calcutta Cup (UAE)**[13] 5617 3-9-0 **65**............................ TonyHamilton 3 57
(Karen McLintock) *keen: trckd ldrs: effrt over 2f out: sn no ex* **40/1**

0/0- **6** *3/4* **Aston Lad**[172] 5789 5-8-8 **55** oh9.................................. GregFairley(3) 9 46
(Micky Hammond) *hld up: rdn 3f out: nvr rchd ldrs* **15/2**

0040 **7** *shd* **Shape Up (IRE)**[10] 5685 6-9-11 **69**.......................................(b) DavidAllan 1 60
(R Craggs) *hld up: effrt u.p 3f out: btn over 1f out* **6/1**[3]

0033 **8** *15* **Melodian**[36] 5064 11-8-8 **57** oh3 ow2........................(b) MarkLawson(5) 10 27
(M Brittain) *chsd ldrs: led over 5f to over 3f out: wknd over 2f out* **12/1**

6-00 **9** *27* **Oman Gulf (USA)**[25] 5354 5-8-11 **55**............................. J-PGuillambert 6 —
(Micky Hammond) *hld up: rdn over 4f out: nvr on terms* **33/1**

0-00 **10** *5* **Jidiya (IRE)**[8] 5723 7-8-8 **55**.................................... StephenDonohoe(3) 7 —
(Mrs H O Graham) *led to over 5f out: sn lost pl* **50/1**

4520 **11** *27* **Kristiansand**[43] 4351 6-8-11 **55** oh7................................ PatCosgrave 11 —
(P Monteith) *w ldr: rdn 5f out: wknd over 3f out* **12/1**

2m 48.38s (4.83) **Going Correction** +0.50s/f (Yiel)
WFA 3 from 4yo+ 7lb **11** Ran SP% **120.6**
Speed ratings (Par 103):103,101,101,97,95 95,95,85,67,64 46
CSF £8.39 CT £117.61 TOTE £2.80: £1.20, £1.90, £6.60; EX 8.00 Place 6 £57.50, Place 5 £9.12.
Owner Seymour Bloodstock (uk) Ltd **Bred** J M Greetham **Trained** Patching, W Sussex
FOCUS
A moderate handicap and the form looks fair rated through the runner-up. There could be a bit more to come from the winner.
T/Plt: £13.60 to a £1 stake. Pool: £45,846.55. 2,460.55 winning tickets. T/Qpdt: £5.20 to a £1 stake. Pool: £3,687.50. 523.05 winning tickets. RY

5780 LINGFIELD (L-H)
Wednesday, October 11

OFFICIAL GOING: Standard
Wind: almost nil

5906 DAWSON NEWS E B F MAIDEN STKS 7f (P)
2:20 (2:21) (Class 5) 2-Y-0 **£3,886** (£1,156; £577; £288) **Stalls** Low

Form RPR

2 **1** **Tybalt (USA)**[22] 5458 2-9-3 .... JimmyFortune 12 88
(J H M Gosden) *pressed ldrs: effrt 2f out: pushed into ld jst over 1f out: drew clr last 100yds* **4/7**[1]

2 *2* **Dance Spiel** 2-9-3 .... LDettori 10 83+
(J Noseda) *mde most and dictated stdy pce: qcknd whn pressed 3f out: rn green over 1f out: sn hdd: wkng nr fin* **11/1**[3]

3 *1/2* **Folk Opera (IRE)** 2-8-12 .... PhilipRobinson 8 77
(M A Jarvis) *trckd ldrs: styd wl in tch whn pce lifted 3f out: shkn up over 1f out: styd on ins fnl f* **14/1**

43 **4** *1/2* **History Boy**[31] 5218 2-9-3 .... TedDurcan 14 81
(D J Coakley) *racd wd: trckd ldrs: prog to chal 3f out: drvn over 1f out: styd on same pce* **16/1**

0 **5** *3* **Niqaab**[106] 2958 2-8-12 .... RHills 9 68
(B W Hills) *hld up towards rr: wl outpcd 3f out: prog 2f out: reminder over 1f out: r.o fnl f: do bttr* **33/1**

2330 **6** *1/2* **Queen Noverre (IRE)**[22] 5464 2-8-12 77...................... RichardMullen 3 67
(E J O'Neill) *cl up: drvn over 2f out: btn over 1f out: fdd* **12/1**

2640 **7** *3 1/2* **Benchmark**[35] 5106 2-9-3 75.. RyanMoore 6 63
(R Hannon) *settled in midfield: rdn and outpcd 3f out: no ch after* **33/1**

0 **8** *1/2* **Kanonkop**[8] 5754 2-8-9 .... EdwardCreighton(3) 5 57
(Miss J R Gibney) *s.i.s: a towards rr: outpcd and rdn 3f out: no ch after* **100/1**

00 **9** *nk* **What Budget**[26] 5339 2-8-12 .... SteveDrowne 4 56
(B J Meehan) *in tch in midfield tl outpcd 3f out: sn struggling* **66/1**

3 **10** *hd* **Elhareer (IRE)**[23] 5424 2-8-12 .... IanMongan 2 56
(B J Meehan) *t.k.h: w ldrs: rdn 2f out: wknd rapidly fnl f* **11/2**[2]

11 *3* **Pappas Image** 2-9-0 .... StephenDonohoe(3) 11 53
(A J McCabe) *a in last trio: outpcd fr 1/2-way* **66/1**

006 **12** *1 1/4* **Poor Nelly**[62] 4292 2-8-12 55.. SebSanders 7 45
(J L Dunlop) *dwlt: a in rr: outpcd fr 1/2-way* **66/1**

00 **13** *shd* **Sadler's Hill (IRE)**[20] 5495 2-9-3 .... ChrisCatlin 13 50
(N A Callaghan) *stdd s and dropped in fr wd draw: a bhd* **100/1**

1m 26.13s (0.24) **Going Correction** -0.075s/f (Stan) **13** Ran SP% **120.0**
Speed ratings (Par 95):95,92,92,91,88 87,83,82,82,82 79,77,77
CSF £7.92 TOTE £1.70: £1.10, £2.10, £3.80; EX 10.00 Trifecta £41.20 Pool £436.96 - 7.52 winning units.
Owner Stonerside Stable Llc **Bred** Stonerside Stable **Trained** Newmarket, Suffolk
FOCUS
The pace was not great early but they really picked up the speed in the final stages. The winner had the form to win and duly did so, while the runner-up and third especially have improvement to come.
NOTEBOOK
Tybalt(USA) could only play second fiddle to Adagio on his debut, which might turn out to be no disgrace, but made no mistake this time. Sweating a touch in paddock before the race, he was always up with the pace and quickened clear once taking up the lead inside the final furlong. He holds a Derby entry but will obviously need to make significant improvement to have any aspirations in a higher grade. (op 1-2 tchd 4-6)
Dance Spiel got to the head of affairs early and ran a perfectly satisfactory race on his racecourse debut. Any ordinary maiden will be within is scope. (tchd 10-1)

Folk Opera(IRE) kept on well after being pushed along just behind the leaders for much of the early part of the race. She looks to have some improvement to come. (tchd 16-1)
History Boy, third in a German Listed race last time on soft ground, showed he is still going the right way with a sound effort. He was another who was warm before the race.
Niqaab, a filly with some scope for physical improvement, was never really close enough to the leading bunch to cause them any worries. One suspects she will be better over middle distances next season.
Queen Noverre(IRE), a really nice looker, could not mix it with some decent fillies last time in a sales race in Ireland but kept on respectably from off the pace. She can win races. (op 16-1)
Elhareer(IRE) weakened dramatically inside the final furlong, losing quite a few places in the process. (op 7-1 tchd 5-1)

5907 SMITH NEWS CLAIMING STKS 7f (P)
2:55 (2:57) (Class 6) 3-Y-0+ £2,730 (£806; £403) Stalls Low

Form RPR
-602 **1** **Prince Dayjur (USA)**[11] 5688 7-9-0 68 DeanMcKeown 10 73
(J Pearce) *prom: led over 2f out: drvn 2 l clr over 1f out: all out* **15/2**[3]
0404 **2** *3/4* **Top Mark**[11] 5670 4-9-6 76 SteveDrowne 7 77
(H Morrison) *rn in snatches: chsd ldrs: rdn to chse wnr 2f out: nt qckn over 1f out: kpt on nr fin* **7/4**[1]
3000 **3** *1 1/2* **Highland Cascade**[14] 5619 4-9-5 68 JTate 6 72
(J M P Eustace) *uns rdr and bolted bef s: wl in tch: effrt over 2f out: drvn and nt qckn over 1f out: veered sharply last stride* **20/1**
3000 **4** *nk* **Fast Heart**[14] 5627 5-9-10 81 (t) JoeFanning 13 76
(D Nicholls) *racd wd: hld up in rr: sme prog over 2f out: rdn and nt qckn over 1f out: styd on ins fnl f* **13/2**[2]
0346 **5** *nk* **Ciccone**[62] 4305 3-8-5 62 PaulDoe 4 59
(W Jarvis) *settled in last trio: same pl 2f out: rdn jst over 1f out: r.o wl last 100yds: no ch* **33/1**
2614 **6** *nk* **Sovereignty (JPN)**[6] 5775 4-8-13 63 JamesMillman(7) 12 71
(D K Ivory) *hld up towards rr: sme prog over 2f out: rdn and nt qckn over 1f out: styd on ins fnl f* **9/1**
0060 **7** *1 3/4* **Sigismundus (IRE)**[8] 5755 3-8-11 66 AmirQuinn(3) 3 62
(J R Boyle) *prom: chal 3f out: stl chsng ldrs u.p over 1f out: wknd fnl f* **33/1**
0604 **8** *1 1/4* **Renderoc (USA)**[29] 5270 3-9-8 65 (p) LPKeniry 9 67
(J S Moore) *hld up in rr: stdy prog 3f out: drvn and fnd nil over 1f out: wknd* **15/2**[3]
3416 **9** *1 1/2* **Marmooq**[11] 5688 3-9-1 73 SaleemGolam(3) 2 59
(A M Hales) *prom: drvn and steadily lost pl fr 1/2-way: n.d fnl 2f* **9/1**
3000 **10** *1 1/2* **What-A-Dancer (IRE)**[29] 5269 9-8-12 64 (b) TedDurcan 1 47
(R A Harris) *s.i.s and drvn in last: a bhd* **20/1**
4140 **11** *3 1/2* **Donna Giovanna**[11] 5689 3-9-3 73 (b) EddieAhern 11 45
(J A Osborne) *mde most to over 2f out: wknd rapidly* **16/1**
130 **12** *5* **Ask No More**[89] 3487 3-8-12 68 (e[1]) BrianReilly 5 27
(P L Gilligan) *lost pl and rdn 5f out: sn struggling in last pair* **11/1**

1m 25.38s (-0.51) **Going Correction** -0.075s/f (Stan)
WFA 3 from 4yo+ 2lb 12 Ran SP% **122.8**
Speed ratings (Par 101):99,98,96,96,95 95,93,91,90,88 84,78
CSF £20.75 TOTE £9.50: £2.50, £1.40, £6.30; EX 24.40 Trifecta £305.80 Part won. Pool £430.71 - 0.60 winning units..There was no bid for the winner. Top Mark was claimed by Mustafa Khan for £12,000. Ciccone was claimed by A Grinder for £6,000
Owner sportaracing.com **Bred** Golden Gate Stud **Trained** Newmarket, Suffolk

FOCUS
Probably only a modest claimer. The form does not look solid and is limited by the sixth.
Donna Giovanna Official explanation: vet said filly returned lame right-fore

5908 MENZIES DISTRIBUTION H'CAP 1m (P)
3:25 (3:26) (Class 5) (0-75,75) 3-Y-0+ £3,238 (£963; £481; £240) Stalls High

Form RPR
0114 **1** **Rakata (USA)**[23] 5436 4-9-2 **70** JimmyFortune 12 80
(P F I Cole) *racd wd and hld up in tch: prog 2f out: led jst over 1f out and drvn 3 l clr: hld on* **5/1**[1]
4300 **2** *1* **Arctic Desert**[37] 5058 6-9-2 **70** LDettori 10 77+
(A M Balding) *dwlt: hld up wl in rr: smooth prog over 2f out: bmpd over 1f out: chsd wnr fnl f: clsd but nvr able to chal* **5/1**[1]
1600 **3** *nk* **Punjabi**[11] 5689 3-9-2 **73** EddieAhern 6 86+
(Mrs G S Rees) *hld up towards rr: prog 2f out: nt clr run: swtchd lft and bmpd rival over 1f out: r.o wl last 150yds: nt rcvr* **5/1**[1]
3000 **4** *nk* **Smokin Joe**[6] 5778 5-9-2 **70** GeorgeBaker 9 76
(J R Best) *hld up in last pair: effrt over 2f out: nt clr run briefly over 1f out: r.o fnl f: nvr gng to rch ldrs* **13/2**[2]
0050 **5** *4* **Liakoura (GER)**[15] 5590 4-9-6 **74** (b[1]) RyanMoore 4 71
(Mrs A J Perrett) *trckd ldrs: wnt 2nd 2f out: upsides over 1f out: sn wknd rapidly u.p* **11/1**[3]
5024 **6** *nk* **Cursum Perficio**[11] 5689 4-9-6 **74** (p) MartinDwyer 7 70
(W R Muir) *trckd ldr 5f out: rdn over 3f out: lost 2nd 2f out: drvn and led briefly over 1f out: fnd nil and wknd rapidly* **5/1**[1]
4040 **7** *3* **Farewell Gift**[33] 5149 5-9-3 **74** (b) StephaneBreux(3) 2 63
(R Hannon) *chsd ldr for 3f: lost pl 1/2-way: u.p and struggling fr 3f out* **20/1**
2120 **8** *1/2* **Chalentina**[23] 5436 3-9-3 **74** TedDurcan 8 62
(H R A Cecil) *chsd ldrs: rdn over 3f out: cl enough 2f out: sn wknd rapidly* **12/1**
0000 **9** *3* **Kabeer**[97] 3212 8-9-2 **73** (t) StephenDonohoe(3) 5 54
(A J McCabe) *led: 3 l clr fr 1/2-way to 2f out: hdd & wknd rapidly over 1f out* **25/1**
1060 **10** *1/2* **Baylaw Star**[3] 5833 5-9-6 **74** SebSanders 3 54
(I W McInnes) *prominent: rdn over 3f out: wknd over 2f out* **14/1**
4-00 **11** *12* **Belly Dancer (IRE)**[11] 5670 4-9-7 **75** JoeFanning 1 27
(P F I Cole) *a in rr: last and struggling sn after 1/2-way: t.o* **16/1**

1m 38.53s (-0.90) **Going Correction** -0.075s/f (Stan)
WFA 3 from 4yo+ 3lb 11 Ran SP% **117.2**
Speed ratings (Par 103):101,100,99,99,95 95,92,91,88,88 76
CSF £28.97 CT £134.97 TOTE £6.20: £2.60, £1.70, £2.00; EX 40.50 Trifecta £277.10 Part won. Pool £390.39 - 0.70 winning units..
Owner A H Robinson **Bred** Mike G Rutherford Sr **Trained** Whatcombe, Oxon

FOCUS
There was little to choose between all of the field on official figures, so a tight finish was always on the cards. However, after a strong early pace set by Kabeer a whole collection of horses got stacked up with a furlong to go, resulting in a messy finish. The fourth is the best guide to the form.
Liakoura(GER) Official explanation: jockey said gelding hung left under pressure
Belly Dancer(IRE) Official explanation: vet said filly had struck into itself left-fore

5909 SUN CONDITIONS STKS 6f (P)
3:55 (3:56) (Class 4) 2-Y-0 £4,533 (£1,348; £674; £336) Stalls Low

Form RPR
124 **1** **Resplendent Alpha**[22] 5455 2-9-4 86 SteveDrowne 6 95
(P Howling) *in tch: pushed along in last pair over 2f out: effrt on wd outside over 1f out: r.o to ld last 75yds: sn clr* **8/1**[3]
2120 **2** *1 1/2* **High Style**[22] 5461 2-8-11 88 RyanMoore 1 83
(R Hannon) *restless stalls: hld up in cl tch: drvn over 2f out: led over 1f out: hdd and outpcd last 75yds* **9/2**[2]
405 **3** *1* **Three Decades (IRE)**[88] 3530 2-8-13 87 EddieAhern 8 82
(C A Cyzer) *t.k.h: hld up in tch and wd: drvn and prog 2f out: tried to chal over 1f out: nt qckn* **16/1**
1 **4** *1 1/4* **Chief Operator (USA)**[14] 5615 2-9-4 LDettori 9 83
(Saeed Bin Suroor) *mde most to over 2f out: sn rdn: stl cl up 1f out: nt qckn* **1/2**[1]
1005 **5** *3/4* **See In The Dark (IRE)**[22] 5461 2-8-11 78 JimmyFortune 4 74
(B J Meehan) *restless stalls: a in rr: last and struggling over 2f out: modest late prog* **16/1**
5063 **6** *1/2* **Tom Paris**[22] 5447 2-8-11 72 (b) MartinDwyer 2 73
(W R Muir) *restless stalls: in tch: rdn over 2f out: no imp over 1f out: wknd fnl f* **25/1**
0400 **7** *shd* **Hythe Bay**[38] 5041 2-8-8 76 JamesDoyle(3) 7 72
(R T Phillips) *cl up: rdn to ld over 2f out: hdd & wknd over 1f out* **33/1**
2600 **8** *shd* **Lord Charles**[9] 5731 2-8-11 87 AmirQuinn(3) 3 75
(W G M Turner) *w ldr to over 2f out: wknd on inner fnl f* **20/1**

1m 12.8s (-0.01) **Going Correction** -0.075s/f (Stan) 8 Ran SP% **119.3**
Speed ratings (Par 97):97,95,93,92,91 90,90,90
CSF £44.47 TOTE £9.80: £1.90, £1.30, £3.30; EX 53.00 Trifecta £152.10 Pool: £544.21 - 2.54 winning units.
Owner Resplendent Racing Limited **Bred** Sunley Stud **Trained** Newmarket, Suffolk

FOCUS
Chief Operator did not run that badly but looked unsuited by the trip, and can be given a chance over further. The winner looks a useful sprinter and should continue to progress with racing. The runner-up ran up to his best and looks the one to rate the race around.

NOTEBOOK
Resplendent Alpha followed the field round in the early part of the race and then flew past most of them inside the last furlong and a half. An all-weather surface obviously suits him well as he scored at the course on his debut, and he will return to the track for the meeting that was transferred from Doncaster later this month.
High Style looked to have nicked it after hitting the front late on, but could not hold the winner as he swooped late. He did little wrong and just bumped into a decent one. (op 5-1 tchd 11-2)
Three Decades(IRE), who was tried in a much higher grade during the summer, was not beaten far and ran well in defeat. She has plenty of ability and can find another race. (op 14-1)
Chief Operator(USA) moved well for much of the race but his effort flattened out under strong pressure before staying on again. His next run will tell us more about him, and a step up in trip is probably likely. (op 4-6)
See In The Dark(IRE) did not break well after getting a bit upset in the stalls, but kept on fairly well in the final stages.

5910 HIGGS INTERNATIONAL H'CAP 2m (P)
4:30 (4:31) (Class 6) (0-65,65) 3-Y-0+ £2,730 (£806; £403) Stalls Low

Form RPR
0201 **1** **Treetops Hotel (IRE)**[12] 5652 7-9-9 **60** RyanMoore 13 68
(B R Johnson) *hld up towards rr: stdy prog over 3f out: effrt to ld jst over 1f out: rdn and styd on wl* **7/2**[2]
-000 **2** *2* **Wait For The Will (USA)**[31] 5213 10-9-5 **61** (b) RobynBrisland(5) 12 67
(G L Moore) *hld up in rr: stdy prog gng wl fr over 3f out: bmpd 2f out: chsd wnr fnl f: shuffled along and no imp* **20/1**
26-0 **3** *3/4* **Desert Image (IRE)**[31] 5213 5-9-11 **62** FrancisNorton 8 67
(C Tinkler) *hld up towards rr and wd: prog 6f out: chsng ldrs whn bmpd 3f out: effrt over 1f out: styd on: nvr able to chal* **20/1**
3603 **4** *4* **Noddies Way**[12] 5651 3-8-12 **60** JimCrowley 2 60
(J F Panvert) *rn in snatches: chsd ldrs: drvn and cl up wl over 2f out: sn nt qckn and lost pl: plugged on* **12/1**
0000 **5** *nk* **Mr Wiseguy**[9] 5725 3-8-12 **60** AdamKirby 5 60
(G C Bravery) *racd wd: hld up in tch: prog to join ldrs over 3f out: led briefly over 1f out: wknd fnl f* **33/1**
0036 **6** *3/4* **Eastborough (IRE)**[31] 5201 7-9-12 **63** DarrylIHolland 7 62
(I A Wood) *dwlt: hld up in last: lft bhd fr 4f out: drvn and effrt over 2f out: kpt on but no ch* **10/1**
0346 **7** *shd* **Amwell Brave**[49] 4702 5-9-11 **62** EddieAhern 14 61+
(J R Jenkins) *hld up in rr: prog on inner whn nt clr run over 2f out: effrt and bdly hmpd over 1f out: nt rcvr* **14/1**
6310 **8** *1* **Montosari**[47] 4764 7-10-0 **65** GeorgeBaker 4 62
(P Mitchell) *w ldrs: led over 2f out to over 1f out: wknd rapidly* **13/2**[3]
-023 **9** *4* **Prince Of Medina**[30] 5235 3-8-10 **58** MartinDwyer 6 51+
(J R Best) *t.k.h: led after 5f: veered rt bnd 9f out: hdd over 2f out: wkng whn bdly hmpd jst over 1f out* **3/1**[1]
0345 **10** *3* **Bobsleigh**[16] 5564 7-9-1 **52** DaneO'Neill 1 41
(H S Howe) *led for 5f: styd prom: rdn over 5f out: sn lost pl and btn* **7/1**
0000 **11** *7* **Beaufort**[23] 5429 4-9-6 **57** FergusSweeney 11 38
(D K Ivory) *t.k.h: trckd ldr after 5f: rdn 4f out: wknd rapidly 2f out* **66/1**
0600 **12** *5* **Play Up Pompey**[90] 3429 4-8-13 **50** SteveDrowne 9 25
(J J Bridger) *dwlt: sn in tch: rdn and wknd over 4f out* **25/1**
3200 **P** **Star Rising**[9] 5736 4-8-13 **50** SebSanders 3 —
(N B King) *a in rr: lost tch u.p over 3f out: p.u and dismntd over 2f out* **16/1**

3m 26.5s (-2.29) **Going Correction** -0.075s/f (Stan)
WFA 3 from 4yo+ 11lb 13 Ran SP% **120.2**
Speed ratings (Par 101):102,101,100,98,98 98,98,97,95,94 90,88,—
CSF £79.52 CT £1247.50 TOTE £3.40: £1.90, £5.20, £6.00; EX 122.70 Trifecta £234.80 Part won. Pool: £330.71 - 0.40 winning units..
Owner Tann Racing **Bred** Miss Jill Finegan **Trained** Ashtead, Surrey
■ Stewards' Enquiry : Jim Crowley two-day ban: careless riding (Oct 23-24)

FOCUS
The pace was sedate early which meant plenty were travelling well for a lot of the race, and many had chances entering the final bend. The form looks pretty solid, rated around the third and fourth, Treetops Hotel won in good fashion and is going the right way.
Desert Image(IRE) Official explanation: jockey said gelding lost its action
Amwell Brave Official explanation: jockey said gelding was denied a clear run

5911 SPORT NEWSPAPERS H'CAP 1m 2f (P)
5:00 (5:01) (Class 5) (0-70,74) 3-Y-O **£3,238** (£963; £481; £240) **Stalls** Low

Form RPR

4501 **1** **Cantabilly (IRE)**[2] 5879 3-9-8 **74** 6ex .... TedDurcan 12 85
(M R Channon) *dwlt: hld up in last pair: gd prog on wd outside fr 3f out: led and hung lft over 1f out: sn drvn clr* **4/1**[1]

0220 **2** *3 1/2* **Lester Leaps In (USA)**[29] 5260 3-9-4 **70** .... RyanMoore 10 75+
(R Hannon) *settled in rr: rdn and prog fr wl over 2f out: styd on to take 2nd nr fin: no ch w wnr* **9/1**

0200 **3** *nk* **Valuta (USA)**[29] 5260 3-8-13 **65** ....(t) SteveDrowne 6 69
(R A Kvisla) *settled wl in rr: pushed along over 3f out: no prog tl effrt on outer over 1f out: styd on wl to take 3rd nr fin* **66/1**

6506 **4** *nk* **Art Investor**[29] 5266 3-9-4 **70** .... SebSanders 14 73
(D R C Elsworth) *hld up in midfield and wd: prog over 4f out: led over 3f out: drvn and hdd over 1f out: lost 2 pls nr fin* **14/1**

5561 **5** *1 1/4* **Ballybeg (IRE)**[121] 2507 3-8-13 **68** .... JamesDoyle[(3)] 4 69
(R J Price) *hld up in midfield: rdn over 2f out: one pce and no imp ldrs over 1f out* **14/1**

1552 **6** *nk* **James Street (IRE)**[27] 5320 3-9-4 **70** .... GeorgeBaker 13 70
(J R Best) *chsd ldrs: u.p fr wl over 3f out: stl in tch: 2f out: one pce after* **9/2**[2]

00-5 **7** *1 1/4* **Chelsea Chelsea**[14] 5612 3-9-1 **67** ....(t) JimmyFortune 11 65
(P F I Cole) *dwlt: hld up in last pair: stl wl bhd and pushed along over 3f out : drvn and wd bnd 2f out: styd on: no ch* **9/1**

3256 **8** *1/2* **High Octave (IRE)**[16] 5568 3-8-13 **65** .... AdamKirby 2 62
(B G Powell) *hld up bhd ldrs: gng wl 3f out: shkn up and cl up whn bdly hmpd over 1f out: nt rcvr and eased* **7/1**[3]

4624 **9** *1* **Siakira**[16] 5574 3-8-13 **65** .... FrancisNorton 9 60
(I A Wood) *settled in midfield: rdn and struggling on inner over 2f out: n.d after* **16/1**

2420 **10** *3* **Benbrook**[16] 5568 3-9-3 **69** .... DaneO'Neill 7 59
(J L Dunlop) *prom: rdn to chse ldr 3f out: wknd rpidly 2f out* **9/2**[2]

0000 **11** *5* **Triple Bluff**[21] 5479 3-8-11 **63** ....(t) JimCrowley 3 43
(Mrs A J Perrett) *t.k.h: prom: rdn 4f out: wknd over 2f out* **25/1**

12 *4* **Quicksharp (IRE)**[18] 5541 3-9-4 **70** .... TPO'Shea 1 42
(Daniel Mark Loughnane, Ire) *t.k.h: led after 2f to over 3f out: wknd* **20/1**

405- **13** *1 1/4* **Thomas Of Bathwick**[461] 3275 3-9-1 **67** .... RobertMiles 5 37
(B G Powell) *led for 2f: wknd over 4f out: last and bhd over 2f out* **66/1**

2m 6.25s (-1.54) **Going Correction** -0.075s/f (Stan) 13 Ran SP% **119.7**
Speed ratings (Par 101):103,100,99,99,98 98,97,97,96,93 89,86,85
CSF £39.08 CT £2058.06 TOTE £5.70: £1.80, £2.90, £14.50; EX 48.80 Trifecta £325.50 Part won. Pool: £330.71 - 0.44 winning units. Place 6 £115.14, Place 5 £88.57.
Owner A R Parrish **Bred** W P Iceton **Trained** West Ilsley, Berks

FOCUS
A fair handicap won in good style by Cantabilly, who is in terrific form. Some of those in behind have various reasons for poor efforts, so apart from the winner the form looks slightly dubious.
High Octave(IRE) Official explanation: jockey said colt was denied a clear run
T/Jkpt: Not won. T/Plt: £285.90 to a £1 stake. Pool: £72,188.80. 184.30 winning tickets. T/Qpdt: £117.00 to a £1 stake. Pool: £3,305.40. 20.90 winning tickets. JN

BORDEAUX LE BOUSCAT (R-H)
Wednesday, October 11

OFFICIAL GOING: Soft

5913a PRIX ANDRE BABOIN (GRAND PRIX DES PROVINCES) (GROUP 3) 1m 1f 110y
2:30 (2:30) 3-Y-0+ **£27,586** (£11,034; £8,276; £5,517; £2,759)

RPR

1 **Doctor Dino (FR)**[35] 5124 4-8-10 .... OPeslier 6 108
(R Gibson, France) *held up in 6th on outside, headway down outside to lead 1f out, ran on strongly* **17/10**[1]

2 *2* **Runaway**[35] 5124 4-8-10 .... SPasquier 2 104
(A Fabre, France) *hld up in last til hdwy down outside over 1f out, jinked lft 120 yds out, soon straightened out and ran on wl, nrst fin* **3/1**[2]

3 *1 1/2* **Barastraight**[25] 5400 3-9-0 ....(b) IMendizabal 7 110
(J-C Rouget, France) *held up in 5th, stayed on under pressure from over 1f out to take 3rd on line* **44/10**[3]

4 *shd* **Afaf (FR)**[41] 4979 4-8-7 .... TJarnet 8 98
(M Delzangles, France) *close up, 3rd straight on outside, led 1 1/2f out to 1f out, one pace* **15/1**

5 *3/4* **Atlantic Air (FR)**[11] 5704 4-9-3 .... J-BEyquem 3 107
(Y De Nicolay, France) *held up in 7th, stayed on from over 1f out but never a factor* **48/10**

6 *snk* **Mister Conway (FR)**[63] 5-8-10 .... RonanThomas 1 100
(P Van De Poele, France) *close up in 4th on inside, one pace final 1 1/2f* **14/1**

7 *2* **Quality Special (BRZ)**[35] 5124 4-8-7 .... C-PLemaire 5 93
(P Bary, France) *pressed leader til led briefly over 1 1/2f out, soon headed and weakened* **12/1**

8 *dist* **Fruhlingssturm**[363] 5863 6-8-10 .... MBlancpain 4 —
(J-L Salas Molto, Spain) *led to over 1 1/2f out, weakened quickly and eased* **30/1**

2m 3.30s
WFA 3 from 4yo+ 4lb 8 Ran SP% **121.6**
PARI-MUTUEL: WIN 2.70; PL 1.20, 1.20, 1.50; DF 3.60.
Owner Dino Nanni **Bred** Ecurie Pelder **Trained** Chantilly, France

5672
NEWMARKET (ROWLEY) (R-H)
Thursday, October 12

OFFICIAL GOING: Good to soft
Wind: Light, across Weather: Sunny and warm

5914 USK VALLEY STUD MEDIAN AUCTION MAIDEN STKS (DIV I) 7f
1:30 (1:33) (Class 4) 2-Y-O **£3,886** (£1,156; £577; £288) **Stalls** Low

Form RPR

2 **1** **Perfect Star**[70] 4084 2-8-12 .... PhilipRobinson 7 77+
(C G Cox) *racd against nr side rail: mde virtually all: rdn 2f out: styd on wl to assert last 100yds* **7/2**[2]

03 **2** *1* **Palamoun**[14] 5640 2-9-3 .... MichaelHills 12 80
(B W Hills) *lw: cl up: prog to join wnr wl over 1f out: upsides ins fnl f: no ex last 100yds* **3/1**[1]

3 *3/4* **Lang Shining (IRE)** 2-9-3 .... RyanMoore 10 78+
(Sir Michael Stoute) *w'like: leggy: lw: hld up in midfield: stdy prog fr 3f out: chsd ldng pair fnl f: clsd but nvr quite able to chal* **11/2**[3]

450 **4** *3* **Messiah Garvey**[46] 4829 2-9-3 67 .... IanMongan 15 70+
(M R Channon) *w wnr to 2f out: rdn and steadily fdd* **33/1**

0 **5** *1 3/4* **Tasweet (IRE)**[13] 5659 2-9-3 .... RHills 5 66+
(J H M Gosden) *trckd ldrs: outpcd fr 3f out: kpt on same pce fnl f* **14/1**

6 *1/2* **Postsprofit (IRE)** 2-9-3 .... EddieAhern 8 65
(N A Callaghan) *w'like: scope: prom: rdn over 2f out: btn over 1f out: fdd* **50/1**

0 **7** *1 1/2* **Sumner (IRE)**[13] 5659 2-9-3 .... TPQueally 2 61+
(M H Tompkins) *settled in midfield: effrt 3f out: outpcd 2f out: n.d after* **50/1**

8 *1 1/4* **Far Seeking** 2-9-3 .... RichardHughes 6 58
(Mrs A J Perrett) *w'like: unf: dwlt: wl in rr tl prog into midfield after 3f: sn pushed along: outpcd over 2f out: keeping on nr fin* **25/1**

9 *3/4* **Raise The Goblet (IRE)** 2-9-3 .... TonyCulhane 14 56
(W J Haggas) *w'like: dwlt: rn green in rr: rdn 3f out: nvr on terms: kpt on* **50/1**

10 *nk* **Good Effect (USA)** 2-9-3 .... DarryllHolland 1 55
(A P Jarvis) *cmpt: dwlt: rn green and sn last: taken to outer 1/2-way and detached fr rest: styd on wl fr over 1f out: nrst fin* **50/1**

3 **11** *1/2* **Gunner's View**[15] 5608 2-9-3 .... LDettori 11 54
(B J Meehan) *lw: t.k.h: pressed ldrs tl wknd u.p over 2f out* **7/2**[2]

0 **12** *shd* **Iolanthe**[16] 5586 2-8-12 .... JamieSpencer 13 49
(B J Meehan) *dwlt: a wl in rr: no prog fnl 2f* **50/1**

0 **13** *1/2* **Sonning Star (IRE)**[23] 5454 2-9-3 .... JohnEgan 16 52
(D R C Elsworth) *veered wildly rt leaving stalls: sn swtchd across to nr side rail: a struggling in rr* **14/1**

0 **14** *1* **Double Banded (IRE)**[26] 5371 2-9-3 .... DaneO'Neill 9 50
(J L Dunlop) *dwlt: nvr beyond midfield: wknd 2f out* **50/1**

15 *shd* **Sell Out** 2-8-12 .... SteveDrowne 4 45
(G Wragg) *gd sort: rn green and sn strugging: a wl in rr* **50/1**

1m 27.65s (1.15) **Going Correction** +0.15s/f (Good) 15 Ran SP% **118.7**
Speed ratings (Par 97):99,97,97,93,91 91,89,87,87,86 86,85,85,84,84
CSF £13.03 TOTE £3.70: £1.40, £2.00, £2.50; EX 14.10.
Owner Dr Bridget Drew & E E Dedman **Bred** Mrs A M Jenkins And E D Kessly **Trained** Lambourn, Berks
■ Stewards' Enquiry : L Dettori caution: careless riding

FOCUS
A pretty ordinary maiden by Newmarket standards and the form is anchored by the performance of Messiah Garvey in fourth.

NOTEBOOK
Perfect Star was no match for Cumin first time out but she improved for that experience and made almost all the running here. She showed plenty of determination to hold off the runner-up and should make up into a middle-distance filly next season. (op 3-1 tchd 11-4)
Palamoun, dropping back a furlong in distance, was ridden more prominently this time and had every chance. He found the filly too strong, though, and does not appear to have progressed much for his previous experience. He is now eligible for a mark. (op 10-3 tchd 7-2)
Lang Shining(IRE), whose dam won over a mile at three and is a sister to top-class miler/ten-furlong performer Spectrum, shaped with promise on his debut. He finished nicely clear of the rest and is likely to do better with a winter behind him. (op 13-2)
Messiah Garvey, who was a beaten favourite on easy ground at Beverley on his last start and has an official rating of 67, ran a better race this time, although his performance does anchor the form somewhat. He would make more appeal in nursery company off that sort of mark.
Tasweet(IRE) again looked less than comfortable on the softish surface. He needs one more run for a mark and could be one to be interested in for handicaps on quicker ground next season.
Postsprofit(IRE), who cost 100,000gns as a yearling, is out of a mare who won five races in all. This should be his trip based on his pedigree, but handicaps look more likely to be his game in time.
Far Seeking, whose dam is an unraced daughter of high-class juvenile and Poule d'Essai des Pouliches winner Houseproud, shaped with a degree of promise. He hails from a stable whose two-year-olds tend to need their debut outings and he should do better in time. (op 33-1)
Good Effect(USA), who was green in rear for much of the race, began to get the hang of things a little towards the end of the race and was staying on at the finish. He needs more time but could be all right next season.

5915 ANGLO HIBERNIAN BLOODSTOCK INSURANCE E B F MAIDEN STKS 6f
2:00 (2:07) (Class 4) 2-Y-O **£5,181** (£1,541; £770; £384) **Stalls** Low

Form RPR

1 **Truly Royal** 2-9-3 .... LDettori 15 91+
(Saeed Bin Suroor) *w'like: scope: bit bkwd: chsd ldrs: shkn up to ld 1f out: r.o wl* **2/1**[1]

2 **2** *3* **Danny Templeton (IRE)**[28] 5326 2-9-3 .... AntonyProcter 11 82
(D R C Elsworth) *lw: sn chsng ldrs: rdn to ld over 1f out: sn hdd: styd on same pce ins fnl f* **11/1**

0 **3** *1* **Shmookh (USA)**[103] 3083 2-9-3 .... RHills 9 79
(J L Dunlop) *w ldr: rdn and ev ch over 1f out: styd on same pce* **20/1**

0 **4** *1 3/4* **Rasaman (IRE)**[26] 5371 2-9-3 .... PhilipRobinson 5 74
(M A Jarvis) *w'like: led: rdn: hung rt and hdd over 1f out: sn btn* **4/1**[3]

5 *1 1/2* **Mutanaseb (USA)** 2-9-3 .... MartinDwyer 16 69+
(M A Jarvis) *w'like: s.i.s: hld up: hdwy over 1f out: nt trble ldrs* **33/1**

6 *hd* **Give Her A Whirl** 2-8-12 .... MichaelHills 7 64
(B W Hills) *leggy: mid-div: rdn over 2f out: hmpd over 1f out: styd on same pce* **8/1**

7 *3/4* **Teasing** 2-8-12 .... JimmyQuinn 4 61
(J Pearce) *leggy: scope: b.hind: hld up in tch: racd keenly: rdn over 2f out: wknd over 1f out* **100/1**

65 **8** *1/2* **Tracer**[98] 3222 2-9-3 .... RichardHughes 17 65
(R Hannon) *lw: hld up: edgd lft 4f out: hdwy over 2f out: hung lft and wknd over 1f out* **8/1**

9 *1/2* **Exit Strategy (IRE)** 2-9-3 .... TonyCulhane 3 63
(W J Haggas) *neat: hld up: rdn over 2f out: sn nt clr run: nvr trbld ldrs* **50/1**

0 **10** *1* **Jete (IRE)**[10] 5735 2-9-0 ....(v) PatrickMathers[(3)] 2 60
(D Shaw) *chsd ldrs over 4f* **100/1**

11 *1/2* **A Peaceful Man** 2-9-3 .... EddieAhern 8 59
(B W Hills) *cmpt: hld up: effrt over 2f out: hmpd and wknd over 1f out* **50/1**

12 *2* **Land's End (IRE)** 2-9-3 .... DarryllHolland 13 53
(J Noseda) *gd sort: hld up in tch: racd keenly: hmpd and lost pl 4f out: n.d after* **7/2**[2]

13 3 **Judge 'n Jury** 2-9-3 .... TedDurcan 12 44
(C A Cyzer) *str: cmpt: hld up: effrt over 2f out: n.m.r and wknd wl over 1f out* **50/1**

14 7 **Jimbobalou** 2-9-3 .... DaleGibson 14 23
(T T Clement) *cmpt: bit bkwd: s.i.s: hmpd over 4f out: a in rr* **100/1**

00 15 ½ **Me Fein**[29] [5297] 2-9-3 .... JamieSpencer 6 21
(B J Curley) *sn outpcd* **100/1**

1m 14.2s (1.10) **Going Correction** +0.15s/f (Good) **15** Ran SP% **123.7**
Speed ratings (Par 97):98,94,92,90,88 88,87,86,85,84 83,81,77,67,67
CSF £26.07 TOTE £3.00: £1.50, £2.50, £3.90; EX 22.10.
Owner Godolphin **Bred** Darley **Trained** Newmarket, Suffolk

FOCUS
A fair maiden won in good style by the Godolphin newcomer Truly Royal, who looks a nice prospect. The placed horses all appeared to show improved form, runbut little reason to question it.

NOTEBOOK
Truly Royal ♦, whose dam was second in the Prix de Diane, is a half-brother to Dignify, a Group 3 winner over a mile, and Attorney General, a dual winner over middle distances. He only had to be pushed out to score in convincing fashion and, while Guineas talk is premature, he clearly has a bright future. A mile should suit him next season. (op 13-8 tchd 85-40 in place)
Danny Templeton(IRE) could not cope with the Godolphin newcomer but ran another solid race in second. Being a son of Namid, he did not find the easier ground an inconvenience, and an ordinary maiden still looks within his ability. (op 16-1)
Shmookh(USA), off the track since July, improved on his debut effort when he was quite green, and appreciated the drop back to six furlongs.
Rasaman(IRE), another son of Namid, should not have been inconvenienced by the easier ground but he was a shade disappointing. One more run will make him eligible for nurseries, though. Official explanation: jockey said colt hung right throughout (op 13-2)
Mutanaseb(USA), who was sold for 135,000gns as a two-year-old, is a brother to Rhumb Line, a triple sprint winner at three in the US. Staying on late in the day, he can build on this. (op 50-1)
Give Her A Whirl, a half-sister to top-class sprinter La Cucaracha, showed speed before weakening in the latter stages. The run should bring her on, but the best of her should be seen next year. (op 17-2 tchd 10-1 in a place)
Tracer Official explanation: jockey said colt hung left throughout
Land's End(IRE) ♦, bought for 200,000gns as a juvenile, is a half-brother to two-year-old winners Kings Mountain and Parole De Star. Keen in the early stages, he got into a bumping match with Tracer after two furlongs and struggled to get into contention afterwards. He is the type who should do better as a three-year-old. (op 4-1 tchd 9-2 in places)

5916 ALEC STEWART NURSERY 1m
2:35 (2:38) (Class 4) (0-95,86) 2-Y-O **£5,181** (£1,541; £770; £384) **Stalls** Low

Form RPR

01 1 **Ladies Best**[15] [5623] 2-9-5 **84** .... KerrinMcEvoy 5 92+
(Sir Michael Stoute) *settled towards rr: stdy prog fr 3f out: rdn to ld ins fnl f: pushed out and in command nr fin* **6/1**[2]

01 2 1 **Buccellati**[45] [4895] 2-9-1 **80** .... FergusSweeney 15 86
(A M Balding) *racd centre: trckd ldrs: prog over 2f out: rdn to ld jst over 1f out to ins fnl f: styd on* **25/1**

612 3 ¾ **Brainy Benny (IRE)**[6] [5783] 2-9-0 **79** .... LDettori 12 83
(N A Callaghan) *sn hld up in centre and towards rr: stdy prog fr 3f out: rdn to chal 1f out: nt qckn last 100yds* **9/2**[1]

3263 4 ¾ **Silca Key**[12] [5676] 2-8-9 **74** .... TPO'Shea 2 77
(M R Channon) *lw: racd against nr side rail: w ldrs: led 3f out to over 2f out: kpt on u.p* **12/1**

056 5 ½ **Balnagore**[29] [5293] 2-8-6 **73** .... JimmyQuinn 11 75
(J L Dunlop) *settled in rr: rdn and prog whn nt clr run wl over 1f out: n.d after: styd on wl last 150yds* **33/1**

1 6 nk **Weld Il Balad (IRE)**[72] [4018] 2-8-12 **77** .... J-PGuillambert 7 78
(M Johnston) *lw: racd nr side: pressed ldrs: lost pl u.p 2f out and struggling: styd on wl again ins fnl f* **16/1**

15 7 shd **Greek Envoy**[24] [5431] 2-9-6 **85** .... MickyFenton 16 86
(T P Tate) *dwlt: racd wdst of all: prog into midfield 1/2-way: rdn over 2f out and in tch: one pce fnl f* **33/1**

21 8 nk **Opera Crown (IRE)**[17] [5565] 2-9-1 **80** .... JimmyFortune 3 80
(P F I Cole) *chsd nr side ldrs: hrd rdn and outpcd over 2f out: styd on again ins fnl f* **12/1**

2301 9 hd **Smokey Oakey (IRE)**[26] [5359] 2-9-4 **86** .... SaleemGolam(3) 1 86
(M H Tompkins) *racd nr side: prom: rdn over 2f out: fdd fnl f* **13/2**[3]

541 10 ½ **Paceman (USA)**[28] [5321] 2-9-3 **82** .... RyanMoore 4 81
(R Hannon) *mde most nr side to 3f out: led again over 2f out to jst over 1f out: wknd* **10/1**

345 11 hd **Loch Tay**[15] [5607] 2-8-9 **74** .... JamieSpencer 9 72
(M L W Bell) *hmpd s: hld up wl in rr: prog in centre over 2f out: no imp over 1f out* **8/1**

0040 12 1 ¼ **Romanov Dynasty (IRE)**[23] [5466] 2-8-13 **78** .... RichardHughes 6 73
(R Hannon) *dwlt: hld up in last trio: effrt over 2f out: hrd rdn and no rspnse over 1f out: btn whn n.m.r last 150yds* **20/1**

5651 13 1 ½ **Our Herbie**[13] [5647] 2-8-10 **75** .... EddieAhern 8 67
(J W Hills) *lw: w ldrs in centre: stl upsides over 1f out: wknd rapidly fnl f* **14/1**

5011 14 9 **The Illies (IRE)**[28] [5322] 2-9-3 **82** .... MichaelHills 10 54
(B W Hills) *t.k.h: prom in centre tl wknd 3f out: t.o* **10/1**

5206 15 nk **Moonwalking**[26] [5359] 2-9-1 **80** .... DaleGibson 13 52
(Jedd O'Keeffe) *a wl in rr: struggling 3f out: t.o* **33/1**

10 16 nk **Emma's Surprise**[111] [2800] 2-8-12 **77** .... CatherineGannon 14 48
(K A Ryan) *plld hrd: racd centre: prom to 1/2-way: sn btn: t.o* **50/1**

1m 40.75s (1.38) **Going Correction** +0.15s/f (Good) **16** Ran SP% **122.4**
Speed ratings (Par 97):99,98,97,96,96 95,95,95,95,94 94,93,91,82,82 82
CSF £160.42 CT £780.31 TOTE £5.00: £1.70, £7.30, £2.00, £3.20; EX 254.80.
Owner Saeed Suhail **Bred** The Lavington Stud **Trained** Newmarket, Suffolk

FOCUS
A competitive nursery featuring a number of unexposed sorts. A strong race which ought to throw up a winner of two before the end of the season.

NOTEBOOK
Ladies Best ♦, a good winner of a Salisbury maiden last time out, did not look too badly rated on his nursery debut off a mark of 84, and while he took a while to get on top, he eventually won a shade cosily. He could do even better on quicker ground and should make up into a smart handicapper next season, when he will get further than this. (tchd 5-1 and 13-2 in a place)
Buccellati, a narrow winner at Warwick last time, is improving with every outing and just ran into an even better handicapped rival in the winner. (op 33-1)
Brainy Benny(IRE) settled better this time and may have got his head in front briefly inside the final furlong before weakening close home. He was already due to go up 4lb in the handicap from Saturday, though, so things are not going to get any easier. (op 3-1)
Silca Key, stepping up a furlong in distance, again made the frame. She is a consistent type and her performance is probably a good guide to the level of the form. (op 10-1)
Balnagore ♦ ran his best race to date on his handicap debut and was staying on well in the closing stages after getting hampered just inside the final two furlongs.
Weld Il Balad(IRE) lost his place two furlongs out but found his feet once they hit the uphill run to the line and rallied well. He looks likely to get further than this in time and will win more races next season. Official explanation: jockey said colt ran very free to post (tchd 20-1)
Greek Envoy looked to have a bit to do off a mark of 85 on his handicap debut, ran a fair race in the circumstances. (tchd 40-1)

5917 LANWADES STUD SEVERALS STKS (LISTED RACE) (F&M) 1m 2f
3:10 (3:13) (Class 1) 3-Y-0+
£15,898 (£6,025; £3,015; £1,503; £753; £378) **Stalls** Low

Form RPR

-554 1 **Innocent Air**[47] [4808] 3-8-11 100 .... MartinDwyer 12 108
(J H M Gosden) *chsd ldrs: led over 7f out: rdn and edgd lft over 1f out: r.o* **16/1**

121 2 1 ¼ **Anna Pavlova**[5] [5803] 3-9-0 106 .... PaulHanagan 7 109+
(R A Fahey) *lw: hld up: hdwy over 1f out: sn rdn to chse wnr: r.o* **6/4**[1]

4426 3 3 ½ **Summer's Eve**[29] [5300] 3-8-11 102 .... DaneO'Neill 13 99
(H Candy) *lw: chsd ldrs: rdn and hung lft over 1f out: no ex fnl f* **12/1**

2220 4 ¾ **Mango Mischief (IRE)**[27] [5342] 5-9-2 105 .... SebSanders 15 98
(J L Dunlop) *hld up: hdwy over 2f out: rdn over 1f out: no ex ins fnl f* **16/1**

-131 5 nk **Portal**[54] [4590] 3-9-0 98 .... JamieSpencer 8 100+
(J R Fanshawe) *hmpd sn after s: hld up: hdwy over 1f out: sn rdn: no ex ins fnl f* **5/1**[2]

1133 6 1 **Princess Nada**[57] [4482] 3-9-0 101 .... NickyMackay 6 98
(L M Cumani) *hld up in tch: swtchd lft 2f out: sn rdn styd on same pce appr fnl f* **12/1**

1232 7 ½ **Grain Of Truth**[19] [5525] 3-8-11 96 .... (v) RyanMoore 10 94
(Sir Michael Stoute) *hld up: hdwy over 1f out: nt trble ldrs* **13/2**[3]

025 8 hd **Giving**[36] [5110] 3-8-11 90 .... SteveDrowne 3 94
(G Wragg) *lw: hld up: hdwy over 1f out: nvr nrr* **66/1**

0122 9 2 ½ **Topatoo**[6] [5787] 4-9-2 91 .... TPQueally 14 89
(M H Tompkins) *lw: hld up: hdwy 1/2-way: rdn and wknd over 1f out* **8/1**

6316 10 hd **Aryaamm (IRE)**[20] [5502] 3-8-11 87 .... PhilipRobinson 4 89
(M A Jarvis) *led: hdd over 7f out: rdn over 2f out: sn edgd rt and wknd* **50/1**

5425 11 1 **Jaish (USA)**[57] [4482] 3-8-11 97 .... RHills 2 87
(J L Dunlop) *chsd ldrs: rdn over 2f out: sn wknd* **33/1**

3621 12 6 **Regal Velvet**[17] [5566] 3-8-11 80 .... JimmyFortune 11 75
(J H M Gosden) *lw: prom: racd keenly: rdn over 3f out: wknd 2f out* **33/1**

2313 13 5 **Pirouetting**[30] [5266] 3-8-11 76 .... MichaelHills 5 66
(B W Hills) *hld up: rdn over 2f out: sn wknd* **66/1**

-160 14 13 **Sandglass**[49] [4741] 3-8-11 99 .... RichardHughes 1 41
(Mrs A J Perrett) *hld up in tch: racd keenly: rdn and wknd over 2f out: eased over 1f out* **50/1**

2m 5.48s (-0.23) **Going Correction** +0.15s/f (Good)
WFA 3 from 4yo+ 5lb **14** Ran SP% **121.0**
Speed ratings (Par 111):106,105,102,101,101 100,100,100,98,97 97,92,88,77
CSF £39.44 TOTE £21.40: £5.30, £1.20, £3.50; EX 88.90.
Owner K Abdulla **Bred** Juddmonte Farms Ltd **Trained** Newmarket, Suffolk

FOCUS
Fairly reliable Listed form based on the performances of the third, fifth and eighth. It was somewhat tactical, however, with fillies racing prominently favoured.

NOTEBOOK
Innocent Air, who looked very fit beforehand, wore the owner's second colours. Taking on front-running duties after two and a half furlongs, she was given a good ride by Dwyer, who saved a bit for the uphill finish. She has not had the season some had expected of her at the end of her juvenile campaign, having been slow to come to hand in the spring, but this Listed-race success is decent compensation.
Anna Pavlova, making a quick reappearance following her success at Ascot five days earlier, had a penalty to carry and was dropping back a couple of furlongs in distance. She was the only one to make a race of it with the winner, but was making no impression close home and perhaps the race came a bit too soon after her Ascot exertions. (tchd 7-4, 2-1 in places and 15-8 in places)
Summer's Eve, who has not had cut in the ground on her last two starts, appreciated the return to a softer surface. She was not far off the pace throughout and, in a rather tactical affair, was fairly well placed for the final dash. (tchd 14-1)
Mango Mischief(IRE) had conditions to suit and ran a better race than at Newbury last time, but she remains vulnerable to less exposed and improving rivals in races like this. (tchd 16-1)
Portal, racing on easy ground for the first time, had a job to do making up ground from well off the pace in a race run in a way that suited those who raced more prominently. She will stay a mile and a half next year, when she could well develop into a Group-class performer. (op 9-2 tchd 4-1 and 11-2)
Princess Nada, whose trainer has only saddled three winners from his last 62 runners, ran a fair race considering that statistic. She is also more effective on quicker ground. (op 14-1)
Grain Of Truth was another asked to challenge from the back in a race mostly dominated by those who raced nearer the pace. She has progressed from handicap company this term but needs to find further improvement to win at this level. (op 7-1 tchd 6-1)

5918 USK VALLEY STUD MEDIAN AUCTION MAIDEN STKS (DIV II) 7f
3:45 (3:52) (Class 4) 2-Y-0 **£3,886** (£1,156; £577; £288) **Stalls** Low

Form RPR

52 1 **Tredegar**[15] [5607] 2-9-3 .... RyanMoore 12 83
(P F I Cole) *lw: w ldr: narrow ld fr over 2f out: drvn and styd on wl fnl f* **7/2**[2]

20 2 ¾ **We'll Come**[13] [5655] 2-9-3 .... PhilipRobinson 16 81
(M A Jarvis) *pressed ldrs: jnd wnr over 2f out and sn clr of rest: rdn and styd on fnl f: a jst hld* **7/4**[1]

00 3 2 **Berkeley Castle (USA)**[48] [4781] 2-9-3 .... RichardHughes 4 76+
(Sir Michael Stoute) *cl up: rdn to chse ldng pair 2f out but sn outpcd: styd on fnl f: unable to chal* **10/1**

0 4 5 **Summer Dancer (IRE)**[23] [5458] 2-9-3 .... AntonyProcter 2 63+
(D R C Elsworth) *t.k.h: hld up in last pair: stmbld over 4f out: prog over 2f out: sn outpcd: kpt on* **20/1**

0 5 nk **Bold Bobby Be (IRE)**[13] [5659] 2-9-3 .... IanMongan 1 62
(J L Dunlop) *hld up towards rr: prog over 2f out: sn outpcd: plugged on fnl f* **66/1**

0 6 1 ¾ **Inchlaggan (IRE)**[13] [5659] 2-9-3 .... MichaelHills 10 58
(B W Hills) *lw: trckd ldrs: rdn over 2f out: sn outpcd and btn* **6/1**[3]

0 7 ½ **Brouhaha**[23] [5460] 2-9-3 .... BrianReilly 8 56
(Miss Diana Weeden) *mde most to over 2f out: sn rdn and btn* **100/1**

8 hd **Henry Bernstein (USA)** 2-9-3 .... TedDurcan 14 56
(H R A Cecil) *gd sort: bkwd: dwlt: in tch in rr: prog 3f out: outpcd 2f out: n.d after* **20/1**

9 1 **Transcend** 2-9-3 .... JimmyFortune 13 53+
(J H M Gosden) *w'like: scope: s.s: hld up in last: sme prog fnl 2f: nvr on terms: bttr for experience* **10/1**

10 ¾ **Troialini** 2-9-3 JTate 15 51
(S W Hall) *w'like: leggy: t.k.h: hld up towards rr: outpcd 2f out: no ch after* **100/1**

0 11 *shd* **Force Group (IRE)**[23] [5460] 2-9-0 SaleemGolam[(3)] 11 51
(M H Tompkins) *t.k.h early and hld up in midfield: lost pl and rdn over 3f out: sn struggling* **25/1**

12 ½ **Golden Folly** 2-9-3 SebSanders 6 50
(Lady Herries) *w'like: unf: uns rdr and cantered off to post: rn green and a wl in rr* **50/1**

13 *nk* **Bussel (USA)** 2-8-12 TonyCulhane 5 44
(W J Haggas) *leggy: scope: trckd ldrs: gng wl enough 3f out: outpcd and pushed along 2f out : eased whn no ch* **50/1**

14 *shd* **Sunburn (IRE)** 2-9-3 JimCrowley 7 49
(Mrs A J Perrett) *w'like: scope: a wl in rr: struggling over 2f out* **50/1**

15 *5* **Hot Shot Hamish (IRE)** 2-9-3 LDettori 9 36
(B J Meehan) *w'like: unf: nvr beyond midfield: wknd 2f out* **12/1**

0 16 *3* **Metropolitan Chief**[23] [5454] 2-9-3 ChrisCatlin 3 28
(D M Simcock) *chsd ldrs: rdn and wknd wl over 2f out* **50/1**

1m 27.57s (1.07) **Going Correction** +0.15s/f (Good) **16** Ran SP% **123.4**
Speed ratings (Par 97):99,98,95,90,89 87,87,87,85,85 84,84,83,83,78 74
CSF £9.26 TOTE £4.60: £1.60, £1.30, £3.70; EX 13.20.
Owner Elite Racing Club **Bred** Elite Racing Club **Trained** Whatcombe, Oxon

FOCUS
No future stars here probably, but sound enough form of its type.

NOTEBOOK
Tredegar has improved with every start and got off the mark at the third time of asking. In all honesty he did not have much to beat, but the family likes softish ground and he made the most of it and his previous experience. (tchd 9-2)
We'll Come, like the winner, having his third start, had every chance and simply met one too good. He got the extra furlong, finished clear of the rest and is now eligible for a handicap mark. (tchd 6-4, 2-1 in places and 9-4 in a place)
Berkeley Castle(USA) ◆, whose dam twice won over middle distances in Listed company, had not shown much on his first two starts, but he was backed at big prices and rewarded each-way support. He will appreciate a stiffer test next season and looks one to bear in mind for handicaps over around ten furlongs. (op 16-1 tchd 20-1)
Summer Dancer(IRE), who was keen early on and stumbled at one stage, stayed on quite well on the stands' side in the closing stages. He looks one who will do better next year when handicapped.
Bold Bobby Be(IRE), a brother to Big Bad Bob, a high-class and prolific winner who stayed ten furlongs, kept on late in the day and is another who will be seen to better effect next year once handicapped.
Inchlaggan(IRE), whose dam is a half-sister to Rockfel Stakes winner Yawl, did not do a lot better than on her debut. (tchd 13-2)
Transcend ◆, who cost 190,000gns, is a half-brother to Suggestive, a seven-furlong specialist who has won in Group 3 company. Pretty friendless in the market beforehand, he was slowly away and ran green in rear before making some headway late on. Better will be seen of him in time. (op 7-1)

5919 E B F BOADICEA FILLIES' STKS (LISTED RACE) 6f
4:20 (4:22) (Class 1) 3-Y-0+
£18,737 (£7,101; £3,554; £1,772; £887; £445) **Stalls** Low

Form RPR

1230 1 **Firenze**[18] [5549] 5-8-13 99 JamieSpencer 1 95
(J R Fanshawe) *lw: hld up and bhd: swtchd lft and hdwy over 1f out: sn hung lft: r.o u.p to ld post* **7/2**[1]

5314 2 *nk* **Ripples Maid**[20] [5501] 3-9-1 92 RichardThomas 16 97
(J A Geake) *chsd ldrs: rdn to ld 1f out: edgd lft: hdd post* **9/1**

1440 3 *hd* **Indian Maiden (IRE)**[12] [5701] 6-9-4 106 TedDurcan 11 99
(M S Saunders) *hld up: hdwy over 1f out: sn rdn: r.o* **5/1**[3]

1010 4 *1* **Mango Music**[14] [5643] 3-8-12 84 ChrisCatlin 17 91
(M R Channon) *lw: chsd ldr: led over 1f out: sn rdn and hdd: styd on same pce ins fnl f* **50/1**

4043 5 *1 ¾* **Leopoldine**[14] [5643] 3-8-12 89 SteveDrowne 9 85
(H Morrison) *led over 4f: no ex ins fnl f* **20/1**

0241 6 *1* **Passion Fruit**[15] [5619] 5-8-13 82 DeanMcKeown 5 82
(C W Fairhurst) *s.i.s: outpcd: r.o ins fnl f: nrst fin* **20/1**

10 7 *shd* **She's My Outsider**[12] [5670] 4-8-13 76 FrancisNorton 4 82
(I A Wood) *hld up: hdwy over 2f out: rdn over 1f out: styd on same pce fnl f* **66/1**

6602 8 ½ **Jeanmaire (IRE)**[92] [3418] 3-8-12 90 JohnEgan 10 80
(H Morrison) *chsd ldrs: rdn over 1f out: wknd fnl f* **22/1**

3215 9 *2* **Madame Medusa (IRE)**[28] [5317] 3-8-12 72 (v) PhilipRobinson 2 74
(J A R Toller) *chsd ldrs: rdn over 1f out: sn wknd* **80/1**

3 10 *shd* **Miss Donovan**[11] [5706] 3-8-12 KerrinMcEvoy 3 74
(Declan Gillespie, Ire) *hld up: hdwy 1/2-way: rdn over 1f out: wknd fnl f* **9/1**

2002 11 *hd* **Nidhaal (IRE)**[25] [5405] 3-8-12 96 RHills 14 74
(E A L Dunlop) *s.i.s: hdwy over 2f out: wknd fnl f* **9/2**[2]

5120 12 *1* **Terentia**[25] [5405] 3-8-12 98 JimmyFortune 8 71
(E S McMahon) *unruly stalls: chsd ldrs over 4f* **6/1**

226 13 *1 ¼* **Indian Steppes (FR)**[19] [5525] 7-8-13 89 EddieAhern 6 67
(P S McEntee) *prom over 4f* **20/1**

3006 14 ¾ **Gamble In Gold (IRE)**[14] [5643] 3-8-12 84 RichardHughes 15 65
(R Hannon) *lw: hld up: bhd fr 1/2-way* **66/1**

100 15 *3 ½* **Tara Too (IRE)**[18] [5550] 3-8-12 87 RyanMoore 12 54
(D W P Arbuthnot) *s.i.s: outpcd* **33/1**

035 16 *9* **Daniella**[16] [5588] 4-8-13 82 (p) FrancisFerris 18 27
(Rae Guest) *dwlt: a in rr: rdn and wknd over 2f out* **33/1**

1m 12.98s (-0.12) **Going Correction** +0.15s/f (Good)
WFA 3 from 4yo+ 1lb **16** Ran SP% **122.1**
Speed ratings (Par 108):106,105,105,104,101 100,100,99,96,96 96,95,93,92,87 75
CSF £31.46 TOTE £4.20: £1.70, £3.60, £2.40; EX 48.20.
Owner Jan and Peter Hopper **Bred** Mrs J P Hopper **Trained** Newmarket, Suffolk

FOCUS
They went a strong gallop here and the winner came from well off the pace. The performances of the relatively lowly-rated fourth, seventh and ninth hold down the form.

NOTEBOOK
Firenze could not go the early pace and was struggling at halfway, but as the leaders tired she found her stride and finished with a real flourish up the stands' side to get up on the line. She needs quicker ground to be at her best and probably won this despite the conditions. She could well make her mark at Group level next year. (tchd 10-3 and 4-1 in places)
Ripples Maid, already a winner at this level at Chester last month, had a 3lb penalty to carry for that success. She posted a good effort in defeat, getting to the front approaching the final furlong and only being denied close home. Since taking over from Toby Balding at the end of the 2004 Flat Turf Season, Jonathan Geake has trained 12 winners, and 11 of those won in April, May, September or October. The stats bare out the impression that the stable is one to have on side when the ground is on the easy side.
Indian Maiden(IRE), giving weight all round, as is often the case with her, was happier back in this company, had the race run to suit and stayed on well from off the pace. Only narrowly denied, her record in Listed races restricted to her own sex now reads 1412191261143. (tchd 11-2 and 6-1 in places)
Mango Music, beaten off a mark of 84 in a handicap last time out, ran a personal best on her first start in Listed company. Her performance, together with one or two others, casts some doubt on the strength of the form, but it could be that she appreciated racing on easier ground for the first time in a while.
Leopoldine ran well considering she set a strong pace in front. She looks sure to be even more effective back over five furlongs.
Passion Fruit, in rear for most of the race, found most of her rivals stopping in front in the latter stages and sailed past a number of them to finish sixth. Five times a winner over seven furlongs already, she will be suited by a return to that distance. (op 22-1)
She's My Outsider was another who was able to perform above herself because of the way the race was run. (tchd 100-1)

5920 NATIONAL STUD H'CAP 1m 4f
4:55 (4:57) (Class 2) (0-100,100) 3-Y-0+
£11,217 (£3,358; £1,679; £840; £419; £210) **Stalls** Centre

Form RPR

11 1 **Counterpunch**[10] [5732] 3-8-7 91 6ex LDettori 15 113+
(Saeed Bin Suroor) *prom: trckd ldr over 2f out: nudged into ld ins fnl f: cleverly* **5/4**[1]

1143 2 *nk* **Alessano**[5] [5804] 4-8-9 86 (b) RichardHughes 10 101
(G L Moore) *led: kicked on over 2f out: sn clr w wnr: hdd ins fnl f: edgd lft but battled on u.p: easily hld* **12/1**

4242 3 *7* **Cool Customer (USA)**[17] [5582] 3-8-9 93 (v[1]) JamieSpencer 1 97
(E A L Dunlop) *hld up in rr: stdy prog fr 7f out to chal 3f out: sn rdn: lft bhd by ldng pair fr 2f out* **14/1**

0421 4 *2* **All The Good (IRE)**[14] [5644] 3-8-5 89 FrancisNorton 4 90
(G A Butler) *t.k.h: hld up in midfield: stl gng strly over 3f out: rdn and wl outpcd fr 2f out: fdd* **18/1**

5064 5 *1 ¼* **Thunder Rock (IRE)**[18] [5548] 4-8-10 87 RyanMoore 11 86
(Sir Michael Stoute) *lw: chsd ldr tl hrd rdn and fdd 3f out* **6/1**[2]

4-15 6 *hd* **Sanchi (IRE)**[28] [5310] 4-9-6 97 KerrinMcEvoy 12 95
(Saeed Bin Suroor) *hld up in rr: prog fr 6f out: in tch over 3f out: sn shkn up and btn* **10/1**

3031 7 *shd* **Mikao (IRE)**[12] [5678] 5-8-10 90 SaleemGolam[(3)] 9 88
(M H Tompkins) *trckd ldrs: rdn over 3f out: wknd 2f out* **7/1**[3]

-445 8 ½ **Orange Touch (GER)**[47] [4797] 6-9-9 100 JimCrowley 7 97
(Mrs A J Perrett) *hld up towards rr: n.m.r over 4f out: wl outpcd fr 3f out: no ch after* **66/1**

3156 9 *1 ¾* **Numeric (GER)**[19] [5530] 3-8-5 89 (b) MartinDwyer 3 84
(J H M Gosden) *hld up in last: rdn and wl bhd 3f out: plugged on* **25/1**

0560 10 *hd* **Red Lancer**[5] [5804] 5-8-6 88 JamieMoriarty[(5)] 5 82
(R A Fahey) *swtg: hld up in rr: rdn 3f out: no rspnse and sn wknd* **50/1**

521 11 *3* **Topjeu (IRE)**[53] [4625] 3-8-8 92 NickyMackay 13 81
(L M Cumani) *hld up in midfield: rdn over 4f out: wknd 3f out* **12/1**

30-0 12 ¾ **Eva Soneva So Fast (IRE)**[20] [5505] 4-8-9 86 oh4 JimmyQuinn 8 74
(J L Dunlop) *dwlt: sn midfield: shkn up over 4f out: wknd 3f out* **100/1**

0-60 13 *13* **Gold Gun (USA)**[19] [5526] 4-8-10 87 (p) PaulHanagan 16 54
(K A Ryan) *hld up in rr: rdn and no prog over 3f out: eased whn no ch fnl f* **100/1**

2m 32.5s (-1.00) **Going Correction** +0.15s/f (Good)
WFA 3 from 4yo+ 7lb **13** Ran SP% **116.9**
Speed ratings (Par 109):109,108,104,102,101 101,101,101,100,100 98,97,88
CSF £17.02 CT £148.80 TOTE £2.00: £1.30, £3.20, £3.00; EX 16.60.
Owner Godolphin **Bred** Darley **Trained** Newmarket, Suffolk

FOCUS
Sound handicap form and another smart effort from the winner, who is now unbeaten in three starts and looks destined for better things.

NOTEBOOK
Counterpunch was 7lb well in under a penalty for his easy Windsor success and won with a good deal in hand again. His rider seemed unnecessarily keen to win by a cocky margin but there can be no doubt that had he wanted to his mount could have won by a clear margin. Unbeaten now in three starts, his handicap days are numbered and he looks likely to make up into a Pattern-class performer next season. (op 10-11 tchd 11-8 in places)
Alessano enjoyed the run of the race and kept the improving and well-handicapped winner up to his job in the latter stages, albeit he was always going to be beaten. He finished a long way clear of the third and this has been rated a personal best, but he has now been beaten three times in a row off marks in the mid to high 80s and is going to have to contend with an even higher mark in future. (op 11-1)
Cool Customer(USA) has improved all season and only twice failed to make the frame in his last ten starts now. Wearing a visor for the first time, he gave vain chase to the front two and posted a respectable effort without suggesting that he is any closer to defying a mark in the low 90s. (op 16-1)
All The Good(IRE), a winner over two furlongs further here last time out, loomed up travelling well on the outside three furlongs out, but when the button was pressed he could only find the one pace. He clearly needs further than this and is still sufficiently lightly raced to have more improvement in him. (op 25-1)
Thunder Rock(IRE) again ran all right but not well enough to justify the fact that he was once again sent off at a relatively short price. (op 7-1 tchc 8-1 in a place)
Sanchi(IRE), the stable's second-string, did not have the race run to suit and was not disgraced in the circumstances. He might well do better on a quicker surface next year. (tchd 11-1)
Mikao(IRE) is on a pretty stiff mark now having been put up 6lb for his success over this course and distance 12 days earlier. (op 15-2 tchd 8-1)
Topjeu(IRE) was disappointing, but the ground may have been too soft for him and his stable is struggling for winners, so he is not one to give up on. (op 16-1)

5921 SPORTING INDEX H'CAP 5f
5:25 (5:28) (Class 2) (0-110,103) 3-Y-0+
£11,217 (£3,358; £1,679; £840; £419; £210) **Stalls** Low

Form RPR

5065 1 **Mecca's Mate**[5] [5812] 5-8-12 97 JamieSpencer 9 107
(D W Barker) *outpcd: hdwy over 1f out: r.o to ld post* **7/2**[1]

0104 2 *shd* **Bond City (IRE)**[23] [5443] 4-9-2 101 LDettori 1 111
(B Smart) *disp ld tl led 1/2-way: rdn over 1f out: hdd post* **12/1**

0001 3 *2* **Sierra Vista**[19] [5535] 6-9-3 102 JohnEgan 2 104
(D W Barker) *lw: chsd ldrs: rdn over 1f out: styd on* **7/1**[2]

0010 4 *nk* **Angus Newz**[14] [5643] 3-8-8 93 (v) FrancisNorton 8 94
(M Quinn) *lw: disp ld to 1/2-way: rdn and hung lft over 1f out: styd on same pce* **16/1**

0012 5 *hd* **Fonthill Road (IRE)**[17] [5578] 6-9-3 102 PaulHanagan 7 103
(R A Fahey) *s.i.s: outpcd: swtchd rt over 1f out: r.o ins fnl f: nt rch ldrs* **7/2**[1]

2603 **6** ½ **Cape Royal**[4] 5832 6-8-9 **94**......(bt) SteveDrowne 4 93
(J M Bradley) *chsd ldrs: rdn over 1f out: wknd towards fin* **12/1**
0540 **7** ¾ **Corridor Creeper (FR)**[5] 5807 9-9-1 **100**......(p) RyanMoore 6 96
(J M Bradley) *b.nr hind: disp ld to 1/2-way: hmpd over 1f out: wknd ins fnl f* **15/2**[3]
4010 **8** *nk* **Philharmonic**[14] 5642 5-8-11 **101**...... JamieMoriarty(5) 3 96
(R A Fahey) *b: hld up: rdn over 1f out: n.d* **12/1**
0005 **9** 1 ¼ **Connect**[5] 5807 9-8-2 **90**......(b) SaleemGolam(3) 10 81
(M H Tompkins) *outpcd* **14/1**
6606 **10** 1 ¼ **The Tatling (IRE)**[14] 5642 9-9-4 **103**...... JimmyQuinn 11 89
(J M Bradley) *s.i.s: outpcd* **10/1**
0600 **11** *nk* **Empress Jain**[14] 5642 3-8-10 **95**...... PhilipRobinson 5 80
(M A Jarvis) *disp ld to 1/2-way: wknd fnl f* **40/1**

60.08 secs (-0.39) **Going Correction** +0.15s/f (Good) **11** Ran SP% **115.9**
Speed ratings (Par 109):109,108,105,105,104 104,102,102,100,98 97
CSF £47.56 CT £285.53 TOTE £4.50: £1.60, £3.40, £2.70; EX 68.90 Place 6 £24.08, Place 5 £16.10.
Owner David T J Metcalfe **Bred** Miss C Tagart **Trained** Scorton, N Yorks

FOCUS
A quality sprint handicap in which the winner and third ran to similar marks as when filling the first two places in this race 12 months earlier.

NOTEBOOK
Mecca's Mate, runner-up to her stablemate Sierra Vista in this race last year off a 3lb higher mark, needs a strong pace to be seen at her best and that's what she got here. She finished to good effect under Spencer, who did not resort to his whip, and just edged it on the line. It was good to see her back in the winner's enclosure for the first time since July 2005, but her performances this season suggest she may struggle again once reassessed. (op 4-1 tchd 10-3 and 9-2 in a place)
Bond City(IRE) likes to have his own way in front and he made most of the running next to the near-side rail. Only headed on the line, he ran his best race of the season. (op 14-1)
Sierra Vista, who won this race last year off 97, had a 5lb higher mark to overcome this time. She ran a solid race, but she found it impossible to confirm last year's placings with her stablemate Mecca's Mate on 8lb worse terms.
Angus Newz, a winner of three Listed races this season, appreciated the return to five furlongs and helped set the strong pace. She would have been happier to have been granted an uncontested lead, though. (op 10-1)
Fonthill Road(IRE), 5lb higher than when winning the Ayr Gold Cup and running over a distance short of his optimum, saw his race out strongly, having predictably struggled to go the early pace. He is running well now that his back problems have been fixed. (op 11-4 tchd 4-1)
Cape Royal has never scored off a mark higher than 90 and is difficult to win with. (op 16-1)
Corridor Creeper(FR) won a conditions race earlier in the season but has struggled in handicaps this term and probably needs some further help from the assessor. (op 10-1 tchd 7-1)
T/Jkpt: Not won. T/Plt: £13.30 to a £1 stake. Pool: £89,435.00. 4,878.80 winning tickets. T/Qpdt: £6.10 to a £1 stake. Pool: £4,178.50. 505.05 winning tickets. CR

5139 SOUTHWELL (L-H)
Thursday, October 12

OFFICIAL GOING: Standard
The jockeys reckoned the surface was riding a shade slower than usual.
Wind: Light, half-against Weather: Fine and warm

5922 BASE 4 MAIDEN CLAIMING STKS 1m (F)
1:50 (1:50) (Class 7) 3-Y-O+ **£1,774** (£523; £262) **Stalls** Low

Form RPR
3000 **1** **Dream Forest (IRE)**[10] 5733 3-9-1 60...... PaulEddery 14 63+
(Mrs P N Dutfield) *a cl up: led 2f out: rdn clr appr last* **11/2**[3]
0060 **2** 5 **Hippolyte (USA)**[26] 5363 3-8-10 46...... JamieMackay 11 48
(J G Given) *midfield: hdwy 3f out: rdn wl over 1f out: kpt on ins last* **14/1**
00-0 **3** 7 **Circumspect (IRE)**[28] 5311 4-9-4 52...... MichaelTebbutt 4 38
(P C Haslam) *midfield: hdwy 3f out: rdn along 2f out: plugged on same pce* **4/1**[1]
00/0 **4** 3 ½ **Royal Approach**[12] 5683 5-8-13 50...... PatCosgrave 10 25
(J R Norton) *chsd ldrs: rdn along over 3f out: drvn 2f out and sn outpcd* **40/1**
060 **5** ¾ **City Minx**[29] 5298 4-8-9 45...... DerekMcGaffin 6 20
(D Morris) *led 2f: cl up on inner: rdn over 2f out: sn drvn and grad wknd* **8/1**
0030 **6** *shd* **Franky'N'Jonny**[8] 5767 3-8-5 47...... AdrianMcCarthy 9 19
(Mrs C A Dunnett) *cl up: led after 2f: rdn along over 2f out: sn hdd: drvn and wknd wl over 1f out* **5/1**[2]
7 2 **Hoofbeats Tour** 4-9-4...... MatthewHenry 7 24
(Miss J Feilden) *s.i.s and bhd tl sme late hdwy* **16/1**
0300 **8** 2 ½ **Lucky Lil**[26] 5363 4-8-13 45...... VHalliday 3 14
(R M Whitaker) *a towards rr* **12/1**
04-0 **9** ½ **Global Guardian**[10] 5737 3-9-1 63...... DavidKinsella 5 18
(Mrs G S Rees) *keen: chsd ldrs: rdn along 1/2-way: drvn over 2f out and sn wknd* **11/2**[3]
00 **10** 16 **Just Jasmin**[38] 5056 3-8-8...... GylesParkin 13 —
(P D Evans) *chsd ldrs: rdn along over 3f out: sn wknd* **33/1**
60 **11** 5 **Talpour (IRE)**[42] 4945 6-9-4...... RobertMiles 12 —
(M C Chapman) *a bhd* **50/1**
046/ **12** 8 **French Gigolo**[782] 4940 6-9-4 50...... BrettDoyle 2 —
(C N Allen) *s.i.s: a bhd* **10/1**

1m 43.88s (-0.72) **Going Correction** -0.375s/f (Stan)
WFA 3 from 4yo+ 3lb **12** Ran SP% **115.2**
Speed ratings (Par 97):88,83,76,72,71 71,69,67,66,50 45,37
CSF £76.51 TOTE £6.20: £1.80, £4.60, £2.10; EX 80.90 TRIFECTA Not won. Pool £181.66.The winner was claimed by M. S. Saunders for £5,000. City Minx was claimed by S. R. Bowring for £3,000. Franky'n'jonny was claimed by M. Attwater for £2,500.
Owner Simon Dutfield **Bred** Mrs Margaret Sinanan **Trained** Axmouth, Devon

FOCUS
A poor maiden claimer run in a time 1.27sec slower than the later banded contest over the same trip and the winner is the best guide to some weak form.
Talpour(IRE) Official explanation: jockey said gelding finished lame

5923 LADBROKES.COM MEDIAN AUCTION MAIDEN STKS 7f (F)
2:20 (2:21) (Class 7) 2-Y-O **£1,638** (£483; £241) **Stalls** Low

Form RPR
4330 **1** **Greyt Big Stuff (USA)**[13] 5655 2-9-3 81...... RobertHavlin 5 75
(B J Meehan) *trckd ldr: led over 2f out: edgd rt fnl f: hld on towards fin* **11/10**[1]
53 **2** ½ **Chasing Memories (IRE)**[29] 5289 2-8-12...... RoystonFfrench 10 69
(B Smart) *chsd ldrs: drvn over 4f out: wnt 2nd 2f out: carried rt and no ex ins last* **7/2**[2]
0 **3** 8 **Sheriff's Silk**[22] 5481 2-9-3...... DerekMcGaffin 11 54
(B Smart) *racd wd: effrt over 2f out: edgd rt: one pce* **100/1**
5440 **4** 3 ½ **Three No Trumps**[28] 5323 2-8-12 54...... HayleyTurner 7 40
(D Morris) *sn outpcd: lost pl over 4f out: kpt on fnl 2f* **40/1**
050 **5** ½ **The Geester**[15] 5613 2-9-0 52......(p) StephenDonohoe(3) 1 44
(S R Bowring) *led tl over 2f out: hung rt: one pce* **33/1**
0 **6** 2 ½ **Burningfold Babe**[38] 5052 2-8-12...... AdrianMcCarthy 6 33
(P Winkworth) *chsd ldrs: hung lft 2f out: one pce* **150/1**
02 **7** 4 **High Five Society**[15] 5614 2-9-3...... PaulEddery 2 28
(S R Bowring) *sn drvn along: lost pl over 4f out: no threat after* **8/1**[3]
02 **8** ½ **Bar Humbug**[12] 5687 2-9-3...... TonyHamilton 4 26
(R A Fahey) *chsd ldrs: outpcd over 3f out: sn btn* **8/1**[3]
540 **9** 2 ½ **Little Hotpotch**[119] 2588 2-8-12 55...... GrahamGibbons 9 15
(J R Jenkins) *lost pl over 4f out: sn bhd* **40/1**
040 **10** 5 **Sahara Dawn (IRE)**[63] 4295 2-8-12 50...... AdamKirby 3 3
(C G Cox) *sn drvn along: chsd ldrs: lost pl over 4f out: sn bhd* **11/1**

1m 29.56s (-1.24) **Going Correction** -0.375s/f (Stan) **10** Ran SP% **109.9**
Speed ratings (Par 89):92,91,82,78,77 74,70,69,66,61
CSF £4.11 TOTE £1.70: £1.10, £1.40, £18.60; EX 5.10 TRIFECTA Not won. Pool £140.02.
Owner Stephen Dartnell **Bred** West Lodge Stud **Trained** Manton, Wilts
■ Inflagrantedelicto was withdrawn (15/2, vet's advice). R4 applies, deduct 10p in the £.
■ Stewards' Enquiry : Royston Ffrench two-day ban: used whip with excessive frequency (Oct 23-24)

FOCUS
A moderate maiden auction and the form is anchored by the fifth.

NOTEBOOK
Greyt Big Stuff(USA), who is aptly named, had the blinkers left off. He made very hard work of it and came off a straight line but was always doing just enough. (op 7-4 tchd 2-1)
Chasing Memories(IRE) went in pursuit of the winner and ran her heart out under extreme pressure but was never doing quite enough. She richly deserves to go one better. (tchd 3-1)
Sheriff's Silk, who stands over plenty of ground, stepped up on his debut effort. Worst drawn, in the end the first two ran right away from him.
Three No Trumps, who had a stone and a half to find with the winner, stayed in in her own time and being hopelessly outpaced. (op 33-1)
The Geester, fitted with cheekpieces for the first time, took them along from his inside draw but he hung badly right when headed and ended up under the stands'-side rail. He does not look straight forward by any means. Official explanation: jockey said colt hung right-handed throughout
Burningfold Babe had finished last on her debut on turf five weeks earlier.

5924 LADBROKESCASINO.COM BANDED STKS (DIV I) 7f (F)
2:55 (2:55) (Class 7) 3-Y-O+ **£2,013** (£594; £297) **Stalls** Low

Form RPR
4005 **1** **Zamhrear**[17] 5571 3-9-0 48...... BrettDoyle 9 60+
(C E Brittain) *s.i.s: sn rdn along and bhd: wd st and gd hdwy 2f out: str run ent last: edgd lft and led last 100 yds* **10/1**
0205 **2** 1 **Priorina (IRE)**[38] 5054 4-9-1 47......(v) RobertHavlin 6 56
(D Haydn Jones) *in tch: gd hdwy on inner over 2f out: led wl over 1f out: rdn clr ent last: hdd and no ex last 100 yds* **9/2**[3]
0020 **3** 1 ½ **Thornaby Green**[12] 5683 5-8-11 50...... NeilBrown(7) 8 56
(T D Barron) *chsd ldrs: effrt and n.m.r 2f out: sn rdn and kpt on ins last* **7/2**[1]
4200 **4** 1 ½ **Monkey Madge**[242] 391 4-9-2 48...... RoystonFfrench 1 50
(B Smart) *midfield: hdwy 2f out: sn rdn and styd on ins last: nrst fin* **12/1**
0240 **5** ½ **Sarah's Prince (IRE)**[73] 3995 3-8-9 50...... JamesMillman(7) 10 50
(D K Ivory) *in tch: hdwy on outer over 2f out: sn rdn and wknd over 1f out* **20/1**
-410 **6** 2 **Government (IRE)**[11] 5240 5-9-0 49...... StephenDonohoe(3) 2 44
(M C Chapman) *led 2f: cl up tl rdn along over 2f out and grad wknd* **11/1**
6000 **7** 1 **Yorkie**[65] 4233 7-9-2 48...... MichaelTebbutt 5 41
(J Pearce) *trckd ldrs: hdwy over 2f out: rdn wl over 1f out and sn one pce* **9/1**
6030 **8** 1 **Mid Valley**[63] 4291 3-9-0 48......(v) GrahamGibbons 3 38
(J R Jenkins) *chsd ldrs on inner: hdwy over 2f out and sn rdn: drvn over 1f out and sn wknd* **10/1**
050 **9** 1 **Inchmarlow (IRE)**[8] 5770 3-8-9 48...... DuranFentiman(5) 12 35
(T H Caldwell) *chsd ldrs: rdn along 2f out: sn wknd* **25/1**
2640 **10** 2 **Baby Barry**[31] 5248 9-9-4 50...... RobbieFitzpatrick 14 32
(M J Attwater) *cl up: led after 2f: rdn along over 2f out: drvn and hdd wl over 1f out: sn wknd* **4/1**[2]
00-0 **11** 5 **Regal Lass**[26] 5368 3-8-13 47...... JamieMackay 11 16
(J G Given) *prom: rdn along wl over 2f out: sn wknd* **80/1**
6000 **12** 7 **Whisper Inthe Wind (IRE)**[23] 5453 3-8-13 50......(t) DeanCorby(3) 7 —
(Miss J Feilden) *a rr* **28/1**
0000 **13** 28 **Star Fern**[57] 4496 5-9-2 48...... PatCosgrave 13 —
(M J Attwater) *v.s.a and a wl t.o* **20/1**

1m 29.62s (-1.18) **Going Correction** -0.375s/f (Stan)
WFA 3 from 4yo+ 2lb **13** Ran SP% **122.7**
Speed ratings (Par 97):91,89,88,86,85 83,82,81,80,77 72,64,32
CSF £52.67 TOTE £12.80: £3.70, £1.90, £1.80; EX 83.90 Trifecta £123.60 Pool £174.15. 0.80 winning units - part won..
Owner Saeed Manana **Bred** Darley **Trained** Newmarket, Suffolk

FOCUS
A typical event of its type but the slowest of three over the trip on the day. The form looks believable with the placed horses to form.
Baby Barry Official explanation: jockey said gelding ran too free

5925 GB LIFTS LTD BANDED STKS 1m 3f (F)
3:30 (3:31) (Class 7) 4-Y-O+ **£2,013** (£594; £297) **Stalls** Low

Form RPR
2600 **1** **Kirkhammerton (IRE)**[4] 5840 4-8-12 48......(b) StephenDonohoe(3) 8 62
(A J McCabe) *hld up in rr: gd hdwy over 3f out: led over 1f out: sn clr: readily* **11/2**[3]
0303 **2** 7 **Justcallmehandsome**[30] 5267 4-9-2 49...... HayleyTurner 9 51
(D J S Ffrench Davis) *in tch: hdwy to chse ldrs over 3f out: wnt 2nd 1f out: no ch w wnr* **13/2**
0002 **3** 1 ¼ **Channel Crossing**[4] 5837 4-8-11 45 ow2......(p) DNolan(3) 1 47
(W M Brisbourne) *mde most: hdd over 1f out: one pce* **6/1**
635/ **4** ½ **Glen Vale Walk (IRE)**[850] 2939 9-8-12 45...... FrankieMcDonald 5 44
(Mrs G S Rees) *s.i.s: hld up in rr: hdwy on ins over 3f out: led 2f out: sn hdd: one pce* **25/1**
-000 **5** ¾ **Red River Rock (IRE)**[4] 5838 4-8-12 45......(be[1]) PatCosgrave 13 43
(T J Fitzgerald) *chsd ldrs: effrt on wd outside over 2f out: one pce* **33/1**
-000 **6** 4 **Laurollie**[86] 3615 4-8-12 45...... GrahamGibbons 2 36
(B P J Baugh) *hld up in rr: hdwy to chse ldrs over 3f out: wknd over 1f out* **28/1**

0-20 **7** *nk* **Trysting Grove (IRE)**[127] 2345 5-8-12 45 PhillipMakin 10 36
(E G Bevan) *in tch: drvn over 3f out: wknd over 1f out* **14/1**

2460 **8** *1¾* **Nakwa (IRE)**[42] 4954 8-8-12 45 DavidAllan 12 33
(E J Alston) *chsd ldrs: led over 2f out: sn hdd: wknd over 1f out* **5/1**[2]

6635 **9** *10* **Ming Vase**[31] 5240 4-8-13 46 RobbieFitzpatrick 7 17
(P T Midgley) *in rr: drvn over 4f out: nvr a factor* **8/1**

005- **10** *¾* **Showtime Annie**[304] 6555 5-8-12 45 (p) JoeFanning 6 15
(A Bailey) *w ldr: wknd over 2f out* **33/1**

500- **11** *½* **Captain Smoothy**[258] 5683 6-8-12 45 LPKeniry 4 14
(M J Gingell) *chsd ldrs: drvn over 5f out: lost pl 4f out* **50/1**

5300 **12** *1¼* **String Serenade (IRE)**[25] 5097 5-8-12 45 MichaelTebbutt 3 12
(V Smith) *chsd ldrs: lost pl 4f out: sn bhd* **22/1**

4240 **13** *6* **Tetragon (IRE)**[43] 4924 6-9-2 49 DanielTudhope 11 6
(D Carroll) *hld up in rr: drvn over 4f out: hung rt and lost pl 3f out: sn bhd* **7/2**[1]

4-40 **14** *42* **Power Glory**[25] 3900 4-8-12 45 AdrianTNicholls 14 —
(M J Gingell) *s.i.s: sn detached in last and drvn: t.o over 4f out: btn 42l* **40/1**

2m 24.76s (-4.14) **Going Correction** -0.375s/f (Stan) **14** Ran SP% **121.6**
Speed ratings (Par 97):100,94,94,93,93 90,89,88,81,80 80,79,75,44
CSF £38.53 TOTE £7.10: £2.10, £3.40, £2.40; EX 36.40 Trifecta £114.10 Pool £160.74. 0.54 winning units - part won.

Owner Paul J Dixon **Bred** Barronstown Stud And Orpendale **Trained** Babworth, Notts

FOCUS
A sound pace and the well-backed winner bounced back to something like his old form for his new trainer. The form does not look that solid.

Tetragon(IRE) Official explanation: jockey said gelding would not face kick back

5926 LADBROKESPOKER.COM BANDED STKS 1m (F)

4:05 (4:09) (Class 7) 3-Y-0+ **£1,911** (£564; £282) **Stalls** Low

Form RPR

6500 **1** **Silver Mont (IRE)**[15] 5618 3-8-11 45 (bt) PaulEddery 6 54
(S R Bowring) *towards rr and pushed along 1/2-way: gd hdwy on inner over 2f out: rdn to ld over 1f out: styd on wl fnl f* **9/1**

5000 **2** *1* **Machhapuchhare**[23] 5452 3-8-11 45 (p) DavidAllan 12 52
(W M Brisbourne) *dwlt and towards rr: hdwy and wd st: rdn wl over 1f out: chsd wnr ins last: kpt on* **11/2**[2]

6606 **3** *3* **Elms Schoolboy**[37] 5097 4-8-11 45 (b) DeanCorby(3) 5 46
(P Howling) *dwlt and towards rr: hdwy on outer 1/2-way: rdn to ld 2f out: drvn and hdd over 1f out: kpt on same pce* **12/1**

6530 **4** *3½* **Sea Frolic (IRE)**[37] 5085 5-9-0 45 (v) RobbieFitzpatrick 9 38
(Jennie Candlish) *towards rr and rdn along ½-way: hdwy over 2f out: sn rdn and edgd lft: styd on ins last: nrst fin* **12/1**

0003 **5** *2½* **Preskani**[134] 2137 4-9-0 45 (p) MichaelTebbutt 11 33
(Mrs N Macauley) *midfield and rdn along 1/2-way: hdwy 2f out: styd on u.p appr last: nrst fin* **5/2**[1]

5040 **6** *¾* **Wodhill Be**[17] 5573 6-9-0 45 DerekMcGaffin 2 31
(D Morris) *trckd ldrs: smooth hdwy over 2f out and sn ev ch: rdn wl over 1f out and wknd appr last* **25/1**

6000 **7** *nk* **Savoy Chapel**[119] 2137 4-8-7 45 MarkCoumbe(7) 4 31
(A W Carroll) *towards rr: wd st: hdwy 2f out: sn rdn and no imp* **8/1**[3]

5010 **8** *4* **Aqua**[4] 5838 4-8-9 45 RoryMoore(5) 14 22
(P T Midgley) *midfeild: hdwy 3f out: rdn over 2f out and sn btn* **12/1**

000- **9** *nk* **Queenstown (IRE)**[312] 6495 5-9-0 45 RobertHavlin 1 22
(J E Long) *c lose up: rdn along 1/2-way: sn wknd* **28/1**

056- **10** *shd* **Cross My Shadow (IRE)**[309] 6524 4-9-0 45 (t) DavidKinsella 10 22
(M F Harris) *bolted bef s: led: rdn along over 2f out: sn hdd & wknd* **16/1**

000 **11** *shd* **King Nicholas (USA)**[66] 4194 7-8-11 45 (tp) NeilChalmers(3) 3 21
(J Parkes) *a rr* **33/1**

-320 **12** *3½* **Frenchgate**[22] 5485 5-8-9 45 NataliaGemelova(5) 13 14
(I W McInnes) *chsd ldrs: rdn along 3f out: sn wknd* **11/2**[2]

000 **13** *5* **Spirit Guide (FR)**[13] 2926 4-9-0 45 JoeFanning 7 3
(R C Guest) *cl up: rdn along 3f out: sn wknd* **33/1**

6640 **14** *11* **Virginia Plain**[18] 5550 3-8-6 45 (b) EmmettStack(5) 8 —
(Miss Diana Weeden) *cl up: rdn along over 3f out: sn wknd* **33/1**

1m 42.61s (-1.99) **Going Correction** -0.375s/f (Stan)
WFA 3 from 4yo+ 3lb **14** Ran SP% **125.5**
Speed ratings (Par 97):94,93,90,86,84 83,82,78,78,78 78,74,69,58
CSF £57.39 TOTE £13.60: £4.50, £2.20, £3.70; EX 83.20 TRIFECTA Not won. Pool £185.99.

Owner Clark Industrial Services Partnership **Bred** Clark Industrial Services Partnership **Trained** Edwinstowe, Notts

FOCUS
A typical contest of its type rated through the winner and limited by the time.

Frenchgate Official explanation: jockey said gelding was unsuited by the standard ground

5927 LADBROKES FREEPHONE ON 0800 777 888 BANDED STKS 2m (F)

4:40 (4:41) (Class 7) 4-Y-0+ **£2,013** (£594; £297) **Stalls** Low

Form RPR

3360 **1** **Bulberry Hill**[73] 3998 5-8-9 45 EdwardCreighton(3) 14 55
(R W Price) *hld up in rr: smooth hdwy 6f out: led on bit 3f out: kpt on u.p fnl f* **5/1**[1]

4266 **2** *1¾* **Red River Rebel**[43] 4924 8-8-12 45 PaulMulrennan 4 53
(J R Norton) *chsd ldrs: kpt on fnl 3f: tk 2nd nr fin* **14/1**

4563 **3** *½* **Lennel**[27] 5338 8-9-0 47 (v) JoeFanning 8 54
(A Bailey) *s.i.s: sn chsng ldrs: led over 4f out: hdd 3f out: styd on same pce* **8/1**

3454 **4** *1* **True (IRE)**[9] 5750 5-9-1 48 RoystonFfrench 1 54
(Mrs S Lamyman) *hld up in tch: effrt over 3f out: one pce fnl 2f* **6/1**[2]

4302 **5** *11* **Makarim (IRE)**[149] 1766 10-8-12 45 (p) LPKeniry 10 38
(M R Bosley) *hld up in rr: hdwy over 7f out: outpcd fnl 3f* **15/2**[3]

0050 **6** *6* **Step Perfect (USA)**[16] 4960 5-8-12 45 (p) DanielTudhope 9 31
(G M Moore) *trckd ldrs: led 6f out tl over 4f out: wknd over 2f out* **6/1**[2]

6600 **7** *¾* **Kirstys Lad**[10] 5741 4-8-12 40 AdrianTNicholls 3 30
(M Mullineaux) *hld up and bhd: effrt over 4f out: nvr on terms* **80/1**

0000 **8** *½* **Indian Chase**[59] 4438 9-8-12 45 AdamKirby 12 29
(Dr J R J Naylor) *hld up in rr: effrt over 4f out: nvr a factor* **15/2**[3]

0046 **9** *7* **Esquillon**[58] 4451 4-8-5 40 MarkCoumbe(7) 6 21
(S Parr) *led: hdd 6f out: lost pl 4f out* **50/1**

2234 **10** *1¾* **Logger Rhythm (USA)**[14] 688 6-8-12 45 (b[1]) AlanDaly 13 19
(Dr J R J Naylor) *s.i.s: nvr on terms* **16/1**

14-0 **11** *1½* **Bongoali**[40] 5033 4-8-12 45 HayleyTurner 7 17
(Mrs C A Dunnett) *in tch: lost pl over 3f out* **25/1**

00-0 **12** *14* **Penalty Clause (IRE)**[17] 5564 6-8-5 40 JPFeatherstone(7) 2 —
(P Howling) *s.i.s: hdwy to chse ldrs after 4f: drvn over 7f out: lost pl over 5f out: t.o 3f out* **40/1**

33-4 **P** **Johnny Alljays (IRE)**[45] 4438 5-8-13 46 PatCosgrave 11 —
(S Lycett) *chsd ldrs: rdn after 6f: lost pl over 8f out: sn t.o: p.u 6f out* **5/1**[1]

3m 39.82s (-4.72) **Going Correction** -0.375s/f (Stan) **13** Ran SP% **118.6**
Speed ratings (Par 97):96,95,94,94,88 85,85,85,81,80 80,73,—
CSF £74.33 TOTE £6.00: £1.80, £5.50, £2.90; EX 139.20 TRIFECTA Not won. Pool of £165.29.

Owner Miss D Hutchinson **Bred** Mrs Ian Pilkington **Trained** Newmarket, Suffolk

FOCUS
Sound form and an improved effort from the strong-travelling winner.

Johnny Alljays(IRE) Official explanation: trainer said gelding lost its action having knocked the inside rail

5928 EXPERIENCE NOTTINGHAMSHIRE BANDED STKS 6f (F)

5:15 (5:15) (Class 7) 3-Y-0+ **£2,013** (£594; £297) **Stalls** Low

Form RPR

0330 **1** **Hamaasy**[56] 4511 5-9-1 47 StephenCarson 2 62+
(D Nicholls) *trckd ldrs: smooth hdwy 2f out: rdn to ld appr last: kpt on strly* **13/2**[2]

005 **2** *3½* **Granakey (IRE)**[71] 4045 3-9-0 50 DominicFox(3) 6 55
(M G Quinlan) *a.p: effrt over 2f out and ev ch: rdn wl over 1f out and kpt on same pce* **20/1**

5320 **3** *2½* **Blakeshall Quest**[62] 4329 6-9-4 50 (b) PatCosgrave 9 47
(R Brotherton) *a cl up: rdn to ld briefly over 1f out: sn drvn: hdd & wknd* **7/1**[3]

3050 **4** *¾* **Estoille**[23] 5443 5-9-4 50 CatherineGannon 14 45
(Mrs S Lamyman) *led: rdn along 2f out: hdd & wknd over 1f out* **8/1**

-000 **5** *1* **Madam Patti**[41] 4984 3-9-0 50 NeilChalmers(3) 4 42
(B Palling) *in tch: hdwy 2f out: sn rdn and no imp* **33/1**

360 **6** *1½* **Harrington Bates**[3] 5865 5-9-1 47 (v) VHalliday 7 34
(R M Whitaker) *a midfield* **7/1**[3]

0000 **7** *nk* **Angelofthenorth**[4] 5834 4-9-4 50 MichaelTebbutt 12 36
(C J Teague) *in tch: rdn along wl over 2f out: sn btn* **12/1**

0440 **8** *¾* **Seesawmilu (IRE)**[50] 4695 3-9-2 49 JosedeSouza 10 33
(E J Alston) *chsd ldrs: rdn along wl over 2f out: sn drvn and wknd* **9/1**

1145 **9** *2½* **Piddies Pride (IRE)**[27] 5350 4-9-2 48 (v) AdrianMcCarthy 1 25
(Miss Gay Kelleway) *a bhd* **4/1**[1]

0350 **10** *½* **A Teen**[68] 4141 8-9-2 48 MatthewHenry 3 23
(P Howling) *a towards rr* **14/1**

3000 **11** *1* **Orchestration (IRE)**[93] 3389 5-9-4 50 DaleGibson 13 22
(M J Attwater) *a towards rr* **7/1**[3]

0000 **12** *3½* **Penny Whisper (IRE)**[14] 5636 3-8-12 50 NataliaGemelova(5) 5 12
(I W McInnes) *a towards rr* **33/1**

4400 **13** *5* **Axis Shield (IRE)**[76] 3913 3-9-1 48 RobertMiles 11 —
(M C Chapman) *chsd ldrs: rdn along wl over 2f out: sn wknd* **40/1**

1m 15.47s (-1.44) **Going Correction** -0.375s/f (Stan)
WFA 3 from 4yo+ 1lb **13** Ran SP% **119.4**
Speed ratings (Par 97):94,89,86,85,83 81,81,80,76,76 74,70,63
CSF £135.09 TOTE £7.10: £2.70, £6.30, £2.30; EX 208.70 TRIFECTA Not won. Pool of £152.92.

Owner J P Honeyman **Bred** Shadwell Estate Company Limited **Trained** Sessay, N Yorks

FOCUS
An ordinary sprint dominated by a pair who were unexposed on the surface but the placed form is not rock sold.

Piddies Pride(IRE) Official explanation: jockey said filly did not face the kick back

5929 LADBROKESCASINO.COM BANDED STKS (DIV II) 7f (F)

5:45 (5:45) (Class 7) 3-Y-0+ **£2,013** (£594; £297) **Stalls** Low

Form RPR

0033 **1** **Keon (IRE)**[31] 5248 4-8-9 48 RussellKennemore(7) 11 60
(R Hollinshead) *trckd ldrs: smooth hdwy to ld 2f out: drvn out* **11/2**[1]

0505 **2** *¾* **Wodhill Gold**[31] 5248 5-9-1 47 DerekMcGaffin 8 57
(D Morris) *chsd ldrs: kpt on wl fnl 2f: no ex ins last* **10/1**

1530 **3** *½* **Start Of Authority**[23] 5450 5-9-1 47 LPKeniry 6 56
(J Gallagher) *chsd ldrs: hung lft over 1f out: nt qckn ins last* **6/1**[2]

0-00 **4** *4* **Suffolk House**[259] 196 4-9-4 50 DanielTudhope 10 48
(M Brittain) *trckd ldrs on outer: one pce fnl 2f* **50/1**

0000 **5** *nk* **Sonderborg**[42] 4974 5-9-2 48 (p) DaleGibson 9 46
(J Mackie) *sn in rr and drvn along on oter: hdwy 2f out: kpt on: nvr rchd ldrs* **10/1**

6000 **6** *¾* **Almowj**[23] 5450 3-9-2 50 BrettDoyle 4 46
(C E Brittain) *in rr: hmpd bnd over 4f out: sme hdwy on outer 2f out: nvr a threat* **8/1**

0623 **7** *shd* **Chickado (IRE)**[97] 3262 5-9-4 50 RobertHavlin 14 45
(D Haydn Jones) *trckd ldrs on outside: effrt over 2f out: one pce* **11/2**[1]

0566 **8** *1½* **Nassar (IRE)**[31] 5247 3-8-9 50 KirstyMilczarek(7) 3 41
(G Prodromou) *sn detached in last: hdwy on inner and n.m.r over 1f out: nvr on terms* **15/2**[3]

5000 **9** *2½* **Filey Buoy**[22] 5483 4-9-4 50 HayleyTurner 12 35
(R M Whitaker) *chsd ldrs on outer: lost pl over 2f out* **14/1**

0000 **10** *shd* **Ronnies Lad**[57] 4467 4-9-1 47 (v) PaulMulrennan 13 32
(J R Norton) *chsd ldrs on outer: outpcd over 3f out: no ch after* **66/1**

3000 **11** *1* **Immaculate Red**[50] 4690 3-9-2 50 RoystonFfrench 1 32
(R Bastiman) *a in rr* **9/1**

3335 **12** *1¼* **Flashing Floozie**[14] 5637 3-9-0 48 (b[1]) JamieMackay 2 27
(J G Given) *s.i.s: sn chsng ldrs on inner: edgd lft and wknd 2f out* **11/1**

1350 **13** *½* **Wilford Maverick (IRE)**[185] 940 4-8-9 48 StacyRenwick(7) 7 26
(M J Attwater) *s.i.s: nvr on terms* **16/1**

0605 **14** *hd* **Kissi Kissi**[3] 5873 3-9-2 50 (v[1]) RobbieFitzpatrick 5 27
(M J Attwater) *led tl hdd & wknd 2f out* **20/1**

1m 28.71s (-2.09) **Going Correction** -0.375s/f (Stan)
WFA 3 from 4yo+ 2lb **14** Ran SP% **125.2**
Speed ratings (Par 97):96,95,94,90,89 88,88,86,84,84 82,81,80,80
CSF £61.89 TOTE £6.20: £2.20, £2.50, £3.10; EX 87.00 Trifecta £100.40 Part won. Pool £141.41 - 0.78 winning units. Place 6 £137.66, Place 5 £59.11.

Owner Chasetown Civil Engineering Ltd **Bred** P F Headon **Trained** Upper Longdon, Staffs

FOCUS
The first three finished clear and could all rate about a stone higher. The form looks rock solid at this level.

T/Plt: £479.50 to a £1 stake. Pool: £49,076.70. 74.70 winning tickets. T/Qpdt: £48.90 to a £1 stake. Pool: £3,499.60. 52.90 winning tickets. JR

5930 - 5932a (Foreign Racing) - See Raceform Interactive

[5570]BRIGHTON (L-H)

Friday, October 13

OFFICIAL GOING: Good to soft

They raced middle to stands' side in all races, but only four horses in serious contention came all the way over to the stands' rail, and three of them won.

Wind: Almost nil Weather: Sunny and warm

5933 EUROPEAN BREEDERS FUND MEDIAN AUCTION MAIDEN STKS 7f 214y

2:25 (2:26) (Class 5) 2-Y-0 **£3,238** (£963; £481; £240) **Stalls** Low

Form RPR

622 **1** **Malyana**[20] 5536 2-8-9 72 MatthewHenry 11 73
(M A Jarvis) *racd freely and restrained in front: mde all: qcknd 3f out: hung lft over 1f out: rdn out* **9/2**[3]

3026 **2** *1* **Colchium (IRE)**[29] 5322 2-8-9 69 LPKeniry 2 71
(H Morrison) *t.k.h: hld up in midfield: hdwy 2f out: drvn to take 2nd ins fnl f: nt rch wnr* **20/1**

255 **3** *1 ¼* **Baltic Belle (IRE)**[13] 5676 2-8-9 80 SebSanders 3 68
(R Hannon) *cl up: chsd wnr over 5f out: hrd rdn and swtchd rt over 1f out: one pce: lost 2nd ins fnl f* **15/8**[1]

3 **4** *1* **Filios (IRE)**[25] 5423 2-9-0 MartinDwyer 6 71
(L M Cumani) *chsd wnr over 2f: rdn and outpcd 4f out: rallied and r.o again fnl f* **2/1**[2]

4426 **5** *½* **Beech Games**[36] 5126 2-9-0 76 RichardMullen 10 70
(E J O'Neill) *s.s: t.k.h and sn prom: hrd rdn and one pce fnl 2f* **9/1**

065 **6** *6* **Amazing King (IRE)**[27] 5379 2-8-11 66 AmirQuinn(3) 8 57
(W G M Turner) *in tch: c alone to stands' rail ent st: outpcd fnl 2f* **66/1**

0500 **7** *2* **Musical Award (IRE)**[14] 5655 2-9-0 66 OscarUrbina 1 52
(M G Quinlan) *sn outpcd in rr: nvr trbld ldrs* **14/1**

5006 **8** *shd* **Pace Telecom Flyer (IRE)**[20] 5527 2-8-11 58 JamesDoyle(3) 9 52
(J W Hills) *towards rr: carried wd and swtchd lft ent st: n.d* **66/1**

000 **9** *2 ½* **Field Sport (FR)**[29] 5321 2-9-0 52 BrettDoyle 7 47
(C E Brittain) *dwlt: sn in tch: wknd over 2f out* **66/1**

000 **10** *hd* **Elmasong**[18] 5570 2-8-9 49 ow3 StephenDonohoe(3) 5 44
(J J Bridger) *dwlt: drvn along 3f out: a towards rr* **66/1**

0 **11** *nk* **Clytha**[69] 4148 2-8-9 JamieMackay 4 41
(M L W Bell) *s.s: a bhd* **33/1**

1m 37.16s (2.12) **Going Correction** +0.125s/f (Good) 11 Ran SP% **116.6**

Speed ratings (Par 95):94,93,91,90,90 84,82,82,79,79 79

CSF £91.29 TOTE £5.30: £2.10, £5.40, £1.10; EX 61.00 Trifecta £162.80 Pool £335.89, 2.06 w/u.

Owner Sheikh Ahmed Al Maktoum **Bred** Darley **Trained** Newmarket, Suffolk

FOCUS

A fair maiden, with the first five home all having reasonable previous form and solid enough rated around the runner-up and eighth. The field, with the exception of Amazing King (who came to the stands' rail) raced centre-track in the home straight.

NOTEBOOK

Malyana dictated her own pace and held on a shade comfortably despite hanging down the camber in the final quarter-mile. She is now likely to be put away for next season and looks the type to train on as long as she is not aimed too high. (op 5-1 tchd 11-2)

Colchium(IRE) again raced too keenly for her own good. Swinging off the bridle for a long way, she was ultimately not good enough to beat the winner but deserves to get off the mark in modest maiden or handicap company. (op 16-1)

Baltic Belle(IRE), sweating, has been running consistently well all season, but has had plenty of chances. Although races over this trip are an option from now on, she is becoming very frustrating. (op 7-4 tchd 9-4)

Filios(IRE) has been staying on over this trip, and looks as if a mile and a quarter will suit, particularly when his stable is back in form. Next season he should get a mile and a half. (op 11-4 tchd 15-8)

Beech Games is struggling to win his maiden, but he has run well in all five races and looks ready to have a crack at handicaps. (op 8-1 tchd 10-1)

Amazing King(IRE) was the only runner to come all the way across to the stands' rail - the others stayed in the centre - though that was at least in part because he took his jockey there by hanging. These tactics often pay dividends here on softish ground, as they did later in the day, but he was nowhere near good enough to take advantage. Official explanation: jockey said colt hung right

5934 RB SOLUTIONS MAIDEN STKS 1m 3f 196y

3:00 (3:00) (Class 5) 3-Y-0+ **£3,238** (£963; £481; £240) **Stalls** High

Form RPR

522 **1** **Red Gala**[9] 5770 3-9-3 MartinDwyer 1 90+
(Sir Michael Stoute) *chsd clr ldr: led wl over 1f out: rdn clr* **4/7**[1]

2 *9* **Flame Creek (IRE)**[350] 10-9-10 OscarUrbina 6 76
(E J Creighton) *led: sn 8l clr: hdd wl over 1f out: sn outpcd* **16/1**

5 **3** *4* **Lunar Landscape (USA)**[13] 5669 3-9-3 SebSanders 3 69
(Saeed Bin Suroor) *a mod 3rd: rdn over 5f out: no imp* **5/2**[2]

623- **4** *30* **Marc Of Brilliance (USA)**[26] 6246 3-9-3 80 GeorgeBaker 4 21+
(G L Moore) *mod 4th: rdn over 4f out: n.d after: bhd whn eased over 1f out* **8/1**[3]

5 *46* **Old Golden Grey**[1007] 9-9-3 FrankiePickard(7) 5 —
(M Wellings) *s.s: a last: t.o fr 1/2-way* **100/1**

2m 32.27s (0.07) **Going Correction** +0.125s/f (Good)

WFA 3 from 4yo+ 7lb 5 Ran SP% **110.2**

Speed ratings (Par 103):104,98,95,75,44

CSF £11.38 TOTE £1.50: £1.30, £5.10; EX 14.30.

Owner Cheveley Park Stud **Bred** Cheveley Park Stud Ltd **Trained** Newmarket, Suffolk

FOCUS

An odd line-up, comprising two runners from powerful Newmarket stables and two veterans making their Flat debuts, with the field strung out from the start despite an ordinary pace. The winner sets the standard but the race did not take much winning

5935 FOSTER'S SUPER CHILLED H'CAP 1m 3f 196y

3:35 (3:35) (Class 5) (0-75,73) 3-Y-0+ **£4,210** (£1,252; £625; £312) **Stalls** High

Form RPR

5526 **1** **And Again (USA)**[35] 5152 3-9-5 73 OscarUrbina 3 80
(J R Fanshawe) *led at modest pce: qcknd 4f out: hld off runner-up tl narrowly hdd nr fin: got bk up on line* **8/1**

5045 **2** *shd* **Nawow**[26] 3935 6-9-3 64 MartinDwyer 5 71
(P D Cundell) *pressed wnr: chalng whn hung lft over 1f out: drvn to take narrow ld nr fin: jst tched off* **11/1**

0400 **3** *2 ½* **Karlu (GER)**[20] 5533 4-9-9 70 RichardMullen 4 73
(Pat Eddery) *in tch: hrd rdn 2f out: styd on same pce* **8/1**

2101 **4** *hd* **Mull Of Dubai**[4] 5868 3-9-4 72 6ex LPKeniry 7 75
(J S Moore) *hld up in rr: nt clr run over 2f out: hdwy whn swtchd lft and nt clr run over 1f out tl ins fnl f: hung lft: no ex* **5/1**[3]

U514 **5** *2 ½* **Serramanna**[3] 5897 5-8-6 56 oh1 JamesDoyle(3) 6 55
(Ms J S Doyle) *hld up towards rr: effrt on outside 3f out: sn hrd rdn and no imp* **9/2**[2]

0451 **6** *8* **Cape Diamond (IRE)**[40] 5047 3-9-2 70 AdamKirby 1 56
(W R Swinburn) *plld hrd: prom: hrd rdn over 2f out: wknd wl over 1f out* **15/2**

4623 **7** *5* **Prime Contender**[99] 3214 4-9-8 69 SebSanders 8 47
(G L Moore) *chsd ldrs tl wknd 2f out* **7/2**[1]

1312 **8** *1 ¾* **Jackie Kiely**[29] 5314 5-9-6 70 (t) StephenDonohoe(3) 2 45
(R Brotherton) *in tch: outpcd over 3f out: sn bhd* **11/2**

2m 34.41s (2.21) **Going Correction** +0.125s/f (Good)

WFA 3 from 4yo+ 7lb 8 Ran SP% **114.8**

Speed ratings (Par 103):97,96,95,95,93 88,84,83

CSF £90.26 CT £726.94 TOTE £10.00: £2.60, £3.50, £2.60; EX 130.10 TRIFECTA Not won..

Owner Prince A A Faisal **Bred** Nawara Stud **Trained** Newmarket, Suffolk

FOCUS

A routine, but competitive, handicap, run at a modest pace. The form is ordinary and has not been rated too positively.

Serramanna Official explanation: jockey said mare ran flat

Cape Diamond(IRE) Official explanation: jockey said gelding ran too free

5936 BBI INSURANCE GROUP H'CAP 7f 214y

4:10 (4:11) (Class 6) (0-58,59) 3-Y-0 **£2,914** (£867; £433; £216) **Stalls** Low

Form RPR

0441 **1** **Under Fire (IRE)**[49] 4757 3-8-6 51 JamesDoyle(3) 5 59
(A W Carroll) *prom: led over 3f out: c alone to stands' rail fr 2f out: rdn and hld on wl* **10/1**

6024 **2** *1 ½* **Moyoko (IRE)**[49] 4772 3-8-8 50 RichardMullen 7 55
(M Blanshard) *sn in midfield: drvn to chse ldrs 2f out: kpt on to take 2nd ins fnl f* **7/1**[3]

0-00 **3** *¾* **Shropshirelass**[18] 5567 3-8-8 50 FJohansson 2 53
(Mrs Norma Pook) *prom: rdn to chse wnr over 1f out: nt qckn fnl f* **40/1**

3504 **4** *shd* **Some Diva**[27] 5370 3-9-2 58 (p) AdamKirby 12 61
(W R Swinburn) *in rr: rdn 1/2-way: r.o fnl 2f: nrst fin* **12/1**

5204 **5** *¾* **Taranis**[15] 5637 3-8-9 51 SebSanders 14 52
(Sir Mark Prescott) *s.s and early reminders: sn chsng ldrs: hrd rdn over 2f out: one pce* **4/1**[1]

5424 **6** *nk* **Hot Agnes**[33] 5210 3-9-1 57 (t) MichaelTebbutt 4 57
(H J Collingridge) *hld up in rr: gd hdwy to chse ldrs 2f out: no ex fnl f* **7/1**[3]

0000 **7** *shd* **Orphina (IRE)**[78] 3869 3-8-11 53 SilvestreDeSousa 9 53
(Pat Eddery) *towards rr: sn pushed along: hdwy 2f out: no imp* **16/1**

2500 **8** *1* **Salvestro**[23] 5474 3-9-2 58 MartinDwyer 13 56
(Mrs A J Perrett) *mid-div: hrd rdn 3f out: hdwy and in tch 2f out: wknd fnl f* **9/1**

5160 **9** *12* **Grand Palace (IRE)**[15] 5637 3-8-9 54 PatrickMathers(3) 3 24
(D Shaw) *sn chsng ldrs: drvn along over 4f out: wknd 2f out: eased whn no ch fnl f* **33/1**

2020 **10** *9* **Never Say Deya**[15] 5637 3-8-9 51 BrettDoyle 11 —
(M R Channon) *t.k.h: prom over 5f: eased whn no ch fnl f* **12/1**

3650 **11** *2* **Cape Of Storms**[51] 4700 3-9-2 58 LPKeniry 15 —
(R Brotherton) *chsd ldrs 5f: eased whn no ch fnl f* **33/1**

006 **12** *¾* **Pleasing Gift**[16] 5611 3-8-9 54 StephenDonohoe(3) 8 —
(J M P Eustace) *a bhd: eased whn no ch fnl f* **25/1**

0033 **13** *1 ½* **Zafantage**[25] 5418 3-9-1 57 (b[1]) GeorgeBaker 1 —
(S Kirk) *drvn to ld: hdd over 3f out: rdn and nt run on fnl 2f* **7/1**[3]

0001 **14** *¾* **North Fleet**[11] 5728 3-8-11 59 6ex AmirQuinn(3) 10 —
(J M Bradley) *plld hrd: prom 5f: eased whn no ch fnl f* **13/2**[2]

1m 36.66s (1.62) **Going Correction** +0.125s/f (Good) 14 Ran SP% **123.4**

Speed ratings (Par 99):96,94,93,93,92 92,92,91,79,70 68,67,66,65

CSF £77.89 CT £2719.91 TOTE £14.70: £4.10, £2.10, £16.40; EX 134.90 TRIFECTA Not won..

Owner Marita Bayley and Trevor Turner **Bred** Mrs M Bayley **Trained** Cropthorne, Worcs

FOCUS

A modest handicap, barely better than a seller, with the winner grabbing the stands' rail. The form appears solid enough with those in the frame behind the winner close to their marks.

Some Diva Official explanation: jockey said filly never travelled

North Fleet Official explanation: jockey said gelding was unsuited by the track

5937 TRADES & LABOUR CLUB LITTLEHAMPTON H'CAP 6f 209y

4:45 (4:46) (Class 5) (0-70,70) 3-Y-0+ **£3,368** (£1,002; £500; £250) **Stalls** Low

Form RPR

6200 **1** **Resplendent Nova**[11] 5739 4-9-1 70 DeanCorby(3) 13 82
(P Howling) *chsd ldrs: c to stands' rail and led 2f out: rdn clr 1f out: edgd lft twrds centre: readily* **12/1**

6200 **2** *3* **Halfwaytoparadise**[31] 5269 3-8-6 60 (p) MatthewHenry 6 64
(W G M Turner) *led tl 2f out: nt qckn fnl f* **66/1**

1320 **3** *1* **Moon Forest (IRE)**[18] 5576 4-8-0 59 oh2 ow3 (p) JamieJones(7) 2 61
(J M Bradley) *prom: rdn and one pce fnl 2f* **25/1**

0401 **4** *¾* **Middleton Grey**[10] 5755 8-8-8 67 (b) LukeMorris(7) 15 67
(A G Newcombe) *in rr tl r.o u.p fnl 2f: nrst fin* **7/1**[3]

0003 **5** *shd* **Flint River**[18] 5572 8-9-2 68 LPKeniry 16 67
(H Morrison) *mid-div: effrt over 2f out: no imp fnl f* **8/1**

6152 **6** *1 ¾* **Kavachi (IRE)**[18] 5574 3-9-0 68 GeorgeBaker 4 63+
(G L Moore) *mid-div: rdn over 2f out: styd on same pce* **6/1**[2]

-021 **7** *nk* **Ebraam (USA)**[27] 5368 3-8-11 65 MartinDwyer 12 59+
(E A L Dunlop) *hld up in midfield: hdwy to press ldrs 2f out: wknd fnl f* **7/2**[1]

5605 **8** *1* **Pure Imagination (IRE)**[13] 5688 5-8-11 66 (b) StephenDonohoe(3) 9 57
(J M Bradley) *prom tl wknd over 1f out* **9/1**

0430 **9** *¾* **Dvinsky (USA)**[8] 5778 5-8-13 68 AmirQuinn(3) 5 61+
(M A Allen) *s.s: sn in midfield: effrt over 2f out: no imp whn eased fnl 100 yds* **12/1**

0002 **10** *¾* **Mythical Charm**[31] 5267 7-7-13 56 (t) EmmettStack(5) 10 44
(J J Bridger) *towards rr: pushed along 3f out: edgd lft over 1f out: n.d* **20/1**

3036 **11** *1 ½* **Danehill Stroller (IRE)**[10] 5755 6-8-2 57 oh1 ow1 JamesDoyle(3) 14 41
(A M Hales) *mid-div: hrd rdn 3f out: outpcd fnl 2f* **16/1**

1210 **12** *1 ¼* **Prince Valentine**[24] 5450 5-8-4 56 oh2 (p) RichardMullen 7 36
(G L Moore) *mid-div: rdn over 2f out: sn btn* **11/1**

4000 **13** *3* **Doctor Dennis (IRE)**[30] 5302 9-8-4 56 (v) JamieMackay 11 29
(J Pearce) *a bhd* **25/1**

0000 **14** *12* **Hey Presto**[111] 2860 6-7-11 56 oh2 RichardRowe(7) 1 —
(R Rowe) *a bhd* **100/1**

40-3 **15** *29* **Dona Vitoria**[162] 1431 3-8-13 **67** .... SebSanders 3 —
(S Kirk) *sn rdn along and wl bhd* **16/1**

1m 22.58s (-0.12) **Going Correction** +0.125s/f (Good)
WFA 3 from 4yo+ 2lb **15** Ran SP% **120.5**
Speed ratings (Par 103):105,101,100,99,99 97,97,95,95,94 92,91,87,73,40
CSF £670.84 CT £18052.33 TOTE £17.30: £5.50, £11.80, £8.30; EX 1517.00 TRIFECTA Not won..
Owner Resplendent Racing Limited **Bred** A Turner **Trained** Newmarket, Suffolk

FOCUS
A run-of-the-mill Brighton handicap, with the winner grabbing the stands' rail in the straight. The form looks sound enough with the placed horses close to recent form.
Danehill Stroller(IRE) Official explanation: trainer said gelding was unsuited by the good to soft ground

5938 HORSEMART.CO.UK H'CAP 5f 59y
5:15 (5:18) (Class 5) (0-70,70) 3-Y-O+ **£3,238** (£963; £481; £240) **Stalls** Low

Form RPR
021 **1** **Dancing Mystery**[23] 5480 12-9-1 **67** .... (b) SebSanders 10 75
(E A Wheeler) *sn chsng ldr: led 3f out and c to stands' rail: 3l clr 2f out: hld on gamely fnl f* **6/1**
3300 **2** *shd* **Musical Script (USA)**[62] 4365 3-8-4 **56** oh1 .... JamieMackay 2 64
(Mrs A J Hamilton-Fairley) *in tch: rdn to go 2nd 2f out: clsd on wnr fnl f: jst hld* **50/1**
0310 **3** *1* **Harrison's Flyer (IRE)**[7] 5791 5-9-2 **68** .... (p) GeorgeBaker 11 72
(J M Bradley) *towards rr: rdn and r.o fnl 2f: nrst fin* **8/1**
2014 **4** *nk* **Zazous**[23] 5480 5-8-8 **60** .... LPKeniry 8 63
(J J Bridger) *chsd ldrs: rdn over 2f out: kpt on* **12/1**
0001 **5** *shd* **Chatshow (USA)**[18] 5569 5-8-4 **63** .... MarkCoumbe(7) 1 66+
(A W Carroll) *in tch: rdn to chse ldrs 2f out: nt qckn fnl f* **5/1**[2]
4020 **6** *1 1/4* **Summer Recluse (USA)**[5] 5842 7-9-4 **70** .... OscarUrbina 16 68
(J M Bradley) *outpcd in rr: r.o u.p fnl 2f: nvr nrr* **8/1**
0350 **7** *1/2* **Supercast (IRE)**[4] 5872 3-9-4 **70** .... MartinDwyer 13 67
(J S Moore) *towards rr tl styd on u.p fnl 2f: nt rch ldrs* **10/1**
6660 **8** *hd* **Semenovskii**[18] 5575 6-8-9 **64** .... JamesDoyle(3) 6 60
(Mrs N Smith) *chsd ldrs: one pce appr fnl f* **11/2**[3]
0002 **9** *5* **Danjet (IRE)**[7] 5791 3-9-0 **69** .... StephenDonohoe(3) 4 47
(J M Bradley) *led tl 3f out: wknd ins fnl 2f* **7/2**[1]
0510 **10** *3* **Namir (IRE)**[16] 5620 4-8-12 **67** .... (vt) PatrickMathers(3) 3 34
(D Shaw) *in tch: hmpd and lost pl bnd over 4f out: nt rcvr* **25/1**
4230 **11** *1/2* **Mister Incredible**[15] 5631 3-8-4 **56** oh1 .... (p) SilvestreDeSousa 5 21
(V Smith) *sn in tch: rdn to chse ldrs 2f out: wknd 1f out* **25/1**
-000 **12** *hd* **Beau Jazz**[110] 2898 5-8-1 **58** oh11 ow2 .... RoryMoore(5) 9 23
(W De Best-Turner) *n.m.r s: mid-div tl wknd 2f out* **66/1**
6000 **13** *1/2* **Vegas Boys**[13] 5684 3-8-11 **63** .... MichaelTebbutt 14 26
(M Wigham) *stmbld s and lost grnd: a outpcd and bhd* **20/1**
6-00 **14** *nk* **Make It Happen Now**[54] 4629 4-8-0 **57** oh11 ow1. KevinGhunowa(5) 12 19
(P A Blockley) *a outpcd and bhd* **66/1**

62.53 secs (0.23) **Going Correction** +0.125s/f (Good) **14** Ran SP% **125.0**
Speed ratings (Par 103):103,102,101,100,100 98,97,97,89,84 83,83,82,82
CSF £301.66 CT £2500.34 TOTE £8.20: £2.00, £9.30, £3.30; EX 319.20 TRIFECTA Not won.
Place 6 £ 8482.52, Place 5 £4718.40.
Owner Astrod TA Austin Stroud & Co **Bred** Mrs D Price **Trained** Whitchurch-on-Thames, Oxon

FOCUS
A competitive sprint, typical of the track, in which the winner again grabbed the stands' rail. The form looks reasonable with the winner, third and fourth close to previous form.
Danjet(IRE) Official explanation: jockey said filly hung right
T/Plt: £7,916.40 to a £1 stake. Pool: £69,946.50. 6.45 winning tickets. T/Qpdt: £3,420.20 to a £1 stake. Pool: £4,622.00. 1.00 winning ticket. LM

5914
NEWMARKET (ROWLEY) (R-H)
Friday, October 13

OFFICIAL GOING: Good to soft
Wind: Almost nil Weather: Sunny and warm

5939 GRAND PRIX WHITE TURF ST MORITZ E B F MAIDEN STKS 1m
1:30 (1:31) (Class 4) 2-Y-O **£5,181** (£1,541; £770; £384) **Stalls** High

Form RPR
56 **1** **Sam Lord**[24] 5454 2-9-3 .... JimmyFortune 8 80
(J H M Gosden) *lw: led 6f: rallied to ld ins fnl f: edgd rt: r.o* **12/1**[3]
2 *3/4* **Diamond Tycoon (USA)** 2-9-3 .... RichardHughes 11 78
(B J Meehan) *leggy: scope: swtg: s.i.s: hld up: hdwy over 3f out: rdn over 1f out: r.o* **12/1**[3]
3 *1 1/4* **Fort Amhurst (IRE)** 2-9-3 .... JamieSpencer 13 75
(E A L Dunlop) *w'like: leggy: s.s: hld up: hdwy 1/2-way: led 2f out: rdn over 1f out: hdd and no ex ins fnl f* **40/1**
4 *1* **Noisy Silence (IRE)** 2-9-3 .... RyanMoore 5 73
(P W Chapple-Hyam) *neat: s.i.s: hdwy over 6f out: rdn over 2f out: n.m.r and no ex ins fnl f* **20/1**
5 *shd* **Dance Of Light (USA)** 2-8-12 .... KerrinMcEvoy 2 68+
(Sir Michael Stoute) *w'like: scope: dwlt: hld up: outpcd over 2f out: r.o ins fnl f: nrst fin* **8/1**[2]
6 *hd* **Jalil (USA)** 2-9-3 .... LDettori 10 72
(Saeed Bin Suroor) *gd sort: bkwd: chsd ldrs: edgd rt and outpcd over 1f out: styd on ins fnl f* **4/6**[1]
7 *3/4* **Madaarek (USA)** 2-9-3 .... RHills 1 71+
(E A L Dunlop) *gd sort: chsd ldrs: rdn over 2f out: outpcd over 1f out: styd on ins fnl f* **33/1**
05 **8** *3/4* **Morning Farewell**[24] 5457 2-9-3 .... EddieAhern 9 69
(P W Chapple-Hyam) *chsd ldrs: rdn over 3f out: nt clr run over 1f out: styd on same pce* **20/1**
9 *hd* **Chunky's Choice (IRE)** 2-9-3 .... DarryllHolland 14 69
(J Noseda) *gd sort: bkwd: hld up: rdn over 2f out: nvr trbld ldrs* **33/1**
10 *2* **Rambling Light** 2-9-3 .... FergusSweeney 4 64
(A M Balding) *cmpct: bit bkwd: hld up: a in rr* **100/1**
04 **11** *1 1/2* **Rock Anthem (IRE)**[28] 5339 2-9-3 .... KDarley 12 60
(J L Dunlop) *hld up in tch: rdn over 2f out: wknd fnl f* **12/1**[3]
0 **12** *1* **Giovanni D'Oro (IRE)**[14] 5658 2-9-3 .... JohnEgan 6 58
(N A Callaghan) *hld up: rdn over 3f out: n.d* **100/1**
5006 **13** *hd* **Mint State**[56] 4572 2-9-3 72 .... AntonyProcter 7 58
(D R C Elsworth) *plld hrd and prom: wknd over 2f out* **66/1**

1m 43.48s (4.11) **Going Correction** +0.35s/f (Good) **13** Ran SP% **115.5**
Speed ratings (Par 97):93,92,91,90,89 89,88,88,88,86 84,83,83
CSF £129.76 TOTE £12.90: £3.20, £4.10, £8.60; EX 279.60.
Owner Anthony Speelman **Bred** Wickfield Farm Partnership **Trained** Newmarket, Suffolk
■ Unplaced Jalil was the most expensive horse ever to step on to a British racecourse.

FOCUS
Difficult to know what to make of the form in this maiden, in which they went 12/1 bar two, with $9.7m yearling Jalil odds on for a winning debut. There were some nice specimens on show, but the pace was steady and the time was 1.66sec slower than the later conditions stakes.

NOTEBOOK
Sam Lord, sixth in a maiden here that had already produced three subsequent winners, again ran free but had clearly learnt a lot. After leading early he came through to show ahead again on reaching the rising ground and galloped on resolutely to score. He should make a decent handicapper next season. (op 11-1)
Diamond Tycoon(USA) ◆, from the family of French Derby winner Polytain, made an encouraging debut, arriving between rivals at the bottom of the hill and then keeping on well but always being held by the more experienced winner. He looks sure to win his maiden before long and can develop into a useful sort next season. (op 11-1 tchd 14-1)
Fort Amhurst(IRE) ◆, who has a fair amount of speed on his dam's side, may have inherited his stamina from his sire Halling. He was slowly into his stride, but moved into contention before halfway and moved ahead three furlongs out looking the likely winner. He was eventually run out of it up the hill but this was a good effort and he looks the sort who will do even better with this experience under his belt. (tchd 33-1)
Noisy Silence(IRE), a Derby entry from a decent American family, ran well and did not have a lot of room in the closing stages. He wore the second colours of his owner, so presumably not much was expected, and he is another who can make his mark over middle distances next year.
Dance Of Light(USA) ◆, a $340,000 sister to Dr Massini, caught the eye, staying on really well having been behind and outpaced at halfway. The only filly in the line-up and in the right hands, she should have learned a lot and will be a different proposition next season. (op 7-1)
Jalil(USA), a $9.7m yearling with a high-class American pedigree and odds on for this debut, travelled well up with the pace but was being pushed along soon after halfway and got outpaced before staying on again on when he met the rising ground. If it wasn't for the hype, this might be construed a reasonably promising debut, especially as the steady pace and dead ground wouldn't have been in his favour, and also because he is a backward sort who ought to be stronger next year. However, he hardly looked an obvious future Group 1 winner, and connections must have been hoping for better. (op 8-11 tchd 8-13)
Madaarek(USA) ◆, a half-brother to Nasij who was reportedly in need of the experience to wake him up, was unsettled in the stalls and ran as well as connections could have expected. He's a nice type and ought to be a fair bit better nex year.
Chunky's Choice(IRE), a 115,000gns half-brother to Telemachus, showed a fair amount on this debut and his pedigree suggests he will improve with age and middle distances.
Rock Anthem(IRE), with previous experience in similar company, had his chance but faded up the hill may do better in handicaps next season.

5940 FEDERATION OF BLOODSTOCK AGENTS NURSERY 6f
2:00 (2:09) (Class 4) (0-95,89) 2-Y-O **£5,181** (£1,541; £770; £384) **Stalls** High

Form RPR
4110 **1** **Cheap Street**[27] 5372 2-9-2 **84** .... NickyMackay 13 90
(J G Portman) *mid-div: hdwy 1/2-way: led over 1f out: sn rdn: jst hld on* **17/2**
10 **2** *shd* **Mystery Ocean**[25] 5434 2-8-12 **80** .... NelsonDeSouza 7 86+
(R M Beckett) *hld up: hmpd over 2f out: hdwy over 1f out: r.o wl* **25/1**
0101 **3** *1 3/4* **Retaliate**[14] 5646 2-8-5 **73** .... FrancisNorton 10 73
(M Quinn) *chsd ldr tl led 2f out: sn rdn and hdd: styd on same pce ins fnl f* **25/1**
211 **4** *3/4* **Adaptation**[91] 3481 2-9-6 **88** .... KDarley 6 86
(M Johnston) *dwlt: outpcd: swtchd lft and hdwy over 1f out: nt rch ldrs* **15/2**[3]
1361 **5** *1/2* **Disco Dan**[24] 5447 2-9-0 **82** .... RyanMoore 12 79
(D M Simcock) *hld up: hdwy over 1f out: sn rdn: styd on same pce ins fnl f* **5/1**[1]
5463 **6** *1/2* **Massenzio (IRE)**[24] 5449 2-8-5 **73** .... DavidKinsella 5 68
(J H M Gosden) *lw: unruly in stalls: dwlt: hld up: hdwy 1/2-way: rdn over 1f out: styd on same pce fnl f* **16/1**
3460 **7** *3/4* **Fares (IRE)**[19] 5546 2-8-0 **68** .... HayleyTurner 9 61
(C E Brittain) *lw: chsd ldrs: outpcd 1/2-way: hung lft over 1f out: n.d after* **25/1**
1004 **8** *nk* **Okikoki**[27] 5372 2-8-12 **80** .... (b) KerrinMcEvoy 3 72
(W R Muir) *prom: rdn over 1f out: sn wknd* **10/1**
014 **9** *3 1/2* **Ava's World (IRE)**[10] 5748 2-8-12 **83** .... GregFairley(3) 4 65
(M Johnston) *chsd ldrs over 4f* **14/1**
134 **10** *nk* **Ede's Dot Com (IRE)**[24] 5461 2-9-0 **82** .... PaulDoe 2 63
(W J Knight) *prom over 4f* **16/1**
6513 **11** *3/4* **Reebal**[11] 5731 2-9-7 **89** .... (b) LDettori 1 67
(B J Meehan) *led over 4f: sn wknd* **13/2**[2]
3021 **12** *1 1/2* **Just Dust**[19] 5546 2-9-0 **85** .... MarcHalford(3) 11 59
(D R C Elsworth) *chsd ldrs 4f* **13/2**[2]

1m 14.73s (1.63) **Going Correction** +0.35s/f (Good) **12** Ran SP% **104.7**
Speed ratings (Par 97):103,102,100,99,98 98,97,96,92,91 90,88
CSF £167.17 CT £3662.07 TOTE £8.50: £2.80, £5.80, £5.90; EX 279.00.
Owner A S B Portman **Bred** Catridge Farm Stud Ltd **Trained** Compton, Berks
■ Roodolph (13/2) withdrawn (broke out of his stall and bolted). Rule 4 applies; deduction 10p in £.

FOCUS
A decent nursery, even though the top weight was rated 6lb below the handicap ceiling, and it was run in a respectable time for the grade. The race was delayed by Roodolph breaking out of his stall.

NOTEBOOK
Cheap Street bounced back from a disappointing run at Newbury to gain his third win in his last four starts. He looked like winning decisively when striking the front and did not really stop, but the runner-up flew up the hill and the post came only just in time. (op 11-1)
Mystery Ocean ◆, a shock winner on her debut, disappointed on fast ground in a nursery next time but bounced back in good fashion and was unlucky not to get up. She was held up off the pace and was hampered when looking for an opening, so it was not until she hit the rising ground that she found her stride, from which point she rapidly cut into the winner's lead. She looks more than capable of gaining compensation if turned out again before the season's end.
Retaliate, raised 5lb for her win in a claimer at Lingfield, really appreciates soft ground and ran above herself, having run keen up with the pace from the start. She could pick up a run-of-the-mill nursery on this evidence. (op 20-1)
Adaptation, having her first outing for three months and tackling much softer ground, was doing her best work at the end and looks in need of a longer trip now. (op 6-1)
Disco Dan, whose two wins have come at Brighton, went off favourite and followed the winner through, but could produce no extra up the hill and may be more effective on a sounder surface. (op 6-1 tchd 9-2 in places)
Massenzio(IRE) got very upset in the stalls and it was a little surprising he was not withdrawn. However, he clearly came to no harm and ran a decent race, doing his best work in the closing stages without ever looking likely to make the frame. (op 20-1)
Reebal went off fast in front but was in trouble at the top of the hill. (op 7-1)
Just Dust, who has been running well, appeared to have every chance but dropped out and may have had enough after a busy and productive season. Official explanation: jockey said gelding hung left throughout (op 9-2)

5941 RACING SOUTH AFRICA HOUGHTON CONDITIONS STKS — 1m
2:35 (2:36) (Class 2) 2-Y-O — £8,101 (£2,425; £1,212; £607) Stalls High

Form	Pos	Dist	Horse	RPR
1	1		**Proponent (IRE)**[28] 5340 2-9-3 ... SteveDrowne 4 (R Charlton) *lw: mde all: shkn up over 1f out: r.o wl* **2/7**[1]	92+
5210	2	6	**Minos (IRE)**[24] 5466 2-9-3 83 ... RichardHughes 3 (R Hannon) *lw: a.p: chsd wnr 2f out: rdn over 1f out: sn outpcd: eased whn btn ins fnl f* **3/1**[2]	78+
3540	3	1 1/4	**Only Hope**[13] 5676 2-8-7 63 ... (v) JohnEgan 2 (Ernst Oertel) *dwlt: sn prom: chsd wnr 1/2-way tl rdn over 2f out: wknd over 1f out* **33/1**[3]	65
0	4	13	**Above And Below (IRE)**[24] 5456 2-8-7 ... FrancisNorton 1 (M Quinn) *w wnr tl rdn 1/2-way: wknd over 2f out* **66/1**	35

1m 41.82s (2.45) **Going Correction** +0.35s/f (Good) — 4 Ran SP% **107.2**
Speed ratings (Par 101):101,95,93,80
CSF £1.39 TOTE £1.30; EX 1.30.
Owner B E Nielsen **Bred** Fortbarrington Stud **Trained** Beckhampton, Wilts
■ With this meeting due to be cut to two days next year, this could well have been the last running of the Houghton Stakes.

FOCUS
An uncompetitive renewal of this decent conditions event, but still run 1.66 sec faster than the opening maiden.

NOTEBOOK
Proponent(IRE), a 160,000gns yearling with a good middle-distance pedigree and Derby and Irish Derby entries, landed the odds in impressive fashion, making most of the running and coming right away. His time was decent and he looks an interesting prospect for next year. (op 1-3)
Minos(IRE), who was well beaten in a sales race last time but whose maiden win is working out reasonably well, tracked the winner throughout but had no answer once that rival went for home. He may prefer a sounder surface but probably ran into a Group horse in the making. (op 11-4)
Only Hopewas well out of her depth on what she had previously achieved and ran about as well as could be expected.
Above And Below(IRE) showed up early but was beaten off quickly once the race began in earnest.

5942 IGLOOS BENTINCK STKS (GROUP 3) — 6f
3:10 (3:10) (Class 1) 3-Y-O+ — £28,390 (£10,760; £5,385; £2,685; £1,345; £675) Stalls High

Form	Pos	Dist	Horse	RPR
2021	1		**Bygone Days**[18] 5578 5-9-1 107 ... LDettori 6 (Saeed Bin Suroor) *hld up: hdwy over 1f out: r.o to ld post* **7/2**[1]	119+
2126	2	shd	**Borderlescott**[8] 5779 4-9-1 106 ... RoystonFfrench 12 (R Bastiman) *chsd ldrs: rdn to ld and hung lft wl ins fnl f: hdd post* **7/1**	118
411	3	3/4	**Tax Free (IRE)**[34] 5179 4-9-1 107 ... AdrianTNicholls 11 (D Nicholls) *chsd ldr tl led over 1f out: sn rdn: hdd wl ins fnl f: hmpd nr fin* **13/2**[3]	116
14-6	4	1	**Great Britain**[13] 5682 4-9-1 100 ... KerrinMcEvoy 10 (Saeed Bin Suroor) *b: led over 4f: styng on same pce whn hmpd nr fin* **25/1**	113
5043	5	1	**Fayr Jag (IRE)**[19] 5549 7-9-5 109 ... DavidAllan 14 (T D Easterby) *lw: mid-div: hdwy 2f out: swtchd rt ins fnl f: styd on same pce* **16/1**	114
4100	6	3/4	**Presto Shinko (IRE)**[19] 5549 5-9-5 107 ... RichardHughes 13 (R Hannon) *lw: hld up in tch: rdn over 1f out: styd on same pce* **25/1**	112
5212	7	3/4	**Fullandby (IRE)**[20] 5523 4-9-1 95 ... PaulMulrennan 15 (T J Etherington) *lw: sn outpcd: r.o ins fnl f: nrst fin* **25/1**	106
1101	8	1 1/4	**Fantasy Believer**[15] 5642 8-9-1 104 ... JimmyQuinn 16 (J J Quinn) *hld up: hdwy 2f out: rdn over 1f out: wknd ins fnl f* **14/1**	102
111	9	3 1/2	**Bustin Justin (USA)**[69] 4144 3-9-0 88 ... DarryllHolland 8 (J Noseda) *chsd ldrs: rdn 1/2-way: wknd over 1f out* **16/1**	91
5012	10	1/2	**Baltic King**[19] 5549 6-9-1 112 ... (t) JimmyFortune 1 (H Morrison) *hld up: rdn over 1f out: n.d* **4/1**[2]	90
430	11	2	**Tawaassol (USA)**[48] 4803 3-9-0 106 ... (t) RHills 2 (Sir Michael Stoute) *chsed ldrs: rdn over 2f out: wknd over 1f out* **40/1**	84
3602	12	1 1/4	**Ashdown Express (IRE)**[34] 5179 7-9-1 114 ... SteveDrowne 4 (C F Wall) *hld up: nt clr run fr over 2f out to over 1f out: n.d* **16/1**	80
0203	13	1	**Eisteddfod**[18] 5578 5-9-1 107 ... RyanMoore 3 (P F I Cole) *chsd ldrs: rdn over 2f out: sn hung rt and wknd* **12/1**	77
2100	14	1	**Quito (IRE)**[17] 5588 9-9-1 114 ... (b) TonyCulhane 5 (D W Chapman) *b: lw: hld up: hdwy 1/2-way: wknd 2f out* **11/1**	74

1m 12.89s (-0.21) **Going Correction** +0.35s/f (Good)
WFA 3 from 4yo+ 1lb — 14 Ran SP% **122.4**
Speed ratings (Par 113):115,114,113,112,111 110,109,107,102,102 99,97,96,95
CSF £27.10 TOTE £4.20: £1.80, £3.40, £2.80; EX 35.80.
Owner Godolphin **Bred** J A E Hobby **Trained** Newmarket, Suffolk
■ Stewards' Enquiry : Royston Ffrench two-day ban: careless riding; two-day ban: excessive use of whip (Oct 25-28)

FOCUS
A competitive renewal of this Group sprint run in a good time and 1.84 sec faster than the earlier nursery. Those drawn lower than the winner and racing away from the action were all well below form, however.

NOTEBOOK
Bygone Days ◆ has returned to action this autumn in fine fettle, having beaten the Ayr Gold Cup winner Fonthill Road at Hamilton last month. He travelled well but, after hitting a flat spot in the dip, ran on really well up the hill to get up near the line. With this under his belt he could well develop into a top sprinter in 2007, and the fact that he handles any ground gives him plenty of options. (op 4-1)
Borderlescott ◆ bounced back after being drawn on the wrong side in France last time. He ran another fine race despite not being able to dominate, but having fought his way to the front he hung left and was collared on the line by the winner, who raced wide of him. He is a credit to his trainer and went very close to winning a Group race at the first attempt. He should be able to make amends before long. (tchd 8-1)
Tax Free(IRE), who has rediscovered his best form of late, ran another good race and only got outbattled up the hill. He was slightly squeezed out near the finish but it did not affect the result, and if he can get a sounder surface before the season's end could add to his score. (op 15-2)
Great Britain, dropping back in trip, set a good pace for his stable companion, but took a deal of pegging back and only tired up the hill. This was his first encounter with soft ground and he handled it well enough, so this lightly-raced individual could well be able to hold his own in Pattern company with this under his belt.
Fayr Jag(IRE) is a reliable old yardstick who has become more effective on easy ground as he has got older. He ran well again, and looked a big threat running into the dip, but had nothing in reserve on the climb to the line. (op 25-1)
Presto Shinko(IRE) has been able to make the step up to Group company this season without setting the world alight, but bounced back from a couple of below-par runs and, after a relatively light campaign, connections will be looking out for another opportunity before the end of the season (op 40-1)
Fullandby(IRE), a consistent sort stepping up from handicaps into Group company, found this tough but was doing his best work late on. He looks capable of making up into a Group performer next season, especially given soft ground, and the fact that he stays seven furlongs means connections can be selective.
Fantasy Believer, who has been in good heart recently, made his run at the top of the hill but could never get close enough to land a blow. The ground was probably a little too soft for him. (op 10-1)
Bustin Justin(USA), a winner of his only three starts, had a mountain to climb on official ratings, plus he was dropping back in trip and encountering soft going for the first time. In the circumstances this was a fair effort and he has time on his side.
Baltic King, taking part in this for the fourth time, having been runner-up a year ago, was never able to get in a significant blow and a Group-race win continues to elude him. (op 5-1)

5943 SPECIAL EVENTS H'CAP — 7f
3:45 (3:46) (Class 2) (0-100,99) 3-Y-O+
£11,217 (£3,358; £1,679; £840; £419; £210) Stalls High

Form	Pos	Dist	Horse	RPR
0013	1		**King's Caprice**[20] 5523 5-9-1 99 ... (t) TravisBlock(5) 14 (J A Geake) *mde all: rdn over 1f out: styd on gamely* **12/1**	110
6110	2	nk	**Woodcote Place**[7] 5785 3-8-5 86 ... JohnEgan 5 (P R Chamings) *s.i.s: hld up: hdwy over 1f out: rdn to chse wnr ins fnl f: r.o* **20/1**	96+
1014	3	1 1/4	**Muzher (IRE)**[13] 5677 3-8-7 88 ... RHills 11 (B W Hills) *hld up: hdwy over 1f out: sn rdn: styd on* **12/1**	95
0026	4	1 1/2	**Arm Candy (IRE)**[21] 5512 3-8-7 88 ... KDarley 3 (J A R Toller) *lw: hld up: hdwy 1/2-way: outpcd over 2f out: r.o ins fnl f* **33/1**	91
3030	5	1/2	**Arminius (IRE)**[20] 5520 3-9-1 96 ... RichardHughes 1 (R Hannon) *dwlt: hld up: nt clr run and swtchd lft over 1f out: r.o ins fnl f: nrst fin* **50/1**	98+
3231	6	nk	**Signor Peltro**[58] 4488 3-8-6 87 ... FergusSweeney 15 (H Candy) *chsd ldrs: rdn over 1f out: hung lft and wknd ins fnl f* **8/1**[3]	88
0205	7	nk	**Kenmore**[13] 5677 4-8-8 87 ... EddieAhern 8 (D Nicholls) *lw; hld up in tch: rdn over 1f out: wkng whn hmpd ins fnl f* **14/1**	87
11-	8	shd	**Desert Chief**[498] 2239 4-8-13 92 ... LDettori 13 (Saeed Bin Suroor) *hld up: hdwy 2f out: sn rdn: no ex ins fnl f* **5/2**[1]	92
0060	9	hd	**Namid Reprobate (IRE)**[41] 5019 3-8-4 85 oh4 ... NelsonDeSouza 6 (P F I Cole) *chsd ldrs: rdn over 2f out: wknd fnl f* **66/1**	84
0665	10	1 1/4	**Trafalgar Bay (IRE)**[21] 5501 3-8-11 92 ... JamieSpencer 9 (S Kirk) *hld up: rdn over 2f out: nt rch ldrs* **12/1**	92+
0000	11	3/4	**Marshman (IRE)**[27] 5355 7-8-3 85 oh3 ... SaleemGolam(3) 18 (M H Tompkins) *hld up: hdwy over 1f out: wknd ins fnl f* **20/1**	79
20	12	1/2	**South Cape**[15] 5639 3-8-9 90 ... TonyCulhane 7 (M R Channon) *chsd ldrs: edgd rt and wknd over 1f out* **12/1**	83
0130	13	1/2	**Minority Report**[13] 5677 6-9-2 95 ... NickyMackay 12 (L M Cumani) *hld up: rdn over 1f out: nvr trbld ldrs* **20/1**	87
4010	14	1/2	**Phluke**[7] 5785 5-8-7 86 ... StephenCarson 16 (R F Johnson Houghton) *chsd wnr to 1/2-way: outpcd over 2f out: n.d after* **50/1**	76
6102	15	1 1/4	**Wavertree Warrior (IRE)**[7] 5789 4-8-11 90 ow1 ... JimmyFortune 17 (N P Littmoden) *prom: rdn over 2f out: wknd fnl f* **11/2**[2]	77
0-10	16	6	**Visionist (IRE)**[153] 1667 4-9-6 99 ... DarryllHolland 10 (Pat Eddery) *lw: hld up: hdwy 2f out: rdn and wknd over 1f out* **25/1**	70
1114	17	3/4	**Glenbuck (IRE)**[7] 5789 3-8-5 86 ... (v) FrancisNorton 4 (A Bailey) *chsd ldrs over 5f* **14/1**	56
5000	18	2 1/2	**Steel Blue**[20] 5535 6-8-6 85 oh4 ... HayleyTurner 19 (R M Whitaker) *chsd ldrs over 5f* **66/1**	48
3020	19	4	**Grizedale (IRE)**[17] 5591 7-8-6 85 oh8 ... (t) JimmyQuinn 2 (J Akehurst) *hld up: rdn over 2f out: sn wknd* **100/1**	38

1m 27.14s (0.64) **Going Correction** +0.35s/f (Good)
WFA 3 from 4yo+ 2lb — 19 Ran SP% **128.1**
Speed ratings (Par 109):110,109,108,106,105 105,105,105,104,103 102,102,101,100,99 92,91,88,84
CSF £242.19 CT £3038.01 TOTE £17.20: £3.30, £3.40, £3.10, £5.60; EX 481.00.
Owner Miss B Swire **Bred** Miss B Swire **Trained** Kimpton, Hants

FOCUS
A decent handicap run at a sound gallop. The winner keeps improving and recorded a clear personal best. The placed horses are relatively lightly raced, improving types.

NOTEBOOK
King's Caprice has been steadily progressive this season and was racing off a mark 12lb higher than when scoring over course and distance in the spring. He made all of the running and stuck on bravely to improve on his runner-up spot in the corresponding race two years ago. He will not find this easy in handicaps in the future off a mark in the low 100s, but his dam developed into a Pattern performer and he may be capable of doing the same. In the meantime, cConnections are eyeing a trip to the Dubai Carnival. (tchd 14-1)
Woodcote Place, another progressive sort, is now a stone higher than when winning his maiden in August. He looked a little unlucky as he came from some way back, but he could not find that extra gear needed to catch the winner. He looks capable of winning good handicaps, possibly on a sounder surface, but also handles Polytrack.
Muzher(IRE), with the cheekpieces he wore last time left off, looked more co-operative and ran his race, but possibly may need a mile unless the ground is really testing.
Arm Candy(IRE), whose sole win was gained over course and distance more than a year ago, stayed on well up the hill having looked unlikely to figure going into the dip. She is consistent but looks in the Handicapper's grip.
Arminius(IRE) ◆, like Arm Candy, only started to make an impression on the climb to the finish. Having been held up, he looked likely to finish at the back until finding his stride late on. He has not had much racing and there looks to be a decent contest in him on the evidence of a couple of runs since his return from a break.
Signor Peltro, whose most recent win was on fast ground, does handle soft but he seemed to race too freely on this occasion and did not get home. (op 9-1)
Kenmore, last year's winner, showed signs of a revivial when just behind Muzher at the last meeting here, but finished further behind that rival despite meeting him on better terms. He was racing off the same mark as when successful for Barry Hills last season, but has not won for new connections and may be worth another try on a flatter track.
Desert Chief, whose yard has been in good form recently, was made favourite despite having been absent since June 2005. He ran a fair race but never looked as if he was going to score, although the outing should bring him on and his old form suggests a sounder surface is ideal. (op 11-4 tchd 3-1 and 10-3 in places)
Namid Reprobate(IRE) has been struggling to form since returning to turf after a successful spell on the All-Weather, had the blinkers he wore last time left off and ran close to previous form with Muzher, despite being 4lb out of the handicap. Soft ground on turf suits and he might be worth trying back at six furlongs.
Wavertree Warrior(IRE) showed up early but was in trouble at the top of the hill. Interestingly, he has done all his winning on turning tracks. Official explanation: jockey said gelding hung left-handed (tchd 6-1 in a place)

5944 JOHN WILSONCROFT LIFETIME IN RACING "PREMIER" CLAIMING STKS 1m 4f

4:20 (4:21) (Class 4) 3-5-Y-0 **£5,505** (£1,637; £818; £408) **Stalls** Centre

Form RPR

0404 **1** **Top Spec (IRE)**[21] 5513 5-8-12 66 JimmyQuinn 2 75+
(J Pearce) *hld up: hdwy over 3f out: edgd lft and led over 2f out: clr over 1f out: comf* **13/2**[3]

0003 **2** *6* **Incidentally (IRE)**[16] 5625 3-9-2 75 RyanMoore 8 76
(R Hannon) *chsd ldr: rdn and ev ch over 2f out: wknd over 1f out* **3/1**[1]

006 **3** *hd* **Chronomatic**[6] 5815 3-8-8 70 SaleemGolam(3) 4 71
(M H Tompkins) *chsd ldrs: nt clr run over 2f out: sn rdn: hung rt and wknd over 1f out* **15/2**

01 **4** *5* **Penryn**[28] 5353 3-9-7 71 AntonyProcter 1 73
(D R C Elsworth) *lw: hld up: hdwy over 3f out: swtchd rt over 2f out: sn rdn and wknd* **14/1**

5104 **5** *2 1/2* **Villa Sonata**[11] 5732 3-8-9 74 ow1 JamieSpencer 7 57
(J R Fanshawe) *led over 9f: sn rdn and wknd* **10/3**[2]

-405 **6** *13* **Well Established (IRE)**[13] 5671 4-9-9 79 PhilipRobinson 6 43
(M A Jarvis) *lw: prom: rdn: edgd rt and wknd over 2f out* **3/1**[1]

2020 **7** *10* **Dik Dik**[18] 5574 3-8-6 57 (v) KDarley 5 17
(C N Allen) *hld up in tch: rdn over 3f out: sn wknd* **33/1**

2m 37.33s (3.83) **Going Correction** +0.35s/f (Good)
WFA 3 from 4yo+ 7lb **7** Ran SP% **107.8**
Speed ratings (Par 105):101,97,96,93,91 83,76
CSF £23.24 TOTE £8.00: £3.20, £2.00; EX 24.60.
Owner G Whorton **Bred** Mrs Jacqueline Donnelly **Trained** Newmarket, Suffolk

FOCUS
A fair claimer run at a steady gallop but ultimately an easy winner.

5945 TAITTINGER CHAMPAGNE H'CAP 1m

4:55 (4:56) (Class 2) (0-100,99) 3-Y-0+
£11,217 (£3,358; £1,679; £840; £419; £210) **Stalls** High

Form RPR

0102 **1** **Rain Stops Play (IRE)**[15] 5639 4-8-7 **85** oh3 FrancisNorton 21 96
(M Quinn) *led far side: rdn and hdd over 1f out: rallied to ld wl ins fnl f: 1st of 4 in gp* **20/1**

0050 **2** *3/4* **Salinja (USA)**[13] 5675 4-9-1 **93** (b[1]) JimmyFortune 22 102
(Mrs A J Perrett) *racd far side: chsd ldr: rdn to ld and edgd rt over 1f out: hdd wl ins fnl f: 2nd of 4 in gp* **18/1**

4040 **3** *1* **Private Business (USA)**[48] 4791 3-9-3 **98** RichardHughes 14 105
(B W Hills) *lw: racd centre: chsd ldrs: rdn over 2f out: r.o to ld that gp nr fin: 1st of 16 in gp* **20/1**

1150 **4** *shd* **Harvest Queen (IRE)**[93] 3418 3-8-11 **92** EddieAhern 3 99+
(P J Makin) *racd centre: chsd ldrs: led that gp over 1f out: rdn and edgd rt ins fnl f: hdd that gp nr fin: 2nd of 16 in grp* **25/1**

5646 **5** *1/2* **Seulement (USA)**[13] 5675 4-8-12 **90** NickyMackay 20 96
(L M Cumani) *lw: racd far side: chsd ldrs: rdn over 1f out: styd on: 3rd of 4 in gp* **8/1**

4154 **6** *nk* **Joseph Henry**[69] 4131 4-8-7 **85** KDarley 1 90+
(M Johnston) *racd centre: hld up: hdwy over 1f out: r.o: 3rd of 16 in gp* **33/1**

5363 **7** *1/2* **Cactus King**[69] 4160 3-8-4 **85** oh1 DavidKinsella 10 89
(J H M Gosden) *racd centre: s.i.s: hdwy to ld that gp over 6f: styng on same pce whn hmpd ins fnl f: 4th of 16 in gp* **12/1**

2004 **8** *1 1/2* **Motaraqeb**[15] 5639 3-8-4 **85** RHills 9 85
(Sir Michael Stoute) *racd centre: hld up in tch: rdn over 1f out: styd on: 5th of 16 in gp* **15/2**[3]

2306 **9** *shd* **Cross My Mind**[20] 5523 4-8-7 **85** KerrinMcEvoy 4 85
(T Keddy) *s.i.s: racd centre: hld up: rdn over 1f out: nt rch ldrs: 6th of 16 in gp* **11/2**[1]

-132 **10** *nk* **Count Trevisio (IRE)**[64] 4298 3-8-13 **94** LDettori 2 93
(Saeed Bin Suroor) *racd centre: chsd ldrs: rdn over 1f out: no ex: 7th of 16 in gp* **6/1**[2]

2311 **11** *nk* **Nanton (USA)**[13] 5680 4-8-8 **86** JimmyQuinn 12 85
(N Wilson) *b: s.i.s: racd centre: hld up: effrt over 3f out: no ex fnl f: 8th of 16 in gp* **12/1**

0460 **12** *hd* **Bustan (IRE)**[13] 5675 7-9-1 **93** PhilipRobinson 19 91
(G C Bravery) *racd far side: prom: rdn over 1f out: wknd ins fnl f: last of 4 in gp* **33/1**

6200 **13** *hd* **Ace Of Hearts**[13] 5675 7-9-7 **99** SteveDrowne 11 97
(C F Wall) *racd centre: hld up in tch: rdn over 1f out: sn wknd: 9th of 16 in gp* **20/1**

-300 **14** *1* **Queen Of Fire**[93] 3418 3-8-4 **85** JohnEgan 8 80
(D R C Elsworth) *lw: racd centre: hld up: rdn over 2f out: n.d: 10th of 16 in gp* **20/1**

2016 **15** *nk* **Plum Pudding (IRE)**[13] 5677 3-9-2 **97** RyanMoore 16 92
(R Hannon) *racd centre: prom: rdn over 1f out: sn wknd: 11th of 16 in gp* **9/1**

0000 **16** *nk* **Johnny Jumpup (IRE)**[15] 5639 4-9-0 **92** NelsonDeSouza 5 86
(R M Beckett) *racd centre: hld up: rdn and wknd over 1f out: 12th of 16 in gp* **25/1**

0252 **17** *4* **Grimes Faith**[17] 5590 3-8-1 **85** oh3 StephaneBreux(3) 18 70
(R Hannon) *racd centre: prom over 6f: 13th of 16 in gp* **20/1**

2100 **18** *5* **Audience**[20] 5520 6-8-13 **91** (p) PaulDoe 17 64
(J Akehurst) *lw: racd centre: chsd ldrs over 6f: 14th of 16 in gp* **40/1**

5320 **19** *shd* **St Petersburg**[7] 5789 6-9-3 **98** SaleemGolam(3) 13 71
(M H Tompkins) *racd centre: prom over 6f: 15th of 16 in gp* **16/1**

5016 **20** *2 1/2* **Silver Dip**[20] 5529 3-8-4 **85** RoystonFfrench 15 52
(B W Hills) *racd centre: chsd ldrs over 5f: last of 16 in gp* **50/1**

1m 40.26s (0.89) **Going Correction** +0.35s/f (Good)
WFA 3 from 4yo+ 3lb **20** Ran SP% **130.9**
Speed ratings (Par 109):109,108,107,107,106 106,105,104,104,103 103,103,103,102,101 101,97,92,92,90
CSF £315.60 CT £7282.56 TOTE £24.20: £3.50, £6.10, £5.00, £6.10; EX 473.00.
Owner Paul Montgomery & Brian Morton **Bred** Lucayan Stud Ltd **Trained** Newmarket, Suffolk

FOCUS
Another good handicap run at a sound gallop, being 1.56sec faster than the quickest of the two earlier juvenile events. Four of the field raced far side with the rest coming up the middle and the smaller group had the advantage.

NOTEBOOK
Rain Stops Play(IRE) ◆, runner-up to Plum Pudding here last month when he raced alone on the far side, had a little company this time and, after making much of the running, outbattled the runner-up in typically game fashion. He was 3lb out of the handicap and, although likely to go up again, may have more to offer.

Salinja(USA), fitted with blinkers for the first time after a couple of below-par performances interspersed with decent efforts, responded positively to the headgear and looked sure to win when going to the front in the dip, however, he faltered on the climb to the line and the more resolute winner rallied to get back up. He is clearly useful but not one to rely on totally. (op 20-1)

Private Business(USA), who has been struggling in Pattern company over longer trips, had the headgear dispensed with and found the drop into handicaps much more his level. He 'won' the race up the centre and finished well, but the principals on the far rail had gone beyond recall.

Harvest Queen(IRE) ◆, who had failed to shine in top handicap company since winning twice at Nottingham in the late spring, bounced back, having been given a three-month break. She is clearly a useful filly and looks capable of winning a good race around this trip. She handles Polytrack, which gives her trainer options, and is one to bear in mind. (op 20-1)

Seulement(USA), who ran so well in the Cambridgeshire, having originally been a reserve, raced in the group on the far rail that contained the first two, but never looked like getting past them. (op 9-1)

Joseph Henry has form on soft ground but had not encountered it recently. He ran well on this return from ten weeks off and looks fairly handicapped at present.

Cactus King ◆, who has been tried over various trips and on differing ground, ran his race from 1lb out of the handicap and overcame having the blindfold removed fractionally late. He is still relatively unexposed, and could be one to watch if returning to Polytrack, where he gained his only previous success.

Motaraqeb, 5lb better off with the winner for a length defeat here last time, finished further behind that rival this time but still ran a reasonable race. (op 13-2)

Cross My Mind, made favourite on the back of several good efforts, missed the break and never got into contention. He is better than this effort suggests. (tchd 6-1)

Count Trevisio(IRE), whose only disappointing run was on soft, appeared to have his chance in the main group, but faded up the hill. (op 11-2 tchd 13-2 in places)

Plum Pudding(IRE), who beat the winner here earlier in the month, was higher in the weights, but his run two days after that victory may have taken its toll. (op 12-1)

5946 NEWMARKET CHALLENGE WHIP (H'CAP) 1m 2f

5:25 (5:25) (Class 6) (0-85,75) 3-Y-0+ **£0Stalls** High

Form RPR

-003 **1** **Hazelnut**[65] 4245 3-8-0 59 JimmyQuinn 3 68
(J R Fanshawe) *dwlt: hld up in tch: shkn up to ld over 1f out: styd on* **2/1**[2]

4210 **2** *2* **Buster Hyvonen (IRE)**[23] 5479 4-9-7 75 JamieSpencer 5 80
(J R Fanshawe) *lw: led: rdn and hdd over 1f out: unable qckn ins fnl f* **10/11**[1]

5535 **3** *2* **Kylkenny**[18] 5581 11-8-9 63 (t) SteveDrowne 2 65+
(H Morrison) *chsd ldr: rdn and ev ch over 1f out: no ex ins fnl f* **7/2**[3]

2m 9.97s (4.26) **Going Correction** +0.35s/f (Good)
WFA 3 from 4yo+ 5lb **3** Ran SP% **107.9**
Speed ratings (Par 101):96,94,92
CSF £4.25 TOTE £2.70; EX 4.00 Place 6 £ 1320.75, Place 5 £ 190.42.
Owner The Hon William Vestey **Bred** Stowell Park Stud **Trained** Newmarket, Suffolk

FOCUS
A modest renewal of this traditional event and the time was very ordinary.
T/Jkpt: Not won. T/Plt: £1,127.50 to a £1 stake. Pool: £90,284.30. 58.45 winning tickets. T/Qpdt: £47.10 to a £1 stake. Pool: £7,374.10. 115.80 winning tickets. CR

5378 WARWICK (L-H)

Friday, October 13

OFFICIAL GOING: Soft
Wind: Nil

5947 RACING UK AND SETANTA FOR £15 MEDIAN AUCTION MAIDEN STKS 1m 22y

1:45 (1:47) (Class 6) 2-Y-0 **£2,388** (£705; £352) **Stalls** Low

Form RPR

5 **1** **Cat De Mille (USA)**[14] 5658 2-9-3 AdrianMcCarthy 10 77+
(P W Chapple-Hyam) *trckd ldrs: led ins fnl 2f: pushed out: readily* **5/6**[1]

4 **2** *1 1/4* **Strikeen (IRE)**[16] 5622 2-9-3 IanMongan 5 74+
(T G Mills) *prom: chsd wnr 4f out: drvn and effrt to cl over 1f out: but a readily hld ins last* **5/2**[2]

64 **3** *3 1/2* **Coyote Creek**[16] 5616 2-9-3 DaneO'Neill 7 67
(E F Vaughan) *sn in tch: hdwy 3f out: rdn and styd on fnl 2f: nvr gng pce to rch ldrs* **11/1**[3]

4 *shd* **Lord Oroko** 2-9-3 CatherineGannon 3 66
(K A Ryan) *s.i.s: sn in tch: hdwy: 3f out: chsd ldrs over 2f out: kpt on same pce* **66/1**

5 **5** *11* **Path To Glory**[30] 5292 2-9-0 NeilChalmers(3) 1 42
(Miss Z C Davison) *sn led: rdn and hdd ins fnl 2f: hung rt and wknd fnl f* **100/1**

0563 **6** *7* **Hemispear**[17] 5596 2-8-12 66 PaulFitzsimons 11 22
(Miss J R Tooth) *sn towards rr: no ch whn hmpd bnd over 2f out: mod late prog* **16/1**

7 *nk* **Wilde Thing** 2-8-12 MickyFenton 2 21
(S Curran) *bhd fr 1/2-way: no ch whn hung bdly rt bnd over 2f out* **66/1**

8 *2 1/2* **Pigeon Flight** 2-9-3 J-PGuillambert 13 21
(M L W Bell) *sn drvn in rr: no ch whn carried bdly rt bnd over 2f out* **33/1**

9 *nk* **Cobra King (IRE)** 2-9-3 JimCrowley 14 20
(P Winkworth) *sn bhd* **66/1**

00 **10** *nk* **Polly Jones (USA)**[77] 3893 2-8-12 DeanMcKeown 9 14
(G L Moore) *v.s.a: a in rr* **50/1**

066 **11** *6* **Mr Forthright**[18] 5570 2-8-10 63 BarrySavage(7) 8 6
(J M Bradley) *sn bhd* **66/1**

4 **12** *6* **Vallemeldee (IRE)**[25] 5425 2-8-12 TPQueally 12 —
(P W D'Arcy) *chsd ldrs to 1/2-way* **11/1**[3]

0 **13** *5* **Butlers Best**[20] 5537 2-9-3 ChrisCatlin 6 —
(E J O'Neill) *slowly away: rcvrd and in tch 1/2-way: no ch whn carried bdly rt bnd over 2f out* **33/1**

0035 **P** **Bathwick Style**[49] 4773 2-8-12 55 GrahamGibbons 4 —
(B R Millman) *t.k.h: hung rt and chsd ldrs tl wnt bdly lame and p.u bnd over 2f out* **33/1**

1m 44.85s (5.25) **Going Correction** +0.50s/f (Yiel) **14** Ran SP% **123.4**
Speed ratings (Par 93):93,91,88,88,77 70,69,67,67,66 60,54,49,—
CSF £2.75 TOTE £1.70: £1.10, £1.20, £2.70; EX 4.00.
Owner R J Arculli **Bred** E P Evans **Trained** Newmarket, Suffolk

FOCUS
An uncompetitive maiden, with some very moderate horses among the also-rans and best rated through the third.

NOTEBOOK
Cat De Mille(USA) set the standard on his debut fifth in a Newmarket maiden last month and, having shown that soft ground held no terrors for him, he handled similar conditions here without a problem and probably did not need to improve to win with a bit to spare. (op 4-5 tchd 8-11)

Strikeen(IRE), a fair fourth on his debut on good ground at Salisbury last month, travelled at least as well as the winner turning for home, but was inclined to carry his head a bit high in the straight and he found the Chapple-Hyam colt too good on the run to the line. He can improve again with experience. (op 7-2)
Coyote Creek kept on for a respectable third on ground that was probably on the slow side for him. (op 14-1)
Lord Oroko recovered quickly from a tardy start and, having raced in mid-division, ran on to the line. He is bred to be a middle-distance horse, and this was an encouraging start to his career. (op 33-1)
Path To Glory, who had shown nothing after being unruly before the start at Sandown on his debut, shaped better here but tired in the closing stages, causing him to hang badly right.
Polly Jones(USA) Official explanation: jockey said filly dwelt in stalls
Vallemeldee(IRE) Official explanation: jockey said filly lost its action

5948 ENTERTAIN CLIENTS AT WARWICK RACECOURSE CLAIMING STKS — 7f 26y
2:15 (2:17) (Class 6) 2-Y-O — **£2,388** (£705; £352) **Stalls** Low

Form — RPR
6060 **1** **Copper King**[39] 5065 2-8-9 58 ....(v) ChrisCatlin 7 — 68+
(A M Balding) *led after 2f: c readily clr fr 3 out: eased cl home* **9/1**
0050 **2** *3 ½* **Peppin's Gold (IRE)**[27] 5387 2-8-0 55 .... AdrianMcCarthy 3 — 48
(B R Millman) *bhd: hdwy fr 3f out: hrd drvn and styd on fr over 1f out: kpt on to take n.d 2nd last strides* **16/1**
5140 **3** *nk* **Goose Green (IRE)**[14] 5647 2-8-10 68 .... EdwardCreighton(3) 6 — 61
(M R Channon) *chsd ldrs: wnt 2nd u.p over 1f out but nvr any ch w wnr: lost 2nd last strides* **15/8**[1]
6 **4** *1 ¾* **Raquel White**[14] 5646 2-8-4 .... FrankieMcDonald 5 — 47
(S Kirk) *in tch: rdn over 2f out: r.o ins last and gng on cl home: nvr a danger* **4/1**[2]
0300 **5** *hd* **Blackwater Stream (IRE)**[28] 5349 2-8-7 65 .... RobertHavlin 14 — 50
(Mrs P N Dutfield) *chsd ldrs: rdn 3f out: styd on same pce fnl 2f* **6/1**[3]
6500 **6** *nk* **Global Traffic**[23] 5482 2-8-3 54 .... TPO'Shea 1 — 45
(P F I Cole) *bhd: hday and drvn 2f out r.o ins last and gng on cl home: nvr in contention* **12/1**
3105 **7** *nk* **Sunstroke (IRE)**[23] 5482 2-8-6 60 .... TPQueally 10 — 47
(M G Quinlan) *chsd ldrs: wnt 2nd 3f out but nvr any ch w wnr: sn hrd drvn: wknd fnl f* **7/1**
050 **8** *¾* **Musical Affair**[39] 5068 2-8-4 57 .... JoeFanning 8 — 44
(F Jordan) *chsd ldrs: rdn over 3f out: wknd over 1f out* **50/1**
6030 **9** *2 ½* **Little Tiny Tom**[17] 5597 2-8-2 55 ....(p) PaulPickard(7) 4 — 42
(C N Kellett) *in tch: rdn and sme hdwy over 2f out: nvr gng pce to rch ldrs and sn btn* **66/1**
060 **10** *¾* **Prima Luna**[4] 5876 2-8-4 .... CatherineGannon 2 — 36
(K R Burke) *rr tl sme hdwy u.p fr 2f out: nvr in contention* **50/1**
0240 **11** *6* **Soffooh (USA)**[60] 4436 2-8-9 55 .... JDSmith 12 — 26
(W J Musson) *sn bhd: no ch whn rn wd bnd over 2f out* **22/1**
050 **12** *5* **Yearning (IRE)**[39] 5052 2-8-6 53 oh5 .... NeilChalmers(3) 13 — 14
(J G Portman) *led 2f: chsd wnr to 1/2-way: wknd fr 3f out* **66/1**
1100 **13** *18* **Feisty**[23] 5482 2-8-8 64 .... FrancisFerris 11 — —
(Rae Guest) *early spd: sn bhd: no ch whn wd bnd over 2f out* **18/1**
0 **14** *4* **Go Dude**[14] 5646 2-8-13 .... BrianReilly 9 — —
(J Ryan) *s.i.s: a bhd* **25/1**

1m 28.59s (3.59) **Going Correction** +0.50s/f (Yiel) **14 Ran SP% 125.5**
Speed ratings (Par 93):99,95,94,92,92 92,91,90,88,87 80,74,54,49
CSF £142.04 TOTE £13.60: £3.60, £4.90, £1.30; EX 128.10.Copper King was claimed by P. D. Evans for £8,000. Goose Green (IRE) was claimed by R. J. Hodges for £10,000. Raquel White was claimed by P. D. Evans for £8,000
Owner Miss A V Hill **Bred** Miss A V Hill **Trained** Kingsclere, Hants

FOCUS
A weak claimer and very few ever got into it. The race could be rated higher but mainly regressive types in behind.

NOTEBOOK
Copper King has had plenty of chances and had something to find on official figures, but he had run well in a first-time visor last time and, tackling a longer trip here, he maintained the improvement to win well under a positive ride.
Peppin's Gold(IRE), who showed some promise early in the season but has been very disappointing of late, was put in on a realistic low mark and ran creditably, suggesting she can win a similar race if connections keep her at the bottom of the weight range. (tchd 14-1)
Goose Green(IRE), winner of a nursery here last month and the top-rated horse in the field, confirmed subsequent Redcar placings with Sunstroke, Global Traffic and Feisty, but took too long to pick up off the turn and could never get in a blow at the enterprisingly ridden winner. (op 9-4)
Raquel White, less exposed than most of her rivals, shaped with some promise and she and the winner were claimed by David Evans. (tchd 7-2)
Blackwater Stream(IRE), trying a longer trip and softer ground, seemed to be beaten more for pace than for stamina. (op 15-2)
Feisty Official explanation: jockey said filly was hampered shortly after start

5949 ANDYLOOS LAST DASH OF THE SEASON MAIDEN STKS (DIV I) — 6f 21y
2:50 (2:50) (Class 5) 3-Y-O+ — **£2,590** (£770; £385; £192) **Stalls** Low

Form — RPR
2 **1** **La Colline (GER)**[11] 5728 3-8-12 .... JoeFanning 10 — 59
(W J Haggas) *sn trcking ldr: chal trav wl 2f out: led wl over 1f out: edgd rt and rdn ins last: kpt on wl* **7/4**[1]
0050 **2** *¾* **The Grey One (IRE)**[24] 5453 3-9-0 49 ....(p) NeilChalmers(3) 11 — 62
(J M Bradley) *chsd ldrs: hung rt u.p and chsd wnr fnl f: kpt on but hld whn carried rt nr fin* **12/1**
004 **3** *5* **Left Nostril (IRE)**[169] 1263 3-8-12 47 .... BrianReilly 9 — 42
(P S McEntee) *sn led: rdn 2f out: hdd over 1f out: styd far side and led that gp: wknd and no ch w stands side fnl f* **33/1**
0000 **4** *7* **Miss Ruby**[58] 4497 4-8-13 45 .... IanMongan 6 — 21
(Rae Guest) *in tch: rdn and styd on same pce fnl 2f* **33/1**
006- **5** *nk* **Boppys Dream**[377] 5622 4-8-13 45 .... MickyFenton 2 — 20
(P T Midgley) *s.i.s: bhd: mod prog fnl f* **25/1**
50-0 **6** *2 ½* **Indian Sundance (IRE)**[43] 4948 3-8-12 45 .... JamieMoriarty(5) 12 — 18
(R A Fahey) *chsd ldrs: rdn 3f out: sn btn* **20/1**
0042 **7** *hd* **Vibrato (USA)**[5] 5840 4-9-4 45 ....(p) PhillipMakin 8 — 17
(C J Teague) *sn in tch: rdn 1/2-way: no ch w ldrs fnl 2f* **8/1**
0000 **8** *5* **Bellanora**[29] 5309 3-8-12 50 ....(b) TPQueally 4 — —
(R F Johnson Houghton) *no ch fr 1/2-way* **7/1**[3]
9 *1 ½* **Thornbill** 3-9-3 .... DaneO'Neill 1 — —
(H Candy) *slowly away: styd far side fnl 2f: a wl bhd* **3/1**[2]
0600 **10** *1 ¾* **Burnt Orange (IRE)**[51] 4690 3-9-3 46 ....(b[1]) RobbieFitzpatrick 3 — —
(T D McCarthy) *in tch early: bhd fr 1/2-way: styd far side and no ch fnl 2f* **66/1**
0500 **11** *3 ½* **Tay Bridge (IRE)**[61] 4389 3-9-0 35 .... DominicFox(3) 7 — —
(G F Bridgwater) *a bhd: styd far side and no ch fnl 2f* **80/1**
4450 **12** *10* **Dragon Flame (IRE)**[16] 5605 3-9-3 62 .... ChrisCatlin 5 — —
(M Quinn) *early spd: sn bhd: s far side and no ch fnl 2f* **8/1**

1m 14.6s (2.50) **Going Correction** +0.50s/f (Yiel)
WFA 3 from 4yo 1lb **12 Ran SP% 121.0**
Speed ratings (Par 103):103,102,95,86,85 82,82,75,73,71 66,53
CSF £23.83 TOTE £2.40: £1.20, £3.70, £8.10; EX 24.90.
Owner Snowdrop Stud Co Limited **Bred** Graf And Grafin Von Stauffenberg **Trained** Newmarket, Suffolk

FOCUS
A weak maiden with only one horse rated above 50. Despite the winning time being 0.45 seconds faster than the second division, the form is unlikely to amount to much.

5950 EUROPEAN BREEDERS FUND MAIDEN FILLIES' STKS — 6f 21y
3:25 (3:25) (Class 5) 2-Y-O — **£3,886** (£1,156; £577; £288) **Stalls** Low

Form — RPR
52 **1** **Gentle Guru**[17] 5586 2-9-0 .... TPQueally 5 — 73
(R T Phillips) *prom: trckd ldr 3f out: led over 1f out: hrd drvn and idled cl home: all out* **2/1**[1]
5300 **2** *hd* **Tee Off (IRE)**[25] 5434 2-9-0 74 ....(t) MichaelHills 11 — 72
(B W Hills) *chsd ldrs: rdn 2f out: styd on u.p to press wnr ins last: no ex cl home* **10/3**[2]
0 **3** *2 ½* **Launch It Lily**[18] 5563 2-8-7 .... JackDean(7) 8 — 65
(W G M Turner) *led after 2f: rdn over 2f out: hdd over 1f out: wknd and lost 2nd ins last* **80/1**
25 **4** *1 ¾* **Twitch Hill**[31] 5264 2-9-0 .... DaneO'Neill 12 — 59
(H Candy) *led 2f: styd chsng ldrs: rdn over 2f out: wknd fnl f* **5/1**[3]
5 *½* **Dancing Jest (IRE)** 2-9-0 .... ChrisCatlin 6 — 58
(Rae Guest) *chsd ldrs: rdn over 2f out: styd on same pce fnl f* **40/1**
46 **6** *hd* **Glen Avon Girl (IRE)**[10] 5753 2-9-0 .... GrahamGibbons 7 — 57
(T D Easterby) *chsd ldrs: rdn over 2f out: wknd fnl f* **18/1**
06 **7** *½* **Knapton Hill**[21] 5507 2-9-0 .... RobertHavlin 14 — 56
(H Morrison) *chsd ldrs: rdn over 2f out: wknd appr fnl f* **14/1**
8 *1 ¼* **Lawyers Choice** 2-9-0 .... JoeFanning 3 — 52+
(Pat Eddery) *s.i.s: bhd: pushed along and kpt on fr over 1f out: nvr nr ldrs* **16/1**
9 *1 ¼* **Slo Mo Shun** 2-9-0 .... JimCrowley 1 — 48
(B R Millman) *s.i.s: a bhd* **33/1**
10 *5* **Day By Day** 2-9-0 .... TPO'Shea 2 — 33
(B J Meehan) *sn outpcd and green in rr: nvr in contention* **6/1**
11 *3* **Winning Smile (USA)** 2-9-0 .... AdrianMcCarthy 10 — 24
(P W Chapple-Hyam) *s.i.s: sn rdn and a bhd* **14/1**
12 *3* **Mirin** 2-9-0 .... WSupple 9 — 15
(G Wragg) *s.i.s: a bhd* **18/1**
13 *2 ½* **Lady Kintyre** 2-9-0 .... RichardThomas 4 — 8
(A W Carroll) *s.i.s: a bhd* **33/1**

1m 15.49s (3.39) **Going Correction** +0.50s/f (Yiel) **13 Ran SP% 126.7**
Speed ratings (Par 92):97,96,93,91,90 90,89,87,86,79 75,71,68
CSF £8.68 TOTE £2.90: £1.10, £1.60, £20.20; EX 12.10.
Owner Flying Tiger Partnership **Bred** R Phillips And Tweenhills Farm And Stud **Trained** Adlestrop, Gloucs

FOCUS
Another weak maiden and the winner probably did not need to improve to score. The form appears solid rated around the fourth and seventh.

NOTEBOOK
Gentle Guru, who had made most of the running when second at Goodwood last time, did not have to improve much on that form to score here and was always going like a winner in the straight after getting a handy lead from Launch It Lily. She did idle in front and had to be kept up to her work to hold the challenge of Tee Off, but she kept finding enough and will probably be put away until next season. (op 11-4 tchd 3-1)
Tee Off(IRE), a good third at Newbury in June, stopped quickly at Ascot next time and was fitted with a tongue tie at Leicester on her latest outing, when she met trouble in running, and was also reported to have hung on the firmish ground. She had no problems on this surface, but ran as if a seventh furlong would suit her. (op 3-1)
Launch It Lily, who had shown nothing when a 100-1 shot on her recent Bath debut, was driven into an early lead and did not give up once headed. However, her prominent showing does raise questions about the overall value of the form. (op 66-1)
Twitch Hill should have appreciated the extra furlong and softer ground, but performed like a non-stayer. (op 11-2)
Dancing Jest(IRE), a 31,000gns half-sister to three winners including The Kiddykid, did not run badly on this debut but is likely to come to herself once handicapped next season.

5951 ANDYLOOS LAST DASH OF THE SEASON MAIDEN STKS (DIV II) — 6f 21y
4:00 (4:01) (Class 5) 3-Y-O+ — **£2,590** (£770; £385; £192) **Stalls** Low

Form — RPR
03 **1** **Efisio Princess**[11] 5729 3-8-12 .... RichardThomas 11 — 55
(J E Long) *trckd ldr: rdn over 1f out: styd on u.p to ld ins last: hung rt cl home: drvn out* **9/1**
6000 **2** *1 ¼* **Tagula Bay (IRE)**[16] 5620 4-8-13 47 ....(b[1]) J-PGuillambert 9 — 52+
(T D Easterby) *sn led: rdn over 1f out: flashed tail u.p and hdd ins last: btn whn hmpd cl home* **9/2**[3]
0 **3** *2* **Palmistry**[11] 5728 3-9-0 .... NeilChalmers(3) 12 — 53+
(A M Balding) *s.i.s: sn rdn and rcvrd to chse ldrs: kpt on same pce fnl f* **13/2**
0060 **4** *8* **Megavegas**[4] 5873 3-8-12 40 .... MickyFenton 1 — 21
(P T Midgley) *chsd ldrs: rdn over 2f out and sn wknd* **66/1**
0230 **5** *1 ¾* **Mujeak (IRE)**[26] 5401 3-9-3 66 .... GrahamGibbons 6 — 21
(J J Quinn) *rdn in mid-div 1/2-way: sn btn* **7/4**[1]
0-00 **6** *2 ½* **Spinning Dancer (IRE)**[130] 2304 3-8-5 30 .... ChrisGlenister(7) 8 — 9
(J R Holt) *s.i.s: outpcd most of way* **66/1**
7 *2* **Ragad** 3-9-3 .... WSupple 3 — 8
(W Jarvis) *slowly away: sn drvn and rcvrd to chse ldrs: wknd fr 2f out* **9/4**[2]
00 **8** *11* **Lucky Tern**[5] 5847 3-9-3 .... ChrisCatlin 4 — —
(J M Bradley) *sn bhd* **33/1**
0506 **9** *6* **Musical Chimes**[91] 3488 3-8-12 46 .... RobbieFitzpatrick 7 — —
(W M Brisbourne) *bhd: no ch whn lost action and stmbld bdly 2f out* **12/1**
00 **10** *12* **Tatillius (IRE)**[11] 5729 3-8-10 .... BarrySavage(7) 5 — —
(J M Bradley) *chsd ldrs to 1/2-way: sn wknd* **50/1**

1m 15.05s (2.95) **Going Correction** +0.50s/f (Yiel)
WFA 3 from 4yo 1lb **10 Ran SP% 124.2**
Speed ratings (Par 103):100,98,95,85,82 79,76,62,54,38
CSF £51.97 TOTE £10.10: £2.40, £1.80, £2.10; EX 44.60.
Owner Miss M B Fernandes **Bred** Mrs A Yearley **Trained** Caterham, Surrey

FOCUS
Another moderate contest and the time was 0.45 seconds slower than the first division.
Musical Chimes Official explanation: jockey said filly lost its action

5952 SUBSCRIBE ONLINE @ RACINGUK.TV H'CAP 1m 6f 213y
4:35 (4:36) (Class 5) (0-75,74) 3-Y-0+ £3,238 (£963; £481; £240) Stalls Low

Form RPR

3212 1 At The Money[136] 2117 3-8-10 66 ... MickyFenton 4 80
(J M P Eustace) *chsd ldr 12f out: drvn to ld 5f out: hdd over 1f out: rallied to ld again ins last: drvn out* 6/1

1350 2 1 3/4 Squirtle (IRE)[20] 5531 3-8-8 64 ... RobbieFitzpatrick 6 76
(W M Brisbourne) *hld up in rr: hdwy 6f out: chsd wnr 3f out: rdn to ld over 1f out: no ex u.p and hdd ins last: sn btn* 8/1

1101 3 6 Leslingtaylor (IRE)[7] 5792 4-9-7 74 ... SladeO'Hara(7) 10 78
(J J Quinn) *hld up in rr tl t.k.h and rapid hdwy to trck ldrs 7f out: drvn and c wd bnd 3f out: outpcd by ldng duo fnl 2f* 11/4[1]

2040 4 2 Jolizero[39] 5061 5-8-9 55 oh1 ... RobertHavlin 13 56
(John Berry) *bhd: hdwy to chse ldrs 5f out: rdn over 3f out: wknd fr 2f out* 14/1

0600 5 4 Bill Bennett (FR)[6] 5815 5-9-3 63 ... PaulEddery 11 58
(J Jay) *bhd: rdn 4f out: styd on fnl 3f but nvr rchd ldrs* 33/1

300 6 1 Dundry[18] 5564 5-9-12 72 ... (p) IanMongan 8 66
(G L Moore) *in tch: hdwy and wd 1m out: rdn 3f out: wknd over 2f out* 9/2[2]

3654 7 18 Primitive Academy[14] 5651 4-9-12 72 ... ChrisCatlin 14 41
(H R A Cecil) *sn led: rdn and hdd 5f out: wknd fr 3f out* 40/1

0-14 8 2 1/2 Precious Mystery (IRE)[185] 966 6-9-8 68 ... (v) DaneO'Neill 5 33
(A King) *chsd ldrs: rdn over 4f out: wknd 3f out* 11/2[3]

10-0 9 1/2 Treason Trial[184] 990 5-9-5 65 ... TPQueally 3 29
(W M Brisbourne) *t.k.h: in tch: rdn and wknd 4f out* 25/1

20-0 10 6 Hawk Arrow (IRE)[160] 1478 4-9-2 65 ... NeilChalmers(3) 2 21
(Miss Sheena West) *chsd ldrs to 5f out* 33/1

015 11 8 Robbie Can Can[9] 3894 7-8-9 55 oh1 ... WSupple 1 —
(A W Carroll) *chsd ldrs: wknd 1/2-way* 14/1

0365 12 3/4 Karshaan (FR)[17] 5587 3-8-7 63 ... JimCrowley 7 7
(P Winkworth) *chsd ldrs: rdn 6f out: sn wknd* 12/1

650/ 13 6 Dangerously Good[656] 1367 8-9-3 63 ... JoeFanning 9 —
(G L Moore) *chsd ldrs 11f: sn wknd* 20/1

2000 14 1 Isa'Af (IRE)[106] 3028 7-9-9 69 ... PhillipMakin 12 —
(P W Hiatt) *in tch to 1/2-way: sn wknd* 20/1

3m 28.15s (12.25) **Going Correction** +0.875s/f (Soft)
WFA 3 from 4yo+ 10lb 14 Ran SP% 128.3
Speed ratings (Par 103):102,101,97,96,94 94,84,83,82,79 75,75,71,71
CSF £52.35 CT £168.30 TOTE £8.00: £2.20, £2.90, £1.30; EX 76.10.
Owner Harold Nass **Bred** Rockville Pike Partnership **Trained** Newmarket, Suffolk

FOCUS
This was run at a decent clip, putting stamina at a premium.
Precious Mystery(IRE) Official explanation: jockey said mare had no more to give

5953 WARWICKRACECOURSE.CO.UK H'CAP 7f 26y
5:05 (5:06) (Class 5) (0-70,70) 3-Y-0 £3,238 (£963; £481; £240) Stalls Low

Form RPR

3045 1 Valentino Swing (IRE)[18] 5568 3-8-8 67 ... JamesMillman(7) 5 74
(J L Spearing) *hld up in rr: gd hdwy over 2f out: str run to ld ins last: kpt on wl cl home* 8/1

0300 2 3/4 River Kintyre[27] 5377 3-9-3 69 ... MichaelHills 12 74
(B W Hills) *sn led: rdn whn chal fr 3f out: hdd ins last: no ex* 11/2[3]

1605 3 1 1/2 The London Gang[15] 5635 3-8-10 62 ... (v) J-PGuillambert 9 64+
(P D Evans) *s.i.s: bhd: hdwy 3f out: styng on whn carried rt and hmpd 1f out: one pce after* 16/1

1300 4 3/4 Jellytot (USA)[27] 5386 3-8-10 62 ... CatherineGannon 11 61
(K A Ryan) *chsd ldrs: rdn and effrt over 2f out: wknd ins fnl f* 40/1

0300 5 nk Princess Lavinia[29] 5320 3-8-13 65 ... WSupple 14 63
(G Wragg) *chsd ldrs: chal over 3f out: stl upsides whn rdn and hung rt 1f out: sn btn* 20/1

0022 6 1 3/4 Smart Ass (IRE)[16] 5619 3-8-13 65 ... TPO'Shea 2 59
(J S Moore) *hld up mid-div: hdwy 3f out: styd on fr over 1f out but nvr gng pce to trble ldrs* 5/1[2]

2253 7 1 1/4 Turkish Sultan (IRE)[10] 5761 3-9-4 70 ... MickyFenton 3 61
(T D Easterby) *in tch: rdn to chse ldrs over 3f out: wknd over 1f out* 9/1

0025 8 2 Charlton[31] 5268 3-9-3 69 ... (v) IanMongan 1 54
(T G Mills) *in tch: rdn 3f out: wknd over 1f out* 4/1[1]

500 9 1 1/4 Fairdonna[16] 5612 3-8-10 62 ... TPQueally 4 44
(D J Coakley) *s.i.s: rdn over 2f out: mod late hdwy* 14/1

5402 10 4 Way To The Stars[10] 5755 3-8-8 67 ... WilliamBuick(7) 10 39
(A M Balding) *bhd: sme hdwy on outside 3f out: nvr in contention* 7/1

-120 11 hd Apply Dapply[74] 3996 3-9-4 70 ... ChrisCatlin 8 41
(H Morrison) *chsd ldrs: rdn 3f out: sn wknd* 11/2[3]

4400 12 6 Regal Sunset (IRE)[27] 5391 3-9-4 70 ... (p) JoeFanning 13 26
(W R Swinburn) *chsd ldrs: rdn 3f out: sn wknd* 33/1

0200 13 4 Boldinor[18] 5568 3-8-11 63 ... AlanDaly 6 8
(N E Berry) *chsd ldrs over 4f* 66/1

1m 28.81s (3.81) **Going Correction** +0.50s/f (Yiel) 13 Ran SP% 125.2
Speed ratings (Par 101):98,97,95,94,94 92,90,88,87,82 82,75,70
CSF £52.69 CT £732.57 TOTE £10.40: £3.90, £2.50, £4.50; EX 90.00.
Owner Mrs Anita Quinn **Bred** Sean P Bourke **Trained** Kinnersley, Worcs

FOCUS
A moderate but competitive little handicap with the seventh the best guide to the form.
Princess Lavinia Official explanation: jockey said filly hung right closing stages

5954 JUMPS SEASON NEXT H'CAP 1m 2f 188y
5:35 (5:35) (Class 6) (0-60,60) 3-Y-0+ £2,388 (£705; £352) Stalls Low

Form RPR

3410 1 Royal Flynn[3] 5904 4-9-7 59 ... JimCrowley 6 67
(M Dods) *hld up in rr: staedy hdwy fr 3f out: str run fr 2f out to ld fnl 100yds* 5/1[1]

4-00 2 3/4 Persona (IRE)[25] 5422 4-9-6 58 ... AdrianMcCarthy 14 65
(B J McMath) *led: rdn 2f out: hdd and no ex fnl 100yds* 14/1

0400 3 2 1/2 Summer Bounty[28] 5354 10-9-6 58 ... JoeFanning 9 61
(F Jordan) *mid-div: hdwy 4f out: chsd ldrs 2f out: chal u.p 1f out: one pce ins last* 10/1

3040 4 hd Plenty Cried Wolf[43] 4947 4-9-0 57 ... JamieMoriarty(5) 10 59
(R A Fahey) *chsd ldrs: rdn 3f out: styd on same pce appr fnl f* 16/1

44-3 5 nk Elopement (IRE)[165] 1353 4-9-2 54 ... DaneO'Neill 8 56
(W M Brisbourne) *mid-div: hdwy 5f: chsd ldrs over 3f out: styd on same pce fnl f* 16/1

0450 6 1/2 Mixing[56] 4565 4-9-2 54 ... MickyFenton 1 55
(W Jarvis) *chsd ldrs: rdn over 3f out: one pce appr fnl f* 14/1

0000 7 1 Adobe[24] 5450 11-8-7 52 ... WilliamBuick(7) 15 51
(W M Brisbourne) *sn chsng ldr: pushed along over 2f out: wknd ins last* 25/1

0-60 8 4 Count Boris[184] 990 5-9-2 54 ... RichardThomas 7 46
(J A Geake) *in tch: outpcd and lost position 6f out: styd on again fr over 1f out* 11/2[2]

0216 9 3 1/2 Rotuma (IRE)[24] 5445 7-9-2 54 ... (b) PhillipMakin 13 39
(M Dods) *chsd ldrs: rdn 3f out: wknd fr 2f out* 7/1[3]

6662 10 shd Native American[46] 4869 4-9-2 54 ... RobbieFitzpatrick 2 39
(T D McCarthy) *chsd ldrs: rdn 3f out: wknd 2f out* 12/1

5255 11 2 1/2 Ermine Grey[16] 5621 5-9-6 58 ... (v) WSupple 17 39
(A W Carroll) *t.k.h: hld up in rr: rdn over 3f out: nvr rchd ldrs* 10/1

3466 12 3/4 Lady Taverner[33] 5213 5-9-6 58 ... J-PGuillambert 11 37
(J E Long) *bhd: hdwy 3f out: chsd ldrs and rdn 2f out: wknd fnl f: dismntd* 14/1

0100 13 9 Le Soleil (GER)[28] 5354 5-9-6 58 ... TPQueally 16 21
(B J Curley) *chsd ldrs tl wknd 3f out* 5/1[1]

06/0 14 7 Gagarin (FR)[11] 5725 6-9-3 55 ... DeanMcKeown 12 6
(Miss L C Siddall) *a in rr* 100/1

00-0 15 1 3/4 Musardiere[44] 4925 4-9-1 53 ... (p) BrianReilly 4 —
(J Balding) *chsd ldrs 7f* 20/1

0001 16 1 3/4 Lady Edge (IRE)[39] 5071 4-9-8 60 ... ChrisCatlin 5 4
(A W Carroll) *a in rr* 25/1

500 17 9 Theologicum[43] 4945 3-8-12 59 ... EdwardCreighton(3) 3 —
(Miss J R Gibney) *a in rr* 66/1

2m 28.5s (9.10) **Going Correction** +0.875s/f (Soft)
WFA 3 from 4yo+ 6lb 17 Ran SP% 133.8
Speed ratings (Par 101):101,100,98,98,98 97,97,94,91,91 89,89,82,77,76 75,68
CSF £78.91 CT £712.94 TOTE £8.50: £2.10, £1.30, £4.10, £5.00; EX 173.10 Place 6 £ 35.37, Place 5 £ 31.41.
Owner J A Wynn-Williams **Bred** Highclere Stud Ltd **Trained** Denton, Co Durham

FOCUS
A modest if competitive handicap and straightforward form, rated around the runner-up and fifth.
Lady Taverner Official explanation: jockey said mare lost its action
Theologicum Official explanation: jockey said filly was unsuited by the soft ground
T/Plt: £13.10 to a £1 stake. Pool: £42,304.05. 2,348.35 winning tickets. T/Qpdt: £8.90 to a £1 stake. Pool: £2,789.70. 230.30 winning tickets. ST

5746 CATTERICK (L-H)
Saturday, October 14

OFFICIAL GOING: Soft (good to soft in places)
After 23mm rain over the previous ten days the ground was described as 'good to soft, softer than that in places'.
Wind: Almost nil Weather: Fine and warm

5955 TOTEPLACEPOT APPRENTICE CLAIMING STKS 1m 3f 214y
2:15 (2:16) (Class 6) 3-Y-0+ £2,730 (£806; £403) Stalls Low

Form RPR

0501 1 Maria Antonia (IRE)[11] 5757 3-7-13 54 ow2 ... KevinGhunowa(5) 1 59
(P A Blockley) *in tch: hdwy 4f out: rdn to ld over 1f out: rider dropped whip ins last: styd on wl* 15/2

1542 2 1 1/4 Court Of Appeal[57] 4544 9-8-13 68 ... (tp) StephenDonohoe 6 59
(B Ellison) *a prom: effrt to chse ldr 4f out: wd st: rdn and over 1f out: sn drvn and kpt on* 3/1[1]

000 3 1 3/4 Explode[6] 5838 9-8-3 45 ... (b) DawnRankin(7) 5 54
(Miss L C Siddall) *in tch: hdwy to ld 7f out: rdn along over 2f out: hdd over 1f out: edgd lft and kpt on same pce* 100/1

0-20 4 nk Danebank (IRE)[27] 4960 6-9-1 54 ... (p) DNolan 4 59
(J Mackie) *hld up in midfield: hdwy 4f out: rdn to chse ldrs 2f out: sn drvn and kpt on ins last: nrst fin* 8/1

0114 5 1 Tedstale (USA)[59] 4475 8-8-8 70 ... (b) NSLawes(7) 15 57
(K A Ryan) *hld up in tch: hdwy 4f out: rdn to chse ldrs 2f out: drvn and no imp appr last* 13/2[3]

6351 6 1/2 Evolution Ex (USA)[22] 5510 4-8-10 65 ... AndrewElliott(3) 2 54
(K R Burke) *cl up: rdn along 4f out: drvn 3f out and sn one pce* 4/1[2]

650 7 1 1/2 Scotty's Future (IRE)[19] 5579 8-8-10 53 ... MarkLawson(3) 9 52
(A Berry) *hld up and bhd tl styd on fnl 3f: nvr rch ldrs* 25/1

430 8 3 Donna's Double[19] 5581 11-8-11 49 ... (p) PaulMulrennan 14 46
(Karen McLintock) *hld up and bhd: hdwy 4f out: rdn along wl over 2f out: nt rch ldrs* 14/1

0004 9 2 Captivate[23] 5497 3-7-8 45 ... (p) MCGeran(7) 13 40
(A J McCabe) *a rr* 25/1

0220 10 nk Yenaled[12] 5725 9-8-10 53 ... LukeMorris(5) 7 47
(J M Bradley) *trckd ldrs: rdn along 4f out: sn wknd* 7/1

0000 11 3/4 Mobane Flyer[39] 5090 6-8-7 53 ... JamieMoriarty(3) 8 41
(R A Fahey) *led 5f: rdn along over 4f out and sn wknd* 16/1

0-00 12 21 Pont Neuf (IRE)[180] 1045 6-8-5 50 ow2 ... (t) SladeO'Hara(5) 10 12
(A Crook) *a towards rr* 50/1

-600 13 27 Ullah Pendragon (IRE)[227] 548 3-8-2 49 ow3 ... AdamCarter(7) 12 —
(A J McCabe) *a bhd* 66/1

0-40 14 11 Good Investment[8] 5683 4-8-12 52 ... AndrewMullen 3 —
(Miss Tracy Waggott) *a bhd* 40/1

350 15 15 Encrypt (IRE)[78] 3919 4-8-3 50 ... JosephWalsh(7) 11 —
(O Brennan) *sddle slipped after 2f: sn t.o* 33/1

2m 45.4s (6.40) **Going Correction** +0.425s/f (Yiel)
WFA 3 from 4yo+ 7lb 15 Ran SP% 123.8
Speed ratings (Par 101):95,94,93,92,92 91,90,88,87,87 86,72,54,47,37
CSF £29.41 TOTE £8.00: £2.80, £1.70, £42.70; EX 48.70.
Owner Pedro Rosas **Bred** J McElroy **Trained** Lambourn, Berks
■ Stewards' Enquiry : Stephen Donohoe two-day ban: used whip with excessive frequency (Oct 25-26)

FOCUS
No gallop to halfway and they were spread out right across the track in the home straight. The proximity of the 45-rated Explode severely limits the overall value of the form.
Encrypt(IRE) Official explanation: jockey said saddle slipped

5956 TOTECOURSE TO COURSE E B F NOVICE STKS 5f
2:45 (2:45) (Class 5) 2-Y-0 £4,210 (£1,252; £625; £312) Stalls Low

Form RPR

5051 1 Luscivious[11] 5753 2-9-2 81 ... (b) StephenDonohoe(3) 9 93+
(A J McCabe) *s.i.s: hdwy to ld over 3f out: drew clr appr fnl f: readily* 6/1[3]

304 2 3 Spoof Master (IRE)[92] 3476 2-9-2 89 ... AmirQuinn(3) 6 82
(W G M Turner) *led over 1f: chsd wnr: kpt on same pce appr fnl f* 8/1

2461 **3** *1* **The Nifty Fox**[11] 5746 2-9-5 79 .... DavidAllan 8 79
(T D Easterby) *prom: rdn over 2f out: kpt on same pce* **8/1**

0050 **4** *1 ½* **Chjimes (IRE)**[14] 5681 2-9-5 87 .... PatCosgrave 5 73
(K R Burke) *chsd ldrs: kpt on same pce fnl 2f* **7/1**

U443 **5** *2 ½* **Princess Ellis**[21] 5528 2-8-7 60 .... PaulQuinn 13 52
(E J Alston) *in rr: kpt on fnl 2f: nvr nr ldrs* **33/1**

22 **6** *hd* **Morristown Music (IRE)**[16] 5632 2-8-7 .... TonyHamilton 12 51
(J S Wainwright) *in rr: hdwy 2f out: nvr nr ldrs* **12/1**

0336 **7** *¾* **Ingleby Image**[29] 5334 2-8-11 77 .... PhillipMakin 3 53+
(T D Barron) *racd alone far side: cl up: edgd rt and fdd fnl f* **9/2**[1]

1440 **8** *nk* **Eloquent Rose (IRE)**[14] 5681 2-9-4 80 .... TPQueally 7 59
(Mrs A Duffield) *trckd ldrs: kpt on same pce fnl 2f* **11/2**[2]

4000 **9** *10* **First Valentini**[8] 5790 2-8-5 51 ow1 ....(b) GregFairley(3) 2 —
(N Bycroft) *swtchd rt after 1f: chsd ldrs: lost pl over 1f out* **66/1**

0010 **10** *1* **Morinqua (IRE)**[14] 5676 2-8-8 78 .... AndrewMullen(3) 4 —
(K A Ryan) *swtchd rt after 1f: chsd ldrs: lost pl 2f out* **12/1**

0 **11** *2* **Bayshambles (IRE)**[11] 5753 2-8-8 ow1 .... MarkLawson(5) 11 —
(R E Barr) *swtchd rt after 1f: sn outpcd and in rr* **125/1**

3212 **12** *nk* **Durova (IRE)**[21] 5528 2-8-9 74 .... RobertWinston 1 —
(T D Easterby) *swtchd rt after 1f: chsd ldrs: lost pl 2f out* **6/1**[3]

61.07 secs (0.47) **Going Correction** +0.125s/f (Good) 12 Ran SP% **117.5**
Speed ratings (Par 95):101,96,94,92,88 87,86,86,70,68 65,64
CSF £52.63 TOTE £6.70: £1.60, £2.90, £2.40; EX 46.20.
Owner Paul J Dixon And Keith Barratt **Bred** R J Turner **Trained** Babworth, Notts

FOCUS
An improved effort from the winner and the race could be rated even higher.

NOTEBOOK
Luscivious has finally come good and with the blinkers on again he took this in fine style. He claimed the favoured stands' side and had this won in a matter of strides. (op 15-2)
Spoof Master(IRE) had 8lb in hand of the unexposed winner on official rtaings but on his first outing for three months in the end was very much second best. (tchd 7-1)
The Nifty Fox , off the mark at the 11th attempt, ran creditably without ever really threatening to follow up his course win . (op 17-2)
Chjimes(IRE), with the visor left off, continues to under-perform and his nursery mark, 87, flatters him. (op 10-1)
Princess Ellis had a mountain to climb and found this much too sharp.
Morristown Music(IRE), having her third outing, will no doubt step back up to six furlongs in nursery company. (op 14-1)
Ingleby Image, back over the minimum trip, was left alone to race down the far side. Looking for company, she edged towards the centre and her chance soon slipped. (op 11-2)
Eloquent Rose(IRE) looked very wintry and was well below her best. (op 9-2)
Durova(IRE), who is only small, became badly upset in the stalls. Official explanation: jockey said filly boiled over at start (op 8-1)

5957 TOTESPORT.COM CATTERICK DASH (H'CAP) 5f
3:15 (3:16) (Class 2) (0-100,102) 3-Y-O+**£14,573** (£4,335; £2,166; £1,082) **Stalls** Low

Form RPR

0216 **1** **Dhaular Dhar (IRE)**[7] 5812 4-8-10 **89** .... DanielTudhope 15 99
(J S Goldie) *trckd ldrs: hdwy on inner wl over 1f out: rdn and squeezed through ent last: led last 100 yds* **15/2**

4140 **2** *½* **Inter Vision (USA)**[7] 5812 6-8-6 **88** .... EdwardCreighton(3) 9 96
(A Dickman) *trckd ldrs: effrt and nt clr run over 1f out: swtchd lft and hdwy ent last: styd on wl* **11/1**

5400 **3** *1 ¼* **Corridor Creeper (FR)**[2] 5921 9-9-2 **98** ....(p) GregFairley(3) 14 102
(J M Bradley) *led: rdn along wl over 1f out: drvn and edgd lft ent last: hdd and nt qckn last 100 yds* **8/1**

0651 **4** *½* **Mecca's Mate**[2] 5921 5-9-4 **102** 6ex .... MarkLawson(5) 2 104
(D W Barker) *midfield: rdn along on outer 2f out: styd on u.p ent last: nrst fin* **9/2**[1]

3006 **5** *hd* **Prince Namid**[7] 5807 4-8-10 **89** .... TPQueally 1 90
(Mrs A Duffield) *cl up: rdn along and ev ch wl over 1f out: drvn and one pce ins last* **8/1**

0504 **6** *1* **Campo Bueno (FR)**[11] 5749 4-8-4 **86** oh3 ....(b) AndrewMullen(3) 8 84
(A Berry) *towards rr and rdn along 1/2-way: swtchd lft and hdwy over 1f out: styd on ins last: nrst fin* **25/1**

1100 **7** *hd* **The Lord**[36] 5158 6-9-4 **100** .... AmirQuinn(3) 7 97
(W G M Turner) *cl up: rdn and ev ch over 1f out: wknd ins last* **16/1**

4200 **8** *¾* **Gallery Girl (IRE)**[22] 5501 3-8-8 **87** .... DavidAllan 13 82
(T D Easterby) *trckd ldrs: effrt wl over 1f out: sn rdn and btn* **12/1**

0604 **9** *nk* **Green Park (IRE)**[7] 5807 3-8-7 **86** .... TonyHamilton 4 80
(R A Fahey) *a rr* **8/1**

4000 **10** *1 ¾* **Westbrook Blue**[49] 4793 4-8-0 **86** oh10 .... JackDean(7) 11 74
(W G M Turner) *trckd ldrs: rdn along wl over 1f out: sn wknd* **33/1**

6036 **11** *½* **Cape Royal**[2] 5921 6-8-10 **92** ....(bt) StephenDonohoe(3) 12 78
(J M Bradley) *s.i.s: a rr* **11/2**[2]

6000 **12** *2* **Dazzling Bay**[21] 5534 6-8-7 **86** .... MickyFenton 3 65
(T D Easterby) *hld up in rr: hmpd after 1f and bhd after* **33/1**

000- **13** *16* **Justalord**[343] 6264 8-8-5 **91** oh14 ow5 ....(p) SladeO'Hara(7) 5 16
(A Crook) *chsd ldrs on outer: rdn along 1/2-way: sn wknd* **100/1**

5030 **P** **Lafi (IRE)**[7] 5807 7-9-5 **98** .... RobertWinston 6 —
(D Nicholls) *towards rr whn broke leg and p.u after 1f: dead* **13/2**[3]

60.97 secs (0.37) **Going Correction** +0.125s/f (Good) 14 Ran SP% **124.6**
Speed ratings (Par 109):102,101,99,98,98 96,96,94,94,91 90,87,62,—
CSF £88.34 CT £695.01 TOTE £8.20: £3.40, £4.50, £5.00; EX 143.50.
Owner J S Goldie **Bred** Gainsborough Stud Management Ltd **Trained** Uplawmoor, E Renfrews
■ The richest Flat prize ever run at Catterick.
■ Stewards' Enquiry : T P Queally five-day ban: careless riding (Oct 25-29)

FOCUS
A tight sprint handicap but the stands' side was the place to be and those drawn low were at a serious disadvantage.

NOTEBOOK
Dhaular Dhar(IRE), dropping back to the minimum trip, had the plum stands' side draw. He never left the running rail and bravely put his head in front where it matters most.
Inter Vision(USA) did well on ground plenty soft enough for him. He had to search for an opening and in the end was just held. (op 12-1)
Corridor Creeper(FR), having his second outing in three days, has slipped to a lenient mark. He showed bags of toe to take them along but hung off the fence leaving the door open for the winner. (op 15-2 tchd 9-1)
Mecca's Mate, making a quick return to action under her penalty, had an unfavourable draw and did very well to finish as close. She is clearly right at the top of her form. (op 5-1)
Prince Namid, warm beforehand, had the worst of the draw. He made his way across, at a cost as it turned out to his rider, but was never going to quite pull it off. (op 9-1)
Campo Bueno(FR) is at last finding his feet here. He likes to get his toe in but is much better served by a sixth furlong. (op 22-1 tchd 28-1)
Cape Royal, normally quickly into his stride, blew it leaving the traps this time. (op 6-1 tchd 5-1)
Lafi(IRE), the 2004 Wokingham winner, came to a sad end. His four career victories netted over £122,000. (op 15-2)

5958 TOTEEXACTA NURSERY 7f
3:55 (3:55) (Class 4) (0-85,84) 2-Y-O **£6,477** (£1,927; £963; £481) **Stalls** Low

Form RPR

013 **1** **Celtic Step**[16] 5633 2-8-13 **79** ....(b[1]) GregFairley(3) 3 80
(M Johnston) *mde all: drvn clr over 2f out: wandered: jst hld on* **3/1**[2]

2320 **2** *hd* **Nota Liberata**[8] 5788 2-8-4 **67** .... DaleGibson 1 68+
(G M Moore) *in rr: hdwy and nt clr run over 1f out: swtchd lft ins last: fin wl: nt quite get up* **8/1**

5005 **3** *1* **Spirited Speedfit (IRE)**[15] 5647 2-7-9 **61** oh2 .... DominicFox(3) 6 59
(G G Margarson) *chsd ldrs: sn drvn along: one pce fnl 2f* **33/1**

0533 **4** *¾* **Bert's Memory**[11] 5747 2-8-1 **67** .... AndrewMullen(3) 10 63
(K A Ryan) *chsd ldrs: one pce fnl 2f* **18/1**

1512 **5** *3* **Fractured Foxy**[14] 5676 2-8-1 **69** .... NataliaGemelova(5) 8 58
(J J Quinn) *chsd ldrs: outpcd over 2f out: no real threat after* **11/4**[1]

464 **6** *nk* **My Valerina (IRE)**[27] 5404 2-8-8 **71** .... TPO'Shea 2 59
(Mrs A Duffield) *chsd ldrs: outpcd 3f out: n.d after* **18/1**

4202 **7** *nk* **Jord (IRE)**[12] 5738 2-8-0 **66** ow1 .... EdwardCreighton(3) 13 53
(A J McCabe) *chsd ldrs: outpcd over 3f out: n.d after* **16/1**

030 **8** *1 ½* **Cheery Cat (USA)**[17] 5613 2-7-12 **66** ow3 .... AndrewElliott(5) 12 49
(D W Barker) *in rr: drvn 4f out: nvr on terms* **66/1**

3102 **9** *¾* **Lemon Silk (IRE)**[16] 5633 2-8-13 **76** .... MickyFenton 11 58
(T P Tate) *dwlt: mid-div and drvn over 3f: swtchd lft over 1f out: nvr on terms* **15/2**

040 **10** *nk* **Prince Noel**[17] 5614 2-7-8 **64** ow2 .... LanceBetts(7) 9 45
(N Wilson) *chsd ldrs: lost pl over 1f out* **80/1**

1214 **11** *10* **Rosbay (IRE)**[28] 5359 2-9-7 **84** .... DavidAllan 4 40+
(T D Easterby) *prom: lost pl 4f out: bhd whn eased fnl f* **5/1**[3]

0000 **12** *shd* **Speedfit World**[12] 5721 2-7-12 **61** oh4 ....(b[1]) JamieMackay 7 17
(G G Margarson) *s.i.s: a in rr: detached 3f out* **50/1**

1m 31.11s (3.75) **Going Correction** +0.425s/f (Yiel) 12 Ran SP% **115.2**
Speed ratings (Par 97):95,94,93,92,89 89,88,86,86,85 74,74
CSF £26.09 CT £656.51 TOTE £3.90: £1.90, £2.30, £8.50; EX 35.10.
Owner S R Counsell **Bred** Woodcote Stud Ltd **Trained** Middleham Moor, N Yorks

FOCUS
A modest nursery in which the winner stole it under a fine front-running ride.

NOTEBOOK
Celtic Step, dropping back in trip and blinkered for the first time, took them along at a strong pace. He came wide off the home turn but ducked and dived and carried his head high and in the end the line came just in time. (tchd 11-4 and 10-3)
Nota Liberata had no luck in running. Pulled wide inside the last he would have made it in two more strides. He is still a maiden after a dozen attempts but will surely put the record straight sooner rather than later.
Spirited Speedfit(IRE), 2lb out of the handicap, was soon making hard work of it. He stuck on all the way to the line and will be better served by a mile.
Bert's Memory, stepping up in trip and encountering easy ground for the first time, stuck on in game fashion but looks rated to the limit. (op 22-1 tchd 14-1)
Fractured Foxy, 7lb higher than her win here two outings ago, is as tough as old boots but she was at a disadvantage here, finding herself rather marooned towards the centre in the home straight. (op 5-2 tchd 7-2)
Rosbay(IRE) was struggling after being left short of room exiting the back straight. (op 6-1)

5959 TOTE TEXT BETTING 60021 MEDIAN AUCTION MAIDEN STKS 7f
4:25 (4:26) (Class 6) 2-Y-O **£2,730** (£806; £403) **Stalls** Low

Form RPR

2 **1** **Musca (IRE)**[112] 2854 2-9-3 .... RobertWinston 6 83+
(J Howard Johnson) *sn led: rdn clr wl over 1f out: styd on wl* **5/4**[1]

344 **2** *6* **Princess Palatine (IRE)**[21] 5536 2-8-12 69 .... PatCosgrave 8 63
(K R Burke) *trckd ldrs on inner: hdwy to chse wnr 1/2-way: rdn 2f out and kpt on same pce* **6/1**[3]

22 **3** *shd* **Cedarlea (IRE)**[52] 4693 2-8-12 .... JamieMoriarty(5) 2 68
(R A Fahey) *chsd ldrs: rdn along wl over 2f out: kpt on same pce* **15/2**

02 **4** *2 ½* **Run Free**[8] 5790 2-9-3 .... TPQueally 1 62
(N Wilson) *midfield: hdwy over 2f out: rdn wl over 1f out: sn no imp* **13/2**

0 **5** *2 ½* **Graceful Steps (IRE)**[24] 5481 2-8-12 .... MickyFenton 5 51
(E J O'Neill) *towards rr tl styd on fnl 2f* **28/1**

0006 **6** *3* **Ellies Faith**[4] 5899 2-8-12 40 ....(b[1]) J-PGuillambert 7 43
(N Bycroft) *chsd ldrs: rdn along 1/2-way: sn outpcd* **80/1**

0043 **7** *1 ¾* **Hunting Call**[17] 5614 2-9-3 72 ....(b) PaulMulrennan 12 44
(K A Ryan) *prom: rdn along 1/2-way: sn wknd* **12/1**

0 **8** *nk* **Kentucky Boy (IRE)**[17] 5614 2-9-0 .... GregFairley(3) 13 43
(Jedd O'Keeffe) *s.i.s: a rr* **100/1**

0 **9** *3* **Presque Perdre**[17] 5615 2-9-3 .... DavidAllan 3 35
(K G Reveley) *s.i.s: a bhd* **100/1**

0 **10** *hd* **Forsters Plantin**[14] 5679 2-8-12 .... TonyHamilton 4 30
(J J Quinn) *a rr* **66/1**

60 **11** *6* **Skye But N Ben**[129] 2361 2-9-3 .... PhillipMakin 9 20
(T D Barron) *a bhd* **33/1**

12 *7* **Veils Of Salome** 2-8-9 .... StephenDonohoe(3) 10 —
(A J McCabe) *a bhd* **33/1**

6 **13** *16* **Oh Gracious Me (IRE)**[105] 3080 2-9-3 .... TPO'Shea 11 —
(P A Blockley) *cl up: rdn along over 3f out: sn wknd* **11/2**[2]

1m 31.37s (4.01) **Going Correction** +0.425s/f (Yiel) 13 Ran SP% **120.9**
Speed ratings (Par 93):94,87,87,84,81 77,75,75,72,71 65,57,38
CSF £8.78 TOTE £2.20: £1.30, £2.30, £2.20; EX 11.70.
Owner Transcend Bloodstock LLP **Bred** Yakup Demir Tokdemir **Trained** Billy Row, Co Durham

FOCUS
A modest event in which the third and sixth dictate the level for the form. The ground does temper enthusiasm for the form.

NOTEBOOK
Musca(IRE) had no Silent Waves standing in his way this time. He forced the pace and had this won some way from home. He will improve again and could prove useful at three. (op 7-4 tchd 15-8, tchd 2-1 in places)
Princess Palatine(IRE), dropping back in trip, went in pursuit of the winner but once in line for home it was soon clear it was a mismatch. (op 5-1)
Cedarlea(IRE), stepping up in trip and encountering soft ground for the first time, stuck on in his own time and this opens up the handicap route for him. (op 8-1)
Run Free, stepping up in trip, did nothing for the form of the York maiden in which he was runner-up a week earlier. (op 6-1)
Graceful Steps(IRE) improved on her debut effort three weeks earlier. She still looks very inexperienced and there should be even better to come. (op 25-1)
Oh Gracious Me(IRE) Official explanation: trainer said colt had mucus in its larynx

5960 TOTESPORT 0800 221 221 H'CAP — 1m 5f 175y
5:00 (5:00) (Class 6) (0-60,60) 3-Y-O+ — £3,238 (£963; £481; £240) Stalls Low

Form — RPR

0305 **1** **Saluscraggie**[4] 5903 4-8-11 **46** .... DavidAllan 5 — 56
(K G Reveley) *dwlt: in rr:hdwy over 4f out: sn hrd drvn: carried hd high: kpt on to ld nr fin* — **12/1**

1402 **2** *nk* **Onyergo (IRE)**[11] 5750 4-9-7 **56** .... PhillipMakin 11 — 66
(J R Weymes) *hld up in rr: hdwy over 6f out: led over 1f out: hdd and no ex nr fin* — **11/2**[2]

43F6 **3** *6* **Impeccable Guest (IRE)**[19] 5581 3-8-6 **55** .... LeanneKershaw(5) 10 — 56
(P C Haslam) *trckd ldrs: led over 2f out: hung lft and hdd over 1f out: one pce* — **14/1**

5412 **4** *2* **Pee Jay's Dream**[4] 5905 4-9-9 **58** .... PaulMulrennan 4 — 56
(M W Easterby) *prom: effrt and ev ch over 2f out: fdd over 1f out* — **7/4**[1]

/00- **5** *6* **Faraway Echo**[18] 1286 5-8-12 **52** .... MarkLawson(5) 8 — 42
(James Moffatt) *in rr: hdwy over 4f out: nvr nr ldrs* — **66/1**

0006 **6** *hd* **Rajam**[39] 5080 8-8-12 **47** ....(v) RobertWinston 6 — 37
(G A Harker) *prom: hung rt and wknd over 1f out* — **8/1**[3]

5004 **7** *2* **Give It Time**[17] 5618 3-9-2 **60** .... J-PGuillambert 14 — 47
(J G Given) *racd wd 5f: led: hdd 4f out: lost pl over 1f out* — **12/1**

6040 **8** *¾* **Zed Candy (FR)**[43] 4982 3-9-1 **59** .... MickyFenton 3 — 45
(J T Stimpson) *chsd ldr: led 4f out: hdd over 2f out: lost pl over 1f out* — **33/1**

4665 **9** *2* **Sweet Lavinia**[17] 5618 3-7-12 **47** .... AndrewElliott(5) 9 — 30
(J D Bethell) *in rr: effrt over 4f out: nvr on terms* — **9/1**

0500 **10** *9* **Shamrock Bay**[12] 5736 4-9-0 **52** ....(t) StephenDonohoe(3) 13 — 22
(C R Dore) *mid-div: lost pl over 4f out* — **28/1**

0500 **11** *1 ½* **Celtic Carisma**[12] 5725 4-9-3 **52** .... PatCosgrave 12 — 20
(K G Reveley) *hld up in rr: drvn over 4f out: nvr on terms* — **18/1**

0066 **12** *18* **Padre Nostro (IRE)**[12] 5725 7-8-9 **51** .... ChrisGlenister(7) 1 — —
(J R Holt) *chsd ldrs: lost pl over 5f out: sn bhd* — **16/1**

-000 **13** *28* **Bramantino (IRE)**[113] 2812 6-9-8 **60** .... GregFairley(3) 7 — —
(T A K Cuthbert) *mid-div: lost pl over 6f out: t.o 3f out* — **66/1**

0/1- **P** **Junkanoo**[556] 912 10-9-0 **56** .... JamesReveley(7) 2 — —
(K G Reveley) *dwlt: in rr: lost pl and p.u over 5f out* — **9/1**

3m 10.25s (5.75) **Going Correction** +0.425s/f (Yiel)
WFA 3 from 4yo+ 9lb — 14 Ran SP% **125.4**
Speed ratings (Par 101):100,99,96,95,91 91,90,90,89,83 83,72,56,—
CSF £78.59 CT £963.09 TOTE £15.90: £3.70, £2.60, £4.00; EX 133.80.
Owner H B E Van Cutsem **Bred** Hilborough Stud Farm Ltd **Trained** Lingdale, Redcar & Cleveland
■ Stewards' Enquiry : David Allan two-day ban: used whip with excessive frequency (Oct 25-26)

FOCUS
A very moderate handicap, little better than banded class, but the first two came clear.

5961 TOTESPORTCASINO.COM H'CAP — 7f
5:35 (5:35) (Class 5) (0-75,75) 3-Y-O+ — £3,238 (£963; £481; £240) Stalls Low

Form — RPR

4064 **1** **Bold Marc (IRE)**[5] 5861 4-8-12 **67** ....(p) PatCosgrave 9 — 86+
(K R Burke) *mde all: wnt clr over 1f out: eased towards fin* — **15/2**[3]

4033 **2** *6* **Efidium**[14] 5680 8-8-8 **70** ....(b) LukeMorris(7) 14 — 73
(N Bycroft) *bhd: hdwy on inner over 2f out: styd on to take 2nd ins last* — **10/1**

5624 **3** *¾* **Flying Bantam (IRE)**[30] 5313 5-8-7 **67** .... JamieMoriarty(5) 5 — 68
(R A Fahey) *chsd ldrs: one pce fnl 2f* — **8/1**

-002 **4** *¾* **Vanilla Delight (IRE)**[43] 4989 3-9-1 **72** .... RobertWinston 10 — 71
(J Howard Johnson) *chsd ldrs: kpt on same pce fnl 2f* — **13/2**[2]

0410 **5** *4* **Rigat**[44] 4958 3-9-2 **73** .... PhillipMakin 12 — 62
(T D Barron) *chsd ldrs: fdd over 1f out* — **33/1**

2200 **6** *¾* **Angaric (IRE)**[62] 4403 3-8-13 **75** .... MarkLawson(5) 8 — 62
(B Smart) *mid-div: kpt on fnl 2f: nvr nr ldrs* — **11/1**

0003 **7** *3* **John Keats**[4] 5902 3-8-13 **70** .... PaulMulrennan 15 — 49
(I Semple) *mid-div on outer: nt clr run 2f out tl appr fnl f: no threat* — **17/2**

500 **8** *nk* **Fair Shake (IRE)**[57] 4569 6-8-10 **65** ....(v) TonyHamilton 1 — 43
(Karen McLintock) *mid-div on inner: effrt on ins over 2f out: nvr a factor* — **14/1**

6440 **9** *nk* **Cornus**[10] 5765 4-8-11 **69** .... StephenDonohoe(3) 6 — 46
(A J McCabe) *in tch: lost pl 2f out* — **9/2**[1]

3260 **10** *½* **Sentiero Rosso (USA)**[30] 5313 4-8-10 **65** ....(t) LeeEnstone 11 — 41
(B Ellison) *s.s: detached in rr: sme hdwy and swtchd lft over 1f out: nvr on terms* — **10/1**

3523 **11** *1 ½* **Viva Volta**[94] 3395 3-9-1 **72** .... DavidAllan 4 — 44
(T D Easterby) *chsd ldrs: lost pl over 1f out* — **11/1**

412/ **12** *2 ½* **Reyadi (IRE)**[1144] 4496 6-9-5 **74** .... MickyFenton 7 — 40
(T D Easterby) *a in rr* — **33/1**

2200 **13** *5* **Up Tempo (IRE)**[32] 5263 8-8-13 **68** ....(b) TPQueally 2 — 21
(C R Dore) *a towards rr* — **16/1**

0100 **14** *10* **Jordans Elect**[54] 4653 6-8-8 **66** .... GregFairley(3) 3 — —
(T J Pitt) *bhd: detached fnl 2f* — **16/1**

1m 29.42s (2.06) **Going Correction** +0.425s/f (Yiel)
WFA 3 from 4yo+ 2lb — 14 Ran SP% **124.1**
Speed ratings (Par 103):105,98,97,96,91 91,87,87,86,86 84,81,76,64
CSF £83.17 CT £643.57 TOTE £9.60: £2.90, £3.90, £4.00; EX 119.60 Place 6 £526.67, Place 5 £200.77.
Owner Market Avenue Racing Club Ltd **Bred** Eamon D Delany **Trained** Middleham Moor, N Yorks

FOCUS
A fair handicap turned into a procession by the all-the-way winner, who is value for further.
John Keats Official explanation: jockey said gelding was denied a clear run
Sentiero Rosso(USA) Official explanation: jockey said gelding missed the break
T/Plt: £551.60 to a £1 stake. Pool: £60,229.35. 79.70 winning tickets. T/Qpdt: £69.60 to a £1 stake. Pool: £2,681.60. 28.50 winning tickets. JR

5939 NEWMARKET (ROWLEY) (R-H)
Saturday, October 14

OFFICIAL GOING: Good to soft
Wind: Light, against Weather: Sunny spells

5962 VC BET CHALLENGE STKS (GROUP 2) — 7f
2:10 (2:10) (Class 1) 3-Y-O+
£51,102 (£19,368; £9,693; £4,833; £2,421; £1,215) Stalls Low

Form — RPR

2-10 **1** **Sleeping Indian**[14] 5701 5-9-3 113 .... JimmyFortune 11 — 121
(J H M Gosden) *lw: chsd ldr: led over 2f out: drvn out* — **9/2**[1]

4024 **2** *1* **Killybegs (IRE)**[21] 5524 3-9-1 113 .... MichaelHills 3 — 119
(B W Hills) *a.p: rdn to chse wnr and edgd rt over 1f out: styd on* — **7/1**[2]

1231 **3** *hd* **Satchem (IRE)**[14] 5673 4-9-3 112 ....(t) KerrinMcEvoy 8 — 118
(Saeed Bin Suroor) *chsd ldrs: rdn and edgd rt over 1f out: styd on* — **8/1**[3]

4426 **4** *2* **Somnus**[20] 5549 6-9-3 112 .... KDarley 13 — 113
(T D Easterby) *a.p: rdn 1/2-way: styd on same pce fnl f* — **28/1**

0210 **5** *¾* **Silver Touch (IRE)**[14] 5701 3-8-12 107 .... RyanMoore 16 — 108
(M R Channon) *hmpd s: hld up: hdwy over 2f out: rdn over 1f out: no ex fnl f* — **12/1**

3444 **6** *1* **Polar Ben**[18] 5588 7-9-3 109 .... JamieSpencer 14 — 109+
(J R Fanshawe) *hld up: hdwy and n.m.r over 1f out: sn rdn: edgd rt ins fnl f: nt rch ldrs* — **25/1**

\- **7** *2 ½* **Art Museum (USA)**[15] 5663 3-9-1 .... JAHeffernan 10 — 102
(A P O'Brien, Ire) *lw: chsd ldrs: rdn over 2f out: wknd fnl f* — **7/1**[2]

1000 **8** *½* **Quito (IRE)**[1] 5942 9-9-3 114 ....(b) TonyCulhane 15 — 101
(D W Chapman) *wnt rt s: hld up: rdn over 1f out: nvr nrr* — **50/1**

1200 **9** *shd* **Jedburgh**[18] 5588 5-9-3 106 ....(b) SebSanders 6 — 101
(J L Dunlop) *chsd ldrs: rdn over 2f out: wknd fnl f* — **100/1**

0102 **10** *nk* **Welsh Emperor (IRE)**[14] 5701 7-9-7 113 .... DarryllHolland 9 — 104
(T P Tate) *lw: led over 4f: wknd over 1f out* — **22/1**

6052 **11** *4* **Suggestive**[14] 5682 8-9-3 108 ....(b) NickyMackay 2 — 89
(W J Haggas) *chsd ldr: rdn over 2f out: wknd over 1f out* — **66/1**

1162 **12** *1 ¾* **Jeremy (USA)**[56] 4596 3-9-1 112 .... MJKinane 5 — 85
(Sir Michael Stoute) *lw: hld up: rdn and nt clr run over 2f out: hmpd over 1f out: n.d* — **8/1**[3]

1401 **13** *2* **Aeroplane**[38] 5116 3-9-1 105 .... EddieAhern 4 — 80
(P W Chapple-Hyam) *sn chsng ldrs: rdn over 2f out: wknd over 1f out* — **16/1**

2241 **14** *¾* **Stronghold**[18] 5588 4-9-3 115 .... RichardHughes 7 — 78
(J H M Gosden) *mid-div: rdn over 2f out: n.m.r and wknd over 1f out* — **17/2**

3321 **15** *2* **Makderah (IRE)**[20] 5550 3-8-12 104 ....(b1) RHills 1 — 70
(M P Tregoning) *chsd ldrs: ev ch over 2f out: wknd over 1f out* — **14/1**

26-2 **16** *37* **Byron**[18] 5588 5-9-3 111 ....(t) LDettori 12 — —
(Saeed Bin Suroor) *chsd ldrs over 4f: eased* — **8/1**[3]

1m 26.16s (-0.34) **Going Correction** +0.35s/f (Good)
WFA 3 from 4yo+ 2lb — 16 Ran SP% **123.4**
Speed ratings (Par 115):115,113,113,111,110 109,106,105,105,105 100,98,96,95,93 51
CSF £32.95 TOTE £4.90: £2.00, £3.30, £3.10; EX 32.00 Trifecta £211.20 Pool: £1,844.86 - 6.20 winning tickets..
Owner George Strawbridge **Bred** George Strawbridge **Trained** Newmarket, Suffolk

FOCUS
A decent renewal of this Group 2 in which the field split into two groups and those towards the centre of the track held the advantage.

NOTEBOOK
Sleeping Indian, who didn't get a run in the Prix de la Foret last time, gained compensation and in the process improved on his second in this race last year. He will now be retired to stud, and as the winner of six of his 11 races and blessed with a fine pedigree, could prove a useful addition to the British-based stallion ranks. (op 4-1 tchd 7-2 in places)
Killybegs(IRE) has rediscovered his form after appearing to lose his way somewhat in the summer. He stuck to his task well but his older rival was always holding him. He looks more than capable of scoring at Group 2 level next season, when he may be tried at up to 10f.
Satchem(IRE), dropping back in trip and stepping up in grade, ran close to previous form with the winner and helps set a solid standard. His best chance of scoring in this grade may be over a mile. (op 9-1)
Somnus has been around a long time but continues to pay his way in Group company. He helps set a reliable standard for the form. (op 33-1)
Silver Touch(IRE), a Listed winner last month, has faced a couple of stiff tasks since and ran quite well in the circumstances. She may be flattered by this but should continue to hold her own agains her own sex.
Polar Ben, who is considered to be at his best with some cut, did not get the best of runs and ended up racing on the less favoured nearside. In the circumstances this was a fair performance.
Art Museum(USA), unbeaten in three outings, was taking a big step up in grade and got rather isolated between the two groups, seeing too much daylight in the process. He could well prove better than this in time. (op 16-1 after 20-1 in places)
Quito(IRE), having his second outing in successive days, is struggling a little at present but could bounce back at any time.
Welsh Emperor(IRE), under a penalty, finished ahead of the winner in the Foret and tried to set the pace as usual, but was never going that well at the head of affairs. He was below his best and may be feeling the effects of his hard race in France. (op 25-1)
Jeremy(USA), who had a solid chance on previous form, was held up in the stands'-side group but failed to get a clear run when he needed it. He was not knocked about when his chance had gone. (tchd 15-2 and 17-2)
Stronghold Official explanation: jockey said colt was unsuited by the good to soft ground
Byron played up beforehand, showed very little in the race and was eased down a long way from home. Official explanation: jockey said horse lost its action

5963 TOTESPORT CESAREWITCH (HERITAGE H'CAP) — 2m 2f
2:50 (2:56) (Class 2) 3-Y-O+
£93,480 (£27,990; £13,995; £7,005; £3,495; £1,755) Stalls High

Form — RPR

612- **1** **Detroit City (USA)**[191] 3242 4-9-1 **94** ....(b1) JamieSpencer 29 — 105
(P J Hobbs) *chsd ldrs early: sn settled in midfield: rdn and hdwy 3f out: styd on u.p to ld jst ins fnl f: rdn out* — **9/2**[1]

-000 **2** *1* **Inchnadamph**[47] 4883 6-8-3 **82** ....(t) RichardMullen 32 — 92
(T J Fitzgerald) *b. nr hind: hld up in midfield: hdwy gng wl 5f out: chsd ldr and rdn over 2f out: led over 1f out tl ins fnl f: kpt on same pce* — **25/1**

0000 **3** *2* **Dr Sharp (IRE)**[7] 5811 6-8-3 **82** .... AdrianTNicholls 11 — 90
(T P Tate) *lw: sn crossed over to ld: jnd and rdn 3f out: hdd 2f out: kpt on same pce fnl f* — **100/1**

0034 **4** *nk* **Ski Jump (USA)**[7] 5811 6-8-0 **79** ....(v) PaulHanagan 20 — 86
(R A Fahey) *chsd ldrs: rdn 3f out: kpt on u.p ins fnl f: edgd rt last 100 yds* — **25/1**

6423 **5** *¾* **Trance (IRE)**[7] 5811 6-8-1 **80** .... SilvestreDeSousa 21 — 87
(T D Barron) *hld up wl bhd: hdwy 6f out: rdn and outpcd over 4f out: styd on u.p last 2f: edgd rt last 100 yds: nvr nrr* — **25/1**

2140 **6** *hd* **Whispering Death**[14] 5678 4-8-4 **83** ....(v) KerrinMcEvoy 31 — 89
(W J Haggas) *hld up on rail: hdwy 3f out: rdn 2f out: kpt on ins fnl f: nt rch ldrs* — **14/1**

3221 **7** *1 ½* **Theatre (USA)**[21] 5526 7-8-0 **79** 4ex .... FrancisNorton 2 — 84+
(Jamie Poulton) *hld up wl bhd: rdn and struggling 6f out: styd on wl over 1f out: nvr trbld ldrs* — **14/1**

0400 **8** *½* **Odiham**[20] 5548 5-9-1 **94** .... JimmyFortune 13 — 98
(H Morrison) *swtg: hld up bhd: hdwy whn short of room 4f out: styd on fnl f: nvr trbld ldrs* — **40/1**

The Form Book, Raceform Ltd, Compton, RG20 6NL

5356 **9** *shd* **Vinando**[91] 3551 5-9-7 **100**..........(bt) JohnEgan 27 105+
(C R Egerton) *w.w in midfield: hdwy 5f out: rdn 3f out: keeping on same pce whn squeezed out wl ins fnl f* **22/1**

4031 **10** *nk* **Mirjan (IRE)**[47] 4883 10-9-1 **94** 4ex..........(b) JimCrowley 26 98
(L Lungo) *hld up wl bhd: hdwy on rail 4f out: kpt on u.p over 1f out: nvr rchd ldrs* **25/1**

1112 **11** *¾* **Key Time (IRE)**[59] 4469 4-8-9 **88**.......... SebSanders 17 93+
(Sir Mark Prescott) *trckd ldrs gng wl: jnd ldr 3f out: led and rdn 2f out: hdd over 1f out: wkng whn squeezed out wl ins fnl f* **8/1**[2]

1U52 **12** *1 ½* **Lightning Strike (GER)**[21] 5526 3-8-2 **93**.......... JimmyQuinn 24 94
(T G Mills) *lw: hld up in tch: hdwy 5f out: rdn wl over 3f out: wknd over 1f out: btn whn short of room ins fnl f* **12/1**

1/65 **13** *shd* **Saint Alebe**[20] 5551 7-8-13 **92**.......... AntonyProcter 18 93
(D R C Elsworth) *swtg: hld up in midfield: hdwy over 5f out: rdn over 3f out: no hdwy last 2f* **17/2**[3]

2010 **14** *4* **High Point (IRE)**[28] 5383 8-7-7 **77** oh3.......... RobynBrisland(5) 10 74
(G P Enright) *lw: hld up bhd: hdwy on outer 6f out: rdn and outpcd over 4f out: no ch after* **100/1**

/01- **15** *5* **Dont Call Me Derek**[217] 6250 5-8-11 **90**.......... GrahamGibbons 25 81
(J J Quinn) *chsd ldrs on rail: rdn over 2f out: wknd over 1f out: eased* **28/1**

-310 **16** *7* **Monolith**[21] 5533 8-8-6 **85** ow2.......... C-PLemaire 3 69
(L Lungo) *hld up in tch: hdwy to chse ldr 10f out: rdn over 3f out: wknd 2f out* **50/1**

2260 **17** *1 ¼* **Boxhall (IRE)**[28] 5383 4-7-12 **77** oh5..........(t) CatherineGannon 19 59
(W R Swinburn) *t.k.h: chsd ldrs: rdn wl over 3f out: wknd over 2f out* **100/1**

5560 **18** *2 ½* **Madiba**[14] 4996 7-7-13 **78** oh27 ow1.......... FrankieMcDonald 5 57
(P Howling) *swtg: hld up bhd: rdn and effrt over 4f out: sn no ch* **200/1**

4002 **19** *nk* **Ebtikaar (IRE)**[30] 5318 4-9-2 **95**.......... RHills 30 74
(J L Dunlop) *hld up wl bhd: rdn over 5f out: no ch last 3f* **16/1**

1104 **20** *1 ½* **Cold Turkey**[14] 5678 6-9-2 **95**.......... RyanMoore 8 72
(G L Moore) *hld up bhd: stdy prog 7f out: chsng ldrs and rdn over 2f out: sn wknd: eased* **25/1**

0515 **21** *¾* **Lets Roll**[19] 5582 5-8-11 **93** 4ex.......... SaleemGolam(3) 15 70
(C W Thornton) *chsd ldrs: rdn over 4f out: wknd over 3f out: sn bhd* **28/1**

0-00 **22** *1* **Mr Ed (IRE)**[14] 5678 8-8-4 **83**..........(p) ChrisCatlin 28 59
(P Bowen) *hld up wl bhd: hdwy 5f out: rdn over 3f out: no prog* **50/1**

0042 **23** *hd* **Laggan Bay (IRE)**[12] 5723 6-7-7 **77** oh11..........(b) DuranFentiman(5) 23 52
(J S Moore) *in tch tl rdn over 4f out: sn wknd* **100/1**

020 **24** *¾* **Quizzene (USA)**[21] 5533 4-8-2 **81**.......... RoystonFfrench 14 56
(M Johnston) *hld up in tch: rdn and wknd over 3f out: sn no ch* **25/1**

/414 **25** *½* **Full House (IRE)**[84] 2723 7-8-1 **80**.......... NelsonDeSouza 1 54
(P R Webber) *tk v k.h: chsd ldrs tl rdn over 4f out: sn wknd* **50/1**

5530 **26** *9* **Baddam**[13] 5711 4-9-10 **103**.......... IanMongan 4 67
(M R Channon) *hld up wl bhd: rdn over 4f out: sn no ch: eased: t.o* **33/1**

1101 **27** *4* **Finalmente**[91] 3533 4-9-8 **101**.......... LDettori 12 61
(N A Callaghan) *lw: hld up bhd: stdy hdwy 6f out: rdn over 4f out: sn struggling and no ch: eased: t.o* **10/1**

0513 **28** *5* **Sir Monty (USA)**[35] 5180 4-8-0 **79**.......... NickyMackay 16 33
(Mrs A J Perrett) *lw: w.w wl in tch: rdn and lost pl qckly 6f out: no ch last 4f: eased: t.o* **25/1**

0-06 **29** *2* **Contact Dancer (IRE)**[19] 5582 7-8-10 **89**.......... KDarley 7 41
(M Johnston) *a bhd: rdn 8f out: no rspnse: t.o last 4f: eased* **33/1**

0/00 **30** *1 ½* **Barathea Blazer**[7] 5808 7-9-2 **95**.......... MJKinane 22 45
(K McAuliffe) *b: chsd ldrs tl over 5f out: wl bhd last 3f: eased: t.o* **100/1**

4500 **31** *18* **Tarandot (IRE)**[63] 4346 5-8-12 **91**..........(v[1]) EddieAhern 9 22
(G G Margarson) *w.w in tch: rdn over 5f out: sn wknd: t.o and eased last 2f* **50/1**

3m 57.84s (5.22) **Going Correction** +0.35s/f (Good)
WFA 3 from 4yo+ 12lb **31** Ran SP% **135.6**
Speed ratings (Par 109):107,106,105,105,105 105,104,104,104,104 103,103,103,101,99 95,95,94,94,93 93,92,92,92,92 88,8
CSF £122.04 CT £9891.50 TOTE £5.60: £2.20, £7.70, £21.10, £6.30; EX 180.10 Trifecta £19938.70 Part won. Pool: £28,028.72 - 0.30 winning tickets..
Owner Terry Warner **Bred** E J Kelly **Trained** Withycombe, Somerset
■ Jamie Spencer is the first jockey since 1885 to land both legs of the 'Autumn Double'.

FOCUS
A typically competitive renewal of this top staying handicap, although the pace was unexceptional.

NOTEBOOK
Detroit City(USA) ◆, last season's champion juvenile hurder, was well backed ante-post and went off a strong favourite. He had not had an official run since April, but had a warm-up in a charity race so lacked nothing in fitness. After settling off the pace on the inside, he hit a flat spot inside the last half mile and did not have the clearest of runs, but once out he powered through to join the leaders and from that point the result was never in doubt. He did give the runner-up a bump when going past, but it did not affect the result. Clearly still on the upgrade and with few miles on the clock, he will presumably be aimed at the Champion Hurdle, but could prove a force in staying races if returning to the level next summer. (tchd 5-1 and 4-1 in places)
Inchnadamph, third in this last year, had been lightly raced and had shown very little since. However, he had clearly been laid out for this and moved up to the leaders travelling ominously well. However, his rider did not want to go for home too soon and held on to him, only to find the favourite ranging alongside when he did make his effort. Had he gone for home earlier he may have poached sufficient advantage to hold on, but that is merely conjecture. He was racing off the same rating as last season and looks reasonably handicapped, although that is still 8lb above his last winning mark. (op 20-1)
Dr Sharp(IRE) was another who had not shown much this season but looked as if this had been the aim. He ran a fine race from the front and stuck to his task really well when headed by the first two. He is 1lb below his last winning mark and there may be a race for him before the year is out.
Ski Jump(USA) is a reliable sort in this grade and was keeping on steadily in the closing stages. Unfortunately he needs all of this trip and will have very few opportunities to add to his score until next year. (op 40-1)
Trance(IRE) finished ahead of today's third and fourth last time and again ran well, although he appeared to hang fire in the closing stages otherwise he may have finished closer. It may be that he does not truly stay this far, and 14 furlongs on the All-Weather may see him adding to his score.
Whispering Death, who seems at his best on a sound surface, was keeping on really well in the closing stages to finish on the heels of the placed horses. He looks worth aiming at Royal Ascot's and Goodwood's long-distance staying handicaps next season, providing he comes to hand early enough. (op 16-1)
Theatre(USA), carrying a penalty for his win in one of the traditional trials for this at Ascot, was the only runner from a single-figure draw to finish in the first 15, coming from a long way back and was doing his best work late on. He is a pretty good yardstick in this sort of contest, and despite his advancing age, may be able to win one next season. (tchd 16-1 in a place)
Odiham, who did not appear to stay in this race last season when ridden positively, had the headgear left off, was held up at the back this time and got the trip much better, closing on the leaders up the hill. (tchd 50-1)
Vinando, who ran so well in this race last season, did so again and would have been closer but for being the worst sufferer from scrimmaging in the closing stages. He has not won for two years though and could do with some leniency from the Handicapper. (op 25-1)
Mirjan(IRE), seventh in the last two runnings, was another doing his best work when the race was over. (op 20-1)
Key Time(IRE), winner of the Goodwood Stakes over an even longer trip, moved into contention going really well but is best on fast ground and did not get home on the easier surface. He was another who was squeezed out in the closing stages. (op 9-1)
Lightning Strike(GER), who has progressed into a useful stayer this season, appeared to find this trip too far on the ground. He seems most effective around Ascot and looks one to bear in mind for next year's Royal Meeting. (op 16-1 tchd 22-1 in a place)
Saint Alebe, who has shown he retains his ability since returning from over three years off this autumn, raced in about the same position as the first two in the early stages but was unable to pick up as well as that pair. (op 15-2 tchd 9-1 in a place)
Lets Roll Official explanation: trainer said gelding finished distressed

5964 EMIRATES AIRLINE CHAMPION STKS (GROUP 1) 1m 2f
3:30 (3:36) (Class 1) 3-Y-O+

£198,730 (£75,320; £37,695; £18,795; £9,415; £4,725) **Stalls** Low

Form RPR

1132 **1** **Pride (FR)**[13] 5716 6-9-0.......... C-PLemaire 2 123+
(A De Royer-Dupre, France) *lw: hld up in tch: shkn up to ld over 1f out: r.o wl* **7/2**[3]

1636 **2** *3* **Rob Roy (USA)**[48] 4839 4-9-3 114.......... KerrinMcEvoy 4 120
(Sir Michael Stoute) *hld up: hdwy over 1f out: sn rdn: styd on same pce ins fnl f* **20/1**

2124 **3** *hd* **Hurricane Run (IRE)**[13] 5716 4-9-3.......... MJKinane 6 120
(A Fabre, France) *lw: led over 6f: sn rdn: ev ch over 1f out: styd on same pce* **9/4**[1]

3035 **4** *1 ½* **Olympian Odyssey**[14] 5673 3-8-12 113.......... JamieSpencer 5 117
(B W Hills) *hld up: swtchd lft and hdwy over 1f out: no ex ins fnl f* **33/1**

2615 **5** *2 ½* **Confidential Lady**[90] 3575 3-8-9 113.......... SebSanders 8 109
(Sir Mark Prescott) *chsd ldrs: rdn over 2f out: wkng whn edgd lft fnl f* **14/1**

1152 **6** *shd* **Maraahel (IRE)**[53] 4679 5-9-3 121..........(v) RHills 7 112
(Sir Michael Stoute) *lw: dwlt: sn chsng ldrs: rdn over 2f out: wknd fnl f* **11/1**

1-21 **7** *½* **Sir Percy**[133] 2228 3-8-12 121.......... MartinDwyer 1 111
(M P Tregoning) *swtg: chsd ldrs: rdn and ev ch over 2f out: edgd lft over 1f out : wknd fnl f* **11/4**[2]

1521 **8** *1 ¾* **Notnowcato**[53] 4679 4-9-3 122.......... RyanMoore 3 108
(Sir Michael Stoute) *b: w ldr tl led over 3f out: rdn and hdd over 1f out: wknd fnl f* **7/1**

2m 6.81s (1.10) **Going Correction** +0.35s/f (Good)
WFA 3 from 4yo+ 5lb **8** Ran SP% **114.9**
Speed ratings (Par 117):109,106,106,105,103 103,102,101
CSF £67.69 TOTE £3.90: £1.10, £6.00, £1.10; EX 114.10 Trifecta £246.20 Pool: £2,538.83 - 7.32 winning tickets..
Owner N P Bloodstock **Bred** N P Bloodstock Ltd **Trained** Chantilly, France
■ Pride is the oldest winner of the Champion Stakes since seven-year-old Bendigo in 1887.

FOCUS
On paper a quality renewal of this contest, despite a few notable absentees, but the the time was modest for the grade and the form does not appear as strong as it could have been, with the Derby winner and the International principals all well below their best. The race has been rated around the fourth.

NOTEBOOK
Pride(FR), runner-up in this last year and a slightly unlucky second in the Arc last time out, was ridden a bit handier this time. Everything fell right and she scooted up the hill for a decisive victory. Having beaten Hurricane Run on two of the three occasions they have met this season she can be rated the best mare in Europe, and she may attempt to end her career in a blaze of glory by winning the Hong Kong Cup, a race in which she was runner-up last season. (tchd 4-1 and 100-30 in places)
Rob Roy(USA), who ran disappointingly in this race last season, fared much better this time. He has yet to prove he is truly Group 1 class, but he seems to be maturing and may finally live up to expectations if kept in training next year. (op 25-1)
Hurricane Run(IRE), who looked unlucky when fourth in the Arc, had to make the running on this drop in trip and hit a flat spot when the pace quickened. He did well to stay on again and finish in the frame, but is really a mile and a half horse and could well end his career with a win if turning up in the Breeders' Cup Turf or the Japan Cup. (op 3-1 tchd 100-30 in places)
Olympian Odyssey bounced back from a disappointing effort last time with different tactics employed. This was more like his 2000 Guineas form and he could well make up into a very useful four-year-old. (op 40-1)
Confidential Lady, having her first outing since the Irish Oaks, travelled well enough but could not find the extra gear in the closing stages. Connections may be looking at a Group 1 abroad for her, something like the Premio Roma, before the end of the year. (op 12-1)
Maraahel(IRE), third in this last year, never really got in a blow this time and may have been another suited by a stronger gallop. He has yet to win at this level. (op 14-1)
Sir Percy, having his first outing since winning the Derby in June, raced up with the pace but when the race began in earnest had nothing more to give. He will be kept in training having had his problems this season, but has to prove himself again after this below-par effort. Official explanation: jockey said colt had no more to give (tchd 3-1 and 100-30 in places)
Notnowcato, who has progressed into a Group 1 performer this season, travelled well up with the pace and was the first to kick for home. However, when challenged he dropped away tamely and something may have been amiss. In any case, along with his stable companion Maraahel, he does not do much for the Juddmonte International form. (op 6-1 tchd 15-2)

5965 DARLEY DEWHURST STKS (GROUP 1) (ENTIRE COLTS & FILLIES) 7f
4:10 (4:11) (Class 1) 2-Y-O

£141,950 (£53,800; £26,925; £13,425; £6,725; £3,375) **Stalls** Low

Form RPR

111 **1** **Teofilo (IRE)**[27] 5410 2-9-1.......... KJManning 4 124+
(J S Bolger, Ire) *gd sort: s.i.s: hdwy over 5f out: rdn to ld over 1f out: edgd rt and hdd wl ins fnl f: rallied to ld nr fin* **11/8**[1]

1121 **2** *hd* **Holy Roman Emperor (IRE)**[13] 5715 2-9-1.......... MJKinane 9 124+
(A P O'Brien, Ire) *lw: wnt rt s: hld up: hdwy and nt clr run over 1f out: swtchd rt: rdn to ld and bmpd wl ins fnl f: hdd nr fin* **3/1**[2]

1511 **3** *2 ½* **Strategic Prince**[73] 4037 2-9-1 114.......... EddieAhern 5 117
(P F I Cole) *h.d.w: trckd ldrs: rdn and ev ch over 1f out: styd on same pce ins fnl f* **9/1**[3]

4 *nk* **Haatef (USA)**[48] 4856 2-9-1.......... DPMcDonogh 7 116+
(Kevin Prendergast, Ire) *hld up: hdwy over 2f out: hmpd 1f out: styd on same pce* **22/1**

1113 **5** *hd* **Vital Equine (IRE)**[13] 5715 2-9-1 113..........(t) RichardMullen 3 115
(E J O'Neill) *lw: plld hrd: w ldr: led 1/2-way: rdn and hdd over 1f out: styd on same pce ins fnl f* **20/1**

141 **6** *1* **Rallying Cry (USA)**[14] 5665 2-9-1 .... JimmyFortune 1 113
(J H M Gosden) *chsd ldrs: ev ch over 1f out: sn rdn: styd on same pce*
40/1

1 **7** *nk* **Adagio**[25] 5458 2-9-1 .... KerrinMcEvoy 11 112
(Sir Michael Stoute) *s.i.s: hld up: hdwy over 1f out: no imp fnl f* **25/1**

1204 **8** *3 ½* **He's A Decoy (IRE)**[13] 5715 2-9-1 .... RyanMoore 8 103
(David Wachman, Ire) *gd sort: mid-div: rdn 1/2-way: wknd over 1f out*
40/1

11 **9** *2 ½* **Traffic Guard (USA)**[25] 5455 2-9-1 99 .... JohnEgan 10 96
(J S Moore) *s.i.s: hld up: rdn over 2f out: wknd over 1f out* **40/1**

0131 **10** *shd* **Dubai Builder**[17] 5626 2-9-1 104 .... MartinDwyer 2 96
(J S Moore) *h.d.w: hld up: rdn and wknd over 1f out* **100/1**

213 **11** *shd* **Prime Defender**[51] 4736 2-9-1 106 .... MichaelHills 13 96
(B W Hills) *hld up: hdwy over 2f out: rdn and wknd over 1f out* **20/1**

6 **12** *1 ¾* **Mount Parnassus**[15] 5658 2-9-1 .... JAHeffernan 12 91
(A P O'Brien, Ire) *lw: chsd ldrs over 5f* **200/1**

11 **13** *nk* **Hamoody (USA)**[71] 4099 2-9-1 .... LDettori 6 90
(P W Chapple-Hyam) *lw: hld up: hdwy and nt clr run over 1f out: sn hung rt and wknd* **9/1**[3]

11 **14** *2 ½* **Halicarnassus (IRE)**[92] 3492 2-9-1 .... TonyCulhane 15 84
(M R Channon) *lw: prom: rdn 1/2-way: wknd over 1f out* **20/1**

15 *3* **Naigani (USA)**[14] 5694 2-9-1 .... DavidMcCabe 14 76
(A P O'Brien, Ire) *w'like: leggy: led to 1/2-way: wknd over 2f out* **200/1**

1m 26.12s (-0.38) **Going Correction** +0.35s/f (Good) **15** Ran SP% **118.9**
Speed ratings (Par 109):116,115,112,112,112 111,110,106,104,103 103,101,101,98,95
CSF £4.17 TOTE £2.20: £1.10, £1.70, £3.20; EX 6.00 Trifecta £35.40 Pool: £1,815.16 - 36.33 winning tickets..

Owner Mrs J S Bolger **Bred** J S Bolger **Trained** Coolcullen, Co Carlow

■ Stewards' Enquiry : K J Manning one-day ban: used whip with excessive frequency (Oct 25)

FOCUS

A cracking renewal of what is traditionally the top juvenile race, and it was run in an exceptional time - faster than the older horses in the opening race. The form looks outstanding, with the first two clear and the third and fifth already good Group 2 winners, and the RPR of 124 awarded to the two principals has been bettered in recent seasons only by this race's 2004 winner Shamardal.

NOTEBOOK

Teofilo(IRE) ◆ retained his unbeaten record with his second successive defeat of the runner-up, but it was much closer than in the National Stakes and he had to pull out all the stops once headed. He is very good and also proved his gameness, and with more physical scope than his main rival could well justify what on the face of it look ludicrously short prices for next season's Classics. (op 13-8 tchd 7-4 and 15-8 in a place)

Holy Roman Emperor(IRE) ◆ has proved himself a top juvenile this season, winning twice at Group 1 level, and on this occasion can be considered unlucky. Settled after running free early on, he was carried back and had to switch a couple of times before getting a run. He showed really good acceleration to get to the front but then flattened out and could not quite resist the renewed effort of the winner. Connections will consider they have every right to gain revenge next season, but he has had a hard campaign and does not have the physical scope of the winner, so there is a possibility he may not train on quite as well. (op 9-4 tchd 2-1 and 100-30 in a place)

Strategic Prince, the winner of Group 2s at six and seven furlongs, travelled really well on this step up in grade but was left behind by the principals in the last furlong. He is a very useful colt in his own right, and helps set a very strong standard for the form. He is bred to get at least a mile and deserves to be trained for the Guineas, although he has a fair amount of improvement to find to trouble the principals here. (op 10-1 tchd 12-1)

Haatef(USA) ◆, a speedily-bred colt stepping up in trip, ran a fine race against more experienced rivals. He looks a decent prospect for next season, although there must be doubts about him getting the Guineas mile, and he may well turn out to be best at sprint trips. (op 33-1)

Vital Equine(IRE) is another decent guide to the form, having won the Champagne Stakes before finishing third to Holy Roman Emperor in the Prix Jean Luc Lagardere. He ran a fine race from the front and was only seen off on the climb to the line. However, he is just below the very best and connections may well have to look to the continent for his best chance of picking up a Classic next season.

Rallying Cry(USA) has been held on both attempts in Group company but that is not to take anything away from a solid performance. Being American-bred and having already won on sand, he could be the ideal sort for Godolphin to take over and aim at the American Triple Crown next season.

Adagio ◆, who was green when scoring on his debut less than a month ago, ran well considering his inexperience and the slow start he made. His dam improved hand over fist at three and it would be no surprise to see him do the same once he steps up to middle distances.

He's A Decoy(IRE), who finished fourth to the runner-up in France last time, did not run as well but his form suggests he is not as effective on a soft surface as he is on fast ground. (op 33-1)

Hamoody(USA), held up on this step up in trip and on softer ground, got carried back with the runner-up and then failed to get a clear run. He can be forgiven this effort. (op 11-1)

Halicarnassus(IRE) lost his unbeaten record and was well below form, but he had been off the course since July and there is every likelihood the ground was against him.

5966 "IN THE PINK" ROCKFEL STKS (SPONSORED BY OWEN BROWN) (GROUP 2) (FILLIES) 7f

4:45 (4:46) (Class 1) 2-Y-O

£39,746 (£15,064; £7,539; £3,759; £1,883; £945) **Stalls** Low

Form RPR

61 **1** **Finsceal Beo (IRE)**[13] 5714 2-9-2 .... KJManning 1 120+
(J S Bolger, Ire) *nice filly: chsd ldrs: led over 1f out: r.o wl* **9/4**[1]

21 **2** *3* **Rahiyah (USA)**[56] 4588 2-8-12 .... LDettori 14 108
(J Noseda) *lw: hld up: hdwy over 2f out: rdn to chse wnr fnl f: styd on same pce* **7/1**[3]

12 **3** *3 ½* **Puggy (IRE)**[14] 5672 2-8-12 97 .... (t) FJohansson 9 99
(R A Kvisla) *hld up: hdwy over 1f out: sn hung lft: nt rch ldrs* **25/1**

1 **4** *nk* **Shorthand**[18] 5595 2-8-12 .... KerrinMcEvoy 7 98
(Sir Michael Stoute) *led 5f: sn rdn: wknd ins fnl f* **8/1**

1123 **5** *1* **English Ballet (IRE)**[21] 5522 2-8-12 108 .... MichaelHills 8 96
(B W Hills) *chsd ldr: led 2f out: rdn and hdd over 1f out: wknd ins fnl f*
4/1[2]

2512 **6** *1 ¼* **Dhanyata (IRE)**[15] 5654 2-8-12 112 .... JimmyFortune 10 92
(B J Meehan) *plld hrd and prom: rdn and wknd over 1f out* **7/1**[3]

1 **7** *shd* **Kaseema (USA)**[31] 5296 2-8-12 .... MartinDwyer 13 92
(Sir Michael Stoute) *h.d.w: s.i.s: hld up: hdwy over 1f out: nt clr run ins fnl f: n.d* **12/1**

14 **8** *2 ½* **Passified**[15] 5655 2-8-12 82 .... JohnEgan 11 86
(D R C Elsworth) *hld up in tch: rdn over 2f out: wknd over 1f out* **25/1**

30 **9** *shd* **Impetious**[13] 5714 2-8-12 .... DPMcDonogh 2 85
(Eamon Tyrrell, Ire) *neat: unruly in stalls: s.i.s: hld up: hdwy 1/2-way: rdn over 2f out: wknd over 1f out* **66/1**

10 *nk* **Queen Of France (USA)**[15] 5661 2-8-12 .... WMLordan 5 85
(David Wachman, Ire) *gd sort: hld up in tch: nt clr run and lost pl 2f out: n.d after* **16/1**

115 **11** *½* **Sudoor**[35] 5187 2-8-12 102 .... RHills 3 83
(J L Dunlop) *hld up: nt clr run 1/2-way: effrt over 2f out: wknd over 1f out*
18/1

2 **12** *1 ¾* **Awwal Malika (USA)**[16] 5638 2-8-12 .... RyanMoore 12 79
(C E Brittain) *lw: chsd ldrs over 5f* **66/1**

4201 **13** *5* **Onida (IRE)**[11] 5760 2-8-12 87 .... MJKinane 6 66
(C G Cox) *chsd ldrs over 5f* **50/1**

01 **14** *4* **Fontana Amorosa**[148] 1824 2-8-12 79 .... KDarley 4 55
(K A Ryan) *chsd ldrs 5f* **33/1**

1m 27.12s (0.62) **Going Correction** +0.35s/f (Good) **14** Ran SP% **121.3**
Speed ratings (Par 104):110,106,102,102,101 99,99,96,96,96 95,93,87,83
CSF £17.24 TOTE £3.30: £1.30, £2.50, £4.40; EX 17.70.

Owner M A Ryan **Bred** Rathbarry Stud **Trained** Coolcullen, Co Carlow

FOCUS

This event has become one of the strongest trials for the year's fillies' Classics and could well be so again. The winner was impressive again and the time, although a second slower than the colts in the preceding race, was very good for the grade. It was an exceptional performance from Finsceal Beo to give weight and a thrashing to a decent field, and her RPR of 120 is superior to that achieved by recent high the best recent European filly Six Perfections (118), and also to Attraction, Divine Proportions and Russian Rhythm, who were all rated 117 at the same stage.

NOTEBOOK

Finsceal Beo(IRE) ◆ has improved considerably of late and proved her Prix Marcel Boussac romp was no fluke, coming right away under her penalty and completing a memorable double for trainer and jockey. She has every right to be favourite for next year's Guineas on this showing, having deposed Sander Camillo at the head of many lists, and it will take a good one to beat her. (tchd 11-4 and 2-1 in places)

Rahiyah(USA) ◆, stepping up in trip and grade, came through to chase home the winner and drew well clear of the rest in the process. Her granddam won the Coronation Stakes and this filly looks the sort who could make her mark in Group company over a mile next season. She will also give her trainer a good line as to how the winner compares with his other good fillies Sander Camillo and Simply Perfect. (op 11-2 tchd 5-1 and 8-1 in a place)

Puggy(IRE) is a likeable sort and ran well again, if only staying on past beaten rivals to reach her final position. She looks well up to winning in Pattern company, but connections will probably have to look abroad if they are thinking in terms of Classics next season.

Shorthand ◆, a sister to Musidora winner Short Skirt and a number of other useful sorts, followed up her good debut with another fine run for one so inexperienced. She will appreciate further next season and has every chance of emulating her sister before going on to run in the Oaks. (op 9-1 tchd 15-2 and 10-1 in places)

English Ballet(IRE) has some pretty solid Group form to her name and ran her race. She is a good guide to the abilities of another Noseda filly, Simply Perfect, who beat her in the May Hill and Fillies' Mile. (op 6-1)

Dhanyata(IRE) represents the Cheveley Park form, but did not help her chance by failing to settle in the early stages on this step up in trip. (op 8-1)

Kaseema(USA) ◆, who cost $1.1m, was slowly away when winning her maiden and did the same again. She ran with credit thereafter and did not get the clearest of passages, so can be expected to improve a good deal with this experience behind her. (tchd 11-1)

Passified was far too keen for her own good in the early stages and did well to finish where she did.

5967 DAVID WILSON HOMES JOCKEY CLUB CUP (GROUP 3) 2m

5:20 (5:22) (Class 1) 3-Y-O+

£28,390 (£10,760; £5,385; £2,685; £1,345; £675) **Stalls** High

Form RPR

0511 **1** **Hawridge Prince**[20] 5551 6-9-0 109 .... JimCrowley 3 112+
(B R Millman) *s.s: hld up: hdwy 5f out: led and hung rt over 1f out: styd on wl* **6/5**[1]

3044 **2** *6* **Bulwark (IRE)**[20] 5551 4-9-0 101 .... (be) RyanMoore 2 105
(Mrs A J Perrett) *lw: hld up: hdwy over 3f out: hung lft and ev ch whn bmpd over 1f out: sn rdn: nt run on* **9/1**

1020 **3** *shd* **Balkan Knight**[72] 4081 6-9-0 108 .... JohnEgan 1 105
(D R C Elsworth) *b. hind: hld up: hdwy 5f out: rdn 2f out: styd on same pce* **11/2**[3]

1222 **4** *¾* **Zurbaran (IRE)**[16] 5641 3-8-3 103 .... JoeFanning 7 104
(B J Meehan) *chsd ldr tl led 3f out: sn hung lft: rdn and hdd over 1f out: wknd ins fnl f* **4/1**[2]

-200 **5** *14* **Franklins Gardens**[20] 5551 6-9-0 107 .... RHills 6 87
(M H Tompkins) *led: hdd 3f out: sn wknd* **13/2**

60-6 **6** *23* **Midas Way**[20] 5551 6-9-0 100 .... MartinDwyer 4 60
(P R Chamings) *lw: chsd ldrs: racd keenly: wknd over 2f out* **33/1**

3-04 **7** *2 ½* **Kasthari (IRE)**[36] 5156 7-9-0 106 .... DarryllHolland 5 57
(J Howard Johnson) *racd alone 6f: prom: rdn 6f out: wknd over 3f out*
16/1

3m 31.21s (4.29) **Going Correction** +0.35s/f (Good)
WFA 3 from 4yo+ 11lb **7** Ran SP% **113.0**
Speed ratings (Par 113):103,100,99,99,92 81,79
CSF £12.89 TOTE £1.90: £1.40, £4.30; EX 16.40.

Owner Eric Gadsden **Bred** Downclose Stud **Trained** Kentisbeare, Devon

FOCUS

An ordinary renewal run at a modest gallop, and Hawridge Prince didn't need to improve to win impressively.

NOTEBOOK

Hawridge Prince ◆ has really found his metier since upped to two miles and completed the hat-trick in runaway fashion, despite hanging right. His form ties in quite well with the Cesarewitch run earlier in the afternoon and he confirmed recent Ascot form with the runner-up. With this Group 3 under his belt connections can think about the Cup races next season, although it remains to be seen if he gets any further than this and he has yet to prove as effective on fast ground. (op 11-10, tchd 5-4 in places and evens in places)

Bulwark(IRE), a quirky character but with plenty of ability, again looked a difficult ride but was the only one to give the winner any sort of race. The pair ran pretty close to their Ascot form, from which the runner-up has since beaten last year's St Leger winner in Ireland, so it looks reasonably solid. Bulwark,though, is not one to trust. (tchd 17-2)

Balkan Knight continues to run well and showed he stays this trip with a running-on third. he looks capable of winning a Listed race, and seems most effective at around 14 furlongs. (op 6-1 tchd 13-2)

Zurbaran(IRE) is a decent young stayer who has made the step into Pattern company of late, but this longer trip on softer ground seemed to find him out. He has time on his side however, and may be able to get home on a sounder surface. (op 6-1)

Franklins Gardens set the pace, but was in trouble as soon as the principals made their moves. (op 15-2, tchd 8-1 in places)

5968 **UNICORN ASSET MANAGEMENT DARLEY STKS (GROUP 3)** **1m 1f**
5:55 (5:55) (Class 1) 3-Y-O+
£28,390 (£10,760; £5,385; £2,685; £1,345; £675) **Stalls** Low

Form RPR
1102 **1** **Stage Gift (IRE)**[35] [5186] 3-8-13 109 .... RyanMoore 5 115+
(Sir Michael Stoute) *trckd ldrs: rdn and hdwy over 2f out: hrd rdn to chse ldr wl over 1f out: led last 50 yds: all out* **11/4**[2]
2214 **2** *hd* **Windsor Knot (IRE)**[49] [4817] 4-9-3 106 .... EddieAhern 1 115
(Saeed Bin Suroor) *lw: chsd ldr tl led after 2f: rdn wl 1f out: kpt on wl tl hdd and no ex last 50 yds* **10/1**
1620 **3** *3* **Bahia Breeze**[35] [5191] 4-9-0 106 .... DarryllHolland 2 106
(Rae Guest) *trckd ldrs: rdn over 2f out: outpcd by ldng pair fnl f* **25/1**
1513 **4** *1 1/4* **Mashaahed**[15] [5657] 3-8-13 110 .... RHills 4 107
(B W Hills) *hld up in midfield: hdwy over 2f out: rdn and no prog over 1f out* **11/2**[3]
6003 **5** *3/4* **Snoqualmie Boy**[28] [5376] 3-8-13 110 .... JohnEgan 8 105
(D R C Elsworth) *hld up in rr: n.m.r over 2f out: sn rdn: kpt on but nvr pce to rch ldrs* **33/1**
0064 **6** *1 1/4* **Babodana**[14] [5673] 6-9-3 107 .... MichaelHills 7 103
(M H Tompkins) *hld up in rr: effrt and rdn 2f out: kpt on same pce* **33/1**
054 **7** *nk* **Tau Ceti**[49] [4818] 7-9-3 105 .... SebSanders 3 102
(R M Beckett) *lw: hld up in rr: rdn and effrt wl over 1f out: nvr trbld ldrs* **33/1**
6156 **8** *5* **Weightless**[99] [3254] 6-9-3 105 .... JimCrowley 9 92
(Mrs A J Perrett) *lw: led for 2f: chsd ldr: rdn over 2f out: wknd wl over 1f out* **100/1**
0003 **9** *8* **Championship Point (IRE)**[24] [5477] 3-8-13 109 .... MartinDwyer 10 76
(M R Channon) *chsd ldrs: rdn over 3f out: wknd over 2f out: eased fnl f* **16/1**
0234 **10** *1 3/4* **Musicanna**[14] [5674] 5-9-0 109 .... (t) JamieSpencer 6 69
(J R Fanshawe) *lw: hld up in midfield: hdwy over 2f out: ev ch u.p 2f out: sn wknd: eased ins fnl f* **12/1**
10-2 **11** *4* **Pinson (IRE)**[14] [5673] 4-9-3 118 .... LDettori 12 64
(Saeed Bin Suroor) *stdd s: hld up in rr: hdwy on outer over 2f out: sn hung rt and btn: eased fnl f* **6/4**[1]
0403 **12** *2 1/2* **St Andrews (IRE)**[6] [5845] 6-9-3 100 .... (p) JimmyFortune 11 59
(M A Jarvis) *hld up in midfield: rdn 3f out: sn struggling: no ch and eased fnl f* **50/1**

1m 53.69s (1.74) **Going Correction** +0.35s/f (Good)
WFA 3 from 4yo+ 4lb 12 Ran SP% **120.3**
Speed ratings (Par 113):106,105,103,102,101 100,100,95,88,86 83,81
CSF £28.92 TOTE £4.00: £1.70, £3.80, £4.90; EX 54.50 Place 6 £37.70, Place 5 £14.70.
Owner Ballymacoll Stud **Bred** Ballymacoll Stud Farm Ltd **Trained** Newmarket, Suffolk

FOCUS
A solid renewal of this Group 3 in which the first two came clear.

NOTEBOOK
Stage Gift(IRE) ◆ stays further than this and showed he could handle the ground with a battling victory, just getting the better of the persistent runner-up to gain his first Group win. He is from a good family and it would be no surprise if he improved considerably from three to four, especially in the hands of a trainer who has done so well with similar types. (tchd 3-1 in places and 5-2 in places)
Windsor Knot(IRE) ◆, another who stays further, has gone close several times in Listed company since returning from a series of problems and fully deserves to win a Pattern race on this showing. Setting the pace, he refused to give in when tackled and galloped on gamely to the line. He handles any ground so connections may look for another opportunity for him before the end of the season. (tchd 11-1 in places)
Bahia Breeze is running well at present and this softer ground appeared to suit, as she was close to the pace throughout and then stuck on despite being no match for the principals. She may be off to the paddocks now but this dual Listed winner takes with her a decent c.v. (op 33-1)
Mashaahed, who was stepped up to a mile and a half last time, was dropped back three furlongs and ran a reasonable race without having the pace to trouble the principals. He may come into his own over further next season. (op 8-1 tchd 9-1)
Snoqualmie Boy came from some way off the pace and never landed a blow, but he did not get the clearest of runs. He should get further and seems to prefer a sounder surface. (tchd 28-1)
Babodana continues to run well and helps set the level for the form. (op 40-1)
Tau Ceti, a surprise winner of a Listed race here last autumn, has not won since despite some fair efforts, and no doubt connections will be aiming at the same race again at the last meeting of the season. (op 40-1)
Musicanna Official explanation: jockey said mare ran flat
Pinson(IRE), who ran so well against his stable companion at the last meeting after an absence, wandered around when asked for his effort and ended up racing wide of the others in the middle of the track. This was a disappointing effort, as he is clearly better than this. He may have 'bounced'. Official explanation: jockey said colt hung right throughout (op 7-4 tchd 11-8 in places)
T/Jkpt: £273.20 to a £1 stake. Pool: £32,323.00. 84.00 winning tickets. T/Plt: £27.10 to a £1 stake. Pool: £205,352.00. 5,530.55 winning tickets. T/Qpdt: £4.40 to a £1 stake. Pool: £7,335.20. 1,214.20 winning tickets. CR

5873 WOLVERHAMPTON (A.W) (L-H)
Saturday, October 14

OFFICIAL GOING: Standard changing to standard to fast after race 2 (7.30pm)
Wind: Almost nil

5969 **HOLIDAY INN DUNSTALL PARK MAIDEN STKS** **5f 20y(P)**
7:00 (7:00) (Class 5) 3-Y-O+ **£3,238** (£963; £481; £240) **Stalls** Low

Form RPR
6 **1** **Fastrac Boy**[94] [3406] 3-9-3 .... GeorgeBaker 5 60+
(J R Best) *sn led: rdn whn hung rt appr fnl f: r.o to hold on nr fin* **9/1**
600 **2** *hd* **Tajjree**[94] [3406] 3-8-12 48 .... (tp) AdamKirby 8 54
(Miss K B Boutflower) *hld up in mid-div: hdwy over 1f out: r.o fnl f to press wnr to line* **50/1**
0023 **3** *nk* **Ceredig**[5] [5874] 3-9-3 60 .... (t) SteveDrowne 10 58
(W R Muir) *chsd ldrs: rdn 2f out: r.o wl fnl f* **7/2**[2]
-002 **4** *3/4* **Benny The Bus**[12] [5737] 4-9-3 65 .... GrahamGibbons 13 55
(Mrs G S Rees) *chsd ldrs: rdn 2f out: kpt on wl fnl f* **11/8**[1]
00-0 **5** *2* **Bond Puccini**[6] [5834] 4-8-12 48 .... DuranFentiman(5) 4 48
(G R Oldroyd) *mid-div: rdn 1/2-way: kpt on but nvr threatened ldrs* **50/1**
0000 **6** *hd* **Height Of Esteem**[5] [5865] 3-9-3 45 .... (p) JimmyQuinn 1 47
(M Mullineaux) *slowly away: in rr: sme prog fnl f* **40/1**
0020 **7** *1/2* **Desert Dust**[6] [5834] 3-9-3 53 .... (v[1]) BrettDoyle 7 46
(R M H Cowell) *slowly away: in rr tl sme late hdwy* **22/1**
3500 **8** *nk* **All Clued Up (IRE)**[56] [4611] 3-8-12 48 .... ChrisCatlin 3 39
(Rae Guest) *chsd ldrs tl rdn and weaken ed wl over 1f out* **25/1**
0006 **9** *2* **Batchworth Blaise**[12] [5729] 3-9-3 45 .... (b) PaulFitzsimons 11 37
(E A Wheeler) *a towards rr* **50/1**
0400 **10** *3/4* **Precautionary**[32] [5273] 3-8-9 47 .... (b[1]) DeanCorby(3) 9 30
(Miss J Feilden) *a towards rr* **33/1**
4-65 **11** *3/4* **Targer Place**[40] [5060] 3-9-3 60 .... DaleGibson 12 32
(T T Clement) *a struggling in rr* **9/1**
2200 **12** *1* **Weakest Link**[24] [5486] 5-9-3 47 .... (p) PaulQuinn 2 28
(E J Alston) *broke wl: sn hdd and dropped rr* **8/1**[3]
00 **13** *2 1/2* **Petite Boulangere (IRE)**[73] [4045] 3-8-12 .... PatDobbs 6 14
(S Kirk) *w wnr: hung rt 3f out and sn dropped rr* **66/1**

61.79 secs (-1.03) **Going Correction** -0.25s/f (Stan) 13 Ran SP% **116.4**
Speed ratings (Par 103):98,97,97,96,92 92,91,91,88,86 85,84,80
CSF £390.73 TOTE £6.90: £2.70, £17.10, £1.20; EX 374.30.
Owner P O'Connell **Bred** Matches Syndicate **Trained** Hucking, Kent
■ Stewards' Enquiry : Paul Fitzsimons caution: used whip down the shoulder in the forehand position

FOCUS
A weak maiden limited by the proximity of the runner-up, fifth and sixth.
Targer Place Official explanation: vet said gelding pulled up lame
Petite Boulangere(IRE) Official explanation: jockey said filly hung badly right-handed

5970 **CORPORATE HOSPITALITY AT DUNSTALL PARK CLAIMING STKS** **5f 20y(P)**
7:30 (7:30) (Class 6) 3-Y-O+ **£2,730** (£806; £403) **Stalls** Low

Form RPR
0200 **1** **Howards Princess**[17] [5620] 4-8-2 57 .... (v[1]) PaulHanagan 1 60
(I Semple) *s.i.s: in rr tl hdwy and n.m.r wl over 1f out: r.o u.p to ld wl ins fnl f* **8/1**
0031 **2** *1 1/4* **Special Gold**[17] [5620] 4-8-11 56 .... (b) GrahamGibbons 5 65
(T D Easterby) *chsd ldrs: rdn to ld ent fnl f: kpt on but nt qckn and hdd wl ins* **6/1**[3]
3500 **3** *1* **Diamond Josh**[25] [5453] 4-7-12 52 .... MCGeran(7) 10 55
(P D Evans) *chsd ldr: rdn and kpt on one pce fnl f* **20/1**
0531 **4** *1 1/2* **City For Conquest (IRE)**[33] [5250] 3-8-10 71 .... (v) FrancisNorton 11 55
(K R Burke) *slowly away and swtchd lft sn after s: hdwy over 1f out: r.o: nvr nrr* **9/4**[1]
6500 **5** *hd* **Johnston's Diamond (IRE)**[19] [5578] 8-9-5 68 .... JimmyQuinn 6 63
(E J Alston) *bhd tl hdwy 2f out: rdn and one pce fnl f* **6/1**[3]
2060 **6** *1/2* **Sounds Simla (IRE)**[24] [5480] 3-8-3 54 .... (p) TolleyDean(7) 9 52
(R A Harris) *mid-div: rdn over 1f out and one pce after* **50/1**
4500 **7** *hd* **Blue Knight (IRE)**[5] [5878] 7-8-11 60 .... (vt) DanielTudhope 2 52
(D Carroll) *mid-div: rdn over 3f out: one pce ins fnl 2f* **10/1**
4520 **8** *shd* **Mystic Queen (IRE)**[17] [5620] 3-8-10 53 .... DaneO'Neill 7 51
(A P Jarvis) *towards rr: effrt over 1f out but nvr on terms* **33/1**
5323 **9** *3/4* **Our Little Secret (IRE)**[14] [5684] 4-9-0 67 .... FergusSweeney 8 52
(A Berry) *led tl rdn and hdd ent fnl f: wknd ins* **7/2**[2]
0646 **10** *nk* **Dutch Key Card (IRE)**[32] [5274] 5-8-11 55 .... (v) RobbieFitzpatrick 13 48
(C Smith) *trckd ldr: rdn 2f out: wknd over 1f out* **40/1**
0/00 **11** *6* **Spliff**[117] [2711] 5-9-1 72 .... SteveDrowne 12 31
(M S Saunders) *a struggling in rr* **33/1**
0 **12** *nk* **Broadfield Lady (IRE)**[19] [5576] 6-8-3 55 .... SCreighton(7) 4 24
(E J Creighton) *slowly away: a bhd* **80/1**

61.57 secs (-1.25) **Going Correction** -0.25s/f (Stan) 12 Ran SP% **118.0**
Speed ratings (Par 101):100,98,96,94,93 92,92,91,90 81,80
CSF £51.84 TOTE £8.60: £2.20, £2.60, £5.00; EX 62.40.Wnr clmd K. C. West £6,000.
Owner Gordon McDowall **Bred** New Hall Stud **Trained** Carluke, S Lanarks

FOCUS
A fair claimer and quite a competitive event, although the form horses were not at their best. The second and sixth limit the form.

5971 **CHRISTMAS PARTIES AT DUNSTALL PARK H'CAP** **2m 119y(P)**
8:00 (8:00) (Class 6) (0-65,65) 3-Y-O+ **£2,730** (£806; £403) **Stalls** Low

Form RPR
1320 **1** **Rehearsed (IRE)**[30] [5324] 3-9-3 **63** .... SteveDrowne 2 74
(H Morrison) *mid-div: rdn and hdwy to ld over 1f out: drvn out* **8/1**[3]
6002 **2** *1/2* **Montage (IRE)**[12] [5736] 4-9-6 **55** .... (p) JimmyQuinn 4 65
(J Akehurst) *hld up: hdwy on outside voer 2f out: styd on to go 2nd ins fnl f: kpt on* **10/3**[1]
4440 **3** *2* **Easibet Dot Net**[51] [4723] 6-9-7 **56** .... (p) PaulHanagan 1 64
(I Semple) *trckd ldrs: rdn 3f out: styd on one pce fnl f* **25/1**
2510 **4** *2 1/2* **Jadeeron**[30] [5324] 7-8-12 **47** .... (p) ChrisCatlin 6 52
(Miss D A McHale) *chsd ldrs: rdn to ld over 2f out: hdd over 1f out: fdd ins fnl f* **16/1**
3404 **5** *nk* **Dickie's Dream (IRE)**[6] [5846] 3-9-5 **65** .... TonyCulhane 5 69
(P J McBride) *mid-div: rdn and hdwy over 1f out: one pce fnl f* **4/1**[2]
2000 **6** *nk* **Zaville**[14] [5683] 4-8-13 **55** .... (p) JamesO'Reilly(7) 11 59
(J O'Reilly) *trckd ldr: led 1/2-way: hdd over 2f out: no imp appr fnl f* **100/1**
5633 **7** *3/4* **Lennel**[2] [5927] 8-8-12 **47** .... (v) FrancisNorton 3 50
(A Bailey) *hld up in tch: sme hdwy over 1f out: sn one pce* **14/1**
0640 **8** *5* **Moon Emperor**[10] [5324] 9-10-0 **63** .... (v) AdamKirby 7 60
(J R Jenkins) *hld up: a bhd* **16/1**
2000 **9** *2* **Our Choice (IRE)**[60] [4451] 4-9-8 **60** .... JamesDoyle(3) 10 55
(N P Littmoden) *mid-div: rdn over 3f out: sn btn* **22/1**
514 **10** *1 1/4* **Swords**[14] [5691] 4-9-12 **61** .... JoeFanning 9 54
(Heather Dalton) *hld up: a bhd* **10/3**[1]
1100 **11** *13* **Vice Admiral**[12] [5723] 3-9-2 **62** .... DaleGibson 12 39
(M W Easterby) *led on outside to 1/2-way: wknd over 3f out* **16/1**
6-00 **12** *2* **Dovedale**[6] [5846] 6-9-7 **56** .... DaneO'Neill 13 31
(H S Howe) *trckd ldrs tl rdn and wknd over 3f out* **33/1**
1440 **P** **Zalkani (IRE)**[15] [5652] 6-9-5 **54** .... DeanMcKeown 8 —
(J Pearce) *bhd: t.o over 5f out: sn p.u and dismntd* **20/1**

3m 38.25s (-4.88) **Going Correction** -0.25s/f (Stan)
WFA 3 from 4yo+ 11lb 13 Ran SP% **118.5**
Speed ratings (Par 101):101,100,99,98,98 98,98,95,94,94 88,87,—
CSF £32.41 CT £652.00 TOTE £12.30: £3.40, £1.90, £3.10; EX 53.10.
Owner Mrs G C Maxwell & J D N Tillyard **Bred** J C Condon **Trained** East Ilsley, Berks

FOCUS
Just a steady pace for this moderate handicap. There are positives to be taken from the first three, as the winner is progressive, the second on a fair mark and the third well-in on his turf form.
Lennel Official explanation: jockey said gelding was denied a clear run
Zalkani(IRE) Official explanation: jockey said gelding was lame

5972 TWILIGHT RACING - MISS THE TRAFFIC H'CAP — 1m 1f 103y(P)
8:30 (8:31) (Class 6) (0-65,65) 3-Y-0+ — **£2,730** (£806; £403) **Stalls** Low

Form				RPR
3320	1		**Floodlight Fantasy**[28] 5388 3-9-3 **64**.....................(p) GrahamGibbons 12 (E S McMahon) *in tch: rdn to go 2nd over 1f out: led ins fnl f: jst hld on* **7/1**	73
0236	2	shd	**Peruvian Prince (USA)**[24] 5479 4-9-7 **64**............................ TPO'Shea 8 (J A R Toller) *trckd ldr: led over 3f out: rdn and hdd ins fnl f: rallied gamely: jst failed* **9/2**[1]	73
0240	3	shd	**Bowled Out (GER)**[17] 5610 4-9-5 **62**.............................. TonyCulhane 7 (P J McBride) *mid-div: hdwy 2f out: r.o u.p to press first 2 cl home* **10/1**	71
0016	4	4	**New England**[12] 5740 4-9-7 **64**.................... RobbieFitzpatrick 10 (W M Brisbourne) *mid-div: rdn over 2f out: kpt on but nt pce to chal* **11/2**[3]	65
2212	5	3/4	**Able Mind**[30] 5316 6-8-13 **59**.. DNolan(3) 2 (D W Thompson) *in tch tl rdn and one pce fr over 1f out* **13/2**	59
0663	6	1	**Western Roots**[12] 5740 5-9-5 **62**........................... GeorgeBaker 3 (M Appleby) *in rr: sme late hdwy but nvr on terms* **5/1**[2]	60
00/0	7	3 1/2	**Rifleman (IRE)**[11] 5755 6-9-3 **60**.............................(tp) JimmyQuinn 11 (B Ellison) *mid-div: rdn over 3f out: wknd 2f out* **25/1**	51
	8	1 3/4	**Sword's Edge (IRE)**[14] 5696 5-9-3 **60**........................... SteveDrowne 9 (W A Murphy, Ire) *slowly away: rdn over 3f out: nvr on terms* **66/1**	48
6304	9	shd	**Scutch Mill (IRE)**[17] 5621 4-9-1 **65**.............................(t) JamieJones(7) 1 (Karen George) *stdd s: a bhd* **16/1**	53
0	10	1	**Princely Ted (IRE)**[19] 5572 5-8-10 **60**........................(vt[1]) SCreighton(7) 6 (E J Creighton) *led tl hdd over 3f out: sn wknd* **50/1**	46
4160	11	1	**Lauro**[12] 5740 6-8-11 **61**..(p) DawnRankin(7) 5 (Miss J A Camacho) *towards rr: hdwy over 5f out: wknd over 2f out* **22/1**	45
0002	12	1	**Gallego**[6] 5831 4-9-3 **60**.. MatthewHenry 4 (R J Price) *slowly away: a bhd* **11/2**[3]	42
600-	13	11	**Art Historian (IRE)**[397] 5171 3-9-2 **63**........................ FrancisNorton 13 (T J Pitt) *plld hrd: trckd ldrs: rdn over 3f out: sn wknd* **25/1**	24

2m 0.13s (-2.49) **Going Correction** -0.25s/f (Stan)
WFA 3 from 4yo+ 4lb — 13 Ran SP% **121.9**
Speed ratings (Par 101):101,100,100,97,96 95,92,91,90,90 89,88,78
CSF £37.37 CT £324.63 TOTE £9.20: £2.40, £2.50, £3.30; EX 73.00.
Owner R L Bedding **Bred** Freynestown Stud **Trained** Hopwas, Staffs
■ Stewards' Enquiry : Dawn Rankin two-day ban: careless riding (Oct 25-26)
Graham Gibbons two-day ban: used whip without allowing colt time to respond (Oct 25-26)

FOCUS
A competitive affair, producing a cracking finish with a couple of short heads separating the first three. Sound form from that trio, who finished clear of the reliable form.

5973 BOOK NOW FOR CHRISTMAS FILLIES' H'CAP — 1m 141y(P)
9:00 (9:01) (Class 5) (0-70,70) 3-Y-0+ — **£3,886** (£1,156; £577; £288) **Stalls** Low

Form				RPR
2340	1		**Bavarica**[12] 5740 4-8-12 **59**.............................. JamesDoyle(3) 2 (Miss J Feilden) *hld up: rdn and hdwy over 2f out: r.o to ld ins fnl f* **4/1**[1]	66
2600	2	1 1/4	**Gelder**[31] 5294 3-9-6 **68**.. SteveDrowne 10 (H Morrison) *sn trckd ldr: led 3f out: rdn and hdd ins fnl f: no ex nr fin* **10/1**	73
4160	3	1 1/4	**Our Faye**[17] 5619 3-9-8 **70**.. GeorgeBaker 1 (S Kirk) *mid-div: hdwy over 2f out: ev ch appr fnl f: nt qckn ins* **8/1**[3]	72
043	4	1/2	**Tipsy Me**[18] 5598 3-9-4 **66**.. HayleyTurner 8 (M L W Bell) *trckd ldr to over 1f out: rdden and one pce after* **5/1**[2]	67
0600	5	nk	**Dyanita**[19] 5566 3-9-4 **66**.. TonyCulhane 4 (B W Hills) *trckd ldrs: rdn over 1f out: kpt on one pce* **14/1**	66
0446	6	nk	**Wasalat (USA)**[14] 5685 4-9-7 **65**............................ PaulHanagan 3 (D W Barker) *in rr: styd on fr over 1f out but nvr nr to chal* **5/1**[2]	65
6314	7	1/2	**Muscari**[24] 5474 4-9-3 **61**.. DaneO'Neill 6 (A P Jarvis) *mid-div: hdwy over 2f out: rdn over 1f out: sn btn* **4/1**[1]	60
-000	8	6	**Rashida**[28] 5384 4-9-2 **60**..............................(p) RobbieFitzpatrick 12 (M Appleby) *towards rr: effrt over 2f out but nvr on terms* **50/1**	46
-600	9	1	**Sophie'Jo**[94] 3400 3-8-12 **63**.................................. DeanCorby(3) 5 (Miss J Feilden) *prom: rdn over 2f out: sn wknd* **50/1**	47
00-0	10	4	**Korolieva (IRE)**[57] 4567 3-9-0 **65**......................... AndrewMullen(3) 13 (K A Ryan) *s.i.s: a bhd* **50/1**	41
0130	11	1 3/4	**Tiber Tilly**[32] 5268 3-9-5 **67**.................................. ChrisCatlin 7 (N P Littmoden) *led tl hdd 3f out: wknd over 1f out* **14/1**	39
3100	12	14	**Oporto (UAE)**[17] 5629 3-9-7 **69**.............................. TPO'Shea 9 (D M Fogarty, Ire) *slowly away: a bhd* **28/1**	11

1m 49.85s (-1.91) **Going Correction** -0.25s/f (Stan)
WFA 3 from 4yo 4lb — 12 Ran SP% **116.2**
Speed ratings (Par 100):98,96,95,95,95 94,94,89,88,84 83,70
CSF £43.06 CT £305.59 TOTE £5.40: £2.00, £3.40, £3.30; EX 75.90.
Owner Mr & Mrs M Jenner, E Jenner **Bred** Juddmonte Farms **Trained** Exning, Suffolk
■ Stewards' Enquiry : George Baker caution: used whip down the shoulder in the forehand position

FOCUS
Another keenly contested handicap and although the form is modest, it looks sound enough rated around the third and fourth.
Oporto(UAE) Official explanation: jockey said filly missed the break

5974 WOLVERHAMPTON-RACECOURSE.CO.UK H'CAP — 1m 141y(P)
9:30 (9:32) (Class 6) (0-65,65) 3-Y-0+ — **£2,730** (£806; £403) **Stalls** Low

Form				RPR
2306	1		**Writ (IRE)**[16] 5636 4-9-4 **61**.................................... PaulHanagan 1 (I Semple) *mde all: rdn clr over 1f out: unchal* **9/1**	75
-341	2	2 1/2	**Primo Gold**[34] 5210 3-9-1 **62**..................................(p) AdamKirby 6 (W R Swinburn) *mid-div: rdn and hdwy over 2f out: chsd wnr fnl f but no imp* **3/1**[1]	71+
1336	3	1 1/2	**Greenmeadow**[35] 5166 4-9-4 **61**............................ GeorgeBaker 13 (S Kirk) *bhd tl hdwy on outside over 2f out: kpt on one pce fr over 1f out* **9/1**	67
3300	4	1/2	**Holiday Cocktail**[22] 5510 4-9-7 **64**........................(t) FJohansson 3 (Miss J Feilden) *a.p: rdn over 3f out: one pce fnl f* **14/1**	69
0100	5	3	**Anduril**[28] 5362 5-9-8 **65**.......................................(b) ChrisCatlin 2 (Miss M E Rowland) *towards rr: kpt on one pce ins fnl 2f but nvr nr to chal* **16/1**	64
2240	6	nk	**Joshua's Gold (IRE)**[26] 5436 5-9-8 **65**....................(v) DanielTudhope 4 (D Carroll) *in tch: rdn over 2f out: wknd over 1f out* **11/2**[3]	63
4105	7	nk	**Magic Warrior**[32] 5267 6-9-5 **62**.............................. PatDobbs 12 (J C Fox) *trckd ldrs tl hung lft and wknd over 1f out* **12/1**	59
562	8	1 3/4	**Nashaab (USA)**[37] 5130 9-9-7 **64**...........................(v) SteveDrowne 7 (P D Evans) *a towards rr* **8/1**	58
2232	9	shd	**Sedge (USA)**[28] 5386 6-9-4 **61**...............................(p) TonyCulhane 9 (P T Midgley) *towards rr: hdwy on outside over 2f out: wknd over 1f out* **9/2**[2]	55
-0RR	10	5	**Arabie**[128] 2387 8-9-7 **64**... RobbieFitzpatrick 11 (Peter Grayson) *slowly away: a bhd* **50/1**	47
5406	11	1/2	**The Gaikwar (IRE)**[19] 5572 7-8-12 **62**.....................(b) TolleyDean(7) 10 (R A Harris) *trckd ldrs tl wknd over 2f out* **12/1**	44
1250	12	4	**Burnley Al (IRE)**[22] 5510 4-9-6 **63**..........................(b) FergusSweeney 8 (A Berry) *prom tl wknd over 2f out* **14/1**	37

1m 48.51s (-3.25) **Going Correction** -0.25s/f (Stan)
WFA 3 from 4yo+ 4lb — 12 Ran SP% **126.2**
Speed ratings (Par 101):104,101,100,100,97 97,96,95,95,90 90,86
CSF £38.51 CT £270.14 TOTE £15.80: £4.50, £2.80, £3.60; EX 80.10 Place 6 £589.47, Place 5 £134.46.
Owner Clarke Boon **Bred** Sean Collins **Trained** Carluke, S Lanarks

FOCUS
A modest handicap but run at a good pace and rated positively.
T/Plt: £1,375.30 to a £1 stake. Pool: £58,029.35. 30.80 winning tickets. T/Qpdt: £69.90 to a £1 stake. Pool: £2,940.80. 31.10 winning tickets. JS

5975 - 5981a (Foreign Racing) - See Raceform Interactive

5858 SAN SIRO (R-H)
Saturday, October 14

OFFICIAL GOING: Good

5982a PREMIO VITTORIO DI CAPUA (GROUP 1) — 1m
3:20 (3:26) 3-Y-0+ — **£97,076** (£47,152; £27,021; £13,510)

			RPR
1		**Ramonti (FR)**[62] 4416 4-8-12 .... EBotti 7 (A Botti, Italy) *made all, ridden clear inside final f (3.63/1)* **363/100**[2]	120
2	2 1/2	**Notability (IRE)**[14] 5703 4-8-12 .... PhilipRobinson 1 (M A Jarvis) *raced in 2nd, ridden over 1 1/2f out, lost 2nd over 1f out, regained 2nd on line* **11/20**[1]	115
3	nse	**Caradak (IRE)**[14] 5701 5-8-12 .... TedDurcan 2 (Saeed Bin Suroor) *raced in 3rd, pushed along 3f out, ridden 2 1/2f out, stayed on under pressure to take 2nd over 1f out, lost 2nd on line* **11/20**[1]	115
4	3	**Distant Way (USA)**[153] 1712 5-8-12 .... MDemuro 3 (L Brogi, Italy) *raced in 4th, ridden over 2f out, soon lost 4th, stayed on at one pace to regain 4th 1f out but never near leaders* **11/2**	109
5	2 1/2	**Arcadio (GER)**[21] 5543 4-8-12 .... THellier 8 (P Schiergen, Germany) *raced in 5th, effort over 2f out, one pace* **48/10**[3]	104
6	hd	**Icelandic** 4-8-12 .... PConvertino 4 (Frank Sheridan, Italy) *held up in last, headway on inside to go 4th 2f out, lost 4th 1f out, eased & lost 5th on line* **136/10**	104
7	hd	**Nordhal**[134] 2217 7-8-12 .... DVargiu 5 (B Grizzetti, Italy) *raced in 6th, never a factor* **64/1**	103
8	7	**Bening (FR)**[134] 2217 6-8-12 .... MMonteriso 6 (O Pessi, Italy) *raced in 7th, always in rear* **27/1**	89

1m 37.8s — 8 Ran SP% **195.2**
(including one euro stakes): WIN 4.63; PL 1.37, 1.69, 1.13; DF 26.89.
Owner Scuderia Antezzate **Bred** Scuderia Siba **Trained** Italy

NOTEBOOK
Ramonti(FR) returned to what he does best - setting a strong pace from the outset. The faster ground was in his favour, after defeats behind Librettist on very soft at Deauville and when trying to give 7lb to Icelandic (only seventh this time) on heavy ground over this mile last month. He galloped on to the end and never allowed the raiders to get near enough to challenge. He goes to Rome for the Premio Ribot on November 5th and will probably end the season in Hong Kong.
Notability(IRE) lost second to Caradak but stayed on to regain that place on the line. He keeps his form well.
Caradak(IRE) was bidding to become Godolphin's fifth winner of this race in eight years. He was always well placed but was the first to come under pressure. He rallied enough to go second but even that was taken from him at the end.

5818 BELMONT PARK (L-H)
Saturday, October 14

OFFICIAL GOING: Fast

5983a CHAMPAGNE STKS (GRADE 1) (DIRT) — 1m
10:15 (10:17) 2-Y-0
£139,535 (£46,512; £23,256; £11,628; £6,977; £930)

			RPR
1		**Scat Daddy (USA)**[40] 2-8-10 .... JRVelazquez 5 (T Pletcher, U.S.A) **27/10**[2]	112
2	3/4	**Nobiz Like Shobiz (USA)** 2-8-10 .... CVelasquez 2 (B Tagg, U.S.A) **29/20**[1]	110
3	1/2	**Pegasus Wind (USA)**[40] 2-8-10 ....(b) MLuzzi 4 (D Wayne Lukas, U.S.A) **216/10**	109
4	8 3/4	**My Golden Opinion (USA)** 2-8-10 .... FJara 3 (E G Harty, U.S.A) **49/1**	89
5	3 1/2	**Got The Last Laugh (USA)**[34] 5230 2-8-10 .... KDesormeaux 8 (W Mott, U.S.A) **72/10**	81
6	hd	**Xchanger (USA)**[40] 2-8-10 ....(b) JBravo 6 (M Shuman, U.S.A) **37/1**	80
7	hd	**I'm A Numbers Guy (USA)** 2-8-10 .... StewartElliott 10 (T F Ritchey, U.S.A) **6/1**[3]	80
8	1 3/4	**Buffalo Man (CAN)**[40] 2-8-10 .... JCastellano 9 (C Gambolati, U.S.A) **48/1**	76
9	3	**Liquidity (USA)** 2-8-10 .... ECoa 1 (Doug O'Neill, U.S.A) **14/1**	69
10	42	**Big Timer (USA)**[53] 4680 2-8-10 .... TomEaves 7 (I Semple) *raced in 6th, weakened quickly from 4f out, eased* **145/10**	—

1m 36.97s — 10 Ran SP% **118.5**
PARI-MUTUEL: WIN 7.40; PL (1-2) 3.60, 3.10; SHOW (1-2-3) 3.00, 2.50,7.80; SF 23.00.
Owner J Scatuorchio & M Tabor **Bred** Axel Wend **Trained** USA

NOTEBOOK
Big Timer(USA) flopped big time on his dirt bow and plans to run in the Breeders' Cup Juvenile have been shelved.

The Form Book, Raceform Ltd, Compton, RG20 6NL

5823 KEENELAND (L-H)
Saturday, October 14

OFFICIAL GOING: Firm

5984a QUEEN ELIZABETH II CHALLENGE CUP (GRADE 1) (FILLIES) 1m 1f (T)
10:35 (10:36) 3-Y-O **£180,233** (£58,140; £29,070; £14,535; £8,721)

RPR
1 **Vacare (USA)**[35] 3-8-9 .... CHMarquezJr 9 113
(C Block, U.S.A) **68/10**
2 ½ **Mauralakana (FR)**[21] 3-8-9 .... JRLeparoux 11 112
(P L Biancone, U.S.A) **54/10**[3]
3 1 ¼ **Quiet Royal (USA)**[41] 5049 3-8-9 .... OPeslier 10 110
(C Laffon-Parias, France) **225/10**
4 1 **Germance (USA)**[55] 4645 3-8-9 .... IMendizabal 7 108
(J-C Rouget, France) **23/10**[1]
5 2 ¼ **Take The Ribbon (USA)**[35] 5198 3-8-9 .... VEspinoza 1 104
(W Dollase, U.S.A) **12/1**
6 nse **Magnificent Song (USA)**[35] 5198 3-8-9 .... (b) GKGomez 3 104
(T Pletcher, U.S.A) **28/10**[2]
7 nk **Vague (USA)**[84] 3757 3-8-9 .... TBaze 4 103
(J Noseda) *led til headed approaching final f, weakened* **544/10**
8 2 ½ **Maxxi Arte (IRE)**[35] 5198 3-8-9 .... PValenzuela 8 98
(J Cassidy, U.S.A) **253/10**
9 ¾ **Citronnade (USA)** 3-8-9 .... EPrado 2 97
(R J Frankel, U.S.A) **101/10**
10 6 **Foxysox**[55] 3-8-9 .... CNakatani 6 86
(Carla Gaines, U.S.A) **129/10**
11 4 ¾ **Trick's Pic (USA)**[271] 3-8-9 .... WillieMartinez 5 77
(P L Biancone, U.S.A) **763/10**

1m 48.42s **11** Ran SP% **120.1**
PARI-MUTUEL (incluing $2 stake): WIN 15.60; PL (1-2) 7.00, 6.00;SHOW (1-2-3) 5.20, 5.00, 10.00; SF 106.20.
Owner Lothenbach Stables Inc **Bred** Lothenbach Stables Inc **Trained** USA

NOTEBOOK
Vague(USA) dropped out in the closing stages having tried to make all. A return to a shorter trip might help.

5825 SANTA ANITA (R-H)
Saturday, October 14

OFFICIAL GOING: Firm

5985a OAK TREE DERBY (GRADE 2) 1m 1f
12:07 (12:08) 3-Y-O **£52,326** (£17,442; £10,465; £5,233; £1,744)

RPR
1 **Dark Islander (IRE)**[35] 5165 3-8-6 .... JValdiviaJr 2 116
(J W Hills) *last early, headway to go 4th after 4f, led under 2f out, ridden out* **34/10**[3]
2 1 ¼ **Obrigado (FR)**[41] 3-8-6 .... (b) ASolis 5 114
(N Drysdale, U.S.A) **17/10**[2]
3 2 ¼ **A. P. Warrior (USA)**[63] 3-8-8 .... DFlores 1 112
(J Shirreffs, U.S.A) **13/10**[1]
4 ½ **Icy Ridge (IRE)**[63] 3-8-6 .... (b) JKCourt 3 109
(M Puhich, U.S.A) **338/10**
5 3 ½ **Potential (USA)**[98] 3-8-6 .... MPedroza 4 102
(Laura Wohlers, U.S.A) **111/10**
6 1 **Refinery (USA)**[210] 3-8-6 .... (b) AGryder 6 100
(Richard E Mandella, U.S.A) **154/10**

1m 46.21s **6** Ran SP% **120.5**
PARI-MUTUEL (including $2 stake): WIN 8.80; PL (1-2) 4.60, 3.00;SHOW (1-2-3) 2.60, 2.40, 2.20; SF 28.00.
Owner Donald M Kerr **Bred** Addison Racing Ltd Inc **Trained** Upper Lambourn, Berks

NOTEBOOK
Dark Islander(IRE) made a fine US debut despite appearing to lose his concentration and gawking at the big screen after hitting the front. Firm ground is his forte and the Hollywood Derby on November 26 is his next target, and he will then have a break before having a campaign in Dubai.

5906 LINGFIELD (L-H)
Sunday, October 15

OFFICIAL GOING: Standard
Wind: Moderate, half-against Weather: Hazy sunshine

5986 LINGFIELDPARK.CO.UK MAIDEN STKS (DIV I) 7f (P)
1:50 (1:54) (Class 5) 3-5-Y-O **£3,886** (£1,156; £577; £288) **Stalls** Low

Form RPR
0003 1 **Reeling N' Rocking (IRE)**[20] 5568 3-8-12 65 .... MichaelHills 5 68+
(B W Hills) *slowly away: sn settled in tch: hdwy over 2f out: rdn to ld jst ins fnl f: sn clr readily* **6/1**[3]
0002 2 2 ½ **Atwirl**[73] 4069 3-8-12 50 .... (v[1]) ChrisCatlin 2 62
(D J Daly) *slowly into sride: sn in midfield: rdn and hdwy over 2f out: chsd wnr ins fnl f: no imp* **20/1**
-044 3 1 ½ **Ribh**[16] 5649 3-8-12 74 .... RyanMoore 14 58
(C E Brittain) *hld up in rr: hdwy 3f out: swtchd rt over 1f out: r.o ins fnl f: nt rch ldrs* **5/2**[2]
4 nk **Soul Blazer (USA)** 3-9-3 .... RichardHughes 12 62
(A M Balding) *stdd s and dropped in bhd: hdwy 3f out: kpt on u.p fnl f: nt rch ldrs* **10/1**
0463 5 ½ **Mambonow (USA)**[66] 4287 3-9-3 70 .... (v[1]) TPQueally 8 61
(J Noseda) *led for 1f: chsd ldr tl led again over 2f out: sn rdn: hdd jst ins fnl f: wknd last 100 yds* **6/1**[3]
0-50 6 ¾ **You're My Son**[30] 5354 4-9-5 57 .... SteveDrowne 7 59
(A B Haynes) *racd in mifield on outer: rdn and effrt over 2f out: kpt on same pce fnl f* **40/1**
00 7 ½ **Grand Assault**[240] 445 3-9-3 .... BrianReilly 9 58
(P S McEntee) *prom: rdn 3f out: chsd ldr 2f out tl over 1f out: wkng whn sltly hmpd 1f out* **100/1**
0000 8 ½ **Laugh 'n Cry**[26] 5450 5-9-0 57 .... RobertWinston 6 51
(C A Cyzer) *hld up bhd: rdn over 2f out: hung lft and kpt on same pce over 1f out* **33/1**
00 9 5 **Ifatfirst (IRE)**[7] 5847 3-9-3 .... MartinDwyer 13 43
(M P Tregoning) *hld up in midfield on outer: rdn wl over 2f out: sn struggling and no ch after* **20/1**
3-64 10 1 ¼ **Alsadaa (USA)**[113] 2868 3-9-3 77 .... (t) RHills 1 40
(J H M Gosden) *s.i.s: sn pushed up and led after 1f: hdd over 2f out: sn btn* **7/4**[1]
0-00 11 nk **Red Pride (IRE)**[7] 5844 3-9-0 52 .... JamesDoyle(3) 11 39
(Miss J Feilden) *a bhd: no ch last 2f* **100/1**
000 12 15 **Cut To (USA)**[6] 5870 3-9-0 .... DeanCorby(3) 4 —
(J Akehurst) *a bhd: t.o* **100/1**
3500 13 1 ½ **Final Award (IRE)**[45] 4961 3-8-12 52 .... JohnEgan 3 —
(G M Moore) *t.k.h in midfield: rdn 3f out: no ch last 2f: t.o* **25/1**

1m 24.64s (-1.25) **Going Correction** -0.10s/f (Stan)
WFA 3 from 4yo+ 2lb **13** Ran SP% **124.3**
Speed ratings (Par 103):103,100,98,98,97 96,96,95,89,88 88,70,69
CSF £123.43 TOTE £6.40: £2.20, £7.90, £1.10; EX 70.40 TRIFECTA Not won..
Owner D M James **Bred** Richard F Barnes **Trained** Lambourn, Berks

FOCUS
This looked like just a modest maiden with 50-rated Atwirl in second. The winning time was 0.14 seconds slower than the second division, but 1.45 seconds quicker than the later juvenile novice event. The form may not prove reliable, with the favourite not running his race and the second, sixth and seventh less than solid.
Laugh 'n Cry Official explanation: jockey said mare hung left

5987 HALLOWEEN FAMILY FUN DAY OCTOBER 26TH H'CAP 6f (P)
2:20 (2:21) (Class 6) (0-65,65) 3-Y-O+ **£2,914** (£867; £433; £108; £108) **Stalls** Low

Form RPR
6503 1 **Sweetest Revenge (IRE)**[13] 5737 5-9-4 **64** .... HayleyTurner 4 74+
(M D I Usher) *racd in midfield: lost pl 3f out: swtchd to outer over 2f out: str run over 1f out: led last 100 yds: sn clr: readily* **8/1**[3]
0004 2 1 ½ **Linda Green**[6] 5872 5-9-5 **65** .... ChrisCatlin 5 71
(M R Channon) *w.w in midfield: rdn over 2f out: ev ch over 1f out: kpt on but outpcd by wnr last 100 yds* **8/1**[3]
2234 3 hd **Small Stakes (IRE)**[13] 5729 4-9-3 **63** .... (t) SebSanders 11 68
(P J Makin) *sn pushed along in rr: hdwy on outer 3f out: ev ch over 1f out: kpt on same pce ins fnl f* **9/2**[2]
4264 4 nk **Unlimited**[33] 5269 4-9-0 **60** .... TedDurcan 1 64
(R Simpson) *slowly away: sn chsng ldrs: rdn over 2f out: led over 1f out tl hdd and no ex last 100 yds* **9/2**[2]
4052 4 dht **Fateful Attraction**[18] 5605 3-8-12 **62** .... (b) JamesDoyle(3) 12 71+
(I A Wood) *slowly away and dropped in bhd: rdn 4f out: hdwy whn clipped heels and stmbld over 1f out: r.o strly last 100 yds* **9/1**
0000 6 1 ½ **Piccostar**[18] 5605 3-9-3 **64** .... DaneO'Neill 10 64
(A B Haynes) *in tch on outer: rdn and hdwy over 2f out: fdd last 100 yds* **25/1**
0000 7 1 ¼ **Bens Georgie (IRE)**[29] 5378 4-8-7 **60** .... JamesMillman(7) 9 56
(D K Ivory) *chsd ldrs on inner: rdn over 2f out: nvr pce to trble ldrs* **12/1**
6122 8 ¾ **Tamino (IRE)**[29] 5378 3-9-3 **64** .... SteveDrowne 3 58
(H Morrison) *mde most tl rdn and hdd over 1f out: wknd fnl f* **4/1**[1]
2206 9 ½ **Light Mozart**[18] 5605 3-9-2 **63** .... RyanMoore 7 55
(C E Brittain) *chsd ldrs: rdn over 2f out: no prog over 1f out* **11/1**
0000 10 1 **Polar Force**[13] 5737 6-9-0 **60** .... JohnEgan 2 49
(Mrs C A Dunnett) *chsd ldrs: rdn over 2f out: wknd over 1f out* **28/1**
5000 11 ¾ **Tiviski (IRE)**[31] 5327 4-9-2 **62** .... (v[1]) JimmyQuinn 8 49
(Miss Gay Kelleway) *bhd: rdn 3f out: no ch last 2f* **25/1**
0110 12 5 **Multahab**[33] 5275 7-9-4 **64** .... (t) BrianReilly 6 36
(Miss D A McHale) *pressed ldr evey ch over 2f out: wkng whn n.m.r over 1f out* **16/1**

1m 12.12s (-0.69) **Going Correction** -0.10s/f (Stan)
WFA 3 from 4yo+ 1lb **12** Ran SP% **121.6**
Speed ratings (Par 101):100,98,97,97,97 95,93,92,92,90 89,83
CSF £70.92 CT £334.15 TOTE £10.50: £3.30, £2.00, £2.80; EX 44.20 Trifecta £135.00 Part won. Pool: £190.20 - 0.67 winning units..
Owner The Ridgeway Partnership **Bred** Joza Partnership **Trained** Upper Lambourn, Berks

FOCUS
A modest but competitive handicap run at a very fast pace. The winner was back to something like his best. The runner-up used to be of similar ability on turf.
Fateful Attraction ◆ Official explanation: jockey said filly was denied a clear run 1 1/2f out
Multahab Official explanation: jockey said gelding hung right throughout

5988 LINGFIELDPARK.CO.UK MAIDEN STKS (DIV II) 7f (P)
2:55 (2:55) (Class 5) 3-5-Y-O **£3,886** (£1,156; £577; £288) **Stalls** Low

Form RPR
1 **Mayonga (IRE)**[386] 5474 3-8-12 83 .... SebSanders 6 75+
(Sir Mark Prescott) *chsd ldrs: rdn over 2f out: drvn to chse ldr over 1f out: led ins fnl f: sn clr: readily* **2/1**[2]
2203 2 2 **Mumaathel (IRE)**[48] 4899 3-9-3 78 .... RHills 5 75+
(M P Tregoning) *chsd ldr tl led 2f out: rdn wl over 1f out: hdd ins fnl f: nt pce of wnr* **15/8**[1]
3-0 3 1 ½ **Iannis (IRE)**[12] 5761 3-9-3 .... TPQueally 11 71+
(J Noseda) *t.k.h: hed up in tch: hdwy 3f out: chsd ldng pair over 1f out: kpt on* **10/1**
5000 4 5 **Grand Design**[16] 5651 4-9-0 46 .... TedDurcan 10 53
(C A Cyzer) *chsd ldrs: rdn wl over 2f out: outpcd by ldrs over 1f out* **33/1**
6053 5 ½ **Special Place**[10] 5774 3-9-3 58 .... MartinDwyer 4 57
(J A R Toller) *t.k.h: sn led: hdd 2f out: wknd wl over 1f out* **16/1**
-00 6 shd **Opus Magnus (IRE)**[18] 5611 3-9-3 .... FergusSweeney 8 57
(P J Makin) *sn outpcd in rr: styd on last 2f: n.d* **50/1**
5060 7 hd **Footstepsinthesnow (IRE)**[12] 5761 3-8-12 48 .... JoeFanning 3 51
(M A Buckley) *slowly away: bhd: styd on over 1f out: n.d* **50/1**
6 8 1 ¾ **Pikaboo**[62] 4431 3-8-12 .... JimmyFortune 13 46
(J H M Gosden) *outpcd in rr: nvr on terms* **4/1**[3]
5-00 9 shd **Take It There**[12] 5756 4-9-0 60 .... RichardThomas 2 46
(A J Lidderdale) *slowly away: racd in midfield: rdn wl over 2f out: no ch after* **66/1**
0500 10 1 ¾ **Penny Glitters**[66] 4306 3-8-7 49 .... DuranFentiman(5) 14 42
(S Parr) *led briefly early: racd in midfield after: rdn and struggling 3f out: no ch w ldrs after* **50/1**
4050 11 2 **Waddon (IRE)**[27] 5418 3-9-3 63 .... (p) AdamKirby 1 41
(C G Cox) *slowly away: sn chsng ldrs: reminder after 1f: rdn wl over 2f out: sn wknd* **16/1**
00 12 2 **Natacha Rostow**[10] 5774 3-8-12 .... JDSmith 7 31
(C A Dwyer) *slowly away: a bhd: nvr a factor* **66/1**

000- **13** *22* **Secret Cavern (USA)**[393] 5305 4-9-5 48 .... DaneO'Neill 12 —
(Mrs Barbara Waring) *racd wd: chsd ldrs tl 4f out: t.o last 2f* **80/1**
14 *14* **Fake Left** 3-9-3 .... JimmyQuinn 9 —
(B P J Baugh) *s.i.s: sn outpcd: t.o fr 1/2-way* **66/1**

1m 24.5s (-1.39) **Going Correction** -0.10s/f (Stan)
WFA 3 from 4yo 2lb **14** Ran SP% **123.5**
Speed ratings (Par 103):103,100,99,93,92 92,92,90,90,88 85,83,58,42
CSF £6.12 TOTE £3.50: £1.50, £1.40, £2.80; EX 11.10 Trifecta £88.70 Pool: £273.77 - 2.19 winning units..
Owner Miss A H Marshall **Bred** Frank Dunne **Trained** Newmarket, Suffolk

FOCUS
A weak maiden, as the proximity of the 46-rated fifth suggests, but the first three can do better. The winning time was 0.14 seconds quicker than the first division, and 1.59 seconds faster than the later juvenile novice event.
Waddon(IRE) Official explanation: jockey said gelding was never travelling
Secret Cavern(USA) Official explanation: jockey said gelding lost its action

5989 EUROPEAN BREEDERS FUND NOVICE STKS — 7f (P)
3:25 (3:25) (Class 4) 2-Y-O — **£5,181** (£1,541; £770; £384) **Stalls** Low

Form — RPR

61 **1** **Ekhtiaar**[9] 5784 2-9-4 91 .... RHills 6 91+
(J H M Gosden) *trckd ldrs: pushed along 2f out: hanging lft fr over 1f out: r.o to ld nr fin* **4/9**[1]

0530 **2** *hd* **Deadshot Keen (IRE)**[26] 5466 2-9-2 84 .... RyanMoore 4 87
(B J Meehan) *racd keenly: chsd ldr: rdn and ev ch over 2f out: led wl ins fnl f: hdd nr fin* **16/1**

4205 **3** *nk* **Codeword (IRE)**[8] 5806 2-9-7 93 .... JoeFanning 1 92
(M Johnston) *qckly away: stdd pce over 4f out: rdn and qcknd over 2f out: hung rt wl over 1f out: hdd and no ex ins fnl f* **10/3**[2]

0160 **4** *5* **Lunces Lad (IRE)**[21] 5546 2-9-7 87 .... TedDurcan 5 79
(M R Channon) *hld up in last pair: rdn and effrt 2f out: outpcd over 1f out* **14/1**

651 **5** *1 1/2* **Murrin (IRE)**[18] 5608 2-9-7 78 .... IanMongan 2 75
(T G Mills) *t.k.h: trckd ldrs: rdn 2f out: outpcd over 1f out* **10/1**[3]

6030 **6** *2* **Urban Warrior**[19] 5585 2-9-2 66 .... MartinDwyer 3 65
(Mrs Norma Pook) *t.k.h: hld up in last pair: rdn over 2f out: sn outpcd* **40/1**

1m 26.09s (0.20) **Going Correction** -0.10s/f (Stan) **6** Ran SP% **116.4**
Speed ratings (Par 97):94,93,93,87,86 83
CSF £10.75 TOTE £1.40: £1.10, £3.50; EX 8.40.
Owner Hamdan Al Maktoum **Bred** Mrs M L Parry And P M Steele-Mortimer **Trained** Newmarket, Suffolk

FOCUS
A good novice event, but it was quite tactical affair and, unsurprisingly, the winning time was around a second and a half slower than both divisions of the older-horse maiden.

NOTEBOOK
Ekhtiaar appeared to hang left under pressure and made hard work of following up his recent course-and-distance maiden success. Still, this represents a useful level of form and he could do even better in a stronger-run race. (op 8-13)
Deadshot Keen(IRE), well beaten in first-time blinkers in the Goffs Million at the Curragh on his previous start, found this easier and made the favourite work hard. (op 14-1)
Codeword(IRE), given a positive ride, ran a good race on his Polytrack debut. He was clear of the rest, but might not be the easiest to place in the longer term. (tchd 7-2)
Lunces Lad(IRE) was no match for the front thee on his Polytrack debut and ran some way below his official mark of 87. (op 12-1)
Murrin(IRE) could not follow up his recent course-and-distance maiden success and will surely be better suited by racing in nurseries.

5990 BOOK ONLINE FOR A £2 DISCOUNT H'CAP — 1m (P)
4:00 (4:00) (Class 3) (0-90,88) 3-Y-O+
£8,101 (£2,425; £1,212; £607; £302; £152) **Stalls** High

Form — RPR

056 **1** **Zato (IRE)**[15] 5666 3-9-4 88 .... JohnEgan 11 98
(M R Channon) *hld up in midfield on outer: hdwy over 2f out: r.o strly u.p to ld nr fin* **14/1**

0210 **2** *nk* **Cross The Line (IRE)**[17] 5639 4-9-5 86 .... JimmyFortune 5 95
(A P Jarvis) *hld up in tch: hdwy gng wl 2f out: rdn to ld last 75 yds: hdd cl home* **8/1**

0406 **3** *1* **Orchard Supreme**[30] 5345 3-9-4 88 .... RichardHughes 12 95
(R Hannon) *hld up in rr: hdwy over 2f out: swtchd rt over 1f out: r.o strly u.p fnl f: nt rch ldrs* **9/1**

1006 **4** *shd* **Adeje Park (IRE)**[70] 4172 3-9-4 88 .... AdrianMcCarthy 8 94
(P W Chapple-Hyam) *trckd ldrs: rdn and chsd ldr 2f out: led over 1f out: hdd and no ex last 75 yds* **25/1**

2-1 **5** *nk* **Juror (USA)**[170] 1274 3-9-4 88 .... RobertWinston 9 94+
(Sir Michael Stoute) *t.k.h: hld up in midfield: rdn over 2f out: n.m.r and swtchd rt over 1f out: kpt on: nt pce to rch ldrs* **7/2**[1]

0110 **6** *1 1/4* **Killena Boy (IRE)**[17] 5639 4-9-4 85 .... PaulDoe 1 88
(W Jarvis) *chsd ldrs: rdn over 2f out: ev ch over 1f out: wknd fnl f* **10/1**

11-6 **7** *2* **Obezyana (USA)**[270] 140 4-9-4 85 .... MartinDwyer 6 83
(G A Huffer) *slowly away: hld up in rr: effrt and short of room over 2f out: nvr trbld ldrs* **16/1**

1505 **8** *1/2* **Kelucia (IRE)**[22] 5520 5-9-7 88 .... SebSanders 10 85
(R M Beckett) *taken down early: hld up in rr: rdn and effrt on outer over 2f out: no imp* **10/1**

0425 **9** *2 1/2* **Mina A Salem**[63] 4399 4-9-2 83 .... RyanMoore 7 74
(C E Brittain) *led: rdn over 2f out: hdd over 1f out: wknd quckly fnl f* **9/2**[2]

2425 **10** *4* **Obrigado (USA)**[27] 5430 6-9-5 86 .... DarryllHolland 3 68
(Karen George) *pressed ldr: rdn over 2f out: wknd wl over 1f out* **10/1**

01 **11** *2* **Bee Stinger**[34] 5233 4-9-2 83 .... TPQueally 4 61
(I A Wood) *slowly away: hld up in midfield: rdn wl over 2f out: sn struggling* **5/1**[3]

5000 **12** *6* **Northern Desert (IRE)**[9] 5785 7-9-2 83 .... ChrisCatlin 2 47
(P W Hiatt) *slowly away: a bhd: lost tch wl over 2f out* **33/1**

1m 36.86s (-2.57) **Going Correction** -0.10s/f (Stan)
WFA 3 from 4yo+ 3lb **12** Ran SP% **124.8**
Speed ratings (Par 107):108,107,106,106,106 105,103,102,100,96 94,88
CSF £128.05 CT £1103.62 TOTE £15.60: £3.50, £3.10, £3.40; EX 159.70 TRIFECTA Not won..
Owner Derek And Jean Clee **Bred** D D And Mrs Jean P Clee **Trained** West Ilsley, Berks

FOCUS
A good, competitive handicap and this form should work out on the sand this winter. The winner was back to something like his best.

NOTEBOOK
Zato(IRE) took advantage of a career-low mark to gain his first success since landing a Listed race in France as a juvenile. He should not go up too much for this and could have more to offer on Polytrack. (op 16-1)
Cross The Line(IRE) appreciated the return to Polytrack and was just held. His record on sand now reads 422312212 and he is one keep in mind for the forthcoming All-Weather season.
Orchard Supreme, the winner of four his last six starts on Polytrack, appreciated the return to his favoured surface and ran well off a career-high mark. He had to be switched with his run and might have finished even closer. (op 8-1 tchd 10-1)
Adeje Park(IRE), back up in trip and switched to Polytrack for the first time, ran well and should be sharper for this first run in just over two months.
Juror(USA) ◆, off the track since winning a seven-furlong Wolverhampton maiden 170 days previously, did not get the best of trips and looks better than the bare form. On this evidence an official mark of 88 is not too harsh and he should have more to offer. (tchd 9-2)
Mina A Salem has a good reord on Polytrack but he was not at his best this time. (op 6-1)
Bee Stinger has enjoyed a fine season, but this was a disappointing effort with no obvious excuse. (tchd 11-2)

5991 LINGFIELDPARK.CO.UK H'CAP — 1m 5f (P)
4:30 (4:30) (Class 4) (0-85,83) 3-Y-O+
£5,608 (£1,679; £839; £420; £209; £105) **Stalls** Low

Form — RPR

5001 **1** **Captain General**[18] 5610 4-8-12 68 .... MartinDwyer 8 79
(J A R Toller) *t.k.h: hld up in midfied: gd hdwy over 2f out: ev ch 1f out: r.o strly to ld nr fin* **9/2**[2]

6054 **2** *hd* **Nawamees (IRE)**[15] 5430 8-9-10 80 .... (p) RyanMoore 3 91
(G L Moore) *hld up in rr: hdwy over 2f out: swtchd lft over 1f out: drvn to ld last 100 yds: hdd nr fin* **6/1**[3]

5440 **3** *nk* **Wise Owl**[15] 5678 4-9-10 80 .... JimmyQuinn 9 90
(J Pearce) *trckd ldrs: chsd ldr over 2f out: hrd drvn to chal over 1f out: nt qucken fnl f* **9/1**

2431 **4** *1/2* **Particle (IRE)**[16] 5651 3-9-2 83 .... GregFairley(3) 10 93
(M Johnston) *chsd ldr tl led 3f out: rdn over 2f out: hdd and no ex last 100 yds* **6/1**[3]

0313 **5** *5* **Linden Lime**[18] 5610 4-9-0 70 .... FrancisNorton 5 72
(Jamie Poulton) *t.k.h: chsd ldrs: rdn over 2f out: outpcd fnl f* **6/1**[3]

2111 **6** *5* **Ardea Brave (IRE)**[15] 5671 4-9-4 74 .... (p) TedDurcan 6 69
(M Botti) *led tl hdd 3f out: sn rdn: wknd wl over 1f out* **7/2**[1]

1415 **7** *2 1/2* **Wild Pitch**[122] 2585 5-9-1 71 .... (b) RichardHughes 7 62
(P Mitchell) *t.k.h: hld up in rr: effrt and rdn over 2f out: hung lft and no imp last 2f* **14/1**

0614 **8** *2* **Boot 'n Toot**[15] 5671 5-9-5 75 .... RobertWinston 2 63
(C A Cyzer) *t.k.h: hld up in midfield: rdn wl over 2f out: wknd wl over 1f out* **12/1**

6203 **9** *1* **Most Definitely (IRE)**[29] 5383 6-9-10 80 .... JimCrowley 4 66
(R M Stronge) *stdd s: plld hrd and hld up in rr: rdn over 2f out: no prog* **12/1**

2m 46.09s (-2.21) **Going Correction** -0.10s/f (Stan)
WFA 3 from 4yo+ 8lb **9** Ran SP% **115.3**
Speed ratings (Par 105):102,101,101,101,98 95,93,92,91
CSF £31.59 CT £232.79 TOTE £5.60: £2.10, £2.00, £1.90; EX 44.30 Trifecta £259.60 Part won. Pool: £365.72 - 0.84 winning units..
Owner M E Wates **Bred** M E Wates **Trained** Newmarket, Suffolk

FOCUS
A good handicap for the grade and the form looks very strong.

5992 VISIT THE TRACKSIDE CARVERY H'CAP — 1m 2f (P)
5:05 (5:06) (Class 6) (0-65,64) 3-Y-O — **£2,914** (£867; £433; £216) **Stalls** Low

Form — RPR

5604 **1** **Blacktoft (USA)**[13] 5740 3-9-3 63 .... (e[1]) J-PGuillambert 8 72
(S C Williams) *stdd s: hld up in rr: gd hdwy over 2f out: chsd ldng pair over 1f out: drvn to ld on inner last 100 yds: r.o* **8/1**

2531 **2** *1/2* **Dab Hand (IRE)**[10] 5774 3-9-4 64 .... RyanMoore 3 72
(D M Simcock) *t.k.h: hld up in tch: rdn to chse ldng pair over 2f out: led ins fnl f: hdd and no ex last 50 yds* **13/2**[3]

2012 **3** *3* **Sanctity**[13] 5740 3-9-4 64 .... (v) MartinDwyer 6 66
(J R Fanshawe) *racd keenly: trckd ldrs: wnt 2nd gng wl over 2f out: led and over 1f out: hdd ins fnl f: sn btn* **5/2**[1]

-060 **4** *2* **Lennoxtown (IRE)**[155] 1681 3-9-2 62 .... MatthewHenry 10 61
(J Ryan) *hld up in rr: hdwy on wd outside over 2f out: no ex u.p over 1f out* **33/1**

-560 **5** *1 1/2* **Sea Of Calm (USA)**[18] 5619 3-9-0 60 .... JimmyFortune 14 56
(E A L Dunlop) *stdd s: hld up bhd: effrt and rdn on wd outside bnd over 2f out: styd on wl fnl f: nvr nrr* **16/1**

0201 **6** *1/2* **Princess Danah (IRE)**[15] 5690 3-9-1 61 .... (tp) AdamKirby 12 56
(W R Swinburn) *prom: wnt 2nd over 7f out tl led over 3f out: rdn over 2f out: hdd over 1f out: fdd fnl f* **6/1**[2]

6140 **7** *3 1/2* **Pothos Way (GR)**[38] 5129 3-9-4 64 .... JimCrowley 2 52
(P R Chamings) *hld up in midfield: rdn and effrt over 2f out: no prog* **14/1**

50-6 **8** *1/2* **Ennobling**[172] 1240 3-9-3 63 .... DaneO'Neill 7 50
(E F Vaughan) *hld up towards rr: rdn over 4f out: n.d after* **14/1**

0006 **9** *2* **Razed**[12] 5751 3-9-0 60 .... JoeFanning 11 43
(M Johnston) *hld up on outer in rr: rdn 4f out: no ch last 2f* **16/1**

5000 **10** *1/2* **In On The Act (IRE)**[34] 5235 3-9-1 61 .... (v[1]) FrancisNorton 13 43
(Jamie Poulton) *chsd ldrs: drvn over 4f: lost pl wl over 2f out: no ch after* **25/1**

5634 **11** *1 1/4* **Can Can Star**[33] 5258 3-9-2 62 .... (b[1]) JamieMackay 9 42
(J G Given) *t.k.h: hld up in rr: nvr on terms* **16/1**

0430 **12** *3/4* **Henchman**[44] 4982 3-9-0 60 .... (p) SebSanders 5 39
(Lady Herries) *rrd in stalls: led after 1f tl hdd and rdn over 3f out: wknd over 2f out* **13/2**[3]

6-00 **13** *11* **Blandford Flyer**[18] 5621 3-9-0 60 .... TedDurcan 1 18
(W R Swinburn) *racd in midfield: lost pl and rdn wl over 3f out: no ch after* **33/1**

1-00 **14** *32* **Pip's Baby**[53] 4700 3-9-2 62 .... RichardHughes 4 —
(S Kirk) *t.k.h: led for 1f: chsd ldrs tl lost pl 4f out: no ch after: eased last 2f* **25/1**

2m 5.82s (-1.97) **Going Correction** -0.10s/f (Stan) **14** Ran SP% **125.2**
Speed ratings (Par 99):103,102,100,98,97 97,94,93,92,91 90,90,81,55
CSF £59.44 CT £171.73 TOTE £11.20: £2.20, £4.10, £1.70; EX 63.60 TRIFECTA Not won. Place 6 £130.75, Place 5 £57.21..
Owner Chris Watkins And David N Reynolds **Bred** Paradigm Thoroughbreds Inc **Trained** Newmarket, Suffolk

FOCUS
Just a modest handicap, but the form should prove reliable.
T/Plt: £162.00 to a £1 stake. Pool: £63,529.40. 286.25 winning tickets. T/Qpdt: £31.60 to a £1 stake. Pool: £3,880.80. 90.70 winning tickets. SP

5993 - 5995a (Foreign Racing) - See Raceform Interactive

4216 NAAS (L-H)

Sunday, October 15

OFFICIAL GOING: Yielding to soft

5996a ALI RETZA & MAMADI SOUDAVAR EUROPEAN BREEDERS FUND GARNET STKS (LISTED RACE) (F&M) — 1m

4:35 (4:37) 3-Y-0+ **£33,672** (£9,879; £4,706; £1,603)

RPR

1 **Sina Cova (IRE)**[26] 5465 4-9-6 107 .... KJManning 7 — 115
(Peter Casey, Ire) *settled 4th: hdwy ent st: led under 2 1/2f out: rdn and styd on wl* **11/2**[2]

2 — 2 1/2 **Cheyenne Star (IRE)**[7] 5849 3-8-12 101 .... MJLane 18 — 105
(Ms F M Crowley, Ire) *hld up: hdwy early st: 5th 2f out: 2nd over 1f out: kpt on* **10/1**

3 — 4 **Paris Winds (IRE)**[26] 5465 3-8-12 104 .... DJCondon 15 — 97
(David Wachman, Ire) *settled 3rd: 2nd 2f out: kpt on same pce fr over 1f out* **7/1**

4 — 1/2 **Eastern Appeal (IRE)**[36] 5192 3-8-12 94 .... JMurtagh 3 — 96
(M Halford, Ire) *towards rr: hdwy on outer early st: 5th 1f out: kpt on* **12/1**

5 — 1 **Danehill Music (IRE)**[97] 3371 3-9-3 100 .... WMLordan 6 — 99
(David Wachman, Ire) *towards rr: rdn st: styd on fr 1 1/2f out* **6/1**[3]

6 — hd **Sacrosanct (IRE)**[7] 5854 3-8-12 94 .... DavidMcCabe 5 — 94
(A P O'Brien, Ire) *s.i.s and hld up towards rr: rdn and styd on fr 2f out* **20/1**

7 — 3/4 **Be My Queen (IRE)**[26] 5465 3-8-12 100 .... JAHeffernan 13 — 92
(A P O'Brien, Ire) *trckd ldrs: 5th into st: rdn and no imp fr over 2f out* **8/1**

8 — 1 3/4 **Moyenne (IRE)**[16] 5663 4-9-1 82 .... RPCleary 1 — 89
(Timothy Doyle, Ire) *mid-div: rdn and no imp st* **50/1**

9 — 3/4 **Chenchikova (IRE)**[26] 5465 3-8-12 94 .... CO'Donoghue 11 — 87
(A P O'Brien, Ire) *towards rr: rdn on inner early st: kpt on fr 1 1/2f out* **14/1**

10 — shd **Blessyourpinksox (IRE)**[15] 5697 5-9-4 101 .... FMBerry 14 — 90
(Peter Casey, Ire) *mid-div: effrt on outer early st: no imp fr 2f out* **12/1**

11 — 2 1/2 **Ardbrae Lady**[15] 5697 3-8-12 105 .... WSupple 17 — 82
(Joseph G Murphy, Ire) *hld up: no imp st* **9/1**

12 — hd **Skerries (IRE)**[23] 5517 5-9-1 87 .... CDHayes 2 — 82
(H Rogers, Ire) *sn led: hdd under 2 1/2f out: wknd over 1 1/2f out* **25/1**

13 — 1 1/4 **Michikabu (IRE)**[26] 5468 3-8-12 89 .... PJSmullen 10 — 79
(D K Weld, Ire) *chsd ldrs: 5th early: mid-div and rdn st: no ex fr 2f out* **10/1**

14 — 3 **Tamazug**[15] 5697 3-8-12 102 .... DPMcDonogh 8 — 73
(Kevin Prendergast, Ire) *trckd ldrs: 5th appr st: rdn and no imp fr over 2f out: eased over 1f out* **5/1**[1]

15 — 2 1/2 **Valentina Guest (IRE)**[36] 5194 5-9-1 92 .... NGMcCullagh 4 — 68
(Peter Casey, Ire) *a towards rr* **25/1**

16 — 3 1/2 **Sweet Petite (IRE)**[9] 5799 3-8-12 83 ....(b) CPGeoghegan 12 — 61
(Kevin F O'Donnell, Ire) *cl up: 2nd early st: 2nd u.p appr st: sn wknd* **16/1**

17 — 4 **Sharapova (IRE)**[33] 5280 3-8-12 82 .... SMGorey 16 — 53
(M J Grassick, Ire) *a bhd* **33/1**

1m 39.4s
WFA 3 from 4yo+ 3lb — **18** Ran SP% **143.4**
CSF £66.95 TOTE £6.80: £2.20, £4.90, £2.80, £2.80; DF 148.90.
Owner Basil Brindley **Bred** Basil Brindley **Trained** Stamullen, Co Meath

FOCUS
A race that has been rated through the second and fourth. The winner has been progressing all season.

NOTEBOOK
Sina Cova(IRE) put up a game performance under her Group 3 penalty. A winner over a mile and half and runner-up in the Blandford Stakes over 1m2f, the slow ground here helped her cause over this shorter trip and she ran on well for a decisive win. She is to be kept in training next year, according to her trainer. (op 5/1)
Cheyenne Star(IRE) is another who should do well next season. She has performed consistently well this year and with her rider unable to claim his 7lb allowance, she came out of this race with her reputation enhanced. (op 8/1)
Paris Winds(IRE), who showed improved form when third in the Blandford Stakes on her previous start, was always well placed but finished further behind the winner despite meeting her on better terms.
Eastern Appeal(IRE) had a bit to find on official ratings and she produced a decent effort having had only a few behind her turning into the straight. (op 12/1 tchd 14/1)
Danehill Music(IRE), absent since July, has shown her best form on testing ground and, although never in serious contention, she ran well enough to suggest she might do better next time. (op 11/2)

5997 - (Foreign Racing) - See Raceform Interactive

5560 COLOGNE (R-H)

Sunday, October 15

OFFICIAL GOING: Good

5998a PREIS DES WINTERFAVORITEN (GROUP 3) — 1m

4:15 (4:40) 2-Y-0
£58,621 (£21,379; £14,138; £7,103; £3,793; £1,862)

RPR

1 **Molly Max (GER)** 2-9-2 .... FilipMinarik 3 — 105
(Frau K Haustein, Germany) *made all, ridden 2 lengths clear 1f out, driven out, held on well* **83/10**

2 — nk **Global Dream (GER)**[44] 5007 2-9-2 .... ABoschert 4 — 104
(U Ostmann, Germany) *held up towards rear, 5th straight, ridden over 1f out, went 2nd inisde final f, stayed on well closing stages, nearest fin* **13/10**[1]

3 — 1 1/4 **Lucky It Is (HOL)**[35] 5218 2-9-2 .... ADeVries 6 — 101
(A Trybuhl, Germany) *raced in 2nd, ridden over 1 1/2f out, stayed on at one pace* **88/10**

4 — 3/4 **Persian Storm (GER)** 2-9-2 .... THellier 8 — 99
(P Schiergen, Germany) *raced in 4th, ridden over 1 1/2f out, unable to quicken* **17/10**[2]

5 — 3 1/2 **Lovely Tiger (GER)** 2-9-2 .... WMongil 1 — 91
(P Schiergen, Germany) *raced in 3rd on inside, outpaced from over 1 1/2f out* **8/1**

6 — 1 3/4 **Monreale (GER)** 2-9-2 .... JPalik 5 — 87
(T Horwart, Germany) *raced in 6th, reminders and dropped back to last over 3f out, no danger after* **22/1**

7 — 1/2 **Global Champion** 2-9-2 .... AStarke 2 — 86
(Mario Hofer, Germany) *raced in 7th, 6th straight, always in rear* **13/2**[3]

1m 38.16s — **7** Ran SP% **130.3**
(including 10 Euro stake): WIN 93; PL 16, 13, 18; SF 225.
Owner Gestut Auenquelle **Bred** Gestut Auenquelle **Trained** Germany

5711 LONGCHAMP (R-H)

Sunday, October 15

OFFICIAL GOING: Good

5999a PRIX DU CONSEIL DE PARIS (GROUP 2) — 1m 4f

2:20 (2:26) 3-Y-0+ **£51,103** (£19,724; £9,414; £6,276; £3,138)

RPR

1 **Daramsar (FR)**[29] 5400 3-8-9 .... CSoumillon 1 — 115
(A De Royer-Dupre, France) *made all, ridden well over 1f out, ran on well* **22/10**[1]

2 — nk **Alix Road (FR)**[15] 5702 3-8-6 .... TThulliez 4 — 112
(Mme M Bollack-Badel, France) *always close up, 3rd on inside straight, chased winner final f, ran on under pressure but too late to be dangerous* **39/10**[3]

3 — 1 **Baby First (FR)**[20] 5584 3-8-9 .... OPeslier 5 — 114
(J-M Beguigne, France) *always close up, 4th straight, ridden well over 1f out, ran on one pace* **73/10**

4 — 1/2 **Kocab**[71] 4169 4-9-3 .... JVictoire 7 — 114
(A Fabre, France) *tracked winner, 2nd straight, every chance 2f out, soon ridden & wandered under poressure, one pace final f* **64/10**

5 — 3 **Oracle West (SAF)**[204] 741 5-9-5 .... FSpanu 6 — 111
(J E Hammond, France) *held up in rear, last straight, ran on final f, never nearer* **15/1**

6 — 1 **Numide (FR)**[93] 3517 3-9-0 .... IMendizabal 2 — 112
(J-C Rouget, France) *held up in rear, 7th straight, effort well over 1f out, never a factor* **38/10**[2]

7 — hd **Policy Maker (IRE)**[35] 5223 6-9-7 ....(b) SPasquier 8 — 111
(E Lellouche, France) *6th straight, 5th & ridden over 1f out, beaten approaching final f* **46/10**

8 — 2 1/2 **Blip**[23] 5519 4-9-3 .... DBoeuf 3 — 104
(D Smaga, France) *broke well, restrained in 5th, 5th straight, ridden 2f out, soon beaten* **64/10**

2m 30.9s **Going Correction** 0.0s/f (Good)
WFA 3 from 4yo+ 7lb — **8** Ran SP% **135.7**
Speed ratings: 113,112,112,111,109 109,109,107
PARI-MUTUEL: WIN 3.20; PL 1.20, 1.50, 1.80; DF 7.50.
Owner H H Aga Khan **Bred** H H The Aga Khan's Studs S C **Trained** Chantilly, France

NOTEBOOK
Daramsar(FR) was running over his best distance and was given an inspired ride by Soumillon. The other seven runners were reluctant to take the lead so Daramsar went to the head of affairs after a couple of furlongs and was never headed. He quickened well in the straight and proved courageous when holding off the challenge of the runner up. Further improvement can be expected and he stays in training next year.
Alix Road(FR), a very game and consistent filly, became outpaced early on in the straight but finished very well. Her connections are hoping for an invitation to the Japan Cup and she will remain in training next year.
Baby First(FR) came with a progressive run from half way up the straight and stayed on at the finish. He should make a very decent four-year-old.
Kocab tracked the winner soon after the start but could not quicken when things warmed up early in the straight. He gradually dropped out of contention but still ran a good race.

6000a PRIX DE CONDE (GROUP 3) — 1m 1f

2:50 (2:55) 2-Y-0 **£27,586** (£11,034; £8,276; £5,517; £2,759)

RPR

1 **Midnight Beauty (IRE)** 2-8-11 .... C-PLemaire 1 — 100
(M Delcher-Sanchez, Spain) *held up in 5th, headway between rivals to go 2nd 120yds out, hard driven to lead post* **8/1**

2 — nse **Massive (IRE)**[12] 5759 2-8-11 .... TonyCulhane 6 — 100
(M R Channon) *led, ridden 1 1/2f out, headed post* **44/10**

3 — 2 1/2 **Ailton (GER)**[20] 2-8-11 .... DBoeuf 2 — 95
(W Baltromei, Germany) *raced in 3rd, ridden on inside over 1f out, stayed on at one pace, just held on for 3rd* **72/10**

4 — nk **Apophis (IRE)**[67] 2-8-11 .... CSoumillon 5 — 94
(A Fabre, France) *raced in 4th, ridden over 1f out, kept on at same pace* **2/1**[1]

5 — hd **Lykios (IRE)**[42] 5048 2-8-11 .... MBlancpain 3 — 94
(C Laffon-Parias, France) *raced in 2nd, effort and unable to quicken over 1f out* **32/10**[2]

6 — 3 **Prototype**[35] 2-8-8 .... TThulliez 4 — 85
(P Bary, France) *last throughout* **33/10**[3]

1m 54.2s **Going Correction** -0.375s/f (Firm) — **6** Ran SP% **122.2**
Speed ratings: 105,104,102,102,102 99
PARI-MUTUEL: WIN 9.00; PL 3.80, 3.10; SF 55.40.
Owner J Postigo Silva **Bred** Michael Lyons **Trained** Spain

NOTEBOOK
Midnight Beauty(IRE) looks a very decent sort in the making. Dropped in at the deep end having landed easy victories at San Sabastian, he quickened well at the furlong and a half marker and got up in the final stride. He will not race again this year and will probably be campaigned in France next year.
Massive(IRE) put up a very brave performance and failed by inches. He looked to have the race at his mercy until the final 50 yards and was literally caught on the post.
Ailton(GER) lengthened his stride in the straight and then stayed on at the one pace to the line up the far rail.
Apophis(IRE), still quite green, did not really get into the race until the final stages. Fourth early on, he made his challenge up the centre of the track and took fourth place well inside the final furlong. He remains worth following and should make an even better three-year-old over this distance and further.

5982 SAN SIRO (R-H)
Sunday, October 15

OFFICIAL GOING: Good

6002a PREMIO SERGIO CUMANI (GROUP 3) (F&M) — 1m
2:50 (2:59) 3-Y-O+ — **£33,486** (£15,493; £8,674; £4,337)

RPR

1 — **Desert Quiet (IRE)** 4-8-13 .... SLandi 4 — 107
(P Giannotti, Italy) *held up, 6th straight, headway over 2f out to track 3rd, challenged approaching final f, led 100y out, driven out* **125/10**

2 — 1 1/2 — **Musa Golosa**[119] 2694 3-8-9 .... DVargiu 6 — 103
(B Grizzetti, Italy) *always close up, 2nd straight, led 3f out to 100y out, ran on same pace* **42/10**[2]

3 — 1 1/2 — **Mrs Snow**[133] 2279 3-8-9 .... ASuborics 7 — 100
(Mario Hofer, Germany) *always close up, 3rd straight, every chance 1f out, one pace* **1/1**[1]

4 — 3/4 — **Kykuit (IRE)**[133] 2280 4-9-2 .... MDemuro 5 — 103
(L Brogi, Italy) *held up, last straight, headway on outside well over 1f out, kept on at one pace final f* **46/10**

5 — snk — **Saishu (IRE)**[132] 2313 4-8-13 .... PConvertino 2 — 99
(E Libaud, France) *4th straight, effort on inside 2f out, one pace from over 1f out* **43/10**[3]

6 — 2 1/2 — **Martines (FR)**[398] 4-8-13 .... SMulas 3 — 94
(B Grizzetti, Italy) *tracked leader early, 5th straight, oen pace final 2f* **49/1**

7 — 6 — **Stella Celtica (ITY)**[154] 1713 3-8-9 .... EBotti 1 — 81
(A Botti, Italy) *led 5f* **63/10**

1m 39.9s
WFA 3 from 4yo 3lb — 7 Ran SP% **129.1**
(including 1 Euro stake): WIN 13.47; PL 3.66, 3.08; DF 24.86.
Owner P Giannotti **Bred** Pierluigi Giannotti **Trained** Italy

6003a GRAN CRITERIUM (GROUP 1) (C&F) — 1m
3:25 (3:31) 2-Y-O — **£177,480** (£95,910; £57,620; £28,810)

RPR

1 — **Kirklees (IRE)**[22] 5521 2-8-11 .... LDettori 7 — 110
(M Johnston) *led over 5f out to 2f out, rallied under pressure to lead again on line* **76/100**[1]

2 — shd — **Strobilus**[9] 5783 2-8-11 .... PhilipRobinson 5 — 110
(M A Jarvis) *led over 2f, 2nd straight, led again 2f out, swished tail when ridden, went one length up 1f out, caught on line* **76/100**[1]

3 — 1 — **Chinese Whisper (IRE)**[14] 5707 2-8-11 .... KFallon 11 — 107
(A P O'Brien, Ire) *always prominent, 4th straight,every chance on outside over 1f out, kept on same pace* **32/10**[2]

4 — 1 — **Golden Titus (IRE)**[56] 4644 2-8-11 .... SLandi 2 — 105
(A Renzoni, Italy) *6th straight, reached 4th 2f out, one pace* **68/10**

5 — 4 — **Amante Latino**[120] 2670 2-8-11 .... MEsposito 4 — 96
(V Caruso, Italy) *10th straight, headway 2f out, never near to challenge* **26/1**

6 — 1 1/2 — **Depp (ITY)**[127] 2474 2-8-11 .... MDemuro 10 — 93
(L D'Auria, Italy) *held up, last straight, headway over 2f out, never a factor* **89/10**

7 — 2 — **Moriwood (ITY)** 2-8-11 .... EBotti 9 — 88
(A Botti, Italy) *midfield, headway over 3f out, weakened well over 1f out* **6/1**[3]

8 — 1/2 — **Golden Dynamic (IRE)**[142] 2-8-11 .... GTemperini 1 — 87
(G Di Chio, Italy) *7th straight, beaten 2f out* **103/10**

9 — 1/2 — **Walharer** 2-8-11 .... DVargiu 3 — 86
(B Grizzetti, Italy) *always towards rear* **46/1**

10 — 3/4 — **Polar Wind (ITY)** 2-8-11 .... LManiezzi 8 — 84
(R Menichetti, Italy) *chased leaders, 3rd straight, weakened well over 2f out* **86/1**

11 — 12 — **Notturno Di Chopin (IRE)**[57] 4622 2-8-11 .... MJKinane 6 — 56
(J Heloury, Italy) *5th straight, weakened well over 2f out* **26/1**

1m 39.9s — 11 Ran SP% **194.2**
WIN 1.76 (coupled with Strobilus); PL 1.29, 1.63, 1.54; DF 5.94.
Owner Sheikh Mohammed **Bred** Darley **Trained** Middleham Moor, N Yorks

FOCUS
Improved form from the first three.

NOTEBOOK
Kirklees(IRE) ran a most determined race, refusing to accept defeat after being headed two furlongs out. He was his trainer's third winner of this contest but will need to step up on this if he is to prosper under his Group 1 penalty.
Strobilus swished his tail when first put under pressure but appeared likely to hold on until the final strides. He should continue to improve.
Chinese Whisper(IRE), well beaten on heavy ground at Tipperary two weeks earlier, was much more at home in these conditions. Close up on the outstde coming into the straight, he never looked like wearing down the first two but never gave up trying.
Golden Titus(IRE), a fair fifth in the Morny, was running beyond six furlongs for the first time. He stayed on gamely to the end and can build on this.

6004a GRAN PREMIO DEL JOCKEY CLUB ITALIANO (GROUP 1) — 1m 4f
4:05 (4:12) 3-Y-O+ — **£161,760** (£84,120; £49,680; £24,840)

RPR

1 — **Laverock (IRE)**[54] 4679 4-9-5 .... DBonilla 3 — 122
(C Laffon-Parias, France) *held up in 6th behind slow pace, closed up halfway, 4th straight, led well over 1f out, ridden out* **84/100**[1]

2 — hd — **Fair Nashwan**[14] 5718 4-9-2 .... DVargiu 1 — 118
(B Grizzetti, Italy) *held up in 3rd, closed up halfway, close 6th on outside straight, ridden 2f out, headway approaching final f, finished well* **16/1**

3 — 1 1/2 — **Cherry Mix (FR)**[54] 4679 5-9-5 .... LDettori 7 — 119
(Saeed Bin Suroor) *allowed clear lead, set moderate pace, taken wide after 5f, quickened over 5f out, headed well over 1f out, kept on at one pce* **84/100**[1]

4 — nk — **Egerton (GER)**[21] 5561 5-9-5 .... TMundry 2 — 119
(P Rau, Germany) *2nd behind clear leader, closed up at halfway, 3rd straight, every chance well over 1f out, disputed 2nd final f, no extra* **11/2**

5 — nk — **Sweet Stream (ITY)**[56] 4646 6-9-2 .... TGillet 8 — 115
(J E Hammond, France) *held up, 7th straight, headway to go 4th 2f out, soon one pace* **28/10**[2]

6 — 5 — **Dickens (GER)**[42] 5051 3-8-12 .... ASuborics 6 — 111
(H Blume, Germany) *held up, closed up rapidly to go 23nd halfway, ridden and beaten 2f out* **97/10**

7 — 1 1/2 — **Groom Tesse**[14] 5718 5-9-5 .... (b) SLandi 5 — 108
(L Camici, Italy) *broke well, restrained in 4th, close up halfway, 5th straight, weakened 2f out* **5/1**[3]

8 — 10 — **Miles Gloriosus (USA)**[14] 5718 3-8-12 .... MDemuro 4 — 93
(R Menichetti, Italy) *last throughout, well behind final 2f* **57/1**

2m 29.8s
WFA 3 from 4yo+ 7lb — 8 Ran SP% **184.0**
WIN 1.84 (coupled with Cherry Mix); PL 2.23, 3.49, 1.57; DF 61.24.
Owner Sheikh Mohammed **Bred** Gainsborough Stud Management Ltd **Trained** Chantilly, France

NOTEBOOK
Laverock(IRE) appreciated the faster ground. He took the lead earlier than his jockey intended and would have struggled if he had been obliged to travel much further. He began the season at Sha Tin and is likely to end it either there or in Japan.
Fair Nashwan, a Group 3 winner over 11 furlongs at this course two weeks earlier, was going nowhere with over a furlong to run but was closing fast at the end. She has recovered well from the tendon injury she suffered last year and is now in the form of her life.
Cherry Mix(FR), last year's winner, was handed a clear lead but his rivals closed up rapidly at halfway. He stayed on creditably to outlast Egerton for third.
Sweet Stream(ITY), running for only the second time this year, stayed on to the end but needed a much stronger pace. She has not got much time left but is certainly capable of winning another big race.

6005a PREMIO OMENONI (GROUP 3) — 5f
5:15 (5:22) 3-Y-O+ — **£29,439** (£13,421; £7,458; £3,729)

RPR

1 — **Champion Place**[112] 3-8-11 .... MDemuro 2 — 98
(R Menichetti, Italy) *raced in centre, led or disputed throughout, definite leader 2f out, just held on* **19/1**

2 — shd — **Krisman (IRE)**[147] 1871 7-9-0 .... WGambarota 1 — 101
(M Ciciarelli, Italy) *always in touch on rails, ran on final f, just failed* **56/10**[3]

3 — snk — **Sacho (GER)**[91] 8-9-0 .... ASuborics 4 — 100
(W Kujath, Germany) *midfield, 4th over 1f out, ran on under pressure, nearest at finish* **73/10**

4 — 1/2 — **Agata Laguna (IRE)** 3-8-11 .... DVargiu 5 — 96
(R Brogi, Italy) *always in touch, kept on well final f* **33/2**

5 — 1 1/2 — **Crucial**[147] 1871 6-9-0 .... PConvertino 8 — 93
(Frank Sheridan, Italy) *pressed winner on outside til weakened over 1f out* **57/10**

6 — 3/4 — **One Putra (IRE)**[10] 5779 4-9-0 .... PhilipRobinson 3 — 91
(M A Jarvis) *prominent near rails, one pace from approaching final f* **4/5**[1]

7 — 1 1/2 — **Velvet Revolver (IRE)**[73] 4095 3-8-11 .... GMarcelli 6 — 82
(L Riccardi, Italy) *tracked leaders, one pace final 1 1/2f* **44/10**[2]

8 — 3 — **Kuaicoss (IRE)**[92] 3564 4-9-0 .... MEsposito 7 — 74
(A Renzoni, Italy) *prominent on outside til weakened over 1f out* **124/10**

58.50 secs — 8 Ran SP% **134.4**
WIN 20.05; PL 4.73, 2.65, 3.13; DF 61.16.
Owner Razza Dell'Olmo **Bred** Larkwood Stud **Trained** Italy

NOTEBOOK
Champion Place showed good speed throughout and and was just able to hang on. She is the third Group 3 winner in Italy for her sire, Compton Place, and all three have been trained by Riccardo Menichetti.
One Putra(IRE) was not beaten far and deserves another chance.

5983 BELMONT PARK (L-H)
Sunday, October 15

OFFICIAL GOING: Firm

6006a CLAIMER — 1m 110y
7:33 (7:34) 4-Y-O+
£15,349 (£5,116; £2,558; £1,279; £767; £128)

RPR

1 — **Tiverton (USA)** 4-8-8 .... (b) GKGomez 9 — 93
(D Donk, U.S.A) **67/10**

2 — 1 3/4 — **Chilly Rooster (USA)**[540] 6-8-8 .... (b) CHill 6 — 89
(D Schettino, U.S.A) **63/10**

3 — 1 1/2 — **Si O No (CHI)** 4-8-8 .... RMigliore 1 — 86
(Patrick L Reynolds, U.S.A) **128/10**

4 — 1 3/4 — **Privy Seal (IRE)**[379] 5634 5-8-8 .... EPrado 3 — 83
(R Dutrow Jr, U.S.A) **51/20**[1]

5 — 4 — **Approved By Dylan (USA)** 4-8-8 .... (b) JBravo 2 — 75
(Kelly Breen, U.S.A) **52/10**[3]

6 — nk — **Fire Path (USA)**[652] 4-8-8 .... (b) ECoa 4 — 74
(J Rogers, U.S.A) **229/10**

7 — 3/4 — **Touched By Madness (USA)**[22] 4-8-8 .... JCastellano 8 — 73
(E Allard, U.S.A) **67/10**

8 — 3/4 — **Grand (IRE)**[1470] 5177 6-8-8 .... JRVelazquez 5 — 71
(Dale Romans, U.S.A) **79/20**[2]

9 — 7 — **Defi (IRE)**[34] 5249 4-8-8 .... (b) TomEaves 7 — 57
(I Semple) *mid-division til lost place approaching straight, 9th and weakening straight SP 40-1* **40/1**

1m 41.75s — 9 Ran SP% **118.0**
PARI-MUTUEL (Including $2 stake): WIN 15.40; PL (1-2) 8.30, 7.30;SHOW (1-2-3) 6.10, 4.40, 9.60; SF 138.00.
Owner W Punk Jr **Bred** Paul Tackett **Trained** USA

NOTEBOOK
Defi(IRE) presumably travelled over with his stablemate Big Timer, but he failed to take racing in the US.

5720 PONTEFRACT (L-H)

Monday, October 16

OFFICIAL GOING: Good to soft

After five dry days the going for the final meeting in 2006 was described as 'soft, sticky and holding'.

Wind: almost nil Weather: fine

6007 TOTEPLACEPOT NURSERY 1m 4y
2:20 (2:20) (Class 5) (0-75,73) 2-Y-O **£3,886** (£1,156; £577; £288) **Stalls** Low

Form RPR

0303 **1** **Doubly Guest**[25] 5492 2-8-13 **65** .... TonyCulhane 5 72
(G G Margarson) *mid-div: hdwa on ins over 2f out: led 1f out: drvn out* **8/1**

2032 **2** *1 ¾* **Fongs Gazelle**[25] 5492 2-8-13 **68** .... GregFairley(3) 11 71
(M Johnston) *w ldrs: led over 2f out: hung lft and hdd 1f out: no ex* **13/2**[3]

0604 **3** *1 ¼* **Revisionist (IRE)**[20] 5597 2-8-12 **64** .... KDarley 1 64
(R Hannon) *chsd ldrs: drvn over 2f out: styd on same pce fnl f* **20/1**

6441 **4** *nk* **Fiumicino**[25] 5492 2-9-7 **73** .... RobertWinston 12 72
(M R Channon) *mid-div: hdwy to chse ldrs over 2f out: kpt on same pce appr fnl f* **4/1**[1]

3534 **5** *2* **Angeletta**[7] 5866 2-9-3 **69** .... SebSanders 16 64
(E S McMahon) *chsd ldrs: n.m.r over 1f out: one pce* **8/1**

5520 **6** *½* **Muncaster Castle (IRE)**[7] 5860 2-8-4 **56** .... PaulHanagan 6 50
(R F Fisher) *chsd ldrs: one pce fnl 2f* **33/1**

0600 **7** *nk* **Salto Chico**[26] 5482 2-8-3 **55** .... RoystonFfrench 8 48
(W M Brisbourne) *s.i.s: kpt on fnl 2f: nvr nr to chal* **100/1**

454 **8** *½* **Firestorm (IRE)**[44] 5014 2-8-8 **60** .... DeanMcKeown 15 52
(C W Fairhurst) *bhd: sme hdwy 2f out: nvr a factor* **40/1**

6055 **9** *shd* **Dee Cee Elle**[25] 5492 2-8-3 **55** .... JoeFanning 4 46
(M Johnston) *in tch: effrt over 2f out: lost pl over 1f out* **20/1**

0004 **10** *3 ½* **Diggs Lane (IRE)**[34] 5262 2-8-0 **55** ....(b) MarcHalford(3) 13 38
(N A Callaghan) *mid-div: effrt over 2f out: nvr a factor* **5/1**[2]

6341 **11** *hd* **Centenary (IRE)**[19] 5616 2-9-4 **70** .... TomEaves 7 53
(J S Wainwright) *chsd ldrs: lost pl over 2f out* **12/1**

100 **12** *1* **Slavonic Lake**[26] 5482 2-8-8 **60** ....(b[1]) DavidAllan 18 41
(I A Wood) *in tch: wknd 2f out* **100/1**

606 **13** *1* **Downbeat**[23] 5537 2-8-13 **65** .... JimmyQuinn 9 43
(J L Dunlop) *rrd s: sme hdwy over 2f out: sn btn* **9/1**

6043 **14** *11* **Deccan Express (IRE)**[52] 4767 2-9-0 **66** .... DarryllHolland 14 19
(R Hannon) *led 1f: swtchd wd 6f out: lost pl over 2f out: eased* **20/1**

3200 **15** *6* **Hair Of The Dog**[14] 5720 2-8-9 **61** .... JamieMackay 10 —
(J G Given) *dwlt: hdwy to ld after 1f: hdd over 2f out: lost pl over 1f out: eased* **50/1**

6541 **16** *44* **Foxxy**[18] 5633 2-9-6 **72** .... PaulMulrennan 2 —
(K A Ryan) *rr-div: lost pl 3f out: sn t.o: virtually p.u: btn 44 l* **12/1**

1m 51.75s (6.05) **Going Correction** +0.60s/f (Yiel) 16 Ran SP% **121.2**

Speed ratings (Par 95):93,91,90,89,87 87,86,86,86,82 82,81,80,69,63 19

CSF £53.95 CT £1058.87 TOTE £11.80: £2.20, £2.00, £3.20, £2.10; EX 53.00.

Owner John Guest **Bred** John Guest Mbe M Univ **Trained** Newmarket, Suffolk

■ A 100th training success for George Margarson, and a first winner in Britain for sire Barathea Guest, who Margarson trained.

■ Stewards' Enquiry : Darryll Holland caution: used whip when out of contention

FOCUS

An ordinary nursery but the form looks solid.

NOTEBOOK

Doubly Guest, out of luck here last time, appreciated getting her toe in and was right on top at the finish. (tchd 17-2)

Fongs Gazelle, renewing rivalry with the winner and the fourth, made little appeal in the paddock. She hung left-handed once in front and at the line was very much second best. (op 11-2 tchd 7-1)

Revisionist(IRE), a solidly-made individual, has a pronounced knee action. Dropping back in trip, he simply proved too slow in the home straight.

Fiumicino, who defeated the winner and the second over course and distance last month, has gone in her coat since and was very edgy beforehand. (op 5-1)

Angeletta, knocking on the door, was edgy in the paddock. From her outside draw, she had little more to give when tightened up between horses coming to the final furlong. (op 15-2)

Muncaster Castle(IRE), on his toes beforehand, had finished runner-up in selling company two outings earlier.

6008 TOTEEXACTA H'CAP 1m 2f 6y
2:50 (2:50) (Class 5) (0-70,76) 3-Y-O+ **£4,533** (£1,348; £674; £336) **Stalls** Low

Form RPR

6231 **1** **Dium Mac**[6] 5904 5-9-6 **76** 6ex .... SuzzanneFrance(7) 14 85
(N Bycroft) *hld up: hdwy on wd outside 4f out: styd on gamely to ld ins fnl f: hld on wl* **15/2**

0562 **2** *¾* **Height Of Fury (IRE)**[50] 4842 3-9-1 **69** .... JimmyQuinn 4 77
(J L Dunlop) *promient: led over 1f out: hdd and no ex ins last* **13/2**[3]

062 **3** *1* **Stolen Glance**[7] 5862 3-8-12 **66** .... PaulMulrennan 8 72
(M W Easterby) *promient: hdwy to chal over 1f out: styd on same pce ins last* **20/1**

0046 **4** *½* **Trans Sonic**[19] 5617 3-9-1 **69** ....(v) SebSanders 6 74
(A P Jarvis) *s.s: hdwy to chse ldrs 5f out: dropped bk 2f out: styd on wl fnl f* **16/1**

5011 **5** *1 ¾* **Cantabilly (IRE)**[5] 5911 3-9-6 **74** 6ex .... TonyCulhane 17 75
(M R Channon) *hld up in rr: hdwy on ins over 2f out: styd on fnl f: nvr rchd ldrs* **7/1**

3353 **6** *2 ½* **Bollin Dolly**[14] 5727 3-8-13 **67** .... DavidAllan 7 64
(T D Easterby) *w ldrs: led after 2f: hdd over 1f out: one pce* **12/1**

2425 **7** *1 ¾* **Contemplation**[7] 5879 3-8-11 **65** .... PaulHanagan 3 58
(G A Swinbank) *mid-div: hdwy to chse ldrs over 2f out: fdd oveer 1f out* **9/2**[1]

6530 **8** *1* **Tidy (IRE)**[6] 5904 6-9-1 **67** .... GregFairley(3) 9 58
(Micky Hammond) *mid-div: kpt on fnl 2f: nvr nr to chal* **22/1**

-240 **9** *¾* **Generator**[58] 4606 4-9-0 **63** .... DarryllHolland 5 53
(Dr J D Scargill) *led 2f: sn stdd: hdwy over 2f out: edgd rt over 1f out: n.d* **40/1**

1122 **10** *12* **Sudden Impulse**[6] 5904 5-9-0 **63** .... SilvestreDeSousa 12 30
(A D Brown) *trckd ldrs: wknd appr fnl f* **11/2**[2]

4010 **11** *nk* **Hawkit (USA)**[7] 5863 5-9-7 **70** .... RobertWinston 18 37
(P Monteith) *a in rr* **18/1**

1000 **12** *6* **My Obsession (IRE)**[43] 5042 4-8-11 **60** .... MickyFenton 11 15
(John Berry) *hld up in rr: hdwy on ins over 2f out: sn wknd* **40/1**

004- **13** *2 ½* **Miss Pebbles (IRE)**[155] 5940 6-9-7 **70** ....(v) RoystonFfrench 2 20
(R Dickin) *chsd ldrs: lost pl over 1f out* **25/1**

000- **14** *1 ½* **Dante's Diamond (IRE)**[347] 5893 4-9-2 **65** .... DeanMcKeown 1 13
(G A Swinbank) *hld up towards rr: bhd fnl 2f* **50/1**

5500 **15** *1 ½* **Mayadeen (IRE)**[18] 4871 4-9-2 **65** ....(v[1]) JoeFanning 15 10
(J G M O'Shea) *chsd ldrs: lost pl over 2f out: sn bhd* **66/1**

0210 **16** *2* **Asaateel (IRE)**[14] 5734 4-9-0 **63** ....(b) TomEaves 13 4
(G L Moore) *chsd ldrs: lost pl over 2f* **25/1**

U513 **17** *18* **Ruby Legend**[25] 5497 8-8-10 **59** ....(p) KDarley 16 —
(K G Reveley) *chsd ldrs on outer: wknd 3f out: sn bhd: eased* **20/1**

2m 19.38s (5.30) **Going Correction** +0.60s/f (Yiel)

WFA 3 from 4yo+ 5lb 17 Ran SP% **119.9**

Speed ratings (Par 103):102,101,100,100,98 96,95,94,94,84 84,79,77,76,74 73,58

CSF £47.36 CT £950.56 TOTE £9.80: £2.70, £1.80, £4.70, £4.90; EX 75.50.

Owner J A Swinburne **Bred** T Umpleby **Trained** Brandsby, N Yorks

FOCUS

A good handicap for the grade, the first two progressive types. It was run at a steady pace to the halfway mark. The winner deserves full marks.

Ruby Legend Official explanation: jockey said gelding was unsuited by the good to soft going

6009 TOTEQUADPOT H'CAP 5f
3:20 (3:21) (Class 4) (0-85,84) 3-Y-O+ **£7,772** (£2,312; £1,155; £577) **Stalls** Low

Form RPR

0051 **1** **Kay Two (IRE)**[10] 5791 4-8-12 **78** .... PhilipRobinson 10 93
(R J Price) *chsd ldrs: led ins last: drvn out* **11/2**[1]

5200 **2** *1* **Rainbow Rising (IRE)**[31] 5336 4-8-11 **82** .... JamieMoriarty(5) 1 93
(J Howard Johnson) *w ldrs: led over 2f out: hdd and no ex ins last* **15/2**[2]

1531 **3** *¾* **Geojimali**[31] 5336 4-8-12 **81** .... SaleemGolam(3) 9 90+
(J S Goldie) *s.i.s: hdwy on outside over 1f out: fin wl* **11/2**[1]

2043 **4** *nk* **Charlie Delta**[8] 5842 3-8-13 **79** .... DarryllHolland 14 87+
(D Carroll) *mid-div: nt clr run over 1f out: hdwy and swtchd rt jst ins last: fin strly* **33/1**

4504 **5** *shd* **Bond Boy**[52] 4771 9-9-0 **80** ....(v) RobertWinston 5 87
(B Smart) *in rr: hdwy over 1f out: styd on ins last* **9/1**[3]

6004 **6** *1* **Bo McGinty (IRE)**[23] 5532 5-8-13 **79** ....(b) PaulHanagan 7 83
(R A Fahey) *in tch: hdwy over 1f out: kpt on same pce* **10/1**

0103 **7** *nk* **Oranmore Castle (IRE)**[31] 5333 4-9-0 **80** ....(t) AdrianTNicholls 3 83
(D Nicholls) *w ldrs: chal over 2f out: kpt on same pce fnl f* **10/1**

0000 **8** *1* **Highland Warrior**[23] 5535 7-9-0 **80** ....(p) DanielTudhope 4 79
(J S Goldie) *s.i.s: hdwy on ins whn nt clr run appr fnl f: nvr on terms* **25/1**

000 **9** *nk* **Crimson Silk**[31] 5336 6-9-0 **80** ....(v[1]) PaulEddery 2 80+
(B Smart) *chsd ldrs: one pce appr fnl f* **28/1**

6010 **10** *shd* **Sea Salt**[31] 5333 3-9-0 **80** .... PhillipMakin 6 81+
(T D Barron) *chsd ldrs: fdd appr fnl f* **33/1**

0021 **11** *1* **Sir Nod**[33] 5286 4-8-11 **77** .... TomEaves 15 71
(Miss J A Camacho) *led on outside: hdd over 2f out: fdd appr fnl f* **9/1**[3]

3300 **12** *1 ¼* **Raymond's Pride**[31] 5336 6-8-11 **80** ....(b) AndrewMullen(3) 17 69
(K A Ryan) *s.i.s: sme hdwy on outside over 1f out: nvr on terms* **25/1**

0050 **13** *2* **Enchantment**[28] 5433 5-8-9 **78** .... StephenDonohoe(3) 11 60
(J M Bradley) *mid-div: drvn over 2f out: nvr a threat* **20/1**

5000 **14** *1 ¼* **Malapropism**[23] 5532 6-8-12 **78** .... TonyCulhane 12 63+
(M R Channon) *in tch: no imp whn bdly hmpd jst ins last* **33/1**

6226 **15** *2* **After The Show**[36] 5212 5-8-12 **78** .... SebSanders 16 49
(Rae Guest) *s.i.s: nvr a factor* **14/1**

0060 **16** *1 ¼* **Peopleton Brook**[8] 5832 4-9-1 **84** .... GregFairley(3) 8 50
(J M Bradley) *w ldrs: wknd appr fnl f* **40/1**

4050 **17** *½* **Matty Tun**[23] 5535 7-8-11 **77** .... DeanMcKeown 18 41
(J Balding) *chsd ldrs on outer: wknd over 1f out* **20/1**

1240 **18** *3 ½* **Shes Minnie**[23] 5532 3-8-10 **76** ....(p) JoeFanning 13 28
(J G M O'Shea) *chsd ldrs: wknd and eased over 1f out* **20/1**

66.02 secs (2.22) **Going Correction** +0.60s/f (Yiel) 18 Ran SP% **124.1**

Speed ratings (Par 105):106,104,103,102,102 100,100,98,98,98 96,94,91,89,86 84,83,77

CSF £38.39 CT £252.52 TOTE £7.70: £2.50, £3.00, £1.70, £4.60; EX 71.20.

Owner H McGahon, D McCarthy & B Llewellyn **Bred** Roger A Ryan **Trained** Ullingswick, H'fords

■ Stewards' Enquiry : Darryll Holland three-day ban: careless riding (Oct 27-29)

FOCUS

A competitive sprint handicap and strong form for the grade. The winner has ended the season in great heart and will be still be fairly treated on old form after this.

6010 TOTESPORT.COM SILVER TANKARD STKS (LISTED RACE) 1m 4y
3:50 (3:50) (Class 1) 2-Y-O

£22,712 (£8,608; £4,308; £2,148; £1,076; £540) **Stalls** Low

Form RPR

1114 **1** **Sweet Lilly**[37] 5187 2-8-11 102 .... TonyCulhane 8 103+
(M R Channon) *hld up gng wl: smooth hdwy over 2f out: led 1f out: edgd rt and swished tail: styd on strly* **4/1**[3]

3104 **2** *1 ¾* **Champlain**[23] 5521 2-9-5 105 .... PhilipRobinson 5 107
(M A Jarvis) *hld up in rr: hdwy on outside over 3f out: chal 1f out: no ex ins last* **11/8**[1]

1 **3** *3* **Empire Day (UAE)**[27] 5460 2-9-2 .... JoeFanning 10 97
(M Johnston) *chsd ldr: led 2f out: hung lft and hdd 1f out: kpt on same pce* **7/2**[2]

123 **4** *2 ½* **Bid For Glory**[27] 5459 2-9-2 82 .... JimmyQuinn 9 91
(H J Collingridge) *hld up in tch: nt clr run over 2f out and over 1f out: kpt on same pce* **20/1**

046 **5** *4* **New Beginning (IRE)**[14] 5720 2-9-2 76 .... MickyFenton 2 82
(Mrs S Lamyman) *chsd ldrs: outpcd 2f out: no threat after* **200/1**

341 **6** *4* **Dream Lodge (IRE)**[8] 5841 2-9-2 .... JamieMackay 6 73
(J G Given) *sn chsng ldrs: rdn and outpcd 3f out: sn wknd* **100/1**

5021 **7** *½* **Zafonical Storm (USA)**[15] 5707 2-9-5 99 .... DJMoran 4 75
(B W Duke) *set str pce: hdd 2f out: sn wknd* **8/1**

2105 **8** *3 ½* **Fishforcompliments**[37] 5183 2-9-2 106 .... PaulHanagan 3 64
(R A Fahey) *trckd ldrs: lost pl wl over 1f out* **13/2**

1m 49.32s (3.62) **Going Correction** +0.60s/f (Yiel) 8 Ran SP% **115.0**

Speed ratings (Par 103):105,103,100,97,93 89,89,85

CSF £9.94 TOTE £5.00: £1.60, £1.30, £1.40; EX 10.00.

Owner Jaber Abdullah **Bred** Red House Stud **Trained** West Ilsley, Berks

FOCUS

Strong form for the grade and the highly progressive winner deserves full marks. The pace was not strong.

NOTEBOOK

Sweet Lilly, on the back of an improved effort in the May Hill at York, is thriving. She came there travelling easily best and, despite as usual being very free with her tail, she stuck on strongly and was right on top at the line. (op 9-2 tchd 5-1)

Champlain, a bonny colt, was put to sleep at the back. Making his effort on the outside, he made the winner dig deep but was definitely the silver medallist at the line. (op 7-4)

Empire Day(UAE), attempting to give his trainer his fourth success in this Listed event in the last nine years, was racing on totally different ground. His inexperience showed in front and in the end the first two were simply too good. He should make a better three-year-old. (op 11-4)

Bid For Glory, who had 25lb to find with the winner on official figures, is a grand type and he did not really have the rub of the green here. However, after this he might struggle for winning opportunities.
New Beginning(IRE), a nice type, was given a big ask on just his fourth career start and he will start 2007 from a stiff handicap mark. (op 150-1)
Dream Lodge(IRE), back on turf after his Polytrack maiden-race success, had a mountain to climb. (op 66-1)
Zafonical Storm(USA), fresh from his Tipperary Listed-race success, set a strong pace and had no more to give turning in. (op 10-1)
Fishforcompliments, who had the blinkers left off, does not impress with his attitude. He will need to turn over a new leaf at three. (op 15-2)

6011 TOTESPORT 0800 221 221 BLUFF COVE H'CAP — 2m 1f 216y

4:20 (4:20) (Class 5) (0-75,69) 3-Y-0+ — **£5,181** (£1,541; £770; £384) **Stalls** Low

Form — RPR
0012 **1** **Esprit De Corps**[30] 5369 4-9-12 **66** ..... SebSanders 5 — 79+
(Sir Mark Prescott) *hld up in tch: stdy hdwy over 4f out: led and hung lft over 1f out: drvn clr* **2/1**[1]
2225 **2** *3½* **Kayf Aramis**[9] 5811 4-9-10 **67** ..... (p) MarcHalford(3) 8 — 76
(J L Spearing) *trckd ldr: chal 8f out: led 5f out tl over 1f out: kpt on same pce* **9/2**[2]
1346 **3** *4* **Great As Gold (IRE)**[14] 5723 7-9-9 **63** ..... (p) TomEaves 12 — 68
(B Ellison) *sn trcking ldrs: chal over 4f out: one pce fnl 2f* **12/1**
06-6 **4** *2½* **Calfraz**[166] 1415 4-8-6 **49** ..... GregFairley(3) 9 — 51
(Micky Hammond) *hld up in rr: effrt over 4f out: kpt on fnl 2f: nvr a threat* **33/1**
2123 **5** *½* **Mister Arjay (USA)**[14] 5723 6-9-9 **68** ..... PJMcDonald(5) 11 — 69
(B Ellison) *chsd ldrs: chal 6f out: one pce fnl 2f* **16/1**
0001 **6** *½* **Dan's Heir**[13] 5750 4-8-11 **58** ..... (p) AshleyHamblett(7) 1 — 59
(P C Haslam) *hld up in rr: hdwy 4f out: one pce* **14/1**
4453 **7** *1* **Totally Scottish**[8] 5836 10-8-9 **49** oh1 ..... DavidAllan 3 — 49
(K G Reveley) *hld up in rr: drvn 6f out: one pce fnl 3f* **20/1**
0321 **8** *nk* **Thewhirlingdervish (IRE)**[14] 5723 8-9-6 **65** ..... DuranFentiman(5) 4 — 64
(T D Easterby) *hld up towards rr: hdwy 6f out: effrt over 2f out: nvr trbld ldrs* **11/2**[3]
3405 **9** *½* **Great Tidings**[20] 5594 3-9-4 **69** ..... JoeFanning 6 — 68
(M Johnston) *led 1f: sn hld up in mid-field: effrt over 3f out: one pce* **10/1**
0553 **10** *45* **Halland**[9] 5815 8-9-7 **61** ..... MickyFenton 2 — —
(T J Fitzgerald) *hld up in rr: drvn 9f out: nvr on terms: eased over 1f out: t.o* **14/1**
1250 **11** *4* **Rare Coincidence**[14] 5736 5-9-4 **58** ..... (p) PaulHanagan 10 — —
(R F Fisher) *led after 1f: hdd 5f out: sn lost pl: t.o 2f out: virtually p.u* **40/1**
41-0 **12** *15* **Grasp**[9] 5587 4-9-6 **60** ..... (b) RobertWinston 7 — —
(G L Moore) *s.i.s: hdwy to chse ldrs after 2f: chal over 4f out: lost pl over 2f out: sn bhd and eased: t.o* **33/1**

4m 9.91s (6.91) **Going Correction** +0.60s/f (Yiel)
WFA 3 from 4yo+ 11lb — **12** Ran SP% **116.0**
Speed ratings (Par 103):108,106,104,103,103 103,102,102,102,76 46,10
CSF £9.47 CT £84.94 TOTE £3.00: £1.50, £2.00, £3.90; EX 15.30.
Owner W E Sturt - Osborne House II **Bred** Miss K Rausing **Trained** Newmarket, Suffolk

FOCUS
A sound gallop and a severe test of stamina in the conditions. Ordinary form, but the winner is progressing well.
Halland Official explanation: jockey said gelding had no more to give

6012 TOTE TEXT BETTING 60021 MAIDEN AUCTION STKS (DIV I) — 6f

4:50 (4:50) (Class 5) 2-Y-0 — **£3,238** (£963; £481; £240) **Stalls** Low

Form — RPR
4040 **1** **Our Blessing (IRE)**[16] 5681 2-8-13 68 ..... SebSanders 7 — 72
(A P Jarvis) *trckd ldrs: led over 2f out: drvn rt out* **10/3**[1]
2 *1* **Giant Slalom** 2-8-12 ..... PaulHanagan 6 — 68+
(W J Haggas) *hld up in rr: hdwy over 2f out: styd on to take 2nd ins last: kpt on wl* **9/2**
50 **3** *1½* **Captain Nemo (USA)**[30] 5379 2-8-11 ..... PhillipMakin 9 — 63
(T D Barron) *in rr: hdwy over 1f out: styd on ins last: tk 3rd on line* **4/1**[3]
6 **4** *shd* **News Of The Day (IRE)**[13] 5760 2-8-5 ..... JoeFanning 3 — 56
(M Johnston) *chsd ldrs: chal over 2f out: edgd rt 1f out: one pce* **7/2**[2]
4000 **5** *5* **The Dandy Fox**[16] 5687 2-8-5 48 ..... JimmyQuinn 8 — 41
(R Bastiman) *trckd ldrs: t.k.h early: effrt over 2f out: fdd appr fnl f* **20/1**
05 **6** *½* **Grethel (IRE)**[10] 5790 2-8-6 ..... TonyHamilton 1 — 41
(A Berry) *chsd ldrs: chal over 2f out: wknd 1f out* **12/1**
7 *3½* **Meathop (IRE)** 2-8-11 ow3 ..... DNolan(3) 5 — 38
(R F Fisher) *s.i.s: nvr a factor* **33/1**
8 *3* **Falcon's Fire (IRE)** 2-8-13 ..... RoystonFfrench 4 — 28
(Mrs A Duffield) *s.s: mid-div: lost pl over 1f out* **7/1**
0 **9** *11* **Moondine (IRE)**[33] 5283 2-8-1 ..... AndrewMullen(3) 10 — —
(B S Rothwell) *s.i.s: lost pl over 2f out: sn bhd* **200/1**
0 **10** *1¾* **Soylent Green**[25] 5491 2-8-8 ow4 ..... MickyFenton 2 — —
(S Parr) *led tl hdd & wknd qckly over 2f out: sn bhd* **200/1**

1m 22.11s (4.71) **Going Correction** +0.60s/f (Yiel) — **10** Ran SP% **112.4**
Speed ratings (Par 95):92,90,88,88,81 81,76,72,57,55
CSF £17.49 TOTE £4.70: £1.80, £1.90, £1.70; EX 22.00.
Owner Geoffrey Bishop and Ann Jarvis **Bred** Mrs N Quinn **Trained** Twyford, Bucks

FOCUS
Marginally the slower of the two divisions. Weak form, the winner matching his current official rating.

NOTEBOOK
Our Blessing(IRE), better over six furlongs, travelled strongly and was always doing more than enough to get off the mark at the fifth attempt. (op 5-1)
Giant Slalom, whose dam was a stayer, is long in the back. He picked up ground once in line for home and finished with quite a flourish. He will be much more the finished article next year. (op 4-1 tchd 5-1)
Captain Nemo(USA), having his third outing, stayed on from the rear and was putting in his best work at the finish. He should make his mark in handicap company over further at three.
News Of The Day(IRE), a slip of a thing, was in the thick of the action from the off. She still showed her inexperience and there is still time for her to make her mark. (op 3-1)
The Dandy Fox, with the blinkers left off, was much too keen and selling company is her right class. (op 14-1)
Grethel(IRE) was another to let down the form of Kafuu's maiden race at York. (op 9-1)

6013 TOTE TEXT BETTING 60021 MAIDEN AUCTION STKS (DIV II) — 6f

5:20 (5:20) (Class 5) 2-Y-0 — **£3,238** (£963; £481; £240) **Stalls** Low

Form — RPR
4 **1** **Flores Sea (USA)**[32] 5307 2-8-9 ..... PhillipMakin 5 — 70
(T D Barron) *w ldrs: led over 2f out: drvn out* **11/10**[1]
3 **2** *¾* **Snow Dancer (IRE)**[18] 5632 2-8-5 ..... PaulQuinn 7 — 64
(A Berry) *in rr: hdwy on outside over 2f out: styd on to take 2nd nr fin* **33/1**
4 **3** *nk* **Hanbrin Bhoy (IRE)**[28] 5431 2-8-12 ..... RoystonFfrench 4 — 70
(R Dickin) *trckd ldrs: t.k.h: outpcd over 2f out: styd on fnl f* **14/1**
033 **4** *3½* **Multitude (IRE)**[12] 5766 2-8-11 67 ..... DavidAllan 6 — 59
(T D Easterby) *chsd ldrs: drvn over 2f out: one pce* **9/2**[3]
0040 **5** *hd* **Silly Gilly (IRE)**[23] 5528 2-8-4 51 ..... (p) AdrianTNicholls 1 — 51
(A Berry) *w ldrs: chal over 2f out: wknd fnl f* **66/1**
430 **6** *2½* **Lusolly**[19] 5613 2-8-12 ..... PaulHanagan 8 — 52
(M G Quinlan) *led tl over 2f out: wknd over 1f out* **8/1**
2434 **7** *2* **Reem Al Fallah (IRE)**[34] 5271 2-8-8 67 ..... TonyCulhane 3 — 42
(M R Channon) *in tch: outpcd over 2f out: no threat after* **4/1**[2]
0 **8** *3* **Chicamia**[24] 5507 2-8-8 ow2 ..... MickyFenton 2 — 33
(M Mullineaux) *sn outpcd and in rr: nvr on terms* **150/1**
00 **9** *1¼* **Dream On Dreamers (IRE)**[19] 5615 2-8-13 ..... PaulEddery 10 — 34
(R C Guest) *s.i.s: nvr on terms* **200/1**
30 **10** *6* **Telling**[8] 5835 2-8-9 ..... SebSanders 9 — 12
(Mrs A Duffield) *chsd ldrs on outer: lost pl over 1f out* **16/1**

1m 22.02s (4.62) **Going Correction** +0.60s/f (Yiel) — **10** Ran SP% **115.1**
Speed ratings (Par 95):93,92,91,86,86 83,80,76,75,67
CSF £48.50 TOTE £2.20: £1.20, £3.10, £3.50; EX 68.30 Place 6 £72.40, Place 5 £12.60.
Owner C A Washbourn **Bred** Mrs B McLay-Irons **Trained** Maunby, N Yorks

FOCUS
Just the quicker of the two parts but average form, the proximity of 51-rated Silly Gilly is a worry.

NOTEBOOK
Flores Sea(USA), easily the paddock pick, was heavily supported. He made hard work of it in the end but will improve again and should make a good-class handicapper at three. (op 13-8 tchd 7-4)
Snow Dancer(IRE) improved on her Ayr debut effort, staying on down the wide outside to snatch second spot near the line. Her close proximity to the winner may well flatter her however.
Hanbrin Bhoy(IRE), a decent type, stuck on after being tapped for toe and will improve over middle-distances at three. (op 18-1)
Multitude(IRE) never looked a real threat and probably needs further and possibly better ground. (op 5-1 tchd 6-1)
Silly Gilly(IRE), with the cheekpieces retained, was having her ninth start and, rated just 51, her proximity ties down the overall level of the form. (op 50-1)
Lusolly went off very hard, and despite dropping back in trip failed to see it out. (op 5-1)
Reem Al Fallah(IRE), who has already been tried over a mile, is proving costly to follow and the drop back to six was definitely not the answer. (op 7-2 tchd 9-2)
T/Jkpt: Not won. T/Plt: £36.90 to a £1 stake. Pool: £67,176.90. 1,326.25 winning tickets. T/Qpdt: £6.40 to a £1 stake. Pool: £4,135.00. 471.00 winning tickets. WG

5866 WINDSOR (R-H)

Monday, October 16

OFFICIAL GOING: Good to soft (soft in places)
Wind: nil

6014 EUROPEAN BREEDERS FUND MAIDEN STKS (DIV I) — 6f

2:00 (2:00) (Class 5) 2-Y-O — **£3,886** (£1,156; £577; £288) **Stalls** High

Form — RPR
40 **1** **Sandrey (IRE)**[27] 5454 2-9-3 ..... EddieAhern 8 — 78
(P W Chapple-Hyam) *mde all: hrd drvn and responded wl whn chal ins fnl f: kpt on strly cl home* **2/1**[2]
332 **2** *nk* **Kyle (IRE)**[7] 5867 2-9-3 ..... RichardHughes 4 — 77
(R Hannon) *hld up rr but in tch: hdwy 3f out: trckd wnr 1f out:drvn to chal ins last: no ex u.p fnl 110yds* **11/8**[1]
3 *¾* **Sunoverregun** 2-9-0 ..... AmirQuinn(3) 9 — 75
(J R Boyle) *bhd: shkn up and gd hdwy over 2f out: styd on to chse ldrs and edgd rt ins last: kpt on but nt pce of first two* **66/1**
30 **4** *1½* **Den's Gift (IRE)**[17] 5655 2-9-3 ..... AdamKirby 2 — 71
(C G Cox) *chsd ldrs: wnt 2nd and rdn 2f out: outpcd fnl f* **4/1**[3]
0 **5** *3* **Danehill Kikin (IRE)**[18] 5638 2-8-12 ..... MichaelHills 6 — 57
(B W Hills) *chsd ldrs: rdn over 2f out: wknd ins fnl f* **10/1**
4000 **6** *½* **Eastern Princess**[28] 5419 2-8-12 56 ..... RichardThomas 10 — 55
(J A Geake) *in tch: rdn 1/2-way: wknd fnl f* **28/1**
0 **7** *3* **Stars Above**[7] 5871 2-8-12 ..... TPQueally 7 — 51+
(Sir Mark Prescott) *rr but in tch: pushed along 3f out: no ch fnl 2f* **50/1**
00 **8** *2* **Bellehurst**[30] 5380 2-8-5 ..... KMay(7) 3 — 40
(B J Meehan) *chsd wnr 4f: sn wknd* **50/1**
0 **9** *¾* **Shrewd Dude**[12] 5766 2-9-3 ..... GeorgeBaker 1 — 43
(Carl Llewellyn) *s.i.s: a in rr* **40/1**
00 **10** *2½* **Divalini**[17] 5648 2-8-12 ..... DaneO'Neill 11 — 30
(J Akehurst) *a in rr* **100/1**

1m 15.6s (1.93) **Going Correction** +0.275s/f (Good) — **10** Ran SP% **116.8**
Speed ratings (Par 95):98,97,96,94,90 89,85,83,82,78
CSF £4.97 TOTE £3.70: £1.20, £1.10, £4.90; EX 6.50 Trifecta £68.70 Pool £455.99 - 4.71 winning units.
Owner Nizar Anwar **Bred** Mohammad Al-Qatami **Trained** Newmarket, Suffolk

FOCUS
Just an ordinary sprint maiden in which they raced far side in the straight. The form looks pretty solid despite the conditions. The winning time was 0.38 seconds quicker than the second division, and 0.11 seconds faster than the handicap for older horses.

NOTEBOOK
Sandrey(IRE), an Irish Guineas entry, was a beaten favourite at Newmarket on his previous start but left that form behind to confirm the promise he had shown on his debut. (op 9-4)
Kyle(IRE) ran just as he did over course and distance the previous week, travelling strongly but not quite having the stamina to see out six furlongs on rain-softened ground. (tchd 6-4)
Sunoverregun, a half-brother to four winners, including prolific seven-furlong winner Millennium Force, out of a useful ten-furlong winner, was the only debutant in the field and shaped with plenty of promise.
Den's Gift(IRE), 12th of 28 in a sales race at Newmarket on his previous start, could not take advantage of the return to maiden company.
Danehill Kikin(IRE) was again well held but is the type to do better once handicapped. (op 11-1)
Shrewd Dude Official explanation: jockey said colt missed the break

6015 EUROPEAN BREEDERS FUND MAIDEN STKS (DIV II) — 6f

2:30 (2:30) (Class 5) 2-Y-O — **£3,886** (£1,156; £577; £288) **Stalls** High

Form — RPR
0364 **1** **Vitznau (IRE)**[38] 5147 2-9-3 71 ..... RichardHughes 8 — 73+
(R Hannon) *hld up in tch: hdwy 2f out: qckn to chal 1f out: drvn to ld last strides: all out* **5/6**[1]
6 **2** *shd* **Genki (IRE)**[10] 5780 2-9-3 ..... SteveDrowne 1 — 73+
(R Charlton) *s.i.s: sn trcking ldrs: led ins fnl 2f: rdn and kpt on wl whn chal fnl f: hdd last strides* **11/2**[2]

				RPR
	3	3	**Vesuvio** 2-9-3 .... MichaelHills 7 (B W Hills) *trckd ldrs: rdn to chal 1f out: wknd fnl 110yds* **7/1**[3]	64
00	4	*shd*	**Dressed To Dance (IRE)**[13] 5760 2-8-12 .... JamieSpencer 3 (B J Meehan) *chsd ldrs: slt ld 2f out: sn hdd: stl ev ch over 1f out: wknd ins last* **17/2**	58
0203	5	4	**Show Trial (IRE)**[10] 5780 2-8-12 54........ ChrisCatlin 10 (D J S Ffrench Davis) *rr but in tch: hdwy 2f out: kpt on fr over 1f out but nvr in contention* **20/1**	46
	6	1 ½	**Katie Kingfisher** 2-8-12 .... NelsonDeSouza 9 (R M Beckett) *s.i.s: bhd: pushed along over 2f out: kpt on fnl f but nvr in contention* **20/1**	42
	7	1	**Miss Hoolie** 2-8-12 .... AdamKirby 2 (W R Swinburn) *in tch: chsd ldrs 1/2-way: wknd appr fnl f* **20/1**	39
4	8	1 ¾	**So Shy (IRE)**[131] 2354 2-8-12 .... EddieAhern 4 (J R Boyle) *slt led tl hdd 2f out: sn btn* **14/1**	34
6000	9	1	**Purple Sands (IRE)**[34] 5261 2-9-3 56........ RyanMoore 6 (B J Meehan) *disp ld 4f: sn btn* **22/1**	36
060	10	8	**Yve Sam La Champ**[7] 5871 2-8-10 .... MarkCoumbe(7) 11 (A W Carroll) *a in rr* **100/1**	12
54	11	6	**Weet In Line**[16] 5687 2-8-12 .... TPQueally 5 (K J Burke) *early spd: sn bhd: collapsed after line: dead* **50/1**	—

1m 15.98s (2.31) **Going Correction** +0.275s/f (Good) **11** Ran SP% **121.2**
Speed ratings (Par 95):95,94,90,90,85 83,82,79,78,67 59
CSF £5.08 TOTE £1.90: £1.10, £1.70, £2.20; EX 5.70 Trifecta £21.30 Pool £439.99 - 14.61 winning units.
Owner Louis Stalder **Bred** John McLoughlin **Trained** East Everleigh, Wilts

FOCUS
Another ordinary sprint maiden and they again raced towards the far side. Not easy to set the level of the form, but it could prove better than this. The winning time was 0.38 seconds slower than the first division and 0.27 seconds off the time recorded by Linda Green in the older-horse handicap.

NOTEBOOK
Vitznau(IRE), back up in trip and returned to easy ground, proved good enough to gain his first success at the sixth attempt. He appeals as one to take on in better company. (op 5-4 tchd 11-8 in a place)
Genki(IRE), very green on his debut over seven furlongs at Lingfield, showed the benefit of that experience and was just held. He was clear of the remainder. (op 6-1 tchd 13-2)
Vesuvio, a brother to Stephano, a dual ten-furlong winner, out of a middle-distance scorer, made a pleasing introduction and should do better over further next year. (op 8-1 tchd 9-1)
Dressed To Dance(IRE) did not run badly and will have more options now she is qualified for a handicap mark. (op 15-2 tchd 10-1)
Show Trial(IRE) will surely be better off in low-grade nurseries. (op 16-1)

6016 JOHN NASH LIFETIME IN RACING (S) STKS — 1m 67y
3:00 (3:01) (Class 5) 2-Y-O **£3,238** (£963; £481; £240) **Stalls** High

Form				RPR
6252	1		**Emergency Services**[56] 4665 2-8-12 56........(p) RichardThomas 4 (Tom Dascombe) *sn chsng ldr: rdn over 2f out: led wl over 1f out: drvn and hld on wl fnl f* **12/1**	56
5006	2	1 ¼	**Global Traffic**[3] 5948 2-8-12 54........ JosedeSouza 8 (P F I Cole) *chsd ldrs: rdn 3f out: styd on to chse wnr ins fnl f but a hld* **5/1**[2]	53
0000	3	1	**Daring You**[34] 5262 2-8-12 53........ NelsonDeSouza 3 (P F I Cole) *chsd ldrs: rdn 3f out: styd on fnl 2f but nvr quite gng pce to chal* **10/1**	51
00	4	1 ¼	**Fighting Mood**[14] 5730 2-8-12 .... MartinDwyer 2 (A M Balding) *in tch: hdwy 4f out and wnt towards far side: styd on u.p fnl 3f: no ex fr over 1f out* **6/1**[3]	48
2003	5	*hd*	**Gifted Heir (IRE)**[26] 5482 2-8-12 54........ RichardMullen 1 (I A Wood) *chsd ldrs: rdn fr 4f out: one pce fnl 2f* **6/1**[3]	47
0500	6	½	**Rowan Venture**[14] 5738 2-8-12 58........(b) TPQueally 10 (M H Tompkins) *led: sn clr: rdn 3f out: hdd wl over 1f out: wandered u.p 1f out and sn wknd* **16/1**	46
6033	7	*nk*	**Grimes Glory**[32] 5323 2-8-12 54........ RyanMoore 13 (R Hannon) *rr: hdwy 4f out: wnt far side 3f out: sn drvn to chse ldrs: one pce fr over 1f out* **3/1**[1]	46
	8	2	**King Of Magic** 2-8-5 .... JackDean(7) 12 (W G M Turner) *bhd: rdn over 3f out: kpt on fnl 2f but nvr in contention* **50/1**	41
510	9	1 ¾	**Distant Flash**[28] 5419 2-8-13 53........ EddieAhern 6 (G L Moore) *mid-div: rdn and effrt twoards far side 3f out: nvr gng pce to trble ldrs: sn btn* **9/1**	38
0	10	13	**Break 'N' Dish**[28] 5423 2-8-9 .... NeilChalmers(3) 9 (B R Johnson) *a in rr* **66/1**	7
0000	11	*shd*	**Garrya**[32] 5323 2-8-12 55........ RichardSmith 14 (R Hannon) *chsd ldrs 5f* **40/1**	7
5020	12	4	**Readyforone**[122] 2626 2-8-12 58........(b) SteveDrowne 5 (P D Evans) *sn bhd* **20/1**	—
0000	13	*shd*	**Last Dog Standing (IRE)**[31] 5349 2-8-12 52........(b1) MichaelHills 11 (B G Powell) *s.i.s: a bhd* **22/1**	—
0500	14	2	**Saxenberg**[82] 3844 2-8-7 54........ JohnEgan 7 (Miss J R Gibney) *sn bhd* **25/1**	—

1m 47.82s (2.22) **Going Correction** +0.075s/f (Good) **14** Ran SP% **121.8**
Speed ratings (Par 95):91,89,88,87,87 86,86,84,82,69 69,65,65,63
CSF £67.09 TOTE £7.60: £2.50, £2.30, £3.50; EX 94.70 Trifecta £258.70 Part won. Pool £364.41 - 0.34 winning units..There was no bid for the winner. Global Traffic was claimed by P D Evans for £6,000.
Owner Sideways Racing IV **Bred** Bearstone Stud **Trained** Lambourn, Berks
■ Stewards' Enquiry : Nelson De Souza one-day ban: careless riding (Oct 27)

FOCUS
A weak race. They probably went off a little too fast and the winning time was fully two seconds slower than the later nursery. They tended to race middle to far side in the straight.

NOTEBOOK
Emergency Services was a maiden after ten starts coming into this, but he had never previously raced over a trip this far and the step up in distance clearly suited.
Global Traffic, back up in trip and returned to selling company, was making a quick reappearance having run just three days earlier. This was a creditable effort and he might find a similar event. (op 9-2)
Daring You, a stablemate of the runner-up, seemed to benefit from the step up in trip and drop in grade. He also seemed fine without the blinkers this time.
Fighting Mood had shown little in a couple of runs in maidens and this grade looks more suitable. (op 13-2)
Gifted Heir(IRE), returned to selling company, was probably a touch below his best and this easy ground may not have been ideal.
Rowan Venture might have gone off a bit too fast. (op 14-1)
Grimes Glory, who raced more towards the far side than many of these, failed to run up to his best and may not have been suited by the easy ground. (op 7-2)
Readyforone Official explanation: jockey said gelding was hampered at start

6017 LINDEN HOMES H'CAP — 1m 2f 7y
3:30 (3:31) (Class 4) (0-85,91) 3-Y-O+ **£6,477** (£1,927; £963; £481) **Stalls** Low

Form				RPR
-151	1		**Abhisheka (IRE)**[6] 5895 3-9-8 91 6ex........ TedDurcan 10 (Saeed Bin Suroor) *trckd ldrs: slifgr led 3f out: edgd lft over 2f out: pushed clr fnl f: easily* **1/1**[1]	108+
4511	2	3	**Kingsholm**[8] 5833 4-9-5 83 6ex........ SteveDrowne 4 (A M Balding) *chsd ldrs: rdn to go 2nd over 1f out: kpt on ins last but no ch w wnr* **5/1**[2]	91
1234	3	¾	**Prince Ary**[7] 5869 3-8-11 80........ MichaelHills 14 (B W Hills) *chsd ldrs: rdn 3f out: kpt on fnl 2f: one pce ins last* **10/1**	87
4512	4	½	**Trouble Mountain (USA)**[6] 5889 9-8-7 71........(bt) DaleGibson 16 (M W Easterby) *bhd: rdn over 3f out: kpt on fnl 2f: gng on cl home but nt pce to rch ldrs* **16/1**	77+
4034	5	½	**Optimus (USA)**[19] 5625 4-8-13 77........ AdamKirby 13 (B G Powell) *lost gd early pitch and bhd after 3f: rdn and kpt on fnl 2f but nt rch ldrs* **25/1**	82
1-00	6	1 ½	**Zabeel Palace**[11] 5776 4-9-7 85........(t) MartinDwyer 3 (Saeed Bin Suroor) *led 1f: styd chsng ldr tl slt ld 5f out: hdd 3f out: wknd fnl f* **20/1**	87
2135	7	1 ¼	**Forthright**[9] 5810 5-8-13 80........ JamesDoyle(3) 1 (A W Carroll) *bhd: hdwy over 3f out: kpt on fnl 2f but nvr pce to get in contention* **11/1**	80
0000	8	*nk*	**Silver Blue (IRE)**[7] 5869 3-9-1 84........(b1) RyanMoore 5 (R Hannon) *led after 1f: narrowly hdd 5f out: sn rdn: wknd over 1f out* **50/1**	83
1536	9	½	**Vale De Lobo**[33] 5295 4-8-10 74........ JimCrowley 12 (B R Millman) *bhd: pushed along 4f out: styd on fnl 2f: nvr in contention* **40/1**	72
0002	10	*hd*	**Wellington Hall (GER)**[24] 5506 8-8-13 77........ EddieAhern 6 (P W Chapple-Hyam) *chsd ldrs: rdn 3f out: wknd ins fnl 2f* **16/1**	75
-000	11	½	**Arry Dash**[14] 5739 6-8-10 74........ DaneO'Neill 8 (M J Wallace) *bhd tl sme prog fnl 2f* **40/1**	71
-620	12	2 ½	**Ned Ludd (IRE)**[72] 4125 3-8-10 79........ RichardHughes 7 (R Hannon) *mid-div: rdn 3f out: n.d after* **33/1**	71
1422	13	8	**Moon On A Spoon**[19] 5610 3-8-9 78........ JamieSpencer 9 (J R Fanshawe) *chsd ldrs early: lost pl after 3f: rdn and sme hdwy 3f out: wknd 2f out* **7/1**[3]	55
P000	14	11	**El Tiger (GER)**[24] 5511 5-8-11 75........ TPQueally 2 (B J Curley) *mid-div: effrt 5f out: sn btn* **50/1**	31

2m 9.63s (1.33) **Going Correction** +0.225s/f (Good)
WFA 3 from 4yo+ 5lb **14** Ran SP% **128.7**
Speed ratings (Par 105):103,100,100,99,99 98,97,96,96,96 95,93,87,78
CSF £5.93 CT £37.88 TOTE £2.30: £1.10, £2.50, £2.80; EX 9.80 Trifecta £28.00 Pool £491.10 - 12.42 winning units.
Owner Godolphin **Bred** Gainsborough Stud Management Ltd **Trained** Newmarket, Suffolk

FOCUS
Quite a good handicap for the grade, with another improved run from the winner and sound form from the placed horses. They raced far side in the straight. Another improved run from the winner, with sound form from the placed horses.
Forthright Official explanation: jockey said gelding was unsuited by the good to soft (soft in places) ground
Moon On A Spoon Official explanation: jockey said filly never travelled

6018 ARENA LEISURE PLC NURSERY — 1m 67y
4:00 (4:00) (Class 4) (0-85,84) 2-Y-O **£4,533** (£1,348; £674; £336) **Stalls** High

Form				RPR
5046	1		**Oakley Heffert (IRE)**[17] 5647 2-8-11 74........ RichardHughes 2 (R Hannon) *hld up rr but in tch: hdwy 2f out: drvn to ld 1f: rdn out* **11/1**	80
2542	2	¾	**Italian Stallion (IRE)**[7] 5866 2-8-12 75........ RyanMoore 1 (R Hannon) *led 1f: lost position 6f out: hdwy 3f out: sn rdn: chsd wnr and effrt ins last but a hld* **2/1**[1]	79
0023	3	¾	**Always Best**[20] 5597 2-8-3 66........ MartinDwyer 7 (M Johnston) *led after 1f: kpt narrow ld and rdn 3f out: hdd 1f out: kpt on ame pce u.p* **9/2**	69
432	4	1 ¾	**Flying Encore (IRE)**[41] 5095 2-9-2 79........ AdamKirby 4 (W R Swinburn) *hld up rr but in tch: hdwy 3f out: drvn to chse ldrs over 2f out: wknd ins last* **7/2**[2]	78
01	5	1 ½	**Victor Trumper**[30] 5381 2-9-1 78........ PaulDoe 8 (P W Chapple-Hyam) *chsd ldrs: rdn and effrt over 2f out: nvr quite gng pce to chal: wknd fnl f* **4/1**[3]	73
526	6	6	**Sophia Gardens**[13] 5754 2-8-8 70 ow1........ DaneO'Neill 3 (D W P Arbuthnot) *w ldrs 1f: styd pressing ldrs tl wknd ins fnl 2f* **10/1**	52
000	7	24	**Allroundtheoutside**[10] 5780 2-7-12 61 oh1........ HayleyTurner 5 (P R Chamings) *in tch whn hmpd bnd 6f out: sn rdn: wknd 3f out* **25/1**	—

1m 45.82s (0.22) **Going Correction** +0.075s/f (Good) **7** Ran SP% **115.0**
Speed ratings (Par 97):101,100,99,97,96 90,66
CSF £33.85 CT £117.08 TOTE £16.10: £5.70, £1.80; EX 33.90 Trifecta £233.80 Pool £543.43 - 1.65 winning units.
Owner Brian C Oakley **Bred** Barouche Stud Ireland Ltd **Trained** East Everleigh, Wilts

FOCUS
A fair nursery in which they raced middle to far side in the straight. Improved form from the first two with a sound run from the third. The winning time was good; faster than the juvenile seller and both divisions of the older-horse maiden over the same trip.

NOTEBOOK
Oakley Heffert(IRE) benefited from the step up to a mile and upset his better-fancied stablemate in determined fashion. The winning time was good and he could have more to offer over this sort of distance. (op 10-1 tchd 12-1)
Italian Stallion(IRE), a good second over course and distance the previous week, again just found one too good. Still, this represents a solid effort and he should do well over further next year. (tchd 15-8, 9-4 in a place)
Always Best, dropped in trip, gave his all but basically looked to find a couple too good. (op 4-1)
Flying Encore(IRE), upped in trip on her handicap debut having shown promise in maiden company, ran a respectable enough race against the colts. Official explanation: jockey said filly suffered interference at start (op 4-1 tchd 9-2)
Victor Trumper could not build on his recent Warwick maiden success.

6019 WINDSOR FIREWORKS EXTRAVAGANZA SATURDAY 28TH OCTOBER MAIDEN STKS (DIV I) — 1m 67y
4:30 (4:30) (Class 5) 3-Y-O+ **£3,238** (£963; £481; £240) **Stalls** High

Form				RPR
6	1		**Sound Of Nature (USA)**[20] 5598 3-9-3 .... RichardHughes 13 (H R A Cecil) *t.k.h: trckd ldrs: wnt 2nd travelling smoothly over 1f out: drvn ins last: styd on to assert cl home* **4/5**[1]	74+

4000 **2** *nk* **Feu D'Artifice (USA)**[96] 3404 3-9-3 68 .... JimmyFortune 10 73
(R Hannon) *disp ld tl slt ld appr fnl 2f: hrd rdn and hld on u.p ins last tl hdd cl home* **8/1**

6 **3** *3* **Depraux (IRE)**[11] 5774 3-9-3 .... MichaelHills 12 66
(W J Haggas) *in tch: hdwy 3f out: pressed ldrs and rdn 2f out: wknd ins last* **16/1**

4- **4** *3 ½* **Oscar Snowman**[480] 2857 3-9-3 .... MartinDwyer 7 58+
(M P Tregoning) *s.i.s: bhd: pushed along and hdwy 2f out: nvr gng pce to rch ldrs* **9/2**[2]

-304 **5** *1* **Gravinsky (USA)**[16] 5669 3-9-3 76 ....(b) RyanMoore 5 56
(Mrs A J Perrett) *plld hrd: slt ld after 1f tl hdd over 2f out: wknd wl over 1f out* **5/1**[3]

6 *½* **Intersky Music (USA)** 3-9-3 .... AdrianMcCarthy 9 55+
(P W Chapple-Hyam) *s.i.s: bhd: styd on fnl 2f but nvr in contention* **25/1**

0 **7** *5* **Osiris Way**[95] 3458 4-9-6 .... JimCrowley 2 43
(P R Chamings) *t.k.h: chsd ldrs: rdn 3f out: wknd 2f out* **40/1**

6550 **8** *½* **Girandola**[11] 5774 3-9-3 54 ....(b[1]) DaneO'Neill 11 42
(R F Johnson Houghton) *rr: hdwy 4f out: sn rdn: wknd over 2f out* **33/1**

9 *2* **Book Of Days (IRE)** 3-8-12 .... NelsonDeSouza 4 33
(R M Beckett) *s.i.s: a bhd* **25/1**

0 **10** *nk* **Kia Ora**[19] 5611 3-9-3 ....(p) PaulDoe 3 37
(J Akehurst) *rdn over 5f out: a bhd* **100/1**

0-00 **11** *3 ½* **Simpsons Gamble (IRE)**[28] 5427 3-9-0 35 .... JamesDoyle(3) 6 29
(R M Flower) *in tch: rdn 5f out: sn wknd* **66/1**

0-00 **12** *21* **Rocket (IRE)**[43] 3948 5-8-13 40 .... MCGeran(7) 1 —
(H J Manners) *sn bhd* **100/1**

0-50 **13** *9* **Eldori**[168] 1355 3-8-12 45 .... RobertHavlin 8 —
(M S Saunders) *plld hrd: pressed ldrs to 1/2-way* **100/1**

1m 46.92s (1.32) **Going Correction** +0.075s/f (Good)
WFA 3 from 4yo+ 3lb **13** Ran SP% **124.9**
Speed ratings (Par 103):96,95,92,89,88 87,82,82,80,79 76,55,46
CSF £8.37 TOTE £1.90: £1.10, £3.60, £4.20; EX 9.80 Trifecta £97.70 Pool £374.29 - 2.72 winning units.
Owner K Abdulla **Bred** Juddmonte Farms Inc **Trained** Newmarket, Suffolk

FOCUS
A weak maiden, as one would expect at this stage of the season, in which they raced far side in the straight. The runner-up limits the form but the winner is bound to do better. The winning time was modest for the grade, despite being half a second quicker than the second division, as it was still 1.1 seconds slower than the nursery.

6020 AT THE RACES H'CAP — 6f
5:00 (5:01) (Class 5) (0-75,77) 3-Y-O+ **£3,886** (£1,156; £577; £288) **Stalls** High

Form RPR

0042 **1** **Linda Green**[1] 5987 5-8-8 65 .... ChrisCatlin 4 77
(M R Channon) *rr and racd towards centre: gd hdwy and rdn over 1f out: styd on strly u.p to ld last strides* **10/1**

0015 **2** *nk* **Chatshow (USA)**[3] 5938 5-8-3 63 .... JamesDoyle(3) 6 74
(A W Carroll) *racd towards centre and chsd ldrs: led overall over 1f out: kpt on u.p: ct last strides* **7/1**

0006 **3** *1 ¾* **Exmoor**[6] 5896 4-9-4 75 ....(b[1]) SteveDrowne 11 81
(R Charlton) *s.i.s: bhd towards stands side: hdwy fr 2f out:chsd ldrs ins last: kpt on same pce* **15/2**

2500 **4** *¾* **Patavium Prince (IRE)**[7] 5872 3-8-11 69 .... DaneO'Neill 3 73
(J R Best) *racd toards far side: chsd ldrs: drvn to chal over 1f out: one pce ins last* **33/1**

1111 **5** *¾* **Forces Sweetheart**[6] 5902 3-8-12 77 6ex ....(v) LukeMorris(7) 8 78+
(M L W Bell) *racd towards far side: rr: hdwy and nt clr run over 1f out: styng on whn n.m.r and swtchd rt wl ins last: kpt on* **9/2**[2]

5012 **6** *nk* **Word Perfect**[13] 5756 4-8-13 70 ....(b) DaleGibson 10 70
(M W Easterby) *racd towards far side and pressed ldrs under t.k.h: rdn 2f out: wknd fnl f* **7/2**[1]

3006 **7** *½* **Cesar Manrique (IRE)**[7] 5872 4-8-5 69 .... PatrickHills(7) 5 68
(B W Hills) *racd towards centre crse: in tch: rdn 2f out: sn one pce* **12/1**

4165 **8** *hd* **Caustic Wit (IRE)**[14] 5737 8-8-6 70 ....(p) TolleyDean(7) 12 68
(M S Saunders) *racd towards stands side: chsd ldrs 1/2-way: sn rdn: wknd ins last* **22/1**

4400 **9** *shd* **Kensington (IRE)**[175] 1188 5-7-13 63 .... MCGeran(7) 14 61
(P D Evans) *racd towards stands side: chsd ldrs: rdn 2f out: wknd ins fnl f* **33/1**

0060 **10** *hd* **Auwitesweetheart**[19] 5627 4-8-11 75 .... JamesMillman(7) 13 72
(B R Millman) *racd towards centre crse: spd over 3f* **33/1**

0633 **11** *nk* **Chinalea (IRE)**[10] 5791 4-9-3 74 ....(p) AdamKirby 16 71
(C G Cox) *racd towards stands side and led overall tl hdd over 1f out: sn btn* **6/1**[3]

4400 **12** *nk* **His Master's Voice (IRE)**[17] 5649 3-9-1 73 .... JimmyFortune 2 69
(D W P Arbuthnot) *ravced along far side 2f: chsd ldrs: outpcd fr over 1f out* **25/1**

6300 **13** *3 ½* **Polliwilline (IRE)**[20] 5591 3-9-3 75 .... RyanMoore 15 60
(R Hannon) *racd towards stands side: sn outpcd* **20/1**

0050 **14** *hd* **Rydal Mount (IRE)**[50] 4837 3-9-3 75 .... FergusSweeney 9 60
(W S Kittow) *racd centre crse: sn outpcd* **40/1**

1m 15.71s (2.04) **Going Correction** +0.275s/f (Good)
WFA 3 from 4yo+ 1lb **14** Ran SP% **120.0**
Speed ratings (Par 103):97,96,94,93,92 91,91,90,90,90 90,89,85,84
CSF £71.64 CT £582.45 TOTE £9.10: £1.80, £2.90, £3.10; EX 55.70 TRIFECTA Not won..
Owner Stephen Roots **Bred** Colin Tinkler **Trained** West Ilsley, Berks
■ Stewards' Enquiry : Luke Morris one-day ban: careless riding (Oct 27)

FOCUS
A modest sprint handicap and is doubtful if the form will prove too solid. They were spread out all over the track and those who raced stands' side seemed at a disadvantage. The winning time was ordinary; slower than the first division of the two-year-old maiden.

6021 WINDSOR FIREWORKS EXTRAVAGANZA SATURDAY 28TH OCTOBER MAIDEN STKS (DIV II) — 1m 67y
5:30 (5:30) (Class 5) 3-Y-O+ **£3,238** (£963; £481; £240) **Stalls** High

Form RPR

2240 **1** **Accompanist**[12] 5770 3-9-3 ....(b[1]) JimmyFortune 11 78
(J H M Gosden) *hld up towards rr: hdwy over 2f out: hrd rdn and styd on u.p to ld fnl 50yds: all out* **10/3**[2]

-456 **2** *¾* **Tennis Star (IRE)**[12] 5770 3-9-3 .... SteveDrowne 9 76
(R Charlton) *trckd ldr: rdn to ld 1f out: hdd and no ex fnl 50yds* **11/2**

42-5 **3** *3 ½* **Mitanni (USA)**[31] 5353 3-9-3 .... RyanMoore 10 68
(Mrs A J Perrett) *chsd ldrs: rdn to chal over 1f out: wknd ins last* **7/2**[3]

60 **4** *1* **Bonnie Belle**[21] 5566 3-8-9 .... AmirQuinn(3) 3 61
(J R Boyle) *led: rdn over 2f out: hdd over 1f out: wknd ins last* **100/1**

00 **5** *nk* **Desert Island Miss**[19] 5611 3-8-12 .... TedDurcan 6 60
(W R Swinburn) *trckd ldrs: rdn 2f out: sn one pce* **33/1**

360- **6** *nk* **Darusso**[373] 5733 3-9-3 .... JohnEgan 12 65
(J S Moore) *bhd: drvn over 2f out: styd on ins last: nt rch ldrs* **20/1**

0500 **7** *1 ¼* **Beckett Hall (IRE)**[43] 5045 3-9-3 .... RichardHughes 8 62
(R Hannon) *chsd ldrs: rdn over 2f out: wkng whn nt clr run 1f out* **12/1**

4- **8** *3 ½* **Ashes Regained**[381] 5592 3-9-3 .... JamieSpencer 1 54+
(B W Hills) *gd sort: h.d.w: scope: bit bkwd: wnt bdly lft s and lost 8l: stdy hdwy fr over 3f out to trck ldrs over 2f out: wknd over 1* **9/4**[1]

5400 **9** *hd* **Blu Manruna**[20] 5590 3-9-3 ....(p) PaulDoe 13 53
(J Akehurst) *bhd most of way* **20/1**

0000 **10** *2 ½* **Mystic Roll**[13] 5755 3-9-3 .... RobertHavlin 4 47
(Jane Chapple-Hyam) *chsd ldrs: rdn 3f out: sn wknd* **33/1**

53-0 **11** *9* **Zagreus (GER)**[8] 5844 4-9-1 ....(p) EmmettStack(5) 7 27
(H J Manners) *t.k.h: chsd ldrs over 5f* **100/1**

060 **12** *1 ¾* **Jose Bove**[205] 720 4-9-6 .... DaneO'Neill 5 23
(R Dickin) *slowly away: sme hdwy 4f out: wknd 3f out* **80/1**

0-0 **13** *shd* **Poliama**[8] 5830 4-9-1 .... ChrisCatlin 2 17
(Evan Williams) *chsd ldrs tl wknd qckly 3f out* **66/1**

1m 47.42s (1.82) **Going Correction** +0.075s/f (Good)
WFA 3 from 4yo 3lb **13** Ran SP% **119.3**
Speed ratings (Par 103):93,92,88,87,87 87,85,82,82,79 70,68,68
CSF £20.45 TOTE £3.90: £1.10, £2.00, £1.60; EX 20.40 Trifecta £64.10 Pool £316.41 - 3.50 winning units. Place 6 £15.58, Place 5 £11.65.
Owner H R H Princess Haya Of Jordan **Bred** Cheveley Park Stud Ltd **Trained** Newmarket, Suffolk

FOCUS
An ordinary maiden in which they raced far side. The winning time was moderate for the grade; half a second slower than the first division, 1.6 seconds slower than the nursery and only 0.4 seconds faster than the two-year-old seller. Similar in standard to division one, judged around the fourth and fifth.
Ashes Regained Official explanation: jockey said colt ducked left shortly after leaving stalls
Zagreus(GER) Official explanation: jockey said gelding hung left
T/Plt: £14.90 to a £1 stake. Pool: £56,629.10. 2,771.50 winning tickets. T/Qpdt: £15.10 to a £1 stake. Pool: £2,968.50. 144.90 winning tickets. ST

5828 BATH (L-H)
Tuesday, October 17
OFFICIAL GOING: Good to soft (meeting abandoned after race 5 (4.00) due to fog)
Wind: Virtually nil Weather: Poor visibilty for races 4 & 5

6023 JOHN SMITH'S NO NONSENSE/E.B.F. MAIDEN STKS — 1m 5y
2:00 (2:04) (Class 5) 2-Y-O **£3,238** (£963; £481; £240) **Stalls** Low

Form RPR

6 **1** **Grey Rover**[41] 5106 2-9-3 .... JimmyFortune 4 73
(R Hannon) *mde virtually all: hrd rdn and styd on gamely thrght fnl f* **20/1**

2 *¾* **Murdoch** 2-9-0 .... DominicFox(3) 14 71
(E S McMahon) *chsd ldrs: rdn to chal 1f out: kpt on but a jst hld by wnr ins last* **50/1**

5 **3** *1 ¾* **Inchnacardoch (IRE)**[24] 5537 2-9-3 .... FergusSweeney 9 67
(A King) *sn chsng wnr: rdn over 2f out: chal over 1f out: one pce ins last* **11/1**

5 **4** *2* **Duty Free (IRE)**[9] 5828 2-9-3 .... SteveDrowne 7 62
(H Morrison) *in tch: hdwy to chse ldrs 3f out: outpcd over 1f out* **7/2**[2]

04 **5** *2* **Private Reason (USA)**[34] 5293 2-9-3 .... RichardHughes 16 58
(R Hannon) *chsd ldrs: drvn along 4f out: pressed ldrs 2f out: wknd fnl f* **9/2**[3]

423 **6** *½* **Emerald Wilderness (IRE)**[34] 5293 2-9-3 84 .... JohnEgan 13 57
(M R Channon) *chsd ldrs: rdn over 2f out: sn btn* **11/4**[1]

00 **7** *nk* **Lightning Queen (USA)**[28] 5456 2-8-12 .... MartinDwyer 5 51
(B W Hills) *in tch: rdn 3f out: wknd fr 2f out* **33/1**

63 **8** *½* **Moorlander (USA)**[43] 5067 2-9-3 .... JimCrowley 11 55
(Mrs A J Perrett) *in tch: rdn to chse ldrs 3f out: wknd fr 2f out* **17/2**

0 **9** *nk* **Muffett's Dream**[32] 5344 2-8-12 .... RichardThomas 12 49
(J A Geake) *bhd: kpt on fnl 2f: nvr in contention* **25/1**

10 *½* **Yeoman Leap** 2-9-3 .... FrancisNorton 6 53
(A M Balding) *slowly away: bhd tl styd on fnl 2f but nvr in contention* **40/1**

0 **11** *7* **Solo City**[7] 5886 2-9-3 .... TPO'Shea 3 37
(P A Blockley) *chsd ldrs: rdn 3f out: wknd 2f out* **100/1**

564 **12** *2* **Christalini**[20] 5624 2-9-3 84 .... PatDobbs 8 32
(J C Fox) *chsd ldrs: rdn over 2f out: sn btn* **11/2**

13 *6* **Polish Prospect (IRE)** 2-8-12 .... JimmyQuinn 15 13
(H S Howe) *s.i.s: a bhd* **100/1**

14 *11* **Pelleas** 2-9-3 .... ChrisCatlin 1 —
(R Charlton) *s.i.s: a bhd* **40/1**

15 *3* **Monkshill** 2-8-12 .... SebSanders 10 —
(Miss Tor Sturgis) *s.i.s: a bhd* **66/1**

1m 43.46s (2.36) **Going Correction** +0.175s/f (Good) **15** Ran SP% **123.2**
Speed ratings (Par 95):95,94,92,90,88 88,87,87,86,86 79,77,71,60,57
CSF £753.15 TOTE £22.50: £4.90, £16.30, £3.90; EX 639.80 TRIFECTA Not won..
Owner The Queen **Bred** The Queen **Trained** East Everleigh, Wilts

FOCUS
A routine maiden and not that many got into it.

NOTEBOOK
Grey Rover, up a furlong from his Polytrack debut, was given a positive ride this time and showed the right attitude to keep his rivals at bay down the home straight. This may not have been the strongest of races, but this was encouraging considering that the family tend to improve with age so even better can be expected next season. (op 16-1)
Murdoch, bred to stay, kept battling away and emerged by far the best of the newcomers. This was an encouraging start and he will appreciate going up in trip. (op 40-1)
Inchnacardoch(IRE), always there or thereabouts, ran another creditable race and just lacked a bit of finishing pace. His pedigree suggests he may get a bit further than this, but the best of him is likely to come when he is handicapped. (op 10-1 tchd 9-1 and 12-1)
Duty Free(IRE), who faced a stiff task against previous winners on his debut, performed a bit better in this company but is another likely to come to himself in handicap company over further in time. (op 11-2)
Private Reason(USA), after racing prominently, again failed to get home but there is a fair amount of speed in his pedigree and it appears that he does not stay this trip as yet. He does now qualify for a mark, however. (op 9-1)
Emerald Wilderness(IRE), more experienced than most in this field and already rated 84, failed to confirm Sandown running with Private Reason and does not appear to be going forward. (op 9-4 tchd 2-1 and 3-1)

6024 HADEN YOUNG / E B F MAIDEN STKS (DIV I) — 5f 11y
2:30 (2:36) (Class 5) 2-Y-O — £2,590 (£770; £385; £192) Stalls Low

Form — RPR

4220 1 **Ishi Adiva**[54] 4736 2-8-12 86 ... RichardThomas 5 — 80
(Tom Dascombe) *trckd ldrs: drvn and qcknd appr fnl f: edgd towards far side ins last: led fnl 50yds: hld on wl* **15/8**[1]

62 2 *nk* **Gower**[18] 5645 2-9-3 ... SteveDrowne 12 — 84
(R Charlton) *chsd ldrs: led over 2f out: rdn over 1f out: edgd towards far side: hdd and no ex fnl 50yds* **2/1**[2]

64 3 *4* **Money For Fun**[17] 5686 2-8-12 ... JohnEgan 3 — 64
(J S Moore) *rr but in tch: rdn over 2f out: styd on to chse ldrs fnl f but no ch* **40/1**

064 4 *1 3/4* **Blue Bamboo**[37] 5206 2-8-12 67 ... JimCrowley 9 — 58
(Mrs A J Perrett) *sn in tch: rdn 1/2-way: kpt on fr over 1f out but nvr gng pce to trble ldrs* **10/1**[3]

5 *4* **Futuristic Dragon (IRE)** 2-9-3 ... TPO'Shea 11 — 49
(P A Blockley) *s.i.s: bhd: pushed along 1/2-way: r.o fnl f but nvr in contention* **33/1**

6 *nk* **Millsini** 2-8-12 ... JimmyFortune 2 — 43
(Rae Guest) *bhd: pushed along 1/2-way: sme prog fnl f but nvr in contention* **20/1**

05 7 *1* **Miss Autumnal (IRE)**[12] 5773 2-8-12 ... (b) ChrisCatlin 6 — 39
(N A Callaghan) *chsd ldrs: rdn to chal 2f out: wknd apoproaching fnl f* **33/1**

8 *1 1/2* **Apache Scout (IRE)** 2-9-3 ... SebSanders 1 — 39
(R M Beckett) *chsd ldrs: sn pushed along: wknd fr 2f out* **10/1**[3]

0 9 *3/4* **Croeso Bach**[22] 5563 2-8-12 ... MickyFenton 4 — 31
(J L Spearing) *sn led: hdd over 2f out: wknd qckly over 1f out* **66/1**

10 *2 1/2* **Good Luck Chip (IRE)** 2-8-5 ... SophieDoyle(7) 7 — 22
(I A Wood) *s.i.s: outpcd* **100/1**

62.37 secs (-0.13) **Going Correction** -0.15s/f (Firm) — 10 Ran SP% **101.9**

Speed ratings (Par 95):95,94,88,85,78 78,76,74,73,69

CSF £4.05 TOTE £2.50: £1.10, £1.10, £4.70; EX 5.30 Trifecta £65.10 Pool: £296.56 - 3.23 winning units..

Owner Stephen Bayless **Bred** S H And Mrs A M Bayless **Trained** Lambourn, Berks

■ Star Strider was withdrawn (11/2, refused to enter stalls). R4 applies, deduct 15p in the £.

FOCUS

Some interesting contenders in this maiden and the front pair pulled well clear. The winning time was 0.12 seconds faster than the second division.

NOTEBOOK

Ishi Adiva, back in maiden company after her brilliant effort in the Weatherbys Super Sprint and less inspiring performance in the St Leger Yearling Stakes, finally got off the mark with a battling victory on ground that may have been a little easier than ideal. She will probably need to progress again in order to be competitive in sprint handicaps off her current mark. (op 7-4 tchd 9-4)

Gower, who has already shown that he can handle easy ground, did little wrong and just ran into a rival with form in better company than this. His winning turn is merely delayed, but whether he has done his handicap mark any good by finishing so close to a filly rated 86 remains to be seen. (op 11-4 tchd 15-8)

Money For Fun was very much best of the rest, but the drop in trip was probably not in her favour. She may progress now that she can be handicapped.

Blue Bamboo, dropped to the minimum trip after three outings over six, lacked the speed to trouble the front pair and will surely appreciate a switch to handicaps off this mark. (tchd 9-1)

Futuristic Dragon(IRE), who fetched 32,000gns as a two-year-old, is by a sprinter but his half-sister won over 14 furlongs and this debut effort suggests he will improve for both the experience and a longer trip. (op 25-1)

Millsini, related to several winning sprinters, is likely to do better with time and experience. (op 14-1)

6025 HADEN YOUNG / E B F MAIDEN STKS (DIV II) — 5f 11y
3:00 (3:03) (Class 5) 2-Y-O — £2,590 (£770; £385; £192) Stalls Low

Form — RPR

3025 1 **Pernomente (IRE)**[17] 5668 2-9-3 71 ... (t) JohnEgan 2 — 76
(J S Moore) *mde all: rdn 2f out: styd on u.p ins last and edgd lft: hld on wl* **6/1**

02 2 *3/4* **Izabela Hannah**[22] 5563 2-8-12 ... SebSanders 1 — 68
(R M Beckett) *wnt lft s: bhd: rdn 1/2-way: kpt on under perssure to chse wnr ins last: hld whn carried lft cl home* **9/4**[1]

050 3 *1 1/2* **Ocean Blaze**[21] 5592 2-8-12 73 ... JimCrowley 3 — 63
(B R Millman) *chsd wnr: rdn 2f out: no imp and outpcd fnl f* **10/1**

640 4 *1/2* **Mo (USA)**[7] 5891 2-9-3 ... (t) FJohansson 10 — 66
(R A Kvisla) *chsd ldrs: rdn and one pce fnl 2f* **7/2**[2]

5 *1* **Ellablue** 2-8-12 ... JimmyFortune 8 — 58
(Rae Guest) *bhd: pushed along and hdwy fr 2f out: kpt on ins last but nvr gng pce to rch ldrs* **20/1**

4400 6 *1* **Miss Kool Kat (USA)**[24] 5528 2-8-12 64 ... CatherineGannon 5 — 54
(K A Ryan) *chsd ldrs: rdn 1/2-way: wknd fnl f* **25/1**

7 *1/2* **Fluttering Rose** 2-8-12 ... SteveDrowne 6 — 52
(R Charlton) *s.i.s: bhd: kpt on ins fnl f but nvr in contention* **10/1**

6 8 *2 1/2* **Tasleem (IRE)**[19] 5638 2-8-12 ... MartinDwyer 7 — 43
(B W Hills) *in tch: rdn halfwway: fnd nthing and sn btn* **5/1**[3]

00 9 *10* **Alonso De Guzman (IRE)**[18] 5648 2-9-3 ... NickyMackay 11 — 12
(J R Boyle) *s.i.s: a outpcd* **100/1**

10 *3* **Royal Obsession (IRE)** 2-8-12 ... FergusSweeney 4 — —
(J G M O'Shea) *s.i.s: a bhd* **66/1**

62.49 secs (-0.01) **Going Correction** -0.15s/f (Firm) — 10 Ran SP% **113.2**

Speed ratings (Par 95):94,92,90,89,88 86,85,81,65,60

CSF £18.72 TOTE £7.70: £2.00, £1.30, £3.60; EX 22.20 Trifecta £190.00 Pool: £447.10 - 1.67 winning units..

Owner Tom Yates,Mrs Evelyn Yates,J S Moore **Bred** Pier House Stud **Trained** Upper Lambourn, Berks

■ Stewards' Enquiry : John Egan caution: careless riding

FOCUS

This did not look as strong as the first division and the time was 0.12 seconds slower.

NOTEBOOK

Pernomente(IRE), by far the most experienced in the field, made it count under a positive ride and saw his race out well despite hanging late on. He will presumably return to handicaps now, but lacks scope. (tchd 15-2)

Izabela Hannah, not for the first time, did not begin too well but stayed on in the latter half of the contest. She needs a return to further. (op 7-2)

Ocean Blaze, unplaced in her three previous starts but not without ability, was never that far away and kept on to take minor honours. On a line through the winner, her current handicap mark looks stiff enough. (op 11-1 tchd 9-1)

Mo(USA) was not beaten far, but lacked toe where it mattered and does not appear to be progressing now. He finished behind two lower-rated rivals here, so will need to find improvement from somewhere if he is to break his duck. Official explanation: jockey said colt hung right (op 4-1)

Ellablue, a half-sister to four winners including the smart Espartero, did best of the newcomers and is likely to improve a good deal on this in time. Official explanation: jockey said filly hung right (op 11-1)

Tasleem(IRE) looked an awkward ride on her Newmarket debut and fared no better here. She has plenty of questions to answer now. (op 4-1)

6026 OCCAM DIRECT MARKETING MAIDEN FILLIES' STKS — 1m 2f 46y
3:30 (3:33) (Class 5) 3-Y-O+ — £3,238 (£963; £481; £240) Stalls Low

Form — RPR

32 1 **Mowazana (IRE)**[22] 5566 3-8-12 ... MartinDwyer 5 — 77
(M P Tregoning) *trckd ldr tl slt advantage over 2f out: hrd drvn fnl f: rdn clr* **5/4**[1]

0-6 2 *4* **Wonderful One (IRE)**[20] 5612 3-8-12 ... JimmyFortune 10 — 69
(J H M Gosden) *led tl narrowly hdd over 2f out: styd pressing wnr and upsides u.p over 1f out: no ex and btn fnl f* **6/1**[3]

5 3 *nk* **Blend**[8] 5870 3-8-12 ... RichardHughes 1 — 69
(J H M Gosden) *chsd ldrs: rdn over 2f out: styd on u.p ins last to press for 2nd cl home but no imp on wnr* **5/2**[2]

0022 4 *5* **Tabulate**[17] 5690 3-8-12 58 ... ChrisCatlin 14 — 59
(P L Gilligan) *bhd: hdwy and pushed along over 2f out: nvr nr ldrs* **10/1**

0- 5 *5* **Cithogue (IRE)**[352] 6178 3-8-12 ... TPO'Shea 8 — 50
(J R Fanshawe) *in tch: effrt 3f out: nvr nr ldrs: sn bhd* **14/1**

0 6 *6* **Coppington Melody (IRE)**[9] 5830 3-8-12 ... MickyFenton 15 — 38
(B W Duke) *s.i.s: a in rr* **66/1**

06 7 *1/2* **Mamonta**[22] 5567 3-8-12 ... FergusSweeney 11 — 37
(D M Simcock) *chsd ldrs: rdn over 3f out: wknd over 2f out* **12/1**

50-0 8 *6* **Dolly**[165] 1462 4-9-3 40 ... SteveDrowne 2 — 26
(Tom Dascombe) *s.i.s: sn in tch: wknd 3f out* **66/1**

0-00 9 *1/2* **Vixen Virago**[124] 2575 3-8-9 45 ... EdwardCreighton(3) 3 — 25
(Jane Southcombe) *chsd ldrs over 6f* **66/1**

0 10 *1/2* **Good Intentions**[194] 894 4-9-3 ... LPKeniry 6 — 24
(P W Hiatt) *in tch to 1/2-way* **50/1**

11 *hd* **Satintheslip (IRE)**[19] 5-9-3 ... CatherineGannon 12 — 23
(Mrs P Ford) *s.i.s: bhd most of way* **66/1**

2m 11.35s (0.35) **Going Correction** +0.175s/f (Good)

WFA 3 from 4yo+ 5lb — 11 Ran SP% **118.7**

Speed ratings (Par 100):105,101,101,97,93 88,88,83,82,82 82

CSF £9.53 TOTE £2.00: £1.10, £2.30, £1.30; EX 9.70 Trifecta £23.10 Pool: £393.22 - 12.08 winning units..

Owner Hamdan Al Maktoum **Bred** Shadwell Estate Company Limited **Trained** Lambourn, Berks

FOCUS

Little strength in depth to this fillies' maiden and only the first three were ever in the race. The runners tacked over to the stands' side in the straight.

6027 WEATHERBYS PRINTING H'CAP — 2m 1f 34y
4:00 (4:01) (Class 5) (0-75,68) 3-Y-O — £3,368 (£1,002; £500; £250) Stalls Low

Form — RPR

346 1 **Malakiya (IRE)**[43] 5057 3-9-4 65 ... FJohansson 9 — 73
(G A Butler) *bhd: hrd drvn and hdwy over 2f out: led ins fnl f: all out* **9/1**

5063 2 *1/2* **Coda Agency**[42] 5097 3-8-6 53 ... JimCrowley 3 — 60
(D W P Arbuthnot) *sn trcking ldr: led gng wl appr fnl 2f: rdn: hdd and no ex ins last* **33/1**

5466 3 *5* **Gallileo Figaro (USA)**[20] 5618 3-9-4 65 ... MartinDwyer 8 — 66
(W M Brisbourne) *led tl rdn and hdd appr fnl 2f: sn one pce* **33/1**

2144 4 *4* **La Via Ferrata (IRE)**[20] 5628 3-8-13 60 ... FergusSweeney 7 — 56
(A G Newcombe) *chsd ldrs: rdn 3f out: sn wknd* **9/1**

1442 5 *shd* **Leo McGarry (IRE)**[20] 5618 3-8-12 62 ... SaleemGolam(3) 2 — 58
(S C Williams) *in tch: rdn over 3f out: sn wknd* **3/1**[2]

4421 6 *nk* **Synonymy**[9] 5846 3-9-4 65 6ex ... NickyMackay 6 — 61
(M Blanshard) *chsd ldrs: rdn over 3f out: wknd over 2f out* **4/1**[3]

-351 7 *3* **Picacho (IRE)**[52] 4800 3-9-7 68 ... JimmyQuinn 10 — 60
(J L Dunlop) *in tch: hdwy over 4f out: sn rdn: wknd qckly ins fnl 2f* **15/8**[1]

4136 8 *5* **Scuzme (IRE)**[124] 2568 3-8-5 55 ow2 ... NeilChalmers(3) 5 — 41
(Miss Sheena West) *bhd most of way* **33/1**

0006 9 *30* **Indian Girl**[31] 5369 3-8-2 49 oh4 ... ChrisCatlin 1 — —
(M R Channon) *chsd ldrs tl wknd qckly 3f out* **20/1**

6060 10 *8* **Kokila**[15] 5741 3-8-2 56 ow6 ... PatrickHills(7) 4 — —
(M H Tompkins) *bhd most of way: no ch fnl 4f* **66/1**

3m 54.95s (5.35) **Going Correction** +0.175s/f (Good) — 10 Ran SP% **114.9**

Speed ratings (Par 101):94,93,91,89,89 89,87,85,71,67

CSF £262.97 CT £8949.73 TOTE £12.80: £4.50, £6.40, £5.80; EX 228.60 TRIFECTA Not won. Place 6 £804.62, Place 5 £36.96.

Owner Future In Mind Partnership **Bred** Mrs F Schwarzenbach **Trained** Blewbury, Oxon

FOCUS

Visibility was poor by this stage. The pace was steady and the time a moderate one for the grade.

6028 INDIAN MAIDEN - GROUP WIN SUCCESS 2006 H'CAP — 1m 3f 144y
() (Class 4) (0-80,) 3-Y-O+ — £

6029 SOMERSET COUNTY POPPY SUPPORT H'CAP — 1m 5y
() (Class 5) (0-75,) 3-Y-O+ — £

6030 RON AND LIZ HOGSTON RETIREMENT APPRENTICE H'CAP — 5f 161y
() (Class 6) (0-58,) 3-Y-O+ — £

T/Jkpt: Not won. T/Plt: £423.70 to a £1 stake. Pool: £66,951.90. 115.35 winning tickets. T/Qpdt: £24.30 to a £1 stake. Pool: £5,253.90. 159.80 winning tickets. ST

5986 LINGFIELD (L-H)
Tuesday, October 17

OFFICIAL GOING: Standard

Wind: Moderate, behind Weather: Overcast becoming fine

6031 BOOK ONLINE FOR A £2 DISCOUNT MAIDEN AUCTION STKS (DIV I) — 7f (P)
1:50 (1:51) (Class 5) 2-Y-O — £2,590 (£770; £385; £192) Stalls Low

Form — RPR

53 1 **Diamond Diva**[25] 5503 2-8-5 ow1 ... EddieAhern 8 — 74+
(J W Hills) *lw: t.k.h: prom: led 2f out: sn clr: pushed out* **11/10**[1]

2 *5* **Toucantini** 2-8-6 ... OscarUrbina 11 — 62
(R Charlton) *w'like: settled towards rr: hdwy on outside over 2f out: chsd comfortable wnr fnl f* **33/1**

4 3 *1/2* **House Maiden (IRE)**[36] 5231 2-8-6 ... AdrianMcCarthy 9 — 61
(D M Simcock) *w'like: lw: dwlt: hld up in rr: rdn and r.o fnl 2f: nrst fin* **9/1**[3]

52 **4** *1* **Minnis Bay (CAN)**[9] 5841 2-9-1 TedDurcan 5 67
(E F Vaughan) *sn rdn up to chse ldrs: no ex over 1f out* **5/2**[2]

2203 **5** *shd* **Drifting Gold**[53] 4753 2-8-4 70 NelsonDeSouza 6 56
(C G Cox) *plld hrd: chsd ldrs: edgd lft and no ex over 1f out* **11/1**

0 **6** *nk* **Dansil In Distress**[29] 5417 2-8-3 JamesDoyle(3) 7 57
(S Kirk) *leggy: hld up towards rr: rdn and outpcd over 2f out: kpt on fnl f* **25/1**

5000 **7** *1/2* **Lay The Cash (USA)**[21] 5585 2-8-9 50 AdamKirby 1 59
(J S Moore) *led tl 2f out: hrd rdn and wknd 1f out* **66/1**

4 **8** *2* **Sweet World**[11] 5780 2-8-11 DarryllHolland 4 56+
(A P Jarvis) *pressed ldr 5f: btn whn squeezed out over 1f out* **14/1**

9 *nk* **Fealeview Lady (USA)** 2-8-10 RobertHavlin 3 54
(H Morrison) *w'like: bit bkwd: s.s: sn chsng ldrs: wknd 2f out* **66/1**

0 **10** *3 1/2* **Art Of Poker (IRE)**[7] 5890 2-9-1 RyanMoore 10 50
(B W Hills) *hrd rdn 3f out: a bhd* **25/1**

1m 24.78s (-1.11) **Going Correction** -0.175s/f (Stan) **10** Ran SP% **114.8**
Speed ratings (Par 95):99,93,92,91,91 91,90,88,87,83
CSF £53.63 TOTE £2.10: £1.10, £8.40, £1.90; EX 54.40.
Owner Mrs Lynne P Meagher **Bred** Glebe Stud And Mrs F Woodd **Trained** Upper Lambourn, Berks

FOCUS
An above-average maiden for the track, the stronger of the two divisions.

NOTEBOOK
Diamond Diva had run well in two decent races on turf, and outclassed the opposition. She will now be put away for the 2007 turf season, since she is considered "too good" to campaign on the All-Weather during the winter. (op 4-5 tchd 6-5)
Toucantini, an attractive 11,000gns yearling who is related to two All-Weather winners, made a promising debut. Though not a match for the winner, there was no disgrace in that and she looks likely to add to the family's successes on sand. (tchd 40-1)
House Maiden(IRE), an athletic sort, was keen to post but settled well enough in the race. Staying on nicely in the straight, she looks capable of winning a similar race at this trip or slightly longer. (op 10-1 tchd 8-1)
Minnis Bay(CAN) has run respectably in all three races to date and is now qualified for handicaps, in which he should be quite effective. (op 11-4 tchd 9-4)
Drifting Gold was trying a longer trip and, though running with credit for a long way, remains hard to win with in maiden company. A switch back to handicaps looks likely. (op 14-1)
Dansil In Distress looks set to come into her own at a mile and beyond in handicap company following one more run. (op 33-1)
Sweet World was already beaten when running out of room on the run to the final furlong, but he had run a fair race until then and looks likely to be at home in handicaps after one more run. (op 20-1)

6032 BOOK ONLINE FOR A £2 DISCOUNT MAIDEN AUCTION STKS (DIV II) 7f (P)
2:20 (2:22) (Class 5) 2-Y-O **£2,590** (£770; £385; £192) **Stalls** Low

Form RPR

30 **1** **Aegean Prince**[18] 5655 2-8-13 RyanMoore 7 80
(R Hannon) *trckd ldrs: effrt 2f out: led ins fnl f: rdn out* **5/2**[2]

630 **2** *1 1/2* **Seven Steps (IRE)**[25] 5503 2-8-8 73 EddieAhern 2 71
(J W Hills) *hld up in tch: hdwy to chse ldr 2f out: led 1f out: hdd and nt qckn ins fnl f* **2/1**[1]

6 **3** *3 1/2* **Give Evidence**[11] 5784 2-9-1 DarryllHolland 10 69
(A P Jarvis) *wd: t.k.h in rr: rdn and r.o fnl 2f: nrst fin* **7/2**[3]

020 **4** *1* **Early Promise (IRE)**[12] 5772 2-8-8 63 ow4 BrianReilly 6 59
(P L Gilligan) *swtg: t.k.h: prom: led over 2f out tl wknd 1f out* **8/1**

5 *2* **Murrisk** 2-8-13 (t) TPQueally 9 59
(Eamon Tyrrell, Ire) *w'like: hld up in tch: rdn over 2f out: sn outpcd* **12/1**

0 **6** *1 1/2* **Palmetto Point**[7] 5890 2-9-1 RobertHavlin 1 57
(H Morrison) *lw: s.s and lost 8 l: in tch in rr after 2f: pushed along 1/2-way: n.d* **66/1**

0 **7** *1* **Noddledoddle (IRE)**[19] 5638 2-8-4 (t) JamieMackay 4 44
(J Ryan) *chsd ldrs over 4f* **25/1**

5000 **8** *2 1/2* **Tumble Jill (IRE)**[11] 5780 2-8-4 50 HayleyTurner 3 37
(J J Bridger) *uns rdr to post: pushed along 3f out: a bhd* **66/1**

2355 **9** *1* **House Arrest**[9] 5835 2-8-4 55 (p) AdrianMcCarthy 5 35
(A J McCabe) *led tl 2f out: sn wknd* **25/1**

1m 25.63s (-0.26) **Going Correction** -0.175s/f (Stan) **9** Ran SP% **113.6**
Speed ratings (Par 95):94,92,88,87,84 83,82,79,78
CSF £7.52 TOTE £3.60: £1.02, £1.70, £1.70; EX 9.60.
Owner Theobalds Stud **Bred** Theobalds Stud **Trained** East Everleigh, Wilts

FOCUS
The weaker of the two divisions, but run at a decent gallop.

NOTEBOOK
Aegean Prince got a clean break this time and seems to be learning his trade, knuckling down well to get on top in the final furlong. (op 15-8)
Seven Steps(IRE) has run well in her two races on Polytrack and is capable of winning a similar maiden. If not, she is already qualified for handicaps and should do well in that sphere. (op 9-4 tchd 5-2)
Give Evidence ran encouragingly from a wide draw, coming on nicely from behind. He is qualified for handicaps after one more run, and is one to bear in mind on Polytrack in the coming months. (op 4-1)
Early Promise(IRE), sweating badly, was trying a longer trip but appeared not to stay it as well as connections might have hoped. (tchd 10-1)
Murrisk, an Irish challenger, has winners in the family from five furlongs to a mile. He made a satisfactory debut but needs to improve a bit to win in similar company. (tchd 11-1)
Palmetto Point blew it at the start, but is worth keeping an eye on for signs of improvement.

6033 LINGFIELDPARK.CO.UK (S) STKS 6f (P)
2:50 (2:50) (Class 6) 3-Y-O **£2,388** (£705; £352) **Stalls** Low

Form RPR

3634 **1** **Cool Sting (IRE)**[35] 5273 3-9-5 60 (v[1]) BrianReilly 6 68
(P S McEntee) *bhd: hdwy on outside 3f out: led over 2f out and kicked clr: drvn to hold on fnl f* **8/1**

0003 **2** *1* **Solicitude**[11] 5781 3-8-9 57 RobertHavlin 10 55
(D Haydn Jones) *lw: hld up in tch: effrt 3f out: styd on to take 2nd nr fin* **16/1**

3460 **3** *1/2* **Balian**[34] 5291 3-9-0 60 (be) RyanMoore 5 58
(G L Moore) *chsd ldrs: n.m.r and sltly outpcd over 2f out: rallied to chse wnr ins fnl f: lost 2nd nr fin* **10/1**

0012 **4** *3/4* **Ockums Razor (IRE)**[11] 5781 3-9-5 63 DarryllHolland 11 61
(C A Dwyer) *wd: prom: rdn 2f out: nt qckn* **13/2**[3]

0004 **5** *3/4* **Danish Blues (IRE)**[11] 5781 3-9-0 55 (p) TedDurcan 8 61+
(N P Littmoden) *s.s: bhd: 5th and styng on whn nt clr run twice ins fnl f* **16/1**

3656 **6** *1 1/2* **Shunkawakhan (IRE)**[11] 5781 3-9-0 54 (b) RobertWinston 7 49
(G C H Chung) *mid-div: effrt over 2f out: no imp fnl f* **9/1**

0304 **7** *2* **Crafty Fox**[8] 5874 3-9-0 59 (v[1]) DaneO'Neill 3 43
(A P Jarvis) *led tl over 2f out: hrd rdn and wknd over 1f out* **14/1**

5552 **8** *1 3/4* **Gift Aid**[8] 5873 3-8-11 49 AmirQuinn(3) 9 38
(P J Makin) *chsd ldrs: pushed along whn hmpd jst ins fnl 3f: n.d after* **20/1**

1001 **9** *1* **Came Back (IRE)**[11] 5781 3-9-5 65 EddieAhern 2 40
(J A Osborne) *prom over 3f: eased whn no ch fnl f: fin lame* **3/1**[1]

5235 **10** *nk* **Memphis Man**[17] 5684 3-9-5 68 J-PGuillambert 1 39
(Miss V Haigh) *in tch: outpcd 3f out: sn btn* **7/2**[2]

11 *1/2* **Tapping Toes (IRE)** 3-8-9 HayleyTurner 4 28
(J R Best) *w'like: leggy: bit bkwd: dwlt: plld hrd early: a in rr* **66/1**

0000 **12** *10* **Aboyne (IRE)**[34] 5298 3-8-9 52 ow2 (p) JonjoMilczarek(7) 12 5
(K F Clutterbuck) *wd: rdn 3f out: a bhd* **66/1**

1m 12.08s (-0.73) **Going Correction** -0.175s/f (Stan) **12** Ran SP% **116.9**
Speed ratings (Par 99):97,95,95,94,93 91,88,86,84,84 83,70
CSF £124.93 TOTE £12.60: £4.10, £4.40, £2.80; EX 461.20.There was no bid for the winner. Memphis Man was claimed by David Bridgwater for £6,000.
Owner Eventmaker Racehorses **Bred** John Foley **Trained** Newmarket, Suffolk

FOCUS
A fair seller, with the winner having contested much better races earlier in the year. He was back to something like his best here.
Danish Blues(IRE) Official explanation: jockey said gelding was denied a clear run
Gift Aid Official explanation: jockey said colt was hampered on bend
Came Back(IRE) Official explanation: vet said colt returned lame

6034 LINGFIELDPARK.CO.UK MEDIAN AUCTION MAIDEN STKS 6f (P)
3:20 (3:20) (Class 5) 2-Y-O **£3,238** (£963; £481; £240) **Stalls** Low

Form RPR

43 **1** **Genuine Call**[12] 5773 2-8-12 TedDurcan 8 72
(C F Wall) *trckd ldrs: led 1f out: rdn out* **5/6**[1]

03 **2** *1 1/2* **Le Singe Noir**[15] 5735 2-9-3 DaneO'Neill 5 73
(D M Simcock) *chsd ldrs: effrt over 2f out: wnt 2nd ins fnl f: kpt on: a hld* **5/2**[2]

3 *2 1/2* **Iza Coming (IRE)** 2-8-12 TPQueally 2 60
(M G Quinlan) *unf: scope: lengthy: dwlt: hld up in tch: effrt 2f out: nt qckn fnl f* **10/1**[3]

00 **4** *1 3/4* **Hereford Boy**[8] 5867 2-9-3 RobertHavlin 11 60
(D K Ivory) *prom: led over 2f out tl wknd 1f out* **66/1**

0 **5** *2* **Golden Prospect**[20] 5623 2-9-3 EddieAhern 9 54
(J W Hills) *w'like: scope: towards rr: pushed along over 3f out: sme late hdwy* **20/1**

6 *1* **Bantry Bere (IRE)** 2-9-3 BrettDoyle 7 51
(J R Best) *leggy: dwlt: sn in midfield: rdn over 2f out: no imp* **33/1**

00 **7** *1* **Kilvickeon (IRE)**[9] 5841 2-9-3 RobbieFitzpatrick 6 48
(Peter Grayson) *mid-div: rdn and no hdwy fnl 3f* **66/1**

0 **8** *3 1/2* **Ishismart**[29] 5424 2-8-5 RussellKennemore(7) 1 32
(R Hollinshead) *leggy: dwlt: sn prom: wknd over 2f out* **33/1**

9 *2* **Golden Ribbons** 2-8-9 AmirQuinn(3) 3 26
(J R Boyle) *leggy: s.s: bhd: rdn 3f out: n.d whn n.m.r on rail over 1f out* **33/1**

10 *hd* **Just A Flash (IRE)** 2-9-3 AdamKirby 12 31
(B R Johnson) *w'like: bit bkwd: swvd rt s: wd: rdn 3f out: a bhd* **40/1**

00 **11** *5* **Tafis Beach**[79] 3979 2-8-12 (v[1]) PaulDoe 4 11
(J R Jenkins) *led tl over 2f out: wknd wl over 1f out* **66/1**

12 *1 1/4* **The Dagger** 2-9-3 GeorgeBaker 10 12
(J R Best) *w'like: bit bkwd: a bhd: eased whn no ch fnl 2f* **16/1**

1m 12.54s (-0.27) **Going Correction** -0.175s/f (Stan) **12** Ran SP% **118.6**
Speed ratings (Par 95):94,92,88,86,83 82,81,76,73,73 66,65
CSF £2.57 TOTE £1.80: £1.10, £1.30, £2.10; EX 3.90.
Owner Mervyn Ayers **Bred** Mervyn Ayers And Richard Brunger **Trained** Newmarket, Suffolk

FOCUS
An ordinary race on the whole, with the winner likely to be a cut above the rest.

NOTEBOOK
Genuine Call had run two solid races before this, and completed a professional - if unspectacular - job in this modest contest. She will be kept going and should continue to pay her way. (op 8-11 tchd Evens)
Le Singe Noir did well to chase home the odds-on favourite, and has shown enough to have another go in maiden company. However, he is already qualified for handicaps, and that is an alternative option. (op 11-4 tchd 9-4)
Iza Coming(IRE), a daughter of Fasliyev, made an encouraging debut. She has plenty of speed in her pedigree and should be dangerous at this level when putting it to full use. (tchd 9-1)
Hereford Boy ran by far his best race to date on this sand debut, and would not be without a chance in handicap company if reproducing this.
Golden Prospect was not knocked about, but neither was he nearly good enough. However, he could be interesting when put back to longer trips, and in handicap company, after one more run.. (op 25-1)
Bantry Bere(IRE) has winners in the family at a mile and beyond, and will improve for longer trips following this satisfactory debut.

6035 MIKE CONSTABLE H'CAP 5f (P)
3:50 (3:50) (Class 5) (0-75,75) 3-Y-O+ **£3,886** (£1,156; £577; £288) **Stalls** High

Form RPR

5122 **1** **Forest Dane**[11] 5782 6-9-0 **74** JamesDoyle(3) 7 81+
(Mrs N Smith) *hld up towards rr: effrt and wd st: r.o to ld fnl 100 yds* **9/4**[1]

1003 **2** *3/4* **Little Edward**[34] 5291 8-9-2 **73** GeorgeBaker 6 77
(R J Hodges) *t.k.h: hld up in midfield: rdn to chal fnl f: nt qckn fnl 50 yds* **14/1**

0322 **3** *hd* **Millinsky (USA)**[35] 5275 5-9-4 **75** J-PGuillambert 10 79+
(Rae Guest) *lw: s.i.s: hld up towards rr on outside: effrt and v wd st: r.o fnl f: nrst fin* **11/2**[3]

3442 **4** *nk* **Xaluna Bay (IRE)**[9] 5842 3-9-1 **72** RyanMoore 1 75
(W R Muir) *prom: rdn to ld 1f out: hdd and one pce fnl 100 yds* **10/3**[2]

210 **5** *hd* **Overwing (IRE)**[33] 5317 3-9-4 **75** EddieAhern 4 77
(R M H Cowell) *led and restrained in front: set modest pce: qcknd 2f out: hdd 1f out: no ex ins fnl f* **14/1**

211 **6** *hd* **Taboor (IRE)**[138] 2182 8-8-13 **70** RobertWinston 5 71
(R M H Cowell) *plld hrd: prom: drvn to chal over 1f out: no ex ins fnl f* **10/1**

1000 **7** *1/2* **Anfield Dream**[37] 5212 4-9-2 **73** TedDurcan 3 72
(J R Jenkins) *in tch: hmpd and lost pl over 2f out: rallied to press ldrs over 1f out: no imp* **10/1**

0000 **8** *1/2* **Zarzu**[12] 5777 7-9-4 **75** DaneO'Neill 8 75+
(C R Dore) *b: s.i.s: in rr tl styd on appr fnl f: 7th and no imp whn nt clr run fnl 75 yds* **10/1**

1600 **9** *1/2* **Silver Dane (IRE)**[11] 5782 4-9-1 **72** (v) TPQueally 9 68
(Mrs C A Dunnett) *t.k.h: prom tl wknd over 1f out* **25/1**

The Form Book, Raceform Ltd, Compton, RG20 6NL

40 **10** ¾ **Lady Bahia (IRE)**[11] 5791 5-8-13 **70**........................(b) RobbieFitzpatrick 2 63
(Peter Grayson) *s.s and lost 7 l: bhd: sme hdwy on rail ent st: no ex fnl f* **14/1**

59.38 secs (-0.40) **Going Correction** -0.175s/f (Stan) **10** Ran SP% **120.4**
Speed ratings (Par 103):96,94,94,94,93 93,92,91,90,89
CSF £37.83 CT £162.41 TOTE £3.20: £1.20, £4.60, £2.70; EX 44.80.
Owner The Ember Partnership **Bred** Loan And Development Corporation **Trained** Bury, W Sussex

FOCUS
A decent sprint for the money, but the weak tempo produced a blanket finish. The progressive winner did not need to improve here. The fifth limits the form.
Zarzu Official explanation: jockey said gelding was denied a clear run
Lady Bahia(IRE) Official explanation: jockey said mare missed the break

6036 LINGFIELDPARK.CO.UK H'CAP 6f (P)
4:20 (4:20) (Class 5) (0-70,71) 3-Y-O+ **£3,238** (£963; £481; £240) **Stalls** Low

Form RPR
0001 **1** **Keyaki (IRE)**[12] 5778 5-9-4 **70**.. GeorgeBaker 9 82+
(C F Wall) *trckd ldrs: led ent st: drvn 2 l clr: hld on wl fnl f* **9/2**[2]
01 **2** 1¼ **Hello Man (IRE)**[8] 5874 3-9-4 **71** 6ex.................................... TPQueally 4 79+
(Eamon Tyrrell, Ire) *stdd s: t.k.h towards rr: hdwy 2f out: hung lft in st: r.o to take 2nd ins fnl f* **14/1**
0300 **3** 1 **Jayanjay**[11] 5782 7-9-3 **69**.. BrettDoyle 12 74
(P Mitchell) *t.k.h towards rr: rdn and hdwy over 1f out: styd on to take 3rd ins fnl f* **16/1**
2606 **4** nk **Mandarin Spirit (IRE)**[36] 5246 6-9-1 **67**......................(b) OscarUrbina 10 71
(G C H Chung) *hld up in rr: rdn and r.o appr fnl f: nrst fin: too much to do* **16/1**
2543 **5** ¾ **Gwilym (GER)**[29] 5427 3-9-1 **68**.. TedDurcan 11 70
(D Haydn Jones) *wd: t.k.h in midfield: rdn and styd on same pce fnl 2f* **16/1**
35-0 **6** hd **Look Of Eagles**[287] 17 4-9-1 **67**.................................. NelsonDeSouza 8 69
(P F I Cole) *hld up in rr: effrt and swtchd wd ent st: styd on* **16/1**
6040 **7** ½ **Roman Quintet (IRE)**[12] 5778 6-9-2 **68**............................... EddieAhern 7 68
(D W P Arbuthnot) *mid-div: effrt 2f out: no imp* **15/2**[3]
1-20 **8** shd **Shade Cozy (USA)**[72] 4180 4-9-1 **67**.................................. DaneO'Neill 2 67
(A M Balding) *rrd s: t.k.h towards rr: hdwy to chse ldrs over 1f out: no ex fnl f* **9/2**[2]
5326 **9** 1½ **H Harrison (IRE)**[33] 5313 6-9-0 **66**.............................. RoystonFfrench 6 61
(I W McInnes) *led and set modest pce: hdd ent st: wknd fnl f* **10/1**
2153 **10** 1¼ **Young Bertie**[20] 5605 3-8-10 **68**..................................(v) TravisBlock(5) 3 59
(H Morrison) *w ldrs tl wknd 1f out* **10/3**[1]
6145 **11** 2 **Lii Najma**[57] 4666 3-9-1 **68**.. RyanMoore 1 53
(C E Brittain) *mid-div: rdn over 2f out: sn outpcd* **25/1**
3601 **12** ½ **Duke Of Milan (IRE)**[20] 5605 3-9-3 **70**................................ AdamKirby 5 54
(G C Bravery) *lw: w ldrs tl wknd over 1f out* **11/1**

1m 11.66s (-1.15) **Going Correction** -0.175s/f (Stan)
WFA 3 from 4yo+ 1lb **12** Ran SP% **122.7**
Speed ratings (Par 103):100,98,97,96,95 95,94,94,92,90 88,87
CSF £68.82 CT £960.02 TOTE £5.80: £2.30, £5.50, £5.40; EX 93.90.
Owner S Oldroyd **Bred** Rathbarry Stud **Trained** Newmarket, Suffolk

FOCUS
A fair sprint race, but the pace was disappointing. Ordinary form overall, but positives to be taken from the first two.
H Harrison(IRE) Official explanation: jockey said gelding ran too free
Duke Of Milan(IRE) Official explanation: jockey said gelding ran too free

6037 HALLOWEEN FAMILY FUN DAY OCTOBER 26TH H'CAP 1m 4f (P)
4:50 (4:50) (Class 6) (0-60,66) 3-Y-O+ **£2,388** (£705; £352) **Stalls** Low

Form RPR
0060 **1** **Maximix**[51] 4847 3-9-0 **58**.. RyanMoore 9 70
(B W Hills) *hld up in midfield: hdwy over 2f out: styd on to ld ins fnl f: rdn clr* **9/1**
0113 **2** 2½ **Lolla's Spirit (IRE)**[18] 5652 3-8-10 **59**......................... AndrewElliott(5) 7 67
(M L W Bell) *prom: led over 2f out tl ins fnl f: one pce* **5/1**[2]
0200 **3** ½ **Missie Baileys**[18] 5652 4-9-0 **54**..................................(p) AmirQuinn(3) 10 61
(Mrs L J Mongan) *hld up in tch: hdwy 4f out: rdn to chal 2f out: one pce fnl f* **16/1**
2011 **4** 1½ **Treetops Hotel (IRE)**[6] 5910 7-9-10 **66** 6ex.............. LiamTreadwell(5) 6 71
(B R Johnson) *hld up in midfield: hdwy 4f out: rdn to press ldrs over 1f out: no ex fnl f* **7/4**[1]
2025 **5** 3½ **Agilete**[17] 5683 4-9-9 **60**.. EddieAhern 13 59
(J Pearce) *hld up towards rr: sme hdwy 3f out: styd on steadily fnl 2f: nvr rchd chalng position* **8/1**[3]
0500 **6** 2 **Lady Pilot**[15] 5736 4-9-6 **57**... GeorgeBaker 5 53
(Ms J S Doyle) *chsd ldrs: outpcd 3f out: steadily fdd* **16/1**
00/0 **7** 2½ **Electrique (IRE)**[12] 5775 6-9-6 **57**............................(b) RobertWinston 14 49
(A J McCabe) *stdd s: t.k.h in rr: hdwy into midfield 3f out: no imp* **66/1**
3-00 **8** 2½ **Escoffier**[25] 5513 4-8-13 **55**.. EmmettStack(5) 2 43
(Pat Eddery) *lw: chsd ldrs tl wknd over 4f out* **100/1**
0060 **9** nk **Mister Completely (IRE)**[7] 5897 5-8-13 **53**.................... JamesDoyle(3) 8 40
(Ms J S Doyle) *lw: bhd: rdn and modest hdwy fnl 3f* **12/1**
55-0 **10** 2½ **Huggle**[81] 3906 3-9-0 **58**.. BrianReilly 15 41
(P S McEntee) *bhd: rdn over 5f out: nvr trbld ldrs* **100/1**
5550 **11** hd **Qualitair Wings**[15] 5725 7-9-3 **54**..................................... DerekMcGaffin 4 37
(J Hetherton) *mid-div: rdn and btn over 3f out* **11/1**
3530 **12** nk **The Iron Giant (IRE)**[9] 5831 4-9-4 **55**................................. RobertMiles 11 38
(B G Powell) *pressed ldr: led over 5f out tl over 2f out: wknd qckly* **11/1**
530- **13** 1¼ **Hathlen (IRE)**[408] 4664 5-9-7 **58**.................................. RoystonFfrench 16 39
(Mrs N Smith) *hld up towards rr: shkn up 3f out: nvr nr ldrs* **33/1**
3000 **14** hd **Competitor**[9] 5831 5-9-7 **58**..(vt) DaneO'Neill 1 38
(J Akehurst) *in tch tl wknd 5f out* **25/1**
4600 **15** 15 **Pukka Tique**[10] 5815 3-8-9 **60**..........................(b[1]) RussellKennemore(7) 3 16
(R Hollinshead) *led tl over 5f out: wknd rapidly 4f out* **33/1**

2m 30.81s (-3.58) **Going Correction** -0.175s/f (Stan)
WFA 3 from 4yo+ 7lb **15** Ran SP% **123.5**
Speed ratings (Par 101):104,102,102,101,98 97,95,94,93,92 92,91,90,90,80
CSF £52.74 CT £730.36 TOTE £11.70: £3.00, £2.30, £6.60; EX 66.80 Place 6 £69.08, Place 5 £47.16.
Owner Enton Thoroughbred Racing & Cavendish Investing **Bred** C G A Liesack And S N C Lagardere Elevage **Trained** Lambourn, Berks

FOCUS
A modest race, but run at a strong gallop with the field soon strung out. Solid form, with the unexposed winner possibly capbale of better.
Qualitair Wings Official explanation: jockey said gelding stopped very quickly 4f out
Hathlen(IRE) Official explanation: jockey said gelding hung left
T/Plt: £162.30 to a £1 stake. Pool: £54,467.65. 244.85 winning tickets. T/Qpdt: £111.20 to a £1 stake. Pool: £2,962.60. 19.70 winning tickets. LM

6038 - 6045a (Foreign Racing) - See Raceform Interactive

6022 DEAUVILLE (R-H)
Tuesday, October 17
OFFICIAL GOING: Turf course - soft; all-weather - standard

6046a PRIX DES RESEVOIRS (GROUP 3) (FILLIES) (ROUND) 1m (R)
2:00 (2:01) 2-Y-O **£27,586** (£11,034; £8,276; £5,517; £2,759)

RPR
1 **Chinandega (FR)**[12] 2-8-9 .... SPasquier 1 102
(P Demercastel, France) *held up in last, headway down outside 2f out, challenged final f, led 100yds out, pushed out* **15/2**
2 ¾ **Cicerole (FR)**[44] 5048 2-8-9 .... IMendizabal 7 100
(J-C Rouget, France) *towards rr early, hdwy appr str, disp 3rd str, rdn & ran on to led over 1f out, hdd 100yds out* **36/10**[2]
3 ¾ **Kahyasola (FR)**[65] 4415 2-8-9 .... TJarnet 5 99
(G Doleuze, France) *in touch, disputing 3rd straight, ridden 1 1/2f out, stayed on* **17/1**
4 nk **Vadapolina (FR)**[31] 2-8-9 .... CSoumillon 3 98
(A Fabre, France) *held up, disputing 6th straight, ridden 1 1/2f out, stayed on at one pace* **2/1**[1]
5 1½ **Sismix (IRE)**[16] 5714 2-8-9 .... OPeslier 9 95
(C Laffon-Parias, France) *prominent, 2nd straight, disputed lead 1 1/2f out, no extra close home* **14/1**
6 2½ **Ikat (IRE)**[16] 5714 2-8-9 .... C-PLemaire 8 89
(D Sepulchre, France) *mid-division, disputing 6th straight, pushed along 1 1/2f out, never in challenging position* **53/10**[3]
7 1 **Eclisse (FR)** 2-8-9 .... JVictoire 2 87
(Y De Nicolay, France) *towards rear, disputing 6th straight, never dangerous* **25/1**
8 5 **Galaxie Des Sables (FR)**[31] 2-8-9 .... DBoeuf 6 76
(Mme N Rossio, France) *led to over 1f out, weakened* **12/1**
9 3 **Sans Reward (IRE)**[38] 5187 2-8-9 ....(b) TThulliez 4 69
(B J Meehan) *tracked leader, niggled along 3f out & lost place, still close 5th straight but soon ridden & beaten* **53/10**[3]

1m 43.8s **9** Ran SP% **122.3**
PARI-MUTUEL: WIN 8.50; PL 2.90, 1.70, 4.10; DF 24.80.
Owner Mme P Demercastel **Bred** Philippe Demercastel **Trained** France

NOTEBOOK
Chinandega(FR), a very nice filly in the making, should get further than a mile next year in decent company. Outpaced in the early stages, she was still last entering the straight but picked up well from three furlongs out and made her challenge up the centre of the track. She finally won with something in hand, but will not be seen out again this year and her trainer hinted that she might be sold before next season.
Cicerole(FR), a very consistent individual, was given every possible chance. She was always close up and took the advantage at the furlong marker, but was unable to hold the winner. Better ground would have helped.
Kahyasola(FR), in mid-division early, progressed from two furlongs out and battled on gamely to the line. A longer trip would probably suit her.
Vadapolina(FR), still a maiden, was made favourite but was given plenty to do. She did run on, but never looked like ending up in the winners' enclosure. Undoubtedly a filly with talent and scope, she is still very green and did not look at home in the soft ground.
Sans Reward(IRE), up there early, her stride began to shorten some three furlongs from home and she finally dropped out of contention to finish a well-beaten last. Her jockey felt it was one race too many after a long season.

5764 NOTTINGHAM (L-H)
Wednesday, October 18
OFFICIAL GOING: Soft (good to soft in places)
After five dry days the ground was described as 'very soft, tacky and holding'.
Wind: almost nil Weather: overcast and dull

6047 WBX.COM WORLD BET EXCHANGE MEDIAN AUCTION MAIDEN STKS 5f 13y
2:00 (2:02) (Class 6) 2-Y-O **£2,388** (£705; £352) **Stalls** High

Form RPR
30 **1** **Kompete**[18] 5681 2-8-12 .... MichaelTebbutt 11 77
(V Smith) *chsd ldrs: rdn 1/2-way: sn hung lft: led ins fnl f: styd on wl* **11/8**[1]
30 **2** 3½ **Kilcusnin Queen (IRE)**[37] 5237 2-8-12 .... JohnEgan 10 64
(Adrian Sexton, Ire) *mid-div: hdwy 1/2-way: rdn over 1f out: styd on* **17/2**[3]
5 **3** ½ **Superjain**[18] 5686 2-8-5 .... PaulPickard(7) 1 62
(J M Jefferson) *led: hdd and no ex ins fnl f* **66/1**
4 1¼ **Off The Record** 2-9-3 .... JamieMackay 4 63
(J G Given) *s.s: outpcd: hdwy over 1f out: nrst fin* **33/1**
00 **5** 5 **Jete (IRE)**[6] 5915 2-9-0 ....(v) PatrickMathers(3) 8 45
(D Shaw) *sn outpcd: styd on ins fnl f: nvr nrr* **66/1**
6 1½ **Ingleby Hill (IRE)** 2-9-3 .... PhillipMakin 12 39
(T D Barron) *prom: outpcd over 3f out: sme late hdwy* **25/1**
222 **7** 1½ **Rippling River**[171] 1309 2-9-3 **79**.. TedDurcan 7 34
(W Jarvis) *chsd ldrs over 3f* **5/2**[2]
8 1¾ **Go Imperial (IRE)** 2-9-3 .... TPQueally 2 28
(M G Quinlan) *s.i.s: outpcd: in rr whn hung lft over 3f out* **16/1**
9 4 **Beechside (IRE)**[32] 5392 2-8-12 .... RobertHavlin 5 8
(W A Murphy, Ire) *chsd ldrs over 3f* **66/1**
00 **10** 5 **Woodland Symphony**[26] 5508 2-9-3 .... KimTinkler 6 —
(N Tinkler) *prom: stmbld 4f out: sn pushed along: wknd 1/2-way* **100/1**
0 **11** nk **O'Dwyer (IRE)**[15] 5746 2-9-3 .... SilvestreDeSousa 9 —
(A D Brown) *chsd ldrs: rdn 1/2-way: wknd over 1f out* **66/1**
0000 **12** 4 **Delta Queen**[18] 5686 2-8-12 **40**................................ RobbieFitzpatrick 13 —
(C N Kellett) *sn outpcd* **150/1**

63.15 secs (1.35) **Going Correction** +0.20s/f (Good) **12** Ran SP% **101.5**
Speed ratings (Par 93):97,91,90,88,80 78,75,73,66,58 58,51
CSF £9.46 TOTE £2.10: £1.10, £1.70, £5.90; EX 13.50.
Owner David Jenkins **Bred** Capt J H Wilson **Trained** Exning, Suffolk
■ Princess Ileana (9/2) was withdrawn after proving unruly in the stalls. R4 applies, deduct 15p in the £.

FOCUS
A moderate contest with the marker horse Rippling River well beaten. The form looks dubious.

NOTEBOOK

Kompete had the necessary form to take an ordinary maiden after a fair effort in the Redcar Two-Year-Old Trophy last time. She fairly routed her rivals down the usually favoured stands'-side rail, and probably had to run nowhere near her best to score. With a bit more scope for improvement, she may have a try on the All-Weather next. (op 2-1)

Kilcusnin Queen(IRE) stayed on fairly well behind the runaway winner after being fairly prominent throughout. She is worth another chance over six furlongs. (op 10-1)

Superjain , who showed very little on her debut, displayed a lot of early toe to hold an advantage down the middle of the course for much of the race. However, left on her own for virtually all the way, she understandably got lonely and idled inside the final furlong before being well beaten by the winner. She deserves a lot of credit for the run and should not be rated too far behind the winner, considering the path she took. (op 50-1)

Off The Record looked clueless early but kept on encouragingly throughout the final stages, down the middle of the course, to give encouragement for the future. He will obviously be sharper for the run and is entitled to consideration next time in a similarly weak maiden.

Jete(IRE) was never going the pace early but kept on reasonably well through weakening horses. He now qualifies for a handicap mark and looks like a horse that will get at least another furlong, albeit at a low level. (op 50-1)

Ingleby Hill(IRE), making his racecourse debut, did not shape without promise but will need to find plenty of improvement for the run to have an obvious chance next time. (op 20-1 tchd 33-1)

Rippling River was beaten by the halfway marker and ran nowhere near any of his previous efforts. The suggestion must be that soft ground is against him, as his best effort came on a faster surface. Official explanation: trainer said colt was unsuited by the soft (good to soft in places) ground (op 9-4)

6048 OVAL H'CAP — 6f 15y

2:30 (2:30) (Class 5) (0-75,75) 3-Y-0+ **£3,238** (£963; £481; £240) **Stalls** High

Form — RPR

0356 **1** **Bel Cantor**[37] 5250 3-8-5 **66** .... RichardKingscote(3) 11 — 83
(W J H Ratcliffe) *mde all stands' side: wnt clr over 1f out: r.o wl* **40/1**

0036 **2** *5* **Digital**[12] 5782 9-8-13 **70** .... JohnEgan 13 — 72
(M R Channon) *hdwy to chse ldrs over 3f out: kpt on to take 2nd ins last: no ch w wnr* **7/1**[3]

1400 **3** *¾* **Joy And Pain**[14] 5765 5-8-6 **68** .... (p) KevinGhunowa(5) 12 — 68
(R A Harris) *chsd ldrs: kpt on same pce fnl 2f* **50/1**

203 **4** *½* **Countdown**[24] 5554 4-9-4 **75** .... DavidAllan 2 — 73+
(T D Easterby) *racd far side w 3 others: hdwy over 2f out: led that side over 1f out: edgd rt: kpt on* **11/1**

4004 **5** *1 ½* **Balakiref**[14] 5765 7-9-3 **74** .... JamieSpencer 14 — 68
(M Dods) *hld up in rr: hdwy over 2f out: nvr trbld ldrs* **11/4**[1]

0400 **6** *¾* **Greenwood**[8] 5896 8-9-0 **71** .... RobertHavlin 15 — 63
(P G Murphy) *mid-div: kpt on fnl 2f: nvr nr ldrs* **16/1**

4340 **7** *2 ½* **Sir Orpen (IRE)**[14] 5765 3-8-11 **69** .... PhillipMakin 4 — 53
(T D Barron) *swtchd rt after s: in rr: sme hdwy 2f out: nvr a factor* **12/1**

4642 **8** *hd* **Lizarazu (GER)**[14] 5765 7-8-10 **74** .... (p) TolleyDean(7) 7 — 57
(R A Harris) *mid-div: effrt on outer over 2f out: nvr a factor* **16/1**

5400 **9** *nk* **Kennington**[14] 5765 6-8-10 **67** .... (b) AdamKirby 3 — 50+
(Mrs C A Dunnett) *racd far side: chsd ldr: led that side 2f out: sn hdd & wknd* **33/1**

6-20 **10** *½* **Morse (IRE)**[18] 5670 5-9-4 **75** .... LDettori 10 — 56
(J A Osborne) *chsd ldrs: wknd 2f out* **9/2**[2]

500 **11** *1 ¾* **Orphan (IRE)**[12] 5791 4-8-13 **70** .... PatCosgrave 16 — 46
(K R Burke) *mid-div: effrt over 2f out: nvr a factor* **9/1**

0050 **12** *1 ¼* **Norcroft**[12] 5782 4-8-13 **70** .... (p) TPQueally 5 — 42+
(Mrs C A Dunnett) *swtchd lft s and led other 3 far side: hdd 2f out: sn wknd* **50/1**

0145 **13** *½* **Vanadium**[15] 5749 4-8-11 **75** .... PatrickHills(7) 1 — 46+
(J G Given) *chsd ldr far side: wknd over 2f out* **11/1**

5100 **14** *6* **Namir (IRE)**[5] 5938 4-8-7 **67** .... (vt) PatrickMathers(3) 6 — 20
(D Shaw) *swtchd rt after s: chsd ldrs: lost pl 2f out* **40/1**

000 **15** *21* **Ascot Lady (IRE)**[20] 5643 3-9-0 **72** .... RobertWinston 9 — —
(J Balding) *s.i.s: detached last and eased 2f out* **66/1**

1m 16.43s (1.43) **Going Correction** +0.20s/f (Good)
WFA 3 from 4yo+ 1lb — **15** Ran SP% **116.7**
Speed ratings (Par 103):98,91,90,89,87 86,83,83,82,82 79,78,77,69,41
CSF £285.68 CT £13331.70 TOTE £46.10: £8.30, £2.60, £9.60; EX 239.10.
Owner W J H Ratcliffe **Bred** Henry And Mrs Rosemary Moszkowicz **Trained** Leyburn, N Yorks

FOCUS

The stands' side was the place to be and the shock winner had the best ground, but it might not have been a fluke even though the first winner also raced on the stands' rail and it is rated to his best previous form. The winning time was modest for the grade.

Ascot Lady(IRE) Official explanation: jockey said filly was unsuited by the soft (good to soft in places) ground

6049 DAVID ASHLEY CONSTRUCTION LTD MAIDEN STKS (DIV I) — 1m 54y

3:00 (3:00) (Class 5) 2-Y-O **£2,590** (£770; £385; £192) **Stalls** Centre

Form — RPR

1 **Metaphoric (IRE)** 2-9-3 .... JamieSpencer 12 — 80
(M L W Bell) *hld up: hdwy over 2f out: sn edgd lft: shkn up to ld ins fnl f: comf* **10/1**

0 **2** *nk* **Toccata (IRE)**[30] 5425 2-8-12 .... MartinDwyer 7 — 74
(D M Simcock) *led 7f out: rdn over 1f out: hdd ins fnl f: kpt on* **50/1**

6 **3** *2* **Kahara**[33] 5352 2-8-12 .... NickyMackay 2 — 70
(L M Cumani) *led: hdd 7f out: chsd ldrs: rdn over 2f out: swtchd lft over 1f out: styd on same pce* **11/2**

4 *1 ½* **Teodora Adivina** 2-8-12 .... TedDurcan 5 — 67
(H R A Cecil) *dwlt: hld up: hdwy and hmpd over 3f out: sn rdn: nt clr run over 1f out: nvr trbld ldrs* **20/1**

2 **5** *1* **Ashn Thunder**[31] 5402 2-9-3 .... KDarley 11 — 69
(M Johnston) *chsd ldrs: rdn over 1f out: no ex fnl f* **9/2**[3]

6 *3* **Hall Of Fame** 2-9-3 .... LDettori 6 — 63
(Saeed Bin Suroor) *s.i.s: hld up: hdwy over 2f out: n.m.r and lost pl sn after: nvr trbld ldrs* **4/1**[2]

00 **7** *1* **Cushat Law (IRE)**[29] 5456 2-8-12 .... MickyFenton 4 — 56
(W Jarvis) *hld up in tch: hmpd and lost pl over 3f out: n.d after* **100/1**

662 **8** *2* **Priory Bay (USA)**[12] 5780 2-9-3 71 .... SebSanders 3 — 56
(E A L Dunlop) *trckd ldrs: rdn over 2f out: hmpd and wknd over 1f out* **5/1**

9 *nk* **All Of Me (IRE)** 2-9-3 .... JohnEgan 8 — 56
(T G Mills) *s.i.s: hld up: hdwy over 2f out: sn hung lft: wknd fnl f* **33/1**

0 **10** *10* **Chord**[29] 5457 2-9-3 .... RobertWinston 1 — 34
(Sir Michael Stoute) *prom over 5f* **7/2**[1]

0600 **11** *9* **Taran Tregarth**[16] 5720 2-8-12 35 .... (b[1]) PaulQuinn 9 — 9
(A Bailey) *plld hrd and prom: wknd over 2f out* **200/1**

1m 51.15s (4.75) **Going Correction** +0.60s/f (Yiel) — **11** Ran SP% **112.7**
Speed ratings (Par 95):100,99,97,96,95 92,91,89,88,78 69
CSF £418.47 TOTE £14.00: £3.20, £5.90, £1.80; EX 292.90.

Owner The Royal Ascot Racing Club **Bred** Gerrardstown House Stud **Trained** Newmarket, Suffolk
■ Stewards' Enquiry : Nicky Mackay two-day ban: careless riding (Oct 29-30)

FOCUS

A fair-looking maiden though the winning time was 0.2 seconds slower than the second division. Priory Bay did not run anywhere near his official mark so the race is not easy to evaluate, but the winner looks capable of better.

NOTEBOOK

Metaphoric(IRE) got behind early but really picked up well down the home straight to win with a bit more in hand than the official margin suggests. Bred to make a three-year-old, he is definitely one to remember for next season and he could make up into a classy performer. (op 14-1)

Toccata(IRE) almost stole it from the front and is not one to plunge on next time, considering the slow time of the race. That said, it was an improvement in form and she has clearly progressed for her first effort. (tchd 66-1)

Kahara never really had a clear sight of the leaders up the straight and was impeded a couple times, before stopping the eventual fourth in her run when switched to the inside. She is going the right way and ought to come into her own over middle distances next year. (tchd 6-1)

Teodora Adivina ◆ would have finished closer had she not met trouble virtually all the way up the home straight. She can be rated in front of the third. (tchd 25-1)

Ashn Thunder raced prominently and was never far away, but does not have a turn of foot and looks one-paced at two. He does, however, look the sort that will make up into a decent staying handicapper next season. (op 7-2)

Hall Of Fame did not get away cleanly and failed to land a serious blow. However, he was not disgraced and should have learnt plenty for the experience. Already gelded despite a top-drawer pedigree, he may not be totally straightforward. (op 3-1)

Priory Bay(USA) ran poorly again back on turf and is bred to need a quicker surface. (op 9-2)

All Of Me(IRE) Official explanation: jockey said colt hung left-handed

Chord, who did not show a great deal on his debut but was still made favourite, dropped out very quickly and probably needs more time. (op 9-2 tchd 5-1)

6050 DAVID ASHLEY CONSTRUCTION LTD MAIDEN STKS (DIV II) — 1m 54y

3:30 (3:32) (Class 5) 2-Y-O **£2,590** (£770; £385; £192) **Stalls** Centre

Form — RPR

1 **Eastern Anthem (IRE)** 2-9-3 .... LDettori 5 — 85+
(Saeed Bin Suroor) *prom: smooth hdwy to ld over 2f out: shkn up and wnt clr pver 1f out: heavily eased ins last* **8/11**[1]

4 **2** *5* **Sagredo (USA)**[10] 5841 2-9-3 .... SebSanders 6 — 74
(Sir Mark Prescott) *chsd ldr: lft in ld bnd over 4f out: hdd over 2f out: kpt on same pce* **5/1**[2]

0 **3** *½* **Hurricane Thomas (IRE)**[20] 5640 2-9-3 .... KDarley 4 — 73
(M Johnston) *chsd ldrs: kpt on same pce fnl 2f* **7/1**[3]

0 **4** *3 ½* **Danehill Silver**[25] 5537 2-9-3 .... MickyFenton 8 — 65
(R Hollinshead) *prom: one pce fnl 3f* **66/1**

0 **5** *3* **Encircled**[21] 5623 2-8-12 .... RobertHavlin 11 — 54
(D Haydn Jones) *s.i.s: hdwy over 3f out: kpt on: nvr nr ldrs* **66/1**

6 *1 ¼* **Intiquilla (IRE)** 2-8-12 .... TedDurcan 3 — 51
(Mrs A J Perrett) *s.s: outpcd and in rr: sme hdwy 3f out: nvr nr ldrs* **12/1**

0 **7** *2* **Berbatov**[25] 5527 2-9-3 .... EddieAhern 10 — 52
(Ms Deborah J Evans) *in rr: sme hdwy over 2f out: nvr on terms* **100/1**

8 *1 ¾* **Astrolibra** 2-8-12 .... TPQueally 1 — 43
(M H Tompkins) *s.i.s: kpt on fnl 3f: nvr on terms* **50/1**

50 **9** *1 ½* **Wee Ellie Coburn**[21] 5616 2-8-12 .... RobertWinston 9 — 39
(A Bailey) *led: hung bdly rt bnd and hdd over 4f out: lost pl over 2f out* **66/1**

10 *4* **Galloise (IRE)** 2-8-12 .... AdamKirby 12 — 31
(C G Cox) *sn in rr and drvn along* **12/1**

11 *¾* **Sven (SWE)** 2-9-3 .... JimCrowley 13 — 34
(B I Case) *hld up in rr: nvr a factor* **100/1**

50 **12** *6* **Little Tommy Fella**[172] 1284 2-9-3 .... DavidAllan 7 — 21
(S C Williams) *chsd ldrs: wknd over 2f out: sn bhd* **33/1**

0 **13** *24* **Follow The Buzz**[10] 5841 2-8-10 .... (p) BarrySavage(7) 2 — —
(J M Bradley) *s.s: a bhd: t.o 4f out* **300/1**

1m 50.95s (4.55) **Going Correction** +0.60s/f (Yiel) — **13** Ran SP% **114.1**
Speed ratings (Par 95):101,96,95,92,89 87,85,84,82,78 77,71,47
CSF £3.98 TOTE £1.50: £1.10, £1.70, £2.30; EX 4.40.
Owner Godolphin **Bred** Darley **Trained** Newmarket, Suffolk

FOCUS

No strength in depth, but the classically-bred winner could hardly have made a bigger impression on his debut and the winning time was 0.2 seconds faster than the first division.

NOTEBOOK

Eastern Anthem(IRE), the first foal of Kazzia, who won both the 1000 Guineas and the Oaks in 2002, is a most attractive individual. He had only to be put about his job to put his stamp on the race and, heavily eased in the end, was value for double the official margin. He will now return to Dubai and only time will tell how good he is. (op 10-11 tchd Evens and 11-10 in places)

Sagredo(USA), a likeable type, was left in front turning in. He proved no match whatsoever for the winner but is the type to make his mark in handicap company over middle-distances at three. (op 9-2)

Hurricane Thomas(IRE), quite a big type, showed a fair bit more than on his debut three weeks earlier and can improve again. (op 5-1)

Danehill Silver, an immature type, did not shape at all badly but will be much more the finished article with another winter over his head. (op 50-1)

Encircled, still carrying tons of condition, stayed on steadily up the home straight and will be seen in a better light at three. (op 50-1)

Intiquilla(IRE), a lengthy, backward-looking newcomer, was clueless. She kept on in her own time in the home straight and can be expected to do better over further next year. (op 11-1 tchd 10-1)

Astrolibra Official explanation: vet said filly had lost a shoe and finished lame; jockey said, regarding the running and riding, his orders were to take his time on the filly - a big backward sort - and let her to get into her stride, adding that the pace had been plenty quick enough on soft ground, and having asked her for an effort early in the straight he felt filly's stride shorten and felt it prudent not to be too hard on her

6051 SAVILLS NOTTINGHAM H'CAP — 1m 1f 213y

4:00 (4:01) (Class 3) (0-90,90) 3-Y-O **£8,096** (£2,408; £1,203; £601) **Stalls** Low

Form — RPR

1166 **1** **Baskerville**[35] 5301 3-8-11 **83** .... EddieAhern 7 — 95+
(P W Chapple-Hyam) *led 1f: chsd ldrs: led over 1f out: rdn out* **12/1**

6040 **2** *2 ½* **Lake Poet (IRE)**[24] 5548 3-9-2 **88** .... SebSanders 13 — 95
(C E Brittain) *hld up: hdwy over 2f out: rdn and hung lft over 1f out: styd on same pce* **12/1**

0000 **3** *shd* **Idarah (USA)**[60] 4612 3-8-13 **85** .... MartinDwyer 2 — 92
(W J Haggas) *prom: outpcd 3f out: hdwy over 1f out: sn hung lft: styd on* **16/1**

221 **4** *¾* **Woolly Bully**[16] 5726 3-8-4 **76** oh2 .... RichardMullen 8 — 81
(G A Huffer) *prom: rdn over 2f out: hung lft 1f out: no ex whn hung rt wl ins fnl f* **5/2**[1]

313 **5** *1 3/4* **Speedy Sam**[26] 5505 3-8-11 **88** AndrewElliott(5) 6 — 90
(K R Burke) *trckd ldrs: led over 6f out: rdn and hdd over 1f out: rdr sn dropped whip: wknd ins fnl f* **9/2**[3]

2020 **6** *4* **Top Jaro (FR)**[18] 5685 3-8-4 **76** oh2 FrancisFerris 1 — 71
(T P Tate) *led 9f out: hdd over 6f out: rdn and wknd over 1f out* **40/1**

5266 **7** *3/4* **Quince (IRE)**[19] 5660 3-8-11 **83** (v) RobertWinston 12 — 77
(J Pearce) *hld up: hdwy 3f out: rdn and wknd over 1f out* **12/1**

-243 **8** *shd* **John Terry (IRE)**[112] 2986 3-9-1 **87** JimCrowley 11 — 81
(Mrs A J Perrett) *hld up: rdn over 2f out: n.d* **10/1**

3560 **9** *hd* **Barodine**[19] 5660 3-8-10 **82** KDarley 5 — 75
(H R A Cecil) *hld up: racd keenly: hdwy over 2f out: rdn and wknd over 1f out* **33/1**

1 **10** *8* **Moonlit Skies**[22] 5589 3-9-4 **90** LDettori 3 — 69
(Saeed Bin Suroor) *chsd ldrs: rdn over 4f out: wknd 2f out* **4/1**[2]

1560 **11** *9* **Lady Disdain**[14] 5769 3-8-4 **76** oh1 JohnEgan 9 — 39
(G M Moore) *hld up: effrt over 3f out: sn hung lft and wknd* **25/1**

124- **12** *20* **Sciatin (IRE)**[396] 5289 3-9-3 **89** NickyMackay 10 — 16
(L M Cumani) *hld up: bhd fnl 3f* **40/1**

11-0 **13** *2* **Natural Force (IRE)**[106] 3176 3-9-3 **89** TedDurcan 4 — 12
(Saeed Bin Suroor) *chsd ldrs over 7f* **40/1**

2m 14.79s (5.09) **Going Correction** +0.60s/f (Yiel) **13** Ran SP% **118.9**
Speed ratings (Par 105):103,101,100,100,98 95,95,95,94,88 81,65,63
CSF £140.16 CT £2293.07 TOTE £13.10: £3.60, £3.70, £5.00; EX 155.00.
Owner Hintlesham Racing **Bred** Mrs J A Prescott **Trained** Newmarket, Suffolk

FOCUS
A useful handicap won in good style by Baskerville. The form looks solid enough with the placed horses to their marks.

NOTEBOOK
Baskerville, who has form on soft ground, ran right away from his rivals from around the furlong pole to win easily. He could do with being turned out quickly before the Handicapper reacts too harshly, as he clearly handles ease and can be found another race before the end of the season. (tchd 11-1)
Lake Poet(IRE) kept plugging away down the home straight but never landed a telling blow. He needs to come down the weights before being of any serious interest. (op 10-1)
Idarah(USA) finally recaptured some of his early-season form, staying on quite well after getting outpaced when the tempo was increased. However, he is still well above the rating he won off in April, which has to be a concern. (op 20-1)
Woolly Bully had every chance but came up short when the pressure was fully applied. The form of his maiden success was dubious and he did not help his chances by hanging under pressure. (op 11-4 after 3-1 in places and 10-3 in a place tchd 9-4)
Speedy Sam has been in fine form during the season and ran well under his apprentice jockey, who has won on him before but who dropped his whip in the latter stages here. The ten-furlong trip seemed to stretch his stamina to the limit in the soft ground. (op 6-1 tchd 7-1)
Moonlit Skies won a weak-looking maiden on his debut and was saddled with what looked a massive official mark. He was not up to the task and needs to come down the handicap to a more realistic level. (op 3-1)

6052 WBX.COM WORLD BET EXCHANGE MAIDEN STKS (DIV I) — 1m 1f 213y
4:30 (4:31) (Class 5) 3-Y-O — **£2,590** (£770; £385; £192) **Stalls** Low

Form — RPR

1 **Emirates Line (USA)** 3-9-3 (t) LDettori 11 — 88+
(Saeed Bin Suroor) *trckd ldrs: drvn to ld over 2f out: kpt on ins last* **4/6**[1]

24 **2** *1* **Sculastic**[14] 5770 3-9-3 NickyMackay 14 — 81
(L M Cumani) *mid-div: hdwy to chse ldrs 4f out: chal over 2f out: no ex ins last* **10/3**[2]

6-62 **3** *3 1/2* **Nawaadi**[21] 5612 3-9-3 79 MartinDwyer 4 — 75
(M P Tregoning) *w ldr: kpt on same pce fnl 2f* **9/2**[3]

0 **4** *3* **Miss Provence**[16] 5727 3-8-12 KDarley 12 — 67+
(G Wragg) *hld up in rr: hdwy and prom 4f out: wknd and eased wl ins last* **33/1**

5 *1 1/4* **Trailmix (FR)** 3-9-3 JohnEgan 13 — 67
(D R C Elsworth) *s.v.s: hdwy and in tch over 4f out: kpt on fnl 2f* **28/1**

0 **6** *5* **Right To Play (USA)**[18] 5669 3-9-3 RobertHavlin 8 — 58
(J H M Gosden) *trckd ldrs: wknd 2f out* **12/1**

-060 **7** *7* **Colinette**[134] 2332 3-8-12 61 FergusSweeney 10 — 40
(H Candy) *mid-div: sme hdwy 4f out: wknd over 2f out* **50/1**

0-0 **8** *9* **Alkhabar (USA)**[22] 5598 3-9-3 SebSanders 1 — 29
(J L Dunlop) *led tl over 2f out: lost pl over 1f out* **100/1**

00 **9** *1/2* **Dream Master (IRE)**[22] 5598 3-9-3 MickyFenton 3 — 28
(J Ryan) *s.i.s: hdwy to chse ldrs after 2f: drvn over 4f out: lost pl over 3f out* **100/1**

10 *7* **Dichoh** 3-9-3 MatthewHenry 7 — 16
(M A Jarvis) *mid-div: lost pl 3f out* **40/1**

0 **11** *2 1/2* **Asleep At The Back (IRE)**[195] 897 3-9-3 (t) JamieMackay 6 — 11
(J G Given) *plld hrd in rr: bhd fnl 3f* **150/1**

12 *58* **Lady Althea** 3-8-12 TPQueally 5 — —
(Mrs C A Dunnett) *s.i.s: sn bhd: t.o 4f out* **100/1**

2m 15.76s (6.06) **Going Correction** +0.60s/f (Yiel) **12** Ran SP% **123.4**
Speed ratings (Par 101):99,98,95,93,92 88,82,75,74,69 67,20
CSF £3.20 TOTE £1.50: £1.10, £1.30, £1.60; EX 4.00.
Owner Godolphin **Bred** W S Farish **Trained** Newmarket, Suffolk

FOCUS
Just an ordinary backend maiden and the winner made hard work of it on his racecourse debut. The winning time was 0.8 seconds quicker than the second division and the runner-up sets the standard.
Trailmix(FR) Official explanation: jockey said gelding missed the break and tired in the latter stages

6053 WBX.COM WORLD BET EXCHANGE MAIDEN STKS (DIV II) — 1m 1f 213y
5:00 (5:03) (Class 5) 3-Y-O — **£2,590** (£770; £385; £192) **Stalls** Low

Form — RPR

5-2 **1** **Galactic Star**[14] 5768 3-9-3 RobertWinston 5 — 80+
(Sir Michael Stoute) *a.p: rdn to ld ins fnl f: r.o* **5/6**[1]

4232 **2** *1* **Conservation (FR)**[9] 5870 3-9-3 72 EddieAhern 11 — 78
(P W Chapple-Hyam) *led: hdd over 8f out: led over 4f out: rdn and hdd over 1f out: ev ch ins fnl f: unable qckn* **4/1**[2]

3 *1 1/4* **Fringe** 3-8-5 MarkWaite(7) 6 — 71+
(Jane Chapple-Hyam) *dwlt: hld up: hdwy over 4f out: outpcd over 2f out: r.o ins fnl f* **100/1**

4 *3/4* **Sahara Sphinx (USA)** 3-9-3 LDettori 13 — 74
(Saeed Bin Suroor) *a.p: led over 1f out: sn rdn: hdd and no ex ins fnl f* **5/1**[3]

422 **5** *1 1/2* **Valverde (IRE)**[72] 4210 3-9-3 77 SebSanders 4 — 72
(J L Dunlop) *hld up: hdwy over 3f out: rdn and ev ch over 1f out: wknd ins fnl f* **7/1**

05 **6** *1 1/4* **La Estrella (USA)**[183] 1070 3-9-3 JamieMackay 9 — 69+
(J G Given) *hld up: r.o ins fnl f: nvr nrr* **50/1**

04 **7** *5* **Broughtons Folly**[30] 5426 3-8-12 TPQueally 7 — 55+
(W J Musson) *hld up: rdn 1/2-way: nvr nrr* **66/1**

000 **8** *5* **Lady Galadriel (USA)**[114] 2934 3-8-12 62 MickyFenton 12 — 46
(J M P Eustace) *chsd ldr: led over 8f out: hdd over 4f out: wknd 3f out* **150/1**

4 **9** *2* **Maraakez**[38] 5203 3-9-3 MartinDwyer 1 — 48
(J H M Gosden) *chsd ldrs over 7f* **14/1**

0000 **10** *1 1/4* **Bacharach (IRE)**[146] 1950 3-9-3 53 JohnEgan 2 — 46
(R F Fisher) *s.s: hld up: plld hrd: effrt over 3f out: sn wknd* **100/1**

00 **11** *1 1/4* **Alujawill (IRE)**[10] 5830 3-9-3 FergusSweeney 10 — 43
(J G M O'Shea) *prom: racd keenly: rdn over 3f out: sn wknd* **200/1**

2m 16.58s (6.88) **Going Correction** +0.60s/f (Yiel) **11** Ran SP% **117.0**
Speed ratings (Par 101):96,95,94,93,92 91,87,83,81,80 79
CSF £4.40 TOTE £1.70: £1.10, £1.80, £19.70; EX 5.80.
Owner Saeed Suhail **Bred** Hascombe And Valiant Studs **Trained** Newmarket, Suffolk

FOCUS
The winning time was 0.8 seconds slower than the first division. The form is held down by the 72-rated runner-up but the winner shaped better than the bare form.

6054 WBX.COM WORLD BET EXCHANGE APPRENTICE H'CAP — 1m 54y
5:30 (5:31) (Class 5) (0-70,70) 3-Y-0+ — **£3,238** (£963; £481; £240) **Stalls** Centre

Form — RPR

6050 **1** **Pure Imagination (IRE)**[5] 5937 5-8-12 **66** (b) BarrySavage(8) 13 — 77+
(J M Bradley) *hld up in mid-field: hdwy over 3f out: led jst ins last: kpt on* **12/1**

0403 **2** *2* **Dispol Isle (IRE)**[9] 5865 4-8-11 **60** NeilBrown(3) 6 — 67
(T D Barron) *hld up towards rr: hdwy on outer over 3f out: edgd lft and led appr fnl f: sn hdd and no ex* **9/1**

505 **3** *hd* **Vacation (IRE)**[15] 5761 3-9-7 **70** JonjoMilczarek 2 — 77
(V Smith) *prom: led 3f out: hdd appr fnl f: kpt on same pce* **8/1**[3]

041 **4** *5* **Bank On Benny**[21] 5621 4-9-0 **63** WilliamBuick(3) 1 — 60+
(P W D'Arcy) *hld up in rr: hdwy on ins 4f out: kpt on same pce fnl 2f: nvr able chal* **3/1**[2]

0411 **5** *1* **Apache Nation (IRE)**[20] 5637 3-9-3 **66** WilliamCarson 4 — 61
(M Dods) *w ldrs: chal 3f out: fdd fnl f* **11/4**[1]

2020 **6** *hd* **Emperor's Well**[28] 5484 7-8-5 **57** (b) AdeleRothery(6) 11 — 52
(M W Easterby) *prom: effrt on outside over 3f out: one pce* **33/1**

1050 **7** *5* **Alfridini**[38] 5205 5-9-7 **67** KMay 12 — 52
(D R C Elsworth) *led tl 3f out: wknd over 1f out* **16/1**

0100 **8** *2 1/2* **Jaassey**[18] 5680 3-8-6 **58** JamesRogers(3) 8 — 38
(A Crook) *rr-div: sme hdwy 3f out: nvr on terms* **25/1**

0000 **9** *3/4* **Right Ted (IRE)**[32] 5386 3-8-9 **61** MarkWaite(3) 10 — 39
(T Wall) *sn detached in rr: hdwy on wd outside 3f out: nvr on terms* **66/1**

2405 **10** *4* **Deeper In Debt**[48] 4968 8-9-8 **68** MarkCoumbe 7 — 38
(J Akehurst) *rr-div: pushed along over 5f out: nvr a factor* **18/1**

2430 **11** *2* **Elidore**[32] 5384 6-8-9 **58** RichardRowe(3) 9 — 24
(B Palling) *w ldrs: lost pl over 2f out* **20/1**

6300 **12** *8* **Capricho (IRE)**[14] 5765 9-9-6 **66** JackMitchell 16 — 16
(J Akehurst) *s.i.s: hdwy and prom over 4f out: lost pl 3f out* **28/1**

1114 **13** *1* **Apres Ski (IRE)**[16] 5739 3-9-4 **67** AlanRutter 5 — 15
(J F Coupland) *bolted gng to s: trckd ldrs: lost pl over 2f out: eased* **8/1**[3]

0100 **14** *1/2* **Primeshade Promise**[29] 5450 5-8-10 **56** JamieHamblett 3 — —
(J M Bradley) *chsd ldrs: lost pl over 2f out: eased* **40/1**

/560 **15** *4* **Johannian**[41] 5130 8-8-6 **60** PietroRomeo(8) 15 — —
(J M Bradley) *s.i.s: hdwy on ins 4f out: lost pl over 2f out* **100/1**

00 **16** *13* **Alocin (IRE)**[8] 5902 3-9-0 **66** (p) PatrickDonaghy(3) 14 — —
(A D Brown) *w ldrs: lost pl over 3f out: sn bhd* **125/1**

1m 50.93s (4.53) **Going Correction** +0.60s/f (Yiel)
WFA 3 from 4yo+ 3lb **16** Ran SP% **123.4**
Speed ratings (Par 103):101,99,98,93,92 92,87,85,84,80 78,70,69,68,64 51
CSF £110.06 CT £968.15 TOTE £14.70: £3.30, £1.60, £1.80, £1.40; EX 123.30 Place 6 £467.35, Place 5 £280.26.
Owner Dab Hand Racing **Bred** Azienda Agricola Valle Falcone Srl **Trained** Sedbury, Gloucs
■ A first winner for 19-year-old Barry Savage on his 99th mount.

FOCUS
A modest apprentice handicap but the form looks sound rated around the placed horses.
Apres Ski(IRE) Official explanation: jockey said colt had been unsuited by the soft (good to soft in places) ground
T/Plt: £190.90 to a £1 stake. Pool: £53,870.45. 206.00 winning tickets. T/Qpdt: £22.00 to a £1 stake. Pool: £3,247.90. 108.85 winning tickets. CR

5321 YARMOUTH (L-H)
Wednesday, October 18

OFFICIAL GOING: Good to soft changing to soft after race 2 (2.40)
Wind: nil

6055 EUROPEAN BREEDERS FUND MAIDEN STKS — 6f 3y
2:10 (2:12) (Class 5) 2-Y-O — **£3,886** (£1,156; £577; £288) **Stalls** High

Form — RPR

1 **Undertone (IRE)** 2-8-12 BrettDoyle 6 — 79
(C E Brittain) *chsd ldr: rdn wl over 1f out: kpt on to ld last 100yds: r.o* **25/1**

00 **2** *1/2* **Atlantic Light**[35] 5297 2-8-12 J-PGuillambert 7 — 77
(M Johnston) *led: rdn wl over 1f out: hdd last 100yds: no ex* **22/1**

332 **3** *3* **Hazzard County (USA)**[29] 5449 2-9-3 78 DaneO'Neill 13 — 73
(D M Simcock) *hld up in tch: hdwy to chse ldng pair 2f out: sn hanging lft: no imp fnl f* **9/4**[2]

00 **4** *5* **Ice Box (IRE)**[18] 5679 2-8-12 JoeFanning 2 — 53
(M Johnston) *hld up in tch: rdn and effrt over 2f out: no ch w ldrs fnl f* **10/1**

0 **5** *1* **Benayoun**[19] 5646 2-9-3 NCallan 10 — 55
(M H Tompkins) *chsd ldrs: rdn and outpcd wl over 2f out: kpt on again ins fnl f: no ch w ldrs* **66/1**

0 **6** *nk* **High Lite**[9] 5867 2-8-12 HayleyTurner 8 — 49
(M L W Bell) *slowly away: rr in tch: rdn and struggling 3f out: kpt on ins fnl f: n.d* **66/1**

3 **7** *1* **Nabra**[63] 4492 2-8-12 RHills 9 — 46
(J H M Gosden) *trckd ldrs: rdn and wknd qckly 2f out: no ch after* **6/4**[1]

00 **8** *shd* **Kyloe Belle (USA)**[9] 5867 2-8-12 OscarUrbina 11 — 46
(Mrs A J Perrett) *bhd: rdn 3f out: nvr on terms* **33/1**

9 *nk* **Kind Of Fizzy** 2-8-12 ChrisCatlin 3 — 45
(Rae Guest) *s.i.s: sn pushed along in rr: nvr on terms* **50/1**

	10	1 1/2	**Pearls Of Wisdom** 2-8-12 ... JimmyFortune 5	40
			(J H M Gosden) *slowly away: t.k.h and sn chsng ldrs: rdn over 2f out: sn wknd* **8/1[3]**	
064	11	3/4	**Napoleon Dynamite (IRE)**[19] [5648] 2-9-3 68... MichaelHills 1	43
			(J W Hills) *t.k.h: hld up in tch on outer: rdn over 2f out: sn btn* **9/1**	
0	12	3	**Savanagh Forest (IRE)**[13] [5773] 2-8-12 ... TPO'Shea 14	29
			(M Quinn) *s.i.s: a bhd: no ch wl over 2f out* **66/1**	

1m 15.74s (2.04) **Going Correction** +0.225s/f (Good) **12** Ran SP% **118.5**
Speed ratings (Par 95):95,94,90,83,82 81,80,80,80,78 77,73
CSF £449.51 TOTE £36.00: £6.60, £5.80, £1.20; EX 545.00 TRIFECTA Not won..
Owner Sheikh Marwan Al Maktoum **Bred** Darley **Trained** Newmarket, Suffolk
■ Stewards' Enquiry : Dane O'Neill caution: used whip down the shoulder in the forehand position

FOCUS
An ordinary maiden for the track and field came down the centre of the track. There was a healthy gap between the front three and the rest.

NOTEBOOK
Undertone(IRE) knew what to do at the first time of asking and showed the right attitude to get on top of the runner-up inside the last furlong. By Noverre and from the family of the Sun Chariot winner Warning Shadows on the distaff side, she should stay a bit further and is entitled to improve from this. (op 28-1)
Atlantic Light was not certain to appreciate dropping back a furlong on breeding, but the evidence of her first two starts was that it would help and, once again given a positive ride, she managed to keep all bar the winner at bay. She is no great shakes, but does now qualify for a mark which opens up a few more options. (op 20-1)
Hazzard County(USA) had every chance and pulled clear of the main body of the field, but he could never quite summon the pace to take him to the front over this shorter trip. He is the benchmark for the form, but will remain vulnerable to unexposed types in races like this. Official explanation: jockey said colt hung left (op 3-1 tchd 2-1)
Ice Box(IRE), like her stable companion the runner-up, was dropping a furlong in her third outing and though she achieved her best placing so far, was still well adrift of the front trio and probably did not improve much. She also now qualifies for a mark and, on the evidence so far, it should be a modest one.
Benayoun did not step up much from his debut effort and looks one for modest handicaps later on. (tchd 80-1)
Nabra did not confirm the promise of her debut effort over course and distance back in August, being amongst the first beaten. The ground was softer this time, but this was still a moderate effort. (op 7-4 tchd 15-8)

6056 RACING WELFARE NURSERY 5f 43y
2:40 (2:40) (Class 5) (0-75,75) 2-Y-O **£3,886** (£1,156; £577; £288) **Stalls** High

Form				RPR
3226	1		**Malaaq**[18] [5668] 2-9-3 71... RHills 11	72
			(M A Jarvis) *hld up in tch: hdwy to ld wl over 1f out: sn rdn: wnt lft 1f out: jnd ins fnl f: fnd ex nr fin* **5/1[1]**	
0445	2	hd	**Aquilegia (IRE)**[15] [5753] 2-8-10 64... GrahamGibbons 7	65
			(E S McMahon) *slowly away: bhd: drvn and hdwy 2f out: w wnr wl ins fnl f: unable qckn nr fin* **12/1**	
3551	3	1	**Hephaestus**[13] [5772] 2-9-0 68... TPO'Shea 5	65
			(M R Channon) *bhd and sn pushed along: gd hdwy 2f out: chsd ldng pair fnl f: kpt on same pce* **9/1[3]**	
0420	4	2 1/2	**Hucking Hope (IRE)**[18] [5668] 2-9-1 69... SteveDrowne 4	57
			(J R Best) *hld up in midfield: effrt u.p 2f out: no imp fnl f* **14/1**	
2041	5	1/2	**Only A Grand**[10] [5835] 2-8-7 61 6ex...(b) RoystonFfrench 13	47
			(R Bastiman) *in rr and drvn 3f out: kpt on fnl f: nvr trbld ldrs* **5/1[1]**	
4202	6	3	**Violet's Pride**[10] [5835] 2-8-8 67... DuranFentiman(5) 12	42
			(S Parr) *w ldrs travelling wl: ev ch wl over 1f out: sn rdn and btn* **40/1**	
4506	7	hd	**Queen Of Narnia**[16] [5731] 2-8-13 67... TonyCulhane 6	42
			(M R Channon) *slowly away: hld up bhd: rdn over 2f out: nvr pce to rch ldrs* **16/1**	
4030	8	nk	**Minimum Fuss (IRE)**[16] [5721] 2-8-2 61... AurelioMedeiros(5) 1	35
			(M C Chapman) *s.i.s: chsd ldrs tl rdn over 2f out: wknd wl over 1f out* **50/1**	
13	9	shd	**Russian Silk**[29] [5442] 2-9-7 75... TomEaves 9	48
			(Jedd O'Keeffe) *led tl wl over 1f out: wknd qckly 1f out* **11/2[2]**	
6320	10	5	**Convivial Spirit**[19] [5655] 2-8-13 67...(t) DaneO'Neill 15	22
			(E F Vaughan) *racd stands' side: nvr on terms* **16/1**	
4200	11	1/2	**Stir Crazy (IRE)**[10] [5829] 2-8-13 67... JoeFanning 2	20
			(M R Channon) *pressed ldr: rdn 2f out: led briefly wl over 1f out: sn hdd & wknd qckly* **14/1**	
331	12	1 3/4	**Baileys Outshine**[19] [5645] 2-9-7 75... J-PGuillambert 14	22
			(J G Given) *led stands' side trio: prom overall tl rdn over 2f out: sn wl btn* **5/1[1]**	
1100	13	22	**Inflight (IRE)**[39] [5162] 2-9-5 73... GeorgeBaker 16	—
			(R M Beckett) *rrd s and slowly away: a wl bhd on stands' side: eased: t.o* **25/1**	

64.63 secs (1.83) **Going Correction** +0.225s/f (Good) **13** Ran SP% **116.4**
Speed ratings (Par 95):94,93,92,88,87 82,82,81,81,73 72,69,34
CSF £62.42 CT £527.35 TOTE £5.90: £2.40, £4.10, £3.60; EX 97.30 TRIFECTA Not won..
Owner Hamdan Al Maktoum **Bred** Shadwell Estate Company Limited **Trained** Newmarket, Suffolk

FOCUS
An ordinary nursery, though competitive nonetheless. The bulk of the field came down the middle, but the three draw highest stayed against the stands' rail and the fact that they finished amongst the last four home strongly suggests that was not the place to be.

NOTEBOOK
Malaaq appreciated this return to a straight track and battled on really well after looking likely to get swamped on both sides. The softer ground was obviously not a problem and she is now due to go to the sales.
Aquilegia(IRE) ◆, making her nursery debut, appreciated the easy ground and looked like scoring when produced with her effort entering the last furlong, but although she never gave up her rival kept on pulling out a bit more. She should be able to win a similar race off this sort of mark.
Hephaestus, whose two wins have been on the Lingfield Polytrack, looked dangerous when produced with his effort on the far side over a furlong from home but was just found wanting for a bit of finishing speed. He seems to take his racing well and looks the ideal fun horse for the sand this winter. (op 10-1)
Hucking Hope(IRE), who finished just behind Malaaq on the Kempton Polytrack last time, was actually 1lb worse off with her on this return to turf and was beaten much further. She does look better on sand. (op 12-1)
Only A Grand, carrying a 6lb penalty for her Musselburgh maiden victory, could never land a blow and may need another furlong in this sort of company. (op 11-2 tchd 9-2)
Baileys Outshine, making her nursery debut under joint top weight, had a progressive profile coming into this but blew out badly. In her defence, she and two of her rivals stayed against the stands' rail from their high draws and that appeared to be a major disadvantage, though her rider reported that she had a breathing problem. Either way, she is better than this. Official explanation: jockey said filly had a breathing problem (op 11-2 tchd 6-1)
Inflight(IRE) Official explanation: jockey said filly was slowly away

6057 GREAT YARMOUTH AND CAISTER GOLF CLUB (S) STKS 1m 3f 101y
3:10 (3:19) (Class 6) 3-Y-O **£2,266** (£674; £337; £168) **Stalls** Low

Form				RPR
0436	1		**Shaika**[14] [5767] 3-8-11 47... SaleemGolam(3) 10	56
			(G Prodromou) *dwlt: in rr: hdwy over 3f out: led 2f out: rdn and hung ins fnl f* **12/1**	
304	2	2	**Hill Of Almhuim (IRE)**[9] [5862] 3-8-12 57...(p) NCallan 11	50
			(K R Burke) *bhd: hdwy over 3f out: led over 2f out: sn hdd: kpt on same pce* **11/2[2]**	
06-5	3	1 1/2	**Josh You Are**[14] [5767] 3-8-12 48... ChrisCatlin 13	48
			(M J Wallace) *hld up: hdwy over 2f out: styd on fnl f* **7/1**	
2000	4	1 3/4	**Fonic Rock (IRE)**[29] [5451] 3-8-7 53...(v1) HayleyTurner 8	40
			(M L W Bell) *hld up: hdwy to chse ldrs over 3f out: kpt on* **5/1[1]**	
0006	5	2	**Coffin Dodger**[15] [5757] 3-8-7 46... KirstyMilczarek(7) 16	44
			(C N Allen) *s.i.s and bhd: sme hdwy over 2f out: nt rch ldrs* **20/1**	
5630	6	4	**Rockatorri**[15] [5757] 3-8-4 35...(b) DominicFox(3) 15	31
			(G G Margarson) *bhd: hdwy over 2f out: nvr nr to chal* **50/1**	
0560	7	1	**Lucy Babe**[85] [3823] 3-8-7 40... AdrianMcCarthy 1	29
			(G Prodromou) *in tch: effrt over 3f out: kpt on one pce* **66/1**	
3300	8	4	**Zizou (IRE)**[11] [4800] 3-8-12 45...(t) PaulHanagan 7	28
			(J J Bridger) *hld up: nvr a factor* **14/1**	
0003	9	4	**Pickwick Miss (USA)**[15] [5757] 3-8-7 46... LPKeniry 2	16
			(D M Simcock) *prom: rdn to chal over 3f out: sn wknd* **11/1**	
0005	10	nk	**Louise Dupin (IRE)**[18] [5690] 3-8-7 49... NelsonDeSouza 3	16
			(R M Beckett) *trckd ldrs: rdn to chal over 2f out: wknd over 1f out* **13/2[3]**	
0006	11	1 1/2	**Bournonville**[30] [5432] 3-8-7 40... NicolPolli(5) 4	18
			(M Wigham) *in tch tl rdn and wknd over 2f out* **50/1**	
1040	12	12	**Peephole**[40] [4173] 3-9-2 59...(b1) StephenDonohoe(3) 12	6
			(A Bailey) *prom tl led 8f out: rdn and hdd over 2f out: sn wknd* **18/1**	
0000	13	5	**Night Reveller (IRE)**[9] [5874] 3-8-2 30... AurelioMedeiros(5) 6	—
			(M C Chapman) *led to 8f out: u.p fr over 4f out: sn wknd* **100/1**	
0000	14	1 1/2	**Saxon Star (IRE)**[69] [4278] 3-8-5 35... JPFeatherstone(7) 5	—
			(P Howling) *nvr a factor* **100/1**	
0060	15	10	**Cragganmore Creek**[125] [2591] 3-8-12 48... DerekMcGaffin 9	—
			(D Morris) *towards rr: nvr a factor* **33/1**	

2m 33.85s **Going Correction** +0.50s/f (Yiel) **15** Ran SP% **100.9**
Speed ratings (Par 99):96,94,93,92,90 87,87,84,81,81 79,71,67,66,59
CSF £52.29 TOTE £11.60: £3.30, £1.90, £2.40; EX 74.90 TRIFECTA Not won..The winner was bought in for 6,000gns. Hill of Almhuim was claimed by P. Grayson for £6,000. Josh You Are was claimed by Don Cantillon for £6,000.
Owner Faisal Al-Nassar **Bred** Ellis Stud Partnership **Trained** East Harling, Norfolk
■ Always Stylish (5/1) was withdrawn on vet's advice. R4 applies, deduct 15p in the £.

FOCUS
The start was delayed for nine minutes due to a stalls malfunction when the six lowest stalls opened but all the others remained shut. This was a modest seller rated through the runner-up and is unlikely to produce many future winners.
Fonic Rock(IRE) Official explanation: jockey said filly was unsuited by the soft ground

6058 BANHAM POULTRY MAIDEN STKS 1m 2f 21y
3:40 (3:43) (Class 5) 2-Y-O **£3,238** (£963; £481; £240) **Stalls** Low

Form				RPR
0	1		**Shimoni**[29] [5456] 2-8-12 ... PaulDoe 14	73
			(W J Knight) *slowly away: sn rcvrd to chse ldrs: led over 1f out: pushed out* **20/1**	
0	2	1 1/2	**Cordwain**[29] [5460] 2-9-3 ...(b1) JimmyFortune 13	75
			(J H M Gosden) *s.i.s and in rr: rdn over 3f out: hung rt over 1f out: r.o and edgd lft ins fnl f* **20/1**	
262	3	1 1/4	**Audit (IRE)**[8] [5886] 2-9-3 ... RHills 5	73
			(Sir Michael Stoute) *hld up: hdwy u.p 3f out: effrt and rn green over 1f out: hung lft ins fnl f: no ex towards fin* **7/2[2]**	
23	4	2	**Yossi (IRE)**[16] [5720] 2-9-3 ... NCallan 6	69
			(M H Tompkins) *mid-div: hdwy u.p 3f out: swtchd rt 2f out: kpt on one pce* **1/1[1]**	
062	5	4	**Here Comes Buster (IRE)**[23] [5565] 2-9-3 79... DaneO'Neill 9	62
			(R Hannon) *led tl hdd 6f out: led again 4f out: rdn and hdd over 1f out: sn wknd* **7/1[3]**	
43	6	5	**Petrosian**[69] [4303] 2-9-3 ... J-PGuillambert 4	53
			(M Johnston) *t.k.h: prom: ev ch whn hung lft over 2f out: wknd fnl f* **20/1**	
	7	9	**Double Exposure** 2-9-3 ... MichaelHills 10	37
			(Jamie Poulton) *mid-div: rdn and no imp fr 3f out* **80/1**	
05	8	10	**Isabella's Best (IRE)**[21] [5613] 2-8-12 ... ChrisCatlin 8	14
			(E J O'Neill) *hld up in mid-div: rdn and wknd 3f out* **40/1**	
45	9	7	**Nothing Is Forever (IRE)**[42] [5105] 2-9-3 ... PhilipRobinson 1	6
			(Mrs A J Perrett) *trckd ldr tl led 6f: hdd 4f out: wknd qckly and sn eased* **14/1**	
0	10	14	**Spellbinding (IRE)**[8] [5882] 2-8-12 ... JTate 12	—
			(J M P Eustace) *wnt rt s: nvr a factor* **100/1**	
0	11	3	**Atlantic Coast (IRE)**[16] [5720] 2-9-3 ... JoeFanning 7	—
			(M Johnston) *chsd ldrs tl wknd fr 1/2-way* **50/1**	
0040	12	8	**Catweasel**[142] [2064] 2-9-3 50... HayleyTurner 11	—
			(L A Dace) *a in rr* **150/1**	

2m 13.5s **Going Correction** +0.50s/f (Yiel) **12** Ran SP% **113.0**
Speed ratings (Par 95):98,96,95,94,91 87,79,71,66,55 52,46
CSF £316.00 TOTE £27.30: £4.70, £4.80, £1.50; EX 365.90 Trifecta £394.40 Part won. Pool £555.58 - 0.10 winning units..
Owner The Welldiggers Partnership **Bred** Lakin Bloodstock And H And W Thornton **Trained** Patching, W Sussex

FOCUS
Not as competitive as the size of the field might suggest with only three horses starting at less than 14-1. This also proved a real test for these juveniles and several of them were found out by it.

NOTEBOOK
Shimoni ◆, appreciating the extra two furlongs and much more testing ground than on her debut, turned this into a war of attrition and kept on finding a bit more when it was needed. The Zetland Stakes at this end of this month looks the obvious target if connections wish to turn her out again this year, but in any case she should make up into a nice staying handicapper next term. (op 18-1 tchd 22-1)
Cordwain, tried in blinkers, had a lot to do for most of way but once finding himself out in the centre of the track, he stayed on strongly only to find the winner had flown. His final effort may have been exacerbated by others coming to the end of their tether, but considering he is related to the likes of Altay and Distant Prospect on the dam's side it is reasonable to assume he will come into his own over middle distances next season. (op 16-1)
Audit(IRE), upped in trip again, had every chance but not for the first time did not convince that he was trying his hardest when asked the question. He has already been tried in headgear and perhaps being gelded might now have to be an option. (op 11-4)

Yossi(IRE) has already run with credit under similar conditions on a stiffer track than this, so it was disappointing to see him deliver so little despite plenty of urging from the saddle. He now qualifies for a mark, but this was a step backwards. (op 11-8)

Here Comes Buster(IRE), runner-up over this trip last time, was given a positive ride but this softer ground appeared to find him out.

Nothing Is Forever(IRE) was up there for much of the way, but did not see out the longer trip in the ground. Official explanation: jockey said colt was unsuited by the soft ground; jockey said, regarding the running and riding, his orders were to have gelding handy as it is one paced; having done so, in trying to show that the horse had no more to give on the soft ground he aggravated an old groin injury and could not ride more vigorously (op 12-1)

6059 GREAT YARMOUTH MERCURY CLAIMING STKS — 1m 3y

4:10 (4:11) (Class 6) 3-Y-O+ — £2,364 (£703; £351; £175) Stalls High

Form				RPR
0360	1		**Rowan Lodge (IRE)**[8] 5904 4-9-7 69 .... (v[1]) NCallan 8 (M H Tompkins) *bmpd s: sn prom: led over 1f out: hung lft: pushed out* **6/1**[2]	71
1300	2	*2*	**Stormy Monday**[22] 5591 3-9-5 72 .... MichaelHills 4 (J W Hills) *mid-div: chsd ldrs over 1f out: styd on* **11/1**	67
0342	3	*hd*	**Outer Hebrides**[18] 5670 5-9-10 77 .... (vt) AmirQuinn(3) 9 (J R Boyle) *hmpd s: hld up: hdwy over 3f out: rdn to chse ldrs over 1f out: one pce* **13/2**[3]	72
2423	4	*nk*	**Band**[35] 5285 6-9-3 54 .... GrahamGibbons 13 (E S McMahon) *hld up: hdwy over 2f out: styd on ins fnl f: nt rch ldrs* **10/1**	61
1010	5	*nk*	**Ellesappelle**[8] 5895 3-8-13 71 .... JimmyFortune 2 (G L Moore) *led: rdn and hdd over 1f out: kpt on one pce* **6/1**[2]	59
0050	6	*2½*	**Divisive**[16] 5724 3-9-1 50 .... SteveDrowne 3 (G Wragg) *chsd ldrs: effrt fr over 2f out tl wknd over 1f out* **50/1**	56
0604	7	*nk*	**La Viola**[37] 5248 4-7-9 50 .... (v) LukeMorris(7) 10 (K R Burke) *wnt lft s: mid-div: rdn to chse ldrs over 2f out: sn one pce* **33/1**	39
620	8	*¾*	**Nashaab (USA)**[4] 5974 9-9-1 67 .... (v) TonyCulhane 11 (P D Evans) *dwlt: nvr a factor* **8/1**	50
0054	9	*nk*	**Kilmeena Magic**[43] 5092 4-8-2 45 .... AdrianMcCarthy 6 (J C Fox) *a bhd* **100/1**	36
6005	10	*2*	**Wild Lass**[58] 4667 5-8-2 45 .... (p) NelsonDeSouza 5 (J C Fox) *towards rr: rdn fr 1/2-way: nvr a factor* **80/1**	32
000	11	*4*	**Midshipman**[32] 5385 8-9-7 50 .... (t) PaulDoe 12 (T Keddy) *prom: rdn to chal over 3f out: wknd over 1f out* **33/1**	42
4305	12	*1¼*	**Shrine Mountain (USA)**[32] 5385 4-9-7 52 .... (v) DaneO'Neill 7 (J R Holt) *wnt rt s: trcking ldr tl rdn and wknd over 2f out* **20/1**	39
000	13	*2*	**Namroud (USA)**[12] 5789 7-9-7 81 .... PaulHanagan 14 (R A Fahey) *in tch tl wknd over 2f out* **9/4**[1]	34
4054	14	*hd*	**Snow Symphony (IRE)**[23] 5571 3-8-6 55 .... ChrisCatlin 15 (D M Simcock) *mid-div tl wknd over 2f out* **50/1**	22
0500	15	*16*	**Wolf Pack**[14] 5768 4-8-6 45 .... EdwardCreighton(3) 16 (R W Price) *a in rr* **150/1**	—

1m 43.6s **Going Correction** +0.425s/f (Yiel)
WFA 3 from 4yo+ 3lb — **15** Ran SP% **118.7**
Speed ratings (Par 101):98,96,95,95,95 92,92,91,91,89 85,84,82,81,65
CSF £65.08 TOTE £8.20: £2.80, £4.70, £2.30; EX 101.80 Trifecta £275.20 Part won. Pool £387.67 - 0.34 winning units..The winner was the subject of a friendly claim.
Owner The Rowan Stud and Clique Partnership **Bred** M P B Bloodstock Ltd **Trained** Newmarket, Suffolk

FOCUS
An ordinary claimer, with the placed horses not quite at their best. The third sets the standard on his course-and-distance form.

6060 AYLSHAM SLURRY SERVICES H'CAP — 7f 3y

4:40 (4:48) (Class 6) (0-65,65) 3-Y-O+ — £3,238 (£963; £481; £240) Stalls High

Form				RPR
2441	1		**Gracie's Gift (IRE)**[28] 5474 4-8-12 59 .... DaneO'Neill 6 (A G Newcombe) *hld up: rdn 3f out: hdwy fr over 1f out to ld nr fin* **3/1**[1]	68
0643	2	*nk*	**Ektimaal**[23] 5571 3-9-1 64 .... (t) RHills 10 (E A L Dunlop) *prom: rdn to ld over 1f out: hdd nr fin* **10/1**	73
0024	3	*1*	**Redwood Rocks (IRE)**[29] 5444 5-8-13 65 .... MarkLawson(5) 9 (B Smart) *led: rdn 3f out: hdd over 1f out: kpt on same pce* **14/1**	71
5450	4	*1¾*	**Great Chieftain (IRE)**[18] 5691 3-9-0 63 .... PaulHanagan 1 (R A Fahey) *w ldr: rdn to chal 2f out: wknd fnl f* **16/1**	64
5243	5	*nk*	**Al Rayanah**[15] 5755 3-8-6 62 .... KirstyMilczarek(7) 3 (G Prodromou) *t.k.h: prom tl wknd over 1f out* **8/1**[3]	63
1645	6	*2*	**Brigadore**[9] 5872 7-9-4 65 .... OscarUrbina 15 (J G Given) *hld up in rr: rdn and sltly hmpd over 2f out: styd on* **8/1**[2]	60
005	7	*hd*	**Hits Only Jude (IRE)**[46] 5036 3-9-0 63 .... PaulMulrennan 14 (J Pearce) *hld up in rr: rdn over 1f out: no imp* **20/1**	58
0030	8	*2½*	**Dispol Katie**[15] 5756 5-9-1 62 .... JoeFanning 16 (T D Barron) *mid-div: rdn and short of room 3f out: wknd fnl f* **8/1**[2]	50
0626	9	*3*	**Border Artist**[13] 5775 7-9-4 65 .... J-PGuillambert 8 (J Pearce) *mid-div: rdn 3f out: wknd ins fnl 2f* **10/1**	46
5163	10	*nk*	**Captain Darling (IRE)**[32] 5386 6-9-1 65 .... EdwardCreighton(3) 12 (R W Price) *chsd ldrs tl rdn and wknd over 1f out* **12/1**	45
2000	11	*¾*	**Dr Synn**[22] 5591 5-9-4 65 .... HayleyTurner 13 (J Akehurst) *t.k.h in rr: nvr a factor* **12/1**	43
-006	12	*hd*	**River Mist Image (USA)**[79] 4010 4-8-13 60 .... (t) TPO'Shea 5 (J R Fanshawe) *chsd ldrs: rdn 1/2-way: wknd over 1f out* **50/1**	37
0056	13	*hd*	**The Crooked Ring**[16] 5737 4-8-12 62 .... (v) StephenDonohoe(3) 11 (P D Evans) *mid-div tl wknd over 1f out* **9/1**[3]	39
2-50	14	*1½*	**Final Bid (IRE)**[259] 269 3-8-10 64 .... JerryO'Dwyer(5) 4 (M G Quinlan) *slowly away: a in rr* **66/1**	37

1m 29.18s **Going Correction** +0.425s/f (Yiel)
WFA 3 from 4yo+ 2lb — **14** Ran SP% **122.7**
Speed ratings (Par 101):102,101,100,98,98 95,95,92,89,89 88,87,87,86
CSF £33.41 CT £378.85 TOTE £3.50: £1.80, £2.70, £6.30; EX 35.70 Trifecta £316.40 Part won. Pool £455.74 - 0.77 winning units..
Owner Samuel Jefford **Bred** Richard O'Hara **Trained** Yarnscombe, Devon

FOCUS
Just a modest handicap. A personal best from the in-form winner with the third close to recent form.

Al Rayanah Official explanation: jockey said filly lost a tooth in stalls
Hits Only Jude(IRE) Official explanation: jockey said gelding hung left in closing stages
Captain Darling(IRE) Official explanation: jockey said gelding hung right on the soft ground

6061 CRYSTAL CLEANING H'CAP — 6f 3y

5:10 (5:13) (Class 6) (0-60,66) 3-Y-O+ — £2,914 (£867; £433; £216) Stalls High

Form				RPR
-040	1		**Black Sea Pearl**[130] 2466 3-8-10 57 .... SaleemGolam(3) 15 (P W D'Arcy) *towards rr: hdwy fr over 1f out to ld fnl strides* **10/1**	68
-254	2	*hd*	**Mina**[139] 2160 4-9-1 58 .... SteveDrowne 10 (Rae Guest) *hld up in mid-div: hdwy over 1f out: led ins fnl f: hdd fnl strides* **7/1**[3]	68
0006	3	*nk*	**Observatory Star (IRE)**[28] 5487 3-9-0 58 .... (b[1]) GrahamGibbons 9 (T D Easterby) *mid-div: hdwy u.p fr over 2f out to ld 1f out: hdd nr fin* **16/1**	68
030	4	*1¼*	**Middle Eastern**[18] 5684 4-9-1 58 .... TPO'Shea 5 (P A Blockley) *chsd ldrs: ev ch over 1f out: one pce* **10/1**	64
1453	5	*¾*	**Mugeba**[15] 5756 5-8-13 56 .... (t) NCallan 11 (Miss Gay Kelleway) *hld up: hdwy to chal ins fnl f: nrst fin* **3/1**[1]	60
0000	6	*¾*	**Polar Force**[3] 5987 6-9-3 60 .... ChrisCatlin 4 (Mrs C A Dunnett) *led tl hdd fnl f: sn wknd* **12/1**	61
0144	7	*1*	**Zazous**[5] 5938 5-9-0 60 .... MarcHalford(3) 1 (J J Bridger) *chsd ldrs: effrt fr over 1f out: one pce* **6/1**[2]	58
4002	8	*2*	**Desert Opal**[9] 5878 6-8-12 58 .... EdwardCreighton(3) 3 (C R Dore) *bhd: n.d* **9/1**	50
0000	9	*½*	**Hits Only Cash**[20] 5635 4-9-3 60 .... J-PGuillambert 8 (J Pearce) *nvr a factor* **11/1**	51
6341	10	*5*	**Cool Sting (IRE)**[1] 6033 3-9-8 66 6ex .... (v) BrianReilly 6 (P S McEntee) *slowly away: a in rr* **7/1**[3]	42
03	11	*2*	**Butterfly Bud (IRE)**[43] 5077 3-8-9 60 .... JamesO'Reilly(7) 12 (J O'Reilly) *prom tl rdn and wknd fr over 2f out* **25/1**	30
4100	12	*1¾*	**Atlantic Viking (IRE)**[44] 5058 11-9-0 60 .... StephenDonohoe(3) 2 (P D Evans) *a bhd* **22/1**	25
-045	13	*2½*	**Miss Sure Bond (IRE)**[8] 5902 3-9-2 60 .... (b) TomEaves 13 (B Smart) *hld up in mid-div: lost pl fr over 2f out* **33/1**	17

1m 16.01s **Going Correction** +0.425s/f (Yiel)
WFA 3 from 4yo+ 1lb — **13** Ran SP% **125.5**
Speed ratings (Par 101):101,100,100,98,97 96,95,92,92,85 82,80,77
CSF £80.77 CT £1142.50 TOTE £9.50: £2.90, £2.40, £4.20; EX 110.00 Trifecta £213.90 Part won. Pool £301.38 - 0.10 winning units. Place 6 £515.66, Place 5 £175.67.
Owner Mrs Jan Harris **Bred** Cheveley Park Stud Ltd **Trained** Newmarket, Suffolk

FOCUS
A moderate but typically competitive sprint handicap. Fairly sound form but the pick of the latter straight races on time.

Cool Sting(IRE) Official explanation: trainer said gelding was unsuited by the soft ground
T/Jkpt: Not won. T/Plt: £270.50 to a £1 stake. Pool: £67,391.55. 181.85 winning tickets. T/Qpdt: £48.30 to a £1 stake. Pool: £4,983.00. 76.20 winning tickets. SP

6046 DEAUVILLE (R-H)

Wednesday, October 18

OFFICIAL GOING: Turf course - soft; all-weather - standard

6062a PRIX VULCAIN (LISTED RACE) — 1m 4f 110y

2:15 (2:17) 3-Y-O — £17,241 (£6,897; £5,172; £3,448; £1,724)

			RPR
1		**Morna (FR)**[142] 3-8-8 .... YBarberot 2 (S Wattel, France)	100
2	*2½*	**Onerous**[123] 3-9-2 .... IMendizabal 8 (J-C Rouget, France)	104
3	*2*	**King Luna (FR)**[139] 3-8-8 .... CSoumillon 5 (A Fabre, France)	93
4	*nk*	**Bremen**[38] 5221 3-9-2 .... SPasquier 1 (A Fabre, France)	101
5	*nk*	**Shahdawar (FR)**[156] 3-8-11 .... DBoeuf 7 (M Pimbonnet, France)	95
6	*2½*	**Hotel Du Cap**[30] 5429 3-8-11 .... DarryllHolland 6 (G Wragg) *racd in 3rd, tk closer order 4f out, pushed along and led str, hdd 1 1/2f out, rdn & stayed on tl no ex fnl 100y (59/10)* **59/10**[1]	91
7	*snk*	**Brodimix (IRE)**[23] 5584 3-8-11 .... DBonilla 3 (A Chaille-Chaille, France)	91
8	*1½*	**Leitmotiv (IRE)**[26] 3-8-11 .... OPeslier 9 (A Fabre, France)	89
9	*6*	**Armand**[41] 5145 3-9-2 .... TThulliez 4 (P Bary, France)	85

2m 50.2s — **9** Ran SP% **14.5**
PARI-MUTUEL: WIN 12.20; PL 2.70, 1.80, 2.10; DF 35.90.
Owner Haras De La Perelle **Bred** Haras De La Perelle **Trained** France

NOTEBOOK
Hotel Du Cap, a winner of a Polytrack maiden last time out, did not run badly on this step up in class, but the testing conditions took their toll in the closing stages. He would be of more interest in handicap company.

5933 BRIGHTON (L-H)

Thursday, October 19

OFFICIAL GOING: Good to soft
Wind: strong against

6063 FINAL MEDIAN AUCTION MAIDEN STKS — 6f 209y

2:30 (2:31) (Class 5) 2-Y-O — £3,238 (£963; £481; £240) Stalls Low

Form				RPR
	1		**Manaal (USA)** 2-8-9 .... RHills 2 (Sir Michael Stoute) *trckd ldr: led wl over 1f out: pushed out fnl f* **10/11**[1]	73
0444	2	*2½*	**Benllech**[24] 5570 2-9-0 71 .... LPKeniry 8 (S Kirk) *a in tch: rdn to chse wnr fnl f* **8/1**[3]	71
0206	3	*1¾*	**Wilmington**[37] 5262 2-9-0 71 .... (b[1]) RyanMoore 3 (R Hannon) *led tl rdn and hdd wl over 1f out: one pce fnl f* **5/2**[2]	66
660	4	*2*	**Sherjawy (IRE)**[43] 5106 2-9-0 58 .... NickyMackay 10 (L M Cumani) *chsd ldrs tl rdn and one pce fr over 1f out* **20/1**	61
00	5	*nk*	**Clytha**[6] 5933 2-8-9 .... JamieMackay 1 (M L W Bell) *in tch: rdn over 2f out: sn btn* **66/1**	55
566	6	*2*	**River Tarrant**[37] 5264 2-8-2 66 .... MCGeran(7) 6 (P W Chapple-Hyam) *plld hrd: trckd ldrs: wknd wl over 1f out* **20/1**	50
0	7	*7*	**Francesco**[30] 5460 2-9-0 .... HayleyTurner 4 (M L W Bell) *slowly away: a bhd* **12/1**	36

00 8 *shd* **Ishimagic**[9] 5890 2-8-9 TPQueally 7 31
(J J Bridger) *outpcd and a bhd* **50/1**
1m 25.59s (2.89) **Going Correction** +0.30s/f (Good) **8** Ran SP% **112.7**
Speed ratings (Par 95):95,92,90,87,87 85,77,77
CSF £8.53 TOTE £1.70: £1.10, £1.60, £1.50; EX 8.40 Trifecta £14.60 Pool £593.54 - 28.84 winning units.
Owner Hamdan Al Maktoum **Bred** Shadwell Farm LLC **Trained** Newmarket, Suffolk

FOCUS
There was no real strength in depth to this juvenile maiden and paddock inspection more than confirmed that opinion. The winner can rate higher, however with the runner-up dictating the level.

NOTEBOOK
Manaal(USA), whose dam was second in the 1000 Guineas, got her career off to a perfect start with a workmanlike display. She proved green in the preliminaries and on the way to post, but she still had enough class to emerge on top and is value for a little further than the winning margin. She will get a mile next year without much fuss and obviously enjoys some ease in the ground. (op 8-11 tchd Evens)
Benllech, who already has an official rating of 71, was the only one to really give the winner a serious race and finished nicely clear in second. This was the softest ground he has encountered to date and he helps to set the level of this form. Official explanation: jockey said colt lost an off-fore shoe (op 7-1)
Wilmington, whose stable has a decent record in this event, failed to raise his game for the application of first-time blinkers and his fate was sealed before the final furlong. He is one to have reservations about and does look flattered by his official rating of 71. (op 7-2)
Sherjawy(IRE), returning from a 43-day break, found it all too hot passing the two-furlong pole and is clearly one of his yard's lesser lights. He should find life easier in nurseries from his current rating. (op 16-1)
Clytha, unplaced over course and distance six days previously, showed a bit more enthusiasm and now has the option of nurseries. (op 50-1)
River Tarrant did not look suited by this softer ground, but she is only moderate and still looks to be very much learning her trade.

6064 SPORTING INDEX NURSERY 6f 209y
3:00 (3:00) (Class 5) (0-75,75) 2-Y-0 **£3,238** (£963; £481; £240) **Stalls** Low

Form				RPR
656	1		**Ask Don't Tell (IRE)**[14] 5772 2-8-1 **58** EdwardCreighton(3) 6 (Tom Dascombe) *a.p: rdn and led whn rdr dropped whip over 1f out: kpt on wl* **25/1**	60
2430	2	1 ½	**Diamond Light (USA)**[33] 5382 2-8-12 **66** SebSanders 7 (J L Dunlop) *a.p: rdn to chse wnr fnl f* **12/1**	64
0552	3	*shd*	**Golan Way**[20] 5647 2-9-5 **73** NCallan 14 (I A Wood) *mid-div: hdwy 1/2-way to chse ldrs: swtchd lft over 1f out: r.o fnl f* **6/1**[2]	71
6250	4	½	**Eager Igor (USA)**[35] 5307 2-9-3 **71** (b[1]) StephenCarson 11 (R F Johnson Houghton) *a.p: came over to stands' side to ld briefly 1/2-way: sn rdn but r.o wl fnl f* **20/1**	67
46	5	¾	**Lawyer To World**[22] 5607 2-8-12 **66** RyanMoore 1 (N A Callaghan) *prom: led 3f out tl rdn and hdd over 1f out: kpt on one pce* **6/1**[2]	60
065	6	*nk*	**Rajeef Ashog**[27] 5508 2-8-13 **67** NickyMackay 10 (L M Cumani) *mid-div: rdn and outpcd 2f out: r.o wl fnl f* **10/1**	60
2241	7	4	**Shebang (IRE)**[24] 5570 2-9-7 **75** TPQueally 3 (M G Quinlan) *prom: rdn and ev ch 2f out: wknd fnl f* **5/1**[1]	58
0564	8	*shd*	**Flying Grey (IRE)**[17] 5738 2-8-6 **60** TPO'Shea 16 (P A Blockley) *in rr: nvr nr to chal* **14/1**	42
5210	9	1 ¾	**Spinning Crystal (IRE)**[17] 5721 2-8-11 **65** MichaelHills 15 (B W Hills) *nvr bttr than mid-div* **11/1**	43
3602	10	¾	**Atheneum (IRE)**[33] 5366 2-9-7 **75** JoeFanning 5 (M Johnston) *led tl hdd 4f out: wknd over 1f out* **8/1**[3]	51
1000	11	6	**Feisty**[6] 5948 2-8-10 **64** FrancisFerris 9 (Rae Guest) *a bhd* **50/1**	23
003	12	1 ¼	**Rumbled**[23] 5592 2-9-4 **72** RichardThomas 13 (J A Geake) *a bhd* **25/1**	28
0605	13	10	**Pas De Trois**[35] 5323 2-7-12 **52** oh6 AdrianMcCarthy 2 (J Pearce) *slowly away: a bhd* **66/1**	—
6120	14	½	**Suhayl Star (IRE)**[20] 5647 2-9-5 **73** JDSmith 4 (W J Musson) *w ldr early: wknd 2f out* **16/1**	1
4003	15	1 ½	**Astroangel**[17] 5721 2-9-0 **68** (b) RHills 12 (M H Tompkins) *slowly away: a bhd* **10/1**	—

1m 24.88s (2.18) **Going Correction** +0.30s/f (Good) **15** Ran SP% **119.0**
Speed ratings (Par 95):99,97,97,96,95 95,90,90,88,87 81,79,68,67,65
CSF £283.93 CT £2086.42 TOTE £26.70: £6.40, £3.70, £2.60; EX 352.00 TRIFECTA Not won..
Owner Sideways Racing V **Bred** Tally-Ho Stud **Trained** Lambourn, Berks

FOCUS
A fairly competitive nursery for the class, run at a sound pace, and the runners tacked over to the stands' side in the home straight. The form is modest but looks reliable, rated around the principals.

NOTEBOOK
Ask Don't Tell(IRE) emerged down the outside of the pack to score readily, despite her rider losing his whip nearing the final furlong. Her yard is having a great time of it at present and the step back up to this trip on easy ground was clearly to her liking. She may have a little more to offer despite a future weight rise and is likely to be kept on the go through the impending All-Weather season.
Diamond Light(USA) posted an improved effort and looked suited by the switch to this softer ground. It may be little coincidence that she remains a maiden after eight outings now, however. (op 14-1)
Golan Way kept to his task gamely under maximum pressure and was only just run out of second place at the line. He is going the right way and likes this sort of ground, but will no doubt go up another few pounds again for this. (op 13-2 tchd 7-1)
Eager Igor(USA) showed improved form in the first-time blinkers and got home well over the longer trip. That said, whether the headgear has the same effect next time remains to be seen.
Lawyer To World, making his nursery debut, was not disgraced yet left the impression he is ready to tackle a mile now. The return to a sound surface may also see him in a better light. (tchd 13-2)
Rajeef Ashog, another having his first outing in this sphere, hit a flat spot before keeping on again all too late and is a little better than the bare form suggests. He ought to fare better next year. (op 7-1)
Shebang(IRE) was ridden with more restraint on this step back up in trip, but still failed to get home on this deep surface. (tchd 9-2)
Rumbled Official explanation: jockey said filly missed the break
Astroangel Official explanation: jockey said filly missed the break

6065 WEATHERBYS INSURANCE STKS (H'CAP) 5f 213y
3:30 (3:30) (Class 4) (0-85,84) 3-Y-0+ **£5,505** (£1,637; £818; £408) **Stalls** Low

Form				RPR
1563	1		**Mujood**[19] 5670 3-8-13 **78** (b) StephenCarson 1 (R F Johnson Houghton) *mde all: styd towards far side: clr over 1f out: easily* **8/1**[3]	91
2000	2	4	**Polish Emperor (USA)**[23] 5593 6-8-9 **73** (p) AdamKirby 6 (W R Swinburn) *a.p: rdn to chse wnr fnl f: jst hld on for 2nd* **25/1**	74
4005	3	*shd*	**Kaveri (USA)**[21] 5643 3-8-10 **75** SebSanders 5 (C E Brittain) *a.p: nt qckn over 1f out but r.o ins fnl f* **9/1**	76
6400	4	½	**Night Prospector**[29] 5476 6-9-2 **80** GeorgeBaker 11 (G L Moore) *plld hrd: cme over to stands' side alone bef 1/2-way: plenty to do 2f out: r.o wl fnl f* **8/1**[3]	79
4000	5	1	**Angel Sprints**[29] 5476 4-8-12 **79** SaleemGolam(3) 7 (C J Down) *prom: rdn 2f out: stayed on one pce* **16/1**	75
4203	6	1	**Who's Winning (IRE)**[24] 5575 5-8-12 **76** RyanMoore 12 (B G Powell) *bhd: rdn over 2f out: r.o fnl f: nvr nrr* **9/2**[2]	69
0060	7	*shd*	**River Thames**[14] 5777 3-9-1 **80** TPO'Shea 10 (J A R Toller) *bhd: rdn over 2f out: mde sme late hdwy* **8/1**[3]	73
4406	8	½	**Gavarnie Beau (IRE)**[31] 5427 3-9-5 **84** NCallan 8 (M Blanshard) *a towards rr* **16/1**	75
1221	9	*nk*	**Forest Dane**[2] 6035 6-8-13 **80** 6ex JamesDoyle(3) 9 (Mrs N Smith) *hld up: effrt over 2f out: wknd over 1f out* **7/2**[1]	71
0604	10	½	**Wainwright (IRE)**[17] 5737 6-8-5 **69** oh14 HayleyTurner 4 (P A Blockley) *hld up in rr: nvr on terms* **66/1**	58
2100	11	½	**Royal Envoy (IRE)**[117] 2863 3-8-11 **76** MichaelHills 13 (B W Hills) *in tch tl wknd 2f out* **16/1**	64
5431	12	3	**Violet Ballerina (IRE)**[31] 5427 3-8-12 **77** (b) RobertHavlin 2 (B J Meehan) *in tch tl wknd 2f out* **10/1**	56
0000	13	*nk*	**Campbeltown (IRE)**[11] 5832 3-9-0 **82** StephenDonohoe(3) 3 (R A Harris) *in tch tl wknd over 2f out* **50/1**	60

1m 11.19s (1.09) **Going Correction** +0.30s/f (Good)
WFA 3 from 4yo+ 1lb **13** Ran SP% **117.8**
Speed ratings (Par 105):104,98,98,97,96 95,95,94,94,93 92,88,88
CSF £193.00 CT £1834.35 TOTE £9.50: £3.10, £7.70, £3.20; EX 180.90 TRIFECTA Not won..
Owner Eden Racing **Bred** Bloomsbury Stud And The Hon Sir David Sieff **Trained** Blewbury, Oxon

FOCUS
A competitive enough sprint handicap for the grade which the field split across the track in the final two furlongs. The winner is full value for his winning margin with the third to her recent level.
Night Prospector Official explanation: jockey said gelding hung violently right
Forest Dane Official explanation: jockey said gelding was unsuited by the good to soft ground

6066 EUROPEAN BREEDERS FUND MAIDEN STKS 7f 214y
4:00 (4:00) (Class 5) 2-Y-0 **£4,533** (£1,348; £674; £336) **Stalls** Low

Form				RPR
33	1		**Hunting Tower**[55] 4781 2-9-3 RyanMoore 8 (R Hannon) *hld up in tch: hdwy on outside 3f out: led wl over 1f out: r.o fnl f* **7/4**[1]	80
4246	2	2 ½	**Jawaab (IRE)**[23] 5585 2-9-3 74 RHills 6 (E A L Dunlop) *led tl hdd 3f out: styd prom: kpt on fnl f but nt pce of wnr* **9/2**[3]	74
006	3	2 ½	**Mujahaz (IRE)**[22] 5622 2-9-3 60 DaneO'Neill 2 (J L Dunlop) *tracd ldr: outpcd 2f out: r.o ins fnl f* **20/1**	68
05	4	*nk*	**Arabian Word**[33] 5381 2-9-3 SebSanders 5 (Sir Michael Stoute) *trckd ldr: led 3f out: rdn and hdd wl over 1f out: wknd ins fnl f* **7/2**[2]	67
0355	5	1 ½	**King Joshua (IRE)**[20] 5648 2-9-3 81 FJohansson 4 (G A Butler) *plld hrd: in tch: hung lft fr 2f out and no further hdwy* **5/1**	64
46	6	10	**My Super Bird (USA)**[9] 5882 2-9-3 JoeFanning 1 (M Johnston) *prom: rdn 3f out: sn bhd: eased over 1f out* **16/1**	41
6	7	¾	**Postsprofit (IRE)**[7] 5914 2-9-3 (p) NCallan 3 (N A Callaghan) *t.k.h: hld up in tch: rdn over 2f out: sn bhd and eased over 1f out* **8/1**	39
000	8	17	**Dancing Reva (IRE)**[34] 5340 2-9-0 45 StephenDonohoe(3) 7 (J J Bridger) *slowly away: outpcd and a bhd* **125/1**	—

1m 37.13s (2.09) **Going Correction** +0.30s/f (Good) **8** Ran SP% **116.0**
Speed ratings (Par 95):101,98,96,95,94 84,83,66
CSF £10.15 TOTE £2.20: £1.10, £1.90, £5.30; EX 9.20 Trifecta £62.40 Pool £607.27 - 6.90 winning units.
Owner The Queen **Bred** The Queen **Trained** East Everleigh, Wilts

FOCUS
No more than a fair juvenile maiden. The field came home fairly strung out and the form can be rated through the consistent runner-up.

NOTEBOOK
Hunting Tower, despite not looking too happy on this unconventional track, duly outclassed his rivals to get off the mark at the third attempt. He handled the softer ground without fuss, proved well suited by the step up to this longer distance and is value for further than his winning margin. It is likely that he will now be put away for the season and he can be expected to stay up to ten furlongs as a three-year-old. (op 2-1 tchd 13-8 and 9-4 in places)
Jawaab(IRE), beaten from a mark of 74 in nurseries the last twice, was put in his place by the winner yet again did not appear to do a great deal wrong in defeat. He is not going to prove easy to place successfully, but still helps to set the level of this form. (op 5-1)
Mujahaz(IRE) ran his best race to date in defeat, but really appeals as the type who will not come into his own until upped in trip next year. (op 16-1)
Arabian Word, easy to back, had no more to offer inside the final furlong and failed to see out the extra furlong as well as expected. He has an abundance of scope, however, and it would be no surprise to see him fare much better in handicaps as a three-year-old. (op 11-4 tchd 4-1)
King Joshua(IRE) paid for running too freely through the early stages and has become disappointing. (op 15-2)
Postsprofit(IRE), equipped with first-time cheekpieces after showing a degree of promise at Newmarket on his debut a week previously, was another who ran too freely under restraint and should become of greater interest when he is eligible for a handicap mark after his next assignment. (op 7-1)

6067 HOP HOP (S) H'CAP 1m 1f 209y
4:30 (4:32) (Class 6) (0-60,58) 3-Y-0+ **£2,388** (£705; £352) **Stalls** High

Form				RPR
3050	1		**Makai**[15] 5767 3-8-8 **50** (b) RoystonFfrench 16 (M Johnston) *wl bhd: rdn over 4f out: picked up appr fnl f: r.o to ld nr fin* **11/2**[3]	54
-000	2	*shd*	**Dream Mountain**[35] 5312 3-9-1 **57** JoeFanning 3 (M Johnston) *a in tch: wnt 2nd over 1f out: led ins fnl f: hdd nr fin* **10/1**	61
0004	3	2	**Earl Kraul (IRE)**[17] 5733 3-8-3 **45** (b) RichardMullen 9 (G L Moore) *hld up in rr: hdwy over 1f out: styd on ins fnl f* **9/1**	45
0000	4	¾	**Thomas A Beckett (IRE)**[45] 5071 3-8-1 **50** PNolan(7) 11 (P R Chamings) *a.p: rdn and no ex ins fnl f* **33/1**	49
00	5	2	**Princely Ted (IRE)**[5] 5972 5-9-1 **55** (t) EdwardCreighton(3) 4 (E J Creighton) *led tl rdn and hdd ins fnl f: no ex* **25/1**	50
5625	6	1	**Sriology (IRE)**[44] 5097 5-8-6 **46** (t) SaleemGolam(3) 8 (G Prodromou) *slowly away: sn wl bhd: mde sme late hdwy* **9/2**[2]	39
3050	7	*shd*	**Top Level (IRE)**[15] 5767 3-8-0 **45** DominicFox(3) 13 (M G Quinlan) *a.p: chal 2f out: wknd fnl f* **14/1**	38

2054 **8** *1 ½* **Milk And Sultana**[44] 5097 6-8-10 **47**.............................. SebSanders 14 38
(G A Ham) *bhd: effrt on far side 2f out: sn btn* **13/2**
0300 **9** *5* **Zinging**[61] 4585 7-8-8 **48** ow3..............................(v) StephenDonohoe[(3)] 2 30
(J J Bridger) *prom tl wknd over 2f out* **11/1**
4003 **10** *1* **Summer Bounty**[6] 5954 10-9-7 **58**.............................. NCallan 10 38
(F Jordan) *prom: rdn to chal 2f out: hung lft and sn wknd* **4/1**[1]
0-00 **11** *6* **Norwegian**[70] 4301 5-8-8 **45**..............................(p) FergusSweeney 1 14
(Ian Williams) *sn cl up: wknd 2f out* **20/1**
1200 **12** *16* **Musical Gift**[26] 2245 6-8-11 **48**..............................(v) TPO'Shea 5 —
(P A Blockley) *in tch tl wknd over 2f out* **16/1**

2m 6.31s (3.71) **Going Correction** +0.30s/f (Good)
WFA 3 from 4yo+ 5lb **12** Ran SP% **118.4**
Speed ratings (Par 101):97,96,95,94,93 92,92,91,87,86 81,68
CSF £57.98 CT £492.51 TOTE £5.60: £2.60, £3.80, £2.40; EX 46.40 Trifecta £56.90 Pool £269.49 - 3.36 winning units..The winner was sold to J Bridger for 6,000gns. Dream Mountain was claimed by Ms J S Doyle for £6,000. Sriology was claimed by Jeff Pearce for £ 6,000.
Owner C H Greensit & W A Greensit **Bred** C H And W A Greensit **Trained** Middleham Moor, N Yorks

FOCUS
A typically weak selling handicap, run at no more than a modest early tempo and the field came home fairly strung out behind the winner, who is the best guide to the form.
Princely Ted(IRE) Official explanation: jockey said gelding hung left

6068 ROGER CURRELL - BARNET 'TIL I DIE APPRENTICE H'CAP 1m 3f 196y
5:00 (5:01) (Class 6) (0-55,60) 3-Y-O+ **£2,266** (£674; £337; £168) **Stalls** High

Form RPR
0002 **1** **Kick And Prance**[38] 5247 3-8-8 **52**..............................(t) TravisBlock 2 63+
(J A Geake) *mde virtually all: pushed out appr fnl f: r.o: comf* **9/1**
2053 **2** *¾* **Gigs Magic (USA)**[24] 5581 3-8-7 **51**.............................. AndrewElliott 1 57
(M Johnston) *a.p: outpcd 3f out: r.o fnl f* **7/2**[1]
0065 **3** *½* **Adage**[9] 5887 3-8-5 **52**..............................(t) AshleyHamblett[(3)] 5 57
(David Pinder) *in rr: hdwy 3f out: hdwy 2f out: styd on fnl f* **16/1**
2045 **4** *shd* **Taranis**[6] 5936 3-8-7 **51**.............................. SMGorey 6 56
(Sir Mark Prescott) *a.p: ev ch over 1f out: fdd ins fnl f* **4/1**[2]
0000 **5** *6* **Sirbrit**[15] 5767 3-7-9 **46**.............................. DebraEngland[(7)] 9 41
(W J Musson) *bhd tl hdwy on stands' side over 2f out: r.o: nvr nrr* **33/1**
6450 **6** *hd* **Garston Star**[30] 5451 5-8-4 **46** oh1.............................. JosephWalsh[(5)] 8 41
(J S Moore) *chsd wnr rdn 2f out: wknd over 1f out* **14/1**
2000 **7** *1* **Plain Champagne (IRE)**[30] 5451 4-8-9 **49**.............................. LukeMorris[(3)] 11 43
(Dr J R J Naylor) *towards rr: sme late hdwy but nvr on terms* **20/1**
6600 **8** *½* **Lady Cree (IRE)**[24] 5574 3-8-4 **51**..............................(p) TolleyDean[(3)] 15 44
(W R Muir) *in rr: mde sme late hdwy* **16/1**
0562 **9** *4* **Arsad (IRE)**[30] 5445 3-8-6 **55**.............................. WilliamCarson[(5)] 10 41
(C E Brittain) *in tch tl wknd over 2f out* **5/1**[3]
/0-0 **10** *8* **Montecristo**[20] 5652 13-8-11 **55**.............................. LukeMcJannet[(7)] 13 29
(Rae Guest) *a in rr* **66/1**
0100 **11** *1* **Unasuming (IRE)**[128] 2529 3-8-6 **57** ow3.............................. StevenCorrigan[(7)] 3 29
(J Pearce) *prom tl wknd over 2f out: eased ins fnl f* **20/1**
000 **12** *¾* **Spiritwind (IRE)**[19] 5669 3-8-5 **54**..............................(tp) WilliamBuick[(5)] 12 25
(W R Swinburn) *a bhd* **33/1**
-340 **13** *1 ¾* **Mademoiselle**[34] 5354 4-8-10 **50**.............................. JamieJones[(3)] 16 18
(R Curtis) *in tch tl wknd over 2f out* **66/1**
5011 **14** *3 ½* **Maria Antonia (IRE)**[5] 5955 3-8-13 **60** 6ex.............................. KevinGhunowa[(3)] 14 22
(P A Blockley) *prom tl wknd over 2f out* **7/2**[1]
00 **15** *16* **April Attraction (FR)**[12] 5390 4-9-1 **55**..............................(t) JamesMillman[(3)] 7 —
(C J Down) *a bhd: eased over 1f out* **33/1**

2m 36.06s (3.86) **Going Correction** +0.30s/f (Good)
WFA 3 from 4yo+ 7lb **15** Ran SP% **130.9**
Speed ratings (Par 101):99,98,98,98,94 93,93,92,90,84 84,83,82,80,69
CSF £41.29 CT £528.80 TOTE £12.40: £3.40, £2.20, £5.90; EX 63.50 TRIFECTA Not won..
Owner Sideways Racing III **Bred** S R Hope And D Erwin **Trained** Kimpton, Hants

FOCUS
A moderate amateur riders' handicap that was run at just a modest early pace and very few got into it from off the pace. The form looks fair enough for the class and solid, with those in teh frame behind the winner close to form.
Maria Antonia(IRE) Official explanation: jockey said filly ran too free

6069 SDS EVENTS & PROMOTIONS H'CAP 7f 214y
5:30 (5:30) (Class 6) (0-63,63) 3-Y-O+ **£2,590** (£770; £385; £192) **Stalls** Low

Form RPR
0602 **1** **Border Edge**[9] 5897 8-8-9 **62**.............................. JamesMillman[(7)] 11 71
(J J Bridger) *a.p: rdn over 1f out: r.o fnl f to ld nr fin* **9/2**[2]
4015 **2** *nk* **Legal Lover (IRE)**[35] 5316 4-8-7 **60**.............................. RussellKennemore[(7)] 2 68
(R Hollinshead) *plld hrd early: mde most tl rdn and hdd nr fin* **12/1**
4640 **3** *1 ¾* **Pleasing**[42] 5130 3-8-13 **62**.............................. DaneO'Neill 13 66
(J L Dunlop) *hld up towards stands'side: rdn 2f out: kpt on u.p fnl f* **7/1**
5005 **4** *1* **Cabourg (IRE)**[25] 5553 3-9-0 **63**.............................. RoystonFfrench 1 65
(R Bastiman) *a prom: chsd wnr over 2f out tl no ex ins fnl f* **20/1**
0020 **5** *1 ¼* **Mythical Charm**[6] 5937 7-8-7 **56**..............................(t) MarcHalford[(3)] 10 55
(J J Bridger) *bhd rdn over 3f out: kpt on one pce on far side fnl f but nvr nr to chal* **12/1**
0/ **6** *¾* **Tamworth (IRE)**[221] 4-8-8 **57**.............................. EdwardCreighton[(3)] 3 54
(E J Creighton) *trckd ldr to over 2f out: no hdwy after* **25/1**
0223 **7** *5* **Sincerely**[14] 5775 4-9-2 **62**.............................. OscarUrbina 14 48
(B W Hills) *hld up: effrt over 2f out: sn btn* **3/1**[1]
500 **8** *2 ½* **Drawback (IRE)**[24] 5568 3-8-12 **61**.............................. RichardThomas 9 41
(R A Harris) *towards rr: rdn 2f out: sn btn* **16/1**
2060 **9** *nk* **Christmas Truce (IRE)**[22] 5621 7-8-10 **59**..............................(p) JamesDoyle[(3)] 15 38
(Ms J S Doyle) *in tch: rdn 1/2-way: no hdwy after* **11/1**
3210 **10** *12* **Lockstock (IRE)**[22] 5621 8-9-1 **61**..............................(p) JimCrowley 5 13
(M S Saunders) *in tch tl wknd qckly over 2f out: eased whn no ch* **9/1**
3000 **11** *3* **Ohana**[17] 5740 3-8-11 **60**.............................. SebSanders 7 5
(Miss Gay Kelleway) *a bhd* **16/1**
3030 **12** *1 ½* **Libre**[9] 5889 6-9-3 **63**.............................. NCallan 6 4
(F Jordan) *a struggling in rr* **11/2**[3]
0450 **13** *5* **Tiz Timely (USA)**[46] 5046 3-8-11 **60**..............................(v[1]) FergusSweeney 8 —
(A M Balding) *t.k.h: prom tl wknd 3f out* **20/1**

1m 39.17s (4.13) **Going Correction** +0.30s/f (Good)
WFA 3 from 4yo+ 3lb **13** Ran SP% **129.9**
Speed ratings (Par 101):91,90,88,87,86 85,80,78,78,66 63,61,56
CSF £61.66 CT £403.28 TOTE £6.40: £2.00, £3.40, £3.30; EX 59.40 Trifecta £149.80 Part won. Pool £211.05 - 0.34 winning units. Place 6 £330.34, Place 5 £299.66.
Owner Allsorts **Bred** R Hutt **Trained** Liphook, Hants

FOCUS
A moderate handicap that was run at just an average pace. The form is rated around the third.
Christmas Truce(IRE) Official explanation: jockey said gelding hung left

T/Jkpt: Not won. T/Plt: £607.00 to a £1 stake. Pool: £75,422.00. 90.70 winning tickets. T/Qpdt: £146.90 to a £1 stake. Pool: £4,567.70. 23.00 winning tickets. JS

6031 LINGFIELD (L-H)
Friday, October 20

OFFICIAL GOING: Standard
Wind: Moderate, half-behind

6070 JUMPING HERE ON NOVEMBER 8TH APPRENTICE H'CAP 1m 2f (P)
1:50 (1:51) (Class 5) (0-70,74) 3-Y-O+ **£3,238** (£963; £481; £240) **Stalls** Low

Form RPR
1003 **1** **Lisathedaddy**[47] 5047 4-9-7 **70**.............................. RichardKingscote 11 79
(B G Powell) *mid-div: hdwy over 2f out: led appr fnl f: rdn: jst hld on* **10/1**
5264 **2** *shd* **Northside Lodge (IRE)**[23] 5610 8-9-2 **65**..............................(p) JamesDoyle 5 74
(W R Swinburn) *mid-div: hdwy over 2f out: str run fnl f: jst failed* **8/1**[3]
0165 **3** *1 ¼* **Lenoir (GER)**[29] 5497 3-8-7 **68**..............................(v) WilliamBuick[(7)] 14 74
(V Smith) *hld up: hdwy 2f out: rdn and r.o to go 3rd cl home* **20/1**
0115 **4** *½* **Cantabilly (IRE)**[4] 6008 3-9-6 **74** 6ex.............................. EdwardCreighton 6 79
(M R Channon) *led tl rdn and hdd appr fnl f: no ex ins* **2/1**[1]
4000 **5** *1 ½* **Just Fly**[190] 1002 6-8-13 **67**.............................. KevinGhunowa[(5)] 12 70
(Dr J R J Naylor) *trckd ldr tl rdn and wknd appr fnl f* **33/1**
6323 **6** *hd* **Burgundy**[72] 4244 9-9-1 **69**..............................(b) JackMitchell[(5)] 8 71
(P Mitchell) *slowly away: rdn and hdwy on outside over 2f out: nt qckn fnl f* **12/1**
4501 **7** *shd* **Inch Lodge**[20] 5691 4-9-0 **68**.............................. KirstyMilczarek[(5)] 10 70
(Miss D Mountain) *led tl rdn and hdd appr fnl f: wknd* **9/1**
1110 **8** *1* **Good Article (IRE)**[10] 5904 5-8-11 **65**.............................. JamesMillman[(5)] 1 65
(D K Ivory) *hld up: sltly hmpd 4f out: nvr on terms* **11/1**
2050 **9** *2* **Wester Lodge (IRE)**[23] 5610 4-9-1 **64**.............................. NelsonDeSouza 9 60
(J M P Eustace) *chsd ldrs: rdn 3f out: sn wknd* **16/1**
0165 **10** *6* **Follow The Colours (IRE)**[63] 4565 3-8-10 **69**.............................. PatrickHills[(5)] 4 54
(J W Hills) *mid-div: rdn 3f out: wknd 2f out* **15/2**[2]
006 **11** *1* **Smooth Jazz**[14] 5786 4-9-2 **70**.............................. PJMcDonald[(5)] 2 53
(R M Beckett) *hld up: rdn 1/2-way: sn bhd* **10/1**
3060 **12** *5* **Catskill**[63] 4575 4-9-0 **66**.............................. RoryMoore[(3)] 13 40
(E F Vaughan) *sn prom: rdn over 3f out and wknd over 2f out* **20/1**
5510 **13** *23* **Airbound (USA)**[23] 5610 3-9-2 **70**.............................. GregFairley 7 —
(M Johnston) *prom but rdn and losing pl whn hmpd on bnd 4f out: nt rcvr* **20/1**

2m 5.19s (-2.60) **Going Correction** -0.25s/f (Stan)
WFA 3 from 4yo+ 5lb **13** Ran SP% **123.5**
Speed ratings (Par 103):100,99,98,98,97 97,97,96,94,89 89,85,66
CSF £85.94 CT £1598.32 TOTE £9.50: £3.10, £2.80, £5.00; EX 99.70 TRIFECTA Not won..
Owner Mrs Patricia Wilson **Bred** M Barrett **Trained** Morestead, Hants

FOCUS
An average apprentice riders' handicap which was run at just a modest pace. The first two came clear.
Airbound(USA) Official explanation: jockey said colt suffered interference in running

6071 LINGFIELDPARK.CO.UK MAIDEN FILLIES' STKS (DIV I) 1m (P)
2:20 (2:22) (Class 5) 2-Y-O **£3,238** (£963; £481; £240) **Stalls** High

Form RPR
2 **1** **Sunlight (IRE)**[31] 5456 2-9-0.............................. PhilipRobinson 4 81+
(M A Jarvis) *mde all: pushed out fnl f: a in command* **4/6**[1]
5 **2** *1 ¼* **Gold Hush (USA)**[45] 5095 2-9-0.............................. SebSanders 1 78
(Sir Michael Stoute) *slowly away: in tch after 2f: chsd wnr wl over 1f out but no imp ins fnl f* **10/1**[3]
063 **3** *3 ½* **Mystery River (USA)**[18] 5730 2-9-0 73.............................. EddieAhern 2 70
(B J Meehan) *trckd wnr tl rdn wl over 1f out: one pce after* **12/1**
4 *1* **Elyaadi** 2-9-0.............................. TonyCulhane 5 68
(M R Channon) *s.i.s: sn mid-div: styd on fnl 2f but nvr nr to chal* **7/2**[2]
5 *1* **Full Of Promise (USA)** 2-9-0.............................. JimCrowley 7 65
(Mrs A J Perrett) *s.i.s: sn in tch: rdn over 3f out: one pce fnl 2f* **33/1**
0 **6** *nk* **Indigo Rose (IRE)**[69] 4373 2-9-0.............................. JimmyFortune 12 65
(J H M Gosden) *in rr: mde sme late hdwy* **12/1**
5 **7** *1 ¾* **Final Curtain**[10] 5899 2-9-0.............................. FJohansson 9 61
(M A Magnusson) *trckd wnr to over 3f out: wknd over 2f out* **33/1**
8 *3 ½* **Susie May** 2-9-0.............................. J-PGuillambert 8 53
(C A Cyzer) *a on outside: sn pushed along and nvr on terms* **50/1**
0 **9** *½* **Chiff Chaff**[17] 5754 2-9-0.............................. JamieMackay 11 52
(M L W Bell) *a struggling in rr* **50/1**
00 **10** *3* **Kanonkop**[9] 5906 2-8-11.............................. EdwardCreighton[(3)] 3 45
(Miss J R Gibney) *s.i.s: sn mid-div: wknd over 2f out* **66/1**
11 *shd* **On The Map** 2-9-0.............................. JohnEgan 6 44
(A P Jarvis) *s.i.s: a bhd* **40/1**

1m 38.0s (-1.43) **Going Correction** -0.25s/f (Stan) **11** Ran SP% **120.4**
Speed ratings (Par 92):97,95,92,91,90 89,88,84,84,81 81
CSF £8.63 TOTE £1.60: £1.10, £2.00, £2.00; EX 7.10 Trifecta £30.10 Pool: £382.86 - 9.03 winning tickets..
Owner Lord Harrington **Bred** The Earl Of Harrington **Trained** Newmarket, Suffolk

FOCUS
This first division of the fillies' maiden lacked any real stength in depth but the form appears solid enough. The winner can rate higher, however.

NOTEBOOK
Sunlight(IRE) ◆, runner-up on debut over this trip at Newmarket 31 days previously, went one better with a comfortable display from the front. She was always holding the runner-up in the home straight and has the makings of a very nice middle-distance performer for next year. (op 8-13)
Gold Hush(USA) ◆, fifth over seven at this track on her debut 45 days previously, was the one to give the winner a serious race and saw out the extra furlong well enough. She ought not to be too long in going one better on this evidence and, like the winner, will appreciate a longer trip as a three-year-old. (op 9-1)
Mystery River(USA) eventually paid for trying to go with the winner turning for home and was made to look one paced. She is in decent enough form at present, and does stay this trip well enough, but her official mark of 73 looks flattering.
Elyaadi, bred to make her mark over a longer trip next year, was always playing catch-up after a sluggish start yet still caught the eye finishing her race with promise. She is entitled to improve for the experience and has a similar race within her compass.
Full Of Promise(USA), a $190,000 half-sister to eight winners in the US, kept on with a degree of promise after her sluggish start and should benefit for this debut experience.
Indigo Rose(IRE), well beaten on her debut at Newmarket 69 days previously, was never a serious factor on this switch to the sand and does not look like living up to her choice pedigree at this stage. She did seem better suited by the extra furlong, however. (op 14-1 tchd 16-1)

6072 EUROPEAN BREEDERS FUND MAIDEN STKS (C&G) 7f (P)

2:50 (2:51) (Class 5) 2-Y-O **£3,886** (£1,156; £577; £288) **Stalls** Low

Form RPR

1 **Escape Route (USA)** 2-9-0 .... JimmyFortune 4 87+
(J H M Gosden) *trckd ldrs: wnt 2nd over 1f out: r.o wl to ld ins fnl f: pushed out* **6/1**[3]

5 **2** *2 ½* **Mystic Dancer**[21] 5659 2-9-0 .... RyanMoore 9 80
(Sir Michael Stoute) *led after 2f: rdn and hdd ins fnl f: nt pce of wnr* **10/11**[1]

0 **3** *3* **Leon Knights**[46] 5066 2-9-0 .... FJohansson 5 72
(G A Butler) *towards rr: hdwy wl over 1f out: r.o to go 3rd ins fnl f* **20/1**

3 **4** *2* **Subadar**[14] 5784 2-9-0 .... RichardHughes 1 67
(R Charlton) *hld up in tch: hdwy 3f out: chal 2f out: wknd ins fnl f* **10/3**[2]

0 **5** *4* **Bergonzi (IRE)**[10] 5883 2-9-0 .... KDarley 6 57
(J H M Gosden) *towards rr: sme late hdwy but nvr on terms* **16/1**

0 **6** *¾* **Polish World (USA)**[10] 5890 2-9-0 .... SebSanders 2 55
(E A L Dunlop) *t.k.h early: a towards rr* **12/1**

7 *5* **Three Half Crowns (IRE)** 2-9-0 .... TonyCulhane 8 42
(P Howling) *a in rr* **50/1**

0 **8** *nk* **Botham (USA)**[119] 2821 2-9-0 .... JohnEgan 3 41
(T J Pitt) *led for 2f: wknd rapidly over 2f out* **14/1**

0 **9** *¾* **Philandering**[10] 5890 2-9-0 .... StephenCarson 11 39
(R F Johnson Houghton) *slowly away: sn prom on outside: wknd over 2f out* **66/1**

10 *6* **Little Rutland** 2-9-0 .... RichardMullen 7 23
(E J O'Neill) *a bhd* **50/1**

1m 25.07s (-0.82) **Going Correction** -0.25s/f (Stan) **10** Ran SP% **120.2**

Speed ratings (Par 95):94,91,87,85,80 80,74,73,73,66

CSF £11.98 TOTE £7.90: £2.30, £1.10, £4.10; EX 16.10 Trifecta £280.30 Pool: £438.36 - 1.11 winning tickets..

Owner H R H Princess Haya Of Jordan **Bred** R N Clay & Serengeti Stable **Trained** Newmarket, Suffolk

FOCUS

This should work out to be a fair maiden and the winner can rate higher in due course.

NOTEBOOK

Escape Route(USA) ◆, a $170,000 first foal of a very useful performer at up to this trip in the US, clearly knew his job and showed a likeable attitiude to win at the first attempt in ready fashion. He has an abundance of scope, not surprisingly with his US pedigree enjoyed this surface, and looks to have a bright future. (op 5-1)

Mystic Dancer, a beaten favourite on his debut at Newmarket 21 days previously, did nothing wrong in defeat yet was put in his place by the debutant winner inside the final furlong. He finished nicely clear of the remainder, and looks certain to win races for his connections in due course, but his future looks to lie with the Handicapper at this stage. (op 11-10 tchd 5-4)

Leon Knights, seventh over this trip at Warwick on his debut 46 days previously, ran freely through the early parts and did well to finish as he did in the circumstances. This was a definite step in the right direction and he will be eligible for nurseries after his next assignment. A mile will also be within his compass before too long.

Subadar, third over course and distance on his debut a fortnight previously, had no more to offer in the final two furlongs and proved a little disappointing. On the evidence of both his outings to date, he really needs to drop back in trip. (op 3-1 tchd 11-4)

Bergonzi(IRE) never seriously threatened from off the pace, but was keeping on with some promise when the race was effectively over and showed the benefit of his recent debut at Leicester. This 190,000euros purchase already looks in need of a mile. (op 14-1)

Polish World(USA), as was the case on his recent Newbury debut, ran too keen through the early parts and eventually paid the price after briefly threatening to get involved turning into the home straight. He will need to learn to settle much better, but he has scope and is not one to totally write off by any means. (op 16-1)

6073 LINGFIELDPARK.CO.UK MAIDEN FILLIES' STKS (DIV II) 1m (P)

3:25 (3:26) (Class 5) 2-Y-O **£3,238** (£963; £481; £240) **Stalls** High

Form RPR

1 **Fragrancy (IRE)** 2-9-0 .... MatthewHenry 10 70+
(M A Jarvis) *s.i.s: hdwy on outside over 3f out: rdn 2f out: styd on strly to ld wl ins fnl f* **10/1**

05 **2** *¾* **Divine Love (IRE)**[23] 5608 2-9-0 .... RichardMullen 1 68
(E J O'Neill) *chsd ldrs: rdn to dispute ld ins fnl f: kpt on* **25/1**

0 **3** *½* **Towy Girl (IRE)**[12] 5828 2-9-0 .... SebSanders 9 67
(I A Wood) *a.p: led over 2f out: rdn and hdd ins fnl f* **16/1**

55 **4** *2* **Satin Braid**[31] 5456 2-9-0 .... KDarley 3 63
(B J Meehan) *t.k.h: trckd ldr: led 3f out: hdd 2f out: no ex fnl f* **11/2**[3]

5 *shd* **Tebee** 2-9-0 .... JimmyFortune 6 70+
(J H M Gosden) *slowly away: in rr tl styd on appr fnl f: nvr nrr* **3/1**[2]

6 *3* **Lady Traill** 2-9-0 .... TonyCulhane 8 55
(B W Hills) *slowly away: in rr and nvr nr to chal* **20/1**

2 **7** *1 ½* **Extravagance (IRE)**[37] 5296 2-9-0 .... NickyMackay 5 52
(L M Cumani) *t.k.h: led tl hdd over 2f out: wknd qckly* **6/4**[1]

8 *2 ½* **Mutoon (IRE)** 2-9-0 .... BrettDoyle 12 46
(E A L Dunlop) *in tch: rdn 1/2-way: wknd over 1f out* **10/1**

9 *½* **Time Upon Time** 2-9-0 .... PaulDoe 4 45
(W J Knight) *s.i.s: a bhd* **20/1**

0 **10** *5* **Atlantic Dame (USA)**[14] 5784 2-9-0 .... JimCrowley 11 34
(Mrs A J Perrett) *a bhd* **33/1**

0 **11** *7* **Guilty Pleasure**[24] 5596 2-9-0 .... JohnEgan 2 17
(G C Bravery) *sn bhd and nvr on terms* **50/1**

1m 38.95s (-0.48) **Going Correction** -0.25s/f (Stan) **11** Ran SP% **122.7**

Speed ratings (Par 92):92,91,90,88,88 85,84,81,81,76 69

CSF £241.63 TOTE £12.30: £3.30, £5.40, £4.40; EX 328.40 TRIFECTA Not won..

Owner Mohammed Al Nabouda **Bred** Darley **Trained** Newmarket, Suffolk

FOCUS

This second division of the fillies' maiden looked the weaker of the pair. The first three came clear.

NOTEBOOK

Fragrancy(IRE), whose stable landed the first division of this maiden, picked up strongly from off the pace and mowed down her rivals inside the closing stages to get her career off to a perfect start. Considering she was allowed to go off at double-figure odds it is fair to expect a deal of improvement for this experience, but it should be noted that she is not certain to get much further than this trip next year on breeding. (old market op 16-1, new market op 12-1)

Divine Love(IRE) was ridden early to attain a handy position and proved game under pressure. She was not beaten at all far, and this must rate as her best effort to date, plus she now has the option of nurseries. (old market op 33-1)

Towy Girl(IRE) ◆, seventh in a conditions event at Bath on her debut 12 days previously, looked the most likely winner when extending on the turn for home yet failed to sustain her effort when it mattered and was just held. She may well have prevailed with a more patient ride and this half-sister to her yard's useful filly She's My Outsider is clearly going the right way. (old market op 25-1)

Satin Braid, fifth on both her previous two outings on turf, was given a positive ride on this All-Weather bow and helps to set the level of this form. She now becomes eligible for a nursery rating and may just benefit for the drop back to seven furlongs in the short term. (old market tchd 9-2)

Tebee ◆, a 110,000gns purchase whose dam was a smart six-furlong winner, was given a considerate ride after missing the break and, considering she was not far from the winner off the pace when that rival made her move, she must rate a lot better than the bare form suggests. It would be a surprise were she not to get closer with this experience under her belt. Official explanation: jockey said filly did not face the kickback (old market op 9-2, new market op 7-2)

Lady Traill, who cost 120,000gns as a yearling and is from the family of Old Vic, took an age to find her full stride and left the clear impression that this debut experience would be of real benefit. She is another who should go closer next time. (old market op 25-1 tchd 16-1)

Extravagance(IRE), runner-up on her debut at Yarmouth 37 days previously, was given a positive ride on this step up in trip and has to rate as disappointing. Her yard is struggling for form at present and she ought to be capable of better in time, however. Official explanation: trainer said filly ran too free early (old market op 13-8, new market op 11-8)

6074 LINGFIELD PARK GOLF CLUB NURSERY 1m (P)

4:00 (4:00) (Class 3) 2-Y-O **£9,715** (£2,890; £1,444; £721) **Stalls** High

Form RPR

515 **1** **Lady Grace (IRE)**[12] 5843 2-9-1 **83** .... TonyCulhane 10 89
(W J Haggas) *in tch on outside: hdwy over 3f out: r.o on outside to ld jst ins fnl f* **8/1**

3212 **2** *1 ¼* **Aaim To Prosper (IRE)**[12] 5828 2-9-2 **84** .... JohnEgan 1 87
(M R Channon) *hld up: hdwy 3f out: wnt 2nd ins fnl f: r.o* **15/2**[3]

10 **3** *1 ¾* **Hanging On**[54] 4840 2-9-4 **89** .... JamesDoyle(3) 5 88
(W R Swinburn) *s.i.s: hld up: hdwy over 2f out: kpt on fnl f to go 3rd nr fin* **16/1**

021 **4** *hd* **Rose Of Petra (IRE)**[31] 5449 2-9-0 **82** .... SebSanders 11 81
(Sir Michael Stoute) *trckd ldrs: rdn over 1f out: wknd ins fnl f* **4/1**[2]

033 **5** *2* **Castara Bay**[41] 5168 2-8-10 **78** .... RyanMoore 9 72
(R Hannon) *in rr: rdn over 2f out: kpt on fnl f but nvr nr to chal* **14/1**

506 **6** *½* **Inquisitress**[20] 5679 2-8-3 **71** .... NelsonDeSouza 7 64
(J M P Eustace) *outpcd: mde sme late hdwy ins fnl 2f* **16/1**

6123 **7** *2* **Brainy Benny (IRE)**[8] 5916 2-9-1 **83** .... JimmyFortune 8 71
(N A Callaghan) *led tl rdn and hdd jst ins fnl f: wknd qckly* **7/4**[1]

1520 **8** *3 ½* **Crumbs Of Comfort (USA)**[20] 5676 2-9-2 **84** .... NickyMackay 12 64
(L M Cumani) *racd wd in mid-div: rdn 3f out: sn wknd* **25/1**

535 **9** *shd* **Grand Art (IRE)**[58] 4688 2-7-12 **69** .... MarcHalford(3) 2 49
(M H Tompkins) *s.i.s: hld up: a bhd* **16/1**

6360 **10** *shd* **Hucking Hill (IRE)**[23] 5606 2-8-2 **70** .... RichardMullen 6 50
(J R Best) *prom: rdn over 3f out: wknd wl over 1f out* **50/1**

4100 **11** *¾* **Mayor Of London (USA)**[31] 5459 2-8-8 **76** .... KDarley 3 54
(M Johnston) *chsd ldrs tl wknd over 1f out* **14/1**

16 **12** *½* **Monachello (USA)**[90] 3735 2-8-13 **81** .... JimCrowley 4 58
(Mrs A J Perrett) *in tch for 5f* **16/1**

1m 37.43s (-2.00) **Going Correction** -0.25s/f (Stan) **12** Ran SP% **121.9**

Speed ratings (Par 99):100,98,97,96,94 94,92,88,88,88 87,87

CSF £68.86 CT £970.05 TOTE £9.80: £2.90, £2.30, £4.90; EX 60.70 Trifecta £385.20 Part won. Pool: £542.66 - 0.67 winning tickets..

Owner F C T Wilson **Bred** Frank Barry **Trained** Newmarket, Suffolk

FOCUS

A competitive nursery that was run at a sound pace. The form looks solid enough rated through the runner-up.

NOTEBOOK

Lady Grace(IRE), despite proving a little keen through the early parts, deservedly got back to winning ways and looked better the further she went. She is clearly right at home on this surface, saw out the extra furlong without fuss and remains open to further improvement in this sphere. (op 13-2)

Aaim To Prosper(IRE), making his nursery debut, ran a solid race in defeat and shaped slightly better than his finishing position suggests, as he was forced to switch wide with his effort in the home straight. He is well worth riding more prominently over this trip again in the future and looks a nice handicapper in the making. (op 9-1)

Hanging On, dropping down from Group 3 company, was doing all of her best work towards the finish and may have given the first two more to think about had she not blown the start. This was a respectable performance under top weight on her All-Weather debut.

Rose Of Petra(IRE), off the mark at Brighton last time, was given a positive ride and held every chance. On this evidence she has begun handicap life on no more than a fair mark, but does appeal as the type who may find further improvement when upped to a longer trip as a three-year-old. (op 7-2)

Castara Bay, making his nursery debut, kept on without threatening in the final furlong and still looks to be learning his trade. He can find a race on this surface during the winter. (tchd 16-1)

Inquisitress, having her first start in this sphere, lacked the speed to get involved and clearly needs a stiffer test now.

Brainy Benny(IRE) was allowed his head through the early parts, but this headstrong colt eventually paid for his exertions at the head of affairs and disappointed. He will need to learn to settle if he is to progress any further. Official explanation: jockey said colt ran too free (op 2-1)

6075 LINGFIELD PARK FOR CHRISTMAS PARTIES H'CAP 2m (P)

4:30 (4:31) (Class 4) (0-85,80) 3-Y-O+ **£6,477** (£1,927; £963; £481) **Stalls** Low

Form RPR

2400 **1** **Archduke Ferdinand (FR)**[107] 3203 8-9-6 **75** ... RichardKingscote(3) 11 83
(A King) *hld up: hdwy on outside 3f out: sn led: styd on wl fnl f* **8/1**

3401 **2** *1 ½* **Maystock**[25] 5564 6-10-0 **80** .... RyanMoore 8 86
(B G Powell) *hld up: hdwy 3f out: chsd wnr 1f out: kpt on but no imp* **11/1**

3-05 **3** *hd* **Turn 'n Burn**[14] 5786 5-9-1 **67** .... JimmyFortune 5 73
(C A Cyzer) *rrd up leaving stalls: hld up: hdwy over 3f out: styd on fnl f* **12/1**

0340 **4** *hd* **Billich**[32] 5421 3-8-10 **72** .... RichardMullen 7 78
(E J O'Neill) *bhd tl hdwy over 3f out: styd on wl ins fnl 2f* **10/1**

6053 **5** *1* **Escayola (IRE)**[41] 5174 6-10-0 **80** ....(b) JohnEgan 9 85
(W J Haggas) *hld up in rr: hdwy on ins over 1f out: fdd ins fnl f* **9/2**[1]

020 **6** *3 ½* **Mersey Sound (IRE)**[63] 4560 8-9-13 **79** .... SebSanders 1 79
(D R C Elsworth) *hld up: hdwy over 2f out: nvr on terms* **7/1**[3]

4050 **7** *nk* **Great Tidings**[4] 6011 3-8-7 **69** .... KDarley 10 69
(M Johnston) *sn led: hdd 6f out: wknd over 2f out* **10/1**

1463 **8** *6* **Takafu (USA)**[25] 5564 4-9-9 **75** .... JimCrowley 2 68
(W S Kittow) *trckd ldr: led 6f out tl hdd over 2f out: wknd qckly wl over 1f out* **7/1**[3]

0140 **9** *5* **Jack Dawson (IRE)**[27] 5531 9-9-8 **74** .... GeorgeBaker 4 61
(John Berry) *in tch tl lost pl over 2f out* **9/1**

5051 **10** *5* **Santando**[11] 5875 6-9-4 **70** 6ex..(b) EddieAhern 3 51
(C E Brittain) *mid-div: rdn 4f out: sn bhd* **11/2**[2]

The Form Book, Raceform Ltd, Compton, RG20 6NL

5210 **11** *5* **Profitable**[22] [5644] 3-9-1 **77** .... TonyCulhane 6 52
(B W Hills) *chsd ldrs: rdn 3f out: sn wknd* **9/1**

3m 23.81s (-4.98) **Going Correction** -0.25s/f (Stan)
WFA 3 from 4yo+ 10lb **11** Ran SP% **123.9**
Speed ratings (Par 105):102,101,101,101,100 98,98,95,93,90 88
CSF £97.80 CT £1071.89 TOTE £9.80: £3.60, £4.00, £3.40; EX 143.30 TRIFECTA Not won..
Owner David Sewell **Bred** Eric Lombard, Marius Bertella And Classic Breeding **Trained** Barbury Castle, Wilts

FOCUS
A fair staying handicap and the winner is value for further.

6076 LINGFIELDPARK.CO.UK H'CAP 1m 2f (P)
5:05 (5:06) (Class 4) (0-80,80) 3-Y-O **£4,202** (£4,202; £963; £481) **Stalls** Low

Form				RPR
1245	**1**		**Tommy Toogood (IRE)**[22] [5639] 3-9-4 **80** .... RyanMoore 8 (B W Hills) *a in tch: led ins fnl f: jnd on line* **5/2**[1]	88
2620	**1**	*dht*	**Go Figure (IRE)**[11] [5869] 3-9-4 **80** .... (t) NelsonDeSouza 14 (B J Meehan) *hld up in rr: hdwy over 1f out: r.o to dead-heat on line* **25/1**	88
0064	**3**	*1 ¼*	**Royal Amnesty**[48] [5016] 3-9-0 **76** .... (b[1]) OscarUrbina 10 (G C H Chung) *hld up: hdwy on ins over 1f out: r.o fnl f* **16/1**	82
2301	**4**	*nk*	**Street Warrior (IRE)**[32] [5436] 3-9-3 **79** .... KDarley 9 (M Johnston) *in tch on outside: rdn over 2f out: kpt on but nt qckn ins fnl f* **9/1**[3]	84
4010	**5**	*½*	**Ahmedy (IRE)**[24] [5599] 3-9-1 **77** .... TPO'Shea 11 (M R Channon) *s.i.s: hld up: hdwy and fin fast ins fnl f* **25/1**	81
0620	**6**	*nk*	**Jebel Ali (IRE)**[56] [4784] 3-8-11 **76** .... JamesDoyle(3) 7 (B Gubby) *trckd ldrs: effrt 3f out: kpt on tl wknd ins fnl f* **25/1**	80
3540	**7**	*shd*	**Snark (IRE)**[10] [5889] 3-9-0 **76** .... FergusSweeney 3 (P J Makin) *trckd ldr: led over 2f out: hdd & wknd ins fnl f* **20/1**	79
3212	**8**	*3*	**Benandonner (USA)**[11] [5869] 3-9-2 **78** .... JimmyFortune 2 (E A L Dunlop) *led tl hdd over 2f out: wknd fnl f* **7/2**[2]	76
1000	**9**	*shd*	**Royal Reservation**[32] [5428] 3-9-1 **77** .... EddieAhern 12 (P W Chapple-Hyam) *mid-div: effrt 2f out: wkng whn bmpd appr fnl f* **9/1**[3]	74
6230	**10**	*1*	**Sharplaw Autumn (USA)**[79] [4040] 3-9-1 **77** .... (v[1]) TonyCulhane 6 (W J Haggas) *hld up in rr: nvr on terms* **20/1**	73
1030	**11**	*nk*	**Southport Star (IRE)**[15] [5778] 3-8-8 **75** .... RoryMoore(5) 4 (J R Fanshawe) *nid-div on ins: rdn 3f out: sn wknd* **25/1**	70
4516	**12**	*nk*	**Cape Diamond (IRE)**[7] [5935] 3-9-2 **78** .... SebSanders 13 (W R Swinburn) *prom on outside tl rdn 3f out: sn wknd* **12/1**	72
3520	**13**	*6*	**Gracechurch (IRE)**[20] [5685] 3-8-12 **74** .... JohnEgan 1 (M R Channon) *prom tl rdn and wknd 3f out* **9/1**[3]	57
635	**14**	*53*	**The Aldbury Flyer**[16] [5770] 3-8-13 **75** .... StephenCarson 5 (W R Swinburn) *bhd: sn rdn virtually p.u 2f out: t.o* **20/1**	—

2m 5.23s (-2.56) **Going Correction** -0.25s/f (Stan) **14** Ran SP% **124.0**
Speed ratings (Par 103): **100,100,99,98,98 98,98,95,95,94 94,94,89,47**WIN: Tommy Toogood £1.70, Go Figure £20.00. PL: TT £1.60, GF £8.50, Royal Amnesty £4.90. EX: TT/GF £66.90, GF/TT £51.20. CSF: TT/GF £38.94, GF/TT £41.31. TRIC: TT/GF/RA £409.53, GF/TT/RA £529.70. TRIF: Not won. Pool of £474.98 carried forward to today. TOTE £27: £Owner, £O'Donnell And Associates, £Bred, £Irish National StudTrained Manton, Wilts.
Owner Rick Barnes **Bred** Barronstown Stud And Orpendale **Trained** Lambourn, Berks

FOCUS
A fair three-year-old handicap that saw the first seven fairly closely covered at the finish.
The Aldbury Flyer Official explanation: jockey said gelding lost its action
T/Plt: £5,169.80 to a £1 stake. Pool: £76,839.10. 10.85 winning tickets. T/Qpdt: £1,076.60 to a £1 stake. Pool: £5,819.90. 4.00 winning tickets. JS

5890 NEWBURY (L-H)
Friday, October 20
6077 Meeting Abandoned - Waterlogged.

6084 - 6091a (Foreign Racing) - See Raceform Interactive

5051 BADEN-BADEN (L-H)
Friday, October 20

OFFICIAL GOING: Soft

6092a FERDINAND LEISTEN MEMORIAL (BBAG AUKTIONSRENNEN) 7f
1:10 (1:18) 2-Y-0
£55,172 (£20,690; £13,793; £6,897; £4,138; £2,759)

			RPR
1		**Smokejumper (GER)** 2-8-9 .... VSchulepov 11 (Frau E Mader, Germany) **272/10**	79
2	*¾*	**Simon Magus (GER)** 2-8-9 .... ABoschert 6 (U Ostmann, Germany) **6/5**[1]	77
3	*nk*	**Ibris (GER)** 2-9-4 .... FilipMinarik 3 (U Ostmann, Germany) **17/2**	85
4	*1 ¼*	**Event Music (IRE)**[57] [4731] 2-8-9 .... ChrisCatlin 4 (M R Channon) *held up, 10th straight, went 4th just inside final furlong, stayed on at one pace* **27/10**[2]	73
5	*1 ¼*	**Caracho Directa (GER)** 2-8-9 .... EPedroza 9 (Andreas Lowe, Germany) **13/1**	70
6	*1 ¾*	**Tipperary (GER)** 2-8-9 .... JVictoire 2 (P Vovcenko, Germany) **24/1**	66
7	*hd*	**All My Life (GER)** 2-8-9 .... J-LSilverio 1 (N Sauer, Germany) **33/1**	65
8	*hd*	**Aleandros (GER)**[40] [5218] 2-8-13 .... (b) J-PCarvalho 5 (Mario Hofer, Germany) **8/1**	69
9	*7*	**Super Eagle (GER)** 2-8-9 .... JBojko 10 (S Wegner, Germany) **47/1**	47
10	*½*	**Aturo (FR)** 2-8-9 .... LHammer-Hansen 8 (C Sprengel, Germany) **27/1**	46
11	*2 ½*	**Man On Fire (IRE)** 2-8-13 .... AStarke 13 (C Von Der Recke, Germany) **77/10**[3]	44
12	*14*	**Lord Hill (GER)** 2-8-9 .... WMongil 7 (C Zeitz) **46/1**	5

1m 27.33s **12** Ran SP% **131.0**
(including ten euro stakes): WIN 282; PL 62, 12, 21; SF 867.
Owner Stall Capricorn **Bred** Peter Baron Von Kap-Herr **Trained** Germany

NOTEBOOK
Event Music(IRE), a Redcar maiden winner last time out, got the longer trip well enough and ran a reasonable race.

6093a BADENER SPRINT CUP (GROUP 3) 7f
3:00 (3:09) 3-Y-0+ **£24,138** (£10,345; £4,138; £2,759)

			RPR
1		**Garnica (FR)**[59] 3-8-9 .... IMendizabal 10 (J-C Rouget, France) *pressed leader, smooth headway to lead over 1f out, ran on well, easily* **13/10**[1]	114
2	*2*	**Donatello (GER)**[54] [4858] 5-8-13 .... JVictoire 4 (W Baltromei, Germany) *held up, 6th straight, stayed on well to take 2nd inside final f but no chance with winner* **68/10**[3]	111
3	*1 ¼*	**Soave (GER)**[54] [4858] 7-9-1 .... ADeVries 2 (A Trybuhl, Germany) *raced in 4th, stayed on steadily under pressure from over 1f out* **43/10**[2]	110
4	*3 ½*	**Polish Magic**[152] [1871] 6-8-13 .... (b) EPedroza 3 (A Wohler, Germany) *led to over 1f out, one pace* **22/1**	98
5	*hd*	**Raptor (GER)**[27] [5543] 3-8-9 .... AStarke 12 (Mario Hofer, Germany) *held up in rear, stayed on well from over 1f out, nearest at finish* **94/10**	96
6	*1 ¼*	**Deauville (GER)**[19] [5710] 3-8-5 .... (b) VSchulepov 1 (Frau E Mader, Germany) *never better than midfield* **8/1**	88
7	*½*	**Shinko's Best (IRE)**[68] [4418] 5-9-1 .... MTimpelan 6 (A Kleinkorres, Germany) *in touch, 5th straight, soon ridden and one pace* **23/1**	95
8	*nk*	**Prince Of Thebes (IRE)**[27] [5523] 5-8-13 .... JimmyQuinn 9 (J Akehurst) *towards rear, 11th half-way, never a factor* **117/10**	92
9	*hd*	**Diable**[90] [3755] 7-8-10 .... THellier 13 (H Hesse, Germany) *never a factor* **50/1**	89
10	*1*	**Magic Dancer (GER)**[110] 5-8-13 .... ABoschert 5 (D Ronge, Germany) **22/1**	89
11	*nse*	**Mercury Chief (SAF)**[253] [357] 5-8-10 .... (b) TMundry 7 (Diego Lowther, France) *raced in 3rd on outside til weakened 2f out* **46/1**	86
12	*4 ½*	**Swing The Ring (IRE)**[36] 3-8-7 .... (b) J-PCarvalho 11 (Bruce Hellier, Germany) *midfield early, beaten over 1 1/2f out* **66/1**	74
13	*1 ½*	**Arc De Triomphe (GER)**[15] 4-8-13 .... FForesi 8 (D Fechner, Germany) *close up to over 3f out* **119/10**	74

1m 24.5s
WFA 3 from 4yo+ 2lb **13** Ran SP% **130.0**
WIN 23; PL 14, 22, 16; SF 126.
Owner E A Gann **Bred** Jean-Pierre Dubois **Trained** Pau, France

NOTEBOOK
Prince Of Thebes(IRE) did not like the tacky ground and is best at a mile. He was not at his best and may have done enough for the year.

6070 LINGFIELD (L-H)
Saturday, October 21

OFFICIAL GOING: Standard
Wind: Fresh, behind

6094 TELETEXT RACING "HANDS AND HEELS" APPRENTICE SERIES FINAL H'CAP 7f (P)
1:50 (1:51) (Class 4) (0-85,85) 3-Y-0 **£6,477** (£1,927; £963; £481) **Stalls** Low

Form				RPR
5065	**1**		**Rubenstar (IRE)**[13] [5833] 3-8-8 **75** .... PatrickHills 3 (M H Tompkins) *hld up in tch: rdn to ld jst ins fnl f: r.o wl* **5/1**[2]	84
1232	**2**	*¾*	**Scrummage**[39] [5268] 3-8-10 **77** .... (v) JamieHamblett 1 (Sir Michael Stoute) *chsd ldr: slightly outpcd appr fnl f: r.o wl u.p ins* **10/3**[1]	84
1100	**3**	*nk*	**Kasumi**[11] [5896] 3-8-3 **73** .... NBazeley(3) 4 (H Morrison) *racd wd in mid-div: r.o wl fnl f* **14/1**	79
2306	**4**	*½*	**Jimmy The Guesser**[22] [5649] 3-9-1 **82** .... AlanRutter 9 (N P Littmoden) *chsd ldrs thrght: rdn over 1f out: r.o one pce fnl f* **14/1**	87
3306	**5**	*½*	**Louie Louie (IRE)**[43] [5150] 3-8-11 **81** .... JosephWalsh(3) 10 (N A Callaghan) *hld up in rr: hdwy appr fnl f: nvr nrr* **9/1**	85
5602	**6**	*½*	**Carmenero (GER)**[22] [5649] 3-8-8 **75** .... JackMitchell 7 (W R Muir) *slowly away: towards rr: hdwy over 1f out but nvr nr to chal* **9/1**	77
5340	**7**	*nk*	**Sleeping Storm (IRE)**[35] [5377] 3-8-4 **71** .... KMay 2 (B J Meehan) *chsd ldrs: rdn over 2f out: wknd over 1f out* **25/1**	73
5461	**8**	*nk*	**Tamagin (USA)**[149] [1963] 3-9-2 **83** .... (p) KevinGhunowa 8 (P D Evans) *led tl rdn and hdd jst ins fnl f: wknd qckly* **9/1**	84
0310	**9**	*nk*	**I'm In Love (USA)**[36] [5345] 3-8-8 **78** .... (p) WilliamBuick(3) 12 (M A Magnusson) *s.i.s: sme late hdwy but nvr on terms* **7/1**[3]	78
5210	**10**	*¾*	**Inaminute (IRE)**[55] [4837] 3-8-8 **78** .... PatrickDonaghy(3) 14 (K R Burke) *a bhd* **25/1**	76
4365	**11**	*1 ½*	**Zennerman (IRE)**[28] [5529] 3-8-9 **76** .... LukeMorris 5 (W M Brisbourne) *a in rr* **12/1**	70
0230	**12**	*5*	**Dune Melody (IRE)**[120] [2818] 3-8-6 **78** .... StevenGibson(5) 11 (J S Moore) *racd wd: in tch tl wknd over 2f out* **66/1**	59
1300	**13**	*5*	**Guest Connections**[15] [5785] 3-9-4 **85** .... (v) ThomasO'Brien 6 (M R Channon) *chsd ldrs tl wknd wl over 1f out* **25/1**	53

1m 24.17s (-1.72) **Going Correction** -0.15s/f (Stan) **13** Ran SP% **116.3**
Speed ratings (Par 103):103,102,101,101,100 100,99,99,99,98 96,90,85
CSF £20.42 CT £191.09 TOTE £6.30: £2.00, £1.60, £4.00; EX 28.70 Trifecta £220.30 Pool: £443.78 - 1.43 winning units..
Owner Ben Allen **Bred** Schwindibode Ag **Trained** Newmarket, Suffolk
■ Kirsty Milczarek won this apprentices' series despite not having a ride in this final.

FOCUS
A competitive handicap run at a good pace and the form looks solid and reliable with the first four to their marks.

6095 24 HOUR LADBROKES FREEPHONE BETTING ON 0800 777888 H'CAP 5f (P)
2:20 (2:20) (Class 2) (0-100,100) 3-Y-0+
£12,464 (£3,732; £1,866; £934; £466; £234) **Stalls** High

Form				RPR
4505	**1**		**Texas Gold**[21] [5667] 8-9-0 **96** .... MartinDwyer 9 (W R Muir) *mid-div: rdn and hdwy to ld wl ins fnl f: r.o wl* **5/1**[2]	108
021	**2**	*1 ½*	**Intrepid Jack**[13] [5832] 4-9-4 **100** .... SebSanders 7 (H Morrison) *in rr: hdwy whn nt clr run wl over 1f out: r.o strly ins fnl f to go 2nd cl home* **10/3**[1]	112+

0062 **3** ¾ **Judd Street**[13] [5832] 4-8-11 **93** .... StephenCarson 2 97+
(R F Johnson Houghton) *disp ld: clr ld 1/2-way: rdn and hdd wl ins fnl f: lost 2nd cl home* **5/1**[2]

6004 **4** shd **Maltese Falcon**[13] [5832] 6-8-9 **91** .... (t) TedDurcan 10 95
(P F I Cole) *s.i.s: outpcd: rdn and r.o fnl f* **13/2**[3]

0600 **5** hd **Qadar (IRE)**[21] [5667] 4-8-13 **98** .... JamesDoyle(3) 8 101
(N P Littmoden) *outpcd: hdwy whn swtchd lft jst ins fnl f: r.o* **14/1**

1000 **6** shd **The Lord**[7] [5957] 6-8-7 **89** .... AlanDaly 4 91
(W G M Turner) *chsd ldrs: hrd rdn over 1f out: kpt on but nt qckn ins fnl f* **16/1**

1500 **7** 1 ½ **King Orchisios (IRE)**[29] [5501] 3-8-12 **94** .... (p) PaulHanagan 3 91
(K A Ryan) *disp ld: chsd ldr 1/2-way tl wknd fnl f* **8/1**

5606 **8** nk **Mr Wolf**[32] [5443] 5-8-11 **93** .... (p) TomEaves 5 89
(D W Barker) *disp ld for over 2f: rdn and wknd appr fnl f* **10/1**

0060 **9** 1 ¼ **Treasure Cay**[33] [5433] 5-8-10 **92** .... (t) IanMongan 6 83
(P W D'Arcy) *mid-div: rdn and wknd 1/2-way* **12/1**

30-4 **10** 1 **Rare Cross (IRE)**[178] [1236] 4-8-5 **87** .... NickyMackay 1 75
(P Mitchell) *disp ld to 1/2-way: in tch tl wknd and hmpd ins fnl f* **20/1**

57.75 secs (-2.03) **Going Correction** -0.15s/f (Stan) **10** Ran SP% **115.0**
Speed ratings (Par 109):110,107,106,106,105 105,103,102,100,99
CSF £21.68 CT £89.06 TOTE £3.70: £1.10, £1.90, £2.20; EX 15.20 Trifecta £28.00 Pool: £630.10 - 15.97 winning units..
Owner C L A Edginton **Bred** Coln Valley Stud **Trained** Lambourn, Berks

FOCUS
A decent sprint handicap run at a strong pace and in a good time, just 0.4sec outside the course record.

NOTEBOOK
Texas Gold has an unbelievable record over this course and distance, which now reads an impressive 2112121221. He had the race run to suit and won well, leaving behind recent lesser efforts at other venues. Clearly he should always demand consideration at this track, but he is likely to have only one more outing this term before being put away for the year. (op 11-2)
Intrepid Jack, running off a three-figure mark for the first time in his career, ran well in defeat against a true course specialist. He did not enjoy the best of luck in running but finished with some purpose and, despite a seemingly stiff mark, could well go one better in similar company. (op 7-2)
Judd Street, runner-up to Intrepid Jack at Bath last time out, was 5lb better off with that rival here, but the result was very similar. He did by far the best of those who helped set the strong pace, though, and is clearly very effective around here. (op 7-2)
Maltese Falcon, making his All-Weather debut, has dropped a fair way in the handicap this term, having been rated 17lb higher when making his seasonal reappearance in July. His last two efforts have hinted that he is returning to a more realisitc mark, although on this occasion the race was very much run to suit him and he was still unable to reverse Bath form with Intrepid Jack despite a 7lb turnaround in the weights. (op 6-1)
Qadar(IRE), successful in two of his previous three starts over this course and distance, is another who is seen at his best in a strongly-run race.
The Lord, who is at his best with give on turf, has only one win on the All-Weather to his name, and that was on the deeper Fibresand surface. (op 14-1)
Rare Cross(IRE) Official explanation: jockey said filly lost two shoes

6096 LADBROKES.COM DONCASTER STKS (LISTED RACE) 6f (P)
2:55 (3:00) (Class 1) 2-Y-O **£14,817** (£5,602; £2,800; £1,400) **Stalls** Low

Form RPR
1612 **1** **Hinton Admiral**[14] [5809] 2-9-1 98 .... J-PGuillambert 6 103
(M Johnston) *trckd ldr: led over 2f out: rdn out fnl f* **3/1**[1]

1241 **2** 1 ¼ **Resplendent Alpha**[10] [5909] 2-9-1 86 .... DeanCorby 12 99
(P Howling) *in rr: hdwy on outside over 1f out: r.o strly to go 2nd cl home* **4/1**[2]

4011 **3** shd **Lady Lily (IRE)**[33] [5434] 2-8-10 80 .... TedDurcan 5 94
(H R A Cecil) *chsd ldrs: wnt 2nd 1f out: rdn and lost 2nd cl home* **9/1**

422 **4** 1 ¼ **Resignation (IRE)**[24] [5626] 2-9-1 98 .... PatDobbs 8 95
(R Hannon) *hld up: rdn and hdwy on ins over 1f out: kpt on but nt pce to chal* **4/1**[2]

053 **5** 2 ½ **Three Decades (IRE)**[10] [5909] 2-8-10 87 .... RoystonFfrench 10 83
(C A Cyzer) *t.k.h: towards rr: effrt over 1f out but nvr nr to chal* **33/1**

1143 **6** 1 ½ **Onenightinlisbon (IRE)**[51] [4946] 2-8-10 82 .... LeeEnstone 7 78
(K R Burke) *racd wd in mid-div: wknd ins fnl f* **50/1**

105 **7** ½ **Pelican Key (IRE)**[63] [4594] 2-8-10 83 .... MartinDwyer 11 77
(D M Simcock) *s.i.s: a in rr* **25/1**

3133 **8** shd **Bazroy (IRE)**[21] [5681] 2-9-1 98 .... StephenDonohoe 2 81
(P D Evans) *led tl rdn and hdd over 2f out: wknd ins fnl f* **8/1**

423U **9** nk **La Neige**[22] [5655] 2-9-1 104 .... IanMongan 9 81
(M R Channon) *a towards rr* **15/2**[3]

1064 **10** ¾ **Scented Present**[24] [5626] 2-9-1 95 .... PJSmullen 3 78
(B J Meehan) *mid-div: wknd appr fnl f* **33/1**

1202 **11** 9 **High Style**[10] [5909] 2-9-1 88 .... SebSanders 4 51
(R Hannon) *prom on ins: rdn over 2f out: wknd over 1f out: eased* **16/1**

1m 11.14s (-1.67) **Going Correction** -0.15s/f (Stan) 2y crse rec **11** Ran SP% **115.4**
Speed ratings (Par 103):105,103,103,101,98 96,95,95,95,94 82
CSF £13.93 TOTE £3.60: £1.40, £1.90, £2.30; EX 14.10 Trifecta £56.70 Pool: £833.87 - 10.44 winning units..
Owner Gainsborough **Bred** Gainsborough Stud Management Ltd **Trained** Middleham Moor, N Yorks
■ A temporary change of home for this race, usually run at Doncaster.

FOCUS
The performance of the third puts a question mark on the form of this Listed race, but the time was decent and it looks sound enough.

NOTEBOOK
Hinton Admiral, runner-up on his first start in Listed company on soft ground last time out, went one better on his All-Weather debut. This quicker surface was more to his liking and he was given a good ride by Guillambert, who stole a march on his rivals by kicking decisively approaching the two-furlong pole. (op 11-4)
Resplendent Alpha, successful on his previous two starts here, finished well down the outside after sweeping wide into the straight, but the winner had got first run and he was never going to be able to bridge the gap. He remains progressive, though. (tchd 9-2)
Lady Lily(IRE) had a lot to find on this step up in class and ran particularly well in the circumstances, securing valuable black type in the process. Her performance casts a slight doubt on the form but she had looked progressive at a lower level and clearly the artificial surface brought about further improvement.
Resignation(IRE), who has run to a fairly consistent level on his last three starts now, is probably a fair guide to the level of the form. He picked up well once in the clear and is unlucky to only have a maiden win to his name so far. (tchd 9-2)
Three Decades(IRE), two and a half lengths behind Resplendent Alpha over this course and distance last time, reopposed on the same terms and was beaten a little further by that rival this time.
Onenightinlisbon(IRE) looked to face a pretty stiff task and was not disgraced in the circumstances.

6097 DEAL OR NO DEAL NOW AT LADBROKES.COM H'CAP 1m 4f (P)
3:30 (3:31) (Class 3) (0-95,95) 3-Y-O+ **£11,658** (£3,468; £1,733; £865) **Stalls** Low

Form RPR
1305 **1** **Millville**[27] [5548] 6-9-9 **95** .... IanMongan 8 111+
(M A Jarvis) *in tch on outside: led over 3f out: rdn clr wl over 1f out: easily* **12/1**

031 **2** 5 **Hasayaz (IRE)**[150] [1940] 3-8-9 **88** .... SebSanders 2 96+
(Sir Michael Stoute) *in tch on outside: chsd wnr fnl f but no imp* **25/1**

0223 **3** 1 ¼ **Royal Jet**[16] [5776] 4-9-4 **90** .... TPO'Shea 13 96
(M R Channon) *hld up in mid-div: riddden and hdwy on outside to chse wnr 2f out: no ex fnl f* **9/1**[3]

2532 **4** hd **Transvestite (IRE)**[16] [5776] 4-8-6 **85** .... PatrickHills(7) 11 91
(J W Hills) *mid-div: hdwy over 1f out: nvr nr to chal* **10/1**

4416 **5** 1 **Pevensey (IRE)**[14] [5804] 4-9-1 **87** .... DavidAllan 1 91
(M A Buckley) *in rr: hdwy over 1f out but nvr nr to chal* **12/1**

-213 **6** hd **Country Pursuit (USA)**[167] [1511] 4-9-0 **86** .... BrettDoyle 9 90
(C E Brittain) *chsd ldrs: no hdwy fnl 2f* **11/1**

0254 **7** shd **Diktatorial**[62] [4626] 4-8-11 **83** .... (t) PaulHanagan 10 87
(G A Butler) *hld up: a bhd* **20/1**

0401 **8** 1 ½ **Florimund**[22] [5650] 3-8-9 **88** .... MartinDwyer 7 89
(Sir Michael Stoute) *hld up: nvr on terms* **8/1**[2]

1-03 **9** 5 **Sacranun**[29] [5511] 4-9-0 **86** .... (v) NickyMackay 3 79
(L M Cumani) *trckd ldrs: t.k.h: wknd over 1f out* **16/1**

0000 **10** 6 **Gig Harbor**[33] [5430] 7-9-4 **90** .... GeorgeBaker 5 74
(Miss E C Lavelle) *hld up: a in rr* **50/1**

3000 **11** ¾ **Day To Remember**[14] [5808] 5-9-4 **90** .... (vt[1]) PatDobbs 14 72
(E F Vaughan) *sn led: hdd over 4f out: wknd over 2f out* **66/1**

2051 **12** 1 ¼ **Robustian**[31] [5478] 3-8-4 **83** ow1 .... StephenCarson 6 63
(R F Johnson Houghton) *mid-div: wknd over 3f out* **33/1**

1/1 **13** shd **Descartes**[16] [5776] 4-9-9 **95** .... TedDurcan 12 75+
(Saeed Bin Suroor) *plld v hrd: trckd ldr: led over 3f out to over 3f out: wknd qckly and eased whn btn* **5/4**[1]

2m 31.58s (-2.81) **Going Correction** -0.15s/f (Stan)
WFA 3 from 4yo+ 7lb **13** Ran SP% **119.2**
Speed ratings (Par 107):103,99,98,98,98 97,97,96,93,89 89,88,88
CSF £288.08 CT £2816.72 TOTE £12.00: £2.70, £4.70, £2.80; EX 309.00 Trifecta £3531.10 Pool: £87,881.17 - 17.67 winning units..
Owner T G Warner **Bred** Red House Stud **Trained** Newmarket, Suffolk

FOCUS
A decent handicap but it was not truly run and, with the favourite running no sort of race, took less winning than had looked likely beforehand. That said, the winner looked impressive.

NOTEBOOK
Millville, a winner of three of his previous five starts on sand, showed improved form on this return to the All-Weather, bolting clear in the straight to score by a clear margin. He was no doubt helped by the fact that the steady early pace played into the hands of those who raced towards the fore, but it was still an impressive performance.
Hasayaz(IRE), not seen since landing a Kempton maiden over this trip back in May, could not hold a candle to the clear winner but this was still a promising effort from one so lightly raced. There is scope for further improvement and he could be worth bearing in mind for decent handicaps next season.
Royal Jet does not find winning easy but he is a reliable sort who has a very good record of placing, having now done so in half of his 26 career starts. (op 11-1)
Transvestite(IRE), runner-up to Descartes here last time, would have probably been suited by a stronger pace, as the leaders got away from him somewhat. He saw his race out well, though, and clearly remains in good form.
Pevensey(IRE), a come-from-behind performer who needs a good pace to be seen at his best, did not have the race run to suit and fared as well as could be expected in the circumstances. (op 11-1)
Country Pursuit(USA), successful on his two previous starts over this course and distance, was another having his first outing since the spring. He has been ridden more prominently in the past and, given the way this race panned out, he would perhaps have done better racing from the front.
Descartes, an impressive winner over the course and distance on his return from almost two years on the sidelines earlier this month, was in danger of bouncing just 16 days later, but he was a well-backed favourite. He threw away any chance he had by pulling very hard in the early stages, though, and was beaten some way out. Official explanation: jockey said colt stopped quickly 4f out (op 6-4)

6098 BACKGAMMON NOW AT LADBROKES.COM E B F MAIDEN FILLIES' STKS (DIV I) 7f (P)
4:00 (4:00) (Class 5) 2-Y-O **£3,562** (£1,059; £529; £264) **Stalls** Low

Form RPR
1 **Malaath (IRE)** 2-9-0 .... MartinDwyer 8 74+
(Saeed Bin Suroor) *hld up in rr: hdwy over 2f out: r.o to ld nr fin* **5/4**[1]

2 ½ **Luck Will Come (IRE)** 2-9-0 .... TPO'Shea 9 71
(M J Wallace) *chsd ldrs: ev ch ins fnl f: nt pce of wnr cl home* **20/1**

4 **3** ½ **Londolozi (USA)**[16] [5773] 2-9-0 .... MatthewHenry 5 70
(M A Jarvis) *trckd ldr: led 2f out: hdd ins fnl f: nt qckn cl home* **3/1**[3]

0 **4** nk **Gwyllion (USA)**[16] [5773] 2-9-0 .... RobertHavlin 3 71+
(J H M Gosden) *bhd: r.o fnl f: nvr nrr* **14/1**

00 **5** 4 **Grangehurst**[11] [5882] 2-9-0 .... IanMongan 6 59
(Miss J R Gibney) *in tch: rdn 1/2-way: wknd over 1f out* **66/1**

2 **6** nk **Thunderousapplause**[21] [5679] 2-9-0 .... PaulHanagan 2 58
(K A Ryan) *led tl hdd 2f out: wknd appr fnl f* **11/4**[2]

7 2 ½ **Lindy Lou** 2-9-0 .... J-PGuillambert 4 51
(C A Cyzer) *prom tl rdn and wknd over 2f out* **25/1**

0 **8** 5 **Edgefour (IRE)**[25] [5592] 2-9-0 .... JimCrowley 1 38
(B I Case) *hld up: a bhd* **66/1**

9 1 **Hora** 2-9-0 .... SebSanders 7 36
(Sir Mark Prescott) *v.s.a: a wl in rr* **40/1**

1m 26.26s (0.37) **Going Correction** -0.15s/f (Stan) **9** Ran SP% **116.8**
Speed ratings (Par 92):91,90,89,89,84 84,81,76,74
CSF £32.90 TOTE £2.70: £1.50, £3.50, £1.70; EX 29.30 Trifecta £69.60 Pool: £370.99 - 3.78 winning units..
Owner Godolphin **Bred** Shadwell Estate Company Limited **Trained** Newmarket, Suffolk

FOCUS
Just a fair maiden, run in a time almost a second slower than the second division and difficult to assess with confidence at this stage.

NOTEBOOK
Malaath(IRE), whose dam is a half-sister to Tasneef, a multiple winner over middle distances, made a fairly promising debut without setting the world alight. Her rider did not have to get too serious and she has the pedigree to do better next year, but the bare form looks no more than fair at present. (tchd 11-10 and 11-8)
Luck Will Come(IRE), a brother to Under My Thumb, a triple seven-furlong winner at two, and half-brother to multiple sprinting winner Pipadash, responded well to pressure on her debut to keep on for second place. She looks capable of better in time and may have bumped into a fair type in the winner.

Londolozi(USA) had the benefit of previous experience but could not make it tell over this extra furlong, despite leading the field into the straight and holding every chance. (op 7-2 tchd 4-1)

Gwyllion(USA) ran on well for fourth place without being given a hard time. She has shaped with promise on both her starts now and will certainly win races in handicap company next season over further. (op 11-1)

Grangehurst has shown a modest level of ability in three starts to date and should find things easier in handicap company. (op 50-1)

Thunderousapplause failed to build on her debut promise, again shaping as though she would appreciate dropping back to a sprint distance, as her pedigree would suggest. (op 5-2)

6099 BACKGAMMON NOW AT LADBROKES.COM EBF MAIDEN FILLIES' STKS (DIV II) 7f (P)

4:30 (4:30) (Class 5) 2-Y-O £3,562 (£1,059; £529; £264) Stalls Low

Form				RPR
222	1		**Cast In Gold (USA)**[36] 5344 2-9-0 87 PJSmullen 1 (B J Meehan) *sn led: rdn and out and in command fnl f* 4/9[1]	85+
	2	2 ½	**Loulwa (IRE)** 2-9-0 PaulHanagan 10 (J Noseda) *bhd: hdwy 2f out: styd on to 2nd ins fnl f but nvr threatened wnr* 5/1[2]	79
	3	nk	**Clouded Leopard (USA)** 2-9-0 RobertHavlin 7 (J H M Gosden) *in rr: hdwy to chse wnr over 2f out: no ex and lost 2nd ins fnl f* 14/1[3]	78
55	4	2 ½	**Duskiness (FR)**[136] 2355 2-9-0 TPO'Shea 8 (M J Wallace) *chsd ldrs: rdn and no ex fnl f* 66/1	71
0	5	2 ½	**Dream Again**[36] 5352 2-9-0 TomEaves 4 (Sir Michael Stoute) *mid-div: lost pl over 2f out: nvr on terms after* 40/1	65
	6	7	**Alleviate (IRE)** 2-9-0 SebSanders 5 (Sir Mark Prescott) *slowly away: a bhd* 50/1	47
	7	¾	**Royal Tiara (UAE)** 2-9-0 TedDurcan 2 (Saeed Bin Suroor) *in tch: rdn 1/2-way: sn bhd* 5/1[2]	45
00	8	5	**Dubai's Fairy**[61] 4657 2-9-0 PatDobbs 6 (R Hannon) *chsd wnr to over 2f out: sn wknd* 100/1	32

1m 25.28s (-0.61) **Going Correction** -0.15s/f (Stan) 8 Ran SP% **116.1**

Speed ratings (Par 92):97,94,93,90,88 80,79,73

CSF £3.23 TOTE £1.50: £1.02, £1.20, £3.70; EX 3.90 Trifecta £26.70 Pool: £441.54 - 11.70 winning units..

Owner Sangster Family & Ben Sangster **Bred** R E Sangster & Ben Stangster **Trained** Manton, Wilts

FOCUS

A good fillies' maiden that should produce some winners. The winning time was almost a second quicker than the first division.

NOTEBOOK

Cast In Gold(USA), second twice in good maiden company before running subsequent Marcel Boussac runner-up Darrfonah to a short-head in a decent conditions event at Newbury, found this a straightforward opportunity to get off the mark at the fourth attempt. She is a nice three-year-old prospect. (tchd 1-2)

Loulwa(IRE) ◆, a 370,000gns half-sister to among others high-class triple sprint juvenile winner Galeota, who was Group-1 placed at three, out of a dual sprint two-year-old scorer, made a very pleasing debut behind the very useful winner. She should win her maiden before stepping up in class. (op 7-1 tchd 8-1)

Clouded Leopard(USA) ◆, a sister to Celtic Cat, a quite useful sprint winner at two, out of a mile scorer, shaped with plenty of promise on her racecourse introduction. She is open to plenty of improvement and, like the second, should win her maiden before stepping up in class. (tchd 16-1)

Duskiness(FR), returning from a 136-day break, improved on the form she showed in a couple of sprint maidens on turf. She is now qualified for a handicap mark and could do well in that sphere.

Dream Again stepped up on the form she showed on her debut in a mile maiden at Nottingham.

Royal Tiara(UAE), a sister to Augustine, a multiple mile to ten-furlong winner, and a half-sister to the useful Balkan Knight, out of a seven-furlong juvenile scorer who was high-class over middle-distances at three, was well held on her racecourse debut. Her powerful stable took the first division with a newcomer, but this one was seemingly in need of the experience. (op 4-1)

6100 POKER AT LADBROKES.COM NURSERY 7f (P)

5:00 (5:00) (Class 2) 2-Y-O £12,954 (£3,854; £1,926; £962) Stalls Low

Form				RPR
1450	1		**Market Day**[29] 5503 2-9-5 **95** NickyMackay 7 (L M Cumani) *slowly away: hld up: hdwy 2f out: rdn to ld ent fnl f: hld on wl* 10/1	100
41	2	hd	**Count Ceprano (IRE)**[22] 5648 2-8-4 **80** StephenCarson 9 (W R Swinburn) *racd on outside: chsd wnr over 1f out: ev ch ins fnl f: no ex cl home* 5/1[1]	84
2510	3	2	**Jo'Burg (USA)**[80] 4037 2-9-7 **97** SebSanders 5 (Mrs A J Perrett) *mid-div: hdwy over 1f out: r.o: nvr nrr* 13/2[2]	96
4000	4	1 ¼	**Mubaashir (IRE)**[21] 5681 2-9-7 **97** MartinDwyer 14 (E A L Dunlop) *hld up in rr: r.o fnl f: nvr nrr* 14/1	93
0200	5	½	**Dubai Magic (USA)**[13] 5843 2-8-8 **84** BrettDoyle 10 (C E Brittain) *in tch: racd wd: one pce fr over 1f out* 33/1	79
2610	6	hd	**Miss Jenny (IRE)**[21] 5676 2-8-7 **83** PJSmullen 6 (B J Meehan) *trckd ldr: led over 2f out: hdd & wknd ins fnl f* 10/1	77
0400	7	1 ¾	**Slipasearcher (IRE)**[32] 5447 2-7-8 **77** (b[1]) MCGeran[(7)] 11 (P D Evans) *a towards rr* 33/1	67
3010	8	nk	**Smokey Oakey (IRE)**[9] 5916 2-8-3 **86** PatrickHills[(7)] 3 (M H Tompkins) *nvr bttr than mid-div* 15/2[3]	75
1162	9	nk	**Heywood**[13] 5843 2-8-12 **88** TPO'Shea 13 (M R Channon) *a bhd* 5/1[1]	76
0200	10	1	**Top Royelle**[17] 5764 2-8-1 **77** RichardSmith 4 (R Hannon) *prom: rdn over 2f out: sn wknd* 25/1	63
31	11	1	**Plane Painter (IRE)**[42] 5168 2-8-5 **81** RoystonFfrench 1 (M Johnston) *sn led: hdd over 2f out: sn wknd* 5/1[1]	64
4250	12	2	**Part Timer (IRE)**[14] 5809 2-8-9 **85** TedDurcan 2 (M R Channon) *chsd ldrs on ins: rdn and wknd qckly 2f out* 20/1	63
0140	13	2	**Ava's World (IRE)**[8] 5940 2-8-4 **83** GregFairley[(3)] 8 (M Johnston) *cl up tl rdn and wknd qckly over 2f out* 16/1	56

1m 24.67s (-1.22) **Going Correction** -0.15s/f (Stan) 13 Ran SP% **120.3**

Speed ratings (Par 101):100,99,97,96,95 95,93,92,92,91 90,88,85

CSF £57.30 CT £355.95 TOTE £15.50: £5.70, £2.20, £2.10; EX 90.10 TRIFECTA Not won..

Owner Allevamento Gialloblu **Bred** Biddestone Stud **Trained** Newmarket, Suffolk

FOCUS

A good nursery in which the front two pulled nicely clear of some useful types. The form looks sound rated around the winner, third and fourth.

NOTEBOOK

Market Day looked a potential Pattern-class filly when winning twice on the Polytrack earlier in the season, but had not progressed on the turf recently, including when only mid-division in a valuable sales race at Ascot on her latest start. However, returned to sand, she was able to show her best and produced a fine effort against the colts to defy an 11lb higher mark than when winning round here in the summer. She arguably ended up getting first run on Count Ceprano, but that one appeared quite leniently treated and this must rate as a very useful performance. She looks well up to picking up some black type, but opportunities to do so on this surface in this country are likely to be limited, and it remains to be seen if she is as effective on turf.

Count Ceprano(IRE) ◆, off the mark in a six-furlong maiden round here on his previous start, did not look too harshly treated for his nursery debut and probably should have followed up. Always travelling the strongest, despite being caught a little wide, his rider took an age to get after him and handed the initiative to Market Day, who was able to build up crucial momentum when kicking off the bend. He was coming back at the winner towards the finish and probably would have won had his rider got after him sooner. He will go up in the weights, but is progressing and looks capable of winning in handicap company. In the longer term, he does have to prove his effectiveness on turf. (op 4-1 tchd 11-2)

Jo'Burg(USA), eighth of ten in the Vintage Stakes when last seen nearly three months previously, posted a fine effort off joint-top weight on his nursery and Polytrack debut. (op 8-1)

Mubaashir(IRE), stepped up to seven furlongs for the first time on his nursery debut, had no easy task under joint-top weight but ran with credit. (op 16-1)

Dubai Magic(USA) ran better than when down the field at Wolverhampton on his previous start. Official explanation: jockey said gelding hung left throughout

Heywood, 2lb higher, was well below the form he showed when second at Wolverhampton on his previous start. Official explanation: jockey said colt was denied a clear run (op 9-2)

Top Royelle Official explanation: trainer's rep said filly was struck into

Plane Painter(IRE) had the best draw when winning his maiden at Chester, but this was a lot tougher and he was well beaten.

Part Timer(IRE) Official explanation: jockey said colt was denied a clear run

6101 PLAY BINGO AT LADBROKES.COM CONDITIONS STKS 7f (P)

5:30 (5:30) (Class 3) 3-Y-O+

£7,790 (£2,332; £1,166; £583; £291; £146) Stalls Low

Form				RPR
4025	1		**Mostashaar (FR)**[35] 5376 4-8-11 102 MartinDwyer 5 (Sir Michael Stoute) *hld up hdwy over 1f out: rdn and r.o to ins fnl f to ld cl home* 7/2[2]	104+
510-	2	nk	**Council Member (USA)**[371] 5900 4-8-11 109 TedDurcan 9 (Saeed Bin Suroor) *s.i.s: hld up: hld up: rdn 2f out: led ins fnl f: cught cl home* 5/2[1]	98
5600	3	2 ½	**Manston (IRE)**[122] 2739 3-8-12 95 PJSmullen 7 (B J Meehan) *a.p: chsd ldr over 1f out: fdd ins fnl f* 16/1	95
5540	4	shd	**Red Cape (FR)**[15] 5785 3-8-9 85 RobertHavlin 8 (Jane Chapple-Hyam) *sn led: rdn: hdd and fdd ins fnl f* 25/1	91
3-60	5	nk	**Violette**[105] 3322 3-8-6 107 ow2 (b[1]) SebSanders 6 (Sir Mark Prescott) *hld up in rr: hdwy 2f out: styd on one pce fnl f* 9/2[3]	87
0505	6	½	**Regal Royale**[83] 3985 3-8-9 92 NickyMackay 4 (Sir Michael Stoute) *hld up in tch: wknd ins fnl f* 9/1	89
520	7	½	**Vortex**[21] 5682 7-8-11 100 (vt) TomEaves 3 (Miss Gay Kelleway) *chsd ldrs tl rdn and wknd ent fnl f* 8/1	88
2650	8	1	**Musicmaestroplease (IRE)**[35] 5384 3-8-2 57 MarkCoumbe[(7)] 2 (S Parr) *bhd: lost tch over 2f out: effrt over 1f out but nvr on terms* 100/1	85?
0002	9	3	**Party Boss**[13] 5845 4-8-11 102 BrettDoyle 1 (C E Brittain) *trckd ldr: rdn over 2f out: wknd ent fnl f* 7/2[2]	77

1m 23.58s (-2.31) **Going Correction** -0.15s/f (Stan)

WFA 3 from 4yo+ 2lb 9 Ran SP% **123.0**

Speed ratings (Par 107):107,106,103,103,103 102,102,101,97

CSF £13.67 TOTE £4.20: £1.50, £1.50, £2.90; EX 16.40 Trifecta £185.90 Pool: £508.11 - 1.94 winning units. Place 6 £28.51, Place 5 £15.34.

Owner Hamdan Al Maktoum **Bred** Shadwell Estate Company Limited **Trained** Newmarket, Suffolk

FOCUS

A decent event but it was run at a steady early pace and turned into something of a sprint. The form is dubious owing to the relative proximity of the eighth.

NOTEBOOK

Mostashaar(FR) overcame a troubled run to lead close home and win for the first time since he took the Britannia at Royal Ascot at York last summer. He has not had things go his way this season and, as they entered the straight, it looked as though his miserable campaign was going to continue as he looked destined not to get a clear run, but to his credit he found a very good turn of foot once switched, and the talent is clearly still there. Perhaps he will fulfill his potential next season. (op 4-1)

Council Member(USA), off the track for over a year, was second best in at the weights and well backed to make a belated winning reappearance. He looked the likely beneficiary of Mostashaar's luckless run until that rival swept by him close home, but it was still a good effort on the back of such a long lay-off. (op 10-3)

Manston(IRE) had a good campaign at two but he has not shown a lot this season and faced a stiff task here giving weight all round. In the circumstances he performed with credit, although racing prominently throughout in a race lacking early pace probably helped in that regard. (op 25-1)

Red Cape(FR), who could only finish in mid-division in a handicap over this course and distance last time off a mark of 87, enjoyed the huge benefit of dictating his own pace out in front. He set a pretty moderate gallop and is almost certainly flattered by his proximity to the principals at the finish.

Violette, best in at the weights, was blinkered for the first time on this first outing since July. Held up at the back of the field in a race run at a steady early pace, she was not well positioned for the sprint for home. (op 5-1 tchd 7-1)

Regal Royale, having his first outing since July and debuting on the All-Weather, may be something of a twilight horse nowadays. (op 10-1)

Vortex was well positioned entering the straight and it was disappointing that he was unable to pick up under pressure. (op 13-2)

Party Boss was another who has good All-Weather form to his name but was unable to capitalise on racing prominently in a steadily-run race.

T/Plt: £69.40 to a £1 stake. Pool: £68,265.65. 717.10 winning tickets. T/Qpdt: £19.50 to a £1 stake. Pool: £3,073.00. 116.20 winning tickets. JS

5890 NEWBURY (L-H)

Saturday, October 21

OFFICIAL GOING: Heavy

Wind: Strong, across

6102 STAN JAMES HORRIS HILL STKS (GROUP 3) (C&G) 7f (S)

2:05 (2:11) (Class 1) 2-Y-O

£22,712 (£8,608; £4,308; £2,148; £1,076; £540) **Stalls** Centre

Form RPR

212 **1** **Dijeerr (USA)**[22] 5653 2-8-12 106 PhilipRobinson 9 106
(M A Jarvis) *lw: a.p: led 2f out: sn rdn: hdd ins fnl f: edgd lft but rallied gamely: led again line* **9/2[3]**

1 **2** *shd* **Mythical Kid (USA)**[11] 5891 2-8-12 RyanMoore 2 106
(Sir Michael Stoute) *lw: hld up: swtchd lft over 2f out: sn rdn and hdwy: led ins fnl f and edgd rt: ct line* **11/4[1]**

321 **3** *4* **Striving Storm (USA)**[49] 5014 2-8-12 106 EddieAhern 7 96
(P W Chapple-Hyam) *lw: in tch: rdn and hung lft fr over 1f out: styd on to go 3rd ins fnl f* **6/1**

21 **4** *1 1/4* **Opera Music**[36] 5339 2-8-12 88 JohnEgan 6 93
(S Kirk) *led tl narrowly hdd 2f out: sn rdn: kpt on pce fnl f* **11/1**

31 **5** *2 1/2* **Heroes**[12] 5867 2-8-12 BrianReilly 5 87
(G A Huffer) *prom: rdn and ev ch 2f out: wknd ins fnl f* **16/1**

1112 **6** *nk* **Tobosa**[22] 5655 2-8-12 102 LDettori 10 86
(W Jarvis) *hld up: hdwy 3f out: sn rdn: no further imp* **3/1[2]**

5321 **7** *1 1/2* **Karoo Blue (IRE)**[31] 5481 2-8-12 81 DarryllHolland 4 82
(C E Brittain) *hld up: rdn 3f out: no imp* **50/1**

61 **8** *9* **Desert Dew (IRE)**[22] 5658 2-8-12 97 MichaelHills 3 60
(B W Hills) *lw: in tch: rdn over 2f out: wknd over 1f out* **8/1**

0504 **9** *3* **Chjimes (IRE)**[7] 5956 2-8-12 87 PatCosgrave 8 53
(K R Burke) *mid div: rdn over 2f out: wknd over 1f out* **66/1**

1331 **10** *8* **Dubai's Touch**[64] 4561 2-8-12 102 JoeFanning 11 33
(M Johnston) *nvr really travelling: in tch tl wknd 2f out* **12/1**

1m 30.66s (3.66) **Going Correction** +0.625s/f (Yiel) **10** Ran SP% **120.6**

Speed ratings (Par 105):104,103,99,97,95 94,92,82,79,70

CSF £17.95 TOTE £6.10: £2.20, £1.60, £1.90; EX 23.40 Trifecta £161.30 Pool: £681.86 - 3.00 winning units..

Owner Sheikh Ahmed Al Maktoum **Bred** Monticule **Trained** Newmarket, Suffolk

FOCUS

This looked close to the level expected for the grade, with the winner setting the standard. The middle of the track was the place to be on some very testing ground.

NOTEBOOK

Dijeerr(USA) travelled really well throughout the race and moved into the lead going easily with a quarter of a mile to go. However, once under pressure he started to idle and was passed by the eventual runner-up inside the final furlong. The jockey managed to conjure another effort out of him and he rallied bravely to get his head back in front on the line. Progressing with every race, a mile should be within his scope and he could be aimed at a Guineas next season. (op 5-1)

Mythical Kid(USA) came through to win the race in the final furlong, looking sure to collect with half a furlong to go. As the winning post loomed, he was just worried out of it by the far more experienced Dijeerr, who had hit full stride again. It was a fine effort for a once-raced horse and one must believe we will be hearing a lot more from him next season. (op 7-2)

Striving Storm(USA), who was well supported in the market, kept on in resolute style to claim a clear third place despite not helping his jockey by hanging. If he strengthens up during the winter, he could make a decent sort next season. (op 8-1)

Opera Music was always close to the pace in the early stages and kept on in determined style when joined at about the two-furlong marker. It was a solid effort on ground he had not encountered before. (op 10-1 tchd 12-1)

Heroes had plenty to find with a few in the field on form but emerged with plenty of credit after keeping on well from a prominent early position. However, on the negative side, he may not be the easiest horse to place next season if he gets handed an official mark in the 90s, as it would seem unlikely that he is a genuine Group-class performer. (op 28-1 tchd 33-1)

Tobosa, who spread a plate on the way to the start, was going really nicely with two furlongs to go but failed to pick up when his jockey asked him to catch the leaders. He has had plenty of hard races this season and is certainly not one to give up on. (op 11-4 tchd 7-2)

Karoo Blue(IRE) was niggled along early but always kept in touch. He did not have the smoothest of passages and can be rated a little bit better than his final position suggests. (tchd 66-1)

Desert Dew(IRE) was prominent early in the race but dropped right away when the tempo was increased. (tchd 9-1)

Chjimes(IRE) was the most exposed horse in the race and was never a factor.

Dubai's Touch, who was returning from a two-month break, was the only one to come up the stands'-side rail which, in hindsight, was not the place to be. It could not have been his true running and something may have been amiss. (op 14-1)

6103 STAN JAMES ST SIMON STKS (GROUP 3) 1m 4f 5y

2:40 (2:42) (Class 1) 3-Y-O+

£28,390 (£10,760; £5,385; £2,685; £1,345; £675) **Stalls** Centre

Form RPR

1326 **1** **Short Skirt**[21] 5702 3-8-10 108 RyanMoore 6 115
(Sir Michael Stoute) *lw: hld up towards rr: stdy prog fr over 4f out: styd on to ld ins fnl f: edgd rt: rdn out* **13/2[3]**

0600 **2** *2* **Mountain (IRE)**[21] 5697 3-8-10 JAHeffernan 4 112
(A P O'Brien, Ire) *in tch: rdn over 3f out: styd on to go 2nd cl home* **9/2[2]**

0236 **3** *hd* **Orcadian**[147] 2010 5-9-3 105 RichardHughes 10 112
(J M P Eustace) *led: rdn 2f out: hdd ins fnl f: no ex: lost 2nd cl home* **14/1**

1633 **4** *7* **The Whistling Teal**[35] 5395 10-9-6 108 SteveDrowne 3 105
(G Wragg) *mid-div: niggled along fr 7f out: dropped rr over 4f out: styd on again fr 2f out* **20/1**

2032 **5** *8* **Munsef**[27] 5547 4-9-3 111 RHills 7 91
(J L Dunlop) *lw: hld up bhd: rdn and sme hdwy into mid-div over 2f out: wknd over 1f out* **13/2[3]**

2424 **6** *4* **Dragon Dancer**[41] 5221 3-8-10 119 DarryllHolland 11 85
(G Wragg) *a towards rr* **4/1[1]**

-204 **7** *3 1/2* **Fracas (IRE)**[35] 5395 4-9-3 (v[1]) WMLordan 8 80
(David Wachman, Ire) *lw: chsd ldrs: rdn over 3f out: wknd jst over 1f out: eased* **12/1**

4355 **8** *2* **Akarem**[22] 5657 5-9-3 108 PatCosgrave 12 78
(K R Burke) *mid-div: drvn along 4f out: wknd over 2f out* **25/1**

2014 **9** *shd* **Foxhaven**[27] 5547 4-9-3 105 FrancisNorton 1 77
(P R Chamings) *chsd ldrs: rdn 4f out: grad fdd* **20/1**

1213 **10** *2* **Alfie Flits**[106] 3254 4-9-3 107 RobertWinston 5 75
(G A Swinbank) *chsd ldrs tl wknd over 2f out* **9/2[2]**

2005 **11** *dist* **Franklins Gardens**[7] 5967 6-9-3 107 NCallan 9 —
(M H Tompkins) *sn punched along in mid-div: dropped rr over 4f out: sn t.o: virtually p.u fnl f* **33/1**

2m 41.74s (5.75) **Going Correction** +0.825s/f (Soft)

WFA 3 from 4yo+ 7lb **11** Ran SP% **113.7**

Speed ratings (Par 113):113,111,111,106,101 98,96,95,95,93 —

CSF £32.61 TOTE £7.00: £2.60, £1.90, £3.60; EX 49.10 Trifecta £147.20 Pool: £1,119.88 - 5.40 winning units..

Owner J M Greetham **Bred** J M Greetham **Trained** Newmarket, Suffolk

FOCUS

A good renewal of a well-established race. Not many got into contention after Orcadian set a good pace in front and the form is rated through the runner-up.

NOTEBOOK

Short Skirt still had plenty to do at the top of the straight, but kept on in great style to wear down the long-time leader Orcadian inside the final furlong. She has been a tough sort during the season and finally dispelled any worries about stamina limitations in the heavy ground. There are plenty of valuable races for older fillies now, so one hopes to see her again next season despite her date at the December Sales. (op 6-1 tchd 15-2)

Mountain(IRE) kept plugging away up the straight to grab second place from Orcadian in the final furlong. He has taken plenty of racing during the season, so emerges with credit in such demanding conditions. If the stable keeps him in training, he could make up into a Cup horse. (op 5-1)

Orcadian looked like landing the race for the second time in three years when pressing for home up the straight. Even with a furlong to go he looked like holding on, but the ground took its toll and he finished very weary. Returning from a long break, he is still clearly up to Group 3 class at his best. (op 12-1)

The Whistling Teal, who was very awkward before going into the stalls, never looked to be helping his jockey during the race and only really consented to run on late in the day. He is not one to trust despite his undoubted talent. (op 16-1)

Munsef was not given the best ride in the prevailing going, as he was never able to bridge the gap to the leaders when asked to make up ground. It is fair to say, however, that he is a much better horse on a sound surface. (op 8-1)

Dragon Dancer was another in the race not given the most advantageous ride in the ground and never posed a threat at any stage. It seems a long time since his brave effort in the Derby and it will be a shame if connections do not try and find a maiden for him soon, so that he can at least get his head in front. (op 7-2)

Fracas(IRE), who was fitted with a visor for the first time, held every chance coming into the home straight but failed to pick up when asked. If headgear is tried again, he is worth one more chance on better ground. (op 14-1 tchd 16-1)

Alfie Flits, having his first race since early July, was given every chance but did not get home after racing very freely in the early stages. The obvious conclusion to draw is that he will benefit for the race. (op 7-2)

Franklins Gardens Official explanation: jockey said horse lost its action; vet said horse lost front shoe

6104 RACING POST TROPHY (GROUP 1) (ENTIRE COLTS & FILLIES) 1m (S)

3:15 (3:19) (Class 1) 2-Y-O

£93,687 (£35,508; £17,770; £8,860; £4,438; £2,227) **Stalls** Centre

Form RPR

3 **1** **Authorized (IRE)**[36] 5343 2-9-0 LDettori 8 117+
(P W Chapple-Hyam) *lw: travelled wl: hld up towards rr: smooth hdwy fr over 2f out: qcknd to ld 1f out: r.o wl: readily* **25/1**

1501 **2** *1 1/4* **Charlie Farnsbarns (IRE)**[14] 5806 2-9-0 95 RyanMoore 7 114
(B J Meehan) *trckd ldrs: led 2f out: sn rdn: edgd rt and hdd 1f out: kpt on but nt pce of wnr* **33/1**

152 **3** *2* **Medicine Path**[28] 5521 2-9-0 109 RichardMullen 11 110
(E J O'Neill) *mid-div: drvn along fr over 2f out: no imp tl styd on fr over 1f out: wnt 3rd fnl f* **20/1**

221 **4** *nk* **Eagle Mountain**[13] 5851 2-9-0 MJKinane 9 110
(A P O'Brien, Ire) *mid-div: lost pl 5f out: hdwy and nt clr run over 1f out: swtchd rt: styd on ins fnl f* **8/11[1]**

1161 **5** *1 3/4* **Thousand Words**[22] 5653 2-9-0 111 RichardHughes 14 106
(B W Hills) *lw: hld up towards rr: stdy prog fr 2f out: rdn to chse ldrs over 1f out: kpt on* **7/1[2]**

21 **6** *5* **Sunshine Kid (USA)**[11] 5893 2-9-0 JimmyFortune 10 95
(J H M Gosden) *lw: chsd ldrs: rdn and ev ch over 1f out: kpt on same pce* **11/1**

412 **7** *1 3/4* **Regime (IRE)**[32] 5466 2-9-0 108 JamieSpencer 5 92
(M L W Bell) *mid-div: trckd ldrs 2f out: sn rdn: one pce fnl f* **15/2[3]**

3 **8** *hd* **Red Rock Canyon (IRE)**[15] 5794 2-9-0 JAHeffernan 4 91
(A P O'Brien, Ire) *hld up bhd: hdwy 2f out: sn rdn: wknd fnl f* **25/1**

221 **9** *hd* **Teslin (IRE)**[36] 5343 2-9-0 91 KDarley 2 91
(M Johnston) *trckd ldrs: rdn over 2f out: wknd fnl f* **40/1**

01 **10** *nk* **Petara Bay (IRE)**[28] 5537 2-9-0 86 DaneO'Neill 6 90
(T G Mills) *lw: prom: led briefly over 2f out: sn rdn: wknd 1f out* **16/1**

1213 **11** *17* **Drumfire (IRE)**[32] 5466 2-9-0 103 JoeFanning 3 55
(M Johnston) *prom: rdn over 2f out: sn wknd* **25/1**

12 *2* **Great Sphinx (USA)**[6] 5995 2-9-0 DavidMcCabe 1 50
(A P O'Brien, Ire) *lw: veered lft s: trckd ldrs: hung lft virtually thrght:wknd 2f out* **100/1**

4 **13** *13* **Malacara**[13] 5851 2-9-0 CO'Donoghue 12 23
(A P O'Brien, Ire) *prom: rdn 3f out: sn btn* **100/1**

4100 **14** *3* **Prince Golan (IRE)**[56] 4809 2-9-0 94 NCallan 13 17
(K A Ryan) *led tl over 2f out: sn wknd* **100/1**

1m 43.74s (3.12) **Going Correction** +0.625s/f (Yiel) **14** Ran SP% **121.0**

Speed ratings (Par 109):109,107,105,105,103 98,96,96,96,96 79,77,64,61

CSF £637.50 TOTE £24.40: £5.20, £5.30, £4.40; EX 472.10 Trifecta £1538.70 Part won. Pool: £2,167.26 - 0.10 winning units..

Owner Saleh Al Homaizi & Imad Al Sagar **Bred** Marengo Investments And Knighton House Ltd And M **Trained** Newmarket, Suffolk

■ This event was run at Newbury due to redevelopment at Doncaster.

FOCUS

One of the biggest fields for the final domestic Group 1 of the season for some time, and the form looks up to scratch despite the starting prices of the first three home. Plenty of decent middle distance performers at three look sure to come out of the race.

NOTEBOOK

Authorized(IRE) ◆ became the first maiden since Dilshaan in 2000 to win the final domestic Group 1 race of the season, powering down the stands' side to win in the manner of a top-quality horse, comprehensively reversing positions with Teslin on their Haynes, Hanson & Clark running. The trainer said after the race that the winner did not really like the ground, and then went on to suggest that his horse may line up in the 2,000 Guineas if straight enough - which is quite a statement considering that he looks after the well-fancied Guineas contender Dutch Art as well. The Derby will be the primary aim and, if turning up fit and well, he must have a great chance, considering the recent record of this race as an Epsom pointer.

Charlie Farnsbarns(IRE), who had not shown a level of form prior to the race which suggested he would be good enough to take a well contested Group 1, looked all set to score when his jockey went for home just over two furlongs from home. However, Authorized swept past him easily when hitting full stride, meaning a honourable runner-up spot was his only reward. While the winner was most impressive and looks a horse to follow, it does seem a bit difficult to believe that Charliefarnsbarns is a true Group 1 competitor considering his previous form. Unless continuing his apparent improvement throughout the winter, he might not be the easiest horse to win with at three. (op 50-1)

Medicine Path ◆, who went close to landing the Group 2 Royal Lodge last time, a race that has already produced a subsequent Group 1 winner, travelled well but could only find one pace under pressure. He looks every inch a decent middle-distance sort in the making and could surprise a few next season in decent company.

Eagle Mountain, who was sent off a very warm favourite after landing the Beresford Stakes last time, did not get the smoothest of passages after being settled in between horses, but pretty much had every chance in the end. In hindsight, his chance may have been enhanced had he been allowed to bowl along somewhere near the front, as he does stay well. (op 4-5 tchd 5-6 and 4-6 in places)

Thousand Words tracked Authorized but didn't quicken as well as the impressive winner when asked to get closer. He finished nicely clear of the fifth and has the physical scope for some improvement at three. (op 8-1)

Sunshine Kid(USA), who was taking a huge step up in class after landing a course and distance maiden last time, did not disgrace himself but did not get home as well as some others in the final furlong after racing towards the head of affairs. There will be other days for him. (op 10-1 tchd 12-1)

Regime(IRE), who became stirred up in the paddock, travelled nicely on the far side of the field and came to have every chance at the two-furlong pole before fading right out of contention. He was a long way in front of the runner-up last time at the Curragh, and one suspects he is much better than he showed. (tchd 7-1)

Red Rock Canyon(IRE) has been the subject of quite a bit of hype this season and ran as well as he was entitled to. Connections will surely be just looking to get a win out of him before making any firm plans. (op 33-1)

Teslin(IRE), who beat Authorized last time, did not seem to get home on the ground. He can be given another chance on a better surface.

Petara Bay(IRE), who has quite a knee action, was prominent in the early stages before being passed by the chasing pack two furlongs from home. To his credit, he never gave up, but he looks a notch or two below Group 1 level.

Drumfire(IRE), another who finished in front of the runner-up in Ireland, helped to set the early tempo but dropped out alarmingly when the pressure was applied. All of his good early-season form came on much quicker ground, so it is easy to excuse a poor effort on heavy ground. (op 33-1)

6105 RACING POST RADLEY STKS (LISTED RACE) (FILLIES) 7f (S)

3:50 (3:53) (Class 1) 2-Y-O

£13,343 (£5,057; £2,530; £1,261; £632; £317) **Stalls** Centre

Form	Pos	Btn	Horse	Jockey	RPR
2421	**1**		**Party (IRE)**[11] 5894 2-8-12 80 ... RyanMoore 3 (R Hannon) *lw: hld up in tch: rdn to ld over 1f out: kpt on gamely: drvn out* **6/1**		92
1	**2**	½	**Hollow Ridge**[11] 5890 2-8-12 ... RichardHughes 5 (B W Hills) *plld hrd: sn in tch: rdn to chse ldrs over 1f out: kpt on to snatch 2nd fnl stride* **7/2**[2]		91
3410	**3**	*shd*	**Easy Lover**[42] 5187 2-8-12 91 ... JamieSpencer 11 (J A Osborne) *hld up bhd: swtchd lft and gd hdwy over 1f out: kpt on to chse wnr ins fnl f: lost 2nd fnl stride* **3/1**[1]		91
1	**4**	¾	**Ransom Captive (USA)**[21] 5679 2-8-12 ... EddieAhern 7 (M A Magnusson) *lw: trckd ldrs: swtchd lft and sltly outpcd 2f out: styd on again ins fnl f* **4/1**[3]		89
362	**5**	½	**Lady Alize (USA)**[11] 5894 2-8-12 ... (t) FJohansson 1 (R A Kvisla) *hld up towards rr: hdwy over 2f out: effrt over 1f out: no ex ins fnl f* **20/1**		87
2114	**6**	3	**Adaptation**[8] 5940 2-8-12 88 ... JoeFanning 10 (M Johnston) *prom: led over 2f out: sn rdn: hdd over 1f out: wknd ins fnl f* **7/1**		80
4216	**7**	½	**Elusive Flash (USA)**[15] 5783 2-8-12 83 ... NelsonDeSouza 8 (P F I Cole) *lw: led: rdn and hdd over 2f out: hung lft over 1f out: wknd ins fnl f* **14/1**		79
6126	**8**	5	**Sparkling Eyes**[32] 5442 2-8-12 80 ... DarryllHolland 6 (C E Brittain) *racd keenly: trckd ldrs: rdn 2f out: sn wknd* **16/1**		67
1360	**9**	*hd*	**Eliza May**[29] 5503 2-8-12 88 ... NCallan 9 (K A Ryan) *restrained s: racd keenly towards rr: nt clr run over 1f out: sn rdn: no imp* **22/1**		66

1m 33.25s (6.25) **Going Correction** +0.925s/f (Soft) **9** Ran SP% **115.7**

Speed ratings (Par 100):101,100,100,99,98 95,94,89,88

CSF £27.35 TOTE £6.40: £1.50, £1.70, £1.70; EX 18.30 Trifecta £36.60 Pool: £659.96 - 12.80 winning units..

Owner Highclere Thoroughbred Racing XXXV **Bred** Al Ca Torre Di Canicarao **Trained** East Everleigh, Wilts

FOCUS

A below average renewal run in a slower time than the Horris Hill, mainly due to the steady early tempo. The first four look capable of progressing as three-year-olds but not a race to have total faith in.

NOTEBOOK

Party(IRE) ◆, who only lost her maiden tag recently, showed herself to be a decent staying filly in the making with another hard-fought success. She looks a filly with real heart and those types can often improve out of all recognition when their confidence is up. A place in a Classic trial next season has been more than earned and it is not beyond the realms of possibility that she could turn out to be a decent sort next season. (op 7-1 tchd 11-2)

Hollow Ridge ◆, who was keen early and a bit green during the race, can only improve with experience, as she was a late foal, and can develop into a nice sort. She has a pedigree that suggests a mile plus will suit her next year. (op 3-1 tchd 4-1)

Easy Lover was unlucky not to go a bit closer, as she had nowhere to go from the rear of the field when her jockey wanted to make his move. Once finding room, she stayed on dourly to catch the winner inside the final furlong, despite losing second late in the race. She should stay well next season. (op 7-2)

Ransom Captive(USA) ◆ was going as well as anything two furlongs from home, but her inexperience started to show under pressure and she tended to run about before staying on again down the stands'-side rail. The run will bring her on mentally again and she is well worth another chance. (op 9-2 tchd 5-1 in a place)

Lady Alize(USA) was only beaten a short head by the winner last time, but that was over six furlongs and she was never able to get that close over a furlong further. She has plenty of decent form but it cannot be certain yet whether six or seven furlongs ideally suits her.

Adaptation took the field along at a steady pace early and kept on respectably when joined and passed a furlong from home. She ran her race but is not quite up to Listed standard. (op 9-2)

Elusive Flash(USA) is a useful sort without being up to Listed grade quite yet. She also did herself no favours by hanging once under pressure. (tchd 16-1)

Sparkling Eyes has given no indication that seven furlongs is what she requires, especially on heavy ground. (op 25-1)

6106 HEROS AND BAYER HEALTHCARE NURSERY 1m (S)

4:20 (4:25) (Class 4) (0-85,82) 2-Y-O

£6,477 (£1,927; £963; £481) **Stalls** Centre

Form	Pos	Btn	Horse	RPR
6401	**1**		**Bed Fellow (IRE)**[12] 5866 2-8-12 73 ... DarryllHolland 12 (A P Jarvis) *swtg: a.p: led 2f out: veered lft and hdd over 1f out: rdn and hung lft after: kpt on: led fnl strides* **8/1**	75
5001	**2**	*nk*	**Mastership (IRE)**[31] 5482 2-8-4 65 ... (b) HayleyTurner 4 (C E Brittain) *lw: t.k.h: hld up: smooth hdwy on bit over 2f out: led over 1f out : sn rdn: idled wl ins fnl f: ct fnl strides* **12/1**	66
0333	**3**	*shd*	**Spiderback (IRE)**[12] 5866 2-8-9 70 ... (b) RichardHughes 5 (R Hannon) *lw: in tch: rdn over 2f out: squeezed out wl over 1f out: chalng whn bmpd ins fnl f: kpt on cl home* **9/2**[1]	71
053	**4**	1	**Sunley Peace**[11] 5892 2-8-13 74 ... LPKeniry 10 (D R C Elsworth) *chsd ldrs: rdn 2f out: sltly hmpd and swtchd lft over 1f out: styd on wl ins fnl f* **5/1**[2]	73
0131	**5**	½	**Celtic Step**[7] 5958 2-9-7 82 ... (b) JoeFanning 8 (M Johnston) *lw: racd freely: led: hdd 2f out: sn rdn: cl up whn bmpd jst ins fnl f: no ex* **5/1**[2]	80
1	**6**	¾	**Magic Echo**[11] 5898 2-8-12 73 ... PhillipMakin 2 (M Dods) *chsd ldrs: rdn over 2f out: kpt on same pce* **5/1**[2]	70
210	**7**	7	**Opera Crown (IRE)**[9] 5916 2-9-5 80 ... (b[1]) JimmyFortune 6 (P F I Cole) *chsd ldrs: rdn over 2f out: wknd fnl f* **15/2**[3]	63
003	**8**	9	**Breezeway (IRE)**[35] 5380 2-8-13 74 ... LDettori 1 (B J Meehan) *a towards rr* **8/1**	39
2200	**9**	13	**Al Raahi**[15] 5783 2-8-13 74 ... TonyCulhane 3 (M R Channon) *a towards rr* **20/1**	13
0040	**10**	*hd*	**Venir Rouge**[44] 5125 2-8-7 68 ... ChrisCatlin 7 (M Salaman) *chsd ldrs for 5f* **33/1**	6
3005	**11**	17	**Prince Of Charm (USA)**[25] 5585 2-7-12 59 ... (b[1]) JimmyQuinn 11 (P Mitchell) *a towards rr* **14/1**	—

1m 48.33s (7.71) **Going Correction** +0.925s/f (Soft) **11** Ran SP% **124.2**

Speed ratings (Par 97):98,97,97,96,96 95,88,79,66,66 49

CSF £105.70 CT £504.08 TOTE £10.70: £2.60, £3.50, £1.90; EX 94.20.

Owner Geoffrey Bishop and Ann Jarvis **Bred** Rathasker Stud **Trained** Twyford, Bucks

FOCUS

A messy finish to a real stamina test and the form not sure to work out.

NOTEBOOK

Bed Fellow(IRE) hung violently away from the stands'-side rail under pressure, causing chaos when getting over to the main pack. It is not the first time he has done this, as the jockey who rode him at Windsor last time was cautioned for something similar. Probably the best horse in the race on the day, he was allowed to keep the race but is obviously one to be wary of. The trainer suggested that he may try earplugs on the horse in the future. (op 15-2)

Mastership(IRE) ◆ was clear of the trouble that went on in the latter stages and only just got worried out of it close to the line after arriving there on the bit. It was a fine effort on vastly different ground than he won on last time, and he is progressing. He might be the sort to try on the Polytrack again over the winter. (tchd 14-1)

Spiderback(IRE) got bumped twice in the concertina effect caused by Bed Fellow and would have made it interesting for the Stewards had he managed to get runners-up spot, as it could easily be argued that he may have won the race without the interference he received. A race can be won with him soon. (op 6-1 tchd 13-2)

Sunley Peace ◆ was the first to be hampered by Bed Fellow's antics when staying on nicely. Once finding his stride again, he stuck to his task well and was a fast-finishing fourth. He seems sure to stay further and can make a nice handicapper next season. (op 4-1)

Celtic Step was much too keen in front but still went really close under his big weight. He received two hefty bumps when still in contention, despite looking tired, and was a bit unlucky not to have gone closer. A really tough sort in the mould of many of his stable companions, he looks like making a decent handicapper next season. (op 13-2)

Magic Echo was given a couple of bumps in the barging match that ensued to the side of her but cannot be called unlucky. She ran a decent race against the boys but did not see out the final furlong. (tchd 11-2)

Opera Crown(IRE), wearing first-time blinkers, faded tamely out of the picture from the two-furlong pole after racing towards the head of affairs early. Well clear of the seventh, it was a disappointing performance after a good effort last time and one can only conclude that he did not appreciate the blinkers being fitted. (op 8-1)

6107 RACINGPOST.CO.UK H'CAP 1m 2f 6y

4:50 (4:55) (Class 3) (0-95,95) 3-Y-O+

£8,724 (£2,612; £1,306; £653; £326; £163) **Stalls** Centre

Form	Pos	Btn	Horse	RPR
0620	**1**		**Best Prospect (IRE)**[15] 5787 4-8-11 85 ... (t) JamieSpencer 7 (M Dods) *lw: hld up towards rr: smooth hdwy fr 2f out: waited for gap bhd ldrs 1f out: sn eased into ld: comf* **9/1**	100+
1-30	**2**	2	**Red Admiral (USA)**[26] 5582 4-9-4 92 ... LDettori 1 (Saeed Bin Suroor) *lw: s.i.s: rcvrd to trck ldr after 2f: led 2f out: sn rdn: hdd ins fnl f: no ex* **13/2**[3]	98
3620	**3**	½	**Folio (IRE)**[15] 5787 6-8-11 85 ... PhilipRobinson 2 (W J Musson) *trckd ldrs: rdn and ev ch fr 2f out: no ex fnl 50yds* **10/1**	90
0000	**4**	*nk*	**Fortunate Isle (USA)**[21] 5678 4-8-12 86 ... MichaelHills 4 (B W Hills) *swtg: mid-div: hdwy over 2f out: rdn to chal over 1f out: kpt on same pce* **11/1**	91
1000	**5**	*nk*	**Public Forum**[59] 4713 4-9-7 95 ... RichardHughes 14 (Sir Michael Stoute) *lw: sn mid-div: rdn and hdwy over 2f out: hung lft 1f out: kpt on same pce* **5/1**[1]	99
6146	**6**	*hd*	**Resonate (IRE)**[27] 5548 8-8-7 81 oh2 ... FergusSweeney 13 (A G Newcombe) *hld up towards rr: hdwy over 2f out: continually hmpd and nt clr run tl ins fnl f: styd on but nvr able to chal* **16/1**	89+
0000	**7**	*shd*	**Silver Blue (IRE)**[5] 6017 3-8-2 81 oh1 ... (b) FrancisNorton 10 (R Hannon) *lw: in tch: effrt 2f out: kpt on same pce ins fnl f* **25/1**	84
31-	**8**	2	**Austrian (UAE)**[378] 5748 3-9-2 95 ... RobertWinston 3 (Saeed Bin Suroor) *lw: t.k.h trcking ldrs: rdn 2f out: sn one pce* **8/1**	95
1005	**9**	½	**Layazaal (IRE)**[22] 5660 3-9-0 93 ... SteveDrowne 12 (J L Dunlop) *towards rr: sme hdwy over 2f out: nvr a factor* **12/1**	92
0015	**10**	½	**Krugerrand (USA)**[15] 5787 7-8-11 88 ... StephenDonohoe(3) 15 (W J Musson) *swtg: hld up towards rr: rdn and hdwy into mid-div 2f out: no further imp* **12/1**	86
1-6	**11**	1¼	**Shelhom**[13] 5845 3-9-0 93 ... RichardMullen 5 (Saeed Bin Suroor) *mid-div: rdn to chse ldrs whn squeezed up 1f out: one pce after* **25/1**	89
4010	**12**	4	**Punta Galera (IRE)**[28] 5530 3-8-8 87 ... (b) RyanMoore 6 (R Hannon) *led tl 2f out: sn rdn: hld whn hmpd 1f out* **25/1**	76
4160	**13**	3	**Inchloch**[29] 5505 4-8-12 86 ... KDarley 11 (B G Powell) *towards rr: hdwy on inner over 5f out: wknd over 1f out* **16/1**	69
3003	**14**	1¾	**Spear Thistle**[21] 5678 4-8-4 81 oh1 ... JamesDoyle(3) 9 (Mrs N Smith) *trckd ldrs: rdn over 2f out: fading whn bdly hmpd wl over 1f out* **11/2**[2]	61

52/0 **15** *15* **Fantasy Ride**[22] 5657 4-9-2 **90** .... JimmyQuinn 19 43
(J Pearce) *a towards rr* **33/1**

2m 14.72s (6.01) **Going Correction** +0.825s/f (Soft)
WFA 3 from 4yo+ 5lb **15** Ran SP% **125.5**
Speed ratings (Par 107): 108,106,106,105,105 105,105,103,103,102 101,98,96,94,82
CSF £66.05 CT £616.40 TOTE £13.90: £3.90, £2.10, £4.40; EX 97.90.

Owner D Neale **Bred** Farmers Hill Stud **Trained** Denton, Co Durham

FOCUS
A strong and competitive handicap that had its share of scrimmaging. A couple looked unlucky, none more so than Resonate, a nd the form may not be totally reliable.

NOTEBOOK
Best Prospect(IRE) came home a very easy winner under an ultra-confident ride. Scything between his rivals inside the final two furlongs, Spencer never got serious with him at any stage and they came home at their leisure. The Handicapper will not be very impressed by the manner of his victory, so he can expect a reasonable rise in the weights for the success. Official explanation: trainer said, regarding apparent improvement in form, gelding was poorly drawn previously at York, and was suited by the tactics employed here (op 11-1)

Red Admiral(USA) ran a solid race under his big weight but had little chance against the winner. His proven stamina over further undoubtedly helped him in such a strong race. (tchd 6-1 and 7-1)

Folio(IRE) was never far from the leaders and kept on in good fashion under pressure. He is much too high in the weights to have an obvious winning chance, which is mainly due to his consistency since his last success, so this performance will not help him drop down the ratings, making his life very difficult in competitive handicaps.

Fortunate Isle(USA) found the drop back to ten furlongs much more to his liking and battled on well under pressure. He has become nicely handicapped again after a spell in the wilderness. (op 9-1)

Public Forum, who is usually strong in the market wherever he runs, ran somewhere close to his best after a few indifferent efforts during the season. He could do with coming down the weights a couple of pounds to make him really interesting next time. (op 4-1)

Resonate(IRE) met all sorts of trouble when making his bid for victory, and can certainly be rated somewhere close to the runner-up. He is a bit high in the weights to have an obvious chance of winning, but he does seems more than capable of going close off his current mark and could not be ruled out next time with any confidence. Official explanation: jockey said horse was denied a clear run (op 14-1)

Silver Blue(IRE) ◆ is steadily coming back to form, which coincides with the blinkers being fitted, and is extremely well handicapped if maintaining his current level of form. He looks poised to strike. (tchd 33-1)

Austrian(UAE) ◆ caught the eye just behind the leaders and was not given an overly hard time in the final furlong. It was his first run for a very long time and, as long as he does not go the wrong way after such a fine effort, can go very close next time. (tchd 9-1)

Layazaal(IRE) is a bit better than his final position suggests, as he had to come around the field to make his challenge after being held up. (op 16-1)

Krugerrand(USA) needs coaxing into a race and did not find a great deal off the bridle when asked to challenge. He is the sort of horse who probably enjoys coming through a field rather than down the outside of it.

Spear Thistle was a big disappointment on a course he often runs well at, and was already losing ground when hampered. (op 6-1 tchd 13-2)

6108 STANJAMESUK.COM LADY JOCKEYS' CHAMPIONSHIP H'CAP 1m 4f 5y

5:20 (5:21) (Class 5) (0-75,75) 3-Y-0+ **£4,996** (£1,549; £774; £387) **Stalls** Centre

Form RPR

5403 **1** **Great View (IRE)**[21] 5671 7-10-7 **72** ....(p) MissLEllison 19 83
(Mrs A L M King) *lw: chsd ldr: led 4f out: clr over 2f out: rdn over 1f out: all out* **9/1**

4022 **2** *½* **Acknowledgement**[24] 5628 4-10-2 **67** ....(b) MissSBrotherton 12 77
(D R C Elsworth) *lw: hld up towards rr: stdy prog fr 4f out: chsd wnr 2f out: rdn over 1f out: styd on strly cl home* **13/2**[2]

6255 **3** *11* **Cormorant Wharf (IRE)**[40] 5236 6-9-13 **69** ow1........ MissJPowell(5) 11 63
(G L Moore) *hld up bhd: stdy prog fr over 4f out: styd on: nt rch ldrs* **10/1**

3150 **4** *hd* **Lake Wakatipu**[18] 5750 4-9-5 **61** oh3.................... MissMMullineaux(5) 3 54
(M Mullineaux) *s.i.s: bhd: stdy hdwy fr over 4f out: styd on: nvr trbld ldrs* **20/1**

6255 **5** *1 ¼* **Duroob**[14] 5815 4-9-5 **61** .... MissKellyBurke(5) 18 53
(K R Burke) *chsd ldr: drew clr wth wnr 4f out: lost 2nd 2f out: wknd fnl f* **8/1**

5353 **6** *1 ¾* **Kylkenny**[8] 5946 11-9-5 **61** ....(t) MissVCartmel(5) 5 50
(H Morrison) *lw: towards rr: styd on past btn horses fr 2f out: n.d* **12/1**

5066 **7** *1 ¾* **Free To Air**[25] 5594 3-9-10 **75** .... MissCAllen(7) 2 61
(A M Balding) *s.i.s: towards rr: styd on past btn horses fr 2f out: n.d* **10/1**

0000 **8** *1 ½* **Hills Of Aran**[19] 5723 4-9-9 **65** ....(b) MissJodieHughes(5) 15 49
(W K Goldsworthy) *led tl 4f out: grad fdd* **33/1**

0560 **9** *shd* **Berkhamsted (IRE)**[14] 5815 4-10-0 **70** .... MissMSowerby(5) 16 54
(Tom Dascombe) *chsd ldrs tl over 3f out* **14/1**

056- **10** *1 ¼* **Sole Agent (IRE)**[205] 5973 4-9-6 **62** ....(b[1]) MissHayleyMoore(5) 6 44
(G L Moore) *in tch tl wknd over 2f out* **12/1**

-232 **11** *4* **Mantle**[19] 5741 4-10-7 **72** .... MrsSBosley 20 48
(J R Fanshawe) *in tch: rdn over 3f out: grad wknd* **7/1**[3]

1213 **12** *4* **Champagne Shadow (IRE)**[52] 4935 5-9-9 **65** .... MissARyan(5) 17 35
(K A Ryan) *a towards rr* **9/2**[1]

0000 **13** *7* **Isa'Af (IRE)**[8] 5952 7-9-9 **65** .... MrsMarieKing(5) 13 25
(P W Hiatt) *mid-div tl wknd over 3f out* **20/1**

/005 **14** *2* **Sea Holly (IRE)**[46] 5090 6-9-8 **66** oh2 ow5........... MissKMargarson(7) 10 23
(G G Margarson) *in tch tl wknd over 3f out* **33/1**

300/ **15** *½* **Time To Shine**[175] 1282 7-9-4 **62** oh2 ow1............... MissSSawyer(7) 14 18
(Mrs L J Mongan) *bhd fnl 5f* **33/1**

3364 **16** *4* **Alexian**[119] 2882 3-9-0 **65** .... MissBKilloran(7) 1 15
(D W P Arbuthnot) *towards rr: t.k.h and advanced into mid-div 7f out: wknd over 3f out* **18/1**

2m 45.43s (9.44) **Going Correction** +0.825s/f (Soft)
WFA 3 from 4yo+ 7lb **16** Ran SP% **129.0**
Speed ratings (Par 103): 101,100,93,93,92 91,90,89,88,88 85,82,78,76,76 73
CSF £65.98 CT £612.58 TOTE £10.50: £2.30, £1.80, £3.00, £5.90; EX 61.80 Place 6 £2,287.05, Place 5 £1,333.15.

Owner All The Kings Horses **Bred** Terry McGrath **Trained** Wilmcote, Warwicks

FOCUS
Not a very good race, made less competitive by some ordinary riding performances. The winner sets the standard.

Champagne Shadow(IRE) Official explanation: jockey said gelding was unsuited by the heavy ground

T/Jkpt: Not won. T/Plt: £2,404.70 to a £1 stake. Pool: £140,825.91. 42.75 winning tickets. T/Qpdt: £325.90 to a £1 stake. Pool: £5,198.00. 11.80 winning tickets. TM

6092 BADEN-BADEN (L-H)

Saturday, October 21

OFFICIAL GOING: Soft

6109a HEEL - BADEN-WURTTEMBERG-TROPHY (GROUP 3) 1m 3f

3:35 (3:44) 3-Y-0+ **£24,138** (£10,345; £4,138; £2,759)

RPR

1 **Simonas (IRE)**[20] 5718 7-9-0 .... EPedroza 13 108
(A Wohler, Germany) *held up, running on and 7th straight, good headway 1 1/2f out to lead 150 yards out, ran on well* **17/2**

2 *¾* **Mohandas (FR)**[29] 5519 5-9-2 .... THellier 7 109
(W Hefter, Germany) *in touch, 4th straight, ran on 1 1/2f out to lead briefly 1f out to 150 yards out, ran on* **43/10**[2]

3 *½* **Kiton (GER)**[83] 3992 5-9-2 .... TMundry 2 108
(P Rau, Germany) *mid-division, finished well from over 1f out, nearest at finish* **131/10**

4 *3* **Chiron (GER)**[146] 2061 5-9-0 .... ABoschert 1 101
(Dr A Bolte, Germany) *close up, 2nd straight, led 2f out, ridden and ran on, headed 1f out, one pace* **23/1**

5 *hd* **Soterio (GER)**[12] 5881 6-9-0 ....(b) JVictoire 12 101
(W Baltromei, Germany) *mid-division, shaken up approaching straight, kept on steadily* **20/1**

6 *¾* **White Lightning (GER)**[18] 5762 4-9-4 .... RJuracek 4 104
(U Stech, Norway) *in touch, effort 2f out, kept on but never in challenging position* **105/10**

7 *hd* **Storm Trooper (GER)**[22] 5657 6-9-0 .... WMongil 5 100
(P Schiergen, Germany) *never better than mid-division* **171/10**

8 *1* **Brisant (GER)**[27] 5561 4-9-0 .... AHelfenbein 9 98
(M Trybuhl, Germany) *held up, effort on outside 2f out, no extra inside final furlong* **68/10**[3]

9 *nse* **Glavalcour (FR)**[174] 6-9-0 .... OPlacais 3 98
(K Schafflutzel, Switzerland) *led, driven straight, headed 2f out, no extra under pressure* **119/10**

10 *3 ½* **Spatzolita (GER)**[13] 5857 7-8-9 ....(b) J-PCarvalho 8 87
(D K Richardson, Germany) *mid-division, never a threat* **24/1**

11 *1 ¾* **Dwilano (GER)**[18] 5762 3-8-7 .... WPanov 11 88
(P Remmert, Germany) *held up, never a threat* **151/10**

12 *½* **Bailamos (GER)**[34] 5414 6-9-2 .... AStarke 10 91
(H Hesse, Germany) *mid-division, ridden 2f out, no impression* **27/10**[1]

13 *7* **Inter Mondo (GER)**[20] 5718 3-8-7 .... FilipMinarik 6 76
(P Rau, Germany) *prominent, 5th straight, one pace final 1 1/2f* **7/1**

2m 22.1s
WFA 3 from 4yo+ 6lb **13** Ran SP% **129.9**
(Including 10 Euros stake): WIN 95; PL 34, 21, 32; SF 855.
Owner Gary A Tanaka **Bred** Gestut Rottgen **Trained** Germany

5544 CAULFIELD (R-H)

Saturday, October 21

OFFICIAL GOING: Good

6110a BMW CAULFIELD CUP (GROUP 1) (H'CAP) 1m 4f

7:00 (7:00) 3-Y-0+

£647,436 (£160,256; £85,470; £47,009; £38,462; £32,051)

RPR

1 **Tawqeet (USA)**[14] 5-8-6 .... DDunn 3 117
(D Hayes, Australia)

2 *nk* **Aqua D'Amore (AUS)**[14] 4-8-3 .... SBaster 4 113
(Mrs Gai Waterhouse, Australia)

3 *nk* **Delta Blues (JPN)**[174] 1329 5-8-11 .... NashRawiller 17 121
(Katsuhiko Sumii, Japan)

4 *hd* **Activation (NZ)**[14] 5-8-5 .... MRodd 5 115
(G Rogerson, Australia)

5 *nk* **Sphenophyta (NZ)**[14] 6-7-12 .... DNikolic 8 107
(Lee Freedman, Australia)

6 *shd* **Our Smoking Joe (AUS)**[14] 6-8-8 .... JimCassidy 2 117
(Lee Freedman, Australia)

7 *shd* **Pop Rock (JPN)** 5-8-5 .... DMOliver 11 114
(Katsuhiko Sumii, Japan)

8 *snk* **Dizelle (AUS)**[14] 5-8-3 .... BShinn 20 112
(J Hawkes, Australia)

9 *1* **Serenade Rose (AUS)**[14] 4-8-4 .... StevenKing 15 111
(Lee Freedman, Australia)

10 *1 ½* **Railings (AUS)**[14] 5-8-10 .... GChilds 7 115
(J Hawkes, Australia)

11 *shd* **Grand Zulu (AUS)**[7] 5-8-6 ....(b) KerrinMcEvoy 12 111
(J Size, Hong Kong)

12 *shd* **Zipping (AUS)**[14] 5-8-4 .... GBoss 21 109
(G Rogerson, Australia)

13 *½* **Growl (NZ)** 4-7-10 .... CraigAWilliams 9 100
(D Hayes, Australia)

14 *3 ¼* **Headturner (AUS)**[14] 4-8-7 .... DBeadman 18 106
(J Hawkes, Australia)

15 *¾* **Ice Chariot (AUS)**[133] 4-8-3 ....(b) JByrne 19 108
(R Maund, Australia)

16 *2 ¼* **Roman Arch (AUS)**[7] 7-8-9 ....(b) NCallow 10 104
(R Laing, Australia)

17 *2 ¾* **Short Pause**[14] 7-8-6 .... MZahra 6 96
(D Hayes, Australia)

18 *1 ¾* **Land 'n Stars**[79] 4081 6-8-5 .... NicholasRyan 16 93
(Jamie Poulton) *broke in tch but was caught three wd in rr third of field 8l off ld, rdn 4f out, dropped to last appr str, sn btn* **100/1**[1]

2m 27.69s
WFA 3 from 4yo+ 7lb **18** Ran SP% **1.0**
SP's: 16-1, 30-1, 80-1, 7-1 (Sphenophyta 34-10F).
Owner Shadwell Australia Ltd Syndicate **Bred** 6 C Stallions Limited **Trained** Australia

FOCUS
A mess of a race, in which many of the field seemed to be given rides with Flemington in mind. There were any amount of eyecatching performances, and it would be no surprise if the Melbourne Cup winner is somewhere in the field.

NOTEBOOK

Tawqeet(USA), who was trained by John Dunlop last season and finished third in the St Leger, has continued his improvement out in Australia and now heads the market for the Melbourne Cup in early November. Travelling really well into the straight, the jockey seemed to have nowhere to go until a gap opened and, once in the clear, won in good style. He has to prove he stays two miles, which is not guarenteed, but he is in terrific form. It should also be noted that he was wearing headgear and picks up a 2kg penalty for Flemington, after already picking up a 1kg penalty for winning the Metropolitan Handicap last time.

Aqua D'Amore(AUS) has been in fine form in recent months but had no chance against the winner as he rushed by him late on. He led for almost all of the straight but had nothing left to hold off the winner. A couple behind him would have run him close for second with clearer runs.

Delta Blues(JPN) looked a bit unlucky and would have given the winner plenty to think about with a clear run. Winner of the Japanese St Leger in 2004, the Melbourne Cup trip of two miles will hold no fears for him, but the trainer has stated that a rider from Japan will take the ride in the big race, which could hinder his chance in such a rough race.

Activation(NZ) must be getting sick of the sight of Tawqeet, as he finished behind him in the Metropolitan Handicap previously, but yet again showed clear signs of being a leading contender for the Melbourne Cup. Whilst not proven at two miles, it looks like the extended trip will suit him and he can go close at Flemington.

Sphenophyta(NZ), a Group 1 winner in his own right, always gives his all and ran a sound race. He did not catch the eye in the way some of the others did, however.

Our Smoking Joe(AUS) was right there with a furlong to go but got swallowed up by the closing pack. Narrowly beaten by Sphenophyta last time in Group 1 company, his chance is not as obvious as some others for Melbourne in a couple of weeks.

Pop Rock(JPN) was not given the most positive of rides. Not looking to get involved at any stage, he came home really strongly and appeared to have plenty in the locker at the end of the race. With a more forceful ride, he must be a leading contender at Flemington.

Dizelle(AUS) finished nicely from off the pace and did not seem to be given a really hard time by her jockey. Fillies and mares have run well in the Melbourne Cup, and it would be no surprise to see this former Australian Oaks winner go much closer in this year's renewal than in 2005.

Serenade Rose(AUS), another in the race to land the Australian Oaks, has been running reasonable well during the season but was one of the only horses weakening late on. She was retired after the race.

Railings(AUS) was finishing quite well behind the leaders after getting outpaced on the final bend. It would be no great surprise to see him run well over half a mile further in the Cup.

Grand Zulu(AUS) was badly hampered when making his challenge and can be rated a bit better than his finishing position suggests.

Zipping(AUS), who was ridden by the jockey who enjoyed so much success on Makybe Diva, finished strongly down the middle of the track, but was never in the hunt. One suspects he is better than he showed.

6111 - 6112a (Foreign Racing) - See Raceform Interactive

5848 CURRAGH (R-H)

Sunday, October 22

OFFICIAL GOING: Round course - soft to heavy; straight course - heavy

6113a LANWADES & STAFFORDSTOWN STUDS SILKEN GLIDER STKS (LISTED RACE) (FILLIES) — 1m

3:00 (3:00) 2-Y-O — **£24,693** (£7,244; £2,313; £2,313)

Pos	Dist	Horse	Jockey	RPR
1		**Boca Dancer (IRE)**[8] 5981 2-8-12 (Kevin Prendergast, Ire) *trckd ldrs in 5th: smooth hdwy over 2f out: led over 1f out: rdn clr: easily* **7/4**[2]	DPMcDonogh 4	100+
2	3 1/2	**Sensible Lady**[22] 5695 2-8-12 (C Collins, Ire) *hld up: 6th and pushed along 1/2-way: 7th u.p early st: mod 5th 1f out: styd on to go 2nd nr fin* **7/1**	PShanahan 7	93
3	1/2	**La Conquistadora**[16] 5798 2-8-12 (J S Bolger, Ire) *trckd ldrs in 4th: 3rd 1/2-way: cl 2nd and chal 2f out: no imp fr over 1f out: kpt on same pce* **6/4**[1]	KJManning 6	92
3	dht	**Essexford (IRE)**[21] 5707 2-8-12 89 (John M Oxx, Ire) *settled 2nd: chal st: led over 2f out: sn strly pressed: hdd over 1f out: kpt on same pce* **13/2**[3]	FMBerry 3	92
5	3/4	**Amusing (IRE)**[16] 5797 2-8-12 78 (John Joseph Murphy, Ire) *settled 3rd: 4th 1/2-way: rdn st: kpt on same pce u.p fr over 1f out* **33/1**	WSupple 8	91?
6	1 1/4	**Hugs 'n Kisses (IRE)**[7] 5994 2-8-12 (John Joseph Murphy, Ire) *a towards rr: no imp st* **66/1**	DMGrant 1	88?
7	3 1/2	**Air Twist (IRE)**[182] 1168 2-8-12 (Edward Lynam, Ire) *hld up: 6th and effrt ent st: no ex fr 1 1/2f out* **16/1**	CDHayes 2	81
8	9	**Uluru (IRE)**[5] 6041 2-8-12 (A P O'Brien, Ire) *sn led: rdn st: hdd 2f out: no ex whn eased ins fnl f* **25/1**	JAHeffernan 5	63

1m 45.8s **Going Correction** +0.60s/f (Yiel) — **8** Ran SP% **116.4**

Speed ratings: 105,101,101,101,100 99,95,86

CSF £14.61 TOTE £2.30: £1.70, £1.60, £1.70; DF 15.90 TRIFECTA PL: Essexford 0.70; La Conquistadora 0.70.

Owner Cathal M Ryan **Bred** Swordlestown Stud **Trained** Friarstown, Co Kildare

NOTEBOOK

Boca Dancer(IRE) ◆, off the mark on her debut in a seven-furlong maiden at Cork, showed improved form stepped up in grade and trip and ran out an impressive winner. She looks a smart prospect. (op 6/4)

Sensible Lady would have found this much tougher than the seven-furlong Fairyhouse maiden she won on her previous start, but ran well and picked up some valuable black type. (op 8/1)

La Conquistadora looked a good prospect when winning a mile maiden at Gowran on her previous start, but failed to build on that on this step up to Listed company and was a touch disappointing. (op 9/2)

Essexford(IRE), fourth of five in an extended seven-furlong Listed race at Tipperary on her previous start, managed to pick up some black type this time. (op 9/2)

6114 - 6118a (Foreign Racing) - See Raceform Interactive

5999 LONGCHAMP (R-H)

Sunday, October 22

OFFICIAL GOING: Good

6119a PRIX ROYAL-OAK (GROUP 1) — 1m 7f 110y

3:10 (3:09) 3-Y-0+ — **£98,517** (£39,414; £19,707; £9,845; £4,931)

Pos	Dist	Horse	Jockey	RPR
1		**Montare (IRE)**[22] 5702 4-9-1 (J E Pease, France) *mid-division, 6th straight, headway on outside 1 1/2f out, driven to lead 100yds out, ran on* **58/10**	(p) OPeslier 6	116+
2	snk	**Bellamy Cay**[56] 4861 4-9-4 (A Fabre, France) *disputed 4th, 4th straight, every chance 100yds out, unable to quicken closing stages* **67/10**	SPasquier 10	118
3	1	**Sergeant Cecil**[21] 5711 7-9-4 (B R Millman) *held up in rear, 8th straight, still 7th inside final f, ran on to take 3rd close home* **27/10**[2]	RyanMoore 1	117+
4	3/4	**Lord Du Sud (FR)**[63] 4647 5-9-4 (J-C Rouget, France) *led after 2f, headed 100yds out, lost 3rd close home* **21/10**[1]	IMendizabal 9	116
5	1/2	**Rising Cross**[22] 5702 3-8-6 (J R Best) *disputed 4th, 5th straight, hard ridden 2f out, kept on same pace* **36/1**	MartinDwyer 3	114
6	2	**Loup De Mer (GER)**[16] 4-9-4 (W Baltromei, Germany) *towards rear, last straight, stayed on final furlong but never a factor* **25/1**	DBoeuf 8	114?
7	hd	**Shamdala (IRE)**[21] 5711 4-9-1 (A De Royer-Dupre, France) *held up, 7th straight, headway on inside 2f out, stayed on under pressure to dispute 4th approaching final f, no extra* **42/10**[3]	CSoumillon 5	111
8	3/4	**Soledad (IRE)**[42] 5223 6-9-4 (G Cherel, France) *led 2f, 3rd straight, weakened approaching final f* **33/1**	FSpanu 2	113
9	4	**Petite Speciale (USA)**[21] 5711 7-9-1 (E Lecoiffier, France) *held up in rear, 9th straight, never a factor* **30/1**	TJarnet 11	106
10	15	**Frank Sonata**[14] 5854 5-9-4 (M G Quinlan) *prominent, went 2nd one mile out, ridden approaching straight, weakened 2f out* **29/1**	TPQueally 7	94

3m 20.3s **Going Correction** -0.05s/f (Good)

WFA 3 from 4yo+ 9lb — **10** Ran SP% **122.3**

Speed ratings: 113,112,112,112,111 110,110,110,108,100

PARI-MUTUEL: WIN 6.80; PL 2.10, 2.60, 1.80; DF 16.70.

Owner George Strawbridge **Bred** George Strawbridge **Trained** Chantilly, France

NOTEBOOK

Montare(IRE) gained her first success at the highest level, fully justifying the decision to keep her in training as a four-year-old. She was being niggled along before the straight and was slightly hampered on two occasions, but that could not stop from quickening well from one and a half out. She is likely to remain in training again next year and could be adding to her Group 1 haul.

Bellamy Cay, on this better ground, ran right up to expectations and was just held. Placed just behind the leaders for much of the way, he began to make his move running into the last two furlongs and looked the likeliest winner a furlong out, but he was just edged out of it close home. He stays in training and one of his main targets will be the Ascot Gold Cup.

Sergeant Cecil, the Prix du Cadran winner, ran a fine race in defeat. Dropped out in last place for much of the way, he still had plenty to do in the straight and did not really engage top gear until the final furlong, running on strongly but just too late. His jockey felt that, having switched off due to a lack of early pace, he hit a flat spot in the straight. Next season his main targets are likely to include the Ascot Gold Cup and a repeat bid in the Cadran.

Lord Du Sud(FR)'s connections feel he goes on any ground, but this was probably a bit quicker than he likes. Having set out to make all the running at a reasonable pace, he quickened in the straight to hold the advantage a furlong and a half out and kept on well to the line. He is likely to be kept in training as a six-year-old.

Rising Cross put up an honourable performance and was beaten just over a couple of lengths into fifth. She was the only three-year-old in the race and emerges with real credit. She is another who will remain in training next year.

Frank Sonata was given every chance but proved disappointing. He was still there at the top of the straight, but dropped out of contention to finally finish in last place and was finally beaten 25 lengths by the winner.

6109 BADEN-BADEN (L-H)

Sunday, October 22

OFFICIAL GOING: Soft

6121a FLIEGER-PREIS (LISTED RACE) — 5f

1:10 (1:17) 3-Y-O+ — **£12,414** (£5,172; £2,069; £1,034)

Pos	Dist	Horse	Jockey	RPR
1		**Fantastica (GER)**[175] 1328 3-8-7 (U Ostmann, Germany)	ABoschert 2	101
2	1/2	**Omasheriff (IRE)**[56] 4858 4-8-11 (W Baltromei, Germany)	JVictoire 1	103
3	1/2	**Fulminant (IRE)**[344] 5-8-11 (W Kujath, Germany)	(b) AHelfenbein 12	101
4	3/4	**World's Mission (GER)**[161] 1715 3-8-11 (Mario Hofer, Germany)	J-PCarvalho 6	99
5	1 1/4	**Sidonius (GER)**[460] 7-8-11 (P Vovcenko, Germany)	(b) LHammer-Hansen 9	94
6	1 3/4	**Portmeirion**[35] 5405 5-8-7 (S C Williams) *mid-division, 7th straight, came stands side, ridden 1 1/2f out, never nearer SP 72-10* **72/10**[1]	FilipMinarik 11	84
7	1/2	**Austrian (GER)**[70] 4418 5-8-11 (M Sowa, Germany)	THellier 3	86
8	1 3/4	**The Yellow (GER)**[400] 3-8-7 (M Sowa, Germany)	WPanov 5	76
9	1 1/4	**De Boxter (FR)**[17] 6-8-11 (A Trybuhl, Germany)	ADeVries 13	75
10	1 3/4	**Lavarone (ARG)** 3-8-11 (Diego Lowther, France)	TMundry 7	69
11	1/2	**Aristaios (GER)**[841] 3552 5-8-11 (Bruce Hellier, Germany)	J-LSilverio 8	67
12	1/2	**Tiberius Caesar (FR)**[56] 4864 6-8-11 (F Reuterskiold, Sweden)	AStarke 4	65
13	2	**Mike Stone**[245] 455 6-8-11 (F Fuhrmann)	ABest 10	58

59.74 secs — **13** Ran SP% **12.2**

(Including 10 Euros stake): WIN 56; PL 16, 22, 18; SF 314.

Owner Stall Dipoli **Bred** Saturn Stable **Trained** Germany

NOTEBOOK

Portmeirion had been running well in ordinary Listed company in her homeland lately and this was a respectable effort.

6122a PREIS DER WINTERKONIGIN (GROUP 3) (FILLIES) — 1m
3:35 (3:54) 2-Y-O

£41,379 (£15,862; £7,586; £4,138; £2,069; £1,379)

RPR

1 **Shane (GER)** 2-9-0 .... AHelfenbein 7 — 98
(Andreas Lowe, Germany) *mid-div, hdwy appr str, 3rd str, qcknd to chal 1 1/2f out, led jst ins fnl f, ran on wl* **11/2**[3]

2 *2 1/2* **Touch My Soul (FR)** 2-9-0 .... AStarke 12 — 93
(P Schiergen, Germany) *held up, effort 2f out, ran on to challenge approaching final furlong, kept on but not pace of winner* **18/10**[1]

3 *1 3/4* **Hashbrown (GER)** 2-9-0 .... WPanov 8 — 89
(C Sprengel, Germany) *in touch, 6th and driven straight, ran on from 1 1/2f out, went 3rd inside last* **39/1**

4 *1* **Pakama (GER)**[19] [5763] 2-9-0 .... J-PCarvalho 9 — 87
(Mario Hofer, Germany) *towards rear, stayed on well from 1 1/2f out, nearest at finish* **22/1**

5 *3* **Laeya Star (GER)** 2-9-0 .... ABoschert 11 — 81
(U Ostmann, Germany) *close up, 5th straight, stayed on same pace* **23/1**

6 *nk* **Sybilia (GER)** 2-9-0 .... THellier 2 — 80
(Mario Hofer, Germany) *prom and running freely early, led appr str, joined 1 1/2f out, hdd just ins fnl f, wknd* **22/10**[2]

7 *2 1/2* **Naomia (GER)** 2-9-0 .... TMundry 10 — 75
(P Rau, Germany) *towards rear, on inside, shaken up 2f out, never in challenging position* **137/10**

8 *1 3/4* **Foreign Music (FR)** 2-9-0 .... LHammer-Hansen 5 — 72
(H J Groschel, Germany) *held up, pushed along 3f out, never dangerous* **30/1**

9 *12* **Pacific Sun (GER)** 2-9-0 .... HGrewe 1 — 48
(P Rau, Germany) *led to approaching straight, 4th straight, one pace from over 1f out* **56/1**

10 *1 1/4* **Sasphee (GER)**[96] 2-9-0 .... JVictoire 3 — 45
(E Kurdu, Germany) *never better than mid-division* **15/1**

11 *2* **Sternenkonigin (IRE)** 2-9-0 .... FilipMinarik 6 — 41
(W Hickst, Germany) *in touch, ridden on outside entering straight, unable to quicken* **145/10**

12 *6* **Desabina (GER)** 2-9-0 .... ADeVries 4 — 29
(H Blume, Germany) *towards rear, never dangerous* **72/10**

1m 41.63s — **12** Ran SP% **130.0**
WIN 65; PL 21, 20, 65; SF 277.
Owner U Zerrath **Bred** Gestut Schaffauer - Hof - Granum Zucht **Trained** Germany

5473 CAPANNELLE (R-H)
Sunday, October 22

OFFICIAL GOING: Heavy

6123a PREMIO GUIDO BERARDELLI (GROUP 3) — 1m 1f
3:10 (3:31) 2-Y-O £33,703 (£15,657; £8,534; £4,392)

RPR

1 **Il Cadetto** 2-8-11 .... DBonilla 7 — 105
(L Di Dio, Italy) *in touch, 5th straight, progress 3f out, ran on to lead 2f out, ridden and ran on well to go clear final furlong, easily* **52/10**[2]

2 *5 1/2* **Rob's Love (ITY)** 2-8-11 .... LDettori 3 — 94
(R Menichetti, Italy) *trckd ldr til led approaching straight, ridden 3f out, headed 2f out, ran on under pressure but lost 2nd close home* **9/10**[1]

3 *hd* **Next King (ITY)** 2-8-11 .... EBotti 1 — 94
(A Botti, Italy) *led to appr str, pushed along 3 1/2f out, ev ch 2f out, hard rdn and stayed on fnl f to tk 2nd cl home* **59/10**

4 *1 1/2* **Lucky Choice (ITY)** 2-8-11 ....(b) FBranca 14 — 91
(A Candi, Italy) *held up, pushed along and headway straight, ridden 2 1/2f out, ran on steadily, nearest at finish* **33/1**

5 *1* **Sopran Promo (IRE)**[18] [5771] 2-8-11 .... DVargiu 5 — 89
(B Grizzetti, Italy) *mid-division, ridden and headway 2f out, nearest at finish* **81/10**

6 *2 1/2* **Koening (ITY)** 2-8-11 .... SLandi 13 — 84
(L Camici, Italy) *towards rear, driven 2f out, stayed on final stages* **52/10**[2]

7 *1* **Selmis** 2-8-11 .... MEsposito 4 — 82
(V Caruso, Italy) *mid-division, some late headway* **78/10**

8 *6* **Cottonmouth (IRE)** 2-8-8 .... MMonteriso 9 — 67
(A Botti, Italy) *mid-division, effort and some progress straight, one pace final 2f* **14/1**

9 *1/2* **Ancus Martius (FR)** 2-8-11 .... MDemuro 8 — 69
(R Biondi, Italy) *held up, pushed along straight, never dangerous* **54/10**[3]

10 *1 1/4* **Jade Hill (IRE)** 2-8-11 .... GMarcelli 6 — 66
(L Riccardi, Italy) *prominent, 3rd straight, ridden and outpaced from 3f out* **127/1**

11 *11* **Golden Event (USA)** 2-8-11 .... MTellini 11 — 44
(M Fratini, Italy) *towards rear, last straight, never dangerous* **32/1**

12 *1 1/2* **Golden Rob'S (IRE)** 2-8-11 .... PBorrelli 12 — 41
(G Di Chio, Italy) *held up, never dangerous* **24/1**

13 *nk* **Danao (USA)** 2-8-11 .... CFiocchi 10 — 41
(R Menichetti, Italy) *in touch, 7th straight, soon driven along, one pace* **9/10**[1]

1m 55.6s — **13** Ran SP% **207.4**
(Including 1 Euro stake): WIN 6.20 (coupled with Koening); PL 2.30, 1.32, 1.69; DF 8.48.
Owner L Colasanti **Bred** Jock Strap Partners **Trained** Italy

6124a PREMIO LYDIA TESIO (GROUP 1) (F&M) — 1m 2f
3:40 (4:05) 3-Y-O+ £95,421 (£45,910; £26,193; £13,097)

RPR

1 **Floriot (IRE)**[140] [2280] 4-9-0 .... KKerekes 9 — 117
(Werner Glanz, Germany) *held up, last straight, headway on stands side 2f out, led just inside final furlong, ran on well* **123/10**

2 *1 1/4* **Confidential Lady**[8] [5964] 3-8-10 .... SebSanders 11 — 116
(Sir Mark Prescott) *disputed 3rd, 4th straight, driven to lead briefly approaching final furlong, ran on* **17/10**[2]

3 *1 1/2* **Musical Way (FR)**[30] [5519] 4-9-0 .... RonanThomas 7 — 112
(P Van De Poele, France) *mid-division, 6th straight, headway towards far side 2f out, kept on same pace final furlong* **21/2**

4 *2 1/2* **Time On**[42] [5220] 3-8-10 .... TedDurcan 1 — 109
(J L Dunlop) *led til approaching final furlong, one pace* **15/2**

5 *2* **Pictavia (IRE)**[42] [5204] 4-9-0 .... LDettori 10 — 104
(Saeed Bin Suroor) *pressed leader, 2nd straight, hard ridden well over 1f out, soon beaten* **16/10**[1]

6 *snk* **Acts Of Grace (USA)**[30] [5502] 3-8-10 .... DBonilla 4 — 105
(J L Dunlop) *held up in rear, 10th straight, headway on outside over 3f out, one pace final 2f* **67/10**

7 *5* **Hands Clean (IRE)**[127] [2671] 3-8-10 .... FBranca 3 — 96
(A Candi, Italy) *held up, last at half-way, headway on inside and 8th straight, beaten 2f out* **43/1**

8 *5* **Opatja**[140] [2280] 4-9-0 .... SLandi 6 — 86
(L Camici, Italy) *mid-division to half-way,9th straight & behind final 2f* **84/1**

9 *shd* **La Vriga**[140] [2280] 5-9-0 .... DVargiu 2 — 86
(B Grizzetti, Italy) *mid-division, 7th straight, behind final 2f* **29/1**

10 *1 3/4* **Rave Reviews (IRE)**[28] [5560] 5-9-0 .... EPedroza 8 — 83
(A Wohler, Germany) *disputed 3rd, 5th straight, weakened over 2f out* **63/10**[3]

11 *15* **Ira Funesta (IRE)**[168] 3-8-10 .... MTellini 5 — 57
(G Angellotti, Italy) *disputed 3rd, 3rd straight, weakened 2f out* **49/1**

2m 6.40s
WFA 3 from 4yo+ 5lb — **11** Ran SP% **138.9**
WIN 13.31; PL 2.69, 1.53, 2.68; DF 24.67.
Owner Clarissa Hiddemann **Bred** K Nercessian **Trained** Germany

NOTEBOOK
Floriot(IRE) had won over course and distance on her only previous visit, in Listed company last November, and the ground was heavy on that occasion too. She came well over to the stands side to make her run in the final quarter-mile and stayed on strongly. The only time that she has finished out of the first two in 13 outings was when she was third on her debut. This was a big step up in class, but the going made the difference.
Confidential Lady has kept her form well and put in another fine effort, especially considering that she had run in the Champion Stakes only eight days earlier. It was probably her final race.
Musical Way(FR), who improved to win the Coupe de Maisons-Laffitte last month, showed that success was no fluke.
Time On set a good pace and stayed on to the end.
Pictavia(IRE) had every chance but was in trouble inside the final two furlongs. All her best form is on good or good to firm going.
Acts Of Grace(USA) was at the back with the winner as far as the straight. She led Floriot up the outside but never looked capable of reaching the leaders.

5415 WOODBINE (L-H)
Sunday, October 22

OFFICIAL GOING: Soft

6125a E P TAYLOR STKS (GRADE 1) (F&M) — 1m 2f (T)
8:00 (8:01) 3-Y-O+

£300,000 (£100,000; £55,000; £30,000; £15,000; £200)

RPR

1 **Arravale (USA)**[35] 3-8-6 .... JValdiviaJr 3 — 117
(M Benson, Canada) *always in touch, 6th straight on inside, led 1 1/2f out, driven out* **19/4**[3]

2 *1* **Barancella (FR)**[30] 5-8-11 .... JCastellano 8 — 116
(R J Frankel, U.S.A) *mid-division, closed up to dispute 3rd 5f out, 2nd straight, every chance over 1f out, kept on same pace* **132/10**

3 *nk* **Naissance Royale (IRE)**[29] 4-8-11 .... GKGomez 6 — 115
(Christophe Clement, U.S.A) *hld up, clr last til over 3f out, still last str, hdwy wl over 1f out, angled out & reached 3rd appr fnl f, kpt on steadily* **9/1**

4 *2 3/4* **Ambitious Cat (USA)**[35] 5-8-11 .... TKabel 1 — 110
(E Coatrieux, Canada) *raced in 8th, 7th straight, edged to outside, ran on from over 1f out, one pace in final f* **16/1**

5 *1/2* **Latice (IRE)**[48] 5-8-11 .... CVelasquez 9 — 109
(J E Sheppard, U.S.A) *always in touch, 5th on outside straight, one pace final 2f* **119/10**

6 *3* **Red Bloom**[33] [5465] 5-8-11 .... MJKinane 5 — 104
(Sir Michael Stoute) *a cl up, 4th str, trying to edge out when slightly hmpd wl over 1f out, rdn when bumped by 3rd over 1f out, sn btn* **37/20**[1]

7 *3* **Ready's Gal (USA)**[35] 4-8-11 .... JRVelazquez 10 — 98
(T Pletcher, U.S.A) *soon tracking leader, led over 3f out to 1 1/2f out, weakened quickly* **126/10**

8 *1/2* **Angara**[15] [5819] 5-8-11 .... FJara 7 — 97
(W Mott, U.S.A) *9th straight, never a factor* **9/2**[2]

9 *3/4* **Almerita (GER)**[35] 3-8-6 .... PHusbands 2 — 96
(W Hickst, Germany) *closed up on outside over 3f out, close 8th straight, soon beaten* **14/1**

10 *7 1/4* **Live Life (FR)**[22] 4-8-11 .... PValenzuela 4 — 83
(N Drysdale, U.S.A) *led to over 3f out, 3rd straight, soon weakened* **174/10**

2m 10.34s
WFA 3 from 4yo+ 5lb — **10** Ran SP% **120.8**
PARI-MUTUEL (including $2 stakes): WIN 11.50; PL (1-2) 6.20, 16.70; SHOW (1-2-3) 4.30, 9.00, 6.90; SF 233.30.
Owner R Costigan **Bred** Bruce Lunsford **Trained** Canada

NOTEBOOK
Arravale(USA) had started odds-on when beaten half a length by Ready's Gal over nine furlongs at this course on firm going last month. It was a different story on this ground, which she had never experienced before. Most races are taken off the turf when the going is soft or worse but she will be tough to beat if she has these conditions again.
Barancella(FR), accustomed to soft going from her days in France, was always close up and stayed on to the end.
Latice(IRE), another ex-French, would have been suited by the easy ground and ran well.
Red Bloom was well in touch but soon found herself in trouble. She first brushed with Latice and then Naissance Royale cut across her and she faltered. She did not seem to be going that well even before the second incident however.

6126a PATTISON CANADIAN INTERNATIONAL (GRADE 1) — 1m 4f (T)
9:05 (9:16) 3-Y-O+

£600,000 (£200,000; £110,000; £60,000; £30,000; £200)

RPR

1 **Collier Hill**[42] [5226] 8-9-0 .... DeanMcKeown 8 — 118
(G A Swinbank) *disputed 2nd, definite 2nd & closed on leader from 4f out, led 2f out, all out* **43/4**

2 *nse* **Go Deputy (USA)**[43] 5199 6-9-0 JRVelazquez 7 118
(T Pletcher, U.S.A) *raced in 5th to straight, headway from 2f out, every chance inside final furlong, unable to quicken last strides* **7/2**[2]

3 *3 ½* **Sky Conqueror (CAN)**[14] 4-9-0 TKabel 1 113
(Darwin D Banach, Canada) *hld up, 9th str, hdwy 2f out, not clr run over 1f out, switched outside & ran on to take 3rd wl ins fnl f* **84/10**

4 *½* **Blue Monday**[37] 5342 5-9-0 SteveDrowne 3 112
(R Charlton) *towards rear, 7th straight, tracking 2nd 2f out, ran on under pressure to go 3rd inside final f, no extra close home* **57/10**

5 *½* **Meteor Storm**[22] 7-9-0 (b) JCastellano 6 111
(W Dollase, U.S.A) *held up, 8th straight, stayed on final 2f, never near to challenge* **45/4**

6 *¾* **Last Answer (CAN)**[28] 6-9-0 ERamsammy 5 110
(M Keogh, Canada) *led to 2f out* **31/1**

7 *1 ¼* **The Last Drop (IRE)**[43] 5185 3-8-7 RHills 9 108
(B W Hills) *dwelt start, soon racing in 4th, went 3rd on turn, soon one pace* **26/1**

8 *2* **Kastoria (IRE)**[36] 5395 5-8-11 MJKinane 2 102
(John M Oxx, Ire) *held up in rear, headway & 6th straight, effort on outside from 2f out, beaten over 1f out* **24/10**[1]

9 *4 ½* **Jambalaya (CAN)**[28] 4-9-0 JCJones 4 98
(Catherine Day Phillips, Canada) *disputed 2nd to 4f out, 4th straight, weakened well over 1f out* **27/1**

10 *1* **Relaxed Gesture (IRE)**[43] 5199 5-9-0 GKGomez 10 97
(Christophe Clement, U.S.A) *last virtually throughout* **5/1**[3]

2m 37.34s
WFA 3 from 4yo+ 7lb **10** Ran SP% **120.9**
PARI-MUTUEL: WIN 23.50; PL (1-2) 9.70, 5.00; SHOW (1-2-3) 5.70, 3.50, 5.10; SF 143.40.
Owner R H Hall J D Abell R Crowe **Bred** George Strawbridge **Trained** Melsonby, N Yorks

NOTEBOOK
Collier Hill was always well in touch and went for home early in the straight. He was one of the proven stayers in this field and the lead he took at that point just proved sufficient. A nose in North America is not quite so thin a margin as in Europe, but it was still very tight at the end. He is likely to end his remarkable season in Hong Kong.
Go Deputy(USA) had plenty of form at this distance, including a Grade 1 victory at Saratoga in August. He was with the winner throughout the final half furlong and lost nothing in defeat.
Sky Conqueror(CAN) had won his last three, all at Woodbine and including a Grade 2 over the distance and on soft ground. He would have finished closer if he had not been stopped in his run.
Blue Monday ran his usual game race but this was a little too far for him in these conditions. He gave everything and was tiring at the end.
The Last Drop(IRE) missed a beat at the start but soon recovered. He ran as well as could be expected.
Kastoria(IRE) was sent off favourite on the strength of her defeat of Yeats in the Irish St Leger. She had nothing in hand of Collier Hill on their running in the Curragh Cup on July 1 and the assumed improvement was never revealed.

6127a NEARCTIC STKS (GRADE 2) 6f
10:08 (10:22) 3-Y-O+

£150,000 (£50,000; £27,500; £15,000; £7,500; £200)

RPR

1 **Fast Parade (USA)**[67] 3-8-6 (b) PValenzuela 7 118
(Peter Miller, U.S.A) *pressed leader on outside after 2f, 2nd straight, led 2f out, 3 lengths clear 1f out, driven out* **47/20**[1]

2 *¾* **In Summation (USA)**[232] 3-8-4 GKGomez 10 113
(Christophe Clement, U.S.A) *always close up, 4th straight, driven to take 2nd 150yds out, ran on but could not reach winner* **106/10**

3 *1 ¾* **Old Dodge (BRZ)**[15] 5824 5-8-5 JValdiviaJr 12 108
(R Horgan, Canada) *7th straight, headway final 2f, nearest at finish* **11/1**

4 *1* **Terrific Challenge (USA)** 4-8-5 (b) JBravo 9 105
(S Hough, U.S.A) *outpaced early, last straight, moved outside 2f out, ran on to take 4th well inside final furlong* **102/10**

5 *1 ½* **Moss Vale (IRE)**[21] 5712 5-8-9 MJKinane 1 105
(D Nicholls) *led to 2f out, gradually weakened* **67/20**[2]

6 *3 ¼* **Atticus Kristy (USA)**[119] 5-8-7 (b) JCastellano 3 93
(M Scherer, U.S.A) *9th straight, never a factor* **53/10**[3]

7 *1* **Metro Meteor (USA)**[414] 3-8-4 (b) CVelasquez 6 88
(Linda Rice, U.S.A) *8th straight, never a factor* **107/10**

8 *1* **Silver Timber (USA)** 3-8-4 (b) TKabel 5 85
(Linda Rice, U.S.A) *pressed leader, 3rd straight, weakened well over 1f out* **30/1**

9 *½* **Dark Cheetah (USA)**[58] 4787 4-8-6 PHusbands 2 84
(R Dutrow Jr, U.S.A) *11th straight, always towards rear* **31/1**

10 *1 ¼* **Man Of Illusion (AUS)**[119] 5-8-7 RHills 8 82
(P L Biancone, U.S.A) *10th straight, always outpaced* **33/1**

11 *1 ¾* **Sgt. Bert (USA)**[170] 5-8-5 JRVelazquez 4 74
(Gary Montgomery, U.S.A) *chased leaders, 6th & weakening straight* **157/10**

12 *10 ½* **Peace Offering (IRE)**[21] 5706 6-8-5 AdrianTNicholls 11 43
(D Nicholls) *chased leaders, ridden 3f out, 5th & weakening straight* **362/10**

1m 12.41s
WFA 3 from 4yo+ 1lb **12** Ran SP% **121.1**
PARI-MUTUEL: WIN 6.70; PL 91-2) 4.30, 9.10; SHOW (1-2-3) 3.60, 6.60, 7.90; SF 65.30.
Owner Gary and Cecil Barber **Bred** Dr Michael John Konecny **Trained** USA

NOTEBOOK
Fast Parade(USA) was never far away and gained a winning lead early in the straight.
Moss Vale(IRE) broke fast from his inside draw and held the lead as far as the straight, but his chance soon evaporated.
Peace Offering(IRE) was being rousted along on the turn and soon gave way.

5665 KEMPTON (A.W) (R-H)
Monday, October 23

OFFICIAL GOING: Standard
Wind: light behind

6128 INTEL LEAP AHEAD BANDED STKS 1m 2f (P)
2:30 (2:30) (Class 7) 3-Y-O+ **£2,047** (£604; £302) **Stalls** High

Form RPR

0540 **1** **Milk And Sultana**[4] 6067 6-9-2 47 StephenDonohoe(3) 13 56
(G A Ham) *hld up in midfield: prog over 2f out: rdn to ld over 1f out: drvn clr* **7/1**

5000 **2** *2* **Ballare (IRE)**[48] 5097 7-9-5 47 FergusSweeney 10 52
(P J Makin) *trckd ldrs: effrt over 2f out: rdn to chal over 1f out: sn brushed aside by wnr* **14/1**

6603 **3** *1* **Wood Fern (UAE)**[44] 5166 6-8-12 47 AshleyHamblett(7) 2 50+
(W M Brisbourne) *hld up in last pair: sme prog 3f out: stl plenty to do whn nt clr run 2f out: r.o strly fnl f: hopeless task* **4/1**[1]

0000 **4** *4* **Must Be Keen**[51] 5035 7-9-8 50 (tp) JohnEgan 12 46
(Ernst Oertel) *plld hrd early and sn led: rdn and hdd over 1f out: wknd* **25/1**

5004 **5** *nk* **Malibu (IRE)**[26] 5609 5-9-8 50 DaneO'Neill 9 45
(M Appleby) *prom: chsd ldr 5f out to wl over 1f out: wknd fnl f* **20/1**

1124 **6** *½* **Revolve**[86] 3934 6-9-7 49 (p) IanMongan 14 43
(Mrs L J Mongan) *trckd ldr to 5f out: cl up over 2f out: wknd over 1f out* **9/2**[2]

3032 **7** *1 ¼* **Justcallmehandsome**[11] 5925 4-9-7 49 HayleyTurner 11 41
(D J S Ffrench Davis) *rrd s: hld up in midfield: rdn over 2f out: no real prog* **5/1**[3]

2001 **8** *¾* **By Storm**[19] 5767 3-8-9 49 KirstyMilczarek(7) 6 39
(John Berry) *hld up in midfield: gng wl enough 3f out: rdn and no rspnse over 2f out* **12/1**

00-0 **9** *½* **Up At Dawn**[63] 4661 3-9-2 49 (t) StephenCarson 3 38
(C F Wall) *chsd ldrs: rdn 3f out: no imp 2f out: wknd over 1f out* **20/1**

5001 **10** *½* **Silver Mont (IRE)**[11] 5926 3-9-3 50 (bt) PaulEddery 4 38
(S R Bowring) *towards rr: rdn 5f out: effrt u.p on inner 2f out: sn no prog* **8/1**

0600 **11** *½* **Footstepsinthesnow (IRE)**[8] 5988 3-8-12 48 RichardKingscote(3) 1 36
(Mrs P N Dutfield) *hld up in last pair: rdn and no rspnse 3f out* **16/1**

0406 **12** *2* **Kinsman (IRE)**[161] 1725 9-9-5 47 RobertMiles 7 31
(T D McCarthy) *dwlt: hld up in midfield: rdn over 2f out: wknd over 1f out* **16/1**

0600 **13** *2 ½* **Catherines Cafe (IRE)**[13] 5885 3-8-10 50 JamesMillman(7) 5 29
(Mrs P N Dutfield) *racd wd towards rr: rdn 4f out: sn struggling* **14/1**

000 **14** *hd* **Votive Daniel (IRE)**[18] 5774 3-9-0 47 JTate 8 26
(Simon Earle) *nvr beyond midfield: wknd 2f out* **50/1**

2m 8.02s (-0.98) **Going Correction** -0.05s/f (Stan)
WFA 3 from 4yo+ 5lb **14** Ran SP% **126.6**
Speed ratings (Par 97):101,99,98,95,95 94,93,93,92,92 91,90,88,88
CSF £101.70 TOTE £8.10: £2.50, £6.70, £1.80; EX 134.40.
Owner Rose Farm Developments (UK) Ltd **Bred** D Malcolm Drury **Trained** Rooks Bridge, Somerset

FOCUS
A reasonable enough race by banded standards and, with the pace fair almost from the start, the form looks sound and should work out at a similar level.
Justcallmehandsome Official explanation: jockey said gelding missed the break
Footstepsinthesnow(IRE) Official explanation: jockey said filly lost a hind shoe

6129 COLLINGWOOD TEAM SERVICE MAIDEN CLAIMING STKS 6f (P)
3:00 (3:00) (Class 7) 3-Y-O+ **£2,047** (£604; £302) **Stalls** High

Form RPR

0045 **1** **Danish Blues (IRE)**[6] 6033 3-9-0 55 (p) IanMongan 4 69
(N P Littmoden) *hld up in midfield: nt clr run briefly over 2f out: prog to ld jst over 1f out: drew rt away* **9/2**[3]

4603 **2** *7* **Balian**[6] 6033 3-8-11 60 (be) RichardKingscote(3) 1 48+
(G L Moore) *hld up towards rr: effrt on wd outside over 2f out: styd on to take modest 2nd nr fin* **4/1**[2]

5200 **3** *hd* **Mystic Queen (IRE)**[9] 5970 3-8-9 53 JohnEgan 12 42
(A P Jarvis) *chsd ldr: rdn and no imp over 2f out: plugged on steadily* **7/2**[1]

62-0 **4** *hd* **Rambling Socks**[13] 5885 3-8-9 57 (b) PaulEddery 6 42
(S R Bowring) *awkward s: hld up in rr: effrt over 2f out: kpt on fnl f: n.d* **11/1**

0200 **5** *1 ¼* **Desert Dust**[9] 5969 3-9-0 50 (v) BrettDoyle 11 43
(R M H Cowell) *led at str pce: 3l clr over 2f out: hdd jst over 1f out: wknd and lost 3rd pls nr fin* **12/1**

5500 **6** *2* **Girandola**[7] 6019 3-8-12 54 (b) DaneO'Neill 9 35
(R F Johnson Houghton) *pushed along early to rch midfield: u.p and struggling over 2f out: no ch after* **9/1**

0005 **7** *shd* **Quote Unquote**[35] 5432 3-8-6 45 NeilChalmers(3) 10 32
(J Parkes) *trckd ldrs: rdn and hung lft over 2f out: wknd* **16/1**

5500 **8** *1 ½* **Straight As A Die**[40] 5291 3-8-6 45 ow1 LPKeniry 7 24
(R J Hodges) *prom tl wknd wl over 1f out* **33/1**

5000 **9** *½* **All Clued Up (IRE)**[9] 5969 3-8-9 48 AdamKirby 5 26
(Rae Guest) *chsd ldrs: u.p on outer over 2f out: wknd over 1f out* **12/1**

060 **10** *2 ½* **Sister Gee (IRE)**[79] 4155 4-8-3 45 RussellKennemore(7) 2 18
(R Hollinshead) *a towards rr: rdn bef 1/2-way: struggling after* **14/1**

0605 **11** *1* **Kings Cavalier (USA)**[74] 4304 3-8-12 45 (b) HayleyTurner 3 18
(I W McInnes) *settled in last: detached and rdn over 3f out: no rspnse* **12/1**

2405 **12** *1 ¾* **Sarah's Prince (IRE)**[11] 5924 3-8-8 48 ow1 JamesMillman(7) 8 16
(D K Ivory) *nvr gng wl and a towards rr: rdn and no prog 1/2-way* **7/1**

1m 13.12s (-0.58) **Going Correction** -0.05s/f (Stan)
WFA 3 from 4yo 1lb **12** Ran SP% **129.8**
Speed ratings (Par 97):101,91,91,91,89 86,86,84,84,80 79,77
CSF £25.31 TOTE £6.20: £2.10, £1.90, £1.40; EX 19.10.The winner was claimed by Don Cantillon for £5,000. Balian was bought by Mrs P M Sly for £5,000.
Owner Nigel Shields **Bred** Tally-Ho Stud **Trained** Newmarket, Suffolk

FOCUS
They went a strong pace and the form looks reliable, but maiden claimers at banded meetings are arguably the weakest races in the calendar, with Young Mick's success at Wolverhampton earlier in the year an obvious exception! The winning time offered some encouragement; 0.82 seconds quicker than the event won by Jennverse and the race could be rated higher.
Sarah's Prince(IRE) Official explanation: vet said gelding returned lame

6130 KEMPTON FOR HOSPITALITY BANDED STKS 7f (P)
3:30 (3:30) (Class 7) 3-Y-O+ **£2,047** (£604; £302) **Stalls** High

Form RPR

0022 **1** **Atwirl**[8] 5986 3-9-3 50 (v) DaneO'Neill 11 65+
(D J Daly) *trckd ldrs: prog and edgd rt 2f out: led over 1f out: sn wl clr: pushed out* **11/4**[1]

-000 **2** *4* **Eccollo (IRE)**[131] 2546 4-9-4 49 JohnEgan 3 55+
(T J Pitt) *sn chsd ldr: effrt whn hmpd 2f out: kpt on u.p to snatch modest 2nd last stride* **8/1**

0005 **3** *shd* **Four Amigos (USA)**[202] 864 5-9-5 50 LeeEnstone 10 51
(I A Wood) *prom: rdn and effrt on inner over 2f out: no ch w wnr over 1f out: kpt on* **12/1**

000 **4** *shd* **Free Silver (IRE)**[73] 4329 3-9-3 50 AdamKirby 1 51
(Miss K B Boutflower) *dwlt: hld up wl in rr: prog on wd outside over 2f out: kpt on fnl f: n.d* **25/1**

0205 **5** *1¼* **Mythical Charm**[4] 6069 7-9-2 50 (t) MarcHalford(3) 12 47
(J J Bridger) *hld up towards rr: prog 1/2-way: rdn over 2f out: nt qckn and btn sn after* **13/2[3]**

/300 **6** *1¾* **Charlottebutterfly**[37] 5370 6-9-2 50 NeilChalmers(3) 13 43
(P J McBride) *settled wl in rr: prog on inner over 2f out: chsd ldrs wl over 1f out: no hdwy after* **16/1**

0331 **7** *½* **Keon (IRE)**[11] 5929 4-8-12 50 RussellKennemore(7) 9 42
(R Hollinshead) *nvr beyond midfield: outpcd and btn 2f out: kpt on again fnl f* **3/1[2]**

0540 **8** *½* **Buckle And Hyde**[52] 4984 3-9-0 50 AmirQuinn(3) 8 40
(Mrs A L M King) *dwlt: wl in rr: sme prog on outer over 2f out: no imp over 1f out* **12/1**

5300 **9** *1½* **Arculinge**[52] 4984 3-9-3 50 FergusSweeney 4 36
(M Blanshard) *racd on outer in midfield: rdn over 2f out: fdd over 1f out* **16/1**

3501 **10** *nk* **Cut Ridge (IRE)**[15] 5840 7-9-5 50 (p) TonyHamilton 5 36
(J S Wainwright) *pushed up to ld: hdd over 1f out: wknd rapidly fnl f* **8/1**

500- **11** *2* **Overdrawn (IRE)**[137] 5566 5-9-1 49 (t) StephenDonohoe(3) 14 29
(A J McCabe) *sn struggling in last: nvr a factor* **10/1**

5000 **12** *4* **Penny Glitters**[8] 5988 3-8-11 49 DuranFentiman(5) 2 19
(S Parr) *prom tl wknd rapidly 2f out* **33/1**

0-00 **13** *3½* **Glitterati**[20] 5761 3-9-2 49 LPKeniry 7 10
(J S Moore) *prom to 1/2-way: wknd over 2f out* **33/1**

000P **14** *81* **Catherine Medici**[64] 4627 3-9-3 50 BrettDoyle 6 —
(R M H Cowell) *in tch tl hung bdly lft bnd 3f out and virtually rn off the crse: t.o* **33/1**

1m 26.34s (-0.46) **Going Correction** -0.05s/f (Stan)
WFA 3 from 4yo+ 2lb **14** Ran SP% **136.1**
Speed ratings (Par 97):100,95,95,95,93 91,91,90,88,88 86,81,77,—
CSF £28.50 TOTE £3.70: £1.80, £2.70, £5.10; EX 39.80.
Owner Sir Evelyn De Rothschild **Bred** Southcourt Stud **Trained** Newmarket, Suffolk

FOCUS
This looked a reasonable race by banded standards and the form might work out, with the third and fourth close to their marks.
Catherine Medici Official explanation: jockey said filly was unsteerable

6131 BOOK YOUR CHRISTMAS PARTY HERE BANDED STKS 6f (P)
4:00 (4:01) (Class 7) 3-Y-0+ £2,047 (£604; £302) Stalls High

Form RPR

0503 **1** **Jennverse**[66] 4554 4-8-13 45 JamieMackay 12 48+
(D K Ivory) *dwlt: hld up wl in rr: hmpd wl over 2f out: prog sn after : rdn to ld narrowly ins fnl f: hld on wl* **3/1[1]**

0003 **2** *½* **Firework**[72] 4365 8-8-13 45 StephenCarson 1 47+
(E A Wheeler) *hld up wl in rr: nt clr run on inner wl over 2f out: prog over 1f out: drvn to chal fnl f: nt qckn* **7/1**

540 **3** *shd* **Teyaar**[42] 5243 10-8-13 45 PaulDoe 7 46
(M Wellings) *dwlt: wl in rr: rdn and prog on outer over 2f out: jnd ldr over 1f out: nt qckn last 100yds* **12/1**

0300 **4** *½* **Nilsatisoptimum (USA)**[15] 5840 3-8-12 45 (p) LeeEnstone 10 45
(M Mullineaux) *mde most: kpt on wl whn hrd pressed over 1f out: hdd ins fnl f: no ex nr fin* **10/1**

0665 **5** *2* **My Girl Pearl (IRE)**[66] 4554 6-8-13 45 RichardThomas 4 39+
(M S Saunders) *hld up towards rr: nt clr run briefly over 2f out: sn lost pl: nt qckn wl over 1f out: kpt on ins fnl f* **5/1[2]**

0430 **6** *nk* **Cuesta Canyon (IRE)**[143] 2195 3-8-7 45 (be) NataliaGemelova(5) 11 38
(A J McCabe) *trckd ldrs: drvn and cl up 2f out: nt qckn: fdd fnl f* **14/1**

0060 **7** *1* **Princess Arwen**[161] 1727 4-8-10 45 NeilChalmers(3) 2 35
(Mrs Barbara Waring) *wl in rr: effrt on wd outside over 2f out: tried to cl over 1f out: wknd fnl f* **33/1**

0000 **8** *1¼* **Flaran**[90] 3825 6-8-13 45 (v[1]) JTate 8 31
(J A R Toller) *hld up in midfield: cl up whn nt clr run over 2f out: no prog after* **10/1**

6100 **9** *¾* **Secret Vision (USA)**[95] 3683 5-8-13 45 BrettDoyle 5 29
(R M H Cowell) *prom: rdn to chse ldr briefly 2f out: wknd over 1f out* **8/1**

6050 **10** *nk* **Crystal Mystic (IRE)**[79] 4157 4-8-13 45 AdrianMcCarthy 6 28
(B Palling) *pressed ldr to 2f out: sn lost pl u.p* **11/2[3]**

4300 **11** *6* **Ace Club**[72] 4363 5-8-13 45 (v[1]) DaleGibson 9 10
(M J Attwater) *prom tl wknd rapidly on inner wl over 1f out* **8/1**

0000 **12** *12* **Binty**[62] 4670 4-8-13 45 RobertMiles 3 —
(A J Chamberlain) *dwlt: sn detached in last and struggling bdly: no ch whn eased over 1f out* **20/1**

1m 13.94s (0.24) **Going Correction** -0.05s/f (Stan)
WFA 3 from 4yo+ 1lb **12** Ran SP% **132.0**
Speed ratings (Par 97):96,95,95,94,91 91,90,88,87,87 79,63
CSF £27.33 TOTE £3.90: £1.50, £2.50, £4.60; EX 23.30.
Owner Mrs J A Cornwell **Bred** Mrs J A Cornwell **Trained** Radlett, Herts
■ Stewards' Enquiry : Lee Enstone one-day ban: used whip with excessive frequency (Nov 3)

FOCUS
A weak event, run at a sound enough pace and the first four came clear. The third and fourth set the standard with the first two slightly better than the bare form.

6132 HP ADVANTAGE BANDED STKS 2m (P)
4:30 (4:32) (Class 7) 3-Y-0+ £2,047 (£604; £302) Stalls High

Form RPR

3546 **1** **Ganymede**[34] 5451 5-9-11 48 IanMongan 8 56
(Mrs L J Mongan) *hld up in tch: effrt on inner 3f out: rdn to ld jst over 2f out: clr ins fnl f: all out* **6/1[3]**

1050 **2** *¾* **Lysander's Quest (IRE)**[27] 5587 8-9-10 47 FergusSweeney 3 54+
(R Ingram) *hld up in midfield: nt qckn over 2f out: r.o over 1f out: chsd wnr ins fnl f: clsng at fin* **6/1[3]**

0600 **3** *2½* **Whoopsie**[20] 5750 4-9-5 47 DuranFentiman(5) 9 51
(S Parr) *pressed ldr: led briefly over 2f out: sn hrd rdn and outpcd: kpt on* **10/1**

5104 **4** *nk* **Jadeeron**[9] 5971 7-9-8 45 (p) AdamKirby 12 49
(Miss D A McHale) *trckd ldng pair: poised to chal gng easily over 2f out: sn rdn and fnd nil* **11/4[1]**

0-01 **5** *1¾* **Sharaab (USA)**[18] 4423 5-9-11 48 (t) DaleGibson 6 50+
(D E Cantillon) *hld up bhd ldrs: rdn and nt qckn whn short of room 2f out: one pce after* **7/2[2]**

416- **6** *3½* **Avanti**[504] 2335 10-9-12 49 AlanDaly 1 46
(Dr J R J Naylor) *hld up in rr: nt on terms w ldng gp 3f out: plugged on: n.d* **25/1**

5005 **7** *½* **Go Amwell**[21] 5741 3-9-3 50 PaulDoe 11 47
(J R Jenkins) *hld up in rr: prog 9f out: pressed ldrs 5f out: chal over 2f out: wknd over 1f out* **20/1**

3420 **8** *¾* **Lenwade**[39] 5324 5-9-5 45 (v[1]) DominicFox(3) 13 41
(G G Margarson) *dwlt: hld up wl in rr: nt on terms w ldng gp 3f out: no ch fnl 2f* **7/1**

0000 **9** *3½* **Plain Champagne (IRE)**[4] 6068 4-9-12 49 RichardThomas 2 41
(Dr J R J Naylor) *s.v.s: hld up wl in rr: prog 6f out: nt on terms 3f out: n.d fnl 2f* **12/1**

-001 **10** *5* **Our Glenard**[75] 4239 7-9-3 40 NataliaGemelova(5) 14 31
(J E Long) *hld up: prog 8f out: poised to chal on outer 3f out: wknd rapidly 2f out* **16/1**

40/0 **11** *2½* **City Affair**[26] 5609 5-9-12 49 LPKeniry 4 32
(J G M O'Shea) *led to over 2f out: wknd rapidly* **33/1**

4/ **12** *7* **Dueling B'Anjiz (USA)**[8] 7-9-5 45 EdwardCreighton(3) 10 19
(E J Creighton) *chsd ldrs: rdn 6f out: wknd 4f out* **25/1**

0-00 **13** *10* **Noble Calling (FR)**[35] 5422 9-9-4 48 JamesMillman(7) 7 10
(R J Hodges) *dwlt: a in last trio: rdn 6f out: t.o over 3f out* **20/1**

065- **14** *72* **Madison Avenue (GER)**[473] 3264 9-9-5 45 NeilChalmers(3) 5 —
(T M Jones) *trckd ldrs tl wknd rapidly over 4f out: sn t.o and eased* **25/1**

3m 34.11s (2.71) **Going Correction** -0.05s/f (Stan)
WFA 3 from 4yo+ 10lb **14** Ran SP% **136.6**
Speed ratings (Par 97):91,90,89,89,88 86,86,85,84,81 80,76,71,35
CSF £43.77 TOTE £6.80: £2.80, £2.00, £6.20; EX 43.20.
Owner Condover Racing **Bred** Mrs A M Jenkins **Trained** Epsom, Surrey

FOCUS
Another poor affair, run at just a modest pace and the first two came clear. The form looks sound rated through the third.
Sharaab(USA) Official explanation: jockey said gelding was denied a clear run
Go Amwell Official explanation: jockey said gelding hung both ways in straight
Noble Calling(FR) Official explanation: jockey said gelding never travelled
Madison Avenue(GER) Official explanation: jockey said gelding hung right-handed

6133 REUTERS PERFORMANCE BANDED STKS 1m 4f (P)
5:00 (5:04) (Class 7) 3-Y-0+ £2,047 (£604; £302) Stalls Centre

Form RPR

2310 **1** **Guadiana (GER)**[49] 5072 4-9-5 45 (v) FrancisNorton 12 47
(A W Carroll) *t.k.h: hld up in rr: effrt 3f out: hanging bdly and sharp reminders: prog 2f out: forced ahd u.p last 75yds* **7/2[2]**

0040 **2** *1* **Captivate**[9] 5955 3-8-9 45 (p) StephenDonohoe(3) 10 45
(A J McCabe) *dwlt: hld up wl in rr: rdn over 3f out: prog fr over 2f out: styd on to take 2nd last stride* **9/1**

004 **3** *shd* **Lady Suffragette (IRE)**[20] 5757 3-8-12 45 BrettDoyle 4 45
(John Berry) *t.k.h: prom: effrt to ld over 2f out: hrd pressed fr over 1f out: hdd last 75yds* **12/1**

5-00 **4** *shd* **Sahf London**[142] 2246 3-8-12 45 AdamKirby 8 45
(G L Moore) *t.k.h: prom: effrt and cl up 2f out: rdn and kpt on after: a jst hld* **12/1**

0000 **5** *1¾* **Diafa (USA)**[16] 5435 4-9-2 45 EdwardCreighton(3) 2 42
(J G M O'Shea) *sn prom: rdn to chal over 2f out: one pce fr over 1f out* **50/1**

6 *½* **River Beau (IRE)**[194] 998 3-8-12 45 JamieMackay 5 41
(E J O'Neill) *t.k.h: pressed ldr: led over 4f out to over 2f out: fdd fnl f* **13/2[3]**

00-2 **7** *1* **Monte Major (GER)**[201] 887 3-8-12 45 DaneO'Neill 3 40
(D J Daly) *dwlt: hld up in rr: prog over 2f out to chse ldrs over 1f out: nt qckn and no hdwy after* **10/1**

0600 **8** *2* **Larad (IRE)**[117] 2966 5-8-12 45 (b) StevenGibson(7) 14 37
(J S Moore) *t.k.h: hld up in midfield: effrt 3f out: bmpd along and no prog fnl 2f* **10/1**

6/0- **9** *3* **Big Smoke (IRE)**[651] 77 6-9-2 45 NeilChalmers(3) 7 32
(J C Tuck) *hld up wl in rr: shuffled along over 2f out: no real prog* **33/1**

0004 **10** *¾* **Queen Of Diamonds (IRE)**[20] 5757 3-8-12 45 PaulEddery 13 31
(Mrs P N Dutfield) *hld up towards rr: sme prog on inner over 2f out: urged along and wknd fnl f* **16/1**

1054 **11** *nk* **Opera Knight**[49] 5072 6-9-5 45 HayleyTurner 11 30
(A W Carroll) *t.k.h: prom: wknd u.p wl over 1f out* **3/1[1]**

00-0 **12** *¾* **Sahara Sun (IRE)**[28] 5567 3-8-12 45 FergusSweeney 9 29
(A King) *restrained s: hld up wl in rr: prog on outer to press ldrs 1/2-way: wknd wl over 1f out* **20/1**

0-00 **13** *8* **Owners Biscuits**[46] 5127 3-8-9 45 GregFairley(3) 6 16
(M Johnston) *mde most to over 4f out: wknd rapidly 3f out* **12/1**

202- **14** *29* **Muqtadi (IRE)**[580] 687 8-9-0 45 DuranFentiman(5) 1 —
(Mrs Barbara Waring) *rel to r then plld hrd: hld up in last: wknd rapidly over 3f out: t.o* **25/1**

2m 38.41s (1.51) **Going Correction** -0.05s/f (Stan)
WFA 3 from 4yo+ 7lb **14** Ran SP% **131.2**
Speed ratings (Par 97):92,91,91,91,90 89,89,87,85,85 85,84,79,59
CSF £37.54 TOTE £5.40: £1.90, £2.90, £3.20; EX 62.80.
Owner The Gumley Gropers **Bred** F Oettingen-Wallerstein **Trained** Cropthorne, Worcs

FOCUS
A typically competitive heat for the level, but they went no pace and the form is weak and not solid.

6134 KEMPTON.CO.UK BANDED STKS 1m (P)
5:30 (5:35) (Class 7) 3-Y-0+ £2,047 (£604; £302) Stalls High

Form RPR

0030 **1** **Tartan Special**[79] 4157 4-9-1 45 LeeEnstone 9 52
(K R Burke) *trckd ldrs: chal gng wl 2f out: rdn to ld over 1f out: in command and pushed out last 100yds* **10/1**

0000 **2** *1¼* **Savoy Chapel**[11] 5926 4-9-1 45 RichardMullen 10 49
(A W Carroll) *wl in tch: prog 3f out gng wl: rdn to chal 2f out: chsd wnr jst over 1f out: kpt on but no imp* **6/1[3]**

3542 **3** *1½* **Spring Time Girl**[63] 4667 4-9-1 45 (p) MichaelTebbutt 14 46+
(B Ellison) *settled wl in rr: taken to wd outside and effrt over 2f out: prog over 1f out: styd on to take 3rd last stride: no ch* **3/1[1]**

6000 **4** *shd* **Warden Warren**[28] 5573 8-9-1 45 (p) AdrianMcCarthy 5 45
(Mrs C A Dunnett) *chsd ldrs: rdn over 3f out: effrt over 2f out: kpt on fr over 1f out: nvr able to chal* **11/1**

0540 **5** *½* **Kilmeena Magic**[5] 6059 4-9-1 45 PatDobbs 12 44
(J C Fox) *hld up wl in rr: prog on inner over 2f out: styd on fnl 2f: nt pce to rch ldrs* **9/1**

0054 **6** *1* **Barzak (IRE)**[167] 1575 6-9-1 45 (bt) PaulEddery 8 42
(S R Bowring) *mde most to over 1f out: fdd fnl f* **8/1**

6063 **7** *2½* **Elms Schoolboy**[11] 5926 4-9-1 45 (b) PaulDoe 3 36
(P Howling) *s.s and rdn early: wl in rr: no ch fnl 2f: plugged on* **5/1[2]**

0600 **8** *1 1/2* **Piquet**[136] 2401 8-9-1 45 .... RobertMiles 4 33
(J J Bridger) *hld up and racd wd: prog over 3f out: nt qckn over 2f out: n.d over 1f out* **20/1**

0000 **9** *5* **Pyramid**[28] 5573 4-9-1 45 .... (tp) BrettDoyle 7 21
(A J Lidderdale) *t.k.h: mostly pressed ldr to over 2f out: wknd rapidly over 1f out* **20/1**

4000 **10** *3 1/2* **Southern Tide (USA)**[36] 3999 4-9-1 45 .... JamieMackay 1 13
(J Pearce) *t.k.h: pressed ldng pair: wknd rapidly 2f out* **8/1**

4500 **11** *2* **Devon Ruby**[18] 3338 3-8-7 45 .... (t) EmmettStack(5) 6 9
(C L Popham) *s.s: a in rr: rdn and struggling 3f out: wknd* **33/1**

-500 **12** *3/4* **Eldori**[7] 6019 3-8-12 45 .... RichardThomas 2 7
(M S Saunders) *t.k.h: hld up in rr: rdn and no prog 3f out: wknd* **100/1**

00-0 **13** *4* **Caspian Rose**[20] 5761 3-8-12 45 .... DaleGibson 13 —
(M J Attwater) *chsd ldrs tl wknd over 3f out* **50/1**

1m 41.41s (0.61) **Going Correction** -0.05s/f (Stan)
WFA 3 from 4yo+ 3lb **13** Ran SP% **121.0**
Speed ratings (Par 97):94,92,91,91,90 89,87,85,80,77 75,74,70
CSF £66.40 TOTE £12.40: £3.70, £2.70, £1.40; EX 127.10 Place 6 £193.05, Place 5 £69.30.
Owner Colin Bryce **Bred** John And Susan Davis **Trained** Middleham Moor, N Yorks

FOCUS
A modest heat for the grade in which Tartan Special was winning at the 18th attempt. The time was moderate and the form, rated around the principals, is not strong.
T/Plt: £257.60 to a £1 stake. Pool: £57,878.90. 164.00 winning tickets. T/Qpdt: £63.20 to a £1 stake. Pool: £4,411.60. 51.60 winning tickets. JN

5882 LEICESTER (R-H)
Monday, October 23
6135 Meeting Abandoned - Waterlogged

6094 LINGFIELD (L-H)
Monday, October 23

OFFICIAL GOING: Standard
Wind: Almost nil Weather: Overcast becoming wet

6142 BOOK ONLINE FOR A £2 DISCOUNT APPRENTICE H'CAP — 6f (P)
1:50 (1:50) (Class 6) (0-53,54) 3-Y-O+ **£2,730** (£806; £403) **Stalls** Low

Form RPR

6064 **1** **Cayman Breeze**[34] 5453 6-8-8 52 .... BarrySavage(5) 8 60
(J M Bradley) *hld up in tch: effrt 2f out: r.o to ld fnl 100 yds: drvn out* **9/2**[2]

4035 **2** *nk* **Supreme Kiss**[28] 5569 3-8-10 54 .... DanielleMcCreery(3) 10 60
(Mrs N Smith) *s.s: bhd tl hdwy over 1f out: fin wl* **10/1**

-405 **3** *nk* **Larky's Lob**[251] 411 7-8-13 52 .... JamesO'Reilly 5 58
(J O'Reilly) *slt ld most of way tl ins fnl f: kpt on same pce* **25/1**

5003 **4** *shd* **Diamond Josh**[9] 5970 4-8-8 52 .... MCGeran(5) 4 58
(P D Evans) *w ldr: rdn to ld ins fnl f: hdd and nt qckn fnl 100 yds* **4/1**[1]

100 **5** *1/2* **Dannabelle (IRE)**[33] 5474 6-8-10 52 .... JackMitchell(3) 11 56
(John A Quinn, Ire) *mid-div: rdn over 3f out: styd on fnl 2f* **7/1**

2300 **6** *shd* **Knead The Dough**[21] 5729 5-8-8 52 .... JonjoMilczarek(5) 9 56
(A E Price) *trckd ldng pair: rdn to chal over 1f out: no ex fnl f* **12/1**

0406 **7** *1 1/2* **Vindication**[28] 5573 6-9-0 53 .... DeanWilliams 7 53
(R M H Cowell) *dwlt: towards rr: sme hdwy over 2f out: rdn and hung lft over 1f out: one pce* **10/1**

3003 **8** *nk* **Diamond Katie (IRE)**[28] 5569 4-8-13 52 .... KevinGhunowa 6 51
(N Tinkler) *outpcd towards rr: hrd rdn and sme hdwy over 1f out: no imp* **11/2**[3]

0500 **9** *2* **Doctor's Cave**[115] 3052 4-8-8 52 .... (b) JosephWalsh(5) 2 45
(K O Cunningham-Brown) *in tch: outpcd 2f out: sn btn* **20/1**

0100 **10** *nk* **Fen Guest**[61] 4691 3-8-12 52 .... PatrickHills 3 44
(Rae Guest) *outpcd towards rr: n.m.r on rail over 2f out: n.d* **9/1**

1005 **11** *nk* **Double M**[118] 2955 9-8-8 52 .... (v) WilliamCarson(5) 12 43
(Mrs L Richards) *dwlt: outpcd: a bhd* **16/1**

0000 **12** *14* **Elgin Marbles**[18] 5775 4-9-0 53 .... (p) ThomasO'Brien 1 2
(A B Haynes) *chsd ldrs: hrd rdn and outpcd whn hit rail over 2f out: wknd qckly* **50/1**

1m 12.48s (-0.33) **Going Correction** -0.075s/f (Stan)
WFA 3 from 4yo+ 1lb **12** Ran SP% **118.4**
Speed ratings (Par 101):99,98,98,98,97 97,95,94,92,91 91,72
CSF £47.93 CT £1035.25 TOTE £5.90: £1.80, £2.80, £3.30; EX 63.80.
Owner G & L Johnson **Bred** M P B Bloodstock Ltd **Trained** Sedbury, Gloucs

FOCUS
A typically modest line-up for a race of this type, but competitive, and run at a good pace. The form is moderate but sound, rated around the third and sixth.

6143 COME JUMPING HERE ON NOVEMBER 8TH MEDIAN AUCTION MAIDEN STKS (DIV I) — 1m (P)
2:20 (2:21) (Class 5) 2-Y-O **£3,238** (£963; £481; £240) **Stalls** High

Form RPR

00 **1** **Guiseppe Verdi (USA)**[13] 5890 2-9-3 .... JimmyFortune 9 78
(J H M Gosden) *chsd ldrs: wnt 2nd over 2f out: led over 1f out: rdn and r.o wl* **13/8**[1]

03 **2** *1 1/2* **Hurricane Thomas (IRE)**[5] 6050 2-9-3 .... KDarley 11 75
(M Johnston) *led tl over 1f out: kpt on: nt pce of wnr fnl f* **2/1**[2]

0 **3** *6* **Good Effect (USA)**[11] 5914 2-9-3 .... DarryllHolland 4 61
(A P Jarvis) *mid-div: n.m.r and lost pl over 2f out: styd on steadily fr over 1f out* **7/1**[3]

4 *shd* **Geordie's Pool** 2-9-3 .... EddieAhern 8 61
(J W Hills) *s.i.s: towards rr: rdn 3f out: styd on to take mod 4th over 1f out: no imp* **20/1**

5 *1* **The Fifth Member (IRE)** 2-9-3 .... RobbieFitzpatrick 5 58
(R M Flower) *prom: outpcd by ldng pair 2f out: lost 3rd pl fnl 100 yds* **66/1**

0 **6** *2* **Hatton Flight**[44] 5178 2-9-3 .... FrancisNorton 1 54
(A M Balding) *s.s: hdwy to chse ldrs after 2f: outpcd and lost pl 3f out: kpt on fnl f* **10/1**

0 **7** *1/2* **Whaxaar (IRE)**[46] 5126 2-9-3 .... PatDobbs 2 52
(S Kirk) *s.s: sn in midfield: rdn and btn 3f out* **20/1**

000 **8** *3/4* **Polly Jones (USA)**[10] 5947 2-8-12 47 .... RyanMoore 6 46
(G L Moore) *t.k.h: in tch: rdn over 2f out: sn btn* **33/1**

0 **9** *1* **Cobra King (IRE)**[10] 5947 2-9-3 .... GeorgeBaker 7 48
(P Winkworth) *wd: hld up towards rr: effrt on outside 3f out: wknd ent st* **33/1**

0004 **10** *4* **Sagassa**[13] 5899 2-8-7 51 .... RoryMoore(5) 3 34+
(W De Best-Turner) *prom tl wknd 2f out* **66/1**

11 *3/4* **Royal Tender (IRE)** 2-8-12 .... MichaelTebbutt 10 33
(V Smith) *s.s: a bhd* **50/1**

1m 39.13s (-0.30) **Going Correction** -0.075s/f (Stan) **11** Ran SP% **113.4**
Speed ratings (Par 95):98,96,90,90,89 87,86,86,85,81 80
CSF £4.29 TOTE £2.60: £1.10, £1.20, £1.80; EX 5.40.
Owner H R H Princess Haya Of Jordan **Bred** Runnymede Farm Inc And Catesby W Clay **Trained** Newmarket, Suffolk

FOCUS
An ordinary maiden run at a modest pace, but form appears decent and the winner and runner-up are likely to prove a cut above their rivals.

NOTEBOOK
Guiseppe Verdi(USA) had run in two better maidens on turf at Newbury and Newmarket. A good-sized, scopey sort, he looks a fair recruit to the All-Weather scene. (op 7-4 tchd 6-4)
Hurricane Thomas(IRE) made a creditable All-Weather debut, since it was no disgrace to be beaten by the above-average winner. He looks sure to pay his way on the surface if campaigned during the winter. (op 6-4)
Good Effect(USA) shaped nicely considering the traffic problems he encountered just before the home straight. Coming home well under hands and heels, he looks to have a future at this level, and will be qualified for handicaps after one more run. (op 8-1)
Geordie's Pool has winners at distances up to a mile and a half in the family, on sand as well as on turf. He made a satisfactory debut, but looks as if he will be suited by a stiffer test of stamina.
The Fifth Member(IRE) has middle-distance stamina on his dam's side, but he showed plenty of pace until tying up in the home straight. He will be more at home when qualified for handicaps. (op 50-1)
Hatton Flight, a 28,000 guinea son of Kahyasi, is bred to stay middle distances. He will be one to consider for handicaps over longer trips when qualified after one more run. (op 8-1)
Polly Jones(USA) Official explanation: jockey said filly ran too free
Sagassa Official explanation: trainer said filly had broken a tooth on leaving stalls

6144 NEXT MEETING ON THURSDAY MAIDEN STKS — 7f (P)
2:50 (2:50) (Class 5) 3-Y-O+ **£3,562** (£1,059; £529; £264) **Stalls** Low

Form RPR

3-03 **1** **Iannis (IRE)**[8] 5988 3-9-5 .... KDarley 7 67+
(J Noseda) *hld up in tch: effrt 2f out: led 1f out: rdn out* **13/8**[1]

05 **2** *nk* **Cordelia**[21] 5728 3-9-0 60 .... FrancisNorton 9 61
(B W Hills) *settled in rr: rdn over 2f out: hdwy over 1f out: pressed wnr ins fnl f: a hld* **9/1**

22 **3** *1 1/2* **Conservative**[41] 5270 3-9-5 .... SteveDrowne 3 62
(P G Murphy) *in tch: outpcd 1/2-way: plld wd and styd on fr over 1f out: nt rch ldrs* **9/2**[3]

2-53 **4** *1/2* **Mitanni (USA)**[7] 6021 3-9-5 70 .... RyanMoore 5 61
(Mrs A J Perrett) *hld up in tch: effrt 2f out: nt clr run 1f out: swtchd rt: kpt on* **7/4**[2]

-000 **5** *3/4* **Simpsons Gamble (IRE)**[7] 6019 3-9-5 35 .... PatDobbs 8 59
(R M Flower) *wd: plld hrd: prom: led briefly over 1f out: no ex fnl f* **100/1**

0000 **6** *1* **Laugh 'n Cry**[8] 5986 5-9-2 57 .... (b[1]) J-PGuillambert 2 51
(C A Cyzer) *sn led and restrained in front: set modest pce: qcknd over 2f out: hdd over 1f out: wknd fnl f* **25/1**

- **7** *7* **El Hogar (IRE)** 3-9-5 .... JimmyFortune 4 37
(S Kirk) *prom 4f* **12/1**

0000 **8** *3* **Prima Markova**[35] 5435 3-9-0 45 .... TPO'Shea 1 24
(D J Daly) *hld up in tch: wknd 3f out* **100/1**

1m 26.77s (0.88) **Going Correction** -0.075s/f (Stan)
WFA 3 from 5yo 2lb **8** Ran SP% **116.2**
Speed ratings (Par 103):91,90,88,88,87 86,78,74
CSF £17.34 TOTE £3.60: £1.10, £2.10, £1.60; EX 19.00.
Owner Saleh Al Homaizi & Imad Al Sagar **Bred** Anthony Kirwan **Trained** Newmarket, Suffolk

FOCUS
A modest pace, and the form is suspect and held down by the proximity of poor turf maiden Simpsons Gamble.
Conservative Official explanation: jockey said gelding hung left

6145 COME JUMPING HERE ON NOVEMBER 8TH MEDIAN AUCTION MAIDEN STKS (DIV II) — 1m (P)
3:20 (3:22) (Class 5) 2-Y-O **£3,238** (£963; £481; £240) **Stalls** High

Form RPR

64 **1** **Pairumani Princess (IRE)**[27] 5595 2-8-12 .... RyanMoore 7 70
(E A L Dunlop) *towards rr: hrd drvn over 2f out: styd on to ld fnl 75 yds* **7/2**[2]

6 **2** *hd* **Heights Of Golan**[13] 5892 2-9-3 .... FrancisNorton 6 75
(I A Wood) *unruly bef s: hld up in midfield: rdn 3f out: styd on to press wnr fnl 75 yds: kpt on* **9/1**

00 **3** *1 1/2* **Find Me (USA)**[21] 5730 2-9-3 .... KDarley 8 71
(M Johnston) *led 1f: pressed ldr after: drvn to ld 1f out: hdd and no ex fnl 75 yds* **9/1**

4 *1 1/4* **Jaady (USA)** 2-9-3 .... MartinDwyer 4 68
(J H M Gosden) *s.s: hld up and bhd: shkn up and stdy hdwy fnl 2f: improve* **3/1**[1]

5 **5** *3* **Ardmaddy (IRE)**[17] 5780 2-9-3 .... TPO'Shea 5 61
(J A R Toller) *prom tl wknd over 1f out* **9/1**

6 *shd* **Anne Bonney** 2-8-12 .... RichardMullen 2 56
(E J O'Neill) *dwlt: hdwy to ld after 1f: hdd & wknd over 1f out* **9/2**[3]

7 *3* **Four Tel** 2-9-3 .... JimmyFortune 1 54
(J H M Gosden) *s.s: bhd: rdn 3f out: n.d* **6/1**

8 *1 1/4* **Mafeking (UAE)** 2-9-3 .... JosedeSouza 10 51
(M R Hoad) *s.s: wd: sn in midfield: effrt on outside 3f out: wknd 2f out* **80/1**

9 *3* **Mirko** 2-9-3 .... SteveDrowne 9 44
(Pat Eddery) *dwlt: plld hrd and sn chsng ldrs: wknd 2f out* **25/1**

0 **10** *64* **Iamtheone (IRE)**[35] 5417 2-9-3 .... MichaelTebbutt 3 —
(Bob Jones) *dwlt: sn in tch: wknd 3f out: wl bhd whn virtually p.u fnl 2f* **66/1**

1m 39.64s (0.21) **Going Correction** -0.075s/f (Stan) **10** Ran SP% **116.3**
Speed ratings (Par 95):95,94,93,92,89 88,85,84,81,17
CSF £34.52 TOTE £4.70: £1.70, £3.00, £4.20; EX 41.40.
Owner Anamoine Ltd **Bred** Windflower Overseas **Trained** Newmarket, Suffolk
■ Stewards' Enquiry : T P O'Shea one-day ban; failed to keep straight from stalls (Nov 3)

FOCUS
Mainly unexposed runners, making this hard to weigh up with the winner rated to debut form. The pace was pedestrian until quickening from the three-furlong pole.

NOTEBOOK

Pairumani Princess(IRE) did well to come from behind in a moderately-run race. She will be even better suited by a stiffer test. (op 4-1)

Heights Of Golan made a good All-Weather debut, on only his second outing, and is capable of winning a similar event. (op 10-1)

Find Me(USA) ran with credit on this All-Weather debut. He is capable of winning a little maiden, but is now also qualified for handicaps, so should find a race of some description. (op 8-1 tchd 10-1)

Jaady(USA), a brother to Royal Lodge winner Al Jadeed, shaped well on this racecourse debut. Green on the way to post, he should improve and find a race soon, with trips from a mile to ten furlongs likely to suit best in the long term. (tchd 11-4)

Ardmaddy(IRE) handles the surface well enough, but looked more effective over seven furlongs on his debut. (op 10-1)

Anne Bonney, a 30,000gns yearling from a decent family with winners from sprints to middle-distances, was intent on making the running, so missing the break was a handicap. That said, she performed satisfactorily for a long way, and ought to be capable of handling a drop to seven furlongs. (op 15-2)

Four Tel, a son of French Guineas winner Vettori, ought to be livened up a bit by this debut appearance, but more is needed. (op 4-1)

Mirko Official explanation: jockey said colt ran too free

6146 ARENALEISUREPLC.COM NOVICE STKS — 6f (P)

3:50 (3:50) (Class 4) 2-Y-O — **£4,857** (£1,445; £722; £360) **Stalls** Low

Form				RPR
2040	**1**		**Palo Verde**[17] 5788 2-9-5 83 ... J-PGuillambert 4 (M Johnston) *prom: effrt 2f out: led ins fnl f: edgd rt: rdn out* **11/2**[2]	83
1000	**2**	¾	**Espartano**[24] 5655 2-9-9 88 ... JimmyFortune 1 (M J Wallace) *hld up towards rr: swtchd lft and hdwy over 1f out: r.o to press wnr fnl 100 yds: nt qckn* **9/1**	85
4125	**3**	1	**Argentine (IRE)**[79] 4130 2-9-2 85 ... KDarley 9 (M Johnston) *dwlt: sn prom: led 2f out: hrd rdn and hdd ins fnl f: one pce* **8/1**	75
2461	**4**	nk	**Non Compliant**[23] 5686 2-9-2 88 ... EddieAhern 8 (J W Hills) *s.s: wd: hdwy over 3f out: hrd rdn over 1f out: one pce* **10/11**[1]	74+
1642	**5**	¾	**Mac Gille Eoin**[18] 5772 2-9-2 67 ... SteveDrowne 2 (J Gallagher) *bmpd s: sn in tch: outpcd 3f out: kpt on again fnl f* **25/1**	72
0	**6**	½	**Johannesburg Cat (USA)**[57] 4857 2-8-9 ... RyanMoore 7 (N P Littmoden) *outpcd in rr: rdn 3f out: r.o fnl f: nrst fin* **16/1**	63
5513	**7**	nk	**Hephaestus**[5] 6056 2-9-4 68 ... RichardHughes 5 (M R Channon) *mid-div: effrt 2f out: hrd rdn over 1f out: no imp* **11/1**	71
0221	**8**	shd	**Swift Cut (IRE)**[17] 5780 2-9-2 76 ... DarryllHolland 6 (A P Jarvis) *led tl 2f out: wknd 1f out* **6/1**[3]	69
0040	**9**	nk	**Fort Worth (IRE)**[69] 4460 2-8-12 69 ... JosedeSouza 3 (B Gubby) *in tch: rdn over 2f out: sn outpcd* **100/1**	64

1m 12.63s (-0.18) **Going Correction** -0.075s/f (Stan) — **9** Ran SP% **122.2**

Speed ratings (Par 97):98,97,95,95,94 93,93,93,92

CSF £57.18 TOTE £8.30: £2.20, £4.00, £1.50; EX 75.00.

Owner Sheikh Mohammed **Bred** Darley **Trained** Middleham Moor, N Yorks

FOCUS

A decent contest for the money, but no pace, producing a bunched finish. The winner sets the level but the fifth limits it.

NOTEBOOK

Palo Verde seems best on good or fast ground, and looked well at home in this first outing on Polytrack. He is relatively unexposed, and can improve a bit more. (op 6-1)

Espartano has been highly tried on turf, but retains all his early-season promise on the evidence of this All-Weather debut. He looks certain to pay his way if returning this winter. (op 10-1 tchd 11-1)

Argentine(IRE) made a sound All-Weather debut. His form on turf was good enough to suggest that the future is bright on sand too. (op 7-1)

Non Compliant, top on official ratings, was always battling against the draw, especially having missed the break and then being stuck wide throughout. He can be rated several pounds better than this. (op 5-4 tchd 11-8 in places)

Mac Gille Eoin was not favoured by the weights, but ran well enough, and looked as if seven furlongs might suit him on this surface. (tchd 33-1)

Johannesburg Cat(USA), an ex-German daughter of Johannesburg, is bred to be pretty speedy at trips up to a mile. Though getting going too late on this British debut, she should do better next time, with seven furlongs an option. (op 14-1)

Hephaestus had won both his previous attempts on sand at this track, but had an almost impossible task at the weights. In the circumstances, he was not disgraced, and would probably have finished sixth but for being eased near the finish. (op 10-1 tchd 9-1)

Swift Cut(IRE), forced into making the running over this shorter trip , was not favoured by the weights. (op 13-2)

6147 LINGFIELD PARK GOLF CLUB H'CAP — 1m (P)

4:20 (4:20) (Class 5) (0-70,70) 3-Y-O+ — **£3,238** (£963; £481; £240) **Stalls** High

Form				RPR
3-0	**1**		**Da Bookie (IRE)**[15] 5845 6-9-2 67 ... TPO'Shea 3 (P A Blockley) *hld up detached last: taken wd: rapid hdwy fnl f: led nr fin* **16/1**	75
0000	**2**	½	**Kabeer**[12] 5908 8-9-4 69 ...(t) JimmyFortune 2 (A J McCabe) *prom: led ins fnl 3f: rdn 3l ahd 1f out and looked wnr: tied up and hdd nr fin* **14/1**	76
0004	**3**	nk	**Smokin Joe**[12] 5908 5-9-5 70 ...(b) GeorgeBaker 7 (J R Best) *s.s: bhd tl hdwy into midfield 3f out: styd on strly fnl f* **7/2**[2]	76
5526	**4**	nk	**James Street (IRE)**[12] 5911 3-9-2 70 ...(b[1]) SteveDrowne 12 (J R Best) *hld up in midfield: rdn 3f out: r.o fnl f* **7/1**[3]	75
5000	**5**	1¼	**Sands Of Barra (IRE)**[18] 5778 3-9-0 68 ... FJohansson 6 (N A Callaghan) *t.k.h in midfield: rdn and outpcd over 2f out: styd on fnl f* **10/1**	71+
4651	**6**	shd	**Molem**[18] 5775 4-9-5 70 ...(tp) RyanMoore 11 (Lady Herries) *chsd ldrs: wnt 2nd ent st: no ex fnl f* **10/3**[1]	72
3033	**7**	1½	**Hollow Jo**[72] 4368 6-8-13 64 ... J-PGuillambert 4 (J R Jenkins) *mid-div: outpcd 3f out: kpt on fnl f* **8/1**	63
2100	**8**	½	**Coalpark (IRE)**[14] 5879 3-9-1 69 ...(t) KDarley 9 (M Johnston) *prom: n.m.r and lost pl after 3f: sn rdn in midfield: n.d after* **8/1**	67
6000	**9**	hd	**First Friend (IRE)**[14] 5877 5-9-5 70 ... DarryllHolland 10 (P Mitchell) *prom tl wknd over 1f out* **9/1**	67
0-10	**10**	1½	**Paradise Expected**[94] 3706 3-9-0 68 ... EddieAhern 8 (P W Chapple-Hyam) *rdn 1/2-way: a towards rr* **20/1**	62
4400	**11**	1½	**Wrighty Almighty (IRE)**[34] 5453 4-8-8 66 ...(p) PNolan(7) 1 (P R Chamings) *t.k.h: chsd ldrs over 5f* **22/1**	56
0000	**12**	17	**Wild Academy (IRE)**[21] 5734 3-8-11 65 ...(b[1]) RobbieFitzpatrick 5 (G C Bravery) *sn led: hdd ins fnl 3f: wknd 2f out* **25/1**	16

1m 37.72s (-1.71) **Going Correction** -0.075s/f (Stan)

WFA 3 from 4yo+ 3lb — **12** Ran SP% **124.6**

Speed ratings (Par 103):105,104,104,103,102 102,101,100,100,98 97,80

CSF £226.51 CT £991.28 TOTE £23.00: £5.60, £4.50, £1.60; EX 241.20.

Owner Sean Dalton **Bred** T P Burns **Trained** Lambourn, Berks

FOCUS

A routine handicap won in anything but routine fashion. The form looks sound overall with the third to his recent mark.

6148 LINGFIELDPARK.CO.UK H'CAP — 1m 4f (P)

4:50 (4:51) (Class 4) (0-85,84) 3-Y-O+ — **£5,505** (£1,637; £818; £408) **Stalls** Low

Form				RPR
-005	**1**		**Kyles Prince (IRE)**[13] 5897 4-8-11 72 ... J-PGuillambert 8 (P J Makin) *hld up in tch: effrt 3f out: led ent st: edgd lft: rdn wl clr* **11/2**[3]	86+
2244	**2**	3	**Velvet Heights (IRE)**[25] 5634 4-9-8 83 ... RichardHughes 6 (J L Dunlop) *trckd ldng pair: led briefly 2f out: nt pce of wnr over 1f out* **9/2**[2]	89
0345	**3**	hd	**Optimus (USA)**[7] 6017 4-9-2 77 ... RyanMoore 9 (B G Powell) *bhd: drvn along over 2f out: styd on to chal for 2nd fnl 50 yds: no ch w wnr* **13/2**	82
2130	**4**	4	**Polish Power (GER)**[128] 2656 6-9-2 77 ... RobbieFitzpatrick 7 (J S Moore) *dwlt: bhd: hdwy on outside 3f out: one pce fnl 2f* **9/1**	76
-253	**5**	3	**Tromp**[235] 556 5-8-12 73 ... EddieAhern 2 (D J Coakley) *t.k.h early: chsd ldrs tl wknd fnl 2f* **8/1**	67+
4531	**6**	shd	**My Princess (IRE)**[28] 5572 4-8-13 74 ... JimmyFortune 3 (N A Callaghan) *hld up in midfield to rr: nt clr run bnd 2f out: nvr in chalng position* **14/1**	68
160	**7**	2	**Newnham (IRE)**[17] 5786 5-8-13 74 ... SteveDrowne 5 (J R Boyle) *towards rr: rdn and n.d fnl 3f* **14/1**	65
1005	**8**	¾	**Given A Choice (IRE)**[18] 5776 4-9-4 84 ... JamieMoriarty(5) 4 (R A Fahey) *disp ld tl wknd 2f out* **4/1**[1]	74
3000	**9**	2	**In Full Cry**[17] 5787 3-8-11 79 ... KDarley 10 (M Johnston) *disp ld tl wknd 2f out* **6/1**	65

2m 32.3s (-2.09) **Going Correction** -0.075s/f (Stan)

WFA 3 from 4yo+ 7lb — **9** Ran SP% **115.6**

Speed ratings (Par 105):103,101,100,98,96 96,94,94,92

CSF £30.51 CT £164.88 TOTE £7.70: £2.20, £2.10, £2.50; EX 41.30 Place 6 £174.61, Place 5 £47.89.

Owner Weldspec Glasgow Limited **Bred** Norelands Bloodstock **Trained** Ogbourne Maisey, Wilts

FOCUS

A fair handicap, run at a sound gallop, but the form is not rock-solid.

T/Jkpt: Part won. £37,228.30 to a £1 stake. Pool: £52,434.24. 0.50 winning tickets. T/Plt: £107.70 to a £1 stake. Pool: £78,737.65. 533.30 winning tickets. T/Qpdt: £34.00 to a £1 stake. Pool: £6,711.80. 146.00 winning tickets. LM

6149 - 6156a (Foreign Racing) - See Raceform Interactive

5955 CATTERICK (L-H)

Tuesday, October 24

OFFICIAL GOING: Soft

Wind: virtually nil

6157 COWTHORPE MEDIAN AUCTION MAIDEN STKS — 5f 212y

2:25 (2:26) (Class 5) 2-Y-O — **£3,412** (£1,007; £504) **Stalls** Low

Form				RPR
	1		**Valery Borzov (IRE)** 2-9-0 ... AdrianTNicholls 11 (D Nicholls) *stdd and swtchd lft s: gd hdwy 1/2-way: chal over 1f out: rdn ent last: styd on to ld last 75 yds* **7/2**[2]	68
502	**2**	nk	**Onatopp (IRE)**[14] 5899 2-8-9 65 ... DavidAllan 6 (T D Easterby) *cl up: led over 2f out: rdn wl over 1f out: drvn ent last: hdd and no ex last 75 yds* **5/2**[1]	62
3064	**3**	3	**Rue Soleil**[22] 5721 2-8-9 64 ... PaulHanagan 5 (J R Weymes) *chsd ldrs: effrt over 2f out: sn rdn and kpt on same pce appr last* **5/1**[3]	53
5640	**4**	10	**Lovers Kiss**[15] 5860 2-8-9 46 ...(b[1]) SilvestreDeSousa 13 (N Wilson) *chsd ldrs: rdn along 1/2-way and sn one pce* **50/1**	23
000	**5**	2½	**Mandriano (ITY)**[14] 5900 2-9-0 35 ... RobertWinston 2 (D W Barker) *towards rr tl styd on fnl 2f: nrst fin* **40/1**	21
00	**6**	1	**Stars Above**[8] 6014 2-8-10 ow1 ... SebSanders 4 (Sir Mark Prescott) *dwlt and towards rr: hdwy over 2f out: nt clr run over 1f out: kpt on ins last: nrst fin* **14/1**	14
00	**7**	1¼	**Baybshambles (IRE)**[10] 5956 2-9-0 ... PhillipMakin 7 (R E Barr) *s.i.s and bhd: hdwy and in tch 1/2-way: rdn along 2f out and sn wknd* **100/1**	14
5400	**8**	½	**Perilore (IRE)**[15] 5860 2-8-8 35 ow2 ...(b[1]) StephenDonohoe(3) 3 (A Berry) *a rr* **100/1**	9
0	**9**	¾	**Sparky Vixen**[83] 4053 2-8-4 ... DuranFentiman(5) 8 (S Parr) *chsd ldrs: rdn along 1/2-way: wknd over 2f out* **100/1**	5
000	**10**	3	**Molto Duro (IRE)**[49] 5076 2-8-2 35 ...(b[1]) LanceBetts(7) 10 (N Wilson) *led: rdn along and hdd over 2f out: sn wknd* **150/1**	—
03	**11**	5	**Delta Shuttle (IRE)**[27] 5613 2-9-0 ... PatCosgrave 9 (K R Burke) *in tch and sn chsd along: rdn 1/2-way and sn bhd* **7/2**[2]	—
	12	2½	**Time Dancer (IRE)** 2-9-0 ... PaulQuinn 1 (A Berry) *s.i.s: a bhd* **33/1**	—
00	**13**	10	**Mambomoon**[82] 4066 2-9-0 ... TonyHamilton 14 (T D Easterby) *bhd fr 1/2-way* **40/1**	—
030	**14**	4	**Mr Wall Street**[105] 3385 2-9-0 61 ...(p) TomEaves 12 (Mrs L Williamson) *bhd fr 1/2-way* **12/1**	—

1m 18.6s (4.60) **Going Correction** +0.70s/f (Yiel) — **14** Ran SP% **117.5**

Speed ratings (Par 95):97,96,92,79,75 74,72,72,71,67 60,57,43,38

CSF £11.96 TOTE £4.80: £1.70, £1.30, £1.80; EX 13.70.

Owner D Kilburn/I Hewitson/J & D Nicholls **Bred** Vincent Harrington **Trained** Sessay, N Yorks

FOCUS

A weak maiden in which they came stands' side in the straight. The winning time was almost a second slower than the later 0-75 handicap and the form is best rated through the runner-up.

NOTEBOOK

Valery Borzov(IRE), a 26,000gns half-brother to Craic Sa Ceili, a minor seven-furlong/mile winner at two and three on sand, out of a multiple sprint scorer, justified strong market support on his racecourse debut with a narrow victory. This was not much of a race and he appeared to know his job, although he ran a little green once in front, so it remains to be seen just how much improvement there is to come. (op 3-1 tchd 5-2)

Onatopp(IRE) improved for the switch to soft ground when second at Newcastle on her previous start and this was another good effort in defeat. She looks up to winning a modest maiden, but she is also eligible for nurseries now. (op 7-2)

Rue Soleil, returned to maiden company, proved no match for the front two but was well clear of the remainder. (op 6-1 tchd 7-1)

Lovers Kiss did not improve for the fitting of blinkers and will surely be better off in low-grade handicaps or even sellers.

Delta Shuttle(IRE) shaped well over seven furlongs at Newcastle on his previous start, but proved a major disappointment this time.

6158 "JOHN MCCORMACK LIFETIME IN RACING" H'CAP — 1m 3f 214y

3:00 (3:00) (Class 6) (0-60,60) 3-Y-0+ — £2,730 (£806; £403) Stalls Low

Form — RPR

6032 **1** **Ego Trip**[105] 3382 5-9-8 **59**................(b) DaleGibson 2 — 71
(M W Easterby) *a cl up: led 2f out: rdn clr appr last and styd on wl* **9/1**

4022 **2** 5 **Onyergo (IRE)**[10] 5960 4-9-9 **60**................ PhillipMakin 10 — 65
(J R Weymes) *midfield: hdwy to chse ldrs over 3f out: rdn wl over 1f out: kpt on fnl f* **5/1**[1]

500 **3** ½ **Scotty's Future (IRE)**[10] 5955 8-8-11 **51**........ StephenDonohoe(3) 12 — 55
(A Berry) *sn pushed along in rr: hdwy 4f out: rdn to chse ldrs over 1f out: drvn and kpt on ins last* **50/1**

2360 **4** 1 ¾ **Platinum Charmer (IRE)**[21] 5751 6-8-9 **51**........(p) AndrewElliott(5) 7 — 53
(K R Burke) *midfield: rdn along 4f out: styd on u.p fnl 2f: nrst fin* **18/1**

-002 **5** nk **Persona (IRE)**[11] 5954 4-9-6 **60**................ SaleemGolam(3) 1 — 61
(B J McMath) *led: rdn along 3f out: hdd 2f out and grad wknd* **9/1**

0544 **6** 1 ¾ **Melvino**[35] 5451 4-9-1 **59**................ NeilBrown(7) 9 — 58
(T D Barron) *keen: hld up in rr: hdwy 4f out: rdn to chse ldrs wl over 1f out: sn no imp* **10/1**

0404 **7** ¾ **Plenty Cried Wolf**[11] 5954 4-9-5 **56**................ PaulHanagan 13 — 54
(R A Fahey) *chsd ldrs: rdn along over 3f out: grad wknd fnl 2f* **9/1**

2003 **8** 3 **Mystical Ayr (IRE)**[14] 5904 4-9-3 **57**........(p) AndrewMullen(3) 11 — 51
(Miss L A Perratt) *nvr bttr than midfield* **12/1**

0025 **9** 3 ½ **Royal Melbourne (IRE)**[21] 5750 6-9-7 **58**................ TomEaves 15 — 47
(Miss J A Camacho) *hld up in rr: gd hdwy over 4f out: rdn along to chse ldrs over 2f out: sn btn* **7/1**[2]

0600 **10** 4 **George's Flyer (IRE)**[35] 5446 3-8-9 **58**........(b) JamieMoriarty(5) 5 — 41
(R A Fahey) *chsd ldrs: rdn along 3f out: sn drvn and wknd* **33/1**

6005 **11** 2 **Bill Bennett (FR)**[11] 5952 5-9-9 **60**................ RobertWinston 3 — 40
(J Jay) *nvr nr ldrs* **8/1**

/000 **12** 1 ½ **Miss Holly**[21] 5751 7-9-0 **58**................ KellyHarrison(7) 14 — 36
(D Carroll) *nvr bttr than midfield* **100/1**

3160 **13** 27 **Star Sign**[35] 5445 4-9-6 **57**................(p) TonyHamilton 4 — —
(D W Barker) *prom: hung rt and rdn along 1/2-way: wknd 4f out* **100/1**

6004 **14** 34 **Balwearie (IRE)**[14] 5905 5-9-2 **53**................(p) PatCosgrave 8 — —
(Miss L A Perratt) *chsd ldrs: rdn along over 5f out: sn wknd* **14/1**

6300 **15** 2 ½ **Darghan (IRE)**[14] 5897 6-9-8 **59**................ TonyCulhane 6 — —
(W J Musson) *hld up: a rr* **15/2**[3]

2m 48.56s (9.56) **Going Correction** +0.70s/f (Yiel)
WFA 3 from 4yo+ 7lb — **15** Ran SP% **117.6**
Speed ratings (Par 101):96,92,92,91,90 89,89,87,84,82 80,79,61,39,37
CSF £51.31 CT £2137.79 TOTE £9.10: £3.70, £1.80, £8.50; EX 59.80.
Owner K Hodgson & Mrs J Hodgson **Bred** K And Mrs Hodgson **Trained** Sheriff Hutton, N Yorks

FOCUS
A moderate middle-distance handicap run at just an ordinary early gallop and rated through the second to recent form.
Star Sign Official explanation: jockey said filly hung right throughout

6159 GO RACING AT WETHERBY THIS FRIDAY H'CAP — 5f 212y

3:35 (3:35) (Class 5) (0-75,71) 3-Y-0 — £3,886 (£1,156; £577; £288) Stalls Low

Form — RPR

0063 **1** **Observatory Star (IRE)**[6] 6061 3-8-5 **58**........(b) GrahamGibbons 12 — 69
(T D Easterby) *trckd ldrs: hdwy 1/2-way: led 2f out: rdn over 1f out: drvn ins last: hdd nr fin: rallied to ld on line* **7/2**[1]

0024 **2** hd **Charles Parnell (IRE)**[14] 5902 3-9-0 **67**................ TonyCulhane 11 — 77
(M Dods) *in tch: gd hdwy over 2f out: swtchd lft and rdn ent last: drvn to ld nr fin: hdd on line* **4/1**[2]

4000 **3** 3 **Choysia**[27] 5619 3-9-3 **70**................ TomEaves 10 — 71
(D W Barker) *s.i.s and bhd: styd to race alone far side: rdn and hdwy wl over 1f out: drvn and kpt on ins last: nrst fin* **16/1**

0100 **4** 1 ½ **The Salwick Flyer (IRE)**[21] 5752 3-7-13 **57** oh7...... DuranFentiman(5) 2 — 54
(A Berry) *chsd ldng pair: rdn along 2f out: drvn over 1f out: kpt on same pce* **40/1**

6660 **5** shd **Making Music**[14] 5902 3-8-7 **60**................ DavidAllan 4 — 57
(T D Easterby) *in tch: rdn along over 2f out: drvn over 1f out and kpt on same pce* **11/1**

0030 **6** 4 **John Keats**[10] 5961 3-9-2 **69**................ PaulHanagan 8 — 54
(I Semple) *bhd tl styd on fnl 2f* **6/1**[3]

035 **7** nk **Hotham**[27] 5605 3-8-13 **66**................ PatCosgrave 7 — 50
(N Wilson) *cl up: led 1/2-way: rdn and hdd 2f out: sn drvn and grad wknd* **9/1**

260 **8** 7 **Welcome Approach**[28] 5593 3-9-4 **71**................ PhillipMakin 9 — 34
(J R Weymes) *a rr* **20/1**

3506 **9** 3 **Amber Glory**[15] 5864 3-8-4 **60**................(p) AndrewMullen(3) 6 — 14
(K A Ryan) *led: rdn along and hdd 1/2-way: sn wknd* **25/1**

6010 **10** 19 **Duke Of Milan (IRE)**[7] 6036 3-9-3 **70**................ NCallan 3 — —
(G C Bravery) *dwlt: effrt and sme hdwy 3f out: sn rdn and wknd* **11/1**

1034 **11** 2 **Highland Song (IRE)**[15] 5864 3-9-0 **67**................ RobertWinston 5 — —
(R F Fisher) *chsd ldrs: rdn along over 2f out: hmpd and lost action wl over 1f out: virtually p.u* **10/1**

1m 17.64s (3.64) **Going Correction** +0.70s/f (Yiel) — **11** Ran SP% **115.8**
Speed ratings (Par 101):103,102,98,96,96 91,90,81,77,52 49
CSF £16.50 CT £87.92 TOTE £5.00: £1.50, £1.60, £3.00; EX 15.10.
Owner and Mrs J D Cotton **Bred** C J Foy **Trained** Great Habton, N Yorks

FOCUS
A modest handicap rated around the first two and the fourth.
Welcome Approach Official explanation: jockey said gelding was unsuited by the soft ground
Highland Song(IRE) Official explanation: jockey said gelding lost its action

6160 JOHN LAYFIELD'S 41 YEARS AT WILLIAM HILL H'CAP — 7f

4:10 (4:10) (Class 4) (0-85,80) 3-Y-0+ — £6,477 (£1,927; £963; £481) Stalls Low

Form — RPR

2034 **1** **Countdown**[6] 6048 4-8-13 **75**................ DavidAllan 13 — 85
(T D Easterby) *in tch: hdwy over 2f out: swtchd lft and rdn ent last: drvn: hung rt and led last 50 yds* **5/1**[2]

0641 **2** ¾ **Bold Marc (IRE)**[10] 5961 4-8-13 **75**................(p) PatCosgrave 9 — 83
(K R Burke) *cl up: led 2f out: sn rdn: drvn and edgd lft ins last: hdd and no ex last 50 yds* **3/1**[1]

1410 **3** 1 ¼ **King Harson**[15] 5877 7-9-2 **78**................ PaulHanagan 8 — 85+
(J D Bethell) *led: rdn along and hdd 2f out: drvn and rallied ins last and ev ch tl hmpd last 50 yds and nt rcvr* **14/1**

5100 **4** 1 **Hiccups**[21] 5749 6-8-10 **75**................ StephenDonohoe(3) 6 — 77
(M Dods) *hld up: hdwy over 2f out: rdn to chse ldrs ent last: sn drvn and one pce* **14/1**

6426 **5** ½ **Titinius (IRE)**[57] 4885 6-8-8 **70**................ DeanMcKeown 2 — 71
(Micky Hammond) *chsd ldrs: rdn along wl over 1f out: kpt on same pce appr last* **16/1**

0013 **6** 1 ¼ **Paris Bell**[21] 5749 4-9-1 **77**................ PaulQuinn 11 — 75+
(T D Easterby) *dwlt: hdwy over 2f out: sn rdn and kpt on ins last: nrst fin* **12/1**

3016 **7** 8 **Trojan Flight**[21] 5749 5-8-12 **74**................(p) TonyCulhane 14 — 51
(D W Chapman) *a towards rr* **8/1**

0332 **8** 1 **Efidium**[10] 5961 8-8-1 **70**................(b) LukeMorris(7) 15 — 44
(N Bycroft) *a towards rr* **16/1**

0600 **9** 3 **Baylaw Star**[13] 5908 5-8-11 **76**................ AndrewMullen(3) 7 — 42
(I W McInnes) *chsd ldrs: rdn along over 2f out: sn wknd* **80/1**

4300 **10** 1 ½ **North Walk (IRE)**[25] 5649 3-9-0 **78**................ NCallan 12 — 41
(K A Ryan) *chsd ldrs: rdn along over 2f out: grad wknd* **12/1**

1240 **11** 1 ¾ **Moody Tunes**[26] 5639 3-9-0 **78**................ PhillipMakin 10 — 36
(K R Burke) *a rr* **11/2**[3]

3050 **12** ¾ **Fiefdom (IRE)**[15] 5877 4-9-4 **80**................ TomEaves 1 — 36
(I W McInnes) *a rr* **40/1**

L/0- **13** 1 ¼ **Akinola (IRE)**[116] 3062 5-8-10 **72**................ CatherineGannon 4 — 25
(K A Ryan) *s.i.s: a rr* **33/1**

3421 **14** 20 **Flying Edge (IRE)**[77] 4230 6-8-8 **70**................ AdrianTNicholls 5 — —
(E J Alston) *chsd ldrs: rdn along 1/2-way: sn wknd* **28/1**

1m 31.48s (4.12) **Going Correction** +0.70s/f (Yiel)
WFA 3 from 4yo+ 2lb — **14** Ran SP% **118.7**
Speed ratings (Par 105):104,103,101,100,100 98,89,88,84,83 81,80,78,56
CSF £19.43 CT £200.69 TOTE £5.70: £1.80, £1.50, £5.50; EX 25.50.
Owner David W Armstrong **Bred** Lady Fairhaven **Trained** Great Habton, N Yorks
■ Stewards' Enquiry : Pat Cosgrave caution: used whip down the shoulder in the forehand position

FOCUS
A fair handicap run at a good pace and the form looks straightforward and sound, rated around the winner and the third.
Titinius(IRE) Official explanation: jockey said gelding hung badly left in straight
North Walk(IRE) Official explanation: jockey said gelding lost its action
Moody Tunes Official explanation: jockey said gelding was unsuited by the track
Flying Edge(IRE) Official explanation: jockey said gelding was unsuited by the soft ground

6161 BOOK RACEDAY HOSPITALITY ON 01748 810165 H'CAP — 1m 7f 177y

4:45 (4:45) (Class 5) (0-70,65) 3-Y-0+ — £3,886 (£1,156; £577; £288) Stalls Low

Form — RPR

/0-6 **1** **Aston Lad**[14] 5905 5-8-9 **46**................ PaulHanagan 3 — 54+
(Micky Hammond) *trckd ldrs: smooth hdwy 4f out: led 2f out: rdn over 1f out: styd on gamely ins last* **4/1**[2]

3210 **2** 1 ¼ **Thewhirlingdervish (IRE)**[8] 6011 8-9-9 **65**........ DuranFentiman(5) 4 — 71
(T D Easterby) *hld up: gd hdwy 3f ouit: rdn to chal over 1f out and ev ch tl drvn and no ex wl ins last* **5/1**[3]

6020 **3** 8 **Ferrando**[146] 2150 4-8-13 **50**................ DeanMcKeown 6 — 46
(G A Swinbank) *hld up in rr: hdwy 3f out: rdn to chse ldrs wl over 1f out: kpt on u.p ins last: nrst fin* **7/1**

4544 **4** nk **True (IRE)**[12] 5927 5-8-11 **48** ow2................ TonyCulhane 2 — 44
(Mrs S Lamyman) *hld up in rr: hdwy over 3f out: rdn to chse ldrs wl: over 1f out: sn drvn and one pce* **7/1**

0004 **5** 5 **Scurra**[50] 5061 7-8-6 **46** oh6................ AndrewMullen(3) 9 — 36
(A C Whillans) *prom: hdwy to ld over 3f out: rdn and hdd 2f out: sn drvn and wknd* **25/1**

0005 **6** ¾ **Mr Wiseguy**[13] 5910 3-8-10 **57** ow2................ NCallan 1 — 46
(G C Bravery) *trckd ldrs: hdwy over 3f out: ev ch wl over 1f out: sn rdn and wknd* **11/1**

5-43 **7** 8 **Cava Bien**[28] 5587 4-8-9 **49**................ StephenDonohoe(3) 7 — 29
(B J Llewellyn) *trckd ldrs: hdwy over 3f out: ev ch 2f out: sn rdn and wknd over 1f out* **11/4**[1]

0552 **8** 8 **Mystified (IRE)**[16] 5836 3-8-0 **52** ow4........(b) AndrewElliott(5) 5 — 22
(R F Fisher) *keen: prom tl led after 5f and sn clr: hdd over 3f out and sn wknd* **12/1**

1000 **9** 11 **Vice Admiral**[10] 5971 3-8-13 **60**................ DaleGibson 8 — 17
(M W Easterby) *led 5f: chsd clr ldr tl rdn along over 4f out and sn wknd* **16/1**

3m 51.82s (20.42) **Going Correction** +0.70s/f (Yiel)
WFA 3 from 4yo+ 10lb — **9** Ran SP% **114.1**
Speed ratings (Par 103):76,75,71,71,68 68,64,60,54
CSF £24.02 CT £134.26 TOTE £5.00: £1.40, £1.80, £3.10; EX 26.50.
Owner S T Brankin **Bred** Micky Hammond Racing Ltd And S Branklin **Trained** Middleham Moor, N Yorks

FOCUS
A low-grade staying handicap best rated through the runner-up.
Ferrando Official explanation: jockey said gelding lost its action
Cava Bien Official explanation: trainer had no explanation for the poor form shown

6162 COME RACING AGAIN NEXT TUESDAY H'CAP — 5f

5:15 (5:16) (Class 6) (0-65,65) 3-Y-0+ — £2,730 (£806; £403) Stalls Low

Form — RPR

3431 **1** **Alugat (IRE)**[21] 5752 3-8-12 **62**................(p) SaleemGolam(3) 6 — 75
(Mrs A Duffield) *racd centre: mde virtually all: rdn clr and edgd lft ent last: styd on strly* **11/2**[2]

0660 **2** 1 ¼ **Conjecture**[24] 5684 4-9-4 **65**................ PatCosgrave 1 — 74
(R Bastiman) *chsd ldr far side gp: rdn over 1f out: kpt on to ld that gp ins last* **12/1**

2600 **3** ½ **Throw The Dice**[15] 5865 4-8-13 **60**................(p) CatherineGannon 5 — 67
(D W Barker) *led far side gp: rdn along 2f out: drvn and one pce ent last* **12/1**

3002 **4** ½ **Viewforth**[26] 5635 8-9-1 **62**................(b) TomEaves 7 — 67
(I Semple) *racd centre: rdn along: outpcd and bhd after 2f: hdwy over 1f out: styd on ins last: nrst fin* **13/2**[3]

2001 **5** 2 **Howards Princess**[10] 5970 4-8-10 **57**................(v) DaleGibson 14 — 55
(J Hetherton) *dwlt and bhd: swtchd to stands rail after 1f: hdwy 2f out: sn rdn and kpt on same pce ins last* **12/1**

00 **6** 1 **Tartatartufata**[58] 4834 4-8-13 **63**................(v) PatrickMathers(3) 15 — 57
(D Shaw) *prom towards stands side: rdn 2f out: grad wknd* **18/1**

4200 **7** 2 **The Leather Wedge (IRE)**[24] 5684 7-8-12 **62**.... StephenDonohoe(3) 11 — 49
(R Johnson) *prom towards stands rail: rdn 2f out: grad wknd* **17/2**

0000 **8** 1 ½ **Rothesay Dancer**[24] 5684 3-9-1 **62**................(p) TonyCulhane 8 — 44
(J S Goldie) *chsd wnr centre: rdn 2f out: drvn and wknd ent last* **20/1**

2000 **9** hd **Ashes (IRE)**[39] 5333 4-8-13 **65**................ AndrewElliott(5) 3 — 46
(K R Burke) *chsd ldng pair far side: rdn along 2f out: grad wknd* **16/1**

U265 **10** 1 ½ **Harrys House**[15] 5865 4-8-13 **60**................(p) GrahamGibbons 9 — 35
(J J Quinn) *racd centre: a towards rr* **7/2**[1]

6000 **11** *2 ½* **Colonel Cotton (IRE)**[29] 5577 7-8-10 **62**................(v) JamieMoriarty[(5)] 4 28
(R A Fahey) *racd centre: a towards rr* **14/1**
5000 **12** *1* **Betsen (IRE)**[33] 5493 4-8-13 **60**.................................. AdrianTNicholls 12 23
(D Nicholls) *racd towards stands side: a towards rr* **16/1**
3-05 **13** *10* **The Fisio**[281] 126 6-9-2 **63**..(v) NCallan 10 —
(S Gollings) *in tch stands side: rdn along 1/2-way: sn wknd* **33/1**
000 **14** *nk* **Almaty Express**[15] 5878 4-8-13 **60**..............................(b) PaulHanagan 13 —
(J R Weymes) *prom stands side: rdn along after 2f: sn wknd* **20/1**

63.35 secs (2.75) **Going Correction** +0.575s/f (Yiel) **14** Ran SP% **120.7**
Speed ratings (Par 101):101,99,98,97,94 92,89,87,86,84 80,78,62,62
CSF £68.39 CT £551.24 TOTE £6.60: £2.50, £2.90, £5.70; EX 114.30 Place 6 £69.09, Place 5 £47.36.
Owner Ian West & Partners **Bred** Rathbarry Stud **Trained** Constable Burton, N Yorks

FOCUS
A modest sprint handicap in which they raced all over the track and the winner came up the centre. The placed horses, who raced far side, were close to form.
T/Plt: £131.40 to a £1 stake. Pool: £71,202.45. 395.30 winning tickets. T/Qpdt: £51.50 to a £1 stake. Pool: £4,936.60. 70.80 winning tickets. JR

6055 YARMOUTH (L-H)
Tuesday, October 24
6163 Meeting Abandoned - Waterlogged

5801 SAINT-CLOUD (L-H)
Tuesday, October 24

OFFICIAL GOING: Soft

6171a PRIX DE FLORE (GROUP 3) (F&M) 1m 2f 110y
2:30 (2:34) 3-Y-0+ **£27,586** (£11,034; £8,276; £5,517; £2,759)

RPR
1 **Miss Salvador (FR)**[70] 3-8-7 .... TJarnet 3 108
(S Wattel, France) *hld up in last, wnt 6th 5f out, hdwy on outside 2f out, rdn to go 2nd just ins fnl f, ran on strongly to ld on line* **5/1**[3]
2 *nse* **Wingspan (USA)**[143] 2257 3-8-7 .... OPeslier 4 108
(A Fabre, France) *raced in 6th, dropped back to last and not settled 5f out, headway over 1 1/2f out, led 1f out, caught on line* **82/10**
3 *3* **Bastet (IRE)**[148] 2092 4-8-11 ....(b) SPasquier 7 101
(E Lellouche, France) *led, set steady pace, headed 1f out, one pace* **32/10**[2]
4 *½* **Anna Mona (GER)**[68] 4543 3-8-7 .... C-PLemaire 2 102
(A De Royer-Dupre, France) *unruly & reluctant to load, raced in 3rd, went 2nd over 3f out, every chance 2f out til one pace from 1f out* **9/1**
5 *hd* **Dynaforce (USA)**[25] 3-8-7 .... CSoumillon 5 102
(A Fabre, France) *racd in 2nd til edged rt & dropped bck to 3rd over 3f out, still edging rt & dropped bck to last 1 1/2f out, some late hdwy* **7/5**[1]
6 *snk* **Bird Of Paradise (FR)**[125] 4-8-11 .... IMendizabal 1 99
(E Libaud, France) *towards rear on inside, 5th straight, chasing leader & in contention when n.m.r on inside 1f out, one pace* **6/1**
7 *1* **Princess Jones**[58] 6-8-11 .... FVeron 6 98
(J-L Guillochon, France) *raced in 4th, effort to dispute 2nd 2f out, weakened 1f out* **19/1**

2m 19.7s
WFA 3 from 4yo+ 5lb **7** Ran SP% **122.3**
PARI-MUTUEL: WIN 6.00; PL 2.70, 3.80; SF 37.70.
Owner J-L Pariente **Bred** J-L Pariente **Trained** France

NOTEBOOK
Miss Salvador(FR) was disqualified in her previous race at Deauville having passed the post on her own so deserved this compensation. Dropped out early on, she came with a beautifully timed late run up the centre of the track to win in the last stride. This race had been her target for some time and she is now finished for the season, but she remains in training next year.
Wingspan(USA) was much better suited to this distance than the mile and a half she ran over last time. She quickened well from two out to lead at the furlong marker, where she looked to have the race in the bag, only to be robbed by inches at the post.
Bastet(IRE) was racing for the first time in five months and was wearing blinkers for the first time. Soon at the head of affairs, she slowed things down on the far side of the track. She led until a furlong and a half out but was then one-paced to the line.
Anna Mona(GER) played up considerably before the start and the handlers were very patient with her. Always well up, she was in with a chance halfway up the straight but could only stay on at the one pace.

6047 NOTTINGHAM (L-H)
Wednesday, October 25

OFFICIAL GOING: Straight course - heavy; inner course - soft
Apart from the 3.10, all races took place on the inner (formerly jumps) track.
Wind: Light, across Weather: Raining

6172 LITTLE JOHN (S) STKS 1m 54y
2:00 (2:03) (Class 6) 2-Y-0 **£2,388** (£705; £352) **Stalls** Centre

Form RPR
05 **1** **Benayoun**[7] 6055 2-8-11 .... JoeFanning 2 55
(M H Tompkins) *sn chsng ldrs: rdn over 2f out: led ins fnl f: styd on* **4/1**[2]
2521 **2** *¾* **Emergency Services**[9] 6016 2-9-2 56....................(p) RichardThomas 16 58
(Tom Dascombe) *a.p: hung lft over 2f out: sn n.m.r and hmpd: hmpd over 1f out: sn hung rt: r.o* **7/2**[1]
346 **3** *½* **Generist**[68] 4545 2-8-3 54.. DominicFox[(3)] 12 47
(M J Attwater) *chsd ldr: led and hung rt 2f out: sn rdn: hung rt and hdd ins fnl f: no ex* **14/1**
56 **4** *1* **Noverfancy (IRE)**[106] 3385 2-8-6 ....(t) OscarUrbina 6 45
(M Botti) *hld up: hdwy over 3f out: hung lft and bumped 2f out: hmpd again over 1f out: styd on same pce ins fnl f* **6/1**[3]
2000 **5** *nk* **Hair Of The Dog**[9] 6007 2-8-11 61................................ MickyFenton 15 49
(J G Given) *hld up: hdwy u.p over 2f out: r.o: nt rch ldrs* **14/1**
2500 **6** *1* **Only A Splash**[17] 5843 2-8-11 50.. PaulQuinn 5 47
(D W Chapman) *led: hung rt and hdd 2f out: wknd wl ins fnl f* **33/1**
4106 **7** *4* **Mollyanko**[117] 3054 2-8-6 55... LiamJones[(5)] 11 39
(W G M Turner) *hld up: hrd rdn over 3f out: sn hung lft: nt rch ldrs* **14/1**
0000 **8** *nk* **Field Sport (FR)**[12] 5933 2-8-11 52................................(p) SebSanders 10 39
(C E Brittain) *prom: rdn over 3f out: wknd 2f out* **10/1**
0 **9** *1* **King Of Magic**[9] 6016 2-8-4 .... JackDean[(7)] 13 37
(W G M Turner) *hld up in tch: rdn over 3f out: wknd 2f out* **25/1**
0300 **10** *4* **Little Tiny Tom**[12] 5948 2-8-4 52................................(p) PaulPickard[(7)] 17 29
(C N Kellett) *hld up: a in rr* **50/1**
0620 **11** *7* **Dansilver**[15] 5891 2-8-4 57.. JosephWalsh[(7)] 3 15
(D J Wintle) *hld up: a in rr* **9/1**
60 **12** *3* **Haut La Vie**[15] 5893 2-8-11 .... StephenCarson 4 9
(R F Johnson Houghton) *chsd ldrs: rdn over 3f out: sn wknd* **12/1**
0 **13** *1 ¾* **Monkshill**[8] 6023 2-8-6 .... PaulDoe 9 —
(Miss Tor Sturgis) *sn outpcd* **66/1**
0000 **14** *13* **Allroundtheoutside**[9] 6018 2-8-4 60... PNolan[(7)] 1 —
(P R Chamings) *unruly in stalls: s.s: sn prom: n.m.r and lost pl 6f out: sn bhd* **25/1**
4404 **15** *8* **Three No Trumps**[13] 5923 2-8-6 54.................................. HayleyTurner 7 —
(D Morris) *s.i.s: outpcd* **25/1**

1m 50.95s (4.55) **Going Correction** +0.475s/f (Yiel) **15** Ran SP% **121.2**
Speed ratings (Par 93):96,95,94,93,93 92,88,88,87,83 76,73,71,58,50
CSF £17.00 TOTE £3.50: £2.10, £1.50, £5.00; EX 15.00.The winner was bought in for 11,000gns
Owner Sakal Family **Bred** P A And Mrs D G Sakal **Trained** Newmarket, Suffolk
■ Stewards' Enquiry : Dominic Fox two-day ban: careless riding (Nov 5-6)

FOCUS
A weak seller unlikely to produce many future winners.

NOTEBOOK
Benayoun had run a reasonable race in the context of this event when fifth in a maiden last time, and the step up to a mile promised to suit on this drop in grade. While his rivals wandered off a straight line in the closing stages, he had the far-side rail to help and kept straight under pressure. The form is nothing to write home about, however. (op 9-2 tchd 7-2)
Emergency Services, a winner over this trip at Windsor last time, had a penalty to carry for that win, but it was not that that got him beaten here but his tendency to hang in the straight. He got into a bit of a bumping match with the eventual third and fourth, too, which did not help. (tchd 9-2)
Generist, stepping up to a mile for the first time, was another unable to keep to a straight line in the final two furlongs. She continually hung right despite her rider attempting corrective action with the whip. Official explanation: jockey said filly hung right-handed (op 16-1)
Noverfancy(IRE), wearing a tongue strap for the first time on this drop in grade, received a few bumps from the eventual runner-up and appeared somewhat intimidated by that. This was only her third-ever start and she might be capable of a bit better. (tchd 5-1)
Hair Of The Dog, disappointing since being sent off favourite for a Redcar nursery last month, ran a bit better without suggesting that he is about to break his maiden tag anytime soon. (op 12-1)

6173 OATH MAIDEN STKS (C&G) 1m 54y
2:35 (2:38) (Class 5) 2-Y-0 **£4,404** (£1,310; £654; £327) **Stalls** Centre

Form RPR
260 **1** **Sahrati**[36] 5457 2-9-0 78.. SebSanders 7 78
(C E Brittain) *mde all: rdn over 2f out: drvn over 1f out: kpt on gamely ins last* **7/2**[2]
3 **2** *hd* **Marriaj (USA)**[15] 5901 2-9-0 .... MickyFenton 11 78
(B Smart) *a cl up: chal 3f out: rdn over 2f out: drvn over 1f out and ev ch tl no ex towards fin* **8/1**
0 **3** *6* **Pigeon Flight**[12] 5947 2-9-0 .... HayleyTurner 12 66
(M L W Bell) *chsd ldrs: rdn along and sltly outpcd 3f out: styd on u.p appr last* **66/1**
0 **4** *2 ½* **Highland Legacy**[15] 5882 2-9-0 .... DarryllHolland 4 61
(M L W Bell) *midfield: hdwy over 3f out: rdn along wl over 2f out: kpt on same pce u.p* **33/1**
00 **5** *½* **Perfect Reward**[15] 5891 2-9-0 .... EddieAhern 14 60
(Mrs A J Perrett) *chsd ldrs: hdwy on outer 3f out and sn rdn to chse ldng pair: drvn 2f out and sn wknd* **20/1**
6 *1 ½* **Wyeth** 2-9-0 .... JamieSpencer 9 57+
(J R Fanshawe) *green and sn pushed along in rr: hdwy 3f out: styd on fnl 2f: nvr a factor* **5/1**[3]
7 *½* **Squadron** 2-9-0 .... RyanMoore 10 56
(Mrs A J Perrett) *rr and pushed along after 3f: hdwy 3f out: sn rdn and plugged on: nvr a factor* **9/1**
8 *2 ½* **Beck** 2-9-0 .... LDettori 1 51
(M L W Bell) *sn prom: rdn along over 3f out: wknd 2f out* **10/3**[1]
9 *3* **Book Of Facts (FR)** 2-9-0 .... JoeFanning 5 45
(M Johnston) *s.i.s and tl sme hdwy fnl 2f* **12/1**
10 *10* **Spartan Dance** 2-9-0 .... RichardThomas 6 25
(J A Geake) *a rr* **33/1**
00 **11** *9* **Kings Shillings**[34] 5491 2-9-0 ....(b[1]) DanielTudhope 13 7
(D Carroll) *midfield: rdn along 4f out: sn wknd* **100/1**
0 **12** *2* **Majestic Chief**[15] 5900 2-9-0 .... NCallan 8 3
(K A Ryan) *chsd ldrs: rdn along 4f out: sn wknd* **25/1**
0 **13** *49* **Crystal Prince**[18] 5814 2-9-0 .... TonyCulhane 3 —
(T P Tate) *a rr* **25/1**

1m 50.47s (4.07) **Going Correction** +0.475s/f (Yiel) **13** Ran SP% **111.6**
Speed ratings (Par 95):98,97,91,89,88 87,86,84,81,71 62,60,11
CSF £26.73 TOTE £4.00: £1.80, £1.70, £18.20; EX 25.10.
Owner Saeed Manana **Bred** Darley **Trained** Newmarket, Suffolk

FOCUS
Fair maiden form rated around the winner.

NOTEBOOK
Sahrati had the best form coming into the race and coped well enough with the softer ground to get off the mark at the fourth attempt. He had to battle to win, and he and the runner-up pulled clear of the rest, but the form looks no better than fair. (op 10-3 tchd 3-1)
Marriaj(USA), beaten a long way into third behind two useful rivals at Newcastle last time, showed improved form on his second start. He pushed the more experienced winner all the way to the line and, on this evidence, should have no trouble winning an ordinary maiden, either on turf or on the All-Weather, before the year is out. (op 10-1 tchd 11-1)
Pigeon Flight, a half-brother to a couple of hurdles winners in Lemagarut and Fantastic Star, tracked the pace for most of the way and, after getting outpaced early in the straight, kept on again for a modest third place at the finish. He looks to be crying out for a longer trip already.
Highland Legacy, a half-brother to high-class middle-distance performer High Accolade, showed the benefit of his debut 15 days earlier and kept on fairly well from off the pace. He will not come into his own until stepped up to middle distances next season. (op 50-1)
Perfect Reward went in pursuit of the first two early in the straight but was soon beaten off and dropped out of contention for the minor placing. He has now had the three runs required for a mark and should do better in handicap company next year. (op 25-1)
Wyeth, a brother to top-class middle-distance older horse Grandera, and half-brother to 2000 Guineas winner George Washington, was too green to do himself justice on this debut, although he made up some ground in the closing stages. He will know more next time. (op 7-2 tchd 11-2)
Beck, a half-brother to three winners over a mile plus, namely Araglin, Ciel and Rill, looked the pick of the Michael Bell representatives, but he proved disappointing on this debut. Clearly thought capable of better than this, he is not one to give up on yet. (op 3-1 tchd 11-4)
Crystal Prince Official explanation: jockey said colt stumbled 2 1/2f out

6174 WILL YOU MARRY ME LUCY BEARDSALL H'CAP — 6f 15y

3:10 (3:11) (Class 5) (0-70,71) 3-Y-0+ £3,238 (£963; £481; £240) Stalls Low

Form / RPR

3561 **1** **Bel Cantor**[7] [6048] 3-9-1 **71** 6ex RichardKingscote(3) 5 — 85
(W J H Ratcliffe) *mde all far side: rdn clr over 1f out: eased nr fin* **3/1**[1]

1200 **2** *2* **Apply Dapply**[12] [5953] 3-9-1 **68** SteveDrowne 10 — 76
(H Morrison) *racd far side: hld up: hdwy over 1f out: swtchd lft ins fnl f: r.o: no ch w wnr: 2nd of 9 in gp* **16/1**

6301 **3** *1* **Pamir (IRE)**[16] [5872] 4-9-1 **67** (b) JimCrowley 6 — 72
(P R Chamings) *racd far side: chsd wnr: rdn over 1f out: no ex ins fnl f: 3rd of 9 in gp* **15/2**[3]

0101 **4** *3* **George The Best (IRE)**[16] [5865] 5-8-10 **62** PaulHanagan 7 — 58
(Micky Hammond) *racd far side: s.i.s: hld up: r.o ins fnl f: nt trble ldrs: 4th of 9 in gp* **9/1**

0000 **5** *nk* **Anfield Dream**[8] [6035] 4-9-4 **70** EddieAhern 9 — 65
(J R Jenkins) *racd far side: chsd ldrs: rdn over 2f out: wknd over 1f out: 5th of 9 in gp* **28/1**

2000 **6** *hd* **Up Tempo (IRE)**[11] [5961] 8-8-9 **66** (b) LiamJones(5) 4 — 61
(C R Dore) *racd far side: s.i.s: outpcd: r.o ins fnl f: nrst fin: 6th of 9 in gp* **33/1**

4003 **7** *5* **Joy And Pain**[7] [6048] 5-8-11 **68** (p) KevinGhunowa(5) 13 — 48
(R A Harris) *racd stands' side: chsd ldrs: led that side 4f out: rdn 2f out: wknd over 1f out: 1st of 6 in gp* **14/1**

0-50 **8** *1 ¼* **Cyfrwys (IRE)**[232] [608] 5-8-12 **64** FergusSweeney 1 — 40
(B Palling) *racd far side: prom over 3f: 7th of 9 in gp* **66/1**

5000 **9** *nk* **Sabrina Brown**[16] [5872] 5-8-12 **64** (t) RichardThomas 15 — 39
(J A Geake) *racd stands' side: prom: chsd ldr of that gp 4f out: rdn and wknd over 1f out: 2nd of 6 in gp* **6/1**[2]

2002 **10** *2* **Greek Secret**[15] [5902] 3-8-6 **66** JamesO'Reilly(7) 11 — 35
(J O'Reilly) *racd stands' side: prom: rdn 1/2-way: wknd 2f out: 3rd of 6 in gp* **10/1**

0320 **11** *5* **Briery Lane (IRE)**[27] [5635] 5-8-9 **61** (p) MickyFenton 8 — 15
(Mrs K Walton) *racd far side: outpcd: 8th of 9 in gp* **20/1**

000 **12** *12* **Sundance (IRE)**[19] [5791] 4-9-3 **69** JimmyQuinn 3 — —
(H J Collingridge) *racd far side: prom to 1/2-way: last of 9 in gp* **16/1**

0461 **13** *2* **Paddywack (IRE)**[16] [5878] 9-8-10 **62** (b) TonyCulhane 16 — —
(D W Chapman) *led stands' side 2f: wknd over 2f out: 4th of 6 in gp* **12/1**

3400 **14** *19* **Calabaza**[29] [5593] 4-8-13 **65** (b) PaulDoe 17 — —
(W Jarvis) *racd stands' side: chsd ldrs to 1/2-way: 5th of 6 in gp* **25/1**

0630 **15** *11* **My Only Sunshine**[16] [5872] 7-8-9 **61** ChrisCatlin 14 — —
(M J Wallace) *racd stands' side: prom to 1/2-way: last of 6 in gp* **12/1**

1m 17.92s (2.92) **Going Correction** +0.575s/f (Yiel)
WFA 3 from 4yo+ 1lb **15** Ran SP% **120.4**
Speed ratings (Par 103):103,100,99,95,94 94,87,86,85,82 76,60,57,32,17
CSF £50.99 CT £340.14 TOTE £3.20: £1.70, £6.70, £2.60; EX 61.70.
Owner W J H Ratcliffe **Bred** Henry And Mrs Rosemary Moszkowicz **Trained** Leyburn, N Yorks

FOCUS
A modest sprint handicap in which the field split and those drawn low held a distinct advantage due to the fact that the far-side rail had been moved back.
Paddywack(IRE) Official explanation: jockey said gelding had no more to give

6175 FRIAR TUCK MAIDEN STKS — 5f 13y

3:45 (3:45) (Class 5) 2-Y-0 £3,238 (£963; £481; £240) Stalls High

Form / RPR

6 **1** **Dramatic Turn**[15] [5894] 2-8-12 EddieAhern 10 — 82+
(Mrs A J Perrett) *led stands side gp: overall ldr 2f out: sn rdn and styd on strly* **11/8**[1]

3630 **2** *2 ½* **Goodbye Cash (IRE)**[23] [5735] 2-8-12 73 NCallan 2 — 74
(P D Evans) *overall ldr far side: rdn along and hdd 2f out: sn drvn and kpt on same pce ent last* **4/1**[3]

0 **3** *2 ½* **Come What May**[26] [5645] 2-8-12 ChrisCatlin 9 — 65
(Rae Guest) *chsd ldrs stands side: rdn along over 2f out: kpt on u.p ins last* **10/1**

3 **4** *nk* **Excessive**[26] [5645] 2-8-12 PaulDoe 12 — 64
(W Jarvis) *chsd ldrs stands side: rdn over 2f out: kpt on ins last: nrst fin* **10/3**[2]

0 **5** *shd* **Sangreal**[29] [5592] 2-8-12 PatCosgrave 1 — 64
(K R Burke) *cl up far side: rdn along 1/2-way: sn wknd* **33/1**

0006 **6** *5* **Answer Back**[21] [5766] 2-8-9 45 RichardKingscote(3) 8 — 46
(Miss J R Tooth) *cl up stands side: rdn over 2f out and sn wknd* **66/1**

7 *nk* **A Big Sky Brewing (USA)** 2-9-3 PhillipMakin 3 — 50
(T D Barron) *chsd ldng pair far side: rdn along 1/2-way: sn outpcd* **20/1**

0 **8** *¾* **Sun Of The Sea**[141] [2315] 2-9-0 JamesDoyle(3) 5 — 47
(N P Littmoden) *dwlt and wnt rt s: a rr stands side* **9/1**

00 **9** *2 ½* **O'Dwyer (IRE)**[7] [6047] 2-9-3 SilvestreDeSousa 7 — 39
(A D Brown) *a towards rr stands side* **100/1**

10 *3 ½* **River Club** 2-9-3 DanielTudhope 6 — 26
(A Dickman) *v.s.a: a bhd far side* **33/1**

6 **11** *½* **Ingleby Hill (IRE)**[7] [6047] 2-9-3 FrancisNorton 11 — 25
(T D Barron) *a bhd stands side* **16/1**

12 *3* **Master William** 2-8-10 JackDean(7) 4 — 14
(W G M Turner) *a bhd stands side* **100/1**

61.75 secs (-0.05) **Going Correction** -0.125s/f (Firm) **12** Ran SP% **124.3**
Speed ratings (Par 95):95,91,87,86,86 78,77,76,72,67 66,61
CSF £7.07 TOTE £2.10: £1.40, £1.50, £3.20; EX 9.30.
Owner Lisselan Farms Ltd **Bred** Mrs M J Blackburn **Trained** Pulborough, W Sussex

FOCUS
Run on the other sprint course, this looks pretty solid maiden form based on the performances of the runner-up and sixth.

NOTEBOOK
Dramatic Turn bagged the stands'-side rail and made every yard on her side of the track, moving into the overall lead with two furlongs to run and drawing clear for a fairly comfortable win. Dropping back to five furlongs caused this speedily-bred filly few problems and it will be interesting to see whether connections try and pick up a nursery with her before the season comes to an end, or whether they leave her alone now. Either way, she looks one to bear in mind for sprint handicaps next season. (op 7-4)
Goodbye Cash(IRE) is still a maiden but she has the ability to win a race, and the drop back to the minimum trip for the first time saw her run very close to her best. It is doubtful that she was on the wrong side of a track bias, and her performance is probably a good guide to the level of the form. (op 9-2 tchd 7-2)
Come What May, who caught the eye at Lingfield on her debut, ran on well for third place. She needs one more run for a mark and will be of interest once she is eligible to run in handicaps.
Excessive, another who shaped with promise on her debut, again put in her best work at the finish. She looks as though she will appreciate a step up to six furlongs and may also be one who will not be seen at her best until she gets an official rating. (op 3-1 tchd 7-2)
Sangreal, whose dam won over this distance and is from the family of Cherry Hinton winner Crime Of Passion, came home second of those that raced on the far side. A very late foal, she looks the type who will do better next year.
Answer Back Official explanation: jockey said filly had no more to give

6176 HARRY BUCKLE "LIFETIME IN RACING" H'CAP — 1m 54y

4:20 (4:20) (Class 4) (0-80,80) 3-Y-0+ £6,477 (£1,927; £963; £481) Stalls Centre

Form / RPR

6010 **1** **Mezuzah**[25] [5680] 6-9-3 **78** PaulMulrennan 10 — 92
(M W Easterby) *led: hdd 7f out: chsd ldrs: led 2f out: rdn clr fnl f* **10/1**

0664 **2** *4* **Dower House**[15] [5889] 11-8-5 **66** (t) ChrisCatlin 1 — 73
(Andrew Turnell) *a.p: rdn to chse wnr fnl f: no imp* **22/1**

300 **3** *4* **Speed Dial Harry (IRE)**[40] [5337] 4-8-13 **74** (v) RyanMoore 3 — 74
(K R Burke) *prom: rdn over 2f out: wknd fnl f* **14/1**

6002 **4** *hd* **Indian Edge**[15] [5896] 5-8-11 **72** FergusSweeney 11 — 71
(B Palling) *chsd ldr: led 1/2-way: rdn and hdd 2f out: wknd fnl f* **14/1**

5001 **5** *shd* **Parnassian**[23] [5734] 6-8-9 **70** RichardThomas 2 — 69+
(J A Geake) *hld up: hdwy 1/2-way: n.m.r and lost pl 3f out: swtchd rt over 1f out: styd on ins fnl f: nvr able to chal* **7/4**[1]

2133 **6** *1* **Barons Spy (IRE)**[37] [5436] 5-8-8 **72** JamesDoyle(3) 12 — 69
(R J Price) *hld up: hdwy over 3f out: wknd fnl f* **15/2**[3]

000 **7** *nk* **Boundless Prospect (USA)**[77] [4241] 7-9-3 **78** DarryllHolland 16 — 75
(Miss Gay Kelleway) *hld up: hdwy u.p and hung lft over 2f out: wknd fnl f* **50/1**

0234 **8** *½* **Breaking Shadow (IRE)**[18] [5810] 4-8-12 **73** JimmyQuinn 9 — 69+
(T D Barron) *hld up: hdwy over 3f out: sn n.m.r: effrt and swtchd lft over 1f out: sn wknd* **9/2**[2]

0300 **9** *1 ¼* **Davenport (IRE)**[17] [5833] 4-8-11 **79** JamesMillman(7) 14 — 73
(B R Millman) *hld up: rdn over 1f out: n.d* **12/1**

0630 **10** *6* **Skyelady**[29] [5590] 3-8-12 **76** TomEaves 7 — 59
(Miss J A Camacho) *chsd ldrs: rdn over 2f out: sn wknd* **22/1**

6106 **11** *hd* **Glenmuir (IRE)**[17] [5833] 3-9-2 **80** DaneO'Neill 5 — 63
(B R Millman) *s.i.s: hld up: n.d* **33/1**

3601 **12** *nk* **Rowan Lodge (IRE)**[7] [6059] 4-8-13 **74** 6ex (v) NCallan 8 — 56
(M H Tompkins) *hld up: hdwy over 3f out: wkng whn hmpd over 1f out: eased* **12/1**

0/0- **13** *11* **Golden Chalice (IRE)**[402] [4174] 7-9-5 **80** JimCrowley 6 — 42
(P R Chamings) *hld up: nt clr run and wknd over 3f out* **66/1**

00 **14** *14* **Stolen Summer (IRE)**[23] [5722] 3-8-11 **75** MickyFenton 4 — 12
(B S Rothwell) *s.i.s: hdwy to ld 7f out: hdd 1/2-way: sn rdn and wknd* **100/1**

1m 48.86s (2.46) **Going Correction** +0.475s/f (Yiel)
WFA 3 from 4yo+ 3lb **14** Ran SP% **120.2**
Speed ratings (Par 105):106,102,98,97,97 96,96,95,94,88 88,88,77,63
CSF £220.97 CT £3144.13 TOTE £12.80: £2.90, £5.50, £3.50; EX 234.60.
Owner Woodford Group Plc **Bred** Mrs Rebecca Philipps **Trained** Sheriff Hutton, N Yorks

FOCUS
A fair handicap in which the ready winner was full value for his winning margin.

6177 RACING UK ON CHANNEL 432 MAIDEN STKS — 1m 54y

4:55 (4:57) (Class 5) 3-Y-0 £4,210 (£1,252; £625; £312) Stalls Centre

Form / RPR

6233 **1** **Show Winner**[16] [5870] 3-9-3 80 RyanMoore 10 — 75
(J Noseda) *racd wd: cl up: led over 4f out: rdn clr over 1f out: styd on strly* **7/4**[2]

0502 **2** *5* **The Grey One (IRE)**[12] [5949] 3-9-0 54 (p) NeilChalmers(3) 15 — 64
(J M Bradley) *keen: trckd ldrs: hdwy 3f out: rdn to chse wnr 2f out: drvn and one pce appr last* **20/1**

00-0 **3** *6* **Art Historian (IRE)**[11] [5972] 3-9-3 58 RobbieFitzpatrick 9 — 51
(T J Pitt) *bhd: hdwy 3f out: rdn 2f out: styd on strly ins last: nrst fin* **66/1**

63-0 **4** *nk* **Hilltop Destiny**[16] [5879] 3-9-3 65 MichaelTebbutt 2 — 51
(V Smith) *chsd ldrs: rdn along 3f out: drvn 2f out and kpt on same pce* **25/1**

4 **5** *½* **Khyberie**[20] [5774] 3-8-12 SteveDrowne 7 — 45
(G Wragg) *chsd ldrs: swtchd rt and rdn to chse ldng pair 3f out: drvn over 2f out and grad wknd* **12/1**[3]

6 *11* **Monashee River (IRE)** 3-8-5 JamesO'Reilly(7) 16 — 22
(Miss V Haigh) *s.i.s and bhd tl styd on fnl 3f* **125/1**

2050 **7** *½* **Vampyrus**[23] [5726] 3-9-3 62 DaneO'Neill 1 — 26
(H Candy) *led: rdn along and hdd over 4f out: drvn 3f out and sn wknd* **28/1**

066 **8** *½* **Boppys Dancer**[23] [5726] 3-9-3 45 MickyFenton 13 — 25
(P T Midgley) *bhd tl sme hdwy fnl 3f* **150/1**

4 **9** *1 ¼* **Sahara Sphinx (USA)**[7] [6053] 3-9-3 LDettori 6 — 22
(Saeed Bin Suroor) *trckd ldrs: effrt to chse ldng pair 4f out: rdn 3f out and sn wknd* **1/1**[1]

10 *nk* **Cinders Spark** 3-8-12 RichardMullen 12 — 16
(G L Moore) *s.i.s and bhd: hdwy into midfield 1/2-way: sn rdn along and wknd* **66/1**

11 *2 ½* **Ratzia (IRE)** 3-8-12 SebSanders 5 — 11
(C E Brittain) *a rr* **20/1**

00 **12** *3* **Thou Shalt Not**[21] [5768] 3-9-3 JimCrowley 14 — 10
(P S Felgate) *s.i.s: a rr* **200/1**

13 *13* **Keep A Welcome** 3-9-3 DanielTudhope 8 — —
(S Parr) *a towards rr* **100/1**

00 **14** *4* **Mika's Fable (FR)**[165] [1691] 3-8-12 FrancisNorton 4 — —
(Miss Tor Sturgis) *midfield: rdn along ½-way and sn wknd* **125/1**

05- **15** *13* **Politkovskaya**[410] [5110] 3-8-12 PaulHanagan 17 — —
(T H Caldwell) *a bhd* **200/1**

16 *3* **Merlins Dreams** 3-8-12 DuranFentiman(5) 3 — —
(S Parr) *s.i.s: a bhd* **100/1**

1m 50.92s (4.52) **Going Correction** +0.475s/f (Yiel) **16** Ran SP% **119.1**
Speed ratings (Par 101):96,91,85,84,84 73,72,72,70,70 68,65,52,48,35 32
CSF £41.50 TOTE £2.80: £1.20, £4.20, £13.70; EX 31.00.
Owner Sir Gordon Brunton **Bred** Sir Gordon Brunton **Trained** Newmarket, Suffolk

FOCUS
A weak three-year-old maiden that saw the field finish fairly strung out. The form is limited by the proximity of the placed horses.
Sahara Sphinx(USA) Official explanation: jockey said gelding was unsuited by soft ground

6178 WILL SCARLET H'CAP — 2m 9y

5:30 (5:33) (Class 6) (0-65,65) 3-Y-0+ £2,730 (£806; £403) Stalls Far side

Form / RPR

-210 **1** **Desert Storm (DEN)**[30] [5564] 4-10-0 **65** NCallan 16 — 76
(Rae Guest) *a.p: rdn to ld over 1f out: all out* **11/2**[3]

0040 **2** *2* **Give It Time**[11] 5960 3-8-11 **58** .... J-PGuillambert 6 67
(J G Given) *chsd ldrs: rdn over 2f out: no ex ins fnl f* **22/1**

1-00 **3** *10* **Grasp**[9] 6011 4-9-9 **60** .... (bt) RyanMoore 3 57
(G L Moore) *led 2f: chsd ldr: led over 5f out: rdn over 2f out: hdd over 1f out: wknd fnl f* **25/1**

0003 **4** *11* **Jazrawy**[15] 5887 4-8-8 **52** .... WilliamCarson(7) 5 36
(P W Hiatt) *led 14f out: hdd over 5f out: rdn and wknd over 3f out* **33/1**

060/ **5** *nk* **Columbus (IRE)**[186] 4502 9-9-4 **55** .... HayleyTurner 2 38
(Jennie Candlish) *chsd ldrs: racd keenly: lost pl 6f out: n.d after* **80/1**

44-6 **6** *½* **Woodford Consult**[183] 1219 4-9-2 **53** .... PaulMulrennan 8 36
(M W Easterby) *prom: rdn 6f out: wknd over 4f out* **28/1**

3463 **7** *nk* **Great As Gold (IRE)**[9] 6011 7-9-12 **63** .... (p) TomEaves 13 45
(B Ellison) *hld up: rdn over 5f out: n.d* **4/1**[1]

0010 **8** *2* **Fair Spin**[23] 5723 6-8-12 **49** .... (p) PaulHanagan 14 29
(Micky Hammond) *hld up: hdwy 6f out: rdn and wknd over 4f out* **12/1**

324 **9** *10* **Ha'Penny Beacon**[23] 5741 3-9-4 **65** .... DanielTudhope 7 33
(D Carroll) *mid-div: hdwy 1/2-way: rdn and wknd over 3f out* **14/1**

5145 **10** *19* **Serramanna**[12] 5935 5-9-4 **58** .... JamesDoyle(3) 1 3
(Ms J S Doyle) *hld up: sme hdwy 7f out: wknd 5f out* **9/1**

0600 **11** *6* **Montana Sky (IRE)**[29] 5589 3-8-8 **55** ow1 .... SteveDrowne 4 —
(R A Harris) *chsd ldrs 10f* **40/1**

3205 **12** *5* **Accordello (IRE)**[23] 5723 5-9-7 **58** .... JimCrowley 15 —
(K G Reveley) *hld up: rdn over 5f out: a in rr* **5/1**[2]

0420 **13** *2½* **Laggan Bay (IRE)**[11] 5963 6-9-12 **63** .... (b) LPKeniry 12 —
(J S Moore) *hld up: hdwy 6f out: wknd over 4f out* **15/2**

/0-3 **14** *12* **Baranook (IRE)**[25] 5691 5-9-9 **60** .... ChrisCatlin 17 —
(D J Wintle) *hld up: bhd fr 1/2-way* **20/1**

50/0 **15** *2½* **Dangerously Good**[12] 5952 8-9-9 **60** .... JoeFanning 9 —
(G L Moore) *hld up: bhd fnl 10f* **40/1**

0326 **16** *11* **Jayer Gilles**[30] 5564 6-9-5 **56** .... DaneO'Neill 10 —
(Dr J R J Naylor) *mid-div: hdwy 1/2-way: wknd 5f out* **11/1**

3m 51.15s (17.65) **Going Correction** +0.475s/f (Yiel)
WFA 3 from 4yo+ 10lb **16** Ran SP% **122.0**
Speed ratings (Par 101):74,73,68,62,62 62,61,60,55,46 43,40,39,33,32 26
CSF £128.36 CT £2807.83 TOTE £8.10: £2.20, £4.90, £4.30, £5.80; EX 292.30 Place 6 £242.00, Place 5 £144.52.
Owner A Elsass **Bred** York Stutteri **Trained** Newmarket, Suffolk

FOCUS
A moderate staying handicap that saw the field trail home on the testing surface. The first two came well clear.
Great As Gold(IRE) Official explanation: jockey said gelding never travelled
Serramanna Official explanation: jockey said mare was unsuited by soft ground
T/Plt: £257.90 to a £1 stake. Pool: £51,551.45. 145.90 winning tickets. T/Qpdt: £55.00 to a £1 stake. Pool: £3,391.10. 45.60 winning tickets. CR

6179 - 6185a (Foreign Racing) - See Raceform Interactive

6142
LINGFIELD (L-H)
Thursday, October 26

OFFICIAL GOING: Standard
Wind: Moderate, behind Weather: Fine but cloudy

6186 EBF LADBROKES.COM MAIDEN FILLIES' STKS (DIV I) 7f (P)
1:50 (1:51) (Class 5) 2-Y-O **£3,886** (£1,156; £577; £288) **Stalls** Low

Form RPR

1 **Dalvina** 2-9-0 .... JamieSpencer 14 81+
(E A L Dunlop) *athletic: s.i.s: settled in rr and racd wd: plenty to do 2f out: gd prog over 1f out: r.o to ld last 100yds: cleverly* **12/1**

4 **2** *1¼* **Salsa Steps (USA)**[16] 5894 2-9-0 .... SteveDrowne 11 76
(H Morrison) *w'like: racd wd: trckd ldrs: awkward bnd 4f out: effrt 2f out: rdn to ld briefly ins fnl f: outpcd by wnr nr fin* **11/4**[1]

3 *1* **Ballroom Dancer (IRE)** 2-9-0 .... DarryllHolland 5 73
(J Noseda) *w'like: trckd ldrs: shkn up and nt qckn 2f out: r.o again ins fnl f* **9/2**[2]

4 *hd* **Royal Choir** 2-9-0 .... SebSanders 8 73
(C E Brittain) *w'like: pressed ldrs: rdn to chal over 1f out: upsides ent fnl f: one pce* **50/1**

5 *¾* **Scarlet Ibis** 2-9-0 .... LDettori 3 71
(Saeed Bin Suroor) *w'like: athletic: mde most: shkn up and hrd pressed over 1f out: hdd and nt qckn ins fnl f* **5/1**[3]

6 *shd* **Ventura (USA)** 2-9-0 .... JimmyFortune 1 71
(Mrs A J Perrett) *w'like: scope: bit bkwd: wl in tch on inner: effrt 2f out: rdn to chal and nrly upsides ent fnl f: fdd* **25/1**

7 *½* **High 'n Dry (IRE)** 2-9-0 .... TedDurcan 9 69
(C A Cyzer) *w'like: scope: str: t.k.h: hld up in midfield: shkn up 2f out: green and hanging over 1f out: styd on steadily fnl f* **66/1**

8 *3* **Expedience (USA)** 2-9-0 .... RyanMoore 6 62
(Sir Michael Stoute) *leggy: bit bkwd: nvr beyond midfield: rdn and no prog over 2f out* **10/1**

9 *nk* **Zawariq (IRE)** 2-9-0 .... MartinDwyer 12 61
(M P Tregoning) *leggy: s.s: last tl 3f out: pushed along and nvr a factor: modest late prog* **16/1**

10 *4* **Mariaverdi** 2-9-0 .... NCallan 10 50
(B J Meehan) *w'like: bit bkwd: s.s: a towards rr: rdn and no real prog over 2f out* **33/1**

30 **11** *½* **Nabra**[8] 6055 2-9-0 .... RHills 7 49
(J H M Gosden) *w'like: pressed ldr: led briefly 1/2-way: wknd rapidly wl over 1f out* **11/1**

12 *1* **Zaafira (SPA)** 2-8-7 .... SCreighton(7) 4 46
(E J Creighton) *leggy: s.i.s: sn cl up: wknd 2f out* **100/1**

04 **13** *4* **Virginia Reel**[23] 5760 2-9-0 .... KDarley 2 36
(M Johnston) *a wl in rr: rdn and struggling 1/2-way* **20/1**

14 *nk* **Piano Key** 2-9-0 .... RichardHughes 13 35
(R Charlton) *w'like: scope: bit bkwd: s.i.s: rn green and rdn in rr 5f out: eased whn no ch 2f out* **20/1**

1m 25.02s (-0.87) **Going Correction** -0.15s/f (Stan) **14** Ran SP% **113.3**
Speed ratings (Par 92):98,96,95,95,94 94,93,90,89,85 84,83,79,78
CSF £39.44 TOTE £14.10: £3.80, £1.30, £2.20; EX 63.30 Trifecta £147.60 Part won. Pool: £208.92 - 0.67 winning units..
Owner St Albans Bloodstock LLP **Bred** Normandie Stud Ltd **Trained** Newmarket, Suffolk

FOCUS
Quite a decent maiden run in a time 0.06 seconds quicker than the second division, but 0.26 seconds slower than the later juvenile event won by Cabinet. The runner-up sets a reasonable standard.

NOTEBOOK
Dalvina was restrained early in the race from her wide draw, but came home to good effect, winning easily. A nice-looking sort in the paddock, it remains to be seen how good she will turn out to be, but first impressions would suggest that she is very useful. (op 8-1)
Salsa Steps(USA), quite a nice type, was always being niggled just off the pace. She responded well to her jockey's pressure to look a likely winner inside the final furlong, before Dalvina swept past wide and late. One suspects she will be better over further, as her pedigree suggests, and a more galloping track. (op 5-2 tchd 3-1)
Ballroom Dancer(IRE) was never far away and kept on well for pressure. She is nicely bred and looked as though she would improve for the run. (op 5-1)
Royal Choir, who looked quite fit, showed no signs of greenness on her debut and shaped nicely.
Scarlet Ibis, wearing a noseband and cross-noseband, clearly knew her job and was the leader early. She looked physically ready to do her best but will come on mentally for the experience. (op 4-1 tchd 7-2)
Ventura(USA) ◆ was very green in the paddock but ran a race full of promise. A bit keen early, she came up the inside rail to have every chance before not getting home. With some growing to do, she will be a nice sort next year.
High 'n Dry(IRE), green beforehand, was another who was keen during the race but showed distinct promise despite hanging. She looks good enough to pick up a race at two. (op 100-1)
Expedience(USA) looked very green in the paddock and ran accordingly during the race. The run will not be lost on her and a better effort can be expected next time. (op 12-1)
Zawariq(IRE) was noted staying on nicely after getting away slowly. She is almost certainly capable of better. (op 14-1)
Mariaverdi, not over-big, was green beforehand and probably needed this first run.
Zaafira(SPA) looked a bit weak and was very green beforehand.
Piano Key looked quite a good type but might just have needed the run.

6187 EBF LADBROKES.COM MAIDEN FILLIES' STKS (DIV II) 7f (P)
2:20 (2:22) (Class 5) 2-Y-O **£3,886** (£1,156; £577; £288) **Stalls** Low

Form RPR

32 **1** **Baylini**[73] 4434 2-8-11 .... JamesDoyle(3) 2 77+
(Ms J S Doyle) *leggy: scope: trckd ldr after 2f: led 2f out: shkn up over 1f out: hung rt but drew clr fnl f* **9/1**

2 *2½* **Sharp Dresser (USA)** 2-9-0 .... RichardHughes 9 71
(Mrs A J Perrett) *w'like: scope: bit bkwd: s.i.s: wl in rr and off the pce: pushed along 1/2-way: prog 2f out: rdn and styd on wl* **25/1**

3 *nk* **Fabine** 2-9-0 .... JamieSpencer 10 70
(B J Meehan) *leggy: lw: prom: chsd wnr wl over 1f out: sn nt qckn and no imp: lost 2nd nr fin* **2/1**[1]

0 **4** *½* **Lawyers Choice**[13] 5950 2-9-0 .... DaneO'Neill 7 68
(Pat Eddery) *w'like: leggy: wl in tch: effrt and swtchd to inner over 1f out: kpt on same pce fnl f* **16/1**

33 **5** *1¼* **Millisecond**[23] 5760 2-9-0 .... PhilipRobinson 11 65
(M A Jarvis) *fast away: led to 2f out: wknd fnl f* **5/2**[2]

6 *¾* **Furbeseta** 2-9-0 .... JimmyFortune 5 63
(L M Cumani) *unf: scope: bit bkwd: trckd ldrs: outpcd 2f out: shkn up and kpt on again fnl f : n.d* **33/1**

7 *2½* **Penny Post (IRE)** 2-9-0 .... JoeFanning 1 57
(M Johnston) *w'like: leggy: chsd ldr for 2f: prom tl wknd 2f out* **20/1**

8 *nk* **Fuschia** 2-9-0 .... SteveDrowne 8 56
(R Charlton) *w'like: scope: bit bkwd: off the pce in midfield: pushed along 3f out: no prog*

9 *shd* **Kimono Kiss (USA)** 2-9-0 .... MartinDwyer 12 56
(M P Tregoning) *w'like: a off the pce towards rr: no ch fnl 2f* **16/1**

10 *1½* **Oriental Dance** 2-9-0 .... LDettori 6 52
(Saeed Bin Suroor) *leggy: wl in rr and off the pce: effrt on outer over 2f out: sn no prog* **9/2**[3]

0 **11** *2* **Fealeview Lady (USA)**[9] 6031 2-9-0 .... MickyFenton 14 47
(H Morrison) *a wl in rr: wl off the pce and no ch fr 3f out* **100/1**

12 *4* **Pivotalia (IRE)** 2-9-0 .... AdamKirby 4 36
(W R Swinburn) *w'like: scope: s.i.s: a wl off the pce in rr* **33/1**

0 **13** *hd* **Golden Ribbons**[9] 6034 2-8-11 .... AmirQuinn(3) 13 36
(J R Boyle) *str: cmpt: b.hind: chsd ldrs to 1/2-way: wknd rapidly* **100/1**

14 *10* **Childish Thoughts** 2-9-0 .... FJohansson 3 10
(Mrs Norma Pook) *leggy: s.v.s: sn t.o: hung bdly rt fnl f* **66/1**

1m 25.08s (-0.81) **Going Correction** -0.15s/f (Stan) **65** Ran SP% **122.3**
Speed ratings (Par 92):98,95,94,94,92 91,89,88,88,86 84,80,79,68
CSF £219.80 TOTE £11.40: £2.80, £9.60, £1.40; EX 266.90 TRIFECTA Not won..
Owner Ms J S Doyle **Bred** Templeton Stud **Trained** Upper Lambourn, Berks

FOCUS
The winning time was 0.06 seconds slower than the first division and 0.32 seconds slower than the following juvenile event won by Cabinet, but this still looked like quite a good maiden with the winner improving on previous form.

NOTEBOOK
Baylini ◆, upped in trip, tracked the leader throughout and was sent on off the final turn. That move proved decisive and she came away in good style. The winning trainer thinks plenty of her and a nice race can come her way. (op 12-1)
Sharp Dresser(USA) ◆ was not the best away but came through her rivals really strongly to catch the eye in no uncertain terms. With this experience behind her, she ought to go very close next time. (op 20-1 tchd 33-1)
Fabine, quite an attractive type, was never far away but got a bit tired in the home straight, keeping on at only one pace. She has some scope for physical improvement and looks sure to win her maiden in time. (tchd 9-4)
Lawyers Choice, who was supported in the market before the off, ran a much better race than on her debut. A step up in trip looks required. (op 50-1)
Millisecond, who got warm, may have gone off too quickly in front. She needs to learn to settle a bit better. (op 11-4 tchd 3-1)
Furbeseta, from the family of Falbrav, shaped with some promise on debut and can be expected to improve for the run. Official explanation: jockey said filly ran green
Penny Post(IRE), very green in the paddock, tried to go with the early pace, and paid for it late on.
Kimono Kiss(USA) looked fit for her debut. (op 25-1)
Oriental Dance, quite an attractive type, is really nicely bred but disappointed badly, never getting into the race at any stage. Official explanation: jockey said filly ran green (op 4-1 tchd 7-2)
Childish Thoughts Official explanation: jockey said filly missed break and hung right throughout

6188 EBF LADBROKES 24 HOUR BETTING 0800 777 888 MAIDEN STKS 7f (P)
2:50 (2:51) (Class 5) 2-Y-O **£4,533** (£1,348; £674; £336) **Stalls** Low

Form RPR

2 **1** **Cabinet (IRE)**[16] 5883 2-9-3 .... RyanMoore 14 85
(Sir Michael Stoute) *w'like: lw: chsd ldrs: pushed along and prog wl over 2f out: rdn to ld jst ins fnl f: r.o wl* **8/13**[1]

2 *3½* **Sea Land (FR)** 2-9-3 .... MartinDwyer 4 76
(M P Tregoning) *w'like: scope: bit bkwd: str: a in ldng trio: led jst over 2f out: hdd and hanging rt jst ins fnl f: outpcd* **16/1**

3 1 1/2 **Common Purpose (USA)** 2-9-3 .... RichardHughes 5 72
(J H M Gosden) *w'like: scope: str: prog to ld over 4f out: hdd jst over 2f out and sn outpcd: kpt on* **10/1**

0 4 *nk* **All Of Me (IRE)**[8] [6049] 2-9-3 .... JohnEgan 6 71
(T G Mills) *unf: scope: chsd ldrs: effrt over 2f out: sn outpcd: styd on fnl f* **20/1**

5 2 **Greyfriars Abbey** 2-9-3 .... JoeFanning 10 66
(M Johnston) *w'like: wl in rr and wd: gd prog 4f out: chsd ldrs over 2f out: veered wildly wd bnd sn after and lost all ch: v green* **25/1**

0 6 *nk* **Mujma**[16] [5883] 2-9-3 .... RHills 13 65
(Sir Michael Stoute) *w'like: settled in rr and towards outer: sme prog 2f out: shuffled along and kpt on steadily: n.d* **7/1**[2]

0 7 3/4 **Hard As Iron**[70] [4525] 2-9-3 .... NCallan 8 63
(M Blanshard) *w'like: lengthy: bit bkwd: drvn in midfield 4f out: no prog after: plugged on* **100/1**

8 1 3/4 **Russki (IRE)** 2-9-3 .... JimCrowley 3 59+
(Mrs A J Perrett) *w'like: scope: bit bkwd: dwlt: mostly last to 3f out: kpt on fnl f: nvr a factor* **50/1**

9 *hd* **Tawaagg** 2-9-3 .... PhilipRobinson 9 58
(M A Jarvis) *w'like: lw: s.i.s: a towards rr: shkn up and hanging lft over 1f out: no real prog* **8/1**[3]

0 10 1/2 **Sularno**[16] [5892] 2-9-3 .... DaneO'Neill 11 57
(H Morrison) *w'like: nvr beyond midfield: pushed along 3f out: outpcd over 2f out: fdd* **100/1**

0 11 2 1/2 **Golden Folly**[14] [5918] 2-9-3 .... SebSanders 12 50
(Lady Herries) *unf: scope: v green and a wl in rr* **66/1**

06 12 1 **Palmetto Point**[9] [6032] 2-9-3 .... SteveDrowne 7 48
(H Morrison) *w'like: scope: bit bkwd: s.i.s: nvr beyond midfield: rdn 3f out: wknd* **66/1**

0 13 2 **Judge 'n Jury**[14] [5915] 2-9-3 .... TedDurcan 1 43
(C A Cyzer) *w'like: str: trckd ldrs tl wknd over 2f out* **100/1**

0 14 6 **Hot Shot Hamish (IRE)**[14] [5918] 2-9-3 .... LDettori 2 27
(B J Meehan) *w'like: bit bkwd: taken down early: led to over 4f out: wknd rapidly 2f out* **33/1**

1m 24.76s (-1.13) **Going Correction** -0.15s/f (Stan) 14 Ran SP% **120.0**
Speed ratings (Par 95):100,96,94,93,91 91,90,88,88,87 84,83,81,74
CSF £11.60 TOTE £1.70: £1.10, £2.00, £2.70; EX 18.00 Trifecta £74.00 Pool: £475.69 - 4.56 winning units..
Owner The Royal Ascot Racing Club **Bred** Hascombe And Valiant Studs **Trained** Newmarket, Suffolk

FOCUS
The winning time was just over a quarter of a second quicker than both divisions of the fillies maiden and this form looks decent. They certainly appeared a very good-looking bunch in the paddock and the winner sets the standard.

NOTEBOOK
Cabinet(IRE) ◆, despite having the benefit of previous experience, took a fair while to hit top stride but he was well on top at the end and won in decisive fashion. He should appreciate longer trips next season and, quite a good type, he should make up into a decent sort. (op 4-6 tchd 8-11 in places)
Sea Land(FR), a 140,000gns half-brother to three winners, looked to be carrying quite a bit of condition, so this must rate as a very pleasing debut. He looked like winning when regaining the lead off the home turn, but had no answer once the winner swept by. He should not be long in winning his maiden.
Common Purpose(USA), who is bred to be suited by this sort of trip, was ridden positively on his debut but could not respond when the principals attacked on the home turn and looked as though he would improve for the run. (op 11-1)
All Of Me(IRE) again showed promise and will be interesting once qualified for handicaps. (op 25-1)
Greyfriars Abbey ◆, who was very green to post, was the real eye-catcher of the race. Drawn wide, he recovered well from a slow start to get on to the heels of the leaders, but failed to negotiate the bend into the straight and lost all chance. He should be much better for the experience and is one to keep an eye on, especially on a more galloping track.
Mujma finished a little closer than he had at Leicester but never really got into the argument. (tchd 13-2)
Russki(IRE) appeared to be carrying quite a lot of condition and should improve.
Tawaagg, in the owner's first colours, failed to make an impression and, despite his sire being a sprinter, may need longer trips. Official explanation: jockey said colt ran green (tchd 9-1)

6189 POKER AT LADBROKES.COM H'CAP 1m 2f (P)
3:20 (3:21) (Class 5) (0-75,73) 3-Y-0+ **£3,238** (£963; £481; £240) **Stalls** Low

Form RPR

41 1 **Khun John (IRE)**[18] [5847] 3-9-3 **72** .... LDettori 9 80+
(B J Meehan) *lw: mostly pressed ldr: drvn to ld wl over 1f out: styd on wl fnl f and a holding on* **9/2**[1]

250 2 3/4 **Logsdail**[30] [5590] 6-9-3 **67** .... (p) OscarUrbina 11 74
(G L Moore) *b: prom: rdn to chal over 1f out: fnd little and a hld* **11/1**

0000 3 3/4 **Sekula Pata (NZ)**[30] [5590] 7-9-2 **66** .... TPO'Shea 13 71
(Christian Wroe, UAE) *hld up in midfield and wd: sltly outpcd 2f out: styd on wl fnl f* **66/1**

2144 4 *hd* **Veiled Applause**[17] [5879] 3-8-13 **68** .... SebSanders 3 73
(R M Beckett) *prom: tried to chal on inner over 1f out: kpt on same pce* **5/1**[2]

3236 5 *shd* **Burgundy**[6] [6070] 9-9-5 **69** .... (b) RyanMoore 5 74+
(P Mitchell) *lw: dwlt: wl in rr: effrt 2f out: nt clr run and swtchd rt over 1f out: r.o wl last 150yds: nt rch ldrs* **13/2**[3]

1005 6 *nk* **Anduril**[12] [5974] 5-8-10 **63** .... (b) SaleemGolam(3) 6 70+
(Miss M E Rowland) *trckd ldrs: gng strly 2f out: hmpd jst over 1f out: nt rcvr* **25/1**

0005 7 1 **Lord Of Dreams (IRE)**[24] [5740] 4-8-12 **62** .... JimCrowley 7 64
(D W P Arbuthnot) *settled in rr and wd: prog over 2f out: wd bnd sn after and lost grnd: kpt on fnl f* **14/1**

5413 8 1/2 **Barbirolli**[16] [5897] 4-9-4 **68** .... EddieAhern 12 69
(W M Brisbourne) *nvr beyond midfield: rdn over 2f out: kpt on u.p fnl f: nt pce to threaten* **9/2**[1]

1603 9 1/2 **Our Faye**[12] [5973] 3-9-1 **70** .... MartinDwyer 10 70
(S Kirk) *nvr beyond midfield: n.m.r briefly over 2f out: no prog* **16/1**

0/16 10 1 1/2 **Alasil (USA)**[22] [5769] 6-9-1 **70** .... LiamJones(5) 4 67
(R J Price) *mde most to wl over 1f out: wknd* **12/1**

0000 11 *nk* **Barry Island**[20] [5786] 7-9-8 **72** .... NeilPollard 8 69
(D R C Elsworth) *dwlt: mostly in last pair: rdn and no prog 3f out: kpt on fnl f* **16/1**

3320 12 *nk* **Captain Margaret**[20] [5786] 4-9-9 **73** .... JimmyQuinn 14 69
(J Pearce) *mostly last: u.p and no prog over 3f out: kpt on* **16/1**

4030 13 *nk* **Oakley Absolute**[18] [5831] 4-9-4 **68** .... RichardHughes 1 64
(R Hannon) *lw: chsd ldrs tl wknd 2f out* **16/1**

00- 14 1/2 **Lorikeet**[401] [5041] 7-9-1 **65** .... LPKeniry 2 60
(Noel T Chance) *a towards rr: wknd over 1f out* **100/1**

2m 6.38s (-1.41) **Going Correction** -0.15s/f (Stan)
WFA 3 from 4yo+ 5lb 14 Ran SP% **118.9**
Speed ratings (Par 103):99,98,97,97,97 97,96,96,95,94 94,94,93,93
CSF £53.07 CT £2872.63 TOTE £4.40: £1.60, £4.10, £12.40; EX 60.00 TRIFECTA Not won..
Owner The Strawberries To A Donkey Partnership **Bred** Sti Engineering Srl **Trained** Manton, Wilts

FOCUS
This looked a decent handicap for the grade but the pace was modest and it paid to be handy. The third and fourth are the best guides to the form.

6190 EBF FLEUR DE LYS FILLIES' STKS (LISTED RACE) 1m (P)
3:50 (3:51) (Class 1) 3-Y-0+
£17,034 (£6,456; £3,231; £1,611; £807; £405) **Stalls** High

Form RPR

1 1 **Mayonga (IRE)**[11] [5988] 3-8-11 **83** .... SebSanders 6 104+
(Sir Mark Prescott) *lw: hld up: prog on outer fr 3f out: chsd ldr wl over 1f out: drvn and r.o to ld ins fnl f* **12/1**

1- 2 1 **Emily Bronte**[373] [5967] 3-8-11 .... EddieAhern 9 102
(Saeed Bin Suroor) *leggy: hld up: prog and prom over 4f out: led over 2f out: drvn and pressed over 1f out: hdd ins fnl f: kpt on* **6/1**[3]

5406 3 *nk* **Kindlelight Debut**[20] [5785] 6-9-0 **89** .... JamesDoyle 7 101+
(N P Littmoden) *lw: hld up in rr: hmpd wl over 2f out and rdn after: wd bnd 2f out: storming run fnl f: gaining fast at fin* **33/1**

2663 4 1 1/4 **Mamela (GER)**[33] [5525] 5-9-0 **97** .... JimmyFortune 4 98
(L M Cumani) *trckd ldrs: rdn and nt qckn 2f out: styd on fnl f: unable to chal* **8/1**

5016 5 2 **Three Wrens (IRE)**[32] [5550] 4-9-3 **97** .... NickyMackay 10 97
(D J Daly) *hld up towards rr: effrt whn outpcd 2f out: drvn to dispute 3rd over 1f out: one pce after* **12/1**

15-1 6 *shd* **Pure Illusion (IRE)**[16] [5888] 3-8-11 **96** .... LDettori 1 93
(Saeed Bin Suroor) *lw: hld up in midfield: nt clr run over 2f out: drvn to dispute 3rd over 1f out: one pce after* **4/1**[1]

2003 7 1 **Bouboulina**[20] [5785] 3-8-11 **92** .... JamieSpencer 5 91+
(E A L Dunlop) *t.k.h: hld up in last: effrt on outer 3f out: outpcd 2f out: hanging and no prog over 1f out* **4/1**[1]

4632 8 2 1/2 **Kahlua Kiss**[36] [5477] 3-8-11 **96** .... MartinDwyer 2 85
(W R Muir) *hld up on inner: last and rdn 3f out: no real prog* **10/1**

2032 9 2 **Highway To Glory (IRE)**[32] [5550] 3-8-11 **100** .... OscarUrbina 11 81
(M Botti) *t.k.h: hld up bhd ldrs: rdn over 2f out: outpcd whn nt clr run over 1f out: wknd* **9/2**[2]

2504 10 5 **Home Sweet Home (IRE)**[32] [5550] 3-8-11 **92** .... (p) RobertWinston 3 69
(P D Evans) *pressed ldrs tl wknd 2f out* **50/1**

2000 11 3/4 **Pintle**[56] [4965] 6-9-0 **85** .... SteveDrowne 8 67
(J L Spearing) *mde most to over 2f out: wkng whn n.m.r sn after* **66/1**

534- 12 *hd* **Antique (IRE)**[431] [4619] 4-9-0 **107** .... TedDurcan 12 67
(Saeed Bin Suroor) *leggy: lt-f: b: sn pressed ldr: upsides over 2f out: wknd rapidly over 1f out* **16/1**

1m 37.76s (-1.67) **Going Correction** -0.15s/f (Stan)
WFA 3 from 4yo+ 3lb 12 Ran SP% **120.3**
Speed ratings (Par 108):102,101,100,99,97 97,96,93,91,86 86,85
CSF £83.03 TOTE £13.70: £2.90, £2.30, £9.30; EX 87.40 TRIFECTA Not won..
Owner Miss A H Marshall **Bred** Frank Dunne **Trained** Newmarket, Suffolk

FOCUS
Just an ordinary fillies' Listed event, but quite competitive, although the form is only fair for the grade.

NOTEBOOK
Mayonga(IRE), off the mark on her debut for her current connections in a seven-furlong maiden round here on her previous start, improved significantly on the bare form of that success to gain some all-important black type. There could be more to come if connections persevere with her on the track. (op 11-1)
Emily Bronte, unbeaten in two starts over a mile as a juvenile when trained by Andre Fabre, ran a blinder on her debut for Godolphin off the back of a year-long absence. She is open to plenty of improvement. (tchd 13-2)
Kindlelight Debut got in the clear just too late having been stopped in her run and was unlucky not to have finished even closer. (op 25-1)
Mamela(GER), who looked to be going in her coat, ran a good race on her Polytrack debut and just missed out on some black type. (op 15-2)
Three Wrens(IRE) is a good sort on the surface and looked to be going well off the final bend, but she did not find quite as much as had looked likely. (op 14-1)
Pure Illusion(IRE), making her Polytrack debut, proved a shade disappointing and may benefit from a step up in trip. (op 11-2)
Bouboulina, winner of the opening maiden on the card last season, was wide throughout and never got home under pressure. She did not seem to help her jockey either, hanging under pressure. Official explanation: jockey said filly ran too free (op 7-2 tchd 9-2)
Kahlua Kiss was on her toes beforehand. (op 8-1)
Highway To Glory(IRE) looked to be going well for much of the race but found very little under pressure and was allowed to come home in her own time. (op 6-1)
Pintle looked as though she would improve for her first run in 56 days.

6191 EUROPEAN BREEDERS FUND RIVER EDEN FILLIES' STKS (LISTED RACE) 1m 5f (P)
4:20 (4:20) (Class 1) 3-Y-0+
£17,034 (£6,456; £3,231; £1,611; £807; £405) **Stalls** Low

Form RPR

3534 1 **High Heel Sneakers**[126] [2772] 3-8-8 **101** .... RyanMoore 6 109
(P F I Cole) *lw: hld up in rr: stdy prog fr 3f out: rdn to chal on inner 1f out: battled on wl to ld nr fin* **9/2**[2]

2 *hd* **Taranto**[368] 3-8-8 .... TedDurcan 9 109
(Saeed Bin Suroor) *leggy: lean: angular: hld up in last pair: prog on outer 3f out: rdn to ld jst ins fnl f: hdd nr fin* **12/1**

43- 3 2 **Lake Toya (USA)**[366] [6104] 4-9-2 **102** .... LDettori 5 106
(Saeed Bin Suroor) *rangy: t.k.h: hld up in tch: effrt over 2f out: cl up over 1f out: one pce fnl f* **15/8**[1]

2443 4 3/4 **Cresta Gold**[28] [5641] 3-8-8 **100** .... MartinDwyer 10 105
(A Bailey) *lw: sn prom: led wl over 2f out: hdd and fdd jst ins fnl f* **6/1**[3]

2560 5 2 1/2 **Guilia**[34] [5502] 3-8-8 **100** .... SebSanders 1 101
(Rae Guest) *lw: hld up in rr: taken to outer and drvn over 2f out: no prog tl kpt on fnl f* **14/1**

1222 6 3/4 **Trick Or Treat**[19] [5803] 3-8-8 **95** .... JamieMackay 3 100
(J G Given) *led for 2f: prom tl outpcd fr 2f out* **8/1**

3023 7 1 **Ti Adora (IRE)**[19] [5803] 4-9-2 **94** .... DarryllHolland 8 98
(P W D'Arcy) *lw: t.k.h: led after 2f to wl over 2f out: wknd over 1f out* **8/1**

5010 8 1 1/4 **Spirit Of The Fen (IRE)**[43] [5300] 3-8-8 **81** .... DaneO'Neill 7 96
(J H M Gosden) *b: hld up in rr: drvn and struggling wl over 2f out* **50/1**

2020 **9** *1 ½* **Fusili (IRE)**[19] 5803 3-8-8 90 ... NCallan 11 94
(N P Littmoden) *cl up: rdn and struggling over 2f out* **25/1**

0004 **10** *8* **Kassiopeia (IRE)**[28] 5641 3-8-8 88 ... TonyCulhane 4 82
(M R Channon) *hld up: last 5f out: no prog 3f out: wknd* **25/1**

4050 **11** *18* **Idealistic (IRE)**[19] 5803 5-9-2 93 ... JamieSpencer 2 55
(L M Cumani) *lw: trckd ldrs tl wknd 4f out: t.o* **20/1**

2m 44.48s (-3.82) **Going Correction** -0.15s/f (Stan)
WFA 3 from 4yo+ 8lb **11** Ran SP% **118.2**
Speed ratings (Par 108):105,104,103,103,101 101,100,99,98,93 82
CSF £54.53 TOTE £5.90: £1.80, £4.30, £1.30; EX 104.30 Trifecta £357.20 Part won. Pool: £503.18 - 0.94 winning units..
Owner Mr & Mrs C Wright & P F I Cole **Bred** Stratford Place Stud **Trained** Whatcombe, Oxon

FOCUS
A competitive fillies' Listed race with seven of the 11 runners rated within 9lb of each other. THe form is not sure to prove reliable, but is rated at face value for now.

NOTEBOOK
High Heel Sneakers, who had the second highest rating, gained her first victory of the season and only the second of her career in slightly more comfortable fashion than the winning margin suggests. She was having her first run since Royal Ascot but looked in fine condition and clearly has more to offer. Connections were suggesting she may go to Hong Kong now, but she will remain in training next season as there are plenty of options for older fillies nowadays. (op 11-2)
Taranto, one of three in the race from the Godolphin yard, came into this unbeaten in two races at up to nine furlongs and looked very fit, despite having been off the track for a year. Held up at the back, she swept into contention down the hill and had every chance, but the winner was just too good over this longer trip. (op 14-1)
Lake Toya(USA) was a strong favourite and had her chance, but she may just have paid the penalty in the straight for being a little keen early on. There could be better to come, as she looked as though the run would bring her on. (op 9-4)
Cresta Gold stays further than this and her rider tried to exploit her stamina by kicking on off the bend, but ultimately she was outpaced and would prefer a more galloping track. (op 7-1 tchd 8-1)
Guilia was held up but lost her place at the top bend five furlongs from home and dropped to the rear before running on in the closing stages. She is relatively lightly raced and could well have more to give with another winter behind her. (op 10-1)
Trick Or Treat was a market drifter, but set the pace early and stayed in contention until left behind in the straight. It may be that she is not as effective on the All-Weather, as her two previous efforts on sand were very moderate. (op 13-2 tchd 6-1)

6192 WEATHERBYS BANK H'CAP 7f (P)
4:50 (4:50) (Class 3) (0-95,95) 3-Y-0+ **£8,096** (£2,408; £1,203; £601) Stalls Low

Form RPR

235 **1** **Areyoutalkingtome**[18] 5845 3-9-1 94 ... EddieAhern 9 105
(C A Cyzer) *lw: cl up: rdn and effrt 2f out: led 1f out and drvn 2l clr: kpt on wl* **33/1**

-503 **2** *1 ¼* **Viking Spirit**[26] 5667 4-9-3 94 ... AdamKirby 2 101
(W R Swinburn) *lw: t.k.h: hld up wl in rr: off the pce over 2f out: rapid prog on outer fnl f: grabbed 2nd on line* **9/1**[2]

2355 **3** *shd* **Secret Night**[61] 4798 3-8-6 85 ... OscarUrbina 4 93+
(J A R Toller) *hld up: last over 4f out: prog over 2f out: clsng whn nt clr run 1f out: r.o last 100yds: nt rcvr* **50/1**

20 **4** *shd* **Easy Air**[61] 4790 3-9-2 95 ... JamieSpencer 6 102+
(E A L Dunlop) *lw: s.i.s: hld up in last pair: off the pce over 2f out: rapid prog on wd outside fnl f: nrst fin* **5/2**[1]

0006 **5** *shd* **Beaver Patrol (IRE)**[26] 5667 4-8-13 90 ... StephenCarson 14 96
(R F Johnson Houghton) *racd on outer: hld up in midfield: rdn and prog 2f out: nt qckn over 1f out: styd on* **25/1**

4063 **6** *shd* **Orchard Supreme**[11] 5990 3-8-9 88 ... RichardHughes 12 94
(R Hannon) *lw: hld up in rr: prog 3f out: effrt on inner and nrly on terms jst ins fnl f: one pce nr fin* **10/1**[3]

21- **7** *shd* **Scandal Keeper (USA)**[378] 5847 3-8-8 87 ... (t) TedDurcan 13 93
(Saeed Bin Suroor) *lw: hld up in midfield and racd on outer: effrt and cl up over 1f out: nt qckn fnl f* **14/1**

0501 **8** *½* **Malcheek (IRE)**[17] 5877 4-8-10 87 ... RobertWinston 8 92
(T D Easterby) *chsd ldr: rdn to chal over 1f out: nt qckn and btn ent fnl f: lost several pls nr fin* **16/1**

2100 **9** *¾* **Mr Lambros**[33] 5523 5-9-4 95 ... RyanMoore 10 98
(A M Balding) *led at decent pce: hdd 1f out: wknd last 100yds* **12/1**

0115 **10** *nk* **Royal Oath (USA)**[90] 3889 3-9-0 93 ... (t) JimmyFortune 5 95+
(J H M Gosden) *lw: hld up towards rr: nt clr run briefly over 2f out: nvr on terms after: styd on ins fnl f* **5/2**[1]

3055 **11** *nk* **King Marju (IRE)**[40] 5355 4-8-10 87 ... NCallan 7 88
(K R Burke) *trckd ldrs: effrt on inner 2f out: one pce u.p over 1f out and sn lost pl* **33/1**

6500 **12** *7* **Will He Wish**[70] 4535 10-8-8 85 ... DarryllHolland 1 68
(S Gollings) *prom tl wknd over 2f out* **66/1**

1-36 **13** *17* **Power Politics (USA)**[24] 5722 3-9-0 93 ... LDettori 3 32
(Saeed Bin Suroor) *lw: hld up in rr: wknd tamely over 2f out: t.o* **9/1**[2]

-660 **14** *shd* **Black Charmer (IRE)**[31] 5578 3-9-2 95 ... KDarley 11 33
(M Johnston) *prom for 3f: sn lost pl: eased whn nt ch 2f out: t.o* **33/1**

1m 23.21s (-2.68) **Going Correction** -0.15s/f (Stan)
WFA 3 from 4yo+ 2lb **14** Ran SP% **122.6**
Speed ratings (Par 107):109,107,107,107,107 107,107,106,105,105 104,96,77,77
CSF £301.09 CT £14363.68 TOTE £29.60: £7.10, £2.80, £8.50; EX 406.70 TRIFECTA Not won..
Owner Mrs Charles Cyzer **Bred** C A Cyzer **Trained** Maplehurst, W Sussex
■ Stewards' Enquiry : Ted Durcan caution: careless riding

FOCUS
A very good handicap and competitive with the runner-up to seventh separated by just a short-heads. The winning time was 1.59 seconds quicker than the following 0-60 handicap, and much faster than the three juvenile maidens and the form looks solid despite the race getting messy in the straight.

NOTEBOOK
Areyoutalkingtome avoided all of the trouble and got a nice lead on his rivals up the straight, winning nicely. He did not look the easiest conveyance earlier in the season, but he has really found his form and is a good sort for these competitive handicaps.
Viking Spirit had plenty to do off the final bend and did well to finish where he did. (op 7-1)
Secret Night ◆ was one of the unlucky runners in the race, as she was short of room when trying to throw down her challenge. She may have won with a clearer effort, but the winner was not stopping in front.
Easy Air ◆ was on the inside rail coming into the final bend, but was forced to switch to the wide outside when short of room. He was finishing well and was another who was unlucky not to be closer. (op 3-1)
Beaver Patrol(IRE) had every chance and ran up to his best.
Orchard Supreme stuck his neck out for his jockey all the way up the straight and was doing his best work at the end. The Handicapper does seem to have his measure, however. (tchd 11-1)
Scandal Keeper(USA) did nothing wrong on his return to the track but needed stoking along off the home bend.
Royal Oath(USA) was in the rear early and did not get the clearest of passages when needed. However, he did not look as unlucky as some in the race and was not given a hard time when his chance was gone. (tchd 11-4)
Power Politics(USA) was extremely disappointing and was well below his best. (op 11-1)

6193 DEAL OR NO DEAL AT LADBROKES.COM H'CAP 7f (P)
5:20 (5:20) (Class 6) (0-60,60) 3-Y-0+ **£3,412** (£1,007; £504) Stalls Low

Form RPR

1645 **1** **Final Tune (IRE)**[44] 5258 3-9-2 60 ... AdamKirby 3 70
(Miss M E Rowland) *hld up towards rr: prog over 2f out: rdn to chse ldr jst over 1f out: styd on wl to ld nr fin* **16/1**

0/6 **2** *½* **Tamworth (IRE)**[7] 6069 4-8-12 57 ... EdwardCreighton(3) 7 66
(E J Creighton) *trckd ldr: led over 2f out and sn kicked 2l clr: kpt on fnl f: hdd nr fin* **12/1**

0020 **3** *1 ¼* **Gallego**[12] 5972 4-9-1 60 ... JamesDoyle(3) 14 65
(R J Price) *dropped in fr wd draw and wl in rr: last over 2f out: rapid prog on wd outside over 1f out: r.o wl to take 3rd nr fin* **14/1**

2644 **4** *½* **Unlimited**[11] 5987 4-9-4 60 ... TedDurcan 12 64
(R Simpson) *t.k.h: hld up in rr: swtchd to inner and prog 2f out: chsd ldng pair fnl f: no imp: lost 3rd nr fin* **13/2**[3]

3003 **5** *1* **Humility**[53] 5046 5-9-3 59 ... EddieAhern 4 61
(C A Cyzer) *trckd ldrs: rdn over 3f out: effrt u.p 2f out: no hdwy over 1f out* **11/2**[2]

6005 **6** *½* **Whitbarrow (IRE)**[23] 5755 7-8-8 57 ... JamesMillman(7) 6 57
(B R Millman) *led at decent pce: hdd over 2f out: wknd fnl f* **7/1**

0113 **7** *hd* **Mountain Pass (USA)**[31] 5573 4-9-1 57 ... (p) DaneO'Neill 10 57
(M J Wallace) *t.k.h early: hld up in midfield: rn in snatches fr 4f out: effrt over 2f out: sn no prog* **3/1**[1]

5065 **8** *1* **Discotheque (USA)**[40] 5370 3-8-11 58 ... DeanCorby(3) 13 55
(P Howling) *v s.i.s: hld up wl in rr: effrt on inner over 2f out: no prog over 1f out* **25/1**

535 **9** *1* **Buzzin'Boyzee (IRE)**[139] 2418 3-9-2 60 ... RobertWinston 9 55
(P D Evans) *t.k.h: hld up: effrt on outer 3f out: no prog 2f out* **14/1**

210 **10** *nk* **Only If I Laugh**[43] 5302 5-9-1 57 ... RobbieFitzpatrick 1 51
(R A Harris) *hld up in midfield on inner: lost pl and virtually last 2f out: shuffled along and kpt on: nvr nr ldrs* **8/1**

2300 **11** *nk* **Blue Beacon**[16] 5902 3-9-2 60 ... NCallan 8 53
(K A Ryan) *sn restrained and in rr: rdn over 2f out: no prog over 1f out* **25/1**

2000 **12** *1 ¼* **Boldinor**[13] 5953 3-9-2 60 ... AlanDaly 11 50
(N E Berry) *t.k.h: hld up bhd ldrs on outer: lost pl over 2f out: struggling over 1f out* **50/1**

1460 **13** *shd* **Dado Mush**[38] 5418 3-8-11 58 ... SaleemGolam(3) 5 47
(G Prodromou) *trckd ldrs tl wknd 2f out* **20/1**

600- **14** *11* **Tee Jay Kassidy**[496] 2657 6-9-2 58 ... BrianReilly 2 19
(P S McEntee) *prom tl wknd rapidly over 2f out: t.o* **25/1**

1m 24.8s (-1.09) **Going Correction** -0.15s/f (Stan)
WFA 3 from 4yo+ 2lb **14** Ran SP% **122.5**
Speed ratings (Par 101):100,99,98,97,96 95,95,94,93,92 92,91,90,78
CSF £186.24 CT £2833.08 TOTE £17.60: £4.20, £3.30, £5.20; EX 184.30 TRIFECTA Not won. Place 6 £89.19, Place 5 £55.06..
Owner M Armstrong Miss M E Rowland **Bred** Shortgrove Manor Stud **Trained** Lower Blidworth, Notts

FOCUS
Just a modest handicap run in a time 1.59 seconds slower than the previous race but the form looks sound rated around the third, fourth and fifth.
T/Jkpt: Not won. T/Plt: £294.90 to a £1 stake. Pool: £64,642.20. 160.00 winning tickets. T/Qpdt: £52.40 to a £1 stake. Pool: £4,630.50. 65.30 winning tickets. JN

6194 - 6198a (Foreign Racing) - See Raceform Interactive

5962
NEWMARKET (ROWLEY) (R-H)
Friday, October 27

OFFICIAL GOING: Good to soft (soft in places)
All the races were named after horses owned by the Queen, to mark her 80th birthday earlier in the year.
Wind: light, across Weather: Overcast

6199 MONAVEEN EBF STKS (MAIDEN) (DIV I) 6f
1:00 (1:02) (Class 5) 2-Y-0 **£2,590** (£770; £385; £192) Stalls High

Form RPR

2 **1** **Princess Valerina**[18] 5871 2-8-12 ... MichaelHills 10 89+
(B W Hills) *leggy: sn led: pushed clr over 1f out: eased nr fin* **7/4**[2]

03 **2** *2 ½* **Shmookh (USA)**[15] 5915 2-9-3 ... RHills 9 85+
(J L Dunlop) *chsd wnr: edgd lft and outpcd over 1f out: styd on ins fnl f* **6/1**[3]

3 **3** *shd* **Shevchenko (IRE)**[38] 5457 2-9-3 ... RyanMoore 8 84+
(J Noseda) *lw: hld up in tch: swtchd lft 2f out: sn rdn: styd on same pce ins fnl f* **11/8**[1]

4 *5* **Little Eskimo** 2-9-3 ... TedDurcan 4 69
(B Smart) *unf: scope: b.bkwd: chsd ldrs: rdn over 2f out: wknd ins fnl f* **16/1**

65 **5** *¾* **Kashmir Lady (FR)**[24] 5754 2-8-12 ... DaneO'Neill 1 62
(H Candy) *lw: strong: plld hrd and prom: rdn over 2f out: wknd fnl f* **20/1**

0 **6** *hd* **Trickle (USA)**[143] 2328 2-8-12 ... (t) BrettDoyle 11 61
(E A L Dunlop) *lw: unf: chsd ldrs: rdn over 2f out: wknd fnl f* **33/1**

0 **7** *2 ½* **Teasing**[15] 5915 2-8-12 ... JimmyQuinn 13 54
(J Pearce) *lw: b.hind: chsd ldrs over 4f* **33/1**

5 **8** *5* **Dancing Jest (IRE)**[14] 5950 2-8-12 ... ChrisCatlin 6 39
(Rae Guest) *w'like: chsd ldrs: lost pl over 4f out: sn bhd* **40/1**

9 *1 ½* **Zain (IRE)** 2-9-3 ... JamieMackay 12 39
(J G Given) *b.bkwd: dwlt: outpcd* **100/1**

10 *hd* **Millyjean** 2-8-5 ... MJMurphy(7) 3 34
(John Berry) *w'like: b.bkwd: dwlt: outpcd* **100/1**

11 *1 ¾* **Pickering** 2-9-3 ... DavidAllan 2 34
(E J Alston) *w'like: b.bkwd: s.i.s: hdwy over 4f out: rdn over 2f out: sn hung rt and wknd* **66/1**

12 *2 ½* **Pleasure Pursuit** 2-9-3 ... MartinDwyer 7 26
(B W Hills) *w'like: b.bkwd: scope: dwlt: outpcd* **50/1**

1m 14.23s (1.13) **Going Correction** +0.275s/f (Good) **12** Ran SP% **117.2**
Speed ratings (Par 95):103,99,99,92,91 91,88,81,79,79 77,73
CSF £11.71 TOTE £2.60: £1.40, £1.60, £1.20; EX 11.30.
Owner G J Hicks **Bred** George Joseph Hicks **Trained** Lambourn, Berks

FOCUS
Not a very competitive maiden and the principals in the market dominated the finish. They set the standard for the form.

The Form Book, Raceform Ltd, Compton, RG20 6NL

NOTEBOOK

Princess Valerina, an athletic type, had run with plenty of promise on her debut at Windsor and had no trouble going one better in this pretty uncompetitive affair. She should get seven furlongs in time and will no doubt be chasing some black type next term. (op 9-4)

Shmookh(USA), who is improving with every outing, is now eligible for a handicap mark, and could be interesting on faster ground in that sphere next season. (op 5-1)

Shevchenko(IRE) looked likely to appreciate the drop back in trip as he had failed to see out seven furlongs on his debut, but in the event he ran as though needing a bit further. He has the ability to win his maiden, and a mile should be his trip next year. (op 5-4)

Little Eskimo, who cost 120,000gns as a foal, is out of a mare who was quite a useful winner in the US and is sister to the smart, prolific winner Sweetness Herself. He ran well for a long way and looks the type to progress next season.

Kashmir Lady(FR), despite dropping back in distance, again pulled too hard, and as a result she failed to get home. Now eligible for handicaps, she should find life easier in that company.

Trickle(USA), whose dam is a half-sister to smart triple winning miler Grazalema and to multiple winning Japanese/French sprinter/miler Princess Carla, had been off the track since making her debut at Windsor in June. The fitting of a tongue tie for the first time indicates that she has had a breathing problem.

6200 MONAVEEN EBF STKS (MAIDEN) (DIV II) 6f

1:30 (1:32) (Class 5) 2-Y-O **£2,590** (£770; £385; £192) **Stalls** High

Form				RPR
3	**1**		**Miss Lucifer (FR)**[17] 5894 2-8-12 ... MichaelHills 2 (B W Hills) *lw: mde all: rdn and edgd rt over 1f out: r.o* **4/7**[1]	81
	2	*2*	**Marozi (USA)** 2-9-3 ... PhilipRobinson 3 (M A Jarvis) *unf: scope: swtchd to racd alone centre 5f out: w ldrs: hung rt thrght: rdn over 2f out: styd on same pce fnl f* **9/2**[2]	80+
0	**3**	*nk*	**Rule Of Life**[106] 3445 2-9-3 ... RichardHughes 11 (B W Hills) *w'like: chsd ldrs: rdn over 2f out: styd on same pce fnl f* **14/1**[3]	79
	4	*2 ½*	**Mutajarred** 2-9-3 ... RHills 9 (W J Haggas) *strong: w'like: scope: dwlt: hld up: r.o ins fnl f: nrst fin* **16/1**	72+
00	**5**	*2 ½*	**Brouhaha**[15] 5918 2-9-3 ... BrianReilly 5 (Miss Diana Weeden) *chsd wnr 4f out: rdn over 2f out: wknd fnl f* **66/1**	64
	6	*1 ¼*	**Spice Gardens (IRE)** 2-8-12 ... LDettori 7 (W Jarvis) *w'like: b.bkwd: s.s: hdwy 5f out: rdn and wknd over 1f out* **14/1**[3]	55
0	**7**	*¾*	**Kind Of Fizzy**[9] 6055 2-8-12 ... ChrisCatlin 10 (Rae Guest) *unf: mid-div: effrt over 2f out: wknd over 1f out* **100/1**	53
	8	*1 ½*	**Doonigan (IRE)** 2-9-0 ... NeilChalmers(3) 1 (A M Balding) *w'like: leggy: b.bkwd: s.s: hdwy over 3f out: rdn and wknd over 1f out* **66/1**	54
0	**9**	*nk*	**Mountain Cat (IRE)**[18] 5867 2-9-3 ... BrettDoyle 4 (W J Musson) *w'like: hld up: plld hrd: n.d* **100/1**	53
04	**10**	*2*	**Tomorrow's Dancer**[30] 5615 2-9-3 ... NCallan 12 (K A Ryan) *mid-div: rdn over 2f out: sn wknd* **25/1**	47
36	**11**	*5*	**Froissee**[84] 4109 2-8-12 ... OscarUrbina 6 (N A Callaghan) *hld up: a in rr* **25/1**	27
0	**12**	*8*	**Step To The Stars (IRE)**[24] 5754 2-8-12 ... JoeFanning 8 (M Johnston) *leggy: chsd wnr 2f: wknd over 2f out* **25/1**	3

1m 14.54s (1.44) **Going Correction** +0.275s/f (Good) 12 Ran SP% **117.6**
Speed ratings (Par 95):101,98,97,94,91 89,88,86,86,83 76,66
CSF £2.88 TOTE £1.60: £1.10, £1.50, £3.10; EX 5.20.
Owner Gainsborough **Bred** Gainsborough Stud Management Ltd **Trained** Lambourn, Berks

FOCUS

Another fairly uncompetitive maiden, and marginally the slower of the two divisions. The winner is the best guide to the level.

NOTEBOOK

Miss Lucifer(FR), whose third behind subsequent Listed race winner Party on her debut made her look difficult to beat here, had no trouble getting off the mark under a positive ride. Her rider thought she had won despite the conditions, though, and this daughter of Noverre is likely to be more at home on quicker ground next season, when she could well make her mark at Listed level. (op 8-13 tchd 4-6 in places)

Marozi(USA), a half-brother to a US sprint winner out of a mare who was a useful multiple sprint winner in the US, made a promising debut. Brought down the centre of the track in search of better ground, he displayed signs of greenness but kept on well for second behind a more experienced and potentially useful filly. He will do better next year, and faster ground should help him, too. (tchd 5-1)

Rule Of Life, last of eight on his debut on the July Course in the summer, had been given time to strengthen up since and ran much better on this easier ground. He has an attractive pedigree and looks sure to make up into a useful three-year-old.

Mutajarred, a half-brother to Mozafin, a mile winner at two, and Arm Candy, a seven-furlong winner at two, got the hang of things late on and was running on at the finish. He should get further than this next year and the experience should have done him the world of good. Official explanation: jockey said colt missed the break (op 20-1)

Brouhaha, who only cost 800gns, has been far from disgraced in three Newmarket maidens now, and is clearly not devoid of ability. He can make his mark in more modest company at a lesser track.

Spice Gardens(IRE), who cost 80,000gns, is out of a mare who won over seven furlongs at two and was later a Group 3 winner over 12 furlongs at three. Bred to get at least ten furlongs next season, she ran well enough on her debut over six. (op 12-1)

6201 HIGHCLERE EBF FILLIES' STKS (REGISTERED AS THE BOSRA SHAM FILLIES' STAKES) (LISTED RACE) 6f

2:05 (2:09) (Class 1) 2-Y-O **£16,182** (£6,133; £3,069; £1,530; £766; £384) **Stalls** High

Form				RPR
5213	**1**		**Blue Echo**[30] 5626 2-8-12 88 ... PhilipRobinson 8 (M A Jarvis) *lw: led 4f: sn rdn and hung rt: rallied to ld nr fin* **16/1**	96
2134	**2**	*shd*	**La Presse (USA)**[28] 5654 2-8-12 109 ... MichaelHills 4 (B W Hills) *chsd wnr tl rdn to ld 2f out: edgd rt over 1f out: hdd nr fin* **11/10**[1]	96
211	**3**	*1 ¼*	**Doric Charm**[23] 5764 2-8-12 80 ... RyanMoore 1 (B Smart) *str: lw: chsd ldrs: outpcd 2f out: r.o ins fnl f* **8/1**[3]	92
301	**4**	*nk*	**Kompete**[9] 6047 2-8-12 ... MichaelTebbutt 6 (V Smith) *w'like: leggy: chsd ldrs: rdn over 1f out: edgd rt ins fnl f: styd on* **25/1**	92
130	**5**	*3 ½*	**Boreal Applause**[27] 5672 2-8-12 89 ... MartinDwyer 10 (E A L Dunlop) *lw: s.i.s: hld up: hdwy over 2f out: rdn and edgd rt over 1f out: wknd fnl f* **50/1**	81
2163	**6**	*hd*	**Final Dynasty**[20] 5809 2-8-12 85 ... TedDurcan 9 (Mrs G S Rees) *chsd ldrs: rdn over 2f out: wknd fnl f* **50/1**	80
102	**7**	*¾*	**Mystery Ocean**[14] 5940 2-8-12 85 ... SebSanders 2 (R M Beckett) *hld up: rdn over 2f out: styd on ins fnl f: nvr trbld ldrs* **8/1**[3]	78
1544	**8**	*¾*	**Zanida (IRE)**[20] 5809 2-8-12 93 ... PatCosgrave 12 (K R Burke) *racd alone far side: chsd ldrs over 4f* **25/1**	76
3421	**9**	*½*	**Mimisel**[17] 5899 2-8-12 84 ... SteveDrowne 5 (Rae Guest) *s.i.s: hld up: effrt over 2f out: wknd over 1f out* **40/1**	74
001	**10**	*9*	**Apache Dream (IRE)**[18] 5871 2-8-12 79 ... LDettori 7 (B J Meehan) *swtg: prom: rdn over 2f out: edgd rt and wknd over 1f out* **9/2**[2]	47
2	**11**	*12*	**Laura's Best (IRE)**[22] 5773 2-8-12 ... PaulHanagan 3 (W J Haggas) *lw: prom over 3f* **25/1**	11

1m 13.78s (0.68) **Going Correction** +0.275s/f (Good) **11** Ran SP% **111.8**
Speed ratings (Par 100):106,105,104,103,99 98,97,96,96,84 68
CSF £30.73 TOTE £19.80: £3.40, £1.10, £1.90; EX 42.50.
Owner Mrs Mary Taylor **Bred** Mrs Mary Taylor And James F Taylor **Trained** Newmarket, Suffolk

FOCUS

Ordinary Listed form in which the favourite failed to run to her best. The whole field bar Zanida came up the centre of the track.

NOTEBOOK

Blue Echo, whose Salisbury effort may have been underestimated, appreciated the soft ground and showed admirable determination to rally and get her nose back in front after being headed. She is all speed and from a family that improves with age, so she could well challenge for further Pattern success over sprint distances next season. (op 33-1)

La Presse(USA), whose fourth in the Cheveley Park Stakes made her the one to beat, had every chance and simply found the determined winner too strong. This may have been one race too many for her, though, and it seems clear that she failed to run up to her Cheveley Park form. (op 10-11 tchd 6-5 in places)

Doric Charm had only beaten trees on her last two starts but she had done so easily and it was difficult to know how she would perform upped in grade. In the event she ran a super race, staying on strongly from the Dip, and soft ground clearly suits her well.

Kompete, who had a draw advantage when winning an ordinary maiden at Nottingham easily last time out, had a good deal more to do in this company and in the circumstances she ran well. She certainly seemed to get the sixth furlong well enough. (op 20-1)

Boreal Applause, who did not get home over seven furlongs last time, has not really progressed as expected since making a winning debut at Nottingham in July. Faster ground may be required to see her at her best.

Final Dynasty, who ran above herself to gain black type in a Listed race at York last time, could not repeat the trick here.

Apache Dream(IRE), an easy winner of a Windsor maiden last time on her first encounter with soft ground, a race in which she beat the winner of the opening maiden on this card into second, was a well-backed second-favourite, but she dropped out tamely and proved most disappointing. This was clearly not her running and she looked to have gone in her coat beforehand. Official explanation: jockey said filly ran too free (op 13-2)

6202 DUNFERMLINE EBF FILLIES' STKS (H'CAP) 1m 4f

2:40 (2:44) (Class 3) (0-90,85) 3-Y-0+
£8,724 (£2,612; £1,306; £653; £326; £163) **Stalls** High

Form				RPR
5210	**1**		**Piety (IRE)**[23] 5769 3-9-5 **80** ... KDarley 3 (M Johnston) *chsd ldrs: led over 3f out: rdn over 1f out: styd on wl* **20/1**	94+
1322	**2**	*3 ½*	**Wannabe Posh (IRE)**[25] 5732 3-9-10 **85** ... EddieAhern 2 (J L Dunlop) *lw: hld up: hdwy 1/2-way: chsd wnr 3f out: sn rdn: styd on same pce fnl f* **13/2**[3]	93
3132	**3**	*½*	**Quantum (IRE)**[29] 5644 3-9-6 **81** ...(b[1]) LDettori 11 (J H M Gosden) *lw: hld up: hdwy and swtchd lft over 3f out: rdn over 1f out: styd on same pce* **5/1**[1]	89
4162	**4**	*5*	**Adraaj (USA)**[17] 5895 3-9-6 **81** ...(b[1]) RHills 8 (E A L Dunlop) *hmpd s: hld up: hdwy over 2f out: sn rdn and hung lft: wknd ins fnl f* **14/1**	81
5630	**5**	*2 ½*	**Power Of Future (GER)**[41] 5383 3-9-1 **76** ... TedDurcan 16 (H R A Cecil) *lw: hld up: hdwy over 4f out: rdn over 2f out: hung lft and wknd over 1f out* **33/1**	72
3P02	**6**	*1 ½*	**Flying Clarets (IRE)**[21] 5792 3-9-3 **78** ... PaulHanagan 5 (R A Fahey) *chsd ldrs: chal over 3f out: sn rdn and hung lft: wknd 2f out* **25/1**	71
4431	**7**	*7*	**Spinning Coin**[30] 5628 4-9-10 **78** ...(p) RyanMoore 13 (J G Portman) *hld up: hdwy 5f out: rdn and wknd over 1f out* **12/1**	60
044	**8**	*¾*	**Detente**[43] 5319 3-8-11 **72** ... JamieSpencer 10 (J R Fanshawe) *lw: prom: rdn 1/2-way: wknd over 2f out* **11/1**	53
1130	**9**	*3*	**Island Odyssey**[22] 5776 3-9-10 **85** ... SteveDrowne 14 (E A L Dunlop) *hld up: rdn over 3f out: n.d* **25/1**	61
2212	**10**	*10*	**Kerriemuir Lass (IRE)**[34] 5538 3-9-10 **85** ... PhilipRobinson 12 (M A Jarvis) *lw: led over 8f: wknd over 2f out* **7/1**	45
0202	**11**	*2 ½*	**Candle**[34] 5533 3-9-6 **81** ... DaneO'Neill 15 (H Candy) *chsd ldrs over 8f* **6/1**[2]	37
2050	**12**	*4*	**Simonda**[69] 4604 5-9-11 **79** ...(b) JimCrowley 4 (Mrs A J Perrett) *b.hind: hld up in tch: rdn over 4f out: wknd 3f out* **33/1**	29
2120	**13**	*2*	**Kibara**[63] 4778 3-9-3 **78** ... NickyMackay 6 (L M Cumani) *prom 8f* **12/1**	24
1	**14**	*2 ½*	**Heart Of Svetlana (IRE)**[29] 5634 3-9-10 **85** ... JoeFanning 7 (M Johnston) *leggy: unf: s.i.s and hmpd s: hld up: hdwy 1/2-way: wknd over 3f out* **10/1**	27
1661	**15**	*2 ½*	**Fear To Tread (USA)**[60] 4900 3-9-3 **78** ... JimmyQuinn 1 (J L Dunlop) *prom: lost pl 1/2-way: wknd 4f out* **25/1**	16
0040	**16**	*8*	**Tcherina (IRE)**[21] 5792 4-9-4 **72** ... DavidAllan 9 (T D Easterby) *chsd ldrs over 8f* **14/1**	—

2m 35.62s (2.12) **Going Correction** +0.275s/f (Good)
WFA 3 from 4yo+ 7lb **16** Ran SP% **125.1**
Speed ratings (Par 104):103,100,100,97,95 94,89,89,87,80 78,76,74,73,71 66
CSF £139.06 CT £771.05 TOTE £25.40: £4.20, £1.90, £1.50, £4.70; EX 287.30 Trifecta £773.80 Part won. Pool £1,089.86 - 0.10 winning units..
Owner Highclere Thoroughbred Racing XXXI **Bred** Baronrath And Baroda Studs **Trained** Middleham Moor, N Yorks

FOCUS

A decent, competitive handicap on paper but they finished pretty strung out in the testing ground. The form looks solid with the placed horses to their marks.

NOTEBOOK

Piety(IRE) has stamina on the dam's side of her pedigree and she found the step up in trip just what she wanted. Bouncing back to winning form in style, connections are apparently now on the look out for black-type opportunities on the continent. (op 16-1)

Wannabe Posh(IRE), who won a handicap off a mark of 61 back in June, has progressed into a useful filly this season but her improvement has been matched by an ever-increasing handicap mark, which means she keeps running well without winning. (op 6-1)

Quantum(IRE), wearing blinkers instead of the visor she wore when runner-up over two furlongs further here last time, ran another solid race, finishing clear of the rest, but she is another who remains vulnerable off her current mark. (op 7-1)

Adraaj(USA) was another swapping a visor for blinkers. She did not see this longer trip out as well as the principals, but was one of the lightest raced fillies in the line-up and possibly still has scope for improvement.

Power Of Future(GER), who has been exposed in handicaps over further this term, ran a better race back down in trip on this soft surface, but she does not look an obvious candidate to improve.
Flying Clarets(IRE) was flattered by her performance at York last time and this run is probably a truer reflection of her ability. (op 33-1)
Kerriemuir Lass(IRE), normally such a consistent filly, ran well on easy ground on her seasonal reappearance but she folded tamely and it may be that she has just had enough for the year.
Official explanation: jockey said filly was unsuited by the good to soft, soft in places ground (op 15-2 tchd 8-1)
Tcherina(IRE) Official explanation: jockey said filly was never travelling

6203 PALL MALL STKS (REGISTERED AS THE JAMES SEYMOUR STAKES) (LISTED RACE) 1m 2f
3:15 (3:17) (Class 1) 3-Y-0+

£15,898 (£6,025; £3,015; £1,503; £753; £378) **Stalls** High

Form	Pos	Dist	Horse / details	RPR
3-52	1		**Into The Dark**[28] 5657 5-9-2 106 ....(t) LDettori 1 (Saeed Bin Suroor) *lw: hld up in tch: led 3f out: pushed clr over 1f out* 11/4[1]	116+
0001	2	6	**Ofaraby**[20] 5813 6-9-2 99 .... PhilipRobinson 3 (M A Jarvis) *b. hld up: hdwy and hung rt over 1f out: rdr dropped reins ent fnl f: r.o: no ch w wnr* 15/2	105
-651	3	shd	**Kilworth (IRE)**[19] 5845 3-8-11 107 .... RyanMoore 7 (Saeed Bin Suroor) *lw: trckd ldrs: racd keenly: jnd wnr 3f out: sn rdn: styd on same pce appr fnl f* 12/1	105
3344	4	1	**Take A Bow**[27] 5675 5-9-2 102 .... JimCrowley 6 (P R Chamings) *hld up: rdn over 3f out: outpcd 2f out: styd on ins fnl f: nvr able to chal* 5/1[3]	103
1-55	5	½	**Nakheel**[37] 5477 3-8-11 107 .... RHills 5 (M Johnston) *lw: s.i.s: sn prom: rdn and hung lft over 1f out: wknd fnl f* 7/2[2]	102
3406	6	½	**Markovitch**[41] 5400 3-8-11 105 .... EddieAhern 8 (P W Chapple-Hyam) *led 7f: wknd over 1f out* 16/1	101
11/2	7	12	**Northern Splendour (USA)**[20] 5813 4-9-2 102 .... TedDurcan 2 (Saeed Bin Suroor) *chsd ldr 7f: wknd 2f out* 12/1	80
540	8	28	**Tau Ceti**[13] 5968 7-9-2 105 .... SebSanders 4 (R M Beckett) *s.i.s: hld up: effrt over 2f out: sn wknd* 7/1	29

2m 7.39s (1.68) **Going Correction** +0.275s/f (Good)
WFA 3 from 4yo+ 5lb **8** Ran SP% **111.1**
Speed ratings (Par 111):104,99,99,98,97 97,87,65
CSF £22.37 TOTE £3.00: £1.40, £2.40, £3.90; EX 24.50.
Owner Godolphin **Bred** Gainsborough Stud Management Ltd **Trained** Newmarket, Suffolk

FOCUS
A fair Listed contest resulting in a runaway victory for Into The Dark which suggests he is deserving of a return to Group company. The form makes sense rated around the placed horses.

NOTEBOOK
Into The Dark has been an expensive horse to follow over the past two seasons as he had failed to win in his last six starts despite being sent off favourite or joint-favourite for five of those races. Indeed, he was beaten at 7-4 in this race last year. Those failures were forgotten on this occasion, though, as he won in great style, pulling clear in the latter stages for an authoritative success. He will travel to Dubai for the winter and looks a likely type for the Carnival in early spring. (op 3-1)
Ofaraby, who beat some higher-rated rivals when successful in a conditions event at York last time, could not live with the impressive winner but can still take plenty of credit for finishing second, as he was again officially rated the worst horse in the field going into the race. He has bounced back to form on soft ground this autumn and it is a shame for him that the season is coming to an end. (tchd 9-1)
Kilworth(IRE), who won a conditions race on the Wolverhampton Polytrack on his recent return from a seven-month layoff, was probably not entirely at home in these testing conditions. His best form is on good ground.
Take A Bow, who ran well to finish fourth in the Cambridgeshire last time, is a consistent performer, but the result of that is a poor strike-rate - he has only won one of his last 14 starts. He is likely to remain difficult to place off his current rating.
Nakheel has yet to prove that he retains the ability he showed at two for Mark Johnston. A pelvic injury this spring appears to have set him back quite a bit. (op 3-1 tchd 4-1 in a place)
Northern Splendour(USA) looks to have bounced on his second run back following a lengthy absence, as his York form suggested he should finish close to Ofaraby. (tchd 14-1)
Tau Ceti, who has been held in Pattern company this term, was unable to repeat last year's shock win in this event. Official explanation: jockey said horse lost its action (op 15-2 tchd 6-1)

6204 DOUTELLE STKS (CONDITIONS RACE) 6f
3:50 (3:50) (Class 4) 2-3-Y-0

£5,297 (£1,586; £793; £396; £198; £99) **Stalls** High

Form	Pos	Dist	Horse / details	RPR
4115	1		**College Scholar (GER)**[27] 5681 2-8-6 87 .... TPO'Shea 7 (M R Channon) *lw: sn chsng ldrs: rdn to ld 1f out: r.o* 7/2[2]	92
1	2	1¼	**Dream Scheme**[29] 5638 2-8-1 .... MartinDwyer 1 (E A L Dunlop) *s.i.s: hld up: hdwy 1/2-way: rdn over 1f out: hung rt ins fnl f: styd on same pce* 13/8[1]	83
4213	3	1¼	**Ebn Reem**[62] 4804 2-8-6 85 .... PhilipRobinson 5 (M A Jarvis) *lw: led: rdn and hdd 1f out: styd on same pce* 9/2[3]	85
2150	4	3½	**Madame Medusa (IRE)**[15] 5919 3-9-6 72 ....(v) RyanMoore 2 (J A R Toller) *prom: chsd ldr 4f out: rdn over 1f out: wknd fnl f* 20/1	69
6020	5	shd	**Jeanmaire (IRE)**[15] 5919 3-9-6 90 .... SteveDrowne 3 (H Morrison) *chsd ldr 2f: rdn over 2f out: wknd over 1f out* 6/1	69
5631	6	4	**Mujood**[8] 6065 3-9-8 78 ....(b) StephenCarson 6 (R F Johnson Houghton) *prom: lost pl over 4f out: bhd fr 1/2-way* 8/1	59
4201	7	4	**Goodwood March**[25] 5729 3-9-6 58 .... IanMongan 4 (J L Dunlop) *hld up: plld hrd: rdn over 2f out: hung rt and wknd over 1f out* 33/1	45

1m 13.94s (0.84) **Going Correction** +0.275s/f (Good) **7** Ran SP% **111.6**
Speed ratings: 105,103,101,97,96 91,86
CSF £9.12 TOTE £4.80: £2.40, £1.40; EX 10.70.
Owner Mohammed Jaber **Bred** Stiftung Gestut Fahrhof **Trained** West Ilsley, Berks

FOCUS
A fascinating clash between the two and three-year-olds that was dominated by the younger generation. The race has been rated conservatively around the placed horses.

NOTEBOOK
College Scholar(GER), a progressive colt who has winning form with some give underfoot, looked a big danger to the favourite if his Redcar Two-Year-Old Trophy fifth was anything to go by and, having been nudged along to hold his position early on, he picked up really strongly inside the final quarter mile to win with a little bit in hand, staying on too well for the favourite. He should develop into a useful handicapper next year, especially when getting his favoured conditions, and is one to be with again. (op 4-1 tchd 5-1)
Dream Scheme, although impressive on her debut over course and distance, had very different conditions to contend with here and she looked short enough at 13-8. Kept towards the outside, she had every chance, but hung a little under pressure and did not see her race out as strongly as the winner. She still looked green and this was a decent effort considering, so there may be more to come at three. (op 11-8 tchd 6-5 and 7-4 in places)
Ebn Reem made it a clean sweep for the juveniles and ran his race, but was always going to be left vulnerable by making the running. He has taken his racing well and is another who should pay his way next season. (op 5-1)

6205 AUREOLE STKS (H'CAP) 2m
4:25 (4:29) (Class 3) (0-90,90) 3-Y-0+ **£8,096** (£2,408; £1,203; £601) **Stalls** High

Form	Pos	Dist	Horse / details	RPR
0003	1		**Dr Sharp (IRE)**[13] 5963 6-9-7 83 .... TonyCulhane 14 (T P Tate) *lw: mde all: rdn over 3f out: styd on gamely* 9/1	93
2252	2	1¼	**Kayf Aramis**[11] 6011 4-8-6 71 oh4 ....(p) MarcHalford(3) 3 (J L Spearing) *lw: a.p: chsd wnr over 4f out: sn rdn: edgd rt over 1f out: kpt on* 10/1	80
2121	3	4	**At The Money**[14] 5952 3-7-13 71 .... FrancisNorton 9 (J M P Eustace) *swtg: chsd ldrs: rdn over 6f out: styd on same pce fnl 2f* 11/4[1]	75
1165	4	1½	**Remember Ramon (USA)**[131] 2717 3-9-3 89 .... JamieSpencer 7 (M J Wallace) *lw: s.i.s: hld up: hdwy over 4f out: rdn over 2f out: no ex fnl f* 10/1	91
3125	5	nk	**Establishment**[34] 5526 9-9-3 79 .... TedDurcan 15 (C A Cyzer) *hld up: rdn over 4f out: styd on fnl 2f: swtchd rt ins fnl f: nt pce to chal* 20/1	81
2030	6	14	**Most Definitely (IRE)**[12] 5991 6-9-3 79 .... JimCrowley 1 (R M Stronge) *hld up: hdwy over 6f out: rdn and wknd over 1f out* 50/1	64
5130	7	4	**Sir Monty (USA)**[13] 5963 4-9-2 78 .... RyanMoore 6 (Mrs A J Perrett) *s.i.s: hld up: hdwy over 4f out: sn rdn: wknd over 2f out* 12/1	58
2534	8	nk	**Sybella**[31] 5594 3-8-5 77 .... JimmyQuinn 11 (J L Dunlop) *hld up in tch: rdn over 4f out: wknd over 2f out* 25/1	57
0342	9	2½	**Salute (IRE)**[19] 5846 7-9-3 79 .... SteveDrowne 12 (P G Murphy) *chsd ldrs: rdn and wknd over 2f out* 33/1	56
3344	10	¾	**Gee Dee Nen**[21] 5792 3-8-6 78 ....(v[1]) EddieAhern 5 (M H Tompkins) *warm: hld up in tch: rdn and wknd over 3f out* 15/2[2]	54
-026	11	8	**Colloquial**[114] 3203 5-10-0 90 ....(v) DaneO'Neill 16 (H Candy) *hld up: rdn over 6f out: son wknd* 16/1	56
206	12	7	**Mersey Sound (IRE)**[7] 6075 8-9-3 79 .... JohnEgan 4 (D R C Elsworth) *hld up: rdn over 6f out: sn wknd* 25/1	37
4235	13	21	**Trance (IRE)**[13] 5963 6-9-4 80 .... NCallan 2 (T D Barron) *s.i.s: hld up: rdn over 6f out: sn wknd* 8/1[3]	12
001-	14	2½	**Pocketwood**[327] 6029 4-9-2 78 .... J-PGuillambert 13 (Jean-Rene Auvray) *chsd ldrs over 10f* 50/1	7
4314	15	33	**Particle (IRE)**[12] 5991 3-8-8 83 .... GregFairley(3) 8 (M Johnston) *lw: prom 11f* 10/1	—
5-	16	35	**Nation State**[392] 5586 5-9-4 80 ....(p) GeorgeBaker 10 (G L Moore) *b. prom 10f* 66/1	—

3m 31.78s (4.86) **Going Correction** +0.275s/f (Good)
WFA 3 from 4yo+ 10lb **16** Ran SP% **121.2**
Speed ratings (Par 107):98,97,95,94,94 87,85,85,84,83 79,76,65,64,47 30
CSF £89.07 CT £318.47 TOTE £10.40: £2.10, £2.60, £1.60, £3.70; EX 129.20.
Owner The Ivy Syndicate **Bred** Mrs Ann Fortune **Trained** Tadcaster, N Yorks

FOCUS
Very few got into this staying handicap, which on paper had looked pretty competitive. The field ended up racing up the stands' side in the straight.

NOTEBOOK
Dr Sharp(IRE), sent off at 100-1 when third in the Cesarewitch 13 days earlier, had gone up 1lb for that effort, leaving him on the same mark as when last successful. Making every yard, he relishes these conditions and was never going to be headed. It will be interesting to see if connections decide to have another go hurdling with him this winter.
Kayf Aramis, not for the first time this season, was asked to race from out of the handicap. He ran well but could not get past the game winner and had to settle for finishing runner-up for the fifth time in his last six starts. (tchd 11-1)
At The Money, a progressive three-year-old at the right end of the weights, had returned from a summer break to record a career best when successful at Warwick a fortnight earlier, but he was 5lb higher here in what was a tougher race, and he came up a bit short. He remains relatively unexposed, however, and is open to further improvement. (tchd 5-2 and 3-1)
Remember Ramon(USA), stepping up in trip from a mile and a half, had been off the track since competing in the Swiss Derby back in June. Having won his maiden on his seasonal reappearance, the absence was not a worry, but the longer distance did appear to find him out. (op 8-1 tchd 11-1)
Establishment could not be said to be well handicapped at present and he probably ran as well as could be expected. (op 16-1)
Particle(IRE) Official explanation: jockey said gelding had no more to give
Nation State Official explanation: jockey said gelding had no more to give

6206 CANISBAY APPRENTICE STKS (H'CAP) 1m
5:00 (5:01) (Class 5) (0-75,74) 3-Y-0 **£3,238** (£963; £481; £240) **Stalls** High

Form	Pos	Dist	Horse / details	RPR
6403	1		**Pleasing**[8] 6069 3-8-4 62 .... AshleyHamblett(3) 4 (J L Dunlop) *hld up: swtchd rt and hdwy over 3f out: rdn to ld and hung lft over 1f out: hung lft ins fnl f: r.o* 11/1	75
0050	2	2½	**Wassfa**[18] 5879 3-8-4 64 ow2 .... WilliamCarson(5) 12 (C E Brittain) *chsd ldr: led over 2f out: rdn and hdd over 1f out: styd on same pce* 33/1	71
053	3	1	**Vacation (IRE)**[9] 6054 3-8-10 70 .... WilliamBuick(5) 10 (V Smith) *lw: hld up: swtchd rt and hdwy over 1f out: hung lft ins fnl f: r.o* 13/2[3]	75
2435	4	½	**Al Rayanah**[9] 6060 3-8-4 62 .... KirstyMilczarek(3) 18 (G Prodromou) *hld up: hdwy over 3f out: rdn over 1f out: styd on same pce* 22/1	66
6206	5	1¾	**Jebel Ali (IRE)**[7] 6076 3-9-1 73 ....(v[1]) JamesMillman(3) 20 (B Gubby) *chsd ldrs: rdn over 1f out: styd on same pce fnl f* 33/1	73
4115	6	nk	**Apache Nation (IRE)**[9] 6054 3-8-11 66 .... MarkLawson 16 (M Dods) *chsd ldrs: rdn over 2f out: no ex fnl f* 12/1	65
-265	7	shd	**Birkside**[35] 5511 3-9-5 74 ....(t) LiamJones 5 (W R Swinburn) *lw: hld up: nt clr run over 1f out: r.o ins fnl f: nt trble ldrs* 6/1[2]	73+
500	8	½	**The Osteopath (IRE)**[18] 5863 3-9-3 72 ....(p) AndrewElliott 11 (M Dods) *lw: mid-div: nt clr run and swtchd lft over 1f out: r.o: nt trble ldrs* 12/1	70
1003	9	shd	**Conrad**[25] 5724 3-9-1 70 .... JamieMoriarty 8 (R A Fahey) *prom: rdn 2f out: sn outpcd* 50/1	67

1-00 **10** ½ **Prince Of Love (IRE)**^{17} [5889] 3-8-11 **66**.......................... TravisBlock 14 62
(Jedd O'Keeffe) *chsd ldrs over 6f* **20/1**

3036 **11** *nk* **Murrumbidgee (IRE)**^{30} [5621] 3-7-13 **61**.......................... BillyCray$^{(7)}$ 19 57
(J W Hills) *hld up: hdwy over 3f out: wknd fnl f* **33/1**

3002 **12** 2 ½ **Stormy Monday**^{9} [6059] 3-9-0 **72**.......................... PatrickHills$^{(3)}$ 9 62
(J W Hills) *s.i.s: hdwy over 3f out: wknd over 1f out* **16/1**

1526 **13** ½ **Kavachi (IRE)**^{14} [5937] 3-8-10 **68**.......................... JamieJones$^{(3)}$ 1 57
(G L Moore) *hld up: rdn over 2f out: n.d* **20/1**

214 **14** 2 ½ **Woolly Bully**^{9} [6051] 3-9-5 **74**.......................... CPGeoghegan 15 57
(G A Huffer) *lw: b.hind: mid-div: rdn over 3f out: wknd 2f out* **11/4**^{1}

1201 **15** ½ **Mataram (USA)**^{47} [5211] 3-8-12 **72**.......................... BRoper$^{(5)}$ 2 54
(W Jarvis) *hld up: effrt over 2f out: sn wknd* **16/1**

1000 **16** *5* **Debord (FR)**^{47} [5211] 3-8-9 **64**.......................... RoryMoore 17 34
(Jamie Poulton) *sn outpcd* **50/1**

1 **17** *nk* **Bucharest**^{77} [4325] 3-8-4 **62**.......................... StephanieHollinshead$^{(3)}$ 13 32
(M Wigham) *lw: sn led: hdd over 2f out: wknd wl over 1f out* **20/1**

05-0 **18** *hd* **Thomas Of Bathwick**^{16} [5911] 3-8-4 **62**.......................... NicolPolli$^{(3)}$ 3 31
(B G Powell) *s.i.s: a in rr* **100/1**

06-6 **19** 1 ¼ **Greytown**^{19} [5844] 3-8-5 **67**.......................... DanielRobinson$^{(7)}$ 7 33
(M A Jarvis) *chsd ldrs 5f* **50/1**

1650 **20** 3 ½ **Sir Douglas**^{125} [2863] 3-9-4 **73**.......................... JerryO'Dwyer 6 31
(J A Osborne) *hld up in tch: rdn and wknd over 2f out* **100/1**

1m 41.52s (2.15) **Going Correction** +0.275s/f (Good) **20** Ran SP% **125.1**
Speed ratings (Par 101):100,97,96,96,94 93,93,93,93,92 92,89,89,86,86 81,81,80,79,76
CSF £344.36 CT £2609.32 TOTE £12.30: £2.90, £7.50, £1.70, £3.90; EX 502.70 Place 6 £6.58, Place 5 £6.19.
Owner Mrs W H Carson & Mrs J L Dunlop **Bred** Minster Enterprises Ltd **Trained** Arundel, W Sussex

FOCUS
A competitive handicap but only modest form.
Woolly Bully Official explanation: jockey said colt ran flat
T/Jkpt: Not won. T/Plt: £8.20 to a £1 stake. Pool: £80,033.25. 7,079.40 winning tickets. T/Qpdt: £7.60 to a £1 stake. Pool: £4,382.80. 423.50 winning tickets. CR

5859 AYR (L-H)
Saturday, October 28

OFFICIAL GOING: Heavy
With conditions very testing, the bare form of all races at this meeting should be treated with caution.
Wind: Fresh, half against

6207 JOHN SMITH'S MAIDEN STKS — 7f 50y
1:55 (1:55) (Class 5) 2-Y-O **£3,886** (£1,156; £577; £288) **Stalls** Far side

Form RPR

55 **1** **Bayonyx (IRE)**^{26} [5720] 2-9-3 .... TomEaves 2 72
(J Howard Johnson) *trckd ldrs: effrt over 2f out: led over 1f out: edgd lft ins fnl f: styd on wl* **13/8**^{1}

6 **2** *1* **Amicus Meus (IRE)**^{43} [5332] 2-8-12 .... JamieMoriarty$^{(5)}$ 8 70
(A Bailey) *cl up: led over 2f to over 1f out: kpt on ins fnl f* **7/1**

00 **3** *9* **Milson's Point (IRE)**^{44} [5307] 2-9-3 .... PaulHanagan 5 49
(I Semple) *led to over 2f out: outpcd over 1f out* **14/1**

0 **4** ½ **Shady Green (IRE)**^{26} [5720] 2-9-3 .... PaulMulrennan 10 47
(M W Easterby) *s.i.s: bhd tl kpt on fr 2f out: nrst fin* **7/1**

03 **5** *6* **My Secrets**^{99} [3713] 2-9-0 .... GregFairley$^{(3)}$ 3 33
(M Johnston) *chsd ldrs tl wknd wl over 1f out* **5/1**^{3}

0 **6** *35* **Senora Lenorah**^{20} [5835] 2-8-12 .... DavidAllan 7 —
(D A Nolan) *in tch: hung bdly to stands rail ent st: sn lost tch* **150/1**

7 *hd* **Thornylee** 2-9-3 .... J-PGuillambert 9 —
(M Johnston) *s.i.s: sn niggled in rr: shortlived effrt towards stands side ent st: sn lost tch* **7/2**^{2}

1m 45.5s (12.78) **Going Correction** +1.65s/f (Heavy) **7** Ran SP% **109.3**
Speed ratings (Par 95):92,90,80,80,73 33,32
CSF £12.44 TOTE £2.80: £1.30, £3.20; EX 16.20.
Owner Transcend Bloodstock LLP **Bred** Dermot Brennan And Associates Ltd **Trained** Billy Row, Co Durham
■ Stewards' Enquiry : Tom Eaves three-day ban: used whip with excessive frequency (Nov 8-10)

FOCUS
Litte strength in depth and not surprisingly just a sensible gallop in the conditions with the third setting the standard. The race was started using a flip start, and hand timed.

NOTEBOOK
Bayonyx(IRE), down in trip, handled the conditions well and confirmed previous promise. Although the bare form of this is ordinary, he will be interesting in modest company in middle-distance handicaps next year. (op 7-4 tchd 6-4)
Amicus Meus(IRE), who hinted at ability over course and distance on his debut, had the run of the race and fared better on this second outing. He was clear of the remainder and, although this bare form should be treated with caution, looks capable of winning a small event in due course. (op 15-2 tchd 8-1)
Milson's Point(IRE) turned in his best effort yet and, while he was well beaten after enjoying the run of the race, is in good hands and will be of more interest in ordinary handicap company next year. (op 20-1)
Shady Green(IRE), dropping in distance, finished further behind the winner than he had done at Pontefract on his debut. He is another who will be of more interest in modest handicaps over middle distances next year. (tchd 6-1)
My Secrets, having his first run since July and his first over this trip and in conditions this testing, was never travelling with much fluency and was below the form of his last run. He should do better back on a sound surface next term.
Senora Lenorah Official explanation: jockey said filly hung right-handed turning into the straight
Thornylee, who cost 32,000 guineas and is the first foal of an unraced half-sister to a seven-furlong winner, floundered badly in these very testing conditions on this racecourse debut.

6208 JOHN SMITH'S NURSERY — 6f
2:30 (2:30) (Class 5) (0-75,75) 2-Y-O **£3,886** (£1,156; £577; £288) **Stalls** Centre

Form RPR

6302 **1** **Goodbye Cash (IRE)**^{3} [6175] 2-9-2 **73**.......................... StephenDonohoe$^{(3)}$ 3 74
(P D Evans) *led to 1f out: rallied gamely to regain ld nr fin* **2/1**^{1}

654 **2** *shd* **Hansomis (IRE)**^{18} [5898] 2-8-12 **66**.......................... PaulHanagan 7 67
(B Mactaggart) *in tch: hdwy to ld 1f out: kpt on u.p: hdd cl home* **4/1**^{2}

604 **3** *3* **Pietersen (IRE)**^{18} [5901] 2-8-9 **63**..........................(b) PhillipMakin 8 55
(T D Barron) *cl up: effrt over 2f out: one pce over 1f out* **9/1**

0415 **4** *4* **Only A Grand**^{10} [6056] 2-8-13 **67**..........................(b) PatCosgrave 5 47
(R Bastiman) *chsd ldrs tl wknd appr fnl f* **8/1**^{3}

065 **5** *3* **Billy Ruffian**^{25} [5746] 2-8-13 **67**.......................... DavidAllan 1 39
(T D Easterby) *trckd ldrs: rdn over 2f out: wknd wl over 1f out* **14/1**

0430 **6** ½ **Hunting Call**^{14} [5959] 2-9-0 **68**..........................(b) CatherineGannon 2 38
(K A Ryan) *in tch tl rdn and wknd fr 2f out* **11/1**

016 **7** ¾ **Redcliff (GER)**^{55} [5041] 2-9-7 **75**.......................... PaulMulrennan 9 43
(M W Easterby) *sn wl bhd: nvr on terms* **8/1**^{3}

0040 **8** *4* **Homes By Woodford**^{19} [5860] 2-7-12 **52**..........................(b^{1}) DaleGibson 4 8
(M W Easterby) *dwlt: a bhd* **8/1**^{3}

1m 22.7s (9.03) **Going Correction** +1.325s/f (Soft) **8** Ran SP% **111.7**
Speed ratings (Par 95):92,91,87,82,78 77,76,71
CSF £9.30 CT £54.83 TOTE £2.50: £1.10, £1.80, £3.30; EX 9.20.
Owner D Healy **Bred** Mrs A C Peters **Trained** Pandy, Abergavenny
■ Stewards' Enquiry : David Allan two-day ban: careless riding (Nov 8-9)
Stephen Donohoe one-day ban: used whip with excessive frequency (Nov 8)

FOCUS
An ordinary event in which the field raced on the stands' rail. The winner is the best guide to the form.

NOTEBOOK
Goodbye Cash(IRE), who ran well in heavy ground at Nottingham three days earlier, confirmed that promise and showed a good attitude back over this longer trip. She is a tough and consistent sort who should continue to give a good account. (op 9-4, tchd 5-2 in places)
Hansomis(IRE), a progressive sort, turned in her best effort yet back in distance and on this nursery debut. Effective over seven furlongs, she looks capable of picking up a similar event with cut in the ground.
Pietersen(IRE), with the blinkers on again for this handicap debut, ran creditably after enjoying the run of the race and should be suited by the return to seven furlongs. (op 8-1)
Only A Grand was not totally disgraced on only her second start on heavy ground but, given she is fully exposed and is not the most consistent, may have to come down the weights before returning to winning ways. (tchd 12-1 in a place)
Billy Ruffian failed to improve for the step up to this trip on his first run in heavy ground but is only lightly raced and is worth another chance in similar company on a sound surface next year. (op 12-1)
Hunting Call had his limitations exposed on this handicap debut but, as his best form had been on a sound surface, will be worth another chance on such ground next year when coming down the handicap. (op 10-1 tchd 9-1, tchd 12-1 in a place)

6209 JOHN SMITH'S EXTRA COLD H'CAP — 1m 1f 20y
3:00 (3:00) (Class 4) (0-85,84) 3-Y-O+
£6,232 (£1,866; £933; £467; £233; £117) **Stalls** Low

Form RPR

0206 **1** **Top Jaro (FR)**^{10} [6051] 3-8-7 **73**.......................... GregFairley$^{(3)}$ 7 83
(T P Tate) *mde virtually all: hrd pressed over 1f out: kpt on gamely fnl f* **6/1**^{3}

2421 **2** 2 ½ **Charlie Tokyo (IRE)**^{19} [5869] 3-9-2 **84**..........................(b) JamieMoriarty$^{(5)}$ 1 89
(R A Fahey) *hld up in tch: smooth hdwy to chal over 1f out: sn rdn: kpt on same pce fnl f* **9/4**^{1}

0100 **3** *3* **Hawkit (USA)**^{12} [6008] 5-8-8 **67** oh1.......................... DaleGibson 5 66
(P Monteith) *hld up in tch: pushed along over 4f out: styd on fnl 2f: nt rch ldrs* **14/1**

6401 **4** *hd* **Chief Scout**^{19} [5863] 4-9-8 **81**.......................... TomEaves 6 80
(I Semple) *chsd ldrs tl rdn and nt qckn fr 2f out* **11/4**^{2}

5344 **5** 1 ¼ **Ulysees (IRE)**^{18} [5904] 7-8-8 **67** oh5.......................... PaulHanagan 8 63
(I Semple) *hld up in tch: pushed along and outpcd over 3f out: n.d after* **13/2**

5200 **6** ¾ **Kristiansand**^{18} [5905] 6-8-9 **73** oh20 ow6.......................... MarkLawson$^{(5)}$ 2 68?
(P Monteith) *dwlt: bhd: hdwy over 2f out: sn no imp* **50/1**

003 **7** ¾ **Little Bob**^{19} [5863] 5-8-8 **67** oh3..........................(b) PatCosgrave 4 60
(J D Bethell) *chsd ldrs: rdn over 3f out: wknd 2f out* **7/1**

2-00 **8** *64* **Maggies Farm (USA)**^{45} [5299] 3-9-2 **79**.......................... J-PGuillambert 3 —
(M Johnston) *pressed wnr tl wknd over 3f out: virtually p.u* **14/1**

2m 12.65s (12.65) **Going Correction** +1.65s/f (Heavy)
WFA 3 from 4yo+ 4lb **8** Ran SP% **112.8**
Speed ratings (Par 105):109,106,104,103,102 102,101,44
CSF £19.38 CT £178.96 TOTE £7.30: £2.10, £2.60, £2.50; EX 38.00.
Owner T T Racing **Bred** J Biraben And Robert Labeyrie **Trained** Tadcaster, N Yorks

FOCUS
A run-of-the-mill handicap in which the pace seemed sound in the conditions. The form looks dubious with the sixth close up from well out of the handicap.

6210 JOHN SMITH'S EXTRA SMOOTH H'CAP — 1m
3:35 (3:36) (Class 3) (0-90,87) 3-Y-O+ **£10,363** (£3,083; £1,540; £769) **Stalls** Far side

Form RPR

6131 **1** **Compromiznotension (IRE)**^{26} [5724] 3-8-7 **75**.......................... TomEaves 3 84
(I Semple) *mde all: rdn over 2f out: kpt on gamely fnl f* **9/2**^{3}

3623 **2** *1* **Collateral Damage (IRE)**^{22} [5789] 3-9-5 **87**.......................... DavidAllan 5 94
(T D Easterby) *cl up: rdn over 2f out: kpt on ins fnl f* **7/4**^{1}

0101 **3** *shd* **Mezuzah**^{3} [6176] 6-9-4 **83** 5ex.......................... PaulMulrennan 6 90
(M W Easterby) *trckd ldrs: ev ch over 1f out: sn rdn: no ex wl ins fnl f* **15/8**^{2}

4610 **4** *10* **Wigwam Willie (IRE)**^{30} [5639] 4-9-4 **83**..........................(p) CatherineGannon 2 70
(K A Ryan) *in tch: rdn and outpcd over 3f out: sn n.d* **9/2**^{3}

00- **5** *29* **Terlan (GER)**^{400} [5434] 8-8-8 **73** oh17 ow1.......................... PatCosgrave 4 2
(P Monteith) *in tch tl rdn and wknd wl over 2f out* **50/1**

1m 56.0s (12.51) **Going Correction** +1.65s/f (Heavy)
WFA 3 from 4yo+ 3lb **5** Ran SP% **109.5**
Speed ratings (Par 107):103,102,101,91,62
CSF £12.69 TOTE £6.00: £2.30, £1.70; EX 14.60.
Owner R Hyndman **Bred** Corduff Stud **Trained** Carluke, S Lanarks

FOCUS
Flip start and hand timed. Not the most competitive of races and just an ordinary gallop in the conditions. The placed horses suggest the form is sound enough.

NOTEBOOK
Compromiznotension(IRE) has been in good form and made it three out of four wins with a gutsy success. He goes really well with give in the ground and, as he should not be going up too much for this win, may be capable of better next term. (op 5-1)
Collateral Damage(IRE) goes well with cut in the ground and ran another gutsy race. He is a reliable sort in this type of event but has little margin for error from his current mark. (op 9-4)
Mezuzah looked the one to beat, even with a penalty for his ready Nottingham success but, while running creditably in terms of form, did not find as much off the bridle as seemed likely. Nevertheless this is his ground and he is the type to win again granted suitable conditions. (op 6-4 tchd 2-1)
Wigwam Willie(IRE) has won in testing ground and over this trip but, although he has little room for manoeuvre from this mark, was a fair way below his best this time.
Terlan(GER) was well beaten on this first run for over a year carrying 18lb more than his long handicap mark. This should have put him spot on for a tilt over hurdles, though. (tchd 40-1)

6211 JOHN SMITH'S FILLIES' H'CAP — 7f 50y

4:10 (4:11) (Class 5) (0-70,70) 3-Y-O+ **£3,238** (£963; £481; £240) **Stalls** Far side

Form — RPR

4001 **1** **Amy Louise (IRE)**[19] 5861 3-9-4 **70** ... TomEaves 4 — 88
(T D Barron) *prom gng wl: shkn up to ld ent fnl f: sn clr* **5/1**[2]

0012 **2** *5* **Scotland The Brave**[19] 5861 6-9-5 **69** ... (v) PatCosgrave 3 — 75
(J D Bethell) *cl up: led over 3f out: hdd ent fnl f: no ch w wnr* **3/1**[1]

2533 **3** *13* **Coronation Flight**[20] 5838 3-8-0 **57** oh7 ow1 ... RoryMoore(5) 6 — 32
(F P Murtagh) *bhd: rdn 3f out: hdwy to chse first two over 1f out: no imp* **33/1**

5063 **4** *½* **Queen's Echo**[30] 5636 5-8-6 **56** oh3 ... PaulMulrennan 9 — 30
(M Dods) *chsd ldrs: effrt 3f out: no ex fr 2f out* **6/1**[3]

0062 **5** *1½* **Hansomelle (IRE)**[30] 5636 4-8-4 **57** oh5 ow1 ... GregFairley(3) 5 — 27
(B Mactaggart) *hld up: rdn and effrt over 2f out: btn wl over 1f out* **9/1**

1334 **6** *5* **Tequila Sheila (IRE)**[30] 5636 4-8-6 **56** oh4 ... CatherineGannon 11 — 14
(K R Burke) *keen: led to over 3f out: wknd 2f out* **14/1**

1220 **7** *10* **Touch Of Ivory (IRE)**[38] 4476 3-8-11 **63** ... (p) DaleGibson 8 — —
(P Monteith) *in tch: rdn after 3f: wknd over 2f out* **10/1**

1300 **8** *8* **Celtic Spa (IRE)**[32] 5590 4-9-3 **70** ... StephenDonohoe(3) 10 — —
(P D Evans) *hld up in tch: rdn and wd st: sn wknd* **16/1**

0005 **9** *65* **Bellsbank (IRE)**[19] 5861 3-8-5 **57** ... PaulQuinn 2 — —
(A Bailey) *s.i.s: sn chsng ldrs: rdn over 3f out: sn btn: virtually p.u fnl f* **6/1**[3]

1m 42.9s (10.18) **Going Correction** +1.65s/f (Heavy)
WFA 3 from 4yo+ 2lb — **9** Ran SP% **104.8**
Speed ratings (Par 100):107,101,86,85,84 78,67,57,—
CSF £16.90 CT £317.82 TOTE £4.20: £1.70, £1.40, £4.90; EX 8.10.
Owner P D Savill **Bred** P D Savill **Trained** Maunby, N Yorks
■ Mystical Ayr (13/2) was withdrawn on vet's advice. R4 applies, deduct 10p in the £.

FOCUS
Flip start and hand timed. Mainly exposed performers, the exception being the winner, who scored with plenty in hand. The runner-up is the best guide to the form.
Bellsbank(IRE) Official explanation: jockey said filly had a breathing problem

6212 JOHN SMITH'S NO NONSENSE H'CAP — 6f

4:45 (4:45) (Class 4) (0-80,80) 3-Y-O+
£6,232 (£1,866; £933; £467; £233; £117) **Stalls** Centre

Form — RPR

5004 **1** **Yorkshire Blue**[42] 5355 7-9-2 **77** ... J-PGuillambert 13 — 89
(J S Goldie) *hld up: effrt and swtchd lft over 1f out: kpt on to ld towards fin* **20/1**

0112 **2** *¾* **Ten Shun**[19] 5872 3-8-7 **72** ... StephenDonohoe(3) 7 — 82
(P D Evans) *trckd ldrs: led over 1f out: kpt on: hdd towards fin* **4/1**[1]

0045 **3** *hd* **Balakiref**[10] 6048 7-8-11 **72** ... PhillipMakin 1 — 81
(M Dods) *hld up bhd: n.m.r over 2f out: hdwy over 1f out: effrt ent fnl f: keeping on whn n.m.r wl ins last* **11/2**[2]

0434 **4** *¾* **Charlie Delta**[12] 6009 3-8-10 **79** ... KellyHarrison(7) 5 — 86
(D Carroll) *in tch: effrt and chsd wnr over 1f out to ins fnl f: nt qckn* **20/1**

0042 **5** *6* **Misphire**[30] 5643 3-9-2 **78** ... TomEaves 10 — 67
(M Dods) *mde most to over 1f out: sn outpcd* **7/1**[3]

2104 **6** *5* **Stellite**[34] 5554 6-9-0 **75** ... LeeEnstone 11 — 49
(J S Goldie) *hld up midfield: effrt over 2f out: outpcd wl over 1f out* **9/1**

0115 **7** *3* **Wanchai Lad**[22] 5791 5-9-5 **80** ... (t) DavidAllan 12 — 45
(T D Easterby) *chsd ldrs to 2f out: sn rdn and btn* **8/1**

6243 **8** *3½* **Flying Bantam (IRE)**[14] 5961 5-8-5 **66** ... PaulHanagan 4 — 20
(R A Fahey) *midfield: outpcd over 2f out: no ch after* **8/1**

0-0 **9** *1¼* **Katie Boo (IRE)**[194] 1042 4-8-9 **70** ... PaulQuinn 8 — 21
(A Berry) *bhd and outpcd: nvr on terms* **100/1**

3000 **10** *¾* **Raymond's Pride**[12] 6009 6-9-2 **77** ... (b) CatherineGannon 2 — 25
(K A Ryan) *w ldrs on outside: wknd fr 2f out* **10/1**

6020 **11** *shd* **Spiritual Peace (IRE)**[35] 5532 3-9-2 **78** ... (p) PaulMulrennan 9 — 26
(K A Ryan) *w ldrs to over 2f out: sn wknd* **40/1**

0126 **12** *nk* **Word Perfect**[12] 6020 4-8-9 **70** ... (b) DaleGibson 6 — 17
(M W Easterby) *w ldrs: hung lft and wknd over 2f out* **8/1**

3012 **13** *36* **Ptarmigan Ridge**[35] 5532 10-8-13 **77** ... GregFairley(3) 3 — —
(Miss L A Perratt) *w ldrs: rdn 1/2-way: sn lost pl* **11/1**

1m 20.43s (6.76) **Going Correction** +1.325s/f (Soft)
WFA 3 from 4yo+ 1lb — **13** Ran SP% **121.6**
Speed ratings (Par 105):107,106,105,104,96 90,86,81,79,78 78,78,30
CSF £97.49 CT £538.04 TOTE £19.50: £6.50, £1.90, £3.00; EX 133.50.
Owner Thoroughbred Leisure Racing Club 2 **Bred** R T And Mrs Watson **Trained** Uplawmoor, E Renfrews

FOCUS
Another ordinary handicap but a decent gallop throughout and the runner-up looks better than the bare form. The fourth is rated to recent form and sets the standard.

6213 JOHN SMITH'S AT AYR RACECOURSE H'CAP — 1m 1f 20y

5:20 (5:20) (Class 6) (0-55,55) 3-Y-O+ **£3,238** (£963; £481; £240) **Stalls** Low

Form — RPR

00-3 **1** **Boppys Pride**[42] 5363 3-8-4 **50** ow3 ... JamieMoriarty(5) 3 — 58
(R A Fahey) *prom: lost pl 1/2-way: plenty to do 2f out: styd on to ld wl ins fnl f: r.o* **20/1**

0001 **2** *1* **Komreyev Star**[20] 5838 4-8-13 **50** ... SilvestreDeSousa 1 — 56
(M Mullineaux) *a cl up: led gng wl over 2f out: rdn over 1f out: kpt on: hdd and no ex wl ins fnl f* **5/1**[2]

1006 **3** *6* **Wizby**[30] 5637 3-8-9 **53** ... StephenDonohoe(3) 5 — 47
(P D Evans) *midfield: effrt over 3f out: rallied over 2f out: no ex fnl f* **20/1**

0650 **4** *3½* **Riverhill (IRE)**[36] 5510 3-8-12 **53** ... TomEaves 13 — 40
(J Howard Johnson) *hld up: hdwy and in tch 1/2-way: effrt over 2f out: hung lft and wknd over 1f out* **14/1**

0100 **5** *5* **Aqua**[16] 5926 4-8-3 **45** ... RoryMoore(5) 11 — 22
(P T Midgley) *mde most to over 2f out: edgd lft and wknd wl over 1f out* **33/1**

5003 **6** *¾* **Scotty's Future (IRE)**[4] 6158 8-9-0 **51** ... DaleGibson 10 — 27
(A Berry) *s.i.s: outpcd tl hdwy 2f out: nvr rchd ldrs* **12/1**

1230 **7** *3½* **Jordans Spark**[33] 5581 5-8-12 **54** ... MarkLawson(5) 14 — 23
(P Monteith) *hld up: hdwy and prom 3f out: hung lft and wknd wl over 1f out* **10/1**

0060 **8** *23* **Time To Regret**[62] 4845 6-8-10 **47** ... DavidAllan 8 — —
(I W McInnes) *in tch: hdwy over 3f out: wknd 2f out* **14/1**

3014 **9** *3½* **Hows That**[20] 5840 4-8-8 **45** ... (p) PhillipMakin 12 — —
(K R Burke) *hld up: pushed along over 3f out: sn btn* **11/1**

0002 **10** *10* **Barataria**[20] 5839 4-8-13 **50** ... PatCosgrave 7 — —
(R Bastiman) *chsd ldrs tl wknd over 2f out* **7/1**[3]

2-66 **11** *16* **Dramatic Review (IRE)**[29] 2808 4-8-10 **47** ... (bt) J-PGuillambert 4 — —
(J Barclay) *towards rr: struggling over 4f out: eased whn no ch* **33/1**

12 *1¼* **Victors Prize (IRE)**[433] 4609 4-9-3 **54** ... PaulMulrennan 2 — —
(T J Pitt) *chsd ldrs: rdn over 4f out: sn wknd* **9/2**[1]

0532 **13** *33* **Gigs Magic (USA)**[9] 6068 3-8-8 **52** ... GregFairley(3) 9 — —
(M Johnston) *towards rr: drvn 1/2-way: sn lost tch* **7/1**[3]

004 **14** *7* **Shardia (IRE)**[24] 5768 3-9-0 **55** ... PaulHanagan 6 — —
(J Jay) *cl up tl wknd over 3f out: t.o* **9/1**

2m 15.13s (15.13) **Going Correction** +1.65s/f (Heavy)
WFA 3 from 4yo+ 4lb — **14** Ran SP% **123.7**
Speed ratings (Par 101):98,97,91,88,84 83,80,60,56,48 33,32,3,—
CSF £116.11 CT £2070.20 TOTE £27.80: £6.30, £3.20, £5.70; EX 211.50 Place 6 £22.10, Place 5 £11.44..
Owner Mrs S Bond **Bred** Sylvia Vokes Bloodstock **Trained** Musley Bank, N Yorks
■ Stewards' Enquiry : Silvestre De Sousa five-day ban: used whip with excessive frequency (Nov 8-11,16)

FOCUS
Modest stuff but a fair gallop and an improved effort from the lightly-raced winner, who is capable of better. The runner-up is rated to last year's form in this contest.
Shardia(IRE) Official explanation: jockey said filly was unsuited by the heavy ground
T/Plt: £20.40 to a £1 stake. Pool: £51,784.45. 1,845.80 winning tickets. T/Qpdt: £10.20 to a £1 stake. Pool: £2,844.80. 204.40 winning tickets. RY

6199 NEWMARKET (ROWLEY) (R-H)

Saturday, October 28

OFFICIAL GOING: Soft
Wind: Fresh, across. Weather: Overcast

6214 BET365 CALL 08000 322365 EBF MAIDEN STKS (C&G) (DIV I) — 7f

1:00 (1:11) (Class 5) 2-Y-O **£2,590** (£770; £385; £192) **Stalls** Low

Form — RPR

2 **1** **Mr Napper Tandy**[18] 5890 2-9-0 ... JamieSpencer 7 — 84
(M R Channon) *lw: chsd ldrs: led 5f out: rdn over 1f out: r.o* **11/8**[1]

2 *½* **Walking Talking** 2-9-0 ... RichardHughes 19 — 83+
(H R A Cecil) *gd sort: scope: chsd ldrs: rdn and ev ch over 1f out: r.o* **15/2**[2]

3 *½* **American Spin** 2-9-0 ... LDettori 9 — 82+
(B J Meehan) *gd sort: s.s: hld up: hdwy 2f out: rdn over 1f out: edgd lft ins fnl f: r.o* **12/1**

4 *1½* **Wester Ross (IRE)** 2-9-0 ... MickyFenton 8 — 78+
(J M P Eustace) *wl grwn: b.bkwd: led 2f: chsd ldrs: rdn over 1f out: stayed on same pce ins fnl f* **100/1**

5 *½* **Hannicean** 2-9-0 ... PhilipRobinson 3 — 77+
(M A Jarvis) *cmpt: scope: chsd ldrs: rdn over 1f out: styd on same pce* **33/1**

6 **6** *1* **The Carlton Cannes**[18] 5883 2-9-0 ... TedDurcan 12 — 74
(G Wragg) *w'like: scope: b.bkwd: prom: rdn 1/2-way: styd on same pce appr fnl f* **9/1**

7 *hd* **Arabian Gulf** 2-9-0 ... RyanMoore 16 — 74+
(Sir Michael Stoute) *gd sort: b.bkwd: chsd ldrs: nt clr run over 1f out: styd on same pce* **8/1**[3]

8 *nk* **Risque Heights** 2-9-0 ... FJohansson 13 — 73+
(G A Butler) *neat: s.i.s: sn mid-div: swtchd rt and hdwy over 1f out: nt trble ldrs* **66/1**

9 *nk* **Mutual Friend (USA)** 2-9-0 ... SteveDrowne 4 — 72
(E A L Dunlop) *tall: scope: s.i.s: sn prom: rdn 2f out: styd on same pce* **66/1**

0 **10** *1* **Chunky's Choice (IRE)**[15] 5939 2-9-0 ... SebSanders 20 — 70
(J Noseda) *lw: chsd ldrs: rdn over 2f out: wknd over 1f out* **20/1**

3 **11** *½* **Limbo King**[18] 5891 2-9-0 ... EddieAhern 15 — 69
(J W Hills) *prom 5f* **9/1**

12 *shd* **Alaghiraar (IRE)** 2-9-0 ... RHills 1 — 69
(J L Dunlop) *leggy: scope: hld up: rdn and hung rt over 2f out: n.d* **25/1**

13 *5* **Silmi** 2-9-0 ... MartinDwyer 10 — 57
(E A L Dunlop) *cmpt: sn pushed along: a in rr:* **33/1**

14 *2½* **Tirade** 2-9-0 ... KDarley 17 — 51
(J H M Gosden) *b.bkwd: a in rr* **20/1**

15 *¾* **Mumbleswerve (IRE)** 2-9-0 ... RobertWinston 2 — 49
(W Jarvis) *w'like: scope: s.s: a in rr* **66/1**

0 **16** *½* **Adversane**[18] 5890 2-9-0 ... IanMongan 11 — 48
(J L Dunlop) *mid-div: lost pl 1/2-way: sn bhd* **66/1**

17 *hd* **Spice Bar** 2-9-0 ... FrancisNorton 5 — 47
(A M Balding) *s.s: hld up: wknd over 2f out* **33/1**

18 *4* **George Henson (IRE)** 2-8-11 ... SaleemGolam(3) 14 — 38
(M H Tompkins) *leggy: b.bkwd: dwlt: outpcd* **66/1**

19 *5* **Maraca (IRE)** 2-9-0 ... MichaelHills 18 — 26
(J H M Gosden) *gd sort: dwlt: sn in mid-div: wknd 1/2-way* **14/1**

1m 29.15s (2.65) **Going Correction** +0.175s/f (Good) — **19** Ran SP% **130.0**
Speed ratings (Par 95):91,90,89,88,87 86,86,85,85,84 83,83,77,75,74 73,73,68,63
CSF £10.58 TOTE £2.30: £1.20, £2.80, £4.20; EX 15.00.
Owner Five Arrows Racing **Bred** Mrs N F M Sampson **Trained** West Ilsley, Berks

FOCUS
A useful-looking maiden on paper, but the form is slightly dubious, with a 100-1 shot in fourth and the winning time almost two seconds slower than the second division. It will be no surprise if several beaten horses improve past the winner.

NOTEBOOK
Mr Napper Tandy, who had run with plenty of promise on his debut at Newbury when a narrow second to a subsequent Listed runner-up, put that experience to good use and found plenty when challenged. He should make a nice three-year-old next year, when he ought to be effective at around this trip and a mile. (op 15-8 tchd 2-1 in places)
Walking Talking is by Rainbow Quest but there is speed on the other side of his pedigree as his dam won a French Listed race over six furlongs at two. Sent off second favourite for this debut, he had clearly been showing something at home, and he ran well, only going down narrowly to a more experienced rival. Faster ground could help next year. (op 11-2)
American Spin, who is a half-brother to quite useful Worchester, a dual six-furlong winner in France, ran an encouraging race on his debut. He was not given too hard a time and looks sure to make up into a nice three-year-old over the winter.
Wester Ross(IRE), a half-brother to Ailincara, a multiple winner over a mile, and to two winners over hurdles, belied his odds to run well on his racecourse debut, although he probably benefited from racing up with the pace. His pedigree suggests he will progress as a three-year-old. (tchd 125-1)
Hannicean, a half-brother to Russian Music, quite a useful winner over seven furlongs and a mile, and to Wax Lyrical, a six-furlong winner at three, shaped with promise and should be effective at around a mile next season.

The Form Book, Raceform Ltd, Compton, RG20 6NL

The Carlton Cannes, who had the benefit of previous experience, was able to race more prominently this time, but he did not have the pace to remain in touch in the latter stages. Bred more for stamina than speed, 12 furlongs is likely to suit him next year. (op 14-1 tchd 8-1)
Arabian Gulf, whose rider wore the owner's second colours, is a brother to Yorkshire Oaks winner Quiff and should have been at home in this ground. He is bred to make a middle-distance three-year-old, and this debut experience should have done him the world of good.
Risque Heights, a brother to Chris Corsa, a seven-furlong winner at two, has more speed in his pedigree than many in this field, and a mile should suit him next year.

6215 BET365.COM EBF MAIDEN FILLIES' STKS 7f
1:30 (1:45) (Class 5) 2-Y-O **£3,238** (£963; £481; £240) **Stalls** Low

Form				RPR
	1		**Measured Tempo** 2-9-0 ... LDettori 5 (Saeed Bin Suroor) *hld up: hdwy over 2f out: led over 1f out: edgd rt: r.o wl* **4/1**[2]	89+
32	2	3	**Siamese Cat (IRE)**[36] 5503 2-9-0 ... PJSmullen 9 (B J Meehan) *led: rdn and hdd over 1f out: edgd rt and styd on same pce fnl f* **6/4**[1]	82
	3	¾	**Eternal Path (USA)** 2-9-0 ... RobertWinston 19 (Sir Michael Stoute) *hld up: hdwy and nt clr run over 1f out: nt trble ldrs* **12/1**	80+
	4	2 ½	**Bonne D'Argent (IRE)** 2-9-0 ... JoeFanning 14 (J R Boyle) *chsd ldrs: rdn and ev ch over 1f out: edgd lft and wknd ins fnl f* **100/1**	74
	5	1	**Silver Pivotal (IRE)** 2-9-0 ... FJohansson 13 (G A Butler) *chsd ldrs: rdn over 2f out: hmpd and wknd over 1f out* **40/1**	72
	6	hd	**Valrhona (IRE)** 2-9-0 ... SteveDrowne 8 (J Noseda) *hld up in tch: outpcd over 2f out: styd on ins fnl f: nt trble ldrs* **20/1**	71+
	7	nk	**Hypoteneuse (IRE)** 2-9-0 ... RyanMoore 12 (Sir Michael Stoute) *chsd ldrs over 5f* **12/1**	70
	8	3 ½	**Elounda (IRE)** 2-9-0 ... TedDurcan 17 (H R A Cecil) *prom: rdn 1/2-way: wknd over 1f out* **25/1**	62
	9	nk	**Lucy Rebecca** 2-9-0 ... KDarley 18 (M R Channon) *s.s: nvr nrr* **33/1**	61
62	10	shd	**Comma (USA)**[18] 5898 2-9-0 ... RichardHughes 11 (Sir Michael Stoute) *chsd ldrs over 5f* **10/1**[3]	61
	11	1 ¼	**Kailasha (IRE)** 2-9-0 ... SebSanders 10 (C F Wall) *dwlt: sn in tch: wknd 2f out* **25/1**	58
	12	hd	**Storm Petrel** 2-8-11 ... JamesDoyle(3) 2 (N P Littmoden) *chsd ldrs: rdn over 2f out: edgd rt and wknd over 1f out* **100/1**	58
	13	½	**Baltic Gift** 2-9-0 ... JamieSpencer 15 (M L W Bell) *s.s: rdn over 2f out: a in rr* **20/1**	56+
0	14	½	**Lindy Lou**[7] 6098 2-9-0 ... DeanMcKeown 20 (C A Cyzer) *hld up: effrt over 2f out: sn wknd* **150/1**	55
	15	hd	**Ashmal (USA)** 2-9-0 ... RHills 16 (J L Dunlop) *sn outpcd* **20/1**	55
	16	½	**Josephine Malines** 2-9-0 ... PhilipRobinson 1 (C G Cox) *prom over 3f* **25/1**	53
	17	½	**Inchinata (IRE)** 2-9-0 ... MichaelHills 6 (B W Hills) *hld up: wknd over 2f out* **33/1**	52
	18	nk	**Starparty (USA)** 2-9-0 ... JimCrowley 4 (Mrs A J Perrett) *a in rr* **66/1**	52
	19	¾	**Evita** 2-9-0 ... NickyMackay 7 (L M Cumani) *s.s: outpcd* **33/1**	50
	20	6	**Fancy Woman** 2-9-0 ... IanMongan 3 (J L Dunlop) *s.s: outpcd* **80/1**	35

1m 28.3s (1.80) **Going Correction** +0.175s/f (Good) **20** Ran SP% **126.9**
Speed ratings (Par 92):96,92,91,88,87 87,87,83,82,82 81,81,80,79,79 79,78,78,77,70
CSF £8.61 TOTE £5.10: £2.30, £1.40, £4.70; EX 13.70.
Owner Godolphin **Bred** Darley **Trained** Newmarket, Suffolk

FOCUS
Run in a faster time than the preceding maiden for colts, this looked a decent maiden on paper, and though the runner-up was below form the winner looks a very useful filly in the making.

NOTEBOOK
Measured Tempo ♦, a half-sister to Prix du Jockey-Club winner Anabaa Blue, was backed beforehand and justified the support in style, drawing away once she hit the rising ground to win by a clear margin from a fair yardstick in second. Her pedigree suggests that she should not be seen at her best until she tackles middle distances next season, so this was highly encouraging. She looks a smart filly in the making and could well develop into an Oaks candidate. (op 11-2)
Siamese Cat(IRE), runner-up to subsequent Cheveley Park winner Indian Ink in the Watership Down Sales Stakes last time out, looked to hold solid claims back in maiden company on that performance. She was perhaps unlucky to run into a potentially smart rival in the winner, but this was nothing like the Ascot form, judged on which she certainly has the ability to win the majority of fillies' maidens. (op 13-8)
Eternal Path(USA) ♦, whose dam won over ten furlongs at three and is a sister to Machiavellian, did not enjoy the best of luck in running but saw her race out well and shaped with a good deal of promise. Another who should make her mark over middle distances next year, she looks to have a bright future. (tchd 14-1)
Bonne D'Argent(IRE), a half-sister to a number of multiple winners in the shape of Winged D'Argent, Greta D'Argent, Desert D'Argent, and Mana D'Argent, hails from a stable not noted for winning with juveniles first time out and was consequently desregarded in the betting. She ran well, though, showing good pace throughout, and will likely keep up the family tradition of success next season.
Silver Pivotal(IRE), who is out of a Listed winner, cost 130,000gns and is a half-sister to Gold Queen, a seven-furlong winner at two. Bred to go on the ground, she was another who showed up well for a long way until getting a bit tired late on.
Valrhona(IRE), whose dam is an unraced half-sister to Sword Dance, a high-class performer in the US, was staying on again in the closing stages after losing her position when the pace quickened. (tchd 16-1)
Hypoteneuse(IRE), a sister to Flight Of Fancy, a seven-furlong winner at two and later placed in the Oaks, shaped encouragingly, as she was in the front rank for a long way.
Elounda(IRE), a half-sister to two winners abroad, has a middle-distance pedigree and should make her mark next year.
Comma(USA) has only shown modest maiden form to date, but at least she is now eligible for a mark. (op 8-1)
Storm Petrel Official explanation: jockey said filly was unsuited by the soft ground

6216 BET365 ZETLAND STKS (LISTED RACE) 1m 2f
2:05 (2:17) (Class 1) 2-Y-O **£13,343** (£5,057; £2,530; £1,261; £632; £317) **Stalls** Low

Form				RPR
13	1		**Empire Day (UAE)**[12] 6010 2-9-2 ... KDarley 5 (M Johnston) *a.p: chsd ldr 7f out: led over 3f out: rdn clr fnl f* **4/1**[1]	97+
2122	2	4	**Aaim To Prosper (IRE)**[8] 6074 2-9-2 87 ... TonyCulhane 1 (M R Channon) *lw: rn in snatches in rr: hdwy u.p over 1f out: no ch w wnr* **8/1**	90
041	3	½	**Fashion Statement**[19] 5859 2-8-11 82 ... RobertWinston 7 (M A Jarvis) *lw: chsd ldrs: rdn and ev 2f out: no ex fnl f* **13/2**[3]	84
02	4	5	**Cordwain**[10] 6058 2-9-2 ... (b) LDettori 8 (J H M Gosden) *s.i.s: hld up: hdwy over 4f out: rdn and wknd over 1f out* **12/1**	80
4011	5	nk	**Bed Fellow (IRE)**[7] 6106 2-9-2 73 ... SebSanders 2 (A P Jarvis) *lw: chsd ldrs: rdn over 1f out: wknd fnl f* **16/1**	80
4124	6	4	**Guacamole**[39] 5459 2-8-11 83 ... MichaelHills 3 (B W Hills) *hld up: rdn over 3f out: wknd 2f out* **7/1**	67
1	7	nk	**One To Follow**[92] 3892 2-9-2 ... PhilipRobinson 6 (C G Cox) *led over 6f: rdn and wknd over 1f out* **9/2**[2]	72
011	8	14	**Philanthropy**[25] 5759 2-9-2 84 ... JoeFanning 4 (M Johnston) *chsd ldr 3f: remained handy tl rdn and wknd wl over 2f out* **9/2**[2]	47
01	9	14	**Clarricien (IRE)**[41] 5402 2-9-2 79 ... RyanMoore 9 (E J O'Neill) *hld up: rdn and wknd over 2f out* **10/1**	21

2m 7.03s (1.32) **Going Correction** +0.175s/f (Good) **9** Ran SP% **116.0**
Speed ratings (Par 103):101,97,97,93,93 89,89,78,67
CSF £36.38 TOTE £3.90: £1.80, £2.20, £2.60; EX 42.80 Trifecta £173.70 Pool £538.36. - 2.20 winning units..
Owner Sheikh Maktoum Bin Mohammed Al Maktoum **Bred** Darley **Trained** Middleham Moor, N Yorks

FOCUS
Not a strong Listed race but ten furlongs on soft ground is a stiff test for two-year-olds and the winner looks one for decent stayers' events next season. The standard in behind is questionable, but the second, third and fourth all appear to have improved too.

NOTEBOOK
Empire Day(UAE), third in a stronger race over a mile at Pontefract last time, got this longer trip well and stayed on strongly from the Dip to record a clear-cut success. On this evidence he has the makings of a very useful stayer next season - possibly a Queen's Vase type. (op 7-2)
Aaim To Prosper(IRE) has been shaping as though he would be suited by a step up in trip, and although he came on and off the bridle throughout the race, he really got it together in the latter stages and saw the trip out well. He is another who can make up into a stayer next season. (op 12-1)
Fashion Statement, a heavy-ground maiden winner at Ayr last time, did not see the trip out as well as the first two but finished clear of the rest and picked up some valuable black type in the process. (op 7-1 tchd 6-1)
Cordwain, runner-up over this trip in a Yarmouth maiden last time out, got tired in the closing stages, but he is bred to stay well and will not have any trouble getting further than this next term. (op 16-1)
Bed Fellow(IRE), a winner of nurseries on his last two starts, copes with soft ground well but this step up in distance was not sure to suit him as well as some of his more stoutly bred rivals, and that is how it transpired.
Guacamole had finished close behind Bid For Glory, who subsequently ran Empire Day to two and a half lengths in a Listed race at Pontefract, in a mile nursery here last month, and that form appeared to give her a chance of running well in this contest, but it proved misleading. (op 5-1)
One To Follow, off the track since winning his maiden at Ascot in July, had much softer ground to deal with on this step up in trip. Official explanation: trainer said colt was unsuited by the soft ground (tchd 5-1)
Philanthropy did not run his race for one reason or another. (op 6-1)
Clarricien(IRE) Official explanation: trainer said colt was unsuited by the soft ground

6217 EBF BET365.COM MONTROSE FILLIES' STKS (LISTED RACE) 1m
2:35 (2:49) (Class 1) 2-Y-O **£13,343** (£5,057; £2,530; £1,261; £632; £317) **Stalls** Low

Form				RPR
51	1		**Passage Of Time**[77] 4373 2-8-12 83 ... RichardHughes 10 (H R A Cecil) *lw: chsd ldrs: led over 2f out: rdn clr over 1f out* **5/1**[3]	100+
4	2	5	**Sues Surprise (IRE)**[43] 5344 2-8-12 ... MichaelHills 1 (B W Hills) *chsd ldrs: hmpd and lost pl over 2f out: r.o wl ins fnl f: no ch w wnr* **8/1**	89+
411	3	nk	**Laurentina**[25] 5748 2-8-12 84 ... LDettori 5 (B J Meehan) *chsd ldrs: rdn over 2f out: styd on same pce appr fnl f* **8/1**	88
5151	4	2 ½	**Lady Grace (IRE)**[8] 6074 2-8-12 83 ... TonyCulhane 6 (W J Haggas) *plld hrd and prom: hmpd and lost pl 7f out: hdwy over 2f out: sn rdn: wknd ins fnl f* **8/1**	83
3625	5	2 ½	**Lady Alize (USA)**[7] 6105 2-8-12 78 ... (t) FJohansson 2 (R A Kvisla) *hld up in tch: lost pl 1/2-way: n.d after* **25/1**	77
041	6	2 ½	**Tarteel (USA)**[35] 5536 2-8-12 86 ... RHills 4 (J L Dunlop) *lw: hld up: plld hrd: hdwy and edgd lft over 2f out: sn rdn: hung rt and wknd fnl f* **4/1**[1]	72
01	7	6	**Hi Calypso (IRE)**[25] 5754 2-8-12 78 ... RyanMoore 9 (Sir Michael Stoute) *mid-div: rdn 1/2-way: wknd wl over 1f out* **7/1**	58
01	8	8	**Maid To Believe**[18] 5882 2-8-12 72 ... EddieAhern 3 (J L Dunlop) *hld up: rdn over 3f out: wknd over 2f out* **25/1**	41
41	9	shd	**Porcelain (IRE)**[35] 5527 2-8-12 78 ... RobertWinston 11 (A Dickman) *lw: led over 5f: wknd over 1f out* **66/1**	40
0215	10	6	**Millestan (IRE)**[28] 5672 2-8-12 92 ... TedDurcan 8 (H R A Cecil) *hld up: rdn and wknd over 2f out* **11/1**	27
4103	11	4	**Easy Lover**[7] 6105 2-8-12 91 ... JamieSpencer 7 (J A Osborne) *s.i.s: hld up: rdn over 2f out: wknd and eased over 1f out* **9/2**[2]	18
5403	12	7	**Only Hope**[15] 5941 2-8-12 66 ... (b[1]) JohnEgan 12 (Ernst Oertel) *chsd ldrs: edgd lft 1/2-way: rdn and wknd over 2f out* **150/1**	—

1m 40.16s (0.79) **Going Correction** +0.175s/f (Good) **12** Ran SP% **118.9**
Speed ratings (Par 100):103,98,97,95,92 90,84,76,76,70 66,59
CSF £43.77 TOTE £6.80: £2.40, £2.40, £2.50; EX 60.90 Trifecta £265.40 Pool £859.76. - 2.30 winning units..
Owner K Abdulla **Bred** Juddmonte Farms Ltd **Trained** Newmarket, Suffolk

FOCUS
An open Listed race on paper, but Passage Of Time routed the opposition. The overall standard looked below par however. and she will need to improve again to pay her way year.

NOTEBOOK
Passage Of Time bounded clear once she hit the rising ground and ran out an impressive winner of what had looked an open, albeit modest, Listed race. The step up in trip suited her, she clearly handles soft ground very well, and there seems no reason why she should not develop into a Group-class filly next year. (tchd 11-2)
Sues Surprise(IRE), who ran well when making her debut in a conditions race at Newbury, was again pushed in at the deep end - all but two of her rivals already had a win to their names - but she performed with great credit. An everyday maiden should be easy pickings for her before a return to better company. (op 7-1)
Laurentina, who had been withdrawn from an intended engagement earlier in the season on account of good to soft ground, may not have been totally at home on this testing surface, so she probably did not run badly in the circumstances. (op 9-1)

Lady Grace(IRE), twice a winner on Polytrack, was racing on turf for the first time and did herself few favours by failing to settle. She was not disgraced in the circumstances but will be of more interest when reverting to the sand. (op 9-1)

Lady Alize(USA) tracked the eventual runner-up on the rail for much of the race and encountered some minor traffic problems once switched out. She ran on well enough and should be able to find a maiden, perhaps on the All-Weather.

Tarteel(USA), running on soft ground for the first time, also failed to settle and gave herself little chance of getting home. Connections also had another excuse after the race. Official explanation: jockey said filly made a noise; vet said filly scoped dirty post race (op 5-1 tchd 11-2 in a place)

Hi Calypso(IRE), whose maiden win came in a slow time, was under pressure from a long way out. (op 6-1)

Porcelain(IRE) Official explanation: jockey said filly lost her action

Millestan(IRE) probably needs quicker ground. Official explanation: jockey said filly was unsuited by the soft ground (op 10-1)

Easy Lover travelled well enough to two furlongs out but found absolutely nothing under pressure. Official explanation: jockey said filly was never travelling (op 5-1 tchd 11-2 in places)

6218 BET365 BEN MARSHALL STKS (LISTED RACE) 1m

3:10 (3:18) (Class 1) 3-Y-O+

£15,898 (£6,025; £3,015; £1,503; £753; £378) **Stalls** Low

Form — RPR

4021 **1** **Blue Ksar (FR)**[42] 5376 3-8-10 104 ....(t) TedDurcan 5 114
(Saeed Bin Suroor) *lw: chsd ldr: led over 6f out: edgd lft ins fnl f: rdn out* **10/1**

0-11 **2** *2 ½* **Army Of Angels (IRE)**[22] 5789 4-8-13 110 .... LDettori 4 109
(Saeed Bin Suroor) *lw: a.p: rdn to chse wnr over 1f out: no imp fnl f* **5/4**[1]

6203 **3** *¾* **Bahia Breeze**[14] 5968 4-8-11 106 .... RobertWinston 7 105
(Rae Guest) *led: hdd over 6f out: chsd wnr to over 1f out: no ex ins fnl f* **14/1**

4264 **4** *shd* **Somnus**[14] 5962 6-8-13 112 .... KDarley 2 107
(T D Easterby) *chsd ldrs: rdn over 2f out: hung lft over 1f out: styd on* **10/1**

4446 **5** *6* **Polar Ben**[14] 5962 7-8-13 109 .... JamieSpencer 9 95
(J R Fanshawe) *hld up: swtchd rt over 1f out: nvr nr to chal* **9/1**[3]

0000 **6** *hd* **Quito (IRE)**[14] 5962 9-9-2 112 ....(b) TonyCulhane 1 97
(D W Chapman) *b. hld up: racd keenly: rdn over 2f out: hmpd over 1f out: n.d* **25/1**

0646 **7** *2* **Babodana**[14] 5968 6-8-13 105 .... JoeFanning 3 90
(M H Tompkins) *chsd ldrs: rdn over 2f out: hmpd and wknd over 1f out* **20/1**

4406 **8** *¾* **Nayyir**[49] 5186 8-9-5 108 .... EddieAhern 8 95
(G A Butler) *b.hind: hld up: rdn over 2f out: wknd over 1f out* **20/1**

2-61 **9** *9* **Final Verse**[156] 1953 3-8-13 109 .... RyanMoore 6 74
(Sir Michael Stoute) *b.hind: lw: hld up in tch: rdn over 2f out: sn wknd* **10/3**[2]

1m 40.28s (0.91) **Going Correction** +0.175s/f (Good)
WFA 3 from 4yo+ 3lb **9** Ran SP% **115.7**
Speed ratings (Par 111):102,99,98,98,92 92,90,89,80
CSF £22.42 TOTE £13.50: £2.30, £1.20, £3.10; EX 25.60 Trifecta £155.80 Pool £1,053.47. - 4.80 winning units..

Owner Godolphin **Bred** Merdian Stud **Trained** Newmarket, Suffolk

■ Stewards' Enquiry : K Darley two-day ban: careless riding (Nov 8-9)

FOCUS

The pace was steady in this Listed race and those who raced handily were at a clear advantage. The winner appears to have improved again by around 8lb, but this is not a race one can be entirely confident about.

NOTEBOOK

Blue Ksar(FR) upstaged a shorter-priced stablemate at Newbury last time, and repeated the trick here. Always up with the gallop in what was a steadily-run race, he picked up well when asked for his effort and saw out the trip strongly. The race was run to suit him, but he has really returned to form this autumn. (op 11-1)

Army Of Angels(IRE) tracked the winner for most of the way and had every chance if good enough, but his stablemate proved the stronger in the closing stages. He had little excuse on account of the trip or ground, but a faster pace may have suited him. (op 11-8)

Bahia Breeze, who ran well in a Group 3 event here a fortnight earlier, gained another piece of black type to add to her résumé. She benefited greatly from being able to set a steady pace in front, though. (tchd 16-1)

Somnus did best of the hold-up horses, his six-furlong pace helping in this steadily-run affair. He has struggled over the past two seasons, winning only once, and that was only a conditions race, but he has thrown in some good performances in defeat, including second, third and fourth placings in Group 2 company this year, which suggests he is no back number yet. (op 9-1)

Polar Ben needs a good gallop, and he did not get that here.

Quito(IRE) was too keen in this steadily-run affair and failed to run his race. It proved an inconclusive trial as to whether he can be as effective over a mile in the future as he is already over shorter.

Final Verse had looked a promising colt in the spring but had been off since May with a foot injury. He was short enough in the market to suggest a decent run was expected, so it looks as if his problems may not be over. (op 7-2 tchd 3-1)

6219 BET365 H'CAP 1m

3:45 (3:47) (Class 2) (0-100,100) 3-Y-O+

£18,696 (£5,598; £2,799; £1,401; £699; £351) **Stalls** Low

Form — RPR

0264 **1** **Arm Candy (IRE)**[15] 5943 3-8-5 87 .... KDarley 13 100
(J A R Toller) *racd far side: chsd ldrs: rdn to ld over 1f out: edgd lft ins fnl f: r.o* **10/1**

142 **2** *3* **Rio Riva**[28] 5680 4-9-4 97 .... TonyCulhane 15 104
(Miss J A Camacho) *lw: racd far side: hld up: hdwy u.p over 2f out: rdn to chse wnr fnl f: styd on same pce: 2nd of 5 in gp* **7/1**[2]

1021 **3** *1 ¾* **Rain Stops Play (IRE)**[15] 5945 4-8-10 89 .... FrancisNorton 12 92
(M Quinn) *racd far side: led: rdn and hdd over 1f out: no ex: 3rd of 5 in gp* **15/2**[3]

0045 **4** *shd* **Gentleman's Deal (IRE)**[22] 5789 5-8-11 90 .... RobertWinston 11 93
(M W Easterby) *racd far side: hld up in tch: rdn over 2f out: hung rt over 1f out: styd on same pce: 4th of 5 in gp* **7/1**[2]

1504 **5** *3* **Harvest Queen (IRE)**[15] 5945 3-8-10 92 .... SebSanders 14 89
(P J Makin) *racd far side: chsd ldrs: rdn over 2f out: wknd fnl f: last of 5 in gp* **15/2**[3]

21-0 **6** *½* **Gramm**[49] 5165 3-8-9 91 .... RichardHughes 3 86
(L M Cumani) *lw: racd stands' side: chsd ldrs: led that gp over 3f out: rdn and hung rt fr over 1f out: no ch w far side: 1st of 10 in g* **16/1**

1000 **7** *2 ½* **Audience**[15] 5945 6-8-11 90 .... PaulDoe 8 80
(J Akehurst) *racd stands' side: hld up: hdwy over 1f out: nrst fin: 2nd of 10 in gp* **33/1**

3006 **8** *½* **Unshakable (IRE)**[22] 5789 7-8-2 88 ow2 .... AshleyHamblett(7) 5 77
(Bob Jones) *racd stands' side: chsd ldrs: rdn over 2f out: wknd over 1f out: 3rd of 10 in gp* **12/1**

0160 **9** *11* **Plum Pudding (IRE)**[15] 5945 3-9-0 96 .... RyanMoore 10 62
(R Hannon) *racd stands' side: hld up: hdwy over 2f out: wknd over 1f out: 4th of 10 in gp* **16/1**

0502 **10** *3* **Salinja (USA)**[15] 5945 4-9-2 95 ....(b) OscarUrbina 6 55
(Mrs A J Perrett) *racd stands' side: chsd ldrs: rdn over 2f out: sn wknd: 5th of 10 in gp* **12/1**

0000 **11** *4* **Blue Spinnaker (IRE)**[28] 5675 7-9-1 94 .... MartinDwyer 4 45
(M W Easterby) *racd stands' side: hld up: rdn 1/2-way: wknd over 2f out: 6th of 10 in gp* **9/1**

3200 **12** *nk* **St Petersburg**[15] 5945 6-8-13 95 ....(t) SaleemGolam(3) 7 46
(M H Tompkins) *racd stands's ide: chsd ldrs over 5f: 7th of 10 in gp* **20/1**

260 **13** *nk* **Indian Steppes (FR)**[16] 5919 7-8-10 89 .... JamieSpencer 1 39
(P S McEntee) *racd stands' side: hld up: wknd over 2f out: 8th of 10 in gp* **20/1**

0015 **14** *¾* **Supaseus**[26] 5722 3-8-11 93 .... SteveDrowne 9 42
(H Morrison) *racd stands' side: chsd ldrs: rdn over 3f out: wknd over 2f out: 9th of 10 in gp* **6/1**[1]

15 *5* **Sailor King (IRE)**[386] 5729 4-9-7 100 .... DaneO'Neill 2 38
(D K Ivory) *b. led stands' side: over 4f: sn wknd: last of 10 in gp* **80/1**

1m 38.58s (-0.79) **Going Correction** +0.175s/f (Good)
WFA 3 from 4yo+ 3lb **15** Ran SP% **122.8**
Speed ratings (Par 109):110,107,105,105,102 101,99,98,87,84 80,80,80,79,74
CSF £76.31 CT £417.64 TOTE £10.70: £2.80, £3.30, £2.80; EX 79.40 Trifecta £139.70 Pool £1,496.02. - 7.60 winning units..

Owner J Charrington & Partners **Bred** Floors Farming And Beckhampton Stables Ltd **Trained** Newmarket, Suffolk

FOCUS

A decent enough handicap, but the field split and the five who raced next to the far-side rail benefited from racing on much faster ground. They filled the first five places.

NOTEBOOK

Arm Candy(IRE) won her maiden at this track last autumn on easy ground and clearly loves to get her toe in. She had shaped as though likely to appreciate a return to a mile as well when running on over seven furlongs here last time, and unsurprisingly she really saw her race out strongly, having been one of five to race on the far side. She certainly benefited from a track bias here, however, so it may not pay to get carried away with the form. (op 11-1 tchd 12-1)

Rio Riva chased the winner home on the far side but was found out by his career-high handicap mark, 9lb higher than it was at the beginning of the season.

Rain Stops Play(IRE), who won a similar affair at the last meeting here, had a 4lb higher mark to deal with. He set a good pace on the far side but ultimately set it up for his companions, who got a good tow from him. (op 17-2 tchd 10-1 in a place)

Gentleman's Deal(IRE), held on turf this season off marks in the 90s, might do better back on the All-Weather this winter. (op 8-1)

Harvest Queen(IRE), two lengths behind Rain Stops Play at the last meeting here, ran close to that form, but she was last of the five who raced on the favoured far side so her finishing position in the race as a whole probably flatters her. (op 7-1)

Gramm ◆, only seen out once previously this season, when finishing last on his debut for his new stable in a firm-ground Bath handicap last month, had conditions much more in his favour this time and bounced back to form in good style, winning the ten-horse race on the stands' side by a clear margin. He clearly has the ability to win a race off his current mark and it is a shame for his connections that the season is drawing to a close. (op 20-1)

Audience, fourth in this race last year off the same mark, kept on well from off the pace to finish second on his side this time. He had not shown much on his last three starts but has often shown that he has the ability to be competitive off this sort of mark when on a going day.

Supaseus is a good horse when on form but he is proving inconsistent and had a bad day at the office this time.

6220 BET365 CALL 08000 322365 EBF MAIDEN STKS (C&G) (DIV II) 7f

4:20 (4:23) (Class 5) 2-Y-O **£2,590** (£770; £385; £192) **Stalls** Low

Form — RPR

1 **Spanish Moon (USA)** 2-9-0 .... RichardHughes 11 90+
(Sir Michael Stoute) *w'like: scope: chsd ldrs: rdn to ld over 1f out: r.o wl* **6/1**[3]

2 *1 ¾* **Mofarij** 2-9-0 .... LDettori 1 86+
(Saeed Bin Suroor) *gd sort: chsd ldrs: rdn and ev ch over 1f out: styd on same pce ins fnl f* **7/2**[1]

5 **3** *1 ¾* **Mutanaseb (USA)**[16] 5915 2-9-0 .... RHills 20 81
(M A Jarvis) *chsd ldrs: rdn and ev ch over 1f out: no ex ins fnl f* **7/1**

0 **4** *¾* **Transcend**[16] 5918 2-9-0 .... DavidKinsella 5 80
(J H M Gosden) *dwlt: hld up: hdwy over 2f out: rdn and hung rt over 1f out: styd on same pce* **9/1**

5 *2* **Wandle** 2-9-0 .... IanMongan 12 75
(T G Mills) *w'like: b.bkwd: s.s: hdwy over 1f out: nrst fin* **25/1**

4 **6** *hd* **Noisy Silence (IRE)**[15] 5939 2-9-0 .... EddieAhern 15 74
(P W Chapple-Hyam) *chsd ldrs: rdn over 2f out: styd on same pce appr fnl f* **4/1**[2]

5 **7** *1* **Seal Point (USA)**[18] 5893 2-8-11 .... SaleemGolam(3) 18 72
(Christian Wroe, UAE) *lw: sn led: rdn and hdd over 1f out: wknd ins fnl f* **15/2**

8 *1 ¾* **Harry Tricker** 2-9-0 .... TedDurcan 14 67+
(Mrs A J Perrett) *w'like: unf: hld up: hdwy over 2f out: nt trble ldrs* **80/1**

04 **9** *nk* **Summer Dancer (IRE)**[16] 5918 2-9-0 .... JohnEgan 4 67
(D R C Elsworth) *hld up: plld hrd: hdwy and swtchd lft over 1f out: n.d* **20/1**

10 *1 ¾* **Earl Marshal (USA)** 2-9-0 .... RyanMoore 3 62
(Sir Michael Stoute) *neat: scope: hld up: nvr nrr* **20/1**

0 **11** *2* **Madaarek (USA)**[15] 5939 2-9-0 .... MartinDwyer 16 58
(E A L Dunlop) *chsd ldrs over 5f* **20/1**

25 **12** *1* **Ashn Thunder**[10] 6049 2-9-0 .... KDarley 9 55
(M Johnston) *lw: s.i.s: sn mid-div: rdn over 2f out: wkng whn hung rt over 1f out* **16/1**

13 *hd* **Venerable** 2-9-0 .... RobertWinston 8 55
(J H M Gosden) *gd sort: sn outpcd* **40/1**

14 *shd* **Buckthorn** 2-9-0 .... SteveDrowne 2 54
(G Wragg) *w'like: b.bkwd: chsd ldrs to 1/2-way* **100/1**

15 *nk* **Art Gallery** 2-9-0 .... SebSanders 7 54
(G L Moore) *leggy: scope: lw: mid-div: wknd over 2f out* **100/1**

16 *hd* **Samuel** 2-9-0 .... DaneO'Neill 19 53
(J L Dunlop) *w'like: leggy: chsd ldrs 5f* **40/1**

0 **17** *3* **I Predict A Riot (IRE)**[18] 5892 2-9-0 .... MichaelHills 13 46
(J W Hills) *lw: hdwy over 4f out: wkng whn stmbld 2f out* **50/1**

18 ½ **Iceman George** 2-9-0 .... DerekMcGaffin 6 45
(D Morris) *w'like: outpcd* **125/1**

19 *1* **Chiave** 2-9-0 .... JamieSpencer 17 42
(M A Jarvis) *cmpt: s.i.s: sn chsng ldrs: rdn and wknd over 2f out* **20/1**

1m 27.16s (0.66) **Going Correction** +0.175s/f (Good) **58** Ran SP% **130.4**
Speed ratings (Par 95):103,101,99,98,95 95,94,92,92,90 87,86,86,86,86 85,82,81,80
CSF £25.20 TOTE £7.00: £2.70, £2.10, £3.00; EX 37.00.
Owner K Abdulla **Bred** Juddmonte Farms **Trained** Newmarket, Suffolk

FOCUS
The faster of the two divisions, by almost two seconds, and probably sound maiden form. The winner looks a particularly nice prospect.

NOTEBOOK
Spanish Moon(USA) ◆, a brother to Ribblesdale Stakes winner Spanish Sun, who also won on her only start over this trip at two, made a highly promising debut. He picked up really well once he hit the rising ground and shaped like a nice middle-distance prospect for next year. Indeed, there were one or two 33-1 quotes for the Derby flying around after the race. (tchd 13-2 in a place)
Mofarij, a half-brother to Iffraaj, was not well drawn as, following the result of the previous race, the whole field raced towards the far side. He ran well, though, especially as the ground might have been plenty soft enough for him. (op 5-1)
Mutanaseb(USA) had the benefit of previous experience and the highest draw in a race in which the whole field elected to race towards the far side. He is by Mr Greeley, who has not had many runners in this country, but did sire Finsceal Beo, who won the Rockfel over this course and distance earlier in the month, and the 2003 Sussex Stakes winner Reel Buddy.. (op 15-2 tchd 8-1)
Transcend, another drawn unfavourably low, showed the benefit of his debut run and finished his race well, despite hanging. He should do better at three and will get a bit further next year. (op 8-1)
Wandle, a half-brother to a three-year-old winner in Japan, kept galloping to the line and will be seen to better effect when stepped up to middle distances next season.
Noisy Silence(IRE) had run with plenty of promise on his debut over a mile but had not shaped as though likely to be particularly suited by a drop back to seven furlongs. He was keeping on well at the finish and will appreciate a return to further. (op 7-2 tchd 9-2)
Seal Point(USA) had run surprisingly well on his debut when sent off a 66-1 shot but, under a more positive ride, was a little disappointing this time. (op 10-1 tchd 11-1 in a place)
Harry Tricker, who is out of Cambridgeshire winner Katy Nowaitee, has a pedigree which suggests he will improve with age.
Venerable Official explanation: jockey said colt ran green

6221 BET365.COM H'CAP 7f
4:55 (4:55) (Class 4) (0-85,85) 3-Y-0+ **£5,505** (£1,637; £818; £408) **Stalls** Low

Form RPR

1321 **1** **Trimlestown (IRE)**[42] 5377 3-8-11 **78** .... DaneO'Neill 10 89
(H Candy) *in tch: effrt 3f out: led over 1f out: rdn out* **8/1**[3]

2001 **2** *1 ¼* **Resplendent Nova**[15] 5937 4-8-9 **77** .... DeanCorby(3) 14 85
(P Howling) *w ldrs: led over 3f out to over 1f out: nt qckn* **11/1**

2340 **3** *½* **Breaking Shadow (IRE)**[3] 6176 4-8-8 **73** .... JimmyQuinn 16 80
(T D Barron) *lw: in tch: rdn over 2f out: styd on fnl f* **6/1**[2]

2100 **4** *2* **Inaminute (IRE)**[7] 6094 3-8-4 **76** .... AndrewElliott(5) 1 78
(K R Burke) *w ldrs: rdn over 2f out: one pce appr fnl f* **16/1**

4000 **5** *½* **Blue Java**[18] 5896 5-8-8 **73** .... LPKeniry 17 73
(H Morrison) *prom: hrd rdn over 1f out: no ex* **12/1**

0100 **6** *hd* **Phluke**[15] 5943 5-9-6 **85** .... StephenCarson 15 85
(R F Johnson Houghton) *led over 3f: wknd over 1f out* **33/1**

0201 **7** *¾* **Fabrian**[18] 5889 8-8-9 **77** .... JamesDoyle(3) 5 75
(R J Price) *chsd ldrs: outpcd over 2f out: kpt on fnl f* **10/1**

2122 **8** *5* **Blues In The Night (IRE)**[42] 5377 3-8-13 **80** .... (t) SebSanders 13 66
(P J Makin) *chsd ldrs: hrd rdn over 2f out: sn wknd* **11/2**[1]

0304 **9** *½* **Makfly**[26] 5724 3-8-9 **76** .... (p) MartinDwyer 11 60
(R Hollinshead) *chsd ldrs 4f* **25/1**

1545 **10** *¾* **Starlight Gazer**[114] 3226 3-8-8 **75** .... RichardThomas 12 57
(J A Geake) *lw: dwlt: nvr rchd ldrs* **20/1**

0610 **11** *hd* **Sun Catcher (IRE)**[66] 4703 3-8-10 **77** .... RyanMoore 20 59
(R Hannon) *prom 5f* **33/1**

4060 **12** *1 ¾* **Gavarnie Beau (IRE)**[9] 6065 3-9-1 **82** .... FrancisNorton 8 60
(M Blanshard) *mid-div: rdn 3f out: sn btn* **33/1**

2300 **13** *1* **Dune Melody (IRE)**[7] 6094 3-8-10 **77** .... (p) JohnEgan 3 52
(J S Moore) *lw: outpcd in rr: nvr nr ldrs* **50/1**

00-5 **14** *1 ½* **Littleton Telchar (USA)**[76] 4411 6-8-13 **78** .... EddieAhern 7 49
(S W Hall) *bhd fnl 3f* **33/1**

2416 **15** *shd* **Passion Fruit**[16] 5919 5-9-3 **82** .... DeanMcKeown 19 53
(C W Fairhurst) *bhd fnl 3f* **6/1**[2]

0000 **16** *3 ½* **Marshman (IRE)**[15] 5943 7-8-12 **80** .... SaleemGolam(3) 4 42
(M H Tompkins) *a bhd* **8/1**[3]

0600 **17** *1 ¼* **Marajaa (IRE)**[19] 5877 4-9-3 **82** .... TonyCulhane 6 41
(W J Musson) *lw: a bhd* **33/1**

0200 **18** *nk* **Grizedale (IRE)**[15] 5943 7-8-12 **77** .... (t) PaulDoe 9 35
(J Akehurst) *bhd fnl 3f* **33/1**

1m 26.67s (0.17) **Going Correction** +0.175s/f (Good)
WFA 3 from 4yo+ 2lb **18** Ran SP% **125.4**
Speed ratings (Par 105):106,104,104,101,101 100,100,94,93,92 92,90,89,87,87 83,82,81
CSF £84.34 CT £580.62 TOTE £9.20: £2.00, £2.70, £2.50, £4.50; EX 105.40 Place 6 £55.73, Place 5 £42.30..
Owner Thurloe Thoroughbreds XVI **Bred** Liam Brennan **Trained** Kingston Warren, Oxon

FOCUS
Another competitive handicap on paper but dominated by two of three last-time-out winners in the field. Trimlestown remains relatively unexposed and is progressing.
Dune Melody(IRE) Official explanation: jockey said filly was never travelling
T/Plt: £34.10 to a £1 stake. Pool: £97,529.20. 2,087.65 winning tickets. T/Qpdt: £26.30 to a £1 stake. Pool: £5,574.10. 156.30 winning tickets. CR

5969 WOLVERHAMPTON (A.W) (L-H)
Saturday, October 28

OFFICIAL GOING: Standard
Wind: Moderate behind

6222 LADBROKES.COM MEDIAN AUCTION MAIDEN STKS 5f 216y(P)
7:00 (7:00) (Class 5) 2-Y-O **£3,238** (£963; £481; £240) **Stalls** Low

Form RPR

0023 **1** **Juncea**[46] 5261 2-8-12 74 .... SteveDrowne 4 69+
(H Morrison) *mde all: pushed clr over 1f out: comf* **2/1**[2]

06 **2** *5* **Burningfold Babe**[16] 5923 2-8-12 .... AdrianMcCarthy 3 54
(P Winkworth) *in tch: rdn 2f out: chsd easy wnr over 1f out* **100/1**

3 *1* **Agitator** 2-9-3 .... GrahamGibbons 7 56
(Mrs G S Rees) *mid-div: rdn 1/2-way: swtchd rt over 1f out: nvr nrr* **40/1**

0 **4** *¾* **Incony**[19] 5867 2-8-12 .... TedDurcan 8 49
(W R Swinburn) *outpcd: rdn and hdwy outside over 2f out: carried rt over 1f out: styd on fnl f* **14/1**

6 **5** *4* **Give Her A Whirl**[16] 5915 2-8-12 .... RichardHughes 6 37
(B W Hills) *sn chsd wnr tl rdn and wknd over 1f out: eased ins fnl f* **5/6**[1]

6 *2 ½* **Pretty Selma** 2-8-12 .... BrettDoyle 5 29
(R M H Cowell) *s.i.s: c wd and hung rt over 1f out: nvr on terms* **66/1**

0 **7** *nk* **Good Luck Chip (IRE)**[11] 6024 2-8-12 .... RichardMullen 11 28
(I A Wood) *in tch: rdn over 2f out: sn btn* **100/1**

0 **8** *½* **Inverted**[25] 5753 2-9-3 .... MickyFenton 9 32
(Mrs A Duffield) *chsd ldrs tl rdn and wknd 2f out* **66/1**

0 **9** *¾* **Lady Kintyre**[15] 5950 2-8-5 .... MarkCoumbe(7) 1 25
(A W Carroll) *outpcd thrght* **100/1**

10 *2 ½* **Wibbadune (IRE)** 2-8-12 .... RobbieFitzpatrick 10 17
(Peter Grayson) *prom on outside tl wknd over 2f out* **100/1**

64 **11** *21* **One White Sock**[43] 5348 2-8-12 .... AdrianTNicholls 2 —
(J L Spearing) *outpcd and nvr on terms: t.o* **6/1**[3]

1m 15.34s (-0.47) **Going Correction** -0.25s/f (Stan) **11** Ran SP% **118.2**
Speed ratings (Par 95):93,86,85,84,78 75,74,74,73,69 41
CSF £189.92 TOTE £3.40: £1.10, £21.70, £7.90; EX 245.40.
Owner Mrs B Oppenheimer **Bred** Mrs B D Oppenheimer **Trained** East Ilsley, Berks

FOCUS
An uncompetitive maiden rated through the winner in a race that took little winning.

NOTEBOOK
Juncea, placed on her two previous outings on this surface, when held up behind the leaders, was allowed to stride on this time. Coming clear in the straight, she slammed some ordinary opposition. (op 5-2 tchd 11-4)
Burningfold Babe, sent off at a three-figure price again, ran her best race to date but had only a remote view of the winner in the latter stages. A step back back up to seven furlongs should suit her. (op 125-1)
Agitator, out of a seven-furlong winner, is a half-brother to Stagecoach Ruby who won at up to ten furlongs. He stayed on pleasingly in the straight and should come on for the experience. (tchd 33-1)
Incony is out of a mile winner and, as she did on her debut at Windsor, shaped as if in need of seven furlongs plus. (op 12-1)
Give Her A Whirl, sent off a warm favourite after a promising debut at Newmarket, chased the winner until fading rather tamely going to the final furlong. A drop to the minimum trip may help. Official explanation: jockey said filly was not moving well (tchd 8-11 and 10-11)
Pretty Selma, a half-sister to Polytrack scorer Simiola, was noticeably green on this debut but did not shape without promise under a fairly sympathetic ride. Official explanation: jockey said, regarding the running and riding, his orders were to jump well but if filly missed the break to ride his own race, adding that filly was slowly away but when ridden early took a very keen hold, then hung right on the final bend and found nothing when asked in the home straight (op 50-1)
One White Sock Official explanation: jockey said filly resented the kick-back

6223 LADBROKES BETTING IN PLAY H'CAP 5f 216y(P)
7:30 (7:31) (Class 5) (0-75,75) 3-Y-0+ **£3,238** (£963; £481; £240) **Stalls** Low

Form RPR

0000 **1** **Briannsta (IRE)**[162] 1820 4-9-1 **72** .... AdamKirby 9 82
(C G Cox) *trckd ldr: rdn to ld over 1f out: edgd lft and drvn out fnl f* **8/1**

0000 **2** *hd* **Zarzu**[11] 6035 7-8-11 **73** .... LiamJones(5) 2 82
(C R Dore) *a in tch: rdn and hdwy on ins 2f out: chsd wnr fnl f* **12/1**

1450 **3** *¾* **Vanadium**[10] 6048 4-9-3 **74** .... TedDurcan 3 81
(J G Given) *mid-div: rdn and hdwy 2f out: edgd lft u.p over 1f out: kpt on ins fnl f* **6/1**[3]

0300 **4** *nk* **Bonne De Fleur**[45] 5286 5-8-12 **69** .... RobertWinston 1 75
(B Smart) *led: rdn 1/2-way: hdd over 1f out: r.o one pce fnl f* **10/1**

012 **5** *nk* **Hello Man (IRE)**[11] 6036 3-9-0 **72** .... JimmyQuinn 12 77
(Eamon Tyrrell, Ire) *t.k.h: in tch on outside: rdn over 2f out: kpt on fnl f* **7/1**

0-10 **6** *1* **Premier Fantasy**[131] 2705 4-8-13 **70** .... RobbieFitzpatrick 13 72
(T J Pitt) *v.s.a: hdwy on ins 2f out: kpt on fnl f but nvr nr to chal* **28/1**

0030 **7** *shd* **Prince Tum Tum (USA)**[20] 5842 6-9-3 **74** .... DeanMcKeown 4 76
(D Shaw) *bhd: rdn and hdwy 2f out: nt clr run and hmpd over 1f out: running on whn hmpd and stmbld wl ins fnl f* **15/2**

0011 **8** *¾* **Keyaki (IRE)**[11] 6036 5-9-4 **75** .... GeorgeBaker 11 75
(C F Wall) *prom: rdn 1/2-way: wkng whn hmpd appr fnl f* **7/2**[1]

0000 **9** *1 ¾* **Glencairn Star**[22] 5791 5-9-1 **72** .... (p) DanielTudhope 5 67
(J S Goldie) *a towards rr* **4/1**[2]

4400 **10** *hd* **Ever Cheerful**[28] 5688 5-8-9 **73** .... MarkCoumbe(7) 10 67
(D G Bridgwater) *a bhd* **33/1**

-060 **11** *hd* **Safari Sunset (IRE)**[92] 3904 4-9-2 **73** .... AdrianMcCarthy 6 66
(P Winkworth) *chsd ldrs tl rdn and wknd 2f out* **25/1**

0066 **12** *3* **Melalchrist**[119] 3097 4-8-13 **70** .... GrahamGibbons 8 54
(J J Quinn) *mid-div: rdn 1/2-way: sn btn* **20/1**

1m 13.93s (-1.88) **Going Correction** -0.25s/f (Stan)
WFA 3 from 4yo+ 1lb **12** Ran SP% **123.7**
Speed ratings (Par 103):102,101,100,100,99 98,98,97,95,94 94,90
CSF £99.37 CT £638.31 TOTE £12.40: £3.40, £4.00, £2.60; EX 307.90.
Owner B Brooks **Bred** Anthony M Cahill **Trained** Lambourn, Berks
■ Stewards' Enquiry : Ted Durcan two-day ban: careless riding (Nov 8,9)
Jimmy Quinn caution: careless riding

FOCUS
Quite a competitive handicap but a somewhat rough race in the home straight.
Prince Tum Tum(USA) Official explanation: jockey said gelding was denied a clear run

6224 LADBROKES IN QUINTON MAIDEN AUCTION STKS 1m 141y(P)
8:00 (8:01) (Class 5) 2-Y-O **£3,238** (£963; £481; £240) **Stalls** Low

Form RPR

1 **Aypeeyes (IRE)** 2-8-9 .... RichardHughes 2 68
(S Kirk) *s.i.s: hdwy on outside over 1f out: r.o u.p to ld wl ins fnl f* **15/2**

30 **2** *½* **Robert The Brave**[18] 5900 2-8-9 .... SteveDrowne 9 67
(A J McCabe) *s.i.s: rdn and hdwy over 2f out: r.o and ev ch wl ins fnl f* **4/1**[1]

2660 **3** *hd* **Callisto Moon**[32] 5585 2-8-4 73 .... KevinGhunowa(5) 4 67
(P A Blockley) *mid-div: hdwy to chse ldrs 4f out: ev ch ins fnl f: no ex cl home* **10/1**

5 **4** *nk* **Murrisk**[11] 6032 2-9-1 .... JimmyQuinn 5 72
(Eamon Tyrrell, Ire) *led after 2f: rdn over 2f out: no ex and hdd wl ins fnl f* **8/1**

0330 **5** *2 ½* **Monsieur Dumas (IRE)**[32] 5597 2-9-1 70 .... TonyCulhane 1 67
(T P Tate) *led for 2f: rdn and fdd over 1f out* **9/2**[2]

00 **6** *¾* **Mineral Rights (USA)**[31] 5613 2-8-12 .... RobertWinston 10 62
(I Semple) *s.i.s: hdwy to chse ldr 2f out tl hung lft and wknd fnl f* **20/1**

0053 **7** *¾* **Right Option (IRE)**[42] 5387 2-8-12 61 .... (p) MickyFenton 3 61
(J R Weymes) *in tch: rdn over 2f out: c wd and wknd over 1f out* **6/1**

0 **8** 1 1/2 **Little Rutland**[8] 6072 2-8-9 .... RichardMullen 12 54
(E J O'Neill) *bhd: effrt over 2f out: nvr on terms* **50/1**
40 **9** 3/4 **Sweet World**[11] 6031 2-8-12 .... DeanMcKeown 11 56
(A P Jarvis) *a towards rr* **14/1**
55 **10** nk **Sosueme Now**[33] 5565 2-8-4 .... ChrisCatlin 6 47
(A B Haynes) *wnt 2nd after 3f: rdn over 3f out: wknd over 2f out* **33/1**
11 3 **Norman The Great** 2-8-12 .... BrettDoyle 7 49
(Jane Chapple-Hyam) *s.i.s: a bhd* **5/1**[3]
40 **12** 16 **Charlotte Grey**[22] 5784 2-8-4 .... NickyMackay 8 7
(C N Allen) *hld up in mid-div: rdn over 2f out: sn wknd: eased* **33/1**

1m 51.26s (-0.50) **Going Correction** -0.25s/f (Stan) 12 Ran SP% **120.4**
Speed ratings (Par 95):92,91,91,91,88 88,87,86,85,85 82,68
CSF £36.88 TOTE £7.70: £3.10, £1.90, £3.10; EX 42.60.
Owner The www.mortgages.tv Partnership **Bred** John Malone **Trained** Upper Lambourn, Berks

FOCUS
The pace was only steady in this moderate maiden but the form looks solid rated through the second, seventh and ninth.

NOTEBOOK
Aypeeyes(IRE) is a half-brother to Killeena Boy, a fair handicapper on this surface. He had a lot to do on straightening up, but came with a strong run down the outside to win going away. This was a pleasing debut and he should be capable of better still, perhaps over further. (op 5-1 tchd 8-1)
Robert The Brave had made an encouraging debut on this surface but was well beaten in soft ground on his second start. After coming under pressure before the turn out of the back straight, he found his stride once in line for home but no sooner had he got his head in front than he was cut down by the winner on his outside. His turn should come. (op 11-2)
Callisto Moon, well beaten on his debut for this yard a month ago, had earlier proved he acted on this surface. He will be suited by the return to handicaps. (op 7-1)
Murrisk was without the tongue tie on this second outing. Soon in front, he tried to kick away from his pursuers on the home turn but was gathered in towards the finish. (op 10-1)
Monsieur Dumas(IRE) appeared to handle the surface well enough but did not shape as if this drop in trip was required. (op 5-1)
Mineral Rights(USA) showed ability on this All-Weather bow and was only run out of second place inside the final furlong. He is now eligible for nurseries, and a drop back in trip should help him. Official explanation: jockey said gelding tied up in the closing stages (tchd 22-1)
Norman The Great, out of a middle-distance winner, was well supported, but could never get into the hunt after a tardy start. (op 14-1)
Charlotte Grey Official explanation: jockey said filly ran too free in the early stages

6225 LADBROKES BREEDERS CUP NIGHT MAIDEN STKS 1m 1f 103y(P)
8:30 (8:31) (Class 5) 3-Y-O+ **£3,238** (£963; £481; £240) **Stalls** Low

Form RPR
220 **1** **Indication**[44] 5319 3-8-12 75 .... (t) RichardHughes 5 72
(J H M Gosden) *hld up in mid-div: hdwy over 2f out: edgd lft and led over 1f out: rdn clr* **7/4**[1]
2 3 **Emirates First (IRE)** 3-8-12 .... TedDurcan 1 66
(Saeed Bin Suroor) *a.p: ev ch whn hmpd and swtchd rt over 1f out: kpt on one pce after* **15/8**[2]
00 **3** 1 1/2 **Jeu D'Esprit (IRE)**[29] 5651 3-8-12 .... MickyFenton 12 63
(J G Given) *trckd ldr: led over 5f out: rdn and hdd over 1f out: nt qckn after* **100/1**
2305 **4** 1 **Tafiya**[64] 4759 3-8-12 67 .... FJohansson 7 62
(G A Butler) *hmpd s: bhd tl hdwy 4f out: hung rt on bnd 2f out: kpt on one pce after* **16/1**
3220 **5** 1 1/2 **Majestic Halo**[56] 5024 3-8-12 75 .... SteveDrowne 2 59
(E A L Dunlop) *chsd ldrs tl rdn and fdd wl over 1f out* **4/1**[3]
2333 **6** 1 **Summer Lodge**[18] 5903 3-9-0 72 .... (b) SaleemGolam(3) 8 62
(A J McCabe) *wnt lft s: sn in tch: rdn and one pce fr over 1f out* **13/2**
7 6 **Love And Affection** 3-9-3 .... BrianReilly 4 50
(P S McEntee) *in rr: rdn 3f out: no hdwy after* **100/1**
06 **8** 1/2 **Coppington Melody (IRE)**[11] 6026 3-8-12 .... AdamKirby 6 44
(B W Duke) *mid-div tl rdn and wknd over 3f out* **100/1**
9 8 **Out Of This Way** 3-9-0 .... JamesDoyle(3) 13 34
(I A Wood) *slowly away: sn trckd ldrs: rdn 3f out: wknd qckly* **50/1**
00 **10** 21 **Ticking**[124] 2934 3-9-3 .... ChrisCatlin 11 —
(T Keddy) *a bhd: lost tch 3f out* **100/1**
0 **11** 14 **Fake Left**[13] 5988 3-8-10 .... (b[1]) SoniaEaton(7) 9 —
(B P J Baugh) *led tl hdd over 5f out: steadily wknd after* **200/1**
12 nk **Fine Deed**[30] 5-9-0 .... StuartHaddon(7) 10 —
(Ian Williams) *mid-div on outside: rdn over 4f out: sn wl bhd* **200/1**

1m 59.99s (-2.63) **Going Correction** -0.25s/f (Stan)
WFA 3 from 5yo 4lb 12 Ran SP% **117.3**
Speed ratings (Par 103):101,98,97,96,94 93,88,88,81,62 49,49
CSF £5.25 TOTE £3.20: £1.20, £1.60, £8.70; EX 7.10.
Owner K Abdulla **Bred** Juddmonte Farms Ltd **Trained** Newmarket, Suffolk

FOCUS
A modest maiden with little strength in depth, but the winner did it quite well.
Ticking Official explanation: jockey said gelding hung right-handed; vet said gelding finished lame

6226 LADBROKES EXTRA H'CAP 1m 1f 103y(P)
9:00 (9:00) (Class 3) (0-90,91) 3-Y-O+ **£8,096** (£2,408; £1,203; £601) **Stalls** Low

Form RPR
0500 **1** **Bahar Shumaal (IRE)**[45] 5299 4-8-13 80 .... (b) BrettDoyle 7 100+
(C E Brittain) *chsd ldrs: led over 2f out: rdn clr: easily* **33/1**
561 **2** 7 **Zato (IRE)**[13] 5990 3-9-6 91 .... TonyCulhane 2 98
(M R Channon) *chsd ldrs: rdn over 3f out: wnt 2nd over 1f out but no ch w wnr* **6/1**[3]
11-2 **3** 1 **Alpine Reel (IRE)**[26] 5739 5-9-1 82 .... AdamKirby 12 87
(W R Swinburn) *hld up in rr: hdwy 3f out: styd on one pce fnl 2f* **11/4**[1]
1/0 **4** 1/2 **Ballinteni**[26] 5739 4-9-1 82 .... TedDurcan 8 86
(Saeed Bin Suroor) *chsd ldrs: rdn over 3f out: one pce after* **15/2**
6602 **5** 1/2 **Regent's Secret (USA)**[41] 5406 6-8-12 79 .... DanielTudhope 10 82
(J S Goldie) *bhd: styd on fnl 2f: nvr nr to chal* **20/1**
3021 **6** hd **Montpellier (IRE)**[33] 5583 3-9-3 88 .... SteveDrowne 13 91
(E A L Dunlop) *t.k.h: hld up in rr: hdwy over 2f out: styd on one pce* **5/1**[2]
3060 **7** shd **Cross My Mind**[15] 5945 4-9-0 84 .... EdwardCreighton(3) 3 86
(T Keddy) *nvr bttr than mid-div* **13/2**
5520 **8** 1 1/4 **Del Mar Sunset**[23] 5776 7-8-10 80 .... SaleemGolam(3) 11 80
(W J Haggas) *trckd ldr: led briefly 3f out: wknd qckly* **12/1**
5600 **9** 1/2 **Spring Goddess (IRE)**[28] 5680 5-8-12 79 .... DeanMcKeown 9 78
(A P Jarvis) *a towards rr* **10/1**
/0-0 **10** 17 **Never Will**[21] 5810 5-8-13 80 .... JimmyQuinn 6 47
(K A Ryan) *led tl hdd & wknd qckly 3f out* **66/1**
11 1 **Lord Of Beauty (FR)**[567] 6-9-1 82 .... ChrisCatlin 1 47
(Noel T Chance) *a struggling wl in rr* **66/1**
030 **12** shd **El Coto**[9] 5310 6-9-6 87 .... RobertWinston 4 52
(K A Ryan) *mid-div tl wknd rapidly 3f out* **16/1**
6/40 **13** 4 **Aunty Euro (IRE)**[73] 4502 4-9-3 84 .... RichardHughes 5 41
(Patrick Morris, Ire) *mid-div: wknd over 3f out* **25/1**

1m 57.34s (-5.28) **Going Correction** -0.25s/f (Stan)
WFA 3 from 4yo+ 4lb 13 Ran SP% **119.9**
Speed ratings (Par 107):113,106,105,105,105 104,104,103,103,88 87,87,83
CSF £215.14 CT £741.67 TOTE £26.70: £7.10, £2.50, £2.00; EX 264.10.
Owner Saeed Manana **Bred** Airlie Stud And Sir Thomas Pilkington **Trained** Newmarket, Suffolk

FOCUS
This looked competitive beforehand but turned into a one-horse race.

NOTEBOOK
Bahar Shumaal(IRE) ◆, fifth to Hurricane Run in last year's Irish Derby, had become very disappointing on turf, finishing last on his two most recent runs. Making his Polytrack debut, he was no less than 25lb lower than at the start of the year and took full advantage, leading off the home turn and pulling well clear. He will still be well treated after the Handicapper has assessed this performance and there is more to come from him on this surface.
Zato(IRE), 3lb higher than when scoring at Lingfield, ran a sound race but was no match for a very well-treated opponent. (op 5-1 tchd 13-2)
Alpine Reel(IRE), a half-brother to the smart Road To Love, was tackling his longest trip to date. He was forced wide on the home turn and could never get in a blow at the winner, but did stick on to confirm recent placings with today's fourth. (op 7-2)
Ballinteni won a soft-ground Doncaster maiden on his only run at two but was then off the track for almost two years prior to his recent reappearance. He ran respectably on this second run back but is going to prove hard to place. (op 7-1 tchd 9-1)
Regent's Secret(USA), who won this event two years ago when 21lb lower, stayed on from off the pace in his usual style and was never nearer than at the line. (tchd 16-1 and 22-1)
Montpellier(IRE), put up 8lb for winning an uncompetitive Hamilton maiden, was making his sand debut. Held up in rear, by the time he made his move the winner had gone clear and, after temporarily challenging for a place, his effort flattened out in the final furlong. (op 4-1)
Spring Goddess(IRE), the subject of market support, was again rather too keen for her own good early on and was struggling before the home turn. (op 25-1)
Aunty Euro(IRE) Official explanation: jockey said filly stopped very quickly in the closing stages; vet said filly had a breathing problem

6227 LADBROKES FIRST FOR CUSTOMER SERVICE H'CAP 7f 32y(P)
9:30 (9:31) (Class 6) (0-68,68) 3-Y-O+ **£3,238** (£963; £481; £240) **Stalls** High

Form RPR
-043 **1** **Climate (IRE)**[44] 5313 7-8-12 64 .... (p) RobertWinston 9 73
(K A Ryan) *hld up: rdn and hdwy 2f out: r.o gamely to ld ins fnl f: all out* **9/2**[3]
3050 **2** hd **Foreplay (IRE)**[63] 4820 3-9-0 68 .... (p) BrettDoyle 1 76
(E A L Dunlop) *trckd ldrs: rdn 2f out: hdwy over 1f out: led briefly ins fnl f: jst failed* **8/1**
4300 **3** 1 **Dvinsky (USA)**[15] 5937 5-9-0 66 .... PaulDoe 11 72
(M A Allen) *sn trckd ldr: rdn and ev ch 1f out: no ex nr fin* **16/1**
1450 **4** nk **Lii Najma**[11] 6036 3-8-12 66 .... HayleyTurner 5 71
(C E Brittain) *t.k.h: in tch: rdn 3f out: r.o wl ins fnl f* **16/1**
431 **5** shd **Vino**[72] 4527 3-8-13 67 .... RichardHughes 3 72
(B W Hills) *led for 2f: sltly hmpd on ins 1f out: swtchd rt: kpt on fnl f* **11/4**[1]
6064 **6** 1/2 **Mandarin Spirit (IRE)**[11] 6036 6-9-1 67 .... (b) OscarUrbina 8 71
(G C H Chung) *mid-div: rdn 2f out: kpt on one pce fnl f* **10/3**[2]
2600 **7** hd **Sentiero Rosso (USA)**[14] 5961 4-8-13 65 .... (t) MickyFenton 10 68
(B Ellison) *led after 2f: rdn and hdd ins fnl f: no ex* **8/1**
2100 **8** 3/4 **Tuscarora (IRE)**[33] 5572 7-8-11 66 .... JamesDoyle(3) 2 67
(A W Carroll) *towards rr: hdwy over 1f out: nvr nr to chal* **14/1**
6000 **9** nk **Happy As Larry (USA)**[77] 4368 4-8-12 64 .... RobbieFitzpatrick 4 64
(T J Pitt) *a towards rr* **14/1**
020 **10** hd **Perfect Treasure (IRE)**[29] 5649 3-9-0 68 .... (t) TedDurcan 12 68
(J A R Toller) *in tch: rdn over 2f out: wknd fnl f* **25/1**
-000 **11** 1 3/4 **Anchor Date**[32] 5593 4-8-10 65 .... (t) PatrickMathers(3) 7 60
(D Shaw) *hmpd s: a bhd* **40/1**
0606 **12** 17 **Goodwood Spirit**[71] 4557 4-9-2 68 .... SteveDrowne 6 19
(J M Bradley) *a bhd* **40/1**

1m 28.78s (-1.62) **Going Correction** -0.25s/f (Stan)
WFA 3 from 4yo+ 2lb 12 Ran SP% **124.0**
Speed ratings (Par 101):99,98,97,97,97 96,96,95,95,94 92,73
CSF £41.93 CT £548.20 TOTE £6.00: £2.20, £2.80, £5.70; EX 49.00 Place 6 £255.08, Place 5 £79.85.
Owner J Nattrass M Howard R Fawcett T Fawcett **Bred** Mrs A Naughton **Trained** Hambleton, N Yorks

FOCUS
A modest handicap.
Goodwood Spirit Official explanation: jockey said gelding had no more to give
T/Plt: £485.30 to a £1 stake. Pool: £68,216.50. 102.60 winning tickets. T/Qpdt: £24.40 to a £1 stake. Pool: £3,358.00. 101.60 winning tickets. JS

5816 MAISONS-LAFFITTE (R-H)
Saturday, October 28

OFFICIAL GOING: Soft

6228a PRIX MIESQUE (GROUP 3) (FILLIES) 7f (S)
1:00 (1:01) 2-Y-O **£27,586** (£11,034; £8,276; £5,517; £2,759)

RPR
1 **Magic America (USA)**[29] 5654 2-8-11 .... C-PLemaire 7 104+
(Mme C Head-Maarek, France) *held up in midfield, headway on outside to lead over 1f out, pushed out, easily* **6/4**[1]
2 1 1/2 **Nuqoosh**[33] 2-8-11 .... DBonilla 9 100
(F Head, France) *led til headed over 1f out, one pace* **5/1**[2]
3 1 1/2 **Zut Alors (IRE)**[8] 2-8-11 .... CSoumillon 1 96
(Robert Collet, France) *always prominent on inside, stayed on at one pace from over 1f out* **54/10**[3]
4 3/4 **Maria Gabriella (IRE)**[17] 5912 2-8-11 .... MBlancpain 5 94
(C Laffon-Parias, France) *held up tracking leaders, stayed on at same pace final 1 1/2f* **18/1**
5 shd **America Nova (FR)**[17] 5912 2-8-11 .... OPeslier 3 94
(R Gibson, France) *midfield on inside, stayed on at same pace from over 1f out* **66/10**
6 3/4 **Testama (FR)**[39] 5471 2-8-11 .... SPasquier 6 92
(J De Roualle, France) *held up in last, headway on outside to dispute 4th under 1 1/2f out, one pace final f* **12/1**
7 3 **Selinea (FR)**[11] 2-8-11 .... JAuge 2 85
(D Prod'Homme, France) *raced in 7th, never a factor* **12/1**
8 1 1/2 **Bleue Doloise (FR)**[21] 2-8-11 .... TJarnet 4 81
(A Bonin, France) *raced in 8th, always in rear* **87/10**

The Form Book, Raceform Ltd, Compton, RG20 6NL

9 5 **Mpumalanga**[29] 5664 2-8-11 ....(b) TThulliez 8 69
(R Gibson, France) *prominent til weakened quickly 1 1/2f out* **18/1**

1m 24.9s 9 Ran SP% **121.7**
PARI-MUTUEL: WIN 2.50; PL 1.30, 1.60, 1.80; DF 6.60.
Owner Dr T A Ryan **Bred** Castleton Group **Trained** Chantilly, France

NOTEBOOK
Magic America(USA) is turning into a really smart racehorse and she really appreciated this longer trip. Settled behind the leading group on the outside, she made a forward move one and a half out and was not extended in the final stages. A mile looks well within her range and targets now are either the 1000 Guineas or the Pouliches. The decision will be taken during the winter and further improvement can be expected.
Nuqoosh is another filly going the right way and she was running at this level for the first time. Asked to set the pace, she only went at a moderate gallop and was outpaced inside the final furlong. She also looks progressive.
Zut Alors(IRE) ran a sound race and was always on the stands' rail. She ran on well but could not quicken when things warmed up. She is probably not quite in this league.
Maria Gabriella(IRE) was tucked in behind the leaders on the outside before making her challenge running into the final two furlongs. She battled on gamely to hold fourth place by a narrow margin.

6229a CRITERIUM DE MAISONS-LAFFITTE (GROUP 2) 6f (S)
1:30 (1:31) 2-Y-O **£74,690** (£28,828; £13,759; £9,172; £4,586)

RPR

1 **Captain Marvelous (IRE)**[29] 5656 2-9-0 .... CSoumillon 1 115+
(B W Hills) *made all, driven clear final f* **13/10**[1]

2 3 **Baby Strange**[21] 5809 2-9-0 .... TPO'Shea 2 106
(P A Blockley) *missed break, recovered to race in 2nd after 2f, ridden 1 1/2f out, kept on but not pace of winner* **44/10**[3]

3 nk **Iron Lips**[29] 5664 2-8-11 .... OPeslier 6 102
(C Laffon-Parias, France) *held up, ridden to go 3rd 1f out, kept on* **27/10**[2]

4 1 **Fairy Dress (USA)**[4] 2-8-11 .... C-PLemaire 8 99
(Robert Collet, France) *always close up on outside, 3rd halfway, one pace from over 1f out* **11/1**

5 snk **Out Of Time (FR)**[29] 5664 2-8-11 .... IMendizabal 3 99
(J-C Rouget, France) *raced in 3rd early, 4th halfway, one pace final 1 1/2f* **77/10**

6 snk **Finikas**[6] 6118 2-9-0 .... YBarberot 4 101
(S Wattel, France) *held up in last, never a factor* **14/1**

7 ¾ **Right Place (FR)**[11] 2-9-0 ....(b) JAuge 5 99
(Robert Collet, France) *midfield, pushed along before halfway, one pace under pressure final 2f* **11/1**

8 1 **We'll Confer**[43] 5335 2-9-0 .... NCallan 7 96
(K A Ryan) *held up towards rear, never a factor* **14/1**

1m 11.6s 8 Ran SP% **130.5**
PARI-MUTUEL: WIN 2.30; PL 1.10, 1.40, 1.20; DF 4.60.
Owner R J Arculli **Bred** Duncan A McGregor **Trained** Lambourn, Berks

NOTEBOOK
Captain Marvelous(IRE) was in a class of his own and always looked like ending up in the winner's enclosure. The colt was asked to go from pillar to post and he quickened when asked a furlong and a half from the line. He passed the post on his own and made his rivals look rather average. This colt has improved all season and he should continue to in the future. His jockey was impressed and thought that his mount could turn into a Group 1 colt at three.
Baby Strange did not have the best of journeys over from England and sweated up in the paddock, and on the way to the start. He did very little wrong in the race, though. He was behind the winner on the rail at the halfway stage, could not quicken when things warmed up but battled on gamely to hold second place. His trainer felt that there was not enough pace and feels he will stay further in the future.
Iron Lips did not really get into this race until it was over. Held up in the early stages, she made a forward move on the rail at the furlong marker but could not quite make it to the runner-up position. A longer trip could be of benefit in the future.
Fairy Dress(USA), smartly into her stride, raced on the outside. She tried to quicken when the pace was injected a furlong and a half out and then stayed on onepaced.
We'll Confer was rather disappointing. Checked soon after the start, he raced in seventh position and could not go the pace in the final stages. He was never a factor and finally finished last.

6230a PRIX DE SEINE-ET-OISE (GROUP 3) 6f (S)
2:30 (2:31) 3-Y-O+ **£27,586** (£11,034; £8,276; £5,517; £2,759)

RPR

1 **New Girlfriend (IRE)**[28] 5701 3-8-7 .... JAuge 2 113
(Robert Collet, France) *in touch on inside in 4th, headway to lead 1f out, driven out* **6/1**

2 ½ **Advanced**[42] 5358 3-8-10 .... NCallan 1 114
(K A Ryan) *raced in 2nd til led 2f out, headed 1f out, stayed on gamely under pressure final f* **81/10**

3 nk **Luisant**[12] 3-8-10 .... TThulliez 3 113
(F Doumen, France) *held up, effort and slightly outpaced over 1f out, stayed on strongly closing stages to take 3rd close home* **5/1**[2]

4 hd **Linngari (IRE)**[28] 5701 4-9-2 .... GSchofield 7 118
(Diego Lowther, France) *always in touch on outside, ridden and 3rd over 1f out, one pace, lost 3rd close home* **13/10**[1]

5 2 ½ **Sabasha (FR)**[28] 5701 3-8-7 .... RMarchelli 9 102
(F Rohaut, France) *held up in 3rd, sone late headway on inside but never near leaders* **25/1**

6 ¾ **Omasheriff (IRE)**[6] 6121 4-8-11 .... JVictoire 4 103
(W Baltromei, Germany) *3rd early, close up til outpaced from under 2f out* **20/1**

7 nk **Matrix (GER)**[23] 5779 5-8-11 .... DBoeuf 5 102
(W Baltromei, Germany) *led to 2f out, weakened* **8/1**

8 5 **Indian Maiden (IRE)**[16] 5919 6-8-10 .... CSoumillon 8 86
(M S Saunders) *held up towards rear, effort over 2f out, no response* **57/10**[3]

9 dist **Just Queen**[139] 3-8-7 .... MBlancpain 6 —
(M Nigge, France) *misssed break, recovered to race towards rear, weakened over 3f out, eased* **38/1**

1m 10.8s
WFA 3 from 4yo+ 1lb 9 Ran SP% **122.6**
PARI-MUTUEL: WIN 7.00; PL 2.30, 2.60, 2.30; DF 31.60.
Owner R C Strauss **Bred** Kilfrush Stud **Trained** Chantilly, France

NOTEBOOK
New Girlfriend(IRE), a classy filly, got back to her best and also over the trip where she can show her talents to the full. Tucked in behind the leading group early on, she went for the line one and a half out, led at the furlong marker and ran on really well. She was winning for the first time in 15 months and looked in great shape. With this Group 3 victory under her belt connections are now hoping for an invitation for the Hong Kong Sprint in December.
Advanced looked set to gain a first Group success until the winner arrived on the scene. He is still relatively inexperienced compared to the others and this performance augurs well for the future. He followed the leader until taking control a furlong and a half out but, although he battled on gamely, he could not resist the late challenge of the winner, who had been a Group 2 winner at this track as a juvenile. He looks to have a very bright future as a four-year-old.
Luisant lost nothing in defeat and is a colt going from strength to strength. This was his first attempt in a Group event, having previously won two minor races and a handicap. He was given a waiting race and was outpaced when things quickened, but he ran on well as the race came to a close and took third place in the final few strides.
Linngari(IRE) should have been closer if he had repeated his previous form but nevertheless ran a decent race. Quickly into his stride, he raced up the centre of the track, looked to have a great chance at the furlong marker but could not quite go the pace as the race came to an end. Although he is a Group 2 winner over six at Baden-Baden, maybe a longer trip is better for this smart four-year-old.
Indian Maiden(IRE) was disappointing on this occasion and was well beaten. She never looked like finishing in the frame, although she did flatter a little on the outside at the two-furlong marker. She has had a long season and this wonderful mare will now be retired to stud at the end of the year.

6128 KEMPTON (A.W) (R-H)
Sunday, October 29

OFFICIAL GOING: Standard
Wind: Almost nil. Weather: Sunny.

6232 KEMPTON FOR HOSPITALITY BANDED STKS 1m 2f (P)
1:00 (1:00) (Class 7) 3-Y-O+ **£2,047** (£604; £302) **Stalls** High

Form RPR

0505 1 **Majehar**[21] 5838 4-9-3 45 .... AdrianMcCarthy 10 53
(A G Newcombe) *wl plcd: slipped through on inner to ld jst over 2f out and sn 3l clr: hrd pressed fnl f: jst lasted* **11/2**[2]

5060 2 shd **Busy Man (IRE)**[85] 4139 7-9-3 45 .... PaulDoe 6 53
(J R Jenkins) *s.s: wl in rr: gd prog 3f out: swtchd to outer and effrt over 1f out: chsd wnr and clsd fnl f: jst failed* **12/1**

16-0 3 1 **Artzola (IRE)**[159] 1911 6-9-3 45 .... PaulEddery 14 51
(C A Horgan) *towards rr: prog 3f out: rdn to dispute 2nd wl over 1f out but outpcd: kpt on* **20/1**

6361 4 nk **Fairy Monarch (IRE)**[21] 5839 7-9-3 45 ....(b) LeeEnstone 11 51
(P T Midgley) *hld up in midfield on inner: prog over 2f out: disp 2nd over 1f out but outpcd: kpt on* **5/1**[1]

0100 5 2 ½ **Wind Chime (IRE)**[50] 5166 9-9-3 45 .... RichardThomas 1 46
(A G Newcombe) *settled in last pair: pushed along over 3f out: prog whn nt clr run over 1f out and swtchd outside: r.o: hopeless task* **6/1**[3]

6000 6 nk **Piquet**[6] 6134 8-9-3 45 .... BrettDoyle 7 45
(J J Bridger) *hld up in midfield: gng wl 3f out: outpcd 2f out: nt clr run over 1f out: one pce after* **25/1**

0006 7 1 ½ **Saucy**[80] 4289 5-9-3 45 .... JDSmith 4 42
(A W Carroll) *trckd ldrs: rdn and outpcd 2f out: wknd fnl f* **7/1**

3000 8 shd **Louve Heureuse (IRE)**[121] 3036 5-9-3 45 .... RobertMiles 8 42
(B G Powell) *t.k.h: cl up: rdn and outpcd 2f out: wknd fnl f* **25/1**

0430 9 2 **Gran Clicquot**[71] 4585 11-8-12 45 .... RobynBrisland(5) 3 38
(G P Enright) *dwlt: settled in last pair: struggling and outpcd over 2f out: n.d* **25/1**

0000 10 hd **Adobe**[16] 5954 11-8-12 45 .... EmmettStack(5) 5 38
(W M Brisbourne) *towards rr: wd and outpcd 2f out: sn wknd u.p* **7/1**

3-40 11 ¾ **Insignia (IRE)**[282] 162 4-9-3 45 .... DerekMcGaffin 12 37
(W M Brisbourne) *t.k.h: led to jst over 2f out: wknd* **16/1**

0000 12 3 **Didnt Tell My Wife**[151] 2132 7-9-3 45 .... TPO'Shea 9 31
(P S McEntee) *prom: chsd ldr 1/2-way to 3f out: wknd rapidly over 1f out* **25/1**

2500 13 3 **Expected Bonus (USA)**[69] 4667 7-9-3 45 .... JamieMackay 2 25
(Jamie Poulton) *racd wd: in tch: dropped to rr and struggling 3f out: wknd* **8/1**

6/00 14 20 **Gagarin (FR)**[16] 5954 6-9-3 45 .... DavidKinsella 13 —
(Miss L C Siddall) *chsd ldr to 1/2-way: wknd rapidly over 3f out: t.o* **66/1**

2m 9.80s (0.80) **Going Correction** -0.05s/f (Stan) 14 Ran SP% **117.7**
Speed ratings (Par 97):94,93,93,92,90 90,89,89,87,87 87,84,82,66
CSF £61.28 TOTE £5.40: £1.80, £5.90, £11.20; EX 87.20.
Owner J R Salter **Bred** Darley **Trained** Yarnscombe, Devon
■ Stewards' Enquiry : Adrian McCarthy four-day ban: used whip with excessive frequency and without allowing sufficient time to respond (Nov 9-11,13)

FOCUS
They went just a modest gallop and many were finishing fast from off the pace.
Gagarin(FR) Official explanation: jockey said gelding moved poorly throughout

6233 SPONSORS AT KEMPTON BANDED STKS 5f (P)
1:35 (1:36) (Class 7) 3-Y-O+ **£2,047** (£604; £302) **Stalls** High

Form RPR

0006 1 **Jahia (NZ)**[77] 4401 7-8-12 45 .... LeeEnstone 9 58
(P T Midgley) *mde all: drew 5l clr 2f out: rdn out: unchal* **7/1**

060 2 3 ½ **Kindallachan**[32] 5611 3-8-12 45 .... PaulEddery 8 45
(G C Bravery) *s.i.s and bustled along early: prog on inner 1/2-way: kpt on fr over 1f out to take 2nd nr fin: no ch w wnr* **20/1**

1000 3 ½ **Secret Vision (USA)**[6] 6131 5-8-12 45 .... BrettDoyle 12 44
(R M H Cowell) *prom: chsd wnr 1/2-way: drvn and no imp 2f out: lost 2nd nr fin* **13/2**[3]

0206 4 nk **Freshwinds**[251] 465 4-8-7 45 ....(b[1]) EmmettStack(5) 4 43
(Miss Diana Weeden) *racd awkwardly in rr: outpcd fr 1/2-way: prog fr 2f out: kpt on: nrst fin* **14/1**

-005 5 nk **Marron Flore**[214] 790 3-8-12 45 .... RichardThomas 7 41
(A J Lidderdale) *settled in midfield: effrt but outpcd fr 2f out: plugged on: n.d* **25/1**

-552 6 1 ¼ **Fern House (IRE)**[72] 4551 4-8-12 45 .... RobertMiles 5 37
(Peter Grayson) *towards rr: outpcd and struggling over 2f out: no ch after: kpt on* **9/4**[1]

0004 7 1 ¼ **College Queen**[72] 4551 8-8-12 45 .... TPO'Shea 2 32
(S Gollings) *a towards rr: wd and wl off the pce bnd 2f out: no ch* **14/1**

0000 8 shd **Arfinnit (IRE)**[78] 4365 5-8-12 45 ....(p) JamieMackay 10 32
(Mrs A L M King) *hld up in last pair: outpcd and wl off the pce 1/2-way: brief effrt over 1f out: sn no prog* **14/1**

0600 9 ½ **Waggledance (IRE)**[59] 4948 4-8-12 45 .... AdrianMcCarthy 3 30
(D Carroll) *nvr beyond midfield: outpcd and struggling fr 1/2-way* **14/1**

40-6 10 4 **Molotov**[21] 5834 6-8-12 45 .... PaulDoe 6 16
(M Dods) *prom 2f: sn struggling and outpcd: wknd over 1f out* **5/1**[2]

0000 **11** *1 1/4* **Pyramid**[6] 6134 4-8-12 45.....(tp) DavidKinsella 1 11
(A J Lidderdale) *a struggling in rr: v wd bnd 2f out: bhd after* **16/1**

0400 **12** *3* **Jackie Francis (IRE)**[55] 5055 3-8-12 45..... DerekMcGaffin 11 —
(R Brotherton) *chsd wnr to 1/2-way: reluctant and wknd rapidly* **33/1**

60.33 secs (-0.07) **Going Correction** -0.05s/f (Stan) 12 Ran SP% **117.4**
Speed ratings (Par 97):98,92,91,91,90 88,86,86,85,79 77,72
CSF £140.25 TOTE £8.60: £2.70, £7.00, £2.50; EX 161.60.
Owner Enjoy A Day Out Partnership **Bred** A K Illston **Trained** Westow, N Yorks

FOCUS
An authoritative performance by Jahia who blew her rivals away.
Fern House(IRE) Official explanation: jockey said gelding missed the break
Jackie Francis(IRE) Official explanation: jockey said gelding had no more to give

6234 KEMPTON FOR WEDDINGS BANDED STKS 6f (P)
2:10 (2:10) (Class 7) 3-Y-0+ **£2,047** (£604; £302) **Stalls** High

Form RPR

0123 **1** **Imperium**[68] 4675 5-9-4 50.....(p) DaneO'Neill 6 63
(Jean-Rene Auvray) *hld up towards rr: prog on outer over 2f out: led jst over 1f out: drvn and kpt on wl* **6/1**[3]

0045 **2** *1/2* **Decider (USA)**[47] 5272 3-9-3 50..... LPKeniry 12 61
(J M Bradley) *hld up bhd ldrs: nt clr run briefly over 2f out: effrt to chal and w wnr 1f out: kpt on but hld last 75yds* **16/1**

0052 **3** *3* **Granakey (IRE)**[17] 5928 3-8-13 49..... DominicFox(3) 9 51
(M G Quinlan) *led for 1f: styd prom: chal and upsides over 1f out: hrd rdn and one pce* **9/2**[2]

0053 **4** *shd* **Four Amigos (USA)**[6] 6130 5-9-4 50..... LeeEnstone 8 52
(I A Wood) *taken down early: trckd ldrs: led over 2f out: hdd jst over 1f out : hrd rdn and fnd nil* **7/2**[1]

5000 **5** *2 1/2* **Burhaan (IRE)**[23] 5781 4-9-0 49..... AmirQuinn(3) 5 43
(J R Boyle) *trckd ldrs: n.m.r and snatched up over 2f out: no imp over 1f out* **14/1**

0456 **6** *3/4* **Twinned (IRE)**[65] 4756 3-8-10 50..... JamieJones(7) 10 42
(Karen George) *t.k.h: hld up towards rr: effrt and nt clr run briefly over 2f out: one pce and btn over 1f out: fdd* **16/1**

0006 **7** *1* **Height Of Esteem**[15] 5969 3-9-3 50.....(p) JimmyQuinn 4 39
(M Mullineaux) *s.i.s: hld up in last pair: effrt on outer over 2f out: no rspnse and sn btn* **14/1**

3203 **8** *1* **Blakeshall Quest**[17] 5928 6-9-2 48.....(b) RoystonFfrench 3 34
(R Brotherton) *pressed ldrs: rdn fr 1/2-way: wknd over 1f out* **13/2**

1206 **9** *6* **Glenargo (USA)**[77] 4398 3-9-2 49.....(p) AdrianMcCarthy 2 17
(R A Harris) *pressed ldrs tl wknd rapidly 2f out* **10/1**

5106 **10** *1/2* **Stanley Wolfe (IRE)**[132] 2701 3-9-2 49..... RobertMiles 7 15
(Peter Grayson) *mounted on crse: led after 1f to over 2f out: wknd rapidly* **20/1**

06-0 **11** *5* **Daughters World**[49] 5210 3-9-3 50..... GeorgeBaker 11 —
(J R Best) *s.i.s: a wl in rr: struggling over 2f out: t.o* **33/1**

3006 **12** *6* **Pantomime Prince**[131] 2730 3-9-3 50..... FrancisNorton 1 —
(C A Dwyer) *s.i.s: wd and a in last pair: bhd fr 1/2-way: t.o* **12/1**

1m 13.57s (-0.13) **Going Correction** -0.05s/f (Stan)
WFA 3 from 4yo+ 1lb 12 Ran SP% **117.6**
Speed ratings (Par 97):98,97,93,93,89 88,87,86,78,77 70,62
CSF £97.23 TOTE £5.90: £2.10, £4.40, £2.40; EX 83.90.
Owner The Cross Keys Racing Club **Bred** Mrs H B Raw **Trained** Upper Lambourn, Berks
■ Stewards' Enquiry : Royston Ffrench caution: careless riding

FOCUS
Not a bad race for the grade and it should produce winners.
Burhaan(IRE) Official explanation: jockey said colt was denied a clear run
Pantomime Prince Official explanation: jockey said gelding moved poorly throughout

6235 PANORAMIC BAR & RESTAURANT BANDED STKS 1m (P)
2:45 (2:46) (Class 7) 3-Y-0+ **£2,047** (£604; £302) **Stalls** High

Form RPR

0002 **1** **Eccollo (IRE)**[6] 6130 4-9-5 49..... FrancisNorton 7 66
(T J Pitt) *wl in rr: pushed along over 3f out: gd prog on outer sn after: led 2f out: styd on wl and in n.d fnl f* **5/2**[1]

2055 **2** *2 1/2* **Mythical Charm**[6] 6130 7-9-3 50.....(t) MarcHalford(3) 10 61
(J J Bridger) *hld up bhd ldrs: nt clr run briefly over 2f out: prog sn after: styd on wl to chse wnr fnl f: no imp* **11/2**[2]

004 **3** *2 1/2* **Free Silver (IRE)**[6] 6130 3-9-3 50..... AdrianMcCarthy 5 55
(Miss K B Boutflower) *trckd ldrs: nt clr run briefly over 2f out: got through to chse wnr wl over 1f out and racd against far rail: one pce after* **9/1**

0200 **4** *2 1/2* **Never Say Deya**[16] 5936 3-9-1 48..... TPO'Shea 2 47
(M R Channon) *pressed ldrs: hrd rdn to ld briefly over 2f out: sn outpcd* **12/1**

0060 **5** *3 1/2* **Wanna Shout**[118] 3142 8-9-6 50..... JimmyQuinn 9 41
(R Dickin) *hld up towards rr on inner: effrt 3f out: drvn and cl enough 2f out: plugged on one pce* **16/1**

1000 **6** *3/4* **Fantasy Defender (IRE)**[40] 5450 4-9-4 48.....(v) LPKeniry 1 37
(Ernst Oertel) *hld up wl in rr: nt clr run over 2f out: taken to outer and pushed along: kpt on fnl f: no ch* **10/1**

6000 **7** *hd* **Play Up Pompey**[18] 5910 4-8-13 50..... JamesMillman(7) 8 39
(J J Bridger) *prom on outer: lost pl 1/2-way: struggling in rr over 2f out: no ch after* **20/1**

0660 **8** *1 1/2* **Calamari (IRE)**[118] 3142 4-9-6 50..... RoystonFfrench 3 36
(Mrs A Duffield) *towards rr: rdn and looked reluctant fr 3f out: hanging and no real prog* **14/1**

0062 **9** *1/2* **Ailsa**[21] 5838 4-9-5 49..... PaulMulrennan 4 33
(C W Thornton) *dwlt: hld up in last: effrt on inner 3f out: sn outpcd and btn* **10/1**

10 *2* **Freda's Choice (IRE)**[33] 5600 3-9-2 49..... DaneO'Neill 12 29
(Patrick Morris, Ire) *w ldrs: chal 3f out: stl upsides over 2f out: wknd rapidly* **8/1**[3]

600 **11** *1 1/4* **Green Pirate**[96] 3817 4-9-1 50..... EmmettStack(5) 11 27
(W M Brisbourne) *w ldrs: led 3f out to over 2f out: wknd rapidly over 1f out* **12/1**

0004 **12** *hd* **Must Be Keen**[6] 6128 7-9-6 50..... MickyFenton 6 26
(Ernst Oertel) *w ldrs: chal 3f out: stl upsides jst over 2f out: wknd rapidly* **25/1**

4440 **13** *2* **Zafarshah (IRE)**[47] 5267 7-8-11 48.....(b) TolleyDean(7) 13 20
(R A Harris) *pushed along in midfield: effrt on inner and cl enough wl over 2f out: sn wknd rapidly* **14/1**

5400 **14** *26* **Buckle And Hyde**[6] 6130 3-9-0 50.....(p) AmirQuinn(3) 14 —
(Mrs A L M King) *dwlt: pushed up to ld: hdd & wknd rapidly 3f out: t.o* **25/1**

1m 40.49s (-0.31) **Going Correction** -0.05s/f (Stan)
WFA 3 from 4yo+ 3lb 14 Ran SP% **130.3**
Speed ratings (Par 97):99,96,94,91,88 87,87,85,85,83 81,81,79,53
CSF £15.94 TOTE £3.20: £1.50, £2.50, £3.30; EX 28.10.
Owner Stephen Pearson & David Marshall **Bred** Swettenham Stud **Trained** Bawtry, S Yorks

FOCUS
Not a very good race, although the winner remains capable of better.
Fantasy Defender(IRE) Official explanation: jockey said gelding was denied a clear run
Buckle And Hyde Official explanation: trainer said filly finished distressed

6236 RACING UK FOR £15 PER MONTH TRI-BANDED STKS 1m (P)
3:20 (3:21) (Class 7) 3-Y-0 **£2,047** (£604; £302) **Stalls** High

Form RPR

0000 **1** **Island Green (USA)**[122] 3006 3-8-9 40..... TPO'Shea 11 47
(B J Curley) *pressed ldng pair: trapped on inner and lost pl over 2f out: rallied over 1f out: led last 100yds: in command after* **9/1**

6400 **2** *3/4* **Bollywood (IRE)**[46] 5291 3-9-0 45..... DaneO'Neill 5 50
(J J Bridger) *chsd ldrs: rdn over 3f out: prog u.p over 2f out: led over 1f out: hdd and no ex last 75yds* **7/2**[1]

0306 **3** *1 1/2* **Franky'N'Jonny**[17] 5922 3-9-0 45.....(t) IanMongan 8 47
(M J Attwater) *rdn in midfield 1/2-way: prog over 2f out: tried to chal jst over 1f out: one pce fnl f* **5/1**[3]

0660 **4** *nk* **Just Tilly**[141] 2463 3-8-9 40..... JimCrowley 12 41
(L Montague Hall) *hld up towards rr: sme prog and gng wl enough over 3f out: rdn to cl on ldrs 2f out: one pce fnl f* **10/1**

0060 **5** *1* **Bournonville**[11] 6057 3-8-6 40..... DominicFox(3) 4 39
(M Wigham) *towards rr: rdn over 3f out: prog u.p and cl enough 2f out: nt qckn over 1f out: one pce* **16/1**

0300 **6** *3/4* **Mid Valley**[17] 5924 3-9-0 45.....(v) MickyFenton 9 42
(J R Jenkins) *pressed ldrs: led over 2f out to over 1f out: wknd last 150yds* **9/2**[2]

00 **7** *1 1/4* **Capital Lass**[46] 5291 3-8-6 40 ow4..... JamesMillman(7) 10 38
(D K Ivory) *v s.i.s: wl in rr: prog to chse ldng gp 2f out: no imp after* **33/1**

0000 **8** *2 1/2* **Saxon Star (IRE)**[11] 6057 3-8-9 40.....(v) PaulDoe 6 29
(P Howling) *wl in rr: rdn on outer and out of tch 3f out: no ch after* **33/1**

-006 **9** *shd* **Pertemps Heroine**[20] 5873 3-9-0 45..... JimmyQuinn 13 33
(A D Smith) *pressed ldrs: drvn over 2f out: btn over 1f out: sn wknd* **11/1**

0406 **10** *nk* **Song Huntress**[21] 5840 3-9-0 45..... FergusSweeney 7 33
(A G Newcombe) *a in rr: rdn and struggling on outer over 2f out: sn no ch* **14/1**

000 **11** *nk* **Haughton Hope**[26] 5761 3-9-0 45..... FrancisNorton 3 32
(T J Pitt) *mostly last: rdn over 2f out: plugged on: no ch* **9/1**

0006 **12** *10* **Orchard House (FR)**[21] 5830 3-8-9 40.....(b[1]) PaulEddery 2 4
(J Jay) *chsd ldr to 3f out: wknd rapidly 2f out* **20/1**

0000 **13** *15* **Hahns Peak**[27] 5733 3-8-11 45.....(p) AmirQuinn(3) 1 —
(Mrs A L M King) *led and crossed fr wdst draw: hdd & wknd rapidly over 2f out: t.o* **40/1**

1m 41.75s (0.95) **Going Correction** -0.05s/f (Stan) 13 Ran SP% **120.1**
Speed ratings (Par 95):93,92,90,90,89 88,87,84,84,84 84,74,59
CSF £39.24 TOTE £9.70: £3.60, £2.00, £2.00; EX 48.40.
Owner Curley Leisure **Bred** Gainsborough Farm Llc **Trained** Newmarket, Suffolk
■ Stewards' Enquiry : T P O'Shea one-day ban: careless riding (Nov 9)

FOCUS
An improved display by Island Green.
Hahns Peak Official explanation: jockey said gelding stopped very quickly

6237 TRAINS FROM WATERLOO BANDED STKS 7f (P)
3:55 (3:56) (Class 7) 3-Y-0+ **£2,047** (£604; £302) **Stalls** High

Form RPR

0004 **1** **Warden Warren**[6] 6134 8-9-0 45.....(b) AdrianMcCarthy 9 53
(Mrs C A Dunnett) *trckd ldng trio: effrt 3f out: rdn to ld over 1f out: styd on wl* **9/2**[2]

-600 **2** *1 1/2* **Binnion Bay (IRE)**[239] 576 5-8-11 45.....(v) AmirQuinn(3) 10 49
(J J Bridger) *hld up in midfield: effrt on inner over 2f out: chsd wnr ins fnl f: styd on but no real imp* **33/1**

55/- **3** *2 1/2* **Shava**[678] 6935 6-9-0 45..... FrancisNorton 5 43
(H J Evans) *t.k.h: hld up bhd ldrs: effrt over 2f out: nt qckn over 1f out: one pce after* **16/1**

5031 **4** *nk* **Jennverse**[6] 6131 4-9-6 45..... JamieMackay 3 48
(D K Ivory) *rrd s: hld up in rr: gng wl enough but plenty to do 2f out: plld out and effrt over 1f out: kpt on same pce: no ch* **2/1**[1]

0040 **5** *3/4* **Bogaz (IRE)**[71] 4585 4-8-11 45.....(v) RichardKingscote(3) 11 40
(Mrs H Sweeting) *led after 1f to over 1f out: fdd fnl f* **10/1**

5405 **6** *shd* **Kilmeena Magic**[6] 6134 4-9-0 45..... LPKeniry 13 40
(J C Fox) *hld up in midfield: effrt on inner over 2f out: nt qckn and btn over 1f out: one pce after* **9/1**

56-0 **7** *shd* **Cross My Shadow (IRE)**[17] 5926 4-9-0 45.....(t) DavidKinsella 4 39
(M F Harris) *pressed ldr: rdn over 2f out: grad wknd fr over 1f out* **20/1**

0006 **8** *nk* **Wodhill Schnaps**[34] 5571 5-9-0 45.....(b[1]) DerekMcGaffin 1 39
(D Morris) *dwlt: rdn towards rr 3f out: nt look keen and no real prog fnl 2f* **25/1**

5403 **9** *1* **Teyaar**[6] 6131 10-9-0 45..... PaulDoe 2 36
(M Wellings) *s.s: wl in rr: nt clr run over 2f out: no prog after* **6/1**[3]

0000 **10** *nk* **Meddle**[18] 4734 3-8-12 45.....(t) PaulEddery 6 35
(J Jay) *settled in last: struggling u.p 3f out: kpt on ins fnl f* **50/1**

0060 **11** *hd* **Aintnecessarilyso**[128] 2813 8-9-0 45.....(p) DaneO'Neill 12 35
(J M Bradley) *hld up in midfield: effrt 3f out: hanging bdly and wknd over 1f out* **12/1**

402/ **12** *4* **Scorch**[930] 1375 5-9-0 45..... RossStudholme 14 24
(V Smith) *led for 1f: prom tl wknd over 2f out* **16/1**

0 **13** *47* **Johnnie Black (IRE)**[34] 5573 4-8-11 45.....(t) EdwardCreighton(3) 8 —
(E J Creighton) *in tch 3f: sn t.o* **33/1**

1m 27.05s (0.25) **Going Correction** -0.05s/f (Stan)
WFA 3 from 4yo+ 2lb 13 Ran SP% **120.8**
Speed ratings (Par 97):96,94,91,91,90 90,90,89,88,88 87,83,29
CSF £157.63 TOTE £5.50: £2.00, £8.10, £6.60; EX 146.50.
Owner Annwell Inn Syndicate **Bred** R G Percival **Trained** Hingham, Norfolk

FOCUS
A drab affair.
Johnnie Black(IRE) Official explanation: jockey said gelding finished lame

6238 SUBSCRIBE ONLINE @RACINGUK.TV BANDED STKS 1m 4f (P)
4:25 (4:25) (Class 7) 3-Y-O+ **£2,047** (£604; £302) **Stalls** Centre

Form RPR
6054 **1** **Ocean Rock**[104] [3597] 5-9-10 50 GeorgeBaker 5 58
(C A Horgan) *dwlt and stdd s: hld up in last: prog to trck ldrs 2f out : sn rdn: drvn ahd last 100yds* **10/1**

0050 **2** *1* **Go Amwell**[6] [6132] 3-9-3 50 PaulDoe 14 56
(J R Jenkins) *hld up in rr: effrt on outer over 2f out: drvn and styd on fnl f to take 2nd nr fin* **25/1**

4503 **3** *nk* **Three Boars**[26] [5750] 4-9-9 49 (b) SilvestreDeSousa 3 54
(S Gollings) *trckd ldrs: rdn to ld 2f out: hdd and one pce last 100yds* **6/1**[2]

1246 **4** *nk* **Revolve**[6] [6128] 6-9-9 49 (p) IanMongan 2 54
(Mrs L J Mongan) *wl in tch: effrt 3f out: hrd rdn to chal and upsides 1f out: nt qckn* **8/1**[3]

0045 **5** *1 1/4* **Malibu (IRE)**[6] [6128] 5-9-10 50 DaneO'Neill 8 53
(M Appleby) *hld up in last pair: prog on wd outside over 2f out: chsd ldrs over 1f out: one pce after* **25/1**

5401 **6** *2 1/2* **Milk And Sultana**[6] [6128] 6-9-13 47 JimmyQuinn 7 52
(G A Ham) *wl in tch on inner: effrt and rdn over 2f out: no imp over 1f out* **5/1**[1]

05-0 **7** *1* **Flaming Weapon**[202] [939] 4-9-5 45 JimCrowley 10 42
(G L Moore) *wl in rr: drvn on outer over 2f out: plugged on fr over 1f out: nt pce to rch ldrs* **5/1**[1]

0023 **8** *2* **Channel Crossing**[17] [5925] 4-9-3 48 (p) EmmettStack(5) 1 42
(W M Brisbourne) *led for 3f: pressed ldr: led again briefly over 2f out: hanging bdly and sn btn* **10/1**

0201 **9** *1/2* **Cool Isle**[40] [5441] 3-8-8 48 (b) JPFeatherstone(7) 13 41
(P Howling) *trckd ldrs: bmpd along and wknd over 1f out* **16/1**

0016 **10** *1/2* **Ndola**[159] [1910] 7-9-7 47 TPO'Shea 4 40
(B J Curley) *settled in midfield: rdn 3f out: sn lost pl and btn* **8/1**[3]

0003 **11** *3/4* **Explode**[15] [5955] 9-9-2 49 (b) DawnRankin(7) 6 40
(Miss L C Siddall) *hld up in rr: prog on outer and prom 5f out: wknd over 2f out* **40/1**

0222 **12** *16* **Alqaayid**[36] [5562] 5-9-1 48 JamesMillman(7) 11 14
(P W Hiatt) *led after 3f to over 2f out: wknd rapidly: t.o* **6/1**[2]

2m 37.31s (0.41) **Going Correction** -0.05s/f (Stan)
WFA 3 from 4yo+ 7lb 12 Ran SP% **118.3**
Speed ratings (Par 97):96,95,95,94,94 92,91,90,90,89 89,78
CSF £238.59 TOTE £14.50: £3.10, £8.60, £2.30; EX 234.10 Place 6 £380.09, Place 5 £111.98..
Owner Mrs B Sumner **Bred** Mrs B Sumner **Trained** Uffcott, Wilts

FOCUS
A competitive heat.
Channel Crossing Official explanation: jockey said gelding hung right throughout
Alqaayid Official explanation: jockey said gelding had no more to give
T/Plt: £530.50 to a £1 stake. Pool: £42,918.90. 59.05 winning tickets. T/Qpdt: £35.90 to a £1 stake. Pool: £3,944.60. 81.30 winning tickets. JN

6222 WOLVERHAMPTON (A.W) (L-H)
Sunday, October 29

OFFICIAL GOING: Standard
Wind: Moderate becoming slight, across.

6239 MASON BROTHERS H'CAP 7f 32y(P)
1:10 (1:10) (Class 5) (0-75,75) 3-Y-O+ **£4,210** (£1,252; £625; £312) **Stalls** High

Form RPR
6021 **1** **Prince Dayjur (USA)**[18] [5907] 7-8-13 70 DeanMcKeown 5 76
(J Pearce) *trckd ldrs: rdn wl over 1f out: r.o to ld last strides* **7/1**

3136 **2** *shd* **Middlemarch (IRE)**[29] [5680] 6-9-0 71 (b) PhillipMakin 11 77
(J S Goldie) *in rr: rdn 1/2-way: hdwy over 1f out: r.o strly fnl f to snatch 2nd cl home* **6/1**[3]

5454 **3** *nk* **Rezzago (USA)**[20] [5877] 6-9-4 75 AdamKirby 10 80
(W R Swinburn) *towards rr: hmpd over 2f out: swtchd lft over 1f out: r.o to ld ins fnl f: hdd and lost 2nd cl home* **4/1**[1]

2006 **4** *nk* **Angaric (IRE)**[15] [5961] 3-9-0 73 RobertWinston 4 77
(B Smart) *mid-div: rdn 3f out: styd on wl fnl f* **12/1**

3000 **5** *hd* **Blue Maeve**[23] [5791] 6-9-1 72 SilvestreDeSousa 2 76
(A D Brown) *led tl hdd 3f out: styd prom: nt qckn ins fnl f* **33/1**

0226 **6** *shd* **Smart Ass (IRE)**[16] [5953] 3-8-9 68 ChrisCatlin 7 71
(J S Moore) *mid-div: rdn over 2f out: hdwy over 1f out: swtchd lft ins fnl f: r.o* **16/1**

7 *1 3/4* **Breaker Morant (IRE)**[23] [5796] 4-9-4 75 (b) DanielTudhope 1 74
(Patrick Morris, Ire) *trckd ldr: led 3f out: hdd & wknd ins fins fnl f* **16/1**

0451 **8** *4* **Valentino Swing (IRE)**[16] [5953] 3-8-8 70 StephenDonohoe(3) 9 58
(J L Spearing) *towards rr: nvr on terms* **9/1**

4042 **9** *1* **Top Mark**[18] [5907] 4-9-4 75 PatCosgrave 8 61
(J R Boyle) *prom early: sn rdn along and bhd fr 1/2-way* **8/1**

0050 **10** *5* **Cardinal Venture (IRE)**[52] [5144] 8-9-2 73 (p) NCallan 12 46
(K A Ryan) *mid-div: rdn 3f out: sn wknd* **28/1**

0040 **11** *2 1/2* **Material Witness (IRE)**[33] [5591] 9-9-2 73 MartinDwyer 6 39
(W R Muir) *chsd ldrs: rdn 3f out: wknd 2f out* **11/2**[2]

0210 **12** *3 1/2* **Corrib (IRE)**[54] [5079] 3-9-1 74 TonyCulhane 3 31
(B Palling) *s.i.s: sn chsd ldrs: wknd 2f out* **16/1**

1m 27.78s (-2.62) **Going Correction** -0.275s/f (Stan)
WFA 3 from 4yo+ 2lb 12 Ran SP% **115.0**
Speed ratings (Par 103):103,102,102,102,101 101,99,95,94,88 85,81
CSF £47.12 CT £194.20 TOTE £5.50: £1.60, £2.00, £1.90; EX 135.40 TRIFECTA Not won..
Owner sportaracing.com **Bred** Golden Gate Stud **Trained** Newmarket, Suffolk

FOCUS
A bunch finish to an ordinary handicap. The form looks solid enough.
Material Witness(IRE) Official explanation: jockey said gelding had no more to give

6240 MILLIE FILLY WALKER H'CAP 1m 141y(P)
1:45 (1:45) (Class 5) (0-70,72) 3-Y-O+ **£3,886** (£1,156; £577; £288) **Stalls** Low

Form RPR
3061 **1** **Writ (IRE)**[15] [5974] 4-9-2 66 TomEaves 7 79
(I Semple) *trckd ldrs: wnt 2nd over 2f out: rdn to ld ins fnl f: kpt up to work* **4/1**[1]

4156 **2** *3/4* **Pab Special (IRE)**[20] [5863] 3-8-9 68 AndrewElliott(5) 3 79
(K R Burke) *trckd ldr closely: led 3f out: rdn and hdd ins fnl f: no ex* **12/1**

0401 **3** *5* **Kildare Sun (IRE)**[27] [5740] 4-9-3 67 DaleGibson 5 68
(J Mackie) *in tch: rdn over 3f out: edgd lft over 1f out: styd on fnl f but no ch w first 2* **11/1**

3-22 **4** *hd* **Esthlos (FR)**[20] [5879] 3-9-2 70 NCallan 10 70
(J Jay) *mid-div: bmpd over 3f out: rdn and hdwy over 2f out: nt pce to chal* **7/1**[3]

0164 **5** *1 3/4* **New England**[15] [5972] 4-8-10 63 StephenDonohoe(3) 9 59
(W M Brisbourne) *slowly away: in rr whn rdn 3f out: effrt 2f out but nvr on terms* **8/1**

0501 **6** *1 1/2* **Pure Imagination (IRE)**[11] [6054] 5-9-1 72 (b) BarrySavage(7) 6 65
(J M Bradley) *hld up: rdn over 2f out: nt clr run and swtchd rt over 1f out: nvr nr to chal* **10/1**

0006 **7** *1* **Greenbelt**[19] [5904] 5-9-0 64 DanielTudhope 4 55
(G M Moore) *bhd and pushed along fr 5f out: sme hdwy whn n.m.r over 1f out* **5/1**[2]

0/50 **8** *10* **Unicorn Reward (IRE)**[23] [5786] 6-9-6 70 (b[1]) AdamKirby 13 40
(Mrs L C Jewell) *bmpd s: a bhd* **100/1**

0000 **9** *hd* **Jakarmi**[19] [5889] 5-9-1 65 TonyCulhane 2 35
(B Palling) *led tl hdd 3f out: sn wknd* **14/1**

3005 **10** *nk* **Bijou Dan**[29] [5689] 5-9-1 70 (v) DuranFentiman(5) 1 39
(W G Harrison) *a bhd* **8/1**

1000 **11** *5* **Jordans Elect**[15] [5961] 6-9-0 64 (v) RobbieFitzpatrick 11 23
(T J Pitt) *bmpd s: sn chsd ldrs: rdn over 3f out: wknd qckly* **33/1**

4252 **12** *6* **Million Percent**[24] [5775] 7-8-9 64 LiamJones(5) 8 10
(C R Dore) *in tch tl rdn and wknd 3f out* **8/1**

1m 48.13s (-3.63) **Going Correction** -0.275s/f (Stan)
WFA 3 from 4yo+ 4lb 12 Ran SP% **118.2**
Speed ratings (Par 103):105,104,99,99,98 96,95,87,86,86 82,76
CSF £53.00 CT £495.22 TOTE £3.80: £1.60, £4.30, £6.10; EX 90.80 TRIFECTA Not won..
Owner Clarke Boon **Bred** Sean Collins **Trained** Carluke, S Lanarks

FOCUS
The first two came clear here and, with the runner-up appearing to run a career-best in defeat, the winner looks to have improved again for his new yard.
Writ(IRE) Official explanation: jockey said gelding hung right throughout
Jakarmi Official explanation: vet said gelding finished lame on its right hind leg; jockey said he eased gelding 1f out
Million Percent Official explanation: jockey said gelding hung throughout

6241 VAUGHAN'S MIDNIGHT BROOMSTICKS CLAIMING STKS 1m 1f 103y(P)
2:20 (2:20) (Class 6) 3-Y-O+ **£3,238** (£963; £481; £240) **Stalls** Low

Form RPR
0431 **1** **Climate (IRE)**[1] [6227] 7-9-6 64 (p) NCallan 10 71
(K A Ryan) *mid-div: hdwy 3f out: rdn and squeezed way through to ld appr fnl f: edgd rt and drvn out* **7/2**[2]

5235 **2** *2* **Ballyhurry (USA)**[28] [5553] 9-9-2 58 DanielTudhope 11 63
(J S Goldie) *bhd tl hdwy on outside over 2f out: styd on fnl f to go 2nd nr fin* **8/1**

3310 **3** *hd* **Risk Free**[27] [5740] 9-8-7 56 (bt) StephenDonohoe(3) 13 57
(P D Evans) *bhd tl hdwy over 2f out: edgd lft appr fnl f: kpt on one pce* **12/1**

4605 **4** *1/2* **Templet (USA)**[38] [2548] 6-9-6 59 (v) RobertWinston 12 68+
(W G Harrison) *bhd and sn reminders in rr: hdwy on ins whn hmpd appr fnl f: nt rcvr* **25/1**

0600 **5** *1 1/2* **Bessemer (JPN)**[29] [5688] 5-9-6 73 (p) SteveDrowne 1 63
(D Carroll) *trckd ldrs: led over 2f out: rdn and hdd over 1f out: wknd ins fnl f* **4/1**[3]

0040 **6** *3/4* **Toshi (USA)**[42] [5406] 4-9-2 64 (v[1]) TomEaves 3 57
(I Semple) *in tch: rdn 3f out: wkng whn hmpd ins fnl f* **5/1**

0000 **7** *3/4* **Namroud (USA)**[11] [6059] 7-9-5 70 (p) JamieMoriarty(5) 8 64
(R A Fahey) *mid-div: hdwy to chse ldrs over 3f out: swtchd lft appr fnl f: one pce after* **11/1**

100- **8** *1 1/2* **Speagle (IRE)**[54] [5101] 4-9-2 PatCosgrave 5 53
(Adrian McGuinness, Ire) *led tl hdd over 2f out: wknd appr fnl f* **3/1**[1]

0000 **9** *7* **Cadeaux Des Mages**[35] [5553] 6-8-12 62 (b[1]) J-PGuillambert 2 36
(J G Given) *chsd ldrs: rdn 1/2-way: wknd 3f out* **20/1**

0- **10** *4* **Nebdi (IRE)**[83] [4216] 5-9-2 56 DavidAllan 4 32
(E J Alston) *rdn 1/2-way: nvr on terms* **66/1**

0600 **11** *6* **Dawaleeb (IRE)**[41] [5418] 3-8-0 59 (v[1]) MarkWaite(7) 7 16
(Jane Chapple-Hyam) *trckd ldr: rdn 3f out: wknd qckly* **66/1**

0 **12** *20* **Satintheslip (IRE)**[12] [6026] 5-8-8 GregFairley(3) 9 —
(Mrs P Ford) *a bhd* **100/1**

-000 **13** *10* **Pip's Baby**[14] [5992] 3-8-8 55 MartinDwyer 6 —
(S Kirk) *in tch: rdn 4f out: sn wl bhd* **25/1**

2m 0.97s (-1.65) **Going Correction** -0.275s/f (Stan)
WFA 3 from 4yo+ 4lb 13 Ran SP% **127.5**
Speed ratings (Par 101):96,94,94,93,92 91,90,89,83,79 74,56,47
CSF £32.19 TOTE £5.20: £2.30, £2.00, £3.30; EX 52.00 Trifecta £60.60 Part won. Pool £85.36 - 0.50 winning units..Toshi (no.8) was claimed by E. Nisbet for £8,000.
Owner J Nattrass M Howard R Fawcett T Fawcett **Bred** Mrs A Naughton **Trained** Hambleton, N Yorks

■ Stewards' Enquiry : Stephen Donohoe three-day ban: careless riding (Nov 9-11)
N Callan caution: careless riding

FOCUS
An ordinary claimer in which the winner did not need to improve on his performance the previous day to win by a clear margin. The race was run at a good early pace, suiting the hold-up horses, and has been rated through the runner-up.

6242 SUSAN SMITH 35TH WEDDING ANNIVERSARY MAIDEN FILLIES' STKS 1m 141y(P)
2:55 (2:56) (Class 4) 2-Y-O **£5,505** (£1,637; £818; £408) **Stalls** Low

Form RPR
62 **1** **Gull Wing (IRE)**[33] [5595] 2-9-0 HayleyTurner 4 76
(M L W Bell) *chsd ldrs: rdn to ld 1f out: hld on gamely* **10/11**[1]

2 *hd* **Katy Carr** 2-9-0 PatCosgrave 9 76
(M J Wallace) *slowly away: in rr tl hdwy 2f out: swtchd lft appr fnl f: ev ch ins: jst failed* **20/1**

03 **3** *hd* **Usk Melody**[54] [5095] 2-9-0 RichardHughes 11 75
(B J Meehan) *led for 2f: styd prom: ev ch u.p ins fnl f: no ex fnl strides* **10/3**[2]

64 **4** *1 3/4* **Raquel White**[16] [5948] 2-9-0 RobertWinston 6 71
(P D Evans) *led after 2f: rdn and hdd 1f out: fdd ins fnl f* **15/2**[3]

0 **5** *hd* **Legend House (FR)**[33] [5595] 2-9-0 JoeFanning 3 71
(M Johnston) *mid-div: rdn 3f out: wknd ins fnl f* **33/1**

6 *1/2* **Penny From Heaven (IRE)** 2-9-0 MartinDwyer 1 70
(E A L Dunlop) *slowly away: in rr: hdwy on ins 3f out: hung lft 1f out: one pce after* **12/1**

7 *2 1/2* **Antrim Rose** 2-9-0 DaleGibson 7 65
(J H M Gosden) *bhd tl mde sme late hdwy* **20/1**

0 **8** 2 **Milla's Rocket (IRE)**[40] 5456 2-9-0 .... ChrisCatlin 13 61
(D J Daly) *nvr bttr than mid-div* **50/1**

0 **9** ½ **Molly Pitcher (IRE)**[124] 2958 2-9-0 .... PaulHanagan 8 60
(M A Jarvis) *a towards rr* **8/1**

0 **10** ½ **Summer Of Love (IRE)**[100] 3707 2-9-0 .... NelsonDeSouza 12 58
(P F I Cole) *a bhd* **40/1**

0 **11** 3 **Night Falcon**[19] 5891 2-9-0 .... SteveDrowne 10 52
(H Morrison) *trckd ldrs: rdn over 3f out: sn btn* **33/1**

12 2 **Miss Charismatic** 2-9-0 .... RobbieFitzpatrick 5 48
(Eamon Tyrrell, Ire) *in tch: rdn 4f out: wknd over 2f out* **50/1**

1m 51.26s (-0.50) **Going Correction** -0.275s/f (Stan) **12** Ran SP% **127.8**
Speed ratings (Par 94):91,90,90,89,88 88,86,84,84,83 80,79
CSF £30.07 TOTE £1.90: £1.10, £7.00, £1.60; EX 31.40 Trifecta £58.80 Part won. Pool £82.82 - 0.20 winning units..
Owner Lady Bamford **Bred** Lady Bamford **Trained** Newmarket, Suffolk
■ Michael Bell's 800th training success.
■ Stewards' Enquiry : Richard Hughes three-day ban: used whip with excessive frequency (Nov 9-11)

FOCUS
A fair maiden but the pace was not that fast early on and it resulted in a tight finish. The winner did not need to reproduce her sound turf form.

NOTEBOOK
Gull Wing(IRE), runner-up last time to a filly who subsequently went on to finish fourth in the Rockfel Stakes, looked to have been found an attractive opportunity to get off the mark. She travelled well and, although she was made to work for her win in the end, she is a middle-distance filly in the making and should do better next year. (op 6-5 tchd 5-4)
Katy Carr, a half-sister to Hardwicke Stakes winner Predappio, shaped with plenty of promise on her debut, running a far more experienced filly very close. She is bred to do better as a three-year-old and will get further in time. (op 10-1)
Usk Melody had shaped as though worth a try over this distance and, having raced up with the pace throughout in what was a steadily-run affair, she would not go down without a fight. Handicaps are now an option for her. (op 9-2 tchd 3-1)
Raquel White, beaten in claimers on her first two starts, has changed stables since and was backed beforehand to put up an improved performance on her All-Weather debut. She ran well, but is probably flattered by the bare form as she benefited from being allowed to set a steady pace in front. (op 25-1)
Legend House(FR), a sister to Inch Lodge, a seven-furlong winner on her juvenile debut, finished a long way behind Gull Wing on her debut at Nottingham but showed the benefit of that outing here in what was a steadily-run contest. (op 28-1 tchd 25-1)
Penny From Heaven(IRE), a half-sister to Sun Kissed, a six-furlong winner at two, and to fair hurdler Flying Enterprise, shaped encouragingly and should benefit from the experience. (op 10-1 tchd 8-1)

6243 I'M GOING TO BE GRANDPA PAYNE H'CAP 5f 20y(P)
3:30 (3:30) (Class 2) (0-100,100) 3-Y-0+
£11,217 (£3,358; £1,679; £840; £419; £210) **Stalls** Low

Form RPR

5000 **1** **King Orchisios (IRE)**[8] 6095 3-8-10 **92**.................................(p) NCallan 5 106
(K A Ryan) *mde all: clr over 1f out: rdn out* **20/1**

0623 **2** 1 **Judd Street**[8] 6095 4-8-10 **92**.. StephenCarson 1 102
(R F Johnson Houghton) *chsd ldrs: rdn to go 2nd ins fnl f* **11/2**[2]

4030 **3** 1½ **First Order**[26] 5749 5-8-6 **88** oh2 ow2..............................(v[1]) TomEaves 6 93
(I Semple) *chsd wnr tl edgd rt and lost 2nd ins fnl f* **20/1**

5233 **4** nk **Charles Darwin (IRE)**[22] 5807 3-8-7 **89**........................ PaulHanagan 10 93
(M Blanshard) *in tch: riden 2f out: swtchd rt ins fnl f: kpt on* **10/1**

212 **5** nk **Intrepid Jack**[8] 6095 4-9-4 **100**... SteveDrowne 9 102
(H Morrison) *mid-div: rdn and styd on fr over 1f out* **2/1**[1]

0511 **6** shd **Grand Show**[24] 5777 4-8-4 **86**... JoeFanning 3 88
(W R Swinburn) *hld up in rr: hdwy on ins fr over 1f out but nvr nr to chal* **8/1**

6044 **7** shd **River Falcon**[22] 5812 6-8-9 **91**....................................... TonyCulhane 13 93
(J S Goldie) *bhd tl mde sme late hdwy* **10/1**

6005 **8** nk **Qadar (IRE)**[8] 6095 4-8-11 **96**... JamesDoyle(3) 7 97
(N P Littmoden) *in tch: rdn 2f out: wknd ins fnl f* **10/1**

2161 **9** ¾ **Dhaular Dhar (IRE)**[15] 5957 4-8-13 **95**......................... DanielTudhope 4 93
(J S Goldie) *towards rr: nvr on terms* **7/1**[3]

0600 **10** 1½ **Graze On**[78] 4360 4-8-8 **90**... RobbieFitzpatrick 8 83
(Peter Grayson) *mid-div: no hdwy fnl 2f* **40/1**

5051 **11** ½ **Texas Gold**[8] 6095 8-9-4 **100**.. MartinDwyer 11 91
(W R Muir) *a towards rr* **8/1**

-000 **12** ¾ **Classic Encounter (IRE)**[67] 4717 3-8-13 **95**.............. RichardHughes 2 83
(D M Simcock) *t.k.h: mid-div: bhd fr 1/2-way* **40/1**

0006 **13** 2 **The Lord**[8] 6095 6-8-6 **88**... DaleGibson 12 69
(W G M Turner) *mid-div tl rdn and wknd 2f out* **33/1**

60.56 secs (-2.26) **Going Correction** -0.275s/f (Stan) **13** Ran SP% **128.1**
Speed ratings (Par 109):107,105,103,102,102 101,101,101,100,97 96,95,92
CSF £129.36 CT £2288.84 TOTE £27.30: £7.10, £2.80, £5.30; EX 176.40 TRIFECTA Not won..
Owner Mr & Mrs Julian And Rosie Richer **Bred** Rathbarry Stud **Trained** Hambleton, N Yorks

FOCUS
A decent handicap run in a course record time, and solid form despite the improvement in form from the winner.

NOTEBOOK
King Orchisios(IRE) was bounced out quickly and, unlike at Lingfield last time, soon secured an uncontested lead. He made every yard to post a personal best and, while he has been somewhat disappointing this season despite two wins, he could really fulfil his potential at four. Official explanation: jockey said colt ducked left out of the stalls (tchd 25-1)
Judd Street came out of the pack to chase the winner home. He, along with four others in the field, had finished in front of King Orchisios eight days earlier at Lingfield, but the winner enjoyed an uncontested lead this time and second was not a bad result in the circumstances. He deserves a change of luck. (op 6-1)
First Order, visored for the first time, not only carried 2lb overweight but was also racing from 2lb out of the handicap. He tracked King Orchisios throughout and benefited from the even gallop set by Callan on the winner. (op 16-1 tchd 22-1)
Charles Darwin(IRE) kept battling away without looking like getting to the winner. He remains vulnerable off this sort of mark but is admirably consistent. (op 11-1 tchd 12-1)
Intrepid Jack, runner-up in the Lingfield race in which King Orchisios went off too fast and helped set it up for closers, ran on quite well from off the pace considering that the winner's rider was able to set perfect fractions to suit himself this time. (op 5-2)
Grand Show was found out by the drop back in distance in a race that was not run to suit those held up. He kept on well in the straight to finish where he did and probably ran a better race than his finishing position suggests. Official explanation: jockey said gelding was hampered leaving the stalls (op 13-2)
Texas Gold had five of today's rivals behind him at Lingfield last time, but this is not his track and he was comfortably held. Official explanation: jockey said gelding did not act on the slow surface (op 9-1)

6244 EXPRESS AND STAR H'CAP 1m 4f 50y(P)
4:05 (4:05) (Class 5) (0-75,75) 3-Y-0 **£3,886** (£1,156; £577; £288) **Stalls** Low

Form RPR

530 **1** **Junior**[29] 5669 3-9-4 **75**.. RichardHughes 6 87+
(B J Meehan) *trckd ldr: rdn over 4f out: led ins fnl f: kpt on* **6/1**

2224 **2** ½ **Osolomio (IRE)**[69] 4668 3-8-4 **61** oh1................................ DaleGibson 1 72
(G A Swinbank) *led tl rdn and hdd ins fnl f* **5/2**[1]

3502 **3** 3 **Squirtle (IRE)**[16] 5952 3-8-7 **67**.......................(v[1]) StephenDonohoe(3) 11 73+
(W M Brisbourne) *dropped out in rr: rdn 3f out: hdwy in ins over 1f out: styd on but no ch w first 2* **11/2**[3]

2632 **4** 1½ **Sgt Schultz (IRE)**[59] 4972 3-8-13 **70**.............................. MartinDwyer 9 74
(J S Moore) *mid-div: edgd lft after 3f: rdn 3f out: styd on one pce* **7/2**[2]

-005 **5** nk **Entranced**[117] 3169 3-8-8 **65**.. TomEaves 4 68
(Miss J A Camacho) *chsd ldrs: rdn 3f out: rdn and hung lft over 1f out: sn wknd* **14/1**

0350 **6** 3 **Ransom Strip (USA)**[22] 5815 3-8-8 **65** ow1............. RobbieFitzpatrick 7 64
(M Brittain) *trckd ldrs: rdn 3f out: wknd 2f out* **16/1**

5615 **7** 7 **Ballybeg (IRE)**[18] 5911 3-8-8 **68**................................ JamesDoyle(3) 3 55
(R J Price) *in tch: rdn over 4f out: sn btn* **10/1**

6016 **8** 4 **Odessa Star (USA)**[84] 4181 3-9-1 **72**.............................. OscarUrbina 10 53
(J G Portman) *bhd: rdn 4f out: nvr on terms* **14/1**

3610 **9** 5 **Kentucky Warbler (IRE)**[32] 5628 3-8-12 **69**.................. SteveDrowne 8 42
(H Morrison) *mid-div: rdn and wknd over 2f out* **9/1**

5605 **10** 10 **Sea Of Calm (USA)**[14] 5992 3-8-4 **61** oh2......................... PaulHanagan 5 18
(E A L Dunlop) *in tch whn bdly hmpd after 3f: sn bhd and c home in own time* **12/1**

2m 38.84s (-3.58) **Going Correction** -0.275s/f (Stan) **10** Ran SP% **126.5**
Speed ratings (Par 101):100,99,97,96,96 94,89,87,83,77
CSF £23.34 CT £93.36 TOTE £8.40: £2.90, £2.50, £2.90; EX 26.10 Trifecta £61.00 Pool £223.52 - 2.60 winning units. Place 6 £163.89, Place 5 £86.74. .
Owner Paul & Jenny Green **Bred** P C Green **Trained** Manton, Wilts

FOCUS
A modest handicap but notable for a successful gamble on the unexposed winner. The form looks ordinary but sound rated through the third and fourth.
T/Jkpt: Not won. T/Plt: £109.90 to a £1 stake. Pool: £65,953.10. 438.00 winning tickets. T/Qpdt: £25.10 to a £1 stake. Pool: £4,894.90. 143.80 winning tickets. JS

6245 - 6247a (Foreign Racing) - See Raceform Interactive

5160 BREMEN
Sunday, October 29

OFFICIAL GOING: Good

6248a GROSSER PREIS DER FREIEN HANSESTADT BREMEN (GROUP 3) 1m
2:25 (2:22) 3-Y-0+ **£22,069** (£6,897; £3,448; £2,069)

RPR

1 **Lucidor (GER)**[21] 5856 3-8-9 .... EPedroza 8 104
(Frau E Mader, Germany) *s.i.s, last to halfway, 7th str and came widest, headway 2f out, hung right under pressure, led 1f out, ridden out* **29/10**[2]

2 1½ **Madresal (GER)**[22] 5816 7-8-13 .... WMongil 7 102
(P Schiergen, Germany) *held up, 6th straight, headway over 1f out, stayed on at one pace for 2nd* **32/10**[3]

3 2 **Apollo Star (GER)**[21] 5856 4-8-13 .... ABoschert 2 98
(Mario Hofer, Germany) *led to 1f out, one pace* **81/10**

4 2½ **Idealist (GER)**[161] 1869 4-9-3 .... THellier 5 97
(P Schiergen, Germany) *mid-division, 5th straight, reached 3rd approaching final furlong, one pace* **9/10**[1]

5 7 **Mharadono (GER)**[21] 5856 3-8-11 .... WPanov 1 80
(P Hirschberger, Germany) *disputed 2nd to half-way, 3rd straight, ridden over 2f out, soon weakened* **98/10**

6 ½ **Amy Storm (GER)**[155] 2059 3-8-4 .... ABest 4 72
(P Vovcenko, Germany) *raced in 4th to straight, weakened well over 1f out* **24/1**

7 10 **Blueberry Forest (IRE)**[21] 5856 8-8-13 .... EFrank 3 58
(P Hirschberger, Germany) *held up in rear, last straight, never a factor* **24/1**

8 shd **First Royal (GER)** 3-8-4 .... JBojko 6 52
(P Vovcenko, Germany) *disputed 2nd to half-way, 2nd straight, weakened well over 1f out* **34/1**

1m 37.39s
WFA 3 from 4yo+ 3lb **8** Ran SP% **133.2**
(Including 10 Euros stake): WIN 39; PL 13, 13, 16; SF 160.
Owner Stall Capricorn **Bred** Graf & Grafin Von Stauffenberg **Trained** Germany

6171 SAINT-CLOUD (L-H)
Sunday, October 29

OFFICIAL GOING: Good to soft

6249a CRITERIUM INTERNATIONAL (GROUP 1) (C&F) 1m
2:20 (2:22) 2-Y-0 **£98,517** (£39,414; £19,707; £9,845; £4,931)

RPR

1 **Mount Nelson**[7] 6116 2-9-0 .... JAHeffernan 9 115
(A P O'Brien, Ire) *hld up in mid-div, 7th str, pushed along & ran on over 2f out, rdn to chal 1 1/2f out, led app fnl f, hard rdn to line* **109/10**

2 hd **Spirit One (FR)**[43] 5399 2-9-0 .... DBoeuf 6 115
(P Demercastel, France) *led, hdd briefly 2f out, sn pushed along and ran on, hdd appr fnl f, rdn and kept on to press winner to line* **3/5**[1]

3 1½ **Yellowstone (IRE)**[64] 4825 2-9-0 .... CO'Donoghue 10 111
(A P O'Brien, Ire) *held up, 8th and pushed along straight, ridden and stayed on down outside 1 1/2f out, took 3rd final strides* **109/10**

4 ¾ **Friston Forest (IRE)**[33] 2-9-0 .... CSoumillon 3 109
(A Fabre, France) *held up, disputing last straight, ridden and ran on on inside 2f out, stayed on steadily and took 4th on line* **17/2**[3]

5 shd **Rallying Cry (USA)**[15] 5965 2-9-0 .... OPeslier 2 109
(J H M Gosden) *mid-div, hdwy on ins 3f out, 2nd str, led briefly 2f out, rdn over 1 1/2f out, kept on under pressure, no ex cl home* **19/1**

6 snk **Makaan (USA)**[23] 5801 2-9-0 .... DBonilla 7 109
(F Head, France) *prominent early, disputing 5th straight, ridden 2f out, ran on down outside, narrowly missed 4th* **82/10**[2]

7 3/4 **Holocene (USA)**[23] [5801] 2-9-0 .... C-PLemaire 1 107
(P Bary, France) *mid-division, disputing 5th straight, one pace final 1 1/2f* **9/1**

8 3/4 **Vital Equine (IRE)**[15] [5965] 2-9-0 .... RichardMullen 5 105
(E J O'Neill) *in touch, disputing 3rd straight, ridden 2f out, stayed on til no extra from over 1f out* **9/1**

9 4 **Beltanus (GER)**[49] [5218] 2-9-0 .... SPasquier 11 96
(Tim Gibson, Germany) *towards rear, disputing last straight, outpaced 2f out, never dangerous* **30/1**

10 3 **Teslin (IRE)**[8] [6104] 2-9-0 .... KDarley 4 89
(M Johnston) *prominent, disputing 3rd and pushed along straight, under pressure 2f out, weakened* **56/1**

1m 41.3s **Going Correction** -0.55s/f (Hard) **10** Ran SP% **130.7**
Speed ratings: 109,108,107,106,106 106,105,104,100,97
PARI-MUTUEL: WIN 11.90 (coupled with Yellowstone); PL 3.40, 1.20,1.80; DF 11.00.
Owner Derrick Smith **Bred** Cliveden Stud Ltd **Trained** Ballydoyle, Co Tipperary

NOTEBOOK
Mount Nelson, who was turned out in great shape, has gone from the winner of a maiden to a Group 1 hero in a period of just one week. He looked magnificent in the paddock and did nothing wrong in the race. The colt was also given a fine professional ride by his jockey and is now in the betting for next year's Vodafone Derby. Settled in fifth position early on, he made his challenge early in the straight and led at the furlong marker. For such an inexperienced individual he showed great courage in the latter stages to hold off the renewed challenge of the runner-up. He has boundless scope for improvement and will certainly be a classic prospect in 2007.
Spirit One(FR) had the whole of France behind him following two spectacular performances. At one time he had been 1-10 for a win with the Pari Mutuel but he did ease a little before the off. Taken directly into the lead, he set a sensible pace and things appeared to be going according to plan until the winner came alongside at the furlong marker. He seemed to hesitate a little before running on again at the end. Next season he will go for races between ten and 12 furlongs, and his jockey felt the colt was surprised at being put under pressure for the first time in his career.
Yellowstone(IRE), a stablemate of the winner, also put up a great performance. Towards the tail of the field early on, he was brought with a progressive run up the centre of the track and was putting in his best effort at the end. Certainly another with a bright future, he looks certain to stay a longer trip.
Friston Forest(IRE), who put up a respectable performance, was one of the backmarkers soon after the start. Gradually moved up to be well placed in the straight, he made his effort up the far rail and then ran on at the end after looking beaten a furlong and a half out. He will improve and should have no problems staying further than a mile.
Rallying Cry(USA) still had plenty to do rounding the final turn, but he ran on extremely well on the far rail throughout the straight and only missed fourth place by a narrow margin. He should turn into a decent three-year-old.
Vital Equine(IRE) looked very one-paced in the final stages having been beautifully placed to make his challenge in the straight. This performance was below his best as he should have finished close to the fifth placed horse on previous form.
Teslin(IRE) was given every possible chance, but this was a disappointing effort as the colt finally finished last and beaten over ten lengths. He was always well up but was in trouble soon after entering the straight and this could not have been his true form.

6250a PRIX PERTH (GROUP 3) 1m
2:50 (2:53) 3-Y-O+ **£27,586** (£11,034; £8,276; £5,517; £2,759)

RPR

1 **Passager (FR)**[14] [6001] 3-8-11 .... DBoeuf 5 113
(Mme C Head-Maarek, France) *close up, 3rd straight, ran on to lead 1 1/2f* **out, ridden over 1f out, ran on under pressure to hold challenge of 2nd** **36/10**[2]

2 1/2 **Gwenseb (FR)**[29] [5701] 3-8-8 .... OPeslier 4 109
(C Laffon-Parias, France) *in tch, disp 4th str, rdn to chal over 1f out, ev ch ins fnl f, ran on but just held by winner* **36/10**[2]

3 2 1/2 **Svedov (FR)**[29] [5703] 5-9-4 .... SPasquier 12 111
(E Lellouche, France) *mid-division, pushed along and close 7th straight, ridden and ran on 1 1/2f out, took 3rd 100 yards out* **13/1**

4 hd **Krataios (FR)**[140] [2490] 6-9-6 .... MBlancpain 10 113
(C Laffon-Parias, France) *prominent, 2nd straight, ridden and every chance 1 1/2f out, stayed on at one pace* **78/10**

5 nk **Daltaya (FR)**[43] [5400] 3-8-11 .... CSoumillon 7 106
(A De Royer-Dupre, France) *held up, ridden and finished well final furlong, nearest at finish* **69/10**

6 1/2 **Gharir (IRE)**[22] [5816] 4-9-1 .... FSpanu 1 106
(J E Hammond, France) *mid-division, disputing 4th straight, ridden and stayed on final furlong, never able to challenge leaders* **3/1**[1]

7 1 1/2 **Hello Sunday (FR)**[29] [5703] 3-9-1 .... C-PLemaire 9 106
(Mme C Head-Maarek, France) *mid-division, effort to chase leaders 1 1/2f out, one pace final 150 yards* **57/10**[3]

8 1 **Atlantic Air (FR)**[18] [5913] 4-9-4 .... TThulliez 13 104
(Y De Nicolay, France) *mid-division, 6th and pushed along straight, ridden over 1f out, never able to challenge* **19/1**

9 hd **Here She Comes (FR)**[22] 4-8-11 .... SFargeat 8 97
(Mme C Martens, France) *held up, never a factor* **37/1**

10 1 **Together (FR)**[63] [4862] 6-8-11 .... (b) SMaillot 11 95
(Mme C Vergne, France) *held up, effort 2f out, stayed on but never dangerous* **54/1**

11 hd **Boris De Deauville (IRE)**[29] [5704] 3-9-1 .... YBarberot 3 101
(S Wattel, France) *held up on inside, never a factor* **8/1**

12 3 **Kalken (FR)**[29] 3-8-11 .... TJarnet 6 91
(L Planard, France) *led to 1 1/2f out, soon ridden and weakened* **10/1**

1m 41.6s **Going Correction** -0.55s/f (Hard)
WFA 3 from 4yo+ 3lb **12** Ran SP% **144.2**
Speed ratings: 107,106,104,103,103 103,101,100,100,99 99,96
PARI-MUTUEL: WIN 4.60 (coupled with Gwenseb); PL 3.30, 2.70, 4.00; DF 28.60.
Owner Alec Head **Bred** Alec Head & Wertheimer Et Frere **Trained** Chantilly, France

NOTEBOOK
Passager(FR) never puts in a poor performance and has never been out of the first three in his last six outings. He was given an excellent ride and was always handy before taking the advantage at the furlong marker. He was then all out to hold off the runner-up, which he did in a game fashion. He had a setback in the summer so was a fresh horse for this race. Definitely going the right way, he looks sure to have a successful season in events over a mile next year.
Gwenseb(FR) as usual, was not interested in the first part of the race. She bowled along at the tail of the field before switching on halfway up the straight. Her usual late turn of foot nearly took her into the lead but she could never get past the game winner.
Svedov(FR) ran a sound race on his favourite track but he still had quite a lot to do at the entrance to the straight, where he made his move up the centre. He stayed on but could not quicken.
Krataios(FR), who had previously won a Group 2 race over the course and distance, had been off the track since mid-June so this was a fine effort. Her was dropped in behind the leader early on and led at the beginning of the straight, before staying on one-paced. This race will have brought him on considerably and connections are hoping for an invitation to run in the Hong Kong Mile.

[6002]SAN SIRO (R-H)
Sunday, October 29

OFFICIAL GOING: Heavy

6251a PREMIO GIOVANNI FALCK (LISTED RACE) (F&M) 1m 4f
2:50 (2:55) 3-Y-O+ **£21,724** (£9,559; £5,214; £2,607)

RPR

1 **Green Room (FR)**[26] [5758] 3-8-9 .... RyanMoore 6 109
(J L Dunlop) *always close up, 3rd straight, led inside final f, ran on* **41/20**[2]

2 1 3/4 **Penelope Star (GER)**[35] [5560] 3-8-9 .... MDemuro 1 106
(H Blume, Germany) **39/20**[1]

3 3 1/4 **Soul Of Magic (IRE)**[155] 7-9-3 .... TCastanheira 4 102
(Karin Suter, Switzerland) **39/10**[3]

4 5 **Tech Engine (GER)**[51] [5160] 3-8-9 .... AStarke 3 94
(P Schiergen, Germany) **121/10**

5 5 **Miola (IRE)** 3-8-9 .... MEsposito 9 86
(V Caruso, Italy) **20/1**

6 1/2 **Chiswick Park** 3-8-9 .... SMulas 8 85
(R Brogi, Italy) **83/1**

7 7 **Wickwing**[133] [2694] 3-8-9 .... EBotti 5 75
(A & G Botti, Italy) **52/10**

8 3 **Dyaphora (IRE)** 3-8-9 .... (b) PConvertino 10 70
(A Mataresi, Italy) **85/1**

9 15 **Riabouchinska**[155] [2043] 3-8-9 .... MMonteriso 2 48
(E Borromeo, Italy) **77/10**

10 8 **Antarctica (GER)** 4-9-1 .... KKerekes 11 35
(M Weber, Germany) **22/1**

11 1 1/2 **Implicita (IRE)**[421] 3-8-9 .... DVargiu 7 34
(B Grizzetti, Italy) **25/1**

2m 35.4s
WFA 3 from 4yo+ 7lb **11** Ran SP% **137.7**
(including one euro stakes): WIN 3.05; PL 1.33, 1.31, 1.54; DF 3.41.
Owner Nigel & Carolyn Elwes **Bred** Aylesfield Farms Stud Ltd **Trained** Arundel, W Sussex

NOTEBOOK
Green Room(FR) was always covering the leader in the straight and nailed her inside the final furlong. She ran on strongly and her trainer believes she will continue to improve next year.

6252a PREMIO CHIUSURA (GROUP 3) 7f
3:20 (3:33) 2-Y-O+ **£30,697** (£14,363; £8,086; £4,043)

RPR

1 **Breath Of Love (USA)**[75] [4463] 4-9-5 .... IMendizabal 8 109
(J-C Rouget, France) *mid-division, headway half-way, led 1 1/2f out, driven out* **54/10**[3]

2 hd **Ricine (IRE)**[63] [4860] 4-9-5 .... F-XBertras 6 108
(F Rohaut, France) *always promt, pressed ldr from halfway, led 2f out to 1 1/2f out, ev ch fnl f, unable to quicken close home* **87/10**

3 6 1/2 **Amante Latino**[14] [6003] 2-8-1 .... MEsposito 7 95
(V Caruso, Italy) *chased leaders, kept on one pace final 2f* **9/2**[2]

4 3 1/2 **Glad To Be Fast (IRE)**[21] [5856] 6-9-9 .... (b) AStarke 5 86
(Mario Hofer, Germany) *mid-division, never near to challenge* **76/10**

5 4 **Jacky Jack (ITY)** 4-9-9 .... SMulas 1 76
(P Paciello, Italy) *last but one to half-way, some progress final 2f, never nearer* **41/1**

6 2 1/2 **Tuxedomoon (GER)** 5-9-9 .... MMonteriso 3 69
(Frau Jutta Mayer, Germany) *in touch til weakening from 2f out* **50/1**

7 3 **Musa Golosa**[14] [6002] 3-9-4 .... DVargiu 9 58
(B Grizzetti, Italy) *in touch on outside to over 2f out* **74/10**

8 1/2 **Arrears (USA)**[721] [6584] 6-9-9 .... LManiezzi 2 60
(R Menichetti, Italy) *always towards rear, eased in final f* **54/1**

9 3 **New Seeker**[29] [5682] 6-9-9 .... (b) RyanMoore 10 52
(P F I Cole) *led to 2f out* **11/10**[1]

10 3 **Arc Bleu (GER)**[490] 5-9-9 .... EBotti 12 44
(Frau Jutta Mayer, Germany) *prominent to over 2f out* **63/1**

11 1 **Villa Sciarra (IRE)**[40] [5473] 3-9-8 .... MDemuro 4 43
(A Peraino, Italy) *always behind* **83/10**

12 1/2 **Mister Pennekamp (IRE)** 4-9-9 .... GBietolini 11 41
(G Colella, Italy) *prominent to half-way* **25/1**

1m 25.5s
WFA 2 from 3yo 22lb 3 from 4yo+ 2lb **12** Ran SP% **137.6**
WIN 6.37; PL 2.30, 2.77, 2.06; DF 22.41.
Owner N Radwan **Bred** Janus Bloodstock Inc **Trained** Pau, France

NOTEBOOK
Breath Of Love(USA) was contesting a Group race for the first time. It looked as if he might win decisively when he took it up but he was forced to fight hard. He had scored three times over one mile last year but his only previous success this term was over seven furlongs.
Ricine(IRE) was no match for Indian Maiden and company in the Prix de Meautry over six furlongs. She had previously won the Group 3 Polar Cup over 6f 165y in Norway and saw out this seven furlongs in the gamest possible style.
Amante Latino was beaten slightly further than he had been when fifth to Kirklees in the Gran Criterium. He was returning from a three months break there and this race may have come a little too soon. He had no chance with the first two in the last 300yds but kept on steadily to the end.
New Seeker was never able to establish a clear lead and dropped out once headed. His rider blamed the heavy going.

[5985]SANTA ANITA (R-H)
Sunday, October 29

OFFICIAL GOING: Firm

6253a LAS PALMAS H'CAP (GRADE 2) (F&M) 1m (T)
12:07 (12:08) 3-Y-O+ **£52,326** (£17,442; £10,465; £5,233; £1,744)

RPR

1 **Beautyandthebeast**[186] 4-8-5 .... CNakatani 2 108
(N Drysdale, U.S.A) **2/1**[1]

2 hd **Clinet (IRE)**[241] [564] 4-8-3 .... ASolis 8 106
(J W Hills) *hld up on ins, 6th towards outside straight, ran on strongly to challenge, just held by winner near finish* **27/10**[2]

3 ½ **Quemar (NZ)** 4-7-13 .... VEspinoza 5 101
(Roger Stein, U.S.A) **235/10**
4 1 ¾ **Movie Star (BRZ)**[294] 5-8-2 .... PValenzuela 1 100
(R J Frankel, U.S.A) **78/10**
5 ½ **Strong Faith (USA)**[32] 5-8-3 .... NArroyoJr 6 100
(Darrell Vienna, U.S.A) **30/1**
6 nk **Berbatim (USA)**[57] 4-8-3 ....(b) AGryder 7 99
(Richard E Mandella, U.S.A) **57/10**
7 3 ½ **Singalong**[29] 4-8-3 .... DFlores 4 92
(P Gallagher, U.S.A) **52/10**[3]
8 2 ½ **Sandra's Rose (USA)**[32] 4-8-3 .... MPedroza 3 87
(M Machowsky, U.S.A) **9/1**

1m 33.33s **8** Ran SP% **120.1**
PARI-MUTUEL (Including $2 stake): WIN 6.00; PL (1-2) 3.40, 4.00;SHOW (1-2-3) 3.00, 3.60, 5.60; SF 25.00.
Owner Abergwaun Farms **Bred** Abergwaun Farm **Trained** USA

NOTEBOOK
Clinet(IRE), a progressive filly last season and earlier this year but off the track since March when she was running in Dubai, made a promising debut in the US, only narrowly being denied in this Grade 2 contest. She should be capable of winning in this company with this experience under her belt.

6239 WOLVERHAMPTON (A.W) (L-H)
Monday, October 30

OFFICIAL GOING: Standard to fast
Wind: fresh, half behind

6254 ENJOY EXECUTIVE HOSPITALITY AT WOLVERHAMPTON MAIDEN STKS (DIV I) 7f 32y(P)
1:00 (1:02) (Class 5) 2-Y-O **£2,590** (£770; £385; £192) **Stalls** High

Form RPR
1 **Phoenix Tower (USA)** 2-9-3 .... RichardHughes 1 80+
(H R A Cecil) *chsd ldrs: wnt 2nd over 2f out: gng wl whn ld appr fnl f but jinked sharply lft: r.o* **5/1**[3]
2 1 ½ **Calabash Cove (USA)** 2-9-3 .... LDettori 11 76
(Saeed Bin Suroor) *mid-div: rdn 3f out: hdwy on outside 2f out: edgd lft bef wnt 2nd ins fnl f* **2/1**[1]
3 1 **Gyroscope** 2-8-12 .... RyanMoore 2 69
(Sir Michael Stoute) *mid-div: rdn 1/2-way: styd on fr over 1f out: nvr nrr* **3/1**[2]
434 4 ½ **History Boy**[19] [5906] 2-9-3 .... LPKeniry 12 73+
(D J Coakley) *towards rr tl hdwy over 1f out: styd on but nvr on terms* **11/2**
5 1 ¼ **Caernarvon (IRE)** 2-9-3 .... MatthewHenry 4 69
(M A Jarvis) *chsd ldr to over 2f out: one pce appr fnl f* **28/1**
0 6 hd **Tivers Song (USA)**[20] [5890] 2-9-3 .... JimCrowley 6 69
(Mrs A J Perrett) *mid-div: rdn 1/2-way: styd on fnl f: nvr nrr* **66/1**
7 1 ¾ **Barkass (UAE)** 2-9-3 .... MartinDwyer 5 65+
(M P Tregoning) *chsd ldrs tl rdn and wknd over 1f out* **16/1**
8 2 ½ **Premio Loco (USA)** 2-9-3 .... GeorgeBaker 7 58
(C F Wall) *slowly away: a towards rr* **66/1**
06 9 2 **Anatolian Prince**[32] [5640] 2-9-0 .... StephenDonohoe(3) 8 53
(J M P Eustace) *mid-div: rdn 3f out: sn wknd* **50/1**
0 10 7 **Hora**[9] [6098] 2-8-12 .... SebSanders 9 31
(Sir Mark Prescott) *a in rr* **80/1**
11 ½ **Whos Counting** 2-8-12 .... SteveDrowne 10 30
(R J Hodges) *a bhd on outside* **100/1**
3020 B **Elizabeth Street (USA)**[52] [5157] 2-8-12 77 .... NelsonDeSouza 3 71+
(P F I Cole) *led tl hdd appr fnl f: sn b.d by wnr* **9/1**

1m 29.17s (-1.23) **Going Correction** -0.30s/f (Stan) **12** Ran SP% **116.9**
Speed ratings (Par 95):95,93,92,91,90 89,87,85,82,74 74,—
CSF £14.87 TOTE £6.70: £2.50, £1.30, £1.30; EX 27.60 Trifecta £102.80 Pool £276.56 - 1.91 winning units.
Owner K Abdulla **Bred** Juddmonte Farms Inc **Trained** Newmarket, Suffolk

FOCUS
This looked a fair maiden for the track with several top yards represented and the winning time was fractionally faster than the second division. Few ever got into it and the winner could be a useful sort, but the race was marred by the incident over a furlong from home when the winner jinked left, sending Elizabeth Street crashing through the inside rail.

NOTEBOOK
Phoenix Tower(USA) ◆, a half-brother to two winners out of a winning half-sister to Day Flight, travelled like a dream and seemed to just have gained the upper hand when he lost concentration, jinked left, and sent Elizabeth Street crashing through the inside rail. He was the best horse in the race and his antics were almost certainly caused by greenness, so he should be capable of progressing and winning something a bit better. (op 6-1 tchd 7-1)
Calabash Cove(USA), whose dam is a half-sister to three winners over middle distances, took a long time to get into gear and, though he stayed on to eventually finish second, he was never a threat to the winner. He should improve as he goes up in trip. (tchd 15-8 and 9-4 in places)
Gyroscope ◆, a 180,000euros half-sister to Arakan, was noted doing some good late work down the centre of the track. She should come on for the experience and her pedigree suggests a mile will be as far as she wants to go. (op 11-4)
History Boy, one of the most experienced in the field, kept on down the outside in the home straight but could not get on terms with the three newcomers. Although this was his fourth outing, one of his previous starts was in Germany and it is only now that he qualifies for a handicap mark. That may be his best option now as he will avoid the progressive types he met here. (op 7-1)
Caernarvon(IRE), a full-brother to a winner over 12 furlongs and a half-brother to five other winners, showed up prominently for a long way before fading. He seems to have some ability and should come on for the run. (op 25-1)
Elizabeth Street(USA), the most experienced in the field, tried to make it count under a positive ride and had most of her rivals in trouble turning in. The winner was the exception though, and he had just got the better of her when he jinked left into her, sending her though the inside rail and her rider crashing to the ground.

6255 WOLVERHAMPTON-RACECOURSE.CO.UK MEDIAN AUCTION MAIDEN STKS 5f 20y(P)
1:30 (1:30) (Class 5) 2-Y-O **£3,238** (£963; £481; £240) **Stalls** Low

Form RPR
0325 1 **Bookiesindex Boy**[28] [5735] 2-9-3 73 ....(b) RyanMoore 10 73
(J R Jenkins) *w ldr: led over 2f out: hung bdly rt fr over 1f out* **8/1**
2422 2 nk **Mazin Lady**[27] [5753] 2-8-12 68 .... TomEaves 8 67
(Miss J A Camacho) *s.i.s: swtchd lft to ins: hdwy over 1f out and r.o to go 2nd ins fnl f* **7/1**
643 3 1 ½ **Money For Fun**[13] [6024] 2-8-12 70 .... LPKeniry 3 62
(J S Moore) *chsd ldrs: rdn and nt qckn ins fnl f* **14/1**
3036 4 ¾ **Feelin Foxy**[72] [4594] 2-8-9 76 .... PatrickMathers(3) 2 59
(D Shaw) *s.i.s: sn mid-div: hdwy wl over 1f out: no ex ins fnl f* **11/2**[3]
554 5 ½ **Duskiness (FR)**[9] [6099] 2-8-12 70 .... PatCosgrave 5 57
(M J Wallace) *led tl hdd over 2f out: rdn and nt qckn ins fnl f* **4/1**[2]
6 1 **Piccolo Diamante (USA)** 2-9-3 .... FrancisNorton 1 58
(T J Pitt) *slowly away: rdn over 2f out: hdwy over 1f out: nvr nrr* **13/2**
005 7 nk **Darling Belinda**[21] [5867] 2-8-12 .... FergusSweeney 11 52
(D K Ivory) *chsd ldrs: rdn and fdd ins fnl f* **20/1**
00 8 shd **Sun Of The Sea**[5] [6175] 2-9-0 .... JamesDoyle(3) 7 57
(N P Littmoden) *slowly away: mde sme late hdwy* **40/1**
2026 9 1 ½ **Violet's Pride**[12] [6056] 2-8-7 59 .... DuranFentiman(5) 4 47+
(S Parr) *mid-div: wknd wl over 1f out* **33/1**
0022 10 1 ¾ **Stargazy**[97] [3822] 2-9-3 76 .... SteveDrowne 12 45+
(R Charlton) *racd wd: no ch fnl 2f* **7/2**[1]
11 5 **Foxy Music** 2-9-3 .... RobbieFitzpatrick 13 27
(Peter Grayson) *racd wd: a bhd* **50/1**
5203 12 nk **Fly Time**[30] [5687] 2-8-5 53 .... MCGeran(7) 6 21
(Mrs L Williamson) *chsd ldrs tl wknd 1/2-way* **40/1**
0 13 hd **La Cuvee**[34] [5586] 2-8-12 .... SebSanders 9 20
(R M Beckett) *a bhd* **28/1**

62.01 secs (-0.81) **Going Correction** -0.30s/f (Stan) **13** Ran SP% **119.2**
Speed ratings (Par 95):94,93,91,89,89 87,87,86,84,81 73,73,72
CSF £58.52 TOTE £10.70: £3.40, £2.10, £6.50; EX 63.30 TRIFECTA Not won..
Owner Bookmakers Index Ltd **Bred** D R Tucker **Trained** Royston, Herts

FOCUS
A modest maiden with several exposed sorts in opposition. The front pair had already raced 15 times previously between them without success, so the form looks ordinary rated through the runner-up.

NOTEBOOK
Bookiesindex Boy, who has plenty of experience under his belt including on this track, was not best drawn but he broke well enough in order to move across and take a handy position. He looked the winner turning for home, but nearly threw it away by hanging violently over to the stands' rail despite the best efforts of his rider to keep him straight. He is hardly one to place maximum faith in when switched to handicaps. (op 9-1)
Mazin Lady, on sand for the first time, was again doing her best work late but was just unable to take advantage of the winner's antics. This was the fourth time in her last five outings that she has finished second, but she seems genuine enough and a longer trip is all she needs. (op 13-2 tchd 15-2)
Money For Fun was never far away and kept on, but was another who seems to find this trip a bit too short. She is less exposed than those that finished around her, so may find a modest race. (op 12-1)
Feelin Foxy, who has faced some stiff tasks in Pattern company in most of her races to date, had been absent for over two months but did not progress for this switch to sand. She will remain very hard to place and as she finished behind three lower-rated rivals here, handicaps do not look an attractive option at this stage either. (op 9-2)
Duskiness(FR), dropping back from seven furlongs, was given a positive ride but was exposed for lack of speed in the home straight. (op 9-2 tchd 7-2)
Stargazy did not have a great draw, but still should have done much better and perhaps this surface was not to his liking. (op 13-2)

6256 WORLD BET EXCHANGE WBX.COM H'CAP 1m 5f 194y(P)
2:00 (2:00) (Class 6) (0-65,65) 3-Y-O+ **£2,730** (£806; £403) **Stalls** Low

Form RPR
0006 1 **Zaville**[16] [5971] 4-8-9 53 ....(p) JamesO'Reilly(7) 9 66
(J O'Reilly) *mde all: styd on wl fr over 1f out* **25/1**
1440 2 3 ½ **Sovereign Spirit (IRE)**[46] [5324] 4-10-0 65 .... AdamKirby 1 73
(W R Swinburn) *hld up in tch: swtchd rt over 3f out: wnt 2nd 2f out: edgd lft and no imp appr fnl f* **4/1**[1]
0366 3 3 **Eastborough (IRE)**[19] [5910] 7-9-10 61 .... EddieAhern 2 65
(J R Jenkins) *slowly away: hld up in rr: styd on past btn horses fnl 2f: nvr nr to chal* **10/1**
0 4 1 ½ **Phoenix Hill (IRE)**[21] [5875] 4-9-9 60 .... SteveDrowne 8 62
(D R Gandolfo) *mid-div whn hmpd over 3f out: styd on ins fnl 2f* **14/1**
6231 5 1 **Kyle Of Lochalsh**[11] [4478] 6-9-4 55 .... DanielTudhope 3 55
(J S Goldie) *in tch but no hdwy fr over 2f out* **10/1**
4403 6 hd **Easibet Dot Net**[16] [5971] 6-9-5 56 ....(p) TomEaves 4 56
(I Semple) *trckd ldr: rdn 4f out: outpcd fnl 2f* **11/2**[2]
6001 7 ½ **Kirkhammerton (IRE)**[18] [5925] 4-9-2 56 ....(b) StephenDonohoe(3) 10 55
(A J McCabe) *hld up: rdn 3f out: no imp after* **8/1**
0500 8 ¾ **Wester Lodge (IRE)**[10] [6070] 4-9-11 62 .... MickyFenton 6 60
(J M P Eustace) *a towards rr* **22/1**
3045 9 4 **Gaze**[21] [5875] 3-9-5 65 .... RyanMoore 13 58
(W Jarvis) *a towards rr* **7/1**[3]
0000 10 ¾ **Beaufort**[19] [5910] 4-9-2 53 .... FergusSweeney 7 45
(D K Ivory) *a bhd* **66/1**
1523 11 6 **Bienheureux**[21] [5875] 5-9-13 64 ....(t) SebSanders 11 47
(Miss Gay Kelleway) *mid-div: rdn and hdwy on outside over 2f out: wknd qckly over 2f out* **11/2**[2]
2100 12 3 **Arch Folly**[32] [5069] 4-8-13 55 .... LiamJones(5) 5 34
(R J Price) *mid-div: rdn 5f out: sn btn* **33/1**
0600 13 21 **Mister Completely (IRE)**[13] [6037] 5-8-10 50 .... JamesDoyle(3) 12 —
(Ms J S Doyle) *chsd ldrs tl wknd qckly 4f out* **12/1**

3m 2.58s (-4.79) **Going Correction** -0.30s/f (Stan)
WFA 3 from 4yo+ 9lb **13** Ran SP% **119.5**
Speed ratings (Par 101):101,99,97,96,95 95,95,95,92,92 88,87,75
CSF £119.69 CT £1102.64 TOTE £28.60: £9.40, £2.60, £3.10; EX 192.80 TRIFECTA Not won..
Owner T Marshall **Bred** K G Powter **Trained** Doncaster, S Yorks
■ Stewards' Enquiry : Adam Kirby two-day ban: careless riding (Nov 10-11)

FOCUS
Just a modest gallop for the majority of this staying event and it came down to a test of speed from the home bend. As a result the guaranteed stayers were not suited by the way the race was run and the form is best rated through the second.
Kirkhammerton(IRE) Official explanation: vet said gelding returned lame on left-fore
Wester Lodge(IRE) Official explanation: jockey said gelding was denied a clear run
Mister Completely(IRE) Official explanation: trainer said gelding finished lame

6257 ENJOY EXECUTIVE HOSPITALITY AT WOLVERHAMPTON MAIDEN STKS (DIV II) 7f 32y(P)
2:30 (2:31) (Class 5) 2-Y-O **£2,590** (£770; £385; £192) **Stalls** High

Form RPR
6 1 **Wait For The Light**[20] [5886] 2-9-3 .... RyanMoore 9 77
(E A L Dunlop) *mid-div: rdn and hdwy wl over 1f out: led wl ins fnl f: hld on* **14/1**
506 2 nk **Royal Rationale (IRE)**[31] [5648] 2-9-3 .... EddieAhern 4 76
(W J Haggas) *chsd ldrs: rdn over 2f out: led ins fnl f: edgd rt and sn hdd* **13/2**[2]

5 **3** *1 1/2* **Not Another Cat (USA)**[61] 4934 2-9-3 .... PatCosgrave 8 72
(K R Burke) *broke wl: sn hdd: led tl hdd over 2f out: rdn and hdd ins fnl f: no ex nr fin* **9/1**
42 **4** *nk* **Strikeen (IRE)**[17] 5947 2-9-3 .... IanMongan 5 71
(T G Mills) *sn led: hdd over 2f out: rdn and nt qckn ins fnl f* **5/6**[1]
30 **5** *3 1/2* **Bidable**[35] 5563 2-8-12 .... FergusSweeney 2 58
(B Palling) *mid-div: rdn 3f out: sme hdwy 2f out but nvr nr to chal* **25/1**
3330 **6** *1 1/2* **Howards Tipple**[21] 5860 2-9-3 72 .... TomEaves 12 59
(I Semple) *chsd ldrs on outside tl wknd over 1f out* **14/1**
0 **7** *1 3/4* **Royal Guest**[38] 5508 2-9-3 .... TonyCulhane 1 54+
(M R Channon) *mid-div: rdn 1/2-way: sn btn* **8/1**[3]
2466 **8** *1/2* **Montemayorprincess (IRE)**[91] 3997 2-8-12 58 .... FrancisNorton 10 48
(D Haydn Jones) *chsd ldrs tl rdn and wknd wl over 1f out* **25/1**
9 *3* **Me No Puppet** 2-8-12 .... DavidAllan 3 41
(E J Alston) *slowly away: a bhd* **100/1**
0005 **10** *6* **Wilde Jasmine (IRE)**[60] 4950 2-8-12 40 .... PhillipMakin 6 26
(J R Weymes) *slowly away: a in rr* **100/1**
6 **11** *6* **Alleviate (IRE)**[9] 6099 2-8-12 .... SebSanders 11 11
(Sir Mark Prescott) *s.i.s: rdn 1/2-way: a bhd* **50/1**
12 *1/2* **Cnoc Moy (IRE)** 2-9-3 .... GeorgeBaker 7 14
(C F Wall) *a bhd* **66/1**

1m 29.21s (-1.19) **Going Correction** -0.30s/f (Stan) **50** Ran SP% **115.5**
Speed ratings (Par 95):94,93,91,91,87 85,83,83,79,73 66,65
CSF £95.44 TOTE £17.70: £2.70, £1.60, £2.80; EX 138.40 TRIFECTA Not won..
Owner Khalifa Sultan **Bred** Pegasus Racing **Trained** Newmarket, Suffolk

FOCUS
Fewer big stables represented than in the first division, but the winning time was only fractionally slower and the front four pulled nicely clear. The form looks reasonable with the fourth the best guide.

NOTEBOOK
Wait For The Light, down a furlong from his debut, knew more this time and was produced with precision timing to score. He is bred to stay further and should develop into a nice middle-distance handicapper next season. (op 16-1)
Royal Rationale(IRE), who landed his apprentice rider in hot water on his third outing last time, took a long time to get on top of the two pace-setters and no sooner had he done so than the winner came up on his outside to snatch the race from him. This is more his trip and he has the option of switching to handicaps. (op 7-1 tchd 6-1)
Not Another Cat(USA), who showed some promise on his debut in a race that has since produced a couple of winners here in August, was given a more positive ride this time but was given no peace by Strikeen, Despite that, he never stopped trying and there should be a race for him on this surface. (op 8-1 tchd 10-1)
Strikeen(IRE) was given a positive ride on this step down from a mile, but had the attentions of Not Another Cat throughout and neither of them could resist the finishing pace of the front pair. He now qualifies for handicaps. (op 4-5 tchd 10-11)
Bidable was not disgraced on this switch to sand and should find easier opportunities than this now that he qualifies for handicaps.
Howards Tipple does not seem to be progressing and this switch to sand failed to make much difference. (op 12-1)

6258 NAME A RACE TO ENHANCE YOUR BRAND (S) STKS 7f 32y(P)
3:00 (3:05) (Class 6) 2-Y-O **£2,388** (£705; £352) **Stalls** High

Form RPR
006 **1** **Dancing Duo**[21] 5867 2-8-6 62 .... EddieAhern 5 61+
(W J Haggas) *trckd ldr: led over 1f out: rdn clr* **9/4**[1]
3062 **2** *3* **Tokyo Jo (IRE)**[60] 4969 2-8-11 58 .... PatCosgrave 1 58
(K R Burke) *a.p: rdn and r.o to go 2nd ins fnl f* **6/1**[3]
0 **3** *3/4* **For Eileen**[191] 1136 2-8-6 .... JimmyQuinn 3 51
(M G Quinlan) *slowly away: hdwy on ins 2f out: swtchd lft over 1f out: kpt on one pce* **16/1**
463 **4** *1/2* **Generist**[5] 6172 2-8-3 54 .... DominicFox(3) 4 50
(M J Attwater) *led tl rdn and hdd over 1f out: fdd ins fnl f* **7/1**
0502 **5** *1* **Peppin's Gold (IRE)**[17] 5948 2-8-6 55 .... AdrianMcCarthy 6 47
(B R Millman) *in tch: rdn over 2f out: no hdwy ins fnl 2f* **7/1**
0520 **6** *2 1/2* **Put It On The Card**[115] 3246 2-8-8 66 .... (v) StephenDonohoe(3) 11 46
(P D Evans) *racd wd: nvr on terms* **9/2**[2]
060 **7** *1 3/4* **Fistral**[35] 5570 2-8-11 54 .... ChrisCatlin 8 42
(M R Channon) *a towards rr* **10/1**
1060 **8** *2* **Mollyanko**[5] 6172 2-8-6 55 .... (b[1]) LiamJones(5) 9 37
(W G M Turner) *slowly away: sme hdwy on outside over 2f out: sn btn* **28/1**
0 **9** *2* **Beshairt**[33] 5608 2-8-7 ow1 .... FergusSweeney 12 28
(D K Ivory) *a towards rr* **50/1**
10 *2* **Short Stuff** 2-8-11 .... LPKeniry 7 27
(R J Hodges) *v.s.a: a bhd* **66/1**
5400 **11** *16* **Top Tier**[30] 5687 2-8-11 55 .... (b) RobbieFitzpatrick 2 —
(Peter Grayson) *trckd ldrs tl wknd over 2f out* **20/1**

1m 31.23s (0.83) **Going Correction** -0.30s/f (Stan) **11** Ran SP% **114.9**
Speed ratings (Par 93):83,79,78,78,77 74,72,69,67,65 47
CSF £14.71 TOTE £3.30: £1.70, £1.90, £2.80; EX 16.80 Trifecta £41.50 Pool £758.22 - 12.95 winning units.The winner was bought for 7,000gns. Tokyo Jo was claimed for £6,000 by T Clement
Owner Mrs Denis Haynes **Bred** Wretham Stud **Trained** Newmarket, Suffolk

FOCUS
A poor contest and the winning time was over two seconds slower than both divisions of the maiden. Not many got into it and the runner-up sets the standard.

NOTEBOOK
Dancing Duo, dropped in grade on this switch to sand, was never far away and had little trouble in pulling away from a dire field. She probably did not need to improve on her turf efforts to win this and she will need to find more in order to follow up. (op 5-2)
Tokyo Jo(IRE) stayed on to snatch second, but was never a threat to the less-exposed winner. She seemed to get the trip well enough this time, but this is good as she is. (tchd 11-2 and 13-2)
For Eileen, not seen since making her debut for a different yard in April, stayed on against the inside rail in the straight and at least she is entitled to still have some improvement in her. (op 12-1)
Generist was given a positive ride on this return to sand, but failed to see it out and looks exposed. (op 13-2)
Peppin's Gold(IRE) was close enough if good enough turning in, but then had nothing more to offer. His efforts on sand do not as yet match up to some of his form on turf. (op 11-2)
Put It On The Card should have done better on official ratings, but a combination of a near four-month layoff, a wide draw and the longer trip probably did for him. (op 5-1 tchd 11-2)
Mollyanko Official explanation: jockey said filly was slow into stride

6259 WBX.COM WORLD BET EXCHANGE H'CAP 1m 141y(P)
3:30 (3:31) (Class 5) (0-75,75) 3-Y-O+ **£3,886** (£1,156; £577; £288) **Stalls** Low

Form RPR
1362 **1** **Middlemarch (IRE)**[1] 6239 6-9-2 71 .... (b) PhillipMakin 9 81
(J S Goldie) *mid-div: rdn to ld over 2f out: in command fnl f* **11/4**[1]
4466 **2** *1 1/2* **Wasalat (USA)**[16] 5973 4-8-8 63 .... TomEaves 4 70
(D W Barker) *mid-div: hdwy wl over 1f out: r.o to go 2nd wl ins fnl f* **12/1**
3645 **3** *nk* **Merrymadcap (IRE)**[28] 5739 4-9-6 75 .... FrancisNorton 8 81
(M Blanshard) *mid-div: hdwy over 2f out: ev ch 1f out but nt qckn* **5/1**[3]
1304 **4** *shd* **Colton**[30] 5680 3-9-0 73 .... DaleGibson 5 79
(J M P Eustace) *trckd ldrs: rdn and nt qckn ins fnl f* **6/1**
44-4 **5** *1/2* **Master Mahogany**[22] 5833 5-9-6 75 .... SteveDrowne 7 80
(R J Hodges) *trckd ldr: ev ch 2f out: nt qckn ins fnl f* **8/1**
3540 **6** *3 1/2* **Hurricane Coast**[113] 3337 7-8-12 70 .... (b) JamesDoyle(3) 3 68
(Ms J S Doyle) *hld up in rr: styd on ins rfnl 2f but nvr nr to chal* **20/1**
0024 **7** *1 3/4* **Indian Edge**[5] 6176 5-8-12 67 .... FergusSweeney 2 61
(B Palling) *led: rdn over 3f out: hdd over 2f out: sn btn* **9/2**[2]
00-0 **8** *1 1/2* **Dante's Diamond (IRE)**[14] 6008 4-8-7 62 oh1 ow1.. RobbieFitzpatrick 1 53
(G A Swinbank) *mid-div: lost pl 5f out: nvr on terms after* **25/1**
0443 **9** *3* **Ribh**[15] 5986 3-9-1 74 .... (b[1]) RyanMoore 11 58
(C E Brittain) *s.i.s: a bhd* **9/1**
0020 **10** *1/2* **Pommes Frites**[28] 5724 3-9-0 73 .... PaulDoe 6 56
(W R Muir) *trckd ldrs: hmpd over 2f out: sn btn* **33/1**
60-0 **11** *8* **Parisette**[37] 5525 4-9-3 72 .... (t) JimmyQuinn 10 39
(A J Lidderdale) *a towards rr on outside* **40/1**

1m 48.75s (-3.01) **Going Correction** -0.30s/f (Stan)
WFA 3 from 4yo+ 4lb **11** Ran SP% **118.6**
Speed ratings (Par 103):101,99,99,99,98 95,94,92,90,89 82
CSF £36.62 CT £163.56 TOTE £3.50: £1.40, £3.70, £2.20; EX 56.00 TRIFECTA Not won..
Owner W M Johnstone **Bred** Swettenham Stud And Hugo Lascelles **Trained** Uplawmoor, E Renfrews

FOCUS
A fair handicap of its type though the pace was not that strong.
Parisette Official explanation: jockey said filly would not face kick-back

6260 TWILIGHT RACING AND SUPPER H'CAP 1m 141y(P)
4:00 (4:00) (Class 6) (0-67,67) 3-Y-O **£2,730** (£806; £403) **Stalls** Low

Form RPR
6005 **1** **Dyanita**[16] 5973 3-8-13 64 .... MichaelHills 7 70
(B W Hills) *mde all: rdn out fnl f and hld on* **7/1**
1006 **2** *nk* **Tender The Great (IRE)**[34] 5590 3-8-11 62 .... EddieAhern 2 67
(V Smith) *chsd ldrs: wnt 2nd wl over 1f out: ev ch ins: nt get up* **13/2**[3]
4350 **3** *hd* **Flylowflylong (IRE)**[21] 5861 3-8-12 63 .... TomEaves 5 68
(I Semple) *trckd wnr hung rt and lost 2nd ins fnl f* **6/1**[2]
110 **4** *1* **Emily's Place (IRE)**[35] 5568 3-9-0 65 .... PatCosgrave 9 68
(J Pearce) *in rr tl hdwy over 2f out: rdn and r.o: nvr nrr* **15/2**
3300 **5** *1 1/2* **Ruffie (IRE)**[75] 4491 3-9-0 65 .... JimmyQuinn 4 65
(Miss Gay Kelleway) *towards rr: hdwy 2f out: one pce fnl f* **20/1**
2541 **6** *shd* **Golden Sprite**[22] 5831 3-8-13 64 .... JimCrowley 3 63
(B R Millman) *in tch tl rdn and one pce fnl f* **11/2**[1]
4040 **7** *2 1/2* **Cheviot Heights**[47] 5284 3-8-13 64 .... DanielTudhope 12 58
(J S Goldie) *bhd tl mde sme late hdwy* **25/1**
6330 **8** *1/2* **Casual Affair**[44] 5388 3-9-2 67 .... ChrisCatlin 6 60
(E J O'Neill) *trckd ldrs: t.k.h: wknd 1f out* **7/1**
60-6 **9** *2 1/2* **Darusso**[14] 6021 3-9-1 66 .... LPKeniry 1 54
(J S Moore) *a towards rr* **14/1**
000 **10** *1 1/2* **Drawback (IRE)**[11] 6069 3-9-2 67 .... RichardThomas 8 52
(R A Harris) *slowly away: a bhd* **40/1**
-000 **11** *hd* **Nimrana Fort**[46] 5311 3-8-5 61 .... AndrewElliott(5) 10 45
(G A Swinbank) *in tch tl rdn and wknd over 3f out* **12/1**
3300 **12** *4* **Sinner Or Saint (IRE)**[46] 5312 3-9-0 65 .... DavidAllan 13 41
(T D Easterby) *racd wd: a bhd* **20/1**
2300 **13** *17* **Beldon Hill (USA)**[44] 5388 3-9-0 65 .... (p) SebSanders 11 5
(C E Brittain) *racd wd: in tch tl wknd rapidly 3f out* **15/2**

1m 49.35s (-2.41) **Going Correction** -0.30s/f (Stan) **13** Ran SP% **121.7**
Speed ratings (Par 99):98,97,97,96,95 95,93,92,90,89 88,85,70
CSF £50.43 CT £296.51 TOTE £6.00: £1.90, £2.90, £2.20; EX 86.40 TRIFECTA Not won. Place 6 £263.15, Place 5 £213.66.
Owner Mrs L Alexander **Bred** Britton House Stud Ltd **Trained** Lambourn, Berks

FOCUS
A moderate handicap in which the pace was ordinary. It paid to race handily and not that many got into it. The form looks fairly sound with the winner the best guide backed up by the runner-up and fifth.
Beldon Hill(USA) Official explanation: jockey said gelding never travelled
T/Jkpt: Not won. T/Plt: £292.00 to a £1 stake. Pool: £51,390.85. 128.45 winning tickets. T/Qpdt: £47.70 to a £1 stake. Pool: £4,169.10. 64.60 winning tickets. JS

6261 - (Foreign Racing) - See Raceform Interactive

5189 LEOPARDSTOWN (L-H)
Monday, October 30
OFFICIAL GOING: Soft (soft to heavy in places)

6262a KILLAVULLAN STKS (GROUP 3) 7f
1:15 (1:15) 2-Y-O **£31,427** (£9,220; £4,393; £1,496)

RPR
1 **Confuchias (IRE)**[15] 5993 2-9-1 .... WSupple 3 103
(Francis Ennis, Ire) *hld up in tch: 4th into st: sltly hmpd 1 1/2f out: chal and led ins fnl f: styd on wl: comf* **7/2**[3]
2 *3/4* **Albert Einstein (IRE)**[16] 5981 2-9-1 .... CO'Donoghue 5 101
(A P O'Brien, Ire) *led: rdn and swvd rt 1 1/2f out: hdd ins fnl f: kpt on* **2/1**[1]
3 *1 1/4* **Frederick Ozanam (IRE)**[16] 5976 2-9-1 86 .... JAHeffernan 4 98
(A P O'Brien, Ire) *sn 2nd: 3rd and rdn ent st: sltly hmpd 1 1/2f out: kpt on same pce fnl f* **7/1**
4 *3 1/2* **Warriors Key (IRE)**[29] 5707 2-9-1 92 .... DPMcDonogh 2 90
(Kevin Prendergast, Ire) *hld up in tch: last into st: kpt on same pce fr 1 1/2f out* **4/1**
5 *1 3/4* **Blue Coral (IRE)**[41] 5466 2-9-1 93 .... (b[1]) PJSmullen 1 85
(D K Weld, Ire) *s.i.s: sn prom: 3rd 1/2-way: cl up whn swtchd to inner early st: effrt 1 1/2f out: wknd fnl f* **3/1**[2]

1m 35.7s **Going Correction** +0.65s/f (Yiel) **5** Ran SP% **113.1**
Speed ratings: 106,105,103,99,97
CSF £11.25 TOTE £4.20: £1.80, £2.80; DF 18.60.
Owner Mrs Annette O'Callaghan **Bred** Mrs Vanessa Hutch **Trained** the Curragh, Co Kildare

FOCUS
This was a weak race at this level, in terms of both quantity and quality. It lacked a runner of the same calibre as subsequent Classic winners Grey Swallow and Footstepsinthesand, successful in 2003 and 2004 respectively.

NOTEBOOK

Confuchias(IRE), a Naas maiden winner over six furlongs earlier in the month on his second start, was not bothered by a touch of interference as the leader jinked to the right around a furlong and a half down, and picked up inside the final furlong to win with a bit to spare. His ability to handle soft ground suggests that he will be ready early next season, and on this evidence he should stay a mile. (op 3/1)

Albert Einstein(IRE) set off to make all, but began to look vulnerable when coming off a straight line just after he had been asked to raise the tempo, and was collared readily in the end. He is a near-certainty to pick up a maiden, but has plenty to prove in order to make the grade at Pattern level. (op 2/1 tchd 7/4)

Frederick Ozanam(IRE) ran a respectable race for a horse rated only 86 and stepping up in class after winning an auction maiden, but will need to improve to be anything better than a decent handicapper in 2007. (op 13/2)

6157 CATTERICK (L-H)

Tuesday, October 31

OFFICIAL GOING: Soft (heavy in places)

Wind: Fresh, against

6270 ROBIN HOOD'S BAY MAIDEN AUCTION STKS — 7f

1:30 (1:30) (Class 5) 2-Y-O — **£3,412** (£1,007; £504) **Stalls** Low

Form	Pos	Dist	Horse / Comment	Jockey	RPR
	1		**Feeling Wonderful (IRE)** 2-8-4 (M Johnston) *cl up on inner: hung rt home turn: wd st to stands rail and led 2f out: sn rdn and kpt on wl fnl f* **25/1**	AdrianTNicholls 2	67
3202	**2**	1 1/4	**Nota Liberata**[17] 5958 2-8-9 69 (G M Moore) *prom on outer: pushed along whn n.m.r and sltly hmpd 2f out: swtchd lft and rdn to chse wnr over 1f out: sn one pce* **5/4**[1]	JimmyQuinn 9	69
32	**3**	1/2	**Snow Dancer (IRE)**[15] 6013 2-7-13 ow2 (A Berry) *led 2f: cl up and ev ch whn n.m.r and sltly hmpd 2f out: rdn and hung lft over 1f out: kpt on same pce* **11/2**[3]	AndrewElliott(5) 8	63
5334	**4**	1	**Bert's Memory**[17] 5958 2-8-4 66 (K A Ryan) *cl up: led after 2f: pushed along whn hmpd: hdd and snatched up 2f out: sn rdn and kpt on same pce after* **9/2**[2]	CatherineGannon 7	60+
05	**5**	3	**Graceful Steps (IRE)**[17] 5959 2-8-9 (E J O'Neill) *trckd ldrs tl pushed along and sltly outpcd 1/2-way: sn rdn along and kpt on appr last* **14/1**	RichardMullen 6	58+
6	**6**	1 3/4	**Streamer**[154] 2106 2-8-2 (M Johnston) *chsd ldrs: rdn along over 2f out: sn wknd* **7/1**	RoystonFfrench 4	47+
0	**7**	4	**Blue Jet (USA)**[24] 5814 2-8-9 (R M Whitaker) *chsd ldrs on inner: rdn along wl over 2f out and sn wknd* **66/1**	VHalliday 1	44
0	**8**	1	**Bold Nevison (IRE)**[34] 5614 2-8-11 (B Smart) *a rr* **12/1**	TomEaves 3	43
00	**9**	7	**Kentucky Boy (IRE)**[17] 5959 2-8-9 (Jedd O'Keeffe) *a rr* **100/1**	PatCosgrave 5	24

1m 33.85s (6.49) **Going Correction** +0.825s/f (Soft) — **9** Ran SP% **111.2**

Speed ratings (Par 95):95,93,93,91,88 86,81,80,72

CSF £54.02 TOTE £16.80: £3.60, £1.10, £1.80; EX 62.30.

Owner Jim McGrath And Reg Griffin **Bred** Glending Bloodstock **Trained** Middleham Moor, N Yorks

■ Stewards' Enquiry : Adrian T Nicholls two-day ban: careless riding (Nov 11, 13)

FOCUS

A modest juvenile maiden and the form looks straightforward rated through the exposed runner-up and the fourth.

NOTEBOOK

Feeling Wonderful(IRE), a 14,000gns purchase whose dam was a six-furlong winner on her debut at two, got her career off to a perfect start in ready fashion - despite taking a big walk in the market. She looked suited by the soft surface, left the impression she would benefit a deal for this debut experience and should have no trouble in tackling a mile next term. (op 11-1)

Nota Liberata had every chance but was ultimately put in his place by the winner. He is exposed, and with an official rating of 69 helps to put this form into perspective, yet it may be no coincidence that he remains winless after 13 outings. (op 15-8)

Snow Dancer(IRE) was given a positive ride and had her chance over this extra furlong. She now qualifies for nurseries and this consistent filly can expect a mark of around 65 when switching to that sphere. (op 7-1)

Bert's Memory was not done too many favours when the runners tracked over stands' side, but she had enough time to recover and never seriously threatened. She still ran very close to her recent course and distance form with the runner-up. (op 7-2 tchd 5-1 in a place)

Graceful Steps(IRE) is going to appreciate stepping up in trip as a three-year-old and now becomes eligible for a handicap rating. (op 10-1)

Streamer failed to raise her game over the extra furlong and looks in need of more time. (op 11-2)

6271 RENEW YOUR ANNUAL MEMBERSHIP TODAY NURSERY — 5f 212y

2:00 (2:00) (Class 4) (0-85,78) 2-Y-O — **£6,477** (£1,927; £963; £481) **Stalls** Low

Form	Pos	Dist	Horse / Comment	Jockey	RPR
002	**1**		**Atlantic Light**[13] 6055 2-9-6 77 (M Johnston) *cl up: led after 2f: rdn clr over 1f out: styd on strly* **5/2**[1]	KDarley 1	91+
1013	**2**	12	**Retaliate**[18] 5940 2-9-3 74 (M Quinn) *led 2f: cl up tl rdn along over 2f out: sn drvn and one pce* **10/3**[3]	SebSanders 6	52
3002	**3**	1 3/4	**Tee Off (IRE)**[18] 5950 2-9-1 72 (B W Hills) *hld up in tch: hdwy to chse ldng pair 3f out: rdn along over 2f out: sn drvn and one pce* **11/4**[2]	(t) SteveDrowne 4	45
4640	**4**	1 1/2	**Baltimore Jack (IRE)**[31] 5681 2-9-7 78 (M W Easterby) *trckd ldrs tl pushed along and outpcd 1/2-way: hdwy whn n.m.r over 1f out: kpt on ins last* **9/2**	DaleGibson 3	46
2100	**5**	1	**Cherri Fosfate**[23] 5828 2-8-6 68 (W G M Turner) *dwlt: hdwy and cl up 1/2-way: rdn along over 2f out: sn wandered and wknd wl over 1f out* **16/1**	(v[1]) LiamJones(5) 2	33
445	**6**	3	**Catlivius (IRE)**[62] 4920 2-8-9 66 (K A Ryan) *a rr* **12/1**	(p) CatherineGannon 5	22

1m 19.18s (5.18) **Going Correction** +0.825s/f (Soft) — **6** Ran SP% **110.1**

Speed ratings (Par 97):98,82,79,77,76 72

CSF £10.67 TOTE £2.40: £1.90, £1.80; EX 9.30.

Owner Mrs R J Jacobs **Bred** Newsells Park Stud Limited **Trained** Middleham Moor, N Yorks

FOCUS

A modest nursery in which the progressive winner proved in a different league to her rivals, but it is difficult to be confident as to the value of the form.

NOTEBOOK

Atlantic Light, making her nursery debut, got off the mark at the fourth attempt with a most decisive display. She is evidently progressing well, looks ready to tackle another furlong now, and it would come as little surprise to see her out under a penalty before the Handicapper has the chance to reassess her. (op 2-1 tchd 15-8)

Retaliate was left trailing by the clear-cut winner, but still kept to her task well enough and remains in good heart. Whether she is quite up to her current official rating remains to be seen, however. (op 4-1)

Tee Off(IRE), runner-up on this sort of ground in maiden company last time, was not suited by being held up over this trip and should be rated better than the bare form. She really looks to be crying out for another furlong or at least a more positive ride over this trip in the future. (op 10-3)

Baltimore Jack(IRE) looks too high in the weights, but left the impression he may need to step back up to another furlong now. (op 11-2 tchd 7-1)

6272 HAMBLETON MAIDEN STKS — 1m 3f 214y

2:30 (2:31) (Class 5) 3-Y-O+ — **£3,886** (£1,156; £577; £288) **Stalls** Low

Form	Pos	Dist	Horse / Comment	Jockey	RPR
5622	**1**		**Height Of Fury (IRE)**[15] 6008 3-9-3 70 (J L Dunlop) *hld up: smooth hdwy 1/2-way: trckd ldrs 4f out: wd st to stands rail: shkn up 2f out: sn led: clr ent last: kpt on wl* **5/4**[1]	JimmyQuinn 8	83+
2	**2**	9	**Flame Creek (IRE)**[18] 5934 10-9-7 (E J Creighton) *led: rdn along over 3f out: styd towards far side home st: hdd wl over 1f out and sn one pce* **12/1**	EdwardCreighton(3) 5	70+
0400	**3**	8	**Zed Candy (FR)**[17] 5960 3-9-3 56 (J T Stimpson) *in tch: rdn along and outpcd 1/2-way: plugged on fnl 3f* **40/1**	DaleGibson 2	59
3200	**4**	7	**Moonshadow**[35] 5594 3-8-12 77 (H R A Cecil) *chsd ldrs: rdn along over 4f out: sn drvn and wknd* **7/1**[3]	KDarley 9	44
250-	**5**	1	**Valiant Shadow (GER)**[398] 5550 4-9-10 53 (W Jarvis) *prom: cl up 1/2-way: rdn along over 3f out: drvn an d wknd over 2f out* **50/1**	RichardMullen 1	48
/56-	**6**	10	**Karathaena (IRE)**[281] 5244 6-9-0 51 (M E Sowersby) *bhd tl sme hdwy fnl 4f* **66/1**	JamieMoriarty(5) 7	29
403	**7**	21	**Shout (IRE)**[36] 5566 3-8-12 75 (R Charlton) *chsd ldrs: rdn along over 4f out and sn wknd* **9/4**[2]	SteveDrowne 12	—
	8	2 1/2	**Funny Times**[20] 5-9-5 (N G Richards) *slowly away and a wl bhd* **17/2**	TomEaves 10	—
00	**9**	26	**La Grande Zoa (IRE)**[22] 5870 3-8-12 (R M Beckett) *in tch: rdn along 1/2-way: sn wknd* **20/1**	SebSanders 4	—
0000	**10**	25	**Roonah (FR)**[114] 3330 3-8-12 45 (Karen McLintock) *a bhd: trailed off fnl 4f* **150/1**	RoystonFfrench 11	—
5-00	**11**	76	**Huggle**[14] 6037 3-9-3 55 (P S McEntee) *chsd ldrs: lost pl after 4f and sn bhd: t.o fnl 4f* **100/1**	(v[1]) BrianReilly 3	—

2m 48.75s (9.75) **Going Correction** +0.825s/f (Soft)

WFA 3 from 4yo+ 7lb — **11** Ran SP% **118.2**

Speed ratings (Par 103):100,94,88,84,83 76,62,61,43,27 —

CSF £17.93 TOTE £2.20: £1.10, £2.70, £5.00; EX 13.70.

Owner Windflower Overseas Holdings Inc **Bred** Windflower Overseas **Trained** Arundel, W Sussex

FOCUS

No real strength in depth to this maiden. The field came home strung out and the form is best rated through the third.

Shout(IRE) Official explanation: jockey said filly was unsuited by the soft (heavy in places) ground

La Grande Zoa(IRE) Official explanation: jockey said filly had no more to give

Roonah(FR) Official explanation: jockey said filly had no more to give

6273 BOOK ON-LINE AT CATTERICKBRIDGE.CO.UK H'CAP — 7f

3:00 (3:00) (Class 4) (0-80,81) 3-Y-O+ — **£6,477** (£1,927; £963; £481) **Stalls** Low

Form	Pos	Dist	Horse / Comment	Jockey	RPR
1004	**1**		**Hiccups**[7] 6160 6-9-0 75 (M Dods) *trckd ldrs: hdwy 2f out: rdn to chal ent last: sn hung lft: styd on u.p to ld nr fin* **11/1**	SteveDrowne 13	87
6412	**2**	nk	**Bold Marc (IRE)**[7] 6160 4-8-9 75 (K R Burke) *racd wd: led: rdn along 2f out: drvn and edgd lft ent last: hdd and no ex nr fin* **2/1**[1]	(p) AndrewElliott(5) 9	86
0341	**3**	4	**Countdown**[7] 6160 4-9-6 81 6ex (T D Easterby) *trckd ldrs: hdwy to chse ldng pair 2f out: sn drvn and kpt on same pce fnl f* **4/1**[2]	DavidAllan 6	82
6000	**4**	3 1/2	**Sentiero Rosso (USA)**[3] 6227 4-8-4 65 (B Ellison) *prom: effrt over 2f out and sn rdn: ev ch tl drvn and wknd over 1f out* **10/1**	(t) RichardMullen 4	57
6200	**5**	1 1/4	**Zhitomir**[22] 5861 8-8-4 65 oh4 (M Dods) *towards rr: hdwy 1/2-way: rdn 2f out: styd on ins last: nt rch ldrs* **16/1**	JimmyQuinn 1	53
0006	**6**	2	**Up Tempo (IRE)**[6] 6174 8-8-0 66 (C R Dore) *bhd: rdn along and hdwy over 2f out: styd on ins last: nt rch ldrs* **20/1**	(b) LiamJones(5) 7	49
0300	**7**	3/4	**Primo Way**[39] 5512 5-9-4 79 (I Semple) *midfield: rdn along and sme hdwy over 2f out: sn drvn and no imp* **14/1**	(b) TomEaves 5	60
4103	**8**	3/4	**King Harson**[7] 6160 7-9-3 78 (J D Bethell) *cl up: rdn along 2f out: drvn and wknd over 1f out* **13/2**[3]	PatCosgrave 12	57
0000	**9**	2 1/2	**Sam's Secret**[42] 5444 4-7-11 65 oh1 (G A Swinbank) *s.i.s: a bhd* **40/1**	KellyHarrison(7) 8	38
000	**10**	2 1/2	**Stolen Summer (IRE)**[6] 6176 3-8-12 75 (B S Rothwell) *a bhd* **66/1**	SilvestreDeSousa 10	41
4265	**11**	1 1/4	**Titinius (IRE)**[7] 6160 6-8-9 70 (Micky Hammond) *chsd ldrs: rdn along over 2f out: sn wknd* **17/2**	(p) KDarley 3	33
6000	**12**	nk	**Baylaw Star**[7] 6160 5-8-10 76 (I W McInnes) *a rr* **40/1**	MarkLawson(5) 2	38

1m 32.43s (5.07) **Going Correction** +0.825s/f (Soft)

WFA 3 from 4yo+ 2lb — **12** Ran SP% **118.3**

Speed ratings (Par 105):104,103,99,95,93 91,90,89,86,83 82,82

CSF £32.30 CT £109.73 TOTE £11.10: £3.00, £1.40, £1.50; EX 40.00.

Owner J M & Mrs E E Ranson **Bred** Mrs Susan Corbett **Trained** Denton, Co Durham

FOCUS

A fair handicap, run at a sound pace and the form is straightforward rated through the winner. The first two came clear.

6274 GO RACING IN YORKSHIRE CLAIMING STKS — 5f

3:30 (3:31) (Class 6) 3-Y-O+ — **£2,730** (£806; £403) **Stalls** Low

Form	Pos	Dist	Horse / Comment	Jockey	RPR
0301	**1**		**Trinculo (IRE)**[74] 4546 9-9-10 90 (D Nicholls) *mde all far side: rdn 2f out: drvn ins last and kpt on wl* **3/1**[2]	AdrianTNicholls 5	78
0000	**2**	nk	**Westbrook Blue**[17] 5957 4-9-5 76 (W G M Turner) *trckd ldng pair far side: hdwy to chse wnr and hung rt over 1f out: drvn and edgd lft ins last: styd on wl towards fin* **15/2**	(tp) LiamJones(5) 1	77
1002	**3**	shd	**Witchry**[48] 5291 4-9-10 69 (A G Newcombe) *trckd ldrs stands side: hdwy 2f out: rdn and ev ch ins last: no ex nr fin* **14/1**	LPKeniry 10	77

1004 **4** 1 ½ **Dark Champion**[28] 5752 6-8-6 55 ....(v) DavidAllan 14 54
(R E Barr) *led stands side gp: rdn along 2f out and ev ch tl wknd ins last* **11/1**

6040 **5** ¾ **The Keep**[69] 4694 4-7-8 40 ....(v) NataliaGemelova(5) 2 44
(R E Barr) *in tch far side: hdwy 2f out: sn rdn and kpt on ins last* **66/1**

0024 **6** 1 ½ **Viewforth**[7] 6162 8-8-6 62 ow2 ....(b) TomEaves 6 46
(I Semple) *chsd wnr far side: rdn along over 2f out: drvn and one pce fr wl over 1f out* **11/4**[1]

6003 **7** 1 ½ **Throw The Dice**[7] 6162 4-8-9 60 ....(p) MarkLawson(5) 15 49
(D W Barker) *rrd s: in tch stands side: hdwy 2f out: sn rdn and no imp appr last* **7/2**[3]

606 **8** 4 **Harrington Bates**[19] 5928 5-8-4 45 ....(v) JimmyQuinn 9 25
(R M Whitaker) *in tch centre: rdn along over 2f out: sn wknd* **22/1**

000 **9** 2 ½ **Stokesies Wish**[60] 4985 6-8-1 47 .... DaleGibson 7 14
(J L Spearing) *in tch far side: rdn along over 2f out: sn wknd* **33/1**

000 **10** ½ **Alexia Rose (IRE)**[40] 5493 4-9-5 54 .... PatCosgrave 4 30
(A Berry) *in tch far side: rdn over 2f out: sn wknd* **66/1**

3500 **11** 2 ½ **She's Our Beauty (IRE)**[23] 5834 3-7-10 47 ow2 ....(v) LanceBetts(7) 13 5
(S T Mason) *s.i.s: sn chsng ldrs towards stands side: rdn along over 2f out and sn wknd* **80/1**

0106 **12** 4 **Miss Mujahid Times**[28] 5752 3-7-13 50 ....(b) SilvestreDeSousa 8 —
(A D Brown) *prom centre: chsd ldrs to 1/2-way: sn wknd* **16/1**

0-2 **13** nk **Tipsy Lillie**[74] 4554 4-8-2 45 .... MarcHalford(3) 12 —
(P S McEntee) *racd centre: a bhd* **25/1**

00 **14** ¾ **Broadfield Lady (IRE)**[17] 5970 6-8-0 52 ow4 ....(p) EdwardCreighton(3) 3 —
(E J Creighton) *a rr far side* **66/1**

65.37 secs (4.77) **Going Correction** +1.00s/f (Soft) **14** Ran SP% **123.4**
Speed ratings (Par 101):101,100,100,97,96 94,91,85,81,80 76,70,69,68
CSF £25.42 TOTE £4.10: £1.40, £3.30, £3.10; EX 43.10.Viewforth was claimed by M. A. Buckley for £5,000.
Owner Nigel Shields **Bred** Humphrey Okeke **Trained** Sessay, N Yorks

FOCUS
A moderate affair that saw those racing on the far side emerge on top. The form is not strong and is weakened by the proximity of the 40-rated fifth.
Tipsy Lillie Official explanation: jockey said filly was unsuited by the soft (heavy in places) ground

6275 NATIONAL HUNT SEASON STARTS ON 29TH NOVEMBER H'CAP 1m 5f 175y
4:00 (4:01) (Class 5) (0-75,71) 3-Y-0+ **£3,886** (£1,156; £577; £288) **Stalls** Low

Form RPR

0123 **1** **Mighty Moon**[49] 5276 3-8-9 **66** ....(bt) JamesO'Reilly(7) 1 89
(J O'Reilly) *trckd ldrs: smooth hdwy to ld 3f out: styd far rails and rdn clr wl over 1f out: styd on strly* **9/2**[3]

4030 **2** 27 **Charlotte Vale**[25] 5792 5-9-13 **68** .... JimmyQuinn 6 53
(Micky Hammond) *hld up: hdwy to trck ldrs 5f out: rdn along and outpcd over 3f out: styd far side and drvn 2f out: kpt on: no ch w wnr* **4/1**[2]

4124 **3** 4 **Pee Jay's Dream**[17] 5960 4-9-6 **61** .... DaleGibson 3 41
(M W Easterby) *trckd ldr: cl up 1/2-way: rdn along and c wd to stands rail home st: sn drvn and plugged on* **10/3**[1]

0650 **4** 8 **Patavium (IRE)**[96] 3869 3-8-8 **58** .... RoystonFfrench 5 26
(E W Tuer) *led: rdn along 4f out: hdd 3f out and sn wknd* **16/1**

3000 **5** nk **Categorical**[30] 5284 3-9-7 **71** .... PatCosgrave 2 39
(K G Reveley) *hld up: effrt and hdwy 5f out: rdn along and outpcd wl over 3f out* **9/1**

131 **6** ¾ **Bronze Dancer (IRE)**[84] 4231 4-9-9 **69** .... AndrewElliott(5) 4 36
(G A Swinbank) *trckd ldrs: rdn along over 4f out and sn wknd* **10/3**[1]

0005 **7** 26 **Epicurean**[21] 5904 4-9-1 **61** .... JamieMoriarty(5) 7 —
(Mrs K Walton) *a towards rr: rdn along and outpcd over 5f out* **9/1**

3m 13.31s (8.81) **Going Correction** +0.825s/f (Soft)
WFA 3 from 4yo+ 9lb **7** Ran SP% **110.2**
Speed ratings (Par 103):107,91,89,84,84 84,69
CSF £21.02 TOTE £3.70: £2.50, £3.30; EX 20.20 Place 6 £55.47, Place 5 £40.75.
Owner Sunpak Potatoes **Bred** Angmering Park Stud **Trained** Doncaster, S Yorks
■ Stewards' Enquiry : James O'Reilly four-day ban: used whip when clearly winning (Nov 11, 13-15)

FOCUS
A modest handicap that produced a hugely decisive winner. The form has been rated relatively positively but should be treated with a little caution.
Bronze Dancer(IRE) Official explanation: jockey said gelding was unsuited by the soft (heavy in places) ground
T/Plt: £27.90 to a £1 stake. Pool: £43,553.75. 1,139.35 winning tickets. T/Qpdt: £12.30 to a £1 stake. Pool: £2,194.30. 131.85 winning tickets. JR

5922 SOUTHWELL (L-H)
Tuesday, October 31

OFFICIAL GOING: Standard to fast
After a wet spell the surface was reported to be riding ' much quicker than usual'.
Wind: Fresh, behind Weather: Cool, overcast and windy. Occasional blustery showers.

6276 WBX.COM WORLD BET EXCHANGE BANDED STKS 5f (F)
1:20 (1:20) (Class 7) 3-Y-0+ **£1,876** (£554; £277) **Stalls** High

Form RPR

00 **1** **Borzoi Maestro**[41] 5480 5-9-1 48 ....(p) AdamKirby 1 61
(M Wellings) *mde all: drew clr fnl f: readily* **15/2**

2005 **2** 2 **Desert Dust**[8] 6129 3-9-3 50 ....(v) BrettDoyle 8 56
(R M H Cowell) *chsd ldrs: styd on fnl f: tk 2nd nr line* **25/1**

0040 **3** hd **Campeon (IRE)**[64] 4872 4-8-11 47 .... StephenDonohoe(3) 3 53
(J M Bradley) *chsd ldrs: kpt on same pce fnl f* **5/1**[2]

0000 **4** ¾ **Orchestration (IRE)**[19] 5928 5-8-8 48 .... StacyRenwick(7) 2 51
(M J Attwater) *chsd ldrs on outside: kpt on same pce fnl f* **8/1**

0000 **5** 3 ½ **Hout Bay**[22] 5865 9-9-0 47 ....(b) PaulQuinn 10 38
(D W Chapman) *sn in rr and drvn along: hdwy over 2f out: hung lft: nvr rchd ldrs* **14/1**

3500 **6** 1 ½ **Trombone Tom**[34] 5620 3-9-2 49 .... PaulMulrennan 6 35
(J R Norton) *prom: one pce fnl 2f* **16/1**

3034 **7** ¾ **Seven No Trumps**[61] 4962 9-8-10 50 .... BarrySavage(7) 11 33
(J M Bradley) *dwlt: hld up in rr: sme hdwy 2f out: nvr nr ldrs* **7/1**

0000 **8** ¾ **Developer (IRE)**[25] 5781 3-8-10 50 ....(v[1]) MarkCoumbe(7) 13 31
(G F Bridgwater) *in rr: sme hdwy 2f out: nvr on terms* **66/1**

0002 **9** ¾ **Tagula Bay (IRE)**[18] 5951 4-9-0 47 ....(b) FrancisNorton 4 25
(T D Easterby) *chsd ldrs on outer: hung lft and wknd over 1f out* **7/2**[1]

6064 **10** 1 **Stoneacre Fred (IRE)**[69] 4690 3-9-0 47 .... RobbieFitzpatrick 5 22
(Peter Grayson) *s.i.s: nvr on terms* **10/1**

0400 **11** nk **Quadrophenia**[28] 5756 3-9-3 50 .... JamieMackay 9 24
(J G Given) *sn outpcd and in rr* **25/1**

0000 **12** ½ **Danethorpe (IRE)**[164] 1859 3-8-12 48 ....(v[1]) PatrickMathers(3) 12 20
(D Shaw) *reminders after s: nvr wnt pce: a in rr* **125/1**

0032 **13** 1 ½ **Sharp Hat**[23] 5834 12-9-2 49 .... TonyCulhane 7 16
(D W Chapman) *mid-div: sn drvn along: lost pl over 1f out* **6/1**[3]

57.85 secs (-2.45) **Going Correction** -0.55s/f (Fast) **13** Ran SP% **120.2**
Speed ratings (Par 97):97,93,93,92,86 84,83,81,80,79 78,77,75
CSF £188.10 TOTE £11.00: £3.30, £5.50, £2.60; EX 318.00 TRIFECTA Not won..
Owner Mrs Ruth M Serrell **Bred** B A Beale & Bbb Computer Services Ltd **Trained** Six Ashes, Shropshire

FOCUS
A fair banded sprint where very few got into it from off the pace and the winner made all, aided by a tail wind. As is often the case those drawn low, racing in the centre of the track, dominated. The form looks solid enough for the grade with the first three close to their marks.
Tagula Bay(IRE) Official explanation: jockey said filly finished distressed

6277 EXPERIENCE NOTTINGHAMSHIRE MAIDEN CLAIMING STKS 7f (F)
1:50 (1:50) (Class 7) 3-Y-0+ **£1,569** (£463; £231) **Stalls** Low

Form RPR

3040 **1** **Crafty Fox**[14] 6033 3-9-5 54 .... AdamKirby 6 61
(A P Jarvis) *sn drvn along: hdwy to ld after 1f: kpt on wl ins last* **5/1**[3]

6503 **2** ¾ **Mucho Loco (IRE)**[21] 5885 3-9-5 52 ....(b) JimCrowley 3 59
(J G Portman) *hld up in tch: effrt over 2f out: chal jst ins last: no ex* **15/8**[1]

6000 **3** 1 ¼ **Hilltop Fantasy**[49] 5272 5-8-1 40 .... WilliamBuick(7) 14 43
(V Smith) *chsd ldrs on outer: wnt 2nd over 2f out: kpt on wl fnl f* **12/1**

5020 **4** 2 **Lottie**[41] 5483 5-8-12 45 .... PhillipMakin 12 42
(G Woodward) *prom: outpcd over 4f out: styd on fnl f* **9/2**[2]

600 **5** 1 ¼ **Sister Gee (IRE)**[8] 6129 4-8-12 45 .... MickyFenton 5 38
(R Hollinshead) *led 1f: chsd ldrs: one pce fnl 2f* **16/1**

5-30 **6** 5 **Sion Hill (IRE)**[94] 3947 5-9-7 45 ....(p) DanielTudhope 8 34
(Mrs N Macauley) *prom: one pce fnl 2f* **16/1**

000- **7** 1 ½ **Young Thomas (IRE)**[322] 6572 4-8-9 40 .... PaulMulrennan 2 18
(B Storey) *mid-div: kpt on fnl 2f: nvr a factor* **80/1**

0506 **8** 3 **Compton Bay**[74] 4548 6-9-3 40 .... DeanMernagh 7 19
(M Brittain) *prom: wknd over 2f out* **18/1**

0000 **9** 1 ½ **Ruby Sunrise (IRE)**[23] 5844 4-8-9 40 .... SoniaEaton(7) 13 14
(B P J Baugh) *slowly away: nvr on terms* **100/1**

006- **10** nk **Guanyin**[326] 6521 3-8-11 45 ....(b[1]) JamesDoyle(3) 10 13
(Ms J S Doyle) *sn outpcd and in rr* **10/1**

2000 **11** shd **Weakest Link**[17] 5969 5-9-7 45 ....(p) PaulQuinn 9 18
(E J Alston) *chsd ldrs on outer: wknd over 2f out* **14/1**

6000 **12** 8 **Active Audience (IRE)**[45] 5363 3-8-11 40 .... StephenDonohoe(3) 11 —
(A Berry) *sn in rr and drvn along: bhd fnl 3f* **28/1**

0/0- **13** 32 **Devil's Bite**[565] 1013 5-8-8 45 .... NicolPolli(5) 4 —
(M C Chapman) *in tch: lost pl over 4f out: sn wl bhd: virtually p.u: t.o* **100/1**

1m 30.59s (-0.21) **Going Correction** -0.15s/f (Stan)
WFA 3 from 4yo+ 2lb **13** Ran SP% **116.8**
Speed ratings (Par 97):95,94,92,90,89 83,81,78,76,76 75,66,30
CSF £14.16 TOTE £7.20: £2.40, £1.40, £4.10; EX 16.20 Trifecta £121.00 Part won. Pool: £170.52 - 0.97 winning units..
Owner A P Jarvis **Bred** Bearstone Stud **Trained** Twyford, Bucks
■ Stewards' Enquiry : Nicol Polli two-day ban: careless riding (Nov 11, 13)

FOCUS
Rock bottom stuff but the winner was entitled to win and the form looks sound with four of the first five close to their marks.
Devil's Bite Official explanation: jockey said gelding had bled from the nose

6278 WBX.COM WORLD BET EXCHANGE MAIDEN AUCTION STKS 6f (F)
2:20 (2:20) (Class 7) 2-Y-O **£1,501** (£443; £221) **Stalls** Low

Form RPR

3443 **1** **Bahamian Love**[50] 5231 2-8-8 67 .... MichaelHills 7 62+
(B W Hills) *trckd ldrs: wnt 2nd 3f out: led over 1f out: styd on strly: eased towards fin* **1/1**[1]

2000 **2** 3 **Gibsons**[29] 5735 2-8-8 51 .... JamesDoyle(3) 3 53
(Mrs P N Dutfield) *led tl over 1f out: kpt on: no ch w wnr* **14/1**

000 **3** 2 ½ **Shouldntbethere (IRE)**[34] 5622 2-8-12 45 .... JamieMackay 10 47
(Mrs P N Dutfield) *reminders after s: in rr: hdwy over 2f out: kpt on fnl f* **50/1**

4 2 ½ **Cape Free** 2-8-3 ow1 .... SaleemGolam(3) 8 33
(E F Vaughan) *s.s: bhd tl hdwy on outer 2f out: styd on fnl f* **18/1**

0000 **5** ¾ **Kyoto City**[23] 5835 2-7-11 30 .... DanielleMcCreery(7) 1 29
(D W Chapman) *chsd ldrs: lost pl over 1f out* **125/1**

6424 **6** ½ **Dispol Truly (IRE)**[119] 3174 2-8-4 50 .... StephenCarson 6 27
(A G Newcombe) *dwlt: effrt on ins over 2f out: nvr nr ldrs* **12/1**[3]

0643 **7** ¾ **Rue Soleil**[7] 6157 2-8-3 64 ow3 .... MichaelJStainton(5) 12 29
(J R Weymes) *mid-div: drvn over 2f out: nvr a threat* **10/3**[2]

00 **8** nk **My Maite Mickey**[23] 5835 2-8-11 .... FergusSweeney 4 31
(R C Guest) *chsd ldrs: wknd 2f out* **22/1**

000 **9** shd **Lady Toyah (IRE)**[31] 5687 2-8-2 35 ow1 .... PatrickMathers(3) 11 25
(Mrs L Williamson) *mid-div: lost pl over 3f out* **125/1**

000 **10** 4 **Littlemadgebob**[34] 5615 2-8-6 40 .... PaulMulrennan 5 14
(J R Norton) *chsd ldrs: lost pl over 2f out* **50/1**

11 3 ½ **Emerald Sky** 2-8-5 .... AdrianMcCarthy 9 2
(R Brotherton) *s.i.s: a in rr* **33/1**

5006 **12** ¾ **Only A Splash**[6] 6172 2-8-12 50 .... PaulQuinn 13 7
(D W Chapman) *chsd ldrs on outer: outpcd and rdn over 3f out: lost pl over 2f out* **12/1**[3]

1m 16.54s (-0.36) **Going Correction** -0.15s/f (Stan) **12** Ran SP% **113.2**
Speed ratings (Par 89):96,92,88,85,84 83,82,82,82,76 72,71
CSF £15.65 TOTE £1.90: £1.10, £3.70, £11.30; EX 14.10 TRIFECTA Not won..
Owner The Anglo Irish Choral Society **Bred** The Anglo Irish Choral Society **Trained** Lambourn, Berks

FOCUS
The winner made this look very simple on her All-Weather debut and could rate higher.

NOTEBOOK
Bahamian Love travelled strongly and made this look very straightforward. She was value for at least five lengths. (op 4-5)
Gibsons, who had 19lb to find with the winner, took them along but was very readily picked off.
Shouldntbethere(IRE), on his toes beforehand, is rated just 45 after being well beaten in three outings on turf. Given some sharp reminders soon after the start, he stayed on in his own time in the home straight. (tchd 40-1)
Cape Free, a lengthy newcomer, stood still when the stalls opened. She made ground on the wide outside once in line for home and was putting in some pleasing work at the line. This should have taught her plenty. (op 16-1)
Kyoto City, rated just 30, showed her first real signs of ability. (op 150-1)

Dispol Truly(IRE) played up in the stalls and missed the break slightly. (op 14-1)
Rue Soleil, who had the same chance as the winner on official ratings, never fired on her All-Weather debut. (op 9-2)
Littlemadgebob Official explanation: jockey said filly was unable to handle the bend

6279 WORLD BET EXCHANGE BANDED STKS 1m 4f (F)
2:50 (2:50) (Class 7) 3-Y-0+ **£1,501** (£443; £221) **Stalls** Low

Form RPR
2050 **1** **Blue Opal**[150] 2242 4-9-5 45 MickyFenton 8 — 54
(Miss S E Hall) *mid-div: hdwy over 3f out: led over 2f out: edgd rt fnl f: hld on towards fin* **6/1**[2]
0030 **2** ½ **Iamback**[47] 5324 6-9-5 40 (t) AdamKirby 13 — 53
(Miss D A McHale) *in tch: hdwy to chalr over 2f out: no ex towards fin* **11/2**[1]
0006 **3** nk **Laurollie**[19] 5925 4-9-5 45 DeanMcKeown 5 — 53
(B P J Baugh) *prom: styd on appr fnl f: kpt on wl towards fin* **33/1**
0050 **4** ¾ **Missouri (USA)**[56] 5082 3-8-12 45 DanielTudhope 4 — 52
(G M Moore) *chsd ldrs: led over 4f out: hdd over 2f out: hung lft and one pce fnl f* **8/1**[3]
0204 **5** nk **Kentucky Bullet (USA)**[168] 1767 10-9-5 40 FergusSweeney 7 — 51
(A G Newcombe) *hld up: stdy hdwy on wd outside over 2f out: kpt on same pce fnl f* **8/1**[3]
-404 **6** 3½ **Phlaunt**[23] 5830 4-9-5 45 StephenCarson 6 — 45
(R F Johnson Houghton) *mid-div: hdwy over 2f out: kpt on fnl f* **12/1**
4600 **7** ½ **Nakwa (IRE)**[19] 5925 8-9-5 45 PaulQuinn 1 — 45
(E J Alston) *led 1f: chsd ldrs: styd far side: edgd rt and wknd fnl f* **10/1**
4361 **8** 5 **Shaika**[13] 6057 3-8-9 45 SaleemGolam(3) 12 — 37
(G Prodromou) *s.i.s: in rr: sme hdwy over 4f out: nvr on terms* **6/1**[2]
6006 **9** ½ **Madame Constanze (IRE)**[32] 5651 3-8-9 45 DominicFox(3) 3 — 36
(Miss Gay Kelleway) *slowly away: nvr on terms* **20/1**
0-06 **10** 2½ **Lihusn Al Haz (USA)**[116] 3258 3-8-12 45 (p) BrettDoyle 14 — 32
(C E Brittain) *mid-div: outpcd over 4f out: sn wknd* **10/1**
0340 **11** 1¼ **Gypsy Royal (IRE)**[50] 5240 4-9-5 40 FrancisNorton 10 — 30
(G Woodward) *a in rr* **10/1**
0024 **12** 20 **House Martin**[11] 3941 4-9-5 45 (b) RobbieFitzpatrick 11 — —
(C R Dore) *led after 1f: hdd over 4f out: sn wknd: eased over 1f out: sn bhd* **9/1**
50-0 **13** 14 **Georgie's Lass (IRE)**[13] 5768 7-9-2 45 JamesDoyle(3) 9 — —
(R J Price) *bhd: t.o 3f out* **100/1**
6000 **14** nk **Kirstys Lad**[19] 5927 4-9-5 40 (e[1]) LeeEnstone 2 — —
(M Mullineaux) *chsd ldrs: rdn over 5f out: sn lost pl: t.o 3f out* **50/1**

2m 41.84s (-0.25) **Going Correction** -0.15s/f (Stan)
WFA 3 from 4yo+ 7lb **14** Ran SP% **121.8**
Speed ratings (Par 97):94,93,93,92,92 90,90,86,86,84 83,70,61,61
CSF £38.41 TOTE £7.10: £2.90, £2.60, £6.00; EX 77.30 TRIFECTA Not won..
Owner C Platts **Bred** Miss S E Hall **Trained** Middleham Moor, N Yorks
■ Stewards' Enquiry : Micky Fenton three-day ban: careless riding (Nov 11, 13-14)

FOCUS
A fair contest and the form looks pretty sound with the winner, second and fifth to form

6280 ERIC ROLLINSON MEMORIAL BANDED STKS 1m 3f (F)
3:20 (3:20) (Class 7) 4-Y-0+ **£1,911** (£564; £282) **Stalls** Low

Form RPR
1044 **1** **Jadeeron**[8] 6132 7-8-12 45 (p) RobbieFitzpatrick 2 — 53+
(Miss D A McHale) *chsd ldrs: rdn to ld over 1f out: eased towards fin* **7/2**[1]
0005 **2** nk **Red River Rock (IRE)**[19] 5925 4-8-12 45 (be) PaulMulrennan 10 — 52
(T J Fitzgerald) *led after 1f: hdd over 1f out: kpt on wl towards fin* **16/1**
0400 **3** 5 **Abbeygate**[78] 4439 5-9-1 48 MickyFenton 3 — 47
(T Keddy) *in rr: hdwy on outside over 2f out: kpt on: nvr a threat to 1st 2* **8/1**
0-00 **4** hd **Musardiere**[18] 5954 4-8-12 48 SaleemGolam(3) 12 — 47
(J Balding) *bhd: hdwy on wd outside over 2f out: edgd lft: kpt on same pce* **14/1**
-010 **5** 3 **Cotton Easter**[154] 2099 5-9-1 48 (t) FrancisNorton 11 — 42
(Mrs A J Bowlby) *s.i.s: kpt on fnl 3f: nvr nr ldrs* **17/2**
3005 **6** ¾ **Sorbiesharry (IRE)**[92] 3998 7-8-12 45 DanielTudhope 14 — 37
(Mrs N Macauley) *hld up in rr: hdwy over 3f out: nvr nr ldrs* **15/2**[3]
2002 **7** 1¼ **Emperor Cat (IRE)**[54] 5127 5-9-0 47 TonyCulhane 13 — 37
(Mrs N S Evans) *prom: effrt over 3f out: wknd over 1f out* **12/1**
35/4 **8** hd **Glen Vale Walk (IRE)**[19] 5925 9-8-12 45 JamieMackay 7 — 35
(Mrs G S Rees) *hld up in rr: effrt on outer over 2f out: nvr a factor* **8/1**
0000 **9** ¾ **Futoo (IRE)**[94] 3941 5-8-12 45 PaulQuinn 1 — 34
(D W Chapman) *prom: effrt over 4f out: sn wknd* **40/1**
0000 **10** 3 **Filey Buoy**[19] 5929 4-8-9 47 MichaelJStainton(5) 4 — 31
(R M Whitaker) *led 1f: chsd ldrs: wknd 2f out* **33/1**
05-5 **11** 5 **Manhattan Jack**[23] 5837 5-9-3 50 DeanMcKeown 9 — 25
(G A Swinbank) *in rr: hdwy on outer over 4f out: lost pl 3f out* **13/2**[2]
352- **12** ¾ **Aggi Mac**[337] 6442 5-8-5 40 SuzzanneFrance(7) 5 — 19
(N Bycroft) *mid-div: lost pl over 4f out* **16/1**
-200 **13** shd **Trysting Grove (IRE)**[19] 5925 5-8-12 45 PhillipMakin 8 — 19
(E G Bevan) *sn chsng ldrs: lost pl over 3f out* **20/1**
00-0 **14** 18 **Swinton**[85] 4205 5-8-12 40 DeanMernagh 6 — —
(M Brittain) *mid-div: lost pl over 4f out: bhd whn eased over 1f out* **66/1**

2m 27.88s (-1.02) **Going Correction** -0.15s/f (Stan) **14** Ran SP% **117.8**
Speed ratings (Par 97):97,96,93,93,90 90,89,89,88,86 82,82,82,69
CSF £60.31 TOTE £3.80: £1.40, £5.10, £3.60; EX 78.00 TRIFECTA Not won..
Owner N Bashir **Bred** Aziz Merza **Trained** Newmarket, Suffolk

FOCUS
The form of this contest does not look strong with the second and fourth having shown little of late and the winner, over a trip shorter than his optimium, the best guide.
Trysting Grove(IRE) Official explanation: trainer said mare was found to have a virus

6281 WBX.COM BANDED STKS 1m (F)
3:50 (3:50) (Class 7) 3-Y-0+ **£1,876** (£554; £277) **Stalls** Low

Form RPR
0420 **1** **Vibrato (USA)**[18] 5949 4-9-0 45 RobbieFitzpatrick 11 — 54
(C J Teague) *s.s: gd hdwy on ins over 2f out: led jst ins last: styd on strly: readily* **16/1**
0035 **2** 3½ **Preskani**[19] 5926 4-9-0 45 (p) DanielTudhope 3 — 47+
(Mrs N Macauley) *prom: reminders over 4f out: led over 2f out: edgd rt: hdd and no ex jst ins last* **11/2**[3]
0500 **3** ½ **Top Level (IRE)**[12] 6067 3-8-8 45 DominicFox(3) 5 — 46
(M G Quinlan) *mid-div: hdwy over 2f out: edgd rt over 1f out: kpt on wl* **18/1**
0630 **4** shd **Tacid**[76] 4497 4-8-11 45 JamesDoyle(3) 7 — 45
(Dr J D Scargill) *s.s: hdwy over 2f out: styd on fnl f* **13/2**
-000 **5** nk **Owners Biscuits**[8] 6133 3-8-8 45 (b[1]) GregFairley(3) 4 — 45
(M Johnston) *w ldr: led over 4f out: hdd over 2f out: one pce* **25/1**
0301 **6** 1¾ **Tartan Special**[8] 6134 4-9-6 45 LeeEnstone 9 — 47
(K R Burke) *trckd ldrs: wknd and eased wl ins last* **4/1**[1]
160- **7** 2 **Scorchio (IRE)**[307] 6680 5-9-0 45 MickyFenton 1 — 37
(B Smart) *s.i.s: kpt on fnl 2f: nvr nr ldrs* **14/1**
5423 **8** shd **Spring Time Girl**[8] 6134 4-9-0 45 (p) PaulMulrennan 12 — 37
(B Ellison) *bhd: kpt on fnl 2f: nvr on terms* **5/1**[2]
0405 **9** shd **Bogaz (IRE)**[2] 6237 4-8-11 45 (v) RichardKingscote(3) 8 — 36
(Mrs H Sweeting) *mid-div: outpcd over 4f out: n.d after* **15/2**
5304 **10** 5 **Sea Frolic (IRE)**[19] 5926 5-8-9 45 (v) RoryMoore(5) 10 — 26
(Jennie Candlish) *rr-div: sme hdwy over 3f out: nvr a factor* **10/1**
0006 **11** nk **Mycenean Prince (USA)**[23] 5838 3-8-11 45 FergusSweeney 14 — 25
(R C Guest) *a in rr* **8/1**
-000 **12** 7 **Layed Back Rocky**[225] 684 4-9-0 45 AdrianMcCarthy 6 — 11
(M Mullineaux) *led tl over 4f out: lost pl 3f out* **100/1**
0000 **13** 1¾ **Tilen (IRE)**[23] 5840 3-8-11 45 TonyCulhane 2 — 7
(S Parr) *chsd ldrs: hrd drvn over 4f out: sn lost pl* **80/1**

1m 44.43s (-0.17) **Going Correction** -0.15s/f (Stan)
WFA 3 from 4yo+ 3lb **13** Ran SP% **121.2**
Speed ratings (Par 97):94,90,90,89,89 87,85,85,85,80 80,73,71
CSF £102.60 TOTE £18.00: £4.90, £2.00, £6.90; EX 143.00 Trifecta £95.70 Part won. Pool: £134.81 - 0.10 winning units..
Owner Richardson Kelly Smith **Bred** Holtsinger Inc **Trained** Station Town, Co Durham

FOCUS
An ordinary contest but the winner came from well back. the form looks slightly dubious rated through the fourth, with third and fifth havinge no recent form.
Tacid ◆ Official explanation: jockey said he had difficulty in removing blindfold
Spring Time Girl Official explanation: jockey said filly never travelled

6282 VISIT WBX.COM BANDED STKS 6f (F)
4:20 (4:21) (Class 7) 3-Y-0+ **£1,876** (£554; £277) **Stalls** Low

Form RPR
0546 **1** **Barzak (IRE)**[8] 6134 6-9-0 45 (bt) PhillipMakin 5 — 54
(S R Bowring) *chsd ldrs: led over 1f out: rdn out: readily* **4/1**[1]
0500 **2** 2 **Mister Jingles**[69] 4695 3-8-8 45 MichaelJStainton(5) 9 — 48
(R M Whitaker) *w ldrs: styd on same pce fnl f* **10/1**
0050 **3** shd **Quote Unquote**[8] 6129 3-8-10 45 NeilChalmers(3) 14 — 48
(J Parkes) *sn w ldrs: kpt on same pce fnl f* **33/1**
3000 **4** 2 **Straffan (IRE)**[22] 5865 4-9-0 45 (p) AdrianMcCarthy 6 — 42
(J Hetherton) *led: qcknd 3f out: hdd over 1f out: wknd wl ins last* **8/1**[3]
3000 **5** 2½ **Ace Club**[8] 6131 5-9-0 45 (b) RobbieFitzpatrick 10 — 34
(M J Attwater) *rr-div: styd far side in home st: hdwy over 2f out: nvr trbld ldrs* **10/1**
0000 **6** ½ **Spinetail Rufous (IRE)**[48] 5291 8-8-11 45 SaleemGolam(3) 12 — 33
(Miss Z C Davison) *s.i.s: in rr tl kpt on fnl 2f* **7/1**[2]
0-00 **7** nk **Caspian Rose**[8] 6134 3-8-13 45 MickyFenton 13 — 32
(M J Attwater) *in rr: c stands' side over 2f out: kpt on: nvr nr ldrs* **50/1**
0055 **8** hd **Jabraan (USA)**[45] 5363 4-9-0 45 TonyCulhane 1 — 31
(D W Chapman) *rr-div: effrt over 2f out: nvr on terms* **8/1**[3]
000 **9** 1½ **Pro Tempore**[60] 4984 4-9-0 45 FergusSweeney 3 — 27
(David Pinder) *chsd ldrs: hrd drvn 3f out: sn btn* **11/1**
0060 **10** ¾ **Fraternity**[120] 3158 9-8-7 45 JamieHamblett(7) 11 — 24
(J A Pickering) *prom: rdn and outpcd over 3f out: n.d after* **10/1**
3004 **11** ½ **Nilsatisoptimum (USA)**[8] 6131 3-8-13 45 (e[1]) LeeEnstone 4 — 23
(M Mullineaux) *in tch: lost pl 2f out* **7/1**[2]
00-0 **12** nk **Young Valentino**[36] 5569 4-9-0 45 FrancisNorton 2 — 22
(A W Carroll) *stdd s: hld up in rr: nvr on terms* **11/1**
-000 **13** 1¾ **Compton Micky**[75] 4511 5-8-7 45 ChrisHough(7) 8 — 17
(R F Marvin) *t.k.h in rr: nvr a factor* **28/1**
0-00 **14** 28 **Flaming Shot (IRE)**[43] 5435 4-8-9 45 (b[1]) RoryMoore(5) 7 — —
(Jennie Candlish) *bhd: heavily eased 2f out: virtually p.u* **100/1**

1m 16.29s (-0.61) **Going Correction** -0.15s/f (Stan)
WFA 3 from 4yo+ 1lb **14** Ran SP% **120.5**
Speed ratings (Par 97):98,95,95,92,89 88,88,87,85,84 84,83,81,44
CSF £43.53 TOTE £4.10: £1.90, £3.50, £8.20; EX 64.40 TRIFECTA Not won. Place 6 £200.50, Place 5 £47.96.
Owner Clark Industrial Services Partnership **Bred** Clarks Industrial Services Partnership **Trained** Edwinstowe, Notts

FOCUS
A sprint in which few got into contention from off the pace. The form is rated as average for the grade.
T/Jkpt: Not won. T/Plt: £273.50 to a £1 stake. Pool: £49,626.45. 132.45 winning tickets. T/Qpdt: £36.40 to a £1 stake. Pool: £3,239.00. 65.80 winning tickets. WG

6254 WOLVERHAMPTON (A.W) (L-H)
Tuesday, October 31

OFFICIAL GOING: Standard to fast
Wind: Fresh, across Weather: Fine

6283 THE ZONGALERO RESTAURANT OVERLOOKS THE TRACK MAIDEN AUCTION STKS 1m 1f 103y(P)
3:55 (3:56) (Class 6) 2-Y-0 **£2,730** (£806; £403) **Stalls** Low

Form RPR
635 **1** **Lets Get Cracking (FR)**[24] 5814 2-8-11 72 NCallan 3 — 72
(K A Ryan) *mde all: hung rt over 2f out: sn rdn: hung rt ins fnl f: styd on* **5/2**[1]
4220 **2** ¾ **Aussie Cricket (FR)**[22] 5866 2-8-8 69 EddieAhern 11 — 68
(D J Coakley) *plld hrd and prom: rdn 2f out: hung lft ins fnl f: styd on* **11/4**[2]
305 **3** nk **Stanley George (IRE)**[23] 5841 2-9-1 75 MatthewHenry 1 — 74
(M A Jarvis) *chsd ldrs: rdn and edgd rt over 1f out: styd on* **11/4**[2]
4 4 **Miss Fancy Pants** 2-8-10 JoeFanning 10 — 61
(M Johnston) *s.s: hdwy over 6f out: outpcd 3f out: r.o ins fnl f* **12/1**[3]
003 **5** ½ **Law Of The Land (IRE)**[29] 5738 2-8-13 62 DaneO'Neill 4 — 63
(W R Muir) *trckd ldr: rdn 2f out: hung lft and wknd ins fnl f* **12/1**[3]
00 **6** 4 **Go Dude**[18] 5948 2-8-9 (p) MichaelTebbutt 2 — 52
(J Ryan) *hld up: hmpd 7f out: hdwy over 2f out: rdn and wknd over 1f out* **100/1**
00 **7** 8 **Grand Officer (IRE)**[52] 5178 2-8-11 HayleyTurner 5 — 39
(D J S Ffrench Davis) *chsd ldrs 7f* **100/1**
8 1¼ **Rebel Pearl (IRE)** 2-8-8 TPQueally 7 — 33
(M G Quinlan) *hld up: hdwy 1/2-way: wknd 2f out* **16/1**

9 ½ **Dr Light (IRE)** 2-9-1 .... GeorgeBaker 9 39
(S Kirk) *s.s: a in rr* **12/1**[3]

0300 10 16 **Mr Wall Street**[7] 6157 2-8-8 61 .... KevinGhunowa(5) 8 7
(Mrs L Williamson) *hld up in tch: dropped rr 5f out: wknd 3f out* **66/1**

2m 1.83s (-0.79) **Going Correction** -0.25s/f (Stan) 10 Ran SP% **114.3**
Speed ratings (Par 93):93,92,92,88,88 84,77,76,75,61
CSF £9.34 TOTE £2.40: £1.10, £1.80, £1.30; EX 10.90.
Owner Mrs Jackie Love and Mrs T Marnane **Bred** B Ducasse Et Al **Trained** Hambleton, N Yorks
■ Stewards' Enquiry : Kevin Ghunowa one-day ban: careless riding (Nov 11)

FOCUS
An unremarkable maiden auction event in which the result panned out very much as adjusted official ratings suggested they would, making the form look solid. The pace was only fair, which rather played into the hands of the favourite.

NOTEBOOK
Lets Get Cracking(FR), taking on rather modest company than in his three turf maidens, again adopted forcing tactics and they worked the oracle against these rivals over this longer trip. Despite hanging right in the straight, he kept on finding enough and as he did no more than he was entitled to on official ratings, his current mark should not be affected when he goes into handicaps. (op 11-4 tchd 3-1)
Aussie Cricket(FR), appreciating the return to a sounder surface, did not help her chances by taking a grip and probably did well to grab second under the circumstances. Now runner-up in three of her five outings, a stronger gallop and possibly a switch back to handicaps may see her go one better. (op 3-1 tchd 10-3)
Stanley George(IRE) was stepping up over two furlongs in trip, but even this did not seem far enough. He does not look anything out of the ordinary and perhaps a switch to handicaps may help him. (op 5-2)
Miss Fancy Pants, a 21,000gns half-sister to Jagger, gave away ground at the start and looked very much in need of the experience. Her pedigree is all about stamina, so it was not a surprise to see her keeping on in her own time at the end and she ought to improve as she goes up in trip. (op 8-1)
Law Of The Land(IRE), the most experienced in the field, failed to see out this longer trip and was up against it on official ratings in any case. (op 16-1)
Dr Light(IRE) Official explanation: jockey said gelding missed the break

6284 RINGSIDE SUITE MEDIAN AUCTION MAIDEN STKS 1m 141y(P)
4:20 (4:22) (Class 6) 2-Y-O £2,559 (£755; £378) Stalls Low

Form RPR

34 1 **Filios (IRE)**[18] 5933 2-9-3 .... NickyMackay 9 70+
(L M Cumani) *hld up: hmpd 7f out: hdwy over 3f out: sn edgd lft: rdn to ld ins fnl f: hung rt: styd on u.p* **4/7**[1]

6603 2 1 ¾ **Callisto Moon**[3] 6224 2-8-12 73 ....(b[1]) KevinGhunowa(5) 7 66
(P A Blockley) *dwlt: hmpd 7f out: hdwy over 5f out: rdn and hung rt 2f out: led 1f out: sn hdd: styng on same pce whn nt clr run nr fin* **10/1**[3]

0 3 3 ½ **Four Tel**[8] 6145 2-9-3 .... DaneO'Neill 10 59
(J H M Gosden) *s.i.s: hdwy 6f out: led over 2f out: rdn: edgd lft an hdd 1f out: no ex* **5/1**[2]

4 1 ¼ **Jocheski (IRE)** 2-9-3 .... EddieAhern 3 56
(M J Wallace) *s.i.s: sn chsng ldrs: rdn 1/2-way: n.m.r and lost pl 3f out: n.d after* **14/1**

00 5 1 **Francesco**[12] 6063 2-9-3 .... HayleyTurner 6 54
(M L W Bell) *outpcd: rdn 1/2-way: hdwy over 1f out: nrst fin* **33/1**

5564 6 nk **Poyle Kiera**[60] 4980 2-8-12 49 .... NCallan 4 48
(M Blanshard) *chsd ldrs: led over 3f out: rdn and hdd over 2f out: wknd over 1f out* **28/1**

0 7 11 **Inflagrantedelicto (USA)**[112] 3385 2-9-3 .... JoeFanning 1 30
(M Johnston) *led: rdn and hdd over 3f out: wknd over 1f out* **14/1**

6 8 4 **Ancient Site (USA)**[45] 5389 2-9-3 .... PaulEddery 5 22
(B P J Baugh) *hld up in tch: edgd rt 7f out: lost pl over 5f out: bhd fnl 3f* **100/1**

0 9 1 ¾ **Mountain Call (IRE)**[42] 5457 2-9-3 ....(b[1]) JimCrowley 8 18
(Mrs A J Perrett) *chsd ldrs 7f* **33/1**

0 10 11 **Fara's Kingdom**[34] 5615 2-9-3 .... GeorgeBaker 11 —
(Miss J A Camacho) *chsd ldrs to 1/2-way* **100/1**

1m 51.12s (-0.64) **Going Correction** -0.25s/f (Stan) 10 Ran SP% **114.1**
Speed ratings (Par 93):92,90,87,86,85 85,75,71,70,60
CSF £6.63 TOTE £1.60: £1.02, £2.80, £1.30; EX 6.30.
Owner L Marinopoulos **Bred** Bluegate Stud **Trained** Newmarket, Suffolk

FOCUS
Another modest maiden auction event limited by the runner-up and sixth, though a couple may have some improvement in them.

NOTEBOOK
Filios(IRE) was well backed at skinny odds, but his supporters must have feared the worse when he came under pressure rounding the home bend and seemed to be going nowhere, but the further they went the better he was going and he was well on top at the line. Handicap now beckon and he can probably continue to improve, whilst a bit further may not come amiss either. (op 8-11)
Callisto Moon was the most experienced in the field so it was a surprise to see him run so wide rounding the home bend, but he still had every chance and was beaten fair and square. He is the benchmark to the form. (op 8-1)
Four Tel played an active role until outpaced by the front pair inside the last furlong, but this was still an improvement from his debut. The best of him may not be seen until he is handicapped. (tchd 11-2)
Jocheski(IRE) ◆, a half-brother to five winners including the multiple Fibresand winner Weet-A-Minute, showed a little ability and was far from disgraced considering he was the only newcomer in the race. He is one to watch out for, especially when the money is down. (tchd 12-1)
Francesco plugged on late and was never nearer at the line. He now qualifies for handicaps and it would be no surprise to see him step up formwise when he does. (tchd 40-1)
Poyle Kiera showed up for a long way, but did not get home and is starting to look exposed. (tchd 33-1)
Fara's Kingdom Official explanation: trainer's rep said gelding was struck into

6285 TWILIGHT RACING MISS THE TRAFFIC NURSERY 1m 141y(P)
4:50 (4:51) (Class 5) (0-75,73) 2-Y-O £4,533 (£1,348; £674; £336) Stalls Low

Form RPR

0636 1 **Tom Paris**[20] 5909 2-9-6 72 .... DaneO'Neill 9 73
(W R Muir) *hld up: hdwy over 2f out: rdn to ld ins fnl f: jst hld on* **20/1**

4265 2 shd **Beech Games**[18] 5933 2-9-7 73 .... ChrisCatlin 3 74
(E J O'Neill) *hld up: hdwy over 1f out: sn hung rt: rdn and ev ch ins fnl f: r.o* **9/1**

056 3 1 ½ **Kon Tiki**[43] 5424 2-9-1 67 .... J-PGuillambert 4 65
(M Johnston) *led over 7f out: rdn 2f out: hung rt and hdd ins fnl f: styd on same pce* **16/1**

5636 4 nk **Hemispear**[18] 5947 2-9-0 66 .... PaulFitzsimons 10 63
(Miss J R Tooth) *a.p: rdn over 1f out: sn hung rt: styd on* **50/1**

0601 5 nk **Copper King**[18] 5948 2-8-13 72 .... MCGeran(7) 2 68
(P D Evans) *hld up: racd keenly: hdwy and nt clr run over 1f out: r.o* **14/1**

023 6 1 ¾ **Keidas (FR)**[55] 5106 2-9-6 72 .... EddieAhern 5 65+
(C F Wall) *chsd ldrs: rdn over 2f out: no clr run over 1f out: styd on same pce* **11/8**[1]

0300 7 hd **Cheery Cat (USA)**[17] 5958 2-8-8 60 .... DarryllHolland 6 52
(D W Barker) *chsd ldrs: ev ch 2f out: sn rdn and hung lft: hung rt 1f out: no ex* **33/1**

5066 8 1 **Inquisitress**[11] 6074 2-9-0 69 .... StephenDonohoe(3) 7 59
(J M P Eustace) *chsd ldrs: rdn over 2f out: wknd over 1f out* **8/1**[3]

4501 9 1 **Nicada (IRE)**[29] 5738 2-9-2 68 .... NCallan 1 56
(Miss Gay Kelleway) *hld up: hmpd 7f out: effrt over 2f out: nt trble ldrs* **13/2**[2]

020 10 1 ¼ **High Five Society**[19] 5923 2-8-10 62 .... PaulEddery 11 47
(S R Bowring) *hld up: a in rr* **25/1**

436 11 2 ½ **Petrosian**[13] 6058 2-8-10 62 .... JoeFanning 8 42
(M Johnston) *chsd ldrs: rdn over 2f out: wknd over 1f out* **10/1**

0000 12 hd **Rikochet**[35] 5597 2-9-0 66 .... JimCrowley 12 46
(Mrs A J Perrett) *hld up in tch: rdn and wknd over 2f out* **33/1**

000 13 12 **Oscarshall (IRE)**[24] 5814 2-8-13 65 .... TPQueally 13 20
(M H Tompkins) *hld up: rn wd 7f out: hdwy 1/2-way: wknd over 2f out* **14/1**

1m 50.62s (-1.14) **Going Correction** -0.25s/f (Stan) 13 Ran SP% **121.3**
Speed ratings (Par 95):95,94,93,93,93 91,91,90,89,88 86,86,75
CSF £184.49 CT £3057.58 TOTE £14.90: £3.60, £2.50, £3.90; EX 161.60.
Owner M J Caddy **Bred** Lostford Manor Stud **Trained** Lambourn, Berks
■ Stewards' Enquiry : Chris Catlin two-day ban: used whip with excessive force (Nov 11, 13)

FOCUS
A fair nursery, but something of a messy race with bunching on the first bend and then several coming very wide into the home straight, which left a huge gap for the front pair to exploit on the inside. The form appears reasonable on paper, with the placed horses to form

NOTEBOOK
Tom Paris, who had not raced beyond six furlongs in 11 previous outings, proved well suited by this longer trip and was helped by the majority of his rivals swinging wide off the final bend and giving him a clear run on the inside. Giving his all, he just managed to hang on by the skin of his teeth. (tchd 25-1)
Beech Games, making his nursery debut, like the winner obtained a clear run on the inside as most of his rivals hung right from the home bend, but despite plenty of encouragement from the saddle he just failed to get up. (op 8-1 tchd 10-1)
Kon Tiki, making her nursery debut after three runs in maidens, was not guaranteed to appreciate this longer trip judged on her previous efforts, but she ran a gritty race from the front until hanging and giving best to the front pair entering the last furlong. Stamina did not appear to be an issue and she remains relatively unexposed. (tchd 18-1)
Hemispear, who got bogged down in the soft ground at Warwick last time, appreciated the return to a sound surface and ran a fair race at a massive price. She does not have much in the way of scope, but looks capable of winning a modest race on this surface.
Copper King, claimed by current connections after winning a Warwick claimer earlier this month, had little room to play with when trying to improve halfway up the home straight but was staying on well at the line. The longer trip did not appear to be a problem and an opportunity should be found for him on this surface in the coming months. (op 12-1 tchd 16-1)
Keidas(FR), making her nursery debut after showing promise in a couple of maidens, travelled very well but did not find anything like as much off the bridle as had seemed likely. The longer trip cannot really be blamed and this was just plain disappointing. (op 6-4 tchd 13-8 in places)

6286 STAY AT THE WOLVERHAMPTON HOLIDAY INN MEDIAN AUCTION MAIDEN STKS 7f 32y(P)
5:20 (5:22) (Class 6) 3-4-Y-O £2,388 (£705; £352) Stalls High

Form RPR

3-02 1 **One Night In Paris (IRE)**[22] 5874 3-8-12 62 .... EddieAhern 7 66
(M J Wallace) *hld up in tch: rdn to ld and edgd rt ins fnl f: r.o* **7/2**[2]

3304 2 2 ½ **Ours (IRE)**[23] 5847 3-9-3 58 ....(b[1]) DarryllHolland 8 65
(J D Bethell) *hld up: hdwy u.p and hung rt over 1f out: nt rch wnr* **9/1**

-540 3 shd **Just Bond (IRE)**[152] 2165 4-9-0 53 .... DuranFentiman(5) 11 64
(G R Oldroyd) *hld up: plld hrd: hdwy 4f out: rdn and ev ch 1f out: no ex wl ins fnl f* **33/1**

050 4 1 ¾ **Mill End (IRE)**[35] 5598 4-9-5 62 .... NCallan 3 60
(R M H Cowell) *hld up: rdn over 2f out: r.o ins fnl f: nrst fin* **14/1**

5 hd **Spoilsport**[68] 4752 3-8-5 .... MCGeran(7) 4 54
(P D Evans) *hld up: rdn over 2f out: r.o ins fnl f: nrst fin* **28/1**

0024 6 1 ½ **Benny The Bus**[17] 5969 4-9-5 64 .... ChrisCatlin 6 55
(Mrs G S Rees) *chsd ldr: led 2f out: sn rdn: hdd 1f out: sn wknd* **9/4**[1]

7 1 ¾ **Tornadodancer (IRE)**[25] 5795 3-8-12 .... OCasey(5) 1 51
(T G McCourt, Ire) *led 5f: rdn to ld 1f out: sn hdd & wknd* **20/1**

53 8 1 ¼ **Kilgary (USA)**[23] 5847 3-8-12 .... TPQueally 5 42
(J Noseda) *s.s: hld up: n.d* **4/1**[3]

0-00 9 nk **Cleveland**[64] 4870 4-8-12 53 .... RussellKennemore(7) 10 47
(R Hollinshead) *plld hrd and prom: hung rt and wknd wl over 1f out* **66/1**

4500 10 5 **Moonstreaker**[42] 5444 3-9-3 57 .... J-PGuillambert 2 34
(R M Whitaker) *chsd ldrs: rdn 1/2-way: wknd over 1f out* **10/1**

2400 11 2 ½ **Creme Brulee**[36] 5576 3-8-12 54 .... JoeFanning 9 22
(C R Egerton) *chsd ldrs over 5f* **18/1**

12 5 **Joe Draper**[59] 4-9-2 .... StephenDonohoe(3) 12 14
(P D Evans) *s.s: outpcd* **100/1**

1m 28.4s (-2.00) **Going Correction** -0.25s/f (Stan)
WFA 3 from 4yo 2lb 12 Ran SP% **117.6**
Speed ratings (Par 101):101,98,98,96,95 94,92,90,90,84 81,76
CSF £33.01 TOTE £4.70: £1.40, £3.00, £16.10; EX 26.20.
Owner D Teevan **Bred** Ken Carroll **Trained** Newmarket, Suffolk

FOCUS
Maidens for older horses at this stage of the season are usually moderate and this was no exception, as these runners had previously raced 93 times between them without success. The third looks the best guide to the level, but not many winners are likely to emerge from it.

6287 WOLVERHAMPTON-RACECOURSE.CO.UK H'CAP 1m 4f 50y(P)
5:50 (5:50) (Class 4) (0-85,77) 3-Y-O+ £5,505 (£1,637; £818; £408) Stalls Low

Form RPR

4040 1 **Heathyards Pride**[103] 3686 6-9-9 77 .... JimCrowley 2 84+
(R Hollinshead) *hld up: nt clr run wl over 1f out: swtchd lft: rdn to ld wl ins fnl f* **18/1**

331 2 ½ **Nando's Dream**[29] 5741 3-8-11 72 .... TPQueally 6 78+
(J Noseda) *chsd ldr tl led over 2f out: rdn and hdd wl ins fnl f* **4/1**[3]

2116 3 ½ **Fossgate**[39] 5506 5-9-8 76 .... NCallan 4 81
(J D Bethell) *prom: outpcd over 2f out: rallied over 1f out: r.o* **7/1**

600 4 1 ½ **Newnham (IRE)**[8] 6148 5-9-6 74 .... GeorgeBaker 1 77
(J R Boyle) *chsd ldrs: rdn over 2f out: styd on same pce fnl f* **11/2**

1660 5 ½ **Pass The Port**[25] 5792 5-9-7 75 .... EddieAhern 3 77
(D Haydn Jones) *dwlt: sn prom: rdn over 2f out: no ex fnl f* **7/2**[2]

-000 **6** 2½ **Supreme Charter**[22] 5869 3-8-12 73 .... JoeFanning 5 71
(M Johnston) *led over 8f: swtchd rt over 1f out: wknd fnl f* **16/1**
0245 **7** 1½ **Stretton (IRE)**[25] 5792 8-9-2 70 .... DarryllHolland 7 66
(J D Bethell) *hld up: rdn over 2f out: sme hdwy over 1f out: wknd fnl f* **11/4**[1]
0353 **8** *nk* **Grave Matters (USA)**[25] 5799 3-8-11 77 .... OCasey(5) 8 72
(T G McCourt, Ire) *hld up: hdwy over 4f out: wknd over 2f out* **33/1**

2m 41.25s (-1.17) **Going Correction** -0.25s/f (Stan)
WFA 3 from 5yo+ 7lb **8** Ran SP% **110.9**
Speed ratings (Par 105):93,92,92,91,91 89,88,88
CSF £83.23 CT £540.99 TOTE £19.40: £6.30, £1.10, £3.00; EX 80.30.
Owner L A Morgan **Bred** L A Morgan **Trained** Upper Longdon, Staffs

FOCUS
A fair little handicap in terms of quality, but a modest early pace resulted in a moderate winning time for a race like this. The form looks weak for the grade with the third the best guide.
Stretton(IRE) Official explanation: jockey said gelding was unsuited by the slow early pace

6288 SPONSOR A RACE TO ENHANCE YOUR BRAND H'CAP 5f 216y(P)
6:20 (6:21) (Class 6) (0-60,60) 3-Y-O+ **£2,388** (£705; £352) **Stalls** Low

Form RPR
3002 **1** **Musical Script (USA)**[18] 5938 3-9-1 58 .... JamieMackay 9 66
(Mrs A J Hamilton-Fairley) *chsd ldrs: rdn over 1f out: hung lft ins fnl f: r.o to ld nr fin* **11/2**[2]
3200 **2** *nk* **Bond Playboy**[33] 5635 6-8-13 60 .... (p) DuranFentiman(5) 5 67
(G R Oldroyd) *mid-div: hdwy to ld 1f out: rdn and hdd nr fin* **7/1**[3]
304 **3** ¾ **Middle Eastern**[13] 6061 4-9-3 59 .... TPO'Shea 1 64
(P A Blockley) *chsd ldrs: swtchd lft over 1f out: sn rdn: styd on* **3/1**[1]
0205 **4** *1* **Val De Maal (IRE)**[61] 4970 6-9-2 58 .... (b) JimCrowley 12 60+
(Miss J A Camacho) *s.i.s: hld up: hdwy over 1f out: nt rch ldrs* **9/1**
0600 **5** ½ **George The Second**[45] 5378 3-9-1 58 .... J-PGuillambert 7 58
(Mrs H Sweeting) *sn led: hdd over 4f out: led 2f out: rdn and hdd 1f out: no ex* **10/1**
0550 **6** *hd* **Cosmic Destiny (IRE)**[22] 5878 4-9-1 57 .... DaneO'Neill 10 57+
(E F Vaughan) *plld hrd and prom: rdn over 1f out: no ex ins fnl f* **11/1**
2300 **7** ½ **Mister Incredible**[18] 5938 3-9-1 58 .... (p) DarryllHolland 3 56
(V Smith) *hld up: effrt over 1f out: nvr trbld ldrs* **12/1**
0000 **8** ¾ **Tiviski (IRE)**[16] 5987 4-9-3 59 .... ChrisCatlin 8 55
(Miss Gay Kelleway) *chsd ldrs: rdn over 1f out: styd on same pce* **18/1**
1000 **9** ½ **Atlantic Viking (IRE)**[13] 6061 11-8-13 58 .... StephenDonohoe(3) 4 53
(P D Evans) *s.i.s: outpcd: nvr nrr* **12/1**
-000 **10** 1¼ **Vlasta Weiner**[45] 5386 6-8-9 58 .... (b) BarrySavage(7) 2 49
(J M Bradley) *s.s: outpcd* **28/1**
0-00 **11** *nk* **Bernie's Beau (IRE)**[28] 5756 3-8-10 60 .... RussellKennemore(7) 13 50
(R Hollinshead) *hld up: plld hrd: rdn over 2f out: wknd over 1f out* **40/1**
0060 **12** 1¾ **Patternmaker (USA)**[171] 1689 4-9-2 58 .... EddieAhern 11 43
(A M Hales) *led over 4f out: hdd over 2f out: rdn and wknd fnl f* **12/1**
0000 **13** *shd* **Boldinor**[5] 6193 3-8-12 60 .... OCasey(5) 6 44
(N E Berry) *mid-div: rdn 1/2-way: wknd over 1f out* **12/1**

1m 14.06s (-1.75) **Going Correction** -0.25s/f (Stan)
WFA 3 from 4yo+ 1lb **13** Ran SP% **122.2**
Speed ratings (Par 101):101,100,99,98,97 97,96,95,95,93 92,90,90
CSF £44.97 CT £144.39 TOTE £6.70: £1.90, £2.60, £1.30; EX 39.80 Place 6 £149.48, Place 5 £124.57.
Owner The Composers **Bred** Juddmonte Farms Inc **Trained** Bramshill, Hants

FOCUS
A modest if competitive-enough sprint and there was not much separating the whole field at the line. The form looks straightforward, rated around the placed horses to recent marks.
T/Plt: £100.00 to a £1 stake. Pool: £48,636.35. 354.95 winning tickets. T/Qpdt: £56.60 to a £1 stake. Pool: £3,267.20. 42.70 winning tickets. CR

6232 KEMPTON (A.W) (R-H)
Wednesday, November 1

OFFICIAL GOING: Standard
Wind: almost nil

6289 DAY TIME, NIGHT TIME, GREAT TIME H'CAP 1m 2f (P)
3:50 (3:51) (Class 6) (0-65,65) 3-Y-O+ **£2,388** (£705; £352) **Stalls** High

Form RPR
2000 **1** **Alekhine (IRE)**[26] 5786 5-9-7 64 .... (p) EddieAhern 3 72
(J R Boyle) *dwlt: in tch in rr: stdy prog fr 4f out: rdn to ld jst over 1f out: hld on wl* **7/1**[3]
2403 **2** *nk* **Bowled Out (GER)**[18] 5972 4-9-6 63 .... RichardMullen 14 70
(P J McBride) *prom: effrt on inner 2f out: chal and upsides over 1f out: pressed wnr fnl f: nt qckn* **5/1**[2]
6021 **3** ¾ **Border Edge**[13] 6069 8-9-1 65 .... JamesMillman(7) 9 71
(J J Bridger) *pressed ldr: led after 4f: drvn and hdd jst over 1f out: hld whn n.m.r ins fnl f* **4/1**[1]
3620 **4** *2* **Siena Star (IRE)**[32] 5691 8-9-4 61 .... PatCosgrave 11 63
(J R Boyle) *chsd ldrs: pushed along 4f out: kpt on same pce u.p fnl 2f: nvr able to chal* **14/1**
3160 **5** 2½ **Sarwin (USA)**[23] 5868 3-8-6 60 .... DebraEngland(7) 4 57
(W J Musson) *sn detached in last: prog on outside fr 3f out: nudged along and styd on steadily: no ch* **12/1**
300 **6** 2½ **Ali D**[42] 5484 8-9-1 58 .... FergusSweeney 13 51
(G Woodward) *settled in midfield: hrd rdn and nt on terms w ldrs 2f out: n.d after* **20/1**
2560 **7** ½ **High Octave (IRE)**[21] 5911 3-9-4 65 .... RichardHughes 2 57
(B G Powell) *n.m.r after 2f: hld up in midfield: clsd on ldrs 3f out: rdn and no rspnse over 1f out: wknd* **4/1**[1]
0004 **8** 1¼ **Street Life (IRE)**[154] 2149 8-9-5 62 .... TPQueally 1 51
(W J Musson) *hld up wl in rr: shuffled along fnl 2f: nvr nr ldrs* **10/1**
0 **9** *2* **Lalina (GER)**[61] 5008 3-8-13 60 .... SteveDrowne 12 46
(Jane Chapple-Hyam) *led for 4f: pressed ldrs tl wknd rapidly wl over 1f out* **12/1**
600 **10** *nk* **Secret Moment**[125] 3029 4-9-5 62 .... AdamKirby 6 47
(C G Cox) *chsd ldrs: wknd rapidly u.p wl over 1f out* **12/1**
3005 **11** 2½ **Dispol Veleta**[22] 5889 5-9-8 65 .... JamieMackay 7 45
(Miss T Spearing) *nvr bttr than midfield: lost tch w ldng gp 2f out: wknd* **20/1**
4000 **12** *11* **Eclipse Park**[115] 3339 3-9-4 65 .... LPKeniry 8 24
(M J McGrath) *a wl in rr: struggling and rdn 6f out: wknd over 2f out* **50/1**
506 **13** *17* **Pearl Of Esteem**[37] 5566 3-8-13 60 .... TedDurcan 5 —
(J Pearce) *rousted along early to rch midfield: struggling and rdn 1/2-way: sn wknd: t.o* **10/1**

2m 7.40s (-1.60) **Going Correction** -0.125s/f (Stan)
WFA 3 from 4yo+ 4lb **13** Ran SP% **128.6**
Speed ratings (Par 101):101,100,100,98,96 94,94,93,91,91 89,80,66
CSF £44.34 CT £167.41 TOTE £10.40: £3.50, £3.00, £1.50; EX 61.70.
Owner James Burley and Jon Hughes **Bred** Mrs S Dalton **Trained** Epsom, Surrey

FOCUS
A pretty modest handicap.

6290 HAMPTON COURT MAIDEN AUCTION STKS 7f (P)
4:20 (4:22) (Class 6) 2-Y-O **£2,388** (£705; £352) **Stalls** High

Form RPR
43 **1** **Hanbrin Bhoy (IRE)**[16] 6013 2-8-12 .... RoystonFfrench 6 70
(R Dickin) *trckd ldrs: wnt 2nd over 1f out: drvn and r.o fnl f to ld nr fin* **8/1**
4540 **2** *hd* **Buddies Girl (IRE)**[40] 5503 2-8-9 68 ow1 .... RichardHughes 12 66
(R Hannon) *led: rdn over 1f out: styd on: collared nr fin* **6/1**[3]
3 ½ **Blue Charm** 2-8-12 .... LPKeniry 3 68
(S Kirk) *dwlt: wl in rr tl prog over 2f out: shkn up over 1f out: r.o wl fnl f: gaining at fin* **10/1**
4 1¼ **Swing On A Star (IRE)** 2-8-8 .... AdamKirby 2 61+
(W R Swinburn) *dwlt: hld up in last pair: brought to wd outside and prog over 2f out: styd on fnl f: nrst fin* **20/1**
0 **5** ½ **Bold Saxon (IRE)**[22] 5890 2-8-13 .... IanMongan 7 65
(M D I Usher) *trckd ldrs: effrt over 2f out: sn hanging and nt qckn: one pce* **6/1**[3]
64 **6** ½ **News Of The Day (IRE)**[16] 6012 2-8-5 .... JoeFanning 4 55
(M Johnston) *racd wd thrght: in tch: effrt 2f out: kpt on: nvr rchd ldrs* **12/1**
7 *hd* **Balanchine Moon** 2-8-0 .... LiamJones(5) 14 55
(W J Haggas) *sn cl up on inner: shkn up and effrt over 2f out: no imp over 1f out: fdd* **25/1**
2 **8** *nk* **Toucantini**[15] 6031 2-8-7 .... SteveDrowne 8 56
(R Charlton) *t.k.h: prom: chsd ldr over 2f out to over 1f out: wknd* **11/4**[1]
00 **9** ¾ **Sumner (IRE)**[20] 5914 2-8-10 .... TPQueally 5 61+
(M H Tompkins) *hld up in rr: nudged along and styd on steadily fnl 2f: nvr nr ldrs: do bttr* **25/1**
2 **10** *hd* **Giant Slalom**[16] 6012 2-8-12 .... MartinDwyer 1 59
(W J Haggas) *hld up in rr: shkn up over 2f out: one pce and no prog* **10/3**[2]
11 *3* **Kiss Chase (IRE)** 2-8-13 .... DaneO'Neill 13 52
(P Mitchell) *v s.i.s and rousted along early: a wl in rr* **33/1**
0 **12** *shd* **Hayley's Flower (IRE)**[22] 5894 2-8-8 ow1 .... PatDobbs 10 47
(J C Fox) *prom tl wknd rapidly 2f out* **50/1**
13 *nk* **Wisdom's Kiss** 2-8-12 .... PatCosgrave 9 50
(J D Bethell) *dwlt: rousted along to rch midfield early: lost pl on inner 3f out: wknd over 1f out* **50/1**
14 *4* **Fiona's Wonder** 2-8-13 .... TedDurcan 11 40
(R A Harris) *chsd ldr to over 2f out: green and wknd rapidly* **66/1**

1m 28.53s (1.73) **Going Correction** -0.125s/f (Stan) **14** Ran SP% **127.0**
Speed ratings (Par 94):85,84,84,82,82 81,81,81,80,79 76,76,76,71
CSF £55.15 TOTE £9.40: £3.00, £3.70, £2.30; EX 63.30.
Owner H & E Scaffolding Ltd **Bred** A Lyons Bloodstock **Trained** Atherstone on Stour, Warwicks

FOCUS
Just an ordinary maiden in which they went a noticeably steady pace pretty much until they straightened for home; the winning time was unsurprisingly moderate and the form is best rated through the runner-up. The majority of the runners tended to drift to their left in the closing stages and ended up racing middle to stands' side.

NOTEBOOK
Hanbrin Bhoy(IRE) had shown plenty of ability on both his previous starts, including when third over six furlongs at Pontefract on his last outing and, back up in trip, he proved good enough to get off the mark at the third attempt. This was probably a decent effort, as the steady early pace is unlikely to have suited, and he should progress. His trainer is confident he will make a jumper in time. (tchd 9-1)
Buddies Girl(IRE), making her sand debut, was given a peach of a ride by Hughes, leading at just a steady pace and stacking up the field on the turn into the straight, but she was just run out of it close home. She has had plenty of chances now. (op 15-2)
Blue Charm, a 10,500gns half-brother to Threezedzz, a five-furlong juvenile scorer who was later a multiple winner over seven furlongs and a mile, made a very pleasing debut, staying on nicely for pressure in the straight.
Swing On A Star(IRE), a 15,000gns purchase, made an encouraging introduction from a poor draw and is open to plenty of improvement. (op 16-1)
Bold Saxon(IRE) could not build on the promise he showed on his debut at Newbury, but the steady pace did not appear to suit and he can leave this effort behind in time. (op 9-1)
News Of The Day(IRE) will have more options now she is qualified for a handicap mark.
Toucantini took a little bit of a grip early and failed to build on the promise she showed when second on her debut at Lingfield. (op 5-2 tchd 3-1)
Sumner(IRE) is now qualified for a handicap mark and could be capable of making an impact in that sphere.
Giant Slalom could not build on the promise he showed on his debut at Pontefract, but had the worst of the draw. (op 11-4 tchd 7-2 in places)
Kiss Chase(IRE) Official explanation: jockey said colt hung left

6291 DIGIBET.COM NURSERY 6f (P)
4:50 (4:53) (Class 6) (0-65,65) 2-Y-O **£2,388** (£705; £352) **Stalls** High

Form RPR
0000 **1** **Lay The Cash (USA)**[15] 6031 2-9-2 60 .... (b¹) MartinDwyer 11 64
(J S Moore) *led: hrd rdn 2f out: narrowly hdd 1f out: battled on wl to ld again nr fin* **12/1**
0640 **2** *hd* **Napoleon Dynamite (IRE)**[14] 6055 2-9-6 64 .... EddieAhern 9 67
(J W Hills) *wl plcd: effrt 2f out: rdn to ld narrowly 1f out: kpt on but hdd nr fin* **15/2**
5566 **3** 1½ **Lake Pontchartrain (IRE)**[30] 5738 2-9-2 60 .... RichardHughes 5 59+
(S Kirk) *settled wl in rr: prog 2f out: rdn and r.o fnl f: too much to do* **11/2**[2]
3200 **4** *1* **Convivial Spirit**[14] 6056 2-9-6 64 .... (t) TPQueally 6 60
(E F Vaughan) *pressed wnr: chal and hanging rt 2f out: hanging rt and nt qckn fnl f* **10/1**
300 **5** *1* **Ishibee (IRE)**[29] 5747 2-9-4 62 .... RoystonFfrench 2 55
(Mrs A Duffield) *trckd ldrs: rdn 2f out: stl cl up over 1f out: fdd fnl f* **20/1**
3600 **6** ¾ **Hucking Hill (IRE)**[12] 6074 2-9-6 64 .... (b¹) DaneO'Neill 3 55
(J R Best) *racd wd: pushed along in rr 4f out: styd on fr over 1f out: nvr rchd ldrs* **12/1**
0056 **7** *hd* **Le Masque**[30] 5721 2-9-5 63 .... TedDurcan 1 53
(B Smart) *effrt into midfield over 3f out: outpcd over 2f out: no imp after* **14/1**

0515 **8** *shd* **Back In The Red (IRE)**[29] 5747 2-9-4 **62** NCallan 8 52+
(M Wellings) *chsd ldrs: drvn and cl up over 1f out: wknd ins fnl f: eased nr fin* **4/1**[1]
5640 **9** *1 1/4* **Flying Grey (IRE)**[13] 6064 2-9-1 **59** TPO'Shea 10 45
(P A Blockley) *drvn and struggling to go the pce over 3f out: nvr a factor* **11/2**[2]
1300 **10** *1 1/2* **Movethegoalposts**[30] 5721 2-9-7 **65** (b) JoeFanning 4 47
(M Johnston) *sn last: rdn and nt look keen 1/2-way: swtchd to inner 2f out: no prog* **16/1**
3100 **11** *hd* **Party Palace**[87] 4178 2-8-12 **59** RichardKingscote(3) 7 40
(J A Osborne) *drvn and lost pl after 2f: toiling in rr after* **12/1**
0224 **12** *4* **Queensgate**[27] 5772 2-9-1 **59** SteveDrowne 12 28+
(M Blanshard) *chsd ldrs: wknd rapidly wl over 1f out: eased* **7/1**[3]

1m 13.59s (-0.11) **Going Correction** -0.125s/f (Stan) **12** Ran SP% **124.5**
Speed ratings (Par 94):95,94,92,91,90 89,88,88,87,85 84,79
CSF £104.24 CT £575.47 TOTE £14.90: £3.90, £2.50, £2.20; EX 86.70.
Owner Peter Webb & Peter Lay **Bred** B C Jones **Trained** Upper Lambourn, Berks

FOCUS
A modest sprint nursery, but certainly competitive enough and sound with the placed horses to form.

NOTEBOOK
Lay The Cash(USA) had shown pretty limited form on his first five previous starts but the application of blinkers for the first time, combined with a return to sprinting, did the trick. Having been given a really positive ride from the start, he looked held when Napoleon Dynamite went past him about a furlong out, but battled back well near the line. He might just be the type who likes to keep something back for himself, but he is getting the hang of things now and could add to this if the headgear continues to have a positive effect. (op 11-1)
Napoleon Dynamite(IRE) looked all over the winner when hitting the front about a furlong out, but he could not resist Lay The Cash's late rally. Still, this was a respectable effort and he might be able to find a similar event. (op 7-1 tchd 8-1)
Lake Pontchartrain(IRE) seemingly failed to see out seven furlongs at Wolverhampton on her previous start, but she basically got going too late on this drop back in trip. A slightly more positive ride may suit better in future. (op 4-1)
Convivial Spirit stuck on at the one pace without ever really looking likely to do enough to win. He might just be seen at his best when getting an uncontested lead. (op 12-1 tchd 14-1)
Ishibee(IRE) was not ideally drawn but ran a respectable race. (op 16-1)
Hucking Hill(IRE) ran reasonably in first-time blinkers. (tchd 14-1)
Back In The Red(IRE) failed to show his best form switched to Polytrack for the first time and was a little disappointing. Official explanation: jockey said colt hung left (op 5-1)

6292 DIGIBET.CO.UK H'CAP 6f (P)
5:20 (5:22) (Class 3) (0-90,90) 3-Y-0+
£7,790 (£2,332; £1,166; £583; £291; £146) **Stalls** High

Form RPR
0406 **1** **Saviours Spirit**[35] 5627 5-9-0 **86** IanMongan 4 95
(T G Mills) *squeezed out s: hld up in last pair: gd prog on outer over 1f out: led last 100yds: pushed out* **9/1**
0000 **2** *3/4* **Don Pele (IRE)**[81] 4357 4-9-0 **86** NCallan 3 93
(K A Ryan) *settled towards rr: prog on outer 2f out: rdn to ld last 150yds: sn hdd and nt qckn* **20/1**
5112 **3** *shd* **Diane's Choice**[44] 5420 3-8-13 **85** DaneO'Neill 11 91
(J Akehurst) *trckd ldrs: nt clr run over 1f out: drvn and r.o fnl f: nrst fin* **10/1**
5116 **4** *1/2* **Grand Show**[3] 6243 4-9-0 **86** TedDurcan 6 96+
(W R Swinburn) *towards rr: hanging rt fr over 2f out: prog over 1f out: running on whn nowhere to go 100yds out: swtchd and styd on* **3/1**[1]
1- **5** *shd* **Mr Garston**[448] 4260 3-8-12 **84** MartinDwyer 12 89
(M P Tregoning) *settled in rr: gd prog on inner fr 2f out: chal 1f out: no ex last 75yds* **14/1**
0405 **6** *1 1/4* **Pieter Brueghel (USA)**[39] 5534 7-9-0 **86** JoeFanning 8 87
(D Nicholls) *led: rdn 2f out: hdd last 150yds: wknd nr fin* **10/1**
0053 **7** *1/2* **Kaveri (USA)**[13] 6065 3-8-13 **85** (b[1]) BrettDoyle 5 84
(C E Brittain) *drvn in last trio early and struggling: no prog tl styd on fr over 1f out: nrst fin* **25/1**
2100 **8** *shd* **Idle Power (IRE)**[25] 5807 8-8-11 **83** PatCosgrave 9 82
(J R Boyle) *pressed ldng pair: rdn over 2f out: btn 1f out: wknd last 100yds* **8/1**
0044 **9** *1 1/2* **Maltese Falcon**[11] 6095 6-9-4 **90** (t) EddieAhern 1 85
(P F I Cole) *chsd ldrs: rdn and effrt 2f out: wknd fnl f* **7/1**
0065 **10** *3/4* **Prince Namid**[18] 5957 4-9-2 **88** RoystonFfrench 10 80
(Mrs A Duffield) *trckd ldrs: effrt 2f out: cl up over 1f out: wknd fnl f* **11/2**[2]
5416 **11** *4* **Hoh Hoh Hoh**[24] 5832 4-8-12 **84** RichardHughes 7 64
(R J Price) *pressed ldr to over 1f out: wknd and eased* **13/2**[3]

1m 11.49s (-2.21) **Going Correction** -0.125s/f (Stan) **11** Ran SP% **120.8**
Speed ratings (Par 107):109,108,107,107,107 105,104,104,102,101 96
CSF £178.18 CT £1880.23 TOTE £11.60: £3.10, £6.90, £2.90; EX 415.10.
Owner J E Harley **Bred** Mrs S Shaw **Trained** Headley, Surrey

FOCUS
A good, competitive sprint handicap run in a new course record time.

NOTEBOOK
Saviours Spirit gained his fourth win of the year in determined fashion, just defying a mark 7lb higher than when last winning in March. His five career victories prior to this had all come on Lingfield's Polytrack, but he is clearly just as effective round Kempton. He is likely to be kept on the go for the time being and should go well in some of the valuable sprints handicaps run on sand this winter. (op 10-1 tchd 11-1)
Don Pele(IRE) was not in much form when last seen, but ran a fine race off the back of a near three-month break. This was his first run on Polytrack and the surface clearly suited.
Diane's Choice is holding her form really well and this was another cracking effort. She will probably go up in the weights for this, but remains one to keep on the right side of. (op 9-1)
Grand Show ◆ was unlucky at Wolverhampton three days earlier and he again failed to get the run of things. He remains progressive, but perhaps Lingfield just suits better. (op 11-4 tchd 10-3 in places)
Mr Garston, off the track since winning a maiden at Sandown on his only previous start in August 2005, ran a fine race against some useful types for the grade. If he goes the right way from this, he could develop into a decent sprinter. (tchd 12-1 and 20-1 in places)
Pieter Brueghel(USA) could not take advantage of a lower sand mark.
Maltese Falcon raced keenly from his unfavourable draw.
Hoh Hoh Hoh dropped out tamely and something was presumably amiss. Official explanation: vet said gelding finished lame (op 8-1)

6293 DIGIBET SPORTS BETTING H'CAP 7f (P)
5:50 (5:52) (Class 6) (0-63,63) 3-Y-0+ **£2,388** (£705; £352) **Stalls** High

Form RPR
0524 **1** **Fateful Attraction**[17] 5987 3-8-12 **62** (b) JamesDoyle(3) 14 73
(I A Wood) *hld up wl in rr: prog on inner over 2f out: rdn to ld over 1f out: r.o wl* **3/1**[1]
052 **2** *2 1/2* **Cordelia**[9] 6144 3-8-13 **60** OscarUrbina 13 65
(B W Hills) *hld up in midfield: nt clr run briefly over 2f out: prog over 1f out: chsd wnr last 150yds: kpt on but no imp* **8/1**
6146 **3** *1 1/4* **Sovereignty (JPN)**[21] 5907 4-8-10 **63** JamesMillman(7) 7 64
(D K Ivory) *prom: rdn to ld 2f out: hdd over 1f out: sn btn: clung on for 3rd* **7/1**[3]
0560 **4** *hd* **The Crooked Ring**[14] 6060 4-9-0 **60** (p) NCallan 8 61
(P D Evans) *hld up wl in rr: nt clr run briefly over 2f out: drvn and styd on fr over 1f out: nrst fin* **10/1**
2542 **5** *hd* **Mina**[14] 6061 4-9-0 **60** SteveDrowne 2 60
(Rae Guest) *trckd ldrs: effrt 2f out: rdn and nt qckn over 1f out: kpt on same pce* **15/2**
4600 **6** *1/2* **Hang Loose**[22] 5902 3-9-1 **62** EddieAhern 5 61
(S W Hall) *pressed ldr: led 3f out to 2f out: styd cl up tl wknd fnl f* **50/1**
0000 **7** *1 1/4* **What-A-Dancer (IRE)**[21] 5907 9-9-1 **61** (b) TedDurcan 10 57
(R A Harris) *dwlt and reminder: wl in rr: hanging rt over 2f out: styd on fr over 1f out: n.d* **25/1**
000 **8** *1 3/4* **Island Prince (IRE)**[57] 5081 3-8-13 **60** RoystonFfrench 12 51
(Mrs A Duffield) *prom: rdn over 2f out: stl chsng ldrs over 1f out: wknd* **20/1**
0401 **9** *shd* **Black Sea Pearl**[14] 6061 3-8-10 **60** SaleemGolam(3) 1 51
(P W D'Arcy) *wl in rr: effrt on outer over 2f out: no real prog* **8/1**
0505 **10** *2* **Marker**[28] 5765 6-9-2 **62** DaneO'Neill 9 48
(J A Geake) *mostly midfield: nt clr run briefly over 2f out: no prog after: fdd* **6/1**[2]
6654 **11** *2 1/2* **Dallma (IRE)**[63] 4930 3-9-1 **62** (b[1]) BrettDoyle 6 41
(C E Brittain) *nvr beyond midfield: rdn and struggling over 2f out* **16/1**
-002 **12** *4* **Double Carpet (IRE)**[29] 5761 3-8-13 **60** JoeFanning 3 29
(G Woodward) *dwlt: a wl in rr: brought to wd outside over 2f out: no prog* **16/1**
1300 **13** *3 1/2* **Hillbilly Cat (USA)**[30] 5737 3-9-0 **61** FergusSweeney 11 21
(R Ingram) *led to 3f out: wknd over 2f out* **33/1**
0-30 **14** *1* **Dona Vitoria**[19] 5937 3-8-13 **60** RichardHughes 4 17
(S Kirk) *prom tl wknd wl over 2f out* **25/1**

1m 25.53s (-1.27) **Going Correction** -0.125s/f (Stan)
WFA 3 from 4yo+ 1lb **14** Ran SP% **125.8**
Speed ratings (Par 101):102,99,97,97,97 96,95,93,93,90 88,83,79,78
CSF £26.46 CT £168.73 TOTE £4.40: £1.90, £2.90, £2.60; EX 34.10.
Owner M I Forbes **Bred** Vidin Gate Stud **Trained** Upper Lambourn, Berks

FOCUS
Just an ordinary handicap.
Sovereignty(JPN) Official explanation: jockey said gelding hung left

6294 BOOK YOUR CHRISTMAS PARTY AT KEMPTON PARK H'CAP 1m (P)
6:20 (6:20) (Class 6) (0-63,62) 3-Y-0+ **£2,388** (£705; £352) **Stalls** High

Form RPR
1050 **1** **Magic Warrior**[18] 5974 6-9-2 **61** PatDobbs 8 68
(J C Fox) *hld up in rr and wl off the pce: prog over 2f out: drvn and styd on fnl f: won on the nod* **5/1**[2]
0530 **2** *shd* **Chia (IRE)**[63] 4933 3-8-13 **60** SteveDrowne 6 67
(D Haydn Jones) *t.k.h: trckd ldng pair: rdn and effrt 2f out: led jst over 1f out: styd on: pipped on the post* **12/1**
2230 **3** *hd* **Sincerely**[13] 6069 4-9-1 **60** OscarUrbina 1 66
(B W Hills) *t.k.h: trckd clr ldrs: drvn and effrt 2f out: styd on to chal ins fnl f: jst hld* **9/2**[1]
6260 **4** *1 1/4* **Border Artist**[14] 6060 7-9-2 **61** RichardHughes 9 64
(J Pearce) *settled off the pce towards rr: effrt over 2f out: drvn and styd on fr over 1f out: unable to chal* **8/1**
005 **5** *1/2* **Desert Island Miss**[16] 6021 3-9-1 **62** TedDurcan 14 64
(W R Swinburn) *trckd ldng pair: drvn on inner to chal 2f out: fdd fnl f* **8/1**
2400 **6** *1/2* **Generator**[16] 6008 4-9-1 **60** JoeFanning 2 61
(Dr J D Scargill) *pressed ldr: rdn to ld wl over 1f out to jst over 1f out: wknd and n.m.r last 100yds* **12/1**
0604 **7** *1* **Lennoxtown (IRE)**[17] 5992 3-9-0 **61** MatthewHenry 11 60
(J Ryan) *hmpd and snatched up after 1f: wl in rr after: kpt on fnl 2f: no ch* **12/1**
3203 **8** *1 1/2* **Moon Forest (IRE)**[19] 5937 4-8-12 **57** (p) DaneO'Neill 5 52
(J M Bradley) *racd freely: led to wl over 1f out: wknd fnl f* **7/1**
3465 **9** *1/2* **Ciccone**[21] 5907 3-8-13 **60** J-PGuillambert 4 54
(G L Moore) *dwlt: wl in rr: rdn and hanging over 2f out: no real prog* **6/1**[3]
2110 **10** *3* **Bold Phoenix (IRE)**[30] 5740 5-8-13 **58** TPQueally 12 45
(B J Curley) *settled in midfield: rdn and no rspnse over 2f out: sn btn* **7/1**
046- **11** *5* **Cherokee Vision**[447] 4285 3-9-0 **61** JamieMackay 7 37
(Miss T Spearing) *a wl in rr: shkn up and struggling over 2f out* **66/1**
606 **12** *2 1/2* **Measured Response**[83] 4287 4-8-12 **57** FergusSweeney 10 27
(J G M O'Shea) *dwlt: a in last pair: struggling fnl 3f* **25/1**

1m 40.24s (-0.56) **Going Correction** -0.125s/f (Stan)
WFA 3 from 4yo+ 2lb **12** Ran SP% **124.8**
Speed ratings (Par 101):97,96,96,95,94 94,93,91,91,88 83,80
CSF £67.59 CT £302.38 TOTE £6.70: £2.50, £3.40, £1.60; EX 91.90 Place 6 £959.63, Place 5 £460.60 .
Owner Miss H J Flower **Bred** Patrick Eddery Ltd **Trained** Collingbourne Ducis, Wilts

FOCUS
A moderate handicap.
T/Plt: £1,211.20 to a £1 stake. Pool: £45,794.55. 27.60 winning tickets. T/Qpdt: £58.10 to a £1 stake. Pool: £5,890.90. 75.00 winning tickets. JN

6172 NOTTINGHAM (L-H)
Wednesday, November 1

OFFICIAL GOING: 5f course - good to soft; round course - soft (heavy in places)
All races run on inner track. The five furlong course was described as ' holding, very sticky'. The round track was described as 'heavy'.
Wind: light, half behind Weather: fine and sunny but turning cold

6295 RANGEMASTER MAIDEN STKS 5f 13y
12:50 (12:51) (Class 5) 2-Y-0 **£4,210** (£1,252; £625; £312) **Stalls** High

Form RPR
4452 **1** **Aquilegia (IRE)**[14] 6056 2-8-12 69 GrahamGibbons 7 72+
(E S McMahon) *w ldr: led over 2f out: rdn clr fnl f* **10/11**[1]
004 **2** *5* **Hereford Boy**[15] 6034 2-9-3 62 PhilipRobinson 9 62+
(D K Ivory) *led tl over 2f out: heavily eased whn wl hld by wnr last 75yds* **13/2**[2]

0 **3** 2 **The Bronx**[98] 3843 2-9-3 .... AdrianMcCarthy 8 52+
(M J Wallace) *dwlt: hdwy 2f out: kpt on to take modest 3rd ins last* **12/1**

0 **4** 1 **Zain (IRE)**[5] 6199 2-9-3 .... DeanMcKeown 11 48
(J G Given) *chsd ldrs: one pce fnl 2f* **22/1**

5 hd **Remark (IRE)**[71] 2-9-3 .... (t) PaulMulrennan 2 47
(M W Easterby) *chsd ldrs: one pce and wandered fnl 2f* **16/1**

00 **6** ½ **Botham (USA)**[12] 6072 2-9-3 .... RobbieFitzpatrick 10 46
(T J Pitt) *sn outpcd and in rr: kpt on fnl 2f: nvr nr ldrs* **16/1**

0 **7** 1 **Classic Blue (IRE)**[44] 5417 2-8-12 .... ChrisCatlin 1 37
(E J O'Neill) *mid-div: effrt on outside over 2f out: nvr on terms* **16/1**

06 **8** 1 ¼ **High Lite**[14] 6055 2-8-12 .... HayleyTurner 12 33
(M L W Bell) *dwlt: a outpcd and bhd* **8/1**[3]

50 **9** 1 **Mangano**[29] 5753 2-9-0 .... StephenDonohoe(3) 5 34
(A Berry) *chsd ldrs: wknd 2f out* **40/1**

10 14 **Nellie** 2-8-7 .... MichaelJStainton(5) 6 —
(R M Whitaker) *s.s: a detached in last* **33/1**

62.09 secs (0.29) **Going Correction** 0.0s/f (Good) **10** Ran SP% **111.9**
Speed ratings (Par 96):97,89,85,84,83 83,81,79,77,55
CSF £6.25 TOTE £1.80: £1.20, £1.30, £3.00; EX 7.00.
Owner J P Hames,G Pickering & P Saxton **Bred** Yeomanstown Stud **Trained** Hopwas, Staffs

FOCUS
A modest backend maiden and the form is limited. The second was heavily eased inside the last flattering those following him home.

NOTEBOOK
Aquilegia(IRE) jumped off bang on terms and had the leader covered. Her rider left nothing at all to chance. (op 5-6 tchd Evens)
Hereford Boy, back over the minimum trip, took them along and was booked for second spot about three lengths down on the winner when heavily eased. (op 8-1 tchd 6-1)
The Bronx, absent since making his debut in July, did just enough to secure a modest third spot. He still has a bit to learn. (op 9-1)
Zain(IRE), who made his debut just five days earlier, showed a bit more but will not be the finished article until next year. (op 25-1)
Remark(IRE), who looked unhappy in the first time tongue strap in the paddock, wandered under pressure, rather getting in the way of the third and the sixth. (op 12-1)
Botham(USA), a keen type, struggled to go the pace and was then slightly messed about. He is bred to need much further once he learn to settle.

6296 BLUES CONSULTANTS LTD NURSERY 5f 13y
1:25 (1:25) (Class 6) (0-65,63) 2-Y-O **£3,238** (£963; £481; £240) **Stalls** High

Form RPR

1605 **1** **Baytown Paikea**[27] 5772 2-9-0 **56** .... BrianReilly 6 60
(P S McEntee) *mde all: hld on wl* **8/1**

540 **2** ½ **Galaxy Of Stars**[64] 4913 2-8-8 **53** .... PatrickMathers(3) 7 55
(D Shaw) *s.i.s: hdwy 2f out: kpt on same pce ins last* **25/1**

0065 **3** nk **Mujart**[28] 5764 2-8-7 **56** .... RussellKennemore(7) 2 57
(J A Pickering) *hld up: swtchd rt after s: hdwy and nt clr run over 1f out: styd on same pce ins last* **9/1**

6510 **4** ½ **Joseph Locke (IRE)**[47] 5334 2-9-7 **63** .... (p) KDarley 9 62+
(M Dods) *sn outpcd and bhd: hdwy and swtchd wd outside over 2f out: styd on same pce ins last* **10/3**[1]

0405 **5** 1 **Silly Gilly (IRE)**[16] 6013 2-8-8 **53** .... (p) StephenDonohoe(3) 12 49
(A Berry) *chsd wnr stands' side: outpcd 2f out: kpt on ins last* **7/1**[3]

0000 **6** ¾ **Molto Duro (IRE)**[8] 6157 2-7-9 **44** oh5 ow4 .... (b) LanceBetts(7) 4 37
(N Wilson) *chsd ldrs: fdd fnl f* **80/1**

5035 **7** 1 ½ **King Of Tricks**[33] 5645 2-9-4 **60** .... HayleyTurner 1 48
(M D I Usher) *chsd ldrs: wknd appr fnl f* **10/1**

0052 **8** nk **Merlins Quest**[29] 5747 2-9-1 **60** .... GregFairley(3) 5 47
(J M Bradley) *mid-div: drvn 2f out: nvr rchd ldrs* **7/2**[2]

0500 **9** 1 ½ **Musical Affair**[19] 5948 2-8-9 **51** .... JimmyQuinn 3 32
(F Jordan) *chsd ldrs on outer: wknd over 1f out* **9/1**

0000 **10** 1 ½ **Spinning Game**[57] 5084 2-8-4 **46** .... PaulQuinn 11 22
(D W Chapman) *nvr wnt pce* **8/1**

000 **11** 10 **Frill A Minute**[28] 5766 2-7-12 **40** oh10 .... AdrianMcCarthy 8 —
(Miss L C Siddall) *sn outpcd and in rr: bhd and eased 1f out* **100/1**

62.72 secs (0.92) **Going Correction** 0.0s/f (Good) **11** Ran SP% **115.2**
Speed ratings (Par 94):92,91,90,89,88 87,84,84,81,79 63
CSF £182.86 CT £1859.28 TOTE £10.30: £2.70, £3.00, £2.40; EX 147.90.
Owner Eventmaker Racehorses **Bred** Launceston Stud **Trained** Newmarket, Suffolk

FOCUS
Modest nursery form but fairly solid and could be rated a fraction higher.

NOTEBOOK
Baytown Paikea, the smallest in the line-up, benefited from a 2lb lower mark. Racing hard against the stands'-side rail, she was always doing just enough. (op 15-2)
Galaxy Of Stars, back after a two-month break, recovered from a tardy start. She went second inside the last but was never quite going to overhaul the winner. (op 20-1)
Mujart, who had a low draw to overcome, met traffic problems. Keeping on in her own time inside the last, she really needs six furlongs. (op 15-2)
Joseph Locke(IRE), who has slipped to a favourable mark, failed hopelessly to go the pace. Pulled wide, he could only keep on at his own pace in the final furlong. (op 3-1 tchd 11-4)
Silly Gilly(IRE) chased the winner up the stands'-side rail. Tapped for toe soon after halfway, she was sticking on at the finish and will appreciate a return to six. (op 9-1 tchd 6-1)
Merlins Quest, the biggest in the line-up, could never take a hand. (op 3-1)

6297 MAWDSLEYS MAIDEN STKS (DIV I) 1m 54y
2:00 (2:00) (Class 5) 2-Y-O **£2,590** (£770; £385; £192) **Stalls** High

Form RPR

42 **1** **Sagredo (USA)**[14] 6050 2-9-3 .... SebSanders 12 86+
(Sir Mark Prescott) *chsd ldrs: led 3f out: pushed clr over 1f out: eased towards fin* **7/2**[2]

33 **2** 4 **Sivota (IRE)**[22] 5900 2-9-3 .... TonyCulhane 9 73+
(T P Tate) *chsd ldrs: chal 3f out: kpt on same pce* **8/1**

3 4 **Petroglyph** 2-9-3 .... LDettori 14 64+
(Saeed Bin Suroor) *hld up towards rr: hdwy over 3f out: edghed lft and wnt laboured 3rd over 1f out: one pce* **11/8**[1]

4 1 ¼ **Passarelle (USA)** 2-8-12 .... RyanMoore 10 57
(R M Beckett) *in rr: hdwy on wd outside 2f out: styd on ins last* **22/1**

0 **5** ½ **Spartan Dance**[7] 6173 2-9-3 .... RichardThomas 3 61
(J A Geake) *chsd ldrs: outpcd over 4f out: kpt on fnl 2f* **80/1**

0 **6** 2 **Magdalene**[47] 5352 2-8-12 .... ChrisCatlin 4 51+
(Rae Guest) *s.i.s: bhd tl kpt on fnl 3f* **66/1**

7 2 **Linlithgow (IRE)** 2-9-3 .... MichaelHills 2 52
(J L Dunlop) *s.s: bhd tl styd on fnl 2f: nvr nr ldrs* **25/1**

6 **8** ½ **Intiquilla (IRE)**[14] 6050 2-8-12 .... JimCrowley 7 46+
(Mrs A J Perrett) *hld up in rr: shkn up and hdwy 4f out: wknd over 1f out* **16/1**

04 **9** ½ **Danehill Silver**[14] 6050 2-9-3 .... MickyFenton 11 50
(R Hollinshead) *rr-div: effrt over 3f out: wknd over 1f out* **33/1**

10 hd **Adonita** 2-8-12 .... RHills 5 44+
(Saeed Bin Suroor) *led tl 3f out: wknd wl over 1f out* **13/2**[3]

0 **11** 2 **Nassmaan (IRE)**[34] 5640 2-9-3 .... AdrianMcCarthy 6 45
(P W Chapple-Hyam) *chsd ldrs: lost pl over 2f out* **33/1**

6 **12** hd **Voss**[23] 5859 2-8-12 .... KDarley 13 39
(M Johnston) *chsd ldrs: lost pl over 2f out* **25/1**

00 **13** hd **Credit Slip**[22] 5893 2-9-3 .... JimmyQuinn 1 44
(J L Dunlop) *s.i.s: sme hdwy on ins over 3f out: sn wknd* **50/1**

0 **14** 42 **Time Dancer (IRE)**[8] 6157 2-9-3 .... PaulQuinn 8 —
(A Berry) *a in rr: detached 3f out: t.o* **150/1**

1m 47.18s (0.78) **Going Correction** +0.175s/f (Good) **14** Ran SP% **117.9**
Speed ratings (Par 96):103,99,95,93,93 91,89,88,88,88 86,85,85,43
CSF £27.88 TOTE £4.90: £1.40, £2.00, £1.40; EX 23.50.
Owner Dr Catherine Wills **Bred** Dr Catherine Wills **Trained** Newmarket, Suffolk
■ Stewards' Enquiry : Richard Thomas caution: careless riding

FOCUS
A run-of-the-mill maiden race but the winner scored with plenty in hand and will progress further at three. Overall the form looks sound backed up by the quicker time of the two divisions.

NOTEBOOK
Sagredo(USA) went on and stepped up the gallop. In the end he was able to take things very easily and should make a useful staying handicapper at three. (tchd 10-3 and 4-1)
Sivota(IRE), who lacks size and scope, went down fighting and deserves to find a race at some stage. (op 7-1 tchd 6-1)
Petroglyph, a big, long-backed individual, had an outside draw to overcome. He was making hard work of it some way out and in the end was a modest third. He will surely be stronger next year. (op 6-4 tchd 7-4)
Passarelle(USA), a rangy newcomer, made ground down the wide outside late in the day. She will surely to better at three. (op 20-1)
Spartan Dance, tapped for toe turning in, kept on in his own time in the final quarter mile and is bred to do better next year. (op 66-1)
Linlithgow(IRE), a narrow newcomer, stayed on from way off the pace late in the day and his future lies in handicap company over much further at three.
Danehill Silver Official explanation: jockey said gelding hung left-handed

6298 MAWDSLEYS MAIDEN STKS (DIV II) 1m 54y
2:35 (2:36) (Class 5) 2-Y-O **£2,590** (£770; £385; £192) **Stalls** High

Form RPR

42 **1** **Regal Flush**[68] 4781 2-9-3 .... RyanMoore 9 81+
(Sir Michael Stoute) *chsd ldr: led 3f out: rdn clr fnl f* **2/5**[1]

2 4 **Dawn Sky** 2-9-3 .... JimmyQuinn 10 72
(M A Jarvis) *mid-div: hdwy over 3f out: styd on to take 2nd ins last: improve* **14/1**

60 **3** 1 **Highland Harvest**[52] 5206 2-9-0 .... MarcHalford(3) 1 70
(D R C Elsworth) *stdd s: t.k.h: wnt prom 5f out: hung lft and styd alone far side: kpt on same pce fnl f* **66/1**

6 **4** shd **Hall Of Fame**[14] 6049 2-9-3 .... LDettori 4 70
(Saeed Bin Suroor) *led tl 3f out: rdr lost whip over 1f out: one pce* **6/1**[2]

06 **5** 6 **Isola Madre**[22] 5898 2-8-12 .... KDarley 13 52
(M Johnston) *in rr: drvn 4f out: nvr nr ldrs* **50/1**

00 **6** ¾ **April Fool**[23] 5867 2-9-3 .... RichardThomas 12 55
(J A Geake) *prom: outpcd fnl 3f* **33/1**

7 ½ **Heart Of Cornwall (IRE)** 2-9-3 .... RHills 8 54
(Saeed Bin Suroor) *hld up in rr: sme hdwy 2f out: nvr nr ldrs* **11/1**[3]

8 6 **Elusory** 2-9-3 .... SebSanders 7 41
(J L Dunlop) *a in rr* **28/1**

9 5 **Heart Of Glass (IRE)** 2-8-5 .... LukeMorris(7) 6 25
(M L W Bell) *a in rr* **28/1**

0 **10** 3 **Wilde Thing**[19] 5947 2-8-12 .... MickyFenton 3 18
(S Curran) *chsd ldrs: lost pl over 3f out* **150/1**

00 **11** ¾ **Sparky Vixen**[8] 6157 2-8-7 .... DuranFentiman(5) 5 16
(S Parr) *a towards rr* **200/1**

00 **12** 23 **Mid Ocean**[57] 5095 2-8-12 .... FrancisNorton 2 —+
(P W D'Arcy) *t.k.h in rr: sddle slipped 6f out: eased rt up fnl 2f* **66/1**

1m 48.69s (2.29) **Going Correction** +0.175s/f (Good) **12** Ran SP% **116.7**
Speed ratings (Par 96):95,91,90,89,83 83,82,76,71,68 67,44
CSF £6.80 TOTE £1.30: £1.10, £2.40, £10.00; EX 8.90.
Owner Cheveley Park Stud **Bred** Cheveley Park Stud Ltd **Trained** Newmarket, Suffolk

FOCUS
Much the slower of the two divisions and the first four finished well clear. The third, fourth and fifth set the standard.

NOTEBOOK
Regal Flush, better for his two-month break, made quite hard work of it but was firmly in command at the line. (op 8-13 after 4-6 in places)
Dawn Sky ◆, related to the Arc winner Marienbard who started life in this stable, is a medium-sized, likeable sort. She stayed on nicely to secure second spot inside the last and looks sure to improve and make his mark over middle-distances at three. (op 15-2)
Highland Harvest, keen to get on with it, stuck to the inner but he tended to hang left and ended up on the far side rail. He kept on in his own time and is very immature at present.
Hall Of Fame, who showed some ability on his debut here two weeks earlier, was clinging onto second spot when Dettori dropped his whip. He is obviously nothing out of the ordinary but can be expected to do a shade better at three. (op 11-2)
Isola Madre, who lacks size, was having her third outing and looks fairly paceless.
Heart Of Cornwall(IRE), a lengthy, good-bodied newcomer, showed a glimmer of ability under a very patient ride. He will surely step up on this at three. (op 12-1)
Mid Ocean Official explanation: jockey said saddle slipped

6299 FRANK HASLAM MILAN CONDITIONS STKS 1m 54y
3:10 (3:10) (Class 2) 3-Y-O+ **£12,464** (£3,732; £1,866; £934; £466) **Stalls** High

Form RPR

1- **1** **With Interest**[390] 5708 3-8-8 **94** .... LDettori 2 108+
(Saeed Bin Suroor) *hld up in last: shkn up over 4f out: led 1f out: cheekily* **11/4**[2]

6460 **2** 1 **Babodana**[4] 6218 6-8-10 **105** .... SebSanders 1 106
(M H Tompkins) *trckd ldrs: led 3f out: hdd 1f out: no ex* **9/2**[3]

0605 **3** 6 **Grand Passion (IRE)**[25] 5813 6-9-6 **97** .... KDarley 6 103
(G Wragg) *led 1f: chsd ldrs: drvn over 3f out: wknd over 1f out* **28/1**

4600 **4** 1 **Bustan (IRE)**[19] 5945 7-8-10 **90** .... MichaelHills 3 91
(G C Bravery) *trckd ldrs: drvn 4f out: one pce* **25/1**

1121 **5** 1 ¾ **Shumookh (IRE)**[30] 5722 3-8-8 **102** .... RHills 4 88
(M A Jarvis) *led after 1f: hdd 3f out: wknd over 1f out* **4/6**[1]

1m 45.66s (-0.74) **Going Correction** +0.175s/f (Good)
WFA 3 from 6yo+ 2lb **5** Ran SP% **112.1**
Speed ratings (Par 109):110,109,103,102,100
CSF £15.21 TOTE £3.00: £2.00, £1.30; EX 14.00.

Owner Godolphin **Bred** George Strawbridge **Trained** Newmarket, Suffolk

FOCUS

A classy little conditions event. Despite the small field, the pace was decent and the winning time was solid for the grade. The front two pulled a long way clear of the rest and the form is best assessed through the placed horses.

NOTEBOOK

With Interest ◆, not seen for over a year since making a winning racecourse debut, had a bit to find with some of these strictly on official ratings, but he was by some way the least-exposed of the quintet. Given a patient ride, he had to battle very hard to get the better of the much more streetwise runner-up, but he impressed in the way he did so and looks capable of winning something a bit better as a four-year-old. (op 7-2)

Babodana, down in grade and best in at the weights, made a bold bid for glory once reaching the home straight. He did nothing wrong and put plenty of daylight between himself and the rest, but was unfortunate to come up against a completely unexposed rival. He is not an easy horse to place these days, hence a losing run of more than two and a half years. (op 4-1 tchd 5-1)

Grand Passion(IRE), worst in at the weights thanks to his penalty, needs faster ground than this and was comfortably held by the front pair. (op 16-1)

Bustan(IRE), successful in his first two career starts in the spring of 2002 but winless since, is dropping down the handicap but had little chance in this company on these terms and was easily seen off. (op 16-1)

Shumookh(IRE) should have had no problem with these conditions and came into this looking a very progressive sort, but after making the early running he folded most disappointingly. This was too bad to be true. Official explanation: trainer had no explanation for the poor form shown (op 4-5 tchd 5-6)

6300 EVENTMASTERS CORPORATE HOSPITALITY H'CAP — 1m 54y

3:45 (3:45) (Class 6) (0-57,57) 3-Y-O+ — **£2,730** (£806; £403) **Stalls** High

Form — RPR

4234 **1** — **Band**[14] [6059] 6-8-12 **54** .... GrahamGibbons 10 — 62
(E S McMahon) *trckd ldrs: styd on: edgd lft and led last 75yds: all out* **11/2**[2]

0000 **2** *hd* **Kathleen Kennet**[46] [5390] 6-8-10 **52** .... ChrisCatlin 1 — 60
(Mrs H Sweeting) *t.k.h: trckd ldrs: no ex towards fin* **40/1**

200 **3** *hd* **Wizard Of Us**[48] [5316] 6-8-13 **55** .... AdrianMcCarthy 4 — 62
(M Mullineaux) *mid-div: hdwy to ld over 2f out: edgd lft and hdd wl ins last: no ex* **9/1**

0200 **4** *shd* **Credential**[28] [5768] 4-8-10 **55** .... StephenDonohoe(3) 9 — 62
(John A Harris) *bhd: gd hdwy on wd outside over 2f out: no ex wl ins last* **40/1**

2550 **5** *nk* **Ermine Grey**[19] [5954] 5-8-13 **55** .... FrancisNorton 17 — 61
(A W Carroll) *in rr: hdwy and hung lft over 3f out: c wd: styd on fnl f* **9/1**

6002 **6** *¾* **Convince (USA)**[37] [5573] 5-8-6 **55** .... BarrySavage(7) 5 — 60
(J M Bradley) *in tch: chal on outer over 2f out: nt qckn ins last* **20/1**

4405 **7** *7* **Atlantic Story (USA)**[43] [5445] 4-9-1 **57** ....(t) DaleGibson 3 — 47
(M W Easterby) *led tl over 4f out: wknd over 1f out* **7/2**[1]

403- **8** *hd* **Topiary Ted**[412] [5256] 4-8-8 **55** ....(t) TravisBlock(5) 6 — 45
(H Morrison) *w ldrs: led over 4f out tl over 2f out: wknd over 1f out* **16/1**

0063 **9** *shd* **Wizby**[4] [6213] 3-8-9 **53** .... RyanMoore 2 — 42
(P D Evans) *dwlt: hdwy on ins over 3f out: sn chsng ldrs: wknd and eased over 1f out* **8/1**[3]

0003 **10** *7* **Morgan Lewis (IRE)**[67] [4795] 5-8-13 **55** .... RichardThomas 16 — 30
(J A Geake) *w ldrs: c wd over 3f out: wknd over 1f out* **20/1**

5022 **11** *nk* **The Grey One (IRE)**[7] [6177] 3-8-10 **54** ....(p) KDarley 13 — 28
(J M Bradley) *w ldrs: ev ch tl wknd over 2f out* **11/2**[2]

2050 **12** *1¼* **Foolish Groom**[31] [4983] 5-9-1 **57** ....(v) JimCrowley 8 — 28
(R Hollinshead) *rr-div: effrt over 3f out: nvr a factor* **20/1**

4506 **13** *2½* **Mixing**[19] [5954] 4-8-10 **52** .... MickyFenton 7 — 18
(W Jarvis) *a towards rr* **12/1**

0202 **14** *1½* **Bold Haze**[22] [5885] 4-8-8 **55** ....(v) MichaelJStainton(5) 12 — 18
(Miss S E Hall) *trckd ldrs: wknd 2f out* **22/1**

600 **15** *29* **Aberlady Bay (IRE)**[32] [5669] 3-8-13 **57** .... HayleyTurner 15 — —
(T T Clement) *bhd and swtchd lft after s: a detached in last: t.o 2f out* **100/1**

1m 47.71s (1.31) **Going Correction** +0.175s/f (Good)
WFA 3 from 4yo+ 2lb — **15** Ran SP% **122.2**
Speed ratings (Par 101):100,99,99,99,99 98,91,91,91,84 83,82,80,78,49
CSF £220.91 CT £2010.18 TOTE £8.10: £2.10, £10.00, £2.80; EX 405.50.
Owner D J Allen **Bred** Mrs J McMahon **Trained** Hopwas, Staffs

■ Stewards' Enquiry : Adrian McCarthy three-day ban: used whip with excessive frequency without giving gelding time to respond (Nov 13-15)

FOCUS

A competitive if low-grade handicap and, though the front six finished in a heap, they pulled a very long way clear of the rest. The form looks straightforward and sound with the third and fourth to form.

6301 BLUES CONSULTANTS LTD H'CAP — 1m 1f 213y

4:15 (4:15) (Class 5) (0-75,75) 3-Y-O+ — **£3,886** (£1,156; £577; £288) **Stalls** Low

Form — RPR

4611 **1** — **Cleaver**[22] [5905] 5-9-3 **71** .... SebSanders 2 — 81+
(Lady Herries) *hld up in rr: hdwy on ins over 3f out: led 1f out: styd on strly: readily* **11/4**[1]

4041 **2** *2½* **Top Spec (IRE)**[19] [5944] 5-9-6 **74** .... JimmyQuinn 9 — 80
(J Pearce) *s.i.s: hdwy on wd outside 3f out: wnt 2nd 1f out: kpt on: no ch w wnr* **14/1**

0000 **3** *2½* **Arry Dash**[16] [6017] 6-9-2 **70** ....(v) HayleyTurner 1 — 71
(M J Wallace) *s.i.s: hdwy on ins 3f out: kpt on same pce appr fnl f* **22/1**

4101 **4** *nk* **Royal Flynn**[19] [5954] 4-8-10 **64** .... JimCrowley 6 — 64
(M Dods) *hld up towards rr: hdwy over 3f out: kpt on same pce fnl 2f* **11/1**

5124 **5** *shd* **Trouble Mountain (USA)**[16] [6017] 9-9-5 **73** ....(t) DaleGibson 12 — 73
(M W Easterby) *s.i.s: in rr and drvn along 5f out: styd on fnl 2f* **9/1**[3]

030 **6** *nk* **Little Bob**[4] [6209] 5-8-10 **64** ....(b) GrahamGibbons 8 — 64
(J D Bethell) *w ldrs: led over 6f out tl 1f out: wknd ins last* **16/1**

6560 **7** *1¼* **Bentley Brook (IRE)**[26] [5792] 4-8-7 **66** ....(b) KevinGhunowa(5) 16 — 63
(P A Blockley) *chsd ldrs: effrt on outside over 3f out: one pce* **50/1**

0015 **8** *nk* **Parnassian**[7] [6176] 6-8-11 **70** .... TravisBlock(5) 11 — 67
(J A Geake) *mid-div: effrt on outside 3f out: kpt on same pce* **7/2**[2]

5260 **9** *½* **Kavachi (IRE)**[5] [6206] 3-8-10 **68** .... TonyCulhane 5 — 64
(G L Moore) *chsd ldrs: one pce fnl 3f* **25/1**

4635 **10** *nk* **Dumaran (IRE)**[105] [3639] 8-9-2 **73** .... StephenDonohoe(3) 3 — 69
(W J Musson) *hld up in rr: hdwy over 3f out: nvr nr ldrs* **16/1**

5016 **11** *nk* **Pure Imagination (IRE)**[3] [6240] 5-8-11 **72** ....(b) BarrySavage(7) 4 — 67
(J M Bradley) *s.i.s: sn mid-field: one pce fnl 3f* **20/1**

0600 **12** *1* **Press Express (IRE)**[36] [5599] 4-8-8 **67** .... JamieMoriarty(5) 13 — 60
(R A Fahey) *hld up in rr: sme hdwy on wd outside 3f out: nvr a factor* **28/1**

2502 **13** *9* **Logsdail**[6] [6189] 6-9-0 **68** ....(p) ChrisCatlin 10 — 45
(G L Moore) *chsd ldrs: lost pl over 1f out* **16/1**

342 **14** *4* **Red Countess**[24] [5844] 3-9-3 **75** .... RyanMoore 15 — 45
(Mrs A J Perrett) *chsd ldrs: wknd over 2f out* **12/1**

1000 **15** *18* **Danelor (IRE)**[30] [5739] 8-8-11 **68** .... PatrickMathers(3) 7 — 5
(D Shaw) *chsd ldrs: lost pl over 3f out: sn bhd: eased* **100/1**

4652 **16** *2½* **Dream Shared**[33] [5651] 3-8-10 **68** .... LDettori 14 — —
(E A L Dunlop) *led tl over 6f out: wknd over 2f: sn bhd and eased* **12/1**

2m 13.35s (3.65) **Going Correction** +0.175s/f (Good)
WFA 3 from 4yo+ 4lb — **16** Ran SP% **126.3**
Speed ratings (Par 103):92,90,88,87,87 87,86,86,85,85 85,84,77,74,59 57
CSF £41.23 CT £748.65 TOTE £3.30: £1.90, £1.50, £3.60, £2.60; EX 56.90 Place 6 £133.60 Place 5 £103.42.
Owner Seymour Bloodstock (uk) Ltd **Bred** J M Greetham **Trained** Patching, W Sussex

FOCUS

A competitive handicap, but the pace was not strong hence the moderate winning time. Almost the entire field were still within a couple of lengths of each other passing the two-furlong pole. The form could be rated slightly higher.

T/Jkpt: £9,477.20 to a £1 stake. Pool: £53,393.00. 4.00 winning tickets. T/Plt: £100.80 to a £1 stake. Pool: £40,980.95. 296.50 winning tickets. T/Qpdt: £13.00 to a £1 stake. Pool: £3,121.80. 176.80 winning tickets. WG

6276 SOUTHWELL (L-H)

Thursday, November 2

OFFICIAL GOING: Standard

After a dry spell the surface had dried out and was back to normal after being on the fast side two days earlier.

Wind: light, half behind Weather: fine and sunny

6302 WBX.COM WORLD BET EXCHANGE MAIDEN CLAIMING STKS — 1m 3f (F)

1:00 (1:05) (Class 7) 3-Y-O+ — **£1,706** (£503; £252) **Stalls** Low

Form — RPR

5465 **1** — **Bolckow**[24] [5862] 3-8-12 50 .... CatherineGannon 4 — 58
(K A Ryan) *sn trcking ldrs: led 3f out: clr over 1f out: styd on strly* **3/1**[2]

3402 **2** *6* **Glory Be (ITY)**[69] [4755] 4-8-12 40 ....(p) RichardThomas 2 — 43
(J L Spearing) *mid-div: hdwy over 5f out: kpt on to take 2nd over 1f out: no ch w wnr* **5/1**[3]

0040 **3** *3* **Queen Of Diamonds (IRE)**[10] [6133] 3-8-7 45 .... RichardMullen 9 — 38
(Mrs P N Dutfield) *sn drvn along: hdwy over 7f out: sn chsng ldrs: one pce fnl 2f* **14/1**

00 **4** *4* **Asleep At The Back (IRE)**[15] [6052] 3-8-12 ....(t) JamieMackay 5 — 36+
(J G Given) *reminders after s: hmpd bnd after 2f: rn in snatches: hdwy over 3f out: rdr dropped whip 2f out: no imp* **50/1**

0605 **5** *hd* **City Minx**[21] [5922] 4-8-12 45 .... PaulEddery 8 — 31
(S R Bowring) *in rr: hdwy over 5f out: sn chsng ldrs: one pce fnl 3f* **25/1**

5022 **6** *2½* **Lanfredo**[23] [5887] 3-8-12 52 ....(p) DaleGibson 10 — 31
(Miss M E Rowland) *keen: w ldrs: led after 3f tl 3f out: sn wknd* **5/2**[1]

0 **7** *17* **Hoofbeats Tour**[21] [5922] 4-9-1 .... MatthewHenry 11 — —
(Miss J Feilden) *sn chsng ldrs: lost pl over 3f out* **100/1**

053/ **8** *10* **Integration**[422] [5041] 6-9-3 45 .... AdrianMcCarthy 13 — —
(Ronald Thompson) *trckd ldrs: lost pl over 3f out* **16/1**

0/04 **9** *8* **Royal Approach**[21] [5922] 5-8-12 45 .... PaulMulrennan 1 — —
(J R Norton) *led 3f: chsd ldrs: wknd 3f out* **80/1**

-000 **10** *36* **Red Pride (IRE)**[18] [5986] 3-8-10 45 .... MichaelTebbutt 14 — —
(Miss J Feilden) *chsd ldrs: drvn over 4f out: sn lost pl: t.o* **33/1**

0030 **11** *5* **Sunset Dreamer (USA)**[135] [2725] 5-8-12 40 ....(b[1]) FJohansson 6 — —
(P Mitchell) *in rr: bhd fnl 5f: t.o 2f out* **20/1**

0-00 **12** *35* **Bright**[268] [333] 3-8-10 45 .... LeeEnstone 7 — —
(Robert Gray) *chsd ldrs: stmbld and lost pl over 5f out: t.o over 3f out: virtually p.u* **50/1**

4664 **13** *3* **Campbells Lad**[81] [4404] 5-9-3 40 .... TPO'Shea 3 — —
(Mrs G S Rees) *s.s: a bhd: t.o 3f out: virtually p.u* **10/1**

2m 28.88s (-0.02) **Going Correction** -0.10s/f (Stan)
WFA 3 from 4yo+ 5lb — **13** Ran SP% **109.6**
Speed ratings (Par 97):96,91,89,86,86 84,72,64,59,32 29,3,1
CSF £14.86 TOTE £3.80: £1.70, £1.70, £3.20; EX 22.30 Trifecta £108.90 Pool 153.48 - 1.00 winning unit.The winner was claimed by J T Stimpson for £6,000.
Owner Graham Frankland **Bred** Khorshed And Ian Deane **Trained** Hambleton, N Yorks

FOCUS

A poor claimer but the back-to-form winner scored in clear-cut fashion and sets the level on his summer form.

6303 EXPERIENCE NOTTINGHAMSHIRE MEDIAN AUCTION MAIDEN STKS — 1m (F)

1:30 (1:32) (Class 7) 2-Y-O — **£1,911** (£564; £282) **Stalls** Low

Form — RPR

2 **1** — **Docofthebay (IRE)**[68] [4794] 2-9-0 .... StephenDonohoe(3) 9 — 73
(J A Osborne) *chsd ldrs: hung rt over 2f out: led on stands' side and hit rail over 1f out: hrd rdn and hld on towards fin* **9/4**[1]

00 **2** *¾* **River Deuce**[35] [5640] 2-9-0 .... SaleemGolam(3) 1 — 71
(M H Tompkins) *s.i.s: bhd tl hdwy over 3f out: styd far side: upsides 1f out: no ex nr fin* **50/1**

63 **3** *¾* **Four Miracles**[23] [5899] 2-8-12 .... TPQueally 3 — 65
(M H Tompkins) *chsd ldrs: edgd rt and kpt on same pce ins last* **7/1**

4 **4** *1¾* **Lord Oroko**[20] [5947] 2-9-3 .... CatherineGannon 2 — 66
(K A Ryan) *sn chsng ldrs: led over 5f out tl over 2f out: kpt on same pce* **11/4**[3]

03 **5** *1¾* **Sheriff's Silk**[21] [5923] 2-9-3 .... PaulEddery 12 — 62
(B Smart) *led tl over 5f out: led over 2f out tl over 1f out: wknd wl ins last* **50/1**

532 **6** *6* **Chasing Memories (IRE)**[21] [5923] 2-8-12 73 .... RoystonFfrench 5 — 43
(B Smart) *sn out of tch and drvn along: hdwy 2f out: styd on ins last* **5/2**[2]

000 **7** *4* **Cavendish**[95] [3979] 2-9-3 45 .... MickyFenton 7 — 39
(J M P Eustace) *chsd ldrs: wknd over 2f out* **80/1**

8 *5* **Alice Howe** 2-8-12 .... RichardMullen 4 — 22
(W R Muir) *sn drvn along in rr: lost pl over 4f out: sn bhd* **33/1**

0 **9** *5* **Jazz Festival (USA)**[23] [5900] 2-9-3 .... PhillipMakin 10 — 16
(T D Barron) *chsd ldrs: lost pl over 3f out* **33/1**

0 **10** *1½* **Spanish Affair**[23] [5900] 2-9-3 .... TomEaves 11 — 12
(Jedd O'Keeffe) *mid-div: lost pl 4f out: sn bhd* **100/1**

11 5 **Heaven's Gates** 2-9-3 .... PaulMulrennan 8 1
(K A Ryan) *s.i.s: sn bhd* **33/1**

1m 45.02s (0.42) **Going Correction** -0.10s/f (Stan) 11 Ran SP% **113.5**
Speed ratings (Par 90):93,92,91,89,88 82,78,73,68,66 61
CSF £113.40 TOTE £3.40: £1.40, £7.80, £1.90; EX 101.10 TRIFECTA Not won..
Owner Paul J Dixon **Bred** G And Mrs Middlebrook **Trained** Upper Lambourn, Berks
■ Stewards' Enquiry : Stephen Donohoe three-day ban: used whip with excessive frequency (Nov 13-15)

FOCUS
Just modest maiden form but it has a fairly solid look about it with the winner and fourth close to pre-race marks.

NOTEBOOK
Docofthebay(IRE), runner-up on his debut at Goodwood in August, hung badly right once in line for home. He hit the running rail and the champion apprentice elect had to use his whip in vigorous fashion to keep him going in a straight line. In the end he did just enough but at the cost of a three-day whip ban. (op 5-2 tchd 11-4 and 3-1 in a place)
River Deuce, playing away from home for the first time and the stable's neglected, travelled strongly on the inner. He stuck to the far side and in the end just missed out with the winner racing on the opposite wing. (op 33-1)
Four Miracles, making her All-Weather debut and returned to a mile, was just found lacking edging towards the centre in the home straight. (op 6-1)
Lord Oroko confirmed the promise shown on his debut. He kept on stoutly when headed and should be able to make his mark in handicap company at three. (tchd 3-1)
Sheriff's Silk, on his third start, showed improved form but in the end the mile on this surface seemed to stretch his stamina to breaking point.
Chasing Memories(IRE), left short of room, clipped heels and lost all chance soon after the start. Official explanation: jockey said filly was hampered and clipped heels shortly after leaving stalls (op 11-4 tchd 9-4)
Cavendish Official explanation: jockey said gelding hung left

6304 WBX.COM WORLD BET EXCHANGE BANDED STKS 1m (F)
2:00 (2:00) (Class 7) 3-Y-0+ £1,945 (£574; £287) **Stalls** Low

Form RPR
0152 **1** **Legal Lover (IRE)**[14] [6069] 4-8-12 50 .... RussellKennemore[(7)] 2 63
(R Hollinshead) *mde all: clr over 1f out: unchal* **2/1**[1]
2606 **2** 1 ½ **Paso Doble**[96] [3948] 8-8-11 49 .... JamesMillman[(7)] 5 59
(B R Millman) *in rr: hdwy 2f out: styd on wl to go 2nd ins last: nt rch wnr* **8/1**[3]
0030 **3** 3 **Perfect Order (USA)**[73] [4667] 3-9-1 48 .... (p) GeorgeBaker 6 52
(N A Callaghan) *s.i.s: hld up: stdy hdwy over 4f out: wnt 2nd over 1f out: kpt on same pce* **14/1**
0203 **4** 2 **Thornaby Green**[21] [5924] 5-8-12 50 .... DeanHeslop[(7)] 12 49
(T D Barron) *w ldrs: one pce fnl 2f* **9/2**[2]
-004 **5** 2 **Suffolk House**[21] [5929] 4-9-3 48 .... DeanMcKeown 4 43
(M Brittain) *chsd ldrs: one pce fnl 2f* **16/1**
0460 **6** ¾ **Fun Time**[70] [4728] 3-9-3 50 .... TPO'Shea 1 44
(M R Channon) *chsd ldrs: drvn 3f out: one pce* **16/1**
6-53 **7** shd **Josh You Are**[15] [6057] 3-9-1 48 .... DaleGibson 7 41
(D E Cantillon) *s.i.s: in rr tl styd on fnl 2f* **10/1**
2004 **8** ½ **Monkey Madge**[21] [5924] 4-9-3 48 .... RoystonFfrench 13 40
(B Smart) *mid-div: lost pl over 4f out: kpt on fnl 2f* **9/1**
0000 **9** 6 **Star Fern**[21] [5924] 5-9-3 48 .... MickyFenton 11 28
(M J Attwater) *racd wd: sn in rr* **25/1**
006- **10** 8 **Maynooth Prince (IRE)**[383] [5896] 4-9-4 49 .... DanielTudhope 9 12
(A Dickman) *prom: lost pl 5f out* **25/1**
6505 **11** 1 ¾ **Josarty**[85] [4262] 3-9-3 50 .... (e[1]) GrahamGibbons 8 9
(J J Quinn) *chsd ldrs: lost pl over 3f out* **8/1**[3]
0000 **12** 5 **Goodenough Prince**[24] [5870] 3-9-0 50 .... RichardKingscote[(3)] 3 —
(Andrew Turnell) *mid-div: effrt on inner over 2f out: sn wknd* **25/1**
5000 **13** 12 **Spanish Story**[77] [4531] 3-9-1 48 .... TonyCulhane 14 —
(J G Portman) *chsd ldrs on outer: lost pl over 3f out: eased whn bhd fnl f* **20/1**

1m 44.32s (-0.28) **Going Correction** -0.10s/f (Stan)
WFA 3 from 4yo+ 2lb 13 Ran SP% **127.6**
Speed ratings (Par 97):97,95,92,90,88 87,87,87,81,73 71,66,54
CSF £18.76 TOTE £2.60: £1.60, £3.10, £3.20; EX 18.50 TRIFECTA Not won..
Owner Tim Leadbeater **Bred** Ballyhane Stud **Trained** Upper Longdon, Staffs

FOCUS
The winner was entitled to take this on his recent turf form and the race has a solid look about it.
Josh You Are Official explanation: jockey said gelding would not face the kick-back
Star Fern Official explanation: jockey said gelding missed the break
Goodenough Prince Official explanation: jockey said gelding was unsuited by the fibresand surface

6305 DINE IN THE QUEEN MOTHER RESTAURANT BANDED STKS 1m 6f (F)
2:35 (2:35) (Class 7) 3-Y-0+ £1,945 (£574; £287) **Stalls** Low

Form RPR
4410 **1** **Ice And Fire**[80] [4438] 7-9-2 48 .... (b) AshleyHamblett[(7)] 3 61
(J T Stimpson) *hld up: smooth hdwy over 4f out: wnt 2nd over 2f out: shkn up to ld appr fnl f: sn pushed clr: readily* **8/1**
2662 **2** 5 **Red River Rebel**[21] [5927] 8-9-6 45 .... PaulMulrennan 12 51
(J R Norton) *chsd ldrs: led over 8f out tl appr fnl f: no ch w wnr* **4/1**[2]
0010 **3** 2 **Silver Mont (IRE)**[10] [6128] 3-9-3 50 .... (bt) PaulEddery 7 53
(S R Bowring) *hld up in rr: hdwy over 4f out: styd on fnl 2f* **14/1**
0660 **4** 5 **Padre Nostro (IRE)**[19] [5960] 7-9-2 48 .... ChrisGlenister[(7)] 13 44
(J R Holt) *in rr: drvn 8f out: kpt on fnl 3f: nvr nr ldrs* **16/1**
0000 **5** 1 ½ **Celtic Empire (IRE)**[52] [5247] 3-9-1 48 .... DaleGibson 4 42
(Jedd O'Keeffe) *mid-div: hdwy u.p over 4f out: nvr nr ldrs* **33/1**
4-00 **6** 7 **Bongoali**[21] [5927] 4-9-6 40 .... AdrianMcCarthy 8 29
(Mrs C A Dunnett) *in tch: effrt over 3f out: sn wknd* **33/1**
3601 **7** 2 **Bulberry Hill**[21] [5927] 5-9-8 50 .... EdwardCreighton[(3)] 11 32
(R W Price) *in tch: hdwy to trck ldrs over 8f out: wknd 3f out* **3/1**[1]
3025 **8** 2 **Makarim (IRE)**[21] [5927] 10-9-6 45 .... (p) GeorgeBaker 6 24
(M R Bosley) *hld up in rr: stdy hdwy outside over 5f out: wknd over 2f out* **13/2**[3]
60-0 **9** 12 **Lady Lucinda**[11] [5768] 5-9-6 40 .... RichardMullen 2 7
(J R Holt) *led 3f: chsd ldrs: lost pl over 3f out* **100/1**
2304 **10** 2 **High Frequency (IRE)**[12] [5369] 5-8-13 45 .... (p) SladeO'Hara[(7)] 14 4
(A Crook) *sn in rr and drvn along: nvr a factor* **9/1**
0/0- **11** 3 **Mr Kayos**[661] [74] 4-9-6 45 .... DeanMcKeown 9 —
(Mrs G S Rees) *prom: lost pl over 5f out* **25/1**
6650 **12** 26 **Sweet Lavinia**[19] [5960] 3-8-12 45 .... PatCosgrave 10 —
(J D Bethell) *trckd ldrs: lost pl over 4f out: bhd and eased 2f out: t.o* **8/1**
0230 **13** 10 **Channel Crossing**[4] [6238] 4-9-9 48 .... (p) RobbieFitzpatrick 5 —
(W M Brisbourne) *hung rt thrght: w ldrs: led after 3f: hdd over 8f out: lost pl over 3f out: ended up stands' side: t.o* **14/1**
/000 **14** 43 **Love Academy**[82] [4363] 11-9-6 40 .... TPO'Shea 1 —
(Luke Comer, Ire) *in rr: t.o 5f out: virtually p.u: hopelessly t.o* **66/1**

3m 8.90s (-0.70) **Going Correction** -0.10s/f (Stan)
WFA 3 from 4yo+ 8lb 14 Ran SP% **122.0**
Speed ratings (Par 97):98,95,94,91,90 86,85,84,77,76 74,59,53,29
CSF £39.22 TOTE £9.00: £2.90, £2.10, £6.60; EX 41.00 Trifecta £190.00 Part won. Pool £267.70 - 0.67 winning units..
Owner J T Stimpson & B Trubshaw **Bred** Abdullah Saeed Bul Hab **Trained** Newcastle-Under-Lyme, Staffs

FOCUS
The winner had one of his good days and the form has a solid look about it.
Makarim(IRE) Official explanation: jockey said gelding hung right
High Frequency(IRE) Official explanation: jockey said gelding never travelled

6306 WBX.COM WORLD BET EXCHANGE TRI-BANDED STKS 7f (F)
3:10 (3:10) (Class 7) 3-Y-0 £1,945 (£574; £287) **Stalls** Low

Form RPR
5003 **1** **Top Level (IRE)**[2] [6281] 3-8-9 45 .... JerryO'Dwyer[(5)] 8 55
(M G Quinlan) *s.i.s: bhd: gd hdwy on outer 2f out: led last 75 yds: drew clr: readily* **7/2**[1]
3063 **2** 2 ½ **Franky'N'Jonny**[4] [6236] 3-9-0 45 .... (p) RobbieFitzpatrick 7 49
(M J Attwater) *s.i.s: hdwy over 3f out: led over 1f out: hdd and no ex ins last* **7/2**[1]
4000 **3** ¾ **Bowl Of Cherries**[29] [5767] 3-8-9 40 .... (b[1]) RichardMullen 12 42
(I A Wood) *chsd ldrs: led 3f out: hdd over 1f out: kpt on same pce* **6/1**[3]
0000 **4** 1 ¼ **No Inkling (IRE)**[29] [5767] 3-8-1 35 .... (p) DominicFox[(3)] 3 33
(John A Harris) *chsd ldrs: outpcd over 2f out: kpt on fnl f* **18/1**
0010 **5** 1 **Bold Love**[69] [4769] 3-8-11 45 .... JasonEdmunds[(3)] 6 41
(J Balding) *sn chsng ldrs: chal over 1f out: one pce* **8/1**
0000 **6** 5 **Tilen (IRE)**[2] [6281] 3-9-0 45 .... MatthewHenry 5 28
(S Parr) *in rr: sme hdwy 2f out: nvr on terms* **66/1**
-060 **7** 1 ¾ **Jenise (IRE)**[76] [4548] 3-8-9 45 .... DuranFentiman[(5)] 11 23
(Mark Campion) *mid-div: drvn 3f out: sn outpcd* **25/1**
5000 **8** 1 ¼ **Tay Bridge (IRE)**[20] [5949] 3-7-13 35 .... (bt) NicolPolli[(5)] 4 10
(G F Bridgwater) *s.i.s: effrt and styd far side over 2f out: nvr on terms* **50/1**
0604 **9** 6 **Megavegas**[20] [5951] 3-8-9 40 .... MickyFenton 2 —
(P T Midgley) *led tl hdd & wknd 3f out* **18/1**
0040 **10** 2 ½ **Nilsatisoptimum (USA)**[2] [6282] 3-9-0 45 .... (p) LeeEnstone 1 —
(M Mullineaux) *w ldrs: reminders after 1f: lost pl over 2f out* **10/1**
3600 **11** 2 **Distant Vision (IRE)**[52] [5244] 3-8-9 40 .... (v[1]) PaulQuinn 9 —
(A Berry) *chsd ldrs: lost pl over 3f out* **11/1**
0000 **12** 3 ½ **Active Audience (IRE)**[2] [6277] 3-8-8 42 ow2 ...... StephenDonohoe[(3)] 13 —
(A Berry) *in tch: lost pl over 4f out* **66/1**
-050 **13** 1 **Double Oh Seven (IRE)**[84] [4297] 3-9-0 45 .... (bt[1]) AdrianMcCarthy 10 —
(J W Unett) *chsd ldrs: lost pl over 3f out* **20/1**
5005 **14** 13 **Quintin**[47] [5368] 3-9-0 45 .... J-PGuillambert 14 —
(T D Easterby) *chsd ldrs on wd outside: hung rt: rn wd and lost pl bnd over 3f out: sn lost pl and eased* **11/2**[2]

1m 31.44s (0.64) **Going Correction** -0.10s/f (Stan) 14 Ran SP% **126.7**
Speed ratings (Par 96):92,89,88,86,85 80,78,76,69,66 64,60,59,44
CSF £14.86 TOTE £4.90: £2.00, £1.70, £2.70; EX 16.80 Trifecta £47.60 Pool £155.60 - 2.32 winning units.
Owner Mrs Jeanette Johnson **Bred** Kildare Racing Syndicate **Trained** Newmarket, Suffolk

FOCUS
The winner was confirming her improved effort here two days earlier and there may be even better to come. The race has been rated positively.
Quintin Official explanation: jockey said filly felt wrong behind 3f out

6307 BOOK YOUR CHRISTMAS PARTY HERE BANDED STKS 7f (F)
3:40 (3:41) (Class 7) 4-Y-0+ £1,945 (£574; £287) **Stalls** Low

Form RPR
0352 **1** **Preskani**[2] [6281] 4-8-12 45 .... (p) DanielTudhope 12 56+
(Mrs N Macauley) *hld up in rr: nt clr run over 3f out: gd hdwy on outer over 2f out: styd on wl to ld ins last: readily* **13/8**[1]
0000 **2** 2 **I Wish**[148] [2347] 8-8-12 45 .... PaulFitzsimons 10 51
(Miss J R Tooth) *trckd ldrs: led over 2f out: edgd rt over 1f out: hdd ins last: no ex* **16/1**
3040 **3** 1 **Sea Frolic (IRE)**[2] [6281] 5-8-7 45 .... (v) RoryMoore[(5)] 1 48+
(Jennie Candlish) *lost pl on inner over 4f out: hdwy over 2f out: kpt on wl ins last* **16/1**
4201 **4** shd **Vibrato (USA)**[2] [6281] 4-9-4 45 .... RobbieFitzpatrick 11 54
(C J Teague) *swtchd lft after s: hdwy on ins over 4f out: chal over 1f out: carried hd high: kpt on same pce ins last* **11/4**[2]
0630 **5** hd **Elms Schoolboy**[10] [6134] 4-8-9 45 .... (b) DeanCorby[(3)] 2 47
(P Howling) *s.i.s: hdwy on wd outside over 2f out: styd on fnl f* **6/1**[3]
0000 **6** 8 **Compton Micky**[2] [6282] 5-8-5 45 .... AshleyHamblett[(7)] 14 27
(R F Marvin) *trckd ldrs: lost pl over 1f out* **50/1**
0204 **7** 1 ¼ **Lottie**[2] [6277] 5-8-12 45 .... (p) PhillipMakin 8 23
(G Woodward) *led tl over 2f out: wknd over 1f out* **8/1**
0600 **8** 6 **Fraternity**[2] [6282] 9-8-5 45 .... RussellKennemore[(7)] 9 8
(J A Pickering) *trckd ldrs: wknd over 2f out* **16/1**
000/ **9** 10 **Carlburg (IRE)**[754] [6061] 5-8-12 45 .... AdrianMcCarthy 3 —
(Mrs C A Dunnett) *a in rr* **50/1**
050 **10** 8 **Always A Story**[58] [5093] 4-8-12 45 .... (b[1]) PaulEddery 13 —
(Miss D Mountain) *prom on outer: lost pl over 4f out: bhd whn hung lft over 2f out* **20/1**

1m 31.13s (0.33) **Going Correction** -0.10s/f (Stan) 10 Ran SP% **116.5**
Speed ratings (Par 97):94,91,90,90,90 81,79,72,61,52
CSF £30.48 TOTE £2.30: £1.20, £4.60, £2.90; EX 46.90 Trifecta £106.60 Part won. Pool £150.17 - 0.30 winning units..
Owner Godfrey Horsford **Bred** P And Mrs Venner **Trained** Sproxton, Leics

FOCUS
An ordinary contest but the winner and third were not far off form.
Elms Schoolboy Official explanation: vet said gelding had bled from the nose

6308 WBX.COM BANDED STKS 6f (F)
4:10 (4:10) (Class 7) 3-Y-0+ £1,945 (£574; £287) **Stalls** Low

Form RPR
0523 **1** **Granakey (IRE)**[4] [6234] 3-8-11 49 .... JerryO'Dwyer[(5)] 8 59
(M G Quinlan) *mid-div: gd hdwy over 1f out: styd on wl to ld ins last* **4/1**[2]
2030 **2** 1 **Blakeshall Quest**[4] [6234] 6-9-1 48 .... (b) PatCosgrave 7 55
(R Brotherton) *mde most: hdd and no ex ins last* **9/1**
0000 **3** 2 **Danethorpe (IRE)**[2] [6276] 3-9-1 48 .... (v[1]) DanielTudhope 2 49
(D Shaw) *in rr: hdwy on ins over 2f out: styd on same pce fnl f* **66/1**
0203 **4** ½ **Cree**[38] [5576] 4-9-3 50 .... RichardMullen 3 50
(W R Muir) *chsd ldrs: sn drvn along: styd on same pce fnl 2f* **3/1**[1]

0534 **5** *3* **Four Amigos (USA)**4 [6234] 5-9-3 50 .... LeeEnstone 4 41
(I A Wood) *chsd ldrs: fdd appr fnl f* **13/2**

3000 **6** *1 1/4* **Far Note (USA)**94 [3995] 8-9-0 50 .... (bt) AmirQuinn(3) 1 37
(S R Bowring) *chsd ldrs: wknd over 1f out* **10/1**

6050 **7** *1 3/4* **Kissi Kissi**21 [5929] 3-9-0 47 .... (vt) RobbieFitzpatrick 5 29
(M J Attwater) *s.i.s: hdwy on inner over 2f out: nvr nr ldrs* **20/1**

0000 **8** *5* **Developer (IRE)**2 [6276] 3-8-10 50 .... (v1) MarkCoumbe(7) 12 17
(G F Bridgwater) *in rr: nvr on terms* **33/1**

0-05 **9** *shd* **Bond Puccini**19 [5969] 4-8-12 50 .... DuranFentiman(5) 14 16
(G R Oldroyd) *mid-div on outer: effrt on outer over 2f out: nvr a factor* **40/1**

-001 **10** *shd* **Alistair John**24 [5873] 3-9-3 50 .... DeanMcKeown 6 16
(Mrs G S Rees) *mid-div: lost pl over 3f out* **6/1**3

000 **11** *1* **Stokesies Wish**2 [6274] 6-9-0 47 .... AdrianTNicholls 10 10
(J L Spearing) *hld up: effrt on wd outside over 2f out: nvr on terms* **12/1**

30-0 **12** *hd* **Tancred Times**30 [5752] 11-9-0 47 .... TomEaves 13 9
(D W Barker) *in tch: effrt on outer over 2f out: no threat* **33/1**

000 **13** *nk* **Obe Bold (IRE)**43 [5486] 5-8-12 48 .... StephenDonohoe(3) 11 9
(A Berry) *rrd s: a in rr* **14/1**

0060 **14** *13* **Height Of Esteem**4 [6234] 3-9-3 50 .... (p) AdrianMcCarthy 9 —
(M Mullineaux) *w ldr: wknd over 2f out: eased and bhd over 1f out* **50/1**

1m 16.85s (-0.05) **Going Correction** -0.10s/f (Stan) **14** Ran SP% **122.6**
Speed ratings (Par 97):96,94,92,91,87 85,83,76,76,76 75,74,74,57
CSF £38.27 TOTE £5.80: £1.90, £3.30, £15.20; EX 49.20 TRIFECTA Not won. Place 6 £68.82, Place 5 £27.61.
Owner The Colourful Bunch **Bred** Mrs Lorraine Castle **Trained** Newmarket, Suffolk
■ A double for apprentice Jerry O'Dwyer.

FOCUS
The form, rated around the first two, looks sound.
Bond Puccini Official explanation: vet said gelding finished lame
T/Plt: £40.00 to a £1 stake. Pool: £43,492.40. 793.70 winning tickets. T/Qpdt: £7.80 to a £1 stake. Pool: £2,316.10. 219.00 winning tickets. WG

6283 WOLVERHAMPTON (A.W) (L-H)
Thursday, November 2

OFFICIAL GOING: Standard to fast
Wind: nil Weather: fine and cold

6309 NAME A RACE TO ENHANCE YOUR BRAND MEDIAN AUCTION MAIDEN FILLIES' STKS 7f 32y(P)
3:45 (3:46) (Class 6) 2-Y-O £2,730 (£806; £403) Stalls High

Form RPR

1 **Situla (IRE)**114 [3391] 2-9-0 .... DaneO'Neill 3 70+
(H J L Dunlop) *mde all: rdn wl over 1f out: r.o wl* **8/1**

2 *2 1/2* **Mankanja (IRE)** 2-9-0 .... ChrisCatlin 5 63
(D J Daly) *s.i.s: hld up in mid-div: hdwy on ins 2f out: sn rdn: kpt on to take 2nd nr fin: nt trble wnr* **66/1**

3302 **3** *shd* **Cantique (IRE)**24 [5876] 2-9-0 62 .... FergusSweeney 2 63
(A G Newcombe) *trckd ldrs: rdn to chse wnr over 1f out: kpt on same fnl f* **25/1**

4230 **4** *1/2* **Miss Saafend Plaza (IRE)**33 [5676] 2-9-0 79 .... RyanMoore 10 62
(R Hannon) *hld up and bhd: rdn over 3f out: c wd st: hdwy and hung lft fnl f: r.o* **15/8**1

554 **5** *1 1/2* **Satin Braid**13 [6073] 2-9-0 70 .... EddieAhern 9 58
(B J Meehan) *sn chsng ldrs: rdn over 2f out: edgd lft ins fnl f: one pce* **13/2**

6 **6** *1 3/4* **Tinted View (USA)**53 [5206] 2-9-0 .... RichardHughes 4 54
(B W Hills) *prom: rdn over 2f out: wknd over 1f out* **9/2**3

5022 **7** *hd* **Onatopp (IRE)**9 [6157] 2-9-0 65 .... DavidAllan 7 53
(T D Easterby) *w wnr: rdn 2f out: wknd fnl f* **16/1**

3 **8** *shd* **Red Current**59 [5068] 2-9-0 .... OscarUrbina 6 53
(J R Fanshawe) *wnt lft s: hld up in mid-div: rdn and no imp fnl 2f* **7/2**2

0 **9** *1/2* **Fruits D'Amour (IRE)**23 [5894] 2-9-0 .... LPKeniry 8 52
(S Kirk) *s.i.s: a bhd* **66/1**

10 *11* **Los Cristianos** 2-9-0 .... DeanMernagh 1 24
(M Brittain) *broke wl: sn outpcd and bhd* **66/1**

1m 28.61s (-1.79) **Going Correction** -0.375s/f (Stan) **10** Ran SP% **113.8**
Speed ratings (Par 91):95,92,92,91,89 87,87,87,86,74
CSF £425.99 TOTE £7.00: £3.50, £7.50, £8.90; EX 174.00.
Owner Anamoine Ltd **Bred** Anamoine Ltd **Trained** Lambourn, Berks
■ A winner with his first runner for Harry Dunlop, son of John and brother of Ed.

FOCUS
A modest event, with the exposed third helping to set the standard.

NOTEBOOK
Situla(IRE) dictated only a steady pace. Increasing the tempo in the straight, she showed a good attitude to her work and was never going to be caught. Her trainer's first runner, she was in the frame in a couple of maidens for Ger Lyons in Ireland over the summer and was switched to this country for the extra opportunities on the sand. (op 7-1)
Mankanja(IRE) shaped with plenty of promise, having to wait for a run before keeping on nicely against the inside rail to snatch second on the line. Out of a half-sister to Chester Cup winner Top Cees, she should improve for a step up in trip. Official explanation: vet said filly had bled from the nose (op 40-1)
Cantique(IRE), claimed from the Ralph Beckett stable after finishing second in a course-and-distance seller, ran her race and just missed out on second. Officially rated 62, she looks a decent pointer to the form's worth. (op 20-1)
Miss Saafend Plaza(IRE), the most experienced filly in the line-up, has some decent placed form in nurseries to her name, but she did not really take to the surface on this first try on Polytrack. From her wide draw, she improved under pressure on the outer in the straight but was hanging left and not helping her rider in the final furlong. (op 7-4)
Satin Braid, reverting to this trip after a couple of tries over a mile, lacked a change of gear in the straight. (op 8-1)
Tinted View(USA), who was staying on over six furlongs at Goodwood on her racecourse bow, faded rather tamely after tracking the pace. (op 5-1 tchd 6-1)
Onatopp(IRE), runner-up in a couple of soft-ground maidens, was stepping back up in trip and the extra yardage caught her out as she faded after matching strides with the winner. (op 14-1)
Red Current had shaped well on her debut at Warwick but was disappointing on this different surface. (tchd 4-1)

6310 TWILIGHT RACING AND SUPPER - RELAX AND ENJOY NURSERY 7f 32y(P)
4:15 (4:16) (Class 5) (0-75,75) 2-Y-O £3,886 (£1,156; £577; £288) Stalls High

Form RPR

225 **1** **Abbotts Ann**73 [4657] 2-9-4 72 .... MichaelHills 2 77
(B W Hills) *mde all: rdn wl over 1f out: drvn out* **11/4**1

4442 **2** *nk* **Benllech**14 [6063] 2-9-3 71 .... LPKeniry 12 75
(S Kirk) *hld up and bhd: hdwy whn swtchd rt over 1f out: r.o wl ins fnl f* **20/1**

000 **3** *shd* **Alittlebitleft (IRE)**47 [5371] 2-8-13 67 .... RichardHughes 3 71
(R Hannon) *hld up in mid-div: rdn and hdwy over 3f out: r.o ins fnl f* **7/2**2

6510 **4** *shd* **Our Herbie**21 [5916] 2-9-7 75 .... EddieAhern 4 79
(J W Hills) *hld up and bhd: hdwy on ins 3f out: rdn 2f out: kpt on ins fnl f* **6/1**3

0401 **5** *1* **Our Blessing (IRE)**17 [6012] 2-9-5 73 .... SebSanders 6 74
(A P Jarvis) *chsd wnr: ev ch over 2f out: sn rdn: no ex wl ins fnl f* **9/1**

005 **6** *3* **Kyllachy Storm**38 [5563] 2-8-13 67 .... SteveDrowne 1 61+
(R J Hodges) *prom: rdn over 2f out: wknd ins fnl f* **20/1**

003 **7** *nk* **Bluebelle Dancer (IRE)**52 [5237] 2-9-5 73 .... RyanMoore 9 66
(W R Muir) *hld up and bhd: rdn 3f out: hdwy on ins wl over 1f out: no imp fnl f* **12/1**

024 **8** *3/4* **Call Me Rosy (IRE)**31 [5735] 2-9-0 68 .... TedDurcan 8 59
(C F Wall) *mid-div: lost pl over 3f out: n.d after* **11/1**

0030 **9** *hd* **Astroangel**14 [6064] 2-8-10 71 .... PatrickHills(7) 7 62
(M H Tompkins) *s.i.s: hdwy 3f out: wknd wl over 1f out* **25/1**

3240 **10** *5* **Love Dubai (USA)**27 [5790] 2-9-5 73 .... JoeFanning 5 51
(M Johnston) *chsd ldrs: rdn 4f out: sn wknd* **8/1**

0245 **11** *1 3/4* **Weyba Downs (IRE)**71 [4699] 2-8-13 67 .... BrettDoyle 11 41
(J R Best) *bhd fnl 3f* **25/1**

0440 **12** *6* **Ensign's Trick**41 [5509] 2-8-8 67 .... LiamJones(5) 10 26+
(W M Brisbourne) *chsd ldrs tl rdn and wknd over 3f out* **50/1**

1m 28.22s (-2.18) **Going Correction** -0.375s/f (Stan) **12** Ran SP% **119.5**
Speed ratings (Par 96):97,96,96,96,95 91,91,90,90,84 82,75
CSF £66.26 CT £205.29 TOTE £2.70: £1.10, £6.50, £2.80; EX 37.60.
Owner Gainsborough **Bred** Gainsborough Stud Management Ltd **Trained** Lambourn, Berks
■ Stewards' Enquiry : Richard Hughes caution: used whip with excessive frequency

FOCUS
A fair nursery run in a slightly quicker time than the opening maiden over the same trip.

NOTEBOOK
Abbotts Ann made all the running, sticking her neck out well for pressure when she appeared set to be swamped inside the last. She has twice been a beaten favourite at Windsor since a promising debut on the Lingfield Polytrack but has been freshened up by a break since her last run and the return to this trip helped. (op 7-2)
Benllech came into this looking fairly exposed but this was an encouraging debut on this surface. He had to be switched out for a run before finishing to good effect, and would have got up with a little further to go. (op 16-1)
Alittlebitleft(IRE), whose promising performance at Newbury last time did not escape the attention of the Stewards, was reverting to seven furlongs and looked to need all of that trip as he stayed on after coming under pressure before the end of the back straight. (op 5-1)
Our Herbie stuck on well against the inside rail in the straight and is worth another chance over a mile ridden more patiently like he was here. (op 7-1 tchd 15-2)
Our Blessing(IRE), who landed an ordinary maiden over six furlongs at Pontefract last month, was running on sand for the first time since his debut. He showed up well for a long way but had been a little keen early on and faded out of the frame in the final furlong. (op 11-1)
Love Dubai(USA) looked a nailed-on future winner after his promising debut in the Convivial maiden at the Ebor meeting, but has been a serious disappointment since and looks one to be wary of. (op 15-2)
Ensign's Trick Official explanation: jockey said filly hung right

6311 SPONSOR A RACE BY CALLING 0870 220 2442 NURSERY 5f 20y(P)
4:45 (4:45) (Class 6) (0-65,65) 2-Y-O £2,388 (£705; £352) Stalls Low

Form RPR

053 **1** **Yungaburra (IRE)**33 [5686] 2-9-5 63 .... FrancisNorton 6 72+
(T J Pitt) *t.k.h: a.p: rdn to ld 1f out: r.o wl* **2/1**1

6430 **2** *1 1/2* **The Italian Job**24 [5860] 2-9-1 59 .... DavidAllan 9 63
(T D Easterby) *led: rdn and hdd whn struck on hd by winning jockey's whip: nt qckn* **11/1**

5060 **3** *3* **Queen Of Narnia**15 [6056] 2-9-6 64 .... RichardHughes 12 57+
(M R Channon) *hld up and bhd: rdn and hdwy whn swtchd rt over 1f out: r.o ins fnl f* **8/1**

600 **4** *1 1/2* **Damhsoir (IRE)**28 [5773] 2-8-12 56 .... DarryllHolland 5 43
(H S Howe) *chsd ldr 2f: rdn over 2f out: wknd over 1f out* **33/1**

5020 **5** *1 1/4* **Totally Free**50 [5290] 2-8-13 57 .... (v) HayleyTurner 4 40
(M D I Usher) *wnt lft s: hld up towards rr: rdn over 2f out: hdwy on ins wl over 1f out: nvr trbld ldrs* **33/1**

6600 **6** *3/4* **Bentley**35 [5633] 2-8-5 52 .... (v1) PatrickMathers(3) 3 32
(D Shaw) *bmpd s: outpcd: late hdwy: nrst fin* **40/1**

2350 **7** *nk* **Shreddy Shrimpster**45 [5419] 2-8-10 54 .... SteveDrowne 11 33
(A B Haynes) *hld up in tch: rdn whn hung lft and wknd over 1f out* **11/1**

4000 **8** *2 1/2* **Mrs Crossy (IRE)**28 [5772] 2-8-8 55 .... JamesDoyle(3) 7 25
(A W Carroll) *bhd: rdn over 3f out: n.d* **15/2**3

3034 **9** *shd* **Mr Mini Scule**44 [5448] 2-8-13 57 .... DaneO'Neill 10 27
(A B Haynes) *prom: rdn over 2f out: wknd wl over 1f out* **16/1**

2203 **10** *3* **Granny Peel (IRE)**63 [4971] 2-9-2 60 .... DeanMernagh 13 19
(M Brittain) *prom tl rdn and wknd over 2f out* **10/1**

506 **11** *3* **Auction Boy**98 [3860] 2-9-4 65 .... MarcHalford(3) 8 13
(B Palling) *mid-div: rdn over 2f out: sn bhd* **50/1**

5666 **12** *11* **River Tarrant**14 [6063] 2-8-11 62 .... MCGeran(7) 1 —
(P W Chapple-Hyam) *rel to r: a wl bhd* **11/1**

050 **13** *shd* **Miss Autumnal (IRE)**16 [6024] 2-9-6 64 .... (b) ChrisCatlin 2 —
(N A Callaghan) *a bhd* **13/2**2

61.67 secs (-1.15) **Going Correction** -0.375s/f (Stan) **13** Ran SP% **119.8**
Speed ratings (Par 94):94,91,86,84,82 81,80,76,76,71 66,49,49
CSF £24.73 CT £158.14 TOTE £3.40: £1.90, £2.80, £2.90; EX 36.80.
Owner J David Abell **Bred** Newlands House Stud **Trained** Bawtry, S Yorks

FOCUS
Few got into this nursery, which only concerned two in the home straight. There should be more to come from the winner with the runner-up the best guide to the level.

NOTEBOOK
Yungaburra(IRE) ◆, previously with Alan Swinbank, successfully reverted to the minimum trip after a couple runs over six. Delivering his challenge off the turn, he had to fight to see off the runner-up but was nicely on top near the finish. He looks progressive and there should be more races to be won with him. (op 3-1)
The Italian Job had been largely consistent prior to a well-beaten effort over six furlongs in bad ground at Ayr. After trying to make all, she received a smack across the nose from the winning rider's whip with a furlong to go and soon had to concede defeat. She clearly acts on this surface and should pay her way over the winter. (op 17-2)
Queen Of Narnia ran a better race than of late but her high draw was no help and she was never nearer than at the line.
Damhsoir(IRE), on her handicap bow, showed a lot more than she had on her recent sand debut when her saddle slipped. (op 40-1)
Totally Free, who ran perhaps his best race when runner-up in a seller in a first-time visor in July, was never a factor but did appear to act on this surface.

Bentley, visored for the first time, flew home too late on this drop to the minimum trip.
River Tarrant, who failed to get home over seven furlongs last time, lost all chance when very reluctant to leave the stalls. (op 9-1)
Miss Autumnal(IRE), back on an artificial surface for this nursery bow, was always at the back of the field. (tchd 6-1 and 7-1)

6312 WOLVERHAMPTON-RACECOURSE.CO.UK H'CAP — 1m 5f 194y(P)
5:20 (5:20) (Class 5) (0-70,70) 3-Y-0+ — **£3,238** (£963; £481; £240) **Stalls** Low

Form				RPR
3201	1		**Rehearsed (IRE)**^{19} [5971] 3-9-2 **66** ... SteveDrowne 4 (H Morrison) *set modest pce after 1f: qckd 2f out: sn rdn: jst hld on* **5/4**^{1}	69+
2130	2	*shd*	**Champagne Shadow (IRE)**^{12} [6108] 5-10-0 **70** ... NCallan 5 (K A Ryan) *prom: chsd wnr after 4f: rdn 2f out: r.o wl towards fin: jst failed* **11/4**^{2}	73+
2250	3	*1/2*	**Tranquilizer**^{36} [5610] 4-10-0 **70** ...(t) EddieAhern 1 (D J Coakley) *set slow pce 1f: a.p: rdn wl over 1f out: nt qckn ins fnl f* **5/1**^{3}	72+
0300	4	*1 3/4*	**Russian Dream (IRE)**^{33} [5691] 3-9-4 **68** ... AdamKirby 2 (W R Swinburn) *hld up in tch: edgd lft over 1f out: one pce* **10/1**	68
5041	5	*1*	**Abstract Folly (IRE)**^{47} [5390] 4-9-6 **62** ... DarryllHolland 3 (J D Bethell) *hld up in rr: hdwy over 3f out: rdn over 2f out: wknd wl over 1f out* **11/2**	60
6006	6	*1 3/4*	**Bubbling Fun**^{39} [4869] 5-8-9 **51** oh6 ... JimmyQuinn 6 (T Wall) *hld up: rdn over 1f out: no rspnse* **50/1**	47

3m 17.07s (9.70) **Going Correction** -0.375s/f (Stan)
WFA 3 from 4yo+ 8lb — **6** Ran SP% **114.2**
Speed ratings (Par 103):57,56,56,55,55 54
CSF £5.07 TOTE £2.00: £1.10, £2.10; EX 6.10.
Owner Mrs G C Maxwell & J D N Tillyard **Bred** J C Condon **Trained** East Ilsley, Berks
FOCUS
Something of a tactical affair with Steve Drowne dictating a very modest pace on the winner. The winning time was painfully slow for a race of this grade and the form is of very limited value.

6313 NORTHERN TRUST GROUP H'CAP — 1m 1f 103y(P)
5:50 (5:50) (Class 4) (0-85,84) 3-Y-0+ — **£5,505** (£1,637; £818; £408) **Stalls** Low

Form				RPR
41-0	1		**Stargazer Jim (FR)**^{33} [5685] 4-8-8 **78** ... LiamJones(5) 4 (W J Haggas) *chsd ldrs: rdn over 3f out: r.o to ld nr fin* **14/1**	87
3452	2	*hd*	**Consonant (IRE)**^{33} [5689] 9-8-12 **77** ... DarryllHolland 2 (D G Bridgwater) *hld up in mid-div: hdwy on ins 2f out: rdn to ld ins fnl f: hdd nr fin* **9/1**	86+
4031	3	*1*	**Woolfall Blue (IRE)**^{33} [5669] 3-8-11 **79** ... IanMongan 3 (G G Margarson) *hld up and bhd: hdwy and edgd lft 1f out: r.o* **25/1**	86
2120	4	*shd*	**Nevada Desert (IRE)**^{33} [5680] 6-8-9 **79** ... MichaelJStainton(5) 11 (R M Whitaker) *hld up towards rr: hdwy 4f out: rdn and edgd lft ins fnl f: kpt on* **12/1**	86
-021	5	*1*	**King Of Argos**^{152} [2220] 3-8-12 **80** ... SebSanders 12 (E A L Dunlop) *t.k.h: a.p: led over 2f out: rdn and hung lft over 1f out: hdd ins fnl f: 3rd and hld whn n.m.r* **11/2**^{2}	85
6642	6	*shd*	**Dower House**^{8} [6176] 11-8-13 **78** ...(t) ChrisCatlin 9 (Andrew Turnell) *hld up and bhd: rdn over 3f out: hdwy on ins wl over 1f out: nt clr run ins fnl f: nt rch ldrs* **14/1**	83+
3630	7	*3 1/2*	**Cactus King**^{20} [5945] 3-9-2 **84** ... RyanMoore 1 (J H M Gosden) *led early: prom: nt clr run and lost pl over 4f out: hrd rdn over 2f out: rallying whn nt clr run and eased ins fnl f* **15/8**^{1}	85+
3110	8	*1 1/4*	**Nanton (USA)**^{20} [5945] 4-9-5 **84** ... JimmyQuinn 13 (N Wilson) *hld up in mid-div: hdwy over 4f out: rdn over 2f out: wknd 1f out* **8/1**^{3}	79
3014	9	*nk*	**Street Warrior (IRE)**^{13} [6076] 3-8-11 **79** ... JoeFanning 5 (M Johnston) *sn chsng ldr: led 5f out: rdn and hdd over 2f out: wkng whn n.m.r jst ins fnl f* **9/1**	74
205-	10	*1*	**Black Falcon (IRE)**^{400} [5553] 6-9-3 **82** ... MickyFenton 10 (P T Midgley) *hld up and bhd: hdwy over 3f out: wknd fnl f* **66/1**	75
211/	11	*10*	**King's Account (USA)**^{751} [6140] 4-9-1 **80** ... EddieAhern 6 (S Gollings) *bhd fnl 3f* **28/1**	54
0605	12	*nk*	**Atlantic Quest (USA)**^{130} [2900] 7-9-1 **83** ...(p) JamesDoyle(3) 7 (Miss Venetia Williams) *s.s: a bhd* **12/1**	56
-000	13	*70*	**Habanero**^{187} [1281] 5-8-13 **78** ... RichardHughes 8 (Miss S J Wilton) *sn led: hdd 5f out: sn rdn and wknd qckly: eased fnl 3f* **66/1**	—

1m 57.94s (-4.68) **Going Correction** -0.375s/f (Stan)
WFA 3 from 4yo+ 3lb — **13** Ran SP% **120.3**
Speed ratings (Par 105):105,104,103,103,102 102,99,98,98,97 88,88,26
CSF £132.14 CT £3116.16 TOTE £17.10: £7.40, £2.40, £5.20; EX 160.90.
Owner Nicholas J Hughes **Bred** Sarl Le Lieu Calice And Peter Kavanagh **Trained** Newmarket, Suffolk
FOCUS
A competitive handicap that should throw up a few winners. The winner is progressive, the second ran as well as he has done for a year and the third and fourth were to form.
Atlantic Quest(USA) Official explanation: jockey said gelding missed the break

6314 BOOK YOUR CHRISTMAS PARTY NOW MEDIAN AUCTION MAIDEN STKS — 1m 1f 103y(P)
6:20 (6:20) (Class 6) 3-5-Y-0 — **£2,388** (£705; £352) **Stalls** Low

Form				RPR
04	1		**Miss Provence**^{15} [6052] 3-8-12 ... DarryllHolland 10 (G Wragg) *a.p: jnd ldr over 2f out: rdn wl over 1f out: r.o to ld cl home* **6/1**^{3}	70
0035	2	*1/2*	**Chasing A Dream**^{25} [5844] 3-8-12 67 ... MichaelHills 5 (B W Hills) *chsd ldr: led over 5f out: rdn over 2f out: hdd cl home* **13/2**	69
3403	3	*2*	**Moves Goodenough**^{25} [5830] 3-9-3 68 ... ChrisCatlin 9 (Andrew Turnell) *keen early: hdwy over 5f out: rdn 4f out: one pce fnl 2f* **7/1**	70
63	4	*3*	**Depraux (IRE)**^{17} [6019] 3-9-3 ... RyanMoore 8 (W J Haggas) *chsd ldrs: rdn 3f out: wknd ins fnl f* **9/4**^{1}	65
0	5	*5*	**Out Of This Way**^{5} [6225] 3-9-3 ...(t) AdamKirby 3 (I A Wood) *hld up in mid-div: hmpd and lost pl over 5f out: n.d after* **50/1**	55+
/000	6	*2 1/2*	**Miss Sudbrook (IRE)**^{92} [4054] 4-9-1 35 ... FrancisNorton 4 (A W Carroll) *rdn 4f out: a bhd* **100/1**	45
2363	7	*3/4*	**Jenny Soba**^{44} [5446] 3-8-7 60 ... MichaelJStainton(5) 6 (R M Whitaker) *a bhd* **9/1**	44
0046	8	*24*	**Laheen (IRE)**^{23} [5903] 3-8-5 54 ...(b^{1}) PatrickHills(7) 7 (M H Tompkins) *s.i.s: last whn bdly hmpd over 5f out: sn t.o* **28/1**	—
	9	*3 1/2*	**Rolons Advice**^{21} 5-9-6 ... SebSanders 2 (V Smith) *hld up in tch: hmpd and lost pl over 5f out: t.o* **40/1**	—
-043	P		**Royle Dancer**^{47} [5384] 3-9-3 61 ... RichardHughes 1 (R Hollinshead) *led: hdd whn b.b.v and eased over 5f out: sn p.u* **3/1**^{2}	—

1m 59.77s (-2.85) **Going Correction** -0.375s/f (Stan)
WFA 3 from 4yo+ 3lb — **10** Ran SP% **114.7**
Speed ratings (Par 101):97,96,94,92,87 85,84,63,60,—
CSF £42.84 TOTE £7.90: £2.40, £1.80, £3.10; EX 18.40 Place 6 £1120.44, Place 5 £86.68.
Owner J L C Pearce **Bred** J L C Pearce **Trained** Newmarket, Suffolk
FOCUS
A weakly contested maiden but the form makes sense with the first four basically to form.
Chasing A Dream Official explanation: jockey said filly had bled from the nose
Royle Dancer Official explanation: jockey said gelding lost its action
T/Plt: £332.80 to a £1 stake. Pool: £51,866.00. 113.75 winning tickets. T/Qpdt: £21.90 to a £1 stake. Pool: £6,972.60. 235.00 winning tickets. KH

5834 MUSSELBURGH (R-H)
Friday, November 3
OFFICIAL GOING: Good to soft (good in places on round course)
Wind: Virtually nil

6315 TOTEPLACEPOT H'CAP — 5f
1:00 (1:01) (Class 6) (0-65,71) 3-Y-0+ — **£3,238** (£963; £481; £240) **Stalls** Low

Form				RPR
1212	1		**How's She Cuttin' (IRE)**^{25} [5864] 3-8-12 **59** ... PhillipMakin 2 (T D Barron) *a.p: hdwy 2f out: rdn to ld appr last: sn edgd rt and drvn out* **4/1**^{1}	69
5132	2	*1/2*	**Compton Classic**^{25} [5865] 4-8-8 **55** ...(p) PaulHanagan 15 (J S Goldie) *towards rr: gd hdwy 2f out: rdn over 1f out: styd on to chal ins last: sn drvn and nt qckn* **7/1**^{3}	63
06	3	*3/4*	**Tartatartufata**^{10} [6162] 4-8-13 **63** ...(v) PatrickMathers(3) 9 (D Shaw) *cl up: rdn along and ev ch over 1f out: drvn and kpt on ins last* **33/1**	68
5524	4	*hd*	**Joyeaux**^{31} [5756] 4-9-1 **62** ...(v) DerekMcGaffin 14 (J Hetherton) *bhd: gd hdwy wl over 1f out: sn rdn and styd on ins last* **12/1**	66
0044	5	*1*	**Ryedane (IRE)**^{34} [5684] 4-8-13 **65** ... DuranFentiman(5) 1 (T D Easterby) *chsd ldrs: rdn along wl over 1f out: kpt on same pce ent last* **14/1**	66
6602	6	*nk*	**Conjecture**^{10} [6162] 4-9-4 **65** ... RoystonFfrench 17 (R Bastiman) *chsd ldrs: rdn along 2f out: drvn and kpt on same pce fnl f* **7/1**^{3}	65
4	7	*3/4*	**Controvento (IRE)**^{9} [6180] 4-9-3 **71** 6ex ...(b) CDTimmons(7) 11 (Eamon Tyrrell, Ire) *midfield and edgd lft after 1f: swtchd rt: rdn and hdwy over 1f out: kpt on ins last* **12/1**	68
2200	8	*1*	**Strawberry Patch (IRE)**^{39} [5577] 7-8-7 **59** ...(p) AndrewElliott(5) 7 (J S Goldie) *broke wl: sn pushed along & outpcd whn hmpd after 1f: swtchd wd & hdwy 1/2-way: in tch wl over 1f out: sn rdn & btn* **14/1**	52
2000	9	*shd*	**The Leather Wedge (IRE)**^{10} [6162] 7-8-12 **62** ... StephenDonohoe(3) 16 (R Johnson) *cl up: rdn along 2f out: drvn and wknd appr last* **20/1**	55
4311	10	*1 1/4*	**Alugat (IRE)**^{10} [6162] 3-9-4 **68** 6ex ...(p) GregFairley(3) 10 (Mrs A Duffield) *sn led: rdn along wl over 1f out: drvn and hdd appr last: sn wknd* **11/2**^{2}	56
0000	11	*1/2*	**Vegas Boys**^{21} [5938] 3-8-13 **60** ... FrancisNorton 13 (M Wigham) *s.i.s and bhd tl sme late hdwy* **25/1**	47
0000	12	*1/2*	**Rothesay Dancer**^{10} [6162] 3-8-10 **62** ...(p) KevinGhunowa(5) 12 (J S Goldie) *chsd ldrs: rdn along 2f out: sn wknd* **40/1**	47
2345	13	*4*	**Newkeylets**^{25} [5864] 3-8-7 **54** ...(p) TomEaves 4 (I Semple) *nvr bttr than midfield* **16/1**	24
0030	14	*shd*	**Throw The Dice**^{3} [6274] 4-8-13 **60** ... DeanMcKeown 5 (D W Barker) *in tch: effrt whn n.m.r wl over 1f out: sn rdn and btn* **14/1**	30
0000	15	*1/2*	**Ashes (IRE)**^{10} [6162] 4-9-4 **65** ... PaulMulrennan 8 (K R Burke) *a rr* **33/1**	33
0050	16	*nk*	**Canadian Danehill (IRE)**^{38} [5593] 4-9-4 **65** ... JoeFanning 6 (R M H Cowell) *prom: rdn along over 2f out and sn wknd* **20/1**	32
5060	17	*3 1/2*	**Amber Glory**^{10} [6159] 3-8-13 **60** ...(b) CatherineGannon 3 (K A Ryan) *prom: rdn along over 2f out: wkg whn hmpd over 1f out and bhd after* **50/1**	15

63.03 secs (2.53) **Going Correction** +0.525s/f (Yiel) — **17** Ran SP% **125.3**
Speed ratings (Par 101):100,99,98,97,96 95,94,92,92,90 89,89,82,82,81 81,75
CSF £28.69 CT £869.91 TOTE £3.70: £1.80, £2.40, £5.50, £2.50; EX 34.10.
Owner Christopher McHale **Bred** A M Burke **Trained** Maunby, N Yorks
FOCUS
Moderate handicap form but solid enough for the grade rated around the runner-up and fourth.
The Leather Wedge(IRE) Official explanation: jockey said gelding hung left-handed throughout

6316 TOTECOURSE TO COURSE EBF MEDIAN AUCTION MAIDEN STKS — 7f 30y
1:30 (1:32) (Class 5) 2-Y-0 — **£4,210** (£1,252; £625; £312) **Stalls** High

Form				RPR
2035	1		**Show Trial (IRE)**^{18} [6015] 2-8-9 52 ... StephenDonohoe(3) 7 (D J S Ffrench Davis) *trckd ldrs: hdwy over 2f out: rdn to ld over 1f out: drvn and edgd rt ins last: kpt on wl* **14/1**	59
0	2	*1/2*	**Risque Heights**^{6} [6214] 2-9-3 ... FJohansson 13 (G A Butler) *stdd s: hld up and bhd: gd hdwy on outer 2f out: rdn and hung rt ins last: kpt on* **6/4**^{1}	63+
4304	3	*1 1/2*	**Chookie Hamilton**^{40} [5552] 2-9-3 62 ... TomEaves 3 (I Semple) *cl up: led 3f out: rdn and hdd over 1f out: kpt on same pce* **12/1**	59
	4	*nk*	**Letham Island (IRE)** 2-8-12 ... KDarley 5 (M Johnston) *trckd ldrs: hdwy 3f out: rdn over 1f out: keeping on whn hmpd wl ins last: nrst fin* **7/1**^{3}	53
0	5	*shd*	**Falcon's Fire (IRE)**^{18} [6012] 2-9-3 ... RoystonFfrench 12 (Mrs A Duffield) *chsd ldng pair: hdwy 3f out: rdn 2f out and ev ch tl drvn and one pce ent last* **33/1**	58
0	6	*2 1/2*	**Caviar Heights (IRE)**^{36} [5632] 2-9-3 ... PaulHanagan 10 (Miss L A Perratt) *bhd tl styd on fnl 2f: nrst fin* **50/1**	52
5	7	*1 1/4*	**Greyfriars Abbey**^{9} [6188] 2-9-3 ... JoeFanning 4 (M Johnston) *in tch: hdwy over 2f out: rdn wl over 1f out and sn no imp* **7/4**^{2}	49
600	8	*hd*	**Skye But N Ben**^{20} [5959] 2-8-10 50 ... DeanHeslop(7) 9 (T D Barron) *a towards rr* **66/1**	48
60	9	*2*	**Ingleby Hill (IRE)**^{9} [6175] 2-9-3 ... PhillipMakin 1 (T D Barron) *bhd: hdwy over 2f out: rdn and in tch wl over 1f out: sn wknd* **28/1**	43
	10	*2*	**La Chesneraie** 2-8-12 ...(t) PaulMulrennan 2 (P C Haslam) *chsd ldrs: rdn along wl over 2f out: sn wknd* **50/1**	33

11 *6* **Kyrhena** 2-8-12 .... DeanMcKeown 8 18
(C W Thornton) *s.i.s: a rr* **40/1**

06 **12** *18* **Senora Lenorah**[6] 6207 2-8-12 .... SilvestreDeSousa 6 —
(D A Nolan) *led: rdn along and hdd 3f out: sn wknd* **150/1**

1m 34.92s (4.98) **Going Correction** +0.525s/f (Yiel) **12** Ran SP% **118.1**
Speed ratings (Par 96):92,91,89,89,89 86,84,84,82,80 73,52
CSF £34.49 TOTE £18.40: £3.40, £1.10, £2.70; EX 64.70.
Owner Zaha Racing Syndicate **Bred** Darley **Trained** Lambourn, Berks

FOCUS
A moderate maiden and strictly plating-class form rated around the winner and third.

NOTEBOOK
Show Trial(IRE) has had a few chances including when beaten in a seller in September, so it does not say a lot for the quality of the opposition that this 52-rated filly proved good enough to win a maiden on her seventh career start. The return to seven furlongs clearly suited her, though. Official explanation: trainer's rep said, regarding apparent improvement in form, that the filly was suited by the return to 7f (op 12-1)
Risque Heights, whose rider made no attempt to use his high draw to his advantage, held the gelding up in last place and basically gave his mount far too much to do around this sharp track. Turning in he had an awful amount of ground to make up and, with his mount understandably running a little green - this was only his second-ever start - he was never quite going to get there. He really should have won, and an opening will now have to be found on the All-Weather. (op 9-4 tchd 5-2 in a place)
Chookie Hamilton, dropping back from nine furlongs, was up there throughout and had every chance. He appears flattered by his current mark. (op 11-1)
Letham Island(IRE), who cost 10,500gns, is a half-sister to Wovoka, who was heavily raced at two, winning four times between five and nine furlongs, including in Listed company. She was being introduced at a very ordinary level so it was a pity that she could not make more of a mark. (tchd 8-1)
Falcon's Fire(IRE), a half-brother to Beauty Queen, a winner over a mile at three in France, and also a winner over jumps, showed the benefit of his debut outing at Pontefract and knew more about what was required this time. (op 40-1)
Greyfriars Abbey had run with promise on his debut on the All-Weather, and this looked an ideal opportunity for him to get off the mark. He loomed up looking a big threat two furlongs out but his effort soon flattened out and he did not get home. This was surprising as, while he is by Fasliyev, his dam won over 11 furlongs at three. (op 11-8)

6317 TOTEQUADPOT H'CAP — 1m 4f
2:00 (2:00) (Class 5) (0-70,69) 3-Y-O+ **£3,886** (£1,156; £577; £288) **Stalls** High

Form RPR

6601 **1** **Virginia Rose (IRE)**[26] 5836 3-8-4 **55** oh2 .... PaulHanagan 10 64
(J G Given) *trckd ldrs on inner: hdwy 3f out: swtchd lft and rdn to ld over 1f out: kpt on wl u.p ins last* **4/1**[1]

6005 **2** *1* **Calcutta Cup (UAE)**[24] 5905 3-8-9 **60** .... RoystonFfrench 7 67
(Karen McLintock) *cl up: led over 5f out: rdn along 2f out: drvn and hdd over 1f out: kpt on u.p ins last* **20/1**

0360 **3** *2* **Sporting Gesture**[28] 5792 9-9-10 **69** .... PaulMulrennan 12 73
(M W Easterby) *led: pushed along and hdd over 5f out: rdn wl over 2f out: drvn and one pce fr over 1f out* **9/1**

3604 **4** *2* **Platinum Charmer (IRE)**[10] 6158 6-8-5 **55** oh4 ......(p) AndrewElliott[(5)] 6 56
(K R Burke) *towards rr: swtchd outside and hdwy over 2f out: sn rdn and kpt on ins last: nrst fin* **10/1**

1500 **5** *3/4* **Dispol Peto**[60] 5064 6-8-9 **57** oh5 ow2 .... StephenDonohoe[(3)] 9 57
(R Johnson) *bhd: hdwy over 2f out: sn rdn and kpt on ins last: nrst fin* **50/1**

2315 **6** *1 1/2* **Kyle Of Lochalsh**[4] 6256 6-8-12 **57** ow2 .... DanielTudhope 11 54
(J S Goldie) *trckd ldrs: hdwy over 3f out: rdn over 2f out and sn one pce* **8/1**[3]

3445 **7** *nk* **Ulysees (IRE)**[6] 6209 7-9-3 **62** .... PhillipMakin 8 59
(I Semple) *hld up and bhd: hdwy 3f out: rdn and n.m.r 2f out: sn btn* **10/1**

0001 **8** *2* **King's Fable (USA)**[59] 5082 3-8-4 **55** .... JoeFanning 4 49
(M Johnston) *in tch: rdn along 3f out: drvn and wknd over 2f out* **7/1**[2]

1220 **9** *hd* **Sudden Impulse**[18] 6008 5-9-3 **62** .... SilvestreDeSousa 5 55
(A D Brown) *hld up in tch: swtchd outside and hdwy 3f out: rdn 2f out and sn no imp* **4/1**[1]

5446 **10** *3/4* **Melvino**[10] 6158 4-8-7 **59** ....(p) NeilBrown[(7)] 1 51
(T D Barron) *hld up towards rr: effrt and sme hdwy on outer 3f out: rdn and btn over 2f out* **8/1**[3]

0036 **11** *3* **Scotty's Future (IRE)**[6] 6213 8-8-10 **55** oh4 .... TedDurcan 3 42
(A Berry) *a bhd* **22/1**

5150 **12** *1 1/2* **Final Esteem**[32] 5724 3-9-1 **66** .... TomEaves 2 51
(I Semple) *cl up: rdn along over 4f out and sn wknd* **33/1**

2m 43.6s (6.70) **Going Correction** +0.525s/f (Yiel)
WFA 3 from 4yo+ 6lb **12** Ran SP% **116.9**
Speed ratings (Par 103):98,97,96,94,94 93,92,91,91,91 89,88
CSF £91.13 CT £684.11 TOTE £4.50: £1.90, £4.60, £2.90; EX 115.80.
Owner The Living Legend Racing Partnership II **Bred** Abbeville & Meadow Court Studs & Tower Bloodstock **Trained** Willoughton, Lincs

FOCUS
Moderate handicap form that looks somewhat dubious with few coming into this in form.

6318 TOTESPORT 0800 221 221 EBF MAIDEN STKS — 1m
2:30 (2:32) (Class 4) 2-Y-O **£5,505** (£1,637; £818; £408) **Stalls** High

Form RPR

2 **1** **Hohlethelonely**[39] 5580 2-8-12 .... AndrewElliott[(5)] 8 80
(M L W Bell) *chsd ldr: sn pushed along: rdn 3f out: drvn and styd on to ld 1f out: kpt on wl* **2/1**[1]

4 **2** *3* **Salaasa (USA)**[36] 5640 2-9-3 .... RHills 10 73+
(M Johnston) *led: pushed along wl over 2f out: rdn and wandered wl over 1f out: hdd 1f out: sn one pce* **5/2**[2]

3 *1 1/2* **Dark Energy** 2-9-3 .... TedDurcan 3 70
(B Smart) *hld up towards rr: hdwy 3f out: swtchd lft and rdn 2f out: styd on ins last: nrst fin* **18/1**

032 **4** *3 1/2* **Hurricane Thomas (IRE)**[11] 6143 2-9-3 .... KDarley 6 62+
(M Johnston) *trckd ldng pair: effrt 3f out: rdn over 2f out: hung rt wl over 1f out and sn btn* **5/2**[2]

5 *3* **Tommy Tobougg** 2-9-3 .... DanielTudhope 1 55
(I Semple) *bhd: hdwy over 2f out: styd on appr last: nrst fin* **50/1**

4022 **6** *1* **Musical Land (IRE)**[40] 5552 2-9-3 72 .... PaulHanagan 5 52
(J R Weymes) *in tch: hdwy 3f out: rdn 2f out and sn btn* **9/1**[3]

7 *2 1/2* **Freya Tricks** 2-8-12 .... TomEaves 2 42
(I Semple) *a bhd* **16/1**

056 **8** *1/2* **Grethel (IRE)**[18] 6012 2-8-9 54 .... StephenDonohoe[(3)] 9 41
(A Berry) *keen: midfield: hdwy and in tch 2f out: sn rdn and wknd ent last* **66/1**

0 **9** *3* **Bishop Auckland (IRE)**[24] 5900 2-9-3 .... RoystonFfrench 11 39
(Mrs A Duffield) *chsd ldrs: rdn along 3f out: sn wknd* **40/1**

10 *2 1/2* **Forrest Flyer (IRE)** 2-9-3 .... PaulMulrennan 7 33
(Miss L A Perratt) *chsd ldrs: rdn along wl over 2f out and sn wknd* **50/1**

1m 45.88s (3.38) **Going Correction** +0.525s/f (Yiel) **10** Ran SP% **119.5**
Speed ratings (Par 98):104,101,99,96,93 92,89,89,86,83
CSF £7.32 TOTE £2.90: £1.40, £1.30, £3.80; EX 8.80.
Owner Estate of the Late D F Allport **Bred** D F Allport **Trained** Newmarket, Suffolk

FOCUS
A fair maiden for the track and solid form rated around the winner.

NOTEBOOK
Hohlethelonely had run with promise behind an odds-on shot from the Mark Johnston yard on his debut, and had clearly learnt plenty from that experience. He did it really nicely in the end and looks a decent candidate for middle-distance handicaps next season. (op 9-4 tchd 15-8)
Salaasa(USA), fourth in a Newmarket maiden first time up, was still green and wandered about under pressure in the straight. He is bound to improve with racing though, and is another who will be seen in a better light next season when stepped up in distance. (op 9-4 tchd 11-4 and 3-1 in a place)
Dark Energy, a half-brother to Maid Of Camelot, a dual ten-furlong winner at three, made a promising debut behind two rivals who had the edge on him in experience. He is bred to make a better three-year-old than a juvenile and can only improve. (op 16-1)
Hurricane Thomas(IRE) had been improving with every run and this looked like a bit of a step back, as he ran quite close to his debut form with stablemate Salaasa, whom he finished behind at Newmarket. (op 3-1 tchd 10-3)
Tommy Tobougg, a half-brother to Esposito, a triple winner between six and eight furlongs in Germany, was friendless in the market beforehand but ran with some promise, getting the hang of things late on. He should do better next year in handicap company.
Musical Land(IRE), the most experienced in the field, is beginning to look distinctly exposed now. (op 11-1)

6319 TOTESPORT.COM WILLIE PARK H'CAP — 1m 6f
3:00 (3:00) (Class 2) (0-100,97) 3-Y-O+
£15,580 (£4,665; £2,332; £1,167; £582; £292) **Stalls** High

Form RPR

4214 **1** **All The Good (IRE)**[22] 5920 3-9-4 **89** .... FJohansson 8 100+
(G A Butler) *trckd ldrs gng wl: hdwy over 2f out: led over 1f out: rdn and edgd rt ins last: sn clr* **10/1**

2101 **2** *2* **Piety (IRE)**[7] 6202 3-9-1 **86** 6ex .... KDarley 6 94
(M Johnston) *in tch: hdwy over 4f out: swtchd outside and effrt whn hung lft over 2f out: rdn to chse wnr and hung rt ins last: kpt on* **7/4**[1]

10 **3** *2 1/2* **Heart Of Svetlana (IRE)**[7] 6202 3-9-0 **85** .... JoeFanning 7 90
(M Johnston) *led: rdn along 3f out: drvn and hdd over 1f out: one pce ins last* **25/1**

5150 **4** *1* **Lets Roll**[20] 5963 5-10-0 **91** .... DeanMcKeown 3 94
(C W Thornton) *hld up in rr: hdwy on inner over 2f out: sn rdn and kpt on ins last: nrst fin* **16/1**

3150 **5** *1/2* **Ermine Sea**[34] 5700 3-9-8 **93** ....(b[1]) NCallan 5 95
(J H M Gosden) *cl up: chal over 2f out: rdn and ev ch over 1f out: drvn and one pce appr last* **7/1**

3303 **6** *9* **Tilt**[39] 5582 4-9-10 **87** .... FrancisNorton 4 77
(B Ellison) *hld up towards rr: hdwy over 4f out: rdn over 2f out: sn edgd rt and btn* **7/2**[2]

3410 **7** *3* **Luna Landing**[28] 5792 3-8-12 **83** .... DaleGibson 1 69
(Jedd O'Keeffe) *a rr* **50/1**

0310 **8** *2 1/2* **Mirjan (IRE)**[20] 5963 10-10-0 **91** ....(b) PaulHanagan 2 73
(L Lungo) *chsd ldrs: rdn along over 3f out: sn wknd* **14/1**

3-26 **9** *20* **Priors Hill (IRE)**[28] 5787 3-9-12 **97** ....(t) TedDurcan 9 51
(Saeed Bin Suroor) *hld up towards rr: effrt over 3f out: sn rdn and wknd* **9/2**[3]

3m 9.51s (3.81) **Going Correction** +0.525s/f (Yiel)
WFA 3 from 4yo+ 8lb **9** Ran SP% **116.7**
Speed ratings (Par 109):110,108,107,106,106 101,99,98,86
CSF £28.21 CT £442.13 TOTE £13.00: £2.20, £1.20, £5.50; EX 38.50.
Owner Future In Mind Partnership **Bred** Mount Coote Partnership **Trained** Blewbury, Oxon

FOCUS
A good quality handicap, and pretty competitive on paper, but it was quite steadily-run, so although the form is sound it may not prove that strong.

NOTEBOOK
All The Good(IRE) travelled well and picked up when asked to take up the running approaching the final furlong. He ran out a good winner, appreciating the return to a mile six after finding 12 furlongs on the short side at Newmarket last time. An improving three-year-old, he already has a Polytrack win to his name, so he could find another opportunity on the All-Weather in the coming weeks. (op 9-1 tchd 12-1 in a place)
Piety(IRE), a winner at Newmarket a week earlier, carried a 6lb penalty for that success, but the step up to a mile six looked likely to suit her. She finished well, and although she hung under pressure and found the winner just too strong, there looks likely to be better to come from her next season, so hopefully she is kept in training. (op 15-8 tchd 2-1)
Heart Of Svetlana(IRE), who was hampered at the start at Newmarket last time and forced to be held up, was able to revert this time to the front-running tactics that saw her off the mark for the year at Ayr in September. She seems to be at her best when able to race prominently. (op 28-1 tchd 33-1)
Lets Roll was at a disadvantage given the pace of the race in being held up at the back of the field. Although now on a mark 5lb higher mark than when last successful, he has the ability to win more races when things fall right.
Ermine Sea, who ran down the field in a French Group 2 last time out, was disappointing on his return to handicap company, the first-time blinkers appearing to have no clearly positive effect. (op 8-1)
Tilt, who needs a strong pace to be seen at his best, again failed to have the race run to suit. (op 11-4)
Priors Hill(IRE) whose performance was too bad to be true, ran as though something was amiss. (op 13-2 tchd 4-1)

6320 TOTEEXACTA H'CAP — 5f
3:30 (3:31) (Class 4) (0-80,79) 3-Y-O+ **£6,477** (£1,927; £963; £481) **Stalls** Low

Form RPR

4004 **1** **Blazing Heights**[28] 5791 3-9-0 **75** .... DanielTudhope 11 87
(J S Goldie) *trckd ldrs: led 2f out: pushed clr over 1f out: rdn ins last: jst hld on* **5/1**[2]

0560 **2** *shd* **Westport**[47] 5401 3-8-12 **73** .... NCallan 7 85
(K A Ryan) *midfield: hdwy over 2f out: rdn to chse wnr and hung rt ins last: drvn and styd on strly towards fin: jst failed* **6/1**[3]

0000 **3** *1 1/2* **Glencairn Star**[6] 6223 5-8-6 **72** ....(p) DuranFentiman[(5)] 12 78
(J S Goldie) *chsd ldrs on outer: hdwy wl over 1f out: sn rdn and kpt on ins last* **18/1**

0100 **4** *2* **Sea Salt**[18] 6009 3-9-3 **78** .... PhillipMakin 9 77
(T D Barron) *cl up: rdn 2f out: drvn and one pce ent last* **12/1**

0120 **5** *shd* **Ptarmigan Ridge**[6] 6212 10-9-2 **77**............................ RoystonFfrench 13 76
(Miss L A Perratt) *towards rr: hdwy over 2f out: rdn to chse ldrs over 1f out: kpt on same pce* **8/1**
5045 **6** *1 1/2* **Bond Boy**[18] 6009 9-9-4 **79**..(v) TedDurcan 1 72
(B Smart) *bhd: hdwy wl over 1f out: sn rdn and no imp ins last* **4/1**[1]
160 **7** *shd* **Mormeatmic**[79] 4468 3-9-1 **76**...................................... PaulMulrennan 10 69
(M W Easterby) *led: rdn along and hdd 2f out: grad wknd* **40/1**
5026 **8** *1/2* **Lyndalee (IRE)**[11] 6150 3-8-6 **67** ow1...................................... KDarley 2 58
(T Hogan, Ire) *dwlt: bhd tl sme late hdwy* **8/1**
0340 **9** *3/4* **Highland Song (IRE)**[10] 6159 3-8-1 **67**................... KevinGhunowa(5) 3 55
(R F Fisher) *a towards rr* **33/1**
0000 **10** *3/4* **Highland Warrior**[18] 6009 7-9-3 **78**..................................(p) TomEaves 8 64
(J S Goldie) *s.i.s: a rr* **7/1**
116 **11** *1* **Taboor (IRE)**[17] 6035 8-8-9 **70**.. PaulHanagan 5 52
(R M H Cowell) *nvr nr ldrs* **11/1**
-560 **12** *14* **Sokoke**[39] 5577 5-8-4 **65** oh20.................................(t) SilvestreDeSousa 4 —
(D A Nolan) *in tch: rdn along 2f out: sn wknd* **100/1**
0002 **13** *1 1/2* **Polish Emperor (USA)**[15] 6065 6-8-12 **73**........................ JoeFanning 6 —
(D W Barker) *cl up: rdn along over 2f out: sn wknd* **9/1**

62.40 secs (1.90) **Going Correction** +0.525s/f (Yiel) **13** Ran SP% **123.3**
Speed ratings (Par 105):105,104,102,99,99 96,96,95,94,93 91,69,66
CSF £36.10 CT £515.79 TOTE £6.30: £2.30, £2.10, £4.70; EX 48.30.
Owner Thoroughbred Leisure Racing Club 2 **Bred** Jim Goldie **Trained** Uplawmoor, E Renfrews

FOCUS
A fair sprint handicap and solid enough form, although pretty ordinary.

6321 TOTESPORTCASINO.COM H'CAP 2m
4:00 (4:01) (Class 4) (0-80,80) 3-Y-0+
£6,232 (£1,866; £933; £467; £233; £117) **Stalls** Low

Form RPR
0535 **1** **Escayola (IRE)**[14] 6075 6-9-9 **80**..............................(v) MarkLawson(5) 11 89
(Grant Tuer) *hld up towards rr: smooth hdwy 4f out: swtchd lft and effrt 3f out: led 2f out: rdn clr appr last: styd on strly* **6/1**[2]
3642 **2** *4* **Reluctant Suitor**[36] 5634 4-9-7 **73**..........................(p) DanielTudhope 10 77
(J S Goldie) *in tch: smooth hdwy on inner over 3f out: rdn to ld briefly over 2f out: sn hdd: drvn and kpt on same pce* **4/1**[1]
4431 **3** *nk* **Grey Outlook**[24] 5903 3-8-3 **64**.................................... RoystonFfrench 6 68
(Miss L A Perratt) *midfield: smooth hdwy over 3f out: rdn along 2f out: sn drvn and kpt on same pce* **7/1**[3]
-100 **4** *1/2* **Millagros (IRE)**[31] 5751 6-8-13 **65**.................................. PaulHanagan 2 68
(I Semple) *hld up and bhd: gd hdwy on inner over 2f out: rdn to chse ldrs over 1f out: sn drvn and one pce* **16/1**
0222 **5** *1/2* **Onyergo (IRE)**[10] 6158 4-8-9 **61** oh1................................. PhillipMakin 5 63
(J R Weymes) *hld up towards rr: hdwy over 3f out: rdn along 2f out: sn drvn and no imp* **8/1**
2102 **6** *1 1/2* **Thewhirlingdervish (IRE)**[10] 6161 8-8-7 **64**........... DuranFentiman(5) 4 65
(T D Easterby) *hld up in rr: hdwy 3f out: rdn along over 2f out: sn drvn and no imp* **6/1**[2]
-244 **7** *5* **Trinity Rose**[157] 2102 3-8-6 **67**... JoeFanning 12 62
(M Johnston) *prom: rdn along over 4f out: sn wknd* **6/1**[2]
1506 **8** *3 1/2* **Silvertown**[64] 4951 11-9-12 **78**.. TomEaves 8 68
(L Lungo) *led: rdn along 3f out: drvn and hdd 2f out: sn wknd* **8/1**
2500 **9** *3 1/2* **Rare Coincidence**[18] 6011 5-8-4 **61** oh5..............(p) KevinGhunowa(5) 7 47
(R F Fisher) *chsd ldrs: rdn along 3f out: sn wknd* **40/1**
-000 **10** *4* **Prince Zafonic**[140] 2620 3-8-5 **66**.. DaleGibson 3 47
(M W Easterby) *a rr: bhd fr 1/2-way* **25/1**
1235 **11** *1 1/2* **Mister Arjay (USA)**[18] 6011 6-8-12 **67**.................. StephenDonohoe(3) 9 47
(B Ellison) *chsd ldrs: rdn along over 5f out: sn lost pl and bhd fnl 4f* **7/1**[3]
12 *47* **Stolen Light (IRE)**[45] 5470 5-9-8 **74**............................ PaulMulrennan 1 —
(A Crook) *prom: rdn along over 4f out: sn wknd* **14/1**

3m 40.05s (6.15) **Going Correction** +0.525s/f (Yiel)
WFA 3 from 4yo+ 9lb **12** Ran SP% **128.9**
Speed ratings (Par 105):105,103,102,102,102 101,99,97,95,93 92,69
CSF £33.07 CT £182.62 TOTE £7.50: £2.60, £2.20, £3.30; EX 54.30 Place 6 £81.68, Place 5 £33.66.
Owner Nice To See You Euro-Racing **Bred** Rozelle Bloodstock **Trained** Great Smeaton, N Yorks

FOCUS
A modest staying handicap but the form appears sound. Escayola was Grant Tuer's first runner on the Flat.
T/Jkpt: Not won. T/Plt: £153.50 to a £1 stake. Pool: £53,018.40. 252.05 winning tickets. T/Qpdt: £37.90 to a £1 stake. Pool: £3,334.40. 65.00 winning tickets. JR

6309 WOLVERHAMPTON (A.W) (L-H)
Friday, November 3

OFFICIAL GOING: Standard to fast
Wind: Nil Weather: Fine

6322 WBX.COM WORLD BET EXCHANGE NURSERY 1m 141y(P)
3:45 (3:47) (Class 5) (0-75,72) 2-Y-0 **£4,533** (£1,348; £674; £336) **Stalls** Low

Form RPR
0040 **1** **Habalwatan (IRE)**[37] 5608 2-9-7 **72**...............................(b) AdamKirby 10 75
(C E Brittain) *bhd: reminders after 1f: hdwy 2f out: c wd st: edgd lft fr over 1f out: led wl ins fnl f: r.o wl* **12/1**
0530 **2** *1 1/4* **Right Option (IRE)**[6] 6224 2-8-10 **61**................................ JimCrowley 6 61
(J R Weymes) *hld up in mid-div: hdwy over 2f out: rdn wl over 1f out: kpt on ins fnl f* **12/1**
0030 **3** *hd* **Boogie Dancer**[34] 5676 2-9-0 **65**... DaneO'Neill 5 65
(H S Howe) *sn w ldr: rdn 2f out: ev ch wl ins fnl f: nt qckn* **12/1**
0004 **4** *1/2* **Featherlight**[43] 5492 2-8-2 **53**.. HayleyTurner 4 52
(N A Callaghan) *a.p: rdn over 3f out: one pce fnl f* **14/1**
6400 **5** *3/4* **Flying Grey (IRE)**[2] 6291 2-8-8 **59**............................ RobbieFitzpatrick 3 56
(P A Blockley) *led: rdn over 2f out: hdd and no ex wl ins fnl f* **6/1**[3]
1360 **6** *1/2* **Beau Sancy**[38] 5597 2-8-9 **60**.. EddieAhern 7 56
(R A Harris) *hld up towards rr: hdwy over 1f out: r.o* **16/1**
465 **7** *shd* **Lawyer To World**[15] 6064 2-8-13 **64**.................................... ChrisCatlin 2 60
(N A Callaghan) *hld up in tch: rdn wl over 1f out: no imp fnl f* **7/1**
0233 **8** *1 1/2* **Always Best**[18] 6018 2-9-1 **66**...................................... J-PGuillambert 13 59
(M Johnston) *prom: rdn 4f out: btn whn edgd lft ins fnl f* **7/2**[1]
6043 **9** *6* **Revisionist (IRE)**[18] 6007 2-8-13 **64**.............................. RichardHughes 11 44
(R Hannon) *hld up towards rr: rdn and hdwy 3f out: 4th wd st: wknd over 1f out* **9/2**[2]
3016 **10** *2 1/2* **Group Force (IRE)**[43] 5492 2-8-7 **58**................................... TPQueally 9 33
(M H Tompkins) *a bhd* **16/1**
5410 **11** *1 1/2* **Foxxy**[18] 6007 2-9-7 **72**...(p) JimmyQuinn 12 44
(K A Ryan) *hld up in tch: rdn and wknd over 3f out* **16/1**
0020 **12** *1 1/4* **Grazie Mille**[38] 5592 2-8-6 **60**... JamesDoyle(3) 8 29
(R Brotherton) *stmbld and lost pl sn after s: sn bhd* **25/1**

1m 49.43s (-2.33) **Going Correction** -0.40s/f (Stan) **12** Ran SP% **118.4**
Speed ratings (Par 96):94,92,92,92,91 91,91,89,84,82 80,79
CSF £147.97 CT £1791.62 TOTE £15.70: £4.30, £4.50, £2.40; EX 154.10 TRIFECTA Not won..
Owner Mohammed Rashid **Bred** Darley **Trained** Newmarket, Suffolk

FOCUS
They went a decent gallop in this typically competitive nursery and the form appears sound with those in the frame behind the winner to their marks.

NOTEBOOK
Habalwatan(IRE), who went off too quickly on his sand debut at Lingfield last time, had to come the scenic route. Appreciating the step up from seven, he was nicely on top in the end despite drifting markedly left in the home straight. (tchd 14-1)
Right Option(IRE), claimed from Alan Jarvis after finishing third in a seven furlong seller here in September, had been tried in cheekpieces over course and distance last week. He stuck to his task on this handicap debut and secured the runner-up spot near the line. (op 14-1)
Boogie Dancer, dropped 4lb, was back up in distance for her All-Weather debut. She ran a sound race but could not hold the second let alone cope with the winner.
Featherlight had the blinkers left off on this switch to sand having been dropped a total of 7lb. (op 9-1)
Flying Grey(IRE), taken off his legs over six at Kempton two days earlier, possibly had too much use made of him on his first attempt beyond seven furlongs. (op 7-1)
Beau Sancy ◆ had lost ground at the start when fitted with cheekpieces and then blinkers on this last two runs. A winner of a firm-ground seller, he has been given a big chance by the Handicapper and gave notice he could be returning to form. (op 25-1)

6323 THE ZONGALERO RESTAURANT OVERLOOKS THE TRACK H'CAP 7f 32y(P)
4:20 (4:20) (Class 6) (0-63,69) 3-Y-0+ **£2,730** (£806; £403) **Stalls** High

Form RPR
3630 **1** **Shy Glance (USA)**[39] 5579 4-9-2 **62**................................ SteveDrowne 6 74
(G A Swinbank) *a.p: rdn and wandered fr over 1f out: r.o to ld cl home* **11/4**[1]
6451 **2** *1/2* **Final Tune (IRE)**[8] 6193 3-9-6 **67** 7ex................................ AdamKirby 2 78
(Miss M E Rowland) *a.p: rdn to ld wl over 1f out: hdd and no ex cl home* **4/1**[3]
0203 **3** *2 1/2* **Gallego**[8] 6193 4-8-11 **60**.. JamesDoyle(3) 3 64
(R J Price) *s.i.s: bhd: rdn over 2f out: hdwy over 1f out: r.o ins fnl f* **7/2**[2]
3200 **4** *shd* **Briery Lane (IRE)**[9] 6174 5-9-1 **61**...............................(p) MickyFenton 4 65
(Mrs K Walton) *mid-div: rdn 4f out: hdwy on ins wl over 1f out: kpt on same pce fnl f* **12/1**
3050 **5** *3/4* **Tamatave (IRE)**[110] 3565 4-9-0 **60**.................................... JimmyQuinn 12 62
(K A Ryan) *t.k.h towards rr: hdwy on outside over 2f out: rdn wl over 1f out: edgd lft and one pce fnl f* **20/1**
0400 **6** *1/2* **Prettilini**[49] 5350 3-9-0 **61**.. J-PGuillambert 10 62
(R Brotherton) *t.k.h: w ldr: ev ch over 2f out: sn rdn: fdd towards fin* **40/1**
3040 **7** *1/2* **Scutch Mill (IRE)**[20] 5972 4-9-0 **60**..............................(t) DarryllHolland 9 59
(Karen George) *s.i.s: bhd: rdn over 2f out: c wd st: nvr nrr* **16/1**
0330 **8** *shd* **Bathwick Emma (IRE)**[31] 5755 3-9-1 **62**............................ JimCrowley 8 61
(P D Evans) *hld up in tch: rdn over 3f out: wknd over 2f out* **33/1**
4504 **9** *hd* **Great Chieftain (IRE)**[16] 6060 3-8-10 **62**.................. JamieMoriarty(5) 11 61
(R A Fahey) *hdwy over 5f out: rdn over 2f out: wknd over 1f out* **15/2**
6040 **10** *1/2* **Wainwright (IRE)**[15] 6065 6-9-2 **62**................................... HayleyTurner 7 59
(P A Blockley) *hld up in mid-div: rdn 2f out: no rspnse* **16/1**
4210 **11** *2 1/2* **Flying Edge (IRE)**[10] 6160 6-9-2 **62**..................................... DavidAllan 5 53
(E J Alston) *led: rdn and hdd wl over 1f out: wkng whn hung lft ins fnl f* **11/1**

1m 28.31s (-2.09) **Going Correction** -0.40s/f (Stan)
WFA 3 from 4yo+ 1lb **11** Ran SP% **118.6**
Speed ratings (Par 101):95,94,91,91,90 90,89,89,89,88 85
CSF £13.45 CT £39.66 TOTE £2.50: £1.60, £1.20, £2.00; EX 19.20 Trifecta £45.20 Pool: £165.21 - 2.59 winning units..
Owner Walcal Property Development Ltd **Bred** R D Hubbard And Constance Sczesny **Trained** Melsonby, N Yorks

FOCUS
A strongly-run and tightly-knit modest handicap rated around the placed horses.
Scutch Mill(IRE) Official explanation: jockey said gelding missed the break

6324 HOTEL & CONFERENCING AT WOLVERHAMPTON RACECOURSE MAIDEN STKS 7f 32y(P)
4:50 (4:51) (Class 5) 2-Y-0 **£3,886** (£1,156; £577; £288) **Stalls** High

Form RPR
606 **1** **Majestic Cheer**[24] 5891 2-9-3 70.. ChrisCatlin 3 75
(M R Channon) *wnt rt s: chsd ldr: rdn and hung rt over 1f out: r.o to ld last strides* **11/1**
2 *nk* **Flying Goose (IRE)** 2-9-3 .... NickyMackay 1 74
(L M Cumani) *s.i.s: sn prom: rdn over 2f out: led ins fnl f: hdd last strides* **9/4**[1]
365 **3** *3/4* **Cool Box (USA)**[48] 5371 2-9-3 77.. JimCrowley 2 72
(Mrs A J Perrett) *led: rdn wl over 1f out: hdd ins fnl f: nt qckn* **9/2**[3]
0 **4** *2* **Pickering**[7] 6199 2-9-3 .... DavidAllan 5 67
(E J Alston) *hld up and bhd: hdwy over 3f out: hung rt and c wd ent st: r.o one pce fnl f* **66/1**
05 **5** *hd* **Putra Laju (IRE)**[28] 5784 2-9-3 .... EddieAhern 10 67
(J W Hills) *t.k.h in tch: lost pl over 3f out: rdn over 2f out: kpt on ins fnl f* **14/1**
60 **6** *1/2* **Postsprofit (IRE)**[15] 6066 2-9-3 .... DarryllHolland 7 65
(N A Callaghan) *hld up in mid-div: hdwy over 1f out: kpt on ins fnl f* **33/1**
7 *1* **Grande Caiman (IRE)** 2-9-3 .... RichardHughes 9 63
(R Hannon) *bhd: pshd along over 4f out: c wd st: nvr nrr* **16/1**
00 **8** *1/2* **Force Group (IRE)**[22] 5918 2-9-3 .... TPQueally 8 62
(M H Tompkins) *hld up and bhd: reminder over 1f out and ins fnl f: nrst fin* **50/1**
3 **9** *1* **Vesuvio**[18] 6015 2-9-3 .... MichaelHills 12 59
(B W Hills) *s.i.s: hdwy on outside over 3f out: wknd over 2f out* **5/2**[2]
10 *hd* **Maeve (IRE)** 2-8-5 .... SCreighton(7) 4 54
(E J Creighton) *s.i.s: a bhd* **66/1**
0 **11** *1 1/2* **Exit Strategy (IRE)**[22] 5915 2-9-3 .... TonyCulhane 6 55
(W J Haggas) *chsd ldrs: rdn over 2f out: sn wknd* **9/1**
05 **12** *3 1/2* **Encircled**[16] 6050 2-8-12 .... SteveDrowne 11 42
(D Haydn Jones) *prom tl wknd over 2f out* **28/1**

1m 29.22s (-1.18) **Going Correction** -0.40s/f (Stan) **12** Ran SP% **119.7**
Speed ratings (Par 96):90,89,88,86,86 85,84,84,82,82 80,76
CSF £35.53 TOTE £15.30: £3.30, £1.90, £1.80; EX 66.00 Trifecta £259.20 Part won. Pool: £365.10 - 0.87 winning units..

Owner Mohammed Jaber **Bred** Gainsborough Stud Management Ltd **Trained** West Ilsley, Berks

FOCUS

There were several top stables represented in this maiden and only time will show the value of the form. It is best rated through the third backed up by the fifth and sixth.

NOTEBOOK

Majestic Cheer, dropped in grade, had finished eight lengths behind Cool Box at Newbury in September. He turned around the form over the extra furlong despite drifting into the centre of the course. (op 16-1)

Flying Goose(IRE) ◆, a half-brother to the miler Glencalvie, was a well-backed favourite on his debut. He will not have to improve much to take a similar contest. (op 11-4 tchd 3-1)

Cool Box(USA) could not confirm his eight length superiority over Majestic Cheer at Newbury in September. He had plenty of use made of him over this extra furlong and the winner did have previous experience of the surface. (op 4-1)

Pickering stepped up on his debut over six at Newmarket a week earlier despite again showing a tendency to hang right. Official explanation: jockey said colt hung right in home straight

Putra Laju(IRE), a half-brother to the winning juvenile hurdler Ever Special, could have settled better and should appreciate a longer trip. (op 12-1)

Postsprofit(IRE) had the cheekpieces left off for his sand debut.

6325 TWILIGHT RACING - MISS THE TRAFFIC H'CAP 5f 20y(P)

5:20 (5:20) (Class 6) (0-60,60) 3-Y-O+ **£2,730** (£806; £403) **Stalls** Low

Form				RPR
0020	1		**Desert Opal**[16] 6061 6-8-11 **58** ....(p) LiamJones(5) 4 (C R Dore) *chsd ldrs: rdn over 1f out: r.o u.p to ld nr fin* **5/1**[2]	71
0006	2	½	**Polar Force**[16] 6061 6-9-2 **58** .... ChrisCatlin 1 (Mrs C A Dunnett) *led: rdn over 1f out: hdd nr fin* **8/1**	69
2220	3	1	**Carcinetto (IRE)**[36] 5631 4-8-13 **55** .... J-PGuillambert 9 (P D Evans) *hdwy over 3f out: rdn over 2f out: nt qckn fnl f* **6/1**[3]	62
0312	4	2	**Special Gold**[20] 5970 4-9-4 **60** ....(b) DavidAllan 12 (A D Brown) *prom: rdn over 2f out: hung lft over 1f out: one pce* **17/2**	60
5004	5	hd	**Patavium Prince (IRE)**[18] 6020 3-9-4 **60** .... DaneO'Neill 7 (J R Best) *bhd: swtchd rt over 1f out: r.o fnl f: nvr nrr* **4/1**[1]	59
0000	6	shd	**Almaty Express**[10] 6162 4-9-4 **60** ....(b) DarryllHolland 5 (J R Weymes) *t.k.h in mid-div: hdwy whn nt clr run wl over 1f out: one pce fnl f* **13/2**	59
0606	7	2 ½	**Sounds Simla (IRE)**[20] 5970 3-8-5 **54** ....(p) TolleyDean(7) 3 (R A Harris) *towards rr: rdn 3f out: nvr nr ldrs* **33/1**	44
0004	8	½	**Mystery Pips**[25] 5878 6-8-13 **55** ....(v) KimTinkler 6 (N Tinkler) *towards rr: n.m.r over 3f out: rdn over 2f out: n.d* **7/1**	43
0150	9	hd	**Henry Tun**[154] 2207 8-8-12 **57** ....(b) JasonEdmunds(3) 2 (J Balding) *s.i.s: a bhd* **16/1**	45
0000	10	1	**Golband**[44] 5487 4-8-6 **55** .... AshleyHamblett(7) 11 (R F Marvin) *w ldr: rdn over 1f out: sn wknd* **50/1**	39
0215	11	5	**Tilsworth Charlie**[39] 5576 3-8-13 **55** ....(v) NickyMackay 8 (J R Jenkins) *hmpd over 3f out: a bhd* **16/1**	21

60.92 secs (-1.90) **Going Correction** -0.40s/f (Stan) **11** Ran SP% **115.1**

Speed ratings (Par 101):99,98,96,93,93 92,88,88,87,86 78

CSF £43.75 CT £250.18 TOTE £6.00: £2.20, £2.30, £1.60; EX 58.60 TRIFECTA Not won..

Owner Page, Ward, Marsh **Bred** Juddmonte Farms **Trained** West Pinchbeck, Lincs

FOCUS

A fast-run closely-knit low-grade sprint handicap and the form appears sound, rated around the placed horses.

6326 WORLD BET EXCHANGE WBX.COM H'CAP 5f 216y(P)

5:50 (5:51) (Class 5) (0-70,70) 3-Y-O+ **£3,886** (£1,156; £577; £288) **Stalls** Low

Form				RPR
-106	1		**Premier Fantasy**[6] 6223 4-9-4 **70** .... RobbieFitzpatrick 3 (T J Pitt) *s.i.s: rdn and hdwy over 1f out: squeezed through to ld ins fnl f: r.o* **8/1**	81+
2123	2	1	**Mr Cellophane**[25] 5872 3-9-3 **69** .... EddieAhern 9 (J R Jenkins) *hld up in mid-div: hdwy whn hung lft over 1f out: r.o ins fnl f* **13/2**	77
0100	3	1 ½	**Duke Of Milan (IRE)**[10] 6159 3-9-3 **69** .... AdamKirby 10 (G C Bravery) *hld up and bhd: nt clr run and swtchd rt 1f out: r.o ins fnl f: nt rch ldrs* **40/1**	72
3003	4	nk	**Dvinsky (USA)**[6] 6227 5-9-0 **66** .... PaulDoe 13 (M A Allen) *chsd ldrs: rdn over 2f out: led over 1f out: edgd lft and hdd ins fnl f: one pce* **18/1**	68
5005	5	nk	**Johnston's Diamond (IRE)**[20] 5970 8-9-0 **66** .... JimmyQuinn 5 (E J Alston) *led early: chsd ldrs: rdn and ev ch 1f out: one pce* **12/1**	67
0242	6	½	**Charles Parnell (IRE)**[10] 6159 3-9-1 **67** .... TonyCulhane 2 (M Dods) *hld up in tch: hung lft over 1f out: nt clr run jst ins fnl f: one pce* **10/3**[1]	76+
0362	7	nk	**Digital**[16] 6048 9-9-2 **68** .... ChrisCatlin 11 (M R Channon) *s.i.s: rdn over 1f out: nvr nrr* **11/1**	67
0500	8	nk	**Norcroft**[16] 6048 4-8-12 **67** ....(p) JamesDoyle(3) 4 (Mrs C A Dunnett) *mid-div: rdn over 3f out: hdwy over 2f out: no imp fnl f* **6/1**[3]	65
0000	9	nk	**Steel Blue**[21] 5943 6-8-12 **69** .... MichaelJStainton(5) 7 (R M Whitaker) *prom: rdn and ev ch 1f out: eased whn btn wl ins fnl f* **11/2**[2]	66
0206	10	1	**Summer Recluse (USA)**[21] 5938 7-9-2 **68** ....(t) SteveDrowne 1 (J M Bradley) *mid-div: hdwy on ins wl over 1f out: rdn whn hmpd ent fnl f: nt rcvr* **16/1**	62+
4204	11	1 ¾	**Winthorpe (IRE)**[43] 5493 6-9-2 **68** .... GrahamGibbons 12 (J J Quinn) *s.i.s: a bhd* **10/1**	57
0410	12	2 ½	**Count Cougar (USA)**[48] 5391 6-9-0 **66** .... LPKeniry 6 (S P Griffiths) *sn led: rdn and hdd over 1f out: wkng whn n.m.r jst ins fnl f* **20/1**	47

1m 13.19s (-2.62) **Going Correction** -0.40s/f (Stan) **12** Ran SP% **120.7**

Speed ratings (Par 103):101,99,97,97,96 95,95,95,95,93 91,88

CSF £60.38 CT £2011.76 TOTE £9.30: £3.70, £2.20, £8.60; EX 94.40 TRIFECTA Not won..

Owner Cadell Overseas Ltd **Bred** P G Jacobs, J Osborne And A Briam **Trained** Bawtry, S Yorks

■ Stewards' Enquiry : Robbie Fitzpatrick one-day ban: careless riding (Nov 14)

FOCUS

A modest handicap but sound overall form and the course record was broken by 0.13 seconds.

6327 BOOK ONLINE AT WOLVERHAMPTON-RACECOURSE.CO.UK MEDIAN AUCTION MAIDEN STKS 1m 141y(P)

6:20 (6:21) (Class 6) 3-5-Y-O **£2,388** (£705; £352) **Stalls** Low

Form				RPR
0533	1		**Vacation (IRE)**[7] 6206 3-8-10 72 .... WilliamBuick(7) 11 (V Smith) *hld up and bhd: hdwy over 3f out: rdn and hung lft fr over 2f out: led over 1f out: sn clr* **11/8**[1]	80+
0620	2	8	**King's Spear (IRE)**[25] 5879 3-9-3 64 .... EddieAhern 5 (P W Chapple-Hyam) *sn chsng ldr: rdn 3f out: hung lft over 1f out: sn wnt 2nd: no ch w wnr* **11/2**[3]	63
3020	3	shd	**Golden Alchemist**[81] 4437 3-9-3 74 .... HayleyTurner 2 (M D I Usher) *s.i.s: bhd: rdn and hdwy over 2f out: r.o ins fnl f* **7/4**[2]	63+
50	4	4	**Pagano (IRE)**[81] 4431 3-9-3 .... AdamKirby 8 (W R Swinburn) *bhd tl styd on fnl 2f: n.d* **8/1**	55+
0060	5	½	**Pleasing Gift**[21] 5936 3-8-5 54 ....(b[1]) KirstyMilczarek(7) 10 (J M P Eustace) *chsd ldrs: rdn over 2f out: wkng whn hung lft wl over 1f out* **33/1**	49
0000	6	¾	**Hiats**[24] 5903 4-8-13 30 .... JamesO'Reilly(7) 3 (J O'Reilly) *led: clr over 3f out: sn rdn: hdd over 1f out: sn wknd* **80/1**	52
000	7	4	**Special Ballot (IRE)**[59] 5077 5-9-1 35 .... SteveDrowne 7 (G A Swinbank) *chsd ldrs tl wknd 3f out* **25/1**	39
006	8	hd	**Red Lantern**[91] 4114 5-9-6 40 ....(vt[1]) RobbieFitzpatrick 13 (M J Attwater) *hld up in mid-div: hdwy over 3f out: wknd over 2f out* **80/1**	43
00	9	6	**Good Intentions**[17] 6026 4-9-1 .... LPKeniry 1 (P W Hiatt) *chsd ldrs: rdn 4f out: wknd over 2f out* **50/1**	26
	10	hd	**Second City** 3-8-12 .... DavidAllan 6 (E J Alston) *s.i.s: a bhd* **20/1**	25
00	11	31	**Tapsalteerie**[249] 536 3-8-12 .... MickyFenton 4 (M J Attwater) *mid-div: rdn 4f out: sn bhd: t.o* **100/1**	—

1m 48.12s (-3.64) **Going Correction** -0.40s/f (Stan)

WFA 3 from 4yo+ 3lb **11** Ran SP% **121.9**

Speed ratings (Par 101):100,92,92,89,88 88,84,84,79,78 51

CSF £9.71 TOTE £2.10: £1.10, £2.20, £1.10; EX 12.50 Trifecta £15.30 Pool: £310.28 - 14.31 winning units. Place 6 £125.84, Place 5 £22.95.

Owner Dave Clayton **Bred** Norelands Bloodstock **Trained** Exning, Suffolk

FOCUS

There was no hanging about in this poor maiden and the winner scored easily.

Pagano(IRE) Official explanation: jockey said gelding hung left throughout

T/Plt: £550.30 to a £1 stake. Pool: £58,425.75. 77.50 winning tickets. T/Qpdt: £32.10 to a £1 stake. Pool: £8,077.60. 186.10 winning tickets. KH

6249 SAINT-CLOUD (L-H)

Friday, November 3

OFFICIAL GOING: Good

6328a PRIX ISOLA BELLA (LISTED RACE) (FILLIES) 1m

2:25 (2:25) 3-Y-O **£17,241** (£6,897; £5,172; £3,448; £1,724)

			RPR
1		**Trip To The Moon**[148] 3-9-2 .... J-LMartinez-Tejera 10 (Y Durepaire, France)	103
2	nk	**Samsa (FR)**[16] 3-8-12 ....(b) FSpanu 11 (R Gibson, France)	98
3	shd	**Polysheba (FR)**[12] 6120 3-8-12 .... SPasquier 4 (A Fabre, France)	98
4	2	**Kezia (FR)**[38] 5604 3-8-12 .... MBlancpain 8 (C Laffon-Parias, France)	94
5	hd	**Tokyo Rose (UAE)**[12] 6120 3-8-12 .... RonanThomas 5 (H-A Pantall, France)	94
6	½	**Grand Vadla (FR)**[18] 6022 3-9-2 .... JVictoire 6 (A Fabre, France)	97
7	1 ½	**Miss Sissy (FR)**[160] 3-8-12 .... TJarnet 9 (H-A Pantall, France)	90
8	hd	**Hollywood Starlet (FR)**[38] 5604 3-8-12 .... MCherel 7 (Y De Nicolay, France)	89
9	1 ½	**Dorelia (IRE)**[37] 5611 3-8-12 .... DBonilla 3 (J H M Gosden) *slowly into stride, soon in midfield, 8th straight, effort on inside from over 2f out, one pace from over 1f out* **15/2**[1]	86
10	6	**Koanga (FR)**[38] 5604 3-8-12 .... DBoeuf 1 (U Suter, France)	74

1m 41.4s **10** Ran SP% **11.8**

PARI-MUTUEL: WIN 9.10; PL 3.50, 3.20, 2.70; DF 39.70.

Owner Y Maroto-Satli **Bred** Blackfoot Bloodstock & Mid Group Holdings Ltd **Trained** France

NOTEBOOK

Dorelia(IRE), winner of a Polytrack maiden over this trip on her previous start, missed the break and a brief effort off the turn petered out in the closing stages.

1498 CHURCHILL DOWNS (L-H)

Friday, November 3

OFFICIAL GOING: Firm

6329a RIVER CITY H'CAP (GRADE 3) 1m 1f (T)

9:43 (9:48) 3-Y-O+

£51,907 (£16,744; £8,372; £4,186; £2,512; £872)

			RPR
1		**Bayeux (USA)**[55] 5175 5-7-13 .... JRVelazquez 2 (G A Butler) *held up early, 3rd ½-way, driven and finished strongly to lead 100 yards out* **234/10**	110
2	1 ½	**Lord Admiral (USA)**[27] 5825 5-8-3 ....(b) MJKinane 5 (Charles O'Brien, Ire) *held up, last half-way, progress over 2f out and 4th straight, driven and finished well to take 2nd close home* **5/1**	111
3	nk	**Ballast (IRE)**[47] 5416 5-8-3 .... GKGomez 4 (H G Motion, U.S.A) **9/2**[2]	110
4	3 ¼	**Victory Design (IRE)**[497] 2890 4-7-13 ....(b) JRLeparoux 3 (P L Biancone, U.S.A) **101/10**	100
5	nk	**Silver Whistle (USA)**[40] 4-8-6 .... RBejarano 6 (W Mott, U.S.A) **67/10**	107
6	1 ¼	**Courtnall (USA)**[27] 5825 5-8-3 ....(b) PValenzuela 1 (Craig Dollase, U.S.A) **48/10**[3]	101
7	½	**Art Master (USA)**[34] 5-8-4 .... EPrado 8 (R J Frankel, U.S.A) **19/10**[1]	101
8	nse	**Erroneous I D (USA)** 5-8-1 .... RAlbarado 9 (P Mouton, U.S.A) **186/10**	98
9	6 ½	**Chief Export (USA)** 4-7-12 .... CHBorel 7 (W Bradley, U.S.A) **427/10**	83

1m 48.77s **9** Ran SP% **120.1**

PARI-MUTUEL (Including $2 stake): WIN 48.80; PL (1-2) 19.40, 6.00;SHOW (1-2-3) 11.40, 4.00, 4.00; SF 286.80.

Owner Michael Tabor **Bred** Darley **Trained** Blewbury, Oxon

NOTEBOOK
Bayeux(USA), who has been campaigned mainly at sprint trips since joining current connections from Godolphin, had no problem staying this longer trip and produced his trademark strong finish too deny the other European raider. A shock winner, it would be no surprise to see him continue his career in America.
Lord Admiral(USA), having his second run in the USA, had blinkers fitted for the first time. He finished well but the winner got first run and he has now finished second or third in all of his ten races this season.

6014 WINDSOR (R-H)

Saturday, November 4

OFFICIAL GOING: Good to soft
Meeting transferred from Doncaster.
Wind: Almost nil Weather: Sunny and crisp.

6330 EUROPEAN BREEDERS FUND MAIDEN STKS (DIV I) 6f
12:20 (12:20) (Class 5) 2-Y-O £3,238 (£963; £481; £240) Stalls High

Form RPR
3 1 **Sunoverregun**[19] 6014 2-9-0 .... AmirQuinn(3) 6 79
(J R Boyle) *w ldr: led 2f out: drvn and hrd pressed fnl f: styd on wl* **4/1**[2]
3322 2 ½ **Kyle (IRE)**[19] 6014 2-9-3 78 .... (p) RichardHughes 1 78
(R Hannon) *wl in tch: trckd ldr gng easily over 1f out: chal fnl f: sn hrd rdn and fnd nil: hld nr fin* **1/1**[1]
0 3 2½ **Bussel (USA)**[23] 5918 2-8-12 .... TonyCulhane 15 65
(W J Haggas) *trckd ldrs: shkn up and outpcd over 1f out: styd on steadily* **11/1**
4 5 **Sofia Royale** 2-8-12 .... FergusSweeney 8 50
(B Palling) *dwlt: towards rr: taken to outer and sme prog 2f out: sn wl outpcd: kpt on* **50/1**
0 5 5 **Art Gallery**[7] 6220 2-9-3 .... RyanMoore 7 40
(G L Moore) *trckd ldrs: shkn up and wknd wl over 1f out* **8/1**[3]
6 nk **Edge End** 2-9-3 .... EddieAhern 4 39
(D J S Ffrench Davis) *trckd ldrs: rdn and wknd wl over 1f out* **40/1**
6 7 1 **Katie Kingfisher**[19] 6015 2-8-12 .... SebSanders 5 31
(R M Beckett) *dwlt: wl in rr: sme prog over 1f out but hanging lft: nvr on terms* **16/1**
0 8 nk **Little Carmela**[26] 5867 2-8-12 .... JamieMackay 3 30
(S C Williams) *s.s: wl in rr: taken to outer over 2f out: prog wl over 1f out but wl outpcd: n.d* **50/1**
00 9 ½ **Cosimo Primo**[25] 5891 2-9-3 .... RichardThomas 12 34
(J A Geake) *prom over 2f: sn bdly outpcd and pushed along: no ch after: plugged on* **80/1**
0 10 nk **Royal Obsession (IRE)**[18] 6025 2-8-12 .... DaneO'Neill 9 28
(J G M O'Shea) *mde most to 2f out: wknd rapidly* **100/1**
0 11 1¼ **A Peaceful Man**[23] 5915 2-9-3 .... MichaelHills 16 29
(B W Hills) *a towards rr: effrt but no ch whn nt clr run over 1f out: no prog* **8/1**[3]
55 12 4 **Path To Glory**[22] 5947 2-9-3 .... AdrianMcCarthy 2 17
(Miss Z C Davison) *w ldrs to over 2f out: wknd rapidly* **50/1**
13 hd **Rogers Lodger** 2-9-3 .... JimmyQuinn 13 16
(J Akehurst) *dwlt: wl in rr: no ch 2f out: reminder over 1f out: nt clr run and no prog* **66/1**
14 7 **Papradon** 2-9-3 .... GeorgeBaker 14 —
(J R Best) *s.s: t.o in last pair after 2f* **33/1**
15 1½ **Fluters House** 2-9-0 .... JamesDoyle(3) 10 —
(S Woodman) *dwlt: t.o in last pair after 2f* **66/1**

1m 13.08s (-0.59) **Going Correction** -0.15s/f (Firm) 15 Ran SP% **122.9**
Speed ratings (Par 96):97,96,93,86,79 79,77,77,76,76 74,69,69,59,57
CSF £8.12 TOTE £6.30: £1.40, £1.20, £3.50; EX 11.30 Trifecta £111.50 Pool £210.48. - 1.34 winning units..
Owner Inside Track Racing Club **Bred** Howard Barton Stud **Trained** Epsom, Surrey
■ Stewards' Enquiry : Richard Hughes caution: used whip with excessive frequency

FOCUS
Just a modest maiden but the quicker of the two divisions by 0.59sec and the level looks reasonable. They came up the stands' side, despite the fact that the ground was on the soft side, as there was a fresh strip of ground there.

NOTEBOOK
Sunoverregun, less than a length behind Kyle on his debut here last month, looked a sitting duck for that rival inside the final furlong, but he found more under pressure than the favourite and held on well. His breeding suggests he should do even better at three. (op 3-1)
Kyle(IRE), who wore cheekpieces, stalked the eventual winner and, not for the first time, looked to be travelling well, but he found disappointingly little under pressure and is one to be seriously wary of. (op 11-8)
Bussel(USA), whose dam was a winner over sprint distances in the US, showed the benefit of her debut at Newmarket and could well find an opening on the All-Weather in the coming weeks. (op 9-1 tchd 12-1)
Sofia Royale, a half-sister to Genius, a triple mile winner at three and four, and to The Good Life, a 12-furlong winner in France, stayed on down the centre of the track and should be more effective when stepped up in distance next year.
Art Gallery, a half-brother to high-class juvenile Titus Livius, came in for a bit of support and ran a better race on this drop back in distance. One more run will qualify him for a handicap mark. (op 12-1)
Edge End, a half-brother to fair two-mile chaser Colliers Court and to Stagecoach Opal, a dual winner over hurdles, showed a fair degree of speed, surprisingly.

6331 EUROPEAN BREEDERS FUND MAIDEN STKS (DIV II) 6f
12:50 (12:51) (Class 5) 2-Y-O £3,238 (£963; £481; £240) Stalls High

Form RPR
1 **Edge Closer** 2-9-3 .... RichardHughes 16 72
(R Hannon) *s.i.s: sn rcvrd and trckd ldr after 2f: effrt to ld over 1f out: drvn and kpt on wl* **6/1**[2]
432 2 ¾ **Danehillsundance (IRE)**[44] 5491 2-9-3 75 .... RyanMoore 12 70
(R Hannon) *free and awkward to post: led: hrd rdn and hdd over 1f out: pressed wnr fnl f: nt qckn* **5/6**[1]
0400 3 ¾ **Fort Worth (IRE)**[12] 6146 2-9-0 67 .... JamesDoyle(3) 13 68
(B Gubby) *trckd ldrs: rdn 2f out: crowded 1f out: styd on but unable to chal* **12/1**
0 4 nk **Effigy**[64] 4987 2-9-3 .... DaneO'Neill 8 67
(H Candy) *wl in tch: outpcd wl over 1f out: shkn up and styd on fnl f: gng on at fin* **11/1**[3]
0 5 shd **Compton Charlie**[26] 5871 2-9-3 .... TPQueally 1 66
(J G Portman) *crossed fr low draw to join rest after 2f and prom: rdn 2f out: edgd rt 1f out: kpt on* **50/1**
0 6 5 **Doonigan (IRE)**[8] 6200 2-8-10 .... WilliamBuick(7) 2 51
(A M Balding) *wl in rr: prog on outer fr over 2f out but nvr on terms w ldrs: shkn up over 1f ot: one pce* **14/1**
0 7 ½ **Slo Mo Shun**[22] 5950 2-8-12 .... JimCrowley 14 45
(B R Millman) *trckd ldr for 2f: styd pressing ldrs tl wknd over 1f out* **25/1**
8 1¼ **Decision Day** 2-8-12 .... RichardThomas 7 41
(J A Geake) *dwlt: wl in rr: shkn up and sme prog fr over 1f out: n.d* **50/1**
9 ¾ **Hope Your Safe** 2-8-12 .... SteveDrowne 15 39
(J R Best) *nvr beyond midfield: outpcd fr 2f out: hanging lft over 1f out* **50/1**
10 nk **She's A Softie (IRE)** 2-8-12 .... SebSanders 3 38
(C F Wall) *racd towards outer: in tch in midfield tl wknd fr 2f out* **22/1**
6 11 nk **Bantry Bere (IRE)**[18] 6034 2-9-3 .... BrettDoyle 5 42
(J R Best) *hld up: a wl in rr: outpcd fr 2f out* **50/1**
0 12 shd **Silent Beauty (IRE)**[25] 5899 2-8-12 .... J-PGuillambert 9 37
(S C Williams) *dwlt: a wl in rr: struggling fr 1/2-way* **40/1**
13 1¾ **Sea Cookie** 2-8-12 .... AdrianMcCarthy 4 31
(W De Best-Turner) *in tch in midfield: rdn over 2f out: wknd wl over 1f out* **66/1**
0 14 3½ **Raise The Goblet (IRE)**[23] 5914 2-9-3 .... TonyCulhane 10 26
(W J Haggas) *a wl in rr: struggling fr 1/2-way* **12/1**
5 15 9 **Remark (IRE)**[3] 6295 2-9-3 .... (t) PaulMulrennan 11 —
(M W Easterby) *a in rr: wknd 1/2-way: t.o* **33/1**
0 16 5 **Pleasure Pursuit**[8] 6199 2-9-3 .... MichaelHills 6 —
(B W Hills) *struggling after 1f: t.o over 2f out* **20/1**

1m 13.67s **Going Correction** -0.15s/f (Firm) 16 Ran SP% **126.9**
Speed ratings (Par 96):94,93,92,91,91 84,84,82,81,81 80,80,78,73,61 54
CSF £10.73 TOTE £9.00: £2.40, £1.10, £3.70; EX 12.30 Trifecta £69.40 Pool £238.53 - 2.44 winning units..
Owner Lady Whent And Friends **Bred** Caroline Wilson **Trained** East Everleigh, Wilts

FOCUS
Another modest maiden, and the slower of the two divisions by 0.59sec, but the winner got it done a shade cosily and is open to improvement and the third sets a solid standard.

NOTEBOOK
Edge Closer is a brother to Edge Of Blue, who was placed over the minimum trip at two and three, out of a mare who was a triple winner over six furlongs as a juvenile. He got the better of his more fancied and more experienced stablemate here, winning a shade cosily after idling in front, and he should make up into a nice handicapper next season. (op 7-1 tchd 15-2)
Danehillsundance(IRE) again looked to have been found a good opportunity, but he was free to post and, in the race itself, found his stablemate too strong for him. He will always be vulnerable in this sort of company to a rival with more potential, and it is doubtful whether he ran to his official mark of 75 here. (op 4-5 tchd 10-11 and evens in places)
Fort Worth(IRE), the most exposed runner in the field, has a mark of 67, and his performance is probably a fair guide to the level of the form. (op 11-1)
Effigy, a half-brother to Prosperine, a winner over a mile at two, to Chelsea Barracks, a dual winner at a mile and 12 furlongs, and to the stayer Guard Duty, is bred to appreciate further in time so it was encouraging to see him seeing his race out well over six furlongs. (op 14-1)
Compton Charlie, whose dam won over five furlongs, knew his job a lot better this time and was up with the pace throughout. He may have fared even better had he enjoyed more luck with the draw. (tchd 66-1)
Doonigan(IRE) is a half-brother to seven winners and is likely to do better next year once handicapped.

6332 LETHEBY & CHRISTOPHER NURSERY 6f
1:20 (1:24) (Class 4) (0-85,85) 2-Y-O £5,181 (£1,541; £770; £384) Stalls High

Form RPR
546 1 **Solid Rock (IRE)**[27] 5841 2-8-10 74 .... DaneO'Neill 1 80+
(T G Mills) *hld up in midfield: shkn up and prog fr 2f out: rdn to ld last 150yds: sn clr* **16/1**
6010 2 2 **Bertoliver**[36] 5655 2-8-11 75 .... SebSanders 3 75
(D K Ivory) *hanging rt thrght: led after 2f: hdd and outpcd last 150yds* **8/1**[3]
1260 3 2½ **Sparkling Eyes**[14] 6105 2-8-12 76 .... RyanMoore 4 69
(C E Brittain) *trckd ldrs: drvn wl over 1f out: one pce fnl f* **10/1**
5130 4 nk **Reebal**[22] 5940 2-9-7 85 .... (b) RichardHughes 5 77
(B J Meehan) *towards rr: prog on wd outside fr over 2f out: nt on terms w ldrs fnl f: kpt on* **16/1**
3021 5 1¼ **Goodbye Cash (IRE)**[7] 6208 2-8-10 77 .... StephenDonohoe(3) 13 65
(P D Evans) *s.i.s: towards rr: swtchd lft 2f out: rdn and kpt on one pce after* **9/1**
1 6 1 **Now Look Out**[31] 5766 2-8-13 77 .... GrahamGibbons 11 62
(E S McMahon) *trckd ldrs: rdn 2f out: outpcd fr over 1f out* **4/1**[2]
5402 7 3 **Buddies Girl (IRE)**[3] 6290 2-8-4 68 .... MartinDwyer 7 44
(R Hannon) *led for 2f: prom tl wknd over 1f out* **9/1**
000 8 2½ **Ishimagic**[16] 6063 2-7-12 62 oh15 .... NickyMackay 9 30
(J J Bridger) *wl in rr: struggling 1/2-way: passed wkng rivals fnl f* **100/1**
0021 9 hd **Atlantic Light**[4] 6271 2-9-6 84 7ex .... KDarley 10 52
(M Johnston) *lost pl and pushed along in midfield over 3f out: struggling over 2f out* **9/4**[1]
3260 10 1¾ **Silkie Smooth (IRE)**[35] 5676 2-8-7 78 .... PatrickHills(7) 14 41
(B W Hills) *s.i.s: nvr beyond midfield: shkn up and no prog 2f out* **14/1**
1300 11 3 **Racing Stripes (IRE)**[87] 4246 2-8-12 76 .... SteveDrowne 2 30
(Miss E C Lavelle) *prom tl wknd wl over 1f out* **33/1**
6604 12 nk **Sherjawy (IRE)**[16] 6063 2-7-12 62 .... AdrianMcCarthy 12 15
(Miss Z C Davison) *lost pl and in midfield over 3f out: struggling over 2f out* **66/1**
003 13 3 **Barley Moon**[37] 5638 2-8-2 69 ow1 .... JamesDoyle(3) 8 13
(T Keddy) *a wl in rr: wl btn over 2f out* **16/1**
0160 14 7 **Redcliff (GER)**[7] 6208 2-8-7 71 .... DaleGibson 6 —
(M W Easterby) *s.i.s: sn t.o* **66/1**

1m 12.7s (-0.97) **Going Correction** -0.15s/f (Firm) 14 Ran SP% **122.2**
Speed ratings (Par 98):100,97,94,93,91 90,86,83,83,80 76,76,72,62
CSF £139.73 CT £914.74 TOTE £14.90: £3.80, £2.90, £4.00; EX 160.70 Trifecta £342.50 Part won. Pool £482.49 - 0.10 winning units..
Owner Mrs L M Askew **Bred** Max Morris **Trained** Headley, Surrey

FOCUS
A fair nursery in which they again came stands' side in the straight and the form looks solid rated through the runner-up.

NOTEBOOK
Solid Rock(IRE), dropping back to six furlongs on his handicap debut, took time to wear down the leader, who had the rail to help, but eventually ran out a clear winner. He was going further away at the line and shapes as though he will not mind returning to seven furlongs. (op 20-1)

Bertoliver grabbed the favoured stands'-side rail in the straight and looked to have most of his rivals in trouble until the winner loomed up. Versatile with regard to ground, it would not be a surprise to see him have another go on the All-Weather soon, and be more successful than he was on his first attempt on the surface, when running over a longer trip than ideal. (tchd 9-1)
Sparkling Eyes appreciated the drop back to sprinting in this more realistic company, and showed that she can be competitive at the right level. (op 20-1)
Reebal did not run too badly considering that he challenged down the centre of the track when the best ground appeared to be on the fresh strip near the stands' rail.
Goodbye Cash(IRE), 4lb higher than when successful at Ayr, was having her third outing on testing ground in 11 days and may just have found this one race too many in such a short space of time. (op 16-1)
Now Look Out, winner of a Nottingham maiden over five furlongs in soft ground on his only previous start, looked to have been given a fair mark for his handicap debut, but he was a bit disappointing, perhaps finding the extra furlong stretching him at this stage of his career. (tchd 9-2)
Ishimagic Official explanation: jockey said filly hung left in early stages
Atlantic Light, who bolted up in a weak affair at Catterick four days earlier, had a 7lb penalty to shoulder in this stronger race and was not up to it. She is surely better than this run suggests, though, and perhaps it just came a bit quick. (op 6-4)
Barley Moon Official explanation: jockey said filly was unsuited by the good to soft ground

6333 E B F TOTESPORT 0800 221 221 GILLIES FILLIES' STKS (LISTED RACE) 1m 2f 7y

1:55 (1:57) (Class 1) 3-Y-O+ **£16,595** (£6,274; £3,136; £1,568) **Stalls** Low

Form RPR
43-3 **1** **Lake Toya (USA)**[9] 6191 4-9-0 102 RHills 12 106
(Saeed Bin Suroor) *mde virtually all: hanging lft 3f out: shkn up over 1f out: pushed out and a holding on fnl f* **5/1**[2]
2204 **2** *¾* **Mango Mischief (IRE)**[23] 5917 5-9-0 105 RichardHughes 10 105
(J L Dunlop) *t.k.h: prom: rdn wl over 2f out: rallied against nr side rail fnl f: a hld* **15/2**
-655 **3** *¾* **Under The Rainbow**[28] 5803 3-8-10 88 EddieAhern 9 104+
(P W Chapple-Hyam) *hld up wl in rr: plenty to do whn nt clr run 3f out: prog jst over 2f out: r.o wl fnl f: nrst fin* **12/1**
1511 **4** *hd* **Abhisheka (IRE)**[19] 6017 3-8-10 100 TedDurcan 2 103
(Saeed Bin Suroor) *prom: drvn to chal over 2f out: nt qckn over 1f out: one pce after* **13/8**[1]
2 **5** *¾* **Taranto**[9] 6191 3-8-10 RichardMullen 4 102
(Saeed Bin Suroor) *hld up in midfield: prog 3f out: rdn over 2f out: kpt on same pce fr over 1f out* **6/1**[3]
1336 **6** *shd* **Princess Nada**[23] 5917 3-8-13 100 NickyMackay 6 105
(L M Cumani) *hld up in midfield: effrt over 2f out: rdn over 1f out: kpt on but nt rch ldrs* **12/1**
4031 **7** *2* **Pleasing**[8] 6206 3-8-10 62 MartinDwyer 14 98?
(J L Dunlop) *dwlt: hld up wl in rr: prog against nr side rail over 2f out: chsd ldrs 1f out: one pce* **33/1**
0200 **8** *1* **Fusili (IRE)**[9] 6191 3-8-10 90 NCallan 5 96
(N P Littmoden) *cl up: rdn 3f out: one pce u.p fnl 2f* **33/1**
2211 **9** *8* **Dayrose**[42] 5538 3-8-10 89 RyanMoore 3 82
(Sir Michael Stoute) *trckd ldrs: rdn 3f out: wknd wl over 1f out* **8/1**
6605 **10** *6* **Trials 'n Tribs**[27] 5847 4-9-0 45 J-PGuillambert 11 71?
(C A Cyzer) *towards rr: rdn on outer 5f out: sn struggling* **100/1**
1112 **11** *4* **Air Biscuit (IRE)**[25] 5888 3-8-10 85 (t) KDarley 1 64
(C F Wall) *prom tl wknd wl over 2f out* **33/1**
12 *5* **Expert Witness (IRE)**[35] 3-8-10 TonyCulhane 8 55
(M R Channon) *restrained to rr after 3f: rdn over 3f out: no prog: wknd over 2f out* **100/1**
0051 **13** *shd* **Zamhrear**[23] 5924 3-8-10 54 BrettDoyle 13 55
(C E Brittain) *wl in tch tl wknd wl over 2f out* **100/1**
41-0 **14** *19* **Manbala (FR)**[222] 773 3-8-10 99 SebSanders 7 21
(J L Dunlop) *v unruly preliminaries: dwlt: hld up in last: brief effrt over 3f out : sn wknd and eased: t.o* **33/1**

2m 9.03s (0.73) **Going Correction** +0.15s/f (Good)
WFA 3 from 4yo+ 4lb **14** Ran SP% **122.0**
Speed ratings (Par 108):103,102,101,101,101 100,99,98,92,87 84,80,80,64
CSF £41.50 TOTE £7.20: £2.20, £2.70, £4.30; EX 53.10 Trifecta £504.50 Part won. Pool £710.59. - 0.77 winning units..
Owner Godolphin **Bred** Darley **Trained** Newmarket, Suffolk

FOCUS
A tactical affair and a front-running masterclass from Richard Hills. The form looks shaky although it makes sense through the first two.

NOTEBOOK
Lake Toya(USA), the stable's second string according to riding arrangements, was given a good front-running ride by Hills, who is at his best when dictating matters. She had been sent off favourite when finishing behind her stablemate Taranto on the Polytrack last time and had no trouble reversing the form back on turf under these circumstances. (op 7-1 tchd 15-2)
Mango Mischief(IRE) had the rail to help in the straight and ran another honest race in defeat. As at Newmarket, though, she showed that she is vulnerable to younger rivals with more potential. (op 8-1)
Under The Rainbow looked to have plenty to do on the ratings but she likes this ground, came good in the autumn last year, and stays well. She finished well from off the pace for third, would have been better suited by a stronger-run race, and the suspicion is that the best of her has yet to be seen. (op 10-1)
Abhisheka(IRE), a progressive handicapper this autumn, was taking a step up in class but sent off favourite for this Listed event. Up there throughout, she could never quite get past her lesser-fancied stablemate and weakened in the closing stages, but she clearly deserves her place in this grade now. (op 6-4 tchd 7-4 and 15-8 in a place)
Taranto, who was second in the Polytrack race in which Lake Toya finished third, two lengths adrift, failed to confirm that form with her stablemate in these very different conditions. (op 13-2 tchd 7-1)
Princess Nada, who has done her winning on fast ground, was below her best, but she can be excused this late-season effort. (op 14-1)

6334 CELEBRATED ARTIST PIRAN STRANGE PAINTS FOR SPARKS STKS (REGISTERED AS SERLBY STAKES) (LISTED RACE) 1m 3f 135y

2:30 (2:30) (Class 1) 3-Y-O+ **£16,595** (£6,274; £3,136; £1,568) **Stalls** Low

Form RPR
2130 **1** **Alfie Flits**[14] 6103 4-9-8 107 RobbieFitzpatrick 8 121+
(G A Swinbank) *waited with in rr: prog fr 3f out: shkn up to ld over 1f out: forged clr* **8/1**[3]
2363 **2** *5* **Orcadian**[14] 6103 5-9-3 108 RichardHughes 5 107
(J M P Eustace) *led: kicked on wl over 3f out: pressed 2f out: hdd and outpcd over 1f out* **3/1**[2]
2230 **3** *3½* **Camrose**[36] 5657 5-9-3 102 (b) EddieAhern 3 101
(J L Dunlop) *prom: trckd ldr 1/2-way: rdn over 3f out: chal 2f out: wknd over 1f out* **16/1**
3444 **4** *nk* **Take A Bow**[8] 6203 5-9-3 102 JimCrowley 7 101
(P R Chamings) *hld up in tch: effrt against nr side rail and nt clr run briefly 2f out: rdn and one pce over 1f out: fdd fnl f* **12/1**
0-66 **5** *2* **Midas Way**[21] 5967 6-9-3 97 GeorgeBaker 6 97
(P R Chamings) *dwlt: hld up in detached last: effrt over 3f out: one pce and no ch w ldrs* **33/1**
11/ **6** *4* **Bull Run (IRE)**[927] 1538 5-9-3 114 RHills 9 91
(Saeed Bin Suroor) *sn settled in last pair: shkn up and no prog 3f out: btn after* **3/1**[2]
132- **7** *1* **Centaurus**[401] 5569 4-9-3 107 TedDurcan 1 89
(Saeed Bin Suroor) *trckd ldrs: disp 2nd 3f out: rdn over 2f out and wknd* **2/1**[1]
4450 **8** *23* **Orange Touch (GER)**[23] 5920 6-9-3 95 DarryllHolland 4 50
(Mrs A J Perrett) *t.k.h: trckd ldr to 1/2-way: rdn and wknd 4f out: t.o* **33/1**

2m 27.83s (-2.27) **Going Correction** +0.15s/f (Good) **8** Ran SP% **113.9**
Speed ratings (Par 111):113,109,107,107,105 103,102,87
CSF £32.01 TOTE £7.80: £1.90, £1.60, £2.70; EX 23.90 Trifecta £120.40 Pool £627.75. - 3.70 winning units..
Owner Dom Flit **Bred** Shadwell Estate Company Limited **Trained** Melsonby, N Yorks

FOCUS
In contrast to the previous race, the gallop in this staying event was strong and the winner came from off the pace. The form looks sound with the runner-up to previous course form.

NOTEBOOK
Alfie Flits disappointed at Newbury last time but that was not his true form and he showed what he is capable of here, travelling well and drawing clear in the closing stages to run out an easy winner. The race was run to suit him, as the leader went off too fast, but he is lightly raced and improving, so should make his mark at Group level next year. The plan is to go to Dubai for the Carnival. (op 11-2)
Orcadian, who has made all in Listed company around here in the past, is a difficult horse to catch when given an easy time of it in front, but on this occasion he perhaps set too strong a gallop as the winner, who was held up towards the back of the field for much of the race, came sailing by inside the final two furlongs. (tchd 11-4 and 10-3)
Camrose usually runs his race, and did so again here, but he is not easy to place and finds winning difficult. (tchd 20-1)
Take A Bow is another who falls a bit short at this level and is burdened with big weights in handicap company. (op 10-1)
Midas Way, dropping back from two miles, had the race run to suit him, but he last won on the Flat in June 2003 and he had a difficult job on his hands at these weights. He ran as well as could be expected in the circumstances. (tchd 40-1)
Bull Run(IRE), off the track since winning the Blue Riband Trial at Epsom in April 2004, likes soft ground, but he was under pressure a long way out and never really made any progress from the rear. This was not a promising return to action and one has to question whether he retains any of his old ability. (op 4-1 tchd 11-4)
Centaurus, who was well supported on his belated seasonal reappearance, was missing the tongue strap he wore on each of his starts last year. He came to challenge early in the straight but his effort did not last long. Along with his stablemate, he has plenty of questions to answer now.

6335 TOTESCOOP6 WENTWORTH STKS (LISTED RACE) 6f

3:05 (3:05) (Class 1) 3-Y-O+ **£16,595** (£6,274; £3,136; £1,568) **Stalls** High

Form RPR
4341 **1** **Rising Shadow (IRE)**[28] 5812 5-9-3 99 FrancisNorton 9 112
(T D Barron) *s.i.s: hld up in rr: rdn and prog 2f out: styd on wl fnl f to ld nr fin* **11/2**[3]
1006 **2** *hd* **Presto Shinko (IRE)**[22] 5942 5-9-9 106 (p) RichardHughes 2 117
(R Hannon) *chsd ldrs: effrt 2f out: rdn to ld last 150yds: collared nr fin* **11/2**[3]
4-64 **3** *¾* **Great Britain**[22] 5942 4-9-3 105 TedDurcan 5 109
(Saeed Bin Suroor) *led over 4f out: gng best 2f out: rdn over 1f out: hdd and nt qckn last 150yds* **11/4**[1]
2550 **4** *½* **Andronikos**[28] 5812 4-9-3 102 (t) JoeFanning 11 107
(P F I Cole) *hld up in last pair: prog 2f out: chsd ldrs ent fnl f: kpt on same pce* **11/1**
2030 **5** *¾* **Eisteddfod**[22] 5942 5-9-3 105 RyanMoore 10 105
(P F I Cole) *led for 1f: lost pl bdly bef 1/2-way: rallied u.p over 1f out: n.m.r and kpt on same pce* **4/1**[2]
-605 **6** *¾* **Violette**[14] 6101 3-8-12 100 SebSanders 1 98
(Sir Mark Prescott) *trckd ldr 4f out: rdn over 2f out: nt qckn over 1f out: fdd fnl f* **10/1**
0103 **7** *3* **Greenslades**[82] 4430 7-9-3 97 DarryllHolland 8 94
(P J Makin) *t.k.h: led briefly after 1f: lost pl 1/2-way: wknd over 1f out* **8/1**
0003 **8** *1¼* **Zowington**[42] 5534 4-9-3 90 GeorgeBaker 6 90
(C F Wall) *rrd s: hld up in last pair: shkn up and no prog 2f out* **16/1**
1115 **9** *6* **Forces Sweetheart**[19] 6020 3-8-12 79 (v) HayleyTurner 4 67
(V Smith) *t.k.h: prom 2f: wknd 2f out* **33/1**
414- **10** *5* **Danzili Bay**[469] 3756 4-9-3 90 EddieAhern 3 57
(P W Chapple-Hyam) *in tch tl wknd over 2f out* **25/1**

1m 13.0s (-0.67) **Going Correction** -0.15s/f (Firm) **10** Ran SP% **118.6**
Speed ratings (Par 111):98,97,96,96,95 94,90,88,80,73
CSF £36.54 TOTE £7.90: £2.20, £1.80, £1.90; EX 38.30 Trifecta £300.80 Pool £707.65. - 1.67 winning units..
Owner G Morrill **Bred** 6c Stallions Ltd **Trained** Maunby, N Yorks

FOCUS
There was a steady early pace to this Listed race and that contributed to a final time that was actually slower than that recorded by the winner of the nursery earlier on the card. The first two set the standard.

NOTEBOOK
Rising Shadow(IRE) has progressed through the handicapping ranks and made his first start in Listed company a winning one with his trademark late finish. It was a particularly praiseworthy effort in as much as the steady early pace would hardly have been ideal for a gelding better known for his exploits in strongly-run big-field handicaps. (op 15-2)
Presto Shinko(IRE), who won this race last year at Doncaster, had a 6lb penalty to carry as a result of his Group 3 win in France in the summer, and ran really well, only getting touched off close home. Two wins and a narrow second on each of his last three seasonal debuts suggests he is one to keep in mind for when next season's campaign gets underway in the spring. (op 6-1)
Great Britain, fourth in a Group 3 last time on his first start over six furlongs, looked to have a good chance here and his rider certainly did little wrong, as his mount enjoyed the run of the race, bagged the stands' rail in the straight and simply was not good enough. It would not come as a surprise if this lightly-raced colt improves for better ground next season. (op 2-1 tchd 3-1)
Andronikos was another staying on late and he finished a lot closer to Rising Shadow this time than when beaten eight lengths giving him 9lb in a York handicap last time. He remains difficult to place, though. (op 10-1)
Eisteddfod had been successful on his previous two starts at this track, but he was disappointing at Newmarket last time and this was another lacklustre effort. He has had a number of tough races this season and simply looks to have had enough for the year. (op 7-2 tchd 10-1)
Violette, along with the favourite, benefited from racing prominently in a steadily-run race, but she failed to capitalise and the evidence points to her having failed to train on. (op 12-1)
Zowington Official explanation: jockey said colt reared on leaving stalls

6336 TOTESPORT.COM NOVEMBER STKS (HERITAGE H'CAP) 1m 3f 135y

3:40 (3:41) (Class 2) 3-Y-0+

£31,160 (£9,330; £4,665; £2,335; £1,165; £585) **Stalls** Low

Form RPR

0132 **1** **Group Captain**[41] 5548 4-9-5 **99** RichardHughes 20 110
(R Charlton) *hld up in midfield: smooth prog fr over 2f out: hung rt fr over 1f out: led 1f out: drvn out* **10/1**

1466 **2** 1 ¼ **Resonate (IRE)**[14] 6107 8-7-11 **80** CDHayes(3) 1 89
(A G Newcombe) *hld up in midfield: smooth prog 3f out: led 2f out: drvn and hdd 1f out: kpt on but hld whn hmpd on line* **20/1**

2031 **3** 1 ½ **Book Of Music (IRE)**[28] 5808 3-9-0 **100** RyanMoore 2 106
(Sir Michael Stoute) *settled in midfield: n.m.r 4f out: rdn and prog over 2f out: styd on u.p: nvr able to chal* **13/2**[3]

4050 **4** hd **Castle Howard (IRE)**[63] 5010 4-7-12 **85** DebraEngland(7) 16 91
(W J Musson) *hld up wl in rr: stdy prog on outer fr over 3f out: clsng on ldrs whn n.m.r jst over 1f out: styd on same pce* **50/1**

5324 **5** 6 **Transvestite (IRE)**[14] 6097 4-8-4 **91** ow6 PatrickHills(7) 19 87
(J W Hills) *trckd ldng gp: hmpd 4f out: effrt 3f out: outpcd fr wl over 1f out* **25/1**

00-0 **6** 1 ¼ **Big Moment**[178] 1584 8-8-9 **89** JimCrowley 17 83
(Mrs A J Perrett) *s.i.s: hld up in last trio: rdn over 3f out: gd prog fnl 2f: no ch* **50/1**

11-1 **7** 1 ½ **Scriptwriter (IRE)**[29] 5787 4-9-3 **97** (p) TedDurcan 7 88
(Saeed Bin Suroor) *trckd ldrs: rdn over 2f out: sn wknd and wandered* **2/1**[1]

1202 **8** ¾ **St Savarin (FR)**[28] 5804 5-8-10 **90** PaulHanagan 12 80
(R A Fahey) *trckd ldrs: rdn 3f out: stl chsng 2f out: wknd over 1f out* **12/1**

1040 **9** 1 ½ **Cold Turkey**[21] 5963 6-8-13 **93** EddieAhern 15 81
(G L Moore) *stdd s: hld up in last pair: wl off the pce whn rdn over 3f out: kpt on: no ch* **20/1**

10 shd **Ursis (FR)**[200] 5854 5-8-12 **92** DaneO'Neill 5 80
(Jonjo O'Neill) *hld up towards rr: plenty to do 3f out: shkn up 2f out: kpt on: no ch* **50/1**

01-0 **11** nk **Come On Jonny (IRE)**[28] 5804 4-9-7 **101** SebSanders 4 88
(R M Beckett) *trckd ldrs: prog to ld over 3f out to 2f out: wknd rapidly* **20/1**

4031 **12** 4 **Great View (IRE)**[14] 6108 7-8-0 **80** (p) JimmyQuinn 18 60
(Mrs A L M King) *hld up in midfield: rdn and struggling 3f out: no ch whn n.m.r over 2f out* **33/1**

0100 **13** shd **Chancellor (IRE)**[49] 5374 8-8-11 **91** DarryllHolland 3 71
(D K Ivory) *settled wl in rr: rdn over 3f out and wl off the pce: modest effrt on outer over 2f out: no prog* **33/1**

0014 **14** 1 **Zero Tolerance (IRE)**[28] 5808 6-9-10 **104** MickyFenton 11 83
(T D Barron) *lost pl and towards rr 6f out: modest effrt on outer 3f out: sn no prog and btn* **25/1**

1131 **15** 3 **Peppertree Lane (IRE)**[28] 5804 3-9-5 **105** KDarley 13 78
(M Johnston) *prom: led over 4f out to over 3f out: wknd rapidly over 2f out* **5/1**[2]

0005 **16** 2 ½ **Hearthstead Wings**[28] 5804 4-9-2 **96** (v) JoeFanning 14 65
(M Johnston) *struggling in last after 4f: nvr a factor* **25/1**

2136 **17** 5 **Country Pursuit (USA)**[14] 6097 4-8-6 **86** RichardMullen 8 47
(C E Brittain) *prom tl wknd u.p fr 3f out* **14/1**

0320 **18** 10 **Beau Nash (USA)**[28] 5804 3-8-1 **87** AdrianMcCarthy 9 31
(P W Chapple-Hyam) *prom tl wknd rapidly 3f out* **14/1**

-302 **19** 1 ¼ **Red Admiral (USA)**[14] 6107 4-8-13 **93** RHills 10 35
(Saeed Bin Suroor) *mostly trckd ldr to over 4f out: wknd rapidly over 3f out* **16/1**

53/- **20** 38 **Shambar (IRE)**[849] 3661 7-8-7 **87** MartinDwyer 6 —
(Miss E C Lavelle) *racd freely: led and clr: wknd rapidly and hdd over 4f out: sn t.o* **66/1**

2m 29.16s (-0.94) **Going Correction** +0.15s/f (Good)
WFA 3 from 4yo+ 6lb **20** Ran SP% **138.4**
Speed ratings (Par 109):109,108,107,107,103 102,101,100,99,99 99,96,96,96,94 92,89,82,81,56
CSF £210.06 CT £1445.00 TOTE £12.10: £2.80, £3.00, £2.70, £16.80; EX 207.00 Trifecta £2873.80 Pool £25,500.15. - 6.30 winning units..
Owner Peter Webb **Bred** Hascombe And Valiant Studs **Trained** Beckhampton, Wilts

FOCUS
A decent renewal of this traditional turf season finale handicap, usually run at Doncaster. The gallop was reasonable and the form looks sound, with the first four clear.

NOTEBOOK
Group Captain was travelling well early in the straight and, when put under pressure, delivered, albeit while hanging to his right. Not over-raced this season, he came here having only had five previous starts during the campaign, and he has clearly progressed since joining his current stable. An inevitable rise in the handicap for this success means that his connections will have to look at Listed races for him next season, but he could well make the leap. (tchd 12-1)
Resonate(IRE) took up the running with over two furlongs to run and had the rail to help, but the winner proved just too strong in the closing stages. He certainly got the trip well enough, though. He acts well on Polytrack, and over the past three years he has been given a few spins on the All-Weather during the winter, so his racing year might not be over yet.
Book Of Music(IRE), a lightly-raced three-year-old who won last time out and was only 2lb higher in the weights, looked to have a good chance coming into the race and did not do a lot wrong in defeat. Still relatively unexposed, he looks like the type his trainer does well with and can improve again as a four-year-old, when he should get a bit further. (op 6-1)
Castle Howard(IRE) ran his best race since leaving Andre Fabre's stable and finished well clear of the rest. It has perhaps taken him until now to settle in to his new surroundings, and on this evidence there will be races to be won with him next season when the ground is on the easy side. (tchd 66-1)
Transvestite(IRE), who last won a race in the summer off 75, was effectively racing off a 16lb higher mark here as his rider put up 6lb overweight. He ran a sound race in the circumstances.
Big Moment, having his first outing since finishing down the field in the Chester Cup, stayed on well in the closing stages, but this trip would be on the short side for him these days. Nevertheless, it should have sharpened him up for a return to the winter game. (tchd 66-1)
Scriptwriter(IRE), who won well on his return from a 15-month absence at York last month, wore cheekpieces for the first time, was only 6lb higher and came in for good support. He disappointed, though, despite having every chance, and it is difficult to say that he bounced, as he had had four weeks off since York. (op 11-4 tchd 3-1 in a place)
St Savarin(FR) appears to be in the grip of the Handicapper now. (op 14-1)
Cold Turkey has the All-Weather season to look forward to now.
Ursis(FR), better known as a useful hurdler these days, was having his first start on the Flat for 767 days. He ran quite well, and this should put an edge on him prior to a return to hurdling.
Come On Jonny(IRE), having only his second start in a truncated season, was running off an 8lb higher mark than when successful in this race last year. (tchd 22-1)
Great View(IRE) Official explanation: jockey said gelding was denied a clear run
Peppertree Lane(IRE) has been in good form this autumn, but this looked like one race too many at the end of a long season. (op 6-1)
Shambar(IRE) Official explanation: jockey said gelding ran too free

6337 TOTE TEXT BETTING 60021 H'CAP 1m 2f 7y

4:10 (4:14) (Class 2) (0-100,100) 3-Y-0+ **£12,954** (£3,854; £1,926; £962) **Stalls** Low

Form RPR

6203 **1** **Folio (IRE)**[14] 6107 6-8-6 **86** oh1 TPQueally 10 93
(W J Musson) *settled in rr: prog on outer fr 3f out: rdn to ld over 1f out: jst hld on* **28/1**

1-1 **2** shd **Rampallion**[36] 5660 3-8-12 **96** EddieAhern 2 102
(Saeed Bin Suroor) *trckd ldrs: effrt over 2f out: drvn and hanging lft wl over 1f out: r.o wl fnl f: jst failed* **10/3**[1]

0012 **3** hd **Ofaraby**[8] 6203 6-9-5 **99** NCallan 5 105
(M A Jarvis) *hld up in midfield: effrt 2f out: rdn and r.o wl fnl f: gaining fast at fin* **12/1**

6201 **4** ½ **Best Prospect (IRE)**[14] 6107 4-9-2 **96** (t) RichardHughes 14 101
(M Dods) *hld up wl in rr: prog on wd outside gng easily 3f out: rdn over 1f out: r.o u.p ins fnl f: a hld* **12/1**

0402 **5** nk **Lake Poet (IRE)**[17] 6051 3-8-6 **90** ow1 DarryllHolland 16 94
(C E Brittain) *trckd ldrs: effrt nr side over 2f out: wl on terms over 1f out: styd on same pce* **14/1**

1- **6** nk **Narvik (IRE)**[410] 5392 3-8-10 **94** RHills 8 98
(Saeed Bin Suroor) *mde most to over 1f out: kpt on same pce fnl f* **7/1**[3]

0454 **7** shd **Gentleman's Deal (IRE)**[7] 6219 5-8-9 **89** PaulMulrennan 7 93
(M W Easterby) *wl in tch: urged along and looked to be struggling over 2f out: rallied fnl f: styd on* **12/1**

4613 **8** nk **Pinpoint (IRE)**[35] 5675 4-9-6 **100** TedDurcan 3 103+
(W R Swinburn) *settled wl in rr: sme prog over 2f out: rdn over 1f out: r.o wl last 150yds: nrst fin* **7/2**[2]

/000 **9** nk **Barathea Blazer**[21] 5963 7-8-7 **87** JoeFanning 6 90+
(K McAuliffe) *dwlt: hld up wl in rr: prog on wd outside 2f out: rdn and styd on: nt rch ldrs* **66/1**

0100 **10** ¾ **Punta Galera (IRE)**[14] 6107 3-8-2 **86** ChrisCatlin 1 87
(R Hannon) *w ldr: drvn over 2f out: fdd jst over 1f out* **50/1**

1120 **11** shd **Reem Three**[105] 3739 3-8-13 **97** NickyMackay 13 98
(L M Cumani) *hld up in midfield: effrt 3f out: nvr much room and no imp on ldrs fnl 2f: kpt on* **20/1**

31-0 **12** hd **Austrian (UAE)**[14] 6107 3-8-10 **94** MartinDwyer 9 95
(Saeed Bin Suroor) *hld up in midfield: effrt on outer 3f out: no prog and rdn 2f out: one pce after* **25/1**

4212 **13** 1 ½ **Charlie Tokyo (IRE)**[7] 6209 3-8-2 **86** oh2 (v[1]) PaulHanagan 18 84
(R A Fahey) *hld up wl in rr: effrt against nr side rail over 2f out: no real prog* **12/1**

5112 **14** hd **Kingsholm**[19] 6017 4-8-6 **86** oh1 FrancisNorton 4 83
(A M Balding) *t.k.h: pressed ldrs: stl chalng 2f out: wknd over 1f out* **18/1**

0150 **15** hd **Krugerrand (USA)**[14] 6107 7-8-6 **89** ow1 StephenDonohoe(3) 15 86
(W J Musson) *hld up in last: n.m.r after 2f: effrt 3f out: no prog* **25/1**

0000 **16** ¾ **Blue Spinnaker (IRE)**[7] 6219 7-8-10 **90** DaleGibson 17 86
(M W Easterby) *settled wl in rr: rdn and no prog 3f out* **28/1**

1620 **17** 5 **Corum (IRE)**[42] 5533 3-8-2 **86** oh1 RichardMullen 11 72
(J H M Gosden) *pressed ldrs tl wknd rapidly over 2f out* **20/1**

0665 **18** 8 **Before You Go (IRE)**[28] 5808 3-9-2 **100** RyanMoore 12 71
(T G Mills) *wl in tch: rdn and n.m.r over 2f out: wknd and eased over 1f out* **25/1**

2m 9.39s (1.09) **Going Correction** +0.15s/f (Good)
WFA 3 from 4yo+ 4lb **18** Ran SP% **131.9**
Speed ratings (Par 109):101,100,100,100,100 99,99,99,99,98 98,98,97,97,96 96,92,85
CSF £116.38 CT £1263.20 TOTE £34.80: £5.30, £1.50, £3.20, £3.30; EX 265.30 Trifecta £543.60 Part won. Pool £765.72. - 0.40 winning units. Place 6 £98.42, Place 5 £74.12..
Owner Goodey and Broughton **Bred** Lord Rothschild **Trained** Newmarket, Suffolk

FOCUS
A competitive handicap run at an ordinary gallop resulted in a tight finish to round off the 2006 Flat turf season. The form is nothing exceptional with the third the best guide.

NOTEBOOK
Folio(IRE) did not look well handicapped coming into the race, and the fact that he was 1lb wrong at the weights only added to that view. However, he has been in good form of late, tends to go well in big fields and is adaptable with regard to ground conditions. He found a good turn of foot and just prevailed in a tight finish. (op 25-1)
Rampallion made a successful return from almost a year on the sidelines at Newmarket last time, and a 5lb higher mark here did not look too harsh. In another stride or two he would have been in front and maintained his unbeaten record, but in the event he was narrowly denied. He has the makings of a smart four-year-old if he can be kept healthy. (op 7-2 tchd 4-1 in a place)
Ofaraby, who has remained stubbornly on a mark of 99 for most of the season, comes good in the autumn and was another who was finishing strongly as the line approached.
Best Prospect(IRE) stayed on well down the outside, justifying the Handicapper's reaction in putting him up 11lb for his recent Newbury win in heavy ground. (op 11-1)
Lake Poet(IRE) ran well in a less-competitive affair at Nottingham last time and this effort was not bad either, but he continues to look vulnerable off his current mark of 90, 6lb higher than when last successful. (tchd 16-1)
Narvik(IRE), not seen since winning a good maiden at Newmarket for Michael Jarvis in September 2005, made most of the running on this debut for Godolphin. He ran alright, but will likely be seen to better effect on quicker ground. (op 11-2)
Gentleman's Deal(IRE) needs a strong gallop to be seen at his best over a mile, but over this longer trip he coped quite well with the less-than blistering pace.
Pinpoint(IRE), who ran so well in the Cambridgeshire last time, is another who needs a strong pace to be seen at his best. He was finishing well at this end but, off this ordinary gallop, it was all too late. (op 4-1 tchd 9-2)
T/Jkpt: Not won. T/Plt: £100.00 to a £1 stake. Pool: £76,019.60. 554.75 winning tickets. T/Qpdt: £111.60 to a £1 stake. Pool: £4,827.30. 32.00 winning tickets. JN

6329 CHURCHILL DOWNS (L-H)

Saturday, November 4

OFFICIAL GOING: Turf course - firm; dirt course - fast

There was a significant track bias on the dirt favouring those racing near the inside rail.

6338a BREEDERS' CUP JUVENILE FILLIES (GRADE 1) 1m 110y(D)

5:30 (5:34) 2-Y-0 **£627,907** (£232,558; £116,279; £59,302; £29,070)

RPR

1 **Dreaming Of Anna (USA)**[48] 5415 2-8-7 RDouglas 1 116
(W Catalano, U.S.A) *made all, ridden out* **10/3**[2]

2 1 ½ **Octave (USA)**[42] 2-8-7 GKGomez 4 113
(T Pletcher, U.S.A) *prominent, close 3rd straight, soon ridden and went 2nd, ran on but always held by winner* **7/1**[3]

3 1 1/4 **Cotton Blossom (USA)**[29] 2-8-7 .... JRVelazquez 7 111
(T Pletcher, U.S.A) *prominent, 4th straight, stayed on final f, took 3rd close home* **16/1**
4 1 1/4 **Appealing Zophie (USA)**[29] 2-8-7 .... SBridgmohan 12 108
(S Blasi, U.S.A) *clase 2nd, ridden to chase leaders straight, stayed on at one pace* **20/1**
5 3 1/2 **Cash Included (USA)**[35] 2-8-7 .... CNakatani 3 101
(Craig Dollase, U.S.A) *midfield, 5th straight, ridden and kept on one pace, never in challenging position* **5/2**[1]
6 7 1/2 **She's Included (USA)**[29] 2-8-7 .... VEspinoza 5 86
(C S Paasch, U.S.A) *towards rear on rail, never a factor* **28/1**
7 hd **Adhrhythm (USA)**[21] 2-8-7 .... EPrado 9 86
(E Plesa, U.S.A) *towards rear, never dangerous* **14/1**
8 nk **Bel Air Beauty (USA)**[29] 2-8-7 .... FJara 6 85
(F Brothers, U.S.A) *midfield, 7th straight, no impression* **8/1**
9 2 1/2 **Sutra (USA)**[21] 2-8-7 .... MLuzzi 2 80
(M Stidham, U.S.A) *never dangerous* **14/1**
10 nk **Quick Little Miss (USA)**[35] 2-8-7 .... JKCourt 13 79
(M Stute, U.S.A) *in touch, 5th halfway, 6th straight, soon one pace* **33/1**
11 3 1/2 **Satulagi (USA)**[42] 5522 2-8-7 .... JohnEgan 11 72
(J S Moore) *towards rear, 9th and ridden straight, never a factor* **33/1**
12 4 1/2 **Gatorize (USA)**[29] 2-8-7 .... MGuidry 14 63
(Helen Pitts, U.S.A) *always in rear* **40/1**
13 3 **Her Majesty (USA)**[29] 2-8-7 ....(b) JRLeparoux 10 57
(P L Biancone, U.S.A) *reluctant to load, always behind* **16/1**
14 14 1/2 **Lilly Carson (USA)**[21] 2-8-7 .... CVelasquez 8 28
(Ralph E Nicks, U.S.A) *prominent early, lost place from halfway, last and beaten straight* **33/1**

1m 43.81s **14** Ran SP% **119.8**
PARI-MUTUEL (including $2 stake): WIN 7.20; PL (1-2) 4.60, 5.80;SHOW (1-2-3) 3.40, 4.40, 9.00; SF 50.80.
Owner Frank C Calabrese **Bred** Frank C Calabrese **Trained** USA
■ A first Breeders' Cup success for jockey Rene Douglas and trainer Wayne Catalano.

FOCUS
On paper this was just an ordinary renewal the Juvenile Fillies, and the race itself was unsatisfactory. Dreaming Of Anna was gifted the lead from the hugely advantageous inside stall (four of the five dirt races went to stall one) and made all at just an ordinary pace. Unsurprisingly, the winning time was 1.22 seconds slower than the following colts' version.

NOTEBOOK
Dreaming Of Anna(USA) won on the dirt on her debut, but her two subsequent victories came on turf, including when she beat the colts in a Grade 3 at Woodbine on her previous start. Back on the sand, she was ideally berthed in stall one (four of the five winners of the races run on the dirt course had the inside stall) and was absolutely gifted the lead, not having to over exert herself to take the field along pretty much from the start. It was clear from some way out that she was unlikely to be passed and she stayed on strongest of all to readily hold off Octave's challenge in the straight, taking her unbeaten record to four in the process. She is clearly a high-class filly, but everything fell into place for her in what looked like just an ordinary renewal, and she is likely to face much tougher tests in future. Her rider was making bullish noises afterwards, and suggested she could well be up to running in the Kentucky Derby, rather than the Kentucky Oaks.
Octave(USA), stepped up a furlong and a half in trip, ran a fine race in defeat considering the steady plays would not have suited. She was the only filly to throw down a serious challenge to the eventual winner, who had been allowed a very soft lead, and she emerges with plenty of credit.
Cotton Blossom(USA), a stablemate of the runner-up, had to come wider into the straight than the front two and ran a good race on this return to dirt (ran on Polytrack last time). Like the second home, and many in behind, a stronger pace would surely have suited better.
Appealing Zophie(USA) was always on the pace but failed to put any pressure on the leader and was soon left behind. Still, she fared best of those in double-figure stalls by some way.
Cash Included(USA) could not repeat the form she showed to win the Grade 1 Oak Leaf Stakes on her previous start and was totally unsuited by the way the race was run.
Satulagi(USA), a smart sort on turf in the UK who was fourth in the Fillies' Mile at Ascot on her previous start, was never seen with a chance on her US debut.
Her Majesty(USA) did not look happy beforehand - she was very reluctant to load - and this run is best forgotten.

6339a BESSEMER TRUST BREEDERS' CUP JUVENILE (C&G) (GRADE 1) 1m110y (D)
6:10 (6:11) 2-Y-0 **£627,907** (£232,558; £116,279; £59,302; £29,070)

RPR
1 **Street Sense (USA)**[28] 5823 2-8-10 .... CHBorel 1 123+
(C Nafzger, U.S.A) *racd in 12th, rapid hdwy on ins 3f out, 4th str, squeezed through on rail to ld over 1 1/2f out, sn clr, rdn out* **16/1**
2 10 **Circular Quay (USA)**[28] 5823 2-8-10 .... GKGomez 9 104
(T Pletcher, U.S.A) *squeezed out s & dropped back to last, hdwy over 3f out, 6th str on outside, wnt 2nd ins fnl f, no ch with wnr* **10/3**[1]
3 2 1/4 **Great Hunter (USA)**[28] 5823 2-8-10 ....(b) CNakatani 7 100
(Doug O'Neill, U.S.A) *held up in 9th, close 5th towards outside straight, went 2nd 1 1/2f out, lost 2nd inside final f* **5/1**[3]
4 2 3/4 **Scat Daddy (USA)**[21] 5983 2-8-10 .... JRVelazquez 3 95
(T Pletcher, U.S.A) *close up, went 3rd 4f out, every chance entering straight, one pace* **7/2**[2]
5 3/4 **Stormello (USA)**[27] 2-8-10 ....(b) KDesormeaux 2 93
(W Currin, U.S.A) *pressed leader on inside til disputed lead from over 4f out, headed over 1 1/2f out, one pace* **9/1**
6 6 1/4 **C P West (USA)**[42] 2-8-10 .... RBejarano 5 81
(N Zito, U.S.A) *raced in 8th, 7th straight, switched outside 1 1/2f out, one pace* **12/1**
7 6 3/4 **U D Ghetto (USA)**[35] 2-8-10 .... MESmith 12 68
(A Reinstedler, U.S.A) *held up in 13th, 12th straight, never a factor* **50/1**
8 9 3/4 **King Of The Roxy (USA)**[42] 2-8-10 ....(b) EPrado 4 50
(T Pletcher, U.S.A) *raced in 7th, 13th and beaten straight* **14/1**
9 1 1/4 **Skip Code (USA)**[26] 2-8-10 ....(b) PHusbands 14 47
(M Casse, Canada) *raced in 11th, always towards rear* **40/1**
10 hd **Teuflesberg (USA)**[13] 2-8-10 ....(b) RAlbarado 8 47
(Jamie Sanders, U.S.A) *raced in 10th, always towards rear* **66/1**
11 2 1/4 **Pegasus Wind (USA)**[21] 5983 2-8-10 ....(b) MLuzzi 10 43
(D Wayne Lukas, U.S.A) *pressed leader til disputed lead over 4f out, headed over 1 1/2f out, weakened quickly* **16/1**
12 2 3/4 **Malt Magic (USA)**[27] 2-8-10 ....(b) JKCourt 13 38
(B Baffert, U.S.A) *in touch, 8th & beaten straight* **33/1**
13 9 **Got The Last Laugh (USA)**[21] 5983 2-8-10 .... RDouglas 11 20
(W Mott, U.S.A) *in touch, 7th & beaten straight* **40/1**
14 dist **Principle Secret (USA)**[27] 2-8-10 .... VEspinoza 6 —
(C S Paasch, U.S.A) *set fast pace til headed over 4f out, weakened quickly, eased* **6/1**

1m 42.59s **14** Ran SP% **123.6**
PARI-MUTUEL: WIN 32.40; PL (1-2) 12.60, 5.00; SHOW (1-2-3) 8.00, 3.20,4.40; SF 181.20.
Owner J B Tafel **Bred** James B Tafel **Trained** USA
■ A first Breeders' Cup success for jockey Calvin Borel.

FOCUS
This looked a competitive renewal on paper but the leaders went off at such a strong pace that it was inevitable that the winner would come from well off the pace. That said, Street Sense won by a record winning distance for this race. The winning time was 1.22 seconds quicker than the Juvenile Fillies'.

NOTEBOOK
Street Sense(USA), ridden by a rider known for liking to keep to the inside rail, was well drawn in stall one and held up well off the frantic early gallop. He enjoyed a wonderful, trouble-free trip on the inside and powered clear in the straight for an easy win, but the chances are he is flattered by the bare result. He did win, however, by the biggest margin in 23 runnings of the Juvenile and is now 14-1 with Coral for next year's Kentucky Derby. His trainer won that race with Unbridled in 1990, but no horse has yet completed the Juvenile-Derby double.
Circular Quay(USA), whose style of racing was suited by the way this race was run, was in last early on but made good headway when the leaders began to flag in front. Unlike the winner, who made his move on the fastest ground next to the inside rail, he challenged wide around horses, and while he beat the rest well enough, the winner had gone beyond recall. He has the potential to develop into a live Kentucky Derby hope next season.
Great Hunter(USA), who had beaten Circular Quay and Street Sense in the Futurity Stakes last time out, also raced off the fast pace in the early stages and came through to have his chance in the straight. He could not have too many excuses.
Scat Daddy(USA), winner of the Champagne Stakes last time out, was well drawn but, along with a number of horses in the line up, had far too much use made of him in the early stages. He did best of those who raced near the strong pace, and as such he deserves extra credit. He should be in the mix for the Kentucky Derby next year.
Stormello(USA), prominent from the off, went too fast to maintain that position and he paid for it in the closing stages. To finish so far clear of the rest, having been ridden so injudiciously, suggests he has plenty of ability, though.
C P West(USA), the least experienced runner in the field, had shown that stamina is his forte over inadequate distances previously this season, and he looked likely to improve for the step up to an extended mile for the first time. He had the race run to suit, but was perhaps lacking in the experience required to land a blow at this level at this stage in his career. He can only improve.
U D Ghetto(USA) was another who benefited from being held up towards the rear and merely stayed on past beaten horses.
Pegasus Wind(USA) helped contribute to the ridiculously fast early gallop.
Principle Secret(USA) burnt himself out at the head of affairs, setting a furious gallop.

6340a EMIRATES AIRLINE BREEDERS' CUP FILLY & MARE TURF (GRADE 1) 1m 3f (T)
6:55 (6:56) 3-Y-0+ **£690,698** (£255,814; £127,907; £65,233; £31,977)

RPR
1 **Ouija Board**[56] 5193 5-8-11 .... LDettori 2 123
(E A L Dunlop) *mid-div on rail, 6th at hlf-way, 4th on outside straight, quickened to challenge appr fnl f, led just inside fnl f, ran on* **6/4**[1]
2 2 1/4 **Film Maker (USA)**[28] 5819 6-8-11 ....(b) EPrado 4 119
(H G Motion, U.S.A) *prominent, disputing 4th half-way, 3rd straight, ridden & soon ran on to go 2nd 1f out, not pace of winner* **10/1**
3 nk **Honey Ryder (USA)**[28] 5819 5-8-11 ....(b) JRVelazquez 5 119
(T Pletcher, U.S.A) *held up, 9th straight, ridden & stayed on well from over 1f out, nearest at finish* **8/1**
4 1 3/4 **Wait A While (USA)**[35] 3-8-7 .... GKGomez 7 117
(T Pletcher, U.S.A) *tracked leaders, disputing 4th half-way, 2nd & driven to challenge straight, not pace of winner* **5/2**[2]
5 1 **Satwa Queen (FR)**[34] 5713 4-8-11 .... TThulliez 9 114
(J De Roualle, France) *held up, disputing 6th straight, driven to chase leaders, never in challenging position* **7/1**[3]
6 nk **My Typhoon (IRE)**[21] 4-8-11 .... RAlbarado 8 114
(W Mott, U.S.A) *raced in close 2nd, led 4f out, headed just inside final f, no extra* **33/1**
7 4 1/2 **Mauralakana (FR)**[21] 5984 3-8-7 .... JRLeparoux 3 107
(P L Biancone, U.S.A) *held up, last half-way, 8th straight, soon ridden and one pace* **20/1**
8 2 1/4 **Dancing Edie (USA)**[35] 4-8-11 .... CNakatani 1 103
(Craig Dollase, U.S.A) *led to 4f out, 5th & beaten straight* **40/1**
9 6 1/2 **Quiet Royal (USA)**[21] 5984 3-8-7 .... OPeslier 6 93
(T Pletcher, U.S.A) *held up, last straight, never dangerous* **33/1**
10 12 3/4 **Germance (USA)**[21] 5984 3-8-7 .... CSoumillon 10 73
(J-C Rouget, France) *prominent, 3rd half-way, disputing 6th straight, one pace from over 1f out* **16/1**

2m 14.55s
WFA 3 from 4yo+ 5lb **10** Ran SP% **120.2**
PARI-MUTUEL: WIN 4.80; PL (1-2) 3.40, 5.80; SHOW (1-2-3) 2.60, 4.40,4.40; SF 33.20.
Owner Lord Derby **Bred** Stanley Estate & Stud Co **Trained** Newmarket, Suffolk
■ Ouija Board was the seventh horse to win multiple Breeders' Cups; only Da Hoss had won races separated by more than a year.

FOCUS
There are no stars among US distaff turf horses, and Ouija Board totally outclassed her field to take her second Filly & Mare Turf. They went just an ordinary pace for much of the way.

NOTEBOOK
Ouija Board, successful in this race in 2004 and second last year, returned to the US off the back of a terrific season in Europe, where she won both the Prince Of Wales's Stakes and the Nassau, as well as running Dylan Thomas to a neck in the Irish Champion Stakes on her latest outing. In all honesty this probably represented her easiest task of the season, but to be able to produce such a high level of form on her eighth start of the year, having been on the go since March, reaffirmed her status as a truly exceptional mare. Always travelling well off what was by no means a frantic pace, she was still going very strongly when manoeuvred into the clear at the top of straight and soon pulled away without Dettori having to ask for everything. She may have two more races this year before she is retired, with connections eyeing both the Japan Cup and the Hong Kong Vase. She was fifth in the former last season before winning the latter. In the longer term, she has been booked to Kingmambo for the 2007 breeding season.
Film Maker(USA), second to Ouija Board in this race in 2004, and again a place behind that one when third in last year's renewal, ran a terrific race but was always going to struggle to reverse form with the English mare. She is likely to be kept in training next year, when her connections will no doubt be pleased she will not have Ouija Board to contend with.
Honey Ryder(USA), just in front of Film Maker when winning the Grade 1 Flower Bowl Stakes at Belmont on her previous start, was asked to come from a long way back and a stronger gallop would have suited better.
Wait A While(USA), the leading US turf filly, came up short faced with her toughest task to date. She does, though, have time on her side.
Satwa Queen(FR) was one of the few dangers to Ouija Board judged on her recent second to the classy Mandesha in the Prix de l'Opera at Longchamp, but she failed to produce her best.
Germance(USA) pulled her way into a prominent position and was beaten a mile.

6341a TVG BREEDERS' CUP SPRINT (GRADE 1) 6f (D)

7:35 (7:38) 3-Y-0+ **£668,721** (£247,674; £123,837; £63,157; £30,959)

RPR

1 **Thor's Echo (USA)**^{28} [5827] 4-9-0 ....(b) CNakatani 1 124
(Doug O'Neill, U.S.A) *tracked leaders in 3rd on inside, switched outside to challenge halfway, led 1 12/f out, driven out* **14/1**

2 *4* **Friendly Island (USA)**^{35} 5-9-0 .... RADominguez 2 112
(T Pletcher, U.S.A) *6th early, 4th straight, stayed on to take 2nd inside final f* **40/1**

3 *½* **Nightmare Affair (USA)**^{63} 5-9-0 ....(b) EPrado 7 110
(M J Azpurua, U.S.A) *7th early, 6th straight, kep on to take 3rd close home* **25/1**

4 *hd* **Bordonaro (USA)**^{28} [5827] 5-9-0 .... PValenzuela 6 109
(B Spawr, U.S.A) *disputed lead til headed 1 1/2f out, one pace* **4/1**^{2}

5 *nk* **Attila's Storm (USA)**^{28} [5820] 4-9-0 ....(b) CVelasquez 13 109
(R Schosberg, U.S.A) *disputed lead til headed 1 1/2f out, one pace* **20/1**

6 *2 ¼* **Too Much Bling (USA)**^{112} 3-8-12 ....(b) GKGomez 9 100
(B Baffert, U.S.A) *8th early, 9th straight, never a factor* **9/1**

7 *nse* **War Front (USA)**^{28} [5820] 4-9-0 .... JSantos 10 102
(H A Jerkens, U.S.A) *5th early, 7th straight, soon one pace* **16/1**

8 *2* **Siren Lure (USA)**^{76} 5-9-0 .... ASolis 11 96
(Art Sherman, U.S.A) *last early, 13th straight, never a factor* **11/2**^{3}

9 *1 ¼* **Pomeroy (USA)**^{63} 5-9-0 ....(b) ECastro 8 92
(M D Wolfson, U.S.A) *close up, 5th straight, soon weakened* **10/1**

10 *hd* **Kelly's Landing (USA)**^{28} 5-9-0 .... RBejarano 14 92
(E Kenneally, U.S.A) *broke sharply, shuffled back to midfield before halfway, 8th straight, no headway* **20/1**

11 *½* **Lewis Michael (USA)**^{22} 3-8-12 ....(b) RDouglas 3 88
(W Catalano, U.S.A) *12th early, never a factor* **50/1**

12 *¾* **Malibu Mint (USA)**^{21} 4-8-11 .... KKaenel 12 85
(Jim Chapman, U.S.A) *10th early, never a factor* **33/1**

13 *1 ½* **Areyoutalkintome (USA)**^{28} 5-9-0 ....(b) VEspinoza 5 84
(Doug O'Neill, U.S.A) *always in rear* **33/1**

14 *3 ¼* **Henny Hughes (USA)**^{28} [5820] 3-8-12 .... JRVelazquez 4 72
(K McLaughlin, U.S.A) *shuffled back towards rear start, never a factor* **2/1**^{1}

68.80 secs **14** Ran SP% **124.0**
PARI-MUTUEL: WIN 33.20; PL (1-2) 15.80, 50.00; SHOW (1-2-3) 10.20,32.80, 15.20; SF 955.40.

Owner Royce S Jaime Racing Stable & Suarez Racing I **Bred** Fast Lane Farms & Block & Forman **Trained** USA

FOCUS

The leaders did not go mad, as they can often do in this race, but the advantage of an inside draw was once again shown up.

NOTEBOOK

Thor's Echo(USA), drawn best of all on a day when the inside rail was a big advantage, edged out to challenge three wide entering the straight, and soon put the race to bed. He did hang in towards the rail from over a furlong out, but that was hardly a bad thing, and he drew nicely clear for an authoritative success. His last win came in a race restricted to California-breds back in August 2005, but he was only a length behind Bordonaro in a Grade 1 at Santa Anita last time, so he came here in good form.

Friendly Island(USA) enjoyed a perfect trip on the inside for most of the way and only had to edge off the rail in the straight. The winner showed more pace than him but he stayed on well to complete a low-draw exacta.

Nightmare Affair(USA) raced one off the rail until the entrance to the straight when he was switched out. He kept on better than most to claim the minor placing and seems to be improving as he gets older.

Bordonaro(USA), whose style of running is to be up with the pace, had beaten Thor's Echo a length when granted an uncontested lead in a Grade 1 race at Santa Anita last time out, but he was not given such an easy time of it here and the battle for the pace-making role eventually took its toll. He remains a high-class sprinter, though, and will win many more races.

Attila's Storm(USA), who fractured a leg after finishing fourth in this race last year and had only had a couple of previous starts this season as a result, ran a blinder from his outside stall position. He broke well and got over to dispute the lead soon after the start, only tiring inside the last. It goes without saying that he would have fared even better had he not had to battle so hard for the lead.

Too Much Bling(USA), whose last outing came in July, had been kept fresh by his trainer for this, but he was struggling to go the pace rounding the turn into the straight and never really got involved. A winner of three Graded races already this year, he is better than this performance suggests.

War Front(USA) was poorly drawn and ran quite well given that he raced wide most of the way on a day when the track bias favoured those who raced on the inside.

Siren Lure(USA), a winner of his last three starts on dirt, each in Graded company and the last two over seven furlongs, was another who had been kept fresh for this big day, having not raced since August. Poorly drawn out wide, he was out the back early in the race and swung widest of all into the straight. He passed a few beaten horses but never really got competitive, and the leaders probably did not go off fast enough for his liking.

Pomeroy(USA) is a Saratoga course specialist and has not achieved the same level of form away from that track.

Henny Hughes(USA), sent off favourite on the back of impressive wins in his last three starts, including in Grade 1 company, has disappointed before when returning to the track on the back of an insufficient break, and four weeks since his last race may well have been too short an absence this time. This was clearly not his true running.

6342a NETJETS BREEDERS' CUP MILE (GRADE 1) 1m (T)

8:15 (8:18) 3-Y-0+ **£681,279** (£252,326; £126,163; £64,343; £31,541)

RPR

1 **Miesque's Approval (USA)**^{28} [5824] 7-9-0 .... ECastro 10 124
(M D Wolfson, U.S.A) *held up, headway on outside and 10th straight, driven to lead inside final f, driven out* **25/1**

2 *2 ¾* **Aragorn (IRE)**^{28} [5825] 4-9-0 .... CNakatani 7 117
(N Drysdale, U.S.A) *midfield, 8th straight on outside, headway well over 1f out, ran on steadily to take 2nd last stride* **4/1**^{2}

3 *hd* **Badge Of Silver (USA)**^{307} 6-9-0 .... EPrado 8 117
(R J Frankel, U.S.A) *tracked leader, 2nd straight, kept on under pressure, lost 2nd last stride* **20/1**

4 *nk* **Sleeping Indian**^{21} [5962] 5-9-0 .... ASolis 4 117+
(J H M Gosden) *held up, 11th straight on inside, moved right well over 1f out, 12th 1f out, finished well* **12/1**

5 *nk* **Rob Roy (USA)**^{21} [5964] 4-9-0 .... RADominguez 9 116+
(Sir Michael Stoute) *slowly into stride, outpaced for 5f, last straight, headway on outside final 1 1/2f, finished well* **16/1**

6 *hd* **Silent Name (JPN)**^{28} [5824] 4-9-0 .... VEspinoza 2 115
(G Mandella, U.S.A) *led to inside final f, one pace* **33/1**

7 *hd* **Gorella (FR)**^{21} 4-8-11 .... JRLeparoux 12 112
(P L Biancone, U.S.A) *12th straight, headway 1 1/2f out, no extra closing stages* **5/1**^{3}

8 *1 ¼* **Aussie Rules (USA)**^{28} [5824] 3-8-11 ....(v) GKGomez 14 111
(A P O'Brien, Ire) *9th straight, never a factor* **16/1**

9 *nk* **Araafa (IRE)**^{42} [5524] 3-8-11 .... JRVelazquez 3 110
(J Noseda) *always in touch, 7th straight towards outside, ridden to go 3rd over 1f out, weakened inside final f* **11/4**^{1}

10 *1 ¼* **Librettist (USA)**^{42} [5524] 4-9-0 .... CSoumillon 13 108
(Saeed Bin Suroor) *midfield, 6th straight on inside, hard ridden and never able to challenge, weakened inside final f* **14/1**

11 *4 ¼* **Free Thinking (USA)**^{35} 5-9-0 .... JSantos 5 98
(D Danner, U.S.A) *disputed 3rd, 5th straight, beaten approaching final f* **33/1**

12 *nk* **Super Frolic (USA)**^{28} [5826] 6-9-0 .... SBridgmohan 11 98
(S Blasi, U.S.A) *always towards rear* **50/1**

13 *1* **Ad Valorem (USA)**^{48} [5416] 4-9-0 .... JamieSpencer 1 95
(A P O'Brien, Ire) *disputed 3rd, 3rd straight, soon beaten* **16/1**

14 *hd* **Echo Of Light**^{35} [5703] 4-9-0 .... LDettori 6 95
(Saeed Bin Suroor) *disputed 3rd, 4th straight, beaten 1 1/2f out* **7/1**

1m 34.75s
WFA 3 from 4yo+ 2lb **14** Ran SP% **124.3**
PARI-MUTUEL: WIN 50.60; PL (1-2) 17.20, 5.80; SHOW (1-2-3) 10.40,4.40, 9.80; SF 246.00.
Owner Live Oak Plantation **Bred** Live Oak Stud **Trained** North America
■ A first Breeders' Cup success for jockey Eddie Castro and trainer Marty Wolfson.

FOCUS

With Europe's Champion Miler running in the Classic, the foreign representation in this race was numerically strong but lacking a top-notch representative. Fast ground also counted against many of the raiders, and the first three home were all American-trained. The pace was strong and suited those who were held up.

NOTEBOOK

Miesque's Approval(USA), who became the oldest horse to ever win this race, is a come-from-behind performer who needs a strong pace to be seen at his best. A steady gallop caught him out when he could only finish fourth behind Aussie Rules last time, but he had won four of his previous five starts and has a good turn of foot when getting a race run to suit. He swept past most of the field on the outside in the straight, eventually running out a clear winner and made a mockery of his odds of 25-1.

Aragorn(IRE), a much-improved performer since moving to the US and a winner of his last four starts, was in a similar position to the eventual winner a furlong and a half out, but he could not match that rival's turn of speed. He still edged the bunch finish for second, though, and all in all it was a solid effort. He now retires to stud.

Badge Of Silver(USA), who made all to win a Grade 2 handicap on his turf debut back in January, had been off the track since with foot problems, so it was some training performance to get him fit to run so well at this big meeting. In addition, the fact that he raced up with the strong gallop in a race in which the four horses who finished around him came from behind, suggests he put up a big effort, and further success on this surface looks assured providing he can be kept sound.

Sleeping Indian, winner of the Challenge Stakes last time out, had something to prove over this trip, but a sharp mile such as this was always going to present him with his best chance of getting home. Held up off the strong gallop, he was towards the rear on the inside turning into the straight and was denied a clear run until switched out wide. He finished well, but it was all too late. Coming here was an afterthought, for he was due to be retired to stud after the Challenge. Connections were frustrated he didn't finish second, but at least he advertised his versatility.

Rob Roy(USA), runner-up in the Champion Stakes on his previous start, missed the break slightly but his rider was happy to anchor him at the rear of the field. Soon outpaced, he was detached in last until he found the leaders coming back to him in the straight. He finished strongly, as befits a colt who gets ten furlongs, but the way the race panned out certainly flattered him. He is to continue his career with Neil Drysdale in the States.

Silent Name(JPN), who was responsible for the fast pace of this race, enjoyed an uncontested lead. He did not fold up without a battle, and was not beaten far by the runner-up, suggesting that he ran right up to his best in defeat.

Gorella(FR), third in this race last year, had the race pan out as she would have wanted as her trademark is a late finish off a good pace. She failed to deliver this time, though, and can have little excuse.

Aussie Rules(USA) has two wins to his name at the top level, but both his French Guineas win and Shadwell Turf Mile success came in races in which he found the best turn of foot in races run at a steady early gallop. The pace was anything but steady on this occasion, though, and he was exposed.

Araafa(IRE), winner of the Irish Guineas and runner-up to George Washington in the QEII last time out, looked to be the best of the European-trained horses in the race, but his best form is definitely on softish ground so these conditions were not ideal, and in the race itself he was ridden plenty close enough to the pace, and pretty wide, in a race run at a strong gallop.

Librettist(USA), disappointing in the QEII, is another who has shown his best form with some give, and he could not make the most of what looked a nice run through on the inside in the home straight.

Ad Valorem(USA), whose best form is on straight tracks, paid the price for chasing the fast gallop.

Echo Of Light, a progressive performer this season who won a French Group 2 last time out, had been successful on his previous four starts on left-handed tracks. However, on the flip side, he has now only beaten one horse home in three starts at Group/Grade 1 level. Probably best with some cut and when allowed his own way in front, this time his cause was harmed by racing too freely close to a strong pace.

6343a EMIRATES AIRLINE BREEDERS' CUP DISTAFF (GRADE 1) (F&M) 1m 1f (D)

8:55 (8:59) 3-Y-0+ **£709,535** (£262,791; £131,395; £67,012; £32,849)

RPR

1 **Round Pond (USA)**^{28} [5818] 4-8-11 .... EPrado 1 121
(M Matz, U.S.A) *always close up, 3rd on inside straight, led 1 1/2f out, driven out* **16/1**

2 *4 ¾* **Happy Ticket (USA)**^{27} 5-8-11 .... GKGomez 13 120
(A Leggio Jr, U.S.A) *mid-div, hdwy over 2f out, 4th str, hrd rdn to go 2nd 1f out, lost 2nd close home, finished 3rd, 4¼l & ½l placed 2nd* **14/1**

3 *1* **Balletto (UAE)**^{28} [5818] 4-8-11 .... CNakatani 14 118
(T Albertrani, U.S.A) *hld up in rear, hdwy on outside & 6th str, rdn & hung left wl over 1f out, hung lft in fnl f, kept on one pace, fin 4th, pl 3rd* **7/1**^{3}

4 **Asi Siempre (USA)**^{27} 4-8-11 ....(b) JRLeparoux 12 120
(P L Biancone, U.S.A) *held up, headway & 7th straight, brushed with 4th 1f out, ran on to take 2nd close home, disqualified & placed 4th* **12/1**

5 *nk* **Lemons Forever (USA)**^{27} 3-8-8 .... MGuidry 5 109
(D Stewart, U.S.A) *outpaced, 11th straight, nearest at finish* **25/1**

6 *½* **Sharp Lisa (USA)**^{27} 4-8-11 ....(b) PValenzuela 4 109
(Doug O'Neill, U.S.A) *prominent, pressed leader well over 2f out, 2nd straight, one pace final f* **50/1**

7 *nk* **Baghdaria (USA)**^{29} 3-8-8 .... RBejarano 8 108
(T Amoss, U.S.A) *chased leaders, 4th straight, no extra final f* **33/1**

8 *2 ¾* **Spun Sugar (USA)**^{27} 4-8-11 .... MLuzzi 6 103
(T Pletcher, U.S.A) *mid-division, 8th & beaten straight* **9/1**

9 6 1/4 **Pool Land (USA)**[55] [5228] 4-8-11 .... JRVelazquez 9 90
(T Pletcher, U.S.A) *pressed leaders, led 3f out to 1 1/2f out, soon weakened* **14/1**

10 4 1/4 **Hollywood Story (USA)**[34] 5-8-11 ....(b) DFlores 10 82
(J Shirreffs, U.S.A) *slowly into stride, outpaced, last to straight, always behind* **33/1**

11 20 **Bushfire (USA)**[56] 3-8-8 .... ASolis 11 44
(E Kenneally, U.S.A) *prominent 6f, 9th & beaten straight, eased* **33/1**

12 2 3/4 **Healthy Addiction (USA)**[34] 5-8-11 ....(b) VEspinoza 3 39
(J W Sadler, U.S.A) *led to 3f out, eased* **12/1**

F **Pine Island (USA)**[56] 3-8-8 .... JCastellano 2 —
(C McGaughey III, U.S.A) *12th when stumbled & fell 6f out, put down* **7/2**[2]

P **Fleet Indian (USA)**[28] [5818] 5-8-11 .... JSantos 7 —
(T Pletcher, U.S.A) *mid-division, eased from over 3f out, pulled up* **5/2**[1]

1m 50.5s
WFA 3 from 4yo+ 3lb **14** Ran SP% **122.5**
PARI-MUTUEL: WIN 29.80; PL (1-2) 14.00, 14.20; SHOW (1-2-3) 9.00,9.20, 5.60; SF 446.00.
Owner Fox Hill Farm **Bred** Trudy McCafferty & John Toffan **Trained** USA

FOCUS
Plenty of incident in the latest renewal of the Distaff, with two horses sadly going wrong and the second past the post disqualified. Round Pond won by four and a half lengths, but had the best draw and this was more competitive than the bare result might suggest.

NOTEBOOK
Round Pond(USA) had the best of the draw (four of the five winners on the dirt course won from stall one) and was given a good ride by Edgar Prado, who stuck to the inside rail whenever possible. Things would have been a lot closer had Asi Siempre got a clear run in the straight, and the bare result surely flatters her, but all that will be irrelevant when she becomes a broodmare - she is worth a fortune now.
Happy Ticket(USA), 11th in this race last year, ran a good race considering she had to come wide with her challenge but was no match whatsoever for the winner.
Balletto(UAE) did not get the best of trips - she was subsequently placed third by stewards having deemed to be hampered by Asi Siempre - but she was not unlucky.
Asi Siempre(USA) ◆, an ex-French filly who was campaigned exclusively on turf prior to her Grade 1 success on the Polytrack at Keenland on her previous start, looked most unlucky not to have won on this her first try on 'dirt'. She was flying in the straight, but had absolutely nowhere to go and had to be switched round the entire field with her run. It is a measure of her ability that she still managed to get up for second, but the stewards' deemed she interfered with Balletto, and disqualified her from the runner-up's spot and placed her behind the aforementioned Balletto. She could have much more to offer on sand if persevered with on the track.
Lemons Forever(USA) came wide into the straight from well off the pace and was never a danger.
Fleet Indian(USA), the leading older mare on the dirt in the US, was pulled up over three furlongs from the finish. She sadly suffered injuries to the suspensory ligament in her left front fetlock joint, but is expected to survive.
Pine Island(USA), a Grade 1 winner on her last two starts, met with a very sad ending. She stumbled and fell six furlongs from the finish and had to be put down after dislocating the fetlock joint in her left foreleg.

6344a JOHN DEERE BREEDERS' CUP TURF (GRADE 1) 1m 4f (T)
9:35 (9:43) 3-Y-0+ **£941,860** (£348,837; £174,419; £88,953; £43,605)

RPR

1 **Red Rocks (IRE)**[56] [5185] 3-8-10 .... LDettori 9 124
(B J Meehan) *hld up in 9th well off pace, headway over 3f out, 4th straight, strong run down outside to lead 200 yards out, driven out* **8/1**

2 1/2 **Better Talk Now (USA)**[41] 7-9-0 ....(b) RADominguez 8 121
(H G Motion, U.S.A) *held up well off pace in 10th, 8th straight, stayed on down outside to go 2nd 150 yards out, no extra last 50 yards* **16/1**

3 2 1/4 **English Channel (USA)**[28] [5821] 4-9-0 .... JRVelazquez 10 118
(T Pletcher, U.S.A) *in touch in 5th on outside, close 3rd straight, every chance 1f out, one pace* **4/1**[2]

4 1 1/2 **Rush Bay (USA)**[29] 4-9-0 .... RBejarano 5 115
(T Amoss, U.S.A) *disputed 2nd on outside, led under 4f out, headed 200 yards out, one pace* **40/1**

5 3/4 **Scorpion (IRE)**[27] [5854] 4-9-0 .... MJKinane 4 114
(A P O'Brien, Ire) *disputed 2nd on inside, 2nd straight, one pace fianl 1 1/2f* **5/1**[3]

6 1/2 **Hurricane Run (IRE)**[21] [5964] 4-9-0 .... CSoumillon 7 114
(A Fabre, France) *raced in 6th, pushed along and lost place over 2f out, 9th straight, wandered under strong pressure but kept on last 1 1/2f* **3/1**[1]

7 3/4 **Go Deputy (USA)**[13] [6126] 6-9-0 .... OPeslier 1 112
(T Pletcher, U.S.A) *raced in 4th, 7th straight, soon ridden and not quicken* **12/1**

8 3/4 **T. H. Approval (USA)**[35] 5-9-0 ....(b) ASolis 2 111
(E Inda, U.S.A) *raced in 8th, headway on inside and 5th straight, soon weakened* **11/1**

9 1 3/4 **Silverfoot (USA)**[39] 6-9-0 .... MGuidry 11 109
(D Stewart, U.S.A) *always behind* **40/1**

10 2 3/4 **Cacique (IRE)**[56] [5199] 5-9-0 .... EPrado 6 105
(R J Frankel, U.S.A) *raced in 4th, 6th straight, soon weakened* **4/1**[2]

11 29 **Icy Atlantic (USA)**[28] [5821] 5-9-0 .... MLuzzi 3 61
(T Pletcher, U.S.A) *set fast pace til headed under 4f out, eased* **50/1**

2m 27.32s
WFA 3 from 4yo+ 6lb **11** Ran SP% **121.5**
PARI-MUTUEL: WIN 23.60; PL (1-2) 11.20, 17.40; SHOW (1-2-3) 6.20,10.00, 4.20; SF 450.80.
Owner J Paul Reddam **Bred** Ballylinch Stud **Trained** Manton, Wilts
■ A first Breeders' Cup success for trainer Brian Meehan, and a Grade 1 double on the day for Frankie Dettori.

FOCUS
Not a very strong renewal of the Breeders' Cup Turf and the leader went off too fast, setting the race up for the closers. Red Rocks, the only three-year-old in the race, showed much improved form under a cool waiting ride.

NOTEBOOK
Red Rocks(IRE) ◆ had produced some terrific efforts in top company prior to this, including when second to subsequent Arc winner Rail Link in the Grand Prix de Paris, and when maybe not quite seeing out just short of a mile six in the St Leger behind Sixties Icon on his latest start. Dropped back in trip, this success owes a lot to a fine ride from Frankie Dettori, who held his mount up a long way off the pace, and produced him with a well-timed challenge to win in determined fashion. It is easy enough to knock this form and say everything fell into place on the day, but he promises to make an even better four-year-old. He may start his season in Dubai and could go very close if taking his chance in the Sheema Classic.
Better Talk Now(USA), the winner of this race in 2004 but only seventh last year, was another to benefit from the strong pace and ran a huge race. He was clear of the remainder and really is a fine servant.
English Channel(USA), the easy winner of the Joe Hirsch Turf Classic Invitational on his previous start, fared best of those to race close to the strong pace and emerges with a bundle of credit.
Rush Bay(USA) had plenty to find with most of these and his chance would not have been helped by racing so close to the strong gallop, so this must rate as a huge effort. It is hard to seen where this came from, though, and for the time being he anchors the form.
Scorpion(IRE) ran a terrific race on his return from a serious injury when second in a Listed race at the Curragh on his previous start, but this was always going to be a big ask turned out again so soon. Although running with credit, he was below his best and probably just paid late on for chasing the silly pace. He can do better again.
Hurricane Run(IRE) continues to follow in the footsteps of his sire Montjeu, who landed the Arc as a three-year-old, but was beaten in the race at four before failing in the Champion Stakes and again in the Breeders' Cup Turf. Many will be quick to knock him for not reproducing his very best form as his career nears its conclusion, but there are valid excuses for his last three defeats, with the ground too quick for him this time and his rider reporting he was not comfortable on the track. Whatever connections decide to do with him now, it should not be forgotten that he was quite brilliant on his day.
Icy Atlantic(USA) went off too fast and set this up for the closers.

6345a BREEDERS' CUP CLASSIC - POWERED BY DODGE (GRADE 1) 1m 2f (D)
10:20 (10:31) 3-Y-0£**1,569,767** (£581,395; £290,698; £148,256; £72,674)

RPR

1 **Invasor (ARG)**[91] 4-9-0 ....(b) FJara 11 127+
(K McLaughlin, U.S.A) *mid-division, headway from 4f out, 5th on outside straight, driven to lead 150yds out, ran on well* **11/2**[3]

2 1 **Bernardini (USA)**[28] [5822] 3-8-10 .... JCastellano 3 125
(T Albertrani, U.S.A) *a in tch, smooth headway from 3f out, 2nd straight, led well over 1f out, ridden & headed 150yds out, one pace* **5/4**[1]

3 2 1/2 **Premium Tap (USA)**[35] 4-9-0 .... EPrado 2 121
(J Kimmel, U.S.A) *always prominent, 3rd straight, kept on same pace under pressure* **33/1**

4 1 **Giacomo (USA)**[28] [5826] 4-9-0 .... MESmith 9 119
(J Shirreffs, U.S.A) *in rear, 11th straight, ran on under pressure to take 4th close home* **40/1**

5 1/2 **Brother Derek (USA)**[28] [5826] 3-8-10 .... ASolis 1 118
(Dan L Hendricks, U.S.A) *led to well over 1f out, kept on one pace* **20/1**

6 2 **George Washington (IRE)**[42] [5524] 3-8-10 .... MJKinane 4 115
(A P O'Brien, Ire) *mid-division, 6th & not much room straight, soon ridden & one pace* **4/1**[2]

7 8 3/4 **Lava Man (USA)**[28] [5826] 5-9-0 ....(b) CNakatani 8 99
(Doug O'Neill, U.S.A) *tracked leaders to over 3f out, 8th & beaten straight* **9/1**

8 hd **Perfect Drift (USA)**[35] 7-9-0 .... GKGomez 6 98
(Murray W Johnson, U.S.A) *in rear to half-way, 7th on inside & ridden straight, never a factor* **40/1**

9 1/2 **Lawyer Ron (USA)**[42] 3-8-10 .... PValenzuela 5 97
(T Pletcher, U.S.A) *pressed leader til over 2f out, 4th & hung right straight, weakened steadily* **33/1**

10 3/4 **Sun King (USA)**[63] 4-9-0 ....(b) RBejarano 13 96
(N Zito, U.S.A) *10th straight, always behind* **25/1**

11 1 1/2 **Flower Alley (USA)**[63] 4-9-0 ....(b) JRVelazquez 10 93
(T Pletcher, U.S.A) *prominent 6f, 9th & beaten straight* **25/1**

12 25 **Suave (USA)**[63] 5-9-0 ....(b) KDesormeaux 12 48
(P McGee, U.S.A) *always towards rear* **50/1**

13 dist **David Junior (USA)**[119] [3314] 4-9-0 .... JamieSpencer 7 —
(B J Meehan) *mid-division til weakening 4f out, tailed off* **10/1**

2m 2.18s
WFA 3 from 4yo+ 4lb **13** Ran SP% **124.1**
PARI-MUTUEL: WIN 15.40; PL (1-2) 5.80, 3.40; SHOW (1-2-3) 4.60, 3.00,8.80; SF 39.60.
Owner Shadwell Stable **Bred** Haras Clausan **Trained** USA
■ Fernando Jara, 18, became the youngest rider ever to win a Breeders' Cup race.

FOCUS
They went a decent pace here and, while the track bias in favour of those drawn low was still significant, both the winner and fourth, who were drawn out wider, managed to overcome it, mainly as result of the strong gallop.

NOTEBOOK
Invasor(ARG), only beaten in one of his previous nine career starts (by the very promising Discreet Cat in Dubai), overcame a severe track bias to win from a double-figure stall. He may have been suited by the strong pace, but he was forced wide turning into the straight and had to battle to stay on past the three lowest-drawn horses, who entered the straight in front. He is clearly a very smart performer on dirt and the Dubai World Cup is now a possible target.
Bernardini(USA), winner of his last six starts, including the Preakness, raced a bit wider than he had to - his rider had taken a heavy fall in the Distaff when racing near the inside rail - and raced close enough to the pace given that they went a fair lick in front. Asked for his effort a good way from home, he did not draw clear as he has been used to, and found himself in unfamiliar territory as he was forced to battle up the straight. Although beaten by the more patiently ridden Invasor, he still finished clear of the rest, and he probably did not run much below his best, if at all, in defeat. It could be worth his connections persevering with him as a four-year-old as he could well improve again next year, but the plan is apparently to send him to stud now.
Premium Tap(USA), who had his excuses when finishing seven lengths behind Invasor in the Whitney Handicap earlier in the season, was well drawn and his rider made the most of it, scraping paint most of the way and only finding a couple of the market leaders too strong. He ran right up to his best, but there is a suspicion he was flattered by being able to race on the inside.
Giacomo(USA), who was a shock winner of last year's Kentucky Derby, has not done a lot since, but he does not get his conditions very often. A proper come-from-behind horse, he needs the leaders to go off like scalded cats for him to show his best. The pace was strong this time, and he stayed on in good style from well off the pace to take fourth, but he would have liked it even fiercer.
Brother Derek(USA), fourth in both the Kentucky Derby and Preakness earlier in the season, is probably more effective over a bit shorter than this, but he was not ridden like a non-stayer as his rider made the most of his good stall position in one and tried to make every yard. He set a strong pace and Bernardini took a while to get past him, but he faltered late on, paying for his earlier efforts. His good draw and the route he took on the faster ground on the inside were a big advantage and contributed greatly to him being able to hold on to fifth place.
George Washington(IRE), Europe's Champion Miler, was thought by connections to have nothing left to prove on turf so, for commercial reasons, they opted to run him in this race. Debuting on dirt and tackling ten furlongs for the first time, he had plenty to prove, and in the circumstances he ran a fine race. His rider did not put a foot wrong, making the most of his low draw and keeping him close to the favoured inside rail until swinging wide into the straight. It was at that point that the three-year-old's stamina began to give out, but he certainly did not have any problems with the dirt surface.
Lava Man(USA), a winner on his last six starts, had run poorly on each of his three previous trips outside of California, and that trend continued here, despite the fact that he had been brought over early to acclimatise.
Perfect Drift(USA), who has run in this race for the past four years, improving from finishing last on his first appearance, to finishing sixth in 2003, fourth in 2004 and third last year, failed to continue that progressive trend despite having the race run to suit.
David Junior(USA) had been kept fresh for this as he had not raced since winning the Eclipse in July, and his American pedigree offered hope that he would take to this surface, but in the event he failed to run any sort of race and it is difficult to believe that something was not amiss.

5817 FLEMINGTON (L-H)
Saturday, November 4

OFFICIAL GOING: Soft

6346a SAAB QUALITY H'CAP (GROUP 3) 1m 4f 110y
12:55 (12:55) 4-Y-0+

£65,812 (£19,231; £9,615; £4,808; £2,671; £2,137)

RPR
1 **Maybe Better (AUS)**[21] 4-9-0 .... SArnold 20 111
(B Mayfield-Smith, Australia) **17/2**[2]
2 nk **Irazu (AUS)**[28] 5817 3-8-2 .... DDunn 3 106
(S J Richards, Australia) **25/1**
3 2 ¼ **Vanquished (AUS)**[10] 6-8-11 ....(b) KerrinMcEvoy 4 105
(B Murray, Australia) **38/10**[1]
4 1 ½ **Grand Zulu (AUS)**[14] 6110 5-9-2 ....(b) DBeadman 2 107
(J Size, Hong Kong) **10/1**[3]
5 2 ¾ **Magic Instinct**[28] 4-8-2 ....(b) CMunce 6 89
(P Moody, New Zealand)
6 1 **Soulacroix**[41] 5548 5-8-7 .... SSeamer 13 93
(L M Cumani) *broke well racing in 6th, 3l off lead, was 9th, 6 lengths back 5f out, came 5 wide and stayed on in straight* **40/1**
7 1 ¼ **Sarrera (AUS)** 6-8-11 .... GChilds 14 95
(M Moroney, Australia)
8 shd **Cefalu (CHI)**[10] 5-8-6 .... JimCassidy 19 90
(Lee Freedman, Australia)
9 nk **Loanhead (NZ)**[147] 3-8-2 .... GBoss 11 92
(P Moody, New Zealand)
10 nk **Aznavour (NZ)**[28] 5817 4-8-2 .... SBaster 17 85
(Danny O'Brien, Australia)
11 ½ **Genebel (AUS)**[28] 5817 5-8-2 .... BMelham 9 84
(M Moroney & A Scott, New Zealand)
12 1 ¼ **Dracs Back (AUS)**[10] 5-8-2 ....(b) BShinn 1 82
(D Weir, Australia)
13 8 **On The Up (AUS)** 5-8-2 .... DGauci 15 70
(J Hawkes, Australia)
14 1 **Ice Chariot (AUS)**[14] 6110 4-8-10 .... JimByrne 10 84
(R Maund, Australia)
15 1 **Lord Erin (NZ)**[901] 7-8-2 ....(b) BPark 16 67
(G Dalziel, Australia)
16 2 **Defining**[400] 5589 7-8-9 ....(b) CraigAWilliams 12 71
(D Hayes, Australia)
17 8 **Roanoke (AUS)** 4-8-2 .... DMoor 21 52
(A Cummings, Australia)
18 1 **Zabeat (NZ)**[196] 7-9-0 ....(b) CoreyBrown 8 63
(Donna Logan, New Zealand)

2m 35.86s
WFA 3 from 4yo+ 6lb **18** Ran SP% **46.7**

.

Owner J Horvat & B Da Silva Jorge **Bred** J & Mrs N Horvat & B & Mrs A Da Silva Jorge **Trained** Australia

NOTEBOOK
Soulacroix has not thrived since arriving in Australia and ran only a fair race, keeping on steadily in the home straight.

6347a MOTOROLA MACKINNON STKS (GROUP 1) 1m 2f
4:45 (4:45) 3-Y-0+

£194,444 (£57,692; £28,846; £14,423; £8,013; £6,410)

RPR
1 **Desert War (AUS)**[28] 5-9-2 ....(b) CMunce 7 121
(Mrs Gai Waterhouse, Australia) **6/1**[2]
2 2 ¼ **Growl (NZ)**[14] 6110 4-9-1 .... CraigAWilliams 1 116
(D Hayes, Australia) **13/1**
3 hd **Aqua D'Amore (AUS)**[7] 6231 4-8-10 .... SBaster 6 111
(Mrs Gai Waterhouse, Australia) **8/1**[3]
4 4 **El Segundo (NZ)**[7] 6231 5-9-2 .... DGauci 9 109
(C Little, Australia) **18/10**[1]
5 1 ½ **Roman Arch (AUS)**[14] 6110 7-9-2 ....(b) CNewitt 8 107
(R Laing, Australia)
6 1 ¼ **Legs (NZ)**[28] 4-8-9 .... SArnold 3 97
(K Gray, New Zealand)
7 1 ¾ **Headturner (AUS)**[14] 6110 4-9-1 .... DBeadman 4 100
(J Hawkes, Australia)
8 shd **Imperial Stride**[45] 5477 5-9-2 .... KerrinMcEvoy 5 101
(Saeed Bin Suroor) *broke wl enough: rdn to hold place, raced in 11th 8l off lead, effort wide 7f out, ridden entering straight, no extra* **11/1**
9 snk **King Of Ashford (NZ)**[252] 6-9-2 .... NashRawiller 14 101
(Karen Zimmerman, New Zealand)
10 1 ½ **Railings (AUS)**[14] 6110 5-9-2 .... GChilds 15 98
(J Hawkes, Australia)
11 2 ½ **Temple Hills (NZ)**[21] 4-9-2 ....(b) LNolen 12 94
(P Moody, New Zealand)
12 shd **Purde (NZ)**[42] 5544 3-8-9 .... DDunn 13 90
(P Gatt, France)
13 snk **Sphenophyta (NZ)**[14] 6110 6-9-2 .... GBoss 2 93
(Lee Freedman, Australia)
14 3 ½ **Molotov (AUS)**[28] 4-9-2 .... MZahra 10 87
(J Conlan, Australia)
15 4 **Accumulate (NZ)**[28] 5-9-2 ....(b) StevenKing 11 80
(J B Cummings, Australia)

2m 2.38s
WFA 3 from 4yo+ 4lb **15** Ran SP% **76.6**

.

Owner Gooree Pastoral Company Syndicate **Bred** Gooree Park Stud Pty Ltd **Trained** Australia

NOTEBOOK
Imperial Stride ran without sparkle and it transpired that he had struck into himself. He will be sent to Dubai to recover.

6186 LINGFIELD (L-H)
Sunday, November 5

OFFICIAL GOING: Standard
Wind: Virtually nil

6348 GUY FAWKES (S) STKS 6f (P)
1:30 (1:30) (Class 6) 3-4-Y-0 **£2,590** (£770; £385; £192) **Stalls** Low

Form RPR
2203 1 **Carcinetto (IRE)**[2] 6325 4-8-12 55 .... J-PGuillambert 6 63
(P D Evans) *led tl rdn and hdd over 2f out: led again last 100 yds: hung lft and bmpd rival nr fin* **7/2**[1]
6566 2 ½ **Shunkawakhan (IRE)**[19] 6033 3-8-12 52 ....(b) OscarUrbina 3 61
(G C H Chung) *trckd ldrs: hdwy to chse ldng pair over 2f out: rdn over 1f out: ev ch ins fnl f: jst hld whn bmpd nr fin* **20/1**
0010 3 1 ½ **Came Back (IRE)**[19] 6033 3-9-3 64 .... JimCrowley 12 64+
(J A Osborne) *t.k.h: trckd ldrs: hdwy to ld over 2f out: rdn wl over 1f out: hdd last 100 yds: btn whn short of room nr fin* **14/1**
1130 4 nk **Mountain Pass (USA)**[10] 6193 4-9-3 56 ....(p) DaneO'Neill 7 61+
(M J Wallace) *slowly away: hld up in rr: rdn and hdwy over 2f out: r.o wl fnl f: nt rch ldrs* **7/1**
6005 5 1 ½ **What Do You Know**[66] 4943 3-8-12 68 ....(t) FJohansson 11 51
(G A Butler) *racd in midfield: effrt u.p over 2f out: chsd ldng trio over 1f out: no imp* **4/1**[2]
3410 6 1 ¼ **Cool Sting (IRE)**[18] 6061 3-9-3 65 ....(v) BrianReilly 10 52
(P S McEntee) *slowly away: sn in tch in midfield on outer: hdwy u.p over 2f out: no hdwy wl over 1f out* **5/1**[3]
006 7 ½ **Rowe Park**[61] 5093 3-8-12 55 .... AdamKirby 2 46
(Mrs L C Jewell) *slowly away: sn rcvrd and chsng ldrs: rdn over 2f out: wknd wl over 1f out* **50/1**
2350 8 hd **Memphis Man**[19] 6033 3-8-12 66 .... RoryMoore(5) 5 50
(D G Bridgwater) *taken down early: slowly away: a bhd: no ch last 2f* **10/1**
0034 9 shd **Diamond Josh**[13] 6142 4-9-0 53 .... StephenDonohoe(3) 1 50
(P D Evans) *racd in midfield on inner: rdn over 2f out: wknd over 1f out* **15/2**
0401 10 5 **Crafty Fox**[5] 6277 3-9-3 54 .... DarryllHolland 4 35
(A P Jarvis) *a bhd: last and rdn over 2f out: nvr on terms* **7/1**
5060 11 5 **Titus Maximus (IRE)**[78] 4587 3-8-7 60 .... EmmettStack(5) 8 15
(H J Manners) *t.k.h: chsd wnr tl hmpd wl over 3f out: rdn and wknd qckly wl over 2f out* **66/1**
2060 12 10 **Glenargo (USA)**[7] 6234 3-8-10 49 ....(p) TolleyDean(7) 9 —
(R A Harris) *w ldrs: chsd wnr wl over 3f out tl over 2f out: sn wknd: eased fnl f: t.o* **50/1**

1m 11.85s (-0.96) **Going Correction** -0.05s/f (Stan) **12** Ran SP% **121.6**
Speed ratings (Par 101):104,103,101,100,98 97,96,96,96,89 82,69
CSF £79.48 TOTE £3.80: £1.50, £5.90, £6.60; EX 103.00 TRIFECTA Not won..The winner was bought in for 6,200gns. Diamond Josh was claimed by Michael Mullineaux for £6,000.
Owner J L Guillambert **Bred** M A Doyle **Trained** Pandy, Abergavenny
■ Stewards' Enquiry : J-P Guillambert 17-day ban (takes into account previous offences; three days deferred): careless riding (Nov 23-Dec 8)

FOCUS
A modest event, as is to be expected in selling company. The time was reasonable for the grade and the form looks sound, rated around the first two.

6349 LINGFIELD PARK FOR CHRISTMAS PARTIES MAIDEN FILLIES' STKS 1m (P)
2:00 (2:01) (Class 5) 2-Y-0 **£4,416** (£1,321; £660; £330; £164) **Stalls** High

Form RPR
1 **Happy Go Lily** 2-9-0 .... AdamKirby 4 74+
(W R Swinburn) *slowly away: wl bhd: pushed along and gd hdwy over 2f out: qcknd to ld wl ins fnl f: readily* **12/1**
2 1 **Lacework** 2-9-0 .... RyanMoore 6 72
(Sir Michael Stoute) *chsd ldrs: rdn and hdwy on outer over 2f out: ev ch: 1f out: nt pce of wnr wl ins fnl f* **5/2**[1]
6 3 ¾ **Penny From Heaven (IRE)**[7] 6242 2-9-0 .... BrettDoyle 11 70
(E A L Dunlop) *chsd ldr: rdn over 2f out: led over 1f out: hdd wl ins fnl f: fdd cl home* **4/1**[2]
4 hd **Market Forces** 2-9-0 .... RichardHughes 8 70
(H R A Cecil) *slowly away: bhd: outpcd and pushed along wl over 3f out: styd on over 1f out: nrst fin* **5/2**[1]
5 nk **Set The Scene (IRE)** 2-9-0 .... DavidKinsella 1 69+
(J H M Gosden) *v.s.a: sn in tch in rr: hdwy 3f out: chsd ldrs 2f out: no ex ins fnl f* **9/1**
0 6 2 ½ **On The Map**[16] 6071 2-9-0 .... DarryllHolland 12 63
(A P Jarvis) *racd in midfield: rdn and outpcd wl over 2f out: kpt on over 1f out: nt pce to trble ldrs* **33/1**
00 7 1 ¾ **Muffett's Dream**[19] 6023 2-9-0 .... RichardThomas 9 59
(J A Geake) *sn led rdn and hdd over 1f out: wknd ins fnl f* **33/1**
00 8 nk **Chiff Chaff**[16] 6071 2-9-0 .... JamieMackay 7 58
(M L W Bell) *chsd ldrs on inner: rdn over 2f out: wknd over 1f out* **33/1**
0 9 2 ½ **Polyquest (IRE)**[69] 4866 2-9-0 .... JoeFanning 10 53
(P F I Cole) *slowly away: hld up in rr on outer: outpcd wl over 3f out: n.d after* **25/1**
0 10 ½ **Susie May**[16] 6071 2-9-0 .... AbdulAziz 5 51
(C A Cyzer) *rn green and sn struggling in rr: no ch whn hung rt last 2f* **50/1**
6 11 3 ½ **Lady Traill**[16] 6073 2-9-0 .... MichaelHills 3 43
(B W Hills) *a bhd: rdn over 4f out: no ch last 3f* **8/1**[3]
12 1 ¾ **Pink Salmon** 2-9-0 .... IanMongan 2 39
(Mrs L J Mongan) *slowly away: sn rcvrd and in tch in midfield: rdn and lost pl 3f out: sn bhd* **33/1**

1m 40.65s (1.22) **Going Correction** -0.05s/f (Stan) **12** Ran SP% **123.5**
Speed ratings (Par 93):91,90,89,89,88 86,84,84,81,81 77,75
CSF £41.76 TOTE £15.80: £3.60, £1.90, £1.30; EX 59.90 Trifecta £105.40 Part won. Pool £148.48 - 0.53 winning units..
Owner Donal Cunningham **Bred** Razza Pallorsi **Trained** Aldbury, Herts

FOCUS
The bare form is probably just fair but there were some encouraging efforts from nicely-bred newcomers.

The Form Book, Raceform Ltd, Compton, RG20 6NL

NOTEBOOK

Happy Go Lily ◆, a 65,000gns purchase, closely related to quite useful Paris Winds, out of a triple seven-furlong juvenile scorer who also won the Group 3 Nell Gwyn Stakes at three, was given a patient ride by Kirby and, without being harassed, made good headway onto the heels of the leading bunch before quickening nicely when the gap opened inside the distance. Her rider was never at any point forced to use his whip and she gave the impression there is a deal more to come next year. Connections rate her highly and she is regarded as 'something to look forward to next season' by her trainer. (op 11-1 tchd 14-1)

Lacework is a full sister to Cyclical and Envision and she shaped nicely on debut, staying on for pressure in the closing stages, although she did not ever have the turn of foot of the winner. (op 2-1 tchd 11-4)

Penny From Heaven(IRE) did not shape too badly on her debut and built on that, quickening to the front on the turn for home before being readily brushed aside by the winner.

Market Forces came under pressure some way out having been held up off the pace but it was not until she straightened up for home that she began to pick up down the middle of the track. (op 4-1)

Set The Scene(IRE) ◆ was another newcomer to catch the eye in defeat, making good headway from off the pace before keeping on. She is the first foal of Irish Oaks winner Margarula and looks the type to do much better upped in trip next year.

6350 LINGFIELD PARK GOLF COURSE FILLIES' H'CAP — 1m (P)

2:30 (2:30) (Class 4) (0-85,83) 3-Y-O+

£7,478 (£2,239; £1,119; £560; £279; £140) **Stalls** High

Form	Pos	Dist	Horse / Details	Odds	RPR
5141	1		**Persian Express (USA)**[36] 5666 3-9-4 **83** MichaelHills 4 (B W Hills) *chsd ldrs: wnt 2nd over 2f out: rdn to ld over 1f: styd on wl and in command fnl f*	4/1[2]	94
2323	2	¾	**Neardown Beauty (IRE)**[26] 5896 3-8-7 **75** JamesDoyle(3) 5 (I A Wood) *stdd s: hld up in rr: hdwy over 2f out: weaved through over 1f out: wnt 2nd wl ins fnl f: r.o: nt rch wnr*	6/1[3]	84+
1003	3	¾	**Kasumi**[15] 6094 3-8-9 **74** SteveDrowne 1 (H Morrison) *chsd ldrs: rdn wl over 3f out:chsd wnr ins fnl f: no imp and demoted wl ins fnl f*	14/1	82
3333	4	¾	**All Quiet**[28] 5833 5-8-12 **75** RichardHughes 6 (R Hannon) *hld up in rr: hdwy on outer over jst over 1f out: r.o ins fnl f: nt rch ldrs*	4/1[2]	81+
6000	5	2	**Spring Goddess (IRE)**[8] 6226 5-9-0 **77** DarryllHolland 2 (A P Jarvis) *t.k.h: hld up in midfield: rdn and outpcd over 2f out: styd on ins fnl f: nt trble ldrs*	13/2	78+
6560	6	hd	**Night Storm**[48] 5436 5-8-7 **70** PaulDoe 8 (S Dow) *slowly away: hld up: rdn and hdwy over 2f out: chsd ldrs over 1f out: wknd 1f out*	14/1	71
-161	7	1 ¾	**Felicitous**[37] 5649 3-9-4 **83** NCallan 11 (Saeed Bin Suroor) *t.k.h: hld up in tch: rdn and effrt over 2f out: wknd over 1f out*	7/2[1]	80
0200	8	nk	**Pommes Frites**[6] 6259 3-8-9 **74** ow1 AdamKirby 10 (W R Muir) *sn chsng ldr: qcknd to ld 3f out: drvn over 2f out: hdd over 1f out: fdd*	40/1	70
1600	9	1 ¼	**Virtuosity**[32] 5769 3-9-3 **82** RyanMoore 3 (Sir Michael Stoute) *t.k.h: hld up in rr: rdn and effrt over 2f out: wknd wl over 1f out*	12/1	75
6165	10	1	**Tawaajud (USA)**[53] 5294 3-8-11 **76** RHills 9 (B W Hills) *led at stdy pce: hdd and rdn 3f out: wknd 2f out*	12/1	67

1m 39.46s (0.03) **Going Correction** -0.05s/f (Stan) 10 Ran SP% **121.0**
WFA 3 from 4yo+ 2lb
Speed ratings (Par 102):97,96,95,94,92 92,90,90,89,88
CSF £29.57 CT £313.65 TOTE £5.70: £3.10, £2.00, £5.90; EX 36.40 TRIFECTA Not won..
Owner D M James **Bred** Kingswood Farm **Trained** Lambourn, Berks

FOCUS
A reasonable handicap, but they did not go particularly quick early on and a few were pulling for their heads. The form may not prove that reliable but has been rated reasonably positively.

6351 JUMPING HERE ON WEDNESDAY H'CAP — 1m 4f (P)

3:00 (3:01) (Class 4) (0-85,85) 3-Y-O+

£7,478 (£2,239; £1,119; £560; £279; £140) **Stalls** Low

Form	Pos	Dist	Horse / Details	Odds	RPR
1003	1		**Sweet Indulgence (IRE)**[30] 5792 5-8-13 **79** StephenDonohoe(3) 13 (W J Musson) *hld up in rr: hdwy over 2f out: rdn over 1f out: str run to ld last 50 yds*	9/2[2]	89
0031	2	¾	**Lisathedaddy**[16] 6070 4-8-7 **73** RichardKingscote(3) 2 (B G Powell) *trckd ldrs on inner: rdn and sltly outpce over 2f out: rallied over 1f out: wnt 2nd and ev ch wl ins fnl f: no ex*	15/2[3]	82
0300	3	1	**Solo Flight**[44] 5511 9-9-3 **80** SteveDrowne 3 (H Morrison) *t.k.h: w.w in tch: hdwy over 2f out: ever ch over 1f out: onepced u.p wl ins fnl f*	16/1	87
0643	4	¾	**Royal Amnesty**[16] 6076 3-8-8 **77** (b) OscarUrbina 10 (G C H Chung) *hld up in tch: hdwy gng wl 3f out: rdn to chal 2f out: led 1f out: hdd last 50 yds: fdd nr fin*	10/1	83
0-00	5	¾	**Eva Soneva So Fast (IRE)**[24] 5920 4-9-2 **79** JimmyQuinn 9 (J L Dunlop) *stdd s: plld hrd and hld up: hdwy into midfield 7f out: rdn and outpcd 2f out: kpt on u.p last 100 yds*	14/1	84
0464	6	1 ½	**Trans Sonic**[20] 6008 3-8-9 **78** (v) DarryllHolland 11 (A P Jarvis) *stdd s: hld up in rr: hdwy on outer 3f out: kpt on same pce over 1f out*	11/1	80
0051	7	hd	**Kyles Prince (IRE)**[13] 6148 4-9-1 **78** J-PGuillambert 6 (P J Makin) *t.k.h: hld up in midfield: hdwy over 3f out: rdn to ld wl over 2f out: hdd 1f out: wknd ins fnl f*	11/8[1]	80
1304	8	2 ½	**Polish Power (GER)**[13] 6148 6-8-13 **76** LPKeniry 5 (J S Moore) *slowly away: hld up in rr: pushed along 4f out: no ch after*	12/1	74
042	9	5	**Top Seed (IRE)**[36] 5671 5-8-7 **77** MarkCoumbe(7) 12 (A J Chamberlain) *hld up in tch in rr: effrt u.p over 2f out: no hdwy last 2f*	14/1	67
056	10	nk	**La Estrella (USA)**[18] 6053 3-9-0 **83** JamieMackay 1 (J G Given) *t.k.h: sn led tl hdd after 2f: chsd ldr tl over 4f out: sn lost pl and no ch after*	12/1	73
0000	11	¾	**Gig Harbor**[15] 6097 7-9-8 **85** NCallan 8 (Miss E C Lavelle) *t.k.h: trckd ldrs: ev ch 3f out: sn rdn: wknd over 1f out*	20/1	73
0-1	12	3 ½	**Jidaar (IRE)**[184] 1458 3-8-11 **80** RobertMiles 4 (P W Hiatt) *t.k.h: trckd ldrs: wnt 2nd over 4f out: led 3f out: sn hdd: wknd qckly*	25/1	63
3536	13	1 ¼	**Kylkenny**[15] 6108 11-9-1 **83** (t) CAdamson(5) 7 (H Morrison) *led after 2f tl 3f out: sn wknd*	33/1	64

2m 32.74s (-1.65) **Going Correction** -0.05s/f (Stan) 13 Ran SP% **135.6**
WFA 3 from 4yo+ 6lb
Speed ratings (Par 105):103,102,101,101,100 99,99,98,94,94 94,91,90
CSF £43.27 CT £534.82 TOTE £7.60: £1.40, £3.60, £5.60; EX 86.60 Trifecta £141.40 Part won. Pool £199.29 - 0.52 winning units..
Owner Broughton Thermal Insulation **Bred** Mrs M Campbell-Andenaes **Trained** Newmarket, Suffolk

FOCUS
They went a steady early pace here before Kylkenny took up the running, but it resulted in something of a sprint finish and the form looks somewhat shaky.

Eva Soneva So Fast(IRE) Official explanation: jockey said gelding missed the break

Trans Sonic Official explanation: jockey said gelding ran too free

6352 LINGFIELDPARK.CO.UK H'CAP — 6f (P)

3:30 (3:30) (Class 4) (0-85,84) 3-Y-O+

£7,478 (£2,239; £1,119; £560; £279; £140) **Stalls** Low

Form	Pos	Dist	Horse / Details	Odds	RPR
2430	1		**Matuza (IRE)**[93] 4102 3-8-13 **79** DarryllHolland 10 (W R Muir) *racd in midfield: pushed along and outpcd over 2f out: hdwy on outer over 1f out: str run to ld on line*	13/2[3]	87
0640	2	nk	**Brandywell Boy (IRE)**[28] 5842 3-8-11 **77** (p) JimCrowley 8 (D J S Ffrench Davis) *in tch: effrt and swtchd rt 2f out: kpt on u.p:wnt 2nd on line*	12/1	84
2441	3	shd	**Woodnook**[30] 5782 3-9-0 **80** JoeFanning 9 (J A R Toller) *chsd ldrs: wnt 2nd 3f out: rdn to ld jst over 1f out: hdd cl home*	6/1[2]	87
3064	4	½	**Jimmy The Guesser**[15] 6094 3-8-13 **82** (b) JamesDoyle(3) 6 (N P Littmoden) *in tch: drvn and effrt over 2f out: hrd rdn and nt qckn over 1f out: kpt on nr fin*	6/1[2]	87
2210	5	1	**Forest Dane**[17] 6065 6-8-4 **77** WilliamBuick(7) 5 (Mrs N Smith) *hld up in tch: hdwy over 2f out: ch over 1f out: kpt on same pce wl ins fnl f*	17/2	79
0050	6	nk	**Bobski (IRE)**[80] 4535 4-9-0 **80** AdamKirby 1 (G A Huffer) *v.s.a: wl bhd: styd on u.p over 1f out: nt rch ldrs*	6/1[2]	81
2500	7	2	**Harry Up**[33] 5749 5-9-4 **84** NCallan 11 (K A Ryan) *led: rdn wl over 2f out: hdd jst over 1f out: wknd fnl f*	10/1	79+
0033	8	2	**Marko Jadeo (IRE)**[145] 2531 8-9-2 **82** DaneO'Neill 7 (S Dow) *slowly away: a bhd: nvr on terms*	16/1	71
1320	9	shd	**Sant Elena**[39] 5627 3-9-0 **80** SteveDrowne 12 (G Wragg) *a bhd: no hdwy u.p over 2f out*	7/1	69
3055	10	nk	**Hammer Of The Gods (IRE)**[31] 5777 6-8-13 **79** (bt) BrianReilly 4 (P S McEntee) *chsd ldr tl 1/2-way: wknd 2f out*	11/2[1]	67
0P05	11	1 ¼	**Chief Exec**[54] 5263 4-8-12 **78** AbdulAziz 2 (C A Cyzer) *hld up in rr: n.d*	20/1	62
0000	12	7	**Ocean Pride (IRE)**[40] 5591 3-9-0 **80** RichardHughes 3 (R Hannon) *chsd ldrs: rdn 3f out: sn struggling: eased ins fnl f: t.o*	16/1	43

1m 10.82s (-1.99) **Going Correction** -0.05s/f (Stan) 12 Ran SP% **127.9**
Speed ratings (Par 105):111,110,110,109,108 108,105,102,102,102 100,91
CSF £89.00 CT £509.66 TOTE £6.20: £2.10, £6.60, £2.30; EX 124.00 TRIFECTA Not won..
Owner The Eastwood Partnership **Bred** Round Hill Stud **Trained** Lambourn, Berks
■ Stewards' Enquiry : William Buick caution: careless riding

FOCUS
Another blanket finish dominated by horses finishing fast from off the pace, and the winning time was decent for the grade. The form looks sound with those in the frame behind the winner to their marks.

Bobski(IRE) Official explanation: jockey said gelding was slowly away

6353 NEXT MEETING AT FOLKESTONE NOVEMBER 14TH H'CAP — 5f (P)

4:00 (4:01) (Class 5) (0-75,75) 3-Y-O+ **£5,181** (£1,541; £770; £384) **Stalls** High

Form	Pos	Dist	Horse / Details	Odds	RPR
0032	1		**Little Edward**[19] 6035 8-9-3 **74** GeorgeBaker 7 (R J Hodges) *hld up in tch on outer: smooth run over 1f out: shkn up to ld last 100 yds: comf*	11/2[3]	84
1301	2	1 ½	**Heavens Walk**[78] 4587 5-8-12 **69** (t) SteveDrowne 8 (P J Makin) *t.k.h early: hld up hdwy over 2f out: swtchd rt wl over 1f out: r.o and wnt 2nd last 50 yds: no ch w wnr*	2/1[1]	74+
0400	3	¾	**Quality Street**[30] 5791 4-8-4 **68** (p) JosephWalsh(7) 1 (P Butler) *led: rdn over 1f out: hdd last 100 yds: no ch w wnr: lost 2nd last 50 yds*	25/1	70
2105	4	shd	**Overwing (IRE)**[19] 6035 3-9-4 **75** NCallan 6 (R M H Cowell) *in tch on outer: rdn over 2f out: ev ch u.p over 1f out: kpt on same pce*	9/1	77
4000	5	½	**Ever Cheerful**[8] 6223 5-8-6 **70** MarkCoumbe(7) 2 (D G Bridgwater) *bhd: rdn and outpcd wl over 2f out: styd on wl fnl f: nt trble ldrs*	11/1	70
2161	6	½	**Smiddy Hill**[66] 4952 4-8-13 **70** PatCosgrave 4 (R Bastiman) *s.i.s: sn rcvrd and chsng ldrs: wnt 2nd wl over 2f out: jnd ldr 2f out: no ex ins fnl f*	11/1	68
1504	7	shd	**Madame Medusa (IRE)**[9] 6204 3-9-1 **72** (b[1]) DarryllHolland 9 (J A R Toller) *hld up in rr: effrt on inner over 1f out: kpt on same pce fnl f*	5/1[2]	70
0020	8	¾	**Danjet (IRE)**[23] 5938 3-8-13 **73** StephenDonohoe(3) 5 (J M Bradley) *pressed ldr tl wl over 2f out: kpt on same pce u.p*	8/1	68
400	9	1 ½	**Lady Bahia (IRE)**[19] 6035 5-8-13 **70** RobertMiles 10 (Peter Grayson) *rrd s and v.s.a: nt rcvr and nvr on terms*	20/1	60
5005	10	nk	**Plateau**[53] 5291 7-8-12 **74** LiamJones(5) 3 (C R Dore) *broke wl: sn settled in tch: rdn and struggling over 2f out: no ch after*	9/1	63

58.84 secs (-0.94) **Going Correction** -0.05s/f (Stan) 10 Ran SP% **121.8**
Speed ratings (Par 103):105,102,101,101,100 99,99,98,95,95
CSF £17.69 CT £270.97 TOTE £6.10: £2.10, £1.60, £7.70; EX 16.10 Trifecta £261.80 Part won. Pool £368.85 - 0.67 winning units. Place 6 £269.28, Place 5 £ 85.39.
Owner J W Mursell **Bred** J W Mursell **Trained** Charlton Adam, Somerset

FOCUS
A fair handicap in which a strong pace resulted in the leaders stopping in front. The race is rated around the winner and fourth.

Lady Bahia(IRE) Official explanation: jockey said mare missed the break

T/Jkpt: Not won. T/Plt: £415.40 to a £1 stake. Pool: £65,587.10. 115.25 winning tickets. T/Qpdt: £37.40 to a £1 stake. Pool: £4,742.90. 93.80 winning tickets. SP

6354 - 6355a (Foreign Racing) - See Raceform Interactive

6261 LEOPARDSTOWN (L-H)

Sunday, November 5

OFFICIAL GOING: Yielding to soft

6356a KNOCKAIRE STKS (LISTED RACE) 7f

1:35 (1:36) 3-Y-O+ **£22,448** (£6,586; £3,137; £1,068)

			RPR
1		**Modeeroch (IRE)**[35] 5708 3-9-1 103................................(t) KJManning 2 (J S Bolger, Ire) *mid-div: 8th 3f out: 5th under 2f out: rdn to ld over 1f out: sn clr: comf* **8/1**[3]	108
2	2 ½	**Ugo Fire (IRE)**[28] 5849 3-8-12 105.................................. DPMcDonogh 7 (Kevin Prendergast, Ire) *mid-div: 8th under 3f out: impr into 4th early st: 2nd and chal over 1f out: kpt on wout troubling wnr* **6/4**[1]	98
3	1 ¼	**Eastern Appeal (IRE)**[21] 5996 3-8-12 94............................ JMurtagh 5 (M Halford, Ire) *hld up: rdn and kpt on wl fr over 1 1/2f out* **8/1**[3]	95
4	1 ½	**Ardbrae Lady**[21] 5996 3-8-12 105......................................(b[1]) WSupple 4 (Joseph G Murphy, Ire) *mid-div on inner: kpt on fr 2f out to go mod 4th cl home* **14/1**	91
5	nk	**Danehill Music (IRE)**[6] 6267 3-9-3 100..........................(b) WMLordan 3 (David Wachman, Ire) *hld up towards rr: kpt on st* **16/1**	95
6	¾	**Lee Applause**[22] 5979 4-8-13 63.............................. NGMcCullagh 12 (Edward P Harty, Ire) *towards rr: kpt on u.p st* **100/1**	88?
7	1	**Chenchikova (IRE)**[6] 6267 3-8-12 95............................. JAHeffernan 10 (A P O'Brien, Ire) *towards rr: kpt on one pce st* **10/1**	86
8	nk	**Cheyenne Star (IRE)**[21] 5996 3-8-12 101....................... PShanahan 13 (Ms F M Crowley, Ire) *mid-div: prog into 5th ent st: mod 4th over 1f out: sn no ex* **11/2**[2]	85
9	hd	**Sacrosanct (IRE)**[6] 6267 3-8-12 94............................. CO'Donoghue 14 (A P O'Brien, Ire) *sn chsd ldrs: 5th 1/2-way: no ex early st* **33/1**	84
10	½	**Crooked Throw (IRE)**[13] 6154 7-9-2 96................................ WJLee 15 (C F Swan, Ire) *sn trckd ldrs on outer: 2nd 1/2-way: chal st: no ex fr over 1f out* **11/1**	86
11	½	**Senor Benny (USA)**[14] 6112 7-9-2 103.............................. FMBerry 11 (M McDonagh, Ire) *hld up: no imp st* **12/1**	85
12	2 ½	**Be My Queen (IRE)**[6] 6267 3-8-12 100........................ DavidMcCabe 16 (A P O'Brien, Ire) *sn prom: led appr 1/2-way: rdn st: hdd over 1f out: wknd* **14/1**	75
13	1 ½	**Ireland's Call (IRE)**[14] 6112 5-9-2 96.............................. OCasey 8 (Peter Casey, Ire) *led early: hdd bef 1/2-way: 4th into st: sn rdn and no imp: nt clr run ins fnl f* **14/1**	74
14	nk	**Yellow Ridge (IRE)**[28] 5854 3-9-1 75....................... FranciscoDaSilva 1 (Luke Comer, Ire) *hld up: mid-div and effrt on inner early st: no ex u.p fnl f* **100/1**	73
15	6	**Queen Of Rap (IRE)**[175] 1709 3-8-12 92............................ PJSmullen 6 (D K Weld, Ire) *chsd ldrs: 4th 1/2-way: wknd bef st* **16/1**	55

1m 30.8s **Going Correction** -0.175s/f (Firm)
WFA 3 from 4yo+ 1lb **16** Ran SP% **139.4**
Speed ratings: 101,98,96,95,94 93,92,92,92,91 90,88,86,86,79
CSF £23.28 TOTE £7.70: £2.20, £1.30, £4.10; DF 21.60.
Owner Ballylinch Stud **Bred** Ballylinch Stud **Trained** Coolcullen, Co Carlow

NOTEBOOK

Modeeroch(IRE) may not have quite lived up to the expectations raised by a juvenile career during which she won twice and finished fourth in the Cheveley Park, but she is a very useful type who has run some good races in smart company. Heavy ground was probably against her when she was fifth to Noelani in a Group 3 event at Tipperary early last month, and she was much better in these less demanding conditions, picking up well when asked for her effort and going clear to reverse Tipperary form with the favourite. (op 7/1)

Ugo Fire(IRE), who stayed on but without looking like closing the gap, has shown good form recently and helps to put the race in a solid context. (op 6/4 tchd 7/4)

Eastern Appeal(IRE) had a fair bit to find with some of these on official figures but maintained the improvement she had shown when fourth to Sina Cova at Naas. There may be more to come from her. (op 8/1)

Ardbrae Lady, who has never been able to match her excellent second to Nightime in the Irish 1000 Guineas, ran her best race for a while. She has plenty of ability, but it has been disappointing that she has failed to add to the single win she recorded as a two-year-old. (op 12/1)

Danehill Music(IRE), who has generally struggled since a productive spell in the early part of the season, stayed on without posing a serious threat.

6357a EYREFIELD STKS (LISTED RACE) 1m 1f

2:05 (2:05) 2-Y-O **£22,448** (£6,586; £3,137; £1,068)

			RPR
1		**Anton Chekhov**[37] 5662 2-9-1 .... CO'Donoghue 4 (A P O'Brien, Ire) *mde all: rdn clr fr under 3f out: styd on wl: eased cl home* **9/2**[2]	108+
2	4 ½	**Star Inside (IRE)**[30] 5797 2-9-1 102............................ DPMcDonogh 1 (Kevin Prendergast, Ire) *mid-div: 6th 3f out: nt clr run ent st: swtchd lft over 1 1/2f out: mod 2nd over 1f out: kpt on* **5/2**[1]	99
3	2 ½	**Luminous One (IRE)**[13] 6153 2-8-12 ....(p) KJManning 5 (J S Bolger, Ire) *settled 2nd: rdn and outpcd ent st: kpt on same pce fr 1 1/2f out* **10/1**	91
4	1 ½	**The Ethiopian (IRE)**[19] 6042 2-9-1 .... JAHeffernan 3 (A P O'Brien, Ire) *chsd ldrs: 5th 1/2-way: 4th 3f out: kpt on same pce st* **9/2**[2]	91
5	1 ¼	**Liscanna (IRE)**[21] 5995 2-8-12 88...................................(b) WMLordan 11 (David Wachman, Ire) *trckd ldrs: 4th 1/2-way: prog into 3rd 3f out: rdn and no imp st: kpt on same pce* **8/1**	86
6	1	**Keep It Cool (IRE)** 2-9-1 .... PJSmullen 6 (D K Weld, Ire) *hld up: 8th 1/2-way: 6th early st: no imp fr over 1f out* **12/1**	87
7	2 ½	**Rock Lily**[13] 6153 2-8-12 .... FMBerry 8 (Charles O'Brien, Ire) *hld up in rr: kpt on one pce st* **8/1**	79
8	2	**Sensible Lady**[14] 6113 2-8-12 89.................................. PShanahan 7 (C Collins, Ire) *mid-div: 7th 1/2-way: rdn and no imp st* **7/1**[3]	75
9	5	**Divine Design (IRE)**[13] 6153 2-8-12 .... RMBurke 2 (Joseph G Murphy, Ire) *dwlt: hld up: no ex fr 3f out* **33/1**	65
10	½	**Uluru (IRE)**[14] 6113 2-8-12 .... AmeliaHegarty 10 (A P O'Brien, Ire) *chsd ldrs in 3rd: wknd appr st* **50/1**	64
11	3 ½	**Hugs 'n Kisses (IRE)**[14] 6113 2-8-12 .... DMGrant 9 (John Joseph Murphy, Ire) *a towards rr* **40/1**	57

1m 59.0s **Going Correction** +0.275s/f (Good) **11** Ran SP% **123.8**
Speed ratings: 104,100,97,96,95 94,92,90,86,85 82
CSF £16.92 TOTE £8.10: £2.70, £1.40, £2.50; DF 18.60.
Owner Michael Tabor **Bred** W And R Barnett Ltd **Trained** Ballydoyle, Co Tipperary

NOTEBOOK

Anton Chekhov, a promising third to the impressive Consul General at Cork on his debut in September, can be rated a bright three-year-old prospect, though it is hard to be sure of where he will fit into the scheme of things next season, when O'Brien will be hoping at least some of the superbly-bred juveniles who have emerged during a successful late-season spell can improve enough to challenge for significant honours.

Star Inside(IRE) had a strong claim as the form horse even though this represented a step up in class from the nurseries in which he had proved a tough and improving competitor. He did not get the best of runs in the straight, and by the time he was switched to the outside to go in pursuit, Anton Chekhov was in control up front. (op 2/1)

Luminous One(IRE) ends the season still a maiden but seems to be going the right way. She readily reversed form with Rock Lily, to whom she had finished third in a maiden at the Curragh, and should pay her way as a three-year-old. (op 10/1)

The Ethiopian(IRE), High Chaparral's brother, did not make as much improvement from his first run as Anton Chekhov but is still a name to keep in mind for next year, with the likelihood that he will prosper when stepping up towards a mile and a half. (op 5/1)

Liscanna(IRE) was not disgraced but probably needs to improve at least 7lb to 10lb to be competitive in Listed races next season.

6358 - 6361a (Foreign Racing) - See Raceform Interactive

6123 CAPANNELLE (R-H)

Sunday, November 5

OFFICIAL GOING: Good

6362a PREMIO GIUSEPPE VALIANI (EX BUONTALENTA) (LISTED RACE) (F&M) 1m 2f

1:30 (1:32) 3-Y-O+ **£21,724** (£9,559; £5,214; £2,607)

			RPR
1		**Mount Eliza (IRE)**[27] 4-8-11 .... MEsposito 3 (J E Hammond, France) **64/10**	99
2	4	**Cockayne (IRE)** 3-8-9 .... CColombi 1 (V Valiani, Italy) **88/10**	94
3	nk	**Penfection (IRE)**[26] 5888 3-8-9 .... EBotti 11 (M Botti) *held up towards rear to straight, brought wide, ran on steadily from over 3f out to take 3rd close home* **31/10**[2]	93
4	½	**Hands Clean (IRE)**[14] 6124 3-9-3 .... FBranca 2 (A Candi, Italy) **53/10**	100
5	1 ¼	**Mia Kross (IRE)** 3-8-12 .... DVargiu 10 (B Grizzetti, Italy) **5/2**[1]	93
6	2	**Rhodagna (IRE)**[505] 2734 4-9-1 ....(b) NPinna 5 (V Valiani, Italy) **88/10**	88
7	2 ½	**La Vriga**[14] 6124 5-8-11 .... SMulas 9 (B Grizzetti, Italy) **71/10**	80
8	1	**Sharp's Queen (IRE)** 6-8-11 .... CFiocchi 6 (C Adaldo) **58/1**	78
9	1 ½	**Annaly (ITY)**[505] 2734 4-8-11 .... TedDurcan 12 (O Pessi, Italy) **17/1**	75
10	6	**Vanitosa (IRE)** 3-8-12 .... MDemuro 8 (L Brogi, Italy) **7/2**[3]	69
11	6	**Opatja**[14] 6124 4-9-1 .... SLandi 4 (L Camici, Italy) **18/1**	58
12	8	**Sunsemperchi**[154] 2280 4-9-1 ....(b) MMonteriso 7 (E Borromeo, Italy) **29/1**	43

2m 0.10s
WFA 3 from 4yo+ 4lb **12** Ran SP% **153.2**
(including one euro stakes): WIN 7.44; PL 3.04, 4.88, 2.17; DF 58.94.
Owner Mme L Shanahan **Bred** Dr M V O'Brien **Trained** France

NOTEBOOK

Penfection(IRE) stuck on well down the outside in the closing stages to grab third, and all-important black type, in the last few strides.

6363a PREMIO UMBRIA (GROUP 3) 6f

2:30 (2:36) 2-Y-O+ **£30,417** (£14,154; £7,945; £3,973)

			RPR
1		**Patapan (USA)**[112] 4-9-8 .... FBranca 6 (R Brogi, Italy) *always in touch, went 3rd half-way, led just inside final 2f, driven out* **76/10**	106
2	1	**Velvet Revolver (IRE)**[21] 6005 3-9-5 .... MDemuro 10 (L Riccardi, Italy) *always prominent, pressed winner well over 1f out, every chance 1f out, kept on same pace* **113/10**	100
3	nk	**Santiago Atitlan** 4-9-8 .... EPedroza 9 (A Wohler, Germany) *outpaced to half-way, headway 2f out, stayed on final f, nearest at finish* **43/10**[2]	102
4	1 ¾	**Lady Marmelade (ITY)** 3-9-5 .... PBorrelli 14 (D Ducci, Italy) *mid-division, headway 2f out, ran on final f, nearest at finish* **33/1**	94
5	1 ¼	**Krisman (IRE)**[21] 6005 7-9-8 .... WGambarota 5 (M Ciciarelli, Italy) *chased leaders, one pace final 2f* **47/10**[3]	93
6	nk	**Thinking Robins (IRE)**[196] 1175 3-9-8 ....(b) PAragoni 1 (P Martometti, Italy) *went left start, outpaced early, never near to challenge* **16/1**	92
7	½	**Chantilly Beauty (FR)**[113] 3564 4-9-5 ....(b) TJarnet 11 (R Pritchard-Gordon, France) *outpaced & in rear, hard ridden 2f out, ran on final f, nearest at finish* **63/10**	88
8	2 ½	**Titus Shadow (IRE)** 2-8-5 .... DVargiu 4 (B Grizzetti, Italy) *disputed lead til weakening from well over 1f out* **2/1**[1]	85
9	½	**Agata Laguna (IRE)**[21] 6005 3-9-5 .... OFancera 12 (R Brogi, Italy) *never nearer than mid-division* **76/10**	79
10	nk	**Chalin**[1260] 1857 6-9-8 .... SBasile 7 (S Deledda, Italy) *never in contention* **84/1**	81
11	1 ½	**Champion Place**[21] 6005 3-9-8 .... CFiocchi 3 (R Menichetti, Italy) *led to just inside final 2f* **18/1**	76
12	3 ½	**San Dany (IRE)**[168] 1871 6-9-8 .... GBietolini 15 (M Massimi Jr, Italy) *prominent on outside to half-way* **81/1**	66
13	nse	**Great Uncle Ted (USA)**[168] 1871 3-9-8 .... SMulas 13 (B Grizzetti, Italy) *speed to half-way* **25/1**	66
14	½	**Shoshiba (IRE)** 3-9-5 .... PConvertino 16 (P Martometti, Italy) *prominent on outside to half-way* **16/1**	61
15	1	**Blu Delta Force**[364] 6277 4-9-8 .... MEsposito 2 (V Caruso, Italy) *chased leaders to half-way, weakened quickly* **99/10**	61

16 1 1/4 **Bahalita (IRE)**[60] [5123] 3-9-5 ....(b) GMarcelli 8 54
(L Riccardi, Italy) *last most of way* **23/1**

68.00 secs **16** Ran SP% **154.4**
WIN 8.62 (coupled with Agata Laguna); PL 3.45, 4.03, 3.26; DF 75.73.

Owner Scuderia Archi Romani **Bred** Scuderia Archi Romani **Trained** Italy

6364a PREMIO RIBOT (GROUP 2) 1m
3:05 (3:14) 3-Y-0+ **£47,241** (£21,795; £12,189; £6,095)

RPR

1 **Ramonti (FR)**[22] [5982] 4-9-2 .... EBotti 12 117
(A Botti, Italy) *made all, two or three lengths clear most of way, went further clear from over 2f out, ran on strongly* **2/5**[1]

2 5 **Mullins Bay**[386] [5906] 5-9-2 .... MDemuro 2 107
(J E Hammond, France) *tracked winner after 2f, kept on one pace from over 2f out* **73/20**[2]

3 2 **Rumsfeld (ITY)**[47] [5473] 3-9-1 .... DVargiu 4 104
(A & G Botti, Italy) *held up, headway & 6th straight, stayed on final 2f to take 3rd well inside final f* **141/10**

4 3/4 **Margine Rosso (IRE)**[196] [1175] 3-9-1 .... OFancera 1 103
(R Brogi, Italy) *prominent, 3rd straight, one pace final 2f, lost 3rd well inside final f* **59/1**

5 2 1/2 **Ceprin (IRE)**[156] [2217] 5-9-2 .... MMonteriso 6 97
(A & G Botti, Italy) *tracked winner for 2f, 4th straight, one pace final 3f* **2/5**[1]

6 nk **Desert Quiet (IRE)**[21] [6002] 4-8-13 .... SLandi 5 93
(P Giannotti, Italy) *towards rear to straight, headway on inside over 3f out, reached 5th 2f out, one pace* **15/1**

7 3/4 **Kill Cat (IRE)**[156] [2217] 5-9-2 .... GBietolini 3 94
(A Peraino, Italy) *7th straight, never a factor* **24/1**

8 2 1/2 **Honey Bunny**[712] 6-9-2 .... MEsposito 10 89
(V Caruso, Italy) *always in rear* **23/1**

9 1/2 **Icelandic**[22] [5982] 4-9-2 .... PConvertino 7 88
(Frank Sheridan, Italy) *always towards rear, behind final 3f* **132/10**

10 6 **Mister Fasliyev (IRE)**[176] 4-9-2 .... FBranca 11 76
(G Colella, Italy) *always in rear* **144/10**

11 2 **Poderoso Kike (ARG)** 3-9-1 .... SBasile 8 73
(M Grassi, Italy) *5th straight, weakened 3f out* **104/10**[3]

1m 35.4s
WFA 3 from 4yo+ 2lb **11** Ran SP% **209.4**
WIN 1.41 (coupled with Ceprin); PL 1.08, 1.35, 1.66; DF 3.14.

Owner Scuderia Antezzate **Bred** Scuderia Siba **Trained** Italy

NOTEBOOK
Ramonti(FR) posted another dominant front-running display. He is a top-notch miler on fast ground and deserves a chance to prove himself on the international stage in the Hong Kong Mile.

6365a PREMIO ROMA (GROUP 1) 1m 2f
3:35 (3:51) 3-Y-0+ **£111,448** (£57,703; £34,055; £17,028)

RPR

1 **Cherry Mix (FR)**[21] [6004] 5-9-2 .... TedDurcan 4 121
(Saeed Bin Suroor) *made all, driven out* **34/10**[3]

2 4 **Hattan (IRE)**[51] [5342] 4-9-2 .... SebSanders 3 113
(C E Brittain) *hld up in midfield on ins, 6th str, rdn 3f out, hdwy on ins to go 2nd 1 1/2f out, kept on but no chance with winner* **98/10**

3 1 3/4 **Distant Way (USA)**[22] [5982] 5-9-2 .... MDemuro 5 110
(L Brogi, Italy) *held up in last, ridden on outside over 2f out, stayed on steadily to take 3rd close home* **28/10**[2]

4 nk **Soldier Hollow**[36] [5704] 6-9-2 .... SPasquier 10 109
(P Schiergen, Germany) *held up in rear, 9th straight, ridden 2f out, headway down outside to dispute 3rd 1f out, one pace* **17/10**[1]

5 1 1/4 **Vol De Nuit**[85] [4358] 5-9-2 .... FBranca 1 107
(L M Cumani) *raced in 4th on inside, went 2nd 4f out, lost 2nd 1 1/2f out, one pace* **28/10**[2]

6 1 1/2 **Donaldson (GER)**[63] [5051] 4-9-2 .... TMundry 2 104
(P Rau, Germany) *close up, 2nd straight, ridden and one pace from over 2f out* **13/2**

7 nk **Fair Nashwan**[21] [6004] 4-8-12 .... DVargiu 8 99
(B Grizzetti, Italy) *held up in rear, 8th straight, effort and unable to quicken from over 2f out* **43/10**

8 1 3/4 **Lauro (GER)**[105] [3776] 3-9-0 .... AStarke 9 102
(P Schiergen, Germany) *held up, 7th straight, ridden well over 2f out, not quicken* **13/2**

9 1/2 **Cocodrail (IRE)**[168] [1870] 5-9-2 .... TJarnet 6 99
(F Brogi, Italy) *midfield, 5th straight, weakened over 1f out* **42/1**

10 20 **Emily Bronte**[10] [6190] 3-8-10 .... TPQueally 7 59
(Saeed Bin Suroor) *prominent, 3rd straight, weakened quickly 4f out* **34/10**[3]

1m 59.4s
WFA 3 from 4yo+ 4lb **10** Ran SP% **192.2**
WIN 4.36 (coupled with Emily Bronte); PL 2.04, 3.01, 1.97; DF 41.20.

Owner Godolphin **Bred** S N C Lagardere Elevage **Trained** Newmarket, Suffolk

NOTEBOOK
Cherry Mix(FR) ran so much better than in Milan three weeks ago despite fast ground that he was supposed not to like. He set a strong, though not uncontested, pace before drawing clear approaching the quarter-mile pole. He is inconsistent, but it highly talented on his day.

Hattan(IRE) ran his best race for some time, staying on under strong pressure down the inside rail to take a clear, if distant, second place.

Distant Way(USA) failed in his bid to win this for a third straight year, flattening out having looked likely to stay on into second approaching the furlong marker.

Vol De Nuit could only keep on at the same pace in the last three furlongs.

Emily Bronte dropped away quickly with fully half a mile to run.

5998 COLOGNE (R-H)
Sunday, November 5

OFFICIAL GOING: Soft

6366a KOLNER HERBST STUTEN MEILE (GROUP 3) (F&M) 1m
2:05 (2:08) 3-Y-0+ **£22,069** (£6,897; £3,448; £2,069)

RPR

1 **Turning Light (GER)**[140] [2694] 3-8-13 .... ADeVries 8 108
(Mario Hofer, Germany) *held up in 7th, headway on outside to lead narrowly just inside final f, ran on under pressure, asserted close home* **103/10**

2 1/2 **Danzon (USA)**[20] [6022] 3-8-13 .... IMendizabal 5 107
(J-C Rouget, France) *held up in 6th, headway between rivals to challenge 1f out, soon hard ridden, still every chance til no extra last 50yds* **13/10**[1]

3 4 **Molly Art (GER)**[85] [4383] 4-9-2 ....(b) ABoschert 7 100
(U Ostmann, Germany) *tracked leaders in 4th, headway on inside to lead narrowly 2f out, headed just inside final f, one pace* **36/10**[2]

4 3/4 **The Spring Flower (GER)**[119] 4-9-2 .... CarinaFey 6 99
(Andreas Lowe, Germany) *pressed leader on outside, close 3rd straight, effort 2f out, one pace* **88/10**

5 4 **Mrs Snow**[21] [6002] 3-8-13 .... AHelfenbein 2 90
(Mario Hofer, Germany) *pressed leader, close 2nd straight, weakened over 1 1/2f out* **15/2**[3]

6 4 1/2 **Drosia (IRE)**[20] [6022] 3-8-13 .... MBlancpain 1 81
(C Laffon-Parias, France) *led narrowly til headed 2f out, weakened steadily* **36/10**[2]

7 1/2 **Heat Of The Night**[58] [5160] 4-9-2 .... FilipMinarik 4 81
(P W Chapple-Hyam) *raced in 5th, outpaced final 2f* **97/10**

8 12 **Orissa (GER)** 4-9-2 .... MTimpelan 3 57
(W Hickst, Germany) *always behind* **31/1**

1m 40.09s
WFA 3 from 4yo 2lb **8** Ran SP% **130.2**
(including ten euro stakes): WIN 113; PL 21, 16, 18: SF 408.

Owner Stall Anima Negra Gmbh & Co Kg **Bred** Stall Anima Negra Gmbh & Co Kg **Trained** Germany

NOTEBOOK
Heat Of The Night never threatened in what looked like a decent quality event for such a late season Group 3.

6367 - 6589a (Foreign Racing) - See Raceform Interactive

6338 CHURCHILL DOWNS (L-H)
Sunday, November 5

OFFICIAL GOING: Firm

6368a CARDINAL H'CAP (GRADE 3) (F&M) 1m 1f (T)
9:46 (9:47) 3-Y-0+

£58,198 (£18,773; £9,386; £4,693; £2,816; £998)

RPR

1 **Sabellina (USA)**[43] 5-8-3 .... JRLeparoux 107
(C Simon, U.S.A) **93/10**

2 nse **Silca's Sister**[135] [2802] 3-8-4 ow2.................................... RAlbarado 111
(Saeed Bin Suroor) *led, headed breifly over 5f out, headed again over 1f out, rallied gamely under pressure final f, just failed (47/10)* **47/10**[2]

3 2 1/4 **Royal Copenhagen (FR)**[85] [4385] 4-8-3 .... ECastro 103
(C Block, U.S.A) **126/10**

4 1/2 **Rich In Spirit (USA)**[85] [4385] 4-8-6 ....(b) MGuidry 105
(T Proctor, U.S.A) **7/2**[1]

5 1/2 **More Than Promised (USA)**[113] 4-8-2 ow1.................... SBridgmohan 100
(S Blasi, U.S.A) **298/10**

6 hd **Dash Of Humor (USA)**[22] 6-8-4 ow1.................................... CHBorel 101
(Hal R Wiggins, U.S.A) **113/10**

7 1 1/4 **Stormina (USA)**[88] 4-8-4 .... JRVelazquez 99
(T Pletcher, U.S.A) **49/10**[3]

8 1/2 **Black Java (USA)** 4-8-4 ow4.................................... JamesGraham 98
(D Galvin, U.S.A) **51/1**

9 1/2 **Amorama (FR)**[64] 5-8-6 ....(b) RBejarano 99
(R J Frankel, U.S.A) **51/10**

10 3 3/4 **Beautiful Bets (USA)**[36] 6-8-0 .... WillieMartinez 86
(G Wismer, U.S.A) **219/10**

11 4 **Carolina Sky (USA)** 4-8-3 ....(b) LMelancon 81
(M Nicks, U.S.A) **76/10**

1m 49.96s
WFA 3 from 4yo+ 3lb **11** Ran SP% **119.5**
PARI-MUTUEL (including $2 stake): WIN 20.60; PL (1-2) 8.60, 6.20;SHOW (1-2-3) 6.80, 5.20, 7.80; SF 139.00.

Owner J Lieberman **Bred** John Valentino **Trained** USA

NOTEBOOK
Silca's Sister, last seen finishing sixth in the Coronation Stakes, set out to make all and was only worn down close home. She rallied once headed but could not quite get back up, and in theory the 2lb overweight her rider put up cost her the win.

6289 KEMPTON (A.W) (R-H)
Monday, November 6

OFFICIAL GOING: Standard
Wind: Nil Weather: Sunny

6370 SPONSOR AT KEMPTON BANDED STKS 1m (P)
1:00 (1:02) (Class 7) 3-Y-0+ **£1,365** (£403; £201) **Stalls** High

Form RPR

0005 1 **Owners Biscuits**[6] [6281] 3-8-9 45....................................(b) GregFairley(3) 3 57
(M Johnston) *hld up in midfield on outer: prog 3f out: led wl over 1f out: rdn and clr fnl f* **14/1**

100/ 2 2 1/2 **Shahm (IRE)**[973] [988] 7-9-0 45.................................... TPQueally 11 51
(B J Curley) *wl in tch: lost pl sltly over 3f out: effrt and hanging over 2f out: drvn and prog to chse wnr 1f out: kpt on one pce* **15/8**[1]

3350 **3** *1* **Flashing Floozie**[25] 5929 3-8-12 45 JamieMackay 8 49
(J G Given) *t.k.h: cl up: gng wl enough over 2f out: rdn and kpt on same pce fr over 1f out* **16/1**

0002 **4** *3/4* **Savoy Chapel**[14] 6134 4-8-7 45 MarkCoumbe(7) 5 47
(A W Carroll) *hld up wl in rr: gng wl but stl in last pair over 2f out: prog over 1f out: shkn up and kpt on same pce fnl f* **8/1**

3200 **5** *1 1/2* **Frenchgate**[25] 5926 5-8-9 45 (v1) NataliaGemelova(5) 4 44
(I W McInnes) *t.k.h: trckd ldr after 3f: chal and upsides over 2f out: hanging bdly and reluctant: one pce after* **20/1**

4002 **6** *nk* **Bollywood (IRE)**[8] 6236 3-8-12 45 DaneO'Neill 14 43
(J J Bridger) *t.k.h: hld up bhd ldrs: gng wl but nt clr run over 2f out: rdn and one pce over 1f out* **9/2**[3]

4060 **7** *1* **Kinsman (IRE)**[14] 6128 9-9-0 45 RobertMiles 13 41
(T D McCarthy) *t.k.h: hld up towards rr: effrt on inner over 2f out: hrd rdn and sme prog over 1f out: one pce fnl f* **20/1**

0012 **8** *1* **Komreyev Star**[9] 6213 4-9-0 45 IanMongan 12 38
(M Mullineaux) *led for 1f: lost pl 1/2-way: drvn over 2f out: no imp over 1f out: fdd* **3/1**[2]

0050 **9** *1* **Wild Lass**[19] 6059 5-9-0 45 (b) LPKeniry 2 36
(J C Fox) *s.i.s: hld up in rr: effrt on outer over 2f out: no prog over 1f out* **40/1**

/06- **10** *1/2* **Over To You Bert**[529] 2029 7-9-0 45 SteveDrowne 6 35
(R J Hodges) *led after 1f to over 2f out: stl upsides over 1f out: wknd fnl f* **33/1**

00-0 **11** *nk* **Queenstown (IRE)**[25] 5926 5-9-0 45 (p) BrianReilly 10 34
(J E Long) *trckd ldrs: led over 2f out to wl over 1f out: wknd rapidly fnl f* **33/1**

3040 **12** *nk* **Legacy (JPN)**[167] 1911 6-8-7 45 (v1) MCGeran(7) 1 34
(P D Evans) *s.v.s: hld up in last pair: c v wd bnd 3f out: urged along and no real prog* **20/1**

00/0 **13** *10* **Carlburg (IRE)**[4] 6307 5-9-0 45 AdrianMcCarthy 9 11
(Mrs C A Dunnett) *s.i.s: plld hrd: hld up in rr: wknd rapidly 2f out* **50/1**

1m 40.3s (-0.50) **Going Correction** -0.125s/f (Stan)
WFA 3 from 4yo+ 2lb 13 Ran SP% **126.2**
Speed ratings (Par 97):97,94,93,92,91 90,89,88,87,87 87,86,76
CSF £39.84 TOTE £19.40: £3.90, £1.60, £4.40; EX 72.60.
Owner Mark Johnston Racing Ltd **Bred** P Cutler **Trained** Middleham Moor, N Yorks

FOCUS
A routine banded contest in many ways, but notable for a big gamble on Shahm which was foiled. A big improvement from the winner, but the form should stand up.
Kinsman(IRE) Official explanation: jockey said gelding stumbled on leaving stalls

6371 DAY TIME, NIGHT TIME, GREAT TIME BANDED STKS 7f (P)
1:30 (1:30) (Class 7) 3-Y-0+ **£1,365** (£403; £201) **Stalls** High

Form RPR

6000 **1** **Stagnite**[25] 4670 6-8-11 50 JamieJones(7) 7 59
(Karen George) *hld up in midfield: prog over 2f out: hrd rdn over 1f out: styd on fnl f to ld nr fin* **20/1**

4606 **2** *1/2* **Fun Time**[4] 6304 3-9-3 50 IanMongan 11 58
(M R Channon) *trckd ldrs: effrt over 2f out: rdn to ld over 1f out: kpt on u.p: hdd nr fin* **8/1**

043 **3** *1 1/2* **Free Silver (IRE)**[8] 6235 3-9-3 50 AdrianMcCarthy 9 54+
(Miss K B Boutflower) *hld up towards rr: prog over 2f out: nt clr run 2f out tl ent fnl f: nt qckn whn in the clr last 150yds* **4/1**[1]

2666 **4** *nk* **Miss Porcia**[80] 4554 5-8-11 48 KevinGhunowa(5) 12 51
(P A Blockley) *mde most: hrd rdn and hdd over 1f out: wknd nr fin* **7/1**

4035 **5** *2* **Siraj**[86] 4365 7-9-2 48 (p) MichaelTebbutt 8 46
(J Ryan) *wl in rr: rdn and struggling wl over 2f out: prog u.p over 1f out: kpt on but n.d* **7/1**

0006 **6** *nk* **Fantasy Defender (IRE)**[8] 6235 4-9-2 48 (v) DaneO'Neill 6 45
(Ernst Oertel) *hld up towards rr: rdn over 2f out: plugged on fr over 1f out: n.d* **6/1**[3]

0300 **7** *1 1/2* **Dora's Green**[58] 5167 3-8-10 48 LiamJones(5) 14 41
(S W Hall) *t.k.h: cl up: chal and upsides over 2f out to over 1f out : wknd ins fnl f* **25/1**

4-00 **8** *1 1/2* **Premier Cru**[146] 2535 3-9-2 49 LPKeniry 10 38
(Andrew Turnell) *chsd ldrs: effrt 3f out: no imp 2f out: wknd fnl f* **33/1**

-000 **9** *hd* **Astorygoeswithit**[222] 797 3-9-3 50 (p) BrianReilly 4 39
(P S McEntee) *sn trckd ldr: wknd u.p wl over 1f out* **40/1**

3006 **10** *1* **Charlottebutterfly**[14] 6130 6-9-2 48 (v1) MickyFenton 1 34
(P J McBride) *dwlt: wl in rr: bhd 3f out: plugged on fnl 2f* **12/1**

4400 **11** *1 3/4* **Zafarshah (IRE)**[8] 6235 7-9-2 48 (b) SteveDrowne 13 30
(R A Harris) *pushed along in midfield after 3f: brief effrt on inner over 2f out: sn btn* **14/1**

3000 **12** *1 1/2* **Be My Charm**[47] 5480 3-8-10 50 LauraReynolds(7) 5 28
(M Blanshard) *dwlt: a wl in rr: nudged along and no prog over 2f out* **16/1**

13 *7* **Affirmed Native (USA)**[148] 3-9-2 49 TPQueally 2 8
(J A Osborne) *racd wd: a in rr: nt keen and losing tch over 2f out* **11/2**[2]

0620 **14** *25* **Attitude Annie**[80] 4554 3-9-1 48 PaulDoe 3 —
(S Dow) *chsd ldrs tl wknd rapidly 1/2-way: t.o* **14/1**

1m 26.98s (0.18) **Going Correction** -0.125s/f (Stan)
WFA 3 from 4yo+ 1lb 14 Ran SP% **126.7**
Speed ratings (Par 97):93,92,90,90,88 87,86,84,84,82 80,79,71,42
CSF £175.48 TOTE £29.30: £6.80, £2.20, £2.30; EX 213.00.
Owner P J H George **Bred** D A And Mrs Hicks **Trained** Higher Easington, Devon
■ Stewards' Enquiry : Adrian McCarthy one-day ban: careless riding (Nov 17)

FOCUS
This looked a modest race of its type, the early pace was ordinary, and there were four in a line across the track half a furlong from home. Sound form.
Fantasy Defender(IRE) Official explanation: trainer said gelding had been struck into front and behind
Attitude Annie Official explanation: jockey said filly never travelled

6372 MCCARTHY & STONE LEADING RETIREMENT BUILDERS BANDED STKS 6f (P)
2:05 (2:05) (Class 7) 3-Y-0+ **£1,365** (£403; £201) **Stalls** High

Form RPR

4200 **1** **Midmaar (IRE)**[167] 1913 5-8-12 45 (b) SteveDrowne 12 53
(M Wigham) *trckd ldr: rdn to ld jst over 1f out: drvn to hold on to rapidly dwindling advantage nr fin* **4/1**[2]

0050 **2** *nk* **Task Complete**[70] 4872 3-8-9 45 (b) NeilChalmers(3) 8 52+
(Jean-Rene Auvray) *dwlt: hld up in last: gng wl but stl last over 2f out: rapid prog over 1f out: clsng fast at fin: too much to do* **33/1**

0032 **3** *nk* **Firework**[14] 6131 8-8-12 45 StephenCarson 6 51
(E A Wheeler) *hld up in rr: prog and weaved through on inner fr 2f out: chsd wnr ins fnl f: clsd but lost 2nd nr fin* **5/2**[1]

0006 **4** *1/2* **Spinetail Rufous (IRE)**[6] 6282 8-8-12 45 IanMongan 4 50
(Miss Z C Davison) *prom: rdn over 2f out: tried to chal over 1f out: nt qckn: kpt on same pce* **12/1**

2000 **5** *shd* **Gaudalpin (IRE)**[144] 2574 4-8-12 45 (t) FergusSweeney 7 49
(Ernst Oertel) *trckd ldrs: cl up 2f out: rdn and nt qckn over 1f out: kpt on* **14/1**

0000 **6** *2* **Beau Jazz**[24] 5938 5-8-12 45 AdrianMcCarthy 2 43
(W De Best-Turner) *led at fast pce: hdd jst over 1f out: sn wknd* **33/1**

6002 **7** *shd* **Binnion Bay (IRE)**[8] 6237 5-8-9 45 (v) AmirQuinn(3) 5 43
(J J Bridger) *settled in midfield: rdn over 2f out: no imp ldrs over 1f out: plugged on* **15/2**

0000 **8** *1* **Yorkie**[25] 5924 7-8-12 45 MichaelTebbutt 11 40
(J Pearce) *prom: rdn over 2f out: lost pl and btn over 1f out* **10/1**

5000 **9** *1/2* **Imtalkinggibberish**[109] 3683 5-8-5 45 (p) WilliamBuick(7) 3 39
(V Smith) *a towards rr: rdn and no real prog over 2f out* **8/1**

0602 **10** *1 3/4* **Kindallachan**[8] 6233 3-8-12 45 PaulEddery 1 33
(G C Bravery) *racd on outer in midfield: rdn over 2f out: btn wl over 1f out: fdd* **14/1**

6002 **11** *1 1/4* **Noble Mount**[88] 4278 5-8-12 45 (p) DaneO'Neill 10 30
(A B Haynes) *dwlt: a wl in rr: last and wl btn over 1f out* **7/1**[3]

0-00 **12** *2* **Young Valentino**[6] 6282 4-8-12 45 TPQueally 9 24
(A W Carroll) *awkward s: sn in midfield: hanging and wknd 2f out* **40/1**

1m 13.52s (-0.18) **Going Correction** -0.125s/f (Stan) 12 Ran SP% **122.4**
Speed ratings (Par 97):96,95,95,94,94 91,91,90,89,87 85,82
CSF £137.61 TOTE £4.90: £1.90, £4.40, £1.30; EX 189.00.
Owner A Dunmore M Wigham **Bred** Shadwell Estate Company Limited **Trained** Newmarket, Suffolk

FOCUS
A reasonable banded contest run at a fair pace and not that many got into it. Fairly sound form at this level.
Kindallachan Official explanation: jockey said filly moved poorly throughout

6373 KEMPTON FOR CONFERENCES BANDED STKS 1m 3f (P)
2:40 (2:41) (Class 7) 3-Y-0+ **£1,365** (£403; £201) **Stalls** High

Form RPR

6-03 **1** **Artzola (IRE)**[8] 6232 6-9-3 45 PaulEddery 12 50+
(C A Horgan) *mounted on crse: hld up in rr: smooth prog to trck ldrs over 2f out: led over 1f out: rdn and r.o wl* **9/2**[2]

4022 **2** *1 1/4* **Glory Be (ITY)**[4] 6302 4-9-3 40 SteveDrowne 8 48
(J L Spearing) *settled in midfield: rdn 3f out: prog 2f out: chsd wnr 1f out: styd on but no imp* **7/2**[1]

-006 **3** *1 3/4* **Bongoali**[4] 6305 4-9-3 40 AdrianMcCarthy 6 45
(Mrs C A Dunnett) *trckd ldrs: pushed along over 3f out: n.m.r wl over 1f out: styd on to take 3rd ins fnl f* **14/1**

4056 **4** *3/4* **Kilmeena Magic**[8] 6237 4-9-3 45 LPKeniry 7 44
(J C Fox) *t.k.h: hld up wl in rr: effrt whn nt clr run over 2f out : kpt on fr over 1f out: n.d to ldrs* **12/1**

0300 **5** *1/2* **Sunset Dreamer (USA)**[4] 6302 5-8-10 40 JackMitchell(7) 5 43
(P Mitchell) *dwlt: hld up towards rr: effrt over 2f out: kpt on fr over 1f out: nt pce to threaten* **25/1**

4300 **6** *1* **Gran Clicquot**[8] 6232 11-8-12 45 RobynBrisland(5) 4 41
(G P Enright) *racd on outer: hld up in midfield: effrt over 2f out: one pce fr over 1f out* **16/1**

3610 **7** *shd* **Shaika**[6] 6279 3-8-7 45 (p) LiamJones(5) 1 41
(G Prodromou) *s.s: detached in last early: stl in last pair and rdn 2f out: styd on fr over 1f out: nrst fin* **11/2**[3]

4046 **8** *3/4* **Phlaunt**[6] 6279 4-9-3 45 (b1) StephenCarson 9 40
(R F Johnson Houghton) *prom: effrt on inner to chal over 2f out: wknd jst over 1f out* **7/1**

/0-0 **9** *shd* **Big Smoke (IRE)**[14] 6133 6-9-0 45 (t) NeilChalmers(3) 14 40
(J C Tuck) *hld up in midfield: prog to chse ldrs 2f out: nt qckn over 1f out: wknd fnl f* **10/1**

0000 **10** *1* **Fortunes Favourite**[33] 5769 6-8-12 40 NataliaGemelova(5) 3 38
(J E Long) *dwlt: rcvrd and prom after 2f: led over 2f out: hdd & wknd over 1f out* **33/1**

0000 **11** *2* **Haughton Hope**[8] 6236 3-8-9 45 GregFairley(3) 2 35
(T J Pitt) *t.k.h: pressed ldr: led over 4f out to over 2f out: wknd* **20/1**

0-00 **12** *nk* **Sahara Sun (IRE)**[14] 6133 3-8-12 45 DaneO'Neill 13 34
(A King) *s.s: hld up in last pair: shkn up over 3f out: no real prog* **20/1**

6 **13** *15* **River Beau (IRE)**[14] 6133 3-8-12 45 JamieMackay 11 9
(E J O'Neill) *led to over 4f out: wknd rapidly over 2f out: t.o* **8/1**

2m 23.03s
WFA 3 from 4yo+ 5lb 13 Ran SP% **125.0**
CSF £20.54 TOTE £4.80: £2.70, £1.50, £5.10; EX 20.20.
Owner Mrs B Sumner **Bred** Mrs B Sumner **Trained** Uffcott, Wilts

FOCUS
A moderate banded contest and the winning time was 0.35 seconds slower than the following contest over the same trip. The winner did not need to improve, the fourth and fifth limiting the form.

6374 JUMP RACING HERE TOMORROW BANDED STKS 1m 3f (P)
3:15 (3:16) (Class 7) 3-Y-0+ **£1,295** (£385; £192; £96) **Stalls** High

Form RPR

5033 **1** **Three Boars**[8] 6238 4-9-7 49 (b) SilvestreDeSousa 13 55
(S Gollings) *prom: trckd ldr over 3f out: led gng easily over 2f out and sn 3 l clr: all out fnl f as pack clsd at fin* **11/2**[3]

4003 **2** *nk* **Abbeygate**[6] 6280 5-9-6 48 MickyFenton 8 53
(T Keddy) *hld up towards rr: prog over 2f out: drvn to chse wnr 1f out: styd on but jst hld* **9/1**

0600 **3** *hd* **Cragganmore Creek**[19] 6057 3-9-3 50 (b1) DerekMcGaffin 6 55
(D Morris) *cl up: rdn to chse wnr wl over 1f out: hanging and nt qckn: styd on ins fnl f but a hld* **66/1**

4016 **4** *nk* **Milk And Sultana**[8] 6238 6-9-8 50 SteveDrowne 1 58+
(G A Ham) *hld up in last trio: effrt whn nt clr run over 2f out and swtchd to outer: r.o wl fr over 1f out: gaining at fin* **7/1**

2464 **5** *shd* **Revolve**[8] 6238 6-9-6 48 (p) IanMongan 7 52
(Mrs L J Mongan) *settled in midfield: effrt over 2f out: nt clr run over 1f out: styd on ins fnl f: nrst fin* **9/2**[1]

0541 **6** *1 1/2* **Ocean Rock**[8] 6238 5-10-0 50 GeorgeBaker 10 58
(C A Horgan) *dwlt: hld up in last trio: prog 4f out: effrt on inner to dispute 2nd over 1f out: nt qckn fnl f: eased nr fin* **9/2**[1]

-150 **7** *1 3/4* **Indigo Dancer**[128] 3075 3-8-13 46 TPQueally 2 45
(C F Wall) *trckd ldrs: rdn and nt qckn over 2f out: wknd ins fnl f* **5/1**[2]

3250 **8** *3 1/2* **Diktatorship (IRE)**[42] 5574 3-9-3 50 DaneO'Neill 4 43
(Ernst Oertel) *settled towards rr: rdn wl over 2f out: no real prog* **10/1**

0000 **9** *1/2* **Play Up Pompey**[8] 6235 4-9-5 50 AmirQuinn(3) 14 42
(J J Bridger) *led to over 2f out: wknd over 1f out* **16/1**

500 **10** *1* **Lady Ambitious**[162] 2048 3-8-10 50 .... JamesMillman(7) 9 41
(D K Ivory) *dwlt: hld up in last trio: effrt on inner and prog whn chopped off against rail wl over 1f out: no ch after* **33/1**

0020 **11** *5* **Height Of Spirits**[57] 5205 4-9-8 50 .... NickyMackay 5 32
(T D McCarthy) *t.k.h: prom: wkng whn squeezed out over 2f out* **10/1**

00/0 **12** *3/4* **Riverweld**[68] 4925 4-9-4 46 .... JosedeSouza 12 27
(J R Holt) *t.k.h: trckd ldr to over 3f out: wknd over 2f out* **33/1**

0000 **13** *4* **Smart Golden Boy (IRE)**[128] 3073 3-8-12 45 .... (p) LPKeniry 11 19
(Mrs L C Jewell) *prom tl wknd 3f out* **50/1**

2m 22.68s
WFA 3 from 4yo+ 5lb **13** Ran SP% **124.3**
CSF £55.63 TOTE £7.10: £1.80, £2.60, £19.30; EX 68.90.
Owner P Whinham **Bred** J M Greetham **Trained** Scamblesby, Lincs
■ Stewards' Enquiry : George Baker two-day ban: careless riding (Nov 17-18)

FOCUS
This looks a stronger contest than the preceding one over the same trip and the time was 0.35 seconds quicker. There was less than a length covering the front five at the line. Very ordinary form, but it does seem to make sense.
Milk And Sultana Official explanation: jockey said mare was denied a clear run
Revolve Official explanation: jockey said gelding was denied a clear run
Diktatorship(IRE) Official explanation: jockey said gelding lost a shoe

6375 KEMPTON FOR OUTDOOR EVENTS BANDED STKS 2m (P)
3:50 (3:51) (Class 7) 3-Y-O+ **£1,365** (£403; £201) **Stalls** High

Form RPR

5461 **1** **Ganymede**[14] 6132 5-9-12 50 .... IanMongan 2 61
(Mrs L J Mongan) *hld up in rr: prog to trck ldrs over 4f out: rdn 3f out: led over 2f out and hung rt after: drvn clr over 1f out* **7/2**[1]

0502 **2** *4* **Lysander's Quest (IRE)**[14] 6132 8-9-10 48 .... FergusSweeney 5 54
(R Ingram) *settled in midfield: prog to trck ldr 5f out: gng easily 3f out but surprised by wnr over 2f out: hmpd over 1f out: btn aft* **7/2**[1]

0441 **3** *1/2* **Jadeeron**[6] 6280 7-9-13 45 .... (p) OscarUrbina 8 61+
(Miss D A McHale) *hld up in midfield: gng wl 3f out: nt clr run over 2f out jst as ldrs wnt for home: r.o fnl f to take 3rd nr fin* **13/2**[3]

521/ **4** *1 1/2* **Silvaani (USA)**[1658] 997 8-9-4 45 .... NeilChalmers(3) 3 49
(B Forsey) *hld up wl in rr: gd prog on inner over 2f out: chsd ldng pair over 1f out: no imp: lost 3rd nr fin* **40/1**

0-20 **5** *7* **Monte Major (GER)**[14] 6133 3-8-12 45 .... DaneO'Neill 4 40
(D J Daly) *hld up in midfield: effrt over 3f out: chsd ldrs over 2f out: sn outpcd: wknd fnl f* **11/1**

6003 **6** *6* **Whoopsie**[14] 6132 4-9-2 45 .... DuranFentiman(5) 11 33
(S Parr) *rdn to ld and set str pce: hdd over 2f out: wkng whn n.m.r over 1f out* **11/2**[2]

-000 **7** *shd* **King Cugat Kid (USA)**[29] 5830 3-8-12 40 .... PaulEddery 7 33
(Simon Earle) *t.k.h: hld up in last: wl outpcd over 2f out: plugged on* **66/1**

-200 **8** *2 1/2* **Ben Bacchus (IRE)**[152] 2362 4-9-7 45 .... RobertMiles 9 30
(P W Hiatt) *hld up towards rr: prog on outer and prom 5f out: wknd rapidly 2f out* **33/1**

00/5 **9** *8* **Habitual (IRE)**[38] 5652 5-9-11 49 .... TPQueally 12 24
(John A Quinn, Ire) *chsd ldrs: rdn over 3f out: wknd rapidly 2f out* **13/2**[3]

30-0 **10** *3* **Hereditary**[203] 457 4-9-12 50 .... (p) LPKeniry 14 22
(Mrs L C Jewell) *trckd ldrs: lost pl on inner and struggling over 3f out: wknd* **25/1**

11 *8* **Sean Og (IRE)**[55] 5279 4-9-9 50 .... EdwardCreighton(3) 1 12
(E J Creighton) *in tch: prog to chse ldr 6f out to 5f out: sn wknd u.p* **25/1**

0050 **12** *4* **War Feather**[38] 5650 4-9-7 40 .... NickyMackay 6 2
(T D McCarthy) *chsd ldr to 6f out: sn rdn: wknd 4f out* **25/1**

53-1 **13** *1 1/4* **Trebello**[209] 688 5-9-6 47 .... AmirQuinn(3) 13 3
(J R Boyle) *prom tl wknd u.p 7f out: wl bhd 4f out* **8/1**

3m 30.68s (-0.72) **Going Correction** -0.125s/f (Stan)
WFA 3 from 4yo+ 9lb **13** Ran SP% **124.4**
Speed ratings (Par 97):96,94,93,93,89 86,86,85,81,79 75,73,73
CSF £14.53 TOTE £3.90: £1.90, £2.10, £2.50; EX 21.20 Place 6 £117.30, Place 5 £50.73.
Owner Condover Racing **Bred** Mrs A M Jenkins **Trained** Epsom, Surrey
■ Stewards' Enquiry : Ian Mongan two-day ban: careless riding (Nov 17-18)

FOCUS
This proved a real test of stamina thanks to the pace set by Whoopsie and there were some decent margins separating the field at the line. This was almost a carbon copy of the course-and-distance banded contest here two weeks earlier with the front four from that contest in opposition once again, and the one-two was exactly the same. The form is more solid than most staying races on sand.
Whoopsie Official explanation: jockey said filly hung left-handed under pressure
T/Jkpt: Not won. T/Plt: £236.70 to a £1 stake. Pool: £43,230.70. 133.30 winning tickets. T/Qpdt: £9.30 to a £1 stake. Pool: £4,269.60. 339.20 winning tickets. JN

6322 WOLVERHAMPTON (A.W) (L-H)
Monday, November 6

OFFICIAL GOING: Standard to fast
Wind: Light, behind Weather: Sunny

6376 DUNSTALL PARK CENTRE AMATEUR RIDERS' H'CAP (DIV I) 1m 5f 194y(P)
1:20 (1:20) (Class 6) (0-65,64) 3-Y-O+ **£1,977** (£608; £304) **Stalls** Low

Form RPR

0002 **1** **Wait For The Will (USA)**[26] 5910 10-11-2 61 .... (b) MrDHutchison(5) 3 69
(G L Moore) *hld up: hdwy over 5f out: led and hung lft wl ins fnl f: styd on* **7/2**[2]

440P **2** *1 1/2* **Zalkani (IRE)**[23] 5971 6-10-11 54 .... MrSPearce(3) 1 60
(J Pearce) *s.s: hld up: hdwy over 2f out: rdn over 1f out: edgd lft ins fnl f: styd on* **13/2**

3640 **3** *shd* **Alexian**[16] 6108 3-10-9 64 .... MissBKilloran(7) 11 70
(D W P Arbuthnot) *plld hrd and prom: led over 2f out: hdd wl ins fnl f* **33/1**

3325 **4** *1 1/4* **Regency Red (IRE)**[44] 5531 8-10-7 52 .... MrBenBrisbourne(5) 6 56
(W M Brisbourne) *hld up: hdwy 7f out: rdn and hung lft ins fnl f: no ex* **9/2**[3]

0040 **5** *1/2* **Cumbrian Knight (IRE)**[10] 4544 8-10-9 54 .... MissNJefferson(5) 4 57
(J M Jefferson) *s.s: hld up: hdwy and hung lft fr over 1f out: nt trble ldrs* **10/3**[1]

2006 **6** *6* **Scottish River (USA)**[27] 5897 7-11-4 58 .... MrLeeNewnes 5 53
(M D I Usher) *s.s: hld up and bhd: rdn over 1f out: n.d* **8/1**

0500 **7** *shd* **Bramcote Lorne**[27] 5903 3-9-12 53 .... MrRRamloll(7) 7 48
(S Parr) *prom: chsd ldr over 8f out: led over 5f out: hdd over 2f out: wknd fnl f* **20/1**

02B **8** *1* **Love You Always (USA)**[45] 5506 6-9-13 46 .... (t) MrRBirkett(7) 2 39
(Miss J Feilden) *s.s: hld up: plld hrd: n.d* **14/1**

0034 **9** *1 1/2* **Jazrawy**[12] 6178 4-10-5 50 .... MrsMarieKing(5) 8 41
(P W Hiatt) *led and sn clr: hdd over 5f out: wknd over 1f out* **11/2**

0-00 **10** *22* **Lady Lucinda**[4] 6305 5-9-9 42 oh2 .... MissJessicaHolt(7) 9 2
(J R Holt) *chsd ldr over 5f: wknd 4f out* **100/1**

0/06 **11** *28* **Luferton Lane (IRE)**[81] 4506 9-9-9 42 oh12 .... MissAColley(7) 10 —
(R F Marvin) *mid-div: dropped rr over 7f out: sn bhd* **100/1**

3m 4.03s (-3.34) **Going Correction** -0.30s/f (Stan)
WFA 3 from 4yo+ 8lb **11** Ran SP% **119.7**
Speed ratings (Par 101):97,96,96,95,95 91,91,91,90,77 61
CSF £26.49 CT £651.48 TOTE £5.20: £1.90, £2.90, £4.50; EX 41.30 TRIFECTA Not won..
Owner Rdm Racing **Bred** Paul Mellon **Trained** Woodingdean, E Sussex

FOCUS
Just a moderate amateur riders' handicap, but they went a good pace and the winning time was 1.56 seconds faster than the second division. The first two have rated higher in the past and are on fair marks currently, but the third limits this form.
Luferton Lane(IRE) Official explanation: jockey said mare felt wrong

6377 EUROPEAN BREEDERS FUND MAIDEN STKS 5f 216y(P)
1:55 (1:56) (Class 5) 2-Y-O **£3,886** (£1,156; £577; £288) **Stalls** Low

Form RPR

0 **1** **Penny Post (IRE)**[11] 6187 2-8-12 .... JoeFanning 6 80+
(M Johnston) *chsd ldr tl led over 1f out: edgd lft ins fnl f: rdn out* **17/2**

2 **2** *2 1/2* **Herotozero (IRE)**[35] 5735 2-9-0 .... StephenDonohoe(3) 1 77
(Gerard O'Leary, Ire) *hld up: led over 4f: no ex ins fnl f* **7/4**[1]

2600 **3** *2* **Silkie Smooth (IRE)**[2] 6332 2-8-12 78 .... SebSanders 2 66
(B W Hills) *chsd ldrs: rdn and hung lft over 1f out: styd on same pce* **3/1**[2]

6 **4** *nk* **Caught You Looking**[28] 5871 2-8-12 .... AdamKirby 5 65
(W R Swinburn) *hld up: hdwy u.p over 1f out: nt rch ldrs* **11/2**[3]

06 **5** *1 1/2* **Trickle (USA)**[10] 6199 2-8-12 .... (t) BrettDoyle 9 61
(E A L Dunlop) *chsd ldrs: rdn over 2f out: hung lft and wknd over 1f out* **12/1**

302 **6** *1 1/2* **Kilcusnin Queen (IRE)**[19] 6047 2-8-12 .... DarryllHolland 4 56
(Adrian Sexton, Ire) *s.i.s: hld up: hdwy 1/2-way: sn rdn: wknd over 1f out* **8/1**

00 **7** *2 1/2* **Giovanni D'Oro (IRE)**[24] 5939 2-9-3 .... J-PGuillambert 7 54
(N A Callaghan) *hld up: effrt over 2f out: n.d* **25/1**

04 **8** *1 1/4* **Pickering**[3] 6324 2-9-3 .... DavidAllan 10 50
(E J Alston) *dwlt: hdwy over 2f out: rdn and wknd over 1f out* **20/1**

00 **9** *3 1/2* **Axis Mundi (IRE)**[48] 5442 2-8-12 .... PaulMulrennan 8 34
(T J Etherington) *chsd ldrs over 3f* **150/1**

10 *5* **Churchtown** 2-9-3 .... PatCosgrave 3 24
(K R Burke) *sn pushed along and prom: lost pl 4f out: bhd fr 1/2-way* **66/1**

1m 14.1s (-1.71) **Going Correction** -0.30s/f (Stan) **10** Ran SP% **116.8**
Speed ratings (Par 96):99,95,93,92,90 88,85,83,78,72
CSF £23.32 TOTE £10.90: £2.70, £1.20, £1.40; EX 39.30 Trifecta £53.90 Pool £223.46 - 2.94 winning units..
Owner Sheikh Mohammed **Bred** Darley **Trained** Middleham Moor, N Yorks

FOCUS
Just ordinary form but solid nonetheless. The winner was much improved, with the second and third setting the standard.

NOTEBOOK
Penny Post(IRE) shaped with some promise on her debut in a better maiden than this over seven furlongs at Lingfield and has clearly gone the right way since. Very well bred, this will have boosted her paddock value and her connections would no doubt love to add a bit of black type to her record at some point, but the bare form of this success is only fair. (op 9-1 tchd 11-1 and 8-1)
Herotozero(IRE) ran well to take second in a similar event over course and distance on his previous start and this was another fair effort. He helps give the form a solid look. (op 15-8 tchd 9-4)
Silkie Smooth(IRE), switched to Polytrack for the first time and returned to maiden company, did not convince off the bridle and looks one to keep taking on. (op 7-2 tchd 11-4)
Caught You Looking probably failed to improve significantly on the form she showed on her debut at Windsor. (op 5-1 tchd 9-2)
Trickle(USA) was well held and did not do enough to warrant following, even though she is now qualified for a handicap mark.
Kilcusnin Queen(IRE) Official explanation: jockey said filly did not face the kick-back
Pickering Official explanation: jockey said colt hung right

6378 DUNSTALL PARK CENTRE AMATEUR RIDERS' H'CAP (DIV II) 1m 5f 194y(P)
2:30 (2:30) (Class 6) (0-65,65) 3-Y-O+ **£1,977** (£608; £304) **Stalls** Low

Form RPR

2040 **1** **Blue Hedges**[35] 5725 4-10-8 54 .... MissALHutchinson(5) 8 66
(H J Collingridge) *hld up: plld hrd: hdwy over 6f out: led over 2f out: styd on wl* **7/1**

1041 **2** *2 1/2* **Sol Rojo**[66] 4991 4-11-4 62 .... (v) MrSPearce(3) 10 71
(J Pearce) *hld up: hdwy over 2f out: rdn to chse wnr over 1f out: styd on* **5/1**[2]

0056 **3** *1 3/4* **Mr Wiseguy**[13] 6161 3-10-2 54 .... MissFayeBramley(3) 6 60
(G C Bravery) *chsd ldrs: nt clr run over 2f out: sn rdn: styd on* **13/2**[3]

-204 **4** *3* **Danebank (IRE)**[23] 5955 6-10-8 54 .... (p) MrStephenHarrison(5) 1 56
(J Mackie) *chsd ldr: ev ch over 2f out: wknd over 1f out* **8/1**

4210 **5** *7* **Equilibria (USA)**[17] 5201 4-10-7 53 .... MissHayleyMoore(5) 5 45
(G L Moore) *hld up: hmpd over 8f out: hdwy over 5f out: wknd over 2f out* **5/1**[2]

0605 **6** *7* **Bournonville**[8] 6236 3-9-4 44 oh3 ow1 .... MrSRees(5) 9 26
(M Wigham) *led: rdn and hdd over 2f out: sn wknd* **28/1**

3-00 **7** *74* **Zagreus (GER)**[21] 6021 4-9-13 45 .... (p) MrFelixDeGiles(5) 2 —
(H J Manners) *plld hrd and prom: hung rt: wknd over 4f out* **66/1**

0-00 **U** **Commander Wish**[57] 5210 3-9-12 54 ow2 .... MrJDown(7) 7 —
(P Howling) *hld up: hmpd and uns rdr over 8f out* **66/1**

1444 **F** **La Via Ferrata (IRE)**[20] 6027 3-11-2 65 .... MissCHannaford 3 —
(A G Newcombe) *hld up: hdwy whn fell over 8f out: dead* **7/4**[1]

0060 **U** **Cordage (IRE)**[137] 2789 4-10-4 52 .... MissKJames(7) 11 —
(J A Pickering) *plld hrd and prom: stdd and lost pl over 11f out: hmpd and uns rdr over 8f out* **40/1**

3m 5.59s (-1.78) **Going Correction** -0.30s/f (Stan)
WFA 3 from 4yo+ 8lb **10** Ran SP% **115.5**
Speed ratings (Par 101):93,91,90,88,84 80,38,—,—,—
CSF £40.65 CT £238.34 TOTE £14.50: £2.80, £1.60, £2.30; EX 54.30 Trifecta £135.60 Pool £286.55 - 1.50 winning units..
Owner N H Gardner **Bred** S C E A Des Bissons **Trained** Exning, Suffolk

FOCUS
A very weak amateur riders' handicap but plenty of incident with the favourite, La Via Ferrata, falling a mile out and forcing a couple of outsiders to lose their jockeys. The winning time was 1.56 seconds slower than the first division.

6379 BOOK ONLINE AT WOLVERHAMPTON-RACECOURSE.CO.UK NOVICE STKS 7f 32y(P)
3:05 (3:12) (Class 5) 2-Y-O £3,238 (£963; £481; £240) Stalls High

Form RPR
521 1 **Tredegar**25 5918 2-9-5 82 JoeFanning 5 87
(P F I Cole) *a.p: chsd ldr over 4f out: rdn over 2f out: hung lft over 1f out: styd on to ld wl ins fnl f* 5/4²
421 2 1 ¼ **Sagredo (USA)**5 6297 2-9-5 SebSanders 1 84
(Sir Mark Prescott) *wnt lft s: rcvrd to ld 6f out: rdn and hdd wl ins fnl f* 6/5¹
1 3 7 **Social Rhythm**84 4433 2-8-11 74 JimmyQuinn 4 58
(H J Collingridge) *chsd ldrs: rdn over 1f out: wknd ins fnl f* 12/1
06 4 3 **Johannesburg Cat (USA)**14 6146 2-8-6 JamesDoyle(3) 3 49
(N P Littmoden) *led 1f: chsd ldrs: rdn and wknd over 2f out* 10/1³
5 4 **Youbetterbegood (IRE)**7 6263 2-8-7 JerryO'Dwyer(5) 2 42
(Adrian Sexton, Ire) *prom 5f* 150/1

1m 28.27s (-2.13) **Going Correction** -0.30s/f (Stan) 5 Ran SP% 107.3
Speed ratings (Par 96):100,98,90,87,82
CSF £2.88 TOTE £2.60: £1.50, £1.10; EX 3.40.
Owner Elite Racing Club **Bred** Elite Racing Club **Trained** Whatcombe, Oxon

FOCUS
Just the five runners, but a decent novice event for the course/time of year. The first two finished clear and the form should work out.

NOTEBOOK
Tredegar showed improved form to get off the mark in a Newmarket maiden over this trip on his previous start and continued his progression with another decent effort. A tough sort, he should have more to offer. (tchd 6-5 and 11-8)
Sagredo(USA), off the mark over a mile at Nottingham on his previous start, had every chance on this drop in distance and switch to Polytrack. (op 5-4 tchd 11-8 and 11-10)
Social Rhythm would have found this much tougher than the six-furlong maiden she won round here on her debut and was no match for the front two off the back of a near three-month break. (op 10-1 tchd 9-1 and 14-1)
Johannesburg Cat(USA) is not bred for this sort of trip and should do better when returned to shorter. (op 9-1 tchd 8-1 and 12-1)

6380 WOLVERHAMPTON-RACECOURSE.CO.UK H'CAP (DIV I) 1m 1f 103y(P)
3:40 (3:40) (Class 6) (0-58,58) 3-Y-O+ £2,047 (£604; £302) Stalls Low

Form RPR
5044 1 **Some Diva**24 5936 3-9-1 58 (v¹) AdamKirby 11 72
(W R Swinburn) *led 1f: chsd ldrs: rdn to ld and hung lft over 1f out: r.o* 7/1³
0000 2 5 **Right Ted (IRE)**19 6054 3-8-8 58 SladeO'Hara(7) 3 63
(T Wall) *mid-div: hdwy over 2f out: rdn over 1f out: styd on same pce fnl f* 22/1
3000 3 1 ½ **Blue Beacon**11 6193 3-9-0 57 PaulHanagan 7 59
(K A Ryan) *hld up: hmpd after 1f: hdwy u.p over 1f out: nvr trbld ldrs* 16/1
4320 4 nk **Lobengula (IRE)**27 5904 4-9-1 55 TomEaves 12 56
(I W McInnes) *prom: chsd ldr over 6f out: led over 2f out: rdn and hdd over 1f out: wknd ins fnl f* 7/1³
3103 5 ¾ **Risk Free**8 6241 9-8-13 56 (vt) StephenDonohoe(3) 8 56
(P D Evans) *dwlt: hld up: hdwy over 1f out: nvr nrr* 8/1
0000 6 1 ½ **Rashida**23 5973 4-9-1 55 (p) JimCrowley 1 52
(M Appleby) *chsd ldrs: rdn over 2f out: wknd fnl f* 33/1
2025 7 1 **Leighton Buzzard**49 5422 4-9-3 57 DanielTudhope 2 52
(N B King) *hld up: hdwy u.p over 1f out: wknd fnl f* 3/1¹
3100 8 2 ½ **Pawn In Life (IRE)**159 2141 8-9-0 55 (v) JoeFanning 5 44
(M J Attwater) *sn pushed along in rr: n.d* 20/1
0-01 9 1 ¼ **Mighty Splash**76 4672 3-8-11 57 RichardKingscote(3) 9 45
(R Charlton) *s.i.s: hdwy over 3f out: wknd over 2f out* 7/2²
0206 10 1 ½ **Emperor's Well**19 6054 7-9-1 55 (b) PaulMulrennan 13 40
(M W Easterby) *led over 8f out: hdd over 2f out: wknd fnl f* 25/1
0150 11 5 **Fantasy Crusader**49 5422 7-9-0 54 JimmyQuinn 10 29
(R M H Cowell) *chsd ldrs: rdn over 3f out: wknd 2f out* 17/2
3000 12 13 **Penwell Hill (USA)**244 606 7-9-1 55 RobbieFitzpatrick 6 6
(Ian Williams) *prom: hmpd and lost pl over 8f out: hdwy 6f out: wknd over 2f out* 20/1

1m 59.01s (-3.61) **Going Correction** -0.30s/f (Stan)
WFA 3 from 4yo+ 3lb 12 Ran SP% 120.4
Speed ratings (Par 101):104,99,98,97,97 95,95,92,91,90 85,74
CSF £157.86 CT £2382.93 TOTE £6.60: £2.20, £6.80, £5.10; EX 115.90 TRIFECTA Not won..
Owner Mrs P W Harris **Bred** Pendley Farm **Trained** Aldbury, Herts
■ Stewards' Enquiry : Jimmy Quinn one-day ban: careless riding (Nov 17)

FOCUS
The winning time was 0.36 seconds faster than the second divison. A weak handicap which looked quite open beforehand, but the winner was much improved. The placed form looks shaky.
Mighty Splash Official explanation: jockey said filly was outpaced throughout

6381 HOTEL AND CONFERENCING AT DUNSTALL PARK H'CAP 2m 119y(P)
4:15 (4:15) (Class 4) (0-85,85) 3-Y-O+ £5,505 (£1,637; £818; £408) Stalls Low

Form RPR
3404 1 **Billich**17 6075 3-8-6 72 JoeFanning 3 79
(E J O'Neill) *hld up: hdwy 5f out: chsd ldr 2f out: shkn up to ld and edgd lft ins fnl f: styd on wl* 5/2²
3326 2 2 **Reinstated (IRE)**29 5846 3-8-6 72 PaulHanagan 4 77
(B W Hills) *led: rdn and hdd ins fnl f: unable qckn* 5/2²
4001 3 2 **Archduke Ferdinand (FR)**17 6075 8-9-6 80 RichardKingscote(3) 1 82
(A King) *hld up: plld hrd: hdwy 11f out: chsd ldr over 3f out tl rdn 2f out: styd on same pce appr fnl f* 13/8¹
01-0 4 6 **Pocketwood**10 6205 4-9-6 77 JimmyQuinn 2 72
(Jean-Rene Auvray) *chsd ldrs: lost pl 11f out: wknd over 3f out* 14/1
B0-0 5 4 **Garden Society (IRE)**44 5526 9-10-0 85 AdamKirby 6 75
(T T Clement) *sn chsng ldr: rdn over 3f out: sn wknd* 12/1³
00-0 6 1 ¾ **Zacatecas (GER)**51 5383 6-9-9 80 DeanMcKeown 5 68
(A J Chamberlain) *chsd ldrs over 11f* 80/1

3m 40.39s (-2.74) **Going Correction** -0.30s/f (Stan)
WFA 3 from 4yo+ 9lb 6 Ran SP% 110.8
Speed ratings (Par 105):94,93,92,89,87 86
CSF £8.93 TOTE £3.70: £1.90, £1.30; EX 9.40.
Owner Mrs Julie Mitchell **Bred** Mrs S J Hearn **Trained** Averham Park, Notts

FOCUS
No great pace on here, so there was less of an emphasis on stamina than there might have been. A moderate winning time for the grade, and the form is not strong, the winner not needing to improve.
Archduke Ferdinand(FR) Official explanation: jockey said gelding ran too free

6382 HOLIDAY INN WOLVERHAMPTON H'CAP 1m 4f 50y(P)
4:45 (4:45) (Class 6) (0-65,64) 3-Y-O+ £2,730 (£806; £403) Stalls Low

Form RPR
2242 1 **Osolomio (IRE)**8 6244 3-8-12 60 DaleGibson 4 70+
(G A Swinbank) *mde all: rdn over 1f out: r.o* 13/8¹
50/0 2 1 ¾ **Saltrio**188 1385 8-9-6 62 DavidAllan 7 69
(W M Brisbourne) *hld up: hdwy over 2f out: rdn and edgd lft over 1f out: r.o: nt rch wnr* 28/1
0-03 3 ¾ **Art Historian (IRE)**12 6177 3-8-9 57 RobbieFitzpatrick 1 63
(T J Pitt) *a.p: chsd wnr over 3f out: rdn over 1f out: styd on same pce* 9/1
6054 4 3 ½ **Templet (USA)**8 6241 6-9-3 59 (v) PaulHanagan 5 59
(W G Harrison) *chsd ldrs: outpcd over 2f out: styd on ins fnl f* 12/1
5230 5 nk **Bienheureux**7 6256 5-9-8 64 (vt) DarryllHolland 2 64
(Miss Gay Kelleway) *hld up: hdwy over 2f out: sn rdn: wknd fnl f* 7/2²
0400 6 shd **Garibaldi (GER)**27 5904 4-8-13 62 JamesO'Reilly(7) 11 62
(J O'Reilly) *s.i.s: hld up: hdwy u.p over 1f out: nvr nrr* 25/1
1553 7 ½ **Finished Article (IRE)**35 5736 9-8-11 53 J-PGuillambert 9 52
(P A Blockley) *hld up: hdwy u.p over 1f out: nrst fin* 7/1³
2200 8 1 ¾ **Yenaled**23 5955 9-8-7 52 ow1 StephenDonohoe(3) 3 48
(J M Bradley) *hld up: plld hrd: nvr nrr* 16/1
0050 9 13 **Lord Of Dreams (IRE)**11 6189 4-9-5 61 JimCrowley 12 36
(D W P Arbuthnot) *chsd ldrs tl rdn and wknd over 2f out* 25/1
6- 10 shd **Da Pooch (IRE)**11 6197 3-8-10 58 ow2 AdamKirby 6 33
(H Rogers, Ire) *chsd ldr over 8f: wknd over 2f out* 33/1
1000 11 9 **Jaassey**19 6054 3-8-9 57 TomEaves 10 18
(A Crook) *hld up: wknd over 3f out* 28/1
12 14 **Beyond Belief (IRE)**211 929 3-8-7 55 JoeFanning 8 —
(Charles O'Brien, Ire) *prom over 8f* 11/1

2m 36.84s (-5.58) **Going Correction** -0.30s/f (Stan)
WFA 3 from 4yo+ 6lb 12 Ran SP% 122.3
Speed ratings (Par 101):106,104,104,102,101 101,101,100,91,91 85,76
CSF £65.64 CT £345.55 TOTE £2.30: £1.20, £6.20, £3.20; EX 102.60 TRIFECTA Not won..
Owner Hokey Cokey Partnership (2) **Bred** Dr T A Ryan **Trained** Melsonby, N Yorks

FOCUS
A strong pace, and a fair winning time for a race of its class. The winner did it quite well and the form, rated through the third, could work out.
Da Pooch(IRE) Official explanation: jockey said filly had no more to give

6383 WOLVERHAMPTON-RACECOURSE.CO.UK H'CAP (DIV II) 1m 1f 103y(P)
5:15 (5:15) (Class 6) (0-58,58) 3-Y-O+ £2,047 (£604; £302) Stalls Low

Form RPR
0021 1 **Eccollo (IRE)**8 6235 4-9-1 55 6ex RobbieFitzpatrick 7 76+
(T J Pitt) *s.i.s: sn chsng ldrs: led over 1f out: rdn clr: eased ins fnl f* 2/1¹
0415 2 5 **Uhuru Peak**52 5354 5-9-2 56 (bt) PaulMulrennan 3 61
(M W Easterby) *hld up: hdwy u.p over 1f out: no ch w wnr* 16/1
0000 3 1 ½ **Qaasi (USA)**107 3749 4-9-0 54 DeanMernagh 1 56
(M Brittain) *w ldr tl led 3f out: rdn and hdd over 1f out: sn outpcd* 14/1
05 4 ½ **Connotation**83 4446 4-9-1 55 (b) PhillipMakin 8 56
(A G Newcombe) *hld up: r.o ins fnl f: nrst fin* 12/1
-404 5 hd **Qik Dip (IRE)**37 5690 3-8-11 57 StephenDonohoe(3) 5 58
(P D Evans) *chsd ldrs: rdn over 2f out: wknd over 1f out* 10/1
0000 6 ¾ **Ohana**18 6069 3-9-1 58 JimmyQuinn 2 57
(Miss Gay Kelleway) *hld up: rdn over 1f out: nvr trbld ldrs* 40/1
3030 7 shd **Unrestricted**247 586 4-9-1 55 SebSanders 4 54
(C F Wall) *s.i.s: hld up: nt clr run over 1f out: nvr nrr* 15/2³
0610 8 3 ½ **Royal Premier (IRE)**51 5385 3-9-0 57 (v) DarryllHolland 6 50
(H J Collingridge) *mid-div: outpcd 3f out: styd on ins fnl f* 8/1
0421 9 1 **Second Reef**47 5485 4-9-1 55 DavidAllan 12 46
(E J Alston) *hld up: hdwy over 2f out: wknd over 1f out* 13/2²
0060 10 ½ **Monmouthshire**37 5690 3-9-1 58 (v) JoeFanning 11 48
(M L W Bell) *hld up: effrt over 2f out: n.d* 16/1
0303 11 ½ **Red Sail**52 5354 5-9-0 57 (b) RichardKingscote(3) 10 46
(Dr J D Scargill) *mid-div: hdwy over 2f out: wknd over 1f out* 8/1
0200 12 1 ¾ **Newcorp Lad**35 5725 6-9-1 55 J-PGuillambert 9 40
(Mrs G S Rees) *led: rdn and hdd 3f out: wknd over 1f out: eased* 22/1
-000 13 2 **Norwegian**18 6067 5-9-0 54 (p) AdamKirby 13 36
(Ian Williams) *chsd ldrs: rdn over 3f out: wknd over 2f out* 50/1

1m 59.37s (-3.25) **Going Correction** -0.30s/f (Stan)
WFA 3 from 4yo+ 3lb 13 Ran SP% 124.6
Speed ratings (Par 101):102,97,96,95,95 94,94,91,90,90 89,88,86
CSF £40.19 CT £383.45 TOTE £3.00: £1.20, £5.90, £6.60; EX 61.80 TRIFECTA Not won. Place 6 £100.75, Place 5 £39.51.
Owner Stephen Pearson & David Marshall **Bred** Swettenham Stud **Trained** Bawtry, S Yorks

FOCUS
The winning time was 0.36 seconds slower than the first division. The winner was value for extra and the form makes a fair bit of sense through the second and fourth.
Qaasi(USA) Official explanation: jockey said gelding had a breathing problem
Second Reef Official explanation: jockey said gelding ran too keen
Red Sail Official explanation: jockey said mare ran flat
Newcorp Lad Official explanation: jockey said gelding lost its action
T/Plt: £145.10 to a £1 stake. Pool: £52,739.20. 265.25 winning tickets. T/Qpdt: £19.80 to a £1 stake. Pool: £5,186.30. 193.50 winning tickets. CR

5562 LE CROISE-LAROCHE
Monday, November 6

OFFICIAL GOING: Very soft

6384a GRAND PRIX DU NORD (LISTED RACE) 1m 2f 110y
2:40 (2:45) 3-Y-O £17,241 (£6,897; £5,172; £3,448; £1,724)

RPR
1 **Acrobatic (USA)**38 5660 3-9-2 DBoeuf 6 100
(R Charlton) *made all, ridden approaching straight, stayed on well final furlong, driven out SP 84-10* 84/10¹
2 nk **Sureyya (GER)**139 3-8-13 SPasquier 12 97
(E Lellouche, France)
3 shd **Spectaculaire**60 5145 3-9-2 OPeslier 4 100
(A Fabre, France)
4 2 ½ **Tequila Brown (FR)**38 3-8-13 TJarnet 11 92
(M Delzangles, France)
5 1 ½ **Quezon Sun (GER)**202 3-8-13 YBarberot 13 89
(S Wattel, France)

6 5 **Balius (IRE)**[40] 3-9-2 .... MBlancpain 7 83
(C Laffon-Parias, France)
7 1/2 **Royal Pennekamp (FR)**[143] 3-9-2 .... MAndrouin 2 82
(H-A Pantall, France)
8 4 **Serampour (FR)**[21] 3-9-2 .... CSoumillon 9 75
(A De Royer-Dupre, France)
9 15 **Mademoiselle Louna (FR)**[146] 2537 3-8-13 .... RonanThomas 10 45
(J-M Beguigne, France)
10 8 **Kilometre Neuf (FR)**[22] 6001 3-9-2 .... TThulliez 5 34
(F Doumen, France)
0 **Prowess (IRE)**[92] 4179 3-8-13 .... FSpanu 14 —
(R Gibson, France)
0 **Nowisza (FR)**[15] 6120 3-8-13 .... ACrastus 8 —
(Ron Caget, France)
0 **Anna Mona (GER)**[13] 6171 3-8-13 .... IMendizabal 3 —
(A De Royer-Dupre, France)
0 **Mistress Bailey (IRE)**[29] 5852 3-8-13 .... DBonilla 1 —
(R Pritchard-Gordon, France)

2m 16.8s **14** Ran SP% **10.6**
PARI-MUTUEL (Including 1 Euro stake): WIN 9.40; PL 3.40, 3.10, 3.50;DF 51.80.
Owner K Abdulla **Bred** Juddmonte Farms Inc **Trained** Beckhampton, Wilts

NOTEBOOK
Acrobatic(USA), who was rated 79 at the beginning of the season and has progressed through the handicapping ranks, made every yard to win on his first attempt at Listed level. Suited by cut on turf, he had conditions to suit, but he is also very effective on Polytrack, as his three victories at Kempton this season testify, so he might well be one to consider for the more valuable races on the All-Weather this winter.

6376 WOLVERHAMPTON (A.W) (L-H)
Tuesday, November 7

OFFICIAL GOING: Standard
Wind: Light, behind Weather: Fine

6385 BOOK YOUR CHRISTMAS PARTY NOW NURSERY 1m 1f 103y(P)
3:55 (3:55) (Class 6) (0-65,65) 2-Y-O **£2,900** (£856; £428) **Stalls** Low

Form RPR
0550 1 **Dee Cee Elle**[22] 6007 2-8-5 **49** .... JoeFanning 8 54+
(M Johnston) *hmpd s: bhd: hdwy over 2f out: led 1f out: rdn out* **6/1**
050 2 shd **Mud Monkey**[41] 5622 2-9-2 **60** .... GeorgeBaker 2 65+
(B G Powell) *prom: lost pl over 6f out: hdwy and nt clr run over 1f out: r.o* **13/2**
0526 3 3 **Red**[42] 5597 2-9-3 **64** .... JamesDoyle(3) 10 63
(R M Beckett) *in rr: hdwy over 1f out: nt rch ldrs* **5/1**[3]
006 4 3 1/2 **Stars Above**[14] 6157 2-8-6 **50** .... SebSanders 6 42
(Sir Mark Prescott) *hld up: hdwy 1/2-way: rdn over 1f out: wknd ins fnl f* **2/1**[1]
0246 5 2 1/2 **Keep Your Distance**[40] 5633 2-9-7 **65** .... PaulMulrennan 11 53
(K R Burke) *chsd ldr: led over 2f out: hdd & wknd 1f out* **22/1**
0005 6 3/4 **Hair Of The Dog**[13] 6172 2-8-10 **54** .... MickyFenton 13 40
(J G Given) *prom: rdn over 2f out: wknd fnl f* **14/1**
4400 7 hd **Fun Thai**[54] 5323 2-8-0 **47** .... EdwardCreighton(3) 12 33
(M R Channon) *in rr: hdwy 5f out: wknd fnl f* **33/1**
4040 8 1 **Three No Trumps**[13] 6172 2-8-6 **50** .... TPQueally 3 34
(D Morris) *prom: rdn over 2f out: wknd over 1f out* **50/1**
6050 9 2 **Pas De Trois**[19] 6064 2-8-1 **45** .... JimmyQuinn 7 25
(J Pearce) *s.i.s and bmpd s: hdwy to ld 7f out: rdn and hdd over 2f out: sn wknd* **40/1**
0040 10 nk **Diggs Lane (IRE)**[22] 6007 2-8-11 **55** .... (b) SteveDrowne 1 35
(N A Callaghan) *chsd ldrs: rdn over 3f out: wknd over 2f out* **7/2**[2]
000 11 18 **Semahs Holly**[63] 5076 2-7-12 **42** oh12 .... JamieMackay 5 —
(J O'Reilly) *chsd ldrs 6f* **100/1**
6404 12 2 **Lovers Kiss**[14] 6157 2-8-1 **45** .... SilvestreDeSousa 4 —
(N Wilson) *mid-div: hmpd and dropped rr over 7f out: wknd over 4f out* **33/1**
000 13 5 **Queen Of Fools (IRE)**[35] 5760 2-8-6 **50** .... MartinDwyer 9 —
(R Hannon) *prom: rdn 1/2-way: sn wknd* **25/1**

2m 2.11s (-0.51) **Going Correction** -0.175s/f (Stan) **13** Ran SP% **126.0**
Speed ratings (Par 94):95,94,92,89,86 86,86,85,83,83 67,65,60
CSF £44.71 CT £217.85 TOTE £7.90: £3.00, £3.00, £1.90; EX 73.80 TRIFECTA Not won..
Owner Douglas Livingston **Bred** Pollards Stables **Trained** Middleham Moor, N Yorks

FOCUS
A modest nursery where the principals came from off the pace. The form is quite limited but looks sound, rated through the third.

NOTEBOOK
Dee Cee Elle, who had raced on various ground on turf, was having her first experience of the All-Weather and trying her longest trip to-date. Bred to stay middle-distances, she overcame trouble in running and, having hit the front, showed resolution typical of her trainer's charges to hold on. She was racing off a plater's mark and should not go up too much for this, so there may be more to come. (op 7-1)
Mud Monkey, trying his longest trip to date on this handicap debut and going left-handed for the first time, recovered from losing his place to travel well off the pace. He did not get the clearest of runs but had his chance in the straight and just found the winner too determined. (tchd 8-1)
Red has form on fast ground on turf but this was her All-Weather debut and, despite running on in the closing stages, she was never really competitive. She may prefer the faster surface at Lingfield.
Stars Above, making her handicap debut for a shrewd yard having had three runs on turf at shorter trips, got into contention on the home turn but, after having every chance, faded in the closing stages. She may be better at around a mile for the time being. (tchd 9-4 in places)
Keep Your Distance, who had form on good ground at up to a mile, was making his All-Weather debut and ran well under top weight until tiring in the straight. His dam stayed much further but the family produced the miler Observatory and his sire was a sprinter, so it is not easy to determine his best trip.
Hair Of The Dog was close up until fading in the straight, but his best form was over a similar trip on fast turf and he is yet to prove as well suited by sand. (op 16-1 tchd 18-1)
Fun Thai has yet to prove she truly stays this far.
Diggs Lane(IRE), whose best previous effort was on Lingfield's Polytrack, appeared to have his chance but did not get home. (op 9-2)

6386 THE ZONGALERO RESTAURANT MAIDEN STKS 1m 141y(P)
4:20 (4:23) (Class 5) 2-Y-O **£3,886** (£1,156; £577; £288) **Stalls** Low

Form RPR
0 1 **Maraca (IRE)**[10] 6214 2-9-3 .... MartinDwyer 6 76+
(J H M Gosden) *hld up: hdwy 2f out: led ins fnl f: r.o wl* **6/1**
0 2 3 **Arctic Wings (IRE)**[40] 5640 2-9-3 .... DaneO'Neill 4 69
(W R Muir) *chsd ldr: led over 6f out: hdd over 2f out: styd on same pce fnl f* **11/2**[3]
06 3 shd **Tivers Song (USA)**[8] 6254 2-9-3 .... JimCrowley 9 69
(Mrs A J Perrett) *s.i.s: plld hrd and sn prom: outpcd over 3f out: rallied over 1f out: styd on* **11/2**[3]
4 nk **Peregrine Falcon** 2-9-3 .... JoeFanning 5 68
(M Johnston) *led: hdd over 6f out: led over 2f out: hdd and no ex ins fnl f* **7/2**[1]
00 5 1/2 **Summer Of Love (IRE)**[9] 6242 2-8-12 .... DarryllHolland 8 62+
(P F I Cole) *hld up: nt clr run 2f out: hdwy over 1f out: nt trble ldrs* **20/1**
60 6 1 1/2 **Alleviate (IRE)**[8] 6257 2-8-12 .... SebSanders 3 59
(Sir Mark Prescott) *prom: rdn over 2f out: wknd fnl f* **25/1**
7 1 **Born West (USA)** 2-9-3 .... AdrianMcCarthy 10 62
(P W Chapple-Hyam) *hld up: rdn 1/2-way: n.d* **5/1**[2]
8 shd **Cavalry Twill (IRE)** 2-9-3 .... EddieAhern 13 62
(P F I Cole) *s.i.s: a in rr* **7/1**
05 9 nk **Moral Fibre (IRE)**[28] 5901 2-9-3 .... J-PGuillambert 12 61
(M Johnston) *chsd ldrs: rdn and ev ch 2f out: wknd over 1f out* **12/1**
5 10 3/4 **Youbetterbegood (IRE)**[1] 6379 2-8-12 .... JerryO'Dwyer(5) 11 60
(Adrian Sexton, Ire) *hld up: hdwy over 2f out: hung lft and wknd over 1f out* **40/1**
11 3 **Danjoe** 2-9-3 .... TomEaves 1 53
(R Brotherton) *s.s: outpcd* **50/1**
0 12 2 1/2 **Bish Basher (IRE)**[43] 5565 2-9-3 .... FergusSweeney 7 48
(P A Blockley) *chsd ldrs 6f* **100/1**

1m 51.99s (0.23) **Going Correction** -0.175s/f (Stan) **12** Ran SP% **118.1**
Speed ratings (Par 96):91,88,88,87,87 86,85,85,84,84 81,79
CSF £37.04 TOTE £7.30: £2.60, £1.60, £2.50; EX 39.90 TRIFECTA Not won..
Owner The Royal Ascot Racing Club **Bred** Tinnakill Partnership No 1 **Trained** Newmarket, Suffolk
■ Stewards' Enquiry : J-P Guillambert three-day ban: careless riding; one-day ban: failed to ride to draw (Nov 18, 20-22)

FOCUS
An interesting maiden for the track, featuring newcomers from major stables but run 2.68 sec slower than the following older horse handicap. The third is the best guide to the level.

NOTEBOOK
Maraca(IRE) ◆, a 105,000gns Derby entry from the family of Sayedah, had finished last on his debut at Newmarket last month but had clearly learnt for the experience and having travelled well off the pace, came through to win in decisive fashion. He looks the sort to make up into a decent handicapper for connections, who will presumably be thinking of aiming him at next season's Royal meeting. (op 7-1)
Arctic Wings(IRE), a stoutly-bred son of In the Wings, was another to be well beaten in a Newmarket maiden on his debut, but he was ridden positively with that experience behind him and had his chance. However, he allowed the winner through on his inside and had no answer to that rival's finishing kick. He can be expected to win races in handicap company over further. (op 6-1)
Tivers Song(USA), a $110,000 half-brother to seven winners in the USA, missed the break and was too keen early. However, he kept on again in the straight and could be interesting now he is qualified for handicaps, especially if ridden positively over sprint trips. (op 9-2)
Peregrine Falcon ◆, a 160,000gns brother to the top-class German-trained horse Soldier Hollow, was made favourite and showed plenty of promise on this racecourse debut. He broke well and made much of the running, but was headed and weakened halfway up the straight. He looks sure to come on for the experience and promises to make up into a decent sort next year. (op 5-1)
Summer Of Love(IRE) was held up and did not get the clearest of runs, but was noted keeping on at the finish without being given too hard a time, and can make her mark in handicaps.
Alleviate(IRE) ◆, half-sister to the useful Allegretto from a family that has served the trainer very well over the years, was having her third run in less than three weeks and is likely to be a different proposition in middle distance handicaps next season. (op 33-1)
Born West(USA), a $120,000 American-bred colt, drifted in the betting and never reached a challenging position. He is likely to do better with the experience under his belt. (op 7-2)

6387 RINGSIDE SUITE 700 THEATRE STYLE CONFERENCE H'CAP 1m 141y(P)
4:50 (4:50) (Class 6) (0-60,60) 3-Y-O+ **£2,730** (£806; £403) **Stalls** Low

Form RPR
2423 1 **Panic Stations**[58] 5210 3-8-9 **60** .... LukeMorris(7) 3 75
(M L W Bell) *chsd ldrs: nt clr run over 2f out: led over 1f out: sn hung lft: rdn out* **5/2**[1]
6500 2 1 3/4 **Musicmaestroplease (IRE)**[17] 6101 3-8-6 **57** .... MarkCoumbe(7) 9 68
(S Parr) *hld up: hdwy over 2f out: rdn and hung lft over 1f out: sn ev ch: no ex ins fnl f* **8/1**[3]
3240 3 2 **Spark Up**[52] 5370 6-8-13 **54** .... (b) MartinDwyer 7 61
(J W Unett) *hld up: hdwy and hung lft over 1f out: nt rch ldrs* **12/1**
4060 4 1/2 **The Gaikwar (IRE)**[24] 5974 7-9-3 **58** .... (b) EddieAhern 11 64
(R A Harris) *hld up: hdwy over 2f out: rdn and hung lft over 1f out: styd on same pce* **12/1**
1016 5 3 1/2 **Todlea (IRE)**[50] 5436 6-9-1 **56** .... (t) DaneO'Neill 4 55
(Jean-Rene Auvray) *chsd ldrs: rdn and ev ch 2f out: wknd over 1f out* **9/2**[2]
0460 6 shd **Ignition**[121] 3331 4-8-13 **59** .... (p) LiamJones(5) 8 58
(W M Brisbourne) *led: rdn and hdd over 1f out: sn wknd* **20/1**
1240 7 1 1/4 **Mister Maq**[35] 5757 3-9-0 **58** .... (b) DarryllHolland 2 54
(A Crook) *sn outpcd: styd on ins fnl f: nrst fin* **33/1**
0000 8 2 **Loaderfun (IRE)**[29] 5865 4-9-0 **55** .... (t) PatCosgrave 12 47
(N Wilson) *hld up: effrt over 2f out: sn wknd* **50/1**
0002 9 2 **Right Ted (IRE)**[1] 6380 3-8-7 **58** .... SladeO'Hara(7) 13 45
(T Wall) *sn chsng ldr: rdn and ev ch over 2f out: sn hung rt and wknd* **17/2**
0-60 10 3 1/2 **Ennobling**[23] 5992 3-9-2 **60** .... SebSanders 6 40
(E F Vaughan) *prom: rdn over 2f out: sn hung rt and wknd* **16/1**
0-00 11 5 **Korolieva (IRE)**[24] 5973 3-9-2 **60** .... JimmyQuinn 1 30
(K A Ryan) *mid-div: rdn over 2f out: sn wknd* **33/1**
-460 12 3 1/2 **Dispol Foxtrot**[29] 5863 8-9-0 **55** .... SilvestreDeSousa 5 17
(D Nicholls) *rel to r: bhd: sme hdwy 4f out: sn wknd* **9/2**[2]
0RR0 R **Arabie**[24] 5974 8-9-5 **60** .... (b) RobbieFitzpatrick 10 —
(Peter Grayson) *ref to r* **40/1**

1m 49.31s (-2.45) **Going Correction** -0.175s/f (Stan)
WFA 3 from 4yo+ 3lb **13** Ran SP% **122.9**
Speed ratings (Par 101):103,101,99,99,96 96,94,93,91,88 83,80,—
CSF £22.68 CT £218.64 TOTE £3.40: £1.40, £4.30, £3.30; EX 42.60 Trifecta £260.90 Part won. Pool: £367.60 - 0.20 winning units..
Owner D W & L Y Payne **Bred** Wickfield Farm Partnership **Trained** Newmarket, Suffolk

FOCUS
A moderate handicap and not all that strong form, rated through the third.
Mister Maq Official explanation: jockey said gelding did not face the kick-back
Ennobling Official explanation: jockey said filly moved poorly in closing stages

6388 WOLVERHAMPTON-RACECOURSE.CO.UK NURSERY 5f 216y(P)
5:20 (5:20) (Class 5) (0-75,73) 2-Y-O **£4,533** (£1,348; £674; £336) **Stalls** Low

Form RPR

6425 **1** **Mac Gille Eoin**[15] 6146 2-9-6 **72** .... JimCrowley 1 73
(J Gallagher) *chsd ldrs: led over 3f out: clr 2f out: sn rdn: all out* **8/1**

2323 **2** *nk* **Vadinka**[29] 5871 2-9-7 **73** .... KimTinkler 4 73
(N Tinkler) *sn pushed along in rr: hdwy over 2f out: r.o* **11/2**[3]

6006 **3** *nk* **Hucking Hill (IRE)**[6] 6291 2-8-12 **64** ....(b) DaneO'Neill 10 63
(J R Best) *outpcd: hdwy over 1f out: r.o wl* **14/1**

3026 **4** *nk* **Kilcusnin Queen (IRE)**[1] 6377 2-9-4 **70** .... DarryllHolland 6 68
(Adrian Sexton, Ire) *chsd ldrs: rdn over 2f out: sn chsng wnr: edgd rt over 1f out: styd on* **12/1**

5130 **5** *¾* **Hephaestus**[15] 6146 2-9-7 **73** .... DeanMcKeown 2 69
(A J Chamberlain) *sn outpcd: hdwy and nt clr run over 1f out: nvr nrr* **16/1**

100 **6** *nk* **Emma's Surprise**[26] 5916 2-9-6 **72** .... PaulMulrennan 7 67
(K A Ryan) *chsd ldrs: hung rt over 3f out: outpcd over 2f out: hung lft over 1f out: styd on* **12/1**

0205 **7** *nk* **Totally Free**[5] 6311 2-7-12 **57** ....(v) FrankiePickard(7) 3 51
(M D I Usher) *s.i.s: outpcd: hdwy over 1f out: n.d* **50/1**

234 **8** *1 ¼* **Herb Paris (FR)**[41] 5607 2-9-4 **70** .... MartinDwyer 13 61
(M P Tregoning) *trckd ldrs: rdn over 2f out: wknd over 1f out* **5/1**[2]

0402 **9** *1 ½* **Nou Camp**[69] 4921 2-8-4 **56** .... JamieMackay 11 42
(N A Callaghan) *hld up: nvr nrr* **20/1**

3265 **10** *2 ½* **Emefdream**[36] 5721 2-8-8 **60** .... CatherineGannon 9 39
(K A Ryan) *chsd ldrs: carried rt over 2f out: wknd over 1f out* **7/1**

3030 **11** *½* **Silver Appraisal**[35] 5747 2-8-9 **61** .... PaulEddery 5 38
(B Smart) *mid-div: effrt over 2f out: wknd over 1f out* **20/1**

104 **12** *7* **Danetime Music (IRE)**[41] 5606 2-9-7 **73** .... EddieAhern 8 29
(M J Wallace) *mid-div: rdn 1/2-way: wknd 2f out* **4/1**[1]

261 **13** *7* **Auction Oasis**[69] 4926 2-9-1 **67** .... AdrianMcCarthy 12 2
(B Palling) *led: hdd over 3f out: wknd over 2f out* **20/1**

1m 15.4s (-0.41) **Going Correction** -0.175s/f (Stan) 13 Ran SP% **119.8**
Speed ratings (Par 96):95,94,94,93,92 92,92,90,88,85 84,75,65
CSF £49.07 CT £639.46 TOTE £11.90: £4.40, £1.40, £5.90; EX 54.10 Trifecta £209.90 Part won. Pool: £295.77 - 0.34 winning units..
Owner M C S D Racing Partnership **Bred** M C S D Racing Ltd **Trained** Chastleton, Oxon

FOCUS
A fair nursery run 0.60sec slower than the following all-aged maiden. The first seven were closely bunched and the form is limited.

NOTEBOOK
Mac Gille Eoin, with previous experience on Polytrack but not on this course, was given a good ride, taking the lead on the turn and opening up a clear advantage which, although he tired in the final furlong, proved enough for him to hold on. His pace should enable him to continue to win his share. (op 10-1)
Vadinka, who like the winner was having his first run here having performed well on the other two Polytrack courses, ran on well in the latter stages and was closing the winner down all the way to the line. She has now been placed on all of her last five starts and deserves to lose her maiden tag, but she is creeping up the weights and may need to find more to do so. (op 6-1 tchd 13-2)
Hucking Hill(IRE), who was a decent type early on in the year, has been revived by the application of blinkers and finished really well. Considering he made his nursery debut in July off a mark of 82, he could be well handicapped now.
Kilcusnin Queen(IRE), whose best form on turf was over the minimum trip, ran much better than on her Polytrack debut over course and distance the day before. (op 11-1)
Hephaestus, who beat today's winner at Lingfield last month, was 1lb worse off and was not helped by being hampered early in the straight.
Emma's Surprise, making her handicap and All-Weather debut, hung in both directions in the second half of the race but ran her best race since her winning debut. (op 14-1)
Herb Paris(FR), dropping in trip, travelled well on the heels of the leaders but found next to nothing once asked for her effort. (op 11-2 tchd 9-2)
Danetime Music(IRE), made favourite despite shouldering top weight, never got into contention having been held up off the pace. (op 5-2)

6389 DINE AT DUNSTALL PARK MEDIAN AUCTION MAIDEN STKS 5f 216y(P)
5:50 (5:50) (Class 5) 3-5-Y-0 **£3,238** (£963; £481; £240) **Stalls** Low

Form RPR

2343 **1** **Small Stakes (IRE)**[23] 5987 4-9-3 64........(vt[1]) SebSanders 8 60+
(P J Makin) *hld up in tch: n.m.r whn rdn to ld wl ins fnl f: r.o* **11/10**[1]

0300 **2** *nk* **Make My Dream**[49] 5453 3-9-3 56........ JimCrowley 1 59
(J Gallagher) *chsd ldrs: rdn to ld ins fnl f: sn hdd: styd on* **11/2**[3]

/0-0 **3** *1 ½* **Gifted Lass**[64] 5060 4-8-12 45........ DavidAllan 3 50
(J Balding) *led: rdn clr and edgd rt over 1f out: hdd and unable qckn ins fnl f* **40/1**

34-0 **4** *1 ¾* **Nawayea**[56] 5270 3-8-12 67........ EddieAhern 2 44
(C N Allen) *chsd ldrs: rdn over 1f out: styd on same pce* **14/1**

5 *2* **Miss Double Daisy** 3-8-12........ TomEaves 6 38
(B Smart) *sn pushed along in rr: hung lft over 3f out: styd on appr fnl f: nrst fin* **20/1**

4020 **6** *½* **Guadaloup**[64] 5062 4-8-12 51........(b) DeanMernagh 5 37
(M Brittain) *s.s: outpcd: nt clr run over 3f out: hdwy u.p over 1f out: nrst fin* **12/1**

2305 **7** *1* **Mujeak (IRE)**[25] 5951 3-9-3 59........(p) GrahamGibbons 9 39
(J J Quinn) *chsd ldrs: rdn over 2f out: wknd over 1f out* **17/2**

405- **8** *1 ¼* **Alcharinga (IRE)**[473] 3703 4-9-3 59........ PaulMulrennan 10 35
(T J Etherington) *prom over 3f* **28/1**

0233 **9** *2 ½* **Ceredig**[24] 5969 3-9-3 59........(t) MartinDwyer 4 28
(W R Muir) *chsd ldrs: rdn over 2f out: wknd over 1f out* **4/1**[2]

10 *4* **Paper Maite** 5-8-12........ MickyFenton 7 11
(S R Bowring) *s.i.s: outpcd* **80/1**

11 *2 ½* **Thistimesforgood (IRE)**[18] 6089 3-9-3........ DarryllHolland 11 8
(Adrian Sexton, Ire) *s.s: outpcd* **40/1**

0030 **12** *8* **Little Miss Verity**[88] 4329 3-8-12 47........ RichardThomas 13 —
(J A Geake) *a in rr: wknd 1/2-way* **50/1**

1m 14.8s (-1.01) **Going Correction** -0.175s/f (Stan) 12 Ran SP% **124.2**
Speed ratings (Par 103):99,98,96,94,91 90,89,87,84,79 75,65
CSF £7.39 TOTE £2.10: £1.10, £3.00, £7.70; EX 14.30 Trifecta £293.00 Part won. Pool: £412.76 - 0.67 winning units..
Owner J P Carrington with Ahier Marchant Moore **Bred** Brian Williamson **Trained** Ogbourne Maisey, Wilts

FOCUS
A moderate sprint maiden run 0.6sec faster than the preceding nursery. The form is pretty weak.
Thistimesforgood(IRE) Official explanation: jockey said gelding missed the break

6390 ENJOY EXECUTIVE HOSPITALITY AT WOLVERHAMPTON H'CAP 7f 32y(P)
6:20 (6:20) (Class 6) (0-60,60) 3-Y-0+ **£2,730** (£806; £403) **Stalls** High

Form RPR

0243 **1** **Redwood Rocks (IRE)**[20] 6060 5-8-12 **60**........ MarkLawson(5) 6 73+
(B Smart) *racd keenly: led 6f out: rdn clr over 1f out* **5/1**[1]

2030 **2** *3* **Moon Forest (IRE)**[6] 6294 4-9-0 **57**........(p) SteveDrowne 3 62
(J M Bradley) *hld up: hdwy 2f out: nt rch wnr* **12/1**

404 **3** *shd* **Mozakhraf (USA)**[94] 4154 4-9-0 **57**........ PaulHanagan 1 62
(K A Ryan) *led 1f: chsd ldrs: rdn and hung rt over 2f out: styd on same pce fnl f* **8/1**

0000 **4** *½* **Dudley Docker (IRE)**[54] 5316 4-9-1 **58**........ DarryllHolland 7 62+
(D Carroll) *s.i.s: hld up: n.m.r over 3f out: hdwy over 1f out: nt clr run and swtchd lft 1f out: r.o: nrst fin* **5/1**[1]

0050 **5** *nk* **Hits Only Jude (IRE)**[20] 6060 3-9-2 **60**........ DeanMcKeown 8 63
(J Pearce) *chsd ldrs: rdn 1/2-way: styd on same pce fnl f* **6/1**[3]

5000 **6** *shd* **Fairdonna**[25] 5953 3-9-1 **59**........ EddieAhern 5 62
(D J Coakley) *mid-div: hmpd 6f out and over 3f out: styd on appr fnl f: nvr nrr* **10/1**

4000 **7** *2* **Cool Sands (IRE)**[36] 5737 4-9-2 **59**........(v) DaneO'Neill 11 56
(D Shaw) *hld up: effrt over 1f out: n.d* **16/1**

0045 **8** *1 ¾* **Patavium Prince (IRE)**[4] 6325 3-9-2 **60**........ MartinDwyer 4 53
(J R Best) *chsd ldrs: rdn over 2f out: wknd fnl f* **11/2**[2]

0030 **9** *¾* **Dancing Deano (IRE)**[40] 5635 4-9-1 **58**........(v) JamieMackay 12 49
(R M Whitaker) *chsd ldrs: rdn over 2f out: wkng whn hmpd ins fnl f* **20/1**

0000 **10** *4* **Anchor Date**[10] 6227 4-9-3 **60**........(t) MickyFenton 9 41
(D Shaw) *hld up: a in rr* **28/1**

-000 **11** *1 ½* **Bernie's Beau (IRE)**[7] 6288 3-8-9 **60**........ RussellKennemore(7) 10 37
(R Hollinshead) *hld up: rdn and wknd over 2f out* **66/1**

0040 **12** *12* **No Grouse**[48] 5487 6-9-0 **57**........ DavidAllan 2 2
(E J Alston) *chsd ldrs over 4f: eased over 1f out* **6/1**[3]

1m 28.45s (-1.95) **Going Correction** -0.175s/f (Stan)
WFA 3 from 4yo+ 1lb 12 Ran SP% **120.8**
Speed ratings (Par 101):104,100,100,99,99 99,97,95,94,89 88,74
CSF £65.44 CT £489.84 TOTE £5.60: £2.20, £4.60, £3.40; EX 67.50 Trifecta £296.40 Part won. Pool: £417.56 - 0.34 winning units. Place 6 £198.60, Place 5 £64.80.
Owner Dan Hall **Bred** 6c Stallions Ltd **Trained** Hambleton, N Yorks

FOCUS
A moderate handicap run at a sound gallop and won in decisive style. The form is solid backed up by a decent time.
Dudley Docker(IRE) Official explanation: jockey said gelding was denied a clear run
Patavium Prince(IRE) Official explanation: jockey said gelding hung right into first bend and ran too freely early
No Grouse Official explanation: jockey said gelding hung right and lost its action
T/Plt: £164.10 to a £1 stake. Pool: £56,558.15. 251.45 winning tickets. T/Qpdt: £17.40 to a £1 stake. Pool: £6,075.30. 257.70 winning tickets. CR

6346 FLEMINGTON (L-H)
Tuesday, November 7

OFFICIAL GOING: Good

6391a LAVAZZA LONG BLACK STKS (H'CAP) 1m 6f
12:45 (12:00) 4-Y-0+ **£28,419** (£8,547; £3,846; £1,709; £855)

RPR

1 **Southern Courage (NZ)** 4-8-7........ CNewitt 103
(Mick Price, Australia) **13/1**

2 *2* **Bay Story (USA)**[31] 5817 4-8-7........ KFallon 101
(B Ellison) *niggled along early to race in 5th 4l off ld, rdn and 2l 4th ent str, stayed on steadily (4/1F)* **4/1**[1]

3 *1* **Slamun (AUS)** 6-8-9........(b) BShinn 102
(T Vasil, Australia) **11/2**[2]

4 *6* **Vengo (NZ)**[369] 5-8-10........ KerrinMcEvoy 96
(Lee Freedman, Australia) **8/1**[3]

5 *shd* **Diamond Jake (AUS)**[1466] 5622 7-9-0........ LNolen 99
(B Mayfield-Smith, Australia)

6 *¾* **Ista Kareem (NZ)**[239] 5-8-9........ SArnold 94
(J Gask, Australia)

7 *½* **Bugatti Royale (USA)**[1470] 5533 6-8-7........(b) MZahra 91
(Peter Morgan, Australia)

8 *hd* **Shrogginet (NZ)** 6-8-7........(b) DMoor 91
(Tom Hughes, Australia)

9 *1* **Encosta Legend (AUS)** 8-8-7........ NicholasRyan 90
(Allison Bennett, Australia)

10 *nk* **Lady Gulch (AUS)** 4-8-7........ MRodd 89
(G Rogerson, Australia)

11 *1* **Kuniya (NZ)**-8-7........(b) CSymons 88
(T Noonan, Australia)

12 *shd* **Special Scene (AUS)**[584] 7-8-7........ BMelham 88
(Dan O'Sullivan, New Zealand)

13 *5* **Don Raphael (AUS)**[402] 7-8-7........(b) CMunce 82
(B Jenkins, New Zealand)

14 *3 ¼* **The Bavarian (AUS)**[239] 4-8-7........(b) ODoleuze 78
(C Little, Australia)

15 *12* **Pride Of Westbury (AUS)**[184] 3-8-7........ StevenKing 72
(Danny O'Brien, Australia)

16 *3 ¼* **Enzed (AUS)**[731] 6582 8-8-7........(b) GChilds 60
(Allison Bennett, Australia)

2m 55.88s 16 Ran SP% **53.6**

Owner K Neylon & S Barnett **Bred** P Thorburn **Trained** Australia

NOTEBOOK
Bay Story(USA) kept on well in the straight to record another solid effort for his new stable. He stays well but has mile-and-a-half pace as well.

6392a EMIRATES MELBOURNE CUP (GROUP 1) (H'CAP) 2m
4:00 (4:01) 3-Y-0+
£1,324,786 (£320,513; £160,256; £85,470; £53,419; £47,009)

RPR

1 **Delta Blues (JPN)**[17] 6110 5-8-11........ YIwata 11 122
(Katsuhiko Sumii, Japan) *racd in 2nd, 3rd halfway, led over 2f out, 2l clr over 1f out, strongly chal and carried lft closing stages, hld on gamely* **17/1**

2 shd **Pop Rock (JPN)**[17] 6110 5-8-5 .... DMOliver 12 116
(Katsuhiko Sumii, Japan) *midfield, 12th halfway, 9th str, hdwy down outside to go 2nd over 1f out, chal and hung lft last 100 yds, no ex cl home* **5/1**[1]

3 4 1/2 **Maybe Better (AUS)**[3] 6346 4-7-12 .... CMunce 3 104
(B Mayfield-Smith, Australia) *in touch, 7th halfway, 6th straight, hard ridden to dispute 2nd briefly over 1f out, kept on at one pace* **9/1**[3]

4 1 1/2 **Zipping (AUS)**[10] 5-8-4 .... GBoss 20 109
(G Rogerson, Australia) *always prominent, 3rd halfway, 4th straight, went 2nd 1 1/2f out, one pace from over 1f out* **9/1**[3]

5 1 1/2 **Land 'n Stars**[17] 6110 6-8-5 .... JohnEgan 6 108
(Jamie Poulton) *always in touch, 5th halfway, 5th and ridden along entering straight, plugged on at same pace* **200/1**

6 snk **Mahtoum (AUS)**[10] 7-8-5 .... CoreyBrown 7 108
(K Waugh, Australia) *raced in 9th, 8th straight, stayed on at same pace towards inside final 2f* **200/1**

7 nk **Yeats (IRE)**[52] 5395 5-9-4 .... KFallon 4 121
(A P O'Brien, Ire) *missed break, recovered to race midfield, steady hdwy on outside to go 2nd halfway, led over 4f out to over 2f out, one pace* **11/2**[2]

8 1/2 **Activation (NZ)**[17] 6110 5-8-5 .... MRodd 22 107
(G Rogerson, Australia) *towards rear, 17th halfway, 12th straight, headway down outside 2f out, one pace closing stages* **20/1**

9 1 **Mandela (NZ)**[13] 5-8-0 .... CraigAWilliams 14 101
(R Yuill, New Zealand) *prominent, 4th halfway, headway on inside to go 3rd and every chance entering straight, weakened 1 1/2f out* **20/1**

10 3/4 **Glistening**[44] 5547 4-8-0 .... SSeamer 24 101
(L M Cumani) *midfield, 16th straight, kept on steadily last 2f* **80/1**

11 3 **Kerry O'Reilly (NZ)**[13] 6-8-2 ....(b) CELammas 5 100
(J Gibbs, New Zealand) *raced in 10th, 7th straight on inside, soon one pace* **50/1**

12 3 1/4 **Railings (AUS)**[3] 6347 5-8-10 .... DBeadman 2 104
(J Hawkes, Australia) *midfield, 11th straight, soon ridden and one pace* **50/1**

13 2 3/4 **Headturner (AUS)**[3] 6347 4-8-7 .... GChilds 19 99
(J Hawkes, Australia) *14th halfway, 13th straight, never a factor* **70/1**

14 nse **Short Pause**[17] 6110 7-8-6 .... NCallow 17 98
(D Hayes, Australia) *raced in 6th, 10th straight, soon beaten* **20/1**

15 2 **Dolphin Jo (AUS)**[10] 4-7-12 ....(b) ASpiteri 18 88
(Terry & Karina O'Sullivan, Australia) *19th halfway, always in rear* **80/1**

16 3 1/4 **Art Success (NZ)**[10] 5-8-1 .... APattillo 13 87
(John Collins, Australia) *20th halfway, always in rear* **40/1**

17 2 **Dizelle (AUS)**[17] 6110 5-8-2 .... BShinn 21 86
(J Hawkes, Australia) *21st halfway, always in rear* **25/1**

18 1 3/4 **Geordieland (FR)**[76] 4713 5-8-7 .... LDettori 10 90
(J A Osborne) *held up, 14th halfway, 15th straight, soon ridden and beaten* **15/1**

19 3/4 **Tawqeet (USA)**[17] 6110 5-8-10 ....(b) DDunn 9 92
(D Hayes, Australia) *held up, 18th halfway, always in rear* **5/1**[1]

20 nk **On A Jeune (AUS)**[13] 6-8-5 .... DGauci 15 87
(P Montgomerie, Australia) *22nd halfway, always behind* **20/1**

21 shd **Demerger (AUS)**[10] 6-8-1 ow1 ....(b) SBaster 23 83
(Danny O'Brien, Australia) *last to under 2f out, always behind* **100/1**

22 3/4 **Ice Chariot (AUS)**[3] 6346 4-8-2 .... JimByrne 1 83
(R Maund, Australia) *mifdfield, 13th halfway, 18th and beaten straight* **200/1**

23 15 **Zabeat (NZ)**[3] 6346 7-8-2 ....(b) ODoleuze 16 68
(Donna Logan, New Zealand) *soon led, headed over 4f out, weakened* **200/1**

3m 21.42s
WFA 3 from 4yo+ 9lb **23** Ran SP% **112.4**
(including Aus$1 stake): WIN 17.50; PL 5.60, 2.10, 3.90; DF 41.30; SF 91.80.
Owner Sunday Racing Co Ltd **Bred** Northern Farm **Trained** Japan

NOTEBOOK
Delta Blues(JPN), two kilos better in with ante-post favourite Tawqeet for about half a length, started at a wonderful price once the world and his mate had decided that the Australian-ridden Pop Rock was the one to win it for Japan. He only just made it but could not have been more game. Predictions of a wholesale invasion are probably well wide of the mark but there is no doubt that Japanese racing is well stocked with stayers.
Pop Rock(JPN) made a lot of ground down the outside in the straight. He was reaching his limit in the final furlong and hung into the winner, but he only just failed in a tremendous finish and the two came well clear.
Land 'n Stars had clearly not been right when finishing last in the Caulfield Cup and this was much more his form. He was always well in touch and kept on steadily in the straight. He stays on for the Perth Cup on New Year's Day and his trainer is already talking of a return to Flemington in November.
Yeats(IRE) made a lot of ground to take it up more than half a mile out and Fallon was accused of doing too much too quickly. His answer was that he needed to be at the front early because the horse did not have the speed to wait to make his challenge in the straight.
Glistening was drawn on the complete outside and never got into the race, although he was still well rewarded for finishing tenth. His trainer said that he would give any future Cup runner a prep in Australia.
Geordieland(FR) broke blood vessels and this effort can be discounted.
Tawqeet(USA) was always towards the rear and was lame in his near fore afterwards. He is likely to make his next appearance in Dubai.

6370 KEMPTON (A.W) (R-H)
Wednesday, November 8

OFFICIAL GOING: Standard
Wind: almost nil

6393 RACING UK FOR £15 PER MONTH MEDIAN AUCTION MAIDEN STKS 1m (P)
3:50 (3:54) (Class 6) 2-Y-0 **£2,388** (£705; £352) **Stalls** High

Form RPR

0 1 **Mafeking (UAE)**[16] 6145 2-9-3 .... FergusSweeney 8 79+
(M R Hoad) *leggy: scope: tall: hld up in midfield: prog on outer over 2f out: chal fnl f: urged along and styd on wl to ld last stride* **50/1**

2 hd **Sign Of The Cross** 2-9-3 .... OscarUrbina 5 79+
(J R Fanshawe) *w'like: scope: hld up: gng easily whn nt clr run 2f out: swtchd lft and prog to ld jst over 1f out: rn green: hdd last stri* **9/2**[3]

3 4 **Personal Column** 2-9-3 .... IanMongan 6 69
(T G Mills) *w'like: lengthy: trckd ldrs: rdn and effrt towards inner 2f out: outpcd by ldng pair fnl f* **11/2**

5 4 shd **The Fifth Member (IRE)**[16] 6143 2-9-3 .... AdamKirby 4 69
(R M Flower) *str: prom on outer: rdn to chal 2f out: upsides over 1f out: sn outpcd* **33/1**

62 5 2 1/2 **Heights Of Golan**[16] 6145 2-9-0 .... JamesDoyle(3) 2 63
(I A Wood) *w'like: lw: mde most: drvn over 2f out: hdd & wknd jst over 1f out* **3/1**[1]

4 6 1/2 **Geordie's Pool**[16] 6143 2-9-3 .... EddieAhern 13 62
(J W Hills) *w'like: scope: lw: settled in rr: effrt and prog 2f out: styng on whn nt clr run over 1f out: no hdwy after* **13/2**

63 7 nk **Give Evidence**[22] 6032 2-9-3 .... DarryllHolland 11 61
(A P Jarvis) *neat: bmpd after 2f: in tch: effrt against far rail over 2f out: wknd jst over 1f out* **10/3**[2]

0 8 1 3/4 **Deep Cover (IRE)**[95] 4140 2-9-3 .... RichardThomas 3 57
(R M Flower) *s.i.s: hld up in last pair: outpcd fr 2f out* **66/1**

0 9 3/4 **Norman The Great**[11] 6224 2-9-3 .... BrettDoyle 14 56
(Jane Chapple-Hyam) *w'like: prom: rdn wl over 2f out: wknd over 1f out* **20/1**

66 10 hd **Streamer**[8] 6270 2-8-12 .... JoeFanning 1 50
(M Johnston) *leggy: pressed ldr: upsides 2f out: wknd rapidly over 1f out* **16/1**

11 11 **Astral Charmer** 2-9-3 .... TPQueally 7 30
(M H Tompkins) *w'like: bit bkwd: s.i.s: rn green and a in last pair: t.o fnl 2f* **33/1**

0 12 1/2 **Kiss Chase (IRE)**[7] 6290 2-9-3 .... MartinDwyer 9 29
(P Mitchell) *prom 3f: wknd rapidly: t.o 2f out* **33/1**

1m 40.45s (-0.35) **Going Correction** -0.125s/f (Stan) **12** Ran SP% **117.9**
Speed ratings (Par 94):96,95,91,91,89 88,88,86,85,85 74,74
CSF £239.99 TOTE £68.60: £25.40, £1.50, £2.30; EX 614.00.
Owner Mrs J E Taylor **Bred** Darley **Trained** Lewes, E Sussex

FOCUS
A fair maiden run with unexposed horses dominating the finish and could prove a reasonable race.

NOTEBOOK
Mafeking(UAE), a brother to Three Thieves, a nine-furlong winner at two, did not show a lot on his debut at Lingfield, but he improved dramatically on this second start, getting the better of the second-favourite in a close finish. He shapes like a colt that will stay further and do better in time.
Sign Of The Cross, a half-brother to Song Of Songs, a dual ten-furlong winner at three, Rumour, a mile winner at four, Zone, a mile winner at two, and Dare To Dance, a winner over hurdles, looked as if he was going to have a hard-luck story as he struggled to get a clear run two furlongs out, but he got free of trouble early enough to hit the front a furlong out, looking by far the most likely winner. He was outbattled in the end, showing signs of greenness in the process, but compensation surely awaits with this experience under his belt. (op 11-4)
Personal Column, a brother to Embraced, a smart dual winner over a mile, and half-brother to four other winners, including high-class Nowhere To Exit and Royal Hunt Cup winner Cesare, showed the ruight attitude, responding to pressure and keeping on well for third. (op 5-1 tchd 6-1)
The Fifth Member(IRE), whose dam was unraced but is a half-sister to five winners, again raced prominently from the off and managed to reverse Lingfield form with Geordie's Pool. He looks to be going the right way, and will qualify for handicaps after one more run.
Heights Of Golan, who was rushed up to make the running, tried to make this a stamina test as he is bred to make up into a middle-distance handicapper next season. (op 11-4)
Geordie's Pool, who finished in front of The Fifth Member at Lingfield on his debut, could not confirm that form at this different track. His style of racing and pedigree suggest that he will be seen in a much better light over middle distances next season. (op 10-1 tchd 12-1)
Give Evidence Official explanation: jockey said colt was slightly hampered

6394 SHILTON SHARPE QUARRY NURSERY 1m (P)
4:20 (4:23) (Class 6) (0-65,65) 2-Y-0 **£2,388** (£705; £352) **Stalls** High

Form RPR

035 1 **My Secrets**[11] 6207 2-9-7 **65** .... JoeFanning 9 71
(M Johnston) *lw: led: drvn and hdd over 1f out: rallied to ld ins fnl f: jst hld on* **10/1**

0400 2 shd **Venir Rouge**[18] 6106 2-9-0 **65** .... JamesMillman(7) 4 71
(M Salaman) *towards rr: prog on outer over 2f out: drvn to chal ins fnl f: upsides nr fin: jst pipped* **25/1**

4600 3 nk **Fares (IRE)**[26] 5940 2-9-6 **64** ....(b[1]) BrettDoyle 12 69+
(C E Brittain) *hld up towards rr: prog on inner over 2f out: nt qckn over 1f out: r.o fnl f and gaining nr fin* **8/1**

0050 4 1 1/4 **Prince Of Charm (USA)**[18] 6106 2-9-0 **58** ....(b) SteveDrowne 10 60
(P Mitchell) *cl up: prog 2f out: rdn to ld over 1f out: hdd & wknd ins fnl f* **11/1**

360 5 1/2 **Froissee**[12] 6200 2-9-2 **60** .... OscarUrbina 7 61+
(N A Callaghan) *hld up towards rr: prog over 2f out: drvn and nt qckn over 1f out: hld whn nt clr run ins fnl f* **10/1**

051 6 2 **Benayoun**[14] 6172 2-9-2 **60** .... TPQueally 13 56
(M H Tompkins) *lw: towards rr: drvn over 2f out: plugged on fr over 1f out: no imp on ldrs* **8/1**

630 7 1 **Ask Yer Dad**[48] 5496 2-9-7 **65** .... MickyFenton 5 59
(Mrs P Sly) *wl in rr: drvn in last trio over 2f out: kpt on fr over 1f out: n.d* **14/1**

0044 8 nk **Susanna's Prospect (IRE)**[36] 5747 2-9-6 **64** .... EddieAhern 14 57
(B J Meehan) *trckd ldrs on inner: rdn to chal over 2f out: wknd over 1f out* **4/1**[1]

0400 9 4 **Alloro**[53] 5382 2-9-7 **65** .... JimCrowley 1 49
(D J S Ffrench Davis) *s.i.s: a wl in rr: rdn and struggling over 2f out* **33/1**

035 10 1 **Law Of The Land (IRE)**[8] 6283 2-9-4 **62** .... MartinDwyer 11 44+
(W R Muir) *cl up tl wknd wl over 1f out: eased fnl f* **11/2**[2]

4030 11 3/4 **Only Hope**[11] 6217 2-9-1 **59** ....(v) AdamKirby 2 39
(Ernst Oertel) *s.v.s: hld up in last trio: gng wl enough 3f out: shkn up and no prog over 2f out: wknd over 1f out* **12/1**

5212 12 nk **Emergency Services**[14] 6172 2-9-4 **62** ....(p) RichardThomas 6 42
(Tom Dascombe) *w wnr to over 2f out: wknd rapidly* **13/2**[3]

062 13 6 **Burningfold Babe**[11] 6222 2-9-3 **61** .... AdrianMcCarthy 3 27
(P Winkworth) *cl up tl wknd 3f out: t.o* **33/1**

1m 40.45s (-0.35) **Going Correction** -0.125s/f (Stan) **13** Ran SP% **121.5**
Speed ratings (Par 94):96,95,95,94,93 91,90,90,86,85 84,84,78
CSF £243.84 CT £2164.22 TOTE £13.20: £5.20, £6.40, £2.70; EX 343.40.
Owner Ahmed Jaber **Bred** Hascombe And Valiant Studs **Trained** Middleham Moor, N Yorks
■ Stewards' Enquiry : James Millman one-day ban: careless riding (Nov 20)

FOCUS
Run in an identical time to the previous maiden, there was a good pace to this nursery and the form should work out with the first four close to their marks.

NOTEBOOK
My Secrets, running on the All-Weather and in a handicap for the first time, rallied well, as is typical of his stable's runners, when headed by Prince Of Charm and held on for a narrow verdict on the line. He should make up into a middle-distance performer next year when good ground or faster should suit on turf. (op 9-1)
Venir Rouge, another running on the All-Weather for the first time, appreciated the good pace and came with a strong late run which only just failed. He looks the sort who could be worth persevering with on the sand over the winter. Official explanation: jockey said colt hung right
Fares(IRE), blinkered for the first time, was another who benefited from being held up off a decent pace. The return to a mile suited him and he now looks fairly rated compared with the 6lb higher mark he began his handicapping career off back in August.
Prince Of Charm(USA), who was warm before the race, returned to form on this sounder surface but, having got to the front approaching the final furlong, was worn down in the closing stages. He might need dropping back to seven. (op 12-1 tchd 10-1)
Froissee, running in a handicap for the first time and debuting on sand, was denied racing room inside the last, but for which she would have probably finished fourth. She looks likely to get further, in contrast to what her pedigree suggests. Official explanation: jockey said filly suffered interference (op 8-1)
Benayoun, who won a soft-ground seller last time out, kept on from off the pace but never really threatened. She might do better on the Fibresand surface at Southwell. (op 10-1 tchd 15-2)
Susanna's Prospect(IRE), who finished well over six furlongs last time out, found the step up to a mile in a race run at a decent pace putting too much emphasis on stamina, and she failed to get home. (op 3-1)
Law Of The Land(IRE) Official explanation: jockey said colt had no more to give
Only Hope Official explanation: jockey said filly missed the break

6395 DIGIBET.COM H'CAP — 6f (P)
4:50 (4:51) (Class 6) (0-60,64) 3-Y-O+ — **£2,388** (£705; £352) **Stalls** High

Form — RPR
5425 **1** **Mina**[7] 6293 4-9-2 **60** .... SteveDrowne 11 — 70
(Rae Guest) *trckd ldrs: effrt on inner 2f out: drvn to ld ins fnl f: in command whn hung lft last 50yds* **7/1**
0021 **2** 1 ¾ **Musical Script (USA)**[8] 6288 3-8-13 **64** 6ex .... JamesMillman(7) 7 — 69
(Mrs A J Hamilton-Fairley) *lw: pressed ldr: led 2f out: drvn and hdd ins fnl f: one pce* **9/2**[1]
3043 **3** ½ **Middle Eastern**[8] 6288 4-9-1 **59** .... (p) J-PGuillambert 8 — 62
(P A Blockley) *hld up in rr: urged along and effrt 2f out: no great prog tl drvn and r.o last 150yds: nrst fin* **6/1**[3]
4006 **4** *nk* **Greenwood**[21] 6048 8-9-0 **58** .... RobertHavlin 4 — 60
(P G Murphy) *wl in tch: chsd ldng trio over 1f out: one pce u.p* **13/2**
0062 **5** ½ **Polar Force**[5] 6325 6-9-0 **58** .... AdamKirby 5 — 59
(Mrs C A Dunnett) *pressed ldrs: upsides 2f out: nt qckn over 1f out: fdd* **5/1**[2]
0001 **6** ¾ **Turibius**[44] 5576 7-9-0 **58** .... JimCrowley 12 — 57
(T E Powell) *sn settled in rr: effrt on inner 2f out: limited prog over 1f out: no imp fnl f* **16/1**
0451 **7** *nk* **Danish Blues (IRE)**[16] 6129 3-9-2 **60** .... (p) DaleGibson 1 — 58
(D E Cantillon) *t.k.h: hld up towards rr: drvn 2f out: nt qckn and btn over 1f out* **7/1**
3000 **8** ½ **Mister Incredible**[8] 6288 3-9-0 **58** .... (p) DarrylHolland 6 — 54
(V Smith) *hld up in last and swtchd to inner: stl last 2f out: drvn and styd on fr over 1f out: no ch* **20/1**
3050 **9** 3 ½ **King Of Charm (IRE)**[119] 3406 3-8-10 **59** .... RobynBrisland(5) 9 — 45
(G L Moore) *pressed ldrs: lost pl u.p 2f out: n.d after* **66/1**
6005 **10** *nk* **George The Second**[8] 6288 3-8-11 **58** .... RichardKingscote(3) 2 — 43
(Mrs H Sweeting) *racd wd: pressed ldrs: wknd fr over 2f out* **16/1**
0000 **11** 2 ½ **Vlasta Weiner**[8] 6288 6-9-0 **58** .... (b) FergusSweeney 3 — 35
(J M Bradley) *dwlt: prog on wd outside into midfield after 2f: lost pl u.p sn after 1/2-way* **50/1**
4523 **12** *hd* **Feelin Irie (IRE)**[69] 4943 3-9-2 **60** .... MartinDwyer 10 — 37
(J R Boyle) *mde most to 2f out: wknd and eased* **6/1**[3]

1m 12.97s (-0.73) **Going Correction** -0.125s/f (Stan) — **12** Ran SP% **121.7**
Speed ratings (Par 101):99,96,96,95,94 93,93,92,88,87 84,84
CSF £39.11 CT £206.55 TOTE £10.40: £3.10, £2.80, £1.90; EX 81.20.
Owner C J Mills **Bred** C J Mills And The Selkirk Syndicate **Trained** Newmarket, Suffolk

FOCUS
Moderate handicap form in which the long-standing maiden Mina finally broke her duck. The form is rated around the placed horses.
Feelin Irie(IRE) Official explanation: jockey's rep said, regarding easing his mount inside final two furlongs, that jockey had injured his ribs whilst coming out of the stalls

6396 DIGIBET.CO.UK H'CAP — 7f (P)
5:20 (5:22) (Class 6) (0-65,68) 3-Y-O+ — **£2,388** (£705; £352) **Stalls** High

Form — RPR
2520 **1** **Million Percent**[10] 6240 7-8-11 **64** .... LiamJones(5) 8 — 73
(C R Dore) *burst out of stalls: restrained to trck ldrs: effrt 2f out: drvn to ld 1f out: hld on wl* **25/1**
0330 **2** ½ **Hollow Jo**[16] 6147 6-9-0 **62** .... EddieAhern 6 — 70
(J R Jenkins) *hld up wl in rr: prog 2f out: nt clr run briefly 1f out: r.o fnl f to take 2nd last stride* **11/1**
0031 **3** *hd* **Reeling N' Rocking (IRE)**[24] 5986 3-9-2 **65** .... DaleGibson 13 — 72+
(B W Hills) *wl in tch in midfield: effrt 2f out: drvn and r.o fnl f: nt rch wnr* **7/1**
1660 **4** ¾ **Jordan's Light (USA)**[50] 5446 3-8-12 **61** .... (v[1]) SteveDrowne 14 — 66
(T J Pitt) *led for 2f: styd prom on inner: nrly upsides 1f out: one pce* **12/1**
0330 **5** *hd* **Dance To The Blues (IRE)**[36] 5756 5-9-2 **64** .... (p) AdamKirby 11 — 69
(B De Haan) *led after 2f: hrd rdn and hdd 1f out: fdd nr fin* **20/1**
4411 **6** *hd* **Gracie's Gift (IRE)**[21] 6060 4-9-0 **62** .... FergusSweeney 5 — 66
(A G Newcombe) *lw: pushed up into midfield after 1f: rdn and struggling over 2f out: picked up fnl f: styd on* **11/2**[2]
5241 **7** ½ **Fateful Attraction**[7] 6293 3-9-2 **68** 6ex .... (b) JamesDoyle(3) 4 — 71
(I A Wood) *hld up wl in rr: effrt 2f out: swtchd ins and prog over 1f out: one pce fnl f* **4/1**[1]
5604 **8** 1 **The Crooked Ring**[7] 6293 4-8-12 **60** .... (p) JimCrowley 12 — 60
(P D Evans) *pressed ldrs: chalng wl over 1f out: wknd fnl f* **14/1**
2604 **9** 1 ¾ **Border Artist**[7] 6294 7-8-13 **61** .... TPQueally 10 — 57
(J Pearce) *settled towards rr: rdn and nt qckn 2f out: one pce after* **20/1**
0000 **10** 2 **First Friend (IRE)**[16] 6147 5-9-3 **65** .... DarrylHolland 9 — 56
(P Mitchell) *dwlt: wl in rr: effrt on inner 2f out: no prog fr over 1f out* **12/1**
5-06 **11** ¾ **Look Of Eagles**[22] 6036 4-9-3 **65** .... NelsonDeSouza 3 — 54
(P F I Cole) *s.i.s: a wl in rr: rdn and no prog 2f out* **14/1**
0/62 **12** 2 ½ **Tamworth (IRE)**[13] 6193 4-8-12 **60** .... OscarUrbina 7 — 42
(E J Creighton) *chsd ldrs tl wknd 2f out* **10/1**
0030 **13** 4 **Joy And Pain**[14] 6174 5-8-12 **65** .... (p) KevinGhunowa(5) 2 — 37
(R A Harris) *b: prom tl wknd over 2f out* **14/1**

1-12 **14** 3 ½ **Free Angel (USA)**[146] 2574 4-9-2 **64** .... JoeFanning 1 — 27
(M Wigham) *lw: dwlt and restrained s: hld up in last: shkn up and no rspnse 2f out* **6/1**[3]

1m 25.79s (-1.01) **Going Correction** -0.125s/f (Stan)
WFA 3 from 4yo+ 1lb — **14** Ran SP% **128.3**
Speed ratings (Par 101):100,99,99,98,98 97,97,96,94,91 91,88,83,79
CSF £289.57 CT £2215.39 TOTE £28.80: £6.20, £3.70, £3.10; EX 264.50.
Owner Ship Tottenham **Bred** D J And Mrs Deer **Trained** West Pinchbeck, Lincs

FOCUS
A modest handicap run at an ordinary gallop but the form appears sound enough. The winner burst the stalls fractionally early but the result was allowed to stand.

6397 DIGIBET SPORTS BETTING H'CAP — 7f (P)
5:50 (5:51) (Class 3) (0-90,88) 3-Y-O+
£7,790 (£2,332; £1,166; £583; £291; £146) **Stalls** High

Form — RPR
6000 **1** **Marajaa (IRE)**[11] 6221 4-8-10 **80** .... BrettDoyle 3 — 92
(W J Musson) *hld up in midfield: effrt 2f out: squeezed though and r.o to ld jst ins fnl f: r.o wl* **8/1**
-000 **2** 1 ¼ **Cape Greko**[31] 5845 4-8-13 **83** .... (v) FergusSweeney 4 — 92
(A M Balding) *t.k.h: hld up in midfield: prog over 1f out: rdn to chal ent fnl f: r.o but a hld* **33/1**
0064 **3** 1 ¾ **Adeje Park (IRE)**[24] 5990 3-9-3 **88** .... AdrianMcCarthy 5 — 92
(P W Chapple-Hyam) *racd wd: trckd ldrs: effrt 2f out: hanging lft fr over 1f out: nt qckn* **7/2**[1]
4213 **4** *nk* **Landucci**[34] 5778 5-8-6 **79** .... JamesDoyle(3) 7 — 82
(J W Hills) *hld up towards rr: gd prog on inner to chal jst over 1f out: one pce fnl f* **6/1**[2]
0032 **5** *nk* **Gifted Gamble**[36] 5749 4-8-13 **83** .... (b) JoeFanning 9 — 86
(K A Ryan) *hld up towards rr: prog to chse ldrs 1f out: pushed along and styd on same pce* **7/1**[3]
3423 **6** *nk* **Outer Hebrides**[21] 6059 5-8-12 **82** .... (vt) EddieAhern 2 — 84
(J R Boyle) *racd wd: wl in tch: rdn and cl enough over 1f out: one pce* **8/1**
2520 **7** *hd* **Grimes Faith**[26] 5945 3-8-10 **81** .... SteveDrowne 13 — 82
(R Hannon) *trckd ldrs on inner: prog to ld over 1f out: hdd & wknd jst ins fnl f* **7/1**[3]
1000 **8** 1 ¼ **Ludovico**[39] 5666 3-9-0 **85** .... IanMongan 10 — 83
(K A Ryan) *chsd ldr: drvn over 1f out: stl cl up 1f out: wknd* **14/1**
1500 **9** 1 **Purus (IRE)**[34] 5777 4-8-8 **78** .... DarryllHolland 6 — 73
(P Mitchell) *led at decent pce: hdd & wknd over 1f out* **14/1**
010 **10** 1 ½ **Bee Stinger**[24] 5990 4-8-10 **80** .... MickyFenton 14 — 72
(I A Wood) *trckd ldng pair: rdn whn hmpd wl over 1f out: no ch after* **8/1**
0230 **11** *shd* **Jaad**[42] 5627 3-8-5 **79** .... EdwardCreighton(3) 11 — 70
(Christian Wroe, UAE) *hld up in last pair: stl last 2f out: shuffled along over 1f out: running on nr fin* **33/1**
4050 **12** 1 ¼ **Deeper In Debt**[21] 6054 8-8-8 **78** .... DaleGibson 8 — 66
(J Akehurst) *hld up in last: rdn and effrt over 2f out: sn no prog and btn* **33/1**
0000 **13** 2 ½ **Marshman (IRE)**[11] 6221 7-8-8 **78** .... TPQueally 1 — 60
(M H Tompkins) *racd on outer: in tch in midfield: wknd 2f out* **16/1**
0505 **14** *hd* **Desert Dreamer (IRE)**[30] 5877 5-8-9 **79** .... JimCrowley 12 — 60
(P R Chamings) *settled in last trio: brief effrt over 2f out: sn wknd* **12/1**

1m 24.85s (-1.95) **Going Correction** -0.125s/f (Stan)
WFA 3 from 4yo+ 1lb — **14** Ran SP% **130.6**
Speed ratings (Par 107):106,104,102,102,101 101,101,99,98,97 96,95,92,92
CSF £268.69 CT £849.99 TOTE £25.90: £5.20, £9.10, £1.80; EX 550.10.
Owner John D Jacques **Bred** Shadwell Estate Company Limited **Trained** Newmarket, Suffolk
■ Stewards' Enquiry : Steve Drowne one-day ban: careless riding (Nov 20)

FOCUS
A pretty decent handicap run at no more than a fair gallop. The form is rated around the first three but is not totally convincing.

NOTEBOOK
Marajaa(IRE), backed in from 20-1, landed a bit of a gamble, and in style too, as he showed a good turn of foot to take a gap between horses and go clear. He was in the process of running well when hampered on his debut for this yard at this venue back in April, and while his performances elsewhere since have not been noteworthy, he clearly acts well on this surface and appreciated returning here. There should be more to come from him. (op 20-1)
Cape Greko, 12lb lower than when last seen in a handicap, showed more sparkle than of late but could not match the winner's turn of foot. He is at least on a more realistic mark now though, and perhaps he can build on this promise. (op 25-1)
Adeje Park(IRE), made favourite on the back of her promising return to action at Wolverhampton last time following a two-month break, had every chance. Off a mark of 88 she is vulnerable to better-handicapped rivals. (op 10-3 tchd 4-1)
Landucci, back to the scene of his previous two wins, ran on well next to the inside rail, but he could have done with a stronger pace. While he has never won off a mark as high as this before, he could still pop up when the race is run to suit. (op 9-2)
Gifted Gamble, who last ran over this trip in July 2005, normally races over six furlongs, but he seemed to get it well enough.
Outer Hebrides extended his losing run to 23 starts, and his handicap mark has hardly budged during that long barren spell. (tchd 15-2)
Bee Stinger was beginning to struggle when hampered over a furlong out. He would have finished a lot closer without that but would not have been in the places. (op 9-1)
Jaad Official explanation: jockey said colt ran too free early

6398 JOIN THE RACING UK CLUB H'CAP — 2m (P)
6:20 (6:23) (Class 6) (0-65,65) 3-Y-O+ — **£2,388** (£705; £352) **Stalls** High

Form — RPR
-003 **1** **Grasp**[14] 6178 4-9-4 **55** .... (v) GeorgeBaker 7 — 62
(G L Moore) *cl up on outer: trckd ldr over 5f out and gng easily: shkn up to ld over 2f out: rdn and kpt on steadily fnl 2f* **9/2**[2]
060 **2** 1 ¾ **Coppington Melody (IRE)**[11] 6225 3-8-6 **52** .... TPQueally 6 — 57
(B W Duke) *hld up in rr: prog 6f out: drvn to chse ldng pair 3f out: kpt on to take 2nd ins fnl f* **14/1**
0632 **3** ¾ **Coda Agency**[22] 6027 3-8-11 **57** .... JimCrowley 8 — 61
(D W P Arbuthnot) *lw: w ldr: led 6f out: drvn and hdd over 2f out: kpt on but lost 2nd ins fnl f* **5/1**[3]
3460 **4** 3 ½ **Amwell Brave**[28] 5910 5-9-11 **62** .... EddieAhern 10 — 62
(J R Jenkins) *settled in midfield: prog 3f out: sn rdn: kpt on same pce and nvr able to chal* **6/1**
0246 **5** 1 ½ **Phone In**[30] 5875 3-9-3 **63** .... (b[1]) IanMongan 12 — 61
(R Brotherton) *t.k.h: hld up in cl tch: drvn to chse ldrs 3f out: no imp: wknd wl over 1f out* **8/1**
6400 **6** *nk* **Moon Emperor**[25] 5971 9-9-9 **60** .... (p) DarryllHolland 1 — 58
(J R Jenkins) *hld up in rr: outpcd fr 4f out and no ch after: kpt on fr over 2f out* **2/1**[1]

200/ **7** *6* **Find The King (IRE)**[70] 3603 8-9-4 **55** RobertHavlin 9 45
(D W P Arbuthnot) *in tch: drvn 1/2-way: sn lost pl: wl bhd over 3f out: eased but kpt on fnl 2f* **25/1**
006/ **8** *24* **Whist Drive**[674] 1302 6-10-0 **65** BrettDoyle 13 27
(Mrs N Smith) *dwlt: in tch in rr to 5f out: sn bhd: t.o* **33/1**
6000 **9** *5* **Montana Sky (IRE)**[14] 6178 3-8-5 **51** RichardThomas 3 7
(R A Harris) *prom tl wknd u.p 6f out: t.o 3f out* **33/1**
50-5 **10** *nk* **Valiant Shadow (GER)**[8] 6272 4-9-2 **53** MickyFenton 11 8
(W Jarvis) *mde most to 6f out: wknd rapidly: t.o* **16/1**
6034 **11** *dist* **Noddies Way**[28] 5910 3-8-9 **55** (b[1]) SteveDrowne 2 —
(J F Panvert) *reluctant to enter stalls: dwlt: nt keen and sn struggling: t.o over 5f out* **7/1**
0/50 **12** *dist* **Habitual (IRE)**[2] 6375 5-8-12 **49** AdamKirby 5 —
(John A Quinn, Ire) *dwlt: prog fr rr to dispute ld after 6f to over 6f out: wknd rapidly and sn wl t.o* **12/1**
30-0 **P** **Hathlen (IRE)**[22] 6037 5-9-4 **58** (b) JamesDoyle[(3)] 4 —
(Mrs N Smith) *racd wd: hld up in last pair: prog 5f out: rdn to dispute 3rd 3f out: broke down and p.u over 2f out* **33/1**

3m 31.7s (0.30) **Going Correction** -0.125s/f (Stan)
WFA 3 from 4yo+ 9lb **13 Ran SP% 139.0**
Speed ratings (Par 101):94,93,92,91,90 90,87,75,72,72 —,—,—
CSF £75.50 CT £347.05 TOTE £6.50: £2.20, £3.60, £2.30; EX 152.10 Place 6 £1942.54, Place 5 £641.33.
Owner R A Green **Bred** A D G Oldrey **Trained** Woodingdean, E Sussex

FOCUS
A moderate stayers' handicap notable for the rather skewed market resulting from the fact that Moon Emperor had to be backed so heavily by one of the off-course firms to reduce their liabilities on a multiple bet placed in one of their shops. The time was modest and the form looks limited with the third to form.
Phone In Official explanation: jockey said gelding ran too free
Habitual(IRE) Official explanation: jockey said gelding lost its action
T/Plt: £2,513.00 to a £1 stake. Pool: £47,507.85. 13.80 winning tickets. T/Qpdt: £71.20 to a £1 stake. Pool: £6,076.10. 63.10 winning tickets. JN

6385 WOLVERHAMPTON (A.W) (L-H)
Wednesday, November 8

OFFICIAL GOING: Standard to fast
Wind: Moderate, half-behind

6399 HOTEL & CONFERENCING AT DUNSTALL PARK CLAIMING STKS 5f 20y(P)
1:20 (1:20) (Class 6) 3-Y-O+ **£2,730** (£806; £403) **Stalls** Low

Form RPR
4566 **1** **Twinned (IRE)**[10] 6234 3-8-5 50 (p) JimmyQuinn 3 56
(Karen George) *a.p: rdn to ld jst ins fnl f: hld on narrowly* **25/1**
0-03 **2** *shd* **Gifted Lass**[1] 6389 4-8-2 45 ow3 MarcHalford[(3)] 1 56
(J Balding) *sn led: rdn and hdd jst ins fnl f: pressed wnr to line* **12/1**
4004 **3** *nk* **Night Prospector**[20] 6065 6-9-5 74 GeorgeBaker 9 69
(G L Moore) *towards rr: str hdwy on outside appr fnl f: r.o: nvr nrr* **11/4[2]**
3011 **4** *1 1/2* **Trinculo (IRE)**[8] 6274 9-9-11 90 AdrianTNicholls 5 69
(D Nicholls) *a.p: rdn 1/2-way: nt qckn ins fnl f* **2/1[1]**
010 **5** *nk* **Mynd**[30] 5878 6-8-11 60 J-PGuillambert 11 54
(B Palling) *led early on outside: styd prom tl one pce fnl f* **25/1**
0000 **6** *3/4* **Succeed (IRE)**[49] 5480 3-7-11 50 DuranFentiman[(5)] 6 42
(Mrs H Sweeting) *bhd: rdn and hdwy over 1f out but nvr nr to chal* **16/1**
2306 **7** *hd* **Peruvian Style (IRE)**[30] 5878 5-8-4 55 BarrySavage[(7)] 8 51
(J M Bradley) *mid-div: rdn and no hdwy fr over 1f out* **12/1**
0600 **8** *shd* **Rainbow Bay**[41] 5635 3-8-7 64 (b) PaulHanagan 4 46
(R A Fahey) *outpcd in rr: sme hdwy fr over 1f out but nvr nr to chal* **4/1[3]**
6000 **9** *1/2* **Beverley Beau**[58] 5243 4-8-4 46 KristinStubbs[(7)] 13 49
(Mrs L Stubbs) *a towards rr* **50/1**
1500 **10** *1 1/4* **Henry Tun**[5] 6325 8-8-10 57 (b) JasonEdmunds[(3)] 12 46
(J Balding) *bhd on outside: hdwy 1/2-way: wknd over 1f out* **25/1**
6000 **11** *hd* **Waggledance (IRE)**[10] 6233 4-7-12 45 KellyHarrison[(7)] 7 37
(D Carroll) *in tch: rdn 2f out: wknd over 1f out* **100/1**
0600 **12** *nk* **Patternmaker (USA)**[8] 6288 4-8-11 58 DaneO'Neill 2 42
(A M Hales) *a towards rr* **16/1**
360 **13** *2 1/2* **Spirit Of Coniston**[93] 4201 3-8-8 58 ow1 (b) RobbieFitzpatrick 10 30
(Peter Grayson) *mid-div: wknd wl over 1f out* **25/1**

61.57 secs (-1.25) **Going Correction** -0.275s/f (Stan) **13 Ran SP% 125.5**
Speed ratings (Par 101):99,98,98,95,95 94,93,93,93,91 90,90,86
CSF £295.10 TOTE £34.60: £5.30, £5.80, £1.10; EX 265.20 TRIFECTA Not won..The winner was the subject of a friendly claim. Night Prospector was claimed by Ron Harris for £12,000.
Owner A B Parr **Bred** Philip Hore Jnr **Trained** Higher Easington, Devon
■ Stewards' Enquiry : Marc Halford one-day ban: excessive use of the whip (Nov 20)

FOCUS
A reasonably strong-looking claimer on paper fought out by two horses qualified for banded company. The form must be considered suspect and is best assessed through the runner-up.

6400 BOOK ONLINE AT WOLVERHAMPTON-RACECOURSE.CO.UK NURSERY 5f 20y(P)
1:50 (1:50) (Class 5) (0-85,78) 2-Y-O **£3,886** (£1,156; £577; £288) **Stalls** Low

Form RPR
0531 **1** **Yungaburra (IRE)**[6] 6311 2-8-8 **68** 6ex GregFairley[(3)] 3 86+
(T J Pitt) *mde all: clr over 1f out: pushed out fnl f: unchal* **1/1[1]**
4222 **2** *4* **Mazin Lady**[9] 6255 2-8-11 **68** PaulHanagan 5 68
(Miss J A Camacho) *chsd ldrs: kpt on to go 2nd over 1f out but no ch w wnr* **5/1[3]**
0000 **3** *2* **Riverside Dancer (USA)**[47] 5503 2-9-7 **78** (b[1]) CatherineGannon 1 70+
(K A Ryan) *slowly away: bhd tl hdwy on outside 2f out: r.o ins fnl f: nvr nrr* **4/1[2]**
4204 **4** *1/2* **Hucking Hope (IRE)**[21] 6056 2-8-12 **69** DaneO'Neill 6 60
(J R Best) *chsd ldrs: rdn 1/2-way: no hdwy fr over 1f out* **16/1**
4041 **5** *3/4* **Sister Etienne (IRE)**[56] 5282 2-8-13 **70** PhillipMakin 2 58
(T D Barron) *chsd wnr tl rdn over 1f out: wknd ins fnl f* **16/1**
130 **6** *6* **Roheryn (IRE)**[33] 5788 2-9-4 **75** JimmyQuinn 8 41
(John A Quinn, Ire) *s.i.s: outpcd and bhd fr 1/2-way* **6/1**
0504 **7** *5* **Daruma (IRE)**[116] 3521 2-7-7 **55** oh5 (b) DuranFentiman[(5)] 4 —
(Peter Grayson) *chsd ldrs for 2f* **100/1**

61.13 secs (-1.69) **Going Correction** -0.275s/f (Stan) **7 Ran SP% 113.7**
Speed ratings (Par 96):102,95,92,91,90 80,72
CSF £6.40 CT £13.91 TOTE £2.00: £1.60, £2.00; EX 5.40 Trifecta £30.30 Pool: £400.34 - 9.30 winning units.
Owner J David Abell **Bred** Newlands House Stud **Trained** Bawtry, S Yorks

FOCUS
This was very much a one-horse race, with Yungaburra winning easily in a new course-record time and the form appears fairly solid. The second and third did not run without promise and will find easier opportunities.

NOTEBOOK
Yungaburra(IRE) ◆ has really improved recently on his early efforts and won in facile style, breaking the course record in the process. He is due to run again soon and must be followed. (op 5-6 tchd 11-10)
Mazin Lady ◆ ran a really nice race and was a clear second best on the day. There was plenty to like about the run and a step up to six furlongs might be worth trying with her soon. (op 6-1)
Riverside Dancer(USA), wearing first-time blinkers, really messed up the start but finished strongly down the home straight to be gaining on the leaders late on. She had no chance giving weight away to an improving sort and is a fair sort to rate the race around. (op 5-1 tchd 11-2)
Hucking Hope(IRE) was pretty much in the same position throughout and never looked like getting involved at any stage. (op 14-1)
Sister Etienne(IRE) tried her best to go with the winner early and paid for it in the latter stages. (tchd 14-1 and 20-1)
Roheryn(IRE) did not show a great deal on his first run on the All-Weather and will need to improve significantly to have a chance next time on Polytrack. The balance of his form suggests that he is not well handicapped. (op 7-1 tchd 11-2)

6401 THE ZONGALERO RESTAURANT OVERLOOKS THE TRACK (S) STKS 5f 216y(P)
2:20 (2:20) (Class 6) 2-Y-O **£2,388** (£705; £352) **Stalls** Low

Form RPR
2000 **1** **Stir Crazy (IRE)**[21] 6056 2-8-13 61 EdwardCreighton[(3)] 12 65
(M R Channon) *mde all: clr 2f out: strly rdn fnl f: hld on* **7/2[2]**
5206 **2** *nk* **Put It On The Card**[9] 6258 2-8-11 66 (p) GrahamGibbons 8 59
(P D Evans) *trckd ldrs: chsd wnr 2f out: kpt on to press him ins fnl f* **7/1**
3 *1/2* **Amber Isle** 2-8-4 RussellKennemore[(7)] 10 58
(R Hollinshead) *mid-div: rdn 1/2-way: hdwy on outside 2f out: swtchd and edgd lft over 1f out: r.o: nvr nrr* **33/1**
1005 **4** *1 3/4* **Aggbag**[30] 5876 2-8-11 60 AndrewElliott[(5)] 11 60+
(B P J Baugh) *towards rr: hdwy over 1f out: r.o ins fnl f: nvr nrr* **8/1**
400 **5** *1 3/4* **Charlotte Grey**[11] 6224 2-8-3 52 DominicFox[(3)] 9 42
(C N Allen) *prom on outside: outpcd 1/2-way: kpt on ins fnl f* **33/1**
000 **6** *1/2* **Desirable Dancer (IRE)**[39] 5686 2-8-6 54 LPKeniry 3 40
(R A Harris) *mid-div: hung lft 1f out and no hdwy fnl f* **25/1**
020 **7** *nk* **Bar Humbug**[27] 5923 2-8-11 59 (p) PaulHanagan 4 44
(R A Fahey) *towards rr: sme hdwy over 1f out but nvr nr to chal* **6/1[3]**
000 **8** *2 1/2* **Woodland Symphony**[21] 6047 2-8-11 52 (v[1]) KimTinkler 5 37
(N Tinkler) *chsd wnr to 2f out: rdn and wknd over 1f out* **40/1**
4306 **9** *shd* **Hunting Call**[11] 6208 2-8-11 66 (b) MichaelHills 2 52+
(K A Ryan) *outpcd: making hdwy on ins whn hmpd ins fnl f: nt rcvr* **9/4[1]**
0340 **10** *1* **Mr Mini Scule**[6] 6311 2-8-11 57 DaneO'Neill 6 33
(A B Haynes) *mid-div: edgd lft over 1f out: sn btn* **14/1**
2030 **11** *2* **Fly Time**[9] 6255 2-8-6 53 (p) CatherineGannon 7 22
(Mrs L Williamson) *chsd ldrs: rdn 2f out: wknd over 1f out* **20/1**
00 **12** *4* **Temple Air (IRE)**[39] 5687 2-8-4 JackDean[(7)] 13 15
(W G M Turner) *outpcd: a bhd* **100/1**
5360 **13** *shd* **Porjenski**[50] 5448 2-8-6 48 JimmyQuinn 1 10
(A B Haynes) *slowly away: a bhd* **22/1**

1m 15.29s (-0.52) **Going Correction** -0.275s/f (Stan) **13 Ran SP% 119.8**
Speed ratings (Par 94):92,91,90,88,86 85,85,81,81,80 77,72,72
CSF £26.03 TOTE £4.80: £1.50, £2.40, £11.60; EX 35.00 TRIFECTA Not won..The winner was bought in for 5,500gns. Amber Isle was claimed by Declan Carroll for £6,000.
Owner Miss F V Cove & Mrs V Beech **Bred** Paddy Kennedy **Trained** West Ilsley, Berks
■ Stewards' Enquiry : Edward Creighton one-day ban: failed to ride to draw (Nov 22)
Jack Dean one-fay ban: careless riding (Nov 20)

FOCUS
A moderate seller at best. The winner sets the level backed up by the fourth and fifth.

NOTEBOOK
Stir Crazy(IRE), the second highest-rated horse in the race on official figures, was given a positive ride which paid off handsomely. A drop back to five furlongs would not be a problem to him in similar company. (op 9-2 tchd 5-1)
Put It On The Card had every chance to get to Stir Crazy but could never quite bridge the gap. He ran his race again but found one too good and does not look like a horse to rely on. (op 9-1 tchd 10-1)
Amber Isle, from a stable that is not associated with first-time out two-year-olds, showed plenty of promise and seems sure to improve for the run. He is related to a decent All-Weather performer and should make his mark in due course. (op 25-1)
Aggbag was never in a position to challenger and can be rated at least a length better than his final position. (tchd 9-1)
Charlotte Grey ran up to her best and had no excuses.
Hunting Call was staying on down the inside rail when hampered by Woodland Symphony. He might have finished somewhere close to the third with a clear run. (op 13-8)
Porjenski Official explanation: jockey said filly suffered interference in running

6402 HBLB DUNSTALL PARK CONDITIONS STKS 5f 216y(P)
2:50 (2:50) (Class 3) 2-Y-O
£6,855 (£2,052; £1,026; £513; £256; £128) **Stalls** Low

Form RPR
2130 **1** **Prime Defender**[25] 5965 2-9-0 106 MichaelHills 1 105+
(B W Hills) *mde all: kpt up to work fnl 2f: in command whn eased cl home* **30/100[1]**
1436 **2** *2 1/2* **Onenightinlisbon (IRE)**[18] 6096 2-8-9 80 PaulMulrennan 8 87
(K R Burke) *trckd wnr thrght: rdn whn edgd lft appr fnl f: no imp* **16/1[3]**
3014 **3** *3* **Kompete**[12] 6201 2-8-9 90 MichaelTebbutt 5 78
(V Smith) *chsd ldrs: rdn over 1f out: no further hdwy* **4/1[2]**
2410 **4** *3 1/2* **Shebang (IRE)**[20] 6064 2-8-6 75 DominicFox[(3)] 4 67
(M G Quinlan) *chsd ldrs: rdn 2f out: sn btn* **16/1[3]**
1005 **5** *2 1/2* **Cherri Fosfate**[8] 6271 2-9-0 68 (v) PaulHanagan 2 64
(W G M Turner) *in tch: rdn 4f out: sn outpcd* **66/1**
6 *3* **Haoin An Bothar (IRE)**[16] 6151 2-8-9 JerryO'Dwyer[(5)] 6 55
(Adrian Sexton, Ire) *outpcd thrght* **200/1**
7 *15* **El Manx Senorita** 2-8-8 ow2 RobbieFitzpatrick 7 3
(C Smith) *slowly away and nvr got into r* **100/1**
8 *14* **Cragg Lass (IRE)** 2-8-6 PaulQuinn 3 —
(A Berry) *s.i.s and outpcd fr s* **150/1**

1m 12.61s (-3.20) **Going Correction** -0.275s/f (Stan) **8 Ran SP% 112.3**
Speed ratings (Par 100):110,106,102,98,94 90,70,52
CSF £7.00 TOTE £1.20: £1.02, £2.10, £1.30; EX 6.60 Trifecta £20.70 Pool: £377.94 - 12.98 winning units.

Owner S Falle, M Franklin, J Sumsion **Bred** Christopher J Mason **Trained** Lambourn, Berks

FOCUS

Not all one-way traffic for Prime Defender, but he came away from the second towards the end, beating both the older-horse and juvenile track records in the process. The first three seem to have run up to form, but fourth and fifth could be flattered.

NOTEBOOK

Prime Defenderwon as he should have and lowered the course record in the process. Connections indicated that he will now be put away for the winter after the race, but one would suspect he will not be the easiest to place next season if he does not stay seven furlongs, as he could be a sprinter and three-year-olds often find it tough due to lack of opportunities. (op 1-3 tchd 4-11 and 2-7)

Onenightinlisbon(IRE) tracked the winner throughout and emerges from the race with plenty of credit considering her official mark. The Handicapper might step in and make things difficult for her now, but connections did well with Fusili last winter and may have a similar type on their hands again. (op 14-1)

Kompete, trying an All-Weather surface for the first time, was comprehensively beaten off under pressure but gives the form some shape. She could land a similar conditions race on the Polytrack during the winter if not bumping into a horse of the calibre of the winner again. (op 7-2 tchd 5-1)

Shebang(IRE) got as close as she was entitled to and never threatened to cause an upset. (tchd 12-1)

Cherri Fosfate was up against it in strong company and did as well as could have been realistically expected. (tchd 80-1)

6403 SATURDAY NIGHT IS PARTY NIGHT MAIDEN STKS (DIV I) 7f 32y(P)

3:20 (3:21) (Class 5) 3-Y-O **£2,590** (£770; £385; £192) **Stalls** High

Form RPR

0 **1** **Dichoh**[21] 6052 3-9-3 MatthewHenry 2 70
(M A Jarvis) *mde all: kpt up to work fr over 1f out* **5/1**[3]

34 **2** *1* **Cross Of Lorraine (IRE)**[37] 5726 3-9-3 (b) PaulHanagan 4 67
(I Semple) *chsd wnr thrght: rdn over 2f out: hung lft appr fnl f and no imp ins* **2/1**[1]

6 **3** *3* **Monashee River (IRE)**[14] 6177 3-8-5 JamesO'Reilly(7) 6 55
(Miss V Haigh) *in tch: rdn and c wd into st: kpt on fnl f but no ch w first 2* **25/1**

000 **4** *2 1/2* **Grand Assault**[24] 5986 3-9-3 54 (p) BrianReilly 12 53
(P S McEntee) *bhd tl hdwy on outside over 1f out but nvr nr to chal* **10/1**

4004 **5** *4* **Weet For Ever (USA)**[31] 5844 3-9-3 55 DaneO'Neill 5 43
(P A Blockley) *prom on outside tl wknd over 1f out* **9/4**[2]

6 *3/4* **Miss Apricot** 3-8-12 PatCosgrave 3 36
(J D Bethell) *in tch: rdn over 2f out: wknd wl over 1f out* **12/1**

0 **7** *nk* **Dodaa (USA)**[37] 5726 3-9-3 JimmyQuinn 10 40
(N Wilson) *bhd: sme hdwy whn nt clr run and swtchd rt 1f out: nvr on terms* **50/1**

6- **8** *7* **Jember Red**[421] 5202 3-8-12 DerekMcGaffin 8 17
(B Smart) *nvr bttr than mid-div* **16/1**

0 **9** *1/2* **Keep A Welcome**[14] 6177 3-9-3 DanielTudhope 7 20
(S Parr) *s.i.s: a in rr* **66/1**

0505 **10** *5* **Optical Seclusion (IRE)**[30] 5874 3-9-3 49 (b) PaulMulrennan 11 7
(T J Etherington) *plld hrd: trckd ldrs tl wknd qckly 1/2-way* **40/1**

11 *1* **Keagles (ITY)** 3-8-12 PhillipMakin 1 —
(J E Long) *v.s.a: a bhd* **20/1**

40 **12** *5* **Dandys Hurricane**[37] 5727 3-9-3 PaulQuinn 9 —
(D Nicholls) *a bhd* **14/1**

1m 28.7s (-1.70) **Going Correction** -0.275s/f (Stan) 12 Ran SP% **124.6**

Speed ratings (Par 102):98,96,93,90,86 85,84,76,76,70 69,63

CSF £15.55 TOTE £6.30: £1.60, £1.20, £10.50; EX 19.80 Trifecta £150.50 Part won. Pool: £212.01 - 0.67 winning units..

Owner T G Warner **Bred** Red House Stud **Trained** Newmarket, Suffolk

FOCUS

Probably just a weak maiden, with the fourth and fifth only rated 54 and 55.

Keep A Welcome Official explanation: jockey said filly hung both ways

Keagles(ITY) Official explanation: jockey said filly had been slowly away

6404 WOLVERHAMPTON-RACECOURSE.CO.UK H'CAP 7f 32y(P)

3:55 (3:55) (Class 6) (0-58,58) 3-Y-O+ **£2,730** (£806; £403) **Stalls** High

Form RPR

0004 **1** **Dudley Docker (IRE)**[1] 6390 4-8-8 58 KellyHarrison(7) 5 69
(D Carroll) *chsd ldrs: rdn to ld over 1f out: edgd lft: r.o u.p* **10/3**[2]

0100 **2** *3/4* **Snow Bunting**[57] 5269 8-9-0 57 PaulHanagan 3 66
(Jedd O'Keeffe) *in tch: racd keenly: rdn and r.o to go 2nd ins fnl f* **10/1**

043 **3** *1* **Mozakhraf (USA)**[1] 6390 4-9-0 57 PatCosgrave 2 66+
(K A Ryan) *a.p: nt clr run 2f out: chalng whn hmpd ins fnl f: sn lost 2nd* **11/4**[1]

0000 **4** *hd* **Hits Only Cash**[21] 6061 4-9-0 57 DeanMcKeown 11 63
(J Pearce) *slowly away: hdwy on ins over 1f out: r.o ins fnl f* **8/1**

0400 **5** *2 1/2* **No Grouse**[1] 6390 6-9-0 57 JimmyQuinn 4 56
(E J Alston) *mid-div: effrt over 1f out: wknd ins fnl f* **6/1**[3]

0020 **6** *hd* **Barry The Brave**[56] 5285 4-8-9 55 GregFairley(3) 7 54
(Micky Hammond) *slowly away: bhd: effrt on outside wl over 1f out: wknd ins fnl f* **11/1**

2100 **7** *1 1/2* **Celtic Thunder**[82] 4571 5-9-0 57 (b) PaulMulrennan 9 52
(T J Etherington) *mid-div: rdn and wknd over 1f out* **28/1**

0230 **8** *nk* **Miskina**[31] 5840 5-8-12 55 DanielTudhope 8 49
(W M Brisbourne) *trckd ldr: led over 2f out: hdd over 1f out: sn wknd* **15/2**

-000 **9** *1* **Take It There**[24] 5988 4-8-12 55 LPKeniry 12 47
(A J Lidderdale) *hld up on outside: a bhd* **40/1**

065 **10** *hd* **Gattuso**[67] 5035 3-8-13 57 PhillipMakin 6 48
(Ms Deborah J Evans) *led: hdd over 2f out: wkng whn hmpd over 1f out* **12/1**

1m 28.56s (-1.84) **Going Correction** -0.275s/f (Stan)

WFA 3 from 4yo+ 1lb 10 Ran SP% **117.9**

Speed ratings (Par 101):99,98,97,96,93 93,91,91,90,90

CSF £37.27 CT £103.41 TOTE £6.10: £2.10, £2.60, £1.60; EX 85.70 Trifecta £104.20 Pool: £205.60 - 1.40 winning units.

Owner J M Walsh **Bred** Nuri Fuat Basak **Trained** Warthill, N Yorks

■ Stewards' Enquiry : Kelly Harrison two-day ban: careless riding (Nov 20-21)

FOCUS

A moderate race in which the form looks sound enough but ordinary. Dudley Docker, Mozakhraf and No Grouse all ran in the same race the day before and two of them got involved in the finish. Mozakhraf can be called slightly unlucky after meeting trouble.

6405 PARADE RESTAURANT H'CAP 1m 4f 50y(P)

4:25 (4:25) (Class 6) (0-55,55) 3-Y-O+ **£2,730** (£806; £403) **Stalls** Low

Form RPR

0003 **1** **Qaasi (USA)**[2] 6383 4-9-2 54 DeanMernagh 11 62
(M Brittain) *trckd ldr: led over 2f out: rdn out fnl f* **15/2**

4660 **2** *1 3/4* **Lady Taverner**[26] 5954 5-9-3 55 PhillipMakin 9 60
(J E Long) *mid-div: hdwy on ins 2f out: wnt 2nd over 1f out: styd on u.p* **8/1**

2003 **3** *1* **Missie Baileys**[22] 6037 4-8-13 54 (p) AmirQuinn(3) 12 58+
(Mrs L J Mongan) *in tch whn hmpd on ins 2f out: styd on ins fnl f* **13/2**[3]

2360 **4** *1 1/4* **Little Richard (IRE)**[228] 733 7-9-1 53 (p) DaneO'Neill 2 55
(M Wellings) *bhd tl hdwy on outside ove 1f out: styd on fnl f: nvr nrr* **8/1**

6400 **5** *nk* **Keshya**[39] 5691 5-9-3 55 GrahamGibbons 4 56
(N P Littmoden) *trckd ldrs: rdn over 1f out: one pce after* **8/1**

00-0 **6** *1 1/2* **Maktu**[7] 5385 4-9-0 52 LPKeniry 10 51
(P G Murphy) *trckd ldrs tl rdn and wknd ent fnl f* **50/1**

4450 **7** *1 1/2* **Ulysees (IRE)**[5] 6317 7-9-3 55 PaulHanagan 7 51
(I Semple) *bhd: effrt over 1f out: nvr on terms* **4/1**[1]

005 **8** *1/2* **Princely Ted (IRE)**[20] 6067 5-8-10 55 (t) SCreighton(7) 3 51
(E J Creighton) *led tl hdd over 2f out: wknd fnl f* **33/1**

4210 **9** *hd* **Second Reef**[2] 6383 4-9-3 55 JimmyQuinn 5 50
(E J Alston) *bhd: effrt over 2f out: wknd appr fnl f* **11/2**[2]

0 **10** *5* **Sword's Edge (IRE)**[25] 5972 5-9-3 55 MichaelHills 6 42
(W A Murphy, Ire) *a bhd* **16/1**

1000 **11** *1/2* **Arch Folly**[9] 6256 4-9-3 55 (p) DanielTudhope 1 41
(R J Price) *in tch tl wknd over 2f out* **14/1**

5503 **12** *2 1/2* **Ronsard (IRE)**[42] 5609 4-8-11 52 NeilChalmers(3) 8 34
(J C Tuck) *t.k.h: hld up: a bhd* **12/1**

2m 38.55s (-3.87) **Going Correction** -0.275s/f (Stan) 12 Ran SP% **119.0**

Speed ratings (Par 101):101,99,99,98,98 97,96,95,95,92 92,90

CSF £66.61 CT £416.87 TOTE £9.70: £2.40, £2.20, £2.60; EX 77.10 TRIFECTA Not won..

Owner Eyes Wide Open Partnership **Bred** G Strawbridge Jr **Trained** Warthill, N Yorks

FOCUS

A moderate race but the form looks reliable for the grade. Dean Mernagh's first winner since his comeback.

Ulysees(IRE) Official explanation: trainer said, regarding poor form shown, gelding had been unsuited by the slow early pace

Second Reef Official explanation: jockey said gelding ran too free early on

Sword's Edge(IRE) Official explanation: trainer said gelding was found to be coughing on return

6406 SATURDAY NIGHT IS PARTY NIGHT MAIDEN STKS (DIV II) 7f 32y(P)

4:55 (4:57) (Class 5) 3-Y-O **£2,590** (£770; £385; £192) **Stalls** High

Form RPR

0 **1** **Thistimesforgood (IRE)**[1] 6389 3-8-12 JerryO'Dwyer(5) 7 60
(Adrian Sexton, Ire) *towards rr: rdn 3f out: hdwy on outside over 1f out: strly rdn to ld post* **66/1**

5442 **2** *shd* **Dixieland Boy (IRE)**[42] 5621 3-9-0 67 AmirQuinn(3) 2 60
(P J Makin) *mid-div: hdwy 1/2-way: rdn to ld jst ins fnl f: hung lft: hdd post* **1/1**[1]

5600 **3** *1 1/2* **Linton Dancer (IRE)**[72] 4892 3-8-12 48 PhillipMakin 9 51
(J R Weymes) *a in tch: led over 1f out: hdd jst ins fnl f: nt qckn fnl stages* **25/1**

0500 **4** *5* **Jumanji (IRE)**[197] 1217 3-8-5 54 StacyRenwick(7) 4 38
(M J Attwater) *t.k.h in mid-div: rdn 2f out: no hdwy fr over 1f out* **20/1**

35 **5** *1* **Light Dreams**[42] 5619 3-8-12 64 PaulDoe 1 35
(W J Knight) *chsd ldrs early: sn outpcd and nvr on terms w ldrs after* **2/1**[2]

6 *nk* **Augustus John (IRE)**[507] 2748 3-9-3 RobbieFitzpatrick 6 39
(T J Pitt) *s.i.s: bhd: sme hdwy over 1f out but nvr on terms* **12/1**

040 **7** *1* **Ten To The Dozen**[53] 5388 3-9-3 67 RobertMiles 8 37
(P W Hiatt) *led after 2f: hdd & wknd over 1f out* **9/1**[3]

0000 **8** *9* **Baron De Hoyland**[176] 1768 3-9-3 35 PaulMulrennan 5 13
(J R Norton) *led for 2f: wknd sn after 1/2-way* **200/1**

0400 **9** *nk* **Nilsatisoptimum (USA)**[6] 6306 3-9-3 45 (p) PatCosgrave 11 13
(M Mullineaux) *w ldrs on outside for 3f* **50/1**

0 **10** *5* **Thornbill**[26] 5949 3-9-3 DaneO'Neill 10 —
(H Candy) *mid-div: bhd fr over 2f out* **14/1**

11 *1* **Existence** 3-8-9 PatrickMathers(3) 12 —
(D Shaw) *slowly away: a bhd* **40/1**

00- **12** *10* **Liverti**[439] 4731 3-8-12 DanielTudhope 3 —
(D Carroll) *chsd ldrs tl wknd 1/2-way* **25/1**

1m 29.37s (-1.03) **Going Correction** -0.275s/f (Stan) 12 Ran SP% **126.5**

Speed ratings (Par 102):94,93,92,86,85 84,83,73,73,67 66,54

CSF £138.59 TOTE £99.00: £14.10, £1.10, £5.20; EX 293.90 TRIFECTA Not won. Place 6 £33.10, Place 5 £7.70.

Owner James Gough **Bred** Peter S McLoughlin **Trained** Athy, Co Kildare

■ Stewards' Enquiry : Daniel Tudhope jockey said filly had been struck into

Jerry O'Dwyer four-day ban: used whip in incorrect place (Nov 20-23)

FOCUS

A very moderate event, probably best rated through the third or fourth, and the slow time makes the form look dubious.

T/Plt: £87.20 to a £1 stake. Pool: £41,555.15. 347.85 winning tickets. T/Qpdt: £19.10 to a £1 stake. Pool: £3,377.25. 130.50 winning tickets. JS

6251 SAN SIRO (R-H)

Wednesday, November 8

OFFICIAL GOING: Good

6407a PREMIO CANTALUPO (MAIDEN) (C&G) 1m 110y

2:45 (2:50) 2-Y-O **£6,897** (£3,034; £1,655; £828)

RPR

1 **Big Sugar (IRE)** 2-9-0 MEsposito 11 —
(B Grizzetti, Italy)

2 *1* **Awelmarduk (IRE)** 2-9-0 EBotti 5 —
(A & G Botti, Italy)

3 *1 3/4* **Bonate (IRE)** 2-9-0 DVargiu 6 —
(B Grizzetti, Italy)

4 *5* **Sharstar (ITY)** 2-9-0 FBossa 10 —
(B Grizzetti, Italy)

5 *2 1/2* **Chicchirichi (IRE)** 2-8-10 NMurru 4 —
(M Gasparini, Italy)

6 *1 1/4* **Magic Tango (ITY)** 2-9-0 MDemuro 8 —
(L D'Auria, Italy)

The Form Book, Raceform Ltd, Compton, RG20 6NL

7 *hd* **Mr Kennedy (IRE)** 2-8-10 .... SMulas 1 —
(B Grizzetti, Italy)
8 *2 ½* **Prince Sakhee** 2-8-10 .... MMonteriso 3 —
(E Borromeo, Italy)
9 *3 ½* **Varro** 2-8-10 .... APolli 2 —
(M G Quinlan) *never better than mid-division SP 5.39-1* **54/10**[1]
10 *nk* **Conto Astronomico (ITY)** 2-8-10 .... WGambarota 9 —
(M Guarnieri, Italy)
11 *2* **Noverenzi (IRE)** 2-9-0 .... APitzalis 7 —
(M Ciciarelli, Italy)
11 Ran SP% **15.6**

(Including 1 Euro stake): WIN 5.70; PL 1.46, 1.21, 1.36; DF 7.48.
Owner Scuderia Incolinx **Bred** Azienda Agricola Rosati Colareti **Trained** Italy

NOTEBOOK
Varro, whose dam placed over ten furlongs at three and is a sister to dual Listed race winner Musha Merr, never really got competitive on his debut.

6348 LINGFIELD (L-H)

Thursday, November 9

OFFICIAL GOING: Standard
Wind: almost nil

6408 DINE IN THE TRACKSIDE CARVERY APPRENTICE H'CAP 1m 5f (P)
1:20 (1:20) (Class 5) (0-75,72) 3-Y-0+ **£3,238** (£963; £481; £240) **Stalls** Low

Form RPR
-250 **1** **Bay Hawk**[21] [5506] 4-9-3 **68** .... JPFeatherstone(5) 8 74
(B G Powell) *w.w in midfield: clsd 6f out: pushed along over 2f out: chsd ldr over 1f out: led ins fnl f: r.o strly* **8/1**
1450 **2** *1 ¾* **Serramanna**[15] [6178] 5-8-7 **58** oh1 .... SophieDoyle(5) 6 61
(Ms J S Doyle) *hld up in rr: clsd 6f out: rdn 3f out: styd on wl fnl f: wnt 2nd nr fin: nt trble wnr* **8/1**
0501 **3** *hd* **Makai**[21] [6067] 3-8-7 **65** .... (b) WilliamBuick(5) 3 68
(J J Bridger) *t.k.h: led for 2f: chsd ldr tl 5f out: rdn 2f out: ev ch over 1f out: kpt on same pce* **14/1**
2440 **4** *shd* **Trinity Rose**[6] [6321] 3-9-0 **67** .... NeilBrown 1 70
(M Johnston) *bhd: rdn and outpcd 4f out: styd on wl over 1f out: nrst fin* **5/1**[3]
6004 **5** *½* **Newnham (IRE)**[9] [6287] 5-9-9 **72** .... WilliamCarson(3) 7 74
(J R Boyle) *hld up in rr: clsd 6f out: chsd ldrs and rdn wl over 2f out: kpt on same pce* **4/1**[2]
3100 **6** *2* **Montosari**[29] [5910] 7-9-4 **64** .... JackMitchell 4 63
(P Mitchell) *lw: chsd clr ldng pair: hdwy to chse ldr 5f out: led gng wl over 2f out: sn rdn: hdd ins fnl f: sn btn* **7/2**[1]
0213 **7** *3* **Border Edge**[8] [6289] 8-9-5 **65** .... AlanRutter 2 60
(J J Bridger) *chsd ldr tl led after 2f: clr 8f out: rdn and hdd wl over 2f out: wknd over 1f out* **7/1**
1614 **8** *4* **Turner's Touch**[168] [1958] 4-8-13 **66** .... KatieOrchin(7) 5 55
(G L Moore) *slowly away: racd in midfield: clsd 6f out: pushed along and struggling 3f out: no ch after* **13/2**

2m 47.7s (-0.60) **Going Correction** -0.10s/f (Stan)
WFA 3 from 4yo+ 7lb 8 Ran SP% **113.6**
Speed ratings (Par 103):97,95,95,95,95 94,92,89
CSF £68.38 CT £878.48 TOTE £13.60: £3.60, £2.40, £4.10; EX 121.20 TRIFECTA Not won..
Owner Miss K E Anderson **Bred** Ashley House Stud **Trained** Morestead, Hants

FOCUS
Not a great race, but no shortage of pace thanks to Makai and Border Edge setting off at rate of knots early. The winner did nto need to improve to score.

6409 EUROPEAN BREEDERS' FUND MEDIAN AUCTION MAIDEN STKS 5f (P)
1:50 (1:50) (Class 5) 2-Y-0 **£3,238** (£963; £481; £240) **Stalls** High

Form RPR
6 **1** **Hurricane Spirit (IRE)**[146] [2623] 2-9-3 .... BrettDoyle 3 81+
(J R Best) *trckd ldng pair: shkn up to ld ins fnl f: pushed out: comf* **9/4**[1]
0 **2** *1 ¼* **Fluttering Rose**[23] [6025] 2-8-12 .... SteveDrowne 1 72
(R Charlton) *leggy: chsd ldr: rdn over 2f out: led jst over 1f out: hdd ins fnl f: one pced* **9/1**
0364 **3** *1 ¼* **Feelin Foxy**[10] [6255] 2-8-9 76 .... (v[1]) PatrickMathers(3) 9 67
(D Shaw) *t.k.h: hld up in midfield: hdwy 3f out: short of room briefly over 2f out: kpt on same pce u.p* **4/1**[3]
4 *3* **Shepherdess (USA)** 2-8-12 .... JoeFanning 4 56
(D M Simcock) *w'like: slowly away: bhd: styd on wl over 1f out: wnt 4th nr fin: n.d* **12/1**
4043 **5** *shd* **Billy Red**[41] [5648] 2-9-3 66 .... EddieAhern 5 61
(J R Jenkins) *sn led: hung bdly lft and hdd jst over 1f out: wknd* **11/4**[2]
3656 **6** *3* **Cyprus Rose**[108] [3801] 2-8-9 45 .... JamesDoyle(3) 10 45
(S Curran) *bhd: rdn wl over 2f out: n.d* **66/1**
00 **7** *1 ¼* **La Cuvee**[10] [6255] 2-8-12 .... NelsonDeSouza 6 41
(R M Beckett) *racd in midfield: pushed along 3f out: sn struggling* **50/1**
00 **8** *¾* **Shrewd Dude**[24] [6014] 2-9-3 .... MickyFenton 8 43
(Carl Llewellyn) *w'like: sn outpcd in rr: rn wd on bnd over 2f out: n.d* **33/1**
5 **9** *hd* **Ellablue**[23] [6025] 2-8-12 .... JimmyFortune 7 37
(Rae Guest) *leggy: chsd ldrs on outer: rdn wl over 2f out: wkng whn rn wd bnd over 2f out: no ch after* **7/1**
40 **10** *3* **So Shy (IRE)**[24] [6015] 2-8-12 .... PaulDoe 2 26
(J R Boyle) *leggy: unf: v.s.a: a bhd* **20/1**

59.38 secs (-0.40) **Going Correction** -0.10s/f (Stan) 10 Ran SP% **118.8**
Speed ratings (Par 96):99,97,95,90,90 85,83,82,81,76
CSF £23.37 TOTE £2.90: £1.40, £2.60, £2.20; EX 19.40 Trifecta £171.30 Pool £171.30 - 3.04 winning units.
Owner The Little House Partnership **Bred** Knocktoran Stud **Trained** Hucking, Kent

FOCUS
An ordinary juvenile maiden for the track and not that many got into it, but probably won by a decent sort. The form looks sound with the principals improving.

NOTEBOOK
Hurricane Spirit(IRE) was racing for the first time since finishing sixth behind the useful Wi Dud on his debut at York in June. The form of that race has worked out particularly well since and the son of Invincible Spirit did not have to be asked a serious question to win comfortably. He is likely to progress again from this and should get further. (op 7-4)
Fluttering Rose was never far off the pace and kept on to the line, reversing Bath debut form with Ellablue. She should find a race. (tchd 10-1)
Feelin Foxy, the most experienced in the field, travelled well in the first-time visor but did not find as much off the bridle as had looked likely. For a filly that was Listed-placed in the spring, she is becoming disappointing. Official explanation: jockey said filly was denied a clear run (op 11-2 tchd 6-1)
Shepherdess(USA) ◆, the only newcomer in the field, caught the eye in staying on for fourth after missing the break. A $62,000 half-sister to winners in the US and Japan, she is one to keep keep in mind for the future. (op 11-1)
Billy Red was given his usual positive ride, but hung badly into the rail once into the home straight and looks totally exposed now. Official explanation: jockey said gelding hung left (op 4-1)
Shrewd Dude Official explanation: jockey said colt hung right

6410 LINGFIELDPARK.CO.UK MAIDEN STKS 1m 4f (P)
2:20 (2:20) (Class 5) 3-Y-0+ **£3,238** (£963; £481; £240) **Stalls** Low

Form RPR
4030 **1** **Shout (IRE)**[9] [6272] 3-8-12 75 .... SteveDrowne 6 80
(R Charlton) *trckd ldr: rdn to ld over 2f out: styd on wl* **11/1**
2 *1* **Abandon (USA)** 3-8-12 .... MichaelHills 10 78
(W J Haggas) *unf: scope: hld up:hdwy 4f out: chsd wnr over 1f out: flashed tail u.p: kpt on nr fin* **9/1**
53 **3** *4* **Blend**[23] [6026] 3-8-12 .... JimmyFortune 8 72
(J H M Gosden) *w'like: str: in tch: hdwy 4f out: chsd ldrs and rdn over 2f out: wknd fnl f* **4/1**[2]
4332 **4** *6* **Shahmina (IRE)**[41] [5650] 3-8-12 72 .... RobertHavlin 9 62
(J H M Gosden) *racd in midfield: in tch: rdn 5f out: outpcd 3f out:plugged on past btn horses fnl f* **7/2**[1]
2-02 **5** *1 ¼* **Scotch Pancake**[40] [5669] 3-8-12 .... EddieAhern 5 60
(D R C Elsworth) *t.k.h: sn led: rdn and hdd over 2f out: sn wknd* **9/2**[3]
2004 **6** *2 ½* **Moonshadow**[9] [6272] 3-8-12 77 .... TPQueally 11 56
(H R A Cecil) *chsd ldrs: rdn 4f out: wknd wl over 2f out* **16/1**
5340 **7** *½* **Sybella**[13] [6205] 3-8-12 75 .... IanMongan 2 56
(J L Dunlop) *trckd ldrs on inner: rdn 4f out: wknd wl over 2f out* **11/2**
0462 **8** *1 ¼* **Peas 'n Beans (IRE)**[45] [5581] 3-8-10 51 .... WilliamBuick(7) 1 59
(T Keddy) *hld up wl bhd: hdwy on inner 3f out: rdn 2f out: sn wknd* **25/1**
0500 **9** *2* **War Feather**[3] [6375] 4-9-6 37 .... EdwardCreighton(3) 7 55
(T D McCarthy) *hld up in tch: rdn 4f out: wknd wl over 2f out* **100/1**
32 **10** *7* **Brocatello (IRE)**[63] [5138] 3-9-3 .... (b) JoeFanning 12 44
(M Johnston) *w'like: racd on outer: hdwy over 5f out: rdn 4f out: sn wl bhd: t.o* **15/2**
0 **11** *21* **Bazil Des Fieffes (FR)**[71] [4931] 4-9-9 .... (b) NancyBloyart 4 11
(J M Plasschaert, Belgium) *slowly away: a bhd: t.o last 2f* **100/1**
00 **12** *38* **St Fris**[40] [5669] 3-9-3 .... MickyFenton 3 —
(J A R Toller) *sn bhd and pushed along: lost tch 4f out: t.o last 3f* **100/1**

2m 31.65s (-2.74) **Going Correction** -0.10s/f (Stan)
WFA 3 from 4yo 6lb 12 Ran SP% **118.6**
Speed ratings (Par 103):105,104,101,97,96 95,94,94,92,88 74,48
CSF £105.12 TOTE £11.00: £2.20, £3.50, £1.60; EX 125.20 TRIFECTA Not won..
Owner Lady Rothschild **Bred** Lord Rothschild **Trained** Beckhampton, Wilts

FOCUS
Some big yards were represented in this maiden though it was not as competitive as the numbers would suggest. The form is probably sound with the first three clear.
Scotch Pancake Official explanation: jockey said filly ran too free

6411 EUROPEAN BREEDERS' FUND FILLIES' H'CAP 1m 2f (P)
2:50 (2:52) (Class 3) (0-90,90) 3-Y-0 **£9,067** (£2,697; £1,348; £673) **Stalls** Low

Form RPR
11-4 **1** **Dubai On**[48] [5505] 3-9-3 **89** .... TPQueally 2 101+
(Saeed Bin Suroor) *lw: s.i.s: t.k.h and sn in tch: stdd to rr 6f out: hdwy and swtchd rt over 1f: str run to ld on line* **5/2**[1]
4205 **2** *hd* **Lake Shabla (USA)**[30] [5895] 3-8-9 **81** .... BrettDoyle 8 88
(E A L Dunlop) *b: hld up bhd: rdn and hdwy over 2f out: led wl ins fnl f: hdd last strides* **5/1**[3]
2000 **3** *½* **Fusili (IRE)**[5] [6333] 3-9-1 **90** .... JamesDoyle(3) 4 96
(N P Littmoden) *led tl over 7f out: lost pl and rdn over 4f out: rallied over 2f out: led ins fnl f: hdd and no ex last 50 yds* **10/1**
250 **4** *1 ½* **Giving**[28] [5917] 3-9-4 **90** .... SteveDrowne 5 93
(G Wragg) *lw: w.w in tch: hdwy to trck ldrs over 4f out: rdn and ev ch wl over 2f out: wknd ins fnl f* **6/1**
2-16 **5** *nk* **Act Friendly (IRE)**[82] [4612] 3-9-2 **88** .... EddieAhern 6 91
(Saeed Bin Suroor) *hld up in tch: hdwy 4f out: chsd ldng pair and rdn over 2f out: ev ch wl over 1f out: wknd ins fnl f* **11/1**
201 **6** *1 ½* **Indication**[12] [6225] 3-8-4 **76** .... (t) DaleGibson 7 76
(J H M Gosden) *chsd ldrs: wnt 2nd 5f out: led wl over 2f out: sn rdn hdd & wknd jst ins fnl f* **12/1**
3130 **7** *½* **Pirouetting**[28] [5917] 3-8-4 **76** .... PaulDoe 1 75+
(B W Hills) *hld up in rr on inner: swtchd rt and rdn over 2f out: kpt on but nvr pce to rch ldrs* **16/1**
3000 **8** *5* **Queen Of Fire**[27] [5945] 3-8-10 **82** .... JoeFanning 9 71
(D R C Elsworth) *t.k.h: hld up in rr: rdn over 2f out: no prog* **25/1**
1-10 **9** *1* **Postage Stampe**[114] [3627] 3-9-4 **90** .... JimmyFortune 3 77
(D M Simcock) *chsd ldr tl 5f out: rdn 4f out: sn bhd* **8/1**
1624 **10** *2 ½* **Adraaj (USA)**[13] [6202] 3-8-9 **81** .... (v) RHills 10 64
(E A L Dunlop) *b: slowly away: racd wd: dashed up on outer to ld over 7f out: rdn 3f out: sn hdd & wknd* **4/1**[2]

2m 5.34s (-2.45) **Going Correction** -0.10s/f (Stan) 10 Ran SP% **125.5**
Speed ratings (Par 103):105,104,104,103,103 101,101,97,96,94
CSF £16.44 CT £114.04 TOTE £3.30: £1.40, £2.60, £2.90; EX 27.00 Trifecta £207.10 Pool £323.88 - 1.11 winning units.
Owner Godolphin **Bred** Darley **Trained** Newmarket, Suffolk

FOCUS
The best contest on the card, and very competitive with virtually five in a line across the track a furlong from home. The form looks pretty sound with the third and fourth the best guides to the level.

NOTEBOOK
Dubai On, given a patient ride, still had a bit to do turning in, but once her rider switched her to the wide outside she flew and got up in the shadow of the post. She looked happier on this surface than on the soft ground at Ascot last time and, still lightly raced, there is probably more to come from her. (op 7-2 tchd 4-1)
Lake Shabla(USA), on Polytrack for the first time since making a winning debut here in February, hit the front well well inside the last furlong, but no sooner had she done so than the winner mugged her near the line. She obviously likes this surface and there should be other days. (op 13-2)
Fusili(IRE), back in a handicap after five runs in Listed events, ran an extremely game race considering she was off the bridle half a mile out, but had put herself back in the picture a furlong from home. She only just lost out and her toughness will always stand her in good stead, though the Handicapper is unlikely to drop her for this. (op 15-2)
Giving came there with every chance, but did not quite see it out. She is another that has faced some stiff tasks in her career, but is not that consistent. (op 7-1)
Act Friendly(IRE), a stable companion of the winner, had every chance on her sand debut but was another who did not quite see the race out. (op 10-1)
Indication, making her handicap debut, led the field into the home straight before getting swamped and found this tougher than the Wolverhampton maiden she won last time. (op 8-1)

6412 WINTER LADIES DAY NOVEMBER 18TH NURSERY 7f (P)
3:20 (3:20) (Class 4) (0-85,79) 2-Y-O £4,533 (£1,348; £674; £336) Stalls Low

Form RPR

601 **1** **Salient**[43] 5607 2-9-6 **79**............ PaulDoe 1 81
(J Akehurst) *lw: mde all: qcknd over 3f out: rdn over 2f out: r.o gamely* **11/4**[3]

15 **2** *hd* **I'm Right (USA)**[34] 5783 2-9-5 **78**............ RHills 2 79
(M P Tregoning) *racd keenly: pressed wnr: rdn and upsides 2f out: unable qck and a jst hld fnl f* **7/4**[1]

004 **3** *2 ½* **Fairly Honest**[51] 5457 2-9-2 **75**............ EddieAhern 5 70
(D R C Elsworth) *stdd s: plld hrd: in tch: hung lft fr over 3f out: outpcd over 2f out: kpt on fnl f* **9/2**

6515 **4** *6* **Murrin (IRE)**[25] 5989 2-9-2 **75**............ RobertHavlin 4 54
(T G Mills) *t.k.h: hld up in tch: rdn and outpcd whn rn wd bnd over 2f out* **5/2**[2]

1m 25.91s (0.02) **Going Correction** -0.10s/f (Stan) **4** Ran SP% **109.8**
Speed ratings (Par 98):95,94,91,85
CSF £8.01 TOTE £3.40; EX 5.60.
Owner Canisbay Bloodstock **Bred** Hesmonds Stud Ltd **Trained** Epsom, Surrey

FOCUS
Just the four runners, but a real war of attrition and there was little separating the front pair throughout the contest. The form is not better than average.

NOTEBOOK
Salient, making his debut for the yard, looked sure to be swallowed up by I'm Right all the way up the home straight, but refused the give in and stuck his neck right out. He shapes as though he will get a mile without too much problem. (op 9-4 tchd 3-1)
I'm Right(USA), fifth in a hot nursery here last time, could never quite get on top of the winner and probably needs a more strongly-run race and a return to a mile. (tchd 6-4 and 15-8)
Fairly Honest, making his sand and handicap debut, did not appear to travel all that well so may have done well to finish as close to the front pair as he did. (op 6-1 tchd 7-1)
Murrin(IRE) already looked booked for fourth when running wide on the home bend. (op 3-1 tchd 9-4)

6413 LINGFIELD PARK FOR CHRISTMAS PARTIES H'CAP 1m (P)
3:50 (3:50) (Class 5) (0-75,75) 3-Y-O+ £3,238 (£963; £481; £240) Stalls High

Form RPR

3232 **1** **Neardown Beauty (IRE)**[4] 6350 3-9-1 **75**............ JamesDoyle(3) 9 86
(I A Wood) *hld up in midfield: shkn up and hdwy over 1f out: qcknd to ld ins fnl f: sn clr* **11/4**[1]

5441 **2** *2 ½* **Hassaad**[45] 5568 3-9-1 **72**............(t) RHills 3 77+
(W J Haggas) *lw: s.i.s: hld up in rr on inner: stl last over 2f out: hdwy on rail over 1f out: r.o: wnt 2nd on line: no ch wwnr* **6/1**[3]

4240 **3** *shd* **Imperial Lucky (IRE)**[118] 3472 3-8-5 **69**............ JamesMillman(7) 2 74
(D K Ivory) *s.i.s: sn in tch in midfield: rdn and hdwy on rail wl over 1f out: led 1f out: hdd ins fnl f: outpcd* **33/1**

0003 **4** *¾* **Zabeel House**[41] 5649 3-9-3 **74**............ MickyFenton 7 77
(J A R Toller) *hld up in rr: hdwy on outer over 2f out: kpt on ins fnl f* **11/2**[2]

0066 **5** *nk* **Up Tempo (IRE)**[9] 6273 8-8-13 **68**............(b) TPQueally 12 71
(C R Dore) *chsd ldr: rdn over 2f out: led wl over 1f out: hdd 1f out: kpt on same pce* **25/1**

3-01 **6** *¾* **Da Bookie (IRE)**[17] 6147 6-8-13 **71**............ EdwardCreighton(3) 8 72
(E J Creighton) *slowly away: hld up in last: hdwy and nt clr run briefly 2f out: hdwy over 1f out: no real prog ins fnl f* **14/1**

4554 **7** *nk* **Marbaa (IRE)**[43] 5611 3-8-13 **70**............ IanMongan 5 70
(S Dow) *s.i.s: hld up in rr: rdn and hdwy 3f out: chsd ldrs 2f out: no imp after* **16/1**

315 **8** *1* **Vino**[12] 6227 3-8-10 **67**............ MichaelHills 1 65
(B W Hills) *t.k.h: chsd ldrs: rdn wl over 2f out: wknd 1f out* **7/1**

5606 **9** *1 ¾* **Night Storm**[4] 6350 5-9-1 **70**............ PaulDoe 6 64
(S Dow) *slowly away: hdwy into midfield 6f out: rdn to chse ldng pair wl over 2f out: wknd over 1f out* **16/1**

0003 **10** *1 ¼* **Aastral Magic**[43] 5621 4-8-12 **67**............ JimmyFortune 4 58
(R Hannon) *lw: chsd ldrs: rdn 3f out: wkng whn hmpd bnd over 2f out: no ch after* **9/1**

1-50 **11** *1* **Stevedore (IRE)**[38] 5734 5-8-13 **68**............ JoeFanning 11 57
(J R Boyle) *lw: led tl rdn and hdd wl over 1f out: wknd* **13/2**

5406 **12** *shd* **Hurricane Coast**[10] 6259 7-8-8 **70**............(b) SophieDoyle(7) 10 58
(Ms J S Doyle) *chsd ldrs: rdn over 2f out: wknd wl over 1f out* **33/1**

1m 37.62s (-1.81) **Going Correction** -0.10s/f (Stan)
WFA 3 from 4yo+ 2lb **12** Ran SP% **120.3**
Speed ratings (Par 103):105,102,102,101,101 100,100,99,97,96 95,95
CSF £18.62 CT £453.92 TOTE £3.60: £1.70, £2.60, £6.00; EX 25.00 Trifecta £257.80 Part won. Pool £363.14 - 0.34 winning units. Place 6 £558.26, Place 5 £65.65.
Owner Ramscove Ltd **Bred** Mrs Joan M Langmead **Trained** Upper Lambourn, Berks
■ Stewards' Enquiry : Paul Doe one-day ban: careless riding (Nov 20)

FOCUS
A fairly competitive handicap best rated around the third and fourth.
Aastral Magic Official explanation: jockey said filly was hampered 2f out
T/Jkpt: Not won. T/Plt: £1,426.90 to a £1 stake. Pool: £51,309.80. 26.25 winning tickets. T/Qpdt: £34.80 to a £1 stake. Pool: £4,521.30. 96.10 winning tickets. SP

6399 WOLVERHAMPTON (A.W) (L-H)
Thursday, November 9

OFFICIAL GOING: Standard to fast
Wind: Almost nil Weather: Fine

6414 HOTEL AND CONFERENCING AT WOLVERHAMPTON RACECOURSE MAIDEN STKS 5f 216y(P)
3:55 (3:55) (Class 5) 2-Y-O £3,886 (£1,156; £577; £288) Stalls Low

Form RPR

0020 **1** **Golden Desert (IRE)**[41] 5655 2-9-3 85............ DaneO'Neill 3 72+
(T G Mills) *chsd ldr: led 2f out: hung lft 1f out: rdn out* **4/5**[1]

6402 **2** *1 ½* **Napoleon Dynamite (IRE)**[8] 6291 2-9-3 64............ FJohansson 1 67
(J W Hills) *a.p: chsd wnr over 1f out: sn nt clr run: swtchd rt: styd on* **13/2**[3]

0653 **3** *1 ¼* **Mujart**[8] 6296 2-8-5 56............ RussellKennemore(7) 4 58
(J A Pickering) *chsd ldrs: rdn over 1f out: styd on same pce* **25/1**

4 *hd* **Voice** 2-8-12............ JimmyQuinn 5 58
(H R A Cecil) *dwlt: hld up: plld hrd: hdwy over 1f out: nt rch ldrs* **11/1**

65 **5** *¾* **Para Siempre**[56] 5307 2-8-12............ PaulEddery 10 55
(B Smart) *chsd ldrs: rdn over 2f out: styd on same pce appr fnl f* **16/1**

6 **6** *¾* **Wadnagin (IRE)**[95] 4177 2-8-12............ DanielTudhope 7 53
(I A Wood) *hld up in tch: outpcd over 2f out: rdn and hung lft ins fnl f: nvr trbld ldrs* **20/1**

3306 **7** *1 ¼* **Howards Tipple**[10] 6257 2-9-3 72............(v[1]) PaulHanagan 6 54
(I Semple) *sn led: hdd 2f out: rdn and hung rt over 1f out: wknd ins fnl f* **14/1**

6 **8** *5* **Piccolo Diamante (USA)**[10] 6255 2-9-3............ RobbieFitzpatrick 8 39
(T J Pitt) *chsd ldrs: rdn over 2f out: wknd over 1f out* **10/3**[2]

0 **9** *11* **Emerald Sky**[9] 6278 2-8-12............ PatCosgrave 9 1
(R Brotherton) *prom: rdn and lost pl 1/2-way: sn bhd* **66/1**

1m 14.36s (-1.45) **Going Correction** -0.40s/f (Stan) **9** Ran SP% **123.0**
Speed ratings (Par 96):93,91,89,89,88 87,85,78,64
CSF £7.32 TOTE £1.90: £1.10, £2.00, £7.60; EX 7.50.
Owner S Parker **Bred** Mervyn Stewkesbury **Trained** Headley, Surrey

FOCUS
Just a modest sprint maiden in which the placed horses look the best guide to the form.

NOTEBOOK
Golden Desert(IRE), a good second in maiden company at Nottingham before running reasonably in a Newmarket sales race, would have found this easier and gained a straightforward victory. Already rated 85, he is likely to find things tougher from now on. (op 13-8)
Napoleon Dynamite(IRE), second in a Kempton nursery off this mark on his previous start, was short of room in the straight but would not have beaten the winner and looks a good guide to the strength of the form. (op 6-1)
Mujart, back up in trip, seemed to run above her official mark of 56. This was a good effort, but she is likely to go up in the weights and things are not going to get any easier.
Voice, the first foal of a six-furlong juvenile winner, raced keenly after missing the kick and showed just modest form on her racecourse debut. She is, though, open to improvement. Official explanation: jockey said filly was slow to get into its stride (op 7-1)
Para Siempre will have more options now she is qualified for a handicap mark. (op 20-1)
Wadnagin(IRE) showed ability on her debut at Newbury, but had not been seen for over three months and looked as though she would be sharper for the run.

6415 TWILIGHT RACING - MISS THE TRAFFIC H'CAP 1m 5f 194y(P)
4:20 (4:21) (Class 5) (0-75,75) 3-Y-O+ £3,238 (£963; £481; £240) Stalls Low

Form RPR

6305 **1** **Power Of Future (GER)**[13] 6202 3-9-13 **75**............ JimmyQuinn 3 85
(H R A Cecil) *a.p: chsd ldr 2f out: led 1f out: rdn out* **5/2**[1]

3663 **2** *2* **Eastborough (IRE)**[10] 6256 7-9-7 **61**............ DarryllHolland 6 68
(J R Jenkins) *hld up: edgd lft 3f out: hdwy 2f out: sn rdn: wnt 2nd ins fnl f: nt trble wnr* **9/2**[2]

6324 **3** *2* **Sgt Schultz (IRE)**[11] 6244 3-9-8 **70**............ LPKeniry 5 74
(J S Moore) *chsd ldr tl led over 2f out: rdn and hdd 1f out: no ex* **11/2**[3]

5600 **4** *5* **Bentley Brook (IRE)**[8] 6301 4-9-6 **60**............ GeorgeBaker 4 57
(P A Blockley) *hld up: hdwy over 3f out: rdn and wknd over 1f out* **11/2**[3]

0000 **5** *1 ½* **Isa'Af (IRE)**[19] 6108 7-9-8 **62**............ PhillipMakin 7 57
(P W Hiatt) *chsd ldrs: rdn over 3f out: wknd over 2f out* **14/1**

4663 **6** *¾* **Galileo Figaro (USA)**[23] 6027 3-8-11 **64**............ LiamJones(5) 2 58
(W M Brisbourne) *led: hung rt thrght: hdd over 2f out: sn wknd* **9/1**

5023 **7** *21* **Squirtle (IRE)**[11] 6244 3-9-5 **67**............(v) RobbieFitzpatrick 1 31
(W M Brisbourne) *hld up: rdn over 4f out: hmpd and wknd 3f out* **9/2**[2]

3m 0.91s (-6.46) **Going Correction** -0.40s/f (Stan)
WFA 3 from 4yo+ 8lb **7** Ran SP% **112.4**
Speed ratings (Par 103):102,100,99,96,96 95,83
CSF £13.35 TOTE £3.50: £1.10, £3.70; EX 14.00.
Owner G Schoeningh **Bred** Gestut Elite **Trained** Newmarket, Suffolk

FOCUS
A modest handicap run at an even pace rated through the third to his latest form.
Squirtle(IRE) Official explanation: jockey said filly never travelled

6416 STAY AT THE WOLVERHAMPTON HOLIDAY INN NURSERY 7f 32y(P)
4:50 (4:50) (Class 6) (0-65,65) 2-Y-O £2,590 (£770; £385; £192) Stalls High

Form RPR

5663 **1** **Lake Pontchartrain (IRE)**[8] 6291 2-9-2 **60**............ GeorgeBaker 4 62
(S Kirk) *hld up: swtchd rt and hdwy over 1f out: rdn to ld last strides* **7/2**[1]

5603 **2** *hd* **Tobago Reef**[31] 5876 2-9-4 **62**............(p) DarryllHolland 10 63
(Mrs L Stubbs) *sn led: edgd lft over 6f out: rdn over 1f out: edgd rt ins fnl f: hdd last strides* **11/1**

3001 **3** *½* **Madam Gaffer**[31] 5876 2-9-0 **65**............ KMay(7) 12 65
(B J Meehan) *hld up: hdwy over 2f out: rdn over 1f out: ev ch ins fnl f: styd on* **8/1**[3]

500 **4** *2* **Sophie's Dream**[122] 3351 2-9-0 **58**............ DeanMcKeown 5 53
(J G Given) *hld up: racd keenly: hdwy over 1f out: nt rch ldrs* **16/1**

3023 **5** *½* **Cantique (IRE)**[7] 6309 2-9-4 **62**............ FergusSweeney 2 56
(A G Newcombe) *chsd ldrs: rdn and edgd lft over 1f out: styd on same pce ins fnl f* **7/2**[1]

005 **6** *1 ¼* **Ishibee (IRE)**[8] 6291 2-8-13 **62**............(p) DuranFentiman(5) 8 52
(Mrs A Duffield) *prom: hmpd over 6f out: rdn and ev ch over 2f out: wknd ins fnl f* **16/1**

6320 **7** *hd* **Tibinta**[54] 5366 2-8-13 **57**............ JimCrowley 11 47
(P D Evans) *s.i.s: hld up: hdwy over 1f out: nvr trbld ldrs* **20/1**

0040 **8** *nk* **Torver**[52] 5419 2-9-0 **58**............ PaulHanagan 1 47
(Dr J D Scargill) *chsd ldrs: rdn 1/2-way: wknd over 1f out* **14/1**

550 **9** *1 ¼* **Solwind (USA)**[40] 5679 2-9-4 **62**............ PaulEddery 3 48
(B Smart) *led early: chsd ldrs: rdn and wknd over 1f out* **9/1**

5U00 **10** *3 ½* **Munster Mountain (IRE)**[54] 5381 2-8-13 **57**............ DaneO'Neill 6 34
(P A Blockley) *s.i.s: hld up: n.m.r 1/2-way: rdn over 1f out: a in rr* **12/1**

4006 **11** *1 ¾* **Beat The Bully**[41] 5645 2-9-1 **59**............(b) DanielTudhope 7 31
(I A Wood) *hld up in tch: rdn over 2f out: sn wknd* **40/1**

1364 **12** *3* **La Marmotte (IRE)**[41] 5646 2-9-6 **64**............ FJohansson 9 28
(J W Hills) *chsd ldrs: hmpd over 6f out: wknd 2f out: eased* **15/2**[2]

1m 29.76s (-0.64) **Going Correction** -0.40s/f (Stan) **12** Ran SP% **119.0**
Speed ratings (Par 94):87,86,86,83,83 81,81,81,79,75 73,70
CSF £44.39 CT £296.49 TOTE £5.00: £2.10, £3.90, £4.40; EX 17.00.
Owner Eddie Tynan **Bred** E Tynan **Trained** Upper Lambourn, Berks
■ Stewards' Enquiry : Darryll Holland seven-day ban: careless riding (Nov 20-26)

FOCUS
A modest but competitive nursery. The winning time was 2.41 seconds slower than the following older-horse 0-75 handicap and the form is ordinary.

NOTEBOOK
Lake Pontchartrain(IRE) got going too late over six furlongs at Kempton on her previous start and, stepped back up in trip, she was able to gain her first success at the seventh attempt. She should remain competitive in modest company. (op 4-1)
Tobago Reef, fitted with cheekpieces for the first time, improved on the form he showed when third to Madam Gaffer in a course and distance seller on his previous start and was just held. (tchd 12-1)
Madam Gaffer would have found this tougher than the course and distance seller she won on her previous start, but was unable to confirm form with Tobago Reef in any case. (op 7-1)

The Form Book, Raceform Ltd, Compton, RG20 6NL

Sophie's Dream, upped in trip and switched to Polytrack for the first time on his handicap debut, ran with promise off the back of a 122-day break. He probably only has to improve a touch to find a similar race.
Cantique(IRE) could confirm recent selling form with Tobago Reef and was below her best. (op 4-1 tchd 9-2)
La Marmotte(IRE) was badly hampered in the early stages and this is best forgotten. (tchd 7-1)

6417 DINE IN THE ZONGALERO RESTAURANT H'CAP 7f 32y(P)
5:20 (5:20) (Class 5) (0-75,75) 3-Y-O+ £3,238 (£963; £481; £240) Stalls High

Form				RPR
0300	1		**Prince Tum Tum (USA)**[12] 6223 6-9-2 74 DeanMcKeown 8 (D Shaw) *hld up: swtchd rt and hdwy over 1f out: edgd lft and r.o to ld wl ins fnl f* 7/1[3]	83
0400	2	1 ½	**Red Contact (USA)**[118] 3469 5-8-12 70 (p) DanielTudhope 4 (A Dickman) *led: rdn over 2f out: hdd wl ins fnl f* 25/1	75
4-45	3	nk	**Master Mahogany**[10] 6259 5-9-3 75 GeorgeBaker 2 (R J Hodges) *chsd ldrs: rdn and hung lft fr over 1f out: styd on* 10/3[1]	79
4510	4	nk	**Valentino Swing (IRE)**[11] 6239 3-8-11 70 AdamKirby 9 (J L Spearing) *s.i.s: hld up: hdwy over 1f out: r.o* 8/1	74
0600	5	1 ¼	**Cape Presto (IRE)**[57] 5301 3-8-8 67 (v) RobbieFitzpatrick 1 (Mrs C A Dunnett) *prom: rdn to chse ldr 2f out: no ex ins fnl f* 14/1	67
1540	6	nk	**Xpres Maite**[43] 5617 3-8-10 72 (b[1]) AmirQuinn(3) 3 (S R Bowring) *s.i.s: hld up: hdwy over 2f out: sn rdn: no ex ins fnl f* 6/1[2]	72
1300	7	½	**Stoic Leader (IRE)**[40] 5680 6-8-11 69 PaulHanagan 12 (R F Fisher) *chsd ldr tl rdn 2f out: wknd ins fnl f* 12/1	67
6005	8	½	**Bessemer (JPN)**[11] 6241 5-9-1 73 (p) DarryllHolland 6 (D Carroll) *hld up: nt clr run over 2f out: styd on ins fnl f: nvr nrr* 8/1	70
201-	9	hd	**Rainbows Guest (IRE)**[359] 6357 3-8-12 74 (v) NeilChalmers(3) 5 (A M Balding) *s.i.s: hld up: rdn over 2f out: n.d* 8/1	70
0034	10	3 ½	**Dvinsky (USA)**[6] 6326 5-8-3 66 LiamJones(5) 11 (M A Allen) *mid-div: rdn and wknd 2f out* 9/1	53
1606	11	shd	**Bollin Edward**[129] 3158 7-8-6 64 CatherineGannon 7 (K A Ryan) *chsd ldrs to 1/2-way* 20/1	51
3040	12	9	**Makfly**[12] 6221 3-8-13 72 (p) GrahamGibbons 10 (R Hollinshead) *chsd ldrs over 4f* 16/1	36

1m 27.35s (-3.05) **Going Correction** -0.40s/f (Stan)
WFA 3 from 5yo+ 1lb 12 Ran SP% 122.0
Speed ratings (Par 103):101,99,98,98,97 96,96,95,95,91 91,81
CSF £172.60 CT £707.72 TOTE £8.20: £1.60, £8.30, £1.30; EX 226.90.
Owner The Circle Bloodstock I Limited **Bred** Clovelly Farms **Trained** Danethorpe, Notts

FOCUS
Just a fair handicap run in a time 2.41 seconds quicker than the earlier 0-65 nursery. The form is ordinary and limited by the fourth.
Bessemer(JPN) Official explanation: jockey said gelding was hampered final bend

6418 BOOK ONLINE AT WOLVERHAMPTON-RACECOURSE.CO.UK H'CAP 1m 1f 103y(P)
5:50 (5:50) (Class 4) (0-85,84) 3-Y-O+ £5,505 (£1,637; £818; £408) Stalls Low

Form				RPR
1-23	1		**Alpine Reel (IRE)**[12] 6226 5-9-4 82 AdamKirby 6 (W R Swinburn) *chsd ldr: led over 1f out: rdn clr and edgd lft ins fnl f* 2/1[1]	96+
5200	2	2 ½	**Del Mar Sunset**[12] 6226 7-8-8 77 LiamJones(5) 1 (W J Haggas) *chsd ldrs: lost pl over 6f out: hdwy 3f out: rdn to chse wnr ins fnl f: styd on* 14/1	86
6025	3	3	**Regent's Secret (USA)**[12] 6226 6-9-1 79 DanielTudhope 5 (J S Goldie) *hld up: hdwy over 2f out: sn rdn: nt rch ldrs* 16/1	83
0200	4	nk	**Wahoo Sam (USA)**[46] 5554 6-8-12 76 CatherineGannon 4 (K A Ryan) *led over 8f out: rdn and hdd over 1f out: wknd ins fnl f* 20/1	79
3222	5	1	**Don Pietro**[32] 5833 3-8-11 78 FJohansson 3 (D J Coakley) *led 1f: chsd ldrs: rdn over 2f out: wknd fnl f* 6/1[2]	79
4522	6	1 ½	**Consonant (IRE)**[7] 6313 9-8-13 77 DarryllHolland 7 (D G Bridgwater) *hld up: styd on ins fnl f: nrst fin* 13/2[3]	75
04-0	7	hd	**Pugilist**[34] 5787 4-8-12 83 KMay(7) 10 (B J Meehan) *hld up in tch: rdn over 2f out: sn wknd* 14/1	81
6426	8	1 ¼	**Dower House**[7] 6313 11-9-0 78 (t) JimCrowley 13 (Andrew Turnell) *hld up: rdn over 1f out: n.d* 11/1	73
3000	9	shd	**Primo Way**[9] 6273 5-8-13 77 PaulHanagan 2 (I Semple) *hld up: rdn over 1f out: n.d* 28/1	72
3453	10	1 ½	**Optimus (USA)**[17] 6148 4-8-13 77 FergusSweeney 11 (B G Powell) *chsd ldrs: rdn over 3f out: wknd 2f out* 16/1	69
6300	11	1 ½	**Cactus King**[7] 6313 3-9-3 84 DaneO'Neill 12 (J H M Gosden) *s.i.s: a bhd* 9/1	74
-306	12	10	**Just Intersky (USA)**[46] 5554 3-8-11 78 DeanMcKeown 9 (K A Ryan) *s.i.s: racd keenly and sn mid-div: rdn over 3f out: wknd over 2f out* 8/1	49

1m 57.17s (-5.45) **Going Correction** -0.40s/f (Stan)
WFA 3 from 4yo+ 3lb 12 Ran SP% 123.7
Speed ratings (Par 105):108,105,103,102,101 100,100,99,99,97 96,87
CSF £35.17 CT £377.60 TOTE £3.40: £1.30, £3.10, £4.40; EX 44.80.
Owner Mrs P W Harris **Bred** South House Stud **Trained** Aldbury, Herts

FOCUS
This looked a decent enough handicap beforehand, but Alpine Reel was in a different league and should be capable of competing at a higher level. The form looks solid rated through the runner-up.

6419 RINGSIDE SUITE 700 THEATRE STYLE CONFERENCE H'CAP 1m 141y(P)
6:20 (6:20) (Class 6) (0-65,65) 3-Y-O+ £2,266 (£674; £337; £168) Stalls Low

Form				RPR
6636	1		**Western Roots**[26] 5972 5-9-1 61 (p) GeorgeBaker 5 (M Appleby) *hld up: hdwy over 2f out: led over 1f out: edgd lft: rdn ins fnl f: jst hld on* 4/1[2]	69+
5000	2	shd	**Tous Les Deux**[31] 5872 3-9-1 64 RobbieFitzpatrick 8 (Peter Grayson) *hld up: hdwy: hung lft over 1f out: r.o wl ins fnl f: jst failed* 12/1	72
3050	3	1 ¾	**Shrine Mountain (USA)**[22] 6059 4-9-2 62 JosedeSouza 9 (J R Holt) *led: rdn and hdd over 1f out: sn hung lft: styd on same pce ins fnl f* 16/1	66
3503	4	1	**Flylowflylong (IRE)**[10] 6260 3-9-0 63 (v[1]) PaulHanagan 2 (I Semple) *hld up in tch: rdn over 2f out: styd on same pce fnl f* 11/8[1]	65
0040	5	¾	**Kingsmaite**[54] 5386 5-8-11 60 (bt) AmirQuinn(3) 3 (S R Bowring) *chsd ldrs: lost pl whn hmpd 2f out: swtchd lft and r.o ins fnl f* 7/1[3]	60
1300	6	¾	**Ask No More**[29] 5907 3-8-13 65 (b[1]) JohnMcAuley(3) 7 (P L Gilligan) *prom: rdn and ev ch 2f out: wknd ins fnl f* 20/1	64
0005	7	1	**Just Fly**[20] 6070 6-9-0 65 (v) KevinGhunowa(5) 12 (Dr J R J Naylor) *hld up: hdwy over 3f out: rdn and wknd fnl f* 8/1	62
0-00	8	½	**Sheriff's Deputy**[26] 5831 6-8-2 53 RoryMoore(5) 1 (C N Kellett) *hld up: nt clr run over 2f out: n.d* 33/1	49
46-0	9	nk	**Cherokee Vision**[8] 6294 3-8-12 61 JimCrowley 11 (Miss T Spearing) *hld up: effrt over 2f out: sn rdn: n.d* 40/1	56
060-	10	nk	**Plausabelle**[528] 2128 5-9-0 60 JamieMackay 13 (G G Margarson) *s.i.s: hld up: hdwy over 2f out: sn rdn and wknd* 12/1	54
00	11	3 ½	**Lalina (GER)**[8] 6289 3-8-11 60 AdamKirby 6 (Jane Chapple-Hyam) *chsd ldrs: rdn over 3f out: nt clr run and wknd 2f out* 14/1	47
1000	12	3 ½	**Life's A Whirl**[57] 5302 4-8-9 55 (p) DarryllHolland 10 (Mrs C A Dunnett) *chsd ldrs 6f* 14/1	35
1035	13	11	**Risk Free**[3] 6380 9-8-3 56 (vt) MCGeran(7) 4 (P D Evans) *in rr: rdn 1/2-way: bhd fnl 3f* 8/1	13

1m 48.66s (-3.10) **Going Correction** -0.40s/f (Stan)
WFA 3 from 4yo+ 3lb 13 Ran SP% 141.6
Speed ratings (Par 101):97,96,95,94,93 93,92,91,91,91 88,85,75
CSF £61.48 CT £760.15 TOTE £5.30: £1.70, £6.10, £5.10; EX 110.70 Place 6 £75.46, Place 5 £50.34.
Owner Sarnian Racing **Bred** Stratford Place Stud **Trained** Shrewley, Warwicks

FOCUS
A modest handicap rated around the placed horses.
Kingsmaite ◆ Official explanation: jockey said gelding was denied a clear run
Lalina(GER) Official explanation: jockey said filly was hampered on bend into home straight
Life's A Whirl Official explanation: jockey said filly was hampered on bend into home straight
T/Plt: £150.80 to a £1 stake. Pool: £60,899.30. 294.80 winning tickets. T/Qpdt: £46.30 to a £1 stake. Pool: £6,929.90. 110.60 winning tickets. CR

6302 SOUTHWELL (L-H)
Friday, November 10

OFFICIAL GOING: Standard
Wind: Virtually nil

6420 BOOK TICKETS ON-LINE MAIDEN AUCTION STKS 5f (F)
12:40 (12:40) (Class 6) 2-Y-O £2,730 (£806; £403) Stalls High

Form				RPR
4302	1		**The Italian Job**[8] 6311 2-8-8 59 DavidAllan 5 (T D Easterby) *mde virtually all: rdn clr wl over 1f out: comf* 11/4[1]	63+
5402	2	2 ½	**Galaxy Of Stars**[9] 6296 2-8-3 53 PatrickMathers(3) 6 (D Shaw) *outpcd in rr: hdwy 2f out: sn rdn and styd on ins last* 14/1	50
0505	3	½	**The Geester**[29] 5923 2-8-11 52 (b[1]) PhillipMakin 1 (S R Bowring) *cl up: effrt over 2f out: sn rdn and ev ch tl drvn and wknd appr last* 12/1	53
6433	4	nk	**Money For Fun**[11] 6255 2-8-5 70 ow1 LPKeniry 7 (J S Moore) *dwlt: sn chsng ldrs: rdn along 2f out: kpt on same pce* 4/1[3]	46
53	5	5	**Superjain**[23] 6047 2-7-11 PaulPickard(7) 9 (J M Jefferson) *pushed along and outpcd towards rr tl kpt on fnl 2f: nvr a factr* 6/1	27
5	6	3 ½	**Stoneacre Gareth (IRE)**[148] 2572 2-8-13 RobbieFitzpatrick 2 (Peter Grayson) *prom: rdn along 1/2-way: sn wknd* 3/1[2]	24
	7	¾	**Miss Kitty** 2-8-10 PaulMulrennan 3 (T D Easterby) *s.i.s: swtchd wd and sn outpcd: hdwy and in tch 2f out: sn rdn and wknd* 28/1	18
050	8	nk	**John Stanley (IRE)**[57] 5315 2-8-9 53 DanielTudhope 4 (D Carroll) *cl up: rdn along after 2f and wknd qckly* 33/1	16
0002	9	nk	**Gibsons**[10] 6278 2-8-6 51 JamesDoyle(3) 8 (Mrs P N Dutfield) *in tch to 1/2-way: sn wknd* 10/1	15

60.87 secs (0.57) **Going Correction** -0.025s/f (Stan) 9 Ran SP% 115.8
Speed ratings (Par 94):94,90,89,88,80 75,73,73,72
CSF £42.25 TOTE £3.30: £1.40, £3.10, £4.20; EX 31.40 TRIFECTA Not won..
Owner P Burton,M Gosse,A Mornin,T Stanley **Bred** J M Gosse **Trained** Great Habton, N Yorks

FOCUS
A very moderate maiden auction event and, as is usually the case over the straight five here, the ability to lay up with the pace was crucial. The form looks solid enough for the grade.

NOTEBOOK
The Italian Job, who performance in finishing second to Yungaburra at Wolverhampton the previous week is looking better and better by the day, bounced out of the stalls and had had little difficulty in disposing of these rivals with the minimum of fuss. This victory and the subsequent exploits of her Wolverhampton conqueror will probably result in a rise in her official mark, and as this was her tenth outing she does not have much scope for improvement. (op 3-1)
Galaxy Of Stars was slow to break yet again, which is usually fatal over this straight five so she can be given plenty of credit for managing to snatch second. She is not completely without hope, but a return to Polytrack and an extra furlong would probably help her.
The Geester, dropping to the minimum trip for the first time, had shown some early pace before now and showed up for a long way from his good draw, but he was inclined to hang left into the slower ground as he got tired late on. (op 20-1)
Money For Fun, who was well in on official ratings, was always in about the same place and appears to need a return to six. (op 9-2)
Superjain, not for the first time, can be considered to have run better than her finishing position as she was drawn next to the stands' rail and over this straight five that is a major disadvantage these days. (op 5-1)
Stoneacre Gareth(IRE) had a decent draw, but was unable to use it to his advantage and failed to see his race out. Perhaps he needs more time. (op 7-2 tchd 11-4)

6421 HOSPITALITY PACKAGES AVAILABLE CLAIMING STKS 1m (F)
1:10 (1:10) (Class 6) 2-Y-O £2,730 (£806; £403) Stalls Low

Form				RPR
0003	1		**Shouldntbethere (IRE)**[10] 6278 2-8-11 45 JamieMackay 7 (Mrs P N Dutfield) *dwlt: sn trcking ldrs: hdwy to chse ldr 3f out: led wl over 1f out: rdn and edgd lft ent last: styd on* 12/1	64
2120	2	nk	**Emergency Services**[2] 6394 2-8-5 62 (p) RichardThomas 9 (Tom Dascombe) *midfield: hdwy 1/2-way: rdn to chal over 1f out and ev ch tl drvn and no ex wl ins last* 5/2[1]	57
0044	3	1 ¼	**Featherlight**[7] 6322 2-7-7 53 (v[1]) MCGeran(7) 11 (N A Callaghan) *stdd s: sn bhd: hdwy and wd st: rdn to chse ldng pair and edgd lft ent last: kpt on* 7/2[2]	49
006	4	8	**Go Dude**[10] 6283 2-8-13 (p) SteveDrowne 3 (J Ryan) *towards rr tl styd on fnl 2f: nvr nr ldrs* 14/1	44
4100	5	1 ¼	**Foxxy**[7] 6322 2-8-12 72 (b[1]) PatCosgrave 8 (K A Ryan) *cl up: led after 1f: rdn along wl over 2f out: hdd wl over 1f out: sn drvn and wknd* 15/2	40
0000	6	6	**Cavendish**[8] 6303 2-8-5 45 PaulHanagan 12 (J M P Eustace) *racd wd: midfield: rdn along 3f out: sn no imp* 16/1	19

4634 **7** 3½ **Generist**[11] [6258] 2-7-11 52................................(p) DominicFox(3) 4 6
(M J Attwater) *chsd ldrs whn hmpd and stmbld after 1f: rdn along 3f out: sn drvn and wknd* **5/1**[3]

0600 **8** 2½ **Jazzanova**[35] [5790] 2-8-3 45.............................. DaleGibson 10 —
(G P Kelly) *a towards rr* **25/1**

00 **9** *nk* **Miss Taboo (IRE)**[58] [5287] 2-8-1 ow2.................. AndrewElliott(5) 6 6
(Miss V Haigh) *prom: rdn along over 3f out: sn wknd* **40/1**

0600 **10** *8* **Gold Response**[98] [4115] 2-8-8 50.....................(v[1]) PatrickMathers(3) 2 —
(D Shaw) *chsd ldrs: rdn along 3f out: sn wknd* **20/1**

3005 **11** *7* **Abdu**[90] [4376] 2-8-9 55.................................. PaulMulrennan 5 —
(G P Kelly) *led 1f: cl up tl rdn along 1/2-way and sn wknd* **28/1**

00 **12** *hd* **Awe**[66] [5089] 2-8-3 ow1.............................. JamesDoyle(3) 1 —
(Mrs C A Dunnett) *a rr: rdn along and wl bhd fr 1/2-way* **40/1**

1m 43.69s (-0.91) **Going Correction** -0.15s/f (Stan) **12** Ran SP% **116.4**
Speed ratings (Par 94):98,97,96,88,87 81,77,75,74,66 59,59
CSF £39.04 TOTE £8.60: £3.00, £1.40, £1.80; EX 72.10 Trifecta £63.20 Pool £149.70 - 1.68 winning units..Featherlight was claimed by Keith Wills for £6,000.
Owner Mrs Kathy Stuart **Bred** Stonethorn Stud Farms Ltd **Trained** Axmouth, Devon
■ Stewards' Enquiry : M C Geran caution: used whip above shoulder height

FOCUS
A moderate claimer, though the pace was solid and few ever got into it. The front three pulled well clear and thwe form appears sound enough, rated through the runner-up.

NOTEBOOK
Shouldntbethere(IRE), who showed his first signs of ability in a Class 7 maiden here last time, with the exception of the pair without official marks was worst in at these weights, but he appreciated this step back up to a mile and, after racing prominently throughout, eventually ground out a dour victory. He seems to have got his act together now, but his future depends entirely on what the Handicapper makes of this. (op 11-1)
Emergency Services, so named because he was lot 999 at the sales, had shown on turf that he was suited by a mile on a testing surface and ran much better than in his two attempts on Polytrack, but he was best in at the weights so was entitled to go close. He did little wrong, but the winner was just that more determined. (op 3-1)
Featherlight, another of those more favoured by the weights, ran a strange race as she hardly went a yard in the first half of the contest and had a mountain to climb turning in, but once switched out wide she made relentless late progress without quite ever looking likely to get there. It is hard to be sure how much effect the application of the visor had and it may be that she is just not straightforward. (op 11-4)
Go Dude, who failed to stay the extended nine furlongs at Wolverhampton last time and had plenty on at the weights, was never in the hunt and probably achieved little in finishing a remote fourth. (op 22-1)
Foxxy, second best in on adjusted official ratings, set a decent pace but faded rather tamely once headed and seems to have gone the wrong way since her September Ayr victory. (op 6-1)
Cavendish Official explanation: jockey said gelding hung left-handed throughout
Generist can be forgiven this to a degree as she was almost on the floor after a furlong. (op 6-1)
Awe Official explanation: jockey said gelding suffered interference in running

6422 EXPERIENCE NOTTINGHAMSHIRE NURSERY 6f (F)
1:45 (1:45) (Class 6) (0-65,61) 2-Y-O **£3,238** (£963; £481; £240) **Stalls** Low

Form RPR

350 **1** **Bridget's Team**[55] [5387] 2-8-11 **51**.............................. DaleGibson 2 55
(P C Haslam) *mde all: rdn over 1f out: styd on* **40/1**

500 **2** 1½ **Wee Ellie Coburn**[23] [6050] 2-9-1 **55**.......................... PaulHanagan 9 55
(A Bailey) *dwlt and n.m.r s:sn towards rr: swtchd wd and hdwy 2f out: sn rdn and str run ins last: nt rch wnr* **20/1**

0443 **3** 1¼ **Diminuto**[52] [5448] 2-8-5 **52**.......................... FrankiePickard(7) 14 48
(M D I Usher) *in tch: hdwy over 2f out: sn rdn and kpt on appr last: nrst fin* **8/1**[3]

5025 **4** ½ **Peppin's Gold (IRE)**[11] [6258] 2-8-6 **53**..................(t) JamesMillman(7) 12 47
(B R Millman) *bmpd s and bhd: swtchd rigfht and gd hdwy wl over 1f out: styd on ins last: nrst fin* **10/1**

6006 **5** *shd* **Bentley**[8] [6311] 2-8-9 **52**..............................(v) PatrickMathers(3) 7 46
(D Shaw) *in tch: rdn along and hdwy over 2f out: drvn and kpt on appr last: nrst fin* **28/1**

0351 **6** 1½ **Show Trial (IRE)**[7] [6316] 2-9-0 **59** 7ex.................. JerryO'Dwyer(5) 1 48
(D J S Ffrench Davis) *chsd ldrs on inner: hdwy over 2f out: sn rdn along and kpt on same pce* **4/1**[1]

3211 **7** 1¼ **Dotty's Daughter**[41] [5687] 2-9-6 **60**..........................(p) JimCrowley 4 46
(Mrs A Duffield) *chsd ldrs: hdwy over 2f out: rdn over 1f out: wknd ins last* **7/1**[2]

0300 **8** *shd* **Silver Appraisal**[3] [6388] 2-9-2 **61**.......................... MarkLawson(5) 6 46
(B Smart) *squeezed out s and bhd: hdwy 2f out: sn rdn and kpt on appr last: nrst fin* **22/1**

5460 **9** *1* **Arabellas Homer**[51] [5482] 2-8-8 **53**...................... AndrewElliott(5) 8 35
(Mrs N Macauley) *midfield: rdn along and outpcd after 3f: styd on u.p fnl 2f: nrst fin* **12/1**

6444 **10** 3½ **Reflective Glory (IRE)**[139] [2870] 2-9-2 **56**............... GrahamGibbons 13 28
(J J Quinn) *chsd ldrs: rdn along 3f out: sn wknd* **14/1**

0000 **11** ¾ **Storm Mission (USA)**[80] [4681] 2-9-5 **59**...................... SteveDrowne 3 29
(Miss V Haigh) *cl up: rdn along over 2f out: sn drvn and wknd* **20/1**

6043 **12** *hd* **Pietersen (IRE)**[13] [6208] 2-9-6 **60**.......................... PhillipMakin 11 29
(T D Barron) *s.i.s: a bhd* **4/1**[1]

2650 **13** *nk* **Emefdream**[3] [6388] 2-9-6 **60**..............................(b[1]) CatherineGannon 10 28
(K A Ryan) *cl up: rdn along over 2f out and ev ch tl drvn and wknd over 1f out* **9/1**

400 **14** ½ **Blakeshall Rose**[60] [5238] 2-8-7 **47** ow1...................... DeanMcKeown 5 14
(A J Chamberlain) *in tch on inner: rdn along 1/2-way: sn wknd* **9/1**

1m 17.49s (0.59) **Going Correction** -0.15s/f (Stan) **14** Ran SP% **126.8**
Speed ratings (Par 94):90,88,86,85,85 83,81,81,80,75 74,74,74,73
CSF £692.75 CT £7043.67 TOTE £26.00: £6.20, £10.20, £2.90; EX 513.10 TRIFECTA Not won..
Owner Middleham Park Racing XIII **Bred** D R Tucker **Trained** Middleham Moor, N Yorks

FOCUS
A modest nursery, but competitive and a solid early pace meant that several were taken off their feet and could never get back into it. THe form looks sound enough with the third to her recent form.

NOTEBOOK
Bridget's Team, who showed that she was not without ability in three maidens on turf and Polytrack, was a different proposition on this nursery debut. Making just about all, she was able to back the perfect position right in the middle of the track turning for home and she was always doing more than enough. Her yard knows how to win races here and it would not be the biggest surprise to see her find another contest like this. (op 33-1)
Wee Ellie Coburn, unplaced in three turf maidens, was another to improve on this switch to Fibresand for her nursery debut. She was attempting the near-impossible in trying to come from so far back at this track, but was finishing to some purpose and looks more than capable of winning a race like this over a bit further. (op 16-1)
Diminuto, who showed that she could cope with this surface when placed a couple of times on it in the spring, ran right up to her best to make the frame without ever offering a threat to the winner. She is vastly more experienced than the pair ahead of her though, and has been beaten several times in sellers so if she is to win again it will be in very modest company. (op 12-1 tchd 14-1)
Peppin's Gold(IRE) soon found herself at the back, and over this shorter trip on a track favouring pace horses that was always going to make things difficult. Under the circumstances she did well to snatch fourth.
Bentley, unplaced in all six of his previous outings, was another doing his best work late. Connections seem to be having some trouble identifying his ideal trip. (op 25-1)
Show Trial(IRE), under a 7lb penalty for her Musselburgh victory, was close enough if good enough starting up the home straight but could never get on terms with the winner and the furlong-shorter trip could not really be blamed. (op 9-2)
Dotty's Daughter, bidding for a hat-trick after winning a couple of sellers, failed to make much impact in this better race and does not seem to stay beyond five furlongs. (op 6-1)
Pietersen(IRE), making his Fibresand debut for a yard with a fine record here, seemed to hate every second of it and was always trailing. (op 9-2 tchd 5-1)

6423 SOUTHWELL-RACECOURSE.CO.UK (S) STKS 1m 4f (F)
2:20 (2:20) (Class 6) 3-5-Y-O **£2,388** (£705; £352) **Stalls** Low

Form RPR

0110 **1** **Maria Antonia (IRE)**[22] [6068] 3-8-5 54...................... KevinGhunowa(5) 5 66+
(P A Blockley) *trckd ldrs: smooth hdwy to ld 3f out: pshd clr over 1f out: easily* **4/1**[2]

0065 **2** 3½ **Coffin Dodger**[23] [6057] 3-8-3 46.......................... KirstyMilczarek(7) 2 49
(C N Allen) *hld up: hdwy on inner 4f out: rdn to chse wnr 2f out: sn drvn and no imp* **8/1**

2010 **3** *5* **Cool Isle**[12] [6238] 3-8-8 48 ow1..............................(b) DeanCorby(3) 3 42
(P Howling) *led: rdn along and hdd 3f out: drvn over 2f out and sn wknd* **4/1**[2]

5220 **4** 3½ **Shaheer (IRE)**[77] [4755] 4-9-7 54..............................(b) JimCrowley 9 40
(J Gallagher) *trckd ldrs: hdwy 4f out: rdn 3f out and sn one pce* **7/1**[3]

0 **5** 1½ **Party Boy (IRE)**[33] [5830] 4-8-10 ....(bt) JerryO'Dwyer(5) 4 32
(Edgar Byrne, Ire) *chsd ldrs on inner: rdn along after 4f: drvn 4f out: sn wknd* **20/1**

6000 **6** *nk* **Fit To Fly (IRE)**[93] [4256] 5-9-1 40..............................(v) PaulHanagan 6 32
(C A Mulhall) *chsd ldng pair: rdn along over 3f out: sn wknd* **10/1**

0105 **7** *5* **Cotton Easter**[10] [6280] 5-9-2 48..............................(t) SteveDrowne 7 25
(Mrs A J Bowlby) *hld up in rr: hdwy over 4f out: rdn along over 3f out: sn wknd* **3/1**[1]

2100 **8** *22* **Dimashq**[38] [5750] 4-9-2 40.. PhillipMakin 1 —
(Ronald Thompson) *cl up: rdn along over 3f out: sn wknd* **11/1**

2m 42.9s (0.81) **Going Correction** -0.15s/f (Stan)
WFA 3 from 4yo+ 6lb **8** Ran SP% **110.8**
Speed ratings (Par 101):91,88,85,83,82 81,78,63
CSF £33.28 TOTE £4.20: £1.30, £2.10, £1.70; EX 23.20 Trifecta £49.90 Pool £254.52 - 3.62 winning units..The winner was bought in for 14,500gns.
Owner Pedro Rosas **Bred** J McElroy **Trained** Lambourn, Berks
■ Stewards' Enquiry : Jerry O'Dwyer four-day ban: used whip with excessive frequency and on a horse showing no response (Nov 24-25, 27-28)

FOCUS
A moderate time, even for a seller, and the form looks decidedly weak with the second the best guide.

6424 ARENA LEISURE H'CAP 1m (F)
2:55 (2:55) (Class 3) (0-90,89) 3-Y-O+
£7,790 (£2,332; £1,166; £583; £291; £146) **Stalls** Low

Form RPR

1204 **1** **Nevada Desert (IRE)**[8] [6313] 6-8-8 **79**...................... DeanMcKeown 2 89
(R M Whitaker) *trckd ldr: hdwy to ld 2f out: sn rdn: drvn and edgd rt ins last: hld on gamely* **10/1**

4122 **2** *nk* **Bold Marc (IRE)**[10] [6273] 4-8-6 **77**..........................(p) PaulHanagan 5 86
(K R Burke) *cl up: effrt 2f out and ev ch tl drvn ins last: n.m.r and no ex nr fin* **7/1**

31- **3** *shd* **Bold Crusader**[393] [5850] 3-8-13 **86**.......................... SteveDrowne 9 95
(Saeed Bin Suroor) *chsd ldrs: hdwy 3f out: rdn wl over 1f out: styd on u.p ins last: jst hld* **10/3**[2]

003 **4** *2* **Speed Dial Harry (IRE)**[16] [6176] 4-7-13 **75** oh1.......(v) AndrewElliott(5) 4 79
(K R Burke) *chsd ldrs: rdn along and outpcd over 2f out: kpt on u.p ins last* **5/2**[1]

3000 **5** *hd* **Davenport (IRE)**[16] [6176] 4-8-6 **77**.............................. JimCrowley 7 81
(B R Millman) *trckd ldrs: hdwy over 2f out: rdn and ev ch over 1f out: kpt on same pce u.p ins last* **12/1**

3000 **6** *10* **North Walk (IRE)**[17] [6160] 3-8-2 **75**...................... CatherineGannon 8 56
(K A Ryan) *rr and sn pushed along: nvr a factor* **33/1**

0213 **7** *10* **Rain Stops Play (IRE)**[13] [6219] 4-8-11 **89**............... ChrisCavanagh(7) 3 47
(M Quinn) *led: rdn along 3f out: hdd 2f out and sn wknd* **6/1**[3]

0003 **8** ¾ **Little Britain (USA)**[55] [5368] 3-7-11 **75** oh22.......(b) DuranFentiman(5) 10 31
(J Howard Johnson) *a rr* **100/1**

5045 **9** *6* **Moi Aussi (USA)**[56] [5337] 3-8-7 **80** ow3......................(v[1]) SebSanders 6 22
(Sir Mark Prescott) *s.i.s: sn chsng ldrs: rdn along over 2f out: sn wknd* **8/1**

1m 41.7s (-2.90) **Going Correction** -0.15s/f (Stan)
WFA 3 from 4yo+ 2lb **9** Ran SP% **110.3**
Speed ratings (Par 107):108,107,107,105,105 95,85,84,78
CSF £72.49 CT £269.72 TOTE £13.20: £2.70, £1.90, £1.50; EX 57.20 Trifecta £201.60 Part won. Pool £284.01 - 0.34 winning units..
Owner J Barry Pemberton **Bred** Bryan Ryan **Trained** Scarcroft, W Yorks

FOCUS
By some way the classiest contest on the card and a cracking finish between the front trio. The form looks rock-solid rated around the runner-up and fourth.

NOTEBOOK
Nevada Desert(IRE) has run a couple of fair on this surface in the past, though his wins have come on turf and Polytrack. However, he is very well suited by a testing surface on grass so there was encouragement that he could produce his best on this surface and that is how it proved, as he had to dig very deep to stay just ahead of his two main rivals. He should not go up much for this and having proved himself on Fibresand opens up all sorts of options. (op 12-1)
Bold Marc(IRE) ◆, making his sand debut, was never far away and never gave an inch in the battle to the line. Although he, like the winner, is proven on soft ground on turf this was only his second try at the trip and he certainly did not fail through lack of stamina. He looks more than capable of winning a decent handicap on sand this winter. (op 15-2)
Bold Crusader, another Godolphin inmate returning from a long layoff, in his case over a year, had every chance and kept on all the way to the line. He looks worth another try on sand this winter. (op 11-4 tchd 7-2)

Speed Dial Harry(IRE), despite being 1lb out of the handicap, was still 1lb lower than when gaining his last win here in February. He did appear a bit short of room rounding the home bend and lost his place as a result, but although he stayed on once switched towards the stands' side he could never make up the ground. He ought to find an opportunity or two again here this winter. (op 3-1 tchd 9-4)
Davenport(IRE) ◆, trying Fibresand for the first time, had every chance and performed better than in his recent outings on turf. A four-time winner on soft ground and placed a couple of times on Polytrack, he seemed to take to the surface well enough and is worth another try. (op 10-1)
North Walk(IRE), without a win in over a year, probably did not achieve much on this switch to Fibresand. (tchd 40-1)
Rain Stops Play(IRE), on sand for the first time, was given his usual positive ride but failed to see his race out and the different surface may have been a bigger problem than his current handicap mark. (tchd 5-1)

6425 JOIN US AGAIN NEXT TUESDAY H'CAP 7f (F)
3:30 (3:30) (Class 5) (0-70,70) 3-Y-0+ **£3,238** (£963; £481; £240) **Stalls** Low

Form RPR
1506 **1** **California Laws**[32] 5861 4-9-0 **66** ... PhillipMakin 10 89+
(T D Barron) *prom: hdwy to ld wl over 1f out: sn rdn clr* **3/1**[1]
1100 **2** *5* **Scuba (IRE)**[32] 5861 4-9-1 **67** ...(b) SteveDrowne 11 74
(H Morrison) *in tch: hdwy over 2f out: sn rdn: styd on appr last: no ch w wnr* **13/2**[3]
3521 **3** *1 1/2* **Preskani**[8] 6307 4-7-12 **52** 7ex...(p) DuranFentiman[(5)] 5 58
(Mrs N Macauley) *midfield: rdn along 3f out: styd on fnl 2f: nrst fin* **13/2**[3]
0004 **4** *shd* **Sentiero Rosso (USA)**[10] 6273 4-8-8 **65** ow1...(t) MarkLawson[(5)] 3 68
(B Ellison) *towards rr and sn rdn along: hdwy over 2f out: styd on wl fnl f: nrst fin* **10/1**
0000 **5** *hd* **Ochre Bay**[138] 2896 3-9-1 **68** ... GrahamGibbons 13 70
(R Hollinshead) *chsd ldrs: hdwy 2f out: sn rdn and kpt on same pce appr last* **20/1**
5611 **6** *hd* **Bel Cantor**[16] 6174 3-9-0 **70** ... RichardKingscote[(3)] 6 72
(W J H Ratcliffe) *led: rdn along wl over 2f out: hdd wl over 1f out: sn drvn and grad wknd* **4/1**[2]
0601 **7** *5* **Shifty**[126] 3262 7-9-3 **69** ... DanielTudhope 7 58
(D Carroll) *towards rr: hdwy over 2f out: sn rdn and no imp* **9/1**
1360 **8** *nk* **Neon Blue**[57] 5313 5-9-1 **67** ... DeanMcKeown 2 55
(R M Whitaker) *chsd ldrs: rdn along 1/2-way: sn wknd* **14/1**
6504 **9** *1 3/4* **Riverhill (IRE)**[13] 6213 3-8-2 **55** oh2... CatherineGannon 1 38
(J Howard Johnson) *prom: rdn along 3f out: sn wknd* **18/1**
0406 **10** *shd* **Wodhill Be**[29] 5926 6-8-3 **55** oh10... DavidKinsella 8 38
(D Morris) *a towards rr* **80/1**
0360 **11** *6* **Set Alight**[162] 2184 5-8-10 **65** ...(p) JamesDoyle[(3)] 4 33
(Mrs C A Dunnett) *s.i.s: a rr* **16/1**
3300 **12** *6* **Woodwee**[32] 5865 3-8-8 **61** ... JimCrowley 12 13
(J R Weymes) *a towards rr* **33/1**
-660 **13** *9* **Aysgarth Flyer (IRE)**[260] 488 3-7-12 **56**...(b) NicolPolli[(5)] 9 —
(James Moffatt) *chsd ldr: rdn along 3f out: sn wknd* **100/1**

1m 28.89s (-1.91) **Going Correction** -0.15s/f (Stan)
WFA 3 from 4yo+ 1lb **13** Ran SP% **118.5**
Speed ratings (Par 103):104,98,96,96,96 96,90,89,87,87 80,74,63
CSF £21.61 CT £124.03 TOTE £3.80: £1.60, £2.50, £2.70; EX 32.70 Trifecta £171.50 Pool £326.22 - 1.35 winning units. Place 6 £267.36, Place 5 £99.51..
Owner Rupert Bear Racing **Bred** P Balding **Trained** Maunby, N Yorks

FOCUS
This looked a competitive, if modest handicap beforehand but it was turned into a procession by the winner. The pace set by Bel Cantor was decent and very few ever got into it, but the form looks sound with the winner value for a little more than the official margin.
Set Alight Official explanation: jockey said mare missed the break
T/Plt: £229.50 to a £1 stake. Pool: £40,540.35. 128.90 winning tickets. T/Qpdt: £94.80 to a £1 stake. Pool: £3,140.20. 24.50 winning tickets. JR

6414 WOLVERHAMPTON (A.W) (L-H)
Friday, November 10

OFFICIAL GOING: Standard
Wind: Fresh behind Weather: Light rain

6426 BOOK YOUR 2007 CONFERENCE NOW H'CAP 1m 4f 50y(P)
3:50 (3:50) (Class 5) (0-75,75) 3-Y-0+ **£3,238** (£963; £481; £240) **Stalls** Low

Form RPR
5010 **1** **Inch Lodge**[21] 6070 4-9-1 **68** ... PaulEddery 3 80+
(Miss D Mountain) *chsd ldrs: led over 1f out: rdn clr* **5/1**[2]
6-30 **2** *3 1/2* **Desert Leader (IRE)**[287] 214 5-9-7 **74** ... DavidAllan 1 79
(W M Brisbourne) *hld up: hdwy over 2f out: styd on same pce fnl f* **12/1**
140 **3** *hd* **Swords**[27] 5971 4-8-8 **61** ... MickyFenton 9 66
(Heather Dalton) *s.i.s: hld up: hdwy over 2f out: sn rdn and ev ch: styd on same pce fnl f* **6/1**[3]
6605 **4** *shd* **Pass The Port**[10] 6287 5-9-8 **75** ... RobertHavlin 8 80
(D Haydn Jones) *hld up: hdwy over 2f out: rdn over 1f out: styd on same pce fnl f* **9/1**
652 **5** *shd* **Edas**[41] 5691 4-8-7 **67** ... SladeO'Hara[(7)] 4 71
(J J Quinn) *chsd ldrs: led over 3f out: rdn and hdd over 1f out: no ex* **3/1**[1]
2535 **6** *8* **Tromp**[18] 6148 5-9-5 **72** ... EddieAhern 10 64
(D J Coakley) *s.i.s: hld up: hdwy over 2f out: rdn: hung lft and wknd over 1f out* **5/1**[2]
3200 **7** *6* **Captain Margaret**[15] 6189 4-9-3 **70** ... JimmyQuinn 2 52
(J Pearce) *prom over 9f* **14/1**
5032 **8** *9* **Special Moment (IRE)**[32] 5868 3-8-8 **67** ... DarryllHolland 7 35
(B W Hills) *mid-div: hdwy 4f out: sn rdn: wknd over 2f out* **15/2**
5040 **9** *20* **William's Way**[31] 5889 4-9-1 **68** ... JimmyFortune 6 4
(I A Wood) *prom: chsd ldr 8f out: rdn whn hmpd and wknd over 3f out* **16/1**
1600 **10** *11* **Empire Dancer (IRE)**[41] 5689 3-8-13 **72** ... BrettDoyle 5 —
(C N Allen) *led over 8f: sn wknd* **28/1**

2m 38.03s (-4.39) **Going Correction** -0.225s/f (Stan)
WFA 3 from 4yo+ 6lb **10** Ran SP% **118.1**
Speed ratings (Par 103):105,102,102,102,102 97,93,87,73,66
CSF £64.22 CT £371.64 TOTE £6.10: £2.10, £5.20, £2.90; EX 100.10.
Owner David Fremel **Bred** Gainsborough Stud Management Ltd **Trained** Newmarket, Suffolk
■ Stewards' Enquiry : Slade O'Hara caution: used whip above shoulder height

FOCUS
A modest handicap run at a fairly steady early gallop but straightforward form rated around the third and fifth.
Captain Margaret Official explanation: jockey said filly suffered interference in running

6427 MISS THE TRAFFIC WITH TWILIGHT RACING NOVICE MEDIAN AUCTION STKS 5f 20y(P)
4:20 (4:20) (Class 5) 2-Y-0 **£3,886** (£1,156; £577; £288) **Stalls** Low

Form RPR
5311 **1** **Yungaburra (IRE)**[2] 6400 2-9-7 62... GregFairley[(3)] 2 83+
(T J Pitt) *led 1f: trckd ldrs: led 1f out: rdn out* **4/11**[1]
3251 **2** *1 3/4* **Bookiesindex Boy**[11] 6255 2-9-6 73...(b) JimmyFortune 4 73
(J R Jenkins) *chsd ldrs: rdn and ev ch 1f out: sn hung rt: nt run on* **3/1**[2]
0042 **3** *3* **Hereford Boy**[9] 6295 2-9-0 62... DarryllHolland 5 56
(D K Ivory) *w ldr tl led 2f out: rdn and hdd 1f out: no ex* **10/1**[3]
00 **4** *11* **Jade's Ballet**[42] 5646 2-8-9 ... StephenCarson 3 11
(E A Wheeler) *led 4f out: hdd 2f out: sn rdn and wknd* **100/1**
00 **P** **Lady Kintyre**[13] 6222 2-8-2 ... MarkCoumbe[(7)] 1 —
(A W Carroll) *s.i.s: outpcd: p.u and dismntd ins fnl f: lame* **100/1**

62.14 secs (-0.68) **Going Correction** -0.225s/f (Stan) **5** Ran SP% **109.4**
Speed ratings (Par 96):96,93,88,70,—
CSF £1.72 TOTE £1.40: £1.10, £1.30; EX 1.70.
Owner J David Abell **Bred** Newlands House Stud **Trained** Bawtry, S Yorks

FOCUS
With the runner-up posting a performance worthy of a rating equal to that he received when a recent course and distance maiden winner, the form looks solid enough, backed up by the second.

NOTEBOOK
Yungaburra(IRE) is being kept busy and looked to hold a strong chance in this minor contest. He quickened up well in the end to win, and is better than the winning margin suggests, but he is already due to go up to a rating of 71 from tomorrow and will have to carry a penalty if turning out at Lingfield, so he might be worth opposing there. (op 1-3 tchd 2-5 in places)
Bookiesindex Boy failed to take advantage of getting first run on the favourite and, like at Wolverhampton last month when winning a maiden, hung right under pressure, giving Yungaburra another chance to get back into the race. (op 7-2)
Hereford Boy had a chance at the weights but he was easily put in his place by the two last-time-out winners from a furlong out. He will not be without hope in handicap company off marks in the low 60s. (tchd 9-1)
Lady Kintyre Official explanation: jockey said filly had pulled up lame behind

6428 WOLVERHAMPTON-RACECOURSE.CO.UK H'CAP 5f 216y(P)
4:50 (4:50) (Class 4) (0-80,79) 3-Y-0+ **£5,505** (£1,637; £818; £408) **Stalls** Low

Form RPR
0002 **1** **Zarzu**[13] 6223 7-8-7 **75** ... LiamJones[(5)] 4 86
(C R Dore) *chsd ldrs: rdn to ld ins fnl f: edgd rt: r.o* **9/1**
0210 **2** *1* **Sir Nod**[25] 6009 4-9-0 **77** ... DavidAllan 10 85
(Miss J A Camacho) *chsd ldrs: rdn to ld over 1f out: hdd and unable qckn ins fnl f* **5/1**[2]
1061 **3** *1/2* **Premier Fantasy**[7] 6326 4-9-0 **77** 7ex... RobbieFitzpatrick 7 84
(T J Pitt) *chsd ldrs: rdn over 1f out: styd on* **13/2**[3]
0151 **4** *1/2* **Rosein**[33] 5842 4-8-13 **76** ... JimmyFortune 3 81+
(Mrs G S Rees) *s.i.s: hld up: edgd lft over 3f out: hdwy u.p over 1f out: hung lft ins fnl f: nt rch ldrs* **7/2**[1]
0050 **5** *1 1/2* **Connect**[29] 5921 9-9-0 **77**...(b) TPQueally 9 78
(M H Tompkins) *sn outpcd: r.o u.p ins fnl f: nrst fin* **7/1**
0-6 **6** *1 1/4* **Turn On The Style**[33] 5842 4-8-12 **78**...(b) MarcHalford[(3)] 6 75
(J Balding) *s.i.s: hld up: hmpd over 2f out: rdn and hung lft over 1f out: nt trble ldrs* **16/1**
4344 **7** *1/2* **Charlie Delta**[13] 6212 3-9-0 **77**... DarryllHolland 13 72
(D Carroll) *prom: rdn 1/2-way: edgd lft over 2f out: hung lft over 1f out: styd on same pce* **7/1**
0204 **8** *shd* **Figaro Flyer (IRE)**[33] 5842 3-8-13 **76**... IanMongan 2 71
(P Howling) *led: rdn and hdd over 1f out: wknd ins fnl f* **14/1**
1000 **9** *5* **Violent Velocity (IRE)**[35] 5791 3-8-7 **77**... SladeO'Hara[(7)] 12 57
(J J Quinn) *sn outpcd* **40/1**
1456 **10** *1 1/4* **Efistorm**[174] 1856 5-9-2 **79**... MickyFenton 11 55
(J Balding) *chsd ldrs: rdn and ev ch 2f out: sn wknd* **33/1**
1131 **11** *nk* **Winning Pleasure (IRE)**[239] 654 8-8-10 **76**... JasonEdmunds[(3)] 5 51
(J Balding) *prom 4f* **25/1**
4-10 **12** *3/4* **Grenane (IRE)**[289] 190 3-8-13 **76**... EddieAhern 1 49
(P D Evans) *broke wl: lost pl 5f out: hmpd over 3f out: sn wknd* **20/1**
0004 **13** *1 3/4* **Fast Heart**[30] 5907 5-9-0 **77**...(t) JoeFanning 8 45
(D Nicholls) *dwlt: outpcd* **11/1**

1m 14.03s (-1.78) **Going Correction** -0.225s/f (Stan) **13** Ran SP% **122.1**
Speed ratings (Par 105):102,100,100,99,97 95,95,94,88,86 86,85,82
CSF £52.63 CT £332.47 TOTE £12.80: £2.30, £2.60, £3.10; EX 80.10.
Owner Page, Pickering, Taylor, Ward, Marsh **Bred** Compton Down Stud **Trained** West Pinchbeck, Lincs

FOCUS
A competitive sprint handicap run at a good pace and sound enough form.
Violent Velocity(IRE) Official explanation: jockey said colt did not face the kick-back
Grenane(IRE) Official explanation: jockey said colt suffered interference in running

6429 THE ZONGALERO RESTAURANT OVERLOOKS THE TRACK MAIDEN STKS 1m 1f 103y(P)
5:20 (5:21) (Class 6) 3-4-Y-0 **£3,412** (£1,007; £504) **Stalls** Low

Form RPR
2 **1** **Emirates First (IRE)**[13] 6225 3-8-12 ... TPQueally 6 68+
(Saeed Bin Suroor) *hld up in tch: hmpd over 2f out: led 1f out: sn clr: eased nr fin* **8/13**[1]
3 **2** *1/2* **Fringe**[23] 6053 3-8-12 ... BrettDoyle 12 60
(Jane Chapple-Hyam) *hld up: hdwy 1/2-way: rdn over 2f out: hmpd and outpcd wl over 1f out: hung lft and styd on ins fnl f* **11/4**[2]
4 **3** *3* **Soul Blazer (USA)**[26] 5986 3-9-3 ... LPKeniry 2 59
(A M Balding) *chsd ldrs: outpcd over 2f out: styd on ins fnl f* **7/1**[3]
0- **4** *1/2* **Daneway**[363] 6319 3-8-12 ... DarryllHolland 5 53
(H R A Cecil) *chsd ldrs: rdn over 2f out: edgd rt wl over 1f out: styd on same pce* **12/1**
05 **5** *hd* **Out Of This Way**[8] 6314 3-9-3 ... MickyFenton 1 58
(I A Wood) *led: rdn and hdd 1f out: sn wknd* **80/1**
000 **6** *1 1/2* **Amron Hill**[38] 5761 3-8-10 55... RussellKennemore[(7)] 9 55
(R Hollinshead) *hld up in tch: rdn whn hung rt wl over 1f out: sn wknd* **33/1**
7 *3/4* **Rinty (NZ)**[254] 4-9-3 ... StephaneBreux[(3)] 13 54
(C G Cox) *chsd ldrs: rdn whn rdr dropped reins over 2f out: wknd fnl f* **50/1**
0 **8** *hd* **Captain Oats (IRE)**[31] 5897 3-9-0 64... GregFairley[(3)] 8 53
(Mrs P Ford) *hld up: rdn over 2f out: n.d* **66/1**
0000 **9** *1* **Ruby Sunrise (IRE)**[10] 6277 4-9-1 40... PaulEddery 4 46
(B P J Baugh) *s.s: bhd: hdwy over 1f out: eased ins fnl f* **200/1**

0 **10** 3 ½ **Love And Affection**[13] [6225] 3-9-3 .... EddieAhern 10 45
(P S McEntee) *hld up: rdn over 2f out: sn wknd* **66/1**
0600 **11** 5 **Jose Bove**[25] [6021] 4-9-6 45.. JimmyQuinn 3 35
(R Dickin) *hld up: plld hrd: rdn 3f out: sn wknd* **200/1**
12 2 ½ **Donnaspear (IRE)** 3-8-12 .... DaleGibson 7 26
(J Mackie) *s.s: outpcd* **66/1**

2m 1.30s (-1.32) **Going Correction** -0.225s/f (Stan)
WFA 3 from 4yo 3lb 12 Ran SP% **120.4**
Speed ratings (Par 101):96,95,92,92,92 90,90,90,89,86 81,79
CSF £2.46 TOTE £1.70: £1.10, £1.40, £1.40; EX 3.00.
Owner Godolphin **Bred** Darley **Trained** Newmarket, Suffolk
■ Stewards' Enquiry : Paul Eddery caution: allowed filly to coast home with no assistance
Stephane Breux caution: allowed horse to coast home with no assistance

FOCUS
A weak maiden won in a modest time, 1.33 seconds slower than the following 51-65 handicap. The form could be rated a little higher but looks dubious.
Ruby Sunrise(IRE) Official explanation: jockey said filly missed the break
Love And Affection Official explanation: trainer's rep said gelding had a breathing problem

6430 STAY AT THE WOLVERHAMPTON HOLIDAY INN H'CAP 1m 1f 103y(P)
5:50 (5:51) (Class 6) (0-65,65) 3-Y-O+ **£2,730** (£806; £403) **Stalls** Low

Form RPR
4662 **1** **Wasalat (USA)**[11] [6259] 4-9-4 63.. PaulHanagan 4 73
(D W Barker) *chsd ldrs: rdn to ld wl ins fnl f: r.o* **3/1**[2]
4032 **2** 1 ½ **Bowled Out (GER)**[9] [6289] 4-9-4 63.................................. JimmyFortune 10 71
(P J McBride) *hld up: hdwy over 3f out: rdn to ld over 1f out: hdd and unable qckn wl ins fnl f* **5/2**[1]
0062 **3** nk **Tender The Great (IRE)**[11] [6260] 3-9-0 62...............(p) DarryllHolland 12 69
(V Smith) *hld up: hdwy u.p over 1f out: r.o* **17/2**
2012 **4** 3 **Desert Lightning (IRE)**[47] [5553] 4-8-7 52.................... PaulMulrennan 8 53
(K R Burke) *plld hrd and prom: led 2f out: sn hdd: wknd ins fnl f* **14/1**
6040 **5** 1 **Lennoxtown (IRE)**[9] [6294] 3-8-13 61.................................. EddieAhern 9 60
(J Ryan) *mid-div: rdn over 2f out: styng on same pce whn rdr dropped whip over 1f out* **14/1**
104 **6** nk **Emily's Place (IRE)**[11] [6260] 3-9-3 65.............................. PatCosgrave 5 64
(J Pearce) *hld up in tch: nt clr run over 2f out: rdn over 1f out: wknd fnl f* **8/1**[3]
500- **7** 1 ¾ **Golda Seek (USA)**[430] [5017] 3-8-7 55............................ RobertHavlin 11 51
(B J Meehan) *s.i.s: hld up: plld hrd: rdn and hung lft over 1f out: n.d* **33/1**
8 1 **Atlantic Gamble (IRE)**[74] [4865] 6-8-1 51 ow1............ AndrewElliott(5) 2 45
(K R Burke) *s.s: hld up: a in rr* **50/1**
4403 **9** ½ **Snake Skin**[37] [5767] 3-7-13 52... EmmettStack(5) 6 45
(J Gallagher) *chsd ldr: led 3f out: rdn and hdd 2f out: wknd over 1f out* **16/1**
0434 **10** 4 **Tipsy Me**[27] [5973] 3-8-10 65.. ChrisHough(7) 13 50
(M L W Bell) *chsd ldrs: ev ch 2f out: sn rdn: hung lft and wknd* **16/1**
3650 **11** 2 **Monte Mayor Junior**[70] [4982] 3-8-6 54..........................(p) JimmyQuinn 1 35
(D Haydn Jones) *chsd ldrs 7f* **50/1**
3-02 **12** nk **Etoile Russe (IRE)**[56] [5354] 4-9-5 64...............................(t) JoeFanning 3 45
(P C Haslam) *led over 6f: wknd 2f out: in rr whn hmpd over 1f out* **9/1**

1m 59.97s (-2.65) **Going Correction** -0.225s/f (Stan)
WFA 3 from 4yo+ 3lb 12 Ran SP% **117.2**
Speed ratings (Par 101):102,100,100,97,96 96,95,94,93,90 88,88
CSF £10.61 CT £55.71 TOTE £2.70: £1.10, £2.10, £1.70; EX 10.10.
Owner Miss Daphne Downes **Bred** Darley **Trained** Scorton, N Yorks

FOCUS
Ordinary handicap form but sound enough based on the performances of the third and fifth.

6431 HOTEL AND CONFERENCING H'CAP 1m 141y(P)
6:20 (6:20) (Class 6) (0-53,53) 3-Y-O+ **£2,388** (£705; £352) **Stalls** Low

Form RPR
5403 **1** **Just Bond (IRE)**[10] [6286] 4-8-9 53.............................. DuranFentiman(5) 12 65+
(G R Oldroyd) *s.s: hld up: hdwy over 2f out: styd on to ld wl ins fnl f* **7/2**[1]
5500 **2** 1 ¼ **Qualitair Wings**[24] [6037] 7-8-13 52................................ DerekMcGaffin 9 61
(J Hetherton) *hld up: hdwy 6f out: rdn over 1f out: ev ch ins fnl f: unable qckn towards fin* **9/2**[2]
0200 **3** 1 ¼ **Wiltshire (IRE)**[31] [5885] 4-8-13 52..................................... MickyFenton 3 58
(P T Midgley) *chsd ldr: led over 1f out: rdn and hdd wl ins fnl f* **14/1**
0500 **4** 3 **Shannon Arms (USA)**[108] [3817] 5-8-12 51.................... PatCosgrave 10 51
(R Brotherton) *led: rdn and hdd over 1f out: no ex* **16/1**
5 3 ½ **Dictation**[21] [6087] 4-8-11 50...(b) EddieAhern 8 43
(Mrs Valerie Keatley, Ire) *chsd ldrs: rdn over 2f out: wknd over 1f out* **13/2**
0054 **6** 2 ½ **Sand Iron (IRE)**[135] [2978] 4-8-8 52.................................... AnnStokell(5) 6 39
(John Allen) *hld up: hmpd 7f out: styd on ins fnl f: nvr nrr* **20/1**
3102 **7** 5 **Wings Of Morning (IRE)**[130] [3158] 5-8-5 51.................. GaryWales(7) 5 28
(D Carroll) *mid-div: rdn over 3f out: wknd over 2f out* **8/1**
0605 **8** 1 **Wanna Shout**[12] [6235] 8-8-11 50.. JimmyQuinn 1 25
(R Dickin) *mid-div: outpcd over 3f out: rallied over 2f out: wknd over 1f out* **11/1**
4063 **9** 2 **Gem Bien (USA)**[71] [4974] 8-9-0 53....................................(b) PaulQuinn 7 24
(D W Chapman) *s.i.s: sn pushed along in rr: hmpd 7f out: hdwy over 2f out: sn hung lft and wknd* **6/1**[3]
0000 **10** 2 **Navigation (IRE)**[90] [4361] 4-8-11 50.................................. DarryllHolland 4 16
(T J Etherington) *hld up: hmpd 7f out: a in rr* **8/1**
-030 **11** ¾ **Food For Thought**[102] [3998] 3-8-4 53............................ SladeO'Hara(7) 13 18
(J J Quinn) *chsd ldrs 6f* **20/1**

1m 49.76s (-2.00) **Going Correction** -0.225s/f (Stan)
WFA 3 from 4yo+ 3lb 11 Ran SP% **120.7**
Speed ratings (Par 101):99,97,96,94,91 88,84,83,81,79 79
CSF £19.32 CT £198.57 TOTE £5.00: £2.10, £2.70, £1.60; EX 32.40 Place 6 £20.59, Place 5 £4.59..
Owner R C Bond **Bred** Schwindibode Ag **Trained** Upper Helmsley, N Yorks
■ Stewards' Enquiry : Derek McGaffin three-day ban: careless riding (Nov 21-23); four-day ban: used whip with excessive frequency (Nov 24-25, 27-28)

FOCUS
A modest handicap, but sound enough based on the second and third having run to form.
Navigation(IRE) Official explanation: jockey said gelding suffered interference in running
T/Plt: £25.70 to a £1 stake. Pool: £54,449.15. 1,543.15 winning tickets. T/Qpdt: £6.90 to a £1 stake. Pool: £6,986.50. 746.10 winning tickets. CR

6393 KEMPTON (A.W) (R-H)
Saturday, November 11

OFFICIAL GOING: Standard
Wind: Light, against.

6432 TFM NETWORKS H'CAP 1m 2f (P)
3:15 (3:15) (Class 5) (0-75,75) 3-Y-O+ **£5,181** (£1,541; £770; £384) **Stalls** High

Form RPR
411 **1** **Khun John (IRE)**[16] [6189] 3-8-11 75.. KMay(7) 8 85+
(B J Meehan) *prom: led after 3f: rn wd and briefly hdd ent st: kpt on gamely: drvn out* **4/1**[2]
2650 **2** nk **Birkside**[15] [6206] 3-9-2 73...(t) IanMongan 7 82
(W R Swinburn) *in tch: tk clsr order 4f out: led briefly ent st: sn rdn: ev ch ins fnl f: no ex nr fin* **9/4**[1]
0003 **3** 1 ¼ **Sekula Pata (NZ)**[16] [6189] 7-8-10 66..................... EdwardCreighton(3) 1 73
(Christian Wroe, UAE) *trckd ldrs: rdn and ev ch jst over 1f out: kpt on same pce* **14/1**
5400 **4** 1 ½ **Snark (IRE)**[22] [6076] 3-9-4 75..................................(t) FergusSweeney 10 79
(P J Makin) *chsd ldrs: rdn 2f out: kpt on same pce* **7/1**[3]
0003 **5** ¾ **Arry Dash**[10] [6301] 6-9-1 68...(v) PatCosgrave 14 71
(M J Wallace) *mid-div: rdn and effrt 2f out: kpt on same pce* **11/1**
040 **6** ½ **Broughtons Folly**[24] [6053] 3-8-9 66................................ BrettDoyle 3 70+
(W J Musson) *s.i.s: bhd: styd on fr over 1f out: nt rch ldrs* **12/1**
4030 **7** 1 ¼ **Bridgewater Boys**[100] [4068] 5-8-11 64...............................(b) LPKeniry 12 63
(K A Ryan) *a mid-div* **25/1**
0160 **8** shd **Odessa Star (USA)**[13] [6244] 3-8-13 70.............................. OscarUrbina 13 69
(J G Portman) *hld up towards rr: sme late prog: nvr a factor* **20/1**
2365 **9** 2 **Burgundy**[16] [6189] 9-9-2 69..(b) TPQueally 5 64
(P Mitchell) *hld up towards rr: hdwy 5f out: rdn over 3f out: wknd over 1f out* **10/1**
3446 **10** 9 **Imperial Harry**[94] [4254] 3-9-1 72.. JimmyQuinn 4 50
(M R Channon) *led for 3f: chsd wnr: rdn 2f out: sn wknd* **20/1**
5360 **11** 6 **Vale De Lobo**[26] [6017] 4-9-8 75... JimCrowley 11 42
(B R Millman) *a bhd* **11/1**
340/ **12** 37 **Circus Dance**[2016] [1051] 9-8-11 64....................................... NickyMackay 9 —
(Luke Comer, Ire) *s.i.s: towards rr: hdwy 5f out: wknd and eased fnl 2f* **66/1**

2m 6.47s (-2.53) **Going Correction** -0.05s/f (Stan)
WFA 3 from 4yo+ 4lb 12 Ran SP% **118.2**
Speed ratings (Par 103):108,107,106,105,104 104,103,103,101,94 89,44
CSF £12.64 CT £115.53 TOTE £3.40: £2.40, £2.40, £4.80; EX 10.60.
Owner The Strawberries To A Donkey Partnership **Bred** Sti Engineering Srl **Trained** Manton, Wilts
■ Stewards' Enquiry : T P Queally caution: used whip above shoulder height
Brett Doyle two-day ban: careless riding (Nov 22-23)

FOCUS
Just a fair handicap run in an alright time for the grade, but few could get involved from off the pace. The form looks solid rated around the fourth and fifth.
Imperial Harry Official explanation: jockey said colt ran too free

6433 EUROPEAN BREEDERS' FUND MAIDEN FILLIES' STKS 7f (P)
3:50 (3:52) (Class 5) 2-Y-O **£3,562** (£1,059; £529; £264) **Stalls** High

Form RPR
0 **1** **Sell Out**[30] [5914] 2-9-0 .... SteveDrowne 9 75
(G Wragg) *mid-div: gd hdwy over 2f out: chal over 1f out: led ins fnl f: r.o wl* **40/1**
0 **2** 1 ¼ **High 'n Dry (IRE)**[16] [6186] 2-9-0 .... JimmyQuinn 10 72
(C A Cyzer) *trckd ldrs: led 2f out: sn rdn and hrd pressed: hdd ins fnl f: no ex* **7/1**[3]
6 **3** 1 ¼ **Furbeseta**[16] [6187] 2-9-0 .... NickyMackay 6 69
(L M Cumani) *in tch: rdn over 2f out: wnt 3rd over 1f out: kpt on* **8/1**
0 **4** 2 **Pivotalia (IRE)**[16] [6187] 2-9-0 .... IanMongan 2 63
(W R Swinburn) *chsd ldrs: outpcd over 2f out: styd on again fr 1f out* **50/1**
5 nk **Red Coronet** 2-9-0 .... TPQueally 14 63
(W J Haggas) *mid-div: rdn over 2f out: hung lft over 1f out: styd on* **20/1**
6 ¾ **Saaratt** 2-9-0 .... RobertHavlin 5 61
(M P Tregoning) *s.i.s: towards rr: hdwy over 2f out: sn rdn and hung lft: styd on: nvr trbld ldrs* **20/1**
0 **7** 1 ¾ **Go Dancing**[44] [5638] 2-8-7 .... MCGeran(7) 7 56
(P W Chapple-Hyam) *towards rr: sme late prog: nvr a danger* **50/1**
8 nk **Capania (IRE)** 2-9-0 .... OscarUrbina 8 55
(J W Hills) *towards rr: sme late hdwy: nvr a danger* **33/1**
0 **9** hd **Kimono My House**[32] [5898] 2-9-0 .... J-PGuillambert 3 55
(J G Given) *mid-div tl outpcd over 2f out* **50/1**
10 nk **Becharm** 2-9-0 .... MatthewHenry 1 54
(M A Jarvis) *in tch: effrt 2f out: sn one pce* **16/1**
0 **11** hd **Pajada**[32] [5894] 2-8-7 .... FrankiePickard(7) 12 53
(M D I Usher) *a towards rr* **66/1**
2 **11** dht **Luck Will Come (IRE)**[21] [6098] 2-9-0 .... PatCosgrave 11 53
(M J Wallace) *led tl 2f out: sn wknd* **5/1**[2]
3 **13** nk **Clouded Leopard (USA)**[21] [6099] 2-9-0 .... JimmyFortune 4 53
(J H M Gosden) *prom: rdn 2f out: sn btn* **10/11**[1]
14 8 **She Knows Too Much** 2-9-0 .... FJohansson 13 32
(G A Butler) *s.i.s: a bhd* **20/1**

1m 27.49s (0.69) **Going Correction** -0.05s/f (Stan) 14 Ran SP% **125.6**
Speed ratings (Par 93):94,92,91,88,88 87,85,85,85,84 84,84,84,75
CSF £290.83 TOTE £72.60: £14.20, £2.50, £3.80; EX 459.40.
Owner T D Rootes **Bred** Shutford Stud **Trained** Newmarket, Suffolk

FOCUS
Some of the more fancied horses failed to give their running and the bare form of this maiden looks modest. They were spread out across the track in the straight, with those who raced towards the far side appearing at an advantage.

NOTEBOOK
Sell Out finished last on her debut at Newmarket but she clearly learnt plenty from that and showed much-improved form to get off the mark. This was not much of a race, but she is likely to be put away for the winter and could progress again next season.
High 'n Dry(IRE) showed ability on her debut at Lingfield and this was another good effort. (op 15-2 tchd 8-1)
Furbeseta, extremely well bred, confirmed the promise she showed on her debut at Lingfield and seems to be going the right way. (tchd 9-1)
Pivotalia(IRE) improved on the form she showed on her debut at Lingfield, but she is probably more of a handicap prospect.
Red Coronet, a half-sister to Argent, a mile winner at four, offered some promise on her debut in a modest race. (op 25-1)

Luck Will Come(IRE) ran nowhere near the form she showed on her debut at Lingfield and was disappointing. (op 6-1 tchd 7-1)
Clouded Leopard(USA) could not confirm the promise she showed on her debut at Lingfield and was a major disappointment. Official explanation: trainer's rep had no explanation for the poor form shown (tchd 5-6 and Evens)

6434 EUROPEAN BREEDERS' FUND MAIDEN STKS (C&G) 7f (P)
4:20 (4:22) (Class 5) 2-Y-0 £3,562 (£1,059; £529; £264) Stalls High

Form				RPR
0	1		**Russki (IRE)**[16] 6188 2-9-0 JimCrowley 12 (Mrs A J Perrett) *set gd pce: mde all: qcknd clr 2f out: r.o wl* 20/1	76+
03	2	3	**Rule Of Life**[15] 6200 2-9-0 OscarUrbina 13 (B W Hills) *trckd ldrs: hmpd and swtchd lft 2f out: sn rdn: styd on: fin 3rd, 3l & shd: plcd 2nd* 8/11[1]	79+
00	3	shd	**Nassmaan (IRE)**[10] 6297 2-8-7 MCGeran(7) 8 (P W Chapple-Hyam) *chsd wnr thrght: rdn and hung rt 2f out:kpt on same pce: fin 2nd, 3l: plcd 3rd* 50/1	68
	4	4	**Last Sovereign** 2-9-0 RobertHavlin 9 (R Charlton) *mid-div: hdwy on rails 4f out: rdn 3f out: kpt on same pce* 16/1	58
0	5	hd	**Grande Caiman (IRE)**[8] 6324 2-8-11 StephaneBreux(3) 2 (R Hannon) *towards rr: rdn and no imp 3f out: styd on fr over 1f out: nt rch ldrs* 14/1	57
0	6	1 ½	**Spice Bar**[14] 6214 2-9-0 LPKeniry 6 (A M Balding) *s.i.s: towards rr: hdwy over 3f out: sn rdn: one pce after* 33/1	53
	7	½	**Shine And Rise (IRE)** 2-9-0 JimmyFortune 5 (C G Cox) *s.i.s: bhd: making hdwy whn swtchd lft over 2f out: no further imp* 12/1[3]	52
00	8	3	**Double Banded (IRE)**[30] 5914 2-9-0 JimmyQuinn 1 (J L Dunlop) *a towards rr* 40/1	44
00	9	½	**Potentiale (IRE)**[45] 5607 2-9-0 WandersonD'Avila 10 (J W Hills) *mid-div tl hung lft on bnd over 3f out* 66/1	43
0	10	1	**Linlithgow (IRE)**[10] 6297 2-9-0 IanMongan 4 (J L Dunlop) *a towards rr* 25/1	40
	11	3	**Kurumda** 2-9-0 SteveDrowne 11 (C R Egerton) *in tch tl 3f out* 4/1[2]	32
	12	19	**Demolition** 2-9-0 AbdulAziz 3 (C A Cyzer) *towards rr: lost tch 3f out* 50/1	—

1m 27.31s (0.51) **Going Correction** -0.05s/f (Stan) 12 Ran SP% **117.5**
Speed ratings (Par 96):95,91,91,86,86 84,84,80,80,79 75,54
CSF £33.58 TOTE £30.60: £4.40, £1.10, £16.40; EX 70.10.
Owner John E Bodie **Bred** Mark Commins **Trained** Pulborough, W Sussex
■ Stewards' Enquiry : M C Geran one-day ban: careless riding (Nov 22)

FOCUS
Like the fillies' maiden, the bare form is just modest and it was uncompetitive, with nothing able to get to Russki.

NOTEBOOK
Russki(IRE) looked to be carrying quite a lot of condition when only mid-division on his debut at Lingfield and that run clearly put him right. Whilst this did not look like a fluke, he was allowed his own way up front and things are likely to be tougher from now on.
Rule Of Life, with Urbina taking over from Hughes, he could not build on the form he showed when third in a six-furlong maiden at Newmarket on his previous start. It was by no means his jockey's finest moment, as he was badly hampered when going for a run up the far rail, but he would not have beaten the winner. He has something to prove now, but could yet confirm that initial promise next year. (op Evens tchd 4-6)
Nassmaan(IRE) showed very little in a couple of turf maidens and this was a much-improved effort. Having hung across Rule Of Life under pressure, he was rightly demoted to third, but this was still encouraging and he will have more options now he is qualified for a handicap mark.
Last Sovereign, an 80,000gns first foal of an unraced half-sister to smart Premiere Cuvee, a triple sprint winner, showed ability but was beaten over seven lengths.
Grande Caiman(IRE) did not really improve on the form he showed on his debut at Wolverhampton and looks more of a handicap prospect. (op 10-1)
Kurumda, a 400,000gns purchase, out of a dual seven to nine-furlong winner, was solid in the market on his racecourse debut but was never going the pace. (op 3-1 tchd 11-4)

6435 DIGIBET.CO.UK H'CAP 1m 4f (P)
4:50 (4:51) (Class 6) (0-60,61) 3-Y-0+ £2,388 (£705; £352) Stalls Centre

Form				RPR
-000	1		**Escoffier**[25] 6037 4-9-2 52 DaneO'Neill 10 (Pat Eddery) *led for 2f: prom: rdn to ld over 2f out: edgd rt ins fnl f: rdn out* 20/1	59
0-31	2	1 ½	**Boppys Pride**[14] 6213 3-8-8 55 JamieMoriarty(5) 11 (R A Fahey) *mid-div: hdwy over 2f out: sn rdn: styd on to go 2nd ins fnl f* 8/1[3]	60
6011	3	hd	**Virginia Rose (IRE)**[8] 6317 3-9-5 61 SebSanders 7 (J G Given) *hld up bhd: sltly hmpd on bnd after 3f: swtchd lft 3f out:sn rdn: styd on strly: wnt 3rd wl ins fnl f: nrst fin* 7/2[2]	69+
5620	4	1	**Arsad (IRE)**[23] 6068 3-9-0 56 BrettDoyle 13 (C E Brittain) *in tch: n.m.r briefly over 2f out: sn rdn: styng on whn n.m.r and snatched up over 1f out: kpt on but no ch after* 8/1[3]	62+
0000	5	½	**Dinner Date**[42] 5691 4-9-5 55 J-PGuillambert 5 (T Keddy) *mid-div: hdwy over 4f out: rdn to chse wnr over 2f: no ex ins fnl f* 20/1	57
150	6	¾	**Robbie Can Can**[20] 5952 7-9-2 52 JimmyFortune 12 (A W Carroll) *hld up towards rr: rdn and stdy prog fr over 2f out: short of room briefly over 1f out: styd on* 9/1	53
0050	7	¾	**Raise The Heights (IRE)**[43] 5652 3-9-2 58 FergusSweeney 14 (C Tinkler) *towards rr: sltly hmpd on bnd after 3f: rdn and hdwy over 2f out: one pce fr over 1f out* 10/1	58
1132	8	¾	**Lolla's Spirit (IRE)**[25] 6037 3-8-13 60 AndrewElliott(5) 2 (M L W Bell) *led after 2f: rdn and hdd over 2f out: edgd rt over 1f out: fdd ins fnl f* 9/4[1]	59
60-0	9	2	**Recalcitrant**[201] 1193 3-9-1 57 LPKeniry 8 (S Dow) *towards rr: sme hdwy over 2f out: sn rdn: no further imp fr over 1f out* 50/1	52
0-	10	3	**Penny Rich (IRE)**[22] 6091 12-9-0 50 (t) FMBerry 1 (T Hogan, Ire) *slowly away: sn swtchd rt: bhd: sltly hmpd on bnd after 3f: short lived effrt over 2f out* 20/1	41
606-	11	nk	**Atlantic City**[419] 5074 5-9-10 60 (e) RichardThomas 6 (Mrs L Richards) *trckd ldrs: rdn over 2f out: sn wknd* 33/1	50
4060	12	5	**Future Deal**[52] 5474 5-9-4 54 SteveDrowne 9 (C A Horgan) *mid-div: effrt 3f out: wknd 2f out* 25/1	36
603-	13	9	**Backstreet Lad**[220] 3615 4-8-13 49 IanMongan 4 (Evan Williams) *chsd ldrs: rdn 4f out: sn btn* 16/1	17

2m 36.73s (-0.17) **Going Correction** -0.05s/f (Stan)
WFA 3 from 4yo+ 6lb 13 Ran SP% **123.2**
Speed ratings (Par 101):98,97,96,96,95 95,94,94,93,91 90,87,81
CSF £164.53 CT £710.15 TOTE £23.70: £5.10, £2.20, £3.30; EX 227.10.
Owner Pat Eddery Racing (Quest For Fame) **Bred** Mrs A J Brudenell **Trained** Nether Winchendon, Bucks
■ Stewards' Enquiry : Andrew Elliott two-day ban: careless riding (Nov 22-23)

FOCUS
Probably not bad form for the grade, rated around the fourth and fifth, despite a few of these not getting the best of trips.
Escoffier Official explanation: trainer said, regarding apparent improvement in form, that the gelding was better suited by a right-handed track
Backstreet Lad Official explanation: jockey said gelding suffered interference in running

6436 DIGIBET.COM H'CAP 1m (P)
5:20 (5:20) (Class 6) (0-58,61) 3-Y-0+ £2,388 (£705; £352) Stalls High

Form				RPR
0211	1		**Eccollo (IRE)**[5] 6383 4-9-6 61 6ex JohnEgan 12 (T J Pitt) *a in tch: qcknd up wl to ld wl over 1f out: sn clr: readily* 8/13[1]	82+
5224	2	5	**Jomus**[71] 4995 5-9-1 56 (b) GeorgeBaker 2 (L Montague Hall) *restrained s: bhd: hdwy on outer over 3f out: rdn 2f out: styd on: wnt 2nd fnl stride* 10/1[2]	61
0560	3	shd	**Myths And Verses**[44] 5637 3-8-12 55 DarryllHolland 11 (K A Ryan) *chsd ldrs: rdn over 2f out: chsd wnr 1f out: kpt on same pce: lost 2nd fnl stride* 33/1	59
3204	4	½	**Lobengula (IRE)**[5] 6380 4-9-0 55 JimmyQuinn 1 (I W McInnes) *mid-div: hdwy over 2f out: sn rdn: styd on* 25/1	58
0001	5	1	**Trevian**[53] 5450 5-8-13 54 DaneO'Neill 7 (J M Bradley) *mid-div: hdwy and nt clr run 2f out: styd on but nt a danger after* 14/1	55+
1245	6	nk	**Hadath (IRE)**[47] 5573 9-8-6 54 (b) PatrickHills(7) 14 (B G Powell) *towards rr: hdwy 3f out: sn rdn: styng on whn nt clr run on rails ins fnl f* 20/1	54
4411	7	shd	**Under Fire (IRE)**[29] 5936 3-8-10 56 JamesDoyle(3) 8 (A W Carroll) *sn led: rdn and hdd wl over 1f out: sn one pce* 12/1[3]	56
0003	8	3	**Picture Show (USA)**[42] 5690 3-8-12 55 (b[1]) SebSanders 6 (C E Brittain) *chsd ldrs: rdn and hung rt over 2f out: wknd fnl f* 12/1[3]	48
-506	9	shd	**You're My Son**[27] 5986 4-9-2 57 FergusSweeney 9 (A B Haynes) *t.k.h after 2f: a towards rr* 33/1	50
1000	10	½	**Primeshade Promise**[24] 6054 5-8-6 54 BarrySavage(7) 13 (J M Bradley) *hld up towards rr: hdwy over 2f out: wknd 1f out* 50/1	46
6010	11	½	**Hallings Overture (USA)**[60] 5267 7-9-0 55 SteveDrowne 5 (C A Horgan) *a towards rr* 14/1	45
0250	12	3	**Penang Cinta**[112] 3730 3-8-13 56 LPKeniry 10 (A J Chamberlain) *chsd ldrs: rdn over 2f out: sn wknd* 66/1	40
6000	13	¾	**Aberlady Bay (IRE)**[10] 6300 3-8-12 55 TPQueally 4 (T T Clement) *in tch tl wknd 2f out* 40/1	37
0000	14	1 ¼	**Boldinor**[11] 6288 3-8-12 55 AlanDaly 3 (N E Berry) *in tch: effrt 3f out: sn wknd* 50/1	34

1m 39.23s (-1.57) **Going Correction** -0.05s/f (Stan)
WFA 3 from 4yo+ 2lb 14 Ran SP% **122.1**
Speed ratings (Par 101):105,100,99,99,98 98,98,95,94,94 93,90,90,88
CSF £6.50 CT £127.58 TOTE £1.60: £1.10, £3.00, £5.70; EX 7.40.
Owner Stephen Pearson & David Marshall **Bred** Swettenham Stud **Trained** Bawtry, S Yorks

FOCUS
Eccollo totally outclassed a bunch of moderate handicappers. The form looks reliable rated around the runner-up and fourth.
You're My Son Official explanation: jockey said gelding hung badly left

6437 ABACUS LIGHTING H'CAP 6f (P)
5:50 (5:50) (Class 5) (0-75,75) 3-Y-0+ £3,238 (£963; £481; £240) Stalls High

Form				RPR
0646	1		**Mandarin Spirit (IRE)**[14] 6227 6-8-7 66 (b) OscarUrbina 12 (G C H Chung) *in tch: trcking ldrs and nt clr run fr over 2f out: qcknd up wl whn gap appeared ins fnl f: led cl home* 13/2[3]	76
0005	2	hd	**Tanforan**[42] 5685 4-8-2 68 (b) SophieDoyle(7) 9 (Ms J S Doyle) *towards rr: n.m.r briefly 2f out: r.o strly ins fnl f: jst failed* 12/1	77
0152	3	nk	**Chatshow (USA)**[26] 6020 5-8-3 65 JamesDoyle(3) 8 (A W Carroll) *t.k.h in mid-div: smooth prog fr over 2f out: led 1f out: no ex whn ct cl home* 7/2[1]	74
2060	4	1	**Summer Recluse (USA)**[8] 6326 7-8-8 67 (t) SteveDrowne 11 (J M Bradley) *towards rr: hdwy 2f out: sn rdn: styng on whn nt clr run ins fnl f* 16/1	73
0421	5	1 ¼	**Linda Green**[26] 6020 5-8-10 69 JimmyQuinn 5 (M R Channon) *towards rr: styd on fnl f: nvr trbld ldrs* 8/1	71
4503	6	nk	**Vanadium**[14] 6223 4-9-1 74 J-PGuillambert 6 (J G Given) *mid-div: rdn over 2f out: kpt on same pce* 9/2[2]	75
000	7	shd	**Fizzlephut (IRE)**[78] 4780 4-8-6 65 PaulFitzsimons 7 (Miss J R Tooth) *led: rdn and hdd 1f out: kpt on same pce* 33/1	66
3003	8	nk	**Jayanjay**[25] 6036 7-8-10 69 SebSanders 10 (P Mitchell) *chsd ldrs: rdn to chal over 2f out: cl up whn short of room on rails 1f out: no ch after* 9/1	69+
5060	9	¾	**Prince Cyrano**[38] 5765 7-8-7 66 TPQueally 4 (W J Musson) *chsd ldrs: rdn over 2f out: sn one pce* 10/1	63
1003	10	¾	**Duke Of Milan (IRE)**[8] 6326 3-8-3 69 PatrickHills(7) 2 (G C Bravery) *chsd ldrs: rdn 2f out: grad wknd* 12/1	64
2036	11	4	**Who's Winning (IRE)**[23] 6065 5-9-2 75 GeorgeBaker 3 (B G Powell) *towards rr: hdwy over 3f out: rdn over 2f out: sn wknd* 11/1	58

1m 13.24s (-0.46) **Going Correction** -0.05s/f (Stan) 11 Ran SP% **116.5**
Speed ratings (Par 103):101,100,100,99,97 96,96,96,95,94 89
CSF £81.07 CT £318.02 TOTE £7.80: £2.80, £3.90, £2.30; EX 97.60.
Owner Peter Tsim **Bred** W Haggas And W Jarvis **Trained** Newmarket, Suffolk

FOCUS
Just a modest handicap, but good form for the grade and sound, rated through the third, and it should produce a few winners this winter.

6438 DIGIBET SPORTS BETTING FLOODLIT STKS (LISTED RACE) 2m (P)
6:20 (6:20) (Class 1) 3-Y-0+
£15,898 (£6,025; £3,015; £1,503; £753; £378) Stalls High

Form				RPR
4000	1		**Odiham**[28] 5963 5-9-4 99 (v) SteveDrowne 3 (H Morrison) *trckd ldrs: niggled along to hold position fr 6f out: rdn to ld over 2f out: sn hrd pressed: styd on wl ins fnl f* 7/2[2]	101

130 **2** 1 ½ **Mudawin (IRE)**[34] 5853 5-9-4 92 .... JohnEgan 6 99
(Jane Chapple-Hyam) *hld up: hdwy 4f out: rdn to chal fr over 2f out: ev ch whn hung rt over 1f out: no ex* **9/2**[3]
4524 **3** 5 **Barolo**[64] 5153 7-9-4 108 .... (p) JimmyFortune 1 93
(W R Swinburn) *led: qckn pce whn jnd 6f out: rdn and hdd over 2f out: sn one pce* **13/8**[1]
5143 **4** 4 **Kiswahili**[48] 5560 4-9-3 96 .... SebSanders 7 87
(Sir Mark Prescott) *trckd ldrs: rdn over 2f out: kpt on same pce* **9/2**[3]
4012 **5** 1 ¼ **Maystock**[22] 6075 6-8-13 80 .... RichardKingscote 8 82
(B G Powell) *chsd ldrs: struggled whn pce qckn 6f out and dropped rr: styd on again fnl 2f* **25/1**
4500 **6** ½ **Orange Touch (GER)**[7] 6334 6-9-4 95 .... DarryllHolland 5 86
(Mrs A J Perrett) *t.k.h early: hld up: short lived effrt over 2f out* **16/1**
1255 **7** 3 **Establishment**[15] 6205 9-9-4 78 .... J-PGuillambert 2 83
(C A Cyzer) *t.k.h in tch: rdn over 2f out: sn wknd* **20/1**
22 **8** 22 **Flame Creek (IRE)**[7] 6272 10-9-4 .... EdwardCreighton 4 56
(E J Creighton) *hld up: hdwy to join ldr 6f out: rdn 3f out: sn wknd* **50/1**

3m 30.98s (-0.42) **Going Correction** -0.05s/f (Stan) **8 Ran SP% 113.1**
Speed ratings (Par 111):99,98,95,93,93 92,91,80
CSF £18.88 TOTE £4.60: £1.60, £2.00, £1.10; EX 20.90 Place 6 £67.48, Place 5 £45.20.
Owner D L Brooks, J F Dean, Mrs J Scott **Bred** Glebe Stud **Trained** East Ilsley, Berks

FOCUS
A weak Listed race run and the pace was somewhat muddling, with a steady tempo increased to a very fast gallop at around halfway. As a result, the winning time was only moderate for the grade. The form is not strong with the first two the best guides.

NOTEBOOK
Odiham showed himself at the top of his game when eighth of 31 in the Cesarewitch on his previous start and, just as effective on Polytrack, he again produced his best to pick up a weak Listed race. He has not always convinced under pressure, but there was no faulting his attitude this time. (op 11-2)
Mudawin(IRE), the Ebor winner, is a huge out-and-out galloper, so one would not expect Kempton to suit, but he was a winner on his only previous start here and again ran well. He did, though, continually hang to his right in the straight and his rider was seemingly unable to throw absolutely everything at him as a result. It will have to be hoped whatever was making him hang can be corrected, and in the longer term, it would be fascinating to see him given a chance over hurdles, especially on a galloping track. (op 11-2)
Barolo, back up to two miles and switched to Polytrack for the first time, could not produce his best, the cheekpieces he has been fitted with for his last three starts seem to be having little effect. (op 5-4 tchd 6-5)
Kiswahili, back up in trip and making her Polytrack debut, was below form and might be better suited by shorter on turf. (op 7-2 tchd 5-1)
Maystock was trying to nick some black type, but she just came up short. (op 20-1)
T/Plt: £200.60 to a £1 stake. Pool: £32,007.85. 116.45 winning tickets. T/Qpdt: £13.50 to a £1 stake. Pool: £3,374.10. 184.40 winning tickets. TM

6408 LINGFIELD (L-H)

Saturday, November 11

OFFICIAL GOING: Standard
Wind: Fresh, across.

6439 LINGFIELD PARK GOLF COURSE H'CAP (DIV I) 7f (P)

12:05 (12:05) (Class 6) (0-60,62) 3-Y-0+ **£1,706** (£503; £252) **Stalls** Low

Form RPR
2303 **1** **Sincerely**[10] 6294 4-9-5 62 .... (b[1]) OscarUrbina 4 73
(B W Hills) *hld up in tch: hdwy over 2f out: rdn to ld ins fnl f: sn in command: pushed out* **5/1**[2]
1304 **2** 1 ¼ **Mountain Pass (USA)**[6] 6348 4-8-13 56 .... (p) EddieAhern 7 64
(M J Wallace) *t.k.h: hld up in tch: rdn over 2f out: ev ch over 1f out: nt pce of wnr ins fnl f* **7/2**[1]
0035 **3** nk **Humility**[16] 6193 5-9-1 58 .... DarryllHolland 9 65
(C A Cyzer) *hld up in midfield: hdwy over 2f out: kpt on u.p fnl f: no ch w wnr* **11/2**[3]
4246 **4** nk **Hot Agnes**[29] 5936 3-8-8 55 .... (t) JamesDoyle(3) 10 61
(H J Collingridge) *sn bhd and niggled along: hdwy 2f out: swtchd rt ins fnl f: fin wl: nvr nrr* **7/1**
0641 **5** nk **Cayman Breeze**[19] 6142 6-8-5 55 .... BarrySavage(7) 6 60
(J M Bradley) *hld up towards rr: pushed along and hdwy over 2f out: kpt on u.p ins fnl f: nt rch ldrs* **14/1**
0044 **6** shd **Millfields Dreams**[47] 5576 7-8-7 55 .... (p) JerryO'Dwyer(5) 5 60
(M G Quinlan) *pressed ldrs: led wl over 3f out: rdn over 2f out: hdd ins fnl f: wknd nr fin* **10/1**
3206 **7** ½ **Mine The Balance (IRE)**[227] 796 3-8-11 55 .... BrettDoyle 12 59
(J R Best) *t.k.h: hld up in tch: hdwy on outer 3f out: rdn and ev ch 2f out: wknd 1f out* **20/1**
006 **8** 6 **Mustammer**[77] 4806 3-8-10 54 .... (v[1]) PaulHanagan 13 42
(D Shaw) *t.k.h: hld up in rr: effrt and rdn 2f out: no real hdwy* **33/1**
3540 **9** hd **Danawi (IRE)**[36] 5781 3-8-11 55 .... FergusSweeney 14 43
(M R Hoad) *dropped in s and hld up in rr: n.d* **33/1**
0000 **10** nk **Lucius Verrus (USA)**[197] 1276 6-8-13 56 .... (v) DaneO'Neill 8 43
(D Shaw) *hld up towards rr: rdn and outpcd over 2f out* **25/1**
4000 **11** shd **Blu Manruna**[26] 6021 3-9-1 59 .... PaulDoe 2 46
(J Akehurst) *sn led: hdd wl over 3f out: sn rdn wknd over 2f out* **20/1**
3332 **12** hd **Fulvio (USA)**[70] 5031 6-8-12 55 .... (v) J-PGuillambert 3 41
(P Howling) *chsd ldrs: pushed along over 3f out: wknd 2f out* **7/1**
454- **13** 11 **Caragh Mia (IRE)**[139] 2907 4-9-3 60 .... IanMongan 1 18
(G G Margarson) *pressed ldrs tl rdn 3f out: sn wknd: eased fnl f: t.o* **16/1**

1m 24.43s (-1.46) **Going Correction** -0.15s/f (Stan)
WFA 3 from 4yo+ 1lb **13 Ran SP% 120.2**
Speed ratings (Par 101):102,100,100,99,99 99,98,92,91,91 91,91,78
CSF £21.20 CT £100.57 TOTE £5.20: £1.20, £3.40, £4.70; EX 23.00 Trifecta £97.50 Pool: £160.69 - 1.17 winning units..
Owner Guy Reed **Bred** Theakston Stud **Trained** Lambourn, Berks

FOCUS
A moderate handicap in which they went a fair pace in this and there seemed to be no real hard-luck stories. The winning time was 0.44 seconds faster than the second division and the form looks sound, rated around the third and fifth.
Fulvio(USA) Official explanation: jockey said gelding never travelled

6440 BOOK ONLINE FOR A £2 DISCOUNT MEDIAN AUCTION MAIDEN STKS 5f (P)

12:35 (12:36) (Class 6) 3-4-Y-0 **£2,388** (£705; £352) **Stalls** High

Form RPR
0060 **1** **Rowe Park**[6] 6348 3-9-3 55 .... LPKeniry 3 60
(Mrs L C Jewell) *chsd ldrs: rdn 2f out: kpt on u.p to ld last 100 yds: all out* **20/1**
2 hd **Staceymac (IRE)** 3-8-12 .... DaneO'Neill 6 54
(B R Johnson) *s.i.s: bhd: hdwy over 2f out: swtchd rt over 1f out: r.o strly fnl f: jst hld* **4/1**[3]
2330 **3** 1 **Ceredig**[4] 6389 3-9-3 59 .... (t) SebSanders 2 56
(W R Muir) *hld up in tch: rdn and effrt on inner over 1f out: ev ch ins fnl f: no ex last 50 yds* **11/4**[2]
0052 **4** nk **Desert Dust**[11] 6276 3-9-3 50 .... (v) EddieAhern 1 55
(R M H Cowell) *rrd in stalls: chsd ldrs tl over 2f out: sn rdn: ev ch over 1f out: no ex ins fnl f* **13/2**
0000 **5** hd **All Clued Up (IRE)**[19] 6129 3-8-12 45 .... SteveDrowne 5 49
(Rae Guest) *sn led: rdn over 2f out: hdd last 100 yds: fdd nr fin* **20/1**
0-60 **6** 2 ½ **Mill End Chateau**[106] 3916 4-8-10 40 .... (t) JamesMillman(7) 4 45
(D K Ivory) *in tch in midfield: effrt and c wd bnd over 2f out: no imp* **66/1**
0055 **7** 1 **Marron Flore**[13] 6233 3-8-12 45 .... RichardThomas 7 36
(A J Lidderdale) *prom: chsd ldr over 2f out: sn rdn: wknd over 1f out* **33/1**
6002 **8** 1 ½ **Tajjree**[28] 5969 3-8-12 53 .... (tp) JimmyFortune 10 31
(Miss K B Boutflower) *hld up in tch: effrt and sltly hmpd 2f out: no prog after* **13/2**
0352 **9** 1 ¼ **Supreme Kiss**[19] 6142 3-8-9 55 .... JamesDoyle(3) 8 26
(Mrs N Smith) *missed break and lost many lengths: no ch after: sme late hdwy* **9/4**[1]
10 18 **Triple Point (IRE)** 4-9-3 .... NancyBloyart 9 —
(J M Plasschaert, Belgium) *sn outpcd: t.o fr 1/2-way* **40/1**

59.09 secs **Going Correction** -0.15s/f (Stan) **10 Ran SP% 120.5**
Speed ratings (Par 101):99,98,97,96,96 92,90,88,86,57
CSF £97.42 TOTE £34.60: £4.20, £1.70, £1.30; EX 247.10 TRIFECTA Not won..
Owner R I B Young and Mrs F J Meekins **Bred** J Baker **Trained** Sutton Valence, Kent
■ Stewards' Enquiry : Dane O'Neill one-day ban: careless riding (Nov 22)

FOCUS
Maidens for older horses at this time of year are never going to be anything special and this was no exception. Add to that the favourite losing all chance at the start and the front five finishing in a heap and, although the form makes sense, it seems likely that very few winners will emerge from this.
Mill End Chateau Official explanation: jockey said gelding hung right throughout
Supreme Kiss Official explanation: jockey said filly planted in the stalls

6441 RACING ALL YEAR ROUND AT LINGFIELD PARK MAIDEN AUCTION STKS 7f (P)

1:05 (1:05) (Class 6) 2-Y-0 **£2,388** (£705; £352) **Stalls** Low

Form RPR
5 **1** **Sharpazmax (IRE)**[105] 3949 2-8-13 .... SebSanders 5 75
(P J Makin) *racd in midfield: hdwy 4f out: ev ch over 2f out: rdn 2f out: led jst over 1f out: styd on wl* **5/1**[3]
0 **2** 1 ¼ **First Buddy**[32] 5891 2-9-0 .... JimmyFortune 4 73
(W J Haggas) *slowly away: bhd: hdwy over 2f out: swtchd rt bnd over 2f out: r.o fnl f: wnt 2nd wl ins fnl f: nt rch ldr* **5/2**[1]
60 **3** ¾ **Bantry Bere (IRE)**[7] 6331 2-8-11 .... BrettDoyle 3 68
(J R Best) *slowly away: sn pushed up to chse ldrs: rdn wl over 2f out: kpt on last 100 yds: wnt 3rd nr fin* **10/1**
4 **4** nk **First Princess (IRE)**[136] 2980 2-8-7 .... FergusSweeney 13 63
(C Tinkler) *chsd ldr: ev ch aand rdn over 2f out: kpt on same pce ins fnl f* **6/1**
5 hd **Play Straight** 2-8-5 .... NelsonDeSouza 8 61
(R M Beckett) *slowly away: bhd: rdn and hdwy on inner over 2f out: styd on fnl f: nrst fin* **20/1**
00 **6** 1 ½ **Hard As Iron**[16] 6188 2-8-10 .... PaulHanagan 9 62
(M Blanshard) *broke wl: sn stdd into midfield: rdn and outpcd over 2f out: styd on fnl f: nt rch ldrs* **14/1**
4020 **7** hd **Buddies Girl (IRE)**[7] 6332 2-8-7 70 ow1 .... SteveDrowne 1 58
(R Hannon) *sn led: hrd pressed and rdn 2f out: hdd jst over 1f out: fdd ins fnl f* **4/1**[2]
8 ½ **Daboy (IRE)** 2-8-12 .... LPKeniry 10 62
(John A Quinn, Ire) *rn green and pushed along in midfield: hdwy over 3f out: outpcd over 2f out: kpt on ins fnl f: n.d* **25/1**
9 ½ **Best Selection** 2-8-8 ow1 .... DarryllHolland 7 56
(A P Jarvis) *in tch: rdn wl over 2f out: c wd bnd over 2f out: kpt on same pce* **12/1**
10 ¾ **Miami Tallyce (IRE)** 2-8-9 .... DaneO'Neill 14 56
(E J O'Neill) *sn bhd and pushed along: sme late hdwy: nvr on terms* **14/1**
05 **11** ¾ **Golden Prospect**[25] 6034 2-8-13 .... EddieAhern 2 58
(J W Hills) *chsd ldrs on inner: rdn over 2f out: wknd qckly fnl f* **25/1**
0000 **12** 6 **Elmasong**[29] 5933 2-8-4 49 .... JimmyQuinn 11 33
(J J Bridger) *a bhd: no ch last 2f* **66/1**
00 **13** 17 **Beshairt**[12] 6258 2-8-3 ow6 .... JamieJones(7) 6 —
(D K Ivory) *sn rdn: wl bhd last 3f: t.o and eased fnl f* **50/1**

1m 26.18s (0.29) **Going Correction** -0.15s/f (Stan) **13 Ran SP% 125.5**
Speed ratings (Par 94):92,90,89,89,89 87,87,86,86,85 84,77,58
CSF £17.87 TOTE £7.40: £3.00, £1.50, £3.80; EX 35.90 TRIFECTA Not won..
Owner Weldspec Glasgow Limited **Bred** Tim Bourke **Trained** Ogbourne Maisey, Wilts

FOCUS
Probably an ordinary maiden for the track and not easy to assess. Several still held a chance a furlong from home, but a few of these still have scope for improvement.

NOTEBOOK
Sharpazmax(IRE) ◆, given time since showing some promise on his debut at Salisbury in July, has obviously done well in the meantime and eventually won this with some authority. He is bred to appreciate further and should develop into a fair middle-distance handicapper next season. (op 8-1)
First Buddy found himself rather outpaced rounding the home bend, resulting in him having plenty to do, but stayed on inside the last furlong only to find the winner was home and hosed. He will appreciate stepping up in trip. (op 11-4 tchd 3-1 and 9-4)
Bantry Bere(IRE) stayed on well in the latter stages and seemed to appreciate this extra furlong. He can now be handicapped which widens his options somewhat. (op 8-1 tchd 14-1 in a place)
First Princess(IRE), not seen since an encouraging debut at Kempton in June, raced up with the pace but did not help her chances of seeing out this extra furlong by racing keenly early and once a turn of foot was called for it was not there. This should have brought her on and there should be a race or two in her. (op 9-2)
Play Straight ◆, an 8,500gns half-sister to Arnie De Burgh, did best of the newcomers and offered some promise. Better can be expected.

Buddies Girl(IRE), the most experienced in the field, tried to make it tell under a positive ride but failed to see it out. She is totally exposed now. (tchd 7-2)

6442 LINGFIELD PARK GOLF COURSE H'CAP (DIV II) 7f (P)
1:40 (1:40) (Class 6) (0-60,60) 3-Y-0+ **£1,706** (£503; £252) **Stalls** Low

Form RPR

4006 **1** **Generator**^{10} 6294 4-9-1 **58** JoeFanning 6 — 64
(Dr J D Scargill) *in tch: swtchd rt and hdwy over 2f out: chsd ldr 2f out: led ins fnl f: jst hld on* **4/1**^{1}

1231 **2** *shd* **Imperium**^{13} 6234 5-8-12 **55** (p) DaneO'Neill 5 — 61
(Jean-Rene Auvray) *hld up bhd: stl plenty to do wl over 1f out: swtchd rt 1f out: str run fnl f: jst failed* **7/1**^{3}

5525 **3** *nk* **Hotchpotch (USA)**^{54} 5418 3-8-10 **54** BrettDoyle 9 — 59
(J R Best) *racd in midfield on outer: hdwy 3f out: rdn 2f out: kpt on u.p ins fnl f* **6/1**^{2}

0650 **4** *nk* **Discotheque (USA)**^{16} 6193 3-8-9 **56** DeanCorby$^{(3)}$ 13 — 60
(P Howling) *slowly away: hld up in rr: rdn and hdwy over 2f out: kpt on same pce ins fnl f* **20/1**

0005 **5** *½* **Simpsons Gamble (IRE)**^{19} 6144 3-8-11 **55** JimmyQuinn 10 — 58
(R M Flower) *hld up in rr on outer: pushed along and effrt bnd over 2f out: kpt on ins fnl f: nvr nrr* **33/1**

0000 **6** *shd* **Moon Bird**^{52} 5474 4-9-0 **57** DarryllHolland 4 — 60
(C A Cyzer) *racd in midfield: rdn and hdwy over 2f out: kpt on same pce fnl f* **12/1**

0000 **7** *1 ¼* **Colonel Cotton (IRE)**^{18} 6162 7-8-13 **56** (v) PaulHanagan 7 — 55
(R A Fahey) *hld up in tch: outpcd wl over 2f out: kpt on u.p ins fnl f: nt trble ldrs* **10/1**

2002 **8** *nk* **Halfwaytoparadise**^{29} 5937 3-8-12 **56** (p) MatthewHenry 12 — 55
(W G M Turner) *taken down early: sn led: rdn wl over 1f out: hdd ins fnl f: wknd* **12/1**

0360 **9** *shd* **Danehill Stroller (IRE)**^{29} 5937 6-8-10 **53** LPKeniry 3 — 51
(A M Hales) *slowly away: t.k.h: hld up on inner: rdn and effrt over 2f out: no prog over 1f out* **9/1**

0010 **10** *1 ¼* **North Fleet**^{29} 5936 3-9-0 **58** SteveDrowne 14 — 53
(J M Bradley) *chsd ldrs: rdn 3f out: wknd wl over 1f out* **12/1**

3005 **11** *3 ½* **Fire Of Love**^{37} 5774 3-8-8 **55** JamesDoyle$^{(3)}$ 11 — 41
(N P Littmoden) *trckd ldrs: wnt 2nd over 3f out: rdn over 2f out: wknd wl over 1f out* **16/1**

0100 **12** *1 ¼* **Clearing Sky (IRE)**^{57} 5350 5-8-10 **56** AmirQuinn$^{(3)}$ 2 — 39
(J R Boyle) *chsd ldr tl over 3f out: wknd wl over 2f out* **14/1**

0000 **13** *1 ¼* **Cool Sands (IRE)**^{4} 6390 4-9-2 **59** (v) PaulMulrennan 8 — 38
(D Shaw) *hld up in last: rdn 3f out: no prog* **7/1**^{3}

1m 24.87s (-1.02) **Going Correction** -0.15s/f (Stan)
WFA 3 from 4yo+ 1lb **13** Ran SP% **121.7**
Speed ratings (Par 101):99,98,98,98,97 97,96,95,95,94 90,88,87
CSF £31.51 CT £171.39 TOTE £5.30: £1.70, £3.00, £2.70; EX 27.50 Trifecta £106.60 Pool: £175.69 - 1.17 winning units..
Owner R A Dalton **Bred** R A Dalton **Trained** Newmarket, Suffolk
■ Stewards' Enquiry : Darryll Holland caution: careless riding

FOCUS
A typical finish to a Lingfield handicap that was run at just an average pace and there was little covering the principals at the line. The winning time was 0.44 seconds slower than the first division and the form makes sense but is not strong.
Cool Sands(IRE) Official explanation: jockey said gelding never travelled

6443 HBLB CONDITIONS STKS 1m (P)
2:15 (2:15) (Class 3) 2-Y-0 **£6,855** (£2,052; £1,026; £513) **Stalls** High

Form RPR

0401 **1** **Habalwatan (IRE)**^{8} 6322 2-9-0 72 (b) SebSanders 2 — 75
(C E Brittain) *trckd ldng pair: rdn and sltly outpcd wl over 1f out: str run ins fnl f to ld last 50 yds* **13/2**^{2}

015 **2** *1* **Victor Trumper**^{26} 6018 2-9-3 78 PaulDoe 4 — 76
(P W Chapple-Hyam) *pressed ldr: shkn up over 2f out: led over 1f out: edgd lft ins fnl f: hdd last 50 yds* **9/1**^{3}

12 **3** *1 ¼* **Valiance (USA)**^{85} 4561 2-9-0 JimmyFortune 1 — 72+
(J H M Gosden) *t.k.h: led: jnd and rdn over 2f out: hdd over 1f out: no ex ins fnl f* **1/5**^{1}

0000 **4** *5* **Ishimagic**^{7} 6332 2-8-9 47 DaneO'Neill 3 — 53?
(J J Bridger) *racd in 4th: in tch tl rdn over 2f out: outpcd wl over 1f out* **100/1**

1m 40.41s (0.98) **Going Correction** -0.15s/f (Stan) **4** Ran SP% **107.7**
Speed ratings (Par 100):89,88,86,81
CSF £44.40 TOTE £7.80; EX 16.50 TRIFECTA Not won..
Owner Mohammed Rashid **Bred** Darley **Trained** Newmarket, Suffolk

FOCUS
A small field and a messy contest. The pace was not at all strong which resulted in a very slow winning time for a race of its type, therefore making the form look suspect.

NOTEBOOK
Habalwatan(IRE) came into this in good form, but still appeared to have plenty to do on these terms. However, he was able to sit off the pace whilst Victor Trumper and Valiance went hard at it from some way out and, once they started to wilt, he was produced with a withering run down the centre of the track. He is in great heart just now, but the slow winning time and the way the race was run has to put a question mark over the true value of the form. (tchd 7-1)
Victor Trumper, making his Polytrack debut, proved a nuisance to the red-hot favourite the whole way and eventually succeeded in getting the better of him, but no sooner had he done so than the winner rushed down the middle of the track to nail them both. It is hard to work out just what he achieved and it may be best to assess this performance through the winner rather than through Valiance. (tchd 10-1)
Valiance(USA) seemed to face a straightforward task despite the three-month layoff, but things were not going well for him from some way out as he refused to settle and had Victor Trumper breathing down his neck the whole way. When he was finally asked for maximum effort the result was dismal, but we know he is a great deal better than this and hopefully some explanation will eventually emerge. (tchd 2-9)
Ishimagic looked totally outclassed beforehand and so it proved.

6444 LINGFIELDPARK.CO.UK NURSERY 6f (P)
2:45 (2:45) (Class 3) 2-Y-0 **£9,715** (£2,890; £1,444; £721) **Stalls** Low

Form RPR

3653 **1** **Cool Box (USA)**^{8} 6324 2-8-11 **75** JamesDoyle$^{(3)}$ 11 — 84+
(Mrs A J Perrett) *hld up wl bhd: hdwy 3f out: mod 5th wl over 1f out: str run 1f out: led last 75 yds: sn clr: readily* **8/1**

4362 **2** 2½ **Onenightinlisbon (IRE)**^{3} 6402 2-9-5 **80** PaulMulrennan 1 — 88+
(K R Burke) *led: rdn over 2f out: hdd wl over 1f out: snatched up and swtchd rt 1f out: rallied: fin 3rd, 2 ½l & hd: plcd 2nd* **6/1**^{3}

3111 **3** *hd* **Yungaburra (IRE)**^{1} 6427 2-9-3 **78** 7ex RobbieFitzpatrick 5 — 79
(T J Pitt) *sn chsng ldr: rdn to ld wl over 1f out: edgd lft 1f out: hdd last 75 yds: no ch w wnr: tired nr fin: fin 2nd 2 ½l, plcd 3rd* **3/1**^{1}

5461 **4** *1 ¼* **Solid Rock (IRE)**^{7} 6332 2-9-7 **82** DaneO'Neill 7 — 79
(T G Mills) *racd in midfield: pushed along and hdwy over 3f out: chsd ldrs over 2f out: kpt on same pce* **3/1**^{1}

4431 **5** *¾* **Bahamian Love**^{11} 6278 2-8-6 **67** PaulHanagan 4 — 62
(B W Hills) *hld up in tch: rdn over 2f out: wknd over 1f out* **8/1**

1400 **6** *4* **Ava's World (IRE)**^{21} 6100 2-8-13 **77** GregFairley$^{(3)}$ 9 — 60
(M Johnston) *sn pushed along and struggling in rr: nvr on terms* **25/1**

2251 **7** *4* **Abbotts Ann**^{9} 6310 2-9-4 **79** DarryllHolland 8 — 50
(B W Hills) *wnt rt s: sn pushed along: rdn and dropped to rr over 3f out : no ch after* **10/1**

0500 **8** *2* **Su Doku (USA)**^{70} 5017 2-8-6 **67** (b^{1}) JoeFanning 10 — 32
(N P Littmoden) *v.s.a: a bhd: no ch last 2f* **50/1**

0220 **9** *5* **Stargazy**^{12} 6255 2-8-10 **71** (b^{1}) EddieAhern 2 — 21
(R Charlton) *t.k.h: trckd ldrs on inner: rdn over 2f out: sn wknd : t.o* **12/1**

431 **10** *2* **Genuine Call**^{25} 6034 2-8-12 **73** SebSanders 6 — 17
(C F Wall) *chsd ldrs: rdn wl over 2f out: sn wknd: t.o* **9/2**^{2}

1m 11.72s (-1.09) **Going Correction** -0.15s/f (Stan) **10** Ran SP% **127.3**
Speed ratings (Par 100):101,97,97,95,94 89,84,81,74,72
CSF £60.71 CT £188.69 TOTE £11.50: £3.80, £2.50, £2.30; EX 93.40 TRIFECTA Not won..
Owner G C Stevens **Bred** Windwoods Farm **Trained** Pulborough, W Sussex
■ Stewards' Enquiry : Robbie Fitzpatrick two-day ban: careless riding (Nov 22-23)

FOCUS
A decent nursery run at a good gallop and the field finished well spread out. The form looks rock-solid, underpinned by the third and fourth.

NOTEBOOK
Cool Box(USA) ◆, dropping back to six, was given a much more patient ride than at Wolverhampton and it certainly suited as he fairly bolted up once picking up the two leaders. This was his first win at the fifth attempt and now that he has got his act together he can go in again. (op 10-1 tchd 11-1)
Onenightinlisbon(IRE), who caught a tartar in a Wolverhampton conditions event the previous week, attempted to make all the running from the inside stall but it is debatable whether that suited him or not. Collared by Yungaburra turning for home, he was blown away by the winner's turn of foot in the straight, but would have got back up for second had Yungaburra not pinched him against the inside rail a furlong from home. The Stewards rightly reversed the placings. (op 5-1)
Yungaburra(IRE) was bidding for a remarkable third win in four days and his fourth victory this month, but with his new mark kicking in and the 7lb penalty he was 10lb higher than for his previous win in a nursery. Up there from the start, it looked turning for home as though he might pull it off, but he tired in the home straight, hampered Onenightinlisbon as he hung towards the rail for which he was later demoted, and was swept aside by the winner's finishing burst. He will find life tough from now on, but has more than paid his way since the start of this month. (op 11-4 tchd 7-2)
Solid Rock(IRE), off an 8lb higher mark than for his Windsor victory, had every chance off the final bend but lacked a turn of speed. This trip on a fast surface looks an inadequate test and time may show he was attempting the impossible in trying to concede weight to this field in any case. (op 5-1)
Bahamian Love, easy winner of a poor Southwell maiden auction event last time, did not perform badly in this much better company and should find another opportunity at a more appropriate level. (op 14-1)
Abbotts Ann, raised 7lb for just scraping home at Wolverhampton last time, never looked happy at any stage. Official explanation: jockey said filly hung right (op 8-1)
Genuine Call reportedly moved a shoe during the race and returned sore behind. Official explanation: trainer's rep said filly moved a shoe and was sore behind (op 11-2)

6445 LINGFIELD PARK FOR CHRISTMAS PARTIES H'CAP 6f (P)
3:20 (3:21) (Class 2) (0-100,100) 3-Y-0+
£11,217 (£3,358; £1,679; £840; £419; £210) **Stalls** Low

Form RPR

0440 **1** **Maltese Falcon**^{10} 6292 6-8-4 **88** (t) NelsonDeSouza 4 — 102
(P F I Cole) *plld hrd:w ldr: rdn to ld over 2f out: clr over 1f out: styd on wl: comf* **10/1**

5032 **2** *1 ½* **Viking Spirit**^{16} 6192 4-8-10 **94** DaneO'Neill 5 — 104
(W R Swinburn) *slowly away: hld up bhd: rdn 3f out: hdwy on inner over 2f out: r.o: wnt 2nd ins fnl f: no ch w wnr* **3/1**^{1}

0050 **3** *1* **Qadar (IRE)**^{13} 6243 4-8-8 **95** JamesDoyle$^{(3)}$ 10 — 102
(N P Littmoden) *hld up in rr: rdn and effrt over 2f out: sn swtchd rt: r.o fnl f: wnt 3rd last 75yds: nvr nrr* **10/1**

3000 **4** *1 ¼* **Pic Up Sticks**^{34} 5832 7-8-2 **89** ow2 RichardKingscote$^{(3)}$ 3 — 92
(B G Powell) *led tl hdd over 2f out: sn rdn: btn 1f out: lost 2 pls last 100 yds* **20/1**

4061 **5** *shd* **Saviours Spirit**^{10} 6292 5-8-5 **89** JoeFanning 1 — 91
(T G Mills) *hld up in tch: rdn over 2f out: kpt on same pce* **5/1**^{3}

0002 **6** *¾* **Don Pele (IRE)**^{10} 6292 4-8-2 **86** PaulHanagan 2 — 86
(K A Ryan) *racd in midfield tl rdn and outpcd 3f out: kpt on ins fnl f: nvr threatened ldrs* **13/2**

0510 **7** *¾* **Texas Gold**^{13} 6243 8-9-2 **100** EddieAhern 6 — 98
(W R Muir) *hld up in tch: rdn 2f out: no prog* **6/1**

6232 **8** *½* **Judd Street**^{13} 6243 4-8-9 **93** StephenCarson 7 — 89
(R F Johnson Houghton) *t.k.h: midfield tl hdwy to chse ldrs 4f out: rdn over 2f out: wknd* **4/1**^{2}

0 **9** *2* **Sailor King (IRE)**^{14} 6219 4-8-11 **95** DarryllHolland 8 — 85
(D K Ivory) *trckd ldng pair tl lost pl 3f out: no ch after* **33/1**

1030 **10** *8* **Greenslades**^{7} 6335 7-8-13 **97** SebSanders 9 — 63
(P J Makin) *racd in midfield on outer: rdn 3f out: sn struggling: t.o* **10/1**

1m 10.06s (-2.75) **Going Correction** -0.15s/f (Stan) course record **10** Ran SP% **124.3**
Speed ratings (Par 109):112,110,108,107,106 105,104,104,101,90
CSF £42.89 CT £333.32 TOTE £10.70: £2.20, £2.20, £3.20; EX 39.00 TRIFECTA Not won..
Owner Christopher Wright **Bred** Stratford Place Stud **Trained** Whatcombe, Oxon

FOCUS
A very decent sprint handicap as it should be for the money and the placed form looks sound. The pace was very good and the winner took almost half a second off the course record.

NOTEBOOK
Maltese Falcon ◆ had finished behind quite a few of these rivals in his last two outings both here and at Kempton, but he has been in freefall down the handicap in recent months and had finally reached a mark he was able to exploit. Quick to break, he raced very keenly until his rider gave him his head approaching the home bend and it was not long before he had established an unassailable lead. Now that he has returned to form it would not be a surprise to see him go in again. (op 8-1)
Viking Spirit, given a patient ride, was rather forced to pick his way through traffic and although he finished strongly down the home straight to snatch second, the winner had gone beyond recall. He looks worth another try over seven on this surface. (op 10-3 tchd 7-2)
Qadar(IRE) ran his usual sort of race, finishing strongly from off the pace without looking a threat. Things will drop just right for him one day. (op 12-1 tchd 9-1)
Pic Up Sticks tried to match strides with the eventual winner from the off, but his exertions eventually told. He still improved on his two previous tries on sand though. (op 25-1)

Saviours Spirit, raised 3lb for his Kempton victory, had his chance turning for home but could find little under pressure. He will need to find improvement from somewhere in order to defy this career-high mark. (op 11-2)
Don Pele(IRE) was taken off his feet over this quick six and could never get involved, but he finished exactly the same distance behind Saviours Spirit as at Kempton last time despite meeting him on 3lb better terms. The fact that both were well held shows that this was a much stronger race. (tchd 7-1)
Texas Gold is a real course specialist, but even he found trying to concede weight to this field an impossible task. (tchd 13-2)
Greenslades Official explanation: jockey said horse never travelled

6446 JUMPING HERE ON NOVEMBER 22ND H'CAP — 5f (P)

3:55 (3:56) (Class 4) (0-85,85) 3-Y-0+ **£5,505** (£1,637; £818; £408) **Stalls** High

Form / RPR

0321 **1** **Little Edward**[6] 6353 8-9-0 **81** 7ex GeorgeBaker 1 — 92+
(R J Hodges) *hld up in tch: smooth hdwy 2f out: led 1f out: shkn up and in command last 100 yds: comf* **9/4**[1]

0550 **2** *1 1/2* **Hammer Of The Gods (IRE)**[6] 6352 6-8-12 **79** (bt) BrianReilly 9 — 85
(P S McEntee) *chsd ldrs tl rdn and outpcd over 2f out: rallied u.p fnl f: wnt 2nd nr fin: no ch w wnr* **5/1**[3]

1630 **3** *nk* **Bold Minstrel (IRE)**[49] 5532 4-8-12 **79** PaulHanagan 4 — 84
(M Quinn) *led for 1f: chsd ldr: rdn and ev ch over 2f out: outpcd by wnr last 100 yds: lost 2nd nr fin* **4/1**[2]

211 **4** *1* **Dancing Mystery**[29] 5938 12-9-1 **82** (b) StephenCarson 2 — 83
(E A Wheeler) *led after 1f out: rdn over 2f out: hdd 1f out: no ex* **6/1**

0600 **5** *nk* **Peopleton Brook**[26] 6009 4-8-13 **80** DarryllHolland 3 — 80
(J M Bradley) *racd in midfield: rdn over 2f out: sme hdwy over 1f out: no imp fnl f* **10/1**

1150 **6** *2* **Forces Sweetheart**[7] 6335 3-8-5 **79** (v) WilliamBuick(7) 6 — 72
(V Smith) *bhd: pushed along over 3f out: no imp u.p last 2f* **11/1**

0-40 **7** *2 1/2* **Rare Cross (IRE)**[21] 6095 4-8-10 **84** JackMitchell(7) 5 — 68
(P Mitchell) *racd in midfield: effrt and sme hdwy over 2f out: no imp over 1f out* **11/1**

0330 **8** *shd* **Marko Jadeo (IRE)**[6] 6352 8-9-1 **82** PaulFitzsimons 7 — 65
(S Dow) *v.s.a: a bhd* **10/1**

4000 **9** *2 1/2* **Stoneacre Boy (IRE)**[117] 3595 3-8-11 **78** (b) RobbieFitzpatrick 8 — 52
(Peter Grayson) *a bhd: no ch last 2f* **20/1**

58.02 secs (-1.76) **Going Correction** -0.15s/f (Stan) **9** Ran SP% **121.3**
Speed ratings (Par 105):108,105,105,103,103 99,95,95,91
CSF £14.48 CT £44.53 TOTE £4.30: £1.40, £1.40, £1.70; EX 16.50 Trifecta £92.10 Pool: £201.26 - 1.55 winning units. Place 6 £157.37, Place 5 £101.49..
Owner J W Mursell **Bred** J W Mursell **Trained** Charlton Adam, Somerset

FOCUS
A decent little sprint handicap run at a solid pace and the form looks strong rated around the placed horses. Those that raced close to the pace seemed greatly favoured.
T/Plt: £624.50 to a £1 stake. Pool: £41,021.10. 47.95 winning tickets. T/Qpdt: £99.60 to a £1 stake. Pool: £2,503.90. 18.60 winning tickets. SP

6426 WOLVERHAMPTON (A.W) (L-H)

Saturday, November 11

OFFICIAL GOING: Standard
Wind: Fresh, behind. Weather: Cloudy.

6447 EUROPEAN BREEDERS' FUND MAIDEN STKS — 1m 141y(P)

7:00 (7:01) (Class 5) 2-Y-O **£3,886** (£1,156; £577; £288) **Stalls** Low

Form / RPR

0 **1** **Book Of Facts (FR)**[17] 6173 2-9-0 GregFairley(3) 10 — 79+
(M Johnston) *hld up: hdwy over 3f out: led 2f out: sn rdn: edgd lft ins fnl f: all out* **20/1**

05 **2** *shd* **Bergonzi (IRE)**[22] 6072 2-9-3 RobertHavlin 3 — 79+
(J H M Gosden) *chsd ldrs: ev ch fr 2f out: sn rdn: bmpd ins fnl f: styd on* **8/1**[3]

00 **3** *13* **Atlantic Coast (IRE)**[24] 6058 2-9-3 JoeFanning 6 — 50
(M Johnston) *chsd ldrs: rdn over 5f out: wknd wl over 1f out* **33/1**

00 **4** *1* **Calzaghe (IRE)**[34] 5828 2-9-0 NeilChalmers(3) 5 — 48
(A M Balding) *led over 6f: sn rdn and wknd* **40/1**

20 **5** *2* **Rambo Honours (IRE)**[98] 4140 2-9-3 CatherineGannon 7 — 44
(K A Ryan) *sn pushed along in rr: nvr nrr* **14/1**

2 **6** *3/4* **Katy Carr**[13] 6242 2-8-12 EddieAhern 4 — 37
(M J Wallace) *hld up in tch: rdn over 3f out: wknd over 2f out* **8/13**[1]

5 **7** *1* **Caernarvon (IRE)**[12] 6254 2-9-3 MatthewHenry 8 — 40
(M A Jarvis) *prom: racd keenly: jnd ldr over 6f out: ev ch over 2f out: sn rdn and wknd* **7/2**[2]

8 *8* **Glenridding** 2-9-3 JamieMackay 2 — 22
(J G Given) *s.s: outpcd: effrt over 2f out: sn wknd* **50/1**

9 *2* **Sherafey (IRE)**[167] 2052 2-8-12 (t) PatCosgrave 1 — 13
(Edgar Byrne, Ire) *chsd ldrs: rdn whn n.m.r and lost pl over 4f out: wknd over 3f out* **25/1**

1m 50.07s (-1.69) **Going Correction** -0.225s/f (Stan) **9** Ran SP% **117.9**
Speed ratings (Par 96):98,97,86,85,83 83,82,75,73
CSF £161.91 TOTE £13.70: £2.80, £2.40, £2.30; EX 69.10.
Owner Jumeirah Racing **Bred** Darley Stud Management Co Ltd **Trained** Middleham Moor, N Yorks

FOCUS
A moderate-looking contest, and with the market leaders finishing down the field it remains to be seen just what the form amounts to. The pace looked respectable though nothing special, but it proved all too much for most of the field.

NOTEBOOK
Book Of Facts(FR) always looked to be just holding his nearest rival on the run to the line. He had come on a lot for his debut run at Nottingham last month, when he could never get competitive after a slow break (op 12-1)
Bergonzi(IRE) appreciated the step up in trip and went down with all guns blazing. He can now be handicapped.. (op 7-1 tchd 9-1)
Atlantic Coast(IRE), beaten a total of 95 lengths in his two previous runs, both on turf, was under pressure a long way out but kept on through beaten horses in the straight for a moderate third. Stamina is likely to be his strong suit.
Calzaghe(IRE), also soundly beaten on his two previous outings, did a bit better under a positive ride on this switch to sand. (tchd 50-1)
Rambo Honours(IRE) did not improve for the switch to sand, but can at least now be handicapped. (tchd 12-1)
Katy Carr, an encouraging debut second here last month, ran no sort of race. Official explanation: trainer had no explanation for the poor form shown (op 10-11)
Caernarvon(IRE) dropped out very tamely after showing up for a while and was reported to have a breathing problem. Official explanation: trainer said gelding had a breathing problem (op 10-3)

6448 THE ZONGALERO RESTAURANT OVERLOOKS THE TRACK FILLIES' H'CAP — 1m 1f 103y(P)

7:30 (7:31) (Class 5) (0-70,70) 3-Y-0+ **£3,238** (£963; £481; £240) **Stalls** Low

Form / RPR

1035 **1** **Daring Affair**[49] 5538 5-9-5 **70** PaulMulrennan 12 — 78
(K R Burke) *chsd ldrs: led over 1f out: rdn and hung rt ins fnl f: styd on* **7/1**[3]

3401 **2** *1/2* **Bavarica**[28] 5973 4-8-6 **64** AmyBaker(7) 5 — 74+
(Miss J Feilden) *hld up: nt clr run over 2f out: hdwy and nt clr run over 1f out: sn swtchd rt: r.o wl* **7/1**[3]

0003 **3** *1 1/4* **Teide Lady**[33] 5879 3-8-12 **66** JoeFanning 9 — 71
(Rae Guest) *hld up: hdwy over 2f out: rdn over 1f out: edgd lft ins fnl f: styd on same pce* **9/2**[2]

-021 **4** *hd* **One Night In Paris (IRE)**[11] 6286 3-8-8 **62** EddieAhern 4 — 66+
(M J Wallace) *hld up: nt clr run over 2f out: hdwy over 1f out: nt rch ldrs* **3/1**[1]

5 *shd* **Soizic (NZ)**[238] 4-9-0 **68** StephaneBreux(3) 13 — 72
(C G Cox) *hld up: hdwy over 2f out: sn rdn: styd on* **33/1**

6664 **6** *1 1/4* **Miss Porcia**[5] 6371 5-8-5 **56** oh8 PaulHanagan 3 — 58
(P A Blockley) *led 1f: chsd ldrs: rdn over 2f out: styd on same pce fnl f* **14/1**

1200 **7** *1 1/2* **Madhavi**[86] 4528 4-9-1 **66** TomEaves 10 — 65
(B S Rothwell) *chsd ldrs: led over 2f out: rdn and hdd over 1f out: wknd ins fnl f* **22/1**

1/1- **8** *shd* **Our Kes (IRE)**[98] 4-9-3 **68** PaulDoe 1 — 67
(P Howling) *hld up: hdwy and hmpd 1f out: nt rch ldrs* **22/1**

3035 **9** *1/2* **Silken Act (CAN)**[33] 5868 3-9-0 **68** (b) JimCrowley 6 — 66
(Mrs A J Perrett) *hld up: effrt over 2f out: wknd fnl f* **17/2**

0446 **10** *3/4* **Dancing Flame**[33] 5862 3-8-2 **56** oh6 PaulQuinn 11 — 52
(E J Alston) *sn chsng ldr: rdn 3f out: wknd over 1f out* **50/1**

/53- **11** *hd* **Rollerbird**[13] 6246 4-8-7 **58** (p) GrahamGibbons 2 — 54
(T Hogan, Ire) *chsd ldrs: rdn over 3f out: wknd over 1f out* **16/1**

12 *6* **Sehoya (IRE)**[130] 3185 4-8-2 **56** oh1 DominicFox(3) 7 — 41
(Eoin Doyle, Ire) *s.s: outpcd* **25/1**

0-62 **13** *8* **Wonderful One (IRE)**[25] 6026 3-8-12 **66** RobertHavlin 8 — 35
(J H M Gosden) *led over 8f out: rdn and hdd over 2f out: sn wknd* **15/2**

2m 0.91s (-1.71) **Going Correction** -0.225s/f (Stan)
WFA 3 from 4yo+ 3lb **13** Ran SP% **120.5**
Speed ratings (Par 100):98,97,96,96,96 95,93,93,93,92 92,87,79
CSF £52.28 CT £249.76 TOTE £9.10: £2.60, £3.10, £1.90; EX 56.20.
Owner Nigel Shields **Bred** N R Shields And K R Burke **Trained** Middleham Moor, N Yorks
■ Stewards' Enquiry : Amy Baker one-day ban: careless riding (Nov 22)

FOCUS
A well-contested race, and a decent performance from the winner to defy top weight. The form is not rock-solid but the form of those in the frame behind the winner makes sense.
Sehoya(IRE) Official explanation: jockey said filly missed the break

6449 EUROPEAN BREEDERS' FUND AT WOLVERHAMPTON MAIDEN STKS — 1m 1f 103y(P)

8:00 (8:00) (Class 5) 2-Y-0 **£3,886** (£1,156; £577; £288) **Stalls** Low

Form / RPR

0 **1** **Troialini**[30] 5918 2-8-12 LiamJones(5) 3 — 78+
(S W Hall) *a.p: rdn to ld and edgd lft over 1f out: styd on wl* **25/1**

4 **2** *6* **Miss Fancy Pants**[11] 6283 2-8-12 JoeFanning 2 — 62
(M Johnston) *led 1f: chsd ldr: led over 2f out: rdn: edgd lft and hdd over 1f out: swtchd rt 1f out: sn hung rt and wknd* **10/11**[1]

0 **3** *2* **Squadron**[17] 6173 2-9-3 JimCrowley 4 — 63
(Mrs A J Perrett) *chsd ldrs: rdn over 3f out: hung lft and wknd over 1f out* **7/2**[2]

06 **4** *5* **Hatton Flight**[19] 6143 2-9-3 LPKeniry 5 — 54
(A M Balding) *led over 8f out: rdn and hdd over 2f out: sn wknd* **8/1**

06 **5** *6* **Windbeneathmywings (IRE)**[40] 5730 2-8-12 EddieAhern 1 — 37
(J W Hills) *sn bhd: effrt over 3f out: sn wknd* **5/1**[3]

2m 1.29s (-1.33) **Going Correction** -0.225s/f (Stan) **5** Ran SP% **106.2**
Speed ratings (Par 96):96,90,88,84,79
CSF £46.21 TOTE £14.80: £2.40, £1.40; EX 65.90.
Owner Dante Racing (Casserly Partnership) **Bred** Mrs A M Varey **Trained** Newmarket, Suffolk

FOCUS
Not a very competitive maiden, but the pace was sound and the field finished well spread out. It remains to be seen what the form amounts to. This was trainer Steve Hall's first winner.

NOTEBOOK
Troialini had cut little ice at Newmarket on his debut last month, but he found the competition here much more to his liking and, despite hanging under pressure in the straight, came right away from favourite Miss Fancy Pants in the last 150 yards to score by a decisive margin.
Miss Fancy Pants, a moderate fourth on her previous run here at the end of last month, did not look the most straightforward of rides this time as she hung right in the final furlong. (op 8-13 tchd 4-7)
Squadron, never a factor at Nottingham on his debut last month, was struggling on the home turn. (op 9-2 tchd 5-1)
Hatton Flight dropped right away after cutting out just an ordinary pace. (op 7-1 tchd 17-2)
Windbeneathmywings(IRE) was never in the hunt and her jockey reported that she would not face the kickback. Official explanation: jockey said filly did not face the kick-back (op 10-1)

6450 TWILIGHT RACING AND SUPPER - RELAX AND ENJOY MAIDEN STKS — 1m 141y(P)

8:30 (8:30) (Class 5) 3-Y-0+ **£3,238** (£963; £481; £240) **Stalls** Low

Form / RPR

0304 **1** **Salonga (IRE)**[34] 5831 3-8-12 59 JoeFanning 10 — 63
(C F Wall) *chsd ldr: led over 3f out: edgd rt over 1f out: rdn and edgd lft ins fnl f: styd on* **9/2**[3]

0352 **2** *1 1/2* **Chasing A Dream**[9] 6314 3-8-12 67 PaulHanagan 8 — 60
(B W Hills) *a.p: chsd wnr over 2f out: sn rdn and ev ch: styd on same pce fnl f* **11/4**[2]

63 **3** *1* **Monashee River (IRE)**[3] 6403 3-8-7 LiamJones(5) 7 — 58
(Miss V Haigh) *hld up: hdwy over 1f out: r.o: nt rch ldrs* **9/1**

4 *shd* **Dissitation (IRE)**[28] 5979 3-8-12 (p) EddieAhern 2 — 58
(M Halford, Ire) *chsd ldrs: nt clr run over 2f out: sn rdn: styd on same pce fnl f* **2/1**[1]

0006 **5** *nk* **Amron Hill**[1] 6429 3-8-10 55 RussellKennemore(7) 5 — 62
(R Hollinshead) *plld hrd and prom: rdn and hung rt fr over 1f out: no ex ins fnl f* **12/1**

0045 **6** *7* **Weet For Ever (USA)**[3] 6403 3-9-3 55 GeorgeBaker 9 — 47
(P A Blockley) *hld up: hdwy over 2f out: rdn: hung lft and wknd over 1f out* **8/1**

0 **7** 1 3/4 **Book Of Days (IRE)**[26] 6019 3-8-12 .... NelsonDeSouza 3 39
(R M Beckett) *sn pushed along in rr: hdwy 6f out: lost pl over 4f out: sn bhd* **33/1**

0 **8** 7 **Slip Star**[61] 5244 3-8-12 .... PaulMulrennan 4 24
(T J Etherington) *hld up: hmpd 7f out: a in rr* **100/1**

400- **9** 3/4 **Isabella Bay**[413] 5468 6-8-12 40 .... NeilChalmers(3) 1 22
(M Wellings) *led 5f: wknd over 2f out* **100/1**

-006 **10** 2 **Spinning Dancer (IRE)**[29] 5951 3-8-5 30 .... ChrisGlenister(7) 6 18
(J R Holt) *s.i.s: effrt 1/2-way: wknd over 3f out* **100/1**

1m 49.94s (-1.82) **Going Correction** -0.225s/f (Stan)
WFA 3 from 4yo+ 3lb **10** Ran SP% **112.9**
Speed ratings (Par 103):99,97,96,96,96 90,88,82,81,79
CSF £16.62 TOTE £7.40: £1.50, £1.90, £1.30; EX 23.50.
Owner Hintlesham Thoroughbreds **Bred** Kevin Foley **Trained** Newmarket, Suffolk

FOCUS
A weak maiden in which only half the field had any realistic chance and the winner did not have to improve to score.

6451 BOOK ONLINE AT WOLVERHAMPTON-RACECOURSE.CO.UK H'CAP 1m 141y(P)
9:00 (9:00) (Class 6) (0-62,67) 3-Y-0+ **£2,730** (£806; £403) **Stalls** Low

Form RPR

0000 **1** **Happy As Larry (USA)**[14] 6227 4-9-2 **62** .... RobbieFitzpatrick 7 69+
(T J Pitt) *hld up: outpcd over 2f out: nt clr run: swtchd rt and hdwy over 1f out: r.o to ld towards fin* **10/1**

5302 **2** 1/2 **Chia (IRE)**[10] 6294 3-8-13 **62** .... SteveDrowne 5 68
(D Haydn Jones) *chsd ldr: rdn to ld ins fnl f: hdd towards fin* **7/1**[3]

6361 **3** 1 3/4 **Western Roots**[2] 6419 5-9-2 **67** 5ex .... (p) LiamJones(5) 6 69
(M Appleby) *stdd s: hld up: hdwy over 2f out: rdn ins fnl f: styd on same pce* **10/3**[1]

0054 **4** nk **Cabourg (IRE)**[23] 6069 3-8-12 **61** .... PatCosgrave 3 63
(R Bastiman) *chsd ldrs: nt clr run and outpcd over 2f out: rallied over 1f out : hung lft ins fnl f: r.o* **20/1**

040 **5** 1/2 **Another Gladiator (USA)**[75] 4891 3-8-11 **60** .... PaulMulrennan 1 61
(K A Ryan) *led: rdn over 1f out: hdd and no ex ins fnl f* **14/1**

6 1/2 **Open Loop (IRE)**[20] 6117 4-9-2 **62** .... (bt) EddieAhern 8 62
(Edgar Byrne, Ire) *mid-div: nt clr run and lost pl 2f out: hung lft and r.o ins fnl f: nvr trbld ldrs* **28/1**

2341 **7** 1/2 **Band**[10] 6300 6-8-10 **56** .... GrahamGibbons 2 55
(E S McMahon) *chsd ldrs: n.m.r and lost pl over 3f out: rallied over 1f out: wknd ins fnl f* **10/3**[1]

2033 **8** 5 **Gallego**[8] 6323 4-8-10 **59** .... JamesDoyle(3) 12 47
(R J Price) *s.i.s: hld up: hdwy 1/2-way: rdn over 1f out: wknd fnl f* **8/1**

043P **9** hd **Royle Dancer**[9] 6314 3-8-5 **61** .... RussellKennemore(7) 10 49
(R Hollinshead) *chsd ldrs: rdn over 3f out: ev ch over 2f out: hung lft and wknd over 1f out* **16/1**

610/ **10** 3 **Experimental (IRE)**[595] 731 12-9-0 **60** .... DeanMcKeown 4 41
(John A Harris) *hld up: a in rr* **80/1**

6-00 **11** 2 1/2 **Cherokee Vision**[2] 6419 3-8-9 **58** .... (p) JimCrowley 11 34
(Miss T Spearing) *chsd ldr: rdn and ev ch over 2f out: wknd over 1f out* **66/1**

0501 **12** shd **Magic Warrior**[10] 6294 6-9-4 **64** .... GeorgeBaker 9 40
(J C Fox) *hld up: rdn over 2f out: sn wknd* **11/2**[2]

1m 49.88s (-1.88) **Going Correction** -0.225s/f (Stan)
WFA 3 from 4yo+ 3lb **12** Ran SP% **117.7**
Speed ratings (Par 101):99,98,97,96,96 95,95,90,90,88 85,85
CSF £75.59 CT £287.05 TOTE £11.00: £3.10, £2.60, £1.60; EX 108.90.
Owner G Naidu, K Luxon & W McKay **Bred** C H Kitchen And Jeffrey Cook **Trained** Bawtry, S Yorks

FOCUS
A strong pace early, but the final time was only 0.06 of a second faster than the preceding maiden. The form looks fair enough with the placed horses close to their marks.
Magic Warrior Official explanation: trainer said gelding bled from the nose

6452 HOTEL & CONFERENCING AT WOLVERHAMPTON RACECOURSE H'CAP 5f 20y(P)
9:30 (9:31) (Class 5) (0-70,70) 3-Y-0+ **£3,886** (£1,156; £577; £288) **Stalls** Low

Form RPR

1232 **1** **Mr Cellophane**[8] 6326 3-9-4 **70** .... EddieAhern 8 81
(J R Jenkins) *hld up: hdwy over 1f out: rdn to ld ins fnl f: edgd lft: r.o* **4/1**[2]

3012 **2** 1/2 **Heavens Walk**[6] 6353 5-9-3 **69** .... (t) SebSanders 5 78
(P J Makin) *s.i.s: hld up: hdwy over 1f out: rdn and ev ch ins fnl f: edgd lft: styd on* **15/8**[1]

4000 **3** 1 3/4 **Lady Bahia (IRE)**[6] 6353 5-9-4 **70** .... (b) RobbieFitzpatrick 10 73
(Peter Grayson) *hld up: hdwy over 1f out: rdn ins fnl f: styd on same pce* **50/1**

3004 **4** 1 **Bonne De Fleur**[14] 6223 5-8-12 **69** .... (b) MarkLawson(5) 12 68+
(B Smart) *led: hdd over 3f out: rdn over 1f out: edgd lft: styd on same pce* **25/1**

0513 **5** 3/4 **Steel City Boy (IRE)**[131] 3154 3-9-4 **70** .... DanielTudhope 7 67
(D Carroll) *chsd ldr: led over 1f out: sn rdn: hdd and no ex ins fnl f* **11/2**[3]

0021 **6** nk **Tag Team (IRE)**[40] 5737 5-9-0 **66** .... DeanMcKeown 4 62
(John A Harris) *chsd ldrs: rdn and ev ch 1f out: wknd wl ins fnl f* **9/1**

0260 **7** shd **Lyndalee (IRE)**[8] 6320 3-9-4 **70** .... (p) JoeFanning 2 65
(T Hogan, Ire) *dwlt: outpcd: r.o ins fnl f: nrst fin* **25/1**

3103 **8** nk **Harrison's Flyer (IRE)**[29] 5938 5-8-12 **67** .... (p) NeilChalmers(3) 3 61
(J M Bradley) *hld up: hdwy over 1f out: wknd ins fnl f* **14/1**

4000 **9** shd **Kennington**[24] 6048 6-8-10 **65** .... (b) JamesDoyle(3) 9 59
(Mrs C A Dunnett) *chsd ldrs: rdn 1/2-way: wknd over 1f out* **14/1**

4100 **10** 1 1/4 **Count Cougar (USA)**[8] 6326 6-8-13 **65** .... LPKeniry 13 54
(S P Griffiths) *mid-div: rdn over 1f out: sn wknd* **40/1**

1616 **11** 2 **Smiddy Hill**[6] 6353 4-9-4 **70** .... PatCosgrave 1 52
(R Bastiman) *led over 3f out: rdn and hdd over 1f out: wknd ins fnl f* **14/1**

2134 **12** 15 **Garlogs**[196] 1279 3-9-1 **67** .... TomEaves 11 —
(A Bailey) *chsd ldrs 3f* **33/1**

61.23 secs (-1.59) **Going Correction** -0.225s/f (Stan) **12** Ran SP% **115.2**
Speed ratings (Par 103):103,102,99,97,96 96,95,95,95,93 90,66
CSF £10.81 CT £317.45 TOTE £5.70: £1.40, £1.70, £8.00; EX 13.50 Place 6 £156.58, Place 5 £20.96..
Owner R B Hill **Bred** Buy And Sell Partnership **Trained** Royston, Herts
■ Stewards' Enquiry : Seb Sanders one-day ban: used whip without giving horse time to respond (Nov 22)

FOCUS
Not the strongest of handicaps, but won in game fashion by the ultra-consistent winner. The time was reasonable and the form looks solid.
T/Plt: £396.60 to a £1 stake. Pool: £66,532.20. 122.45 winning tickets. T/Qpdt: £9.70 to a £1 stake. Pool: £3,286.90. 249.50 winning tickets. CR

5197 TOULOUSE
Saturday, November 11

OFFICIAL GOING: Good to soft

6453a CRITERIUM DU LANGUEDOC - PRIX PAUL GUICHOU (LISTED RACE) 1m
2:20 (2:26) 2-Y-0 **£17,241** (£6,897; £5,172; £3,448; £1,724)

RPR

1 **Literato (FR)**[81] 2-9-2 .... IMendizabal 2 95
(J-C Rouget, France)

2 3/4 **Laureldean Express**[70] 5034 2-8-9 ow1 .... CSoumillon 4 86
(E J O'Neill) *led, pushed along straight, headed approaching final furlong, stayed on under pressure to line SP 52-10*

3 nk **Prior Warning**[25] 2-8-11 .... DBoeuf 1 88
(D Smaga, France)

4 nk **Gris De Gris (IRE)** 2-8-11 .... TThulliez 5 87
(J-M Capitte, France)

5 1/2 **Sanvic (IRE)**[36] 5801 2-8-11 .... SPasquier 3 86
(J-C Rouget, France)

6 4 **Tio Poppy (IRE)**[26] 2-8-8 .... TJarnet 6 74
(R Gibson, France)

1m 40.47s **6** Ran
PARI-MUTUEL (Including 1 Euro stake): WIN 1.80; PL 1.40, 2.20; SF 11.80.
Owner H Morin **Bred** Bsh Of Administrativa **Trained** Pau, France

NOTEBOOK
Laureldean Express, having set out to make all, was only caught as the race came to an end and ran a brave race in defeat. She did cause interference in the straight when hanging left but the Stewards left the order unchanged. She could now go on to a race in Marseille.

6454a PRIX FILLE DE L'AIR (GROUP 3) (F&M) 1m 2f 110y
2:50 (3:00) 3-Y-0+ **£27,586** (£11,034; £8,276; £5,517; £2,759)

RPR

1 **Afaf (FR)**[31] 5913 4-8-11 .... TJarnet 2 106
(M Delzangles, France) *prom disp 3rd early, 3rd str, rdn to chal appr fnl f, ran on wl to ld 100 yards out, rdn out* **133/10**

2 1 1/2 **In Clover**[35] 5816 4-8-11 .... DBonilla 10 103
(F Head, France) *raced in 2nd, joined ldr appr str, rdn to chal 1 1/2 f out, led appr fnl f, hdd 100 yards out, kept on* **13/2**

3 hd **Sanaya (IRE)**[20] 6120 3-8-8 .... (p) CSoumillon 1 105
(A De Royer-Dupre, France) *hld up in last, 10th halfway, ran on wl fr over 1f out, rdn and fin strongly on outside fnl f, nrst at fin* **18/10**[1]

4 3/4 **Histoire De Moeurs (FR)**[22] 3-8-8 .... DBoeuf 4 104
(Y De Nicolay, France) *prominent, disputing 3rd early, 4th and pushed along straight, stayed on at one pace* **12/1**

5 3/4 **Epatha (IRE)**[63] 5197 3-8-8 .... IMendizabal 3 102
(J-C Rouget, France) *raced in 8th early, 5th towards inside straight, driven to chase leaders, stayed on at one pace* **11/1**

6 nk **Wingspan (USA)**[18] 6171 3-8-8 .... TThulliez 8 102
(A Fabre, France) *held up, last and ridden on outside straight, stayed on final furlong, nearest at finish* **32/10**[2]

7 1 1/2 **Green Girl (FR)**[90] 4417 4-8-11 .... FSpanu 7 97
(J E Hammond, France) *raced in 7th, disputing 7th straight, never in challenging position* **18/1**

8 nk **Bastet (IRE)**[18] 6171 4-8-11 .... (b) SPasquier 5 97
(E Lellouche, France) *mid-division in 6th, disputing 7th straight, soon ridden and one pace* **62/10**[3]

9 nk **Princess Jones**[18] 6171 6-8-11 .... FVeron 6 96
(J-L Guillochon, France) *raced in 9th, disputing 7th straight, never dangerous* **35/1**

10 10 **Chavela (IRE)**[193] 1398 4-8-11 .... CNora 9 78
(R Martin-Sanchez, Spain) *led, joined approaching straight, headed approaching final furlong, quickly weakened* **80/1**

11 10 **Afriketa (IRE)** 3-8-8 .... J-LMartinez 11 62
(R Lopez Gallego, Spain) *prominent in 5th early, 6th and under pressure straight, weakened* **27/1**

2m 13.79s
WFA 3 from 4yo+ 4lb **11** Ran SP% **122.6**
PARI-MUTUEL: WIN 14.30; PL 2.60, 2.20, 1.40; DF 47.10.
Owner Z Hakam **Bred** Z Hakam **Trained** France

NOTEBOOK
Afaf(FR), a highly consistent filly, gained a thoroughly deserved win. Settled in third place for much of the race, she made a forward move halfway up the straight, took the lead a furlong out and finally won with plenty in hand. She may now be campaigned in Dubai next year.
In Clover, always well up there, was given every chance. She took the advantage halfway up the straight but had nothing in reserve when tackled by the winner. Once again she battled on gamely to the line.
Sanaya(IRE), dropped out early on, was given an awful lot to do. She came up the centre of the track but never looked like reaching the first two and is better than this performance showed. She is another who might race in Dubai next year.
Histoire De Moeurs(FR), fourth for most of this race, also came with her run up the centre of the track. She was one-paced throughout the final furlong and a half, though.

6391 FLEMINGTON (L-H)
Saturday, November 11

OFFICIAL GOING: Good

6455a QUEEN ELIZABETH STKS (GROUP 3) (H'CAP) 2m 4f 110y
5:30 (12:00) 3-Y-0+
£64,744 (£19,231; £9,615; £4,808; £2,671; £2,137)

RPR

1 **Gallant Guru (AUS)**[188] 4-8-13 .... (b) SArnold 1 105
(Lee Freedman, Australia)

2 shd **Magic Instinct**[7] 6346 4-8-5 .... CMunce 3 97
(P Moody, New Zealand)

3 3/4 **Fooram (NZ)**[35] 5-9-0 .... DBeadman 7 105
(John O'Shea, Australia)

4 1 3/4 **Bay Story (USA)**[4] 6391 4-8-5 .... KerrinMcEvoy 13 94
(B Ellison) *began well & travelled nicely in 4th 2l off lead, hld position to home turn, outpaced by leaders but stayed on to line*
5 shd **Zavite (NZ)** 4-8-5 .... HBowman 8 94
(A Cummings, Australia)
6 shd **Show Barry (AUS)**[14] 6-9-2 .... NCallow 15 105
(J Rattle, Australia)
7 2 **Blue Collar Jack (AUS)** 5-8-7 .... CSymons 9 94
(K Keys, Australia)
8 1/2 **Vanquished (AUS)**[7] 6346 6-9-1 ....(b) DMOliver 10 102
(B Murray, Australia)
9 1 1/4 **Force Nine (AUS)** 5-8-5 .... GChilds 16 90
(Cliff Brown, Australia)
10 shd **Spinney (AUS)**[210] 3-9-0 .... BShinn 14 110
(J Hawkes, Australia)
11 1 **Pantani (NZ)**[516] 7-9-0 .... NashRawiller 2 98
(R Laing, Australia)
12 2 **Jagger**[413] 5458 6-8-9 .... CraigAWilliams 11 91
(D Hayes, Australia)

2m 40.67s
WFA 3 from 4yo+ 11lb **12** Ran
SP's: 7-1, 11-2, 11-2, 16-1 (Vanquished 3-1F).
Owner B & Mrs C Perks et al **Bred** Toorak Park Stud Pty Ltd **Trained** Australia

NOTEBOOK
Bay Story(USA) ran well on this step up in trip and grade and is building up a nice portfolio of respectable efforts in Australia. He is being aimed at the Perth Cup, to be run over two miles on New Year's Day.

6328 SAINT-CLOUD (L-H)
Sunday, November 12

OFFICIAL GOING: Good

6456a CRITERIUM DE SAINT-CLOUD (GROUP 1) (C&F) 1m 2f
2:20 (2:21) 2-Y-O **£98,517** (£39,414; £19,707; £9,845; £4,931)

RPR
1 **Passage Of Time**[15] 6217 2-8-11 .... RichardHughes 9 112+
(H R A Cecil) *always close up, 5th straight, found gap approaching final f, quickened to lead 150yds out, driven out* **32/10**[2]
2 3/4 **Soldier Of Fortune (IRE)**[26] 6042 2-9-0 .... KFallon 1 114
(A P O'Brien, Ire) *broke well, held up in 4th, 3rd straight, led approaching final f to 150yds out, one pace* **64/10**
3 3 **Empire Day (UAE)**[15] 6216 2-9-0 .... KDarley 2 108
(M Johnston) *first to show, tracked leader, 2nd straight, hard ridden over 1f out, kept on one pace* **17/2**
4 3/4 **Spirit One (FR)**[14] 6249 2-9-0 .... DBoeuf 10 106
(P Demercastel, France) *led after 2f to approaching final f, one pace* **13/10**[1]
5 snk **Red Rock Canyon (IRE)**[22] 6104 2-9-0 .... JAHeffernan 4 106
(A P O'Brien, Ire) *led 2f, 4th straight, ran on one pace under pressure from over 1f out* **64/10**
6 5 **Meridia (GER)** 2-8-11 .... SPasquier 8 94
(Mario Hofer, Germany) *held up, 12th straight, some late progress, never a factor* **18/1**
7 hd **Consul General**[44] 5662 2-9-0 .... PJSmullen 13 96
(D K Weld, Ire) *headway half-way, 6th straight, ridden well over 1f out, one pace from distance* **32/10**[2]
8 shd **Aaim To Prosper (IRE)**[15] 6216 2-9-0 .... JohnEgan 11 96
(M R Channon) *10th straight, always towards rear* **60/1**
9 3/4 **Nommo (FR)**[21] 2-9-0 .... TJarnet 6 95
(R Martens, France) *9th straight, never a factor* **80/1**
10 1/2 **Perdono (USA)**[39] 5771 2-9-0 .... EPedroza 12 94
(A Wohler, Germany) *held up in rear, 11th straight, no headway* **74/1**
11 1 1/2 **Dilshaan's Prize (IRE)** 2-9-0 .... DBonilla 3 91
(R Pritchard-Gordon, France) *soon in rear, last straight* **56/1**
12 8 **Ailton (GER)**[28] 6000 2-9-0 .... JVictoire 5 76
(W Baltromei, Germany) *prominent, 7th straight, ridden & beaten 2f out* **38/1**
13 1/2 **Massive (IRE)**[28] 6000 2-9-0 .... CSoumillon 7 75
(M R Channon) *mid-division, 8th straight, soon weakened* **49/10**[3]

2m 8.90s **13** Ran SP% **159.4**
PARI-MUTUEL: WIN 4.20 (coupled with Consul General); PL 4.00, 2.70, 3.60; DF 34.20.
Owner K Abdulla **Bred** Juddmonte Farms Ltd **Trained** Newmarket, Suffolk

NOTEBOOK
Passage Of Time is certainly a Classic filly in the making and she could not have impressed more in showing both stamina and speed at the end of the race. Her jockey had to be a little patient in the straight but, once he pressed the button just over a furlong out, she produced an outstanding turn of foot to take the lead inside the final furlong. She is likely to start off next year in the Musidora Stakes at York, and her owner will then make a decision as to whether she will be aimed at the Vodafone Oaks or the Prix de Diane Hermes. She is certainly one for the notebook.
Soldier Of Fortune(IRE), considering his relative inexperience, put up a decent effort and can only make progress in the future. He was given a perfect ride, tucked in on the rail, before hitting the front approaching the final furlong. He then idled and was passed by the winner before running on again in the final stages. He will certainly turn into a Group colt next year and may well make it to the Classic scene.
Empire Day(UAE) put up a brave performance but just lacked speed at the end. He was not suited by the unusually good ground as he is a colt who likes to get his toe in. Staying is his main asset and he should turn into a decent three-year-old.
Spirit One(FR), once again made favourite, was soon at the head of affairs. He set a strong and kept up the good work until halfway up the straight, when attacked by several rivals. He was then one-paced to the line. Racing just two weeks after another Group 1 race at this track, he tries to do it the hard way, and his jockey felt that a pacemaker would help in future if he is to show his best. He is likely to be trained for the Prix du Jockey Club next year, with a run before in a trial.
Red Rock Canyon(IRE) is still a maiden, but recorded a personal best on this step up in trip.
Consul General, who looked very promising when strolling away with a good maiden on his debut, did not look to be crying out for this distance and, having moved into contention, failed to get home.
Aaim To Prosper(IRE) was drawn on the outside and then settled in mid-division. His effort petered out early in the straight.
Massive(IRE) made no show on this occasion. He never reached the leading group and was being pushed along some way out. He was already a forlorn hope in the straight and finally finished last.

6439 LINGFIELD (L-H)
Monday, November 13

OFFICIAL GOING: Standard
Wind: Strong, half-behind Weather: Fine but cloudy

6457 EUROPEAN BREEDERS' FUND MAIDEN STKS 6f (P)
1:20 (1:20) (Class 5) 2-Y-O **£3,886** (£1,156; £577; £288) **Stalls** Low

Form RPR
1 **My Love Thomas (IRE)** 2-8-12 .... EddieAhern 5 67+
(E A L Dunlop) *dwlt: sn pressed ldr: carried rt and intimidated fr wl over 1f out: pushed along and r.o to ld last strides* **11/4**[2]
3222 2 shd **Kyle (IRE)**[9] 6330 2-9-3 78 .... JimmyFortune 4 69
(R Hannon) *led at stdy pce: qcknd over 2f out: wnt v wd bnd sn after: hung rt fr over 1f out: hdd last strides* **4/11**[1]
0 3 5 **Hope Your Safe**[9] 6331 2-8-12 .... DaneO'Neill 3 49
(J R Best) *t.k.h: hld up bhd ldng pair: outpcd outpcd fr over 1f out* **16/1**[3]
00 4 3 **Delaporte**[98] 4207 2-8-12 ....(vt[1]) JimmyQuinn 1 40
(M A Buckley) *t.k.h: trckd ldng pair: outpcd wl over 1f out: wknd fnl f* **100/1**
0 5 11 **Papradon**[9] 6330 2-9-3 .... GeorgeBaker 2 12
(J R Best) *a last: rdn and struggling wl over 2f out* **33/1**

1m 16.42s (3.61) **Going Correction** -0.025s/f (Stan) 5 Ran SP% **109.8**
Speed ratings (Par 96):74,73,67,63,48
CSF £4.09 TOTE £3.60: £1.50, £1.02; EX 4.40.
Owner Old Road Securities Plc **Bred** Twelve Oaks Stud Establishment **Trained** Newmarket, Suffolk

FOCUS
This maiden only really concerned two horses, and one of those has a suspect attitude. The time was very poor and the form looks very modest.

NOTEBOOK
My Love Thomas(IRE), a 155,000gns half-sister to Louvain, a high-class seven-furlong/miler, out of a smart sprinter, overcame a very troubled trip to make a winning debut. She was carried over to the near-side rail in the straight by the wayward Kyle and was continually intimidated, so it is to her credit she found enough to get up near the line. If nothing else this will have taught her plenty and she should be able to improve on the bare form. (tchd 3-1)
Kyle(IRE), beaten at short prices on his five previous starts, including over this trip at Windsor on his last three outings, was once again an expensive failure, this time on his Polytrack debut. He threw this away, hanging badly right off the home bend to end up against the near-side rail, and he could offer little when the eventual winner found his stride late on. In his defence this was only the second time he has ever run on a round course - the only other time he had run round a bend he was carried wide - and he does have sufficient ability to win a similar event, but it would be unwise to keep taking short prices. Official explanation: jockey said colt hung badly right (op 2-5 tchd 1-3 and 4-9 in a place)
Hope Your Safe, well held on her debut at Windsor, was no match for the front two, despite having the advantage of not venturing to the near-side rail, and she looks more of a handicap prospect. (tchd 20-1)
Delaporte was well beaten in a couple of runs on turf when last seen over three months previously but, fitted with both a tongue-tie and a visor for the first time, this was better. (op 66-1)

6458 SID LATHAM 90TH BIRTHDAY NURSERY 1m (P)
1:50 (1:50) (Class 4) (0-85,79) 2-Y-O **£4,533** (£1,348; £674; £336) **Stalls** High

Form RPR
3120 1 **Cesc**[38] 5783 2-9-7 79 .... EddieAhern 1 85
(P J Makin) *cl up: trckd ldr over 3f out: led over 2f out: idled whn shkn up 1f out: pushed out and in command after* **2/1**[1]
030 2 1 1/4 **Bajan Pride**[34] 5893 2-8-12 70 .... JimmyFortune 5 73
(R Hannon) *hld up in tch: prog on outer over 3f out: rdn over 2f out: chsd wnr fnl f: no imp* **8/1**
0461 3 1 3/4 **Oakley Heffert (IRE)**[28] 6018 2-9-6 78 .... JimmyQuinn 3 77
(R Hannon) *disp ld tl led after 2f: rdn and hdd over 2f out: styd on inner and one pce* **7/1**
6361 4 nk **Tom Paris**[13] 6285 2-9-4 76 .... DaneO'Neill 7 74
(W R Muir) *hld up in last pair: effrt 3f out: rdn and one pce fr over 2f out* **14/1**
5523 5 1 **Golan Way**[25] 6064 2-8-13 74 .... JamesDoyle[(3)] 4 70
(I A Wood) *disp ld for 2f: chsd ldr tl lost pl u.p over 3f out: last 2f out: plugged on fnl f* **7/1**
5104 6 1 1/2 **Our Herbie**[11] 6310 2-9-4 76 .... J-PGuillambert 6 69
(J W Hills) *hld up in last: effrt over 2f out: rdn and no prog fnl 2f* **6/1**[3]
0450 7 1 3/4 **Lap Of Honour (IRE)**[38] 5788 2-9-0 72 .... TPQueally 2 61
(N A Callaghan) *disp ld for 2f: rdn and lost pl over 3f out: nt look keen and wl btn over 1f out* **7/2**[2]

1m 38.83s (-0.60) **Going Correction** -0.025s/f (Stan) 7 Ran SP% **112.6**
Speed ratings (Par 98):102,100,99,98,97 96,94
CSF £18.12 TOTE £2.60: £1.50, £3.20; EX 23.20.
Owner Keith And Brian Brackpool **Bred** H J P Farr **Trained** Ogbourne Maisey, Wilts

FOCUS
A fair nursery that looks solid rated around those in the frame behind the winner.

NOTEBOOK
Cesc had looked very unlucky on his last couple of starts and gained compensation with a pretty straightforward victory. He is likely to be kept on the go and it will be surprising if he does not add to this. (op 9-4 tchd 5-2)
Bajan Pride, making his handicap debut having shown promise in maiden company, ran well behind the well-handicapped winner. He might be able to do even better over further next year.
Oakley Heffert(IRE), a stablemate of the runner-up, ran reasonablyy but could not defy a 4lb higher mark than when winning at Windsor on his previous start.
Tom Paris, 4lb higher, found this tougher than the Wolverhampton nursery he won on his previous start.
Golan Way, upped to a mile for the first time, stayed on after getting outpaced and seemed unsuited by the way the race was run. (op 8-1)
Our Herbie could not confirm Lingfield form from earlier in the season with Golan Way. (op 11-2)
Lap Of Honour(IRE) did not improve for the step up to a mile and switch to Polytrack. (op 3-1)

6459 WINTER LADIES DAY THIS SATURDAY MAIDEN STKS 1m 2f (P)
2:20 (2:20) (Class 5) 3-Y-O+ **£3,238** (£963; £481; £240) **Stalls** Low

Form RPR
2205 1 **Majestic Halo**[16] 6225 3-8-12 72 .... JimCrowley 7 59+
(E A L Dunlop) *hld up in last trio: prog on outer 2f out: shkn up over 1f out: led ins fnl f: pushed out and hld on* **6/1**
02 2 nk **Calming Waters**[47] 5611 3-9-3 .... EddieAhern 9 64+
(D W P Arbuthnot) *t.k.h: prom: led jst over 2f out: drvn and hdd ins fnl f: styd on wl but jst hld* **4/1**[3]
0002 3 2 **Feu D'Artifice (USA)**[28] 6019 3-9-3 70 .... JimmyFortune 1 60+
(R Hannon) *trckd ldrs: effrt over 2f out: drvn to chal 1f out: sn outpcd* **4/1**[3]

The Form Book, Raceform Ltd, Compton, RG20 6NL

2352 **4** 1 **Muntada**[48] 5589 3-8-12 75 .... DaneO'Neill 8 53
(M P Tregoning) *led to over 7f out: led again over 3f out to jst over 2f out: stl pressing 1f out: outpcd* **11/4**[1]

0064 **5** ½ **Camp Attack**[55] 5452 3-9-3 53 .... LPKeniry 3 57
(S Dow) *hld up in midfield: sltly hmpd on inner over 2f out and off the pce: effrt wl over 1f out: kpt on one pce* **25/1**

6000 **6** ¾ **Footstepsinthesnow (IRE)**[21] 6128 3-8-12 47 .... PaulDoe 4 51
(M A Buckley) *hld up in midfield: rdn over 2f out: sn lost pl: hmpd wl over 1f out: kpt on fnl f: no ch* **100/1**

7 nk **Unquenchable (USA)** 3-8-12 .... TPQueally 2 50
(Saeed Bin Suroor) *s.v.s: hld up in last pair: pushed along and outpcd over 2f out: nvr a factor* **7/2**[2]

0006 **8** 1¼ **Laugh 'n Cry**[21] 6144 5-9-2 50 .... (b) JimmyQuinn 6 48
(C A Cyzer) *t.k.h: hld up in midfield: effrt over 3f out: rdn and no prog 2f out: fdd* **33/1**

9 3 **Apache Fort** 3-9-3 .... J-PGuillambert 5 47
(T Keddy) *s.v.s: hld up in last: nvr a factor* **20/1**

00 **10** 1¾ **Bazil Des Fieffes (FR)**[4] 6410 4-9-7 .... (b) NancyBloyart 10 44
(J M Plasschaert, Belgium) *dwlt: pushed up to ld over 7f out: hdd over 3f out: wknd* **100/1**

2m 6.98s (-0.81) **Going Correction** -0.025s/f (Stan)
WFA 3 from 4yo+ 4lb **10** Ran SP% **116.7**
Speed ratings (Par 103):102,101,100,99,98 98,98,97,94,93
CSF £28.95 TOTE £4.60: £1.60, £2.10, £1.30; EX 37.90 Trifecta £125.70 Pool: £497.64 - 2.81 winning tickets..
Owner Lord Derby **Bred** Stanley Estate And Stud Co **Trained** Newmarket, Suffolk
■ Stewards' Enquiry : Nancy Bloyart caution: used whip when out of contention

FOCUS
An ordinary maiden, as the proximity of the fifth and sixth suggests, although the first three could be better than the form.
Unquenchable(USA) Official explanation: jockey said filly missed the break

6460 JUMPING AT FOLKESTONE TOMORROW CLAIMING STKS 7f (P)
2:50 (2:50) (Class 6) 2-Y-O **£2,266** (£674; £337; £168) **Stalls** Low

Form RPR

00 **1** **Lordswood (IRE)**[58] 5371 2-7-10 .... WilliamBuick(7) 4 61
(A M Balding) *dwlt: t.k.h: trckd ldng pair: effrt to ld over 1f out: shkn up fnl f: hld on wl* **3/1**[2]

450 **2** shd **Marine Parade**[45] 5655 2-8-11 70 .... JimmyFortune 3 69
(R Hannon) *dwlt: hld up in last pair: effrt 2f out: chsd wnr fnl f: hrd rdn and clsd: jst failed* **6/4**[1]

3640 **3** 1¼ **La Marmotte (IRE)**[4] 6416 2-8-3 64 .... NickyMackay 1 57
(J W Hills) *led: sddle slipped after 2f: wd bnd 2f out: hdd over 1f out: one pce* **7/2**[3]

0506 **4** 3 **Vodka Luge**[60] 5323 2-7-13 48 ow1 .... JimmyQuinn 2 46
(J W Hills) *hld up in last pair: rdn wl over 2f out: no imp fnl 2f* **12/1**

4 **5** ¾ **Cape Free**[13] 6278 2-8-1 ow1 .... JamesDoyle(3) 5 49
(E F Vaughan) *mostly chsd ldr: carried wd bnd 2f out: sn wknd* **7/1**

1m 26.46s (0.57) **Going Correction** -0.025s/f (Stan) **5** Ran SP% **107.4**
Speed ratings (Par 94):95,94,93,90,89
CSF £7.53 TOTE £3.80: £2.00, £1.10; EX 8.10.
Owner Lord Roborough & The Lopes Sisters **Bred** Blackdown Stud **Trained** Kingsclere, Hants

FOCUS
Just the five runners and only an ordinary claimer with the first two within a length of pre-race marks.

NOTEBOOK
Lordswood(IRE) showed ability in a couple of six-furlong maidens at Newbury earlier in the season and took advantage of the drop in grade to get off the mark. This is just modest form, but it would not be a total surprise to see him get competitive in handicaps. (tchd 11-4)
Marine Parade, who showed ability in maidens before running down the field in a sales race at Newmarket, was just held on this drop in grade and step up in trip. He may not be the easiest to place outside of this grade. (tchd 13-8 in places)
La Marmotte(IRE)'s saddle slipped and that cost her any chance she had of winning. Official explanation: jockey said saddle slipped (op 5-2)
Vodka Luge, a stablemate of the unlucky third, ran reasonably and might just be better than her official mark of 48. (tchd 11-1)
Cape Free seemingly achieved little when fourth on her debut at Southwell. (op 9-1)

6461 LINGFIELD PARK FOR CHRISTMAS PARTIES H'CAP 7f (P)
3:20 (3:20) (Class 4) (0-85,85) 3-Y-O+ **£5,505** (£1,637; £818; £408) **Stalls** Low

Form RPR

0506 **1** **Bobski (IRE)**[8] 6352 4-8-12 **80** .... AdamKirby 9 89
(G A Huffer) *dwlt: hld up in rr: pushed along and prog fr 3f out: drvn on outer and hanging fnl f: edgd lft but forced ahd last 75yds* **15/2**

0012 **2** hd **Resplendent Nova**[16] 6221 4-8-9 **80** .... DeanCorby(3) 12 88
(P Howling) *pressed ldr: rdn to chal 1f out: upsides ins fnl f: n.m.r and jst hld nr fin* **5/1**[3]

4610 **3** nk **Tamagin (USA)**[23] 6094 3-8-8 **82** .... (p) LiamJones(5) 5 89
(P D Evans) *led at str pce: carried hd awkwardly but battled on whn chal fnl f: edgd rt and hdd last 75yds* **9/1**

5006 **4** ¾ **Bomber Command (USA)**[42] 5739 3-8-10 **79** .... EddieAhern 10 84+
(J W Hills) *settled in midfield: pushed along in 7th whn hmpd and snatched up over 2f out: styd on fr over 1f out: nt rch ldrs* **10/1**

344 **5** ½ **Perfect Story (IRE)**[46] 5643 4-8-11 **79** .... JimmyFortune 3 83
(J A R Toller) *trckd ldrs: poised to chal over 1f out: rdn and fnd nil fnl f* **7/2**[1]

6100 **6** nk **Sun Catcher (IRE)**[16] 6221 3-8-2 **74** .... StephaneBreux(3) 11 77
(R Hannon) *trckd ldrs: rdn and nt qckn over 1f out: styd on same pce* **40/1**

053 **7** ½ **Buy On The Red**[39] 5777 5-8-11 **79** .... PaulDoe 4 81
(W R Muir) *hld up towards rr: effrt on inner 2f out: prog over 1f out: nt qckn and btn fnl f* **11/1**

0401 **8** nk **Ninth House (USA)**[44] 5688 4-9-0 **85** .... (t) JamesDoyle(3) 13 86
(N P Littmoden) *hld up in last: rdn over 2f out: no real prog tl styd on wl last 150yds: no ch* **9/2**[2]

5106 **9** ½ **Deira (USA)**[82] 4689 3-8-7 **76** .... TPQueally 6 76
(C E Brittain) *trckd ldrs: rdn 2f out: nt qckn over 1f out: fdd fnl f* **16/1**

1050 **10** 1½ **Fast Bowler**[44] 5666 3-8-11 **80** .... DaneO'Neill 8 76
(J M P Eustace) *settled towards rr: rdn over 2f out: nt qckn and no prog over 1f out* **10/1**

00-6 **11** 1 **Dart Along (USA)**[22] 6117 4-8-0 **71** oh1 .... (b) DominicFox(3) 1 64
(Eoin Doyle, Ire) *dwlt: rousted along on inner to rch midfield: rdn over 2f out: fdd over 1f out* **20/1**

5050 **12** 2½ **Desert Dreamer (IRE)**[5] 6397 5-8-11 **79** .... JimCrowley 14 66
(P R Chamings) *hld up in last trio: shkn up and no prog over 2f out* **14/1**

P050 **13** ½ **Chief Exec**[8] 6352 4-8-10 **78** .... JimmyQuinn 2 64
(C A Cyzer) *s.s: hld up in last trio: rdn and no prog over 2f out* **25/1**

1m 23.78s (-2.11) **Going Correction** -0.025s/f (Stan)
WFA 3 from 4yo+ 1lb **13** Ran SP% **128.9**
Speed ratings (Par 105):111,110,110,109,109 108,108,107,107,105 104,101,100
CSF £47.62 CT £371.05 TOTE £11.50: £3.90, £2.20, £4.30; EX 67.60 Trifecta £286.40 Part won. Pool: £403.43 - 0.20 winning tickets..
Owner Robert Thomson **Bred** Patrick Kennedy **Trained** Newmarket, Suffolk

FOCUS
This looked like a good handicap, but they finished in a bunch and the bare form should not be taken too literally. The winning time, though, was decent for the grade.
Fast Bowler Official explanation: trainer said gelding was scoped and found to have bled
Chief Exec Official explanation: jockey said gelding missed the break

6462 LINGFIELD PARK GOLF CLUB AMATEUR RIDERS' H'CAP 1m 4f (P)
3:50 (3:50) (Class 5) (0-70,68) 3-Y-O+ **£3,123** (£968; £484; £242) **Stalls** Low

Form RPR

40P2 **1** **Zalkani (IRE)**[7] 6376 6-10-4 **54** .... MrSPearce(3) 1 64
(J Pearce) *dwlt: hld up off the pce: clsd 5f out: trckd ldrs over 2f out: shkn up to ld 1f out: sn in command* **7/2**[1]

2553 **2** 2 **Cormorant Wharf (IRE)**[23] 6108 6-11-1 **67** .... MissJPowell(5) 4 74
(T E Powell) *hld up off the pce: prog on outer over 3f out: led 2f out: pushed along and hdd 1f out: one pce* **7/1**[3]

0401 **3** ¾ **Blue Hedges**[7] 6378 4-10-7 **59** 5ex .... MissALHutchinson(5) 9 65
(H J Collingridge) *dwlt: hld up off the pce: clsd over 3f out: rdn over 1f out: kpt on to take 3rd ins fnl f* **11/2**[2]

5000 **4** 2 **Bramcote Lorne**[7] 6376 3-9-8 **54** oh1 .... MrCAHarris(7) 6 57
(S Parr) *pressed ldrs: led over 3f out to 2f out: nudged along and one pce* **33/1**

0021 **5** 1¼ **Wait For The Will (USA)**[7] 6376 10-11-0 **66** 5ex...(b) MrDHutchison(5) 5 67
(G L Moore) *hld up off the pce: clsd on ldng gp over 2f out: nt qckn over 1f out: one pce after* **7/2**[1]

0066 **6** 2 **Scottish River (USA)**[7] 6376 7-10-11 **58** .... MrLeeNewnes 12 55
(M D I Usher) *s.s: hld up off the pce: prog to trck ldrs over 4f out : cl enough over 2f out: fnd nil* **16/1**

5013 **7** 4 **Makai**[4] 6408 3-10-5 **65** .... (b) RyanBird(7) 8 56
(J J Bridger) *pressed ldrs: squeezed out after 3f: keen after: bmpd along and wknd over 1f out* **12/1**

0006 **8** 1¾ **Piquet**[15] 6232 8-10-2 **54** oh14 .... MrHHaynes(5) 3 42
(J J Bridger) *w ldrs: cl up over 2f out: sn wknd* **100/1**

6403 **9** 2½ **Alexian**[7] 6376 3-10-4 **64** .... MissBKilloran(7) 7 48
(D W P Arbuthnot) *dwlt: hld up off the pce: lost tch w ldng gp 3f out* **8/1**

0310 **10** 5 **Great View (IRE)**[9] 6336 7-11-7 **68** .... (p) MissLEllison 2 44
(Mrs A L M King) *led for 3f: rdn and lost pl rapidly 5f out: sn bhd* **11/2**[2]

00-0 **11** 1½ **Lorikeet**[18] 6189 7-10-13 **60** .... MrJSnowden 11 34
(Noel T Chance) *led after 3f to over 3f out: wknd* **14/1**

4000 **12** 3½ **Colonel Bilko (IRE)**[47] 5625 4-10-0 **54** oh14 .... MrCHughes(7) 10 22
(J J Bridger) *sn trckd ldrs: lost pl over 4f out: sn wknd* **100/1**

2m 34.53s (0.14) **Going Correction** -0.025s/f (Stan)
WFA 3 from 4yo+ 6lb **12** Ran SP% **124.0**
Speed ratings (Par 103):98,96,96,94,94 92,90,88,87,83 82,80
CSF £29.88 CT £137.53 TOTE £4.30: £1.70, £2.90, £2.40; EX 43.40 Trifecta £107.90 Pool: £448.35 - 2.95 winning tickets. Place 6 £30.67, Place 5 £29.76.
Owner Jeff Pearce **Bred** His Highness The Aga Khan's Studs S C **Trained** Newmarket, Suffolk
■ Stewards' Enquiry : Mr J Snowden two-day ban: careless riding (Nov 27,28)

FOCUS
A moderate amateur riders' handicap run at a very muddling tempo. The overall form looks reasonable with the third to recent form.
T/Plt: £75.90 to a £1 stake. Pool: £51,494.90. 494.75 winning tickets. T/Qpdt: £17.90 to a £1 stake. Pool: £3,973.30. 163.90 winning tickets. JN

6420 SOUTHWELL (L-H)
Monday, November 13

OFFICIAL GOING: Standard
Wind: Moderate, behind

6463 BOOK TICKETS ON-LINE MEDIAN AUCTION MAIDEN STKS 5f (F)
1:00 (1:00) (Class 5) 2-Y-O **£3,238** (£963; £481; £240) **Stalls** High

Form RPR

4 **1** **Off The Record**[26] 6047 2-9-3 .... JamieMackay 3 70+
(J G Given) *dwlt and wnt lft s: sn chsng ldrs: led after 2f: pushed clr over 1f out: comf* **8/15**[1]

5200 **2** 4 **Grange Lili (IRE)**[47] 5606 2-8-12 65 .... (b[1]) RobbieFitzpatrick 2 45+
(Peter Grayson) *dwlt and carried lft s: hdwy 1/2-way: rdn to chse wnr wl over 1f out: sn drvn and no imp* **4/1**[2]

0005 **3** ½ **Mandriano (ITY)**[20] 6157 2-8-12 35 .... (p) MarkLawson(5) 1 48
(D W Barker) *cl up: rdn along over 2f out: sn drvn and one pce* **14/1**

0006 **4** 2 **Molto Duro (IRE)**[12] 6296 2-8-5 40 .... (b) LanceBetts(7) 5 36
(N Wilson) *chsd ldrs: rdn along over 2f out: sn one pce* **33/1**

6 **5** nk **Pretty Selma**[16] 6222 2-8-12 .... BrettDoyle 8 35
(R M H Cowell) *dwlt and towards rr: hdwy over 2f out: rdn and hung lft wl over 1f out: no further prog* **11/1**[3]

500 **6** 9 **Mangano**[12] 6295 2-9-3 53 .... TomEaves 7 7
(A Berry) *a outpcd and bhd* **12/1**

0 **7** 7 **Wibbadune (IRE)**[16] 6222 2-8-6 ow1 .... RonanKeogh(7) 4 —
(Peter Grayson) *led 2f: prom tl rdn along 2f out and sn wknd* **33/1**

000 **8** 2 **Tafis Beach**[27] 6034 2-8-12 30 .... (b[1]) RobertHavlin 6 —
(J R Jenkins) *chsd ldrs to 1/2-way: sn wknd* **33/1**

60.06 secs (-0.24) **Going Correction** -0.125s/f (Stan) **8** Ran SP% **116.7**
Speed ratings (Par 96):96,89,88,85,85 70,59,56
CSF £2.96 TOTE £1.50: £1.02, £1.40, £2.50; EX 3.40.
Owner Ian Henderson **Bred** P Onslow **Trained** Willoughton, Lincs

FOCUS
A poor maiden as usual dominated by the lowest drawn horses over this straight five, and the form is limited by the proximity of the third and fourth.

NOTEBOOK
Off The Record probably did not need to improve much from his Nottingham debut in order to win this. He did not start too well, but shifting left leaving the gates meant he had the perfect route down the centre of the track and it was not long before he had put his rivals to the sword. He will find life much tougher from now on, but is entitled to progress again from this. (op 4-6 tchd 8-11 in a place)
Grange Lili(IRE), who had failed to beat a rival in her last two outings, returned to something like her best form in the first-time blinkers, but she did have a decent draw so is still to convince that she has what it takes to win a race. (op 7-2)

Mandriano(ITY), beaten a total of 118 lengths in his previous four outings, appeared to run much better here having raced up with the pace for much of the way, but he did have the plum draw and is rated just 35, so it would be unwise to take too much notice of this performance. (op 16-1)
Molto Duro(IRE), unplaced in all five of her previous starts, is another with a plater's mark and achieved nothing.
Pretty Selma did not progress from her debut as might have been hoped and her only defence may be that she was not well drawn. (op 9-1)

6464 HOSPITALITY PACKAGES AVAILABLE APPRENTICE H'CAP (DIV I) 6f (F)
1:30 (1:30) (Class 6) (0-64,63) 3-Y-0+ **£2,590** (£770; £385; £192) **Stalls** Low

Form RPR
0500 **1** **Windy Prospect**[62] 5267 4-8-0 **50** oh4........................ JosephWalsh(5) 2 63
(P A Blockley) *cl up: led wl over 1f out: sn rdn and kpt on wl u.p fnl f* **9/2**[2]
2460 **2** 1 3/4 **Sweet Pickle**[55] 5453 5-9-4 **63**................................(e) JamesMillman 10 71
(J R Boyle) *hld up in rr: hdwy on outer 3f out: rdn to chse wnr over 1f out: sn drvn and kpt on: nt rch wnr* **6/4**[1]
-054 **3** 6 **Blythe Spirit**[273] 401 7-8-1 **51**..........................(p) JamesRogers(5) 6 41
(R A Fahey) *led: rdn along wl over 2f out: hdd wl over 1f out and sn one pce* **7/1**[3]
1500 **4** 4 **Further Outlook (USA)**[42] 5737 12-8-10 **62**..................(t) TJHowell(7) 4 40
(Miss Gay Kelleway) *prom: pushed along: edgd lft and outpcd 1/2-way: styd on u.p fnl 2f* **10/1**
/620 **5** nk **Tamworth (IRE)**[5] 6396 4-9-1 **60**.................................. SCreighton 1 37
(E J Creighton) *hld up: hdwy on inner whn hmpd 1/2-way: swtchd rt and rdn 2f out: kpt on ins last: nrst fin* **8/1**
0040 **6** shd **Majik**[105] 3995 7-9-0 **59**..(p) KevinGhunowa 8 36
(P T Midgley) *dwlt: hdwy to chse ldrs 1/2-way: rdn along over 2f out and sn one pce* **16/1**
0600 **7** 1 3/4 **Amber Glory**[10] 6315 3-8-10 **55**.................................(b) ThomasO'Brien 9 26
(K A Ryan) *prom: rdn along wl over 2f out and sn wknd* **20/1**
3042 **8** 1 **Hill Of Almhuim (IRE)**[26] 6057 3-8-7 **52**....................(b[1]) RonanKeogh 3 20
(Peter Grayson) *dwlt: sn outpcd and a bhd* **15/2**
0-00 **9** 1 3/4 **Tancred Times**[11] 6308 11-8-5 **50** oh5.......................... DonnaCaldwell 7 13
(D W Barker) *chsd ldrs: rdn along over 2f out: drvn wl over 1f out and sn wknd* **40/1**
6600 **10** 2 1/2 **Amanda's Lad (IRE)**[41] 5752 6-8-7 **52**.......................... RussellKennemore 5 8
(M C Chapman) *sn pushed along and in tch: rdn 1/2-way and sn wknd* **16/1**

1m 16.53s (-0.37) **Going Correction** +0.075s/f (Slow) **10** Ran SP% **121.6**
Speed ratings (Par 101):105,102,94,89,88 88,86,85,82,79
CSF £12.16 CT £49.73 TOTE £5.30: £2.40, £1.10, £2.90; EX 18.30.
Owner Bill Cahill **Bred** T J Cooper **Trained** Lambourn, Berks

FOCUS
A moderate handicap rated through the runner-up. The winning time was more than acceptable for the class of contest, despite being almost a second slower than the second division.

6465 HOSPITALITY PACKAGES AVAILABLE APPRENTICE H'CAP (DIV II) 6f (F)
2:00 (2:00) (Class 6) (0-64,63) 3-Y-0+ **£2,590** (£770; £385; £192) **Stalls** Low

Form RPR
21 **1** **La Colline (GER)**[31] 5949 3-8-7 **52**.................................. PatrickHills 5 71+
(W J Haggas) *trckd ldrs: smooth hdwy over 2f out: rdn to ld over 1f out: clr ins last* **11/8**[1]
0000 **2** 5 **Elusive Warrior (USA)**[60] 5316 3-8-5 **55**...............(p) JamesRogers(5) 1 59
(R A Fahey) *in tch on inner: swtchd rt and hdwy over 2f out: rdn wl over 1f out: styd on fnl f* **20/1**
0500 **3** 1 1/2 **Canadian Danehill (IRE)**[10] 6315 4-9-4 **63**.................... JamieJones 9 63
(R M H Cowell) *prom: hdwy to ld wl over 2f out: sn rdn: edgd rt and hdd over 1f out: wknd ins last* **16/1**
4006 **4** nk **Prettilini**[10] 6323 3-8-11 **59**.. NeilBrown(3) 7 58
(R Brotherton) *in tch: hdwy over 2f out: rdn to chse ldrs over 1f out: kpt on same pce* **17/2**[3]
2002 **5** 1 **Bond Playboy**[13] 6288 6-9-3 **62**.......................................(p) LukeMorris 8 58
(G R Oldroyd) *sn rdn along in rr: hdwy 2f out: styd on u.p appr last: nt rch ldrs* **5/2**[2]
1300 **6** 4 **Muara**[44] 5684 4-8-8 **53**... DonnaCaldwell 2 37
(D W Barker) *chsd ldng pair: rdn along wl over 2f out: grad wknd* **16/1**
2530 **7** 3 1/2 **Favouring (IRE)**[61] 5286 4-8-10 **55**.......................(v) RussellKennemore 3 28
(M C Chapman) *led: rdn along 1/2-way: sn hdd & wknd* **9/1**
0005 **8** 1 1/2 **Hout Bay**[13] 6276 9-8-2 **50** oh5..........................(b) DanielleMcCreery(3) 4 19
(D W Chapman) *s.i.s: a rr* **25/1**
1350 **9** 8 **Dark Moon**[54] 5474 3-8-6 **51**... KellyHarrison 6 —
(D Shaw) *a rr* **20/1**
0605 **10** 3/4 **Geordie Dancer (IRE)**[89] 4473 4-8-0 **50** oh10...............(p) MCGeran(5) 10 —
(A Berry) *a rr* **100/1**

1m 15.57s (-1.33) **Going Correction** +0.075s/f (Slow) **26** Ran SP% **117.3**
Speed ratings (Par 101):111,104,102,101,100 95,90,88,77,76
CSF £37.43 CT £335.97 TOTE £2.00: £1.10, £4.20, £7.00; EX 31.70.
Owner Snowdrop Stud Co Limited **Bred** Graf And Grafin Von Stauffenberg **Trained** Newmarket, Suffolk

FOCUS
A moderate contest with the winner a class apart, and very smart winning time for the grade and almost a second faster than the first division.

6466 EUROPEAN BREEDERS' FUND MAIDEN STKS 7f (F)
2:30 (2:30) (Class 5) 2-Y-0 **£3,562** (£1,059; £529; £264) **Stalls** Low

Form RPR
00 **1** **Sularno**[18] 6188 2-9-3 .... RobertHavlin 4 65
(H Morrison) *trckd ldrs: hdwy on outer 3f out: led 2f out: sn rdn: drvn ins last and hld on wl* **14/1**
4 **2** hd **Letham Island (IRE)**[10] 6316 2-8-12 .... JoeFanning 3 59
(M Johnston) *set stdy pce: pushed along and hdd 2f out: sn rdn: rallied and ev ch ins last: jst hld* **5/2**[2]
4 **3** 3/4 **Little Eskimo**[17] 6199 2-9-3 .... TomEaves 1 63
(B Smart) *trckd ldrs: pushed along and sltly outpcd 3f out: rdn and hdwy wl over 1f out: ch ent last: sn drvn and no ex* **10/11**[1]
05 **4** 5 **Falcon's Fire (IRE)**[10] 6316 2-9-3 .... VHalliday 6 50
(Mrs A Duffield) *keen: cl up: ev ch 2f out tl rdn and wknd ent last* **33/1**
4005 **5** 2 1/2 **Flying Grey (IRE)**[10] 6322 2-8-12 56....................(b[1]) KevinGhunowa(5) 2 43
(P A Blockley) *trckd ldrs: n.m.r after 1f: effrt 3f out: sn rdn and wknd 2f out* **8/1**[3]
00 **6** 2 1/2 **Exit Strategy (IRE)**[10] 6324 2-9-3 .... PaulHanagan 5 37
(W J Haggas) *hld up: effrt over 2f out: sn rdn and no hdwy* **17/2**

1m 32.79s (1.99) **Going Correction** +0.075s/f (Slow) **6** Ran SP% **112.2**
Speed ratings (Par 96):91,90,89,84,81 78
CSF £48.88 TOTE £13.10: £5.40, £1.10; EX 56.80.
Owner Miss B Swire **Bred** Miss B Swire **Trained** East Ilsley, Berks
■ Stewards' Enquiry : Joe Fanning one-day ban: careless riding (Nov 24)

FOCUS
A moderate juvenile maiden and not easy to rate. The first three came clear.

NOTEBOOK
Sularno, who had shown little in two previous outings, relished the switch to the Fibresand and showed a good attitude to get off the mark. He is clearly going the right way now and, while his future lies with the Handicapper, this scopey colt should have no trouble getting a bit further next year. (tchd 12-1)
Letham Island(IRE) had her chance from the front and proved game in defeat. Her dam was a dual 11-furlong winner and the way this filly was coming back towards the finish would suggest she is well worth a step up to a mile now. (op 9-4 tchd 3-1)
Little Eskimo, fourth in a much better contest on debut 17 days previously, was well backed to go one better on this All-Weather bow. However, having travelled kindly through the early parts, he found himself outpaced turning for home, and may have been at a disadvantage in being kept to the far side for his effort in the straight. He is clearly up to finding a race during the winter, but may be better switching to a Polytrack surface next time. (op Evens)
Falcon's Fire(IRE), just behind the runner-up at Musselburgh last time, showed just about his best form to date and now qualifies for a nursery mark. He handled the surface without any fuss, and can be expect to get a mile before too long, but will have to learn to settle better if he is to progress. (op 25-1)

6467 ARENA LEISURE H'CAP 1m 6f (F)
3:00 (3:00) (Class 3) (0-95,85) 3-Y-0+ **£8,096** (£2,408; £1,203; £601) **Stalls** Low

Form RPR
2442 **1** **Velvet Heights (IRE)**[21] 6148 4-9-12 **83**............................ IanMongan 2 96+
(J L Dunlop) *trckd ldg pair: hdwy 5f out: led on bit over 2f out: pushed clr ent last: kpt on wl* **5/2**[2]
0306 **2** 5 **Most Definitely (IRE)**[17] 6205 6-9-5 **76**...................... FergusSweeney 1 82
(R M Stronge) *trckd ldrs: smooth hdwy 4f out: chal 2f out: sn rdn and ev ch tl drvn and one pce ent last* **9/1**
1213 **3** 6 **At The Money**[17] 6205 3-8-5 **70**.. PaulHanagan 4 68
(J M P Eustace) *led: rdn along over 3f out: hdd over 2f out: sn drvn and wknd* **1/1**[1]
1360 **4** 1 3/4 **Country Pursuit (USA)**[9] 6336 4-10-0 **85**........................... BrettDoyle 3 80
(C E Brittain) *trckd ldr: pushed along 4f out: rdn wl over 2f out and sn outpcd* **7/2**[3]

3m 9.73s (0.13) **Going Correction** +0.075s/f (Slow)
WFA 3 from 4yo+ 8lb **4** Ran SP% **110.8**
Speed ratings (Par 107):102,99,95,94
CSF £19.44 TOTE £3.30; EX 17.30.
Owner Windflower Overseas Holdings Inc **Bred** Windflower Overseas **Trained** Arundel, W Sussex

FOCUS
A disappointing turnout for the money and although the winner scored as he liked not easy to say how strong the race was.

NOTEBOOK
Velvet Heights(IRE), back over a more suitable trip, travelled like a dream throughout and, with his rider barely moving a muscle, cantered home to win on the bit. There will not be many opportunities for him on this surface, especially when he is reassessed, but may find something back on Polytrack given a suitable test of stamina. (op 10-3)
Most Definitely(IRE) travelled almost as well as the winner out the back of the field for most of the way, but once asked for his effort he was unable to get his rival off the bridle let alone offer a threat. He is on a lengthy losing run, but this was only his third try on sand and he looks worth another try. (tchd 8-1)
At The Money, 12lb higher than when a beaten favourite in his only previous sand start here in April, was allowed to set his own modest pace yet was still comfortably swept aside. On this evidence his improvement on turf this year has not been matched on sand. (op 11-8)
Country Pursuit(USA) settled well enough behind the leader, but did not find much off the bridle and seemed to find this trip on this slow surface too much for him. (op 9-4 tchd 4-1)

6468 SOUTHWELL-RACECOURSE.CO.UK H'CAP 1m 3f (F)
3:30 (3:30) (Class 2) (0-100,92) 3-Y-0+
£11,217 (£3,358; £1,679; £840; £419; £210) **Stalls** Low

Form RPR
2020 **1** **St Savarin (FR)**[9] 6336 5-9-2 **82**.. PaulHanagan 6 89
(R A Fahey) *trckd ldrs: hdwy on outer over 2f out: rdn and hung lft over 1f out: styd on to ld last 100 yds* **7/4**[1]
0401 **2** 3/4 **Heathyards Pride**[13] 6287 6-9-0 **80**.......................... GrahamGibbons 2 86
(R Hollinshead) *keen: trckd ldrs: effrt and swtchd lft 2f out: rdn to ld 1f out: sn edgd rt and drvn: hdd and no ex last 100 yds* **9/1**
0000 **3** 2 1/2 **Baan (USA)**[60] 5310 3-9-7 **92**... JoeFanning 4 94
(M Johnston) *led: rdn along over 3f out: hdd over 2f out: drvn and kpt on sme pce appr last* **11/2**[3]
3005 **4** 1 1/2 **Bobby Charles**[152] 2540 5-8-13 **79**................................ DarrylHolland 5 78
(Dr J D Scargill) *trckd ldrs: hdwy 3f out: rdn 2f out and ev ch tl drvn and wknd appr last* **7/1**
4025 **5** nk **Lake Poet (IRE)**[9] 6337 3-8-10 **81**.................................... BrettDoyle 1 80
(C E Brittain) *trckd ldr: hdwy 3f out: led over 2f out: sn rdn: drvn and hdd 1f out: sn wknd* **2/1**[2]
/00- **6** 5 **Credit (IRE)**[26] 3365 5-9-4 **80** ow4........................... LiamTreadwell(5) 3 80
(Jennie Candlish) *in tch: rdn along 4f out: outpcd fnl 3f* **100/1**

2m 29.22s (0.32) **Going Correction** +0.075s/f (Slow)
WFA 3 from 5yo+ 5lb **6** Ran SP% **108.6**
Speed ratings (Par 109):101,100,98,97,97 93
CSF £16.44 TOTE £3.20: £1.30, £3.00; EX 12.20.
Owner J H Tattersall **Bred** F W Holtkotter **Trained** Musley Bank, N Yorks

FOCUS
Something of a tactical affair and the front five were all in a line across the track entering the final furlong. The winning time was moderate for a race of its class and the form does not appear that strong.

NOTEBOOK
St Savarin(FR), 6lb higher than when last seen on sand but still 8lb lower than on turf, came off the bridle earlier than the majority of his rivals, but he does stay particularly well and responded to pressure to grind out a determined if narrow victory. He should not go up much for this and may find other opportunities on this surface. (op 15-8 tchd 2-1)
Heathyards Pride, raised 3lb for his Wolverhampton victory, had every chance and did nothing wrong. He stays further than this, is basically consistent, and should win another race or two on this surface this winter. (op 8-1)
Baan(USA), on sand for the first time, was allowed an uncontested lead and fought back in typically brave fashion for a horse from the yard when the challengers arrived, but considering he was contesting Group races in the spring he has become very disappointing and is going to remain hard to place. (op 5-1 tchd 9-2)
Bobby Charles appeared to be travelling better than anything turning for home, but once out under pressure found less than looked likely. This was his first outing since June, but he has won after a similar break in the past so it remains to be seen whether he will come on much for this. (op 6-1 tchd 8-1)

The Form Book, Raceform Ltd, Compton, RG20 6NL

Lake Poet(IRE), rated 8lb lower on sand than on turf, had as good a chance as any starting up the home straight but failed to get home. This testing surface may have just found him out. (op 15-8)

6469 RACING HERE TOMORROW H'CAP 1m (F)
4:00 (4:00) (Class 5) (0-75,75) 3-Y-0+ **£3,238** (£963; £481; £240) **Stalls** Low

Form RPR

4002 **1** **Red Contact (USA)**[4] 6417 5-8-13 **70**........................(p) DanielTudhope 3 86
(A Dickman) *mde all: rdn 2f out: drvn and edgd lft over 1f out: styd on wl* **3/1**[2]

0002 **2** *5* **Kabeer**[21] 6147 8-8-9 **71**..(t) NataliaGemelova(5) 9 77
(A J McCabe) *prom: cl up 1/2-way: effrt over 2f out: sn rdn and ev ch tl drvn and one pce appr last* **6/1**

2362 **3** *6* **Peruvian Prince (USA)**[30] 5972 4-8-8 **65**........................ PaulHanagan 6 58
(R A Fahey) *hld up and bhd: hdwy whn n.m.r over 3f out and wl over 2f out: styd on appr last: nvr nr ldrs* **13/8**[1]

0420 **4** *1 ½* **Top Mark**[15] 6239 4-9-3 **74**..(ve[1]) DarryllHolland 8 64
(J R Boyle) *in tch on outer: rdn along 3f out: drvn and no imp 2f out* **9/2**[3]

0600 **5** *5* **Startori**[51] 5538 3-9-2 **75**..(v[1]) PaulEddery 4 54
(B Smart) *chsd ldng pair: rdn along 3f out: sn drvn and wknd* **16/1**

0000 **6** *8* **Stolen Summer (IRE)**[13] 6273 3-8-6 **65**.................. SilvestreDeSousa 7 27
(B S Rothwell) *a towards rr* **33/1**

3000 **7** *6* **Sinner Or Saint (IRE)**[14] 6260 3-8-3 **62**............................ DaleGibson 5 12
(T D Easterby) *in tch: rdn along and bhd fr 1/2-way* **25/1**

0-00 **8** *4* **Never Will**[16] 6226 5-9-4 **75**.. PatCosgrave 1 16
(K A Ryan) *chsd ldrs on inner: rdn along over 4f out: sn wknd* **16/1**

00/0 **9** *9* **Theme Time (USA)**[77] 4881 10-8-8 **65** oh26 ow4....(t) DerekMcGaffin 10 —
(D Morris) *in tch: rdn along 1/2-way: wkng whn hung lft 3f out: sn bhd* **100/1**

1m 43.37s (-1.23) **Going Correction** +0.075s/f (Slow)
WFA 3 from 4yo+ 2lb **9** Ran SP% **115.1**
Speed ratings (Par 103):109,104,98,96,91 83,77,73,64
CSF £20.99 CT £38.15 TOTE £3.20: £1.40, £1.60, £1.10; EX 15.20 Place 6 £62.50, Place 5 £54.10.
Owner Miss Sini Lehkonen **Bred** Shadwell Farm LLC **Trained** Sandhutton, N Yorks

FOCUS
Very few ever got into this and the front pair had the race to themselves from halfway. A solid pace resulted in a decent winning time for the grade and the race is rated at face value through the runner-up.
T/Plt: £32.90 to a £1 stake. Pool: £42,895.90. 951.60 winning tickets. T/Qpdt: £24.60 to a £1 stake. Pool: £2,128.10. 63.90 winning tickets. JR

6463 SOUTHWELL (L-H)
Tuesday, November 14

OFFICIAL GOING: Standard
Wind: Almost nil Weather: Cool, light drizzle turning to more persistent rain.

6470 BOOK HOSPITALITY HERE H'CAP (DIV I) 6f (F)
12:20 (12:26) (Class 6) (0-55,55) 3-Y-0+ **£2,047** (£604; £302) **Stalls** Low

Form RPR

0206 **1** **Guadaloup**[7] 6389 4-8-10 **51**..(v[1]) DeanMernagh 6 60
(M Brittain) *w ldrs: edgd lft and led over 2f out: styd far side: hrd rdn: kpt on wl* **12/1**

5213 **2** *1 ¾* **Preskani**[4] 6425 4-8-9 **50**..(p) DanielTudhope 11 54
(Mrs N Macauley) *hdwy on outer over 2f out: edgd rt and c stands' side: styd on to take 2nd ins last* **5/2**[1]

-300 **3** *nk* **Glamaraazi (IRE)**[59] 5370 3-8-13 **54**............................ PaulHanagan 10 57+
(R A Fahey) *trckd ldrs: styd on fnl f* **16/1**

0302 **4** *nk* **Blakeshall Quest**[12] 6308 6-8-8 **49**..................................(b) PatCosgrave 2 51
(R Brotherton) *led: hdd: hmpd and swtchd rt over 2f out: kpt on same pce fnl f* **8/1**

0000 **5** *1 ½* **Doctor Dennis (IRE)**[32] 5937 9-9-0 **55**..................(v) MichaelTebbutt 13 52
(J Pearce) *s.i.s: racd wd: styd on wl fnl 2f* **14/1**

03-0 **6** *1 ¼* **Topiary Ted**[13] 6300 4-8-12 **53**..(t) SteveDrowne 1 47
(H Morrison) *lost pl over 4f out: hdwy u.p over 2f out: nvr rchd ldrs: eased towards fin* **4/1**[2]

5345 **7** *1* **Four Amigos (USA)**[12] 6308 5-8-7 **48**.............................. JoeFanning 8 39
(I A Wood) *chsd ldrs: one pce fnl 2f* **10/1**

2100 **8** *2* **Only If I Laugh**[19] 6193 5-9-0 **55**...................................... DaneO'Neill 12 40
(R A Harris) *prom: outpcd 3f out: no threat after* **15/2**[3]

9 *1 ¼* **Claws**[75] 4977 3-8-11 **52**.. RichardThomas 3 33
(A J Lidderdale) *chsd ldrs: lost pl over 1f out* **14/1**

0005 **10** *¾* **Madam Patti**[33] 5928 3-8-3 **47**...................................... NeilChalmers(3) 9 26
(B Palling) *chsd ldrs: wknd over 1f out* **66/1**

2600 **11** *11* **Witchelle**[125] 3398 5-9-0 **55**.. DavidAllan 5 1
(R Craggs) *w ldrs: lost pl 2f out: heavily eased* **16/1**

1m 17.42s (0.52) **Going Correction** -0.075s/f (Stan) **11** Ran SP% **114.8**
Speed ratings (Par 101):93,90,90,89,87 86,84,82,80,79 64
CSF £39.39 CT £432.83 TOTE £15.10: £3.80, £1.50, £5.00; EX 53.20 TRIFECTA Not won..
Owner Northgate Red **Bred** Cheveley Park Stud Ltd **Trained** Warthill, N Yorks

FOCUS
A moderate winning time for the grade, 0.56 seconds slower than the second division. Just modest form rated through the winner.

6471 SOUTHWELL-RACECOURSE.CO.UK CLAIMING STKS 7f (F)
12:50 (12:53) (Class 6) 2-Y-0 **£2,730** (£806; £403) **Stalls** Low

Form RPR

0400 **1** **Homes By Woodford**[17] 6208 2-8-7 48........................ PaulMulrennan 8 52+
(M W Easterby) *w ldrs: led 3f out: edgd rt and rdn clr over 1f out* **4/1**[2]

6000 **2** *6* **Taran Tregarth**[27] 6049 2-8-4 35..(b) PaulQuinn 9 33
(A Bailey) *chsd ldrs: outpcd 3f out: hdwy over 1f out: tk 2nd ins last* **28/1**

0400 **3** *1* **The Light Fandango**[49] 5586 2-9-0 50.............................. DaneO'Neill 3 41
(R A Harris) *s.i.s: hdwy on inner over 4f out: edgd rt and one pce fnl 2f* **11/1**

0500 **4** *4* **Pas De Trois**[7] 6385 2-8-7 45.. DeanMcKeown 4 23
(J Pearce) *s.i.s: hld up: kpt on fnl 2f: nvr trbld ldrs* **6/1**[3]

3000 **5** *½* **Little Tiny Tom**[20] 6172 2-8-8 50..................................(p) RoryMoore(5) 7 28
(C N Kellett) *chsd ldrs: wknd ins last* **14/1**

0006 **6** *2 ½* **Desirable Dancer (IRE)**[6] 6401 2-8-3 54.............. TolleyDean(7) 1 19
(R A Harris) *w ldrs: wknd fnl f* **9/1**

005 **7** *½* **Dazzling Olivia (IRE)**[78] 4887 2-8-6 46.......................... PaulHanagan 5 13
(R A Fahey) *chsd ldrs: drvn 4f out: nvr a threat* **15/8**[1]

5060 **8** *15* **Auction Boy**[12] 6311 2-8-9 58.. PhillipMakin 2 —
(B Palling) *led tl 3f out: sn wknd: bhd and eased 1f out* **12/1**

0 **9** *11* **Zaafira (SPA)**[19] 6186 2-8-10.. JimCrowley 6 —
(E J Creighton) *chsd ldrs: lost pl over 2f out: bhd and heavily eased 1f out* **15/2**

1m 32.05s (1.25) **Going Correction** -0.075s/f (Stan) **9** Ran SP% **117.0**
Speed ratings (Par 94):89,82,81,76,75 73,72,55,42
CSF £105.33 TOTE £5.90: £1.60, £5.50, £3.20; EX 311.20 TRIFECTA Not won..The winner was claimed by R. A. Harris for £4,000.
Owner Woodford Group Plc **Bred** Mrs H B Raw **Trained** Sheriff Hutton, N Yorks

FOCUS
A very moderate claimer but a clear-cut winner.

NOTEBOOK
Homes By Woodford, easily the biggest in the line-up, forged clear up the home straight to account for a poor lot by a wide margin. He was claimed for £4,000. (op 5-1 tchd 6-1)
Taran Tregarth, who had shown precious little previously, is rated just 35 which does not say much for those behind her. (op 20-1)
The Light Fandango, making her All-Weather debut, missed the break slightly. Making her effort on the inner she came way from the rail and lost second inside the last. (op 10-1 tchd 9-1 and 12-1)
Pas De Trois, warm on a cold day, was dropping back in trip but even at this low level she was still found wanting. (op 7-1 tchd 11-2)
Little Tiny Tom, edgy and awkward to mount, seemed to find this trip on this surface too much. (op 12-1)
Dazzling Olivia(IRE), absent for 11 weeks, started to struggle leaving the back stretch and never threatened to be involved. (op 9-4 tchd 5-2 and 7-4)
Zaafira(SPA) Official explanation: trainer said filly caught its mouth on leaving stalls

6472 BOOK YOUR CHRISTMAS PARTY HERE NURSERY 6f (F)
1:20 (1:21) (Class 6) (0-65,65) 2-Y-0 **£2,590** (£770; £385; £192) **Stalls** Low

Form RPR

2020 **1** **Jord (IRE)**[31] 5958 2-9-2 **65**.. NataliaGemelova(5) 3 70
(A J McCabe) *trckd ldrs: styd on wl to ld last 75yds* **7/2**[1]

0560 **2** *1 ¼* **Le Masque**[13] 6291 2-8-11 **60**.. MarkLawson(5) 1 61
(B Smart) *mde most: rdn over 2f out: hdd and no ex ins last* **9/2**[2]

0000 **3** *5* **Spinning Game**[13] 6296 2-8-1 **45**.. PaulQuinn 2 31
(D W Chapman) *dwlt: sn w ldrs: one pce fnl 2f* **20/1**

0000 **4** *1* **Storm Mission (USA)**[4] 6422 2-9-1 **59**........................(b[1]) SteveDrowne 9 42
(Miss V Haigh) *sn w ldrs: one pce fnl 2f* **16/1**

0430 **5** *2 ½* **Pietersen (IRE)**[4] 6422 2-8-9 **60**..................................(b) DeanHeslop(7) 8 36
(T D Barron) *s.i.s: bhd tl hdwy on wd outside over 2f out: kpt on: nvr nr ldrs* **9/2**[2]

0056 **6** *1* **Ishibee (IRE)**[5] 6416 2-9-1 **59**..(p) JimCrowley 10 32
(Mrs A Duffield) *trckd ldrs: rdn over 2f out: one pce* **7/2**[1]

0000 **7** *1 ½* **Hits Only Vic (USA)**[56] 5458 2-8-8 **52**.......................... DeanMcKeown 6 20
(J Pearce) *sn outpcd and bhd: kpt on fnl 2f: nvr on terms* **6/1**[3]

0005 **8** *11* **Kyoto City**[14] 6278 2-7-5 **42** oh7............................ DanielleMcCreery(7) 4 —
(D W Chapman) *swtchd lft after s: lost pl over 4f out: sn bhd* **25/1**

000 **9** *20* **Imperial Style (IRE)**[106] 3994 2-7-13 **43** oh2 ow1........... PaulHanagan 5 —
(D Shaw) *mid-div: outpcd and lost pl over 4f out: sn bhd* **28/1**

1m 17.15s (0.25) **Going Correction** -0.075s/f (Stan) **9** Ran SP% **113.0**
Speed ratings (Par 94):95,93,86,85,82 80,78,64,37
CSF £18.30 CT £233.07 TOTE £3.30: £1.60, £2.00, £5.10; EX 20.40 Trifecta £218.70 Part won. Pool: £308.05 - 0.67 winning tickets..
Owner Paul J Dixon **Bred** M Channon **Trained** Babworth, Notts

FOCUS
A weak nursery and the form is weak, but an improved effort from both the first two.

NOTEBOOK
Jord(IRE), a decent type, travelled very strongly but took an age to gain the upper hand. She took a deal of pulling up. (op 4-1 tchd 9-2)
Le Masque, who came in for sustained support, was very warm on a very cool day. He made the running and really stretched out and battled but the winner had his measure near the line. (op 6-1 tchd 4-1)
Spinning Game, having her first taste of Fibresand, quickly recovered from a tardy start but the first two ran right away from her in the final two furlongs. (op 16-1)
Storm Mission(USA), making a quick return, ran better than on his two most recent outings forced to race on the outside from his high draw. (op 14-1)
Pietersen(IRE), back here after his miserable effort four days earlier, had the blinkers back on. He ran a moody race, staying on down the wide outside after a tardy break. He looks one to have reservations about. (op 4-1)
Ishibee(IRE), despite slipping to a more lenient mark, was unable to get competitive. (op 3-1)

6473 PLAY GOLF COME RACING (S) STKS 1m (F)
1:50 (1:50) (Class 6) 3-Y-0+ **£2,388** (£705; £352) **Stalls** Low

Form RPR

-020 **1** **Formidable Will (FR)**[61] 5316 4-9-0 64........................(tp) DaleGibson 14 64
(M W Easterby) *trckd ldr: led over 2f out: rdn clr fnl f* **4/1**[2]

5005 **2** *4* **For Life (IRE)**[96] 4306 4-9-0 46.. DaneO'Neill 7 55
(A P Jarvis) *led tl over 2f out: kpt on same pce: no ch w wnr* **16/1**

5052 **3** *2 ½* **Wodhill Gold**[33] 5929 5-9-6 47.................................... DerekMcGaffin 10 56
(D Morris) *chsd ldrs: one pce fnl 2f* **8/1**[3]

5040 **4** *¾* **Great Chieftain (IRE)**[11] 6323 3-8-12 60..................(p) PaulHanagan 13 48
(R A Fahey) *trckd ldrs: one pce fnl 2f* **7/2**[1]

0005 **5** *nk* **Sonderborg**[33] 5929 5-8-12 47..................................(p) GregFairley(3) 11 49+
(J Mackie) *in rr: styd on fnl 2f: nt rch ldrs* **11/1**

6062 **6** *1* **Paso Doble**[12] 6304 8-8-7 50.................................... JamesMillman(7) 4 46+
(B R Millman) *in rr: kpt on fnl 2f: nvr on terms* **7/2**[1]

3204 **7** *6* **Crusoe (IRE)**[211] 906 9-9-6 52..(b) DarryllHolland 8 39
(A Sadik) *swtchd wd after 1f: sn chsng ldrs: wknd fnl 2f* **12/1**

4460 **8** *1 ¼* **Dancing Flame**[3] 6448 3-8-7 50..(p) PaulQuinn 2 25
(E J Alston) *n.m.r on inner and lost pl after 1f: sme hdwy on outside over 2f out: nvr on terms* **12/1**

000 **9** *1* **Drawback (IRE)**[15] 6260 3-8-11 59..........................(p) TolleyDean(7) 5 34
(R A Harris) *s.i.s: hdwy into midfield over 4f out: nvr on terms* **16/1**

00 **10** *8* **Hoofbeats Tour**[12] 6302 4-8-7 .... AmyBaker(7) 9 12
(Miss J Feilden) *mid-div: lost pl 3f out* **100/1**

0-00 **11** *10* **Queenstown (IRE)**[8] 6370 5-9-0 45..........................(p) RichardThomas 3 —
(J E Long) *sn drvn along in rr: hmpd on ins 3f out: nvr a factor* **50/1**

0000 **12** *27* **Chilsdown**[59] 5368 3-8-12 47.. PhillipMakin 12 —
(Ronald Thompson) *racd v wd: lost pl 4f out: sn bhd: t.o* **100/1**

0- **13** *16* **The Crunch (IRE)**[78] 4905 5-8-9 ....(t) CatherineGannon 6 —
(Daniel Mark Loughnane, Ire) *chsd ldrs: lost pl over 4f out: bhd and eased over 2f out: t.o* **40/1**

00- **14** *5* **Self Discipline**[11] 2375 4-9-0 .... MichaelTebbutt 1 —
(Mrs L B Normile) *s.i.s: bhd and hung bdly rt after 1f: t.o over 3f out* **66/1**

1m 43.34s (-1.26) **Going Correction** -0.075s/f (Stan)
WFA 3 from 4yo+ 2lb **14** Ran SP% **118.9**
Speed ratings (Par 101):103,99,96,95,95 94,88,87,86,78 68,41,25,20
CSF £64.69 TOTE £5.50: £1.60, £4.30, £2.80; EX 52.40 TRIFECTA Not won..There was no bid for the winner.

Owner Bert and Dilys Kelly **Bred** Gfa Haras Du Hoguenet And Searching Sarl **Trained** Sheriff Hutton, N Yorks

FOCUS

An ordinary seller and the winner had easily the best chance of official ratings. The form has been rated through the third.

6474 EXPERIENCE NOTTINGHAMSHIRE H'CAP 1m 3f (F)

2:20 (2:21) (Class 6) (0-65,65) 3-Y-O+ **£2,590** (£770; £385; £192) **Stalls** Low

Form RPR

4003 **1** **Zed Candy (FR)**[14] 6272 3-8-5 **52** DaleGibson 3 63
(J T Stimpson) *led tl over 5f out: hung rt and led appr fnl f: kpt on* **22/1**

-000 **2** 1 ½ **Prince Of Love (IRE)**[18] 6206 3-9-2 **63** PaulHanagan 4 71
(Jedd O'Keeffe) *chsd ldrs: kpt on to take 2nd ins last* **5/1**[2]

0340 **3** 3 **Jazrawy**[8] 6376 4-8-5 **54** ow4 WilliamCarson(7) 13 57
(P W Hiatt) *chsd ldrs: led over 5f out: hdd appr fnl f: kpt on one pce* **20/1**

623 **4** 2 **Stolen Glance**[29] 6008 3-9-4 **65** PaulMulrennan 7 65
(M W Easterby) *prom: drvn 4f out: hung lft and one pce fnl 2f* **11/2**[3]

2305 **5** 5 **Bienheureux**[8] 6382 5-9-7 **63** (vt) DarryllHolland 6 54
(Miss Gay Kelleway) *mid-div: hdwy u.p over 4f out: wknd over 1f out* **7/1**

0060 **6** 2 ½ **Greenbelt**[16] 6240 5-9-6 **62** DanielTudhope 10 52+
(G M Moore) *bhd: stdy hdwy on outside over 3f out: lost pl over 1f out* **11/4**[1]

0-00 **7** hd **Memphis Belle**[41] 5770 3-8-7 **54** StephenCarson 12 41
(Mrs H Sweeting) *bhd: sme hdwy 4f out: wknd fnl 2f* **80/1**

5416 **8** ¾ **Golden Sprite**[15] 6260 3-9-3 **64** JimCrowley 11 49
(B R Millman) *s.i.s: sme hdwy 4f out: nvr a factor* **16/1**

5530 **9** 5 **Finished Article (IRE)**[8] 6382 9-8-11 **53** J-PGuillambert 9 30
(P A Blockley) *in rr: hdwy on outer 4f out: wknd over 2f out* **9/1**

0302 **10** 1 ¼ **Iamback**[14] 6279 6-8-7 **49** oh4 (t) TPQueally 5 24
(Miss D A McHale) *prom: lost pl over 3f out* **16/1**

2000 **11** 3 **Mi Odds**[141] 2935 10-9-4 **60** PhillipMakin 1 30
(Mrs N Macauley) *mid-div: sme hdwy on outside over 3f out: sn lost pl* **40/1**

4413 **12** 2 ½ **Jadeeron**[8] 6375 7-8-7 **49** oh2 (p) PaulEddery 2 15
(Miss D A McHale) *chsd ldrs: lost pl over 2f out* **7/1**

2330 **13** 16 **Mossmann Gorge**[140] 2956 4-9-3 **59** (v) DaneO'Neill 14 —
(M Wellings) *rr-div: bhd and drvn over 2f out* **25/1**

14 81 **La Commara (IRE)**[20] 6185 4-8-12 **59** (b) JerryO'Dwyer(5) 8 —
(Daniel Mark Loughnane, Ire) *s.i.s: bhd and drvn 7f out: t.o 4f out: virtually p.u* **33/1**

2m 26.89s (-2.01) **Going Correction** -0.075s/f (Stan)
WFA 3 from 4yo+ 5lb **14** Ran SP% **125.1**
Speed ratings (Par 101):104,102,100,99,95 93,93,93,89,88 86,84,72,14
CSF £126.70 CT £2300.61 TOTE £43.80: £11.10, £4.10, £7.00; EX 446.50 TRIFECTA Not won..
Owner J T S (International) Ltd **Bred** Haras De Saint Pair Du Mont **Trained** Newcastle-Under-Lyme, Staffs

FOCUS

A moderate handicap in which nothing was able to get involved from off the pace. The form does not look strong.

Stolen Glance Official explanation: jockey said filly hung left-handed
La Commara(IRE) Official explanation: trainer said filly finished distressed

6475 EUROPEAN BREEDERS' FUND MEDIAN AUCTION MAIDEN STKS 7f (F)

2:50 (2:51) (Class 5) 2-Y-O **£3,238** (£963; £481; £240) **Stalls** Low

Form RPR

0 **1** **Autograph Hunter**[180] 1807 2-9-3 JoeFanning 5 87+
(M Johnston) *s.i.s: sn trcking ldrs: led on bit wl over 1f out: drvn wl clr: v readily* **14/1**

2 8 **Leprechaun's Gold (IRE)** 2-9-3 J-PGuillambert 8 63
(M Johnston) *sn w ldrs: upsides over 2f out: kpt on: no ch w wnr* **5/1**[3]

05 **3** 5 **Compton Charlie**[10] 6331 2-9-3 TPQueally 2 50
(J G Portman) *mde most tl wl over 1f out: wknd fnl f* **3/1**[2]

06 **4** 1 **Doonigan (IRE)**[10] 6331 2-9-3 SteveDrowne 6 48
(A M Balding) *w ldrs: rdn and outpcd over 2f out: kpt on fnl f* **7/1**

2063 **5** hd **Wilmington**[26] 6063 2-9-3 71 DarryllHolland 3 47
(N P Littmoden) *w ldrs: wkng whn hmpd over 1f out* **11/8**[1]

00 **6** 1 ¾ **Golden Folly**[19] 6188 2-9-3 DaleGibson 9 43
(Lady Herries) *hld up in rr: sme hdwy on outside 2f out: nvr trbld ldrs* **25/1**

00 **7** nk **Hora**[15] 6254 2-8-12 JamieMackay 7 37
(Sir Mark Prescott) *hld up in rr: kpt on fnl f: nvr a factor* **50/1**

04 **8** 4 **Shady Green (IRE)**[17] 6207 2-9-3 PaulMulrennan 4 31
(M W Easterby) *sn outpcd and in rr: nvr on terms* **16/1**

1m 30.28s (-0.52) **Going Correction** -0.075s/f (Stan) **8** Ran SP% **114.6**
Speed ratings (Par 96):99,89,84,83,82 80,80,75
CSF £82.27 TOTE £14.60: £4.00, £1.60, £1.50; EX 31.30 Trifecta £448.50 Part won. Pool: £631.73 - 0.77 winning tickets..
Owner A D Spence **Bred** Barry Taylor **Trained** Middleham Moor, N Yorks

FOCUS

A modest maiden but a one-two for trainer Mark Johnston.

NOTEBOOK

Autograph Hunter, who finished tailed off on his debut at York in May and had been absent since, had also been gelded during that time. He was unfancied in the market despite looking to be the stable's first string on jockey bookings, but proved that all wrong by overcoming a slow start and showing signs of greenness to win as he pleased. This was an ordinary race but he has the potential to make up into a fair handicapper. (op 7-1)

Leprechaun's Gold(IRE) was the stable second string on jockey bookings, but was much the stronger in the betting market. He made an encouraging debut but found his stable companion far too strong in the closing stages. He looks to have races in him with this under his belt. (op 9-2 tchd 11-2)

Compton Charlie, who had shown promise on his previous outing, was making his All-Weather debut and trying his longest trip to date. He made much of the running but had no answer when the winner went by halfway up the straight. He know qualifies for a handicap mark and should do better in that sphere. (op 4-1)

Doonigan(IRE) got closer to the third than her had at Windsor last time and, like that rival, is likely to be seen to better effect in handicaps. (op 5-1)

Wilmington with the blinkers left off for this first try on Fibresand, had every chance but faded out of contention in the closing stages. He looks far more effective on turf than the artificial surfaces, having struggled on Polytrack in the past. (op 2-1)

6476 ARENA LEISURE H'CAP 1m (F)

3:20 (3:20) (Class 5) (0-70,69) 3-Y-O+ **£3,238** (£963; £481; £240) **Stalls** Low

Form RPR

000 **1** **Boundless Prospect (USA)**[20] 6176 7-9-3 **68** DarryllHolland 8 80
(Miss Gay Kelleway) *trckd ldrs: styd on to ld last 50yds: drvn out* **4/1**[3]

-500 **2** 1 **Stevedore (IRE)**[5] 6413 5-9-3 **68** PatCosgrave 6 78
(J R Boyle) *w ldrs: led over 4f out: hdd and no ex wl ins last* **5/2**[1]

6010 **3** 2 ½ **Shifty**[4] 6425 7-9-4 **69** DanielTudhope 7 74
(D Carroll) *hld up: effrt 3f out: sn chsng ldrs: kpt on same pce fnl f* **7/2**[2]

/0-0 **4** 5 **Akinola (IRE)**[21] 6160 5-9-2 **67** CatherineGannon 3 62
(K A Ryan) *w ldrs: outpcd and lost pl over 3f out: no threat after* **14/1**

6000 **5** 3 ½ **Sophie'Jo**[31] 5973 3-7-12 **58** AmyBaker(7) 9 45
(Miss J Feilden) *chsd ldrs on outer: lost pl over 2f out* **20/1**

6240 **6** nk **Maud's Cat (IRE)**[73] 5015 3-8-4 **60** NeilChalmers(3) 5 47
(A P Jarvis) *hld up in rr: nvr a threat* **10/1**

0000 **7** 8 **Danelor (IRE)**[13] 6301 8-8-13 **64** DaneO'Neill 2 34
(D Shaw) *sn pushed along in rr: sme hdwy over 2f out: sn btn* **11/1**

6600 **8** 1 **Parkview Love (USA)**[124] 3459 5-8-13 **67** (v) PatrickMathers(3) 1 35
(D Shaw) *s.i.s: sn chsng ldrs: lost pl 2f out* **17/2**

2-04 **9** 3 **Rambling Socks**[22] 6129 3-8-3 **56** ow1 (b) PaulEddery 4 17
(S R Bowring) *t.k.h: led tl over 4f out: lost pl 2f out* **25/1**

1m 42.81s (-1.79) **Going Correction** -0.075s/f (Stan)
WFA 3 from 5yo+ 2lb **9** Ran SP% **114.0**
Speed ratings (Par 103):105,104,101,96,93 92,84,83,80
CSF £14.20 CT £37.27 TOTE £4.40: £1.60, £1.40, £2.20; EX 19.20 Trifecta £40.10 Pool: £429.23 - 7.59 winning tickets..
Owner M M Foulger **Bred** Mrs Edgar Scott Jr & Mrs Lawrence Macelree **Trained** Exning, Suffolk

FOCUS

A decent handicap of its type and run at a true pace also. The field finished well spread out which suggests the form is solid, the third being the best guide.

6477 BOOK HOSPITALITY HERE H'CAP (DIV II) 6f (F)

3:50 (3:51) (Class 6) (0-55,55) 3-Y-O+ **£2,047** (£604; £302) **Stalls** Low

Form RPR

0001 **1** **Bodden Bay**[35] 5885 4-8-13 **54** DarryllHolland 10 63
(D Carroll) *mde virtually all: edgd lft and styd on wl fnl 2f: drvn rt out* **13/2**[3]

5460 **2** 1 ½ **Piccolo Prince**[36] 5865 5-8-12 **53** DavidAllan 2 58+
(E J Alston) *hld up in midfield: effrt over 3f out: kpt on to take 2nd ins last* **8/1**

0004 **3** hd **Orchestration (IRE)**[14] 6276 5-8-6 **47** JoeFanning 5 51+
(M J Attwater) *mid-div: sn pushed along: hdwy on ins to chse ldrs over 1f out: kpt on same pce* **9/1**

2003 **4** shd **Mystic Queen (IRE)**[22] 6129 3-8-11 **52** DaneO'Neill 13 56
(A P Jarvis) *chsd ldrs on outside: kpt on same pce appr fnl f* **18/1**

5461 **5** nk **Barzak (IRE)**[14] 6282 6-8-9 **50** (bt) PhillipMakin 1 53
(S R Bowring) *prom: rdn over 3f out: kpt on wl fnl f* **6/1**[2]

0446 **6** 2 ½ **Millfields Dreams**[3] 6439 7-9-0 **55** (p) TPQueally 9 50
(M G Quinlan) *w ldrs: wknd over 1f out* **7/2**[1]

0015 **7** ¾ **Howards Princess**[21] 6162 4-9-0 **55** (p) DaleGibson 14 48+
(J Hetherton) *racd wd: in rr: styd on fnl 2f: nvr a factor* **18/1**

0314 **8** 2 ½ **Jennverse**[16] 6237 4-8-6 **47** JamieMackay 11 32
(D K Ivory) *chsd ldrs: outpcd 3f out: sn lost pl* **16/1**

0041 **9** ½ **Warden Warren**[16] 6237 8-8-8 **49** (b) SteveDrowne 6 33
(Mrs C A Dunnett) *bhd and drvn along: hdwy on ins over 2f out: wknd over 1f out* **10/1**

0060 **10** 1 ¾ **Mustammer**[3] 6439 3-8-10 **54** (v) PatrickMathers(3) 8 33
(D Shaw) *mid-div: rdn over 3f out: nvr a factor* **33/1**

-500 **11** ½ **Cyfrwys (IRE)**[20] 6174 5-8-6 **50** NeilChalmers(3) 7 27
(B Palling) *w ldrs: wknd over 1f out* **20/1**

1005 **12** 11 **Dannabelle (IRE)**[22] 6142 6-8-11 **52** PatCosgrave 3 —
(John A Quinn, Ire) *mid-div: hmpd and lost pl over 4f out: sn bhd: eased* **11/1**

2040 **L** **Mission Affirmed (USA)**[145] 2793 5-8-10 **51** (b) DanielTudhope 4 —
(Peter Grayson) *reluctant to go to s: virtually ref to r and uns rdr leaving stalls* **17/2**

1m 16.86s (-0.04) **Going Correction** -0.075s/f (Stan) **69** Ran SP% **123.0**
Speed ratings (Par 101):97,95,94,94,94 90,89,86,85,83 82,68,—
CSF £59.64 CT £494.48 TOTE £8.20: £3.30, £4.00, £3.90; EX 67.90 TRIFECTA Not won. Place 6 £486.11, Place 5 £194.18.
Owner Andy Franks & Steve Franks **Bred** Gary Middlemiss **Trained** Warthill, N Yorks

FOCUS

A modest time for a race of its type despite being 0.56 seconds quicker than the first division, and the form looks very ordinary.

T/Jkpt: Not won. T/Plt: £2,029.60 to a £1 stake. Pool: £44,763.80. 16.10 winning tickets. T/Qpdt: £215.20 to a £1 stake. Pool: £3,782.10. 13.00 winning tickets. WG

6447 WOLVERHAMPTON (A.W) (L-H)

Tuesday, November 14

OFFICIAL GOING: Standard

Wind: Light, behind Weather: Overcast with light rain

6478 BOOK ONLINE AT WOLVERHAMPTON-RACECOURSE.CO.UK H'CAP 5f 216y(P)

3:45 (3:49) (Class 5) (0-75,75) 3-Y-O+ **£3,562** (£1,059; £529; £264) **Stalls** Low

Form RPR

0001 **1** **Briannsta (IRE)**[17] 6223 4-9-2 **75** AdamKirby 7 85+
(C G Cox) *chsd ldrs: led 2f out: drvn out* **9/4**[1]

0023 **2** nk **Witchry**[14] 6274 4-8-10 **69** LPKeniry 5 79+
(A G Newcombe) *hld up: hdwy over 2f out: swtchd lft fnl f: sn rdn: r.o* **15/2**

4100 **3** 1 ½ **Inch By Inch**[70] 5096 7-8-11 **73** (b) AmirQuinn(3) 4 78
(P J Makin) *hld up: hmpd wl over 3f out: hdwy over 2f out: rdn and edgd lft ins fnl f: styd on* **14/1**

2426 **4** shd **Charles Parnell (IRE)**[11] 6326 3-8-11 **70** JimmyFortune 3 75
(M Dods) *hld up in tch: rdn over 1f out: styd on same pce ins fnl f* **5/2**[2]

0005 **5** 1 ½ **Ever Cheerful**[9] 6353 5-8-13 **75** ow5 DNolan(3) 12 75
(D G Bridgwater) *s.i.s: outpcd: hdwy over 1f out: nt rch ldrs* **20/1**

2100 **6** 2 ½ **Corrib (IRE)**[16] 6239 3-8-13 **72** FergusSweeney 2 65
(B Palling) *s.i.s: sn prom: rdn 1/2-way: wknd over 1f out* **33/1**

1463 **7** 1 ½ **Sovereignty (JPN)**[13] 6293 4-8-4 **63** ChrisCatlin 9 51
(D K Ivory) *mid-div: rdn 1/2-way: n.d* **12/1**

0005 **8** 1 ¼ **Blue Maeve**[16] 6239 6-8-13 **72** SilvestreDeSousa 11 56
(A D Brown) *chsd ldrs: rdn over 2f out: wknd fnl f: eased* **10/1**

0055 **9** shd **Johnston's Diamond (IRE)**[11] 6326 8-8-6 **65** JimmyQuinn 1 49
(E J Alston) *led: rdn and hdd 2f out: wknd ins fnl f* **13/2**[3]

-00 **10** nk **Katie Boo (IRE)**[17] 6212 4-8-8 **67** ow2 TomEaves 6 50
(A Berry) *s.i.s: and stmbld s: outpcd* **40/1**

0550 **11** ¾ **Kings Heir (IRE)**[72] 5042 3-8-6 **72** (b) RonanKeogh(7) 10 53
(Peter Grayson) *prom: rdn 1/2-way: wknd 2f out* **25/1**

The Form Book, Raceform Ltd, Compton, RG20 6NL

0006 **12** ¾ **Canina**[172] 1983 3-8-6 **65** ow1 .... EddieAhern 8 44
(Ms Deborah J Evans) *chsd ldrs 4f out* **33/1**

1m 14.37s (-1.44) **Going Correction** -0.05s/f (Stan) **12** Ran SP% **124.8**
Speed ratings (Par 103):107,106,104,104,102 99,97,95,95,94 93,92
CSF £19.81 CT £205.67 TOTE £2.60: £1.50, £1.40, £5.40; EX 23.90.
Owner B Brooks **Bred** Anthony M Cahill **Trained** Lambourn, Berks
■ Stewards' Enquiry : Ronan Keogh two-day ban: careless riding (Nov 25,27)

FOCUS
A fair handicap run at a good pace, and rated around the third.

6479 RINGSIDE SUITE 700 THEATRE STYLE CONFERENCE H'CAP 1m 5f 194y(P)
4:20 (4:20) (Class 5) (0-70,70) 3-Y-0+ **£3,412** (£1,007; £504) **Stalls** Low

Form RPR
0000 **1** **Your Amount (IRE)**[36] 5868 3-8-11 **61** .... JDSmith 5 72
(W J Musson) *s.i.s: hld up: hdwy over 3f out: rdn to ld over 1f out: styd on* **16/1**

2503 **2** 1¼ **Tranquilizer**[12] 6312 4-10-0 **70** .... (t) EddieAhern 6 79
(D J Coakley) *led 1f: stdd and sn lost pl: hdwy 4f out: led on bit over 2f out: rdn and hdd over 1f out: styd on same pce* **9/2**[3]

3420 **3** ¾ **Salute (IRE)**[18] 6205 7-9-10 **66** .... RobertHavlin 2 74
(P G Murphy) *hld up in tch: lost pl 8f out: hdwy over 4f out: outpcd over 2f out: edgd lft and styd on u.p ins fnl f* **5/1**

0150 **4** hd **Sendinpost**[52] 5531 3-8-8 **61** .... JamesDoyle(3) 8 69
(S C Williams) *chsd ldrs: rdn and ev ch over 2f out: outpcd over 1f out: rdr dropped reins ins fnl f: styd on* **7/2**[2]

4553 **5** 1 **Taxman (IRE)**[37] 5846 4-10-0 **70** .... (p) JimmyFortune 1 76
(C E Brittain) *chsd ldr 4f: remained handy: rdn and edgd lft over 2f out: no ex fnl f* **15/8**[1]

000 **6** 9 **Ifatfirst (IRE)**[30] 5986 3-8-3 **53** .... (b[1]) JimmyQuinn 3 47
(M P Tregoning) *hld up: plld hrd: hdwy to chse ldr 10f out: led over 5f out: rdn adn hdd whn hmpd over 2f out: sn wknd* **25/1**

1004 **7** hd **Millagros (IRE)**[11] 6321 6-9-9 **65** .... TomEaves 4 58
(I Semple) *hld up: rdn over 4f out: hmpd wl over 3f out: sn wknd* **10/1**

3004 **8** 26 **Russian Dream (IRE)**[12] 6312 3-9-3 **67** .... AdamKirby 7 24
(W R Swinburn) *led after 1f: hdd over 5f out: wknd wl over 3f out* **10/1**

3m 4.37s (-3.00) **Going Correction** -0.05s/f (Stan)
WFA 3 from 4yo+ 8lb **8** Ran SP% **119.8**
Speed ratings (Par 103):106,105,104,104,104 99,98,84
CSF £90.23 CT £425.54 TOTE £32.10: £4.60, £1.50, £1.80; EX 133.00.
Owner The Norf 'N' Sarf Partnership **Bred** C And E Farrell **Trained** Newmarket, Suffolk

FOCUS
An ordinary handicap run at a modest pace, but the form makes sense rated through the consistent runner-up and third/fifth.

6480 HOTEL & CONFERENCING AT WOLVERHAMPTON MAIDEN STKS 5f 216y(P)
4:50 (4:53) (Class 5) 2-3-Y-0 **£3,562** (£1,059; £529; £264) **Stalls** Low

Form RPR
6 **1** **Speedy Suzanne (USA)**[61] 5326 2-8-2 .... JimmyQuinn 8 55+
(B J Meehan) *dwlt: hdwy and edgd lft over 4f out: rdn and nt clr run over 1f out: swtchd lft: r.o u.p to ld post* **11/2**

522 **2** hd **Cordelia**[13] 6293 3-9-7 62 .... TonyCulhane 9 59
(B W Hills) *led: rdn over 1f out: hdd post* **2/1**[1]

3450 **3** ½ **Newkeylets**[11] 6315 3-9-7 53 .... (p) TomEaves 13 58
(I Semple) *chsd ldrs: rdn over 1f out: r.o* **16/1**

0 **4** 1½ **Storm Petrel**[17] 6215 2-8-2 ow3 .... JamesDoyle(3) 3 51+
(N P Littmoden) *sn outpcd: edgd lft and hdwy over 1f out: nrst fin* **9/4**[2]

0 **5** ½ **Ragad**[32] 5951 3-9-12 .... JimmyFortune 5 57
(W Jarvis) *trckd ldrs: rdn over 1f out: no ex ins fnl f* **10/1**

6006 **6** 3 **Hang Loose**[13] 6293 3-9-12 60 .... (p) EddieAhern 2 48
(S W Hall) *mid-div: rdn 1/2-way: styd on same pce fnl 2f* **9/2**[3]

0000 **7** shd **Penny Glitters**[22] 6130 3-9-2 45 .... DuranFentiman(5) 12 42
(S Parr) *chsd ldrs: rdn over 2f out: wknd over 1f out* **100/1**

650 **8** nk **Gattuso**[6] 6404 3-9-12 57 .... GeorgeBaker 1 46
(Ms Deborah J Evans) *sn outpcd: nt clr run over 1f out: nvr nrr* **10/1**

3000 **9** ¾ **Mr Wall Street**[14] 6283 2-8-2 50 .... (b[1]) LiamJones(5) 4 39
(Mrs L Williamson) *mid-div: sn drvn along: n.m.r 4f out: n.d* **66/1**

500 **10** 1 **Inchmarlow (IRE)**[33] 5924 3-9-12 45 .... DeanMcKeown 6 41
(T H Caldwell) *hld up: n.m.r 4f out: effrt over 2f out: n.d* **66/1**

0000 **11** 7 **Galaxy Bound (IRE)**[37] 5847 3-9-12 45 .... (v) LPKeniry 11 20
(D Shaw) *dwlt: outpcd* **100/1**

12 ½ **Whozart (IRE)** 3-9-12 .... AdamKirby 10 19
(A Dickman) *s.s: outpcd* **33/1**

13 3 **Skiddaw Fox** 2-8-7 .... SilvestreDeSousa 7 5
(Mrs L Williamson) *sn outpcd* **50/1**

1m 15.5s (-0.31) **Going Correction** -0.05s/f (Stan) **13** Ran SP% **131.6**
Speed ratings: 100,99,99,97,96 92,92,91,90,89 80,79,75
CSF £18.62 TOTE £9.70: £2.60, £1.30, £3.90; EX 23.20.
Owner Roldvale Limited **Bred** And Mrs A F Regard II Et Al **Trained** Manton, Wilts

FOCUS
A modest maiden but reliable enough form given that the race was run at a good pace, although limited by the third.

NOTEBOOK
Speedy Suzanne(USA), who had shaped with promise on her debut while running green, was always well placed just off the pace. She picked up well when asked to go and win her race and, while she benefited from a generous weight allowance here and the form is no more than modest, there could be a bit of improvement to come from her. (op 7-1 tchd 8-1)
Storm Petrel, whose dam won over a mile at three, had not been disgraced on her debut in a big-field Newmarket maiden, and this was obviously a less-competitive race than that. The drop in trip from seven furlongs did not play to her strengths, though, and she got going far too late. There was promise, however, and she could be interesting in handicaps over further after one more run. (op 5-2 tchd 2-1 and 11-4 in places)

6481 EUROPEAN BREEDERS' FUND MAIDEN FILLIES' STKS 7f 32y(P)
5:20 (5:22) (Class 5) 2-Y-0 **£3,886** (£1,156; £577; £288) **Stalls** High

Form RPR
342 **1** **Whazzis**[39] 5784 2-8-9 82 .... LiamJones(5) 3 81+
(W J Haggas) *chsd ldrs: led over 1f out: rdn out* **4/5**[1]

5 **2** 1 **Scarlet Ibis**[19] 6186 2-9-0 .... JimmyFortune 4 79+
(Saeed Bin Suroor) *a.p: rdn to chse wnr fnl f: styd on* **5/1**[3]

00 **3** 4 **Fealeview Lady (USA)**[19] 6187 2-9-0 .... RobertHavlin 10 69
(H Morrison) *hld up: swtchd rt and hdwy over 2f out: hung lft and no ex fnl f* **100/1**

305 **4** 1 **Bidable**[15] 6257 2-9-0 61 .... FergusSweeney 5 66
(B Palling) *chsd ldrs: led over 2f out: rdn and hdd over 1f out: wknd ins fnl f* **100/1**

5 ¾ **Pearl (IRE)** 2-9-0 .... TonyCulhane 7 66+
(W J Haggas) *s.i.s: outpcd: hdwy and hung lft over 1f out: nt rch ldrs* **20/1**

323 **6** hd **Snow Dancer (IRE)**[14] 6270 2-9-0 65 .... PaulQuinn 1 64
(A Berry) *led 1f: chsd ldrs: rdn over 2f out: hung lft and wknd fnl f* **28/1**

04 **7** 1¾ **Incony**[17] 6222 2-9-0 .... AdamKirby 12 59
(W R Swinburn) *led 6f out: hdd over 2f out: hung lft and wknd fnl f* **25/1**

8 6 **Hint Of Spring** 2-9-0 .... EddieAhern 8 53+
(Saeed Bin Suroor) *sn pushed along and prom: hung lft: wknd and eased over 1f out* **7/2**[2]

50 **9** 3 **Boschendal (IRE)**[49] 5586 2-9-0 .... (t) ChrisCatlin 6 37
(J W Hills) *s.s: outpcd* **150/1**

10 ¾ **Zilli** 2-8-11 .... JamesDoyle(3) 9 35
(N P Littmoden) *s.i.s: outpcd* **100/1**

11 ½ **Rock Diva (IRE)** 2-9-0 .... PaulMulrennan 11 34
(P C Haslam) *hld up: hdwy 1/2-way: wknd over 1f out* **66/1**

12 shd **Theta** 2-9-0 .... JimmyQuinn 2 33
(H R A Cecil) *sn outpcd* **10/1**

1m 29.38s (-1.02) **Going Correction** -0.05s/f (Stan) **12** Ran SP% **120.7**
Speed ratings (Par 93):103,101,97,96,95 95,93,86,82,81 81,81
CSF £5.06 TOTE £1.70: £1.20, £1.40, £16.80; EX 5.70.
Owner W Gredley & The Hon Mrs Peter Stanley **Bred** Eurostrait Ltd **Trained** Newmarket, Suffolk

FOCUS
Not a bad maiden and it was won in a very smart time for a race of its type. The sixth helps set the standard.

NOTEBOOK
Whazzis had done enough in her first three starts to suggest that a race like this was well within her ability, and the market reflected that fact. However, this was a stronger than usual Wolverhampton maiden and she had to be at her best to beat what turned out to be a useful Godolphin rival. (op Evens tchd 11-10)
Scarlet Ibis had run with promise on her debut at Lingfield but she carried the Godolphin second colours here. A half-sister to smart US juvenile performer Anasheed, and also dual mile to ten-furlong winner Marhoob, she is a daughter of the high-class mare Flagbird, and she lost nothing in defeat to a more experienced filly with useful form already in the book. She finished well clear of the rest and can go one better soon. (tchd 9-2)
Fealeview Lady(USA) improved considerably on her first two efforts and kept on steadily in the straight under hands and heels for a very respectable third. She looks likely to benefit from a step up in trip now she can move into handicaps, although this performance is likely to result in her starting off on a higher mark than had looked likely after her first two runs.
Bidable was towards the fore for much of the race but faded out of contention once the big two appeared on the scene.
Pearl(IRE), a sister to Fregate Island, a dual winner over seven furlongs and a mile at two, represented the stable who also had the odds-on favourite in the race. Out the back for much of the race, she got going late on and made up some decent ground, and looks likely to come on plenty for this debut experience. Another furlong will not go amiss. (op 25-1)
Snow Dancer(IRE) would probably be more effective in handicap company. (op 33-1)
Incony, given a more positive ride this time, set a fair pace and was burnt out early in the straight. She will now be eligible for handicaps and should be more effective in that grade. (op 33-1)
Hint Of Spring, whose dam was a top-class performer over six and seven furlongs, winning the Prix Maurice De Gheest and Haydock Park Sprint in 1995, is a half-sister to high-class miler Bowman. Under pressure from an early stage, she hung throughout the race and was not knocked about when clearly beaten in the straight. Official explanation: jockey said filly ran green and hung left (op 5-2)
Theta Official explanation: jockey said filly ran green and hung left

6482 THE ZONGALERO RESTAURANT OVERLOOKS THE TRACK MEDIAN AUCTION MAIDEN STKS 1m 4f 50y(P)
5:50 (5:50) (Class 6) 3-5-Y-0 **£2,730** (£806; £403) **Stalls** Low

Form RPR
1 **Lilakiya (IRE)**[23] 6114 3-8-9 53 .... JamesDoyle(3) 5 41+
(James Leavy, Ire) *chsd ldrs: rdn over 3f out: n.m.r and outpcd over 2f out: rallied over 1f out: hung lft and r.o to ld nr fin* **7/2**[2]

6640 **2** 1¼ **Campbells Lad**[12] 6302 5-9-4 40 .... LiamJones(5) 8 44
(Mrs G S Rees) *hld up: plld hrd: hdwy over 2f out: led over 1f out: rdn and hdd nr fin* **33/1**

6050 **3** nk **Sea Of Calm (USA)**[16] 6244 3-8-12 59 .... JimmyFortune 7 39+
(E A L Dunlop) *hld up: nt clr run over 2f out: hdwy over 1f out: sn rdn and edgd rt: hung lft and no ex wl ins fnl f* **5/2**[1]

0222 **4** 3½ **Glory Be (ITY)**[8] 6373 4-9-4 45 .... (v[1]) JimmyQuinn 1 33+
(J L Spearing) *chsd ldrs: nt clr run over 2f out: rdn over 1f out: styd on same pce* **5/2**[1]

0000 **5** 1 **Special Ballot (IRE)**[11] 6327 5-9-4 40 .... DeanMcKeown 3 31
(G A Swinbank) *s.i.s: hld up: hdwy to ld over 2f out: rdn and hdd over 1f out: wknd ins fnl f* **8/1**

600/ **6** 2½ **Howards Rocket**[26] 4905 5-9-9 35 .... TonyCulhane 2 32
(J S Goldie) *hld up: rdn over 1f out: nvr nrr* **50/1**

0200 **7** 6 **Dik Dik**[32] 5944 3-9-3 55 .... (v) JDSmith 9 23
(C N Allen) *chsd ldrs: rdn and ev ch over 2f out: wknd over 1f out* **7/1**[3]

0 **8** 3½ **Rolons Advice**[12] 6314 5-9-2 .... WilliamBuick(7) 4 17
(V Smith) *led over 9f: wknd over 1f out* **40/1**

0 **9** ½ **Second City**[11] 6327 3-8-12 .... ChrisCatlin 10 11
(E J Alston) *hld up: hdwy over 2f out: sn rdn and wknd* **25/1**

10 19 **Young Emma**[13] 3-8-12 .... EddieAhern 6 —
(G G Margarson) *chsd ldr 9f: wkng whn n.m.r over 2f out* **20/1**

2m 42.55s (0.13) **Going Correction** -0.05s/f (Stan)
WFA 3 from 4yo+ 6lb **10** Ran SP% **118.9**
Speed ratings (Par 101):97,96,95,93,92 91,87,84,84,71
CSF £119.43 TOTE £6.60: £1.80, £7.70, £1.10; EX 79.80.
Owner Morecool Racing Syndicate **Bred** His Highness The Aga Khan's Studs S C **Trained** Friarstown, Co Kildare

FOCUS
A maiden no better than banded class.
Glory Be(ITY) Official explanation: jockey said filly was denied a clear run

6483 STAY AT THE WOLVERHAMPTON HOLIDAY INN FILLIES' H'CAP 1m 141y(P)
6:20 (6:20) (Class 5) (0-70,67) 3-Y-0+ **£3,562** (£1,059; £529; £264) **Stalls** Low

Form RPR
0210 **1** **Gaelic Princess**[52] 5523 6-9-5 **67** .... FergusSweeney 4 74
(A G Newcombe) *hld up in tch: rdn to ld and hung lft wl ins fnl f* **5/1**[3]

0623 **2** 1¼ **Tender The Great (IRE)**[4] 6430 3-8-6 **64** .... (v[1]) WilliamBuick(7) 2 69
(V Smith) *chsd ldr: led over 1f out: rdn: hung lft and hdd wl ins fnl f* **5/2**[2]

4012 **3** 1¼ **Bavarica**[3] 6448 4-8-13 **64** .... JamesDoyle(3) 3 66
(Miss J Feilden) *hld up in tch: rdn over 1f out: styd on same pce ins fnl f* **6/4**[1]

2403 **4** 1 **Spark Up**[7] 6387 6-8-1 **54** .... (b) LiamJones(5) 5 54
(J W Unett) *prom: lost pl over 3f out: hdwy over 1f out: sn rdn: no ex wl ins fnl f* **6/1**

041- **5** *3 1/2* **Baba Ghanoush**[339] 6545 4-9-4 **66** .... PaulDoe 1 59
(W Jarvis) *led: rdn over 2f out: hdd over 1f out: wknd ins fnl f* **10/1**

54-0 **6** *1 1/2* **Caragh Mia (IRE)**[3] 6439 4-8-12 **60** .... EddieAhern 7 49
(G G Margarson) *s.s: hld up: effrt over 1f out: sn wknd* **20/1**

1000 **7** *1 3/4* **Tuscarora (IRE)**[17] 6227 7-9-2 **64** .... ChrisCatlin 8 50
(A W Carroll) *hld up: plld hrd: hdwy over 3f out: wknd over 1f out* **20/1**

0400 **8** *5* **Cheviot Heights**[15] 6260 3-8-6 **62** .... DuranFentiman(5) 9 37
(J S Goldie) *hld up: hdwy over 3f out: wknd 2f out* **20/1**

1m 52.13s (0.37) **Going Correction** -0.05s/f (Stan)
WFA 3 from 4yo+ 3lb **8** Ran SP% **122.9**
Speed ratings (Par 100):96,94,93,92,89 88,86,82
CSF £18.87 CT £26.91 TOTE £7.00: £2.00, £1.50, £1.10; EX 29.20 Place 6 £29.79, Place 5 £13.80.
Owner M K F Seymour **Bred** Mrs N Quinn **Trained** Yarnscombe, Devon

FOCUS
An ordinary handicap run at a modest pace. Even in victory the winner has been rated a stone off the mark she was given when successful at Salisbury in the summer.
Bavarica Official explanation: jockey said filly was unsuited by the slow pace
T/Plt: £18.90 to a £1 stake. Pool: £64,157.50. 2,470.10 winning tickets. T/Qpdt: £4.80 to a £1 stake. Pool: £6,311.40. 958.50 winning tickets. CR

6432 KEMPTON (A.W) (R-H)

Wednesday, November 15

OFFICIAL GOING: Standard
Wind: fresh, half-against

6484 BOOK NOW FOR CHRISTMAS H'CAP — 1m 2f (P)
3:45 (3:46) (Class 6) (0-60,61) 3-Y-0+ **£2,388** (£705; £352) **Stalls** High

Form RPR

2111 **1** **Eccollo (IRE)**[4] 6436 4-9-7 **61** 6ex .... RobertHavlin 8 81+
(T J Pitt) *lw: fly-jmpd s: sn trckd ldrs: prog 4f out: led wl over 1f out: hanging lft and flashed tail but sn drew rt away* **1/2**[1]

5-40 **2** *4* **Bronze Star**[41] 5774 3-9-0 **58** .... OscarUrbina 11 69+
(J R Fanshawe) *hld up in midfield: n.m.r and lost pl 4f out: effrt 2f out: r.o fnl f to take 2nd nr fin* **12/1**[3]

1605 **3** *nk* **Sarwin (USA)**[14] 6289 3-9-2 **60** .... BrettDoyle 12 66
(W J Musson) *t.k.h: hld up bhd ldrs: effrt 2f out: chsd wnr ins fnl f: no imp: lost 2nd nr fin* **10/1**[2]

5006 **4** *1 1/4* **Lady Pilot**[29] 6037 4-8-11 **54** .... JamesDoyle(3) 6 58
(Ms J S Doyle) *settled towards rr: prog on inner over 2f out: drvn and styd on fr over 1f out: n.d* **25/1**

6204 **5** *1* **Siena Star (IRE)**[14] 6289 8-9-2 **59** .... AmirQuinn(3) 9 61
(J R Boyle) *prom: rdn to ld over 2f out to wl over 1f out: wknd ins fnl f* **16/1**

0405 **6** *nk* **Lennoxtown (IRE)**[5] 6430 3-9-1 **59** ....(p) AdamKirby 3 60
(J Ryan) *hld up: prog on outer and prom 4f out: hrd rdn 2f out: sn struggling* **20/1**

0006 **7** *1 1/4* **Ohana**[9] 6383 3-9-0 **58** ....(e[1]) DarryllHolland 1 57
(Miss Gay Kelleway) *b.hind: hld up in last pair: gng wl enough but only 11th 2f out: r.o last 150yds: no ch* **33/1**

0025 **8** *shd* **Persona (IRE)**[22] 6158 4-9-5 **59** .... ChrisCatlin 7 58
(B J McMath) *hld up in rr: pushed along and prog 3f out: chsng ldrs 2f out: wknd fnl f* **25/1**

6000 **9** *hd* **Blackmail (USA)**[50] 5587 8-9-2 **56** .... JoeFanning 5 54
(P Mitchell) *hld up towards rr: effrt over 2f out: sn rdn and nt qckn: one pce after* **33/1**

10 *5* **Cove Mountain (IRE)**[138] 3061 4-9-5 **59** .... LPKeniry 2 48
(S Kirk) *s.s: hld up in last pair: brief effrt 2f out: sn no prog* **25/1**

2100 **11** *4* **Asaateel (IRE)**[30] 6008 4-9-6 **60** ....(b) GeorgeBaker 10 41
(G L Moore) *lw: trckd ldr: led 3f out to over 2f out: hanging bdly and wknd rapidly* **25/1**

-540 **12** *1 3/4* **Swindon (USA)**[109] 3952 4-9-4 **58** ....(t) JimmyFortune 4 36
(P F I Cole) *dwlt: hld up in rr: rdn and no prog over 2f out: sn lost tch* **14/1**

000- **13** *6* **Timberlake**[15] 3976 4-9-6 **60** .... SteveDrowne 13 26
(Miss E C Lavelle) *rousted along to ld: hdd & wknd rapidly 3f out* **66/1**

1100 **14** *12* **Bold Phoenix (IRE)**[14] 6294 5-9-2 **56** .... TPQueally 14 —
(B J Curley) *trckd ldrs tl wknd rapidly 4f out: t.o* **25/1**

2m 6.28s (-2.72) **Going Correction** -0.10s/f (Stan)
WFA 3 from 4yo+ 4lb **14** Ran SP% **127.4**
Speed ratings (Par 101):106,102,102,101,100 100,99,99,99,95 92,90,85,76
CSF £6.39 CT £42.54 TOTE £1.40: £1.10, £3.40, £3.00.
Owner Stephen Pearson & David Marshall **Bred** Swettenham Stud **Trained** Bawtry, S Yorks

FOCUS
A decent winning time for the grade and a one-horse race, very much as the market suggested it would be. The form looks solid with the third and sixth to recent form.

6485 RACINGUK.TV H'CAP — 5f (P)
4:20 (4:21) (Class 5) (0-75,80) 3-Y-0+ **£3,886** (£1,156; £577; £288) **Stalls** High

Form RPR

3211 **1** **Little Edward**[4] 6446 8-9-10 **80** 6ex .... GeorgeBaker 1 88+
(R J Hodges) *hld up and racd wd: prog over 1f out: wl timed run fnl f to ld nr fin* **7/2**[2]

3013 **2** *hd* **Pamir (IRE)**[21] 6174 4-8-11 **67** ....(b) JimCrowley 9 74
(P R Chamings) *rrd s: trckd ldrs: effrt over 1f out: disp ld 1f out: fnd less than looked likely fnl f: hdd nr fin* **6/1**[3]

0122 **3** *nk* **Heavens Walk**[4] 6452 5-8-13 **69** ....(t) SteveDrowne 11 75
(P J Makin) *stdd s but sn trckd ldng pair: effrt on inner to ld jst over 1f out: sn jnd: jst hld nr fin* **6/4**[1]

160 **4** *1* **Taboor (IRE)**[12] 6320 8-8-13 **69** .... BrettDoyle 7 71
(R M H Cowell) *dwlt: settled in rr: rdn and nt qckn over 1f out: styd on ins fnl f* **20/1**

5435 **5** *nk* **Gwilym (GER)**[29] 6036 3-8-11 **67** .... RobertHavlin 6 68
(D Haydn Jones) *lw: towards rr: rdn and struggling wl over 1f out: plugged on* **9/1**

4300 **6** *1 1/4* **Kempsey**[103] 4101 4-8-9 **65** ....(b) LPKeniry 8 62
(J J Bridger) *pressed ldr: rdn over 2f out: led briefly over 1f out: wknd ins fnl f* **50/1**

0030 **7** *1* **Jayanjay**[4] 6437 7-8-13 **69** .... JoeFanning 5 62
(P Mitchell) *hld up in rr: nt clr run over 1f out and hmpd sn after: swtchd lft and no ch* **7/1**

0046 **8** *1 1/2* **Sofinella (IRE)**[67] 5181 3-8-4 **60** oh2 .... ChrisCatlin 12 48
(A W Carroll) *rousted along to ld: hdd over 1f out: losing pl whn squeezed out jst ins fnl f* **50/1**

4003 **9** *nk* **Quality Street**[10] 6353 4-8-5 **68** ....(p) JoesphWalsh(7) 10 55
(P Butler) *trckd ldrs: nt qckn over 1f out: wkng whn stmbld jst ins fnl f* **16/1**

-050 **10** *3* **The Fisio**[22] 6162 6-8-4 **60** oh1 ....(v) SilvestreDeSousa 2 36
(S Gollings) *racd wd: nvr on terms: struggling 2f out* **33/1**

60.16 secs (-0.24) **Going Correction** -0.10s/f (Stan) **10** Ran SP% **116.5**
Speed ratings (Par 103):97,96,96,94,94 92,90,88,87,82
CSF £23.91 CT £43.97 TOTE £4.30: £1.60, £2.20, £1.30; EX 31.60.
Owner J W Mursell **Bred** J W Mursell **Trained** Charlton Adam, Somerset

FOCUS
The pace did not appear to be that strong for this sprint, hence the small margins separating the principals at the line. The winning time was therefore modest for the grade but the form looks sound rated around the placed horses.
Jayanjay Official explanation: jockey said gelding was denied a clear run

6486 DIGIBET.COM E B F MAIDEN FILLIES' STKS — 1m (P)
4:50 (4:55) (Class 5) 2-Y-0 **£3,562** (£1,059; £529; £264) **Stalls** High

Form RPR

1 **Flower Of Kent (USA)** 2-9-0 .... RobertHavlin 8 74+
(J H M Gosden) *w'like: prom: chsd ldr 3f out: rdn and green briefly 2f out: led jst ins fnl f: pushed out and in command nr fin* **13/2**[3]

03 **2** *1 1/2* **Towy Girl (IRE)**[26] 6073 2-9-0 .... AdamKirby 6 71
(I A Wood) *t.k.h: led: carried hd high fr over 2f out: hdd and nt qckn jst ins fnl f* **3/1**[2]

3 **3** *1* **Eulogize**[36] 5882 2-9-0 .... BrettDoyle 13 68+
(E A L Dunlop) *w'like: athletic: trckd ldrs: lost pl 1/2-way: rdn and effrt over 2f out: chsd ldng pair over 1f out: kpt on but nvr able t* **9/4**[1]

0 **4** *hd* **Starparty (USA)**[18] 6215 2-9-0 .... JimCrowley 1 68
(Mrs A J Perrett) *lw: trckd ldrs: rdn over 2f out: styd on same pce and pressed for 3rd fnl f* **14/1**

5 *1 3/4* **Fascinatin Rhythm** 2-9-0 .... MichaelTebbutt 14 64+
(V Smith) *unf: s.i.s: settled at bk of main gp: pushed along and sme prog 2f out: no imp after* **25/1**

6 *1 3/4* **Sweetheart** 2-9-0 .... DarryllHolland 10 60
(M A Jarvis) *w'like: bit bkwd: towards rr: shkn up over 2f out: kpt on same pce and n.d* **10/1**

7 *1* **Wild Gardenia** 2-9-0 .... JimmyFortune 9 57
(J H M Gosden) *leggy: unf: b.hind: prom: rdn over 2f out: grad wknd fr over 1f out* **15/2**

0 **8** *4* **My Jeanie (IRE)**[101] 4177 2-8-11 .... StephaneBreux(3) 2 48
(J C Fox) *chsd ldr to 3f out: wknd rapidly 2f out* **50/1**

9 *2* **Confident** 2-9-0 .... MatthewHenry 4 44
(M A Jarvis) *unf: scope: bit bkwd: towards rr: pushed along over 3f out: sn struggling* **8/1**

10 *4* **Restless Soul** 2-9-0 .... DeanMcKeown 11 34
(C A Cyzer) *unf: detached fr main gp after 2f: bhd after* **20/1**

11 *nk* **Astarte** 2-8-7 .... PNolan(7) 5 34
(P R Chamings) *unf: bolted to post: tk fierce hold: hld up tl plld way up towards ldrs 1/2-way: wknd rapidly over 2f out* **33/1**

12 *12* **Rosemarkie** 2-8-7 .... JamesMillman(7) 12 6
(J L Spearing) *leggy: s.i.s: sn t.o* **33/1**

1m 40.79s (-0.01) **Going Correction** -0.10s/f (Stan) **12** Ran SP% **124.2**
Speed ratings (Par 93):96,94,93,93,91 89,88,84,82,78 78,66
CSF £26.20 TOTE £6.90: £2.10, £1.60, £1.50; EX 26.60.
Owner K Abdulla **Bred** Juddmonte Farms Inc **Trained** Newmarket, Suffolk

FOCUS
An ordinary maiden for the track and it paid to race close to the pace.

NOTEBOOK
Flower Of Kent(USA) ◆, first foal of a high-class miler in the US, came off the bridle sooner than the runner-up but responded really well to pressure and was well on top at the line. She gave the impression that she would benefit from the experience and should go on from here. (op 9-1)
Towy Girl(IRE) tried to make her experience tell from the front though she did not help her chances by racing very keenly. Nonetheless, she found more when asked in the home straight and just came up against a better rival on the day. She can now be handicapped, but should still be up to winning an ordinary maiden. (op 10-3 tchd 11-4)
Eulogize did not find as much off the bridle as had looked likely in the home straight and did not really progress as much from her Leicester debut as might have been hoped. Her breeding does suggest that this is about as far as she wants. (op 2-1 tchd 3-1)
Starparty(USA) ran much better than on her Newmarket debut and seems to have learnt from that effort as many of her stablemates do. She may be the type that will come into her own once handicapped. (op 20-1)
Fascinatin Rhythm ◆, a half-sister to several winners including Winning Venture, did show distinct signs of promise on this debut and, given her breeding, she is likely to appreciate a longer trip. She still looked on the weak side, so this was encouraging.
Sweetheart ◆, a half-sister to a winner in France, is another that is likely to improve for a longer trip with this debut effort under her belt. (op 7-1)
Astarte Official explanation: jockey said filly ran too free to post
Rosemarkie Official explanation: jockey said filly would not face the kickback

6487 DIGIBET.CO.UK NURSERY — 7f (P)
5:20 (5:21) (Class 6) (0-65,64) 2-Y-0 **£2,388** (£705; £352) **Stalls** High

Form RPR

0035 **1** **Gifted Heir (IRE)**[30] 6016 2-8-8 **51** .... JoeFanning 5 54
(I A Wood) *lw: pressed ldr: led over 2f out: sn drvn: styd on wl fr over 1f out* **11/2**[3]

650 **2** *1 3/4* **Lawyer To World**[12] 6322 2-9-7 **64** .... ChrisCatlin 2 62
(N A Callaghan) *lw: pushed along in rr early: prog on wd outside to chal over 2f out: sn rdn and nt qckn: kpt on same pce after* **3/1**[1]

400 **3** *1 1/4* **Sweet World**[18] 6224 2-9-6 **63** .... DarryllHolland 6 58+
(A P Jarvis) *s.i.s: t.k.h and hld up in last pair: effrt on inner 2f out: styd on to take 3rd nr fin: no ch* **11/2**[3]

055 **4** *nk* **A Nod And A Wink (IRE)**[81] 4816 2-8-4 **50** .... StephaneBreux(3) 10 44
(R Hannon) *t.k.h: hld up: n.m.r after 2f: outpcd over 2f out: shkn up and styd on fnl f: nrst fin* **8/1**

000 **5** *nk* **Priceless Melody (USA)**[62] 4774 2-8-2 **48** ow3 ......(b[1]) JamesDoyle(3) 8 42
(Mrs A J Perrett) *cl up: chsd ldng pair wl over 1f out: no imp: lost 2 pls nr fin* **14/1**

2050 **6** *3* **Totally Free**[8] 6388 2-8-9 **52** ....(v) HayleyTurner 7 38
(M D I Usher) *t.k.h: trckd ldrs: wknd wl over 1f out* **9/1**

0006 **7** *nk* **Eastern Princess**[30] 6014 2-8-13 **56** .... RichardThomas 9 41
(J A Geake) *chsd ldrs: rdn and no imp over 2f out: wknd over 1f out* **10/1**

6000 **8** *5* **Gold Response**[5] 6421 2-8-7 **50** ....(v) DeanMcKeown 1 22
(D Shaw) *stdd s: plld hrd and hld up in last: rdn and no prog over 2f out* **40/1**

640 **9** *6* **One White Sock**[18] 6222 2-8-12 **55** ....(v[1]) SteveDrowne 4 11
(J L Spearing) *led to over 2f out: wknd rapidly over 1f out* **20/1**

000 **10** *14* **Bellehurst**^{30} [6014] 2-9-0 **57** .... JimmyFortune 3 —
(B J Meehan) *chsd ldrs: nt keen and wknd rapidly fr over 2f out* **4/1**^{2}

1m 27.2s (0.40) **Going Correction** -0.10s/f (Stan) **10** Ran SP% **119.8**
Speed ratings (Par 94):93,91,89,89,88 85,85,79,72,56
CSF £23.04 CT £97.63 TOTE £7.80: £2.40, £1.70, £2.50; EX 33.90.
Owner M I Forbes **Bred** A Malone **Trained** Upper Lambourn, Berks

FOCUS
An ordinary nursery and the form looks weak outside the placed horses.

NOTEBOOK
Gifted Heir(IRE) was never far off the pace and impressed in the way that he fended off the challenge of the favourite in the latter stages. He has already been beaten in sellers though, so will find it hard to follow up especially as he will go up for this. (op 5-1 tchd 6-1)
Lawyer To World, who had yet to make the first three in five starts coming into this, still started favourite which demonstrates the weakness of the contest. Covering a lot of ground on the wide outside rounding the home bend in order to get into a challenging position, he had every chance but found the winner too determined and is now looking exposed. (op 10-3 tchd 7-2)
Sweet World, making his nursery debut, did not get going until it was too late. He probably needs to return to a mile and is one to note when the money is down. (op 5-1)
A Nod And A Wink(IRE), well beaten in a seller last time, was stepping up in trip for this nursery debut, but shaped as though it was not far enough. (op 15-2 tchd 7-1)
Priceless Melody(USA), beaten out of sight in all three starts on turf, showed up for a long way in the first-time blinkers and had every chance, but did not get home. (tchd 16-1)
Totally Free raced keenly just off the pace, but as a result he failed to see out the extra furlong.
One White Sock, yet another making her nursery debut and stepping up in trip, probably did too much too early in the first-time visor.

6488 DIGIBET SPORTS BETTING NURSERY 6f (P)
5:50 (5:53) (Class 5) (0-75,73) 2-Y-O **£3,238** (£963; £481; £240) **Stalls** High

Form RPR

0063 **1** **Hucking Hill (IRE)**^{8} [6388] 2-8-9 **61** .... (b) BrettDoyle 4 68
(J R Best) *trckd ldrs: effrt on inner to ld 2f out: edgd lft but styd on wl and in n.d fnl f* **6/1**

4015 **2** *2 ½* **Our Blessing (IRE)**^{13} [6310] 2-9-7 **73** .... DarryllHolland 1 73
(A P Jarvis) *racd freely: w ldr: chsd wnr 2f out: nt qckn over 1f out: wl hld after* **4/1**^{2}

4322 **3** *1* **Danehillsundance (IRE)**^{11} [6331] 2-9-7 **73** .... JimmyFortune 3 70
(R Hannon) *racd wd: in tch: effrt over 2f out: chsd ldng pair fnl f : no imp* **2/1**^{1}

4020 **4** *nk* **Nou Camp**^{8} [6388] 2-8-4 **56** .... JamieMackay 6 52
(N A Callaghan) *t.k.h: hld up in tch: prog on inner 2f out: one pce fr over 1f out* **12/1**

5403 **5** *nk* **La Quinta (IRE)**^{41} [5772] 2-9-0 **66** .... PJSmullen 8 61
(B J Meehan) *lw: hld up and sn last: pushed along 1/2-way: nt clr run over 1f out: styd on ins fnl f* **11/2**^{3}

0065 **6** *1* **Bentley**^{5} [6422] 2-8-0 **52** .... (v) HayleyTurner 2 44
(D Shaw) *wnt lft s: plld hrd: pressed ldrs 2f out: wknd fnl f* **16/1**

550 **7** *4* **Path To Glory**^{11} [6330] 2-7-7 **50** oh5 .... NicolPolli$^{(5)}$ 9 30
(Miss Z C Davison) *t.k.h early and hld up in last pair: lost tch u.p 2f out* **50/1**

0240 **8** *4* **Call Me Rosy (IRE)**^{13} [6310] 2-9-1 **67** .... JoeFanning 7 35
(C F Wall) *mde most to 2f out: wknd rapidly* **9/1**

0603 **U** **Queen Of Narnia**^{13} [6311] 2-8-9 **61** .... ChrisCatlin 5 —
(M R Channon) *uns rdr s* **6/1**

1m 12.93s (-0.77) **Going Correction** -0.10s/f (Stan) **9** Ran SP% **122.8**
Speed ratings (Par 96):101,97,96,95,95 94,88,83,—
CSF £32.34 CT £66.87 TOTE £7.30: £1.70, £2.00, £1.30; EX 46.20.
Owner Hucking Horses **Bred** Ballyhane Stud **Trained** Hucking, Kent

FOCUS
A dramatic start with Queen Of Narnia getting rid of her rider at the start. Those that were left set a decent pace which resulted in a fair winning time for a race like this.

NOTEBOOK
Hucking Hill(IRE) ◆, whose only previous victory came here in the spring, has been plummeting down the weights in recent months and had offered plenty of encouragement in his last outing that he was nearing a winning mark. Another 3lb drop sealed it, and the way he bounded home suggested he could cope with a penalty if returned to the track in the near future. (op 4-1)
Our Blessing(IRE) seemed happier back over six and showed up for a long way, but could not match the winner from the furlong pole. (op 6-1)
Danehillsundance(IRE), trying sand for the first time on this nursery debut, had every chance but lacked pace where it mattered and was forced to settle for a place in the frame yet again. He is not progressing. (op 7-2)
Nou Camp tried to get into the race in the home straight, but his effort came to little. His best performances so far, such as they are, have been over the minimum trip. (tchd 10-1)
La Quinta(IRE) tried to come from off the pace, but did not have much room to play with in the straight and failed to land a blow. She is only modest, but would have finished closer with a clear run and may be worth a try over seven. (op 4-1)

6489 FOLLOW YOUR MEETING WITH FLOODLIT RACING H'CAP 7f (P)
6:20 (6:20) (Class 5) (0-75,80) 3-Y-O+ **£4,533** (£1,348; £674; £336) **Stalls** High

Form RPR

3001 **1** **Prince Tum Tum (USA)**^{6} [6417] 6-9-8 **80** 6ex .... DeanMcKeown 12 91+
(D Shaw) *lw: wl plcd: chsd ldr over 1f out: rdn to ld last 150yds: a holding on* **5/1**^{3}

3002 **2** *½* **Arctic Desert**^{35} [5908] 6-9-1 **73** .... (t) DarryllHolland 7 80
(Miss Gay Kelleway) *b.hind: t.k.h: hld up in midfield: effrt 2f out: rdn and r.o fnl f to take 2nd nr fin* **4/1**^{2}

4630 **3** *½* **Sovereignty (JPN)**^{1} [6478] 4-8-5 **63** .... HayleyTurner 11 68
(D K Ivory) *t.k.h: w ldr: led 4f out: rdn over 1f out: hdd last 150yds: kpt on* **14/1**

0600 **4** *shd* **Safari Sunset (IRE)**^{18} [6223] 4-8-12 **70** .... (p) JimCrowley 5 75
(P Winkworth) *chsd ldrs: effrt on outer over 2f out: rdn and styd on fnl f: nvr quite able to chal* **33/1**

4543 **5** *hd* **Rezzago (USA)**^{17} [6239] 6-9-3 **75** .... AdamKirby 2 83+
(W R Swinburn) *lw: dwlt: settled in rr: gd prog on inner 2f out: styng on but hld whn nt clr run ins fnl f: kpt on nr fin* **7/2**^{1}

0005 **6** *1 ½* **Quantum Leap**^{41} [5778] 9-8-12 **70** .... (v) JimmyQuinn 3 71+
(S Dow) *settled towards rr: shuffled along over 2f out: shkn up and styd on fnl f: nvr nr ldrs* **14/1**

1660 **7** *½* **First Approval**^{41} [5778] 3-8-11 **70** .... MichaelHills 9 69
(B W Hills) *prom: pressed ldr over 2f out to over 1f out: wknd ins fnl f* **12/1**

2410 **8** *nk* **Fateful Attraction**^{7} [6396] 3-8-7 **69** .... (b) JamesDoyle$^{(3)}$ 14 68
(I A Wood) *dwlt: hld up towards rr: effrt on inner but plenty to do whn nt clr run over 1f out: styng on nr fin* **15/2**

223 **9** *nk* **Conservative**^{23} [6144] 3-8-8 **67** .... RobertHavlin 10 65
(P G Murphy) *chsd ldrs: pushed along 3f out: no prog and btn 2f out: fdd* **20/1**

0060 **10** *nk* **Cesar Manrique (IRE)**^{30} [6020] 4-8-8 **66** .... (p) LPKeniry 13 63
(A E Jones) *t.k.h: led for 3f: wknd 2f out* **40/1**

5104 **11** *1 ¼* **Valentino Swing (IRE)**^{6} [6417] 3-8-9 **68** .... (v^{1}) SteveDrowne 8 62
(J L Spearing) *s.s: a wl in rr: no prog 2f out* **9/1**

2000 **12** *2* **Pommes Frites**^{10} [6350] 3-8-12 **71** .... ChrisCatlin 4 59
(W R Muir) *hld up in last: nvr a factor* **40/1**

4210 **13** *3 ½* **Torquemada (IRE)**^{57} [5444] 5-8-7 **65** .... (p) PaulDoe 6 44
(W Jarvis) *swtg: t.k.h: a wl in rr: struggling over 2f out* **10/1**

1m 26.29s (-0.51) **Going Correction** -0.10s/f (Stan)
WFA 3 from 4yo+ 1lb **13** Ran SP% **123.4**
Speed ratings (Par 103):98,97,96,96,96 94,94,93,93,93 91,89,85
CSF £25.28 CT £270.04 TOTE £6.60: £2.00, £2.10, £4.30; EX 36.40 Place 6 £5.66, Place 5 £5.09 .
Owner The Circle Bloodstock I Limited **Bred** Clovelly Farms **Trained** Danethorpe, Notts

FOCUS
A competitive handicap, but the pace was ordinary hence a modest winning time for the grade and the form is limited by the third and fourth.
Valentino Swing(IRE) Official explanation: jockey said gelding dwelt in stalls
T/Plt: £4.80 to a £1 stake. Pool: £58,751.00. 8,770.75 winning tickets. T/Qpdt: £5.00 to a £1 stake. Pool: £5,719.60. 834.70 winning tickets. JN

6470 SOUTHWELL (L-H)
Wednesday, November 15

OFFICIAL GOING: Standard
Wind: fresh, half-against Weather: cool, overcast and breezy

6490 GOLF AND RACING AT SOUTHWELL MAIDEN STKS (DIV I) 6f (F)
12:00 (12:00) (Class 5) 3-Y-O+ **£2,590** (£770; £385; £192) **Stalls** Low

Form RPR

0246 **1** **Benny The Bus**^{15} [6286] 4-9-3 63 .... GrahamGibbons 6 55
(Mrs G S Rees) *chsd ldr: led jst ins last: rdn clr* **4/6**^{1}

0020 **2** *2 ½* **Double Carpet (IRE)**^{14} [6293] 3-9-3 55 .... FergusSweeney 2 48
(G Woodward) *in rr: hdwy on wd outside over 2f out: styd on wl fnl f: tk 2nd last stride* **8/1**^{3}

0436 **3** *shd* **Dysonic (USA)**^{112} [3833] 4-9-3 40 .... (v) DavidAllan 7 48
(J Balding) *led: hdd jst ins last: one pce* **14/1**

0000 **4** *2 ½* **Swallow Senora (IRE)**^{71} [5077] 4-8-5 35 .... RussellKennemore$^{(7)}$ 12 35
(M C Chapman) *in tch on outer: edgd lft and one pce fnl 2f* **33/1**

6000 **5** *4* **Distant Vision (IRE)**^{13} [6306] 3-8-12 35 .... (t) PaulQuinn 8 23
(A Berry) *swtchd wd after 1f: hdwy over 3f out: nvr nr ldrs* **66/1**

5002 **6** *1* **Mister Jingles**^{15} [6282] 3-9-3 45 .... TonyCulhane 11 25
(R M Whitaker) *trckd ldrs on outer: edgd lft and wknd over 1f out* **5/1**^{2}

0 **7** *½* **Existence**^{7} [6406] 3-8-9 .... PatrickMathers$^{(3)}$ 9 19
(D Shaw) *chsd ldrs: lost pl over 1f out* **50/1**

0050 **8** *7* **Westlake Bond (IRE)**^{90} [4507] 4-8-7 40 .... (p) DuranFentiman$^{(5)}$ 10 —
(G R Oldroyd) *in tch: rdn and lost pl over 3f out* **16/1**

9 *1 ½* **Grey Vision** 3-8-12 .... (b^{1}) DeanMernagh 1 —
(M Brittain) *dwlt: sn in tch: rdn and lost pl over 3f out* **8/1**^{3}

000 **10** *6* **Tapsalteerie**^{12} [6327] 3-8-12 30 .... DaneO'Neill 3 —
(M J Attwater) *a in rr* **100/1**

0000 **11** *5* **Dancing Moonlight (IRE)**^{95} [4382] 4-8-12 30 .... (p) DanielTudhope 4 —
(Mrs N Macauley) *sn bhd* **100/1**

000/ **12** *59* **Battle Green Lad**^{1985} [2004] 9-8-10 30 .... JamieHamblett$^{(7)}$ 5 —
(R F Marvin) *s.i.s: t.k.h: lost pl over 4f out: eased over 2f out: sn wl bhd: virtually p.u and t.o* **100/1**

1m 18.72s (1.82) **Going Correction** +0.175s/f (Slow) **12** Ran SP% **120.8**
Speed ratings (Par 103):94,90,90,87,81 80,79,70,68,60 53,—
CSF £6.97 TOTE £1.50: £1.10, £2.20, £2.70; EX 6.70 Trifecta £22.10 Pool £133.26 - 4.28 winning units.
Owner Ballard Campbell & D Brady **Bred** Capt J H Wilson **Trained** Sollom, Lancs

FOCUS
The slower of the two divisions and they can hardly come worse than this. The form is anchored by the third.
Mister Jingles Official explanation: jockey said gelding hung left

6491 BOOK TICKETS ON-LINE CLAIMING STKS 6f (F)
12:30 (12:30) (Class 6) 2-Y-O **£2,730** (£806; £403) **Stalls** Low

Form RPR

4040 **1** **Lovers Kiss**^{8} [6385] 2-8-2 45 .... (b) DaleGibson 2 49
(N Wilson) *chsd ldrs: rdn over 2f out: edgd rt and led ins last: all out* **66/1**

0055 **2** *hd* **Cherri Fosfate**^{7} [6402] 2-8-11 64 .... TonyCulhane 1 58
(W G M Turner) *dwlt: hdwy on ins to ld over 4f out: hdd ins last: kpt on wl* **9/2**^{3}

3060 **3** *½* **Hunting Call**^{7} [6401] 2-8-9 66 .... (b) TomEaves 6 54
(K A Ryan) *in rr: hdwy on ins over 2f out: upsides ent last: no ex* **8/1**

000 **4** *7* **Kings Shillings**^{21} [6173] 2-8-9 35 .... (b) DanielTudhope 8 33
(D Carroll) *dwlt: in last tl styd on fnl f: nvr on terms* **66/1**

2062 **5** *½* **Put It On The Card**^{7} [6401] 2-8-9 59 .... (p) GrahamGibbons 5 32
(P D Evans) *chsd ldrs: effrt on outer over 2f out: wknd over 1f out* **10/3**^{2}

0060 **6** *1 ¼* **Vizionary**^{78} [4913] 2-8-4 48 .... PaulQuinn 9 23
(Mrs P Sly) *in tch on outer: effrt over 2f out: lost pl over 1f out* **20/1**

3024 **7** *1 ¼* **Jost Van Dyke**^{37} [5876] 2-8-7 67 .... (p) PatCosgrave 4 22
(J R Boyle) *led tl over 4f out: lost pl over 1f out* **13/8**^{1}

0066 **8** *shd* **Answer Back**^{21} [6175] 2-8-4 45 .... PaulFitzsimons 7 19
(Miss J R Tooth) *chsd ldrs: edgd lft and wknd wl over 1f out* **40/1**

2110 **9** *1 ¼* **Dotty's Daughter**^{5} [6422] 2-8-1 60 .... (p) DuranFentiman$^{(5)}$ 3 17
(Mrs A Duffield) *in rr: hdwy on ins over 2f out: hung rt and lost pl over 1f out* **11/2**

1m 18.71s (1.81) **Going Correction** +0.175s/f (Slow) **9** Ran SP% **116.0**
Speed ratings (Par 94):94,93,93,83,83 81,79,79,77
CSF £338.83 TOTE £41.00: £8.40, £1.50, £2.50; EX 228.00 Trifecta £108.20 Part won. Pool £152.52 - 0.34 winning units..There was no bid for the winner. Hunting Call was claimed by C Bjorling for £8,000
Owner Ian W Glenton **Bred** Newsells Park Stud Limited **Trained** Upper Helmsley, N Yorks

FOCUS
A weak contest rated around the winner and fourth.

NOTEBOOK
Lovers Kiss, who had 14lb to find with the runner-up, at least proved persistent and in the end her and her rider's efforts paid off.
Cherri Fosfate, conceding weight all round, went on leaving the back stretch after missing a beat at the start. He fought back when headed and in the end only just missed out. (op 10-3)
Hunting Call, on his Fibresand debut, was taken to post early. He came there on the inner looking a real threat but was found wanting inside the last. It was sufficient for him to be claimed and he may now head for Spain. (tchd 15-2)

Kings Shillings, making his All-Weather debut, gave away ground at the start and was last until staying on in the final furlong.
Put It On The Card had the cheekpieces on again but struggled to see it out on the much slower surface. (op 4-1 tchd 3-1)
Jost Van Dyke, clear top on official figures, wore cheekpieces but, after jumping out first, in the end he came up a long way short. (op 2-1 tchd 9-4)

6492 GOLF AND RACING AT SOUTHWELL MAIDEN STKS (DIV II) 6f (F)
1:00 (1:00) (Class 5) 3-Y-O+ **£2,590** (£770; £385; £192) **Stalls** Low

Form RPR
0560 **1** **Jabbara (IRE)**^{58} [5418] 3-8-12 55...............................(b^{1}) StephenCarson 2 63+
(C E Brittain) *trckd ldrs gng wl: shkn up to ld over 1f out: hung lft and rdn wl clr: eased towards fin* **3/1^{2}**
043 **2** *6* **Left Nostril (IRE)**^{33} [5949] 3-8-12 40.................................... BrianReilly 4 42
(P S McEntee) *led: hdd over 1f out: hung lft and kpt on same pce* **7/1**
6032 **3** *2* **Balian**^{23} [6129] 3-9-3 55..(p) MickyFenton 1 41
(Mrs P Sly) *drvn along to chse ldrs: one pce fnl 2f* **9/4^{1}**
-000 **4** *nk* **Caspian Rose**^{15} [6282] 3-8-12 40...................................... DaneO'Neill 10 35
(M J Attwater) *mid-div: outpcd over 3f out: edgd lft and kpt on fnl 2f* **25/1**
5 *nk* **Villa Bianca's (IRE)** 3-8-9 .... RichardKingscote$^{(3)}$ 3 34
(J A Osborne) *dwlt: in rr: kpt on u.p fnl 2f: nvr on terms* **9/2^{3}**
-306 **6** *nk* **Sion Hill (IRE)**^{15} [6277] 5-9-3 45.................................(p) DanielTudhope 6 38
(Mrs N Macauley) *trckd ldrs: one pce fnl 2f* **10/1**
00 **7** *5* **Dodaa (USA)**^{7} [6403] 3-8-10 .... LanceBetts$^{(7)}$ 8 23
(N Wilson) *in tch: edgd rt over 1f out: sn wknd* **20/1**
300/ **8** *3 ½* **Poyle Josh**^{73} [3635] 6-8-12 45...................................(p) EmmettStack$^{(5)}$ 9 13
(H J Manners) *nvr wnt pce: a in rr* **80/1**
4000 **9** *½* **Sunny Haze**^{44} [5728] 3-8-12 35.. PaulEddery 11 6
(Mrs P N Dutfield) *mid-div: outpcd over 3f out: sn wknd* **25/1**
0405 **10** *6* **The Keep**^{15} [6274] 4-8-7 40...................................(v) NataliaGemelova$^{(5)}$ 7 —
(R E Barr) *hmpd and lost pl after 1f: sn bhd: t.o 3f out* **12/1**
000- **11** *33* **Indian Kate**^{380} [6196] 3-8-12 30.. TomEaves 5 —
(R Brotherton) *chsd ldrs: lost pl over 3f out: sn bhd and eased: virtually p.u: t.o* **50/1**

1m 18.14s (1.24) **Going Correction** +0.175s/f (Slow) **11** Ran SP% **118.9**
Speed ratings (Par 103):98,90,87,86,86 86,79,74,74,66 22
CSF £23.13 TOTE £3.70: £1.10, £2.20, £1.50; EX 22.70 Trifecta £77.60 Pool £129.06 - 1.18 winning units.
Owner Saeed Manana **Bred** Tower Bloodstock **Trained** Newmarket, Suffolk
■ Stewards' Enquiry : Dane O'Neill one-day ban: careless riding (Nov 27)

FOCUS
The quicker of the two divisions and a very ready winner but it was only a low-grade sprint maiden. The form is weak with banded-class horses close up.

6493 EXPERIENCE NOTTINGHAMSHIRE (S) STKS 7f (F)
1:30 (1:30) (Class 6) 3-Y-O+ **£2,388** (£705; £352) **Stalls** Low

Form RPR
-000 **1** **Cleveland**^{15} [6286] 4-8-8 50.................................... RussellKennemore$^{(7)}$ 4 57
(R Hollinshead) *trckd ldrs: c stands' side and led 2f out: hld on wl* **33/1**
4000 **2** *1* **Kensington (IRE)**^{30} [6020] 5-9-0 60................................(p) MCGeran$^{(7)}$ 9 61
(P D Evans) *hld up in midfield: hdwy over 1f out: styd on to take 2nd nr fin* **9/1**
6600 **3** *nk* **Prince Of Gold**^{91} [4467] 6-9-1 46...........................(e^{1}) FergusSweeney 11 54
(R Hollinshead) *hld up in midfield: hdwy and c wd over 2f out: swtchd lft over 1f out: no ex ins last* **12/1**
0035 **4** *¾* **Flint River**^{33} [5937] 8-9-1 67.. MickyFenton 1 52
(H Morrison) *trckd ldrs on inner: kpt on same pce fnl f* **6/5^{1}**
3300 **5** *2 ½* **Bathwick Emma (IRE)**^{12} [6323] 3-8-9 60................. GrahamGibbons 10 41
(P D Evans) *chsd ldrs: outpcd over 3f out: kpt on same pce fnl 2f* **11/2^{2}**
0004 **6** *1 ½* **Straffan (IRE)**^{15} [6282] 4-9-2 45.................................(p) DaleGibson 3 43
(J Hetherton) *led tl 2f out: one pce* **16/1**
000 **7** *8* **Mulberry Lad (IRE)**^{149} [2702] 4-9-0 46................... WilliamCarson$^{(7)}$ 2 27
(P W Hiatt) *hood removed v late: s.i.s: hdwy to chse ldrs over 4f out: wknd over 1f out* **33/1**
0000 **8** *1 ½* **What-A-Dancer (IRE)**^{14} [6293] 9-9-7 59........................(b) DaneO'Neill 13 23
(R A Harris) *trckd ldrs on outer: outpcd over 3f out: wknd fnl 2f* **14/1**
3000 **9** *3* **Woodwee**^{5} [6425] 3-9-0 61... PhillipMakin 14 9
(J R Weymes) *chsd ldrs: lost pl over 2f out* **25/1**
6053 **10** *2 ½* **The London Gang**^{33} [5953] 3-9-6 58...............................(v) PatCosgrave 6 9
(P D Evans) *s.i.s: nvr on terms* **6/1^{3}**
4000 **11** *2 ½* **Zafarshah (IRE)**^{9} [6371] 7-8-8 45................................(b) TolleyDean$^{(7)}$ 7 —
(R A Harris) *in rr: reminders after 1f: t.o 3f out* **16/1**

1m 32.02s (1.22) **Going Correction** +0.175s/f (Slow)
WFA 3 from 4yo+ 1lb **11** Ran SP% **121.0**
Speed ratings (Par 101):100,98,98,97,94 93,83,82,78,75 73
CSF £309.55 TOTE £49.30: £7.10, £2.80, £3.40; EX 606.70 TRIFECTA Not won..The winner was bought in for 4,250gns.
Owner R Hollinshead **Bred** Darley **Trained** Upper Longdon, Staffs
■ Stewards' Enquiry : Russell Kennemore one-day ban: used whip down the shoulder in the forehand position (Nov 27)

FOCUS
A moderate race as is to be expected for the grade, but the form appears reasonably sound.

6494 BOOK YOUR CHRISTMAS PARTY HERE H'CAP 1m 4f (F)
2:00 (2:00) (Class 5) (0-75,72) 3-Y-O+ **£3,238** (£963; £481; £240) **Stalls** Low

Form RPR
031- **1** **Mr Excel (IRE)**^{366} [6342] 3-8-12 71......................... RichardKingscote$^{(3)}$ 4 80+
(J A Osborne) *t.k.h: trckd ldrs: led 3f out: styd on strly fnl f* **5/1**
0400 **2** *1 ½* **William's Way**^{5} [6426] 4-9-4 68... LeeEnstone 3 75
(I A Wood) *hld up on outer: stdy hdwy over 4f out: chal 3f out: kpt on same pce fnl f* **14/1**
051- **3** *9* **Stravara**^{378} [6228] 3-9-2 72.. GrahamGibbons 5 65
(R Hollinshead) *hld up in prom position: effrt over 3f out: one pce fnl 2f* **13/2**
0400 **4** *2 ½* **Shape Up (IRE)**^{36} [5905] 6-9-2 66..(b) TomEaves 1 55
(R Craggs) *led 2f: chsd ldrs: hung rt and one pce fnl 2f* **11/4^{1}**
0045 **5** *6* **Newnham (IRE)**^{6} [6408] 5-9-8 72.. DavidAllan 6 51
(J R Boyle) *led after 2f: set mod pce: qcknd over 4f out: hdd 3f out: wknd fnl 2f* **7/2^{3}**
311- **6** *½* **Spunger**^{414} [5536] 3-8-10 66.. DaneO'Neill 2 44
(H J L Dunlop) *trckd ldrs: chal 3f out: sn rdn and btn* **3/1^{2}**

2m 42.54s (0.45) **Going Correction** +0.175s/f (Slow)
WFA 3 from 4yo+ 6lb **6** Ran SP% **110.6**
Speed ratings (Par 103):105,104,98,96,92 92
CSF £61.51 TOTE £6.70: £2.40, £4.80; EX 64.50.
Owner A Taylor **Bred** Ellesmere Bloodstock Ltd **Trained** Upper Lambourn, Berks

FOCUS
Quite a good handicap for the grade rated through the runner-up.

6495 VENUE FOR ALL OCCASIONS H'CAP 2m (F)
2:30 (2:30) (Class 5) (0-75,70) 3-Y-O+ **£3,238** (£963; £481; £240) **Stalls** Low

Form RPR
4404 **1** **Trinity Rose**^{6} [6408] 3-9-3 66.. GregFairley$^{(3)}$ 8 86
(M Johnston) *chsd ldrs: pushed along 9f out: hdwy on ins to ld over 3f out: drew rt away* **4/1^{3}**
2133 **2** *18* **At The Money**^{2} [6467] 3-9-10 70... MickyFenton 2 68
(J M P Eustace) *chsd ldr: drvn 7f out: kpt on to take 2nd 2f out: no ch w wnr* **5/2^{1}**
0402 **3** *3* **Give It Time**^{21} [6178] 3-9-2 62... J-PGuillambert 1 56
(J G Given) *led: qcknd 10f out: hdd over 3f out: one pce* **10/3^{2}**
0520 **4** *20* **Bolshoi Ballet**^{25} [3350] 8-8-13 50................................(b) PaulMulrennan 4 20
(Miss J E Foster) *chsd ldrs: outpcd and lost pl over 4f out: plodded on* **33/1**
6010 **5** *26* **Bulberry Hill**^{13} [6305] 5-8-12 49... PaulEddery 7 —
(R W Price) *hld up in tch: drvn over 5f out: sn lost pl and bhd* **6/1**
1002 **6** *17* **Victory Quest (IRE)**^{240} [675] 6-10-0 65...........................(v) DaneO'Neill 3 —
(Mrs S Lamyman) *chsd ldrs: drvn 6f out: sn lost pl and bhd* **12/1**
0005 **7** *21* **Isa'Af (IRE)**^{6} [6415] 7-9-11 62... PhillipMakin 6 —
(P W Hiatt) *hld up in tch: reminders 9f out: lost pl 5f out: sn bhd and eased* **11/2**
5000 **8** *120* **Annies Valentine**^{37} [5870] 3-7-13 50 oh6 ow4............. EmmettStack$^{(5)}$ 5 —
(J Gallagher) *trckd ldrs: pushed along over 8f out: sn wknd: t.o 6f out: completed in own time* **50/1**

3m 45.46s (0.92) **Going Correction** +0.175s/f (Slow)
WFA 3 from 5yo+ 9lb **8** Ran SP% **113.9**
Speed ratings (Par 103):104,95,93,83,70 62,51,—
CSF £14.32 CT £35.86 TOTE £4.70: £1.40, £1.40, £1.40; EX 13.80 Trifecta £39.80 Pool £162.68 - 2.90 winning units.
Owner T P M McDonagh **Bred** T P And M McDonagh **Trained** Middleham Moor, N Yorks

FOCUS
A modest handicap and very uncompetitive, with this testing two miles seemingly proving too much for some of these. The runner-up to recent form is the best guide.

6496 ARENA LEISURE H'CAP 5f (F)
3:00 (3:00) (Class 3) (0-95,90) 3-Y-O+ **£8,096** (£2,408; £1,203; £601) **Stalls** High

Form RPR
114 **1** **Dancing Mystery**^{4} [6446] 12-8-10 82.........................(b) StephenCarson 5 88
(E A Wheeler) *mde all: hld on gamely* **6/1**
0005 **2** *hd* **Anfield Dream**^{21} [6174] 4-7-11 76 oh7.......................... WilliamBuick$^{(7)}$ 7 81
(J R Jenkins) *hld up in tch: hdwy over 2f out: chal appr fnl f: edgd lft ins last: jst hld* **10/1**
4301 **3** *½* **Matuza (IRE)**^{10} [6352] 3-8-13 85 6ex.................................. DaneO'Neill 6 92+
(W R Muir) *trckd ldrs: n.m.r and swtchd rt ins last: styd on wl nr fin* **3/1^{1}**
6000 **4** *½* **Graze On**^{17} [6243] 4-9-2 88...(b) GrahamGibbons 3 90
(Peter Grayson) *wnt rt s: chsd ldrs: kpt on same pce fnl f* **16/1**
4560 **5** *nk* **Efistorm**^{5} [6428] 5-8-2 79 .... AndrewElliott$^{(5)}$ 2 80
(J Balding) *w ldrs: kpt on same pce fnl f* **8/1**
003 **6** *hd* **Stoneacre Lad (IRE)**^{74} [5009] 3-8-13 85................(b) RobbieFitzpatrick 1 85
(Peter Grayson) *racd alone far side: w ldrs: no ex fnl f* **9/2^{2}**
0-66 **7** *6* **Turn On The Style**^{5} [6428] 4-8-6 78................................(b) DavidAllan 10 58
(J Balding) *dwlt: bhd and drvn along: nvr on terms* **12/1**
0030 **8** *12* **Zowington**^{11} [6335] 4-9-4 90... TonyCulhane 9 29
(C F Wall) *hld up: effrt 2f out: sn btn* **5/1^{3}**
0540 **9** *nk* **Pawan (IRE)**^{43} [5749] 6-8-3 80 oh1 ow4.........................(b) AnnStokell$^{(5)}$ 4 18
(Miss A Stokell) *ducked lft: bmpd and rdr lost irons s: nvr on terms: virtually p.u ins last* **20/1**
0020 **10** *1 ¼* **Polish Emperor (USA)**^{12} [6320] 6-8-8 85...............(p) MarkLawson$^{(5)}$ 11 19
(D W Barker) *racd stands' side: chsd ldrs: lost pl over 1f out* **20/1**
0-00 **11** *23* **Distinctly Game**^{144} [2847] 4-9-4 90 .... CatherineGannon 8 —
(K A Ryan) *bhd: drvn and lost pl over 2f: eased* **25/1**

60.06 secs (-0.24) **Going Correction** +0.15s/f (Slow) **11** Ran SP% **121.3**
Speed ratings (Par 107):107,106,105,105,104 104,94,75,75,73 36
CSF £64.71 CT £219.17 TOTE £6.10: £2.40, £3.20, £1.60; EX 60.80 Trifecta £222.00 Pool £838.10 - 2.90 winning units.
Owner Astrod TA Austin Stroud & Co **Bred** Mrs D Price **Trained** Whitchurch-on-Thames, Oxon

FOCUS
A fair handicap in which 'old boy' Dancing Mystery recorded his fifth course and distance win. The form is not that strong for the grade but makes sense.

NOTEBOOK
Dancing Mystery, who failed to land the hat-trick back on the All-Weather off a much higher mark compared with turf at Lingfield last time, had four course and distance wins to his name coming into the race and the near 13-year-old blazed the trail in his usual fashion before sticking his neck out to hold the persistent challenge of Anfield Dream. He is obviously not the force of old, but still enjoys his racing and will remain a threat over this straight five. (op 9-2)
Anfield Dream, racing from 7lb out of the handicap, was given a well-judged ride and came through with his challenge, but was unable to get past the veteran, who is three times his age. This was an improved run, but the likelihood now is that he will go up a fair bit for this. (op 8-1)
Matuza(IRE), back to form over a furlong further at Lingfield earlier in the month, was probably unfortunate not to defy a penalty, getting short of room at a vital stage and then not being able to quicken over this furlong shorter trip. He looks to be progressing again and the three-year-old is a sprinter to keep on-side. (op 10-3 tchd 11-4)
Graze On was doing his best work late on, but never looked like winning. This was a better effort with the blinkers back on.
Efistorm was unable to lead with the winner in the opposition and the money that came for him beforehand never looked like coming good. (op 12-1)
Stoneacre Lad(IRE) went across to the far rail, probably unfavoured, and he may have been involved in the finish had he raced with the pack. (op 5-1 tchd 6-1)
Zowington flopped on this Fibresand debut, never getting involved having been held up, and clearly needs switching back to a different surface. Official explanation: jockey said colt lost its action (op 6-1)
Distinctly Game Official explanation: jockey said gelding finished distressed

6497 JOIN US ON THE 20TH H'CAP 1m (F)
3:30 (3:30) (Class 6) (0-66,66) 3-Y-O+ **£2,730** (£806; £403) **Stalls** Low

Form RPR
6604 **1** **Jordan's Light (USA)**^{7} [6396] 3-8-8 61.................(v) RobbieFitzpatrick 10 73+
(T J Pitt) *in tch: hdwy on inner over 2f out: hrd rdn and styd on to ld last 75yds* **7/4^{1}**
0041 **2** *1* **Dudley Docker (IRE)**^{7} [6404] 4-8-6 64 6ex................. KellyHarrison$^{(7)}$ 8 74
(D Carroll) *trckd ldrs: racd keenly: smooth hdwy to ld over 1f out: edgd lft and hdd ins last: no ex* **11/2^{3}**

4504 **3** 5 **Lii Najma**^{18} 6227 3-8-13 **66** J-PGuillambert 14 66
(C E Brittain) *trckd ldrs: hung lft and one pce fnl 2f* **9/2**^{2}
0630 **4** 5 **Gem Bien (USA)**^{5} 6431 8-8-4 **55** oh2 (b) PaulQuinn 11 44
(D W Chapman) *s.i.s: hdwy to chse ldrs 4f out: one pce fnl 2f* **16/1**
0604 **5** 3/4 **The Gaikwar (IRE)**^{8} 6387 7-8-7 **58** (b) DaleGibson 2 45
(R A Harris) *s.i.s: bhd tl styd on fnl 2f: nt rch ldrs* **14/1**
5300 **6** nk **Favouring (IRE)**^{2} 6465 4-7-11 **55** (v) MCGeran$^{(7)}$ 12 42
(M C Chapman) *trckd ldrs: led over 3f out: hdd over 1f out: edgd lft and fdd* **12/1**
3050 **7** 2 1/2 **Tour D'Amour (IRE)**^{56} 5484 3-8-10 **63** TomEaves 3 45
(R Craggs) *s.i.s: hdwy to ld after 1f: hdd over 4f out: wknd 2f out* **16/1**
5505 **8** 1/2 **Ermine Grey**^{14} 6300 5-9-0 **65** FergusSweeney 5 45
(A W Carroll) *in rr: kpt on fnl 2f: nvr a factor* **8/1**
10/0 **9** 2 1/2 **Experimental (IRE)**^{4} 6451 12-8-9 **60** StephenCarson 13 35
(John A Harris) *dwlt: bhd and swtchd lft after s: sme hdwy on ins whn n.m.r 2f out: nvr on terms* **50/1**
2004 **10** 3 1/2 **Never Say Deya**^{17} 6235 3-7-11 **55** oh8 LiamJones$^{(5)}$ 4 23
(M R Channon) *mid-div: lost pl over 4f out* **14/1**
65-0 **11** 6 **Amongst Amigos (IRE)**^{47} 5663 5-8-9 **60** ow2 (b) PhillipMakin 7 15
(Thomas Cleary, Ire) *in tch: lost pl over 2f out* **20/1**
0006 **12** 6 **Stolen Summer (IRE)**^{2} 6469 3-8-12 **65** MickyFenton 9 8
(B S Rothwell) *led 1f: chsd ldrs: lost pl over 2f out* **25/1**
13 1/2 **Randall's Diana (IRE)**^{63} 5305 3-8-2 **55** oh1 CatherineGannon 6 —
(Daniel Mark Loughnane, Ire) *dwlt: a in rr* **33/1**
/500 **14** 6 **Unicorn Reward (IRE)**^{17} 6240 6-9-0 **65** (b) DaneO'Neill 1 —
(Mrs L C Jewell) *sn chsng ldrs: led over 4f out: hdd over 3f out: lost pl over 2f out* **33/1**

1m 44.17s (-0.43) **Going Correction** +0.175s/f (Slow)
WFA 3 from 4yo+ 2lb **14** Ran SP% **130.3**
Speed ratings (Par 101):109,108,103,98,97 96,94,93,91,87 81,75,75,69
CSF £11.35 CT £43.64 TOTE £2.30: £1.50, £2.20, £2.10; EX 18.40 Trifecta £34.20 Pool £278.34 - 5.77 winning units. Place 5 £555.03, Place 5 £396.36 .
Owner B A Jordan **Bred** Lantern Hill Farm Llc **Trained** Bawtry, S Yorks
■ Stewards' Enquiry : Kelly Harrison three-day ban: careless riding (Nov 27-29)

FOCUS
A moderate handicap but a very smart winning time for a race of its class. The runner-up is the best guide to the level.
T/Plt: £720.50 to a £1 stake. Pool: £33,855.55. 34.30 winning tickets. T/Qpdt: £105.20 to a £1 stake. Pool: £2,986.00. 21.00 winning tickets. WG

6478 WOLVERHAMPTON (A.W) (L-H)
Thursday, November 16

OFFICIAL GOING: Standard
Wind: Fresh, behind Weather: Cloudy

6498 DINE IN THE ZONGALERO RESTAURANT MEDIAN AUCTION MAIDEN STKS 1m 1f 103y(P)
3:45 (3:45) (Class 5) 2-Y-O **£3,238** (£963; £481; £240) **Stalls** Low

Form RPR
0465 **1** **New Beginning (IRE)**^{31} 6010 2-9-3 78 RobertWinston 2 75+
(Mrs S Lamyman) *mde all: rdn and hung rt wl over 1f out: r.o: eased nr fin* **2/1**^{2}
005 **2** 2 1/2 **Summer Of Love (IRE)**^{9} 6386 2-8-12 JoeFanning 6 63
(P F I Cole) *chsd ldrs: rdn over 3f out: styd on same pce fnl f* **5/1**^{3}
2202 **3** 1 3/4 **Aussie Cricket (FR)**^{16} 6283 2-8-12 68 EddieAhern 3 60
(D J Coakley) *trckd ldrs: plld hrd: rdn over 1f out: no ex fnl f* **1/1**^{1}
0 **4** 1 **Astral Charmer**^{8} 6393 2-9-3 TPQueally 1 63
(M H Tompkins) *hld up in tch: rdn over 2f out: styd on same pce appr fnl f* **28/1**
00 **5** 2 1/2 **Polyquest (IRE)**^{11} 6349 2-8-12 NelsonDeSouza 8 53
(P F I Cole) *hld up: pushed along 6f out: styd on ins fnl f: n.d* **25/1**
00 **6** 2 1/2 **Little Rutland**^{19} 6224 2-9-3 ChrisCatlin 4 54
(E J O'Neill) *plld hrd: trckd ldr: rdn over 2f out: hung lft and wknd over 1f out* **25/1**
7 1 1/2 **Toboggan Lady** 2-8-12 TonyCulhane 7 46
(Mrs A Duffield) *dwlt: sn pushed along in rr: wknd 3f out* **25/1**

2m 3.68s (1.06) **Going Correction** -0.15s/f (Stan) **7** Ran SP% **115.0**
Speed ratings (Par 96):89,86,85,84,82 79,78
CSF £11.65 TOTE £2.60: £1.20, £1.90; EX 9.80 Trifecta £23.50 Pool £350.15 - 10.55 winning units.
Owner P Lamyman **Bred** Airlie Stud And Sir Thomas Pilkington **Trained** Ruckland, Lincs

FOCUS
A moderate juvenile maiden that was run at a modest pace. The winner is value for further but the standard is pretty weak.

NOTEBOOK
New Beginning(IRE) made all to open his account at the sixth attempt, despite hanging badly on the final turn and ending up on the stands' rail inside the final furlong. He had very much the run of the race out in front, but he still did very well to win as he did despite his antics off the home bend and he must rate value for about double his winning margin. He is clearly still learning his trade. (op 9-4)
Summer Of Love(IRE), easy to back, was another who still looked distinctly green yet posted her best effort to date in defeat. She got the extra distance well enough and should come on again for the experience. (tchd 7-1)
Aussie Cricket(FR) has to rate slightly disappointing. However, she would not have enjoyed the uneven pace, and on recent evidence a drop back in trip now looks in order. (op 6-5 tchd 10-11)
Astral Charmer showed improved form on his Kempton debut eight days previously without ever threatening. He will become eligible for a handicap rating after his next assignment and is another who probably needs a stronger early pace over this trip. (op 20-1)
Polyquest(IRE), up in trip, had plenty to do from off the pace approaching the home turn and ran a little better than her finishing position suggests. She is now eligible for a nursery mark and should be seen in a better light with a more positive ride over this distance. (op 20-1)

6499 TWILIGHT RACING AND SUPPER - RELAX & ENJOY H'CAP 5f 216y(P)
4:20 (4:20) (Class 4) (0-85,84) 3-Y-O+ **£5,505** (£1,637; £818; £408) **Stalls** Low

Form RPR
0505 **1** **Connect**^{6} 6428 9-8-9 **77** (b) TPQueally 9 87
(M H Tompkins) *chsd ldrs: rdn to ld ins fnl f: r.o* **10/1**
5200 **2** 1 **Grimes Faith**^{8} 6397 3-8-13 **81** JimmyFortune 10 88
(R Hannon) *sn outpcd: hdwy over 2f out: rdn and hung lft over 1f out: r.o* **6/1**
4056 **3** 1 1/4 **Pieter Brueghel (USA)**^{15} 6292 7-9-2 **84** JoeFanning 8 87
(D Nicholls) *trckd ldr: racd keenly: rdn to ld over 1f out: hdd and unable qckn ins fnl f* **11/2**^{3}
1514 **4** 1/2 **Rosein**^{6} 6428 4-8-8 **76** SteveDrowne 12 78
(Mrs G S Rees) *hld up: hdwy over 2f out: rdn over 1f out: styd on same pce ins fnl f* **4/1**^{1}
0645 **5** 1 1/4 **Kingscross**^{50} 5627 8-8-1 **76** LauraReynolds$^{(7)}$ 7 74
(M Blanshard) *sn outpcd: r.o wl ins fnl f: nrst fin* **16/1**
5000 **6** nk **Will He Wish**^{21} 6192 10-9-1 **83** IanMongan 4 80
(S Gollings) *sn outpcd: rdn over 2f out: styd on fnl f: nt trble ldrs* **16/1**
-035 **7** 3/4 **Foreign Edition (IRE)**^{39} 5842 4-8-12 **80** TomEaves 6 75
(Miss J A Camacho) *chsd ldrs: rdn 1/2-way: no imp fnl 2f* **9/2**^{2}
5000 **8** 2 **Harry Up**^{11} 6352 5-8-9 **84** DanielRobinson$^{(7)}$ 1 73
(K A Ryan) *led over 4f: wknd ins fnl f* **8/1**
1046 **9** 1/2 **Stellite**^{19} 6212 6-8-2 **75** DuranFentiman$^{(5)}$ 2 62
(J S Goldie) *s.i.s: hdwy over 4f out: wknd over 2f out* **14/1**
004 **10** 2 1/2 **Nusoor (IRE)**^{37} 5896 3-8-6 **74** ow1 RobbieFitzpatrick 3 54
(Peter Grayson) *s.i.s: outpcd* **12/1**
5046 **11** 3 **Campo Bueno (FR)**^{33} 5957 4-9-1 **83** RobertWinston 11 54
(A Berry) *chsd ldrs over 3f* **14/1**

1m 13.61s (-2.20) **Going Correction** -0.15s/f (Stan) **11** Ran SP% **120.8**
Speed ratings (Par 105):108,106,105,104,102 102,101,98,97,94 90
CSF £70.89 CT £372.74 TOTE £7.50: £3.60, £1.40, £3.40; EX 65.20 TRIFECTA Not won..
Owner Mrs P R Bowring **Bred** J A E Hobby **Trained** Newmarket, Suffolk
■ Stewards' Enquiry : Joe Fanning one-day ban: failed to ride to draw (Nov 27)

FOCUS
An open sprint for the grade, run at a sound enough pace and the form looks fairly straightforward, rated around the placed horses.

6500 BOOK ONLINE AT WOLVERHAMPTON-RACECOURSE.CO.UK NURSERY 5f 20y(P)
4:50 (4:50) (Class 6) (0-65,68) 2-Y-O **£2,266** (£674; £337; £168) **Stalls** Low

Form RPR
4022 **1** **Galaxy Of Stars**^{6} 6420 2-8-9 **55** (v^{1}) PatrickMathers$^{(3)}$ 12 60
(D Shaw) *sn outpcd: hdwy over 1f out: rdn to ld wl ins fnl f* **8/1**
6533 **2** 1 1/4 **Mujart**^{7} 6414 2-8-7 **57** RussellKennemore$^{(7)}$ 11 57
(J A Pickering) *hld up: hdwy 1/2-way: rdn to ld and hung lft over 1f out: hdd and unable qckn wl ins fnl f* **8/1**
0050 **3** 1/2 **Darling Belinda**^{17} 6255 2-9-5 **62** FergusSweeney 4 60
(D K Ivory) *s.i.s: sn mid-div: hdwy and hung lft fr over 1f out: r.o* **14/1**
660 **4** 1 1/4 **Minnow**^{73} 5059 2-8-12 **55** AdamKirby 1 49
(S C Williams) *chsd ldrs: rdn and hung lft over 1f out: no ex ins fnl f* **7/2**^{2}
4000 **5** 1 1/2 **Blakeshall Rose**^{6} 6422 2-8-5 **48** ow2 DeanMcKeown 9 36
(A J Chamberlain) *sn outpcd: styd on ins fnl f: nrst fin* **16/1**
0056 **6** hd **Kyllachy Storm**^{14} 6310 2-9-7 **64** SteveDrowne 2 52
(R J Hodges) *prom: hmpd and lost pl 4f out: nt clr run wl over 1f out: hdwy and nt clr run 1f out: swtchd rt: nt trble ldrs* **3/1**^{1}
0053 **7** 1 **Mandriano (ITY)**^{3} 6463 2-7-11 **47** oh6 ow6 (p) DonnaCaldwell$^{(7)}$ 7 31
(D W Barker) *chsd ldr: ev ch 2f out: sn rdn: wknd fnl f* **7/1**^{3}
000 **8** 1 3/4 **Kilvickeon (IRE)**^{30} 6034 2-8-7 **50** (b^{1}) RobbieFitzpatrick 10 28
(Peter Grayson) *s.s: n.d* **20/1**
0001 **9** nk **Stir Crazy (IRE)**^{8} 6401 2-9-11 **68** 7ex ChrisCatlin 8 45
(M R Channon) *led 1f: chsd ldrs: rdn 2f out: wknd fnl f* **7/1**^{3}
5000 **10** nk **Eastern Playboy (IRE)**^{52} 5570 2-8-2 **50** (b^{1}) LiamJones$^{(5)}$ 5 26
(J Jay) *led 4f out: rdn and hdd over 1f out: sn wknd* **16/1**
0000 **11** 3 1/2 **Mrs Crossy (IRE)**^{14} 6311 2-8-7 **53** JamesDoyle$^{(3)}$ 3 16
(A W Carroll) *prom: rdn 1/2-way: wknd over 1f out* **14/1**

62.71 secs (-0.11) **Going Correction** -0.15s/f (Stan) **11** Ran SP% **124.3**
Speed ratings (Par 94):94,92,91,89,86 86,84,82,81,81 75
CSF £74.77 CT £918.65 TOTE £6.60: £1.70, £3.50, £4.60; EX 32.10 Trifecta £182.40 Part won. Pool £257.02 - 0.34 winning units..
Owner Danethorpe Racing Ltd **Bred** Mrs C Regalado-Gonzalez **Trained** Danethorpe, Notts

FOCUS
A moderate nursery and the form looks straightforward rated through the runner-up.

NOTEBOOK
Galaxy Of Stars, runner-up on her previous two outings, deservedly opened her account at the fifth time of asking in ready fashion. The application of a first-time visor had the desired effect and she deserves extra credit for defying her outside stall. She is clearly at the top of her game at present, and has developed into a consistent sort, but her prospects no doubt rely on the headgear having the same effect in the future. (op 10-1)
Mujart came through to have every chance from her wide draw and, while ultimately being put in her place by the winner, ran another sound race in defeat. She helps to set the level of this form, looks best kept to this distance, and deserves a change of fortune.
Darling Belinda, fractious at the start, posted by far her best effort to date on this nursery debut. She has now found her level and, while clearly a little headstrong, is entitled to build on this. (op 16-1)
Minnow, a half-sister to the useful sprinter Enchantment, was all the rage in the betting for this nursery bow. However, she was made to look one paced when it mattered on this drop back to the minimum trip and ultimately proved disappointing. On this evidence she needs another furlong and is presumably thought capable of better from this sort of mark. (op 10-3 tchd 4-1)
Blakeshall Rose was never seriously in the hunt, but still kept on to post her best effort to date.
Kyllachy Storm proved unsuited by the drop back to this trip, but may have been closer with a clearer passage around the final furlong marker. Official explanation: jockey said colt was denied a clear run (op 11-2)
Mandriano(ITY) failed to raise his game on this handicap debut and probably found it coming too soon. (op 13-2 tchd 15-2)

6501 WOLVERHAMPTON RACECOURSE FOR ANY OCCASION MEDIAN AUCTION MAIDEN STKS 1m 5f 194y(P)
5:20 (5:20) (Class 6) 3-4-Y-O **£2,730** (£806; £403) **Stalls** Low

Form RPR
0502 **1** **Go Amwell**^{18} 6238 3-9-3 47 PaulDoe 1 46
(J R Jenkins) *hld up: hdwy over 2f out: sn rdn: lft 2nd ins fnl f: sn led: all out* **6/1**^{2}
-205 **2** shd **Monte Major (GER)**^{10} 6375 3-9-3 45 (v^{1}) DaneO'Neill 10 46
(D J Daly) *hld up: keen: hdwy to chse ldr over 3f out: sn rdn: hld whn hmpd and lft in ld ins fnl f: sn hdd: kpt on* **14/1**^{3}
3 7 **Drumfergus Boy (IRE)**^{30} 6040 4-9-11 JoeFanning 8 36
(Andrew Oliver, Ire) *chsd ldrs: rdn over 2f out: sn outpcd* **25/1**
/0-0 **4** 7 **Mr Kayos**^{14} 6305 4-9-11 40 DeanMcKeown 4 26
(Mrs G S Rees) *prom: hmpd over 3f out: sn wknd* **66/1**
-000 **5** 35 **Vixen Virago**^{30} 6026 3-8-12 40 RobertWinston 9 —
(Jane Southcombe) *led: hdd over 7f out: wknd over 2f out* **100/1**
2320 **P** **Mantle**^{26} 6108 4-9-6 69 OscarUrbina 5 47
(J R Fanshawe) *trckd ldrs: led 4f out: 4 l clr whn broke down and p.u ins fnl f* **1/4**^{1}
000 **P** **Good Intentions**^{13} 6327 4-9-6 35 LPKeniry 6 —
(P W Hiatt) *prom: chsd ldr over 11f out: sddle sn slipped: led over 7f out: hdd 4f out: sn lost pl: p.u over 1f out* **100/1**

3m 9.79s (2.42) **Going Correction** -0.15s/f (Stan)
WFA 3 from 4yo 8lb **7** Ran SP% **108.3**
Speed ratings (Par 101):87,86,82,78,58 —,—
CSF £60.15 TOTE £5.00: £1.80, £3.00; EX 35.60 Trifecta £81.40 Pool £390.10 - 3.40 winning units.

Owner Amwell Racing **Bred** Michael Ng **Trained** Royston, Herts

FOCUS
No strength in depth to this staying maiden, run at a moderate early pace, and the race dramatically changed its complexion when hot favourite Mantle broke down when appearing to have to race in safe keeping entering the final furlong. The form looks dubious and probably worth little.

Vixen Virago Official explanation: jockey said filly lost its action

Good Intentions Official explanation: jockey said saddle slipped

6502 STAY AT THE WOLVERHAMPTON HOLIDAY INN H'CAP 1m 141y(P)
5:50 (5:50) (Class 4) (0-80,80) 3-Y-0+ £5,505 (£1,637; £818; £408) Stalls Low

Form RPR

0461 **1** **Cusoon**[41] [5786] 4-9-3 **78** .... GeorgeBaker 12 — 88
(G L Moore) *hld up: hdwy over 2f out: led and hung lft fr over 1f out: rdn out* **14/1**

0215 **2** *2* **King Of Argos**[14] [6313] 3-9-2 **80** .... JimmyFortune 3 — 86
(E A L Dunlop) *chsd ldrs: rdn and hung lft fnl f: styd on same pce* **7/2**[1]

2010 **3** *1* **Mataram (USA)**[20] [6206] 3-8-12 **76** .... RobertWinston 7 — 80+
(W Jarvis) *hld up: hmpd 7f out: hdwy over 1f out: nt rch ldrs* **14/1**

0611 **4** *nk* **Writ (IRE)**[18] [6240] 4-8-10 **71** .... TomEaves 5 — 74
(I Semple) *chsd ldrs: rdn over 1f out: styd on same pce* **11/2**[2]

1222 **5** *½* **Bold Marc (IRE)**[6] [6424] 4-8-13 **79** .... (p) AndrewElliott(5) 13 — 81
(K R Burke) *chsd ldr tl led over 2f out: rdn and hdd over 1f out: no ex fnl f* **8/1**[3]

3621 **6** *¾* **Middlemarch (IRE)**[17] [6259] 6-9-0 **75** .... (b) PhillipMakin 9 — 76
(J S Goldie) *hld up in tch: rdn over 2f out: styd on same pce appr fnl f* **7/2**[1]

1500 **7** *½* **Tempsford Flyer (IRE)**[47] [5666] 3-9-2 **80** .... EddieAhern 4 — 80
(J W Hills) *hld up: effrt and hung lft over 1f out: n.d* **8/1**[3]

5400 **8** *nk* **Trifti**[45] [5739] 5-8-13 **74** .... JimmyQuinn 1 — 73
(C A Cyzer) *chsd ldrs: rdn over 2f out: wknd fnl f* **20/1**

0140 **9** *3 ½* **Street Warrior (IRE)**[14] [6313] 3-9-0 **78** .... JoeFanning 8 — 70
(M Johnston) *dwlt: hld up: effrt over 1f out: eased whn btn fnl f* **14/1**

-453 **10** *nk* **Master Mahogany**[7] [6417] 5-8-13 **74** .... SteveDrowne 6 — 65
(R J Hodges) *sn led: rdn and hdd over 2f out: wknd over 1f out* **12/1**

05-0 **11** *1 ¾* **Black Falcon (IRE)**[14] [6313] 6-9-5 **80** .... TonyCulhane 2 — 67
(P T Midgley) *hld up: rdn over 2f out: a in rr* **12/1**

11/0 **12** *15* **King's Account (USA)**[14] [6313] 4-9-3 **78** .... IanMongan 11 — 34
(S Gollings) *prom 6f* **50/1**

1m 47.55s (-4.21) **Going Correction** -0.15s/f (Stan)
WFA 3 from 4yo+ 3lb **12** Ran SP% **124.2**
Speed ratings (Par 105):112,110,109,109,108 107,107,107,104,103 102,88
CSF £65.53 CT £741.70 TOTE £14.30: £4.00, £1.90, £3.40; EX 88.60 Trifecta £230.60 Pool £324.92 - 1.00 winning units.

Owner The Winning Hand **Bred** Mrs Dare Wigan And Dominic Wigan **Trained** Woodingdean, E Sussex

FOCUS
A tight handicap for the grade that was run at a decent pace. Sound form rated through the runner-up.

Tempsford Flyer(IRE) Official explanation: jockey said colt hung left

6503 TWILIGHT RACING - BEAT THE TRAFFIC H'CAP 1m 1f 103y(P)
6:20 (6:20) (Class 5) (0-70,70) 3-Y-0+ £3,238 (£963; £481; £240) Stalls Low

Form RPR

4013 **1** **Kildare Sun (IRE)**[18] [6240] 4-9-4 **67** .... DaleGibson 11 — 81
(J Mackie) *sn pushed along in rr: hdwy over 1f out: led ins fnl f: r.o* **8/1**

0002 **2** *hd* **Tous Les Deux**[7] [6419] 3-8-12 **64** .... RobbieFitzpatrick 9 — 78+
(Peter Grayson) *hld up: nt clr run over 2f out: swtchd rt and hdwy over 1f out: r.o* **3/1**[2]

0441 **3** *5* **Some Diva**[10] [6380] 3-8-13 **65** 7ex .... (v) AdamKirby 2 — 69
(W R Swinburn) *led: rdn over 1f out: sn edgd rt: hdd and no ex ins fnl f* **15/8**[1]

0021 **4** *1 ¼* **Port 'n Starboard**[204] [1244] 5-9-2 **65** .... TonyCulhane 7 — 67
(C A Cyzer) *hld up: hdwy over 2f out: rdn over 1f out: wknd ins fnl f* **14/1**

4130 **5** *¾* **Barbirolli**[21] [6189] 4-9-4 **67** .... EddieAhern 1 — 67
(W M Brisbourne) *chsd ldrs: rdn over 2f out: sn outpcd* **7/1**[3]

160 **6** *½* **Alasil (USA)**[21] [6189] 6-9-0 **68** .... LiamJones(5) 5 — 67
(R J Price) *chsd ldrs: rdn over 2f out: wknd fnl f* **25/1**

5-00 **7** *1* **Amongst Amigos (IRE)**[1] [6497] 5-8-9 **58** .... (b) TomEaves 4 — 55
(Thomas Cleary, Ire) *w ldr: rdn and ev ch over 1f out: wknd fnl f* **33/1**

0105 **8** *1 ½* **Ellesappelle**[29] [6059] 3-9-1 **67** .... (be[1]) GeorgeBaker 6 — 62
(G L Moore) *dwlt: n.d* **16/1**

6000 **9** *1 ½* **George's Flyer (IRE)**[23] [6158] 3-8-13 **70** .... (b) JamieMoriarty(5) 10 — 62
(R A Fahey) *hld up: rdn over 2f out: sn wknd* **33/1**

003 **10** *6* **Jeu D'Esprit (IRE)**[19] [6225] 3-9-3 **69** .... JoeFanning 3 — 49
(J G Given) *chsd ldrs tl rdn and wknd over 1f out* **20/1**

0056 **11** *4* **Anduril**[21] [6189] 5-9-0 **63** .... (b) ChrisCatlin 8 — 36
(Miss M E Rowland) *chsd ldrs over 7f* **7/1**[3]

1m 59.89s (-2.73) **Going Correction** -0.15s/f (Stan)
WFA 3 from 4yo+ 3lb **11** Ran SP% **122.9**
Speed ratings (Par 103):106,105,101,100,99 99,98,96,95,90 86
CSF £32.46 CT £65.64 TOTE £15.00: £3.10, £1.30, £1.30; EX 48.50 Trifecta £93.60 Pool £211.05 - 1.60 winning units. Place 6 £795.07, Place 5 £356.97.

Owner Mrs Barbara Woodworth **Bred** Gordan Woodworth **Trained** Church Broughton , Derbys

FOCUS
A modest handicap, run at a fair pace, and the first two came clear. The third is the best guide to the level.

Ellesappelle Official explanation: jockey said filly missed the break

T/Plt: £665.60 to a £1 stake. Pool: £67,839.45. 74.40 winning tickets. T/Qpdt: £54.10 to a £1 stake. Pool: £8,184.80. 111.90 winning tickets. CR

6498 WOLVERHAMPTON (A.W) (L-H)
Friday, November 17

OFFICIAL GOING: Standard
Wind: Light, half-behind Weather: Cloudy

6504 WOLVERHAMPTON-RACECOURSE.CO.UK MAIDEN AUCTION STKS 7f 32y(P)
3:50 (3:51) (Class 5) 2-Y-0 £3,562 (£1,059; £529; £264) Stalls High

Form RPR

20 **1** **Giant Slalom**[16] [6290] 2-8-6 .... LiamJones(5) 6 — 73
(W J Haggas) *trckd ldrs: plld hrd: styd on to ld wl ins fnl f* **9/2**[3]

2 *½* **Cape Thea** 2-8-8 .... AdamKirby 2 — 68
(W R Swinburn) *s.i.s: hld up: hdwy over 2f out: led over 1f out: edgd lft and hdd wl ins fnl f* **10/1**

3 *shd* **Bold Indian (IRE)**[26] [6111] 2-8-11 .... TomEaves 4 — 71
(I Semple) *chsd ldrs: lost pl 1/2-way: hdwy over 1f out: hung rt ins fnl f: r.o* **5/2**[1]

5326 **4** *½* **Chasing Memories (IRE)**[15] [6303] 2-8-4 73 .... JamieMackay 3 — 63
(B Smart) *a.p: hung rt fr over 2f out: rdn and ev ch over 1f out: styd on* **9/2**[3]

0 **5** *shd* **Rebel Pearl (IRE)**[17] [6283] 2-8-8 .... TPQueally 10 — 67
(M G Quinlan) *hld up: hdwy over 1f out: sn rdn: kpt on* **40/1**

56 **6** *½* **Stoneacre Gareth (IRE)**[7] [6420] 2-8-13 .... RobbieFitzpatrick 1 — 71
(Peter Grayson) *led: hung rt thrght: rdn and hdd over 1f out: styd on same pce* **18/1**

3232 **7** *¾* **Vadinka**[10] [6388] 2-8-11 73 .... KimTinkler 9 — 67+
(N Tinkler) *hld up: hdwy 1/2-way: rdn and nt clr run over 1f out: no imp* **11/4**[2]

00 **8** *½* **Classic Blue (IRE)**[16] [6295] 2-8-4 .... ChrisCatlin 7 — 58
(E J O'Neill) *chsd ldrs: rdn and carried rt over 1f out: styd on same pce* **25/1**

00 **9** *2 ½* **Hayley's Flower (IRE)**[16] [6290] 2-8-7 ow1 .... LPKeniry 5 — 55
(J C Fox) *hld up: effrt over 1f out: sn wknd* **66/1**

10 *8* **Strathaird (IRE)** 2-8-9 .... LeeEnstone 11 — 38
(P C Haslam) *s.i.s: hld up: hdwy over 2f out: wknd over 1f out* **40/1**

00 **11** *1* **Time Dancer (IRE)**[16] [6297] 2-8-9 .... PaulQuinn 8 — 35
(A Berry) *prom: hmpd and lost pl 6f out: rdn over 3f out: sn wknd* **100/1**

1m 31.83s (1.43) **Going Correction** -0.25s/f (Stan) **11** Ran SP% **117.2**
Speed ratings (Par 96):81,80,80,79,79 79,78,77,74,65 64
CSF £46.45 TOTE £5.60: £2.20, £3.00, £1.40; EX 52.10 Trifecta £436.20 Pool: £626.69 - 1.02 winning tickets..

Owner B Smith,A Duke,J Netherthorpe,G Goddard **Bred** Old Mill Farm **Trained** Newmarket, Suffolk

FOCUS
A weak juvenile maiden and, with the pace noticeably steady from the start, plenty of these raced keenly. Stoneacre Gareth had the inside draw, but hung right off the final bend and the field ended up spread out across the track at the line. Not an easy race to rate.

NOTEBOOK
Giant Slalom had a poor draw when below form at Kempton last time, but he had previously shaped with plenty of promise on his debut at Pontefract and confirmed that with a determined effort. He raced very keenly in the early stages and a stronger pace would have suited better, so he could yet be capable of better.
Cape Thea, a 14,000gns purchase, out of a seven-furlong juvenile winner who was later successful over middle-distances, shaped with plenty of promise on her racecourse debut, keeping on well in the straight having been a touch slow to start. She is open to plenty of improvement and a similar race should come her way. (op 9-1)
Bold Indian(IRE), who showed ability in a couple of starts in Ireland at up to six furlongs, made an encouraging debut for the Semple yard. He is now qualified for a handicap mark and his more than capable stable will surely find an opening for him at some stage. (op 4-1)
Chasing Memories(IRE) did not have the run of things when below form over a mile at Southwell on her previous start, but she had previously shown plenty of ability over this trip. Switched to Polytrack for the first time, she could not produce her best and might have appreciated a stronger pace. (tchd 4-1 and 5-1)
Rebel Pearl(IRE) did not get the run of things and looks better than the bare form. (op 33-1)
Stoneacre Gareth(IRE) had the inside draw, but hung right off the final bend. Official explanation: jockey said colt hung right-handed throughout (op 12-1)
Vadinka, just held off a mark of 73 over six furlongs round here on his previous start, did not get the best of runs in the straight but did not look unlucky. (tchd 5-2)
Classic Blue(IRE) ◆ is a half-sister to the fair handicapper Tagula Blue and could do better now she is qualified for an official mark. (op 20-1)
Strathaird(IRE) Official explanation: jockey said gelding had steering problems

6505 EUROPEAN BREEDERS' FUND MAIDEN FILLIES' STKS 5f 216y(P)
4:20 (4:22) (Class 5) 2-Y-0 £3,562 (£1,059; £529; £264) Stalls Low

Form RPR

00 **1** **Teasing**[21] [6199] 2-9-0 .... JimmyFortune 6 — 75
(J Pearce) *dwlt: hld up: hdwy over 2f out: swtchd lft over 1f out: rdn to ld wl ins fnl f: hung rt* **16/1**

2 *nk* **Carrie McCurry (IRE)**[18] [6261] 2-9-0 .... TPQueally 5 — 74
(Patrick Martin, Ire) *chsd ldrs: lost pl 5f out: hdwy over 2f out: rdn to ld and hung lft 1f out: hdd wl ins fnl f: carried rt: kpt on* **20/1**

4330 **3** *2 ½* **Isobel Rose (IRE)**[49] [5655] 2-9-0 70 .... TonyCulhane 8 — 67
(E A L Dunlop) *chsd ldrs: rdn over 2f out: edgd lft over 1f out: styd on same pce* **5/1**[3]

3 **4** *hd* **Fabine**[22] [6187] 2-9-0 .... PJSmullen 9 — 66
(B J Meehan) *prom: lost pl over 4f out: hdwy u.p over 1f out: edgd lft: nt rch ldrs* **4/6**[1]

05 **5** *nk* **Sangreal**[23] [6175] 2-9-0 .... PatCosgrave 10 — 65+
(K R Burke) *prom: lost pl over 4f out: hdwy and hung lft over 1f out: nt rch ldrs* **33/1**

43 **6** *2* **Londolozi (USA)**[27] [6098] 2-9-0 .... MatthewHenry 3 — 59
(M A Jarvis) *chsd ldrs: led over 2f out: rdn and hung lft over 1f out: sn hdd and no ex* **3/1**[2]

4 **7** *3* **Shepherdess (USA)**[8] [6409] 2-9-0 .... JoeFanning 1 — 50
(D M Simcock) *led over 3f: rdn and wknd fnl f* **12/1**

8 *shd* **Compton Special** 2-9-0 .... J-PGuillambert 7 — 50
(J G Given) *mid-div: rdn and wknd over 2f out* **33/1**

50 **9** *hd* **Final Curtain**[28] [6071] 2-9-0 .... ChrisCatlin 4 — 49
(M A Magnusson) *hld up: hld up: nvr nr to chal* **25/1**

0 **10** *3* **Maeve (IRE)**[14] [6324] 2-8-7 .... SCreighton(7) 2 — 40
(E J Creighton) *chsd ldrs 4f* **100/1**

1m 15.68s (-0.13) **Going Correction** -0.25s/f (Stan) **10** Ran SP% **130.7**
Speed ratings (Par 93):90,89,86,86,85 82,78,78,78,74
CSF £295.39 TOTE £27.60: £5.10, £3.80, £1.60; EX 347.00 TRIFECTA Not won..

The Form Book, Raceform Ltd, Compton, RG20 6NL

Owner D Leech **Bred** Chippenham Lodge Stud Ltd **Trained** Newmarket, Suffolk

FOCUS

A few of these had previously shown plenty of ability, and this looked like a reasonable enough fillies' maiden for the track and time of year. The third sets the level.

NOTEBOOK

Teasing, although well held, showed plenty ability in a couple of six-furlong maidens at Newmarket on her previous two outings, and confirmed that promise with a determined effort on her Polytrack debut. Having been the slowest away from the stalls, she was soon travelling nicely in behind and responded well when asked to take the gaps in the straight. Her connections said they might keep her going until around Christmas time, and it would be no surprise to see her take a nursery whilst in this form. (op 20-1)

Carrie McCurry(IRE) showed plenty of ability on her debut when sixth of 17 in a seven-furlong maiden at Leopardstown and this was another good effort in defeat. She might be able to find a small maiden on the sand this winter, and should make a fair handicapper in time. (op 16-1)

Isobel Rose(IRE), a beaten favourite in three of her six starts in maiden company before finishing well down the field in a first-time visor in a sales race at Newmarket, ran okay on her Polytrack debut. She has, though, had a few chances now. (op 8-1)

Fabine, a beaten favourite when third on her debut in a decent seven-furlong maiden at Lingfield, had no real worries about the drop in trip on breeding but failed to show any improvement. She has something to prove now (op 10-11 tchd Evens)

Sangreal, well held on her debut before showing improved form when fifth in a five-furlong maiden at Nottingham on her previous start, was caught widest of all for much of the way and looks better than the bare form. She could be one to watch when switched to handicap company. (tchd 40-1)

Londolozi(USA) shaped well behind the highly-regarded Rainbow Promises on her debut before running another good race when third over seven furlongs at Lingfield last time, but she was a little disappointing on this occasion. (op 4-1)

Shepherdess(USA) shaped well when fourth on her debut (she was the only newcomer in that race) over five furlongs at Lingfield, but this was a shade disappointing. She showed plenty of pace and may benefit from a drop back in distance. (op 8-1)

Final Curtain, dropped back to sprinting having finished well held in a couple of runs at up to a mile, was well held but could yet do much better now she is qualified for a handicap mark.

6506 MOORCROFT RACEHORSE WELFARE CENTRE NURSERY 1m 141y(P)

4:50 (4:51) (Class 5) (0-75,70) 2-Y-O £3,886 (£1,156; £577; £288) Stalls Low

Form				RPR
2400	1		**Love Dubai (USA)**[15] 6310 2-9-4 **67** ... JoeFanning 7 (M Johnston) *hld up: hdwy u.p over 1f out: r.o to ld wl ins fnl f* **13/2**	75+
0003	2	1 1/4	**Alittlebitleft (IRE)**[15] 6310 2-9-5 **68** ... JimmyFortune 2 (R Hannon) *chsd ldrs: rdn over 3f out: hung lft fr over 1f out: led ins fnl f: sn hdd and unable qck* **2/1**[2]	73
1	3	1/2	**Aypeeyes (IRE)**[20] 6224 2-9-7 **70** ... JohnEgan 3 (S Kirk) *a.p: rdn to chse ldr over 1f out: ev ch ins fnl f: styd on same pce* **7/4**[1]	74
2465	4	1 1/2	**Keep Your Distance**[10] 6385 2-9-2 **65** ...(p) PaulMulrennan 6 (K R Burke) *led over 7f out: rdn and hung rt over 1f out: rdr dropped whip ins fnl f: sn hdd and no ex* **33/1**	65
6032	5	nk	**Callisto Moon**[17] 6284 2-9-1 **69** ...(b) KevinGhunowa[(5)] 5 (P A Blockley) *s.s: hld up: hdwy 5f out: outpcd over 2f out: styd on u.p fnl f* **11/1**	69
0064	6	1 1/2	**Stars Above**[10] 6385 2-8-1 **50** ... JamieMackay 1 (Sir Mark Prescott) *led 1f: chsd ldr tl rdn over 2f out: hung lft over 1f out: wknd ins fnl f* **4/1**[3]	46
0003	7	13	**Spinning Game**[3] 6472 2-7-12 **47** oh2 ... PaulQuinn 4 (D W Chapman) *hld up: rdn 1/2-way: wknd over 2f out* **33/1**	13

1m 50.4s (-1.36) **Going Correction** -0.25s/f (Stan) 7 Ran SP% **117.2**

Speed ratings (Par 96):96,94,94,93,92 91,79

CSF £20.79 TOTE £5.90: £2.60, £1.20; EX 27.10.

Owner M Doyle **Bred** Foxfield **Trained** Middleham Moor, N Yorks

FOCUS

Just the seven runners, but this looked like a fair nursery for the grade and the form is sound. They seemed to go just an ordinary pace for much of the way, though.

NOTEBOOK

Love Dubai(USA) offered little when well behind Alittlebitleft on his nursery debut over seven furlongs here last time, but interestingly he was the pick of Mark Johnston's four entries in this race. Upped to his furthest trip to date, he picked up nicely under a well-judged ride from the in-form Joe Fanning and there was plenty to like about the way he ran on close home. He might just be value for a little further than the winning margin suggests and could add to this. (op 8-1)

Alittlebitleft(IRE), who caught the attentions of the Newbury stewards' on his third start in maiden company, before showing improved form when narrowly beaten into third on his first try over seven furlongs on his nursery debut round here last time, again just found one too good. He had Love Dubai well behind last time, but the winner has clearly improved significantly for the step up in trip. (op 5-2 tchd 7-4)

Aypeeyes(IRE) defied market weakness to make a winning debut in an ordinary course-and-distance maiden, picking up well when getting the hang of things late, and he did not look overburdened on his handicap debut. This was a solid effort, but he could only plug on at the one pace and gave the impression a stronger-run race will see him in better light. (op 13-8 tchd 9-4)

Keep Your Distance, two and a half lengths behind Stars Above when fifth over a furlong further here on his previous start, had cheekpieces fitted for the first time and was able to reverse form with that rival. He seemed to enjoy being left alone up front in the early stages, but quickly looked vulnerable on the turn into the straight and was probably beaten when his rider dropped his whip inside the final furlong. He was due to be dropped 3lb and that should make things easier. (op 28-1)

Callisto Moon, returned to handicap company following his recent second in a weak course-and-distance maiden (blinkers first time) on his previous start, did not help his chance with a slow start and never posed a serious threat. (op 14-1 tchd 16-1)

Stars Above proved disappointing when sent off favourite on her nursery debut over a furlong further round here last time, having qualified for a handicap mark with three runs over six furlongs, and she again failed to deliver. She is not the biggest and it remains to be seen whether she will progress. (op 9-2 tchd 5-1)

6507 GLOW-WORM FLEXICOM H'CAP 1m 141y(P)

5:20 (5:20) (Class 5) (0-70,70) 3-Y-0+ £3,238 (£963; £481; £240) Stalls Low

Form				RPR
1111	1		**Eccollo (IRE)**[2] 6484 4-8-11 **62** 7ex ... JohnEgan 6 (T J Pitt) *hld up in tch: nt clr run over 2f out: led and hung lft wl over 1f out: sn rdn clr: eased nr fin* **4/7**[1]	87+
-224	2	6	**Esthlos (FR)**[19] 6240 3-9-2 **70** ... ChrisCatlin 11 (J Jay) *chsd ldrs: rdn over 2f out: sn outpcd* **11/1**[3]	74
0022	3	hd	**Tous Les Deux**[1] 6503 3-8-10 **64** ... RobbieFitzpatrick 8 (Peter Grayson) *hld up: plld hrd: hdwy over 2f out: sn outpcd* **7/2**[2]	68
0000	4	hd	**Defi (IRE)**[33] 6006 4-9-4 **69** ...(b) TomEaves 9 (I Semple) *chsd ldr tl led over 2f out: rdn and hdd over 1f out: wknd ins fnl f* **66/1**	72
0-60	5	1	**Dart Along (USA)**[4] 6461 4-9-0 **70** ... JerryO'Dwyer[(5)] 7 (Eoin Doyle, Ire) *hld up: hdwy over 2f out: sn rdn: hung lft and wknd ins fnl f* **25/1**	71
	6	nk	**Symbol Of Peace (IRE)**[28] 6086 3-8-9 **63** ... AdamKirby 2 (J W Unett) *chsd ldrs: rdn over 2f out: wknd over 1f out* **66/1**	63
0330	7	2	**Gallego**[6] 6451 4-8-5 **59** ... JamesDoyle[(3)] 4 (R J Price) *s.s: outpcd: nvr nrr* **20/1**	55
0-00	8	nk	**Dante's Diamond (IRE)**[18] 6259 4-8-7 **58** ... PaulQuinn 5 (G A Swinbank) *hld up: a in rr* **50/1**	54
0030	9	nk	**Aastral Magic**[8] 6413 4-9-2 **67** ...(b[1]) JimmyFortune 12 (R Hannon) *hld up: rdn over 3f out: no rspnse* **33/1**	62
3600	10	5	**Neon Blue**[7] 6425 5-9-2 **67** ... DeanMcKeown 3 (R M Whitaker) *chsd ldrs 6f* **40/1**	51
0240	11	2 1/2	**Indian Edge**[18] 6259 5-9-0 **65** ... FergusSweeney 10 (B Palling) *led: rdn and hdd over 2f out: wknd over 1f out* **33/1**	44

1m 47.45s (-4.31) **Going Correction** -0.25s/f (Stan)

WFA 3 from 4yo+ 3lb 11 Ran SP% **116.1**

Speed ratings (Par 103):109,103,103,103,102 102,100,100,99,95 93

CSF £7.01 CT £14.46 TOTE £1.80: £1.10, £1.90, £1.20; EX 9.80 Trifecta £22.40 Pool: £922.52 - 29.23 winning tickets..

Owner Stephen Pearson & David Marshall **Bred** Swettenham Stud **Trained** Bawtry, S Yorks

FOCUS

Nothing was ever going to beat Eccollo if he turned up in the same form that had seen him rattle up a four-timer in recent weeks, and he duly gained his fifth straight success in the space of just 20 days. Sound form from the placed horses. The winning time was nearly three seconds faster than the earlier nursery.

6508 STAY AT THE WOLVERHAMPTON HOLIDAY INN H'CAP 5f 216y(P)

5:50 (5:54) (Class 5) (0-70,69) 3-Y-O+ £3,238 (£963; £481; £240) Stalls Low

Form				RPR
6005	1		**Cape Presto (IRE)**[8] 6417 3-9-0 **67** ...(v) RobbieFitzpatrick 6 (Mrs C A Dunnett) *chsd ldrs: led over 1f out: drvn out* **9/1**	79
2040	2	2 1/2	**True Magic**[78] 4957 5-8-13 **66** ... DarryllHolland 3 (J D Bethell) *chsd ldrs: rdn over 1f out: styd on same pce* **8/1**	70
3000	3	1 1/2	**Stoic Leader (IRE)**[8] 6417 6-8-13 **69** ... DNolan[(3)] 5 (R F Fisher) *sn outpcd: r.o ins fnl f: nrst fin* **9/2**[1]	69+
0000	4	nk	**Steel Blue**[14] 6326 6-9-0 **67** ... TonyCulhane 7 (R M Whitaker) *mid-div: hdwy over 2f out: sn rdn: styd on same pce fnl f* **8/1**	66
4106	5	3/4	**Cool Sting (IRE)**[12] 6348 3-8-9 **65** ... JamesDoyle[(3)] 12 (P S McEntee) *sn outpcd: r.o ins fnl f: nrst fin* **25/1**	62+
0300	6	1/2	**Catspraddle (USA)**[63] 5350 3-8-13 **66** ... JimmyFortune 1 (R Hannon) *led: rdn and hdd over 1f out: wknd ins fnl f* **14/1**	61
0216	7	nk	**Tag Team (IRE)**[6] 6452 5-8-13 **66** ... DeanMcKeown 10 (John A Harris) *chsd ldrs: rdn over 1f out: wknd fnl f* **11/2**[3]	60
3305	8	shd	**Dance To The Blues (IRE)**[9] 6396 5-8-11 **64** ...(p) AdamKirby 8 (B De Haan) *chsd ldrs over 4f* **5/1**[2]	58
5314	9	2 1/2	**City For Conquest (IRE)**[34] 5970 3-9-1 **68** ... JohnEgan 2 (T J Pitt) *dwlt: in rr: effrt over 1f out: wknd fnl f* **8/1**	55
1000	10	nk	**Count Cougar (USA)**[6] 6452 6-8-12 **65** ... LPKeniry 9 (S P Griffiths) *hld up: sme hdwy over 1f out: sn wknd* **40/1**	51
0550	11	2	**Johnston's Diamond (IRE)**[3] 6478 8-8-12 **65** ... PaulQuinn 11 (E J Alston) *mid-div: wknd over 2f out* **20/1**	45
5/	12	2	**La Motta (IRE)**[56] 5515 6-9-2 **69** ... PatCosgrave 4 (Adrian McGuinness, Ire) *chsd ldrs over 3f* **11/1**	43
400	13	9	**Ten To The Dozen**[9] 6406 3-9-0 **67** ... ChrisCatlin 13 (P W Hiatt) *dwlt: outpcd* **66/1**	14

1m 13.71s (-2.10) **Going Correction** -0.25s/f (Stan) 13 Ran SP% **121.1**

Speed ratings (Par 103):104,100,98,98,97 96,96,96,92,92 89,87,75

CSF £77.56 CT £374.39 TOTE £10.40: £3.30, £4.00, £1.90; EX 116.50 Trifecta £237.50 Part won. Pool: £334.61 - 0.34 winning tickets..

Owner Jaber Ali Alsabah **Bred** C Lilburn **Trained** Hingham, Norfolk

■ Stewards' Enquiry : Robbie Fitzpatrick one-day ban: careless riding (Nov 28)

FOCUS

Just a modest sprint handicap. The winner has slipped a long way this year and this performance was in line with his best form this season. Sound form overall.

City For Conquest(IRE) Official explanation: jockey said filly missed the break

6509 TWILIGHT RACING - MISS THE TRAFFIC H'CAP 1m 5f 194y(P)

6:20 (6:23) (Class 6) (0-60,59) 3-Y-O+ £2,730 (£806; £403) Stalls Low

Form				RPR
0061	1		**Zaville**[18] 6256 4-9-3 **59** ...(p) JamesO'Reilly[(7)] 11 (J O'Reilly) *led over 1f: chsd ldr tl led again 6f out: pushed clr fr over 2f out: rdn out* **6/1**	71
4620	2	3	**Peas 'n Beans (IRE)**[8] 6410 3-8-1 **51** ... WilliamBuick[(7)] 12 (T Keddy) *hld up: hmpd 7f out and over 3f out: hdwy over 2f out: hung lft over 1f out: nt rch wnr* **12/1**	59+
0	3	4	**Atlantic Gamble (IRE)**[7] 6430 6-8-10 **50** ... AndrewElliott[(5)] 6 (K R Burke) *dwlt: hld up: hdwy over 3f out: sn rdn: styd on: nt trble ldrs* **28/1**	52
2044	4	hd	**Danebank (IRE)**[11] 6378 6-9-5 **54** ...(p) TonyCulhane 2 (J Mackie) *prom: chsd wnr over 5f out: rdn and hung lft over 1f out: sn wknd* **16/1**	56
632	5	5	**Lady Georgette (IRE)**[59] 5452 3-8-11 **54** ... ChrisCatlin 1 (E J O'Neill) *hld up: hmpd 7f out: hdwy 6f out: rdn over 2f out: wknd over 1f out* **11/2**[3]	49
4101	6	8	**Ice And Fire**[15] 6305 7-9-2 **56** ...(b) JerryO'Dwyer[(5)] 5 (J T Stimpson) *hld up: hmpd 7f out: n.d* **12/1**	40
-033	7	1/2	**Art Historian (IRE)**[11] 6382 3-9-0 **57** ... JohnEgan 13 (T J Pitt) *hld up: hmpd 7f out: hdwy over 5f out: rdn and wknd over 2f out* **4/1**[2]	40
5520	8	23	**Mystified (IRE)**[9] 6161 3-8-11 **57** ...(b) DNolan[(3)] 9 (R F Fisher) *chsd ldrs: rdn 5f out: edgd lft and wknd over 3f out* **33/1**	8
1000	9	22	**Unasuming (IRE)**[29] 6068 3-8-9 **52** ... DarryllHolland 10 (J Pearce) *chsd ldrs: rdn over 7f out: sn wknd* **33/1**	—
000	10	13	**Lalina (GER)**[8] 6419 3-8-12 **55** ... RobertHavlin 4 (Jane Chapple-Hyam) *plld hrd: led over 12f out: sddle sn slipped: hdd 6f out: wknd wl over 3f out* **50/1**	—
0000	U		**Golden Boot**[9] 4320 7-9-0 **49** ...(v) JimmyFortune 3 (A Bailey) *hld up: hmpd and uns rdr 7f out* **12/1**	—
0022	F		**Montage (IRE)**[34] 5971 4-9-8 **57** ...(p) TPQueally 8 (J Akehurst) *chsd ldrs: cl 3rd whn fell 7f out: dead* **13/8**[1]	—

3m 2.46s (-4.91) **Going Correction** -0.25s/f (Stan)

WFA 3 from 4yo+ 8lb 12 Ran SP% **128.0**

Speed ratings (Par 101):104,102,100,99,97 92,92,79,66,59 —,—

CSF £79.65 CT £1922.84 TOTE £8.80: £3.00, £4.00, £14.30; EX 124.70 TRIFECTA Not won. Place 6 £338.46, Place 5 £176.98.

Owner T Marshall **Bred** K G Powter **Trained** Doncaster, S Yorks
■ Stewards' Enquiry : James O'Reilly caution: used whip when clearly winning

FOCUS
A horrible incident marred this staying handicap, with Montage breaking a leg and bringing down Golden Boot. The race itself, as insignificant as it seems, represents weakish form.
Danebank(IRE) Official explanation: jockey said, in regard to stopping riding, that he was alerted by the sight of a warning flag on the bend and therefore began to take avoiding action, thus being passed for third
T/Plt: £1,022.30 to a £1 stake. Pool: £60,991.50. 43.55 winning tickets. T/Qpdt: £35.50 to a £1 stake. Pool: £8,025.80. 167.20 winning tickets. CR

6457 LINGFIELD (L-H)
Saturday, November 18

OFFICIAL GOING: Standard (meeting abandoned after race 7 (3.15) due to a security alert)
The track seemed to be riding on the quick side and it proved hard to make up ground from off the pace in the first three races.
Wind: Light behind becoming nil after Race 4 (1.40) Weather: Sunny

6510 IBETX.COM MONEY MAN H'CAP (DIV I) — 6f (P)
12:10 (12:12) (Class 6) (0-60,60) 3-Y-0+ — **£2,047** (£604; £302) **Stalls** Low

Form / RPR
0050 **1** **George The Second**[10] 6395 3-8-8 **55** .... RichardKingscote(3) 12 — 66
(Mrs H Sweeting) *wl away and sn pressed ldr: led jst over 2f out: drvn and styd on gamely fnl f* **16/1**
4000 **2** *nk* **Creme Brulee**[18] 6286 3-8-7 **51** .... SteveDrowne 7 — 61
(C R Egerton) *wl plcd: chsd ldng pair over 2f out: rdn and hanging lft over 1f out: wnt 2nd last 150yds: clsd unenthusiastically* **11/1**
012 **3** *1 ½* **Inka Dancer (IRE)**[60] 5453 4-8-11 **55** .... AdrianMcCarthy 10 — 61
(B Palling) *wl away: led and sn across to inner: rdn and hdd jst over 2f out : pressed wnr tl one pce ins fnl f* **6/1**[2]
5662 **4** *2 ½* **Shunkawakhan (IRE)**[13] 6348 3-8-8 **52** .... (b) OscarUrbina 9 — 50
(G C H Chung) *chsd ldrs: rdn over 2f out: sn outpcd: hanging and no imp over 1f out* **9/2**[1]
0246 **5** *1 ¼* **Viewforth**[18] 6274 8-9-2 **60** .... (b) MartinDwyer 4 — 54
(M A Buckley) *chsd ldng pair to over 2f out: sn outpcd and btn* **9/1**
0005 **6** *hd* **Desert Light (IRE)**[40] 5878 5-8-13 **57** .... (v) DaneO'Neill 5 — 51
(D Shaw) *nvr bttr than midfield: rdn wl over 2f out: sn outpcd and btn* **7/1**
3002 **7** *1 ¾* **Make My Dream**[11] 6389 3-8-12 **56** .... JimCrowley 8 — 44
(J Gallagher) *nvr bttr than midfield: rdn whn nt clr run over 2f out: n.d after* **15/2**
0020 **8** *shd* **Halfwaytoparadise**[7] 6442 3-8-10 **54** .... (p) MatthewHenry 6 — 42
(W G M Turner) *taken down early: n.m.r sn after s: a towards rr: brief effrt on wd outside over 2f out* **12/1**
3000 **9** *½* **Hillbilly Cat (USA)**[17] 6293 3-9-0 **58** .... RobertHavlin 11 — 45
(R Ingram) *dwlt: hld up in last: outpcd and struggling over 2f out* **33/1**
1440 **10** *nk* **Zazous**[31] 6061 5-9-0 **58** .... LPKeniry 1 — 44
(J J Bridger) *dwlt: in tch on inner: outpcd over 2f out: wknd fnl f* **13/2**[3]
0000 **11** *hd* **Lucius Verrus (USA)**[7] 6439 6-8-7 **54** .... (v) PatrickMathers(3) 2 — 39
(D Shaw) *sn rdn to stay in tch: struggling fr 1/2-way* **20/1**
-022 **12** *16* **She's Dunnett**[211] 1126 3-8-13 **57** .... JohnEgan 3 — —
(Mrs C A Dunnett) *n.m.r after 1f: wl in rr after: eased 2f out: t.o* **16/1**

1m 11.05s (-1.76) **Going Correction** -0.15s/f (Stan) 12 Ran SP% **115.6**
Speed ratings (Par 101):105,104,102,99,97 97,95,94,94,93 93,72
CSF £176.89 CT £1199.28 TOTE £28.60: £5.30, £5.20, £1.80; EX 282.90 TRIFECTA Not won..
Owner The Kennet Connection **Bred** R Withers **Trained** Lockeridge, Wilts
■ Stewards' Enquiry : Steve Drowne one-day ban: used whip with excessive frequency (Nov 29)

FOCUS
A moderate sprint handicap and, despite the pace appearing strong, it proved hard to make up significant amounts of ground. The winning time was around 0.65 seconds faster than the second division (that race was hand timed), won by State Dilemma. The form looks sound enough.
She's Dunnett Official explanation: jockey said filly did not feel right

6511 IBETX.COM BETTING EXCHANGE (S) STKS — 1m (P)
12:40 (12:41) (Class 6) 2-Y-0 — **£2,388** (£705; £352) **Stalls** High

Form / RPR
0660 **1** **Inquisitress**[18] 6285 2-8-6 66 .... JohnEgan 8 — 60+
(J M P Eustace) *mde virtually all: stdy pce tl qcknd 3f out: pressed over 1f out : steadily drew clr* **4/6**[1]
03 **2** *3* **For Eileen**[19] 6258 2-8-3 .... DominicFox(3) 6 — 53
(M G Quinlan) *prog to trck wnr over 5f out: cl enough 2f out: hld ent fnl f: wkng nr fin* **9/2**[2]
00 **3** *nk* **Noddledoddle (IRE)**[32] 6032 2-8-6 .... (t) OscarUrbina 2 — 52
(J Ryan) *t.k.h early: trckd wnr to over 5f out: nt qckn over 2f out: kpt on fnl f* **13/2**[3]
0400 **4** *1 ¾* **Three No Trumps**[11] 6385 2-8-6 46 .... (t) AdrianMcCarthy 4 — 48
(D Morris) *t.k.h early: chsd ldrs: rdn 3f out: sn outpcd and btn* **33/1**
0 **5** *¾* **Whos Counting**[19] 6254 2-8-6 .... RobertHavlin 1 — 47
(R J Hodges) *in tch to over 3f out: sn struggling u.p: plugged on* **20/1**
0 **6** *2* **Short Stuff**[19] 6258 2-8-11 .... LPKeniry 3 — 47
(R J Hodges) *dwlt: a in last pair: struggling fr 3f out* **50/1**
0 **7** *nk* **Alice Howe**[16] 6303 2-8-6 .... MartinDwyer 7 — 41
(W R Muir) *hld up: rdn over 2f out: no prog* **12/1**

1m 40.76s (1.33) **Going Correction** -0.15s/f (Stan) 7 Ran SP% **108.9**
Speed ratings (Par 94):87,84,83,81,81 79,78
CSF £3.36 TOTE £1.70: £1.10, £2.30; EX 3.10 Trifecta £8.10 Pool £51.72 - 4.50 winning units.The winner was sold to J Bridger for 6,200gns.
Owner J C Smith **Bred** A Saccomando **Trained** Newmarket, Suffolk

FOCUS
No strength in depth to this seller, a race that is unlikely to produce many winners in the coming months. They went a steady gallop for much of the way and it proved hard to make up ground from off the pace.

NOTEBOOK
Inquisitress was faced with by far her easiest take to date and gained a straightforward victory, her first at the sixth attempt. She was sold to John Bridger for 6,200gns and will find things tougher outside of this grade. (op 8-15 tchd 8-11 in a place)
For Eileen could not build on her recent third over seven furlongs in this grade at Wolverhampton and did not stay the mile. (op 7-2)
Noddledoddle(IRE) was not good enough to take advantage of the drop in grade. (op 12-1)
Three No Trumps, fitted with a tongue-tie for the first time on her return to selling company, offered little. (tchd 50-1)

6512 IBETX.COM MONEY MAN EUROPEAN BREEDERS' FUND MAIDEN STKS — 5f (P)
1:10 (1:12) (Class 5) 2-Y-0 — **£3,886** (£1,156; £577; £288) **Stalls** High

Form / RPR
02 **1** **Fluttering Rose**[9] 6409 2-8-12 .... SteveDrowne 10 — 71
(R Charlton) *a in ldng pair: pressed ldr jst over 1f out: drvn and styd on wl: won on the nod* **10/3**[2]
442 **2** *shd* **Shustraya**[80] 4920 2-8-12 70 .... EddieAhern 5 — 71
(P J Makin) *trckd ldrs: prog to ld over 1f out: edgd rt and sn jnd: hdd on the post* **5/4**[1]
3643 **3** *1 ½* **Feelin Foxy**[9] 6409 2-8-12 70 .... (v) DaneO'Neill 9 — 65
(D Shaw) *t.k.h: hld up bhd ldrs: effrt over 1f out: chsd ldng pair ins fnl f: styd on but no imp* **13/2**
45 **4** *3 ½* **Ama De Casa (USA)**[122] 3645 2-8-12 .... (t) DarryllHolland 3 — 53
(J Noseda) *s.i.s: in tch: rdn over 2f out: sn outpcd: plugged on* **9/2**[3]
00 **5** *shd* **Wibbadune (IRE)**[5] 6463 2-8-12 .... RobertMiles 2 — 52
(Peter Grayson) *led to over 1f out: n.m.r sn after: wknd fnl f* **100/1**
6 *2 ½* **Esprit De Nuit (IRE)** 2-9-0 .... GregFairley(3) 4 — 48
(Mrs A Duffield) *hld up in rr: outpcd 2f out: rdn jst over 1f out: one pce* **12/1**
04 **7** *¾* **Zain (IRE)**[17] 6295 2-9-3 .... JamieMackay 6 — 46
(J G Given) *s.i.s: a in rr: struggling over 2f out* **33/1**
6566 **8** *nk* **Cyprus Rose**[9] 6409 2-8-9 48 .... JamesDoyle(3) 1 — 40
(S Curran) *chsd ldrs tl wknd 2f out* **40/1**
0 **9** *½* **Foxy Music**[19] 6255 2-9-3 .... RobbieFitzpatrick 8 — 43
(Peter Grayson) *plld hrd: hld up in last pair: pushed along and no prog 2f out: wknd* **50/1**

59.54 secs (-0.24) **Going Correction** -0.15s/f (Stan) 9 Ran SP% **115.1**
Speed ratings (Par 96):95,94,92,86,86 82,81,81,80
CSF £7.74 TOTE £4.60: £1.40, £1.20, £1.80; EX 11.20 Trifecta £15.70 Pool £73.10 - 3.30 winning units..
Owner The Veterinary Defence Society Ltd **Bred** Stanley Estate And Stud Co And Mount Coote Stud **Trained** Beckhampton, Wilts

FOCUS
An ordinary sprint maiden in which it proved hard to make up ground from off the pace. Sound form.

NOTEBOOK
Fluttering Rose confirmed the promise she showed when second in a similar event over course and distance on her previous start, overcoming her wide draw to gamely get off the mark at the third attempt. (op 5-2 tchd 7-2, tchd 4-1 in a place)
Shustraya, dropped in trip and switched to Polytrack for the first time off the back of a near three-month break, had every chance but basically seemed to be outbattled. She did not look ungenuine, but gave the impression she is still learning. (op 2-1 tchd 9-4)
Feelin Foxy came widest in the straight and found the front two too strong late on. Her yard tend to do okay through the winter and she should find a race at some point. (op 11-2)
Ama De Casa(USA), fitted with a tongue-tie for the first time, started slowly and never threatened in a race that suited those who were prominent. She looks pretty limited, but can be expected to be sharper for this first run in 122 days and is now qualified for a handicap mark. (op 4-1)
Wibbadune(IRE) needed this run for a handicap mark and was not given an over-hard time once beaten. Her trainer does well with his runners on the sand and it would be no surprise to see this one placed to win a small race or two at some point. Official explanation: jockey said filly hung right (op 66-1)

6513 IBETX.COM MONEY MAN H'CAP (DIV II) — 6f (P)
1:40 (1:42) (Class 6) (0-60,65) 3-Y-0+ — **£2,047** (£604; £302) **Stalls** Low

Form / RPR
5054 **1** **State Dilemma (IRE)**[271] 461 5-8-11 **55** .... (v) DaneO'Neill 8 — 63
(D Shaw) *wl in tch in midfield: prog over 1f out: led last 100yds: rdn out* **16/1**
3520 **2** *¾* **Supreme Kiss**[7] 6440 3-8-8 **55** .... JamesDoyle(3) 6 — 61
(Mrs N Smith) *s.s: hld up in last pair: nt wl plcd on inner 2f out: angled out over 1f out: r.o wl to take 2nd nr fin and clsng* **9/1**
4251 **3** *½* **Mina**[10] 6395 4-9-7 **65** .... SteveDrowne 1 — 70
(Rae Guest) *dwlt: towards rr: rdn and prog over 1f out: styd on ins fnl f to take 3rd last stride* **5/1**[2]
0016 **4** *shd* **Turibius**[10] 6395 7-9-0 **58** .... JimCrowley 12 — 62
(T E Powell) *trckd ldrs: gng strly over 1f out: shkn up to ld jst ins fnl f: hdd and nt qckn last 100yds* **14/1**
5123 **5** *1 ¼* **Labelled With Love**[149] 2793 6-8-10 **54** .... (t) FergusSweeney 5 — 54
(J R Boyle) *towards rr and racd wd: effrt over 1f out: styd on ins fnl f: nt rch ldrs* **8/1**
3124 **6** *½* **Special Gold**[15] 6325 4-9-1 **59** .... (p) PaulMulrennan 10 — 58
(A D Brown) *led at stdy pce: hrd pressed fr 2f out: hdd & wknd jst ins fnl f* **9/2**[1]
6000 **7** *1* **Patternmaker (USA)**[10] 6399 4-8-12 **56** .... LPKeniry 7 — 52
(A M Hales) *trckd ldrs: cl enough jst over 1f out: fdd fnl f* **20/1**
4630 **8** *shd* **Gone'N'Dunnett (IRE)**[65] 5327 7-9-0 **58** .... (v) JohnEgan 11 — 54
(Mrs C A Dunnett) *pressed ldr to jst over 1f out: wknd ins fnl f* **9/1**
0001 **9** *¾* **Stagnite**[12] 6371 6-8-2 **53** ow1 .... (p) JamieJones(7) 9 — 46
(Karen George) *t.k.h: trckd ldng pair to over 1f out: wknd fnl f* **10/1**
0000 **10** *2* **Tiviski (IRE)**[18] 6288 4-8-13 **57** .... DarryllHolland 3 — 44
(Miss Gay Kelleway) *prom: lost pl and in midfield after 2f: wknd on inner fnl f* **12/1**
2456 **11** *nk* **Hadath (IRE)**[7] 6436 9-8-2 **53** .... (v) PatrickHills(7) 2 — 40
(B G Powell) *dwlt: sn detached in last: nvr a factor* **11/2**[3]
0050 **12** *3* **Double M**[26] 6142 9-8-5 **49** .... (v) RichardThomas 4 — 27
(Mrs L Richards) *n.m.r after 1f: a in rr after: rdn and struggling over 2f out* **20/1**

1m 11.7s (-1.11) **Going Correction** -0.15s/f (Stan) 12 Ran SP% **120.2**
Speed ratings (Par 101):101,100,99,99,97 96,95,95,94,91 91,87
CSF £155.07 CT £841.95 TOTE £19.50: £5.30, £2.80, £1.70; EX 218.70 TRIFECTA Not won..
Owner Danethorpe Racing Ltd **Bred** Gainsborough Stud Management Ltd **Trained** Danethorpe, Notts

FOCUS
Run-of-the-mill form, similar to division one but, with the pace steady, the winning time was around 0.65 seconds slower (hand timed) and a few of these had troubled runs.

6514 IBETX.COM BETTING EXCHANGE H'CAP — 7f (P)
2:10 (2:12) (Class 2) (0-100,102) 3-Y-0+
£11,217 (£3,358; £1,679; £840; £419; £210) **Stalls** Low

Form / RPR
351 **1** **Areyoutalkingtome**[23] 6192 3-8-13 **97** .... EddieAhern 3 — 109+
(C A Cyzer) *trckd ldrs gng wl: effrt to ld over 1f out: 2l clr ins fnl f: drvn and hld on wl* **4/1**[1]

The Form Book, Raceform Ltd, Compton, RG20 6NL

0636 **2** ½ **Orchard Supreme**[23] [6192] 3-8-1 **88**........................ StephaneBreux(3) 10 99
(R Hannon) *sn last: prog but v wd bnd 2f out: gd hdwy over 1f out: clsd on wnr nr fin: post c too sn* **10/1**

0503 **3** 1 ¼ **Qadar (IRE)**[7] [6445] 4-8-9 **95**.. JamesDoyle(3) 13 102
(N P Littmoden) *hld up in midfield: prog over 1f out: styd on wl fnl f: nvr able to chal* **13/2**

5200 **4** 1 ½ **Vortex**[28] [6101] 7-8-12 **95**..(t) DarryllHolland 8 99
(Miss Gay Kelleway) *wl in tch: prog over 2f out to chse ldng trio: carried wd bnd sn after: styd on one pce fnl f* **6/1**[3]

1000 **5** ½ **Mr Lambros**[23] [6192] 5-8-11 **94**.. MartinDwyer 1 96
(A M Balding) *led after 1f and set str pce: hdd over 1f out: wknd ins fnl f* **15/2**

5504 **6** ½ **Andronikos**[14] [6335] 4-9-3 **100**...(t) SteveDrowne 7 104+
(P F I Cole) *hld up wl in rr: v wd bnd 2f out and n.m.r sn after: running on but no ch whn nt clr run last 75yds* **5/1**[2]

6103 **7** *hd* **Tamagin (USA)**[5] [6461] 3-7-11 **86** oh4..................(p) DuranFentiman(5) 11 86
(P D Evans) *led for 1f: chsd ldr tl over 2f out: hung rt bnd sn after: wknd fnl f* **10/1**

3-60 **8** ½ **Xtra Torrential (USA)**[184] [1806] 4-9-1 **98**.................... FergusSweeney 6 97
(D M Simcock) *settled wl in rr: styd on fr over 1f out: nvr rchd ldrs* **33/1**

3553 **9** ¾ **Secret Night**[23] [6192] 3-8-2 **86** oh1...................................... DaleGibson 4 83
(J A R Toller) *s.s: rchd midfield after 2f: rdn and struggling over 2f out: one pce after* **10/1**

0 **10** ½ **King Nov (ARG)**[20] 4-8-12 **95**...(t) P-AGraberg 12 91
(B Bo, Sweden) *prom: bmpd along and wknd 2f out* **50/1**

00 **11** 3 **Sailor King (IRE)**[7] [6445] 4-8-7 **90**....................................... JohnEgan 14 78
(D K Ivory) *hld up in rr: rdn and struggling wl over 2f out* **50/1**

5056 **12** 4 **Regal Royale**[28] [6101] 3-8-6 **90**.................................. RobbieFitzpatrick 5 68
(Peter Grayson) *hld up wl in rr: no prog over 2f out* **25/1**

0020 **13** ½ **Party Boss**[28] [6101] 4-9-5 **102**.. BrettDoyle 2 78
(C E Brittain) *prom to over 2f out: wknd rapidly* **14/1**

1m 22.92s (-2.97) **Going Correction** -0.15s/f (Stan) course record
WFA 3 from 4yo+ 1lb **13** Ran SP% **120.7**
Speed ratings (Par 109):110,109,108,106,105 105,104,104,103,102 99,94,94
CSF £43.94 CT £267.33 TOTE £5.00: £1.60, £4.20, £2.40; EX 64.30 Trifecta £185.80 Part won. Pool £261.82 - 0.50 winning units..

Owner Mrs Charles Cyzer **Bred** C A Cyzer **Trained** Maplehurst, W Sussex

FOCUS
A high-class handicap run at a very strong pace from the start. The form should prove reliable.

NOTEBOOK
Areyoutalkingtome ◆ has always had bags of ability, but his connections have taken time to work out his optimum conditions. He is ideally suited by a strongly-run seven furlongs (although he could get away with a mile if the pace was good), so this race worked out just as he would have liked, and he was able to follow his recent course-and-distance success off a 3lb higher mark. It is easy to argue the runner-up was unlucky, but Areyoutalkingtome can also be rated better than the bare form, as he chased the frantic pace from the start and took up the running plenty soon enough, before understandably getting tired late on. He is very smart indeed when things fall into place but, while he can be found more opportunities over here, both on Polytrack and turf next year (he is just as effective on grass), he looks made for racing in the US. There is big money to made with this horse. (op 9-2)
Orchard Supreme ◆ had Stephane Breux taking over from Richard Hughes, and the 3lb claimer had a shocker. Still last inside the final three furlongs, he could hardly have come any wider round the final bend and must have forfeited several lengths, certainly considerably more than he was beaten anyway. It is to the horse's credit he managed to get so close, even if the winner was getting tired and, already four times a winner round here, he looks set to develop into a very useful Polytrack performer. (op 9-1 tchd 12-1)
Qadar(IRE), back up in trip, stayed on to the line without ever likely to hit the front. He is not that easy to win with and could be ready for some sort of headgear. (op 8-1)
Vortex has always looked at his best when held up for a late run, so it could be argued he was not given the best of rides by Darryll Holland. He always looked a little closer to the fast pace than was probably ideal, even though the winner tracked the leaders, and he was caught wide throughout to boot. On the turn into the straight, he was forced even further out and it is to his credit he still managed to finish so close. He has dropped to a fair mark and can win a similar race when things fall right. Official explanation: jockey said gelding was taken wide on the bend (op 4-1)
Mr Lambros is at his best when going a good pace from the front over this course and distance, but he was never really left alone by Tamagin and had probably just been softened up by the time he was seriously challenged. (tchd 8-1)
Andronikos ◆, dropped in grade on his Polytrack debut, came wide into the straight (only Orchard Supreme came wider) but still enjoyed little luck in-running. He would have been in the shake up with a clear run and might be able to end a losing run stretching back to April 2005 if kept on the go through the winter. (op 13-2)
Tamagin(USA) could not get to the front, which shows just how fast Mr Lambros was going. Official explanation: jockey said colt hung right (op 11-1 tchd 14-1)
Xtra Torrential(USA), worryingly retained at the sales for just 8,500gns the previous month, ran a big race off the back of a six-month break and offered some hope. He has always been held in high regard and, on this evidence, is not one to write off just yet. (op 50-1)

6515 IBETX.COM £20 FREE BET H'CAP 1m 4f (P)
2:40 (2:40) (Class 2) (0-100,107) 3-Y-0+

£11,217 (£3,358; £1,679; £840; £419; £210) **Stalls** Low

Form RPR
0031 **1** **Sweet Indulgence (IRE)**[13] [6351] 5-8-8 **86** oh2.......... FergusSweeney 1 96
(W J Musson) *hld up in last pair: smooth prog over 3f out: trckd ldr over 2f out: rdn to ld 1f out: styd on wl* **11/2**[3]

0400 **2** 1 ¾ **Cold Turkey**[14] [6336] 6-9-0 **92**... EddieAhern 6 99
(G L Moore) *hld up in last trio: smooth prog over 3f out: led over 2f out: drvn and hdd 1f out: one pce* **7/4**[1]

1000 **3** 3 **Punta Galera (IRE)**[14] [6337] 3-8-2 **86** oh1.......................... DaleGibson 2 88
(R Hannon) *trckd ldrs: drvn to chse ldng pair 2f out: nt qckn and no imp* **11/1**

00 **4** *nk* **Honduras (SWI)**[35] [5526] 5-8-12 **90**.................................. SteveDrowne 3 92
(G L Moore) *hld up in tch: drvn 3f out: nt qckn 2f out: kpt on same pce after* **25/1**

-100 **5** 2 ½ **Postage Stampe**[9] [6411] 3-8-4 **88**..................................... MartinDwyer 7 86
(D M Simcock) *hld up in last: prog on outer over 3f out: drvn and wd bnd 2f out : n.d after* **16/1**

1231 **6** 2 ½ **Mighty Moon**[18] [6275] 3-8-6 **90** oh1 ow4.....................(bt) DarryllHolland 4 84
(J O'Reilly) *chsd ldrs: led over 3f out to over 2f out: sn wknd* **9/1**

3632 **7** 11 **Orcadian**[14] [6334] 5-10-1 **107**.. JohnEgan 8 83
(J M P Eustace) *led after 1f to over 4f out: nt run on and sn bhd: t.o* **3/1**[2]

3604 **8** ½ **Country Pursuit (USA)**[5] [6467] 4-8-8 **86** oh1..................(b) BrettDoyle 5 61
(C E Brittain) *led for 1f: led again over 4f out to over 3f out: wknd rapidly: t.o* **7/1**

2m 29.48s (-4.91) **Going Correction** -0.15s/f (Stan)
WFA 3 from 4yo+ 6lb **8** Ran SP% **117.3**
Speed ratings (Par 109):110,108,106,106,104 103,95,95
CSF £16.01 CT £104.13 TOTE £6.80: £1.30, £1.40, £3.40; EX 16.00 Trifecta £73.30 Part won. Pool £103.26 - 0.10 winning units..

Owner Broughton Thermal Insulation **Bred** Mrs M Campbell-Andenaes **Trained** Newmarket, Suffolk

FOCUS
A good handicap and the pace seemed fair, certainly by Lingfield's usual standards for this sort of distance anyway. A personal best from the winner, but the form is not strong with the runner-up the best guide.

NOTEBOOK
Sweet Indulgence(IRE) ◆ readily defied a 7lb higher mark (5lb rise and 2lb out of the handicap) than when winning over course and distance on his previous start and is quickly developing into a very useful handicapper on Polytrack. His connections suggested last time that he could be sent hurdling at some point, but it would be no surprise to see those plans put on hold and he looks one to keep on the right side of on sand. (op 9-2)
Cold Turkey, a very useful sort indeed on Polytrack, was produced with every chance and did not seem to have any excuses. (tchd 9-4)
Punta Galera(IRE), 1lb out of the handicap, ran very well upped to his furthest trip to date behind two very useful Polytrack handicappers. (op 14-1)
Honduras(SWI), a stablemate of the second, was having just his third start on the Flat in this country having previously been trained in Scandinavia, and ran with some promise. (op 20-1)
Postage Stampe, upped to her furthest trip to date, could make little impression and is not progressing quite as one might have hoped. (tchd 20-1)
Orcadian, making his Polytrack debut, spat his dummy out before the race got serious. Official explanation: jockey said gelding did not handle the surface (op 4-1)

6516 IBETX.COM CHURCHILL STKS (LISTED RACE) 1m 2f (P)
3:15 (3:17) (Class 1) 3-Y-0+

£22,712 (£8,608; £4,308; £2,148; £1,076; £540) **Stalls** Low

Form RPR
4060 **1** **Nayyir**[21] [6218] 8-9-6 103..(b[1]) EddieAhern 1 112
(G A Butler) *hld up in midfield: trckd ldrs gng easily 2f out: led 1f out: hrd pressed last 100yds: hld on gamely* **12/1**

4012 **2** *shd* **Blue Bajan (IRE)**[49] [5675] 4-9-2 98.................................. MichaelHills 12 108
(Andrew Turnell) *dwlt: hld up in rr: prog on wd outside 1/2-way: chsd ldrs 2f out: chal ins fnl f: r.o: jst hld* **13/2**[3]

3120 **3** 1 **Charlie Cool**[49] [5675] 3-8-12 102.. DaleGibson 3 106+
(W J Haggas) *t.k.h: hld up in tch: stl at the bk of main gp 2f out: hanging lft over 1f out: drvn and r.o: nrst fin* **5/1**[2]

4063 **4** *shd* **Kindlelight Debut**[23] [6190] 6-8-11 98................................. JamesDoyle 8 101
(N P Littmoden) *hld up wl in rr: prog over 1f out: r.o fnl f: nvr nrr* **33/1**

6053 **5** 1 **Grand Passion (IRE)**[17] [6299] 6-9-2 104.............................. JohnEgan 4 104
(G Wragg) *hld up towards rr: prog over 1f out: tried to cl fnl f: one pce last 100yds* **8/1**

3051 **6** *shd* **Millville**[28] [6097] 6-9-2 100.. DarryllHolland 2 104+
(M A Jarvis) *dwlt: hld up in last: stl there over 2f out: prog on outer over 1f out: r.o fnl f: hopeless task* **4/1**[1]

1321 **7** *shd* **Group Captain**[14] [6336] 4-9-2 107...................................... SteveDrowne 6 104
(R Charlton) *trckd ldrs: chal over 2f out: led over 1f out to 1f out: fdd* **4/1**[1]

4602 **8** 2 ½ **Babodana**[17] [6299] 6-9-2 101.. JimCrowley 9 99
(M H Tompkins) *dwlt: hld up in midfield: effrt over 2f out: chsng ldrs over 1f out: wknd* **25/1**

5636 **9** *hd* **Simple Exchange (IRE)**[112] [3964] 5-9-4 ....(v[1]) PJSmullen 10 101
(D K Weld, Ire) *led for 2f: styd prom: led jst over 2f out to over 1f out: wknd* **16/1**

-461 **10** 1 ¼ **Maybach**[34] 5-9-4 .... P-AGraberg 5 98
(B Bo, Sweden) *hld up towards rr: pushed along over 3f out: rdn and no prog over 2f out* **66/1**

1560 **11** ¾ **Weightless**[35] [5968] 6-9-2 103... PaulMulrennan 13 95
(N P Littmoden) *dwlt: t.k.h: led after 2f to over 6f out: rdn 4f out: wknd over 1f out* **33/1**

3006 **12** 1 **Kew Green (USA)**[63] [5360] 8-9-2 105.................................. DaneO'Neill 11 93
(P R Webber) *dwlt: sn prom: chal over 2f out: wknd over 1f out* **16/1**

5001 **13** *nk* **Bahar Shumaal (IRE)**[21] [6226] 4-9-2 93..........................(b) BrettDoyle 14 92
(C E Brittain) *t.k.h: prom: led over 6f out to jst over 2f out: wknd over 1f out* **15/2**

2641 **14** 17 **Arm Candy (IRE)**[21] [6219] 3-8-7 93.................................. MartinDwyer 7 55
(J A R Toller) *prom: lost pl on inner 4f out: wkng whn bdly hmpd over 2f out* **16/1**

2m 3.90s (-3.89) **Going Correction** -0.15s/f (Stan)
WFA 3 from 4yo+ 4lb **14** Ran SP% **129.4**
Speed ratings (Par 111):109,108,108,108,107 107,107,105,104,103 103,102,102,88
CSF £92.46 TOTE £15.20: £3.60, £3.00, £2.20; EX 196.00 Trifecta £750.50 Pool £1,057.14 - 1.00 winning unit. Place 6 £61.61, Place 5 £12.32.

Owner Abdulla Al Khalifa **Bred** Saeed Manana **Trained** Blewbury, Oxon

■ Stewards' Enquiry : P-A Graberg two-day ban: careless riding (Nov 29, Dec 1)

FOCUS
A good renewal of the Churchill Stakes on paper, but rather disappointingly the pace was steady for much of the way. Sound form overall, the winner better than this at his peak with a personal best from the runner-up.

NOTEBOOK
Nayyir has been a fine servant to the Butler yard over the years, but has not always been the easiest to win with. Equipped with blinkers for the first time, he was always travelling very strongly and found just enough to gain the ninth win of his career. He is likely to be aimed at the Winter Derby in March where he will try and improve on last year's third-place finish, and it will have to be hoped the headgear works as well. (op 10-1)
Blue Bajan(IRE) ◆ has progressed into a smart sort this season and was stepping up to Listed company following his fine second in the Cambridgeshire. This was another terrific effort, but it could be argued he should have won, with Michael Hills bringing his mount widest of all into the straight and not totally convincing in a driving finish. On this evidence, he is clearly pattern class and it would be no surprise to see him re-oppose the winner in the Winter Derby next March. (op 11-1 tchd 12-1)
Charlie Cool ◆, eighth of 33 and behind Blue Bajan in the Cambridgeshire on his previous start, did not appreciate the steady pace on his Polytrack debut, just getting going too late to get on terms with the front two. He is still lightly raced and can build on this next year. (op 13-2)
Kindlelight Debut put up an improved effort to take third in a fillies' Listed race over a mile here on her previous start and this was another career best. She absolutely loves the Polytrack and could have even more to offer.
Grand Passion(IRE), the Winter Derby runner-up, could never quite get in a serious blow and might have preferred a stronger pace.

Millville ◆, a five-length winner of a 12-furlong handicap round here off a mark of 95 on his previous start, was totally unsuited by the way the race panned out considering he stays much further, and is better than he was able to show. Official explanation: jockey said gelding missed the break (op 5-1)
Group Captain, winner of the November Handicap off a mark of 99 at Windsor on his previous start, was a little disappointing on his return to Polytrack (he won his maiden over course and distance on his only previous try on sand). (tchd 5-1)
Bahar Shumaal(IRE), mightily impressive in a Wolverhampton handicap on his previous start, albeit off a mark of 80, was far too keen in the better race. (op 8-1)
Arm Candy(IRE) Official explanation: jockey said filly was hampered on the bend

6517 IBETX.COM BETTING EXCHANGE EUROPEAN BREEDERS' FUND FILLIES' H'CAP 1m (P)

() (Class 4) (0-85,) 3-Y-0+ £

T/Plt: £37.60 to a £1 stake. Pool: £56,264.00. 1,092.05 winning tickets. T/Qpdt: £11.90 to a £1 stake. Pool: £3,674.70. 226.80 winning tickets. JN

6504 WOLVERHAMPTON (A.W) (L-H)

Saturday, November 18

OFFICIAL GOING: Standard

Wind: Light, behind Weather: Fine

6518 WOLVERHAMPTON RACECOURSE NURSERY 1m 1f 103y(P)

4:10 (4:10) (Class 6) (0-65,62) 2-Y-O **£2,388** (£705; £352) **Stalls** Low

Form RPR
065 **1** **Isola Madre**[17] 6298 2-9-4 **59** JoeFanning 3 62
(M Johnston) *chsd ldrs: rdn to ld and hung lft 1f out: jst hld on* **4/1**[3]
3606 **2** *shd* **Beau Sancy**[15] 6322 2-8-9 **57** TolleyDean(7) 8 60
(R A Harris) *hld up: hdwy over 2f out: rdn and edgd lft over 1f out: r.o* **5/1**
5302 **3** *1 ½* **Right Option (IRE)**[15] 6322 2-9-2 **62** JamieMoriarty(5) 4 62
(J R Weymes) *s.i.s: hld up: nt clr run over 2f out: hdwy over 1f out: swtchd lft ins fnl f: r.o* **3/1**[1]
0443 **4** *¾* **Featherlight**[8] 6421 2-8-6 **52** (v) LiamJones(5) 6 51
(J Jay) *hld up in tch: rdn over 2f out: no ex fnl f* **7/2**[2]
0300 **5** *1* **Only Hope**[10] 6394 2-9-0 **55** (p) AdamKirby 7 52
(Ernst Oertel) *sn chsng ldr: led over 3f out: rdn over 1f out: hdd and no 1f out* **8/1**
5000 **6** *1 ¾* **Best Woman**[152] 2709 2-8-12 **53** TonyCulhane 1 47
(P Howling) *chsd ldrs: lost pl 7f out: n.d after* **28/1**
4000 **7** *16* **Fun Thai**[11] 6385 2-8-5 **46** ow1 RobertHavlin 5 9
(M R Channon) *chsd ldrs: rdn and ev ch over 2f out: sn wknd* **10/1**
0060 **8** *1 ¼* **Only A Splash**[18] 6278 2-8-9 **50** PaulQuinn 2 11
(D W Chapman) *led: rdn and hdd over 3f out: wknd over 2f out* **20/1**

2m 1.85s (-0.77) **Going Correction** -0.25s/f (Stan) 8 Ran SP% **112.3**
Speed ratings (Par 94):93,92,91,90,90 88,74,73
CSF £23.35 CT £66.42 TOTE £4.10: £2.00, £2.30, £1.40; EX 24.90.
Owner Gainsborough **Bred** Gainsborough Stud Management Ltd **Trained** Middleham Moor, N Yorks

FOCUS
A moderate nursery and the form is modest but solid.

NOTEBOOK
Isola Madre showed very moderate form in three runs at up to a mile in maiden company but, upped in trip on her nursery debut, she put up an improved effort to win narrowly. She did not do much in front and might be capable of a little better. (op 3-1 tchd 5-1)
Beau Sancy ◆, back up in trip, very nearly took advantage of his lowest mark yet. He finished very strongly and showed enough to suggest he could find a similar race. (op 11-2)
Right Option(IRE) failed to build on the form he showed when second over an extended mile round here on his previous start. He was short of room close home, but was by no means unlucky. (op 10-3)
Featherlight, third in a claimer over a mile on the Fibresand for Neville Callaghan on her previous start, came widest into the straight and was well held. (op 10-3)
Only Hope was basically not good enough, but she would be of interest if dropped into selling company. (op 12-1)

6519 ENJOY EXECUTIVE HOSPITALITY AT WOLVERHAMPTON RACECOURSE H'CAP 1m 4f 50y(P)

4:40 (4:40) (Class 4) (0-85,80) 3-Y-O+ **£5,505** (£1,637; £818; £408) **Stalls** Low

Form RPR
2660 **1** **Quince (IRE)**[31] 6051 3-8-13 **77** (v) PatCosgrave 5 86
(J Pearce) *hld up in tch: chsd ldr over 2f out: rdn to ld and hung rt ins fnl f: r.o* **11/4**[1]
6054 **2** *nk* **Pass The Port**[8] 6426 5-9-3 **75** RobertHavlin 8 83
(D Haydn Jones) *hld up: hdwy over 2f out: rdn and ev ch whn hung rt ins fnl f: styd on* **7/1**
1116 **3** *1 ½* **Ardea Brave (IRE)**[34] 5991 4-9-2 **74** (p) OscarUrbina 2 80
(M Botti) *led: rdn over 1f out: hdd and unable qckn ins fnl f* **4/1**[2]
1-01 **4** *11* **Stargazer Jim (FR)**[16] 6313 4-9-3 **80** LiamJones(5) 4 68
(W J Haggas) *trckd ldrs: plld hrd: hung lft over 3f out: wknd 2f out* **11/4**[1]
0301 **5** *nk* **Shout (IRE)**[9] 6410 3-9-0 **78** TonyCulhane 3 66
(R Charlton) *chsd ldr 7f: sn rdn: hung lft and wknd wl over 1f out* **5/1**[3]
0 **6** *½* **Lord Of Beauty (FR)**[21] 6226 6-9-5 **77** AdamKirby 7 64
(Noel T Chance) *hld up: rdn over 4f out: wknd wl over 2f out* **50/1**
00-1 **7** *7* **War At Sea (IRE)**[39] 5887 4-9-5 **77** (t) JoeFanning 1 53
(A W Carroll) *prom: rdn over 4f out: wknd over 2f out* **16/1**
0-10 **8** *11* **Jidaar (IRE)**[13] 6351 3-9-2 **80** RobertMiles 6 38
(P W Hiatt) *hld up in tch: rdn over 3f out: sn wknd* **40/1**

2m 37.21s (-5.21) **Going Correction** -0.25s/f (Stan)
WFA 3 from 4yo+ 6lb 8 Ran SP% **112.8**
Speed ratings (Par 105):107,106,105,98,98 97,93,85
CSF £22.22 CT £74.74 TOTE £3.00: £1.80, £1.10, £2.40; EX 20.00.
Owner D Leech **Bred** David Ryan **Trained** Newmarket, Suffolk

FOCUS
A fair handicap run at an even pace and the form looks straightforward rated through the third. The winning time was 2.18 seconds quicker than the later 12-furlong handicap won by the 55-rated Noble Minstrel.
Shout(IRE) Official explanation: jockey said, regarding appearing not to ride as vigorously in final furlong as he had done earlier, he had used his whip earlier on the filly with no response and therefore tried to get it to go forward with hands and heels, adding that it pricked its ears in final furlong and that he could not have finished closer

6520 SATURDAY NIGHT IS PARTY NIGHT MAIDEN STKS 7f 32y(P)

5:10 (5:10) (Class 5) 2-Y-O **£3,238** (£963; £481; £240) **Stalls** High

Form RPR
0 **1** **Ravinia (USA)**[63] 5371 2-8-12 RobertHavlin 5 68+
(B J Meehan) *chsd ldr: rdn 2f out: styd on to ld ins fnl f* **9/2**[2]
54 **2** *½* **Murrisk**[21] 6224 2-9-3 KJManning 2 72
(Eamon Tyrrell, Ire) *led: rdn over 1f out: hdd and unable qckn ins fnl f* **6/1**
6255 **3** *1 ½* **Lady Alize (USA)**[21] 6217 2-8-12 88 (t) FJohansson 7 63+
(R A Kvisla) *chsd ldrs: outpcd over 2f out: styd on ins fnl f* **6/5**[1]
3 **4** *½* **Amber Isle**[10] 6401 2-9-3 DanielTudhope 1 67
(D Carroll) *chsd ldrs: rdn over 2f out: no ex ins fnl f* **14/1**
006 **5** *1* **Mineral Rights (USA)**[21] 6224 2-9-3 63 TomEaves 10 65
(I Semple) *hld up: rdn over 2f out: r.o ins fnl f: nrst fin* **22/1**
040 **6** *hd* **Theoretical**[57] 5503 2-8-12 60 AdamKirby 8 59
(A J McCabe) *s.s: hld up: hdwy over 1f out: no imp ins fnl f* **25/1**
0 **7** *1 ¾* **Beck**[24] 6173 2-9-3 TonyCulhane 3 60
(M L W Bell) *chsd ldrs: rdn over 2f out: sn outpcd* **5/1**[3]
8 *hd* **Dr McFab** 2-9-0 RichardKingscote(3) 6 59
(J A Osborne) *hld up: styd on ins fnl f: nrst fin* **28/1**
4600 **9** *3* **Arabellas Homer**[8] 6422 2-8-5 50 RussellKennemore(7) 4 47
(Mrs N Macauley) *hld up: rdn 1/2-way: hung rt and wknd over 2f out* **66/1**
00 **10** *6* **Ishismart**[32] 6034 2-8-7 HelenKeohane(5) 9 32
(R Hollinshead) *hld up: rdn 1/2-way: sn wknd* **100/1**

1m 30.31s (-0.09) **Going Correction** -0.25s/f (Stan) 10 Ran SP% **115.4**
Speed ratings (Par 96):90,89,87,87,86 85,83,83,80,73
CSF £29.43 TOTE £4.10: £1.50, £2.00, £1.10; EX 34.30.
Owner Arthur Watson **Bred** Burning Daylight Farms Inc **Trained** Manton, Wilts

FOCUS
This looked a reasonable maiden for the time of year, but it proved hard to make up significant amounts of ground and the winning time was 1.55 seconds slower than the later nursery, won by the 66-rated Fares. The form is limited by the proximity of the fifth and sixth.

NOTEBOOK
Ravinia(USA) showed ability when mid-division in a good Newbury maiden on her debut two months previously and confirmed that promise with a narrow victory. This did not look a bad race for the time of year and she should make a nice three-year-old. (op 5-1)
Murrisk, dropped in trip, had the run of the race out in front but basically ran into a better horse on the day. A similar race could come his way, and he also now has the option of switching to handicaps. (op 7-1)
Lady Alize(USA) had shown plenty of ability in both maiden and Listed company on the turf, but she proved a bitter disappointment on her Polytrack debut, running well below her official mark of 88. She seemed unsuited by the drop in trip and should do better back over further. (op 11-10 tchd 13-8)
Amber Isle really caught the eye when running on well to take third in a six-furlong seller on his debut for Reg Hollinshead, and confirmed that promise on his first start for new connections. He might be able to find a maiden and should make an fair handicapper in the longer term.
Mineral Rights(USA) fared best of those held up. (op 25-1 tchd 20-1)
Beck was a beaten favourite on his debut over a mile at Nottingham and he again failed to deliver. (op 9-2 tchd 11-2)

6521 ENJOY AFTER RACING ENTERTAINMENT AT WOLVERHAMPTON H'CAP 5f 20y(P)

5:40 (5:40) (Class 6) (0-60,60) 3-Y-O+ **£2,388** (£705; £352) **Stalls** Low

Form RPR
6520 **1** **Sir Don (IRE)**[98] 4361 7-8-10 **52** (p) GrahamGibbons 6 59
(E S McMahon) *chsd ldrs: drvn along thrght: r.o u.p to ld post* **8/1**[3]
0000 **2** *shd* **Rothesay Dancer**[15] 6315 3-8-12 **59** (p) KevinGhunowa(5) 5 66
(J S Goldie) *led to 1/2-way: hrd rdn fr over 1f out: led wl ins fnl f : hdd post* **18/1**
0040 **3** *shd* **Mystery Pips**[15] 6325 6-8-12 **54** (v) KimTinkler 8 60
(N Tinkler) *w ldr tl led 1/2-way: rdn over 1f out: hdd wl ins fnl f* **14/1**
2031 **4** *nk* **Carcinetto (IRE)**[13] 6348 4-8-6 **55** WilliamBuick(7) 7 60
(P D Evans) *s.i.s: hld up: r.o wl ins fnl f: nrst fin* **7/2**[2]
5506 **5** *½* **Cosmic Destiny (IRE)**[18] 6288 4-9-0 **56** AdamKirby 1 59
(E F Vaughan) *hld up: hmpd over 1f out: r.o wl ins fnl f: nvr able to chal* **8/1**[3]
61 **6** *shd* **Fastrac Boy**[35] 5969 3-8-11 **60** KylieManser(7) 11 63
(J R Best) *chsd ldrs: rdn and edgd lft over 1f out: styng on same pce whn n.m.r wl ins fnl f* **12/1**
0000 **7** *nk* **The Leather Wedge (IRE)**[15] 6315 7-8-11 **60**... RussellKennemore(7) 2 62
(R Johnson) *s.i.s: hld up: plld hrd: rdn and hung lft over 1f out: r.o: nvr trbld ldrs* **8/1**[3]
0460 **8** *shd* **Sofinella (IRE)**[3] 6485 3-8-9 **58** MarkCoumbe(7) 3 60
(A W Carroll) *chsd ldrs: nt clr run 2f out: sn rdn: styd on same pce ins fnl f* **22/1**
1322 **9** *1* **Compton Classic**[15] 6315 4-9-1 **57** (p) DanielTudhope 4 55
(J S Goldie) *chsd ldrs: nt clr run over 2f out: rdn and edgd lft over 1f out: btn whn n.m.r ins fnl f* **11/4**[1]
3600 **10** *½* **Spirit Of Coniston**[10] 6399 3-8-6 **55** (b) RonanKeogh(7) 9 51
(Peter Grayson) *mid-div: lost pl 3f out: rdn over 1f out: n.d after* **33/1**
000 **11** *shd* **Egyptian Lord**[40] 5878 3-9-1 **57** (b) RobbieFitzpatrick 10 53
(Peter Grayson) *hld up in tch: plld hrd: hung rt over 1f out: wknd fnl f* **25/1**
1004 **12** *6* **The Salwick Flyer (IRE)**[25] 6159 3-8-11 **53** ow1 TonyCulhane 13 27
(A Berry) *chsd ldrs: lost pl over 3f out: wknd 1/2-way* **25/1**

61.84 secs (-0.98) **Going Correction** -0.25s/f (Stan) 12 Ran SP% **116.8**
Speed ratings (Par 101):97,96,96,96,95 95,94,94,93,92 92,82
CSF £132.27 CT £1977.23 TOTE £7.70: £3.80, £8.50, £2.30; EX 180.70.
Owner Mrs Dian Plant **Bred** C And R O'Brien **Trained** Hopwas, Staffs

FOCUS
The first 11 home were separated by around only three lengths, so dubious form for this sprint handicap, although it appears sound enough on paper.
Compton Classic Official explanation: jockey said gelding was denied a clear run

6522 BOOK ONLINE AT WOLVERHAMPTON-RACECOURSE.CO.UK CLAIMING STKS 1m 141y(P)

7:00 (7:00) (Class 6) 2-Y-O **£2,730** (£806; £403) **Stalls** Low

Form RPR
3043 **1** **Chookie Hamilton**[15] 6316 2-8-9 61 TomEaves 6 66+
(I Semple) *sn chsng ldr: led 2f out: rdn and hung rt ins fnl f : r.o* **9/2**[2]
6631 **2** *1 ½* **Lake Pontchartrain (IRE)**[9] 6416 2-8-9 64 LPKeniry 8 63
(S Kirk) *hld up: hdwy over 3f out: chsd wnr over 1f out: sn rdn and hung lft: nt clr run ins fnl f: styd on same pce* **7/4**[1]
1000 **3** *2 ½* **Party Palace**[17] 6291 2-7-7 54 WilliamBuick(7) 5 48
(J A Osborne) *chsd ldrs: rdn over 3f out: outpcd over 2f out: styd on ins fnl f* **15/2**[3]

4003 **4** *1 1/2* **The Light Fandango**[4] 6471 2-7-13 50 .... LiamJones(5) 4 49
(R A Harris) *chsd ldrs: rdn over 2f out: wknd fnl f* **14/1**

6340 **5** *1* **Generist**[8] 6421 2-8-0 50 .... (p) DaleGibson 2 43
(M J Attwater) *led: rdn and hdd 2f out: wknd fnl f* **12/1**

1050 **6** *5* **Sunstroke (IRE)**[36] 5948 2-7-12 55 .... DominicFox(3) 1 33
(M G Quinlan) *hld up: rdn and wknd over 2f out* **9/2**[2]

6200 **7** *14* **Dansilver**[24] 6172 2-7-12 60 .... JosephWalsh(7) 7 7
(D J Wintle) *prom: rdn over 3f out: wknd over 2f out* **11/1**

8 *15* **Cocobean** 2-8-11 .... RobbieFitzpatrick 3 —
(M Appleby) *dwlt: outpcd* **40/1**

1m 49.99s (-1.77) **Going Correction** -0.25s/f (Stan) **8** Ran SP% **109.6**
Speed ratings (Par 94):97,95,93,92,91 86,74,61
CSF £11.67 TOTE £5.10: £1.70, £1.30, £2.10; EX 9.90.
Owner Raeburn Brick Limited **Bred** D And J Raeburn **Trained** Carluke, S Lanarks
■ Stewards' Enquiry : Tom Eaves caution: careless riding

FOCUS
Just a moderate claimer, but the winning time was 0.76 seconds quicker than the following maiden won by Peregrine Falcon.

NOTEBOOK
Chookie Hamilton, making his Polytrack debut, benefited from the drop in grade to gain his first success at the seventh attempt. He came across the runner-up close home, but was the winner on merit. (op 4-1)
Lake Pontchartrain(IRE), successful off a mark 60 in a seven-furlong nursery round here on her previous start, failed to follow up on this drop in grade and this trip stretched her stamina. The winner came across her close home, but she was not unlucky. (tchd 13-8)
Party Palace ran reasonably on this drop in class but was no match for the front two. (op 8-1 tchd 13-2)
The Light Fandango could not build on her recent second in this grade over seven furlongs at Southwell. (op 16-1)
Generist had her chance from the front. (op 10-1)
Sunstroke(IRE) was well below the pick of her form and she does not seem to be progressing. (op 6-1 tchd 15-2)

6523 STAY AT THE WOLVERHAMPTON HOLIDAY INN MAIDEN STKS 1m 141y(P)
7:30 (7:31) (Class 5) 2-Y-O **£3,238** (£963; £481; £240) **Stalls** Low

Form RPR

4 **1** **Peregrine Falcon**[11] 6386 2-9-3 .... JoeFanning 6 74+
(M Johnston) *led: hdd 6f out: led over 1f out: edgd lft: rdn out* **15/8**[1]

0 **2** *1 3/4* **Cavalry Twill (IRE)**[11] 6386 2-9-3 .... RobertHavlin 7 70
(P F I Cole) *chsd ldrs: rdn over 2f out: sn outpcd: styd on ins fnl f* **14/1**

3 *hd* **Fired Up (GER)** 2-9-3 .... EddieAhern 5 70
(Saeed Bin Suroor) *hld up: hmpd 7f out: hdwy 5f out: outpcd wl over 2f out: styd on fnl f* **3/1**[2]

30 **4** *1* **Tenancy (IRE)**[42] 5814 2-9-3 .... JimCrowley 8 67
(J A Osborne) *plld hrd and prom: led 6f out: rdn and hdd over 1f out: hung lft and wknd ins fnl f* **9/2**[3]

02 **5** *1* **Arctic Wings (IRE)**[11] 6386 2-9-3 .... MartinDwyer 11 65
(W R Muir) *slowly intos tride: hld up: hdwy 2f out: sn rdn: no imp fnl f* **5/1**

6 *4* **Sundrive (IRE)**[32] 6041 2-8-12 .... KJManning 1 52
(Eamon Tyrrell, Ire) *hld up: hmpd 7f out: hdwy over 5f out: rdn over 2f out: sn hung lft and wknd* **25/1**

00 **7** *1 1/4* **Citrus Chief (USA)**[56] 5527 2-8-10 .... TolleyDean(7) 3 54
(R A Harris) *mid-div: hmpd 7f out: sn lost pl: hung lft over 1f out: n.d* **33/1**

00 **8** *3/4* **King Of The Beers (USA)**[56] 5527 2-9-3 .... RobbieFitzpatrick 13 52
(R A Harris) *sn outpcd* **50/1**

9 *3* **Don't Desert Me (IRE)** 2-9-0 .... RichardKingscote(3) 12 46
(R Charlton) *s.i.s: outpcd* **20/1**

0 **10** *1 3/4* **Churchtown**[12] 6377 2-9-3 .... PatCosgrave 4 42
(K R Burke) *chsd ldrs 6f* **100/1**

11 *10* **Santera (IRE)** 2-8-12 .... TonyCulhane 2 16
(Mrs A Duffield) *sn outpcd* **66/1**

0 **12** *7* **Danjoe**[11] 6386 2-8-12 .... LiamJones(5) 9 —
(R Brotherton) *chsd ldrs 6f* **66/1**

13 *18* **Jewelled Dagger (IRE)** 2-9-3 .... TomEaves 10 —
(I Semple) *dwlt: outpcd* **33/1**

1m 50.75s (-1.01) **Going Correction** -0.25s/f (Stan) **13** Ran SP% **121.7**
Speed ratings (Par 96):94,92,92,91,90 86,85,85,82,80 72,65,49
CSF £30.02 TOTE £2.90: £1.20, £2.30, £2.50; EX 53.10.
Owner Sheikh Mohammed **Bred** Car Colston Hall Stud **Trained** Middleham Moor, N Yorks

FOCUS
Probably not a bad maiden for the time of year, but the winning time was 0.76 seconds slower than the earlier claimer won by Chookie Hamilton.

NOTEBOOK
Peregrine Falcon ◆ confirmed the promise he showed when fourth over course and distance on his debut with a ready success. He should stay further and ought to make a lovely three-year-old. (op 9-4)
Cavalry Twill(IRE) improved on the form he showed when behind today's winner over course and distance on his debut and is going the right way. (tchd 16-1)
Fired Up(GER), a 125,000gns half-brother to very smart juvenile miler Bahamian Dancer, later renamed Industrial Success and high-class over 12 furlongs on Hong Kong, out of a middle-distance winner, made a respectable debut. He should do better over further next year. (op 10-3 tchd 7-2)
Tenancy(IRE) has not really built on the promise he showed on his debut for Warwick, but might do better now he has qualified for a handicap mark. (op 7-1)
Arctic Wings(IRE) could not confirm recent course form with Peregrine Falcon and was obviously disappointing, even allowing for the winner having improved. (op 9-2 tchd 11-2)

6524 WOLVERHAMPTON RACECOURSE FOR ANY OCCASION (S) STKS 1m 141y(P)
8:00 (8:01) (Class 6) 3-5-Y-O **£2,388** (£705; £352) **Stalls** Low

Form RPR

00-0 **1** **Speagle (IRE)**[20] 6241 4-9-3 .... DanielTudhope 7 64
(Adrian McGuinness, Ire) *led: hdd over 6f out: led again over 3f out: rdn clr over 1f out: styd on* **5/1**

2100 **2** *1 1/2* **Second Reef**[10] 6405 4-9-3 55 .... PaulQuinn 6 61
(E J Alston) *hld up: plld hrd: hdwy over 2f out: rdn to chse wnr fnl f: hung lft: styd on* **9/2**[3]

4600 **3** *1 3/4* **Dancing Flame**[4] 6473 3-8-2 50 .... DaleGibson 12 45
(E J Alston) *hld up: rdn over 1f out: r.o ins fnl f: nrst fin* **8/1**

0010 **4** *1/2* **Crush On You**[39] 5885 3-8-3 48 ow1 .... RussellKennemore(7) 4 52
(R Hollinshead) *chsd ldrs: rdn over 2f out: edgd rt fr over 1f out: styd on* **16/1**

0124 **5** *1* **Desert Lightning (IRE)**[8] 6430 4-9-3 52 .... PatCosgrave 8 54
(K R Burke) *a.p: chsd wnr over 2f out: sn rdn: edgd rt and no ex fnl f* **7/2**[2]

6 *hd* **History Prize (IRE)** 3-8-0 .... JosephWalsh(7) 2 47
(D J Wintle) *s.i.s: hld up: rdn and edgd lft over 1f out: nvr trbld ldrs* **50/1**

0000 **7** *2 1/2* **Norwegian**[12] 6383 5-8-10 47 .... (p) AdamKirby 9 42
(Ian Williams) *mid-div: rdn over 3f out: hdwy over 2f out: wknd over 1f out* **33/1**

4045 **8** *6* **Qik Dip (IRE)**[12] 6383 3-8-7 55 .... EddieAhern 3 29
(P D Evans) *chsd ldrs: rdn over 2f out: wknd over 1f out* **10/3**[1]

43-0 **9** *1/2* **Ivans Ride (IRE)**[60] 5446 3-8-7 62 .... GrahamGibbons 5 28
(J J Quinn) *prom 6f* **15/2**

0000 **10** *17* **Mind That Fox**[138] 3155 4-8-10 45 .... JoeFanning 10 —
(T Wall) *s.i.s: a in rr* **66/1**

060 **11** *8* **Red Lantern**[15] 6327 5-8-10 45 .... (vt) RobbieFitzpatrick 13 —
(M J Attwater) *racd keenly: w wnr tl led over 6f out: hdd over 3f out: sn rdn and wknd* **66/1**

1m 48.96s (-2.80) **Going Correction** -0.25s/f (Stan)
WFA 3 from 4yo+ 3lb **11** Ran SP% **116.8**
Speed ratings (Par 101):102,100,99,98,97 97,95,90,89,74 67
CSF £27.18 TOTE £4.40: £2.40, £2.40, £3.30; EX 38.70.The winner was sold to D Carroll for 6,500gns. History Prize was claimed by S F Turton for £6,000.
Owner P Sheridan **Bred** Mrs Sheila Morrissey **Trained** Lusk, Co Dublin

FOCUS
Sound form, a shade above the overall level for the grade.

6525 WOLVERHAMPTON-RACECOURSE.CO.UK NURSERY 7f 32y(P)
8:30 (8:31) (Class 4) (0-85,75) 2-Y-O **£4,533** (£1,348; £674; £336) **Stalls** High

Form RPR

6003 **1** **Fares (IRE)**[10] 6394 2-8-12 66 .... (b) BrettDoyle 6 74+
(C E Brittain) *hld up: hdwy over 2f out: led over 1f out: sn hung lft: rdn out* **3/1**[1]

6015 **2** *1 1/4* **Copper King**[18] 6285 2-8-11 72 .... MCGeran(7) 1 77
(P D Evans) *trckd ldrs: rdn to chse wnr fnl f: edgd lft: styd on* **5/1**[3]

020 **3** *5* **Henry The Seventh**[41] 5841 2-9-1 69 .... (v[1]) EddieAhern 4 61
(J W Hills) *s.i.s: outpcd: rdn 1/2-way: r.o ins fnl f: nvr nrr* **10/1**

434 **4** *shd* **Until When (USA)**[39] 5900 2-9-7 75 .... TomEaves 3 67
(B Smart) *w ldr: rdn and ev ch over 1f out: wknd fnl f* **15/2**

0201 **5** *nk* **Jord (IRE)**[4] 6472 2-8-10 71 6ex .... WilliamBuick(7) 5 62
(A J McCabe) *plld hrd and prom: rdn over 2f out: wknd over 1f out* **7/1**

0001 **6** *1/2* **Lay The Cash (USA)**[17] 6291 2-8-10 64 .... (b) MartinDwyer 2 54
(J S Moore) *led: rdn and hdd over 1f out: wknd fnl f* **4/1**[2]

5010 **7** *nk* **Nicada (IRE)**[18] 6285 2-8-11 68 .... DominicFox(3) 7 57
(Miss Gay Kelleway) *hld up: rdn over 2f out: n.d* **6/1**

1m 28.76s (-1.64) **Going Correction** -0.25s/f (Stan) **7** Ran SP% **109.3**
Speed ratings (Par 98):99,97,91,91,91 90,90
CSF £16.42 TOTE £4.80: £2.10, £2.30; EX 12.50.
Owner Mohammed Rashid **Bred** Darley **Trained** Newmarket, Suffolk

FOCUS
A fair nursery and, with the pace good, the winning time was 1.55 seconds quicker than the earlier maiden won by Ravinia. The first two finished clear.

NOTEBOOK
Fares(IRE) finished to good effect when third over a mile at Kempton on his previous start, so the decent pace would have suited and he gained his first success at the ninth attempt in convincing fashion. In this form, he can win again.
Copper King ran better than when fifth over an extended mile round here on his previous start and proved suited by the drop back to seven furlongs. (tchd 9-2)
Henry The Seventh, fitted with a visor for the first time, never threatened after starting slowly. (op 8-1 tchd 15-2)
Until When(USA), switched to Polytrack for the first time, was well held and is not progressing as one might have expected. (op 6-1 tchd 8-1)
Jord(IRE), carrying a 6lb penalty, could not repeat the form she showed to win over six furlongs at Southwell on her previous start. (op 6-1 tchd 8-1)
Lay The Cash(USA), 4lb higher, was below the form he showed when winning over six furlongs at Kempton on his previous start and the blinkers seemingly failed to work as well this time. (op 9-2)

6526 RINGSIDE SUITE 700 THEATRE STYLE CONFERENCE H'CAP 1m 4f 50y(P)
9:00 (9:00) (Class 6) (0-55,55) 3-Y-O+ **£2,730** (£806; £403) **Stalls** Low

Form RPR

0-00 **1** **Noble Minstrel**[170] 2171 3-8-11 55 .... (t) GrahamGibbons 5 63+
(S C Williams) *hld up in tch: swtchd rt over 1f out: rdn to ld ins fnl f: r.o* **3/1**[1]

4130 **2** *1 3/4* **Jadeeron**[4] 6474 7-8-11 49 .... (p) RobbieFitzpatrick 12 54
(Miss D A McHale) *chsd ldr tl led over 2f out: rdn and hdd 1f out: styd on same pce* **8/1**

3 *nk* **Ilza**[57] 5518 3-8-11 55 .... MartinDwyer 4 60
(Eamon Tyrrell, Ire) *s.i.s: sn prom: chsd ldr over 2f out: sn rdn and hung lft: led 1f out: sn hdd and no ex* **33/1**

3254 **4** *3/4* **Regency Red (IRE)**[12] 6376 8-8-9 52 .... LiamJones(5) 3 55
(W M Brisbourne) *hld up: hdwy 2f out: rdn over 1f out: r.o* **5/1**[3]

5005 **5** *3* **Dispol Peto**[15] 6317 6-8-9 54 .... (p) RussellKennemore(7) 2 53
(R Johnson) *hld up: hdwy over 1f out: edgd lft ins fnl f: nt rch ldrs* **12/1**

3604 **6** *2* **Little Richard (IRE)**[10] 6405 7-8-12 53 .... (p) NeilChalmers(3) 9 48
(M Wellings) *hld up: hdwy 2f out: wknd fnl f* **9/2**[2]

5300 **7** *1 3/4* **Newport Boy (IRE)**[40] 5875 3-8-11 55 .... (p) JimCrowley 6 48
(R A Harris) *chsd ldrs: rdn over 3f out: n.m.r and wknd over 2f out* **16/1**

0000 **8** *shd* **Mystic Roll**[33] 6021 3-8-11 55 .... RobertHavlin 1 47
(Jane Chapple-Hyam) *hld up: hmpd over 2f out: n.d* **16/1**

-606 **9** *1 3/4* **Come What July (IRE)**[293] 243 5-9-0 55 .... PatrickMathers(3) 7 45
(D Shaw) *hld up: n.d* **25/1**

500- **10** *15* **Elle Nino**[29] 6087 4-9-0 52 .... AdamKirby 10 18
(Patrick Morris, Ire) *hld up: hdwy 5f out: rdn and wknd over 2f out* **16/1**

00 **11** *2* **Sword's Edge (IRE)**[10] 6405 5-9-0 52 .... EddieAhern 8 14
(W A Murphy, Ire) *led: rdn and hdd over 2f out: sn wknd* **28/1**

3156 **12** *9* **Kyle Of Lochalsh**[15] 6317 6-9-2 54 .... DanielTudhope 11 2
(J S Goldie) *chsd ldrs: rdn and wkng whn hmpd over 2f out* **8/1**

2m 39.39s (-3.03) **Going Correction** -0.25s/f (Stan)
WFA 3 from 4yo+ 6lb **12** Ran SP% **117.6**
Speed ratings (Par 101):100,98,98,98,96 94,93,93,92,82 81,75
CSF £26.42 CT £666.28 TOTE £4.40: £1.70, £3.10, £12.00; EX 35.10.
Owner Alasdair Simpson **Bred** Mrs M Lavell **Trained** Newmarket, Suffolk

FOCUS
A moderate handicap run in a time 2.18 seconds slower than the earlier 12-furlong handicap won by the 77-rated Quince. The winner is unexposed but the race has not been rated positively.
Elle Nino Official explanation: jockey said filly hung violently left throughout
Sword's Edge(IRE) Official explanation: jockey said gelding finished lame

6527 GET MARRIED AT WOLVERHAMPTON RACECOURSE H'CAP 5f 216y(P)
9:30 (9:31) (Class 5) (0-75,77) 4-Y-0+ £3,238 (£963; £481; £240) Stalls Low

Form RPR
0043 1 Night Prospector[10] 6399 6-8-11 70 (p) JimCrowley 8 79
(R A Harris) *hld up: hdwy over 2f out: rdn to ld towards fin* 5/1[3]
0613 2 ½ Premier Fantasy[8] 6428 4-9-4 77 RobbieFitzpatrick 9 84+
(T J Pitt) *s.i.s: hld up: hdwy over 1f out: r.o wl* 13/8[1]
0400 3 hd Sahara Silk (IRE)[93] 4507 5-8-5 67 (v) PatrickMathers(3) 3 73
(D Shaw) *chsd ldr over 3f out: led over 1f out: rdn and hdd towards fin* 14/1
5/0 4 2½ La Motta (IRE)[1] 6508 6-8-10 69 (bt) PatCosgrave 7 68
(Adrian McGuinness, Ire) *led over 4f: no ex ins fnl f* 13/2
-200 5 3 Morse (IRE)[31] 6048 5-9-1 74 EddieAhern 2 64
(J A Osborne) *chsd ldrs: rdn over 3f out: wknd fnl f* 11/4[2]
0050 6 ½ Plateau[13] 6353 7-8-6 70 LiamJones(5) 4 58
(C R Dore) *chsd ldrs over 4f* 20/1
000 7 shd Katie Boo (IRE)[4] 6478 4-8-6 65 JoeFanning 6 53
(A Berry) *hld up: effrt over 1f out: n.d* 33/1
40 8 5 Controvento (IRE)[15] 6315 4-8-6 65 (b) MartinDwyer 5 38
(Eamon Tyrrell, Ire) *chsd ldrs: rdn over 2f out: wknd over 1f out* 12/1

1m 14.1s (-1.71) **Going Correction** -0.25s/f (Stan) 8 Ran SP% 116.8
Speed ratings (Par 103):101,100,100,96,92 92,91,85
CSF £13.88 CT £108.08 TOTE £5.90: £1.90, £1.30, £2.10; EX 20.80 Place 6 £24.90, Place 5 £15.52.
Owner D Tumman & R F Bloodstock **Bred** Miss S N Ralphs **Trained** Earlswood, Monmouths

FOCUS
A pretty weak sprint handicap, with only the favourite coming into it in much form. The time was modest.
T/Plt: £100.00 to a £1 stake. Pool: £57,902.25. 422.30 winning tickets. T/Qpdt: £19.70 to a £1 stake. Pool: £5,647.50. 212.10 winning tickets. CR

MARSEILLE BORELY (L-H)
Saturday, November 18

OFFICIAL GOING: Soft

6528a PRIX DELAHANTE (LISTED RACE) 1m 1f
12:25 (12:28) 2-Y-0 £17,241 (£6,897; £5,172; £3,448; £1,724)

RPR
1 Al Ken (FR) 2-8-11 TThulliez 7 —
(J-M Capitte, France)
2 1 Palosanto (FR) 2-8-11 IMendizabal 9 —
(J-C Rouget, France)
3 shd All Is Vanity (FR) 2-8-8 FBlondel 6 —
(W J Cargeeg)
4 1 Val D'Ham (FR) 2-8-11 (p) DBoeuf 2 —
(F Forneron, France)
5 shd Paper Profits 2-8-8 MPoirier 4 —
(A De Royer-Dupre, France)
6 5 Laureldean Express[7] 6453 2-8-8 TJarnet 1 —
(E J O'Neill) *led or disputed lead, pushed along 3f out, 2nd and ridden straight, weakened final furlong SP 7-2* 7/2[1]
7 5 Big Bertha (GER)[41] 5858 2-8-8 RonanThomas 5 —
(J-C Rouget, France)
8 ½ Auto Rouge (IRE) 2-8-8 GElorriaga-Santos 8 —
(J-M Capitte, France)

1m 51.63s 8 Ran SP% 22.2
PARI-MUTUEL (Including 1 Euro stake): WIN 4.80; PL 2.10, 2.20, 4.90;DF 16.10.
Owner J C Seroul **Bred** Jean-Claude Seroul **Trained** France

NOTEBOOK
Laureldean Express was smartly into her stride and took the field along until the straight. She was challenged by several opponents a furlong and a half out, though, and quickly dropped out of contention.

5857 FRANKFURT (L-H)
Sunday, November 19

OFFICIAL GOING: Soft

6529a HESSEN-POKAL (GROUP 3) 1m 2f
2:05 (2:11) 3-Y-0+ £22,069 (£6,897; £3,448; £2,069)

RPR
1 Wiesenpfad (FR)[42] 5856 3-9-0 JVictoire 5 109
(W Hickst, Germany) *in touch, headway over 3f out, led entering straight, ran on well final furlong, driven out* 17/10[1]
2 2 Golden Rose (GER)[168] 6-8-8 JBojko 1 96
(H Hesse, Germany) *led, close 3rd half-way, led again 4f out, headed entering straight, kept on but not pace of winner* 59/1
3 2 Ioannina[14] 6367 3-8-5 FilipMinarik 3 93
(P Schiergen, Germany) *raced in 2nd, led half-way to 4f out, close 3rd straight, stayed on at one pace to line* 11/2[3]
4 2 Lucidor (GER)[21] 6248 3-9-0 EPedroza 2 98
(Frau E Mader, Germany) *towards rear, stayed on from over 1f out, nearest at finish* 71/10
5 nk Harar (GER)[183] 1860 4-9-1 (b) WMongil 9 95
(Andreas Lowe, Germany) *mid-division on inside, some late headway* 106/10
6 1 Spatzolita (GER)[29] 6109 7-8-8 AHelfenbein 6 86
(D K Richardson, Germany) *in touch, shaken up to chase leaders approaching straight, stayed on at one pace* 36/1
7 nk Storm Trooper (GER)[29] 6109 6-8-13 (b) AStarke 8 91
(P Schiergen, Germany) *always mid-division* 98/10
8 8 Mharadono (GER)[21] 6248 3-8-12 WPanov 4 79
(P Hirschberger, Germany) *close up, 2nd half-way, ridden approaching straight, stayed on at one pace* 32/1
9 1¼ Bailamos (GER)[29] 6109 6-9-1 ADeVries 15 76
(H Hesse, Germany) *held up, never dangerous* 109/10
10 nse Orange Blue (GER)[311] 97 4-8-13 CarolinLippert 10 74
(C Von Der Recke, Germany) *mid-division towards inside, never in challenging position* 51/1
11 nk Mohandas (FR)[29] 6109 5-9-1 THellier 7 75
(W Hefter, Germany) *towards rear, never dangerous* 5/1[2]
12 hd New Inspiration (GER)[99] 4383 5-8-8 KKerekes 11 68
(W Kujath, Germany) *prominent in 4th, driven entering straight, weakened* 63/1
13 nk Chiron (GER)[29] 6109 5-8-13 ABoschert 13 72
(Dr A Bolte, Germany) *never dangerous* 11/1
14 ½ Obrigado (GER)[47] 5762 5-8-13 EFrank 12 71
(M Sowa, Germany) *in touch on outside, weakened 3f out* 25/1
15 6 Grantley[246] 666 9-9-1 HanaMouchova 14 63
(H Hesse, Germany) *towards rear, never a factor* 68/1

2m 22.69s
WFA 3 from 4yo+ 4lb 15 Ran SP% 132.2
(Including 10 Euros stake): WIN 27; PL 16, 50, 23; SF 1,052.
Owner Frau Heide Harzheim **Bred** Gestut Ravensberg **Trained** Germany

2911 KYOTO (R-H)
Sunday, November 19

OFFICIAL GOING: Firm

6530a MILE CHAMPIONSHIP (GRADE 1) 1m
6:40 (6:40) 3-Y-0+ £513,201 (£203,030; £126,191; £74,027; £49,351)

RPR
1 Daiwa Major (JPN)[21] 5-9-0 KAndo 10 124
(H Uehara, Japan) 13/10[1]
2 nk Dance In The Mood (JPN)[21] 5-8-9 YTake 7 118
(Kazuo Fujisawa, Japan) 57/10[3]
3 1¼ Symboli Gran (IRE)[168] 4-9-0 YShibayama 16 120
(Y Hatakeyama, Japan) 31/1
4 1¼ Meiner Scherzi (JPN)[196] 3-8-12 YShibata 11 117
(R Inaba, Japan) 65/1
5 nk Kinshasa No Kiseki (AUS)[196] 3-8-9 SAkiyama 14 114
(M Horii, Japan) 122/10
6 ½ Precise Machine (JPN)[218] 7-9-0 MMatsuoka 3 115
(K Hagiwara, Japan) 40/1
7 ½ Court Masterpiece[57] 5524 6-9-0 LDettori 1 114
(E A L Dunlop) *in touch, disputing 8th straight, effort over 1f out, one pace final furlong* 51/10[2]
8 ½ Hat Trick (JPN)[21] 5-9-0 YIwata 8 113
(Katsuhiko Sumii, Japan) 123/10
9 ½ Super Hornet (JPN)[175] 3-8-12 HMiyuki 2 112
(Y Yahagi, Japan) 37/1
10 ¾ Camphor Best (JPN)[931] 7-9-0 (b) TEda 6 110
(Y Sato, Japan) 48/1
11 hd Telegnosis (JPN)[168] 7-9-0 MEbina 5 110
(H Sugiura, Japan) 66/1
12 nk Maruka Shenck (JPN)[28] 3-8-12 YFukunaga 15 109
(T Setoguchi, Japan) 99/10
13 ¾ Daring Heart (JPN)[189] 4-8-9 SFujita 18 102
(H Fujiwara, Japan) 26/1
14 ½ Suteki Shinsukekun (USA)[49] 5717 3-8-12 FKomaki 9 106
(Hideyuki Mori, Japan) 36/1
15 ½ Agnes Raspberry (JPN)[189] 5-8-9 KTsunoda 17 100
(Katsuichi Nishiura, Japan) 47/1
16 nse New Very (JPN)[218] 8-9-0 HShii 12 105
(H Otonashi, Japan) 143/1
17 nk Logic (JPN)[175] 3-8-12 C-PLemaire 4 104
(K Hashiguchi, Japan) 36/1
18 5 Kinetics (JPN)[364] 7-9-0 Kenichilkezoe 13 93
(M Shinkawa, Japan) 62/1

1m 32.7s
WFA 3 from 4yo+ 2lb 18 Ran SP% 125.8
(Including 100Y stake): WIN 230; PL 120, 180, 500; DF 650.
Owner K Oshiro **Bred** Shadai Farm **Trained** Japan

NOTEBOOK
Court Masterpiece, last seen finishing third in the QEII, had conditions to suit but never threatened to play a part in the finish.

6490 SOUTHWELL (L-H)
Monday, November 20

OFFICIAL GOING: Standard
Wind: virtually nil

6531 WBX.COM WORLD BET EXCHANGE AMATEUR RIDERS' H'CAP (DIV I) 1m (F)
12:10 (12:10) (Class 6) (0-60,60) 3-Y-0+ £1,977 (£608; £304) Stalls Low

Form RPR
0000 1 Take It There[12] 6404 4-10-6 50 MissZoeLilly(5) 11 61
(A J Lidderdale) *hld up and bhd: smooth hdwy 3f out: rdn to ld over 1f out: edgd lft ins last: kpt on* 16/1
6040 2 1½ Louisiade (IRE)[189] 1735 5-10-6 50 MissARyan(5) 2 58
(K A Ryan) *a.p: effrt 2f out and ev ch: rdn over 1f out: hld in 2nd whn rdr dropped whip ins last* 8/1[3]
0666 3 5 Scottish River (USA)[7] 6462 7-11-3 56 MrLeeNewnes 4 53
(M D I Usher) *s.i.s and bhd: hdwy on outer 3f out: styd on fnl 2f and nrst fin* 10/1
6010 4 1¾ Im Ova Ere Dad (IRE)[103] 4255 3-11-0 58 MrJOwen(3) 5 52
(D E Cantillon) *midfield: hdwy on bit 3f out: led 2f out: sn rdn: hdd and kpt on same pce* 11/4[1]
3042 5 2 Mountain Pass (USA)[9] 6439 4-10-13 57 (p) MrPaulJMcMahon(5) 8 46
(M J Wallace) *s.i.s and bhd: swtchd wd and hdwy 2f out: kpt on u.p appr last: nrst fin* 4/1[2]
0240 6 nk Quiet Reading (USA)[173] 2137 9-11-1 54 (v) MrsSBosley 9 43
(M R Bosley) *in tch: effrt over 2f out: sn rdn and kpt on same pce appr last* 8/1[3]
0000 7 3 Jaassey[14] 6382 3-11-0 55 MrSDobson 7 38
(A Crook) *chsd ldrs: rdn along 1/2-way: sn wknd* 20/1
4600 8 ½ Dado Mush[25] 6193 3-10-8 56 MrDarylChinn(7) 13 37
(G Prodromou) *chsd ldrs: rdn along 3f out: sn wknd* 14/1

9 *1* **Yellow Mane (IRE)**[99] 4413 3-10-7 **53**.......................... MrBMcHugh(5) 6 — 32
(Luke Comer, Ire) *chsd ldrs on inner: rdn along 3f out: sn wknd* **50/1**

00-0 **10** *1* **Tee Jay Kassidy**[25] 6193 6-11-0 **53**.......................... MrSWalker 3 — 30
(P S McEntee) *towards rr: rdn along and hdwy over 2f out: nvr nr ldrs* **16/1**

6304 **11** *2 1/2* **Gem Bien (USA)**[5] 6497 8-10-13 **52**..........................(b) MissADeniel 12 — 24
(D W Chapman) *in tch: hdwy to chse ldrs over 3f out: sn rdn and wknd over 2f out* **8/1**[3]

0000 **12** *5* **Loaderfun (IRE)**[13] 6387 4-10-4 **50**..........................(e[1]) MissWGibson(7) 1 — 12
(N Wilson) *dwlt: sn led on inner: rdn along 3f out: hdd 2f out and sn wknd* **28/1**

-000 **13** *4* **Cherokee Vision**[9] 6451 3-10-13 **54**..........................(b[1]) MissEJJones 14 — 7
(Miss T Spearing) *chsd ldrs: rdn along 3f out: sn wknd* **40/1**

RR0R **R** **Arabie**[13] 6387 8-11-0 **60**..........................(b) MrCEllingham(7) 10 — —
(Peter Grayson) *ref to r* **80/1**

1m 44.77s (0.17) **Going Correction** -0.175s/f (Stan)
WFA 3 from 4yo+ 2lb **14** Ran SP% **121.4**
Speed ratings (Par 101):92,90,85,83,81 81,78,77,76,75 73,68,64,—
CSF £134.29 CT £1403.72 TOTE £25.90: £8.50, £2.80, £3.40; EX 426.30.
Owner Entertainments Committee **Bred** The Queen **Trained** Eastbury, Berks

FOCUS
A moderate amateur riders' handicap run a time 0.69 seconds slower than the second division. The winner was well in on three-year-old form and the first two finished clear.
Scottish River(USA) Official explanation: jockey said gelding missed the break

6532 WBX.COM WORLD BET EXCHANGE AMATEUR RIDERS' H'CAP (DIV II) — 1m (F)
12:40 (12:41) (Class 6) (0-60,61) 3-Y-0+ **£1,977** (£608; £304) **Stalls** Low

Form — RPR

1 **Astronomical Odds (USA)**[86] 4827 3-11-5 **61**.......................... MrJJDoyle 2 — 71+
(T D Barron) *trckd ldrs: smooth hdwy to ld wl over 2f out: sn clr: rdn and kpt on fnl f* **11/1**

0626 **2** *3* **Paso Doble**[6] 6473 8-10-6 **50**.......................... MissDO'Brien(7) 6 — 57
(B R Millman) *bhd: hdwy and wd st: rdn over 2f out: styd on appr last* **8/1**

0400 **3** *3/4* **Benny The Ball (USA)**[96] 4496 5-10-13 **50**....... MrsEmmaLittmoden 11 — 55
(N P Littmoden) *trckd ldrs: hdwy over 2f out: sn rdn: styd on u.p appr last* **15/2**[3]

4152 **4** *3 1/2* **Uhuru Peak**[14] 6383 5-11-5 **56**..........................(bt) MissSBrotherton 9 — 54
(M W Easterby) *midfield: hdwy over 2f out: sn rdn and kpt onm ins last: nrst fin* **3/1**[1]

2014 **5** *1* **Vibrato (USA)**[18] 6307 4-10-13 **50**.......................... MrSWalker 5 — 46
(C J Teague) *midfield: hdwy 3f out: rdn to chse ldrs wl over 2f out: sn drvn and kpt on same pce* **7/1**[2]

0544 **6** *3/4* **Cabourg (IRE)**[9] 6451 3-11-2 **60**.......................... MissRBastiman(5) 12 — 54
(R Bastiman) *in tch: hdwy 3f out: sn rdn and kpt on same pce fnl 2f* **8/1**

3320 **7** *5* **Fulvio (USA)**[9] 6439 6-10-10 **54**..........................(v) MissFGuillambert(7) 7 — 37
(P Howling) *bhd tl styd on fnl 2f* **14/1**

1000 **8** *2* **Pawn In Life (IRE)**[14] 6380 8-10-13 **53**..........(v) MissFayeBramley(3) 13 — 32
(M J Attwater) *cl up: led over 3f out: rdn wl over 2f out: sn hdd and grad wknd* **12/1**

4106 **9** *1* **Government (IRE)**[4] 5924 5-10-3 **47**.......................... MrKJames(7) 4 — 24
(M C Chapman) *cl up: rdn along 3f out: sn wknd* **50/1**

0546 **10** *1* **Sand Iron (IRE)**[10] 6431 4-10-7 **51**.......................... MissHannahWatson(7) 14 — 26
(John Allen) *chsd ldrs: rdn along 1/2-way: sn wknd* **40/1**

0005 **11** *1 1/4* **Doctor Dennis (IRE)**[6] 6470 9-11-1 **55**..........................(v) MrSPearce(3) 1 — 27
(J Pearce) *a rr* **10/1**

0010 **12** *10* **Jewel Of India**[19] 5285 7-11-2 **53**..........................(p) MissLEllison 3 — 4
(Mrs A L M King) *a rr* **9/1**

060U **13** *1 1/4* **Cordage (IRE)**[14] 6378 4-10-8 **52**.......................... MissKJames(7) 8 — 1
(J A Pickering) *sn led: rdn along and hdd over 3f out: sn wknd* **50/1**

1m 44.08s (-0.52) **Going Correction** -0.175s/f (Stan)
WFA 3 from 4yo+ 2lb **13** Ran SP% **119.6**
Speed ratings (Par 101):95,92,91,87,86 86,81,79,78,77 75,65,64
CSF £95.68 CT £730.73 TOTE £9.70: £3.00, £2.40, £2.60; EX 104.30.
Owner J Browne **Bred** S B Coulter **Trained** Maunby, N Yorks

FOCUS
Probably stronger form than the first division and the winning time was 0.69 seconds quicker. The winner was a lot less exposed than the opposition and showed improved form on this surface. Pretty sound form.

6533 WBXTRIPLECROWN.COM H'CAP — 5f (F)
1:10 (1:11) (Class 6) (0-53,53) 3-Y-0+ **£2,730** (£806; £403) **Stalls** High

Form — RPR

4053 **1** **Larky's Lob**[28] 6142 7-8-7 **53**.......................... JamesO'Reilly(7) 11 — 62+
(J O'Reilly) *sn led: rdn wl over 1f out: hdd ent last: drvn and rallied wl to ld nr line* **12/1**

3006 **2** *hd* **Muara**[7] 6465 4-9-0 **53**.......................... TomEaves 2 — 61
(D W Barker) *trckd ldrs: swtchd lft and hdwy over 1f out: rdn to ld wl ins last: sn drvn: hdd and no ex nr fin* **14/1**

6064 **3** *shd* **Jilly Why (IRE)**[151] 2784 5-9-0 **53**.......................... FMBerry 7 — 61
(Ms Deborah J Evans) *cl up: rdn wl over 1f out: led ent last: drvn: hdd and nt qckn wl ins fnl f* **8/1**[3]

0550 **4** *4* **Marron Flore**[9] 6440 3-8-7 **46** oh1..........................(p) RichardThomas 1 — 40
(A J Lidderdale) *chsd ldrs on outer: effrt and cl up 2f out: sn rdn and kpt on same pce ent last* **50/1**

3000 **5** *shd* **Dora's Green**[14] 6371 3-8-2 **46** oh1..........................(p) LiamJones(5) 4 — 40
(S W Hall) *cl up: ev ch 2f out: sn rdn and wknd ent last* **28/1**

0543 **6** *1* **Blythe Spirit**[7] 6464 7-8-7 **51**..........................(tp) JamieMoriarty(5) 8 — 41
(R A Fahey) *rdn along and outpcd towards rr 1/2-way: swtchd rt wl over out: kpt on ins last* **13/2**[1]

0043 **7** *shd* **Orchestration (IRE)**[6] 6477 5-8-8 **47**.......................... ChrisCatlin 14 — 37
(M J Attwater) *in tch: rdn along and outpcd 1/2-way: kpt on u.p appr last* **7/1**[2]

3450 **8** *1/2* **Four Amigos (USA)**[6] 6470 5-8-6 **48**..........................(b) JamesDoyle(3) 13 — 36
(I A Wood) *cl up: rdn and ev ch 2f out: sn drvn and wknd appr last* **12/1**

5000 **9** *3/4* **Henry Tun**[12] 6399 8-8-13 **52**..........................(b) MickyFenton 10 — 38
(J Balding) *midfield: pushed along 1/2-way: swtchd lft and rdn wl over 1f out: no imp* **14/1**

0504 **10** *1 1/4* **Estoille**[39] 5928 5-8-8 **47**.......................... JimmyQuinn 5 — 28
(Mrs S Lamyman) *squeezed out s: a towards rr* **13/2**[1]

01 **11** *1 1/2* **Borzoi Maestro**[20] 6276 5-9-0 **53**..........................(p) AdamKirby 12 — 29
(M Wellings) *chsd ldrs: rdn along 2f out: sn wknd* **7/1**[2]

6000 **12** *nk* **Amanda's Lad (IRE)**[7] 6464 6-8-13 **52**.......................... BrianReilly 3 — 27
(M C Chapman) *chsd ldrs: rdn along 1/2-way: sn wknd* **33/1**

1010 **13** *shd* **Bahamian Bay**[76] 5078 4-8-7 **53**.......................... AndrewHeffernan(7) 9 — 28
(M Brittain) *cl up: rdn along 2f out: sn wknd* **10/1**

0000 **14** *2 1/2* **One Way Ticket**[45] 5791 6-9-0 **53**..........................(p) JohnEgan 6 — 20
(J M Bradley) *chsd ldrs: rdn along 2f out: sn wknd* **8/1**[3]

58.64 secs (-1.64) **Going Correction** -0.30s/f (Stan) **14** Ran SP% **120.0**
Speed ratings (Par 101):101,100,100,94,93 92,92,91,90,88 85,85,85,81
CSF £167.04 CT £1476.12 TOTE £15.60: £3.60, £6.10, £2.30; EX 309.30.
Owner J Morris **Bred** P Balding **Trained** Doncaster, S Yorks

FOCUS
A moderate sprint handicap. Sound form, the first three clear. The winner had become well handicapped and this was his best run for over a year.
Dora's Green Official explanation: jockey said filly was struck into
Henry Tun Official explanation: jockey said gelding was denied a clear run
Estoille Official explanation: jockey said mare missed the break
Borzoi Maestro Official explanation: jockey said gelding never travelled
One Way Ticket Official explanation: jockey said horse never travelled

6534 WBX.COM LAUNCHING 25TH NOVEMBER (S) STKS — 7f (F)
1:40 (1:41) (Class 6) 2-Y-0 **£2,388** (£705; £352) **Stalls** Low

Form — RPR

035 **1** **Sheriff's Silk**[18] 6303 2-8-12 64.......................... PaulEddery 11 — 57
(B Smart) *a.p: hdwy over 2f out: rdn to ld 11.2f out: hdd and edgd lft ent last: drvna nd rallied to ld last 75 yds* **2/1**[1]

4005 **2** *1/2* **Charlotte Grey**[12] 6401 2-8-4 48.......................... EdwardCreighton(3) 10 — 51
(C N Allen) *trckd ldrs: smooth hdwy 2f out: rdn to ld and edgd lft ent last: hdd and no ex last 75 yds* **14/1**

00 **3** *shd* **Inflagrantedelicto (USA)**[20] 6284 2-8-9 .... GregFairley(3) 12 — 55+
(M Johnston) *midfield: pushed along 3f out: rdn over 2f out: swtchd lft and hdwy over 1f out: styd on wl u.p ins last* **5/1**[2]

0401 **4** *3* **Lovers Kiss**[5] 6491 2-8-12 40..........................(b) DaleGibson 5 — 48
(N Wilson) *chsd ldrs: rdn along 2f out: drvn and one pce appr last* **9/1**

4000 **5** *1* **Ella Y Rossa**[59] 5503 2-8-4 48.......................... JamesDoyle(3) 1 — 40
(P D Evans) *bhd and rdn along 1/2-way: swtchd outside and hdwy 2f out: styd on wl u.p ins last: nrst fin* **16/1**

0030 **6** *1* **Spinning Game**[3] 6506 2-8-7 45.......................... LiamJones(5) 4 — 42
(D W Chapman) *midfield and rdn along 1/2-way: gd hdwy on inner 2f out: chsd ldrs tl drvn and wknd ent last* **20/1**

0620 **7** *3 1/2* **Burningfold Babe**[12] 6394 2-8-8 59 ow1.......................... TomEaves 8 — 29
(P Winkworth) *led: rdn along over 2f out: hdd 11/2f out and sn wknd* **14/1**

0 **8** *1* **La Chesneraie**[17] 6316 2-8-7 ....(t) LPKeniry 13 — 26
(P C Haslam) *chsd ldrs: rdn along over 2f out: sn wknd* **40/1**

0002 **9** *1 1/4* **Taran Tregarth**[6] 6471 2-8-7 35..........................(b) PaulQuinn 3 — 22
(A Bailey) *a rr* **33/1**

U000 **10** *nk* **Munster Mountain (IRE)**[11] 6416 2-8-12 57..........................(p) JohnEgan 6 — 27
(P A Blockley) *prom on inner: rdn along 3f out: sn drvn and wknd* **7/1**[3]

0 **11** *7* **Callahan (FR)**[72] 5168 2-8-12 .... FMBerry 2 — 9
(Ms Deborah J Evans) *a rr* **20/1**

0200 **12** *3* **Bar Humbug**[12] 6401 2-8-7 57..........................(p) JamieMoriarty(5) 7 — —
(R A Fahey) *a towards rr* **8/1**

6000 **13** *2 1/2* **Jazzanova**[10] 6421 2-8-12 40..........................(b[1]) MickyFenton 9 — —
(M W Easterby) *s.i.s: racd wd and a rr* **50/1**

1m 31.48s (0.68) **Going Correction** -0.175s/f (Stan) **13** Ran SP% **119.7**
Speed ratings (Par 94):89,88,88,84,83 82,78,77,76,75 67,64,61
CSF £31.12 TOTE £3.10: £1.90, £3.80, £1.80; EX 59.40.There was no bid for the winner. Inflagrantedelicto was claimed by David Chapman for £6,000
Owner Mrs Linda Pestell **Bred** P A Mason **Trained** Hambleton, N Yorks

FOCUS
A weak seller, rated through the second and fourth.

NOTEBOOK
Sheriff's Silk benefited from both the drop in trip and grade and was able to gain his first success at the fourth attempt. This was not much of a race, though, and it remains to be seen if he is as good as his official rating of 64 suggests. (op 15-8 tchd 9-4)
Charlotte Grey, stepped back up in trip, travelled strongly for much of the way but looked a weak finisher. She might to better back over shorter, but is probably not one to place too much faith in. (op 12-1)
Inflagrantedelicto(USA), dropped in grade and trip, stepped up on his two previous efforts. He might be able to find a similar race at some point. (op 9-2 tchd 4-1)
Lovers Kiss ran to a similar level of form as when winning a weak claimer over six furlongs round here on her previous start. (op 7-1)
Ella Y Rossa, dropped significantly in grade after beating only one home in a sales race at Ascot, got going too late. (op 20-1)
Munster Mountain(IRE) Official explanation: jockey said colt had no more to give

6535 WBX.COM WORLD BET EXCHANGE MAIDEN STKS — 1m 4f (F)
2:10 (2:11) (Class 5) 3-Y-0+ **£3,238** (£963; £481; £240) **Stalls** Low

Form — RPR

0-22 **1** **Melpomene**[56] 5583 3-8-9 77.......................... GregFairley(3) 7 — 70+
(M Johnston) *trckd ldrs: hdwy 1/2-way: led over 3f out: clr wl over 1f out: easily* **2/1**[2]

5064 **2** *8* **Art Investor**[40] 5911 3-9-4 69 ow1.......................... AntonyProcter 10 — 63
(D R C Elsworth) *hld up in tch: stdy hdwy over 5f out: rdn to chse wnr wl over 1f out: sn drvn and no imp* **13/2**[3]

0456 **3** *4* **Weet For Ever (USA)**[9] 6450 3-9-3 52.......................... JohnEgan 9 — 56
(P A Blockley) *trckd ldrs: hdwy over 4f out: rdn 3f out: kpt on same pce* **16/1**

0-4 **4** *1 3/4* **Daneway**[10] 6429 3-8-12 .... JimmyQuinn 8 — 48
(H R A Cecil) *chsd ldrs: rdn along over 3f out: sn drvn and wknd over 2f out* **9/1**

3262 **5** *6* **Reinstated (IRE)**[14] 6381 3-8-12 73.......................... MichaelHills 6 — 38
(B W Hills) *cl up: led after 3f: rdn along over 4f out: hdd over 3f out: sn drvn and btn* **1/1**[1]

06-0 **6** *27* **Spartan Odyssey**[118] 3810 5-9-9 35.......................... PaulQuinn 5 — —
(A Bailey) *a rr* **100/1**

7 *10* **Orphir (IRE)** 3-8-12 .... DuranFentiman(5) 2 — —
(Mrs N Macauley) *s.i.s: green and a bhd* **66/1**

0 **8** *2 1/2* **Moonlight Safari (IRE)**[42] 5870 3-8-12 .... DaleGibson 1 — —
(P Winkworth) *prom: rdn along over 5f out: sn wknd* **50/1**

0 **9** *8* **Kai Kuri (IRE)**[18] 5650 5-8-11 .... WilliamCarson(7) 4 — —
(P W Hiatt) *a bhd* **100/1**

3400 **10** *3* **Gypsy Royal (IRE)**[20] 6279 4-9-4 40.......................... MickyFenton 3 — —
(G Woodward) *led 3f: prom tl rdn along over 5f out and sn wknd* **66/1**

2m 36.99s (-5.10) **Going Correction** -0.175s/f (Stan)
WFA 3 from 4yo+ 6lb **10** Ran SP% **119.5**
Speed ratings (Par 103):110,104,102,100,96 78,72,70,65,63
CSF £15.93 TOTE £3.00: £1.10, £2.00, £3.30; EX 11.20.
Owner Mrs Christine E Budden **Bred** Zubieta Ltd **Trained** Middleham Moor, N Yorks

FOCUS
A weakish maiden, but the winning time was smart for a race like this. The winner impressed but it is doubtful she had to improve with the placed horses having disappointing profiles.

6536 EUROPEAN BREEDERS' FUND NOVICE STKS 1m (F)
2:40 (2:40) (Class 5) 2-Y-O £4,533 (£1,348; £674; £336) Stalls Low

Form RPR
05 1 **Legend House (FR)**[22] 6242 2-8-4 GregFairley(3) 4 73
(M Johnston) *cl up: led over 2f out: rdn and hdd over 1f out: rallied to ld again ins last: styd on wl* 15/8[2]
3301 2 1 ½ **Greyt Big Stuff (USA)**[39] 5923 2-8-12 80 JohnEgan 6 75
(Miss Gay Kelleway) *trckd ldrs: hdwy 3f out: rdn: edgd lft and led over 1f out: drvn and hdd ins last: kpt on same pce* 10/11[1]
05 3 2 ½ **Spartan Dance**[19] 6297 2-8-12 RichardThomas 3 69
(J A Geake) *led: rdn along and hdd over 2f out: drvn and hung bdly lft over 1f out: kpt on same pce* 12/1
06 4 1 **Spice Bar**[9] 6434 2-8-12 LPKeniry 2 67
(A M Balding) *trckd ldrs: effrt over 2f out: sn rdn and one pce* 12/1
00 5 2 **Berbatov**[33] 6050 2-8-12 FMBerry 1 62
(Ms Deborah J Evans) *a rr* 40/1
064 6 6 **Johannesburg Cat (USA)**[14] 6379 2-8-6 JamesDoyle(3) 5 45
(N P Littmoden) *hld up: swtchd outside 1/2-way: rdn along wl over 2f out and sn wknd* 11/1[3]

1m 43.37s (-1.23) **Going Correction** -0.175s/f (Stan) 6 Ran SP% 113.3
Speed ratings (Par 96):99,97,95,94,92 86
CSF £3.98 TOTE £3.30: £1.70, £1.10; EX 4.40.
Owner Gainsborough **Bred** Gainsborough Stud Management Ltd **Trained** Middleham Moor, N Yorks

FOCUS
Just an ordinary novice event. The runner-up sets the standard, and the winner can do better.

NOTEBOOK
Legend House(FR), making her debut on Fibresand, stepped up on her two previous efforts with a ready success. She should make a nice three-year-old and it will be interesting to see what handicap mark she is given. (op 11-8 tchd 2-1)
Greyt Big Stuff(USA), off the mark in a seven-furlong maiden round here on his final start for Brian Meehan, ran well in this tougher contest and emerges with plenty of credit. His official mark of 80 looks stiff enough, though, and it remains to be seen how he will fare when switched to handicaps. (op 11-8 tchd 6-4 in places)
Spartan Dance ◆ ran a nice race in third and should do well over further in handicaps next year. (op 14-1 tchd 16-1)
Spice Bar is another who should do better now he is qualified for a handicap mark. (op 18-1)
Berbatov is also qualified for an official mark following his third run. (op 33-1 tchd 50-1)
Johannesburg Cat(USA) did not stay and can probably do better when returned to sprinting. (op 15-2)

6537 WBX.COM H'CAP 1m 6f (F)
3:10 (3:10) (Class 5) (0-75,73) 3-Y-O+ £3,238 (£963; £481; £240) Stalls Low

Form RPR
0 1 **Stolen Light (IRE)**[17] 6321 5-10-0 70 (b) TomEaves 5 78
(A Crook) *in tch: hdwy and cl up 1/2-way: rdn to ld 2f out: drvn over 1f out: kpt on wl* 20/1
4041 2 ¾ **Trinity Rose**[5] 6495 3-9-6 73 6ex GregFairley(3) 1 80+
(M Johnston) *prom tl rdn and outpcd over 5f out: drvn and hdwy 3f out: styng on whn n.m.r and swtchd rt 1f out: kpt on* 4/9[1]
0320 3 ¾ **Special Moment (IRE)**[10] 6426 3-9-0 64 MichaelHills 6 70
(B W Hills) *trckd ldrs: hdwy to chse ldng pair over 4f out: rdn along over 2f out: drvn and kpt on same pce appr last* 10/1[3]
0113 4 ¾ **Virginia Rose (IRE)**[9] 6435 3-8-13 63 MickyFenton 4 68
(J G Given) *cl up: led 1/2-way: rdn along 3f out: hdd 2f out: sn drvn and wknd ins last* 7/2[2]
1600 5 39 **Grand Palace (IRE)**[38] 5936 3-8-4 54 JimmyQuinn 3 4
(D Shaw) *led to 1/2-way: rdn along over 5f out: sn wknd* 33/1
600- 6 16 **Galandora**[335] 4934 6-8-9 51 oh16 RichardThomas 2 —
(Dr J R J Naylor) *chsd ldrs: rdn along over 6f out: sn outpcd and bhd* 150/1

3m 7.11s (-2.49) **Going Correction** -0.175s/f (Stan)
WFA 3 from 5yo+ 8lb 6 Ran SP% 108.9
Speed ratings (Par 103):100,99,99,98,76 67
CSF £28.40 TOTE £15.80: £4.20, £1.10; EX 46.70.
Owner Mrs Helen Sinclair **Bred** Moyglare Stud Farm Ltd **Trained** Middleham Moor, N Yorks

FOCUS
Basically a four-horse race and, with the pace far from furious, they finished in a bunch. The form is not rock solid, with a chance that the winner did not need to improve to beat the below-par favourite.

6538 WBX.COM LAUNCHING 25TH NOVEMBER FILLIES' H'CAP 6f (F)
3:40 (3:40) (Class 5) (0-70,63) 3-Y-O+ £3,562 (£1,059; £529; £264) Stalls Low

Form RPR
211 1 **La Colline (GER)**[7] 6465 3-8-0 52 LiamJones(5) 2 73+
(W J Haggas) *trckd ldrs: n.m.r over 2f out and sn swtchd rt: qcknd to ld wl over 1f out and sn clr* 1/4[1]
0150 2 5 **Howards Princess**[6] 6477 4-8-8 55 (p) TomEaves 5 61
(J Hetherton) *in tch: hdwy over 2f out: sn rdn and styd on ins last: no ch w wnr* 28/1
0434 3 shd **Palais Polaire**[86] 4820 4-8-7 54 RichardThomas 6 60
(J A Geake) *chsd ldrs: rdn 2f out: styd on xsame pce appr last* 11/1[2]
3003 4 3 **Glamaraazi (IRE)**[6] 6470 3-8-7 54 DaleGibson 1 51
(R A Fahey) *cl yup: rdn to ld 2f out: sn edgd lft: hdd & wknd* 20/1
-060 5 shd **Look Of Eagles**[12] 6396 4-9-2 63 NelsonDeSouza 8 59
(P F I Cole) *chsd ldrs: hdwy over 2f out and ev ch: sn rdn and wknd over 1f out* 12/1[3]
3005 6 1 ¼ **Bathwick Emma (IRE)**[5] 6493 3-8-13 60 (p) JohnEgan 3 53
(P D Evans) *chsd ldrs: rdn along over 2f out: sn btn* 25/1
20 7 1 **Tipsy Lillie**[20] 6274 4-8-2 49 oh9 HayleyTurner 7 39
(P S McEntee) *dwlt and a rr* 33/1
0105 8 2 ½ **Bold Love**[18] 6306 3-7-11 49 oh4 DuranFentiman(5) 4 31
(J Balding) *led: rdn along 3f out: hdd & wknd 2f out* 66/1

1m 14.24s (-2.66) **Going Correction** -0.175s/f (Stan) 8 Ran SP% 112.5
Speed ratings (Par 100):110,103,103,99,99 97,96,92
CSF £14.54 CT £32.76 TOTE £1.20: £1.02, £4.40, £1.90; EX 13.10 Place 6 £381.69, Place 5 £78.97.
Owner Snowdrop Stud Co Limited **Bred** Graf And Grafin Von Stauffenberg **Trained** Newmarket, Suffolk

FOCUS
La Colline was differnet class to this lot and recorded a very decent winning time for the type of contest. She was value for extra, while the placed form is sound.
T/Plt: £427.90 to a £1 stake. Pool: £41,388.50. 70.60 winning tickets. T/Qpdt: £17.30 to a £1 stake. Pool: £4,140.80. 176.70 winning tickets. JR

6518 WOLVERHAMPTON (A.W) (L-H)
Monday, November 20

OFFICIAL GOING: Standard
Wind: Fresh, behind Weather: Cloudy

6539 IBETX.COM BANDED STKS 5f 20y(P)
1:30 (1:30) (Class 7) 3-Y-O+ £1,365 (£403; £201) Stalls Low

Form RPR
0524 1 **Desert Dust**[9] 6440 3-9-5 50 (v) BrettDoyle 6 58
(R M H Cowell) *chsd ldrs: rdn to ld ins fnl f: r.o* 13/2
0006 2 nk **Succeed (IRE)**[12] 6399 3-9-5 50 GeorgeBaker 3 57
(Mrs H Sweeting) *hld up: hdwy over 1f out: rdn and ev ch whn hung rt ins fnl f: r.o* 7/1
1052 3 ½ **Davids Mark**[56] 5569 6-8-10 48 WilliamBuick(7) 2 53+
(J R Jenkins) *mid-div: n.m.r over 3f out: hdwy over 1f out: nt clr run ins fnl f: r.o* 10/3[1]
0403 4 ¾ **Campeon (IRE)**[20] 6276 4-9-2 47 FrancisNorton 5 49
(J M Bradley) *led: hdd over 3f out: led over 1f out: rdn and hdd ins fnl f: styd on same pce* 5/1[2]
0320 5 5 **Sharp Hat**[20] 6276 12-9-2 47 TonyCulhane 1 31
(D W Chapman) *chsd ldrs: rdn 1/2-way: wknd over 1f out* 10/1
1000 6 3 ½ **Prime Recreation**[193] 1618 9-9-2 47 PatCosgrave 12 19
(P S Felgate) *led over 3f out: hung rt and hdd over 1f out: wknd fnl f* 33/1
6010 7 1 **Lady Hopeful (IRE)**[85] 4846 4-9-3 48 (b) RobbieFitzpatrick 4 16
(Peter Grayson) *prom: hmpd over 3f out: rdn 1/2-way: wknd over 1f out* 6/1[3]
560- 8 1 ¾ **Howards Call**[466] 4294 3-9-0 50 (b) AndrewElliott(5) 10 12
(W G Harrison) *sn outpcd* 33/1
0433 9 2 **Vicky Pollard**[117] 3842 3-9-3 48 DeanMernagh 9 3
(P Howling) *in rr whn hmpd over 3f out: sn wknd* 16/1
0600 10 ½ **Glenargo (USA)**[15] 6348 3-9-3 48 (p) AdrianMcCarthy 11 —
(R A Harris) *mid-div: hung lft over 3f out: sn rdn: wknd 2f out* 25/1
2000 11 ½ **Percy Douglas**[113] 3988 6-8-13 49 (bt) AnnStokell(5) 7 —
(Miss A Stokell) *in rr whn hmpd over 3f out: sn bhd* 33/1
2236 12 ½ **Montillia (IRE)**[117] 3847 4-9-3 48 MatthewHenry 8 —
(J W Unett) *chsd ldrs 3f* 9/1

62.14 secs (-0.68) **Going Correction** -0.275s/f (Stan) 12 Ran SP% 117.5
Speed ratings (Par 97):94,93,92,91,83 77,76,73,70,69 68,67
CSF £49.09 TOTE £10.00: £2.60, £2.70, £1.40; EX 64.50 Trifecta £79.40 Part won. Pool £111.94 - 0.34 winning units..
Owner Bottisham Heath Stud **Bred** Miss D Birkbeck **Trained** Six Mile Bottom, Cambs

FOCUS
This sprint had a wide-open look to it, and produced a good finish. The form looks sound enough rated around the first four.
Vicky Pollard Official explanation: jockey said filly suffered interference
Percy Douglas Official explanation: trainer said gelding returned lame
Montillia(IRE) Official explanation: jockey said filly hit its head on leaving stalls

6540 IBETX.COM APPRENTICE BANDED STKS 1m 5f 194y(P)
2:00 (2:01) (Class 7) 3-Y-O+ £1,365 (£403; £201) Stalls Low

Form RPR
0331 1 **Three Boars**[14] 6374 4-9-6 50 (b) WilliamBuick(5) 4 61
(S Gollings) *hld up in tch: racd keenly: chsd ldr 2f out: led 1f out: sn hung rt and rdn clr* 2/1[1]
0402 2 6 **Captivate**[28] 6133 3-8-7 45 (p) MCGeran(5) 5 46+
(A J McCabe) *s.s: hld up: hdwy over 1f out: edgd rt ins fnl f: no ch w wnr* 17/2
3 1 ¼ **Definite (IRE)**[31] 6091 8-9-2 46 AmyKathleenParsons(5) 10 46
(T G McCourt, Ire) *prom: chsd ldr over 7f out: rdn over 3f out: ev ch over 1f out: wknd ins fnl f* 11/1
03 4 ½ **Atlantic Gamble (IRE)**[3] 6509 6-9-9 48 AndrewElliott 12 47
(K R Burke) *led: clr 10f out: rdn and hdd 1f out: sn wknd* 9/2[2]
323- 5 4 **Toni Alcala**[329] 6472 7-9-4 46 KevinGhunowa(3) 7 39
(R F Fisher) *chsd ldrs: rdn over 4f out: wknd over 2f out* 15/2[3]
0063 6 1 ½ **Laurollie**[20] 6279 4-9-3 45 PatrickHills(3) 3 36
(B P J Baugh) *hld up in tch: racd keenly: rdn and wknd over 2f out* 10/1
2204 7 1 ½ **Shaheer (IRE)**[10] 6423 4-9-7 49 (v) JamieJones(3) 6 38
(J Gallagher) *hld up: hdwy over 4f out: rdn and wknd over 2f out* 16/1
0000 8 9 **Arch Folly**[12] 6405 4-9-11 50 (p) LiamTreadwell 11 27
(R J Price) *hld up: rdn over 6f out: wknd over 3f out* 22/1
0103 9 1 ½ **Cool Isle**[10] 6423 3-8-9 45 ow2 (b) JPFeatherstone(5) 13 22
(P Howling) *chsd ldrs over 10f* 14/1
10 10 **Mrs Mooney (IRE)**[179] 1970 3-9-0 50 AshleyHamblett(3) 9 11
(E J O'Neill) *chsd ldrs 9f* 12/1
11 83 **Blue Alabama (IRE)**[84] 4903 3-8-12 45 RoryMoore 2 —
(Seamus G O'Donnell, Ire) *hld up: wknd 6f out* 16/1

3m 5.61s (-1.76) **Going Correction** -0.275s/f (Stan)
WFA 3 from 4yo+ 8lb 11 Ran SP% 121.7
Speed ratings (Par 97):94,90,89,89,87 86,85,80,79,73 26
CSF £20.50 TOTE £2.80: £1.20, £2.90, £4.90; EX 20.50 Trifecta £88.20 Part won. Pool £124.30 - 0.88 winning units..
Owner P Whinham **Bred** J M Greetham **Trained** Scamblesby, Lincs

FOCUS
An uncompetitive event and weak form but an easy winner, who was back to his best.

6541 IBETX.COM BETTING EXCHANGE BANDED STKS 5f 216y(P)
2:30 (2:30) (Class 7) 3-Y-O+ £1,365 (£403; £201) Stalls Low

Form RPR
0355 1 **Siraj**[14] 6371 7-9-0 47 (b) BrettDoyle 6 57
(J Ryan) *mid-div: hdwy over 2f out: rdn to ld and hung rt over 1f out: r.o* 8/1
2034 2 1 ¼ **Cree**[18] 6308 4-9-1 48 GeorgeBaker 3 57+
(W R Muir) *hld up: hdwy and hit over hd by rivals whip over 1f out: r.o* 10/3[1]
2061 3 2 **Guadaloup**[6] 6470 4-9-9 50 (v) DeanMernagh 9 56
(M Brittain) *chsd ldrs: rdn and ev ch over 1f out: styd on same pce* 9/2[2]
0000 4 1 ¾ **Beverley Beau**[12] 6399 4-8-8 48 KristinStubbs(7) 7 43
(Mrs L Stubbs) *chsd ldr: led 2f out: rdn and hdd over 1f out: wknd ins fnl f* 16/1
3140 5 shd **Jennverse**[6] 6477 4-9-0 47 JamieMackay 11 41
(D K Ivory) *chsd ldrs: lost pl 5f out: hdwy u.p over 1f out: no imp fnl f* 10/1
5000 6 ¾ **Cyfrwys (IRE)**[6] 6477 5-9-3 50 (p) TonyCulhane 8 42
(B Palling) *hld up: hdwy u.p over 1f out: nt trble ldrs* 11/1

3000 **7** *nk* **Red Vixen (IRE)**[41] 5885 3-8-9 47 NicolPolli(5) 4 38
(C N Allen) *s.i.s: outpcd: r.o ins fnl f: nvr nrr* **12/1**

0020 **8** *1 1/2* **Flying Tackle**[53] 5631 8-8-9 47 (v) MarkLawson(5) 13 34
(I W McInnes) *sn outpcd* **12/1**

0000 **9** *1 1/2* **Mr Cheers**[155] 2678 3-9-0 47 (b) FrancisNorton 12 29
(C A Dwyer) *hld up: a in rr* **33/1**

2036 **10** *hd* **Otis B Driftwood**[171] 2187 3-9-2 49 (b) PaulFitzsimons 5 31
(Miss J R Tooth) *prom rdn over 2f out: wknd over 1f out* **33/1**

0/0- **11** *1 1/4* **Noble Locks (IRE)**[658] 240 8-9-1 48 MatthewHenry 2 26
(J W Unett) *led: hdd 5f out: rdn and wknd over 1f out* **50/1**

0010 **12** *1 1/2* **Alistair John**[18] 6308 3-9-3 50 DeanMcKeown 1 23
(Mrs G S Rees) *led 5f out: rdn and hdd 2f out: sn wknd* **6/1**[3]

6060 **13** *2 1/2* **Sounds Simla (IRE)**[17] 6325 3-8-10 50 (p) TolleyDean(7) 10 16
(R A Harris) *chsd ldrs: rdn over 2f out: sn wknd* **16/1**

1m 14.61s (-1.20) **Going Correction** -0.275s/f (Stan) **13** Ran SP% **119.1**
Speed ratings (Par 97):97,95,92,90,90 89,88,86,84,84 82,80,77
CSF £34.15 TOTE £10.00: £3.00, £1.90, £2.20; EX 26.70 Trifecta £79.60 Pool £249.07 - 2.22 winning units.
Owner T C Gilligan **Bred** Mrs S J Etches **Trained** Newmarket, Suffolk
■ John Ryan's first winner on the Flat.

FOCUS
A moderate sprint but sound form rated around the third.

6542 IBETX.COM MONEY MAN BANDED STKS 7f 32y(P)
3:00 (3:00) (Class 7) 3-Y-0+ **£1,365** (£403; £201) **Stalls** High

Form RPR

0000 **1** **Penny Glitters**[6] 6480 3-8-12 45 DeanMernagh 6 50
(S Parr) *chsd ldrs: rdn 1/2-way: hung lft over 1f out: styd on to ld nr fin* **12/1**

3006 **2** *nk* **Mid Valley**[22] 6236 3-8-12 45 (v) PatCosgrave 7 49
(J R Jenkins) *hld up: hdwy over 2f out: rdn to ld 1f out: edgd rt and hdd nr fin* **4/1**[1]

4060 **3** *3/4* **Wodhill Be**[10] 6425 6-8-13 45 DerekMcGaffin 12 47
(D Morris) *hld up: hdwy over 1f out: r.o* **16/1**

4030 **4** *3/4* **Teyaar**[22] 6237 10-8-13 45 PaulFitzsimons 9 45
(M Wellings) *hld up: hdwy over 2f out: rdn over 1f out: styd on* **12/1**

0565 **5** *1 3/4* **Grezie**[101] 4329 4-8-13 45 AdrianMcCarthy 2 41
(T D McCarthy) *led: rdn and hdd 1f out: no ex* **4/1**[1]

2030 **6** *nk* **Chalice Welcome**[259] 594 3-8-12 45 StephenCarson 11 40
(C F Wall) *prom: lost pl 5f out: rdn over 2f out: hung lft fr over 1f out: styd on* **9/2**[2]

5/-3 **7** *hd* **Shava**[22] 6237 6-8-13 45 (t) BrettDoyle 8 39
(H J Evans) *plld hrd and prom: trckd ldr over 4f out: rdn and ev ch over 1f out: no ex ins fnl f* **11/2**[3]

66-0 **8** *10* **Urban Calm**[280] 402 5-8-13 45 MatthewHenry 3 13
(J W Unett) *hld up: n.d* **14/1**

02/0 **9** *1* **Scorch**[22] 6237 5-8-13 45 MichaelTebbutt 5 11
(V Smith) *hld up: a in rr* **14/1**

6655 **10** *1* **My Girl Pearl (IRE)**[28] 6131 6-8-13 45 JamieMackay 10 8
(M S Saunders) *chsd ldrs over 4f* **9/1**

5060 **11** *1 1/4* **Musical Chimes**[38] 5951 3-8-12 45 PaulMulrennan 1 5
(W M Brisbourne) *chsd ldrs 4f* **25/1**

0006 **12** *6* **Miss Sudbrook (IRE)**[18] 6314 4-8-13 45 (t) LeeEnstone 4 —
(A W Carroll) *s.s: outpcd* **16/1**

1m 29.33s (-1.07) **Going Correction** -0.275s/f (Stan)
WFA 3 from 4yo+ 1lb **12** Ran SP% **127.9**
Speed ratings (Par 97):95,94,93,92,90 90,90,78,77,76 75,68
CSF £64.31 TOTE £21.70: £4.80, £1.60, £6.10; EX 109.60 TRIFECTA Not won..
Owner Adrian Swingler **Bred** Mrs G Slater **Trained** Carburton, Notts

FOCUS
A very moderate contest in which the form is sound but limited.
Musical Chimes Official explanation: jockey said filly hung right throughout

6543 MONEY MAN COMING SOON FROM IBETX.COM BANDED STKS (DIV I) 1m 141y(P)
3:30 (3:31) (Class 7) 3-Y-0+ **£1,365** (£403; £201) **Stalls** Low

Form RPR

6646 **1** **Miss Porcia**[9] 6448 5-9-6 50 BrettDoyle 8 57
(P A Blockley) *chsd ldr: rdn to ld 1f out: edgd lft: r.o* **6/1**[3]

0523 **2** *nk* **Wodhill Gold**[6] 6473 5-9-3 47 (v) DerekMcGaffin 11 53
(D Morris) *hld up in tch: rdn over 2f out: r.o* **7/2**[1]

0410 **3** *1* **Warden Warren**[6] 6477 8-9-5 49 (b) AdrianMcCarthy 1 53
(Mrs C A Dunnett) *chsd ldrs: rdn over 2f out: styd on* **12/1**

1500 **4** *1/2* **Indigo Dancer**[14] 6374 3-8-13 46 (bt[1]) StephenCarson 9 49+
(C F Wall) *hld up: hdwy u.p over 1f out: hung lft: r.o* **4/1**[2]

4020 **5** *1/2* **Boucheen**[43] 5838 3-8-12 45 MichaelTebbutt 7 47
(Ms Deborah J Evans) *led: rdn and hdd 1f out: styng on same pce whn nt clr run wl ins fnl f* **12/1**

2350 **6** *nk* **Frank's Quest (IRE)**[107] 4139 6-9-3 47 SamHitchcott 4 48
(A B Haynes) *hld up: hdwy over 1f out: nt trble ldrs* **8/1**

0303 **7** *nk* **Perfect Order (USA)**[18] 6304 3-9-0 47 (p) JamieMackay 2 48
(N A Callaghan) *hld up: plld hrd: hmpd 7f out: hdwy over 2f out: rdn over 1f out: nt trble ldrs* **12/1**

-400 **8** *3 1/2* **Insignia (IRE)**[22] 6232 4-9-1 45 (p) PatCosgrave 13 38
(W M Brisbourne) *hld up: rdn over 1f out: n.d* **20/1**

6600 **9** *1 3/4* **Calamari (IRE)**[22] 6235 4-9-1 45 (b[1]) PaulFitzsimons 10 35
(Mrs A Duffield) *hld up in tch: racd keenly: rdn over 2f out: hung lft and wknd over 1f out* **25/1**

-050 **10** *7* **Danzar**[68] 5285 4-9-5 49 DeanMernagh 12 24
(M Brittain) *hld up: sme hdwy over 2f out: sn rdn and wknd* **8/1**

6050 **11** *6* **Wanna Shout**[10] 6431 8-9-3 47 RobertMiles 6 9
(R Dickin) *dwlt: hld up: hdwy over 2f out: sn hung rt and wknd* **22/1**

0000 **12** *2* **Bacharach (IRE)**[33] 6053 3-9-3 50 (t) PaulMulrennan 3 8
(R F Fisher) *chsd ldrs: rdn over 2f out: sn wknd* **33/1**

1m 50.77s (-0.99) **Going Correction** -0.275s/f (Stan)
WFA 3 from 4yo+ 3lb **12** Ran SP% **117.7**
Speed ratings (Par 97):93,92,91,91,90 90,90,87,85,79 74,72
CSF £25.62 TOTE £10.10: £2.80, £1.70, £4.00; EX 32.90 Trifecta £71.00 Pool £242.28 - 2.42 winning units.
Owner Miss S Clough **Bred** C N And Mrs Hart **Trained** Lambourn, Berks
■ Stewards' Enquiry : Derek McGaffin two-day ban: careless riding (Dec 1-2); two-day ban: used whip with excessive frequency (Dec 3-4)

FOCUS
A modest time and the form is sound but limited by the third.
Bacharach(IRE) Official explanation: trainer said gelding bled from the nose; jockey said gelding hung right

6544 BET WITH IBETX.COM BANDED STKS 1m 1f 103y(P)
4:00 (4:00) (Class 7) 3-Y-0+ **£1,535** (£453; £226) **Stalls** Low

Form RPR

2034 **1** **Thornaby Green**[18] 6304 5-9-5 49 GrahamGibbons 7 57
(T D Barron) *chsd ldr tl led over 6f out: rdn over 1f out: edgd rt ins fnl f: r.o* **9/2**[3]

0164 **2** *nk* **Milk And Sultana**[14] 6374 6-9-6 50 FrancisNorton 1 57
(G A Ham) *hld up: hdwy over 2f out: rdn to chse wnr over 1f out: r.o* **4/1**[2]

6033 **3** *1 1/4* **Wood Fern (UAE)**[28] 6128 6-8-12 47 AshleyHamblett(5) 12 52
(W M Brisbourne) *hld up: hdwy over 2f out: rdn and swtchd lft ins fnl f: r.o* **3/1**[1]

300- **4** *1* **Jarvo**[380] 5131 5-8-12 47 MarkLawson(5) 4 50
(I W McInnes) *hld up: hdwy over 1f out: hung lft ins fnl f: r.o* **33/1**

0320 **5** *3* **Justcallmehandsome**[28] 6128 4-8-11 48 DonnaCaldwell(7) 5 45
(D J S Ffrench Davis) *chsd ldrs: nt clr run and lost pl over 3f out: hung lft and r.o fnl f* **13/2**

000- **6** *nk* **Blakeshall Hope**[496] 3416 4-9-6 50 DeanMcKeown 6 47
(A J Chamberlain) *chsd ldrs: rdn over 1f out: wknd ins fnl f* **18/1**

0200 **7** *3* **Height Of Spirits**[14] 6374 4-9-4 48 (p) AdamKirby 9 39
(T D McCarthy) *hld up: hdwy and hung lft over 3f out: rdn and wknd over 1f out* **14/1**

0000 **8** *1* **Fuel Cell (IRE)**[43] 5839 5-8-13 50 (p) JamesO'Reilly(7) 13 39
(J O'Reilly) *hld up: hdwy and hung lft over 3f out: rdn and wknd 2f out* **16/1**

0004 **9** *1* **Thomas A Beckett (IRE)**[32] 6067 3-8-9 49 PNolan(7) 2 36
(P R Chamings) *prom: lost pl 4f out: in rr whn hmpd 1f out* **20/1**

5000 **10** *1/2* **Lady Ambitious**[14] 6374 3-9-1 48 BrettDoyle 8 34
(D K Ivory) *s.i.s: hld up: rdn over 3f out: n.d* **25/1**

3000 **11** *1 1/4* **Joe Jo Star**[205] 1305 4-9-6 50 RobbieFitzpatrick 10 34
(B P J Baugh) *sn led: hdd over 6f out: remained handy tl wknd 2f out: in rr whn hmpd 1f out* **14/1**

2000 **12** *1/2* **Musical Gift**[32] 6067 6-9-0 49 (v) KevinGhunowa(5) 11 32
(P A Blockley) *chsd ldrs 7f* **14/1**

-000 **13** *1 1/4* **Sheriff's Deputy**[11] 6419 6-9-1 50 RoryMoore(5) 3 31
(C N Kellett) *hld up: hmpd 7f out: sme hdwy over 2f out: sn wknd* **16/1**

2m 0.82s (-1.80) **Going Correction** -0.275s/f (Stan)
WFA 3 from 4yo+ 3lb **13** Ran SP% **125.1**
Speed ratings (Par 97):97,96,95,94,92 91,89,88,87,86 85,85,84
CSF £23.46 TOTE £6.20: £2.50, £1.80, £1.50; EX 14.90 Trifecta £31.70 Pool £263.25 - 5.89 winning units.
Owner K J Alderson **Bred** Mrs S Broadhurst **Trained** Maunby, N Yorks

FOCUS
A fair time for this contest and solid form with the front three fair types for the grade.
Blakeshall Hope Official explanation: jockey said gelding was struck into
Fuel Cell(IRE) Official explanation: jockey said gelding hung left up the straight

6545 MONEY MAN COMING SOON FROM IBETX.COM BANDED STKS (DIV II) 1m 141y(P)
4:30 (4:31) (Class 7) 3-Y-0+ **£1,365** (£403; £201) **Stalls** Low

Form RPR

3310 **1** **Keon (IRE)**[28] 6130 4-9-6 50 BrettDoyle 4 58+
(R Hollinshead) *chsd ldrs: edgd rt 1f out: rdn to ld ins fnl f: r.o* **9/4**[1]

0600 **2** *1* **Khetaab (IRE)**[57] 5553 4-9-3 47 DavidKinsella 2 52
(E J Alston) *led: hdd 7f out: chsd ldrs: rdn to ld over 1f out: hdd ins fnl f: styd on same pce* **20/1**

3016 **3** *shd* **Tartan Special**[20] 6281 4-9-5 49 LeeEnstone 6 54
(K R Burke) *hld up: plld hrd: nt clr run over 2f out: hdwy over 1f out: swiched lft: r.o* **9/2**[3]

0000 **4** *1/2* **Star Fern**[18] 6304 5-9-1 45 DeanMernagh 9 49
(M J Attwater) *s.s: outpcd: swtchd rt over 1f out: r.o u.p ins fnl f: nrst fin* **40/1**

00 **5** *1 1/2* **Inveraray**[43] 5847 3-9-3 50 StephenCarson 3 51
(P S Felgate) *dwlt: hld up: r.o ins fnl f: nvr nrr* **33/1**

0550 **6** *nk* **Jabraan (USA)**[20] 6282 4-9-1 45 MatthewHenry 7 45
(D W Chapman) *led 7f out: rdn and hdd over 1f out: no ex* **40/1**

7 *3/4* **Spurron (IRE)**[96] 4505 6-9-3 47 PatCosgrave 5 46
(Gerard Keane, Ire) *hld up: rdn over 3f out: hung lft over 1f out: styd on u.p* **12/1**

8 *4* **Mujobliged (IRE)**[103] 4270 3-9-3 50 PaulMulrennan 13 40
(Seamus G O'Donnell, Ire) *trckd ldr: plld hrd: rdn over 2f out: hung lft and wknd over 1f out* **12/1**

0050 **9** *1 3/4* **Madam Patti**[6] 6470 3-9-0 47 AdrianMcCarthy 1 34
(B Palling) *prom: rdn over 2f out: edgd lft and wknd over 1f out* **33/1**

0002 **10** *2* **Ballare (IRE)**[28] 6128 7-9-2 46 MichaelTebbutt 12 29
(P J Makin) *chsd ldrs: rdn over 2f out: wknd over 1f out* **5/1**

4 **11** *5* **Cameo Story**[43] 5839 3-9-1 48 SamHitchcott 11 20
(Andrew Oliver, Ire) *hld up: rdn over 3f out: wknd over 1f out* **14/1**

5303 **12** *nk* **Start Of Authority**[39] 5929 5-9-3 47 JamieMackay 8 18
(J Gallagher) *hld up: plld hrd: hmpd 7f out: wknd over 2f out* **7/2**[2]

1m 50.07s (-1.69) **Going Correction** -0.275s/f (Stan)
WFA 3 from 4yo+ 3lb **12** Ran SP% **125.4**
Speed ratings (Par 97):96,95,95,94,93 92,92,88,87,85 80,80
CSF £58.03 TOTE £3.90: £1.40, £6.70, £1.60; EX 80.30 Trifecta £256.80 Part won. Pool £361.70 - 0.34 winning units. Place 6 £28.84, Place 5 £14.67 .
Owner Chasetown Civil Engineering Ltd **Bred** P F Headon **Trained** Upper Longdon, Staffs
■ A 1,534-1 four-timer for Brett Doyle.

FOCUS
The form looks reasonable rated around the first three, although the proximity of the fifth and sixth limits confidence.
Star Fern Official explanation: jockey said gelding was slowly away
Jabraan(USA) Official explanation: jockey said saddle slipped
Start Of Authority Official explanation: jockey said gelding suffered interference in running
T/Jkpt: Not won. T/Plt: £32.30 to a £1 stake. Pool: £59,042.10. 1,331.60 winning tickets. T/Qpdt: £10.80 to a £1 stake. Pool: £4,609.70. 315.20 winning tickets. CR

6228 MAISONS-LAFFITTE (R-H)

Monday, November 20

OFFICIAL GOING: Very soft

6546a PRIX ZEDDAAN (LISTED RACE) 6f (S)
1:25 (1:28) 2-Y-0 **£17,241** (£6,897; £5,172; £3,448; £1,724)

RPR
1 **Missvinski (USA)**[40] 5912 2-8-8 .... IMendizabal 2 98
(J-C Rouget, France)
2 *nse* **Damdam (FR)**[17] 2-8-11 .... (b) FSpanu 9 101
(J-P Despeyroux, France)
3 *6* **Zut Alors (IRE)**[23] 6228 2-8-12 .... TThulliez 4 84
(Robert Collet, France)
4 *1/2* **Aleandros (GER)**[31] 6092 2-8-11 .... (b) J-PCarvalho 8 82
(Mario Hofer, Germany)
5 *1 1/2* **Place Vendome (FR)**[20] 2-8-8 .... TJarnet 3 74
(Mlle S-V Tarrou, France)
6 *1/2* **Grey Winner (FR)**[20] 2-8-8 .... VVion 1 73
(Rod Collet, France)
7 *3/4* **Adaptation**[30] 6105 2-8-8 .... JoeFanning 5 70
(M Johnston) *mid-division, driven along before half-way, 4th half-way, soon ridden, weakened 1 1/2f out* **14/1**[1]
8 *3* **Punisher (FR)**[27] 2-8-11 .... FSanchez 11 64
(S Loeuillet, France)
9 *nk* **Spirit Of Pearl (IRE)**[88] 4747 2-8-8 .... THuet 10 60
(R Pritchard-Gordon, France)
10 *6* **Right Place (FR)**[23] 6229 2-8-11 .... (b) JAuge 7 45
(Robert Collet, France)
11 *6* **Jailamigraine (IRE)**[42] 5880 2-8-8 .... SPasquier 6 24
(P Bary, France)

1m 13.0s **11** Ran SP% **6.7**
PARI-MUTUEL: WIN 4.50; PL 1.70, 5.40, 1.70; DF 118.10.
Owner J C Gour **Bred** Ray Stark Irrevocable Trust **Trained** Pau, France

NOTEBOOK
Adaptation, well up from the start, was outpaced a little a furlong and a half out before staying on one-paced on ground that was certainly not to her liking.

6547a PRIX CONTESSINA (LISTED RACE) 6f (S)
1:55 (1:55) 3-Y-0+ **£17,241** (£6,897; £5,172; £3,448; £1,724)

RPR
1 **Donatello (GER)**[31] 6093 5-8-11 .... JVictoire 11 101
(W Baltromei, Germany)
2 *nse* **Kourka (FR)**[46] 5779 4-8-8 .... RonanThomas 12 98
(J-M Beguigne, France) *finished 3rd, placed 2nd*
3 *1 1/2* **Fulminant (IRE)**[29] 6121 5-8-11 .... (b) AHelfenbein 6 101
(W Kujath, Germany) *finished 2nd, placed 3rd*
4 *snk* **Derison (USA)**[13] 4-8-11 .... (b) TJarnet 1 96
(H Van De Poele, France)
5 *1 1/2* **Luisant**[23] 6230 3-8-11 .... TThulliez 3 92
(F Doumen, France)
6 *3/4* **Dizzy Dreamer (IRE)**[72] 5171 3-8-8 .... RobertHavlin 9 86
(P W Chapple-Hyam) *led in centre, pushed along half-way and kept finding more when pressed til headed 150 yards out, no extra* **24/1**[1]
7 *3* **Arc De Triomphe (GER)**[31] 6093 4-9-2 .... FForesi 8 85
(D Fechner, Germany)
8 *nk* **Brescello (FR)**[44] 3-8-11 .... THuet 7 79
(J E Pease, France)
9 *nk* **Priere**[50] 5710 4-8-8 .... J-MBreux 4 76
(N Clement, France)
10 *8* **Jardin Bleu**[44] 5816 7-8-11 .... (b) AlxiBadel 2 55
(Mme M Bollack-Badel, France)
11 *8* **Tycoon's Hill (IRE)**[46] 5779 7-9-2 .... JAuge 5 36
(Robert Collet, France)
12 *20* **Alyzea (IRE)**[20] 3-8-8 .... (b) MBlancpain 10 —
(C Laffon-Parias, France)

1m 12.0s **12** Ran SP% **4.0**
PARI-MUTUEL: WIN 3.80; PL 1.90, 4.10, 3.70; DF 37.10.
Owner Rennstall Gestut Hachtsee **Bred** Brigitte Grafin Von Norman **Trained** Germany

NOTEBOOK
Dizzy Dreamer(IRE) tried to make every yard and was still fighting to keep her lead at the furlong marker, but she gradually dropped away from that point. It was a brave effort, though, and the trip appeared to be a furlong too far on this ground.

6531 SOUTHWELL (L-H)

Tuesday, November 21

OFFICIAL GOING: Standard
Wind: Light, behind

6548 HOSPITALITY PACKAGES AVAILABLE BANDED STKS 5f (F)
12:20 (12:22) (Class 7) 3-Y-0+ **£1,365** (£403; £201) **Stalls** High

Form RPR
5000 1 **She's Our Beauty (IRE)**[21] 6274 3-8-7 45 .... (v) DuranFentiman(5) 2 51
(S T Mason) *mde virtually all: rdn wl over 1f out: drvn ins last and hld on wl* **33/1**
0600 2 *hd* **El Potro**[119] 3817 4-8-12 45 .... GrahamGibbons 5 50
(J R Holt) *in tch: rdn along over 2f out: hdwy over 1f out: styd on u.p ins last: jst hld* **10/3**[2]
0005 3 *shd* **All Clued Up (IRE)**[10] 6440 3-8-12 45 .... ChrisCatlin 8 50
(Rae Guest) *towards rr and pushed along halwfay: hdwy over 1f out: rdn and str run ins last: nrst fin* **10/1**
4000 4 *nk* **Axis Shield (IRE)**[40] 5928 3-8-7 45 .... EmmettStack(5) 4 49
(M C Chapman) *cl up: rdn over 1f out and ev ch tl drvn and no ex last 100 yds* **25/1**
0050 5 *3/4* **Hout Bay**[8] 6465 9-8-12 45 .... RobertWinston 7 46
(D W Chapman) *midfield: sn rdn along and outpcd: hdwy 2f out and sn rdn: styd on ins last: nrst fin* **5/1**[3]
000- 6 *3/4* **Ames Souer (IRE)**[347] 6528 3-8-12 45 .... DanielTudhope 1 44
(D Carroll) *cl up: effrt and ev ch over 1f out: sn rdn and wknd wl ins last* **3/1**[1]
0503 7 *1 1/4* **Quote Unquote**[21] 6282 3-8-9 45 .... NeilChalmers(3) 14 40
(J Parkes) *chsd ldrs: rdn along over 2f out: kpt on same pce* **16/1**
-606 8 *1 3/4* **Mill End Chateau**[10] 6440 4-8-12 45 .... (t) RobertHavlin 6 34
(D K Ivory) *midfield: effrt and hdwy 2f out: sn rdn and no imp* **18/1**
5400 9 *1/2* **Eternally**[196] 1571 4-8-12 45 .... (p) FMBerry 10 32
(R M H Cowell) *chsd ldrs: rdn along over 2f out: grad wknd* **16/1**
2403 10 *2* **Comic Tales**[189] 1762 5-8-12 45 .... LeeEnstone 12 25
(M Mullineaux) *in tch: rdn along over 2f out and sn wknd* **18/1**
0000 11 *3* **Valiant Romeo**[75] 5131 6-8-12 45 .... (v) PatCosgrave 11 15
(R Bastiman) *chsd ldrs to 1/2-way: sn wknd* **20/1**
000 12 *3* **Broadfield Lady (IRE)**[21] 6274 6-8-9 45 .... (p) EdwardCreighton(3) 3 5
(E J Creighton) *s.i.s and a bhd* **40/1**
0065 13 *nk* **First Among Equals**[90] 4710 3-9-0 45 ow5 .... DNolan(3) 9 9
(D G Bridgwater) *sn outpcd and a bhd* **25/1**

59.35 secs (-0.95) **Going Correction** -0.25s/f (Stan) **13** Ran SP% **114.0**
Speed ratings (Par 97):97,96,96,96,94 93,91,88,88,84 80,75,74
CSF £115.81 TOTE £33.70: £6.50, £1.70, £2.90; EX 244.00 TRIFECTA Not won..
Owner Tarn Lads Syndicate **Bred** R N Auld **Trained** Lanchester, Co. Durham
■ The first training success for Scott Mason, a former conditional jockey and recently assistant to David Nicholls.
■ Stewards' Enquiry : Graham Gibbons two-day ban; using whip with excessive frequency (Dec 2-3)

FOCUS
Secret Vision (8/1) was withdrawn on vet's advice. R4, deduct 10p in the £. As is usual over this straight five, those drawn low held a big advantage and all the action took place down the centre of the track. Very average banded form.

6549 ARENA LEISURE BANDED STKS (DIV I) 7f (F)
12:50 (12:50) (Class 7) 3-Y-0+ **£1,365** (£403; £201) **Stalls** Low

Form RPR
0001 1 **Cleveland**[6] 6493 4-9-3 50 .... RussellKennemore(7) 14 72+
(R Hollinshead) *prom: hdwy to ld wl over 2f out: rdn clr over 1f out: easily* **7/1**[3]
1400 2 *5* **Haroldini (IRE)**[126] 3617 4-9-0 49 .... (p) JasonEdmunds(3) 5 52
(J Balding) *midfield: hdwy over 2f out: rdn to chse wnr over 1f out: sn no imp* **25/1**
6230 3 *1 3/4* **Chickado (IRE)**[40] 5929 5-9-4 50 .... (p) RobertHavlin 8 48
(D Haydn Jones) *midfield: hdwy 3f out: rdn to chse ldrs over 1f out: sn one pce* **6/1**[2]
5001 4 *hd* **Windy Prospect**[8] 6464 4-9-0 46 .... HayleyTurner 9 43
(P A Blockley) *towards rr: pushed along 3f out: rdn and hdwy 2f out: kpt on appr last: nt rch ldrs* **11/8**[1]
0031 5 *4* **Top Level (IRE)**[19] 6306 3-8-13 49 .... DominicFox(3) 4 36
(M G Quinlan) *towards rr: hdwy and poushed along wl over 2f out: swtchd lft and rdn over 1f out: kpt on ins last* **8/1**
0003 6 *3 1/2* **Danethorpe (IRE)**[19] 6308 3-9-0 47 .... (v) DanielTudhope 10 25
(D Shaw) *towards rr tl styd on fnl 2f: n.d* **12/1**
5004 7 *1/2* **Jumanji (IRE)**[13] 6406 3-9-3 50 .... DaleGibson 13 27
(M J Attwater) *towards rr tl styd on fnl 2f: n.d* **40/1**
-506 8 *nk* **Aboustar**[225] 942 6-8-13 40 .... DeanMernagh 6 21
(M Brittain) *prom: rdn along 3f out: drvn over 2f out and sn wknd* **33/1**
0500 9 *3* **Kissi Kissi**[19] 6308 3-8-12 45 .... (t) FMBerry 1 13
(M J Attwater) *dwlt: chsd ldrs on inner: rdn along 3f out and sn wknd* **33/1**
0300 10 *1 3/4* **Food For Thought**[11] 6431 3-9-0 47 .... (v) GrahamGibbons 3 11
(J J Quinn) *a rr* **16/1**
000 11 *6* **Mulberry Lad (IRE)**[6] 6493 4-8-7 46 .... WilliamCarson(7) 12 —
(P W Hiatt) *cl up: rdn along 3f out: sn drvn and wknd* **18/1**
5010 12 *3 1/2* **Cut Ridge (IRE)**[29] 6130 7-9-4 50 .... (p) RobertWinston 2 —
(J S Wainwright) *led: rdn along 3f out: sn hdd & wknd* **12/1**
5023 13 *6* **Newsround**[135] 3330 4-9-3 49 .... PaulQuinn 11 —
(D W Chapman) *s.i.s: a bhd* **16/1**
0000 U **Didnt Tell My Wife**[23] 6232 7-8-13 40 .... (v[1]) BrianReilly 7 —
(P S McEntee) *towards rr whn n.m.r and uns rdr after 3f* **66/1**

1m 28.58s (-2.22) **Going Correction** -0.30s/f (Stan)
WFA 3 from 4yo+ 1lb **14** Ran SP% **126.1**
Speed ratings (Par 97):100,94,92,92,87 83,82,82,79,77 70,66,59,—
CSF £184.12 TOTE £12.20: £3.80, £7.00, £2.50; EX 256.30 TRIFECTA Not won..
Owner R Hollinshead **Bred** Darley **Trained** Upper Longdon, Staffs

FOCUS
Strong form for the grade. Not many got into this and the winner proved different class, posting a well above-average effort for the grade. The winning time was 1.38 seconds quicker than the second division.

6550 SOUTHWELL-RACECOURSE.CO.UK BANDED STKS 6f (F)
1:25 (1:25) (Class 7) 3-Y-0+ **£1,365** (£403; £201) **Stalls** Low

Form RPR
0000 1 **Cool Tiger**[55] 5609 3-8-12 45 .... FrancisNorton 9 55
(P Howling) *towards rr: hdwy over 2f out: swtchd lft and rdn over 1f out: led ent last: styd on* **8/1**
3066 2 *1 1/4* **Sion Hill (IRE)**[6] 6492 5-8-5 45 .... (p) RussellKennemore(7) 10 51
(Mrs N Macauley) *trckd ldrs: hdwy 2f out: sn rdn: styd on u.p ins last* **12/1**
0046 3 *3/4* **Straffan (IRE)**[6] 6493 4-8-12 45 .... (p) DaleGibson 8 49
(J Hetherton) *prom: effrt 2f out: led 11.2f out: rdn and hdd ent last: kpt on same pce* **7/2**[1]
0323 4 *1* **Firework**[15] 6372 8-8-12 45 .... StephenCarson 6 46
(E A Wheeler) *hld up in tch: swtchd outside and hdwy 2f out: sn rdn and kpt on ins last: nrst fin* **5/1**[2]
3500 5 *2 1/2* **A Teen**[40] 5928 8-8-9 45 .... DeanCorby(3) 1 38
(P Howling) *prom on inner: rdn along wl over 2f out: sn one pce* **14/1**
0000 6 *nk* **Astorygoeswithit**[15] 6371 3-8-12 45 .... (p) AdamKirby 14 37
(P S McEntee) *prom: rdn along wl over 2f out: grad wknd* **28/1**
0002 7 *1 1/2* **I Wish**[19] 6307 8-8-12 45 .... PaulFitzsimons 11 33
(Miss J R Tooth) *nvr bttr than midfield* **6/1**
150 8 *2 1/2* **Drury Lane (IRE)**[105] 4233 6-8-12 45 .... (p) RobertWinston 2 25
(D W Chapman) *rr whn hmpd after 2f and bhd tl sme late hdwy* **12/1**
0600 9 *1/2* **Princess Arwen**[29] 6131 4-8-9 45 .... NeilChalmers(3) 4 24
(Mrs Barbara Waring) *bmpd s: a rr* **33/1**
2064 10 *2 1/2* **Freshwinds**[23] 6233 4-8-7 45 .... (b) EmmettStack(5) 5 16
(Miss Diana Weeden) *bmpd s: led after 1f: rdn along over 2f out: drvn and hdd 11/2f out: sn wknd* **11/2**[3]
0036 11 *3/4* **Sanders Boy**[189] 1768 3-8-12 45 .... PaulMulrennan 7 14
(J R Norton) *rr fr 1/2-way* **18/1**

0000 **12** *10* **Developer (IRE)**[19] 6308 3-8-5 45..........................(b[1]) MarkCoumbe(7) 12 —
(G F Bridgwater) *a rr* **33/1**

0000 **13** *1* **Boisdale (IRE)**[182] 1913 8-8-12 45.................................. MickyFenton 13 —
(P S Felgate) *led 1f: prom tl rdn along 3f out and sn wknd* **18/1**

1m 16.22s (-0.68) **Going Correction** -0.30s/f (Stan) **13** Ran SP% **121.6**
Speed ratings (Par 97):92,90,89,88,84 84,82,78,78,74 73,60,59
CSF £100.46 TOTE £9.90: £3.00, £3.90, £1.80; EX 241.00 TRIFECTA Not won..

Owner Tony Clifford & Claudia Fisher **Bred** G B Partnership **Trained** Newmarket, Suffolk

FOCUS
The early pace looked solid enough, but the winning time was modest and the winner came from well back, which suggests the leaders may have gone off too quick. Average form for the grade, but not particularly sound.

6551 PLAY GOLF COME RACING BANDED STKS — 1m 4f (F)
1:55 (1:55) (Class 7) 3-Y-0+ — **£1,706** (£503; £252) **Stalls** Low

Form RPR

6003 **1** **Cragganmore Creek**[15] 6374 3-9-3 50.........................(b) HayleyTurner 4 65+
(D Morris) *hld up: stdy hdwy over 4f out: swtchd outside and effrt 2f out: rdn to ld over 1f out and sn clr* **14/1**

3F63 **2** *7* **Impeccable Guest (IRE)**[38] 5960 3-9-3 50....................... LeeEnstone 6 51
(P C Haslam) *in tch. hdwy over 4f out: rdn to chse ldrs over 2f out: drvn and kpt on same pce appr last* **5/1**[2]

5236 **3** *nk* **Romil Star (GER)**[113] 3998 9-9-7 48..............................(v) AdamKirby 12 49
(M Wellings) *prom: led after 1f: rdn along wl over 2f out: drvn and hdd over 1f out: kpt on same pce* **6/1**[3]

0160 **4** *3* **Ndola**[23] 6238 7-9-5 46... JimmyQuinn 10 42
(B J Curley) *trckd ldrs: hdwy over 3f out: rdn along over 2f out and kpt on same pce* **8/1**

0032 **5** *2 1/2* **Abbeygate**[15] 6374 5-9-7 48.. FrancisNorton 13 40+
(T Keddy) *bhd: hdwy and wd st: sn rdn and styd on fnl 2f: nvr nr ldrs* **3/1**[1]

0501 **6** *5* **Blue Opal**[21] 6279 4-9-4 45.. MickyFenton 3 29
(Miss S E Hall) *midfield: hdwy and in tch 3f out: sn rdn and no prog fnl 2f* **6/1**[3]

0000 **7** *nk* **Beaufort**[22] 6256 4-9-9 50.. FergusSweeney 14 33
(D K Ivory) *dwlt: sn prom: cl up 1/2-way: rdn along wl over 2f out and grad wknd* **25/1**

0 **8** *3* **Sean Og (IRE)**[15] 6375 4-9-6 47... FMBerry 2 25
(E J Creighton) *a towards rr* **28/1**

0652 **9** *8* **Coffin Dodger**[11] 6423 3-8-8 46... NicolPolli(5) 8 12
(C N Allen) *dwlt: a rr* **14/1**

0005 **10** *2 1/2* **Diafa (USA)**[29] 6133 4-9-4 45... RobertHavlin 7 7
(J G M O'Shea) *cl up: rdn along 4f out: drvn 3f out and sn wknd* **33/1**

0360 **11** *3* **Scotty's Future (IRE)**[18] 6317 8-9-9 50....................... RobertWinston 1 7
(A Berry) *a rr* **12/1**

-000 **12** *1/2* **Fantasy Legend (IRE)**[279] 419 3-9-1 48................. RichardThomas 11 4
(N P Littmoden) *a bhd* **40/1**

00-0 **13** *3 1/2* **Overdrawn (IRE)**[29] 6130 5-9-1 47......................(bt) NataliaGemelova(5) 5 —
(A J McCabe) *chsd ldrs: rdn along over 4f out: wknd 3f out* **20/1**

2m 38.96s (-3.13) **Going Correction** -0.30s/f (Stan)
WFA 3 from 4yo+ 6lb **13** Ran SP% **119.8**
Speed ratings (Par 97):98,93,93,91,89 86,85,83,78,76 74,74,72
CSF £78.04 TOTE £17.00: £4.10, £2.40, £2.60; EX 64.10 TRIFECTA Not won..

Owner Stag And Huntsman **Bred** Grovewood Stud **Trained** Newmarket, Suffolk

FOCUS
A solid pace for this poor contest which made it a proper test of stamina. That proved too much for several of these as they finished well spread out. A much-improved effort from the winner, who was value for a bit extra.

6552 JOIN US ON THE 28TH BANDED STKS — 1m (F)
2:30 (2:30) (Class 7) 3-Y-0+ — **£1,365** (£403; £201) **Stalls** Low

Form RPR

0003 **1** **Bowl Of Cherries**[19] 6306 3-8-12 40...............................(b) LeeEnstone 9 52
(I A Wood) *a.p: rdn to ld 11/2f out: drvn ins last and hld on wl* **7/1**[3]

0060 **2** *nk* **Wodhill Schnaps**[23] 6237 5-9-0 45...............................(b) HayleyTurner 6 51
(D Morris) *in tch: hdwy 2f out: rdn to chal ins last: kpt on* **16/1**

6256 **3** *2 1/2* **Sriology (IRE)**[33] 6067 5-9-0 45.. JimmyQuinn 4 46+
(J Pearce) *towards rr: hdwy on inner 3f out: rdn to chse ldrs over 1f out: sn drvn and kpt on same pce ins last* **4/1**[1]

6305 **4** *1 1/4* **Elms Schoolboy**[19] 6307 4-8-11 45..............................(b) DeanCorby(3) 2 43
(P Howling) *in tch on inner: hdwy 3f out: rdn and edgd lft wl over 1f out: sn drvn and no imp* **9/1**

0003 **5** *4* **Hilltop Fantasy**[21] 6277 5-8-7 40................................. WilliamBuick(7) 8 35
(V Smith) *sn led: rdn along wl over 2f out: hdd 11/2f out and grad wknd* **8/1**

0000 **6** *1/2* **Southern Tide (USA)**[29] 6134 4-9-0 40........................... MickyFenton 14 34
(J Pearce) *cl up: rdn along wl over 2f out: drvn and wknd over 1f out* **22/1**

0056 **7** *1 3/4* **Sorbiesharry (IRE)**[21] 6280 7-9-0 45.......................(p) DanielTudhope 10 30
(Mrs N Macauley) *bhd tl styd on fnl 2f* **13/2**[2]

0000 **8** *shd* **Ronnies Lad**[40] 5929 4-9-0 45...................................... PaulMulrennan 12 30
(J R Norton) *a towards rr* **66/1**

0403 **9** *3 1/2* **Sea Frolic (IRE)**[19] 6307 5-8-9 45.................................(v) RoryMoore(5) 5 22
(Jennie Candlish) *chsd ldrs to 1/2-way: sn wknd* **14/1**

0240 **10** *5* **Tommytyler (IRE)**[185] 1852 7-8-7 45...............................(t) GaryWales(7) 3 12
(D Carroll) *prom: rdn along 3f out: sn wknd* **20/1**

0632 **11** *1 1/4* **Franky'N'Jonny**[19] 6306 3-8-12 45....................................(p) ChrisCatlin 7 9
(M J Attwater) *dwlt: a rr* **7/1**[3]

0020 **12** *6* **Emperor Cat (IRE)**[21] 6280 5-8-11 45.................. EdwardCreighton(3) 1 —
(Mrs N S Evans) *a rr* **12/1**

0064 **13** *1 1/4* **Huxley (IRE)**[44] 5838 7-9-0 40..................................(t) FergusSweeney 11 —
(D J Wintle) *chsd ldrs: rdn along over 3f out: sn wknd* **8/1**

6000 **14** *38* **Parisian Playboy**[6] 5497 6-9-0 40..........................(bt[1]) RobertWinston 13 —
(A D Brown) *chsd ldrs to 1/2-way: sn wknd* **20/1**

1m 42.9s (-1.70) **Going Correction** -0.30s/f (Stan)
WFA 3 from 4yo+ 2lb **14** Ran SP% **126.2**
Speed ratings (Par 97):96,95,93,91,87 87,85,85,82,77 75,69,68,30
CSF £113.91 TOTE £8.00: £2.00, £6.40, £2.10; EX 218.50 TRIFECTA Not won..

Owner Graham Bradbury **Bred** Eurostrait Ltd **Trained** Upper Lambourn, Berks

FOCUS
A routine banded contest run in a slow time, and the form is unlikely to mean much outside this level.

6553 SPONSOR A RACE AT SOUTHWELL BANDED STKS — 1m 6f (F)
3:00 (3:01) (Class 7) 3-Y-0+ — **£1,365** (£403; £201) **Stalls** Low

Form RPR

6622 **1** **Red River Rebel**[19] 6305 8-9-3 45................................ PaulMulrennan 7 52
(J R Norton) *mde virtually all: rdn 3f out: drvn over 1f out: styd on gamely ins last* **4/1**[1]

0052 **2** *3/4* **Red River Rock (IRE)**[21] 6280 4-9-3 45.............(be) CatherineGannon 9 51
(T J Fitzgerald) *a.p: effrt to chal 2f out: sn rdn and ev ch tl drvn ins last and no ex towards fin* **7/1**

2224 **3** *nk* **Glory Be (ITY)**[7] 6482 4-9-3 45....................................(v) SamHitchcott 13 50
(J L Spearing) *in tch: hdwy to trck ldrs 5f out: swtchd rt and rdn wl over 1f out: drvn: ch whn edgd lft ins last: no ex* **11/1**

3020 **4** *3 1/2* **Iamback**[7] 6474 6-9-3 45..(t) AdrianMcCarthy 6 45
(Miss D A McHale) *in tch: hdwy over 4f out: rdn to chse ldrs over 2f out: sn drvn and one pce* **11/1**

3403 **5** *1/2* **Jazrawy**[7] 6474 4-9-5 47... RobertMiles 14 47
(P W Hiatt) *prom: hdwy and cl up over 4f out: rdn along over 2f out and grad wknd* **5/1**[2]

0050 **6** *2 1/2* **Bill Bennett (FR)**[28] 6158 5-9-6 48..................................... PaulEddery 4 44
(J Jay) *midfield: hdwy on inner 4f out: rdn along to chse ldrs 2f out: sn drvn and one pce* **12/1**

6604 **7** *3/4* **Padre Nostro (IRE)**[19] 6305 7-9-4 46............................ JosedeSouza 11 41
(J R Holt) *hld up: hdwy over 4f out: rdn to chse ldrs 2f out: sn drvn and btn* **12/1**

0005 **8** *hd* **Special Ballot (IRE)**[7] 6482 5-9-3 40.................................. PaulQuinn 12 40
(G A Swinbank) *hld up in rr: stdy hdwy over 4f out: in tch and rdn along 2f out: sn drvn and no imp* **14/1**

0004 **9** *1 1/4* **Dynamite Deano**[164] 2463 3-9-0 50................................. JamieMackay 1 43
(D K Ivory) *alwasy towards rr* **33/1**

5444 **10** *1* **True (IRE)**[28] 6161 5-9-3 45... DeanMernagh 8 37
(Mrs S Lamyman) *racd wd: hld up in rr: hdwy 5f out: rdn along wl over 2f out and n.d* **15/2**

-530 **11** *3 1/2* **Josh You Are**[19] 6304 3-8-12 48... DaleGibson 3 35
(D E Cantillon) *a rr* **6/1**[3]

0000 **12** *14* **Saxon Star (IRE)**[23] 6236 3-8-10 35 ow1........................... LeeEnstone 2 13
(P Howling) *cl up: rdn along over 5f out: sn wknd* **100/1**

03-0 **13** *39* **Backstreet Lad**[10] 6435 4-9-5 47.................................... StephenCarson 5 —
(Evan Williams) *chsd ldrs: rdn along and lost pl 6f out: sn bhd* **20/1**

30-0 **14** *6* **Make My Hay**[155] 767 7-8-12 45...............................(b) EmmettStack(5) 10 —
(J Gallagher) *in tch: rdn along and lost pl 1/2-way: sn wl bhd* **40/1**

3m 7.07s (-2.53) **Going Correction** -0.30s/f (Stan)
WFA 3 from 4yo+ 8lb **14** Ran SP% **125.1**
Speed ratings (Par 97):95,94,94,92,92 90,90,90,89,88 86,78,56,53
CSF £32.05 TOTE £4.00: £1.50, £3.30, £5.30; EX 12.90 Trifecta £194.70 Part won. Pool: £274.27 - 0.44 winning tickets..

Owner Jeff Slaney **Bred** J Slaney **Trained** High Hoyland, S Yorks

FOCUS
A real test of stamina for these moderate horses and dominated by those that raced up with the pace. Sound form.

6554 ARENA LEISURE BANDED STKS (DIV II) — 7f (F)
3:35 (3:36) (Class 7) 3-Y-0+ — **£1,365** (£403; £201) **Stalls** Low

Form RPR

000 **1** **Capital Lass**[23] 6236 3-8-12 40.. HayleyTurner 13 50
(D K Ivory) *in tch on outer: hdwy over 2f out: rdn to ld over 1f out: drvn ins last: edgd lft and hld on wl* **33/1**

6003 **2** *shd* **Prince Of Gold**[6] 6493 6-9-0 46..................................(e) FergusSweeney 9 51
(R Hollinshead) *hld up in tch: hdwy on outer 2f out: rdn to chal ent last: snd riven and ev ch: jst hld* **9/4**[1]

2544 **3** *1* **Mon Petite Amour**[42] 5885 3-8-11 47.................(p) EdwardCreighton(3) 4 49
(D W P Arbuthnot) *hld up: hdwy on inner 3f out: rdn and ch over 1f out: drvn and nt qckn ins last* **11/1**

0040 **4** *1* **Monkey Madge**[19] 6304 4-8-8 45.............................. MarkLawson(5) 11 45
(B Smart) *a.p: rdn to ld wl over 1f out: drvn and hdd appr last: one pce* **11/2**[3]

4615 **5** *1* **Barzak (IRE)**[7] 6477 6-9-1 50...(bt) AmirQuinn(3) 6 47
(S R Bowring) *in tch: hdwy to chse ldrs 2f out: sn rdn and kpt on same pce* **7/2**[2]

6003 **6** *8* **Linton Dancer (IRE)**[13] 6406 3-9-3 50........................... PaulMulrennan 5 26
(J R Weymes) *chsd ldrs: rdn over 2f out: sn drvn and wknd* **7/1**

3500 **7** *nk* **Wilford Maverick (IRE)**[40] 5929 4-8-8 47................. StacyRenwick(7) 7 22
(M J Attwater) *led: rdn along 3f out: drvn 2f out: sn hdd & wknd* **20/1**

0400 **8** *3* **Christian Bendix**[174] 2141 4-9-1 50................................ DeanCorby(3) 1 18
(P Howling) *cl up on inner: chal 3f out: sn rdn and wknd fnl 2f* **16/1**

2060 **9** *1 1/2* **Rocky Reppin**[189] 1765 6-8-10 40...........................(b) JasonEdmunds(3) 3 9
(J Balding) *s.i.s: a rr* **20/1**

60-0 **10** *5* **Decent (IRE)**[126] 3609 3-8-11 47........................(b) RichardKingscote(3) 10 —
(W J H Ratcliffe) *s.i.s: a rr* **66/1**

4306 **11** *3/4* **Cuesta Canyon (IRE)**[29] 6131 3-8-7 45............(be) NataliaGemelova(5) 8 —
(A J McCabe) *cl up: rdn along wl over 2f out: sn wknd* **10/1**

0445 **12** *17* **Joking John**[129] 3529 3-8-12 40... LeeEnstone 12 —
(C W Fairhurst) *a rr* **14/1**

1m 29.95s (-0.85) **Going Correction** -0.30s/f (Stan)
WFA 3 from 4yo+ 1lb **12** Ran SP% **124.8**
Speed ratings (Par 97):92,91,90,89,88 79,78,75,73,68 67,47
CSF £109.04 TOTE £38.80: £7.80, £1.40, £3.30; EX 195.60 TRIFECTA Not won. Place 6 £349.56, Place 5 £116.28.

Owner H Schwartz **Bred** Kirtlington Stud Ltd **Trained** Radlett, Herts

FOCUS
This looked inferior to the first division and the time was 1.38 seconds slower. The winner was showing his first form for a long time.

T/Plt: £1,408.10 to a £1 stake. Pool: £40,025.25. 20.75 winning tickets. T/Qpdt: £82.40 to a £1 stake. Pool: £3,755.10. 33.70 winning tickets. JR

6539 WOLVERHAMPTON (A.W) (L-H)

Tuesday, November 21

OFFICIAL GOING: Standard to fast

Wind: Fresh, behind Weather: Cloudy with an odd shower

6555 WBX.COM LAUNCHING 25TH NOVEMBER H'CAP 5f 20y(P)

3:50 (3:50) (Class 5) (0-75,74) 3-Y-O+ £3,238 (£963; £481; £240) Stalls Low

Form RPR

063 1 **Tartatartufata**18 6315 4-8-4 **63**....(v) PatrickMathers(3) 2 77
(D Shaw) led 1f: chsd ldr: led over 1f out: r.o wl **7/1**

0003 2 2 1/2 **Lady Bahia (IRE)**10 6452 5-8-12 **68**....(b) RobbieFitzpatrick 8 73
(Peter Grayson) hld up: hdwy 2f out: r.o **14/1**

2321 3 nk **Mr Cellophane**10 6452 3-9-4 **74**.... PatCosgrave 10 78
(J R Jenkins) hld up: hdwy on outside 1/2-way: rdn and hung lft over 1f out: r.o **11/4**1

1523 4 1/2 **Chatshow (USA)**10 6437 5-8-9 **68**.... JamesDoyle(3) 7 70+
(A W Carroll) hld up: rdn over 1f out: r.o ins fnl f: nvr nrr **5/1**3

0232 5 1/2 **Witchry**7 6478 4-8-13 **69**.... LPKeniry 9 69
(A G Newcombe) hld up: rdn over 1f out: nt trble ldrs **10/3**2

2040 6 nk **Figaro Flyer (IRE)**11 6428 3-9-4 **74**.... IanMongan 4 73
(P Howling) chsd ldrs: rdn 1/2-way: styd on same pce fnl f **6/1**

040 7 hd **Nusoor (IRE)**5 6499 3-9-3 **73**....(b1) TonyCulhane 1 72
(Peter Grayson) chsd ldrs: rdn over 1f out: no ex fnl f **20/1**

1030 8 1 3/4 **Harrison's Flyer (IRE)**10 6452 5-8-6 **65**....(p) NeilChalmers(3) 6 57
(J M Bradley) chsd ldrs: rdn 1/2-way: wknd over 1f out **16/1**

0000 9 nk **Maktavish**46 5791 7-8-13 **69**....(b) TomEaves 5 60
(R Brotherton) led 4f out: rdn and hdd over 1f out: wknd ins fnl f **25/1**

000 10 1 3/4 **Fizzlephut (IRE)**10 6437 4-8-8 **64**.... PaulFitzsimons 11 49
(Miss J R Tooth) chsd ldrs: rdn and hung lft over 1f out: wknd fnl f **14/1**

5000 11 3/4 **Legal Set (IRE)**57 5577 10-8-7 **68** oh20 ow8....(t) AnnStokell(5) 3 50
(Miss A Stokell) chsd ldrs: n.m.r and lost pl 1/2-way: in rr whn hung lft over 1f out **66/1**

0000 12 2 1/2 **New Options**95 4551 9-7-13 **60** oh20....(b) LiamJones(5) 12 33
(Peter Grayson) s.s: outpcd: in rr whn hmpd over 1f out **100/1**

0000 13 2 **Stoneacre Boy (IRE)**10 6446 3-9-4 **74**....(b) GeorgeBaker 13 40
(Peter Grayson) sn outpcd **33/1**

60.68 secs (-2.14) **Going Correction** -0.35s/f (Stan) **13** Ran SP% **126.4**
Speed ratings (Par 103):103,99,98,97,96 96,96,93,92,90 88,84,81
CSF £101.66 CT £353.95 TOTE £12.40: £4.70, £5.70, £1.10; EX 63.10.
Owner Danethorpe Racing Ltd **Bred** Dr A Ramkaran **Trained** Danethorpe, Notts

FOCUS
Modest handicap form, but the pace was decent and the form looks solid enough, rated through the runner-up.
Legal Set(IRE) Official explanation: jockey said gelding suffered interference home straight
New Options Official explanation: jockey said gelding suffered interference home straight
Stoneacre Boy(IRE) Official explanation: jockey said gelding did not face the kickback

6556 HOTEL & CONFERENCING H'CAP 5f 216y(P)

4:20 (4:21) (Class 6) (0-60,60) 3-Y-O+ £2,730 (£806; £403) Stalls Low

Form RPR

0625 1 **Polar Force**13 6395 6-9-1 **59**.... IanMongan 4 69
(Mrs C A Dunnett) chsd ldrs: rdn over 2f out: styd on to ld wl ins fnl f **10/1**

123 2 nk **Inka Dancer (IRE)**3 6510 4-8-11 **55**.... TonyCulhane 8 64
(B Palling) led: hdd 4f out: rdn to ld over 1f out: hdd wl ins fnl f **7/2**1

0040 3 3/4 **Dasheena**42 5902 3-8-8 **59**.... MCGeran(7) 7 66
(A J McCabe) s.i.s: hld up: hdwy over 1f out: r.o **33/1**

0056 4 hd **Desert Light (IRE)**3 6510 5-8-13 **57**....(v) DaneO'Neill 3 63
(D Shaw) hld up in tch: rdn over 1f out: unable qck towards fin **8/1**3

6300 5 3/4 **Gone'N'Dunnett (IRE)**3 6513 7-9-0 **58**....(v) AdamKirby 1 62
(Mrs C A Dunnett) w ldr: led 4f out: rdn: hung rt and hdd over 1f out: no ex ins fnl f **10/1**

2054 6 hd **Val De Maal (IRE)**21 6288 6-8-13 **57**....(b) TomEaves 11 60
(Miss J A Camacho) hld up: plld hrd: r.o ins fnl f: nt rch ldrs **12/1**

5055 7 hd **Nistaki (USA)**62 5487 5-8-13 **60**.... PatrickMathers(3) 10 63
(D Shaw) hld up: rdn over 1f out: r.o ins fnl f: nvr nrr **16/1**

0002 8 nk **Elusive Warrior (USA)**8 6465 3-8-6 **55**....(p) JamieMoriarty(5) 9 57
(R A Fahey) hld up: rdn over 1f out: r.o ins fnl f: nrst fin **8/1**3

0400 9 3/4 **Wainwright (IRE)**18 6323 6-9-2 **60**....(b) GeorgeBaker 2 60
(P A Blockley) s.i.s: hdwy over 4f out: rdn over 1f out: no ex ins fnl f **8/1**3

1306 10 1/2 **Cerulean Rose**49 5756 7-8-13 **57**.... FrancisNorton 5 55
(A W Carroll) prom: rdn 1/2-way: styd on same pce fnl 2f **11/2**2

2300 11 1/2 **Miskina**13 6404 5-8-10 **54**.... RobbieFitzpatrick 13 51
(W M Brisbourne) chsd ldrs: rdn 2fd out: wknd fnl f **25/1**

0100 12 nk **North Fleet**10 6442 3-8-12 **56**.... SteveDrowne 12 52
(J M Bradley) chsd ldrs: rdn over 2f out: hung lft and wknd over 1f out **16/1**

0302 13 3 1/2 **Moon Forest (IRE)**14 6390 4-8-6 **57**....(p) BarrySavage(7) 6 42
(J M Bradley) mid-div: rdn and hung lft over 3f out: bhd fnl 2f **12/1**

1m 13.97s (-1.84) **Going Correction** -0.35s/f (Stan) **13** Ran SP% **123.1**
Speed ratings (Par 101):98,97,96,96,95 95,94,94,93,92 92,91,87
CSF £46.20 CT £1156.09 TOTE £11.80: £2.80, £1.80, £10.60; EX 51.90.
Owner Mrs Christine Dunnett **Bred** Cheveley Park Stud Ltd **Trained** Hingham, Norfolk
■ Stewards' Enquiry : M C Geran one-day ban; using whip above shoulder height (Dec 2)

FOCUS
Sound enough form, albeit moderate, based around the first three home.

6557 PARTY NIGHTS AT WOLVERHAMPTON MEDIAN AUCTION MAIDEN STKS 7f 32y(P)

4:50 (4:51) (Class 6) 3-5-Y-O £2,730 (£806; £403) Stalls High

Form RPR

3042 1 **Ours (IRE)**21 6286 3-9-3 58....(b) PatCosgrave 4 66
(J D Bethell) trckd ldrs: rdn to ld and hung rt fr over 1f out: styd on **5/2**2

2 1/2 **The Tyke** 3-9-3.... AdamKirby 8 65
(C G Cox) led 6f out: hung lft and hdd over 1f out: styd on **16/1**

0 3 2 **Pain In The Neck (IRE)**260 590 3-9-3.... ChrisCatlin 3 60
(M J Wallace) led 1f: chsd ldr: rdn and ev ch 1f out: no ex **7/1**3

0320 4 1/2 **Lilac Star**120 3793 3-8-12 72.... DaneO'Neill 6 53
(Pat Eddery) chsd ldrs: rdn over 2f out: styd on same pce fnl f **8/11**1

0600 5 3 1/2 **Jenise (IRE)**19 6306 3-8-7 40.... DuranFentiman(5) 2 44
(Mark Campion) chsd ldrs: rdn over 2f out: wknd over 1f out **50/1**

06-5 6 4 **Boppys Dream**39 5949 4-8-13 40.... MickyFenton 9 34
(P T Midgley) mid-div: rdn and hung lft 1/2-way: wknd 2f out **25/1**

060 7 2 **It's Gone**93 4635 3-9-3 30.... JoeFanning 7 34
(J G Given) hld up: rdn 1/2-way: a in rr **50/1**

6040 8 3 **Megavegas**19 6306 3-8-12 35.... RobbieFitzpatrick 1 21
(P T Midgley) chsd ldrs: lost pl 6f out: rdn and wknd 3f out **66/1**

-006 9 5 **Charanne**43 5874 3-8-5 35.... BarrySavage(7) 5 8
(J M Bradley) s.i.s: in rr: rdn 1/2-way: wknd wl over 2f out **100/1**

1m 29.99s (-0.41) **Going Correction** -0.35s/f (Stan)
WFA 3 from 4yo 1lb **9** Ran SP% **115.1**
Speed ratings (Par 101):88,87,85,84,80 76,73,70,64
CSF £36.41 TOTE £3.70: £1.10, £2.80, £1.90; EX 38.00.
Owner M J Dawson **Bred** David John Brown **Trained** Middleham Moor, N Yorks

FOCUS
A weak maiden run in a very moderate time for the class. The winner did not need to improve to score, and the favourite was way below her turf form.

6558 E B F STAY AT THE WOLVERHAMPTON HOLIDAY INN MAIDEN FILLIES' STKS 1m 141y(P)

5:20 (5:22) (Class 5) 2-Y-O £3,469 (£1,038; £519; £259; £129) Stalls Low

Form RPR

1 **Stravita** 2-9-0.... GrahamGibbons 5 67
(R Hollinshead) chsd ldrs: rdn to ld ins fnl f: r.o **50/1**

42 2 hd **Letham Island (IRE)**8 6466 2-9-0.... JoeFanning 11 67
(M Johnston) chsd ldr: led over 2f out: rdn over 1f out: edgd rt and hdd ins fnl f: r.o **5/2**2

050 3 1/2 **Encircled**18 6324 2-9-0 55.... RobertHavlin 4 66
(D Haydn Jones) s.i.s: hld up: hdwy over 2f out: rdn and hung lft fr over 1f out: r.o **33/1**

634 4 2 1/2 **Princess Taylor**64 5424 2-9-0 72....(tp) SteveDrowne 8 60
(M Botti) chsd ldrs: ev ch 2f out: sn rdn and hung lft: nt run on **9/4**1

06 5 3 **Dansil In Distress**35 6031 2-9-0.... LPKeniry 6 54
(S Kirk) mid-div: hdwy over 2f out: wknd fnl f **22/1**

5 6 2 **Red Coronet**10 6433 2-9-0.... TonyCulhane 1 49
(W J Haggas) chsd ldrs: rdn over 3f out: wknd over 1f out **7/2**3

00 7 2 1/2 **Kimono My House**10 6433 2-9-0.... MickyFenton 10 44
(J G Given) led: rdn and hdd over 2f out: sn hung rt and wknd **50/1**

8 1 1/2 **Super Sifted (GER)** 2-9-0.... JimmyQuinn 13 41
(H R A Cecil) s.i.s: hdwy over 6f out: wknd over 2f out **16/1**

00 9 2 1/2 **Go Dancing**10 6433 2-8-7.... MCGeran(7) 9 35
(P W Chapple-Hyam) s.i.s: hld up: rdn over 2f out: n.d **33/1**

00 10 1 1/4 **Slo Mo Shun**17 6331 2-9-0.... JimCrowley 7 32
(B R Millman) prom over 5f **33/1**

0 11 1 1/2 **Miami Tallyce (IRE)**10 6441 2-9-0.... ChrisCatlin 12 29
(E J O'Neill) hld up: hmpd over 6f out: a in rr **14/1**

0 12 3 1/2 **Kyrhena**18 6316 2-9-0.... DeanMcKeown 3 21
(C W Thornton) outpcd **100/1**

00 13 6 **Molly Pitcher (IRE)**23 6242 2-9-0.... MatthewHenry 2 —
(M A Jarvis) hld up: in rr fr 1/2-way **10/1**

1m 49.46s (-2.30) **Going Correction** -0.35s/f (Stan) **13** Ran SP% **121.3**
Speed ratings (Par 93):96,95,95,93,90 88,86,85,82,81 80,77,72
CSF £170.97 TOTE £42.60: £9.50, £1.30, £7.40; EX 140.70.
Owner E Bennion **Bred** E Bennion And Miss S Hollinshead **Trained** Upper Longdon, Staffs

FOCUS
A weak maiden in which the third, who is rated 55, provides a benchmark for the form.

NOTEBOOK
Stravita would not have been an obvious choice to win first time out considering her stable and breeding, but there is no doubt that her pedigree screams All-Weather. She did it well, outbattling a Mark Johnston-trained filly to hold on, and given that both parents excelled on Fibresand, she will probably be just as effective at Southwell. (op 40-1)
Letham Island(IRE), whose stable has been in such good form of late, was prominent throughout and only narowly denied. She got the longer trip well and, while nothing special, should be able to find a race in the coming weeks. (op 2-1 tchd 3-1)
Encircled, whose dam was unraced but is a half-sister to Catella, a top-class multiple winner at up to 12 furlongs in Germany, and Lizzey Letti, a useful ten-furlong winner in Germany, shaped as though she is going to appreciate a step up to middle distances herself next year.
Princess Taylor, wearing a tongue strap and cheekpieces for the first time, had every chance entering the straight, but she did not see out this longer trip as well as the first three. Her pedigree suggests that she should have appreciated the extra distance, so her performance must go down as disappointing. (op 11-4)
Dansil In Distress has now had the three runs required for a handicap mark, and she might do better in that sphere. (op 20-1)
Red Coronet, another who should have been seen to better effect over this longer trip, was very disappointing in what was a pretty moderate affair. (op 5-1 tchd 10-3)

6559 WBX.COM LAUNCHING 25TH NOVEMBER CONDITIONS STKS 1m 141y(P)

5:50 (5:50) (Class 4) 3-Y-O+ £5,829 (£1,734; £866; £432) Stalls Low

Form RPR

-145 1 **Cimyla (IRE)**248 666 5-9-7 105.... GeorgeBaker 5 111+
(C F Wall) hld up: hdwy 2f out: led and hung lft fr over 1f out: r.o wl: eased towards fin **6/4**1

135 2 4 **Speedy Sam**34 6051 3-9-0 87.... PatCosgrave 4 94
(K R Burke) led 1f: chsd ldrs: rdn and carried rt wl over 1f out: sn nt clr run: styd on same pce **9/2**2

0200 3 3 **Party Boss**3 6514 4-9-0 102.... BrettDoyle 7 85
(C E Brittain) w ldrs tl led over 6f out: rdn over 2f out: hdd over 1f out: wknd ins fnl f **15/2**

0003 4 1/2 **Fusili (IRE)**12 6411 3-8-3 90.... JamesDoyle(3) 1 79
(N P Littmoden) s.i.s: sn chsng ldrs: outpcd 4f out: styd on ins fnl f **13/2**3

5600 5 3/4 **Weightless**3 6516 6-9-5 103.... IanMongan 2 87
(N P Littmoden) led over 7f out: hdd over 6f out: rdn and ev ch whn hung rt fr over 2f out: wknd fnl f **7/1**

04 6 3/4 **Langford**68 5310 6-9-0 93.... JimCrowley 3 81
(M H Tompkins) s.i.s: hld up: hdwy 4f out: rdn and ev ch over 1f out: wknd fnl f **10/1**

6056 7 2 1/2 **Violette**17 6335 3-8-7 95 ow1.... SebSanders 6 72
(Sir Mark Prescott) hld up: effrt and hung rt over 2f out: sn rdn and wknd **9/1**

1m 47.26s (-4.50) **Going Correction** -0.35s/f (Stan)
WFA 3 from 4yo+ 3lb **7** Ran SP% **114.9**
Speed ratings (Par 105):106,102,99,99,98 98,95
CSF £8.50 TOTE £2.20: £1.30, £2.70; EX 8.60.
Owner Gary A Tanaka **Bred** Dr D G St John And Mrs Sherry Collier **Trained** Newmarket, Suffolk

FOCUS
A quality contest for the track and an impressive win for Cimyla, who showed himself to be one of the best around on Polytrack last winter. The form does not appear all that strong, however.

6560 TWILIGHT RACING AND SUPPER H'CAP 2m 119y(P)
6:20 (6:20) (Class 6) (0-65,65) 3-Y-0+ **£2,730** (£806; £403) **Stalls** Low

Form RPR
0/ **1** **Market Watcher (USA)**[19] [4902] 5-8-11 **53**..............(t) JamieMoriarty[(5)] 7 66+
(Seamus Fahey, Ire) *sn chsng ldr: led 4f out: rdn clr over 1f out* **15/2**
4216 **2** *6* **Synonymy**[35] [6027] 3-9-1 **61**.......................... TonyCulhane 8 67
(M Blanshard) *chsd ldrs: rdn and n.m.r over 3f out: styd on same pce fnl 2f* **7/2**[3]
4402 **3** *1 ¼* **Sovereign Spirit (IRE)**[22] [6256] 4-10-0 **65**......................(t) AdamKirby 1 69+
(W R Swinburn) *prom: chsd wnr over 3f out: sn rdn: wknd fnl f* **5/2**[1]
4006 **4** *1* **Garibaldi (GER)**[15] [6382] 4-9-2 **60**...........................(t) JamesO'Reilly[(7)] 6 63
(J O'Reilly) *s.i.s: sn chsng ldrs: outpcd 3f out: rdn and hung lft over 1f out: styd on* **12/1**
0226 **5** *5* **Lanfredo**[19] [6302] 3-8-4 **50**..(p) ChrisCatlin 4 47
(Miss M E Rowland) *hld up: hdwy over 5f out: rdn over 2f out: sn wknd* **16/1**
3000 **6** *10* **Border Tale**[17] [3810] 6-9-9 **60**.. MickyFenton 9 45
(James Moffatt) *hld up: hdwy 1/2-way: wknd over 2f out* **33/1**
0-06 **7** *7* **Maktu**[13] [6405] 4-9-0 **51**.. SteveDrowne 5 28
(P G Murphy) *sn led: hdd 4f out: sn hmpd and wknd* **33/1**
0602 **8** *nk* **Coppington Melody (IRE)**[13] [6398] 3-8-0 **53**............ SophieDoyle[(7)] 11 29
(B W Duke) *hld up: a in rr: wknd 3f out* **14/1**
4611 **9** *5* **Ganymede**[15] [6375] 5-9-3 **54**.. IanMongan 2 24
(Mrs L J Mongan) *hld up: hdwy over 5f out: rdn and hung rt 2f out: sn wknd: virtually p.u fnl f* **3/1**[2]
/00- **10** *7* **Caliban (IRE)**[473] [3679] 8-8-9 **46** oh1......................... RobbieFitzpatrick 3 8
(Ian Williams) *slwly into stride: hld up: rdn and wknd over 3f out* **40/1**
0000 **11** *nk* **King Cugat Kid (USA)**[15] [6375] 3-7-7 **46** oh6............ WilliamBuick[(7)] 10 8
(Simon Earle) *trckd ldrs: racd keenly: lost pl 7f out: bhd fnl 5f* **66/1**

3m 35.84s (-7.29) **Going Correction** -0.35s/f (Stan)
WFA 3 from 4yo+ 9lb **11** Ran SP% **117.6**
Speed ratings (Par 101):103,100,99,99,96 92,88,88,86,82 82
CSF £33.23 CT £85.65 TOTE £7.70: £2.70, £1.50, £1.50; EX 44.60 Place 6 £98.87, Place 5 £45.35.
Owner J J Bailey **Bred** Phipps Stable **Trained** Monestereven, Co. Kildare
■ Stewards' Enquiry : James O'Reilly three-day ban: used whip with excessive force (Dec 2-4)

FOCUS
An ordinary handicap but the form looks reliable judged on the performance of the runner-up.
Ganymede Official explanation: jockey said gelding had no more to give
T/Plt: £74.00 to a £1 stake. Pool: £56,597.25. 557.65 winning tickets. T/Qpdt: £18.10 to a £1 stake. Pool: £5,494.70. 224.20 winning tickets. CR

6484 KEMPTON (A.W) (R-H)
Wednesday, November 22

OFFICIAL GOING: Standard
Wind: moderate across

6561 RACING UK MAIDEN STKS 7f (P)
3:50 (3:50) (Class 5) 2-Y-0 **£3,238** (£963; £481; £240) **Stalls** High

Form RPR
1 **Boscobel** 2-9-0 .... GregFairley[(3)] 6 76+
(M Johnston) *chsd ldrs: rdn 2f out: hanging and green tl picked up wl to ld 1f out: sn clr: quite promising* **9/2**[2]
0 **2** *3* **Silmi**[25] [6214] 2-9-3 .... RHills 4 69
(E A L Dunlop) *dwlt: wl in rr: pushed along and sme prog 2f out: shkn up and r.o fnl f to take 2nd last 75yds* **6/1**
6404 **3** *1* **Mo (USA)**[36] [6025] 2-9-3 70...(t) FJohansson 9 66
(R A Kvisla) *led: edgd lft and hdd 2f out: kpt on same pce after* **6/1**
64 **4** *½* **Hall Of Fame**[21] [6298] 2-9-3 .... EddieAhern 13 65
(Saeed Bin Suroor) *trckd ldr: swtchd ins and led 2f out: hdd & wknd 1f out* **2/1**[1]
44 **5** *¾* **First Princess (IRE)**[11] [6441] 2-8-12 .... FergusSweeney 7 58
(C Tinkler) *t.k.h: trckd ldrs: outpcd over 1f out: kpt on* **5/1**[3]
00 **6** *2* **Adversane**[25] [6214] 2-9-3 .... IanMongan 8 58
(J L Dunlop) *s.i.s: sn in midfield: shkn up 2f out: no imp after* **20/1**
7 *shd* **Voleris Pearl** 2-8-9 ow4.. JonjoMilczarek[(7)] 12 56
(C F Wall) *s.i.s: sn in tch: shkn up 2f out: no prog* **20/1**
8 *1 ¼* **Mr Aviator (USA)** 2-9-3 .... ChrisCatlin 2 54
(R Hannon) *s.s: hld up wl in rr: shkn up 2f out: no prog* **6/1**
0 **9** *shd* **The Wily Woodcock**[69] [5326] 2-9-3 .... JimmyQuinn 1 54+
(G Wragg) *hld up in last pair: effrt on inner 2f out: sn no prog and btn* **10/1**
05 **10** *6* **Art Gallery**[18] [6330] 2-9-3 .... GeorgeBaker 5 38
(G L Moore) *nvr bttr than midfield: wknd 2f out* **8/1**
11 *1 ¼* **Conny Nobel (IRE)** 2-8-10 ....(t) WilliamBuick[(7)] 11 35
(R A Kvisla) *s.s: rn green and pushed along thrght: a in last pair* **16/1**

1m 25.93s (-0.87) **Going Correction** -0.275s/f (Stan) **11** Ran SP% **146.6**
Speed ratings (Par 96):93,89,88,87,87 84,84,83,83,76 74
CSF £40.62 TOTE £6.50: £2.70, £2.60, £3.10; EX 54.40.
Owner Jumeirah Racing **Bred** Darley **Trained** Middleham Moor, N Yorks

FOCUS
A fair maiden run at a decent tempo. The form should be reliable based on the performances of the third and sixth, and the first two might be much better than the bare result suggests.

NOTEBOOK
Boscobel, who holds a Derby entry, came home a fluent winner on his debut. There was a moment when he was ridden along for a few strides and carried his head awkwardly, but he really got the hang of things just over a furlong from home and was a ready winner. He has the scope to improve and may be seen again soon. The winning time suggests that it was not a bad race, so he is entitled to respect wherever he appears.
Silmi, who also holds a Derby entry, showed very little when the owner's second string at Newmarket back in late October and looked like doing the same again for much of the race. Much like the winner, he finished strongly and promised more for the future.
Mo(USA) has kept some decent company this season and ran a much better race than he had done at Bath last time. A keen sort, he has a mark of 70 and is the one to rate the race around. A drop to six furlongs may help him.
Hall Of Fame is not going to live up to his illustrious parentage, and he did not seem to get home after travelling nicely towards the head of affairs. (tchd 9-4 and 5-2 in a place)
First Princess(IRE) is bred to be smart as she is a half-sister to Storming Home, who famously lost the 2003 Arlington Million in unfortunate circumstances. However, she may have inherited some of his quirkiness, as she did not look entirely straightforward down the home straight after holding every chance. (op 9-2)
Adversane was having his third start - the first two had come on soft ground - and will now be qualified for a handicap mark. He looks like a horse who will appreciate much further in time.
Mr Aviator(USA), who was twice declared a non-runner on turf in the autumn, did not show a great deal from a wide draw and will need to improve. (op 11-2)
The Wily Woodcock was given a very patient ride at the rear and still had plenty to do turning in. His jockey tried to weave his way through but found the path blocked before making some headway under pressure. That effort was shortlived and he came home in his own time.
Art Gallery Official explanation: jockey said, regarding the poor form shown, that his instructions were to jump and travel where he was comfortable in the race. He added that he is a big gross horse and that he followed the eventual winner, before being taken slightly wide on the bend, and between the three and the two furlong markers, when he asked for an effort, the horse became tired in the final furlong, at which time he eased.

6562 FOLLOW YOUR CONFERENCE WITH FLOODLIT RACING MAIDEN AUCTION STKS 6f (P)
4:20 (4:21) (Class 6) 2-Y-0 **£2,388** (£705; £352) **Stalls** High

Form RPR
3230 **1** **Mr Loire**[54] [5647] 2-8-11 69....................................... RichardKingscote[(3)] 2 66
(R Charlton) *dwlt: hld up in last pair: taken to wd outside and gd prog fr 2f out to ld jst over 1f out: pushed out: comf* **6/4**[1]
6000 **2** *1 ¼* **Buckie Massa**[54] [5647] 2-8-13 70... JohnEgan 4 61
(S Kirk) *chsd ldrs: rdn 2f out: styd on to take 2nd ins fnl f: no imp on wnr* **11/4**[2]
3 *¾* **Iron Pearl**[104] [4308] 2-8-6 .... HayleyTurner 3 52
(Jane Chapple-Hyam) *t.k.h: hld up in tch: prog 2f out: tried to chal over 1f out but sn outpcd by wnr: kpt on* **9/2**[3]
50 **4** *nk* **The Jay Factor (IRE)**[128] [3588] 2-8-6 .... EmmettStack[(5)] 5 56
(Pat Eddery) *pressed ldr: led over 2f out: hdd jst over 1f out: one pce* **9/2**[3]
0 **5** *1* **Tumblin Rosie**[174] [2166] 2-8-5 .... FrancisNorton 7 47
(M Blanshard) *plld hrd early: hld up in rr: pushed along and rn green 2f out: prog over 1f out: kpt on* **16/1**
05 **6** *3 ½* **Papradon**[9] [6457] 2-9-0 .... MickyFenton 9 45
(J R Best) *dwlt: cl up tl wknd over 1f out* **33/1**
00 **7** *½* **Golden Ribbons**[27] [6187] 2-8-6 ow1................................... EddieAhern 1 36
(J R Boyle) *racd wd: prom: chal over 2f out: wknd over 1f out* **16/1**
0 **8** *¾* **Go Imperial (IRE)**[35] [6047] 2-8-7 .... DominicFox[(3)] 6 38
(M G Quinlan) *s.v.s: in tch after 2f: no ch whn nt clr run 1f out* **10/1**
0600 **9** *½* **Joint Expectations (IRE)**[115] [3979] 2-8-10 45 ow1.......(v[1]) AdamKirby 8 36
(Mrs C A Dunnett) *led to over 2f out: wknd rapidly over 1f out* **33/1**

1m 13.49s (-0.21) **Going Correction** -0.275s/f (Stan) **9** Ran SP% **129.8**
Speed ratings (Par 94):90,88,87,86,85 80,80,79,78
CSF £6.72 TOTE £2.90: £1.10, £1.30, £2.40; EX 7.10.
Owner Beckhampton Stables Ltd **Bred** Harts Farm And Stud **Trained** Beckhampton, Wilts

FOCUS
A modest looking maiden and the form will probably not amount to a great deal. The winner did not need to improve to score.

NOTEBOOK
Mr Loire was a comfortable winner, despite edging to the right slightly under pressure, and should handle a step back into handicap company. (op 15-8 tchd 2-1)
Buckie Massa pretty much had every chance but never looked like getting to the winner. He has proved a shade disappointing since his debut, but will surely find a race in time. (op 3-1)
Iron Pearl was a bit keen early but stayed on well enough under pressure. This run qualifies her for a handicap mark and she could pick up a weak nursery before the end of the year. (op 6-1 tchd 13-2)
The Jay Factor(IRE) ran much better than he had done last time and also looks like a horse who will do better in handicaps. (op 4-1)
Tumblin Rosie, who looked a shade green under pressure, flew home when the penny dropped and should be a lot wiser next time. (op 14-1)
Go Imperial(IRE) Official explanation: jockey said colt dwelt in stalls

6563 DIGIBET.COM NURSERY 6f (P)
4:50 (4:50) (Class 4) (0-85,84) 2-Y-0 **£4,533** (£1,348; £674; £336) **Stalls** High

Form RPR
01 **1** **Penny Post (IRE)**[16] [6377] 2-9-1 **81**................................ GregFairley[(3)] 3 83+
(M Johnston) *trckd ldr: led jst over 2f out: hung lft fr over 1f out: pushed out and wl in command fnl f* **10/11**[1]
1305 **2** *1 ¼* **Boreal Applause**[26] [6201] 2-9-7 **84**.. JohnEgan 2 82
(E A L Dunlop) *trckd ldng pair: rdn and nt qckn 2f out: wnt 2nd 1f out: no imp on wnr* **7/4**[2]
13 **3** *shd* **Social Rhythm**[16] [6379] 2-8-7 **70**.. JimmyQuinn 1 68
(H J Collingridge) *hld up in last: pushed along over 2f out: kpt on fr over 1f out to press for 2nd nr fin* **7/1**
2603 **4** *2 ½* **Sparkling Eyes**[18] [6332] 2-8-11 **74**....................................... EddieAhern 4 64
(C E Brittain) *led to jst over 2f out: wknd fnl f* **9/2**[3]

1m 12.83s (-0.87) **Going Correction** -0.275s/f (Stan) **4** Ran SP% **119.4**
Speed ratings (Par 98):94,92,92,88
CSF £3.27 TOTE £1.90; EX 3.40.
Owner Sheikh Mohammed **Bred** Darley **Trained** Middleham Moor, N Yorks

FOCUS
A decent contest despite there only being four runners. The tempo was good throughout, so the form should be reliable enough.

NOTEBOOK
Penny Post(IRE) ◆ came home a comfortable winner despite edging left under pressure in the final furlong. She does not look a bad sort for the time of year, and may well be seen out again this winter. (op Evens tchd 11-10 and 4-5)
Boreal Applause was last seen in the Listed Bosra Sham Stakes at Newmarket in late October, shaping well not far behind the principals. Trying Polytrack for the first time, she seemed to take an age to pick up before running on. There was also a hint that she may not be entirely straightforward. (op 13-8)
Social Rhythm ◆ was a cosy winner on her debut over six furlongs but was well held in a fair-looking seven-furlong novice event next time. The drop in trip did not look to help her and she will probably be better back over seven. (op 8-1)
Sparkling Eyes kept some good company during the year but only managed one victory in a busy campaign. She set a decent tempo in front, but was left behind when the progressive fillies went for home. (op 4-1)

6564 DIGIBET.CO.UK H'CAP 1m (P)
5:20 (5:21) (Class 5) (0-75,78) 3-Y-0+ **£3,238** (£963; £481; £240) **Stalls** High

Form RPR
4412 **1** **Hassaad**[13] [6413] 3-9-1 **72**..(t) RHills 13 93+
(W J Haggas) *dwlt: hld up wl in rr: gd prog against rail fr 2f out: led ins fnl f: scooted clr* **10/3**[2]
0060 **2** *2 ½* **Coleridge (AUS)**[53] [5670] 7-9-3 **72**.. GeorgeBaker 4 80
(B G Powell) *hld up in midfield on outer: prog over 2f out: chal wl over 1f out: upsides ent fnl f: no ch w wnr sn after* **20/1**

1111 **3** *½* **Eccollo (IRE)**[5] 6507 4-9-9 **78** 6ex.. JohnEgan 1 85+
(T J Pitt) *racd wd: wl in tch: prog to ld over 2f out: hrd pressed and drvn over 1f out: hung lft and hdd ins fnl f: one pce* **5/4**[1]

3031 **4** *1* **Sincerely**[11] 6439 4-8-12 **67**..(b) OscarUrbina 10 72
(B W Hills) *t.k.h: hld up in rr: prog over 2f out: chsd ldrs over 1f out: kpt on but nvr able to chal* **9/1**

-000 **5** *¾* **Maggies Farm (USA)**[25] 6209 3-9-1 **75**.......................... GregFairley(3) 6 78
(M Johnston) *trckd ldrs: rdn and nt qckn 2f out: kpt on same pce after* **16/1**

5264 **6** *1 ½* **James Street (IRE)**[30] 6147 3-8-13 **70**.......................(b) MickyFenton 11 70
(J R Best) *t.k.h: hld up in midfield: hanging bdly and virtually unrideable over 2f out: styd on fr over 1f out: no ch* **12/1**

1046 **7** *½* **Goose Chase**[13] 1644 4-9-0 **69**... LPKeniry 2 68
(A M Hales) *t.k.h: hld up wl in rr: rdn over 2f out: no prog and btn wl over 1f out: plugged on* **33/1**

6004 **8** *1* **Safari Sunset (IRE)**[7] 6489 4-9-1 **70**............................(p) JimCrowley 12 66
(P Winkworth) *t.k.h: hld up in midfield: rdn and no prog 2f out* **16/1**

4033 **9** *2* **Moves Goodenough**[20] 6314 3-8-11 **68**.......................... HayleyTurner 9 60
(Andrew Turnell) *trckd ldng pair to over 2f out: grad wknd over 1f out* **25/1**

-016 **10** *2 ½* **Da Bookie (IRE)**[13] 6413 6-9-2 **71**... FMBerry 8 57
(E J Creighton) *dwlt: hld up in last trio: rdn and no prog over 2f out* **7/1**[3]

11 *2 ½* **Napoletano (GER)**[67] 5-8-12 **67**... ChrisCatlin 3 47
(S Dow) *w ldr: hanging over 2f out: sn wknd* **16/1**

1-00 **12** *½* **Magadar (USA)**[88] 4807 3-9-1 **72**...................................... EddieAhern 14 51
(C E Brittain) *led to over 2f out: wknd and heavily eased fr over 1f out* **20/1**

13 *nk* **Lit Et Mixe (FR)**[242] 3-8-11 **75**.................................... JosephWalsh(7) 7 53
(Noel T Chance) *s.v.s: a last: rdn and no prog over 2f out* **33/1**

1m 38.02s (-2.78) **Going Correction** -0.275s/f (Stan)
WFA 3 from 4yo+ 2lb **13** Ran SP% **134.6**
Speed ratings (Par 103):102,99,99,98,97 95,95,94,92,89 87,86,86
CSF £81.32 CT £136.42 TOTE £7.00: £1.60, £9.20, £1.10; EX 130.70.
Owner Hamdan Al Maktoum **Bred** Shadwell Estate Company Limited **Trained** Newmarket, Suffolk

FOCUS
A solid-looking handicap that really got going off the final bend. The form looks sound for the grade.
James Street(IRE) Official explanation: jockey said gelding hung right-handed

6565 DIGIBET SPORTS BETTING H'CAP 1m 4f (P)
5:50 (5:52) (Class 6) (0-65,65) 3-Y-0+ **£2,388** (£705; £352) **Stalls** Centre

Form RPR

1050 **1** **Wee Charlie Castle (IRE)**[51] 5740 3-9-3 **61**................. OscarUrbina 13 71
(G C H Chung) *dwlt: hld up wl in rr: last over 3f out: gd prog wl over 2f out: led jst over 1f out: rdn and styd on wl* **14/1**

4502 **2** *1* **Serramanna**[13] 6408 5-9-3 **58**... JamesDoyle(3) 1 66
(Ms J S Doyle) *in tch: trckd ldrs 5f out: poised to chal gng easily 2f out: nt qckn over 1f out: chsd wnr fnl f: a hld* **7/1**

4604 **3** *¾* **Amwell Brave**[14] 6398 5-9-8 **60**.. EddieAhern 7 67
(J R Jenkins) *trckd ldrs: rdn 2f out: nt qckn over 1f out: styd on ins fnl f to take 3rd last 50yds* **6/1**[3]

0-00 **4** *½* **Recalcitrant**[11] 6435 3-8-11 **55**.. LPKeniry 2 61
(S Dow) *hld up in midfield: cl enough over 2f out: outpcd over 1f out: styd on ins fnl f* **20/1**

2003 **5** *hd* **Valuta (USA)**[42] 5911 3-9-7 **65**.......................................(t) FJohansson 11 71
(R A Kvisla) *prom: lost pl fr 5f out: wl in rr and struggling 3f out: styd on again fr over 1f out* **12/1**

6204 **6** *shd* **Arsad (IRE)**[11] 6435 3-8-13 **57**... AdamKirby 3 63
(C E Brittain) *trckd ldrs: cl enough 2f out: kpt on same pce u.p after* **11/2**[2]

0055 **7** *nk* **Entranced**[24] 6244 3-9-6 **64**... TomEaves 14 69
(Miss J A Camacho) *led: kpt on whn pressed 2f out: hdd jst over 1f out: fdd and lost pls last 100yds* **5/1**[1]

0005 **8** *½* **Dinner Date**[11] 6435 4-9-3 **55**...................................... FrancisNorton 12 59
(T Keddy) *trckd ldrs: effrt on inner and cl up over 1f out: fdd fnl f* **8/1**

0000 **9** *nk* **Blackmail (USA)**[7] 6484 8-9-4 **56**............................... RichardThomas 10 60+
(P Mitchell) *towards rr: lost pl and last pair over 3f out: swtchd ins and prog 2f out: nt clr run over 1f out: no ch after* **16/1**

3055 **10** *2* **Bienheureux**[8] 6474 5-9-10 **62**..(vt) JohnEgan 4 63
(Miss Gay Kelleway) *hld up wl in rr: prog on inner over 2f out: cl up over 1f out: nt qckn whn n.m.r sn after: wknd fnl f* **7/1**

0533 **11** *2* **Swainson (USA)**[211] 1213 5-9-8 **60**.............................. GeorgeBaker 5 58
(P Mitchell) *racd wd early: prom: trckd ldr over 6f out to 2f out: wkng whn squeezed out ins fnl f* **15/2**

6100 **12** *5* **Royal Premier (IRE)**[16] 6383 3-8-12 **56**......................(v) MickyFenton 6 46
(H J Collingridge) *dwlt and pushed along early: reminders in rr 7f out: nvr gng wl after* **14/1**

633 **13** *4* **Monashee River (IRE)**[11] 6450 3-8-9 **58**......................... LiamJones(5) 9 41
(Miss V Haigh) *wl in tch tl wknd over 2f out* **14/1**

0450 **14** *8* **Double Bay (USA)**[144] 3095 3-9-7 **65**................................ ChrisCatlin 8 35
(Jane Chapple-Hyam) *chsd ldr to over 6f out: wknd over 5f out: wl bhd fnl 2f* **25/1**

2m 33.73s (-3.17) **Going Correction** -0.275s/f (Stan)
WFA 3 from 4yo+ 6lb **14** Ran SP% **136.4**
Speed ratings (Par 101):99,98,97,97,97 97,97,96,96,95 93,90,87,82
CSF £123.23 CT £684.25 TOTE £16.20: £6.40, £2.70, £2.10; EX 164.20.
Owner The Maybe This Time Partnership **Bred** Bryan Ryan **Trained** Newmarket, Suffolk

FOCUS
A very modest handicap run in a very good time. The form should work out.
Royal Premier(IRE) Official explanation: trainer said colt was never travelling in the first 2f

6566 BURGUNDY'S 100TH RACE H'CAP 1m 3f (P)
6:20 (6:21) (Class 5) (0-75,75) 3-Y-0+ **£3,886** (£1,156; £577; £288) **Stalls** High

Form RPR

6230 **1** **Prime Contender**[40] 5935 4-9-1 **67**................................(b[1]) GeorgeBaker 6 74
(G L Moore) *hld up in midfield: effrt over 2f out: drvn ahd jst ins fnl f: styd on wl* **5/1**

0312 **2** *1 ¼* **Lisathedaddy**[17] 6351 4-9-6 **75**......................... RichardKingscote(3) 10 80+
(B G Powell) *trckd ldr after 3f: chal fr 4f out: led over 2f out: hdd u.p jst ins fnl f: one pce* **3/1**[1]

6041 **3** *½* **Blacktoft (USA)**[38] 5992 3-8-11 **68**....................................(e) AdamKirby 1 72
(S C Williams) *t.k.h: hld up towards rr: gng wl 3f out: effrt over 2f out: rdn and styd on same pce fr over 1f out* **9/2**[3]

-053 **4** *½* **Turn 'n Burn**[33] 6075 5-9-1 **67**.. EddieAhern 3 70
(C A Cyzer) *sn trckd ldrs: rdn 2f out: kpt on one pce and nvr able to chal* **7/2**[2]

0010 **5** *1* **Liberty Run (IRE)**[15] 5725 4-9-4 **70**..................................... ChrisCatlin 5 71
(Mrs A J Hamilton-Fairley) *hld up in last trio: sme prog over 2f out: urged along and styd on: nvr rchd ldrs* **20/1**

3650 **6** *nk* **Burgundy**[11] 6432 9-8-10 **69**.......................................(b) JackMitchell(7) 13 70
(P Mitchell) *hld up in last pair: rdn and no rspnse on outer 2f out: styd on ins fnl f* **14/1**

4444 **7** *2* **Emilion**[156] 2713 3-8-6 **63**.. FrancisNorton 11 61
(W R Muir) *trckd ldr for 3f: styd cl up tl wknd fnl f* **16/1**

0064 **8** *3* **Lady Pilot**[7] 6484 4-8-6 **61** oh7.. JamesDoyle(3) 7 54
(Ms J S Doyle) *le3d: set stdy pce to 4f out: hdd over 2f out: sn lost pl and btn* **12/1**

0000 **9** *½* **Barry Island**[27] 6189 7-9-3 **69**.. AntonyProcter 4 61
(D R C Elsworth) *t.k.h early: hld up in midfield: lost pl 4f out: no prog fnl 2f* **14/1**

1600 **10** *3 ½* **Odessa Star (USA)**[11] 6432 3-8-12 **69**............................ JimCrowley 12 55
(J G Portman) *plld hrd: prom: wkng whn n.m.r jst over 2f out* **14/1**

6140 **11** *12* **Turner's Touch**[13] 6408 4-9-0 **66**...................................... TomEaves 2 32
(G L Moore) *hld up in last pair: rdn and lost tch 3f out: t.o* **10/1**

2m 23.6s
WFA 3 from 4yo+ 5lb **11** Ran SP% **129.5**
CSF £22.66 CT £77.98 TOTE £7.80: £1.60, £1.70, £1.60; EX 23.50 Place 6 £58.27, Place 5 £13.83.
Owner Matthew Green & Richard Green **Bred** Gecko Bloodstock Ltd **Trained** Woodingdean, E Sussex

FOCUS
A modest handicap run in a poor time. The race effectively turned into a two-furlong sprint.
Blacktoft(USA) Official explanation: jockey said gelding ran too freely
T/Plt: £41.80 to a £1 stake. Pool: £52,039.40. 908.40 winning tickets. T/Qpdt: £9.50 to a £1 stake. Pool: £5,811.60. 448.60 winning tickets. JN

6456 SAINT-CLOUD (L-H)
Wednesday, November 22

OFFICIAL GOING: Very soft

6567a PRIX BELLE DE NUIT (LISTED RACE) (F&M) 1m 4f 110y
1:10 (1:11) 3-Y-0+ **£17,241** (£6,897; £5,172; £3,448; £1,724)

RPR

1 **Ponte Tresa (FR)**[53] 5700 3-8-13 .... OPeslier 14 107
(Y De Nicolay, France)

2 *1* **King Luna (FR)**[35] 6062 3-8-8 .... JVictoire 1 101
(A Fabre, France)

3 *1 ½* **Elle Galante (GER)**[375] 3-8-8 .... ABadel 5 98
(W Hickst, Germany)

4 *1 ½* **Mango Mischief (IRE)**[18] 6333 5-9-4 .... DBonilla 2 99
(J L Dunlop) *in touch on inside, dropped back approaching straight, 12th straight, stayed on steadily from 1 1/2f out to take 4th SP 11-* **11/1**[1]

5 *1* **Jeritza**[20] 3-8-8 .... YBarberot 10 95
(S Wattel, France)

6 *2* **Miss Provence**[20] 6314 3-8-8 .... TJarnet 13 92
(G Wragg) *towards rear on outside, 9th straight, soon driven, stayed on final furlong SP 61-1* **61/1**[3]

7 *1 ½* **Ragazza Mio (IRE)**[25] 3-8-8 .... TThulliez 7 89
(N Clement, France)

8 *4* **Pray For Sun (IRE)**[162] 2537 3-8-8 ....(b) RMarchelli 12 83
(F Rohaut, France)

9 *3* **Piety (IRE)**[19] 6319 3-8-8 .... JoeFanning 16 79
(M Johnston) *close up, disputing lead half-way, 2nd and ridden straight, one pace from 1 1/2f out SP 21-1* **21/1**[2]

10 *1 ½* **Nazlia (FR)**[48] 3-8-8 .... DBoeuf 11 77
(A De Royer-Dupre, France)

0 **Salila (IRE)**[125] 3-8-8 ....(b) JAuge 6 —
(R Gibson, France)

0 **Varsity**[175] 3-8-8 .... RonanThomas 3 —
(H-A Pantall, France)

0 **Premiere Note**[34] 3-8-8 .... SPasquier 8 —
(A Fabre, France)

0 **Alethia (IRE)**[144] 3102 3-8-8 .... SMaillot 4 —
(J-C Rouget, France)

0 **Mrs Backshoe (IRE)**[31] 6120 3-8-8 .... MBlancpain 15 —
(F Poulsen, France)

2m 49.5s
WFA 3 from 5yo 6lb **15** Ran SP% **14.5**
PARI-MUTUEL: WIN 2.80; PL 1.20, 1.90, 2.70; DF 11.00.
Owner Mme E Hilger **Bred** Paul Hilger **Trained** France

NOTEBOOK
Mango Mischief(IRE) would not have won, but she could have finished closer had she not been slowly into her stride. She made a forward move from two furlongs out up the centre of the track and was staying on at the end. She stays in training next year.
Miss Provence, given a waiting ride, produced an effort up the centre of the track from a furlong and a half out, but never looked like finishing in the frame.
Piety(IRE), well placed for much of the early part of the race, was a spent force early in the straight.

6555 WOLVERHAMPTON (A.W) (L-H)
Thursday, November 23

OFFICIAL GOING: Standard
Wind: Fresh behind becoming moderate from Race 3 (4.50) onwards Weather: Fine

6568 TWILIGHT RACING AND SUPPER - RELAX & ENJOY AMATEUR RIDERS' H'CAP 1m 141y(P)
3:45 (3:45) (Class 5) (0-70,70) 3-Y-0+ **£3,747** (£1,162; £580; £290) **Stalls** Low

Form RPR

0412 **1** **Sol Rojo**[17] 6378 4-10-11 **63**..(v) MrSPearce(3) 10 71
(J Pearce) *hld up: hdwy over 1f out: r.o to ld post* **12/1**

6041 **2** *hd* **Jordan's Light (USA)**[8] 6497 3-11-1 **67** 6ex....................(v) MrSWalker 2 75
(T J Pitt) *chsd ldrs: nt clr run and swtchd wl over 1f out: rdn to ld 1f out: hdd post* **11/8**[1]

0123 **3** *nk* **Bavarica**[9] 6483 4-10-12 **68**... MrRBirkett(7) 13 75
(Miss J Feilden) *hld up: hdwy over 1f out: edgd lft ins fnl f: r.o* **18/1**

5002 **4** *2* **Stevedore (IRE)**[9] 6476 5-10-11 **65** MrDHutchison(5) 7 — 68
(J R Boyle) *led: rdn over 2f out: hdd and no ex 1f out* **13/2**[2]

3000 **5** *3* **Celtic Spa (IRE)**[26] 6211 4-10-9 **61** MissEFolkes(3) 1 — 58
(P D Evans) *hld up: plld hrd: r.o ins fnl f: nrst fin* **33/1**

0203 **6** *hd* **Golden Alchemist**[20] 6327 3-11-4 **70** MrLeeNewnes 9 — 66
(M D I Usher) *chsd ldr: rdn and ev ch over 2f out: wknd fnl f* **25/1**

0665 **7** *½* **Up Tempo (IRE)**[14] 6413 8-11-1 **67** (b) MrJOwen(3) 4 — 62
(C R Dore) *chsd ldrs: ev ch 2f out: wknd fnl f* **20/1**

0050 **8** *nk* **Bijou Dan**[25] 6240 5-10-13 **69** (b) MrCMcGaffin(7) 8 — 64
(W G Harrison) *hld up: plld hrd: hdwy and hmpd over 3f out: rdn over 2f out: wknd fnl f* **25/1**

4311 **9** *nk* **Climate (IRE)**[25] 6241 7-11-0 **68** (p) MissARyan(5) 5 — 62
(K A Ryan) *s.s: hld up: swtchd rt over 2f out: n.d* **13/2**[2]

2215 **10** *nk* **Red Rudy**[68] 5384 4-11-0 **68** MrMJJSmith(5) 11 — 61
(A W Carroll) *hld up: plld hrd: hdwy over 6f out: ev ch over 2f out: wknd fnl f* **11/1**[3]

053- **11** *1¾* **Forfeiter (USA)**[79] 5101 4-10-6 **62** MissPHermansson(7) 6 — 52
(R Ford) *mid-div: sn pushed laong: rdn over 2f out: wkng whn hung lft over 1f out* **14/1**

04 **12** *1½* **King's Jester (IRE)**[24] 6266 4-11-4 **70** MrDMacAuley(3) 12 — 57
(J J Lambe, Ire) *prom: rdn over 2f out: wknd over 1f out* **25/1**

2100 **13** *10* **Mocha Java**[50] 5765 3-10-9 **68** MissLauraGray(7) 3 — 34
(Mrs L J Mongan) *prom 6f* **40/1**

1m 51.43s (-0.33) **Going Correction** -0.175s/f (Stan)
WFA 3 from 4yo+ 3lb — 13 Ran SP% **118.4**
Speed ratings (Par 103):94,93,93,91,89 88,88,88,87,87 86,84,75
CSF £26.18 CT £327.35 TOTE £11.40: £4.10, £1.10, £7.20; EX 36.30 Trifecta £145.30 Part won. Pool: £204.78 - 0.88 winning tickets..
Owner Mrs Lydia Pearce **Bred** Mrs A Yearley **Trained** Newmarket, Suffolk
■ Stewards' Enquiry : Mr D MacAuley one-day ban: failed to ride to draw (Dec 18)

FOCUS
A run-of-the-mill amateur riders' event that resulted in a good finish. The form is ordinary and best rated through the fourth.

6569 WBX.COM LAUNCHING 25TH NOVEMBER NURSERY — 1m 141y(P)
4:20 (4:22) (Class 5) (0-75,72) 2-Y-O — **£3,886** (£1,156; £577; £288) **Stalls** Low

Form — RPR

0351 **1** **My Secrets**[15] 6394 2-9-4 **69** JoeFanning 10 — 76
(M Johnston) *chsd ldr: rdn to ld over 3f out: edgd rt and clr over 1f out: hung lft towards fin: jst hld on* **9/2**[2]

0012 **2** *nk* **Mastership (IRE)**[33] 6106 2-9-2 **67** (b) EddieAhern 4 — 73+
(C E Brittain) *hld up: nt clr run over 2f out: hdwy over 1f out: sn rdn: r.o* **7/2**[1]

003 **3** *4* **Milson's Point (IRE)**[26] 6207 2-8-4 **55** FrancisNorton 9 — 53
(I Semple) *prom: jnd wnr over 3f out: rdn over 1f out: styd on same pce* **14/1**

302 **4** *2* **Robert The Brave**[26] 6224 2-9-3 **68** SteveDrowne 2 — 61
(A J McCabe) *hld up: rdn 1/2-way: hdwy u.p over 1f out: nrst fin* **9/2**[2]

4000 **5** *1¼* **Slipasearcher (IRE)**[33] 6100 2-9-7 **72** (b) JohnEgan 6 — 62
(P D Evans) *hld up: hdwy u.p over 3f out: wknd over 1f out* **14/1**

4450 **6** *1½* **Intersky Sports (USA)**[87] 4882 2-8-12 **63** DeanMcKeown 7 — 50
(K A Ryan) *hld up: hdwy 1/2-way: rdn and wknd over 1f out* **16/1**

3605 **7** *shd* **Froissee**[15] 6394 2-8-9 **60** (p) ChrisCatlin 3 — 47
(N A Callaghan) *prom 5f* **8/1**[3]

0306 **8** *1¾* **Spinning Game**[3] 6534 2-7-12 **49** oh4 PaulQuinn 8 — 32
(D W Chapman) *chsd ldrs: wkng whn hmpd over 3f out* **66/1**

063 **9** *1½* **Tivers Song (USA)**[16] 6386 2-9-7 **72** JimCrowley 1 — 52
(Mrs A J Perrett) *chsd ldrs: rdn 1/2-way: wknd over 2f out* **9/2**[2]

500 **10** *shd* **Green Day Packer (IRE)**[105] 4295 2-8-12 **68** AshleyHamblett(5) 5 — 48
(P C Haslam) *led: rdn and hdd over 3f out: wkng whn hmpd 2f out* **12/1**

1m 50.21s (-1.55) **Going Correction** -0.175s/f (Stan) — 10 Ran SP% **116.3**
Speed ratings (Par 96):99,98,95,93,92 90,90,89,87,87
CSF £20.58 CT £208.23 TOTE £5.90: £1.10, £2.20, £5.60; EX 17.60 Trifecta £45.80 Pool: £498.53 - 7.72 winning tickets..
Owner Ahmed Jaber **Bred** Hascombe And Valiant Studs **Trained** Middleham Moor, N Yorks

FOCUS
This looked a fair nursery for the time of year. The time was 1.22 seconds faster than the opening amateurs' event and the first two drew clear in the straight. The form looks strong with the first two clear.

NOTEBOOK
My Secrets ran on gamely to hold the late challenge of the favourite and has taken well to Polytrack, supplementing his recent win at Kempton. With his stable in such good form, he could well complete the hat-trick. (op 7-2)
Mastership(IRE) looked unlucky as he was travelling really well on the home turn, but did not get a clear run and by the time he got through he had five lengths to make up on the winner. He did well to finish as close as he did. (op 4-1 tchd 3-1)
Milson's Point(IRE) ran a decent race on this All-Weather and handicap debut, but was left behind from the home turn. (op 10-1)
Robert The Brave was last and being pushed along half a mile out, but was doing his best work in the closing stages. He has a handicap in him on this surface. (op 6-1)
Slipasearcher(IRE) failed to see out the longer trip. She is plummeting down the weights having been punished for contesting Pattern races on turf earlier in the year, but appears to have further to go. (tchd 16-1)

6570 EUROPEAN BREEDERS' FUND MAIDEN STKS — 1m 141y(P)
4:50 (4:52) (Class 5) 2-Y-O — **£3,886** (£1,156; £577; £288) **Stalls** Low

Form — RPR

4344 **1** **History Boy**[24] 6254 2-9-3 83 JimmyQuinn 4 — 84
(D J Coakley) *trckd ldrs: racd keenly: rdn to ld over 1f out: hung rt ins fnl f: drvn out* **3/1**[3]

3053 **2** *1¼* **Stanley George (IRE)**[23] 6283 2-9-3 74 MatthewHenry 9 — 81
(M A Jarvis) *chsd ldrs: led over 3f out: rdn and hdd over 1f out: styd on* **7/1**

0 **3** *5* **Born West (USA)**[16] 6386 2-9-3 RobertHavlin 8 — 70
(P W Chapple-Hyam) *s.s: sn pushed along in rr: hdwy over 5f out: outpcd and hung rt over 2f out: styd on ins fnl f* **5/2**[2]

4 *nk* **Zar Solitario** 2-9-3 JoeFanning 10 — 69
(M Johnston) *prom: chsd ldr over 2f out: sn ev ch: wkng whn hung lft ins fnl f* **13/8**[1]

0043 **5** *¾* **Fairly Honest**[14] 6412 2-9-3 74 AntonyProcter 5 — 68
(D R C Elsworth) *hmpd s: hld up: hmpd 3f out: hdwy over 1f out: nrst fin* **12/1**

00 **6** *1¾* **Butlers Best**[41] 5947 2-9-3 ChrisCatlin 7 — 64
(E J O'Neill) *hld up: hdwy 2f out: nt trble ldrs* **50/1**

0 **7** *14* **Meathop (IRE)**[38] 6012 2-9-0 DNolan(3) 6 — 33
(R F Fisher) *led: hdd over 3f out: wknd over 2f out* **33/1**

004 **8** *shd* **Delaporte**[10] 6457 2-8-12 (vt) DavidAllan 1 — 28
(M A Buckley) *trckd ldrs: racd keenly: wknd 3f out* **66/1**

00 **9** *33* **Wilde Thing**[22] 6298 2-8-9 JamesDoyle(3) 3 — —
(S Curran) *wnt rt s: sn pushed along in rr: rdn and wknd 4f out* **100/1**

1m 49.47s (-2.29) **Going Correction** -0.175s/f (Stan) — 9 Ran SP% **119.2**
Speed ratings (Par 96):103,101,97,97,96 94,82,82,53
CSF £24.65 TOTE £4.40: £1.80, £1.60, £1.10; EX 16.40 Trifecta £42.00 Pool: £556.00 - 9.38 winning tickets..
Owner Chris Van Hoorn **Bred** C T Van Hoorn **Trained** West Ilsley, Berks

FOCUS
A fair juvenile maiden in which the time was 0.74 sec faster than the preceding nursery and nearly two seconds quicker than the opening amateurs' event, but nothing got into contention from off the pace. The form looks solid.

NOTEBOOK
History Boy gained a deserved first success, getting a good split on the rail turning in and proving too strong for the runner-up, despite wandering under pressure. He seemed to appreciate this longer trip and, although his future is likely to be in handicaps, he is not that well treated with an official rating of 83. (op 7-2)
Stanley George(IRE) was dropping in trip having been placed over the trip here last time. He was always close to the pace and tried to make the best of his way home after taking over going into the home turn, but the winner got up his inside straightening up and, although sticking on well could not find any extra. He looks to have a small race in him on this surface. (op 15-2 tchd 6-1)
Born West(USA) missed the break and was pushed along virtually throughout. He ran on steadily in the closing stages and will be seen to better effect in handicaps next year. (op 7-2)
Zar Solitario was green in the paddock beforehand and ran well for a long way. However, after having every chance turning for home, he got tired and faded in the closing stages. He should come on for the experience. (op 6-4 tchd 2-1)
Fairly Honest did not enjoy the smoothest of passages, but he was beaten far enough which makes it difficult to say how much his chance was affected. Stamina did not appear to be an issue over this longer trip though. (op 9-1 tchd 14-1)

6571 WATCH OUT FOR THEMED DAYS H'CAP — 1m 4f 50y(P)
5:20 (5:21) (Class 6) (0-60,60) 3-Y-O+ — **£2,590** (£770; £385; £192) **Stalls** Low

Form — RPR

0033 **1** **Missie Baileys**[15] 6405 4-9-2 **54** IanMongan 5 — 63
(Mrs L J Mongan) *chsd ldrs: rdn to ld and hung lft 1f out: styd on* **15/2**

2544 **2** *2½* **Regency Red (IRE)**[5] 6526 8-8-9 **52** LiamJones(5) 8 — 57
(W M Brisbourne) *hld up in tch: rdn over 2f out: edgd lft and styd on same pce ins fnl f* **10/1**

-312 **3** *hd* **Boppys Pride**[12] 6435 3-8-8 **57** JamieMoriarty(5) 10 — 62
(R A Fahey) *led: hdd over 9f out: chsd ldr: rdn and ev ch 1f out: sn hung lft and no ex* **4/1**[1]

6004 **4** *1½* **Bentley Brook (IRE)**[14] 6415 4-9-6 **58** (t) GeorgeBaker 3 — 61
(P A Blockley) *wnt lft s: hld up: hdwy over 2f out: nt clr run over 1f out: sn rdn and hung lft: styd on same pce* **6/1**[3]

0330 **5** *2½* **Art Historian (IRE)**[6] 6509 3-9-0 **58** JohnEgan 6 — 62+
(T J Pitt) *trckd ldrs: racd keenly: led over 9f out: rdn over 2f out: hdd 1f out: styng on same pce whn hmpd wl ins fnl f: eased* **9/2**[2]

4460 **6** *shd* **Melvino**[20] 6317 4-9-4 **56** GrahamGibbons 7 — 54
(T D Barron) *s.s: hld up: plld hrd: rdn over 3f out: styd on ins fnl f: nrst fin* **17/2**

3300 **7** *1* **Mossmann Gorge**[9] 6474 4-9-7 **59** (v) DaneO'Neill 2 — 56
(M Wellings) *hmpd s: hld up: hdwy over 5f out: rdn over 3f out: wknd over 1f out* **33/1**

2465 **8** *nk* **Phone In**[15] 6398 3-9-2 **60** (b) TomEaves 1 — 56
(R Brotherton) *wnt rt s: sn chsng ldrs: rdn over 2f out: wknd over 1f out* **7/1**

2400 **9** *2½* **Mister Maq**[16] 6387 3-9-0 **58** (b) JoeFanning 11 — 50
(A Crook) *s.s: a in rr* **40/1**

0050 **10** *4* **Epicurean**[23] 6275 4-9-8 **60** MickyFenton 9 — 46
(Mrs K Walton) *hld up: rdn whn hmpd over 3f out: sn wknd* **33/1**

0031 **11** *1½* **Qaasi (USA)**[15] 6405 4-9-8 **60** DeanMernagh 12 — 44
(M Brittain) *chsd ldrs tl rdn over 2f out: wknd over 1f out* **7/1**

2m 41.7s (-0.72) **Going Correction** -0.175s/f (Stan)
WFA 3 from 4yo+ 6lb — 11 Ran SP% **117.2**
Speed ratings (Par 101):95,93,93,92,90 90,89,89,87,85 84
CSF £78.52 CT £345.25 TOTE £9.40: £2.20, £2.20, £2.40; EX 47.90 Trifecta £190.80 Part won. Pool: £268.76 - 0.44 winning tickets..
Owner Mrs P J Sheen **Bred** Mrs J Wotherspoon **Trained** Epsom, Surrey
■ Stewards' Enquiry : Jamie Moriarty three-day ban: careless riding (Dec 4-6)

FOCUS
This moderate handicap was run at a very steady early pace and the time was modest. The form is very ordinary with the winner the best guide.

6572 CALL WOLVERHAMPTON RACECOURSE ON 0870 220 2442 H'CAP — 5f 216y(P)
5:50 (5:53) (Class 6) (0-65,71) 3-Y-O+ — **£2,590** (£770; £385; £192) **Stalls** Low

Form — RPR

-200 **1** **Shade Cozy (USA)**[37] 6036 4-9-2 **65** FrancisNorton 10 — 80+
(A M Balding) *chsd ldr: led wl over 1f out: r.o: eased nr fin* **9/2**[3]

0051 **2** *1¾* **Cape Presto (IRE)**[6] 6508 3-9-8 **71** 6ex (v) JohnEgan 12 — 79
(Mrs C A Dunnett) *hld up in tch: racd keenly: rdn to chse wnr fnl f: edgd lft and no imp* **3/1**[1]

5244 **3** *¾* **Joyeaux**[20] 6315 4-8-13 **62** (v) DavidAllan 8 — 67
(J Hetherton) *prom: hmpd and lost pl 5f out: r.o ins fnl f: nrst fin* **8/1**

0025 **4** *¾* **Bond Playboy**[10] 6465 6-8-8 **62** (v[1]) DuranFentiman(5) 13 — 65
(G R Oldroyd) *hld up: hdwy and hung lft fr over 1f out: nt trble ldrs* **9/1**

3300 **5** *½* **Casual Affair**[24] 6260 3-9-2 **65** ChrisCatlin 4 — 67
(E J O'Neill) *chsd ldrs: rdn over 1f out: hung lft and styd on same pce ins fnl f* **16/1**

6026 **6** *½* **Conjecture**[20] 6315 4-9-2 **65** PatCosgrave 2 — 65
(R Bastiman) *sn led: rdn and hdd wl over 1f out: wknd ins fnl f* **15/2**

0 **7** *½* **Richelieu**[24] 6265 4-9-2 **65** TonyCulhane 7 — 64
(J J Lambe, Ire) *hld up: hdwy over 1f out: nvr nrr* **25/1**

2560 **8** *1¾* **Gilded Cove**[50] 5765 6-8-13 **64** RussellKennemore(7) 1 — 68+
(R Hollinshead) *hld up: hdwy over 1f out: 5th whn rdn and hmpd ins fnl f: nt rcvr* **4/1**[2]

0000 **9** *1¼* **Royal Orissa**[136] 3368 4-8-13 **62** RobertHavlin 3 — 52
(D Haydn Jones) *chsd ldrs over 4f* **16/1**

0060 **10** *1* **Canina**[9] 6478 3-9-1 **64** GeorgeBaker 5 — 51
(Ms Deborah J Evans) *s.s: a in rr* **33/1**

0006 **11** *3½* **Piccostar**[39] 5987 3-8-13 **62** DaneO'Neill 6 — 38
(A B Haynes) *sn outpcd* **22/1**

3400 12 *shd* **Highland Song (IRE)**[20] 6320 3-8-13 **65** .... DNolan(3) 9 41
(R F Fisher) *chsd ldrs: n.m.r over 4f out: sn rdn: wknd 2f out* **50/1**

1m 14.03s (-1.78) **Going Correction** -0.175s/f (Stan) **12** Ran SP% **120.9**
Speed ratings (Par 101):104,101,100,99,99 98,97,95,93,92 87,87
CSF £18.05 CT £108.11 TOTE £6.90: £2.10, £1.90, £2.40; EX 21.70 TRIFECTA Not won..
Owner Mr & Mrs A Hogarth **Bred** London Thoroughbred Services Ltd **Trained** Kingsclere, Hants

FOCUS
A modest sprint which, unusually for this track, was dominated by high-drawn horses. The form looks straightforward with the placed horses the key.
Bond Playboy Official explanation: jockey said gelding hung left

6573 WBX.COM WORLD BET EXCHANGE H'CAP 7f 32y(P)
6:20 (6:21) (Class 5) (0-70,70) 3-Y-0+ **£3,886** (£1,156; £577; £288) **Stalls** High

Form RPR
0502 1 **Foreplay (IRE)**[26] 6227 3-9-2 **70** .... (p) EddieAhern 7 81
(E A L Dunlop) *trckd ldrs: led ins fnl f: pushed out* **9/1**
01 2 *hd* **Dichoh**[15] 6403 3-8-12 **66** .... MatthewHenry 9 77
(M A Jarvis) *chsd ldr: led wl over 1f out: hdd ins fnl f: r.o* **16/1**
2403 3 *1 3/4* **Imperial Lucky (IRE)**[14] 6413 3-9-1 **69** .... DaneO'Neill 5 75
(D K Ivory) *hld up: hdwy over 1f out: nt clr run ins fnl f: r.o* **8/1**[3]
0005 4 *shd* **Ochre Bay**[13] 6425 3-8-12 **66** .... GrahamGibbons 6 72
(R Hollinshead) *in rr: hdwy over 4f out: rdn over 1f out: r.o* **7/1**[2]
0050 5 *1* **Bessemer (JPN)**[14] 6417 5-9-3 **70** .... (p) DanielTudhope 4 73
(D Carroll) *chsd ldrs: rdn over 2f out: no ex ins fnl f* **8/1**[3]
0003 6 *3/4* **Stoic Leader (IRE)**[6] 6508 6-8-12 **68** .... DNolan(3) 3 69
(R F Fisher) *broke wl: sn lost pl: hdwy over 2f out: rdn over 1f out: styng on same pce whn nt clr run ins fnl f* **7/2**[1]
2431 7 *hd* **Redwood Rocks (IRE)**[16] 6390 5-8-9 **67** .... MarkLawson(5) 8 68
(B Smart) *led: rdn and hdd wl over 1f out: no ex ins fnl f* **7/2**[1]
4040 8 *3 1/2* **Play The Ball (USA)**[24] 6266 4-9-2 **69** .... TonyCulhane 11 61
(J J Lambe, Ire) *s.i.s: n.d* **40/1**
0000 9 *1/2* **Tuscarora (IRE)**[9] 6483 7-8-8 **64** .... JamesDoyle(3) 1 55
(A W Carroll) *s.i.s: hung lft over 1f out: n.d* **33/1**
5000 10 *1 1/4* **Takes Tutu (USA)**[66] 5436 7-8-11 **64** .... SteveDrowne 10 51
(C R Dore) *s.i.s: a in rr* **22/1**
1460 11 *1* **Le Chiffre (IRE)**[102] 4399 4-8-9 **69** .... (p) TolleyDean(7) 2 54
(R A Harris) *mid-div: lost pl 5f out: n.d after* **14/1**
0005 12 *shd* **Sands Of Barra (IRE)**[31] 6147 3-8-13 **67** .... TomEaves 12 51
(I W McInnes) *chsd ldrs 5f* **18/1**

1m 28.6s (-1.80) **Going Correction** -0.175s/f (Stan)
WFA 3 from 4yo+ 1lb **12** Ran SP% **116.7**
Speed ratings (Par 103):103,102,100,100,99 98,98,94,93,92 91,91
CSF £138.72 CT £1202.01 TOTE £12.70: £4.40, £1.70, £2.00; EX 57.00 Trifecta £348.00 Part won. Pool: £490.17 - 0.98 winning tickets. Place 6 £147.76, Place 5 £83.83.
Owner St Albans Bloodstock LLP **Bred** Gainsborough Stud Management Ltd **Trained** Newmarket, Suffolk
■ Stewards' Enquiry : Dane O'Neill caution: careless riding

FOCUS
An ordinary handicap but a good finish and the form looks reasonble, rated around the third and fourth.
Tuscarora(IRE) Official explanation: jockey said mare hung left throughout
T/Plt: £33.30 to a £1 stake. Pool: £68,892.75. 1,505.85 winning tickets. T/Qpdt: £13.10 to a £1 stake. Pool: £6,442.30. 362.20 winning tickets. CR

6062 DEAUVILLE (R-H)
Thursday, November 23
OFFICIAL GOING: Standard

6574a PRIX LUTHIER (LISTED) (ALL-WEATHER) 7f 110y
1:40 (1:40) 3-Y-0+ **£17,241** (£6,897; £5,172; £3,448; £1,724)

RPR
1 **Goetot (FR)**[145] 5-9-2 .... TThulliez 14 111
(J-M Beguigne, France)
2 *2* **Mayonga (IRE)**[28] 6190 3-8-11 .... SebSanders 7 104
(Sir Mark Prescott) *mid-division, 7th straight, ran on from over 1f out, took second close home (52/10)* **52/10**[1]
3 *3/4* **Kavafi (IRE)**[35] 4-8-13 .... MBlancpain 12 102
(C Laffon-Parias, France)
4 *1/2* **Adeje Park (IRE)**[15] 6397 3-8-8 .... DBonilla 8 98
(P W Chapple-Hyam) *raced in 3rd on outside, 4th straight, driven 1 1/2f out, stayed on steadily to line (56/1)* **56/1**[2]
5 *nk* **Madresal (GER)**[25] 6248 7-9-2 .... WMongil 15 103
(P Schiergen, Germany)
6 *nk* **Glad To Be Fast (IRE)**[25] 6252 6-8-13 .... (b) JVictoire 6 100
(Mario Hofer, Germany)
7 *shd* **Mister Charm (FR)**[88] 4862 6-9-2 .... IMendizabal 3 103
(J-C Rouget, France)
8 *1/2* **Prokopios (GER)**[349] 4-8-13 .... ADeVries 11 99
(H Blume, Germany)
9 *hd* **Together (FR)**[25] 6250 6-8-13 .... (b) SMaillot 5 98
(Mme C Vergne, France)
10 *1 1/2* **Ryono (USA)**[74] 5227 7-9-5 .... TCastanheira 4 101
(S Smrczek, Germany)
0 **Ganja (FR)**[53] 6-8-9 .... JAuge 9 —
(G Pannier, France)
0 **Take Grace (FR)**[62] 4-8-9 .... ACrastus 1 —
(Y De Nicolay, France)
0 **Bien Partie (FR)**[47] 4-8-9 .... THuet 13 —
(Mlle S-V Tarrou, France)
0 **Apollo Star (GER)**[25] 6248 4-9-2 .... J-PCarvalho 2 —
(Mario Hofer, Germany)
0 **Tigron (USA)**[210] 1266 5-8-13 .... (b) DBoeuf 10 —
(Mme C Barande-Barbe, France)

1m 28.1s
WFA 3 from 4yo+ 1lb **15** Ran SP% **17.9**
PARI-MUTUEL: WIN 8.50; PL 2.60, 2.60, 2.10; DF 36.70.
Owner Mme C Brovedani **Bred** Haras De Preaux **Trained** France

NOTEBOOK
Mayonga(IRE) put up a decent effort. Settled in mid-division on the rail until the straight, she was extracted to challenge a furlong and a half out and was putting in her best work at the finish. She never looked like catching the winner, though. The plan is to come back here in January for the Listed Prix Miss Satamixa.
Adeje Park(IRE) lost nothing in defeat. Racing just behind the leading group, she was given every possible chance, but she could not quicken as well as the others inside the final furlong.

6561 KEMPTON (A.W) (R-H)
Friday, November 24
OFFICIAL GOING: Standard
Wind: Strong, behind Weather: Overcast

6575 LETCHWORTH COURIERS E B F MAIDEN FILLIES' STKS 6f (P)
3:50 (3:50) (Class 5) 2-Y-0 **£3,562** (£1,059; £529; £264) **Stalls** High

Form RPR
03 1 **Bussel (USA)**[20] 6330 2-9-0 .... TonyCulhane 3 73+
(W J Haggas) *w ldr: led wl over 2f out: pushed clr over 1f out: in n.d after* **4/6**[1]
3303 2 *2* **Isobel Rose (IRE)**[7] 6505 2-9-0 70 .... BrettDoyle 5 67
(E A L Dunlop) *off the pce in midfield: prog over 2f out: rdn to chse wnr 1f out: styd on but no imp* **10/3**[2]
3 *3* **Night Rocket (IRE)** 2-9-0 .... LPKeniry 6 58
(A M Balding) *s.s: wl in rr and off the pce: prog on outer fr 2f out: rn green and plugged on to take 3rd ins fnl f* **14/1**
00 4 *1/2* **Regal Curtsy**[45] 5894 2-9-0 .... JimCrowley 9 57
(P R Chamings) *led to wl over 2f out: sn rdn: outpcd over 1f out: plugged on* **14/1**
5 *3/4* **Scarlett Heart (IRE)** 2-9-0 .... FergusSweeney 8 54
(P J Makin) *s.i.s: t.k.h and sn trckd ldrs: rdn to chse wnr briefly over 1f out: wknd ins fnl f* **12/1**
6 *1* **Midnight Sky** 2-9-0 .... SteveDrowne 2 51
(Rae Guest) *t.k.h: trckd ldrs: rdn and fdd fr over 1f out* **10/1**[3]
7 *3/4* **Descargo** 2-9-0 .... AdamKirby 7 49
(C G Cox) *t.k.h: in tch: hanging rt over 2f out: no prog fnl 2f* **16/1**
00 8 *3 1/2* **Fruits D'Amour (IRE)**[22] 6309 2-9-0 .... MickyFenton 1 39
(S Kirk) *hld up and sn last: wl off the pce over 2f out: shuffled along and no prog* **33/1**
00 9 *9* **Respect My Wishes**[130] 3588 2-9-0 .... StephenCarson 4 12
(R Ingram) *in tch to 1/2-way: sn wknd: t.o* **50/1**

1m 13.01s (-0.69) **Going Correction** -0.275s/f (Stan) **9** Ran SP% **124.0**
Speed ratings (Par 93):93,90,86,85,84 83,82,77,65
CSF £3.44 TOTE £1.50: £1.10, £1.10, £5.00; EX 3.20.
Owner W J Haggas **Bred** John Weld **Trained** Newmarket, Suffolk

FOCUS
A modest and uncompetitive maiden in which they bet 10/1 bar two. The runner-up sets the standard but the winner can rate higher.

NOTEBOOK
Bussel(USA), whose breeding suggested she would handle this surface, built on her decent effort at Windsor and, having been up with the pace throughout, went clear early in the straight and from that point had the race in safe keeping. She swished her tail but kept galloping and looks capable of winning handicaps on this surface. (op Evens tchd 11-10 in places)
Isobel Rose(IRE) is quite exposed having been in the frame now in nine of her ten races. She chased the winner to no avail in the last furlong, but gives a good guide to the level of the form. She may be worth trying in handicaps in an attempt to get that elusive victory. (op 3-1 tchd 7-2)
Night Rocket(IRE), a full-sister to Dark Missile, showed promise in running on into the places having been behind early. She should come on for the run. (op 12-1)
Regal Curtsy, a half-sister to the useful Take A Bow, made a bold bid from the front and did not drop out when headed. She now qualifies for a handicap mark and that looks to be where her future lies. (op 12-1)
Scarlett Heart(IRE) ◆, a cheaply-bought first foal from the family of prolific winners Riley Boys and Game Guru, caught the eye having missed the break. She was soon on the heels of the leaders and only faded in the last quarter mile. She looks likely to improve a fair amount for the experience. (op 10-1)
Midnight Sky ◆, from the family of Miss Anabaa, Move it and Out After Dark, ran very free on this debut and not surprisingly got tired in the straight. She looks sure to improve for the experience but will need to learn to settle better.
Descargo Official explanation: jockey said filly hung right throughout

6576 FORTIS BANK NURSERY 1m (P)
4:20 (4:21) (Class 6) (0-65,65) 2-Y-0 **£2,388** (£705; £352) **Stalls** High

Form RPR
6312 1 **Lake Pontchartrain (IRE)**[6] 6522 2-9-6 **64** .... GeorgeBaker 3 70+
(S Kirk) *hld up towards rr: prog on outer wl over 1f out: rdn and r.o fnl f to ld last strides* **4/1**[2]
0504 2 *nk* **Prince Of Charm (USA)**[16] 6394 2-9-0 **58** .... (b) SteveDrowne 6 63
(P Mitchell) *cl up: trckd ldr over 2f out: rdn to ld 1f out: styd on: hdd last strides* **9/2**[3]
0554 3 *3/4* **A Nod And A Wink (IRE)**[9] 6487 2-8-3 **50** .... StephaneBreux(3) 5 53+
(R Hannon) *t.k.h: hld up in rr: nt clr run over 2f out: bmpd along and prog fnl 2f: styd on wl to take 3rd nr fin* **12/1**
6300 4 *shd* **Ask Yer Dad**[16] 6394 2-9-4 **62** .... (p) MickyFenton 12 65
(Mrs P Sly) *rousted along to ld: drvn and pressed 2f out: hdd 1f out: kpt on wl* **10/1**
0000 5 *2 1/2* **Tumble Jill (IRE)**[38] 6032 2-7-10 **47** .... JosephWalsh(7) 4 44
(J J Bridger) *hld up wl in rr: outpcd 2f out: prog on outer jst over 1f out: styng on whn hung rt ins fnl f* **50/1**
065 6 *1 1/2* **Trickle (USA)**[18] 6377 2-9-7 **65** .... (t) BrettDoyle 10 59
(E A L Dunlop) *t.k.h: hld up in midfield: prog and cl up jst over 1f out: wknd ins fnl f* **7/1**
4003 7 *1 1/2* **Sweet World**[9] 6487 2-9-5 **63** .... AdamKirby 14 53
(A P Jarvis) *trckd ldrs: effrt and cl up on inner over 1f out: wknd fnl f* **9/1**
0064 8 *shd* **Go Dude**[14] 6421 2-8-10 **54** .... (p) OscarUrbina 7 44
(J Ryan) *hld up in midfield: prog to chse ldrs over 1f out: wknd ent fnl f* **20/1**
646 9 *1/2* **News Of The Day (IRE)**[23] 6290 2-8-10 **59** .... AndrewElliott(5) 8 48
(M Johnston) *prom: rdn 1/2-way: sn lost pl and struggling* **10/3**[1]
0000 10 *hd* **Fun Thai**[6] 6518 2-8-1 **48** ow3 .... EdwardCreighton(3) 11 37
(M R Channon) *hld up in last pair of main gp: effrt over 2f out: swtchd lft over 1f out: nt pce to trble ldrs* **25/1**
4050 11 *3* **Spence's Choice (IRE)**[65] 5482 2-8-11 **55** .... PaulMulrennan 2 37
(M W Easterby) *nvr bttr than midfield: wd bnd 3f out: sn struggling* **33/1**
0004 12 *5* **Storm Mission (USA)**[10] 6472 2-8-8 **52** .... (b) AdrianMcCarthy 9 22
(Miss V Haigh) *hld up in midfield on inner: hanging over 2f out: sn wknd* **20/1**
3200 13 *5* **Tibinta**[15] 6416 2-8-10 **54** .... FMBerry 1 13
(P D Evans) *pressed ldr tl wknd rapidly over 2f out* **25/1**

The Form Book, Raceform Ltd, Compton, RG20 6NL

0000 **14** *39* **Soundasapound**[80] 5084 2-7-10 **45**.....................(p) DuranFentiman(5) 13 —
(I W McInnes) *veering arnd and t.o after 3f* **66/1**
1m 40.35s (-0.45) **Going Correction** -0.275s/f (Stan) **14** Ran SP% **124.2**
Speed ratings (Par 94):91,90,89,89,87 85,84,84,83,83 80,75,70,31
CSF £21.23 CT £207.51 TOTE £4.80: £2.10, £1.70, £3.20; EX 29.30.
Owner Eddie Tynan **Bred** E Tynan **Trained** Upper Lambourn, Berks

FOCUS
A modest nursery and an ordinary time, but a close finish. The form is modest but solid, rated through the runner-up.

NOTEBOOK
Lake Pontchartrain(IRE) ◆ has really found her forte in handicaps on Polytrack and got up close home to supplement a series of good efforts this month. She was quite keen early and Baker had to settle her, but then the pair found themselves towards the back of the field. Switching wide in the straight, she found plenty for pressure and won slightly more comfortably than the margin suggests. She may be capable of adding to her score, even after re-assessment. (tchd 7-2)
Prince Of Charm(USA) was always in the right place and, hitting the front entering the last furlong, briefly looked as if he would score. However, the winner loomed up on his outside and always looked like catching him. His recent form on this surface stands up pretty well and he should find a race before too long. (op 7-1)
A Nod And A Wink(IRE), stepping up again in trip, came from well off the pace and had to wait for an opening, but was doing her best work late on. She was beaten in sellers on turf, but this surface and the longer distance has improved her (op 10-1)
Ask Yer Dad, with cheekpieces fitted for the first time, got closer to the runner-up than he had over course and distance on their previous meeting. The different tactics may have helped, but something slightly less forceful may enable him to last home.
News Of The Day(IRE), made favourite on this handicap debut, presumably because the stable is in such good form, had every chance but faded in the final quarter mile. She may be better back at shorter trips for now. (op 7-2)
Spence's Choice(IRE) Official explanation: jockey said gelding hung left throughout
Soundasapound Official explanation: jockey said filly hung violently left throughout

6577 MARSHELS OF FARNHAM H'CAP 1m (P)
4:50 (4:53) (Class 6) (0-55,61) 3-Y-O+ **£2,388** (£705; £352) **Stalls** High

Form RPR
4050 **1** **Atlantic Story (USA)**[23] 6300 4-8-11 **55**.....................(t) JamesDoyle(3) 9 74+
(M W Easterby) *wl plcd bhd ldrs: prog to ld over 1f out: r.o wl and drew rt away* **9/2**[1]
0002 **2** *5* **Kathleen Kennet**[23] 6300 6-8-8 **52**........................ RichardKingscote(3) 7 57
(Mrs H Sweeting) *trckd ldr and clr of rest after 3f: rdn to chal 2f out: hung bdly lft after and ended on nr side rail: hld on for 2nd* **10/1**
6050 **3** *nk* **Kareeb (FR)**[72] 5302 9-9-0 **55**.......................................(p) TonyCulhane 11 60
(Miss J Feilden) *hld up wl in rr: stdy prog fr 2f out: rdn to chse clr wnr ins fnl f: no imp* **16/1**
0055 **4** *1 1/4* **Simpsons Gamble (IRE)**[13] 6442 3-8-12 **55**...................... AdamKirby 4 57
(R M Flower) *hld up wl in rr: prog on inner fr 2f out: styd on same pce fnl f* **20/1**
4-06 **5** *nk* **Caragh Mia (IRE)**[10] 6483 4-9-0 **55**................................ OscarUrbina 12 56
(G G Margarson) *towards rr: rdn over 3f out: no prog tl styd on fr over 1f out: nrst fin* **20/1**
1235 **6** *1/2* **Labelled With Love**[6] 6513 6-8-10 **54**............................(t) AmirQuinn(3) 6 54
(J R Boyle) *t.k.h: hld up bhd ldrs: effrt over 2f out: ch of pl 1f out: wknd nr fin* **7/1**[3]
2003 **7** *nk* **Wiltshire (IRE)**[14] 6431 4-8-11 **52**................................... MickyFenton 10 51
(P T Midgley) *in tch in midfield: rdn and prog over 2f out: disp 2nd 1f out: wknd* **10/1**
4560 **8** *1* **Hadath (IRE)**[6] 6513 9-8-12 **53**...(b) FMBerry 3 50
(B G Powell) *hld up in last pair: rdn over 2f out: modest late prog* **16/1**
0015 **9** *2* **Trevian**[13] 6436 5-8-13 **54**.. SteveDrowne 5 46
(J M Bradley) *hld up wl in rr: hanging rt fr over 2f out and no real prog* **7/1**[3]
2044 **10** *3/4* **Lobengula (IRE)**[13] 6436 4-8-8 **54**............................... AndrewElliott(5) 8 45
(I W McInnes) *led at decent pce: hung lft fr 2f out: hdd & wknd over 1f out* **9/2**[1]
0541 **11** *3/4* **State Dilemma (IRE)**[6] 6513 5-9-6 **61** 6ex....................(v) DaneO'Neill 13 50
(D Shaw) *chsd ldrs: hanging bdly bnd over 3f out: wknd wl over 1f out* **13/2**[2]
-300 **12** *2 1/2* **Dona Vitoria**[23] 6293 3-8-12 **55**... LPKeniry 14 38
(S Kirk) *t.k.h: hld up towards rr: brief effrt over 2f out: wknd over 1f out* **33/1**
2060 **13** *2 1/2* **Mine The Balance (IRE)**[13] 6439 3-8-11 **54**........................ BrettDoyle 1 31
(J R Best) *t.k.h: prom tl wknd rapidly 2f out* **10/1**
1m 38.55s (-2.25) **Going Correction** -0.275s/f (Stan)
WFA 3 from 4yo+ 2lb **13** Ran SP% **126.2**
Speed ratings (Par 101):100,95,94,93,93 92,92,91,89,88 87,85,82
CSF £52.04 CT £687.87 TOTE £6.30: £1.80, £3.60, £3.50; EX 80.70.
Owner Matthew Green **Bred** A I Appleton **Trained** Sheriff Hutton, N Yorks

FOCUS
A modest handicap but an impressive winner who can rate higher. The time was modest compared with the preceding nursery.
Kathleen Kennet Official explanation: jockey said mare hung badly left in straight
State Dilemma(IRE) Official explanation: jockey said gelding hung right

6578 MICHAEL O'LEARY MEDIAN AUCTION MAIDEN STKS 1m 4f (P)
5:20 (5:20) (Class 6) 3-4-Y-O **£2,388** (£705; £352) **Stalls** Centre

Form RPR
1 **Night Cruise (IRE)** 3-9-3 .... JimCrowley 7 73+
(J A Osborne) *trckd ldng pair and a gng wl: led over 2f out: stretched clr over 1f out: r.o wl* **8/1**
634 **2** *3 1/2* **Depraux (IRE)**[22] 6314 3-9-3 64.. TonyCulhane 4 67
(W J Haggas) *hld up in 5th: effrt over 2f out: drvn to chse wnr ent fnl f: no imp* **4/6**[1]
0 **3** *1 1/2* **Poseidon's Secret (IRE)**[219] 1088 3-8-12 .... EmmettStack(5) 2 65
(Pat Eddery) *rn in snatches and looked hrd ride: in tch: effrt u.p to chse wnr over 1f out tl ent fnl f: one pce* **4/1**[2]
-500 **4** *6* **Final Bid (IRE)**[37] 6060 3-9-3 59..(b) BrettDoyle 6 55
(M G Quinlan) *rousted along to ld then t.k.h: hdd over 2f out: wknd over 1f out* **7/1**[3]
5000 **5** *2 1/2* **War Feather**[15] 6410 4-9-6 45................................. EdwardCreighton(3) 3 51
(T D McCarthy) *dwlt: hld up in last pair: rdn 3f out: no prog and sn btn* **20/1**
6 *nk* **Coolaw (IRE)**[208] 1317 3-8-12 ....(b[1]) OscarUrbina 5 46
(G G Margarson) *dwlt: hld up in last: rdn 3f out: no prog and sn btn* **25/1**
0000 **7** *5* **Cativo Cavallino**[67] 5426 3-9-3 47.. IanMongan 1 43
(Jamie Poulton) *t.k.h: pressed ldr to over 2f out: wknd rapidly: eased nr fin* **16/1**
2m 33.4s (-3.50) **Going Correction** -0.275s/f (Stan)
WFA 3 from 4yo 6lb **7** Ran SP% **118.1**
Speed ratings (Par 101):100,97,96,92,91 90,87
CSF £14.53 TOTE £7.60: £3.10, £1.10; EX 13.00.
Owner Mr & Mrs G Middlebrook **Bred** G And Mrs Middlebrook **Trained** Upper Lambourn, Berks

FOCUS
A moderate and uncompetitive maiden but a bright start from the debutant winner. The form makes sense through the second and third.

6579 CELTIC CONTRACTORS LTD H'CAP 6f (P)
5:50 (5:51) (Class 5) (0-75,74) 3-Y-O+ **£4,533** (£1,348; £674; £336) **Stalls** High

Form RPR
4215 **1** **Linda Green**[13] 6437 5-8-8 **69**.................................. EdwardCreighton(3) 9 78
(M R Channon) *chsd ldrs: rdn 1/2-way: clsd over 1f out: styd on to ld last 75yds* **12/1**
0300 **2** *nk* **Jayanjay**[9] 6485 7-8-9 **67**.. RichardThomas 11 75
(P Mitchell) *prom: trckd ldr over 2f out: effrt to ld ent fnl f: hdd and nt qckn last 75yds* **8/1**
6461 **3** *nk* **Mandarin Spirit (IRE)**[13] 6437 6-8-13 **71**......................(b) OscarUrbina 6 78
(G C H Chung) *hld up wl in rr: plenty to do and pushed along over 2f out: prog jst over 1f out: styd on to take 3rd nr fin* **5/1**[2]
1006 **4** *nk* **Sun Catcher (IRE)**[11] 6461 3-9-2 **74**.................................. DaneO'Neill 8 80
(R Hannon) *off the pce in midfield bef 1/2-way: drvn over 2f out: styd on wl fnl f: nrst fin* **9/1**
0132 **5** *nk* **Pamir (IRE)**[9] 6485 4-8-9 **67**...(b) JimCrowley 4 72
(P R Chamings) *fast away fr wd draw: led at str pce: 2l clr 2f out: hdd ent fnl f: fdd* **9/2**[1]
0030 **6** *1/2* **Duke Of Milan (IRE)**[13] 6437 3-8-9 **67**............................ AdamKirby 10 71
(G C Bravery) *dwlt: hld up in rr: prog on inner over 2f out: clsd over 1f out: fnd little fnl f* **20/1**
2005 **7** *1/2* **Morse (IRE)**[6] 6527 5-8-13 **74**................................ RichardKingscote(3) 5 76
(J A Osborne) *pressed ldr to over 2f out: sn lost pl u.p: kpt on fnl f* **8/1**
0052 **8** *nk* **Tanforan**[13] 6437 4-8-7 **72**..(b) SophieDoyle(7) 7 73
(Ms J S Doyle) *dwlt: wl in rr: off the pce 1/2-way and wd in st: no prog tl styd on fnl f* **8/1**
1122 **9** *shd* **Ten Shun**[27] 6212 3-9-2 **74**.. FMBerry 1 75
(P D Evans) *off the pce in midfield over 3f out: nt handle bnd sn after: struggling over 2f out: kpt on fnl f* **11/2**[3]
0604 **10** *1* **Summer Recluse (USA)**[13] 6437 7-8-9 **67**...................(t) SteveDrowne 3 65
(J M Bradley) *nvr on terms w ldrs: struggling in rr 2f out* **11/1**
1003 **11** *2* **Inch By Inch**[10] 6478 7-8-12 **73**...(b) AmirQuinn(3) 2 65
(P J Makin) *chsd ldrs: drvn 1/2-way: wknd over 1f out* **12/1**
0000 **12** *4* **Sundance (IRE)**[30] 6174 4-8-4 **65**................................ JamesDoyle(3) 12 45
(H J Collingridge) *nvr on terms: bhd fnl 2f* **33/1**
1m 12.14s (-1.56) **Going Correction** -0.275s/f (Stan) **12** Ran SP% **125.0**
Speed ratings (Par 103):99,98,98,97,97 96,96,95,95,94 91,86
CSF £110.47 CT £566.15 TOTE £14.50: £2.40, £2.10, £2.40; EX 76.60.
Owner Stephen Roots **Bred** Colin Tinkler **Trained** West Ilsley, Berks

FOCUS
A modest sprint but a good finish. The form looks solid and should prove reliable, with a slight personal best from the winner.

6580 AJ MORRISROE & SONS LTD H'CAP 7f (P)
6:20 (6:21) (Class 4) (0-85,84) 3-Y-O+ **£5,505** (£1,637; £818; £408) **Stalls** High

Form RPR
0064 **1** **Bomber Command (USA)**[11] 6461 3-8-4 **79**................ PatrickHills(7) 8 91+
(J W Hills) *trckd ldng pair: effrt to ld 2f out: hrd pressed 1f out: pushed out and a holding on* **9/2**[2]
0122 **2** *3/4* **Resplendent Nova**[11] 6461 4-8-10 **80**............................ DeanCorby(3) 7 90
(P Howling) *fast away: led for 1f: w ldr: led over 3f out to 2f out: pressed wnr but a jst hld fnl f* **5/2**[1]
0325 **3** *1 1/4* **Gifted Gamble**[16] 6397 4-9-1 **82**.......................................(b) DaneO'Neill 6 89
(K A Ryan) *trckd ldrs: rdn over 2f out: prog and cl up over 1f out: kpt on same pce* **6/1**[3]
0530 **4** *nk* **Buy On The Red**[11] 6461 5-8-12 **79**... FMBerry 14 85
(W R Muir) *trckd ldng pair: effrt to chal and n.m.r 2f out: kpt on same pce after* **11/1**
2660 **5** *2* **Samuel Charles**[77] 5149 8-9-0 **81**...................................... AdamKirby 13 82
(C R Dore) *dwlt: sn in tch in midfield: gng wl enough over 2f out: rdn and nt qckn wl over 1f out: no imp after* **20/1**
4236 **6** *1 1/4* **Outer Hebrides**[16] 6397 5-8-12 **82**..............................(vt) AmirQuinn(3) 11 80
(J R Boyle) *hld up towards rr: drvn over 2f out: one pce and no imp on ldrs* **10/1**
100 **7** *nk* **Bee Stinger**[16] 6397 4-8-11 **78**... LeeEnstone 3 75+
(I A Wood) *hld up wl in rr: plenty to do 3f out: modest late prog: n.d* **10/1**
1636 **8** *3/4* **Ivory Lace**[50] 5777 5-8-9 **79**.. JamesDoyle(3) 9 74
(S Woodman) *off the pce in midfield: hrd rdn over 2f out: brief effrt on inner wl over 1f out: sn btn* **20/1**
4014 **9** *1/2* **Middleton Grey**[42] 5937 8-8-10 **77**..........................(b) FergusSweeney 10 71
(A G Newcombe) *dwlt: wl in rr and off the pce: kpt on fr over 1f out: no ch* **16/1**
0500 **10** *1 1/4* **Deeper In Debt**[16] 6397 8-8-9 **76**.. AlanDaly 5 66
(J Akehurst) *wl in rr: last and struggling 3f out: no ch after* **33/1**
B410 **11** *2* **Surwaki (USA)**[70] 5337 4-8-12 **79**...................................... BrettDoyle 2 64
(R M H Cowell) *nvr beyond midfield: u.p and struggling wl over 2f out: wknd* **25/1**
6366 **12** *hd* **Finsbury**[46] 5877 3-8-10 **78** ow1.. TonyCulhane 4 63
(Miss J Feilden) *squeezed out s: a wl in rr: no ch fnl 2f* **12/1**
5000 **13** *nk* **Purus (IRE)**[16] 6397 4-8-9 **76**.. SteveDrowne 12 60
(P Mitchell) *led after 1f to over 3f out: wknd rapidly over 2f out* **12/1**
1006 **14** *1/2* **Phluke**[27] 6221 5-9-3 **84**... StephenCarson 1 66
(R F Johnson Houghton) *fast away: w ldrs to 1/2-way: wknd rapidly over 2f out* **16/1**
1m 23.91s (-2.89) **Going Correction** -0.275s/f (Stan)
WFA 3 from 4yo+ 1lb **14** Ran SP% **131.0**
Speed ratings (Par 105):105,104,102,102,100 98,98,97,96,95 93,92,92,92
CSF £16.79 CT £74.62 TOTE £5.60: £2.40, £1.70, £2.60; EX 16.90 Place 6 £51.72, Place 5 £42.54.
Owner G Woodward **Bred** J B Feins **Trained** Upper Lambourn, Berks

FOCUS
A fair handicap run at a good gallop and the progressive winner broke the course record. The form appears sound with several in-form sorts close up.
T/Plt: £86.20 to a £1 stake. Pool: £54,129.00. 458.15 winning tickets. T/Qpdt: £29.90 to a £1 stake. Pool: £4,431.40. 109.60 winning tickets. JN

6568 WOLVERHAMPTON (A.W) (L-H)

Friday, November 24

OFFICIAL GOING: Standard

Wind: Moderate, behind

6581 WBX.COM LAUNCHING 25TH NOVEMBER MEDIAN AUCTION MAIDEN STKS — 1m 141y(P)

1:10 (1:10) (Class 6) 2-Y-O — £2,730 (£806; £403) Stalls Low

Form				RPR
233	1		**Aureate**[48] 5814 2-9-0 78 ... GregFairley(3) 4 (M Johnston) *mde all: stretched out wl fnl f: comf* 1/2[1]	79+
3236	2	1 ¼	**Snow Dancer (IRE)**[10] 6481 2-8-12 65 ... FrancisNorton 8 (A Berry) *t.k.h: in tch: rdn to chse wnr wl over 1f out: edgd rt fnl f: no imp on wnr* 33/1	71+
	3	5	**Distant Sun (USA)** 2-9-3 ... JimmyFortune 3 (R Charlton) *trckd ldrs: chsd wnr 3f out to wl over 1f out: wknd fnl f* 25/1	65
03	4	1	**Good Effect (USA)**[32] 6143 2-9-3 ... DaneO'Neill 5 (A P Jarvis) *mid-div: rdn sn after 1/2-way: styd on one pce ins fnl 2f* 11/1[3]	63
2652	5	3 ½	**Beech Games**[24] 6285 2-9-3 76 ... ChrisCatlin 7 (E J O'Neill) *racd wd: bhd tl hdwy 4f out: hung lftg and wknd over 1f out* 4/1[2]	55
0	6	1	**Don't Desert Me (IRE)**[6] 6523 2-9-0 ... RichardKingscote(3) 6 (R Charlton) *chsd wnr to 3f out: rdn and wknd 2f out* 50/1	53
0460	7	5	**Pret A Porter (UAE)**[52] 5748 2-8-12 65 ... JohnEgan 1 (P D Evans) *s.i.s: a bhd* 16/1	37
	8	½	**Mr Crystal (FR)** 2-9-3 ... DeanMcKeown 9 (Micky Hammond) *slowly away: a bhd* 100/1	41
	9	nk	**Port Macquairie (IRE)** 2-9-3 ... NelsonDeSouza 10 (R M Beckett) *slowly away: sme hdwy over 6f out: wknd over 2f out* 50/1	40
000	10	59	**Time Dancer (IRE)**[7] 6504 2-9-3 ... PaulQuinn 2 (A Berry) *bhd: lost tch 1/2-way: t.o* 100/1	—

1m 49.46s (-2.30) **Going Correction** -0.20s/f (Stan) — **10** Ran SP% **113.6**

Speed ratings (Par 94):102,100,96,95,92 91,87,86,86,33

CSF £31.53 TOTE £1.20: £1.02, £9.40, £6.40; EX 20.20 Trifecta £178.80 Part won. Pool: £251.88 - 0.68 winning tickets..

Owner Sheikh Mohammed **Bred** Darley **Trained** Middleham Moor, N Yorks

FOCUS

A slight step up in form from the winner, and an improved effort from the runner-up too. Sound form, the pair clear.

NOTEBOOK

Aureate, in the frame in three Class 4 turf maidens, set a fair standard from an official rating of 78 but ran up to that form on this sand debut. Able to dictate the pace, he was sent about his work at the head of the straight and was never going to be caught, although the runner-up was closing the gap at the end. A colt with plenty of scope, he will be suited by middle-distances next year and has already shown that he can handle both fast and soft ground on turf. (op 8-13 tchd 4-6)

Snow Dancer(IRE) was found wanting on her recent Polytrack debut over seven furlongs but this longer trip brought about an improved showing and she was making ground on the winner at the line. A small event should come her way but this effort will not have helped her handicap mark. (op 25-1)

Distant Sun(USA) showed signs of greenness but definitely has ability. Out of a useful sprinter in the United States, he might be happier over a shorter trip. (op 16-1)

Good Effect(USA) was never a serious factor in fourth but can now run in handicaps and is the sort to do better in that sphere. (op 8-1 tchd 12-1)

Beech Games, just denied in a course-and-distance nursery last time, was a shade disappointing. He made headway from the rear towards the end of the back straight but could make no further inroads once in line for home, not appearing to face the kick-back. (op 7-2 tchd 10-3)

Don't Desert Me(IRE), a stablemate of the third, showed more than well beaten after a slow start on his debut here. (op 33-1)

6582 WBX.COM LAUNCHING 25TH NOVEMBER NURSERY — 7f 32y(P)

1:45 (1:45) (Class 5) (0-75,73) 2-Y-O — £3,886 (£1,156; £577; £288) Stalls High

Form				RPR
0032	1		**Alittlebitleft (IRE)**[7] 6506 2-9-2 68 ... (b[1]) JimmyFortune 4 (R Hannon) *led after 1f: rdn clr oer 1f out: r.o strly: easily* 2/1[1]	80
1	2	5	**Situla (IRE)**[22] 6309 2-9-6 72 ... DaneO'Neill 7 (H J L Dunlop) *a front rnk: sn trckd wnr: rdn and nt pce of wnr fr over 1f out but kpt on ins fnl f* 7/2[2]	72
0013	3	1 ¾	**Madam Gaffer**[15] 6416 2-9-1 67 ... EddieAhern 10 (B J Meehan) *towards rr: rdn 1/2-way: hdwy over 2f out: hung lft over 1f out but r.o ins fnl f* 9/2[3]	62
630	4	¾	**Give Evidence**[16] 6393 2-9-4 70 ... ChrisCatlin 3 (A P Jarvis) *iin tch tl outpcd 4f out: styd on fr over 1f out but nvr nr to chal* 9/1	63
3344	5	shd	**Bert's Memory**[24] 6270 2-8-13 65 ... PatCosgrave 1 (K A Ryan) *led for 1f: rdn over 2f out: sn wknd* 16/1	58
644	6	2 ½	**Raquel White**[26] 6242 2-9-4 70 ... JohnEgan 5 (P D Evans) *sltl hmpd after 1f: rdn over 2f out: wknd wl over 1f out* 15/2	57
0005	7	6	**Blakeshall Rose**[8] 6500 2-7-13 54 oh5 ow4 ... PatrickMathers(3) 9 (A J Chamberlain) *slowly away: t.k.h: a bhd* 14/1	26
4440	8	3 ½	**Reflective Glory (IRE)**[14] 6422 2-7-7 50 ... NataliaGemelova(5) 8 (J J Quinn) *a bhd* 33/1	13
1305	9	2	**Hephaestus**[17] 6388 2-9-7 73 ... DeanMcKeown 6 (A J Chamberlain) *racd wd: in cl tch tl rdn and wknd qckly over 2f out* 20/1	31

1m 29.54s (-0.86) **Going Correction** -0.20s/f (Stan) — **9** Ran SP% **115.8**

Speed ratings (Par 96):96,90,88,87,87 84,77,73,71

CSF £8.90 CT £27.65 TOTE £2.50: £1.10, £1.80, £1.30; EX 11.10 Trifecta £19.20 Pool: £297.07 - 10.97 winning tickets..

Owner Team Havana **Bred** T Hyde **Trained** East Everleigh, Wilts

FOCUS

A reasonable race of its type, run at a good clip. The winner has improved of late and won this emphatically. The level looks solid enough in behind.

NOTEBOOK

Alittlebitleft(IRE) ◆, who has been running well in defeat, got off the mark with a clear-cut victory which would have been even more emphatic had Fortune not eased the colt close home with the race in the bag. The first-time blinkers obviously had a positive effect but he can win again, with a step back up in trip unlikely to bother him. (op 9-4)

Situla(IRE), her trainer's first winner when making all in a maiden over course and distance three weeks ago, ran a solid race on this nursery debut, but had enjoyed an easy lead last time and was unable to get to the front here from a less favourable draw. She never stopped trying and finished clear of the others. (tchd 10-3)

Madam Gaffer has now run two creditable races in this grade here since landing a seller. (op 7-1)

Give Evidence, who has shown ability at the other two Polytrack venues, ran respectably on this handicap debut and first start here. (tchd 10-1)

Bert's Memory has had her limitations exposed in a succession of turf events since she made her debut on this surface in June. She ran creditably back on sand but was a spent force in the straight. (op 11-1)

6583 WBX.COM WORLD BET EXCHANGE H'CAP — 5f 216y(P)

2:20 (2:21) (Class 4) (0-85,85) 3-Y-O+ — £5,505 (£1,637; £818; £408) Stalls Low

Form				RPR
0303	1		**First Order**[26] 6243 5-9-2 85 ... (v) TomEaves 10 (I Semple) *trckd ldrs: rdn to ld 1f out: drvn out* 7/1	93
0011	2	½	**Prince Tum Tum (USA)**[9] 6489 6-9-2 85 7ex ... DeanMcKeown 5 (D Shaw) *in rr tl gd hdwy wl over 1f out: r.o to go 2nd ins fnl f* 8/1	92+
6132	3	¾	**Premier Fantasy**[6] 6527 4-8-8 77 ... JohnEgan 11 (T J Pitt) *in rr: rdn and hdwy over 1f out: r.o strly fnl f: nvr nrr* 5/1[2]	81+
0021	4	nk	**Zarzu**[14] 6428 7-8-5 79 ... LiamJones(5) 12 (C R Dore) *a in tch: rdn over 1f out: kpt on one pce ins fnl f* 20/1	82
3013	5	hd	**Matuza (IRE)**[9] 6496 3-8-12 81 ... EddieAhern 4 (W R Muir) *t.k.h: in tch: hdwy 3f out: n.m.r on ins appr fnl f: no ex ins* 5/2[1]	84+
4156	6	nk	**Moorhouse Lad**[102] 4422 3-9-0 83 ... JimmyQuinn 2 (G Woodward) *led tl rdn, edgd lft and hdd 1f out: fdd ins fnl f* 25/1	85
6455	7	nk	**Kingscross**[8] 6499 8-8-0 76 ... LauraReynolds(7) 7 (M Blanshard) *bhd tl hdwy on ins over 1f out: styd on: nvr nrr* 16/1	77
2002	8	1 ¼	**Grimes Faith**[8] 6499 3-8-12 81 ow1 ... JimmyFortune 1 (R Hannon) *mid-div: hdwy on ins whn short of room over 2f out: nvr on terms after* 6/1[3]	78
3440	9	1 ¼	**Charlie Delta**[14] 6428 3-8-7 76 ... DanielTudhope 3 (D Carroll) *a towards rr: rdn and hung rt fr over 1f out* 14/1	69
5502	10	1 ¾	**Hammer Of The Gods (IRE)**[13] 6446 6-8-10 79 ... (bt) HayleyTurner 6 (P S McEntee) *t.k.h: trckd ldr tl wknd 2f out* 14/1	67
2260	11	nk	**After The Show**[39] 6009 5-8-7 76 ... ChrisCatlin 8 (Rae Guest) *t.k.h: mid-div tl wknd over 1f out* 25/1	63
1100	12	8	**Sands Crooner (IRE)**[197] 1604 3-8-6 78 ... (v) PatrickMathers(3) 9 (D Shaw) *a bhd: eased fnl f* 66/1	41

1m 14.51s (-1.30) **Going Correction** -0.20s/f (Stan) — **12** Ran SP% **116.3**

Speed ratings (Par 105):100,99,98,97,97 97,96,95,93,91 90,80

CSF £58.01 CT £310.60 TOTE £8.50: £3.30, £2.70, £1.90; EX 84.70 Trifecta £319.80 Part won. Pool: £450.51 - 0.10 winning tickets..

Owner Gordon McDowall **Bred** Mrs Hazel Conroy **Trained** Carluke, S Lanarks

FOCUS

A well-contested handicap in which the pace was not strong, producing something of a blanket finish. A fair handicap, but the bare form is only ordinary.

Sands Crooner(IRE) Official explanation: jockey said colt lost its action

6584 WBX.COM LAUNCHING 25TH NOVEMBER (S) STKS — 1m 4f 50y(P)

2:50 (2:50) (Class 6) 3-Y-O+ — £2,388 (£705; £352) Stalls Low

Form				RPR
1030	1		**Cool Isle**[4] 6540 3-9-0 45 ... (b) JimmyQuinn 8 (P Howling) *in tch: rdn over 3f out: rdn to ld 1f out: drew clr ins fnl f* 12/1	56
3600	2	3 ½	**Khanjar (USA)**[71] 5311 6-9-6 63 ... PatCosgrave 4 (K R Burke) *led after 3f: rdn and hdd 1f out: nt pce of wnr* 9/4[1]	50
0	3	½	**Willy (SWE)**[11] 5897 4-8-13 68 ... (t) WilliamBuick(7) 12 (R A Kvisla) *stdd wl in rr tl rapid hdwy 6f out: pressed ldr over 3f out tl rdn and no ex fnl f* 10/1[3]	50
606	4	1 ¾	**Alasil (USA)**[8] 6503 6-9-6 68 ... LiamJones(5) 2 (R J Price) *mid-div: styd on fr over 1f out: nvr nrr* 9/4[1]	52
6003	5	¾	**Dancing Flame**[6] 6524 3-8-9 50 ... DaleGibson 5 (E J Alston) *in rr tl hdwy 4f out: rdn over 2f out to chse ldrs: wknd fnl f* 7/1[2]	41
4060	6	3	**Ulshaw**[47] 5846 9-8-13 40 ... BarrySavage(7) 3 (J M Bradley) *in rr: rdn 4f out: one pce fnl 2f* 20/1	41
0605	7	2	**Pleasing Gift**[21] 6327 3-8-9 52 ... JohnEgan 7 (J M P Eustace) *in tch: rdn 3f out: wknd appr fnl f* 11/1	33
	8	nk	**World Supremacy (IRE)**[30] 6183 3-9-0 ... ChrisCatlin 9 (Gerard O'Leary, Ire) *bhd and nvr on terms* 16/1	37
000	9	½	**Oman Gulf (USA)**[45] 5905 5-9-6 48 ... DeanMcKeown 11 (Micky Hammond) *in rr whn swtchd to outside 4f out: wknd 3f out* 20/1	36
0000	10	11	**Saxon Star (IRE)**[3] 6553 3-9-0 35 ... FrancisNorton 1 (P Howling) *led for 3f: wknd over 3f out* 40/1	19
0650	11	6	**Keltic Rainbow (IRE)**[206] 1392 5-9-1 35 ... (v) DavidKinsella 6 (D Haydn Jones) *mid-div: rdn and wknd over 3f out* 33/1	4
0000	12	75	**Tay Bridge (IRE)**[22] 6306 3-8-11 30 ... (b) DominicFox(3) 10 (G F Bridgwater) *trckd ldrs: rdn over 5f out: wknd rapidly: t.o* 80/1	—

2m 40.56s (-1.86) **Going Correction** -0.20s/f (Stan)

WFA 3 from 4yo+ 6lb — **12** Ran SP% **121.2**

Speed ratings (Par 101):98,95,95,94,93 91,90,90,89,82 78,28

CSF £38.19 TOTE £12.20: £2.60, £1.20, £3.30; EX 35.50 Trifecta £113.50 Pool: £215.83 - 1.35 winning tickets..There was no bid for the winner. Khanjar was claimed by J Pearce for £6,000

Owner Rory Murphy **Bred** The C H F Partnership **Trained** Newmarket, Suffolk

FOCUS

A weakish seller with the joint-favourites both below form. A slight personal best from the exposed winner but the form is not too solid.

6585 WBXTRIPLECROWN.COM H'CAP — 5f 20y(P)

3:25 (3:26) (Class 5) (0-70,69) 3-Y-O+ — £3,238 (£963; £481; £240) Stalls Low

Form				RPR
000	1		**Fizzlephut (IRE)**[3] 6555 4-8-13 64 ... PaulFitzsimons 10 (Miss J R Tooth) *chsd ldr: led over 1f out: rdn clr fnl f* 16/1	77
0044	2	2	**Bonne De Fleur**[13] 6452 5-8-11 67 ... (b) MarkLawson(5) 6 (B Smart) *chsd ldrs: rdn 1/2-way: styd on to go 2nd ins fnl f* 7/2[1]	73
4355	3	1	**Gwilym (GER)**[9] 6485 3-9-2 67 ... RobertHavlin 7 (D Haydn Jones) *mid-div: rdn 1/2-way: hdwy over 1f out: r.o: nvr nrr* 17/2[3]	69
0300	4	shd	**Harrison's Flyer (IRE)**[3] 6555 5-8-11 65 ... (b) GregFairley(3) 5 (J M Bradley) *mid-div: hdwy on ins over 1f out: styd on wl fnl f* 11/1	67
3140	5	nk	**City For Conquest (IRE)**[7] 6508 3-9-3 68 ... (b) JohnEgan 2 (T J Pitt) *wnt rt s: towards rr: hdwy and swtchd rt 1f out: r.o: nvr nrr* 9/1	69
3006	6	¾	**Catspraddle (USA)**[7] 6508 3-9-1 66 ... JimmyFortune 4 (R Hannon) *bhd tl rdn and hdwy over 1f out: nvr nrr* 15/2[2]	64
1604	7	½	**Taboor (IRE)**[9] 6485 8-9-4 69 ... ChrisCatlin 12 (R M H Cowell) *bhd: hdwy and swtchd lft over 1f out: nvr nrr* 14/1	65
0052	8	hd	**Anfield Dream**[9] 6496 4-9-4 69 ... EddieAhern 9 (J R Jenkins) *s.i.s: c wd into st: mde sme late hdwy* 7/2[1]	64
0000	9	¾	**Maktavish**[3] 6555 7-9-4 69 ... (b) PatCosgrave 1 (R Brotherton) *led tl rdn and hdd over 1f out: wknd ins fnl f* 20/1	62
2600	10	nk	**Lyndalee (IRE)**[13] 6452 3-9-4 69 ... (p) JimmyQuinn 13 (T Hogan, Ire) *towards rr tl hdwy on outside 1/2-way: wknd over 1f out* 16/1	61

4000 **11** ¾ **Misaro (GER)**[60] 5575 5-8-10 **68**....................(b) TolleyDean(7) 8 57
(R A Harris) *mid-div: rdn over 3f out: wknd over 1f out* **12/1**

1340 **12** ½ **Garlogs**[13] 6452 3-8-11 **62**.................... TomEaves 11 49
(A Bailey) *chsd ldrs: rdn 1/2-way: wknd qckly ent fnl f* **40/1**

61.68 secs (-1.14) **Going Correction** -0.20s/f (Stan) **12** Ran SP% **118.4**
Speed ratings (Par 103):101,97,96,96,95 94,93,93,92,91 90,89
CSF £71.25 CT £525.59 TOTE £24.10: £6.70, £1.70, £2.40; EX 167.40 Trifecta £386.24 Part won. Pool: £544.03 - 0.34 winning tickets..
Owner Warwick Racing Partnership **Bred** Tally-Ho Stud **Trained** Lowsonford, Warwickshire

FOCUS
Not many came into this run-of-the-mill handicap in the best of form. The winner was back to his form of the summer in this ordinary event, rated through the second.
Fizzlephut(IRE) Official explanation: trainer had no explanation for the apparent improvement in form
Anfield Dream Official explanation: jockey said gelding suffered interference shortly after start

6586 WBX.COM LAUNCHING 25TH NOVEMBER HBLB CONDITIONS STKS 7f 32y(P)
4:00 (4:00) (Class 3) 2-Y-O
£6,855 (£2,052; £1,026; £513; £256; £128) **Stalls** High

Form RPR
0031 **1** **Fares (IRE)**[6] 6525 2-9-0 66....................(b) EddieAhern 3 79
(C E Brittain) *chsd ldr: rdn to ld over 1f out: edgd lft: styd on* **11/4**[2]

0152 **2** *nk* **Victor Trumper**[13] 6443 2-9-3 78.................... MichaelHills 2 81
(P W Chapple-Hyam) *in tch: rdn and edgd lft: styd on to go 2nd wl ins fnl f* **11/4**[2]

6011 **3** 1½ **Salient**[15] 6412 2-9-3 82.................... PaulDoe 1 78+
(J Akehurst) *in tch: hdwy on ins over 1f out: swtchd rt and ev ch ins fnl f: no ex and short of room cl home* **5/6**[1]

0005 **4** 2 **Slipasearcher (IRE)**[1] 6569 2-8-9 72....................(b) JohnEgan 5 65
(P D Evans) *led tl rdn and hdd over 1f out: fdd ins fnl f* **14/1**[3]

0 **5** 23 **El Manx Senorita**[16] 6402 2-8-9 .... RobbieFitzpatrick 4 —
(C Smith) *a struggling in rr* **100/1**

0 **6** 1¼ **Cragg Lass (IRE)**[16] 6402 2-8-9 .... PaulQuinn 6 —
(A Berry) *slowly away: sn in tch on outside: wknd 1/2-way* **200/1**

1m 29.43s (-0.97) **Going Correction** -0.20s/f (Stan) **6** Ran SP% **116.0**
Speed ratings (Par 100):97,96,94,92,66 64
CSF £11.26 TOTE £3.10: £1.60, £2.00; EX 16.10.
Owner Mohammed Rashid **Bred** Darley **Trained** Newmarket, Suffolk

FOCUS
A decent little conditions race, but not an easy event to rate. The winner is in great heart though and there could be more to come.

NOTEBOOK
Fares(IRE) has been an improved performer since the blinkers were fitted and was able to supplement his recent win in a course-and-distance nursery. Chasing the clear leader before going to the front with over a furlong to run, he shifted to his left, something he has done in the past, before holding the late challenge of the runner-up. (op 7-2 tchd 4-1)
Victor Trumper lacked a telling change of pace until finding his stride inside the last, but the post came too soon. He has scope to progress and will be suited by a return to a mile. (op 10-3 tchd 7-2)
Salient was seeking a hat-trick after two wins over this trip at Lingfield, most recently a nursery off 79. He appeared to have every chance but could not quicken up at the business end and was held when running out of racing room close home. The step up to a mile should suit him. Official explanation: jockey said colt hung left final stages (tchd Evens)
Slipasearcher(IRE), who had run here the day before, was responsible for the healthy pace and was several lengths clear at one stage, but could only plug on at the same pace when collared. (op 9-1)

6587 WBX.COM LAUNCHING 25TH NOVEMBER MAIDEN STKS (DIV I) 1m 1f 103y(P)
4:30 (4:31) (Class 5) 3-Y-O **£2,590** (£770; £385; £192) **Stalls** Low

Form RPR
0560 **1** **La Estrella (USA)**[19] 6351 3-9-3 80.................... JimmyFortune 7 72
(J G Given) *a in tch: wnt 2nd over 2f out: rdn to ld jst ins fnl f: kpt on* **11/4**[1]

3522 **2** 1¾ **Chasing A Dream**[13] 6450 3-8-12 65.................... MichaelHills 11 64
(B W Hills) *sn chsd ldr: led over 3f out: rdn and hdd jst ins fnl f: kpt on one pce* **11/4**[1]

43 **3** 1½ **Soul Blazer (USA)**[14] 6429 3-9-3 .... FrancisNorton 10 66
(A M Balding) *led after 1f: hdd over 3f out: clr 3rd whn swtchd rt ins fnl f: one pce* **7/2**[2]

5 **4** 2½ **Trailmix (FR)**[37] 6052 3-9-3 .... AntonyProcter 1 61
(D R C Elsworth) *towards rr: styd on ins fnl 2f: nvr nrr* **5/1**[3]

0 **5** *shd* **Ratzia (IRE)**[30] 6177 3-8-12 .... JimmyQuinn 6 56
(C E Brittain) *slowly away: hld up: rdn over 3f out: styd on ins fnl 2f: nvr nr to chal* **25/1**

0 **6** 11 **Apache Fort**[11] 6459 3-9-3 .... PaulDoe 8 40
(T Keddy) *slowly away: a bhd* **33/1**

5 **7** 10 **Spoilsport**[24] 6286 3-8-12 58.................... JohnEgan 5 16
(P D Evans) *prom: rdn over 3f out: sn wknd* **14/1**

0004 **8** 1 **Grand Assault**[16] 6403 3-9-3 54.................... HayleyTurner 3 19
(P S McEntee) *led for 1f: dropping to rr whn rdn 4f out* **25/1**

06 **9** 3½ **Miswadah (IRE)**[149] 2985 3-8-12 .... CatherineGannon 4 7
(Kevin F O'Donnell, Ire) *t.k.h: trckd ldrs tl rdn and wknd qckly wl over 2f out* **20/1**

0 **10** 18 **Keagles (ITY)**[16] 6403 3-8-12 .... RobertHavlin 9 —
(J E Long) *s.i.s: a in rr* **66/1**

2m 0.16s (-2.46) **Going Correction** -0.20s/f (Stan) **10** Ran SP% **115.8**
Speed ratings (Par 102):102,100,99,96,96 87,78,77,74,58
CSF £9.57 TOTE £4.40: £1.30, £1.30, £1.60; EX 12.50 Trifecta £37.70 Pool: £499.40 - 9.39 winning tickets..
Owner The G-Guck Group **Bred** Five Horses Ltd And Theatrical Syndicate **Trained** Willoughton, Lincs

FOCUS
Ordinary form but better than some recent maidens. The winner did not need to improve.
Ratzia(IRE) Official explanation: jockey said filly was slow into stride

6588 WBX.COM LAUNCHING 25TH NOVEMBER MAIDEN STKS (DIV II) 1m 1f 103y(P)
5:00 (5:00) (Class 5) 3-Y-O **£2,590** (£770; £385; £192) **Stalls** Low

Form RPR
03- **1** **Where's Broughton**[393] 6120 3-8-5 .... DebraEngland(7) 2 75+
(W J Musson) *hld up in tch: gd hdwy on outside over 2f out: led ins fnl f: r.o wl* **13/2**

-540 **2** 1¼ **Italian Romance**[176] 2177 3-9-3 77.................... MichaelHills 7 75
(J W Unett) *trckd ldrs: led 4f out: rdn and hdd ins fnl f: no ex* **11/4**[2]

4346 **3** 8 **Izadore (IRE)**[81] 5056 3-8-12 73.................... JimmyFortune 1 55
(E A L Dunlop) *trckd ldrs: disp ld 4f out: rdn over 2f out: wknd appr fnl f* **9/4**[1]

00 **4** 3 **Captain Oats (IRE)**[14] 6429 3-9-0 60.................... GregFairley(3) 8 54
(Mrs P Ford) *in tch: hdwy wl over 2f out: one pce fr over 1f out* **33/1**

3 **5** 2 **Chart Oak**[270] 531 3-9-3 .... FrancisNorton 3 50
(P Howling) *in tch: rdn over 2f out: wknd over 1f out* **8/1**

5056 **6** 3 **Fondness**[144] 3152 3-8-12 66.................... EddieAhern 5 40
(D Carroll) *in rr and nvr on terms* **5/1**[3]

000- **7** 4 **Spinning Gold**[479] 4020 3-8-12 52.................... JimmyQuinn 4 32
(Miss Gay Kelleway) *in tch: rdn 4f out: sn wknd* **14/1**

00 **8** 5 **Gundula (IRE)**[60] 5566 3-8-12 .... PatCosgrave 9 23
(D J S Ffrench Davis) *a bhd* **50/1**

9 13 **War Of The Roses (IRE)** 3-9-3 .... TomEaves 6 —
(R Brotherton) *led tl hdd 4f out: sn wknd* **25/1**

2m 0.24s (-2.38) **Going Correction** -0.20s/f (Stan) **9** Ran SP% **114.0**
Speed ratings (Par 102):102,100,93,91,89 86,83,78,67
CSF £24.03 TOTE £9.80: £2.30, £1.80, £1.50; EX 38.10 Trifecta £149.90 Pool: £356.90 - 1.69 winning tickets. Place 6 £53.13, Place 5 £35.87.
Owner Broughton Thermal Insulation **Bred** Branston Stud Ltd **Trained** Newmarket, Suffolk
■ Debra England's first winner.

FOCUS
A weakish maiden, run in a marginally slower time than division one. The winner should be capabale of better but the second and third are harshly handicapped.
T/Plt: £74.20 to a £1 stake. Pool: £45,463.85. 446.80 winning tickets. T/Qpdt: £40.50 to a £1 stake. Pool: £3,439.00. 62.80 winning tickets. JS

6589 - (Foreign Racing) - See Raceform Interactive

6575 KEMPTON (A.W) (R-H)
Saturday, November 25

OFFICIAL GOING: Standard
Wind: Fresh, half-behind

6590 PANORAMIC BAR & RESTAURANT H'CAP 1m 2f (P)
3:50 (3:54) (Class 6) (0-65,67) 3-Y-0+ **£2,388** (£705; £352) **Stalls** High

Form RPR
0412 **1** **Jordan's Light (USA)**[2] 6568 3-9-4 **67**....................(v) JohnEgan 9 74+
(T J Pitt) *t.k.h: a in tch: rdn 2f out: r.o u.p to ld last strides* **11/8**[1]

2045 **2** *hd* **Siena Star (IRE)**[10] 6484 8-8-12 **57**.................... MickyFenton 2 64
(Stef Liddiard) *prom: led wl over 1f out: rdn and hdd last strides* **8/1**[3]

0000 **3** *nk* **First Friend (IRE)**[17] 6396 5-9-3 **62**.................... GeorgeBaker 10 68
(P Mitchell) *led for 1f: styd prom: ev ch ent fnl f tl no ex cl home* **10/1**

2130 **4** 1½ **Border Edge**[16] 6408 8-8-13 **65**.................... JamesMillman(7) 8 68
(J J Bridger) *sn led: rdn and hdd wl over 1f out: one pce ins fnl f* **10/1**

0050 **5** 2½ **Just Fly**[16] 6419 6-8-13 **63**....................(v) KevinGhunowa(5) 7 61
(Dr J R J Naylor) *trckd ldrs: rdn 2f out: one pce fnl f* **14/1**

504 **6** *shd* **Pagano (IRE)**[22] 6327 3-9-0 **63**.................... AdamKirby 1 61+
(W R Swinburn) *settled in rr: rdn over 2f out: hdwy on ins over 1f out: nvr nrr* **20/1**

6150 **7** 1½ **Ballybeg (IRE)**[27] 6244 3-8-11 **65**....................(b) LiamJones(5) 11 60
(R J Price) *in tch on ins: rdn over 2f out: wknd appr fnl f* **10/1**

3065 **8** 1¼ **Magic Amigo**[90] 4848 5-9-5 **64**.................... PaulDoe 4 57
(J R Jenkins) *slowly away: bhd tl effrt on outside over 2f out: nvr on terms* **20/1**

0214 **9** *shd* **Port 'n Starboard**[9] 6503 5-9-6 **65**.................... TonyCulhane 3 58
(C A Cyzer) *racd wd: effrt over 1f out: nvr on terms* **6/1**[2]

06-0 **10** 2 **Beautiful Mover (USA)**[48] 5831 4-8-5 **55**.................... NataliaGemelova(5) 5 44
(J E Long) *t.k.h in mid-div: wknd over 1f out* **50/1**

1003 **11** *nk* **Ektishaaf**[20] 6360 4-8-12 **57**.................... NelsonDeSouza 6 45
(R McGlinchey, Ire) *a towards rr* **16/1**

0000 **12** *hd* **Danelor (IRE)**[11] 6476 8-9-1 **60**.................... DaneO'Neill 14 48
(D Shaw) *prom tl wknd over 2f out* **25/1**

0-03 **13** 4 **Blue Quiver (IRE)**[309] 163 6-8-12 **57**.................... PaulEddery 13 37
(C A Horgan) *t.k.h: hld up in rr: a bhd* **20/1**

0000 **14** 1¾ **Cool Sands (IRE)**[14] 6442 4-8-9 **57**....................(v) PatrickMathers(3) 12 34
(D Shaw) *a bhd* **33/1**

2m 7.30s (-1.70) **Going Correction** -0.10s/f (Stan)
WFA 3 from 4yo+ 4lb **14** Ran SP% **130.4**
Speed ratings (Par 101):102,101,101,100,98 98,97,96,96,94 94,94,90,89
CSF £12.48 CT £94.17 TOTE £2.10: £1.60, £3.40, £3.00; EX 18.30.
Owner B A Jordan **Bred** Lantern Hill Farm Llc **Trained** Bawtry, S Yorks
■ Stewards' Enquiry : Micky Fenton caution: used whip with excessive frequency

FOCUS
Although there was very little recent winning form on show, plenty of these looked in with a chance in a wide-open race. The race has been rated fairly negatively, through the third, but there should be more to come from the winner.
Pagano(IRE) Official explanation: jockey said gelding hung left

6591 FOLLOW YOUR BUSINESS MEETING WITH FLOODLIT RACING MEDIAN AUCTION MAIDEN STKS 7f (P)
4:20 (4:25) (Class 6) 2-Y-O **£2,266** (£674; £337; £168) **Stalls** High

Form RPR
4422 **1** **Benllech**[23] 6310 2-9-3 72.................... LPKeniry 7 75
(S Kirk) *s.i.s: sn chsd ldrs: swtchd lft to chal 1f out: r.o wl to ld last stride* **3/1**[2]

2553 **2** *shd* **Baltic Belle (IRE)**[43] 5933 2-8-12 78.................... JimmyFortune 5 70
(R Hannon) *prom: led over 1f out: rdn and hdd last stride* **7/4**[1]

3 2 **Trump Call (IRE)** 2-9-3 .... NelsonDeSouza 3 70
(R M Beckett) *a.p on outside: led briefly 2f out: rdn and nt qckn ins fnl f* **8/1**

0 **4** 1½ **Annia Faustina (IRE)**[89] 4895 2-8-12 .... SamHitchcott 4 61
(J L Spearing) *towards rr: hdwy over 2f out: hung lft but styd on ins fnl f* **33/1**

6 **5** 4 **Party Best**[172] 2315 2-8-12 .... HayleyTurner 13 50
(C E Brittain) *led tl hdd 2f out: wknd appr fnl f* **7/1**[3]

6 *shd* **Dancewiththestars (USA)** 2-8-12 .... OscarUrbina 9 50
(J R Fanshawe) *mid-div: outpcd 2f out: nvr on terms w ldrs after* **8/1**

7 1½ **Summerville Star (IRE)**[54] 5742 2-8-12 .... MickyFenton 6 46+
(Michael McElhone, Ire) *trckd ldr: wkng whn short of room over 2f out* **33/1**

00 **8** 1¾ **Pajada**[14] 6433 2-8-5 .... FrankiePickard(7) 12 42
(M D I Usher) *a towards rr on ins* **66/1**

9 *hd* **Rustic Gold** 2-9-3 .... BrettDoyle 11 46
(J R Best) *slowly away: a bhd* **16/1**

10 1 1/2 **Hit The Road (IRE)**[36] 6085 2-9-3 .... DaneO'Neill 2 42
(Michael McElhone, Ire) *t.k.h: in rr: outpcd over 2f out* **40/1**
11 14 **Itsawindup** 2-9-3 .... PaulDoe 1 6
(W J Knight) *slowly away: lost tch 3f out: t.o* **16/1**
1m 27.07s (0.27) **Going Correction** -0.10s/f (Stan) **11** Ran SP% **117.7**
Speed ratings (Par 94):94,93,91,89,85 85,83,81,81,79 63
CSF £8.40 TOTE £4.20: £1.40, £1.40, £1.90; EX 6.90.
Owner Speedlith Group **Bred** Speedlith Group **Trained** Upper Lambourn, Berks

FOCUS

The fron two in the market had the best form of the seven who had raced before, but they had both had plenty of chances and there was a suspicion they could be vulnerable to one of the newcomers. However, in a race run in a blustery winter shower, their previous experience stood them in good stead and they battled out the finish. The winner is back to his early-season best now.

NOTEBOOK

Benllech, runner-up over this trip at Wolverhampton last time, jumped away slowly but was soon chasing the leaders and, having been given a quiet ride just off the pace, was switched over a furlong out to mount his challenge. He showed a good turn of foot late on and this win at the 11th time of asking would have done his confidence the world of good. (op 4-1)

Baltic Belle(IRE) was only headed late in the race after being sent on inside the final two furlongs. Although she has now had nine attempts at losing her maiden tag, she does not look one to give up on yet. (op 15-8, tchd 2-1 in places)

Trump Call(IRE) ◆, a 30,000gns half-brother to two winners including Hurricane Alley, ran best of the newcomers having disputed the lead turning for home and this was an encouraging first start. His trainer has done well with his juveniles this year and he looks a certain winner in the near future. (tchd 7-1)

Annia Faustina(IRE), not seen since her debut in August, came from well off the pace but was hanging late on. (op 25-1)

Party Best, absent since her debut in June, faded after showing up for a long way and may have needed it.

Dancewiththestars(USA), a half-sister to four winners in the US, is likely to come to herself once handicapped next season. (tchd 15-2)

6592 DIGIBET.COM NURSERY 6f (P)
4:50 (4:52) (Class 6) (0-65,68) 2-Y-O **£2,388** (£705; £352) **Stalls** High

Form RPR
0631 1 **Hucking Hill (IRE)**[10] 6488 2-9-10 **68**..............................(b) BrettDoyle 3 76
(J R Best) *mid-div: hdwy on outside and rdn to ld ent fnl f: drvn out* **9/4**[1]
0204 2 1 1/4 **Nou Camp**[10] 6488 2-8-10 **54**.. ChrisCatlin 10 58
(N A Callaghan) *hld up in tch: hdwy to lad over 1f out: hdd ent fnl f: kpt on* **7/1**[3]
0503 3 1/2 **Darling Belinda**[9] 6500 2-9-5 **63**.................................. FergusSweeney 4 66
(D K Ivory) *in rr: hdwy and r.o fnl 2f to go 3rd nr fin* **9/1**
4001 4 3/4 **Homes By Woodford**[11] 6471 2-8-13 **57**........................... DaneO'Neill 8 57
(R A Harris) *trckd ldrs: ev ch over 2f out: kpt on but nt qckn fnl f* **16/1**
603U 5 1 1/2 **Queen Of Narnia**[10] 6488 2-9-0 **61**..................... EdwardCreighton(3) 6 57
(M R Channon) *v.s.a: rdn 2f out: mde sme late hdwy* **15/2**
0221 6 1/2 **Galaxy Of Stars**[9] 6500 2-9-0 **61**..............................(v) PatrickMathers(3) 5 55
(D Shaw) *mid-div: rdn 2f out: no hdwy ins fnl 2f* **7/1**[3]
0060 7 2 **Eastern Princess**[10] 6487 2-8-10 **54**........................... RichardThomas 11 42
(J A Geake) *chsd ldr: led over 2f out: hdd over 1f out: wknd fnl f* **25/1**
0566 8 3/4 **Kyllachy Storm**[9] 6500 2-9-6 **64**...................................(b[1]) GeorgeBaker 7 50
(R J Hodges) *slowly away: in rr: sme hdwy 2f out but nvr on terms* **9/2**[2]
0060 9 2 1/2 **Beat The Bully**[16] 6416 2-8-9 **53**.....................................(b) LeeEnstone 1 32
(I A Wood) *s.i.s: a in rr* **50/1**
5500 10 1/2 **Solwind (USA)**[16] 6416 2-9-0 **58**....................................... PaulEddery 12 35
(B Smart) *led tl hdd over 2f out: sn wknd* **16/1**
1m 13.47s (-0.23) **Going Correction** -0.10s/f (Stan) **10** Ran SP% **113.3**
Speed ratings (Par 94):97,95,94,93,91 91,88,87,84,83
CSF £17.60 CT £120.04 TOTE £3.00: £1.30, £2.80, £3.10; EX 26.90.
Owner Hucking Horses **Bred** Ballyhane Stud **Trained** Hucking, Kent

FOCUS

There were plenty of question marks hanging over a number of these in a trappy looking nursery. The form looks sound enough though and should produce future winners.

NOTEBOOK

Hucking Hill(IRE), up 7lb rise for his win over course and distance last time, came from off a frantic early pace to win reasonably comfortably in a respectable time. He is clearly a tough sort - this was his 16th run of the season - and connections will wait to see what the Handicapper does before deciding where they go next. (op 5-2)

Nou Camp continues to go the right way. He has now come up against the winner three times and, although he is still a maiden, if he continues in this manner he should get his head in front soon. (tchd 15-2)

Darling Belinda snatched third late on and this step back up to six furlongs seemed to suit. (op 7-1)

Homes By Woodford ran respectably on his first start for new connections. (op 14-1)

Queen Of Narnia, who was again unruly in the stalls, was very slow away and put in her best work late on. (op 8-1 tchd 7-1)

6593 DIGIBET.CO.UK MEDIAN AUCTION MAIDEN STKS 1m (P)
5:20 (5:21) (Class 6) 3-4-Y-O **£2,388** (£705; £352) **Stalls** High

Form RPR
2242 1 **Esthlos (FR)**[8] 6507 3-9-3 70.. ChrisCatlin 2 67+
(J Jay) *racd wd: a in tch: rdn to ld narrowly appr fnl f: drvn out* **11/8**[1]
0-0 2 1/2 **Lopinot (IRE)**[163] 2581 3-9-3 69..................................... FergusSweeney 6 66
(P J Makin) *sn led: rdn and hdd appr fnl f: nt qckn ins* **25/1**
3 1/2 **Foreign Language (USA)** 3-8-12 .... EddieAhern 7 60+
(N A Callaghan) *hld up in rr: rdn and hdwy over 1f out: r.o: nvr nrr* **6/1**
0002 4 1 3/4 **Simpsons Ross (IRE)**[51] 5774 3-9-3 59........................... JimmyQuinn 3 61
(R M Flower) *in rr: rdn and hdwy over 2f out: one pce fnl f* **20/1**
0502 5 1 1/2 **Wassfa**[29] 6206 3-8-12 66.. BrettDoyle 1 52
(C E Brittain) *prom on outside: wnt 2nd 1/2-way: rdn over 2f out: one pce appr fnl f* **4/1**[3]
6 nk **Musango** 3-8-12 .... LiamJones(5) 4 57
(B R Johnson) *trckd ldrs tl lost pl over 3f out: nvr on terms after* **10/1**
4422 7 hd **Dixieland Boy (IRE)**[17] 6406 3-9-0 67.......................... AmirQuinn(3) 8 56
(P J Makin) *broke wl: prom tl hung rt and wknd over 1f out* **7/2**[2]
6-06 8 6 **Veba (USA)**[163] 2570 3-9-3 60.. HayleyTurner 9 42
(M D I Usher) *t.k.h in rr: outpcd fr 1/2-way* **66/1**
1m 40.22s (-0.58) **Going Correction** -0.10s/f (Stan) **8** Ran SP% **117.8**
Speed ratings (Par 101):98,97,97,95,93 93,93,87
CSF £45.09 TOTE £2.30: £1.10, £5.50, £1.70; EX 75.00.
Owner Ms Medina Jessop **Bred** J Jay **Trained** Newmarket, Suffolk

FOCUS

A largely moderate bunch at best went to post for this weak maiden, the runner-up limiting the form. The winner was 7lb off his latest mark.

6594 DIGIBET SPORTS BETTING H'CAP 1m (P)
5:50 (5:50) (Class 3) (0-95,91) 3-Y-O+
£7,790 (£2,332; £1,166; £583; £291; £146) **Stalls** High

Form RPR
6362 1 **Orchard Supreme**[7] 6514 3-9-4 **91**.................................. JimmyFortune 6 100+
(R Hannon) *hld up in rr: hdwy 1f out: strly rdn to ld nr fin* **7/2**[1]
2321 2 1/2 **Neardown Beauty (IRE)**[16] 6413 3-8-9 **82** ow1................ LeeEnstone 1 86+
(I A Wood) *hld up: rdn to chal 2f out: ev ch 1f out: kpt on u.p to go 2nd post* **11/2**[2]
0241 3 shd **Freeloader (IRE)**[14] 5362 6-8-8 **84**.......................... JamieMoriarty(5) 8 88
(R A Fahey) *racd on ins: trckd ldrs: led 1f out: rdn: hdd and lost 2nd cl home* **7/1**
1020 4 nk **Wavertree Warrior (IRE)**[43] 5943 4-8-11 **85**.............. JamesDoyle(3) 2 88
(N P Littmoden) *led after 2f: hdd 2f out: ev ch 1f out: no ex fnl 50yds* **13/2**[3]
0002 5 nk **Cape Greko**[17] 6397 4-9-0 **85**..(v) FergusSweeney 3 88+
(A M Balding) *trckd ldrs: outpcd over 1f out: r.o ins fnl f* **7/2**[1]
2134 6 1 1/4 **Landucci**[17] 6397 5-8-1 **79**.. PatrickHills(7) 5 79
(J W Hills) *t.k.h: led for 2f: led again 2f out: hdd 1f out: wknd fnl f* **13/2**[3]
-601 7 nk **Cape Of Luck (IRE)**[154] 2863 3-9-1 **88**.............................. GeorgeBaker 4 87
(P Mitchell) *in rr: sme late hdwy but nvr nr to chal* **14/1**
4010 8 nk **Ninth House (USA)**[12] 6461 4-8-13 **84**...............................(t) IanMongan 7 82
(N P Littmoden) *hld up in rr: rdn 2f out: sme hdwy but nvr on terms* **8/1**
1m 40.87s (0.07) **Going Correction** -0.10s/f (Stan)
WFA 3 from 4yo+ 2lb **8** Ran SP% **116.8**
Speed ratings (Par 107):95,94,94,94,93 92,92,91
CSF £23.45 CT £129.04 TOTE £3.30: £1.40, £2.00, £2.20; EX 12.20.
Owner Brian C Oakley **Bred** Mrs M H Goodrich **Trained** East Everleigh, Wilts

FOCUS

Just the eight runners and a pedestrian early pace, but a competitive handicap nonetheless with arguments possible for the chances of the whole field. In the end little more than a length separated the first five home which rather limits the form.

NOTEBOOK

Orchard Supreme has been running well without getting his head in front recently and this was a well-deserved win following his unlucky second at Lingfield last week. He was given a superb ride, having not looked particularly keen when he got the gap around two furlongs out.

Neardown Beauty(IRE) ◆ was also held up, but had every chance and stayed on well. She is a model of consistency and looks capable of winning again soon. (op 3-1 tchd 6-1)

Freeloader(IRE) had every chance on his first start on sand for more than a year. A step up in trip may suit him.

Wavertree Warrior(IRE), well backed, made much of the running before being headed late on. He may benefit from a drop back in trip. (op 11-1)

Cape Greko was putting in his best work late on. The application of a visor looks to have brought about improvement in him. (op 9-2)

Landucci did himself no favours by taking a keen hold early on. (op 6-1 tchd 7-1)

Cape Of Luck(IRE) Official explanation: jockey said colt hung left

6595 TFM NETWORKS H'CAP 7f (P)
6:20 (6:20) (Class 6) (0-68,68) 3-Y-O+ **£2,388** (£705; £352) **Stalls** High

Form RPR
0313 1 **Reeling N' Rocking (IRE)**[17] 6396 3-8-13 **66**................. MichaelHills 14 75+
(B W Hills) *sn led: made rest: strly rdn appr fnl f: jst hld on* **7/2**[1]
5201 2 nk **Million Percent**[17] 6396 7-8-10 **67**.................................... LiamJones(5) 12 75
(C R Dore) *a in tch: rdn to chal over 1f out: snatched 2nd nr fin* **7/1**[3]
4400 3 nk **Zazous**[7] 6510 5-8-4 **56**.. HayleyTurner 1 64
(J J Bridger) *in rr: swtchd lft over 2f out: r.o strly fnl f to go 3rd nr fin* **25/1**
4005 4 hd **No Grouse**[17] 6404 6-8-3 **55**.. JimmyQuinn 5 62
(E J Alston) *in rr tl hdwy on ins 2f out: ev ch ins fnl f: no ex nr fin* **16/1**
3302 5 1 **Hollow Jo**[17] 6396 6-8-11 **63**.. EddieAhern 10 67
(J R Jenkins) *hld up in tch: ev ch over 1f out: kpt on one pce ins fnl f* **7/2**[1]
5043 6 1 **Lii Najma**[10] 6497 3-8-12 **65**.. BrettDoyle 9 67
(C E Brittain) *in rr tl hdwy on ins to chse ldrs 2f out: nt qckn ins fnl f* **12/1**
0050 7 2 **Sands Of Barra (IRE)**[2] 6573 3-9-0 **67**..................... RobbieFitzpatrick 3 64
(I W McInnes) *s.i.s: r.o fnl 2f but nvr nr to chal* **20/1**
4020 8 hd **Way To The Stars**[43] 5953 3-9-1 **68**..............................(v[1]) MartinDwyer 8 64
(A M Balding) *hld up in mid-div: no hdwy ins fnl 2f* **12/1**
1002 9 1 **Scuba (IRE)**[15] 6425 4-9-1 **67**......................................(b) JimmyFortune 6 60
(H Morrison) *prom: rdn 2f out: wknd appr fnl f* **11/2**[2]
0550 10 2 **Nistaki (USA)**[4] 6556 5-8-5 **60**.............................. PatrickMathers(3) 11 48
(D Shaw) *slowly away: sn trckd ldrs: wknd over 1f out* **12/1**
000/ 11 1 1/4 **Burley Firebrand**[30] 6195 6-8-5 **57**..............................(b) NelsonDeSouza 7 42
(Michael McElhone, Ire) *prom tl rdn and wknd 2f out* **20/1**
6420 12 nk **Lizarazu (GER)**[38] 6048 7-8-6 **65**.................................(p) TolleyDean(7) 13 49
(R A Harris) *chsd ldrs: rdn over 2f out: wknd over 1f out* **12/1**
1000 13 1/2 **Blue Empire (IRE)**[74] 5269 5-8-9 **61**.................................. AdamKirby 4 44
(C R Dore) *chsd ldrs: rdn 3f out: sn wknd* **20/1**
5050 14 shd **Marker**[24] 6293 6-8-8 **60**.. RichardThomas 2 43
(J A Geake) *bhd fnl 3f* **14/1**
1m 25.52s (-1.28) **Going Correction** -0.10s/f (Stan)
WFA 3 from 4yo+ 1lb **14** Ran SP% **133.8**
Speed ratings (Par 101):103,102,102,102,100 99,97,97,96,93 92,92,91,91
CSF £29.59 CT £589.41 TOTE £4.50: £2.10, £2.20, £10.60; EX 23.20 Place 6 £19.80, Place 5 £12.40.
Owner D M James **Bred** Richard F Barnes **Trained** Lambourn, Berks

FOCUS

Another wide-open contest and another in which the first few home finished in a heap, although this time they went a decent gallop early on. A fair race for the grade and the form seems solid.

Scuba(IRE) Official explanation: jockey said gelding hung left on bend

T/Plt: £12.80 to a £1 stake. Pool: £49,579.35. 2,826.25 winning tickets. T/Qpdt: £9.50 to a £1 stake. Pool: £3,388.70. 263.30 winning tickets. JS

6510 LINGFIELD (L-H)
Saturday, November 25

OFFICIAL GOING: Standard

Wind: Moderate behind Weather: Overcast becoming fine

6596 LINGFIELDPARK.CO.UK MAIDEN AUCTION STKS 6f (P)
12:25 (12:25) (Class 6) 2-Y-O **£2,388** (£705; £352) **Stalls** Low

Form RPR
4422 1 **Shustraya**[7] 6512 2-8-5 70.. EddieAhern 2 73+
(P J Makin) *hld up in 3rd tl trckd ldr over 2f out: led over 1f out and gng easily: pushed clr* **1/2**[1]

The Form Book, Raceform Ltd, Compton, RG20 6NL

6433 **2** *4* **Feelin Foxy**[7] 6512 2-8-8 68..........(v) DaneO'Neill 1 64
(D Shaw) *dwlt: sn rcvrd and led: hdd over 1f out: no ch w wnr after* **11/2**[3]
3 **3** *1 ¼* **Iza Coming (IRE)**[39] 6034 2-8-7 ow1.......... BrettDoyle 3 59
(M G Quinlan) *hld up in 4th: rdn over 2f out: kpt on same pce: n.d* **7/2**[2]
2002 **4** *½* **Grange Lili (IRE)**[12] 6463 2-8-9 59..........(b) RobbieFitzpatrick 4 60
(Peter Grayson) *chsd ldr to over 2f out: u.p and btn sn after* **20/1**
0 **5** *2 ½* **Sea Cookie**[21] 6331 2-8-4.......... AdrianMcCarthy 5 47
(W De Best-Turner) *a last: struggling bef 1/2-way* **50/1**
1m 11.74s (-1.07) **Going Correction** -0.125s/f (Stan) 5 Ran SP% **111.0**
Speed ratings (Par 94):102,96,95,94,91
CSF £3.90 TOTE £1.50: £1.02, £3.90; EX 4.00.
Owner Four Leaf Clover **Bred** Millsec Limited **Trained** Ogbourne Maisey, Wilts

FOCUS
A moderate maiden which saw the winner score as she pleased. The form is straightforward.

NOTEBOOK
Shustraya deservedly got off the mark at the fifth time of asking and did the job pretty much as she pleased. She was entitled to win as she did on her previous form, but this will have boosted her confidence and, more importantly, her potential paddock value. She could build on this in nurseries. (op 4-7)
Feelin Foxy was made to look very one paced when the winner asserted, but she got the extra furlong well and still finished nicely clear in second. Her trainer will most likely place her to advantage during the winter and she is a good benchmark for this form. Official explanation: jockey said filly hung throughout (op 5-1)
Iza Coming(IRE) proved easy to back and failed to improve on the level of her debut over course and distance 39 days previously. She ought to be of greater interest when qualifying for nurseries after her next outing. (tchd 3-1)
Grange Lili(IRE), second in a weaker event on Fibresand last time, ran her race and left the impression she really needs a drop in grade.

6597 ARENA LEISURE PLC NOVICE MEDIAN AUCTION STKS 7f (P)
1:00 (1:00) (Class 6) 2-Y-O **£2,388** (£705; £352) **Stalls** Low

Form RPR
51 **1** **Sharpazmax (IRE)**[14] 6441 2-9-1 76.......... EddieAhern 2 79
(P J Makin) *trckd ldr: led over 3f out: hrd pressed fnl 2f: hld on wl* **7/4**[2]
01 **2** *nk* **Autograph Hunter**[11] 6475 2-9-3 81.......... JoeFanning 3 80+
(M Johnston) *s.i.s: cl up: trckd wnr 3f out: chal fr 2f out: hanging and fnd nil over 1f out: clsd reluctantly nr fin* **1/2**[1]
00 **3** *4* **My Jeanie (IRE)**[10] 6486 2-8-7.......... FergusSweeney 4 60
(J C Fox) *hld up in last: pushed along and outpcd 1/2-way: wnt 3rd wl over 1f out: nudged along and no imp ldng pair* **33/1**[3]
0040 **4** *9* **Sagassa**[33] 6143 2-8-7 51.......... AdrianMcCarthy 1 36
(W De Best-Turner) *led at mod pce to over 3f out: sn wknd* **50/1**
1m 26.44s (0.55) **Going Correction** -0.125s/f (Stan) 4 Ran SP% **107.9**
Speed ratings (Par 94):91,90,86,75
CSF £2.97 TOTE £2.40; EX 3.30.
Owner Weldspec Glasgow Limited **Bred** Tim Bourke **Trained** Ogbourne Maisey, Wilts

FOCUS
No strength in depth to this novice event and it was run at a steady early pace. The first two in the betting came clear and the third is the best guide to the level.

NOTEBOOK
Sharpazmax(IRE) followed up his maiden success over course and distance a fortnight previously in tenacious fashion. He is clearly improving, does enjoy this surface, and it will be interesting to see how he copes with a future higher mark. (tchd 13-8 and 15-8)
Autograph Hunter, a clear-cut winner at Southwell last time, would not have enjoyed the lack of early pace on this switch to Polytrack and he did look tricky under pressure when the chips were down. He has scope, but whether he is yet up to his current official mark is in some doubt. (tchd 4-9 and 8-15)
My Jeanie(IRE) was another who did not appear to be suited by the lack of early pace and was never a threat to the first pair. She now has the option of nurseries and ought to fare a little better in that sphere.
Sagassa dictated at a steady pace early on and was not surprisingly left behind when things hotted up. (op 40-1)

6598 SLEIGHT HILL CHALLENGE NURSERY 7f (P)
1:30 (1:31) (Class 3) 2-Y-O
£6,855 (£2,052; £1,026; £513; £256; £128) **Stalls** Low

Form RPR
1201 **1** **Cesc**[12] 6458 2-9-7 **85**.......... EddieAhern 2 90+
(P J Makin) *hld up bhd ldrs: effrt and brought wd in st: pushed into ld 1f out: shkn up and in command after* **10/11**[1]
2304 **2** *1* **Miss Saafend Plaza (IRE)**[23] 6309 2-8-8 **72**.......... DaneO'Neill 3 74
(R Hannon) *mostly trckd ldr tl led wl over 2f out: drvn sn after: hdd 1f out: kpt on wl but a hld* **5/1**[3]
321 **3** *¾* **Baylini**[30] 6187 2-9-0 **81**.......... JamesDoyle(3) 4 81
(Ms J S Doyle) *hld up in 5th: prog 2f out: brought wd in st: nt qckn over 1f out: styd on last 150yds* **7/2**[2]
0023 **4** *1 ½* **Tee Off (IRE)**[25] 6271 2-8-7 **71**..........(t) OscarUrbina 1 67
(B W Hills) *hld up bhd ldrs: tongue-strap c off 3f out: effrt wl over 1f out: kpt on same pce* **8/1**
566 **5** *1 ¾* **Stoneacre Gareth (IRE)**[8] 6504 2-8-9 **73**.......... RobbieFitzpatrick 6 65
(Peter Grayson) *s.s: rdn in last wl over 2f out: one pce and n.d* **11/1**
6403 **6** *1 ¼* **La Marmotte (IRE)**[12] 6460 2-7-12 **62**.......... JimmyQuinn 5 50
(J W Hills) *taken down early: mde most to wl over 2f out: wknd over 1f out* **16/1**
1m 24.9s (-0.99) **Going Correction** -0.125s/f (Stan) 6 Ran SP% **116.6**
Speed ratings (Par 100):100,98,98,96,94 92
CSF £6.39 TOTE £1.70: £1.60, £2.00; EX 9.00.
Owner Keith And Brian Brackpool **Bred** H J P Farr **Trained** Ogbourne Maisey, Wilts

FOCUS
A fair little nursery in which the form looks quite strong and should work out. The winner is progressive and is value for a little further than the winning margin.

NOTEBOOK
Cesc, 6lb higher than when scoring over a mile at this venue 12 days previously, followed up in ready fashion and did the job with something up his sleeve at the finish. He is a useful colt when things go his way, his versatility as regards trip is a real bonus, and he remains capable of further improvement on this surface. (op 5-4 tchd 11-8)
Miss Saafend Plaza(IRE) had her chance yet is a little flattered by her proximity to the winner. She had dropped to a fair mark for this, but there can be no coincidence that she remains a maiden after ten outings, and no doubt she will go back up a few pounds for this effort. (op 11-2 tchd 9-2)
Baylini, well backed when winning her maiden over course and distance 30 days previously, had to come wide for her challenge off the final bend and ultimately shaped as though she may be ready to tackle a seventh furlong now. She looks to have her fair share of weight in this sphere, however. (op 5-2)
Tee Off(IRE), making her All-Weather bow, is proving very hard to catch right yet is probably best forgiven this effort as her tongue strap came off before the turn for home.

6599 HBLB CONDITIONS STKS 1m 2f (P)
2:00 (2:00) (Class 3) 2-Y-O **£6,855** (£2,052; £1,026; £513; £256) **Stalls** Low

Form RPR
0014 **1** **Montalembert (USA)**[53] 5763 2-9-0 79.......... JohnEgan 2 83+
(J S Moore) *cl up: trckd ldr over 2f out: led wl over 1f out: hung rt fnl f: hld on* **11/4**[2]
0335 **2** *½* **Castara Bay**[36] 6074 2-8-11 75.......... StephaneBreux(3) 1 82
(R Hannon) *hld up in last: effrt 2f out: chsd wnr fnl f: clsng at fin but a jst hld* **11/2**
01 **3** *2* **Mafeking (UAE)**[17] 6393 2-9-0 83.......... FergusSweeney 5 78
(M R Hoad) *t.k.h: led over 7f out: rdn and hdd wl over 1f out: one pce* **7/1**
4011 **4** *2 ½* **Habalwatan (IRE)**[14] 6443 2-9-5 77..........(b) BrettDoyle 4 79
(C E Brittain) *reminder s: cl up: effrt 2f out: rdn and nt qckn over 1f out: n.d after* **9/2**[3]
41 **5** *27* **Peregrine Falcon**[7] 6523 2-9-3.......... JoeFanning 3 25
(M Johnston) *led to over 7f out: pressed ldr tl wknd rapidly over 2f out: virtually p.u nr fin* **6/4**[1]
2m 5.25s (-2.54) **Going Correction** -0.125s/f (Stan) 5 Ran SP% **112.7**
Speed ratings (Par 100):105,104,103,101,79
CSF £17.63 TOTE £3.30: £1.80, £1.60; EX 20.10.
Owner Willie McKay **Bred** Delehanty Stock Farm **Trained** Upper Lambourn, Berks

FOCUS
An interesting conditions event in which all of the runners were tackling this trip for the first time. The pace was fair and the form looks sound enough although the winner dod not need to be at his best to prevail.

NOTEBOOK
Montalembert(USA) ♦, fifth in a Listed event in Germany 53 days previously, showed the benefit of this drop in class and resumed winning ways in good style. The switch to this sounder surface was also right up his street, as was the longer trip, and he has the scope to build on this and do better as a three-year-old. (op 5-2 tchd 10-3)
Castara Bay was doing his best work towards the finish yet was never a serious threat to the cosy winner. He enjoyed the step up in distance and should not remain a maiden for too long on this evidence. (op 13-2 tchd 5-1)
Mafeking(UAE), off the mark over a mile at Kempton last time, spoilt his chances of getting this longer trip by running too freely through the early parts. He looks as though he could do better as a three-year-old, but will need to improve through the winter to justify his current official mark. (op 8-1)
Habalwatan(IRE) did not help his cause with a sluggish start and ultimately found the burden of top weight beyond him in this quest for the hat-trick. He may also benefit for the return to a mile on this evidence.
Peregrine Falcon, a Wolverhampton maiden winner a week previously, dropped out after losing his action and it remains to be seen how he recovers from this experience. Official explanation: jockey said colt hung left from 5f out (tchd 11-8, tchd 13-8 in a place)

6600 LINGFIELDPARK.CO.UK H'CAP 1m 2f (P)
2:35 (2:35) (Class 2) (0-100,98) 3-Y-O+
£11,217 (£3,358; £1,679; £840; £419; £210) **Stalls** Low

Form RPR
352 **1** **Speedy Sam**[4] 6559 3-8-0 **87**.......... AndrewElliott(5) 5 101
(K R Burke) *trckd ldng pair: prog to ld over 2f out and kicked on: wd bnd sn after: hung rt but styd on wl fnl f* **11/4**[2]
-231 **2** *2 ½* **Alpine Reel (IRE)**[16] 6418 5-8-11 **89**.......... AdamKirby 4 98
(W R Swinburn) *cl up: prog to chse wnr jst over 2f out: styd on but no real imp fnl f* **13/8**[1]
0010 **3** *1* **Bahar Shumaal (IRE)**[7] 6516 4-9-1 **93**..........(b) BrettDoyle 6 100
(C E Brittain) *dwlt: t.k.h: hld up in midfield: prog over 2f out: chsd ldng pair over 1f out: kpt on but no imp* **5/1**[3]
0634 **4** *½* **Kindlelight Debut**[7] 6516 6-9-3 **98**.......... JamesDoyle(3) 1 104
(N P Littmoden) *hld up in last pair: outpcd over 2f out: prog over 1f out: styd on fnl f: n.d* **10/1**
0003 **5** *6* **Baan (USA)**[12] 6468 3-8-8 **90**.......... JoeFanning 8 85
(M Johnston) *pressed ldr after 2f: led briefly 3f out: wknd wl over 1f out* **8/1**
0003 **6** *½* **Punta Galera (IRE)**[7] 6515 3-8-2 **84**.......... DaleGibson 7 78
(R Hannon) *racd freely: led to 3f out: wknd over 2f out* **10/1**
21-3 **7** *5* **Psychiatrist**[323] 57 5-9-0 **92**.......... PaulFitzsimons 3 76
(Miss J R Tooth) *hld up in midfield: rdn and struggling 3f out: sn lost tch* **25/1**
0560 **8** *½* **Regal Royale**[7] 6514 3-8-5 **87** ow2.......... RobbieFitzpatrick 2 70
(Peter Grayson) *hld up in last pair: rdn and struggling 3f out: sn bhd* **33/1**
2m 3.52s (-4.27) **Going Correction** -0.125s/f (Stan)
WFA 3 from 4yo+ 4lb 8 Ran SP% **117.5**
Speed ratings (Par 109):112,110,109,108,104 103,99,99
CSF £7.87 CT £20.49 TOTE £4.00: £2.20, £1.10, £1.30; EX 8.70 Trifecta £74.50 Pool: £412.91 - 3.93 winning units..
Owner Mrs M Gittins **Bred** Cheveley Park Stud Ltd **Trained** Middleham Moor, N Yorks

FOCUS
A strong handicap for the grade and it looks decent form. The early pace was only modest, however. A positive view has been taken of the form with the first two unexposed on sand.

NOTEBOOK
Speedy Sam ♦, up in trip, deservedly regained the winning thread and was full value for his winning margin. He is likely to take a hike in the weights now, but this consistent three-year-old probably still has more to offer on the All-Weather. (op 4-1)
Alpine Reel(IRE), having his first outing at this track, had his chance yet was ultimately put in his place from this 7lb higher mark. He still managed to reverse his Wolverhampton form with Bahar Shumaal, however, and has developed into a most consistent performer. (op 7-4, tchd 2-1 in a place)
Bahar Shumaal(IRE), down in grade, again ran freely early on and probably needs a stronger early pace over this trip to be seen at his best. The Handicapper looks to have his measure now, however. (op 7-2)
Kindlelight Debut was not disgraced under top weight and helps to set the level of this form. This likeable filly is another who ideally wants a stronger early pace, but is weighted to around her best nowadays all the same. (op 8-1)
Baan(USA) found little when it mattered and failed to raise his game for this switch to this surface. No doubt he is on a fair mark at present, but he is proving very hard to catch right. (op 13-2)

6601 JUMPING HERE ON DECEMBER 9TH H'CAP 1m 4f (P)
3:10 (3:11) (Class 6) (0-65,65) 3-Y-O **£2,388** (£705; £352) **Stalls** Low

Form RPR
0406 **1** **Broughtons Folly**[14] 6432 3-9-3 **64**.......... BrettDoyle 5 69+
(W J Musson) *t.k.h early: hld up in midfield: effrt 2f out: gd prog to ld jst over 1f out: pushed clr* **7/4**[1]
0645 **2** *1 ½* **Camp Attack**[12] 6459 3-8-6 **53**.......... LPKeniry 8 56
(S Dow) *t.k.h: trckd ldr for 4f: styd cl up: effrt to chal and upsides over 1f out: outpcd fnl f* **10/1**

325 **3** ½ **Lady Georgette (IRE)**^{8} [6509] 3-8-5 **52** ChrisCatlin 2 56+
(E J O'Neill) *hld up in midfield: lost pl on inner over 2f out: prog over 1f out: hung rt but styd on fnl f* **7/2**^{2}

0503 **4** *nk* **Sea Of Calm (USA)**^{11} [6482] 3-8-5 **52** EddieAhern 10 54
(E A L Dunlop) *t.k.h early: trckd ldrs: effrt to ld 2f out: hdd and outpcd jst over 1f out* **6/1**^{3}

4650 **5** ½ **Ciccone**^{24} [6294] 3-8-11 **58** FergusSweeney 6 59
(G L Moore) *dwlt: t.k.h: hld up in rr: prog on outer 3f out: jnd ldrs wl over 1f out: sn rdn and fnd nil* **7/1**

5000 **6** 5 **Theologicum**^{43} [5954] 3-8-4 **54** EdwardCreighton(3) 1 47
(Miss J R Gibney) *hld up in last: effrt over 2f out: outpcd over 1f out: wknd* **25/1**

3425 **7** ¾ **Valart**^{61} [5566] 3-9-1 **65** JamesDoyle(3) 4 57
(Ms J S Doyle) *hld up in last pair: effrt over 2f out: wknd over 1f out* **8/1**

0000 **8** 6 **Revolving World (IRE)**^{89} [4884] 3-8-5 **52** (tp) JoeFanning 3 34
(T J Fitzgerald) *dwlt: t.k.h and sn prom: trckd ldr after 4f: led over 2f out to 2f out: wknd rapidly* **16/1**

0010 **9** 5 **By Storm**^{33} [6128] 3-7-13 **51** oh2 AndrewElliott(5) 9 25
(John Berry) *mde most to over 2f out: wknd rapidly* **25/1**

2m 34.53s (0.14) **Going Correction** -0.125s/f (Stan) **9** Ran SP% **119.1**
Speed ratings (Par 98):94,93,92,92,92 88,88,84,80
CSF £21.84 CT £56.45 TOTE £3.00: £1.10, £2.10, £1.70; EX 22.30 Trifecta £44.80 Pool: £369.20 - 5.85 winning units..
Owner Broughton Thermal Insulation **Bred** Broughton Bloodstock **Trained** Newmarket, Suffolk

FOCUS
A weak handicap, in which only one of the runners had previously won a race. The winner is value for further. The second and fifth limit the form.
Lady Georgette(IRE) Official explanation: jockey said filly hung badly right in straight

6602 BOOK ONLINE FOR A £2 DISCOUNT H'CAP 1m 5f (P)
3:40 (3:40) (Class 4) (0-85,85) 3-Y-0+ **£5,362** (£1,604; £802; £401; £199) **Stalls** Low

Form RPR
3312 **1** **Nando's Dream**^{25} [6287] 3-8-4 **73** ChrisCatlin 7 78+
(J Noseda) *trckd ldr: led 3f out: kicked on 2f out: at least 3l clr 1f out: drvn out* **7/2**^{1}

-005 **2** ½ **Eva Soneva So Fast (IRE)**^{20} [6351] 4-9-3 **79** JimmyQuinn 2 86+
(J L Dunlop) *hld up towards rr: trapped on inner fr 3f out tl got through to chse clr wnr last 200yds: r.o: unlucky* **4/1**^{2}

0534 **3** 1½ **Turn 'n Burn**^{3} [6566] 5-8-9 **71** oh4 EddieAhern 5 73
(C A Cyzer) *hld up in rr: effrt over 2f out: drvn and styd on wl to take 3rd ins fnl f: nvr able to chal* **5/1**

0000 **4** 1 **Barathea Blazer**^{21} [6337] 7-9-9 **85** JoeFanning 4 86
(K McAuliffe) *hld up in last: stl last over 2f out: prog on outer wl over 1f out: styd on: no ch* **12/1**

2501 **5** *shd* **Bay Hawk**^{16} [6408] 4-8-9 **71** FMBerry 1 71
(B G Powell) *trckd ldng pair: rdn over 2f out: chsd clr wnr briefly over 1f out: wknd ins fnl f* **9/2**^{3}

3135 **6** 1½ **Linden Lime**^{41} [5991] 4-8-9 **71** oh2 RobertHavlin 8 69
(Jamie Poulton) *plld hrd: hld up in midfield: prog to join ldrs 3f out: nt qckn 2f out: wknd fnl f* **7/1**

5535 **7** 1¼ **Taxman (IRE)**^{11} [6479] 4-8-9 **71** oh2 (p) FergusSweeney 3 67
(C E Brittain) *trckd ldrs: lost pl and outpcd 2f out: wknd* **6/1**

420 **8** ¾ **Top Seed (IRE)**^{20} [6351] 5-8-7 **76** MarkCoumbe(7) 6 71
(A J Chamberlain) *led at mod pce to 3f out: chsd wnr to over 1f out: wknd rapidly* **20/1**

2m 51.1s (2.80) **Going Correction** -0.125s/f (Stan)
WFA 3 from 4yo+ 7lb **8** Ran SP% **116.3**
Speed ratings (Par 105):86,85,84,84,84 83,82,81
CSF £18.00 CT £69.55 TOTE £4.50: £1.50, £1.70, £2.70; EX 24.90 Trifecta £72.30 Pool: £147.67 - 1.45 winning units. Place 6 £24.07, Place 5 £18.20.
Owner Hesmonds Stud **Bred** Hesmonds Stud Ltd **Trained** Newmarket, Suffolk

FOCUS
A weakish handicap which was run at just a steady early pace. The front pair are less exposed than most but neither needed to improve, and the form is worth treating with a little caution.
Eva Soneva So Fast(IRE) ◆ Official explanation: jockey said gelding missed the break
T/Plt: £32.60 to a £1 stake. Pool: £34,291.35. 766.75 winning tickets. T/Qpdt: £8.20 to a £1 stake. Pool: £2,264.20. 204.20 winning tickets. JN

6581 WOLVERHAMPTON (A.W) (L-H)
Saturday, November 25

OFFICIAL GOING: Standard
Wind: Light, behind Weather: Cloudy

6603 IBETX.COM MAIDEN STKS 5f 216y(P)
7:00 (7:01) (Class 5) 2-Y-O **£3,886** (£1,156; £577; £288) **Stalls** Low

Form RPR
1 **Danapali (IRE)**^{56} [5694] 2-8-12 PatCosgrave 5 63+
(P J Prendergast, Ire) *mde all: rdn out* **11/10**^{1}

4022 **2** ½ **Napoleon Dynamite (IRE)**^{16} [6414] 2-9-3 **67** FJohansson 4 66+
(J W Hills) *chsd wnr over 3f: rdn to chse wnr and nt clr run over 1f out: swtchd rt: r.o* **6/5**^{2}

3 2½ **Pont Wood** 2-9-3 FrancisNorton 3 59
(M Blanshard) *dwlt: sn prom: rdn to chse wnr over 2f out: no ex fnl f* **20/1**

00 **4** 5 **Ponte Vecchio (IRE)**^{57} [5659] 2-9-3 JoeFanning 2 44
(J R Boyle) *trckd ldrs: plld hrd: wknd wl over 1f out* **40/1**

00 **5** 1¼ **Raise The Goblet (IRE)**^{21} [6331] 2-9-3 TonyCulhane 1 40
(W J Haggas) *chsd ldrs: outpcd 4f out: sn bhd* **14/1**^{3}

1m 16.71s (0.90) **Going Correction** -0.10s/f (Stan) **5** Ran SP% **106.9**
Speed ratings (Par 96):90,89,86,79,77
CSF £2.49 TOTE £2.00: £1.20, £1.40; EX 2.80.
Owner Ananda Krishnan **Bred** Swettenham Stud **Trained** Melitta Lodge, Co Kildare

FOCUS
A weak maiden which saw the two market rivals come clear. The runner-up sets the standard for the form.

NOTEBOOK
Danapali(IRE), whose prolific half-brother Eccollo was killed later on this card, had to be kept up to her work to hold off her market rival. On this evidence, she could struggle if brought back over for a handicap unless the British assessor shows some leniency. (op 8-11)
Napoleon Dynamite(IRE) ran another sound race but is proving difficult to win with, this being his third successive runner-up placing. (op 9-4)
Pont Wood, a newcomer from a stable not noted for its first-time out scorers, shaped with plenty of promise and can only improve on this effort. (op 16-1)
Ponte Vecchio(IRE) did not help her causes by refusing to settle on this drop in trip. She is now eligible for a handicap mark. (op 33-1)

6604 IBETX.COM BETTING EXCHANGE CLAIMING STKS 1m 5f 194y(P)
7:30 (7:30) (Class 6) 3-Y-0+ **£2,730** (£806; £403) **Stalls** Low

Form RPR
2203 **1** **Zaffeu**^{10} [5033] 5-8-9 **48** AshleyHamblett(5) 7 55
(A G Juckes) *s.s: hdwy 1/2-way: chsd ldr over 2f out: rdn to ld 1f out: styd on wl* **13/2**^{3}

0544 **2** 7 **Templet (USA)**^{19} [6382] 6-9-4 **59** (b) DanielTudhope 6 49
(W G Harrison) *hld up in tch: led over 3f out: clr over 2f out: rdn and hdd 1f out: sn btn* **3/1**^{1}

530- **3** 3 **Haiban**^{26} [6268] 4-9-0 TonyCulhane 2 41
(J J Lambe, Ire) *prom: rdn to chse ldr over 2f out: sn wknd* **9/2**^{2}

100/ **4** 8 **Killing Joke**^{21} [6266] 6-8-12 JohnEgan 8 28
(J J Lambe, Ire) *racd keenly: led 2f: trckd ldr tl rdn over 3f out: wknd over 2f out* **10/1**

0050 **5** 3 **Isa'Af (IRE)**^{10} [6495] 7-8-9 **57** WilliamCarson(7) 9 28
(P W Hiatt) *hld up in tch: rdn over 5f out: wknd over 3f out* **9/2**^{2}

6604 **6** 20 **Is**^{67} [5441] 3-7-8 **35** NicolPolli(5) 5 —
(Rae Guest) *chsd ldrs: lost pl after 3f: wknd 5f out* **25/1**

0444 **7** 2½ **Danebank (IRE)**^{8} [6509] 6-9-4 **51** (v) DaleGibson 1 —
(J Mackie) *led 12f out: rdn and hdd over 3f out: sn wknd* **3/1**^{1}

-000 **8** 62 **Dara Mac**^{26} [3194] 7-8-12 **47** FJohansson 10 —
(M Scudamore) *chsd ldrs: lost pl over 8f out: sn bhd* **33/1**

3m 7.15s (-0.22) **Going Correction** -0.10s/f (Stan)
WFA 3 from 4yo+ 8lb **8** Ran SP% **115.6**
Speed ratings (Par 101):96,92,90,85,84 72,71,35
CSF £26.66 TOTE £6.60: £1.50, £1.90, £2.10; EX 26.40.
Owner Whispering Winds **Bred** Patrick Eddery Ltd **Trained** Abberley, Worcs

FOCUS
A weak affair which saw the field come home fairly strung out. The winner ran to this year's form. The time was very slow.

6605 IBETX.COM BETTING EXCHANGE MAIDEN STKS 5f 20y(P)
8:00 (8:00) (Class 5) 2-Y-O **£3,238** (£963; £481; £240) **Stalls** Low

Form RPR
3224 **1** **Dress To Impress (IRE)**^{94} [4699] 2-9-3 **77** PatCosgrave 7 69+
(J R Boyle) *plld hrd: led 4f out: clr over 1f out: rdn out* **8/11**^{1}

454 **2** 2 **Ama De Casa (USA)**^{7} [6512] 2-8-12 **59** (t) JohnEgan 6 57
(J Noseda) *prom: nt clr run over 2f out: rdn to chse wnr fnl f: no imp* **9/2**^{2}

45 **3** 1¼ **Tang**^{194} [1743] 2-8-12 TonyCulhane 3 52
(W G M Turner) *led: hdd 4f out: rdn over 1f out: edgd lft and no ex fnl f* **7/1**^{3}

0300 **4** 5 **Fly Time**^{17} [6401] 2-8-12 **51** DaleGibson 1 34
(Mrs L Williamson) *sn outpcd: sme hdwy over 1f out: nvr nrr* **50/1**

40 **5** 8 **Shepherdess (USA)**^{8} [6505] 2-8-12 JoeFanning 8 6
(D M Simcock) *chsd ldrs: wkng whn hung lft over 1f out* **15/2**

6 **6** 3½ **Esprit De Nuit (IRE)**^{7} [6512] 2-9-0 GregFairley(3) 5 —
(Mrs A Duffield) *chsd ldrs: rdn 1/2-way: sn wknd* **25/1**

005 **7** *nk* **Wibbadune (IRE)**^{7} [6512] 2-8-12 **56** MickyFenton 4 —
(Peter Grayson) *sn outpcd* **50/1**

62.37 secs (-0.45) **Going Correction** -0.10s/f (Stan) **7** Ran SP% **108.1**
Speed ratings (Par 96):99,95,93,85,73 67,66
CSF £3.62 TOTE £1.50: £1.30, £2.60; EX 4.20.
Owner M Khan X2 **Bred** K Molloy **Trained** Epsom, Surrey

FOCUS
A very uncompetitive maiden. The winner looks flattered by his official rating of 77 and the runner-up sets the level.

NOTEBOOK
Dress To Impress(IRE) was the clear form pick in this uncompetitive maiden and did not need to run up to his best summer form to win with something to spare. A speedy sort, his big test will come when he reverts to handicaps and only time will tell whether he can justify a mark of 77. (op Evens tchd 4-6)
Ama De Casa(USA) who is officially rated 18lb below the winner, ran as well as could be expected, confirming recent Lingfield with the two back markers. (op 7-2)
Tang was put firmly in her place when headed, yet is entitled to come on for the run and now has the option of handicaps. (op 13-2 tchd 8-1)
Fly Time, beaten in selling company of late, looked tricky from off the pace and is in need of an extra furlong now. (op 40-1)

6606 IBETX.COM MONEY MAN (S) STKS 1m 141y(P)
8:30 (8:31) (Class 6) 3-Y-0+ **£2,388** (£705; £352) **Stalls** Low

Form RPR
3-06 **1** **Topiary Ted**^{11} [6470] 4-9-0 **50** RobertHavlin 5 64+
(H Morrison) *hld up: hdwy over 3f out: led over 1f out: rdn clr: eased ins fnl f* **8/1**

1002 **2** 5 **Second Reef**^{7} [6524] 4-9-5 **55** DavidAllan 13 58+
(E J Alston) *hld up and bhd: nt clr run over 2f out: hdwy over 1f out: no ch w wnr* **5/2**^{1}

6400 **3** 5 **Merdiff**^{152} [2936] 7-9-2 **52** DNolan(3) 12 48
(W M Brisbourne) *chsd ldrs: led over 2f out: rdn and hdd over 1f out: wknd fnl f* **14/1**

001- **4** ½ **Prince Vettori**^{415} [5704] 4-9-0 **62** JoeFanning 9 41
(D J Coakley) *chsd ldr tl led over 3f out: rdn and hdd over 2f out: wknd over 1f out* **9/2**^{3}

00 **5** 2 **Domesday (UAE)**^{62} [5553] 5-9-0 DanielTudhope 6 37
(W G Harrison) *chsd ldrs: rdn over 2f out: wknd over 1f out* **25/1**

0055 **6** 3½ **Sonderborg**^{11} [6473] 5-9-0 **45** (p) DaleGibson 4 30
(J Mackie) *hld up: rdn over 3f out: n.d* **14/1**

1245 **7** ¾ **Desert Lightning (IRE)**^{7} [6524] 4-9-5 **50** LeeEnstone 3 33
(K R Burke) *chsd ldrs: nt clr run and lost pl 3f out: swtchd rt and hdwy over 2f out: wknd over 1f out* **3/1**^{2}

2350 **8** *nk* **Danum**^{169} [2413] 6-8-7 **45** (p) RussellKennemore(7) 11 28
(R Hollinshead) *hld up: rdn over 3f out: n.d* **18/1**

0060 **9** 6 **Pantomime Prince**^{27} [6234] 3-8-11 **45** (p) FrancisNorton 8 15
(C A Dwyer) *hld up: rdn over 2f out: wknd and eased over 1f out* **50/1**

4000 **10** ¾ **Cheviot Heights**^{11} [6483] 3-8-1 **57** (p) KevinGhunowa(5) 1 9
(J S Goldie) *mid-div: rdn over 3f out: wkng whn hmpd over 2f out* **10/1**

0/- **11** 2½ **Jenkins Lane (IRE)**^{39} [6044] 4-9-0 (p) TonyCulhane 10 8
(J J Lambe, Ire) *prom: rdn over 3f out: wknd over 2f out* **25/1**

00/0 **12** 30 **Poyle Josh**^{10} [6492] 6-8-9 **45** EmmettStack(5) 2 —
(H J Manners) *led 5f: sn wknd* **100/1**

1m 49.31s (-2.45) **Going Correction** -0.10s/f (Stan)
WFA 3 from 4yo+ 3lb **12** Ran SP% **121.2**
Speed ratings (Par 101):106,101,97,96,94 91,91,90,85,84 82,55
CSF £28.23 TOTE £11.40: £3.50, £2.00, £3.20; EX 50.50.

The Form Book, Raceform Ltd, Compton, RG20 6NL

Owner Ron Plant **Bred** Stowell Hill Ltd And Mrs C Van Straubenzee **Trained** East Ilsley, Berks
FOCUS
A typically moderate seller.

6607 IBETX.COM H'CAP 1m 1f 103y(P)
9:00 (9:01) (Class 4) (0-85,83) 3-Y-0+ **£5,505** (£1,637; £818; £408) **Stalls** Low

Form RPR
0131 **1** **Kildare Sun (IRE)**[9] 6503 4-8-10 **72** DaleGibson 3 80
(J Mackie) *hld up: hdwy over 2f out: rdn to ld wl ins fnl f* **8/1**[3]
5331 **2** ½ **Vacation (IRE)**[22] 6327 3-8-4 **76** WilliamBuick(7) 13 83
(V Smith) *hld up: plld hrd: hdwy and hung lft fr over 1f out: rdn and ev ch ins fnl f: r.o* **17/2**
0351 **3** *nk* **Daring Affair**[14] 6448 5-8-12 **74** PaulMulrennan 9 80
(K R Burke) *chsd ldrs: rdn to ld ins fnl f: sn edgd lft: hdd and unable qckn* **25/1**
0253 **4** *1* **Regent's Secret (USA)**[16] 6418 6-9-2 **78** DanielTudhope 10 82
(J S Goldie) *s.i.s: hld up: hdwy over 1f out: r.o* **16/1**
6050 **5** ¾ **Atlantic Quest (USA)**[23] 6313 7-9-0 **81** (p) LiamJones(5) 7 84
(Miss Venetia Williams) *s.i.s: hld up: hdwy and hung lft fr over 2f out: styd on same pce ins fnl f* **33/1**
045 **6** *2* **Dream Catcher (SWE)**[88] 4919 3-9-1 **83** (t) JamesDoyle(3) 6 82
(R A Kvisla) *hld up: hdwy u.p over 1f out: nt trble ldrs* **50/1**
0005 **7** ½ **Maggies Farm (USA)**[3] 6564 3-8-10 **75** JoeFanning 12 73
(M Johnston) *chsd ldrs: led and edgd lft over 2f out: rdn over 1f out: hdd and no ex ins fnl f* **20/1**
2052 **8** 3½ **Lake Shabla (USA)**[16] 6411 3-9-4 **83** BrettDoyle 8 74
(E A L Dunlop) *hld up in tch: rdn over 1f out: btn whn hmpd ins fnl f* **7/2**[2]
0313 **9** 3½ **Woolfall Blue (IRE)**[23] 6313 3-9-0 **79** IanMongan 5 63
(G G Margarson) *chsd ldrs: hmpd over 2f out: sn wknd* **18/1**
1140 **10** *shd* **Glenbuck (IRE)**[43] 5943 3-9-4 **83** (v) FrancisNorton 11 66
(A Bailey) *chsd ldr tl led over 6f out: rdn and hdd over 2f out: sn hmpd and wknd* **20/1**
4/50 **11** *39* **Spainnash (IRE)**[56] 5699 6-8-13 **75** TonyCulhane 4 —
(J J Lambe, Ire) *hld up: rdn over 3f out: bhd whn hmpd over 2f out: eased* **66/1**
5226 **B** **Consonant (IRE)**[16] 6418 9-8-12 **77** DNolan(3) 1 —
(D G Bridgwater) *hld up: rdn over 3f out: b.d 2f out* **16/1**
1113 **F** **Eccollo (IRE)**[3] 6564 4-9-2 **78** JohnEgan 2 —
(T J Pitt) *chsd ldrs: shkn up and n.m.r over 2f out: stmbld and fell 2f out: dead* **11/8**[1]

1m 59.74s (-2.88) **Going Correction** -0.10s/f (Stan)
WFA 3 from 4yo+ 3lb **13** Ran SP% **122.8**
Speed ratings (Par 105):108,107,107,106,105 103,103,100,97,97 62,—,—
CSF £70.35 CT £1652.04 TOTE £11.70: £3.40, £3.60, £3.70; EX 55.50.
Owner Mrs Barbara Woodworth **Bred** Gordan Woodworth **Trained** Church Broughton , Derbys
FOCUS
A fair handicap but a rough race, with favourite Eccollo taking a fatal fall, bringing down Consonant and badly hampering Spainnash. Not strong form, but the winner continues to impress.

6608 IBETX.COM BETTING EXCHANGE FILLIES' H'CAP 7f 32y(P)
9:30 (9:37) (Class 6) (0-60,60) 3-Y-0+ **£2,730** (£806; £403) **Stalls** High

Form RPR
6504 **1** **Discotheque (USA)**[14] 6442 3-8-10 **56** DeanCorby(3) 2 63
(P Howling) *mid-div: hdwy over 2f out: rdn over 1f out: r.o to ld nr fin* **12/1**
4010 **2** *hd* **Black Sea Pearl**[24] 6293 3-8-10 **60** WilliamBuick(7) 9 66
(P W D'Arcy) *hld up: hdwy over 2f out: rdn over 1f out: hung lft ins fnl f: r.o* **10/1**
0006 **3** *hd* **Fairdonna**[18] 6390 3-9-1 **58** JoeFanning 1 64+
(D J Coakley) *chsd ldrs: nt clr run and lost pl over 3f out: hdwy over 1f sn carried lft: led wl ins fnl f: hdd nr fin* **7/2**[1]
5603 **4** *nk* **Myths And Verses**[14] 6436 3-8-12 **55** FrancisNorton 12 60
(K A Ryan) *hld up: hdwy u.p over 1f out: sn hung lft: nt rch ldrs* **10/1**
3000 **5** ½ **Miskina**[4] 6556 5-8-12 **54** RobbieFitzpatrick 5 58
(W M Brisbourne) *chsd ldrs: rdn over 1f out: hung lft and styd on same pce ins fnl f* **7/1**
5601 **6** ½ **Jabbara (IRE)**[10] 6492 3-8-12 **55** (b) StephenCarson 8 57
(C E Brittain) *s.i.s: sn chsng ldrs: led over 2f out: rdn and hung lft fr over 1f out: hdd wl ins fnl f* **5/1**[2]
0032 **7** 1½ **Solicitude**[39] 6033 3-8-12 **55** RobertHavlin 10 54
(D Haydn Jones) *hld up: hdwy u.p fr over 1f out: edgd lft fnl f: nt trble ldrs* **14/1**
5500 **8** *2* **Stylistic (IRE)**[47] 5865 5-9-0 **56** (p) TonyCulhane 4 49
(J J Lambe, Ire) *hld up: hdwy over 1f out: hmpd ins fnl f: nt trble ldrs* **50/1**
3000 **9** *hd* **True West (USA)**[83] 5046 3-9-3 **60** (v[1]) JimmyQuinn 11 53
(Miss Gay Kelleway) *hld up: nt clr run over 2f out: hmpd ins fnl f: n.d* **25/1**
0522 **10** *nk* **Whistleupthewind**[87] 4930 3-9-3 **60** MickyFenton 3 52
(J M P Eustace) *led: rdn and hdd over 2f out: wknd fnl f* **6/1**[3]
0064 **11** *nk* **Prettilini**[12] 6465 3-8-8 **56** LiamJones(5) 6 47
(R Brotherton) *mid-div: hdwy over 2f out: rdn and wknd over 1f out* **12/1**
6461 **12** *8* **Miss Porcia**[5] 6543 5-9-0 **56** 6ex BrettDoyle 7 26
(P A Blockley) *chsd ldrs: rdn over 2f out: sn wknd* **7/1**

1m 29.86s (-0.54) **Going Correction** -0.10s/f (Stan)
WFA 3 from 5yo 1lb **12** Ran SP% **124.2**
Speed ratings (Par 98):99,98,98,98,97 97,95,93,92,92 92,83
CSF £132.68 CT £528.37 TOTE £17.10: £4.50, £4.10, £3.10; EX 157.00 Place 6 £46.59, Place 5 £44.25.
Owner Waterford Hall Stud Ltd **Bred** Classic Thoroughbred Xviii **Trained** Newmarket, Suffolk
FOCUS
A moderate handicap run at a fair pace. There was little between the first six at the end.
Miss Porcia Official explanation: trainer's rep said race may have come too soon
T/Plt: £91.60 to a £1 stake. Pool: £69,230.90. 551.35 winning tickets. T/Qpdt: £44.10 to a £1 stake. Pool: £3,040.50. 51.00 winning tickets. CR

6567 SAINT-CLOUD (L-H)
Saturday, November 25

OFFICIAL GOING: Heavy

6609a PRIX ISONOMY (LISTED) 1m
1:10 (1:12) 2-Y-0 **£17,241** (£6,897; £5,172; £3,448; £1,724)

RPR
1 **Anabaa's Creation (IRE)** 2-8-8 SPasquier 1 104
(A De Royer-Dupre, France)
2 *hd* **Une Pivoine (FR)**[30] 2-8-8 (p) OPeslier 5 104
(J E Pease, France)
3 *6* **Cadran (FR)**[32] 2-8-11 YLerner 4 93
(C Lerner, France)
4 1½ **My Quentin (FR)** 2-8-11 FBlondel 2 90
(F Demets, France)
5 *3* **Reve D'Ailleur (FR)** 2-8-8 IMendizabal 7 80
(J-M Sauve, France)
6 *3* **Cylindree (IRE)**[13] 2-8-8 TThulliez 3 74
(P Bary, France)
7 *4* **Lets Get Cracking (FR)**[25] 6283 2-8-11 DBoeuf 8 68
(K A Ryan) *drawn on outside, narrow leader for 3f, 3rd straight, soon ridden & beaten (58/10)*
8 ¾ **Bleue Doloise (FR)**[28] 6228 2-8-8 JVictoire 6 63
(A Bonin, France)

1m 48.3s **8** Ran
PARI-MUTUEL: WIN 2.20; PL 1.20, 1.50, 1.50; DF 5.50.
Owner W-J Preston **Bred** Prestonwood Farms **Trained** Chantilly, France

NOTEBOOK
Lets Get Cracking(FR) was given every possible chance but was completely flat footed when things warmed up and a beaten force early in the straight. The ground was of the holding variety.

6610a PRIX DENISY (LISTED) 1m 7f 110y
2:45 (2:48) 3-Y-0+ **£17,241** (£6,897; £5,172; £3,448; £1,724)

RPR
1 **El Tango (GER)**[55] 5718 4-9-4 FilipMinarik 17 106
(P Schiergen, Germany)
2 *4* **Summer Shower**[11] 3-8-4 SPasquier 6 97
(A Fabre, France)
3 *3* **Caprice Meill (FR)**[47] 5881 6-8-11 TJarnet 15 92
(E Leenders, France)
4 ½ **Tirwanako (FR)**[50] 4-9-4 F-XBertras 3 99
(J-L Pelletan, France)
5 *1* **Sentry Duty (FR)**[47] 5881 4-9-1 TThulliez 10 95
(E Libaud, France)
6 1½ **Elasos (FR)**[50] 4-9-4 DBonilla 8 96
(D Sepulchre, France)
7 *6* **La Capitaine (FR)**[13] 6-8-11 OPeslier 14 83
(Y De Nicolay, France)
8 *10* **Petite Speciale (USA)**[34] 6119 7-9-4 IMendizabal 16 80
(E Lecoiffier, France)
9 *4* **Stephenson (FR)**[30] 5-9-1 JAuge 11 73
(W Baltromei, Germany)
10 *6* **Arkando (GER)**[181] 5-9-1 AHelfenbein 13 67
(M Trybuhl, Germany)
11 **Great Tune (FR)**[30] 6-9-1 MBlancpain 12 67
(E Libaud, France)
12 **Carus (GER)**[230] 7-9-4 WMongil 1 70
(D K Richardson, Germany)
13 **Allez Olive (IRE)**[67] 8-9-1 FBlondel 9 67
(F Demets, France)
14 **Trezene (USA)**[50] 4-9-1 DBoeuf 2 67
(D Smaga, France)
15 **Soterio (GER)**[35] 6109 6-9-1 (b) JVictoire 7 67
(W Baltromei, Germany)
16 **Le Carre (USA)**[162] 2629 8-9-1 FSpanu 4 67
(A De Royer-Dupre, France)
17 **Odiham**[14] 6438 5-9-4 (v) SteveDrowne 5 70
(H Morrison) *broke towards rear of midfield, soon pushed along and in rear, tailed off final 6f (31/1)*

3m 36.5s
WFA 3 from 4yo+ 8lb **17** Ran
PARI-MUTUEL: WIN 21.30; PL 7.00, 3.50, 8.50; DF 103.10.
Owner Stall Mydlinghoven **Bred** Gestut Wittekindshof **Trained** Germany

NOTEBOOK
Odiham was never really at the races. Pushed along soon after the start, he was a totally beaten force by the entrance to the straight. The distances between the runners at the finish looked more like ones you would find in a jumping event.

6369 AQUEDUCT (L-H)
Saturday, November 25

OFFICIAL GOING: Fast

6611a HILL 'N' DALE CIGAR MILE (GRADE 1) (H'CAP) (DIRT) 1m
8:48 (8:53) 3-Y-0+ **£104,651** (£34,884; £17,442; £8,721; £5,233)

RPR
1 **Discreet Cat (USA)**[55] 5719 3-8-12 GKGomez 4 131+
(Saeed Bin Suroor) **1/4**[1]
2 3¾ **Badge Of Silver (USA)**[21] 6342 6-8-5 JCastellano 1 115
(R J Frankel, U.S.A) **15/2**[3]
3 *nk* **Silver Train (USA)**[49] 5820 4-8-8 EPrado 2 117
(R Dutrow Jr, U.S.A) **42/10**[2]
4 *6* **Dixie Meister (USA)**[161] 4-8-5 (b) FJara 3 102
(J Canani, U.S.A) **262/10**
5 3¾ **Sharp Humor (USA)**[203] 1498 3-8-4 ow1 CVelasquez 5 97
(Dale Romans, U.S.A) **152/10**

1m 32.46s
WFA 3 from 4yo+ 2lb **5** Ran SP% **120.8**
PARI-MUTUEL (including $2 stakes): WIN 2.50; PL (1-2) 2.10, 4.40; SHOW (1-2-3) 2.10, 2.40, 2.10; SF 8.40.
Owner Godolphin Racing Inc **Bred** E Paul Robsham **Trained** Newmarket, Suffolk

NOTEBOOK
Discreet Cat(USA) ◆ was faced with his toughest task to date, conceding upwards of 4lb to a decent field, but he produced another stunning performance to claim his first Grade 1 victory and stretch his unbeaten record to six. The field were fairly sprinting for home from some way out, but Discreet Cat was always moving with ease - if anything he was a little too keen - and drew away when asked, equalling the track record set by Easy Goer in the 1989 Gotham despite apparently not being touched with the whip. To be fair, he probably came under more pressure than in any of his previous races in the US, but his rider's claim that it was all hands and heels suggests he has even more to offer. He has been recording top-class times from day one, even though he has yet to be fully extended, and there is no doubt he is up there with the very best dirt horses in the world. He will now be trained in Dubai for either the Godolphin Mile or the Dubai World Cup. It would be fascinating to see him in the latter race, although he will have to learn to settle better if he is to see out the ten-furlong trip.

TOKYO (L-H)
Sunday, November 26

OFFICIAL GOING: Firm

6612a JAPAN CUP (GRADE 1) — 1m 4f
6:20 (6.20) 3-Y-O **£1,223,776** 493,510; £310,912; £187,534; £123,378)

Pos	Dist	Horse	Jockey	RPR
1		**Deep Impact (JPN)**[56] 5716 4-9-0 (Y Ikee, Japan) **30/100**[1]	YTake 6	127+
2	2	**Dream Passport (JPN)**[35] 3-8-9 (H Matsuda, Japan) **152/10**	YIwata 7	124
3	1/2	**Ouija Board**[22] 6340 5-8-9 (E A L Dunlop) *held up in 10th, headway over 3f out, 6th straight, stayed on steadily final 2f* **17/2**[3]	LDettori 3	117
4	1	**Cosmo Bulk (JPN)**[28] 5-9-0 (K Tabe, Japan) **40/1**	FIgarashi 10	121
5	1 1/2	**Fusaichi Pandora (JPN)**[14] 3-8-5 (T Shirai, Japan) **52/1**	YFukunaga 8	116
6	nse	**Meisho Samson (JPN)**[35] 3-8-9 (T Setoguchi, Japan) **15/1**	MIshibashi 11	119
7	1/2	**Freedonia**[50] 5821 4-8-9 (J E Hammond, France) *held up in 9th, last straight, headway final f, never nearer* **89/1**	TGillet 9	113
8	3/4	**Swift Current (JPN)**[28] 5-9-0 (Hideyuki Mori, Japan) **42/1**	NYokoyama 2	117
9	3 1/2	**Tosen Shana O (JPN)**[35] 3-8-9 (Hideyuki Mori, Japan) **150/1**	HGoto 5	112
10	6	**Heart's Cry (JPN)**[120] 3927 5-9-0 (K Hashiguchi, Japan) **58/10**[2]	C-PLemaire 1	102
11	3 1/2	**Yukino Sun Royal (JPN)**[574] 9-9-0 (S Masuzawa, Japan) **216/1**	KatsuharuTanaka 4	97

2m 25.1s
WFA 3 from 4yo+ 6lb — 11 Ran SP% **123.5**
TOTE (including 100 yen stakes): WIN 130; PL 110, 210, 190; DF 750; SF 860.
Owner Kaneko Makoto Holdings Co Ltd **Bred** Northern Farm **Trained** Japan

NOTEBOOK
Deep Impact(JPN), back on his own patch, returned to his best form. Held up in last, he quickened up well to mow down his rivals and, despite edging right in the straight, was always going to get there. He won in the style his supporters have grown accustomed to seeing, and it is a shame that the tactical nature of the Arc failed to show him at his best, but he now boasts an impressive record of 11 wins from 13 career starts. His last race before being retired will come in the Arima Kinen at Nakayama on Christmas Eve, the race in which he was unexpectedly beaten into second by Heart's Cry last year.
Ouija Board raced close to Deep Impact throughout and, when Take kicked, Dettori followed him through. Although the mare stayed on up the straight, she could not cope with the impressive colt on his home turf, but it was still a very good effort in defeat. She picked up more prize-money for finishing third here than she did for winning the Prince of Wales's Stakes or Nassau Stakes earlier this year. Her last race before being retired to the paddocks will be the Hong Kong Vase.
Heart's Cry(JPN), the King George third, was very disappointing, as at his best he should have been the main threat to the favourite. After all, he beat Deep Impact in the Arima Kinen last year.

6589 HOLLYWOOD PARK (L-H)
Sunday, November 26

OFFICIAL GOING: Firm

6613a HOLLYWOOD DERBY (GRADE 1) — 1m 2f (T)
11:04 (11:29) 3-Y-O **£174,419** (£58,140; £34,884; £17,442; £5,814)

Pos	Dist	Horse	Jockey	RPR
1		**Showing Up (USA)**[43] 3-8-10 (B Tagg, U.S.A) **4/5**[1]	CVelasquez 6	119
2	2 1/4	**Obrigado (FR)**[43] 5985 3-8-10 (N Drysdale, U.S.A) **17/2**	(b) GKGomez 11	115
3	1 1/2	**Ivan Denisovich (IRE)**[64] 5524 3-8-10 (A P O'Brien, Ire) *raced in 6th, 4th and improving straight, ran on to take 3rd inside final furlong* **59/10**[3]	(v) JRVelazquez 7	112
4	nk	**Crested**[43] 3-8-10 (W Dollase, U.S.A) **265/10**	(b) VEspinoza 4	111
5	3/4	**Zann (USA)** 3-8-10 (M Machowsky, U.S.A) **342/10**	(b) DFlores 8	110
6	4 3/4	**Kip Deville (USA)**[78] 3-8-10 (R Dutrow Jr, U.S.A) **7/1**	(b) JRLeparoux 9	102
7	1/2	**Frost Giant (USA)**[50] 5821 3-8-10 (R Dutrow Jr, U.S.A) **7/1**	EPrado 5	101
8	7	**Dark Islander (IRE)**[43] 5985 3-8-10 (J W Hills) *led or disputed lead on inside, dropped back to 4th 2f out, 8th and weakening straight* **58/10**[2]	JValdiviaJr 1	88
9	nse	**Big Mistake (USA)** 3-8-10 (B Cecil, U.S.A) **31/1**	(b) CNakatani 2	88
10	3 3/4	**Vega's Lord (GER)**[64] 5543 3-8-10 (P Rau, Germany) **69/1**	AGryder 3	81

1m 59.35s (24.56) — 10 Ran SP% **131.3**
PARI-MUTUEL (Including $2 stake): WIN 3.60; PL (1-2) 2.60, 4.80;SHOW (1-2-3) 2.20, 3.40, 3.60; DF 14.60.
Owner Lael Stable **Bred** Nellie M Cox & Rose Retreat Farm **Trained** USA

NOTEBOOK
Ivan Denisovich(IRE), trying 11 furlongs for the first time, did not get the best of trips but stayed on well in the straight to grab a place.
Dark Islander(IRE) came from last position to win a Grade 2 at Santa Anita on his debut in the US, so it is fair to say things did not go to plan this time - he basically ended up setting it up for the closers.

6614a MATRIARCH STKS (GRADE 1) (F&M) — 1m (T)
12:05 (12:37) 3-Y-O+ **£174,442** (£58,140; £34,884; £17,442; £5,814)

Pos	Dist	Horse	Jockey	RPR
1		**Price Tag**[57] 5701 3-8-8 (R J Frankel, U.S.A) **22/10**[1]	EPrado 8	114
2	1/2	**Three Degrees (IRE)**[57] 4-8-11 (P Gallagher, U.S.A) **43/10**[2]	ASolis 7	114
3	hd	**Pommes Frites (USA)**[42] 4-8-11 (W Mott, U.S.A) **8/1**[3]	JSantos 10	114
4	hd	**Mea Domina (USA)**[43] 5-8-11 (R McAnally, U.S.A) **152/10**	TBaze 4	113
5	hd	**Society Hostess (USA)**[111] 4-8-11 (Christophe Clement, U.S.A) **98/10**	(b) GKGomez 9	113
6	1/2	**Ready To Please (USA)**[113] 3-8-8 (T Pletcher, U.S.A) **191/10**	JRVelazquez 2	111
7	3/4	**Beautyandthebeast**[28] 6253 4-8-11 (N Drysdale, U.S.A) **104/10**	CNakatani 5	110
8	nk	**Memorette (USA)**[127] 4-8-11 (W Currin, U.S.A) **313/10**	KDesormeaux 3	110
9	3/4	**Attima**[98] 3-8-11 (J Canani, U.S.A) **12/1**	VEspinoza 1	110
10	hd	**Danzon (USA)**[21] 6366 3-8-8 (J-C Rouget, France) **27/1**	JRLeparoux 14	107
11	1	**Clinet (IRE)**[28] 6253 4-8-11 (J W Hills) *towards rear on outside, 10th half-way, 13th and five wide entering straight, unable to quicken* **104/10**	JValdiviaJr 6	106
12	2 1/4	**Mirabilis (USA)**[169] 4-8-11 (R J Frankel, U.S.A) **22/10**[1]	PValenzuela 13	101
13	1/2	**Cambiocorsa (USA)**[60] 4-8-11 (Doug O'Neill, U.S.A) **313/10**	JKCourt 11	100
14	1	**River's Prayer (USA)**[435] 3-8-8 (Paula Capestro, U.S.A) **504/10**	(b) CLPotts 12	97

1m 34.7s
WFA 3 from 4yo+ 2lb — 14 Ran SP% **149.8**
PARI-MUTUEL: WIN 6.40 (coupled in all pools with Mirabilis); PL (1-2) 4.00, 4.20; SHOW (1-2-3) 2.80, 2.80, 3.80; DF 18.00.
Owner K Abdulla **Bred** Juddmonte Farms Ltd **Trained** USA

NOTEBOOK
Clinet(IRE), second in a Grade 2 at Santa Anita on her debut in the US, did not get the run of things and was unable to produce her best. She is now expected to head to Dubai.

6590 KEMPTON (A.W) (R-H)
Monday, November 27

OFFICIAL GOING: Standard
Wind: Fresh, behind Weather: Overcast

6615 IBETX.COM BANDED STKS — 5f (P)
1:10 (1:10) (Class 7) 3-Y-O+ — **£1,365** (£403; £201) **Stalls** High

Form	Pos	Dist	Horse	Jockey	RPR
0062	1		**Muara**[7] 6533 4-8-12 50 (D W Barker) *rdn along towards rr: hdwy over 1f out: led ins fnl f: drvn out* **3/1**[1]	MarkLawson(5) 11	59
1500	2	3/4	**Muktasb (USA)**[193] 1794 5-9-3 50 (D Shaw) *s.s: hld up in rr: hdwy and nt clr run over 1f out: squeezed through to cse wnr fnl 75 yds: r.o* **14/1**	(v) AdamKirby 1	56+
0064	3	1	**Spinetail Rufous (IRE)**[21] 6372 8-8-12 45 (Miss Z C Davison) *led tl edgd lft and no ex ins fnl f* **20/1**	AdrianMcCarthy 12	48
0523	4	shd	**Davids Mark**[7] 6539 6-9-1 48 (J R Jenkins) *chsd ldrs: nt clr run over 1f out: one pce fnl f* **10/3**[2]	EddieAhern 10	50+
5241	5	hd	**Desert Dust**[7] 6539 3-9-9 50 (R M H Cowell) *swvd lft s: midfield on outside: styng on whn edgd rt ins fnl f* **7/1**	(v) BrettDoyle 3	58
0006	6	hd	**Prime Recreation**[7] 6539 9-9-0 47 (P S Felgate) *towards rr: rdn 2f out: nrst fin* **10/1**	PatCosgrave 8	48
4034	7	3/4	**Campeon (IRE)**[7] 6539 4-9-0 47 (J M Bradley) *chsd ldr tl edgd lft and no ex ins fnl f* **7/1**	SteveDrowne 6	45
5661	8	1/2	**Twinned (IRE)**[19] 6399 3-9-3 50 (Karen George) *trckd ldrs: nowhere to go over 1f out: nt rcvr* **6/1**[3]	(p) JimmyQuinn 7	46+
0062	9	3/4	**Succeed (IRE)**[7] 6539 3-9-3 50 (Mrs H Sweeting) *hld up in midfield: effrt and hmpd over 1f out: in tch and styng on whn bdly squeezed and snatched up ins fnl f* **7/1**	GeorgeBaker 9	44+
0360	10	3/4	**Otis B Driftwood**[7] 6541 3-9-2 49 (Miss J R Tooth) *prom: rdn over 1f out: btn whn squeezed for room ins fnl f* **50/1**	(b) PaulFitzsimons 5	40
4030	11	7	**Comic Tales**[6] 6548 5-8-12 45 (M Mullineaux) *s.v.s: a wl bhd* **50/1**	(e[1]) LeeEnstone 2	11

60.52 secs (0.12) **Going Correction** -0.225s/f (Stan) — 11 Ran SP% **124.3**
Speed ratings (Par 97):90,88,87,87,86 86,85,84,83,82 70
CSF £48.78 TOTE £3.60: £2.00, £5.70, £4.60; EX 84.40.
Owner W R Arblaster **Bred** W R And Mrs Arblaster **Trained** Scorton, N Yorks
■ Stewards' Enquiry : Adrian McCarthy caution: careless riding
Paul Fitzsimons two-day ban: used whip in the incorrect place (Dec 8-9)

FOCUS
Several of these enjoyed little luck in running in what was an ordinary banded heat, rated through the fifth. The time was modest.
Twinned(IRE) Official explanation: jockey said gelding was denied a clear run
Comic Tales Official explanation: jockey said gelding missed the break

6616 IBETX.COM BETTING EXCHANGE BANDED STKS — 1m 2f (P)
1:40 (1:40) (Class 7) 3-Y-O+ — **£1,365** (£403; £201) **Stalls** High

Form	Pos	Dist	Horse	Jockey	RPR
3054	1		**Elms Schoolboy**[6] 6552 4-9-2 45 (P Howling) *t.k.h: chsd ldr: led 2f out: hld on gamely fnl f* **6/1**[2]	(b) IanMongan 4	53
3056	2	1/2	**Weet Yer Tern (IRE)**[243] 793 4-9-2 45 (W M Brisbourne) *prom: drvn to press wnr ins fnl f: nt qckn nr fin* **9/1**	EddieAhern 9	52

The Form Book, Raceform Ltd, Compton, RG20 6NL

0600 **3** ¾ **Kinsman (IRE)**[21] [6370] 9-9-2 45........................(p) AdamKirby 7 51
(T D McCarthy) *hld up towards rr: wd bnd into st: rdn and r.o fnl 2f* **14/1**

0026 **4** nk **Bollywood (IRE)**[21] [6370] 3-8-12 45........................ MatthewHenry 8 50
(J J Bridger) *t.k.h: chsd ldrs: effrt and swtchd lft over 1f out: one pce fnl f* **8/1**[3]

2563 **5** 2 **Sriology (IRE)**[6] [6552] 5-9-2 45........................ JimmyQuinn 3 46
(J Pearce) *in tch: effrt over 2f out: styd on same pce* **9/4**[1]

1005 **6** ½ **Wind Chime (IRE)**[29] [6232] 9-9-2 45........................ RichardThomas 10 45+
(A G Newcombe) *mid-div: lost pl 1/2-way: hrd rdn and r.o fnl 2f* **6/1**[2]

0605 **7** 2 ½ **Discomania**[28] [938] 4-8-9 45........................(b) JonjoMilczarek(7) 6 41
(K F Clutterbuck) *hdwy and in tch on outside after 4f: outpcd fnl 3f* **20/1**

0000 **8** hd **Louve Heureuse (IRE)**[29] [6232] 5-9-2 45........................ RobertMiles 14 40
(B G Powell) *chsd ldrs tl no ex fnl 2f* **14/1**

2005 **9** 1 ¾ **Frenchgate**[5] [6370] 5-8-11 45........................(v) MarkLawson(5) 11 37
(I W McInnes) *s.i.s: t.k.h in midfield: no hdwy fnl 3f* **12/1**

6-0 **10** ½ **Impulsive Madam**[61] [5625] 3-8-12 45........................ LPKeniry 1 36
(S Kirk) *towards rr: sme hdwy 4f out: rdn and btn 2f out* **20/1**

-000 **11** 3 **Premier Cru**[21] [6371] 3-8-12 45........................ FergusSweeney 13 30
(Andrew Turnell) *led tl wknd 2f out* **14/1**

0000 **12** ¾ **Ruby Sunrise (IRE)**[17] [6429] 4-9-2 45........................ PaulEddery 2 29
(B P J Baugh) *s.s: plld hrd early: a bhd* **16/1**

60 **13** 1 ¾ **River Beau (IRE)**[21] [6373] 3-8-12 45........................ SteveDrowne 12 25
(E J O'Neill) *in tch: rdn 4f out: sn wknd* **16/1**

060- **14** 8 **Almisq (USA)**[353] [6534] 5-9-2 45........................(b[1]) BrettDoyle 5 10
(Miss D Mountain) *stdd s: plld hrd early: a bhd: eased whn no ch fnl f* **33/1**

2m 8.25s (-0.75) **Going Correction** -0.225s/f (Stan)
WFA 3 from 4yo+ 4lb **14** Ran SP% **132.4**
Speed ratings (Par 97):94,93,93,92,91 90,88,88,87,86 84,83,82,76
CSF £64.03 TOTE £7.90: £1.90, £3.70, £5.00; EX 63.50.
Owner Paul Howling **Bred** L A C Ashby **Trained** Newmarket, Suffolk

FOCUS
They went a decent gallop in what was a moderate contest even for the grade, rated through the runner-up.
Ruby Sunrise(IRE) Official explanation: jockey said filly had no more to give

6617 BET WTIH IBETX.COM BANDED STKS 1m 2f (P)
2:10 (2:10) (Class 7) 3-Y-O+ **£1,365** (£403; £201) **Stalls** High

Form RPR

2040 **1** **Shaheer (IRE)**[7] [6540] 4-9-5 49........................(v) JimCrowley 13 57
(J Gallagher) *in tch: drvn to ld jst ins fnl f: hld on wl nr fin* **16/1**

1642 **2** nk **Milk And Sultana**[7] [6544] 6-9-6 50........................ SteveDrowne 2 57+
(G A Ham) *hld up in midfield: effrt and hmpd ent st: swtchd lft over 1f out: r.o to press wnr fnl 50 yds: jst hld* **4/1**[2]

5051 **3** 1 ½ **Majehar**[29] [6232] 4-9-2 46........................ AdrianMcCarthy 14 51
(A G Newcombe) *in tch: effrt over 2f out: led briefly 1f out: one pce fnl f* **5/1**

4645 **4** ¾ **Revolve**[21] [6374] 6-9-4 48........................(p) IanMongan 12 51
(Mrs L J Mongan) *prom: led over 1f out: sn hdd and one pce* **9/2**[3]

0333 **5** ½ **Wood Fern (UAE)**[7] [6544] 6-9-3 47........................ EddieAhern 9 49+
(W M Brisbourne) *hld up in midfield: promising hdwy on rail whn nt clr run over 1f out: one pce* **3/1**[1]

0-00 **6** nk **Overdrawn (IRE)**[6] [6551] 5-8-10 47........................(bt) WilliamBuick(7) 6 49
(A J McCabe) *bhd tl rdn and r.o fnl 2f* **25/1**

005 **7** nk **Inveraray**[7] [6545] 3-9-2 50........................ PatCosgrave 1 51
(P S Felgate) *towards rr: hdwy to chse ldrs over 1f out: one pce* **12/1**

00-4 **8** 1 ½ **Jarvo**[7] [6544] 5-8-12 47........................ MarkLawson(5) 11 45
(I W McInnes) *prom in chsng gp: hrd rdn 2f out: wknd over 1f out* **12/1**

2000 **9** ¾ **Height Of Spirits**[7] [6544] 4-9-4 48........................(b[1]) AdamKirby 4 45
(T D McCarthy) *mid-div: effrt 4f out: hrd rdn and hung rt ent st: sn wknd* **20/1**

3030 **10** 10 **Perfect Order (USA)**[7] [6543] 3-8-13 47........................(p) MickyFenton 8 25
(N A Callaghan) *sn led: set str pce: hdd & wknd qckly over 1f out* **12/1**

6000 **11** 1 ¼ **Ullah Pendragon (IRE)**[44] [5955] 3-8-7 46........................ NataliaGemelova(5) 10 21
(A J McCabe) *a bhd* **40/1**

4300 **12** 6 **Noorain**[106] [4389] 4-9-3 47........................ LPKeniry 5 11
(A M Hales) *chsd tearaway ldr tl wknd over 2f out* **20/1**

-060 **13** 1 ¾ **Hometomammy**[280] [457] 4-9-6 50........................ RobertMiles 7 11
(P W Hiatt) *missed break and hmpd s: a bhd* **33/1**

4450 **14** 6 **Phoenix Eye**[165] [2407] 5-9-3 47........................ LeeEnstone 3 —
(M Mullineaux) *s.s: rdn 4f out: a towards rr* **25/1**

2m 6.94s (-2.06) **Going Correction** -0.225s/f (Stan)
WFA 3 from 4yo+ 4lb **14** Ran SP% **131.4**
Speed ratings (Par 97):99,98,97,96,96 96,96,94,94,86 85,80,79,74
CSF £79.73 TOTE £30.10: £8.10, £1.60, £1.40; EX 142.10.
Owner Colin Rashbrook and John Gallagher **Bred** David Crichton-Watt **Trained** Chastleton, Oxon

FOCUS
There was a fair pace on up front and Shaheer had everything go to plan. He ran to this year's turf form in a race run in a decent time.
Wood Fern(UAE) Official explanation: jockey said gelding was denied a clear run

6618 LAY BACK AND RELAX WITH IBETX.COM BANDED STKS 1m (P)
2:40 (2:41) (Class 7) 3-Y-O+ **£1,365** (£403; £201) **Stalls** High

Form RPR

0552 **1** **Mythical Charm**[29] [6235] 7-9-5 50........................(t) MatthewHenry 6 62
(J J Bridger) *hld up towards rr: gd hdwy 2f out: led over 1f out: rdn clr* **9/4**[1]

5000 **2** 2 **Wilford Maverick (IRE)**[6] [6554] 4-9-2 47........................ DaleGibson 10 54
(M J Attwater) *towards rr: gd hdwy over 1f out: r.o to chse wnr ins fnl f* **20/1**

6062 **3** 2 ½ **Fun Time**[21] [6371] 3-9-3 50........................ SamHitchcott 9 51
(M R Channon) *prom: drvn along 2f out: nt qckn appr fnl f* **9/2**[2]

0000 **4** ¾ **Lucius Verrus (USA)**[9] [6510] 6-9-5 50........................(v) RichardThomas 12 50
(D Shaw) *mid-div: effrt over 2f out: styd on same pce* **14/1**

5004 **5** ¾ **Shannon Arms (USA)**[17] [6431] 5-9-4 49........................ PatCosgrave 13 47
(R Brotherton) *led tl over 1f out: no ex* **13/2**[3]

0000 **6** nk **Orphina (IRE)**[45] [5936] 3-9-3 50........................ RobertMiles 7 47
(B G Powell) *in tch: effrt on outside appr st: no imp fnl 2f* **9/1**

5400 **7** 2 ½ **Danawi (IRE)**[16] [6439] 3-9-3 50........................ BrettDoyle 3 41
(M R Hoad) *s.i.s: bhd: rdn 3f out: nvr rchd ldrs* **14/1**

0000 **8** nk **Lady Ambitious**[7] [6544] 3-9-1 48........................ LeeEnstone 8 39
(D K Ivory) *mid-div: rdn and no hdwy fnl 3f* **25/1**

0040 **9** shd **Jumanji (IRE)**[6] [6549] 3-9-3 50........................(v[1]) DeanMernagh 4 40
(M J Attwater) *t.k.h: chsd ldrs tl wknd over 2f out* **33/1**

0050 **10** 1 ¼ **Dannabelle (IRE)**[13] [6477] 6-9-0 50........................ EmmettStack(5) 1 38
(John A Quinn, Ire) *prom tl wknd wl over 1f out* **12/1**

000 **11** 2 **Cankara (IRE)**[122] [3916] 3-9-0 47........................ StephenCarson 2 30
(D Carroll) *s.v.s: rdn 3f out: a bhd* **16/1**

4103 **12** 3 **Warden Warren**[7] [6543] 8-9-4 49........................(b) AdrianMcCarthy 11 25
(Mrs C A Dunnett) *chsd ldrs tl wknd wl over 1f out* **7/1**

500- **13** 22 **Sticky Mint (IRE)**[459] [4691] 3-9-0 47........................ MichaelTebbutt 5 —
(M Blanshard) *a towards rr: wl bhd fnl 3f* **33/1**

1m 39.88s (-0.92) **Going Correction** -0.225s/f (Stan)
WFA 3 from 4yo+ 2lb **13** Ran SP% **126.2**
Speed ratings (Par 97):95,93,90,89,89 88,86,85,85,84 82,79,57
CSF £59.35 TOTE £2.80: £1.40, £6.40, £1.80; EX 57.00.
Owner Tommy Ware **Bred** B J And Mrs Crangle **Trained** Liphook, Hants

FOCUS
Again the pace was good. Ordinary form, the winner not needing to improve and a length off this year's turf best.

6619 IBETX.COM MONEY MAN BANDED STKS 6f (P)
3:10 (3:17) (Class 7) 3-Y-O+ **£1,365** (£403; £201) **Stalls** High

Form RPR

3551 **1** **Siraj**[7] [6541] 7-9-6 47........................(b) BrettDoyle 12 64
(J Ryan) *mde all: hld on wl fnl f* **7/2**[1]

0005 **2** nk **Burhaan (IRE)**[29] [6234] 4-8-11 47........................ AmirQuinn(3) 11 57
(J R Boyle) *prom: drvn to press wnr fnl f: jst hld* **9/1**

3600 **3** hd **Danehill Stroller (IRE)**[16] [6442] 6-9-3 50........................ LPKeniry 9 59
(A M Hales) *bmpd s and s.i.s: bhd tl hdwy 2f out: r.o fnl f* **7/1**[3]

0052 **4** 1 ½ **For Life (IRE)**[13] [6473] 4-9-1 48........................ AdamKirby 10 54
(A P Jarvis) *w wnr tl nt qckn appr fnl f* **5/1**[2]

0430 **5** 3 **Orchestration (IRE)**[7] [6533] 5-9-0 47........................(v) DeanMernagh 6 45
(M J Attwater) *towards rr: nt clr run over 2f out: sn rdn: styd on fnl f* **5/1**[2]

0000 **6** ¾ **African Concerto (IRE)**[52] [5781] 3-9-2 49........................ GeorgeBaker 5 45
(S Kirk) *stdd s: towards rr: drvn along 2f out: nvr rchd ldrs* **5/1**[2]

0600 **7** 1 ¼ **Mustammer**[13] [6477] 3-9-3 50........................(v) MickyFenton 1 43
(D Shaw) *swvd lft s and s.i.s: hld up and bhd: styd on fr over 1f out: nvr nrr* **25/1**

0004 **8** shd **Beverley Beau**[7] [6541] 4-8-8 48........................(p) KristinStubbs(7) 8 40
(Mrs L Stubbs) *chsd ldrs over 3f* **9/1**

0200 **9** 2 **Mostanad**[81] [5131] 4-8-8 48........................(b) BarrySavage(7) 4 35
(J M Bradley) *hld up towards rr: swtchd outside and rdn over 2f out: n.d* **25/1**

3500 **10** 4 **Dark Moon**[14] [6465] 3-9-2 49........................ FergusSweeney 2 26
(D Shaw) *in tch 3f* **25/1**

000 **11** ½ **Mantolini**[53] [5774] 3-9-0 47........................(b[1]) EddieAhern 7 22
(Pat Eddery) *in tch over 3f: eased whn no ch 1f out* **12/1**

1m 12.7s (-1.00) **Going Correction** -0.225s/f (Stan) **11** Ran SP% **124.0**
Speed ratings (Par 97):97,96,96,94,90 89,87,87,84,79 78
CSF £37.37 TOTE £3.70: £1.60, £3.90, £2.60; EX 44.90.
Owner T C Gilligan **Bred** Mrs S J Etches **Trained** Newmarket, Suffolk

FOCUS
High draws were favoured and Siraj was able to make all from stall 12. Solid form, the winner producing his best figure for a long time.

6620 IBETX.COM MONEY MAN COMING SOON BANDED STKS 1m 4f (P)
3:40 (3:43) (Class 7) 3-Y-O+ **£1,365** (£403; £201) **Stalls** Centre

Form RPR

-031 **1** **Artzola (IRE)**[21] [6373] 6-9-4 45........................ PaulEddery 10 52+
(C A Horgan) *dwlt: hld up towards rr: effrt and n.m.r over 2f out: hdwy over 1f out: r.o to ld ins fnl f* **6/4**[1]

604- **2** nk **Gallas (IRE)**[347] [6583] 5-9-4 45........................(b) AdrianMcCarthy 6 51
(S Lycett) *t.k.h: in tch: rdn to ld over 1f out: hdd ins fnl f: kpt on wl* **20/1**

3 1 ½ **Mikimoto (IRE)**[144] [3234] 4-9-4 45........................ LeeEnstone 3 49
(S C Williams) *rrd s: t.k.h: mid-div on outside: effrt over 2f out: styd on fnl f* **14/1**

0564 **4** ½ **Kilmeena Magic**[21] [6373] 4-9-4 45........................ PaulFitzsimons 4 48
(J C Fox) *hld up in rr: hdwy to chal over 1f out: one pce fnl f* **14/1**

2243 **5** 1 ¼ **Glory Be (ITY)**[6] [6553] 4-9-4 45........................(v) SamHitchcott 12 46
(J L Spearing) *chsd ldr: led over 4f out tl over 1f out: no ex* **11/2**[2]

0636 **6** 1 ¼ **Laurollie**[7] [6540] 4-9-4 45........................ RichardThomas 2 44
(B P J Baugh) *chsd ldrs: rdn over 2f out: wknd 1f out* **12/1**

0000 **7** ¾ **Play Up Pompey**[21] [6374] 4-9-4 45........................ MatthewHenry 8 43
(J J Bridger) *stdd s: plld hrd: hld up and bhd: rdn and hdwy 2f out: nt rch ldrs* **20/1**

0036 **8** 3 **Whoopsie**[21] [6375] 4-9-4 45........................ DeanMernagh 14 38
(S Parr) *prom: rdn and lost pl over 3f out: midfield and n.d after* **6/1**[3]

0050 **9** 1 ¼ **Diafa (USA)**[6] [6551] 4-9-4 45........................(b[1]) DaleGibson 11 36
(J G M O'Shea) *cl up: wnt 2nd 3f out: chal on bit 2f out: rdn and wknd over 1f out* **25/1**

4022 **10** 3 **Captivate**[7] [6540] 3-8-7 45........................(p) NataliaGemelova(5) 7 31
(A J McCabe) *s.s: rdn along and bhd: nvr nr ldrs* **11/2**[2]

4460 **11** 11 **Liquid Lover (IRE)**[243] [794] 4-9-4 45........................(p) PatCosgrave 9 14
(W M Brisbourne) *in tch: rdn 5f out: wknd 3f out* **10/1**

0300 **12** 12 **Homebred Star**[188] [1911] 5-8-13 45........................(p) RobynBrisland(5) 5 —
(G P Enright) *a bhd* **25/1**

630- **13** 1 ½ **Delightfully**[604] [575] 5-9-4 45........................(b) BrettDoyle 13 —
(Jean-Rene Auvray) *led tl over 4f out: wknd qckly 3f out* **14/1**

2m 34.77s (-2.13) **Going Correction** -0.225s/f (Stan)
WFA 3 from 4yo+ 6lb **13** Ran SP% **139.1**
Speed ratings (Par 97):98,97,96,96,95 94,94,92,91,89 82,74,73
CSF £48.03 TOTE £2.70: £1.50, £6.70, £6.40; EX 45.40 Place 6 £276.97, Place 5 £93.01.
Owner Mrs B Sumner **Bred** Mrs B Sumner **Trained** Uffcott, Wilts

■ Stewards' Enquiry : Matthew Henry four-day ban: careless riding (Dec 8-11)

FOCUS
A pretty uncompetitive finale and the form is weak even for the grade, although the winner should continue to progress.
Homebred Star Official explanation: trainer said gelding finished lame

T/Plt: £147.20 to a £1 stake. Pool: £48,112.30. 238.55 winning tickets. T/Qpdt: £8.10 to a £1 stake. Pool: £3,640.00. 330.50 winning tickets. LM

[6603] WOLVERHAMPTON (A.W) (L-H)

Monday, November 27

OFFICIAL GOING: Standard

Wind: Fresh, behind Weather: Fresh

6621 BOOK ONLINE AT WOLVERHAMPTON-RACECOURSE.CO.UK H'CAP (FOR AMATEUR RIDERS) (DIV I) 1m 5f 194y(P)

1:20 (1:20) (Class 6) (0-65,69) 3-Y-0+ £1,977 (£608; £304) Stalls Low

Form RPR

4013 1 **Blue Hedges**[14] 6462 4-10-12 **59** MissALHutchinson(5) 10 67
(H J Collingridge) *hld up in rr: hdwy over 3f out: led wl over 1f out: sn rdn: r.o* **15/8**[1]

0405 2 *1* **Cumbrian Knight (IRE)**[21] 6376 8-10-6 **53** MissNJefferson(5) 6 59
(J M Jefferson) *s.s: hld up: hdwy over 8f out: rdn over 2f out: chsd wnr fnl f: styd on* **4/1**[3]

4121 3 *hd* **Sol Rojo**[4] 6568 4-11-10 **69** 6ex (v) MrSPearce(3) 8 75
(J Pearce) *plld hrd towards rr: hdwy 3f out: sn rdn: styd on ins fnl f* **7/2**[2]

4030 4 *3* **Alexian**[14] 6462 3-10-7 **64** MissBKilloran(7) 11 66
(D W P Arbuthnot) *plld hrd: racd wd tl swtchd lft and jnd ldr after 1f: led 5f out: rdn and hdd wl over 1f out: wknd ins fnl f* **16/1**

20-0 5 *3* **Dizzy Future**[64] 733 4-10-9 **51** MrsSBosley 3 49
(M R Bosley) *hld up in tch: rdn over 3f out: sn wknd* **10/1**

6060 6 *9* **Come What July (IRE)**[9] 6526 5-10-11 **53** MrsMMorris 5 38
(D Shaw) *hld up in mid-div: wknd over 3f out* **14/1**

4563 7 *1 1/4* **Weet For Ever (USA)**[7] 6535 3-9-13 **52** MissFayeBramley(3) 2 35
(P A Blockley) *led after 1f: hdd 8f out: rdn and wknd over 2f out* **15/2**

60U0 8 *11* **Cordage (IRE)**[7] 6532 4-10-3 **52** MissKJames(7) 7 20
(J A Pickering) *plld hrd: led 1f: led 8f out to 5f out: wknd 3f out* **50/1**

-030 9 *4* **Hill Of Clare (IRE)**[161] 2702 4-9-11 **46** MissSarah-JayneDavies(7) 1 8
(G H Jones) *prom tl wknd 5f out* **25/1**

3m 11.8s (4.43) **Going Correction** +0.05s/f (Slow)
WFA 3 from 4yo+ 8lb **9** Ran SP% **116.2**
Speed ratings (Par 101):89,88,88,86,84 79,79,72,70
CSF £9.48 CT £23.96 TOTE £2.60: £1.20, £1.80, £1.30; EX 12.50 Trifecta £13.50 Pool: £229.87 - 12.04 winning units..
Owner N H Gardner **Bred** S C E A Des Bissons **Trained** Exning, Suffolk
■ Stewards' Enquiry : Miss K James one-day ban: used whip when out of contention

FOCUS
A modest amateur riders' handicap and, with the pace very steady for much of the way, the winning time was 1.55 seconds slower than the second division. Plenty of these raced keenly. The winner and third produced personal bests, but the form is very ordinary.

6622 TWILIGHT RACING AND DINNER - RELAX AND ENJOY H'CAP 5f 20y(P)

1:50 (1:51) (Class 6) (0-65,71) 3-Y-0+ £2,730 (£806; £403) Stalls Low

Form RPR

631 1 **Tartatartufata**[6] 6555 4-9-5 **69** 6ex (v) PatrickMathers(3) 9 82
(D Shaw) *hld up in tch: rdn wl over 1f out: r.o to ld towards fin* **6/1**[3]

2001 2 *3/4* **Shade Cozy (USA)**[4] 6572 4-9-10 **71** 6ex FrancisNorton 8 81
(A M Balding) *hld up in tch: rdn to ld ins fnl f: hdd towards fin* **5/2**[1]

0201 3 *1/2* **Desert Opal**[24] 6325 6-8-10 **62** (p) LiamJones(5) 2 71
(C R Dore) *hld up in mid-div: rdn and swtchd rt over 1f out: hdwy fnl f: r.o* **5/1**[2]

3330 4 *1* **Blessed Place**[84] 5058 6-9-0 **61** JamieSpencer 3 66
(D J S Ffrench Davis) *chsd ldr: rdn wl over 1f out: nt qckn ins fnl f* **6/1**[3]

006 5 *1 1/4* **Almaty Express**[24] 6325 4-8-10 **57** (b) PaulMulrennan 5 57+
(J R Weymes) *outpcd: rdn and hdwy on ins wl over 1f out: swtchd rt wl ins fnl f: nvr nrr* **12/1**

3004 6 *nk* **Harrison's Flyer (IRE)**[3] 6585 5-9-1 **65** (b) GregFairley(3) 13 64
(J M Bradley) *hld up and bhd: rdn whn carried sltly rt over 1f out: hdwy whn hung lft ins fnl f: nvr trbld ldrs* **16/1**

000 7 *1/2* **Egyptian Lord**[9] 6521 3-8-8 **55** (b) RobbieFitzpatrick 4 53
(Peter Grayson) *n.m.r sn after s: sn chsng ldrs on ins: rdn wl over 1f out: fdd towards fin* **40/1**

3400 8 *shd* **Garlogs**[3] 6585 3-9-1 **62** RobertWinston 1 59
(A Bailey) *led: rdn wl over 1f out: hdd ins fnl f: wknd* **16/1**

1030 9 *3* **Union Jack Jackson (IRE)**[119] 3996 4-8-7 **54** JamieMackay 6 40
(J G Given) *s.i.s: sn wl outpcd: rdn whn swtchd lft wl over 1f out: a bhd* **25/1**

6251 10 *1 1/2* **Polar Force**[6] 6556 6-9-4 **65** 6ex ChrisCatlin 12 46
(Mrs C A Dunnett) *a bhd* **16/1**

0002 11 *3* **Rothesay Dancer**[9] 6521 3-8-8 **60** (p) KevinGhunowa(5) 10 30
(J S Goldie) *chsd ldrs on outside: wknd over 2f out* **20/1**

0000 12 *5* **The Leather Wedge (IRE)**[9] 6521 7-8-13 **60** TomEaves 7 12
(R Johnson) *prom: rdn over 2f out: sn wknd* **16/1**

62.39 secs (-0.43) **Going Correction** +0.05s/f (Slow) **12** Ran SP% **116.1**
Speed ratings (Par 101):105,103,103,101,99 98,98,97,93,90 85,77
CSF £20.28 CT £82.52 TOTE £5.50: £1.80, £1.80, £1.50; EX 20.40 Trifecta £22.30 Pool: £253.92 - 8.05 winning units..
Owner Danethorpe Racing Ltd **Bred** Dr A Ramkaran **Trained** Danethorpe, Notts

FOCUS
Competitive stuff and very good, solid form for the grade. The winner was back to his best.

6623 BOOK ONLINE AT WOLVERHAMPTON-RACECOURSE.CO.UK H'CAP (FOR AMATEUR RIDERS) (DIV II) 1m 5f 194y(P)

2:20 (2:20) (Class 6) (0-65,64) 3-Y-0+ £1,977 (£608; £304) Stalls Low

Form RPR

0/02 1 **Saltrio**[21] 6382 8-11-2 **64** MrBenBrisbourne(5) 1 78
(W M Brisbourne) *hld up and bhd: stdy hdwy over 6f out: led 4f out: edgd rt ins fnl f: r.o* **9/4**[2]

0P21 2 *1* **Zalkani (IRE)**[14] 6462 6-10-13 **59** MrSPearce(3) 11 72
(J Pearce) *hld up and bhd: stdy hdwy over 6f out: rdn and ev ch 2f out: nt qckn ins fnl f* **2/1**[1]

2654 3 *10* **Tip Toes (IRE)**[74] 5324 4-9-10 **46** MrJDown(7) 8 45
(P Howling) *hld up and bhd: hdwy over 3f out: wknd over 1f out* **14/1**

5300 4 *1/2* **Finished Article (IRE)**[13] 6474 9-10-1 **51** MissFGuillambert(7) 2 49
(P A Blockley) *hld up and bhd: hdwy over 3f out: wknd over 1f out* **7/1**

5 *10* **Something Simple (IRE)**[41] 6045 3-10-2 **60** MissPHermansson(7) 5 44
(R Ford) *hld up in tch: wknd 4f out* **25/1**

6 *1/2* **Kyathos (GER)**[13] 5-11-3 **60** MrSWalker 3 44
(M F Harris) *hld up in tch: rdn over 3f out: wknd wl over 2f out* **14/1**

0055 7 *3/4* **Dispol Peto**[9] 6526 6-10-10 **53** (p) MrWHogg 7 36
(R Johnson) *t.k.h: prom: led 8f out to 4f out: wknd over 2f out* **13/2**[3]

6000 8 *10* **Blanc Visage**[58] 5690 3-9-9 **53** MissNMCook(7) 10 22
(Mrs H Sweeting) *t.k.h: sn led: hdd 8f out: wknd 4f out* **33/1**

0-30 9 *2 1/2* **Ashstanza**[139] 3382 5-9-10 **46** MrOPestryy(7) 6 11
(R D E Woodhouse) *led early: prom tl wknd over 4f out* **40/1**

00-0 10 *65* **No Commission (IRE)**[126] 3784 4-10-4 **54** MrGGilbertson(7) 9 —
(R F Fisher) *a towards rr: t.o fnl 4f* **66/1**

035- 11 *28* **Staff Nurse (IRE)**[358] 6495 6-9-9 **45** oh5 MissWGibson(7) 4 —
(N Wilson) *a towards rr: t.o fnl 4f* **25/1**

3m 10.25s (2.88) **Going Correction** +0.05s/f (Slow)
WFA 3 from 4yo+ 8lb **37** Ran SP% **117.8**
Speed ratings (Par 101):93,92,86,86,80 80,80,74,72,35 19
CSF £6.76 CT £49.27 TOTE £3.00: £1.20, £1.20, £2.90; EX 6.10 Trifecta £62.20 Pool: £304.37 - 3.45 winning units..
Owner Raymond McNeill **Bred** Val Di Luna S R L **Trained** Great Ness, Shropshire
■ Stewards' Enquiry : Mr Ben Brisbourne one-day ban: careless riding
Mr O Pestryy three-day ban: used whip with excessive frequency when out of contention

FOCUS
Another modest amateur riders' handicap, but the pace was better this time and the winning time was 1.55 seconds quicker than the first division. The first two finished clear and have been rated positively.

6624 HOTEL AND CONFERENCING AT WOLVERHAMPTON RACECOURSE (S) STKS 7f 32y(P)

2:50 (2:50) (Class 6) 3-Y-0+ £2,388 (£705; £352) Stalls High

Form RPR

0505 1 **Bessemer (JPN)**[4] 6573 5-9-6 **70** (p) DanielTudhope 6 69
(D Carroll) *hld up: hdwy over 2f out: rdn over 2f out: led wl over 1f out: sn hung lft: hung rt ins fnl f: drvn out* **2/1**[1]

0000 2 *1 1/2* **Pommes Frites**[12] 6489 3-8-8 **67** FrancisNorton 1 54
(W R Muir) *chsd ldrs: rdn and ev ch wl over 1f out: nt qckn ins fnl f* **11/2**[3]

0425 3 *hd* **Mountain Pass (USA)**[7] 6531 4-9-6 **57** (p) FMBerry 2 64
(M J Wallace) *hld up and bhd: rdn and hdwy on ins whn nt clr run and plld out wl over 1f out: kpt on ins fnl f* **5/1**[2]

6220 4 *2* **Royal Embrace**[178] 2210 3-8-10 **58** (v) PatrickMathers(3) 5 53
(D Shaw) *hld up and bhd: rdn and hdwy on ins wl over 1f out: one pce fnl f* **20/1**

3200 5 *1/2* **Fulvio (USA)**[7] 6532 6-9-3 **54** (v) DeanCorby(3) 7 58
(P Howling) *hld up: rdn and hdwy over 2f out: one pce fnl f* **16/1**

0-0 6 *1/2* **Nebdi (IRE)**[29] 6241 5-9-0 **55** (p) DavidAllan 10 50
(E J Alston) *led: rdn over 2f out: hdd wl over 1f out: wknd ins fnl f* **50/1**

6060 7 *5* **Bollin Edward**[18] 6417 7-9-6 **60** (p) NCallan 8 43
(K A Ryan) *bhd: sme hdwy whn edgd lft over 1f out: n.d* **12/1**

1065 8 *3* **Cool Sting (IRE)**[10] 6508 3-9-5 **62** (vt) BrianReilly 12 36
(P S McEntee) *sn prom: rdn over 2f out: wknd over 1f out* **20/1**

1630 9 *3/4* **Captain Darling (IRE)**[40] 6060 6-9-3 **65** EdwardCreighton(3) 11 34
(R W Price) *hdwy over 5f out: rdn over 3f out: wknd over 2f out* **7/1**

2303 10 *nk* **Chickado (IRE)**[6] 6549 5-9-1 **50** (p) RobertHavlin 4 28
(D Haydn Jones) *hld up in tch: n.m.r over 3f out: lost pl whn nt clr run over 2f out* **9/1**

0000 11 *13* **Bernie's Beau (IRE)**[20] 6390 3-8-8 **54** GrahamGibbons 3 —
(R Hollinshead) *prom: rdn over 3f out: wknd over 2f out* **33/1**

1m 30.64s (0.24) **Going Correction** +0.05s/f (Slow)
WFA 3 from 4yo+ 1lb **11** Ran SP% **115.9**
Speed ratings (Par 101):100,98,98,95,95 94,88,85,84,84 69
CSF £11.75 TOTE £3.00: £1.80, £1.60, £2.00; EX 18.70 Trifecta £22.60 Pool: £238.17 - 7.45 winning units..The winner was bought in for 8,500gns. Cool Sting was claimed by Mick Quinlan for £6,000. Mountain Pass was claimed by Simon Dow for £6,000.
Owner Mrs B Ramsden **Bred** Darley Stud **Trained** Warthill, N Yorks

FOCUS
Not a bad seller, with the front pair better than this grade on their day. The third is the best guide to the form.
Chickado(IRE) Official explanation: jockey said mare suffered interference on the final bend

6625 STAY AT THE WOLVERHAMPTON HOLIDAY INN NURSERY 1m 141y(P)

3:20 (3:21) (Class 6) (0-65,63) 2-Y-0 £3,238 (£963; £481; £240) Stalls Low

Form RPR

6062 1 **Beau Sancy**[9] 6518 2-8-11 **60** TolleyDean(7) 1 62
(R A Harris) *a.p: rdn over 3f out: led wl over 1f out: sn edgd rt: r.o* **10/3**[1]

4654 2 *shd* **Keep Your Distance**[10] 6506 2-9-7 **63** (p) PaulMulrennan 8 65
(K R Burke) *led: rdn and hdd wl over 1f out: sn hung rt: r.o ins fnl f* **9/2**[2]

3023 3 *1 3/4* **Right Option (IRE)**[9] 6518 2-9-6 **62** NCallan 4 60
(J R Weymes) *hld up in tch: rdn over 3f out: nt qckn ins fnl f* **10/3**[1]

6000 4 *1/2* **Arabellas Homer**[9] 6520 2-8-8 **50** HayleyTurner 3 47
(Mrs N Macauley) *a.p: rdn over 2f out: sltly hmpd over 1f out: one pce fnl f* **25/1**

040 5 *1/2* **Zain (IRE)**[9] 6512 2-8-10 **52** DeanMcKeown 6 48
(J G Given) *hld up: n.m.r sn after s: rdn and hdwy over 2f out: one pce fnl f* **5/1**[3]

6000 6 *1 3/4* **Skye But N Ben**[24] 6316 2-8-8 **50** ChrisCatlin 5 42
(T D Barron) *bhd: rdn over 4f out: hdwy on ins over 1f out: no further prog fnl f* **12/1**

0020 7 *5* **Taran Tregarth**[7] 6534 2-8-3 **45** (b) FrancisNorton 7 27
(A Bailey) *hld up in tch: n.m.r after 1f: wknd over 2f out* **33/1**

3005 8 *6* **Only Hope**[9] 6518 2-8-8 **53** (p) JamesDoyle(3) 9 22
(Ernst Oertel) *prom tl rdn and wknd over 2f out* **7/1**

000 9 *20* **Dream On Dreamers (IRE)**[42] 6013 2-7-12 **40** JamieMackay 2 —
(R C Guest) *nvr gng wl: a in rr: t.o fnl 3f* **40/1**

1m 53.4s (1.64) **Going Correction** +0.05s/f (Slow) **9** Ran SP% **110.4**
Speed ratings (Par 94):94,93,92,91,91 89,85,80,62
CSF £16.93 CT £49.41 TOTE £2.90: £1.40, £1.10, £1.60; EX 14.30 Trifecta £18.90 Pool: £447.09 - 16.74 winning units..
Owner S & A Mares **Bred** Mrs J Keegan **Trained** Earlswood, Monmouths
■ Stewards' Enquiry : Paul Mulrennan three-day ban: used whip with excessive frequency (Dec 8-10)

FOCUS
The pace was no more than ordinary for this nursery and there were almost five in a line at the furlong pole. Modest, but solid form.

NOTEBOOK
Beau Sancy, beaten by the minimum margin over the extra furlong here last time, found the camera favouring him on this occasion. Off the bridle a long way out, he responded to the pressure but looked far from enthusiastic in the home straight and only held on by the skin of his teeth. He probably has a lot more ability than he cares to show, which does not make him an attractive proposition for a follow-up. (op 4-1)
Keep Your Distance, given a positive ride once again, kept battling away once headed but it was mainly the winner's reluctance after taking over from him that enabled him to nearly grab the race back. He is still to win after eight attempts, but there should be a modest race in him. (op 3-1)

Right Option(IRE), dropping back a furlong, came through to hold every chance but lacked a turn of foot and was forced to settle for a place in the frame for the third race running at this track. He is still to win after nine attempts. (tchd 4-1)

Arabellas Homer, trying this trip for the first time, ran her best race so far for her new yard and a modest opportunity can be found. (op 33-1)

Zain(IRE), making his nursery debut after three starts in maidens and taking a big step up in trip, lacked a turn of foot in the straight when holding every chance but did not appear to fail through lack of stamina. (op 9-2 tchd 6-1)

Taran Tregarth Official explanation: jockey said filly suffered interference on the first bend

6626 RINGSIDE SUITE 700 THEATRE STYLE CONFERENCE H'CAP — 2m 119y(P)

3:50 (3:50) (Class 5) (0-75,75) 3-Y-O+ — **£3,238** (£963; £481; £240) **Stalls** Low

Form — RPR

4041 **1** **Billich**[21] 6381 3-9-9 **75** ChrisCatlin 8 — 88
(E J O'Neill) *plld hrd in rr: hdwy over 7f out: led 3f out: sn rdn: edgd rt ins fnl f: drvn out* **9/4**[2]

220 **2** *nk* **Flame Creek (IRE)**[16] 6438 10-9-6 **66** EdwardCreighton(3) 3 — 79
(E J Creighton) *hld up and bhd: hdwy over 6f out: chsd wnr over 2f out: sn rdn: styd on ins fnl f* **11/1**

1302 **3** *3 1/2* **Champagne Shadow (IRE)**[25] 6312 5-10-0 **71** NCallan 10 — 79
(K A Ryan) *a.p: rdn 4f out: edgd lft 1f out: one pce* **15/8**[1]

0026 **4** *6* **Victory Quest (IRE)**[12] 6495 6-9-6 **63** (v) RobertWinston 4 — 64
(Mrs S Lamyman) *chsd ldr: led over 6f out: rdn and hdd 3f out: wknd over 1f out* **28/1**

0-40 **5** *21* **Proprioception (IRE)**[24] 3467 4-8-9 **52** HayleyTurner 2 — 28
(W K Goldsworthy) *hld up in mid-div: lost pl 12f out: n.d after* **18/1**

00/0 **6** *9* **Find The King (IRE)**[19] 6398 8-8-9 **52** RobertHavlin 6 — 17
(D W P Arbuthnot) *prom tl wknd over 6f out* **12/1**

0000 **7** *1* **El Tiger (GER)**[42] 6017 5-9-13 **70** JamieSpencer 7 — 34
(B J Curley) *t.k.h in mid-div: hdwy over 11f out: chsd ldr over 6f out: rdn over 3f out: wknd qckly over 2f out* **9/2**[3]

060- **8** *3 1/2* **Worlaby Dale**[429] 5248 10-8-9 **52** oh22 FrancisNorton 9 — 12
(Mrs S Lamyman) *plld hrd in rr: gd hdwy to ld over 11f out: hdd over 6f out: wknd over 5f out* **50/1**

0-06 **9** *14* **Zacatecas (GER)**[21] 6381 6-9-13 **70** DeanMcKeown 1 — 13
(A J Chamberlain) *led: hdd over 11f out: lost pl over 8f out* **50/1**

3m 43.14s (0.01) **Going Correction** +0.05s/f (Slow)
WFA 3 from 4yo+ 9lb — **9** Ran SP% **112.4**
Speed ratings (Par 103):101,100,99,96,86 82,81,80,73
CSF £25.82 CT £52.92 TOTE £3.20: £1.10, £3.20, £1.10; EX 22.80 Trifecta £68.90 Pool: £407.11 - 4.19 winning units..
Owner Mrs Julie Mitchell **Bred** Mrs S J Hearn **Trained** Averham Park, Notts

FOCUS
Not as competitive as the size of the field might suggest and, despite the ordinary pace set by the Lamyman pair, this proved too much of a test for several. Respectable form, the winner progressing.

6627 FIRST PAST THE POST H'CAP (DIV I) — 1m 1f 103y(P)

4:20 (4:20) (Class 6) (0-55,55) 3-Y-O+ — **£2,047** (£604; £302) **Stalls** Low

Form — RPR

5002 **1** **Qualitair Wings**[17] 6431 7-8-13 **54** DavidAllan 8 — 65
(J Hetherton) *hld up and bhd: rdn and hdwy over 1f out: r.o to ld cl home* **4/1**[3]

000- **2** *nk* **Picador**[406] 5946 3-8-7 **51** JamieMackay 7 — 61
(Sir Mark Prescott) *a.p: rdn over 2f out: edgd lft and led over 1f out: hdd cl home* **7/2**[2]

-000 **3** *1 1/2* **Dante's Diamond (IRE)**[10] 6507 4-9-0 **55** DeanMcKeown 11 — 62
(G A Swinbank) *hld up and bhd: c wd st: hdwy on outside over 1f out: r.o ins fnl f* **16/1**

6213 **4** *1 1/4* **Desert Hawk**[280] 469 5-8-9 **50** (b) RobbieFitzpatrick 3 — 54
(W M Brisbourne) *hld up in tch: rdn and ev ch over 1f out: one pce fnl f* **8/1**

0065 **5** *hd* **Amron Hill**[16] 6450 3-8-11 **55** GrahamGibbons 4 — 59
(R Hollinshead) *a.p: rdn wl over 1f out: one pce fnl f* **11/1**

2100 **6** *1* **Lockstock (IRE)**[39] 6069 8-8-10 **51** (p) FMBerry 2 — 53
(M S Saunders) *w ldr: led over 3f out: rdn over 2f out: hdd over 1f out: wknd ins fnl f* **16/1**

4030 **7** *3 1/2* **Sea Frolic (IRE)**[6] 6552 5-8-0 **46** oh1 (v) RoryMoore(5) 13 — 41
(Jennie Candlish) *hld up in mid-div: hdwy over 5f out: riddn 3f out: wknd wl over 1f out* **50/1**

1500 **8** *shd* **Fantasy Crusader**[21] 6380 7-8-11 **52** RobertWinston 9 — 47
(R M H Cowell) *hld up and bhd: rdn and short-lived effrt over 2f out* **20/1**

0 **9** *11* **Sehoya (IRE)**[16] 6448 4-9-0 **55** NCallan 12 — 28
(Eoin Doyle, Ire) *hld up in mid-div: rdn and wknd over 2f out: bhd whn hmpd over 1f out* **20/1**

4030 **10** *1 1/4* **Snake Skin**[17] 6430 3-8-8 **52** (p) ChrisCatlin 6 — 22
(J Gallagher) *led: hdd over 3f out: rdn over 2f out: wkng whn hmpd over 1f out* **33/1**

2500 **U** **Diktatorship (IRE)**[13] 6374 3-8-3 **50** (v) JamesDoyle(3) 5 — —
(Ernst Oertel) *hld up in mid-div: rdn and sme hdwy whn hmpd and uns rdr over 1f out* **28/1**

-100 **F** **Mad Maurice**[179] 2181 5-8-11 **52** JamieSpencer 10 — —
(B J Curley) *stdd s: sn swtchd lft: t.k.h: sn mid-div: rdn and hdwy whn nt clr run wl over 1f out: sn hmpd and fell: dead* **2/1**[1]

2m 2.07s (-0.55) **Going Correction** +0.05s/f (Slow)
WFA 3 from 4yo+ 3lb — **12** Ran SP% **124.6**
Speed ratings (Par 101):104,103,102,101,101 100,97,97,87,86 —,—
CSF £18.23 CT £212.17 TOTE £5.10: £1.50, £1.80, £4.90; EX 21.60 TRIFECTA Not won..
Owner PSB Holdings Ltd **Bred** C S Tateson **Trained** Norton, N Yorks

■ Stewards' Enquiry : Jamie Mackay three-day ban: careless riding (Dec 8-10)

FOCUS
A messy contest and the field were packed together for much of the way. Because of that, it was not the biggest surprise to see a horse come down, the third time that has happened here in the past 11 days, though none of them appeared to be surface-related. The winning time was just over half a second slower than the second division. Ordinary form, but sound.

Dante's Diamond(IRE) Official explanation: jockey said, regarding running and riding, that her orders were to hold the gelding up, keep him up in the bridle, adding that it lacks confidence and that she was to give it a chance and that it needed to be coaxed to give of its best; trainer's rep was satisfied with the ride given and accorded with instructions, adding that she was well pleased with the performance.

Sehoya(IRE) Official explanation: jockey said filly suffered interference

6628 FIRST PAST THE POST H'CAP (DIV II) — 1m 1f 103y(P)

4:50 (4:50) (Class 6) (0-55,55) 3-Y-O+ — **£2,047** (£604; £302) **Stalls** Low

Form — RPR

0606 **1** **Pop Music (IRE)**[50] 5847 3-8-8 **55** (p) JamesDoyle(3) 12 — 68
(Miss J Feilden) *a.p: rdn over 3f out: led over 2f out: r.o wl* **14/1**

6663 **2** *1 1/4* **Scottish River (USA)**[7] 6531 7-9-0 **55** HayleyTurner 10 — 65
(M D I Usher) *stdd s: hld up in rr: smooth hdwy on outside over 2f out: chsd wnr fnl f: sn edgd lft: nt qckn* **7/2**[2]

0066 **3** *2 1/2* **Fantasy Defender (IRE)**[21] 6371 4-8-5 **46** oh1 (v) ChrisCatlin 7 — 51
(Ernst Oertel) *hld up: hdwy over 5f out: rdn over 3f out: one pce fnl f* **12/1**

3410 **4** *3* **Band**[16] 6451 6-9-0 **55** GrahamGibbons 1 — 54
(E S McMahon) *a.p: chsd ldr wl over 1f out: sn edgd lft: wknd ins fnl f* **2/1**[1]

0045 **5** *3 1/2* **Suffolk House**[25] 6304 4-8-6 **47** oh1 ow1 DeanMcKeown 11 — 39
(M Brittain) *hld up in mid-div: rdn 3f out: no hdwy fnl 2 out* **14/1**

0060 **6** *1 1/4* **Ohana**[12] 6484 3-8-11 **55** TomEaves 4 — 45
(Miss Gay Kelleway) *hld up and bhd: rdn and hdwy on ins over 3f out: wknd over 2f out* **13/2**[3]

0063 **7** *1 1/4* **Bongoali**[21] 6373 4-8-0 **46** oh6 LiamJones(5) 3 — 33
(Mrs C A Dunnett) *hld up and bhd: rdn over 4f out: n.d* **16/1**

0000 **8** *5* **Aberlady Bay (IRE)**[9] 6436 3-8-6 **50** (v[1]) JamieMackay 8 — 27
(T T Clement) *w ldr: led 3f out: sn rdn and hdd: wknd wl over 1f out* **50/1**

0050 **9** *1 1/2* **Princely Ted (IRE)**[19] 6405 5-8-8 **52** (vt) EdwardCreighton(3) 2 — 26
(E J Creighton) *led: rdn and hdd 3f out: wknd 2f out* **14/1**

1005 **10** *6* **Strife (IRE)**[169] 2479 3-8-8 **52** DavidAllan 9 — 14
(W M Brisbourne) *sn bhd: rdn over 6f out: no rspnse* **8/1**

2040 **11** *13* **Crusoe (IRE)**[8] 6473 9-8-9 **50** (b) BrianReilly 5 — —
(A Sadik) *hld up in mid-div: rdn over 4f out: sn bhd* **33/1**

2m 1.50s (-1.12) **Going Correction** +0.05s/f (Slow)
WFA 3 from 4yo+ 3lb — **45** Ran SP% **118.5**
Speed ratings (Par 101):106,104,102,100,96 95,94,90,88,83 72
CSF £63.08 CT £624.60 TOTE £15.50: £4.20, £1.60, £4.00; EX 93.40 Trifecta £267.10 Pool: £376.20 - 1.20 winning units. Place 6 £2.68, Place 5 £2.29.
Owner Michael Jenner **Bred** John Foley **Trained** Exning, Suffolk

FOCUS
Fortunately not the messy contest seen in the previous division and the winning time was over half a second quicker. The winner has slipped a long way in the weights and this was a slight personal best.

Ohana Official explanation: jockey said gelding was never travelling
T/Jkpt: £946.60 to a £1 stake. Pool: £10,000.00. 7.50 winning tickets. T/Plt: £2.50 to a £1 stake. Pool: £58,819.30. 17,088.75 winning tickets. T/Qpdt: £1.70 to a £1 stake. Pool: £3,592.10. 1,492.50 winning tickets. KH

6596 LINGFIELD (L-H)

Tuesday, November 28

OFFICIAL GOING: Standard
Wind: almost nil

6629 ARENA LEISURE PLC H'CAP (DIV I) — 6f (P)

12:20 (12:21) (Class 6) (0-57,57) 3-Y-O+ — **£2,590** (£770; £385; £192) **Stalls** Low

Form — RPR

4003 **1** **Zazous**[3] 6595 5-8-12 **56** MarcHalford(3) 10 — 67+
(J J Bridger) *trckd ldng gp: effrt whn nowhere to go and hmpd wl over 1f out: rallied etering fnl f: r.o wl to ld last 75yds* **13/8**[1]

0000 **2** *1 1/4* **One Way Ticket**[8] 6533 6-8-12 **53** (p) MickyFenton 12 — 57
(J M Bradley) *led at decent pce: kicked 2l clr over 1f out: collared last 75yds* **20/1**

0600 **3** *1* **Mine The Balance (IRE)**[4] 6577 3-8-13 **54** (b[1]) BrettDoyle 9 — 55
(J R Best) *chsd ldrs: rdn and outpcd wl over 1f out: styd on ins fnl f* **9/2**[2]

0050 **4** *nk* **Doctor Dennis (IRE)**[8] 6532 9-8-11 **52** (v) JimmyQuinn 2 — 52
(J Pearce) *lw: bdly outpcd and wl adrift after 2f: r.o fr over 1f out: fin wl* **17/2**

2465 **5** *1 1/2* **Viewforth**[10] 6510 8-9-2 **57** (v) PaulDoe 6 — 53
(M A Buckley) *pressed ldng pair but sn pushed along: wd bnd 2f out and outpcd: plugged on again last 100yds* **15/2**

0000 **6** *1/2* **Patternmaker (USA)**[10] 6513 4-8-13 **54** (v[1]) SteveDrowne 5 — 48
(A M Hales) *pressed ldr: rdn and nt qckn wl over 1f out: wknd rapidly ins fnl f* **7/1**[3]

0500 **7** *nk* **Double M**[10] 6513 9-8-6 **47** (v) AlanDaly 4 — 40
(Mrs L Richards) *chsd ldrs: outpcd 2f out: no imp after: wkng nr fin* **20/1**

0430 **8** *1* **Monte Major (IRE)**[165] 2611 5-8-12 **53** (v) DaneO'Neill 11 — 43
(D Shaw) *trckd ldrs gng wl: n.m.r briefly wl over 1f out: sn rdn and fnd nil: wknd* **12/1**

0-06 **9** *1/2* **The Terminator (IRE)**[89] 4959 4-8-0 **46** oh6 AndrewElliott(5) 1 — 35
(M Mullineaux) *bdly outpcd after 2f: wl adrift after* **66/1**

0000 **10** *1 3/4* **Galaxy Bound (IRE)**[14] 6480 3-8-2 **46** oh1 (v) PatrickMathers(3) 3 — 29
(D Shaw) *restless stalls: dwlt: a outpcd and wl bhd* **66/1**

0000 **11** *hd* **Vlasta Weiner**[20] 6395 6-8-7 **55** (b) BarrySavage(7) 8 — 38
(J M Bradley) *n.m.r after 1f: outpcd and drvn wl over 3f out: no prog after* **20/1**

0-60 **12** *dist* **Free Wheelin (IRE)**[101] 4587 6-8-6 **47** oh6 ow1 StephenCarson 7 — —
(T M Jones) *dwlt: a last: t.o over 3f out* **33/1**

1m 11.66s (-1.15) **Going Correction** -0.10s/f (Stan) — **12** Ran SP% **119.0**
Speed ratings (Par 101):103,101,100,99,97 96,96,95,94,92 91,—
CSF £44.71 CT £130.09 TOTE £2.40: £1.20, £7.20, £1.30; EX 38.30 Trifecta £139.50 Part won. Pool £196.59 - 0.68 winning units..
Owner J J Bridger **Bred** Lordship Stud **Trained** Liphook, Hants
■ Stewards' Enquiry : Brett Doyle two-day ban; careless riding (Dec 9-10)

FOCUS
A moderate handicap run at a very good pace. The form should be reliable for the grade.
Free Wheelin(IRE) Official explanation: jockey said gelding missed the break and hung right

6630 JUMPING HERE ON DECEMBER 9TH AMATEUR RIDERS' H'CAP — 2m (P)

12:50 (12:51) (Class 6) (0-65,63) 3-Y-O+ — **£2,307** (£709; £354) **Stalls** Low

Form — RPR

1006 **1** **Montosari**[19] 6408 7-11-2 **63** MrDHutchison(5) 9 — 72
(P Mitchell) *wl in tch: prog over 4f out: led over 2f out: drew clr fr over 1f out: pushed out* **9/1**

6323 **2** *3 1/2* **Coda Agency**[20] 6398 3-10-6 **57** MrLeeNewnes 5 — 62
(D W P Arbuthnot) *trckd ldr: led 5f out: rdn and hdd over 2f out: no ch w wnr over 1f out* **5/1**

5022 **3** *1 1/4* **Lysander's Quest (IRE)**[22] 6375 8-10-6 **48**........................ MrSWalker 2 52
(R Ingram) *lw: trckd ldrs: rdn and nt qckn 3f out: sn outpcd: styd on fr over 1f out to take 3rd last 75yds* **4/1**[2]

0004 **4** *2* **Bramcote Lorne**[15] 6462 3-9-8 **52**................................ MrCAHarris(7) 12 53
(S Parr) *led at stdy pce: hdd 5f out: outpcd by ldng pair over 2f out: wknd fnl f* **16/1**

21/4 **5** *nk* **Silvaani (USA)**[22] 6375 8-10-3 **45**...................................... MrSDobson 4 46
(B Forsey) *hld up in last pair: prog over 3f out: outpcd wl over 2f out: no ch after: plugged on* **33/1**

0000 **6** *nk* **Cheveley Flyer**[17] 4606 3-9-5 **45**..................................... MrSPearce(3) 3 45
(J Pearce) *lw: hld up in midfield: n.m.r on inner 5f out: wl outpcd fr 3f out: no ch after* **10/3**[1]

0-12 **7** *3/4* **Salut Saint Cloud**[10] 2140 5-11-2 **63**...............(p) MissHayleyMoore(5) 1 62
(G L Moore) *hld up in midfield: shuffled along and outpcd 3f out: no ch after: kpt on* **9/2**[3]

0300 **8** *7* **Full Of Zest**[25] 3305 4-10-8 **57**...............................(b) MissLauraGray(7) 10 48
(Mrs L J Mongan) *prom: lost pl over 5f out: struggling and wl btn over 3f out* **40/1**

3314 **9** *2* **Primondo (IRE)**[63] 5587 4-11-1 **62**.............................. MrMJJSmith(5) 7 51
(A W Carroll) *a towards rr: hmpd 5f out and dropped to last pair: sn btn* **6/1**

025/ **10** *3* **It's Rumoured**[8] 2872 6-10-8 **55**.................................(b) MissZoeLilly(5) 6 40
(Jean-Rene Auvray) *racd wd: prom to 5f out: sn struggling in rr* **33/1**

0250 **11** *shd* **Makarim (IRE)**[26] 6305 10-10-2 **44** oh4..........................(p) MrsSBosley 8 29
(M R Bosley) *b.hind: stdd s: hld up in last pair: no prog over 3f out* **20/1**

3m 28.73s (-0.06) **Going Correction** -0.10s/f (Stan)
WFA 3 from 4yo+ 9lb **11** Ran SP% **121.2**
Speed ratings (Par 101):96,94,93,92,92 92,91,88,87,85 85
CSF £53.33 CT £214.50 TOTE £14.10: £3.80, £1.80, £1.40; EX 82.00 Trifecta £160.30 Part won. Pool £225.84 - 0.84 winning units..
Owner Mrs S Sheldon **Bred** S Gollogly **Trained** Epsom, Surrey

FOCUS
A very moderate handicap run at a slow tempo. The form looks very suspect.
Silvaani(USA) Official explanation: jockey said gelding went lame near-fore
Makarim(IRE) Official explanation: jockey said gelding was struck into and hung right

6631 BOOK ONLINE FOR A £2 DISCOUNT NOVICE STKS 6f (P)
1:20 (1:20) (Class 4) 2-Y-O **£4,533** (£1,348; £674; £336) **Stalls** Low

Form RPR

61 **1** **Hurricane Spirit (IRE)**[19] 6409 2-9-2 80............................. BrettDoyle 3 88+
(J R Best) *lw: mde virtually all: pushed 2 l clr over 1f out: in command after* **4/7**[1]

2 *1* **Corlough Mountain** 2-8-8 .... OscarUrbina 2 71
(N A Callaghan) *leggy: w'like: dwlt: sn cl up: shkn up 2f out: outpcd over 1f out: styd on ins fnl f to take 2nd nr fin* **40/1**

001 **3** *hd* **Teasing**[11] 6505 2-9-0 76.. JimmyQuinn 1 76
(J Pearce) *cl up: rdn 2f out: effrt to chse wnr ins fnl f: no imp: lost 2nd nr fin* **20/1**[3]

3623 **4** *1/2* **Onenightinlisbon (IRE)**[17] 6444 2-8-10 83................ AndrewElliott(5) 4 76
(K R Burke) *w wnr: rdn 2f out: hanging lft and nt qckn over 1f out: fdd and lost 2nd ins fnl f* **7/4**[2]

1m 12.1s (-0.71) **Going Correction** -0.10s/f (Stan) 4 Ran SP% **107.2**
Speed ratings (Par 98):100,98,98,97
CSF £16.99 TOTE £1.80; EX 22.70.
Owner The Little House Partnership **Bred** Knocktoran Stud **Trained** Hucking, Kent

FOCUS
A decent novice event won by an above-average juvenile for the time of year.

NOTEBOOK
Hurricane Spirit(IRE)did it the hard way from the front but still ran out a comfortable winner. The step up in trip proved no hindrance to him and he looks a well above-average juvenile for the time of year. He could run again very soon and should be followed, but his long-term target is the Listed Spring Cup next March. (op 8-11 tchd 8-15 in a place)
Corlough Mountain, a 56,000gns full-brother to Smooch making his debut, was not given a hard race at all and shaped with a degree of promise. However, connections will hope to get a win out of him very soon as his handicap mark could be seriously affected by this effort. (op 25-1)
Teasingkept on quite nicely inside the final furlong but could not get to grips with the leader. The effort was still promising and she should definitely win more races in the coming months if persevered with on the All Weather. (op 14-1)
Onenightinlisbon(IRE) was not beaten that far despite hanging badly under pressure. If the steering can be sorted out, she should still be competitive during the winter. (op 11-8 tchd 15-8 in a place)

6632 ARENA LEISURE PLC H'CAP (DIV II) 6f (P)
1:50 (1:50) (Class 6) (0-57,56) 3-Y-O+ **£1,680** (£1,680; £385; £192) **Stalls** Low

Form RPR

2312 **1** **Imperium**[17] 6442 5-9-2 **56**..(p) DaneO'Neill 10 65
(Jean-Rene Auvray) *s.i.s: sn midfield: prog to chse ldr wl over 1f out: sustained chal fnl f: got up nr fin* **9/2**[2]

000 **1** *dht* **Mulberry Lad (IRE)**[7] 6549 4-8-5 **45**...................................... PaulDoe 6 54
(P W Hiatt) *prom: led wl over 2f out: drvn 2 l clr over 1f out: jnd nr fin* **25/1**

5202 **3** *1 1/4* **Supreme Kiss**[10] 6513 3-9-2 **56**... EddieAhern 4 61
(Mrs N Smith) *s.s: hld up in last: prog 2f out: chsd ldng pair fnl f: threatened to cl but didn't* **11/2**[3]

0564 **4** *nk* **Desert Light (IRE)**[7] 6556 5-9-0 **54**..............................(v) MickyFenton 9 58
(D Shaw) *hld up in midfield: effrt 2f out: chsd ldrs over 1f out: hanging lft and nt qckn* **7/2**[1]

5253 **5** *nk* **Hotchpotch (USA)**[17] 6442 3-8-9 **56** ow2..................... KylieManser(7) 5 59+
(J R Best) *hld up: n.m.r and in last pair over 2f out: taken to outer and urged along over 1f out: r.o: no ch* **6/1**

6415 **6** *1 1/4* **Cayman Breeze**[17] 6439 6-8-8 **55**.................................... BarrySavage(7) 12 55
(J M Bradley) *lw: hld up wl in rr: sme prog 2f out: rdn and no imp on ldrs fnl f* **11/2**[3]

0004 **7** *3/4* **Bella Bertolini**[78] 5250 3-9-0 **54**...(p) IanMongan 2 51
(T G Mills) *hld up wl in rr: nt clr run on inner over 2f out: rdn and nt qckn wl over 1f out: one pce* **16/1**

0000 **8** *1* **Mayden Dawn**[64] 5576 3-8-8 **48**......................................(v) SteveDrowne 7 42
(Miss E C Lavelle) *chsd ldrs: rdn and wkng whn n.m.r 1f out: eased* **50/1**

3234 **9** *1* **Firework**[7] 6550 8-8-5 **45**.. StephenCarson 8 36
(E A Wheeler) *taken down early: prom to 1/2-way: wknd 2f out* **8/1**

0520 **10** *3* **Mind Alert**[120] 3995 5-8-10 **53**....................................(v) PatrickMathers(3) 3 35+
(D Shaw) *lost pl on inner after 2f: hmpd in midfield over 2f out: effrt over 1f out: hld whn bdly hmpd sn after: eased* **10/1**

0000 **11** *1 1/2* **Colonel Bilko (IRE)**[15] 6462 4-8-2 **45** oh5...............(b) MarcHalford(3) 11 23
(J J Bridger) *led to wl over 2f out: wknd wl over 1f out: eased* **50/1**

1m 12.0s (-0.81) **Going Correction** -0.10s/f (Stan) **11** Ran SP% **119.3**
Speed ratings (Par 101):101,101,99,98,98 96,95,94,93,89 87
WIN Imperium £2.40, Mulberry Lad £14.10; PL IM £1.60, ML £7.00, SK £1.50; EX IM/ML £167.40, ML/IM £79.10; CSF - IM/ML £56.96, ML/IM £67.57; TRICAST IM/ML/SK £322.46, ML/IM/SK £368.94 TRIFECTA Not won..
Owner P W Hiatt **Bred** Mountarmstrong Stud **Trained** Hook Norton, Oxon
Owner The Cross Keys Racing Club **Bred** Mrs H B Raw **Trained** Upper Lambourn, Berks

FOCUS
A very moderate sprint handicap, though still competitive for its level..
Mulberry Lad(IRE) Official explanation: trainer said, regarding the apparent improvement in form, that on the gelding's previous run at Southwell it had a wide draw, was unable to get competitive and is better suited by the poly-track surface
Mind Alert Official explanation: jockey said gelding suffered interference in running

6633 LINGFIELD PARK FOR CHRISTMAS PARTIES H'CAP 1m 2f (P)
2:20 (2:20) (Class 4) (0-80,80) 3-Y-O+
£5,297 (£1,586; £793; £396; £198; £99) **Stalls** Low

Form RPR

3003 **1** **Solo Flight**[23] 6351 9-9-6 **80**.. SteveDrowne 9 87
(H Morrison) *hld up in midfield: prog to trck ldng pair over 2f out: led over 1f out: drvn out last 100yds* **9/2**[2]

0000 **2** *3/4* **Activo (FR)**[54] 5776 5-9-6 **80**.. PaulDoe 7 86
(S Dow) *lw: dwlt: hld up in last pair: prog and got through over 1f out: chsd wnr ins fnl f: nudged along and clsd nr fin: lame* **9/2**[2]

0500 **3** *3* **Chief Exec**[15] 6461 4-8-13 **73**... OscarUrbina 8 73
(C A Cyzer) *dwlt: hld up in last pair: prog and pushed along over 2f out: shkn up and one pce over 1f out* **16/1**

2652 **4** *3/4* **Red Birr (IRE)**[53] 5786 5-9-1 **75**.. BrettDoyle 4 74
(P R Webber) *trckd ldrs: effrt over 2f out: nt qckn wl over 1f out: one pce after* **15/8**[1]

0000 **5** *1 1/2* **Silver Blue (IRE)**[38] 6107 3-9-2 **80**...................................(b) DaneO'Neill 5 76
(R Hannon) *trckd ldrs: prog to ld wl over 2f out: hdd & wknd over 1f out* **9/2**[2]

6540 **6** *3/4* **Primitive Academy**[46] 5952 4-8-10 **70**........................... JimmyQuinn 10 65
(H R A Cecil) *lw: trckd ldr: led briefly 3f out: wknd over 1f out* **14/1**

5360 **7** *1* **Kylkenny**[23] 6351 11-9-1 **80**......................................(t) CAdamson(5) 2 73
(H Morrison) *hld up towards rr: rdn and struggling over 2f out* **40/1**

-025 **8** *25* **Scotch Pancake**[19] 6410 3-8-9 **73**..................................... EddieAhern 3 18
(D R C Elsworth) *racd v freely: led to 3f out: wknd rapidly: t.o* **9/1**[3]

2m 4.13s (-3.66) **Going Correction** -0.10s/f (Stan)
WFA 3 from 4yo+ 4lb **8** Ran SP% **114.3**
Speed ratings (Par 105):110,109,107,106,105 104,103,83
CSF £25.01 CT £294.58 TOTE £6.00: £1.20, £2.10, £4.00; EX 20.40 Trifecta £263.70 Part won. Pool £371.43 - 0.10 winning units..
Owner Lady Hardy **Bred** S Wingfield Digby **Trained** East Ilsley, Berks

FOCUS
A fair handicap run at a good pace and in a decent winning time for the class.
Activo(FR) Official explanation: jockey said, regarding running and riding, that his orders were to jump out and ride the gelding to its best ability, adding that it was slowly away, as in previous runs, and that whilst in rear, it was keen and running free; trainer said he was satisfied with the ride and the gelding's performance; vet said gelding returned lame near-fore
Red Birr(IRE) Official explanation: jockey said gelding hung left

6634 LINGFIELD PARK GOLF CLUB NURSERY 1m (P)
2:50 (2:50) (Class 4) (0-95,82) 2-Y-O **£4,857** (£1,445; £722; £360) **Stalls** High

Form RPR

4614 **1** **Solid Rock (IRE)**[17] 6444 2-9-7 **82**...................................... DaneO'Neill 3 86
(T G Mills) *t.k.h: hld up bhd ldng pair: effrt and wd bnd 2f out: rdn to ld 1f out: jst hld on* **2/1**[2]

3450 **2** *shd* **Cry Presto (USA)**[49] 5892 2-9-0 **75**...............................(t) EddieAhern 2 78
(R Hannon) *lw: s.s and reminder: rdn in last over 2f out: wd bnd sn after: drvn and chsd wnr ins fnl f: clsd: jst failed* **13/2**

01 **3** *1 1/2* **Book Of Facts (FR)**[17] 6447 2-9-2 **80**............................ GregFairley(3) 4 80
(M Johnston) *pressed ldr: hrd rdn to chal over 1f out: nt qckn and hld ins fnl f* **11/4**[3]

0113 **4** *hd* **Salient**[4] 6586 2-9-7 **82**.. PaulDoe 1 82
(J Akehurst) *lw: led: rdn wl over 1f out: hdd 1f out: one pce* **7/4**[1]

1m 39.41s (-0.02) **Going Correction** -0.10s/f (Stan) 4 Ran SP% **109.7**
Speed ratings (Par 98):96,95,94,94
CSF £13.19 TOTE £3.00; EX 10.50.
Owner Mrs L M Askew **Bred** Max Morris **Trained** Headley, Surrey

FOCUS
Not a bad little nursery, but the pace was not that good and the race turned into something of a sprint.

NOTEBOOK
Solid Rock(IRE) had been shaping as though in need of a stiffer test but this race was not run at a breakneck gallop, and it turned into something of a sprint from the turn into the straight. He used his six-furlong pace to get to the front but only just held on from the fast-finishing runner-up. He would not be sure to confirm the form if the two met again in the coming weeks. (op 9-4)
Cry Presto(USA), wearing a tongue tie for the first time on his All-Weather debut, gave his rivals all a four-length head start when he missed the break, and was then forced to challenge widest of all turning into the straight. The last to come with his run, he was finishing strongly in the closing stages, and this was a far more promising performance. He may yet break his maiden tag on this surface. (op 5-1 tchd 9-2)
Book Of Facts(FR), a winner over the extended mile at Wolverhampton last time, was not suited by the steady early pace followed by the sprint to the line. He will be more effective in a race run at a more regular tempo. (op 5-2 tchd 3-1)
Salient did not go too fast in front and the race turned into something of a sprint from the home turn. At this track being in front does not help in that situation, and he was done for toe in the closing stages. (op 2-1 tchd 9-4 in a place)

6635 LINGFIELDPARK.CO.UK H'CAP 1m (P)
3:20 (3:20) (Class 4) (0-80,80) 3-Y-O+ **£5,505** (£1,637; £818; £408) **Stalls** High

Form RPR

2-41 **1** **Sotik Star (IRE)**[62] 5612 3-9-3 **79**.......................................(t) EddieAhern 3 85+
(P J Makin) *lw: trckd ldr: hung rt over 1f out: drvn and styd on wl fnl f: narrow ld last 75yds: hld on* **5/2**[1]

1000 **2** *hd* **Bee Stinger**[4] 6580 4-9-4 **78**.. LeeEnstone 1 84+
(I A Wood) *trckd ldrs: effrt over 1f out: drvn to chal and upsides ins fnl f: jst pipped* **7/1**

1000 **3** *hd* **Miss Highjinks (USA)**[217] 1205 3-9-4 **80**........................... DaneO'Neill 7 85
(E J O'Neill) *hld up towards rr: shkn up and prog wl over 1f out: clsd on ldrs ins fnl f: jst hld* **11/1**

0005 **4** ½ **Davenport (IRE)**[18] 6424 4-8-9 **76**..........................(p) JamesMillman(7) 2 80
(B R Millman) *hld up in midfield: rdn wl over 2f out: styd on fr over 1f out: nrst fin* **11/2[3]**

1304 **5** ½ **Border Edge**[3] 6590 8-8-2 **65**.. MarcHalford(3) 5 68
(J J Bridger) *led: drvn 2f out: kpt on wel: hdd and no ex last 75yds* **11/2[3]**

0034 **6** *nk* **Zabeel House**[19] 6413 3-8-12 **74**.. MickyFenton 9 76
(J A R Toller) *hld up in last: effrt on outer 2f out: styd on fnl f: nt rch ldrs* **9/2[2]**

6060 **7** *nk* **Night Storm**[19] 6413 5-8-7 **67**.. PaulDoe 4 69+
(S Dow) *s.v.s: hld up in last pair: prog on inner over 1f out: looked dangerous ins fnl f: wknd last 75yds* **16/1**

5540 **8** 1¼ **Marbaa (IRE)**[19] 6413 3-8-6 **68**.. JimmyQuinn 8 67
(S Dow) *lw: s.i.s: hld up in last trio: prog over 1f out: chsd ldrs ins fnl f: wknd last 100yds* **16/1**

0000 **9** ¾ **Northern Desert (IRE)**[44] 5990 7-9-4 **78**.......................... RobertMiles 6 75
(P W Hiatt) *t.k.h: trckd ldng pair: hanging and fnd nil over 1f out: wknd* **33/1**

01-0 **10** 1¾ **Rainbows Guest (IRE)**[19] 6417 3-8-10 **72**..................(v) SteveDrowne 10 65
(A M Balding) *t.k.h: hld up on outer: no prog over 1f out: wknd* **16/1**

1m 38.54s (-0.89) **Going Correction** -0.10s/f (Stan)
WFA 3 from 4yo+ 2lb **10 Ran SP% 118.9**
Speed ratings (Par 105):100,99,99,99,98 98,98,96,96,94
CSF £20.96 CT £170.39 TOTE £2.60: £1.60, £2.60, £4.10; EX 29.50 Trifecta £172.20 Pool £410.01 - 1.69 winning units. Place 6 £114.01, Place 5 £74.97 .
Owner D Ladhams M Holland J Ritchie G Marchant **Bred** Holborn Trust Co **Trained** Ogbourne Maisey, Wilts

FOCUS
A competitive handicap not run at a strong gallop, which resulted in a sprint to the line and a bunch finish.
T/Plt: £235.80 to a £1 stake. Pool: £41,835.85. 129.50 winning tickets. T/Qpdt: £32.70 to a £1 stake. Pool: £2,232.40. 50.50 winning tickets. JN

6548 SOUTHWELL (L-H)
Tuesday, November 28

OFFICIAL GOING: Standard
Wind: slight across

6636 HOSPITALITY PACKAGES AVAILABLE CLAIMING STKS (DIV I) 6f (F)
12:00 (12:00) (Class 6) 3-Y-O+ **£2,047** (£604; £302) **Stalls** Low

Form RPR

4600 **1** **Le Chiffre (IRE)**[5] 6573 4-8-8 69..........................(b[1]) MichaelJStainton(5) 3 67
(R A Harris) *sn led: rdn clr wl over 1f out: comf* **11/4[1]**

6500 **2** 4 **The City Kid (IRE)**[8] 5636 3-8-2 55..........................(p) FrancisNorton 2 44
(P D Evans) *trckd ldrs: rdn along and outpcd 1/2-way: styd on u.p appr last* **10/3[2]**

0406 **3** ½ **Majik**[15] 6464 7-8-2 57..........................(p) RoryMoore(5) 8 48
(P T Midgley) *towards rr: wd st: hdwy 2f out: sn rdn and kpt on appr last* **10/3[2]**

0000 **4** 2½ **Woodwee**[13] 6493 3-8-8 54 ow1..........................(b[1]) TomEaves 5 41
(J R Weymes) *towards rr: poushed along and hdwy on outer 2f out: styd on appr last: nrst fin* **9/1**

0004 **5** *nk* **Swallow Senora (IRE)**[13] 6490 4-8-5 35.......... RussellKennemore(7) 11 44
(M C Chapman) *trckd ldrs: hdwy to chse wnr 2f out: sn rdn and kpt on same pce* **16/1**

0005 **6** 4 **Ace Club**[28] 6282 5-8-9 45..........................(b) DaleGibson 9 29
(M J Attwater) *cl up: rdn along over 2f out: sn drvn and one pce* **8/1[3]**

00-0 **7** ½ **Steel Grey**[218] 1185 5-9-7 30.. DeanMernagh 6 40
(M Brittain) *s.i.s and bhd tl sme late hdwy* **33/1**

0600 **8** 5 **Aintnecessarilyso**[30] 6237 8-8-7 40..........................(p) LPKeniry 12 11
(J M Bradley) *s.i.s: a rr* **14/1**

0054 **9** 2 **On The Trail**[103] 4523 9-8-7 40.. AdrianTNicholls 10 5
(D W Chapman) *cl up: rdn along wl over 2f out and sn wknd* **9/1**

0000 **10** 1¼ **Baron De Hoyland**[20] 6406 3-8-13 35.. PaulMulrennan 1 7
(J R Norton) *cl up: rdn along 1/2-way: sn wknd* **80/1**

1m 16.36s (-0.54) **Going Correction** -0.20s/f (Stan) **10 Ran SP% 120.7**
Speed ratings (Par 101):95,89,89,85,85 79,79,72,69,68
CSF £12.43 TOTE £3.30: £1.50, £1.20, £1.60; EX 15.40.The winner was claimed by Nigel Shields for £8,000
Owner www.gardenshedracing.com **Bred** Agricola Del Parco **Trained** Earlswood, Monmouths

FOCUS
A routine claimer and the winning time was 0.21 seconds faster than the second division, which is understandable given that the winner was by far the highest-rated horse in either division. They finished very much as adjusted official ratings suggested they should.

6637 BOOK YOUR TICKETS ON LINE MAIDEN STKS 5f (F)
12:30 (12:30) (Class 5) 3-Y-O+ **£3,238** (£963; £481; £240) **Stalls** High

Form RPR

0452 **1** **Decider (USA)**[30] 6234 3-9-3 53.. LPKeniry 10 62
(J M Bradley) *prom on outer: hdwy 2f out: rdn to chal ent last: styd on u.p to ld nr fin* **16/1**

342 **2** *hd* **Cross Of Lorraine (IRE)**[20] 6403 3-9-3 63..........................(b) TomEaves 5 61
(I Semple) *bmpd s: sn prom: led wl over 1f out: rdn and edgd lft ins last: hdd nr fin* **7/4[1]**

0323 **3** 1 **Balian**[13] 6492 3-8-10 52..........................(b) JosephWalsh(7) 9 58
(Mrs P Sly) *in tch: hdwy 2f out: sn rdn and styd on ins last: nrst fin* **14/1**

-032 **4** *nk* **Gifted Lass**[20] 6399 4-8-12 47.. DavidAllan 2 52
(J Balding) *sn led: rdn along over 2f out: hdd wl over 1f out: sn drvn and wknd ins last* **5/2[2]**

4363 **5** 1¼ **Dysonic (USA)**[13] 6490 4-9-0 45..........................(v) JasonEdmunds(3) 3 53
(J Balding) *cl up: effrt 2f out: sn rdn and wknd ent last* **8/1[3]**

0662 **6** 1¼ **Sion Hill (IRE)**[7] 6550 5-8-10 45..........................(p) RussellKennemore(7) 11 48
(Mrs N Macauley) *bmpd s and bhd tl styd on appr last: nrst fin* **25/1**

0053 **7** 2½ **All Clued Up (IRE)**[7] 6548 3-8-12 45.. ChrisCatlin 7 35
(Rae Guest) *in tch: swtchd lft and rdn along 2f out: sn drvn and wknd* **8/1[3]**

-040 **8** *nk* **Rambling Socks**[14] 6476 3-8-7 52..........................(b) AshleyHamblett(5) 12 34
(S R Bowring) *wnt lft s: a bhd* **40/1**

9 2½ **Mikey (IRE)**[36] 6156 3-9-3..........................(t) FrancisNorton 1 30
(Edgar Byrne, Ire) *cl up: rdn along 1/2-way: drvn and wknd fnl 2f* **18/1**

00 **10** ¾ **Existence**[13] 6490 3-8-12.. HayleyTurner 6 23
(D Shaw) *hmpd s: a towards rr* **100/1**

0 **11** 1¾ **Paper Maite**[21] 6389 5-8-12.. DeanMcKeown 4 17
(S R Bowring) *outpcd and bhd fr 1/2-way* **100/1**

12 6 **Our Georgia** 3-8-12.. NCallan 8 —
(T D Barron) *sn outpaced and a bhd* **20/1**

59.69 secs (-0.61) **Going Correction** -0.025s/f (Stan) **12 Ran SP% 118.0**
Speed ratings (Par 103):103,102,101,100,98 96,92,92,88,86 84,74
CSF £42.74 TOTE £19.60: £6.60, £1.10, £3.40; EX 75.30.
Owner Robert Bailey **Bred** Green Willow Farms **Trained** Sedbury, Gloucs

FOCUS
A poor maiden. Despite the winner and the third coming from high draws, they both drifted left throughout the race and the principals all ended up racing towards the far side of the track.

6638 HOSPITALITY PACKAGES AVAILABLE CLAIMING STKS (DIV II) 6f (F)
1:00 (1:01) (Class 6) 3-Y-O+ **£2,047** (£604; £302) **Stalls** Low

Form RPR

0011 **1** **Bodden Bay**[14] 6477 4-8-12 59.. DanielTudhope 1 68
(D Carroll) *mde all: rdn clr over 2f out: drvn out* **13/8[1]**

4602 **2** 2 **Piccolo Prince**[14] 6477 5-8-10 53.. DavidAllan 4 60
(E J Alston) *midfield and sn rdn along: hdwy over 2f out: drvn to chse wnr wl over 1f out: kpt on u.p ins last* **10/3[2]**

0032 **3** 3 **Prince Of Gold**[7] 6554 6-8-13 50..........................(e) FergusSweeney 6 54
(R Hollinshead) *in tch: hdwy on outer over 2f out: sn rdn and kpt on same pce appr last* **10/3[2]**

5004 **4** ¾ **Further Outlook (USA)**[15] 6464 12-8-13 60..........................(t) NCallan 9 52
(Miss Gay Kelleway) *cl up: rdn along over 2f out: sn drvn and kpt on same pce* **13/2[3]**

0505 **5** 2 **Hout Bay**[7] 6548 9-8-7 45.. MatthewHenry 3 40
(D W Chapman) *midfield: hdwy 3f out: rdn along 2f out: kpt on same pce* **18/1**

000- **6** 1¼ **Ligne D'Eau**[358] 6507 5-8-7 47..........................(b) RobertHavlin 10 36
(P D Evans) *dwlt and bhd tl styd on fnl 2f: nrst fin* **80/1**

4500 **7** ¾ **Four Amigos (USA)**[8] 6533 5-8-3 45 ow1..........(b) AshleyHamblett(5) 11 35
(I A Wood) *cl up: rdn along over 2f out: sn drvn and wknd* **16/1**

0500 **8** *hd* **Danzar**[8] 6543 4-9-3 49..........................(b[1]) DeanMernagh 5 43
(M Brittain) *dwlt and bhd: hdwy 1/2-way: rdn and int ouch 2f out: sn drvn and wknd* **66/1**

0000 **9** 3½ **Headland (USA)**[104] 4467 8-8-7 35..........................(be) AdrianTNicholls 12 23
(D W Chapman) *a rr* **40/1**

0000 **10** 13 **Bermuda Beauty (IRE)**[95] 4756 3-8-4 45.. FrancisNorton 8 —
(J M Bradley) *chsd ldrs: rdn along 1/2-way: sn wknd* **66/1**

-500 **11** 23 **John Claude (IRE)**[235] 910 3-8-9 55..........................(v[1]) DaleGibson 2 —
(Ronald Thompson) *cl up: rdn along 1/2-way: sn wknd* **40/1**

1m 16.57s (-0.33) **Going Correction** -0.20s/f (Stan) **11 Ran SP% 117.8**
Speed ratings (Par 101):94,91,87,86,83 82,81,80,76,58 28
CSF £6.94 TOTE £2.40: £1.10, £1.50, £1.90; EX 6.90.The winner was claimed by R A Harris for £7,500.
Owner Andy Franks & Steve Franks **Bred** Gary Middlemiss **Trained** Warthill, N Yorks

FOCUS
A poor and uncompetitive claimer in which the winning time was 0.21 seconds slower than the first division. Again those most favoured by the weights were generally those that made the biggest impression, and the fact that the front two home both raced against the inside rail suggests that part of the track was not quite as bad as it often is here.
John Claude(IRE) Official explanation: jockey said gelding lost its action

6639 SPONSOR A RACE AT SOUTHWELL NURSERY 1m (F)
1:30 (1:31) (Class 5) (0-75,74) 2-Y-O **£3,238** (£963; £481; £240) **Stalls** Low

Form RPR

424 **1** **Strikeen (IRE)**[29] 6257 2-9-7 **74**.. RobertHavlin 4 83+
(T G Mills) *dwlt: switrhed outside and smooth hdwy 1/2-way: rdn to ld wl over 1f out: sn clr* **13/8[1]**

0031 **2** 4 **Shouldntbethere (IRE)**[18] 6421 2-8-13 **66**.......................... JamieMackay 9 64
(Mrs P N Dutfield) *s.i.s and bhd: hdwy over 2f out: rdn to chse wnr and hung bdly lft ins last: no imp* **4/1[2]**

0100 **3** 1½ **Nicada (IRE)**[10] 6525 2-8-11 **67**.. DominicFox(3) 6 62
(Miss Gay Kelleway) *hld up: hdwy over 2f out: sn rdn and kpt on same pce fr over 1f out* **10/1**

0062 **4** 1¾ **Global Traffic**[43] 6016 2-8-2 **55**.. FrancisNorton 8 46
(P D Evans) *prom: effrt 3f out: rdn to ld 2f out: sn drvn and hdd: wknd appr last* **4/1[2]**

2300 **5** 2½ **My Mirasol**[59] 5681 2-8-12 **65**..........................(p) NCallan 5 50
(K A Ryan) *trckd ldrs: rdn along: lost pl and bhd wl over 2f out: swtchd outside and drvn wl over 1f out: kpt on ins last* **20/1**

000 **6** 3 **Citrus Chief (USA)**[10] 6523 2-8-4 **64**.. TolleyDean(7) 3 43
(R A Harris) *in tch on inner: rdn along over 3f out: drvn over 2f out and sn btn* **33/1**

3264 **7** *nk* **Chasing Memories (IRE)**[11] 6504 2-9-2 **69**.. TomEaves 7 47
(B Smart) *cl up: rdn and ev ch over 2f out: sn drvn and wknd* **7/1[3]**

3060 **8** 6 **Spinning Game**[5] 6569 2-7-13 **52** oh11 ow1..................(b[1]) DaleGibson 1 17
(D W Chapman) *led: rdn along 3f out: drvn and hdd over 2f out: sn wknd* **66/1**

040 **9** 4 **Virginia Reel**[33] 6186 2-8-3 **56**.. AdrianTNicholls 2 12
(M Johnston) *cl up: rdn along 1/2-way: sn wknd* **12/1**

1m 43.08s (-1.52) **Going Correction** -0.20s/f (Stan) **9 Ran SP% 116.6**
Speed ratings (Par 96):99,95,93,91,89 86,85,79,75
CSF £8.07 CT £49.12 TOTE £2.30: £1.10, £1.30, £2.70; EX 7.20.
Owner Buxted Partnership **Bred** R N Auld **Trained** Headley, Surrey
■ Stewards' Enquiry : Dominic Fox one-day ban: failed to ride to draw (Dec 9)

FOCUS
Probably not a very competitive nursery with five of the nine runners starting at double-figure prices, but the pace was sound enough and the winner was different class.

NOTEBOOK
Strikeen(IRE), one of the least exposed in the field and making his nursery debut, relished this return to a mile and could be seen running all over his rivals from a long way out. He can expect a stiff ride for this, but would be hard to beat if turned out quickly under a penalty. (op 11-8 tchd 15-8)
Shouldntbethere(IRE), winner of a claimer at disadvantageous terms over course and distance last time, gave his rivals a start and that is far from ideal here. He did travel well enough and tried to slipstream the winner turning for home, but he hung violently left under pressure and could make no impression at all. (op 9-2 tchd 7-2)
Nicada(IRE), down 1lb though still looking high enough in the weights, plodded on without looking a threat and is much more exposed than most of his rivals. (op 12-1 tchd 9-1)
Global Traffic, runner-up in a turf seller over this trip last time, had every chance but this testing surface and better company seemed to find him out. (op 13-2)
My Mirasol, beaten out of sight in the Redcar Two-Year-Old Trophy last time, was trying sand for the first time and stepping up two furlongs in trip. Stamina did not appear to be an issue despite her speedy pedigree, but she was never doing enough to get herself involved. (op 16-1)
Virginia Reel Official explanation: jockey said filly had no more to give

6640 SOUTHWELL-RACECOURSE.CO.UK (S) STKS 6f (F)

2:00 (2:00) (Class 6) 2-Y-O £2,388 (£705; £352) Stalls Low

Form RPR

6500 **1** **Emefdream**[18] 6422 2-9-0 52 (p) NCallan 4 64+
(K A Ryan) *trckd ldrs: hdwy to ld 2f out: rdn clr ins last: r.o* **7/1**[3]

3501 **2** 3½ **Bridget's Team**[18] 6422 2-9-1 58 DaleGibson 7 55
(P C Haslam) *cl up: led 1/2-way: rdn and hdd 2f out: drvn and one pce ent last* **6/5**[1]

0054 **3** 6 **Aggbag**[20] 6401 2-9-6 60 PaulEddery 5 42
(B P J Baugh) *midfield whn n.m.r and lost pl after 2f: hdwy over 2f out: sn rdn and kpt on appr last* **12/1**

4 1 **Ugenius** 2-8-7 TolleyDean(7) 12 33
(R A Harris) *s.i.s and bhd: rdn and hdwy 2f out: styd on u.p appr last: nrst fin* **8/1**

0240 **5** 3½ **Jost Van Dyke**[13] 6491 2-9-6 65 PatCosgrave 9 28
(J R Boyle) *cl up: rdn along over 2f out and sn wknd* **7/2**[2]

0064 **6** nk **Molto Duro (IRE)**[15] 6463 2-8-2 40 (b) LanceBetts(7) 10 16
(N Wilson) *chsd ldrs: riddcen along over 2f out: sn wknd* **33/1**

0050 **7** 3½ **Kyoto City**[14] 6472 2-8-2 35 DanielleMcCreery(7) 8 6
(D W Chapman) *chsd ldrs: rdn along 1/2-way: sn wknd* **100/1**

0000 **8** 2 **Allroundtheoutside**[34] 6172 2-9-0 49 (b[1]) FrancisNorton 3 5
(P R Chamings) *dwlt:sn rdn along and in tch: drvn over 2f out and sn wknd* **22/1**

00 **9** 1¼ **Fly The World**[71] 5425 2-8-9 ChrisCatlin 1 —
(A P Jarvis) *dwlt: sn rdn along and a bhd* **16/1**

0066 **10** ½ **Desirable Dancer (IRE)**[14] 6471 2-8-9 45 (b[1]) LPKeniry 6 —
(R A Harris) *a rr* **40/1**

2030 **11** 4 **Granny Peel (IRE)**[26] 6311 2-9-1 56 DeanMernagh 2 —
(M Brittain) *led: rdn along and hdd 1/2-way: sn drvn and wknd* **12/1**

1m 16.36s (-0.54) **Going Correction** -0.20s/f (Stan) 11 Ran SP% **123.3**
Speed ratings (Par 94):95,90,82,81,76 75,71,68,66,66 60
CSF £16.21 TOTE £9.00: £2.50, £1.10, £3.50; EX 33.20.The winner was sold to Janine Hemphrey for £8,000. Bridget's Team was claimed by D G Bridgwater for £6,000
Owner Mrs M Forsyth and M F Logistics Ltd **Bred** Hollington Stud **Trained** Hambleton, N Yorks

FOCUS
Not a very competitive seller, but the pace was fair and with decent margins separating the first three, the form is probably sound for the grade.

NOTEBOOK
Emefdream, disappointing since showing some ability on turf in the summer but 10lb better off with Bridget's Team for a 12-length beating in a nursery over course and distance last time, travelled well and, once hitting the front at the quarter-mile pole, quickly stamped his authority on the race. He was subsequently sold for 8,000gns and joins Norma Macauley. Official explanation: trainer said, regarding apparent improvement in form, that the gelding gained confidence from the fitting of cheek pieces for the first time (op 15-2)

Bridget's Team, winner of a course-and-distance nursery last time, failed to confirm the form with Emefdream on 10lb worse terms and was comfortably held, but given the margin back to the third it would be harsh to say she did not run to form. She was subsequently claimed by David Bridgewater for £6,000 and should be up to winning another modest event here. (op 6-4)

Aggbag has plenty of experience of Polytrack, but this was his first try on Fibresand and he was found wanting for pace over the last couple of furlongs. He is totally exposed now. (op 9-1)

Ugenius, out of a winning half-sister to Baylaw Star, was a major springer in the market having been back in from 33-1. His supporters soon knew their fate though, as he looked clueless early and did not get going until it was far too late. The market support suggested he was not expected to need it, but his performance smacked of inexperience so it may be best not to give up on him just yet. (op 33-1)

Jost Van Dyke, who was well beaten despite being best in at the weights in a claimer here last time, showed up for a while but it soon became obvious the same fate was going to befall him at this level. (tchd 10-3 and 4-1)

6641 TARGET EXPRESS H'CAP 1m (F)

2:30 (2:34) (Class 6) (0-64,64) 3-Y-O+ £2,730 (£806; £403) Stalls Low

Form RPR

0044 **1** **Sentiero Rosso (USA)**[18] 6425 4-9-2 63 (t) TomEaves 8 69
(B Ellison) *trckd ldrs: hdwy 3f out: rdn to ld wl over 1f out: drvn ins last and styd on wl* **6/1**[3]

3005 **2** ¾ **Ruffie (IRE)**[29] 6260 3-9-1 64 (e[1]) NCallan 7 68
(Miss Gay Kelleway) *chsd ldrs: hdwy over 2f and sn rdn: drvn ent last and no imp towards fin* **28/1**

0405 **3** nk **Kingsmaite**[19] 6419 5-8-12 59 (bt) DeanMcKeown 12 62
(S R Bowring) *cl up: led 3f out: rdn and hdd wl over 1f out: drvn and no ex ins last* **8/1**

0201 **4** 1¼ **Formidable Will (FR)**[14] 6473 4-9-3 64 (tp) DaleGibson 6 65
(M W Easterby) *in tch: hdwy to trck ldrs 3f out: rdn 2f out: drvn and no imp appr last* **4/1**[2]

0503 **5** 3 **Shrine Mountain (USA)**[19] 6419 4-9-1 62 JosedeSouza 5 56
(J R Holt) *c lose up: rdn along 3f out: drvn over 2f out and grad wknd* **13/2**

0001 **6** 1¾ **Dream Forest (IRE)**[47] 5922 3-8-13 62 FrancisNorton 9 53
(M S Saunders) *towards rr: hdwy wl over 2f out: sn rdn and kpt on appr last: nrst fin* **8/1**

2406 **7** 3 **Quiet Reading (USA)**[8] 6531 9-8-7 54 (v) CatherineGannon 10 38
(M R Bosley) *a towards rr* **20/1**

1521 **8** 3 **Legal Lover (IRE)**[26] 6304 4-8-3 57 RussellKennemore(7) 2 35
(R Hollinshead) *sn rdn to ld: hdd 3f out: sn drvn and wknd over 2f out* **3/1**[1]

0001 **9** 3 **Take It There**[8] 6531 4-8-9 56 6ex RichardThomas 4 28
(A J Lidderdale) *towards rr: sme hdwy wl over 2f out: sn rdn and btn* **8/1**

0/00 **10** 2 **Experimental (IRE)**[13] 6497 12-8-8 55 PaulMulrennan 3 23
(John A Harris) *a towards rr* **100/1**

10 **11** 19 **Bucharest**[32] 6206 3-8-13 62 MichaelTebbutt 11 —
(M Wigham) *chsd ldrs to 1/2-way: sn wknd* **16/1**

0000 **12** 1½ **Sunny Haze**[13] 6492 3-8-3 52 oh16 ow1 PaulEddery 1 —
(Mrs P N Dutfield) *a rr* **150/1**

1m 42.6s (-2.00) **Going Correction** -0.20s/f (Stan)
WFA 3 from 4yo+ 2lb 12 Ran SP% **121.7**
Speed ratings (Par 101):102,101,100,99,96 94,91,88,85,83 64,63
CSF £170.31 CT £1389.33 TOTE £8.00: £2.30, £5.50, £2.10; EX 77.00.
Owner Black and White Diamond Partnership **Bred** Thomas And Lakin **Trained** Norton, N Yorks

FOCUS
A modest handicap, but the pace was sound enough and the principals were all close to it throughout.

6642 RACING AGAIN ON SATURDAY H'CAP 7f (F)

3:00 (3:01) (Class 6) (0-63,63) 3-Y-O+ £2,730 (£806; £403) Stalls Low

Form RPR

0501 **1** **Atlantic Story (USA)**[4] 6577 4-9-0 61 6ex (t) DaleGibson 3 84
(M W Easterby) *hld up in tch: gd hdwy 2f out: rdn to ld 1f out: styd on* **6/5**[1]

433 **2** ¾ **Mozakhraf (USA)**[20] 6404 4-8-10 57 NCallan 4 78
(K A Ryan) *keen: cl up on inner: hdwy to ld 2f out: rdn and hdd 1f out: kpt on wl u.p ins last* **9/1**[3]

0011 **3** 5 **Cleveland**[7] 6549 4-8-7 61 6ex RussellKennemore(7) 2 69+
(R Hollinshead) *n.m.r on inner after 1f: hdwy 3f out: effrt and ev ch 2f out: sn rdn and wknd ent last* **9/2**[2]

0000 **4** 2½ **Count Cougar (USA)**[11] 6508 6-8-13 60 SamHitchcott 8 62
(S P Griffiths) *led: rdn along 3f out: hdd 2f out: sn drvn and grad wknd* **40/1**

0433 **5** 1¼ **Middle Eastern**[20] 6395 4-8-10 57 (p) DanielTudhope 1 55
(P A Blockley) *midfield: hdwy 3f out: swtchd rt and rdn to chse ldrs over 2f out: sn drvn and no imp* **10/1**

3006 **6** nk **Favouring (IRE)**[13] 6497 4-7-13 53 ow1 (v) ChrisHough(7) 5 51
(M C Chapman) *prom: rdn along 3f out: wknd 2f out* **33/1**

0000 **7** ½ **Pawn In Life (IRE)**[8] 6532 8-8-6 53 (v) FrancisNorton 10 49
(M J Attwater) *dwlt and bhd tl styd on fnl 2f* **25/1**

2132 **8** 2½ **Preskani**[14] 6470 4-8-0 52 (p) DuranFentiman(5) 7 42
(Mrs N Macauley) *a towards rr* **12/1**

0002 **9** 1¾ **Kensington (IRE)**[13] 6493 5-8-8 60 (p) MichaelJStainton(5) 6 45
(P D Evans) *a towards rr* **16/1**

1505 **10** ¾ **Mister Elegant**[87] 5031 4-8-12 59 AdrianTNicholls 13 42
(J L Spearing) *chsd ldrs: rdn wl over 2f out: drvn and wknd fnl 2f* **20/1**

0613 **11** 2½ **Guadaloup**[8] 6541 4-8-9 56 (v) DeanMernagh 11 33
(M Brittain) *midfield: hdwy to chse ldrs on outer 3f out: sn rdn and btn* **20/1**

0034 **12** nk **Mystic Queen (IRE)**[14] 6477 3-8-4 52 ChrisCatlin 12 28
(A P Jarvis) *prom: rdn along 1/2-way: sn wknd* **33/1**

3600 **13** 1 **Set Alight**[18] 6425 5-9-2 63 (p) BrianReilly 14 36
(Mrs C A Dunnett) *a rr* **33/1**

1m 27.55s (-3.25) **Going Correction** -0.20s/f (Stan)
WFA 3 from 4yo+ 1lb 13 Ran SP% **120.9**
Speed ratings (Par 101):110,109,103,100,99 98,98,95,93,92 89,89,88
CSF £11.38 CT £40.89 TOTE £2.10: £1.10, £2.70, £2.20; EX 15.40.
Owner Matthew Green **Bred** A I Appleton **Trained** Sheriff Hutton, N Yorks
■ Stewards' Enquiry : Sam Hitchcott two-day ban; careless riding (Dec 10-11)

FOCUS
A decent pace and a very smart winning time for a race of its type. With the front pair pulling a long way clear of an in-form rival, the form looks strong.

6643 EXPERIENCE NOTTINGHAMSHIRE H'CAP 6f (F)

3:30 (3:30) (Class 5) (0-75,75) 3-Y-O+ £3,238 (£963; £481; £240) Stalls Low

Form RPR

0431 **1** **Night Prospector**[10] 6527 6-8-9 75 (p) TolleyDean(7) 3 93+
(R A Harris) *mde all: qckned clr 2f out: rdn ent last and styd on strly* **4/1**[2]

2513 **2** 2½ **Mina**[10] 6513 4-8-6 65 JamieMackay 6 72
(Rae Guest) *chsd ldrs on outer: effrt over 2f out: sn rdn and chsd wnr over 1f out: drvn and no imp ins last* **4/1**[2]

4602 **3** 2½ **Sweet Pickle**[15] 6464 5-8-5 64 (e) AdrianTNicholls 8 64
(J R Boyle) *swtchd lft s and hld up: hdwy on inner 3f out: rdn to chse wnr 2f out: sn drvn and one pce appr last* **3/1**[1]

4000 **4** shd **Wainwright (IRE)**[7] 6556 6-7-13 63 oh1 ow2 KevinGhunowa(5) 1 62
(P A Blockley) *chsd ldrs: hdwy over 2f out: rdn wl over 1f out: kpt on same pce appr last* **7/1**[3]

1310 **5** 2 **Winning Pleasure (IRE)**[18] 6428 8-8-13 75 JasonEdmunds(3) 7 68
(J Balding) *trckd ldrs: hdwy 3f out: rdn over 2f out and sn btn* **8/1**

500 **6** ¾ **Drury Lane (IRE)**[7] 6550 6-8-2 61 oh16 (p) MatthewHenry 4 52
(D W Chapman) *chsd ldrs: rdn along 1/2-way: sn wknd* **50/1**

2560 **7** hd **Rose Muwasim**[186] 1997 3-8-5 64 DaleGibson 2 54
(M J Attwater) *chsd ldrs: rdn wl over 2f out: sn wknd* **28/1**

0000 **8** ¾ **Primo Way**[19] 6418 5-9-1 74 (v[1]) TomEaves 5 62
(I Semple) *cl up: rdn along wl over 2f out: sn drvn and wknd* **4/1**[2]

1m 15.34s (-1.56) **Going Correction** -0.20s/f (Stan) 8 Ran SP% **114.0**
Speed ratings (Par 103):102,98,95,95,92 91,91,90
CSF £20.26 CT £53.85 TOTE £4.10: £1.30, £1.40, £1.40; EX 20.00 Place 6 £19.89, Place 5 £15.21.
Owner D Tumman & R F Bloodstock **Bred** Miss S N Ralphs **Trained** Earlswood, Monmouths

FOCUS
An ordinary sprint handicap and very few ever got into it.
T/Jkpt: Not won. T/Plt: £38.80 to a £1 stake. Pool: £36,129.80. 679.40 winning tickets. T/Qpdt: £25.60 to a £1 stake. Pool: £2,648.50. 76.30 winning tickets. JR

6621 WOLVERHAMPTON (A.W) (L-H)

Tuesday, November 28

OFFICIAL GOING: Standard
Wind: Light, behind Weather: Cloudy

6644 STAY AT THE WOLVERHAMPTON HOLIDAY INN MAIDEN STKS 7f 32y(P)

3:50 (3:50) (Class 5) 2-Y-O £3,238 (£963; £481; £240) Stalls High

Form RPR

1 **Brosna Cry (IRE)**[36] 6151 2-9-3 PaulHanagan 6 81+
(J G Burns, Ire) *chsd ldrs: rdn over 2f out: led on bit 1f out: rdn clr* **10/1**

2 3½ **First Bloom (USA)** 2-8-12 RobertHavlin 2 65
(P F I Cole) *chsd ldr tl led over 2f out: rdn and hdd 1f out: styd on same pce* **9/2**

5 **3** 3½ **Mardi**[49] 5892 2-9-3 TonyCulhane 10 62
(W J Haggas) *hld up: hdwy 1/2-way: rdn over 2f out: hung lft and wknd over 1f out* **4/1**[3]

304 **4** ¾ **Tenancy (IRE)**[10] 6523 2-9-3 70 JimCrowley 5 60
(J A Osborne) *led over 4f: wknd fnl f* **2/1**[1]

5 shd **Carefree** 2-8-7 LiamJones(5) 1 54
(W J Haggas) *mid-div: effrt 1/2-way: wknd over 1f out* **20/1**

00 **6** ¾ **Bold Nevison (IRE)**[28] 6270 2-8-12 MarkLawson(5) 3 58
(B Smart) *hmpd s: hdwy over 4f out: rdn 3f out: wknd over 1f out* **40/1**

00 **7** 9 **Beck**[10] 6520 2-9-3 HayleyTurner 7 35
(M L W Bell) *sn pushed along in rr: lost tch fnl 3f* **14/1**

8 1¼ **Gertie (IRE)** 2-8-12 EdwardCreighton 8 27
(E J Creighton) *s.s: outpcd* **66/1**

2 9 *nk* **Leprechaun's Gold (IRE)**[14] 6475 2-9-3 .... JoeFanning 9 31
(M Johnston) *chsd ldrs to 1/2-way* **7/2**[2]
1m 30.42s (0.02) **Going Correction** -0.075s/f (Stan) 9 Ran SP% **118.2**
Speed ratings (Par 96):96,92,88,87,87 86,75,74,74
CSF £55.01 TOTE £14.50: £3.90, £1.20, £2.50; EX 104.20.
Owner M A Kilduff **Bred** D And J Cantillon And C And K Canning **Trained** Curragh, Co Kildare

FOCUS
A good maiden for the time of year run in a time 0.27 seconds quicker than the following four-runner nursery.

NOTEBOOK
Brosna Cry(IRE) ◆ had shown ability in a couple of big-field maidens in Ireland, but this represents much-improved form. By Dubai World Cup winner Street Cry, the switch to Polytrack clearly suited and there was plenty to like about this effort, coming back on the bridle at the top of the straight before clearing away when asked. A Derby entry, he could develop into a useful sort on this surface, or fast turf.
First Bloom(USA) ◆, a $250,000 half-sister to seven winners, most notably Diffident, a high-class multiple six/seven-furlong winner, hails from a stable whose juveniles seem to go well at Wolverhampton and made a pleasing debut. He might just have bumped into a useful sort and should be well up to going one place better. (op 4-1)
Mardi shaped with plenty of promise on his debut in a mile maiden at Newbury, but he would have been totally unsuited by the drop in trip. He is seemingly more of a handicap prospect and can do better over further. (op 6-1)
Tenancy(IRE) did not improve for the drop back in trip and is not progressing. Modest handicaps may be more suitable. (op 11-4)
Carefree, an 8,000gns purchase, out of a multiple winner in Denmark, was well held on her debut but is obviously open to plenty of improvement. (op 33-1)
Gertie(IRE) Official explanation: jockey said filly was slowly away

6645 BOOK ONLINE AT WOLVERHAMPTON-RACECOURSE.CO.UK NURSERY 7f 32y(P)
4:20 (4:23) (Class 4) (0-85,78) 2-Y-O **£3,361** (£3,361; £770; £384) **Stalls** High

Form RPR
0152 **1** **Copper King**[10] 6525 2-8-11 **75** .... MCGeran(7) 4 77
(P D Evans) *trckd ldrs: rdn to ld and edgd lft over 1f out: jnd post* **13/8**[2]
5665 **1** *dht* **Stoneacre Gareth (IRE)**[3] 6598 2-9-2 **73** .... GeorgeBaker 1 75
(Peter Grayson) *trckd ldr: rdn and ev ch fr over 1f out: edgd rt and r.o to join wnr post* **16/1**
055 **3** *3/4* **Putra Laju (IRE)**[25] 6324 2-9-1 **72** .... JoeFanning 3 72
(J W Hills) *dwlt: hld up: hdwy and hmpd over 1f out: r.o: nvr able to chal* **8/1**[3]
1522 **4** *shd* **Victor Trumper**[4] 6586 2-9-7 **78** ....(b[1]) RobertHavlin 2 78
(P W Chapple-Hyam) *led: rdn and hung lft wl over 1f out: sn hdd: styd on* **8/11**[1]
1m 30.69s (0.29) **Going Correction** -0.075s/f (Stan) 4 Ran SP% **113.0**
Speed ratings (Par 98):95,95,94,94
WIN Copper King £1.00, Stoneacre Gareth £24.10; EX SG/CK £14.00, CK/SG £24.10; CSF - SG/CK £21.51, CK/SG £9.51.
Owner R Teatum And Mrs S Grayson **Bred** Robert De Vere Hunt **Trained** Formby, Lancs
Owner Richard Edwards **Bred** Miss A V Hill **Trained** Pandy, Abergavenny

FOCUS
Very suspect form. They went steady - resulting in a time was 0.27 seconds slower than the earlier juvenile maiden - and less than a length covered the four runners at the line.

NOTEBOOK
Copper King defied a 3lb higher mark than when second to the progressive Fares over course and distance on his previous start to share the spoils with Stoneacre Gareth. However, the time was slower than the earlier maiden and, with the field separated by less than a length at the line, the form does not look strong. (tchd 20-1)
Stoneacre Gareth(IRE), turned out just three days after beating only one home in a reasonable six-runner nursery at Lingfield, ran on strongly to grab a share of the spoils. This form does not look very reliable, though. (tchd 20-1)
Putra Laju(IRE) was badly hampered when beginning to get involved over a furlong from the finish and that arguably cost him the race. This form is suspect, but he clearly has plenty of ability and should not be underestimated in similar company. (op 7-1 tchd 9-1)
Victor Trumper, fitted with blinkers for the first time, looked vulnerable at the top of the straight having set only a modest pace, but offered little under pressure in any case, hanging badly left when asked for everything. He has something to prove now. (op 5-6 tchd 10-11 in places)

6646 DINE IN THE ZONGALERO RESTAURANT MAIDEN AUCTION STKS 1m 141y(P)
4:50 (4:50) (Class 5) 2-Y-O **£3,238** (£963; £481; £240) **Stalls** Low

Form RPR
5235 **1** **Golan Way**[15] 6458 2-8-12 72 .... JoeFanning 2 72
(I A Wood) *led: rdn and hdd over 1f out: hmpd ins fnl f: rallied to ld post* **2/1**[1]
0325 **2** *shd* **Callisto Moon**[11] 6506 2-8-9 67 .... GrahamGibbons 1 69
(P A Blockley) *chsd ldrs: rdn to ld over 1f out: edgd rt ins fnl f: hdd post* **9/2**[3]
003 **3** *shd* **Fealeview Lady (USA)**[14] 6481 2-8-8 68 .... RobertHavlin 7 68
(H Morrison) *hld up in tch: rdn and ev ch fr over 1f out: r.o* **3/1**[2]
4 *10* **Hostage** 2-8-6 .... HayleyTurner 3 45
(M L W Bell) *sn pushed along in rr: rdn over 3f out: wkng whn nt clr run over 2f out* **12/1**
0065 **5** *6* **Mineral Rights (USA)**[10] 6520 2-8-11 65 .... PaulHanagan 6 37
(I Semple) *chsd wnr: rdn and ev ch over 2f out: wknd over 1f out* **13/2**
0 **6** *1 1/2* **Daboy (IRE)**[17] 6441 2-8-13 .... LPKeniry 4 36
(John A Quinn, Ire) *s.i.s: sn prom: rdn 5f out: wknd over 2f out* **20/1**
7 *13* **Here's Blue Chip (IRE)** 2-8-13 .... TonyCulhane 5 9
(P W D'Arcy) *hld up: rdn over 3f out: sn wknd* **12/1**
1m 51.29s (-0.47) **Going Correction** -0.075s/f (Stan) 7 Ran SP% **110.0**
Speed ratings (Par 96):99,98,98,89,84 83,71
CSF £10.35 TOTE £2.40: £1.50, £2.70; EX 9.30.
Owner Lewis Caterers **Bred** Lewis Caterers **Trained** Upper Lambourn, Berks
■ Stewards' Enquiry : Graham Gibbons three-day ban; one-day for careless riding, two-days for using whip with excessive frequency (Dec 9-11)

FOCUS
An ordinary maiden that only concerned three of the seven-strong field.

NOTEBOOK
Golan Way, returned to maiden company having been running with credit in nurseries, seemed to get outpaced early in the straight having set just an ordinary pace, and was hampered by the eventual runner-up just inside the final furlong, but he kept on gamely for pressure to get back up literally on the line. This represents just ordinary form, but he should do better over middle-distances next year. (op 9-4)
Callisto Moon, returned to maiden company, wandered around under a hard ride (hampering the eventual winner) and just lost out. He has had a few chances and his attitude is open to question, but he will surely find a race at some point.
Fealeview Lady(USA), who showed improved form over seven furlongs here on her previous start, was just worried out of it over this longer trip. A modest race should come her way at some point. (tchd 11-4)
Hostage, a 10,000gns first foal of an unraced half-sister to the high-class Brave Act, a prolific winner at around a mile, seemed badly in need of this first racecourse experience. (op 10-1)
Mineral Rights(USA) was well below his official mark of 65 and seemed unsuited by the step back up in trip. (op 9-2)

6647 TOP UK LTD POLISH RECRUITMENT SPECIALISTS H'CAP 1m 1f 103y(P)
5:20 (5:20) (Class 5) (0-70,70) 3-Y-O **£3,886** (£1,156; £577; £288) **Stalls** Low

Form RPR
0223 **1** **Tous Les Deux**[11] 6507 3-8-13 **67** .... GrahamGibbons 5 76
(Peter Grayson) *hld up in tch: plld hrd: led ins fnl f: rdn out* **15/8**[1]
31 **2** *1* **Snowy Day (FR)**[215] 1254 3-8-9 **63** .... TonyCulhane 7 70
(W J Haggas) *trckd ldrs: rdn and edgd lft over 1f out: sn ev ch: kpt on* **9/4**[2]
3022 **3** *1/2* **Chia (IRE)**[17] 6451 3-8-9 **63** .... RobertHavlin 2 69
(D Haydn Jones) *hld up: hdwy over 2f out: rdn and edgd lft over 1f out: r.o* **10/1**
6232 **4** *2* **Tender The Great (IRE)**[14] 6483 3-8-11 **65** ....(v) HayleyTurner 4 67
(V Smith) *trckd ldrs: plld hrd: led over 2f out: rdn over 1f out: hdd and no ex ins fnl f* **15/2**[3]
-000 **5** *nk* **Three Thieves (UAE)**[53] 5786 3-8-13 **67** .... JimCrowley 1 68
(M S Saunders) *prom: lost pl over 3f out: r.o ins fnl f* **22/1**
0003 **6** *1 3/4* **Blue Beacon**[22] 6380 3-8-2 **56** .... PaulHanagan 9 54
(K A Ryan) *hld up: hdwy over 2f out: sn rdn: wknd fnl f* **16/1**
-400 **7** *1* **King's Ransom**[117] 4076 3-9-1 **69** ....(b[1]) LPKeniry 8 65
(W R Muir) *dwlt: hld up: effrt over 2f out: hung lft and wknd over 1f out* **33/1**
0006 **8** *9* **Supreme Charter**[28] 6287 3-9-2 **70** ....(b[1]) JoeFanning 6 48
(M Johnston) *chsd ldrs 7f* **10/1**
5500 **9** *1* **Kings Heir (IRE)**[14] 6478 3-9-1 **69** .... AdrianMcCarthy 3 45
(Peter Grayson) *mde most 7f: sn rdn and wknd* **33/1**
2m 0.70s (-1.92) **Going Correction** -0.075s/f (Stan) 9 Ran SP% **111.6**
Speed ratings (Par 102):105,104,103,101,101 100,99,91,90
CSF £5.74 CT £28.89 TOTE £2.70: £1.10, £1.10, £3.20; EX 8.30.
Owner Mrs Sarah Grayson **Bred** G And Mrs Middlebrook **Trained** Formby, Lancs

FOCUS
Just a modest handicap though the time was creditable for the grade..
Kings Heir(IRE) Official explanation: jockey said gelding hung right

6648 HOTEL & CONFERENCING AT WOLVERHAMPTON RACECOURSE H'CAP 1m 1f 103y(P)
5:50 (5:50) (Class 6) (0-60,58) 3-Y-O+ **£2,730** (£806; £403) **Stalls** Low

Form RPR
400 **1** **Buscador (USA)**[168] 2522 7-9-0 **58** .... LiamJones(5) 7 66
(W M Brisbourne) *mde all: rdn over 1f out: edgd rt ins fnl f: all out* **9/2**[2]
2532 **2** *shd* **Keisha Kayleigh (IRE)**[59] 5683 3-8-9 **56** ....(p) MarkLawson(5) 2 64
(B Ellison) *hld up: hdwy over 2f out: rdn to chse wnr fnl f: edgd rt: styd on* **4/1**[1]
0242 **3** *3* **Moyoko (IRE)**[46] 5936 3-8-9 **51** .... FrancisNorton 9 53
(M Blanshard) *chsd ldrs: rdn over 1f out: styd on* **11/2**[3]
0020 **4** *1* **Right Ted (IRE)**[21] 6387 3-9-2 **58** .... JoeFanning 10 58
(T Wall) *chsd wnr: rdn and ev ch over 2f out: wknd fnl f* **12/1**
2500 **5** *1* **Burnley Al (IRE)**[45] 5974 4-9-5 **58** ....(b) GeorgeBaker 4 56
(Peter Grayson) *hld up and bhd: hdwy u.p over 1f out: no imp fnl f* **6/1**
6 *4* **Salthill (IRE)**[33] 6197 3-8-3 **45** .... AdrianMcCarthy 6 35
(Jarlath P Fahey, Ire) *s.i.s: hld up: effrt over 2f out: sn wknd* **33/1**
262- **7** *shd* **Show Me The Lolly (FR)**[379] 6343 6-8-6 **52** .... MJMurphy(7) 3 42
(P J McBride) *chsd ldrs: rdn over 2f out: wknd fnl f* **14/1**
0504 **8** *13* **Mill End (IRE)**[28] 6286 4-9-5 **58** .... ChrisCatlin 1 22
(R M H Cowell) *chsd ldrs: rdn over 3f out: wkng whn n.m.r over 2f out* **11/2**[3]
0206 **9** *1* **Barry The Brave**[20] 6404 4-9-0 **53** .... PaulHanagan 8 15
(Micky Hammond) *hld up: wknd over 2f out: eased over 1f out* **15/2**
10 *7* **Marcosdream (IRE)**[39] 6090 5-8-5 **44** oh4 .... HayleyTurner 5 —
(Jarlath P Fahey, Ire) *plld hrd and prom: rdn over 3f out: wknd over 2f out* **25/1**
2m 2.21s (-0.41) **Going Correction** -0.075s/f (Stan)
WFA 3 from 4yo+ 3lb 10 Ran SP% **116.1**
Speed ratings (Par 101):98,97,95,94,93 89,89,78,77,71
CSF £22.78 CT £101.17 TOTE £6.40: £1.60, £1.70, £1.70; EX 26.10.
Owner David Robson **Bred** William H Floyd **Trained** Great Ness, Shropshire

FOCUS
A weak handicap in which it proved hard to get involved from off the pace.
Barry The Brave Official explanation: jockey said gelding moved poorly throughout

6649 CHRISTMAS PARTY NIGHT THIS SATURDAY MEDIAN AUCTION MAIDEN STKS 5f 216y(P)
6:20 (6:21) (Class 6) 3-4-Y-O **£2,590** (£770; £385; £192) **Stalls** Low

Form RPR
5000 **1** **Kissi Kissi**[7] 6549 3-8-12 45 ....(v) AdrianMcCarthy 8 51
(M J Attwater) *outpcd: hdwy over 2f out: rdn to ld ins fnl f: r.o* **33/1**
0020 **2** *hd* **Make My Dream**[10] 6510 3-9-3 55 .... JimCrowley 3 55
(J Gallagher) *prom: rdn over 2f out: ev ch ins fnl f: r.o* **5/2**[2]
3060 **3** *1/2* **Primarily**[50] 5865 4-9-3 45 .... GeorgeBaker 12 54
(Peter Grayson) *outpcd: hdwy u.p over 1f out: hung lft ins fnl f: r.o* **10/1**
4503 **4** *2 1/2* **Newkeylets**[14] 6480 3-8-12 53 ....(p) TomEaves 5 41
(I Semple) *chsd ldr: rdn to ld over 1f out: hdd and no ex ins fnl f* **15/8**[1]
03 **5** *3* **Pain In The Neck (IRE)**[7] 6557 3-9-3 .... ChrisCatlin 6 37
(M J Wallace) *prom: rdn over 2f out: wknd over 1f out* **7/2**[3]
5504 **6** *nk* **Marron Flore**[8] 6533 3-8-12 45 ....(p) RichardThomas 7 32
(A J Lidderdale) *chsd ldrs: rdn over 2f out: wknd over 1f out* **20/1**
432 **7** *4* **Left Nostril (IRE)**[13] 6492 3-8-12 40 .... BrianReilly 1 20
(P S McEntee) *led: rdn and hdd over 1f out: wknd ins fnl f* **14/1**
5 **8** *5* **Miss Double Daisy**[21] 6389 3-8-7 .... MarkLawson(5) 9 5
(B Smart) *mid-div: sn drvn along: wkng whn hung lft over 2f out* **16/1**
9 *1* **Lady Lucas (IRE)**[275] 3-8-12 .... EdwardCreighton 10 2
(E J Creighton) *slowly intos tride: outpcd* **40/1**
-000 **10** *7* **Lough Arrow (IRE)**[207] 1464 3-9-3 30 .... PaulHanagan 4 —
(P S Felgate) *prom to 1/2-way: in rr whn hmpd over 2f out* **100/1**
1m 15.4s (-0.41) **Going Correction** -0.075s/f (Stan) 10 Ran SP% **118.3**
Speed ratings (Par 101):99,98,98,94,90 90,85,78,77,67
CSF £114.47 TOTE £22.60: £7.40, £1.10, £2.90; EX 193.90 Place 6 £58.66, Place 5 £23.27.
Owner Mrs M Tanner **Bred** G L And Mrs Tanner **Trained** Wysall, Notts

FOCUS
An atrocious maiden though the time was acceptable..
Kissi Kissi Official explanation: trainer said, regarding apparent improvement in form, the filly benefited from a drop in trip, change in riding tactics and being fitted with a new type of bit

Left Nostril(IRE) Official explanation: jockey said filly lost its action
T/Plt: £141.40 to a £1 stake. Pool: £58,421.20. 301.45 winning tickets. T/Qpdt: £27.90 to a £1 stake. Pool: £6,901.00. 182.80 winning tickets. CR

6615 KEMPTON (A.W) (R-H)
Wednesday, November 29

OFFICIAL GOING: Standard
Wind: virtually nil

6650 SPONSOR AT KEMPTON MEDIAN AUCTION MAIDEN STKS — 1m 2f (P)
3:50 (3:50) (Class 6) 2-Y-O — £2,388 (£705; £352) Stalls High

Form — RPR

3 **1** **Personal Column**[21] 6393 2-9-3 .... IanMongan 2 — 71+
(T G Mills) *lw: t.k.h early: trckd ldrs: rdn 2f out: kpt on to ld ins fnl f: rdn out* 4/7[1]

040 **2** 1 1/4 **Into Action**[74] 5389 2-9-3 78 .... DaneO'Neill 6 — 66
(R Hannon) *trckd ldr: rdn over 2f out: kpt on ins fnl f: wnt 2nd fnl stride* 7/2[2]

6364 **3** hd **Hemispear**[29] 6285 2-8-12 65 .... PaulFitzsimons 1 — 61
(Miss J R Tooth) *led: rdn 2f out: no ex whn hdd ins fnl f: lost 2nd fnl stride* 8/1[3]

04 **4** nk **Astral Charmer**[13] 6498 2-8-10 .... PatrickHills(7) 4 — 65
(M H Tompkins) *hld up in tch: rdn over 2f out: styd on fnl f* 14/1

0000 **5** 7 **Elmasong**[18] 6441 2-8-12 49 .... LPKeniry 5 — 47
(J J Bridger) *hld up in tch: rdn 3f out: wknd jst over 1f out* 100/1

00 **6** nk **Deep Cover (IRE)**[21] 6393 2-9-3 .... RichardThomas 8 — 52
(R M Flower) *trckd ldrs: pushed along fr over 4f out: wknd over 1f out* 40/1

055 **7** 4 **Mayireneyrbel**[108] 4394 2-8-12 56 .... JamieSpencer 7 — 39
(R Ingram) *bhd: niggled along fr over 5f out: short lived effrt over 2f out* 9/1

2m 9.87s (0.87) **Going Correction** -0.125s/f (Stan) 7 Ran SP% **117.1**
Speed ratings (Par 94):91,90,89,89,84 83,80
CSF £3.07 TOTE £1.50: £1.50, £1.50; EX 4.40.
Owner Mrs L M Askew **Bred** Cheveley Park Stud Ltd **Trained** Headley, Surrey

FOCUS
An ordinary maiden over the maximum trip for juveniles but not much strength in depth and the time was moderate.

NOTEBOOK
Personal Column took a while to get the better of long-time leader Hemispear but, once in front, kept on to win cosily and should appreciate even further next season. Much will depend on how the Handicapper views this effort. (op 8-11)
Into Action, who was having his first run since September, could not pick up as well as the winner but was staying on again late. This was better than his previous effort on Polytrack, at Wolverhampton. (op 9-2)
Hemispear, who looked very fit, made much of the running and tried to kick off the home turn, but she was unable to resist the winner and got collared for the runner-up spot close home. She is the best guide to the level of the form. (op 7-1)
Astral Charmer, who was held up, got closer to the winner than on their respective debuts here but in truth never looked a serious danger. Now qualified for handicaps, he will be better off in that sphere.

6651 RICHARDS GRAY FIRST PAST THE POST MAIDEN AUCTION STKS — 1m (P)
4:20 (4:20) (Class 6) 2-Y-O — £2,388 (£705; £352) Stalls High

Form — RPR

02 **1** **World Spirit**[63] 5613 2-8-4 .... ChrisCatlin 1 — 68
(Rae Guest) *hld up: hdwy over 2f out: r.o to ld ins fnl f: rdn out* 11/4[2]

02 **2** 1 1/4 **First Buddy**[18] 6441 2-9-1 .... JamieSpencer 8 — 76
(W J Haggas) *lw: trckd ldrs: led after 2f: rdn and hrd pressed fr over 2f out: kpt on but no ex whn hdd ins fnl f* 4/6[1]

04 **3** nk **Starparty (USA)**[14] 6486 2-8-10 .... JimCrowley 2 — 70
(Mrs A J Perrett) *lw: prom: rdn 3f out: ev ch 1f out: kpt on* 8/1[3]

603 **4** 1 1/2 **Bantry Bere (IRE)**[18] 6441 2-8-11 68 .... BrettDoyle 7 — 68
(J R Best) *led for 2f: trckd ldrs: rdn over 2f out: kpt on same pce fnl f* 14/1

5 nk **Hyde Park Flight (IRE)** 2-8-11 .... AdamKirby 5 — 67
(John A Quinn, Ire) *leggy: in tch: nt clr run briefly over 2f out: sn rdn: kpt on same pce* 50/1

00 **6** 1/2 **Whaxaar (IRE)**[37] 6143 2-8-11 .... LPKeniry 6 — 66
(S Kirk) *s.i.s: bhd: rdn 3f out: no imp tl styd on fnl 75yds* 50/1

54 **7** 3/4 **The Fifth Member (IRE)**[21] 6393 2-8-10 .... RobbieFitzpatrick 4 — 63
(R M Flower) *t.k.h early: in tch: effrt over 2f out: wknd ins fnl f* 14/1

1m 42.02s (1.22) **Going Correction** -0.125s/f (Stan) 7 Ran SP% **115.0**
Speed ratings (Par 94):88,86,86,84,84 84,83
CSF £4.96 TOTE £3.30: £1.60, £1.40; EX 7.50.
Owner R J Searle **Bred** Chippenham Lodge Stud Ltd **Trained** Newmarket, Suffolk

FOCUS
A modest juvenile maiden auction, but a good finish following a very steady early gallop.

NOTEBOOK
World Spirit, the only filly in the field, was making her All-Weather debut having been off for nine weeks since finishing runner-up at Newcastle, and she had been cast in her box subsequently. She will not run again this year, but should appreciate at least a mile and a quarter as a three-year-old. (op 7-2)
First Buddy had a clear favourite's chance on his Lingfield second earlier in the month, but was rather forced into making the running after the funereal early gallop, which may not have suited. He kept on to hold off the rest, but the winner finished too powerfully for him. (op 8-11)
Starparty(USA) was always close to the pace but, like the runner-up, could not produce an extra gear in the closing stages.
Bantry Bere(IRE), stepping up in trip, was a reluctant early leader, but after settling close to the pace could not pick up once in line for home and finished further behind the runner-up than on their recent meeting at Lingfield. (op 10-1)
Hyde Park Flight(IRE), an Irish-trained debutant, was running on steadily at the finish and can do better with this experience under his belt.
Whaxaar(IRE) was able to overcome a slow start due to the steady early gallop, but never got into contention.
The Fifth Member(IRE), who finished just behind the winner of the opening race here last time, was pretty keen under restraint and faded after having every chance at the two-furlong pole. (op 11-1)

6652 DIGIBET.COM H'CAP — 1m (P)
4:50 (4:51) (Class 5) (0-70,73) 3-Y-O+ — £3,238 (£963; £481; £240) Stalls High

Form — RPR

3321 **1** **Evident Pride (USA)**[74] 5388 3-9-1 69 .... DaneO'Neill 6 — 81+
(B R Johnson) *slowly away: steadily rcvrd into mid-div: hdwy over 2f out: qcknd to ld over 1f out: r.o: pushed out* 3/1[2]

5600 **2** 3 **Berkhamsted (IRE)**[39] 6108 4-9-1 67 .... (bt[1]) JimCrowley 8 — 72
(Tom Dascombe) *lw: trckd ldrs: led over 2f out: sn rdn: hdd over 1f out: nt pce of wnr* 12/1

2266 **3** 1 **Smart Ass (IRE)**[31] 6239 3-9-0 68 .... NCallan 2 — 71
(J S Moore) *towards rr: hdwy whn hung rt and short of room over 2f out: sn rdn: styd on* 12/1

5010 **4** 1 1/4 **Magic Warrior**[18] 6451 6-8-12 64 .... PaulFitzsimons 7 — 64+
(J C Fox) *towards rr: hdwy whn bdly hmpd and snatched up over 2f out: styd on again fr 1f out but no ch after* 20/1

6000 **5** nk **Parkview Love (USA)**[15] 6476 5-8-10 65 .... (p) PatrickMathers(3) 13 — 64
(D Shaw) *lw: prom: rdn 3f out: kpt on same pce fnl 2f* 25/1

5521 **6** 3/4 **Mythical Charm**[2] 6618 7-8-1 56 6ex .... (t) MarcHalford(3) 12 — 54+
(J J Bridger) *hld up bhd: hdwy over 2f out: nt clr run on rails over 1f out: styd on* 7/1

0043 **7** 1/2 **Smokin Joe**[37] 6147 5-9-4 70 .... (b) GeorgeBaker 4 — 67
(J R Best) *hld up bhd: hung rt over 2f out: styd on fnl f: nvr trbld ldrs* 13/2[3]

4121 **8** 3/4 **Jordan's Light (USA)**[4] 6590 3-9-5 73 6ex .... (v) RobbieFitzpatrick 14 — 68
(T J Pitt) *mid-div: rdn whn nt clr run briefly over 1f out: no further imp* 5/2[1]

3005 **9** 1 3/4 **Princess Lavinia**[47] 5953 3-8-9 63 .... EddieAhern 9 — 54
(G Wragg) *trckd ldrs: rdn and ev ch over 2f out: wknd over 1f out* 9/1

0 **10** 2 **Napoletano (GER)**[7] 6564 5-9-1 67 .... ChrisCatlin 10 — 53
(S Dow) *sn led: rdn and hdd ove 2f out: sn wknd* 33/1

4060 **11** 8 **Hurricane Coast**[20] 6413 7-9-0 66 .... (b) AdamKirby 5 — 34
(Ms J S Doyle) *in tch on outer tl wknd 2f out* 33/1

500- **12** 3/4 **Oranges And Lemons (FR)**[546] 2190 3-8-13 67 .... BrettDoyle 11 — 33
(C E Brittain) *in tch tl wknd over 2f out* 33/1

13 5 **Speckled Hen (IRE)**[234] 3-8-10 64 .... RobertHavlin 1 — 19
(D Haydn Jones) *racd wd and a in rr* 66/1

1m 37.47s (-3.33) **Going Correction** -0.125s/f (Stan)
WFA 3 from 4yo+ 2lb 13 Ran SP% **123.7**
Speed ratings (Par 103):111,108,107,105,105 104,104,103,101,99 91,90,85
CSF £37.19 CT £396.20 TOTE £3.80: £1.60, £3.20, £4.70; EX 62.30.
Owner C Lefevre **Bred** Juddmonte Farms Inc **Trained** Ashtead, Surrey
■ Stewards' Enquiry : Robbie Fitzpatrick three-day ban: careless riding (Dec 10-12)
N Callan four-day ban: careless riding (Dec 10-13)

FOCUS
A modest handicap run 4.55sec faster than the preceding juvenile maiden and a very good time for the grade.

6653 DIGIBET.CO.UK NURSERY — 7f (P)
5:20 (5:23) (Class 6) (0-65,70) 2-Y-O — £2,388 (£705; £352) Stalls High

Form — RPR

5042 **1** **Prince Of Charm (USA)**[5] 6576 2-9-0 58 .... (p) BrettDoyle 2 — 67+
(P Mitchell) *slowly away: towards rr: rapid prog fr wl over 1f out to ld ent fnl f: r.o wl: readily* 7/2[1]

004 **2** 1 1/2 **Dressed To Dance (IRE)**[44] 6015 2-9-0 58 .... JamieSpencer 6 — 63
(B J Meehan) *hld up bhd: qcknd wl to weave way through field fr wl over 1f out: wnt 2nd ent fnl f: kpt on* 6/1[3]

6601 **3** 2 **Inquisitress**[11] 6511 2-9-6 64 .... NCallan 8 — 64
(J J Bridger) *trckd ldrs: snatched up and swtchd lft 2f out: r.o to chal 1f out but nt pce of ldng pair* 10/1

3516 **4** 1 1/2 **Show Trial (IRE)**[19] 6422 2-9-2 60 .... AdamKirby 10 — 56
(D J S Ffrench Davis) *s.i.s: sn rcvrd into mid div: hdwy 3f out: ev ch 2f out tl 1f out: kpt on same pce* 14/1

000 **5** 1/2 **Shrewd Dude**[20] 6409 2-8-9 53 .... MickyFenton 11 — 48
(Carl Llewellyn) *trckd ldrs: effrt over 2f out: kpt on same pce fr over 1f out* 7/2[1]

0656 **6** 1/2 **Bentley**[14] 6488 2-8-3 50 .... (v) PatrickMathers(3) 14 — 43
(D Shaw) *towards rr: hdwy over 2f out: sn rdn: one pce fr 1f out* 14/1

5004 **7** 3/4 **Sophie's Dream**[20] 6416 2-8-12 56 .... EddieAhern 5 — 47
(J G Given) *plld hrd: prom: led over 2f out: sn rdn and hrd pressed: hdd ent fnl f: wknd* 12/1

0014 **8** 2 **Homes By Woodford**[4] 6592 2-8-13 57 .... DaneO'Neill 3 — 43
(R A Harris) *mid-div: effrt on outer ent st: wknd over 1f out* 9/2[2]

003 **9** 1 **Ballyshane Spirit (IRE)**[61] 5646 2-9-0 65 .... DanielRobinson(7) 12 — 49
(N A Callaghan) *hld up bhd: hdwy over 2f out: sn rdn: wknd jst over 1f out* 25/1

500 **10** 3/4 **Final Curtain**[12] 6505 2-9-4 62 .... FJohansson 13 — 44
(M A Magnusson) *mid div tl wknd wl over 1f out* 20/1

0005 **11** 7 **Priceless Melody (USA)**[14] 6487 2-8-3 47 .... (b) JimmyQuinn 9 — 10
(Mrs A J Perrett) *sn led: rdn and hdd over 2f out: sn wknd* 16/1

0000 **12** 6 **Imperial Style (IRE)**[15] 6472 2-7-12 42 oh7 .... JamieMackay 4 — —
(D Shaw) *a bhd* 100/1

1m 26.02s (-0.78) **Going Correction** -0.125s/f (Stan) 12 Ran SP% **122.5**
Speed ratings (Par 94):99,97,95,93,92 92,91,89,87,87 79,72
CSF £24.97 CT £201.42 TOTE £3.80: £1.40, £2.40, £2.90; EX 21.70.
Owner J R Stephens **Bred** Juddmonte Farms Inc **Trained** Epsom, Surrey
■ Stewards' Enquiry : F Johansson three-day ban: careless riding (Dec 10-12)

FOCUS
A moderate nursery in which interest was slightly diminished by the absence of Lake Pontchartrain

NOTEBOOK
Prince Of Charm(USA) ◆, wearing cheekpieces instead the blinkers he has been wearing recently, was narrowly beaten over a mile here last week and gained compensation by sweeping down the outside to record a decisive first success at the tenth time of asking. He is going the right way and looks capable of further success on this surface.
Dressed To Dance(IRE) ◆ came through just behind the winner and drew clear of the remainder without ever looking likely to trouble that rival. This was a good effort on her All-Weather and handicap debuts and she should not be long in winning a similar contest. (op 11-2)
Inquisitress, dropping in trip, tried to put her stamina to good use. She kept on, but was well held by the principals. (op 8-1)
Show Trial(IRE) was slowly away, but had every chance and briefly looked the winner until the first two swept by. (op 12-1)
Shrewd Dude was well supported having been upped in trip for this handicap debut, but after being well-enough placed, could make no impression in the closing stages. (op 4-1)
Sophie's Dream was again far too keen and needs to learn to settle if he is to progress.
Homes By Woodford handles this surface, but seems more effective on Fibresand. (op 6-1)

6654 DIGIBET SPORTS BETTING H'CAP 7f (P)
5:50 (5:53) (Class 5) (0-75,75) 3-Y-0+ £3,886 (£1,156; £577; £288) Stalls High

Form RPR

0-50 **1** **Littleton Telchar (USA)**[32] 6221 6-8-9 **72**.................... LiamJones(5) 2 78
(S W Hall) *hld up bhd: rdn and hdwy jst over 1f out: r.o strly but drifted rt: led fnl stride* **25/1**

2646 **2** *nk* **James Street (IRE)**[7] 6564 3-8-11 **70**..........................(b) BrettDoyle 11 75
(J R Best) *led: rdn 2f out: battled on gamely tl ct fnl stride* **8/1**

0056 **3** *½* **Quantum Leap**[14] 6489 9-8-11 **69**................................(v) JimmyQuinn 1 73
(S Dow) *mid-div: rdn over 2f out: stdy prog to chal 1f out: kpt on* **14/1**

0000 **4** *½* **Purus (IRE)**[5] 6580 4-9-3 **75**.................................... GeorgeBaker 7 77
(P Mitchell) *lw: prom: rdn and ev ch fr 2f out: cl up but hld whn n.m.r cl home* **9/1**

5435 **5** *½* **Rezzago (USA)**[14] 6489 6-9-3 **75**.................................... AdamKirby 5 76
(W R Swinburn) *lw: hld up towards rr: hdwy and nt clr run briefly over 2f out: sn rdn: styd on: nt clr run nr fin* **3/1**[1]

3200 **6** *hd* **Linda's Colin (IRE)**[71] 5444 4-9-3 **75**.......................... DaneO'Neill 8 77+
(R A Harris) *mid-div: hemmed in on rails fr over 2f out: swtchd lft wl over 1f out: kpt on but tight of room thrght fnl f* **50/1**

0520 **7** *hd* **Tanforan**[5] 6579 4-9-0 **72**..(b) JamieSpencer 3 72
(Ms J S Doyle) *lw: stdd s: bhd: rdn and no imp over 2f out: styd on strly fnl f: nrst fin* **7/2**[2]

0125 **8** *shd* **Hello Man (IRE)**[32] 6223 3-8-13 **72**................................ KJManning 10 72
(Eamon Tyrrell, Ire) *chsd ldrs: rdn over 2f out: cl up but hld whn n.m.r nr fin* **13/2**

0003 **9** *2* **Highland Cascade**[49] 5907 4-8-12 **70**..........................(p) MickyFenton 9 65
(J M P Eustace) *mid div: rdn over 2f out: wknd fnl f* **33/1**

4430 **10** *2* **Ribh**[30] 6259 3-8-13 **72**.. EddieAhern 12 61
(C E Brittain) *s.i.s: sn trcking ldrs: rdn 3f out: wknd over 1f out* **16/1**

40-0 **11** *½* **Dig Deep (IRE)**[197] 1760 4-9-3 **75**................................ TonyCulhane 4 63
(W J Haggas) *lw: t.k.h: trckd ldrs: rdn over 2f out: wkng whn n.m.r over 1f out* **11/2**[3]

31- **12** *4* **Haifa (IRE)**[392] 6225 3-9-2 **75**....................................... JimCrowley 6 53
(Mrs A Duffield) *a bhd* **25/1**

1m 24.93s (-1.87) **Going Correction** -0.125s/f (Stan)
WFA 3 from 4yo+ 1lb 12 Ran SP% **122.2**
Speed ratings (Par 103):105,104,104,103,102 102,102,102,100,97 97,92
CSF £213.79 CT £2978.09 TOTE £45.00: £8.90, £3.00, £3.70; EX 290.90.
Owner Dr P O'Driscoll **Bred** Morven Stud Ltd **Trained** Newmarket, Suffolk
■ Stewards' Enquiry : Liam Jones four-day ban: careless riding (Dec 10-13)

FOCUS
A modest handicap run 1.09 sec faster than the preceding nursery, but the field finished in a heap and there were a couple that looked unlucky.

6655 KEMPTON FOR CONFERENCES H'CAP 2m (P)
6:20 (6:20) (Class 4) (0-85,85) 3-Y-0+ £5,505 (£1,637; £818; £408) Stalls High

Form RPR

0100 **1** **High Point (IRE)**[46] 5963 8-9-3 **74**................................ DaneO'Neill 2 81
(G P Enright) *trckd ldrs: led jst over 2f out: styd on strly to assert ins fnl f: rdn out* **9/2**

041 **2** *2* **Valance (IRE)**[8] 4935 6-10-0 **85**................................(t) JamieSpencer 1 89
(C R Egerton) *trckd ldr: rdn and lost 2nd over 2f out: kpt on again ins fnl f: regained 2nd fnl strides* **4/1**[3]

31-1 **3** *shd* **Mr Excel (IRE)**[14] 6494 3-8-7 **76**.......................... RichardKingscote(3) 4 80+
(J A Osborne) *lw: hld up 5th: rdn and hdwy fr over 2f out: jnd wnr jst ins fnl f: wknd cl home* **5/2**[2]

0412 **4** *hd* **Trinity Rose**[9] 6537 3-8-7 **76**.. GregFairley(3) 6 80+
(M Johnston) *led: rdn and hdd over 2f out: kpt on* **6/4**[1]

0360 **5** *¾* **Llamadas**[34] 2176 4-9-8 **79**.. NCallan 5 82
(C Roberts) *trckd ldrs: rdn over 2f out: kpt on same pce* **20/1**

3m 33.25s (1.85) **Going Correction** -0.125s/f (Stan)
WFA 3 from 4yo+ 9lb 5 Ran SP% **111.5**
Speed ratings (Par 105):90,89,88,88,88
CSF £22.13 TOTE £6.00: £2.80, £2.20; EX 30.10 Place 6 £270.44, Place 5 £241.84 .
Owner The Aedean Partnership **Bred** Ballymacoll Stud Farm Ltd **Trained** Lewes, E Sussex

FOCUS
An interesting and tight-knit handicap with only 9lb between the whole field on official ratings; the race developed into something of a sprint in the straight.
T/Plt: £281.80 to a £1 stake. Pool: £59,823.30. 154.95 winning tickets. T/Qpdt: £151.80 to a £1 stake. Pool: £5,192.80. 25.30 winning tickets. TM

6629 LINGFIELD (L-H)
Friday, December 1

OFFICIAL GOING: Standard
Wind: Moderate behind. Weather: Dank and dismal

6656 JUMPING HERE ON DECEMBER 9TH H'CAP 6f (P)
12:50 (12:51) (Class 5) (0-70,71) 3-Y-0+ £3,238 (£963; £481; £240) Stalls Low

Form RPR

3431 **1** **Small Stakes (IRE)**[24] 6389 4-8-10 **63**..........................(vt) EddieAhern 2 74
(P J Makin) *trckd ldrs: rdn over 1f out: r.o fnl f to ld last 75yds: jst hld on* **4/1**[2]

0012 **2** *shd* **Shade Cozy (USA)**[4] 6622 4-9-4 **71** 6ex.................... FrancisNorton 11 82+
(A M Balding) *racd on outer: hld up in midfield: prog 2f out: rdn over 1f out: r.o to chal last 75yds: btn on the nod* **11/8**[1]

0030 **3** *1 ½* **Quality Street**[16] 6485 4-8-5 **65**..............................(p) JosephWalsh(7) 3 71
(P Butler) *led: rdn over 1f out: wknd and hdd last 75yds* **33/1**

0055 **4** *¾* **Ever Cheerful**[17] 6478 5-9-2 **69**...................................... MickyFenton 5 73
(D G Bridgwater) *towards rr and racd wd: rdn over 2f out: r.o fr over 1f out: nrst fin* **15/2**[3]

0605 **5** *shd* **Look Of Eagles**[11] 6538 4-8-11 **64** ow1.................................... NCallan 4 67
(P F I Cole) *pressed ldr: rdn over 2f out: chal over 1f out: wknd ins fnl f* **16/1**

6 *½* **Star Of Russia (IRE)**[32] 6265 4-8-12 **65**.................... MichaelTebbutt 7 67
(V Smith) *n.m.r after 1f: hld up in last pair: gng wl but plenty to do over 1f out: urged along and r.o fnl f: nvr nr ldrs* **33/1**

0306 **7** *¾* **Duke Of Milan (IRE)**[7] 6579 3-9-0 **67**................................ AdamKirby 6 67
(G C Bravery) *dwlt: hld up towards rr: gng wl enough whn hmpd over 1f out: no ch after* **12/1**

0506 **8** *nk* **Plateau**[13] 6527 7-8-9 **67**.. LiamJones(5) 12 66
(C R Dore) *walked to post 15 minutes early: racd wd: chsd ldrs: drvn over 2f out: wknd jst over 1f out* **16/1**

2030 **9** *½* **Monashee Prince (IRE)**[72] 5480 4-8-9 **62**.......................... BrettDoyle 9 59
(J R Best) *nvr bttr than midfield: rdn over 2f out: fdd over 1f out* **8/1**

4003 **10** *¾* **Sahara Silk (IRE)**[13] 6527 5-8-13 **69**..................(v) PatrickMathers(3) 10 64
(D Shaw) *hld up in last pair: rdn and no prog over 2f out* **25/1**

6040 **11** *2* **Taboor (IRE)**[7] 6585 8-9-1 **68**....................................... RobertWinston 1 57
(R M H Cowell) *prom tl wknd rapidly over 1f out* **16/1**

1m 11.31s (-1.50) **Going Correction** -0.125s/f (Stan) 11 Ran SP% **120.0**
Speed ratings (Par 103):105,104,102,101,101 101,100,99,99,98 95
CSF £9.86 CT £159.45 TOTE £4.40: £1.60, £1.20, £7.00; EX 9.90 Trifecta £107.30 Pool £232.82, 1.54 w/u.
Owner J P Carrington with Ahier Marchant Moore **Bred** Brian Williamson **Trained** Ogbourne Maisey, Wilts

FOCUS
An ordinary handicap in which the pace was sound and one in which the two recent winners fought out the finish in the centre of the track. The form is solid with the third to recent form.
Duke Of Milan(IRE) Official explanation: jockey said gelding was denied a clear run

6657 LINGFIELDPARK.CO.UK CLAIMING STKS 1m 4f (P)
1:20 (1:20) (Class 6) 3-Y-0+ £2,388 (£705; £352) Stalls Low

Form RPR

0000 **1** **Ocean Pride (IRE)**[26] 6352 3-9-1 77.................................. DaneO'Neill 2 56+
(R Hannon) *trckd ldrs: prog over 3f out: led over 2f out: rdn 3 l clr over 1f out: eased nr fin* **2/1**[1]

6505 **2** *1 ½* **Ciccone**[6] 6601 3-9-0 58... FergusSweeney 6 53
(G L Moore) *plld hrd: hld up in rr: bmpd 4f out: prog over 3f out: rdn over 1f out: wnt 2nd ins fnl f: no ch w wnr* **7/2**[3]

6520 **3** *1 ¼* **Coffin Dodger**[10] 6551 3-7-9 46.. NicolPolli(5) 8 37
(C N Allen) *hld up in last trio: prog to chse ldrs over 2f out but nt on terms: rdn over 1f out: styd on: no ch to chal* **14/1**

0010 **4** *½* **Our Glenard**[39] 6132 7-8-11 40............................ NataliaGemelova(5) 4 47
(J E Long) *s.s: hld up in last trio: prog on outer 3f out: pressed ldng pair 2f out: sn outpcd and btn* **16/1**

0064 **5** *1* **Life Peer**[138] 3017 3-9-1 56.. JimCrowley 3 50
(J G Portman) *dwlt: hld up in rr: prog over 3f out: pressed wnr 2f out: sn outpcd and btn* **5/2**[2]

0204 **6** *9* **Iamback**[10] 6553 6-9-1 45..(t) ChrisCatlin 5 30
(Miss D A McHale) *trckd ldr: led over 4f out to over 2f out: sn wknd* **6/1**

0-00 **7** *1 ¾* **Yeldham Lady**[58] 5054 4-8-6 40.........................(p) PatrickMathers(3) 1 21
(A J Chamberlain) *trckd ldrs: rdn and wknd rapidly wl over 1f out* **50/1**

-000 **8** *18* **Miracle Baby**[16] 3730 4-8-6 35...................................... MarcHalford(3) 7 —
(A J Chamberlain) *plld hrd: led to over 4f out: sn wknd and t.o* **50/1**

06-0 **9** *3* **Guanyin**[31] 6277 3-7-10 40 ow3................................. JosephWalsh(7) 9 —
(Ms J S Doyle) *prom to 5f out: wknd and sn t.o* **33/1**

2m 35.15s (0.76) **Going Correction** -0.125s/f (Stan)
WFA 3 from 4yo+ 5lb 9 Ran SP% **117.8**
Speed ratings (Par 101):92,91,90,89,89 83,82,70,68
CSF £9.48 TOTE £3.10: £1.60, £1.70, £2.00; EX 9.80 Trifecta £58.80 Pool £341.23, 4.12 w/u.The winner was claimed by D E Pipe for £10,000
Owner D G Churston **Bred** Miss Laura Byrne **Trained** East Everleigh, Wilts

FOCUS
An uncompetitive event in which the pace was just fair and the winning time modest. The form is limited by the proximity of the fourth.
Life Peer Official explanation: vet said gelding returned lame

6658 ARENALEISUREPLC.COM MAIDEN STKS 1m (P)
1:55 (1:57) (Class 5) 2-Y-0 £3,238 (£963; £481; £240) Stalls High

Form RPR

1 **Sweeney (IRE)** 2-9-3 .... NCallan 7 74+
(M A Jarvis) *reluctant to enter stalls: t.k.h: prom: trckd ldr 3f out : green but rdn to ld ent fnl f: jst hld on* **7/4**[1]

2 *shd* **Saviour Sand (IRE)** 2-9-4 ow1.............................. AntonyProcter 12 75+
(D R C Elsworth) *plld way to ld over 6f out: rdn and hdd ent fnl f: rallied: jst failed* **20/1**

0 **3** *nk* **Sister Maria (USA)**[98] 4765 2-8-12 .... BrettDoyle 6 68+
(E A L Dunlop) *in tch: prog over 3f out: chsd ldng pair over 2f out: hanging lft fr over 1f out: clsng at fin* **7/4**[1]

4 **4** *5* **Jocheski (IRE)**[31] 6284 2-9-3 .... EddieAhern 2 62
(M J Wallace) *trckd ldrs: rdn 2f out: wknd jst over 1f out* **20/1**

5 *1 ¾* **Challis (IRE)** 2-9-3 .... DarryllHolland 11 58
(J Noseda) *v green in rr and racd wd: prog 3f out: outpcd 2f out: no ch after: wknd fnl f* **14/1**

0 **6** *hd* **Dr Light (IRE)**[31] 6283 2-9-3 .... LPKeniry 4 57
(S Kirk) *racd wd in rr: sme prog 2f out but sn wl outpcd: n.d after* **66/1**

7 *1 ¼* **Dawn Mystery** 2-8-12 .... ChrisCatlin 10 49
(Rae Guest) *dwlt: hld up in last: pushed along and modest prog on inner over 1f out: nvr a factor* **66/1**

0 **8** *shd* **Antrim Rose**[33] 6242 2-8-12 .... RobertHavlin 5 49
(J H M Gosden) *led to over 6f out: prom tl wknd rapidly over 1f out* **9/1**[3]

03 **9** *¾* **Born West (USA)**[8] 6570 2-9-3 .... AdrianMcCarthy 3 52
(P W Chapple-Hyam) *a towards rr: last and struggling 2f out* **7/1**[2]

10 *½* **Soldier Field** 2-9-3 .... FrancisNorton 1 51
(A M Balding) *dwlt: nvr beyond midfield: brief effrt over 1f out: sn wknd* **33/1**

11 *shd* **Italstar (IRE)** 2-8-12 .... SteveDrowne 8 46
(H Morrison) *rn green and nvr beyond midfield: lost pl and struggling 3f out* **66/1**

12 *3* **Flashing Feet (IRE)** 2-9-3 .... DaneO'Neill 9 44
(R Hannon) *dwlt: a in rr: wknd 2f out* **20/1**

1m 40.49s (1.06) **Going Correction** -0.125s/f (Stan) 12 Ran SP% **123.6**
Speed ratings (Par 96):89,88,88,83,81 81,80,80,79,79 78,75
CSF £48.27 TOTE £3.20: £1.40, £5.00, £1.30; EX 60.80 Trifecta £212.60 Pool £392.37, 1.31 w/u.
Owner Jumeirah Racing **Bred** Darley **Trained** Newmarket, Suffolk

FOCUS
An ordinary looking event in which the pace was fair. The first three pulled clear of the remainder but the race is not easy to rate.

NOTEBOOK
Sweeney(IRE), a half-brother to a winner up to middle distances in France, was green beforehand and during the race but showed a good attitude to make a winning debut. He will stay at least a mile and a quarter and is entitled to improve for the experience. (op 13-8 tchd 6-4 and 15-8)
Saviour Sand(IRE), a half-brother to the useful middle distance performer Profit's Reality, had the run of the race on this racecourse debut but showed a good attitude when tackled and looks capable of winning a similar event.
Sister Maria(USA) fully confirmed the bit of promise shown on her turf debut and turned in a fair effort on this All-Weather debut. However, her tendency to hang in behind the leaders once asked for an effort arguably cost her the race and, although capable of winning races on this surface, may not be one for maximum faith. (op 2-1 tchd 9-4 in places)

Jocheski(IRE) again showed ability on only this second racecourse start and, although likely to remain vulnerable in this type of event, looks the sort that is capable of winning races in ordinary handicap company.
Challis(IRE), a half-brother to a triple winner up to a mile in France, was easy to back but hinted at ability, despite greenness on racecourse debut. He should improve for the experience. (tchd 16-1)
Dr Light(IRE), very easy to back, bettered the form of his debut at Wolverhampton and left the impression he would be capable of further improvement once handicapped.

6659 TOWERGATE UNDERWRITING NURSERY 6f (P)
2:25 (2:25) (Class 5) (0-85,87) 2-Y-0 **£4,210** (£1,252; £625; £312) **Stalls** Low

Form				RPR
611	1		**Hurricane Spirit (IRE)**[3] 6631 2-10-0 **87** 7ex BrettDoyle 2 (J R Best) *t.k.h: hld up in last: prog 2f out: led jst over 1f out: easily drew clr* **4/11**[1]	101+
0013	2	3 ½	**Teasing**[3] 6631 2-9-3 **76** JimmyQuinn 3 (J Pearce) *led: set stdy pce to 1/2-way: 2 l clr 2f out: hdd jst over 1f out and brushed aside* **10/1**[3]	76
021	3	1 ¾	**Fluttering Rose**[13] 6512 2-8-12 **71** SteveDrowne 4 (R Charlton) *cl up: trckd ldr over 3f out to over 1f out: sn outpcd* **7/2**[2]	66
1006	4	4	**Emma's Surprise**[24] 6388 2-8-12 **71** NCallan 1 (K A Ryan) *chsd ldr to over 3f out: sn u.p and btn* **14/1**	54

1m 12.48s (-0.33) **Going Correction** -0.125s/f (Stan) **4** Ran SP% **111.3**
Speed ratings (Par 96):97,92,90,84
CSF £5.10 TOTE £1.60; EX 3.20.
Owner The Little House Partnership **Bred** Knocktoran Stud **Trained** Hucking, Kent
FOCUS
Not the most competitive of races and a muddling gallop but a taking performance from Hurricane Spirit, who turned in a useful performance to maintain his unbeaten record on Polytrack.
NOTEBOOK
Hurricane Spirit(IRE) ◆ again found himself in an uncompetitive event but could hardly have been more impressive ridden with more restraint than has been the case. He is improving rapidly and looks very much the type to hold his own in stronger company. (op 4-7 tchd 8-13 in a place)
Teasing had a big pull in the weights with Hurricane Spirit on previous course and distance form and was allowed her own way in front but was readily put in her place by a most progressive rival. There will be many easier opportunities than this one. (op 6-1)
Fluttering Rose, who beat a subsequent winner and had looked likely to benefit from the step up to this trip on her latest outing over five furlongs, was readily outpointed on this nursery debut. A stronger pace would have suited and she is not one to write off just yet. (op 10-3)
Emma's Surprise, a six-furlong turf winner who did not look an easy ride at Wolverhampton last time, again proved disappointing and will have to improve on what she has shown so far on sand to win in nursery company from this sort of mark. (op 10-1)

6660 BUY YOUR NEW 2007 DIARY AT THERACINGDIARY.COM H'CAP 6f (P)
3:00 (3:00) (Class 3) (0-95,95) 3-Y-0+ **£8,096** (£2,408; £1,203; £601) **Stalls** Low

Form				RPR
4401	1		**Maltese Falcon**[20] 6445 6-9-1 **94** (t) NelsonDeSouza 4 (P F I Cole) *mde all: kicked on wl over 1f out: drvn fnl f: a holding on but all out nr fin* **3/1**[2]	104+
4413	2	nk	**Woodnook**[26] 6352 3-8-2 **81** oh1 JimmyQuinn 7 (J A R Toller) *prom: chsd wnr 1/2-way: cl up 2f out: rdn and nt qckn over 1f out: styd on fnl f: gaining at fin* **7/1**	90
5033	3	1 ½	**Qadar (IRE)**[13] 6514 4-9-2 **95** IanMongan 1 (N P Littmoden) *hld up in last: plenty to do whn prog on wd outside wl over 1f out: styd on strly fnl f: too much to do* **5/1**[3]	100
0615	4	½	**Saviours Spirit**[20] 6445 5-8-10 **89** JoeFanning 5 (T G Mills) *dwlt: t.k.h and hld up: effrt but outpcd wl over 1f out: styd on fnl f: nvr able to chal* **5/1**[3]	92
2111	5	3	**Little Edward**[16] 6485 8-8-8 **87** JimCrowley 6 (R J Hodges) *t.k.h: racd wd and hld up: gng wl enough 2f out: no prog after* **12/1**	81
1164	6	½	**Grand Show**[30] 6292 4-8-7 **86** AdamKirby 8 (W R Swinburn) *prom: rdn over 2f out: outpcd sn after: wknd fnl f* **9/4**[1]	79
000	7	½	**Sailor King (IRE)**[13] 6514 4-8-6 **85** ChrisCatlin 3 (D K Ivory) *a in rr: rdn and struggling over 2f out* **66/1**	76
0004	8	1 ½	**Graze On**[16] 6496 4-8-8 **87** (b) AdrianMcCarthy 2 (Peter Grayson) *chsd wnr to 1/2-way: wknd wl over 1f out* **14/1**	74

1m 10.31s (-2.50) **Going Correction** -0.125s/f (Stan) course record **8** Ran SP% **117.5**
Speed ratings (Par 107):111,110,108,107,103 103,102,100
CSF £25.05 CT £103.82 TOTE £4.50: £1.50, £2.30, £2.30; EX 29.40 Trifecta £93.50 Pool £610.08, 4.63 w/u.
Owner Christopher Wright **Bred** Stratford Place Stud **Trained** Whatcombe, Oxon
■ Stewards' Enquiry : Chris Catlin five-day ban: improper riding (Dec 12-16)
FOCUS
A competitive handicap in which the pace was sound and this form should stand up at a similar level. Those racing closest to the pace held the edge.
NOTEBOOK
Maltese Falcon, 6lb higher than his latest course and distance win turned in a smart performance from the front and won with more in hand than the official margin suggests. He should not be going up too much for this, should prove equally effective over five furlongs and will remain of interest if allowed an uncontested lead after reassessment. (op 11-4 tchd 100-30 in places)
Woodnook, up in the weights and in grade, ran as well as she ever has done on this surface. She travelled really strongly for a long way and, on this evidence, is capable of winning again on this surface. (op 8-1 tchd 13-2)
Qadar(IRE) ran a typical race in that he got behind before sticking on in determined fashion. He is a good guide to the worth of this form and is on a fair mark but his style of racing does mean that he needs things to drop just right. (op 9-2 tchd 4-1)
Saviours Spirit finished closer to the winner than over course and distance last time on these more favourable terms but has little margin for error from his current mark. He looks worth a try over seven furlongs. (op 13-2 tchd 7-1)
Little Edward failed to improve for the step up to this trip and will be much better suited by the return to a strongly-run five furlongs on Polytrack. He goes well for George Baker and is not one to be writing off just yet. (op 9-1)
Grand Show looked to have plenty in his favour returned to the scene of his three previous course and distance wins but proved disappointing having enjoyed the run of the race. Life may be tough in competitive handicaps from now on. (op 11-4 tchd 3-1)

6661 VISIT BRISNET.CO.UK FOR FREE U.S.A. RACECARDS H'CAP 1m 4f (P)
3:30 (3:30) (Class 4) (0-80,79) 3-Y-0+ **£5,505** (£1,637; £818; £408) **Stalls** Low

Form				RPR
3040	1		**Polish Power (GER)**[26] 6351 6-9-3 **75** LPKeniry 4 (J S Moore) *in tch: pushed along and prog over 3f out: chsd ldr wl over 1f out: drvn to ld ins fnl f: hld on* **20/1**	85
0052	2	½	**Eva Soneva So Fast (IRE)**[6] 6602 4-9-7 **79** JimmyQuinn 8 (J L Dunlop) *t.k.h: trckd ldr: led 3f out: drvn and hdd ins fnl f: kpt on: jst hld* **5/4**[1]	88+
0542	3	1 ¼	**Pass The Port**[13] 6519 5-9-5 **77** RobertHavlin 5 (D Haydn Jones) *hld up in rr: prog over 2f out: drvn over 1f out: styd on fnl f: nt rch ldng pair* **9/1**	84
3122	4	shd	**Lisathedaddy**[9] 6566 4-9-0 **75** RichardKingscote(3) 2 (B G Powell) *trckd ldrs: wnt 3rd over 1f out and poised to chal: swtchd to inner and nt qckn fnl f* **6/1**[3]	82
6434	5	5	**Royal Amnesty**[26] 6351 3-8-13 **76** (b) OscarUrbina 1 (G C H Chung) *dwlt: hld up in rr: effrt over 2f out: no imp over 1f out: wknd fnl f* **4/1**[2]	75
6506	6	hd	**Burgundy**[9] 6566 9-8-4 **69** (b) JackMitchell(7) 7 (P Mitchell) *hld up in rr: pushed along and effrt 3f out: outpcd over 2f out: n.d after* **25/1**	68
1400	7	3	**Street Warrior (IRE)**[15] 6502 3-8-13 **76** RobertWinston 3 (M Johnston) *led to 3f out: wknd wl over 1f out* **7/1**	70
0033	8	1 ¾	**Sekula Pata (NZ)**[20] 6432 7-8-5 **66** NeilChalmers(3) 6 (Christian Wroe, UAE) *prom tl wknd wl over 2f out* **14/1**	57

2m 30.9s (-3.49) **Going Correction** -0.125s/f (Stan)
WFA 3 from 4yo+ 5lb **8** Ran SP% **116.5**
Speed ratings (Par 105):106,105,104,104,101 101,99,98
CSF £46.68 CT £261.59 TOTE £23.70: £3.30, £1.10, £3.00; EX 61.20 Trifecta £171.50 Pool £413.28, 1.71 w/u. Place 6 £10.62, Place 5 £7.29.
Owner Mrs Fitri Hay **Bred** Gestut Hofgut Mappen **Trained** Upper Lambourn, Berks
FOCUS
An ordinary handicap and one in which the pace was just fair. The form looks sound rated around the third and fourth.
T/Plt: £18.70 to a £1 stake. Pool: £48,082.25. 1,872.45 winning tickets. T/Qpdt: £12.10 to a £1 stake. Pool: £2,628.00. 159.70 winning tickets. JN

6644 WOLVERHAMPTON (A.W) (L-H)
Friday, December 1

OFFICIAL GOING: Standard
Wind: Moderate behind Weather: Fine

6662 EBF HOTEL & CONFERENCING MAIDEN STKS (C&G) 7f 32y(P)
3:50 (3:51) (Class 5) 2-Y-0 **£4,533** (£1,348; £674; £336) **Stalls** High

Form				RPR
43	1		**Little Eskimo**[18] 6466 2-9-0 TomEaves 5 (B Smart) *a.p: wnt 2nd over 3f out: rdn over 2f out: led 1f out: r.o wl* **1/1**[1]	66+
0	2	1	**Dr McFab**[13] 6520 2-9-0 JamieSpencer 4 (J A Osborne) *hld up in tch: rdn over 2f out: edgd lft over 1f out: sn n.m.r: kpt on ins fnl f: nt trble wnr* **5/2**[2]	64
34	3	4	**Amber Isle**[13] 6520 2-9-0 DanielTudhope 3 (D Carroll) *w ldr: led over 3f out: rdn over 2f out: hdd 1f out: wknd ins fnl f* **11/2**[3]	54
	4	shd	**Not To Know** 2-9-0 SamHitchcott 6 (John A Quinn, Ire) *s.i.s: sn hld up in tch: rdn 3f out: wknd 2f out* **50/1**	53
	5	2	**Blockley (USA)** 2-9-0 PaulHanagan 2 (Ian Williams) *led over 3f: sn rdn: wknd over 2f out* **9/1**	48

1m 31.37s (0.97) **Going Correction** -0.10s/f (Stan) **5** Ran SP% **105.9**
Speed ratings (Par 96):90,88,84,84,81
CSF £3.35 TOTE £1.90: £2.10, £2.10; EX 5.60.
Owner M Barber **Bred** Netherfield House Stud **Trained** Hambleton, N Yorks
FOCUS
A moderate juvenile maiden. The first pair came clear and the form is straightforward.
NOTEBOOK
Little Eskimo got off the mark at the third time of asking in ready fashion and clearly enjoyed this switch to Polytrack. He has should be capable of improving further as a three-year-old, when he can be expected to stay further, and will reportedly now be put away until next year. (op 10-11)
Dr McFab improved a little on his debut effort over course and distance 13 days previously and finished nicely clear of the remainder. At this stage he does look like proving expensive, but he is going the right way and he would be better suited by a more positive ride in the future. He will also have the option of handicaps after his next assignment. (tchd 9-4)
Amber Isle had his chance yet was readily brushed aside by the winner when it mattered and shaped as though he would benefit for a drop back to six furlongs. He is now eligible for a handicap mark and can expect a mark of around 60 in that sphere. (op 9-2 tchd 6-1)
Not To Know, an 8,000gns purchase related to winners over five furlongs and a mile, was doing all of his best work towards the finish after making a sluggish start. He ought to be sharper next time. (op 33-1)
Blockley(USA), whose pedigree suggests he ought to be effective on the sand, was well backed on course for this racecourse debut. However, after racing prominently he dropped out when the tempo became serious and was clearly in need of the run. (op 14-1)

6663 EUROPEAN BREEDERS' FUND MAIDEN FILLIES' STKS 7f 32y(P)
4:20 (4:20) (Class 5) 2-Y-0 **£4,533** (£1,348; £674; £336) **Stalls** High

Form				RPR
2	1		**Lacework**[26] 6349 2-9-0 JamieSpencer 1 (Sir Michael Stoute) *a.p: nt clr run over 2f out: rdn to ld jst over 1f out: sn hung rt: r.o* **1/3**[1]	77
	2	nk	**Fidelia (IRE)** 2-9-0 PaulHanagan 9 (G Wragg) *hld up towards rr: hdwy over 3f out: rdn wl over 1f out: ev ch wl ins fnl f: r.o* **16/1**[3]	76
	3	2	**Musical Beat** 2-9-0 EdwardCreighton 2 (Miss V Haigh) *hld up: sn mid-div: rdn and hdwy 2f out: ev ch 1f out: nt qckn* **66/1**	71
04	4	2	**Lawyers Choice**[36] 6187 2-9-0 TonyCulhane 5 (Pat Eddery) *hld up: hdwy on outside over 4f out: rdn to ld 2f out: sn hdd: wknd ins fnl f* **5/1**[2]	66
	5	nk	**Vincennes** 2-9-0 MatthewHenry 4 (M A Jarvis) *bhd: rdn 3f out: styd on ins fnl f: nt rch ldrs* **18/1**	65+
66	6	2 ½	**Wadnagin (IRE)**[22] 6414 2-9-0 LeeEnstone 7 (I A Wood) *chsd ldr: led 3f out: rdn and hdd 2f out: wknd fnl f* **40/1**	59
0	7	5	**Compton Special**[14] 6505 2-9-0 JamieMackay 10 (J G Given) *t.k.h in tch: rdn and ev ch 2f out: sn hung lft and wknd* **80/1**	47
60	8	10	**Tu Sei Romantica (IRE)**[141] 3457 2-9-0 CatherineGannon 3 (K A Ryan) *led: hdd and rdn 3f out: sn wknd* **100/1**	22
	9	7	**Bali Belony** 2-9-0 StephenCarson 6 (J R Jenkins) *hld up in tch: lost pl over 4f out* **100/1**	4

1m 29.55s (-0.85) **Going Correction** -0.10s/f (Stan) **9** Ran SP% **110.0**
Speed ratings (Par 93):100,99,97,95,94 91,86,74,66
CSF £6.41 TOTE £1.20: £1.10, £2.90, £10.90; EX 7.30.
Owner Cheveley Park Stud **Bred** Cheveley Park Stud Ltd **Trained** Newmarket, Suffolk
FOCUS
A fair juvenile fillies' maiden which was run at a solid pace.

NOTEBOOK
Lacework, runner-up at Lingfield on her debut 26 days previously, just did enough to go one better on this drop back in trip. She ran green after meeting a troubled passage at the top of the home straight, but she was always holding the runner-up when it mattered and looks a useful filly in the making. (op 2-5)
Fidelia(IRE) ◆, whose dam won twice for this yard at seven furlongs and is a half-sister to their top-class filly Rebecca Sharp, posted a very pleasing debut effort and was only just denied. She was nicely clear of the remainder and, considering he stable's juveniles mostly tend to need their first run, a maiden should prove a formaiity for her during the winter. (tchd 22-1)
Musical Beat, a 15,000gns purchase, was found wanting nearing the final furlong yet still turned in a promising debut effort. She will be seen to better effect over a stiffer test in due course and is clearly up to winning races. (op 50-1)
Lawyers Choice failed to improve on the level of her All-Weather debut at Lingfield 36 days previously and was well held. She is now qualified for a handicap mark, however, and it would be little surprise to see her upped in trip in that arena. (op 9-2 tchd 13-2)
Vincennes ◆, who boasts a choice pedigree and is half-sister to Cape Cross among others, proved friendless in the betting ring and duly shaped as though this debut experience was needed. She ought to get plenty closer next time with this experience under her belt and will stay further. (op 11-1)

6664 WBX.COM WORLD BET EXCHANGE H'CAP 7f 32y(P)
4:50 (4:50) (Class 5) (0-70,70) 3-Y-O+ **£3,886** (£1,156; £577; £288) **Stalls** High

Form RPR
040 **1** **Regal Raider (IRE)**[167] 2662 3-9-2 **70**.................................. TomEaves 4 81
(I Semple) *a.p: rdn to ld ins fnl f: r.o* **10/1**
4033 **2** *1 1/4* **Imperial Lucky (IRE)**[8] 6573 3-8-8 **69**..................... JamesMillman(7) 10 77
(D K Ivory) *hld up and bhd: hdwy on outside over 1f out: edgd lft ins fnl f: r.o* **6/1**[3]
1200 **3** *1/2* **Hoh Wotanite**[63] 5649 3-9-0 **68**.................................... GrahamGibbons 5 74
(R Hollinshead) *sn pushed along towards rr: hdwy on ins whn nt clr run over 1f out: r.o ins fnl f* **5/1**[2]
0412 **4** *shd* **Dudley Docker (IRE)**[16] 6497 4-8-7 **68**....................... KellyHarrison(7) 1 74
(D Carroll) *led: rdn over 1f out: hdd and nt qckn ins fnl f* **11/4**[1]
4340 **5** *1 1/4* **Tipsy Me**[21] 6430 3-8-3 **64**.. ChrisHough(7) 8 67
(M L W Bell) *hld up and bhd: hdwy on outside over 2f out: edgd lft fr over 1f out: no ex ins fnl f* **25/1**
2443 **6** *1* **Joyeaux**[8] 6572 4-8-8 **62**..(v) DavidAllan 6 62+
(J Hetherton) *hld up in mid-div: hdwy whn nt clr run 1f out: swtchd rt and nt clr run ins fnl f: nt rcvr* **5/1**[2]
0040 **7** *1 3/4* **Safari Sunset (IRE)**[9] 6564 4-9-2 **70**.........................(p) StephenCarson 7 66
(P Winkworth) *chsd ldr: ev ch over 2f out: sn rdn: wknd ins fnl f* **22/1**
6005 **8** *1 1/2* **Startori**[18] 6469 3-9-2 **70**..(v) PaulEddery 3 62
(B Smart) *n.m.r sn after s: towards rr: nt clr run on ins over 3f out: n.d after* **40/1**
0020 **9** *nk* **Greek Secret**[37] 6174 3-8-6 **67** ow2............................ JamesO'Reilly(7) 2 58
(J O'Reilly) *chsd ldrs: rdn over 2f out: wknd over 1f out* **12/1**
2040 **10** *1 1/2* **Winthorpe (IRE)**[28] 6326 6-8-7 **68** ow1........................ SladeO'Hara(7) 11 55
(J J Quinn) *sn prom: ev ch over 2f out: sn rdn: wknd over 1f out* **33/1**
1006 **11** *3 1/2* **Corrib (IRE)**[17] 6478 3-9-2 **70**... TonyCulhane 12 48
(B Palling) *hld up in mid-div: hdwy over 3f out: nt clr run ent st: sn lost pl* **28/1**
4360 **12** *9* **Desert Lover (IRE)**[181] 2223 4-8-8 **62**....................... CatherineGannon 9 17
(R J Price) *prom: rdn 4f out: sn wknd* **10/1**
1m 29.35s (-1.05) **Going Correction** -0.10s/f (Stan) 12 Ran SP% **117.2**
Speed ratings (Par 103):102,100,100,99,98 97,95,93,93,91 87,77
CSF £63.90 CT £345.52 TOTE £9.00: £2.90, £1.90, £2.90; EX 62.10.
Owner Joseph Leckie & Sons Ltd **Bred** Gerard Callanan **Trained** Carluke, S Lanarks
FOCUS
A modest handicap, but the pace was generous and the form looks sound enough rated through the runner-up.
Joyeaux Official explanation: jockey said filly was denied a clear run

6665 WBXTRIPLECROWN.COM NURSERY 5f 20y(P)
5:20 (5:20) (Class 5) (0-75,64) 2-Y-O **£4,533** (£1,348; £674; £336) **Stalls** Low

Form RPR
0655 **1** **Billy Ruffian**[34] 6208 2-9-7 **64**... DavidAllan 2 70+
(T D Easterby) *a.p: wnt 2nd 2f out: rdn to ld over 1f out: edgd rt fnl f: drvn out* **7/2**[3]
0000 **2** *2* **Kilvickeon (IRE)**[15] 6500 2-7-13 **47**..............................(b) LiamJones(5) 4 46
(Peter Grayson) *swtchd lft sn after s: hdwy on ins 2f out: sn rdn: edgd rt over 1f out: swtchd lft ins fnl f: kpt on* **10/1**
6051 **3** *shd* **Baytown Paikea**[30] 6296 2-9-3 **60**....................................... BrianReilly 1 58
(P S McEntee) *led: rdn and hdd over 1f out: carried rt ins fnl f: nt qckn* **11/2**
0050 **4** *1* **Wibbadune (IRE)**[6] 6605 2-8-13 **56**.......................... RobbieFitzpatrick 5 51
(Peter Grayson) *wnt rt s: chsd ldrs: hung rt fr over 2f out tl over 1f out: one pce fnl f* **33/1**
4334 **5** *nk* **Money For Fun**[21] 6420 2-9-5 **62**..................................... TonyCulhane 6 56
(J S Moore) *carried rt s: bhd: carried wd ent st: hung lft ins fnl f: nvr able to chal* **11/4**[2]
03U5 **6** *1 3/4* **Queen Of Narnia**[6] 6592 2-9-4 **61**............................. EdwardCreighton 7 48
(M R Channon) *hmpd s: hld up: rdn and hdwy over 2f out: edgd lft and wknd fnl f* **9/4**[1]
000 **7** *4* **Suntan Lady (IRE)**[73] 5448 2-7-12 **46**...................... DuranFentiman(5) 3 19
(Miss V Haigh) *w ldr: rdn and wknd wl over 1f out* **25/1**
63.35 secs (0.53) **Going Correction** -0.10s/f (Stan) 7 Ran SP% **110.9**
Speed ratings (Par 96):91,87,87,86,85 82,76
CSF £34.64 TOTE £3.90: £3.30, £4.10; EX 24.80.
Owner Chris & Antonia Deuters **Bred** Slatch Farm Stud **Trained** Great Habton, N Yorks
FOCUS
A weak nursery and the winner is full value for his winning margin.
NOTEBOOK
Billy Ruffian, returning from a 34-day break, broke his duck at the fifth attempt and did the job in good style. The return to a sounder surface proved much to his liking and, while this form is nothing to get carried away with, he should remain competitive from a higher mark now his confidence has been boosted.
Kilvickeon(IRE) again looked tricky, but still showed much-improved form in defeat all the same. His proximity at the finish does hold down this form, but he can find easier opportunities if consenting to build on this. (op 20-1)
Baytown Paikea, 4lb higher than when scoring at Nottingham 30 days previously, had her chance from the front on this return to the All-Weather and was not disgraced. This was her best effort to date on sand, however, she looks to be just in the Handicapper's grip now. (op 5-1 tchd 13-2)
Wibbadune(IRE) Official explanation: jockey said filly hung right-handed throughout
Money For Fun did not have the most enjoyable experience and is capable of better than the bare form would suggest. (op 7-4)
Queen Of Narnia, very well backed on this drop in trip, was beaten before the final furlong marker and ran well below her best. (op 7-2)

6666 COME TO THE WOLVERHAMPTON CHRISTMAS PARTY TOMORROW H'CAP 1m 1f 103y(P)
5:50 (5:50) (Class 6) (0-65,65) 3-Y-O+ **£2,590** (£770; £385; £192) **Stalls** Low

Form RPR
0-01 **1** **Speagle (IRE)**[13] 6524 4-9-4 **65**.................................... DanielTudhope 7 75
(D Carroll) *sn led: rdn over 2f out: drvn out* **8/1**
0214 **2** *3/4* **One Night In Paris (IRE)**[20] 6448 3-8-13 **62**................. JamieSpencer 9 71
(M J Wallace) *hld up in tch: rdn over 2f out: chsd wnr fnl f: kpt on* **11/4**[1]
0101 **3** *1 1/4* **Inside Story (IRE)**[74] 5435 4-9-4 **65**...........................(b) PaulMulrennan 5 71
(G P Kelly) *hld up in mid-div: hdwy over 2f out: hung rt ent st: sn rdn: kpt on towards fin* **14/1**
0-04 **4** *nk* **Akinola (IRE)**[17] 6476 5-9-3 **64**................................(p) CatherineGannon 6 69
(K A Ryan) *a.p: rdn over 3f out: one pce fnl f* **20/1**
0021 **5** *3/4* **Qualitair Wings**[4] 6627 7-9-0 **61** 7ex.............................. DavidAllan 10 65
(J Hetherton) *hld up and bhd: nt clr run ent st: hdwy fnl f: nt rch ldrs* **4/1**[2]
3613 **6** *hd* **Western Roots**[20] 6451 5-9-4 **65**...................................... GeorgeBaker 8 69
(M Appleby) *stdd s: hdwy over 2f out: rdn over 1f out: no imp fnl f* **7/1**
6 **7** *6* **Symbol Of Peace (IRE)**[14] 6507 3-8-12 **61**.................. MatthewHenry 3 53
(J W Unett) *s.i.s: sn mid-div: hdwy over 4f out: rdn over 3f out: wknd wl over 1f out* **33/1**
6632 **8** *1* **Scottish River (USA)**[4] 6628 7-8-2 **56** ow1.............. AshleyMorgan(7) 4 46
(M D I Usher) *stdd s: nvr nr ldrs* **6/1**
0322 **9** *nk* **Bowled Out (GER)**[21] 6430 4-9-3 **64**.............................. TonyCulhane 2 53
(P J McBride) *led early: prom: rdn over 3f out: wknd over 1f out* **5/1**[3]
6330 **10** *7* **Monashee River (IRE)**[9] 6565 3-8-4 **58**......................... LiamJones(5) 1 33
(Miss V Haigh) *hld up in tch: rdn over 4f out: wknd over 3f out* **40/1**
2m 0.20s (-2.42) **Going Correction** -0.10s/f (Stan)
WFA 3 from 4yo+ 2lb 10 Ran SP% **118.0**
Speed ratings (Par 101):106,105,104,103,103 103,97,96,96,90
CSF £30.14 CT £311.47 TOTE £10.90: £4.50, £1.80, £6.10; EX 37.30.
Owner Document Express Ltd **Bred** Mrs Sheila Morrissey **Trained** Warthill, N Yorks
FOCUS
A modest handicap that was run at a sound pace. The form looks fair enough and should prove reliable.

6667 VISIT BRISNET.CO.UK FOR FREE U.S.A. RACECARDS H'CAP 1m 141y(P)
6:20 (6:20) (Class 6) (0-60,62) 3-Y-O+ **£2,730** (£806; £403) **Stalls** Low

Form RPR
5011 **1** **Atlantic Story (USA)**[3] 6642 4-9-6 **62** 7ex...................(t) JamieSpencer 5 76+
(M W Easterby) *hld up and bhd: smooth hdwy over 2f out: rdn over 1f out: r.o to ld cl home* **1/2**[1]
0510 **2** *1/2* **Zamhrear**[27] 6333 3-8-10 **54**.. HayleyTurner 3 67
(C E Brittain) *a.p: rdn to ld over 1f out: hdd cl home* **16/1**
4031 **3** *nk* **Just Bond (IRE)**[21] 6431 4-8-13 **60**......................... DuranFentiman(5) 12 72
(G R Oldroyd) *hld up towards rr: hung rt over 2f out: hdwy wl over 1f out: sn rdn: r.o ins fnl f* **11/2**[2]
0022 **4** *4* **Second Reef**[6] 6606 4-8-13 **55**... DavidAllan 7 59
(E J Alston) *hld up and bhd: hdwy and squeezed through over 2f out: sn rdn: one pce fnl f* **17/2**[3]
4606 **5** *nk* **Ignition**[24] 6387 4-8-11 **58**...................................(p) LiamJones(5) 11 61
(W M Brisbourne) *chsd ldr: led over 4f out: rdn over 2f out: hdd over 1f out: wknd ins fnl f* **28/1**
60-0 **6** *nk* **Plausabelle**[22] 6419 5-9-3 **59**.. JamieMackay 6 61
(G G Margarson) *hld up and bhd: swtchd lft and hdwy over 1f out: nvr trbld ldrs* **33/1**
4350 **7** *1 1/2* **Voice Mail**[101] 4673 7-9-3 **59**...(v) DeanCorby 8 58
(P Howling) *hld up in mid-div: hdwy over 3f out: sn rdn: wknd fnl f* **20/1**
000 **8** *1/2* **Ten To The Dozen**[14] 6508 3-9-2 **60**................................... RobertMiles 4 58
(P W Hiatt) *chsd ldrs: rdn over 2f out: wknd over 1f out* **100/1**
0000 **9** *3 1/2* **Atlantic Viking (IRE)**[31] 6288 11-8-13 **55**....................(v) PaulHanagan 10 46
(P D Evans) *hld up in mid-div: c wd ent st: sn bhd* **40/1**
0000 **10** *hd* **Joe Jo Star**[11] 6544 4-8-8 **50**..................................... RobbieFitzpatrick 1 40
(B P J Baugh) *led: hdd over 4f out: rdn and wknd 2f out* **66/1**
0U66 **11** *1/2* **Miss Imperious**[95] 4891 3-8-7 **51** ow1................................. TomEaves 2 40
(B Smart) *mid-div: nt clr run on ins over 2f out: n.d after* **66/1**
0000 **12** *3/4* **Wahchi (IRE)**[69] 4730 7-8-12 **54**...................................(bt) DaleGibson 13 42
(M W Easterby) *s.i.s: a bhd* **66/1**
1m 50.52s (-1.24) **Going Correction** -0.10s/f (Stan)
WFA 3 from 4yo+ 2lb 12 Ran SP% **117.5**
Speed ratings (Par 101):101,100,100,96,96 96,94,94,91,91 90,90
CSF £9.45 CT £28.03 TOTE £1.40: £1.10, £3.70, £1.30; EX 11.50 Place 6 £43.48, Place 5 £37.94.
Owner Matthew Green **Bred** A I Appleton **Trained** Sheriff Hutton, N Yorks
FOCUS
A moderate handicap and the form looks fair for the class. The in-form winner is value for further than his winning margin and the form is rated fairly positively through the fourth.
T/Plt: £43.70 to a £1 stake. Pool: £61,962.45. 1,034.35 winning tickets. T/Qpdt: £35.80 to a £1 stake. Pool: £5,611.90. 115.80 winning tickets. KH

6650 KEMPTON (A.W) (R-H)
Saturday, December 2

OFFICIAL GOING: Standard
Wind: Nil

6668 KEMPTON.CO.UK MEDIAN AUCTION MAIDEN STKS 1m 2f (P)
3:45 (3:45) (Class 6) 3-5-Y-O **£2,388** (£705; £352) **Stalls** High

Form RPR
0000 **1** **Play Up Pompey**[5] 6620 4-9-6 45................................... MatthewHenry 5 58
(J J Bridger) *stdd s: rr but in tch: hdwy fr 2f out: swtchd rt and qcknd jst ins last: drvn to ld fnl 100yds: kpt on strly* **33/1**
3204 **2** *1/2* **Lilac Star**[11] 6557 3-8-12 65.. DaneO'Neill 4 52
(Pat Eddery) *trckd ldrs: led 2f out: rdn over 1f out: hdd and nt qckn fnl 100yds* **5/1**[3]
0- **3** *1 1/4* **Clear Vision**[398] 6178 3-8-12 .... JimCrowley 2 50
(Mrs A J Perrett) *t.k.h: trckd ldrs: rdn and effrt over 1f out: one pce ins last* **6/1**
62 **4** *shd* **Spinning Reel**[55] 5847 3-8-12 .... AdamKirby 6 49
(W R Swinburn) *trckd ldrs: effrt and n.m.r wl over 1f out: sn one pce* **10/11**[1]
0035 **5** *2 1/2* **Valuta (USA)**[10] 6565 3-9-3 65..(t) SteveDrowne 3 50
(R A Kvisla) *led tl rdn and hdd over 2f out: wknd fnl f* **3/1**[2]

00 6 7 **Love And Affection**[22] [6429] 3-9-3 ....(t) BrianReilly 1 36
(P S McEntee) *pressed ldr tl slt ld over 2f out: sn hdd: wkng whn hdd jst ins fnl f* **66/1**

2m 10.49s (1.49) **Going Correction** 0.0s/f (Stan)
WFA 3 from 4yo 3lb **6** Ran SP% **112.8**
Speed ratings (Par 101):94,93,92,92,90 84
CSF £184.08 TOTE £21.10: £8.50, £2.70; EX 237.90.
Owner Double-R-Racing **Bred** M Pollitt **Trained** Liphook, Hants

FOCUS
A poor maiden run at a steady pace that resulted in something of a sprint to the line. Unreliable form.

Play Up Pompey Official explanation: trainer's rep said, regarding apparent improvement in form, that the gelding was suited by being held up

6669 PAT SMITH ANDOVER 60TH BIRTHDAY MAIDEN STKS 6f (P)
4:20 (4:20) (Class 5) 2-Y-O **£3,238** (£963; £481; £240) **Stalls** High

Form RPR

1 **Estimator** 2-9-3 .... DaneO'Neill 5 70
(Pat Eddery) *trckd ldr: chal 2f out tl drvn to ld appr fnl f: pushed out: readily* **12/1**

4043 2 1 1/4 **Mo (USA)**[10] [6561] 2-9-3 70 ....(t) SteveDrowne 7 66
(R A Kvisla) *led: rdn whn chal fr 2f out: hdd appr fnl f and styd on same pce* **6/4**[1]

3 1/2 **Hollywood George** 2-9-0 .... LiamJones[(3)] 6 65
(W J Haggas) *bmpd s: sn in tch: hdwy over 2f out: styd on wl fnl f but nvr quite gng pce to rch ldrs* **11/2**[3]

4 3/4 **Ginger Pop** 2-9-3 .... RobertWinston 8 62
(G G Margarson) *chsd ldrs: rdn and keeping on whn n.m.r ins last: swtchd lft and kpt on same pce* **12/1**

03 5 1 1/4 **Hope Your Safe**[19] [6457] 2-8-12 .... BrettDoyle 4 54+
(J R Best) *chsd ldrs: rdn over 2f out: one styd on same pce fnl f* **11/1**

4 6 nk **Last Sovereign**[21] [6434] 2-9-0 .... RichardKingscote[(3)] 1 58
(R Charlton) *stdd s: bhd: shkn up over 1f out: kpt on wl fnl f but nvr gng pce to be competitive* **10/3**[2]

7 2 1/2 **Comrade Cotton** 2-9-3 .... EddieAhern 9 50
(N A Callaghan) *bhd: sme prog 2f out: sn fdd* **11/1**

00 8 2 1/2 **Tranquility**[150] [3201] 2-8-12 .... JimmyQuinn 3 38
(J Pearce) *bhd: sme hdwy 2f out: sn fdd* **33/1**

60 9 2 1/2 **Power Alert**[53] [5891] 2-9-3 .... JimCrowley 2 35
(B R Millman) *chsd ldrs: rdn over 2f out: sn wknd* **25/1**

1m 14.26s (0.56) **Going Correction** 0.0s/f (Stan) **9** Ran SP% **117.3**
Speed ratings (Par 96):96,94,93,92,91 90,87,83,80
CSF £30.94 TOTE £10.70: £3.20, £1.30, £1.40; EX 33.90.
Owner Pat Eddery Racing (Moonax) **Bred** Llety Stud **Trained** Nether Winchendon, Bucks

FOCUS
Pretty modest maiden form with the runner-up dictating the level.

NOTEBOOK
Estimator, whose first run had been delayed due to him hurting his pelvis in the summer, overcame greenness to win on his racecourse debut. A half-brother to Tuscarora, a multiple winner between six furlongs and a mile, Euro Route, a six-furlong winner at two, and to Littleton Valar, a winner over hurdles, he looks the type to do better at three. (tchd 11-1)
Mo(USA), officially rated 70 and dropping back in trip after looking to find seven furlongs a bit too far last time, was unlucky to run into a fair newcomer. He will win one of these before long. (op 5-2)
Hollywood George, a half-brother to Border Artist, a multiple winner between six and seven furlongs, Lodge Keeper, a winner over seven furlongs and a mile, and dual seven-furlong winner Doctorate, stayed on late without being given a hard time and is another who should benefit from this outing and do better at three. (op 5-1)
Ginger Pop, whose dam was a dual winner over six furlongs at two, hails from a stable that does not send out many winners first time up, but he showed ability and is likely to come on for this experience. (op 9-1)
Hope Your Safe, who was keen, has now had the three runs required for a mark and she can step up on this when switching to modest handicap company. (op 12-1 tchd 14-1)
Last Sovereign looks likely to appreciate a return to a longer trip. (op 5-2)
Tranquility, a half-sister to Corker, a 12-furlong winner at three, should do better over further in handicap company.

6670 DIGIBET.COM NURSERY 1m (P)
4:50 (4:50) (Class 6) (0-65,64) 2-Y-O **£2,388** (£705; £352) **Stalls** High

Form RPR

6013 1 **Inquisitress**[3] [6653] 2-9-7 64 .... EddieAhern 7 69+
(J J Bridger) *trckd ldrs: hmpd after 2f: smooth hdwy to ld over 2f out: pushed out ins last* **15/8**[2]

5543 2 1 3/4 **A Nod And A Wink (IRE)**[8] [6576] 2-8-5 51 .... StephaneBreux[(3)] 5 52
(R Hannon) *hmpd after 2f: hdwy and pushed wd bnd 3f out: styd on fr 2f out to chse wnr ins last: kpt on but a hld* **11/10**[1]

0565 3 1 3/4 **Ten Black**[77] [5387] 2-9-1 58 .... RobertWinston 6 55
(R Brotherton) *hmpd after 2f: prom: chsd wnr ins fnl 2f but no imp: lost 2nd ins last* **12/1**

000 4 4 **Grand Officer (IRE)**[32] [6283] 2-8-3 49 ....(b[1]) LiamJones[(3)] 1 37
(D J S Ffrench Davis) *chsd ldr: bumper after 2f: slt ld and rdn 3f out: hdd over 2f out: wknd fnl f* **25/1**

205 5 2 1/2 **Rambo Honours (IRE)**[21] [6447] 2-9-3 60 .... CatherineGannon 4 42
(K A Ryan) *stmbld sn after s: hmpd after 2f: rdn and hung lft bnd 3f out: effrt sn after but nvr in contention: wknd over 1f out* **7/1**[3]

0024 6 30 **Grange Lili (IRE)**[7] [6596] 2-9-4 61 ....(b) RobbieFitzpatrick 2 —
(Peter Grayson) *led: veered rt and hit rail after 2f: hdd 3f out: wknd ins fnl 2f: virtually p.u ins last* **10/1**

1m 42.71s (1.91) **Going Correction** 0.0s/f (Stan) **6** Ran SP% **115.5**
Speed ratings (Par 94):90,88,86,82,80 50
CSF £4.49 TOTE £3.20: £1.30, £1.10; EX 4.20.
Owner C Marshall **Bred** A Saccomando **Trained** Liphook, Hants
■ Stewards' Enquiry : Stephane Breux two-day ban: used whip in the incorrect place and with excessive frequency (Dec 13-14)

FOCUS
A modest nursery which lacked strength in depth.

NOTEBOOK
Inquisitress, returning to her best distance of a mile, won easily and provided her in-form stable with its fourth winner from its last ten runners. Her best performance to date was when finishing fifth on her debut at Newmarket in the summer, and this success suggests that her new stable is on the way to getting her back to her best. (op 7-4)
A Nod And A Wink(IRE) again ran on late in the day to grab a place, and she is getting closer bit by bit to recording a first win. Her style of racing would be well suited to Lingfield. (op 11-8 tchd 6-4)
Ten Black, returning from an 11-week break, probably did not improve on his form in a Wolverhampton seller last time. (tchd 14-1)
Grand Officer(IRE), who is out of a half-sister to Derby winner Oath, was blinkered for the first time on his handicap debut, but he showed little.
Rambo Honours(IRE), another making his handicap debut, also failed to show much for the future.

6671 DIGIBET.CO.UK H'CAP 1m (P)
5:20 (5:20) (Class 4) (0-85,83) 3-Y-O+ **£5,505** (£1,637; £818; £408) **Stalls** High

Form RPR

3312 1 **Vacation (IRE)**[7] [6607] 3-8-4 78 .... WilliamBuick[(7)] 2 91+
(V Smith) *hld up rr: hdwy on rails whn swtchd lft to outside ins fnl 2f: str run fr over 1f out: kpt on wl to ld nr fin: readily* **3/1**[2]

0641 2 3/4 **Bomber Command (USA)**[8] [6580] 3-9-2 83 .... EddieAhern 5 92
(J W Hills) *trckd ldrs: drvn and hdwy fr 2f out to ld ins fnl f: hdd and outpcd cl home* **13/8**[1]

2101 3 nk **Gaelic Princess**[18] [6483] 6-8-5 71 .... ChrisCatlin 8 79
(A G Newcombe) *in tch: hdwy 2f out: styd on to chse ldrs ins last but nvr quite gng pce to chal* **6/1**

0303 4 1 1/4 **Magical Music**[63] [5689] 3-8-6 73 .... JimmyQuinn 6 78
(J Pearce) *chsd ldrs: rdn to ld over 1f out: hdd: ins last and sn one pce* **9/1**

0420 5 1 **Norton (IRE)**[55] [5833] 9-9-3 83 .... DaneO'Neill 10 86
(T G Mills) *led tl hdd over 1f out: wknd nr fin* **11/2**[3]

6605 6 nk **Samuel Charles**[8] [6580] 8-8-11 80 .... LiamJones[(3)] 3 82
(C R Dore) *bhd: hdwy on outside fr 2f out: kpt on cl home but nvr in contention* **10/1**

7 1 3/4 **Erra Go On**[41] [6112] 5-9-3 83 .... JimCrowley 7 81
(Adrian McGuinness, Ire) *chsd ldr: ev ch over 2f out: wknd ins fnl f* **16/1**

2 8 2 **Bay Boy**[27] [6359] 4-9-0 80 .... RobertWinston 4 74
(Andrew Oliver, Ire) *chsd ldrs: one pce whn bmpd ins fnl 2f: n.d after* **25/1**

5000 9 1 1/2 **Deeper In Debt**[8] [6580] 8-8-7 73 .... AlanDaly 9 63
(J Akehurst) *chsd ldrs: rdn 3f out: wknd 2f out* **50/1**

6000 10 1/2 **Emilio**[91] [5021] 5-9-0 80 ....(t) DeanMcKeown 1 69
(R A Kvisla) *a towards rr and nvr in contention* **33/1**

1m 39.51s (-1.29) **Going Correction** 0.0s/f (Stan)
WFA 3 from 4yo+ 1lb **10** Ran SP% **126.5**
Speed ratings (Par 105):106,105,104,103,102 102,100,98,97,96
CSF £8.98 CT £30.37 TOTE £5.40: £1.50, £1.20, £2.90; EX 16.20.
Owner Dave Clayton **Bred** Norelands Bloodstock **Trained** Exning, Suffolk

FOCUS
Not a bad handicap and it was won by a progressive type. The second is improving too and put up a slight personal best.

6672 DIGIBET SPORTS BETTING H'CAP 6f (P)
5:50 (5:51) (Class 6) (0-65,65) 3-Y-O+ **£2,388** (£705; £352) **Stalls** High

Form RPR

5511 1 **Siraj**[5] [6619] 7-8-7 56 6ex ....(v[1]) BrettDoyle 10 70
(J Ryan) *trckd ldrs: led over 1f out: qckned ins last: comf* **7/2**[1]

5500 2 3/4 **Nistaki (USA)**[7] [6595] 5-8-9 58 .... DaneO'Neill 8 70
(D Shaw) *n.m.r s: hdwy and nt clr run 2f out: styd on strly to chse wnr fnl f but a hld* **10/1**

3304 3 3 1/2 **Blessed Place**[5] [6622] 6-8-12 61 .... JimCrowley 2 62
(D J S Ffrench Davis) *t.k.h: sn chsng ldr: chal fr 3f out tl slt ld 2f out: hdd wl over 1f out: wknd ins last* **9/1**

2461 4 shd **Benny The Bus**[17] [6490] 4-8-13 62 .... JimmyQuinn 5 63
(Mrs G S Rees) *chsd ldrs tl shkn up and outpcd over 2f out: kpt on again ins last but n.d* **9/2**[2]

5220 5 3/4 **Whistleupthewind**[7] [6608] 3-8-10 59 .... MickyFenton 4 58
(J M P Eustace) *mid-div: rdn over 2f out: kpt on fr over 1f out: styng on cl home but nvr in contention* **25/1**

0003 6 hd **Sparkwell**[54] [5878] 4-8-13 62 .... DeanMcKeown 6 60
(D Shaw) *s.i.s: bhd: hdwy fr 2f out: kpt on fnl f but nvr in contention* **7/1**[3]

6600 7 2 1/2 **Semenovskii**[50] [5938] 6-8-13 62 .... RichardThomas 1 53
(Mrs N Smith) *bhd: kpt on fnl 2f but nvr in contention* **20/1**

0066 8 shd **Catspraddle (USA)**[8] [6585] 3-8-11 63 .... StephaneBreux[(3)] 9 53
(R Hannon) *mid-divisiom: rdn 3f out: nvr gng pce to get competitive* **12/1**

0602 9 1 1/4 **Surely Truly (IRE)**[21] [3488] 3-9-2 65 ....(p) LPKeniry 11 52
(A E Jones) *rrd s: chsd ldrs: wknd over 1f out* **50/1**

232 10 1 **Inka Dancer (IRE)**[11] [6556] 4-8-8 57 .... AdrianMcCarthy 12 41
(B Palling) *led tl hdd 2f out: wknd appr fnl f* **7/1**[3]

16-4 10 dht **Opal Warrior**[327] [68] 3-8-12 61 .... AdamKirby 7 45
(Jane Southcombe) *a towards rr and nvr in contention* **25/1**

5132 12 2 **Mina**[4] [6643] 4-9-2 65 .... JamieMackay 3 43
(Rae Guest) *a outpcd in rr* **9/2**[2]

1m 13.17s (-0.53) **Going Correction** 0.0s/f (Stan) **12** Ran SP% **124.8**
Speed ratings (Par 101):103,102,97,97,96 95,92,92,90,89 89,86
CSF £40.21 CT £308.39 TOTE £5.10: £2.00, £4.40, £3.50; EX 63.00.
Owner T C Gilligan **Bred** Mrs S J Etches **Trained** Newmarket, Suffolk

FOCUS
A modest handicap, but it was strongly run and the first two finished clear. Good form for the grade.

6673 KEMPTON FOR EXHIBITIONS H'CAP 1m 4f (P)
6:20 (6:20) (Class 5) (0-75,75) 3-Y-O+ **£4,210** (£1,252; £625; £312) **Stalls** Centre

Form RPR

2301 1 **Prime Contender**[10] [6566] 4-9-5 71 ....(b) GeorgeBaker 9 81
(G L Moore) *hld up in tch: stdy hdwy to ld ins fnl 2f: shkn up ins last and kpt on strly cl home* **11/4**[1]

052 2 nk **Jeepstar**[70] [5531] 6-9-7 73 .... JimCrowley 10 82
(S C Williams) *led tl hdd ins fnl 2f: kpt on gamely for 2nd but a hld by wnr thrght fnl f* **5/1**[3]

4662 3 1/2 **Resonate (IRE)**[28] [6336] 8-9-4 70 .... DaneO'Neill 5 78
(A G Newcombe) *hld up rr but in tch: hdwy 3f out: drvn to chal ins fnl 2f: no ex and nt qckn ins last* **11/4**[1]

0412 4 3 **Top Spec (IRE)**[31] [6301] 5-9-9 75 .... JimmyQuinn 4 78
(J Pearce) *towards rr: hdwy on ins to trck ldrs 3f out: rdn over 2f out: styd on same pce fr over 1f out* **8/1**

0101 5 2 1/2 **Inch Lodge**[22] [6426] 4-9-8 74 .... PaulEddery 2 73
(Miss D Mountain) *chsd ldr: rdn to chal over 2f out: wknd fnl f* **7/2**[2]

0-10 6 3 **War At Sea (IRE)**[14] [6519] 4-8-13 72 .... MarkCoumbe[(7)] 8 66
(A W Carroll) *bhd: pushed along and kpt on fnl 2f: nvr nr ldrs* **33/1**

5022 7 2 1/2 **Serramanna**[10] [6565] 5-8-9 61 oh2 .... AdamKirby 7 51
(Ms J S Doyle) *chsd ldrs: rdn over 2f out: sn wknd* **9/1**

0 8 1 1/4 **Lit Et Mixe (FR)**[10] [6564] 3-8-13 70 .... LPKeniry 3 58
(Noel T Chance) *a towards rr* **40/1**

06-0 **9** *12* **Atlantic City**[21] 6435 5-8-9 **61** oh2................................(e) RichardThomas 1 30
(Mrs L Richards) *chsd ldrs over a m* **40/1**

2m 34.7s (-2.20) **Going Correction** 0.0s/f (Stan)
WFA 3 from 4yo+ 5lb **9** Ran SP% **121.2**
Speed ratings (Par 103):107,106,106,104,102 100,99,98,90
CSF £17.80 CT £41.54 TOTE £4.70: £1.70, £1.80, £1.50; EX 22.30 Place 6 £45.82, Place 5 £4.53.
Owner Matthew Green & Richard Green **Bred** Gecko Bloodstock Ltd **Trained** Woodingdean, E Sussex
■ Stewards' Enquiry : Jim Crowley one-day ban: failed to ride to draw (Dec 13)
Adam Kirby one-day ban: failed to ride to draw (Dec 13)
Paul Eddery one-day ban: failed to ride to draw (Dec 13)

FOCUS
The first three came clear in this fair handicap and the form looks sound.
T/Plt: £57.60 to a £1 stake. Pool: £39,798.45. 504.00 winning tickets. T/Qpdt: £5.60 to a £1 stake. Pool: £4,508.30. 592.50 winning tickets. ST

6636 SOUTHWELL (L-H)
Saturday, December 2

OFFICIAL GOING: Standard
Wind: Virtually nil.

6674 RACING AGAIN ON THE 5TH H'CAP 7f (F)
12:30 (12:30) (Class 6) (0-60,60) 3-Y-0+ **£3,071** (£906; £453) **Stalls** Low

Form RPR
0020 **1** **Elusive Warrior (USA)**[11] 6556 3-8-9 **53**.....................(p) PaulHanagan 9 68
(R A Fahey) *trckd ldrs gng wl: smooth hdwy to chal wl over 1f out: shkn up to ld ins last: sn rdn and kpt on* **6/1**[3]
0014 **2** *2* **Windy Prospect**[11] 6549 4-8-13 **57**.. NCallan 2 67
(P A Blockley) *cl up: led over 3f out: rdn wl over 1f out: drvn and hdd ins last: kpt on* **10/3**[1]
0402 **3** *3* **Louisiade (IRE)**[12] 6531 5-8-6 **50**.............................. CatherineGannon 3 52
(K A Ryan) *chsd ldrs on inner: hdwy 3f out: effrt 2f out and ev ch tl rdn and one pce appr last* **6/1**[3]
6040 **4** *nk* **Border Artist**[24] 6396 7-9-2 **60**.. TonyCulhane 10 61
(J Pearce) *in tch: hdwy to chse ldrs over 2f out: sn rdn and no imp appr last* **11/1**
0066 **5** *2* **Favouring (IRE)**[4] 6642 4-8-8 **52**...............................(b[1]) HayleyTurner 4 48
(M C Chapman) *dwlt and bhd tl hdwy over 2f out: sn rdn and styd on appr last: nrst fin* **11/1**
0000 **6** *2* **Danelor (IRE)**[7] 6590 8-8-8 **55**.................................(v) PatrickMathers[(3)] 8 46
(D Shaw) *dwlt and rr tl styd on fnl 2f: nrst fin* **33/1**
4343 **7** *1 ¾* **Palais Polaire**[12] 6538 4-8-8 **52**.............................. RichardThomas 6 38
(J A Geake) *midfield: hdwy to chse ldrs wl over 2f out: sn rdn and wknd* **4/1**[2]
3101 **8** *2 ½* **Keon (IRE)**[12] 6545 4-8-1 **50**...................................... HelenKeohane[(5)] 14 30
(R Hollinshead) *midfield: effrt wl over 2f out: sn rdn and no hdwy* **6/1**[3]
0000 **9** *½* **Ten To The Dozen**[1] 6667 3-9-2 **60**................................. RobertMiles 7 39
(P W Hiatt) *s.i.s: a rr* **20/1**
0000 **10** *6* **Xpres Boy (IRE)**[144] 3378 3-8-8 **55**........................... JasonEdmunds[(3)] 12 18
(S R Bowring) *led: pushed along and hdd over 3f out: sn rdn and wknd over 2f out* **50/1**
0000 **11** *7* **Rosthwaite (IRE)**[3] 5370 3-8-5 **49**...............................(b[1]) DaleGibson 11 —
(Ronald Thompson) *midfield: rdn along wl over 2f out and sn wknd* **100/1**
3040 **12** *4* **Gem Bien (USA)**[12] 6531 8-8-6 **50**...................................(b) JoeFanning 1 —
(D W Chapman) *dwlt: a towards rr* **16/1**
3-60 **13** *12* **Grand Sefton**[188] 2050 3-9-2 **60**.................................. TomEaves 13 —
(D Shaw) *prom: rdn along 1/2-way: wknd qckly* **25/1**

1m 30.08s (-0.72) **Going Correction** -0.075s/f (Stan) **13** Ran SP% **123.0**
Speed ratings (Par 101):101,98,95,94,92 90,88,85,84,78 70,65,51
CSF £25.89 CT £134.39 TOTE £9.00: £3.10, £1.80, £2.30; EX 38.10 Trifecta £102.00 Part won. Pool £143.67. - 0.67 winning units..
Owner Northumbria Leisure Ltd & B Morton **Bred** Steve Peskoff **Trained** Musley Bank, N Yorks

FOCUS
A moderate handicap rated through the runner-up to his best.

6675 SPONSOR A RACE MAIDEN AUCTION STKS 1m (F)
1:05 (1:08) (Class 5) 2-Y-0 **£3,238** (£963; £481; £240) **Stalls** Low

Form RPR
422 **1** **Letham Island (IRE)**[11] 6558 2-8-7 74................................ JoeFanning 1 60
(M Johnston) *cl up: led over 4f out: rdn wl over 1f out: drvn ins last: kpt on* **4/11**[1]
3445 **2** *½* **Bert's Memory**[8] 6582 2-8-7 63.....................................(p) PatCosgrave 7 59
(K A Ryan) *sn trcking ldrs: effrt on outer over 2f out: rdn to chal wl over 1f out and ev ch tl drvn and no ex wl ins last* **6/1**[2]
003 **3** *¾* **Inflagrantedelicto (USA)**[12] 6534 2-8-13 57................. TonyCulhane 6 63
(D W Chapman) *sn rdn along in rr: hdwy u.p over 2f out: drvn to chse ldrs over 1f out: kpt on same pce ins last* **12/1**[3]
4 *3* **Barney's Dancer** 2-8-0 ow1....................................... AndrewElliott[(5)] 2 48
(J Balding) *dwlt: sn chsng ldrs: n.m.r on inner and lost pl over 3f out: styd on fnl 2f* **33/1**
5 *nk* **Danish Rebel (IRE)** 2-8-10 .... PaulHanagan 3 52
(J I A Charlton) *dwlt: keen and sn in tch: lost pl and bhd over 3f out: styd on fnl 2f: nrst fin* **20/1**
6 *¾* **Lauder** 2-8-5 ow2.. JasonEdmunds[(3)] 8 49
(J Balding) *chsd ldrs: rdn along 3f out and sn wknd* **40/1**
0 **7** *6* **Glenridding**[21] 6447 2-8-12 .... JamieMackay 5 39
(J G Given) *a bhd* **33/1**
00 **8** *1 ¼* **Solo City**[46] 6023 2-8-4 .... KevinGhunowa[(5)] 10 33
(P A Blockley) *led: hdd over 4f out: rdn along over 3f out: sn drvn and wknd* **25/1**
9 **Out Of Town** 2-8-10 .... DaleGibson 9 34
(Ronald Thompson) *in tch: rdn along over 3f out: sn wknd and bhd fnl 2f* **50/1**

1m 45.99s (1.39) **Going Correction** -0.075s/f (Stan) **9** Ran SP% **114.2**
Speed ratings (Par 96):90,89,88,85,85 84,78,77,77
CSF £2.26 TOTE £1.40: £1.02, £1.30, £2.60; EX 2.30 Trifecta £7.10 Pool £347.76. - 34.71 winning units..
Owner John A Smith **Bred** Rathasker Stud **Trained** Middleham Moor, N Yorks

FOCUS
A modest maiden and the 74-rated Letham Island seemed below her best, despite managing to win. The winning time was 1.28 seconds slower than the following nursery won by the 66-rated Chookie Hamilton.

NOTEBOOK
Letham Island(IRE) made hard work of confirming earlier promise and looked below her best, despite managing to win. However, she should do better over further and ought to leave the bare form of this success behind next year. (op 4-9)
Bert's Memory proved well suited by both the step up in trip and fitting of cheekpieces and just lost out. A minor race may come her way over this sort of distance. (op 11-2 tchd 5-1)
Inflagrantedelicto(USA), third in a seven-furlong seller round here on his final start for Mark Johnston, ran well behind his former stablemate, responding well to pressure to make the frame having been well off the pace. His new trainer does well with cast-offs. (op 16-1)
Barney's Dancer, a half-sister to 12-furlong winner Queen's Fantasy, out of a winning hurdler, stayed on again after losing her place inside the final half mile and clearly has ability. (op 40-1 tchd 50-1)
Danish Rebel(IRE) ◆, a 5,000euros purchase, out of a dual seven-furlong winner who was later successful in Belgium, stayed on from quite a way off the pace without being given too hard a time at all. This is modest form, but he clearly has ability and really should improve. Official explanation: jockey said, regarding running and riding, that the colt had hung badly early stages and only stayed on late when ceased to hang (op 25-1)

6676 EXPERIENCE NOTTINGHAMSHIRE NURSERY 1m (F)
1:40 (1:40) (Class 4) (0-85,81) 2-Y-O **£4,857** (£1,445; £722; £360) **Stalls** Low

Form RPR
0431 **1** **Chookie Hamilton**[14] 6522 2-8-6 **66**.................................... TomEaves 3 66
(I Semple) *trckd ldr: hdwy over 2f out: rdn to ld over 1f out: drvn and styd on gamely inisde last* **7/4**[1]
5224 **2** *shd* **Victor Trumper**[4] 6645 2-9-7 **81**.. RobertHavlin 4 81
(P W Chapple-Hyam) *hld up in tch: smooth hdwy 2f out: rdn to chal ent last and ev ch tl drvn and no ex towards fin* **5/2**[2]
053 **3** *5* **Spartan Dance**[12] 6536 2-8-8 **68**................................ RichardThomas 1 57
(J A Geake) *led: rdn along 2f out: hdd over 1f out: wknd ins last* **3/1**[3]
0233 **4** *7* **Right Option (IRE)**[5] 6625 2-8-2 **62**..............................(b[1]) PaulHanagan 2 34
(J R Weymes) *dwlt: sn rdn along to chse ldng pair: drvn along over 2f out and sn wknd* **4/1**

1m 44.71s (0.11) **Going Correction** -0.075s/f (Stan) **4** Ran SP% **109.9**
Speed ratings (Par 98):96,95,90,83
CSF £6.44 TOTE £2.40; EX 11.00.
Owner Raeburn Brick Limited **Bred** D And J Raeburn **Trained** Carluke, S Lanarks

FOCUS
A disappointing turnout for a nursery worth £7,500 and the form may not prove all that strong, but the winning time was 1.28 seconds quicker than the earlier maiden.

NOTEBOOK
Chookie Hamilton gamely followed up his recent Wolverhampton claiming success, handling the Fibresand just fine and showing himself on a fair mark. He should not go up much for this and ought to remain competitive. (tchd 9-4)
Victor Trumper threw away a winning chance in first-time blinkers at Wolverhampton on his previous start and he once again displayed a suspect attitude, drifting left under pressure. His rider seemed to try and kid him along in the closing stages, rather than go for everything, but he gave the impression he would not have gone by the eventual winner no matter what Havlin tried. (op 2-1 tchd 15-8 and 11-4)
Spartan Dance failed to build on his recent course and distance third and could be considered a little disappointing. (op 7-2 tchd 9-2)
Right Option(IRE) offered nothing in first-time blinkers on his Fibresand debut. (op 9-2 tchd 5-1 and 10-3)

6677 ARENA LEISURE PLC H'CAP 1m 4f (F)
2:10 (2:10) (Class 3) (0-95,89) 3-Y-0+
£7,945 (£2,379; £1,189; £595; £297; £149) **Stalls** Low

Form RPR
4421 **1** **Velvet Heights (IRE)**[19] 6467 4-9-7 **89**............................. IanMongan 10 104+
(J L Dunlop) *a cl up: led wl over 2f out: sn clr: rdn and r.o ins last* **11/10**[1]
2316 **2** *4* **Mighty Moon**[14] 6515 3-8-12 **85**....................................(bt) TonyCulhane 8 91
(J O'Reilly) *led: rdn along over 3f out: hdd wl over 2f out: sn drvn and kpt on same pce* **14/1**
0201 **3** *2* **St Savarin (FR)**[19] 6468 5-9-6 **88**...................................... PaulHanagan 2 91
(R A Fahey) *chsd ldrs tl pushed along and sltly outpcd over 5f out: rdn and hdwy over 2f out: sn drvn and kpt on same pce* **10/3**[2]
3600 **4** *½* **Kylkenny**[4] 6633 11-8-7 **80**...(t) CAdamson[(5)] 6 82
(H Morrison) *in tch: hdwy 4f out: rdn along wl over 2f out: kpt on same pce* **20/1**
4012 **5** *1 ¾* **Heathyards Pride**[19] 6468 6-8-7 **82**..................... RussellKennemore[(7)] 9 81
(R Hollinshead) *hld up in midfield: hdwy over 4f out: rdn along 3f out: drvn 2f out and sn no imp* **8/1**[3]
-302 **6** *1 ½* **Desert Leader (IRE)**[22] 6426 5-8-7 **75**................................ DavidAllan 7 72
(W M Brisbourne) *in tch: hdwy to chse ldng pair over 4f out: rdn along 3f out: sn drvn and wknd over 1f out* **8/1**[3]
3062 **7** *9* **Most Definitely (IRE)**[19] 6467 6-8-7 **75**....................... FergusSweeney 3 58
(R M Stronge) *hld up in rr: effrt over 3f out: sn rdn along and nvr a factor* **20/1**
6130 **8** *nk* **Kames Park (IRE)**[127] 3888 4-9-4 **86**................................... TomEaves 1 68
(I Semple) *a rr* **14/1**
00-6 **9** *4* **Credit (IRE)**[19] 6468 5-9-0 **82**... HayleyTurner 5 58
(Jennie Candlish) *a rr* **100/1**
00-0 **10** *1* **Dance World**[195] 108 6-9-1 **83**.. NCallan 4 57
(Miss J Feilden) *chsd ldrs: rdn along 3f out: wknd fnl 2f* **28/1**

2m 38.94s (-3.15) **Going Correction** -0.075s/f (Stan)
WFA 3 from 4yo+ 5lb **10** Ran SP% **120.2**
Speed ratings (Par 107):107,104,103,102,101 100,94,94,91,90
CSF £19.34 CT £45.20 TOTE £2.10: £1.10, £3.60, £1.80; EX 15.60 Trifecta £71.90 Pool £414.66. - 4.09 winning units..
Owner Windflower Overseas Holdings Inc **Bred** Windflower Overseas **Trained** Arundel, W Sussex

FOCUS
A good middle-distance handicap with a clear winner and the time was sound.

NOTEBOOK
Velvet Heights(IRE) ◆ has been a beaten favourite five times on turf, but he is much more reliable on the sand and is progressing into a smart middle-distance/stayer on his favoured surface. Raised just 6lb for an easy success over a mile six round here on his previous start, he followed up in good style, drawing well clear despite conceding weight all round to some reasonable types for the level. His form figures on Fibresand and Polytrack now read 12211 and he must be kept on the right side of. (op 13-8)
Mighty Moon ◆ is a very strong stayer, so Fibresand was always going to suit much better than Polytrack, and he ran a fine race in second behind the most progressive winner. He could be capable of even better over further. (op 18-1)
St Savarin(FR) ran well off a 6lb higher mark than when winning over a mile three round here on his previous start, keeping on well having become a little outpaced at about halfway. He gives the impression he will stay a little further. (op 3-1 tchd 11-4)
Kylkenny absolutely loves the Southwell Fibresand and this was a decent effort. His form figures round here now read 1132112121114315213241121114. (op 16-1)

Heathyards Pride had no easy task against this class of opposition from a career-high mark and was well held. (tchd 15-2)
Dance World Official explanation: jockey said gelding had no more to give

6678 SOUTHWELL-RACECOURSE.CO.UK H'CAP 1m (F)
2:45 (2:45) (Class 2) (0-100,93) 3-Y-0+
£11,217 (£3,358; £1,679; £840; £419; £210) **Stalls** Low

Form				RPR
4540	**1**		**Gentleman's Deal (IRE)**[28] 6337 5-9-1 **91** .... PaulMulrennan 4 (M W Easterby) *a.p: hdwy to ld wl over 1f out: rdn clr ent last: sn clr* **7/4**[1]	108
2106	**2**	*6*	**Wessex (USA)**[220] 1246 6-9-3 **93** .... IanMongan 8 (P A Blockley) *in tch: hdwy to chse ldrs 3f out: rdn 2f out: kpt on u.p appr last* **14/1**	97
2041	**3**	*1 1/4*	**Nevada Desert (IRE)**[22] 6424 6-8-6 **82** .... HayleyTurner 1 (R M Whitaker) *a.p: rdn along over 2f out: drvn wl over 1f out: kpt on same pce* **8/1**	83
2000	**4**	*shd*	**Paraguay (USA)**[105] 4605 3-8-4 **81** .... EdwardCreighton 9 (Miss V Haigh) *hld up in rr: hdwy 3f out: rdn wl over 1f out: kpt on ins last: nrst fin* **40/1**	82
4550	**5**	*1/2*	**Byron Bay**[77] 5355 4-8-10 **86** .... TomEaves 6 (I Semple) *hld up in rr: hdwy over 2f out: sn rdn and kpt on fnl f nrst fin* **9/1**	86
3500	**6**	*3/4*	**Kamanda Laugh**[63] 5675 5-9-0 **90** .... NCallan 2 (K A Ryan) *led: rdn along wl over 2f out: hdd wl over 1f out: sn drvn and wknd 1f out* **10/3**[2]	89
2413	**7**	*2 1/2*	**Freeloader (IRE)**[7] 6594 6-8-8 **84** .... PaulHanagan 3 (R A Fahey) *cl up: rdn along over 2f out: drvn and wknd wl over 1f out* **7/1**[3]	77
46	**8**	*3/4*	**Langford**[11] 6559 6-8-7 **90** .... PatrickHills(7) 7 (M H Tompkins) *trckd ldrs on outer: effrt 3f out: rdn wl over 1f out: sn edgd lft and wknd* **10/1**	82
1102	**9**	*3 1/2*	**Grey Boy (GER)**[140] 3549 5-8-6 **82** .... DaleGibson 5 (R A Fahey) *a rr* **12/1**	66

1m 41.33s (-3.27) **Going Correction** -0.075s/f (Stan)
WFA 3 from 4yo+ 1lb **9** Ran SP% **118.9**
Speed ratings (Par 109):113,107,105,105,105 104,101,101,97
CSF £30.28 CT £165.64 TOTE £2.80: £1.10, £4.50, £2.90; EX 36.40 Trifecta £191.30 Pool £598.39. - 2.22 winning units..
Owner Stephen J Curtis **Bred** C H Wacker Iii **Trained** Sheriff Hutton, N Yorks

FOCUS
A good handicap and the winning time was decent for the grade. The form looks solid enough overall.

NOTEBOOK
Gentleman's Deal(IRE) ◆ failed to win during the turf season, but he was three out of three on an artificial surface coming into this and extended his unbeaten run to four with an impressive success. Well backed, he was always moving nicely and pulled clear when asked for his effort. He is bred to be pretty special - by Danehill out of Guineas winner Sleepytime - but it is a little surprising he is seems so well suited to racing on sand, as his immediate family were very much turf horses. This represents a Listed class/Group 3-class performance, so he is unlikely to be able to run in handicaps on sand for much longer, and it would be fascinating to see him tried in the US. He is quite a big horse and has presumably had his problems, so perhaps the old-style American tracks would not suit him, but there are surely some decent prizes to be won on their new Polytrack surfaces. If a trip stateside is too unrealistic, he will remain hard to beat when found opportunities on our sand tracks. (op 11-4)
Wessex(USA) ◆ ran a good race behind the smart winner off the back of a 220-day break. He is open to improvement and should be a major player in many of the top handicaps on sand this winter. (op 12-1)
Nevada Desert(IRE) ran a good race off a 3lb higher mark than when winning a lesser race over course and distance on his previous start and emerges with plenty of credit. (op 13-2 tchd 6-1)
Paraguay(USA) showed some useful form during the turf season, albeit without really progressing, and this was a pleasing Fibresand debut. He could have more to offer on sand.
Byron Bay, three out of five on sand coming into this, and unbeaten round here, never posed a serious threat from off the pace and did not really have things go his way. He is better than he showed and can be given another chance. Official explanation: jockey said, regarding running and riding, his orders were to drop the colt in early stages as it had shown a tendency to race too freely, adding that the colt blew up closing stages and would not have responded to the whip; trainer's rep confirmed instructions. (op 10-1)
Kamanda Laugh, seventh in the Cambridgeshire two months previously, failed to show his best form on his Fibresand debut. (op 7-2 tchd 3-1)
Freeloader(IRE) is probably better suited by Polytrack. (op 13-2 tchd 8-1)

6679 PLAY GOLF COME RACING MAIDEN AUCTION STKS 5f (F)
3:15 (3:15) (Class 6) 2-Y-0 **£3,071** (£906; £453) **Stalls** High

Form				RPR
0	**1**		**Zadalla**[38] 6179 2-8-6 .... JoeFanning 5 (Andrew Oliver, Ire) *cl up: effrt to ld wl over 1f out: rdn ent last and kpt on* **11/2**	64
4456	**2**	*1 1/4*	**Catlivius (IRE)**[32] 6271 2-8-6 64 .... (p) PaulHanagan 4 (K A Ryan) *s.i.s and swtchd lft s: rdn along and bhd 1/2-way hdwy wl over 1f out: drvn and edgd rt ins last: kpt on* **3/1**[2]	59+
055	**3**	*nk*	**Sangreal**[15] 6505 2-8-10 68 .... PatCosgrave 3 (K R Burke) *cl up: swtchd lft and rdn 2f out: sn drvn and one pce* **5/4**[1]	62
055	**4**	*1 1/2*	**Silly Gilly (IRE)**[31] 6296 2-8-4 53 .... FrancisNorton 1 (A Berry) *reminders sn after s: chsd ldrs: rdn along 2f out: drvn and wknd over 1f out* **12/1**	51
5053	**5**	*1*	**The Geester**[22] 6420 2-8-11 55 .... (b) NCallan 2 (S R Bowring) *sn led: rdn along and edgd rt 2f out: sn hdd: drvn and hung rt over 1f out: wknd* **5/1**[3]	54

60.35 secs (0.05) **Going Correction** -0.125s/f (Stan) **5** Ran SP% **109.2**
Speed ratings (Par 94):94,92,91,89,87
CSF £21.46 TOTE £7.10: £1.50, £2.30; EX 17.20 Place 6 £24.07, Place 5 £12.76..
Owner Mrs Beatrice Lombard **Bred** Ms C R Sharp **Trained** Caledon, Co. Tyrone

FOCUS
A moderate sprint maiden rated through hte runner-up but the form is modest.

NOTEBOOK
Zadalla had shown pretty limited ability in five runs in Ireland, but this was a weak race and he was able to gain his first-career success and give his trainer his first winner in Britain. (op 9-2)
Catlivius(IRE), dropped in trip and switched to Fibresand for the first time, blew her chance at the start but still managed to come through for second, suggesting those behind her achieved little. (op 10-3 tchd 7-2)
Sangreal, making her debut on Fibresand, could not confirm earlier promise and an official mark of 68 looks harsh on this evidence. (op 6-5 tchd 11-10)
Silly Gilly(IRE) ran a little better without the cheekpieces on her Fibresand debut. (op 16-1)
The Geester is seemingly not progressing. (tchd 9-2 and 11-2)
T/Plt: £27.00 to a £1 stake. Pool: £39,703.35. 1,072.10 winning tickets. T/Qpdt: £17.80 to a £1 stake. Pool: £2,160.20. 89.80 winning tickets. JR

6662 WOLVERHAMPTON (A.W) (L-H)
Saturday, December 2

OFFICIAL GOING: Standard
Wind: Fresh, behind Weather: Cloudy

6680 CHRISTMAS PARTY NIGHT MAIDEN STKS 1m 4f 50y(P)
7:00 (7:00) (Class 5) 3-Y-0+ **£3,238** (£963; £481; £240) **Stalls** Low

Form				RPR
2	**1**		**Abandon (USA)**[23] 6410 3-8-12 .... TonyCulhane 12 (W J Haggas) *trckd ldrs: led 3f out: rdn over 1f out: styd on* **1/3**[1]	70+
0642	**2**	*nk*	**Art Investor**[12] 6535 3-9-3 67 .... AntonyProcter 1 (D R C Elsworth) *a.p: chsd wnr over 2f out: sn rdn and edgd lft: kpt on* **13/2**[2]	73
	3	*5*	**Executive Paddy (IRE)**[18] 7-9-8 .... LeeEnstone 11 (I A Wood) *s.i.s: hld up: racd keenly: hdwy 5f out: rdn over 2f out: styng on same pce whn hung lft ins fnl f* **16/1**	65
	4	*7*	**Mayyas**[34] 6-9-8 .... (t) FrancisNorton 7 (C C Bealby) *s.i.s: hld up: hdwy over 3f out: nt clr run over 2f out : sn rdn and wknd* **100/1**	54
3	**5**	*10*	**Drumfergus Boy (IRE)**[16] 6501 4-9-8 .... AdrianTNicholls 5 (Andrew Oliver, Ire) *hld up in tch: rdn and wknd over 2f out* **50/1**	38
6	**6**	*3 1/2*	**Coolaw (IRE)**[8] 6578 3-8-5 .... (b) DanielRobinson(7) 3 (G G Margarson) *chsd ldrs over 8f* **200/1**	27
	7	*1/2*	**Empor Castle (IRE)**[35] 4-9-3 .... (p) JerryO'Dwyer(5) 2 (Adrian Sexton, Ire) *prom over 7f* **28/1**	31
	8	*4*	**Moneyforcredit (IRE)**[20] 6-9-8 .... PaulDoe 4 (Jarlath P Fahey, Ire) *chsd ldr: led 5f out: hdd 3f out: sn rdn and wknd* **66/1**	25
	9	*2 1/2*	**Aizen Myoo (IRE)**[48] 5931 8-9-3 .... JamieMoriarty(5) 10 (Seamus Fahey, Ire) *s.s and rel to r: hld up: wknd 4f out* **14/1**[3]	21
0	**10**	*1 3/4*	**Fine Deed**[35] 6225 5-9-1 .... StuartHaddon(7) 9 (Ian Williams) *hld up: wknd 4f out* **300/1**	18
0	**11**	*1*	**Donnaspear (IRE)**[22] 6429 3-8-12 .... DaleGibson 6 (J Mackie) *in rr: bhd fnl 4f* **200/1**	12
00	**12**	*1/2*	**Second City**[18] 6482 3-8-12 .... DavidAllan 8 (E J Alston) *led 7f: hung lft and wknd wl over 3f out* **300/1**	11

2m 40.54s (-1.88) **Going Correction** -0.05s/f (Stan)
WFA 3 from 4yo+ 5lb **12** Ran SP% **110.5**
Speed ratings (Par 103):104,103,100,95,89 86,86,83,82,80 80,79
CSF £2.33 TOTE £1.40: £1.02, £1.30, £3.00; EX 3.20.
Owner Cheveley Park Stud **Bred** 6 C Stallions Limited **Trained** Newmarket, Suffolk

FOCUS
An uncompetitive event in which the pace was fair and the form is rated around the first two.

6681 SATURDAY NIGHT IS PARTY NIGHT CLAIMING STKS 5f 216y(P)
7:30 (7:31) (Class 6) 3-Y-0+ **£2,730** (£806; £403) **Stalls** Low

Form				RPR
0026	**1**		**Don Pele (IRE)**[21] 6445 4-9-9 86 .... NCallan 8 (K A Ryan) *trckd ldrs: led ins fnl f: drvn out* **1/1**[1]	87
0114	**2**	*3/4*	**Trinculo (IRE)**[24] 6399 9-9-3 80 .... AdrianTNicholls 7 (D Nicholls) *led: rdn and hdd ins fnl f: kpt on* **8/1**	79
0040	**3**	*2*	**Fast Heart**[22] 6428 5-8-9 73 .... (t) FrancisNorton 2 (D Nicholls) *sn chsng ldr: rdn over 1f out: styd on same pce* **13/2**[2]	65
3500	**4**	*3*	**Supercast (IRE)**[50] 5938 3-8-13 68 .... RobbieFitzpatrick 10 (W M Brisbourne) *sn outpcd: nt clr run over 2f out: nvr nrr* **16/1**	60
6022	**5**	*shd*	**Piccolo Prince**[4] 6638 5-8-7 53 .... DavidAllan 3 (E J Alston) *sn pushed along in rr: effrt over 2f out: n.d* **9/1**	54
0314	**6**	*1/2*	**Carcinetto (IRE)**[14] 6521 4-7-13 55 .... DuranFentiman(5) 6 (P D Evans) *mid-div: outpcd over 2f out: rdn and flashed tail over 1f out: nt trble ldrs* **7/1**[3]	49
5000	**7**	*3*	**Blue Knight (IRE)**[49] 5970 7-8-11 57 .... TonyCulhane 13 (P Howling) *sn outpcd: rdn and hung lft over 1f out: n.d* **33/1**	47
0000	**8**	*1*	**Mind That Fox**[14] 6524 4-8-5 40 .... DaleGibson 1 (T Wall) *chsd ldrs over 3f* **125/1**	38
5500	**9**	*nk*	**Johnston's Diamond (IRE)**[15] 6508 8-8-7 62.... MichaelJStainton(5) 11 (E J Alston) *prom over 3f* **16/1**	44

1m 15.11s (-0.70) **Going Correction** -0.05s/f (Stan) **9** Ran SP% **112.4**
Speed ratings (Par 101):102,101,98,94,94 93,89,88,87
CSF £9.26 TOTE £2.10: £1.20, £1.90, £1.90; EX 6.40.The winner was claimed by Declan Carroll for £15,000. Fast Heart was claimed by C. R. Dore for £8,000.
Owner Pedro Rosas **Bred** John J Cosgrave **Trained** Hambleton, N Yorks

FOCUS
A couple of fair sorts in a claimer that went largely to form. The pace was sound and this form should stand up at a similar level.

6682 ED WEETMAN HAULAGE AND STORAGE LTD H'CAP 5f 20y(P)
8:00 (8:00) (Class 4) (0-80,81) 3-Y-0+ **£5,505** (£1,637; £818; £408) **Stalls** Low

Form				RPR
4311	**1**		**Night Prospector**[4] 6643 6-8-12 **81** 6ex .... (p) TolleyDean(7) 2 (R A Harris) *chsd ldrs: pushed along 1/2-way: hrd rdn to ld ins fnl f: r.o* **15/8**[1]	90
6311	**2**	*nk*	**Tartatartufata**[5] 6622 4-8-12 **77** 6ex .... (v) PatrickMathers(3) 4 (D Shaw) *trckd ldr: hung rt over 3f out: hung lft lft over 1f out: rdn and ev ch ins fnl f: r.o* **9/4**[2]	85
5605	**3**	*1 1/2*	**Efistorm**[17] 6496 5-9-1 **77** .... NCallan 3 (J Balding) *led: rdn over 1f out: hdd and unable qckn ins fnl f* **11/1**	80
463	**4**	*nk*	**Scooby Dude (IRE)**[141] 3475 3-9-4 **80** .... TonyCulhane 1 (Ms Deborah J Evans) *fly-leapt s: hdwy u.p over 1f out: nrst fin* **12/1**	82
3223	**5**	*nk*	**Millinsky (USA)**[46] 6035 5-9-0 **76** .... SteveDrowne 6 (Rae Guest) *prom: rdn and lost pl whn hmpd 2f out: r.o u.p fnl f* **6/1**[3]	77
0000	**6**	*2 1/2*	**New Options**[11] 6555 9-8-1 **66** oh26 .... (b) LiamJones(3) 9 (Peter Grayson) *swtchd lft sn after s: hld up: hdwy u.p over 1f out : no ex fnl f* **150/1**	58
0000	**7**	*3 1/2*	**Stoneacre Boy (IRE)**[11] 6555 3-8-8 **70** .... (b) RobbieFitzpatrick 8 (Peter Grayson) *chsd ldrs to 1/2-way* **40/1**	49
5/04	**8**	*1*	**La Motta (IRE)**[14] 6527 6-8-5 **67** .... (bt) PaulHanagan 7 (Adrian McGuinness, Ire) *chsd ldrs 3f* **9/1**	43
0002	**9**	*2 1/2*	**Westbrook Blue**[32] 6274 4-8-7 **76** .... (tp) JackDean(7) 5 (W G M Turner) *sn outpcd* **20/1**	43

62.26 secs (-0.56) **Going Correction** -0.05s/f (Stan) **9** Ran SP% **113.7**
Speed ratings (Par 105):102,101,99,98,98 94,88,86,82
CSF £5.99 CT £32.97 TOTE £3.10: £1.30, £1.70, £4.30; EX 6.00.
Owner D Tumman & R F Bloodstock **Bred** Miss S N Ralphs **Trained** Earlswood, Monmouths
■ Stewards' Enquiry : Tolley Dean four-day ban: excessive use of the whip (Dec 13-16)

The Form Book, Raceform Ltd, Compton, RG20 6NL

FOCUS
A truly-run race and, with the in-form types filling the first two places, this form should prove reliable.
Millinsky(USA) Official explanation: jockey said mare was denied a clear run
Stoneacre Boy(IRE) Official explanation: jockey said gelding hung right-handed throughout

6683 TWILIGHT RACING - MISS THE TRAFFIC H'CAP 1m 141y(P)
8:30 (8:31) (Class 6) (0-57,58) 3-Y-O+ £2,730 (£806; £403) Stalls Low

Form RPR

4034 **1** **Spark Up**[18] 6483 6-8-8 **53**....(b) RichardKingscote(3) 4 62
(J W Unett) *mde all: rdn over 1f out: styd on* **10/1**

0003 **2** ½ **Dante's Diamond (IRE)**[5] 6627 4-8-13 **55**.... DeanMcKeown 12 63+
(G A Swinbank) *hld up: hdwy over 2f out: rdn and hung lft fr over 1f out: styd on* **10/3**[2]

3 *1* **Send Me Home (IRE)**[37] 6195 4-8-7 **49**.... PatCosgrave 7 55
(Adrian McGuinness, Ire) *a.p: chsd wnr over 3f out: rdn and hung lft fr over 2f out: styd on* **15/2**

2464 **4** 3½ **Hot Agnes**[21] 6439 3-8-11 **55**....(t) MickyFenton 13 54
(H J Collingridge) *hld up: hdwy u.p over 2f out: edgd lft and wknd over 1f out* **16/1**

0102 **5** 1¼ **Harare**[73] 5474 5-8-7 **52**....(b) LiamJones(3) 5 48
(R J Price) *s.i.s: racd keenly and sn prom: hung lft over 3f out: styd on same pce fnl 2f* **12/1**

6-00 **6** *2* **Beautiful Mover (USA)**[7] 6590 4-8-3 **50**.... NataliaGemelova(5) 1 42
(J E Long) *chsd wnr 5f: wknd over 1f out* **66/1**

-061 **7** *shd* **Topiary Ted**[7] 6606 4-9-2 **58**.... SteveDrowne 2 49
(H Morrison) *trckd ldrs: lost pl whn hmpd over 3f out: hung rt fnl 2f: n.d after* **13/8**[1]

6500 **8** ½ **Gattuso**[18] 6480 3-8-8 **52**.... DaleGibson 3 42
(Ms Deborah J Evans) *s.i.s: hld up: plld hrd: a in rr* **33/1**

0341 **9** *1* **Thornaby Green**[12] 6544 5-8-10 **52**.... PaulHanagan 8 40
(T D Barron) *chsd ldrs 6f* **7/1**[3]

6045 **10** 1½ **The Gaikwar (IRE)**[17] 6497 7-9-0 **56**....(b) IanMongan 10 41
(R A Harris) *s.i.s: hdwy 7f out: rdn 4f out: wknd wl over 2f out* **14/1**

1m 50.56s (-1.20) **Going Correction** -0.05s/f (Stan)
WFA 3 from 4yo+ 2lb 10 Ran SP% **119.2**
Speed ratings (Par 101):103,102,101,98,97 95,95,95,94,92
CSF £44.40 CT £278.54 TOTE £9.90: £2.00, £2.10, £2.50; EX 47.60.
Owner Winning Formula Partnership **Bred** Cheveley Park Stud Ltd **Trained** Preston, Shropshire

FOCUS
A run-of-the-mill handicap in which the pace was fair and the winner is the best guide to the level.
Topiary Ted Official explanation: jockey said gelding hung right-handed
Gattuso Official explanation: jockey said gelding hung right-handed
Thornaby Green Official explanation: jockey said gelding hung left-handed

6684 ED WEETMAN (NORTH WEST) LTD H'CAP 1m 1f 103y(P)
9:00 (9:00) (Class 5) (0-70,73) 3-Y-O+ £3,238 (£963; £481; £240) Stalls Low

Form RPR

-605 **1** **Dart Along (USA)**[15] 6507 4-8-12 **69**.... JerryO'Dwyer(5) 6 81
(Eoin Doyle, Ire) *hld up: hdwy over 2f out: rdn to ld ins fnl f: r.o* **10/1**

6621 **2** 1½ **Wasalat (USA)**[22] 6430 4-9-1 **67**.... PaulHanagan 9 76
(D W Barker) *trckd ldrs: rdn to ld and hung lft 1f out: sn hdd and unable qckn* **10/3**[2]

/1-0 **3** 1½ **Our Kes (IRE)**[21] 6448 4-9-2 **68**.... IanMongan 11 74
(P Howling) *mid-div: hdwy over 2f out: rdn and ev ch over 1f out: styng on same pce whn n.m.r ins fnl f* **7/1**[3]

2231 **4** ¾ **Tous Les Deux**[4] 6647 3-9-5 **73** 6ex.... RobbieFitzpatrick 8 78+
(Peter Grayson) *hld up: plld hrd: hdwy over 1f out: sn hung lft: no imp ins fnl f* **2/1**[1]

512- **5** *1* **Lunar Promise (IRE)**[197] 6183 4-9-4 **70**.... SteveDrowne 12 73
(Ian Williams) *hld up: hdwy over 1f out: nt trble ldrs* **25/1**

-000 **6** *nk* **Never Will**[19] 6469 5-9-2 **68**....(p) NCallan 7 70
(K A Ryan) *sn led: clr 7f out: rdn and hdd 1f: sn wknd* **33/1**

6064 **7** 1¼ **Alasil (USA)**[8] 6584 6-8-5 **60**.... LiamJones(3) 2 59
(R J Price) *chsd ldrs: rdn over 2f out: wknd fnl f* **16/1**

1346 **8** *hd* **Out For A Stroll**[92] 4995 7-8-11 **63**.... HayleyTurner 5 62
(S C Williams) *hld up: racd keenly: n.d* **20/1**

1305 **9** ¾ **Barbirolli**[16] 6503 4-8-6 **65**.... TolleyDean(7) 4 63
(W M Brisbourne) *chsd ldr: rdn over 2f out: wknd over 1f out* **8/1**

5406 **10** *nk* **Primitive Academy**[4] 6633 4-9-4 **70**.... TonyCulhane 3 67
(H R A Cecil) *hld up: rdn over 2f out: n.d* **10/1**

5 **11** *12* **Soizic (NZ)**[21] 6448 4-8-13 **68**.... StephaneBreux(3) 1 41
(C G Cox) *mid-div: rdn and wknd 2f out* **16/1**

2m 1.18s (-1.44) **Going Correction** -0.05s/f (Stan)
WFA 3 from 4yo+ 2lb 11 Ran SP% **121.5**
Speed ratings (Par 103):104,102,101,100,99 99,98,98,97,97 86
CSF £43.89 CT £259.15 TOTE £13.90: £4.70, £2.00, £2.20; EX 94.60.
Owner Eoin Doyle **Bred** George Strawbridge And London Thoroughbred Service **Trained** Mooncoin, Co. Kilkenny

FOCUS
An ordinary event in which the pace seemed fair and the form looks sound rated around the first two.

6685 RACING IS FOR EVERYONE AT WOLVERHAMPTON H'CAP 2m 119y(P)
9:30 (9:30) (Class 6) (0-65,62) 3-Y-O+ £2,730 (£806; £403) Stalls Low

Form RPR

0/1 **1** **Market Watcher (USA)**[11] 6560 5-9-9 **61**....(t) JamieMoriarty(5) 1 80+
(Seamus Fahey, Ire) *hld up: hdwy 1/2-way: trckd ldr 4f out: led on bit 1f out: canter* **8/15**[1]

6636 **2** 2½ **Gallileo Figaro (USA)**[23] 6415 3-9-4 **62**.... PatrickMathers(3) 3 68
(W M Brisbourne) *chsd ldrs: led 5f out: rdn and hdd 1f out: no ch w wnr* **16/1**

1016 **3** *8* **Ice And Fire**[15] 6509 7-9-3 **55**....(b) AshleyHamblett(5) 7 52
(J T Stimpson) *s.i.s: hld up: hdwy over 4f out: no imp fnl 2f* **5/1**[2]

0-00 **4** *3* **Montecristo**[44] 6068 13-8-13 **53**.... LukeMcJannet(7) 2 46
(Rae Guest) *hld up: nvr trbld ldrs* **80/1**

2363 **5** *7* **Romil Star (GER)**[11] 6551 9-9-1 **48**....(v) RobbieFitzpatrick 9 33
(M Wellings) *prom: chsd ldr 12f out: led 1/2-way: hdd 5f out: rdn and wknd 3f out* **8/1**[3]

405 **6** 2½ **Proprioception (IRE)**[5] 6626 4-9-5 **52**....(v) HayleyTurner 6 34
(W K Goldsworthy) *sn outpcd: hdwy 12f out: wknd 6f out* **28/1**

5204 **7** *30* **Bolshoi Ballet**[17] 6495 8-8-12 **45**....(b) PaulMulrennan 5 —
(Miss J E Foster) *chsd ldr 4f: wknd over 6f out* **33/1**

0600 **8** *dist* **Ballymena**[58] 4282 5-8-6 **42** oh2.... LiamJones(3) 4 —
(R A Harris) *led: rdn over 11f out: hdd 1/2-way: sn eased: t.o: rdr rode a fin a circ too sn* **40/1**

3m 43.42s (0.29) **Going Correction** -0.05s/f (Stan)
WFA 3 from 4yo+ 8lb 8 Ran SP% **109.0**
Speed ratings (Par 101):97,95,92,90,87 86,72,—
CSF £9.16 CT £20.06 TOTE £1.70: £1.30, £2.20, £1.30; EX 11.50 Place 6 £10.67, Place 5 £9.90.
Owner J J Bailey **Bred** Phipps Stable **Trained** Monestereven, Co. Kildare
■ Stewards' Enquiry : Liam Jones 12-day ban: rode a finish a circuit too early (Dec 14-26)

FOCUS
A modest event run at a fair pace but a very easy winner in Market Watcher, who is capable of better. The winner is rated to his Irish form.
T/Plt: £15.80 to a £1 stake. Pool: £73,190.10. 3,374.05 winning tickets. T/Qpdt: £13.30 to a £1 stake. Pool: £3,280.80. 181.80 winning tickets. CR

6656 LINGFIELD (L-H)
Sunday, December 3

OFFICIAL GOING: Standard
Wind: Strong, behind

6686 RACINGPOST.CO.UK H'CAP (DIV I) 5f (P)
11:50 (11:51) (Class 6) (0-60,59) 3-Y-O+ £1,706 (£503; £252) Stalls High

Form RPR

1246 **1** **Special Gold**[15] 6513 4-9-3 **58**....(b) PaulMulrennan 8 65
(A D Brown) *mde virtually all: rdn 2f out: clr 1f out: hld on u.p cl home: all out* **15/2**

0620 **2** *nk* **Succeed (IRE)**[6] 6615 3-8-6 **50**.... RichardKingscote(3) 4 56
(Mrs H Sweeting) *bhd: effrt on outside over 2f out: r.o u.p fnl f: nt quite rch wnr* **8/1**

2415 **3** 1½ **Desert Dust**[6] 6615 3-8-11 **52**....(v) BrettDoyle 5 53
(R M H Cowell) *chsd ldrs: rdn over 2f out: kpt on fnl f: nt pce to trble wnr* **9/2**[2]

6610 **4** *shd* **Twinned (IRE)**[6] 6615 3-8-9 **50**....(p) DarryllHolland 3 50+
(Karen George) *hld up in midfield: short of room and swtchd wl over 1f out: kpt on fnl f: nt trble ldrs* **13/2**

0000 **4** *dht* **Egyptian Lord**[6] 6622 3-9-0 **55**....(b) RobbieFitzpatrick 2 55
(Peter Grayson) *t.k.h: hld up in midfield inner: n.m.r over 2f out: swtchd rt over 1f out: styd on fnl f: nvr nrr* **12/1**

616 **6** 1¾ **Fastrac Boy**[15] 6521 3-9-4 **59**.... GeorgeBaker 7 53
(J R Best) *pressed wnr: led briefly over 3f out: rdn over 2f out: wknd fnl f* **3/1**[1]

0340 **7** 1¼ **Campeon (IRE)**[6] 6615 4-8-7 **48** ow1.... MickyFenton 6 37
(J M Bradley) *cl up: rdn wl over 2f out: wknd over 1f out* **12/1**

4600 **8** ½ **Sofinella (IRE)**[15] 6521 3-9-2 **57**.... FrancisNorton 9 45
(A W Carroll) *chsd ldrs: rdn over 2f out: wknd over 1f out* **16/1**

3005 **9** ½ **Gone'N'Dunnett (IRE)**[12] 6556 7-9-1 **56**....(b) ChrisCatlin 1 42
(Mrs C A Dunnett) *a bhd: nvr on terms* **6/1**[3]

6000 **10** *4* **Spirit Of Coniston**[15] 6521 3-8-9 **53**....(b) PatrickMathers(3) 10 24
(Peter Grayson) *slowly away: a outpcd in last* **33/1**

58.29 secs (-1.49) **Going Correction** -0.15s/f (Stan) 10 Ran SP% **117.9**
Speed ratings (Par 101):105,104,102,101,101 99,97,96,95,89
CSF £66.89 CT £304.90 TOTE £10.60: £2.70, £2.60, £2.10; EX 41.80 Trifecta £155.80 Part won. Pool £219.57 - 0.87 winning units..
Owner S Pedersen **Bred** Barry Minty **Trained** Pickering, York

FOCUS
Not the strongest sprint handicap run around here, with doubts about a number of them, but the form appears reasonable, rated around the winner and third.
Spirit Of Coniston Official explanation: jockey said gelding missed the break

6687 RACING AND FOOTBALL OUTLOOK H'CAP (DIV I) 1m 2f (P)
12:20 (12:20) (Class 6) (0-60,60) 3-Y-O+ £1,706 (£503; £252) Stalls Low

Form RPR

0022 **1** **Storm Of Arabia (IRE)**[146] 3347 3-9-2 **60**.... AdamKirby 9 66
(W R Swinburn) *hld up in rr: hdwy on outer over 3f out: rdn and ev ch 2f out: led jst over 1f out: kpt on wl* **11/4**[1]

0452 **2** *nk* **Siena Star (IRE)**[8] 6590 8-9-5 **60**.... MickyFenton 4 65
(Stef Liddiard) *chsd ldrs: rdn and hdwy over 2f out: kpt on to chse wnr wl ins fnl f: r.o* **11/4**[1]

0640 **3** *1* **Lady Pilot**[11] 6566 4-8-13 **54**.... DaneO'Neill 11 57
(Ms J S Doyle) *hld up in tch on outer: rdn and c wd 2f out: r.o fnl f: nrst fin* **7/1**[3]

0000 **4** *shd* **Blu Manruna**[22] 6439 3-8-11 **55**.... PaulDoe 10 58
(J Akehurst) *chsd ldrs: rdn 3f out: ev ch 2f out: keeping on same pce whn hung rt ins fnl f* **33/1**

4003 **5** *shd* **Benny The Ball (USA)**[13] 6532 5-8-8 **49**.... HayleyTurner 1 52
(N P Littmoden) *t.k.h: chsd ldr: rdn to ld over 2f out: hdd jst over 1f out: btn whn edgd rt ins fnl f* **8/1**

0 **6** *1* **Cove Mountain (IRE)**[18] 6484 4-9-2 **57**.... LPKeniry 7 58
(S Kirk) *hld up in midfield: rdn wl over 2f out: kpt on over 1f out: btn whn n.m.r nr fin* **10/1**

0400 **7** *hd* **Scutch Mill (IRE)**[30] 6323 4-9-3 **58**....(t) DarryllHolland 6 59
(Karen George) *slowly away: bhd: rdn and effrt 2f out: kpt on: nt pce to trble ldrs* **6/1**[2]

0440 **8** *3* **Lobengula (IRE)**[9] 6577 4-8-12 **53**.... JimmyQuinn 5 48
(I W McInnes) *led tl rdn and hdd over 2f out: wknd qckly over 1f out* **8/1**

0 **9** *3* **Starofthemorning (IRE)**[12] 3192 5-8-5 **46** oh6.... FrancisNorton 8 35
(A W Carroll) *hld up bhd: rdn 4f out: no ch last 2f* **16/1**

0606 **10** 3½ **Come What July (IRE)**[6] 6621 5-8-9 **53**....(v) PatrickMathers(3) 2 35
(D Shaw) *shkn up early: sn racing in midfield: rdn over 4f out: no ch last 2f* **22/1**

2m 6.65s (-1.14) **Going Correction** -0.15s/f (Stan)
WFA 3 from 4yo+ 3lb 10 Ran SP% **124.6**
Speed ratings (Par 101):98,97,96,96,96 96,95,93,91,88
CSF £10.30 CT £50.57 TOTE £5.30: £1.50, £1.40, £1.60; EX 11.50 Trifecta £83.00 Part won. Pool £116.98 - 0.77 winning units..
Owner The Mavericks **Bred** Liam Ormsby **Trained** Aldbury, Herts

FOCUS
A moderate handicap run at a steady pace, and little over a length separated the first five at the line. The form is rated through the runner-up, but does not look that solid.

6688 RACINGPOST.CO.UK H'CAP (DIV II) 5f (P)

12:50 (12:50) (Class 6) (0-60,60) 3-Y-O+ £1,706 (£503; £252) Stalls High

Form RPR

0601 1 **Rowe Park**[22] 6440 3-8-13 **55** LPKeniry 5 66
(Mrs L C Jewell) *chsd ldr: rdn to chal over 2f out: slt ld over 1f out: hld on wl u.p* **12/1**

0002 2 *shd* **One Way Ticket**[5] 6629 6-8-8 **50** (p) MickyFenton 2 60
(J M Bradley) *sn led: rdn over 2f out: hdd over 1f out: kpt on u.p but a jst hld* **3/1**[1]

0500 3 *2* **The Fisio**[18] 6485 6-9-1 **57** (v) NCallan 10 60
(S Gollings) *chsd ldrs: rdn to chse ldng pair over 2f out: kpt on same pce fnl f* **20/1**

0164 4 *1 1/4* **Turibius**[15] 6513 7-9-2 **58** (b) JimCrowley 4 57
(T E Powell) *chsd ldrs: rdn over 2f out: kpt on same pce* **7/1**

6624 5 *3/4* **Shunkawakhan (IRE)**[15] 6510 3-8-10 **52** (b) OscarUrbina 9 48
(G C H Chung) *dwlt: bhd: hdwy on outer over 2f out: kpt on u.p fnl f: n.d* **11/2**

5003 6 *nk* **Canadian Danehill (IRE)**[20] 6465 4-9-4 **60** EddieAhern 3 55
(R M H Cowell) *chsd ldrs: rdn over 2f out: wknd over 1f out* **7/2**[2]

5002 7 *nk* **Muktasb (USA)**[6] 6615 5-8-5 **50** (v) PatrickMathers(3) 8 46+
(D Shaw) *hld up towards rr: effrt wl over 1f out: no real prog: no ch whn nt clr run ins fnl f* **12/1**

100 8 *3/4* **Lady Hopeful (IRE)**[13] 6539 4-8-5 **47** (b) RobbieFitzpatrick 7 38
(Peter Grayson) *dwlt: a bhd: nvr on terms* **50/1**

5065 9 *3/4* **Cosmic Destiny (IRE)**[15] 6521 4-9-0 **56** DaneO'Neill 1 44
(E F Vaughan) *racd in midfield on inner: short of room on inner bnd over 2f out: sn wknd* **5/1**[3]

2016 10 *5* **Epineuse**[107] 4551 3-8-8 **50** BrettDoyle 6 20
(J R Best) *broke wl: sn pushed along and outpcd: no ch and hung rt last 2f* **20/1**

57.85 secs (-1.93) **Going Correction** -0.15s/f (Stan) **33 Ran SP% 118.6**
Speed ratings (Par 101):109,108,105,103,102 101,101,100,99,91
CSF £47.90 CT £751.31 TOTE £15.20: £2.60, £1.50, £2.90; EX 62.40 TRIFECTA Not won..
Owner R I B Young and Mrs F J Meekins **Bred** J Baker **Trained** Sutton Valence, Kent

FOCUS
This looked the stronger division of the sprint handicap, and it was run in a time 0.44sec quicker than the earlier heat. The form appears solid, rated through the third.
Muktasb(USA) Official explanation: jockey said gelding was denied a clear run home straight

6689 EBF RACING POST MAIDEN STKS 7f (P)

1:20 (1:20) (Class 5) 2-Y-O £3,562 (£1,059; £529; £264) Stalls Low

Form RPR

00 1 **Nordic Affair**[54] 5890 2-9-3 AntonyProcter 8 74
(D R C Elsworth) *t.k.h: in tch on outer: rdn to ld 2f out: jst hld on* **25/1**

2 *shd* **Resplendent Ace (IRE)** 2-9-3 DeanCorby 5 73
(P Howling) *slowly away: sn in tch in rr: rdn and effrt 2f out: r.o strly ins fnl f: jst failed* **6/1**[3]

603 3 *1 1/4* **Highland Harvest**[32] 6298 2-9-0 74 MarcHalford(3) 9 70
(D R C Elsworth) *t.k.h: hld up in tch: hdwy over 2f out: chsd wnr over 1f out: hung lft and nt qckn fnl f* **9/1**

3223 4 *2* **Danehillsundance (IRE)**[18] 6488 2-9-3 72 RichardHughes 7 65
(R Hannon) *taken down early: plld hrd: in tch: rdn and kpt on same pce over 1f out* **1/1**[1]

0002 5 *1 1/2* **Buckie Massa**[11] 6562 2-9-3 68 GeorgeBaker 3 61
(S Kirk) *taken down early: t.k.h: hld up in midfield: rdn 2f out: kpt on same pce* **7/1**

6 *1 3/4* **Perfect Practice** 2-8-12 OscarUrbina 1 51
(J A R Toller) *slowly away: bhd: styd on over 1f out: nrst fin* **20/1**

0 7 *3/4* **Rustic Gold**[5] 6591 2-9-3 BrettDoyle 4 54
(J R Best) *led at stdy pce tl 2f out: wknd over 1f out* **33/1**

0 8 *shd* **Itsawindup**[8] 6591 2-9-3 PaulDoe 6 54
(W J Knight) *pressed ldr tl wl over 1f out: wknd* **66/1**

65 9 *nk* **Party Best**[8] 6591 2-8-12 HayleyTurner 2 48
(C E Brittain) *t.k.h: trckd ldrs on inner: rdn and wknd wl over 1f out* **16/1**

05 10 *2 1/2* **Tasweet (IRE)**[52] 5914 2-9-3 IanMongan 10 47
(T G Mills) *broke wl: sn stdd and dropped out in last: no ch last 2f* **5/1**[2]

1m 27.22s (1.33) **Going Correction** -0.15s/f (Stan) **10 Ran SP% 122.4**
Speed ratings (Par 96):86,85,84,82,80 78,77,77,77,74
CSF £170.92 TOTE £36.00: £7.30, £3.00, £4.20; EX 608.50 TRIFECTA Not won..
Owner J C Smith **Bred** Baydon House Stud **Trained** Newmarket, Suffolk

FOCUS
An ordinary-looking maiden where they went no gallop at all, resulting in a slow winning time

NOTEBOOK
Nordic Affair, despite proving reluctant to go into the stalls, jumped off better than on his previous two starts to leave his earlier form behind.
Resplendent Ace(IRE) ◆, a brother to the useful Something and half-brother to Lake Coniston, was slowly into stride on this debut. He flew home to post an encouraging first effort and looks a certain future winner. (op 7-1)
Highland Harvest's limitations are starting to look exposed and after being too keen early on he hung in the straight and could only keep on at the one pace. A return to a mile may help. (op 8-1)
Danehillsundance(IRE), another who took a keen hold, like the third failed to pick up in the straight. (tchd 6-5, 5-4 in a place)
Buckie Massa did not build on his effort on his All-Weather debut at Kempton, but did not help himself by racing too freely. (op 12-1)
Perfect Practice, another debutante, was also slowly into her stride and was doing her best work late on.
Tasweet(IRE) ◆, having jumped away all right, was soon dropped out towards the rear. He was never a factor on his first start for new connections but is eligible for a handicap mark now and looks one to keep a close eye on. (op 4-1)

6690 THE WEEKENDER H'CAP 6f (P)

1:50 (1:51) (Class 4) (0-85,83) 3-Y-O+ £5,505 (£1,637; £818; £408) Stalls Low

Form RPR

445 1 **Perfect Story (IRE)**[20] 6461 4-8-11 **78** OscarUrbina 12 89
(J A R Toller) *hld up bhd on outer: hdwy 2f out: str run on wd outside fnl f to ld nr fin* **13/2**

0000 2 *3/4* **Quiet Times (IRE)**[278] 541 7-9-1 **82** (b) NCallan 2 91
(K A Ryan) *led: rdn over 2f out: battled on wl tl hdd and no ex nr fin* **14/1**

5304 3 *1/2* **Buy On The Red**[9] 6580 5-8-11 **78** (p) DarryllHolland 1 85
(W R Muir) *slowly away: hdwy on inner over 2f out: chsd wnr ins fnl f: kpt on same pce and demoted nr fin* **5/1**[2]

0360 4 *nk* **Who's Winning (IRE)**[22] 6437 5-8-3 **73** RichardKingscote(3) 3 79
(B G Powell) *hld up in midfield: hdwy 2f out: swtchd lft ins fnl f: r.o last 100 yds: nt rch ldrs* **16/1**

6402 5 *hd* **Brandywell Boy (IRE)**[28] 6352 3-8-11 **78** (p) JimCrowley 5 84
(D J S Ffrench Davis) *t.k.h: rdn to chal 2f out: kpt on same pce fnl f* **11/2**[3]

0512 6 *1/2* **Cape Presto (IRE)**[10] 6572 3-8-6 **73** (v) RobbieFitzpatrick 4 77
(Mrs C A Dunnett) *t.k.h: prom: rdn 2f out: unable qck fnl f* **4/1**[1]

4060 7 *1/2* **Pinchbeck**[223] 1183 7-8-9 **83** DanielRobinson(7) 8 86
(M A Jarvis) *chsd ldrs on outer: effrt and rdn over 2f out: wknd ins fnl f* **16/1**

0020 8 *1/2* **Grimes Faith**[9] 6583 3-9-1 **82** RichardHughes 6 83
(R Hannon) *chsd ldr tl wl over 1f out: wknd ins fnl f* **5/1**[2]

6360 9 *hd* **Ivory Lace**[9] 6580 5-8-11 **78** AdamKirby 7 79
(S Woodman) *hld up bhd: rdn and effrt over 2f out: nvr pce to rch ldrs* **14/1**

0 10 *nk* **Erra Go On**[1] 6671 5-9-2 **83** EddieAhern 11 83
(Adrian McGuinness, Ire) *hld up wl bhd: rdn 2f out: nvr threatened ldrs* **12/1**

0214 11 *hd* **Zarzu**[9] 6583 7-8-9 **79** LiamJones(3) 10 78
(C R Dore) *hld up: hdwy over 2f out: wknd ins fnl f* **12/1**

1m 10.79s (-2.02) **Going Correction** -0.15s/f (Stan) **11 Ran SP% 122.5**
Speed ratings (Par 105):107,106,105,104,104 104,103,102,102,102 101
CSF £97.74 CT £511.16 TOTE £7.00: £3.10, £4.30, £1.80; EX 134.40 Trifecta £66.20 Pool £140.00 - 1.50 winning units..
Owner John Drew and Dr Bridget Drew **Bred** Airlie Stud **Trained** Newmarket, Suffolk

FOCUS
Plenty of the usual suspects took their chance in this competitive handicap although it would be unlikely if any of them were hiding anything from the handicapper nowadays. Run in absolutely appalling conditions, there was a little over three lengths separating the 11 runners as they crossed the line in a quick time. A slight personal best from the winner.
Cape Presto(IRE) Official explanation: jockey said colt ran too freely

6691 RACEFORM UPDATE NOVICE STKS 1m (P)

2:20 (2:20) (Class 5) 2-Y-O £3,238 (£963; £481) Stalls High

Form RPR

0321 1 **Alittlebitleft (IRE)**[9] 6582 2-9-4 81 (b) RichardHughes 3 92+
(R Hannon) *w ldr: qcknd to ld wl over 2f out: sn clr: pushed out* **5/6**[1]

012 2 *7* **Autograph Hunter**[8] 6597 2-9-4 81 JoeFanning 1 75
(M Johnston) *sn led: rdn and hdd wel over 2f out: sn btn: hung rt over 1f out* **5/6**[1]

05 3 *8* **Sea Cookie**[8] 6596 2-8-9 AdrianMcCarthy 2 48
(W De Best-Turner) *a 3rd: rdn 4f out: wl outpcd 3f out: no ch after* **66/1**[2]

1m 39.18s (-0.25) **Going Correction** -0.15s/f (Stan) **3 Ran SP% 110.6**
Speed ratings (Par 96):95,88,80
CSF £1.95 TOTE £1.60; EX 1.70.
Owner Team Havana **Bred** T Hyde **Trained** East Everleigh, Wilts

FOCUS
Just the three runners went to post for this novice stakes, but this was effectively a match. Hard to know what the winner's form is worth, with the second well below his best again, but he was impressive once more.

NOTEBOOK
Alittlebitleft(IRE) came home clear from his market rival in his own time. He has come on leaps and bounds since switching to sand and looks to have plenty more to give, with a longer trip looking well within his compass.
Autograph Hunter once again gave the impression he is bit of a character, hanging slightly to the right after he was headed.
Sea Cookie had no chance with the 81-rated pair on what she had shown so far.

6692 RACING POST H'CAP 7f (P)

2:50 (2:51) (Class 2) (0-100,103) 3-Y-O+

£11,217 (£3,358; £1,679; £840; £419; £210) Stalls Low

Form RPR

511 1 **Areyoutalkingtome**[15] 6514 3-9-4 **102** EddieAhern 5 112
(C A Cyzer) *in tch: rdn and hdwy on inner 2f out: drvn to ld ins fnl f: jst hld on* **7/4**[1]

0001 2 *shd* **Marajaa (IRE)**[25] 6397 4-8-2 **86** FrancisNorton 10 96
(W J Musson) *hld up in last pair: c wd over 2f out: str run fnl f: jst failed* **11/2**[3]

2004 3 *1 1/2* **Vortex**[15] 6514 7-8-10 **94** (t) DarryllHolland 9 100
(Miss Gay Kelleway) *chsd ldng pair: rdn over 2f out: led over 1f out tl ins fnl f: kpt on same pce* **8/1**

1030 4 *1* **Tamagin (USA)**[15] 6514 3-7-13 **86** oh3 (p) LiamJones(3) 2 91+
(P D Evans) *taken down early: racd freely: led: hung rt 3f out: rn wd and hdd bnd wl over 1f out: nt rcvr: kpt on again last 100 yds* **14/1**

3621 5 *hd* **Orchard Supreme**[8] 6594 3-8-9 **93** DaneO'Neill 3 96
(R Hannon) *dwlt: sn in tch: rdn over 2f out: kpt on same pce* **7/1**

0040 6 *1 1/2* **Red Spell (IRE)**[64] 5675 5-9-5 **103** RichardHughes 4 102
(R Hannon) *chsd ldr tl lft in ld wl over 1f out: sn hdd & wknd* **7/2**[2]

-600 7 *1/2* **Xtra Torrential (USA)**[15] 6514 4-8-11 **95** FergusSweeney 8 93
(D M Simcock) *hld up in last pair: rdn and effrt over 2f out: no imp* **33/1**

5046 8 *1 3/4* **Andronikos**[15] 6514 4-9-1 **99** (t) JoeFanning 6 92
(P F I Cole) *hld up in midfield: rdn over 2f out: no imp* **7/1**

4000 P **Hidden Dragon (USA)**[88] 5117 7-8-5 **89** ChrisCatlin 11 —
(J Pearce) *hld up in rr tl lost action and p.u after 2f* **50/1**

1m 23.13s (-2.76) **Going Correction** -0.15s/f (Stan) **9 Ran SP% 121.7**
Speed ratings (Par 109):109,108,107,106,105 104,103,101,—
CSF £12.68 CT £65.24 TOTE £2.60: £1.40, £2.50, £2.40; EX 17.00 Trifecta £54.30 Pool £275.60 - 3.60 winning units..
Owner Mrs Charles Cyzer **Bred** C A Cyzer **Trained** Maplehurst, W Sussex

FOCUS
Just the nine runners, but quality wise this was a decent turnout, with a number of in-form sorts taking their chance. It looks sound, with the winner, who is among the best racing on the All Weather at present, as well as the third, fourth and sixth all close to last month's form.

NOTEBOOK
Areyoutalkingtome has developed into a very smart performer since reverting to the Polytrack, with connections putting that down in part to his maturing physically. However, having gone up 5lb for his win over this course and distance two weeks earlier, when he had five of these behind, he was made to work harder this time. There is another race back here for him in two weeks' time, or alternatively he could go to Dubai or to California. Looking further ahead, the Lincoln was mentioned as a possibility. (op 9-4)
Marajaa(IRE) ◆ looks to have got his act together. He ran on strongly and looks capable of adding to his win at Kempton last time soon. (op 6-1 tchd 5-1)
Vortex again had the race run to suit, but he was once again not able to make the most of it. He has been given a chance by the handicapper, but looks some way short of his best. (op 11-2)
Tamagin(USA) was up against it at the weights. He did his chances no good by running very freely early on, and despite the fact he has done his best racing here, he did not look at home coming round the final bend, racing wide into the straight. Official explanation: jockey said colt hung right on bend
Orchard Supreme, who gained a well deserved win at Kempton eight days earlier, may have found this race coming too soon. (op 11-2)

Red Spell(IRE), a stone higher on sand than on turf, held a great position and had every chance but did not get home. (op 5-1)

6693 RACING AND FOOTBALL OUTLOOK H'CAP (DIV II) 1m 2f (P)
3:20 (3:21) (Class 6) (0-60,59) 3-Y-0+ **£1,706** (£503; £252) **Stalls** Low

Form RPR

0100 **1** **Hallings Overture (USA)**[22] 6436 7-9-0 **54** PaulEddery 10 61
(C A Horgan) *slowly away: hld up wl bhd: hdwy and swtchd rt over 1f out: str run ins fnl f to ld on line* **12/1**

4606 **2** *nk* **Melvino**[10] 6571 4-9-0 **54** ChrisCatlin 6 60
(T D Barron) *s.i.s: hld up: hdwy 6f out: swtchd lft over 1f: rdn and led last 100 yds: hdd on line* **4/1**[2]

0060 **3** *shd* **Saucy**[35] 6232 5-8-5 **45** FrancisNorton 8 51
(A W Carroll) *stdd s: t.k.h and hld up bhd: hdwy on outer 3f out: rdn to chal 1f out: no ex nr fin* **6/1**

0000 **4** *1 1/4* **Mystic Roll**[15] 6526 3-8-10 **53** BrettDoyle 9 56
(Jane Chapple-Hyam) *led and sn clr: rdn wl over 1f out: hdd last 100 yds: fdd nr fin* **16/1**

0036 **5** *1/2* **Blue Beacon**[5] 6647 3-8-13 **56** (b[1]) NCallan 7 59+
(K A Ryan) *racd in midfield: hdwy over 3f out: rdn to chse ldng pair over 2f out tl over 1f out: btn whn short of room ins fnl f* **14/1**

3 **6** *hd* **Ilza**[15] 6526 3-8-13 **56** JimmyQuinn 3 58
(Eamon Tyrrell, Ire) *chsd ldr: rdn over 2f out: wknd jst ins fnl f* **7/1**

-065 **7** *1/2* **Caragh Mia (IRE)**[9] 6577 4-8-13 **53** EddieAhern 2 54
(G G Margarson) *racd in midfield: rdn wl over 2f out: kpt on fnl f: nt rch ldrs* **9/1**

0331 **8** *1/2* **Missie Baileys**[10] 6571 4-9-5 **59** IanMongan 1 59
(Mrs L J Mongan) *racd in midfield: rdn and outpcd 4f out: rallied wl over 1f out: kpt on but nt trble ldrs* **11/4**[1]

3300 **9** *1/2* **Gallego**[16] 6507 4-9-0 **57** LiamJones[(3)] 5 56
(R J Price) *slowly away: hld up in last pair: nvr on terms* **11/2**[3]

6-00 **10** *1* **Ile Michel**[158] 2966 9-9-4 **58** RichardHughes 4 55
(Lady Herries) *chsd clr ldng pair tl wl over 2f out: sn btn* **10/1**

2m 7.46s (-0.33) **Going Correction** -0.15s/f (Stan)
WFA 3 from 4yo+ 3lb **33** Ran SP% **128.2**
Speed ratings (Par 101):95,94,94,93,93 93,92,92,91,91
CSF £65.65 CT £334.80 TOTE £15.10: £4.50, £2.20, £2.50; EX 131.30 TRIFECTA Not won. Place 6 £293.31, Place 5 £105.33..
Owner Mrs B Sumner **Bred** Spectrum Bloodstock S A And Partners **Trained** Uffcott, Wilts

FOCUS
Plenty of in-and-out types, and very little recent winning form. A moderate race run in a slower time than the first division. Weak form.
T/Plt: £1,288.60 to a £1 stake. Pool: £41,041.80. 23.25 winning tickets. T/Qpdt: £461.90 to a £1 stake. Pool: £4,120.00. 6.60 winning tickets. SP

6686 LINGFIELD (L-H)
Monday, December 4

OFFICIAL GOING: Standard
Wind: Fresh, half-behind Weather: Overcast

6694 RIVERBELLE.COM/RACES CLAIMING STKS (DIV I) 7f (P)
12:10 (12:10) (Class 6) 3-Y-0+ **£2,047** (£604; £302) **Stalls** Low

Form RPR

0000 **1** **Ludovico**[26] 6397 3-8-12 83 (b[1]) JamieJones[(7)] 11 74
(K A Ryan) *stdd s: plld hrd and sn prom: led over 2f out: sn in command: rdn out* **9/4**[1]

3140 **2** *1 3/4* **Muscari**[51] 5973 4-8-9 59 DarryllHolland 6 59
(A P Jarvis) *t.k.h: prom: led briefly 3f out: nt pce of wnr fnl 2f* **3/1**[2]

0000 **3** *3/4* **George's Flyer (IRE)**[18] 6503 3-8-9 65 (b) JerryO'Dwyer[(5)] 5 62
(R A Fahey) *chsd ldrs on rail: effrt over 2f out: kpt on same pce* **8/1**

0460 **4** *nk* **Goose Chase**[12] 6564 4-8-12 67 RichardHughes 8 59
(A M Hales) *hld up midfield to rr: rdn and styd on fnl 2f: nt pce to chal* **3/1**[2]

4230 **5** *2* **Davidia (IRE)**[164] 2814 3-8-12 60 LPKeniry 4 54
(S Kirk) *plld hrd: hld up towards rr: rdn over 2f out: nvr nrr* **7/1**[3]

0300 **6** *3/4* **Fizzy Lizzy**[171] 2599 6-8-0 45 NicolPolli[(5)] 9 45
(H E Haynes) *in tch on outside: hrd rdn and btn 2f out* **66/1**

0000 **7** *3* **Atlantic Viking (IRE)**[3] 6667 11-8-11 55 (v) SteveDrowne 1 43
(P D Evans) *plld hrd: chsd ldrs 4f* **14/1**

00-0 **8** *shd* **Deirdre's Dilemma (IRE)**[79] 5363 4-7-11 40 JosephWalsh[(7)] 7 36
(G C Bravery) *s.i.s: bhd: hrd rdn over 2f out: n.d* **66/1**

00-0 **9** *1 1/4* **The Loose Screw (IRE)**[57] 5837 8-8-9 35 EddieAhern 10 38
(C W Thornton) *sn led: hdd 3f out: sn wknd* **66/1**

10 *20* **Imperial Glory** 5-8-11 NeilChalmers[(3)] 3 —
(Mrs P Townsley) *dwlt: rdn 1/2-way: a bhd* **66/1**

1m 25.0s (-0.89) **Going Correction** -0.125s/f (Stan) **10** Ran SP% **117.0**
Speed ratings (Par 101):100,98,97,96,94 93,90,90,88,65
CSF £9.14 TOTE £2.60: £1.40, £1.60, £2.70; EX 12.40 Trifecta £70.50 Pool £110.34, 1.11 winning units..The winner was claimed by J. M. Bradley for £15,000. Muscari was claimed by S. Woodman for £10,000.
Owner Pedro Rosas **Bred** M Grant And W Hawkings **Trained** Hambleton, N Yorks

FOCUS
Just an ordinary claimer and the pace was steady, resulting in a time 0.67 seconds slower than the second division. The form is limited by the proximity of the sixth.
Atlantic Viking(IRE) Official explanation: jockey said gelding hung right-handed

6695 GOLF BEFORE RACING AT LINGFIELD PARK (S) STKS 6f (P)
12:40 (12:40) (Class 6) 2-Y-0 **£2,388** (£705; £352) **Stalls** Low

Form RPR

0000 **1** **Polly Jones (USA)**[42] 6143 2-8-6 45 PaulHanagan 4 50
(G L Moore) *hld up in rr: rdn and hdwy over 1f out: r.o to ld on line* **13/2**[2]

2 *shd* **New York Oscar (IRE)** 2-8-6 JerryO'Dwyer[(5)] 6 55
(N A Callaghan) *v green thrght: trckd ldr: rdn to ld over 1f out: looked wnr tl idled and ct on line* **6/5**[1]

05 **3** *1 1/4* **Whos Counting**[16] 6511 2-8-7 ow1 RobertHavlin 5 47
(R J Hodges) *chsd ldrs: hrd rdn over 1f out: kpt on fnl f* **25/1**[3]

2405 **4** *1/2* **Jost Van Dyke**[6] 6640 2-9-2 65 EddieAhern 3 55
(J R Boyle) *led and set modest pce: qcknd 2f out: hrd rdn over 1f out: no ex fnl f* **6/5**[1]

004 **5** *2 1/2* **Jade's Ballet**[24] 6427 2-8-7 35 ow1 PaulFitzsimons 1 38
(E A Wheeler) *hld up in rr: rdn and outpcd whn pce qckngd 2f out: n.d after* **33/1**

06 **6** *1 3/4* **Short Stuff**[16] 6511 2-8-11 LPKeniry 2 37
(R J Hodges) *chsd ldrs tl hrd rdn and wknd over 1f out* **33/1**

1m 13.19s (0.38) **Going Correction** -0.125s/f (Stan) **6** Ran SP% **114.0**
Speed ratings (Par 94):92,91,90,89,86 83
CSF £15.08 TOTE £8.30: £3.60, £1.50; EX 13.60.There was no bid for the winner. New York Oscar was claimed by Paul J. Dixon for £6,000.
Owner Favourites Racing XXV **Bred** Henri Mastey & Golden Gate Stud **Trained** Woodingdean, E Sussex

FOCUS
A very poor race, even by selling standards.

NOTEBOOK
Polly Jones(USA), dropped back in trip from a mile and switched to selling company for the first time, took advantage of New York Oscar's waywardness in the latter stages to get up on the line. A step back up in trip may suit, but she could struggle to add to this. (op 7-1)
New York Oscar(IRE) , a 21,000euros half-brother to Spin King, a seven-furlong winner at two, and Silver And Gold, a prolific seven-furlong/mile winner in Italy, out of an 11 times scorer in the same country, was well backed to make a winning debut in what was a terrible race, but he threw it away. He looked to have the race won when kicking on off the home bend, but carried his head high and was doing nothing in front. He was claimed by Paul Dixon for £6,000 and his new connections will be hoping his inexperience was to blame for his waywardness, because he will need to improve on this form. (op 11-8 tchd 6-4)
Whos Counting probably achieved little dropped to her shortest trip to date.
Jost Van Dyke is regressing fast. (op 11-10 tchd Evens and 5-4)

6696 RIVERBELLE.COM/RACES CLAIMING STKS (DIV II) 7f (P)
1:10 (1:10) (Class 6) 3-Y-0+ **£2,047** (£604; £302) **Stalls** Low

Form RPR

0006 **1** **Moon Bird**[23] 6442 4-8-11 57 OscarUrbina 7 69
(C A Cyzer) *hld up in midfield: rdn and hdwy over 1f out: chal ins fnl f: led nr fin* **16/1**

3300 **2** *shd* **Marko Jadeo (IRE)**[23] 6446 8-8-12 78 PaulFitzsimons 8 70+
(S Dow) *s.s and lost 8l: hld up and bhd: rdn and hdwy over 1f out: jnd ldrs ins fnl f: r.o: jst pipped* **9/4**[2]

2366 **3** *1/2* **Outer Hebrides**[10] 6580 5-9-0 80 (vt) EddieAhern 6 70
(Stef Liddiard) *hld up in midfield: rdn and hdwy over 1f out: jnd ldrs ins fnl f: nt qckn nr fin* **6/5**[1]

0354 **4** *nk* **Flint River**[19] 6493 8-8-10 60 SteveDrowne 5 66
(H Morrison) *chsd ldrs: drvn to ld 1f out: kpt on u.p: hdd nr fin* **10/1**

6320 **5** *3* **Paparaazi (IRE)**[22] 5810 4-9-0 68 PaulHanagan 1 62
(R A Fahey) *trckd ldrs: rdn over 2f out: one pce* **9/2**[3]

0000 **6** *1* **Mystic Man (FR)**[65] 5688 8-9-2 75 (b) BrettDoyle 11 61
(I W McInnes) *prom tl wknd 1f out* **33/1**

0006 **7** *1 1/4* **African Concerto (IRE)**[7] 6619 3-8-9 49 LPKeniry 9 51
(S Kirk) *hld up in rr: rdn over 2f out: nvr rchd ldrs* **33/1**

0524 **8** *1/2* **For Life (IRE)**[7] 6619 4-8-12 48 (v) DarryllHolland 10 53
(A P Jarvis) *led tl wknd 1f out* **14/1**

-000 **9** *3/4* **Compton Express**[121] 4143 3-8-7 49 RobertHavlin 3 46
(Jamie Poulton) *mid-div on rail: rdn over 3f out: sn outpcd* **66/1**

0 **10** *8* **Cinders Spark**[40] 6177 3-7-13 RobynBrisland[(5)] 2 22
(G L Moore) *dwlt: a towards rr: n.d fnl 3f* **66/1**

0000 **11** *5* **Tantien**[63] 5728 4-7-12 35 WilliamBuick[(7)] 4 10
(T Keddy) *prom early: rdn along after 2f: grad lost pl* **66/1**

1m 24.33s (-1.56) **Going Correction** -0.125s/f (Stan) **11** Ran SP% **126.4**
Speed ratings (Par 101):103,102,102,101,98 97,95,95,94,85 79
CSF £55.54 TOTE £18.70: £3.60, £1.20, £1.10; EX 95.40 Trifecta £227.80 Pool £356.19, 1.11 w/u.Marko Jadeo was claimed by R. A. Harris for £8,000. Outer Hebrides was claimed by Clifton Hunt for £10,000
Owner Mrs Charles Cyzer **Bred** C A Cyzer **Trained** Maplehurst, W Sussex

FOCUS
A good claimer; much better than the first division. The winning time was 0.67 seconds quicker than the opening race.

6697 BUY YOUR LADY JOCKEYS CALENDAR - CALL 01635 44 102 MEDIAN AUCTION FILLIES' MAIDEN STKS 1m (P)
1:40 (1:40) (Class 6) 2-Y-0 **£2,590** (£770; £385; £192) **Stalls** High

Form RPR

1 **Les Fazzani (IRE)** 2-9-0 EddieAhern 6 70+
(M J Wallace) *hld up towards rr: hrd rdn and hdwy over 1f out: r.o to ld ins fnl f: readily* **6/1**[3]

3042 **2** *1 1/2* **Miss Saafend Plaza (IRE)**[9] 6598 2-9-0 74 RichardHughes 4 67
(R Hannon) *in tch: rdn 3f out: drvn to chal 1f out: nt qckn ins fnl f* **10/11**[1]

032 **3** *1 1/4* **Towy Girl (IRE)**[19] 6486 2-9-0 70 LeeEnstone 1 64
(I A Wood) *t.k.h: covered up on rail bhd ldr: drvn to chal ins fnl f: no ex fnl 100 yds* **9/4**[2]

4 *3/4* **Rann Na Cille (IRE)**[43] 6111 2-9-0 LPKeniry 3 62
(K A Ryan) *led: hrd rdn over 1f out: hdd & wknd ins fnl f* **20/1**

5 *2 1/2* **Spring Glory** 2-9-0 JamieMackay 2 57
(Sir Mark Prescott) *s.s: rn green: same pl most of way: pushed along 3f out: no imp tl kpt on steadily fnl f* **12/1**

0 **6** *7* **Toboggan Lady**[18] 6498 2-9-0 PaulHanagan 5 40
(Mrs A Duffield) *prom 5f* **33/1**

7 *nk* **Eridani (IRE)** 2-9-0 HayleyTurner 7 40
(M L W Bell) *a last: rdn over 3f out: sn lost tch* **25/1**

1m 40.46s (1.03) **Going Correction** -0.125s/f (Stan) **7** Ran SP% **116.7**
Speed ratings (Par 91):89,87,86,85,83 76,75
CSF £12.18 TOTE £10.60: £3.30, £1.80; EX 15.80.
Owner Mike & Denise Dawes **Bred** J Erhardt And Mrs J Schonwalder **Trained** Newmarket, Suffolk

FOCUS
Just an ordinary fillies' maiden rated around the fourth to her mark.

NOTEBOOK
Les Fazzani(IRE) ◆, a 55,000gns half-sister to the useful Miss Lips, a triple six-furlong/mile winner, and Moody Blues, a sprint winner in Germany, out of a useful seven to ten-furlong scorer, picked up nicely in the straight to make a winning debut. The bare form looks just ordinary, but she is open to improvement and should make a nice three-year-old. (op 5-1 tchd 7-1)
Miss Saafend Plaza(IRE), trying a mile for the first time, seemed to run her race but basically found the winner too good. She has had a few chances. (op 11-10 tchd 5-4 and 6-4 in a place)
Towy Girl(IRE) was a little keen tracking the steady pace and would have preferred a stronger gallop. (op 5-2 tchd 2-1)
Rann Na Cille(IRE) showed limited form in five runs in Ireland and was well held on her debut for new connections. She is likely to be seen to better effect in handicaps. (op 16-1)
Spring Glory, a half-sister to useful middle-distance filly On Call, as well as two-year-old winner Doctor's Glory, Lyrical Bid and Remedy, was badly in need of the experience. (op 10-1)

6698 FRED GIBSON MEMORIAL H'CAP 1m (P)
2:10 (2:10) (Class 5) (0-75,78) 3-Y-0+ **£5,505** (£1,637; £818; £408) **Stalls** High

Form RPR
0022 **1** **Kabeer**[21] 6469 8-8-8 **71**........................(t) NataliaGemelova(5) 11 82
(A J McCabe) *pressed ldr: led 4f out: rdn out* **8/1**
4000 **2** ¾ **Trifti**[18] 6502 5-9-0 **72**........................ EddieAhern 4 81
(C A Cyzer) *chsd ldrs: wnt 2nd over 2f out: kpt on and clsd on wnr fnl f: a hld* **9/2**[2]
3334 **3** 1 ¾ **All Quiet**[29] 6350 5-9-2 **74**........................ RichardHughes 3 79
(R Hannon) *prom: hrd rdn over 1f out: one pce* **11/4**[1]
0430 **4** ¾ **Smokin Joe**[5] 6652 5-8-12 **70**........................ BrettDoyle 8 73
(J R Best) *hld up towards rr: hdwy on outside 2f out: rdn and styd on: nrst fin* **6/1**[3]
0600 **5** ¾ **Night Storm**[6] 6635 5-8-9 **67**........................ SteveDrowne 5 69+
(S Dow) *s.s and lost 8l: bhd: rdn and hdwy over 1f out: no imp fnl f* **12/1**
-501 **6** 1 ¾ **Littleton Telchar (USA)**[5] 6654 6-9-3 **78** 6ex........ LiamJones(3) 12 76
(S W Hall) *plld hrd: chsd ldrs on outside: rdn 3f out: outpcd fnl 2f* **10/1**
5005 **7** ½ **Scroll**[60] 5775 3-7-10 **62**........................(v) WilliamBuick(7) 6 58
(P Howling) *mid-div: squeezed for room and dropped to rr over 4f out: swtchd outside and rdn 3f out: nt rch ldrs* **20/1**
0005 **8** 1 **Celtic Spa (IRE)**[11] 6568 4-8-3 **61** oh2........................ PaulHanagan 1 55
(P D Evans) *mid-div on rail: drvn along 3f out: sn outpcd* **33/1**
0005 **9** nk **Spring Goddess (IRE)**[29] 6350 5-9-3 **75**........................ DarryllHolland 9 68
(A P Jarvis) *plld hrd: in tch: rdn 3f out: sn lost pl* **6/1**[3]
0300 **10** 1 **Aastral Magic**[17] 6507 4-8-1 **62**........................(p) StephaneBreux(3) 7 53
(R Hannon) *sn led: hdd 4f out: wknd 2f out* **33/1**
0006 **11** ¾ **North Walk (IRE)**[24] 6424 3-8-13 **72**........................ LPKeniry 10 61
(K A Ryan) *mid-div tl rdn and wknd 3f out* **16/1**
2036 **12** 5 **Golden Alchemist**[11] 6568 3-8-9 **68**........................ HayleyTurner 2 46
(M D I Usher) *dwlt: hdwy into midfield after 3f: wknd over 3f out* **33/1**

1m 37.37s (-2.06) **Going Correction** -0.125s/f (Stan)
WFA 3 from 4yo+ 1lb **12** Ran SP% **120.8**
Speed ratings (Par 103):105,104,102,101,101 99,98,97,97,96 95,90
CSF £43.06 CT £126.33 TOTE £9.30: £2.30, £2.20, £1.40; EX 64.40 Trifecta £153.90 Pool £401.05, 1.85 w/u.
Owner Placida Racing **Bred** Shadwell Estate Company **Trained** Babworth, Notts
FOCUS
Just an ordinary handicap for the grade but the form looks reasonable.

6699 LINGFIELDPARK.CO.UK NURSERY 7f (P)
2:40 (2:40) (Class 5) (0-85,89) 2-Y-0 **£4,210** (£1,252; £625; £312) **Stalls** Low

Form RPR
6141 **1** **Solid Rock (IRE)**[6] 6634 2-9-7 **89** 7ex........................ PatrickHills(7) 5 94+
(T G Mills) *t.k.h early: pressed ldr: led ent st: rdn clr: in command whn edgd rt ins fnl f* **2/1**[2]
2140 **2** 1 ¼ **Beauchamp Viceroy**[79] 5372 2-9-3 **78**........................ EddieAhern 2 80+
(G A Butler) *t.k.h early: hld up in rr: rdn 3f out: hdwy over 1f out: styd on wl to take 2nd ins fnl f* **15/8**[1]
001 **3** 2 **Lordswood (IRE)**[21] 6460 2-7-12 **66**........................ WilliamBuick(7) 6 63
(A M Balding) *t.k.h: in tch on outside: effrt 2f out: hrd rdn over 1f out: one pce* **7/2**[3]
6034 **4** ½ **Bantry Bere (IRE)**[5] 6651 2-8-7 **68**........................ BrettDoyle 4 63
(J R Best) *sn led: rdn and hdd ent st: no ex fnl f* **20/1**
0054 **5** 1 ½ **Slipasearcher (IRE)**[10] 6586 2-8-7 **68**........................(v[1]) PaulHanagan 3 59
(P D Evans) *plld hrd early: in tch: rdn 3f out: one pce fnl 2f* **12/1**
6304 **6** 6 **Give Evidence**[10] 6582 2-8-7 **68**........................ DarryllHolland 1 44
(A P Jarvis) *chsd ldrs 5f* **9/1**

1m 25.12s (-0.77) **Going Correction** -0.125s/f (Stan) **6** Ran SP% **112.8**
Speed ratings (Par 96):99,97,95,94,93 86
CSF £6.24 TOTE £2.60: £1.80, £1.30; EX 8.20.
Owner Mrs L M Askew **Bred** Max Morris **Trained** Headley, Surrey
FOCUS
An ordinary nursery for the level but the first two look to be going the right way.
NOTEBOOK
Solid Rock(IRE) readily defied a 7lb penalty for his recent course success over a mile, despite having been keen enough early on. This looked like a weak race for the grade and things will be tougher in future, but he is obviously progressing nicely. (op 5-4)
Beauchamp Viceroy, trying seven furlongs for the first time on his return to Polytrack, was never really that well placed and got going too late to pose a threat. He looks a little better than the bare form. (op 5-2 tchd 11-4)
Lordswood(IRE) would have found this tougher than the course and distance claimer he won last time and was well held in third. (op 11-2)
Bantry Bere(IRE) was well held in fourth and looks on a stiff enough mark. (op 14-1)
Slipasearcher(IRE) is exposed and raced too keenly in the first-time visor. (op 10-1 tchd 9-1)

6700 LINGFIELD PARK FOR CHRISTMAS PARTIES H'CAP 1m 2f (P)
3:10 (3:10) (Class 6) (0-52,53) 3-Y-0+ **£2,730** (£806; £403) **Stalls** Low

Form RPR
00-2 **1** **Picador**[7] 6627 3-8-9 **51**........................ JamieMackay 5 59+
(Sir Mark Prescott) *led 1f: trckd ldr: led over 1f out: drvn out* **4/6**[1]
6454 **2** 1 ¼ **Revolve**[7] 6617 6-8-9 **48**........................(b) LPKeniry 3 54
(Mrs L J Mongan) *prom: hrd rdn over 1f out: kpt on* **9/1**[3]
5300 **3** 1 **The Iron Giant (IRE)**[48] 6037 4-8-13 **52**........................ PaulHanagan 6 56
(B G Powell) *led after 1f tl over 1f out: one pce* **11/2**[2]
4500 **4** hd **King Of Knight (IRE)**[210] 1553 5-8-13 **52**........................ OscarUrbina 12 56
(G Prodromou) *hld up in tch: promising effrt on bit over 2f out: rdn and nt qckn fnl f* **14/1**
0060 **5** 1 **Laugh 'n Cry**[21] 6459 5-8-11 **50**........................(b) EddieAhern 2 53+
(C A Cyzer) *hdwy 5f out: rdn and carried hd high over 1f out: n.m.r ent fnl f: kpt on nr fin* **14/1**
0006 **6** hd **Ifatfirst (IRE)**[20] 6479 3-8-11 **53** ow1........................(b) RichardHughes 13 54+
(M P Tregoning) *stdd s: hld up and bhd: rdn over 2f out: styd on strly fnl f: nvr nrr* **12/1**
0006 **7** ¾ **Theologicum**[9] 6601 3-8-7 **52**........................ NeilChalmers(3) 4 52
(Miss J R Gibney) *chsd ldrs: lost pl 1/2-way: rallied 2f out: no imp over 1f out* **33/1**
5000 **8** 1 ½ **Fantasy Crusader**[7] 6627 7-8-13 **52**........................(p) DarryllHolland 7 49
(R M H Cowell) *hld up towards rr: hdwy on outside over 3f out: wd and outpcd ent st: n.d after* **16/1**
-003 **9** 1 **Shropshirelass**[52] 5936 3-8-5 **50**........................ RichardKingscote(3) 9 45
(Mrs Norma Pook) *hld up towards rr: sme hdwy over 1f out: sn hrd rdn and wl hld* **25/1**
500U **10** 3 **Diktatorship (IRE)**[7] 6627 3-8-8 **50**........................(v) BrettDoyle 8 40
(Ernst Oertel) *in tch: effrt over 2f out: wknd wl over 1f out* **33/1**
0000 **11** 2 **Ameliore (IRE)**[116] 4278 3-8-1 **46** oh6........................ LiamJones(3) 1 32
(S Woodman) *in tch: dropped to rr 1/2-way: n.d after* **66/1**

2m 7.44s (-0.35) **Going Correction** -0.125s/f (Stan)
WFA 3 from 4yo+ 3lb **11** Ran SP% **123.5**
Speed ratings (Par 101):96,95,94,94,93 93,92,91,90,88 86
CSF £7.94 CT £24.13 TOTE £1.70: £1.10, £2.30, £3.00; EX 9.00 Trifecta £23.90 Pool £433.54 - 12.83 winning units. Place 6 £5.66, Place 5 £3.75.
Owner Sir Mark Prescott **Bred** Cheveley Park Stud Ltd **Trained** Newmarket, Suffolk
FOCUS
A moderate handicap run at a steady pace and rated through the second to banded form.
Laugh 'n Cry Official explanation: jockey said mare was denied clear run
Diktatorship(IRE) Official explanation: jockey said gelding hung right-handed throughout
T/Plt: £26.10 to a £1 stake. Pool: £37,572.10. 1,050.35 winning tickets. T/Qpdt: £3.60 to a £1 stake. Pool: £3,341.50. 677.40 winning tickets. LM

6680 WOLVERHAMPTON (A.W) (L-H)
Monday, December 4

OFFICIAL GOING: Standard
Wind: Moderate half-behind Weather: Light rain from 3pm

6701 WOLVERHAMPTON-RACECOURSE.CO.UK BANDED STKS 1m 1f 103y(P)
1:00 (1:00) (Class 7) 3-Y-0+ **£1,365** (£403; £201) **Stalls** Low

Form RPR
0000 **1** **Norwegian**[16] 6524 5-9-0 45........................(p) DavidKinsella 13 52
(Ian Williams) *hld up in mid-div: hdwy over 3f out: rdn over 2f out: led ins fnl f: r.o* **20/1**
0562 **2** hd **Weet Yer Tern (IRE)**[7] 6616 4-9-0 45........................ PatCosgrave 8 52
(W M Brisbourne) *hld up in mid-div: hdwy over 3f out: rdn over 2f out: led 1f out tl ins fnl f: r.o* **5/2**[2]
0205 **3** 2 ½ **Boucheen**[14] 6543 3-8-12 45........................ CatherineGannon 9 47
(Ms Deborah J Evans) *led: rdn over 2f out: hdd 1f out: no ex ins fnl f* **9/1**
-030 **4** nk **Iceni Warrior**[213] 1462 4-9-0 45........................ PaulDoe 1 46
(P Howling) *broke wl: t.k.h and stdd: sn bhd: rdn over 3f out: hdwy over 2f out: r.o ins fnl f* **20/1**
0556 **5** ¾ **Sonderborg**[9] 6606 5-9-0 45........................(p) DaleGibson 3 45
(J Mackie) *bhd: rdn over 3f out: hdwy whn hung lft over 1f out: styd on ins fnl f* **10/1**
0066 **6** nk **Bubbling Fun**[32] 6312 5-9-0 45........................ JDSmith 5 44
(T Wall) *prom: rdn over 2f out: wknd over 1f out* **11/1**
5004 **7** shd **Indigo Dancer**[14] 6543 3-8-12 45........................(b) StephenCarson 10 44
(C F Wall) *chsd ldr: rdn 3f out: ev ch over 1f out: wknd fnl f* **9/4**[1]
0000 **8** ¾ **Ruby Sunrise (IRE)**[7] 6616 4-9-0 45........................ RichardThomas 4 46+
(B P J Baugh) *s.v.s: rdn and hdwy on ins wl over 1f out: hung lft fnl f: styng on whn nt clr run towards fin* **50/1**
3500 **9** 25 **Danum**[9] 6606 6-9-0 45........................(p) MatthewHenry 12 —
(R Hollinshead) *prom tl rdn and wknd over 2f out* **20/1**
2/00 **10** 2 **Scorch**[14] 6542 5-9-1 40 ow1........................(e[1]) MichaelTebbutt 6 —
(V Smith) *rdn over 3f out: a bhd* **66/1**
0004 **11** 1 ½ **Star Fern**[14] 6545 5-9-0 45........................ DeanMernagh 7 —
(M J Attwater) *s.v.s: a wl bhd* **15/2**[3]
0-00 **12** ½ **South Hill**[172] 2569 3-8-12 45........................ PaulMulrennan 11 —
(R J Price) *mid-div: rdn 4f out: sn bhd* **40/1**

2m 1.50s (-1.12) **Going Correction** -0.15s/f (Stan)
WFA 3 from 4yo+ 2lb **12** Ran SP% **118.7**
Speed ratings (Par 97):98,97,95,95,94 94,94,93,71,69 68,67
CSF £66.25 TOTE £31.20: £7.80, £1.10, £3.00; EX 222.80.
Owner Robert Bee **Bred** Darley **Trained** Portway, Worcs
FOCUS
A good finish to a moderate contest with the runner-up to recent form setting the standard.
Ruby Sunrise(IRE) Official explanation: jockey said filly missed the break
Star Fern Official explanation: jockey said gelding missed the break

6702 HOTEL & CONFERENCING AT WOLVERHAMPTON BANDED STKS 1m 141y(P)
1:30 (1:30) (Class 7) 3-Y-0+ **£1,365** (£403; £201) **Stalls** Low

Form RPR
643- **1** **Bobering**[348] 6650 6-8-7 40........................ SoniaEaton(7) 6 49
(B P J Baugh) *hld up and bhd: rdn and hdwy on ins wl over 1f out: swtchd rt and r.o to ld wl ins fnl f* **10/1**
0663 **2** 1 **Fantasy Defender (IRE)**[7] 6628 4-9-0 45........................(v) AdamKirby 1 47
(Ernst Oertel) *a.p: rdn over 2f out: led over 1f out tl wl ins fnl f: nt qckn* **6/4**[1]
0300 **3** 1 ¾ **Sea Frolic (IRE)**[7] 6627 5-8-9 45........................(v) RoryMoore(5) 2 43
(Jennie Candlish) *led: rdn over 2f out: hdd over 1f out: no ex ins fnl f* **14/1**
4000 **4** nk **Insignia (IRE)**[14] 6543 4-9-0 45........................(p) PatCosgrave 8 43
(W M Brisbourne) *hld up in mid-div: rdn wl over 1f out: hdwy fnl f: kpt on* **12/1**
0541 **5** hd **Elms Schoolboy**[7] 6616 4-9-6 45........................(b) IanMongan 9 48
(P Howling) *s.i.s: bhd: rdn over 3f out: hdwy fnl f: r.o* **9/2**[2]
0002 **6** hd **Wilford Maverick (IRE)**[7] 6618 4-9-0 45........................ DaleGibson 5 42
(M J Attwater) *t.k.h in tch: rdn wl over 1f out: one pce fnl f* **5/1**[3]
-000 **7** 1 ½ **Young Valentino**[28] 6372 4-9-0 40........................(e[1]) JimCrowley 12 39
(A W Carroll) *hld up in mid-div: hdwy on outside over 2f out: c wd st: nvr trbld ldrs* **66/1**
0500 **8** ½ **Madam Patti**[14] 6545 3-8-12 45........................ AdrianMcCarthy 7 38
(B Palling) *hld up and bhd: rdn over 2f out: c wd st: n.d* **40/1**
6-56 **9** hd **Boppys Dream**[13] 6557 4-9-0 40........................ MickyFenton 10 37
(P T Midgley) *chsd ldr: rdn and ev ch over 2f out: wknd over 1f out* **33/1**
0020 **10** 5 **Ballare (IRE)**[14] 6545 7-9-0 45........................(vt) FergusSweeney 4 27
(P J Makin) *hld up in tch: rdn over 3f out: wknd over 1f out* **13/2**
0500 **11** 17 **Wanna Shout**[14] 6543 8-9-0 45........................ TonyCulhane 13 —
(R Dickin) *hld up in tch: rdn and wknd over 2f out* **20/1**

1m 52.08s (0.32) **Going Correction** -0.15s/f (Stan)
WFA 3 from 4yo+ 2lb **11** Ran SP% **123.3**
Speed ratings (Par 97):92,91,89,89,89 88,87,87,86,82 67
CSF £26.00 TOTE £15.20: £3.60, £1.10, £5.20; EX 72.30.
Owner J H Chrimes And Mr & Mrs G W Hannam **Bred** J H Chrimes **Trained** Audley, Staffs
FOCUS
This was won in a time over a second slower than the subsequent race over this trip. The form is poor and best assessed through the winner.

6703 TWILIGHT RACING AND SUPPER BANDED STKS (DIV I) 7f 32y(P)
2:00 (2:00) (Class 7) 3-Y-0+ £1,706 (£503; £252) Stalls High

Form RPR
4002 1 **Haroldini (IRE)**[13] 6549 4-9-1 49..........................(p) JasonEdmunds(3) 11 56
(J Balding) *hld up and bhd: rdn and hdwy over 1f out: r.o wl to ld last strides* 17/2
6002 2 nk **Khetaab (IRE)**[14] 6545 4-9-3 48...................................... DavidKinsella 10 54
(E J Alston) *hld up in mid-div: rdn and hdwy over 1f out: led wl ins fnl f: hdd last strides* 9/2[2]
000 3 ¾ **Green Pirate**[36] 6235 4-9-3 48... GeorgeBaker 12 52
(W M Brisbourne) *hld up and bhd: plld out wl over 1f out: gd hdwy and hung lft fnl f: fin wl* 13/2[3]
0006 4 nk **Hiats**[31] 6327 4-9-5 50...(p) TonyCulhane 4 53
(J O'Reilly) *led: rdn over 1f out: hdd and no ex wl ins fnl f* 16/1
0001 5 1 **Capital Lass**[13] 6554 3-8-11 49................................... JamesMillman(7) 1 50
(D K Ivory) *t.k.h: chsd ldr: rdn and hung lft over 1f out: nt qckn fnl f* 10/1
0004 6 nk **Lucius Verrus (USA)**[7] 6618 6-9-2 50..................(v) PatrickMathers(3) 2 50
(D Shaw) *mid-div: rdn and hdwy on ins 3f out: one pce whn n.m.r ins fnl f* 15/8[1]
00-6 7 2 ½ **Ligne D'Eau**[6] 6638 5-9-2 47...(b) JimCrowley 8 40
(P D Evans) *s.i.s: rdn over 3f out: hdwy on ins wl over 1f out: no further prog fnl f* 16/1
1020 8 nk **Wings Of Morning (IRE)**[24] 6431 5-8-12 50...........(v) KellyHarrison(7) 6 43
(D Carroll) *prom: rdn over 3f out: wknd wl over 1f out* 8/1
0001 9 3 ½ **Penny Glitters**[14] 6542 3-9-3 48...................................... DeanMernagh 9 31
(S Parr) *mid-div: rdn over 2f out: wknd wl over 1f out* 12/1
1030 10 8 **Warden Warren**[7] 6618 8-9-4 49..............................(b) AdrianMcCarthy 7 12
(Mrs C A Dunnett) *prom: rdn over 3f out: wknd 2f out: eased whn btn over 1f out* 14/1

1m 30.47s (0.07) **Going Correction** -0.15s/f (Stan) 10 Ran SP% **123.1**
Speed ratings (Par 97):93,92,91,91,90 89,87,86,82,73
CSF £49.36 TOTE £11.50: £4.00, £2.40, £3.40; EX 89.60.
Owner Tykes And Terriers Racing Club **Bred** Michael O'Mahony **Trained** Scrooby, Notts

FOCUS
This was 0.63 seconds slower than the other division but looks quite sound overall, rated around the first three.
Warden Warren Official explanation: jockey said gelding lost its action

6704 DINE IN THE ZONGALERO RESTAURANT BANDED STKS 5f 20y(P)
2:30 (2:30) (Class 7) 3-Y-0+ £1,365 (£403; £201) Stalls Low

Form RPR
3635 1 **Dysonic (USA)**[6] 6637 4-8-9 45..............................(v) JasonEdmunds(3) 2 56+
(J Balding) *chsd ldrs: nt clr run over 1f out: rdn to ld cl home* 7/2[1]
6030 2 ½ **Rowanberry**[132] 3825 4-8-12 45.. PatCosgrave 1 52
(R M H Cowell) *hld up in tch: n.m.r and squeezed through over 1f out: rdn to ld ins fnl f: sn hung lft: hdd cl home* 6/1[3]
0603 3 1 ½ **Primarily**[6] 6649 4-8-12 45... MichaelTebbutt 7 47+
(Peter Grayson) *mid-div: rdn and hdwy 1f out: r.o u.p towards fin* 4/1[2]
6020 4 nk **Kindallachan**[28] 6372 3-8-12 45..................................... MatthewHenry 9 46
(G C Bravery) *s.i.s: c wd st: hung lft over 1f out: r.o ins fnl f: nrst fin* 20/1
4330 5 1 ½ **Vicky Pollard**[14] 6539 3-8-12 45.. PaulDoe 13 41
(P Howling) *w ldrs: rdn and ev ch whn edgd lft over 1f out: wknd ins fnl f* 20/1
0643 6 shd **Spinetail Rufous (IRE)**[7] 6615 8-8-12 45............(b) AdrianMcCarthy 10 40
(Miss Z C Davison) *w ldrs: rdn to ld and edgd lft jst over 1f out: hdd ins fnl f: wknd* 10/1
0360 7 shd **Sanders Boy**[13] 6550 3-8-12 45...................................... PaulMulrennan 8 40
(J R Norton) *sn outpcd: hdwy whn nt clr run over 1f out: nt rch ldrs* 50/1
6002 8 ½ **El Potro**[13] 6548 4-8-12 45.. JDSmith 3 41+
(J R Holt) *sn bhd: hdwy whn nt clr run over 1f out: nt rch ldrs* 4/1[2]
0300 9 ½ **Comic Tales**[7] 6615 5-8-12 45.................................. CatherineGannon 11 36
(M Mullineaux) *s.i.s: outpcd: rdn and hdwy on ins wl over 1f out: nt clr run ent fnl f: one pce* 66/1
3150 10 1 ¾ **Katie Killane**[162] 2897 4-8-12 45.................................(v) DaleGibson 6 30
(M Wellings) *w ldrs: rdn and ev ch whn bmpd jst over 1f out: wknd ins fnl f* 12/1
2-50 11 2 ½ **Cark**[265] 633 8-8-12 45..(b[1]) DeanMernagh 4 21
(T J Pitt) *led: rdn and hdd whn bmpd jst over 1f out: wknd qckly ins fnl f* 11/1
2 12 ¾ **Stone Arch (IRE)**[159] 2995 6-8-12 45.......................... StephenCarson 12 18
(Jarlath P Fahey, Ire) *mid-div: rdn over 3f out: c wd st: sn bhd* 11/1

62.95 secs (0.13) **Going Correction** -0.15s/f (Stan) 12 Ran SP% **122.9**
Speed ratings (Par 97):92,91,88,88,85 85,85,84,84,81 77,76
CSF £24.74 TOTE £5.10: £1.60, £2.50, £2.20; EX 39.40.
Owner T R Pearson **Bred** Shadwell Farm LLC **Trained** Scrooby, Notts

FOCUS
This messy race was wide open coming to the furlong pole and the form is anchored by the proximity of the fourth.
Cark Official explanation: jockey said gelding hung right-handed

6705 STAY AT THE WOLVERHAMPTON HOLIDAY INN BANDED STKS 1m 5f 194y(P)
3:00 (3:00) (Class 7) 3-Y-0+ £1,706 (£503; £252) Stalls Low

Form RPR
0220 1 **Captivate**[7] 6620 3-8-5 45..(p) MCGeran(7) 12 53
(A J McCabe) *s.i.s: hdwy over 2f out: rdn and hung lft over 1f out: led ins fnl f: edgd rt: r.o* 16/1
0455 2 nk **Malibu (IRE)**[11] 6238 5-9-5 45... GeorgeBaker 6 53
(M Appleby) *s.i.s: hld up and bhd: hdwy over 3f out: rdn and hung lft over 1f out: led briefly ins fnl f: r.o* 10/1
0-00 3 1 ¼ **Twist Bookie (IRE)**[25] 4845 6-9-7 47................................ ChrisCatlin 11 53
(S Lycett) *led early: t.k.h: prom: led 3f out: rdn and hdd 2f out: ev ch ins fnl f: nt qckn* 4/1[3]
23-5 4 ½ **Toni Alcala**[14] 6540 7-9-6 46... TomEaves 5 54+
(R F Fisher) *mid-div: lost pl and nt clr run over 3f out: sn rdn: rallied over 1f out: hung lft ins fnl f: styd on wl* 14/1
3 5 ½ **Mikimoto (IRE)**[7] 6620 4-9-5 45.. AdamKirby 1 50
(S C Williams) *chsd ldr: rdn to ld 2f out: hdd and no ex ins fnl f* 11/4[1]
2265 6 1 ½ **Lanfredo**[13] 6560 3-8-12 48.....................................(p) PatrickMathers(3) 3 51
(Miss M E Rowland) *hld up in mid-div: hdwy on ins over 3f out: rdn over 2f out: carried lft over 1f out: sn btn* 3/1[2]
0522 7 6 **Red River Rock (IRE)**[13] 6553 4-9-5 45...............(be) PaulMulrennan 13 39
(T J Fitzgerald) *sn led: rdn and hdd 3f out: wknd 2f out* 9/2
3635 8 nk **Romil Star (GER)**[2] 6685 9-9-8 48..................(v) RobbieFitzpatrick 2 42
(M Wellings) *prom: rdn over 4f out: sn wknd* 9/1
6 9 1 ¼ **Salthill (IRE)**[6] 6648 3-8-12 45.................................. AdrianMcCarthy 10 37
(Jarlath P Fahey, Ire) *a towards rr* 33/1
0000 10 18 **Unasuming (IRE)**[17] 6509 3-9-3 50..................................(t) JimmyQuinn 9 17
(J Pearce) *hld up in mid-div: rdn over 5f out: short-lived effrt 4f out: eased whn no ch fnl 2f* 20/1

3m 5.66s (-1.71) **Going Correction** -0.15s/f (Stan)
WFA 3 from 4yo+ 7lb 10 Ran SP% **129.2**
Speed ratings (Par 97):98,97,97,96,96 95,92,92,91,81
CSF £182.81 TOTE £21.80: £4.70, £3.90, £2.60; EX 185.80.
Owner Paul J Dixon and James Kennerley **Bred** Miss K Rausing **Trained** Babworth, Notts

FOCUS
An even gallop made this a reasonable test of stamina and the runner-up is the best guide to the level.
Red River Rock(IRE) Official explanation: jockey said gelding hung right-handed
Unasuming(IRE) Official explanation: jockey said filly had a breathing problem

6706 RINGSIDE SUITE MAIDEN AUCTION STKS 5f 216y(P)
3:30 (3:30) (Class 7) 2-Y-0 £1,365 (£403; £201) Stalls Low

Form RPR
0052 1 **Charlotte Grey**[14] 6534 2-8-6 52.................................. EdwardCreighton 7 60
(C N Allen) *led early: w ldr: led over 3f out: rdn over 1f out: r.o wl* 9/2[2]
6032 2 1 ½ **Tobago Reef**[25] 6416 2-8-13 65..(p) TomEaves 2 63
(Mrs L Stubbs) *sn led: hdd over 3f out: rdn 2f out: nt qckn ins fnl f* 4/7[1]
0 3 3 ½ **Pappas Image**[54] 5906 2-8-10 ....(b[1]) DavidAllan 1 49
(A J McCabe) *chsd ldrs: rdn over 2f out: one pce* 17/2[3]
0 4 5 **Gertie (IRE)**[6] 6644 2-8-8 ow1... MickyFenton 6 32
(E J Creighton) *sn outpcd: sme hdwy over 1f out: n.d* 33/1
0500 5 2 **Kyoto City**[6] 6640 2-8-4 35...(b[1]) MatthewHenry 5 22
(D W Chapman) *s.i.s: nvr nr ldrs* 66/1
00 6 1 ½ **Emerald Sky**[25] 6414 2-8-3 ow1.................................... MarcHalford(3) 8 20
(R Brotherton) *in tch: rdn and wknd over 2f out* 66/1
6000 7 3 **Joint Expectations (IRE)**[12] 6562 2-8-11 45..................(v) AdamKirby 3 16
(Mrs C A Dunnett) *hld up: rdn over 3f out: sn bhd* 14/1
6550 8 1 ½ **Elizabeth Garrett**[122] 4115 2-8-5 46.................................... ChrisCatlin 4 —
(R M H Cowell) *prom: rdn over 3f out: sn wknd* 10/1

1m 15.85s (0.04) **Going Correction** -0.15s/f (Stan) 8 Ran SP% **114.0**
Speed ratings (Par 90):93,91,86,79,77 75,71,69
CSF £7.37 TOTE £7.00: £1.80, £1.02, £1.50; EX 15.90.
Owner Travel Spot Ltd **Bred** Finbar Kent **Trained** Newmarket, Suffolk

FOCUS
A weak maiden, little better than a seller.

NOTEBOOK
Charlotte Grey did not mind a return to this trip after being narrowly beaten over seven in a Southwell seller a fortnight ago. (op 6-1 tchd 13-2 in places)
Tobago Reef, just touched off in a seven-furlong nursery here last time, was well outpointed in the end. Official explanation: jockey said gelding hung right throughout (op 1-2)
Pappas Image was fitted with blinkers and stepped up on his debut. (op 14-1 tchd 8-1)

6707 BEAT THE TRAFFIC AT TWILIGHT RACING TRI-BANDED STKS 1m 141y(P)
4:00 (4:00) (Class 7) 3-Y-0 £1,365 (£403; £201) Stalls Low

Form RPR
0 1 **Freda's Choice (IRE)**[36] 6235 3-9-0 45.................(b[1]) DanielTudhope 11 52
(Patrick Morris, Ire) *hld up and bhd: hdwy on outside over 3f out: rdn to ld and edgd lft jst over 1f out: r.o* 12/1
001 2 1 ¼ **Island Green (USA)**[36] 6236 3-9-0 45........................... FrancisNorton 9 50
(B J Curley) *prom: led 6f out: rdn 2f out: hdd jst over 1f out: nt qckn* 9/4[1]
0640 3 1 ¼ **Stoneacre Fred (IRE)**[34] 6276 3-9-0 45................. RobbieFitzpatrick 13 47
(Peter Grayson) *hld up in rr: hdwy and hung rt over 2f out: edgd lft ins fnl f: nvr able to chal* 20/1
0306 4 2 **Chalice Welcome**[14] 6542 3-9-0 45............................ StephenCarson 1 43
(C F Wall) *led: hdd 6f out: rdn over 3f out: 3rd and btn whn hung lft over 1f out* 3/1[2]
3503 5 3 **Flashing Floozie**[28] 6370 3-8-7 45............................. MarkCoumbe(7) 3 37
(A W Carroll) *prom tl rdn and wknd over 2f out* 9/2[3]
0036 6 ¾ **Danethorpe (IRE)**[13] 6549 3-8-11 45..................(v) PatrickMathers(3) 4 35
(D Shaw) *bhd: rdn and hdwy on ins wl over 1f out: no further prog* 16/1
000 7 2 ½ **Dodaa (USA)**[19] 6492 3-9-0 45.. JimmyQuinn 5 30
(N Wilson) *hld up in mid-div: rdn and lost pl over 4f out: hdwy on ins over 2f out: swtchd rt over 1f out: wknd fnl f* 16/1
0006 8 9 **Astorygoeswithit**[13] 6550 3-9-0 45.................................(p) BrianReilly 6 11
(P S McEntee) *prom: rdn over 3f out: wknd over 2f out* 20/1
0300 9 ½ **Great Composer (IRE)**[108] 4568 3-9-0 45........................(b) AdamKirby 7 10
(M Wellings) *mid-div: rdn over 3f out: sn bhd* 16/1
6604 10 1 ¼ **Just Tilly**[36] 6236 3-8-9 40.. JimCrowley 2 2
(L Montague Hall) *mid-div: rdn 4f out: sn bhd* 16/1
0000 11 ¾ **Red Vixen (IRE)**[14] 6541 3-9-0 45........................... EdwardCreighton 12 6
(C N Allen) *hdwy over 6f out: rdn over 3f out: wknd 2f out* 12/1
0060 12 ½ **Pertemps Heroine**[36] 6236 3-8-9 40.............................. FergusSweeney 8 —
(A G Newcombe) *rdn over 3f out: a bhd* 40/1

1m 51.0s (-0.76) **Going Correction** -0.15s/f (Stan) 12 Ran SP% **124.8**
Speed ratings (Par 96):97,95,94,93,90 89,87,79,79,77 77,76
CSF £40.35 TOTE £11.80: £3.50, £1.50, £5.00; EX 33.70.
Owner D Veitch **Bred** Thomas Heatrick **Trained** Ruanbeg, Co. Kildare

FOCUS
This was over a second faster than the earlier race over this trip and the form makes sense rated around the runner-up and fourth.
Red Vixen(IRE) Official explanation: jockey said filly lost its action

6708 TWILIGHT RACING AND SUPPER BANDED STKS (DIV II) 7f 32y(P)
4:30 (4:31) (Class 7) 3-Y-0+ £1,706 (£503; £252) Stalls High

Form RPR
0 1 **Claws**[20] 6470 3-9-5 50... FrancisNorton 7 60
(A J Lidderdale) *chsd ldrs: rdn over 1f out: led jst ins fnl f: drvn out* 25/1
0342 2 nk **Cree**[14] 6541 4-9-3 48.. GeorgeBaker 3 57
(W R Muir) *hld up and bhd: rdn and hdwy over 2f out: r.o ins fnl f* 3/1[3]
5436 3 1 ¼ **Blythe Spirit**[14] 6533 7-8-11 49.................................(p) JamesRogers(7) 6 55
(R A Fahey) *hld up in tch: led wl over 1f out: sn rdn: hdd jst ins fnl f: nt qckn* 6/1
5443 4 hd **Mon Petite Amour**[13] 6554 3-9-3 48.......................(p) EdwardCreighton 1 53
(D W P Arbuthnot) *hld up and bhd: rdn and hdwy over 1f out: swtchd lft jst ins fnl f: kpt on* 12/1
00-0 5 hd **Oakbridge (IRE)**[335] 22 4-9-5 50...................................... AdamKirby 10 54
(D J Wintle) *t.k.h: sn chsng ldrs: rdn over 2f out: edgd lft over 1f out: kpt on same pce* 11/4[2]
0420 6 2 ½ **Hill Of Almhuim (IRE)**[21] 6464 3-9-5 50................. RobbieFitzpatrick 12 48
(Peter Grayson) *bhd: rdn over 3f out: late hdwy: nvr nrr* 16/1

0045 **7** ½ **Shannon Arms (USA)**[7] 6618 5-9-4 49 (p) PatCosgrave 11 46
(R Brotherton) *led over 5f out: rdn over 2f out: hdd wl over 1f out: wknd fnl f* **16/1**

3 **8** 1 **Send Me Home (IRE)**[2] 6683 4-9-4 49 DanielTudhope 9 43
(Adrian McGuinness, Ire) *chsd ldrs: rdn over 2f out: ev ch wl over 1f out: sn edgd lft: wknd fnl f* **7/4**[1]

3000 **9** shd **Captain Bolsh**[29] 4847 3-9-3 48 JimmyQuinn 4 42
(J Pearce) *mid-div: rdn over 2f out: hdwy over 1f out: wknd ins fnl f* **40/1**

4060 **10** ½ **Dexileos (IRE)**[104] 4670 7-9-5 50 (t) FergusSweeney 8 43
(David Pinder) *led over 1f: rdn and wknd over 2f out* **33/1**

0000 **11** 2 **Aberlady Bay (IRE)**[7] 6628 3-9-5 50 (b[1]) ChrisCatlin 2 37
(T T Clement) *hmpd s: hld up and bhd: short-lived effrt on outside over 3f out* **66/1**

1m 29.84s (-0.56) **Going Correction** -0.15s/f (Stan) 11 Ran SP% **132.5**
Speed ratings (Par 97):97,96,95,95,94 91,91,90,90,89 87
CSF £109.47 TOTE £26.20: £6.30, £1.50, £2.60; EX 89.00 Place 6 £71.87, Place 5 £30.52.
Owner Entertainments Committee **Bred** Mrs P Carter **Trained** Eastbury, Berks

FOCUS
This looked quite competitive and was 0.63 seconds faster than the first division so the form should work out.
T/Jkpt: Not won. T/Plt: £336.30 to a £1 stake. Pool: £51,101.65. 110.90 winning tickets. T/Qpdt: £36.50 to a £1 stake. Pool: £3,838.40. 77.70 winning tickets. KH

6668 KEMPTON (A.W) (R-H)
Tuesday, December 5

OFFICIAL GOING: Standard
Wind: Moderate, hlaf-behind. Weather: Overcast.

6709 BETBROKERS "NEVER MISS A BET" H'CAP 5f (P)
3:50 (3:50) (Class 5) (0-75,75) 3-Y-0+ **£3,886** (£1,156; £577; £288) **Stalls** High

Form RPR

300 **1** **No Time (IRE)**[60] 5782 6-8-10 67 SteveDrowne 8 78
(A J McCabe) *s.i.s: hld up in last trio: swtchd out fr inner jst over 1f out: r.o wl fnl f to ld last 50yds* **10/1**

1223 **2** ¾ **Heavens Walk**[20] 6485 5-8-13 70 (t) EddieAhern 1 78
(P J Makin) *trckd ldrs: effrt over 1f out: led jst ins fnl f: hdd and outpcd last 50yds* **15/8**[1]

1405 **3** ½ **City For Conquest (IRE)**[11] 6585 3-8-9 66 (b) FrancisNorton 4 72
(T J Pitt) *s.i.s: hld up in last trio: rdn and hanging bdly over 1f out: prog ent fnl f: r.o: nt pce to chal* **14/1**

2600 **4** nk **After The Show**[11] 6583 5-9-3 74 ChrisCatlin 6 79
(Rae Guest) *hld up in last trio: rdn and prog jst over 1f out: styd on fnl f: nt pce to chal* **10/1**

3006 **5** 1¼ **Kempsey**[20] 6485 4-8-6 63 ow1 (b) LPKeniry 3 64
(J J Bridger) *mde most: hdd and fdd jst ins fnl f* **20/1**

0046 **6** shd **Harrison's Flyer (IRE)**[8] 6622 5-8-3 63 (b) NeilChalmers(3) 9 63
(J M Bradley) *b: w ldr to jst over 1f out: fdd fnl f* **14/1**

0001 **7** ¾ **Fizzlephut (IRE)**[11] 6585 4-8-13 70 PaulFitzsimons 2 68
(Miss J R Tooth) *taken down early: trckd ldrs: rdn and wknd fnl f* **9/1**

1000 **8** 1 **Sands Crooner (IRE)**[11] 6583 3-9-1 75 (v) PatrickMathers(3) 5 69+
(D Shaw) *b: hld up bhd ldrs: nt clr run fr over 1f out to ins fnl f: no ch after* **50/1**

3002 **9** hd **Jayanjay**[11] 6579 7-8-12 69 BrettDoyle 10 62+
(P Mitchell) *lw: trckd ldrs on inner: effrt over 1f out: nt clr run sn after: no ch whn nowhere to go last 100yds* **9/2**[3]

1325 **10** 1¾ **Pamir (IRE)**[11] 6579 4-8-12 69 (b) JimCrowley 7 56
(P R Chamings) *w ldng pair: sltly impeded jst over 1f out: wknd rapidly* **10/3**[2]

60.65 secs (0.25) **Going Correction** +0.125s/f (Slow) 10 Ran SP% **124.3**
Speed ratings (Par 103):103,101,101,100,98 98,97,95,95,92
CSF £31.08 CT £288.65 TOTE £16.50: £3.00, £1.50, £2.90; EX 52.00.
Owner Paul J Dixon **Bred** Tally-Ho Stud **Trained** Babworth, Notts
■ Stewards' Enquiry : Steve Drowne one-day ban; careless riding (Dec 16)

FOCUS
A fair sprint handicap of its type and as is the norm in races like this around the inside bend, space was at a premium in the home straight. They went a decent pace, but those that helped set it did not figure at the finish, although the form looks sound rated around the runner-up to form.
City For Conquest(IRE) Official explanation: jockey said filly suffered interference just after the start
Sands Crooner(IRE) Official explanation: jockey said colt was denied a clear run
Jayanjay Official explanation: jockey said gelding was denied a clear run

6710 BETBROKERS "BETTING JUST GOT BETTER" MAIDEN AUCTION STKS 6f (P)
4:20 (4:20) (Class 5) 2-Y-0 **£3,238** (£963; £481; £240) **Stalls** High

Form RPR

3 **1** **Blue Charm**[34] 6290 2-8-12 LPKeniry 1 76+
(S Kirk) *lw: trckd ldng pair: led wl over 1f out: sn clr and in n.d: pushed out* **7/4**[1]

00 **2** 3 **Go Imperial (IRE)**[13] 6562 2-8-11 BrettDoyle 6 61
(M G Quinlan) *rrd s: t.k.h: trckd ldrs: outpcd by wnr over 1f out: kpt on to snatch 2nd on post* **25/1**

2320 **3** shd **Vadinka**[18] 6504 2-8-11 73 KimTinkler 4 61
(N Tinkler) *t.k.h: led for 2f: led again 3f out to wl over 1f out: bmpd along and sn outpcd: jst lost battle for 2nd* **5/2**[3]

0 **4** 2 **Mariaverdi**[40] 6186 2-7-11 KMay(7) 5 48
(B J Meehan) *s.i.s: hld up in rr: effrt over 2f out: sn outpcd: kpt on same pce* **20/1**

05 **5** ¾ **Tumblin Rosie**[13] 6562 2-8-5 FrancisNorton 8 46
(M Blanshard) *trckd ldrs: outpcd 2f out: fdd fnl f* **33/1**

604 **6** ¾ **Baytown Rosie (IRE)**[190] 2073 2-8-4 40 HayleyTurner 7 43
(P S McEntee) *towards rr: rdn and outpcd over 2f out: no ch after: plugged on* **50/1**

2 **7** ½ **Mankanja (IRE)**[33] 6309 2-8-5 ChrisCatlin 9 43
(W Jarvis) *unf: hld up in last: outpcd over 2f out: no real prog after* **9/4**[2]

5 **8** ½ **Play Straight**[24] 6441 2-8-6 NelsonDeSouza 2 42
(R M Beckett) *t.k.h: w ldr: led after 2f to 3f out: wknd over 1f out* **6/1**

9 1 **Shaded Edge** 2-8-10 EddieAhern 3 43
(D W P Arbuthnot) *leggy: dwlt: wl in rr: brief effrt over 2f out: sn btn* **20/1**

1m 14.94s (1.24) **Going Correction** +0.125s/f (Slow) 9 Ran SP% **128.3**
Speed ratings (Par 96):96,92,91,89,88 87,86,85,84
CSF £56.48 TOTE £2.80: £1.20, £5.80, £1.20; EX 62.80.
Owner A W Nielsen **Bred** Mrs R Pease **Trained** Upper Lambourn, Berks

FOCUS
Only one newcomer and the other eight all had previous experience of Polytrack. A modest maiden, but the winner was in a different league, although the form is limited by the proximity of the runner-up and sixth.

NOTEBOOK
Blue Charm, who had shown ability over seven furlongs here on his debut, had no problem with the drop in trip against these rivals and pulled right away in the closing stages. Considered a nice scopey sort by his trainer, he may turn out again in a novice event in the near future but the very best of him may not be seen until next year (op 6-4 tchd 2-1, 9-4 in places)
Go Imperial(IRE), despite being firmly put in his place by the winner, still improved considerably on his first two efforts and will be of more interest now that he can be handicapped. (op 33-1)
Vadinka was by far the most experienced in the line-up and ran his race again having been up with the pace throughout. This was his fifth placing on Polytrack, but he is proving very hard to win with. (op 9-2)
Mariaverdi was staying on late and showed a bit more than on her debut. She is nothing special, but may the type for handicaps in due course. (op 16-1)
Mankanja(IRE) has plenty of stamina in her pedigree so she was always likely to struggle over this shorter trip and so it proved. Under the circumstances it may be wise to forgive her this. (op 2-1 tchd 5-2 in a place)

6711 BETBROKERS OPEN AN ACCOUNT ON 0844 855 2111 NURSERY 6f (P)
4:50 (4:52) (Class 6) (0-65,63) 2-Y-0 **£3,238** (£963; £481; £240) **Stalls** High

Form RPR

0406 **1** **Theoretical**[17] 6520 2-8-13 60 NataliaGemelova(5) 5 64+
(A J McCabe) *s.i.s: hld up: prog on inner 3f out: led over 1f out: rdn and kpt on wl* **11/2**[2]

2042 **2** ¾ **Nou Camp**[10] 6592 2-8-13 55 ChrisCatlin 6 58+
(N A Callaghan) *lw: hld up bhd ldrs: nt clr run briefly wl over 1f out: effrt but nt qckn sn after: wnt 2nd last 200yds: clsd on wnr but hl* **1/2**[1]

0030 **3** 1¾ **Sweet World**[11] 6576 2-9-7 63 DaneO'Neill 7 60
(A P Jarvis) *mde most to over 2f out: nt qckn over 1f out: kpt on same pce* **8/1**

0002 **4** nk **Kilvickeon (IRE)**[4] 6665 2-8-5 47 (b) EddieAhern 3 43
(Peter Grayson) *lw: restless in stalls: hld up in last: effrt but outpcd 2f out: kpt on fnl f but n.d* **7/1**[3]

6400 **5** 2 **One White Sock**[20] 6487 2-8-3 48 (b[1]) MarcHalford(3) 4 38
(J L Spearing) *racd wd: pressed ldrs over 3f out: rdn and nt qckn wl over 1f out: edgd rt and wknd fnl f* **40/1**

0600 **6** 2 **Eastern Princess**[10] 6592 2-8-8 50 RichardThomas 1 37+
(J A Geake) *chsd ldrs: rdn over 2f out: sn struggling* **20/1**

0513 **7** 3 **Baytown Paikea**[4] 6665 2-9-4 60 BrianReilly 2 35
(P S McEntee) *pressed ldr: led over 2f out to over 1f out: wknd rapidly* **12/1**

1m 15.05s (1.35) **Going Correction** +0.125s/f (Slow) 7 Ran SP% **120.6**
Speed ratings (Par 94):96,95,92,92,89 86,82
CSF £9.29 TOTE £7.80: £4.20, £1.10; EX 16.80.
Owner Paul J Dixon and Michael F Maguire **Bred** Highclere Stud **Trained** Babworth, Notts

FOCUS
Not a great nursery and only one of the septet was a previous winner. The winning time was 0.11 seconds slower than the preceding maiden and the beaten favourite is the best guide to the level.

NOTEBOOK
Theoretical ◆ was one of the least exposed in the field and made a successful nursery debut under a well-judged ride, who made full use of the inside of the track where the false rail ends and was always holding the favourite from then on. She looks the type that could well go in again under a penalty. (op 6-1)
Nou Camp seemed to be in the perfect position throughout, but had to wait to get a clear run and also seemed to take a crack across the nose from a rival's whip a furlong out. Even so, once daylight appeared he took far too long to get into gear and was never going to get to the winner in time. This looked a decent opportunity for him to break his duck and he has questions to answer now. (op 4-6 tchd 8-11)
Sweet World was always up with the pace, but lacked speed where it mattered and the drop in trip did not seem to suit. (op 9-1 tchd 10-1)
Kilvickeon(IRE) did not help his chances by being unruly in the stalls and that may have contributed to him not confirming the promise of his recent Wolverhampton effort. (op 4-1)
One White Sock, with blinkers replacing the visor, was close enough turning in but did not get home. (tchd 33-1)
Baytown Paikea, the only previous winner in the field, could never dominate on her own and this sixth furlong stretches her. (op 9-1)

6712 BETBROKERS WORLD'S 1ST BET BROKER H'CAP 1m 4f (P)
5:20 (5:21) (Class 5) (0-70,69) 3-Y-0 **£3,886** (£1,156; £577; £288) **Stalls** Centre

Form RPR

5046 **1** **Pagano (IRE)**[10] 6590 3-8-12 63 AdamKirby 1 74
(W R Swinburn) *led at stdy pce: hdd 7f out: led again 4f out: hanging lft fnl 2f but styd on wl* **10/1**

0413 **2** 1½ **Blacktoft (USA)**[13] 6566 3-9-3 68 (e) OscarUrbina 2 77
(S C Williams) *dwlt: plld hrd: hld up: prog to chse wnr over 2f out: nt qckn over 1f out: hld after* **2/1**[2]

4061 **3** 2 **Broughtons Folly**[10] 6601 3-9-4 69 BrettDoyle 7 75
(W J Musson) *b: dwlt: t.k.h: hld up in rr: prog to chse ldng pair 2f out: rdn and one pce after* **6/5**[1]

0355 **4** 1 **Valuta (USA)**[3] 6668 3-8-7 65 (t) WilliamBuick(7) 5 69
(R A Kvisla) *trckd ldr to 7f out: lost pl and n.m.r over 2f out: rdn and one pce after* **10/1**

1552 **5** 6 **High Seasons**[19] 3540 3-8-8 66 JamesMillman(7) 6 60
(B R Millman) *s.s: t.k.h and hld up in rr: lost tch w ldrs over 2f out* **10/1**

-004 **6** 3 **Recalcitrant**[13] 6565 3-8-4 55 ChrisCatlin 8 45
(S Dow) *plld hrd: hld up in rr: rdn and struggling over 3f out: bhd fnl 2f* **8/1**[3]

1500 **7** ¾ **Ballybeg (IRE)**[10] 6590 3-8-9 63 (b) LiamJones(3) 3 51
(R J Price) *plld way through to ld 7f out: hdd 4f out: wknd rapidly over 2f out* **25/1**

11-6 **8** 1½ **Spunger**[20] 6494 3-9-0 65 DaneO'Neill 4 51
(H J L Dunlop) *trckd ldrs tl wknd rapidly over 2f out* **14/1**

2m 39.8s (2.90) **Going Correction** +0.125s/f (Slow) 8 Ran SP% **127.7**
Speed ratings (Par 102):95,94,92,92,88 86,85,84
CSF £34.17 CT £45.02 TOTE £10.50: £2.40, £1.10, £1.20; EX 42.30.
Owner The Chorus Line **Bred** Albert Conneally **Trained** Aldbury, Herts

FOCUS
A fair handicap on paper, but a messy contest as it turned out as nothing wanted to lead early and a few took a fierce grip as a result. The winning time was not surprisingly slow and the form is not easy top rate with confidence.

6713 BETBROKERS.COM H'CAP 6f (P)
5:50 (5:51) (Class 6) (0-53,53) 3-Y-0+ £2,590 (£770; £385; £192) Stalls High

Form RPR

4466 1 **Millfields Dreams**[21] 6477 7-8-12 **53** EddieAhern 8 63
(M G Quinlan) *trckd ldrs: effrt to ld 2f out: sn in command: rdn out* **9/4**[1]

6260 2 1 3/4 **Double Valentine**[156] 3118 3-8-11 **52** SteveDrowne 7 57
(R Ingram) *hld up in rr: prog 2f out: wnt 2nd jst over 1f out: styd on but no imp on wnr* **33/1**

4300 3 1 1/2 **Monte Major (IRE)**[7] 6629 5-8-12 **53** (v) DaneO'Neill 9 53
(D Shaw) *towards rr: rdn and effrt over 2f out: styd on to take 3rd jst ins fnl f: no imp ldng pair* **12/1**

2000 4 1 **Mostanad**[8] 6619 4-8-0 **48** (b) BarrySavage(7) 4 45
(J M Bradley) *wl in rr: effrt over 2f out: urged along on outer and kpt on fnl f* **50/1**

2356 5 1/2 **Labelled With Love**[11] 6577 6-8-11 **52** (t) IanMongan 11 50+
(J R Boyle) *dwlt: hld up in last: effrt 2f out: nt clr run over 1f out and swtchd rt: nt clr run fnl f: no ch* **10/3**[2]

5200 6 2 **Mind Alert**[7] 6632 5-8-9 **53** (v) PatrickMathers(3) 1 43
(D Shaw) *t.k.h: sn trckd ldrs: rdn 2f out: grad wknd* **16/1**

6003 7 1/2 **Mine The Balance (IRE)**[7] 6629 3-8-11 **52** (b) BrettDoyle 5 40
(J R Best) *bmpd s: t.k.h and sn w ldrs: wknd 2f out* **7/2**[3]

0010 8 1 1/2 **Stagnite**[17] 6513 6-8-11 **52** ChrisCatlin 2 36
(Karen George) *chsd ldrs: rdn bef 1/2-way: struggling over 2f out* **12/1**

0340 9 2 1/2 **Mystic Queen (IRE)**[7] 6642 3-8-11 **52** AdamKirby 12 28
(A P Jarvis) *chsd ldrs: rdn wl over 2f out: no prog wl over 1f out: wknd* **12/1**

0001 10 3/4 **Mulberry Lad (IRE)**[7] 6632 4-8-11 **52** 7ex PaulDoe 3 26
(P W Hiatt) *w ldr: led over 3f out to 2f out: wkng rapidly whn hmpd ins fnl f* **9/1**

1000 11 1/2 **Clearing Sky (IRE)**[24] 6442 5-8-9 **53** (p) AmirQuinn(3) 6 26
(J R Boyle) *racd freely: led to over 3f out: styd w ldr: wkng whn bdly bmpd fnl f* **16/1**

3300 12 hd **Thoughtsofstardom**[97] 4927 3-8-11 **52** (v) BrianReilly 10 24
(P S McEntee) *hld up in rr: effrt on inner over 2f out: nt clr run over 1f out: btn after and eased fnl f* **16/1**

1m 13.41s (-0.29) **Going Correction** +0.125s/f (Slow) 12 Ran SP% **131.7**
Speed ratings (Par 101):106,103,101,100,99 97,96,94,91,90 89,89
CSF £100.88 CT £816.06 TOTE £3.50: £1.60, £7.90, £4.00; EX 122.80.

Owner Mrs Theresa Fitsall **Bred** T G Price **Trained** Newmarket, Suffolk

FOCUS
A very tight handicap with 11 of the 12 runners rated within 1lb of each other, and the top weights were rated 53 which made this little better than a banded contest. Nonetheless, the winning time was decent for a race like this and the form appears solid.

Labelled With Love Official explanation: jockey said gelding was denied a clear run

Mine The Balance(IRE) Official explanation: jockey said gelding hung left

Clearing Sky(IRE) Official explanation: jockey said mare lost her action

6714 BETBROKERS BACK HERE ON 10TH APPRENTICE H'CAP 1m (P)
6:20 (6:20) (Class 6) (0-58,58) 3-Y-0+ £2,590 (£770; £385; £192) Stalls High

Form RPR

4000 1 **Scutch Mill (IRE)**[2] 6687 4-9-1 **58** (t) JerryO'Dwyer(3) 5 68
(Karen George) *lw: hld up: prog on outer fr 1/2-way: hanging rt over 2f out: drvn and r.o to ld over 1f out: styd on wl* **5/1**[2]

5355 2 1 3/4 **Beneking**[185] 2223 6-8-10 **55** JosephWalsh(5) 6 61
(D Burchell) *lw: led: rdn over 2f out: hdd over 1f out: kpt on same pce* **9/1**

2242 3 1 3/4 **Jomus**[24] 6436 5-8-11 **56** (b) JamesMillman(5) 12 58
(L Montague Hall) *hld up in rr: prog to trck ldrs over 2f out: rdn and nt qckn over 1f out: kpt on same pce after* **5/2**[1]

0503 4 1 1/2 **Kareeb (FR)**[11] 6577 9-9-1 **55** MarcHalford 7 54
(Miss J Feilden) *prom: trckd ldr over 3f out: poised to chal gng easily over 2f out: rdn and fnd nil over 1f out* **13/2**

0000 5 1 1/4 **True West (USA)**[10] 6608 3-9-0 **55** (v) AdamKirby 1 51
(Miss Gay Kelleway) *wl in tch: effrt on inner over 2f out: drvn and one pce fnl 2f* **20/1**

0 6 1 3/4 **Rinty (NZ)**[25] 6429 4-9-3 **57** StephaneBreux 2 49
(C G Cox) *mostly chsd ldr to over 3f out: sn outpcd and rdn: one pce after* **10/1**

00-0 7 1 1/2 **Sticky Mint (IRE)**[8] 6618 3-7-13 **47** LauraReynolds(7) 9 35
(M Blanshard) *hld up in midfield: urged along and outpcd 3f out: n.d after* **66/1**

0300 8 3/4 **Little Miss Verity**[28] 6389 3-8-5 **46** oh1 RichardKingscote 8 32
(J A Geake) *t.k.h: hld up bhd ldrs: outpcd over 2f out: no ch after* **50/1**

2535 9 2 1/2 **Hotchpotch (USA)**[7] 6632 3-8-8 **54** KylieManser(5) 14 35
(J R Best) *t.k.h: prom tl wknd over 2f out* **10/1**

5600 10 hd **Hadath (IRE)**[11] 6577 9-8-5 **50** (b) PatrickHills(5) 3 30
(B G Powell) *lw: a in rr: urged along and no prog over 2f out* **10/1**

54 11 3 1/2 **Connotation**[29] 6383 4-9-0 **54** AmirQuinn 4 26
(A G Newcombe) *s.s: detached in last: nvr a factor* **11/2**[3]

0/00 12 6 **Electrique (IRE)**[49] 6037 6-8-8 **55** (v) AdamCarter(7) 11 13
(A J McCabe) *lw: chsd ldrs tl wknd rapidly 3f out* **12/1**

-060 13 8 **Veba (USA)**[10] 6593 3-8-7 **55** FrankiePickard(7) 10 —
(M D I Usher) *t.k.h: hld up towards rr: wknd 3f out: sn bhd* **50/1**

1m 42.0s (1.20) **Going Correction** +0.125s/f (Slow)
WFA 3 from 4yo+ 1lb 13 Ran SP% **129.1**
Speed ratings (Par 101):99,97,95,94,92 91,89,88,86,86 82,76,68
CSF £52.80 CT £149.13 TOTE £6.60: £1.90, £4.10, £1.40; EX 114.60 Place 6 £12.09, Place 5 £5.36..

Owner B R Phillips **Bred** Denis McDonnell **Trained** Higher Easington, Devon

FOCUS
Another modest handicap with the top weight rated just 58, but still pretty competitive and the early pace looked decent. The runner-up was rated to form.

True West(USA) Official explanation: jockey said filly hung left up the straight

Veba(USA) Official explanation: jockey said gelding pulled up lame

T/Plt: £27.00 to a £1 stake. Pool: £59,799.45. 1,615.15 winning tickets. T/Qpdt: £9.60 to a £1 stake. Pool: £4,517.40. 346.90 winning tickets. JN

6674 SOUTHWELL (L-H)
Tuesday, December 5

OFFICIAL GOING: Standard
Wind: Moderate, across.

6715 WBX.COM WORLD BET EXCHANGE NURSERY 5f (F)
12:30 (12:30) (Class 5) (0-75,73) 2-Y-O £3,238 (£963; £481; £240) Stalls High

Form RPR

33 1 **Diminuto**[25] 6422 2-7-7 **52** FrankiePickard(7) 4 55
(M D I Usher) *mde all: rdn wl over 1f out: styd on* **7/1**

0406 2 1 1/4 **Cryptic Clue (USA)**[57] 5860 2-8-1 **53** PaulQuinn 7 52
(D W Chapman) *dwlt: hdwy to chse ldrs after 2f: rdn 2f out: styd on u.p ins last: nrst fin* **14/1**

0300 3 shd **Minimum Fuss (IRE)**[48] 6056 2-8-0 **59** MCGeran(7) 3 57
(M C Chapman) *chsd ldrs: hdwy 2f out and sn rdn:drvn and styng on whn hung rt ins last: nrst fin* **9/1**

000 4 3/4 **Suntan Lady (IRE)**[4] 6665 2-7-8 **51** oh4 ow1 (p) DuranFentiman(5) 1 46
(Miss V Haigh) *outpcd and pushed along 1/2-way: rdn 2f out: styd on appr last: nrst fin* **66/1**

6551 5 3 1/2 **Billy Ruffian**[4] 6665 2-9-4 **70** 6ex DavidAllan 8 53
(T D Easterby) *cl up: rdn along over 2f out: sn drvn and wknd wl over 1f out* **15/8**[1]

2436 6 2 1/2 **Perlachy**[82] 5307 2-9-0 **73** RussellKennemore(7) 6 47
(Mrs N Macauley) *cl up: rdn along 1/2-way: sn wknd* **9/2**[3]

453 7 3/4 **Tang**[10] 6605 2-8-9 **61** TonyCulhane 2 32
(W G M Turner) *chsd ldrs on outer: rdn along 1/2-way: sn wknd* **11/4**[2]

4560 8 6 **Lady Chastity**[57] 5876 2-8-3 **55** DaleGibson 5 5
(Mrs L J Young) *sn outpcd and a bhd* **25/1**

61.10 secs (0.80) **Going Correction** -0.025s/f (Stan) 8 Ran SP% **114.1**
Speed ratings (Par 96):92,90,89,88,83 79,77,68
CSF £96.02 CT £890.02 TOTE £8.50: £2.30, £4.20, £3.80; EX 70.90 Trifecta £125.70 Part won. Pool £177.10. - 0.34 winning units..

Owner R H Brookes **Bred** B Minty **Trained** Upper Lambourn, Berks

■ Stewards' Enquiry : M C Geran ten-day ban: failed to ride out (Dec 16, 18-23, 26-28)

FOCUS
A moderate sprint nursery and the form looks fair enough.

NOTEBOOK
Diminuto, third from a high draw over six at this track last time, was rightly given a very positive ride and readily got back to winning ways. This well-named filly rarely does much wrong in her races and she looked well suited by this straight five furlongs. (op 5-1)

Cryptic Clue(USA), making his All-Weather debut after a 57-day break, was always playing catch-up after a sluggish start and never seriously threatened to hit the front at any stage. He is entitled to improve for this outing, however, and left the impression he has a race within him compass from this sort of mark, perhaps back over a sixth furlong. (op 12-1)

Minimum Fuss(IRE), whose only previous success came in a seller over course and distance in July, turned in an improved effort on this return from a 48-day break yet again looked tricky. Her rider appeared to take things a little easy towards the finish - losing second place in the process - and was subsequently banned for failing to ride out to the line. That was perhaps a little harsh, however, as the filly was hanging and did look to duck in behind the winner somewhat. (tchd 10-1)

Suntan Lady(IRE), 4lb out of the handicap, was always struggling to go the pace yet still finished her race with a degree of promise. The first-time cheekpieces looked to have a positive effect. (op 50-1)

Billy Ruffian, off the mark at Wolverhampton four days previously, was a different proposition under his penalty on this deeper surface and ran well below his best. He may have found this coming too soon, but it is more likely that he is a much happier horse on Polytrack. (op 2-1 tchd 5-2)

Perlachy, making his All-Weather debut for new connections, has been gelded during his break and this has to rate a disappointing effort. It may prove that he prefers one of the other All-Weather tracks, and the return to six furlongs, but he does look flattered by his current official rating all the same. (op 6-1)

Tang, making her handicap debut, was unable to get to the front and ran poorly as a result. She could be better off when reverting to Polytrack, but her stable's last winner was back in July and she is one to avoid for win-only purposes. Official explanation: trainer had no explanation for the poor form shown (op 5-2 tchd 9-4 and 3-1 in a place)

6716 WBXTRIPLECROWN.COM H'CAP 1m 3f (F)
1:00 (1:00) (Class 5) (0-75,74) 3-Y-0+ £3,238 (£963; £481; £240) Stalls Low

Form RPR

0031 1 **Zed Candy (FR)**[21] 6474 3-8-2 **60** oh3 DaleGibson 6 69
(J T Stimpson) *trckd ldrs: hdwy over 3f out: sn rdn along: drvn over 1f out kpt on u.p ins last to ld nr fin* **9/2**[3]

4002 2 nk **William's Way**[20] 6494 4-9-2 **70** LeeEnstone 4 78
(I A Wood) *hld up in tch: smooth hdwy 4f out: led over 2f out: sn rdn and hung bdly lft over 1f out: sn drvn: hdd and no ex nr fin* **12/1**

034 3 1 1/4 **Speed Dial Harry (IRE)**[25] 6424 4-9-1 **74** (v) AndrewElliott(5) 7 80
(K R Burke) *trckd ldrs: hdwy 4f out: cl up over 2f out: rdn: sltly hmpd and swtchd rt wl over 1f out: sn drvn and kpt on* **3/1**[2]

0002 4 nk **Prince Of Love (IRE)**[21] 6474 3-8-7 **65** PaulHanagan 8 71
(Jedd O'Keeffe) *keen: cl up: led over 3f out: rdn and hdd over 2f out: drvn and hmpd over 1f out: kpt on u.p ins last* **9/4**[1]

6234 5 10 **Stolen Glance**[21] 6474 3-8-7 **65** PaulMulrennan 9 54
(M W Easterby) *prom tl rdn along and outpcd over 4f out* **9/1**

4000 6 1/2 **Mister Maq**[12] 6571 3-8-2 **60** oh4 (b) JimmyQuinn 5 48
(A Crook) *midfield: hdwy to chse ldrs over 4f out: n.m.r and swtchd rt over 3f out: sn rdn and wknd fnl 2f* **40/1**

51-3 7 9 **Stravara**[20] 6494 3-9-0 **72** GrahamGibbons 3 45
(R Hollinshead) *hld up: a rr* **14/1**

0606 8 8 **Greenbelt**[21] 6474 5-8-7 **61** ow1 (p) TomEaves 1 20
(G M Moore) *led: rdn along and hdd over 3f out: sn wknd* **7/1**

055 9 114 **Out Of This Way**[25] 6429 3-8-5 **63** (t) JoeFanning 2 —
(I A Wood) *outpcd and bhd fr 1/2-way* **22/1**

2m 26.26s (-2.64) **Going Correction** -0.175s/f (Stan)
WFA 3 from 4yo+ 4lb 9 Ran SP% **117.6**
Speed ratings (Par 103):102,101,100,100,93 93,86,80,—
CSF £57.86 CT £188.46 TOTE £6.10: £1.40, £2.40, £1.50; EX 48.40 Trifecta £104.90 Pool £223.14. - 1.51 winning units..

Owner J T S (International) Ltd **Bred** Haras De Saint Pair Du Mont **Trained** Newcastle-Under-Lyme, Staffs

FOCUS
A modest handicap that was run at a solid pace. The form looks sound enough with the first four coming clear and is rated at face value.

Stolen Glance Official explanation: jockey said filly hung left

Greenbelt Official explanation: jockey said gelding hung right

Out Of This Way Official explanation: jockey said colt had a breathing problem

6717 WBX.COM WORLD BET EXCHANGE (S) STKS — 6f (F)

1:30 (1:30) (Class 6) 3-Y-0+ — £2,388 (£705; £352) — Stalls Low

Form — RPR

00-0 **1** — **Skip Of Colour**[58] 5842 6-9-0 55 ....(t) PaulHanagan 8 — 56
(P A Blockley) *cl up: led 2f out: sn rdn: edgd lft and drvn ent last: styd on* — 11/4[1]

6626 **2** 1 ¾ **Sion Hill (IRE)**[7] 6637 5-8-7 45 ....(p) RussellKennemore(7) 10 — 51
(Mrs N Macauley) *trckd ldrs: hdwy over 2f out: rdn to chal over 1f out and ev ch till drvn and no ex ins last* — 12/1

0056 **3** nk **Ace Club**[7] 6636 5-9-0 45 ....(b) RobbieFitzpatrick 5 — 50
(M J Attwater) *in tch: hdwy 2f out: sn rdn: styd on ins last: nrst fin* — 33/1

5002 **4** ½ **The City Kid (IRE)**[7] 6636 3-8-9 55 ....(p) TonyCulhane 13 — 44
(P D Evans) *sn pushed along and towards rr: rdn 1/2-way: hdwy 2f out: styd on wl fnl f: nrst fin* — 11/2

5005 **5** 2 ½ **A Teen**[14] 6550 8-9-0 45 .... DeanCorby 7 — 41
(P Howling) *towards rr: hdwy over 2f out: sn rdn and kpt on same pce appr last* — 16/1

0044 **6** 3 **Further Outlook (USA)**[7] 6638 12-9-7 60 ....(tp) DarryllHolland 9 — 39
(Miss Gay Kelleway) *chsd ldrs: rdn over 2f out: kpt on same pce* — 4/1[2]

3233 **7** nk **Balian**[7] 6637 3-9-0 52 ....(b) MickyFenton 2 — 31
(Mrs P Sly) *led: rdn along over 2f out: sn hdd and grad wknd* — 5/1[3]

0530 **8** ½ **The London Gang**[20] 6493 3-9-0 55 ....(p) MCGeran(7) 11 — 37
(P D Evans) *s.i.s and bhd tl sme late hdwy* — 9/1

0600 **9** 1 ¼ **Sounds Simla (IRE)**[15] 6541 3-8-11 48 ....(b[1]) JerryO'Dwyer(5) 4 — 28
(R A Harris) *sn outpcd in rr: hdwy 1/2-way: rdn along over 2f out and sn no imp* — 33/1

0004 **10** 1 ½ **Woodwee**[7] 6636 3-9-0 54 ....(b) TomEaves 12 — 21
(J R Weymes) *a midfield* — 33/1

0005 **11** 3 **Phinerine**[114] 4398 3-9-0 62 ....(b) TolleyDean(7) 6 — 19
(R A Harris) *cl up: rdn wl over 2f out and sn btn* — 16/1

3000 **12** 12 **Sweetly Sharp (IRE)**[57] 5864 3-8-9 40 .... PaulQuinn 14 — —
(A Berry) *s.i.s: a bhd* — 66/1

00-0 **13** 3 **Liverti**[27] 6406 3-8-10 35 ow1 .... DanielTudhope 1 — —
(D Carroll) *a rr* — 100/1

0400 **14** 42 **Jumanji (IRE)**[8] 6618 3-8-9 45 ....(v) DeanMernagh 3 — —
(M J Attwater) *in tch on inner: bit slipped and hung rt 1/2-way: sn bhd* — 33/1

1m 17.3s (0.40) **Going Correction** -0.175s/f (Stan) — **14** Ran SP% **122.4**
Speed ratings (Par 101):90,87,87,86,83 79,78,78,76,74 70,54,50,—
CSF £37.09 TOTE £2.80: £1.10, £3.40, £6.10; EX 58.40 TRIFECTA Not won..There was no bid for the winner.
Owner Mrs Joanna Hughes **Bred** Juddmonte Farms **Trained** Lambourn, Berks

FOCUS
A very moderate time, even for a seller, and the form is weak. The well-backed winner did not have to run up to his mark to score and the next three home represent better guides to the level.
Jumanji(IRE) Official explanation: jockey said bit slipped through filly's mouth

6718 WBX.COM H'CAP — 1m 6f (F)

2:00 (2:01) (Class 5) (0-75,74) 3-Y-0+ — £3,238 (£963; £481; £240) — Stalls Low

Form — RPR

2202 **1** — **Flame Creek (IRE)**[8] 6626 10-9-6 66 .... EdwardCreighton 2 — 92+
(E J Creighton) *hld up: stdy hdwy 5f out: led 3f out: sn rdn clr: easily* — 8/1

6043 **2** 14 **Amwell Brave**[13] 6565 5-9-0 60 .... PaulHanagan 3 — 63
(J R Jenkins) *hld up in tch: hdwy over 4f out: rdn along 3f out: drvn to chse wnr over 2f out: sn no imp* — 5/1[1]

0550 **3** 5 **Bienheureux**[13] 6565 5-8-9 58 ....(t[1]) DominicFox(3) 8 — 54
(Miss Gay Kelleway) *hld up in rr: hdwy over 3f out: styd on fnl 2f: nvr a factor* — 8/1

0031 **4** 1 ½ **Cragganmore Creek**[14] 6551 3-8-10 63 ....(b) DerekMcGaffin 6 — 57
(D Morris) *prom: effrt 4f out: rdn along 3f out and sn outpcd* — 5/1[1]

0550 **5** 4 **Entranced**[13] 6565 3-8-10 63 .... TomEaves 9 — 51
(Miss J A Camacho) *trckd ldr: led over 4f out: rdn and hdd 3f out: sn drvn and wknd* — 5/1[1]

0100 **6** ½ **Optimum (IRE)**[14] 5390 4-8-11 57 .... MickyFenton 5 — 45
(J T Stimpson) *trckd ldrs: rdn along over 5f out: sn btn* — 6/1[2]

5200 **7** 5 **Sand Repeal (IRE)**[188] 2140 4-9-1 68 .... AmyBaker(7) 1 — 49
(Miss J Feilden) *chsd ldrs: rdn along and outpcd fr 1/2-way* — 16/1

0264 **8** 1 ¼ **Victory Quest (IRE)**[8] 6626 6-9-3 63 ....(v) PatCosgrave 10 — 42
(Mrs S Lamyman) *led: rdn along 5f out: sn hdd & wknd* — 8/1

01 **9** 43 **Stolen Light (IRE)**[15] 6537 5-10-0 74 ....(b) DarryllHolland 7 — —
(A Crook) *chsd ldrs on outer: rdn along over 4f out: wknd over 3f out* — 13/2[3]

60-0 **10** 1 ¼ **Worlaby Dale**[8] 6626 10-8-9 55 oh25 .... CatherineGannon 11 — —
(Mrs S Lamyman) *a bhd* — 100/1

0000 **P** — **Legal Set (IRE)**[14] 6555 10-8-6 57 oh15 ow2 ....(t) AnnStokell(5) 4 — —
(Miss A Stokell) *in tch: lost pl after 5f: t.o 1/2-way: p.u over 3f out and dismntd* — 100/1

3m 5.33s (-4.27) **Going Correction** -0.175s/f (Stan)
WFA 3 from 4yo+ 7lb — **11** Ran SP% **118.8**
Speed ratings (Par 103):105,97,94,93,91 90,87,87,62,61 —
CSF £48.29 CT £335.95 TOTE £7.80: £2.80, £2.40, £2.60; EX 38.30 Trifecta £210.10 Part won. Pool £295.99 - 0.84 winning units..
Owner Estrella Partners **Bred** Kilcornan Stables **Trained** East Garston, Berks

FOCUS
A modest handicap which was run at a strong early pace rated through the second to his recent mark. Eddie Creighton's first winner in Britain since a spell training in Spain.
Stolen Light(IRE) Official explanation: jockey said gelding hung right-handed throughout
Legal Set(IRE) Official explanation: vet said gelding finished distressed

6719 EXPERIENCE NOTTINGHAMSHIRE H'CAP — 6f (F)

2:30 (2:31) (Class 6) (0-57,57) 3-Y-0+ — £2,730 (£806; £403) — Stalls Low

Form — RPR

0531 **1** — **Larky's Lob**[15] 6533 7-9-1 56 .... TonyCulhane 11 — 71
(J O'Reilly) *cl up: led 1/2-way: rdn clr wl over 1f out: styd on strly* — 11/2[2]

4063 **2** 5 **Majik**[7] 6636 7-8-11 57 ....(p) RoryMoore(5) 6 — 57
(P T Midgley) *in tch: hdwy 2f out: sn rdn and kpt on ins last: no ch w wnr* — 18/1

3040 **3** shd **Rancho Cucamonga (IRE)**[81] 5350 4-8-6 54 ....(b) NeilBrown(7) 1 — 54+
(T D Barron) *dwlt and bhd tl styd on fnl 2f: nrst fin* — 9/1

4000 **4** 1 ½ **Christian Bendix**[14] 6554 4-8-7 48 .... DeanCorby 13 — 43
(P Howling) *prom: rdn along over 2f out: sn drvn and kpt on same pce* — 25/1

0000 **5** 1 ¾ **Tiviski (IRE)**[17] 6513 4-8-13 54 .... TinaSmith 5 — 44
(Miss Gay Kelleway) *in tch: rdn along wl over 2f out: sn no imp* — 40/1

4305 **6** 2 **Orchestration (IRE)**[8] 6619 5-8-7 48 ow2 ....(v) RobbieFitzpatrick 12 — 32
(M J Attwater) *towards rr: hdwy on inenr 1/2-way: rdn over 2f out: sn no imp* — 5/1[1]

0000 **7** ½ **Hillbilly Cat (USA)**[17] 6510 3-9-0 55 .... RobertHavlin 2 — 37
(R Ingram) *chsd ldrs: rdn along wl over 2f out: grad wknd* — 7/1

0300 **8** ½ **Dancing Deano (IRE)**[28] 6390 4-8-9 55 ....(v) MichaelJStainton(5) 3 — 36
(R M Whitaker) *bhd tl sme late hdwy* — 6/1[3]

6000 **9** ½ **Amber Glory**[22] 6464 3-8-11 52 ....(b) CatherineGannon 8 — 31
(K A Ryan) *led: hdd 1/2-way: sn rdn along and wknd* — 33/1

0400 **10** ½ **Rambling Socks**[7] 6637 3-8-8 52 ....(p) JasonEdmunds(3) 10 — 30
(S R Bowring) *towards rr: swtchd rt and effrt 1/2-way: sn rdn and no hdwy* — 100/1

1502 **11** ½ **Howards Princess**[15] 6538 4-8-12 53 ....(p) DaleGibson 4 — 29
(J Hetherton) *chsd ldrs: rdn along 1/2-way: sn wknd* — 8/1

6130 **12** 1 ¼ **Guadaloup**[7] 6642 4-9-0 55 ....(v) DeanMernagh 9 — 28
(M Brittain) *s.i.s and swtchd outside s: rdn wl over 2f out and nvr a factor* — 12/1

0546 **13** 2 **Val De Maal (IRE)**[14] 6556 6-9-0 55 ....(b) TomEaves 7 — 22
(Miss J A Camacho) *midfield: effrt and in tch over 2f out: sn rdn and btn* — 11/2[2]

000 **14** 5 **Obe Bold (IRE)**[33] 6308 5-8-5 46 oh1 .... AdrianTNicholls 14 — —
(A Berry) *midfield on outer: n.m.r 1/2-way: sn rdn and wknd* — 50/1

1m 15.99s (-0.91) **Going Correction** -0.175s/f (Stan) — **14** Ran SP% **120.5**
Speed ratings (Par 101):99,92,92,90,87 85,84,83,83,82 81,80,77,70
CSF £96.19 CT £911.01 TOTE £5.40: £2.20, £3.80, £3.20; EX 41.70 Trifecta £144.60 Part won. Pool £203.67 - 0.20 winning units..
Owner J Morris **Bred** P Balding **Trained** Doncaster, S Yorks

FOCUS
A weak sprint handicap that was run at a fair pace with the winner back to his best.
Val De Maal(IRE) Official explanation: jockey said gelding ran too keen early on

6720 WBX.COM WORLD BET EXCHANGE H'CAP — 5f (F)

3:00 (3:00) (Class 3) (0-90,90) 3-Y-0+ — £8,096 (£2,408; £1,203; £601) — Stalls High

Form — RPR

036 **1** — **Stoneacre Lad (IRE)**[20] 6496 3-8-11 83 ....(b) RobbieFitzpatrick 7 — 92+
(Peter Grayson) *wnt rt s: prom: rdn to ld over 1f out: hung lft ins last: kpt on wl* — 22/1

1566 **2** 1 **Moorhouse Lad**[11] 6583 3-8-11 83 .... JimmyQuinn 6 — 89
(G Woodward) *a cl up: led wl over 1f out: sn rdn and hdd appr last: kpt on same pce* — 12/1

5400 **3** ¾ **Pawan (IRE)**[20] 6496 6-8-6 83 oh1 ow7 ....(b) AnnStokell(5) 5 — 86
(Miss A Stokell) *chsd ldrs: rdn wl over 1f out: kpt on ins last* — 66/1

0135 **4** ¾ **Matuza (IRE)**[11] 6583 3-8-11 83 .... DarryllHolland 4 — 84
(W R Muir) *in tch: swtchd lft 1/2-way: rdn to chse ldrs wl over 1f out: sn drvn and one pce fnl f* — 11/4[2]

141 **5** 2 ½ **Dancing Mystery**[20] 6496 12-8-11 83 ....(b) StephenCarson 1 — 75
(E A Wheeler) *led: rdn along 2f out: sn hdd and grad wknd* — 7/1[3]

3111 **6** ½ **Night Prospector**[3] 6682 6-8-2 81 6ex ....(p) TolleyDean(7) 2 — 72
(R A Harris) *in tch whn hmpd and swtchd rt 2f out: sn rdn and no imp* — 2/1[1]

6053 **7** nk **Efistorm**[3] 6682 5-8-0 77 .... DuranFentiman(5) 9 — 67
(J Balding) *chsd ldrs: rdn 2f out: grad wknd* — 8/1

0520 **8** 1 **Anfield Dream**[11] 6585 4-8-4 76 oh1 .... PaulHanagan 10 — 62
(J R Jenkins) *chsd ldrs: hdwy 2f out: sn rdn and wknd appr last* — 20/1

3031 **9** 1 ¾ **First Order**[11] 6583 5-9-4 90 ....(v) TomEaves 8 — 70
(I Semple) *bmpd s: sn rdn along: a outpcd in rr* — 7/1[3]

6001 **10** ¾ **Le Chiffre (IRE)**[7] 6636 4-7-13 73 6ex ....(b) AndrewElliott(5) 3 — 54
(K R Burke) *a rr* — 20/1

58.71 secs (-1.59) **Going Correction** -0.025s/f (Stan) — **10** Ran SP% **119.2**
Speed ratings (Par 107):111,109,108,107,103 102,101,100,97,96
CSF £254.48 CT £15895.13 TOTE £19.70: £4.00, £3.00, £7.30; EX 109.70 TRIFECTA Not won..
Owner Richard Teatum **Bred** Mrs Annie Hughes **Trained** Formby, Lancs

FOCUS
A decent sprint and the form looks solid.

NOTEBOOK
Stoneacre Lad(IRE) had clearly done well since his return from a break behind Dancing Mystery at this venue last time and he bounced back to his best with a ready success. He is clearly a useful sprinter when the mood takes him and was racing from a 2lb lower mark than when successful at Leicester during the summer. While the Handicapper will now have his say, he should be high on confidence now and should at least remain competitive. (op 14-1)
Moorhouse Lad, nibbled at in the betting ring, showed much-improved form and had every chance. This was his best effort since winning on the turf ealier in the year, he looked suited by this surface and can build on this. (op 14-1)
Pawan(IRE) came through to run an improved race and showed his true colours in defeat. His trainer/rider often carries overweight, and he has in the past run very well in the face of some stiff tasks, so the form should not be downgraded despite his proximity from a 1lb out of the handicap.
Matuza(IRE), most unlucky not to have finished closer at Wolverhampton last time, met support in the betting ring yet was never really looking happy on this drop back to the minimum distance. This was disappointing, but it could well be that this imposing sprinter may need all of six furlongs now. (op 10-3 tchd 7-2 in places)
Dancing Mystery, in great form of late, was soon at the head of affairs as he prefers yet he was unable to sustain his effort when it really mattered. He is a decent benchmark for the form. (op 8-1 tchd 9-1)
Night Prospector, searching for a four-timer, was not done any favours when hampered nearing the two furlong marker. However, he was not travelling as well has he can at that stage and it is more likely that his recent busy period is catching up with him now. It will be interesting to see how he fares from his new future mark. Official explanation: trainer said gelding never travelled (tchd 15-8 and 5-2 in places)

6721 WORLD BET EXCHANGE H'CAP — 7f (F)

3:30 (3:30) (Class 6) (0-60,65) 3-Y-0+ — £2,730 (£806; £403) — Stalls Low

Form — RPR

332 **1** — **Mozakhraf (USA)**[7] 6642 4-8-7 57 .... JamieJones(7) 4 — 74
(K A Ryan) *trckd ldrs: smooth hdwy to ld 2f out: rdn over 1f out: hung rt ins last: drvn out* — 1/1[1]

0505 **2** 1 ¼ **Tamatave (IRE)**[32] 6323 4-9-2 59 .... CatherineGannon 5 — 73
(K A Ryan) *trckd ldrs: hdwy to chse wnr wl over 1f out: sn rdn: kpt on ins last: n.m.r towards fin* — 20/1

0320 **3** 5 **Solicitude**[10] 6608 3-8-10 53 .... RobertHavlin 10 — 54
(D Haydn Jones) *midfield: hdwy 2f out: sn rdn: styd on u.p ins last* — 16/1

0142 **4** nk **Windy Prospect**[3] 6674 4-9-0 57 .... PaulHanagan 11 — 57
(P A Blockley) *cl up: led 1/2-way: rdn and hdd 2f out: sn drvn and grad wknd* — 11/4[2]

3030 **5** 2 **Chickado (IRE)**[8] 6624 5-8-6 49 ....(p) JamieMackay 13 — 44
(D Haydn Jones) *bhd tl styd on fnl 2f* — 25/1

6 1 **Mouseen (IRE)**[104] 4721 3-8-8 **58**....(p) TolleyDean[(7)] 3 — 50
(R A Harris) *s.i.s and bhd tl styd on fnl 2f* **50/1**

6205 7 ½ **Tamworth (IRE)**[22] 6464 4-9-1 **58**.... EdwardCreighton 7 — 49
(E J Creighton) *hld up in rr: effrt over 2f out: sn rdn and no imp* **20/1**

060 8 2 **Miswadah (IRE)**[11] 6587 3-9-1 **58**.... JoeFanning 14 — 44
(Kevin F O'Donnell, Ire) *prom: rdn along wl over 2f out: sn drvn and wknd* **66/1**

0202 9 hd **Double Carpet (IRE)**[20] 6490 3-8-9 **52**.... TomEaves 9 — 37
(G Woodward) *midfield: rdn along 1/2-way: nvr a factor* **25/1**

6500 10 nk **Cape Of Storms**[53] 5936 3-8-11 **54**.... PatCosgrave 12 — 39
(R Brotherton) *chsd ldrs on outer: rdn along wl over 2f out: sn wknd* **50/1**

0000 11 1 **Grafton (IRE)**[147] 3378 3-8-12 **55**.... TonyCulhane 1 — 37
(J O'Reilly) *keen: in tch on inner: rdn along over 2f out and sn wknd* **66/1**

0400 12 ¾ **Crusoe (IRE)**[8] 6628 9-8-0 **50**....(b) AmyBaker[(7)] 6 — 30
(A Sadik) *a rr* **50/1**

0111 13 6 **Bodden Bay**[7] 6638 4-9-8 **65** 6ex.... DarryllHolland 2 — 29
(Miss Gay Kelleway) *led: rdn along and hdd 1/2-way: sn wknd* **13/2**[3]

1m 29.11s (-1.69) **Going Correction** -0.175s/f (Stan) **13** Ran SP% **122.0**
Speed ratings (Par 101):102,100,94,94,92 91,90,88,88,87 86,85,78
CSF £30.75 CT £227.66 TOTE £1.60: £1.10, £4.50, £3.90; EX 30.70 Trifecta £342.10 Pool £486.71 - 1.01 winning units. Place 6 £7,749.55, Place 5 £1,330.93..
Owner Mrs J Ryan **Bred** Audley Farm Inc **Trained** Hambleton, N Yorks
■ Stewards' Enquiry : Jamie Jones caution: careless riding

FOCUS
A moderate handicap which saw the first two - stable companions - come clear. The form is strong for the grade and rated around the fourth.
T/Jkpt: Not won. T/Plt: £16,715.10 to a £1 stake. Pool: £48,084.80. 2.10 winning tickets. T/Qpdt: £818.40 to a £1 stake. Pool: £3,649.70. 3.30 winning tickets. JR

6609 SAINT-CLOUD (L-H)
Tuesday, December 5

OFFICIAL GOING: Heavy

6722a PRIX PETITE ETOILE (LISTED RACE) (FILLIES) 1m 2f 110y
1:55 (2:00) 3-Y-O **£17,241** (£6,897; £5,172; £3,448; £1,724)

RPR

1 **Pearl Sky (FR)**[10] 3-8-11 .... ACrastus 5 — 97
(Y De Nicolay, France)

2 2 **Ragazza Mio (IRE)**[13] 6567 3-8-11 .... YLetondeur 13 — 93
(N Clement, France)

3 1 **Quezon Sun (GER)**[29] 6384 3-8-11 .... YBarberot 8 — 92
(S Wattel, France)

4 ¾ **Fringe**[25] 6429 3-8-11 .... WMLordan 9 — 90
(Jane Chapple-Hyam) *niggled along early, rcd in 4th, pushed along 4f out, brought wide and rdn to press ldr over 2f out, no ex fnl f* **22/1**[2]

5 4 **Tequila Brown (FR)**[29] 6384 3-8-11 .... TJarnet 7 — 83
(M Delzangles, France)

6 1 ½ **Under The Rainbow**[31] 6333 3-8-11 .... IMendizabal 6 — 80
(P W Chapple-Hyam) *prom on inside, led narrowly over 2f out to over 1 1/2f out, weakened* **41/10**[1]

7 1 **Negra Del Oro (GER)**[67] 3-8-11 .... JAuge 12 — 79
(A Lund, Norway)

8 2 **Beiramar (IRE)**[30] 6367 3-8-11 .... J-PCarvalho 3 — 75
(W Hickst, Germany)

9 2 ½ **Partly Sunny**[32] 3-8-11 .... THuet 11 — 70
(J E Pease, France)

10 ½ **Maisha (GER)**[46] 3-8-11 .... GBenoist 10 — 70
(D Smaga, France)

0 **Sureyya (GER)**[29] 6384 3-8-11 .... GFaucon 1 — —
(E Lellouche, France)

0 **Tech Engine (GER)**[37] 6251 3-8-11 .... WMongil 4 — —
(P Schiergen, Germany)

0 **Ballymore Lady (USA)**[93] 5050 3-8-11 .... CSoumillon 2 — —
(Rod Collet, France)

2m 25.6s **13** Ran SP% **24.0**
PARI-MUTUEL: WIN 10.90; PL 3.40, 10.10, 4.40; DF 257.70.
Owner H Hogg **Bred** Mme Patricia Beck **Trained** France

NOTEBOOK
Fringe, who is relatively inexperienced, struggled to get involved early and, after having a chance at the quarter-mile pole, tired late on, just missing out on black type.
Under The Rainbow handles soft ground and was ridden close to the pace, but she gradually weakened out of contention in the straight.

6709 KEMPTON (A.W) (R-H)
Wednesday, December 6

OFFICIAL GOING: Standard
Wind: moderate, behind

6723 KEMPTON FOR TEAM BUILDING BANDED STKS 5f (P)
1:10 (1:10) (Class 7) 3-Y-O+ **£1,365** (£403; £201) **Stalls** High

Form RPR

5234 1 **Davids Mark**[9] 6615 6-9-1 48.... HayleyTurner 3 — 58
(J R Jenkins) *mid-div: hdwy over 1f out: styd on to ld fnl 100yds: readily* **6/1**

0020 2 1 ¼ **Muktasb (USA)**[3] 6688 5-9-3 50....(v) DaneO'Neill 6 — 55
(D Shaw) *in tch: hdwy fr 2f out to take slt ld appr fnl f: outpcd fnl 100yds* **7/2**[2]

6436 3 shd **Spinetail Rufous (IRE)**[2] 6704 8-8-12 45....(b) AdrianMcCarthy 10 — 50
(Miss Z C Davison) *chsd ldrs: drvn to chal appr fnl f: kpt on same pce ins last* **10/1**

1500 4 2 ½ **Katie Killane**[2] 6704 4-8-12 45....(v) AdamKirby 9 — 41
(M Wellings) *chsd ldrs: rdn, hung rt and chal over 1f out: wknd ins last* **7/1**

0000 5 ½ **He's A Rocket (IRE)**[149] 3356 5-8-12 45.... LeeEnstone 1 — 39
(K R Burke) *bhd: stl plenty to do over 1f out: r.o fnl f but nvr in contention* **16/1**

0050 6 ¾ **Instinct**[135] 3781 5-8-12 35.... JimmyQuinn 5 — 37
(Micky Hammond) *bhd: stl plenty to do over 1f out: r.o fnl f but nvr in contention* **33/1**

6104 7 hd **Twinned (IRE)**[3] 6686 3-8-10 50....(p) JamieJones[(7)] 4 — 41
(Karen George) *chsd ldrs: rdn over 2f out: wknd fnl f* **3/1**[1]

0/ 8 ½ **Kurkova (IRE)**[104] 4744 4-8-12 45....(t) LPKeniry 12 — 34
(John A Quinn, Ire) *chsd ldrs: rdn over 2f out: wknd fnl f* **11/1**

0003 9 shd **Secret Vision (USA)**[38] 6233 5-8-12 45....(p) ChrisCatlin 11 — 34
(R M H Cowell) *mid-div: rdn 1/2-way and n.d* **11/2**[3]

2600 10 3 **Princess Kai (IRE)**[106] 4670 5-8-12 40.... RobertHavlin 2 — 23
(R Ingram) *s.i.s: outpcd* **33/1**

3600 11 ¾ **Otis B Driftwood**[9] 6615 3-9-0 47....(p) PaulFitzsimons 7 — 22
(Miss J R Tooth) *a outpcd* **25/1**

0066 12 1 ¼ **Prime Recreation**[9] 6615 9-8-12 45.... PatCosgrave 8 — 16
(P S Felgate) *led tl hdd appr fnl f: wknd qckly* **8/1**

60.83 secs (0.43) **Going Correction** -0.05s/f (Stan) **12** Ran SP% **133.5**
Speed ratings (Par 97):94,92,91,87,87 85,85,84,84,79 78,76
CSF £30.55 TOTE £5.30: £2.40, £1.50, £2.60; EX 16.90.
Owner Mrs Wendy Jenkins **Bred** D Lowe **Trained** Royston, Herts

FOCUS
A race over course and distance back in November held the key to this race with the first three home and beaten favourite Twinned all contesting it. The form looks straightforward rated around the third and fifth.
Otis B Driftwood Official explanation: jockey said gelding suffered interference in runing

6724 KEMPTON FOR EXHIBITIONS BANDED STKS 1m 2f (P)
1:40 (1:40) (Class 7) 3-Y-O+ **£1,365** (£403; £201) **Stalls** High

Form RPR

0401 1 **Shaheer (IRE)**[9] 6617 4-9-8 46....(v) JimCrowley 2 — 61
(J Gallagher) *trckd ldr: led 2f out: rdn and hld on wl fnl f* **11/2**

3335 2 nk **Wood Fern (UAE)**[9] 6617 6-8-12 47.... AshleyHamblett[(5)] 7 — 55
(W M Brisbourne) *chsd ldrs: styd on to press wnr ins last but a jst hld* **7/2**[2]

5644 3 1 **Kilmeena Magic**[9] 6620 4-9-1 45.... PaulFitzsimons 8 — 51
(J C Fox) *t.k.h mid-div: rdn and styd on fr over 1f out: kpt on ins last but nvr quite gng pce to chal* **12/1**

0001 4 nk **Play Up Pompey**[4] 6668 4-9-7 45.... MatthewHenry 4 — 57
(J J Bridger) *stdd s: bhd: hdwy into mid-div: rdn and styd on fnl f but a jst hld* **5/1**[3]

0/ 5 hd **Proud Ruler (IRE)**[1264] 2597 6-9-1 40....(vt[1]) RobertHavlin 10 — 50
(Niall Moran, Ire) *trckd ldrs: hdwy on rails fr 2f out: styd on u.p but nvr gng pce to chal* **9/4**[1]

5444 6 shd **Hiawatha (IRE)**[117] 888 7-9-4 48.... DaneO'Neill 13 — 54+
(A M Hales) *t.k.h in mid-div: hdwy fr 2f out: kpt on fnl f but nvr gng pce to chal* **10/1**

2B0 7 1 ½ **Love You Always (USA)**[30] 6376 6-8-8 45....(t) AmyBaker[(7)] 3 — 47
(Miss J Feilden) *slowly away: bhd: impr on outer 3f out: styd on fnl f but nvr in contention* **9/1**

0264 8 1 **Bollywood (IRE)**[9] 6616 3-8-12 45....(p) PaulEddery 1 — 45
(J J Bridger) *led: t.k.h: hdd 2f out: wknd ins fnl f* **10/1**

5000 9 ½ **Expected Bonus (USA)**[38] 6232 7-9-1 40.... SteveDrowne 6 — 44
(Jamie Poulton) *bhd tl sme hdwy fnl f* **12/1**

3534 10 1 **Simplified**[55] 5298 3-8-12 45.... MickyFenton 11 — 42
(N B King) *chsd ldrs: rdn 3f out: wknd ins fnl f* **12/1**

0050 11 1 ½ **Inveraray**[9] 6617 3-9-2 49.... PatCosgrave 5 — 44
(P S Felgate) *a towards rr* **12/1**

0006 12 3 **Orphina (IRE)**[9] 6618 3-9-3 50.... GeorgeBaker 12 — 39
(B G Powell) *sn bhd* **12/1**

2m 10.08s (1.08) **Going Correction** -0.05s/f (Stan)
WFA 3 from 4yo+ 3lb **12** Ran SP% **151.7**
Speed ratings (Par 97):93,92,91,91,91 91,90,89,89,88 87,84
CSF £32.76 TOTE £7.10: £2.70, £1.90, £4.60; EX 34.40.
Owner Colin Rashbrook and John Gallagher **Bred** David Crichton-Watt **Trained** Chastleton, Oxon

FOCUS
A competitive heat for the grade rated around the placed horses.
Orphina(IRE) Official explanation: jockey said filly had a breathing problem

6725 KEMPTON FOR CONFERENCES BANDED STKS 1m (P)
2:10 (2:11) (Class 7) 3-Y-O+ **£1,365** (£403; £201) **Stalls** High

Form RPR

5216 1 **Mythical Charm**[7] 6652 7-9-10 50....(t) MatthewHenry 12 — 65+
(J J Bridger) *hld up in rr: hdwy and nt clr run over 2f out: swtchd lft and qcknd over 1f out: drvn to ld fnl 75yds: kpt on wl* **7/4**[1]

3506 2 ¾ **Frank's Quest (IRE)**[16] 6543 6-9-1 47.... SamHitchcott 5 — 54
(A B Haynes) *hld up in rr: gd hdwy on ins fr 2f out: str chal thrght fnl f tl outpcd by wnr cl home* **8/1**

0000 3 1 ¼ **Wayward Shot (IRE)**[84] 5285 4-9-4 50.... DaleGibson 9 — 54
(G P Kelly) *chsd ldrs: drvn to chal over 1f out tl slt ld jst ins last: hdd and no ex fnl 75yds* **4/1**[3]

0163 4 1 ¼ **Tartan Special**[16] 6545 4-9-4 50.... LeeEnstone 6 — 51
(K R Burke) *bhd: gd hdwy fr 3f out to ld appr fnl 2f: hdd jst ins last: kpt on same pce* **3/1**[2]

0000 5 3 ½ **Musical Gift**[16] 6544 6-8-13 45....(v) CatherineGannon 3 — 38
(P A Blockley) *chsd ldrs: effrt fr 2f out: wknd ins fnl f* **14/1**

0062 6 1 ½ **Mid Valley**[16] 6542 3-9-0 47....(v) PaulDoe 11 — 37
(J R Jenkins) *s.i.s: hld up in rr: kpt on fr over 1f out but nvr gng pce to trble ldrs* **8/1**

0500 7 ½ **Wild Lass**[30] 6370 5-8-13 40....(p) PaulFitzsimons 4 — 36+
(J C Fox) *t.k.h in mid-div: hdwy whn nt clr run and hmpd over 1f out: sn btn* **20/1**

0010 8 8 **Penny Glitters**[2] 6703 3-9-1 48.... DeanMernagh 8 — 18
(S Parr) *chsd ldrs: led 3f out: hdd appr fnl 2f: wknd qckly* **12/1**

0005 9 3 **Vixen Virago**[20] 6501 3-8-12 35.... AdrianMcCarthy 10 — 8
(Jane Southcombe) *led 1f: wknd fr 3f out* **33/1**

3000 10 1 **Noorain**[9] 6617 4-9-1 47....(t) DavidKinsella 1 — 8
(A M Hales) *led after 1f tl hdd 3f out: sn wknd* **25/1**

1m 41.21s (0.41) **Going Correction** -0.05s/f (Stan)
WFA 3 from 4yo+ 1lb **10** Ran SP% **129.5**
Speed ratings (Par 97):95,94,93,91,88 86,86,78,75,74
CSF £19.13 TOTE £2.40: £1.50, £2.40, £1.90; EX 13.00.
Owner Tommy Ware **Bred** B J And Mrs Crangle **Trained** Liphook, Hants
■ Stewards' Enquiry : Michael Tebbutt two-day ban: careless riding (Dec 18-19)

FOCUS
Mythical Charm is in top form at the minute and won readily although she did not need to improve to do so. The fourth is the best guide to the level.

6726 RACINGUK.TV BANDED STKS 7f (P)
2:40 (2:41) (Class 7) 3-Y-0+ £1,365 (£403; £201) **Stalls** High

Form RPR

0020 **1** **Binnion Bay (IRE)**[30] 6372 5-8-9 45 (b[1]) AmirQuinn(3) 2 58+
(J J Bridger) *s.i.s: hld up: hdwy over 2f out: nt clr run over 1f out: qcknd to ld ins last: sn clr: comf* **9/1**

5340 **2** *3* **Limit Down (IRE)**[107] 4667 5-8-12 40 RobertHavlin 8 48
(John Berry) *in tch: chsd ldrs 3f out: led 2f out: hdd and outpcd ins last* **6/1**[3]

/-30 **3** *hd* **Shava**[16] 6542 6-8-12 45 SteveDrowne 1 47
(H J Evans) *in tch: chsd ldrs over 2f out: kpt on ins last but nvr gng pce to chal* **9/1**

035 **4** *3* **Hilltop Fantasy**[15] 6552 5-8-12 40 MichaelTebbutt 11 39
(V Smith) *bhd: hdwy over 2f out: kpt on fnl f but nvr gng pce to be competitive* **10/1**

0006 **5** *nk* **Southern Tide (USA)**[15] 6552 4-8-12 40 JimmyQuinn 12 38
(J Pearce) *mid-div: hdwy over 2f out: one pce fnl f* **10/1**

0502 **6** *¾* **Task Complete**[30] 6372 3-8-12 45 (b) DaneO'Neill 3 36
(Jean-Rene Auvray) *bhd: hdwy over 2f out: sn one pce* **4/1**[1]

0300 **7** *1 ¼* **Angel River**[116] 4363 4-8-5 40 (b) WilliamBuick(7) 9 33
(J Ryan) *bhd: drvn along over 2f out: kpt on fnl f but nvr in contention* **14/1**

0004 **8** *nk* **Danielle's Lad**[64] 5755 10-8-12 45 (b) AdrianMcCarthy 4 32
(B Palling) *sn led: hdd 2f out: wknd fnl f* **11/2**[2]

4050 **9** *1 ¾* **Bogaz (IRE)**[36] 6281 4-8-9 45 (v) RichardKingscote(3) 6 28
(Mrs H Sweeting) *chsd ldrs: rdn over 2f out: wknd fnl f* **12/1**

0020 **10** *hd* **I Wish**[15] 6550 8-8-12 45 PaulFitzsimons 10 27
(Miss J R Tooth) *chsd ldrs: rdn 3f out: wknd qckly fnl f* **8/1**

0000 **11** *3* **Galaxy Bound (IRE)**[8] 6629 3-8-12 45 AdamKirby 13 20
(D Shaw) *chsd ldrs: rdn 3f out: wknd 2f out* **50/1**

0000 **12** *nk* **Colonel Bilko (IRE)**[8] 6632 4-8-12 40 ChrisCatlin 5 19
(J J Bridger) *bhd: effrt on outside over 3f out: nvr in contention* **25/1**

-060 **13** *2* **The Terminator (IRE)**[8] 6629 4-8-12 40 (p) DeanMernagh 7 14
(M Mullineaux) *chsd ldrs over 4f* **66/1**

600- **14** *4* **Good Wee Girl (IRE)**[341] 6693 4-8-12 40 (b) MickyFenton 14 —
(S Woodman) *chsd ldrs over 4f* **16/1**

1m 26.74s (-0.06) **Going Correction** -0.05s/f (Stan) 14 Ran SP% **126.5**
Speed ratings (Par 97):98,94,94,90,90 89,88,87,85,85 82,81,79,75
CSF £64.81 TOTE £11.10: £3.10, £2.40, £3.10; EX 111.80.
Owner J J Bridger **Bred** Fieldspring Ltd **Trained** Liphook, Hants

FOCUS
A rampant display by the revitalised Binnion Bay and the form looks sound.

6727 FOLLOW YOUR MEETING WITH RACING BANDED STKS 6f (P)
3:10 (3:10) (Class 7) 3-Y-0+ £1,365 (£403; £201) **Stalls** High

Form RPR

0010 **1** **Mulberry Lad (IRE)**[1] 6713 4-9-4 45 PaulDoe 10 56
(P W Hiatt) *trckd ldrs: rdn to ld fnl 100yds: drvn out* **6/1**[2]

0020 **2** *¾* **El Potro**[2] 6704 4-8-12 45 JosedeSouza 9 48
(J R Holt) *chsd ldrs: led 2f out: sn rdn: hdd and no ex fnl 100yds* **10/3**[1]

2340 **3** *shd* **Firework**[8] 6632 8-8-12 45 StephenCarson 7 49+
(E A Wheeler) *bhd: hdwy fr 2f out: rdn and styng on whn tight for room ins last: kpt on again cl home but a jst hld* **13/2**[3]

0304 **4** *¾* **Teyaar**[16] 6542 10-8-12 45 PaulFitzsimons 8 48+
(M Wellings) *in tch: hdwy fr 2f out: styng on whn nt clr run ins last: swtchd lft and kpt on but nvr gng pce to rch ldrs after* **8/1**

0640 **5** *nk* **Freshwinds**[15] 6550 4-8-7 45 (b) EmmettStack(5) 12 44
(Miss Diana Weeden) *chsd ldrs 3f out: drvn to chal over 1f out: no ex nr fin* **10/1**

0020 **6** *1* **Noble Mount**[30] 6372 5-8-12 45 (p) SamHitchcott 6 41
(A B Haynes) *chsd ldrs: rdn and outpcd over 2f out: styd on again fnl f* **14/1**

0060 **7** *hd* **Charlottebutterfly**[30] 6371 6-8-12 45 PaulEddery 3 41
(P J McBride) *t.k.h: hld up in rr: hdwy on ins fr over 1f out: nvr gng pce to be competitive* **12/1**

1050 **8** *1 ½* **Bold Love**[16] 6538 3-8-9 45 JasonEdmunds(3) 5 36
(J Balding) *bhd: kpt on fr over 1f out: n.d* **10/1**

0463 **9** *hd* **Straffan (IRE)**[15] 6550 4-8-12 45 (p) DaleGibson 1 36
(J Hetherton) *chsd ldrs: rdn over 2f out: wknd fnl f* **8/1**

0000 **10** *1 ¼* **Boisdale (IRE)**[15] 6550 8-8-12 45 RichardThomas 11 32
(P S Felgate) *led: hdd 2f out: wknd fnl f* **25/1**

6050 **11** *shd* **Kings Cavalier (USA)**[44] 6129 3-8-12 45 (v) LeeEnstone 4 32
(I W McInnes) *a outpcd* **16/1**

5300 **12** *7* **Peggys First**[168] 2758 4-8-12 45 (b[1]) MichaelTebbutt 2 11
(D E Cantillon) *racd on outside: a towards rr* **14/1**

1m 13.83s (0.13) **Going Correction** -0.05s/f (Stan) 12 Ran SP% **121.9**
Speed ratings (Par 97):97,96,95,94,94 93,92,90,90,88 88,79
CSF £27.02 TOTE £6.80: £2.20, £1.60, £1.90; EX 30.60.
Owner P W Hiatt **Bred** Mountarmstrong Stud **Trained** Hook Norton, Oxon
■ Stewards' Enquiry : Jose de Souza two-day ban: used whip with excessive frequency (Dec 18-19)

FOCUS
The whole field was not covered by many lengths, and more than one horse was unlucky in running, so the form is a little messy.
Mulberry Lad(IRE) Official explanation: trainer said, regarding apparent improvement in form, that the gelding saw too much daylight on its previous run

6728 KEMPTON.CO.UK BANDED STKS 6f (P)
3:40 (3:41) (Class 7) 3-Y-0+ £1,365 (£403; £201) **Stalls** High

Form RPR

3422 **1** **Cree**[2] 6708 4-9-1 48 GeorgeBaker 8 56
(W R Muir) *hld up in rr: stdy hdwy to ld jst ins last: drvn and hld on wl cl home* **5/2**[2]

0004 **2** *hd* **Black Oval**[59] 5834 5-8-13 46 DeanMernagh 2 53
(S Parr) *hld up in rr: str run fnl f: fin wl: nt quite get up* **25/1**

0052 **3** *¾* **Burhaan (IRE)**[9] 6619 4-8-11 47 AmirQuinn(3) 6 52
(J R Boyle) *chsd ldrs: chal ins fnl f: outpcd nr fin* **8/1**

5111 **4** *¾* **Siraj**[4] 6672 7-9-2 50 (v) WilliamBuick(7) 1 59
(J Ryan) *w ldr: led after 2f: rdn over 2f out: hdd jst ins last: kpt on same pce* **5/4**[1]

6003 **5** *nk* **Danehill Stroller (IRE)**[9] 6619 6-9-3 50 DaneO'Neill 5 52
(A M Hales) *in tch: hdwy over 2f out: rdn: effrt and hung rt appr fnl f: one pce* **7/1**[3]

1405 **6** *1 ¾* **Jennverse**[16] 6541 4-8-13 46 HayleyTurner 9 42
(D K Ivory) *prom: n.m.r and edgd lft 2f out: kpt on fnl f but nvr gng pce to rch ldrs* **14/1**

0004 **7** *3* **Mostanad**[1] 6713 4-8-8 48 (b) BarrySavage(7) 7 35
(J M Bradley) *chsd ldrs: bmpd 2f out: wknd appr fnl f* **16/1**

6000 **8** *¾* **Princess Arwen**[15] 6550 4-8-9 45 NeilChalmers(3) 11 30
(Mrs Barbara Waring) *led 2f: styd chsng ldrs: rdn and edgd lft 2f out: sn btn* **50/1**

6000 **9** *3 ½* **Mustammer**[9] 6619 3-9-3 50 (v) MickyFenton 4 25
(D Shaw) *chsd ldrs tl bdly hmpd 2f out: sn bhd* **33/1**

4003 **10** *4* **Shirley Oaks (IRE)**[246] 872 8-8-6 46 JemmaMarshall(7) 3 9
(Miss Z C Davison) *in tch early: sn outpcd* **33/1**

1m 13.61s (-0.09) **Going Correction** -0.05s/f (Stan) 10 Ran SP% **120.9**
Speed ratings (Par 97):98,97,96,95,95 93,89,88,83,78
CSF £70.20 TOTE £4.60: £1.30, £4.00, £2.30; EX 90.20.
Owner Inflite Partners **Bred** Miss G J Abbey **Trained** Lambourn, Berks

FOCUS
A decent contest for the grade and sound form rated around the first two. The first two home were the back two entering the home straight, and Black Oval would have won in a couple more strides.

6729 FOLLOW YOUR CONFERENCE WITH RACING BANDED STKS 1m 4f (P)
4:10 (4:10) (Class 7) 3-Y-0+ £1,365 (£403; £201) **Stalls** Low

Form RPR

5416 **1** **Ocean Rock**[30] 6374 5-9-8 50 GeorgeBaker 5 59+
(C A Horgan) *hld up in rr: gd hdwy over 1f out: str run ins last to ld nr fin* **3/1**[1]

5021 **2** *½* **Go Amwell**[20] 6501 3-9-0 47 PaulDoe 2 55
(J R Jenkins) *bhd: hdwy 4f out: chal 3f out: slt ld 2f out: kpt on u.p whn chal fnl f: hdd last nr fin* **6/1**[3]

0325 **3** *¾* **Abbeygate**[15] 6551 5-9-5 47 MickyFenton 6 54
(T Keddy) *chsd ldrs: chal over 2f out: stl upsides ins last: no ex nr fin* **9/1**

034 **4** *½* **Atlantic Gamble (IRE)**[16] 6540 6-9-4 46 (p) LeeEnstone 8 55+
(K R Burke) *hdwy 4f out: in tch whn hmpd and lost position over 2f out: rdn and styd on again ins last: nt rch ldrs* **10/1**

04-2 **5** *nk* **Gallas (IRE)**[9] 6620 5-9-3 45 (b) AdrianMcCarthy 12 51
(S Lycett) *in tch: rdn to chse ldrs 3f out: one pce fnl f* **4/1**[2]

6046 **6** *2 ½* **Little Richard (IRE)**[18] 6526 7-9-8 50 (p) DaneO'Neill 4 52
(M Wellings) *bhd: hdwy 3f out: rdn: hung rt and no imp fnl 2f* **13/2**

6050 **7** *3 ½* **Discomania**[9] 6616 4-8-10 45 (b) JonjoMilczarek(7) 7 41
(K F Clutterbuck) *chsd ldrs: slt ld 3f out tl hdd 2f out: wknd fnl f* **50/1**

0600 **8** *1 ¼* **Hometomammy**[9] 6617 4-9-5 50 AmirQuinn(3) 11 44
(P W Hiatt) *chsd ldrs: rdn 3f out: wknd ins fnl 2f* **50/1**

6000 **9** *4* **Larad (IRE)**[44] 6133 5-9-3 45 (b) LPKeniry 14 33
(J S Moore) *bhd: rdn 4f out: nvr gng pce to rch ldrs* **16/1**

30-0 **10** *5* **Delightfully**[9] 6620 5-8-10 45 (b) SophieDoyle(7) 3 25
(Jean-Rene Auvray) *chsd ldrs: chal fr 3f out to 2f out: sn wknd* **50/1**

0- **11** *3* **Chaco (IRE)**[55] 5930 3-8-12 45 (vt[1]) RichardThomas 10 20
(Niall Moran, Ire) *led after 1f: hdd 3f out: sn wknd* **16/1**

0500 **12** *nk* **Cantrip**[51] 4530 6-9-6 48 SteveDrowne 9 22
(S Dow) *led 1f: chsd ldrs 9f* **25/1**

0005 **13** *14* **War Feather**[12] 6578 4-9-3 45 RobertHavlin 13 —
(T D McCarthy) *nvr bttr than mid-div* **25/1**

-004 **14** *3 ½* **Musardiere**[36] 6280 4-9-0 45 JasonEdmunds(3) 1 —
(J Balding) *bhd most of way* **10/1**

2m 35.48s (-1.42) **Going Correction** -0.05s/f (Stan)
WFA 3 from 4yo+ 5lb 14 Ran SP% **126.1**
Speed ratings (Par 97):102,101,101,100,100 98,96,95,93,89 87,87,78,75
CSF £21.10 TOTE £5.30: £1.60, £2.10, £2.80; EX 26.50 Place 6 £150.29, Place 5 £56.88.
Owner Mrs B Sumner **Bred** Mrs B Sumner **Trained** Uffcott, Wilts
■ Stewards' Enquiry : Jonjo Milczarek one-day ban: used whip when out of contention

FOCUS
A decent gallop from the off and the form looks solid enough with four of the first five close to form and the first five nicely clear of the the rest.
Chaco(IRE) Official explanation: trainer said colt was struck into behind
Musardiere Official explanation: jockey said filly moved poorly
T/Jkpt: Not won. T/Plt: £142.60 to a £1 stake. Pool: £46,170.70. 236.30 winning tickets. T/Qpdt: £30.20 to a £1 stake. Pool: £2,479.70. 60.70 winning tickets. ST

6701 WOLVERHAMPTON (A.W) (L-H)
Wednesday, December 6

OFFICIAL GOING: Standard
Wind: moderate, behind

6730 DINE IN THE ZONGALERO RESTAURANT MAIDEN AUCTION STKS 5f 216y(P)
3:50 (3:50) (Class 5) 2-Y-0 £3,238 (£963; £481; £240) **Stalls** Low

Form RPR

233 **1** **Eau Good**[61] 5790 2-8-9 76 RussellKennemore(7) 4 88+
(M C Chapman) *a.p: rdn over 2f out: led wl over 1f out: sn clr: r.o wl* **11/4**[2]

5002 **2** *6* **Wee Ellie Coburn**[26] 6422 2-8-4 58 FrancisNorton 2 58
(A Bailey) *led 1f: w ldr tl hung rt fr over 3f out: rn wd ent st: rdn and hung lft over 1f out: wnt 2nd 1f out: no ch w* **3/1**[3]

3 *5* **High Tribute** 2-9-1 JamieMackay 1 54+
(Sir Mark Prescott) *s.i.s: led after 1f: rdn and hdd wl over 1f out: wknd fnl f* **7/1**

0 **4** *½* **Strathaird (IRE)**[19] 6504 2-8-9 AdrianTNicholls 7 47
(P C Haslam) *outpcd: n.d* **12/1**

5006 **5** *3 ½* **Mangano**[23] 6463 2-8-10 48 PaulQuinn 6 37
(A Berry) *broke wl: sn stdd and lost pl: rdn over 2f out: sn struggling* **40/1**

3032 **6** *2 ½* **Isobel Rose (IRE)**[12] 6575 2-8-11 71 EddieAhern 3 31
(E A L Dunlop) *sn chsng ldrs: rdn and wknd over 2f out* **7/4**[1]

00 **7** *5* **Meathop (IRE)**[13] 6570 2-8-11 PaulHanagan 5 16
(R F Fisher) *hld up: rdn and bhd fnl 3f* **40/1**

1m 15.1s (-0.71) **Going Correction** -0.025s/f (Stan) 7 Ran SP% **113.1**
Speed ratings (Par 96):103,95,88,87,83 79,73
CSF £11.19 TOTE £4.00: £1.30, £2.20; EX 13.30.
Owner Sir Clement Freud **Bred** Baydon House Stud **Trained** Market Rasen, Lincs

FOCUS
A weak juvenile sprint maiden, but a decent winning time - over half a second quicker than the following maiden for three-year-olds over the same trip amd the form looks solid rated through the runner-up.

NOTEBOOK

Eau Good has clearly gone the right way since joining the Chapman yard. He had shown plenty of ability for Mark Johnston, but basically failed to progress and was beaten in first-time blinkers at York when last seen two months previously. Switched to Polytrack for the first time with the headgear left off, he handled the surface well and picked up in good style when asked to go on at the top of the straight. The bare form is not worth a great deal, but there was plenty to like about the manner of his victory and he should not be underestimated in better company. (op 9-4 tchd 3-1 and 100-30 in places)

Wee Ellie Coburn's recent second off a mark of 55 in a six-furlong nursery at Southwell on her previous start represented just moderate form, but she was getting plenty of weight. However, she blew any chance she may have had of threatening the winner by hanging to her right rounding the final bend, and then going left in the straight. Official explanation: jockey said filly hung right (op 7-2 tchd 11-4)

High Tribute, a half-brother to a few winners, including the stable's very useful six to seven-furlong winner Flying Officer, out of Area Girl, who was a triple five-furlong juvenile scorer for the Prescott yard, finished up well held in third but showed ability. The slowest away from the stalls, he was soon driven to the front and seemed in a good rhythm for much of the way, but he could offer little when strongly challenged at the top of the straight. He was easy to back and should leave this effort behind in time. (op 4-1)

Strathaird(IRE) is nicely bred - by Medicean out of a mare who was placed in the Group 1 Moyglare Stud Stakes as a juvenile - but he was well beaten on his debut over seven furlongs round here. Dropped in trip, he seemed to struggle to go the pace for much of the way, but stayed on in the straight and gave the impression the penny is just beginning to drop. He only needs one more run for a handicap mark and should find his level in time. (op 14-1)

Isobel Rose(IRE) is fully exposed and ran a poor race. (op 9-4 tchd 5-2)

6731 CONFERENCING AT WOLVERHAMPTON RACECOURSE MAIDEN STKS — 5f 216y(P)

4:20 (4:20) (Class 5) 3-Y-O — **£3,238** (£963; £481; £240) **Stalls** Low

Form	Pos	Dist	Horse / Trainer / Comment	Jockey	RPR
3422	**1**		**Cross Of Lorraine (IRE)**[8] 6637 3-9-3 63 ....(b) (I Semple) *sn led: clr wl over 1f out: pushed out* **8/15**[1]	TomEaves 1	69
05	**2**	4	**Ragad**[22] 6480 3-9-3 .... (W Jarvis) *t.k.h: sn w wnr: rdn wl over 1f out: sn btn* **9/4**[2]	BrettDoyle 4	57
5	**3**	1 ¾	**Villa Bianca's (IRE)**[21] 6492 3-8-12 .... (J A Osborne) *hld up: rdn and outpcd over 2f out: styd on fnl f* **12/1**[3]	EddieAhern 5	47
6	**4**	1 ¼	**Miss Apricot**[28] 6403 3-8-12 .... (J D Bethell) *hld up and bhd: hdwy on ins over 3f out: rdn over 2f out: sn wknd* **20/1**	DarryllHolland 2	43
000	**5**	8	**Existence**[8] 6637 3-8-9 .... (D Shaw) *rdn over 3f out: a bhd* **50/1**	PatrickMathers(3) 6	19
0000	**6**	1 ¾	**Night Reveller (IRE)**[6] 6057 3-8-5 30 .... (M C Chapman) *led early: rdn and wknd 3f out* **100/1**	RussellKennemore(7) 3	14

1m 15.63s (-0.18) **Going Correction** -0.025s/f (Stan) **6** Ran SP% **111.4**

Speed ratings (Par 102):100,94,92,90,80 77

CSF £1.89 TOTE £1.50: £1.02, £1.60; EX 2.00.

Owner Semple Racing **Bred** Kildaragh Stud **Trained** Carluke, S Lanarks

FOCUS

A very weak sprint maiden although the winner scored well and is rated slightly positively.

6732 BOOK ONLINE AT WOLVERHAMPTON-RACECOURSE.CO.UK NURSERY — 5f 20y(P)

4:50 (4:50) (Class 4) (0-85,85) 2-Y-O — **£4,533** (£1,348; £674; £336) **Stalls** Low

Form	Pos	Dist	Horse / Trainer / Comment	Jockey	RPR
1112	**1**		**Yungaburra (IRE)**[25] 6444 2-9-7 85 .... (T J Pitt) *a.p: swtchd rt wl over 1f out: led wl ins fnl f: pushed clr* **11/10**[1]	RobbieFitzpatrick 1	95+
2241	**2**	5	**Dress To Impress (IRE)**[11] 6605 2-8-13 77 .... (J R Boyle) *rrd stalls: t.k.h: jnd ldr over 2f out: rdn to ld 1f out: hdd ins fnl f: no ch w wnr* **5/4**[2]	PatCosgrave 3	69+
5130	**3**	2 ½	**Baytown Paikea**[1] 6711 2-7-7 62 oh2 .... (P S McEntee) *led: rdn over 2f out: hdd 1f out: sn wknd* **12/1**[3]	DuranFentiman(5) 2	45
3050	**4**	½	**Hephaestus**[12] 6582 2-8-3 74 ow3 .... (A J Chamberlain) *sn pushed along: a in rr* **14/1**	MarkCoumbe(7) 4	55+

63.22 secs (0.40) **Going Correction** -0.025s/f (Stan) **4** Ran SP% **106.4**

Speed ratings (Par 98):95,87,83,82

CSF £2.68 TOTE £1.50; EX 2.80.

Owner J David Abell **Bred** Newlands House Stud **Trained** Bawtry, S Yorks

■ Stewards' Enquiry : Mark Coumbe seven-day ban: failed to ride out (Dec 18-23, 26)

FOCUS

A poor turnout with just the four runners taking their chance and the form needs treating with caution.

NOTEBOOK

Yungaburra(IRE) ◆ found this pretty straightforward, with both the third and fourth home clearly of limited ability, and the runner-up compromising his chance by racing keenly, but this must still rate as a decent effort off a career-high mark. He progressed tremendously well last month, winning three races in nine days, before just finding six furlongs stretching his stamina when last seen just over three weeks previously, and he is clearly still improving. His trainer said there is nothing for him now and he will be put away until next year. A really tough sort, he should make a very useful three-year-old in the sprint division.

Dress To Impress(IRE) probably did not have to be at his best to win a course and distance maiden on his previous start and he was far too keen on this switch to nursery company. He will have to settle better in future. (tchd 11-8)

Baytown Paikea, down the field at Kempton the previous day, was no match for the front two from 2lb out of the handicap. She will benefit from a drop in grade, but has been kept very busy. (op 9-1)

Hephaestus, another who has had a busy campaign, can be rated a little better than the bare form as he was by no means given a hard time in the final furlong and his jockey put up 3lb overweight. Official explanation: jockey said, regarding running and riding, his orders were to try to make the running but he had been outpaced in home straight and the gelding hung left, he had therefore not ridden out vigorously to the line (op 12-1)

6733 WBXTRIPLECROWN.COM H'CAP — 7f 32y(P)

5:20 (5:20) (Class 4) (0-85,84) 3-Y-O+ — **£5,297** (£1,586; £793; £396; £198; £99) **Stalls** High

Form	Pos	Dist	Horse / Trainer / Comment	Jockey	RPR
0-00	**1**		**Dig Deep (IRE)**[7] 6654 4-8-7 75 .... (W J Haggas) *hld up towards rr: hdwy 2f out: rdn to ld ins fnl f: r.o wl* **5/1**[2]	GrahamGibbons 3	92+
300	**2**	2 ½	**El Coto**[39] 6226 6-9-2 84 ....(p) (K A Ryan) *hld up in tch: rdn over 2f out: kpt on ins fnl f: tk 2nd post* **12/1**	PatCosgrave 4	90
1560	**3**	shd	**Magic Rush**[61] 5785 4-9-0 82 .... (Mrs Norma Pook) *sn chsng ldr: rdn to ld wl over 1f out: hdd ins fnl f: nt qckn* **7/1**	BrettDoyle 5	88
0006	**4**	½	**Will He Wish**[20] 6499 10-8-13 81 .... (S Gollings) *bhd: rdn 3f out: swtchd lft and hdwy over 1f out: r.o one pce fnl f* **8/1**	DarryllHolland 7	86
1400	**5**	1 ¾	**Glenbuck (IRE)**[11] 6607 3-8-13 81 ....(v) (A Bailey) *sn led: rdn and hdd wl over 1f out: wknd ins fnl f* **11/2**[3]	FrancisNorton 2	81
546	**6**	1 ¾	**Methusaleh (IRE)**[77] 5483 3-8-3 74 .... (D Shaw) *in rr: rdn 2f out: nvr nr ldrs* **28/1**	PatrickMathers(3) 8	70
1346	**7**	nk	**Landucci**[11] 6594 5-8-3 78 .... (J W Hills) *racd wd: hld up in mid-div: rdn wl over 1f out: no rspnse* **6/1**	PatrickHills(7) 9	73
6040	**8**	nk	**Josh**[74] 5529 4-9-0 82 .... (K A Ryan) *hld up in tch: rdn over 2f out: wknd wl over 1f out* **7/1**	TomEaves 6	76
0036	**9**	nk	**Stoic Leader (IRE)**[13] 6573 6-8-2 70 oh3 .... (R F Fisher) *led early: prom: rdn over 2f out: wknd wl over 1f out* **9/2**[1]	PaulHanagan 1	63

1m 29.21s (-1.19) **Going Correction** -0.025s/f (Stan) **9** Ran SP% **111.8**

Speed ratings (Par 105):105,102,102,101,99 97,97,96,96

CSF £59.90 CT £412.05 TOTE £6.00: £3.00, £3.20, £3.80; EX 111.20 Trifecta £495.20 Part won. Pool £697.52 - 0.20 winning units..

Owner G Roberts/F Green/Tessona Racing **Bred** Sir Eric Parker **Trained** Newmarket, Suffolk

FOCUS

Just a fair handicap rated through the third, although the race could be better than assessed.

Magic Rush Official explanation: jockey said gelding hung left

6734 ICI GLIDDEN TRADE H'CAP — 1m 141y(P)

5:50 (5:52) (Class 5) (0-70,73) 3-Y-O+ — **£3,238** (£963; £481; £240) **Stalls** Low

Form	Pos	Dist	Horse / Trainer / Comment	Jockey	RPR
0001	**1**		**Happy As Larry (USA)**[25] 6451 4-9-0 66 .... (T J Pitt) *led early: hld up in tch: rdn to ld 2f out: clr 1f out: eased considerably ins fnl f* **9/4**[1]	FrancisNorton 2	84+
	2	3 ½	**Exit To Luck (GER)**[80] 5-9-2 68 .... (S Gollings) *bhd: rdn over 3f out: styd on to take 2nd nr fin: no ch w wnr* **16/1**	DarryllHolland 6	74
6002	**3**	½	**Berkhamsted (IRE)**[7] 6652 4-9-1 67 ....(b) (Tom Dascombe) *sn led: hdd over 6f out: led 4f out: rdn and hdd 2f out: sn btn* **10/3**[3]	JimCrowley 3	72
6136	**4**	2	**Western Roots**[5] 6666 5-8-13 65 ....(p) (M Appleby) *hld up in tch: jnd ldrs over 5f out: rdn 3f out: wknd 2f out* **15/2**	EddieAhern 5	66
2314	**5**	3 ½	**Tous Les Deux**[4] 6684 3-9-5 73 6ex .... (Peter Grayson) *sn w ldr: led over 6f out to 4f out: rdn 3f out: wknd 2f out* **5/2**[2]	RobbieFitzpatrick 4	66

1m 50.33s (-1.43) **Going Correction** -0.025s/f (Stan)

WFA 3 from 4yo+ 2lb **5** Ran SP% **100.1**

Speed ratings (Par 103):105,101,101,99,96

CSF £25.58 TOTE £3.90: £1.60, £7.50; EX 37.50.

Owner G Naidu, K Luxon & W McKay **Bred** C H Kitchen And Jeffrey Cook **Trained** Bawtry, S Yorks

FOCUS

This looked like quite competitive beforehand, despite the small field, but Happy As Larry absolutely hacked up. The form is sound enough, backed up by the time, but not that strong.

6735 WBX.COM WORLD BET EXCHANGE H'CAP — 1m 4f 50y(P)

6:20 (6:20) (Class 5) (0-70,69) 3-Y-O+ — **£3,238** (£963; £481; £240) **Stalls** Low

Form	Pos	Dist	Horse / Trainer / Comment	Jockey	RPR
3-04	**1**		**Hilltop Destiny**[42] 6177 3-8-9 65 .... (V Smith) *mde all: clr after 3f: rdn over 2f out: r.o wl* **20/1**	JerryO'Dwyer(5) 5	73
6053	**2**	1 ½	**Sarwin (USA)**[21] 6484 3-8-10 61 .... (W J Musson) *hld up in mid-div: hdwy 3f out: swtchd rt over 1f out: edgd lft and wnt 2nd ins fnl f: nt rch wnr* **5/2**[2]	BrettDoyle 1	67
/021	**3**	1	**Saltrio**[9] 6623 8-9-9 69 5ex .... (W M Brisbourne) *a.p: rdn over 1f out: styd on same pce fnl f* **7/2**[3]	EddieAhern 7	73
0415	**4**	shd	**Abstract Folly (IRE)**[34] 6312 4-9-2 62 .... (J D Bethell) *hld up in tch: rdn 3f out: styd on one pce fnl f* **12/1**	DarryllHolland 3	66
-001	**5**	3	**Noble Minstrel**[18] 6526 3-8-9 60 ....(t) (S C Williams) *t.k.h: chsd wnr: rdn 3f out: wknd over 1f out* **15/8**[1]	GrahamGibbons 4	59
3406	**6**	2 ½	**River City (IRE)**[137] 3743 9-9-7 67 .... (Noel T Chance) *hld up and bhd: hdwy 4f out: rdn 3f out: wknd over 1f out* **20/1**	JimCrowley 8	62
0016	**7**	3 ½	**Dan's Heir**[29] 6011 4-8-6 57 ....(p) (P C Haslam) *a bhd* **16/1**	LeanneKershaw(5) 2	47
0400	**8**	3 ½	**Makfly**[27] 6417 3-8-10 68 .... (R Hollinshead) *hld up in mid-div: rdn over 3f out: sn struggling* **40/1**	RussellKennemore(7) 9	52
432-	**9**	4	**Spence Appeal (IRE)**[8] 4065 4-9-7 67 .... (C Roberts) *rdn over 5f out: a bhd* **40/1**	AdrianTNicholls 6	45

2m 40.93s (-1.49) **Going Correction** -0.025s/f (Stan)

WFA 3 from 4yo+ 5lb **9** Ran SP% **113.6**

Speed ratings (Par 103):103,102,101,101,99 97,95,92,90

CSF £66.69 CT £222.30 TOTE £22.90: £4.70, £3.00, £1.20; EX 140.90 Trifecta £382.80 Part won. Pool £539.17 - 0.10 winning units. Place 6 £539.34, Place 5 £27.20 .

Owner G Noble **Bred** G Noble **Trained** Exning, Suffolk

■ Stewards' Enquiry : Graham Gibbons one-day ban: careless riding (Dec 18)

FOCUS

Just a modest middle-distance handicap and the form is quite straightforward, rated around the runner-up and fourth.

T/Plt: £146.40 to a £1 stake. Pool: £52,598.40. 262.20 winning tickets. T/Qpdt: £66.10 to a £1 stake. Pool: £4,691.70. 52.50 winning tickets. KH

6730 WOLVERHAMPTON (A.W) (L-H)

Thursday, December 7

OFFICIAL GOING: Standard

Wind: Strong, behind Weather: Fine

6736 WBXTRIPLECROWN.COM NURSERY — 7f 32y(P)

3:45 (3:45) (Class 6) (0-65,65) 2-Y-O — **£3,412** (£1,007; £504) **Stalls** High

Form	Pos	Dist	Horse / Trainer / Comment	Jockey	RPR
0140	**1**		**Homes By Woodford**[8] 6653 2-8-11 55 .... (R A Harris) *hld up in mid-div: lost pl over 5f out: swtchd lft and hdwy wl over 1f out: r.o wl to ld post* **13/2**[2]	DaneO'Neill 1	57
0042	**2**	shd	**Dressed To Dance (IRE)**[8] 6653 2-9-0 58 .... (B J Meehan) *hld up in mid-div: hdwy over 2f out: rdn to ld 1f out: hdd post* **5/6**[1]	RobertHavlin 8	60
0656	**3**	nk	**Trickle (USA)**[13] 6576 2-9-5 63 .... (Miss D Mountain) *hld up and bhd: hdwy over 2f out: sn rdn: r.o ins fnl f* **16/1**	PaulEddery 10	64
065	**4**	nk	**Imprimis Tagula (IRE)**[145] 3521 2-9-2 60 .... (A Bailey) *led early: prom: rdn and edgd rt over 1f out: kpt on ins fnl f* **14/1**	PaulHanagan 6	60

4506 **5** *nk* **Intersky Sports (USA)**[14] 6569 2-9-2 **60**............(p) CatherineGannon 12 60
(K A Ryan) *sn prom: led over 2f out: sn rdn: edgd rt and hdd 1f out: no ex towards fin* **16/1**

5000 **6** *3/4* **Green Day Packer (IRE)**[14] 6569 2-9-7 **65**...................... LeeEnstone 4 63
(P C Haslam) *hld up in tch: lost pl over 4f out: rdn and hdwy on ins wl over 1f out: one pce fnl f* **18/1**

4305 **7** *3/4* **Pietersen (IRE)**[23] 6472 2-8-5 **56**..................................(b) NeilBrown(7) 5 52
(T D Barron) *hld up and bhd: gd hdwy on wd outside over 2f out: one pce fnl f* **14/1**

2200 **8** *1 1/4* **Stargazy**[26] 6444 2-9-4 **65**....................................... RichardKingscote(3) 2 58
(R Charlton) *hld up and bhd: effrt whn hmpd wl over 1f out: nvr trbld ldrs* **8/1**[3]

000 **9** *7* **Fruits D'Amour (IRE)**[13] 6575 2-8-11 **55**............................... LPKeniry 3 30
(S Kirk) *hld up in mid-div: rdn over 3f out: wknd over 1f out* **11/1**

0622 **10** *4* **Tokyo Jo (IRE)**[38] 6258 2-9-0 **58**..................................... PatCosgrave 9 23
(T T Clement) *hld up in mid-div: hdwy over 5f out: rdn 3f out: wkng whn n.m.r and carried lft wl over 1f out* **14/1**

000 **11** *2 1/2* **O'Dwyer (IRE)**[43] 6175 2-8-10 **54**................................ PaulMulrennan 11 13
(A D Brown) *sn w ldr: led 3f out tl over 2f out: wknd over 1f out* **66/1**

6200 **12** *3 1/2* **Burningfold Babe**[17] 6534 2-9-1 **59**......................(b[1]) AdrianMcCarthy 7 9
(P Winkworth) *w ldr: led over 5f out to 3f out: rdn and wknd 2f out* **100/1**

1m 31.95s (1.55) **Going Correction** +0.025s/f (Slow) **12** Ran SP% **126.8**
Speed ratings (Par 94):92,91,91,91,90 90,89,87,79,75 72,68
CSF £13.05 CT £98.87 TOTE £11.60: £3.40, £1.02, £7.40; EX 23.40 Trifecta £152.10 Part won. Pool: £214.27 - 0.34 winning tickets..

Owner Mrs Ruth M Serrell **Bred** Mrs H B Raw **Trained** Earlswood, Monmouths

FOCUS
Not a great nursery, but competitive nonetheless and despite a decent early pace several still had a chance entering the last furlong. The form looks solid enough but modest.

NOTEBOOK
Homes By Woodford, whose only previous win came in a Fibresand claimer, may have been more suited by going this way round after a couple of spins around Kempton. The decent early pace certainly suited him and he was produced between horses to snatch the race right on the line. (op 8-1)

Dressed To Dance(IRE), who had the winner well behind her when runner-up at Kempton the previous week, failed by a whisker to confirm the form on just 2lb worse terms and can have few excuses as she was given a nice tow by the pacesetters and was sent to the front in plenty of time. (op 4-5 tchd 10-11)

Trickle(USA), who failed to see out the mile at Kempton last time, was putting in some good late work down the middle of the track and ran her best race to date from a moderate draw.

Imprimis Tagula(IRE), making his nursery and sand debuts and racing beyond the minimum trip for the first time, was not ridden as though stamina was going to be an issue and that certainly seemed to be the case. He was one of the least exposed in the field so may be able to improve again on this. (op 16-1)

Intersky Sports(USA), always there or thereabouts, seemed happier back over this trip and ran better than of late, but he has still not really confirmed early promise.

Pietersen(IRE) did not help his chances by trying to making his effort five-wide off the home bend. (tchd 16-1)

Stargazy Official explanation: jockey said colt was denied a clear run

6737 WBXTRIPLECROWN.COM MAIDEN STKS 1m 1f 103y(P)
4:20 (4:22) (Class 5) 2-Y-O **£3,412** (£1,007; £504) **Stalls** Low

Form RPR

0503 **1** **Encircled**[16] 6558 2-8-12 73... RobertHavlin 5 67+
(D Haydn Jones) *hld up in mid-div: hdwy over 2f out: rdn to ld and hung lft jst over 1f out: hung lft ins fnl f: r.o wl* **11/4**[2]

44 **2** *1 1/4* **Lord Oroko**[35] 6303 2-9-3 .... CatherineGannon 8 68+
(K A Ryan) *t.k.h in tch: rdn over 2f out: r.o ins fnl f: nt trble wnr* **9/1**

42 **3** *1 1/4* **Miss Fancy Pants**[26] 6449 2-8-12 .... JoeFanning 7 61
(M Johnston) *led: rdn over 2f out: hdd jst over 1f out: nt qckn* **7/2**[3]

6 **4** *hd* **Sweetheart**[22] 6486 2-8-12 .... MatthewHenry 2 60
(M A Jarvis) *a.p: rdn over 2f out: ev ch over 1f out: one pce fnl f* **6/1**

03 **5** *nk* **Squadron**[26] 6449 2-9-3 .... JimCrowley 9 65
(Mrs A J Perrett) *a.p: rdn and ev ch over 1f out: one pce* **8/1**

6 *1 1/2* **Moral Code (IRE)** 2-9-3 .... ChrisCatlin 6 62
(E J O'Neill) *s.s: in rr: rdn over 3f out: swtchd rt over 1f out: late hdwy: nvr nrr* **5/2**[1]

000 **7** *2 1/2* **King Of The Beers (USA)**[19] 6523 2-9-3 58.................. DaneO'Neill 10 57
(R A Harris) *prom: rdn and ev ch over 2f out: wknd over 1f out* **33/1**

0004 **8** *3/4* **Arabellas Homer**[10] 6625 2-8-12 50............................... HayleyTurner 4 51
(Mrs N Macauley) *plld hrd in mid-div: rdn over 2f out: sn bhd* **25/1**

0 **9** *hd* **Royal Tender (IRE)**[45] 6143 2-8-12 .... MichaelTebbutt 3 50
(V Smith) *s.i.s: rdn 3f out: a bhd* **66/1**

00 **10** *17* **Kyrhena**[16] 6558 2-8-12 .... IanMongan 1 18
(C W Thornton) *rdn 3f out: a bhd* **100/1**

2m 4.36s (1.74) **Going Correction** +0.025s/f (Slow) **10** Ran SP% **122.1**
Speed ratings (Par 96):93,91,90,90,90 89,86,86,85,70
CSF £28.58 TOTE £4.90: £1.10, £4.70, £1.10; EX 32.40 Trifecta £111.40 Pool: £635.61 - 4.05 winning tickets..

Owner Mrs M L Parry **Bred** M H Ings **Trained** Efail Isaf, Rhondda C Taff

FOCUS
An ordinary maiden, especially with the well-backed newcomer not running particularly well. The form is limited although the winner looks capable of a little better.

NOTEBOOK
Encircled duly appreciated stepping up in trip again and the further they went the better she was going. The way she put the race to bed suggests she can be competitive off her current mark in middle-distance handicaps in the New Year. (op 7-2)

Lord Oroko was another to appreciate this longer trip and plugged on to finish a clear second best. He looks capable of winning an ordinary maiden on sand, but can also now be handicapped which will open up a few more opportunities. (op 13-2)

Miss Fancy Pants, whose three outings including this one have all been over this course and distance, can have few excuses as she was able to lead for most of the way but was found wanting for a change of pace in the home straight. She can also now be handicapped. (op 11-4)

Sweetheart had every chance on the inside starting up the home straight, but could never find the required turn of foot. This was an improvement from her debut, but she does not look anything special. (op 7-2 tchd 10-3)

Squadron was always close to the pace, but was completely exposed for a turn of foot down the home straight. He can now be handicapped, but will need to find improvement from somewhere in order to get off the mark. (op 12-1)

Moral Code(IRE), an 82,000euros half-brother to Critic, was backed right down to favouritism but his supporters soon knew their fate, as he was slow to break and was struggling to stay in touch for most of the contest. He did make some progress over the last couple of furlongs, but it was a slow process and he could never get competitive. (op 8-1)

6738 WBXTRIPLECROWN.COM MEDIAN AUCTION MAIDEN STKS 5f 216y(P)
4:50 (4:50) (Class 6) 3-5-Y-O **£3,412** (£1,007; £504) **Stalls** Low

Form RPR

0002 **1** **Creme Brulee**[19] 6510 3-8-12 54.................................... SteveDrowne 2 60
(C R Egerton) *led early: prom: rdn to ld and hung lft over 1f out: r.o wl* **9/4**[3]

3005 **2** *2* **Casual Affair**[14] 6572 3-9-3 63.. ChrisCatlin 5 59
(E J O'Neill) *w ldr: led over 2f out: rdn and hdd over 1f out: nt qckn* **15/8**[1]

3000 **3** *3* **Comic Tales**[3] 6704 5-9-3 45....................................... CatherineGannon 1 50
(M Mullineaux) *dwlt: hld up in rr: rdn over 2f out: hdwy over 1f out: edgd lft and one pce ins fnl f* **66/1**

4 *4* **Xocolatl** 3-8-12 .... RobbieFitzpatrick 3 33
(Peter Grayson) *s.i.s: hld up: short-lived effrt on ins 2f out* **14/1**

2 **5** *2* **The Tyke**[16] 6557 3-9-3 .... AdamKirby 4 32
(C G Cox) *sn led: rdn and hdd over 2f out: wknd over 1f out* **2/1**[2]

0 **6** *7* **Our Georgia**[9] 6637 3-8-5 .... DeanHeslop(7) 6 6
(T D Barron) *chsd ldrs: rdn over 2f out: sn wknd: b.b.v* **33/1**

1m 16.53s (0.72) **Going Correction** +0.025s/f (Slow) **6** Ran SP% **110.0**
Speed ratings (Par 101):96,93,89,84,81 72
CSF £6.57 TOTE £3.20: £3.50, £1.20; EX 7.70.

Owner Mrs Julie Martin And David R Martin **Bred** Mrs Julie Routledge-Martin **Trained** Chaddleworth, Berks

FOCUS
A moderate maiden with the winner rated just 54, and the form probably adds up to little.

Our Georgia Official explanation: trainer said filly bled from the nose

6739 WBXTRIPLECROWN.COM H'CAP 5f 20y(P)
5:20 (5:20) (Class 6) (0-65,65) 3-Y-O+ **£2,730** (£806; £403) **Stalls** Low

Form RPR

2013 **1** **Desert Opal**[10] 6622 6-8-12 **62**.......................................(p) LiamJones(3) 1 71
(C R Dore) *hld up in mid-div: hdwy over 2f out: rdn over 1f out: edgd lft and r.o to ld towards fin* **2/1**[1]

0006 **2** *nk* **New Options**[5] 6682 9-8-6 **53** oh11 ow2................(b) RobbieFitzpatrick 3 61
(Peter Grayson) *hld up: hdwy 2f out: rdn to ld jst ins fnl f: hdd towards fin* **20/1**

0254 **3** *nk* **Bond Playboy**[14] 6572 6-8-8 **60**..............................(v) DuranFentiman(5) 2 73+
(G R Oldroyd) *hld up and bhd: nt clr run 2f out: rdn and hdwy on ins wl over 1f out: r.o wl towards fin* **7/1**[3]

5201 **4** *1* **Sir Don (IRE)**[19] 6521 7-8-7 **54**.................................(p) GrahamGibbons 6 57
(E S McMahon) *a.p: rdn over 2f out: nt qckn ins fnl f* **9/1**

0036 **5** *nk* **Sparkwell**[5] 6672 4-9-1 **62**.. SteveDrowne 4 64
(D Shaw) *hld up in mid-div: hdwy over 2f out: sn rdn: kpt on ins fnl f* **7/2**[2]

0643 **6** *nk* **Jilly Why (IRE)**[17] 6533 5-8-8 **55**.............................. CatherineGannon 7 56
(Ms Deborah J Evans) *a.p: rdn wl over 1f out: one pce fnl f* **9/1**

3043 **7** *1* **Blessed Place**[5] 6672 6-9-0 **61**.. JimCrowley 13 59
(D J S Ffrench Davis) *led: rdn wl over 1f out: hdd jst ins fnl f: fdd* **8/1**

0050 **8** *1/2* **Phinerine**[2] 6717 3-8-8 **62**...(b) TolleyDean(7) 10 58
(R A Harris) *bhd: hung lft over 3f out: rdn and hdwy over 1f out: no imp fnl f* **50/1**

0000 **9** *1 3/4* **White Ledger (IRE)**[149] 3389 7-8-4 **51** oh3................(p) HayleyTurner 8 40
(R E Peacock) *w ldrs: rdn over 2f out: sn wknd* **80/1**

0000 **10** *1 1/4* **General Feeling (IRE)**[163] 2947 5-8-13 **65**................. AndrewElliott(5) 9 50
(M Mullineaux) *s.i.s: a bhd* **25/1**

0000 **11** *2* **Misaro (GER)**[13] 6585 5-9-4 **65**.......................................(b) DaneO'Neill 12 43
(R A Harris) *chsd ldrs on outside: rdn over 2f out: sn lost pl: hung lft over 1f out* **16/1**

0-00 **12** *3 1/2* **Best Lead**[304] 317 7-8-4 **54**...................................(b) PatrickMathers(3) 11 19
(Ian Emmerson) *chsd ldrs: rdn 3f out: sn wknd* **80/1**

2360 **13** *3* **Montillia (IRE)**[17] 6539 4-8-4 **51** oh4............................. MatthewHenry 5 5
(J W Unett) *prom: rdn 3f out: wknd 2f out* **40/1**

62.85 secs (0.03) **Going Correction** +0.025s/f (Slow) **13** Ran SP% **120.5**
Speed ratings (Par 101):100,99,99,97,96 96,94,94,91,89 86,80,75
CSF £51.62 CT £224.68 TOTE £3.00: £1.40, £4.10, £4.20; EX 45.30 Trifecta £302.60 Part won. Pool: £426.21 - 0.34 winning tickets..

Owner Page, Ward, Marsh **Bred** Juddmonte Farms **Trained** West Pinchbeck, Lincs

FOCUS
A typically strongly-run sprint handicap, and the draw played its part with the front six all starting from stall seven or lower, so the form is not that strong. The winner's stall opened a fraction early after he had charged it, but the result stood after the Stewards decided he had gained no advantage.

6740 WORLD BET EXCHANGE WBX.COM H'CAP 5f 20y(P)
5:50 (5:51) (Class 4) (0-80,80) 3-Y-O+ **£6,477** (£1,927; £963; £481) **Stalls** Low

Form RPR

0030 **1** **Sahara Silk (IRE)**[6] 6656 5-8-4 **69**..........................(v) PatrickMathers(3) 7 79
(D Shaw) *chsd ldrs: rdn and outpcd over 3f out: rallied over 1f out: swtchd edgd ins fnl f: r.o to ld towards fin* **14/1**

0010 **2** *1/2* **Fizzlephut (IRE)**[2] 6709 4-8-8 **70**................................... RichardThomas 6 78
(Miss J R Tooth) *chsd ldr: rdn over 1f out: led ins fnl f: hdd towards fin* **13/2**[3]

0011 **3** *1 1/4* **Briannsta (IRE)**[23] 6478 4-9-3 **79**.. AdamKirby 1 83
(C G Cox) *mid-div: rdn over 2f out: hdwy over 1f out: kpt on ins fnl f* **10/11**[1]

634 **4** *1 1/4* **Scooby Dude (IRE)**[5] 6682 3-9-4 **80**............................... TonyCulhane 2 79
(Ms Deborah J Evans) *a.p: rdn to ld wl over 1f out: edgd rt and hdd ins fnl f: no ex* **4/1**[2]

0000 **5** *2 1/2* **Maktavish**[13] 6585 7-8-4 **66**...(b) PaulHanagan 4 56
(R Brotherton) *led: rdn and hdd wl over 1f out: wkng whn bmpd ins fnl f* **25/1**

00-6 **6** *3/4* **Loyal Tycoon (IRE)**[213] 1545 8-8-6 **75**...................... JamesMillman(7) 8 62
(D K Ivory) *hld up and bhd: rdn over 2f out: sme late prog: n.d: fin lame* **22/1**

0032 **7** *4* **Lady Bahia (IRE)**[16] 6555 5-8-6 **68**........................(b) RobbieFitzpatrick 3 41
(Peter Grayson) *a bhd* **13/2**[3]

5350 **8** *hd* **Lucayos**[144] 3568 3-8-7 **72**..................................(b) RichardKingscote(3) 5 44
(Mrs H Sweeting) *s.s: outpcd* **22/1**

61.89 secs (-0.93) **Going Correction** +0.025s/f (Slow) **8** Ran SP% **118.3**
Speed ratings (Par 105):108,107,105,103,99 98,91,91
CSF £100.44 CT £169.61 TOTE £17.80: £3.00, £2.30, £1.10; EX 136.10 Trifecta £318.70 Part won. Pool: £448.88 - 0.44 winning tickets..

Owner Danethorpe Racing Ltd **Bred** John Cullinan **Trained** Danethorpe, Notts

■ Stewards' Enquiry : Patrick Mathers caution: careless riding

FOCUS
A fair little sprint handicap and thanks to a decent pace the winning time was nearly a second quicker than the preceding Class 6 handicap. Despite that the form, rated through the runner-up, does not look that strong.
Loyal Tycoon(IRE) Official explanation: trainer's rep said gelding finished lame
Lucayos Official explanation: jockey said gelding missed the break

6741 WBX.COM WORLD BET EXCHANGE H'CAP — 1m 1f 103y(P)
6:20 (6:20) (Class 5) (0-75,75) 3-Y-0+ — **£3,886** (£1,156; £577; £288) **Stalls** Low

Form — RPR
3034 **1** **Magical Music**[5] 6671 3-9-0 **73** .... JimmyQuinn 3 — 83
(J Pearce) *hld up: hdwy over 2f out: rdn to ld 1f out: drvn out* **5/1**[3]
4260 **2** ½ **Dower House**[28] 6418 11-9-4 **75** .... (t) ChrisCatlin 5 — 84
(Andrew Turnell) *hld up: rdn and hdwy over 1f out: r.o ins fnl f: nt rch wnr* **4/1**[2]
1233 **3** nk **Bavarica**[14] 6568 4-8-5 **69** .... AmyBaker(7) 8 — 77
(Miss J Feilden) *hld up in rr: nt clr run and swtchd rt wl over 1f out: sn rdn: r.o wl towards fin* **10/1**
5402 **4** 1 **Italian Romance**[13] 6588 3-8-7 **73** .... PatrickHills(7) 2 — 79
(J W Unett) *prom: rdn and outpcd over 2f out: rallied 1f out: no ex ins fnl f* **10/1**
6114 **5** 3 **Writ (IRE)**[21] 6502 4-9-0 **71** .... TomEaves 1 — 71
(I Semple) *led 1f: prom: rdn to ld over 2f out: hdd 1f out: wknd wl ins fnl f* **13/8**[1]
1-03 **6** 6 **Our Kes (IRE)**[5] 6684 4-8-11 **68** .... IanMongan 6 — 56
(P Howling) *led after 1f: rdn and hdd over 2f out: wknd over 1f out* **8/1**
0160 **7** 19 **Da Bookie (IRE)**[15] 6564 6-8-13 **70** .... EdwardCreighton 4 — 20
(E J Creighton) *s.i.s: hdwy over 5f out: rdn over 3f out: sn wknd* **16/1**
0660 **8** 30 **Following Flow (USA)**[189] 2170 4-9-4 **75** .... GrahamGibbons 7 — —
(R Hollinshead) *a bhd: rdn 4f out: eased whn no ch wl over 1f out* **25/1**

2m 0.30s (-2.32) **Going Correction** +0.025s/f (Slow)
WFA 3 from 4yo+ 2lb — **8** Ran SP% **113.8**
Speed ratings (Par 103):111,110,110,109,106 101,84,57
CSF £25.02 CT £190.77 TOTE £8.80: £1.80, £2.00, £1.60; EX 29.50 Trifecta £98.60 Pool: £411.35 - 2.96 winning tickets. Place 6 £25.25, Place 5 £17.65.
Owner Killarney Glen & Mrs E M Clarke **Bred** Peter Taplin **Trained** Newmarket, Suffolk

FOCUS
No hanging around thanks to Our Kes and as a result a decent winning time for a race of its class. The form looks solid rated through the runner-up.
T/Plt: £14.80 to a £1 stake. Pool: £66,094.70. 3,259.00 winning tickets. T/Qpdt: £8.30 to a £1 stake. Pool: £5,616.50. 500.70 winning tickets. KH

6723 KEMPTON (A.W) (R-H)
Friday, December 8

OFFICIAL GOING: Standard
Wind: Light across Weather: Fine

6742 CSPARKING.COM MEDIAN AUCTION MAIDEN STKS — 5f (P)
3:15 (3:16) (Class 6) 2-Y-0 — **£2,388** (£705; £352) **Stalls** High

Form — RPR
4332 **1** **Feelin Foxy**[13] 6596 2-8-12 66 .... (v) DaneO'Neill 5 — 62+
(D Shaw) *wnt lft s: t.k.h: prom: led 1/2-way: narrow ld after: drvn over 1f out: fnd jst enough to hold on* **1/1**[1]
0423 **2** nk **Hereford Boy**[28] 6427 2-9-3 63 .... RobertHavlin 1 — 66
(D K Ivory) *prom: pressed wnr fr 1/2-way: jst hld u.p fnl f* **9/4**[2]
5500 **3** 6 **Path To Glory**[23] 6488 2-9-3 45 .... (p) IanMongan 8 — 44
(Miss Z C Davison) *led to 1/2-way: sn u.p and btn: struggled home to hold on for 3rd* **50/1**
0533 **4** ½ **Splendidio**[143] 3624 2-8-5 52 .... JamesMillman(7) 2 — 38
(D K Ivory) *wnt rt s: t.k.h: trckd ldrs to 1/2-way: sn btn* **10/1**
5 hd **Lady Warning** 2-8-5 .... JackDean(7) 4 — 37
(W G M Turner) *squeezed out s: outpcd in 5th: hanging and green 2f out: nvr a factor* **25/1**
6 4 **Redflo** 2-8-9 .... JamesDoyle(3) 6 — 22
(Ms J S Doyle) *bdly outpcd in last after 1f: no ch* **25/1**
7 7 **Lost All Alone** 2-9-3 .... AdamKirby 7 — 2
(D M Simcock) *rn green in last pair and sn bhd* **6/1**[3]

61.48 secs (1.08) **Going Correction** -0.025s/f (Stan) — **7** Ran SP% **113.8**
Speed ratings (Par 94):90,89,79,79,78 72,61
CSF £3.35 TOTE £2.00: £1.10, £2.00; EX 2.80.
Owner Danethorpe Racing Ltd **Bred** Bearstone Stud **Trained** Danethorpe, Notts

FOCUS
A very weak sprint maiden and the first two came clear. The form is moderate.

NOTEBOOK
Feelin Foxy had been running well in defeat lately and found this a good opportunity to gain a deserved first success at the 12th attempt. She should remain competitive in handicap company. (op 1-2)
Hereford Boy found this easier than the novice event he ran third in at Wolverhampton on his previous start and was just held. A similar race should come his way at some point. (op 3-1)
Path To Glory, fitted with cheekpieces for the first time, was no match for the front two. He will probably be better in banded races or low-grade handicaps.
Splendidio will surely be better off in selling company. (op 16-1)
Lady Warning, the first foal of an unraced sister to the very smart Lord Smith, a multiple six/seven-furlong winner at two and later smart at around a mile in the US, showed some ability on her racecourse debut.
Lost All Alone, a 13,500gns half-brother to among others Leofric, a dual seven-furlong/mile winner, out of a successful sprinter, attracted support on his racecourse debut, but seemed badly in need of the experience. Surely he is capable of significantly better. (op 10-1)

6743 DAVE AUSTIN CSP H'CAP — 1m 2f (P)
3:50 (3:52) (Class 6) (0-60,60) 3-Y-0+ — **£2,388** (£705; £352) **Stalls** High

Form — RPR
00 **1** **Generous Lad (IRE)**[98] 4982 3-9-0 **58** .... (p) DaneO'Neill 7 — 70+
(A B Haynes) *dwlt: t.k.h and hld up in rr: brought wd and prog over 1f out: led jst ins fnl f: r.o wl* **50/1**
530 **2** 2½ **Kilgary (USA)**[38] 6286 3-9-2 **60** .... SteveDrowne 3 — 66+
(J Noseda) *hld up in midfield: effrt 2f out: prog and cl up over 1f out: hanging and nt qckn: chsd wnr last 100yds: no imp* **11/1**
6452 **3** 2 **Camp Attack**[13] 6601 3-8-10 **54** .... LPKeniry 1 — 56
(S Dow) *trckd ldr after 3f: rdn to ld wl over 1f out: hdd and outpcd jst ins fnl f* **10/1**[3]
2305 **4** 1¼ **Davidia (IRE)**[4] 6694 3-9-2 **60** .... GeorgeBaker 9 — 60
(S Kirk) *trckd ldrs: rdn over 2f out: lost pl and btn over 1f out: plugged on* **9/1**[2]
0-21 **5** nk **Picador**[4] 6700 3-8-13 **57** 6ex .... EddieAhern 10 — 57
(Sir Mark Prescott) *t.k.h: trckd ldr for 3f: styd cl up: effrt on inner to chal over 1f out: sn nt qckn: fdd fnl f* **2/5**[1]
0002 **6** ¾ **Dream Mountain**[50] 6067 3-8-8 **55** .... JamesDoyle(3) 11 — 53
(Ms J S Doyle) *in tch in midfield: rdn 3f out: no imp over 1f out* **10/1**[3]
-030 **7** 1 **Blue Quiver (IRE)**[13] 6590 6-9-1 **56** .... PaulEddery 4 — 52
(C A Horgan) *walked to post: s.s: hld up in last: shuffled along and limited prog over 1f out: nvr nr ldrs: eased nr fin* **33/1**
6060 **8** 1¾ **Come What July (IRE)**[5] 6687 5-8-12 **53** .... HayleyTurner 2 — 46
(D Shaw) *hld up in rr: sme prog on outer 4f out: lost pl and struggling over 2f out* **33/1**
5000 **9** ¾ **Unicorn Reward (IRE)**[23] 6497 6-9-5 **60** .... (v[1]) AdamKirby 8 — 52
(Mrs L C Jewell) *mde most to wl over 1f out: sn wknd* **50/1**
0000 **10** 1 **Blanc Visage**[11] 6623 3-8-9 **53** .... JimCrowley 6 — 43
(Mrs H Sweeting) *hld up: plld way through to chse ldng pair 1/2-way: wknd over 2f out* **50/1**

2m 8.06s (-0.94) **Going Correction** -0.025s/f (Stan)
WFA 3 from 4yo+ 3lb — **10** Ran SP% **119.7**
Speed ratings (Par 101):102,100,98,97,97 96,95,94,93,92
CSF £513.53 CT £5859.32 TOTE £62.90: £13.90, £1.80, £2.80; EX 815.60.
Owner Mike Bowden **Bred** Frank Towey **Trained** Collingbourne Ducis, Wilts

FOCUS
This looked like a reasonable enough race for the grade and the winning time was not too bad, only 1.24 seconds slower than the following handicap and the form looks straightforward rate around the third and fifth.
Camp Attack Official explanation: jockey said gelding hung right
Picador Official explanation: jockey said gelding ran flat

6744 DIGIBET.COM H'CAP — 1m 2f (P)
4:20 (4:21) (Class 3) (0-95,90) 3-Y-0+
£7,790 (£2,332; £1,166; £583; £291; £146) **Stalls** High

Form — RPR
2312 **1** **Alpine Reel (IRE)**[13] 6600 5-9-7 **90** .... AdamKirby 2 — 99+
(W R Swinburn) *trckd ldr: led over 2f out: drvn and hrd pressed on all sides fnl f: battled on wl* **10/11**[1]
0034 **2** hd **Fusili (IRE)**[17] 6559 3-9-4 **90** .... IanMongan 8 — 98
(N P Littmoden) *chsd ldng pair: rdn over 2f out: chsd wnr wl over 1f out: upsides fnl f: kpt on wl but jst hld* **11/1**
0054 **3** hd **Bobby Charles**[25] 6468 5-8-9 **78** .... RobertHavlin 7 — 86
(Dr J D Scargill) *hld up in last pair: prog 3f out: rdn to chal 1f out: upsides fnl f: nt qckn nr fin* **10/1**[3]
3130 **4** ¾ **Woolfall Blue (IRE)**[13] 6607 3-8-7 **79** .... OscarUrbina 3 — 86
(G G Margarson) *trckd ldrs: effrt on wd outside over 1f out: kpt on fnl f but nvr able to chal* **14/1**
460 **5** 1 **Langford**[6] 6678 6-9-7 **90** .... JimCrowley 6 — 95
(M H Tompkins) *hld up in midfield: clsd on ldrs over 1f out: rdn and one pce after* **16/1**
0002 **6** nk **Activo (FR)**[10] 6633 5-8-11 **80** .... SteveDrowne 10 — 84
(S Dow) *hld up in last pair: prog wl over 1f out: chsd ldrs ent fnl f: rdn and fnd nil* **7/2**[2]
004 **7** 4 **Honduras (SWI)**[20] 6515 5-9-5 **88** .... GeorgeBaker 4 — 85
(G L Moore) *led to over 2f out: carried hd high and wknd over 1f out* **10/1**[3]
3-00 **8** ¾ **Crocodile Bay (IRE)**[30] 3852 3-8-10 **82** .... HayleyTurner 9 — 78
(Carl Llewellyn) *plld hrd early: hld up in tch: rdn and lost pl qckly 3f out: no ch after* **50/1**
6010 **9** 8 **Cape Of Luck (IRE)**[13] 6594 3-9-2 **88** .... BrettDoyle 5 — 69
(P Mitchell) *in tch to over 3f out: sn last and bhd* **20/1**

2m 6.82s (-2.18) **Going Correction** -0.025s/f (Stan)
WFA 3 from 4yo+ 3lb — **9** Ran SP% **120.4**
Speed ratings (Par 107):107,106,106,106,105 105,101,101,94
CSF £13.68 CT £70.55 TOTE £2.00: £1.10, £3.20, £3.00; EX 16.90.
Owner Mrs P W Harris **Bred** South House Stud **Trained** Aldbury, Herts

FOCUS
Not that strong a race for the grade, although the winning time was 1.24 seconds quicker than the earlier handicap. The form looks sound enough with the third and fourth running to form.

NOTEBOOK
Alpine Reel(IRE) could have been considered a little disappointing not to have won a similar event at Lingfield on his previous start, but he just prevailed this time. Considering this was probably not the strongest of races for the grade, he could have been expected to win a little more convincingly, but it would be harsh to knock him and there is no doubting he remains most progressive. He will remain worthy of respect in this sort of event, but it might be that this trip just stretches him and he could be worth a try over a mile - there is plenty of speed in his pedigree. (op 11-10 tchd 5-4 in places and 6-4 in a place)
Fusili(IRE), a really tough sort, ran a fine race behind the progressive winner. She should continue to run well in similar events and could pick up some more black type this All-Weather season, with some new Listed events added to the calendar next year. (op 10-1 tchd 12-1)
Bobby Charles improved on the form he showed on his return from a break at Southwell and was just held in third. There could be even more to come. (op 8-1)
Woolfall Blue(IRE) ran much better than when down the field at Wolverhampton on his previous start and is clearly well suited by this course and distance. (op 12-1)
Langford's last four wins have come over a mile and may just benefit from a drop back in trip. (tchd 20-1)
Activo(FR), who apparently finished lame when second under a sympathetic ride at Lingfield on his previous start, offered little under pressure and looks best watched for the time being. Official explanation: jockey said gelding hung right (op 3-1)
Honduras(SWI) Official explanation: jockey said gelding hung left throughout

6745 DIGIBET.CO.UK MAIDEN AUCTION STKS — 1m (P)
4:50 (4:52) (Class 6) 2-Y-0 — **£2,388** (£705; £352) **Stalls** High

Form — RPR
040 **1** **Summer Dancer (IRE)**[41] 6220 2-8-10 68 .... MarcHalford(3) 2 — 67+
(D R C Elsworth) *hld up in last: prog 3f out: led over 1f out: sn clr: easily* **8/13**[1]
0640 **2** 2½ **Go Dude**[14] 6576 2-8-10 51 .... (v[1]) BrettDoyle 5 — 52
(J Ryan) *hld up in tch: rdn over 2f out: styd on fr over 1f out to take 2nd last 150yds: no ch w wnr* **16/1**
3 1 **Scar Tissue** 2-8-6 .... RichardThomas 6 — 46
(Tom Dascombe) *restless stalls: wl in tch: rdn and rn green 2f out: outpcd over 1f out: plugged on* **16/1**
04 **4** 1 **Annia Faustina (IRE)**[13] 6591 2-8-5 .... JimmyQuinn 3 — 43
(J L Spearing) *t.k.h: trckd ldr: led over 2f out to over 1f out: wknd fnl f* **3/1**[2]
3550 **5** 4 **Tres Hombres**[114] 4480 2-8-11 55 .... SteveDrowne 4 — 39
(Tom Dascombe) *led to over 2f out: wknd over 1f out* **7/1**[3]

0005 **6** 5 **Elmasong**[9] 6650 2-8-4 49 .... HayleyTurner 1 21
(J J Bridger) *t.k.h: cl up to over 2f out: sn wknd* **33/1**
1m 42.87s (2.07) **Going Correction** -0.025s/f (Stan) **6** Ran SP% **114.1**
Speed ratings (Par 94):88,85,84,83,79 74
CSF £13.28 TOTE £1.60: £1.40, £2.60; EX 10.00.
Owner The Sunday Lunch Partnership **Bred** Eddie O'Leary **Trained** Newmarket, Suffolk

FOCUS
A very weak maiden and a steady pace resulted in a time 3.51 seconds slower than the following conditions event. The runner-up sets the standard.

NOTEBOOK
Summer Dancer(IRE) had shown plenty of ability in three starts in maiden company at Newmarket and, faced with by far his easiest task to date, he ran out a comfortable winner. He will apparently now be gelded and reappear in the spring. (op 4-6)
Go Dude, with a visor replacing cheekpieces, had 14lb to find with Summer Dancer and was well held in second. He will surely be better off in handicap company. (op 14-1)
Scar Tissue, a 9,000gns half-sister to among others the Group 3-placed Protectorate, who won over five and six furlongs, out of a dual-mile winner at three, made a satisfactory debut and is open to plenty of improvement.
Annia Faustina(IRE) could not build on the form she showed when third over seven furlongs round here on her previous start, but she is now qualified for a handicap mark. (op 5-2)
Tres Hombres, a stablemate of the third, was well held on his Polytrack debut off the back of a 114-day break.

6746 DIGIBET SPORTS BETTING CONDITIONS STKS 1m (P)
5:20 (5:22) (Class 3) 2-Y-O £6,855 (£2,052; £1,026; £513) Stalls High

Form RPR
2011 **1** **Cesc**[13] 6598 2-9-0 90 .... EddieAhern 2 90+
(P J Makin) *trckd ldr: led jst over 1f out: pushed out and wl in command fnl f* **4/9**[1]
3211 **2** 2 ½ **Alittlebitleft (IRE)**[5] 6691 2-9-3 81 ....(b) RichardHughes 4 87
(R Hannon) *led: rdn and hdd jst over 1f out: kpt on but no ch w wnr ins fnl f* **2/1**[2]
5 **3** 5 **Fascinatin Rhythm**[23] 6486 2-8-9 .... MichaelTebbutt 1 68
(V Smith) *cl up: rdn over 2f out: lft bhd fr over 1f out* **20/1**[3]
004 **4** 19 **Ponte Vecchio (IRE)**[13] 6603 2-9-0 52 .... PatCosgrave 3 29
(J R Boyle) *cl up: rdn over 3f out: wknd 2f out: t.o* **50/1**
1m 39.36s (-1.44) **Going Correction** -0.025s/f (Stan) **4** Ran SP% **109.3**
Speed ratings (Par 100):106,103,98,79
CSF £1.61 TOTE £1.50; EX 1.50.
Owner Keith And Brian Brackpool **Bred** H J P Farr **Trained** Ogbourne Maisey, Wilts

FOCUS
Basically a two-horse race and a disappointing turnout. The winning time was 3.51 seconds quicker than the earlier maiden and the winner put up a solid effort with the form capable of being rated higher.

NOTEBOOK
Cesc ◆ only really had Alittlebitleft to worry about and readily brushed that rival aside when it mattered. He has been well placed to win his last three starts and could bid for the four-timer in a similar race on December 20. (op 8-15 tchd 4-7 and 4-6 in a place)
Alittlebitleft(IRE) was chasing the hat-trick following a success in a Wolverhampton nursery off a mark of 68 and an easy win in a three-runner novice event at Lingfield, but he was 12lb wrong with Cesc and proved no match for that rival. (op 13-8)
Fascinatin Rhythm showed some ability in a course and distance maiden on her debut, but this was asking a bit much. She ran well in the circumstances and can do even better when returned to maiden company. (op 16-1)
Ponte Vecchio(IRE) will be better off in low-grade handicaps.

6747 ALF WOODS CSP H'CAP 7f (P)
5:50 (5:50) (Class 5) (0-67,67) 3-Y-O+ £3,412 (£1,007; £504) Stalls High

Form RPR
0061 **1** **Generator**[27] 6442 4-8-7 60 .... JoeFanning 11 71+
(Dr J D Scargill) *trckd ldrs gng wl: effrt over 1f out: led jst ins fnl f: bustled along and wl in command nr fin* **4/1**[2]
0340 **2** 1 ¼ **Dvinsky (USA)**[29] 6417 5-8-11 64 .... PaulDoe 3 72
(P Howling) *prom: effrt to ld 2f out: hdd jst ins fnl f: kpt on same pce* **12/1**
0314 **3** hd **Sincerely**[16] 6564 4-9-0 67 ....(b) OscarUrbina 2 74
(B W Hills) *trckd ldrs: effrt to chal over 1f out: sn rdn and nt qckn: kpt on same pce after* **7/2**[1]
0054 **4** hd **No Grouse**[13] 6595 6-8-3 56 oh1 .... JimmyQuinn 1 62
(E J Alston) *hld up in midfield on outer: prog 2f out: chsd ldrs fnl f: styd on same pce* **12/1**
6303 **5** 1 **Sovereignty (JPN)**[23] 6489 4-8-3 63 .... JamesMillman(7) 9 67
(D K Ivory) *hld up in midfield: effrt and cl enough over 1f out: one pce after* **9/1**
0020 **6** 1 ½ **Scuba (IRE)**[13] 6595 4-8-13 66 ....(b) SteveDrowne 8 65
(H Morrison) *hld up in rr: shuffled along 2f out: kpt on steadily fr over 1f out: nvr nr ldrs* **6/1**[3]
0500 **7** ½ **Sands Of Barra (IRE)**[13] 6595 3-8-12 65 .... BrettDoyle 12 63
(I W McInnes) *t.k.h: hld up wl in rr: pushed along and kpt on fnl 2f: n.d* **12/1**
00 **8** nk **Napoletano (GER)**[9] 6652 5-8-12 65 .... LPKeniry 14 62
(S Dow) *t.k.h: hld up in last: effrt on inner over 2f out: prog over 1f out: no hdwy fnl f* **33/1**
0353 **9** ½ **Humility**[27] 6439 5-8-5 58 .... EddieAhern 10 54
(C A Cyzer) *hld up in midfield: clsd on ldrs and swtchd towards inner 2f out: no prog fnl f* **7/1**
0000 **10** ¾ **Blue Empire (IRE)**[13] 6595 5-8-6 59 .... RichardThomas 6 53
(C R Dore) *hld up wl in rr: rdn and no prog over 2f out: one pce after* **50/1**
0000 **11** 1 ½ **Takes Tutu (USA)**[15] 6573 7-8-9 62 ....(p) AdamKirby 13 51
(C R Dore) *hld up in rr: swtchd to inner and sme prog 2f out: shuffled along and lost pls fnl f* **16/1**
3000 **12** nk **Aastral Magic**[4] 6698 4-8-9 62 ....(p) DaneO'Neill 7 51
(R Hannon) *s.i.s: hld up in rr: rdn 3f out: no real prog* **20/1**
5-46 **13** ½ **Night Wolf (IRE)**[303] 343 6-8-3 56 oh3 .... HayleyTurner 5 43
(Jamie Poulton) *led after 3f to 2f out: wknd rapidly jst over 1f out* **20/1**
1000 **14** 6 **Mocha Java**[15] 6568 3-9-0 67 .... IanMongan 4 37
(Mrs L J Mongan) *led for 3f: wknd 3f out: sn bhd* **33/1**
1m 25.85s (-0.95) **Going Correction** -0.025s/f (Stan) **14** Ran SP% **125.3**
Speed ratings (Par 103):104,102,102,102,100 99,98,98,97,96 95,94,94,87
CSF £50.44 CT £195.88 TOTE £6.10: £1.70, £5.30, £2.00; EX 92.70.
Owner R A Dalton **Bred** R A Dalton **Trained** Newmarket, Suffolk

FOCUS
A modest handicap but the form looks solid rated through the runner-up.
Takes Tutu(USA) Official explanation: jockey said gelding was denied a clear run

6748 CSPARKING CHRISTMAS DINNER H'CAP 1m 4f (P)
6:20 (6:20) (Class 6) (0-65,65) 3-Y-O+ £2,388 (£705; £352) Stalls Low

Form RPR
1400 **1** **Turner's Touch**[16] 6566 4-9-7 63 ....(be) GeorgeBaker 4 77+
(G L Moore) *dwlt: hld up in last: prog on outside 4f out: cruised up to ldrs over 2f out: led over 1f out: drvn 2l clr: idled last 100y* **5/1**[3]
1504 **2** ½ **Sendinpost**[24] 6479 3-9-0 61 .... AdamKirby 1 72
(S C Williams) *hld up towards rr: effrt over 2f out: rdn and prog to take 2nd 1f out: clsd as wnr idled: a hld* **4/1**[1]
1013 **3** ¾ **Inside Story (IRE)**[7] 6666 4-9-6 65 ....(b) JamesDoyle(3) 7 75
(G P Kelly) *dwlt: hld up in last pair: stl there 3f out: prog u.p wl over 1f out: r.o fnl f: too much to do* **6/1**
3500 **4** 1 ¾ **Duelling Banjos**[199] 1926 7-9-6 62 .... DaneO'Neill 9 69
(J Akehurst) *hld up towards rr: prog over 2f out: rdn to dispute 2nd 1f out: fdd ins fnl f* **16/1**
0114 **5** hd **Treetops Hotel (IRE)**[52] 6037 7-9-6 65 .... LiamJones(3) 8 72
(B R Johnson) *hld up in last trio: effrt over 2f out: styd on fr over 1f out: no ch* **9/2**[2]
0046 **6** 2 **Recalcitrant**[3] 6712 3-8-8 55 .... LPKeniry 10 59
(S Dow) *led for 1f: chsd clr ldr tl led again over 2f out to over 1f out: wknd fnl f* **33/1**
4452 **7** nk **Ruse**[61] 5830 3-8-11 58 .... OscarUrbina 3 62
(J R Fanshawe) *prom in chsng gp: shkn up over 2f out: nt qckn and btn wl over 1f out: fdd* **11/2**
0000 **8** 2 ½ **Blackmail (USA)**[16] 6565 8-8-12 54 .... EddieAhern 11 54
(P Mitchell) *wl plcd in chsng gp: effrt on inner and cl enough 2f out: wknd jst over 1f out* **7/1**
4650 **9** 1 ¼ **Phone In**[15] 6571 3-8-11 58 ....(b) PatCosgrave 6 56
(R Brotherton) *plld hrd: led after 1f and sn clr: hdd & wknd over 2f out* **20/1**
4056 **10** 2 **Lennoxtown (IRE)**[23] 6484 3-8-9 56 ....(p) BrettDoyle 2 51
(J Ryan) *hld up towards rr: gng wl enough whn stmbld wl over 2f out: sn rdn and btn* **10/1**
3516 **11** 1 ¾ **Evolution Ex (USA)**[55] 5955 4-9-6 62 .... JimmyQuinn 5 54
(I W McInnes) *prom in chsng gp: rdn 3f out: sn lost pl and btn* **20/1**
2m 35.57s (-1.33) **Going Correction** -0.025s/f (Stan)
WFA 3 from 4yo+ 5lb **11** Ran SP% **124.5**
Speed ratings (Par 101):103,102,102,101,100 99,99,97,96,95 94
CSF £26.29 CT £128.23 TOTE £5.30: £1.90, £1.70, £3.50; EX 26.60 Place 6 £33.17, Place 5 £29.28.
Owner The Wacko Partnership **Bred** Hedgeholme Stud **Trained** Woodingdean, E Sussex

FOCUS
A modest but very competitive middle-distance handicap and rated positively through the third and fifth, with those behind close to their marks
Turner's Touch Official explanation: trainer said, regarding apparent improvement in form, that the gelding benefited from the refitting of eyeshield and blinkers
Inside Story(IRE) ◆ Official explanation: jockey said gelding was denied a clear run
Lennoxtown(IRE) Official explanation: jockey said gelding clipped heels
T/Plt: £89.40 to a £1 stake. Pool: £42,667.90. 348.05 winning tickets. T/Qpdt: £5.60 to a £1 stake. Pool: £5,421.90. 715.20 winning tickets. JN

6736 WOLVERHAMPTON (A.W) (L-H)
Friday, December 8

OFFICIAL GOING: Standard
Wind: Light, half-behind Weather: Fine

6749 WBX.COM WORLD BET EXCHANGE MEDIAN AUCTION MAIDEN STKS 5f 216y(P)
12:25 (12:26) (Class 6) 2-Y-O £2,730 (£806; £403) Stalls Low

Form RPR
0025 **1** **Buckie Massa**[5] 6689 2-9-3 68 .... GeorgeBaker 2 75+
(S Kirk) *chsd ldrs: hung rt fr over 2f out: rdn to ld over 1f out: r.o* **3/1**[1]
655 **2** 4 **Para Siempre**[29] 6414 2-8-12 58 .... PaulEddery 1 58
(B Smart) *w ldr tl led 1/2-way: rdn and hdd over 1f out: styd on same pce* **7/2**[2]
33 **3** ¾ **Iza Coming (IRE)**[13] 6596 2-8-7 .... JerryO'Dwyer(5) 5 56
(M G Quinlan) *chsd ldrs: rdn over 2f out: styng on same pce whn hung lft fnl f* **5/1**[3]
4 3 ½ **Tilapia (IRE)** 2-9-3 .... EddieAhern 9 50+
(Sir Mark Prescott) *sn outpcd: styd on ins fnl f: nrst fin* **16/1**
3 **5** ¾ **Pont Wood**[13] 6603 2-9-3 .... FrancisNorton 4 48
(M Blanshard) *s.i.s: sn pushed along in rr: sme hdwy u.p over 1f out: n.d* **7/2**[2]
6 2 **Ardennes (IRE)** 2-9-3 ....(t) OscarUrbina 8 42
(M Botti) *s.i.s: hld up: hdwy over 2f out: rdn: edgd lft and wknd over 1f out* **11/2**
65 **7** 3 **Pretty Selma**[25] 6463 2-8-12 ....(p) ChrisCatlin 3 28
(R M H Cowell) *led to 1/2-way: sn rdn and hung rt: wknd over 1f out* **25/1**
00 **8** ½ **Churchtown**[20] 6523 2-9-3 .... PatCosgrave 7 32
(K R Burke) *in tch: rdn 1/2-way: wknd 2f out* **50/1**
00 **9** 3 **Foxy Music**[20] 6512 2-9-3 .... RobbieFitzpatrick 6 23
(Peter Grayson) *mid-div: rdn whn n.m.r 2f out: sn hung rt and wknd* **66/1**
1m 14.84s (-0.97) **Going Correction** -0.075s/f (Stan) **9** Ran SP% **114.7**
Speed ratings (Par 94):103,97,96,92,91 88,84,83,79
CSF £13.42 TOTE £3.60: £1.20, £2.10, £2.40; EX 21.50 Trifecta £87.40 Pool £187.31, 1.52 w/u.

Owner M M Matalon **Bred** Vernon Matalon **Trained** Upper Lambourn, Berks

FOCUS
A modest maiden in which the pace was just fair but the form looks solid. The winner edged into the centre of the track in the straight.

NOTEBOOK
Buckie Massa proved suited by the return to sprinting and turned in his best effort yet to win an ordinary maiden. He had looked exposed, though, so will find things tougher after reassessment in handicaps. (op 4-1)
Para Siempre is a consistent sort who had the run of the race and looks a fair guide to the level of this form. While likely to remain vulnerable in this grade, she will be of more interest over seven furlongs in modest handicaps. (op 9-2 tchd 5-1)
Iza Coming(IRE) has now run to a similar level of form on all three starts and, on this evidence, will be suited by the step up to seven furlongs and the switch to modest handicaps. She is in good hands and is capable of winning a race. (op 10-3 tchd 6-1)
Tilapia(IRE), related to several winners from six furlongs to middle distances, was easy to back but shaped with a hint of promise on this racecourse debut. He is in very good hands and can be expected to leave this form a long way behind in due course. (op 9-1 tchd 8-1)

Pont Wood failed to build on his fairly encouraging debut effort over this course and distance and, on this evidence, he is likely to continue to look vulnerable in this type of race. (op 9-2)
Ardennes(IRE), the first foal of an unraced half-sister to a fairly useful winner up to middle distances, sported a tongue-tie for this racecourse debut and shaped as though a bit better than the distance beaten implies after attracting support and travelling strongly for a long way. He is likely to improve for this experience. (op 7-1 tchd 9-2)
Foxy Music Official explanation: jockey said gelding hung right in home straight

6750 WBXTRIPLECROWN.COM NURSERY 5f 216y(P)
1:00 (1:00) (Class 5) (0-75,73) 2-Y-O **£3,886** (£1,156; £577; £288) **Stalls** Low

Form RPR
4221 **1** **Shustraya**[13] [6596] 2-9-7 **73** EddieAhern 2 75
(P J Makin) *trckd ldrs: led over 2f out: rdn and hung rt fr over 1f out: r.o* **10/11**[1]
133 **2** ½ **Social Rhythm**[16] [6563] 2-9-3 **69** JimmyQuinn 5 70
(H J Collingridge) *hld up in tch: rdn over 1f out: r.o* **5/1**[2]
2301 **3** ½ **Mr Loire**[16] [6562] 2-9-3 **72** RichardKingscote[(3)] 7 71
(R Charlton) *s.s: hdwy and hung lft over 1f out: r.o* **6/1**[3]
2015 **4** ¾ **Jord (IRE)**[20] [6525] 2-9-0 **71** NataliaGemelova[(5)] 4 68
(A J McCabe) *racd keenly: a.p: rdn and hung rt over 1f out: styd on same pce ins fnl f* **7/1**
2216 **5** 1 ¾ **Galaxy Of Stars**[13] [6592] 2-8-6 **61** (v) PatrickMathers[(3)] 1 53
(D Shaw) *hld up in tch: rdn over 1f out: no ex fnl f* **12/1**
0264 **6** 2 ½ **Kilcusnin Queen (IRE)**[31] [6388] 2-8-12 **69** JerryO'Dwyer[(5)] 3 53
(Adrian Sexton, Ire) *prom: lost pl 4f out: n.d after* **20/1**
4035 **7** ¾ **La Quinta (IRE)**[23] [6488] 2-8-7 **66** KMay[(7)] 6 48
(B J Meehan) *chsd ldrs: rdn over 2f out: wknd over 1f out* **14/1**
535 **8** nk **Superjain**[28] [6420] 2-8-1 **60** PaulPickard[(7)] 8 41
(J M Jefferson) *sn led: hdd over 2f out: hung lft and wknd over 1f out* **40/1**

1m 15.41s (-0.40) **Going Correction** -0.075s/f (Stan) 8 Ran SP% **117.4**
Speed ratings (Par 96):99,98,97,96,94 91,90,89
CSF £6.02 CT £18.43 TOTE £1.70: £1.10, £1.50, £1.80; EX 5.90 Trifecta £19.40 Pool £291.01, 10.61 w/u.
Owner Four Leaf Clover **Bred** Millsec Limited **Trained** Ogbourne Maisey, Wilts

FOCUS
An ordinary nursery in which the pace was just fair and the form is sound rated through the third to previous form. The winner came up the centre.

NOTEBOOK
Shustraya is a progressive sort who had the run of the race from a decent draw but turned in an improved effort on this handicap debut. She should not be going up too much for this win and may be capable of a bit better. (op 6-4)
Social Rhythm, who won her only previous start over this course and distance on her debut, lost little in defeat against a progressive rival. She still takes a fair grip in her races but is capable of winning again away from improving sorts. (op 11-2 tchd 6-1 and 9-2)
Mr Loire, who beat the winner of the opener in ready fashion at Kempton last time, is not entirely straightforward and spoiled his chance this time with a slow start. On this evidence he is capable of winning a similar event when jumping off on terms. (op 5-1 tchd 7-1)
Jord(IRE) ran creditably in terms of form but again looked less than straightforward when failing to settle and hanging under pressure. She looks worth another try over seven furlongs and on Fibresand. (op 8-1)
Galaxy Of Stars, a five-furlong winner from a wide draw at this course last month, was much better berthed returned to Wolverhampton. She was not disgraced in this higher grade but looked beaten on merit and will have to improve to win from this mark. (op 10-1 tchd 14-1)
Kilcusnin Queen(IRE), who ran well on her handicap debut over course and distance early last month, was well beaten on her first run since. Consistency does not look to be her strongest suit. (op 12-1)

6751 WBX.COM WORLD BET EXCHANGE MAIDEN STKS 7f 32y(P)
1:35 (1:36) (Class 5) 2-Y-O **£3,886** (£1,156; £577; £288) **Stalls** High

Form RPR
1 **Leonard Charles** 2-9-3 PaulHanagan 3 72
(Sir Mark Prescott) *s.i.s: sn prom: rdn and hung lft over 1f out: led and hung rt ins fnl f: styd on* **6/1**[3]
3 **2** ¾ **Bold Indian (IRE)**[21] [6504] 2-9-3 TomEaves 4 70
(I Semple) *chsd ldrs: rdn over 1f out: r.o* **10/11**[1]
3 1 **Poisiedon (IRE)** 2-9-3 MickyFenton 8 68
(Liam McAteer, Ire) *led 6f out: rdn and hung rt over 1f out: hdd and unable qckn ins fnl f* **10/1**
00 **4** ½ **Briarwood Bear**[186] [2287] 2-9-3 FrancisNorton 7 66
(M Blanshard) *chsd ldrs: rdn over 1f out: styd on same pce ins fnl f* **33/1**
06 **5** nk **Don't Desert Me (IRE)**[14] [6581] 2-9-0 RichardKingscote[(3)] 5 66
(R Charlton) *hld up: rdn over 2f out: styd on fnl f: nt trble ldrs* **4/1**[2]
5 **6** 2 **Dear One (IRE)**[237] [1019] 2-8-12 ChrisCatlin 1 56
(P A Blockley) *led: hdd 6f out: chsd ldrs: rdn over 2f out: wknd fnl f* **9/1**
7 11 **Jemima Godfrey** 2-8-7 ow2 (t) StevenCorrigan[(7)] 2 30
(J Pearce) *s.i.s: outpcd* **33/1**

1m 32.17s (1.77) **Going Correction** -0.075s/f (Stan) 7 Ran SP% **111.6**
Speed ratings (Par 96):86,85,84,83,83 80,68
CSF £11.32 TOTE £7.60: £2.60, £1.50; EX 14.00 Trifecta £65.70 Pool £360.46, 3.89 w/u.
Owner John Brown & Megan Dennis **Bred** John Brown & Megan Dennis **Trained** Newmarket, Suffolk

FOCUS
Little strength in depth but the winner won despite his greenness and is the type to improve again. The runner-up sets the level for the form.

NOTEBOOK
Leonard Charles ◆, a half-brother to dual five-furlong and mile winner Joseph Henry and five-furlong juvenile scorer Royal Engineer, turned in a fair effort to get off the mark at the first attempt, despite his apparent greenness. He should have no problems with a mile and is the type to improve and win another race. (op 13-2 tchd 11-2)
Bold Indian(IRE) ran a similar race to that on his first run for these connections over this course and distance on his All-Weather debut last time in that he lost his place before staying on in the closing stages. He will be well suited by the step up to a mile and is capable of wining a race this winter. (op 5-6 tchd Evens)
Poisiedon(IRE), out of an unraced half-sister to a top class performer in the US, had the run of the race but ran creditably on this racecourse debut. This was an ordinary event but he is entitled to improve for the experience. (op 8-1 tchd 7-1)
Briarwood Bear, who had been soundly beaten on his two previous starts on turf, fared much better this time but his proximity does hold this form down to a degree and he is likely to remain vulnerable in this type of race. (tchd 40-1)
Don't Desert Me(IRE) ran his best race to date in this ordinary maiden. He will be suited by the switch to modest handicap company and the return to a mile and he is one to keep an eye on in the coming weeks. (op 6-1 tchd 13-2)
Dear One(IRE), having her first start since April, again showed ability at a modest level on this first run over seven furlongs. She is likely to remain vulnerable in this grade but will be of more interest once handicapped. (op 7-1)

6752 WORLD BET EXCHANGE WBX.COM H'CAP 1m 141y(P)
2:10 (2:10) (Class 4) (0-85,82) 3-Y-O+ **£5,505** (£1,637; £818; £408) **Stalls** Low

Form RPR
-003 **1** **Very Wise**[155] [3218] 4-9-4 **82** TonyCulhane 1 89+
(W J Haggas) *hld up in tch: rdn over 1f out: styd on u.p to ld nr fin* **9/4**[1]
0505 **2** hd **Atlantic Quest (USA)**[13] [6607] 7-8-13 **80** AmirQuinn[(3)] 4 87
(Miss Venetia Williams) *sn led: rdn and edgd rt over 1f out: hung lft ins fnl f: hdd nr fin* **7/1**
3253 **3** shd **Gifted Gamble**[14] [6580] 4-9-4 **82** (b) FrancisNorton 3 88
(K A Ryan) *chsd ldr: rdn and hung rt over 1f out: ev ch ins fnl f: styd on* **3/1**[2]
0644 **4** ¾ **Jimmy The Guesser**[33] [6352] 3-9-2 **82** MickyFenton 7 87
(N P Littmoden) *chsd ldrs: rdn and hung lft fr over 1f out: styd on* **6/1**
0000 **5** 1 ¼ **Primo Way**[10] [6643] 5-8-10 **74** (b) TomEaves 8 76
(I Semple) *hld up: rdn over 2f out: nt trble ldrs* **10/1**
2324 **6** 1 ¾ **Tender The Great (IRE)**[10] [6647] 3-7-9 **68** oh3 (v) WilliamBuick[(7)] 2 67
(V Smith) *s.i.s: hld up: rdn over 2f out: n.d* **11/2**[3]

1m 51.42s (-0.34) **Going Correction** -0.075s/f (Stan)
WFA 3 from 4yo+ 2lb 6 Ran SP% **107.0**
Speed ratings (Par 105):98,97,97,97,95 94
CSF £16.30 CT £38.52 TOTE £3.00: £1.90, £3.20; EX 10.50 Trifecta £43.30 Pool £315.22, 5.16 w/u.
Owner J M Greetham **Bred** J M Greetham **Trained** Newmarket, Suffolk

FOCUS
Mainly exposed performers and a muddling gallop means this bare form does not look entirely reliable, although the third, fourth and sixth were close to recent form. The winner, who looks better than the bare result, raced towards the far rail in the straight.

6753 WBX.COM WORLD BET EXCHANGE H'CAP (DIV I) 5f 20y(P)
2:45 (2:46) (Class 6) (0-52,52) 3-Y-O+ **£2,047** (£604; £302) **Stalls** Low

Form RPR
0324 **1** **Gifted Lass**[10] [6637] 4-8-7 **47** DavidAllan 1 56
(J Balding) *w ldr: rdn over 1f out: led wl ins fnl f: r.o* **7/2**[3]
0202 **2** shd **Muktasb (USA)**[2] [6723] 5-8-7 **50** (v) PatrickMathers[(3)] 6 59
(D Shaw) *outpcd: hdwy u.p over 1f out: r.o* **3/1**[2]
0022 **3** ½ **One Way Ticket**[5] [6688] 6-8-10 **50** (p) MickyFenton 7 57
(J M Bradley) *led: rdn and hung fr over 1f out: hdd wl ins fnl f* **15/8**[1]
010 **4** 3 ½ **Borzoi Maestro**[18] [6533] 5-8-12 **52** (b[1]) DaleGibson 2 47
(M Wellings) *chsd ldrs: rdn 1/2-way: hung lft and wknd fnl f* **10/1**
4153 **5** ½ **Desert Dust**[5] [6686] 3-8-12 **52** ChrisCatlin 10 45
(R M H Cowell) *chsd ldrs: rdn 1/2-way: wknd fnl f* **6/1**
6000 **6** 3 **Otis B Driftwood**[2] [6723] 3-8-7 **47** (p) StephenCarson 4 29
(Miss J R Tooth) *sn pushed along and prom: rdn over 3f out: wknd 1/2-way* **28/1**
0540 **7** ¾ **On The Trail**[10] [6636] 9-8-6 **46** oh6 PaulQuinn 3 25
(D W Chapman) *s.s: hdwy 1/2-way: rdn and wkng whne n.m.r over 1f out* **40/1**
3600 **8** 6 **Montillia (IRE)**[1] [6739] 4-8-1 **48** ow1 PatrickHills[(7)] 9 5
(J W Unett) *mid-div: rdn 1/2-way: sn wknd* **25/1**

62.05 secs (-0.77) **Going Correction** -0.075s/f (Stan) 8 Ran SP% **115.1**
Speed ratings (Par 101):103,102,102,96,95 90,89,80
CSF £14.28 CT £24.80 TOTE £4.50: £1.50, £1.20, £1.40; EX 17.00 Trifecta £52.50 Pool £474.15, 6.41 w/u.
Owner Bawtry Racing Partnership **Bred** Charles Castle **Trained** Scrooby, Notts

FOCUS
A low-grade sprint in which the gallop was sound throughout and the form looks solid enough, rated around the first three. The winner raced towards the inside rail in the straight.

6754 WBX.COM WORLD BET EXCHANGE APPRENTICE H'CAP 1m 5f 194y(P)
3:20 (3:21) (Class 6) (0-65,65) 3-Y-O+ **£2,730** (£806; £403) **Stalls** Low

Form RPR
1 **Share The Feeling (IRE)**[75] [5559] 4-9-3 **54** RichardKingscote 4 63
(J W Unett) *a.p: chsd ldr over 3f out: led over 2f out: rdn out* **40/1**
6500 **2** nk **Capitalise (IRE)**[24] [5839] 3-7-9 **46** oh1 WilliamBuick[(7)] 2 55
(V Smith) *hld up: hdwy over 4f out: hmpd over 3f out: chsd wnr over 1f out: swtchd rt ins fnl f: r.o* **14/1**
0001 **3** 5 **Your Amount (IRE)**[24] [6479] 3-9-1 **64** AlanRutter[(5)] 3 69+
(W J Musson) *hld up: hdwy over 2f out: nt clr run over 1f out: styd on ins fnl f: nvr able to chal* **11/4**[1]
4-50 **4** ½ **Rajayoga**[69] [4252] 5-8-4 **46** oh6 PatrickHills[(5)] 6 47
(M H Tompkins) *prom: lost pl over 10f out: hdwy over 1f out: nt trble ldrs* **14/1**
0000 **5** nk **Mustakhlas (USA)**[154] [3270] 5-8-2 **46** oh6 SoniaEaton[(7)] 10 47
(B P J Baugh) *plld hrd: w ldrs: rdn over 1f out: wknd ins fnl f* **66/1**
4023 **6** nk **Sovereign Spirit (IRE)**[17] [6560] 4-9-9 **65** (t) JackMitchell[(5)] 7 65
(W R Swinburn) *hld up: hdwy 1/2-way: rdn over 1f out: sn hung lft wknd* **3/1**[2]
6202 **7** 1 **Peas 'n Beans (IRE)**[21] [6509] 3-8-6 **53** DuranFentiman[(3)] 1 52
(T Keddy) *hld up: rdn over 3f out: n.d* **9/1**
4651 **8** 1 **Bolckow**[36] [6302] 3-8-4 **53** AshleyHamblett[(5)] 12 51
(J T Stimpson) *plld hrd and prom: rdn over 2f out: hung lft fr over 1f out: wknd ins fnl f* **9/1**
2201 **9** shd **Captivate**[4] [6705] 3-8-0 **51** 6ex (p) MCGeran[(7)] 11 49
(A J McCabe) *s.i.s: a in rr* **16/1**
0606 **10** ½ **Ulshaw**[14] [6584] 9-8-4 **46** oh6 JamieJones[(5)] 8 44
(J M Bradley) *hld up: hdwy over 5f out: rdn over 2f out: wknd wl over 1f out* **100/1**
0611 **11** hd **Zaville**[21] [6509] 4-9-8 **64** (p) JamesO'Reilly[(5)] 5 61
(J O'Reilly) *mde most over 11f: wknd fnl f* **7/2**[3]
0504 **12** 9 **Missouri (USA)**[16] [6279] 3-7-12 **47** oh1 ow1 KellyHarrison[(5)] 9 31
(G M Moore) *chsd ldrs: wkng whn hung lft over 1f out* **33/1**
13 19 **Saitama**[457] 4-9-2 **60** JosephWalsh[(7)] 13 17
(A M Hales) *hld up: hdwy 8f out: wknd 4f out* **100/1**

3m 6.38s (-0.99) **Going Correction** -0.075s/f (Stan)
WFA 3 from 4yo+ 7lb 13 Ran SP% **122.0**
Speed ratings (Par 101):99,98,95,95,95 95,94,94,94,93 93,88,77
CSF £527.32 CT £2071.21 TOTE £47.10: £8.80, £4.90, £1.60; EX 274.30 TRIFECTA Not won..
Owner John Malone **Bred** John Malone **Trained** Preston, Shropshire

FOCUS
A modest handicap in which the early pace was just fair and the form looks reasonable but limited. The winner raced towards the far rail in the straight.

6755 WBX.COM WORLD BET EXCHANGE H'CAP (DIV II) 5f 20y(P)
3:55 (3:56) (Class 6) (0-52,52) 3-Y-0+ £2,047 (£604; £302) Stalls Low

Form RPR
6202 1 **Succeed (IRE)**[5] [6686] 3-8-7 50 RichardKingscote(3) 2 59+
(Mrs H Sweeting) *chsd ldrs: led over 1f out: rdn out* 3/1[1]
1000 2 1 1/4 **Lady Hopeful (IRE)**[5] [6688] 4-8-7 47 (b) RobbieFitzpatrick 3 50
(Peter Grayson) *s.i.s: hld up: hdwy over 1f out: r.o* 8/1
3400 3 1/2 **Campeon (IRE)**[5] [6686] 4-8-8 48 ow1 MickyFenton 8 49
(J M Bradley) *prom: chsd ldr 1/2-way: rdn and ev ch over 1f out: styd on same pce ins fnl f* 9/1
0062 4 1/2 **New Options**[1] [6739] 9-8-3 46 oh6 (b) PatrickMathers(3) 7 45
(Peter Grayson) *hld up: hdwy over 1f out: r.o* 9/2[2]
0000 5 1 3/4 **Mustammer**[2] [6728] 3-8-10 50 (v) PaulHanagan 10 43
(D Shaw) *dwlt: outpcd: hung lft over 1f out: nt clr run ins fnl f: r.o: nrst fin* 33/1
6 hd **Chapelizod (IRE)**[44] [6180] 3-8-6 46 oh1 FrancisNorton 5 38
(Liam McAteer, Ire) *chsd ldrs: lost pl wl over 2f out: r.o ins fnl f* 8/1
0001 7 1 **She's Our Beauty (IRE)**[17] [6548] 3-8-1 46 (v) DuranFentiman(5) 4 35
(S T Mason) *sn led: rdn and hdd over 1f out: wknd ins fnl f* 11/1
0340 8 2 1/2 **Diamond Josh**[33] [6348] 4-8-12 52 (p) TomEaves 6 32
(M Mullineaux) *chsd ldrs over 3f* 6/1[3]
0006 9 shd **Luloah**[239] [1003] 3-8-12 52 (p) BrianReilly 11 31
(P S McEntee) *chsd ldrs: rdn over 1f out: hung lft and wknd fnl f* 66/1
0000 10 3 **Henry Tun**[18] [6533] 8-8-7 50 (v) JasonEdmunds(3) 1 18
(J Balding) *sn pushed along in rr: bhd fr 1/2-way* 13/2

62.16 secs (-0.66) **Going Correction** -0.075s/f (Stan) 10 Ran SP% 115.8
Speed ratings (Par 101):102,100,99,98,95 95,93,89,89,84
CSF £27.43 CT £198.67 TOTE £3.70: £1.70, £2.70, £2.50; EX 29.60 Trifecta £113.30 Pool £159.69 - 1.00 winning unit. Place 6 £9.35, Place 5 £5.99.
Owner P Sweeting **Bred** M Downey And Glending Bloodstock **Trained** Lockeridge, Wilts
FOCUS
Another low-grade handicap but one in which the pace was sound and the form is moderate rated around the third and fifth. The winner ended up in the centre of the track.
T/Plt: £13.60 to a £1 stake. Pool: £38,812.70. 2,075.00 winning tickets. T/Qpdt: £7.20 to a £1 stake. Pool: £2,566.30. 262.10 winning tickets. CR

6715 SOUTHWELL (L-H)
Saturday, December 9

OFFICIAL GOING: Standard
Wind: Moderate, behind. Weather: Fine.

6756 JOIN US ON NEW YEARS DAY H'CAP (DIV I) 7f (F)
11:30 (11:30) (Class 6) (0-53,59) 3-Y-0+ £2,047 (£604; £302) Stalls Low

Form RPR
0201 1 **Elusive Warrior (USA)**[7] [6674] 3-9-6 59 (p) PaulHanagan 12 69+
(R A Fahey) *hld up in mid-div: hdwy on outside 3f out: rdn over 1f out: r.o to ld last strides* 4/6[1]
0640 2 hd **Prettilini**[14] [6608] 3-9-0 53 PatCosgrave 10 62
(R Brotherton) *a.p: led over 2f out: sn rdn: hdd last strides* 12/1
6155 3 3 **Barzak (IRE)**[18] [6554] 6-8-7 49 (bt) JasonEdmunds(3) 6 50
(S R Bowring) *hld up towards rr: hdwy over 3f out: rdn over 2f out: r.o one pce fnl f* 9/1[3]
4000 4 3 **Borodinsky**[89] [5243] 5-8-7 46 TomEaves 4 39
(R E Barr) *a.p: rdn 3f out: wknd fnl f* 33/1
6005 5 3/4 **Grand Palace (IRE)**[19] [6537] 3-8-13 52 (v[1]) DaneO'Neill 1 43
(D Shaw) *s.i.s: bhd tl rdn and hdwy on ins over 2f out: no real prog fnl f* 16/1
0003 6 shd **Wayward Shot (IRE)**[3] [6725] 4-8-11 50 JimmyQuinn 3 41
(G P Kelly) *led 2f: sn lost pl: rdn and rallied over 2f out: no imp fnl f* 8/1[2]
4434 7 3/4 **Mon Petite Amour**[5] [6708] 3-8-9 48 (p) EdwardCreighton 11 36
(D W P Arbuthnot) *bhd: sme hdwy over 2f out: swtchd rt wl over 1f out: nvr nr ldrs* 8/1[2]
5060 8 3 **Aboustar**[18] [6549] 6-8-7 46 oh6 DeanMernagh 9 26
(M Brittain) *led after 2f: rdn and hdd over 2f out: wknd over 1f out* 66/1
5 9 1/2 **Dictation**[29] [6431] 4-8-8 47 (b) ChrisCatlin 7 26
(Mrs Valerie Keatley, Ire) *hld up in mid-div: rdn over 3f out: no rspnse* 25/1
0026 10 1/2 **Wilford Maverick (IRE)**[5] [6702] 4-8-8 47 DaleGibson 5 25
(M J Attwater) *s.i.s: sn chsng ldrs: rdn over 2f out: wknd over 1f out* 16/1
-000 11 12 **Korolieva (IRE)**[32] [6387] 3-9-0 53 (b) CatherineGannon 13 —
(K A Ryan) *s.s: a bhd: eased whn no ch fnl f* 50/1
-000 12 6 **Lord Conyers (IRE)**[219] [1443] 7-8-8 47 oh11 ow1 FergusSweeney 2 —
(G Woodward) *prom 2f: eased whn no ch fnl f* 66/1
00-0 13 1 1/2 **Isabella Bay**[28] [6450] 6-8-4 48 oh6 ow2 (p) KevinGhunowa(5) 8 —
(M Wellings) *prom: rdn over 4f out: wknd over 3f out: eased whn no ch fnl f* 80/1

1m 30.83s (0.03) **Going Correction** -0.075s/f (Stan) 13 Ran SP% 124.6
Speed ratings (Par 101):96,95,92,88,88 87,87,83,83,82 68,61,60
CSF £10.48 CT £52.87 TOTE £1.60: £1.10, £2.70, £2.90; EX 11.40 Trifecta £51.00 Pool £78.31. - 1.09 winning units..
Owner Northumbria Leisure Ltd & B Morton **Bred** Steve Peskoff **Trained** Musley Bank, N Yorks
FOCUS
This banded-class handicap was run almost a second slower than the other division and the winner did not need to improve to score.

6757 EUROPEAN BREEDERS' FUND MAIDEN STKS 1m (F)
12:00 (12:00) (Class 5) 2-Y-0 £3,886 (£1,156; £577; £288) Stalls Low

Form RPR
53 1 **Mardi**[11] [6644] 2-9-3 TonyCulhane 6 73
(W J Haggas) *w ldr: led 4f out: sn rdn: narrowly hdd 2f out: led 1f out: drvn out* 9/4[2]
2 nk **Algarade** 2-8-12 J-PGuillambert 14 67
(Sir Mark Prescott) *w ldrs: slt ld 2f out to 1f out: r.o* 1/1[1]
033 3 4 **Inflagrantedelicto (USA)**[7] [6675] 2-9-3 67 PaulQuinn 10 63
(D W Chapman) *hld up in mid-div: rdn and hdwy 4f out: kpt on same pce fnl 2f* 10/1[3]
4 1 1/2 **Strabinios King** 2-9-3 AdrianTNicholls 13 60
(P C Haslam) *racd wd: prom: rdn over 3f out: wkng whn edgd lft over 1f out* 33/1
5 3 1/2 **Acece** 2-8-12 KevinGhunowa(5) 8 52
(M Appleby) *bhd: rdn and hdwy on ins over 2f out: nvr trbld ldrs* 100/1
6 shd **Riguez Dancer** 2-9-3 LeeEnstone 3 51
(P C Haslam) *bhd: rdn over 3f out: hdwy on ins over 2f out: nvr trbld ldrs* 20/1
5 7 3 1/2 **Danish Rebel (IRE)**[7] [6675] 2-9-3 PaulHanagan 11 43
(J I A Charlton) *nvr nr ldrs* 10/1[3]
340 8 1 1/2 **Calloff The Search**[192] [2130] 2-9-3 63 (p) DaleGibson 2 40
(W G M Turner) *led 4f: sn rdn and wknd* 40/1
0 9 2 1/2 **Heaven's Gates**[37] [6303] 2-9-3 PatCosgrave 12 34
(K A Ryan) *w ldrs: rdn over 3f out: wkng whn edgd rt wl over 1f out* 80/1
0 10 6 **Confident**[24] [6486] 2-8-12 JimmyQuinn 1 15
(M A Jarvis) *s.i.s: sn chsng ldrs: rdn and wknd 3f out* 16/1
11 11 **Athea Lad (IRE)**[83] [5409] 2-9-3 HayleyTurner 9 —
(W K Goldsworthy) *chsd ldrs: rdn over 5f out: sn lost pl* 33/1
12 7 **Intensifier (IRE)** 2-9-3 ChrisCatlin 5 —
(P A Blockley) *s.i.s: sn wl in rr* 20/1
00 13 2 1/2 **Mr Chocolate Drop (IRE)**[149] [3448] 2-9-3 RobbieFitzpatrick 4 —
(M J Attwater) *trckd ldrs tl wknd over 3f out* 100/1

1m 45.46s (0.86) **Going Correction** -0.075s/f (Stan) 13 Ran SP% 125.9
Speed ratings (Par 96):92,91,87,86,82 82,79,77,75,69 58,51,48
CSF £4.76 TOTE £3.20: £1.10, £1.20, £2.10; EX 8.20 Trifecta £37.10 Pool £107.33. - 2.05 winning units..
Owner B Haggas **Bred** J B Haggas **Trained** Newmarket, Suffolk
FOCUS
A reasonable Fibresand maiden for the time of the year rated through the third.
NOTEBOOK
Mardi duly handled the switch from Polytrack after making a promising debut in the soft at Newbury. Putting his previous experience to good use against a promising newcomer, he will be put away after an impending gelding operation. (op 5-2 tchd 3-1 and 100-30 in a place)
Algarade ◆ was a well-touted half-sister to the staying handicapper Alambic. Worried out of it by the more experienced winner, there are races to be won with her. (op 5-4 tchd 6-4 and 11-8 in places)
Inflagrantedelicto(USA) did appear to have more to do than when third over course and distance last time. (tchd 9-1)
Strabinios King, a half-brother to the dual Polytrack scorer Strawberry Lolly, showed that he possesses some ability on his debut. (op 25-1)
Acece was another debutant to run a lot better than his starting price suggested.
Riguez Dancer was yet another newcomer who hopefully will be better for the experience. (tchd 16-1)

6758 SOUTHWELL-RACECOURSE.CO.UK CLAIMING STKS 1m 3f (F)
12:35 (12:35) (Class 6) 3-4-Y-0 £2,730 (£806; £403) Stalls Low

Form RPR
4035 1 **Jazrawy**[18] [6553] 4-8-6 50 ow2 WilliamCarson(7) 11 59
(P W Hiatt) *sn led: rdn clr 3f out: drvn out* 7/2[3]
3000 2 2 1/2 **Mossmann Gorge**[16] [6571] 4-9-3 56 (b) DaneO'Neill 4 59+
(M Wellings) *hld up towards rr: smooth hdwy 4f out: chsd wnr over 2f out: rdn over 1f out: fnd little* 11/1
6342 3 1 1/4 **Depraux (IRE)**[15] [6578] 3-8-9 64 TonyCulhane 1 53
(W J Haggas) *hld up in mid-div: rdn 5f out: hdwy 2f out: one pce fnl f* 11/8[1]
03 4 3 **Willy (SWE)**[15] [6584] 4-9-2 60 (t) PatCosgrave 2 51
(R Brotherton) *hld up in tch: rdn over 4f out: one pce fnl 2f* 12/1
1101 5 9 **Maria Antonia (IRE)**[29] [6423] 3-8-11 54 KevinGhunowa(5) 5 41
(P A Blockley) *t.k.h towards rr: hdwy over 6f out: rdn over 3f out: wknd 2f out* 3/1[2]
000 6 shd **Hoofbeats Tour**[25] [6473] 4-8-0 35 AmyBaker(7) 10 28
(Miss J Feilden) *sn chsng ldr: rdn over 3f out: wknd wl over 1f out* 100/1
0006 7 16 **Mister Maq**[4] [6716] 3-8-7 56 (b) JimmyQuinn 9 6
(A Crook) *s.i.s: rdn over 5f out: a bhd* 12/1
6055 8 3/4 **City Minx**[37] [6302] 4-8-2 40 PaulEddery 3 —
(S R Bowring) *led early: prom: rdn over 4f out: sn wknd* 33/1
-000 9 7 **Elli Lewtia**[79] [3357] 3-8-1 35 ow1 ChrisCatlin 8 —
(J Jay) *a bhd* 100/1
000 10 9 **Westcourt Phoenix**[89] [5241] 3-8-4 30 (b) DaleGibson 7 —
(M W Easterby) *rdn over 5f out: a bhd* 100/1
-000 11 24 **Bright**[37] [6302] 3-8-3 40 HayleyTurner 6 —
(Robert Gray) *prom: rdn over 6f out: wknd over 5f out: t.o* 100/1

2m 27.53s (-1.37) **Going Correction** -0.075s/f (Stan)
WFA 3 from 4yo 4lb 11 Ran SP% 119.9
Speed ratings (Par 101):101,99,98,96,89 89,77,77,72,65 48
CSF £41.78 TOTE £5.00: £1.70, £3.00, £1.30; EX 50.20 Trifecta £73.80 Pool £351.70. - 3.38 winning units..Depraux was claimed by D McCain Jnr for £8,000.
Owner P W Hiatt **Bred** Scuderia Antonella S R L **Trained** Hook Norton, Oxon
FOCUS
Few could be seriously considered in this ordinary claimer and the form has been rated cautiously with the fourth and sixth closest to form.

6759 ANN JARVIS' CELEBRATION MAIDEN STKS 1m 4f (F)
1:05 (1:10) (Class 5) 3-4-Y-0 £3,238 (£963; £481; £240) Stalls Low

Form RPR
0353 1 **Aphorism**[72] [5644] 3-8-12 68 OscarUrbina 5 73+
(J R Fanshawe) *hld up in tch: led on bit over 3f out: shkn up over 2f out: clr over 1f out: easily* 4/9[1]
-400 2 8 **Stagecoach Emerald**[249] [882] 4-9-8 57 EdwardCreighton 8 60
(R W Price) *a.p: led over 5f out: rdn and hdd over 3f out: one pce fnl 2f* 12/1[3]
5630 3 1 1/4 **Weet For Ever (USA)**[12] [6621] 3-9-3 52 PaulHanagan 9 58
(P A Blockley) *dwlt: plld hrd in rr: hdwy 5f out: rdn over 3f out: one pce fnl 2f* 5/1[2]
004 4 6 **Asleep At The Back (IRE)**[37] [6302] 3-9-3 40 J-PGuillambert 10 49
(J G Given) *hdwy over 7f out: rdn over 3f out: wknd wl over 1f out* 20/1
0005 5 3 1/2 **Sophie'Jo**[25] [6476] 3-8-5 55 AmyBaker(7) 1 39
(Miss J Feilden) *led: hdd over 6f out: wknd over 3f out* 16/1
00-0 6 5 **Spinning Gold**[15] [6588] 3-8-12 50 JimmyQuinn 3 31
(Miss Gay Kelleway) *w ldrs: led over 6f out tl over 5f out: wknd over 3f out* 33/1
0 7 shd **Orphir (IRE)**[19] [6535] 3-8-12 DuranFentiman(5) 4 36
(Mrs N Macauley) *s.i.s: a bhd* 66/1
0630 8 3 **Prophet Preacher (IRE)**[138] [3791] 3-8-12 45 DaleGibson 7 27
(M Wellings) *s.i.s: bhd: rdn over 5f out: short-lived effrt over 3f out* 14/1
9 38 **Watermill (IRE)**[10] 3-9-3 PaulQuinn 6 —
(D W Chapman) *a bhd: rdn over 6f out: t.o fnl 3f* 12/1[3]

 The Form Book, Raceform Ltd, Compton, RG20 6NL

10 38 **Grey Finale**[17] 4-9-3 .... DeanMernagh 2 —
(M Brittain) *w ldr tl wknd over 6f out: t.o fnl 3f* **50/1**

2m 39.77s (-2.32) **Going Correction** -0.075s/f (Stan)
WFA 3 from 4yo 5lb **10** Ran SP% **125.0**
Speed ratings (Par 103):104,98,97,93,91 88,88,86,60,35
CSF £8.27 TOTE £1.60: £1.10, £2.80, £1.70; EX 9.40 Trifecta £66.70 Pool £430.76. - 4.58 winning units..
Owner Dr Catherine Wills **Bred** St Clare Hall Stud **Trained** Newmarket, Suffolk

FOCUS
A weak maiden apart from the winner and rated through the third to his best form.

6760 PERSONALISED CARDS FROM BONUSPRINT.COM NURSERY 1m (F)
1:40 (1:40) (Class 5) (0-75,85) 2-Y-O **£3,238** (£963; £481; £240) **Stalls** Low

Form RPR
1003 1 **Nicada (IRE)**[11] 6639 2-8-12 **66** ....(p) JimmyQuinn 4 70
(Miss Gay Kelleway) *hld up: hdwy over 4f out: rdn 2f out: led 1f out: sn edgd rt: r.o* **9/1**[3]

4241 2 nk **Strikeen (IRE)**[11] 6639 2-9-10 **85** .... PatrickHills(7) 5 88
(T G Mills) *a.p: rdn 2f out: ev ch whn edgd lft jst ins fnl f: carried rt towards fin: r.o* **4/6**[1]

4062 3 3 ½ **Cryptic Clue (USA)**[4] 6715 2-7-13 **53** .... PaulQuinn 8 48
(D W Chapman) *a.p: led over 2f out: sn rdn: edgd rt over 1f out: hung lft and hdd 1f out: hld whn sn squeezed out* **12/1**

3005 4 1 ¼ **My Mirasol**[11] 6639 2-8-8 **62** ....(p) FrancisNorton 6 54
(K A Ryan) *led over 1f: prom: rdn and wkng whn swtchd rt 2f out* **25/1**

0624 5 1 ¼ **Global Traffic**[11] 6639 2-7-8 **55** .... WilliamBuick(7) 1 45
(P D Evans) *hld up in rr: rdn and hdwy over 2f out: no imp fnl f* **12/1**

6566 6 5 **Bentley**[10] 6653 2-7-13 **53** oh4 ow1 ....(v) HayleyTurner 7 31
(D Shaw) *t.k.h: led over 6f out tl over 2f out: sn rdn and wknd* **25/1**

6446 7 12 **Raquel White**[15] 6582 2-9-0 **68** .... JimCrowley 3 18
(P D Evans) *a bhd* **18/1**

0351 8 hd **Sheriff's Silk**[19] 6534 2-8-8 **62** .... PaulEddery 2 12
(B Smart) *bhd: rdn over 5f out: no ch whn hung lft 2f out* **11/2**[2]

0005 9 6 **Up The Pole**[144] 3619 2-8-3 **57** .... DaleGibson 9 —
(M W Easterby) *s.i.s: rdn over 3f out: sn struggling* **25/1**

1m 43.16s (-1.44) **Going Correction** -0.075s/f (Stan) **9** Ran SP% **117.6**
Speed ratings (Par 96):104,103,100,98,97 92,80,80,74
CSF £15.40 CT £74.75 TOTE £8.50: £1.80, £1.10, £3.50; EX 27.80 Trifecta £119.50 Pool £441.33. - 2.62 winning units..
Owner S P Cook **Bred** Peadar Kelly **Trained** Exning, Suffolk
■ Stewards' Enquiry : Jimmy Quinn one-day ban: careless riding (Dec 20)

FOCUS
A good finish to a race that was not that competitive by nursery standards but the form looks solid overall.

NOTEBOOK
Nicada(IRE), back in cheekpieces, reversed a five and a half length defeat by Strikeen over course and distance on 12lb better terms. His rider picked up a one-day ban after he carried the runner-up across the course. (op 8-1)
Strikeen(IRE) could not confirm his five and a half length superiority over the winner when landing a similar event here on 12lb worse terms. With his old rival forcing him off a true line, he lost nothing in defeat. (op 8-11 tchd 4-5 in places)
Cryptic Clue(USA), back up to a mile, did not prove to be a straightforward ride. He did not look like solving this puzzle when becoming the meat in the sandwich. (op 10-1)
My Mirasol was 2lb better off than when just over four lengths behind the winner here last time. (op 12-1)
Global Traffic had finished ahead of My Mirasol when behind the first two over course and distance last time.

6761 RACING AGAIN ON THE 12TH H'CAP 1m 6f (F)
2:15 (2:16) (Class 5) (0-75,76) 3-Y-0+ **£3,238** (£963; £481; £240) **Stalls** Low

Form RPR
2021 1 **Flame Creek (IRE)**[4] 6718 10-10-1 **76** 6ex........ EdwardCreighton 1 89+
(E J Creighton) *hld up in tch: led 3f out: sn pushed clr: easily* **30/100**[1]

010 2 9 **Stolen Light (IRE)**[4] 6718 5-9-13 **74**........(b) TomEaves 4 71
(A Crook) *hld up in tch: led over 4f out: rdn and hdd 3f out: sn btn* **13/2**[2]

0505 3 5 **Isa'Af (IRE)**[14] 6604 7-8-9 **56** oh1........ ChrisCatlin 5 47
(P W Hiatt) *chsd ldr: led over 7f out: rdn and hdd over 4f out: wknd over 3f out* **12/1**[3]

0000 4 11 **Kalush**[17] 5751 5-8-7 **59** oh21 ow3........ AnnStokell(5) 3 36
(Miss A Stokell) *hld up in tch: wknd 4f out* **100/1**

200 5 1 **Top Seed (IRE)**[14] 6602 5-9-7 **75**........ MarkCoumbe(7) 2 50
(A J Chamberlain) *led: rdn and hdd over 4f out: wknd over 3f out* **13/2**[2]

3m 8.83s (-0.77) **Going Correction** -0.075s/f (Stan) **5** Ran SP% **112.3**
Speed ratings (Par 103):99,93,91,84,84
CSF £3.04 TOTE £1.30: £1.10, £2.50; EX 2.50.
Owner Estrella Partners **Bred** Kilcornan Stables **Trained** East Garston, Berks

FOCUS
This turned out to be the expected one-horse race and the winner is value for at least 12 lengths, although the third limits the form.

6762 PHOTO GIFTS FROM BONUSPRINT.COM H'CAP 1m (F)
2:50 (2:50) (Class 6) (0-65,66) 3-Y-0+ **£2,590** (£770; £385; £192) **Stalls** Low

Form RPR
4053 1 **Kingsmaite**[11] 6641 5-8-8 **59**........(bt) JasonEdmunds(3) 9 69+
(S R Bowring) *chsd ldr: led over 6f out: rdn wl over 1f out: r.o* **6/1**

0441 2 ¾ **Sentiero Rosso (USA)**[11] 6641 4-9-4 **66**........(t) TomEaves 12 74
(B Ellison) *hld up in tch: rdn over 2f out: ev ch over 1f out: nt qckn ins fnl f* **3/1**[2]

4116 3 1 ¼ **Gracie's Gift (IRE)**[31] 6396 4-9-0 **62**........ DaneO'Neill 7 68
(A G Newcombe) *hld up in tch: rdn over 3f out: r.o one pce fnl f* **4/1**[3]

1 4 ½ **Astronomical Odds (USA)**[19] 6532 3-9-1 **64**........ PaulHanagan 3 69
(T D Barron) *a.p: rdn and hung lft fr over 2f out: kpt on same pce* **11/4**[1]

00 5 1 ¼ **Mohawk Star (IRE)**[7] 5590 5-9-2 **64**........(b) LeeEnstone 6 66+
(I A Wood) *sn in rr: rdn over 4f out: hdwy on outside fnl f: nrst fin* **14/1**

0600 6 ½ **Cesar Manrique (IRE)**[24] 6489 4-9-2 **64**........(p) LPKeniry 5 65
(A E Jones) *hld up and bhd: hdwy 4f out: rdn and one pce fnl 2f* **50/1**

5035 7 2 **Shrine Mountain (USA)**[11] 6641 4-9-0 **62**........ JosedeSouza 8 59
(J R Holt) *led over 1f: wknd over 2f out* **12/1**

0630 8 nk **Wizby**[38] 6300 3-7-9 **51** oh6........ WilliamBuick(7) 13 47
(P D Evans) *hld up towards rr: rdn over 4f out: nvr trbld ldrs* **40/1**

4000 9 ½ **Tyrone Sam**[259] 737 4-9-0 **62**........(b) CatherineGannon 4 57
(K A Ryan) *hld up in tch: rdn over 3f out: eased whn btn ins fnl f* **66/1**

0052 10 1 ¼ **Ruffie (IRE)**[11] 6641 3-9-2 **65**........(e) JimmyQuinn 2 58
(Miss Gay Kelleway) *mid-div: rdn over 3f out: wknd over 1f out* **12/1**

0006 11 2 ½ **Danelor (IRE)**[7] 6674 8-8-3 **51** oh1........(v) HayleyTurner 11 39
(D Shaw) *a bhd* **25/1**

6000 12 6 **Dado Mush**[19] 6531 3-7-11 **53**........ JosephWalsh(7) 1 29
(G Prodromou) *s.i.s: a bhd* **50/1**

5446 13 8 **Cabourg (IRE)**[19] 6532 3-8-10 **59**........ PatCosgrave 10 19
(R Bastiman) *hld up in mid-div: rdn over 4f out: sn lost pl: eased whn no ch fnl f* **20/1**

1m 42.76s (-1.84) **Going Correction** -0.075s/f (Stan)
WFA 3 from 4yo+ 1lb **13** Ran SP% **124.5**
Speed ratings (Par 101):106,105,104,103,102 101,99,99,98,97 95,89,81
CSF £24.09 CT £84.79 TOTE £7.20: £2.50, £1.70, £2.00; EX 39.80 Trifecta £132.10 Pool £323.85. - 1.74 winning units..
Owner S R Bowring **Bred** S R Bowring **Trained** Edwinstowe, Notts

FOCUS
A modest handicap and the form looks solid with the majority of those immediately behind the first two running close to previous marks.

6763 JOIN US ON NEW YEARS DAY H'CAP (DIV II) 7f (F)
3:25 (3:25) (Class 6) (0-53,56) 3-Y-0+ **£2,047** (£604; £302) **Stalls** Low

Form RPR
0000 1 **Cool Sands (IRE)**[14] 6590 4-9-0 **53**........(v) DaneO'Neill 6 62
(D Shaw) *a.p: rdn wl over 1f out: led ins fnl f: r.o* **15/2**

0021 2 ¾ **Haroldini (IRE)**[5] 6703 4-9-0 **56** 7ex........(p) JasonEdmunds(3) 11 63
(J Balding) *hld up in mid-div: hdwy on outside over 3f out: led on bit over 2f out: rdn over 1f out: hdd and nt qckn ins fnl f* **10/3**[2]

5231 3 ½ **Granakey (IRE)**[37] 6308 3-8-9 **53**........ JerryO'Dwyer(5) 9 59
(M G Quinlan) *led early: a.p: rdn over 3f out: n.m.r 2f out: sn edgd lft: kpt on ins fnl f* **5/2**[1]

00 4 3 **Tipsy Lillie**[19] 6538 4-8-7 **46** oh6........ HayleyTurner 8 44
(P S McEntee) *bhd: rdn over 4f out: hdwy on outside 2f out: kpt on same pce fnl f* **33/1**

0000 5 nk **Pawn In Life (IRE)**[11] 6642 8-8-11 **50**........(v) JoeFanning 5 47
(M J Attwater) *hld up in tch: lost pl over 4f out: rallied 2f out: kpt on same pce fnl f* **6/1**[3]

0323 6 1 **Prince Of Gold**[11] 6638 6-8-10 **49**........(e) FergusSweeney 3 43
(R Hollinshead) *hld up and bhd: nt clr run 2f out: hdwy over 1f out: one pce fnl f* **6/1**[3]

0400 7 1 ¼ **Gem Bien (USA)**[7] 6674 8-8-9 **48**........(b) PaulQuinn 4 39
(D W Chapman) *prom: rdn over 2f out: wknd fnl f* **16/1**

4000 8 7 **Crusoe (IRE)**[4] 6721 9-8-9 **48** ow1........(b) BrianReilly 1 20
(A Sadik) *sn prom: rdn over 3f out: wknd over 2f out* **20/1**

200 9 1 ½ **Halfwaytoparadise**[21] 6510 3-8-13 **52**........(p) DaleGibson 7 20
(W G M Turner) *sn led: hdd over 3f out: rdn and wknd over 2f out* **14/1**

0/00 10 5 **Theme Time (USA)**[26] 6469 10-8-10 **49** oh11 ow3..(t) DerekMcGaffin 12 3
(D Morris) *sn prom: led over 3f out: rdn and hdd over 2f out: wknd over 1f out* **100/1**

040- 11 14 **First Generation**[50] 6087 4-8-8 **47**........ JimCrowley 2 —
(P D Evans) *prom: rdn over 3f out: wknd 2f out* **20/1**

0000 12 1 ¼ **Teddy Monty (IRE)**[122] 4263 3-8-7 **46** oh6........ PaulHanagan 10 —
(R E Barr) *a bhd* **50/1**

1m 29.88s (-0.92) **Going Correction** -0.075s/f (Stan) **12** Ran SP% **120.0**
Speed ratings (Par 101):102,101,100,97,96 95,94,86,84,78 62,61
CSF £31.48 CT £83.53 TOTE £8.70: £3.30, £1.40, £1.60; EX 42.60 Trifecta £124.20 Pool £409.34. - 2.34 winning units. Place 6 £1.95, Place 5 £1.52..
Owner Peter Swann **Bred** Rathasker Stud **Trained** Danethorpe, Notts

FOCUS
This was nearly a second faster than the first division with the first two running top previous marks.
Cool Sands(IRE) Official explanation: trainer said, regarding apparent improvement in form, that the gelding was suited by a drop in trip and grade
T/Plt: £2.30 to a £1 stake. Pool: £35,995.60. 11,150.35 winning tickets. T/Qpdt: £1.90 to a £1 stake. Pool: £2,646.80. 1,013.00 winning tickets. KH

6749 WOLVERHAMPTON (A.W) (L-H)
Saturday, December 9

OFFICIAL GOING: Standard
Wind: Light, half behind Weather: Cold, overcast

6764 GREETINGS CARDS FROM BONUSPRINT.COM NURSERY 7f 32y(P)
4:00 (4:02) (Class 5) (0-75,77) 2-Y-O **£4,533** (£1,348; £674; £336) **Stalls** High

Form RPR
0033 1 **Milson's Point (IRE)**[16] 6569 2-7-13 **53**........ DavidKinsella 4 58
(I Semple) *chsd ldr: led over 2f out: rdn out* **3/1**[1]

0654 2 1 ½ **Imprimis Tagula (IRE)**[2] 6736 2-8-6 **60**........ FrancisNorton 3 61
(A Bailey) *hld up: rdn and hdd over 2f out: no ex towards fin* **9/2**[2]

0203 3 shd **Henry The Seventh**[21] 6525 2-8-12 **66**........ J-PGuillambert 2 67
(J W Hills) *chsd ldrs: rdn 3f out: edgd lft ins fnl f: styd on* **9/2**[2]

1005 4 4 **Foxxy**[29] 6421 2-8-2 **61** ow1........(p) JamieJones(5) 5 51
(K A Ryan) *midfield: outpcd 4f out: hung lft u.p 1f out: kpt on: nt trble ldrs* **33/1**

544 5 3 ½ **Racing Times**[99] 4992 2-9-7 **75**........ RobertHavlin 9 56
(B J Meehan) *midfield: hdwy 4f out: rdn 3f out: wknd over 1f out* **3/1**[1]

0500 6 ¾ **Juvenescent (USA)**[67] 5747 2-7-11 **56**........ DuranFentiman(5) 6 35
(R D E Woodhouse) *rdn 4f out: a bhd* **25/1**

0646 7 2 ½ **Johannesburg Cat (USA)**[19] 6536 2-8-10 **67**........ JamesDoyle(3) 1 40
(N P Littmoden) *rdn 4f out: a bhd* **20/1**

1521 8 shd **Copper King**[11] 6645 2-9-6 **77**........ PatrickMathers(3) 7 50
(P D Evans) *chsd ldrs: rdn over 3f out: wknd wl over 1f out* **5/1**[3]

1m 29.35s (-1.05) **Going Correction** -0.225s/f (Stan) **8** Ran SP% **114.6**
Speed ratings (Par 96):97,95,95,90,86 85,82,82
CSF £16.40 CT £58.94 TOTE £5.80: £2.10, £2.60, £1.20; EX 34.20.
Owner D G Savala **Bred** John B O'Connor **Trained** Carluke, S Lanarks

FOCUS
A modest nursery but solid enough form rated around the winner and third.

NOTEBOOK
Milson's Point(IRE), third over an extended mile round here on his previous start, seemed to benefit from the drop back to seven furlongs and won in decent-enough style. He may well be put away until next year and should continue his progression at three. (op 11-4 tchd 5-2 and 7-2)
Imprimis Tagula(IRE) confirmed the promise he showed when a close fourth over course and distance just two days previously but basically found the winner too good. (tchd 5-1)
Henry The Seventh ran much better with the visor left off this time. (op 13-2 tchd 7-1)
Foxxy has been given a real chance by the Handicapper, but this trip was too short for her. (op 25-1)
Racing Times, dropped a furlong in trip on his nursery debut, did not find as much as had looked likely and has to be considered disappointing. (op 10-3 tchd 11-4)
Copper King ran a stinker and was well below the form he showed when winning over course and distance on his previous start. (op 4-1 tchd 6-1)

6765 PONTIN'S HOLIDAYS MAIDEN STKS — 1m 141y(P)
4:30 (4:31) (Class 5) 3-4-Y-O **£3,238** (£963; £481; £240) **Stalls** Low

Form RPR

1 **Rapid City**[56] 3-9-0 68 ...... JamesDoyle(3) 8 73+
(Miss J Feilden) *hld up: hdwy gng wl over 3f out: led over 1f out: rdn clr ins fnl f: eased towards fin* **15/8**[2]

3 2 3 ½ **Foreign Language (USA)**[14] 6593 3-8-12 ...... SteveDrowne 4 59+
(N A Callaghan) *chsd ldrs: rdn to take 2nd 2f out: ev ch over 1f out: no ch w wnr ins fnl f* **10/11**[1]

000 3 7 **Layed Back Rocky**[39] 6281 4-9-5 40 ...... MickyFenton 7 50
(M Mullineaux) *prom: rdn to ld over 2f out: hdd over 1f out: wknd fnl f* **66/1**

0036 4 2 ½ **Linton Dancer (IRE)**[18] 6554 3-8-5 48 ...... PatrickHills(7) 5 40
(J R Weymes) *led: rdn and hdd over 2f out: wknd over 1f out* **9/1**[3]

0 5 shd **Champion's Way (IRE)**[68] 5728 4-8-12 ...... JamesMillman(7) 2 45
(B R Millman) *midfield: rdn 4f out: sn wknd* **25/1**

000 6 5 **Useful**[90] 5210 3-8-12 54 ...... FrancisNorton 3 30
(A W Carroll) *rdn over 3f out: a bhd* **10/1**

0060 7 14 **Spinning Dancer (IRE)**[28] 6450 3-8-12 30 ...... J-PGuillambert 1 —
(J R Holt) *racd keenly: prom: rdn over 3f out: wknd over 2f out: eased whn btn fnl f* **100/1**

0 8 2 **Lady Lucas (IRE)**[11] 6649 3-8-5 ...... SCreighton(7) 6 —
(E J Creighton) *midfield: lost pl over 5f out: bhd fnl 4f* **100/1**

1m 49.47s (-2.29) **Going Correction** -0.225s/f (Stan)
WFA 3 from 4yo 2lb 8 Ran SP% **113.6**
Speed ratings (Par 103):101,97,91,89,89 84,72,70
CSF £3.82 TOTE £2.40: £1.10, £1.10, £12.90; EX 4.50.
Owner Good Company Partnership **Bred** Juddmonte Farms Ltd **Trained** Exning, Suffolk

FOCUS
A very weak maiden and not worth dwelling on with neither of the first two having solid form.

6766 PHOTO GIFTS FROM BONUSPRINT.COM H'CAP — 2m 119y(P)
5:00 (5:00) (Class 5) (0-75,80) 3-Y-O+ **£3,886** (£1,156; £577; £288) **Stalls** Low

Form RPR

4203 1 **Salute (IRE)**[25] 6479 7-9-8 66 ...... RobertHavlin 4 76+
(P G Murphy) *a.p: rdn to ld over 1f out: r.o* **5/1**[3]

2 1 ½ **Marikhar (IRE)**[21] 5629 4-9-3 66 ...... JamieMoriarty(5) 3 74
(Seamus Fahey, Ire) *hld up: hdwy 3f out: sn rdn: wnt 2nd ins fnl f: styd on: a hld* **6/1**

3023 3 1 ¼ **Champagne Shadow (IRE)**[12] 6626 5-9-8 71 ...... JamieJones(5) 2 78+
(K A Ryan) *midfield: hdwy over 6f out: rdn 4f out: hung lft fr over 1f out: swtchd rt ins fnl f: styd on towards fin* **4/1**[2]

411 4 1 ¼ **Billich**[12] 6626 3-10-0 80 ...... ChrisCatlin 6 85
(E J O'Neill) *sn led: rdn over 2f out: hdd over 1f out: no ex ins fnl f* **11/8**[1]

6362 5 11 **Gallileo Figaro (USA)**[7] 6685 3-8-9 64 ...... PatrickMathers(3) 1 57
(W M Brisbourne) *racd keenly: in tch: rdn 4f out: wknd over 3f out* **16/1**

4610 6 15 **Ariodante**[103] 4900 4-9-8 66 ...... MickyFenton 7 43
(J M P Eustace) *prom: rdn 4f out: losing pl whn bmpd over 2f out: sn wknd* **25/1**

5015 7 3 **Bay Hawk**[14] 6602 4-9-13 71 ...... GeorgeBaker 8 44
(B G Powell) *bhd: rdn over 3f out: sn btn* **10/1**

3m 40.2s (-2.93) **Going Correction** -0.225s/f (Stan)
WFA 3 from 4yo+ 8lb 7 Ran SP% **111.9**
Speed ratings (Par 103):97,96,95,95,89 82,81
CSF £32.89 CT £128.80 TOTE £6.70: £5.00, £7.40; EX 42.80.
Owner The Golden Anorak Partnership **Bred** Ahmed M Foustok **Trained** East Garston, Berks

FOCUS
Just an ordinary staying handicap for the grade but the winner had a bit in hand and the runner-up was close to his form.
Bay Hawk Official explanation: jockey said gelding had no more to give

6767 PONTIN'S HOLIDAYS H'CAP — 1m 1f 103y(P)
5:30 (5:30) (Class 6) (0-65,63) 3-Y-O+ **£2,590** (£770; £385; £192) **Stalls** Low

Form RPR

0313 1 **Just Bond (IRE)**[8] 6667 4-8-12 62 ...... DuranFentiman(5) 8 79+
(G R Oldroyd) *stdd s: hld up: swtchd rt and hdwy on wd outside over 2f out: rdn over 1f out: led ins fnl f: hung rt and r.o* **5/2**[1]

0300 2 1 ¾ **Bridgewater Boys**[28] 6432 5-9-4 63 ......(b) CatherineGannon 12 71
(K A Ryan) *chsd ldrs: rdn 2f out: hung rt ins fnl f: styd on to take 2nd towards fin* **22/1**

6061 3 nk **Pop Music (IRE)**[12] 6628 3-8-9 59 ......(p) JamesDoyle(3) 13 66
(Miss J Feilden) *a.p: rdn over 2f out: led over 1f out: hdd ins fnl f: sn hung rt: no ex towards fin* **9/2**[2]

0215 4 1 ¼ **Qualitair Wings**[8] 6666 7-9-1 60 ...... DavidAllan 10 65
(J Hetherton) *hld up: hdwy over 3f out: nt clr run over 2f out: swtchd lft over 1f out: hung rt whn keeping on same pce wl ins fnl f* **6/1**[3]

0000 5 ¾ **Tuscarora (IRE)**[16] 6573 7-9-3 62 ...... RichardThomas 7 66
(A W Carroll) *midfield: rdn and hdwy 2f out: one pce ins fnl f* **40/1**

6 6 1 **Open Loop (IRE)**[28] 6451 4-9-1 60 ......(bt) FrancisNorton 6 62
(Edgar Byrne, Ire) *j. awkwardly fr stalls: hld up: nt clr run fr over 3f out tl rdn over 1f out: kpt on ins fnl f: nt trble ldrs* **12/1**

0040 7 1 ¼ **Street Life (IRE)**[38] 6289 8-9-1 60 ...... TonyCulhane 5 60
(W J Musson) *bhd: rdn over 1f out: styd on fnl f: nvr rchd ldrs* **16/1**

5322 8 ½ **Keisha Kayleigh (IRE)**[11] 6648 3-8-11 58 ......(p) TomEaves 2 57
(B Ellison) *midfield: hdwy 4f out: rdn over 2f out: wknd fnl f* **7/1**

0005 9 2 **Parkview Love (USA)**[10] 6652 5-9-1 63 ......(v) PatrickMathers(3) 11 58
(D Shaw) *prom: led over 3f out: sn rdn: hdd over 1f out: wknd ins fnl f* **20/1**

00-0 10 5 **Golda Seek (USA)**[29] 6430 3-8-6 53 ...... ChrisCatlin 1 39
(B J Meehan) *rdn over 4f out: a bhd* **16/1**

0016 11 8 **Dream Forest (IRE)**[11] 6641 3-8-6 60 ...... TolleyDean(7) 3 32
(M S Saunders) *in tch: pushed along over 6f out: wknd over 2f out* **20/1**

01 12 3 ½ **Thistimesforgood (IRE)**[31] 6406 3-9-2 63 ...... J-PGuillambert 9 29
(Adrian Sexton, Ire) *midfield: effrt over 3f out: wknd over 2f out: eased whn btn over 1f out* **20/1**

6000 13 1 ¼ **Secret Moment**[38] 6289 4-9-1 60 ...... AdamKirby 4 23
(C G Cox) *led: hdd over 3f out: wkng whn hmpd over 2f out* **28/1**

2m 0.28s (-2.34) **Going Correction** -0.225s/f (Stan)
WFA 3 from 4yo+ 2lb 13 Ran SP% **117.5**
Speed ratings (Par 101):101,99,99,98,97 96,95,94,93,88 81,78,77
CSF £69.05 CT £241.04 TOTE £4.40: £1.60, £6.60, £1.90; EX 80.70.
Owner R C Bond **Bred** Schwindibode Ag **Trained** Upper Helmsley, N Yorks
■ Stewards' Enquiry : Catherine Gannon one-day ban: careless riding (Dec 20)

FOCUS
Just a modest handicap, but they went a very good pace and the form looks decent for the grade with the fourth and sixth the best guides.
Street Life(IRE) Official explanation: jockey said gelding hung left final bend

6768 PONTIN'S HOLIDAYS CLAIMING STKS — 1m 1f 103y(P)
7:00 (7:00) (Class 5) 2-Y-O **£3,238** (£963; £481; £120; £120) **Stalls** Low

Form RPR

4600 1 **Pret A Porter (UAE)**[15] 6581 2-9-0 58 ......(b[1]) JimCrowley 10 66
(P D Evans) *midfield: hdwy over 3f out: led 1f out: r.o ins fnl f: won gng away* **12/1**

2334 2 3 **Right Option (IRE)**[7] 6676 2-8-6 62 ...... JamieMoriarty(5) 3 57
(J R Weymes) *hld up: rdn and hdwy over 2f out: wnt 2nd ins fnl f: no imp on wnr* **7/2**[1]

0646 3 2 ½ **Stars Above**[22] 6506 2-8-2 47 ...... JimmyQuinn 8 44
(Sir Mark Prescott) *led after 1f: hdd over 6f out: regained ld 4f out: hdd 1f out: no ex ins fnl f* **7/2**[1]

6 4 ½ **Haoin An Bothar (IRE)**[31] 6402 2-9-0 ...... JerryO'Dwyer(5) 9 60
(Adrian Sexton, Ire) *prom: led over 6f out: hdd 4f out: stl ev ch over 1f out: sn hung lft: no ex ins fnl fulong* **8/1**

0003 4 dht **Party Palace**[21] 6522 2-8-2 51 ...... ChrisCatlin 6 43
(J A Osborne) *in tch: rdn over 3f out: kpt on same pce fr over 1f out* **5/1**[2]

00 6 ½ **La Chesneraie**[19] 6534 2-8-4 ...... JoeFanning 4 44
(P C Haslam) *in tch: rdn over 3f out: sn outpcd: edgd rt fr over 1f out: kpt on ins fnl f* **33/1**

0200 7 8 **Taran Tregarth**[12] 6625 2-8-1 40 ow1 ......(p) FrancisNorton 1 25
(A Bailey) *led 1f: continued to trck ldrs: rdn over 3f out: wknd over 2f out* **20/1**

4 8 1 ¾ **Ugenius**[11] 6640 2-8-8 ...... TolleyDean(7) 2 36
(R A Harris) *hld up: rdn over 3f out: no imp* **11/2**[3]

0 9 5 **Flashing Feet (IRE)**[8] 6658 2-9-5 ...... DaneO'Neill 5 31
(R Hannon) *racd keenly: in tch: rdn 4f out: wknd over 3f out* **7/1**

00 10 10 **Alice Howe**[21] 6511 2-8-2 ...... PaulHanagan 7 —
(W R Muir) *rdn over 3f out: a bhd* **33/1**

2m 1.68s (-0.94) **Going Correction** -0.225s/f (Stan) 10 Ran SP% **118.4**
Speed ratings (Par 96):95,92,90,89,89 89,82,80,76,67
CSF £53.70 TOTE £14.70: £4.10, £1.50, £1.30; EX 104.30.Right Option (IRE) was claimed by S. Dow for £8,000
Owner John P Jones **Bred** Darley **Trained** Pandy, Abergavenny

FOCUS
A weak juvenile event that was run at a fair pace. The winner did the job readily and the form is rated conservatively through the placed horses.

NOTEBOOK
Pret A Porter(UAE), equipped with first-time blinkers, produced her best effort to date and got off the mark with a cosy success. Her current trainer tends to do well with this type of performer, and she should be high on confidence now, but her future hopes probably rely on the headgear having the same effect in the future.
Right Option(IRE), with the blinkers abandoned, showed improved form on this return to Polytrack and can have no real excuses. He helps to set the standard of this form, but he still looks flattered by his current official rating and is not one for win-only purposes. (tchd 10-3)
Stars Above turned in a more encouraging effort on this drop in class, but she is ultimately struggling to find her ideal trip at present and looks very one paced.
Haoin An Bothar(IRE), up in trip, did not get home under a positive ride and looks to need more patient tactics at around this distance. He can build on this. (op 16-1)
Party Palace ran below her best and is another who has yet to really prove her stamina for this trip. (op 16-1)
Alice Howe Official explanation: jockey said filly hung right throughout

6769 PONTINS.COM H'CAP — 1m 4f 50y(P)
7:30 (7:32) (Class 6) (0-60,60) 3-Y-O+ **£2,730** (£806; £403) **Stalls** Low

Form RPR

6062 1 **Melvino**[6] 6693 4-9-2 54 ...... ChrisCatlin 2 63
(T D Barron) *hld up: hdwy over 3f out: rdn over 2f out: led ins fnl f: r.o* **4/1**[2]

500 2 2 **Opera Writer (IRE)**[10] 5248 3-9-3 60 ...... GeorgeBaker 9 66
(R Hollinshead) *hld up: hung lft whn rdn and hdwy over 1f out: styd on to take 2nd ins fnl f: nt trble wnr* **12/1**

5442 3 ½ **Regency Red (IRE)**[16] 6571 8-8-11 52 ...... LiamJones(3) 3 57
(W M Brisbourne) *midfield: rdn and hdwy over 2f out: styd on ins fnl f* **6/1**[3]

0310 4 1 ½ **Qaasi (USA)**[16] 6571 4-9-7 59 ...... DeanMernagh 7 62
(M Brittain) *a.p: led over 2f out: hdd ins fnl f: no ex* **11/1**

3310 5 1 ¼ **Missie Baileys**[6] 6693 4-9-7 59 ...... IanMongan 6 60
(Mrs L J Mongan) *trckd ldrs: rdn 3f out: one pce fnl f* **7/1**

3003 6 2 ½ **The Iron Giant (IRE)**[5] 6700 4-9-0 52 ...... PaulHanagan 1 49
(B G Powell) *led: rdn and hdd over 2f out: wknd ins fnl f* **2/1**[1]

6602 7 5 **Lady Taverner**[31] 6405 5-9-0 57 ...... NataliaGemelova(5) 4 47
(J E Long) *racd keenly: hld up: rdn 3f out: no imp* **6/1**[3]

6500 8 7 **Monte Mayor Junior**[29] 6430 3-8-9 52 ......(v) JimmyQuinn 5 31
(D Haydn Jones) *trckd ldrs: rdn and hung lft over 3f out: sn wknd* **33/1**

2m 38.83s (-3.59) **Going Correction** -0.225s/f (Stan)
WFA 3 from 4yo+ 5lb 8 Ran SP% **113.4**
Speed ratings (Par 101):102,100,100,99,98 96,93,88
CSF £49.02 CT £282.91 TOTE £6.00: £2.00, £3.10, £1.80; EX 56.70.
Owner Theo Williams and Charles Mocatta **Bred** T J Cooper **Trained** Maunby, N Yorks

FOCUS
A moderate handicap that was run at a solid pace. The form is rated around the third/fourth horses.

6770 BLANK CANVAS EVENTS LTD H'CAP — 7f 32y(P)
8:00 (8:04) (Class 5) (0-75,75) 3-Y-O+ **£3,238** (£963; £481; £240) **Stalls** High

Form RPR

4613 1 **Mandarin Spirit (IRE)**[15] 6579 6-8-13 72 ......(b) OscarUrbina 6 84
(G C H Chung) *hld up: rdn and hdwy over 1f out: led ins fnl f: r.o* **6/1**[3]

0211 2 1 ¼ **Prince Dayjur (USA)**[41] 6239 7-8-13 72 ...... JimmyQuinn 5 81
(J Pearce) *chsd ldrs: rdn to ld over 1f out: hdd ins fnl f: nt qckn* **9/2**[2]

0004 3 3 ½ **Purus (IRE)**[10] 6654 4-9-1 74 ...... GeorgeBaker 2 73
(P Mitchell) *led: rdn and hdd over 1f out: no ex ins fnl f* **13/2**

4400 4 1 **Charlie Delta**[15] 6583 3-9-1 74 ...... DanielTudhope 1 71
(D Carroll) *rr div: rdn 2f out: hdwy over 1f out: no ex ins fnl f* **12/1**

5540 5 1 ¾ **Danetime Lord (IRE)**[60] 5902 3-8-13 72 ......(p) CatherineGannon 11 64
(K A Ryan) *in tch: pushed along over 3f out: outpcd over 1f out* **25/1**

4550 6 shd **Kingscross**[15] 6583 8-9-2 75 ...... FergusSweeney 9 67
(M Blanshard) *hld up: effrt over 1f out: nvr trbld ldrs* **10/1**

2006 7 3 **Linda's Colin (IRE)**[10] 6654 4-9-1 74 ...... DaneO'Neill 4 58
(R A Harris) *rr div: rdn and hdwy over 2f out: nt clr run over 1f out: sn swtchd lft: hung lft and wknd ins fnl f* **8/1**

0401 8 1 **Regal Raider (IRE)**[8] 6664 3-9-2 75 ...... TomEaves 8 56
(I Semple) *chsd ldrs: rdn 2f out: wknd 1f out* **3/1**[1]

0030 **9** 1 1/4 **Highland Cascade**[10] 6654 4-8-9 **68**............................(p) MickyFenton 7 46
(J M P Eustace) *w ldr: rdn and ev ch 2f out: wknd 1f out* **28/1**
1m 27.96s (-2.44) **Going Correction** -0.225s/f (Stan) 9 Ran SP% **106.0**
Speed ratings (Par 103):104,102,98,97,95 95,91,90,89
CSF £27.64 CT £132.87 TOTE £6.00: £1.70, £1.50, £2.40; EX 30.00.
Owner Peter Tsim **Bred** W Haggas And W Jarvis **Trained** Newmarket, Suffolk
■ Foreplay (IRE) (6/1) was withdrawn on vet's advice. Rule 4 applies, deduction 10p in £.

FOCUS
A fair handicap for the class. The pace was solid and the form looks sound.
Linda's Colin(IRE) Official explanation: jockey said gelding lost its action; vet said gelding bled from the nose
Regal Raider(IRE) Official explanation: vet said gelding finished lame near-fore

6771 PONTINS.COM MAIDEN STKS 7f 32y(P)
8:30 (8:33) (Class 5) 3-Y-0+ **£3,238** (£963; £481; £240) **Stalls** High

Form RPR
0 **1** **Barney McGrew (IRE)**[95] 5092 3-9-3 .... OscarUrbina 8 75+
(J A R Toller) *chsd ldr: led jst over 1f out: edgd lft ins fnl f: r.o wl: won gng away* **8/1**
0063 **2** 3 1/2 **Fairdonna**[14] 6608 3-8-12 59............................ JoeFanning 3 61+
(D J Coakley) *chsd ldrs: rdn over 2f out: swtchd rt over 1f out: styd on to take 2nd cl home: no ch w wnr* **7/4**[1]
0 **3** 1/2 **Mikey (IRE)**[11] 6637 3-9-3 ....(t) FrancisNorton 7 65
(Edgar Byrne, Ire) *led: rdn and hdd jst over 1f out: no ex ins fnl f* **16/1**
4 4 **Priceoflove (IRE)**[47] 6156 3-8-12 75............................ FergusSweeney 5 49
(P J Makin) *chsd ldrs: rdn over 2f out: wknd over 1f out* **7/2**[2]
5600 **5** 3/4 **Rose Muwasim**[11] 6643 3-8-12 60............................ DaleGibson 10 47
(M J Attwater) *towards rr: rdn 3f out: hdwy 2f out: one pce fnl f* **14/1**
6 3 1/2 **Global Strategy**[231] 1160 3-9-3 .... ChrisCatlin 6 42
(Rae Guest) *bhd: kpt on fnl f: nvr rchd ldrs* **7/1**[3]
4000 **7** 1/2 **Jumanji (IRE)**[4] 6717 3-8-12 45............................(b[1]) MickyFenton 4 36
(M J Attwater) *midfield: rdn 3f out: wknd over 1f out* **28/1**
06 **8** 1/2 **Apache Fort**[15] 6587 3-9-3 .... PaulDoe 11 40
(T Keddy) *s.i.s: midfield: rdn over 3f out: wknd over 1f out* **28/1**
9 1/2 **Inscribed (IRE)** 3-8-12 .... PatCosgrave 9 33
(G A Huffer) *s.i.s: a towards rr* **7/1**[3]
0 **10** 2 **Whozart (IRE)**[25] 6480 3-9-3 .... DanielTudhope 1 33
(A Dickman) *midfield: rdn and wknd over 2f out* **50/1**
11 shd **Risk Challenge (USA)**[30] 4-9-3 .... TonyCulhane 2 33
(C J Price) *s.i.s: a bhd* **8/1**
1m 28.75s (-1.65) **Going Correction** -0.225s/f (Stan) 11 Ran SP% **127.2**
Speed ratings (Par 103):100,96,95,90,90 86,85,84,84,82 81
CSF £23.96 TOTE £9.20: £2.50, £1.80, £3.60; EX 22.90.
Owner M A Whelton **Bred** Mrs H B Raw **Trained** Newmarket, Suffolk

FOCUS
A poor maiden that lacked any strength in depth. The winner can rate higher but the seventh tends to limit the form.
Priceoflove(IRE) Official explanation: jockey said filly seemed to be going short on off-fore

6772 FOCUS MULTIMEDIA'S CHRISTMAS H'CAP 1m 1f 103y(P)
9:00 (9:01) (Class 4) (0-85,83) 3-Y-0+ **£5,505** (£1,637; £818; £408) **Stalls** Low

Form RPR
3513 **1** **Daring Affair**[14] 6607 5-8-10 **75**............................ IanMongan 9 85
(K R Burke) *chsd ldrs: rdn 3f out: nt clr run 2f out: r.o ins fnl f to ld fnl strides* **11/1**
2152 **2** nk **King Of Argos**[23] 6502 3-9-1 **82**............................(v[1]) SteveDrowne 4 91
(E A L Dunlop) *racd keenly: chsd ldrs: rdn to ld over 1f out: hung lft ins fnl f: hdd fnl strides* **7/2**[2]
5052 **3** 1/2 **Atlantic Quest (USA)**[1] 6752 7-8-12 **80**............................ AmirQuinn[(3)] 5 88
(Miss Venetia Williams) *hld up: hdwy over 2f out: rdn over 1f out and carried hd to one side: r.o ins fnl f* **8/1**
-014 **4** 1 **Stargazer Jim (FR)**[21] 6519 4-8-12 **80**............................ LiamJones[(3)] 7 86
(W J Haggas) *midfield: pushed along over 3f out: hdwy over 1f out: styd on ins fnl f: edgd lft towards fin* **4/1**[3]
0460 **5** shd **Sew'N'So Character (IRE)**[64] 5787 5-9-2 **81**............................ TonyCulhane 8 87
(M Blanshard) *hld up: rdn and hdwy over 1f out: styd on ins fnl f* **9/1**
0100 **6** 1 3/4 **Ninth House (USA)**[14] 6594 4-9-1 **83**............................(t) JamesDoyle[(3)] 10 86
(N P Littmoden) *hld up: rdn 3f out: effrt whn edgd lft over 1f out: styd on ins fnl f: nt rch ldrs* **10/1**
2004 **7** 3/4 **Wahoo Sam (USA)**[30] 6418 6-8-9 **74**............................(p) CatherineGannon 3 76
(K A Ryan) *prom: led after 1f: rdn over 2f out: hdd over 1f out: wknd ins fnl f* **11/1**
2/00 **8** 3 1/2 **Fantasy Ride**[49] 6107 4-9-4 **83**............................ JimmyQuinn 6 78
(J Pearce) *s.i.s: rdn 3f out: a bhd* **33/1**
1311 **9** 5 **Kildare Sun (IRE)**[14] 6607 4-8-11 **76**............................ DaleGibson 2 82+
(J Mackie) *midfield: rdn and hdwy over 2f out: styng on whn n.m.r and bdly hmpd 1f out: rdr lost irons and nt rcvr* **10/3**[1]
0021 **10** 3/4 **Red Contact (USA)**[26] 6469 5-8-13 **78**............................(p) DanielTudhope 1 63
(A Dickman) *led 1f: chsd ldr: rdn 2f out: wknd over 1f out* **12/1**
1m 59.17s (-3.45) **Going Correction** -0.225s/f (Stan)
WFA 3 from 4yo+ 2lb 10 Ran SP% **122.8**
Speed ratings (Par 105):106,105,105,104,104 102,102,98,94,93
CSF £52.14 CT £339.83 TOTE £11.10: £2.60, £2.40, £3.10; EX 56.30.
Owner Nigel Shields **Bred** N R Shields And K R Burke **Trained** Middleham Moor, N Yorks
■ Stewards' Enquiry : Catherine Gannon two-day ban: careless riding (Dec 21-22)

FOCUS
A decent handicap for the class that was run at a strong pace. The first three came clear and the form is solid.

6773 GO PONTIN'S H'CAP 5f 216y(P)
9:30 (9:30) (Class 5) (0-75,74) 3-Y-0+ **£3,238** (£963; £481; £240) **Stalls** Low

Form RPR
0406 **1** **Figaro Flyer (IRE)**[18] 6555 3-9-0 **72**............................ IanMongan 11 81
(P Howling) *hld up: hdwy 2f out: r.o ins fnl f to ld fnl stride* **11/1**
1250 **2** hd **Hello Man (IRE)**[10] 6654 3-8-8 **71**............................ JerryO'Dwyer[(5)] 12 79
(Eamon Tyrrell, Ire) *a.p: led over 2f out: rdn over 1f out: hdd fnl stride* **7/1**
4300 **3** 1/2 **Hypocrisy**[120] 4328 3-8-9 **74**............................ GaryWales[(7)] 10 81
(D Carroll) *in rr: hdwy over 3f out: styd on ins fnl f* **25/1**
5036 **4** hd **Vanadium**[28] 6437 4-9-1 **73**............................(p) J-PGuillambert 13 79
(J G Given) *stdd and swtchd lft s: hld up: hdwy on ins over 1f out: styd on ins fnl f* **10/1**
0554 **5** 1/2 **Ever Cheerful**[8] 6656 5-8-8 **69**............................ JamesDoyle[(3)] 7 73
(D G Bridgwater) *led early: chsd ldrs: rdn over 2f out: styd on same pce ins fnl f* **7/1**
4124 **6** hd **Dudley Docker (IRE)**[8] 6664 4-8-3 **68**............................ KellyHarrison[(7)] 6 72
(D Carroll) *in tch: rdn over 1f out: kpt on ins fnl f* **6/1**[3]

2151 **7** 1/2 **Linda Green**[15] 6579 5-9-0 **72**............................ EdwardCreighton 1 74
(M R Channon) *in rr: rdn over 2f out: r.o ins fnl f: nrst fin* **9/2**[2]
5002 **8** 1/2 **Nistaki (USA)**[7] 6672 5-8-2 **60** oh1............................ FrancisNorton 4 61
(D Shaw) *midfield: lost pl over 2f out: nt clr run over 1f out: swtchd lft ins fnl f: kpt on* **4/1**[1]
3553 **9** 3/4 **Gwilym (GER)**[15] 6585 3-8-7 **65**............................ RobertHavlin 5 64
(D Haydn Jones) *prom: rdn over 2f out: wknd fnl f* **10/1**
0402 **10** 1 1/2 **True Magic**[22] 6508 5-8-8 **66**............................ PatCosgrave 9 60
(J D Bethell) *chsd ldrs: rdn 3f out: wknd over 1f out* **13/2**
6000 **11** 9 **Lyndalee (IRE)**[15] 6585 3-8-9 **67**............................(p) JimCrowley 2 34
(P D Evans) *s.i.s: sn racd keenly in midfield: rdn and wknd over 2f out* **20/1**
560- **12** 1 1/4 **Melandre**[451] 5222 4-8-8 **66**............................ DeanMernagh 8 29
(M Brittain) *sn led: rdn and hdd over 2f out: wknd over 1f out* **40/1**
1m 14.21s (-1.60) **Going Correction** -0.225s/f (Stan) 12 Ran SP% **128.4**
Speed ratings (Par 103):101,100,100,99,99 98,98,97,96,94 82,80
CSF £91.40 CT £1292.92 TOTE £15.30: £3.70, £2.30, £5.90; EX 118.50 Place 6 £57.37, Place 5 £35.63.
Owner Mark Entwistle **Bred** Mohammad Al Qatami **Trained** Newmarket, Suffolk

FOCUS
A modest sprint that was run at a strong pace and the form looks sound enough rated through the fourth and fifth. Those to be held up were at an advantage.
T/Plt: £138.40 to a £1 stake. Pool: £64,699.20. 341.20 winning tickets. T/Qpdt: £54.90 to a £1 stake. Pool: £5,048.40. 68.00 winning tickets. DO

6742 KEMPTON (A.W) (R-H)
Sunday, December 10

OFFICIAL GOING: Standard
Wind: Fresh, half-behind. Weather: Dull

6774 BETBROKERS OPEN AN ACCOUNT ON 0844 855 2111 MEDIAN AUCTION MAIDEN STKS 5f (P)
1:00 (1:00) (Class 6) 3-5-Y-0 **£2,590** (£770; £385; £192) **Stalls** High

Form RPR
2 **1** **Staceymac (IRE)**[29] 6440 3-8-12 .... DaneO'Neill 6 50+
(B R Johnson) *t.k.h: chsd ldrs: rdn 2f out: r.o to ld fnl 75 yds* **2/5**[1]
320 **2** 1 **Left Nostril (IRE)**[12] 6649 3-8-12 40............................ BrianReilly 2 45
(P S McEntee) *led: hrd rdn over 1f out: hdd and nt qckn fnl 75 yds* **16/1**[3]
4-04 **3** 2 **Nawayea**[33] 6389 3-8-12 62............................ EdwardCreighton 7 38
(C N Allen) *in tch: outpcd and rdn 3f out: styd on fnl f* **7/2**[2]
0006 **4** nk **Beau Jazz**[34] 6372 5-9-3 45............................ AdrianMcCarthy 4 42
(W De Best-Turner) *chsd ldr tl no ex ins fnl f* **33/1**
0-00 **5** 3 1/2 **Dancing Beauty (IRE)**[227] 1261 4-8-12 35............................ JoeFanning 3 24
(T T Clement) *in tch in rr whn rn wd bnd after 1f: sn struggling: no ch whn rn wd bnd into st* **66/1**
6060 **6** 3/4 **Wotavadun (IRE)**[146] 3595 3-8-10 40............................(b) SophieDoyle[(7)] 5 26
(Ms J S Doyle) *t.k.h: chsd ldrs tl wknd over 1f out* **50/1**
7 5 **Brief Engagement (IRE)** 3-8-12 .... AdamKirby 8 —
(T D McCarthy) *s.i.s: rn v green: sn wl bhd: no ch whn hung lft in st* **16/1**[3]
0 **8** 10 **Imperial Glory**[6] 6694 5-9-0 .... NeilChalmers[(3)] 1 —
(Mrs P Townsley) *in tch in rr whn carried wd bnd after 1f: sn rdn and bhd* **100/1**
60.57 secs (0.17) **Going Correction** -0.025s/f (Stan) 8 Ran SP% **112.8**
Speed ratings (Par 101):97,95,92,91,86 84,76,60
CSF £8.61 TOTE £1.60: £1.02, £2.60, £1.10; EX 6.20.
Owner Paul Naughton **Bred** Mick McGinn And James Waldron **Trained** Ashtead, Surrey

FOCUS
A weak race with no pace until the tempo increased after two furlongs. The winner did not need to reproduce her debut effort and is better than the bare form.

6775 BETBROKERS.COM FILLIES' H'CAP 1m 2f (P)
1:30 (1:30) (Class 6) (0-65,64) 3-Y-0+ **£2,590** (£770; £385; £192) **Stalls** High

Form RPR
-402 **1** **Bronze Star**[25] 6484 3-9-3 **60**............................ OscarUrbina 7 70
(J R Fanshawe) *chsd ldrs: effrt over 2f out: chal 1f out: drvn to ld fnl strides* **6/4**[1]
06 **2** shd **Cove Mountain (IRE)**[7] 6687 4-9-3 **57**............................ LPKeniry 1 66
(S Kirk) *prom: drvn to ld ins fnl f: kpt on: hdd fnl strides* **16/1**
5603 **3** 3/4 **Danzare**[82] 5450 4-8-10 **50**............................ FrancisNorton 14 58
(J L Spearing) *in tch: drvn to chse ldrs over 1f out: styd on wl fnl f* **16/1**
5025 **4** 1 1/4 **Wassfa**[15] 6593 3-9-6 **63**............................ RichardHughes 12 69
(C E Brittain) *led 2f: chsd clr ldr after tl led over 2f out: hdd ins fnl f: no ex* **12/1**
3030 **5** 1 **Red Sail**[34] 6383 5-9-1 **55**............................(b) RobertHavlin 13 59
(Dr J D Scargill) *a.p: rdn and one pce fnl 2f* **14/1**
0-00 **6** hd **Proud Scholar (USA)**[12] 4005 4-8-8 **55**............................ WilliamBuick[(7)] 2 59+
(R A Kvisla) *wd in midfield: rdn over 3f out: styd on fnl f* **66/1**
7 1 **Asian Alliance (IRE)**[27] 6317 5-9-0 **54**............................ CatherineGannon 10 56
(K A Ryan) *bhd: pushed along 1/2-way: nrst fin* **25/1**
6403 **8** nk **Lady Pilot**[7] 6687 4-9-0 **54**............................ DaneO'Neill 11 55
(Ms J S Doyle) *hld up towards rr: rdn and kpt on fnl 2f: nt rch ldrs* **10/1**
4440 **9** 1/2 **Emilion**[18] 6566 3-9-5 **62**............................ JoeFanning 9 62
(W R Muir) *stdd s: hld up towards rr: rdn 4f out: sme late hdwy* **9/1**
00-0 **10** 1/2 **Tecktal (FR)**[124] 4225 3-9-6 **63**............................ IanMongan 6 62
(P M Phelan) *in tch: rdn over 2f out: sn outpcd* **50/1**
5460 **11** 1/2 **Sand Iron (IRE)**[20] 6532 4-8-4 **51** ow3............................ SladeO'Hara[(7)] 3 50
(John Allen) *a towards rr* **33/1**
6530 **12** 1 1/2 **Fratt'n Park (IRE)**[61] 5895 3-9-7 **64**............................ J-PGuillambert 8 60
(J J Bridger) *mid-div: rdn over 2f out: sn btn* **15/2**[3]
6422 **13** 3/4 **Milk And Sultana**[13] 6617 6-8-12 **52**............................ SteveDrowne 5 47
(G A Ham) *hld up midfield to rr: rdn 3f out: n.d* **7/1**[2]
1050 **14** 11 **Ellesappelle**[24] 6503 3-9-7 **64**............................(b) GeorgeBaker 4 39
(G L Moore) *dwlt: rdn to ld after 2f: sn 8 l clr: hdd & wknd over 2f out: eased whn no ch fnl f* **10/1**
2m 6.61s (-2.39) **Going Correction** -0.025s/f (Stan)
WFA 3 from 4yo+ 3lb 14 Ran SP% **128.8**
Speed ratings (Par 98):108,107,107,106,105 105,104,104,103,103 103,101,101,92
CSF £31.52 CT £320.31 TOTE £2.20: £1.20, £4.10, £4.00.
Owner J M Greetham **Bred** J M Greetham **Trained** Newmarket, Suffolk
■ Stewards' Enquiry : L P Keniry one-day ban: used whip with excessive frequency (Dec 21)
J-P Guillambert caution: careless riding

FOCUS
A moderate line-up. The field ignored the tearaway leader, but it paid to be handy in the chasing group. The winner is progressive, and the second, third, fifth and sixth ran to their 2006 turf level.

6776 BETBROKERS "NEVER MISS A BET" H'CAP — 5f (P)

2:00 (2:02) (Class 3) (0-95,92) 3-Y-0+

£7,790 (£2,332; £1,166; £583; £291; £146) Stalls High

Form				RPR
0000	1		**Harry Up**[24] 6499 5-8-7 **81** .... CatherineGannon 1 — (K A Ryan) *trckd ldr: drvn to ld jst over 1f out: rdn out* **17/2**	90
2000	2	¾	**Talbot Avenue**[120] 4360 8-9-2 **90** .... SteveDrowne 7 — (M Blanshard) *chsd ldrs: n.m.r on rail over 3f out: rdn 2f out: r.o to chse wnr ins fnl f: a hld* **9/2**[3]	97
0000	3	1¼	**Classic Encounter (IRE)**[42] 6243 3-9-4 **92** .... RichardHughes 8 — (D M Simcock) *t.k.h in 5th: effrt and nt clr run over 1f out: 3rd and running on whn nt best of runs ins fnl f* **16/1**	94
1003	4	nk	**Smokin Beau**[78] 5535 9-9-0 **88** .... JoeFanning 5 — (N P Littmoden) *in tch: hmpd and forced v wd over 3f out: rallied 2f out: one pce appr fnl f* **7/1**	89
0040	5	shd	**Graze On**[9] 6660 4-8-10 **84** .... (b) AdrianMcCarthy 6 — (Peter Grayson) *chsd ldrs: hmpd over 3f out: one pce fnl 2f* **6/1**	85
4025	6	shd	**Brandywell Boy (IRE)**[7] 6690 3-7-11 **78** .... (v[1]) WilliamBuick(7) 4 — (D J S Ffrench Davis) *dwlt: hld up in rr: nt clr run and swtchd lft ent st: nrst fin* **5/2**[1]	78
-400	7	½	**Rare Cross (IRE)**[29] 6446 4-8-6 **80** .... JimmyQuinn 2 — (P Mitchell) *led tl jst over 1f out: no ex fnl f* **16/1**	78
3112	8	hd	**Tartatartufata**[8] 6682 4-8-3 **80** .... (v) PatrickMathers(3) 3 — (D Shaw) *in tch: hmpd and forced wd over 3f out: n.d after: kept on fnl 2f* **3/1**[2]	78

59.77 secs (-0.63) **Going Correction** -0.025s/f (Stan) **8** Ran SP% **120.8**
Speed ratings (Par 107):104,102,100,100,100 100,99,98
CSF £49.15 CT £621.90 TOTE £12.20: £2.30, £1.90, £4.70; EX 70.00.
Owner The Fishermen **Bred** J E Rose **Trained** Hambleton, N Yorks
■ Stewards' Enquiry : Catherine Gannon two-day ban: careless riding (Dec 23, 26)

FOCUS
A messy race, in which the track record was surprisingly broken despite a modest early tempo. There was plenty of trouble in running and the form has a shaky look to it.

NOTEBOOK
Harry Up, despite winning twice over six furlongs, is quite happy at this trip too, and received a nice tow from the leader from the start. With several rivals behind suffering interference, he was in the perfect position to strike, and his rider - who deserves more opportunities - looked both strong and stylish in the process. (op 10-1)
Talbot Avenue is a smart sprinter on his day, and he had been dropped 5lb for this belated All-Weather debut. He adapted well to the new surface, and looks capable of adding to his four victories on turf. (op 7-1)
Classic Encounter(IRE) is dropping to a more realistic mark, and gave notice that he is recapturing some of his old form, as he endured a difficult passage in the home straight. Official explanation: jockey said gelding was denied a clear run (tchd 14-1)
Smokin Beau has re-joined trainer Littmoden after a spell elsewhere, and did well to recover from an incident on the first bend which forced him very wide. There is plenty of life in him yet. (op 4-1)
Graze On has slipped back to a competitive mark after a largely barren spell during the summer, and is not far off regaining the winning thread. (op 15-2)
Brandywell Boy(IRE)'s only victory was over this trip, but six furlongs probably suits him best these days. That said, he did well off an ordinary early pace and with little luck in running, so was not disgraced despite failing to justify favoritism. (op 7-2 tchd 4-1)
Tartatartufata deserves another chance after being hampered in a domino effect, started by the winner, on the turn out of the back straight. (op 11-4 tchd 10-3)

6777 BETBROKERS ONE ACCOUNT NOVICE MEDIAN AUCTION STKS — 7f (P)

2:30 (2:30) (Class 5) 2-Y-0 £3,238 (£963; £481; £240) Stalls High

Form				RPR
1		**Circus Polka (USA)** 2-9-0 .... (t) JosedeSouza 2 — (P F I Cole) *t.k.h: chsd ldr: rdn over 2f out: led and qcknd clr ins fnl f: rn green* **8/1**[2]	66+
6220	2	2½	**Tokyo Jo (IRE)**[3] 6736 2-8-13 58 .... AdamKirby 3 — (T T Clement) *in tch: rdn over 3f out: hung rt fnl 2f: r.o to take 2nd nr fin* **20/1**	58
12	3	nk	**Situla (IRE)**[16] 6582 2-8-13 74 .... DaneO'Neill 5 — (H J L Dunlop) *w ldr: led wl over 1f out tl ins fnl f: one pce* **1/3**[1]	57
0004	4	4	**Ishimagic**[29] 6443 2-8-9 51 .... SteveDrowne 6 — (J J Bridger) *dwlt: chsd ldr: hrd rdn 2f out: wknd over 1f out* **33/1**	43
5001	5	2½	**Emefdream**[12] 6640 2-9-4 65 .... (p) LeeEnstone 4 — (Mrs N Macauley) *led: rdn and hdd wl over 1f out: sn wknd* **8/1**[2]	45
6	7	**Shea's Round** 2-9-0 .... GeorgeBaker 1 — (G L Moore) *s.s: rn green in rr: pushed along 1/2-way: sn no ch* **11/1**[3]	23

1m 27.0s (0.20) **Going Correction** -0.025s/f (Stan) **6** Ran SP% **113.3**
Speed ratings (Par 96):97,94,93,89,86 78
CSF £127.01 TOTE £7.20: £2.10, £5.60; EX 55.40.
Owner Allport, Jefferson, Meyrick, Thomas **Bred** Hedgewood Farm **Trained** Whatcombe, Oxon

FOCUS
A mixed bunch, with no early pace. With the odds-on favourite finishing behind a selling plater, the race took little winning.

NOTEBOOK
Circus Polka(USA), a 27,000 guinea son of Stravinsky out of an unraced mare, made a stylish start to his career, though the opposition was not strong. Despite showing obvious signs of inexperience, he showed a smart turn of foot to settle it and is one to keep an eye around this trip and a little farther. (tchd 9-1 and 10-1 in a place)
Tokyo Jo(IRE) is essentially selling and claiming quality, so holds the form down a bit. She only grabbed second as others tired, but this was a creditable second run for her new stable.
Situla(IRE) did not live up to the promise of previous outings. To be beaten by the unexposed winner may have been no disgrace, but the runner-up has been beaten in sellers and claimers. She may be more effective at Wolverhampton, where she has run well in two recent races. (op 4-11)
Ishimagic has improved a bit, but she still faced a tough task here.
Emefdream could not handle the step up from selling company, and capitulated quickly when the race began in earnest.
Shea's Round, related to several winners from seven furlongs to middle distances, should do better than this as she gains experience. Official explanation: jockey said colt missed the break (op 10-1 tchd 12-1)

6778 BETBROKERS WORLD'S 1ST BET BROKER EBF MAIDEN STKS — 1m (P)

3:00 (3:01) (Class 4) 2-Y-0 £4,857 (£1,445; £722; £360) Stalls High

Form				RPR
0	1		**Mr Aviator (USA)**[18] 6561 2-9-3 .... RichardHughes 5 — (R Hannon) *prom: led over 3f out: shkn up and qcknd clr wl over 1f out: readily* **5/6**[1]	76+
02	2	2	**Risque Heights**[37] 6316 2-9-3 .... (b[1]) SteveDrowne 1 — (G A Butler) *s.i.s: plld hrd in rr: stdy hdwy 3f out: pressed wnr 2f out: sn outpcd* **9/4**[2]	67
3	6	**Fowey (USA)** 2-8-12 .... J-PGuillambert 6 — (Sir Mark Prescott) *rn green: sn bhd: rdn and styd on fnl 2f: edgd rt: nt rch ldrs* **6/1**[3]	48
00	4	1	**Zaafira (SPA)**[26] 6471 2-8-5 .... SCreighton(7) 2 — (E J Creighton) *hdwy to join ldrs on outside after 3f: wknd 2f out* **100/1**	46
0	5	3	**Conny Nobel (IRE)**[18] 6561 2-8-10 .... (t) WilliamBuick(7) 9 — (R A Kvisla) *prom: lost pl on rail over 3f out: eased outside and hung rt over 2f out: no hdwy* **50/1**	44
0	6	1	**Childish Thoughts**[45] 6187 2-8-12 .... CatherineGannon 4 — (Mrs Norma Pook) *chsd ldrs: hrd rdn over 2f out: sn wknd* **66/1**	37
00	7	19	**Maeve (IRE)**[23] 6505 2-8-12 .... EdwardCreighton 7 — (E J Creighton) *led tl over 3f out: wknd qckly* **66/1**	—
00	8	nk	**Linlithgow (IRE)**[29] 6434 2-9-3 .... IanMongan 8 — (J L Dunlop) *mid-div: n.m.r on rail and lost pl over 4f out: trying to rally whn hmpd and snatched up over 3f out: n.d after* **14/1**	—
0	9	nk	**Italstar (IRE)**[9] 6658 2-8-12 .... RobertHavlin 3 — (H Morrison) *towards rr: rdn 4f out: sn bhd* **25/1**	—

1m 40.21s (-0.59) **Going Correction** -0.025s/f (Stan) **9** Ran SP% **116.1**
Speed ratings (Par 98):101,99,93,92,89 88,69,68,68
CSF £2.79 TOTE £2.00: £1.10, £1.10, £1.70; EX 4.80.
Owner Mrs Sue Brendish **Bred** Dr T Keenan & Dr H G White Jr **Trained** East Everleigh, Wilts
■ Stewards' Enquiry : William Buick two-day ban: careless riding (Dec 21-22)

FOCUS
A routine maiden, run at a medium pace.

NOTEBOOK
Mr Aviator(USA), the subject of strong support on the exchanges, travelled well and swiftly put the result beyond doubt when asked to quicken. He has improved since his first race, and clearly has ability, but will be tested more strongly than this in future races. (op 11-10 tchd 5-4 in places)
Risque Heights, blinkered for the first time, was unlucky to run into a well-backed favourite. He is now qualified for handicaps, where he should do well, but looks capable of winning in routine maiden company if remaining there instead for the time being. (op 2-1)
Fowey(USA), a 250,000 dollar daughter of Gone West, has a good American pedigree and should do well on this surface. Her dam was a high-class winner around a mile on both dirt and turf, so she could well pick up a race or two on the All-Weather before switching to grass next year. (op 4-1)
Zaafira(SPA) ran her best race to date, but will be more at home in handicaps now she is qualified.
Conny Nobel(IRE) needs a few more races to harden him up. He looked a difficult ride here, and needs to improve to become genuinely competitive. (op 66-1)
Childish Thoughts ran better than on her debut, but looks a modest handicapper at best in the long term.
Linlithgow(IRE), who had a nightmare in running, is now qualified for handicaps and should do much better over middle distances.

6779 BETBROKERS H'CAP (DIV I) — 1m (P)

3:30 (3:30) (Class 6) (0-52,52) 3-Y-0+ £1,706 (£503; £252) Stalls High

Form				RPR
2423	1		**Moyoko (IRE)**[12] 6648 3-8-12 **51** .... FrancisNorton 5 — (M Blanshard) *hld up in midfield: smooth hdwy over 2f out: led wl over 1f out: qcknd clr: comf* **3/1**[1]	58+
0000	2	2	**Rowan Warning**[61] 5885 4-9-0 **52** .... SteveDrowne 1 — (J R Boyle) *towards rr: rdn and styd on fnl 2f: tk 2nd on line: nt trble ldr* **13/2**	52
0354	3	shd	**Hilltop Fantasy**[4] 6726 5-8-1 **46** oh6 .... WilliamBuick(7) 6 — (V Smith) *w ldrs: led 2f out: sn hdd and nt pce of wnr: lost 2nd on line* **5/1**[3]	46
200/	4	3	**Lady Korrianda**[770] 6493 5-8-10 **48** .... DaneO'Neill 4 — (B R Johnson) *mid-div: outpcd 3f out: hrd rdn and styd on fr over 1f out* **16/1**	42
6300	5	hd	**Secam (POL)**[13] 1245 7-9-0 **52** .... (b) DeanCorby 9 — (Mrs P Townsley) *hld up in tch: rdn over 2f out: one pce* **12/1**	45
2B00	6	hd	**Love You Always (USA)**[4] 6724 6-8-1 **46** oh1 .... (t) AmyBaker(7) 7 — (Miss J Feilden) *s.i.s: plld hrd in rr: gd hdwy on rail over 2f out: no ex over 1f out* **5/1**[3]	39
0006	7	3½	**Almowj**[59] 5929 3-8-2 **48** .... WilliamCarson(7) 3 — (C E Brittain) *prom: led over 4f out tl wknd 2f out* **4/1**[2]	34
0050	8	8	**Vixen Virago**[4] 6725 3-8-7 **46** oh11 .... AdrianMcCarthy 10 — (Jane Southcombe) *led tl over 4f out: wknd over 3f out* **66/1**	16
000	9	¾	**Bazil Des Fieffes (FR)**[27] 6459 4-8-11 **49** oh1 ow3 .... (b) CDehens 8 — (J M Plasschaert, Belgium) *s.i.s: rdn over 3f out: a bhd* **25/1**	8
4400	10	5	**Renegade (IRE)**[101] 4970 5-9-0 **52** .... (b) IanMongan 2 — (Mrs L J Mongan) *chsd ldrs: hung rt and wknd over 2f out* **12/1**	11

1m 40.19s (-0.61) **Going Correction** -0.025s/f (Stan)
WFA 3 from 4yo+ 1lb **10** Ran SP% **118.3**
Speed ratings (Par 101):102,100,99,96,96 96,93,85,84,79
CSF £23.32 CT £98.61 TOTE £3.30: £1.50, £2.20, £1.50; EX 31.90.
Owner Mrs N L Young **Bred** P F Headon **Trained** Upper Lambourn, Berks

FOCUS
Little better than a seller, with a modest early tempo, but the winner is on the upgrade and was value for further.

6780 BETBROKERS H'CAP (DIV II) — 1m (P)

4:00 (4:00) (Class 6) (0-52,52) 3-Y-0+ £1,706 (£503; £252) Stalls High

Form				RPR
0031	1		**Bowl Of Cherries**[19] 6552 3-8-11 **50** .... (b) LeeEnstone 8 — (I A Wood) *hld up in midfield: hdwy to ld 2f out: rdn clr: readily* **11/2**[3]	63+
5004	2	2	**King Of Knight (IRE)**[6] 6700 5-9-0 **52** .... OscarUrbina 9 — (G Prodromou) *hld up towards rr: hdwy and nt clr run 2f out: styd on to take 2nd on line* **5/1**[2]	59
0022	3	shd	**Kathleen Kennet**[16] 6577 6-9-0 **52** .... GeorgeBaker 2 — (Mrs H Sweeting) *trckd ldrs: chal over 2f out: sn rdn: edgd lft and kpt on same pce: lost 2nd on line* **11/4**[1]	59
6262	4	½	**Paso Doble**[20] 6532 8-8-5 **50** .... JamesMillman(7) 4 — (D K Ivory) *chsd ldrs: hrd rdn over 2f out: styd on same pce* **7/1**	56
6632	5	1¾	**Fantasy Defender (IRE)**[6] 6702 4-8-9 **47** oh1 ow1 .... (v) AdamKirby 3 — (Ernst Oertel) *in tch: rdn 3f out: styd on same pce* **11/4**[1]	50
0000	6	½	**Colonel Bilko (IRE)**[4] 6726 4-8-5 **46** oh6 .... MarcHalford(3) 1 — (J J Bridger) *stdd s: hld up in rr: rapid hdwy on rail over 2f out: hrd rdn and wknd over 1f out* **33/1**	48
0-00	7	5	**Filliemou (IRE)**[64] 5566 5-8-8 **46** oh11 .... FergusSweeney 10 — (A W Carroll) *pressed ldr tl wknd 2f out* **66/1**	38
0000	8	¾	**Sprinkle**[61] 5885 3-8-13 **52** .... DaneO'Neill 5 — (B R Johnson) *towards rr: rdn 3f out: sn bhd* **12/1**	42
000-	9	1¼	**Shergael (IRE)**[12] 5996 5-8-9 **47** .... (b[1]) FrancisNorton 7 — (J L Spearing) *led tl wknd 2f out* **16/1**	35

4455 **10** *6* **Jazz At The Sands (USA)**[219] 1464 3-8-4 **46** oh6... PatrickMathers(3) 6 22
(D Shaw) *plld hrd: in tch tl wknd over 2f out* **20/1**

1m 40.24s (-0.56) **Going Correction** -0.025s/f (Stan)
WFA 3 from 4yo+ 1lb **35** Ran SP% **120.7**
Speed ratings (Par 101):101,99,98,98,96 96,91,90,89,83
CSF £33.86 CT £95.38 TOTE £7.50: £1.80, £1.90, £1.50; EX 31.10.
Owner Graham Bradbury **Bred** Eurostrait Ltd **Trained** Upper Lambourn, Berks

FOCUS
Like division one, little better than a seller, and run at a modest pace, but the winner is at least improving for the addition of blinkers.
Shergael(IRE) Official explanation: jockey said gelding ran too free early

6781 BETBROKERS BACK HERE ON THE 16TH H'CAP 7f (P)
4:30 (4:30) (Class 5) (0-70,77) 3-Y-0+ **£4,857** (£1,445; £722; £360) **Stalls** High

Form RPR

012 **1** **Dichoh**[17] 6573 3-9-2 **70** RichardHughes 3 79+
(M A Jarvis) *hld up towards rr: hdwy and hung rt over 2f out: qckn to ld ins fnl f: readily* **7/1**[3]

3211 **2** *1* **Evident Pride (USA)**[11] 6652 3-9-9 **77** DaneO'Neill 9 82
(B R Johnson) *dwlt: hld up towards rr: rdn 3f out: styd on wl fnl 2f: tk 2nd nr fin: nt rch wnr* **5/4**[1]

0300 **3** *hd* **Monashee Prince (IRE)**[9] 6656 4-8-6 **60** StephenCarson 14 65
(J R Best) *t.k.h: prom: led 2f out: hdd and nt qckn ins fnl f* **33/1**

4304 **4** *nk* **Smokin Joe**[6] 6698 5-9-1 **69** (b) GeorgeBaker 11 73
(J R Best) *hld up and bhd: shkn up over 2f out: gd late hdwy* **12/1**

4100 **5** *½* **Fateful Attraction**[25] 6489 3-9-0 **68** (b) LeeEnstone 2 71
(I A Wood) *chsd ldrs: rdn 2f out: kpt on same pce* **33/1**

0600 **6** *nk* **Hurricane Coast**[11] 6652 7-8-1 **62** (tp) SophieDoyle(7) 10 64
(Ms J S Doyle) *led tl 2f out: no ex fnl f* **66/1**

3321 **7** *½* **Mozakhraf (USA)**[5] 6721 4-8-8 **67** 6ex JamieJones(5) 4 67
(K A Ryan) *chsd ldrs: effrt over 2f out: one pce appr fnl f* **5/1**[2]

0563 **8** *shd* **Quantum Leap**[11] 6654 9-9-1 **69** (v) JimmyQuinn 12 69
(S Dow) *t.k.h: hld up in midfield: drvn to chse ldrs 2f out: hld whn n.m.r ins fnl f* **16/1**

0332 **9** *½* **Imperial Lucky (IRE)**[9] 6664 3-8-9 **70** JamesMillman(7) 7 69
(D K Ivory) *hld up towards rr: gd hdwy on rail over 2f out: no ex appr fnl f* **10/1**

6055 **10** *hd* **Look Of Eagles**[9] 6656 4-8-6 **60** NelsonDeSouza 13 58
(P F I Cole) *mid-div: rdn and no imp fnl 2f* **20/1**

6462 **11** *½* **James Street (IRE)**[11] 6654 3-9-3 **71** (p) SteveDrowne 5 68
(J R Best) *chsd ldr tl over 2f out: grad fdd* **12/1**

2-10 **12** *3* **Woodsley House (IRE)**[89] 5263 4-9-2 **70** AdamKirby 8 59
(Miss Gay Kelleway) *t.k.h: sn in midfield: rdn 3f out: outpcd fnl 2f* **66/1**

6 **13** *5* **Star Of Russia (IRE)**[9] 6656 4-8-2 **63** WilliamBuick(7) 6 38
(V Smith) *wd in midfield: rdn over 2f out: sn wknd* **8/1**

1m 26.82s (0.02) **Going Correction** -0.025s/f (Stan) **13** Ran SP% **128.7**
Speed ratings (Par 103):98,96,96,96,95 95,94,94,94,93 93,89,84
CSF £16.77 CT £315.83 TOTE £5.90: £1.90, £1.30, £9.80; EX 22.60 Place 6 £115.63, Place 5 £109.00..
Owner T G Warner **Bred** Red House Stud **Trained** Newmarket, Suffolk

FOCUS
A competitive race, with two lightly-raced and progressive sorts filling the first two places, but run at an ordinary pace, with a disappointing time.
Woodsley House(IRE) Official explanation: jockey said gelding ran too free
T/Plt: £202.40 to a £1 stake. Pool: £54,317.60. 195.85 winning tickets. T/Qpdt: £52.60 to a £1 stake. Pool: £3,410.70. 47.90 winning tickets. LM

1527 SHA TIN (R-H)
Sunday, December 10
OFFICIAL GOING: Good to firm Race times are a.m. British time

6782a CATHAY PACIFIC HONG KONG VASE (GROUP 1) 1m 4f
6:00 (6:00) 3-Y-0+
£599,549 (£231,405; £105,184; £60,105; £34,560; £21,037)

RPR

1 **Collier Hill**[49] 6126 8-9-0 DeanMcKeown 10 122
(G A Swinbank) *close up in 4th, niggled along from ½-way, hdwy on outside to ld 2f out, sn hrd rdn, went 2l clear, just held on* **11/1**

2 *nse* **Kastoria (IRE)**[49] 6126 5-8-10 MJKinane 1 118+
(John M Oxx, Ire) *midfield, 5th on inside 3f out, squeezed up and dropped back to last 2f out, still last over 1f out, fin wl, jst failed, unlucky* **69/10**[3]

3 *1* **Shamdala (IRE)**[49] 6119 4-8-10 CSoumillon 3 116
(A De Royer-Dupre, France) *held up, 7th straight, n.m.r 2f out to over 1f out, headway to go 2nd briefly 100y out, kept on* **11/1**

4 *¾* **Song Of Wind (JPN)**[49] 3-8-9 KTake 6 119
(Hidekazu Asami, Japan) *held up and behind, headway around outside from 4f out, 4th straight, went 2nd 1 1/2f out, lost 2nd 100y out, one pace* **7/2**[2]

5 *1 ½* **Maraahel (IRE)**[57] 5964 5-9-0 (v) RHills 9 117
(Sir Michael Stoute) *missed break, raced in 9th, last straight, headway down outside to go 4th briefly over 1f out, stayed on at same pace* **10/1**

6 *1 ½* **Egerton (GER)**[56] 6004 5-9-0 TMundry 7 114
(P Rau, Germany) *raced in 6th, went 3rd 1 1/2f out, soon hard ridden and edged right to inside rail, one pace final f* **56/1**

7 *¾* **Scorpion (IRE)**[36] 6344 4-9-0 JAHeffernan 5 113
(A P O'Brien, Ire) *tracked leader in 3rd, 5th straight towards inside, one pace final 2f* **78/10**

8 *7 ½* **Admire Main (JPN)**[49] 3-8-9 YTake 4 102
(M Hashida, Japan) *set strong gallop til steadied pace after 4f, headed 2f out, weakened* **13/10**[1]

9 *6 ¾* **Saturn (IRE)**[28] 6-9-0 DNikolic 8 92
(C Fownes, Hong Kong) *pulled hard early in 2nd on outside, pressed leader entering straight, weakened over 1 1/2f out, eased* **21/1**

2m 27.1s
WFA 3 from 4yo+ 5lb **9** Ran SP% **121.8**
(including HK$10 stake): WIN 120.50; PL 45.00, 30.00, 39.50; DF 471.50.
Owner R H Hall J D Abell R Crowe **Bred** George Strawbridge **Trained** Melsonby, N Yorks

FOCUS
A high-class contest and another success for the globetrotting Collier Hill.

NOTEBOOK
Collier Hill produced another amazing performance, especially given that he was in danger of missing the race through dehydration 48 hours beforehand. McKeown gave him a never-say-die ride, getting busy with fully six furlongs to run. He responded gamely, coming three wide to hit the front at the top of the straight. Forging clear, he carried his head to one side as if feeling the ground in the closing stages, but had just enough in hand to ward off the unlucky runner-up. A third crack at the Dubai Sheema Classic is the next port of call for this indomitable warrior.
Kastoria(IRE) should have won. Badly squeezed and dropping back to last two furlongs out, she finished with a rare rattle, relishing the return to a sound surface after soggy Woodbine. She will now be covered, but may have a final start in the Sheema Classic and try to level the score with Collier Hill at 2-2.
Maraahel(IRE) was out the back after a tardy start but moved up to have a chance halfway up the straight before his effort flattened out.
Scorpion(IRE) was well enough placed for much of the race, but could not pick up off the turn.

6783a CATHAY PACIFIC HONG KONG SPRINT (GROUP 1) 6f
7:10 (7:10) 3-Y-0+
£513,899 (£198,347; £90,158; £51,089; £30,053; £18,032)

RPR

1 **Absolute Champion (AUS)**[42] 5-9-0 BPrebble 5 129
(D Hall, Hong Kong) *raced in 6th, 4th straight, led over 1f out, soon clear, impressive* **54/10**[3]

2 *4 ¼* **Silent Witness (AUS)**[21] 7-9-0 FCoetzee 2 117
(A S Cruz, Hong Kong) *midfield, 6th straight, went 2nd inside final f, kept on but no chance with winner* **6/1**

3 *¾* **Benbaun (IRE)**[70] 5717 5-9-0 (v) JamieSpencer 3 115
(M J Wallace) *towards rear, 8thb and pushed along halfway, ridden over 1f out, went 3rd 120 yards out, kept on* **38/1**

4 *1 ¼* **Down Town (AUS)**[21] 4-9-0 ODoleuze 13 111
(C H Yip, Hong Kong) *in rear, last straight, stayed on well down outside to take 4th closing stages* **39/10**[2]

5 *1* **Sunny Sing (IRE)**[21] 4-9-0 CSoumillon 8 108
(J Moore, Hong Kong) *close up early, 8th straight, stayed on at one pace final 2f* **16/10**[1]

6 *¾* **Billet Express (AUS)**[21] 5-9-0 DWhyte 10 106
(J Moore, Hong Kong) *towards rear, 10th straight, some late headway* **48/1**

7 *1 ¾* **Able Prince (AUS)**[21] 5-9-0 (b) MNunes 9 101
(J Moore, Hong Kong) *3rd early, 5th straight, soon one pace* **30/1**

8 *shd* **Scintillation (AUS)**[21] 6-9-0 GMosse 6 100
(C S Shum, Hong Kong) *in touch, chasing clear leaders in 3rd halfway, led over 1 1/2f out to over 1f out, weakened* **17/1**

9 *2 ¾* **Red Oog (AUS)**[43] 6-9-0 HBowman 14 92
(J Pride, Australia) *always in rear* **34/1**

10 *nk* **She Is Tosho (JPN)**[70] 5717 6-8-10 KenichiIkezoe 11 87
(A Tsurudome, Japan) *always in rear* **22/1**

11 *3 ½* **Natural Blitz I (AUS)**[21] 6-9-0 ADelpech 1 81
(D Cruz, Hong Kong) *set rapid pace til headed 2 1/2f out, weakened 2f out* **40/1**

12 *nse* **Desert Lord**[70] 5712 6-9-0 (b) NCallan 4 80
(K A Ryan) *pressed leader and soon 3l clear of remainder, led 2 1/2f out to over 1 1/2f out, weakened* **30/1**

R **Meisho Bowler (JPN)**[43] 5-9-0 YFukunaga 7 —
(T Shirai, Japan) *refused to race* **12/1**

67.80 secs **13** Ran SP% **122.7**
WIN 64.00; PL 21.00, 22.00, 100.00; DF 224.50.
Owner Mr & Mrs Eddie Wong Ming Chak **Bred** J W Kelly, Suffolk Vale & Co **Trained** Hong Kong

NOTEBOOK
Absolute Champion(AUS) lived up to his name with a dominant performance, sweeping past the tiring leaders in the straight and leaving some high-class rivals in his wake.
Silent Witness(AUS), who has not been the same horse since getting a virus in Japan, at least showed signs of a revival, although he never got near the winner.
Benbaun(IRE) ran a personal best, keeping on stoutly in the final quarter mile having failed to keep up with the fierce early pace. He deserves to win one of Europe's top sprint prizes in 2007.
Desert Lord helped force a suicidal early pace and, Callan having been forced to pull with both hands on the right rein to get round the bend, predictably ran out of puff in the closing stages. Five furlongs suits him better.

6784a CATHAY PACIFIC HONG KONG MILE (GROUP 1) 1m
8:20 (8:20) 3-Y-0+
£685,199 (£264,463; £120,210; £68,370; £39,820; £24,042)

RPR

1 **The Duke (AUS)**[21] 6-9-0 ODoleuze 4 120
(C Fownes, Hong Kong) *raced in 3rd behind clear leaders, led over 1f out, driven 1l clear, just held on* **142/10**

2 *hd* **Armada (NZ)**[21] 5-9-0 DWhyte 5 120
(J Size, Hong Kong) *midfield, pushed along over 2 1/2f out, 6th straight, still 6th 1f out, finished strongly, just failed* **6/5**[1]

3 *1 ¼* **Ramonti (FR)**[35] 6364 4-9-0 EBotti 12 117
(A & G Botti, Italy) *set strong pace til headed over 1f out, kept on* **16/1**

4 *½* **Bullish Luck (USA)**[21] 7-9-0 (b) BPrebble 7 116
(A S Cruz, Hong Kong) *held up, 10th straight, brought left to find room over 1 1/2f out, stayed on down outside to take 4th on line* **15/2**[3]

5 *shd* **Linngari (IRE)**[43] 6230 4-9-0 GSchofield 13 116
(H J Brown, South Africa) *held up in rear, last straight, headway through field 1 1/2f out, switched towards inside 80 yards out, finished well* **66/1**

6 *hd* **Joyful Winner (AUS)**[21] 6-9-0 CSoumillon 2 115
(J Moore, Hong Kong) *raced in 5th, went 3rd over 1f out, lost 3rd close home* **14/1**

7 *shd* **Floral Pegasus (AUS)**[21] 4-9-0 LDettori 6 115
(A S Cruz, Hong Kong) *raced in 4th, disputed 3rd 1 1/2f out, kept on at one pace* **5/1**[2]

8 *2 ½* **Rebel Rebel (IRE)**[42] 4-9-0 EPrado 3 110
(R Dutrow Jr, U.S.A) *raced in 8th, 8th straight, one pace final 2f* **44/1**

9 *nk* **Sir Ernesto (AUS)**[21] 5-9-0 FCoetzee 1 110
(D Cruz, Hong Kong) *pressed leader 3 lengths clear of remainder, 2nd straight, weakened 1 1/2f out* **16/1**

10 *½* **Russian Pearl (NZ)**[21] 6-9-0 ESaint-Martin 10 109
(A S Cruz, Hong Kong) *held up in rear, 12th straight, never a factor* **37/1**

11 *¾* **Bowman's Crossing (IRE)**[21] 7-9-0 GMosse 8 107
(C Fownes, Hong Kong) *11th straight, always in rear* **40/1**

12 *shd* **Dance In The Mood (JPN)**[21] 6530 5-8-10 YTake 14 103
(Kazuo Fujisawa, Japan) *towards rear on outside, 9th straight, never a factor* **9/1**

13 1 ¾ **Dave's Best**[21] 6-9-0 .... MJKinane 9 103
(C H Yip, Hong Kong) *always in rear* **55/1**
14 1 ¼ **Mustameet (USA)**[92] 5193 5-9-0 .... DPMcDonogh 11 101
(Kevin Prendergast, Ire) *midfield, pushed along 3f out, 7th straight, looked beaten when hampered over 1 1/2f out, not recover* **29/1**
1m 33.4s **14** Ran SP% **122.8**
WIN 152.00; PL 29.50, 13.50, 37.00; DF 182.00.
Owner Eddie Yau Jr **Bred** Caradale Pty Ltd **Trained** Hong Kong

6785a CATHAY PACIFIC HONG KONG CUP (GROUP 1) 1m 2f
9:00 (9:00) 3-Y-O+
£856,499 (£330,579; £150,263; £85,650; £49,587; £30,053)

RPR
1 **Pride (FR)**[57] 5964 6-8-10 .... C-PLemaire 9 121
(A De Royer-Dupre, France) *last til hdwy around outside 4f out, close 7th straight on outside, led just ins fnl f, went 1l clear, just held on* **51/20**[2]
2 *shd* **Admire Moon (JPN)**[42] 3-8-11 .... YTake 4 125
(H Matsuda, Japan) *raced in 10th, 11th straight only 3 lengths off lead, 6th 1f out, finished well, just failed* **10/1**
3 1 ¾ **Vengeance Of Rain (NZ)**[21] 5-9-0 .... ADelpech 2 121
(D Ferraris, Hong Kong) *raced in 5th, headway around outside to lead narrowly 2 1/2f out, headed just inside final f, one pace* **4/1**[3]
4 1 ½ **Viva Pataca**[28] 4-9-0 .... CSoumillon 8 118
(J Moore, Hong Kong) *missed break, recovered to track leaders in 4th, 6th straight, went 2nd briefly 1 1/2f out, stayed on at same pace* **73/10**
5 ¾ **Art Trader (USA)**[21] 5-9-0 .... ESaint-Martin 12 117
(J Moore, Hong Kong) *raced in 6th, close 9th straight, kept on steadily final 2f* **73/1**
6 *hd* **Satwa Queen (FR)**[36] 6340 4-8-10 .... LDettori 5 113
(J De Roualle, France) *raced in 8th, 5th straight, soon ridden, stayed on at one pace* **26/1**
7 *nk* **Dia De La Novia (JPN)**[28] 4-8-10 .... YFukunaga 11 112
(Katsuhiko Sumii, Japan) *11th early, last straight, some late headway* **37/1**
8 *nk* **Hello Pretty (AUS)**[28] 4-9-0 .... BPrebble 6 115
(A S Cruz, Hong Kong) *always prominent, 2nd straight, one pace final 2f* **23/10**[1]
9 2 ½ **Alexander Goldrun (IRE)**[71] 5674 5-8-10 .... KJManning 10 107
(J S Bolger, Ire) *raced wide in 9th, headway on outside to be close 4th straight, soon ridden and unable to quicken* **9/1**
10 1 ½ **Musical Way (FR)**[49] 6124 4-8-10 .... RonanThomas 3 104
(P Van De Poele, France) *raced in 7th, 10th straight, never a factor* **100/1**
11 4 **Growl (NZ)**[36] 6347 4-9-0 .... CraigAWilliams 7 100
(D Hayes, Australia) *pressed leader, 3rd straight, soon weakened* **28/1**
12 4 **High Intelligent (AUS)**[28] 6-9-0 ....(b) DWhyte 1 93
(J Size, Hong Kong) *set steady pace til headed 2 1/2f out, weakened 2f out, eased* **50/1**
2m 1.60s
WFA 3 from 4yo+ 3lb **12** Ran SP% **123.7**
PARI-MUTUEL: WIN 35.50; PL 16.50, 30.00, 17.50; DF 218.00.
Owner N P Bloodstock **Bred** N P Bloodstock Ltd **Trained** Chantilly, France

FOCUS
This event saw the final runs before retirement of the top mares Pride and Alexander Goldrun, with the former just holding on to end her career in a blaze of glory.

NOTEBOOK
Pride(FR) signed off her brilliant career with another win, albeit by the smallest possible margin. This trip round a sharp track is near her minimum, and a slow pace did not help. Coming from last but beginning her run earlier than usual, she got a smooth passage around the outside to gwet to the front, but was coming to the end of her tether late on and barely held off the slightly unlucky runner-up.
Alexander Goldrun(IRE), who had reportedly not travelled well, was given every chance to emulate her 2004 win in this race, but was unable to run up to her best on her final outing before retirement.

6453 TOULOUSE
Sunday, December 10
OFFICIAL GOING: Very heavy

6786a PRIX DE L'EUROPE (PRIX MAX SICARD) (LISTED RACE) 1m 4f
2:35 (2:37) 3-Y-O+ **£20,690** (£8,276; £6,207; £4,138; £2,069)

RPR
1 **Mister Conway (FR)**[40] 5-9-3 .... SPasquier 9 109
(P Van De Poele, France)
2 3 **Vert Helice (SPA)**[15] 4-9-0 .... RMarchelli 4 102
(M Rolland, France)
3 3 **Varevees**[82] 5472 3-8-9 .... DMichaux 5 97
(J Boisnard, France)
4 1 ½ **Belcantista (FR)**[262] 759 4-9-0 .... F-XBertras 3 95
(L Urbano-Grajales, France)
5 1 ½ **Cyr Cry (FR)**[626] 715 6-9-0 .... LHuart 2 93
(C Le Lay, France)
6 *hd* **Sentry Duty (FR)**[15] 6610 4-9-0 .... MBlancpain 7 92
(E Libaud, France)
7 *hd* **Blushing King (FR)**[65] 4-9-0 .... FVeron 14 92
(J-L Guillochon, France)
8 10 **Epatha (IRE)**[29] 6454 3-8-13 .... WMongil 11 81
(J-C Rouget, France)
9 5 **Tunduru (IRE)**[224] 1332 5-9-3 .... CNora 1 72
(R Martin-Sanchez, Spain)
10 6 **Limatus (GER)**[68] 5-9-0 .... RJuracek 16 60
(P Vovcenko, Germany)
11 **Lilakiya (IRE)**[26] 6482 3-8-6 .... JamesDoyle 12 57
(James Leavy, Ire) *soon ridden along in mid-division, reminders over 7f out, last over 5f out, finished 11th, beaten a distance* **98/1**[1]
12 **Atlantique Nord (FR)**[62] 5881 6-9-3 .... IMendizabal 13 63
(D De Watrigant, France)
13 **Kalahari King (FR)**[626] 715 5-9-3 .... TJarnet 15 63
(H-A Pantall, France)
14 **Benta Berri (FR)**[62] 5881 4-9-3 ....(b) OTrigodet 8 63
(R Martin-Sanchez, Spain)
15 **Resleon (FR)**[48] 3-8-9 .... GToupel 6 60
(H-A Pantall, France)
16 **Belle Epine (FR)**[271] 4-8-10 .... GHeurtault 10 56
(C Dufreche, France)
2m 38.89s
WFA 3 from 4yo+ 5lb **16** Ran SP% **1.0**
PARI-MUTUEL (including one euro stakes): WIN 4.90; PL 2.20, 2.60, 3.40; DF 14.90.
Owner S Constantinidis **Bred** J Van Der Weide **Trained** France

6764 WOLVERHAMPTON (A.W) (L-H)
Monday, December 11
OFFICIAL GOING: Standard
Racing was delayed by 30 minutes after a pile-up in the 2.05 resulted in insufficient ambulance cover.
Wind: Moderate behind becoming almost nil Weather: Fine

6787 WBXTRIPLECROWN.COM H'CAP (DIV I) 1m 141y(P)
1:00 (1:02) (Class 6) (0-55,55) 3-Y-O+ **£2,047** (£604; £302) **Stalls** Low

Form RPR
004 1 **Mozie Cat (IRE)**[117] 4495 3-8-12 **55** .... BrettDoyle 7 63
(John Berry) *a.p: rdn over 2f out: led over 1f out: edgd rt ins fnl f: r.o* **16/1**
0003 2 *nk* **Green Pirate**[7] 6703 4-8-0 **48** .... WilliamBuick(7) 2 55+
(W M Brisbourne) *t.k.h in rr: nt clr run on ins fr over 3f out tl plld out ent st: hdwy and n.m.r over 1f out: rdn and r.o wl ins fnl f: unl* **10/3**[1]
2500 3 2 **Penang Cinta**[30] 6436 3-8-10 **53** .... LPKeniry 10 56
(A J Chamberlain) *hld up and bhd: rdn and hdwy 2f out: edgd rt ins fnl f: kpt on* **33/1**
0030 4 1 **Wiltshire (IRE)**[17] 6577 4-8-11 **52** .... MickyFenton 1 53
(P T Midgley) *led early: a.p: rdn over 2f out: edgd rt jst over 1f out: one pce fnl f* **11/2**[3]
4110 5 *shd* **Under Fire (IRE)**[30] 6436 3-8-12 **55** .... FrancisNorton 6 56
(A W Carroll) *sn led: hdd over 5f out: led over 3f out: rdn over 2f out: hdd and edgd rt over 1f out: fdd towards fin* **8/1**
0145 6 *hd* **Vibrato (USA)**[21] 6532 4-8-8 **49** .... PaulHanagan 3 49
(C J Teague) *hld up: sn mid-div: lost pl over 4f out: rdn and r.o ins fnl f* **5/1**[2]
0450 7 *nk* **The Gaikwar (IRE)**[9] 6683 7-8-13 **54** ....(b) AdamKirby 4 54
(R A Harris) *hld up and bhd: hdwy on ins 4f out: rdn 2f out: carried rt jst over 1f out: one pce* **7/1**
0000 8 4 **Joe Jo Star**[10] 6667 4-8-5 **46** .... JimmyQuinn 8 37
(B P J Baugh) *hld up in mid-div: rdn and hdwy 2f out: wkng whn n.m.r jst over 1f out: edgd rt ins fnl f* **12/1**
000U 9 3 ½ **Didnt Tell My Wife**[20] 6549 7-8-5 **46** oh6 ....(v) HayleyTurner 5 30
(P S McEntee) *hld up and bhd: hdwy on ins over 2f out: wknd 1f out* **66/1**
0004 10 3 ½ **Insignia (IRE)**[7] 6702 4-8-5 **46** oh1 ....(p) CatherineGannon 11 23
(W M Brisbourne) *prom: led over 5f out tl over 3f out: rdn over 2f out: wknd wl over 1f out* **22/1**
0640 11 *hd* **My Pension (IRE)**[282] 582 5-9-0 **55** .... DeanCorby 13 31
(P Howling) *c wd over 2f out: a bhd* **9/1**
P- 12 7 **Brogue Lanterns (IRE)**[302] 4-9-0 **55** .... EdwardCreighton 9 16
(E J Creighton) *prom tl over 3f out* **33/1**
0300 13 5 **Union Jack Jackson (IRE)**[14] 6622 4-8-11 **52** .... J-PGuillambert 12 3
(J G Given) *mid-div: rdn over 3f out: wknd over 2f out* **14/1**
1m 51.2s (-0.56) **Going Correction** -0.075s/f (Stan)
WFA 3 from 4yo+ 2lb **13** Ran SP% **120.7**
Speed ratings (Par 101):99,98,96,96,95 95,95,91,88,85 85,79,74
CSF £67.63 CT £1851.42 TOTE £16.90: £5.00, £1.60, £9.50; EX 67.80 Trifecta £8.00 Pool: £113.78 - 10.00 winning units..
Owner Norcroft Park Stud **Bred** Western Bloodstock **Trained** Newmarket, Suffolk
■ Stewards' Enquiry : William Buick one-day ban: used whip without giving time to respond (Dec 23)

FOCUS
This modest handicap was run 1.42 seconds slower than the second division and the form is very ordinary rated around the third and fifth.

6788 WBXTRIPLECROWN.COM MAIDEN AUCTION STKS 5f 20y(P)
1:35 (1:36) (Class 6) 2-Y-O **£2,730** (£806; £403) **Stalls** Low

Form RPR
046 1 **Bungie**[64] 5835 2-8-10 62 ow1 .... J-PGuillambert 5 63
(Ms Deborah J Evans) *sn w ldr: led over 2f out: hrd rdn and hung lft wl over 1f out: r.o* **13/2**[3]
5 2 1 **Scarlett Heart (IRE)**[17] 6575 2-8-4 .... JoeFanning 1 53
(P J Makin) *led early: chsd ldrs: rdn and wnt 2nd over 1f out: nt qckn ins fnl f* **13/8**[2]
0504 3 *shd* **Wibbadune (IRE)**[10] 6665 2-8-4 54 .... JimmyQuinn 4 53
(Peter Grayson) *n.m.r sn after s: sn outpcd: hdwy 2f out: kpt on towards fin* **16/1**
5332 4 1 ¼ **Mujart**[25] 6500 2-8-6 59 .... ChrisCatlin 2 50
(J A Pickering) *hld up in tch: rdn and one pce fnl 2f* **11/10**[1]
5334 5 6 **Splendidio**[3] 6742 2-8-3 52 ow2 .... JamesMillman(7) 3 33
(D K Ivory) *wnt rt s: sn led: hdd over 2f out: wknd over 1f out: eased fnl f* **20/1**
63.16 secs (0.34) **Going Correction** -0.075s/f (Stan) **5** Ran SP% **109.7**
Speed ratings (Par 94):94,92,92,90,80
CSF £17.46 TOTE £7.20: £4.10, £1.10; EX 23.50.
Owner R Trimmer & Evie McHugh **Bred** P A Mason **Trained** Lydiate, Merseyside

FOCUS
A weak maiden rated around the winner and third.

NOTEBOOK
Bungie found a switch to sand doing the trick and saw it out after appearing to resent some liberal use of the whip once in line for home. (op 10-1)
Scarlett Heart(IRE) had to be content to play second fiddle once the winner got back on an even keel. (op 11-10 tchd Evens and 7-4)
Wibbadune(IRE) got taken off her legs after she was rather squeezed out at the start. Although only moderate, she would have been second in another stride. (tchd 22-1)
Mujart was not beaten as far as seemed likely at the quarter-mile marker but this was still a disappointing performance. (op 6-4 tchd 15-8, 2-1 in places)

6789 WBXTRIPLECROWN.COM (S) STKS 5f 216y(P)
2:05 (2:05) (Class 6) 2-Y-O **£2,388** (£705; £352) **Stalls** Low

Form RPR
0300 1 **Pirner's Brig**[89] 5282 2-8-12 50 .... PaulMulrennan 8 61
(M W Easterby) *mde all: clr whn rdn over 1f out: r.o* **20/1**

0506 **2** *8* **Totally Free**[26] 6487 2-8-5 52....(v) FrankiePickard(7) 12 37
(M D I Usher) *w wnr: rdn 2f out: sn btn* **13/2[3]**
3 *2* **Show Business (IRE)** 2-8-12.... JamieMackay 10 31
(Sir Mark Prescott) *towards rr and rdn whn hmpd over 3f out: r.o fnl f: n.d* **7/1**
6046 **4** *1 ¾* **Baytown Rosie (IRE)**[6] 6710 2-8-7 40.... HayleyTurner 6 21
(P S McEntee) *chsd ldrs: bdly hmpd over 3f out: nt rcvr* **25/1**
000 **5** *2 ½* **Byanita (IRE)**[63] 5876 2-8-7 35.... AdrianMcCarthy 2 13
(B Palling) *mid-div whn lft 3rd over 3f out: rdn over 2f out: wknd over 1f out* **66/1**
5005 **6** *21* **Kyoto City**[7] 6706 2-8-7 35....(b) PaulQuinn 7 —
(D W Chapman) *s.s: bhd whn carried wd over 3f out: t.o* **66/1**
B **Polly Rocket** 2-8-7.... PaulHanagan 1 —
(P D Niven) *s.s: last whn b.d over 3f out* **14/1**
3345 **F** **Money For Fun**[10] 6665 2-8-0 60....(b[1]) JosephWalsh(7) 4 —
(J S Moore) *prom: 3rd whn fell over 3f out: dead* **5/2[1]**
0543 **U** **Aggbag**[13] 6640 2-8-10 60.... SoniaEaton(7) 5 —
(B P J Baugh) *plld hrd in rr: hmpd and uns rdr over 3f out* **7/1**
3004 **U** **Fly Time**[16] 6605 2-8-8 48 ow1.... TomEaves 3 —
(Mrs L Williamson) *hld up towards rr: hmpd and uns rdr over 3f out* **14/1**
0625 **U** **Put It On The Card**[26] 6491 2-8-12 60....(b[1]) JimCrowley 11 —
(P D Evans) *chsd ldrs: lft 3rd whn hmpd and uns rdr over 3f out* **7/2[2]**

1m 16.16s (0.35) **Going Correction** -0.075s/f (Stan) **11** Ran SP% **114.1**
Speed ratings (Par 94):94,83,80,78,75 47,—,—,—,— —
CSF £137.30 TOTE £20.80: £5.20, £2.00, £2.30; EX 237.20 TRIFECTA Not won..There was no bid for the winner.
Owner Mrs E Rhind **Bred** C F Spence & Mrs E Rhind **Trained** Sheriff Hutton, N Yorks

FOCUS
The first two were left clear after a pile-up before halfway and not a race to dwell on.

NOTEBOOK
Pirner's Brig only had the runner-up to worry about after the carnage before halfway and drew away from the two-furlong pole. (op 22-1 tchd 25-1)
Totally Free, like the winner, missed all the trouble but could not live with his rival in the final quarter-mile. (op 8-1)
Show Business(IRE) was certainly starting his career at the basement level. Already scrubbed along when caught up in the melee, this form is best forgotten although he may well want further. (op 4-1)
Baytown Rosie(IRE)'s rider did well to stay in the plate when he jumped a prostrate faller. (op 33-1)

6790 WBX.COM WORLD BET EXCHANGE H'CAP — 1m 5f 194y(P)
2:35 (3:07) (Class 6) (0-55,55) 3-Y-O+ **£2,730** (£806; £403) **Stalls** Low

Form RPR
0466 **1** **Little Richard (IRE)**[5] 6729 7-8-13 **50**....(p) AdamKirby 1 58
(M Wellings) *a.p: rdn over 2f out: styd on to ld wl ins fnl f* **9/1**
1 **2** *½* **Share The Feeling (IRE)**[3] 6754 4-9-0 **54**.... RichardKingscote(3) 8 61
(J W Unett) *a.p: led over 4f out: rdn over 2f out: hdd and nt qckn wl ins fnl f* **9/2[2]**
-003 **3** *¾* **Twist Bookie (IRE)**[7] 6705 6-8-10 **47**.... ChrisCatlin 12 53
(S Lycett) *hld up and bhd: hdwy over 4f out: rdn over 2f out: styd on ins fnl f* **14/1**
5002 **4** *1 ¾* **Capitalise (IRE)**[3] 6754 3-7-9 **46** oh1.... WilliamBuick(7) 9 50
(V Smith) *hld up and bhd: hdwy on outside over 2f out: hung lft fr wl over 1f out: one pce fnl f* **11/4[1]**
2031 **5** *1 ½* **Zaffeu**[16] 6604 5-8-11 **55**.... RussellKennemore(7) 10 56
(A G Juckes) *s.i.s: hld up and bhd: nt clr run on ins wl over 1f out: hdwy fnl f: nrst fin* **10/1**
0344 **6** *½* **Atlantic Gamble (IRE)**[5] 6729 6-8-9 **46**....(p) LeeEnstone 2 47
(K R Burke) *hld up in tch: chsd ldr 3f out: sn rdn: lost 2nd 1f out: fdd* **9/2[2]**
2020 **7** *nk* **Peas 'n Beans (IRE)**[3] 6754 3-8-4 **53**.... DuranFentiman(5) 7 53
(T Keddy) *hld up in mid-div: rdn over 2f out: no hdwy* **11/1**
3305 **8** *3* **Art Historian (IRE)**[18] 6571 3-8-10 **54**.... FrancisNorton 13 50
(T J Pitt) *t.k.h in mid-div: hung lft fr wl over 1f out: no imp* **8/1[3]**
0000 **9** *nk* **Fuel Cell (IRE)**[21] 6544 5-8-10 **47**.... PaulQuinn 4 43
(J O'Reilly) *t.k.h: rdn over 3f out: a towards rr* **66/1**
4440 **10** *1* **True (IRE)**[20] 6553 5-8-10 **47** oh1 ow1.... MickyFenton 11 41
(Mrs S Lamyman) *hld up towards rr: rdn over 3f out: no rspnse* **20/1**
0-05 **11** *6* **Dizzy Future**[14] 6621 4-8-13 **50**.... FergusSweeney 6 36
(M R Bosley) *w ldr: led over 5f out tl over 4f out: rdn over 3f out: wknd over 2f out* **25/1**
3604 **12** *27* **Matinee Idol**[36] 5318 3-8-3 **47**.... JimmyQuinn 3 —
(Mrs S Lamyman) *set slow pce tl qcknd over 6f out: hdd over 5f out: sn lost pl: t.o* **33/1**

3m 7.13s (-0.24) **Going Correction** -0.075s/f (Stan)
WFA 3 from 4yo+ 7lb **12** Ran SP% **121.3**
Speed ratings (Par 101):97,96,96,95,94 94,93,92,92,91 88,72
CSF £48.68 CT £579.61 TOTE £11.70: £3.20, £2.60, £3.20; EX 63.30 TRIFECTA Not won..
Owner Mark Wellings Racing **Bred** Rathbarry Stud **Trained** Six Ashes, Shropshire

FOCUS
They went no gallop until the tempo picked up at around halfway in this moderate affair. The form is plating-class but makes sense through the third and fifth.
Art Historian(IRE) Official explanation: jockey said gelding hung left in home straight
True(IRE) Official explanation: jockey said mare hung left in home straight; trainer said mare was later found to be lame owing to a pulled muscle in her off hindquarter

6791 WORLD BET EXCHANGE WBX.COM H'CAP — 1m 1f 103y(P)
3:10 (3:40) (Class 5) (0-75,75) 3-Y-O+ **£3,238** (£963; £481; £240) **Stalls** Low

Form RPR
3623 **1** **Peruvian Prince (USA)**[28] 6469 4-8-8 **65**.... DaleGibson 1 79
(R A Fahey) *led 1f: a.p: led wl over 1f out: sn edgd rt: hrd rdn: drvn out* **4/1[2]**
0011 **2** *1 ¾* **Happy As Larry (USA)**[5] 6734 4-9-1 **72** 6ex.... FrancisNorton 5 82
(T J Pitt) *hld up and bhd: rdn and hdwy on outside over 1f out: chsd wnr fnl f: nt qckn* **8/13[1]**
1013 **3** *1 ½* **Gaelic Princess**[9] 6671 6-9-1 **72**.... FergusSweeney 6 79
(A G Newcombe) *hld up in mid-div: hdwy over 3f out: sn rdn: one pce fnl f* **10/1**
3336 **4** *¾* **Summer Lodge**[44] 6225 3-8-4 **68**....(b) NataliaGemelova(5) 3 74
(A J McCabe) *t.k.h: sn chsng ldr: rdn and ev ch 2f out: no ex fnl f* **20/1**
0343 **5** *½* **Speed Dial Harry (IRE)**[6] 6716 4-9-3 **74**....(v) IanMongan 4 79
(K R Burke) *hld up: sn bhd: nt clr run over 2f out: rdn over 1f out: nvr able to chal* **15/2[3]**
0505 **6** *3* **Just Fly**[16] 6590 6-8-4 **61**.... JimmyQuinn 8 60
(Dr J R J Naylor) *stdd s: sn swtchd lft: hdwy on ins over 2f out: sn rdn: wknd fnl f* **18/1**
5-00 **7** *13* **Black Falcon (IRE)**[25] 6502 6-9-4 **75**.... MickyFenton 2 48
(P T Midgley) *led after 1f: rdn over 2f out: hdd wl over 1f out: sn wknd* **40/1**
00 **8** *13* **Ma'Am (USA)**[76] 5599 4-8-13 **70**.... LeeEnstone 7 17
(I A Wood) *hld up in tch: rdn 4f out: sn wknd* **50/1**

2m 0.50s (-2.12) **Going Correction** -0.075s/f (Stan)
WFA 3 from 4yo+ 2lb **8** Ran SP% **117.2**
Speed ratings (Par 103):106,104,103,102,102 99,87,76
CSF £6.90 CT £22.18 TOTE £6.50: £1.80, £1.10, £2.00; EX 12.50 Trifecta £64.10 Pool: £534.51 - 5.92 winning units..
Owner R G Leatham **Bred** Alexander-Groves Thoroughbreds **Trained** Musley Bank, N Yorks

FOCUS
An uncompetitive handicap rated at face value but not rock-solid.

6792 WBX.COM WORLD BET EXCHANGE MAIDEN STKS — 1m 1f 103y(P)
3:40 (4:11) (Class 5) 3-Y-O+ **£3,238** (£963; £481; £240) **Stalls** Low

Form RPR
60 **1** **Symbol Of Peace (IRE)**[10] 6666 3-8-9 60.... RichardKingscote(3) 7 69
(J W Unett) *hld up: hdwy over 5f out: rdn to ld 2f out: r.o wl* **12/1**
5222 **2** *1 ¼* **Chasing A Dream**[17] 6587 3-8-12 67.... TonyCulhane 3 66
(B W Hills) *led: rdn and hdd 2f out: ev ch 1f out: nt qckn* **4/1[3]**
0-6 **3** *nk* **Flyingit (USA)**[36] 6360 3-8-12....(p) CatherineGannon 2 65
(K A Ryan) *a.p: rdn over 3f out: outpcd over 2f out: styd on ins fnl f* **2/1[1]**
3 **4** *3* **Executive Paddy (IRE)**[9] 6680 7-9-5.... LeeEnstone 1 64
(I A Wood) *s.i.s: hld up and bhd: hdwy 3f out: sn rdn: one pce fnl 2f* **11/2**
3463 **5** *3* **Izadore (IRE)**[17] 6588 3-8-12 68....(b[1]) SteveDrowne 4 53
(E A L Dunlop) *prom: rdn and wknd 2f out* **8/1**
0000 **6** *2 ½* **Ruby Sunrise (IRE)**[7] 6701 4-9-0 40....(b[1]) RichardThomas 10 48
(B P J Baugh) *s.i.s: t.k.h: hdwy over 5f out: wknd over 2f out* **100/1**
6 **7** *5* **History Prize (IRE)**[23] 6524 3-9-3.... SamHitchcott 5 43
(A G Newcombe) *wnt rt s: hld up in mid-div: rdn over 4f out: sn struggling* **33/1**
00 **8** *1* **Book Of Days (IRE)**[30] 6450 3-8-12.... MickyFenton 6 36
(R M Beckett) *bmpd s: pushed along over 5f out: a bhd* **50/1**
9 *48* **Village Storm (IRE)**[445] 5424 3-9-3.... PaulQuinn 8 —
(C J Teague) *t.k.h: prom: rdn over 5f out: sn lost pl: t.o* **150/1**
624 **10** *4* **Spinning Reel**[9] 6668 3-8-12 65.... AdamKirby 9 —
(W R Swinburn) *hld up in mid-div: rdn 4f out: sn bhd: t.o: b.b.v* **7/2[2]**

2m 1.38s (-1.24) **Going Correction** -0.075s/f (Stan)
WFA 3 from 4yo+ 2lb **10** Ran SP% **116.3**
Speed ratings (Par 103):102,100,100,97,95 93,88,87,45,41
CSF £59.10 TOTE £15.50: £4.60, £1.30, £1.30; EX 79.80 Trifecta £338.80 Part won. Pool: £477.23 - 0.67 winning units..
Owner John Malone **Bred** Calley House Syndicate **Trained** Preston, Shropshire

FOCUS
A very ordinary maiden and although the form is sound enough it is limited.
Spinning Reel Official explanation: vet said filly had bled from the nose

6793 WBXTRIPLECROWN.COM H'CAP (DIV II) — 1m 141y(P)
4:10 (4:41) (Class 6) (0-55,55) 3-Y-O+ **£2,047** (£604; £302) **Stalls** Low

Form RPR
1025 **1** **Harare**[9] 6683 5-8-8 **52**....(b) JamesDoyle(3) 6 63
(R J Price) *hld up and bhd: hdwy over 3f out: rdn to ld wl ins fnl f: r.o wl* **13/2**
2005 **2** *2 ½* **Fulvio (USA)**[14] 6624 6-8-11 **52**....(v) J-PGuillambert 9 58
(P Howling) *chsd ldr: led over 4f out: rdn over 2f out: hdd and no ex wl ins fnl f* **8/1**
1010 **3** *1 ¼* **Keon (IRE)**[9] 6674 4-8-6 **54**.... RussellKennemore(7) 2 57
(R Hollinshead) *hld up in tch: chsd ldr over 3f out: rdn over 1f out: 3rd and btn whn hung rt ins fnl f* **9/2[2]**
5034 **4** *1 ¼* **Kareeb (FR)**[6] 6714 9-9-0 **55**....(p) TonyCulhane 8 56
(Miss J Feilden) *hld up and bhd: rdn and hdwy over 2f out: kpt on same pce fnl f* **11/2[3]**
4003 **5** *5* **Merdiff**[16] 6606 7-8-8 **52**.... PatrickMathers(3) 3 42
(W M Brisbourne) *hld up in mid-div: nt clr run on ins over 3f out: nvr trbld ldrs* **12/1**
0000 **6** *hd* **King After**[88] 5316 4-8-12 **53**.... IanMongan 5 43
(J R Best) *hld up and bhd: rdn over 2f out: n.d* **3/1[1]**
6000 **7** *½* **Tip Top Style**[34] 5319 3-8-7 **50**....(t) DaleGibson 7 39
(J Mackie) *hld up towards rr: rdn over 3f out: n.d* **25/1**
5060 **8** *6* **You're My Son**[30] 6436 4-8-13 **54**.... SteveDrowne 12 30
(A B Haynes) *hld up in mid-div: hdwy over 6f out: rdn over 4f out: sddle sn slipped: eased over 2f out* **15/2**
0040 **9** *3* **Danielle's Lad**[5] 6726 10-8-5 **46** oh1....(p) AdrianMcCarthy 1 16
(B Palling) *led: hdd over 4f out: rdn over 3f out: wknd over 2f out* **16/1**
5506 **10** *17* **Jabraan (USA)**[21] 6545 4-8-5 **46** oh1....(b) PaulQuinn 11 —
(D W Chapman) *t.k.h: prom: rdn over 4f out: sn lost pl* **66/1**

1m 49.78s (-1.98) **Going Correction** -0.075s/f (Stan)
WFA 3 from 4yo+ 2lb **10** Ran SP% **113.7**
Speed ratings (Par 101):105,102,101,100,96 95,95,90,87,72
CSF £56.05 CT £262.52 TOTE £9.50: £2.90, £2.40, £2.00; EX 45.00 TRIFECTA Not won. Place 6 £150.86, Place 5 £44.35.
Owner Mrs P A Wallis **Bred** Limestone Stud **Trained** Ullingswick, H'fords

FOCUS
A moderate handicap and the winning time was 1.42 seconds faster than the first division. The form is solid enough but limited.
You're My Son Official explanation: jockey said saddle slipped
Jabraan(USA) Official explanation: jockey said gelding had a breathing problem
T/Jkpt: Not won. T/Plt: £126.60 to a £1 stake. Pool: £51,852.35. 298.90 winning tickets. T/Qpdt: £25.00 to a £1 stake. Pool: £4,353.50. 128.70 winning tickets. KH

6756 SOUTHWELL (L-H)
Tuesday, December 12

OFFICIAL GOING: Standard
Wind: Fresh, across Weather: Overcast with the odd shower

6794 BUY YOUR LADY JOCKEYS CALENDAR 01635 44102 TRI-BANDED STKS — 7f (F)
1:00 (1:02) (Class 7) 3-Y-0 **£2,047** (£604; £302) **Stalls** Low

Form RPR
6403 **1** **Stoneacre Fred (IRE)**[8] 6707 3-8-12 45.... GrahamGibbons 4 48+
(Peter Grayson) *a.p: led on bit over 1f out: rdn and hung lft ins fnl f: r.o* **11/4[1]**

0060 **2** *1 ¾* **Astorygoeswithit**[8] 6707 3-8-12 45..................................(b) AdamKirby 5 43
(P S McEntee) *chsd ldrs: rdn to ld over 2f out: hdd over 1f out: styd on same pce ins fnl f* **25/1**

0366 **3** *nk* **Danethorpe (IRE)**[8] 6707 3-8-12 45......................(v) AdrianMcCarthy 12 42
(D Shaw) *sn outpcd: hdwy and hung rt over 1f out: rdn and hung lft ins fnl f: styd on* **7/1**[3]

5046 **4** *nk* **Marron Flore**[14] 6649 3-8-12 45..................................(tp) FrancisNorton 3 41
(A J Lidderdale) *hld up: hdwy over 2f out: rdn over 1f out: styd on same pce ins fnl f* **8/1**

0500 **5** *5* **Bold Love**[6] 6727 3-8-9 45......................................(p) JasonEdmunds[(3)] 9 28
(J Balding) *mid-div: rdn 1/2-way: hdwy over 2f out: hung lft and wknd over 1f out* **5/1**[2]

6320 **6** *2 ½* **Franky'N'Jonny**[21] 6552 3-8-12 45..................................(p) DaleGibson 7 22
(M J Attwater) *s.i.s: outpcd: hdwy and hung lft over 1f out: nvr nrr* **7/1**[3]

6005 **7** *1 ½* **Jenise (IRE)**[21] 6557 3-8-12 45...................................... J-PGuillambert 8 18
(Mark Campion) *mid-div: rdn 4f out: nt clr run 1/2-way: hung lft over 1f out: n.d* **25/1**

00-6 **8** *10* **Ames Souer (IRE)**[21] 6548 3-8-5 45............................ KellyHarrison[(7)] 2 —
(D Carroll) *dwlt: plld hrd and sn prom: hung lft and wknd over 1f out* **9/1**

5030 **9** *hd* **Quote Unquote**[21] 6548 3-8-12 45.................................. DeanMernagh 1 —
(M Brittain) *prom: rdn 1/2-way: wknd 2f out: eased fnl f* **9/1**

3000 **10** *1* **Great Composer (IRE)**[8] 6707 3-8-12 45..................(t) MickyFenton 14 —
(M Wellings) *s.i.s: sn pushed along and prom: rdn 4f out: wknd 1/2-way* **18/1**

0000 **11** *2* **Aberlady Bay (IRE)**[8] 6708 3-8-12 45..............................(b) DavidAllan 6 —
(T T Clement) *dwlt: outpcd* **18/1**

0000 **12** *1 ½* **Dodaa (USA)**[8] 6707 3-8-12 45....................................(b[1]) PatCosgrave 10 —
(N Wilson) *led over 4f: wknd wl over 1f out* **16/1**

0000 **13** *7* **Prima Markova**[50] 6144 3-8-12 45................................. TonyCulhane 11 —
(J Jay) *sn outpcd* **33/1**

1m 32.07s (1.27) **Going Correction** +0.025s/f (Slow) **13** Ran SP% **126.5**
Speed ratings (Par 96):93,91,90,90,84 81,80,68,68,67 64,63,55
CSF £89.16 TOTE £3.40: £1.60, £7.40, £2.60; EX 78.60 TRIFECTA Not won..
Owner R Teatum And Mrs S Grayson **Bred** John And Mrs Susan Flavin **Trained** Formby, Lancs

FOCUS
A typically ordinary event featuring only two previous winners and the winner is value for a little extra.
Quote Unquote Official explanation: jockey said filly lost its action

6795 PONTINS.COM BANDED STKS 1m 4f (F)
1:30 (1:31) (Class 7) 3-Y-0+ **£2,047** (£604; £302) **Stalls** Low

Form RPR

2045 **1** **Kentucky Bullet (USA)**[42] 6279 10-9-3 45.................. SamHitchcott 10 51
(A G Newcombe) *hld up: rdn 4f out: hdwy over 2f out: styd on to ld wl ins fnl f* **9/2**[2]

5016 **2** *½* **Blue Opal**[21] 6551 4-9-3 45...(p) PaulEddery 8 50
(Miss S E Hall) *chsd ldrs: led 3f out: rdn over 1f out: hdd wl ins fnl f* **4/1**[1]

6060 **3** *shd* **Ulshaw**[4] 6754 9-9-3 40.. BrettDoyle 6 50
(J M Bradley) *hld up: hdwy 1/2-way: rdn: edgd rt and ev ch fr over 1f out: styd on* **12/1**

0560 **4** *4* **Sorbiesharry (IRE)**[21] 6552 7-9-3 40........................... DeanMernagh 12 44
(Mrs N Macauley) *hld up: hdwy 4f out: rdn over 1f out: wknd ins fnl f* **12/1**

4600 **5** *1 ¼* **Liquid Lover (IRE)**[15] 6620 4-9-3 45.......................(p) MatthewHenry 13 42
(W M Brisbourne) *s.i.s: hdwy 10f out: rdn over 1f out: wknd fnl f* **8/1**

5/40 **6** *2* **Glen Vale Walk (IRE)**[42] 6280 9-9-3 45.................. CatherineGannon 3 39
(Mrs G S Rees) *s.i.s: hld up: hdwy 1/2-way: nt clr run and lost pl over 4f out: n.d after* **16/1**

60-0 **7** *¾* **Scorchio (IRE)**[42] 6281 5-9-3 45.. PatCosgrave 7 38
(B Smart) *chsd ldr: led 5f out: rdn and hdd 3f out: wknd over 1f out* **10/1**

5635 **8** *2* **Sriology (IRE)**[15] 6616 5-9-3 45................................... MichaelTebbutt 4 35
(J Pearce) *hld up in tch: rdn over 3f out: wknd over 1f out* **11/2**[3]

2046 **9** *nk* **Iamback**[11] 6657 6-9-3 40...(t) JamieMackay 1 35
(Miss D A McHale) *hld up: sme hdwy over 3f out: nvr trbld ldrs* **12/1**

40-0 **10** *10* **In Rhubarb**[201] 1947 4-9-3 40...................................... AdrianMcCarthy 14 20
(P Howling) *mid-div: hdwy over 4f out: wknd 2f out* **66/1**

000 **11** *3 ½* **Gundula (IRE)**[18] 6588 3-8-12 40................................ RichardThomas 5 14
(D J S Ffrench Davis) *chsd ldrs: rdn 1/2-way: wknd 4f out* **25/1**

35-0 **12** *dist* **Staff Nurse (IRE)**[15] 6623 6-9-3 40...................................(p) LeeEnstone 2 —
(N Wilson) *chsd ldrs: rdn 1/2-way: wknd over 4f out* **33/1**

400/ **13** *nk* **Flyoff (IRE)**[880] 3885 9-9-3 40..(p) PaulMulrennan 11 —
(Mrs N Macauley) *led 7f: wknd 4f out* **100/1**

2m 43.18s (1.09) **Going Correction** +0.025s/f (Slow)
WFA 3 from 4yo+ 5lb **13** Ran SP% **112.0**
Speed ratings (Par 97):97,96,96,93,93 91,91,89,89,83 80,—,—
CSF £19.88 TOTE £5.50: £1.90, £1.70, £3.10; EX 17.20 TRIFECTA Not won..
Owner Mrs B J Sherwin **Bred** Foxfield **Trained** Yarnscombe, Devon

FOCUS
Ordinary form given the performance of the third, but he was dropping in class and the form is better rated around the first two.
Sorbiesharry(IRE) Official explanation: jockey said gelding hung right in home straight

6796 GO PONTINS BANDED STKS 6f (F)
2:00 (2:01) (Class 7) 3-Y-0+ **£2,047** (£604; £302) **Stalls** Low

Form RPR

3024 **1** **Blakeshall Quest**[28] 6470 6-9-2 49.................................(b) PatCosgrave 9 57
(R Brotherton) *chsd ldr: led 4f out: rdn and edgd lft over 1f out: all out* **15/2**[3]

0-06 **2** *shd* **Nebdi (IRE)**[15] 6624 5-9-3 50..(p) DavidAllan 10 58
(E J Alston) *a.p: rdn to chse wnr over 2f out: hung lft over 1f out: sn ev ch: styd on* **12/1**

0004 **3** *2* **Christian Bendix**[7] 6719 4-9-1 48.. DeanCorby 8 50
(P Howling) *hld up in tch: n.m.r over 4f out. rdn over 1f out: styd on* **8/1**

0040 **4** *nk* **Woodwee**[7] 6717 3-8-12 50.. JamieMoriarty[(5)] 7 51
(J R Weymes) *sn outpcd: rdn over 2f out: sn swtchd rt r.o ins fnl f: nrst fin* **33/1**

6262 **5** *shd* **Sion Hill (IRE)**[7] 6717 5-8-5 45.........................(p) RussellKennemore[(7)] 4 46
(Mrs N Macauley) *s.i.s: plld hrd and sn prom: rdn over 2f out: styd on same pce fnl f* **15/2**[3]

0015 **6** *¾* **Capital Lass**[8] 6703 3-8-9 49.. JamesMillman[(7)] 14 47
(D K Ivory) *hld up: hdwy over 1f out: sn edgd lft: styd on: nt trble ldrs* **16/1**

0101 **7** *2 ½* **Mulberry Lad (IRE)**[6] 6727 4-9-1 49........................ WilliamCarson[(7)] 12 46
(P W Hiatt) *mid-div: rdn over 2f out: wknd fnl f* **5/1**[2]

0000 **8** *½* **Vlasta Weiner**[14] 6629 6-8-10 50................................(b) BarrySavage[(7)] 1 39
(J M Bradley) *hld up: hdwy 2f out: wknd fnl f* **33/1**

9 *1 ½* **Deneuve**[48] 6180 3-8-11 47.. JerryO'Dwyer[(3)] 2 32
(M G Quinlan) *sn outpcd: nvr nrr* **10/1**

0001 **10** *1* **Cool Tiger**[21] 6550 3-9-2 49... FrancisNorton 11 31
(P Howling) *s.i.s: swtchd lft sn after s: outpcd: nvr nrr* **3/1**[1]

0000 **11** *1 ½* **Time N Time Again**[232] 1196 8-9-0 47.....................(b) GrahamGibbons 3 24
(Peter Grayson) *chsd ldrs: rdn over 2f out: wknd over 1f out* **28/1**

6201 **12** *1 ¾* **Tuscan Flyer**[124] 4278 8-9-0 47...................................(b) PaulMulrennan 6 19
(R Bastiman) *hld up: a in rr* **20/1**

0000 **13** *1 ½* **Amanda's Lad (IRE)**[22] 6533 6-9-3 50.................................. BrianReilly 5 18
(M C Chapman) *led: hdd 4f out: wknd 2f out* **33/1**

0064 **14** *3* **Hiats**[8] 6703 4-9-3 50...(p) TonyCulhane 13 9
(J O'Reilly) *chsd ldrs over 3f* **12/1**

1m 17.58s (0.68) **Going Correction** +0.025s/f (Slow) **14** Ran SP% **123.7**
Speed ratings (Par 97):96,95,93,92,92 91,88,87,85,84 82,80,78,74
CSF £91.10 TOTE £8.60: £2.00, £6.60, £3.90; EX 122.30 TRIFECTA Not won..
Owner Droitwich Jokers **Bred** M P Bishop **Trained** Elmley Castle, Worcs

FOCUS
Sound form and quite straightforward to rate, with the winner rated close to her best performance of the last two years.
Cool Tiger Official explanation: jockey said gelding would not face the kickback

6797 LADY JOCKEYS CHARITY CALENDAR 01635 44102 BANDED STKS 2m (F)
2:30 (2:30) (Class 7) 3-Y-0+ **£2,047** (£604; £302) **Stalls** Low

Form RPR

0105 **1** **Bulberry Hill**[27] 6495 5-9-8 47.................................... EdwardCreighton 10 55
(R W Price) *trckd ldrs: led over 3f out: rdn 2f out: styd on: eased nr fin* **5/1**[3]

6221 **2** *¾* **Red River Rebel**[21] 6553 8-9-7 46.................................. PaulMulrennan 8 53
(J R Norton) *mde most tl over 3f out: sn rdn: edgd rt over 1f out: styd on* **15/8**[1]

/3-4 **3** *18* **Misbehaviour**[7] 1541 7-9-6 40.. GeorgeBaker 6 30
(G L Moore) *hld up: hdwy 6f out: wknd over 3f out* **10/3**[2]

0000 **4** *3* **Lawood (IRE)**[7] 3196 6-9-8 47..................................(vt) AdrianTNicholls 9 29
(M Scudamore) *mid-div: rdn 10f out: wknd 4f out* **16/1**

0/06 **5** *¾* **Find The King (IRE)**[15] 6626 8-9-9 48.............................(p) RobertHavlin 2 29
(D W P Arbuthnot) *outpcd: t.o 1/2-way: nvr nrr* **11/1**

3203 **6** *1 ¾* **Alisdanza**[65] 5837 4-8-13 45... LanceBetts[(7)] 7 24
(N Wilson) *chsd ldrs: rdn and wknd over 3f out* **16/1**

2040 **7** *1* **Bolshoi Ballet**[10] 6685 8-9-6 45......................................(p) SamHitchcott 1 23
(Miss J E Foster) *chsd ldrs 12f* **40/1**

0000 **8** *6* **Indian Chase**[23] 5927 9-9-6 40.......................................(v) RichardThomas 5 15
(Dr J R J Naylor) *hld up: a bhd* **12/1**

6543 **9** *32* **Tip Toes (IRE)**[15] 6623 4-9-6 45.. DeanCorby 3 —
(P Howling) *outpcd* **8/1**

L/0- **10** *43* **Moyne Pleasure (IRE)**[188] 5826 8-8-13 40.............. ChrisCavanagh[(7)] 4 —
(R Johnson) *w ldr 10f: sn wknd* **20/1**

3m 47.59s (3.05) **Going Correction** +0.025s/f (Slow) **10** Ran SP% **120.6**
Speed ratings (Par 97):93,92,83,82,81 80,80,77,61,39
CSF £15.30 TOTE £7.60: £1.80, £1.30, £1.60; EX 24.50 Trifecta £103.20 Pool £215.13 - 1.48 winning units.
Owner Miss D Hutchinson **Bred** Mrs Ian Pilkington **Trained** Newmarket, Suffolk

FOCUS
A weak staying contest which concerned only two horses from some way out and rated to previous banded form.
Indian Chase Official explanation: jockey said gelding never travelled
Tip Toes(IRE) Official explanation: jockey said filly never travelled

6798 PONTINS BANDED STKS 7f (F)
3:00 (3:02) (Class 7) 3-Y-0+ **£2,047** (£604; £302) **Stalls** Low

Form RPR

0-00 **1** **Tee Jay Kassidy**[22] 6531 6-9-2 49...............................(v) AntonyProcter 13 61
(P S McEntee) *mid-div: hdwy over 2f out: rdn to ld and hung lft 1f out: styd on* **33/1**

0212 **2** *1 ¼* **Haroldini (IRE)**[3] 6763 4-9-5 49..............................(p) JasonEdmunds[(3)] 6 64
(J Balding) *trckd ldrs: led over 1f out: sn rdn and hdd: styd on same pce* **13/8**[1]

0046 **3** *1 ½* **Lucius Verrus (USA)**[8] 6703 6-9-2 49..................(v) AdrianMcCarthy 10 54
(D Shaw) *prom: rdn over 2f out: styd on* **8/1**[3]

0665 **4** *1* **Favouring (IRE)**[10] 6674 4-9-3 50..............................(v) MatthewHenry 7 53
(M C Chapman) *chsd ldr: rdn and ev ch over 1f out: no ex ins fnl f* **8/1**[3]

5240 **5** *2* **For Life (IRE)**[8] 6696 4-9-1 48.....................................(v) SamHitchcott 2 45
(A P Jarvis) *led: clr 1/2-way: rdn and hdd over 1f out: wknd ins fnl f* **9/1**

0550 **6** *1 ½* **Dispol Peto**[15] 6623 6-8-12 50 ow2........................(p) ChrisCavanagh[(7)] 1 45
(R Johnson) *sn outpcd: styd on ins fnl f: nvr nrr* **8/1**[3]

0200 **7** *3* **I Wish**[6] 6726 8-8-12 45... PaulFitzsimons 5 31
(Miss J R Tooth) *chsd ldrs: rdn 1/2-way: wknd over 2f out* **33/1**

40 **8** *2 ½* **Cameo Story**[22] 6545 3-8-13 46.. JamieMackay 12 25
(Andrew Oliver, Ire) *mid-div: rdn 1/2-way: n.d* **40/1**

0504 **9** *1 ¼* **Doctor Dennis (IRE)**[14] 6629 9-9-3 50.....................(v) MichaelTebbutt 3 26
(J Pearce) *s.i.s: a in rr* **12/1**

1006 **10** *7* **Lockstock (IRE)**[15] 6627 8-9-3 50.....................................(p) BrettDoyle 8 8
(M S Saunders) *a in rr* **7/1**[2]

0005 **11** *9* **Pawn In Life (IRE)**[3] 6763 8-9-3 50.................................(v) DaleGibson 4 —
(M J Attwater) *sn outpcd* **10/1**

401/ **12** *20* **Ally Makbul**[1029] 810 6-9-3 50... DeanMernagh 11 —
(Ian Emmerson) *prom: lost pl 5f out: bhd fr 1/2-way* **50/1**

1m 30.02s (-0.78) **Going Correction** +0.025s/f (Slow) **12** Ran SP% **121.0**
Speed ratings (Par 97):105,103,101,100,98 96,93,90,89,81 70,47
CSF £87.32 TOTE £64.70: £9.60, £1.60, £2.90; EX 180.90 TRIFECTA Not won..
Owner Danny Berry **Bred** Miss Jeanne M Brooks **Trained** Newmarket, Suffolk

FOCUS
Above-average form for the grade and a decent time for a banded event, just over two seconds quicker than the earlier tri-banded contest over the same trip and rated through the runner-up to his recent best.
Tee Jay Kassidy Official explanation: trainer said, regarding apparent improvement in form, the gelding possibly improved because of the reapplication of visors
Doctor Dennis(IRE) Official explanation: jockey said gelding finished lame

6799 PONTINS HOLIDAYS BANDED STKS 1m (F)
3:30 (3:35) (Class 7) 3-Y-0+ **£2,047** (£604; £302) **Stalls** Low

Form RPR

5565 **1** **Sonderborg**[8] 6701 5-8-13 45..(p) DaleGibson 5 52
(J Mackie) *hld up: hdwy 2f out: sn rdn: hung lft and led wl ins fnl f* **8/1**[3]

6304 **2** 3/4 **Tacid**[42] 6281 4-8-13 45 .... FrancisNorton 11 50+
(Dr J D Scargill) *hld up: hdwy 2f out: rdn to ld 1f out: hung rt and hdd wl ins fnl f* **3/1**[1]

U660 **3** 1 **Miss Imperious**[11] 6667 3-8-12 45 .... DavidAllan 13 48
(B Smart) *hld up: hdwy over 3f out: hung lft 2f out: sn rdn and ev ch: styd on same pce ins fnl f* **20/1**

0040 **4** 1 **Insignia (IRE)**[1] 6787 4-8-13 45 ....(p) PatCosgrave 8 46
(W M Brisbourne) *hld up: hdwy 1/2-way: rdn over 1f out: no ex ins fnl f* **12/1**

0060 **5** 1 1/4 **Mycenean Prince (USA)**[37] 6281 3-8-12 45 ....(v[1]) LPKeniry 10 43
(R C Guest) *chsd ldrs: led over 2f out: rdn and hdd 1f out: no ex* **20/1**

0120 **6** 2 **Komreyev Star**[36] 6370 4-8-13 45 ....(p) JimmyQuinn 7 39
(M Mullineaux) *chsd ldrs: rdn 1/2-way: wknd ins fnl f* **9/2**[2]

0005 **7** 5 **Musical Gift**[6] 6725 6-8-13 45 ....(p) J-PGuillambert 12 29
(P A Blockley) *chsd ldrs: rdn over 2f out: wknd over 1f out* **9/2**[2]

2053 **8** 4 **Boucheen**[8] 6701 3-8-12 45 .... CatherineGannon 3 20
(Ms Deborah J Evans) *prom: nt clr run and lost pl over 4f out: n.d after* **8/1**[3]

3003 **9** 6 **Sea Frolic (IRE)**[8] 6702 5-8-8 45 ....(v) RoryMoore(5) 14 8
(Jennie Candlish) *chsd ldrs over 4f* **10/1**

4000 **10** 2 **Super Dominion**[175] 2728 9-8-8 45 ....(e[1]) HelenKeohane(5) 4 3
(R Hollinshead) *sn outpcd* **33/1**

0040 **11** shd **Blushing Russian (IRE)**[298] 440 4-8-13 45 ....(p) BrettDoyle 6 3
(J M Bradley) *chsd ldrs: chal 3f out: wknd over 1f out* **25/1**

0050 **12** 2 1/2 **Mighty Duel**[142] 3762 3-8-12 45 ....(tp) PaulMulrennan 2 —
(J R Norton) *s.i.s: outpcd* **100/1**

4000 **13** shd **Massey**[252] 876 10-8-13 45 .... AdamKirby 9 —
(C R Dore) *led: rdn and hdd over 2f out: wkng whn hit over hd by rival's whip sn after* **25/1**

5000 **14** 45 **Danzar**[14] 6638 4-8-13 45 ....(b) DeanMernagh 1 —
(M Brittain) *s.i.s: hdwy 6f out: wkng whn n.m.r 1/2-way* **40/1**

1m 44.61s (0.01) **Going Correction** +0.025s/f (Slow)
WFA 3 from 4yo+ 1lb **14** Ran SP% **124.0**
Speed ratings (Par 97):100,99,98,97,96 94,89,85,79,77 76,74,74,—
CSF £30.68 TOTE £10.20: £2.90, £1.90, £4.70; EX 38.20 Trifecta £190.40 Part won. Pool £268.23 - 0.60 winning units. Place 6 57.01, Place 5 £24.59 .
Owner Mrs J Mackie **Bred** M S Griffiths **Trained** Church Broughton , Derbys

FOCUS
Average form for the grade, with the winner back to the level of form she recorded last winter and the third and fifth close to their marks.
T/Jkpt: Not won. T/Plt: £40.50 to a £1 stake. Pool: £54,395.10. 978.80 winning tickets. T/Qpdt: £13.70 to a £1 stake. Pool: £3,605.80. 194.00 winning tickets. CR

6694 LINGFIELD (L-H)
Wednesday, December 13

OFFICIAL GOING: Standard
Wind: Fresh, behind Weather: Overcast

6800 GO PONTINS BANDED STKS — 1m 2f (P)
12:05 (12:05) (Class 7) 3-Y-O+ — **£1,433** (£423; £211) **Stalls** Low

Form — RPR

0603 **1** **Saucy**[10] 6693 5-9-1 45 .... FergusSweeney 2 51
(A W Carroll) *chsd ldrs: led over 2f out: drvn clr over 1f out: hld on wl fnl 100 yds* **7/4**[1]

0-40 **2** 3/4 **Jarvo**[16] 6617 5-9-1 45 .... RobbieFitzpatrick 12 50
(I W McInnes) *t.k.h: in tch: effrt 3f out: rdn to chse wnr over 1f out: ch ins fnl f: nt qckn* **12/1**

0000 **3** 1 1/2 **Louve Heureuse (IRE)**[16] 6616 5-8-12 45 .... RichardKingscote(3) 11 47
(B G Powell) *led tl over 2f out: hrd rdn over 1f out: one pce* **8/1**[3]

5622 **4** 1/2 **Weet Yer Tern (IRE)**[9] 6701 4-9-1 45 .... EddieAhern 6 46
(W M Brisbourne) *t.k.h: prom: outpcd 2f out: kpt on again fnl f* **2/1**[2]

6443 **5** 1 1/4 **Kilmeena Magic**[7] 6724 4-9-1 45 ....(p) PaulFitzsimons 9 44
(J C Fox) *t.k.h: in tch: rdn over 2f out: one pce* **8/1**[3]

6003 **6** 3/4 **Kinsman (IRE)**[16] 6616 9-9-1 45 ....(p) J-PGuillambert 1 42
(T D McCarthy) *mid-div: rdn 3f out: styd on same pce* **14/1**

3000 **7** 1/2 **Homebred Star**[16] 6620 5-8-10 45 ....(p) RobynBrisland(5) 10 41
(G P Enright) *dwlt: hld up in rr: hdwy on outside 3f out: wd bnd into st: no ex over 1f out* **33/1**

000 **8** 2 **Royal Sailor (IRE)**[114] 4667 4-9-1 35 ....(b) BrettDoyle 5 38
(J Ryan) *towards rr: swtchd towards outside and hdwy 3f out: wknd over 1f out* **50/1**

3000 **9** 1 1/2 **Little Miss Verity**[8] 6714 3-8-12 45 .... RichardThomas 3 35
(J A Geake) *a towards rr: n.d fnl 4f* **20/1**

0-00 **10** 5 **Sticky Mint (IRE)**[8] 6714 3-8-5 45 .... LauraReynolds(7) 8 25
(M Blanshard) *prom tl wknd over 2f out* **50/1**

0000 **11** 9 **Tantien**[9] 6696 4-8-10 35 .... JamieJones(5) 4 8
(T Keddy) *rdn over 3f out: a towards rr* **66/1**

3000 **12** 3 1/2 **Zinging**[26] 6067 7-8-8 45 ....(b) RyanBird(7) 7 2
(J J Bridger) *s.s: hld up and bhd: hrd rdn and no ch fnl 3f* **25/1**

2m 10.1s (2.31) **Going Correction** +0.025s/f (Slow)
WFA 3 from 4yo+ 3lb **12** Ran SP% **123.2**
Speed ratings (Par 97):91,90,89,88,87 87,86,85,84,80 72,70
CSF £23.71 TOTE £3.20: £1.10, £3.40, £3.40; EX 33.10 Trifecta £45.20 Part won. Pool £63.67 - 0.10 winning units..
Owner Mrs B Quinn **Bred** Wyck Hall Stud Ltd **Trained** Cropthorne, Worcs

FOCUS
A typical event for the class and the form looks straightforward enough rated through the runner-up to recent form.

6801 PONTINS.COM BANDED STKS — 1m 2f (P)
12:40 (12:41) (Class 7) 3-Y-O+ — **£1,433** (£423; £211) **Stalls** Low

Form — RPR

4542 **1** **Revolve**[9] 6700 6-9-4 48 ....(b) LPKeniry 8 55
(Mrs L J Mongan) *led tl 5f out: prom: drvn bk level fnl f: led fnl strides* **5/2**[1]

3352 **2** hd **Wood Fern (UAE)**[7] 6724 6-9-3 47 .... EddieAhern 10 53
(W M Brisbourne) *prom: led over 2f out: hrd rdn over 1f out: jnd by wnr fnl f: kpt on u.p: jst pipped* **5/2**[1]

0060 **3** 2 1/2 **Orphina (IRE)**[7] 6724 3-8-12 48 ....(t) RichardKingscote(3) 1 50
(B G Powell) *chsd ldrs: rdn and sltly outpcd over 2f out: kpt on appr fnl f* **12/1**[3]

0000 **4** nk **Expected Bonus (USA)**[7] 6724 7-9-1 40 ....(p) RobertHavlin 5 46
(Jamie Poulton) *hld up in tch: jnd ldrs 3f out: one pce fnl f* **14/1**

62-0 **5** 1 1/4 **Show Me The Lolly (FR)**[15] 6648 6-9-6 50 .... TonyCulhane 3 49
(P J McBride) *hld up towards rr: dropped to last over 4f out: shkn up and styd on steadily fnl 2f* **12/1**[3]

0-00 **6** nk **Dolly**[17] 6026 4-9-1 40 .... RichardThomas 2 43
(Tom Dascombe) *in tch: lost pl over 4f out: rdn and no imp fnl 2f* **25/1**

3004 **7** 1/2 **Finished Article (IRE)**[16] 6623 9-9-5 49 .... J-PGuillambert 11 46
(P A Blockley) *hld up in rr: effrt on wd outside 4f out: nvr able to chal* **4/1**[2]

0060 **8** nk **Piquet**[30] 6462 8-8-12 40 .... AmirQuinn(3) 7 42
(J J Bridger) *hld up towards rr: effrt towards outside 4f out: hrd rdn 2f out: no imp* **14/1**

5340 **9** 1/2 **Simplified**[7] 6724 3-8-12 45 .... HayleyTurner 4 41
(N B King) *plld hrd: chsd ldrs: slt ld 5f out tl over 2f out: sn outpcd* **14/1**

0-00 **10** 39 **African Blues**[167] 3006 3-8-12 30 .... FergusSweeney 6 —
(M R Hoad) *stdd s: bhd: pushed along over 4f out: no ch fnl 2f* **80/1**

2m 13.22s (5.43) **Going Correction** +0.025s/f (Slow)
WFA 3 from 4yo+ 3lb **10** Ran SP% **117.6**
Speed ratings (Par 97):79,78,76,76,75 75,74,74,74,43
CSF £8.45 TOTE £3.00: £1.20, £1.50, £3.90; EX 9.60 Trifecta £102.80 Part won. Pool £144.89 - 0.54 winning units..
Owner Mrs P J Sheen **Bred** Wickfield Farm Partnership **Trained** Epsom, Surrey

FOCUS
They went no pace until past halfway and the race developed into a sprint, which did not suit a few. As a result the winning time was pedestrian, more than three seconds slower than the opener and the form is not strong; it is best rated through the principals.
Show Me The Lolly(FR) ◆ Official explanation: jockey said mare was hampered at the start

6802 PONTIN'S HOLIDAYS BANDED STKS — 1m (P)
1:10 (1:10) (Class 7) 3-Y-O+ — **£1,433** (£423; £211) **Stalls** High

Form — RPR

0032 **1** **Green Pirate**[2] 6787 4-9-2 48 .... GeorgeBaker 8 59+
(W M Brisbourne) *hld up in rr: squeezed through and effrt 3f out: gd hdwy on outside over 1f out: rdn to ld ins fnl f: sn clr* **7/4**[1]

311 **2** 1 3/4 **Bowl Of Cherries**[3] 6780 3-9-9 50 ....(b) LeeEnstone 3 63
(I A Wood) *chsd ldrs: drvn to narrow ld over 1f out: hdd and nt pce of wnr ins fnl f* **9/4**[2]

0600 **3** 3/4 **Dexileos (IRE)**[9] 6708 7-9-4 50 ....(t) FergusSweeney 4 55
(David Pinder) *trckd ldr: led over 2f out tl over 1f out: nt qckn fnl f* **33/1**

0006 **4** 2 1/2 **Colonel Bilko (IRE)**[3] 6780 4-8-10 40 .... MarcHalford(3) 10 44
(J J Bridger) *hld up in rr: hdwy on rail ent st: hrd rdn over 1f out: one pce* **25/1**

4206 **5** shd **Hill Of Almhuim (IRE)**[9] 6708 3-9-3 50 .... RobbieFitzpatrick 2 49
(Peter Grayson) *in tch: rdn 3f out: one pce* **11/1**

-006 **6** 1/2 **Beautiful Mover (USA)**[11] 6683 4-8-9 46 .... NataliaGemelova(5) 5 44
(J E Long) *in tch: outpcd 3f out: no imp* **50/1**

5062 **7** hd **Frank's Quest (IRE)**[7] 6725 6-9-1 47 .... SamHitchcott 12 44
(A B Haynes) *wd: towards rr: rdn 3f out: nt pce to chal* **9/1**[3]

5000 **8** 1/2 **Wild Lass**[7] 6725 5-8-13 40 ....(p) PaulFitzsimons 9 41
(J C Fox) *mid-div: rdn and no hdwy fnl 3f* **66/1**

2640 **9** 1/2 **Bollywood (IRE)**[7] 6724 3-8-12 45 ....(b[1]) MatthewHenry 7 40
(J J Bridger) *led tl over 2f out: wknd over 1f out* **12/1**

0000 **10** 1 1/2 **Sprouston (FR)**[128] 4199 3-9-0 47 .... LPKeniry 11 39
(J S Moore) *towards rr: rdn and bmpd 3f out: nvr a factor* **11/1**

5415 **11** shd **Elms Schoolboy**[9] 6702 4-9-1 47 ....(b) TonyCulhane 6 38
(P Howling) *hld up towards rr: rdn and n.d fnl 3f* **10/1**

0-00 **12** dist **Robin Sharp**[182] 2551 8-8-13 35 ....(p) PaulDoe 1 —
(J Akehurst) *prom: rdn and wknd over 3f out: bhd whn virtually p.u over 1f out: walked over line* **66/1**

1m 39.72s (0.29) **Going Correction** +0.025s/f (Slow)
WFA 3 from 4yo+ 1lb **12** Ran SP% **122.3**
Speed ratings (Par 97):99,97,96,94,93 93,93,92,92,90 90,—
CSF £5.66 TOTE £2.90: £1.20, £1.50, £8.60; EX 7.20 Trifecta £94.20 Pool £261.48 - 1.97 winning units.
Owner J Babb **Bred** Hrh Princess Michael Of Kent **Trained** Great Ness, Shropshire
■ Stewards' Enquiry : George Baker one-day ban: careless riding (Dec 26)

FOCUS
A fair pace for this banded contest and the pair that dominated the market duly occupied the first two places. The form makes sense rated through the runner-up.
Dexileos(IRE) Official explanation: vet said gelding had lost a shoe

6803 PONTINSBINGO.COM BANDED STKS — 7f (P)
1:45 (1:45) (Class 7) 3-Y-O+ — **£1,433** (£423; £211) **Stalls** Low

Form — RPR

0201 **1** **Binnion Bay (IRE)**[7] 6726 5-9-1 45 ....(b) AmirQuinn(3) 5 59+
(J J Bridger) *stdd s: patiently rdn fr rr: hdwy on bit fr 2 out: w.w tl shkn up to ld fnl 100 yds* **11/4**[2]

3006 **2** 1 1/4 **Fizzy Lizzy**[9] 6694 6-8-7 45 .... NicolPolli(5) 1 50
(H E Haynes) *w ldr: drvn to ld over 1f out: hdd and nt qckn fnl 100 yds* **14/1**

4056 **3** 1/2 **Jennverse**[7] 6728 4-8-5 45 .... JamesMillman(7) 6 49
(D K Ivory) *hld up towards rr: hrd rdn and hdwy over 1f out: styd on strly fnl f* **9/2**[3]

3402 **4** 2 **Limit Down (IRE)**[7] 6726 5-8-12 40 .... BrettDoyle 9 44
(John Berry) *mid-div: rdn to chse ldng pair 2f out: one pce appr fnl f* **9/4**[1]

3000 **5** nk **Angel River**[7] 6726 4-8-12 40 ....(v) RobertHavlin 8 43
(J Ryan) *in tch: effrt over 2f out: hrd rdn: no imp* **16/1**

060- **6** nk **Calusa Lady (IRE)**[494] 4158 6-8-12 45 ....(t) RichardThomas 4 42
(J A Geake) *led tl over 1f out: no ex* **10/1**

0055 **7** nk **A Teen**[8] 6717 8-8-12 45 .... PaulDoe 2 41
(P Howling) *chsd ldrs: n.m.r over 2f out: sn outpcd* **10/1**

605- **8** 1 **Badou**[575] 1790 6-8-12 40 ....(p) LPKeniry 10 39
(L Montague Hall) *in rr: rdn over 3f out: nvr trbld ldrs* **20/1**

0000 **9** 1 1/4 **Love Academy**[41] 6305 11-8-5 40 .... ChrisHough(7) 3 35
(Luke Comer, Ire) *hld up in midfield: n.m.r and hit rail over 2f out: hmpd ent st: nt rcvr* **33/1**

0060 **10** 1 1/2 **Miss Sudbrook (IRE)**[23] 6542 4-8-12 45 ....(v) FergusSweeney 7 31
(A W Carroll) *prom: rdn 3f out: wknd over 1f out* **25/1**

1m 26.72s (0.83) **Going Correction** +0.025s/f (Slow) **10** Ran SP% **117.9**
Speed ratings (Par 97):96,94,94,91,91 91,90,89,88,86
CSF £40.21 TOTE £3.30: £1.60, £2.40, £2.20; EX 41.50 Trifecta £67.90 Pool £177.16 - 1.85 winning units.
Owner J J Bridger **Bred** Fieldspring Ltd **Trained** Liphook, Hants

FOCUS
A routine banded contest and it proved a bit of a rough race for a couple, including the winner. The form is not strong but looks fair enough.

6804 LYNHURST PRESS BANDED STKS 1m 4f (P)
2:15 (2:15) (Class 7) 3-Y-O+ £1,433 (£423; £211) Stalls Low

Form RPR
0311 1 **Artzola (IRE)**[16] 6620 6-9-4 46.. GeorgeBaker 11 58+
(C A Horgan) *stdd s: patiently rdn fr rr: hdwy on bit over 2f out: led 1f out: cruised clr* **4/6**[1]
0104 2 5 **Our Glenard**[12] 6657 7-8-12 45............................ NataliaGemelova(5) 4 46
(J E Long) *s.s: towards rr: hdwy on outside over 4f out: led 3f out tl 1f out: no ch w easy wnr* **11/1**
16-6 3 nk **Avanti**[51] 6132 10-9-6 48..(v) AlanDaly 10 49
(Dr J R J Naylor) *hld up in midfield: lost pl 5f out: rdn and styd on fnl 2f* **8/1**[2]
0/6- 4 1 1/4 **Nod's Star**[380] 1115 5-9-3 45..(t) LPKeniry 7 44
(Mrs L C Jewell) *in tch: rdn 3f out: styd on same pce* **25/1**
0304 5 1/2 **Iceni Warrior**[9] 6701 4-9-3 45.. PaulDoe 6 43
(P Howling) *hld up in midfield: hdwy to join ldr 3f out: one pce fnl f* **8/1**[2]
6000 6 1 **Mister Completely (IRE)**[44] 6256 5-9-1 50................. SophieDoyle(7) 1 46
(Ms J S Doyle) *prom: led after 2f tl 8f out: led 5f out tl 3f out: wknd 2f out* **9/1**[3]
3006 7 1 **Gran Clicquot**[37] 6373 11-8-12 40............................ RobynBrisland(5) 2 40
(G P Enright) *prom: lost pl 4f out: n.d after* **16/1**
6100 8 5 **Shaika**[37] 6373 3-8-12 45.. TonyCulhane 8 32
(G Prodromou) *hld up in midfield: hdwy to press ldrs 4f out: wknd over 2f out* **11/1**
0000 9 10 **Bazil Des Fieffes (FR)**[3] 6779 4-9-3 45..............................(b) CDehens 5 16
(J M Plasschaert, Belgium) *led 2f: led 8f out tl 5f out: wknd over 3f out: sn eased* **33/1**
000- 10 22 **Hawksmoor (IRE)**[396] 6329 4-9-3 30..............................(t) FergusSweeney 3 —
(L A Dace) *chsd ldrs: rdn and wknd over 3f out: sn bhd* **66/1**

2m 35.48s (1.09) **Going Correction** +0.025s/f (Slow)
WFA 3 from 4yo+ 5lb **10** Ran SP% **123.0**
Speed ratings (Par 97):97,93,93,92,92 91,90,87,80,66
CSF £10.23 TOTE £1.70: £1.10, £2.60, £2.50; EX 8.50 Trifecta £33.10 Pool £383.26 - 8.21 winning units.
Owner Mrs B Sumner **Bred** Mrs B Sumner **Trained** Uffcott, Wilts

FOCUS
An ordinary affair taken apart by Artzola, who won doing handsprings, but the form behind is weak.

6805 PONTIN'S FAMILY HOLIDAYS BANDED STKS 6f (P)
2:50 (2:51) (Class 7) 3-Y-O+ £1,433 (£423; £211) Stalls Low

Form RPR
-303 1 **Shava**[7] 6726 6-8-12 45.. FergusSweeney 1 55
(H J Evans) *hld up in rr: gd hdwy and hung lft over 1f out: led ins fnl f: sn clr* **9/2**[2]
0600 2 1 1/2 **Charlottebutterfly**[7] 6727 6-8-12 45.............................. TonyCulhane 11 50
(P J McBride) *hld up in rr: wd bnd into st: rdn and r.o fnl 2f: nrst fin* **10/1**
0040 3 3/4 **Beverley Beau**[16] 6619 4-8-5 45.................................. KristinStubbs(7) 8 48
(Mrs L Stubbs) *prom: rdn to ld 1f out: sn hdd and nt qckn* **9/1**
3044 4 shd **Teyaar**[7] 6727 10-8-12 45.. PaulFitzsimons 12 47
(M Wellings) *chsd ldrs: rdn 2f out: one pce* **8/1**[3]
-020 5 3/4 **Tiny Tim (IRE)**[113] 4670 8-8-5 40...............................(b) DavidProbert(7) 5 45
(A M Balding) *trckd ldr: rdn to dispute ld over 1f out: no ex fnl f* **20/1**
0206 6 shd **Noble Mount**[7] 6727 5-8-12 45..(p) SamHitchcott 7 45
(A B Haynes) *trckd ldrs: rdn 2f out: no ex over 1f out* **12/1**
0302 7 1 **Rowanberry**[9] 6704 4-8-12 45... BrettDoyle 10 42
(R M H Cowell) *mid-div: effrt over 2f out: styd on same pce* **4/1**[1]
3403 8 1/2 **Firework**[7] 6727 8-8-12 45... StephenCarson 4 40
(E A Wheeler) *dwlt: hld up towards rr: rdn and sme hdwy 2f out: no imp over 1f out* **9/2**[2]
5000 9 3 1/2 **Double M**[15] 6629 9-8-12 45.......................................(v) RichardThomas 6 30
(Mrs L Richards) *towards rr: rdn and n.d fnl 3f* **12/1**
3305 10 1 **Vicky Pollard**[9] 6704 3-8-12 45.. RobertHavlin 3 27
(P Howling) *led tl 1f out: wknd qckly fnl f* **16/1**
0000 11 1 **Smart Golden Boy (IRE)**[24] 6374 3-8-12 45.....................(v[1]) LPKeniry 2 24
(Mrs L C Jewell) *mid-div: hrd rdn 3f out: sn struggling* **33/1**
5006 12 3 **Hello Deauville (FR)**[72] 5728 3-8-12 40................................... PaulDoe 9 15
(J Akehurst) *in tch tl wknd 3f out* **16/1**

1m 12.17s (-0.64) **Going Correction** +0.025s/f (Slow) **12** Ran SP% **121.4**
Speed ratings (Par 97):105,103,102,101,100 100,99,98,94,92 91,87
CSF £50.57 TOTE £5.70: £2.20, £4.50, £4.00; EX 119.00 TRIFECTA Not won..
Owner Mrs J Evans **Bred** Slatch Farm Stud **Trained** Honeybourne, Worcs

FOCUS
An ordinary sprint and a decent winning time for a banded race. The form looks solid and reliable with the third to fifth very close to their marks. A first Flat winner for James Evans.

6806 PONTINS "BOOK EARLY" BANDED STKS 5f (P)
3:20 (3:20) (Class 7) 3-Y-O+ £1,528 (£451; £225) Stalls High

Form RPR
6351 1 **Dysonic (USA)**[9] 6704 4-9-1 45..............................(v) JasonEdmunds(3) 5 59
(J Balding) *hld up in 5th: rdn and hdwy over 1f out: str run to ld on line* **11/4**[1]
0624 2 shd **New Options**[5] 6755 9-9-3 50..(b) GeorgeBaker 1 58
(Peter Grayson) *dwlt: t.k.h in 4th: wnt 2nd 2f out: rdn to ld 1f out: kpt on: hdd on line* **11/4**[1]
0002 3 1/2 **Lady Hopeful (IRE)**[5] 6755 4-9-0 47......................(b) RobbieFitzpatrick 2 53
(Peter Grayson) *blindfold removed late and s.s: bhd: gd hdwy over 1f out: kpt on fnl f* **4/1**[2]
4363 4 nk **Spinetail Rufous (IRE)**[7] 6723 8-8-12 45...................(v[1]) BrettDoyle 4 50
(Miss Z C Davison) *t.k.h: prom in chsng gp: shkn up over 1f out: one pce fnl f* **9/2**[3]
6033 5 3/4 **Primarily**[9] 6704 4-9-0 47.. TonyCulhane 6 49
(Peter Grayson) *prom in chsng gp: outpcd on outside ent st: hld after* **9/2**[3]
0606 6 4 **Wotavadun (IRE)**[3] 6774 3-8-5 40.............................(b) SophieDoyle(7) 3 33
(Ms J S Doyle) *plld hrd: led and restrained in front 3l ahd: rdn over 2f out: hdd & wknd 1f out* **33/1**

59.84 secs (0.06) **Going Correction** +0.025s/f (Slow) **6** Ran SP% **112.6**
Speed ratings (Par 97):100,99,99,98,97 90
CSF £10.58 TOTE £3.20: £1.50, £1.40; EX 10.30 Place 6 £25.88, Place 5 £13.88.
Owner T R Pearson **Bred** Shadwell Farm LLC **Trained** Scrooby, Notts

FOCUS
There was a fairly steady pace to this sprint and the form looks modest, but the gallop would not have suited the winner and he looks to be improving. The form seems sound and the fourth sets the standard.
T/Plt: £41.90 to a £1 stake. Pool: £43,472.60. 757.20 winning tickets. T/Qpdt: £19.00 to a £1 stake. Pool: £3,557.60. 138.20 winning tickets. LM

6787 WOLVERHAMPTON (A.W) (L-H)
Wednesday, December 13

OFFICIAL GOING: Standard
Wind: Strong behind Weather: Cloudy

6807 WBX.COM WORLD BET EXCHANGE NURSERY 5f 216y(P)
3:50 (4:01) (Class 6) (0-65,61) 2-Y-O £2,730 (£806; £403) Stalls Low

Form RPR
0521 1 **Charlotte Grey**[9] 6706 2-9-4 58 6ex........................... EdwardCreighton 2 64
(C N Allen) *chsd ldrs: led over 2f out: sn rdn clr: jst hld on* **7/1**
0004 2 hd **Suntan Lady (IRE)**[8] 6715 2-7-9 40.....................(v[1]) DuranFentiman(5) 5 45
(Miss V Haigh) *hld up: swtchd rt and hdwy over 1f out: r.o wl* **16/1**
5164 3 1/2 **Show Trial (IRE)**[14] 6653 2-9-3 57.................................... SteveDrowne 9 61
(D J S Ffrench Davis) *dwlt: hld up: hdwy over 2f out: rdn over 1f out: r.o* **7/1**
666 4 2 **Wadnagin (IRE)**[12] 6663 2-9-4 61.................................. JamesDoyle(3) 7 59
(I A Wood) *broke wl: stdd and lost pl 5f out: hdwy over 2f out: rdn and hung rt over 1f out: styd on* **11/2**[3]
5000 5 1 **Final Curtain**[14] 6653 2-9-4 58... EddieAhern 6 53
(M A Magnusson) *led early: chsd ldrs: rdn over 1f out: no ex fnl f* **8/1**
5062 6 2 1/2 **Totally Free**[2] 6789 2-8-12 52...(v) HayleyTurner 4 39
(M D I Usher) *hld up in tch: nt clr run over 2f out: nvr trbld ldrs* **8/1**
5600 7 shd **Lady Chastity**[8] 6715 2-8-8 55.. MCGeran(7) 3 42
(Mrs L J Young) *chsd ldrs: rdn over 2f out: wknd over 1f out* **33/1**
4014 8 1/2 **Lovers Kiss**[23] 6534 2-9-1 55...(b) DaneO'Neill 11 40
(N Wilson) *chsd ldrs: rdn over 2f out: wknd fnl f* **14/1**
0040 9 7 **Sophie's Dream**[14] 6653 2-9-1 55.................................. DeanMcKeown 1 19
(J G Given) *sn led: hung rt and hdd over 2f out: wknd over 1f out* **7/2**[1]
506 10 1 1/4 **Ranavalona**[78] 5586 2-8-6 53.. WilliamBuick(7) 10 13
(A M Balding) *mid-div: rdn over 3f out: wknd over 2f out* **5/1**[2]
0535 11 9 **The Geester**[11] 6679 2-9-1 55...(p) PaulQuinn 8 —
(S R Bowring) *hld up: plld hrd: rdn and wknd over 2f out* **14/1**

1m 18.33s (2.52) **Going Correction** +0.30s/f (Slow) **11** Ran SP% **123.7**
Speed ratings (Par 94):95,94,94,91,90 86,86,85,76,74 62
CSF £118.81 CT £842.64 TOTE £6.10: £1.60, £4.30, £3.10; EX 99.20.
Owner Travel Spot Ltd **Bred** Finbar Kent **Trained** Newmarket, Suffolk

FOCUS
A moderate but competitive sprint nursery and the form looks sound enough with those behind the first two close to form.

NOTEBOOK
Charlotte Grey narrowly followed up her recent success in a weak course and distance maiden and is clearly progressing. She should not go up too much for this and can remain competitive. (op 4-1)
Suntan Lady(IRE), with a visor replacing cheekpieces, just got going too late. She is only rated 40 and her current sort of mark can surely be exploited in similar company, maybe over another furlong. (op 12-1)
Show Trial(IRE) was just found out by the drop in trip and can probably do better when ridden from off the pace over slightly further. (op 5-1 tchd 9-2)
Wadnagin(IRE) did not get the run of things - she was forced to come very wide into the straight - and should do better. (op 6-1 tchd 13-2)
Final Curtain, dropped a furlong in trip, offered a little more this time and should be up to finding a similar race at some point. (op 9-1 tchd 10-1)
Sophie's Dream was really well back on this drop in trip, but he offered little under pressure having been ridden positively. Official explanation: jockey said gelding ran too freely early (op 13-2)
Ranavalona, switched on Polytrack for the first time on her handicap debut, failed to confirm the promise she showed in turf maidens. (op 7-1)

6808 PERSONALISED CARDS FROM BONUSPRINT.COM MAIDEN STKS 7f 32y(P)
4:20 (4:24) (Class 5) 2-Y-O £3,886 (£1,156; £577; £288) Stalls High

Form RPR
0553 1 **Putra Laju (IRE)**[15] 6645 2-9-3 72.. EddieAhern 1 70
(J W Hills) *trckd ldrs: rdn to ld over 1f out: all out* **5/4**[1]
05 2 hd **Bold Saxon (IRE)**[42] 6290 2-9-3 .... HayleyTurner 4 70
(M D I Usher) *chsd ldr: led over 2f out: rdn and hdd over 1f out: r.o* **9/2**[3]
4 3 3/4 **Not To Know**[17] 6662 2-9-3 .... DaneO'Neill 7 68
(John A Quinn, Ire) *s.i.s: hld up: hdwy over 1f out: styd on* **25/1**
4 nk **Regal Riband** 2-8-12 .... JamieMackay 5 62
(Sir Mark Prescott) *chsd ldrs: ev ch over 2f out: sn rdn: edgd rt ins fnl f: unable qckn* **7/2**[2]
5 4 **Razzano (IRE)**[121] 4440 2-8-12 .... SteveDrowne 3 52
(P D Evans) *hld up in tch: rdn and wknd over 1f out* **11/1**
4 6 7 **Ginger Pop**[11] 6669 2-9-3 .... MickyFenton 6 39
(G G Margarson) *hld up: plld hrd: hdwy over 4f out: rdn and hung rt 1/2-way: wknd over 1f out* **5/1**
7 15 **Jayzee (IRE)**[125] 4309 2-8-12 .... EdwardCreighton 2 —
(P D Deegan, Ire) *led: hdd & wknd over 2f out* **40/1**

1m 34.22s (3.82) **Going Correction** +0.30s/f (Slow) **7** Ran SP% **116.1**
Speed ratings (Par 96):90,89,88,88,84 76,58
CSF £7.59 TOTE £2.10: £1.10, £2.90; EX 8.20.
Owner F Lee **Bred** Rathasker Stud **Trained** Upper Lambourn, Berks

FOCUS
By no means a bad maiden for the time of year, although not totally solid, with the winner the best guide.

NOTEBOOK
Putra Laju(IRE) had looked unlucky when third in a four-runner nursery over course and distance on his previous start and he was able to get off the mark at the fifth attempt on this return to maiden company. He was forced to work hard, but the runner-up had previously shown plenty of ability and he should not be underestimated when returned to handicaps. (tchd 11-8 in places and 6-4 in a place)
Bold Saxon(IRE) did not get the run of things when only fifth at Kempton last time, but he had previously shown plenty of ability in a Newbury maiden on his debut and confirmed that with a good second. He looks up to winning a maiden, but will also now have the option of going handicapping. (op 7-1)
Not To Know confirmed the ability he showed on his debut over course and distance and is coming along nicely. (op 20-1)
Regal Riband ◆, a half-sister to Regal Royale, a six-furlong winner on juvenile debut, out of a Group 1 Cheveley Park Stakes winner, showed plenty of ability on her racecourse debut. This should have sharpened her up and it will be disappointing if she does not win next time. (op 9-4 tchd 2-1)
Razzano(IRE) had shown only moderate ability in four runs on turf in Ireland and was well held on his debut for new connections. She should be better off in low-grade handicaps. (op 16-1)
Ginger Pop failed to confirm the ability he showed in a weak six-furlong maiden at Kempton on his debut and proved disappointing. (op 6-1 tchd 13-2)

The Form Book, Raceform Ltd, Compton, RG20 6NL

6809 **PONTIN'S HOLIDAYS MEDIAN AUCTION MAIDEN STKS** **1m 141y(P)**
4:50 (4:50) (Class 6) 2-Y-O £2,730 (£806; £403) **Stalls** Low

Form RPR
524 **1** **Benny The Bat**[72] [5730] 2-9-3 76 SteveDrowne 5 73+
(H Morrison) *rrd s: sn chsng ldrs: rdn to ld over 2f out: clr whn hung lft over 1f out: eased ins fnl f* **4/7**[1]
2 *5* **Bewildering (IRE)** 2-9-3 GrahamGibbons 2 60
(E J O'Neill) *trckd ldrs: rdn over 2f out: hung lft and wknd over 1f out: wnt 2nd nr fin* **3/1**[2]
3 *nk* **My Beautaful** 2-8-9 JamesDoyle(3) 4 54
(Miss J S Davis) *dwlt: hld up: hdwy over 2f out: rdn to chse wnr and hung lft over 1f out: wknd fnl f* **33/1**
0 **4** *3/4* **Port Macquairie (IRE)**[19] [6581] 2-9-3 MickyFenton 6 58
(R M Beckett) *led: hdd over 4f out: rdn to ld over 3f out: hdd over 2f out: wknd over 1f out* **20/1**
0040 **5** *3/4* **Arabellas Homer**[6] [6737] 2-8-12 49 HayleyTurner 3 51
(Mrs N Macauley) *hld up in tch: rdn and wknd over 1f out* **25/1**
5 **6** *15* **Hyde Park Flight (IRE)**[14] [6651] 2-9-3 DaneO'Neill 1 23
(John A Quinn, Ire) *w ldr tl led over 4f out: hdd over 3f out: rdn and wknd over 2f out* **6/1**[3]
1m 55.54s (3.78) **Going Correction** +0.30s/f (Slow) 6 Ran SP% **114.5**
Speed ratings (Par 94):95,90,90,89,88 75
CSF £2.58 TOTE £1.50: £1.10, £2.30; EX 3.40.
Owner A J Richards **Bred** Ewar Stud Farms **Trained** East Ilsley, Berks
FOCUS
A very uncompetitive maiden and not a race to dwell on with the fifth the best guide to the level.
NOTEBOOK
Benny The Bat had shown plenty of ability in his three previous starts and, faced with by far his easiest task to date, he ran out a comfortable winner. (op 8-13 tchd 8-11)
Bewildering(IRE), a 45,000euros brother to the quite useful Toldo, a multiple winner from a mile to two miles, out of a seven-furlong scorer, ran to just a moderate level of form on his racecourse debut but is obviously open to improvement. (op 4-1)
My Beautaful, out of a triple winner over staying distances who was also placed over hurdles, made a satisfactory debut but is unlikely to come into his own until sent handicapping over further.
Port Macquairie(IRE) is likely to find things easier when handicapped. (op 14-1)
Arabellas Homer is eligible for banded races. (op 20-1)
Hyde Park Flight(IRE) had shown plenty of ability on his debut at Kempton, so presumably something was amiss this time. (op 11-2 tchd 5-1)

6810 **IAN GRIFFITHS RACEGOERS CLUB H'CAP** **1m 1f 103y(P)**
5:20 (5:20) (Class 6) (0-58,58) 3-Y-0+ £2,730 (£806; £403) **Stalls** Low

Form RPR
0001 **1** **Scutch Mill (IRE)**[8] [6714] 4-8-13 58 (t) JerryO'Dwyer(3) 12 68+
(Karen George) *s.i.s: hld up: hdwy and hung rt over 1f out: rdn to ld and edgd lft ins fnl f: r.o wl* **5/1**[2]
5041 **2** *2* **Discotheque (USA)**[18] [6608] 3-9-0 58 DeanCorby 4 64
(P Howling) *hld up: hdwy and edgd rt over 2f out: rdn to ld 1f out: hung rt: hdd and unable qckn ins fnl f* **12/1**
0400 **3** *1 1/4* **Atticus Trophies (IRE)**[191] [2301] 3-8-9 56 (p) JamesDoyle(3) 6 60
(Ms J S Doyle) *chsd ldr: led over 3f out: rdn: hung rt and hdd 1f out: no ex* **50/1**
1524 **4** *hd* **Uhuru Peak**[23] [6532] 5-9-0 56 (bt) PaulMulrennan 9 59
(M W Easterby) *hld up: hdwy over 2f out: rdn over 1f out: styd on same pce fnl f* **7/1**
000- **5** *hd* **King Gabriel (IRE)**[35] [3177] 4-8-13 55 AdrianTNicholls 10 58
(Andrew Turnell) *hld up: hdwy and hung lft fnl f: nt rch ldrs* **33/1**
0032 **6** *1/2* **Dante's Diamond (IRE)**[11] [6683] 4-9-1 57 SteveDrowne 5 59
(G A Swinbank) *hld up in tch: rdn whn hmpd over 2f out: no ex fnl f* **9/4**[1]
0250 **7** *1 3/4* **Leighton Buzzard**[24] [6380] 4-8-6 55 GaryWales(7) 1 53
(N B King) *chsd ldrs: rdn over 2f out: wknd over 1f out* **16/1**
0-06 **8** *3 1/2* **Plausabelle**[12] [6667] 5-9-0 56 EddieAhern 3 47
(G G Margarson) *chsd ldrs: rdn over 2f out: wkng whn hmpd ins fnl f* **6/1**[3]
0500 **9** *1* **Consuelita**[142] [3793] 3-9-0 58 DaneO'Neill 7 47
(B J Meehan) *s.i.s: hld up: rdn over 2f out: nt clr run ins fnl f: n.d* **25/1**
0006 **10** *3* **King After**[2] [6793] 4-8-4 53 WilliamBuick(7) 2 36
(J R Best) *s.i.s: racd keenly and sn led: hdd over 2f out: sn rdn and wknd* **5/1**[2]
5005 **11** *2* **Burnley Al (IRE)**[15] [6648] 4-9-2 58 (b) GrahamGibbons 13 37
(Peter Grayson) *s.i.s: plld hrd and hdwy over 7f out: wkng whn hmpd over 2f out* **14/1**
2m 4.63s (2.01) **Going Correction** +0.30s/f (Slow)
WFA 3 from 4yo+ 2lb 11 Ran SP% **119.9**
Speed ratings (Par 101):103,101,100,99,99 99,97,94,93,91 89
CSF £63.69 CT £2694.59 TOTE £7.10: £1.60, £4.50, £25.80; EX 35.60.
Owner B R Phillips **Bred** Denis McDonnell **Trained** Higher Easington, Devon
FOCUS
A moderate handicap but the form looks sound for the grade and should prove reliable.

6811 **PERSONALISED CALENDARS FROM BONUSPRINT.COM H'CAP** **1m 4f 50y(P)**
5:50 (5:56) (Class 4) (0-85,83) 3-Y-0+ £5,505 (£1,637; £818; £408) **Stalls** Low

Form RPR
1015 **1** **Inch Lodge**[11] [6673] 4-8-12 74 MickyFenton 4 84
(Miss D Mountain) *hmpd sn after s: hld up: hung rt thrght: hdwy to ld over 9f out: rdn and hung to stands' side over 1f out: all out* **7/2**[2]
5601 **2** *1 1/4* **La Estrella (USA)**[19] [6587] 3-8-13 80 J-PGuillambert 5 88
(J G Given) *edgd lft s: prom: lost pl over 9f out: hdwy over 2f out: rdn to chse wnr and hung lft over 1f out: styd on* **12/1**
5423 **3** *2* **Pass The Port**[12] [6661] 5-8-10 77 AshleyHamblett(5) 12 82
(D Haydn Jones) *hld up: hdwy 6f out: chsd wnr over 3f out: rdn over 1f out: styd on same pce* **3/1**[1]
6601 **4** *1 1/4* **Quince (IRE)**[25] [6519] 3-8-13 80 (v) JimmyQuinn 8 83
(J Pearce) *prom: rdn over 1f out: styd on same pce* **3/1**[1]
0001 **5** *1* **Ocean Pride (IRE)**[12] [6657] 3-8-10 77 AdrianTNicholls 6 78+
(D E Pipe) *chsd ldrs: hmpd and lost pl over 3f out: hdwy over 1f out: hung rt and lft ins fnl f: styd on* **20/1**
0-60 **6** *2 1/2* **Credit (IRE)**[11] [6677] 5-9-2 78 HayleyTurner 7 75
(Jennie Candlish) *hld up: styd on ins fnl f: nvr nrr* **50/1**
0255 **7** *1 1/2* **Lake Poet (IRE)**[30] [6468] 3-9-0 81 EddieAhern 1 76
(C E Brittain) *led: hdd over 9f out: chsd ldrs: rdn and wknd over 1f out* **4/1**[3]
10-0 **8** *4* **Mr Jack Daniells (IRE)**[38] [6360] 5-9-7 83 DJCondon 2 72
(Anthony Mullins, Ire) *chsd ldrs tl wknd over 1f out* **14/1**
010- **9** *shd* **Solarias Quest**[18] [4451] 4-9-6 82 DaneO'Neill 3 70
(A King) *hmpd sn after s: hld up: rdn and wknd over 2f out* **14/1**
620- **10** *15* **Baie Des Flamands (USA)**[38] [5948] 4-8-11 76 (bt) JerryO'Dwyer(3) 11 40
(Miss S J Wilton) *chsd ldrs tl rdn over 3f out: sn wknd* **66/1**
2m 46.18s (3.76) **Going Correction** +0.30s/f (Slow)
WFA 3 from 4yo+ 5lb 10 Ran SP% **121.5**
Speed ratings (Par 105):99,98,96,96,95 93,92,90,89,79
CSF £46.23 CT £144.03 TOTE £5.40: £1.90, £3.20, £1.40; EX 65.40.
Owner David Fremel **Bred** Gainsborough Stud Management Ltd **Trained** Newmarket, Suffolk
FOCUS
A good middle-distance handicap for the grade and the form looks solid rated around the winner and third.

6812 **WBXTRIPLECROWN.COM H'CAP** **1m 4f 50y(P)**
6:20 (6:25) (Class 6) (0-55,61) 3-Y-0+ £2,730 (£806; £403) **Stalls** Low

Form RPR
4423 **1** **Regency Red (IRE)**[4] [6769] 8-8-8 52 AshleyHamblett(5) 8 60
(W M Brisbourne) *s.i.s: hld up: hdwy over 4f out: rdn over 1f out: styd on to ld wl ins fnl f* **9/4**[2]
1000 **2** *3/4* **Royal Premier (IRE)**[21] [6565] 3-8-11 55 (v) MickyFenton 2 62
(H J Collingridge) *chsd ldr: rdn 7f out: led over 3f out: hdd wl ins fnl f* **8/1**[3]
2134 **3** *3/4* **Desert Hawk**[16] [6627] 5-8-11 50 (v[1]) DaneO'Neill 6 56
(W M Brisbourne) *hld up in tch: rdn over 1f out: styd on* **5/4**[1]
0050 **4** *18* **Strife (IRE)**[16] [6628] 3-8-7 51 (p) JimmyQuinn 12 28
(W M Brisbourne) *hld up: hdwy over 2f out: sn wknd* **16/1**
0301 **5** *2* **Cool Isle**[19] [6584] 3-8-11 55 (b) DeanCorby 1 29
(P Howling) *chsd ldrs: rdn over 3f out: wknd over 2f out* **11/1**
0650 **6** *11* **Caragh Mia (IRE)**[10] [6693] 4-9-0 53 J-PGuillambert 3 9
(G G Margarson) *rrd s: hdwy over 7f out: sn rdn: wknd 3f out* **12/1**
-006 **7** *5* **Proud Scholar (USA)**[3] [6775] 4-9-2 55 SteveDrowne 11 3
(R A Kvisla) *chsd ldrs: rdn over 4f out: wknd over 2f out* **10/1**
000P **8** *3 1/2* **Good Intentions**[27] [6501] 4-8-2 48 oh11 ow2 WilliamCarson(7) 4 —
(P W Hiatt) *led over 8f: sn wknd* **40/1**
0000 **9** *25* **Fantasy Legend (IRE)**[22] [6551] 3-8-2 46 oh1 (b[1]) PaulQuinn 9 —
(N P Littmoden) *hld up: rdn and wknd over 3f out* **40/1**
2m 44.84s (2.42) **Going Correction** +0.30s/f (Slow)
WFA 3 from 4yo+ 5lb 9 Ran SP% **122.2**
Speed ratings (Par 101):103,102,102,90,88 81,78,75,59
CSF £22.43 CT £31.80 TOTE £4.00: £1.40, £2.10, £1.10; EX 36.00 Place 6 £59.36, place 5 £9.51.
Owner M J P Arthur **Bred** Patrick J Burke **Trained** Great Ness, Shropshire
FOCUS
This moderate contest was weakened by withdrawals, but the first three came well clear and the form looks fair for the grade and sound enough.
Caragh Mia(IRE) Official explanation: jockey said filly was unsuited by the surface
T/Plt: £25.10 to a £1 stake. Pool: £69,285.35. 2,011.55 winning tickets. T/Qpdt: £6.40 to a £1 stake. Pool: £4,988.20. 570.60 winning tickets. CR

6794 SOUTHWELL (L-H)
Thursday, December 14

OFFICIAL GOING: Standard
Wind: strong across

6813 **PONTIN'S FAMILY HOLIDAYS NURSERY** **5f (F)**
12:30 (12:30) (Class 5) (0-75,66) 2-Y-O £3,238 (£963; £481; £240) **Stalls** High

Form RPR
331 **1** **Diminuto**[9] [6715] 2-8-6 58 6ex FrankiePickard(7) 1 62
(M D I Usher) *wnt lft s: sn led: rdn wl over 1f out: styd on wl fnl f* **7/2**[2]
0415 **2** *1 1/4* **Sister Etienne (IRE)**[36] [6400] 2-9-0 66 DeanHeslop(7) 4 66
(T D Barron) *chsd ldrs: hdwy 1/2-way: rdn to chse wnr and edgd lft 1f out: kpt on same pce* **4/1**[3]
0246 **3** *3/4* **Grange Lili (IRE)**[12] [6670] 2-8-12 57 (b) RobbieFitzpatrick 5 54
(Peter Grayson) *dwlt: in tch: hdwy 2f out: sn rdn and sltly outpcd over 1f out: drvn ent last: edgd lft and kpt on* **5/1**
0042 **4** *3/4* **Suntan Lady (IRE)**[1] [6807] 2-7-7 43 oh3 (v[1]) DuranFentiman(5) 2 37
(Miss V Haigh) *prom: rdn along wl over 1f out: drvn appr last: sn one pce* **4/1**[3]
0623 **5** *nk* **Cryptic Clue (USA)**[5] [6760] 2-8-8 53 TonyCulhane 3 46
(D W Chapman) *cl up: rdn along 2f out: drvn: edgd lft and wknd over 1f out: hld whn n.m.r ent last* **9/4**[1]
61.09 secs (0.79) **Going Correction** +0.075s/f (Slow) 5 Ran SP% **109.7**
Speed ratings (Par 96):96,94,92,91,91
CSF £17.06 TOTE £4.00: £1.40, £2.30; EX 10.80.
Owner R H Brookes **Bred** B Minty **Trained** Upper Lambourn, Berks
■ Stewards' Enquiry : Dean Heslop four-day ban: careless riding (Dec 26) and using whip with excessive frequency without allowing mount time to respond (Dec 27-29)
FOCUS
An ordinary nursery heavily influenced by the draw as races over this straight five usually are. As such the form should be treated with some caution although the winner improved on her previous success.
NOTEBOOK
Diminuto, who was carrying a 6lb penalty for her course-and-distance victory nine days earlier when she had both Suntan Lady and Cryptic Clue behind her, had the plum draw here and the early speed to exploit it. Ploughing a lone furrow down the quicker centre of the track, she always seemed to have matters under control, but the nature of the race means that the form cannot be relied upon. (op 11-4 tchd 4-1)
Sister Etienne(IRE), trying Fibresand for the first time, stayed on to chase the winner home and did best of the quartet to race nearer to the stands' side, but could never get on terms with the winner. She may need an extra furlong on sand. (op 6-1)
Grange Lili(IRE), back over a more suitable trip, was drawn closest to the stands' rail which did her no favours and she was always struggling to get on terms in the slower ground. She should not be judged too harshly on this. (tchd 9-2)
Suntan Lady(IRE), visored for the first time and making a quick reappearance after finishing runner-up at Wolverhampton the previous day, was a stone better off with Diminuto for a beating of just over two lengths over course and distance earlier in the month. However, she had the favoured number one draw then, whilst her old rival had it this time, and she ended up being beaten further. To be fair, she shapes as though she needs much further than this now. (op 7-2 tchd 9-2)
Cryptic Clue(USA), 6lb better off with Diminuto for a beating of just over a length over course and distance earlier this month, had tried a mile here in the meantime and was always struggling for pace back over the trip. His best distance remains a mystery. (tchd 2-1)

6814 **PONTINSBINGO.COM (S) STKS** **1m (F)**
1:00 (1:00) (Class 6) 3-Y-0+ £2,388 (£705; £352) **Stalls** Low

Form RPR
2014 **1** **Formidable Will (FR)**[16] [6641] 4-9-7 63 (bt) DaleGibson 7 71
(M W Easterby) *cl up: led over 3f out: clr wl over 1f out: styd on wl* **15/8**[1]

0000 **2** *5* **Penwell Hill (USA)**[38] 6380 7-9-1 53 ....(b) AdamKirby 3 54
(Miss M E Rowland) *led: rdn along 1/2-way: sn hdd: drvn and kpt on same pce fnl 2f* **14/1**

6300 **3** *3* **Captain Darling (IRE)**[17] 6624 6-9-7 64 .... EdwardCreighton 2 54
(R W Price) *chsd ldrs on inner: rdn along 3f out: drvn and kpt on same pce fnl 2f* **10/1**

0104 **4** *1 1/2* **Crush On You**[26] 6524 3-9-1 48 .... GrahamGibbons 5 46
(R Hollinshead) *chsd ldrs: rdn along 3f out: drvn over 2f out and sn one pce* **25/1**

01-4 **5** *shd* **Prince Vettori**[19] 6606 4-9-1 58 .... JimmyQuinn 12 45
(D J Coakley) *in tch: hdwy to chse ldrs over 2f out: sn drvn and no imp appr last* **5/1**[3]

0600 **6** *6* **Rocky Reppin**[23] 6554 6-8-12 40 ....(b) JasonEdmunds(3) 8 32
(J Balding) *dwlt: sn chsng ldrs: rdn along 3f out: drvn and wknd over 2f out* **40/1**

0600 **7** *7* **Bollin Edward**[17] 6624 7-9-2 55 ....(b) JamieJones(5) 1 23
(K A Ryan) *in tch: rdn along over 3f out: sn drvn and btn* **25/1**

00 **8** *3/4* **Paper Maite**[16] 6637 5-8-10 .... DeanMcKeown 10 11
(S R Bowring) *a towards rr* **100/1**

0003 **9** *6* **George's Flyer (IRE)**[10] 6694 3-9-1 65 ....(b) JamieMoriarty(5) 6 9
(R A Fahey) *a rr: bhd fnl 2f* **7/1**

3035 **10** *32* **Ali Bruce**[204] 1938 6-9-1 75 .... PaulMulrennan 13 —
(P A Blockley) *trckd ldrs gng wl: effrt 3f out: sn rdn and wknd qckly over 2f out: sn bhd and eased* **3/1**[2]

11 *2* **Tellitlikeitis**[20] 5-8-12 .... JerryO'Dwyer(3) 4 —
(Miss Kariana Key) *s.i.s: sn t.o* **100/1**

1m 44.21s (-0.39) **Going Correction** -0.10s/f (Stan)
WFA 3 from 4yo+ 1lb **11** Ran SP% **116.8**
Speed ratings (Par 101):97,92,89,87,87 81,74,73,67,35 33
CSF £29.39 TOTE £2.50: £1.50, £3.20, £2.50; EX 27.60 TRIFECTA Not won..The winner was sold to Gainthorpe Racing for 10,000gns.
Owner Bert and Dilys Kelly **Bred** Gfa Haras Du Hoguenet And Searching Sarl **Trained** Sheriff Hutton, N Yorks

FOCUS
A routine seller in which the principals were always up with the pace and few ever got into it. The winner is rated to his best but several appeared to run below form.
Ali Bruce Official explanation: vet said gelding finished distressed

6815 PONTIN'S BOOK EARLY MAIDEN AUCTION STKS 7f (F)
1:30 (1:31) (Class 6) 2-Y-O **£2,590** (£770; £385; £192) **Stalls** Low

Form RPR

4 **1** **Hostage**[16] 6646 2-8-8 .... HayleyTurner 4 66
(M L W Bell) *cl up: chal 2f out: sn rdn: rn green and hung rt: styd on to ld ent last: sn edgd lft: kpt on* **5/1**[3]

3203 **2** *1 1/4* **Vadinka**[9] 6710 2-8-13 73 .... KimTinkler 2 68
(N Tinkler) *led: rdn 2f out: drvn over 1f out: hdd ent last: kpt on u.p* **11/4**[1]

2640 **3** *5* **Chasing Memories (IRE)**[16] 6639 2-8-5 66 .... AdrianMcCarthy 8 47
(B Smart) *cl up on outer: effrt over 2f out: sn rdn and hung lft over 1f out: one pce* **7/2**[2]

4 *1/2* **Mujamead** 2-8-12 .... LeeEnstone 5 53
(P C Haslam) *trckd ldrs: effrt over 2f out: rdn: green and wandered over 1f out: sn one pce* **8/1**

0 **5** *nk* **Brean Dot Com (IRE)**[126] 4295 2-8-11 .... RobertHavlin 6 51
(Mrs P N Dutfield) *in tch: effrt over 2f out: sn rdn and keeping on same pce whn nt clr run over 1f out* **7/2**[2]

0004 **6** *nk* **Kings Shillings**[29] 6491 2-8-12 45 ....(b) GrahamGibbons 1 51
(D Carroll) *s.i.s: hdwy to chse ldrs 1/2-way: sn rdn and one pce fnl 2f* **33/1**

6 **7** *5* **Lauder**[12] 6675 2-8-4 .... JasonEdmunds(3) 7 33
(J Balding) *in tch: rdn along over 2f out: sn wknd* **16/1**

0 **8** *hd* **Jayzee (IRE)**[1] 6808 2-8-9 .... EdwardCreighton 3 34
(P D Deegan, Ire) *dwlt: a towards rr* **25/1**

0 **9** *nk* **Mr Crystal (FR)**[20] 6581 2-9-1 .... DeanMcKeown 9 40
(Micky Hammond) *in tch: rdn along over 2f out: sn btn* **33/1**

1m 31.41s (0.61) **Going Correction** -0.10s/f (Stan) **9** Ran SP% **114.5**
Speed ratings (Par 94):92,90,84,84,83 83,77,77,77
CSF £18.62 TOTE £4.60: £2.20, £1.10, £1.30; EX 17.90 Trifecta £28.50 Pool £209.28 - 5.21 winning units.
Owner The Dukes of Roxburghe & Devonshire **Bred** The Duke Of Devonshire And Floors Farming **Trained** Newmarket, Suffolk
■ Stewards' Enquiry : Kim Tinkler caution: used whip with excessive frequency

FOCUS
A moderate maiden once again dominated by those that raced up with the pace, and the first two home were the front pair throughout. The form is modest, limited by the sixth, though the winner is entitled to improve.

NOTEBOOK
Hostage ◆ may have had a run but still proved very green, especially over the last couple of furlongs where she hung all over the track. Despite that, she still proved too good for a fairly reliable yardstick and, with further improvement likely, she should make her mark in handicap company. (op 4-1 tchd 11-2)
Vadinka, by far the most experienced in the field, ran his race from the front and kept plugging away but yet again found a less-exposed type too good. He has now made the frame in seven of his last eight starts so is hardly an attractive win-only bet. (tchd 7-2)
Chasing Memories(IRE), back in a maiden after being well beaten in a nursery here last time, made a brief effort soon after turning in but it amounted to little. She seems to have gone the wrong way since her promising sand debut here in October. (op 11-4)
Mujamead, an 8,000gns half-brother to five winners including Cashel Mead, looked in need of the experience and should do better in due course. (op 10-1 tchd 12-1 and 15-2)
Brean Dot Com(IRE), not seen since showing some ability on his Haydock debut in August, may have finished third had he not had to take evasive action entering the last furlong. The market suggested he might have been expected to have done better, but Fibresand does not suit every horse and he may be capable of more on a less-demanding surface, especially once handicapped. (op 9-2)

6816 PROTEC GROUP H'CAP 1m 4f (F)
2:00 (2:00) (Class 5) (0-75,71) 3-Y-O+ **£3,238** (£963; £481; £240) **Stalls** Low

Form RPR

-041 **1** **Hilltop Destiny**[8] 6735 3-9-3 71 6ex .... JerryO'Dwyer(3) 2 86+
(V Smith) *mde all: rdn over 2f out: drvn over 1f out: styd on strly ins last* **2/1**[2]

0024 **2** *3 1/2* **Prince Of Love (IRE)**[9] 6716 3-9-0 65 .... MickyFenton 4 72
(Jedd O'Keeffe) *hld up: hdwy over 4f out: rdn over 2f out: drvn to chse wnr over 1f out: no imp ins last* **11/4**[3]

0311 **3** *1 1/2* **Zed Candy (FR)**[9] 6716 3-8-12 63 6ex .... DaleGibson 3 68
(J T Stimpson) *trckd wnr: effrt and cl up 4f out: rdn along wl over 2f out: sn drvn and one pce fr wl over 1f out* **15/8**[1]

0314 **4** *8* **Cragganmore Creek**[9] 6718 3-8-12 63 ....(b) HayleyTurner 1 55
(D Morris) *hld up: hdwy over 4f out: rdn along 3f out and sn wknd* **15/2**

-060 **5** *13* **Zacatecas (GER)**[17] 6626 6-9-7 67 .... DeanMcKeown 5 38
(A J Chamberlain) *chsd ldng pair: rdn along 4fr out: sn wknd* **66/1**

2m 39.08s (-3.01) **Going Correction** -0.10s/f (Stan)
WFA 3 from 6yo 5lb **5** Ran SP% **108.0**
Speed ratings (Par 103):106,103,102,97,88
CSF £7.53 TOTE £3.40: £1.30, £1.70; EX 12.80.
Owner G Noble **Bred** G Noble **Trained** Exning, Suffolk

FOCUS
A fair handicap and solid pace thanks to the winner who produced a powerful piece of front-running. The form looks sound with the placed horses close to recent form.

6817 PONTIN'S HOLIDAYS MAIDEN STKS 1m 3f (F)
2:30 (2:30) (Class 5) 3-Y-O+ **£3,238** (£963; £481; £240) **Stalls** Low

Form RPR

0-63 **1** **Flyingit (USA)**[3] 6792 3-8-12 ....(p) CatherineGannon 1 57+
(K A Ryan) *plld hrd: mde all: clr whn shkn up and edgd rt wl over 1f out: idled ins last: pushed out* **8/13**[1]

2656 **2** *1 1/4* **Lanfredo**[10] 6705 3-9-3 48 ....(p) AdamKirby 6 55
(Miss M E Rowland) *trckd ldrs: edgd rt and hdwy over 3f out: rdn to chse wnr wl over 1f out: drvn and kpt on ins last* **8/1**[3]

3 *5* **Neshla** 3-8-12 .... BrettDoyle 8 42+
(C E Brittain) *hld up in rr: hdwy on outer whn bmpd 3f out: swtchd lft and hdwy wl over 1f out: styd on ins last* **5/2**[2]

0 **4** *10* **Watermill (IRE)**[5] 6759 3-9-3 .... PaulQuinn 2 30
(D W Chapman) *in tch: hdwy over 3f out: rdn to chse wnr briefly over 2f out: sn drvn and wknd* **66/1**

6-0 **5** *9* **Jember Red**[36] 6403 3-8-9 .... MarkLawson(3) 7 9
(B Smart) *plld hrd: prom tl rdn along 3f out and sn wknd* **66/1**

004 **6** *1 1/2* **Captain Oats (IRE)**[20] 6588 3-9-0 57 .... GregFairley(3) 3 12
(Mrs P Ford) *cl up: rdn along over 4f out: sn wknd* **16/1**

00 **7** *18* **Donnaspear (IRE)**[12] 6680 3-8-12 .... DaleGibson 4 —
(J Mackie) *prom: rdn along over 4f out: wknd over 3f out: sn bhd* **80/1**

2m 27.51s (-1.39) **Going Correction** -0.10s/f (Stan)
WFA 3 from 5yo 4lb **7** Ran SP% **111.7**
Speed ratings (Par 103):101,100,96,89,82 81,68
CSF £6.33 TOTE £1.70: £1.10, £2.90; EX 5.70 Trifecta £15.00 Pool £229.01 - 10.77 winning units..
Owner Mrs Sandra McCarthy **Bred** Patchen Wilkes Farm, Llc **Trained** Hambleton, N Yorks

FOCUS
A moderate maiden run at an ordinary pace in which few gave any sort of encouragement for the future. The runner-up sets the standard but the form is limited.
Neshla Official explanation: jockey said, regarding the running and riding, that his instructions were to sit in the first four, make steady headway and ride a finish from 2f out, but having missed the break he lost his position, found himself in the kickback and that filly ran in snatches throughout. Furthermore, having been bumped on final bend, she became unbalanced, but plugged on past beaten horses in latter stages.

6818 GO PONTIN'S H'CAP 1m (F)
3:00 (3:00) (Class 5) (0-75,72) 3-Y-O+ **£3,238** (£963; £481; £240) **Stalls** Low

Form RPR

2663 **1** **Smart Ass (IRE)**[15] 6652 3-8-12 68 .... BrettDoyle 6 77
(J S Moore) *trckd ldrs on outer: hdwy over 2f out: rdn to ld and edgd lft wl over 1f out: clr ent last: kpt on* **7/2**[3]

0560 **2** *1* **Anduril**[28] 6503 5-8-9 64 ow2 ....(p) AdamKirby 7 71
(Miss M E Rowland) *hld up in rr: hdwy and nt clr 2f out: swtchd rt and rdn over 1f out: styd on strly ins last* **12/1**

0103 **3** *1 1/4* **Shifty**[30] 6476 7-8-6 68 .... KellyHarrison(7) 5 72
(D Carroll) *trckd ldrs: effrt and nt clr run 2f out: sn rdn and kpt on same pce* **17/2**

001 **4** *2 1/2* **Boundless Prospect (USA)**[30] 6476 7-9-3 72 .... JimmyQuinn 2 71
(Miss Gay Kelleway) *trckd ldrs: hdwy on inner 1/2-way: rdn along over 2f out: sn one pce* **10/3**[2]

5252 **5** *3/4* **Little Jimbob**[33] 3812 5-8-10 70 .... JamieMoriarty(5) 1 68
(R A Fahey) *led: rdn along wl over 2f out: hdd wl over 1f out: sn wknd* **7/1**

4412 **6** *nk* **Sentiero Rosso (USA)**[5] 6762 4-8-8 66 ....(t) CatherineGannon(3) 3 63
(B Ellison) *trckd ldrs: hdwy 4f out: effrt and ev ch over 2f out: sn rdn and btn* **15/8**[1]

31-0 **7** *2* **Haifa (IRE)**[15] 6654 3-9-2 72 .... MichaelTebbutt 4 65
(Mrs A Duffield) *cl up: rdn along over 3f out: sn wknd* **50/1**

1m 43.14s (-1.46) **Going Correction** -0.10s/f (Stan)
WFA 3 from 4yo+ 1lb **7** Ran SP% **112.8**
Speed ratings (Par 103):103,102,100,98,97 97,95
CSF £41.56 TOTE £4.70: £2.30, £3.90; EX 56.70.
Owner J Laughton **Bred** M Ervine **Trained** Upper Lambourn, Berks

FOCUS
A tight little handicap in which the early pace was ordinary and the field were still tightly bunched passing the quarter-mile pole. The placed horses were close to recent form and set the level.

6819 PONTINS.COM H'CAP 1m (F)
3:30 (3:31) (Class 6) (0-58,58) 3-Y-O+ **£2,730** (£806; £403) **Stalls** Low

Form RPR

5102 **1** **Zamhrear**[13] 6667 3-9-0 57 .... BrettDoyle 14 69
(C E Brittain) *in tch on outer: smooth hdwy 3f out: slt ld wl over 1f out: rdn ent last: edgd lft and styd on* **11/4**[1]

5210 **2** *1* **Legal Lover (IRE)**[16] 6641 4-9-0 56 .... GrahamGibbons 11 66
(R Hollinshead) *cl up: led over 3f out: rdn along and hdd wl over 1f out: drvn and ev ch tl no ex wl ins last* **3/1**[2]

5000 **3** *2 1/2* **Moonstreaker**[44] 6286 3-8-7 55 .... MichaelJStainton(5) 13 60
(R M Whitaker) *trckd ldrs: effrt over 2f out: sn rdn and kpt on same pce appr last* **50/1**

4400 **4** *1* **Nimello (USA)**[220] 1553 10-8-13 58 .... NeilChalmers(3) 9 61
(A G Newcombe) *s.i.s and bhd: hdwy on inner 2f out: sn rdn and kpt on: nrst fin* **12/1**

0104 **5** *1 1/2* **Im Ova Ere Dad (IRE)**[10] 6531 3-9-0 57 .... DaleGibson 12 56
(D E Cantillon) *trckd ldrs: hdwy over 2f out: sn rdn and no imp* **9/2**[3]

0000 **6** *1/2* **Tip Top Style**[3] 6793 3-8-7 50 ....(tp) PaulMulrennan 8 48
(J Mackie) *cl up: rdn along wl over 2f out: grad wknd* **25/1**

0000 **7** *2 1/2* **Crusoe (IRE)**[5] 6763 9-8-5 47 .... JosedeSouza 2 40
(A Sadik) *prom: rdn along over 3f out: grad wknd* **40/1**

6065 **8** *2* **Ignition**[13] 6667 4-8-9 56 .... JamieMoriarty(5) 4 45
(W M Brisbourne) *in tch: n.m.r 1/2-way: rdn along 3f out and no hdwy* **10/1**

1320 **9** *4* **Preskani**[16] 6642 4-8-9 51 ow1 ....(p) AdamKirby 7 32
(Mrs N Macauley) *midfield: hdwy over 2f out: sn rdn and btn* **6/1**

100 **10** *1 ½* **Bucharest**[16] 6641 3-9-1 **58** ... MichaelTebbutt 5 35
(M Wigham) *led: rdn along and hdd over 3f out: wknd wl over 2f out* **25/1**
0-60 **11** *1 ½* **Ligne D'Eau**[10] 6703 5-8-4 **46** oh1 ... (v) CatherineGannon 10 20
(P D Evans) *in tch: rdn along 1/2-way: sn wknd* **50/1**
0400 **12** *2* **Crimson Flame (IRE)**[85] 5474 3-8-9 **52** ... EdwardCreighton 3 22
(A J Chamberlain) *dwlt: a in rr* **33/1**
1m 43.28s (-1.32) **Going Correction** -0.10s/f (Stan)
WFA 3 from 4yo+ 1lb 12 Ran SP% **117.9**
Speed ratings (Par 101):102,101,98,97,96 95,93,91,87,85 84,82
CSF £10.24 CT £306.71 TOTE £3.40: £1.70, £1.90, £8.00; EX 14.20 Trifecta £199.20 Part won. Pool £280.60 - 0.10 winning units. Place 6 £75.82, Place 5 £33.55.
Owner Saeed Manana **Bred** Darley **Trained** Newmarket, Suffolk

FOCUS
A modest, but pretty competitive, handicap run at just an ordinary pace but the form has been rated positively around the first two.
Crimson Flame(IRE) Official explanation: jockey said gelding would not face the kickback
T/Plt: £65.40 to a £1 stake. Pool: £37,616.25. 419.60 winning tickets. T/Qpdt: £11.50 to a £1 stake. Pool: £2,729.90. 175.60 winning tickets. JR

6807 WOLVERHAMPTON (A.W) (L-H)

Thursday, December 14

OFFICIAL GOING: Standard
Wind: Strong behind Weather: Cloudy

6820 PONTIN'S HOLIDAYS APPRENTICE H'CAP 7f 32y(P)
3:50 (3:50) (Class 6) (0-65,65) 3-Y-O+ £3,238 (£963; £481; £240) Stalls High

Form RPR
3035 **1** **Sovereignty (JPN)**[6] 6747 4-9-3 **63** ... JamesMillman 8 71
(D K Ivory) *mid-div: hdwy over 4f out: led wl over 1f out: edgd lft: rdn out* **6/1**[3]
1002 **2** *1* **Snow Bunting**[36] 6404 8-8-12 **58** ... KevinGhunowa 7 63
(Jedd O'Keeffe) *s.i.s: hld up: racd keenly: hdwy over 2f out: rdn over 1f out: r.o* **14/1**
0102 **3** *1 ¼* **Black Sea Pearl**[19] 6608 3-8-10 **61** ... WilliamBuick[(5)] 4 66+
(P W D'Arcy) *prom: hmpd and lost pl 6f out: hdwy over 1f out: r.o* **11/2**[2]
5050 **4** *shd* **Mister Elegant**[16] 6642 4-8-7 **58** ... JosephWalsh[(5)] 1 60+
(J L Spearing) *chsd ldrs: nt clr run over 1f out: swtchd lft: r.o* **12/1**
0050 **5** *nk* **Scroll**[10] 6698 3-8-11 **62** ... (v) JPFeatherstone[(5)] 11 63
(P Howling) *s.i.s: hld up: hdwy over 1f out: r.o* **33/1**
0403 **6** *hd* **Dasheena**[23] 6556 3-8-13 **59** ... PatrickHills 3 60
(A J McCabe) *mid-div: hdwy over 2f out: rdn over 1f out: styd on same pce ins fnl f* **6/1**[3]
0436 **7** *3 ½* **Lii Najma**[19] 6595 3-8-13 **64** ... WilliamCarson[(5)] 9 55
(C E Brittain) *chsd ldrs: rdn over 1f out: wknd ins fnl f* **13/2**
6650 **8** *1 ½* **Up Tempo (IRE)**[21] 6568 8-9-5 **65** ... (b) JamieJones 2 53
(C R Dore) *led: hdd over 4f out: rdn and ev ch 2f out: wknd fnl f* **8/1**
2060 **9** *shd* **Franksalot (IRE)**[103] 5031 6-8-13 **62** ... NeilBrown[(3)] 6 49
(I W McInnes) *mid-div: effrt over 1f out: wknd fnl f* **25/1**
3544 **10** *½* **Flint River**[10] 6696 8-9-0 **60** ... RussellKennemore 12 46
(H Morrison) *chsd ldrs: rdn and ev ch 2f out: edgd lft over 1f out: wknd fnl f* **9/2**[1]
3600 **11** *2 ½* **Desert Lover (IRE)**[13] 6664 4-8-11 **60** ... AlanRutter[(3)] 5 40
(R J Price) *chsd ldrs: led over 4f out: rdn and hdd wl over 1f out: wkng whn hmpd ins fnl f* **14/1**
0 **12** *26* **Speckled Hen (IRE)**[15] 6652 3-9-0 **60** ... (b) AshleyHamblett 10 —
(D Haydn Jones) *hld up: rdn 1/2-way: sn wknd* **33/1**
1m 32.11s (1.71) **Going Correction** +0.20s/f (Slow) 12 Ran SP% **117.3**
Speed ratings (Par 101):98,96,95,95,94 94,90,89,88,88 85,55
CSF £84.20 CT £486.95 TOTE £9.10: £1.80, £3.10, £1.70; EX 69.50.
Owner Radlett Racing **Bred** Darley Stud Management, L L C **Trained** Radlett, Herts
■ Stewards' Enquiry : Jamie Jones one-day ban: careless riding (Dec 26)

FOCUS
A moderate but competitive handicap and the form looks solid enough rated around the first four.
Black Sea Pearl Official explanation: jockey said filly was denied a clear run
Mister Elegant Official explanation: jockey said colt was denied a clear run

6821 EBF PONTIN'S HOLIDAYS MAIDEN FILLIES' STKS 5f 216y(P)
4:20 (4:22) (Class 5) 2-Y-O £4,210 (£1,252; £625; £312) Stalls Low

Form RPR
1 **Pixie Ring** 2-9-0 ... JamieMackay 2 69+
(Sir Mark Prescott) *chsd ldrs: led over 3f out: rdn and hdd over 2f out: nt clr run and swtchd rt 1f out: r.o to ld wl ins fnl f* **5/1**[3]
5033 **2** *1* **Darling Belinda**[19] 6592 2-9-0 63 ... FergusSweeney 7 66
(D K Ivory) *chsd ldrs: led over 2f out: rdn and hung lft fr over 1f out: hdd wl ins fnl f* **15/8**[1]
3 *3* **Fiona Fox** 2-8-7 ... RussellKennemore[(7)] 4 57
(R Hollinshead) *s.i.s: sn chsng ldrs: rdn and hung lft over 1f out: styd on same pce* **16/1**
4 *2* **Dramatic Touch** 2-9-0 ... SteveDrowne 6 51
(G Wragg) *s.i.s: hld up: hdwy over 1f out: nt rch ldrs* **4/1**[2]
5 *nk* **Bogside Katie**[114] 4683 2-9-0 ... JoeFanning 10 50
(G M Moore) *chsd ldrs: edgd lft over 2f out: sn rdn: styd on same pce* **25/1**
6 *1 ¼* **Meeting Of Minds** 2-8-7 ... BRoper[(7)] 9 46
(W Jarvis) *s.i.s: hld up: hdwy over 1f out: wknd ins fnl f* **14/1**
7 *nk* **Minnie Mill** 2-9-0 ... RobbieFitzpatrick 8 45
(B P J Baugh) *sn outpcd: hdwy over 1f out: sn edgd lft: wknd ins fnl f* **25/1**
8 *2 ½* **Vivi Belle** 2-9-0 ... HayleyTurner 5 38
(M L W Bell) *sn outpcd* **11/2**
0 **9** *shd* **Veils Of Salome**[61] 5959 2-8-9 ... NataliaGemelova[(5)] 3 38
(A J McCabe) *s.i.s: hdwy over 4f out: nt clr run over 2f out: sn wknd* **20/1**
3U30 **10** *21* **Go On Jessica (IRE)**[177] 2731 2-8-9 56 ... (b[1]) AshleyHamblett[(5)] 1 —
(A G Juckes) *sn led: hdd over 3f out: wkng whn hmpd over 2f out* **16/1**
1m 18.2s (2.39) **Going Correction** +0.20s/f (Slow) 10 Ran SP% **117.7**
Speed ratings (Par 93):92,90,86,84,83 81,81,78,78,50
CSF £14.51 TOTE £8.10: £3.00, £1.02, £9.30; EX 21.00.
Owner Nicholas Jones **Bred** Coln Valley Stud **Trained** Newmarket, Suffolk

FOCUS
The bare form of this fillies' maiden is just modest but sound rated through the runner-up and fifth, but the winning time was 1.38 seconds quicker than the following novice event and it should produce some winners.

NOTEBOOK
Pixie Ring ◆ is a half-sister to quite useful Airex, who was placed over middle-distances in smart company in France, dual-mile winner Scaramantich, and six-furlong scorer Dr Dignity. She was easy to back on course, but proved good enough to make a winning debut, staying on strongly in the straight to take full advantage when the favourite began to hang. The bare form is clearly modest, but she is open to loads of improvement and is almost sure to do better over a little further. (op 3-1)
Darling Belinda, rated just 63, was always going to prove vulnerable if any of the newcomers were up to much and she found the Prescott filly too good. She did not help her chance by hanging left under pressure and is clearly no that easy to win with. (op 2-1 tchd 9-4)
Fiona Fox, a half-sister to among others King Of Wolves, a multiple six to ten-furlong winner in Italy, out of a six-furlong scorer, was nibbled at in the market and showed plenty of ability on her racecourse debut. She looked very dangerous turning out of the back straight, but was probably found out by her inexperience when asked for maximum effort in the straight. She should be sharper next time and looks well up to finding a similar event. (op 25-1)
Dramatic Touch, out of a winning miler, was not without support in the market but she looked in need of the experience. She should show improvement next time. (op 9-2)
Bogside Katie did not run badly but is likely to be better off in low-grade handicaps. (op 33-1)
Meeting Of Minds, a 14,000gns first foal of a nine-furlong winner, is almost sure to improve on this. (op 12-1)
Vivi Belle, a 35,000gns first foal of a fair five-furlong juvenile winner, was supported in the market but showed little. Surely she is better than this. (op 15-2)
Go On Jessica(IRE) Official explanation: trainer said filly was showing signs of possibly coming into season post race

6822 WBXTRIPLECROWN.COM NOVICE STKS 5f 216y(P)
4:50 (4:50) (Class 5) 2-Y-O £4,533 (£1,348; £674; £336) Stalls Low

Form RPR
1402 **1** **Beauchamp Viceroy**[10] 6699 2-9-4 78 ... EddieAhern 1 83+
(G A Butler) *led early: trckd ldr: rdn to ld 1f out: r.o* **8/13**[1]
0005 **2** *¾* **Nina Blini**[94] 5234 2-9-2 91 ... SteveDrowne 4 79
(B J Meehan) *s.i.s: sn chsng ldrs: rdn and ev ch 1f out: styd on* **9/4**[2]
3 **3** *½* **Hollywood George**[12] 6669 2-9-0 ... TonyCulhane 3 75
(W J Haggas) *trckd ldrs: rdn and hung lft over 1f out: styd on* **15/2**[3]
0545 **4** *2 ½* **Slipasearcher (IRE)**[10] 6699 2-8-11 68 ... (b) JimCrowley 2 65
(P D Evans) *sn led: rdn and hdd 1f out: no ex* **20/1**
1m 19.58s (3.77) **Going Correction** +0.20s/f (Slow) 4 Ran SP% **109.2**
Speed ratings (Par 96):82,81,80,77
CSF £2.28 TOTE £1.30; EX 2.10.
Owner Erik Penser **Bred** E Penser **Trained** Blewbury, Oxon

FOCUS
Just an ordinary novice event - Nina Blini was clearly well below her official mark of 91 - and a muddling pace resulted in a time 1.38 seconds slower than the preceding fillies' maiden. The form is limited by the fourth but the winner scored quite nicely.

NOTEBOOK
Beauchamp Viceroy, perhaps not given the best of rides when a beaten favourite over seven furlongs at Lingfield on his previous start, coped just fine with the return to sprinting and did enough to gain the second win of his career. The runner-up clearly ran well below her official mark of 91, so the bare form is useful at best and it would be unwise to get carried away. He could bid for a quick follow up back at Wolverhampton. (op 8-11 after 10-11 in a place and 4-5 in a place)
Nina Blini was third in the Queen Mary earlier in the season, but she has not progressed since and was well below her official mark of 91 on her return from a three-month break/debut on Polytrack. (op 2-1 tchd 5-2)
Hollywood George ◆ improved significantly on the form he showed when third in a weak maiden at Kempton on his debut and emerges with plenty of credit. He should have no trouble in winning when returned to maiden company. (op 7-1 tchd 8-1)
Slipasearcher(IRE) enjoyed the run of the race but was still put in her place when it mattered. (tchd 16-1)

6823 WBX.COM WORLD BET EXCHANGE H'CAP 5f 20y(P)
5:20 (5:20) (Class 5) (0-75,74) 3-Y-O+ £4,533 (£1,348; £674; £336) Stalls Low

Form RPR
0365 **1** **Sparkwell**[7] 6739 4-8-8 **62** ... DeanMcKeown 9 69
(D Shaw) *a.p: shkn up to ld wl ins fnl f: r.o* **4/1**[3]
4053 **2** *1 ¼* **City For Conquest (IRE)**[9] 6709 3-8-12 **66** ... (b) FrancisNorton 10 68
(T J Pitt) *chsd ldrs: outpcd 1/2-way: rallied and hung lft ins fnl f: r.o* **13/2**
3500 **3** *nk* **Lucayos**[7] 6740 3-9-1 **72** ... (b) RichardKingscote[(3)] 1 73
(Mrs H Sweeting) *s.i.s: outpcd: swtchd rt over 1f out: r.o ins fnl f: nt rch ldrs* **22/1**
0102 **4** *¾* **Fizzlephut (IRE)**[7] 6740 4-9-2 **70** ... (p) PaulFitzsimons 7 68
(Miss J R Tooth) *trckd ldrs: racd keenly: rdn over 1f out: styd on same pce ins fnl f* **9/4**[1]
0005 **5** *shd* **Maktavish**[7] 6740 7-8-12 **66** ... (b) PatCosgrave 6 64
(R Brotherton) *led: clr 2f out: hdd and unable qckn wl ins fnl f* **14/1**
0000 **6** *¾* **General Feeling (IRE)**[7] 6739 5-8-6 **65** ... AndrewElliott[(5)] 8 60
(M Mullineaux) *s.i.s: outpcd: r.o ins fnl f: nvr nrr* **33/1**
0320 **7** *¾* **Lady Bahia (IRE)**[7] 6740 5-9-0 **68** ... (b) RobbieFitzpatrick 2 61
(Peter Grayson) *outpcd: hdwy over 1f out: styd on same pce ins fnl f* **11/1**
001 **8** *1* **No Time (IRE)**[9] 6709 6-9-6 **74** 7ex ... SteveDrowne 4 63
(A J McCabe) *hld up: rdn over 1f out: n.d* **3/1**[2]
0660 **9** *1 ½* **Hornpipe**[101] 5058 4-9-2 **70** ... MickyFenton 5 54
(M S Saunders) *chsd ldr: rdn 1/2-way: wknd fnl f* **20/1**
63.50 secs (0.68) **Going Correction** +0.20s/f (Slow) 9 Ran SP% **116.2**
Speed ratings (Par 103):102,100,99,98,98 96,95,94,91
CSF £29.40 CT £511.24 TOTE £5.60: £2.10, £1.70, £4.70; EX 32.30.
Owner The Circle Bloodstock I Limited **Bred** Juddmonte Farms **Trained** Danethorpe, Notts

FOCUS
Just a modest sprint surprisingly dominated by the high draws and ordinary form rated through the fifth.

6824 PONTINS.COM NURSERY 1m 1f 103y(P)
5:50 (5:50) (Class 4) (0-85,78) 2-Y-O £6,477 (£1,927; £963; £481) Stalls Low

Form RPR
4001 **1** **Love Dubai (USA)**[27] 6506 2-9-1 **72** ... JoeFanning 8 80
(M Johnston) *sn pushed along in rr: hdwy 1/2-way: chsd ldr over 2f out: sn rdn: led 1f out: styd on* **3/1**[1]
01 **2** *1* **Troialini**[33] 6449 2-9-3 **77** ... JerryO'Dwyer[(3)] 1 83
(S W Hall) *trckd ldrs: outpcd 1/2-way: hdwy over 2f out: sn rdn: edgd lft ins fnl f: styd on* **7/2**[2]
6525 **3** *4* **Beech Games**[20] 6581 2-9-4 **75** ... (b[1]) FrancisNorton 3 74
(E J O'Neill) *sn rdn to ld: hdd 1f out: wknd ins fnl f* **8/1**
13 **4** *shd* **Aypeeyes (IRE)**[27] 6506 2-9-0 **71** ... LPKeniry 6 69
(S Kirk) *prom: rdn over 3f out: hung lft over 1f out: styd on same pce ins fnl f* **9/2**[3]
0621 **5** *12* **Beau Sancy**[17] 6625 2-8-7 **64** ... SteveDrowne 5 40
(R A Harris) *mid-div: rdn 1/2-way: wknd over 2f out* **20/1**

4502 **6** *1 3/4* **Cry Presto (USA)**^{16} [6634] 2-9-6 77....................(t) EddieAhern 2 49
(R Hannon) *hld up and bhd: effrt over 2f out: sn wknd* **5/1**
6651 **7** *5* **Stoneacre Gareth (IRE)**^{16} [6645] 2-9-4 75.............. RobbieFitzpatrick 7 38
(Peter Grayson) *hld up: rdn and wknd over 2f out* **20/1**
4651 **8** *3* **New Beginning (IRE)**^{28} [6498] 2-9-7 78.................. DaneO'Neill 4 35
(Mrs S Lamyman) *trckd ldr: racd keenly: rdn and wknd over 2f out* **7/1**
2m 2.99s (0.37) **Going Correction** +0.20s/f (Slow) **8** Ran SP% **115.2**
Speed ratings (Par 98):106,105,101,101,90 89,84,82
CSF £13.77 CT £72.77 TOTE £3.30: £1.50, £1.10, £3.40; EX 17.40.
Owner M Doyle **Bred** Foxfield **Trained** Middleham Moor, N Yorks

FOCUS
They went a good pace - the winning time was very decent - and this is very solid nursery form.

NOTEBOOK
Love Dubai(USA) ◆, off the mark in a similar event when stepped up to an extended mile for the first time round here on his previous start, benefited from this even longer trip and was able to defy a 5lb higher mark. The strong pace brought his stamina into play having come under some pressure to stay in touch, and he gives the impression he has plenty more to offer. A more galloping track is likely to suit better and he could develop into a useful handicapper on turf next season. (op 5-2)
Troialini ◆ would have found this much tougher than the course and distance maiden he won on his previous start, but he ran a fine race behind the progressive winner. He was well ahead of the rest and is clearly improving. (op 11-2)
Beech Games, with blinkers fitted for the first time and stepped up to his furthest trip to date on his return to handicap company, ran a solid enough race behind two progressive sorts.
Aypeeyes(IRE) would have appreciated the strong pace and he can have few excuses. (tchd 5-1)
Beau Sancy found this much harder than the course and distance nursery he won on his previous start and could not defy a 4lb higher mark.
Cry Presto(USA), upped in trip, could not confirm the promise of his recent Lingfield second. (op 11-2 tchd 9-2)

6825 GO PONTIN'S H'CAP — 1m 4f 50y(P)
6:20 (6:20) (Class 5) (0-75,73) 3-Y-0 — **£4,210** (£1,252; £625; £312) **Stalls** Low

Form RPR
0461 **1** **Pagano (IRE)**^{9} [6712] 3-8-13 **68** 5ex.................... AdamKirby 3 81
(W R Swinburn) *chsd ldr: led over 3f out: rdn and hung lft ins fnl f: styd on* **5/4**^{1}
1 **2** *2 1/2* **Night Cruise (IRE)**^{20} [6578] 3-9-4 **73**.................... JimCrowley 4 82
(J A Osborne) *a.p: chsd wnr over 2f out: rdn and hung lft over 1f out: styd on same pce* **7/2**^{2}
046 **3** *5* **Emily's Place (IRE)**^{34} [6430] 3-8-9 **64**..............(p) PatCosgrave 6 65
(J Pearce) *hld up: hdwy over 2f out: sn rdn and no imp* **8/1**
0624 **4** *3* **Always Baileys (IRE)**^{65} [5887] 3-8-13 **68**.............. JoeFanning 5 64
(T Wall) *chsd ldrs over 9f* **14/1**
0005 **5** *4* **Three Thieves (UAE)**^{16} [6647] 3-8-10 **65**.............. MickyFenton 1 55
(M S Saunders) *led over 8f: wknd 2f out* **13/2**^{3}
4000 **P** **King's Ransom**^{16} [6647] 3-8-12 **67**....................(b) EddieAhern 2 —
(W R Muir) *s.i.s and wnt rt s: hld up: rdn 1/2-way: sn wknd: p.u over 3f out* **7/1**
2m 42.09s (-0.33) **Going Correction** +0.20s/f (Slow) **6** Ran SP% **110.3**
Speed ratings (Par 102):109,107,104,102,99 —
CSF £5.51 TOTE £2.90: £1.10, £2.60; EX 3.80 Place 6 £41.68, Place 5 £10.67.
Owner The Chorus Line **Bred** Albert Conneally **Trained** Aldbury, Herts

FOCUS
Just the five runners, but the winning time was smart for the grade and this looks fair but solid form.
King's Ransom Official explanation: jockey said gelding had a breathing problem
T/Plt: £68.10 to a £1 stake. Pool: £56,596.05. 606.10 winning tickets. T/Qpdt: £28.90 to a £1 stake. Pool: £4,594.90. 117.50 winning tickets. CR

6774 KEMPTON (A.W) (R-H)
Friday, December 15

OFFICIAL GOING: Standard
Wind: moderate, half-behind Weather: overcast

6826 FOLLOW YOUR CONFERENCE WITH TWILIGHT RACING MAIDEN STKS — 7f (P)
3:45 (3:51) (Class 5) 2-Y-0 — **£3,238** (£963; £481; £240) **Stalls** High

Form RPR
4504 **1** **Messiah Garvey**^{64} [5914] 2-9-3 72.................... EdwardCreighton 11 74+
(M R Channon) *mde all: kicked clr 2f out: in n.d after: pushed out* **7/2**^{2}
2 **2** *2 1/2* **Corlough Mountain**^{17} [6631] 2-9-3 .... GeorgeBaker 2 67
(N A Callaghan) *lw: racd wd in midfield and hanging: rdn 3f out: prog to chse wnr jst over 1f out: styd on but no ch* **4/5**^{1}
3 *1* **Not Too Taxing** 2-9-0 .... StephaneBreux$^{(3)}$ 12 64
(R Hannon) *unf: prom: rdn to chse wnr over 2f out: no imp: one pce and lost 2nd jst over 1f out* **20/1**
4 *1 3/4* **Coastal Command** 2-9-3 .... SteveDrowne 5 60+
(R Charlton) *unf: scope: bit bkwd: reluctant to enter stalls: dwlt: in tch in rr: prog whn squeezed out 2f out: styd on fnl f* **9/1**
5 *2 1/2* **Krakatau (FR)** 2-9-3 .... SamHitchcott 8 53
(D J Wintle) *w'like: pressed ldrs: rdn 3f out: fdd fr over 1f out* **40/1**
6 *2* **Spirit Of Adjisa (IRE)** 2-9-3 .... DaneO'Neill 6 48
(Pat Eddery) *lw: s.v.s: in tch in rr after 2f: rdn 3f out: wl outpcd 2f out: kpt on fnl f* **13/2**^{3}
7 *3/4* **Orchestrator (IRE)** 2-9-3 .... RobertHavlin 10 46
(T G Mills) *w'like: bit bkwd: scope: wl in tch: gng easily over 2f out: wknd rapidly on inner over 1f out* **10/1**
06 **8** *2* **Childish Thoughts**^{5} [6778] 2-8-9 .... JamesDoyle$^{(3)}$ 3 36
(Mrs Norma Pook) *prom: rdn over 2f out: wknd rapidly over 1f out* **40/1**
9 *2 1/2* **Dickie Deano** 2-8-10 .... BarrySavage$^{(7)}$ 9 35
(J M Bradley) *leggy: s.i.s: a wl in rr: lost tch over 2f out* **33/1**
10 *3/4* **Otaki (IRE)** 2-8-12 .... J-PGuillambert 7 28
(Sir Mark Prescott) *w'like: bit bkwd: reluctant to enter stalls: chsd wnr to over 2f out: wknd rapidly wl over 1f out* **16/1**
11 *4* **Tobougg Welcome (IRE)** 2-9-3 .... FrancisNorton 13 22
(S C Williams) *leggy: dwlt: a in rr: wknd and bhd over 2f out* **20/1**
12 *1/2* **Eau Sauvage** 2-8-12 .... PaulDoe 4 16
(J Akehurst) *leggy: a in last trio: wl bhd fnl 2f* **40/1**
1m 28.56s (1.76) **Going Correction** +0.175s/f (Slow) **12** Ran SP% **135.9**
Speed ratings (Par 96):96,93,92,90,87 84,84,81,78,78 73,72
CSF £7.25 TOTE £6.20: £1.60, £1.10, £4.30; EX 11.40.
Owner N Martin **Bred** Hascombe And Valiant Studs **Trained** West Ilsley, Berks

FOCUS
A modest maiden and the winner is possibly the best guide to the level.

NOTEBOOK
Messiah Garvey, the most experienced of these, was debuting on the All-Weather and made the most of his high draw, showing speed from the off. Given an uncontested lead, he kicked clear approaching the final furlong and won fairly comfortably. He did not have to run any better than to his official mark to win here, though. (op 4-1)
Corlough Mountain had an extra furlong to help this time but he had a low draw to overcome and ended up having to race on the outside of the bunch. He took a while to understand what was required of him in the straight, but stayed on quite well late in the day, and a stronger pace is likely to suit him better in future. (op 5-4 after 6-4 in places tchd 11-8 in places)
Not Too Taxing, well drawn, was never too far off the steady pace. His dam was a prolific winner between a mile and 12 furlongs, and he should do better with age, too.
Coastal Command, a half-brother to a seven-furlong winner in Daytime, a couple of middle-distance winners in Spinning Top and Virtue, and to useful jumper Locksmith, should get ten furlongs plus himself next year. (op 7-1)
Krakatau(FR) hails from a stable not known for sending out juvenile winners, but he was another who was never too far off the pace in a race not run at a strong gallop.
Spirit Of Adjisa(IRE), a 40,000euros half-brother to Princess Nala, a dual winner over middle distances, lost his race with a very slow start, but to his credit he did stay on in the latter stages. The experience should not be lost on him though, so he should know a bit more next time. (op 9-2)
Orchestrator(IRE), a half-brother to four winners over seven to nine furlongs, notably useful juvenile Mana-Mou Bay, was stuck on the rail behind horses and looked to be going well as they swung into the straight, but he found very little under pressure. (op 11-1 tchd 12-1)
Otaki(IRE), up with the pace to two and a half furlongs out, is out of a mare who stayed two miles and is a half-sister to numerous winners, including Oblique, a multiple winner over nine to 12 furlongs, and to One Off, a multiple 11 to 15-furlong winner. She is likely to do much better next year once handicapped. (op 14-1)
Tobougg Welcome(IRE) is a close-coupled type.

6827 COME RACING BY TRAIN FROM WATERLOO H'CAP — 6f (P)
4:20 (4:21) (Class 6) (0-60,62) 3-Y-0+ — **£2,388** (£705; £352) **Stalls** High

Form RPR
1114 **1** **Siraj**^{9} [6728] 7-9-2 **60**....................(v) BrettDoyle 4 68
(J Ryan) *off the pce in midfield: prog over 2f out: rdn and clsd to ld jst ins fnl f: sn jnd: hld on wl* **11/4**^{1}
3121 **2** *1/2* **Imperium**^{17} [6632] 5-9-2 **60**....................(p) DaneO'Neill 10 66
(Jean-Rene Auvray) *chsd ldrs: rdn over 2f out: prog wl over 1f out: jnd wnr ins fnl f: nt qckn nr fin* **11/4**^{1}
5410 **3** *shd* **State Dilemma (IRE)**^{21} [6577] 5-9-1 **59**....................(v) FrancisNorton 6 65
(D Shaw) *b: wl off the pce in rr: drvn and hanging over 2f out: gd prog on outer over 1f out: clsd on ldrs last 100yds: a hld* **11/1**
1402 **4** *shd* **Muscari**^{11} [6694] 4-8-12 **59**.................... JamesDoyle$^{(3)}$ 8 65
(S Woodman) *off the pce in midfield: rdn over 2f out: clsd fr wl over 1f out: pressed ldrs last 100yds: kpt on* **10/1**
0600 **5** *1 1/2* **Miswadah (IRE)**^{10} [6721] 3-8-9 **58**....................(v^{1}) JamieJones$^{(5)}$ 5 59
(Kevin F O'Donnell, Ire) *sn outpcd and pushed along in last pair: prog u.p 2f out: styd on: nvr able to chal* **50/1**
1650 **6** *1 3/4* **Caustic Wit (IRE)**^{60} [6020] 8-8-9 **60**.................... BenjaminWishart$^{(7)}$ 1 56
(M S Saunders) *wl off the pce in rr and racd wd: rdn over 2f out: plugged on: no ch* **14/1**
6000 **7** *hd* **Semenovskii**^{13} [6672] 6-8-8 **59**....................(bt^{1}) JamesMillman$^{(7)}$ 12 54
(Mrs N Smith) *led: clr over 3f out: wknd and hdd jst ins fnl f* **9/1**^{3}
0004 **8** *nk* **Count Cougar (USA)**^{17} [6642] 6-9-0 **58**.................... AdrianTNicholls 3 52
(S P Griffiths) *chsd ldr: rdn 1/2-way: wknd over 1f out* **9/1**^{3}
0000 **9** *6* **Majestical (IRE)**^{174} [2858] 4-9-2 **60**....................(p) TonyCulhane 11 36
(J M Bradley) *dwlt: a in rr and off the pce: wknd over 1f out* **25/1**
0501 **10** *1/2* **George The Second**^{27} [6510] 3-9-1 **59**.................... GeorgeBaker 9 34
(Mrs H Sweeting) *lw: prom tl wknd rapidly on inner over 2f out* **9/2**^{2}
6-40 **11** *7* **Opal Warrior**^{13} [6672] 3-9-1 **59**.................... SteveDrowne 7 13
(Jane Southcombe) *prom to 1/2-way: wknd rapidly over 2f out* **33/1**
1m 13.56s (-0.14) **Going Correction** +0.175s/f (Slow) **11** Ran SP% **124.4**
Speed ratings (Par 101):107,106,106,106,104 101,101,101,93,92 83
CSF £10.27 CT £76.67 TOTE £3.50: £1.80, £1.40, £3.30; EX 13.70.
Owner T C Gilligan **Bred** Mrs S J Etches **Trained** Newmarket, Suffolk

FOCUS
Just a moderate sprint handicap, but it was run at a strong pace and the finish was dominated by in-form performers. It looks ordinary but solid for the grade.

6828 DIGIBET.COM MEDIAN AUCTION MAIDEN STKS — 1m 4f (P)
4:50 (4:52) (Class 6) 3-4-Y-0 — **£2,266** (£674; £337; £168) **Stalls** Low

Form RPR
0304 **1** **Alexian**^{18} [6621] 3-9-3 62.................... BrettDoyle 4 67
(D W P Arbuthnot) *hld up in last pair: prog 5f out: effrt to ld jst over 1f out: rdn clr* **3/1**^{2}
3340 **2** *2* **Monets Masterpiece (USA)**^{76} [4125] 3-9-3 80.............. GeorgeBaker 1 64
(G L Moore) *restless in stalls: hld up in last pair: effrt over 2f out: sn shkn up and nt qckn: kpt on to take 2nd last stride* **1/1**^{1}
0-3 **3** *shd* **Clear Vision**^{13} [6668] 3-8-12 .... JimCrowley 5 59
(Mrs A J Perrett) *lw: prom: trckd ldr 1/2-way: urged into ld over 2f out: fnd little in front: hdd jst over 1f out: lost 2nd last stride* **7/2**^{3}
4500 **4** *3* **Mighty Kitchener (USA)**^{173} [2895] 3-9-3 57.............. TonyCulhane 7 59
(P Howling) *chsd ldrs: rdn over 2f out: one pce and no imp after* **16/1**
6 **5** *1* **Musango**^{20} [6593] 3-9-3 .... DaneO'Neill 8 57
(B R Johnson) *rel ldr at slow pce: rdn and hdd over 2f out: fdd over 1f out* **14/1**
456 **6** *34* **Artist's Muse (USA)**^{173} [2895] 3-8-12 72.................... FrancisNorton 6 —
(M S Saunders) *chsd ldr to 1/2-way: wknd rapidly over 2f out: t.o* **8/1**
2m 44.05s (7.15) **Going Correction** +0.175s/f (Slow)
WFA 3 from 4yo 5lb **6** Ran SP% **120.9**
Speed ratings (Par 101):83,81,81,79,78 55
CSF £7.06 TOTE £4.90: £1.90, £1.40; EX 8.40.
Owner Miss Samantha Dare **Bred** B L Lay **Trained** Upper Lambourn, Berks

FOCUS
A modest maiden run at a pretty slow gallop that resulted in something of a sprint to the line. The form is far from solid, but makes sense rated through those immediately behind the first two.

6829 DIGIBET.CO.UK H'CAP — 1m (P)
5:20 (5:22) (Class 6) (0-52,56) 3-Y-0+ — **£2,388** (£705; £352) **Stalls** High

Form RPR
0002 **1** **Rowan Warning**^{5} [6779] 4-9-0 **52**.................... SteveDrowne 8 63
(J R Boyle) *lw: settled in midfield: pushed along over 2f out: prog to ld 1f out: sn clr* **5/4**^{1}
0040 **2** *3 1/2* **Grand Assault**^{21} [6587] 3-8-13 **52**....................(b^{1}) CatherineGannon 2 55
(P S McEntee) *t.k.h: pressed ldrs: led over 2f out to 1f out: sn outpcd by wnr* **12/1**

0055 **3** *hd* **Grand Palace (IRE)**[6] [6756] 3-8-13 **52**..........................(v) DaneO'Neill 14 54
(D Shaw) *t.k.h in midfield: pushed along and effrt over 2f out: kpt on to taken 3rd ins fnl f* **7/1**[3]

00U0 **4** *1/2* **Didnt Tell My Wife**[4] [6787] 7-8-8 **46** oh6......................(v) HayleyTurner 4 47
(P S McEntee) *dwlt: t.k.h: hld up in rr: pushed along over 2f out: styd on fr over 1f out: nt rch ldrs* **16/1**

5606 **5** *3/4* **Seldemosa**[106] [4974] 5-9-0 **52**.. TonyCulhane 7 51
(M S Saunders) *hld up in rr: effrt on outer over 2f out: rdn and kpt on fr over 1f out: n.d* **10/1**

0000 **6** *1* **Height Of Spirits**[18] [6617] 4-8-8 **46** oh1.........................(b) RobertHavlin 6 43
(T D McCarthy) *b: hld up in midfield: prog over 2f out: chsd ldr briefly over 1f out: sn btn* **8/1**

0060 **7** *1* **African Concerto (IRE)**[11] [6696] 3-8-9 **48**............................. LPKeniry 3 43
(S Kirk) *plld hrd in midfield early: effrt on outer over 2f out: sn rdn and no real prog* **11/2**[2]

0000 **8** *nk* **Love Academy**[2] [6803] 11-8-8 **46** oh6...................... EdwardCreighton 10 40
(Luke Comer, Ire) *squeezed out s: hld up in rr: sme prog over 2f out to chse ldrs over 1f out: no hdwy after* **50/1**

3005 **9** *7* **Secam (POL)**[5] [6779] 7-9-0 **52**...(b) DeanCorby 13 30
(Mrs P Townsley) *b: t.k.h: wl plcd on inner: effrt and cl up over 2f out: wknd rapidly over 1f out* **10/1**

000- **10** *nk* **Sharp Tune (USA)**[556] [2377] 4-8-4 **49**.......................... HaddenFrost(7) 9 26
(J D Frost) *chsd ldrs: rdn wl over 2f out: wknd wl over 1f out* **50/1**

0300 **11** *6* **Oasis Sun (IRE)**[180] [2678] 3-8-10 **49**................................... BrettDoyle 1 12
(J R Best) *dropped in fr wd draw and sn last: hanging and struggling over 2f out : bhd after* **12/1**

0000 **12** *10* **Young Valentino**[11] [6702] 4-8-8 **46** oh6..........................(e) JimCrowley 11 —
(A W Carroll) *t.k.h: pressed ldr: led 1/2-way to over 2f out: wknd rapidly* **33/1**

0000 **13** *3* **Ameliore (IRE)**[11] [6700] 3-8-4 **46** oh6.......................... JamesDoyle(3) 12 —
(S Woodman) *led to 1/2-way: wknd rapidly* **50/1**

1m 41.82s (1.02) **Going Correction** +0.175s/f (Slow)
WFA 3 from 4yo+ 1lb **13** Ran SP% **131.7**
Speed ratings (Par 101):101,97,97,96,96 95,94,93,86,86 80,70,67
CSF £21.05 CT £93.61 TOTE £2.40: £1.20, £4.70, £2.10; EX 29.60.
Owner Rowan Stud Partnership 2 **Bred** Rowan Farm Stud **Trained** Epsom, Surrey

FOCUS
A weak handicap no better than banded class, and very moderate form that is suspect overall.

6830 DIGIBET SPORTS BETTING H'CAP 7f (P)
5:50 (5:51) (Class 4) (0-85,85) 3-Y-0+ **£5,505** (£1,637; £818; £408) **Stalls** High

Form RPR

6412 **1** **Bomber Command (USA)**[13] [6671] 3-8-9 **85**................ PatrickHills(7) 8 98+
(J W Hills) *prom: trckd ldr 1/2-way: shkn up to ld over 1f out: edgd rt and kpt on* **2/1**[1]

0204 **2** *nk* **Wavertree Warrior (IRE)**[20] [6594] 4-8-13 **85**............. JamesDoyle(3) 10 93
(N P Littmoden) *lw: chsd ldrs: rdn over 2f out: styd on u.p fr over 1f out: lft 2nd nr fin* **6/1**[3]

3660 **3** *nk* **Finsbury**[21] [6580] 3-8-6 **75**.. HayleyTurner 6 86+
(Miss J Feilden) *hld up towards rr: prog on inner over 2f out: cl up whn nt clr run 1f out: styd on and lft 3rd nr fin* **16/1**

0304 **4** *1* **Tamagin (USA)**[12] [6692] 3-9-0 **83**...................................(p) JimCrowley 11 90+
(P D Evans) *led at decent pce: drvn and hdd over 1f out: keeping on but hld in 2nd whn hmpd and lost 2 pls nr fin* **14/1**

5016 **5** *3* **Littleton Telchar (USA)**[11] [6698] 6-8-2 **74**................. MarcHalford(3) 12 71
(S W Hall) *settled wl in rr: prog on inner over 2f out: chsd ldrs over 1f out: no imp fnl f* **16/1**

0550 **6** *3/4* **King Marju (IRE)**[50] [6192] 4-9-2 **85**....................................(v) PJSmullen 4 80
(K R Burke) *hld up in midfield: drvn and fnd nil 2f out: one pce after* **11/1**

0000 **7** *1 1/4* **Northern Desert (IRE)**[17] [6635] 7-8-6 **75**................................ PaulDoe 3 67
(P W Hiatt) *hld up wl in rr: taken to outer and effrt over 2f out: no real prog* **33/1**

004 **8** *nk* **Paraguay (USA)**[13] [6678] 3-8-11 **80**.......................... EdwardCreighton 1 71
(Miss V Haigh) *hld up in rr: plenty to do whn nt clr run over 2f out: no prog over 1f out* **25/1**

-001 **9** *shd* **Dig Deep (IRE)**[9] [6733] 4-8-9 **78** 6ex......................... GrahamGibbons 9 69
(W J Haggas) *lw: s.i.s: sn prom on inner: rdn and wknd wl over 1f out* **5/2**[2]

0200 **10** *1* **Grimes Faith**[12] [6690] 3-8-13 **82**.. DaneO'Neill 5 70
(R Hannon) *hld up in rr: rdn and no rspnse over 2f out* **20/1**

0025 **11** *1 1/4* **Cape Greko**[20] [6594] 4-9-2 **85**.......................................(v) FrancisNorton 2 70
(A M Balding) *lw: hld up in midfield: u.p and struggling wl over 2f out: sn btn* **9/1**

0000 **12** *5* **Grand Jour (IRE)**[76] [5666] 3-8-4 **80**.............................. SophieDoyle(7) 7 52
(Ms J S Doyle) *chsd ldr to 1/2-way: c wd bnd 3f out and wknd* **40/1**

1m 25.7s (-1.10) **Going Correction** +0.175s/f (Slow) **12** Ran SP% **126.9**
Speed ratings (Par 105):113,112,112,111,107 106,105,105,105,103 102,96
CSF £15.15 CT £164.40 TOTE £3.60: £1.40, £2.00, £5.30; EX 11.60.
Owner G Woodward **Bred** J B Feins **Trained** Upper Lambourn, Berks

FOCUS
A fairly competitive handicap run at just an ordinary gallop rated around those in the frame behind the winner. Patrick Hills susp.two days (Dec 26-27) careless riding, interf to Tamagin.

6831 DAY TIME, NIGHT TIME, GREAT TIME H'CAP 2m (P)
6:20 (6:23) (Class 5) (0-75,72) 3-Y-0+ **£4,533** (£1,348; £674; £336) **Stalls** High

Form RPR

2031 **1** **Salute (IRE)**[6] [6766] 7-10-3 **72** 6ex.................................... RobertHavlin 9 78+
(P G Murphy) *trckd ldr: shkn up to ld over 2f out: pressed 1f out: styd on wl and won gng away* **11/4**[1]

/0-0 **2** *1 1/2* **Critical Stage (IRE)**[8] [5201] 7-9-0 **62**......................... HaddenFrost(7) 10 66
(J D Frost) *hld up towards rr: weaved through fr over 2f out: chsd wnr 1f out and looked dangerous: sn one pce and btn* **33/1**

4056 **3** *1 1/4* **Haatmey**[79] [5628] 4-9-5 **60**.. LPKeniry 5 63
(B G Powell) *trckd ldng trio: rdn wl over 2f out: effrt to dispute 2nd over 1f out: one pce after* **9/1**

1356 **4** *nk* **Linden Lime**[20] [6602] 4-9-13 **68**.. FrancisNorton 3 70+
(Jamie Poulton) *plld hrd for most of r: hld up in rr: prog over 2f out: hanging over 1f out: nvr able to chal* **5/1**[3]

-036 **5** *1/2* **Almizan (IRE)**[27] [3116] 6-9-8 **63**....................................(b) GeorgeBaker 8 65
(G L Moore) *trckd ldrs: rdn 3f out: nt qckn 2f out: one pce after* **11/2**

5330 **6** *1 1/2* **Swainson (USA)**[23] [6565] 5-9-4 **59**.................................... DaneO'Neill 12 59
(P Mitchell) *led: rdn and hdd over 2f out: wknd ins fnl f* **11/1**

5343 **7** *1/2* **Turn 'n Burn**[20] [6602] 5-9-9 **69**................................ AshleyHamblett(5) 6 68
(C A Cyzer) *dwlt: hld up in last: prog 7f out to trck ldrs 4f out: shkn up and no rspnse over 2f out: sn btn* **4/1**[2]

4-00 **8** *3/4* **Teorban (POL)**[258] [832] 7-9-5 **60**................................ J-PGuillambert 1 58
(Mrs N S Evans) *awkward s: hld up in last pair: trapped on inner 3f out: no real prog fnl 2f* **40/1**

5600 **9** *1 3/4* **Madiba**[42] [5963] 7-9-5 **60**.. TonyCulhane 4 56
(P Howling) *nvr bttr than midfield: rdn over 3f out: struggling over 2f out* **9/1**

6020 **10** *3 1/2* **Coppington Melody (IRE)**[24] [6560] 3-8-3 **52**.............. HayleyTurner 11 44
(B W Duke) *chsd ldng pair: rdn over 3f out: wknd wl over 1f out* **25/1**

0220 **11** *14* **Serramanna**[13] [6673] 5-9-0 **58**.. JamesDoyle(3) 2 33
(Ms J S Doyle) *plld hrd: hld up: rdn 3f out: sn btn: eased fnl f* **8/1**

3m 35.62s (4.22) **Going Correction** +0.175s/f (Slow)
WFA 3 from 4yo+ 8lb **11** Ran SP% **127.4**
Speed ratings (Par 103):96,95,94,94,94 93,93,92,91,90 83
CSF £114.95 CT £771.18 TOTE £4.00: £1.50, £9.40, £3.50; EX 146.80 Place 6 £10.49, Place 5 £7.87 .
Owner The Golden Anorak Partnership **Bred** Ahmed M Foustok **Trained** East Garston, Berks

FOCUS
Another steadily-run contest that proved more of a test of speed than ought to be the case over two miles. The form looks pretty weak and the winner did not need to improve to score.
T/Plt: £7.30 to a £1 stake. Pool: £55,544.45. 5,536.75 winning tickets. T/Qpdt: £5.30 to a £1 stake. Pool: £4,284.50. 592.25 winning tickets. JN

6820 WOLVERHAMPTON (A.W) (L-H)
Friday, December 15

OFFICIAL GOING: Standard to slow
Wind: strong behind Weather: fine

6832 WBXTRIPLECROWN.COM MAIDEN STKS 1m 141y(P)
1:05 (1:06) (Class 5) 2-Y-0 **£3,886** (£1,156; £577; £288) **Stalls** Low

Form RPR

1 **Serengeti** 2-9-3 .... JoeFanning 2 80+
(M Johnston) *s.i.s and bmpd s: hdwy to ld over 6f out: rdn over 2f out: edgd rt fr over 1f out: drvn out* **5/1**[3]

03 **2** *nk* **Sister Maria (USA)**[14] [6658] 2-8-12 .... BrettDoyle 3 72
(E A L Dunlop) *hld up in tch: rdn and hung lft over 1f out: carried rt ins fnl f: r.o* **4/6**[1]

3 *2* **Red Petal** 2-8-12 .... JamieMackay 4 67
(Sir Mark Prescott) *s.i.s: sn led: hdd over 6f out: chsd wnr: rdn 3f out: hung lft over 1f out: nt qckn ins fnl f* **12/1**

0033 **4** *hd* **Fealeview Lady (USA)**[17] [6646] 2-8-12 68........................ RobertHavlin 1 67
(H Morrison) *hld up in tch: rdn over 2f out: nt qckn ins fnl f* **3/1**[2]

5 *34* **Truly Genuine (IRE)** 2-8-12 .... CatherineGannon 6 —
(K A Ryan) *rn green: led early: sn bhd: rdn over 3f out: sn lost tch: t.o* **50/1**

1m 55.47s (3.71) **Going Correction** +0.20s/f (Slow) **5** Ran SP% **111.3**
Speed ratings (Par 96):91,90,88,88,58
CSF £9.03 TOTE £5.50: £2.30, £1.10; EX 12.50.
Owner Jumeirah Racing **Bred** Darley **Trained** Middleham Moor, N Yorks

FOCUS
A modest maiden run at a dawdle for the first quarter of a mile and not easy to rate, although the winner should rate higher in time.

NOTEBOOK
Serengeti, a well-bred newcomer, seized the initiative after they went no pace for the first two furlongs. He showed the right attitude despite displaying signs of greeness in the home straight and will be better for the experience. (tchd 6-1)
Sister Maria(USA) again showed a tendency to lug in behind when trying to challenge. The winner did take her across the course in the closing stages but she was definitely second best. (op 4-5 after 5-6 and 10-11 in places tchd 8-13)
Red Petal is out of an unraced sister to top-class mile and ten-furlong winner Red Bloom. Easy to back, she showed signs of inexperience and should come on for the outing. (op 8-1)
Fealeview Lady(USA) did nothing wrong but proved vulnerable to some less-exposed sorts. (tchd 7-2)

6833 GO PONTIN'S (S) STKS 5f 216y(P)
1:40 (1:40) (Class 6) 3-Y-0+ **£2,388** (£705; £352) **Stalls** Low

Form RPR

5300 **1** **The London Gang**[10] [6717] 3-9-5 55.......................................(v) NCallan 2 63+
(P D Evans) *sn mid-div: hdwy on ins whn nt clr run briefly 2f out: rdn to ld 1f out: wandered ins fnl f: r.o* **16/1**

0005 **2** *1* **Mustammer**[7] [6755] 3-8-12 48... AdamKirby 13 53
(D Shaw) *hld up and bhd: hdwy on ins over 1f out: hrd rdn and rn ins fnl f* **16/1**

0500 **3** *2* **Phinerine**[8] [6739] 3-9-0 62..............................(b) MichaelJStainton(5) 12 54
(R A Harris) *hld up and bhd: rdn and hdwy on outside whn hung lft over 1f out: kpt on towards fin* **33/1**

-062 **4** *shd* **Nebdi (IRE)**[3] [6796] 5-8-12 50..(p) DavidAllan 8 47
(E J Alston) *chsd ldr: rdn 3f out: led briefly jst over 1f out: no ex ins fnl f* **7/2**[2]

0103 **5** *hd* **Came Back (IRE)**[40] [6348] 3-9-5 62..................................... EddieAhern 4 53
(J A Osborne) *sn prom: rdn over 1f out: one pce* **3/1**[1]

3500 **6** *2 1/2* **Memphis Man**[40] [6348] 3-9-0 63..................................... RoryMoore(5) 3 46
(D G Bridgwater) *s.i.s: hld up and bhd: swtchd rt and hdwy over 1f out: nvr nr to chal* **12/1**

6000 **7** *1 1/4* **Sounds Simla (IRE)**[10] [6717] 3-8-11 48............(b) RichardKingscote(3) 6 37
(R A Harris) *led: rdn over 2f out: hdd jst over 1f out: sn edgd rt: wknd ins fnl f* **50/1**

6020 **8** *1/2* **Surely Truly (IRE)**[13] [6672] 3-8-7 62.........................(p) FergusSweeney 1 28
(A E Jones) *chsd ldrs: rdn over 2f out: wknd ins fnl f* **11/1**

3600 **9** *1 3/4* **Sanders Boy**[11] [6704] 3-8-12 45....................................... PaulMulrennan 5 28
(J R Norton) *sn bhd: rdn and sme hdwy over 2f out: no imp whn hmpd over 1f out* **50/1**

2006 **10** *shd* **Mind Alert**[10] [6713] 5-9-2 52.....................................(v) PatrickMathers(3) 10 35
(D Shaw) *mid-div: bhd fnl 2f* **12/1**

0300 **11** *1 1/4* **Highland Cascade**[6] [6770] 4-8-7 68.................................. MickyFenton 11 19
(J M P Eustace) *chsd ldrs: rdn over 2f out: hung lft fr over 1f out: sn btn* **4/1**[3]

5000 **12** *2 1/2* **Kings Heir (IRE)**[17] [6647] 3-8-12 67.........................(b) RobbieFitzpatrick 7 17
(Peter Grayson) *chsd ldrs: rdn over 3f out: sn lost pl* **14/1**

0000 **13** *23* **Banjo Bay (IRE)**[95] [5232] 8-9-2 62................................(t) JerryO'Dwyer(3) 9 —
(Miss Gay Kelleway) *a bhd: eased whn no ch wl over 1f out* **14/1**

1m 16.75s (0.94) **Going Correction** +0.20s/f (Slow) **13** Ran SP% **122.9**
Speed ratings (Par 101):101,99,97,96,96 93,91,90,88,88 86,83,52
CSF £253.84 TOTE £19.70: £5.60, £6.20, £9.10; EX 233.00 TRIFECTA Not won..There was no bid for the winner.

Owner D Healy **Bred** Lostford Manor Stud **Trained** Pandy, Abergavenny

FOCUS

A typically trappy seller with doubts hanging over the majority of the field but the form appears sound enough rated around the first two.

Sounds Simla(IRE) Official explanation: jockey said filly hung right-handed on bend

Sanders Boy Official explanation: jockey said gelding suffered interference in running

Mind Alert Official explanation: jockey said gelding was unsuited by the standard to slow going

6834 WBX.COM WORLD BET EXCHANGE NURSERY — 5f 216y(P)

2:15 (2:15) (Class 4) (0-95,85) 2-Y-O — **£4,533** (£1,348; £674; £336) **Stalls** Low

Form				RPR
1044	1		**Love In May (IRE)**[148] 3678 2-9-4 **75** ... NCallan 4 (J S Moore) *chsd ldr over 4f out: rdn to ld 1f out: r.o* **33/1**	77
4021	2	1 ½	**Beauchamp Viceroy**[1] 6822 2-10-0 **85** 7ex ... EddieAhern 2 (G A Butler) *chsd ldr over 1f: rdn over 2f out: swtchd rt over 1f out: r.o wl towards fin* **4/7**[1]	83+
3013	3	nk	**Mr Loire**[7] 6750 2-8-12 **72** ... RichardKingscote(3) 5 (R Charlton) *t.k.h: led: rdn and hdd 1f out: no ex towards fin* **7/4**[2]	69
0235	4	3 ½	**Cantique (IRE)**[36] 6416 2-8-7 **64** ... FergusSweeney 1 (A G Newcombe) *hld up: rdn over 2f out: btn whn hung lft over 1f out* **20/1**[3]	50

1m 18.36s (2.55) **Going Correction** +0.20s/f (Slow) — **4** Ran SP% **107.7**

Speed ratings (Par 98):91,89,88,83

CSF £54.69 TOTE £10.20; EX 28.40.

Owner A D Crook **Bred** Weathersfield Ltd **Trained** Upper Lambourn, Berks

FOCUS

Although the winner did touch 50/1 this has to be considered a turn-up. The form is rated through the runner-up to his course form of the previous day.

NOTEBOOK

Love In May(IRE), off course for five months, returned to the sort of form she had shown when taking the first two-year-old race of the year on the Polytrack at Lingfield back in March. (op 20-1 tchd 50-1 in places)

Beauchamp Viceroy, who won a messy affair over course and distance the previous day, got going too late under his big weight, He shaped as though he would not mind a return to seven. (op 8-11)

Mr Loire got away on level terms in this small field and actually looked a rather reluctant leader. (op 2-1)

Cantique(IRE), raised 2lb, was friendless in the market and ran accordingly. (op 8-1)

6835 PONTIN'S HOLIDAYS H'CAP — 5f 216y(P)

2:50 (2:50) (Class 4) (0-85,83) 3-Y-O+ **£5,297** (£1,586; £793; £396; £198) **Stalls** Low

Form				RPR
0002	1		**Quiet Times (IRE)**[12] 6690 7-9-1 **82** ... (b) NCallan 2 (K A Ryan) *mde all: rdn clr over 1f out: r.o wl* **6/4**[1]	94
3043	2	2	**Buy On The Red**[12] 6690 5-8-11 **78** ... (p) EddieAhern 3 (W R Muir) *w wnr: rdn and one pce fnl 2f* **2/1**[2]	84
3604	3	4	**Who's Winning (IRE)**[12] 6690 5-8-6 **73** ... JoeFanning 5 (B G Powell) *s.i.s: hld up: rdn 3f out: wknd 2f out* **8/1**	67
0600	4	½	**Pinchbeck**[12] 6690 7-8-9 **83** ... (p) DanielRobinson(7) 4 (M A Jarvis) *chsd ldrs: rdn and wknd 2f out* **11/2**[3]	76
3002	5	3	**Marko Jadeo (IRE)**[11] 6696 8-8-11 **78** ... MickyFenton 1 (R A Harris) *s.s: sn rcvrd: rdn 3f out: wknd 2f out* **6/1**	62

1m 16.15s (0.34) **Going Correction** +0.20s/f (Slow) — **5** Ran SP% **114.1**

Speed ratings (Par 105):105,102,97,96,92

CSF £5.03 TOTE £2.30: £1.60, £1.40; EX 5.20.

Owner Yorkshire Racing Club and Francis Moll **Bred** Times Of Wigan Ltd **Trained** Hambleton, N Yorks

FOCUS

Quiet Times had finished ahead of three of his rivals at Lingfield on his previous outing and the form is rated around the first two.

Marko Jadeo(IRE) Official explanation: jockey said gelding hung right

6836 PONTINS.COM H'CAP — 1m 4f 50y(P)

3:20 (3:22) (Class 2) (0-100,105) 3-Y-O+

£11,217 (£3,358; £1,679; £840; £419; £210) **Stalls** Low

Form				RPR
0311	1		**Sweet Indulgence (IRE)**[27] 6515 5-8-12 **91** ... FergusSweeney 2 (W J Musson) *hld up in rr: rdn and hdwy over 2f out: led ins fnl f: r.o* **3/1**[2]	98
0516	2	nk	**Millville**[27] 6516 6-9-12 **105** ... NCallan 5 (M A Jarvis) *hld up: hdwy over 5f out: rdn over 3f out: led briefly ins fnl f: r.o* **11/4**[1]	112
4211	3	2 ½	**Velvet Heights (IRE)**[13] 6677 4-9-5 **98** ... IanMongan 4 (J L Dunlop) *hld up: hdwy over 5f out: rdn over 3f out: one pce fnl f* **7/1**	101
3121	4	nk	**Alpine Reel (IRE)**[7] 6744 5-9-3 **96** 6ex ... AdamKirby 3 (W R Swinburn) *hld up in tch: led 3f out: sn rdn: hdd and edgd lft ins fnl f: no ex* **9/2**	99+
3162	5	9	**Mighty Moon**[13] 6677 3-8-2 **86** ... (bt) DaleGibson 7 (J O'Reilly) *chsd ldr: led 5f out to 3f out: wknd over 2f out* **20/1**	74
0103	6	9	**Bahar Shumaal (IRE)**[20] 6600 4-9-0 **93** ... (b) EddieAhern 1 (C E Brittain) *led: rdr lost irons after 1f: hdd 5f out: lost pl over 3f out* **7/2**[3]	67
0035	7	22	**Baan (USA)**[20] 6600 3-8-5 **89** ... JoeFanning 6 (M Johnston) *chsd ldrs tl wknd over 5f out* **12/1**	28

2m 40.33s (-2.09) **Going Correction** +0.20s/f (Slow)

WFA 3 from 4yo+ 5lb — **7** Ran SP% **117.0**

Speed ratings (Par 109):114,113,112,111,105 99,85

CSF £12.21 CT £52.70 TOTE £4.80: £2.20, £1.70; EX 18.60 Trifecta £11.20 Pool £287.64 - 18.21 winning units..

Owner Broughton Thermal Insulation **Bred** Mrs M Campbell-Andenaes **Trained** Newmarket, Suffolk

FOCUS

This valuable handicap was not run at an even pace after Eddie Ahern soon lost his irons on the pacemaker. The fourth sets the standard.

NOTEBOOK

Sweet Indulgence(IRE) is holding his form well and completed a hat-trick despite having been raised a total of 12lb. (op 7-2 tchd 4-1)

Millville, highly tried when finding ten furlongs inadequate last time, could not hold the progressive winner off a mark 10lb higher than when he won at Lingfield in October. (op 9-4 tchd 3-1 and 10-3 in a place)

Velvet Heights(IRE), up a total of 15lb for his back-to-back Fibresand wins, got beaten for speed in this hotter company. (op 5-1)

Alpine Reel(IRE) had plenty on his plate under a penalty in this company over a longer trip. Whether he really stays this distance remains to be seen. (op 5-1 tchd 11-2)

6837 GO PONTIN'S H'CAP — 1m 1f 103y(P)

3:55 (3:58) (Class 6) (0-65,71) 3-Y-O+ — **£2,730** (£806; £403) **Stalls** Low

Form				RPR
6231	1		**Peruvian Prince (USA)**[4] 6791 4-9-5 **71** 6ex ... JamieMoriarty(5) 8 (R A Fahey) *a gng wl: led ins fnl f: shkn up and qcknd clr* **8/13**[1]	88+
0224	2	2	**Second Reef**[14] 6667 4-8-6 **53** ... DavidAllan 10 (E J Alston) *t.k.h in rr: nt clr run on ins over 2f out: hdwy wl over 1f out: rdn to ld 1f out: sn hdd: nt qckn* **7/1**[3]	61
001	3	3	**Buscador (USA)**[17] 6648 7-8-11 **61** ... PatrickMathers(3) 4 (W M Brisbourne) *led: rdn 3f out: hdd 1f out: sn btn* **11/1**	63
50	4	nk	**Spoilsport**[21] 6587 3-8-4 **53** ... DaleGibson 7 (P D Evans) *hld up and bhd: rdn and hdwy on outside over 2f out: edgd lft over 1f out: one pce* **25/1**	54
3050	5	nk	**Barbirolli**[13] 6684 4-9-1 **62** ... (v[1]) FergusSweeney 2 (W M Brisbourne) *hld up in tch: swtchd rt and rdn over 1f out: nvr able to chal* **11/2**[2]	63
6320	6	1 ½	**Scottish River (USA)**[14] 6666 7-8-2 **56** ... AshleyMorgan(7) 6 (M D I Usher) *stdd s: hld up in rr: rdn 1f out: n.d* **10/1**	54
000-	7	½	**Key Partners (IRE)**[534] 3021 5-8-10 **64** ... RussellKennemore(7) 5 (B D Leavy) *s.i.s: t.k.h: sn in tch: rdn 3f out: wnt 2nd briefly 2f: wknd fnl f* **33/1**	61
0204	8	13	**Right Ted (IRE)**[17] 6648 3-8-7 **56** ... JoeFanning 1 (T Wall) *chsd ldr tl rdn 2f out: sn wknd* **16/1**	27

2m 3.58s (0.96) **Going Correction** +0.20s/f (Slow)

WFA 3 from 4yo+ 2lb — **8** Ran SP% **119.9**

Speed ratings (Par 101):103,101,98,98,98 96,96,84

CSF £6.18 CT £28.45 TOTE £1.60: £1.10, £1.60, £2.00; EX 9.90 Trifecta £59.70 Pool £219.82 - 2,61 winning units. Place 6 £1878.79, Place 5 £1334.24.

Owner R G Leatham **Bred** Alexander-Groves Thoroughbreds **Trained** Musley Bank, N Yorks

FOCUS

A steadily-run contest but the form looks sound rated around the second and fourth.

Right Ted(IRE) Official explanation: jockey said filly hung throughout

T/Plt: £1,258.30 to a £1 stake. Pool: £42,233.25. 24.50 winning tickets. T/Qpdt: £87.60 to a £1 stake. Pool: £3,409.90. 28.80 winning tickets. KH

6826 KEMPTON (A.W) (R-H)

Saturday, December 16

OFFICIAL GOING: Standard

Wind: almost nil

6838 BETBROKERS "BETTING JUST GOT BETTER" MAIDEN STKS — 5f (P)

3:50 (3:51) (Class 5) 2-Y-O — **£3,238** (£963; £481; £240) **Stalls** High

Form				RPR
0334	1		**Rocker**[74] 5753 2-8-10 69 ... WilliamBuick(7) 4 (B R Johnson) *mde all: kicked on over 1f out: kpt on fnl f: jst hld on* **5/2**[2]	68
	2	hd	**Telltime (IRE)** 2-8-12 ... FrancisNorton 6 (A M Balding) *hld up in last trio: shkn up over 1f out: r.o ent fnl f: clsng fast at fin* **14/1**	62+
4232	3	½	**Hereford Boy**[8] 6742 2-9-3 63 ... GeorgeBaker 3 (D K Ivory) *chsd wnr after 2f: rdn and nt qckn over 1f out: kpt on fnl f but a hld* **11/8**[1]	65
50	4	nk	**Ellablue**[37] 6409 2-8-12 ... AdamKirby 2 (Rae Guest) *trckd ldrs: rdn and nt qckn over 1f out: kpt on fnl f* **16/1**	59
2	5	1 ¼	**New York Oscar (IRE)**[12] 6695 2-8-12 ... NataliaGemelova(5) 5 (A J McCabe) *trckd wnr for 2f: awkward bnd sn after: lost pl 2f out: one pce after* **6/1**	59
6	6	¾	**Redflo**[8] 6742 2-8-5 ... SophieDoyle(7) 7 (Ms J S Doyle) *hld up in last trio: n.m.r briefly 2f out: pushed along and no prog* **50/1**	52
03	7	¾	**The Bronx**[45] 6295 2-9-3 ... AdrianMcCarthy 1 (M J Wallace) *racd wd: hld up in last trio: rdn and no prog wl over 1f out* **11/2**[3]	54

61.65 secs (1.25) **Going Correction** -0.05s/f (Stan) — **7** Ran SP% **114.9**

Speed ratings (Par 96):88,87,86,86,84 83,82

CSF £35.90 TOTE £3.30: £1.40, £4.30; EX 49.40.

Owner Sir Eric Parker **Bred** Sir Eric Parker **Trained** Ashtead, Surrey

FOCUS

A modest sprint maiden run at a very steady pace and producing a close finish. The winner and third were close to their marks, but the runner-up looks the pick long term.

NOTEBOOK

Rocker, returning from a break and having his first run for his new trainer and first on the All-Weather, made all the running and just did enough to hold off the fast-finishing runner-up. He looks capable of winning handicaps off his current mark. (tchd 9-4)

Telltime(IRE) ◆, a newcomer who is by a sprinter but bred to get further on his dam's side, did not get the best of runs but finished well and very nearly made a winning start. She should not be too long in gaining compensation. (tchd 12-1)

Hereford Boy has had some good chances and had every opportunity to score this time, but he could not find a change of gear under pressure which appears to be his problem. Connections may have to resort to some kind of headgear to get that little extra out of him. (tchd 6-4)

Ellablue, having her third run, was quite keen early but put up arguably her best effort to date and will be more interesting in handicaps off a mark in the high 50s, possibly when upped in trip. (op 20-1)

New York Oscar(IRE), who was touched off in six-furlong seller on his debut at Lingfield, found this step up in grade and drop in trip beyond him, although he did not handle the bend that well and may prefer going the other way around. (op 9-2)

The Bronx failed to build on two reasonable previous efforts but at least now qualifies for a handicap mark. (op 7-1 tchd 5-1)

6839 BETBROKERS.COM NURSERY — 5f (P)

4:20 (4:20) (Class 6) (0-65,61) 2-Y-O — **£2,590** (£770; £385; £192) **Stalls** High

Form				RPR
6604	1		**Minnow**[30] 6500 2-8-13 **53** ... J-PGuillambert 9 (S C Williams) *trckd ldng pair gng wl: effrt to ld jst over 1f out: rdn out* **4/1**[2]	57+
5043	2	¾	**Wibbadune (IRE)**[5] 6788 2-8-13 **53** ... AdamKirby 4 (Peter Grayson) *towards rr whn stmbld over 3f out: plenty to do after: r.o u.p fr over 1f out: tk 2nd and gaining on wnr at fin* **12/1**	54
0422	3	1	**Nou Camp**[11] 6711 2-8-10 **57** ... WilliamBuick(7) 8 (N A Callaghan) *pressed ldr: shkn up and upsides over 1f out: edgd lft and fnd nil* **1/1**[1]	54
6006	4	1 ¾	**Eastern Princess**[11] 6711 2-8-6 **46** ... RichardThomas 1 (J A Geake) *chsd ldrs: pushed along 1/2-way: no imp over 1f out: kpt on* **14/1**	37

6664 **5** ½ **Wadnagin (IRE)**[3] 6807 2-9-7 **61** .... LeeEnstone 3 50
(I A Wood) *dwlt: rn v wd bnd over 3f out: struggling in rr after: styd on ins fnl f* **8/1**[3]

660 **6** 1 **Flushed**[128] 4290 2-8-0 **45** .... NataliaGemelova(5) 6 31
(A J McCabe) *hld up: outpcd after 2f: struggling 2f out: plugged on* **10/1**

000 **7** 1¼ **Foxy Music**[8] 6749 2-8-5 **45** .... (b[1]) AdrianMcCarthy 7 26
(Peter Grayson) *trckd ldrs: cl up on inner over 1f out and gng wl: appeared nt to have clr run and sn lost pl: eased* **16/1**

1303 **8** shd **Baytown Paikea**[10] 6732 2-9-3 **57** .... HayleyTurner 5 38
(P S McEntee) *mde most to jst over 1f out: wknd rapidly* **11/1**

61.27 secs (0.87) **Going Correction** -0.05s/f (Stan) 8 Ran SP% **118.8**
Speed ratings (Par 94):91,89,88,85,84 83,81,80
CSF £52.04 CT £83.51 TOTE £5.20: £1.40, £1.60, £1.20; EX 44.80.
Owner Tweenhills Racing VIII **Bred** Downclose Stud **Trained** Newmarket, Suffolk

FOCUS
A moderate nursery. It was run 0.38 sec faster than the opening maiden, but the form looks pretty weak, despite the winner looking likely to go on from this.

NOTEBOOK
Minnow who was well backed on her handicap debut last time, had been dropped 2lb since and gained compensation for her backers with a somewhat cosy success. She could well follow up in similar company. (op 11-2)
Wibbadune(IRE) ◆, having her seventh run since the end of October, is progressing with her racing and looked unlucky, having stumbled on the turn, and did well to finish as close as she did. She could pick up a similar contest before long on this evidence. Official explanation: jockey said filly was reluctant to turn into the final bend (op 6-1)
Nou Camp has had plenty of chances and this drop in trip did not appear to make any difference. He might be worth another try in headgear. (op 11-10 tchd 6-5)
Eastern Princess ran her best race so far on sand but lacked the extra gear needed to get involved. She probably needs to drop into selling company.
Wadnagin(IRE), dropping in trip, missed the break and ran wide on the turn, so it was no surprise she failed to figure. (op 7-1 tchd 13-2)
Foxy Music, in blinkers for the first time on this handicap debut, was travelling strongly when short of room on the inside early in the straight and his rider did not persevere when his chance had gone. He can be rated better than the bare form and could be one to keep an eye on. Official explanation: jockey said gelding hung right (tchd 20-1)

6840 BETBROKERS WORLD'S 1ST BET BROKER MEDIAN AUCTION MAIDEN FILLIES' STKS 1m (P)
4:50 (4:51) (Class 5) 2-Y-0 **£3,238** (£963; £481; £240) **Stalls** High

Form RPR
0262 **1** **Colchium (IRE)**[64] 5933 2-9-0 73 .... FrancisNorton 7 71
(H Morrison) *chsd ldrs: rdn to ld jst over 2f out: edgd rt and tired fnl f: jst hld on* **15/8**[2]

0422 **2** shd **Miss Saafend Plaza (IRE)**[12] 6697 2-9-0 74 .... (b[1]) RyanMoore 3 71
(R Hannon) *pressed ldr: led 3f out to over 2f out: hrd rdn and nt qckn: styd on as ldng pair faltered ins fnl f: jst failed* **11/8**[1]

3 **3** nk **Musical Beat**[15] 6663 2-9-0 .... EdwardCreighton 9 70
(Miss V Haigh) *cl up: effrt and jinked lft 2f out: chal fnl f: nt qckn u.p nr fin* **5/1**[3]

0 **4** 2 **Mirin**[64] 5950 2-9-0 .... JamieMackay 5 65
(G Wragg) *s.i.s: sn in midfield: outpcd by ldrs over 2f out: reminder ins fnl 2f: styd on steadily fnl f* **16/1**

5 6 **Silver Mitzva (IRE)** 2-9-0 .... (t) J-PGuillambert 8 52
(M Botti) *dwlt: sn in tch: rdn over 3f out: lft wl bhd fr over 2f out* **10/1**

6 1¾ **Auntie Mame** 2-9-0 .... StephenCarson 2 48
(D J Coakley) *s.v.s: in tch in rr after 2f: wknd over 2f out* **25/1**

0030 **7** 3½ **Barley Moon**[42] 6332 2-9-0 67 .... MickyFenton 6 40
(T Keddy) *led at stdy pce to 3f out: wknd rapidly 2f out* **16/1**

0 **8** 1½ **Bali Belony**[15] 6663 2-9-0 .... PatCosgrave 4 36
(J R Jenkins) *s.v.s and awkward: in tch after 2f: wknd wl over 2f out* **100/1**

0 **9** 2½ **Eridani (IRE)**[12] 6697 2-9-0 .... HayleyTurner 1 30
(M L W Bell) *chsd ldrs tl wknd rapidly 3f out* **33/1**

10 3 **First Frost** 2-9-2 ow2 .... AntonyProcter 10 25
(M J Gingell) *s.v.s: in tch after 2f: wknd rapidly wl over 2f out* **66/1**

1m 42.26s (1.46) **Going Correction** -0.05s/f (Stan) 10 Ran SP% **123.7**
Speed ratings (Par 93):90,89,89,87,81 79,76,74,72,69
CSF £5.09 TOTE £2.20: £1.40, £1.40, £1.10; EX 7.90.
Owner Mrs B Oppenheimer **Bred** Mrs B D Oppenheimer **Trained** East Ilsley, Berks
■ Stewards' Enquiry : Francis Norton caution: careless riding

FOCUS
A fair maiden for the time of year, but a very slow early gallop and the time was nearly 3sec slower than the following handicap. The form is not totally convincing.

NOTEBOOK
Colchium(IRE), making her debut on sand, handled it well and did just enough to get off the mark at the seventh attempt. She does not look particularly well treated at present, but may have more improvement in her on this surface. (op 5-2)
Miss Saafend Plaza(IRE), fitted with a blinkers for the first time, was given a positive ride but looked beaten going into the last furlong before rallying late. She has now been runner-up on her last three outings and is finding it tough to get her head in front. (op 2-1)
Musical Beat, stepping up in trip, built on her promising debut effort and, clear of the rest, should be capable of picking up an ordinary maiden. (op 7-2)
Mirin, having only her second outing and her first on sand, was also stepping up in trip. She missed the break but was keeping on steadily in the closing stages and looks one to bear in mind for handicaps in due course.

6841 BETBROKERS OPEN AN ACCOUNT ON 0844 855 2111 H'CAP 1m (P)
5:20 (5:20) (Class 5) (0-70,70) 3-Y-0+ **£3,886** (£1,156; £577; £288) **Stalls** High

Form RPR
0104 **1** **Magic Warrior**[17] 6652 6-8-11 **64** .... PaulFitzsimons 6 72
(J C Fox) *hld up wl in rr: prog on inner over 2f out: rdn to ld 1f out: kpt on* **4/1**[1]

02 **2** nk **Lopinot (IRE)**[21] 6593 3-9-0 **68** .... J-PGuillambert 12 75
(P J Makin) *sn trckd ldr: drvn to ld over 1f out to 1f out: kpt on fnl f but a hld* **10/1**

2423 **3** 1 **Jomus**[11] 6714 5-8-3 **56** oh1 .... (b) HayleyTurner 10 61
(L Montague Hall) *taken down early and mounted on crse: dwlt: hld up in last: brought v wd in st: urged along and styd on nr fin* **11/2**[3]

2012 **4** 1 **Million Percent**[21] 6595 7-9-1 **68** .... GeorgeBaker 5 71
(C R Dore) *trckd ldrs gng wl: rdn 2f out: nt qckn over 1f out: hld after* **9/2**[2]

0051 **5** 1¼ **Dyanita**[47] 6260 3-8-13 **67** .... (b[1]) TonyCulhane 7 67
(B W Hills) *led at decent pce: hdd over 1f out: fdd fnl f* **10/1**

0045 **6** 1 **Samarinda (USA)**[12] 5727 3-8-10 **64** .... MickyFenton 2 62
(Mrs P Sly) *settled in midfield: rdn and lost pl 3f out: struggling after: kpt on again fnl f* **33/1**

5455 **7** nk **Sky Quest (IRE)**[98] 5163 8-9-3 **70** .... RyanMoore 9 67
(J R Boyle) *hld up wl in rr: sme prog into midfield 2f out: no imp on ldrs over 1f out* **13/2**

2161 **8** 1¼ **Mythical Charm**[10] 6725 7-8-2 **58** .... (t) MarcHalford(3) 11 52
(J J Bridger) *stdd s: hld up: prog on outer 1/2-way: wknd 2f out* **6/1**

0000 **9** nk **Deeper In Debt**[14] 6671 8-9-3 **70** .... AlanDaly 3 63
(J Akehurst) *chsd ldrs: rdn and wknd wl over 2f out* **16/1**

433 **10** nk **Soul Blazer (USA)**[22] 6587 3-9-1 **69** .... FrancisNorton 4 62
(A M Balding) *trckd ldng pair: rdn over 2f out: hanging and fnd nil* **7/1**

600- **11** 9 **Epices**[157] 3421 4-8-12 **65** .... StephenCarson 1 37
(R Ingram) *t.k.h: hld up bhd ldrs: rdn and lost pl wl over 2f out: t.o* **50/1**

1m 39.32s (-1.48) **Going Correction** -0.05s/f (Stan)
WFA 3 from 4yo+ 1lb 11 Ran SP% **122.7**
Speed ratings (Par 103):105,104,103,102,101 100,100,98,98,98 89
CSF £46.89 CT £232.51 TOTE £5.80: £2.50, £5.70, £1.50; EX 50.70.
Owner Miss H J Flower **Bred** Patrick Eddery Ltd **Trained** Collingbourne Ducis, Wilts

FOCUS
A modest handicap featuring several horses who are regulars on this track. It was run at a fair gallop and the form should work out.

6842 BETBROKERS ONE ACCOUNT H'CAP 6f (P)
5:50 (5:51) (Class 5) (0-70,68) 3-Y-0+ **£3,886** (£1,156; £577; £288) **Stalls** High

Form RPR
3025 **1** **Hollow Jo**[21] 6595 6-8-11 **63** .... MickyFenton 5 72
(J R Jenkins) *hld up in last trio: prog on outer 2f out: sustained run to ld last 100yds: kpt on wl* **4/1**

0203 **2** ¾ **Bobby Rose**[157] 3406 3-8-12 **64** .... NCallan 6 71+
(D K Ivory) *hld up bhd ldrs: nt clr run 2f out: rdn to chal 1f out: upsides fnl f: nt qckn* **20/1**

3402 **3** hd **Dvinsky (USA)**[8] 6747 5-8-13 **65** .... PaulDoe 8 71
(P Howling) *hld up in midfield: prog on inner 2f out: drvn to ld 1f out: hdd and one pce last 100yds* **7/2**[3]

1320 **4** nk **Mina**[14] 6672 4-8-13 **65** .... JamieMackay 2 70+
(Rae Guest) *dwlt: t.k.h: hld up in last pair: plenty to do over 2f out: prog and swtchd to inner 1f out: kpt on but unable to chal* **20/1**

4311 **5** nk **Small Stakes (IRE)**[15] 6656 4-9-2 **68** .... (vt) J-PGuillambert 9 72
(P J Makin) *settled midfield: lost pl and struggling over 2f out: hanging and plld out over 1f out: styd on wl last 150yds* **3/1**[2]

0040 **6** ¾ **Count Cougar (USA)**[1] 6827 6-8-6 **58** .... AdrianTNicholls 3 60
(S P Griffiths) *led: hrd pressed 2f out: hdd 1f out: wknd last 100yds* **20/1**

0020 **7** 2½ **Jayanjay**[11] 6709 7-9-2 **68** .... RyanMoore 4 62
(P Mitchell) *trckd ldrs: effrt 2f out: rdn and nt qckn over 1f out: fdd* **11/4**[1]

0430 **8** 2½ **Blessed Place**[9] 6739 6-8-7 **59** .... FrancisNorton 1 46
(D J S Ffrench Davis) *t.k.h: pressed ldr to over 1f out: wknd* **10/1**

0040 **9** shd **Auentraum (GER)**[169] 3052 6-8-3 **57** ow2 .... JamesDoyle(3) 7 45
(Ms J S Doyle) *awkward s: hld up in last: rdn and no prog 2f out* **25/1**

1m 12.14s (-1.56) **Going Correction** -0.05s/f (Stan) 9 Ran SP% **121.1**
Speed ratings (Par 103):108,107,106,106,105 104,101,98,98
CSF £84.40 CT £313.46 TOTE £4.50: £1.40, £3.80, £2.30; EX 64.10.
Owner Jim McCarthy **Bred** K J Reddington **Trained** Royston, Herts

FOCUS
A blanket finish, with only around two lengths separating the first six.

6843 BETBROKERS "NEVER MISS A BET" H'CAP 1m 4f (P)
6:20 (6:20) (Class 6) (0-65,65) 3-Y-0+ **£3,238** (£963; £481; £240) **Stalls** Low

Form RPR
5066 **1** **Burgundy**[15] 6661 9-9-7 **65** .... (b) GeorgeBaker 7 75
(P Mitchell) *hld up in last pair: prog on inner over 2f out: squeezed through to ld jst over 1f out: r.o wl* **12/1**

0560 **2** 2½ **Lennoxtown (IRE)**[8] 6748 3-8-7 **56** .... (p) BrettDoyle 11 62
(J Ryan) *trckd ldrs: wnt 2nd gng easily over 2f out: led briefly over 1f out: nt qckn fnl f* **16/1**

0650 **3** ½ **Magic Amigo**[21] 6590 5-9-3 **61** .... NCallan 8 66
(J R Jenkins) *t.k.h: hld up in midfield: effrt over 2f out: drvn to cl on ldrs over 1f out: one pce* **25/1**

-000 **4** ½ **Lord Laing (USA)**[139] 3977 3-8-3 **59** .... WilliamBuick(7) 5 63
(H J Collingridge) *chsd ldrs: pushed along 4f out: brought wd in st: kpt on u.p fnl 2f: n.d* **33/1**

0501 **5** 1¾ **Wee Charlie Castle (IRE)**[24] 6565 3-9-2 **65** .... J-PGuillambert 1 66
(G C H Chung) *stdd s: hld up in last trio: brought v wd in st and effrt over 2f out: chsd ldrs over 1f out: no hdwy after* **4/1**[3]

0001 **6** shd **Escoffier**[35] 6435 4-8-13 **57** .... MickyFenton 9 58
(Pat Eddery) *led for 1f: led again over 6f out to over 1f out: wknd fnl f* **7/2**[2]

0221 **7** 1½ **Storm Of Arabia (IRE)**[13] 6687 3-9-2 **65** .... AdamKirby 4 64
(W R Swinburn) *hld up in midfield: drvn over 2f out: no prog over 1f out: wknd* **6/4**[1]

3021 **8** 3 **Sovietta (IRE)**[201] 2075 5-8-7 **58** .... JamesMillman(7) 6 52
(A G Newcombe) *a towards rr: struggling in last trio over 2f out* **20/1**

6002 **9** 2½ **Khanjar (USA)**[22] 6584 6-9-2 **60** .... MichaelTebbutt 2 50
(J Pearce) *prom: chsd ldr over 6f out tl wknd wl over 2f out* **14/1**

4030 **10** ½ **Lady Pilot**[6] 6775 4-8-7 **54** .... JamesDoyle(3) 3 43
(Ms J S Doyle) *t.k.h: led after 1f to over 6f out: wknd over 2f out* **11/1**

2m 34.47s (-2.43) **Going Correction** -0.05s/f (Stan)
WFA 3 from 4yo+ 5lb 10 Ran SP% **122.3**
Speed ratings (Par 101):106,104,104,103,102 102,101,99,97,97
CSF £188.46 CT £4669.99 TOTE £8.00: £1.60, £3.30, £4.50; EX 86.50 Place 6 £366.33, Place 5 £119..
Owner Mrs S Sheldon **Bred** Cheveley Park Stud Ltd **Trained** Epsom, Surrey

FOCUS
A modest handicap, but it was run at a sound gallop and produced a decisive winner.
T/Plt: £526.20 to a £1 stake. Pool: £56,306.75. 78.10 winning tickets. T/Qpdt: £75.30 to a £1 stake. Pool: £5,275.30. 51.80 winning tickets. JN

6800 LINGFIELD (L-H)
Saturday, December 16

OFFICIAL GOING: Standard
Wind: virtually nil

6844 GO PONTIN'S H'CAP 5f (P)
12:55 (12:59) (Class 5) (0-70,71) 3-Y-0+ **£3,238** (£963; £481; £240) **Stalls** High

Form RPR
0000 **1** **Stoneacre Boy (IRE)**[14] 6682 3-8-13 **65** .... (b) TonyCulhane 5 75
(Peter Grayson) *lw: racd in midfield: pushed along and hdwy over 2f out: rdn over 1f out: styd on wl to ld nr fin* **14/1**

000 **2** *nk* **Financial Times (USA)**[131] 4208 4-9-2 **68**............(t) NCallan 9 76
(Stef Liddiard) *swtg: w ldrs: rdn over 2f out: led wl over 1f out: hdd and no ex nr fin* **13/2**

2461 **3** *shd* **Special Gold**[13] 6686 4-8-11 **63**............(b) PaulMulrennan 7 71
(A D Brown) *pressed ldr: rdn and ev ch fr 2f out: unable qckn wl ins fnl f* **13/2**

2232 **4** *nk* **Heavens Walk**[11] 6709 5-9-5 **71**............(t) J-PGuillambert 10 78
(P J Makin) *lw: in tch on outer: rdn wl over 2f out: styd on wl ins fnl f: nt quite rch ldrs* **11/4**[1]

0403 **5** *1 1/4* **Fast Heart**[14] 6681 5-9-4 **70**............(t) BrettDoyle 4 73
(R A Harris) *dwlt: bhd: swtchd rt wl over 1f out: r.o fnl f: nvr nrr* **7/2**[2]

0000 **6** *nk* **Misaro (GER)**[9] 6739 5-8-10 **62**............(b) MickyFenton 8 63
(R A Harris) *sn pushed along and struggling to go pce: c wd bnd over 2f out: r.o ins fnl f: n.d* **25/1**

0532 **7** *hd* **City For Conquest (IRE)**[2] 6823 3-9-0 **66**............(b) FrancisNorton 6 67
(T J Pitt) *s.i.s: sn drvn to chse ldrs: kpt on same pce ins fnl f* **5/1**[3]

0303 **8** *1/2* **Quality Street**[15] 6656 4-8-5 **64**............(p) PatrickHills(7) 3 63
(P Butler) *led tl wl over 1f out: wknd ins fnl f* **15/2**

0000 **9** *5* **Triskaidekaphobia**[94] 5286 3-8-11 **63**............ PaulFitzsimons 1 44
(Miss J R Tooth) *prom on inner: rdn over 2f out: wknd wl over 1f out* **33/1**

58.99 secs (-0.79) **Going Correction** -0.10s/f (Stan) 9 Ran SP% **117.4**
Speed ratings (Par 103):102,101,101,100,98 98,98,97,89
CSF £103.35 CT £661.99 TOTE £19.50: £3.50, £2.50, £1.80; EX 101.50 TRIFECTA Not won..
Owner Richard Teatum **Bred** Michael Dalton **Trained** Formby, Lancs

FOCUS
A competitive sprint in which there was plenty of pace on. The form looks sound rated through the fourth, with the first two capable of rating higher.
Triskaidekaphobia Official explanation: trainer said gelding finished distressed

6845 PONTIN'S HOLIDAYS (S) STKS 6f (P)
1:30 (1:30) (Class 6) 2-Y-O **£2,388** (£705; £352) **Stalls** Low

Form RPR

0626 **1** **Totally Free**[3] 6807 2-8-11 52............(v) HayleyTurner 3 54
(M D I Usher) *t.k.h: trckd ldrs: rdn wl over 1f out: styd on wl fnl f to ld nr fin* **9/2**[3]

0000 **2** *1/2* **O'Dwyer (IRE)**[9] 6736 2-8-11 50............(p) PaulMulrennan 9 53
(A D Brown) *sn led: rdn 2f out: kpt on wl tl hdd and no ex nr fin* **12/1**

3550 **3** *1* **House Arrest**[60] 6032 2-8-1 50............(b[1]) NataliaGemelova(5) 1 45
(A J McCabe) *lw: w.w in tch on inner: rdn and hdwy wl over 1f out: ch 1f out: one pce last 100 yds* **10/1**

4054 **4** *1/2* **Jost Van Dyke**[12] 6695 2-8-11 56............ BrettDoyle 7 48
(J R Boyle) *prom: wnt 2nd wl over 3f out tl 1f out: fdd last 100 yds* **10/3**[2]

00 **5** *hd* **Mister Always**[111] 4843 2-8-8............(tp) JamesDoyle(3) 6 47
(Ms J S Doyle) *swtg: hld up in tch: effrt and hung lft wl over 1f out: swtchd rt 1f out: styd on wl ins fnl f: nt rch ldrs* **33/1**

0001 **6** *3/4* **Polly Jones (USA)**[12] 6695 2-8-6 48............ JimmyQuinn 4 40+
(G L Moore) *s.i.s: bhd: hdwy over 2f out: rdn over 1f out: kpt on same pce ins fnl f* **7/4**[1]

00 **7** *5* **Flashing Feet (IRE)**[7] 6768 2-8-11............ PaulFitzsimons 5 30
(R Hannon) *sn rdn along in rr: sme late hdwy: nvr trbld ldrs* **15/2**

0045 **8** *hd* **Jade's Ballet**[12] 6695 2-8-6 35............ StephenCarson 2 25
(E A Wheeler) *chsd ldr tl wl over 3f out: rdn over 2f out: wknd qckly 1f out* **33/1**

5 **9** *4* **Lady Warning**[8] 6742 2-8-1 ow2............ JackDean(7) 10 15
(W G M Turner) *chsd ldrs on outer: rdn and wknd wl over 2f out* **50/1**

1m 13.99s (1.18) **Going Correction** -0.10s/f (Stan) 9 Ran SP% **114.0**
Speed ratings (Par 94):88,87,86,85,85 84,77,77,71
CSF £54.38 TOTE £5.00: £1.30, £3.90, £2.70; EX 74.60 Trifecta £142.70 Part won. Pool £201.12 - 0.67 winning units..There was no bid for the winner.
Owner I Sheward **Bred** B Mills **Trained** Upper Lambourn, Berks

FOCUS
Ordinary plating-class form and a race unlikely to have much future impact.

NOTEBOOK
Totally Free, runner-up on two of his previous three career starts in selling company, went one better and lost his maiden tag at the 11th time of asking. The form is pretty moderate, though. (op 4-1 tchd 5-1)
O'Dwyer(IRE), wearing headgear for the first time, tried to quicken from the front entering the straight, but he never got clear of the pack and was worn down close home. (op 11-1)
House Arrest, wearing blinkers this time instead of cheekpieces, was brought to have every chance on the inner inside the last, but she did not go by O'Dwyer, and one can see why she has six placed efforts to her name but no wins from 13 starts. (op 8-1)
Jost Van Dyke found very little at the business end and, although he reversed recent course and distance form with Polly Jones, one should not read much into that. Official explanation: jockey said gelding was bumped at start (op 7-2 tchd 4-1)
Mister Always, one of the less-exposed runners in the line-up, was making his debut for a new stable having been off the track since August. Dropping into a seller for the first time, he had cheekpieces and a tongue tie on to help, but he hung in the straight and did not help his rider.
Polly Jones(USA) did not get much of a run early in the straight and is probably a bit better than the bare form suggests. (op 13-8)

6846 TURNER & GREEN NOVICE STKS 1m (P)
2:00 (2:02) (Class 5) 2-Y-O **£3,886** (£1,156; £577; £288) **Stalls** High

Form RPR

1 **1** **Sweeney (IRE)**[15] 6658 2-9-5............ NCallan 6 85+
(M A Jarvis) *w'like: athletic: str: t.k.h: stdd and dropped rr: hdwy on outer over 3f out: chal 2f out: rdn to ld over 1f out: readily* **4/5**[1]

001 **2** *1 1/4* **Nordic Affair**[13] 6689 2-9-5 78............ AntonyProcter 7 79
(D R C Elsworth) *lw: pressed ldr tl led after 2f: rdn over 2f out: hdd over 1f out: kpt on same pce* **8/1**

6234 **3** *1 1/2* **Onenightinlisbon (IRE)**[18] 6631 2-9-1 81............ RyanMoore 2 72
(K R Burke) *lw: t.k.h: led for 2f: chsd ldrs tl rdn and outpcd over 2f out: rallied over 1f out: kpt on same pce fnl f* **9/2**[3]

3441 **4** *1/2* **History Boy**[23] 6570 2-9-5 81............ JimmyQuinn 1 74
(D J Coakley) *trckd ldrs: wnt 2nd over 4f out: rdn and ev ch 2f out: wknd over 1f out* **11/4**[2]

5 *12* **Kimpton Carer** 2-8-12............ AdrianTNicholls 4 40
(J A Geake) *w'like: leggy: slowly away: sn in tch: rdn wl over 3f out: lost tch over 2f out* **66/1**

1m 39.37s (-0.06) **Going Correction** -0.10s/f (Stan) 5 Ran SP% **113.0**
Speed ratings (Par 96):96,94,93,92,80
CSF £8.46 TOTE £1.70: £1.10, £3.30; EX 6.50.
Owner Jumeirah Racing **Bred** Darley **Trained** Newmarket, Suffolk

FOCUS
A fair contest, but they went quite steady and it turned into a dash from the turn in. The winner can do better but it is difficult to rate higher at present.

NOTEBOOK
Sweeney(IRE), a winner on his debut over this course and distance just over a fortnight earlier, was made a short price to follow up against some fair sorts. He did not do a lot once he was in front but was always holding his rivals at bay and won pretty cosily in the end, suggesting that he is a useful performer in the making. He should get further in time. (op 5-6 tchd 10-11 and evens in places)
Nordic Affair, a seven-furlong maiden winner here earlier in the month, was well positioned in a steadily-run contest, but he could not hold off the favourite when he loomed up approaching the final furlong. It was still a solid effort, though, as he beat two rivals rated 3lb higher. (tchd 9-1)
Onenightinlisbon(IRE), the most experienced runner in the line-up, had never previously run beyond a sprint distance. She raced pretty keenly off the steady early pace and then got outpaced when the leaders began to quicken running to the bend into the straight, so this performance leaves plenty of questions unanswered. (op 5-1 tchd 4-1)
History Boy was not suited by the way the race was run. He looked far better over a bit further off a better pace at Wolverhampton last time, albeit that was only a maiden. (op 3-1 tchd 100-30 in places)
Kimpton Carer, a half-brother to the smart handicapper/Listed winner Bomb Alaska and a number of other winners, faced a stiff task on his debut. He will do better in time and once handicapped. (tchd 50-1)

6847 PONTINS.COM CONDITIONS STKS 1m (P)
2:40 (2:40) (Class 4) 3-Y-O+ **£5,505** (£1,637; £818; £408) **Stalls** High

Form RPR

0043 **1** **Vortex**[13] 6692 7-8-12 94............(t) JimmyQuinn 2 101
(Miss Gay Kelleway) *t.k.h: trckd ldng pair: shkn up to ld jst over 1f out: rdn and hld on wl last 100 yds* **10/3**[3]

0406 **2** *hd* **Red Spell (IRE)**[13] 6692 5-8-12 103............ RyanMoore 3 101+
(R Hannon) *hld up in last: c wd and rdn bnd over 2f out: wnt 2nd ins fnl f: r.o* **5/4**[1]

6344 **3** *1 1/2* **Kindlelight Debut**[21] 6600 6-8-4 98............ JamesDoyle(3) 1 92
(N P Littmoden) *led at stdy pce: shkn up and qcknd wl over 2f out: hdd jst over 1f out: edgd rt and kpt on same pce fnl f* **15/8**[2]

0000 **4** *1* **Curtail (IRE)**[126] 4345 3-8-11 93............ PaulMulrennan 4 95
(I Semple) *chsd ldr: rdn over 2f out: kpt on one pce fr over 1f out* **12/1**

1m 41.27s (1.84) **Going Correction** -0.10s/f (Stan)
WFA 3 from 4yo+ 1lb 4 Ran SP% **110.0**
Speed ratings (Par 105):86,85,84,83
CSF £8.10 TOTE £3.20; EX 5.50.
Owner Coriolis Partnership **Bred** Juddmonte Farms **Trained** Exning, Suffolk

FOCUS
A good quality contest but they went no pace in the early stages before quickening up running down the hill and as a result the race has been rated fairly negatively.

6848 PULSE FIXINGS XMAS RUN AROUND H'CAP 1m 2f (P)
3:10 (3:11) (Class 5) (0-70,78) 3-Y-O+ **£3,238** (£963; £481; £240) **Stalls** Low

Form RPR

1 **1** **Rapid City**[7] 6765 3-8-11 **68**............ JamesDoyle(3) 9 82+
(Miss J Feilden) *w'like: athletic: trckd ldrs: wnt 2nd gng wl over 3f out: led over 2f out: sn rdn: rn green and hung lft ins fnl f: hld on* **4/1**[2]

0112 **2** *hd* **Happy As Larry (USA)**[5] 6791 4-9-6 **78**............ PatrickHills(7) 7 92+
(T J Pitt) *lw: hld up in midfield: hdwy over 3f out: chsd wnr wl over 1f out: ev ch 1f out: unable qckn nr fin* **2/1**[1]

3044 **3** *3* **Smokin Joe**[6] 6781 5-9-3 **68**............(b) BrettDoyle 6 76
(J R Best) *t.k.h: hld up towards rr: hdwy over 3f out: rdn to chse ldng pair over 1f out: no imp* **5/1**[3]

2140 **4** *3* **Port 'n Starboard**[21] 6590 5-8-13 **64**............ TonyCulhane 10 66
(C A Cyzer) *racd in midfield: rdn and outpcd over 2f out: styd on fnl f : no ch w ldrs* **10/1**

4522 **5** *nk* **Siena Star (IRE)**[13] 6687 8-8-11 **62**............ MickyFenton 1 64
(Stef Liddiard) *t.k.h: hld up in tch: rdn over 2f out: sn outpcd* **10/1**

5400 **6** *1/2* **Marbaa (IRE)**[18] 6635 3-8-12 **66**............ LPKeniry 11 67
(S Dow) *slowly away: hld up in rr: hdwy 2f out: sn rdn: nvr trbld ldrs* **22/1**

0000 **7** *1* **Almanshood (USA)**[35] 2647 4-8-12 **66**............ RichardKingscote(3) 8 65
(P L Gilligan) *led tl hdd and rdn over 2f out: wknd over 1f out* **25/1**

0600 **8** *3 1/2* **Christmas Truce (IRE)**[58] 6069 7-7-13 **57**............(p) JosephWalsh(7) 5 49
(Ms J S Doyle) *hld up towards rr on inner: rdn over 2f out: kpt on fnl f: nvr trbld ldrs* **33/1**

04P0 **9** *1 1/2* **Nikki Bea (IRE)**[97] 5210 3-8-5 **59** ow2............ PaulDoe 12 48
(Jamie Poulton) *in tch: rdn wl over 2f out: sn wknd* **33/1**

P212 **10** *shd* **Zalkani (IRE)**[19] 6623 6-8-13 **64**............ MichaelTebbutt 4 53
(J Pearce) *chsd ldrs: rdn over 3f out: wknd over 2f out* **7/1**

5000 **11** *3* **Ballybeg (IRE)**[11] 6712 3-8-6 **60**............(b) DaleGibson 13 43
(R J Price) *hld up in rr on outer: rdn and lost tch over 2f out* **25/1**

4500 **12** *18* **Double Bay (USA)**[24] 6565 3-8-9 **63**............ JoeFanning 2 12
(Jane Chapple-Hyam) *chsd ldr after 1f tl over 3f out: sn wknd: t.o* **50/1**

0000 **13** *1* **Compton Express**[12] 6696 3-8-4 **58** oh7 ow2............ AdrianTNicholls 3 5
(Jamie Poulton) *slowly away: a wl bhd: rdn and lost tch wl over 3f: t.o* **66/1**

2m 4.72s (-3.07) **Going Correction** -0.10s/f (Stan)
WFA 3 from 4yo+ 3lb 13 Ran SP% **122.1**
Speed ratings (Par 103):108,107,105,103,102 102,101,98,97,97 95,80,79
CSF £11.77 CT £42.37 TOTE £4.90: £2.10, £1.60, £2.30; EX 18.40 Trifecta £12.80 Pool £203.47 - 11.27 winning units..
Owner Good Company Partnership **Bred** Juddmonte Farms Ltd **Trained** Exning, Suffolk

FOCUS
modest handicap but there was a fair pace on here and the well-fancied first two came clear, suggesting the form is solid.
Marbaa(IRE) Official explanation: jockey said colt missed the break
Almanshood(USA) Official explanation: jockey said gelding hung right under pressure
Nikki Bea(IRE) Official explanation: jockey said filly hung left throughout
Compton Express Official explanation: jockey said filly moved poorly

6849 PONTIN'S FAMILY HOLIDAYS H'CAP 6f (P)
3:40 (3:41) (Class 2) (0-100,105) 3-Y-O+
£11,217 (£3,358; £1,679; £840; £419; £210) **Stalls** Low

Form RPR

5111 **1** **Areyoutalkingtome**[13] 6692 3-9-7 **105**............ TonyCulhane 6 115
(C A Cyzer) *hld up in rr: swtchd rt and hdwy over 1f out: qcknd to ld wl ins fnl f: readily* **4/1**[2]

0333 **2** *1* **Qadar (IRE)**[15] 6660 4-8-11 **95**............ NCallan 3 102
(N P Littmoden) *lw: chsd ldrs: rdn and hdwy 2f out: swtchd lft over 1f out: led ins fnl f: sn hdd and nt pce of wnr* **4/1**[2]

0310 **3** *1* **First Order**[11] 6720 5-8-8 **92** ow2............(v) PaulMulrennan 5 96
(I Semple) *sn chsng ldr: rdn over 2f out: kpt on same pce wl ins fnl f* **11/1**

2000 **4** *shd* **One More Round (USA)**[91] 5358 8-8-10 **97**.............(b) JamesDoyle(3) 8 101
(N P Littmoden) *sn bhd: pushed along after 2f out: hdwy and nt clr run briefly over 1f out: r.o wl fnl f: n.m.r nr fin* **20/1**

4011 **5** *nk* **Maltese Falcon**[15] 6660 6-9-0 **98**...............................(t) NelsonDeSouza 1 101
(P F I Cole) *led at gd pce: rdn wl over 1f out: hdd ins fnl f: fdd nr fin* **7/2**[1]

4132 **6** *hd* **Woodnook**[15] 6660 3-8-2 **86** oh2.. JimmyQuinn 7 89
(J A R Toller) *chsd ldrs: rdn and effrt over 2f out: kpt on same pce fnl f* **5/1**[3]

451 **7** *1 1/4* **Perfect Story (IRE)**[13] 6690 4-8-2 **86** oh3................. CatherineGannon 4 85
(J A R Toller) *hld up towards rr: rdn wl over 2f out: nt pce to rch ldrs* **14/1**

0034 **8** *2* **Smokin Beau**[6] 6776 9-8-4 **88**... JoeFanning 9 81
(N P Littmoden) *hld up towards rr: rdn over 2f out: bmpd wl over 1f out: no prog after* **16/1**

0002 **9** *1 1/2* **Talbot Avenue**[6] 6776 8-8-6 **90**... DaleGibson 2 78
(M Blanshard) *t.k.h: chsd ldrs tl rdn over 2f out: wknd wl over 1f out* **8/1**

1m 10.08s (-2.73) **Going Correction** -0.10s/f (Stan) course record **9** Ran SP% **115.6**
Speed ratings (Par 109):114,112,111,111,110 110,108,106,104
CSF £20.45 CT £162.21 TOTE £4.60: £2.00, £1.80, £3.20; EX 26.90 Trifecta £318.20 Part won. Pool £448.21 - 0.67 winning units. Place 6 £228.93, Place 5 £63.40.
Owner Mrs Charles Cyzer **Bred** C A Cyzer **Trained** Maplehurst, W Sussex

FOCUS
A decent and competitive sprint run at a fast pace that resulted in a winning time only fractionally outside the track record. The form looks strong and solid rated around the third and fourth.

NOTEBOOK
Areyoutalkingtome, once switched approaching the furlong marker, found a smart turn of foot to mow down those in front of him. He completed a four-timer in style, and on his first try over a trip as short as this. The key to him is a strong pace, as he travels and quickens. (op 11-2)
Qadar(IRE) had the race run to suit and got to the front briefly inside the last, but it was not long before he was overhauled by the fast-finishing winner. He is running to a consistent level at present. (op 10-3 tchd 9-2)
First Order left his poor effort on Fibresand well behind and ran really well considering he raced just off the strong pace set by the leader. His rider also put up 2lb overweight, so it was a solid effort in the circumstances.
One More Round(USA), having his first outing for three months, ran his usual race, staying on late from off the pace. He did not get much luck in running in the straight, so he deserves rating a bit better than his finishing position suggests, but while he remains talented, he is undoubtedly a difficult horse to win with.
Maltese Falcon, 6lb higher than for his last win, attempted to repeat the tactics that had been so successful last time, but he went too fast in front and ended up setting it up for the closers. (op 3-1)
Woodnook was a bit disappointing considering that she has been improving steadily of late and arguably put up a career-best effort last time out, but she was running from 2lb out of the handicap and was effectively worse off with Maltese Falcon despite finishing behind him last time.
T/Plt: £319.80 to a £1 stake. Pool: £53,010.15. 121.00 winning tickets. T/Qpdt: £24.00 to a £1 stake. Pool: £3,233.05. 99.55 winning tickets. SP

HANSHIN (R-H)
Sunday, December 17

OFFICIAL GOING: Firm

6850a HANSHIN CUP (GROUP 2) 7f
6:40 (12:00) 3-Y-0+ **£352,021** (£140,058; £89,770; £54,286; £34,546)

RPR

1 **Fusaichi Richard (JPN)**[22] 3-8-12 .... YFukunaga 10 117
(K Matsuda, Japan)

2 *nk* **Precise Machine (JPN)**[28] 6530 7-9-0 .... MMatsuoka 7 118
(K Hagiwara, Japan)

3 *hd* **Meiner Scherzi (JPN)**[28] 6530 3-8-12 .... YTake 13 115
(R Inaba, Japan)

4 *nk* **Asakusa Den'En**[49] 7-9-0 .... SFujita 11 117
(Michifumi Kono, Japan)

5 *1 1/2* **Symboli Gran (IRE)**[28] 6530 4-9-0 .... YShibayama 16 113
(Y Hatakeyama, Japan)

6 *nk* **New Very (JPN)**[28] 6530 8-9-0 .... HShii 4 112
(H Otonashi, Japan)

7 *nk* **Cheerful Smile (JPN)**[77] 5717 6-8-9 .... YIwata 14 106
(Y Ikee, Japan)

8 *nse* **Venus Line (JPN)**[77] 5717 5-8-9 .... SAkiyama 9 106
(N Hori, Japan)

9 *nse* **Court Masterpiece**[28] 6530 6-9-0 .... OPeslier 6 111
(E A L Dunlop) *missed break, raced towards rear of mid-division, driven to improve position on final turn, one pace straight SP 26-10F* **26/10**[1]

10 *1 3/4* **Tamamo Hot Play (JPN)**[77] 5717 5-9-0 .... KWatanabe 15 106
(K Minai, Japan)

11 *1/2* **Cosmo Schindler (AUS)** 4-9-0 .... KTake 8 105
(T Kayo)

12 *nk* **Tagano Bastille (JPN)**[77] 5717 3-8-11 .... KenichiIkezoe 5 101
(Kaneo Ikezoe, Japan)

13 *nk* **Daiwa Passion (JPN)**[252] 3-8-7 .... KHasegawa 2 96
(S Masuzawa, Japan)

14 *hd* **Blue Shotgun (JPN)**[77] 5717 7-9-0 .... HMiyuki 12 102
(K Take, Japan)

15 *nse* **Orewa Matteruze (JPN)**[77] 5717 6-9-0 .... YShibata 18 102
(H Otonashi, Japan)

16 *2 1/2* **Tsurugaoka Hayate (JPN)** 6-9-0 .... MMonteriso 17 96
(M Ito, Japan)

17 *2* **Daiwa Memphis (JPN)** 5-9-0 .... SKumazawa 3 90
(S Masuzawa, Japan)

1m 20.6s **17** Ran SP% **27.8**
(Including Y100 stake): WIN 1,010; PL 360, 310, 260; DF 5,390.
Owner Fusaro Sekiguchi **Bred** Northern Farm **Trained** Japan

NOTEBOOK
Fusaichi Richard(JPN) took the inagural running of this event in a tight finish. He was last year's champion juvenile in Japan, and improved significantly on his previous start when 13th in the Japan Cup Dirt.
Court Masterpiece probably found things happening a bit too quickly, being slowly away in a race run at a very fast pace. Attempting to make ground to challenge approaching the straight, he found himself shuffled slightly wide and unable to get involved.

[6838] KEMPTON (A.W) (R-H)
Monday, December 18

OFFICIAL GOING: Standard
Wind: Light behind Weather: Fine

6851 STAN JAMES BANDED STKS 5f (P)
1:20 (1:21) (Class 7) 3-Y-0+ **£1,365** (£403; £201) **Stalls** High

Form RPR

6405 **1** **Freshwinds**[12] 6727 4-8-7 45...............................(b) EmmettStack(5) 11 59
(Miss Diana Weeden) *t.k.h: prom: trckd ldr 2f out and gng easily: led ent fnl f: rdn clr* **6/1**[2]

3205 **2** *3* **Sharp Hat**[28] 6539 12-8-12 45.. PaulQuinn 8 48
(D W Chapman) *pushed along in midfield 1/2-way: effrt on inner over 1f out: styd on to take 2nd last 50yds: no ch w wnr* **10/1**

3050 **3** *1/2* **Vicky Pollard**[5] 6805 3-8-12 45..................................... IanMongan 12 46
(P Howling) *uns rdr and bolted bef s: led: drvn over 1f out: hdd and outpcd ent fnl f* **10/1**

0005 **4** *3/4* **Gaudalpin (IRE)**[42] 6372 4-8-9 45..........................(tp) JamesDoyle(3) 4 44
(Ernst Oertel) *sn trckd ldrs gng wl: rdn and fnd nil over 1f out: one pce after* **7/1**[3]

0660 **5** *3/4* **Prime Recreation**[12] 6723 9-8-12 45............................ PatCosgrave 2 41
(P S Felgate) *hld up in rr: prog on inner fr 1/2-way: kpt on fnl f: no ch* **12/1**

0040 **6** *3/4* **College Queen**[50] 6233 8-8-12 45................................. AdamKirby 10 38
(S Gollings) *nvr bttr than midfield: pushed along 1/2-way: one pce and no prog* **25/1**

3000 **7** *nk* **Peggys First**[12] 6727 4-8-12 45....................................(b) DaleGibson 1 37
(D E Cantillon) *taken down early: hld up in last pair and wl off the pce: shuffled along over 1f out: nvr nr ldrs* **16/1**

-000 **8** *1/2* **Tancred Times**[35] 6464 11-8-5 45........................ DonnaCaldwell(7) 5 35
(D W Barker) *rousted along to go prom fr wd draw: wknd over 1f out* **25/1**

0202 **9** *nk* **El Potro**[12] 6727 4-8-7 45...................................... AshleyHamblett(5) 9 34
(J R Holt) *chsd ldr to 2f out: sn wknd* **2/1**[1]

0030 **10** *1 1/4* **Secret Vision (USA)**[12] 6723 5-8-12 45.....................(p) HayleyTurner 7 30
(R M H Cowell) *nvr bttr than midfield: rdn 1/2-way: struggling wl over 1f out* **9/1**

0064 **11** *2 1/2* **Beau Jazz**[8] 6774 5-8-12 45....................................(p) AdrianMcCarthy 6 21
(W De Best-Turner) *a in last trio: struggling fnl 2f* **16/1**

4000 **12** *3/4* **Eternally**[27] 6548 4-8-9 45..(p) AmirQuinn(3) 3 18
(R M H Cowell) *racd wd early fr poor draw: a in rr: no ch fnl 2f* **16/1**

59.87 secs (-0.53) **Going Correction** -0.175s/f (Stan) **12** Ran SP% **121.3**
Speed ratings (Par 97):97,92,91,90,89 87,87,86,86,84 80,78
CSF £66.51 TOTE £11.00: £2.40, £3.70, £3.10; EX 80.70.
Owner The Porcia Partnership **Bred** Hedgeholme Stud **Trained** Newmarket, Suffolk
■ A first winner in Britain for Diana Weeden, who was previously based in Dubai.
■ Stewards' Enquiry : Donna Caldwell one-day ban: careless riding (Dec 29)

FOCUS
An ordinary banded sprint but the form should prove sound with hte placed horses to their marks.
Gaudalpin(IRE) Official explanation: trainer said filly lost a front shoe
Peggys First Official explanation: jockey said gelding hung right

6852 PANORAMIC BAR & RESTAURANT BANDED STKS 1m 2f (P)
1:50 (1:50) (Class 7) 3-Y-0+ **£1,365** (£403; £201) **Stalls** High

Form RPR

0056 **1** **Wind Chime (IRE)**[21] 6616 9-9-1 45........................... RichardThomas 9 52
(A G Newcombe) *settled in midfield: pushed along 3f out: prog 2f out: sustained chal fnl f to ld last strides* **15/2**

4435 **2** *shd* **Kilmeena Magic**[5] 6800 4-9-1 45.......................... StephenCarson 14 52
(J C Fox) *hld up off the pce: stdy prog gng wl fr 3f: rdn to ld on inner over 1f out: hdd last strides* **11/2**[3]

0600 **3** *hd* **Piquet**[5] 6801 8-8-12 40.. AmirQuinn(3) 6 51
(J J Bridger) *hld up wl in rr: stdy prog fr over 3f out: trckd ldrs over 1f out gng wl: drvn to chal: nt qckn last 150yds* **14/1**

3045 **4** *4* **Iceni Warrior**[5] 6804 4-9-1 45....................................... PaulDoe 4 44
(P Howling) *wl plcd: prog to chse ldr 3f out: rdn to dispute ld 2f out to over 1f out: wknd fnl f* **9/2**[2]

35 **5** *1 1/2* **Mikimoto (IRE)**[14] 6705 4-8-8 45.......................... PatrickHills(7) 11 41
(S C Williams) *prom: effrt on inner to dispute ld 2f out to over 1f out: wknd* **15/8**[1]

0006 **6** *3 1/2* **Tilen (IRE)**[46] 6306 3-8-12 40... NCallan 3 34
(V Smith) *hld up in midfield: effrt 3f out: no prog wl over 1f out and sn btn* **14/1**

0000 **7** *1 1/4* **Futoo (IRE)**[19] 6280 5-9-1 40...(p) PaulQuinn 12 32
(D W Chapman) *chsd ldr to 3f out: sn lost pl and btn* **25/1**

00 **8** *nk* **Sean Og (IRE)**[27] 6551 4-8-8 45..............................(p) SCreighton(7) 13 31
(E J Creighton) *led at generous pce to 2f out: wknd rapidly over 1f out* **50/1**

0660 **9** *1 1/4* **Boppys Dancer**[54] 6177 3-8-12 45.................................. MickyFenton 8 29
(P T Midgley) *dwlt: rousted along early to go prom: reminders at several stages and wknd 2f out* **16/1**

0600 **10** *3/4* **Ello Lucky (IRE)**[26] 4755 4-9-1 35............................ AdrianTNicholls 7 28
(C Roberts) *hld up wl in rr: detached fr main gp and struggling 3f out* **16/1**

0004 **11** *2 1/2* **Expected Bonus (USA)**[5] 6801 7-9-1 40...............(p) AdrianMcCarthy 1 23
(Jamie Poulton) *a in rr: hrd rdn and btn over 2f out* **10/1**

12 *1/2* **Richards Claire (IRE)**[7] 4341 5-9-1 45.........................(t) HayleyTurner 5 22
(D P Keane) *s.s: t.k.h: hld up in rr: no prog over 2f out: sn wknd* **25/1**

-000 **13** *14* **Yeldham Lady**[17] 6657 4-8-12 40.................................(p) LPKeniry(3) 10 —
(A J Chamberlain) *t.k.h: prom tl wknd rapidly 4f out: t.o* **33/1**

0000 **14** *16* **Zinging**[5] 6800 7-8-8 45..(b) RyanBird(7) 2 —
(J J Bridger) *hld up in last pair: rdn and lost tch over 5f out: sn t.o* **33/1**

2m 7.81s (-1.19) **Going Correction** -0.175s/f (Stan)
WFA 3 from 4yo+ 3lb **14** Ran SP% **129.8**
Speed ratings (Par 97):97,96,96,93,92 89,88,88,87,86 84,84,73,60
CSF £50.07 TOTE £8.30: £2.60, £1.80, £3.50; EX 51.40.
Owner M K F Seymour **Bred** Saeed Manana **Trained** Yarnscombe, Devon

FOCUS
Moderate banded form but sound enough rated around the first two.
Ello Lucky(IRE) Official explanation: jockey said filly hung left

6853 RUK MAIDEN AUCTION STKS 1m (P)
2:25 (2:26) (Class 7) 2-Y-O £1,365 (£403; £201) Stalls High

Form RPR

0005 1 **Ella Y Rossa**[28] 6534 2-8-4 45 JamesDoyle(3) 1 52
(P D Evans) *chsd ldrs: drvn wl over 2f out: effrt u.p to ld jst over 1f out: styd on wl* **7/1**[3]

003 2 1 **My Jeanie (IRE)**[23] 6597 2-8-5 58 AdrianTNicholls 10 48+
(J C Fox) *t.k.h: hld up in 7th: gng wl enough over 2f out: rdn over 1f out: r.o wl to take 2nd nr fin: too much to do* **2/1**[1]

0005 3 nk **Tumble Jill (IRE)**[24] 6576 2-8-4 45 ow1 AshleyHamblett(5) 7 51
(J J Bridger) *hld up in midfield: prog on inner over 2f out: jinked sn after: rdn to chal and upsides over 1f out: nt qckn* **8/1**

003 4 1 **Noddledoddle (IRE)**[30] 6511 2-8-2 50 (t) MarcHalford(3) 9 45
(J Ryan) *prom: rdn to ld over 2f out: hdd and one pce jst over 1f out* **7/2**[2]

0 5 6 **Athea Lad (IRE)**[9] 6757 2-8-11 AdamKirby 4 37
(W K Goldsworthy) *rdn to ld: hdd over 2f out: sn wknd* **16/1**

0044 6 shd **Ishimagic**[8] 6777 2-8-6 51 MatthewHenry 3 32
(J J Bridger) *pressed ldr: rdn to chal and upsides over 2f out: wknd over 1f out* **7/2**[2]

0464 7 nk **Baytown Rosie (IRE)**[7] 6789 2-8-5 45 HayleyTurner 2 30
(P S McEntee) *in tch in midfield: wknd 2f out* **11/1**

8 1 **Poyle Ruby** 2-8-5 DaleGibson 6 28
(M Blanshard) *s.s: rn green in last: wl adrift 3f out: styd on ins fnl f* **20/1**

000 9 ½ **Respect My Wishes**[24] 6575 2-8-7 35 ow1 LPKeniry 8 29
(R Ingram) *stdd s: hld up in 8th: brief effrt on outer 3f out: sn no prog* **66/1**

1m 41.06s (0.26) **Going Correction** -0.175s/f (Stan) 9 Ran SP% **121.9**
Speed ratings (Par 90):91,90,89,88,82 82,82,81,80
CSF £22.67 TOTE £8.60: £2.40, £1.40, £2.90; EX 41.00.
Owner Miss D L Wisbey & R J Viney **Bred** Miss Deborah Wisbey **Trained** Pandy, Abergavenny

FOCUS
A terrible maiden and the form looks really weak.

NOTEBOOK
Ella Y Rossa got going too late when a beaten favourite in a seven-furlong seller at Southwell on her previous start and the step up in trip suited. She will do well to follow up. (op 10-1)
My Jeanie(IRE), back up in trip, got going too late and can be considered unlucky not to have won. She clearly has ability, but her connections will do well to find a race as weak as this next time. (op 11-8 tchd 9-4)
Tumble Jill(IRE) ran a respectable race returned to maiden company and was not beaten far at all. (op 9-1)
Noddledoddle(IRE) weakened tamely inside the final furlong and did not see out his race. (op 4-1)
Ishimagic was well supported but in the market but ran well below her best. (op 5-1)

6854 FOLLOW YOUR MEETING WITH RACING BANDED STKS 1m (P)
2:55 (2:58) (Class 7) 3-Y-O+ £1,365 (£403; £201) Stalls High

Form RPR

0513 1 **Majehar**[21] 6617 4-8-11 46 AmirQuinn(3) 9 57+
(A G Newcombe) *trckd ldrs: effrt on inner over 2f out: hrd rdn to ld over 1f out: clr fnl f* **11/4**[2]

12 2 2 **Bowl Of Cherries**[5] 6802 3-9-6 50 (b) JamesDoyle(3) 5 61
(I A Wood) *s.i.s and wl in rr: prog 3f out: drvn over 2f out: styd on to take 2nd nr fin: no ch w wnr* **5/4**[1]

6 3 ½ **Tackcoat (IRE)**[216] 1764 6-8-10 40 (p) JerryO'Dwyer(3) 13 49
(Eoin Doyle, Ire) *led at decent pce: drvn and hdd over 1f out: hung lft fnl f: kpt on* **16/1**

0620 4 1¾ **Frank's Quest (IRE)**[5] 6802 6-9-1 47 LPKeniry 8 47
(A B Haynes) *off the pce in midfield: prog over 2f out: hrd rdn to chse ldrs over 1f out: no imp after* **14/1**

004 5 hd **Tipsy Lillie**[9] 6763 4-8-13 40 HayleyTurner 7 45
(P S McEntee) *sn pushed along towards rr: styd on u.p fr over 2f out: nrst fin* **33/1**

5232 6 ½ **Wodhill Gold**[28] 6543 5-9-3 49 (v) AdamKirby 3 47
(D Morris) *trckd ldrs: drvn over 2f out: nt qckn wl over 1f out: fdd fnl f* **8/1**[3]

4150 7 nk **Elms Schoolboy**[5] 6802 4-9-1 47 (b) IanMongan 12 45
(P Howling) *s.i.s: hld up in last trio: rdn over 2f out: hanging and nt qckn: styd on fnl f* **20/1**

0640 8 nk **Huxley (IRE)**[27] 6552 7-8-10 40 (t) NeilChalmers(3) 2 42
(D J Wintle) *hld up in rr: sme prog on outer 2f out: nvr pce to rch ldrs* **33/1**

3543 9 ¾ **Hilltop Fantasy**[8] 6779 5-8-13 40 NCallan 10 40
(V Smith) *prom: chsd ldr 3f out to 2f out: wknd* **11/1**

0064 10 3 **Colonel Bilko (IRE)**[5] 6802 4-8-10 40 (b) MarcHalford(3) 11 33
(J J Bridger) *s.i.s: last trio tl sme prog on outer 3f out: no hdwy and btn 2f out* **33/1**

5000 11 1 **Wanna Shout**[14] 6702 8-8-13 45 (p) MickyFenton 14 31
(R Dickin) *lost pl on inner after 2f and wl in rr: last 3f out: drvn and modest prog 2f out: no ch* **66/1**

6400 12 2½ **Bollywood (IRE)**[5] 6802 3-8-12 45 MatthewHenry 1 25
(J J Bridger) *racd wd towards rr: reminders 1/2-way: sn struggling* **20/1**

4000 13 ½ **Gem Bien (USA)**[9] 6763 8-8-13 45 (p) PaulQuinn 4 24
(D W Chapman) *chsd ldr to 3f out: wknd* **25/1**

0005 14 3 **Angel River**[5] 6803 4-8-13 40 (v) DavidKinsella 6 17
(J Ryan) *chsd ldrs tl wknd rapidly over 2f out* **66/1**

1m 39.32s (-1.48) **Going Correction** -0.175s/f (Stan)
WFA 3 from 4yo+ 1lb 14 Ran SP% **128.3**
Speed ratings (Par 97):100,98,97,95,95 95,94,94,93,90 89,87,86,83
CSF £6.35 TOTE £4.80: £1.40, £1.40, £6.50; EX 11.60.
Owner J R Salter **Bred** Darley **Trained** Yarnscombe, Devon

FOCUS
A decent race by banded standards and they went a good pace. The form looks solid for the grade.

6855 BOOK NOW FOR BOXING DAY BANDED STKS 7f (P)
3:25 (3:28) (Class 7) 3-Y-O+ £1,365 (£403; £201) Stalls High

Form RPR

4340 1 **Mon Petite Amour**[9] 6756 3-9-0 47 (p) AdamKirby 13 55+
(D W P Arbuthnot) *n.m.r after 1f and dropped to last trio: rdn and prog over 2f out: sustained effrt fr over 1f out to ld nr fin* **10/1**

0623 2 ½ **Fun Time**[21] 6618 3-9-3 50 AdrianTNicholls 8 57
(M R Channon) *t.k.h: pressed ldr: led 1/2-way: drvn 2f out: looked like holding on fnl f: hdd nr fin* **5/1**[3]

0050 3 hd **Musical Gift**[6] 6799 6-8-7 45 (v) KevinGhunowa(5) 11 51
(P A Blockley) *hld up in rr: rdn and prog over 2f out: chsd ldrs over 1f out: nt qckn: styd on nr fin* **14/1**

4660 4 ½ **Jools**[125] 4446 8-8-10 48 JamieJones(5) 7 53
(D K Ivory) *t.k.h: hld up in cl tch: effrt over 2f out: pressed ldr over 1f out: nt qckn ins fnl f* **12/1**

4023 5 ½ **Louisiade (IRE)**[16] 6674 5-9-3 50 (p) NCallan 3 53
(K A Ryan) *t.k.h: prom: chsd ldr 3f out: hanging and nt qckn over 1f out: kpt on* **9/4**[1]

0000 6 ½ **Atlantic Viking (IRE)**[14] 6694 11-9-0 50 (v) JamesDoyle(3) 14 55+
(P D Evans) *dwlt and drvn in rr early: prog u.p over 2f out: clsd but hanging and nt keen 1f out: n.m.r last 100yds* **20/1**

0000 7 1¼ **Double M**[5] 6805 9-8-12 45 (b) RichardThomas 12 44
(Mrs L Richards) *wl plcd: effrt on inner over 2f out: tried to chal over 1f out: wknd last 150yds* **33/1**

2011 8 ½ **Binnion Bay (IRE)**[5] 6803 5-9-6 50 AmirQuinn(3) 4 54
(J J Bridger) *dwlt and stdd s: wl in rr: wd bnd 3f out: swtchd to inner and drvn 2f out: kpt on but no ch* **10/3**[2]

00-0 9 1¾ **Junebug Symphony (IRE)**[348] 43 4-8-9 45 JerryO'Dwyer(3) 9 38
(V Smith) *t.k.h: hld up off the pce: prog over 2f out: chsd ldrs over 1f out: wknd fnl f* **50/1**

6003 10 nk **Dexileos (IRE)**[5] 6802 7-8-9 47 (t) AshleyHamblett(5) 10 39
(David Pinder) *t.k.h: hld up towards rr: rdn and no real prog 2f out* **13/2**

0300 11 3 **Warden Warren**[14] 6703 8-9-0 47 (b) AdrianMcCarthy 1 31
(Mrs C A Dunnett) *chsd ldrs: rdn and lost pl wl over 2f out: sn struggling* **25/1**

000 12 5 **Halfwaytoparadise**[9] 6763 3-9-3 50 (p) MatthewHenry 5 21
(W G M Turner) *led to 1/2-way: hung lft bnd sn after and reminders: eased fnl 2f* **25/1**

0000 13 5 **Sprouston (FR)**[5] 6802 3-8-7 47 (b) StevenGibson(7) 2 5
(J S Moore) *still wearing hood whn stalls opened and slowly away: wd and a in trble* **25/1**

1m 26.47s (-0.33) **Going Correction** -0.175s/f (Stan) 13 Ran SP% **128.5**
Speed ratings (Par 97):94,93,93,92,92 91,90,89,87,87 83,78,72
CSF £59.23 TOTE £11.30: £2.70, £1.90, £5.70; EX 68.80.
Owner Noel Cronin **Bred** Branston Stud Ltd **Trained** Upper Lambourn, Berks
■ Stewards' Enquiry : Adrian T Nicholls three-day ban: careless riding (Dec 29-31)

FOCUS
Another ordinary banded race and sound form rated around the first two.
Binnion Bay(IRE) Official explanation: jockey said gelding was slowly away
Dexileos(IRE) Official explanation: trainer said gelding was struck into behind

6856 SPONSOR AT KEMPTON BANDED STKS 6f (P)
3:55 (3:58) (Class 7) 3-Y-O+ £1,365 (£403; £201) Stalls High

Form RPR

0010 1 **Cool Tiger**[6] 6796 3-9-2 49 AlanDaly 8 56
(P Howling) *s.i.s: sn midfield: rdn and prog 2f out: led 1f out: drvn out* **4/1**[2]

0042 2 ¾ **Black Oval**[12] 6728 5-9-1 48 DeanMernagh 5 55+
(S Parr) *hld up in 8th: gng wl but plenty to do 2f out: prog 1f out: nt clr run briefly ins fnl f: pushed along and fin strly* **10/1**

0502 3 hd **Detonate**[113] 4846 4-8-13 49 JamesDoyle(3) 4 53
(Ms J S Doyle) *hld up in last pair: plenty to do 2f out: rapid prog on inner jst over 1f out: looked dangerous 75yds out: nt qckn nr fin* **7/1**[3]

0006 4 1½ **Patternmaker (USA)**[20] 6629 4-9-3 50 LPKeniry 3 50
(A M Hales) *hld up in midfield: effrt 2f out: chsd ldrs 1f out: one pce* **10/1**

0052 5 ½ **Mustammer**[3] 6833 3-9-1 48 MickyFenton 12 46
(D Shaw) *trckd ldrs: hanging 2f out: drvn to chal and upsides 1f out: fdd* **7/2**[1]

0060 6 1 **Almowj**[8] 6779 3-8-8 48 WilliamCarson(7) 1 43+
(C E Brittain) *rrd s: hld up in last pair: rdn and no prog 2f out: r.o wl last 150yds: nrst fin* **14/1**

0060 7 shd **Luloah**[10] 6755 3-9-3 50 HayleyTurner 7 45
(P S McEntee) *trckd ldr: rdn 2f out: effrt to chal and upsides 1f out: wknd* **33/1**

3000 8 hd **Thoughtsofstardom**[13] 6713 3-9-3 50 (p) AdamKirby 11 44
(P S McEntee) *s.i.s: t.k.h and sn chsd ldrs: rdn over 2f out: wknd jst over 1f out* **9/1**

0000 9 ½ **Amber Glory**[13] 6719 3-9-3 50 (b) NCallan 10 43
(K A Ryan) *led to 1f out: wknd* **10/1**

2065 10 1¼ **Hill Of Almhuim (IRE)**[5] 6802 3-9-1 48 DaleGibson 2 37
(Peter Grayson) *a wl in rr: rdn and no prog 2f out* **4/1**[2]

0160 11 30 **Epineuse**[15] 6688 3-9-1 48 (v[1]) StephenCarson 6 —
(J R Best) *prom to 1/2-way: wknd rapidly: t.o* **25/1**

1m 13.13s (-0.57) **Going Correction** -0.175s/f (Stan) 11 Ran SP% **125.4**
Speed ratings (Par 97):96,95,94,92,92 90,90,90,89,88 48
CSF £47.25 TOTE £6.60: £2.30, £2.20, £2.20; EX 56.30.
Owner Tony Clifford & Claudia Fisher **Bred** G B Partnership **Trained** Newmarket, Suffolk

FOCUS
A competitive banded sprint and sound form rated around the first three.
Epineuse Official explanation: jokey said filly hung left

6857 KEMPTON.CO.UK BANDED STKS 2m (P)
4:25 (4:25) (Class 7) 3-Y-O+ £1,365 (£403; £201) Stalls High

Form RPR

0006 1 **Mister Completely (IRE)**[5] 6804 5-9-8 50 JamesDoyle(3) 5 56
(Ms J S Doyle) *prom: trckd ldr over 3f out: rdn over 2f out: led 1f out: hld on u.p* **8/1**

0223 2 1 **Lysander's Quest (IRE)**[20] 6630 8-9-9 48 StephenCarson 6 53
(R Ingram) *led: tried to kick on over 2f out: fnd little and hdd 1f out: kpt on again once hdd* **11/4**[2]

0054 3 hd **Domenico (IRE)**[59] 4268 8-9-10 49 AdamKirby 2 53
(J R Jenkins) *hld up in midfield: effrt over 2f out: drvn and nt qckn over 1f out : kpt on* **10/1**

4552 4 nk **Malibu (IRE)**[14] 6705 5-9-8 47 MickyFenton 9 51
(M Appleby) *hld up: last tl 4f out: effrt on wd outside over 2f out: plugged on fr over 1f out: nvr able to chal* **7/1**

30-0 5 2 **Krasivi's Boy (USA)**[7] 5451 4-9-11 50 (b) GeorgeBaker 8 52
(G L Moore) *hld up in midfield: effrt and swtchd to inner 2f out: one pce and no imp fnl f* **4/1**[3]

-504 6 ½ **Rajayoga**[10] 6754 5-8-13 45 PatrickHills(7) 4 46+
(M H Tompkins) *hld up in last trio: trapped on inner over 2f out and sn outpcd: kpt on fr over 1f out: nt rcvr* **2/1**[1]

0000 7 7 **Indian Chase**[6] 6797 9-9-6 40 AlanDaly 1 38
(Dr J R J Naylor) *t.k.h: hld up in last trio: effrt over 2f out: wknd wl over 1f out* **33/1**

4/0 8 hd **Dueling B'Anjiz (USA)**[13] 6132 7-8-13 45 (p) SCreighton(7) 3 37
(E J Creighton) *chsd ldr to over 3f out: sn lost pl and btn* **66/1**

00-6 **9** *11* **Galandora**[14] 6537 6-9-6 35 ... RichardThomas 7 24
(Dr J R J Naylor) *prom to over 3f out: sn wknd: t.o* **66/1**

3m 35.83s (4.43) **Going Correction** -0.175s/f (Stan) **9** Ran SP% **118.6**
Speed ratings (Par 97):81,80,80,80,79 79,75,75,69
CSF £31.07 TOTE £11.40: £3.20, £1.10, £2.70; EX 40.10 Place 6 £263.87, Place 5 £85.78.
Owner Kevin Pattinson **Bred** Eamonn Griffin **Trained** Upper Lambourn, Berks

FOCUS
An ordinary banded staying event run in a slow time. The form makes sense though with the first two and the fourth close to form.
Galandora Official explanation: jockey said mare hung left in straight
T/Plt: £105.30 to a £1 stake. Pool: £38,909.45. 269.60 winning tickets. T/Qpdt: £15.80 to a £1 stake. Pool: £3,716.80. 173.10 winning tickets. JN

6832 WOLVERHAMPTON (A.W) (L-H)
Monday, December 18

OFFICIAL GOING: Standard to slow
Wind: Nil Weather: Some drizzle

6858 GO PONTIN'S AMATEUR RIDERS' H'CAP 5f 216y(P)
1:30 (1:30) (Class 5) (0-75,75) 3-Y-0+ **£2,045** (£2,045; £484; £242) **Stalls** Low

Form RPR
0025 **1** **Marko Jadeo (IRE)**[3] 6835 8-11-2 **75** ... MrJoshuaHarris(5) 9 86
(R A Harris) *s.i.s: rdn and hdwy on outside over 1f out: r.o wl to join ldr post* **14/1**
5600 **1** *dht* **Gilded Cove**[25] 6572 6-10-3 **62** ... MrStephenHarrison(5) 1 73+
(R Hollinshead) *bhd: rdn over 2f out: swtchd rt and hdwy over 1f out: led ins fnl f: jnd post* **9/1**
1220 **3** *1 ¾* **Ten Shun**[24] 6579 3-10-12 **73** ... MrRichardEvans(7) 3 79+
(P D Evans) *hld up in mid-div: hdwy whn nt clr run over 1f out: r.o ins fnl f* **7/1**[2]
5405 **4** *1* **Danetime Lord (IRE)**[9] 6770 3-10-11 **70** ... (p) MissARyan(5) 7 73+
(K A Ryan) *hld up in mid-div: stmbld over 3f out: swtchd rt over 2f out: hrd rdn and hung lft over 1f out: r.o wl ins fnl f* **15/2**[3]
4004 **5** *½* **Charlie Delta**[9] 6770 3-10-13 **72** ... MrSFMagee(5) 5 73
(D Carroll) *chsd ldrs: rdn and ev ch 1f out: one pce* **7/1**[2]
5234 **6** *½* **Chatshow (USA)**[27] 6555 5-10-8 **67** ... MrMJJSmith(5) 11 67
(A W Carroll) *chsd ldrs: rdn over 2f out: one pce fnl f* **5/1**[1]
0-01 **7** *hd* **Skip Of Colour**[13] 6717 6-10-4 **61** oh6 ... (t) MissFayeBramley(3) 6 60
(P A Blockley) *hld up and bhd: nt clr run over 3f out: rdn and hdwy on ins fnl f: r.o* **10/1**
0442 **8** *1* **Bonne De Fleur**[24] 6585 5-10-13 **67** ... (b) MrSWalker 10 63
(B Smart) *led 1f: chsd ldr: rdn to ld wl over 1f out: hdd & wknd ins fnl f* **7/1**[2]
4035 **9** *shd* **Fast Heart**[2] 6844 5-10-9 **70** ... (t) MissBKilloran(7) 12 66
(R A Harris) *racd wd bk st: chsd ldrs: ev ch over 2f out: wknd ins fnl f* **9/1**
0225 **10** *1 ½* **Piccolo Prince**[16] 6681 5-10-7 **61** oh8 ... MissEJJones 8 52
(P A Blockley) *mid-div: rdn over 2f out: btn whn hung lft over 1f out* **20/1**
0003 **11** *hd* **Comic Tales**[11] 6738 5-10-2 **61** oh16 ... MissMMullineaux(5) 2 52
(M Mullineaux) *s.i.s: a bhd* **66/1**
4300 **12** *1* **Blessed Place**[2] 6842 6-10-6 **67** oh2 ow6 ... (t) MrSJEdwards(7) 4 55
(D J S Ffrench Davis) *s.i.s: sn rcvrd: led after 1f: rdn and hdd wl over 1f out: wknd fnl f* **9/1**

1m 16.2s (0.39) **Going Correction** +0.05s/f (Slow) **12** Ran SP% **117.9**
Speed ratings (Par 103):99,99,96,95,94 94,93,92,92,90 90,88
, £3.50 TRIFECTA Win: MJ 6.00, GC 5.50; Pl: MJ 3.70, GC 2.70; Ex: MJ-GC 42.90, GC-MJ 45.10; CSF: MJ-GC 66.88; GC-MJ 63.89; T/C: MJ-GC-TS 490.52, GC-.
Owner D Tumman & R F Bloodstock **Bred** P Casey **Trained** Earlswood, Monmouths
Owner M Johnson **Bred** R Hollinshead And M Johnson **Trained** Upper Longdon, Staffs
■ Stewards' Enquiry : Mr S F Magee three-day ban: used whip with excessive force (Jan 5, 15, 19)

FOCUS
A modest but very competitive handicap; the form look straightforward and should work out.

6859 GO PONTIN'S CLAIMING STKS 1m 141y(P)
2:00 (2:00) (Class 6) 2-Y-0 **£2,730** (£806; £403) **Stalls** Low

Form RPR
0054 **1** **My Mirasol**[9] 6760 2-9-0 59 ... (p) FrancisNorton 10 58
(K A Ryan) *led: hdd over 6f out: remained prom: rdn 2f out: led wl ins fnl f: r.o* **7/2**[2]
6245 **2** *nk* **Global Traffic**[9] 6760 2-8-9 53 ... (b[1]) JimCrowley 7 52
(P D Evans) *hld up in mid-div: rdn and hdwy over 2f out: nt clr run fr wl over 1f out: tl swtchd rt ins fnl f: r.o wl: unlucky* **7/2**[2]
0034 **3** *nk* **Party Palace**[9] 6768 2-8-2 62 ... ChrisCatlin 12 47+
(J A Osborne) *chsd ldrs: wnt 2nd over 5f out: led over 2f out: rdn and edgd lft wl over 1f out: hdd and nt qckn wl ins fnl f* **11/2**[3]
0000 **4** *5* **Gold Response**[33] 6487 2-8-11 45 ... DeanMcKeown 1 43
(D Shaw) *hld up and bhd: rdn and hdwy whn hung lft over 1f out: nvr trbld ldrs* **40/1**
600 **5** *¾* **Power Alert**[16] 6669 2-8-12 45 ... RichardKingscote(3) 4 45
(B R Millman) *hld up in mid-div: rdn and hdwy over 1f out: nvr trbld ldrs* **33/1**
6463 **6** *¾* **Stars Above**[9] 6768 2-8-0 47 ... JamieMackay 8 29
(Sir Mark Prescott) *wnt rt s: sn pushed along: led over 6f out: rdn and hdd over 2f out: n.m.r on ins wl over 1f out: wknd fnl f* **11/4**[1]
0050 **7** *½* **Up The Pole**[9] 6760 2-8-6 53 ... (b[1]) PaulMulrennan 6 34
(M W Easterby) *wnt lft s: hld up in tch: rdn over 2f out: wknd over 1f out* **20/1**
0000 **8** *2* **Fun Thai**[24] 6576 2-8-3 45 ... EdwardCreighton 5 26
(M R Channon) *hmpd s: rdn over 3f out: a bhd* **16/1**
0000 **9** *2* **Fruits D'Amour (IRE)**[11] 6736 2-8-2 51 ... JimmyQuinn 11 21
(S Kirk) *s.i.s: sn mid-div: rdn over 3f out: sn bhd* **14/1**
0660 **10** *25* **Desirable Dancer (IRE)**[20] 6640 2-7-13 45 ... (p) TolleyDean(7) 3 —
(R A Harris) *hld up in tch: rdn over 3f out: wknd over 2f out* **33/1**
0 **11** *48* **Jewelled Dagger (IRE)**[30] 6523 2-9-5 ... RobertWinston 9 —
(I Semple) *s.i.s: bhd: lost tch 4f out: eased 3f out: t.o* **25/1**

1m 52.04s (0.28) **Going Correction** +0.05s/f (Slow) **11** Ran SP% **116.0**
Speed ratings (Par 94):100,99,99,95,94 93,93,91,89,67 24
CSF £14.83 TOTE £4.10: £1.30, £1.80, £2.00; EX 18.40 Trifecta £48.70 Pool £183.28, 2.67 w/u.Stars Above was claimed by D P Keane for £5,000
Owner Mrs Margaret Forsyth **Bred** J A Forsyth **Trained** Hambleton, N Yorks

FOCUS
Not a great claimer but form looks weak, although they did appear to go a good pace.

NOTEBOOK
My Mirasol was down in grade for this switch from Fibresand to Polytrack. She confirmed her length and a quarter superiority over Global Traffic at Southwell on 2lb better terms but did look rather lucky to do so. (op 10-3 tchd 4-1)
Global Traffic ◆ was well backed in the first-time blinkers and would have won with any sort of luck in running. Providing the headgear works again, losses should soon be recouped. (op 11-2)
Party Palace caused the runner-up and Start Above problems when drifting towards the inside rail once in line for home. She may well have found the extended nine furlongs beyond her last time. (op 8-1 tchd 5-1)
Gold Response had the visor left off on this return to claiming company and did not aid his cause by hanging left. (op 50-1)
Power Alert, down in class and up in distance, was another who could never make his presence felt.
Stars Above did not get home after being scrubbed along to seize the initiative after a quarter of a mile. (op 2-1 tchd 3-1)

6860 PONTINS.COM (S) STKS 1m 4f 50y(P)
2:35 (2:35) (Class 6) 3-Y-0+ **£2,388** (£705; £352) **Stalls** Low

Form RPR
0400 **1** **Saameq (IRE)**[222] 1590 5-9-4 45 ... EddieAhern 6 59
(D W Thompson) *hld up towards rr: smooth hdwy over 3f out: led on bit 2f out: rdn clr 1f out: r.o wl* **15/2**
0040 **2** *6* **Finished Article (IRE)**[5] 6801 9-9-8 49 ... J-PGuillambert 5 53
(P A Blockley) *t.k.h in mid-div: rdn over 3f out: hdwy over 2f out: wnt 2nd over 1f out: no ch w wnr* **6/1**[3]
0600 **3** *2 ½* **Come What July (IRE)**[10] 6743 5-9-4 47 ... DeanMcKeown 9 45
(D Shaw) *hld up and bhd: rdn and hdwy on outside 3f out: hung lft over 1f out: one pce* **25/1**
3015 **4** *1* **Cool Isle**[5] 6812 3-8-12 55 ... (b) DeanCorby 1 43
(P Howling) *led early: a.p: rdn 3f out: wknd fnl f* **5/1**[2]
5442 **5** *2 ½* **Templet (USA)**[23] 6604 6-9-4 57 ... (v) DanielTudhope 11 40+
(W G Harrison) *hld up towards rr: rdn whn n.m.r briefly 3f out: swtchd rt over 1f out: styd on fnl f: n.d* **2/1**[1]
6366 **6** *5* **Laurollie**[21] 6620 4-8-13 40 ... BrettDoyle 7 27
(B P J Baugh) *sn led: hdd 9f out: led 7f out: rdn and hdd 2f out: wknd 1f out* **12/1**
/50- **7** *2* **Saddler's Quest**[18] 524 9-8-11 40 ... SoniaEaton(7) 12 29
(B P J Baugh) *hdwy on outside to ld 9f out: hdd 7f out: wknd over 2f out* **66/1**
62S- **8** *2* **Stallone**[475] 2419 9-9-4 69 ... RobertWinston 3 25
(N Wilson) *hld up and bhd: rdn and short-lived effrt over 2f out* **9/1**
0000 **9** *3 ½* **Elli Lewtia**[9] 6758 3-8-8 35 ... DerekMcGaffin 10 15
(J Jay) *hld up in mid-div: pushed along 7f out: sn bhd: rdn over 4f out: no rspnse* **100/1**
0550 **10** *1* **Out Of This Way**[13] 6716 3-8-13 63 ... LeeEnstone 4 18
(I A Wood) *prom: rdn over 3f out: wknd wl over 1f out* **16/1**
2430 **11** *5* **Moon Shot**[28] 694 10-9-8 54 ... TonyCulhane 8 14
(A G Juckes) *t.k.h in mid-div: hdwy over 4f out: wknd over 3f out* **15/2**
40-0 **12** *¾* **First Generation**[9] 6763 4-9-4 45 ... JimCrowley 2 9
(P D Evans) *hld up in mid-div: rdn and lost pl over 3f out: n.m.r on ins briefly 3f out* **66/1**

2m 42.92s (0.50) **Going Correction** +0.05s/f (Slow)
WFA 3 from 4yo+ 5lb **12** Ran SP% **119.2**
Speed ratings (Par 101):100,96,94,93,92 88,87,86,83,83 79,79
CSF £51.67 TOTE £10.60: £3.00, £2.10, £4.00; EX 53.90 TRIFECTA Not won..The winner was bought in for 7,500gns
Owner Mrs L Irving **Bred** Shadwell Estate Company Limited **Trained** Bolam, Co Durham

FOCUS
An ordinary seller and the form looks weak.
Out Of This Way Official explanation: jockey said colt never travelled

6861 PONTIN'S HOLIDAYS MAIDEN STKS 1m 141y(P)
3:05 (3:07) (Class 5) 3-Y-0+ **£3,238** (£963; £481; £240) **Stalls** Low

Form RPR
32 **1** **Foreign Language (USA)**[9] 6765 3-8-5 ... WilliamBuick(7) 4 56+
(N A Callaghan) *hld up in tch: rdn to ld jst over 1f out: sn clr: r.o wl* **3/1**[2]
0223 **2** *4* **Chia (IRE)**[20] 6647 3-8-12 63 ... FrancisNorton 7 48
(D Haydn Jones) *a.p: rdn and ev ch jst over 2f out: one pce fnl f* **5/4**[1]
003 **3** *1 ½* **Layed Back Rocky**[9] 6765 4-9-5 45 ... EddieAhern 9 50
(M Mullineaux) *a.p: wnt 2nd over 6f out: rdn and ev ch 2f out: no ex fnl f* **40/1**
34 **4** *1 ½* **Executive Paddy (IRE)**[7] 6792 7-9-5 ... LeeEnstone 11 47
(I A Wood) *hld up in mid-div: hdwy 6f out: rdn 3f out: one pce fnl 2f* **14/1**
2 **5** *¾* **Call My Bluff (FR)**[152] 3639 3-9-3 66 ... ChrisCatlin 2 45
(Rae Guest) *led: rdn over 2f out: hdd jst over 2f out: wknd ins fnl f* **11/2**[3]
0600 **6** *shd* **The Terminator (IRE)**[12] 6726 4-8-12 40 ... SoniaEaton(7) 3 45
(M Mullineaux) *prom: lost pl 4f out: sme late prog: n.d* **66/1**
3440 **7** *¾* **Sweet Medicine**[136] 4104 4-9-0 72 ... TonyCulhane 1 38
(P Howling) *hld up towards rr: sme hdwy on outside fnl f: nvr nr ldrs* **9/1**
0 **8** *1 ½* **Inscribed (IRE)**[9] 6771 3-8-12 ... J-PGuillambert 6 35
(G A Huffer) *hld up in mid-div: rdn over 3f out: no hdwy fnl 2f* **33/1**
6 **9** *nk* **Global Strategy**[9] 6771 3-9-3 ... BrettDoyle 13 40
(Rae Guest) *a bhd* **33/1**
05 **10** *2 ½* **Champion's Way (IRE)**[9] 6765 4-9-0 ... JamesMillman(5) 5 34
(B R Millman) *hld up in mid-div: rdn over 3f out: wknd over 2f out* **50/1**
/060 **11** *64* **Inmom (IRE)**[218] 771 5-9-0 40 ... (t) DeanMcKeown 12 —
(S R Bowring) *rrd s: a in rr: rdn 5f out: t.o fnl 4f* **66/1**
12 *dist* **Gizmo** 3-9-3 ... RobertWinston 10 —
(B Smart) *s.i.s: nvr gng wl: t.o fnl 5f* **16/1**

1m 51.39s (-0.37) **Going Correction** +0.05s/f (Slow)
WFA 3 from 4yo+ 2lb **12** Ran SP% **120.6**
Speed ratings (Par 103):103,99,98,96,96 96,95,94,93,91 34,—
CSF £6.75 TOTE £4.60: £1.80, £1.10, £6.00; EX 8.80 Trifecta £86.80 Pool £195.77, 1.60 w/u.
Owner N A Callaghan **Bred** Juddmonte Farms Inc **Trained** Newmarket, Suffolk

FOCUS
A modest maiden limited by the proximity of the third and sixth.
Executive Paddy(IRE) Official explanation: jockey said gelding hung left in home straight
Gizmo Official explanation: jockey said gelding never travelled

6862 WBXTRIPLECROWN.COM H'CAP 1m 1f 103y(P)
3:35 (3:35) (Class 5) (0-75,75) 3-Y-0+ **£3,886** (£1,156; £577; £288) **Stalls** Low

Form RPR
0341 **1** **Magical Music**[11] 6741 3-9-2 **75** ... JimmyQuinn 4 86
(J Pearce) *a.p: rdn to ld jst over 1f out: drvn out* **4/1**[3]

0054 **2** 2 **Davenport (IRE)**[20] 6635 4-8-13 **75**........................(p) JamesMillman(5) 9 82
(B R Millman) *s.i.s: sn swtchd lft: hld up: rdn over 3f out: hdwy over 2f out: swtchd lft wl over 1f out: kpt on ins fnl* **10/1**

0005 **3** nk **Primo Way**[10] 6752 5-8-13 **70**........................(b) RobertWinston 8 76
(I Semple) *chsd ldr: led 2f out: sn rdn: hdd jst over 1f out: nt qckn* **9/1**

03-1 **4** 3 **Where's Broughton**[24] 6588 3-9-2 **75**........................ BrettDoyle 5 75
(W J Musson) *hld up: hdwy over 2f out: edgd lft fnl f: no imp* **9/4**[1]

3026 **5** 1 1/2 **Desert Leader (IRE)**[16] 6677 5-9-3 **74**........................ EddieAhern 2 71
(W M Brisbourne) *prom: rdn over 3f out: hld whn nt clr run briefly wl over 1f out* **11/4**[2]

0531 **6** 3/4 **Kingsmaite**[9] 6762 5-8-6 **63**........................(bt) DeanMcKeown 6 59
(S R Bowring) *led: rdn and hdd 2f out: wknd 1f out* **8/1**

-106 **7** shd **War At Sea (IRE)**[16] 6673 4-8-13 **70**........................ FrancisNorton 1 65
(A W Carroll) *a bhd* **25/1**

1-30 **8** 5 **Stravara**[13] 6716 3-8-3 **69**........................ RussellKennemore(7) 7 54
(R Hollinshead) *t.k.h: rdn over 3f out: sn bhd* **20/1**

2m 3.08s (0.46) **Going Correction** +0.05s/f (Slow)
WFA 3 from 4yo+ 2lb 8 Ran SP% **116.2**
Speed ratings (Par 103):99,97,96,94,92 92,92,87
CSF £43.67 CT £340.97 TOTE £4.90: £1.30, £2.20, £2.30; EX 32.80 Trifecta £189.70 Pool £355.50, 1.33 w/u.
Owner Killarney Glen & Mrs E M Clarke **Bred** Peter Taplin **Trained** Newmarket, Suffolk
FOCUS
A fair handicap in which they went a steady pace for the first half a mile. The form makes sense with the placed horses to recent form.
Where's Broughton Official explanation: jockey said filly hung left throughout

6863 WBX.COM WORLD BET EXCHANGE H'CAP 1m 141y(P)
4:05 (4:05) (Class 5) (0-75,73) 3-Y-0+ **£3,238** (£963; £481; £240) **Stalls** Low

Form RPR

2311 **1** **Peruvian Prince (USA)**[3] 6837 4-8-11 **71** 6ex.......... JamieMoriarty(5) 7 84+
(R A Fahey) *led early: a gng wl: led on bit ins fnl f: easily* **4/11**[1]

0050 **2** 3 **Startori**[17] 6664 3-8-9 **66**........................ RobertWinston 6 69
(B Smart) *sn led: hdd over 7f out: rdn over 3f out: ev ch wl over 1f out: sn edgd rt: one pce fnl f* **40/1**

0515 **3** hd **Dyanita**[2] 6841 3-8-10 **67**........................(b[1]) TonyCulhane 4 70
(B W Hills) *led over 7f out: rdn over 2f out: hdd and no ex ins fnl f* **14/1**[3]

4 1 1/2 **Dapple Dawn (IRE)**[99] 5214 3-8-5 **69** ow1........................ GaryEdwards(7) 3 69
(D Carroll) *sn prom: wnt 2nd 6f out: rdn and ev ch wl over 1f out: one pce* **40/1**

0602 **5** 1 1/2 **Coleridge (AUS)**[26] 6564 7-9-4 **73**........................ EddieAhern 5 70
(B G Powell) *hld up: rdn 3f out: hdwy on ins wl over 1f out: no imp fnl f* **9/2**[2]

0500 **6** 1 **Bijou Dan**[25] 6568 5-8-8 **68**........................(b) DuranFentiman(5) 1 63
(W G Harrison) *hld up in rr: rdn 3f out: nvr trbld ldrs* **20/1**

6400 **P** **My Pension (IRE)**[7] 6787 5-8-4 **59** oh4........................ JimmyQuinn 2 —
(P Howling) *hld up: rdn over 3f out: sn eased: p.u lame over 2f out* **66/1**

1m 50.93s (-0.83) **Going Correction** +0.05s/f (Slow)
WFA 3 from 4yo+ 2lb 7 Ran SP% **109.3**
Speed ratings (Par 103):105,102,102,100,99 98,—
CSF £24.51 TOTE £1.40: £1.10, £8.20; EX 15.10 Place 6 £133.20, Place 5 £35.50.
Owner R G Leatham **Bred** Alexander-Groves Thoroughbreds **Trained** Musley Bank, N Yorks
■ Stewards' Enquiry : Gary Edwards fine: breach of instruction H24, reports of performance by riders £130.
FOCUS
An uncompetitive handicap and the form is not solid, with the third the best guide.
Dapple Dawn(IRE) Official explanation: jockey said, regarding running and riding, that his orders were to jump out and make running, however, he was unable to do so having been slightly squeezed at start, adding that the filly hung left back straight and right home straight when it became tired; trainer confirmed, adding that the filly is temperamental and was not to be knocked about.
T/Plt: £172.70 to a £1 stake. Pool of £53,408.60. 225.70 winning tickets T/Qpdt: £29.40 to a £1 stake. Pool of £4,128.10. 103.70 winning tickets KH

6844 LINGFIELD (L-H)
Tuesday, December 19

OFFICIAL GOING: Standard
Wind: Almost nil Weather: Light mist

6864 PONTIN'S FAMILY HOLIDAYS H'CAP (DIV I) 7f (P)
12:30 (12:32) (Class 6) (0-58,59) 3-Y-0+ **£1,706** (£503; £252) **Stalls** Low

Form RPR

0000 **1** **Super Frank (IRE)**[18] 5129 3-9-0 **55**........................ RichardHughes 12 64
(J Akehurst) *t.k.h: trckd ldr: qcknd to ld over 1f out: rdn clr* **8/1**

0001 **2** 1 **Cool Sands (IRE)**[10] 6763 4-9-2 **57**........................(v) DaneO'Neill 5 63
(D Shaw) *in tch: effrt 2f out: r.o to take 2nd ins fnl f: hld whn edgd lft nr fin* **9/2**[2]

01 **3** 1 1/4 **Claws**[15] 6708 3-8-10 **54**........................ JamesDoyle(3) 2 57
(A J Lidderdale) *chsd ldrs: rdn 2f out: one pce appr fnl f* **9/1**

5350 **4** hd **Hotchpotch (USA)**[14] 6714 3-8-13 **54**........................(v[1]) BrettDoyle 10 57
(J R Best) *plld hrd early: chsd ldrs: rdn 2f out: one pce appr fnl f: hld whn sltly hmpd nr fin* **7/2**[1]

3001 **5** 5 **The London Gang**[4] 6833 3-9-4 **59** 6ex........................(v) JimCrowley 11 49
(P D Evans) *towards rr: rdn 2f out: nt pce to chal* **7/1**

2050 **6** 1 1/4 **Tamworth (IRE)**[14] 6721 4-9-0 **55**........................(t) EdwardCreighton 4 41
(E J Creighton) *in rr: pushed along after 2f: n.d* **9/1**

4253 **7** shd **Mountain Pass (USA)**[22] 6624 4-8-9 **57**........................(p) ThomasBubb(7) 6 43
(S Dow) *rrd s and missed break: hld up in rr: wd fr 4f out: nvr trbld ldrs* **11/2**[3]

0050 **8** 1 3/4 **Secam (POL)**[4] 6829 7-8-12 **53** ow1........................(b) SamHitchcott 1 35
(Mrs P Townsley) *in tch: rdn 3f out: wknd fnl 2f* **10/1**

-460 **9** nk **Night Wolf (IRE)**[11] 6747 6-8-12 **53**........................ PaulDoe 8 34
(Jamie Poulton) *led: rdn 3f out: hdd & wknd qckly over 1f out* **16/1**

1m 23.87s (-2.02) **Going Correction** -0.275s/f (Stan) 9 Ran SP% **114.4**
Speed ratings (Par 101):100,98,97,97,91 90,89,87,87
CSF £43.43 CT £334.06 TOTE £12.80: £3.00, £1.80, £2.50; EX 55.60 Trifecta £88.10 Part won. Pool £124.11 - 0.10 winning units..
Owner A D Spence **Bred** A Butler **Trained** Epsom, Surrey
FOCUS
A modest race, run at a pedestrian tempo, so the fast time may have been due to the texture of the Polytrack surface following a cold night. The form looks solid and could be slightly better than rated.

6865 PHOTO GIFTS FROM BONUSPRINT.COM H'CAP 6f (P)
1:00 (1:00) (Class 5) (0-70,71) 3-Y-0+ **£3,238** (£963; £481; £240) **Stalls** Low

Form RPR

043 **1** **Lethal**[105] 5092 3-9-2 **69**........................ RichardHughes 5 82+
(D K Ivory) *stdd s: sn chsng ldrs: r.o to ld ins fnl f: rdn clr* **12/1**

3121 **2** 2 1/2 **Louphole**[152] 3682 4-9-2 **69**........................ EddieAhern 2 75
(P J Makin) *dwlt: hld up in midfield: rdn over 2f out: styd on to chse wnr over 1f out: no imp* **10/3**[2]

3030 **3** 1 **Quality Street**[3] 6844 4-8-4 **64**........................(p) JosephWalsh(7) 6 67
(P Butler) *led: 4l clr 2f out: rdn and hdd over 1f out: no ex* **11/1**

5644 **4** nk **Desert Light (IRE)**[21] 6632 5-7-10 **56**........................(v) WilliamBuick(7) 8 58
(D Shaw) *bhd: rdn and r.o fnl 2f: nrst fin* **11/2**[3]

00 **5** 1 3/4 **Perfect Treasure (IRE)**[52] 6227 3-8-13 **66**........................ OscarUrbina 3 63
(J A R Toller) *sn rdn along and bhd: sme hdwy 2f out: nvr rchd ldrs* **12/1**

0200 **6** hd **Jayanjay**[3] 6842 7-8-8 **68**........................ JackMitchell(7) 7 64
(P Mitchell) *hld up towards rr: effrt and in tch over 1f out: no ex fnl f* **7/1**

0200 **7** 2 **Greek Secret**[18] 6664 3-8-11 **71** ow8........................(b[1]) JamesO'Reilly(7) 4 61
(J O'Reilly) *t.k.h: prom: chsd ldr after 2f tl wknd over 1f out* **14/1**

3651 **8** 4 **Sparkwell**[5] 6823 4-8-13 **66** 6ex........................ DaneO'Neill 9 44
(D Shaw) *s.s: bhd: rdn 3f out: nvr a factor* **9/4**[1]

2020 **9** 6 **Sarah's Art (IRE)**[154] 3612 3-9-1 **68**........................(b) MickyFenton 1 28
(Miss D A McHale) *rdn to press ldr 2f: wknd 3f out* **33/1**

1m 10.83s (-1.98) **Going Correction** -0.275s/f (Stan) 9 Ran SP% **115.1**
Speed ratings (Par 103):102,98,97,96,94 94,91,86,78
CSF £51.73 CT £463.03 TOTE £13.30: £3.60, £1.40, £3.40; EX 30.20 Trifecta £129.30 Part won. Pool £182.16 - 0.10 winning units..
Owner A S Reid **Bred** A S Reid **Trained** Radlett, Herts
FOCUS
A fair sprint, run at a good gallop, with an unexposed winner and solid form rated through the third and fourth.
Sparkwell Official explanation: vet said colt was distressed

6866 PERSONALISED CARDS FROM BONUSPRINT.COM NURSERY 7f (P)
1:30 (1:31) (Class 4) (0-85,81) 2-Y-O **£4,533** (£1,348; £674; £336) **Stalls** Low

Form RPR

511 **1** **Sharpazmax (IRE)**[24] 6597 2-9-5 **79**........................ EddieAhern 2 83+
(P J Makin) *hld up in midfield: effrt 2f out: str run to ld nr fin* **2/1**[1]

3213 **2** nk **Baylini**[24] 6598 2-9-4 **81**........................ JamesDoyle(3) 5 85
(Ms J S Doyle) *chsd ldrs: wnt 2nd 2f out: drvn to ld wl ins fnl f: hdd and nt qckn nr fin* **5/2**[2]

5445 **3** 1 **Racing Times**[10] 6764 2-9-1 **75**........................ RichardHughes 9 76
(B J Meehan) *sn led and crossed to ins fr wd draw: hrd rdn and hdd wl ins fnl f: no ex nr fin* **8/1**

5210 **4** 3 1/2 **Copper King**[10] 6764 2-9-3 **77**........................ JimCrowley 4 69
(P D Evans) *t.k.h in rr: shkn up and hdwy over 1f out: nt rch ldrs* **16/1**

0152 **5** 1 3/4 **Our Blessing (IRE)**[34] 6488 2-9-1 **75**........................ DaneO'Neill 7 62
(A P Jarvis) *prom tl hrd rdn and wknd over 1f out* **9/2**[3]

6502 **6** 1 1/2 **Lawyer To World**[34] 6487 2-8-7 **67** ow1........................ MickyFenton 8 50
(N A Callaghan) *dwlt: towards rr: rdn over 2f out: n.d* **9/1**

0030 **7** nk **Ballyshane Spirit (IRE)**[20] 6653 2-7-5 **58** oh1........................ WilliamBuick(7) 1 41
(N A Callaghan) *towards rr: rdn 3f out: nvr able to chal* **33/1**

3240 **8** 3 1/2 **Silver Hotspur**[97] 5290 2-8-7 **67**........................ AdrianMcCarthy 6 41
(M Wigham) *chsd ldr tl wknd qckly 2f out* **20/1**

1m 24.27s (-1.62) **Going Correction** -0.275s/f (Stan) 8 Ran SP% **114.8**
Speed ratings (Par 98):98,97,96,92,90 88,88,84
CSF £7.17 CT £31.15 TOTE £2.70: £1.30, £1.10, £2.30; EX 5.50 Trifecta £38.60 Pool £148.14 - 2.72 winning units..
Owner Weldspec Glasgow Limited **Bred** Tim Bourke **Trained** Ogbourne Maisey, Wilts
FOCUS
A decent nursery, though the pace was ordinary as Hughes got across to the rail and dictated it on Racing Times. The form looks sound enough rated through the third with the first two improving.
NOTEBOOK
Sharpazmax(IRE) made a fine start to his handicap career with a rattling late run that just got him there in the nick of time. He is coming on nicely, and should remain on the short-list while he is in such good form. (op 7-4 tchd 9-4)
Baylini has some excellent form round here, and is close to winning her first handicap. On this occasion, she arrived to win the race with a well-timed run, only to be mugged near the finish. (op 3-1 tchd 2-1)
Racing Times ran better than on his handicap debut, showing that his handicap mark is about right. He seemed to enjoy the return to front-running tactics, and - though having the run of the race here - would be one to consider in similar company. (op 7-1)
Copper King was a bit too keen early on, and ended up giving himself a bit too much to do. This was a better run that his his previous outing, but he is not quite in the form he was last month. (op 12-1)
Our Blessing(IRE) looks more effective over six furlongs. (op 11-2)

6867 GO PONTIN'S MAIDEN STKS 1m (P)
2:05 (2:07) (Class 5) 2-Y-O **£3,238** (£963; £481; £240) **Stalls** High

Form RPR

05 **1** **Grande Caiman (IRE)**[38] 6434 2-9-3........................ RichardHughes 10 76
(R Hannon) *led early: chsd ldrs: led 1f out: drvn clr* **12/1**

2 2 1/2 **Salford Mill (IRE)** 2-9-0........................ MarcHalford(3) 9 74+
(D R C Elsworth) *s.s: hld up towards rr: shkn up and hdwy over 1f out: r.o to take 2nd nr fin: promising* **9/1**

3 hd **Man Of Vision (USA)** 2-9-3........................ EdwardCreighton 1 70
(M R Channon) *chsd ldrs: rdn to chal 1f out: one pce* **7/2**[2]

5 **4** 1 1/4 **Spring Glory**[15] 6697 2-8-12........................ DaneO'Neill 8 62
(Sir Mark Prescott) *in tch: rdn 3f out: styd on same pce* **33/1**

22 **5** shd **Corlough Mountain**[4] 6826 2-9-3........................ OscarUrbina 2 67+
(N A Callaghan) *hld up in midfield: stmbld 5f out: drvn to chse ldrs over 1f out: one pce* **4/1**[3]

2 **6** 1 1/4 **Saviour Sand (IRE)**[18] 6658 2-9-3........................ AntonyProcter 3 64
(D R C Elsworth) *dwlt: hdwy to ld after 100 yds: hrd rdn and hdd 1f out: wknd fnl f* **13/8**[1]

3 **7** 1 3/4 **Trump Call (IRE)**[24] 6591 2-9-3........................ EddieAhern 6 60
(R M Beckett) *towards rr: rdn 3f out: n.d* **7/1**

60 **8** 3 **Voss**[48] 6297 2-8-12........................ J-PGuillambert 5 48
(M Johnston) *prom: rdn over 3f out: wknd 2f out* **25/1**

0 **9** 1 1/2 **Double Exposure**[62] 6058 2-9-3........................ RobertHavlin 11 49
(Jamie Poulton) *mid-div: rdn over 2f out: sn outpcd* **100/1**

6 **10** 1/2 **Shea's Round**[9] 6777 2-9-3........................ JimCrowley 4 48
(G L Moore) *dwlt: rdn along in rr: hmpd 5f out: nvr trbld ldrs* **100/1**

11 18 **Lap Of The Gods** 2-9-3 .... IanMongan 7 —
(Miss Z C Davison) *s.i.s: a outpcd and bhd* 100/1

1m 37.43s (-2.00) **Going Correction** -0.275s/f (Stan) 11 Ran SP% **120.3**
Speed ratings (Par 96):99,96,96,95,94 93,91,88,87,86 68
CSF £113.82 TOTE £14.30: £3.20, £2.10, £1.70; EX 141.60 TRIFECTA Not won..
Owner I A N Wight **Bred** Sweet Retreat Syndicate **Trained** East Everleigh, Wilts

FOCUS
This looked above average for a Lingfield All-Weather maiden, and the pace was decent, so the form should work out.

NOTEBOOK
Grande Caiman(IRE) stepped up significantly on previous performances for the extra furlong. A 65,000 guinea son of Grand Lodge, he has the potential to improve with racing and should have a brighter future than many All-Weather performers.
Salford Mill(IRE) ◆, a good-looking son of Peintre Celebre, cost 45,000 guineas as a yearling and is related to several decent three-year-old winners over ten furlongs and a mile and a half. Despite being green in the rear, he ran a race full of promise and looks one to be on next time. Official explanation: vet said colt had been struck into (op 33-1)
Man Of Vision(USA) is a son of the miler Kingmambo, but his dam stayed at least a mile and a half, so he can be expected to do even better at longer trips as he matures. This was an encouraging debut in a decent maiden, from which he should progress. (op 4-1 tchd 10-3)
Spring Glory stepped up on her debut, but shapes as if a mile-and-a-quarter will suit before long. She is capable of winning a routine maiden, and handicaps will also be available after one more run. (op 40-1)
Corlough Mountain stayed the extra furlong alright, and Urbina nearly managed to get him involved despite losing ground when stumbling on the first bend. He could win a typical All-Weather maiden, but is now also qualified for handicaps. (op 11-2 tchd 6-1)
Saviour Sand(IRE) probably found this race tougher than the one in which he finished second on his debut. Though run out of it late on, he is up to winning a less hotly-contested maiden. (op 11-10 tchd 2-1)
Trump Call(IRE) seemed more effective ridden prominently over seven furlongs on his debut. (tchd 15-2)

6868 EGL GROUP LTD H'CAP — 1m (P)
2:35 (2:37) (Class 4) (0-85,85) 3-Y-O+ **£5,505** (£1,637; £818; £408) **Stalls** High

Form RPR
4250 **1** **Mina A Salem**[65] 5990 4-9-1 **83** .... RichardHughes 6 93
(C E Brittain) *trckd ldrs: effrt 2f out: drvn level ins fnl f: wore down runner-up to ld fnl 50 yds* 6/1[3]
3044 **2** ½ **Tamagin (USA)**[4] 6830 3-9-0 **83** ....(p) J-PGuillambert 9 92
(P D Evans) *led at str pce: 6l clr 1/2-way: rdn 3f out: jnd by runner-up ins fnl f: hdd fnl 50 yds: kpt on gamely* 8/1
3121 **3** 1 ¼ **Vacation (IRE)**[17] 6671 3-8-6 **82** .... WilliamBuick(7) 11 88
(V Smith) *dwlt: bhd: rdn 3f out: gd hdwy over 1f out: kpt on fnl f* 13/8[1]
0103 **4** nk **Mataram (USA)**[33] 6502 3-8-7 **76** .... BrettDoyle 2 81+
(W Jarvis) *s.s: towards rr: effrt and hung lft over 1f out: styd on wl: nrst fin* 6/1[3]
2506 **5** shd **Waterline Twenty (IRE)**[101] 5165 3-8-9 **81** .... JamesDoyle(3) 4 86
(P D Evans) *mid-div: rdn over 2f out: styd on fnl f* 33/1
0064 **6** nk **Will He Wish**[13] 6733 10-8-12 **80** .... IanMongan 10 85
(S Gollings) *prom: chsd ldr over 4f out tl over 1f out: one pce* 25/1
411 **7** hd **Sotik Star (IRE)**[21] 6635 3-8-12 **81** ....(t) EddieAhern 7 85
(P J Makin) *mid-div: effrt and hrd rdn over 1f out: styd on same pce* 7/2[2]
1020 **8** ½ **Grey Boy (GER)**[17] 6678 5-8-7 **80** .... JamieMoriarty(5) 8 83
(R A Fahey) *dwlt: bhd: rdn over 2f out: styd on fr over 1f out* 14/1
1/3- **9** ¾ **Daniel Thomas (IRE)**[613] 1023 4-9-3 **85** .... JimCrowley 1 86
(Mrs A J Perrett) *s.s: sn chsng ldrs: hrd rdn and no ex over 1f out* 16/1
6400 **10** 9 **Meditation**[95] 5345 4-8-4 **79** .... SophieDoyle(7) 5 59
(I A Wood) *chsd ldr over 3f: wknd over 2f out: lame* 50/1
0500 **11** 31 **Chateau Nicol**[174] 2981 7-8-7 **75** .... FergusSweeney 3 —
(B G Powell) *s.s: a bhd: no ch fnl 3f: lame* 50/1

1m 35.4s (-4.03) **Going Correction** -0.275s/f (Stan) course record
WFA 3 from 4yo+ 1lb 11 Ran SP% **123.3**
Speed ratings (Par 105):109,108,107,106,106 106,106,105,105,96 65
CSF £54.41 CT £117.32 TOTE £7.70: £2.10, £2.10, £1.50; EX 54.60 Trifecta £164.10 Pool £414.54 - 1.91 winning units..
Owner Saeed Manana **Bred** Darley **Trained** Newmarket, Suffolk

FOCUS
A race of reasonable quality for the track, in which the runner-up set a strong gallop and did well to hold on for so long. The form looks solid and reliable.
Mina A Salem Official explanation: trainer's rep said, regarding the improved form shown, animal had been gelded since its last run
Meditation Official explanation: vet said filly was lame behind
Chateau Nicol Official explanation: jockey said gelding was moving badly; vet said gelding was lame behind

6869 PONTIN'S FAMILY HOLIDAYS H'CAP (DIV II) — 7f (P)
3:10 (3:11) (Class 6) (0-58,58) 3-Y-O+ **£1,706** (£503; £252) **Stalls** Low

Form RPR
0535 **1** **Special Place**[65] 5988 3-9-2 **58** .... OscarUrbina 9 66
(J A R Toller) *s.i.s: patiently rdn fr rr: rdn and hdwy over 1f out: r.o to ld fnl 100 yds* 5/1[3]
0061 **2** ¾ **Moon Bird**[15] 6696 4-9-1 **57** .... EddieAhern 1 63
(C A Cyzer) *hld up in midfield: hdwy 2f out: rdn to ld ins fnl f: hdd fnl 100 yds: kpt on* 5/2[1]
3 ½ **Spot The Subbie (IRE)**[110] 4977 3-8-9 **51** .... RobertHavlin 11 56
(Jamie Poulton) *bhd: rdn 3f out: gd late hdwy* 12/1
4655 **4** nk **Viewforth**[21] 6629 8-8-13 **55** .... J-PGuillambert 12 59
(M A Buckley) *pressed ldr: rdn over 2f out: nt qckn fnl f* 16/1
1010 **5** shd **Mulberry Lad (IRE)**[7] 6796 4-8-12 **54** .... PaulDoe 2 58+
(P W Hiatt) *hld up towards rr: rdn and hdwy over 1f out: swtchd lft ent fnl f: styd on same pce* 16/1
0100 **6** 2 ½ **Stagnite**[14] 6713 6-8-3 **50** ....(p) JamieJones(5) 8 47
(Karen George) *plld hrd: chsd ldrs: rdn 3f out: hld whn edgd lft ins fnl f* 16/1
3552 **7** hd **Beneking**[14] 6714 6-8-7 **56** ....(p) JosephWalsh(7) 4 53
(D Burchell) *mid-div: hdwy to trck ldrs 3f out: wknd 1f out* 13/2
0030 **8** nk **Shirley Oaks (IRE)**[13] 6728 8-8-4 **46** oh1 .... AdrianMcCarthy 5 42
(Miss Z C Davison) *chsd ldrs: rdn and outpcd over 2f out: sn btn* 66/1
2602 **9** 1 ¼ **Double Valentine**[14] 6713 3-8-10 **52** .... DaneO'Neill 6 45
(R Ingram) *s.i.s: towards rr: mod effrt on rail over 2f out: nvr able to chal* 12/1
2205 **10** shd **Whistleupthewind**[17] 6672 3-9-1 **57** ....(b) MickyFenton 7 50
(J M P Eustace) *sn led: hrd rdn and hdd ins fnl f: wknd* 8/1
2313 **11** 1 ½ **Granakey (IRE)**[10] 6763 3-8-8 **53** .... JerryO'Dwyer(3) 3 42
(M G Quinlan) *t.k.h: chsd ldrs: rdn 3f out: wknd over 1f out* 9/2[2]
0500 **12** 7 **King Of Charm (IRE)**[41] 6395 3-8-13 **55** .... JimCrowley 10 26
(G L Moore) *t.k.h: mid-div on outside: rn v wd home turn: nt rcvr* 20/1

1m 24.39s (-1.50) **Going Correction** -0.275s/f (Stan) 12 Ran SP% **127.2**
Speed ratings (Par 101):97,96,95,95,95 92,92,91,90,90 88,80
CSF £19.25 CT £154.25 TOTE £5.50: £1.80, £1.40, £4.00; EX 20.00 Trifecta £185.70 Part won. Pool £261.55 - 0.50 winning units..
Owner Miss Julia Staughton **Bred** Miss J Staughton & Mrs O Staughton **Trained** Newmarket, Suffolk

FOCUS
A low-grade but competitive race, run at a medium gallop and sound enough form rated through the third and fifth.
King Of Charm(IRE) Official explanation: jockey said gelding hung right-handed

6870 PONTINS.COM H'CAP — 1m 2f (P)
3:40 (3:40) (Class 6) (0-62,62) 3-Y-O+ **£2,730** (£806; £403) **Stalls** Low

Form RPR
5225 **1** **Siena Star (IRE)**[3] 6848 8-9-2 **62** .... MickyFenton 1 67
(Stef Liddiard) *t.k.h: prom: led after 3f: pressed by runner-up over 1f out: hrd rdn fnl f: hld on gamely* 5/2[2]
3311 **2** shd **Three Boars**[29] 6540 4-8-12 **58** .... RichardHughes 6 63+
(S Gollings) *trckd ldng pair: chal on bit over 1f out: shkn up ins fnl f: kpt on: nt quite get up* 6/4[1]
0000 **3** 1 **Graft**[237] 1244 7-8-8 **57** ....(p) NeilChalmers(3) 3 60
(Mrs P Townsley) *s.s: hld up and bhd: gd hdwy on rail over 1f out: chsd ldrs ins fnl f: nt qckn fnl 50 yds* 25/1
5052 **4** ½ **Ciccone**[18] 6657 3-8-8 **57** ....(p) FergusSweeney 5 60+
(G L Moore) *hld up in 5th: nt clr run and tried to switch rt over 1f out: swtchd lft ins fnl f: kpt on* 9/1
3003 **5** 1 **Monashee Prince (IRE)**[9] 6781 4-9-0 **60** .... BrettDoyle 7 60
(J R Best) *hld up in rr: effrt on outside 2f out: no imp fnl f* 3/1[3]
6400 **6** 1 **The Great Delaney**[109] 4983 3-8-7 **56** ....(b) EddieAhern 4 54
(Ms J S Doyle) *t.k.h in 4th: pressed ldrs 3f out: no ex fnl f* 11/1
2406 **7** 2 ½ **Maud's Cat (IRE)**[35] 6476 3-8-8 **57** .... LPKeniry 2 50
(A P Jarvis) *led and set slow pce: plld hrd and heavily restrained in front: hdd after 3f: rdn over 2f out: wknd over 1f out* 20/1

2m 8.02s (0.23) **Going Correction** -0.275s/f (Stan)
WFA 3 from 4yo+ 3lb 7 Ran SP% **120.5**
Speed ratings (Par 101):88,87,87,86,85 85,83
CSF £7.21 TOTE £3.90: £1.70, £1.30; EX 8.00 Place 6 £96.80, Place 5 £35.23.
Owner ownarace horse.co.uk (Shefford) **Bred** Mrs A J Brudenell **Trained** Great Shefford, Berks

FOCUS
A modest race, run at a weak tempo until the winner quickened it up going into the home turn. The form is not solid and limited by the third and fourth.
Three Boars Official explanation: jockey said, regarding the running and riding, his orders were to sit as long as he could before asking for an effort, adding that trainer informed him gelding would run around if hitting the front too soon
T/Jkpt: Not won. T/Plt: £389.90 to a £1 stake. Pool: £53,343.40. 99.85 winning tickets. T/Qpdt: £91.20 to a £1 stake. Pool: £3,626.70. 29.40 winning tickets. LM

6813 SOUTHWELL (L-H)
Tuesday, December 19

OFFICIAL GOING: Standard Meeting abandoned after race 3 (fog)
Wind: Almost nil Weather: Thick fog

6871 GO PONTIN'S CLAIMING STKS — 1m 3f (F)
12:40 (12:46) (Class 6) 3-Y-O+ **£2,730** (£806; £403) **Stalls** Low

Form RPR
1432 **1** **Ionian Spring (IRE)**[154] 3626 11-9-4 77 .... DanielTudhope 12 68
(D Carroll) *s.i.s: hld up: hdwy over 4f out: led 3f out: drvn out* 9/2[2]
1560 **2** 1 ¼ **Bethanys Boy (IRE)**[161] 1187 5-9-2 77 .... SteveDrowne 4 64
(A M Hales) *prom: outpcd 5f out: hdwy over 2f out: styd on* 9/2[2]
-000 **3** ½ **Memphis Belle**[35] 6474 3-8-5 52 .... DeanMcKeown 9 56
(G A Swinbank) *chsd ldrs: ev ch 3f out: styd on same pce fnl f* 8/1
0002 **4** 5 **Mossmann Gorge**[10] 6758 4-9-0 55 ....(b) AdamKirby 1 53
(M Wellings) *hld up in tch: rdn over 2f out: wknd over 1f out* 8/1
3446 **5** nk **Atlantic Gamble (IRE)**[8] 6790 6-8-9 46 ....(p) AndrewElliott(5) 7 52
(K R Burke) *chsd ldrs: rdn over 4f out: wknd over 1f out* 6/1[3]
0024 **6** ½ **Stevedore (IRE)**[26] 6568 5-9-6 70 .... PatCosgrave 6 57
(J R Boyle) *chsd ldrs: led 5f out: hdd 3f out: wknd over 1f out* 3/1[1]
43P0 **7** ½ **Royle Dancer**[38] 6451 3-9-2 59 .... GrahamGibbons 5 56
(R Hollinshead) *hld up: styd on ins fnl f: nvr nrr* 16/1
5040 **8** 10 **Missouri (USA)**[11] 6754 3-8-7 45 .... ChrisCatlin 8 30
(G M Moore) *chsd ldr: rdn over 3f out: wknd over 2f out* 14/1
0000 **9** 3 ½ **Mi Odds**[35] 6474 10-8-12 57 .... LeeEnstone 3 25
(Mrs N Macauley) *hld up: bhd fnl 5f* 20/1
000- **10** 1 ¼ **Truckle**[14] 4506 4-9-0 65 .... PaulMulrennan 2 25
(C W Fairhurst) *mde most 6f: wknd over 3f out* 16/1

2m 24.63s (-4.27) **Going Correction** -0.35s/f (Stan)
WFA 3 from 4yo+ 4lb 10 Ran SP% **121.1**
Speed ratings (Par 101):101,100,99,96,95 95,95,87,85,84
CSF £26.21 TOTE £4.00: £2.00, £2.30, £2.70; EX 20.50.There was no bid for the winner.
Owner Diamond Racing Ltd **Bred** Ballymacoll Stud Farm Ltd **Trained** Driffield, E Yorks

FOCUS
An ordinary claimer, best rated through the fairly well-backed but moderate third.
Atlantic Gamble(IRE) Official explanation: trainer said gelding bled from the nose

6872 WBX.COM WORLD BET EXCHANGE NURSERY — 7f (F)
1:10 (1:16) (Class 5) (0-75,71) 2-Y-O **£3,238** (£963; £481; £240) **Stalls** Low

Form RPR
5065 **1** **Intersky Sports (USA)**[12] 6736 2-8-10 **60** ....(p) DeanMcKeown 1 63
(K A Ryan) *in ld over 4f out: drifted rt fr over 1f out: drvn out* 4/1[2]
0154 **2** ½ **Jord (IRE)**[11] 6750 2-9-2 **71** .... NataliaGemelova(5) 5 73
(A J McCabe) *chsd wnr over 4f out: rdn over 2f out: edgd rt fr over 1f out: styd on* 6/1[3]
6542 **3** 4 **Keep Your Distance**[22] 6625 2-9-2 **66** ....(p) PaulMulrennan 4 58
(K R Burke) *chsng ldrs over 4f out: rdn and drifted rt fr over 1f out: styd on same pce* 7/1
0031 **4** 1 **Nicada (IRE)**[10] 6760 2-9-7 **71** ....(p) JimmyQuinn 3 60
(Miss Gay Kelleway) *prom over 4f out: sn rdn: no imp ent st* 5/2[1]
0006 **5** ½ **Green Day Packer (IRE)**[12] 6736 2-8-9 **64** .... AshleyHamblett(5) 2 52
(P C Haslam) *hld up in tch: outpcd 1/2-way: n.d after* 10/1
436 **6** 1 ¼ **Londolozi (USA)**[32] 6505 2-9-4 **66** .... MatthewHenry 7 52
(M A Jarvis) *prom: rdn 1/2-way: styd on same pce fnl 2f* 4/1[2]

0015 7 5 **Emefdream**[9] 6777 2-9-1 **65** LeeEnstone 6 36
(Mrs N Macauley) *in rr over 4f out: hung rt over 2f out: sn wknd* **11/1**

1m 29.68s (-1.12) **Going Correction** -0.35s/f (Stan) **7** Ran SP% **112.8**
Speed ratings (Par 96):92,91,86,85,85 83,78
CSF £27.00 TOTE £5.90: £2.60, £2.80; EX 36.60.
Owner Intersky Bloodstock **Bred** Joseph Lacombe Stables Inc **Trained** Hambleton, N Yorks

FOCUS
A modest handicap but solid enough form for the level.

NOTEBOOK
Intersky Sports(USA) had performed well here on his debut and appreciated running on Fibresand again. Getting off the mark at the ninth time of asking, he probably did not need to run to his very best to win this modest affair. (op 5-1)
Jord(IRE), a winner on his only previous start on this surface, ran a career-best in second, pulling well clear of the rest. She looks better suited to this surface than Polytrack and could well bag another win on the surface soon. (op 7-1 tchd 15-2)
Keep Your Distance is best suited by a mile plus and, despite this more testing surface, he found the trip too short. (op 6-1 tchd 11-2)
Nicada(IRE) won in first-time cheekpieces over a mile here last time, but the combination of a 5lb higher mark and drop in distance found him out. (op 11-4)
Green Day Packer(IRE) was not a long way behind Intersky Sports at Wolverhampton last time, but he did not handle this slower surface as well as that rival. (tchd 9-1)
Londolozi(USA), making her handicap debut after three outings in maidens, could not take advantage of what looked a fairly modest mark for one so well bred. (op 3-1)

6873 NEW CENTURY WINDOWS H'CAP 2m (F)
1:45 (1:46) (Class 5) (0-75,63) 3-Y-0+ **£3,238** (£963; £481; £240) **Stalls** Low

Form RPR
-120 1 **Salut Saint Cloud**[21] 6630 5-10-0 **63** (p) GeorgeBaker 1 71+
(G L Moore) *a.p: in ld over 4f out: pushed out* **5/4**[1]
2640 2 3 ½ **Victory Quest (IRE)**[14] 6718 6-9-9 **58** (v) RobertWinston 6 62
(Mrs S Lamyman) *mde most tl over 4f out: rdn over 2f out: styd on same pce fnl f* **7/2**[2]
6-00 3 3 **Acceleration (IRE)**[14] 4351 6-9-2 **51** (v) ChrisCatlin 5 51
(Karen McLintock) *prom: racd keenly: rdn over 2f out: sn outpcd* **33/1**
6000 4 nk **Madiba**[4] 6831 7-9-11 **60** TonyCulhane 3 60
(P Howling) *chsd ldr: outpcd over 4f out: styd on ins fnl f* **4/1**[3]
1006 5 2 ½ **Optimum (IRE)**[10] 6718 4-9-6 **55** RobbieFitzpatrick 2 52
(J T Stimpson) *hld up: rdn over 4fr out: n.d* **11/2**
0004 6 ¾ **Kalush**[10] 6761 5-8-8 **48** oh4 ow4 AnnStokell(5) 7 44?
(Miss A Stokell) *hld up: hdwy over 4f out: wknd 2f out* **100/1**
5-0 7 5 **Proper Article (IRE)**[23] 5281 4-9-13 **62** (bt) PaulMulrennan 4 52
(Miss J E Foster) *prom over 12f* **25/1**

3m 41.37s (-3.17) **Going Correction** -0.35s/f (Stan) **7** Ran SP% **109.8**
Speed ratings (Par 103):93,91,89,89,88 87,85
CSF £5.27 TOTE £2.00: £1.10, £1.90; EX 5.30 Place 6 £7.90, Place 5 £3.69.
Owner A Grinter **Bred** Mill House Stud **Trained** Woodingdean, E Sussex

FOCUS
Modest handicap form, especially given the performance of the third, with the fifth also limiting.

6874 PONTINS.COM (S) STKS 7f (F)
() (Class 6) 2-Y-0 £

6875 WBXTRIPLECROWN.COM H'CAP 5f (F)
() (Class 4) (0-85,) 3-Y-0+ £

6876 PONTIN'S FAMILY HOLIDAYS H'CAP 7f (F)
() (Class 6) (0-65,) 3-Y-0+ £

CR

6851 KEMPTON (A.W) (R-H)
Wednesday, December 20

OFFICIAL GOING: Standard
Restricted close-ups due to fog.
Wind: virtually nil Weather: fog

6877 BAILEYGOMM BUILDING SERVICES ENGINEERING CONSULTANTS H'CAP 5f (P)
3:15 (3:17) (Class 6) (0-58,55) 3-Y-0+ **£3,412** (£1,007; £504) **Stalls** High

Form RPR
4521 1 **Decider (USA)**[22] 6637 3-9-2 **55** LPKeniry 8 63
(J M Bradley) *in ld 2f out: hrd drvn: hld on all out* **2/1**[1]
6242 2 ½ **New Options**[7] 6806 9-9-2 **55** (b) BrettDoyle 6 61
(Peter Grayson) *chsng ldrs 2f out: str run u.p fnl f but a jst hld* **10/1**
2021 3 nk **Succeed (IRE)**[12] 6755 3-8-12 **54** RichardKingscote(3) 5 59
(Mrs H Sweeting) *in tch 2f out: styd on to chse ldrs over 1f out: kpt on ins last but a hld* **5/1**[2]
0000 4 1 ½ **Spirit Of Coniston**[17] 6686 3-8-8 **50** (b) JerryO'Dwyer(3) 9 50
(Peter Grayson) *broke wl: w ldr 2f out: hung lft u.p fnl f: wknd nr fin* **14/1**
3241 5 ¾ **Gifted Lass**[12] 6753 4-8-11 **50** DavidAllan 3 47
(J Balding) *chsng ldrs 2f out: rdn and styd on same pce fr over 1f out* **5/1**[2]
-005 6 nk **Dancing Beauty (IRE)**[10] 6774 4-8-4 **43** oh8 ChrisCatlin 10 39
(T T Clement) *rr 2f out: styd on fr over 1f out: nt pce to rch ldrs* **66/1**
061 7 ¾ **Jahia (NZ)**[52] 6233 7-8-13 **52** LeeEnstone 2 45
(P T Midgley) *s.i.s: hdwy fr 2f out: kpt on wl fnl f but nt rch ldrs* **8/1**[3]
5003 8 ¾ **The Fisio**[17] 6688 6-9-2 **55** (v) NCallan 1 45
(S Gollings) *bhd fr 2f out and n.d* **5/1**[2]
0640 9 hd **Beau Jazz**[2] 6851 5-8-6 **45** (p) JamieMackay 11 35
(W De Best-Turner) *in tch 2f out: sn rdn and n.d* **50/1**
0050 10 nk **Gone'N'Dunnett (IRE)**[17] 6686 7-9-1 **54** (p) AdamKirby 4 43
(Mrs C A Dunnett) *bhd fr 2f out* **8/1**[3]

59.82 secs (-0.58) **Going Correction** -0.125s/f (Stan) **10** Ran SP% **124.8**
Speed ratings (Par 101):99,98,97,95,94 93,92,91,90,90
CSF £26.52 CT £95.73 TOTE £3.90: £1.50, £3.40, £2.20; EX 30.40.
Owner Robert Bailey **Bred** Green Willow Farms **Trained** Sedbury, Gloucs

FOCUS
Moderate handicap form but the winner is steadily improving.
Spirit Of Coniston Official explanation: jockey said gelding hung left-handed throughout

6878 CANVAS PRINTS FROM BONUSPRINT.COM H'CAP 1m 2f (P)
3:50 (3:52) (Class 5) (0-70,71) 3-Y-0+ **£5,505** (£1,637; £818; £408) **Stalls** High

Form RPR
414 1 **Bank On Benny**[63] 6054 4-9-0 **63** FrancisNorton 8 72
(P W D'Arcy) *hld up in tch: drvn and str run fr over 1f out to ld fnl 75yds: kpt on wl* **4/1**[2]
01 2 1 **Generous Lad (IRE)**[12] 6743 3-8-13 **65** (p) SteveDrowne 2 72
(A B Haynes) *hld up in rr: hdwy over 1f out: str run fnl f: fin wl but nt rch wnr* **13/2**
5004 3 shd **Duelling Banjos**[12] 6748 7-8-13 **62** RobertHavlin 10 69
(J Akehurst) *chsd ldrs: drvn to chal 1f out: stl upsides ins last: outpcd fnl 75yds* **6/1**[3]
0043 4 shd **Luckylover**[16] 5617 3-8-11 **66** (t) JerryO'Dwyer(3) 9 73
(M G Quinlan) *led: hrd drvn fr 2f out: hdd and outpcd fnl 75yds* **9/1**
0532 5 ½ **Sarwin (USA)**[14] 6735 3-8-11 **63** BrettDoyle 11 69
(W J Musson) *bhd: hdwy over 1f out: shkn up and kpt on fnl f but nvr gng pce to rch ldrs* **7/2**[1]
0661 6 hd **Burgundy**[4] 6843 9-9-8 **71** 6ex (b) GeorgeBaker 4 76
(P Mitchell) *bhd: rdn over 1f out: swtchd rt and str run ins last: fin wl but nt rch ldrs* **13/2**
6000 7 hd **Odessa Star (USA)**[28] 6566 3-9-0 **66** NCallan 7 71
(J G Portman) *chsd ldrs: rdn 2f out: one pce fr over 1f out* **25/1**
5525 8 2 **High Seasons**[15] 6712 3-8-13 **65** (b[1]) JimCrowley 1 66
(B R Millman) *chsd ldrs: rdn over 2f out: wknd fnl f* **20/1**
2 9 2 ½ **Exit To Luck (GER)**[14] 6734 5-9-5 **68** IanMongan 3 65
(S Gollings) *chsd ldr: rdn 2f out: wknd qckly fnl f* **14/1**
0443 10 ¾ **Smokin Joe**[4] 6848 5-9-5 **68** (v) LPKeniry 6 63
(J R Best) *bhd: sme hdwy over 2f out: wknd over 1f out* **13/2**

2m 8.54s (-0.46) **Going Correction** -0.125s/f (Stan)
WFA 3 from 4yo+ 3lb **10** Ran SP% **121.8**
Speed ratings (Par 103):96,95,95,95,94 94,94,92,90,90
CSF £31.85 CT £159.25 TOTE £6.00: £1.90, £4.20, £2.50; EX 53.00.
Owner The Golf Oil Partnership **Bred** Gilridge Bloodstock Ltd **Trained** Newmarket, Suffolk

FOCUS
A modest handicap run at a steady early gallop, resulting in a bit of a sprint to the line.
Sarwin(USA) Official explanation: jockey said gelding hung right-handed up straight

6879 DIGIBET.COM EBF MAIDEN FILLIES' STKS 1m (P)
4:20 (4:22) (Class 4) 2-Y-0 **£4,857** (£1,445; £722; £360) **Stalls** High

Form RPR
2 1 **Algarade**[11] 6757 2-9-0 JamieMackay 9 76+
(Sir Mark Prescott) *mde all: rdn over 1f out: styd on strly ins last* **1/2**[1]
5 2 1 **Vincennes**[19] 6663 2-9-0 NCallan 6 74+
(M A Jarvis) *a chsng wnr: rdn and effrt over 2f out but nvr gng pce to chal and a hld ins last* **7/2**[2]
3 7 **Namibian Pink (IRE)** 2-9-0 AdamKirby 7 57
(R M Beckett) *rr: hdwy fr 2f out: kpt on to take 3rd ins last but nvr any ch w ldng pair* **25/1**
00 4 hd **Miami Tallyce (IRE)**[29] 6558 2-9-0 ChrisCatlin 4 57
(E J O'Neill) *sn prom: rdn and outpcd by ldng pair fr over 2f out: outpcd for 3rd ins last* **33/1**
00 5 1 **Antrim Rose**[19] 6658 2-9-0 RobertHavlin 3 55
(J H M Gosden) *bhd: modest prog fr 2f out but nvr in contention* **6/1**[3]
5 6 2 **Carefree**[22] 6644 2-9-0 TonyCulhane 5 50
(W J Haggas) *bhd tl pushed along and modest hdwy 2f out but nvr a factor* **10/1**
0 7 shd **My Monna**[183] 2733 2-9-0 EdwardCreighton 2 50
(Miss Sheena West) *chsd ldrs: rdn 3f out: wknd fr 2f out* **66/1**
00 8 6 **Italstar (IRE)**[10] 6778 2-9-0 SteveDrowne 8 36
(H Morrison) *chsd ldrs tl wknd qckly over 2f out* **66/1**
9 nk **Iceni Princess** 2-9-0 DeanCorby 1 35
(P Howling) *s.i.s: a towards rr* **66/1**

1m 40.11s (-0.69) **Going Correction** -0.125s/f (Stan) **9** Ran SP% **123.5**
Speed ratings (Par 95):98,97,90,89,88 86,86,80,80
CSF £2.82 TOTE £1.50: £1.02, £1.30, £7.00; EX 2.70.
Owner Miss K Rausing **Bred** Miss K Rausing And Mrs S M Rogers **Trained** Newmarket, Suffolk

FOCUS
Not a very competitive maiden with over half the field starting at 25-1 or longer and very few ever got into it. The front pair held those positions throughout and the way they pulled right away from the rest suggests they both have a future.

NOTEBOOK
Algarade ◆ made sure there was no messing about this time and her rider was positive from the start. She only had the runner-up to worry about from a very long way out and, although she was never able to take things easy, she kept on finding as much as was needed. Almost certain to improve even more as a three-year-old, her trainer has had plenty of success at a high level with the dam's family and she seems likely to continue the trend. (tchd 8-15 and 4-7 in places)
Vincennes ◆, who held her place in the market rather better than on her debut, duly improved from that effort and made sure the favourite never had a moment's peace. It should only be a matter of time before she goes one better. (op 3-1 tchd 4-1)
Namibian Pink(IRE), a 12,500gns half-sister to a dual sprint winner in Italy, was given a patient ride before staying on to win the separate race for third. Quite what she achieved is questionable, but she is perfectly entitled to improve for the experience.
Miami Tallyce(IRE), ridden more prominently than in her first two starts, was well and truly left behind by the front pair soon after turning in. She does not appear much, but does at least now qualify for a mark. (op 25-1)
Antrim Rose was never in the race and looks very much one of the stable's lesser lights. (op 10-1)

6880 DIGIBET.CO.UK NURSERY 1m (P)
4:50 (4:51) (Class 4) (0-85,77) 2-Y-0 **£7,772** (£2,312; £1,155; £577) **Stalls** High

Form RPR
0114 1 **Habalwatan (IRE)**[25] 6599 2-9-7 **77** (b) BrettDoyle 3 84+
(C E Brittain) *hld up in cl 4th: str run on outside to ld ins fnl f: sn clr: readily* **13/8**[1]
065 2 3 ½ **Don't Desert Me (IRE)**[12] 6751 2-8-5 **64** RichardKingscote(3) 1 63
(R Charlton) *chsd ldr: chal over 2f out: outpcd appr fnl f: styd on again ins last to take 2nd cl home: no ch w wnr* **3/1**[2]
0131 3 nk **Inquisitress**[18] 6670 2-9-0 **70** EddieAhern 4 68
(J J Bridger) *chsd ldrs: chal over 2f out: sn led: hdd ins last: sn one pce: lost 2nd cl home* **13/8**[1]
6510 4 3 ½ **Stoneacre Gareth (IRE)**[6] 6824 2-9-5 **75** (b[1]) GeorgeBaker 2 65
(Peter Grayson) *led: rdn 2f out: sn hdd: wknd over 1f out* **10/1**[3]

1m 40.39s (-0.41) **Going Correction** -0.125s/f (Stan) **4** Ran SP% **110.3**
Speed ratings (Par 98):97,93,93,89
CSF £6.86 TOTE £2.20; EX 8.90.

Owner Mohammed Rashid **Bred** Darley **Trained** Newmarket, Suffolk

FOCUS
A slightly disappointing turnout for the prizemoney. The pace was no more than ordinary and the winning time was 0.28 seconds slower than the fillies' maiden. The race could be rated higher if assessed through the runner-up.

NOTEBOOK
Habalwatan(IRE), back over probably his best trip, was held up last of the quartet but, when pulled wide for his effort in the home straight, found a turn of foot that proved far too much for his rivals. He may not be totally straightforward, but gets the job done. (op 6-4 tchd 7-4 and 15-8 in a place)
Don't Desert Me(IRE), making his handicap debut after finishing unplaced in three maidens, may have appreciated a stronger pace but still improved on previous efforts. There should be an ordinary nursery in him off this sort of mark. (tchd 5-2)
Inquisitress, raised 6lb for her recent course-and-distance victory, had every chance but found this better company too hot to handle. (op 7-4 tchd 15-8)
Stoneacre Gareth(IRE) tried to make every yard, but did not get home and is still to convince that he stays this far. (tchd 11-1)

6881 DIGIBET SPORTS BETTING CONDITIONS STKS 7f (P)
5:20 (5:20) (Class 3) 2-Y-O **£8,101** (£2,425; £1,212; £607) **Stalls** High

Form RPR
6111 **1** **Hurricane Spirit (IRE)**[19] 6659 2-9-3 102 BrettDoyle 4 86+
(J R Best) *slowly away: sn rcvrd: wnt 3rd 4f out: qcknd over 1f out: led jst ins last: comf* **1/3**[1]
0311 **2** ¾ **Fares (IRE)**[26] 6586 2-9-5 81 (b) RichardHughes 1 86
(C E Brittain) *led: rdn 2f out: hdd jst ins last: sn no ch w wnr but kpt on for clr 2nd* **7/1**[3]
31 **3** 3 **Blue Charm**[15] 6710 2-9-0 76 LPKeniry 2 73
(S Kirk) *chsd ldrs: rdn and wd 3f out: outpcd fnl 2f* **11/2**[2]
6311 **4** 8 **Hucking Hill (IRE)**[25] 6592 2-9-0 73 (b) DaneO'Neill 3 52
(J R Best) *chsd ldr to 3f out: wknd fr 2f out* **14/1**
1m 25.35s (-1.45) **Going Correction** -0.125s/f (Stan) 4 Ran SP% **109.6**
Speed ratings (Par 100):103,102,98,89
CSF £3.31 TOTE £1.30; EX 2.40.
Owner The Little House Partnership **Bred** Knocktoran Stud **Trained** Hucking, Kent

FOCUS
An uncompetitive conditions race in which Hurricane Spirit appeared to run quite a way below his best, despite still managing to win but the runner-up is improving.

NOTEBOOK
Hurricane Spirit(IRE) may have broken the track record on his first try over seven furlongs, but he had to worker harder than many might have expected and failed to confirm what appeared to be a much-improved effort when defying a mark of 87 in a six-furlong nursery at Lingfield on his previous start. It is hard to knock a horse who has just won four races on the bounce - he is obviously very decent - but he has faced just three rivals on his last three starts and has still to prove his is as good as an official mark of 102 suggests. (op 1-4)
Fares(IRE), bidding for the hat-trick following a couple of wins in six furlongs nurseries round here (the first off 61, the second off 68), ran a fine race in defeat over this longer trip considering he had 23lb to find with Hurricane Spirit. He has had plenty of racing, but is clearly still going the right way. (tchd 15-2)
Blue Charm found this much tougher than the six-furlong maiden he won here last time and never really landed a blow. (op 6-1 tchd 13-2)
Hucking Hill(IRE) was chasing the three-timer following two wins in six-furlong nurseries round here (off 61 and 68), but he was out of his depth.

6882 FOLLOW YOUR CONFERENCE WITH TWILIGHT RACING H'CAP 6f (P)
5:50 (5:51) (Class 5) (0-75,75) 3-Y-O+ **£5,505** (£1,637; £818; £408) **Stalls** High

Form RPR
0050 **1** **Morse (IRE)**[26] 6579 5-8-10 72 RichardKingscote(3) 4 82
(J A Osborne) *mde virtually all: drvn out* **10/1**
4061 **2** ¾ **Figaro Flyer (IRE)**[11] 6773 3-9-1 74 IanMongan 6 81
(P Howling) *in tch 2f out: rdn and kpt on fnl f: nt rch wnr* **11/2**[3]
5506 **3** shd **Kingscross**[11] 6770 8-9-1 74 NCallan 10 81
(M Blanshard) *rr 2f out: r.o wl fnl f: fin strly* **15/2**
1500 **4** ½ **Russian Rocket (IRE)**[99] 5263 4-9-2 75 SteveDrowne 12 81
(Mrs C A Dunnett) *hdwy fr 2f out: kpt on ins last: styng on cl home* **25/1**
2325 **5** shd **Witchry**[29] 6555 4-8-12 71 FergusSweeney 5 76
(A G Newcombe) *in tch 2f out: r.o fnl f but nt pce to rch wnr* **9/2**[2]
1510 **6** 1 **Linda Green**[11] 6773 5-8-13 72 EdwardCreighton 11 74
(M R Channon) *in tch 2f out: rdn and kpt on appr fnl f: one pce nr fin* **7/2**[1]
5200 **7** hd **Anfield Dream**[15] 6720 4-8-9 75 WilliamBuick(7) 2 77
(J R Jenkins) *pressing ldrs 2f out: ev ch over 1f out: wknd nr fin* **16/1**
0-66 **8** hd **Loyal Tycoon (IRE)**[13] 6740 8-8-8 72 JamesMillman(5) 9 73
(D K Ivory) *in tch 2f out: r.o fnl f but nvr gng pce to rch ldrs* **25/1**
4000 **9** hd **His Master's Voice (IRE)**[65] 6020 3-8-11 70 BrettDoyle 7 70
(D W P Arbuthnot) *bhd 2f out: str run fnl f but nvr gng pce to be competitive* **8/1**
3500 **10** 1¼ **Effective**[194] 2405 6-9-1 74 DaneO'Neill 3 71
(A P Jarvis) *chsd ldrs over 2f out: wknd fnl f* **12/1**
0064 **11** 2 **Sun Catcher (IRE)**[26] 6579 3-9-2 75 RichardHughes 1 66
(R Hannon) *in rr 2f out* **9/2**[2]
1m 12.28s (-1.42) **Going Correction** -0.125s/f (Stan) 11 Ran SP% **127.2**
Speed ratings (Par 103):104,103,102,102,102 100,100,100,99,98 95
CSF £69.59 CT £458.47 TOTE £13.80: £5.30, £2.90, £2.60; EX 85.50.
Owner Morsethehorse Syndicate **Bred** Auriga Partnership **Trained** Upper Lambourn, Berks

FOCUS
Thick fog resulted in poor vision for this sprint handicap, so some of the comments are not as detailed as they might have been. A fair handicap, and typically competitive for the distance rated through the runner-up to latest form.
Sun Catcher(IRE) Official explanation: jockey said gelding hung left-handed throughout

6883 BAILEYGOMM CHRISTMAS SPECIAL H'CAP 1m 4f (P)
6:20 (6:21) (Class 6) (0-60,66) 3-Y-O+ **£3,412** (£1,007; £504) **Stalls** Centre

Form RPR
0351 **1** **Jazrawy**[11] 6758 4-8-8 52 WilliamCarson(7) 1 64
(P W Hiatt) *10l clr after 2f: stl clr 3f out: drvn out fnl f* **8/1**
0432 **2** 3 **Amwell Brave**[15] 6718 5-9-9 60 EddieAhern 7 67
(J R Jenkins) *prom after 2f: chsng wnr 3f out: no imp fnl f* **11/4**[2]
2200 **3** 2½ **Serramanna**[5] 6831 5-9-0 58 SophieDoyle(7) 9 61
(Ms J S Doyle) *chsng ldrs after 2f: rdn and stl wl there 3f out: one pce fr over 1f out* **14/1**
4021 **4** 1¾ **Bronze Star**[10] 6775 3-9-10 66 6ex NCallan 6 66
(J R Fanshawe) *chsng ldrs after 2f: rdn 3f out: one pce fnl f* **5/4**[1]
0621 **5** ¾ **Melvino**[11] 6769 4-9-8 59 ChrisCatlin 10 58
(T D Barron) *bhd after 2f: sme hdwy 3f out: no ch fr over 1f out* **3/1**[3]
6-00 **6** 2½ **Atlantic City**[18] 6673 5-9-6 57 (p) RichardThomas 3 52
(Mrs L Richards) *chsng wnr after 2f: dropped to 3rd 3f out: no ch fr over 1f out* **40/1**
500 **7** ¾ **Voice Mail**[19] 6667 7-9-7 58 (v) DeanCorby 8 52
(P Howling) *chsng ldrs after 2f: wknd fr 3f out* **20/1**
00/4 **8** ½ **Lady Korrianda**[10] 6779 5-8-11 48 DaneO'Neill 2 41
(B R Johnson) *towards rr after 2f: stl in rr 3f out* **16/1**
2m 35.24s (-1.66) **Going Correction** -0.125s/f (Stan)
WFA 3 from 4yo+ 5lb 8 Ran SP% **127.0**
Speed ratings (Par 101):100,98,96,95,94 93,92,92
CSF £33.89 CT £324.07 TOTE £10.60: £2.00, £1.40, £3.30; EX 54.20 Place 6 £61.42, Place 5 £35.96.
Owner P W Hiatt **Bred** Scuderia Antonella S R L **Trained** Hook Norton, Oxon

FOCUS
Once again, visibility was very poor owing to thick fog. This was a weak middle-distance handicap.
T/Plt: £45.30 to a £1 stake. Pool: £57,438.45. 925.05 winning tickets. T/Qpdt: £13.40 to a £1 stake. Pool: £4,381.90. 240.20 winning tickets. ST

6864 LINGFIELD (L-H)
Wednesday, December 20

OFFICIAL GOING: Standard
Wind: almost nil Weather: sunny and crisp

6884 PONTINSBINGO.COM H'CAP (DIV I) 6f (P)
12:30 (12:30) (Class 6) (0-55,55) 3-Y-O+ **£1,706** (£503; £252) **Stalls** Low

Form RPR
0030 **1** **Mine The Balance (IRE)**[15] 6713 3-8-9 50 (b) BrettDoyle 2 59
(J R Best) *trckd ldng pair: effrt over 1f out: drvn to ld last 100yds: hld on* **5/1**[2]
3146 **2** ½ **Carcinetto (IRE)**[18] 6681 4-9-0 55 J-PGuillambert 11 63
(P D Evans) *rousted along fr wd draw to chse ldr: rdn to ld jst over 1f out: hanging and hdd last 100yds: nt qckn* **5/1**[2]
4156 **3** ½ **Cayman Breeze**[22] 6632 6-8-6 54 BarrySavage(7) 10 60+
(J M Bradley) *hld up in last: stl last 2f out: prog on outer over 1f out: r.o fnl f: too much to do* **13/2**[3]
3003 **4** ½ **Monte Major (IRE)**[15] 6713 5-8-9 50 (v) DaneO'Neill 8 55
(D Shaw) *hld up in midfield: rdn 2f out: styd on fr over 1f out: nvr able to chal* **9/2**[1]
0202 **5** hd **Make My Dream**[22] 6649 3-8-12 53 (b[1]) JimCrowley 5 57
(J Gallagher) *hld up in rr: threaded way through fr over 1f out: n.m.r briefly ins fnl f: nvr rchd ldrs* **5/1**[2]
001 **6** ¾ **Midmaar (IRE)**[44] 6372 5-8-5 46 (b) FrancisNorton 6 48
(M Wigham) *s.i.s: trckd ldrs: rdn and cl up over 1f out: hanging fnl f: fdd last 100yds* **5/1**[2]
53 **7** 1 **Tembladora (IRE)**[72] 5873 3-8-12 53 EddieAhern 4 52
(J W Hills) *dwlt: hmpd and snatched up after 1f: wl in rr after: effrt on inner whn nt clr run over 1f out: styd on last 150yds* **10/1**
0600 **8** 1¼ **Luloah**[2] 6856 3-8-9 50 HayleyTurner 7 45
(P S McEntee) *led to jst over 1f out: wknd* **20/1**
0 **9** 1 **Yellow Mane (IRE)**[30] 6531 3-8-9 50 ChrisCatlin 3 42
(Luke Comer, Ire) *hmpd and snatched up after 1f: rdn over 2f out: sn struggling* **66/1**
6000 **10** 8 **Glenargo (USA)**[30] 6539 3-7-12 46 oh1 (p) WilliamBuick(7) 9 14
(R A Harris) *chsd ldrs to 1/2-way: sn wknd u.p: t.o* **33/1**
1m 11.89s (-0.92) **Going Correction** -0.125s/f (Stan) 10 Ran SP% **116.5**
Speed ratings (Par 101):101,100,99,99,98 97,96,94,93,82
CSF £29.65 CT £168.67 TOTE £8.70: £1.90, £1.90, £2.10; EX 52.10 TRIFECTA Not won..
Owner M Folan & R Lees **Bred** Andrew Sharkey **Trained** Hucking, Kent

FOCUS
A low-grade handicap.
Tembladora(IRE) Official explanation: jockey said filly was hampered shortly after start
Yellow Mane(IRE) Official explanation: jockey said colt was hampered shortly after start

6885 PONTINS.COM H'CAP 1m 4f (P)
1:00 (1:00) (Class 5) (0-75,75) 3-Y-O+ **£3,238** (£963; £481; £240) **Stalls** Low

Form RPR
0452 **1** **Nawow**[47] 5935 6-8-13 67 DaneO'Neill 6 76
(P D Cundell) *hld up in 4th: prog 2f out: rdn to ld jst over 1f out: hld on wl nr fin* **3/1**[2]
4001 **2** hd **Turner's Touch**[12] 6748 4-9-2 70 (be) GeorgeBaker 3 79
(G L Moore) *hld up in last: prog 2f out: rdn to chal 1f out: hanging bdly and nt go by* **2/1**[1]
2602 **3** 1¾ **Dower House**[13] 6741 11-9-7 75 (t) ChrisCatlin 5 81
(Andrew Turnell) *settled in 3rd tl keen and trckd ldr 7f out: led over 2f out to jst over 1f out: one pce* **2/1**[1]
6106 **4** ¾ **Ariodante**[11] 6766 4-8-11 65 MickyFenton 1 70
(J M P Eustace) *trckd ldr to 7f out: rdn 2f out: one pce and btn 1f out* **14/1**
4150 **5** shd **Wild Pitch**[66] 5991 5-9-2 70 (b) RichardHughes 2 75
(P Mitchell) *hld up in 5th: t.k.h after 5f: effrt over 1f out: nvr pce to threaten ldrs after* **7/1**[3]
2005 **6** 8 **Top Seed (IRE)**[11] 6761 5-9-4 72 J-PGuillambert 4 64
(A J Chamberlain) *led: rdn over 3f out: hdd over 2f out: sn btn* **20/1**
2m 35.53s (1.14) **Going Correction** -0.125s/f (Stan) 6 Ran SP% **115.6**
Speed ratings (Par 103):91,90,89,89,89 83
CSF £9.86 TOTE £3.40: £1.70, £1.30; EX 11.40.
Owner Ian M Brown **Bred** Kirtlington Stud Ltd **Trained** Compton, Berks

FOCUS
This was run at a pretty steady pace and the winning time was moderate for a race of this class.

6886 EBF PONTIN'S HOLIDAYS MAIDEN FILLIES' STKS 7f (P)
1:30 (1:30) (Class 5) 2-Y-O **£3,562** (£1,059; £529; £264) **Stalls** Low

Form RPR
3 **1** **Basaata (USA)**[96] 5344 2-9-0 RichardHughes 9 82+
(M P Tregoning) *disp ld tl def advantage over 2f out: shkn up and in command over 1f out: pushed out* **8/13**[1]
2 3 **Barshiba (IRE)** 2-9-0 AntonyProcter 5 75+
(D R C Elsworth) *s.v.s: rn green in last but sn in tch: prog 2f out: r.o to take 2nd last 100yds: no ch w wnr* **5/1**[2]
5540 **3** 1½ **Nicomedia (IRE)**[92] 5464 2-8-11 72 StephaneBreux(3) 6 67
(R Hannon) *disp ld to over 2f out: shkn up and one pce after* **6/1**[3]
0 **4** shd **Becharm**[39] 6433 2-9-0 NCallan 1 67
(M A Jarvis) *hld up bhd ldrs: effrt on inner over 1f out to dispute 2nd: shkn up and one pce* **20/1**

0 **5** 3/4 **Best Selection**[39] [6441] 2-9-0 .... DaneO'Neill 3 65
(A P Jarvis) *disp ld to over 2f out: shkn up and grad fdd* **66/1**
6 3/4 **Soft Morning** 2-9-0 .... J-PGuillambert 10 63
(Sir Mark Prescott) *racd v wd: wl in tch: pushed along 2f out: outpcd over 1f out* **14/1**
7 1 1/2 **Going To Work (IRE)** 2-8-11 .... MarcHalford(3) 2 59
(D R C Elsworth) *dwlt: t.k.h and sn trckd ldrs: pushed along and outpcd over 1f out* **16/1**
6 **8** 2 **Perfect Practice**[17] [6689] 2-9-0 .... EddieAhern 4 58+
(J A R Toller) *hld up in rr: gng wl enough in last pair whn hmpd wl over 1f out: n.d after* **33/1**
9 3 **Grand Symphony** 2-9-0 .... RobertWinston 8 46
(W Jarvis) *racd wd: in tch: pushed along 2f out: wknd over 1f out* **25/1**
4302 **10** 1 3/4 **Diamond Light (USA)**[62] [6064] 2-9-0 67 .... BrettDoyle 7 41
(M Botti) *trckd ldrs to over 2f out: sn wknd* **12/1**

1m 24.8s (-1.09) **Going Correction** -0.125s/f (Stan) **10** Ran SP% **126.2**
Speed ratings (Par 93):101,97,95,95,94 94,92,90,86,84
CSF £4.41 TOTE £1.60: £1.10, £2.60, £1.40; EX 5.40 Trifecta £18.20 Pool £413.31 - 16.08 winning units..
Owner Hamdan Al Maktoum **Bred** Shadwell Farm LLC **Trained** Lambourn, Berks
■ Stewards' Enquiry : Antony Procter two-day ban: careless riding (Dec 31, Jan 1)

FOCUS
The front two are both better than the bare facts imply and can do better.

NOTEBOOK
Basaata(USA) ◆ was a promising third to the smart Darrfonah on her debut at Newbury in September. Switched to Polytrack, she was always in the front rank and quickened nicely in the straight for an authoritative win. Connections think a lot of her and she looks a nice prospect at up to ten furlongs next year.
Barshiba(IRE) ◆, a half-sister to Doctor Dash, a Listed winner for this yard at two, shaped with a deal of promise. After falling out of the stalls, she soon latched on to the main bunch as the early pace was modest. After having to wait for a run, she ran on nicely in the straight for second, although the winner was beyond recall. She should not be long in going one better. (tchd 11-2)
Nicomedia(IRE) was out of her depth in a valuable sales race at the Curragh last time but ran up to the form of her previous try on this surface. (op 8-1)
Becharm was still a little green and lacked a change of gear up the straight, but this was an improvement on her debut effort at Kempton. (tchd 25-1)
Best Selection, a half-sister to some modest winners, showed more than on her debut and looks the type to do better when qualified for handicaps.
Soft Morning, a half-sister to the yard's smart performers Souvenance and Songerie, ran with promise from her outside draw which obliged her to race wide. She looks capable of better. (op 16-1)

6887 EBF GO PONTIN'S MAIDEN STKS (C&G) 7f (P)
2:00 (2:00) (Class 5) 2-Y-O **£3,562** (£1,059; £529; £264) **Stalls** Low

Form RPR
2234 **1** **Danehillsundance (IRE)**[17] [6689] 2-9-0 72 .... RichardHughes 2 71
(R Hannon) *led: rdn and hdd 2f out: kpt on wl to ld again last 100yds* **3/1**[2]
04 **2** nk **All Of Me (IRE)**[55] [6188] 2-9-0 .... DaneO'Neill 7 70
(T G Mills) *trckd ldr: effrt to ld 2f out: fnd little in front: hdd and nt qckn last 100yds* **7/4**[1]
6033 **3** 1 1/4 **Highland Harvest**[17] [6689] 2-8-11 74 .... MarcHalford(3) 8 67
(D R C Elsworth) *t.k.h: trckd ldrs: effrt over 1f out: kpt on same pce and no imp ldng pair* **9/2**[3]
5 **4** hd **Challis (IRE)**[19] [6658] 2-9-0 .... NCallan 3 66+
(J Noseda) *hld up in rr: effrt over 1f out: trying to cl whn nt clr run ins fnl f: kpt on nr fin* **7/1**
3 **5** shd **High Tribute**[14] [6730] 2-9-0 .... J-PGuillambert 1 66
(Sir Mark Prescott) *trckd ldng pair: effrt on inner over 1f out: nt qckn and hld fnl f* **16/1**
6 1/2 **Realy Naughty (IRE)** 2-9-0 .... FergusSweeney 6 65
(B G Powell) *trckd ldrs: rdn over 2f out: lost pl wl over 1f out: kpt on again fnl f* **33/1**
0 **7** shd **Mumbleswerve (IRE)**[53] [6214] 2-9-0 .... RobertWinston 5 69+
(W Jarvis) *dwlt: hld up in last: nudged along and styd on steadily fnl f: do bttr* **14/1**
00 **8** hd **Rustic Gold**[17] [6689] 2-9-0 .... BrettDoyle 9 64
(J R Best) *wl in rr: rdn over 2f out: struggling after: styd on again last 150yds* **33/1**
9 1 1/2 **Leg Sweep** 2-9-0 .... AntonyProcter 4 60
(D R C Elsworth) *dwlt: in tch tl wknd over 1f out* **14/1**

1m 26.16s (0.27) **Going Correction** -0.125s/f (Stan) **9** Ran SP% **117.1**
Speed ratings (Par 96):93,92,91,91,90 90,90,89,88
CSF £8.78 TOTE £3.20: £1.30, £2.00, £1.40; EX 10.60 Trifecta £20.60 Pool £360.39 - 12.41 winning units.
Owner J P Hardiman **Bred** J P Hardiman **Trained** East Everleigh, Wilts

FOCUS
Modest maiden form judged by the time and bunched finish.

NOTEBOOK
Danehillsundance(IRE) has been expensive to follow, getting beaten as favourite on his last four starts, but he put that record right with a win from the front. He did get the run of the race and the form looks modest given the bunched finish, but to his credit he did battle to win. (op 4-1 tchd 11-4)
All Of Me(IRE), fourth in a similar event over this course and distance back in October, was given every chance but was outbattled. A question mark now hangs over his attitude as he found little under pressure. (op 5-4 tchd 11-10)
Highland Harvest ruined his chance by failing to settle, so he had nothing left for the sprint in the straight. He will be happier in a more strongly-run race. Official explanation: jockey said colt ran too free (tchd 4-1)
Challis(IRE) had run with a little promise on his debut and he again shaped as though he is capable of better. He was staying on well when short of room inside the last, and he might well be worth looking out for in handicap company after one more run. (op 8-1)
High Tribute, unfancied in the betting, is another best left alone till running in handicaps next year.
Mumbleswerve(IRE), a half-brother to five winners, was not given a hard time by his rider and looks likely to do better than the bare form suggests in future, most likely once he has achieved a handicap mark. (tchd 16-1)

6888 PONTIN'S "BOOK EARLY" H'CAP 1m 2f (P)
2:30 (2:31) (Class 4) (0-85,85) 3-Y-O+ **£5,505** (£1,637; £818; £408) **Stalls** Low

Form RPR
4611 **1** **Cusoon**[34] [6502] 4-9-4 84 .... GeorgeBaker 2 96
(G L Moore) *hld up in rr: stdy prog fr 3f out: trckd ldrs 2f out: led 1f out: hanging but sn rdn clr* **9/4**[1]
635/ **2** 2 **Watamu (IRE)**[858] [4737] 5-9-0 80 .... EddieAhern 10 88
(P J Makin) *hld up: prog gng wl 3f out: chsd ldr over 2f out to over 1f out: kpt on but easily outpcd by wnr* **8/1**
0144 **3** 1 **Stargazer Jim (FR)**[11] [6772] 4-9-0 80 .... TonyCulhane 3 87
(W J Haggas) *cl up: trckd ldr wl over 3f out: led wl over 2f out and sn kicked 2l clr: hdd and outpcd 1f out* **9/2**[2]
0523 **4** nk **Atlantic Quest (USA)**[11] [6772] 7-8-12 81 .... AmirQuinn(3) 5 87
(Miss Venetia Williams) *hld up in midfield: trapped bhd rivals fr 3 out to 2f out: chsd clr ldng trio over 1f out: rdn and r.o wl: no ch* **14/1**
2000 **5** 5 **Awatuki (IRE)**[114] [4878] 3-8-11 80 .... DaneO'Neill 14 77
(A P Jarvis) *hld up in rr: prog on outer 3f out: outpcd and hanging lft over 1f out: no ch after* **8/1**
0031 **6** 1 1/4 **Solo Flight**[22] [6633] 9-9-4 84 .... SteveDrowne 7 78
(H Morrison) *hld up towards rr: stdy prog on outer 3f out: outpcd 2f out: no ch after* **6/1**[3]
226B **7** 1 1/4 **Consonant (IRE)**[25] [6607] 9-8-8 77 .... JamesDoyle(3) 1 69
(D G Bridgwater) *nvr beyond midfield: pushed along 1/2-way: in tch over 2f out: sn outpcd and btn* **20/1**
6-30 **8** 1/2 **James Caird (IRE)**[158] [3552] 6-9-4 84 .... MickyFenton 6 75
(M H Tompkins) *hld up in rr: last over 3f out: urged along and styd on fr over 1f out: nvr nr ldrs* **12/1**
140- **9** 1 1/2 **Shannon Springs (IRE)**[33] [5767] 4-9-5 85 .... FergusSweeney 9 73
(Andrew Turnell) *prom: rdn over 3f out: steadily lost pl* **25/1**
3610 **10** 1 **Vicious Warrior**[75] [5789] 7-9-0 80 .... DeanMcKeown 4 66
(R M Whitaker) *w ldr to 5f out: sn rdn: wknd over 2f out* **12/1**
/400 **11** 1 3/4 **Aunty Euro (IRE)**[53] [6226] 4-9-4 84 .... RichardHughes 11 67
(Patrick Morris, Ire) *hld up and sn last: brief effrt over 3f out: no prog over 2f out* **33/1**
6004 **12** shd **Kylkenny**[18] [6677] 11-8-6 77 .... (t) CAdamson(5) 8 60
(H Morrison) *dwlt: hld up wl in rr: no prog whn hmpd on inner over 2f out* **50/1**
0000 **13** 8 **Grand Jour (IRE)**[5] [6830] 3-8-4 80 .... SophieDoyle(7) 13 47
(Ms J S Doyle) *mde most to wl over 4f out: wknd 3f out: t.o* **66/1**
0026 **14** 2 **Activo (FR)**[12] [6744] 5-9-2 82 .... PaulDoe 12 46
(S Dow) *dwlt: rushed up to go prom after 2f: led wl over 4f out to wl over 2f out: wknd rapidly: t.o* **11/1**

2m 2.19s (-5.60) **Going Correction** -0.125s/f (Stan) course record
WFA 3 from 4yo+ 3lb **14** Ran SP% **130.8**
Speed ratings (Par 105):117,115,114,114,110 109,108,107,106,105 104,104,98,96
CSF £21.91 CT £83.64 TOTE £3.10: £1.60, £3.00, £2.10; EX 42.20 Trifecta £143.30 Pool £417.84 - 2.07 winning units.
Owner The Winning Hand **Bred** Mrs Dare Wigan And Dominic Wigan **Trained** Woodingdean, E Sussex

FOCUS
A good handicap run in a very impressive winning time for the grade which took 0.41 seconds off the existing course record.
Grand Jour(IRE) Official explanation: trainer said gelding had a breathing problem
Activo(FR) Official explanation: jockey said gelding had no more to give

6889 PONTIN'S FAMILY HOLIDAYS CLAIMING STKS 1m 2f (P)
3:00 (3:00) (Class 6) 3-Y-O+ **£2,388** (£705; £352) **Stalls** Low

Form RPR
0000 **1** **Blackmail (USA)**[12] [6748] 8-9-0 53 .... EddieAhern 4 62
(P Mitchell) *trckd ldng pair to 1/2-way: effrt over 2f out: chsd ldr over 1f out: nt qckn and looked hld tl styd on to ld last strides* **6/1**
6000 **2** hd **Christmas Truce (IRE)**[4] [6848] 7-8-7 57 .... (p) JamesDoyle(3) 3 58
(Ms J S Doyle) *pressed ldr: led 3f out: drvn and hanging fr over 1f out: idled and hdd last strides* **13/2**
0060 **3** hd **Linda's Colin (IRE)**[11] [6770] 4-9-4 72 .... DaneO'Neill 8 66
(R A Harris) *hld up in last pair: effrt over 2f out: rdn and hanging over 1f out: styd on last 100yds: nt quite get up* **4/1**[3]
0000 **4** 1 **Barry Island**[28] [6566] 7-9-8 65 .... AntonyProcter 9 68
(D R C Elsworth) *hld up in last pair: effrt over 2f out: rdn on inner over 1f out: fnd little and btn ins fnl f* **3/1**[2]
3205 **5** 1/2 **Paparaazi (IRE)**[16] [6696] 4-9-4 66 .... (v) RobertWinston 5 63
(R A Fahey) *cl up: chsd ldr over 2f out: drvn and fnd nil over 1f out: lost pl fnl f* **11/8**[1]
1360 **6** 2 1/2 **Scuzme (IRE)**[15] [6027] 3-8-9 52 .... FergusSweeney 7 52
(Miss Sheena West) *trckd ldrs: rdn and losing pl whn n.m.r over 2f out: sn last and no ch: kpt on ins fnl f* **25/1**
060- **7** 10 **East Riding**[588] [1621] 6-8-7 35 ow4 .... DeanMcKeown 2 28
(A J Chamberlain) *mde most to 3f out: wknd over 2f out* **66/1**

2m 8.47s (0.68) **Going Correction** -0.125s/f (Stan)
WFA 3 from 4yo+ 3lb **7** Ran SP% **120.1**
Speed ratings (Par 101):92,91,91,90,90 88,80
CSF £46.53 TOTE £6.80: £2.20, £4.00; EX 35.80 Trifecta £123.50 Pool £464.58 - 2.67 winning units.
Owner Peter Crate **Bred** Skymarc Farm Inc **Trained** Epsom, Surrey

FOCUS
There was a tight finish to this modest claimer and the winning time was moderate for the grade.
Blackmail(USA) Official explanation: jockey said gelding suffered interference in running

6890 PONTINSBINGO.COM H'CAP (DIV II) 6f (P)
3:35 (3:36) (Class 6) (0-55,55) 3-Y-O+ **£1,706** (£503; £252) **Stalls** Low

Form RPR
4221 **1** **Cree**[14] [6728] 4-8-7 51 .... JamesDoyle(3) 2 61
(W R Muir) *s.i.s: outpcd and sn pushed along: clsd 2f out: hanging lft over 1f out: drvn and styd on to ld last stride* **1/1**[1]
4220 **2** shd **Kitchen Sink (IRE)**[110] [4985] 4-9-0 55 .... (e) EddieAhern 5 65
(P J Makin) *hld up bhd ldrs: wnt 3rd 1/2-way: clsd over 1f out: drvn to ld wl ins fnl f: hdd last stride* **3/1**[2]
0105 **3** nk **Mulberry Lad (IRE)**[1] [6869] 4-8-13 54 .... PaulDoe 8 63
(P W Hiatt) *chsd clr ldr: clsd 2f out: led over 1f out: hrd rdn and hdd wl ins fnl f: kpt on* **13/2**[3]
0223 **4** 1 **One Way Ticket**[12] [6753] 6-8-12 53 .... (p) MickyFenton 4 59
(J M Bradley) *led and sn 4l clr: collared over 1f out: wknd last 100yds* **3/1**[2]
0060 **5** hd **Mind Alert**[5] [6833] 5-8-9 50 .... (v) DaneO'Neill 7 55
(D Shaw) *settled off the pce: clsd on ldrs over 1f out: shuffled along and n.m.r ins fnl f: rdn and no imp last 75yds* **9/1**
0000 **6** 2 **Thoughtsofstardom**[2] [6856] 3-8-9 50 .... (p) HayleyTurner 1 49
(P S McEntee) *dwlt: hld up in last pair and wl off the pce: hrd rdn over 1f out: no real imp on ldrs* **20/1**
4550 **7** 3 1/2 **Jazz At The Sands (USA)**[10] [6780] 3-7-12 46 oh6 .... WilliamBuick(7) 9 35
(D Shaw) *chsd ldng pair to 1/2-way: sn u.p: wknd 2f out* **33/1**

8 3 **Ask Jenny (IRE)**[56] 6180 4-7-12 46 oh1..................(p) JosephWalsh(7) 6 26
(Patrick Morris, Ire) *rel to r and sn wl bhd: nvr a factor* **25/1**

1m 11.3s (-1.51) **Going Correction** -0.125s/f (Stan) 8 Ran SP% **134.9**
Speed ratings (Par 101):105,104,104,103,102 100,95,91
CSF £5.40 CT £16.88 TOTE £2.50: £1.20, £1.50, £1.80; EX 8.50 Trifecta £33.70 Pool £811.80 - 15.27 winning units. Place 6 £66.54, Place 5 £20.30.
Owner Inflite Partners **Bred** Miss G J Abbey **Trained** Lambourn, Berks

FOCUS
A moderate handicap but it was run at a good clip thanks to the trail-blazing One Way Ticket, and the form looks sound enough for the grade.
T/Jkpt: £12,796.20 to a £1 stake. Pool: £54,068.50. 3.00 winning tickets. T/Plt: £42.80 to a £1 stake. Pool: £60,778.95. 1,035.50 winning tickets. T/Qpdt: £14.50 to a £1 stake. Pool: £4,487.10. 227.50 winning tickets. JN

6871 SOUTHWELL (L-H)
Thursday, December 21

OFFICIAL GOING: Standard
Wind: Nil

6891 PONTINSBINGO.COM MAIDEN AUCTION STKS 1m (F)
12:30 (12:31) (Class 6) 2-Y-O **£2,730** (£806; £403) **Stalls** Low

Form RPR
0532 **1** **Stanley George (IRE)**[28] 6570 2-8-13 74...................... MatthewHenry 8 78+
(M A Jarvis) *mde virtually all: clr wl over 1f out: easily* **1/2**[1]
6402 **2** 3 **Go Dude**[13] 6745 2-8-10 55...(v) BrettDoyle 2 65
(J Ryan) *hld up in rr: hdwy and wd st: rdn to chse wnr wl over 1f out: sn no imp* **14/1**
4452 **3** 4 **Bert's Memory**[19] 6675 2-8-5 63....................................(p) JimmyQuinn 1 51
(K A Ryan) *hld up: hdwy 3f out: sn rdn and kpt on same pce fnl 2f* **4/1**[2]
0333 **4** 6 **Inflagrantedelicto (USA)**[12] 6757 2-8-11 65................. TonyCulhane 7 43
(D W Chapman) *sn pushed along towards rr: hdwy over 3f out: sn rdn and no prog fnl 2f* **13/2**[3]
000 **5** 5 **Mr Chocolate Drop (IRE)**[12] 6757 2-8-11 40 ow2........... AdamKirby 5 32
(M J Attwater) *chsd ldrs: rdn along over 3f out: sn wknd* **50/1**
0 **6** 1 **Fiona's Wonder**[50] 6290 2-8-4 .... TolleyDean(7) 4 29
(R A Harris) *prom: rdn along 1/2-way: sn wknd* **40/1**
006 **7** ¾ **Bold Nevison (IRE)**[23] 6644 2-8-12 62........................... PatCosgrave 6 29
(B Smart) *chsd ldrs on outer: rdn along over 3f out: sn wknd* **14/1**
8 6 **Bear Essential** 2-8-9 .... RobertHavlin 9 12
(Mrs P N Dutfield) *chsd ldrs: rdn along over 3f out: sn wknd* **40/1**
0600 **9** 2½ **Joella's Lad**[89] 5537 2-8-10 30....................................... J-PGuillambert 3 7
(Ms Deborah J Evans) *chsd ldrs on inner: rdn 1/2-way: sn wknd* **66/1**

1m 42.57s (-2.03) **Going Correction** -0.375s/f (Stan) 9 Ran SP% **121.7**
Speed ratings (Par 94):95,92,88,82,77 76,75,69,66
CSF £10.76 TOTE £1.60: £1.02, £3.40, £1.50; EX 8.90 Trifecta £26.90 Pool: £271.54 - 7.16 winning tickets..
Owner A D Bly **Bred** J Osborne **Trained** Newmarket, Suffolk

FOCUS
Moderate maiden form and the winner did not have to be at his best to score with a big improvement from the runner-up.

NOTEBOOK
Stanley George(IRE) looked to have been found a good opportunity to finally get off the mark, and he took it. The slower surface caused him few problems against this modest opposition and he won easily, but it remains to be seen whether he can compete successfully in handicap company off this sort of mark. (tchd 4-7)
Go Dude, exposed as moderate, has an official rating 19lb lower than the winner, so in the circumstances he did not do badly finishing three lengths down in second, albeit to a comfortable winner.
Bert's Memory finished less than a length in front of Inflagrantedelicto over this course and distance last time and confirmed that form by dealing out a bigger beating to that rival. (op 7-2 tchd 9-2)
Inflagrantedelicto(USA) could not reverse recent course and distance form with Bert's Memory on the same terms. (op 6-1)

6892 PONTIN'S HOLIDAYS (S) STKS 7f (F)
1:00 (1:03) (Class 6) 3-Y-O+ **£2,388** (£705; £352) **Stalls** Low

Form RPR
0350 **1** **Shrine Mountain (USA)**[12] 6762 4-9-4 60................(v) J-PGuillambert 8 73
(J R Holt) *mde all: rdn wl over 1f out: drvn ins last and hld on wl* **6/1**[3]
2445 **2** ¾ **Rafferty (IRE)**[272] 719 7-8-12 85................................ GrahamGibbons 3 65
(T D Barron) *prom: hdwy to chse wnr over 2f out: sn rdn: drvn and ev ch ins last: no ex towards fin* **11/10**[1]
3110 **3** nk **Climate (IRE)**[28] 6568 7-9-4 68...(p) NCallan 9 70
(K A Ryan) *in tch: pushed along and hdwy to chse ldrs over 2f out: sn rdn and ch ent last: sn drvn and kpt on same pce* **4/1**[2]
0156 **4** 4 **Capital Lass**[9] 6796 3-8-13 49... HayleyTurner 13 55
(D K Ivory) *in tch: hdwy over 2f out: sn rdn and kpt on same pce* **20/1**
2624 **5** hd **Paso Doble**[11] 6780 8-8-7 50... JamesMillman(5) 1 53
(D K Ivory) *bhd and rdn along 1/2-way: swtchd wd st and styd on appr last: nrst fin* **9/1**
0024 **6** ½ **The City Kid (IRE)**[16] 6717 3-8-7 47...........................(p) JimmyQuinn 12 47
(P D Evans) *chsd ldrs: rdn along wl over 2f out: sn one pce* **12/1**
0305 **7** 3 **Chickado (IRE)**[16] 6721 5-8-13 47..............................(p) RobertHavlin 10 45
(D Haydn Jones) *bhd: rdn along 1/2-way: styd on fnl 2f: nt rch ldrs* **16/1**
5006 **8** shd **Memphis Man**[6] 6833 3-9-4 63.. DaleGibson 4 50
(D G Bridgwater) *nvr nr ldrs* **20/1**
2000 **9** 5 **I Wish**[9] 6798 8-8-7 45.. PaulFitzsimons 14 26
(Miss J R Tooth) *chaqsed wnr: rdn along 1/2-way: wknd over 2f out* **50/1**
5055 **10** 6 **Hout Bay**[23] 6638 9-8-12 45... TonyCulhane 6 16
(D W Chapman) *midfield: rdn along 3f out: no hdwy* **28/1**
2625 **11** 1½ **Sion Hill (IRE)**[9] 6796 5-8-5 45..................(p) RussellKennemore(7) 2 12
(Mrs N Macauley) *chsd ldrs: rdn wl over 2f out: sn wknd* **33/1**
3000 **12** 2½ **Millbrook Star (IRE)**[37] 5873 3-8-12 40.................(v[1]) AdrianMcCarthy 5 —
(M C Chapman) *a rr* **100/1**
2010 **13** 3½ **Tuscan Flyer**[9] 6796 8-9-4 47..(b) PatCosgrave 11 —
(R Bastiman) *in tch: rdn along 1/2-way: sn wknd* **33/1**
1060 **14** 4 **Government (IRE)**[13] 6532 5-8-11 45....................(b) JamieHamblett(7) 7 —
(M C Chapman) *chsd ldrs: rdn along 1/2-way: sn wknd* **50/1**

1m 28.52s (-2.28) **Going Correction** -0.375s/f (Stan) 14 Ran SP% **129.2**
Speed ratings (Par 101):98,97,96,92,92 91,88,87,82,75 73,70,66,62
CSF £12.94 TOTE £8.50: £2.60, £1.10, £1.90; EX 23.70 Trifecta £125.50 Pool: £236.94 - 1.34 winning tickets..The winner was sold to Ron Harris for 3,500gns. Climate was claimed by Mrs J. B. Pye for £6,000. Memphis Man was claimed by Mr J. Babb for £6,000.
Owner G J Oliver **Bred** WinStar Farm Llc **Trained** Peckleton, Leics

FOCUS
A modest seller that, despite the presence of 85-rated Rafferty, is best rated through the fourth and fifth.
Sion Hill(IRE) Official explanation: jockey said gelding hung right-handed

6893 WBX.COM WORLD BET EXCHANGE H'CAP 1m 4f (F)
1:30 (1:30) (Class 5) (0-70,70) 3-Y-O+ **£3,238** (£963; £481; £240) **Stalls** Low

Form RPR
-011 **1** **Speagle (IRE)**[20] 6666 4-9-7 70..................................... DanielTudhope 3 85
(D Carroll) *trckd ldr: led 3f out: sn rdn clr: styd on wl* **5/2**[2]
002 **2** 6 **Opera Writer (IRE)**[12] 6769 3-8-7 61.................................. PaulQuinn 4 66
(R Hollinshead) *hld up in rr: hdwy over 3f out: rdn and chsd wnr ent last: no imp* **8/1**[3]
0040 **3** 1¾ **Russian Dream (IRE)**[37] 6479 3-8-12 66.......................... AdamKirby 5 68
(W R Swinburn) *trckd ldng pair: hdwy 3f out: rdn and one pce appr last* **8/1**[3]
3531 **4** 3½ **Aphorism**[12] 6759 3-9-0 68.. NCallan 2 65
(J R Fanshawe) *trckd ldrs: hdwy 4f out: rdn wl over 2f out and sn btn* **5/6**[1]
5000 **5** 1 **Gattuso**[19] 6683 3-7-11 56 oh6.................................. DuranFentiman(5) 6 51
(Ms Deborah J Evans) *led: rdn along 4f out: hdd 3f out and sn wknd* **33/1**
500/ **6** 9 **Hathaal (IRE)**[284] 7-9-2 65...(v) MickyFenton 1 46
(E J Creighton) *hld up: a rr* **33/1**

2m 36.7s (-5.39) **Going Correction** -0.375s/f (Stan)
WFA 3 from 4yo+ 5lb 6 Ran SP% **111.2**
Speed ratings (Par 103):102,98,96,94,93 87
CSF £21.40 TOTE £3.40: £1.90, £2.30; EX 16.00.
Owner Document Express Ltd **Bred** Mrs Sheila Morrissey **Trained** Driffield, E Yorks

FOCUS
A modest handicap but it was won in authoritative style by an improving four-year-old.

6894 PONTIN'S BOOK EARLY "PREMIER" CLAIMING STKS 6f (F)
2:00 (2:02) (Class 4) 2-Y-O **£5,181** (£1,541; £770; £384) **Stalls** Low

Form RPR
031 **1** **Bussel (USA)**[27] 6575 2-9-2 75... TonyCulhane 5 75+
(W J Haggas) *trckd ldng pair: hdwy 2f out: rdn over 1f out: styd on to ld ins last* **11/10**[1]
0552 **2** nk **Cherri Fosfate**[36] 6491 2-8-3 63.................................... MatthewHenry 4 61
(W G M Turner) *chsd ldr: hdwy 2f out: rdn to ld appr fnl f: drvn and hdd ins last: kpt on* **10/3**[2]
5012 **3** 2½ **Bridget's Team**[23] 6640 2-7-12 58....................................(t) DaleGibson 6 49
(D G Bridgwater) *led: rdn along 2f out: hdd appr last: kpt on same pce* **9/2**[3]
4562 **4** 1 **Catlivius (IRE)**[19] 6679 2-8-1 63...................................(tp) JimmyQuinn 2 49
(K A Ryan) *in tch: pushed along and hdwy 2f out: sn rdn and no imp* **11/2**

1m 16.06s (-0.84) **Going Correction** -0.375s/f (Stan) 4 Ran SP% **104.3**
Speed ratings (Par 98):90,89,86,84
CSF £4.55 TOTE £2.00; EX 4.20.
Owner W J Haggas **Bred** John Weld **Trained** Newmarket, Suffolk

FOCUS
A competitive claimer, with only 3lb separating the four runners on adjusted official ratings and the form looks fair.

NOTEBOOK
Bussel(USA) won her maiden on the Polytrack at Kempton last time but she is by a sire who has a good record on Fibresand and she handled this more testing surface well. She got home narrowly and probably ran to a similar level as when losing her maiden tag. (op 10-11 tchd 5-4)
Cherri Fosfate, who could only finish runner-up to a plater in a claimer over this course and distance last time out, had to settle for the same position again, but the opposition was stronger this time and it was a better performance. (op 4-1 tchd 9-2 and 3-1)
Bridget's Team was able to dictate, as she had when winning a nursery here in November, but she was below her best in the first-time tongue tie. (op 5-1)
Catlivius(IRE), another fitted with a tongue strap for the first time, could not take advantage of the drop in grade. She might be more effective over the minimum trip. (op 6-1)

6895 CLARENCE CONTRACTORS LTD NOVICE STKS 5f (F)
2:30 (2:30) (Class 4) 2-Y-O **£4,533** (£1,348; £674; £336) **Stalls** High

Form RPR
2323 **1** **Hereford Boy**[5] 6838 2-8-12 63..................................... RobertHavlin 4 68
(D K Ivory) *cl up: rdn to ld over 1f out: kpt on* **8/1**[3]
01 **2** nk **Zadalla**[19] 6679 2-8-9 .... RobertWinston 5 64
(Andrew Oliver, Ire) *led: rdn along 2f out: hdd over 1f out: kpt on u.p ins last* **9/2**[2]
2331 **3** nk **Eau Good**[15] 6730 2-8-9 84.............................. RussellKennemore(7) 3 70
(M C Chapman) *chsd ldrs: pushed along over 2f out: sn rdn: kpt on ins last* **2/5**[1]
461 **4** 1¼ **Bungie**[10] 6788 2-9-0 62.. J-PGuillambert 1 63
(Ms Deborah J Evans) *chsd ldng pair: rdn along 2f out: kpt on same pce* **12/1**
00 **5** 4 **Inverted**[54] 6222 2-8-12 .... MickyFenton 2 47
(Mrs A Duffield) *rdn along and outpcd fr 1/2-way* **66/1**

59.39 secs (-0.91) **Going Correction** -0.225s/f (Stan) 5 Ran SP% **109.9**
Speed ratings (Par 98):98,97,97,95,88
CSF £40.97 TOTE £6.60: £2.90, £1.30; EX 30.70.
Owner T G N Burrage **Bred** Mrs L R Burrage **Trained** Radlett, Herts

FOCUS
With the favourite running well below his best this took less winning than had looked likely. The form is rated around the first two and the fourth.

NOTEBOOK
Hereford Boy has been running to a consistent, albeit modest, level on Polytrack and one could argue that the switch to Fibresand brought about some improvement, but the key to this win was the poor performance of the favourite, and he probably did not need to improve much. (op 15-2 tchd 9-1)
Zadalla won a weak maiden over the course and distance last time and she tried to follow up by making every yard. She looked to give her running and her performance is probably the best guide to the level of the form. (tchd 6-1)
Eau Good won easily at Wolverhampton last time, albeit against modest opposition, and he looked the one to beat on that evidence, despite the drop in trip. However, he failed to run to the same level on this more testing surface. (op 4-9)
Bungie was another switching to Fibresand after winning his maiden on Polytrack. It is difficult to argue that he ran below form though, as he finished close enough to be considered to have run near to his mark. (tchd 11-1)

6896 ARCHER ELECTRICAL H'CAP 6f (F)
3:00 (3:00) (Class 4) (0-85,85) 3-Y-0+ £5,505 (£1,637; £818; £408) Stalls Low

Form RPR
5061 1 **California Laws**[41] 6425 4-8-6 75 MatthewHenry 5 87+
(T D Barron) *towards rr: hdwy over 2f out: rdn to ld ins last* 11/8[1]
6444 2 nk **Jimmy The Guesser**[13] 6752 3-8-12 81 HayleyTurner 9 92
(N P Littmoden) *cl up: led 1/2-way: rdn over 1f out: hdd ins last* 8/1
0045 3 4 **Charlie Delta**[3] 6858 3-7-12 74 ow2 (p) KellyHarrison(7) 1 73
(D Carroll) *chsd ldrs on inner: rdn over 2f out: kpt on same pce* 14/1
0301 4 5 **Sahara Silk (IRE)**[14] 6740 5-8-4 73 (v) AdrianMcCarthy 4 57
(D Shaw) *in tch: pushed along and sltly outpcd 1/2-way: styd on fnl 2f* 18/1
3105 5 ¾ **Winning Pleasure (IRE)**[23] 6643 8-7-13 73 AndrewElliott(5) 7 55
(J Balding) *towards rr: wd st: n.d* 8/1
0000 6 ¾ **Sailor King (IRE)**[20] 6660 4-8-13 82 RobertWinston 6 62
(D K Ivory) *led: rdn along and hdd 1/2-way: grad wknd* 16/1
2605 7 1¾ **Hits Only Heaven (IRE)**[76] 5785 4-8-10 84 (e) MichaelJStainton(5) 10 58
(D Nicholls) *towards rr: wd st: nvr a factor* 5/1[2]
1116 8 hd **Night Prospector**[16] 6720 6-8-9 85 (p) TolleyDean(7) 2 59
(R A Harris) *prom: rdn over 2f out: sn wknd* 15/2[3]
5506 9 nk **King Marju (IRE)**[6] 6830 4-9-2 85 PatCosgrave 3 58
(K R Burke) *chsd ldrs: rdn over 2f out: sn wknd* 8/1
0000 10 5 **Violent Velocity (IRE)**[41] 6428 3-8-4 73 DaleGibson 8 31
(J J Quinn) *wd st: a towards rr* 50/1

1m 14.19s (-2.71) **Going Correction** -0.375s/f (Stan) 10 Ran SP% 123.6
Speed ratings (Par 105):103,102,97,90,89 88,86,86,85,78
CSF £14.38 CT £123.82 TOTE £2.10: £1.20, £2.80, £4.00; EX 12.90 Trifecta £169.90 Pool: £354.35 - 1.48 winning tickets..
Owner Rupert Bear Racing **Bred** P Balding **Trained** Maunby, N Yorks

FOCUS
Not a bad handicap, and the first two came clear, suggesting the form is sound for the grade, with the third setting the standard.

6897 WBXTRIPLECROWN.COM H'CAP 1m (F)
3:30 (3:30) (Class 6) (0-62,61) 3-Y-0+ £2,730 (£806; £403) Stalls Low

Form RPR
0003 1 **Moonstreaker**[7] 6819 3-8-5 55 MichaelJStainton(5) 9 64
(R M Whitaker) *midfield: hdwy 2f out: rdn ins last: styd on to ld nr fin* 10/1
0000 2 nk **Blue Empire (IRE)**[13] 6747 5-8-13 57 RobertWinston 7 65
(C R Dore) *led: rdn along 2f out: drvn ins last: hdd nr fin* 13/2[3]
3203 3 1½ **Solicitude**[16] 6721 3-8-7 52 ow2 (p) RobertHavlin 5 57
(D Haydn Jones) *a.p: rdn 2f out: kpt on sme pce ins last* 8/1
1023 4 1 **Black Sea Pearl**[7] 6820 3-9-2 61 DaleGibson 8 64
(P W D'Arcy) *a.p: chsd ldr over 3f out: sn rdn and kpt on same pce* 5/1[1]
0602 5 nk **Wodhill Schnaps**[30] 6552 5-8-5 49 (b) HayleyTurner 4 51
(D Morris) *bhd tl styd on fnl 2f: nrst fin* 12/1
0463 6 nk **Lucius Verrus (USA)**[9] 6798 6-8-5 49 oh2 (v) AdrianMcCarthy 3 51
(D Shaw) *in tch: rdn along over 2f out: kpt on same pce* 6/1[2]
1105 7 ¾ **Under Fire (IRE)**[10] 6787 3-8-3 55 KellyHarrison(7) 14 55
(A W Carroll) *chsd ldrs: rdn along over 2f out: kpt on same pce* 7/1
40/6 8 3½ **Roman Boy (ARG)**[143] 3995 7-9-2 60 MickyFenton 1 53
(Stef Liddiard) *cl up on inner: rdn wl over 2f out: sn wknd* 10/1
000 9 ½ **Golden Spectrum (IRE)**[178] 2936 7-8-2 53 (p) TolleyDean(7) 11 45
(R A Harris) *bhd tl styd on fnl 2f* 28/1
1553 10 1 **Barzak (IRE)**[12] 6756 6-8-5 49 (bt) MatthewHenry 13 39
(S R Bowring) *chsd ldrs: rdn over 2f out: sn wknd* 13/2[3]
0000 11 4 **Tyrone Sam**[12] 6762 4-9-1 59 (b) PatCosgrave 2 40
(K A Ryan) *in tch: rdn along wl over 2f out: sn btn* 16/1
0000 12 shd **Crusoe (IRE)**[7] 6819 9-8-5 49 oh4 JosedeSouza 12 30
(A Sadik) *a towards rr* 33/1
P-0 13 16 **Brogue Lanterns (IRE)**[10] 6787 4-8-6 55 AndrewElliott(5) 6 3
(E J Creighton) *a bhd* 100/1

1m 41.82s (-2.78) **Going Correction** -0.375s/f (Stan)
WFA 3 from 4yo+ 1lb 13 Ran SP% 120.4
Speed ratings (Par 101):98,97,96,95,94 94,93,90,89,88 84,84,68
CSF £73.45 CT £557.19 TOTE £12.40: £3.10, £3.00, £3.40; EX 98.50 TRIFECTA Not won. Place 6 £51.65, Place 5 £43.16.
Owner Ian B Ender **Bred** Hellwood Stud Farm **Trained** Scarcroft, W Yorks

FOCUS
An ordinary handicap and no more than moderate form rated around the third, fourth and fifth.
T/Plt: £60.20 to a £1 stake. Pool: £37,534.20. 455.00 winning tickets. T/Qpdt: £55.20 to a £1 stake. Pool: £1,911.00. 25.60 winning tickets. JR

6858 WOLVERHAMPTON (A.W) (L-H)
Thursday, December 21

OFFICIAL GOING: Standard to slow changing to standard after race 3 (4.50) (meeting abandoned after race 4 (5.20) due to heavy fog)
Last two races abandoned due to fog.
Wind: Almost nil Weather: Foggy

6898 PONTIN'S HOLIDAYS CLAIMING STKS 1m 141y(P)
3:50 (3:52) (Class 5) 3-4-Y-0 £3,886 (£1,156; £577; £288) Stalls Low

Form RPR
4204 1 **Top Mark**[38] 6469 4-9-8 72 FergusSweeney 2 71
(J R Boyle) *chsd ldrs: rdn to ld ins fnl f: styd on* 9/2[2]
0060 2 ½ **North Walk (IRE)**[17] 6698 3-9-8 69 (p) NCallan 8 72
(K A Ryan) *led 1f: chsd ldr: rdn and ev ch ins fnl f: styd on* 6/1
3006 3 1¼ **Ask No More**[42] 6419 3-8-7 63 (b) DominicFox(3) 13 57
(P L Gilligan) *led over 7f out: rdn over 2f out: hdd and no ex ins fnl f* 11/1
6600 4 hd **Following Flow (USA)**[14] 6741 4-8-13 72 (p) RichardKingscote(3) 9 61
(R Hollinshead) *hld up: hdwy over 2f out: rdn over 1f out: edgd lft fnl f: styd on* 22/1
0000 5 1 **Ronnies Lad**[30] 6552 4-8-12 40 PaulMulrennan 4 55
(J R Norton) *prom: lost pl 6f out: nt clr run over 1f out: r.o ins fnl f* 100/1
4604 6 ¾ **Goose Chase**[17] 6694 4-9-4 67 DaneO'Neill 12 59
(A M Hales) *mid-div: rdn over 3f out: nt clr run over 1f out: r.o: nt trble ldrs* 16/1
0004 7 shd **Defi (IRE)**[34] 6507 4-9-5 69 (b) JamieMoriarty(5) 7 65
(I Semple) *hld up in tch: rdn over 2f out: hung lft and no ex ins fnl f* 11/2[3]
0006 8 1¼ **Ruby Sunrise (IRE)**[10] 6792 4-8-7 40 (b) RichardThomas 11 45
(B P J Baugh) *s.i.s: hld up: hdwy over 1f out: n.d* 100/1
3054 9 1 **Davidia (IRE)**[13] 6743 3-8-12 58 SteveDrowne 5 50
(S Kirk) *trckd ldrs: rdn over 3f out: wknd over 1f out* 11/1
466 10 ½ **Methusaleh (IRE)**[15] 6733 3-9-3 73 JamieJones(5) 6 59
(D Shaw) *hld up in tch: nt clr run over 2f out: sn rdn: wknd over 1f out* 12/1
0030 11 2½ **George's Flyer (IRE)**[7] 6814 3-8-10 65 (b) DavidAllan 1 42
(R A Fahey) *mid-div: rdn 1/2-way: wknd over 1f out* 16/1
6 12 14 **Mouseen (IRE)**[16] 6721 3-9-0 55 (p) BrettDoyle 3 17
(R A Harris) *s.i.s: a in rr: bhd fnl 3f* 33/1
1500 13 26 **Diamonds And Dust**[68] 5301 4-9-10 82 (b) GeorgeBaker 10 —
(N P Littmoden) *hld up: rdn over 3f out: wknd over 2f out: eased* 7/2[1]

1m 51.09s (-0.67) **Going Correction** -0.05s/f (Stan)
WFA 3 from 4yo 2lb 13 Ran SP% 115.5
Speed ratings (Par 103):100,99,98,98,97 96,96,95,94,94 91,79,56
CSF £29.79 TOTE £5.50: £1.50, £1.90, £3.20; EX 41.80.North Walk was claimed by Ms Jennie Candlish for £12,000.
Owner M Khan X2 **Bred** Ewar Stud Farms **Trained** Epsom, Surrey

FOCUS
A moderate claimer and although the visibility was poor, enough of the race could be seen to deduce that those that raced handily were much favoured.
Mouseen(IRE) Official explanation: jockey said gelding never travelled

6899 PONTIN'S HOLIDAYS H'CAP 1m 1f 103y(P)
4:20 (4:21) (Class 6) (0-55,57) 3-Y-0+ £2,590 (£770; £385; £192) Stalls Low

Form RPR
0 1 **Kilimandscharo (USA)**[185] 2708 4-8-11 50 BrettDoyle 4 65+
(P J McBride) *chsd ldrs: led 1f out: rdn out* 15/8[1]
4400 2 3 **Lobengula (IRE)**[18] 6687 4-8-13 52 JimmyQuinn 10 61
(I W McInnes) *led: hdd over 7f out: led again 4f out: rdn and hdd 1f out: no ex* 16/1
1343 3 2½ **Desert Hawk**[8] 6812 5-8-11 50 (b) DaneO'Neill 2 54
(W M Brisbourne) *s.i.s: hld up: hdwy over 1f out: nt rch ldrs* 11/4[2]
3410 4 ¾ **Thornaby Green**[19] 6683 5-8-13 52 GrahamGibbons 5 54
(T D Barron) *chsd ldr: led over 7f out: hdd 4f out: rdn over 2f out: wknd ins fnl f* 9/1
504 5 1½ **Spoilsport**[6] 6837 3-8-12 53 JimCrowley 3 52
(P D Evans) *mid-div: rdn over 2f out: hdwy over 1f out: nvr trbld ldrs* 25/1
4231 6 8 **Moyoko (IRE)**[11] 6779 3-9-2 57 6ex SteveDrowne 9 40
(M Blanshard) *hld up in tch: rdn over 3f out: wknd over 1f out* 5/1[3]
1456 7 1¾ **Vibrato (USA)**[10] 6787 4-8-10 49 DavidAllan 8 29
(C J Teague) *hld up: effrt over 3f out: wknd 2f out* 16/1
2000 8 1½ **Newcorp Lad**[45] 6383 6-9-0 53 TonyCulhane 1 30
(Mrs G S Rees) *prom 7f* 50/1
1000 9 nk **Bold Phoenix (IRE)**[36] 6484 5-9-0 53 PaulMulrennan 7 29
(B J Curley) *hld up: bhd fnl 3f* 20/1
0655 10 hd **Amron Hill**[24] 6627 3-9-0 55 FergusSweeney 11 31
(R Hollinshead) *mid-div: rdn and wknd over 2f out* 25/1
0365 11 2 **Blue Beacon**[18] 6693 3-9-0 55 (b) NCallan 13 27
(K A Ryan) *chsd ldrs: rdn over 3f out: wknd over 2f out* 33/1
300 12 8 **Monashee River (IRE)**[20] 6666 3-8-6 54 JamesO'Reilly(7) 6 10
(Miss V Haigh) *hld up: hdwy 1/2-way: rdn and wknd over 2f out* 50/1
200- 13 15 **Mysteriosa**[562] 2369 4-8-5 49 JamesMillman(5) 12 —
(B R Millman) *s.i.s: a in rr* 66/1

2m 1.34s (-1.28) **Going Correction** -0.05s/f (Stan)
WFA 3 from 4yo+ 2lb 13 Ran SP% 120.7
Speed ratings (Par 101):103,100,98,97,96 89,87,86,85,85 83,76,63
CSF £33.16 CT £86.48 TOTE £2.20: £1.70, £6.50, £1.10; EX 51.50.
Owner P J McBride **Bred** Ron Dufficy **Trained** Newmarket, Suffolk

FOCUS
The visibility was even worse than for the opener and little could be seen. It did however appear that again those that raced handily were at an advantage.
Mysteriosa Official explanation: jockey said filly lost its action

6900 PONTINS.COM NURSERY 7f 32y(P)
4:50 (4:52) (Class 6) (0-65,65) 2-Y-0 £3,238 (£963; £481; £240) Stalls High

Form RPR
0322 1 **Tobago Reef**[17] 6706 2-9-4 62 (p) DaneO'Neill 4 73+
(Mrs L Stubbs) *mde all: rdn clr fnl f* 7/2[2]
445 2 4 **First Princess (IRE)**[29] 6561 2-9-5 63 EddieAhern 3 64
(J S Moore) *prom: chsd wnr 1/2-way: rdn over 1f out: styd on same pce* 6/1
1643 3 1½ **Show Trial (IRE)**[8] 6807 2-8-13 57 AdamKirby 5 54
(D J S Ffrench Davis) *hld up: hdwy 2f out: nt trble ldrs* 3/1[1]
5666 4 1½ **Bentley**[12] 6760 2-8-3 47 (v) ChrisCatlin 2 41
(D Shaw) *mid-div: rdn over 2f out: styd on same pce* 9/1
0424 5 nk **Suntan Lady (IRE)**[7] 6813 2-8-0 49 (v) DuranFentiman(5) 6 42
(Miss V Haigh) *mid-div: rdn over 3f out: styd on same pce fnl 2f* 16/1
01 6 nk **Forced Upon Us**[96] 5387 2-9-3 61 TonyCulhane 10 53
(P J McBride) *dwlt: hdwy 1/2-way: rdn and wknd over 1f out* 9/2[3]
0405 7 2½ **Zain (IRE)**[24] 6625 2-8-7 51 ow1 PaulMulrennan 11 37
(J G Given) *prom over 5f* 8/1
004 8 3 **Briarwood Bear**[13] 6751 2-9-7 65 JimmyQuinn 9 43
(M Blanshard) *mid-div: rdn 1/2-way: wknd over 2f out* 16/1
000 9 10 **Brynris**[208] 2015 2-7-12 42 oh7 PaulQuinn 1 —
(Mrs G S Rees) *prom early: bhd fnl 4f* 66/1
050 10 16 **Heart And Hand (IRE)**[189] 2588 2-8-3 50 DominicFox(3) 7 —
(M G Quinlan) *chsd ldrs over 4f* 25/1

1m 30.07s (-0.33) **Going Correction** -0.05s/f (Stan) 10 Ran SP% 117.9
Speed ratings (Par 94):99,94,92,91,90 90,87,84,72,54
CSF £25.27 CT £70.58 TOTE £5.50: £1.10, £3.90, £1.10; EX 36.50.
Owner Vincent Lee **Bred** M Williams **Trained** Norton, N. Yorks

FOCUS
Very poor visibility for this nursery, but at the few stages where the runners could be picked out the winner was in front, which showed that the pace bias was still going strong. The draw also had an effect, with the first five home starting from stall six or lower.

NOTEBOOK
Tobago Reef, a confirmed front-runner, found that the way the track was riding was helping him no end and ran his rivals into the ground to record a deserved first victory at the ninth attempt. (tchd 10-3)
First Princess(IRE), making her nursery debut, was always in pursuit of the winner but could never get to him. She still has a bit of scope and ought to find a modest contest. (op 5-1 tchd 13-2)
Show Trial(IRE), like all those that tried to come from off the pace at this meeting, found it tough to do so and probably achieved as much as could be expected despite being a beaten favourite. She is more exposed than most of her rivals, however. (tchd 10-3)
Bentley was another not helped by the way the track was riding yet managed to stay on and record his best placing to date, albeit in his 11th outing. (op 12-1)

The Form Book, Raceform Ltd, Compton, RG20 6NL

Suntan Lady(IRE), trying this trip for the first time, was yet another whose style of running was a disadvantage at this meeting. She is still a maiden after 13 attempts, but may be capable of finding a small race over this longer distance when the cards fall better for her. (op 14-1)

6901 PONTIN'S HOLIDAYS AUCTION MAIDEN STKS 7f 32y(P)
5:20 (5:21) (Class 5) 3-4-Y-0 £3,238 (£963; £481; £240) Stalls High

Form RPR
0563 **1** **Networker**[74] 5844 3-9-3 55 TonyCulhane 3 62
(P J McBride) *chsd ldrs: led ins fnl f: r.o* **9/2**[2]
0632 **2** ¾ **Fairdonna**[12] 6771 3-8-12 59 EddieAhern 1 55
(D J Coakley) *chsd ldrs: rdn over 1f out: r.o* **1/1**[1]
5034 **3** 2 ½ **Newkeylets**[23] 6649 3-8-9 53 (p) GregFairley(3) 2 49
(I Semple) *chsd ldrs: led over 2f out: rdn over 1f out: hdd and no ex ins fnl f:* **11/2**[3]
2204 **4** 1 **Royal Embrace**[24] 6624 3-9-3 56 (v) DaneO'Neill 11 51
(D Shaw) *s.s: bhd: r.o ins fnl f: nrst fin* **16/1**
0050 **5** ¾ **Jenise (IRE)**[9] 6794 3-8-12 45 JimCrowley 4 44
(Mark Campion) *mid-div: rdn 1/2-way: styd on same pce fnl 2f* **80/1**
033 **6** shd **Layed Back Rocky**[3] 6861 4-9-3 45 GeorgeBaker 5 49
(M Mullineaux) *in ld 1/2-way: hdd over 2f out: wknd fnl f* **11/1**
7 1 ¼ **Big Ralph**[29] 3-9-3 JimmyQuinn 10 45
(M Wigham) *in rr: hdwy over 1f out: nvr trbld ldrs* **16/1**
0000 **8** 1 ¾ **Obscene**[215] 1859 3-9-3 61 NCallan 9 41
(A J McCabe) *mid-div: rdn and wknd over 1f out* **14/1**
9 1 ½ **Uptown Rosie (IRE)**[177] 2964 3-8-9 DominicFox(3) 7 32
(John Monroe, Ire) *s.s: a in rr* **66/1**
400 **10** 3 ½ **Cameo Story**[9] 6798 3-8-12 BrettDoyle 8 23
(Andrew Oliver, Ire) *chsd ldrs 5f* **40/1**

1m 30.17s (-0.23) **Going Correction** -0.05s/f (Stan) 10 Ran SP% 115.5
Speed ratings (Par 103):99,98,95,94,93 93,91,89,88,84
CSF £9.18 TOTE £5.60: £2.00, £1.10, £1.60; EX 11.30 Place 6 £6.17, Place 5 £2.12.
Owner P J McBride **Bred** T S And Mrs M E Child **Trained** Newmarket, Suffolk

FOCUS
The visibility for this maiden was virtually non-existent, but from what could be seen the principals were all up with the pace throughout. The draw again played its part with the first three home starting from the three inside stalls. The winning time was 1/10 of a second slower than the preceding nursery, albeit in terrible conditions.
Cameo Story Official explanation: jockey said filly hung left

6902 GO PONTIN'S H'CAP 1m 5f 194y(P)
() (Class 4) (0-85,) 3-Y-0+ £

6903 PONTINS.COM H'CAP 5f 216y(P)
() (Class 6) (0-60,) 3-Y-0+ £

T/Plt: £6.20 to a £1 stake. Pool: £59,518.05. 6,948.85 winning tickets. T/Qpdt: £1.10 to a £1 stake. Pool: £6,535.20. 4,080.90 winning tickets. CR

6877 KEMPTON (A.W) (R-H)
Friday, December 22

OFFICIAL GOING: Standard (meeting abandoned after race 4 (2.50) due to heavy fog)
Visibility deteriorated to the point where the 2.50 race was delayed. Though it eventually went ahead, racing was called off before the next could be run.
Wind: Nil Weather: Foggy

6904 WBX.COM BANDED STKS 1m 2f (P)
1:20 (1:20) (Class 7) 3-Y-0+ £1,365 (£403; £201) Stalls High

Form RPR
5421 **1** **Revolve**[9] 6801 6-9-12 50 (b) PaulDoe 7 61
(Mrs L J Mongan) *mde all: set slow pce to 1/2-way: rdn over 1f out: kpt on fnl f: jst hld on* **9/4**[1]
3522 **2** shd **Wood Fern (UAE)**[9] 6801 6-9-5 49 (v) PatCosgrave 8 54
(W M Brisbourne) *trckd wnr for 3f: styd handy: wnt 2nd again jst over 1f out: cajoled along and clsd last 100yds: jst failed* **11/4**[2]
4446 **3** 1 ¾ **Hiawatha (IRE)**[16] 6724 7-9-4 48 SamHitchcott 10 50
(A M Hales) *prom: rdn over 2f out: kpt on same pce fr over 1f out* **10/1**
0040 **4** 1 ½ **Expected Bonus (USA)**[4] 6852 7-9-1 40 (p) DavidKinsella 2 44
(Jamie Poulton) *pushed up to go prom: chsd wnr after 3f to over 4f out: rdn over 2f out: steadily outpcd* **14/1**
6003 **5** nk **Piquet**[4] 6852 8-9-1 40 (p) MatthewHenry 5 43
(J J Bridger) *t.k.h: hld up in last tl rapid prog to press wnr over 4f out: nrly upsides over 1f out: sn wknd* **8/1**
2603 **6** 1 **Pharaoh Prince**[231] 1467 5-9-3 47 AdrianMcCarthy 3 43
(G Prodromou) *t.k.h: hld up: last over 4f out: rdn over 2f out: plugged on: n.d* **6/1**[3]
0-00 **7** 4 **The Rip**[57] 4483 5-9-4 48 JDSmith 6 37
(R M Stronge) *t.k.h: hld up towards rr: rdn and no prog over 2f out* **25/1**
005/ **8** 1 **Grand Welcome (IRE)**[462] 4-9-6 50 (bt) AlanDaly 1 37
(E J Creighton) *t.k.h: trckd ldrs: rdn and wknd rapidly 2f out* **25/1**
0000 **9** 1 ¼ **Fantasy Crusader**[18] 6700 7-9-5 49 (p) PaulMulrennan 9 33
(R M H Cowell) *t.k.h: hld up in rr: rdn 2f out: fnd nil* **9/1**
0000 **10** 2 ½ **Wild Lass**[9] 6802 5-9-1 40 (p) LeeEnstone 4 25
(J C Fox) *t.k.h: hld up in rr: rdn 4f out: sn struggling* **25/1**

2m 12.42s (3.42) **Going Correction** -0.15s/f (Stan) 10 Ran SP% 120.1
Speed ratings (Par 97):80,79,78,77,77 76,73,72,71,69
CSF £8.52 TOTE £2.70: £1.10, £1.90, £2.40; EX 9.00.
Owner Mrs P J Sheen **Bred** Wickfield Farm Partnership **Trained** Epsom, Surrey

FOCUS
The winning jockey dictated a tempo to suit, and he and his partner were able to hang on from a rival who wins infrequently. The winning time was therefore very slow, even for a banded race. The form is not solid, the runner-up looking the best guide.

6905 WBX.COM WORLD BET EXCHANGE MEDIAN AUCTION MAIDEN STKS 6f (P)
1:50 (1:50) (Class 7) 2-Y-0 £1,365 (£403; £201) Stalls High

Form RPR
1 **Galaxy Stars** 2-8-11 (t) AmirQuinn(3) 4 68
(P J Makin) *dwlt: sn rcvrd and trckd ldr after 2f: led wl over 1f out: edgd lft sn after: drvn and hld on wl nr fin* **7/1**[3]
0332 **2** nk **Darling Belinda**[8] 6821 2-8-9 63 (p) FergusSweeney 1 62
(D K Ivory) *carried lft s: settled in rr: prog on outer over 2f out: chsd wnr over 1f out: clsng nr fin but nvr finding enough* **6/4**[2]
3 **3** 1 ¼ **Not Too Taxing**[7] 6826 2-8-11 StephaneBreux(3) 7 63
(R Hannon) *chsd ldr for 2f: sn pushed along: effrt again over 1f out: keeping on but hld whn rn out of room nr fin* **11/8**[1]
0 **4** 3 ½ **Millyjean**[56] 6199 2-8-9 HayleyTurner 8 48
(John Berry) *chsd ldrs: rdn 1/2-way: effrt on inner over 1f out: no prog fnl f* **16/1**
6 **5** ½ **Meeting Of Minds**[8] 6821 2-8-9 PaulDoe 3 46
(W Jarvis) *dwlt: prog fr rr 1/2-way: shkn up and lost pl 2f out: no real hdwy after* **14/1**
4005 **6** 1 ½ **One White Sock**[17] 6711 2-8-6 45 (b) MarcHalford(3) 5 42
(J L Spearing) *led to wl over 1f out: wknd fnl f* **33/1**
00 **7** 7 **Danjoe**[34] 6523 2-9-0 PatCosgrave 2 26
(R Brotherton) *chsd ldrs tl wknd 2f out: t.o* **50/1**

1m 13.45s (-0.25) **Going Correction** -0.15s/f (Stan) 7 Ran SP% 112.1
Speed ratings (Par 90):95,94,92,88,87 85,76
CSF £17.26 TOTE £5.60: £2.40, £1.60; EX 21.80.
Owner Miss Nivin El-Gamal **Bred** The National Stud **Trained** Ogbourne Maisey, Wilts

FOCUS
A fair turnout for the money, and run at a decent gallop. The race has been rated through the placed horses.

NOTEBOOK
Galaxy Stars cost only 8,000 guineas as a yearling, but this gelded son of the top-class Golden Snake has many winners in the family from sprints to middle-distances, including the triple banded race winner Bahamian Boy. He battled well to hold on, and could be something of a bargain, with trips up to ten furlongs on the agenda in the long-term. (tchd 6-1)
Darling Belinda was wearing first-time cheekpieces, but they could not produce the magic required to get her head in front at the eighth attempt. However, though she is a little quirky, it is too early to give up on her, with blinkers or a visor an obvious option. (op 5-4 tchd 13-8)
Not Too Taxing was dropping a furlong in trip from his debut run over six furlongs, but he was soon off the bridle and a return to seven should not inconvenience him. That said, he ran well enough and should be placed to win a little race. (op 6-4 tchd 5-4 and 13-8 in a place)
Millyjean's only previous run was on turf at Newmarket. This is more her level, and as a first effort on sand it was satisfactory enough.
Meeting Of Minds has shown minor ability in her two outings, but looks one for handicap company after another run. (op 10-1)
One White Sock is not up to winning in maidens, but has also been beaten in handicaps. She seems most likely to return to that company, where a drop of several pounds would at least give her a chance. (op 20-1)

6906 TAKE CONTROL WITH WBX.COM BANDED STKS 6f (P)
2:20 (2:20) (Class 7) 3-Y-0+ £1,365 (£403; £201) Stalls High

Form RPR
016 **1** **Midmaar (IRE)**[2] 6884 5-8-13 46 (b) FergusSweeney 11 56
(M Wigham) *in 5th pl after 1f: chsng ldrs over 2f out: in ld ent fnl f: jst hld on* **3/1**[1]
0523 **2** shd **Burhaan (IRE)**[16] 6728 4-8-11 47 AmirQuinn(3) 9 57
(J R Boyle) *hld up: 10th after 1f: prog 2f out: clsd on wnr fnl f: jst failed* **4/1**[2]
0000 **3** 1 ¼ **Vlasta Weiner**[10] 6796 6-8-12 50 (b) JamieJones(5) 3 56
(J M Bradley) *chsng ldng pair after 1f: stl cl up over 2f out: disputing ld jst over 1f out: one pce* **50/1**
0006 **4** ½ **Atlantic Viking (IRE)**[4] 6855 11-9-3 50 (p) PaulMulrennan 6 54
(P D Evans) *hld up: 9th after 1f: stl towards rr over 2f out: r.o fnl f: nrst fin* **16/1**
3634 **5** ½ **Spinetail Rufous (IRE)**[9] 6806 8-9-0 47 (v) AdrianMcCarthy 4 50
(Miss Z C Davison) *7th after 1f: stl midfield over 2f out: kpt on fnl f* **20/1**
0035 **6** 1 **Danehill Stroller (IRE)**[16] 6728 6-8-11 49 (b[1]) AndrewElliott(5) 10 49
(A M Hales) *8th after 1f: stl towards rr over 2f out: r.o ins fnl f* **5/1**[3]
3056 **7** ½ **Orchestration (IRE)**[17] 6719 5-8-12 45 HayleyTurner 1 43
(M J Attwater) *led for 2f: prom over 2f out: fdd* **10/1**
6245 **8** nk **Shunkawakhan (IRE)**[19] 6688 3-8-10 50 (b) MarvinCheung(7) 7 48
(G C H Chung) *plld hrd: led after 2f: sddle sn slipped: wknd over 1f out* **15/2**
0043 **9** 1 ¼ **Christian Bendix**[10] 6796 4-9-0 47 (p) PaulDoe 12 41
(P Howling) *in last pair after 1f: nvr on terms* **9/1**
0023 **10** hd **Lady Hopeful (IRE)**[9] 6806 4-9-0 47 (b) AdamKirby 2 40
(Peter Grayson) *in last pair after 1f: nvr on terms* **12/1**
00-0 **11** ½ **Shergael (IRE)**[12] 6780 5-9-0 47 (p) SamHitchcott 8 39
(J L Spearing) *6th after 1f: stl in midfield over 2f out: in rr fnl f* **25/1**
0563 **12** nk **Ace Club**[17] 6717 5-8-12 45 (b) PatCosgrave 5 36
(M J Attwater) *4th after 1f: wkng 2f out* **33/1**

1m 13.61s (-0.09) **Going Correction** -0.15s/f (Stan) 12 Ran SP% 119.6
Speed ratings (Par 97):94,93,92,91,90 89,88,88,86,86 85,85
CSF £14.04 TOTE £3.00: £1.80, £1.70, £15.80; EX 14.90.
Owner A Dunmore M Wigham **Bred** Shadwell Estate Company Limited **Trained** Newmarket, Suffolk

FOCUS
Run in thickening fog at an ordinary sprint gallop. Just ordinary form for the grade.
Danehill Stroller(IRE) Official explanation: jockey said gelding ran too free
Shunkawakhan(IRE) Official explanation: jockey said saddle slipped
Shergael(IRE) Official explanation: jockey said gelding hung left

6907 WBX.COM COMMITTED TO RACING MAIDEN CLAIMING STKS 1m 3f (P)
2:50 (3:14) (Class 7) 3-Y-0+ £1,365 (£403; £201) Stalls High

Form RPR
5300 **1** **Josh You Are**[18] 6553 3-8-13 46 PatCosgrave 7 59
(D E Cantillon) *hld up: 7th after 1f: prog 4f out: in ld and in command ent fnl f: drvn out* **10/1**
3400 **2** 2 ½ **Simplified**[9] 6801 3-8-8 45 DavidKinsella 6 50
(N B King) *hld up: 11th after 1f: prog and 3rd 4f out: 2nd and wl hld fnl f* **14/1**
4352 **3** ½ **Kilmeena Magic**[4] 6852 4-8-12 45 LeeEnstone 13 49
(J C Fox) *hld up: 8th after 1f: stl same pl 4f out: 3rd and one pce fnl f* **13/8**[1]
00P0 **4** ½ **Good Intentions**[9] 6812 4-8-6 35 JosedeSouza 10 42
(P W Hiatt) *in ld after 1f and 4f out: 4th and keeping on one pce fnl f* **33/1**
0060 **5** 2 **Orchard House (FR)**[18] 6236 3-8-13 40 DerekMcGaffin 9 50
(J Jay) *9th after 1f: stl in rr 4f out: 5th and one pce fnl f* **50/1**
0055 **6** 2 **Sophie'Jo**[13] 6759 3-8-8 47 (p) PaulMulrennan 11 42
(Miss J Feilden) *3rd after 1f: stl prom 4f out: n.d fnl f* **12/1**
5600 **7** 1 ¾ **Lucy Babe**[65] 6057 3-8-3 40 EmmettStack(5) 4 39
(G Prodromou) *10th after 1f: stl wl in rr 4f out: n.d fnl f* **33/1**
0600 **8** 3 **Miss Sudbrook (IRE)**[9] 6803 4-8-12 45 RichardThomas 2 33
(A W Carroll) *chsng ldr after 1f: rdn and losing pl 4f out* **50/1**
-504 **9** hd **Beauchamp United**[29] 3264 3-8-11 54 AdrianMcCarthy 14 36
(B Palling) *5th after 1f: rdn and losing pl 4f out* **8/1**[3]

0450 **10** *7* **Qik Dip (IRE)**[34] 6524 3-8-10 53 ow3 .... JDSmith 12 23
(P D Evans) *t.k.h: hld up in last: prog on outer 4f out: bhd fnl f* **3/1**[2]
0-00 **11** *1 ½* **Golo Gal**[23] 2088 4-9-3 57 .... PaulDoe 3 24
(Mrs L J Mongan) *4th after 1f: chsng ldr and pushed along 4f out: bhd fnl f* **9/1**
0-00 **12** *2 ½* **In Rhubarb**[10] 6795 4-9-3 40 .... AlanDaly 1 19
(P Howling) *6th after 1f: no bttr 4f out: bhd fnl f* **33/1**

2m 21.17s **Going Correction** -0.15s/f (Stan)
WFA 3 from 4yo+ 4lb **12** Ran SP% **120.4**
Speed ratings (Par 97):99,97,96,96,95 93,92,90,89,84 83,81
CSF £136.23 TOTE £14.80: £3.20, £3.20, £1.30; EX 192.90 Place 6 £11.16, Place 5 £7.41.
Owner Mrs Edward Cantillon **Bred** Phil Jen Racing **Trained** Newmarket, Suffolk
■ Restricted to jockeys who rode fewer than 30 winners in 2005. Chicherova was w/d at the s as Hayley Turner was not eligible.

FOCUS
A poor race, but run at a reasonable gallop. However, in thick fog it was hard to see anything by now. An improved effort from the winner who is less exposed than most.
Sophie'Jo Official explanation: jockey said filly hung right
Qik Dip(IRE) Official explanation: jockey said gelding hung left

6908 JOIN WBX.COM TODAY BANDED STKS 1m (P)
() (Class 7) 3-Y-0+ £

6909 WORLD BET EXCHANGE WBX.COM BANDED STKS 7f (P)
() (Class 7) 3-Y-0+ £

6910 WBXTRIPLECROWN.COM BANDED STKS 1m 4f (P)
() (Class 7) 3-Y-0+ £

T/Plt: £4.70 to a £1 stake. Pool: £44,358.05. 6,757.80 winning tickets. T/Qpdt: £1.70 to a £1 stake. Pool: £2,739.40. 1,128.90 winning tickets. JN

6884 LINGFIELD (L-H)
Friday, December 22

OFFICIAL GOING: Standard
Wind: Nil

6911 PONTINSBINGO.COM H'CAP 1m 4f (P)
12:10 (12:10) (Class 6) (0-60,57) 3-Y-0 **£3,238** (£963; £481; £240) **Stalls** Low

Form RPR
0066 **1** **Ifatfirst (IRE)**[18] 6700 3-8-11 **52** .... RichardHughes 8 61
(M P Tregoning) *stdd s: hld up in last: plld wd and hdwy over 2f out: rdn wl over 1f out: styd on to ld nr fin* **5/2**[1]
0466 **2** *nk* **Recalcitrant**[14] 6748 3-8-4 **52** .... WilliamCarson(7) 11 61
(S Dow) *chsd ldrs: wnt 2nd over 3f out: rdn to ld 2f out: hdd and no ex nr fin* **12/1**
253 **3** *nk* **Lady Georgette (IRE)**[27] 6601 3-8-11 **52** .... EddieAhern 5 61
(E J O'Neill) *in tch: hdwy over 3f out: rdn over 2f out: chsd ldr over 1f out: kpt on u.p fnl f: lost 2nd nr fin* **7/2**[2]
0026 **4** *3* **Dream Mountain**[14] 6743 3-8-9 **53** .... JamesDoyle(3) 12 57
(Ms J S Doyle) *s.i.s: sn chsng ldrs: rdn over 2f out: kpt on same pce fnl f* **25/1**
060 **5** *hd* **Mamonta**[66] 6026 3-9-2 **57** .... JamieSpencer 4 60
(M J Wallace) *hld up in rr: rdn and effrt over 2f out: kpt on fnl f: nt pce to rch ldrs* **7/1**[3]
5602 **6** *¾* **Lennoxtown (IRE)**[6] 6843 3-9-1 **56** .... BrettDoyle 3 58
(J Ryan) *in tch: rdn to chse ldrs 2f out: wknd ins fnl f* **7/2**[2]
4523 **7** *2 ½* **Camp Attack**[14] 6743 3-8-13 **54** .... LPKeniry 9 52
(S Dow) *chsd ldr tl led wl over 3f out: rdn and hdd 2f out: wknd fnl f* **16/1**
0006 **8** *5* **Footstepsinthesnow (IRE)**[39] 6459 3-8-6 **47** .... JimmyQuinn 6 37
(M A Buckley) *t.k.h: hld up towards rr: rdn and effrt over 2f out: nvr trbld ldrs* **20/1**
0-44 **9** *3 ½* **Daneway**[32] 6535 3-9-2 **57** .... DeanCorby 7 42
(P Howling) *dwlt: rr but in tch: rdn over 3f out: no ch last 2f* **20/1**
0060 **10** *26* **Theologicum**[18] 6700 3-8-9 **50** .... EdwardCreighton 1 —
(Miss J R Gibney) *led and clr tl 5f out: hdd and rdn wl over 3f out: sn wknd: t.o and eased fnl f* **50/1**

2m 30.64s (-3.75) **Going Correction** -0.15s/f (Stan) **10** Ran SP% **114.4**
Speed ratings (Par 98):106,105,105,103,103 102,101,97,95,78
CSF £31.50 CT £104.90 TOTE £3.60: £1.10, £4.50, £2.50; EX 42.30 TRIFECTA Not won..
Owner Mrs M Horne Mrs W Biggs Nic de Boinville **Bred** Mrs Belinda Strudwick **Trained** Lambourn, Berks

FOCUS
A very poor race on paper with the ten runners only having achieved one solitary previous victory between them. The first two home had never previously been placed, but even so the winning time was very respectable for a race of its type and the form looks sound enough.

6912 IQ PROJECT SOLUTIONS LTD MEDIAN AUCTION MAIDEN STKS 6f (P)
12:40 (12:43) (Class 5) 2-Y-0 **£3,886** (£1,156; £577; £288) **Stalls** Low

Form RPR
3 **1** **Iron Pearl**[30] 6562 2-8-12 .... BrettDoyle 1 57+
(Jane Chapple-Hyam) *trckd ldrs on inner: hdwy over 1f out: led 1f out: pushed clr: readily* **4/1**[2]
4 **2** *2 ½* **Tilapia (IRE)**[14] 6749 2-9-3 .... J-PGuillambert 3 55
(Sir Mark Prescott) *s.i.s: sn pushed up to ld: rdn over 2f out: hdd 1f out: kpt on but nt pce of wnr* **9/2**[3]
3 *hd* **Ravenna** 2-8-12 .... RichardHughes 2 49
(M P Tregoning) *s.i.s: sn trcking ldrs: rdn and briefly outpcd 2f out: kpt on ins fnl f* **7/2**[1]
4 *1* **My Drop (IRE)** 2-9-3 .... ChrisCatlin 5 51
(E J O'Neill) *s.i.s: t.k.h and hld up in midfield: hdwy on inner over 1f out: rdn and kpt on ins fnl f* **10/1**
5003 **5** *nk* **Path To Glory**[14] 6742 2-9-3 46 .... (p) IanMongan 4 50
(Miss Z C Davison) *t.k.h: w ldr: rdn and ev ch over 2f out: kpt on same pce fnl f* **14/1**
0 **6** *shd* **Zilli**[38] 6481 2-8-9 .... JamesDoyle(3) 7 45
(N P Littmoden) *unruly s: s.i.s: bhd: rdn and edgd rt wl over 1f out: swtchd lft over 1f: r.o nr fin: nt rch ldrs* **50/1**
0 **7** *nk* **Shaded Edge**[17] 6710 2-9-3 .... EddieAhern 11 49
(D W P Arbuthnot) *slowly away: hld up in rr: rdn and effrt whn short of room briefly wl over 1f out: r.o last 100 yds: n.d* **25/1**
000 **8** *nk* **Hoh Me Hoh You (IRE)**[139] 4161 2-9-3 56 .... DPMcDonogh 6 48
(S Kirk) *trckd ldrs: rdn and effrt over 2f out: wknd wl ins fnl f* **4/1**[2]
60 **9** *nk* **Katie Kingfisher**[48] 6330 2-8-12 .... AdamKirby 10 42
(R M Beckett) *s.i.s: rr: rdn and hdwy 2f out: kpt on same pce wl ins fnl f* **20/1**
0 **10** *5* **Lost All Alone**[14] 6742 2-9-3 .... LPKeniry 9 32
(D M Simcock) *chsd ldrs: rdn over 2f out: wknd wl over 1f out* **40/1**
11 *15* **Northern Dune (IRE)** 2-9-3 .... JamieSpencer 8 —
(B J Curley) *s.i.s: a wl bhd: no ch whn rn wd bnd over 2f out: t.o* **7/1**

1m 13.07s (0.26) **Going Correction** -0.15s/f (Stan) **11** Ran SP% **121.7**
Speed ratings (Par 96):92,88,88,87,86 86,86,85,85,78 58
CSF £22.40 TOTE £4.30: £2.30, £1.60, £2.30; EX 23.40 Trifecta £28.00 Pool: £155.88 - 3.95 winning tickets..
Owner Miss Vanessa Church **Bred** T J Cooper **Trained** Newmarket, Suffolk

FOCUS
A modest maiden and weak form for the grade, but the winner scored with a little in hand.

NOTEBOOK
Iron Pearl, who ran well on her first start in Britain and first for her current trainer at Kempton last month, settled better this time and that made the difference. She won well but also tends to limit the form. (op 9-2)
Tilapia(IRE), who made a promising debut at Wolverhampton, built on that under a positive ride and should be winning a race before too long. (op 4-1 tchd 7-2)
Ravenna, a half-sister to Don't Call Me Derek but with plenty of speed in her pedigree, was well backed but gave the impression the experience would be of benefit. She will know a lot more next time. (op 10-3 tchd 5-1)
My Drop(IRE), a speedily-bred colt, ran well on this debut and his trainer can be expected to place him to win races. (op 8-1)
Path To Glory raced prominently but was quite keen and that cost him in the last furlong (tchd 16-1)
Hoh Me Hoh You(IRE), having his first run on this surface, tracked the leaders and appeared to have every chance, but had nothing in reserve in the final furlong. (op 13-2)
Katie Kingfisher Official explanation: jockey said filly did not face kickback

6913 IQ STORAGE SOLUTIONS H'CAP 6f (P)
1:10 (1:15) (Class 6) (0-65,69) 3-Y-0+ **£3,238** (£963; £481; £240) **Stalls** Low

Form RPR
0251 **1** **Hollow Jo**[6] 6842 6-9-6 **69** 6ex .... MickyFenton 3 77
(J R Jenkins) *wnt rt s: sn chsng ldrs: rdn to ld wl over 1f out: rdn out* **7/2**[1]
4024 **2** *½* **Muscari**[7] 6827 4-8-7 **59** .... JamesDoyle(3) 10 65
(S Woodman) *rel to enter stalls: bhd: rdn and swtchd rt wl over 1f out: r.o wl ins fnl f: nt rch wnr* **10/1**
5530 **3** *¾* **Gwilym (GER)**[13] 6773 3-9-1 **64** .... (b[1]) RobertHavlin 5 68
(D Haydn Jones) *chsd ldr: rdn and ev ch 2f out: kpt on same pce fnl f* **16/1**
4023 **4** *nk* **Dvinsky (USA)**[6] 6842 5-9-2 **65** .... DeanCorby 6 68
(P Howling) *in tch: hdwy over 2f out: ch jst over 1f out: kpt on same pce ins fnl f* **9/2**[3]
1644 **5** *½* **Turibius**[19] 6688 7-8-8 **57** .... JimCrowley 7 58
(T E Powell) *bhd: rdn over 3f out: sme late hdwy: nvr nrr* **14/1**
0650 **6** *shd* **Cool Sting (IRE)**[25] 6624 3-8-8 **60** .... (b[1]) JerryO'Dwyer(3) 9 61
(M G Quinlan) *in tch: effrt and rdn over 2f out: no imp fnl f* **10/1**
0600 **7** *nk* **Franksalot (IRE)**[8] 6820 6-8-13 **62** .... JimmyQuinn 4 62
(I W McInnes) *hld up in midfield: nt clr run over 2f out: swtchd rt and effrt over 1f out: no imp last 100 yds* **25/1**
3000 **8** *½* **Blessed Place**[4] 6858 6-8-10 **59** .... (t) JamieSpencer 2 58
(D J S Ffrench Davis) *led tl rdn and hdd wl over 1f out: eased whn btn last 100 yds* **17/2**
0065 **9** *1* **Kempsey**[17] 6709 4-8-11 **60** .... (b) EddieAhern 11 56
(J J Bridger) *hld up in rr: effrt and rdn wl 1f out: nvr trbld ldrs* **14/1**
0000 **10** *nk* **Majestical (IRE)**[7] 6827 4-8-11 **60** .... (p) LPKeniry 12 55
(J M Bradley) *stdd s: t.k.h and sn in midfield: rdn over 2f out: sn btn* **50/1**
2032 **11** *1 ½* **Bobby Rose**[6] 6842 3-9-1 **64** .... BrettDoyle 1 54
(D K Ivory) *s.i.s: t.k.h and sn prom: rdn over 2f out: wknd 2f out* **4/1**[2]

1m 11.28s (-1.53) **Going Correction** -0.15s/f (Stan) **11** Ran SP% **114.1**
Speed ratings (Par 101):104,103,102,101,101 101,100,100,98,98 96
CSF £36.28 CT £437.19 TOTE £4.90: £2.70, £2.60, £4.50; EX 37.80 TRIFECTA Not won..
Owner Jim McCarthy **Bred** K J Reddington **Trained** Royston, Herts
■ George The Second (10/1) was withdrawn on vet's advice. R4 applies, deduct 5p in the £.

FOCUS
Ordinary form, not solid through the third and fifth, but an improved run from the winner.

6914 PONTIN'S HOLIDAYS CONDITIONS STKS 7f (P)
1:40 (1:40) (Class 4) 3-Y-0+
£6,232 (£1,866; £933; £467; £233; £117) **Stalls** Low

Form RPR
0431 **1** **Vortex**[6] 6847 7-9-5 93 .... (t) JimmyQuinn 6 108
(Miss Gay Kelleway) *t.k.h: hld up in last pair: hdwy over 3f out: shkn up to chal 1f out: led last 100 yds: r.o wl* **11/2**[3]
4062 **2** *hd* **Red Spell (IRE)**[6] 6847 5-9-0 101 .... RichardHughes 4 102
(R Hannon) *w.w in tch: chsd wnr over 4f out: clsd over 2f out: rdn wl over 1f out: pressed wnr last 100 yds: a hld* **6/4**[1]
122- **3** *1 ¼* **Cupid's Glory**[470] 5073 4-9-0 113 .... J-PGuillambert 1 99
(Sir Mark Prescott) *led: clr after 1f: rdn over 2f out: hdd last 100 yds: no ex: btn and eased nr fin* **15/8**[2]
3443 **4** *2* **Kindlelight Debut**[6] 6847 6-8-6 98 .... JamesDoyle(3) 3 89
(N P Littmoden) *hld up in last pair: hdwy on outer over 3f out: chsd ldng trio and rdn wl over 1f out: one pced* **11/2**[3]
6-4 **5** *15* **Fly By Jove (IRE)**[195] 2445 3-9-0 .... JimCrowley 2 55
(Jane Southcombe) *trckd ldrs tl over 3f out: sn rdn and bhd: t.o* **100/1**
660 **6** *1 ¼* **Savannah**[66] 6043 3-9-3 .... EddieAhern 5 55
(Luke Comer, Ire) *chsd ldr: pushed along over 4f out: demoted and sltly hmpd 4f out: sn bhd: t.o* **25/1**

1m 23.39s (-2.50) **Going Correction** -0.15s/f (Stan) **6** Ran SP% **110.4**
Speed ratings (Par 105):108,107,106,104,86 85
CSF £13.78 TOTE £5.10: £3.00, £1.10; EX 13.00.
Owner Coriolis Partnership **Bred** Juddmonte Farms **Trained** Exning, Suffolk

FOCUS
Almost a carbon copy of the result of the conditions event over an extra furlong here six days earlier, though this race was run at a much stronger pace thanks to Cupid's Glory. The race could have been rated higher but the time was only modest.

6915 PONTINS.COM H'CAP 1m (P)

2:10 (2:10) (Class 3) (0-95,93) 3-Y-0+

£11,092 (£3,321; £1,660; £831; £414; £208) **Stalls** High

Form RPR

6215 **1** **Orchard Supreme**[19] [6692] 3-9-3 **93**............................ RichardHughes 6 103+
(R Hannon) *t.k.h: hld up: shkn up and gd hdwy on outer over 1f out: led ins fnl f: readily* **3/1**[2]

5530 **2** ¾ **Secret Night**[34] [6514] 3-8-9 **85**.. EddieAhern 9 93
(J A R Toller) *t.k.h: hld up in midfield: hdwy 2f out: rdn and ev ch jst over 1f out: kpt on same pce ins fnl f* **8/1**

4121 **3** nk **Bomber Command (USA)**[7] [6830] 3-8-8 **91** 6ex........... PatrickHills(7) 3 98
(J W Hills) *chsd ldrs: wnt 2nd 2f out: sn led and rdn: hdd ins fnl f: no ex* **7/2**[3]

2042 **4** ¾ **Wavertree Warrior (IRE)**[7] [6830] 4-8-7 **85**.................. JamesDoyle(3) 7 91
(N P Littmoden) *hld up in rr: pushed along 2f out: swtchd rt and rdn 1f out: r.o last 100 yds: nvr nrr* **11/4**[1]

040 **5** 1 ½ **Paraguay (USA)**[7] [6830] 3-8-4 **80**.............................. EdwardCreighton 4 82
(Miss V Haigh) *s.i.s: hld up in rr on inner: rdn and hdwy 2f out: no prog fnl f* **16/1**

0112 **6** 1 **Prince Tum Tum (USA)**[28] [6583] 6-8-13 **88**............... DeanMcKeown 1 88+
(D Shaw) *trckd ldrs: nt clr run on inner 2f out tl 1f out: pushed along and no real hdwy wl ins fnl f* **11/1**

1-30 **7** 2 **Psychiatrist**[27] [6600] 5-9-1 **90**... PaulFitzsimons 2 85
(Miss J R Tooth) *t.k.h: chsd ldr tl 2f out: wknd over 1f out* **33/1**

0600 **8** 1 ¼ **Yarqus**[111] [5019] 3-9-2 **92**.. BrettDoyle 5 84
(C E Brittain) *sn pushed up to ld: rdn and hdd wl over 1f out: wknd fnl f* **16/1**

6000 **9** ½ **Xtra Torrential (USA)**[19] [6692] 4-9-3 **92**........................... JimCrowley 8 83
(D M Simcock) *hld up towards rr: rdn over 2f out: no ch over 1f out* **16/1**

1m 35.83s (-3.60) **Going Correction** -0.15s/f (Stan) course record
WFA 3 from 4yo+ 1lb **9** Ran SP% **113.9**
Speed ratings (Par 107):112,111,110,110,108 107,105,104,103
CSF £26.88 CT £86.85 TOTE £3.20: £1.70, £3.20, £1.60; EX 23.30 Trifecta £131.10 Pool: £376.82 - 2.04 winning tickets..
Owner Brian C Oakley **Bred** Mrs M H Goodrich **Trained** East Everleigh, Wilts

FOCUS
A competitive handicap full of talented Polytrack performers and no hanging about thanks to Yarqus, resulting in a decent winning time for the class of contest. Solid form.

NOTEBOOK
Orchard Supreme, a four-time winner around here, was ridden with supreme confidence and when asked for his effort in the home straight he found plenty to go and win his race. He can never be left out of calculations around here and there should be more opportunities for him at this track this winter. (op 7-2 tchd 11-4)
Secret Night, who has already crossed swords with Orchard Supreme a couple of times here in the last two months, was brought through to hold every chance and did little wrong, but her old rival had the greater impetus at the line. As consistent as she is, she has not won for over a year and never over as far as this, which has to be a bit of a worry. (op 7-1)
Bomber Command(USA) came into this in fine form, but with his penalty was 12lb higher than when fifth here on his last visit last month. He had every chance and was only just run out of it so it would be harsh to be negative about this effort, but he may just be better suited by Kempton. (tchd 9-2)
Wavertree Warrior(IRE), 6lb better off with Bomber Command for a neck beating at Kempton last time and 2lb better off for a length defeat by Orchard Supreme at the same track before that, was ridden with a great deal more patience than of late but the tactic did not pay off. He did not respond immediately when first asked for his effort and when he eventually did it was far too late. As he was only a length behind the eventual winner when first coming under pressure, he cannot in any way be considered unlucky. (op 9-4)
Paraguay(USA), making his Polytrack debut, was far from disgraced and seems to handle both sand surfaces, but he is still a few pounds above his last winning mark on turf so may need to drop a bit further. (op 14-1)
Prince Tum Tum(USA), up another 3lb despite getting beaten last time, seemed to hold a good position for much of the way, but he then found himself with no room on the inside as the leader started to fold and when he did get through he had lost all chance. He was by no means beaten up after that and he looks as though he can still be competitive off this sort of mark. (op 9-1 tchd 17-2 and 12-1)

6916 ROSE RUSSELL MEDIAN AUCTION MAIDEN STKS 1m 5f (P)

2:40 (2:40) (Class 5) 3-4-Y-0 **£4,533** (£1,348; £674; £336) **Stalls** Low

Form RPR

520- **1** **Ross Moor**[439] [5773] 4-9-6 61... JamesDoyle(3) 6 74
(N P Littmoden) *trckd ldrs: chsd ldr wl over 2f out: led jst over 2f out: clr 1f out: rdn out* **14/1**

3402 **2** 1 ¾ **Monets Masterpiece (USA)**[7] [6828] 3-9-3 80................ GeorgeBaker 5 71
(G L Moore) *t.k.h: hld up in midfield: hdwy and rdn over 2f out: chsd wnr ins fnl f: no imp* **2/1**[1]

0-33 **3** 4 **Clear Vision**[7] [6828] 3-8-12 .... JimCrowley 3 60
(Mrs A J Perrett) *t.k.h: chsd wnr after 3f: led jst over 3f out: hdd over 2f out: one pce* **8/1**[3]

062 **4** 2 **Cove Mountain (IRE)**[12] [6775] 4-9-4 56........................ DPMcDonogh 8 57
(S Kirk) *t.k.h: hld up in tch: rdn and effrt wl over 2f out: no hdwy over 1f out* **2/1**[1]

4520 **5** ¾ **Ruse**[14] [6748] 3-8-12 57.. JamieSpencer 4 56
(J R Fanshawe) *t.k.h: hld up towards rr: rdn and effrt over 2f out: no hdwy over 1f out: wknd ins fnl f* **3/1**[2]

6 1 ¼ **Scaramoushca** 3-9-3 .... AntonyProcter 7 59
(P S McEntee) *stdd s: hld up in last: pushed along over 3f out: no imp last 2f* **25/1**

00-0 **7** 28 **Eidsfoss (IRE)**[173] [2] 4-9-9 35.. BrianReilly 1 17
(T T Clement) *t.k.h: led tl jst over 3f out: sn rdn and wknd t.o* **100/1**

2m 47.32s (-0.98) **Going Correction** -0.15s/f (Stan)
WFA 3 from 4yo 6lb **7** Ran SP% **114.3**
Speed ratings (Par 103):97,95,93,92,91 91,73
CSF £42.40 TOTE £14.50: £4.40, £1.80; EX 37.30 TRIFECTA Not won..
Owner M Murphy **Bred** R T And Mrs Watson **Trained** Newmarket, Suffolk

FOCUS
A moderate maiden including a few that have been in action over hurdles. The winning time was modest, 2.26 seconds slower than the following handicap, so the form probably does not add up to much.

6917 EUROPA QUALITY PRINT H'CAP 1m 5f (P)

3:10 (3:10) (Class 4) (0-85,84) 3-Y-0+ **£6,477** (£1,927; £963; £481) **Stalls** Low

Form RPR

-221 **1** **Melpomene**[32] [6535] 3-8-6 **77**.. GregFairley(3) 7 87
(M Johnston) *chsd ldr tl led briefly 3f out: rdn over 2f out: 3rd and outpcd wl over 1f out: rallied strly fnl f: led on post* **7/2**[2]

0522 **2** shd **Eva Soneva So Fast (IRE)**[21] [6661] 4-9-5 **81**.................. JimmyQuinn 3 91
(J L Dunlop) *hld up in rr: gd hdwy on inner over 3f out: rdn to ld 2f out: clr 1f out: ct on line* **7/4**[1]

6040 **3** 1 **Country Pursuit (USA)**[34] [6515] 4-9-5 **81**.......................(b) BrettDoyle 2 90
(C E Brittain) *t.k.h: hld up in tch: pushed along and outpcd bnd over 2f out: r.o strly ins fnl f: nt rch ldrs* **14/1**

0401 **4** 1 **Polish Power (GER)**[21] [6661] 6-9-2 **78**.................................... LPKeniry 1 85
(J S Moore) *trckd ldrs: rdn to wl over 2f out: hdd 2f out: kpt on same pce u.p* **7/1**

0015 **5** 2 ½ **Ocean Pride (IRE)**[9] [6811] 3-8-10 **78** ow1.................... RichardHughes 4 81
(D E Pipe) *t.k.h: trckd ldrs: rdn 3f out: kpt on same pce wl over 1f out* **14/1**

4233 **6** shd **Pass The Port**[9] [6811] 5-9-1 **77**.. EddieAhern 6 80
(D Haydn Jones) *hld up bhd: hdwy on outer 3f out: chsd ldrs and rdn 2f out: wknd 1f out* **6/1**[3]

0105 **7** 2 **Liberty Run (IRE)**[30] [6566] 4-8-8 **70** oh1............................. ChrisCatlin 5 70
(Mrs A J Hamilton-Fairley) *t.k.h: hld up in rr: rdn over 2f out: no real hdwy* **33/1**

0004 **8** hd **Barathea Blazer**[27] [6602] 7-9-8 **84**...................................... JamieSpencer 8 84
(K McAuliffe) *led tl jst over 3f out: sn rdn: wknd over 2f out* **8/1**

2m 45.06s (-3.24) **Going Correction** -0.15s/f (Stan)
WFA 3 from 4yo+ 6lb **8** Ran SP% **112.8**
Speed ratings (Par 105):103,102,102,101,100 100,98,98
CSF £9.72 CT £71.59 TOTE £5.10: £2.10, £1.10, £3.10; EX 8.80 Trifecta £68.80 Pool: £513.64 - 5.30 winning tickets..
Owner Mrs Christine E Budden **Bred** Zubieta Ltd **Trained** Middleham Moor, N Yorks

FOCUS
A fair pace for this handicap and it was noticeable that the majority wanted to stay well away from the inside rail throughout. Modest form, but sound.

6918 PONTIN'S "BOOK EARLY" H'CAP 1m 2f (P)

3:40 (3:40) (Class 6) (0-60,60) 3-Y-0+ **£3,238** (£963; £481; £240) **Stalls** Low

Form RPR

0000 **1** **Reaching Out (IRE)**[15] [5450] 4-8-9 **53**.......................(b) JamesDoyle(3) 10 60
(N P Littmoden) *v.s.a: sn in tch in rr: bmpd bnd over 2f out: plld wd and str run to ld wl ins fnl f* **6/1**[3]

0004 **2** ½ **Blu Manruna**[19] [6687] 3-8-11 **55**...............................(b) DeanMcKeown 4 61
(J Akehurst) *led: rdn over 1f out: hdd wl ins fnl f: nt pce of wnr* **7/1**

0300 **3** 1 **Lady Pilot**[6] [6843] 4-8-13 **54**.. LPKeniry 7 58
(Ms J S Doyle) *hld up in tch: chsd ldrs over 2f out: hdwy u.p 1f out: kpt on same pce last 100 yds* **12/1**

0000 **4** 1 **Takes Tutu (USA)**[14] [6747] 7-9-5 **60**.................................. EddieAhern 9 62
(C R Dore) *t.k.h: hld up in rr: hdwy over 2f out: kpt on ins fnl f: nt rch ldrs* **14/1**

0014 **5** ½ **Play Up Pompey**[16] [6724] 4-9-0 **55**.............................. MatthewHenry 2 56
(J J Bridger) *v.s.a: racd in last but in tch: kpt on fr over 1f out: n.d* **14/1**

0524 **6** ¾ **Ciccone**[3] [6870] 3-8-13 **57**... JamieSpencer 1 57+
(G L Moore) *trckd ldrs: rdn over 2f out: btn and eased wl ins fnl f* **7/2**[1]

4011 **7** nk **Shaheer (IRE)**[16] [6724] 4-9-0 **55**......................................(v) JimCrowley 8 54
(J Gallagher) *t.k.h: trckd ldrs on outer: rdn over 2f out: wknd over 1f out* **6/1**[3]

0050 **8** shd **Dinner Date**[30] [6565] 4-8-13 **54**.. ChrisCatlin 5 53
(T Keddy) *chsd ldr: rdn over 2f out: wknd ins fnl f* **4/1**[2]

0003 **9** ¾ **Graft**[3] [6870] 7-8-13 **57**...(p) NeilChalmers(3) 6 55+
(Mrs P Townsley) *v.s.a: sn in tch in rr: nt clr run over 1f out and 1f out: nvr trbld ldrs* **12/1**

0000 **10** nk **Compton Express**[6] [6848] 3-8-5 **49**................................. JimmyQuinn 3 46
(Jamie Poulton) *hld up in midfield: rdn 3f out: no prog fr over 1f out* **50/1**

4003 **11** 1 ½ **Atticus Trophies (IRE)**[9] [6810] 3-8-12 **56**.....................(p) BrettDoyle 11 50
(Ms J S Doyle) *hld up towards rr on outer: rdn over 2f out: no real hdwy* **14/1**

2m 7.64s (-0.15) **Going Correction** -0.15s/f (Stan)
WFA 3 from 4yo+ 3lb **11** Ran SP% **120.6**
Speed ratings (Par 101):94,93,92,92,91 91,90,90,90,89 88
CSF £49.04 CT £498.22 TOTE £10.20: £3.80, £2.70, £4.70; EX 92.20 TRIFECTA Not won. Place 6 £32.79, Place 5 £20.26.
Owner Peter Webb **Bred** Roundhill Stud And Gleadhill House Stud Ltd **Trained** Newmarket, Suffolk

FOCUS
A low-grade handicap, but quite a dramatic contest with three horses, including the eventual winner, giving away a good six lengths at the start. A slow early pace allowed them to soon get back in touch though, and also contributed to a moderate winning time for the class. The winner has slipped a long way in the weights and the race has been rated through the third.
T/Plt: £39.40 to a £1 stake. Pool: £44,987.45. 832.95 winning tickets. T/Qpdt: £14.70 to a £1 stake. Pool: £3,515.80. 176.90 winning tickets. SP

[6898] WOLVERHAMPTON (A.W) (L-H)

Friday, December 22

OFFICIAL GOING: Standard

Wind: Nil Weather: Misty

6919 WBX.COM WORLD BET EXCHANGE H'CAP 7f 32y(P)

3:50 (3:51) (Class 5) (0-70,68) 3-Y-0+ **£5,181** (£1,541; £770; £384) **Stalls** High

Form RPR

0054 **1** **Ochre Bay**[29] [6573] 3-9-0 **66**...(p) GrahamGibbons 2 78
(R Hollinshead) *s.i.s: sn chsng ldrs: led over 1f out: edgd lft ins fnl f: rdn out* **7/2**[2]

4220 **2** ¾ **Dixieland Boy (IRE)**[27] [6593] 3-8-9 **61**............................ SteveDrowne 1 71
(P J Makin) *sn led: rdn and hdd over 1f out: edgd lft ins fnl f: styd on* **7/1**

350 **3** 2 **Buzzin'Boyzee (IRE)**[57] [6193] 3-8-6 **58**............................. DavidAllan 6 63
(P D Evans) *hld up: nt clr run over 2f out: hdwy over 1f out: sn swtchd rt: r.o u.p: nt rch ldrs* **25/1**

5545 **4** ¾ **Ever Cheerful**[13] [6773] 5-9-2 **68**... DaleGibson 3 71
(D G Bridgwater) *plld hrd and prom: rdn 1/2-way: styd on same pce fnl f* **10/1**

5004 **5** nk **Supercast (IRE)**[20] [6681] 3-9-2 **68**... NCallan 8 70
(W M Brisbourne) *trckd ldrs: plld hrd: rdn over 1f out: n.m.r and wknd ins fnl f* **14/1**

0351 **6** ¾ **Sovereignty (JPN)**[8] [6820] 4-8-6 **63**......................... JamesMillman(5) 9 63
(D K Ivory) *s.i.s: hdwy over 5f out: rdn over 2f out: styng on same pce whn whn edgd rt ins fnl f* **9/4**[1]

0022 **7** shd **Snow Bunting**[8] [6820] 8-8-1 **58**.................................. KevinGhunowa(5) 7 58
(Jedd O'Keeffe) *hld up: racd keenly: hdwy over 1f out: nt trble ldrs* **12/1**

0050 **8** 1 ¾ **Parkview Love (USA)**[13] [6767] 5-8-9 **61**.....................(v) JamieMackay 5 56
(D Shaw) *sn w ldr: rdn and ev ch over 2f out: wknd fnl f* **11/1**

0504 **9** *1 ½* **Mister Elegant**[8] 6820 4-8-6 **58** .... AdrianTNicholls 4 49
(J L Spearing) *plld hrd and prom: stdd and lost pl over 4f out: nt clr run and swtchd rt 3f out: n.d after* **8/1**

4200 **10** *1 ¾* **Lizarazu (GER)**[27] 6595 7-8-4 **63** ....(b) TolleyDean(7) 10 50
(R A Harris) *hld up: rdn whn hmpd 3f out: n.d* **20/1**

2011 **11** *7* **Elusive Warrior (USA)**[13] 6756 3-8-7 **64** ....(p) JamieMoriarty(5) 12 33
(R A Fahey) *hld up: wknd over 2f out* **6/1**[3]

1m 29.28s (-1.12) **Going Correction** -0.15s/f (Stan) **11** Ran SP% **131.3**

Speed ratings (Par 103):100,99,96,96,95 94,94,92,90,88 80

CSF £32.33 CT £576.82 TOTE £4.90: £2.50, £2.20, £10.90; EX 25.70.

Owner M Johnson **Bred** R Hollinshead And M Johnson **Trained** Upper Longdon, Staffs

FOCUS

An ordinary handicap in which the pace was only fair and those racing up with the pace held the edge. The principals raced towards the far rail in the straight. Modest form, but it seems to make sense.

6920 EBF PONTINS.COM HOLIDAYS MAIDEN STKS 7f 32y(P)

4:20 (4:21) (Class 5) 2-Y-O **£4,533** (£1,348; £674; £336) **Stalls** High

Form RPR

4 **1** **Regal Riband**[9] 6808 2-8-12 .... JamieMackay 7 75+
(Sir Mark Prescott) *trckd ldr: led 1/2-way: rdn clr and hung lft over 1f out: eased wl ins fnl f* **3/1**[2]

05 **2** *5* **Conny Nobel (IRE)**[12] 6778 2-9-3 ....(t) FrancisNorton 3 65
(R A Kvisla) *broke wl: outpcd 6f out: nt clr run over 2f out: r.o ins fnl f: no ch w wnr* **33/1**

4460 **3** *1 ¼* **Raquel White**[13] 6760 2-8-12 65 .... NCallan 2 56
(P D Evans) *sn led: hdd 1/2-way: rdn over 2f out: wknd fnl f* **13/2**[3]

4 *1* **Countess Majella (IRE)**[53] 6261 2-8-12 .... GrahamGibbons 4 54
(E J O'Neill) *chsd ldrs: rdn whn hmpd 1/2-way: wknd fnl f* **3/1**[2]

3 **5** *2* **Poisiedon (IRE)**[14] 6751 2-9-3 .... DaleGibson 1 54
(Liam McAteer, Ire) *s.i.s: plld hrd and sn trcking ldrs: n.m.r 1/2-way: wkng whn hung rt over 1f out* **11/4**[1]

500 **6** *12* **Animated**[165] 3351 2-9-3 66 .... SteveDrowne 6 24
(A J McCabe) *hld up: racd keenly: wknd 3f out* **10/1**

20 **7** *6* **Leprechaun's Gold (IRE)**[24] 6644 2-9-3 .... AdrianTNicholls 5 9
(M Johnston) *prom: bmpd 1/2-way: sn wknd* **7/1**

1m 30.06s (-0.34) **Going Correction** -0.15s/f (Stan) **7** Ran SP% **114.5**

Speed ratings (Par 96):95,89,87,86,84 70,63

CSF £81.27 TOTE £3.30: £1.40, £19.00; EX 56.40.

Owner Cheveley Park Stud **Bred** Cheveley Park Stud Ltd **Trained** Newmarket, Suffolk

FOCUS

A race lacking strrength and a wide-margin winner in Regal Riband, who is the type to hold her own in better company. The winner raced just off the far rail in the straight.

NOTEBOOK

Regal Riband ◆, who shaped well, despite her apparent greenness on her debut in an ordinary event over course and distance, turned in an improved effort to draw right away in the closing stages. She looks capable of holding her own in better company and is capable of further progress. (op 13-8 tchd 10-3)

Conny Nobel(IRE) had shown precious little in two outings at Kempton but fared much better this time. He will have no problems staying a mile but is likely to remain vulnerable in this type of event. (op 40-1)

Raquel White had not been at her best in handicaps on her last two starts but fared better this time having enjoyed the run of the race. However, she is likely to continue to remain vulnerable in this type of event. (op 9-1)

Countess Majella(IRE), having her first run for new connections and her first on artificial surfaces, was not totally disgraced but looks the type to do better in modest handicap company in due course. (op 8-1)

Poisiedon(IRE), failed to build on his debut run but did spoil his chance by pulling in this moderately-run race. He is worth another chance in modest company. (op 9-4 tchd 3-1)

Animated, from a stable that has done well this winter, failed to settle on this first run beyond five furlongs and first run for this yard. He remains capable of better but is likely to remain vulnerable in this type of event. (op 14-1)

Leprechaun's Gold(IRE) was again a long way below his debut form at Southwell and looks one to tread carefully with at present. (op 8-1 tchd 17-2 and 13-2)

6921 PONTIN'S HOLIDAYS MAIDEN STKS 5f 20y(P)

4:50 (4:50) (Class 4) 2-Y-O **£4,533** (£1,348; £674; £336) **Stalls** Low

Form RPR

30 **1** **Elhareer (IRE)**[72] 5906 2-8-12 .... NCallan 5 67
(B J Meehan) *mde all: clr over 1f out: rdn out* **11/8**[1]

0432 **2** *2 ½* **Wibbadune (IRE)**[6] 6839 2-8-12 53 .... TonyCulhane 3 58
(Peter Grayson) *prom: hung rt 1/2-way: rdn to chse wnr and hung lft fnl f: no imp* **11/1**

3 *2* **Fairnilee** 2-8-12 .... JamieMackay 1 65+
(Sir Mark Prescott) *s.s: outpcd: hung lft over 1f out: r.o ins fnl f: nvr nrr* **9/2**[3]

03 **4** *¾* **Pappas Image**[18] 6706 2-9-3 ....(b) DavidAllan 2 53
(A J McCabe) *chsd wnr: rdn 1/2-way: wknd fnl f* **28/1**

0432 **5** *2 ½* **Mo (USA)**[20] 6669 2-9-3 70 ....(t) SteveDrowne 4 44
(R A Kvisla) *chsd ldrs: hung rt 1/2-way: rdn and wknd over 1f out* **7/4**[2]

0 **6** *½* **Comrade Cotton**[20] 6669 2-9-3 .... FrancisNorton 6 42
(N A Callaghan) *s.i.s: outpcd* **25/1**

62.02 secs (-0.80) **Going Correction** -0.15s/f (Stan) **6** Ran SP% **112.3**

Speed ratings (Par 98):100,96,92,91,87 86

CSF £17.16 TOTE £1.90: £1.50, £2.50; EX 8.90.

Owner Kuwait Racing Syndicate **Bred** Mohammad Al Qatami **Trained** Manton, Wilts

FOCUS

A weak race in which the second favourite disappointed, and the runner-up is the best guide. The pace was ordinary and the winner raced towards the far rail in the straight.

NOTEBOOK

Elhareer(IRE), who disappointed at Lingfield on her previous start, had little to beat when her main market rival failed to run his race but did the job in workmanlike fashion dropped to this trip for the first time. The Handicapper is unlikely to overreact to the defeat of a 53-rated rival and she may progress in handicaps. (tchd 7-4)

Wibbadune(IRE), who looked better than the bare form of her previous start, again showed a tendency to hang but again ran creditably in the face of a stiffish task. She looks worth another try over six furlongs and may do better in modest handicaps. (op 15-2)

Fairnilee ◆, a half-sister to Polytrack winner Fantaisiste, was too green to do herself justice on this racecourse debut but showed enough to suggest she is capable of winning races for shrewd connections. (op 4-1 tchd 5-1)

Pappas Image, dropped again in distance, again showed ability and left the impression that the step into modest handicap company would be to his liking. He is not one to write off just yet. (op 25-1)

Mo(USA), who had been running consistently well on turf and All-Weather, looked a leading player in this company but proved a disappointment. Although he is better than this, he may not be the easiest to place successfully. (op 11-4 tchd 6-4)

Comrade Cotton, down in trip, offered little immediate promise but may be the type to fare better in modest handicap company. (op 18-1)

6922 WBXTRIPLECROWN.COM H'CAP 5f 216y(P)

5:20 (5:20) (Class 6) (0-58,58) 3-Y-O+ **£3,238** (£963; £481; £240) **Stalls** Low

Form RPR

0000 **1** **Vegas Boys**[49] 6315 3-9-2 **57** .... MichaelTebbutt 3 70
(M Wigham) *trckd ldrs: edgd lft 4f out: rdn to ld ins fnl f: hung lft: r.o* **11/4**[1]

2211 **2** *1 ¾* **Cree**[2] 6890 4-9-3 **58** 7ex .... FrancisNorton 2 66
(W R Muir) *trckd ldrs: racd keenly: nt clr run and lost pl 4f out: hdwy 2f out: r.o* **7/2**[2]

0065 **3** *½* **Almaty Express**[25] 6622 4-9-0 **55** ....(b) NCallan 1 62
(J R Weymes) *led: rdn and edgd rt over 1f out: hdd and no ex ins fnl f* **10/1**

6444 **4** *1 ½* **Desert Light (IRE)**[3] 6865 5-9-1 **56** ....(v) JamieMackay 6 58
(D Shaw) *hld up: hdwy over 1f out: swtchd rt ins fnl f: nt rch ldrs* **9/1**

0000 **5** *½* **White Ledger (IRE)**[15] 6739 7-8-7 **48** ....(p) AdrianTNicholls 5 49
(R E Peacock) *s.s: bhd tl r.o ins fnl f: nrst fin* **80/1**

5460 **6** *½* **Val De Maal (IRE)**[17] 6719 6-8-13 **54** ....(b) DavidAllan 9 53
(Miss J A Camacho) *hld up: hmpd wl over 3f out: rdn over 2f out: nt trble ldrs* **12/1**

2014 **7** *nk* **Sir Don (IRE)**[15] 6739 7-8-13 **54** ....(p) GrahamGibbons 4 52
(E S McMahon) *chsd ldrs: rdn over 3f out: styd on same pce appr fnl f* **6/1**[3]

0621 **8** *nk* **Muara**[25] 6615 4-8-11 **55** .... MarkLawson(3) 11 52
(D W Barker) *chsd ldrs: rdn over 2f out: edgd rt over 1f out: styd on same pce* **14/1**

4363 **9** *1 ¼* **Blythe Spirit**[18] 6708 7-8-0 **48** ....(p) JamesRogers(7) 13 41
(R A Fahey) *hld up in tch: rdn over 1f out: wknd fnl f* **11/1**

0000 **10** *¾* **Blue Knight (IRE)**[20] 6681 7-9-2 **57** .... TonyCulhane 7 48
(P Howling) *hld up: effrt over 1f out: n.d* **40/1**

0021 **11** *1 ¾* **Creme Brulee**[15] 6738 3-8-13 **54** .... SteveDrowne 10 40
(C R Egerton) *chsd ldr over 4f out: rdn over 1f out: wknd fnl f* **8/1**

5020 **12** *2* **Howards Princess**[17] 6719 4-8-11 **52** ....(v) DaleGibson 12 32
(J Hetherton) *prom: sn hung lft: rdn over 2f out: wknd over 1f out* **25/1**

1m 14.55s (-1.26) **Going Correction** -0.15s/f (Stan) **12** Ran SP% **123.6**

Speed ratings (Par 101):102,99,99,97,96 95,95,94,93,92 89,87

CSF £12.48 CT £86.29 TOTE £3.70: £1.90, £1.20, £5.70; EX 28.50.

Owner P R Iron **Bred** Brimpton Bloodstock **Trained** Newmarket, Suffolk

FOCUS

An ordinary event in which the pace was fair and the winner, who landed a gamble, raced towards the far rail in the straight. Fair form for the grade.

6923 GO PONTIN'S MAIDEN STKS 1m 4f 50y(P)

5:50 (5:51) (Class 5) 3-4-Y-O **£3,886** (£1,156; £577; £288) **Stalls** Low

Form RPR

4400 **1** **Emilion**[12] 6775 3-8-12 62 .... FrancisNorton 4 57
(W R Muir) *chsd ldrs: rdn over 3f out: led 1f out: sn hung lft: styd on* **11/4**[2]

4002 **2** *nk* **Stagecoach Emerald**[13] 6759 4-9-8 57 ....(t) JamieMackay 5 62
(R W Price) *led: hdd over 5f out: rdn over 3f out: styd on* **12/1**[3]

4024 **3** *1 ¾* **Italian Romance**[15] 6741 3-9-0 72 .... RichardKingscote(3) 6 59
(J W Unett) *racd keenly: prom: chsd ldr 7f out: led over 5f out: rdn and hdd 1f out: styd on same pce* **8/13**[1]

35 **4** *5* **Chart Oak**[28] 6588 3-9-3 .... IanMongan 2 51
(P Howling) *dwlt: hld up: hdwy over 4f out: wknd over 1f out* **18/1**

0 **5** *18* **Risk Challenge (USA)**[13] 6771 4-9-8 .... TonyCulhane 7 22
(C J Price) *wnt rt s: plld hrd and sn trcking ldr: rdn over 5f out: wknd over 3f out* **16/1**

6 *34* **Grafty Green (IRE)**[20] 3-9-3 .... AdrianTNicholls 3 —
(T H Caldwell) *hld up: wknd over 4f out* **66/1**

2m 41.23s (-1.19) **Going Correction** -0.15s/f (Stan)

WFA 3 from 4yo 5lb **6** Ran SP% **108.9**

Speed ratings (Par 103):97,96,95,92,80 57

CSF £30.60 TOTE £3.50: £1.70, £4.30; EX 22.30.

Owner Mr & Mrs G Middlebrook **Bred** G And Mrs Middlebrook **Trained** Lambourn, Berks

FOCUS

An uncompetitive maiden in which the pace was steady, the winning time was modest, and this bare form does not look reliable.

6924 PONTINS.COM H'CAP 1m 1f 103y(P)

6:20 (6:20) (Class 6) (0-68,72) 3-Y-O+ **£3,238** (£963; £481; £240) **Stalls** Low

Form RPR

3131 **1** **Just Bond (IRE)**[13] 6767 4-8-11 **68** .... DuranFentiman(5) 1 86
(G R Oldroyd) *hld up: plld hrd: hdwy over 2f out: rdn to ld 1f out: r.o u.p* **4/1**[2]

3111 **2** *nk* **Peruvian Prince (USA)**[4] 6863 4-9-1 **72** 7ex .... JamieMoriarty(5) 4 89
(R A Fahey) *hld up: hdwy over 2f out: rdn and ev ch fnl f: r.o* **4/11**[1]

0013 **3** *7* **Buscador (USA)**[7] 6837 7-8-4 **61** .... AshleyHamblett(5) 5 64
(W M Brisbourne) *chsd ldr tl rdn to ld over 3f out: hdd 1f out: sn btn* **20/1**[3]

10-0 **4** *10* **Zakfree (IRE)**[58] 6184 5-9-1 **67** ....(b) DaleGibson 6 50
(Liam McAteer, Ire) *trckd ldrs: racd keenly: rdn and wknd 2f out* **33/1**

-036 **5** *nk* **Our Kes (IRE)**[15] 6741 4-9-0 **66** .... IanMongan 2 49
(P Howling) *led: hdd over 3f out: rdn and wknd over 1f out* **20/1**[3]

2120 **6** *6* **Zalkani (IRE)**[6] 6848 6-8-12 **64** .... MichaelTebbutt 7 35
(J Pearce) *chsd ldrs 7f* **25/1**

2m 0.35s (-2.27) **Going Correction** -0.15s/f (Stan)

WFA 3 from 4yo+ 2lb **6** Ran SP% **109.6**

Speed ratings (Par 101):104,103,97,88,88 83

CSF £5.65 TOTE £5.50: £1.70, £1.10; EX 7.00 Place 6 £98.64, Place 5 £33.30.

Owner R C Bond **Bred** Schwindibode Ag **Trained** Upper Helmsley, N Yorks

FOCUS

An ordinary gallop but the two progressive performers - who raced in the centre in the straight - pulled a long way clear of the remainder in the last quarter mile.

T/Plt: £210.90 to a £1 stake. Pool: £65,874.15. 227.95 winning tickets. T/Qpdt: £24.50 to a £1 stake. Pool: £7,097.30. 214.20 winning tickets. CR

6891 SOUTHWELL (L-H)

Saturday, December 23

OFFICIAL GOING: Standard

Wind: Almost nil. Weather: Overcast, cold and dull and misty.

6925 GO PONTIN'S MAIDEN AUCTION STKS 5f (F)

12:55 (12:56) (Class 5) 2-Y-O **£3,238** (£963; £481; £240) **Stalls** High

Form				RPR
25	1		**New York Oscar (IRE)**[7] 6838 2-9-0 NCallan 6 (A J McCabe) *mde all: kpt on wl ins last* **13/2**	62
5350	2	3/4	**The Geester**[10] 6807 2-8-7 55 (bt) JasonEdmunds(3) 3 (S R Bowring) *sn trcking ldrs: wnt 2nd over 1f out: no ex ins last* **25/1**	55
2032	3	4	**Vadinka**[9] 6815 2-8-11 70 KimTinkler 7 (N Tinkler) *dwlt: hdwy 3f out: kpt on same pce* **9/4**[2]	42
2	4	1/2	**Carrie McCurry (IRE)**[36] 6505 2-8-5 JimmyQuinn 2 (Patrick Martin, Ire) *trckd ldrs: outpcd and drvn over 2f out: wknd fnl f* **7/4**[1]	34
4	5	nk	**Mujamead**[9] 6815 2-8-11 LeeEnstone 1 (P C Haslam) *dwlt: sn outpcd and in rr: kpt on fnl 2f: nvr on terms* **5/1**[3]	39
5	6	2	**Bogside Katie**[9] 6821 2-8-5 ChrisCatlin 5 (G M Moore) *trckd ldrs: wknd over 1f out* **14/1**	26
00	7	hd	**Head To Head (IRE)**[180] 2938 2-8-13 (b[1]) TonyCulhane 4 (Peter Grayson) *chsd ldrs: wknd over 1f out* **25/1**	33

61.04 secs (0.74) **Going Correction** +0.05s/f (Slow) 7 Ran SP% **111.5**

Speed ratings (Par 96):96,94,88,87,87 83,83

CSF £127.40 TOTE £7.10: £2.60, £7.20; EX 70.80.

Owner Paul J Dixon **Bred** Corduff Stud And J Judd **Trained** Babworth, Notts

FOCUS

A very modest sprint maiden with the first two clear and the form horses below par. The exposed runner-up has an official rating of just 55 and sets the level for the form.

NOTEBOOK

New York Oscar(IRE), having just his third outing, was much happier on this straight track and was right on top at the finish. He still looked inexperienced and there may be even better to come. (op 11-1)

The Geester, who gave a problem or two beforehand, is full exposed and came into this with an official rating of just 55.

Vadinka missed a beat at the start and seemed to find the drop back to five against him. (op 11-4 tchd 3-1)

Carrie McCurry(IRE), who lacks scope, did not reproduce her Wolverhampton running over this furlong shorter trip on a differnt type of surface. (op 11-10 tchd 15-8 in a place)

Mujamead, a late foal, was dropping back in trip on just his second start and he could never go the pace. He still has plenty to learn. (op 11-2)

6926 PONTINSBINGO.COM NURSERY 6f (F)

1:25 (1:26) (Class 6) (0-65,65) 2-Y-O **£3,238** (£963; £481; £240) **Stalls** Low

Form				RPR
552	1		**Para Siempre**[15] 6749 2-9-1 62 (b[1]) MarkLawson(3) 4 (B Smart) *t.k.h: w ldrs: led over 2f out: clr over 1f out: drvn rt out* **5/1**[1]	75
3001	2	7	**Pirner's Brig**[12] 6789 2-9-6 64 PaulMulrennan 3 (M W Easterby) *led: hung lft and hdd over 2f out: no ch w wnr* **9/1**	56
543U	3	1	**Aggbag**[12] 6789 2-8-9 60 SoniaEaton(7) 14 (B P J Baugh) *in rr: hdwy 3f out: kpt on same pce fnl 2f* **40/1**	49
0500	4	hd	**Spence's Choice (IRE)**[29] 6576 2-8-7 51 BrettDoyle 1 (M W Easterby) *s.i.s: sn chsng ldrs: one pce fnl 2f* **10/1**	39
060	5	shd	**Knapton Hill**[71] 5950 2-9-1 59 GrahamGibbons 7 (R Hollinshead) *swtchd lft after s: in rr: hdwy over 3f out: one pce fnl 2f fnl 2f* **11/1**	47
4245	6	1	**Suntan Lady (IRE)**[2] 6900 2-7-10 45 (v) DuranFentiman(5) 2 (Miss V Haigh) *dwlt: hdwy 3f out: one pce fnl 2f* **16/1**	30
1401	7	4	**Homes By Woodford**[16] 6736 2-8-9 60 TolleyDean(7) 12 (R A Harris) *in rr: sn drvn along: sme hdwy over 2f out: nvr on terms* **11/2**[2]	33
2463	8	1 1/2	**Grange Lili (IRE)**[9] 6813 2-8-13 57 (b) AdamKirby 9 (Peter Grayson) *chsd ldrs on outer: hmpd bnd over 4f out: hung lft and lost pl 2f out* **13/2**[3]	26+
0140	9	2	**Lovers Kiss**[10] 6807 2-8-10 54 ow1 (b) LeeEnstone 8 (N Wilson) *prom: lost pl over 2f out* **20/1**	17
0500	10	2 1/2	**Fire In Cairo (IRE)**[82] 5721 2-8-13 57 AdrianTNicholls 6 (P C Haslam) *in rr: sn drvn along* **16/1**	12
0005	11	hd	**Final Curtain**[10] 6807 2-8-11 55 (t) ChrisCatlin 5 (M A Magnusson) *w ldrs: hung rt bnd over 4f out: lost pl over 2f out* **10/1**	10
6235	12	21	**Cryptic Clue (USA)**[9] 6813 2-8-9 53 TonyCulhane 13 (D W Chapman) *unruly in stalls: chsd ldrs: lost pl over 3f out: sn bhd: eased* **9/1**	—
4061	13	shd	**Theoretical**[18] 6711 2-9-2 65 NataliaGemelova(5) 11 (A J McCabe) *chsd ldrs on outer: bdly hmpd bnd over 4f out: lost pl over 2f out: sn bhd and eased* **7/1**	—

1m 16.1s (-0.80) **Going Correction** -0.15s/f (Stan) 13 Ran SP% **123.4**

Speed ratings (Par 94):99,89,88,88,87 86,81,79,76,73 73,45,44

CSF £51.42 CT £1701.23 TOTE £4.80: £1.80, £2.90, £12.30; EX 52.80 TRIFECTA Not won..

Owner Mrs Linda Pestell **Bred** D R Tucker **Trained** Hambleton, N Yorks

FOCUS

A fair winning time for a race of its type and a step up from the winner, although the form of those behind looks weak.

NOTEBOOK

Para Siempre, fitted with blinkers on her nursery bow, came right away and the boy left nothing to chance. Her rating will shoot up as a result. (op 7-1)

Pirner's Brig, hoisted 9lb after his Wolverhampton success, set a strong pace but was always wanting to hang left and in the end the winner ran right away from him. (op 15-2)

Aggbag, out of luck behind Pirner's Brig at Wolverhampton, stayed on in his own time from off the pace and is better suited by seven. (op 33-1)

Spence's Choice(IRE), dropped 10lb after three outings in nursery company, proved better suited by this left-handed track. (op 16-1)

Knapton Hill, who has changed stables, was making her nursery bow. She shapes as though she would be happier over seven or even a mile. (tchd 12-1)

6927 PONTIN'S FAMILY HOLIDAYS MEDIAN AUCTION MAIDEN FILLIES' STKS 7f (F)

2:00 (2:01) (Class 5) 2-Y-O **£3,238** (£963; £481; £240) **Stalls** Low

Form				RPR
20	1		**Mankanja (IRE)**[18] 6710 2-9-0 BrettDoyle 2 (W Jarvis) *chsd ldrs: nt clr run and swtchd ins jst ins last: styd on to ld last 50yds* **7/1**	69+
33	2	3/4	**Musical Beat**[7] 6840 2-9-0 EdwardCreighton 6 (Miss V Haigh) *w ldrs: t.k.h: chal 2f out: kpt on to take 2nd nr line* **5/2**[2]	65
322	3	1/2	**Belvedere Vixen**[130] 4445 2-9-0 63 GrahamGibbons 1 (M J Wallace) *mde most: hdd & wknd wl ins last* **4/1**[3]	64
4	4	1/2	**Rann Na Cille (IRE)**[19] 6697 2-9-0 NCallan 7 (K A Ryan) *w ldrs: chal 2f out: one pce* **9/4**[1]	63
0022	5	3 1/2	**Wee Ellie Coburn**[17] 6730 2-9-0 58 FrancisNorton 4 (A Bailey) *t.k.h: trckd ldrs: hung rt 3f out: one pce* **11/2**	54
	6	10	**Best Option** 2-9-0 TonyCulhane 3 (W R Muir) *s.i.s: lost pl over 4f out: sn bhd* **33/1**	28
00	7	nk	**Veils Of Salome**[9] 6821 2-8-9 NataliaGemelova(5) 5 (A J McCabe) *s.i.s: hdwy on outer to chse ldrs over 4f out: hung rt bnd 3f out: sn lost pl* **100/1**	27

1m 31.22s (0.42) **Going Correction** -0.15s/f (Stan) 7 Ran SP% **111.2**

Speed ratings (Par 93):91,90,89,89,85 73,73

CSF £23.46 TOTE £8.90: £2.00, £2.10; EX 37.80 Trifecta £81.70 Pool £502.14 - 4.36 winning units..

Owner B Olsson **Bred** Neville O'Byrne And Roderick Ryan **Trained** Newmarket, Suffolk

FOCUS

A low-grade maiden with the third rated just 63 and the form rated through her and the fourth. The winner can improve again especially over further.

NOTEBOOK

Mankanja(IRE), quite a big filly, was back over seven. She made hard work of it but showed a willing attitude and snatched the prize after being switched to the inner. She will be better suited by a mile plus. (op 6-1)

Musical Beat, dropping back in trip, was keen to get on with it. Just as she got the better of a long running argument with the third, the winner slipped past both on their inside near the line. (op 9-4 tchd 11-4)

Belvedere Vixen, who has changed stables, looked as fit as a flea on her first outing since August. She tried hard to make every yard but had no more to give near the line. (tchd 7-2)

Rann Na Cille(IRE), having her second outing here, moved upsides two furlongs out but in the end was simply not good enough. (op 3-1 tchd 2-1 and 7-2 in a place)

Wee Ellie Coburn wanted to do nothing but hang and on one rein throughout, in the end the bit slipped through her mouth. Official explanation: jockey said bit slipped through filly's mouth (op 6-1)

6928 PONTINS.COM H'CAP 1m (F)

2:35 (2:35) (Class 5) (0-70,71) 3-Y-O+ **£3,238** (£963; £481; £240) **Stalls** Low

Form				RPR
6631	1		**Smart Ass (IRE)**[9] 6818 3-9-3 71 BrettDoyle 5 (J S Moore) *trckd ldrs: led over 1f out: hrd rdn: jst hld on* **5/2**[1]	82
0246	2	shd	**Stevedore (IRE)**[4] 6871 5-9-0 70 AmirQuinn(3) 10 (J R Boyle) *sn in rr and pushed along: hdwy on outside over 2f out: edgd lft u.p: chal fnl f: jst failed* **9/2**[3]	81
360	3	1 3/4	**Rebellious Spirit**[201] 2301 3-8-12 66 PhillipMakin 7 (P W Hiatt) *trckd ldrs: crowded 1f out: kpt on same pce* **40/1**	73
0141	4	shd	**Formidable Will (FR)**[9] 6814 4-8-4 64 (vt[1]) PatrickHills(7) 1 (D Shaw) *w ldrs: one pce fnl f* **4/1**[2]	71
1033	5	4	**Shifty**[9] 6818 7-8-7 67 KellyHarrison(7) 2 (D Carroll) *trckd ldrs: wknd fnl f* **12/1**	66+
1-00	6	1 1/4	**Rainbows Guest (IRE)**[25] 6635 3-9-1 69 (v) FrancisNorton 4 (A M Balding) *led over 5f out tl over 1f out: sn wknd* **12/1**	65
1040	7	5	**Exit Smiling**[74] 5889 4-9-2 69 MickyFenton 9 (P T Midgley) *led tl over 5f out: wknd over 1f out* **11/1**	55
2003	8	1 3/4	**Hoh Wotanite**[22] 6664 3-9-0 68 GrahamGibbons 3 (R Hollinshead) *sn outpcd and in rr: nvr a factor* **14/1**	50
-044	9	1 1/4	**Akinola (IRE)**[22] 6666 5-8-11 64 (b[1]) NCallan 6 (K A Ryan) *chsd ldrs: lost pl over 3f out* **5/1**	43
	10	nk	**Buddy Man (IRE)**[10] 3654 8-8-8 64 (t) JerryO'Dwyer(3) 8 (Patrick Martin, Ire) *sn in rr and drvn along: nvr a factor* **33/1**	43

1m 43.07s (-1.53) **Going Correction** -0.15s/f (Stan)

WFA 3 from 4yo+ 1lb 10 Ran SP% **119.2**

Speed ratings (Par 103):101,100,99,99,95 93,88,87,85,85

CSF £14.03 CT £374.78 TOTE £3.60: £1.10, £1.90, £9.50; EX 17.80 Trifecta £492.10 Pool £998.16 - 1.44 winning units..

Owner J Laughton **Bred** M Ervine **Trained** Upper Lambourn, Berks

■ Stewards' Enquiry : Amir Quinn caution: careless riding

Brett Doyle one-day ban: used whip in incorrect position (Jan 3)

6929 PONTIN'S BOOK EARLY H'CAP 1m 4f (F)

3:05 (3:05) (Class 5) (0-75,75) 3-Y-O **£3,886** (£1,156; £577; £288) **Stalls** Low

Form				RPR
21	1		**Abandon (USA)**[21] 6680 3-9-4 75 TonyCulhane 2 (W J Haggas) *hld up: smooth hdwy to ld over 1f out: sn hrd drvn: hld on wl* **10/11**[1]	85+
0022	2	1/2	**Opera Writer (IRE)**[2] 6893 3-8-4 61 PaulQuinn 6 (R Hollinshead) *sn trcking ldrs: chal over 1f out: no ex wl ins last* **9/2**[2]	65
2046	3	hd	**Arsad (IRE)**[31] 6565 3-8-4 61 oh4 ChrisCatlin 5 (C E Brittain) *trckd ldrs: outpcd over 4f out: rallied over 1f out: styd on towards fin* **5/1**[3]	65
3364	4	2 1/2	**Summer Lodge**[12] 6791 3-8-7 69 (b) NataliaGemelova(5) 1 (A J McCabe) *w ldrs: led over 4f out: hdd over 1f out: wknd fnl 150yds* **9/1**	69
1-00	5	nk	**Haifa (IRE)**[9] 6818 3-8-9 66 ow1 MickyFenton 4 (Mrs A Duffield) *led after 1f: hdd over 4f out: hung rt 3f out: wknd fnl f* **50/1**	65
003	6	33	**Moon Empress (FR)**[138] 4210 3-8-10 67 BrettDoyle 7 (W R Muir) *hld up: effrt on outer over 4f out: sn lost pl and bhd: eased fnl f: t.o* **9/1**	13
3000	7	14	**Shaydreambeliever**[46] 5868 3-8-7 64 DaleGibson 3 (R A Fahey) *led 1f: chsd ldrs: lost pl over 3f out: bhd and eased fnl f: t.o* **16/1**	—

2m 39.75s (-2.34) **Going Correction** -0.15s/f (Stan) 7 Ran SP% **115.1**

Speed ratings (Par 102):101,100,100,98,98 76,67

CSF £5.44 TOTE £1.50: £1.30, £1.60; EX 4.80.

Owner Cheveley Park Stud **Bred** 6 C Stallions Limited **Trained** Newmarket, Suffolk

FOCUS

A modest handicap but the winner looks capable of better.

Moon Empress(FR) Official explanation: jockey said filly hung right throughout
Shaydreambeliever Official explanation: jockey said gelding bled from the nose

6930 PONTIN'S HOLIDAYS H'CAP 6f (F)
3:35 (3:35) (Class 5) (0-70,67) 3-Y-0+ **£3,562** (£1,059; £529; £264) **Stalls** Low

Form RPR
111 **1** **La Colline (GER)**[33] 6538 3-8-6 **64**.................... PatrickHills(7) 4 75+
(W J Haggas) *prom: effrt over 2f out: styd on to ld towards fin* **4/6**[1]
2160 **2** *nk* **Tag Team (IRE)**[36] 6508 5-8-13 **64**.................... DaleGibson 5 74
(John A Harris) *chsd ldrs: styd on to ld ins last: hdd and no ex towards fin* **25/1**
5311 **3** *1* **Larky's Lob**[18] 6719 7-8-7 **65**.................... JamesO'Reilly(7) 6 72
(J O'Reilly) *mde most: hdd ins last: kpt on* **8/1**[2]
0406 **4** *1 ½* **Count Cougar (USA)**[7] 6842 6-8-5 **56** ow1.............. AdrianTNicholls 13 59
(S P Griffiths) *w ldrs on outer: chal over 2f out: fdd ins last* **11/1**
4345 **5** *3* **Soba Jones**[145] 3995 9-8-6 **60**.................... JasonEdmunds(3) 2 54
(J Balding) *mid-div: hdwy to chse ldrs over 2f out: one pce* **22/1**
1246 **6** *2* **Dudley Docker (IRE)**[14] 6773 4-8-9 **67**.................... KellyHarrison(7) 9 55
(D Carroll) *prom: n.m.r and lost pl 3f out: kpt on fnl 2f* **12/1**
4310 **7** *nk* **Redwood Rocks (IRE)**[30] 6573 5-8-12 **66**.................... MarkLawson(3) 8 53
(B Smart) *in rr: sme hdwy 2f out: nvr on terms* **10/1**[3]
0600 **8** *½* **Laith (IRE)**[94] 5487 3-8-5 **56**.................... EdwardCreighton 7 41
(Miss V Haigh) *hood stl on whn stalls opened: in rr tl kpt on fnl 2f: nvr a factor* **66/1**
3204 **9** *1* **Mina**[7] 6842 4-9-0 **65**.................... ChrisCatlin 10 47
(Rae Guest) *s.i.s: sn mid-div on outer: lost pl 3f out* **16/1**
0066 **10** *nk* **Cerebus**[319] 332 4-8-7 **63**.................... NataliaGemelova(5) 12 44
(A J McCabe) *w ldrs on outer: lost pl 3f out* **20/1**
6023 **11** *¾* **Sweet Pickle**[25] 6643 5-8-10 **64**....................(e) AmirQuinn(3) 3 43
(J R Boyle) *rrd s: a in rr* **14/1**
5/5- **12** *4* **Branston Tiger**[688] 266 7-9-0 **65**....................(v) DanielTudhope 11 32
(Ian Emmerson) *prom on outer: lost pl over 3f out* **50/1**
6465 **13** *5* **Smile For Us**[147] 3932 3-8-10 **64**....................(b) JerryO'Dwyer(3) 1 16
(C Drew) *s.i.s: a towards rr* **66/1**

1m 15.53s (-1.37) **Going Correction** -0.15s/f (Stan) **13 Ran SP% 126.7**
Speed ratings (Par 103):103,102,101,99,95 92,92,91,90,89 88,83,76
CSF £32.67 CT £99.48 TOTE £2.20: £1.10, £8.60, £1.70; EX 44.00 Trifecta £187.80 Pool £1,002.96 - 3.79 winning units. Place 6 £258.03, Place 5 £17.12..
Owner Snowdrop Stud Co Limited **Bred** Graf And Grafin Von Stauffenberg **Trained** Newmarket, Suffolk
■ Stewards' Enquiry : Patrick Hills two-day ban: used whip with excessive frequency (Jan 3-4)

FOCUS
A modest handicap in which it was very hard to make ground from off the pace.
Sweet Pickle Official explanation: jockey said mare was slowly away
T/Plt: £403.30 to a £1 stake. Pool: £49,169.90. 89.00 winning tickets. T/Qpdt: £5.20 to a £1 stake. Pool: £3,741.60. 529.00 winning tickets. WG

6919 WOLVERHAMPTON (A.W) (L-H)
Saturday, December 23

OFFICIAL GOING: Standard
Wind: Almost nil Weather: Cloudy

6931 PONTINS.COM NOVICE STKS 5f 216y(P)
3:50 (3:50) (Class 5) 2-Y-0 **£4,533** (£1,348; £674; £336) **Stalls** Low

Form RPR
0331 **1** **Milson's Point (IRE)**[14] 6764 2-9-1 59.................... GregFairley(3) 3 69
(I Semple) *sn led: rdn over 1f out: r.o* **10/11**[1]
5211 **2** *1 ¾* **Charlotte Grey**[10] 6807 2-8-8 63.................... DominicFox(3) 6 57
(C N Allen) *chsd wnr: rdn over 1f out: styd on same pce* **6/4**[2]
5 **3** *4* **Krakatau (FR)**[8] 6826 2-9-0 .... SamHitchcott 7 48
(D J Wintle) *prom: rdn over 3f out: styd on same pce fnl 2f* **13/2**[3]
4 *21* **Betty Oxo** 2-8-9 .... DeanMcKeown 4 —
(B P J Baugh) *s.i.s: sn chsng ldrs: rdn and wknd over 2f out* **40/1**

1m 15.09s (-0.72) **Going Correction** -0.20s/f (Stan) **4 Ran SP% 108.2**
Speed ratings (Par 96):96,93,88,60
CSF £2.54 TOTE £1.70; EX 2.30.
Owner D G Savala **Bred** John B O'Connor **Trained** Carluke, S Lanarks

FOCUS
An uncompetitive event in which the gallop was fair and the form can almost be taken at face value. The action unfolded next to the far rail.

NOTEBOOK
Milson's Point(IRE), dropped again in trip, had the run of the race but turned in his best effort to beat an in-form rival in this uncompetitive event. He will not mind the return to seven furlongs and may be capable of better. (op 11-10 tchd 4-5)
Charlotte Grey, a dual course and distance winner, who had a good chance at the weights, seemed to run her race. She is a fair guide to the level of this form and should continue to give a good account in ordinary company. (op 11-8 tchd 15-8)
Krakatau(FR), who was not disgraced on his racecourse debut over seven furlongs at Kempton, had his limitations exposed over this shorter trip but left the impression that he would be capable of better back over further once handicapped. (op 8-1)
Betty Oxo, from a stable not normally associated with debut winners, was easy to back and soundly beaten on this racecourse debut. (op 16-1)

6932 PONTIN'S HOLIDAYS H'CAP 7f 32y(P)
4:20 (4:20) (Class 5) (0-75,81) 3-Y-0+ **£3,238** (£963; £481; £240) **Stalls** High

Form RPR
1145 **1** **Writ (IRE)**[16] 6741 4-8-8 **70**.................... GregFairley(3) 7 79
(I Semple) *chsd ldr: rdn to ld 1f out: edgd lft: r.o* **5/2**[1]
5021 **2** *¾* **Foreplay (IRE)**[30] 6573 3-9-2 **75**....................(p) EddieAhern 4 82
(E A L Dunlop) *hld up: hdwy over 1f out: rdn ins fnl f: r.o* **5/1**[3]
0251 **3** *nk* **Marko Jadeo (IRE)**[5] 6858 8-9-1 **81** 6ex.................... TolleyDean(7) 9 87
(R A Harris) *s.s: hld up: hdwy over 1f out: r.o* **12/1**
2112 **4** *½* **Prince Dayjur (USA)**[14] 6770 7-9-1 **74**.................... JimmyQuinn 5 79
(J Pearce) *sn pushed along in rr: rdn 1/2-way: r.o ins fnl f: nrst fin* **3/1**[2]
0500 **5** *nk* **Casablanca Minx (IRE)**[235] 1381 3-8-11 **73**.................... JamesDoyle(3) 1 77
(N P Littmoden) *chsd ldrs: rdn over 2f out: styd on same pce fnl f* **20/1**
6060 **6** *1* **Zarabad (IRE)**[75] 5861 4-8-0 **64**.................... AndrewElliott(5) 2 65
(K R Burke) *led: rdn and hdd 1f out: no ex* **8/1**
2430 **7** *1 ½* **Flying Bantam (IRE)**[56] 6212 5-7-13 **65**....................(p) JamesRogers(7) 8 62
(R A Fahey) *prom: lost pl 4f out: n.d after* **14/1**
2203 **8** *1 ½* **Ten Shun**[5] 6858 3-9-0 **73**.................... RobertWinston 6 67
(P D Evans) *prom: rdn 2f out: wknd fnl f* **7/1**

1m 28.97s (-1.43) **Going Correction** -0.20s/f (Stan) **8 Ran SP% 113.0**
Speed ratings (Par 103):100,99,98,98,97 96,95,93
CSF £14.92 CT £123.41 TOTE £3.70: £1.60, £1.80, £1.60; EX 16.00.
Owner Clarke Boon **Bred** Sean Collins **Trained** Carluke, S Lanarks
■ Stewards' Enquiry : Tolley Dean one-day ban: used whip with excessive frequency (Jan 3)

FOCUS
An ordinary handicap in which the pace was fair.

6933 GO PONTIN'S NURSERY 1m 141y(P)
4:50 (4:50) (Class 5) (0-75,75) 2-Y-0 **£3,238** (£963; £481; £240) **Stalls** Low

Form RPR
0122 **1** **Mastership (IRE)**[30] 6569 2-9-3 **71**....................(b) EddieAhern 2 79+
(C E Brittain) *trckd ldrs: led on bit towards fin: cleverly* **5/4**[1]
4311 **2** *nk* **Chookie Hamilton**[21] 6676 2-8-12 **69**.................... GregFairley(3) 5 70
(I Semple) *chsd ldrs: rdn to ld over 2f out: hdd nr fin* **6/1**[3]
5253 **3** *1 ¼* **Beech Games**[9] 6824 2-9-7 **75**....................(b) FrancisNorton 7 73
(E J O'Neill) *s.i.s: hld up: hdwy over 1f out: nt rch ldrs* **9/1**
6001 **4** *3* **Pret A Porter (UAE)**[14] 6768 2-9-0 **68**....................(b) RobertWinston 6 60
(P D Evans) *hld up: hdwy u.p over 1f out: nvr nrr* **20/1**
015 **5** *1 ¾* **Strike Force**[134] 4335 2-9-2 **70**.................... AdamKirby 1 58
(M Wellings) *led: rdn and hdd over 2f out: wknd ins fnl f* **33/1**
2033 **6** *5* **Henry The Seventh**[14] 6764 2-9-0 **68**.................... J-PGuillambert 3 45
(J W Hills) *chsd ldrs: rdn 1/2-way: sn outpcd: sme hdwy over 1f out: sn wknd* **8/1**
400 **7** *4* **View From The Top**[109] 5091 2-9-0 **68**.................... JamieMackay 4 37
(Sir Mark Prescott) *plld hrd and prom: rdn over 2f out: sn hung rt and wknd* **7/2**[2]
0030 **8** *1 ¾* **Breezeway (IRE)**[63] 6106 2-9-2 **70**.................... RobertHavlin 8 35
(B J Meehan) *hld up: hdwy over 5f out: wknd over 2f out* **20/1**

1m 50.35s (-1.41) **Going Correction** -0.20s/f (Stan) **8 Ran SP% 114.5**
Speed ratings (Par 96):98,97,96,93,92 87,84,82
CSF £8.96 CT £47.38 TOTE £2.70: £1.10, £1.50, £2.90; EX 9.20.
Owner Sheikh Marwan Al Maktoum **Bred** Darley **Trained** Newmarket, Suffolk

FOCUS
Another ordinary handicap but, although the margin of victory was a neck, Mastership was value for considerably more than that distance suggests and the overall form looks solid.

NOTEBOOK
Mastership(IRE) ◆, an unlucky loser over course and distance on his previous start, turned in his best effort under an ice cool ride and was value for considerably more than the winning margin suggests. He will be of obvious interest if turned out under a penalty. (op 11-8 tchd 6-4, 13-8 in places)
Chookie Hamilton is an honest sort who was greatly flattered by his proximity to the easy winner. However, he did not do much wrong and should continue to go well away from progressive sorts. (op 11-2)
Beech Games fared the best of those attempting to come from off the pace after a tardy start but, although he will be suited by the return to a bit further, would not be one to lump on at short odds until getting his head in front where it matters. (op 11-1)
Pret A Porter(UAE), who won an uncompetitive claimer in first-time blinkers over the extended nine furlongs here last time, found things tougher from this higher mark back in handicap company. (op 16-1)
Strike Force, who won on turf for John Gosden in June, had been off since August but was not disgraced on this All-Weather debut for new connections. He may have to come down in the weights before returning to winning ways, though.
Henry The Seventh, who ran his best race over seven furlongs at this course last time, was below that level on this first outing over this trip. Consistency does not look his strongest suit.
View From The Top, having his first run for Sir Mark Prescott, pulled far too hard to do himself justice on this All-Wweather and handicap debut and first run since early September. He is not one to write off by any means but will have to settle much better if he is to progress. (tchd 4-1)

6934 PONTINS.COM H'CAP 1m 141y(P)
5:20 (5:24) (Class 6) (0-58,60) 3-Y-0+ **£2,914** (£867; £433; £216) **Stalls** Low

Form RPR
0610 **1** **Topiary Ted**[21] 6683 4-9-0 **56**.................... RobertHavlin 3 68+
(H Morrison) *s.s: hld up: hdwy over 2f out: rdn to ld ins fnl f: r.o* **4/1**[1]
6034 **2** *1 ½* **Myths And Verses**[28] 6608 3-8-11 **55**....................(p) NCallan 6 64
(K A Ryan) *chsd ldrs: rdn and ev ch ins fnl f: unable qck* **10/1**
0341 **3** *3 ½* **Spark Up**[21] 6683 6-8-12 **57**....................(b) RichardKingscote(3) 7 59
(J W Unett) *sn led: rdn over 1f out: hdd and no ex ins fnl f* **9/1**
0300 **4** *1 ¼* **Mister Benji**[184] 2794 7-8-13 **55**.................... DeanMcKeown 2 57+
(B P J Baugh) *hld up: nt clr run over 2f out: hdwy over 1f out: nt trble ldrs* **28/1**
0103 **5** *2 ½* **Keon (IRE)**[12] 6793 4-8-5 **54**.................... RussellKennemore(7) 5 48
(R Hollinshead) *hld up: nt clr run 3f out: r.o ins fnl f: nvr nrr* **5/1**[3]
0050 **6** *½* **Burnley Al (IRE)**[10] 6810 4-9-0 **56**....................(b) AdamKirby 9 49
(Peter Grayson) *hmpd s: hld up and bhd: styd on u.p fr over 1f out: n.d* **25/1**
0060 **7** *1* **King After**[10] 6810 4-8-8 **50**.................... HayleyTurner 10 41
(J R Best) *chsd ldrs: rdn over 2f out: wkng whn hung lft fr over 1f out* **25/1**
0412 **8** *2 ½* **Discotheque (USA)**[10] 6810 3-9-0 **58**.................... DeanCorby 8 43
(P Howling) *hld up: rdn over 2f out: n.d* **10/1**
0041 **9** *¾* **Mozie Cat (IRE)**[12] 6787 3-9-2 **60**.................... BrettDoyle 11 44
(John Berry) *rn in snatches: in tch: rdn 5f out: wknd 2f out* **9/2**[2]
0050 **10** *2 ½* **Celtic Spa (IRE)**[19] 6698 4-9-2 **58**.................... RobertWinston 1 37
(P D Evans) *led early: chsd ldr tl wknd wel over 1f out* **14/1**
0002 **11** *¾* **Blue Empire (IRE)**[2] 6897 5-9-1 **57**.................... EddieAhern 13 34
(C R Dore) *chsd ldrs 6f* **5/1**[3]
0404 **12** *1 ¾* **Border Artist**[21] 6674 7-9-2 **58**.................... JimmyQuinn 12 31
(J Pearce) *hld up: hdwy over 3f out: wknd 2f out* **16/1**

1m 49.42s (-2.34) **Going Correction** -0.20s/f (Stan)
WFA 3 from 4yo+ 2lb **12 Ran SP% 123.4**
Speed ratings (Par 101):102,100,97,96,94 93,92,90,90,87 87,85
CSF £45.61 CT £351.67 TOTE £6.10: £1.80, £5.20, £2.10; EX 39.50.
Owner Ron Plant **Bred** Stowell Hill Ltd And Mrs C Van Straubenzee **Trained** East Ilsley, Berks
■ Stewards' Enquiry : Jimmy Quinn jockey said gelding lost its action
Adam Kirby jockey said gelding would not face kickback

FOCUS
A run-of-the-mill handicap in which the pace seemed fair.
Burnley Al(IRE) Official explanation: jockey said gelding would not face the kickback
Border Artist Official explanation: jockey said gelding lost its action

6935 GO PONTIN'S H'CAP 5f 20y(P)
5:50 (5:51) (Class 5) (0-75,73) 3-Y-0+ **£5,181** (£1,541; £770; £384) **Stalls** Low

Form RPR
0131 **1** **Desert Opal**[16] 6739 6-8-8 **65**....................(p) RobertWinston 5 79
(C R Dore) *a.p: chsd ldr over 1f out: rdn to ld wl ins fnl f* **13/8**[1]
002 **2** *¾* **Financial Times (USA)**[7] 6844 4-8-13 **70**....................(t) NCallan 7 81
(Stef Liddiard) *sn led: rdn over 1f out: hdd wl ins fnl f* **5/2**[2]
0001 **3** *4* **Stoneacre Boy (IRE)**[7] 6844 3-8-12 **69**....................(b) TonyCulhane 2 66+
(Peter Grayson) *sn outpcd: r.o ins fnl f: nrst fin* **9/2**[3]

The Form Book, Raceform Ltd, Compton, RG20 6NL

6600 **4** *3/4* **Hornpipe**[9] 6823 4-8-8 **65** ... FrancisNorton 8 59
(M S Saunders) *chsd ldr: rdn 1/2-way: wknd fnl f* **33/1**

0000 **5** *nk* **Sands Crooner (IRE)**[18] 6709 3-9-2 **73** ...(v) DeanMcKeown 3 66
(D Shaw) *hld up: swtchd rt and hdwy over 1f out: wknd ins fnl f* **11/1**

5003 **6** *hd* **Lucayos**[9] 6823 3-8-10 **70** ...(b) RichardKingscote(3) 1 62
(Mrs H Sweeting) *s.s: outpcd: styd on ins fnl f: nvr nrr* **9/1**

0006 **7** *hd* **Misaro (GER)**[7] 6844 5-8-3 **60** ...(b) AdrianMcCarthy 11 51
(R A Harris) *chsd ldrs over 4f* **14/1**

200 **8** *1 3/4* **Lady Bahia (IRE)**[9] 6823 5-8-8 **65** ...(b) JimmyQuinn 6 50
(Peter Grayson) *hld up: hdwy over 1f out: sn rdn: hung lft and nt run on* **12/1**

0000 **9** *1* **Lyndalee (IRE)**[14] 6773 3-8-5 **65** ...(p) JamesDoyle(3) 9 46
(P D Evans) *chsd ldrs: wkng whn hmpd over 1f out* **33/1**

61.44 secs (-1.38) **Going Correction** -0.20s/f (Stan) 9 Ran SP% **123.4**
Speed ratings (Par 103):103,101,95,94,93 93,93,90,88
CSF £6.27 CT £15.58 TOTE £3.00: £1.30, £1.60, £1.60; EX 10.30.
Owner Page, Ward, Marsh **Bred** Juddmonte Farms **Trained** West Pinchbeck, Lincs
■ Stewards' Enquiry : Richard Kingscote jockey said gelding was slowly away
Dean McKeown four-day ban: careless riding (Jan 3-6)

FOCUS
An ordinary handicap run at a decent gallop and one in which a couple of in-form types did well to pull clear of the rest.
Lucayos Official explanation: jockey said gelding was slowly away

6936 PONTINSBINGO.COM H'CAP 1m 4f 50y(P)
6:20 (6:20) (Class 6) (0-55,54) 3-Y-0+ **£3,071** (£906; £453) **Stalls** Low

Form RPR

0033 **1** **Twist Bookie (IRE)**[12] 6790 6-8-9 **47** ... ChrisCatlin 4 57
(S Lycett) *trckd ldrs: racd keenly: rdn to ld wl ins fnl f* **6/1**[3]

4661 **2** *1/2* **Little Richard (IRE)**[12] 6790 7-9-0 **52** ...(p) AdamKirby 6 61
(M Wellings) *chsd ldrs: rdn to ld and hung rt over 1f out: edgd lft and hdd wl ins fnl f* **6/1**[3]

6510 **3** *3 1/2* **Bolckow**[15] 6754 3-8-10 **53** ... DaleGibson 5 56
(J T Stimpson) *plld hrd and prom: rdn and ev ch over 1f out: no ex fnl f* **8/1**

4161 **4** *hd* **Ocean Rock**[17] 6729 5-9-2 **54** ... GeorgeBaker 11 57+
(C A Horgan) *hld up and bhd: styd on u.p fr over 1f out: nvr nrr* **2/1**[1]

006/ **5** *nk* **The Cute Won (USA)**[204] 1658 8-8-8 **49** ...(b) JerryO'Dwyer(3) 2 52
(N Dooly, Ire) *hld up: rdn over 3f out: styd on u.p ins fnl f: nrst fin* **28/1**

4231 **6** *hd* **Regency Red (IRE)**[10] 6812 8-8-10 **53** ... AshleyHamblett(5) 10 55+
(W M Brisbourne) *hld up: hdwy over 4f out: rdn over 1f out: eased whn btn ins fnl f* **11/2**[2]

060 **7** *1 3/4* **Reminiscent (IRE)**[188] 2684 7-8-5 **50** ... SoniaEaton(7) 8 49
(B P J Baugh) *s.i.s: hld up: styd on ins fnl f: nvr nrr* **33/1**

0000 **8** *3/4* **Monkstown Road**[70] 4457 4-8-8 **46** ...(p) JimmyQuinn 1 44
(C N Kellett) *led: rdn 4f out: hdd over 1f out: wknd fnl f* **80/1**

0 **9** *1 1/4* **Asian Alliance (IRE)**[13] 6775 5-9-1 **53** ...(p) NCallan 3 49
(K A Ryan) *plld hrd and prom: rdn over 2f out: sn wknd* **11/2**[2]

6003 **10** *5* **Come What July (IRE)**[5] 6860 5-8-9 **47** ... DeanMcKeown 12 35
(D Shaw) *hld up: rdn and wknd over 2f out* **20/1**

034 **11** *5* **Willy (SWE)**[14] 6758 4-9-2 **54** ...(t) RobertWinston 9 34
(R Brotherton) *trckd ldrs: plld hrd: rdn and ev ch 2f out: sn hung rt and wknd* **12/1**

4454 **12** *1* **Countback (FR)**[319] 328 7-8-12 **50** ... FrancisNorton 7 29
(A W Carroll) *hld up: rdn over 3f out: wknd over 2f out* **20/1**

2m 41.46s (-0.96) **Going Correction** -0.20s/f (Stan)
WFA 3 from 4yo+ 5lb 12 Ran SP% **128.6**
Speed ratings (Par 101):95,94,92,92,92 91,90,90,89,86 82,82
CSF £43.13 CT £304.53 TOTE £10.00: £3.60, £2.60, £3.00; EX 64.90 Place 6 £41.33, Place 5 £21.22.
Owner Frank Dronzek **Bred** Wolfgang Stiltz **Trained** Naunton, Gloucs
■ Stewards' Enquiry : Robert Winston jockey said gelding lost its action

FOCUS
A modest handicap run at only a moderate gallop and one that favoured those that raced up with the pace. This bare form is best treated with caution.
Willy(SWE) Official explanation: jockey said gelding lost its action
T/Plt: £35.80 to a £1 stake. Pool: £65,509.50. 1,332.65 winning tickets. T/Qpdt: £13.70 to a £1 stake. Pool: £5,960.80. 320.60 winning tickets. CR

6931 WOLVERHAMPTON (A.W) (L-H)
Tuesday, December 26

OFFICIAL GOING: Standard
Wind: Almost nil Weather: Overcast and cold

6937 WBX.COM WORLD BET EXCHANGE NOVICE STKS 7f 32y(P)
1:40 (1:40) (Class 5) 2-Y-0 **£3,886** (£1,156; £577) **Stalls** High

Form RPR

4221 **1** **Benllech**[31] 6591 2-9-0 77 ... LPKeniry 1 84+
(S Kirk) *hld up in rr: hdwy 2f out: sn led: rdn clr and edgd lft 1f out: eased cl home* **5/2**[2]

0441 **2** *7* **Love In May (IRE)**[11] 6834 2-9-5 79 ... NCallan 4 72
(J S Moore) *w ldr: led 3f out: rdn and hdd jst under 2f out: no ch w wnr fnl f* **5/1**[3]

41 **3** *3* **Regal Riband**[4] 6920 2-9-0 ... JamieMackay 3 60
(Sir Mark Prescott) *led: rdn and hdd 3f out: hung lft and wknd wl over 1f out* **8/13**[1]

1m 32.33s (1.93) **Going Correction** +0.225s/f (Slow) 3 Ran SP% **107.2**
Speed ratings (Par 96):97,89,85
CSF £10.44 TOTE £3.60; EX 9.10.
Owner Speedlith Group **Bred** Speedlith Group **Trained** Upper Lambourn, Berks

FOCUS
A modest event, weakened further by the withdrawal of Homes By Woodford. With the hot favourite running so poorly it took little winning, but the pace was fair enough and the time was respectable under the circumstances.

NOTEBOOK
Benllech, who only just scraped home in a Kempton median auction event last time to record his first win at the 11th attempt, won this in much more authoritative style and once the favourite folded it was obvious that he was running all over his only remaining rival. The form probably adds up to little, but the time was fair enough and he could hardly have done more than win like he did. (op 9-4 tchd 15-8)
Love In May(IRE), unbeaten in two starts on Polytrack, had no sooner got the better of the disappointing favourite on the home bend than the winner arrived on her outside and it proved no contest from then on. She is still to prove that she gets this far. (op 6-1)
Regal Riband, making a quick reappearance following her clear-cut victory over course and distance four days earlier, tried to make every yard but she came off the bridle as soon as Love In May ranged alongside her on the turn for home and folded most disappointingly. Either this came too soon or the form of the race she won is very poor. Official explanation: trainer was unable to explain the poor run (tchd 8-11)

6938 WBXTRIPLECROWN.COM CLAIMING STKS 7f 32y(P)
2:15 (2:15) (Class 6) 3-Y-0+ **£2,730** (£806; £403) **Stalls** High

Form RPR

0015 **1** **The London Gang**[7] 6864 3-8-0 59 ...(v) WilliamBuick(7) 11 68
(P D Evans) *towards rr: pushed along 4f out: hdwy 2f out: r.o to ld and edgd lft wl ins fnl f: drvn out* **16/1**

0053 **2** *1/2* **Primo Way**[8] 6862 5-9-2 70 ...(b) GregFairley(3) 5 79
(I Semple) *midfield: rdn and hdwy 2f out: ch ins fnl f: styd on* **5/1**[3]

5051 **3** *1/2* **Bessemer (JPN)**[29] 6624 5-9-1 69 ...(p) DanielTudhope 7 73
(D Carroll) *in tch: clsd 3f out: rdn over 2f out: led over 1f out: hdd wl ins fnl f: no ex fnl strides* **13/2**

2513 **4** *1 1/4* **Marko Jadeo (IRE)**[3] 6932 8-8-8 75 ... TolleyDean(7) 1 70
(R A Harris) *s.i.s: towards rr: hdwy 3f out: rdn over 1f out whn chsd ldrs: edgd rt ins fnl f: styd on same pce* **7/4**[1]

2040 **5** *1 1/2* **Mistral Sky**[134] 4437 7-9-1 62 ...(p) RobertHavlin 8 66
(Stef Liddiard) *midfield: outpcd 4f out: hdwy over 1f out: kpt on ins fnl f: nvr able to chal* **25/1**

0006 **6** *1/2* **Mystic Man (FR)**[22] 6696 8-9-1 70 ...(b) JimmyQuinn 2 65
(I W McInnes) *in tch: clsd 3f out: nt clr run 2f out: rdn and ev ch over 1f out: fdd towards fin* **22/1**

0113 **7** *5* **Cleveland**[28] 6642 4-8-12 63 ... RussellKennemore(7) 3 56
(R Hollinshead) *led for 1f: remained prom: rdn and ev ch whn hung rt 2f out: wknd over 1f out* **7/1**

8 *5* **Spotoncon**[19] 5-8-6 ... AndrewElliott(5) 9 35
(A J Lidderdale) *s.s: a bhd* **66/1**

0040 **9** *2* **Wahoo Sam (USA)**[17] 6772 6-9-5 72 ... NCallan 10 38
(K A Ryan) *led after 1f: rdn 2f out: hdd over 1f out: wknd and eased fnl f* **4/1**[2]

0506 **10** *5* **Tamworth (IRE)**[7] 6864 4-8-11 55 ...(b) EdwardCreighton 6 17
(E J Creighton) *trckd ldrs: rdn over 3f out: wknd over 2f out* **33/1**

1m 31.82s (1.42) **Going Correction** +0.225s/f (Slow) 10 Ran SP% **117.4**
Speed ratings (Par 101):100,99,98,97,95 95,89,83,81,75
CSF £91.41 TOTE £15.10: £3.30, £2.40, £1.70; EX 83.80 TRIFECTA Not won..Marko Jadeo was subject to a friendly claim.
Owner D Healy **Bred** Lostford Manor Stud **Trained** Pandy, Abergavenny

FOCUS
An ordinary claimer in which the leaders may well have gone off too quick, setting the race up for the closers.
Wahoo Sam(USA) Official explanation: jockey said gelding hung left-handed from halfway

6939 WBX.COM WORLD BET EXCHANGE NURSERY 5f 20y(P)
2:45 (2:46) (Class 4) (0-85,77) 2-Y-0 **£4,533** (£1,348; £674; £336) **Stalls** Low

Form RPR

6041 **1** **Minnow**[10] 6839 2-7-10 **59** ... WilliamBuick(7) 5 67+
(S C Williams) *a.p: r.o to ld wl ins fnl f: won gng away* **7/4**[2]

4630 **2** *2* **Grange Lili (IRE)**[3] 6926 2-7-10 **57** ...(b) DuranFentiman(5) 3 55
(Peter Grayson) *towards rr: rdn 3f out: hdwy over 1f out: styd on to take 2nd fnl strides: nt pce of wnr* **12/1**

412 **3** *1/2* **Dress To Impress (IRE)**[20] 6732 2-9-7 **77** ... NCallan 1 73
(J R Boyle) *led: rdn over 1f out: hdd wl ins fnl f: no ex cl home* **6/4**[1]

311 **4** *2* **Diminuto**[12] 6813 2-8-0 **63** ... FrankiePickard(7) 7 52
(M D I Usher) *chsd ldrs: rdn over 2f out: one pce fr over 1f out: edgd lft whn wl hld ins fnl f* **7/1**

0000 **5** *1 3/4* **Foxy Music**[10] 6839 2-7-12 **54** oh9 ...(b) AdrianMcCarthy 2 37
(Peter Grayson) *chsd ldrs: n.m.r over 3f out: sn lost pl: no imp after* **16/1**

5454 **6** *1 3/4* **Slipasearcher (IRE)**[12] 6822 2-8-9 **65** ...(p) RobertHavlin 6 41
(P D Evans) *bhd: rdn over 3f out: nvr on terms* **6/1**[3]

63.81 secs (0.99) **Going Correction** +0.225s/f (Slow) 6 Ran SP% **116.7**
Speed ratings (Par 98):101,97,97,93,91 88
CSF £22.97 TOTE £2.80: £1.60, £3.00; EX 24.00.
Owner Tweenhills Racing VIII **Bred** Downclose Stud **Trained** Newmarket, Suffolk
■ Stewards' Enquiry : William Buick one-day remedial training: careless riding (date TBA)

FOCUS
An ordinary nursery, but the time was solid and winner looks progressive.

NOTEBOOK
Minnow ◆, raised 6lb for her Kempton success, was the least exposed of the sextet on sand. Never far away, her rider did not panic when the favourite quickened into a clear lead turning in and eventually picked her rival off to record a cosy success. She seems to be improving and may not have stopped winning yet. (op 13-8 tchd 15-8 and 2-1 in places)
Grange Lili(IRE), who came off the bridle a long way out, responded to pressure to eventually snatch second from the flagging favourite near the line, but was never a threat to the winner. She remains a maiden after 11 attempts, but has the ability to win a small race on sand. (tchd 11-1)
Dress To Impress(IRE) had the ideal draw from which to try and make all and everything seemed to be working out perfectly as he kicked clear rounding the home bend, but he then started to wander and was eventually swamped in the closing stages. He got away with it when winning a maiden here two starts back, but it may be that he is a short runner. (op 5-2)
Diminuto was not ideally drawn to repeat her normal front-running tactics and thanks to the favourite she could never quite get to the front. She looks better suited by Fibresand in any case. (op 8-1)
Foxy Music, who met trouble in running when over six lengths behind Minnow at Kempton last time, again encountered bother on the home bend here. It usually does not pay to make too many excuses, but he is still lightly raced and was 9lb wrong, so may be worth one more chance off his proper mark. (op 12-1)
Slipasearcher(IRE) could never go the pace and the drop back to the minimum trip did her few favours. (op 9-2)

6940 WBXTRIPLECROWN.COM MAIDEN STKS 5f 216y(P)
3:20 (3:20) (Class 5) 2-Y-0 **£3,238** (£963; £481; £240) **Stalls** Low

Form RPR

33 **1** **Hollywood George**[12] 6822 2-9-3 ... TonyCulhane 3 66
(W J Haggas) *trckd ldrs: rdn to ld narrowly 1f out: all out* **4/5**[1]

5602 **2** *shd* **Le Masque**[42] 6472 2-9-0 ... MarkLawson(3) 7 66
(B Smart) *racd keenly: led: rdn and hdd narrowly 1f out: r.o u.p* **7/1**

0 **3** *hd* **Minnie Mill**[12] 6821 2-8-12 ... JimmyQuinn 4 60
(B P J Baugh) *hld up: rdn and hdwy 2f out: edgd lft and r.o towards fin* **25/1**

004 **4** *1 1/2* **Ice Box (IRE)**[69] 6055 2-8-12 62 ... J-PGuillambert 1 56+
(M Johnston) *in tch: rdn and outpcd 3f out: styd on ins fnl f: nt pce to chal* **9/2**[3]

4366 **5** 2 **Perlachy**[21] 6715 2-9-3 68 .... DanielTudhope 5 55
(Mrs N Macauley) *trckd ldrs: rdn and ev ch 2f out: no extra ins fnl f* **20/1**
6 ¾ **Haydock Express (IRE)** 2-9-3 .... AdamKirby 6 52
(Peter Grayson) *s.i.s: bhd: nvr on terms w lesders* **25/1**
42 **7** 2 **Tilapia (IRE)**[4] 6912 2-9-3 .... JamieMackay 2 46
(Sir Mark Prescott) *prom: rdn 3f out: wknd over 1f out* **4/1**[2]
1m 17.34s (1.53) **Going Correction** +0.225s/f (Slow) **7** Ran SP% **118.7**
Speed ratings (Par 96):98,97,97,95,92 91,89
CSF £7.59 TOTE £1.60: £1.20, £3.60; EX 9.00.
Owner W J Gredley **Bred** Chippenham Lodge Stud Ltd **Trained** Newmarket, Suffolk
■ Stewards' Enquiry : Jimmy Quinn one-day ban: used whip with excessive frequency (Jan 6)

FOCUS
Not a great maiden, but a thrilling finish, with very little separating the front three at the line.

NOTEBOOK
Hollywood George, who took on previous winners in a novice event over course and distance last time, appeared to face a straightforward task on this return to maiden company, but he made very hard work of it and it was probably only a strong ride from his jockey in the closing stages that got him home by the skin of his teeth. He now qualifies for a mark which, in theory, should be in the mid 60s, using the runner-up as a guide. A longer trip may suit him better. (tchd 10-11 and Evens in places)
Le Masque, returning to maiden company after three outings in nurseries, tried the same tactics as when running his best race so far as Southwell last time. He again never stopped trying and deserves to win a modest event on sand. (tchd 13-2 and 8-1)
Minnie Mill ran a very similar race to her debut. Making her effort wide, she looked as though she might get to the front but hung in towards her rivals and could never quite get there. Provided her hanging is still due to greenness, there should be a small race in her. (op 40-1)
Ice Box(IRE), making her sand debut after three runs on turf, ran as though finding this trip inadequate and may be better off in modest handicaps over further. (tchd 4-1 and 5-1)
Perlachy again failed to reproduce his turf form and looks to have gone the wrong way. (op 14-1)
Tilapia(IRE) did not run up to his previous form and this was another disappointing performance from a Prescott juvenile following that of the odds-on favourite in the opener. (op 7-1)

6941 WBX.COM WORLD BET EXCHANGE H'CAP 1m 4f 50y(P)
3:50 (3:50) (Class 4) (0-85,85) 3-Y-0+ **£5,505** (£1,637; £818; £408) **Stalls** Low

Form RPR
5032 **1** **Tranquilizer**[42] 6479 4-8-9 **73** ow2 .... (t) AdamKirby 1 82
(D J Coakley) *hld up in tch: rdn to ld over 1f out: r.o* **10/3**[3]
6014 **2** 1 ¾ **Quince (IRE)**[13] 6811 3-8-11 **80** .... (v) JimmyQuinn 6 86
(J Pearce) *led: rdn and hdd over 1f out: nt qckn towards fin* **3/1**[2]
0125 **3** 1 ¾ **Heathyards Pride**[24] 6677 6-9-4 **82** .... TonyCulhane 2 85
(R Hollinshead) *prom: rdn and outpcd over 3f out: rallied over 1f out: one pce ins fnl f* **7/2**
3145 **4** ¾ **Tous Les Deux**[20] 6734 3-8-2 **71** .... AdrianMcCarthy 3 73
(Peter Grayson) *stdd s: hld up: hdwy 3f out: rdn and hung lft whn chsd ldrs over 1f out: no ex ins fnl f* **8/1**
0211 **5** 13 **Flame Creek (IRE)**[17] 6761 10-9-7 **85** .... EdwardCreighton 5 66
(E J Creighton) *in tch: hdwy to take 2nd 1/2-way: ev ch 3f out: rdn and lost 2nd over 2f out: wknd over 1f out* **11/4**[1]
0-00 **6** 8 **Dance World**[24] 6677 6-8-13 **80** .... RichardKingscote(3) 7 48
(Miss J Feilden) *hld up: rdn over 3f out: sn btn* **16/1**
2m 44.73s (2.31) **Going Correction** +0.225s/f (Slow)
WFA 3 from 4yo+ 5lb **6** Ran SP% **114.0**
Speed ratings (Par 105):101,99,98,98,89 84
CSF £14.05 TOTE £4.30: £2.10, £2.40; EX 15.00.
Owner Count Calypso Racing **Bred** Highclere Stud Ltd **Trained** West Ilsley, Berks

FOCUS
The early pace was only modest in this handicap, and it developed into something of a sprint from the home bend. The form has not been rated positively.

6942 WBXTRIPLECROWN.COM FILLIES' H'CAP 1m 1f 103y(P)
4:20 (4:20) (Class 5) (0-70,69) 3-Y-0+ **£3,238** (£963; £481; £240) **Stalls** Low

Form RPR
0000 **1** **Odessa Star (USA)**[6] 6878 3-8-13 **66** .... J-PGuillambert 7 71
(J G Portman) *hld up: hdwy over 3f out: rdn over 1f out: r.o ins fnl f to ld post* **14/1**
2333 **2** shd **Bavarica**[19] 6741 4-8-11 **69** .... AmyBaker(7) 5 74+
(Miss J Feilden) *hld up: hdwy on ins rail 2f out: led over 1f out: rdn ins fnl f: hdd post* **9/4**[1]
601 **3** ½ **Symbol Of Peace (IRE)**[15] 6792 3-8-12 **68** .... RichardKingscote(3) 9 72
(J W Unett) *racd keenly: prom: rdn over 3f out: sltly outpcd over 1f out: styd on ins fnl f* **7/1**
463 **4** ¾ **Emily's Place (IRE)**[12] 6825 3-8-9 **62** .... (p) JimmyQuinn 6 65
(J Pearce) *in tch: nt clr run over 1f out: sn rdn: kpt on ins fnl f* **3/1**[3]
3440 **5** 1 ¼ **Westering Home (IRE)**[97] 5484 3-8-9 **62** .... DaleGibson 8 62
(J Mackie) *in tch: rdn and outpcd over 3f out: no real imp after* **12/1**
0650 **6** ½ **Ignition**[12] 6819 4-7-11 **55** oh1 .... (p) WilliamBuick(7) 1 54
(W M Brisbourne) *led: rdn over 3f out: hdd over 1f out: wknd ins fnl f* **12/1**
0624 **7** 1 ¼ **Cove Mountain (IRE)**[4] 6916 4-8-8 **59** .... LPKeniry 2 56
(S Kirk) *prom: rdn and ev ch 2f out: wknd ins fnl f* **11/4**[2]
5000 **8** 8 **Reveur**[196] 2518 3-8-5 **63** .... AndrewElliott(5) 4 44
(M Mullineaux) *a bhd* **25/1**
2m 4.72s (2.10) **Going Correction** +0.225s/f (Slow)
WFA 3 from 4yo 2lb **8** Ran SP% **120.8**
Speed ratings (Par 100):99,98,98,97,96 96,95,88
CSF £48.52 CT £254.09 TOTE £14.50: £3.40, £1.50, £2.50; EX 72.30 Trifecta £484.20 Pool: £804.89 - 1.18 winning units. Place 6 £198.48, Place 5 £51.07.
Owner Portlee Bloodstock **Bred** Sugar Maple Farm **Trained** Compton, Berks

FOCUS
The early pace looked decent thanks to Ignition, but in the end they finished in a bit of a heap. The form has a weakish look about it.
T/Plt: £330.30 to a £1 stake. Pool: £37,969.95. 83.90 winning tickets. T/Qpdt: £23.10 to a £1 stake. Pool: £2,812.50. 89.80 winning tickets. DO

6925 SOUTHWELL (L-H)
Wednesday, December 27
OFFICIAL GOING: Standard
Wind: Light, half-against Weather: Mainly fine but cold and rain race seven.

6943 PONTIN'S FAMILY HOLIDAYS CLAIMING STKS 5f (F)
12:00 (12:00) (Class 6) 3-Y-0+ **£2,730** (£806; £403) **Stalls** High

Form RPR
0004 **1** **Spirit Of Coniston**[7] 6877 3-8-0 50 .... (b) DuranFentiman(5) 5 57
(Peter Grayson) *mde all: wnt lft over 1f out: kpt on wl* **5/1**[3]
0453 **2** 1 ¼ **Charlie Delta**[6] 6896 3-9-9 72 .... (p) DanielTudhope 2 71
(D Carroll) *chsd ldrs: carried lft and swtchd ins over 1f out: hung lft: kpt on: no real imp* **4/6**[1]
0000 **3** 4 **Kings Heir (IRE)**[12] 6833 3-8-5 60 .... (b) ChrisCatlin 6 39
(Peter Grayson) *chsd ldrs: outpcd after 2f: hdwy over 1f out: kpt on same pce* **10/1**
0005 **4** 2 ½ **He's A Rocket (IRE)**[21] 6723 5-8-0 45 .... AndrewElliott(5) 3 31
(K R Burke) *chsd ldrs: sn drvn along: fdd over 1f out* **9/2**[2]
5400 **5** 1 ¼ **On The Trail**[19] 6753 9-8-3 40 .... MatthewHenry 7 24
(D W Chapman) *w wnr: wknd over 1f out* **22/1**
00 **6** ¾ **Blissphilly**[79] 5865 4-7-11 30 .... DominicFox(3) 1 19
(M Mullineaux) *outpcd after 2f: n.d after* **80/1**
0-00 **7** 5 **Ronnie From Donny (IRE)**[186] 2874 6-8-5 35 ...... (t) CatherineGannon 4 7
(C J Teague) *dwlt: hdwy after 2f: hung lft and lost pl 2f out* **50/1**
59.62 secs (-0.68) **Going Correction** -0.075s/f (Stan) **7** Ran SP% **111.5**
Speed ratings (Par 101):102,100,93,89,87 86,78
CSF £8.33 TOTE £7.60: £2.10, £1.10; EX 14.60.
Owner Richard Teatum **Bred** Green Square Racing **Trained** Formby, Lancs

FOCUS
A weak claimer with the runner-up below his best.

6944 PONTINSBINGO.COM MAIDEN STKS 6f (F)
12:30 (12:33) (Class 5) 3-Y-0+ **£3,238** (£963; £481; £240) **Stalls** Low

Form RPR
052 **1** **Ragad**[21] 6731 3-9-3 53 .... BrettDoyle 7 69+
(W Jarvis) *trckd ldrs: led over 1f out: pushed clr jst ins last* **7/4**[1]
2 5 **Et Dona Ferentes**[105] 5305 3-8-12 .... PhillipMakin 2 49
(T D Barron) *led tl over 1f out: kpt on same pce* **4/1**[2]
653 **3** 5 **Going Skint**[286] 653 3-9-3 63 .... AdamKirby 5 39
(M Wellings) *swvd rt s: hdwy 3f out: kpt on to take modest 3rd ins last* **4/1**[2]
60 **4** nk **Pikaboo**[73] 5988 3-8-12 .... J-PGuillambert 6 33
(S C Williams) *w ldrs: wknd appr fnl f* **4/1**[2]
0030 **5** 5 **Comic Tales**[9] 6858 5-9-3 45 .... CatherineGannon 1 23
(M Mullineaux) *s.i.s: hdwy on ins over 2f out: wknd over 1f out* **16/1**[3]
6 4 **Epidaurian King (IRE)** 3-9-3 .... DanielTudhope 3 11
(D Shaw) *rrd bdly s: t.o 3f out: sme hdwy* **25/1**
000- **7** 1 **Ross Is Boss**[536] 3341 4-9-0 30 .... GregFairley(3) 4 8
(C J Teague) *rrd s: sn chsng ldrs: lost pl over 1f out* **80/1**
3-00 **8** 2 **Nell Tupp**[116] 5023 3-9-3 55 .... (p) DavidAllan 8 2
(G Woodward) *reluctant to go to s: chsd ldrs: drvn over 3f out: lost pl 2f out* **33/1**
1m 15.85s (-1.05) **Going Correction** -0.175s/f (Stan) **8** Ran SP% **110.3**
Speed ratings (Par 103):100,93,86,86,79 74,72,70
CSF £8.16 TOTE £2.60: £1.10, £1.70, £1.50; EX 10.20 Trifecta £24.60 Pool £239.95 - 6.90 winning units..
Owner Ziad A Galadari **Bred** Galadari Sons Stud Company Limited **Trained** Newmarket, Suffolk

FOCUS
A weak maiden but a much-improved effort from the 53-rated winner.

6945 GO PONTIN'S (S) STKS 5f (F)
1:05 (1:05) (Class 6) 2-Y-0 **£2,388** (£705; £352) **Stalls** High

Form RPR
4152 **1** **Sister Etienne (IRE)**[13] 6813 2-8-12 66 .... PhillipMakin 2 64+
(T D Barron) *w ldr: led over 1f out: drvn out* **13/8**[2]
251 **2** 1 ¾ **New York Oscar (IRE)**[4] 6925 2-9-3 .... NCallan 3 63
(A J McCabe) *led: hung rt fr over 2f out: hdd over 1f out: kpt on same pce* **6/5**[1]
3345 **3** 1 ¼ **Splendidio**[16] 6788 2-8-7 47 .... ChrisCatlin 7 48
(D K Ivory) *hld up: effrt over 2f out: hdwy over 1f out: kpt on same pce* **14/1**
005 **4** 3 **Inverted**[6] 6895 2-8-12 .... MickyFenton 8 42
(Mrs A Duffield) *chsd ldrs: edgd rt over 1f out: sn wknd* **16/1**
0646 **5** 1 **Molto Duro (IRE)**[29] 6640 2-8-0 40 .... (b) LanceBetts(7) 6 34
(N Wilson) *swvd rt s: sn outpcd: sme late hdwy* **50/1**
4000 **6** 1 ¾ **Top Tier**[58] 6258 2-8-7 49 .... DuranFentiman(5) 5 33
(Peter Grayson) *chsd ldrs over 2f: sn outpcd and lost pl* **20/1**
0002 **7** 4 **O'Dwyer (IRE)**[11] 6845 2-8-12 56 .... (p) PaulMulrennan 4 18
(A D Brown) *chsd ldrs: hung bdly lft over 2f out: sn lost pl* **13/2**[3]
60.76 secs (0.46) **Going Correction** -0.075s/f (Stan) **7** Ran SP% **116.2**
Speed ratings (Par 94):93,90,88,83,81 79,72
CSF £4.05 TOTE £2.90: £1.30, £1.60; EX 4.90 Trifecta £13.40 Pool £304.68 - 16.09 winning units..There was no bid for the winner. New York Oscar was claimed by G P Martin for £6,000.
Owner S Knighton & A Kundi **Bred** Oghill House Stud **Trained** Maunby, N Yorks

FOCUS
A decent race by selling standards but anchored by the 47-rated third.

NOTEBOOK
Sister Etienne(IRE), who is not very big, is all speed and, racing up the centre of the track, she was always doing too much for the runner-up. (op 6-4 tchd 2-1)
New York Oscar(IRE), making a quick return, was drawn one from the outside. He took them along but hung towards the stands'-side rail and in the end the winner simply proved too good. It was enough to see him being claimed. (op 7-4 tchd 11-10)
Splendidio, happy to be back on Fibresand, was in no hurry to join issue. In the end she was simply not good enough to trouble the winner, whom she had a stone to find with on official rtaings.
Inverted, dropped in grade, had his limitations thoroughly exposed. (op 14-1)
Molto Duro(IRE), a bit of a handful beforehand, was never in the contest. (op 40-1)
O'Dwyer(IRE), down in trip and on a different surface, wanted to do nothing but hang left-handed. Official explanation: jockey said gelding was never travelling (op 8-1 tchd 11-2)

6946 PHOTO GIFTS FROM BONUSPRINT.COM H'CAP 1m (F)
1:40 (1:40) (Class 5) (0-75,78) 3-Y-0+ **£3,238** (£963; £481; £240) **Stalls** Low

Form RPR
0421 **1** **Orpen Wide (IRE)**[12] 5617 4-8-10 **75** .... RussellKennemore(7) 6 83
(M C Chapman) *drvn to chse ldrs: styd on on ins to ld ins last* **8/1**
6311 **2** 1 **Smart Ass (IRE)**[4] 6928 3-8-12 **78** 7ex .... WilliamBuick(7) 4 84
(J S Moore) *trckd ldrs: led 1f out: hdd and no ex ins last* **11/4**[2]
-000 **3** 1 **Black Falcon (IRE)**[16] 6791 6-8-12 **70** .... MickyFenton 3 74
(P T Midgley) *hld up in rr: effrt over 4f out: styd on fnl 2f: kpt on same pce ins last* **40/1**
1210 **4** ½ **Jordan's Light (USA)**[28] 6652 3-8-12 **71** .... (v) FrancisNorton 7 74
(T J Pitt) *chsd ldrs: kpt on same pce fnl 2f* **9/4**[1]
0335 **5** nk **Shifty**[4] 6928 7-8-10 **68** ow1 .... DanielTudhope 8 70
(D Carroll) *chsd ldrs: led over 1f out: sn hdd: fdd towards fin* **6/1**[3]

0014 **6** *6* **Boundless Prospect (USA)**[13] 6818 7-9-0 **72** NCallan 2 62
(Miss Gay Kelleway) *hld up in rr: drvn over 4f out: hdwy on wd outside 2f out: nvr nr ldrs* **6/1**[3]

0502 **7** *½* **Startori**[9] 6863 3-8-7 **66** DavidAllan 5 54
(B Smart) *led 1f: w ldr: led over 2f out: hdd & wknd over 1f out* **16/1**

3060 **8** *5* **Just Intersky (USA)**[48] 6418 3-9-1 **74** DeanMcKeown 1 52
(K A Ryan) *led after 1f: hdd over 2f out: sn wknd* **10/1**

1m 42.57s (-2.03) **Going Correction** -0.175s/f (Stan)
WFA 3 from 4yo+ 1lb **8** Ran SP% **114.5**
Speed ratings (Par 103):103,102,101,100,100 94,93,88
CSF £30.40 CT £834.76 TOTE £7.40: £2.00, £1.30, £11.30; EX 18.30 Trifecta £185.70 Part won. Pool £261.58 - 0.67 winning units..
Owner Andy & Bev Wright **Bred** Mrs Marian Maguire **Trained** Market Rasen, Lincs
■ Stewards' Enquiry : William Buick caution: careless riding

FOCUS
An ordinary handicap but an improved effort from the in-form, penalised runner-up.

6947 PONTINS.COM H'CAP 1m 4f (F)
2:15 (2:15) (Class 5) (0-75,74) 3-Y-0+ **£3,238** (£963; £481; £240) **Stalls** Low

Form RPR

3120 **1** **Jackie Kiely**[75] 5935 5-9-3 **70** (t) PhillipMakin 1 77
(R Brotherton) *hld up in tch: hdwy 4f out: hrd rdn and led over 1f out: hld on gamely* **7/1**

3435 **2** *nk* **Speed Dial Harry (IRE)**[16] 6791 4-9-7 **74** (v) IanMongan 2 81
(K R Burke) *hld up: hdwy over 3f out: upsides fnl f: no ex nr line* **9/4**[1]

-005 **3** *2 ½* **Haifa (IRE)**[4] 6929 3-8-9 **67** ow2 (p) MickyFenton 5 70
(Mrs A Duffield) *led after 1f: stdd over 7f out: qcknd over 4f out: hdd over 1f out: kpt on same pce* **10/1**

113- **4** *3 ½* **Caribbean Dancer (USA)**[516] 3911 4-9-3 **70** (b) J-PGuillambert 6 67
(M Johnston) *led 1f: chsd ldr: chal over 4f out: wknd appr fnl f* **5/1**

2000 **5** *hd* **Sand Repeal (IRE)**[22] 6718 4-8-9 **65** (p) JamesDoyle(3) 3 62
(Miss J Feilden) *trckd ldrs: outpcd over 3f out: lost pl over 1f out* **7/2**[2]

5503 **6** *7* **Bienheureux**[22] 6718 5-8-4 **60** oh3 (vt) DominicFox(3) 4 46
(Miss Gay Kelleway) *hld up: effrt over 4f out: lost pl over 2f out* **9/2**[3]

2m 39.2s (-2.89) **Going Correction** -0.175s/f (Stan)
WFA 3 from 4yo+ 5lb **6** Ran SP% **109.4**
Speed ratings (Par 103):102,101,100,97,97 93
CSF £21.96 TOTE £8.50: £4.10, £1.50; EX 21.50.
Owner P S J Croft **Bred** Mrs M Chaworth Musters **Trained** Elmley Castle, Worcs
■ Stewards' Enquiry : Phillip Makin two-day ban: used whip with excessive frequency (Jan 7-8)

FOCUS
Not a strong pace but a respectable time in the end. A slight personal best from the winner who seemed to outstay the runner-up.

6948 PERSONALISED CARDS FROM BONUSPRINT.COM NURSERY 1m (F)
2:50 (2:50) (Class 4) (0-95,84) 2-Y-0 **£6,477** (£1,927; £963; £481) **Stalls** Low

Form RPR

1 **1** **Circus Polka (USA)**[17] 6777 2-8-9 **72** (t) JosedeSouza 1 81+
(P F I Cole) *trckd ldr: t.k.h: carried hd high: hung lft and led over 1f out: r.o strly: readily* **7/4**[2]

3313 **2** *2 ½* **Eau Good**[6] 6895 2-9-0 **84** RussellKennemore(7) 2 82
(M C Chapman) *hld up wl in tch: stdy hdwy 3f out: rdn and hung lft 1f out: no imp* **9/2**[3]

3334 **3** *1 ½* **Inflagrantedelicto (USA)**[6] 6891 2-8-2 **65** MatthewHenry 3 60
(D W Chapman) *set mod pce: qcknd over 3f out: hdd over 1f out: one pce* **16/1**

2601 **4** *7* **Sahrati**[63] 6173 2-9-0 **77** BrettDoyle 4 56
(C E Brittain) *trckd ldrs: effrt 3f out: sn rdn: lost pl over 1f out: eased* **1/1**[1]

1m 44.5s (-0.10) **Going Correction** -0.175s/f (Stan) **4** Ran SP% **110.4**
Speed ratings (Par 98):93,90,89,82
CSF £9.41 TOTE £2.50; EX 11.20.
Owner Allport, Jefferson, Meyrick, Thomas **Bred** Hedgewood Farm **Trained** Whatcombe, Oxon

FOCUS
They went a steady gallop but the winner scored in some style in the end and can take much higher rank.

NOTEBOOK
Circus Polka(USA) ◆, a tall individual, took a keen hold in a tactical race. He sill showed signs of inexperience but was firmly in command at the line. He is a good deal better than a 72-rated two-year-old. (tchd 13-8 and 2-1)
Eau Good, who looked as fit as a flea, travelled smoothly and looked a real danger at one stage, but under pressure he ducked left and he was very much second best in the end. (op 11-4)
Inflagrantedelicto(USA) dawdled round in front. He kept on to finish a well-rewarded third in a nursery carrying an inflated £10,000 prize. (op 10-1)
Sahrati, encountering a totally different surface, was warm at the start on a cold day. The first under pressure, he dropped right away and eventually completed in his own time. This was not his form. (op 15-8)

6949 PONTIN'S BOOK EARLY H'CAP 1m (F)
3:25 (3:25) (Class 6) (0-58,58) 3-Y-0+ **£2,730** (£806; £403) **Stalls** Low

Form RPR

4560 **1** **Vibrato (USA)**[6] 6899 4-8-6 **49** (v[1]) DavidAllan 3 60+
(C J Teague) *swloly into stride: stdy hdwy over 3f out: carried hd high: hung led 1f out: hld on wl towards fin* **6/1**

2102 **2** *¾* **Legal Lover (IRE)**[13] 6819 4-8-8 **58** RussellKennemore(7) 5 66
(R Hollinshead) *t.k.h: trckd ldrs: led over 3f out: hdd 1f out: no ex* **5/2**[1]

0550 **3** *½* **Look Of Eagles**[17] 6781 4-9-1 **58** JosedeSouza 6 65
(P F I Cole) *sn chsng ldrs: chal over 1f out: nt qckn ins last* **9/1**

1424 **4** *1 ½* **Windy Prospect**[22] 6721 4-8-10 **58** KevinGhunowa(5) 8 62
(P A Blockley) *sn chsng ldrs: effrt over 2f out: styd on same pce appr fnl f* **9/2**[3]

0012 **5** *1 ¼* **Cool Sands (IRE)**[8] 6864 4-9-0 **57** (v) DanielTudhope 9 59
(D Shaw) *trckd ldrs on wd outside: t.k.h: effrt over 2f out: wknd last 100yds* **11/4**[2]

-001 **6** *1 ½* **Tee Jay Kassidy**[15] 6798 6-8-10 **53** (v) CatherineGannon 1 51
(P S McEntee) *trckd ldrs: drvn over 4f out: hdwy on inner over 2f out: wknd fnl f* **9/1**

0060 **7** *½* **Razed**[73] 5992 3-8-8 **55** RichardKingscote(3) 2 52
(P L Gilligan) *hld up wl in tch: effrt over 2f out: lost pl over 1f out* **16/1**

6006 **8** *5* **The Terminator (IRE)**[9] 6861 4-7-12 **46** oh6 DuranFentiman(5) 4 33
(M Mullineaux) *s.i.s: a in rr* **50/1**

000 **9** *5* **Bucharest**[13] 6819 3-8-10 **54** MichaelTebbutt 7 30
(M Wigham) *led tl over 3f out: lost pl over 2f out: eased ins last* **20/1**

1m 42.93s (-1.67) **Going Correction** -0.175s/f (Stan)
WFA 3 from 4yo+ 1lb **9** Ran SP% **120.3**
Speed ratings (Par 101):101,100,99,98,97 95,95,90,85
CSF £22.37 CT £138.93 TOTE £7.30: £1.80, £1.40, £3.00; EX 40.10 Trifecta £111.30 Pool £630.33 - 4.02 winning units. Place 6 £34.15, Place 5 £25.78..
Owner Richardson Kelly Smith **Bred** Holtsinger Inc **Trained** Station Town, Co Durham

FOCUS
The form looks solid rated through the second, third and fourth.
Vibrato(USA) Official explanation: trainer said, regarding the improved form shown, that gelding was better suited by being fitted with a visor for the first time
T/Plt: £15.80 to a £1 stake. Pool: £31,811.90. 1,462.50 winning tickets. T/Qpdt: £10.80 to a £1 stake. Pool: £1,798.40. 122.10 winning tickets. WG

6937 WOLVERHAMPTON (A.W) (L-H)
Wednesday, December 27

OFFICIAL GOING: Standard
Wind: Light, behind Weather: Overcast

6950 EBF PONTINSBINGO.COM MAIDEN STKS 1m 141y(P)
3:50 (3:51) (Class 5) 2-Y-0 **£3,886** (£1,156; £577; £288) **Stalls** Low

Form RPR

0 **1** **Lazy Darren**[89] 5658 2-9-3 GeorgeBaker 2 77+
(R Hannon) *trckd ldrs: rdn to ld 1f out: edgd lft: r.o* **2/1**[1]

442 **2** *3 ½* **Lord Oroko**[20] 6737 2-9-3 71 NCallan 10 70
(K A Ryan) *chsd ldr tl led over 2f out: rdn and hdd 1f out: styd on same pce* **7/2**[2]

3 **3** *1 ¾* **Red Petal**[12] 6832 2-8-12 JamieMackay 12 61
(Sir Mark Prescott) *s.i.s: hdwy over 5f out: rdn and hung lft over 1f out: styd on same pce* **5/1**

5 **4** *5* **Razzano (IRE)**[14] 6808 2-8-12 PaulMulrennan 7 51
(P D Evans) *led 6f: rdn and wknd over 1f out* **40/1**

5 *nk* **No Supper (IRE)** 2-9-3 TPQueally 11 55
(M G Quinlan) *hld up in tch: rdn over 2f out: sn wknd* **4/1**[3]

6 *1 ¾* **Rain And Shade** 2-9-3 DeanMcKeown 9 52
(M Johnston) *prom: lost pl over 5f out: n.d after* **12/1**

5 **7** *shd* **Blockley (USA)**[26] 6662 2-9-3 AdamKirby 5 51
(Ian Williams) *sn pushed along in rr: hdwy u.p over 3f out: wknd over 2f out* **40/1**

8 *hd* **Marju's Gold** 2-9-3 ChrisCatlin 8 51
(E J O'Neill) *slowly in to stride: a in rr* **16/1**

00 **9** *shd* **Heaven's Gates**[18] 6757 2-8-12 JamieJones(5) 3 51
(K A Ryan) *chsd ldrs: rdn 1/2-way: wknd over 2f out: hung lft over 1f out* **66/1**

0000 **10** *1 ¼* **King Of The Beers (USA)**[20] 6737 2-8-10 58 (p) TolleyDean(7) 6 48
(R A Harris) *s.i.s: sn pushed along in rr: nt clr run over 2f out: n.d* **66/1**

5 **11** *5* **Kimpton Carer**[11] 6846 2-9-3 RichardThomas 4 38
(J A Geake) *hld up: n.m.r and dropped rr over 6f out: n.d* **80/1**

5 **12** *15* **Acece**[18] 6757 2-8-12 AndrewElliott(5) 1 6
(M Appleby) *prom to 1/2-way* **33/1**

1m 52.71s (0.95) **Going Correction** +0.15s/f (Slow) **12** Ran SP% **117.8**
Speed ratings (Par 96):101,97,96,91,91 90,89,89,89,88 84,70
CSF £8.53 TOTE £2.10: £2.90, £1.60, £1.80; EX 13.90.
Owner J B R Leisure Ltd **Bred** Henry And Mrs Rosemary Moszkowicz **Trained** East Everleigh, Wilts

FOCUS
A fair pace for this maiden, not many got into it and the first three pulled well clear. The winning time was fair for the type of contest, just 0.2 seconds slower than the later handicap for older horses. The form seems sound.

NOTEBOOK
Lazy Darren ◆, not seen since making a promising debut for Michael Wigham at Newmarket in September, was well backed on this first start for his new yard and the market got it absolutely right, as he travelled well just behind the leaders throughout and found plenty when asked. He should find other opportunities. (op 3-1)
Lord Oroko, dropping back a furlong, was always up with the pace and just found the winner's superior turn of foot too much. He has the ability to win an ordinary maiden or handicap, but may appreciate going back over further. (tchd 10-3)
Red Petal, who was unable to lead this time following a tardy start, nonetheless had every chance turning for home but, as on her debut, she was inclined to hang in behind the two leaders and was never quite doing enough. She is nothing special, but in view of her breeding a victory of any sort is probably the goal. (op 9-2 tchd 11-2)
Razzano(IRE) made much of the running, but found the front trio too classy over the last couple of furlongs. She is beginning to look exposed and may be better off in low-grade handicaps in due course. (op 50-1)
No Supper(IRE), a 30,000gns two-year-old whose dam won at up to ten furlongs, was well supported and did eventually do best of the newcomers, but will need to improve from this if he is to win a race. (op 7-2)

6951 WBX.COM WORLD BET EXCHANGE NURSERY 7f 32y(P)
4:20 (4:23) (Class 6) (0-65,65) 2-Y-0 **£3,238** (£963; £481; £240) **Stalls** High

Form RPR

4010 **1** **Homes By Woodford**[4] 6926 2-9-2 **60** SteveDrowne 4 65+
(R A Harris) *hld up in tch: led over 1f out: pushed out* **10/3**[1]

6563 **2** *1 ¼* **Trickle (USA)**[20] 6736 2-9-7 **65** PaulEddery 6 67
(Miss D Mountain) *hld up: hdwy over 2f out: ev ch over 1f out: unable qck ins fnl f* **11/2**[2]

0024 **3** *2* **Kilvickeon (IRE)**[22] 6711 2-8-1 **45** JimmyQuinn 5 42
(Peter Grayson) *chsd ldrs: rdn over 1f out: hung lft and no ex fnl f* **7/1**[3]

0000 **4** *2 ½* **Brierley Lil**[113] 5094 2-8-9 **53** ow1 AdamKirby 2 44
(J L Spearing) *hld up: rdn 1/2-way: hdwy over 1f out: styd on same pce fnl f* **20/1**

0000 **5** *hd* **Brynris**[6] 6900 2-7-12 **42** oh7 PaulQuinn 8 32
(Mrs G S Rees) *prom: rdn 1/2-way: led over 2f out: hdd over 1f out: sn wknd* **100/1**

5423 **6** *shd* **Keep Your Distance**[8] 6872 2-9-6 **64** (t) PaulMulrennan 10 54
(K R Burke) *s.i.s: hld up: styd on u.p ins fnl f: nvr nrr* **10/3**[1]

6261 **7** *2* **Totally Free**[11] 6845 2-9-0 **58** (p) HayleyTurner 11 43
(M D I Usher) *hld up: rdn over 2f out: nvr trbld ldrs* **14/1**

0404 **8** *1* **Devilfishpoker Com**[118] 4955 2-8-4 **48** (b) JamieMackay 9 31
(R C Guest) *dwlt: hld up: nt clr run over 2f out: nvr trbld ldrs* **40/1**

3400 **9** *hd* **Calloff The Search**[18] 6757 2-8-12 **56** TonyCulhane 1 38
(W G M Turner) *led: hdd 6f out: chsd ldrs: rdn over 2f out: wknd fnl f* **17/2**

3010 **10** *1* **Pat Will (IRE)**[141] 4222 2-9-0 **58** NCallan 3 38
(P D Evans) *mid-div: rdn 1/2-way: wknd over 1f out* **7/1**[3]

060 **11** *hd* **Childish Thoughts**[12] 6826 2-8-1 **45** RichardThomas 7 24
(Mrs Norma Pook) *led 6f out: sn hdd: hung rt and led again 1/2-way: continued to hang rt: hdd over 2f out: wknd wl over 1f out* **40/1**

0060 **12** *31* **Bonny Scotland (IRE)**[138] 4334 2-7-10 **45**.......... NataliaGemelova[(5)] 12 —
(I W McInnes) *racd keenly: led over 5f out: sddle slipped and hdd 1/2-way: wknd over 2f out* **25/1**

1m 32.98s (2.58) **Going Correction** +0.15s/f (Slow) **12** Ran SP% **118.2**
Speed ratings (Par 94):91,89,87,84,84 84,81,80,80,79 79,43
CSF £20.37 CT £122.29 TOTE £6.40: £1.90, £2.40, £1.80; EX 19.70.
Owner Mrs Ruth M Serrell **Bred** Mrs H B Raw **Trained** Earlswood, Monmouths

FOCUS
A modest nursery and unlike in the opener, this race suited those that were held up off the pace. The winner looks well handicapped and there could be more to come, while the overall form looks sound.

NOTEBOOK
Homes By Woodford, who missed an engagement here the previous day having suffered a bout of colic and then been cast in his box over the Christmas period, was back in top form here and appreciated this return to seven furlongs. His only moment of worry was whether he would get a clear run turning for home, but one emerged - partly by him nudging Kilvickeon aside - and he made no mistake from thereon in. (op 7-2 tchd 4-1)
Trickle(USA), 3lb better off with Homes By Woodford for a half-length beating over course and distance earlier in the month, came through to hold every chance in the home straight but her old rival kept pulling out more. She may appreciate a return to a mile. (op 4-1 tchd 6-1)
Kilvickeon(IRE), who ran poorly on his only previous try over this trip, performed better this time. He had every chance turning for home, but after being forced wide as the winner eased him out of the way he was then inclined to lurch to his left under pressure and was not doing anything like enough. (op 6-1)
Brierley Lil, beaten out of sight in four starts on turf, showed a little bit more on this sand debut following a near four-month break and may be capable of winning a modest race. (op 16-1)
Brynris, beaten a long way in all four of his previous starts, responded well to a positive ride and was not beaten off until the last furlong. At first glance his proximity does nothing for the form, but it was probably more of a case of him running above himself. (op 66-1)
Keep Your Distance did his chances no good with a tardy start over a trip he was likely to find on the sharp side in any case. He travelled well at the back, but when asked for his effort it was much too little too late. A sharper exit and a return to further will see him in a better light. Official explanation: jockey said gelding was slowly into stride and lost an early position (op 5-1 tchd 3-1)
Pat Will(IRE) Official explanation: jockey said filly hung right-handed from halfway round bend
Childish Thoughts Official explanation: jockey said filly hung right-handed throughout

6952 WBX.COM WORLD BET EXCHANGE H'CAP 7f 32y(P)
4:50 (4:52) (Class 6) (0-68,68) 3-Y-0+ **£3,238** (£963; £481; £240) **Stalls** High

Form RPR
5060 **1** **Plateau**[26] 6656 7-8-13 **65**.......................... TPQueally 5 77
(C R Dore) *mid-div: rdn 1/2-way: hdwy over 2f out: sn chsng ldr: rdn to ld and edgd lft ins fnl f: r.o* **33/1**
4221 **2** *1* **Cross Of Lorraine (IRE)**[21] 6731 3-8-7 **62**..................(b) GregFairley[(3)] 7 72
(I Semple) *chsd ldrs: led over 2f out: rdn over 1f out: hdd and unable qck ins fnl f* **13/8**[1]
0045 **3** *3* **Supercast (IRE)**[5] 6919 3-9-2 **68**.......................... NCallan 6 70
(W M Brisbourne) *hld up: hdwy 2f out: sn rdn: hung lft and no ex fnl f* **8/1**
3503 **4** *shd* **Buzzin'Boyzee (IRE)**[5] 6919 3-7-13 **58**.................. WilliamBuick[(7)] 3 60
(P D Evans) *hld up: hdwy over 1f out: edgd lft ins fnl f: styd on* **8/1**
0606 **5** *nk* **Zarabad (IRE)**[4] 6932 4-8-12 **64**.......................... PaulMulrennan 4 65
(K R Burke) *hld up: plld hrd: nt clr run over 2f out: hdwy over 1f out: nt trble ldrs* **12/1**
0206 **6** *2 ½* **Scuba (IRE)**[19] 6747 4-8-13 **65**..................(b) SteveDrowne 1 59
(H Morrison) *prom: lost pl 4f out: n.d after* **3/1**[2]
0006 **7** *nk* **General Feeling (IRE)**[13] 6823 5-8-5 **62**.............. AndrewElliott[(5)] 8 56
(M Mullineaux) *s.i.s: hld up: hdwy over 2f out: hung rt and wknd over 1f out* **7/1**[3]
5000 **8** *5* **Sands Of Barra (IRE)**[19] 6747 3-8-11 **63**.................. JimmyQuinn 2 44
(I W McInnes) *chsd ldrs over 5f* **14/1**
0063 **9** *1 ¾* **Ask No More**[6] 6898 3-8-11 **63**..................(b) DeanMcKeown 9 39
(P L Gilligan) *sn led: hdd over 2f out: wknd wl over 1f out* **20/1**
00-0 **10** *42* **Oranges And Lemons (FR)**[28] 6652 3-8-9 **61** ow1........ AdamKirby 10 —
(C E Brittain) *chsd ldrs: rdn 1/2-way: wknd and eased over 2f out* **66/1**

1m 31.4s (1.00) **Going Correction** +0.15s/f (Slow) **10** Ran SP% **121.4**
Speed ratings (Par 101):100,98,95,95,94 92,91,86,84,36
CSF £89.50 CT £517.85 TOTE £35.10: £10.80, £1.20, £3.50; EX 94.50.
Owner Page, Ward, Marsh **Bred** Juddmonte Farms **Trained** West Pinchbeck, Lincs

FOCUS
A moderate handicap and something of a shock result, but the form appears sound enough. The early pace was strong, but those that set it paid for it.

6953 BONUSPRINT.COM H'CAP 5f 20y(P)
5:20 (5:20) (Class 4) (0-80,80) 3-Y-0+ **£6,477** (£1,927; £963; £481) **Stalls** Low

Form RPR
0530 **1** **Efistorm**[22] 6720 5-8-11 **76**.......................... JasonEdmunds[(3)] 7 86
(J Balding) *trckd ldrs: rdn to ld wl ins fnl f: r.o* **11/1**
022 **2** *¾* **Financial Times (USA)**[4] 6935 4-8-8 **70**..................(t) MickyFenton 2 77
(Stef Liddiard) *sn led: rdn and hdd wl ins fnl f* **2/1**[1]
6100 **3** *1 ½* **Magic Glade**[80] 5832 7-8-11 **73**.......................... RichardThomas 3 75
(Tom Dascombe) *chsd ldr: rdn over 1f out: edgd lft and no ex ins fnl f* **11/2**[3]
2235 **4** *1 ¼* **Millinsky (USA)**[25] 6682 5-9-0 **76**.......................... SteveDrowne 5 73
(Rae Guest) *chsd ldrs: rdn over 1f out: no ex ins fnl f* **9/1**
3014 **5** *1 ¼* **Sahara Silk (IRE)**[6] 6896 5-8-4 **73**..................(v) WilliamBuick[(7)] 1 66
(D Shaw) *soon outpcd: styd on ins fnl f: nvr nrr* **7/2**[2]
6510 **6** *½* **Sparkwell**[8] 6865 4-8-6 **68** ow2.......................... DeanMcKeown 8 59
(D Shaw) *hld up: hdwy 1/2-way: hung lft and wknd over 1f out* **8/1**
0200 **7** *¾* **Polish Emperor (USA)**[42] 6496 6-9-4 **80**..................(p) NCallan 6 68
(D W Barker) *trckd ldrs: rdn 1/2-way: wknd over 1f out* **25/1**
1024 **8** *5* **Fizzlephut (IRE)**[13] 6823 4-8-8 **70**.......................... PaulFitzsimons 4 40
(Miss J R Tooth) *chsd ldrs: rdn 1/2-way: wknd 2f out* **11/1**

62.75 secs (-0.07) **Going Correction** +0.15s/f (Slow) **8** Ran SP% **112.6**
Speed ratings (Par 105):106,104,102,100,98 97,96,88
CSF £32.39 CT £137.50 TOTE £14.60: £4.30, £1.10, £2.50; EX 44.20.
Owner Mrs Jo Hardy **Bred** E Duggan And D Churchman **Trained** Scrooby, Notts

FOCUS
A fair handicap of its type and predictably there was no hanging around. The winner returned to the form of his Southwell win in March.

6954 WBXTRIPLECROWN.COM H'CAP 1m 4f 50y(P)
5:50 (5:51) (Class 6) (0-65,68) 3-Y-0+ **£3,071** (£906; £453) **Stalls** Low

Form RPR
6215 **1** **Melvino**[7] 6883 4-9-3 **59**.......................... DeanMcKeown 3 68
(T D Barron) *s.i.s: hld up: hdwy over 3f out: led and hung lft fr over 1f out: styd on* **3/1**[1]
00-0 **2** *1 ¾* **Key Partners (IRE)**[12] 6837 5-9-7 **63**.......................... GeorgeBaker 2 69
(B D Leavy) *hld up: hdwy u.p and hung lft over 1f out: styd on* **16/1**
0505 **3** *1 ¾* **Barbirolli**[12] 6837 4-9-4 **60**..................(v) NCallan 7 63
(W M Brisbourne) *hld up: hdwy over 2f out: chsd wnr over 1f out: no ex ins fnl f* **13/2**[3]
3220 **4** *1 ¼* **Keisha Kayleigh (IRE)**[18] 6767 3-8-7 **57**..................(p) GregFairley[(3)] 11 58
(B Ellison) *hld up: hdwy: hung lft and nt clr run over 1f out: styd on u.p: nt trble ldrs* **9/1**
0055 **5** *hd* **Three Thieves (UAE)**[13] 6825 3-9-2 **63**.......................... TonyCulhane 5 64
(M S Saunders) *hld up: hdwy 7f out: rdn over 2f out: styd on same pce appr fnl f* **8/1**
5/05 **6** *5* **Blushing Prince (IRE)**[54] 4568 8-8-7 **49** oh9............(t) JamieMackay 12 42
(R C Guest) *hld up: plld hrd: hdwy 8f out: chsd ldr 5f out: rdn and ev ch over 1f out: sn wknd* **50/1**
2251 **7** *¾* **Siena Star (IRE)**[8] 6870 8-9-12 **68** 7ex.......................... MickyFenton 1 60
(Stef Liddiard) *chsd ldrs: rdn over 2f out: wknd over 1f out* **10/1**
0254 **8** *1 ¼* **Wassfa**[17] 6775 3-9-1 **62**.......................... BrettDoyle 6 52
(C E Brittain) *sn led: hdd & wknd over 1f out* **11/2**[2]
54-0 **9** *3* **Zonic Boom (FR)**[20] 156 6-8-7 **56**..................(tp) WilliamBuick[(7)] 8 41
(Heather Dalton) *mid-div: lost pl 7f out: n.d after* **9/1**
0666 **10** *10* **Bubbling Fun**[23] 6701 5-8-7 **49** oh4.......................... HayleyTurner 4 18
(T Wall) *prom: rdn over 3f out: wknd over 2f out* **33/1**
101- **11** *2 ½* **Tresor Secret (FR)**[506] 4226 6-9-4 **60**.......................... JimCrowley 10 25
(J Gallagher) *prom over 8f* **13/2**[3]
6- **12** *1 ¼* **Presently Blessed (IRE)**[193] 2667 3-8-7 **54**.......... CatherineGannon 9 17
(K A Ryan) *chsd ldrs over 9f* **40/1**

2m 45.13s (2.71) **Going Correction** +0.15s/f (Slow)
WFA 3 from 4yo+ 5lb **12** Ran SP% **120.5**
Speed ratings (Par 101):96,94,93,92,92 89,88,88,86,79 77,76
CSF £56.50 CT £300.22 TOTE £3.90: £1.40, £6.30, £3.40; EX 85.40.
Owner Theo Williams and Charles Mocatta **Bred** T J Cooper **Trained** Maunby, N Yorks

FOCUS
A modest handicap in which the early pace was ordinary and those that were held up were very much favoured.

6955 PHOTO BOOKS FROM BONUSPRINT.COM H'CAP 1m 141y(P)
6:20 (6:21) (Class 6) (0-53,53) 3-Y-0+ **£2,914** (£867; £433; £216) **Stalls** Low

Form RPR
000 **1** **Golden Spectrum (IRE)**[6] 6897 7-8-7 **53**..................(b) TolleyDean[(7)] 5 63
(R A Harris) *hld up: hdwy over 2f out: rdn to ld and edgd lft ins fnl f: r.o* **40/1**
0553 **2** *1 ¾* **Grand Palace (IRE)**[12] 6829 3-8-9 **50**..................(v) DeanMcKeown 4 56
(D Shaw) *a.p: rdn to chse ldr and hung lft over 1f out: styng on same pce whn n.m.r ins fnl f* **16/1**
4002 **3** *nk* **Lobengula (IRE)**[6] 6899 4-8-13 **52**.......................... JimmyQuinn 9 57
(I W McInnes) *trckd ldrs: racd keenly: led over 2f out: rdn: edgd lft and hdd ins fnl f: no ex* **4/1**[3]
5131 **4** *2 ½* **Majehar**[9] 6854 4-8-11 **53** 7ex.......................... AmirQuinn[(3)] 2 53
(A G Newcombe) *prom: rdn over 1f out: styd on same pce* **3/1**[2]
0321 **5** *2* **Green Pirate**[14] 6802 4-8-7 **53**.......................... WilliamBuick[(7)] 6 49+
(W M Brisbourne) *s.i.s: hld up: nt clr run over 2f out: hdwy over 1f out : nt trble ldrs* **15/8**[1]
600 **6** *5* **Red Raptor**[212] 2063 5-9-0 **53**..................(t) RichardThomas 1 38
(J A Geake) *hld up: hmpd over 3f out: rdn over 1f out: n.d* **50/1**
0035 **7** *2 ½* **Merdiff**[16] 6793 7-8-10 **49**.......................... DavidAllan 7 29
(W M Brisbourne) *hld up: hdwy over 2f out: wknd over 1f out* **14/1**
0344 **8** *1 ½* **Kareeb (FR)**[16] 6793 9-9-0 **53**..................(p) AdamKirby 8 30
(Miss J Feilden) *hld up: rdn over 2f out: n.d* **14/1**
5045 **9** *2* **Spoilsport**[6] 6899 3-8-10 **51**..................(b[1]) JimCrowley 3 24
(P D Evans) *dwlt: hld up: a in rr* **16/1**
4610 **10** *¾* **Miss Porcia**[32] 6608 5-8-11 53.......................... JerryO'Dwyer[(3)] 13 24
(P A Blockley) *chsd ldrs over 6f* **40/1**
6065 **11** *½* **Seldemosa**[12] 6829 5-8-11 **50**.......................... TonyCulhane 11 20
(M S Saunders) *s.i.s: hld up: effrt over 2f out: sn wknd* **25/1**
0304 **12** *5* **Wiltshire (IRE)**[16] 6787 4-8-12 **51**..................(p) MickyFenton 12 11
(P T Midgley) *sn led: hdd over 2f out: wknd over 1f out* **12/1**
-000 **13** *3 ½* **Moors Myth**[237] 606 5-8-6 **52**.......................... KarenKenny[(7)] 10 4
(B G Powell) *prom 6f* **66/1**

1m 52.51s (0.75) **Going Correction** +0.15s/f (Slow)
WFA 3 from 4yo+ 2lb **13** Ran SP% **124.8**
Speed ratings (Par 101):102,100,100,97,96 91,89,88,86,85 85,80,77
CSF £587.34 CT £3140.65 TOTE £62.20: £15.50, £4.10, £1.50; EX 590.80 Place 6 £48.50, Place 5 £34.98.
Owner Peter A Price **Bred** Orpendale And Global Investments **Trained** Earlswood, Monmouths

FOCUS
A modest if competitive handicap and another shock result, but the form looks solid.
T/Plt: £68.30 to a £1 stake. Pool: £64,199.65. 685.70 winning tickets. T/Qpdt: £35.10 to a £1 stake. Pool: £6,344.50. 133.60 winning tickets. CR

6943 SOUTHWELL (L-H)
Thursday, December 28

OFFICIAL GOING: Standard
Wind: Virtually nil

6956 GO PONTIN'S BANDED STKS 5f (F)
12:40 (12:40) (Class 7) 3-Y-0+ **£1,876** (£554; £277) **Stalls** High

Form RPR
2415 **1** **Gifted Lass**[8] 6877 4-9-3 50.......................... DavidAllan 4 69+
(J Balding) *cl up: led over 2f out: rdn clr appr last* **7/2**[1]
0560 **2** *5* **Orchestration (IRE)**[6] 6906 5-8-12 45..................(v) DaleGibson 10 45
(M J Attwater) *midfield: hdwy 2f out: sn rdn and styd on ins last* **9/2**[3]
0000 **3** *½* **Amber Glory**[10] 6856 3-9-0 50..................(b) AndrewMullen[(3)] 1 48
(K A Ryan) *wnt rt s: a.p: rdn along to chse wnr wl over 1f out: sn drvn and one pce* **11/1**
0000 **4** *3* **Tribute (IRE)**[170] 3390 5-9-3 50.......................... PaulMulrennan 5 38
(John A Harris) *bhd: pushed alonga nd hdwy wl over 1f out: sn rdn and kpt on ins last: nrst fin* **22/1**
4003 **5** *2* **Campeon (IRE)**[20] 6755 4-9-0 47.......................... MickyFenton 12 28
(J M Bradley) *chsd ldrs: rdn along 2f out: kpt on same pce* **10/1**
0104 **6** *hd* **Borzoi Maestro**[20] 6753 5-9-3 50..................(b) AdamKirby 6 31
(M Wellings) *led: rdn along 1/2-way: sn hdd: drvn and wknd over 1f out* **4/1**[2]

5040 **7** *1 ½* **Estoille**[38] 6533 5-8-12 45.. RobertWinston 8 — 21
(Mrs S Lamyman) *in tch: hdwy to chse ldrs 1/2-way: sn rdn and wknd over 1f out* **7/1**

0000 **8** *1 ¾* **Percy Douglas**[38] 6539 6-8-11 49................................(b) AnnStokell(5) 2 — 19
(Miss A Stokell) *bmpd s: a rr* **25/1**

0000 **9** *hd* **Xpres Boy (IRE)**[26] 6674 3-9-3 50....................................(t) PhillipMakin 9 — 19
(S R Bowring) *chsd ldrs: rdn along over 2f out: sn wknd* **25/1**

0000 **10** *2* **Golband**[55] 6325 4-8-12 50.. AshleyHamblett(5) 7 — 12
(R F Marvin) *cl up: rdn along 1/2-way: sn wknd* **28/1**

0000 **11** *2* **Henry Tun**[20] 6755 8-8-12 48................................(b) JasonEdmunds(3) 13 — 3
(J Balding) *a towards rr* **12/1**

0010 **12** *1 ¼* **She's Our Beauty (IRE)**[20] 6755 3-8-8 46..........(v) DuranFentiman(5) 14 — —
(S T Mason) *a towards rr* **14/1**

4000 **13** *1* **Rambling Socks**[23] 6719 3-9-2 49...........................(p) MichaelTebbutt 11 — —
(S R Bowring) *dwlt: a bhd* **50/1**

60.42 secs (0.12) **Going Correction** -0.05s/f (Stan) **13** Ran SP% **122.1**
Speed ratings (Par 97):97,89,88,83,80 79,77,74,74,71 67,65,64
CSF £18.17 TOTE £3.50: £1.40, £2.40, £3.90; EX 30.70 TRIFECTA Not won..
Owner Bawtry Racing Partnership **Bred** Charles Castle **Trained** Scrooby, Notts

FOCUS
Not a bad banded sprint, won decisively by the improving Gifted Lass who is better than this grade.
Estoille Official explanation: trainer said mare finished distressed

6957 PERSONALISED CALENDARS FROM BONUSPRINT.COM BANDED STKS — 2m (F)
1:10 (1:10) (Class 7) 3-Y-0+ — **£1,876** (£554; £277) **Stalls** Low

Form — RPR

1000 **1** **Galantos (GER)**[120] 4929 5-9-11 50..................................... BrettDoyle 5 — 63
(G L Moore) *hld up in rr: stdy hdwy over 6f out: led 2f out: sn rdn and kpt on* **2/1**[1]

0044 **2** *1 ½* **Asleep At The Back (IRE)**[19] 6759 3-8-12 45.............. JamieMackay 8 — 56
(J G Given) *midfield: hdwy 6f out: chsd ldr over 4f out: effrt to chal over 2f out: ev ch tl drvn and one pce ins last* **5/1**[3]

5150 **3** *20* **Bold Trump**[140] 4282 5-9-9 48... LeeEnstone 1 — 46+
(Mrs N S Evans) *prom: led over 6f out: rdn along 3f out: hdd 2f out: sn drvn and outpcd* **8/1**

54-1 **4** *6* **Elaala (USA)**[289] 635 4-9-8 50................................ JasonEdmunds(3) 10 — 30
(B D Leavy) *hld up in rr: hdwy over 6f out: chsd ldrs over 3f out: sn rdn and wknd* **10/3**[2]

0000 **5** *1 ¾* **Elli Lewtia**[10] 6860 3-8-12 35.......................................(b[1]) DerekMcGaffin 2 — 23
(J Jay) *chsd ldrs: rdn along 1/2-way: drvn and wknd over 3f out* **66/1**

0364 **6** *1 ½* **Linton Dancer (IRE)**[19] 6765 3-8-12 45............................ DaleGibson 9 — 21
(J R Weymes) *dwlt: keen: hld up in rr: sme hdwy 4f out: sn rdn along and nvr a factor* **12/1**

0440 **7** *8* **Beaumont Girl (IRE)**[117] 5033 4-9-3 40.........................(t) DominicFox(3) 6 — 12
(Miss M E Rowland) *led: rdn along and hdd over 6f out: sn wknd* **20/1**

0-00 **8** *3 ½* **Scorchio (IRE)**[16] 6795 5-9-6 45................................... MatthewHenry 3 — 7
(B Smart) *chsd ldrs: rdn along over 4f out: wknd over 3f out* **8/1**

6040 **9** *5* **Matinee Idol**[17] 6790 3-8-12 45.................................. CatherineGannon 4 — 1
(Mrs S Lamyman) *midfield: lost pl and bhd fnl 4f* **20/1**

0500 **10** *125* **Mighty Duel**[16] 6799 3-8-12 40..(tp) PaulMulrennan 7 — —
(J R Norton) *cl up: rdn along and wknd qckly over 6f out: sn bhd and t.o fnl 3f* **100/1**

0046 **P** **Kalush**[9] 6873 5-9-1 40... AnnStokell(5) 11 — —
(Miss A Stokell) *a rr: bhd whn p.u 2f out: dismntd* **20/1**

3m 46.64s (2.10) **Going Correction** +0.025s/f (Slow)
WFA 3 from 4yo+ 8lb **11** Ran SP% **119.8**
Speed ratings (Par 97):95,94,84,81,80 79,75,73,71,— —
CSF £11.62 TOTE £2.60: £1.10, £1.60, £3.40; EX 10.70 Trifecta £88.20 Pool: £284.68 - 2.29 winning tickets..
Owner Allen & Associates **Bred** R Zimmer **Trained** Woodingdean, E Sussex
■ Stewards' Enquiry : Derek McGaffin two-day ban: used whip in wrong position and without allowing time to respond (Jan 8-9)

FOCUS
A weak banded event, with very few of these having anything like a convincing profile, and the first two pulled a long way clear in the straight.

6958 PONTINS.COM TRI-BANDED STKS — 6f (F)
1:40 (1:40) (Class 7) 3-Y-0 — **£1,876** (£554; £277) **Stalls** Low

Form — RPR

0000 **1** **Dodaa (USA)**[16] 6794 3-8-7 40.. MatthewHenry 6 — 45
(N Wilson) *mde all: rdn 2f out: drvn ent last and styd on* **18/1**

5005 **2** *1 ¼* **Bold Love**[16] 6794 3-8-5 40 ow1..............................(b[1]) JasonEdmunds(3) 3 — 42
(J Balding) *stdd s: hld up in tch: hdwy 2f out: rdn to chse ldrs over 1f out: swtchd lft ins last: styd on wl towards fin* **5/1**

0602 **3** *shd* **Astorygoeswithit**[16] 6794 3-8-12 45...................(b) CatherineGannon 5 — 46
(P S McEntee) *chsd ldrs: rdn to c hase wnr 2f out: swtchd rt over 1f out: sn drvn and hung rt: kpt on* **7/2**[2]

0004 **4** *hd* **No Inkling (IRE)**[56] 6306 3-8-2 35.................................(p) DeanMernagh 4 — 35
(John A Harris) *chsd ldrs on inner: rdn 2f out: styd alone far rail: drvn and ch over 1f out tl no ex wl ins last* **8/1**

0000 **5** *4* **Red Vixen (IRE)**[24] 6707 3-8-9 45...........................(be[1]) DominicFox(3) 2 — 33
(C N Allen) *outpcd and bhd tl styd fnl 2f: nt rch ldrs* **9/1**

0464 **6** *5* **Marron Flore**[16] 6794 3-8-12 45...................................(tp) RichardThomas 1 — 18
(A J Lidderdale) *sn outpcd and a rr* **9/2**[3]

0600 **7** *1 ¼* **Spinning Dancer (IRE)**[19] 6765 3-8-2 30..................(v[1]) JosedeSouza 8 — 4
(J R Holt) *cl up: rdn along 3f out and sn wknd* **50/1**

0060 **8** *nk* **Cate Washington**[146] 4120 3-8-12 45.................................... DaleGibson 7 — 13
(Mrs L Williamson) *a rr* **14/1**

0000 **9** *¾* **Teddy Monty (IRE)**[19] 6763 3-8-7 40.........................(b) PaulMulrennan 10 — 6
(R E Barr) *s.i.s: a rr* **20/1**

0 **10** *½* **Deneuve**[16] 6796 3-8-12 45...(tp) BrettDoyle 9 — 10
(M G Quinlan) *chsd ldrs: rdn along over 2f out: sn drvn and wknd* **11/4**[1]

1m 18.0s (1.10) **Going Correction** +0.025s/f (Slow) **10** Ran SP% **123.5**
Speed ratings (Par 96):93,91,91,90,85 78,77,76,75,75
CSF £111.84 TOTE £23.50: £8.70, £3.00, £1.20; EX 224.90 TRIFECTA Not won..
Owner Ian W Glenton and Paul and Linda Dixon **Bred** Silverleaf Farm Inc **Trained** Flaxton, N Yorks
■ Noel Wilson's first winner from his new yard.
■ Stewards' Enquiry : Jason Edmunds £275 fine: failed to stay in weighing room for five minutes after weighed-in
Catherine Gannon two-day ban: careless riding (Jan 9-10); £275 fine: failed to stay in weighing room for five minutes after weighed-in

FOCUS
Few obvious candidates for another race lacking strength in depth. Typically weak form.

6959 NORKING ALUMINIUM BANDED STKS — 1m 3f (F)
2:10 (2:10) (Class 7) 3-Y-0+ — **£1,672** (£493; £246) **Stalls** Low

Form — RPR

6040 **1** **Padre Nostro (IRE)**[37] 6553 7-8-9 45....................... ChrisGlenister(7) 14 — 56
(J R Holt) *hld up: hdwy and in tch 4f out: effrt wl over 1f out: rdn and styd on strly to ld ins last* **8/1**

6600 **2** *nk* **Boppys Dancer**[10] 6852 3-8-12 45...............................(b[1]) MickyFenton 13 — 55
(P T Midgley) *trckd ldrs: hdwy 4f out: rdn 2f out: led over 1f out: drvn and hdd ins last: kpt on* **66/1**

0451 **3** *3* **Kentucky Bullet (USA)**[16] 6795 10-9-2 45..................... SamHitchcott 8 — 50
(A G Newcombe) *bhd: pushed along over 4f out: hdwy over 2f out: rdn wl over 1f out: styd on ins last: nrst fin* **5/1**[2]

0060 **4** *½* **Danelor (IRE)**[19] 6762 8-9-4 47..(p) AdamKirby 7 — 51
(D Shaw) *trckd ldrs: hdwy 4f out: chal 2f out and sn rdn: drvn and wknd ent last* **10/1**

3253 **5** *nk* **Abbeygate**[22] 6729 5-9-5 48.. J-PGuillambert 10 — 52
(T Keddy) *hld up in rr: hdwy over 4f out: wd st: rdn to chse ldrs wl over 1f out: sn drvn and no impression* **11/4**[1]

0003 **6** *shd* **Louve Heureuse (IRE)**[15] 6800 5-8-13 45........... RichardKingscote(3) 6 — 48
(B G Powell) *prom: led 1/2-way: rdn along 2f out: sn drvn: hdd & wknd over 1f out* **12/1**

0-05 **7** *5* **Krasivi's Boy (USA)**[10] 6857 4-9-7 50..........................(be) GeorgeBaker 5 — 45
(G L Moore) *hld up in rr: pushed along and outpcd over 3f out: styd on fnl 2f: nt rch ldrs* **11/2**[3]

4014 **8** *2* **Tiegs (IRE)**[275] 785 4-8-12 48.................................... WilliamCarson(7) 12 — 40
(P W Hiatt) *midfield: rdn along over 3f out and sn wknd* **16/1**

0455 **9** *nk* **Suffolk House**[31] 6628 4-9-2 45.................................... DeanMcKeown 11 — 36
(M Brittain) *prom: effrt over 3f out: rdn over 2f out and grad wknd* **25/1**

0504 **10** *1* **Jiminor Mack**[85] 5767 3-8-12 45...............................(b[1]) PaulMulrennan 9 — 34
(W J H Ratcliffe) *cl up: rdn along over 4f out: wknd 3f out* **16/1**

050- **11** *21* **Alphun (IRE)**[494] 4239 4-9-7 50...................................... RobertWinston 1 — 4
(G A Swinbank) *keen: chsd ldrs on inner: rdn along 4f out: wknd 3f out* **13/2**

-000 **12** *nk* **Herninski**[57] 4471 3-8-8 48.................................. RussellKennemore(7) 2 — 1
(M C Chapman) *s.i.s: a rr* **66/1**

3445 **13** *23* **Beamsley Beacon**[282] 686 5-8-11 45..................(b) DuranFentiman(5) 4 — —
(S T Mason) *keen: led: poushed along and hdd 1/2-way: wknd 4f out* **18/1**

2m 30.01s (1.11) **Going Correction** +0.025s/f (Slow)
WFA 3 from 4yo+ 4lb **13** Ran SP% **123.8**
Speed ratings (Par 97):96,95,93,93,93 92,89,87,87,86 71,71,54
CSF £471.43 TOTE £9.80: £3.10, £10.40, £1.90; EX 241.40 TRIFECTA Not won..
Owner Mrs E Glenister **Bred** Mrs G P Gaffney **Trained** Peckleton, Leics

FOCUS
Plenty with questions to answer in another uncompetitive race, but they went a good gallop and the form looks sound.

6960 PHOTO GIFTS FROM BONUSPRINT.COM BANDED STKS — 1m (F)
2:40 (2:41) (Class 7) 3-Y-0+ — **£1,876** (£554; £277) **Stalls** Low

Form — RPR

6245 **1** **Paso Doble**[7] 6892 8-8-13 50.. JamesMillman(5) 5 — 58
(D K Ivory) *in tch: hdwy to chse ldr 2f out: sn ridde: drvn and sltly outpcd ent last: styd on wl last 100 yds to ld nr line* **5/1**[1]

0235 **2** *shd* **Louisiade (IRE)**[10] 6855 5-9-1 50............................(p) AndrewMullen(3) 12 — 58
(K A Ryan) *promoinent: led over 3f out: rdn clr wl over 1f out: drvn ins last: hdd and no ex nr line* **5/1**[1]

6025 **3** *1* **Wodhill Schnaps**[7] 6897 5-9-3 49...............................(b) HayleyTurner 13 — 55
(D Morris) *bhd: wd st and gd hdwy over 2f out: rdn to chse wnr ent last: sn drvn and ev ch tl no ex last 100 yds* **13/2**

4636 **4** *5* **Lucius Verrus (USA)**[7] 6897 6-9-1 47.............................(v) AdamKirby 1 — 42
(D Shaw) *chsd ldrs: rdn along 2f out: sn drvn and kpt on same pce* **6/1**[3]

3042 **5** *2* **Tacid**[16] 6799 4-9-0 46..(v[1]) RobertHavlin 10 — 37
(Dr J D Scargill) *hld up in tch: hdwy to chse ldrs over 2f out: sn rdn and kpt on same pce* **11/2**[2]

4060 **6** *1 ¼* **Quiet Reading (USA)**[30] 6641 9-9-4 50..........................(v) GeorgeBaker 4 — 38
(M R Bosley) *cl up: rdn along over 2f out: grad wknd* **8/1**

5651 **7** *2 ½* **Sonderborg**[16] 6799 5-9-2 48...(p) DaleGibson 8 — 31
(J Mackie) *bhd and rdn along 1/2-way: nvr nr ldrs* **7/1**

0000 **8** *1* **Cankara (IRE)**[31] 6618 3-8-12 45.................................... DanielTudhope 7 — 26
(D Carroll) *in tch: rdn along wl over 2f out: sn wknd* **20/1**

6224 **9** *1 ¼* **Weet Yer Tern (IRE)**[15] 6800 4-9-1 47................ RobertWinston 11 — 25
(W M Brisbourne) *chsd ldrs: rdn along wl over 2f out: sn wknd* **15/2**

0000 **10** *3* **Crusoe (IRE)**[7] 6897 9-9-0 45 ow1..................................... BrianReilly 9 — 18
(A Sadik) *chsd ldrs. lost pl after 2f and sn bhd* **33/1**

2400 **11** *14* **Tommytyler (IRE)**[37] 6552 7-8-6 45...............................(t) GaryWales(7) 2 — —
(D Carroll) *led: pushed along and hdd over 3f out: sn rdn and wknd* **40/1**

1m 44.02s (-0.58) **Going Correction** +0.025s/f (Slow)
WFA 3 from 4yo+ 1lb **11** Ran SP% **121.9**
Speed ratings (Par 97):103,102,101,96,94 93,91,90,88,85 71
CSF £30.34 TOTE £7.00: £2.50, £2.30, £3.00; EX 31.00 Trifecta £128.80 Part won. Pool: £181.42 - 0.50 winning tickets..
Owner Mrs H Brain **Bred** P Cutler **Trained** Radlett, Herts

FOCUS
Competitive fare as banded races go, with plenty seemingly having the form to take a hand, and the first three probably did well to pull clear of the rest.
Tommytyler(IRE) Official explanation: trainer said gelding bled from the nose

6961 PONTINSBINGO.COM BANDED STKS — 7f (F)
3:10 (3:11) (Class 7) 3-Y-0+ — **£1,706** (£503; £252) **Stalls** Low

Form — RPR

1564 **1** **Capital Lass**[7] 6892 3-9-1 48... HayleyTurner 2 — 61
(D K Ivory) *trckd ldrs gng wl: smooth bhdwy over 2f out: led 11/2f out: sn rdn clr* **11/1**

6654 **2** *2 ½* **Favouring (IRE)**[16] 6798 4-8-8 48.....................(v) RussellKennemore(7) 8 — 55+
(M C Chapman) *n.m.r after 100 yds: midfield whn n.m.r over 4f out: hdwy on inner 3f out: rdn to chse wnr 1f out: no imp* **4/1**[1]

2060 **3** *1 ¾* **Barry The Brave**[30] 6648 4-9-0 50................................ GregFairley(3) 1 — 52
(Micky Hammond) *cl up: led 1/2-way: rdn wl over 2f out: hdd 11/2f out: sn drvn and kpt on same pce* **25/1**

0603 **4** *1 ¼* **Wodhill Be**[38] 6542 6-8-12 45...................................... DerekMcGaffin 11 — 44
(D Morris) *s.i.s and bhd: hdwy over 2f out: sn rdn and kpt on approachiong last: nrst fin* **20/1**

0606 **5** *hd* **Almowj**[10] 6856 3-8-5 45... WilliamCarson(7) 13 — 43+
(C E Brittain) *bhd: hdwy 2f out: swtchd lft and rdn ent last: styd on wl towards fin* **14/1**

5530 **6** ½ **Barzak (IRE)**[7] 6897 6-9-2 49............(bt) DaleGibson 6 46
(S R Bowring) *chsd ldrs: rdn along wl over 2f out: sn one pce* **10/1**

63 **7** ¾ **Tackcoat (IRE)**[10] 6854 6-8-9 40............(p) JerryO'Dwyer(3) 12 40
(Eoin Doyle, Ire) *cl up: led after 2f: rdn along and hdd 1/2-way: wknd 2f out* **7/1**[3]

0404 **8** 1 **Monkey Madge**[37] 6554 4-8-12 45............ PaulMulrennan 10 37
(B Smart) *chsd ldrs: rdn along wl over 2f out: sn wknd* **8/1**

3236 **9** 3½ **Prince Of Gold**[19] 6763 6-9-1 48............(e) BrettDoyle 9 31
(R Hollinshead) *a towards rr* **9/2**[2]

0446 **10** 1 **Further Outlook (USA)**[23] 6717 12-9-0 50............(tp) TinaSmith(3) 3 31
(Miss Gay Kelleway) *led 2f: prom tl rdn along 3f out and grad wknd* **16/1**

0260 **11** 3½ **Wilford Maverick (IRE)**[19] 6756 4-8-12 45............ MickyFenton 4 17
(M J Attwater) *chased ldrs on inner: rdn along 3f out: grad wknd* **25/1**

0404 **12** 3 **Woodwee**[16] 6796 3-9-2 49............ PhillipMakin 5 13
(J R Weymes) *in tch: rdn along 1/2-way: sn wknd* **16/1**

0200 **13** ¾ **Wings Of Morning (IRE)**[24] 6703 5-8-8 48............(v) KellyHarrison(7) 7 10
(D Carroll) *chsd ldrs 3f: sn rdn along: lost pl and bhd* **16/1**

0004 **14** *hd* **Borodinsky**[19] 6756 5-8-12 45............ RobertWinston 14 6
(R E Barr) *a rr* **12/1**

1m 29.89s (-0.91) **Going Correction** +0.025s/f (Slow) **14** Ran SP% **123.7**
Speed ratings (Par 97):106,103,101,99,99 98,98,96,92,91 87,84,83,83
CSF £54.67 TOTE £14.70: £4.80, £2.20, £9.70; EX 63.70 Trifecta £201.00 Part won. Pool: £283.18 - 0.20 winning tickets..
Owner H Schwartz **Bred** Kirtlington Stud Ltd **Trained** Radlett, Herts

FOCUS
Another decent contest by the standard of banded races in prospect and the time was good, but few got into it. Improved form from the winner.

6962 PONTIN'S FAMILY HOLIDAYS BANDED STKS 6f (F)
3:40 (3:41) (Class 7) 3-Y-0+ **£1,876** (£554; £277) **Stalls** Low

Form RPR

0000 **1** **Massey**[16] 6799 10-8-12 40............ PaulMulrennan 1 49
(C R Dore) *chsd ldrs on inner: hdwyt 3f out: rdn to ld over 1f out: drvn ins last: hld on wl* **16/1**

0600 **2** *nk* **Aboustar**[19] 6756 6-8-12 40............ DeanMernagh 2 48
(M Brittain) *led to 1/2-way: c lose up: effrt to chal and ev ch over 1f out: drvn ins last and kpt on* **8/1**

0000 **3** ½ **Peggys First**[10] 6851 4-8-12 45............ MichaelTebbutt 6 47
(D E Cantillon) *cl up: led 1/2-way: rdn 2f out: drvn and hdd over 1f out: drvn and no ex ins last* **10/1**

5630 **4** ½ **Ace Club**[6] 6906 5-8-12 45............(b) DaleGibson 3 45
(M J Attwater) *in tch: hdwy to chse ldrs 2f out: sn rdn and kpt on same pce ins last* **7/1**[3]

0006 **5** 2½ **Compton Micky**[56] 6307 5-8-7 40............(p) AshleyHamblett(5) 12 38
(R F Marvin) *chsd ldrs on outer: effrt 2f out: sn rdn and kpt onsame pce* **33/1**

0054 **6** *nk* **Gaudalpin (IRE)**[10] 6851 4-8-9 45............(tp) JamesDoyle(3) 11 37
(Ernst Oertel) *towards rr: hdwy 3f out: rdn and in touch wl over 1f out: sn drvn and no imp* **3/1**[1]

0045 **7** ¾ **Swallow Senora (IRE)**[30] 6636 4-8-5 40............ RussellKennemore(7) 8 34
(M C Chapman) *in touc h: rdn along over 2f out: sn btn* **16/1**

-560 **8** 2 **Boppys Dream**[24] 6702 4-8-12 40............ MickyFenton 10 28
(P T Midgley) *a rr* **11/1**

0506 **9** *shd* **Instinct**[22] 6723 5-8-9 40............ GregFairley(3) 13 28
(Micky Hammond) *s.i.s: a rr* **16/1**

6250 **10** ¾ **Sion Hill (IRE)**[7] 6892 5-8-12 45............(p) DanielTudhope 7 26
(Mrs N Macauley) *cl up: rdn along wl over 2f out: sn wknd* **7/2**[2]

0000 **11** 11 **Roko**[137] 4389 4-8-12 35............(bt) PhillipMakin 9 —
(S R Bowring) *chsd ldrs to 1/2-way: sn wknd* **33/1**

006 **12** 5 **Drury Lane (IRE)**[30] 6643 6-8-12 45............(p) MatthewHenry 5 —
(D W Chapman) *a towards rr* **8/1**

0000 **13** 5 **Boisdale (IRE)**[22] 6727 8-8-12 45............ RobertWinston 4 —
(P S Felgate) *stall opened v slowly: a t.o* **10/1**

1m 17.96s (1.06) **Going Correction** +0.025s/f (Slow) **13** Ran SP% **132.0**
Speed ratings (Par 97):93,92,91,91,87 87,86,83,83,82 68,61,54
CSF £152.88 TOTE £25.40: £5.70, £4.10, £3.30; EX 258.30 TRIFECTA Not won. Place 6 £149.55, Place 5 £76.37.
Owner K Nicholls **Bred** Sheikh Mohammed Bin Rashid Al Maktoum **Trained** West Pinchbeck, Lincs

FOCUS
Very few to take seriously judged on recent form. The second and fifth set the standard.
Drury Lane(IRE) Official explanation: jockey said gelding missed the break
Boisdale(IRE) Official explanation: jockey said gelding missed the break having anticipated the start, causing the gate to malfunction
T/Plt: £132.60 to a £1 stake. Pool: £48,473.65. 266.85 winning tickets. T/Qpdt: £44.10 to a £1 stake. Pool: £2,966.20. 49.70 winning tickets. JR

6950 WOLVERHAMPTON (A.W) (L-H)
Thursday, December 28

OFFICIAL GOING: Standard
Wind: Light, half-behind Weather: Dry

6963 PONTINSBINGO.COM MAIDEN AUCTION STKS 7f 32y(P)
3:50 (3:50) (Class 5) 2-Y-0 **£3,238** (£963; £481; £240) **Stalls** High

Form RPR

50 **1** **Play Straight**[23] 6710 2-8-8............ FergusSweeney 7 62
(R M Beckett) *midfield: rdn and outpcd over 3f out: hdwy over 1f out: r.o wl to ld fnl strides* **9/1**[3]

2 *nk* **Doubtful Sound (USA)** 2-8-11............ PaulFessey 4 64
(T D Barron) *led: rdn and hung lft over 1f out: edgd rt ins fnl f: hdd fnl strides* **12/1**

32 **3** *hd* **Bold Indian (IRE)**[20] 6751 2-8-13............ JimmyQuinn 8 66
(I Semple) *dwlt: racd keenly: hdwy over 5f out: rdn over 1f out: hung lft ins fnl f: r.o* **10/11**[1]

6403 **4** *shd* **Chasing Memories (IRE)**[14] 6815 2-8-5 61............(b[1]) AdrianMcCarthy 1 57
(B Smart) *a.p: rdn over 2f out: styd on u.p ins fnl f: hld fnl strides* **7/2**[2]

0034 **5** 5 **Noddledoddle (IRE)**[10] 6853 2-8-4 50............(t) FrancisNorton 6 44
(J Ryan) *chsd ldrs: rdn 3f out: wknd ins fnl f* **20/1**

6 4 **Jousting** 2-8-13............ RossStudholme 9 43
(V Smith) *bhd: pushed along over 5f out: keeping on past btn horses whn hung lft over 1f out: nvr on terms w ldrs* **14/1**

45 **7** ¾ **Mujamead**[5] 6925 2-8-12............ LeeEnstone 2 40
(P C Haslam) *s.i.s: midfield: rdn and wknd 4f out* **9/1**[3]

05 **8** 2½ **Athea Lad (IRE)**[10] 6853 2-8-10............(b) EdwardCreighton 5 32
(W K Goldsworthy) *w ldr: rdn and wknd over 3f out* **33/1**

00 **9** 3 **Jewelled Dagger (IRE)**[10] 6859 2-8-11............(v[1]) DeanCorby 3 25
(I Semple) *sn pushed along and wl bhd* **66/1**

1m 32.3s (1.90) **Going Correction** +0.125s/f (Slow) **9** Ran SP% **118.2**
Speed ratings (Par 96):94,93,93,93,87 83,82,79,75
CSF £108.99 TOTE £10.50: £4.10, £6.20, £1.02; EX 115.90.
Owner Richard Morecombe and Jamie Perryman **Bred** Wyck Hall Stud Ltd **Trained** Whitsbury, Hants

FOCUS
A moderate maiden in which the front four were separated by less than half a length. Weak form.

NOTEBOOK
Play Straight, who failed to build on her debut effort when dropped to six furlongs at Kempton, appreciated the return to this distance and, despite hitting a flat spot, she stayed on strongly inside the final furlong to get there in the final strides. There should be more to come from her and she looks likely to stay a mile. (op 10-1)
Doubtful Sound(USA), who was seemingly not overly fancied for this racecourse debut, certainly knew his job and very nearly made all the running, but was claimed close home by the filly having hung left under pressure. There is every reason to expect him to come on for this and winning an ordinary maiden should not prove a problem.
Bold Indian(IRE) looked the one to beat on the evidence of his recent course and distance form, but he took a keen grip from the outset and then hung under pressure when still in with every chance. He was not beaten far and will find a similar race eventually, but this was disappointing. (tchd 11-10 and 6-5 in a place)
Chasing Memories(IRE) seemed to show improved form in the first-time blinkers and was right in the thick of it, but just lacked that extra gear to propel her into the lead. (op 3-1)
Noddledoddle(IRE) was comfortably held back in fifth and appeals as a more of a low-grade handicap prospect.

6964 PONTIN'S FAMILY HOLIDAYS H'CAP 7f 32y(P)
4:20 (4:21) (Class 6) (0-60,67) 3-4-Y-0 **£2,590** (£770; £385; £192) **Stalls** High

Form RPR

2122 **1** **Haroldini (IRE)**[16] 6798 4-8-9 **56**............(p) JasonEdmunds(3) 10 65
(J Balding) *midfield: hdwy 2f out: rdn over 1f out: hung lft ins fnl f: r.o to ld post* **7/1**[3]

3215 **2** *shd* **Green Pirate**[1] 6955 4-8-2 **53**............ WilliamBuick(7) 3 62
(W M Brisbourne) *hld up: nt clr run over 2f out: swtchd rt and hdwy wl over 1f out: r.o ins fnl f* **5/2**[1]

0403 **3** *shd* **Rancho Cucamonga (IRE)**[23] 6719 4-8-9 **53**............(b) DaneO'Neill 1 61
(T D Barron) *s.i.s: midfield: hdwy 4f out: rdn over 1f out: led ins fnl f: hdd post* **9/1**

5631 **4** 1 **Networker**[7] 6901 3-9-4 **62** 7ex............ TonyCulhane 2 68+
(P J McBride) *sn led: rdn over 1f out: hdd ins fnl f: no ex cl home* **3/1**[2]

0505 **5** *nk* **Scroll**[14] 6820 3-9-2 **60**............(v) DeanCorby 4 65
(P Howling) *towards rr: rdn and hdwy 2f out: swtchd lft ins fnl f: styd on* **12/1**

0000 **6** *nk* **Mister Incredible**[50] 6395 3-8-8 **55**............ SaleemGolam(3) 12 59
(V Smith) *hld up bhd: rdn and hdwy over 1f out: styd on* **50/1**

5034 **7** *nk* **Buzzin'Boyzee (IRE)**[1] 6952 3-9-0 **58**............ JimCrowley 5 62
(P D Evans) *hld up: hdwy over 2f out: nt clr run wl over 1f out: sn rdn: kpt on ins fnl f: nt pce of ldrs* **16/1**

1035 **8** 4 **Keon (IRE)**[5] 6934 4-8-10 **54**............ TPQueally 7 47
(R Hollinshead) *led early: squeezed out after 1f: sn in midfield: hdwy 3f out: rdn over 1f out: wknd ins fnl f* **14/1**

6402 **9** 1½ **Prettilini**[19] 6756 3-8-10 **57**............ MarcHalford(3) 8 46
(R Brotherton) *towards rr: rdn and hdwy over 2f out: wknd ins fnl f* **16/1**

0405 **10** 2 **Another Gladiator (USA)**[47] 6451 3-9-0 **58**............ CatherineGannon 6 42
(K A Ryan) *racd keenly: prom: rdn over 2f out: wkng whn n.m.r and hmpd over 1f out* **10/1**

3501 **11** 10 **Shrine Mountain (USA)**[7] 6892 4-9-2 **67** 7ex............ TolleyDean(7) 11 25
(R A Harris) *bustled along to go prom after 1f: rdn over 3f out: wknd over 2f out* **12/1**

36 **12** 3½ **Ilza**[25] 6693 3-8-11 **55**............ SteveDrowne 9 4
(Eamon Tyrrell, Ire) *prom: rdn 3f out: sn wknd* **33/1**

1m 30.86s (0.46) **Going Correction** +0.125s/f (Slow) **12** Ran SP% **123.9**
Speed ratings (Par 101):102,101,101,100,100 99,99,95,93,91 79,75
CSF £25.90 CT £170.02 TOTE £7.20: £1.70, £1.50, £3.00; EX 40.10.
Owner Tykes And Terriers Racing Club **Bred** Michael O'Mahony **Trained** Scrooby, Notts
■ Stewards' Enquiry : William Buick five-day ban: used whip with excessive frequency and without allowing mount to respond. (Jan 8-12)

FOCUS
A highly competitive handicap run at a decent early pace. The form looks sound and should prove reliable.

6965 WBX.COM WORLD BET EXCHANGE NURSERY 5f 216y(P)
4:50 (4:51) (Class 5) (0-75,75) 2-Y-0 **£4,533** (£1,348; £674; £336) **Stalls** Low

Form RPR

1 **1** **Estimator**[26] 6669 2-9-6 **74**............ DaneO'Neill 1 77+
(Pat Eddery) *mde all: rdn 1f out: r.o* **8/15**[1]

0440 **2** 1 **Bertie Swift**[115] 5065 2-8-13 **67**............ JimCrowley 6 66
(J Gallagher) *hld up bhd ldrs: rdn and hdwy over 1f out: sn hung lft: styd on to take 2nd post: nt pce of wnr* **14/1**[3]

5515 **3** *shd* **Billy Ruffian**[23] 6715 2-9-0 **68**............ DavidAllan 3 67
(T D Easterby) *a.p: rdn over 2f out: styd on* **11/2**[2]

2000 **4** ¾ **Stargazy**[21] 6736 2-8-8 **62**............ SteveDrowne 2 58
(R Charlton) *hld up bhd ldrs: hdwy over 1f out: sn rdn: no ex cl home* **11/2**[2]

5104 **5** 1½ **Stoneacre Gareth (IRE)**[8] 6880 2-9-7 **75**............(b) RobbieFitzpatrick 5 67
(Peter Grayson) *hld up bhd ldrs: rdn over 1f out: one pce fnl f* **14/1**[3]

0100 **6** 5 **Pat Will (IRE)**[1] 6951 2-7-11 **58**............ WilliamBuick(7) 4 35
(P D Evans) *prom: rdn over 2f out: wknd over 1f out: eased whn btn ins fnl f* **25/1**

1m 16.98s (1.17) **Going Correction** +0.125s/f (Slow) **6** Ran SP% **113.2**
Speed ratings (Par 96):97,95,95,94,92 85
CSF £10.00 TOTE £1.20: £1.10, £4.60; EX 11.80.
Owner Pat Eddery Racing (Moonax) **Bred** Llety Stud **Trained** Nether Winchendon, Bucks

FOCUS
A cosy enough win for the well-backed odds-on favourite Estimator. The runner-up stes the level.

NOTEBOOK
Estimator, a tidy winner on his debut at Kempton, looked the standout selection in an uncompetitive event and he bounced out of the stalls to make all the running, staying on strongly to win with a bit in hand. He is clearly a fair sort and can continue to improve. (op 8-11)
Bertie Swift came through late to snatch second, but he never looked like getting to the winner. He seemed to appreciate the change in tactics and can pick up a small race off this sort of mark. (op 8-1)
Billy Ruffian bounced back from a disappointing effort at Southwell and is clearly more effective on this surface. The way he kept on right the way to the line suggests he may be worth a try at seven furlongs. (op 9-2 tchd 6-1)

Stargazy has not really progressed as first expected and, having got himself into contention, he found little. (op 7-1)

Stoneacre Gareth(IRE) never really got into it and the blinkers did not work quite as well this time. (tchd 12-1)

6966 WBXTRIPLECROWN.COM H'CAP 5f 216y(P)
5:20 (5:20) (Class 5) (0-75,75) 3-Y-0+ **£5,181** (£1,541; £770; £384) **Stalls** Low

Form RPR

2502 **1** **Hello Man (IRE)**[19] 6773 3-8-10 **72**............ JerryO'Dwyer(3) 10 **79**
(Eamon Tyrrell, Ire) *a.p: led over 1f out: sn rdn: hld on* **7/2**[2]

0036 **2** *hd* **Lucayos**[5] 6935 3-8-8 **70**............ RichardKingscote(3) 3 **77**
(Mrs H Sweeting) *midfield: rdn over 2f out: hdwy over 1f out: r.o ins fnl f: jst failed* **16/1**

4020 **3** *hd* **True Magic**[19] 6773 5-8-6 **65**............ JimmyQuinn 6 **71**
(J D Bethell) *towards rr: rdn 3f out: hdwy over 1f out: r.o ins fnl f* **9/1**

0612 **4** *1* **Figaro Flyer (IRE)**[8] 6882 3-9-1 **74**............ IanMongan 9 **77**
(P Howling) *midfield: hdwy over 3f out: rdn over 1f out: chsd wnr ins fnl f: tl no ex cl home* **2/1**[1]

0350 **5** *1 1/4* **Fast Heart**[10] 6858 5-8-2 **68**............ TolleyDean(7) 2 **67**
(R A Harris) *a.p: rdn 2f out: one pce ins fnl f* **8/1**

0060 **6** *1/2* **General Feeling (IRE)**[1] 6952 5-7-13 **63** ow1............ AndrewElliott(5) 5 **61**
(M Mullineaux) *bhd: rdn over 1f out: styd on ins fnl f: nvr nrr* **16/1**

5320 **7** *1/2* **City For Conquest (IRE)**[12] 6844 3-8-6 **65**............(b) FrancisNorton 4 **61**
(T J Pitt) *chsd ldrs: rdn 2f out: fdd ins fnl f* **10/1**

5004 **8** *nk* **Russian Rocket (IRE)**[8] 6882 4-9-2 **75**............ SteveDrowne 1 **70**
(Mrs C A Dunnett) *chsd ldrs: lost pl 4f out: renewed effrt whn swtchd lft over 1f out: sn nt clr run: no imp after* **5/1**[3]

2510 **9** *2 1/2* **Polar Force**[31] 6622 6-8-3 **62**............ AdrianMcCarthy 7 **50**
(Mrs C A Dunnett) *led: rdn and hdd over 1f out: wknd ins fnl f* **14/1**

2050 **10** *1/2* **Mambazo**[81] 5842 4-8-7 **73**............(e) FLenclud(7) 8 **59**
(S C Williams) *racd wd: hdwy over 4f out: cl up 3f out: wknd wl over 1f out* **16/1**

1m 15.72s (-0.09) **Going Correction** +0.125s/f (Slow) **10 Ran SP% 126.7**
Speed ratings (Par 103):105,104,104,103,101 100,100,99,96,95
CSF £63.78 CT £498.23 TOTE £4.20: £1.50, £4.90, £2.30; EX 80.00.

Owner Tailor Made Syndicate **Bred** William Moloney **Trained** The Curragh, Co Kildare

FOCUS
Another tight finish, with the front three being separated by two heads. The winner probably didn't have to improve.

6967 GO PONTIN'S MEDIAN AUCTION MAIDEN STKS 1m 4f 50y(P)
5:50 (5:50) (Class 6) 3-5-Y-0 **£2,590** (£770; £385; £192) **Stalls** Low

Form RPR

5302 **1** *shd* **Kilgary (USA)**[20] 6743 3-8-12 62............ SteveDrowne 6 **59**
(J Noseda) *hld up in tch: clsd over 3f out: led over 2f out: sn hdd: swtchd rt ins fnl f: rallied: jst failed: fin 2nd, s.h: awrdd r* **11/8**[1]

5-56 **2** **Foursquare Flyer (IRE)**[175] 3220 4-9-8 70............ DaleGibson 1 **66+**
(J Mackie) *hld up: hdwy 3f out: led 2f out: rdn and hung lft fr over 1f out: jst hld on: fin 1st: disq & plcd 2nd* **5/2**[2]

5004 **3** *3* **Mighty Kitchener (USA)**[13] 6828 3-9-3 57............ IanMongan 4 **59**
(P Howling) *s.i.s: hld up and bhd: hdwy over 2f out: rdn and hung lft whn chsd ldng pair over 1f out: nt run on* **20/1**

4 *3 1/2* **High Ambition**[26] 3-9-3............ FrancisNorton 2 **53**
(P W D'Arcy) *prom: rdn over 2f out: sn wknd* **6/1**

3200 **5** *6* **Chicherova (IRE)**[35] 2249 3-8-12 46............ DavidAllan 5 **39**
(W M Brisbourne) *racd keenly: prom: led over 3f out: hdd over 2f out: wknd over 1f out* **28/1**

4400 **6** *dist* **Sweet Medicine**[10] 6861 4-9-3 72............ TonyCulhane 3 **—**
(P Howling) *led: rdn and hdd over 3f out: sn wknd: eased whn btn wl over 1f out: t.o* **4/1**[3]

2m 43.64s (1.22) **Going Correction** +0.125s/f (Slow)
WFA 3 from 4yo 5lb **6 Ran SP% 113.2**
Speed ratings (Par 101):99,100,97,95,91 —
CSF £5.14 TOTE £2.50: £1.90, £1.30; EX 6.90.

Owner Edward J Kelly Jr & Michael M Kelly **Bred** Warner L Jones Farm Inc **Trained** Newmarket, Suffolk

FOCUS
A weakish maiden and a bizarre race with the Stewards wrongly promoting the short-price favourite. Neither of the front pair were at their best.

6968 WORLD BET EXCHANGE WBX.COM H'CAP 1m 1f 103y(P)
6:20 (6:20) (Class 5) (0-75,81) 3-Y-0+ **£4,533** (£1,348; £674; £336) **Stalls** Low

Form RPR

3411 **1** **Magical Music**[10] 6862 3-9-8 **81** 6ex............ JimmyQuinn 4 **91**
(J Pearce) *racd keenly: a.p: rdn over 1f out: led narrowly and carried rt wl ins fnl f: r.o* **4/1**[2]

1311 **2** *nk* **Just Bond (IRE)**[6] 6924 4-8-12 **74** 6ex............ DuranFentiman(5) 2 **83+**
(G R Oldroyd) *racd keenly: led: rdn over 1f out: hung rt and hdd narrowly wl ins fnl f: hld fnl strides* **10/11**[1]

4345 **3** *1* **Royal Amnesty**[27] 6661 3-8-13 **75**............ SaleemGolam(3) 5 **82**
(G C H Chung) *hld up: hdwy over 1f out: trying to chal whn hung lft ins fnl f: nt qckn towards fin* **5/1**[3]

0542 **4** *hd* **Davenport (IRE)**[10] 6862 4-8-13 **75**............(p) JamesMillman(5) 1 **82**
(B R Millman) *s.i.s: hld up: rdn 3f out: swtchd lft ins fnl f: kpt on: nt pce to chal* **4/1**[2]

30- **5** *6* **Music Celebre (IRE)**[83] 5800 6-8-11 **71**............(p) JamesDoyle(3) 7 **66**
(S Curran) *cl up: rdn over 2f out: wknd over 1f out* **18/1**

2m 5.20s (2.58) **Going Correction** +0.125s/f (Slow)
WFA 3 from 4yo+ 2lb **5 Ran SP% 114.3**
Speed ratings (Par 103):93,92,91,91,86
CSF £8.52 TOTE £2.20: £1.30, £1.50; EX 8.30 Place 6 £14.70, Place 5 £9.66.

Owner Killarney Glen & Mrs E M Clarke **Bred** Peter Taplin **Trained** Newmarket, Suffolk

FOCUS
A very slow early pace, but two bang in-form rivals fought out the finish with the hat-trick seeking filly just coming out on top. The winner is still improving if the form is taken at face value.

T/Plt: £14.60 to a £1 stake. Pool: £72,716.10. 3,624.55 winning tickets. T/Qpdt: £8.40 to a £1 stake. Pool: £6,142.00. 535.10 winning tickets. DO

6956 SOUTHWELL (L-H)
Friday, December 29

OFFICIAL GOING: Standard

The last 'regional' race meeting, banded racing confined to horses rated below 45. A limited number of such races will be run on ordinary cards in future.
Wind: Strong, half-against Weather: Overcast and cold

6969 PHOTO GIFTS FROM BONUSPRINT.COM BANDED STKS 5f (F)
12:50 (12:50) (Class 7) 3-Y-0+ **£1,365** (£403; £201) **Stalls** High

Form RPR

5602 **1** **Orchestration (IRE)**[1] 6956 5-8-12 45............(v) DaleGibson 13 **57**
(M J Attwater) *rr-div: hdwy over 2f out: styd on to ld last 75yds* **10/3**[1]

2020 **2** *1* **El Potro**[11] 6851 4-8-12 45............ JosedeSouza 3 **54**
(J R Holt) *w ldrs: led over 1f out: hdd and no ex wl ins last* **7/2**[2]

0000 **3** *1 1/4* **Amanda's Lad (IRE)**[17] 6796 6-8-12 45............ AdrianMcCarthy 2 **50**
(M C Chapman) *chsd ldrs on outer: kpt on wl fnl f* **11/1**

6002 **4** *1 3/4* **Aboustar**[1] 6962 6-8-12 40............ DeanMernagh 7 **44**
(M Brittain) *chsd ldrs: outpcd over 2f out: hrd rdn and swtchd ins over 1f out: kpt on* **11/2**

4005 **5** *3/4* **On The Trail**[2] 6943 9-8-12 40............(p) PhillipMakin 10 **41**
(D W Chapman) *led tl over 1f out: one pce* **20/1**

2052 **6** *1 3/4* **Sharp Hat**[11] 6851 12-8-12 45............ TonyCulhane 4 **35**
(D W Chapman) *chsd ldrs: fdd fnl f* **5/1**[3]

0503 **7** *1 1/4* **Vicky Pollard**[11] 6851 3-8-12 45............ PaulDoe 12 **31**
(P Howling) *w ldrs: wknd over 1f out* **15/2**

0000 **8** *3/4* **Sounds Simla (IRE)**[14] 6833 3-8-5 45............ TolleyDean(7) 6 **29**
(R A Harris) *chsd ldrs: wknd appr fnl f* **14/1**

0006 **9** *hd* **Torrent**[133] 4546 11-8-5 40............(p) KevinMachent(7) 5 **28**
(J M Saville) *hld up in rr: swtchd rt sn after s: effrt 2f out: nvr a factor* **80/1**

0000 **10** *1/2* **Time N Time Again**[17] 6796 8-8-12 45............(b) RobbieFitzpatrick 14 **26**
(Peter Grayson) *dwlt: nvr nr ldrs* **20/1**

0000 **11** *5* **Laurel Dawn**[183] 3004 8-8-7 45............ AnnStokell(5) 9 **9**
(Miss A Stokell) *s.i.s: a outpcd and in rr* **25/1**

61.71 secs (1.41) **Going Correction** +0.225s/f (Slow) **11 Ran SP% 118.7**
Speed ratings (Par 97):97,95,93,90,89 86,84,83,83,82 74
CSF £14.54 TOTE £5.10: £1.60, £1.60, £3.10; EX 25.80 Trifecta £67.30 Part won. Pool: £94.83 - 0.84 winning units..

Owner Brooklands Racing **Bred** Mrs Anita Rothschild **Trained** Wysall, Notts

FOCUS
Not a bad race of its type. The runner-up and the fourth set the standard.

6970 PONTINS.COM BANDED STKS 1m (F)
1:25 (1:25) (Class 7) 3-Y-0+ **£1,365** (£403; £201) **Stalls** Low

Form RPR

30 **1** **Tackcoat (IRE)**[1] 6961 6-8-8 45............(p) EmmettStack(5) 13 **53**
(Eoin Doyle, Ire) *trckd ldrs: led over 2f out: hrd rdn and hung lft fnl f: jst hld on* **10/3**[1]

0006 **2** *shd* **Tip Top Style**[15] 6819 3-8-12 45............(tp) DaleGibson 12 **52**
(J Mackie) *in rr: sn drvn along: hdwy over 2f out: styd on fnl f: jst ct* **9/2**[2]

1044 **3** *4* **Crush On You**[15] 6814 3-8-12 45............ PaulQuinn 14 **44**
(R Hollinshead) *mid-div: hdwy 3f out: one pce fnl f* **6/1**

6603 **4** *1 1/4* **Miss Imperious**[17] 6799 3-8-12 45............ PaulMulrennan 5 **41**
(B Smart) *sn chsng ldrs: rdn and hung lft over 2f out: one pce* **5/1**[3]

0400 **5** *nk* **Blushing Russian (IRE)**[17] 6799 4-8-13 45............(p) RichardThomas 7 **41**
(J M Bradley) *sn chsng ldrs: chal 3f out: one pce* **25/1**

6006 **6** *1 1/4* **Rocky Reppin**[15] 6814 6-8-10 40............(b) JasonEdmunds(3) 10 **38**
(J Balding) *mid-div: outpcd over 3f out: no threat after* **8/1**

500 **7** *1 1/2* **Liskaveen Beauty**[191] 2763 3-8-12 45............ PaulFessey 3 **35**
(T J Fitzgerald) *chsd ldrs: drvn over 3f out: wknd over 1f out* **11/1**

-000 **8** *1/2* **In Rhubarb**[7] 6907 4-8-13 40............ PaulDoe 1 **34**
(P Howling) *led tl over 2f out: wknd over 1f out* **33/1**

0045 **9** *2* **Tipsy Lillie**[11] 6854 4-8-13 40............(v[1]) CatherineGannon 11 **30**
(P S McEntee) *sn w ldrs: n.m.r over 2f out: wknd over 1f out* **7/1**

0000 **10** *1 3/4* **Millbrook Star (IRE)**[8] 6892 3-8-12 40............(b) AdrianMcCarthy 8 **26**
(M C Chapman) *chsd ldrs: outpcd over 4f out: sn lost pl* **40/1**

0000 **11** *1/2* **Crusoe (IRE)**[1] 6960 9-8-13 45............ MichaelTebbutt 6 **25**
(A Sadik) *in rr: sn drvn along: nvr on terms* **14/1**

1m 44.77s (0.17) **Going Correction** -0.025s/f (Stan)
WFA 3 from 4yo+ 1lb **11 Ran SP% 120.1**
Speed ratings (Par 97):98,97,93,92,92 91,89,89,87,85 84
CSF £18.11 TOTE £3.80: £1.70, £2.10, £2.70; EX 23.90 Trifecta £95.80 Part won. Pool: £134.93 - 0.34 winning units..

Owner Eoin Doyle **Bred** Drumlargan Stud **Trained** Mooncoin, Co. Kilkenny

FOCUS
Very ordinary banded form, in a race run at a modest pace.

Miss Imperious Official explanation: jockey said filly hung right in the straight

6971 GO PONTIN'S MAIDEN CLAIMING STKS 1m 3f (F)
2:00 (2:00) (Class 7) 3-Y-0+ **£1,365** (£403; £201) **Stalls** Low

Form RPR

0400 **1** **Missouri (USA)**[10] 6871 3-8-12 45............ DanielTudhope 13 **50**
(G M Moore) *in tch: effrt and 2nd over 3f out: led 2f out: hung lft: drvn out* **9/2**[3]

4 **2** *2 1/2* **Mayyas**[21] 6680 6-9-2............(t) TonyCulhane 2 **46**
(C C Bealby) *s.i.s: sn chsng ldrs: outpcd over 3f out: kpt on to take 2nd ins last* **4/1**[2]

355 **3** *3/4* **Mikimoto (IRE)**[11] 6852 4-8-11 45............ J-PGuillambert 8 **40**
(S C Williams) *hld up towards rr: hdwy over 4f out: kpt on wl ins last* **4/1**[2]

000 **4** *3/4* **Royal Sailor (IRE)**[16] 6800 4-9-2 35............ RobertHavlin 3 **44**
(J Ryan) *chsd ldrs: one pce fnl 2f* **33/1**

53/0 **5** *nk* **Integration**[57] 6302 6-9-0 45............ DaleGibson 5 **41**
(Ronald Thompson) *in tch: drvn over 4f out: one pce fnl 2f* **12/1**

5000 **6** *1/2* **Count The Trees**[8] 2568 3-8-0 45............ JackDean(7) 9 **37**
(W G M Turner) *t.k.h: trckd ldr: one pce fnl 3f* **16/1**

0000 **7** *nk* **Tantien**[16] 6800 4-8-9 35............(b[1]) PaulDoe 1 **35**
(T Keddy) *led: clr over 6f out: hdd 2f out: wknd ins last* **100/1**

0500 **8** *5* **Discomania**[23] 6729 4-8-9 45............(b) BRoper(7) 7 **34**
(K F Clutterbuck) *mid-div: hdwy over 3f out: lost pl over 1f out* **12/1**

030 **9** *2* **Princess Toto**[7] 5683 3-8-7 54............(v[1]) PaulMulrennan 10 **26**
(P C Haslam) *chsd ldrs: rdn over 4f out: sn lost pl and bhd* **7/2**[1]

000 **10** *1 1/4* **Paper Maite**[15] 6814 5-8-7 30............ DeanMcKeown 12 **20**
(S R Bowring) *in rr: effrt over 4f out: wknd 2f out* **50/1**

0550 **11** *½* **City Minx**[20] 6758 4-8-7 35 PaulEddery 6 19
(S R Bowring) *in rr: hdwy over 4f out: lost pl over 2f out* **10/1**

0-0 **12** *39* **Monte Carrio**[8] 5426 3-8-5 (b[1]) DominicFox(3) 4 —
(C Drew) *bhd and pushed along: t.o 5f out: btn 38 l* **100/1**

0 **P** **Vonnies Night Out**[118] 5023 3-8-12 MickyFenton 11 —
(C J Teague) *s.i.s: bhd and hung rt: t.o 7f out: p.u 5f out* **25/1**

2m 30.12s (1.22) **Going Correction** -0.025s/f (Stan)
WFA 3 from 4yo+ 4lb **13** Ran SP% **121.5**
Speed ratings (Par 97):94,92,91,91,90 90,90,86,85,84 83,55,—
CSF £22.68 TOTE £7.40: £2.10, £2.20, £1.80; EX 32.10 Trifecta £110.40 Part won. Pool £155.60 - 0.94 winning units..The winner was claimed by Bill Turner for £5,000. Integration was claimed by Miss M. E. Rowland for £4,000.
Owner Mrs Susan Moore **Bred** P Newton **Trained** Middleham Moor, N Yorks
■ Stewards' Enquiry : Paul Doe caution: careless riding

FOCUS
A weak claimer and a modest time. The form is held down by the proximity of the 35-rated seventh.
Vonnies Night Out Official explanation: jockey said colt moved poorly throughout

6972 PONTINSBINGO.COM BANDED STKS 1m 4f (F)
2:30 (2:30) (Class 7) 3-Y-0+ **£1,365** (£403; £201) **Stalls** Low

Form RPR

0000 **1** **Miss Holly**[66] 6158 7-9-8 50 DanielTudhope 2 62+
(D Carroll) *hld up in rr: hdwy over 3f out: led 1f out: styd on wl* **6/1**[3]

/000 **2** *2½* **Experimental (IRE)**[31] 6641 12-9-7 49 DaleGibson 9 57
(John A Harris) *t.k.h: w ldr: led over 8f out tl 1f out: kpt on same pce* **16/1**

0212 **3** *½* **Go Amwell**[23] 6729 3-9-2 49 PaulDoe 13 56
(J R Jenkins) *hld up in rr: hdwy on outside over 5f out: chal over 3f out: kpt on same pce fnl f* **9/4**[1]

3666 **4** *2* **Laurollie**[11] 6860 4-9-3 40 RichardThomas 7 49
(B P J Baugh) *hld up in rr: stdy hdwy over 4f out: rdn and hung lft over 1f out: kpt on same pce* **25/1**

6350 **5** *3* **Romil Star (GER)**[25] 6705 9-9-4 46 (v) AdamKirby 3 45
(M Wellings) *chsd ldrs: drvn over 5f out: outpcd over 3f out: no threat after* **8/1**

0162 **6** *5* **Blue Opal**[17] 6795 4-9-3 45 (p) MickyFenton 5 36
(Miss S E Hall) *hld up: hdwy over 3f out: rdn 2f out: sn btn* **11/4**[2]

0466 **7** *2½* **Finnegans Rainbow**[21] 4945 4-9-3 40 AdrianMcCarthy 11 32
(M C Chapman) *sn chsng ldrs: lost pl over 2f out* **25/1**

6005 **8** *2* **Liquid Lover (IRE)**[17] 6795 4-9-3 40 TonyCulhane 10 29
(W M Brisbourne) *mid-div: drvn over 3f out: lost pl over 1f out* **12/1**

0-00 **9** *hd* **Treason Trial**[77] 5952 5-9-8 50 DavidAllan 4 34
(W M Brisbourne) *in rr: hdwy u.p over 4f out: lost pl over 2f out* **7/1**

00/0 **10** *39* **Flyoff (IRE)**[17] 6795 9-9-3 40 (p) PhillipMakin 6 —
(Mrs N Macauley) *led tl over 8f out: lost pl over 3f out: sn bhd and eased: t.o: btn 39 l* **100/1**

0000 **11** *12* **Revolving World (IRE)**[34] 6601 3-9-3 50 (bt) PaulMulrennan 1 —
(T J Fitzgerald) *chsd ldrs: lost pl over 4f out: sn bhd: eased 2f out: t.o* **25/1**

2m 41.89s (-0.20) **Going Correction** -0.025s/f (Stan)
WFA 3 from 4yo+ 5lb **11** Ran SP% **121.4**
Speed ratings (Par 97):99,97,97,95,93 90,88,87,87,61 53
CSF £95.28 TOTE £6.70: £2.80, £3.80, £1.50; EX 82.70 Trifecta £242.80 Pool: £341.98 - 1.00 winning unit..
Owner Mrs B Ramsden **Bred** Vikingstar Bloodstock **Trained** Driffield, E Yorks

FOCUS
Sound form rated through the third and fourth. The winner landed quite a gamble.
Laurollie Official explanation: jockey said filly hung left in the straight
Liquid Lover(IRE) Official explanation: jockey said gelding lost its action in the closing stages
Revolving World(IRE) Official explanation: jockey said colt lost its action

6973 PERSONALISED CARDS FROM BONUSPRINT.COM BANDED STKS 1m 6f (F)
3:00 (3:00) (Class 7) 3-Y-0+ **£1,365** (£403; £201) **Stalls** Low

Form RPR

2212 **1** **Red River Rebel**[17] 6797 8-9-10 50 PaulMulrennan 4 62
(J R Norton) *mde all: clr over 2f out: drvn rt out* **5/6**[1]

-400 **2** *10* **Good Investment**[23] 5955 4-9-5 45 (b) DeanMernagh 2 43
(Miss Tracy Waggott) *sn trcking ldrs: outpcd over 6f out: styd on fnl 2f: tk modest 2nd ins last* **40/1**

0605 **3** *3* **Orchard House (FR)**[7] 6907 3-8-12 40 (b) DerekMcGaffin 5 39
(J Jay) *chsd ldrs: drvn over 4f out: one pce fnl 3f* **20/1**

0200 **4** *2* **Peas 'n Beans (IRE)**[18] 6790 3-9-3 50 PaulDoe 7 41
(T Keddy) *trckd ldrs: wnt 2nd over 5f out: rdn 3f out: wknd fnl f* **13/8**[2]

0000 **5** *2½* **Gavanello**[21] 5618 3-8-12 40 AdrianMcCarthy 6 33
(M C Chapman) *trckd ldrs: drvn over 6f out: outpcd over 4f out* **25/1**

00-0 **6** *42* **Obstreperous Way**[2] 1293 4-9-5 45 (p) MichaelTebbutt 1 —
(Miss Tracy Waggott) *drvn early to chse ldrs: lost pl 5f out: t.o 3f out: btn 42 l* **100/1**

2500 **P** **Makarim (IRE)**[31] 6630 10-9-5 40 (p) AlanDaly 3 —
(M R Bosley) *hld up in last but wl in tch: eased and p.u after 5f* **11/1**[3]

3m 10.06s (0.46) **Going Correction** -0.025s/f (Stan)
WFA 3 from 4yo+ 7lb **7** Ran SP% **113.0**
Speed ratings (Par 97):97,91,89,88,87 63,—
CSF £44.02 TOTE £1.90: £1.30, £5.20; EX 15.90 Trifecta £58.40 Pool: £532.26 - 6.47 winning units..
Owner Jeff Slaney **Bred** J Slaney **Trained** High Hoyland, S Yorks

FOCUS
A weak event that looked a two-horse race beforehand but turned into a one-horse race. An improved run from the winner, though.
Makarim(IRE) Official explanation: jockey said gelding lost its action

6974 PONTIN'S FAMILY HOLIDAYS BANDED STKS 6f (F)
3:30 (3:30) (Class 7) 3-Y-0+ **£1,706** (£503; £252) **Stalls** Low

Form RPR

6304 **1** **Ace Club**[1] 6962 5-8-12 45 (b) DaleGibson 5 51
(M J Attwater) *chsd ldrs: drvn over 4f out: led 1f out: edgd lft: hld on wl* **8/1**

0605 **2** *1* **Mind Alert**[9] 6890 5-9-3 50 (v) AdamKirby 9 53+
(D Shaw) *rt-hand rein bec unattached leaving stalls: hld up in last: hdwy on ins 2f out: styd on wl to take 2nd nr line* **6/1**[3]

3000 **3** *hd* **Union Jack Jackson (IRE)**[18] 6787 4-9-3 50 (b) J-PGuillambert 8 52
(J G Given) *hld up wl in tch: effrt 2f out: kpt on same pce ins last* **4/1**[1]

0035 **4** *nk* **Campeon (IRE)**[1] 6956 4-9-0 47 MickyFenton 7 49
(J M Bradley) *led tl 1f out: no ex* **15/2**

0003 **5** *1½* **Vlasta Weiner**[7] 6906 6-9-0 47 (b) RobertHavlin 3 44
(J M Bradley) *chsd ldrs: kpt on same pce appr fnl f* **7/1**

3630 **6** *1¼* **Blythe Spirit**[7] 6922 7-9-1 48 (p) RobertWinston 10 41
(R A Fahey) *chsd ldrs: effrt 2f out: kpt on same pce* **9/2**[2]

0005 **7** *1* **Tiviski (IRE)**[24] 6719 4-8-12 50 NataliaGemelova(5) 11 40
(Miss Gay Kelleway) *chsd ldrs on outer: rdn and hung lft 2f out: one pce* **10/1**

0430 **8** *hd* **Christian Bendix**[7] 6906 4-9-0 47 (p) AlanDaly 6 37
(P Howling) *sn chsng ldrs: one pce fnl 2f* **7/1**

9 *½* **Breeze In (IRE)**[73] 6038 3-8-5 45 JamesRogers(7) 1 33
(R A Fahey) *dwlt: hld up: effrt 3f out: hung lft over 1f out: nvr a threat* **16/1**

00-0 **10** *11* **Ross Is Boss**[2] 6944 4-8-12 30 PaulMulrennan 4 —
(C J Teague) *chsd ldrs: wknd 2f out: eased ins last* **100/1**

1m 17.39s (0.49) **Going Correction** -0.025s/f (Stan) **10** Ran SP% **116.3**
Speed ratings (Par 97):95,93,93,93,91 89,88,87,87,72
CSF £55.25 TOTE £7.60: £2.50, £2.40, £2.10; EX 58.90 Trifecta £291.70 Pool: £410.90 - 1.67 winning units. Place 6 £22.06, Place 5 £12.48.
Owner Brooklands Racing **Bred** Helescane Stud **Trained** Wysall, Notts

FOCUS
The form looks sound at banded level.
T/Plt: £52.00 to a £1 stake. Pool: £55,568.25. 779.90 winning tickets. T/Qpdt: £17.10 to a £1 stake. Pool: £3,814.80. 165.00 winning tickets. WG

6963 WOLVERHAMPTON (A.W) (L-H)
Friday, December 29

OFFICIAL GOING: Standard
Wind: Fresh, behind Weather: Overcast with the odd light shower

6975 PONTIN'S HOLIDAYS MEDIAN AUCTION MAIDEN STKS 5f 20y(P)
3:45 (3:46) (Class 6) 2-Y-0 **£2,730** (£806; £403) **Stalls** Low

Form RPR

34 **1** **Rebel Duke (IRE)**[189] 2821 2-9-3 TPQueally 6 69+
(M G Quinlan) *mde virtually all: pushed clr fnl f* **1/3**[1]

4322 **2** *4* **Wibbadune (IRE)**[7] 6921 2-8-12 55 RobbieFitzpatrick 3 50+
(Peter Grayson) *prom: chsd wnr 1/2-way: wknd ins fnl f* **9/2**[2]

000 **3** *1½* **Head To Head (IRE)**[6] 6925 2-9-3 GeorgeBaker 7 43
(Peter Grayson) *hung lft thrght: sn outpcd: styd von fr over 1f out: nvr trbld ldrs* **25/1**

00 **4** *1* **Lost All Alone**[7] 6912 2-9-3 LPKeniry 5 39
(D M Simcock) *chsd ldrs to 1/2-way* **66/1**

06 **5** *2½* **Zilli**[7] 6912 2-8-9 JamesDoyle(3) 1 25
(N P Littmoden) *sn outpcd* **10/1**[3]

0000 **6** *shd* **Rubber Duck (IRE)**[120] 4971 2-8-9 30 GregFairley(3) 2 25
(Peter Grayson) *w wnr tl rdn 3f out: wknd 2f out* **40/1**

64.30 secs (1.48) **Going Correction** +0.10s/f (Slow) **6** Ran SP% **110.1**
Speed ratings (Par 94):92,85,83,81,77 77
CSF £2.02 TOTE £1.30: £1.02, £1.90; EX 2.00.
Owner L Cashman **Bred** Rathbarry Stud **Trained** Newmarket, Suffolk

FOCUS
An uncompetitive event in which the pace was fair. The front two are better than the facts but the third, fourth and sixth hold down the form.

NOTEBOOK
Rebel Duke(IRE), off the course since June, did not have to improve too much to open his account on this All-Weather debut returned to the minimum trip. He is only lightly raced and will be interesting in handicaps with the emphasis on speed. (op 4-11 tchd 2-5 in a place)
Wibbadune(IRE) has been running creditably and seemed to give it her best shot once again. She is a good guide to the worth of this form but should appreciate the step back into modest handicap company. (op 7-2)
Head To Head(IRE) ran his best race to date but looked a very tricky ride in the process. He is likely to continue to look vulnerable in this type of event. (op 33-1)
Lost All Alone faced a stiff task on these terms and was soundly beaten but may do better in modest handicap company in due course.
Zilli again had her limitations exposed in this type of event but may be capable of a bit better over further in modest handicap company. (op 11-1 tchd 12-1)
Rubber Duck(IRE), having her first start for four months, again offered no immediate promise. (op 33-1)

6976 WBX.COM WORLD BET EXCHANGE MEDIAN AUCTION MAIDEN STKS 1m 141y(P)
4:20 (4:20) (Class 6) 2-Y-0 **£2,730** (£806; £403) **Stalls** Low

Form RPR

1 **Alfredian Park** 2-9-3 LPKeniry 3 79+
(S Kirk) *a.p: chsd ldr over 3f out: rdn to ld wl ins fnl f* **7/2**[3]

2362 **2** *1¼* **Snow Dancer (IRE)**[35] 6581 2-8-12 68 FrancisNorton 9 71
(A Berry) *led over 7f out: rdn over 1f out: hdd wl ins fnl f* **11/4**[2]

022 **3** *3* **Risque Heights**[19] 6778 2-9-3 70 (b) SteveDrowne 1 70
(G A Butler) *trckd ldrs: rdn over 1f out: no ex fnl f* **5/2**[1]

6 **4** *½* **Spirit Of Adjisa (IRE)**[14] 6826 2-9-3 DaneO'Neill 5 69
(Pat Eddery) *s.i.s: hdwy 4f out: sn rdn: hung lft over 1f out: no ex* **4/1**

4022 **5** *8* **Go Dude**[8] 6891 2-9-3 55 BrettDoyle 4 52
(J Ryan) *chsd ldrs: rdn over 2f out: hung lft and wknd over 1f out* **16/1**

35 **6** *¾* **High Tribute**[9] 6887 2-9-3 JamieMackay 6 50
(Sir Mark Prescott) *s.i.s: hld up: hdwy over 2f out: rdn: hung lft and wknd over 1f out* **9/1**

00 **7** *10* **Eridani (IRE)**[13] 6840 2-8-5 ChrisHough(7) 7 24
(M L W Bell) *hld up: rdn 1/2-way: wknd 3f out* **100/1**

56 **8** *7* **Hyde Park Flight (IRE)**[16] 6809 2-9-3 GeorgeBaker 2 15
(John A Quinn, Ire) *led 1f: trckd ldr to over 3f out: wknd 2f out* **50/1**

9 *18* **Pindar (GER)** 2-9-3 TPQueally 8 —
(B J Curley) *s.s: a in rr: wknd 1/2-way* **50/1**

1m 52.79s (1.03) **Going Correction** +0.10s/f (Slow) **9** Ran SP% **118.3**
Speed ratings (Par 94):99,97,95,94,87 87,78,71,55
CSF £13.93 TOTE £4.30: £2.50, £1.90, £1.10; EX 21.50.
Owner N Pickett **Bred** G J Hamer **Trained** Upper Lambourn, Berks

FOCUS
The pace was only fair. Not a strong race, but the well-backed winner produced a fair effort for the time of year and there could be more to come from him.

NOTEBOOK
Alfredian Park, a brother to fairly useful sprinter Come Out Fighting and out of a dual juvenile five-furlong winner, justified the market support on this racecourse debut. Although this bare form is ordinary and he will find things tougher from now on, he is entitled to improve for this experience. (op 9-2)
Snow Dancer(IRE), largely a consistent sort, had the run of the race and seemed to run up to her best. She looks a good guide to the worth of this form but is likely to remain vulnerable to the more progessive sorts in this type of event. (op 10-3 tchd 7-2)

The Form Book, Raceform Ltd, Compton, RG20 6NL

Risque Heights, with the headgear on again, was not disgraced in terms of form but again looked less than straightforward as he refused to settle and just wanted to hang left when pressure was applied. He remains one to be wary of at a short price in this type of event. (op 9-4 tchd 3-1)
Spirit Of Adjisa(IRE) was again tardy at the gates but nowhere near as markedly so as on his debut at Kempton over seven furlongs. He again showed ability and appeals as the sort to fare better in ordinary handicap company. (op 11-2 tchd 6-1)
Go Dude, an exposed maiden, had his limitations firmly exposed in this type of event and is likely to continue to struggle in this type of race. (op 11-1)
High Tribute, having his third start in less than a month, was well below his previous run at Lingfield but is the type to fare better once switched into handicap company and when attracting market support. (op 11-1 tchd 13-2)

6977 WBXTRIPLECROWN.COM H'CAP 1m 141y(P)
4:50 (4:52) (Class 6) (0-60,60) 3-Y-O+ £2,590 (£770; £385; £192) Stalls Low

Form RPR
2032 1 **Scamperdale**[137] 4439 4-8-6 55 SoniaEaton(7) 13 66
(B P J Baugh) *hld up: hdwy over 2f out: edgd lft and r.o to ld wl ins fnl f* **10/1**
0613 2 1 1/2 **Pop Music (IRE)**[20] 6767 3-8-12 59 (p) JamesDoyle(3) 1 67
(Miss J Feilden) *led: rdn and hdd 2f out: rallied to ld ins fnl f: sn hdd and unable qck* **9/4**[1]
4460 3 1/2 **Cabourg (IRE)**[20] 6762 3-8-10 57 GregFairley(3) 8 64
(R Bastiman) *trckd ldr: racd keenly: rdn to ld 2f out: hdd and edgd lft ins fnl f: styd on same pce* **14/1**
0506 4 nk **Burnley Al (IRE)**[6] 6934 4-9-0 56 (b) RobbieFitzpatrick 11 62+
(Peter Grayson) *mid-div: hdwy 1/2-way: rdn over 2f out: hung lft over 1f out: nt clr run ins fnl f: styd on* **25/1**
3P00 5 4 **Royle Dancer**[10] 6871 3-9-1 59 BrettDoyle 10 57
(R Hollinshead) *prom: rdn over 3f out: hung lft and wknd over 1f out* **20/1**
2240 6 3/4 **Weet Yer Tern (IRE)**[1] 6960 4-7-12 47 WilliamBuick(7) 4 43
(W M Brisbourne) *chsd ldrs: rdn over 2f out: wknd over 1f out* **9/1**
-400 7 2 1/2 **Opal Warrior**[14] 6827 3-8-11 55 SteveDrowne 9 46
(Jane Southcombe) *chsd ldrs: lost pl 1/2-way: n.d after* **66/1**
5052 8 shd **Tamatave (IRE)**[24] 6721 4-9-4 60 CatherineGannon 12 51
(K A Ryan) *hld up: hdwy 1/2-way: nt clr run over 3f out: sn rdn: wknd 2f out* **4/1**[2]
9 1 1/4 **Tancredi (SWE)**[346] 4-9-4 60 JamieMackay 6 48
(N B King) *hld up: racd keenly: n.d* **9/1**
0300 10 5 **Blue Quiver (IRE)**[21] 6743 6-8-12 54 PaulEddery 5 32
(C A Horgan) *mid-div: rdn over 3f out: wknd over 2f out* **7/1**[3]
3206 11 10 **Scottish River (USA)**[14] 6837 7-8-6 55 AshleyMorgan(7) 2 12
(M D I Usher) *s.s: n.m.r wl over 3f out: a in rr* **10/1**
0500 12 10 **Inveraray**[23] 6724 3-8-3 47 FrancisNorton 7 —
(P S Felgate) *s.s: hmpd wl over 3f out: a in rr* **50/1**
1m 51.96s (0.20) **Going Correction** +0.10s/f (Slow)
WFA 3 from 4yo+ 2lb 12 Ran SP% **120.2**
Speed ratings (Par 101):103,101,101,100,97 96,94,94,93,88 79,71
CSF £32.20 CT £334.21 TOTE £12.70: £3.10, £1.10, £5.50; EX 38.50.
Owner Park Lane Thoroughbreds **Bred** Mrs J A Prescott **Trained** Audley, Staffs
FOCUS
An ordinary handicap that was run at just a fair pace.

6978 WBX.COM WORLD BET EXCHANGE NURSERY 7f 32y(P)
5:20 (5:20) (Class 3) (0-95,89) 2-Y-O £7,124 (£2,119; £1,059; £529) Stalls High

Form RPR
0212 1 **Beauchamp Viceroy**[14] 6834 2-9-3 85 BrettDoyle 1 89
(G A Butler) *led: hdd over 5f out: shkn up to ld and edgd lft ins fnl f: r.o* **5/2**[2]
2005 2 2 **Dubai Magic (USA)**[69] 6100 2-8-12 80 SteveDrowne 3 79
(C E Brittain) *prom: chsd ldr over 5f out: edgd lft over 3f out: rdn to ld over 1f out: hdd and unable qck ins fnl f* **13/2**[3]
2112 3 1 1/4 **Alittlebitleft (IRE)**[21] 6746 2-9-7 89 (b) DaneO'Neill 2 85
(R Hannon) *chsd ldr tl led over 5f out: rdn and hdd over 1f out: no ex ins fnl f* **8/11**[1]
4412 4 1 1/4 **Love In May (IRE)**[3] 6937 2-8-4 79 JosephWalsh(7) 4 71
(J S Moore) *dwlt: sn prom: ev ch 2f out: sn rdn and hung lft: wknd ins fnl f* **14/1**
1m 32.06s (1.66) **Going Correction** +0.10s/f (Slow) 4 Ran SP% **106.5**
Speed ratings (Par 100):94,91,90,88
CSF £15.45 TOTE £2.90; EX 17.30.
Owner Erik Penser **Bred** E Penser **Trained** Blewbury, Oxon
FOCUS
A fair event but a muddling pace means this bare form may not be entirely reliable. The race has been rated through the runner-up.
NOTEBOOK
Beauchamp Viceroy proved well suited by the return to seven furlongs and turned in his best effort yet to notch his third win at this course. A stronger pace would have suited him and, although life will be tougher after reassessment, he may well be capable of a bit better. (op 2-1)
Dubai Magic(USA) had the run of the race and ran creditably after a short break, but things went perfectly for him here and he was still beaten and he may continue to look vulnerable against progressive or well handicapped sorts in nursery company from his current mark. (op 8-1 tchd 11-1)
Alittlebitleft(IRE) had been progressing well on Polytrack and had the run of the race but found a 21lb rise in the weights since his last handicap run too much. He was far from disgraced but life is not going to be easy against the more progressive sorts from his current mark.. (op 5-6 after 10-11 in places, tchd 4-6)
Love In May(IRE) again left the impression that a more strongly-run race over six furlongs may see her in a better light and she is worth another chance back over the shorter trip in nursery company. (op 8-1)

6979 PONTINS.COM H'CAP 2m 119y(P)
5:50 (5:50) (Class 6) (0-65,62) 3-Y-O+ £2,730 (£806; £403) Stalls Low

Form RPR
12 1 **Share The Feeling (IRE)**[18] 6790 4-9-7 56 RichardKingscote(3) 8 68
(J W Unett) *a.p: chsd ldr over 3f out: rdn to ld and hung lft over 2f out: hdd over 1f out: rallied to ld nr fin* **7/2**[1]
0024 2 shd **Capitalise (IRE)**[18] 6790 3-8-1 48 WilliamBuick(7) 4 60
(V Smith) *mid-div: hdwy 6f out: rdn to ld and hung lft fr over 1f out : hdd nr fin* **7/2**[1]
-002 3 6 **That Look**[85] 4734 3-8-13 53 DaleGibson 5 58
(D E Cantillon) *chsd ldrs: led 4f out: hdd and n.m.r over 2f out: styd on same pce appr fnl f* **4/1**[2]
5046 4 14 **Rajayoga**[11] 6857 5-8-6 45 PatrickHills(7) 11 35
(M H Tompkins) *hld up: hung lft fr over 4f out: sme hdwy over 2f out: n.d* **9/1**
-000 5 5 **Teorban (POL)**[14] 6831 7-9-12 58 J-PGuillambert 10 42
(Mrs N S Evans) *hld up: hdwy 1/2-way: rdn and wknd over 2f out* **33/1**
0563 6 1 **Haatmey**[14] 6831 4-10-0 60 LPKeniry 6 43
(B G Powell) *chsd ldrs: pushed along 6f out: rdn and wknd over 2f out* **11/2**[3]
4425 7 3 1/2 **Leo McGarry (IRE)**[25] 6027 3-9-8 62 JamieMackay 3 41
(N B King) *hld up: sme hdwy and hung lft over 3f out: sn rdn and wknd* **10/1**
4-00 8 19 **Mahmjra**[93] 5610 4-9-12 58 EdwardCreighton 2 16
(C N Allen) *chsd ldrs tl rdn and wknd over 3f out* **66/1**
50-0 9 5 **Saddler's Quest**[11] 6860 9-8-2 41 oh1 (p) SoniaEaton(7) 7 —
(B P J Baugh) *hld up: a in rr* **66/1**
0065 10 1 **Optimum (IRE)**[10] 6873 4-9-9 55 (v[1]) MickyFenton 12 7
(J T Stimpson) *sn led: hdd & wknd 4f out* **18/1**
/065 11 1 **Find The King (IRE)**[17] 6797 8-8-13 45 BrettDoyle 1 —
(D W P Arbuthnot) *s.s: hdwy 1/2-way: wknd over 6f out* **20/1**
0066 12 2 1/2 **Tilen (IRE)**[11] 6852 3-8-1 41 oh1 FrancisNorton 9 —
(V Smith) *hld up: a in rr: bhd fnl 6f* **66/1**
3m 43.69s (0.56) **Going Correction** +0.10s/f (Slow)
WFA 3 from 4yo+ 8lb 12 Ran SP% **116.4**
Speed ratings (Par 101):102,101,99,92,90 89,88,79,76,76 75,74
CSF £14.69 CT £49.49 TOTE £4.10: £1.50, £2.70, £2.70; EX 21.90.
Owner John Malone **Bred** John Malone **Trained** Preston, Shropshire
FOCUS
A modest event in which the pace was fair. The winner showed a fine attitude.
Find The King(IRE) Official explanation: jockey said gelding missed the break

6980 GO PONTIN'S H'CAP 1m 1f 103y(P)
6:20 (6:21) (Class 6) (0-58,60) 3-Y-O+ £2,730 (£806; £403) Stalls Low

Form RPR
0400 1 **Street Life (IRE)**[20] 6767 8-9-1 57 TonyCulhane 1 67
(W J Musson) *hld up: hdwy over 2f out: rdn to ld over 1f out: r.o* **5/1**[2]
0001 2 2 1/2 **Reaching Out (IRE)**[7] 6918 4-9-1 60 7ex (b) JamesDoyle(3) 2 65
(N P Littmoden) *s.s: hld up: hdwy over 1f out: nt rch wnr* **9/2**[1]
4120 3 shd **Discotheque (USA)**[6] 6934 3-9-0 58 DeanCorby 12 63
(P Howling) *mid-div: hdwy over 3f out: rdn over 1f out: styd on same pce* **14/1**
00-5 4 1/2 **King Gabriel (IRE)**[16] 6810 4-8-13 55 DaneO'Neill 7 59
(Andrew Turnell) *a.p: chsd ldr over 2f out: rdn and ev ch over 1f out: no ex ins fnl f* **8/1**
43-1 5 4 **Bobering**[25] 6702 6-7-13 48 SoniaEaton(7) 5 44
(B P J Baugh) *hld up: racd keenly: hdwy over 2f out: rdn and hung lft over 1f out: sn wknd* **16/1**
6506 6 1 1/4 **Ignition**[3] 6942 4-8-12 54 (p) MickyFenton 13 48
(W M Brisbourne) *led over 8f out: rdn and hdd over 1f out: wknd ins fnl f* **20/1**
3500 7 6 **Zando**[175] 3263 4-8-10 52 PhillipMakin 4 34
(E G Bevan) *hld up: hdwy over 2f out: hung lft and wknd over 1f out* **50/1**
5244 8 2 1/2 **Uhuru Peak**[16] 6810 5-8-13 55 (bt) PaulMulrennan 8 32
(M W Easterby) *chsd ldrs: lost pl 1/2-way: nt clr run over 2f out: n.d after* **7/1**
3104 9 4 **Qaasi (USA)**[20] 6769 4-9-2 58 DeanMernagh 3 27
(M Brittain) *led: hdd over 8f out: wknd over 2f out* **11/2**[3]
4004 10 1 3/4 **Nimello (USA)**[15] 6819 10-9-1 57 FergusSweeney 9 22
(A G Newcombe) *n.d* **10/1**
11 1 1/2 **The Perfect Plan (IRE)**[125] 4827 3-8-12 56 SteveDrowne 6 18
(Tom Dascombe) *prom 7f* **25/1**
6303 12 1 1/2 **Weet For Ever (USA)**[20] 6759 3-8-8 52 J-PGuillambert 10 11
(P A Blockley) *s.s: hld up: plld hrd: effrt over 3f out: wknd over 2f out* **10/1**
0- 13 12 **Faraday (IRE)**[58] 3-8-8 52 TPQueally 11 —
(B J Curley) *mid-div: wknd over 2f out* **16/1**
2m 3.88s (1.26) **Going Correction** +0.10s/f (Slow)
WFA 3 from 4yo+ 2lb 13 Ran SP% **121.0**
Speed ratings (Par 101):98,95,95,95,91 90,85,83,79,77 76,75,64
CSF £27.53 CT £303.56 TOTE £7.00: £3.10, £2.80, £7.00; EX 27.90 Place 6 £20.41, Place 5 £18.68.
Owner W J Musson **Bred** Derek Veitch **Trained** Newmarket, Suffolk
FOCUS
Another run-of-the-mill handicap and one in which the decent gallop suited those coming from off the pace. The form has been rated through the third and fourth.
Nimello(USA) Official explanation: jockey said gelding ran flat
T/Plt: £39.10 to a £1 stake. Pool: £75,980.85. 1,416.20 winning tickets. T/Qpdt: £26.30 to a £1 stake. Pool: £5,725.50. 160.70 winning tickets. CR

6911 LINGFIELD (L-H)
Saturday, December 30

OFFICIAL GOING: Standard
Wind: Moderate, behind Weather: Rain from Race 2 (1.10) onwards

6981 PONTINS.COM H'CAP (DIV I) 7f (P)
12:30 (12:30) (Class 6) (0-54,60) 3-Y-O+ £2,047 (£604; £302) Stalls Low

Form RPR
5232 1 **Burhaan (IRE)**[8] 6906 4-8-7 47 FergusSweeney 3 58
(J R Boyle) *lw: cl up: gng easily 2f out: trckd ldr over 1f out: urged along to ld last 150yds: kpt on* **7/2**[1]
0600 2 3/4 **King After**[7] 6934 4-8-10 50 HayleyTurner 8 59
(J R Best) *pressed ldr: led 4f out: kicked on 2f out: hdd last 150yds: kpt on* **10/1**
6052 3 3/4 **Mind Alert**[1] 6974 5-8-10 50 (v) MickyFenton 12 57+
(D Shaw) *dropped in fr wd draw: t.k.h and hld up in last pair: effrt over 1f out: urged along and r.o wl fnl f: too much to do* **13/2**
0422 4 shd **Black Oval**[12] 6856 5-8-8 48 DeanMernagh 9 55
(S Parr) *lw: plld hrd: hld up in rr: prog 2f out: chsd ldng pair 1f out: hanging lft and fnd nil* **6/1**
0550 5 1 1/2 **A Teen**[17] 6803 8-8-6 46 oh1 PaulDoe 2 49
(P Howling) *b: pressed ldrs: rdn 2f out: one pce and no imp over 1f out* **66/1**
0223 6 1 1/4 **Kathleen Kennet**[20] 6780 6-8-12 52 ChrisCatlin 1 52
(Mrs H Sweeting) *settled in midfield: shuffled along over 1f out: nvr nr ldrs* **8/1**
2000 7 2 1/2 **Wings Of Morning (IRE)**[2] 6961 5-8-1 48 (v) KellyHarrison(7) 6 41
(D Carroll) *led to 4f out: pressed ldr to over 1f out: wknd* **50/1**

3401 **8** *1 1/4* **Mon Petite Amour**[12] 6855 3-8-13 **53** 6ex....................(p) AdamKirby 11 43
(D W P Arbuthnot) *racd wd: hld up in rr: outpcd wl over 1f out: no ch after* **12/1**
21 **9** *shd* **Staceymac (IRE)**[20] 6774 3-8-13 **53**.................................. DaneO'Neill 10 43
(B R Johnson) *t.k.h: trckd ldrs: wknd over 1f out* **4/1**[2]
0563 **10** *1/2* **Jennverse**[17] 6803 4-8-6 **46** oh1.................................. AdrianMcCarthy 7 35
(D K Ivory) *a in rr: u.p and struggling 3f out* **20/1**
4644 **11** *nk* **Hot Agnes**[28] 6683 3-9-0 **54**..(t) TPQueally 5 42
(H J Collingridge) *snatched up over 4f out: sn rdn: struggling in rr over 2f out* **11/2**[3]
1m 24.87s (-1.02) **Going Correction** -0.025s/f (Stan) 11 Ran SP% **121.3**
Speed ratings (Par 101):104,103,102,102,100 99,96,94,94,94 93
CSF £40.25 CT £227.64 TOTE £3.90: £1.80, £4.00, £3.00; EX 107.20 TRIFECTA Not won..
Owner John Hopkins (t/a South Hatch Racing) **Bred** Shadwell Estate Company Limited **Trained** Epsom, Surrey
FOCUS
A modest race, run at a weak early tempo which became more respectable after the first two furlongs. Sound form for the grade.
Staceymac(IRE) Official explanation: jockey said filly ran too free

6982 PONTIN'S "BOOK EARLY" (S) STKS 1m 2f (P)
1:10 (1:10) (Class 6) 3-Y-0+ **£2,388** (£705; £352) **Stalls** Low

Form RPR
5246 **1** **Ciccone**[8] 6918 3-8-6 57..(p) FergusSweeney 5 55
(G L Moore) *hld up in last pair: smooth prog to trck ldr over 2f out: rdn to ld over 1f out: edgd rt: hld on* **11/4**[1]
1-45 **2** *1/2* **Prince Vettori**[16] 6814 4-9-0 54.. MartinDwyer 3 59
(D J Coakley) *hld up in 4th: pushed along to chse ldng pair over 2f out: hrd rdn to chal ins fnl f: nt qckn nr fin* **3/1**[2]
0000 **3** *2 1/2* **Competitor**[74] 6037 5-9-6 55...(vt) DaneO'Neill 6 60
(J Akehurst) *lw: trckd ldng pair: wnt 2nd 4f out and led 3f out: drvn and hdd over 1f out: one pce* **4/1**
0160 **4** *6* **Dream Forest (IRE)**[21] 6767 3-9-3 58........................... FrancisNorton 2 49
(M S Saunders) *lw: hld up in last: pushed along and no prog 4f out: sn lost tch: plugged on into remote 4th over 1f out* **6/1**
0002 **5** *7* **Christmas Truce (IRE)**[10] 6889 7-9-6 54..................(p) AdamKirby 4 35
(Ms J S Doyle) *chsd ldr to 4f out: sn rdn and lost pl: bhd fnl 2f* **10/3**[3]
00-0 **6** *2 1/2* **Epices**[14] 6841 4-9-0 55... MickyFenton 7 25
(R Ingram) *led and sn clr: hdd & wknd rapidly 3f out* **25/1**
2m 6.14s (-1.65) **Going Correction** -0.025s/f (Stan)
WFA 3 from 4yo+ 3lb 6 Ran SP% **112.9**
Speed ratings (Par 101):105,104,102,97,92 90
CSF £11.45 TOTE £3.00: £1.70, £2.00; EX 10.70.The winner was bought in for 6,200gns.
Owner A Grinter **Bred** R C J Manning **Trained** Woodingdean, E Sussex
FOCUS
A weakish seller, in which Epices raced off into an eight-length lead. The others went a more sensible, but still decent enough, pace.

6983 PONTINS.COM H'CAP (DIV II) 7f (P)
1:45 (1:45) (Class 6) (0-54,54) 3-Y-0+ **£2,047** (£604; £302) **Stalls** Low

Form RPR
3504 **1** **Hotchpotch (USA)**[11] 6864 3-9-0 **54**...........................(p) HayleyTurner 5 62
(J R Best) *lw: t.k.h: trckd ldrs: effrt over 1f out: forced ahd last 100yds: hld on* **11/2**[3]
161 **2** *nk* **Midmaar (IRE)**[8] 6906 5-8-12 **52** 6ex........................(b) FergusSweeney 4 59
(M Wigham) *lw: hld up in midfield: smooth prog 2f out: rdn to chal wl ins fnl f: nt qckn and hld nr fin* **5/1**[2]
0052 **3** *nk* **Fulvio (USA)**[19] 6793 6-8-13 **53**................................(v) J-PGuillambert 10 59
(P Howling) *mde most at stdy pce: rdn 2f out: hdd and one pce last 100yds* **5/1**[2]
5023 **4** *1/2* **Detonate**[12] 6856 4-8-9 **49**.. AdamKirby 6 54
(Ms J S Doyle) *hld up in rr: prog on inner wl over 1f out: drvn and styd on: unable to chal* **9/1**
6604 **5** *1/2* **Jools**[12] 6855 8-8-4 **49** ow1... JamieJones(5) 11 53+
(D K Ivory) *hld up in last trio: shuffled along over 1f out: styd on steadily fnl f: nvr nr ldrs* **8/1**
1053 **6** *shd* **Mulberry Lad (IRE)**[10] 6890 4-9-0 **54**.................................... PaulDoe 7 57
(P W Hiatt) *lw: hld up in last pair: nudged along over 1f out: styd on steadily fnl f: nvr in chalng position* **9/2**[1]
5000 **7** *nk* **Sahara Prince (IRE)**[249] 1217 6-8-6 **46** oh1.............(p) PaulFitzsimons 3 49
(K A Morgan) *t.k.h: prom: chsd ldr 3f out tl jst ins fnl f: wknd* **20/1**
4031 **8** *1* **Stoneacre Fred (IRE)**[18] 6794 3-8-10 **50**................. RobbieFitzpatrick 1 52+
(Peter Grayson) *chsd ldr to 3f out: sn rdn: keeping on at one pce whn n.m.r last 75yds* **15/2**
3663 **9** *hd* **Danethorpe (IRE)**[18] 6794 3-8-6 **46** oh1.....................(v) FrancisNorton 2 46
(D Shaw) *trckd ldrs: rdn over 2f out: losing pl whn edgd rt fnl f* **14/1**
/00- **10** *1 3/4* **Blakeshall Boy**[568] 2466 8-8-6 **53** ow5........................ MarkCoumbe(7) 9 48
(A J Chamberlain) *t.k.h: hld up in last pair: rdn over 1f out: no prog* **66/1**
0402 **11** *1/2* **Grand Assault**[15] 6829 3-8-12 **52**.........................(v[1]) CatherineGannon 8 46
(P S McEntee) *t.k.h: prom on outer tl rdn and wknd over 1f out* **12/1**
1m 26.22s (0.33) **Going Correction** -0.025s/f (Stan) 34 Ran SP% **120.4**
Speed ratings (Par 101):97,96,96,95,95 95,94,93,93,91 90
CSF £34.04 CT £152.57 TOTE £6.30: £2.50, £2.20, £2.00; EX 39.40 Trifecta £177.70 Pool: £352.92 - 1.41 winning tickets..
Owner G G Racing **Bred** Runnymeade Farm Inc & Catesby W Clay **Trained** Hucking, Kent
■ Stewards' Enquiry : Adam Kirby one-day ban: careless riding (Jan 10)
FOCUS
A modest contest run at an ordinary gallop. Very ordinary form, the winner less exposed than most.
Mulberry Lad(IRE) Official explanation: jockey said, regarding the running and riding, that his instructions were to drop in and get a lead, but that he suffered interference approx. 5f out and was shuffled back and lost his position. He then had to find a way through the field and finished in the best possible place

6984 PONTIN'S FAMILY HOLIDAYS CLAIMING STKS 6f (P)
2:15 (2:16) (Class 6) 3-Y-0+ **£2,730** (£806; £403) **Stalls** Low

Form RPR
0405 **1** **Mistral Sky**[4] 6938 7-8-9 62..(p) MickyFenton 6 70
(Stef Liddiard) *stwg: mostly chsd ldr: drvn into narrow ld jst over 1f out: hld on wl last 150yds* **12/1**
0261 **2** *hd* **Don Pele (IRE)**[28] 6681 4-9-5 85.................................... DanielTudhope 8 79
(D Carroll) *b: swtg: hld up in 6th: prog on wd outside 2f out: drvn to chal fnl f: nt qckn and a jst hld* **6/4**[1]
6043 **3** *nk* **Who's Winning (IRE)**[15] 6835 5-9-3 72...........................(t) GeorgeBaker 3 76
(B G Powell) *cl up on inner: rdn to chal 1f out: edgd rt and nt qckn last 100yds* **9/2**[3]
0612 **4** *2 1/2* **Moon Bird**[11] 6869 4-8-12 57.. DaneO'Neill 9 64
(C A Cyzer) *hld up in last pair: outpcd wl over 1f out: drvn and kpt on to take modest 4th ins fnl f* **7/1**
2530 **5** *1 3/4* **Mountain Pass (USA)**[11] 6864 4-8-1 57.................(p) ThomasBubb(7) 7 55
(S Dow) *prom: cl up 1f out: bmpd along and wknd* **33/1**
6000 **6** *1/2* **Princess Kai (IRE)**[24] 6723 5-8-0 40 ow1........................ DavidKinsella 5 45
(R Ingram) *t.k.h and sn cl up: rdn and lost pl over 2f out: struggling after* **100/1**
5400 **7** *1 1/2* **Fromsong (IRE)**[195] 2683 8-9-5 94................................. MartinDwyer 4 60
(D K Ivory) *b.bkwd: fast away: led: hdd & wknd jst over 1f out* **9/4**[2]
0400 **8** *nk* **Auentraum (GER)**[14] 6842 6-8-9 55.................................... AdamKirby 2 49
(Ms J S Doyle) *dwlt: hld up in last: effrt on inner over 1f out: sn no prog* **33/1**
1m 11.56s (-1.25) **Going Correction** -0.025s/f (Stan) 8 Ran SP% **116.0**
Speed ratings (Par 101):107,106,106,103,100 100,98,97
CSF £30.93 TOTE £13.90: £2.90, £1.10, £1.70; EX 50.00 Trifecta £332.60 Pool: £801.26 - 1.71 winning tickets..Mountain Pass was claimed by B J Llewellyn for £9,000.
Owner Shefford Valley Stud **Bred** Peter Nelson **Trained** Great Shefford, Berks
FOCUS
A decent claimer, but the disappointing Fromsong - despite breaking well, with his stall opening fractionally before the others - steadied the tempo in mid-race, probably making it an advantage to have raced close to the pace. Sound-enough form.

6985 PHOTO BOOKS FROM BONUSPRINT.COM NURSERY 6f (P)
2:45 (2:45) (Class 4) (0-85,75) 2-Y-0 **£4,533** (£1,348) **Stalls** Low

Form RPR
302 **1** **Grange Lili (IRE)**[4] 6939 2-8-5 **59** ow2...................... RobbieFitzpatrick 4 53+
(Peter Grayson) *chsd rival: rdn and nt qckn over 1f out: styd on u.p to ld nr fin* **2/11**[1]
0005 **2** *nk* **Foxy Music**[4] 6939 2-7-12 **52** oh7................................ AdrianMcCarthy 2 45
(Peter Grayson) *led: gng bttr than rival over 1f out: shkn up last 100yds: hdd nr fin* **7/2**[2]
1m 15.03s (2.22) **Going Correction** -0.025s/f (Stan) 2 Ran SP% **106.8**
Speed ratings (Par 98):84,83
TOTE £1.20.
Owner Mrs M Shaughnessy and Mrs S Grayson **Bred** Jack Ronan And Des Ver Hunt Farm Ltd **Trained** Formby, Lancs
FOCUS
A match between two stablemates run at a modest pace until the final bend. The form should be taken with a large pinch of salt. Incredibly, trainer Peter Grayson had all five runners originally declared for the race, but one was taken out overnight and two more were withdrawn with veterinary certificates during the day.
NOTEBOOK
Grange Lili(IRE) won her first race at the 12th attempt, but she had to work much harder than expected, and this was a hardly a contest from which to draw any firm conclusions. (op 1-4)
Foxy Music made his better-fancied stablemate battle much harder than the betting suggested, and for a while in the home straight it looked as if he might cause an upset. Though this is not a race on which to rely, his trainer reports him to be a slow-maturing type, so it would be no surprise if he were to improve on some modest efforts to date. (op 5-2)

6986 DIGITAL PRINTS FROM BONUSPRINT.COM H'CAP 1m (P)
3:15 (3:16) (Class 4) (0-85,89) 3-Y-0+ **£5,505** (£1,637; £818; £408) **Stalls** High

Form RPR
1122 **1** **Happy As Larry (USA)**[14] 6848 4-9-1 **83**...................... FrancisNorton 2 93+
(T J Pitt) *hld up in midfield: rdn and effrt 2f out: styd on fr over 1f out: led nar fin* **2/1**[1]
0221 **2** *1/2* **Kabeer**[26] 6698 8-8-2 **75**..(t) NataliaGemelova(5) 12 84
(A J McCabe) *lw: prom: trckd ldr over 3f out: led over 2f out: floundered ins fnl f: hdd nr fin* **10/1**
2000 **3** *1/2* **St Petersburg**[63] 6219 6-9-0 **82**.. TPQueally 6 90
(M H Tompkins) *s.i.s: hld up in last trio: rdn on wd outside over 1f out: r.o fnl f: nrst fin* **10/1**
2501 **4** *nk* **Mina A Salem**[11] 6868 4-9-0 **89** 6ex............................ WilliamCarson(7) 8 96
(C E Brittain) *trckd ldrs: rdn to dispute 2nd ent fnl f: kpt on same pce* **11/2**[3]
0002 **5** *1* **Trifti**[26] 6698 5-8-6 **74**.. FergusSweeney 5 79
(C A Cyzer) *settled in midfield: lost pl over 3f out: struggling and wl in rr 2f out: styd on again fnl f* **17/2**
/3-0 **6** *1/2* **Daniel Thomas (IRE)**[11] 6868 4-9-3 **85**............................ JimCrowley 11 89
(Mrs A J Perrett) *hld up in last trio: rdn 2f out: styd on fnl f: nt rch ldrs* **20/1**
0000 **7** *nk* **Northern Desert (IRE)**[15] 6830 7-8-4 **72**............................ ChrisCatlin 3 75
(P W Hiatt) *t.k.h: hld up bhd ldrs: effrt 2f out: rdn to dispute 2nd 1f out: wknd* **10/1**
0442 **8** *2* **Tamagin (USA)**[11] 6868 3-9-0 **83**.................................(p) J-PGuillambert 4 81
(P D Evans) *led after 1f: hdd over 2f out: wknd fnl f* **3/1**[2]
5603 **9** *1* **Magic Rush**[24] 6733 4-9-0 **82**.................................. EdwardCreighton 10 78
(Mrs Norma Pook) *led for 1f: chsd ldr to over 3f out: wl hld whn n.m.r jst ins fnl f* **20/1**
0100 **10** *3/4* **Cape Of Luck (IRE)**[22] 6744 3-9-2 **85**................................. GeorgeBaker 7 79
(P Mitchell) *b.hind: hld up in last trio: prog on outer and in tch 2f out: wknd over 1f out* **20/1**
1000 **11** *6* **Yellow Ridge (IRE)**[55] 6356 3-8-6 **75**........................ CatherineGannon 9 56
(Luke Comer, Ire) *prom: rdn and lost pl 3f out: sn no ch: eased fnl f* **50/1**
6130 **12** *hd* **Wheelavit (IRE)**[118] 5042 3-8-2 **71** oh1............................ HayleyTurner 1 51
(B G Powell) *dwlt: a in last trio: struggling over 2f out: wknd* **66/1**
1m 37.39s (-2.04) **Going Correction** -0.025s/f (Stan)
WFA 3 from 4yo+ 1lb 12 Ran SP% **129.3**
Speed ratings (Par 105):109,108,108,107,106 106,105,103,102,102 96,95
CSF £24.68 CT £183.06 TOTE £4.20: £1.80, £2.80, £4.20; EX 38.60 Trifecta £478.30 Part won. Pool: £673.74 - 0.97 winning tickets..
Owner G Naidu, K Luxon & W McKay **Bred** C H Kitchen And Jeffrey Cook **Trained** Bawtry, S Yorks
FOCUS
A fair handicap, run at a good gallop. The progressive winner did not need to improve to score.
Magic Rush Official explanation: jockey said gelding hung badly left throughout
Cape Of Luck(IRE) Official explanation: jockey said colt hung left-handed from 3 1/2f out

6987 PONTINSBINGO.COM MAIDEN STKS 1m 2f (P)
3:45 (3:46) (Class 5) 3-Y-0 **£3,886** (£1,156; £577; £288) **Stalls** Low

Form RPR
0456 **1** **Samarinda (USA)**[14] 6841 3-9-3 62.................................. MickyFenton 1 66
(Mrs P Sly) *cl up: effrt to press ldr 3f out: sustained chal to ld ins fnl f: edgd rt but kpt on wl* **13/2**[3]

4006 **2** ½ **Marbaa (IRE)**[14] 6848 3-9-3 64 .... LPKeniry 8 65
(S Dow) *mostly trckd ldr: narrow ld fr 3f out: hdd ins fnl f : no ex nr fin* **3/1**[1]

036 **3** *shd* **Moon Empress (FR)**[7] 6929 3-8-12 67 .... MartinDwyer 3 60
(W R Muir) *trckd ldrs: outpcd by ldng pair over 1f out: styd on wl fnl f: gaining at fin* **8/1**

4 3 ½ **Love Ridot (IRE)**[102] 5462 3-8-9 72 .... GregFairley(3) 10 53+
(M Johnston) *trckd ldrs: bdly outpcd fr 2f out: kpt on again ins fnl f* **3/1**[1]

65 **5** ¾ **Musango**[15] 6828 3-9-3 .... FergusSweeney 2 57
(B R Johnson) *hld up wl in rr: sme prog on inner over 1f out: rdn and kpt on fnl f* **20/1**

6300 **6** ¾ **Velvet Valley (USA)**[131] 4662 3-9-3 68 .... DaneO'Neill 4 55
(C E Longsdon) *s.s: sn in tch in midfield: rdn wl over 1f out: one pce* **11/2**[2]

7 *hd* **Wicked Lady (UAE)** 3-8-12 .... SamHitchcott 6 50
(B R Johnson) *unf: hld up last of main gp: effrt on outer 2f out: kpt on but no real imp* **33/1**

000 **8** ½ **Nahlass**[99] 5510 3-8-5 45 .... SophieDoyle(7) 5 49
(Ms J S Doyle) *towards rr: rdn 2f out: one pce and no imp* **50/1**

0030 **9** 2 **Atticus Trophies (IRE)**[8] 6918 3-9-3 56 ....(p) AdamKirby 11 50
(Ms J S Doyle) *leggy: lw: led to 3f out: wknd 2f out* **16/1**

0060 **10** *nk* **Footstepsinthesnow (IRE)**[8] 6911 3-8-12 47 .... PaulDoe 9 45
(M A Buckley) *cl up on outer: rdn 3f out: wknd 2f out* **33/1**

3 **11** 1 ½ **Neshla**[16] 6817 3-8-12 .... HayleyTurner 12 42
(C E Brittain) *dwlt: pushed along after 1f: a in rr: struggling over 2f out* **11/2**[2]

4566 **12** *21* **Artist's Muse (USA)**[15] 6828 3-8-5 70 .... BenjaminWishart(7) 7 2
(M S Saunders) *sn detached in last: t.o bef 1/2-way* **33/1**

2m 8.66s (0.87) **Going Correction** -0.025s/f (Stan) 12 Ran SP% **126.6**
Speed ratings (Par 102):95,94,94,91,91 90,90,89,88,88 86,70
CSF £26.95 TOTE £10.90: £3.50, £1.90, £2.50; EX 53.10 TRIFECTA Not won. Place 6 £20.13, Place 5 £7.94.
Owner D Bayliss, T Davies, G Libson & P Sly **Bred** Gainsborough Farm Llc **Trained** Thorney, Cambs

FOCUS
A routine maiden. The gallop was not strong, and the form looks far from solid.
Love Ridot(IRE) Official explanation: jockey said filly was denied a clear run
Atticus Trophies(IRE) Official explanation: jockey said gelding hung badly right
Neshla Official explanation: jockey said filly ran green
T/Plt: £25.00 to a £1 stake. Pool: £64,797.00. 1,888.35 winning tickets. T/Qpdt: £6.40 to a £1 stake. Pool: £3,258.20. 373.25 winning tickets. JN

6975 WOLVERHAMPTON (A.W) (L-H)
Saturday, December 30

OFFICIAL GOING: Standard
Wind: Light, across Weather: Showers

6988 GO PONTIN'S CLAIMING STKS 1m 141y(P)
3:50 (3:50) (Class 6) 3-Y-0 **£2,590** (£770; £385; £192) **Stalls** Low

Form RPR

0246 **1** **The City Kid (IRE)**[9] 6892 3-8-4 47 ....(b) JimmyQuinn 5 60
(P D Evans) *hld up: hdwy over 1f out: styd on to ld wl ins fnl f* **6/1**[3]

6005 **2** *1* **Rose Muwasim**[21] 6771 3-8-8 57 .... DaleGibson 1 62
(M J Attwater) *chsd ldrs: led over 1f out: hdd wl ins fnl f* **7/1**

0056 **3** ¾ **Bathwick Emma (IRE)**[40] 6538 3-7-11 55 ....(p) WilliamBuick(7) 4 56
(P D Evans) *chsd ldr: rdn over 1f out: sn hung rt: styd on same pce ins fnl f* **5/2**[1]

1200 **4** *4* **Chalentina**[80] 5908 3-8-13 72 .... TonyCulhane 2 57
(P Howling) *hld up in tch: rdn over 2f out: wknd over 1f out* **7/2**[2]

3220 **5** 1 ½ **Night Groove (IRE)**[244] 1314 3-8-9 59 .... JamesDoyle(3) 3 53
(N P Littmoden) *led: rdn and hdd over 1f out: wknd fnl f* **5/2**[1]

1m 52.96s (1.20) **Going Correction** +0.125s/f (Slow) 5 Ran SP% **106.2**
Speed ratings (Par 98):99,98,97,93,92
CSF £39.37 TOTE £9.50: £3.20, £3.10; EX 59.10.
Owner Mrs S J Lawrence **Bred** T B And Mrs T B Russell **Trained** Pandy, Abergavenny

FOCUS
An uncompetitive event in which the gallop picked up around halfway. Shaky form, the outsiders filling the first two places, and it is doubtful whether the winner had to improve.

6989 BONUSPRINT.COM NOVICE STKS 5f 216y(P)
4:20 (4:22) (Class 5) 2-Y-0 **£4,175** (£1,445) **Stalls** Low

Form RPR

1 **1** **Pixie Ring**[16] 6821 2-9-2 73 .... JamieMackay 3 77
(Sir Mark Prescott) *mde all: rdn and hung lft over 1f out: r.o* **11/4**[2]

2211 **2** *hd* **Shustraya**[22] 6750 2-9-1 77 .... SteveDrowne 1 75
(P J Makin) *s.s: sn chsg wnr: hrd rdn and ev ch ins fnl f: r.o* **30/100**[1]

U **Comptonspirit** 2-8-6 .... RichardThomas 2 —
(B P J Baugh) *chsd ldrs: rdn whn hit rails and rdr lost iron over 3f out: uns rdr wl over 2f out* **66/1**[3]

1m 19.22s (3.41) **Going Correction** +0.125s/f (Slow) 3 Ran SP% **105.1**
Speed ratings (Par 96):82,81,—
CSF £4.10 TOTE £3.20; EX 4.00.
Owner Nicholas Jones **Bred** Coln Valley Stud **Trained** Newmarket, Suffolk

FOCUS
A match between the two market leaders and a steady pace means this bare form is not easy to assess and may not prove entirely reliable.

NOTEBOOK
Pixie Ring looked to have a bit to find with the favourite on official ratings but had the run of the race as her main rival blew the start and showed a determined attitude, despite hanging, in the closing stages. She should prove equally effective over seven furlongs, though, is in good hands and remains capable of a bit better. (op 9-4 tchd 10-3)
Shustraya, a progressive sort who knows how to win, looked the one to beat on these terms but blew the start and, although the modest gallop enabled her to be soon back on terms, she just failed to overhaul the unexposed winner, who had the run of the race. She is worth another chance. (op 4-11 tchd 2-7)
Comptonspirit, out of a triple sprint winner, was already starting to struggle when unshipping her rider on the approach to the straight on this racecourse debut. Modest handicaps will offer her best chance of success. (op 40-1)

6990 PONTINS.COM H'CAP 5f 216y(P)
4:50 (4:51) (Class 6) (0-60,64) 3-Y-0+ **£2,590** (£770; £385; £192) **Stalls** Low

Form RPR

2543 **1** **Bond Playboy**[23] 6739 6-8-11 60 ....(v) DuranFentiman(5) 12 69
(G R Oldroyd) *hld up: hdwy over 2f out: led and edgd lft fr over 1f out: drvn out* **7/2**[1]

0001 **2** *nk* **Vegas Boys**[8] 6922 3-9-6 64 7ex .... MichaelTebbutt 13 72
(M Wigham) *mid-div: hdwy over 2f out: bmpd wl over 1f out: sn rdn and ev ch: r.o* **11/2**[3]

1462 **3** ½ **Carcinetto (IRE)**[10] 6884 4-8-4 55 .... WilliamBuick(7) 2 62
(P D Evans) *chsd ldrs: lost pl over 3f out: swtchd rt and hdwy over 1f out: sn hung rt: r.o u.p despite swishing tail* **11/2**[3]

4661 **4** *nk* **Millfields Dreams**[25] 6713 7-9-1 59 .... DaleGibson 10 65
(M G Quinlan) *chsd ldrs: rdn and ev ch over 1f out: styd on same pce ins fnl f* **9/2**[2]

6506 **5** *nk* **Caustic Wit (IRE)**[15] 6827 8-8-11 58 ....(p) JamesDoyle(3) 9 63
(M S Saunders) *hld up: hdwy over 2f out: sn rdn: edgd lft ins fnl f: styd on* **10/1**

4103 **6** *3* **State Dilemma (IRE)**[15] 6827 5-9-2 60 ....(v) PaulHanagan 4 56
(D Shaw) *mid-div: hdwy over 2f out: styd on same pce appr fnl f* **13/2**

5003 **7** *2* **Phinerine**[15] 6833 3-8-4 55 ....(b) TolleyDean(7) 6 45
(R A Harris) *s.i.s: plld hrd and sn prom: rdn over 2f out: wknd over 1f out* **33/1**

0000 **8** *nk* **Blue Knight (IRE)**[8] 6922 7-8-13 57 .... TonyCulhane 1 46
(P Howling) *hld up: rdn over 1f out: nvr trbld ldrs* **33/1**

0466 **9** ½ **Harrison's Flyer (IRE)**[25] 6709 5-9-2 60 ....(b) SteveDrowne 11 48
(J M Bradley) *hld up: rdn over 1f out: hung lft fnl f: n.d* **16/1**

0000 **10** *hd* **Majestical (IRE)**[8] 6913 4-8-13 57 ....(b) JimmyQuinn 3 44
(J M Bradley) *s.i.s: a in rr* **16/1**

3400 **11** *nk* **Diamond Josh**[22] 6755 4-8-6 50 .... SilvestreDeSousa 7 36
(M Mullineaux) *led early: chsd ldrs: rdn over 2f out: wknd over 1f out* **33/1**

0610 **12** *hd* **Jahia (NZ)**[10] 6877 7-8-3 52 .... RoryMoore(5) 5 38
(P T Midgley) *sn rdn to ld: hdd over 1f out: wknd ins fnl f* **25/1**

1m 15.43s (-0.38) **Going Correction** +0.125s/f (Slow) 12 Ran SP% **118.0**
Speed ratings (Par 101):107,106,105,105,105 101,98,98,97,97 96,96
CSF £21.51 CT £102.33 TOTE £6.70: £2.00, £2.00, £1.40; EX 24.50.
Owner R C Bond **Bred** P A Mason **Trained** Upper Helmsley, N Yorks

FOCUS
An ordinary handicap in which the gallop was fair and those drawn high fared best. The action unfolded in the centre in the straight. Solid form, the third and fourth the best guide.
Majestical(IRE) Official explanation: jockey said gelding was slow into his stride from leaving the stalls

6991 PONTIN'S FAMILY HOLIDAYS NURSERY 7f 32y(P)
5:20 (5:20) (Class 5) (0-75,74) 2-Y-0 **£3,886** (£1,156; £577; £288) **Stalls** High

Form RPR

3221 **1** **Tobago Reef**[9] 6900 2-8-9 69 7ex ....(p) KristinStubbs(7) 4 75
(Mrs L Stubbs) *mde all: sn rdn clr: jst hld on* **11/4**[2]

1332 **2** ½ **Social Rhythm**[22] 6750 2-9-4 71 .... JimmyQuinn 1 76
(H J Collingridge) *hld up: hdwy and n.m.r over 1f out: r.o u.p* **9/4**[1]

1 **3** *shd* **Leonard Charles**[22] 6751 2-9-7 74 .... JamieMackay 3 79+
(Sir Mark Prescott) *s.i.s: sn prom: rdn to chse wnr over 2f out: sn hung lft: r.o* **7/2**[3]

3223 **4** 1 ¼ **Belvedere Vixen**[7] 6927 2-8-3 63 .... WilliamBuick(7) 2 64
(M J Wallace) *hld up in tch: rdn over 2f out: styd on* **7/1**

004 **5** 3 ½ **My Sara**[187] 2938 2-8-2 55 .... PaulHanagan 6 48
(R A Fahey) *sn pushed along in rr: rdn 1/2-way: n.d* **8/1**

123 **6** ½ **Bridget's Team**[9] 6894 2-8-5 58 ....(t) DaleGibson 5 49
(D G Bridgwater) *chsd wnr over 4f: wknd over 1f out* **25/1**

1m 30.82s (0.42) **Going Correction** +0.125s/f (Slow) 6 Ran SP% **107.1**
Speed ratings (Par 96):102,101,101,99,95 95
CSF £8.43 TOTE £3.90: £2.40, £1.90; EX 9.40.
Owner Vincent Lee **Bred** M Williams **Trained** Norton, N. Yorks

FOCUS
An ordinary event but an enterprising ride aboard the winner, who is a progressive sort on this surface. An improved effort from the second.

NOTEBOOK
Tobago Reef, up in grade and under a penalty for his recent win, was given an enterprising ride to notch his second victory over this course and distance. Although life will be tougher after reassessment, he will remain of interest when it looks as though he will be allowed his own way in front. (tchd 5-2 and 3-1)
Social Rhythm is a consistent sort who ran as well as she ever has done returned to seven furlongs. She settled better than has been the case and would have gone very close with a clear run. She looks capable of making amends. (op 7-2)
Leonard Charles, the most inexperienced member of the field, ran at least as well as he had when winning his maiden on this handicap debut. There were still definite signs of greenness and he left the impression that the step up to a mile would bring about further improvement. (op 2-1)
Belvedere Vixen, a consistent sort who had run creditably on her All-Weather debut at Southwell, was not disgraced on this handicap bow and first start on Polytrack. She will have to improve to win from her current mark, though. (op 8-1 tchd 10-1)
My Sara, up in distance, was not totally disgraced on this first run for over six months on this handicap debut. She is in good hands and left the impression that a stiffer test of stamina would have been in her favour. (op 7-1 tchd 13-2)
Bridget's Team had been running creditably in low-grade events on Fibresand but had her limitations exposed back in fair nursery company returned to Polytrack. The return to Southwell should be to her liking. (op 22-1)

6992 PHOTO BOOKS FROM BONUSPRINT.COM H'CAP 1m 1f 103y(P)
5:50 (5:50) (Class 4) (0-85,84) 3-Y-0+ **£5,362** (£1,604; £802; £401; £199) **Stalls** Low

Form RPR

1000 **1** **Chicken Soup**[82] 5877 4-8-4 77 .... WilliamBuick(7) 1 91
(T J Pitt) *chsd ldrs: rdn to ld and edgd rt wl over 1f out: clr fnl f* **4/1**[3]

3110 **2** *5* **Kildare Sun (IRE)**[21] 6772 4-8-10 76 .... DaleGibson 6 80
(J Mackie) *chsd ldr tl led 3f out: rdn and hdd wl over 1f out: edgd lft: outpcd fnl f* **7/2**[2]

5234 **3** 1 ¼ **Atlantic Quest (USA)**[10] 6888 7-8-12 81 .... AmirQuinn(3) 9 82
(Miss Venetia Williams) *hld up: hdwy over 1f out: nt rch ldrs* **4/1**[3]

2000 **4** *shd* **Master Of The Race**[148] 4112 4-8-10 76 .... SteveDrowne 10 77
(Tom Dascombe) *hld up: plld hrd: hdwy over 1f out: edgd lft fnl f: nt rch ldrs* **20/1**

4605 **5** 1 ¾ **Sew'N'So Character (IRE)**[21] 6772 5-9-1 81 .... TonyCulhane 7 79
(M Blanshard) *hld up in tch: ev ch over 2f out: wknd fnl f* **13/2**

4010 **6** *shd* **Prince Charlemagne (IRE)**[190] 2805 3-8-13 84 .... JamesDoyle(3) 5 81
(N P Littmoden) *hld up: hdwy over 2f out: rdn and wknd over 1f out* **3/1**[1]

-300 **7** ½ **James Caird (IRE)**[10] 6888 6-9-1 **84**........................ SaleemGolam(3) 3 80
(M H Tompkins) *chsd ldrs: rdn over 2f out: wknd over 1f out* **11/1**

0265 **8** ½ **Desert Leader (IRE)**[12] 6862 5-8-8 **74**........................ JamieMackay 8 69
(W M Brisbourne) *s.i.s: hld up: effrt and n.m.r over 1f out: hmpd ins fnl f: n.d* **25/1**

26B0 **9** 2 **Consonant (IRE)**[10] 6888 9-8-6 **77**........................ RoryMoore(5) 4 68
(D G Bridgwater) *led 6f: edgd rt and wknd over 1f out* **20/1**

2m 5.16s (2.54) **Going Correction** +0.125s/f (Slow)
WFA 3 from 4yo+ 2lb **9** Ran SP% **122.3**
Speed ratings (Par 105):93,88,87,87,85 85,85,84,83
CSF £19.10 CT £61.59 TOTE £5.70: £1.50, £1.50, £1.70; EX 26.20.
Owner Fishlake Commercial Motors Ltd **Bred** Limestone Stud **Trained** Bawtry, S Yorks

FOCUS
A fair handicap but an ordinary pace suited those racing prominently. The winner won well but the form does not have a solid look to it.
Prince Charlemagne(IRE) Official explanation: jockey said gelding was unsuited by the slow early pace

6993 PONTINSBINGO.COM H'CAP 1m 141y(P)
6:20 (6:20) (Class 6) (0-65,65) 3-Y-O+ **£2,590** (£770; £385; £192) **Stalls** Low

Form RPR

5600 **1** **Bold Diktator**[86] 5778 4-9-4 **65**........................ SteveDrowne 2 74
(Tom Dascombe) *led 1f: chsd ldrs: rdn to ld ins fnl f: edgd lft: r.o* **4/1**[3]

3413 **2** 1¾ **Spark Up**[7] 6934 6-8-7 **57**........................(b) RichardKingscote(3) 9 62
(J W Unett) *chsd ldrs: led 3f out: rdn over 1f out: hdd and unable qck ins fnl f* **7/4**[1]

3000 **3** 2 **Sir Bond (IRE)**[135] 4518 5-8-8 **60**........................ DuranFentiman(5) 5 61+
(G R Oldroyd) *hld up: hdwy over 2f out swtchd lft over 1f out: sn rdn: no imp fnl f* **2/1**[2]

-060 **4** 8 **Plausabelle**[17] 6810 5-8-10 **57** ow2........................ TonyCulhane 7 41
(G G Margarson) *hld up in tch: rdn over 2f out: wknd over 1f out* **13/2**

0-60 **5** 2½ **Cumberland Road**[105] 5363 3-7-13 **51** oh3........................ DominicFox(3) 1 30
(C A Mulhall) *hld up: rdn over 3f out: sn wknd* **100/1**

0-00 **6** ¾ **The Loose Screw (IRE)**[26] 6694 8-8-4 **51** oh16........................ DaleGibson 6 28
(C W Thornton) *chsd ldrs: rdn 1/2-way: wknd over 2f out* **150/1**

0000 **7** 2½ **Reveur**[4] 6942 3-9-0 **63**........................ SilvestreDeSousa 3 35
(M Mullineaux) *led over 7f out: rdn and hdd 3f out: wknd over 1f out* **33/1**

0/0- **8** 5 **Double Mystery (FR)**[115] 5121 6-8-7 **59**........................(tp) EmmettStack(5) 8 20
(K J Burke) *hld up: rdn over 3f out: sn wknd* **20/1**

1m 51.5s (-0.26) **Going Correction** +0.125s/f (Slow)
WFA 3 from 4yo+ 2lb **8** Ran SP% **112.4**
Speed ratings (Par 101):106,104,102,95,93 92,90,86
CSF £11.00 CT £17.05 TOTE £5.60: £1.50, £2.30, £1.10; EX 23.90 Place 6 £150.67, Place 5 £14.77.
Owner Oneway RSM Racing Club **Bred** T J And Mrs Heywood **Trained** Lambourn, Berks

FOCUS
A run-of-the-mill handicap in which the pace was fair. Only the first three were ever involved and the form seems sound enough.
T/Plt: £63.80 to a £1 stake. Pool: £51,861.30. 592.90 winning tickets. T/Qpdt: £4.40 to a £1 stake. Pool: £7,932.40. 1,319.00 winning tickets CR

6988 WOLVERHAMPTON (A.W) (L-H)
Sunday, December 31

OFFICIAL GOING: Standard
Wind: Strong, half-behind. Weather: Showers.

6994 PONTINSBINGO.COM H'CAP 5f 20y(P)
1:25 (1:25) (Class 6) (0-60,59) 3-Y-O+ **£2,730** (£806; £403) **Stalls** Low

Form RPR

6011 **1** **Rowe Park**[28] 6688 3-9-4 **59**........................ LPKeniry 1 74
(Mrs L C Jewell) *chsd ldr: rdn and hung lft fr over 1f out: styd on to ld wl ins fnl f* **10/3**[1]

0653 **2** 1 **Almaty Express**[9] 6922 4-9-0 **55**........................(b) TPQueally 4 66
(J R Weymes) *sn led: rdn adn edgd rt over 1f out: hdd and unable qck ins fnl f* **4/1**[2]

0034 **3** 1¾ **Monte Major (IRE)**[11] 6884 5-8-9 **50**........................(v) FrancisNorton 12 55
(D Shaw) *hld up: r.o ins fnl f: nrst fin* **14/1**

2022 **4** ½ **Muktasb (USA)**[23] 6753 5-8-11 **52**........................(v) DaneO'Neill 8 55+
(D Shaw) *hld up: r.o ins fnl f: nrst fin* **9/2**[3]

6016 **5** nk **Jabbara (IRE)**[36] 6608 3-9-0 **55**........................(b) HayleyTurner 3 57
(C E Brittain) *hld up: rdn over 1f out: r.o ins fnl f: nvr nrr* **11/2**

0030 **6** shd **Phinerine**[1] 6990 3-8-9 **55**........................(b) TolleyDean(5) 11 56
(R A Harris) *prom: rdn 1/2-way: styd on same pce fnl f* **20/1**

0000 **7** ½ **Triskaidekaphobia**[15] 6844 3-9-3 **58**........................ PaulFitzsimons 9 58
(Miss J R Tooth) *chsd ldrs: rdn over 1f out: no ex fnl f* **50/1**

0230 **8** 1¼ **Lady Hopeful (IRE)**[9] 6906 4-8-6 **47**........................(b) RobbieFitzpatrick 10 42
(Peter Grayson) *dwlt: hld up: r.o ins fnl f: nvr nrr* **14/1**

1040 **9** ½ **Twinned (IRE)**[25] 6723 3-8-8 **49**........................(p) ChrisCatlin 7 42
(Karen George) *chsd ldrs over 3f* **20/1**

2422 **10** nk **New Options**[11] 6877 9-8-13 **57**........................(b) JerryO'Dwyer(3) 2 49
(Peter Grayson) *hmpd s: sn chasng ldrs: rdn 1/2-way: wknd fnl f* **10/1**

2630 **11** 2½ **Jun Fan (USA)**[174] 3356 4-9-3 **58**........................(t) PaulMulrennan 5 41
(B Ellison) *mid-div: sn drvn along: wknd over 1f out* **20/1**

5410 **12** 5 **Signor Whippee**[83] 5864 3-9-0 **55**........................(b) PaulQuinn 6 20
(A Berry) *hld up: a in rr* **50/1**

62.96 secs (0.14) **Going Correction** +0.075s/f (Slow) **12** Ran SP% **117.3**
Speed ratings (Par 101):101,99,96,95,95 95,94,92,91,91 87,79
CSF £14.96 CT £164.74 TOTE £2.30: £1.10, £1.80, £5.20; EX 13.70 Trifecta £93.10 Pool £202.15 - 1.54 winning units..
Owner R I B Young and Mrs F J Meekins **Bred** J Baker **Trained** Sutton Valence, Kent

FOCUS
A moderate handicap and ordinary form for the grade.

6995 PONTIN'S FAMILY HOLIDAYS H'CAP 1m 5f 194y(P)
1:55 (1:55) (Class 6) (0-60,60) 3-Y-O+ **£2,730** (£806; £403) **Stalls** Low

Form RPR

6612 **1** **Little Richard (IRE)**[8] 6936 7-9-1 **52**........................(p) AdamKirby 4 62
(M Wellings) *a.p: chsd ldr over 1f out: styd on u.p to ld wl ins fnl f* **15/8**[1]

0463 **2** ½ **Arsad (IRE)**[8] 6929 3-8-13 **57**........................ J-PGuillambert 7 66
(C E Brittain) *led: hdd 10f out: chsd ldr tl led again over 3f out: rdn clr 2f out: hdd and unable qck wl ins fnl f* **4/1**[2]

0000 **3** 4 **Pocket Too**[15] 5897 3-8-9 **53**........................ JimmyQuinn 3 57
(M Salaman) *hld up: rdn over 5f out: hdwy over 2f out: nt rch ldrs* **20/1**

0005 **4** shd **Mustakhlas (USA)**[23] 6754 5-8-2 **45** oh1........................ SoniaEaton(7) 6 50
(B P J Baugh) *a.p: chsd ldr over 2f out tl styd on same pce appr fnl f* **12/1**

0315 **5** hd **Zaffeu**[20] 6790 5-8-10 **52**........................ RussellKennemore(5) 10 55
(A G Juckes) *s.i.s: hld up: nt clr run over 2f out: hdwy over 1f out : nrst fin* **13/2**

4322 **6** 3½ **Amwell Brave**[11] 6883 5-9-9 **60**........................ PaulHanagan 12 58
(J R Jenkins) *hld up: plld hrd: hdwy over 1f out: n.d* **11/2**[3]

5430 **7** ½ **Tip Toes (IRE)**[19] 6797 4-8-9 **44** oh1........................ DeanCorby 2 44
(P Howling) *hld up: rdn over 3f out: hdwy over 1f out: nvr nrr* **33/1**

6-63 **8** 2 **Avanti**[18] 6804 10-8-11 **48**........................(v) AlanDaly 1 43
(Dr J R J Naylor) *s.i.s: hld up: hdwy over 3f out: wknd over 2f out* **33/1**

4000 **9** 1¼ **Crimson Flame (IRE)**[17] 6819 3-8-7 **51** ow3........................ DeanMcKeown 8 44
(A J Chamberlain) *slowly in to stride: hld up: hdwy over 4f out: wknd 2f out* **66/1**

2006 **10** ½ **Blue Hills**[168] 3454 5-9-2 **56**........................(p) AmirQuinn(3) 5 48
(P W Hiatt) *chsd ldr tl led 10f out: hdd over 3f out: wknd over 1f out* **16/1**

5524 **11** 1 **Malibu (IRE)**[13] 6857 5-8-10 **47**........................ DaneO'Neill 11 38
(M Appleby) *prom: rdn over 3f out: wknd 2f out* **10/1**

6000 **12** 32 **Hometomammy**[25] 6729 4-8-10 **47** ow1........................ PhillipMakin 9 —
(P W Hiatt) *chsd ldrs: rdn over 3f out: sn wknd* **50/1**

3m 7.36s (-0.01) **Going Correction** +0.075s/f (Slow)
WFA 3 from 4yo+ 7lb **12** Ran SP% **120.3**
Speed ratings (Par 101):103,102,100,100,100 98,97,96,96,95 95,76
CSF £8.65 CT £116.79 TOTE £2.60: £1.50, £1.70, £7.10; EX 10.20 TRIFECTA Not won..
Owner Mark Wellings Racing **Bred** Rathbarry Stud **Trained** Six Ashes, Shropshire

FOCUS
Just a fair pace on here for this moderate staying handicap.

6996 PONTIN'S HOLIDAYS (S) STKS 1m 141y(P)
2:25 (2:25) (Class 6) 2-Y-O **£2,730** (£806; £403) **Stalls** Low

Form RPR

0004 **1** **Gold Response**[13] 6859 2-8-12 45........................ DeanMcKeown 2 55+
(D Shaw) *hld up: hdwy and hmpd 2f out: wandered over 1f out: styd on u.p to ld nr fin* **7/1**[3]

0034 **2** nk **The Light Fandango**[43] 6522 2-8-2 48........................ TolleyDean(5) 5 49
(R A Harris) *chsd ldrs: hung lft over 1f out: rdn to ld ins fnl f: hdd nr fin* **10/1**

004 **3** 1 **Zaafira (SPA)**[21] 6778 2-8-7 53........................ EdwardCreighton 6 47
(E J Creighton) *a.p: led wl over 1f out: sn rdn and hung rt: hdd 1f out: styd on same pce* **18/1**

0343 **4** ¾ **Party Palace**[13] 6859 2-8-10 47........................ RichardKingscote(3) 3 52
(J A Osborne) *led: hdd over 5f out: led again over 3f out: hdd wl over 1f out: rallied to ld 1f out: sn hdd and no ex* **3/1**[1]

6005 **5** 2½ **Power Alert**[13] 6859 2-8-12 47........................ JimCrowley 9 45
(B R Millman) *plld hrd and prom: lost pl over 6f out: hdwy over 2f out: rdn and hung lft fr over 1f out: styd on same pce* **10/1**

0054 **6** 4 **Foxxy**[22] 6764 2-8-10 58........................(b) AndrewMullen(3) 8 38
(K A Ryan) *s.i.s: sn prom: led over 5f out: hdd over 3f out: rdn and wknd over 2f out* **3/1**[1]

032 **7** nk **For Eileen**[43] 6511 2-8-7 51........................ TPQueally 4 31
(M G Quinlan) *chsd ldrs: rdn over 3f out: wknd 2f out* **4/1**[2]

40 **8** 8 **Ugenius**[22] 6768 2-8-7........................ MichaelJStainton(5) 7 20
(R A Harris) *chsd ldrs: rdn and ev ch whn hung rt over 2f out: wknd over 1f out* **16/1**

6000 **9** 1¾ **Lady Chastity**[18] 6807 2-8-7 47........................ HayleyTurner 10 11
(Mrs L J Young) *prom: lost pl over 7f out: effrt over 3f out: sn wknd* **50/1**

0000 **10** dist **Time Dancer (IRE)**[37] 6581 2-8-12 45........................(b[1]) PaulQuinn 1 —
(A Berry) *sn pushed along in rr: bhd fr 1/2-way* **66/1**

1m 53.33s (1.57) **Going Correction** +0.075s/f (Slow) **10** Ran SP% **115.3**
Speed ratings (Par 94):96,95,94,94,91 88,88,81,79,—
CSF £73.89 TOTE £6.40: £2.00, £3.10, £5.00; EX 79.30 TRIFECTA Not won..There was no bid for the winner.
Owner Danethorpe Racing Ltd **Bred** J C S Wilson **Trained** Danethorpe, Notts

FOCUS
A moderate seller, the runner-up helping to set the level. The winner is capable of better but looks tricky.

NOTEBOOK
Gold Response, who had shown a hint of ability when fourth in a claimer here last time and was now meeting third-placed Party Palace on 10lb better terms, was well supported to reverse the placings and did so despite running about under pressure in the straight. He is evidently not the most straightforward, but should be able to win again at this level. (op 16-1)
The Light Fandango, another who had finished behind Party Palace here recently and was weighted to turn the tables, managed to do so but did not help her chances of victory by hanging on the run to the line. (op 9-1)
Zaafira(SPA), best in on official figures, hung under pressure through the final furlong and, on this evidence, is not worth even her modest mark of 53. (op 12-1)
Party Palace, who has finished in front of both of today's first two in claiming company here in recent weeks, was given a positive ride but was never left alone in front and that eventually told in the run to the line. (tchd 11-4)
Power Alert, who was inclined to race in snatches, finished behind Gold Response and Party Palace in a claimer here last time and did so again, which suggests this is as good as he is. (op 9-1)
Foxxy, dropped into a seller for the first time, may have won over a mile in soft ground on turf but this was the second time she has performed like a non-stayer over this trip on sand. (tchd 7-2)

6997 PONTINS.COM H'CAP 1m 1f 103y(P)
2:55 (2:55) (Class 2) (0-100,98) 3-Y-O+
£11,217 (£3,358; £1,679; £840; £419; £210) **Stalls** Low

Form RPR

1036 **1** **Bahar Shumaal (IRE)**[16] 6836 4-8-13 **93**........................(b) J-PGuillambert 8 104
(C E Brittain) *a.p: chsd ldr 6f out: led 3f out: rdn over 1f out: all out* **3/1**[2]

1213 **2** shd **Vacation (IRE)**[12] 6868 3-7-9 **84** oh1........................ WilliamBuick(7) 9 95+
(V Smith) *hld up: hdwy u.p and hung lft over 1f out: swtchd lft ins fnl f: r.o wl* **15/8**[1]

605 **3** 2 **Langford**[23] 6744 6-8-8 **88**........................ TPQueally 2 95
(M H Tompkins) *chsd ldrs: rdn over 1f out: styd on same pce ins fnl f* **12/1**

4434 **4** nk **Kindlelight Debut**[9] 6914 6-9-0 **97**........................ JamesDoyle(3) 4 103
(N P Littmoden) *mid-div: rdn over 3f out: hdwy over 2f out: hmpd ins fnl f: rdr sn dropped whip: styd on* **7/1**

5000 **5** 3½ **Boo**[106] 5374 4-9-1 **95**........................(v) PatCosgrave 7 94
(K R Burke) *trckd ldrs: rdn over 2f out: wknd fnl f* **11/1**

5505 **6** 5 **Byron Bay**[29] 6678 4-8-6 **86**........................ PaulHanagan 5 75
(I Semple) *hld up: rdn over 3f out: n.d* **6/1**[3]

6005 **7** *5* **Weightless**[40] 6559 6-9-4 **98** .... PaulMulrennan 3 77
(N P Littmoden) *rdn to ld after 1f: hung rt fnl 6f: hdd 3f out: wknd over 1f out* **16/1**
405 **8** *½* **Paraguay (USA)**[9] 6915 3-7-11 **84** oh6 .... DuranFentiman(5) 6 62
(Miss V Haigh) *hld up: wknd 2f out* **20/1**
-300 **9** *2½* **Psychiatrist**[9] 6915 5-8-10 **90** .... (b1) PaulFitzsimons 1 63
(Miss J R Tooth) *trckd ldrs: plld hrd: rdn over 3f out: wknd over 2f out* **40/1**

2m 1.23s (-1.39) **Going Correction** +0.075s/f (Slow)
WFA 3 from 4yo+ 2lb **9** Ran SP% **115.7**
Speed ratings (Par 109):109,108,107,106,103 99,94,94,92
CSF £9.03 CT £56.62 TOTE £4.00: £1.20, £1.40, £3.30; EX 10.70 Trifecta £166.60 Pool £640.75 - 2.73 winning units..
Owner Saeed Manana **Bred** Airlie Stud And Sir Thomas Pilkington **Trained** Newmarket, Suffolk
■ Stewards' Enquiry : William Buick three-day ban: used whip with excessive frequency and without allowing time to respond (Jan 13-15)

FOCUS
A respectable field for this good prize, and the form looks sound rated around the third and fourth.

NOTEBOOK
Bahar Shumaal(IRE), who had taken advantage of a plummeting handicap mark when scoring here in October, has had excuses since but he bounced back to form to score off a 13lb higher mark than when last successful. He got first run on Vacation and Langford in the straight, and the line came just in time. (op 5-2)
Vacation(IRE) ◆, a come-from-behind horse who needs things to drop just right for him, hung left when first put under pressure but was running on strongly in the last 100 yards and would have got up in another stride. He remains in good heart and should soon be winning again. (op 2-1 tchd 9-4 and 5-2 in places)
Langford has been in the grip of the handicapper all year and, although now slipping down the weights from a mark in the mid-90s, he is still finding it difficult to get his head in front. (op 10-1)
Kindlelight Debut has been struggling from her present mark, having taken a hike after a couple of good runs in Listed races, but she ran a decent race. (tchd 13-2)
Boo did not see his race out on this first start in three months, but he won after a similar break the previous year so it is more likely that he remains a few pounds too high in the weights. (op 10-1)
Weightless hung for much of the race and looked far from keen. Official explanation: jockey said gelding hung right throughout
Psychiatrist was wearing first-time blinkers, but that caused him to race even more freely and he was a spent force turning for home.

6998 DADDY'S LITTLE GIRL - JORJA HUGHES MEMORIAL MAIDEN STKS 7f 32y(P)
3:25 (3:25) (Class 5) 2-Y-0 **£3,886** (£1,156; £577; £288) **Stalls** High

Form RPR
042 **1** **All Of Me (IRE)**[11] 6887 2-9-3 72 .... DaneO'Neill 5 74+
(T G Mills) *hld up in tch: rdn and hung lft fr over 1f out: r.o to ld post* **9/4**[2]
6 **2** *shd* **Soft Morning**[11] 6886 2-8-12 .... JamieMackay 9 69
(Sir Mark Prescott) *led: rdn over 1f out: edgd lft and hdd post* **7/4**[1]
0 **3** *1½* **Lascelles**[220] 1959 2-9-3 .... JimCrowley 2 70
(J A Osborne) *hld up: hdwy over 2f out: styd on same pce ins fnl f* **5/1**[3]
6 **4** *3½* **Realy Naughty (IRE)**[11] 6887 2-9-3 .... FergusSweeney 1 61
(B G Powell) *prom: chsd ldr over 2f out: rdn over 1f out: wknd ins fnl f* **10/1**
5 *6* **Lady Cartuccia** 2-8-12 .... JimmyQuinn 6 41
(J J Quinn) *s.s: bhd: shkn up over 1f out: nvr trbld ldrs* **7/1**
60 **6** *3* **Ancient Site (USA)**[61] 6284 2-9-3 .... DeanMcKeown 7 39
(B P J Baugh) *hld up: rdn over 2f out: n.d* **80/1**
7 *5* **Isn't It Grand (IRE)** 2-8-12 .... J-PGuillambert 10 21
(Miss V Haigh) *dwlt: plld hrd and sn prom: rdn over 2f out: wknd qckly* **50/1**
6 **8** *hd* **Wiseton Dancer (IRE)**[281] 727 2-9-3 .... EdwardCreighton 4 26
(Miss V Haigh) *chsd ldr tl rdn over 2f out: sn wknd* **16/1**
06 **9** *36* **Cragg Lass (IRE)**[37] 6586 2-8-12 .... PaulQuinn 3 —
(A Berry) *hld up: bhd fr 1/2-way* **100/1**

1m 31.85s (1.45) **Going Correction** +0.075s/f (Slow) **9** Ran SP% **115.5**
Speed ratings (Par 96):94,93,92,88,81 77,72,71,30
CSF £6.57 TOTE £3.40: £1.20, £1.10, £1.70; EX 8.30 Trifecta £17.40 Pool £837.74 - 34.06 winning units..
Owner John Humphreys **Bred** Lynn Lodge Stud **Trained** Headley, Surrey

FOCUS
The winner showed slight improvement to beat the improved runner-up and the form appears sound.

NOTEBOOK
All Of Me(IRE) set the standard in this moderate maiden on the strength of his second at Lingfield last time, although he had not found a lot for pressure when touched off there. He made hard work of wearing down Soft Morning, hanging left all the way down the straight, and O'Neill was seen at his strongest to get him up in the last stride. (tchd 15-8)
Soft Morning, forced to race wide from her high draw on her recent debut at Lingfield, managed to get across early from her high berth and ran a sound race from the front. Though just touched off, she does not need to improve much to pick up a little race. (op 5-4 tchd 2-1)
Lascelles, a 42,000gns purchase who was having his first run since May, was well supported but could not pick up as required in the straight. He is entitled to come on for this first outing in seven months and should make his mark in time. (op 10-1)
Realy Naughty(IRE) finished further behind today's winner than he had on his debut at Lingfield. (op 12-1)
Lady Cartuccia is out of an unraced half-sister to Derby runner-up City Honours. She lost ground at the start and ran green, but the penny looked to be dropping for her in the closing stages and she should be all the better for the experience. Official explanation: jockey said filly missed the break (op 9-1 tchd 13-2)

6999 GO PONTIN'S H'CAP 7f 32y(P)
3:55 (3:55) (Class 4) (0-85,84) 3-Y-0+ **£5,505** (£1,637; £818; £408) **Stalls** High

Form RPR
0432 **1** **Buy On The Red**[16] 6835 5-8-7 **78** .... (p) JamesDoyle(3) 8 87
(W R Muir) *sn led: rdn over 1f out: all out* **15/2**
6131 **2** *¾* **Mandarin Spirit (IRE)**[22] 6770 6-8-6 **77** .... (b) SaleemGolam(3) 4 84
(G C H Chung) *hld up: swtchd lft and hdwy over 1f out: sn rdn: r.o* **11/2**[2]
4010 **3** *1* **Regal Raider (IRE)**[22] 6770 3-8-7 **75** .... PaulHanagan 3 79
(I Semple) *chsd ldrs: rdn over 2f out: styd on u.p* **11/2**[2]
2533 **4** *shd* **Gifted Gamble**[23] 6752 4-9-0 **82** .... (b) FrancisNorton 7 86
(K A Ryan) *prom: rdn over 2f out: styd on* **5/1**[1]
6056 **5** *shd* **Samuel Charles**[29] 6671 8-8-10 **78** .... TPQueally 6 82
(C R Dore) *mid-div: hdwy over 2f out: rdn and hung lft fr over 1f out: styd on* **7/1**[3]
030 **6** *1½* **Inch By Inch**[37] 6579 7-8-4 **72** .... ChrisCatlin 1 72
(P J Makin) *led early: chsd ldrs: outpcd over 2f out: styd on udner press fnl f* **25/1**
5060 **7** *2* **King Marju (IRE)**[10] 6896 4-8-12 **80** .... (v) PatCosgrave 10 75
(K R Burke) *hld up: rdn over 1f out: nvr trbld ldrs* **16/1**
20 **8** *nk* **Bay Boy**[29] 6671 4-8-7 **78** .... GregFairley(3) 5 72
(M Johnston) *chsd ldrs: rdn over 2f out: wknd over 1f out* **7/1**[3]
002 **9** *1½* **El Coto**[25] 6733 6-9-2 **84** .... (p) PaulMulrennan 2 74
(K A Ryan) *hld up: hdwy 1/2-way: nt clr run over 2f out: sn rdn and wknd* **7/1**[3]
6603 **10** *nk* **Finsbury**[16] 6830 3-8-8 **76** .... HayleyTurner 9 65
(Miss J Feilden) *dwlt: hld up: nt clr run over 1f out: n.d* **10/1**

1m 30.3s (-0.10) **Going Correction** +0.075s/f (Slow) **10** Ran SP% **115.5**
Speed ratings (Par 105):103,102,101,100,100 99,96,96,94,94
CSF £47.98 CT £252.30 TOTE £7.90: £2.90, £1.50, £2.10; EX 30.70 Trifecta £219.80 Pool £938.22 - 3.03 winning units. Place 6 £55.01, Place 5 £34.15..
Owner R Haim **Bred** J Gittins And Capt J H Wilson **Trained** Lambourn, Berks
■ Stewards' Enquiry : Saleem Golam caution: careless riding

FOCUS
Not a strongly-run race. The winner is rated to his best form of the past two years.
T/Plt: £87.20 to a £1 stake. Pool: £92,020.05. 770.20 winning tickets. T/Qpdt: £26.30 to a £1 stake. Pool: £6,543.40. 183.90 winning tickets. CR

5802 ASCOT (AUS) (R-H)
Wednesday, December 20

OFFICIAL GOING: Good

7000a C B COX STKS (GROUP 2) 1m 4f
9:20 (12:00) 3-Y-0+
£34,423 (£34,423; £7,692; £3,419; £2,137; £1,282)

RPR
1 **Scenic Shot (AUS)**[11] 4-9-0 .... DMOliver 6 —
(D Morton, Australia) **19/10**[1]
1 *dht* **Daka's Gem (AUS)**[11] 7-9-2 .... PatrickCarbery 10 —
(A Mathews, Australia) **10/1**[3]
3 *1¼* **Ramiro (AUS)** 4-9-0 .... RStewart 4 —
(M Dillon) **16/1**
4 *nse* **Zero Engagement (AUS)** 6-9-2 .... DStaeck 7 —
(T Roney, Australia) **18/1**
5 *hd* **Black Tom (AUS)**[282] 5-9-2 .... PHall 14 —
(F Maynard, Australia) **8/1**[2]
6 *nk* **Purde (NZ)**[11] 3-8-8 .... SParnham 1 —
(P Gatt, France) **10/1**[3]
7 *nse* **Bay Story (USA)**[39] 6455 4-9-2 .... MZahra 8 —
(B Ellison) *raced in 3rd to straight, went 2nd approaching final f, one pace* **14/1**
8 *1* **Respect (NZ)** 7-9-2 .... JWhiting 11 —
(P Cave, Australia) **20/1**
9 *nk* **Laetare (AUS)**[583] 6-9-2 .... LaneMoloney 9 —
(E Martinovich, Australia) **70/1**
10 *nse* **Coalseam (AUS)** 5-9-2 .... JasonBrown 12 —
(Jim Taylor, Australia) **15/1**
11 *1¼* **Woodala (AUS)** 5-8-10 .... LCamilleri 2 —
(A Mathews, Australia) **25/1**
12 *nk* **Zoometric (AUS)**[11] 6-9-2 .... TroyTurner 3 —
(G Webster Snr, New Zealand) **8/1**[2]
13 *2½* **Kia Ora Miss (AUS)** 3-8-8 .... SMcgruddy 13 —
(A Durrant, Australia) **20/1**
14 *nk* **Land 'n Stars**[43] 6392 6-9-2 .... WPike 5 —
(Jamie Poulton) *tracked leader to over 2f out, one pace* **15/1**

2m 32.54s
WFA 3 from 4yo+ 5lb **14** Ran SP% **120.0**
(including $AUS1 stakes): Daka's Gem WIN 6.20, PL 3.00; Scenic Shot WIN 1.20, PL 1.50; Ramiro PL 5.90; DF 15.60.
Owner D Morton et al **Bred** R & Mrs A Anderson **Trained** Australia
Owner G Nicholls, Mrs C Archibald et al **Bred** Kendel Park Stud **Trained** Australia

INDEX TO MEETINGS FLAT 2006

† Abandoned
* All-Weather
(M) Mixed meeting

INDEX TO FLAT RACING

Horses are shown in alphabetical order; the trainer's name follows the name of the horse. The figures to the right are current master ratings for all-weather and turf; the all-weather rating is preceded by the letter 'a'.Underneath the horse's name is its age, colour and sex in abbreviated format e.g. 6 b g indicates the horse is six-years-old, bay in colour, and a gelding.The descriptive details are followed by the race numbers of the races in which it has taken part in chronological order; a superscript figure indicates its finishing position in that race (brackets indicate it was the winner of the race).

Aahayson *K R Burke* 89
2 b c Noverre(USA) —See You Later (Emarati (USA))
(2191) 2724[13] 4088[2] (4519) 4893[2] 5334[2] 5655[3]

Aahgowangowan (IRE) *M Dods* a50 87
7 b m Tagula(IRE) —Cabcharge Princess (IRE) (Rambo Dancer (CAN))
2856[3] (3172) 3267[4] (3478) (3783) (3912) 4003[3] (4119) 4589[2]4952[5] 5117[5] 5336[13]

Aaim To Prosper (IRE) *M R Channon* a87 96
2 br c Val Royal(FR) —Bint Al Balad (IRE) (Ahonoora)
4572[4] 4867[3] 5126[2] (5389) 5828[2] 6074[2]6216[2] 6456a[8]

Aamaaq *J L Dunlop* 84+
3 b c Danehill(USA) —Alabaq (USA) (Riverman (USA))
1095[10] 1490[7] (2734)

Aaron's Way *A W Carroll* 61
2 gb f Act One—Always On My Mind (Distant Relative)
4920[6] 5417[5] 5764[2]

Aastral Magic *R Hannon* a76 73
4 b m Magic Ring(IRE) —Robanna (Robellino (USA))
721[12] 985[2]1338[7] 1692[4] 1962[2]2259[6] 2708[14] 2954[4] 4564[8] 5042[11]5384[13] 5621[3] 6413[10]6507[9] 6698[10]6747[12]

Abaconian (IRE) *M J Wallace* a71
3 b c Danehill(USA) —Double Grange (IRE) (Double Schwartz)
590[6] 703[2](802)

Abandon (USA) *W J Haggas* a80
3 ch f Rahy(USA) —Caerless (IRE) (Caerleon (USA))
6410[2] (6680) (6929)

Abbey Cat (IRE) *G A Swinbank* 86
3 b f Indian Danehill(IRE) —Catfoot Lane (Batshoof)
1122[6] (1592) 1734[3] 2297[7] 3282[5] (5512) 5724[U]

Abbeygate *T Keddy* a54 46
5 b g Unfuwain(USA) —Ayunli (Chief Singer)
72[12] 156[8]423[4] 697[6]889[5] (1201) 1537[7] 1725[4]2820[16] 4439[7] 6280[3]6374[2] 6551[5]6729[3] 6959[5]

Abbondanza (IRE) *J Howard Johnson* 75
3 b g Cape Cross(IRE) —Ninth Wonder (USA) (Forty Niner (USA))
(1343) 2659[8] 4711[16]

Abbotts Account (USA) *Mrs A J Perrett* 55
2 b g Mr Greeley(USA) —Agenda (USA) (Private Account (USA))
4705[11] 5379[7] 5640[11]

Abbotts Ann *B W Hills* a76 70
2 b f Marju(IRE) —Anne Boleyn (Rainbow Quest (USA))
3843[2] 4207[2] 4657[5](6310) 6444[7]

Abby Road (IRE) *B J Meehan* 101
2 b f Danehill(USA) —Bells Are Ringing (USA) (Sadler's Wells (USA))
2703[2] 3216[4] (3745) (4594) 5154[6] 5802[8]

Abdu *G P Kelly* a25 52
2 ch g Kyllachy—Better Still (IRE) (Glenstal (USA))
1096[8] 2072[3] 2321[8] 3917[10]4376[5] 6421[11]

Aberdeen Park *Mrs H Sweeting* a58 60
4 gr m Environment Friend—Michelee (Merdon Melody)
697[10] 1194[7]1537[9] (3379) 4139[13] 4439[4]4869[10] 5474[12]

Aberlady Bay (IRE) *T T Clement* a59
3 ch f Selkirk(USA) —Desert Serenade (USA) (Green Desert (USA))
4701[6] 5426[10]5669[8] 6300[15] 6436[13]6628[8] 6708[11]6794[11]

Abeurbe Condita (IRE) *E S McMahon* 66
3 ch g Titus Livius(FR) —Avantage Service (IRE) (Exactly Sharp (USA))
4891[3] 5138[3] 5862[3]

Abhisheka (IRE) *Saeed Bin Suroor* 108+
3 b f Sadler's Wells(USA) —Snow Bride (USA) (Blushing Groom (FR))
(1649) 2679[5] (5895) (6017) 6333[4]

Abide With Me (USA) *A P O'Brien* 91
2 b c Danehill(USA) —Sequoyah (IRE) (Sadler's Wells (USA))
3574a[7] 5521[6]

Abigail Pett *J S Bolger* 107
3 ch f Medicean—Kalindi (Efisio)
2054a[5] 3129a[6] 5849a[5]

A Big Sky Brewing (USA) *T D Barron* 50
2 b c Arch(USA) —Runalpharun (USA) (Thunder Rumble (USA))
6175[7]

A Bit Of Fun *J T Stimpson* a47 33
5 ch g Unfuwain(USA) —Horseshoe Reef (Mill Reef (USA))
788[7]

Able Baker Charlie (IRE) *J R Fanshawea83* 102
7 b g Sri Pekan(USA) —Lavezzola (IRE) (Salmon Leap (USA))
5639[14]

Able Mind *D W Thompson* a59 66
6 b g Mind Games—Chlo-Jo (Belmez (USA))
2286[5] 2966[10] 3386[3]3815[2] 4194[2] (5285) 5316[2] 5972[5]

Able Prince (AUS) *J Moore* 115
5 b h Hurricane Sky(AUS) —Queen's Choir (NZ) (Palace Music (USA))
6783a[7]

Abounding *R M Beckett* a53 56
2 b f Generous(IRE) —Ecstasy (Pursuit Of Love)
2478[8] 3010[3] 3435[10]5597[5]

Aboustar *M Brittain* a53 39
6 b g Abou Zouz(USA) —Three Star Rated (IRE) (Pips Pride)
691[5] 784[8]942[6] 6549[8]6756[8] 6962[2]6969[4]

Above And Below (IRE) *M Quinn* 36
2 b f Key Of Luck(USA) —Saramacca (IRE) (Kahyasi)
5456[14] 5941[4]

Aboyne (IRE) *K F Clutterbuck* a66 65
3 b g Mull Of Kintyre(USA) —Never End (Alzao (USA))
447[4] 538[5]945[8] 1424[8] 1829[11] 5298[15] 6033[12]

Abraham (IRE) *Michael Cunningham* 75
4 b g Orpen(USA) —We've Just Begun (USA) (Huguenot (USA))
273[6] (Dead)

Abraham Lincoln (IRE) *A P O'Brien* 89+
2 b c Danehill(USA) —Moon Drop (Dominion)
1807[2]

Absent Love *G G Margarson* 49
2 bb f Diktat—Jolis Absent (Primo Dominie)
1181[8] 1675[6] 5083[13]

Absolute Champion (AUS) *D Hall* 129
5 br g Marauding(NZ) —Beauty Belle (AUS) (Ideal Planet (AUS))
(6783a)

Absolute Image (IRE) *D K Weld* 99
4 gr g Indian Ridge—Absolute Glee (USA) (Kenmare (FR))
3123a[2] 4031a[2]

Absolutelyfabulous (IRE) *David Wachman* 100+
3 b f Mozart(IRE) —Lady Windermere (IRE) (Lake Coniston (IRE))
3967a[4] 4633[4] 4855a[4] 5393a[7]

Absolutelythebest (IRE) *J G M O'Shea* a75 81
5 b g Anabaa(USA) —Recherchee (Rainbow Quest (USA))
1502[8]

Abstract Art (USA) *N A Callaghan* a76 78
3 ch g Distorted Humor(USA) —Code From Heaven (USA) (Lost Code (USA))
(62) 294[6] 448[7]583[4] (695) 805[4] 1077[4] (1738)

Abstract Folly (IRE) *J D Bethell* a66 62
4 b g Rossini(USA) —Cochiti (Kris)
1152[6] 1425[12] 1996[5]2697[7] (3192) 3674[5] 4472[7] 4925[4] (5390) 6312[5] 6735[4]

Abunai *R Charlton* 82
2 ch f Pivotal—Ingozi (Warning)
2328[6] 2710[2] (3344) (4603) (5140) 5809[5]

Abundance (USA) *Mme C Head-Maarek* 109
4 b m Anabaa(USA) —Gorgeous (USA) (Slew O'Gold (USA))
3564a[7] 4860a[4] 5779a[8]

Abwaab *R F Johnson Houghton* a53 88
3 b g Agnes World(USA) —Flitteriss Park (Beldale Flutter (USA))
2048[3] (3219) 3973[10] 4429[3] 4923[4] 5377[8]5666[12]

Abyla *M P Tregoning* 60
2 b f Rock Of Gibraltar(IRE) —Animatrice (USA) (Alleged (USA))
4964[10]

Academy Reward (IRE) *Mario Hofer* 91
6 ch g Peintre Celebre(USA) —Avigail (USA) (Miswaki (USA))
4414a[9]

Acca Larentia (IRE) *Mrs H O Graham* a29 42
5 gr m Titus Livius(FR) —Daisy Grey (Nordance (USA))
2751[6] 3135[10] 3350[8] 3675[6]

Acceleration (IRE) *Karen McLintock* a51
6 b g Groom Dancer(USA) —Overdrive (Shirley Heights)
414[8] 4351[11] 6873[3]

Accent (IRE) *Sir Mark Prescott* a45 32
3 b g Beckett(IRE) —Umlaut (Zafonic (USA))
5574[14]

Accompanist *J H M Gosden* 82
3 b c Pivotal—Abscond (USA) (Unbridled (USA))
1476[7] 2118[2] 4300[2] 4776[2] 5151[4]5770[7] (6021)

Accordello (IRE) *K G Reveley* 60
5 b m Accordion—Marello (Supreme Leader)
1034[4] 1503[3] 1827[2] 3019[9] 5723[5]6178[12]

According To Pete *J M Jefferson* 73
5 b g Accordion—Magic Bloom (Full Of Hope)
5086[8] 5319[8] 5770[3]

Accountforthegold (USA) *G Contessa* a103
4 b h Successful Appeal(USA) —Accountess (USA) (Private Account (USA))
4787a[2]

Accumulate (NZ) *J B Cummings* 109
5 b g Zabeel(NZ) —Enhancer (NZ) (Red Tempo (NZ))
6347a[15]

Accumulus *Noel T Chance* 37
6 b g Cloudings(IRE) —Norstock (Norwick (USA))
5086[14]

Ace (IRE) *A P O'Brien* 124
5 b h Danehill(USA) —Tea House (Sassafras (FR))
1365a[2] 2202[4] 2741[7] 3559a[2] 4386a[6]5193a[5]

Ace Baby *K J Burke* 62
3 b g First Trump—Mise En Scene (Lugana Beach)
5863[7]

Acece *M Appleby* a52
2 b c Muthahb(IRE) —Berry Brook (Magic Ring (IRE))
6757[5] 6950[12]

Ace Club *M J Attwater* a51 39
5 ch g Indian Rocket—Presently (Cadeaux Genereux)
27[4] 127[11]260[11] 529[9]618[11] 691[6]873[4] 942[3]1054[13] 4363[13] 6131[11]6282[5] 6636[6]6717[3] 6906[12]6962[4] (6974)

Ace Of Hearts *C F Wall* a76 109
7 b g Magic Ring(IRE) —Lonely Heart (Midyan (USA))
1129[17] 1678[7] 2079[2] 2742[14] 3313[2]3733[6] 4145[2] 4739[15] 5675[23] 5945[13]

Acheekyone (IRE) *B J Meehan* a75 94
3 b g Indian Ridge—Tafrah (IRE) (Sadler's Wells (USA))
1115[2] 1490[4] 1841[7] 3224[2]

Acknowledgement *D R C Elsworth* a60 77
4 b g Josr Algarhoud(IRE) —On Request (IRE) (Be My Guest (USA))
3122[6] 3850[6] 4210[4] 4472[11] 5276[2]5628[2] 6108[2]

Acomb *Mrs L Richards* a69 67
6 b g Shaamit(IRE) —Aurora Bay (IRE) (Night Shift (USA))
662[9] 846[12]1382[9] 2405[9] 2606[9]2954[6] 3337[9] 3845[12]

Acorazado (IRE) *C P Morlock* a41 43
7 b g Petorius—Jaldi (IRE) (Nordico (USA))
82[10] 156[12]328[8] 417[7]498[6]

Acosta *Dr J R J Naylor* 52
2 b c Foxhound(USA) —Dancing Heights (IRE) (High Estate)
4526[10] 4980[11] 5622[10]

Acrobatic (USA) *R Charlton* a102 106
3 ch c Storm Boot(USA) —Alvernia (USA) (Alydar (USA))
(963) 1190[5] 2177[4] (2754) (3401) (4997) 5110[2]5660[3] (6384a)

Acropolis (IRE) *J Howard Johnson* 112
5 b g Sadler's Wells(USA) —Dedicated Lady (IRE) (Pennine Walk)
2010[7] 3078[17]

Act Friendly (IRE) *Saeed Bin Suroor* a91 80
3 b f Sadler's Wells(USA) —Ozone Friendly (USA) (Green Forest (USA))
(3620) 4612[6] 6411[5]

Activation (NZ) *G Rogerson* 115
5 b g Zabeel(NZ) —Coogee Walk (NZ) (Success Express (USA))
6110a[4] 6392a[8]

Active Account (USA) *J R Holt* a58d 55
9 bb g Unaccounted For(USA) —Ameritop (USA) (Topsider (USA))
156[11] 328[6]423[9] 2137[12]2245[12]

Active Asset (IRE) *M R Channon* 90
4 ch g Sinndar(IRE) —Sacristy (Godswalk (USA))
800[9] (1281) 1992[7] 2079[3] 2387[13] 2761[3](3081) 3151[3] 3747[3] 4023[7] 4370[8] 4878[7]5511[2] 5787[13]

Active Audience (IRE) *A Berry* a21 39
3 b f Fasliyev(USA) —Luisa Demon (IRE) (Barathea (IRE))
1036[8] 1609[7] 3384[4]3698[6] 4071[8] 4728[10] 5363[10] 6277[12]6306[12]

Activist *D Carroll* a65 65
8 ch g Diesis—Shicklah (USA) (The Minstrel (CAN))
52[6] (103) 283[7]

Activo (FR) *S Dow* a93 96
5 b g Trempolino(USA) —Acerbis (GER) (Rainbow Quest (USA))
116[5] 222[4]4805[9] 5177[8] 5511[11] 5776[8]6633[2] 6744[6]6888[14]

Actodos (IRE) *B R Millman* 73
2 ch c Act One—Really Gifted (IRE) (Cadeaux Genereux)
4526[4] 5125[6] 5623[2]

Act Sirius (IRE) *J Howard Johnson* 77
2 ch g Grand Lodge(USA) —Folgore (USA) (Irish River (FR))
5025[8] (5552)

Acts Of Grace (USA) *J L Dunlop* 106
3 b f Bahri(USA) —Rafha (Kris)
2118[6] 2580[2] (3146) 4482[5] (4979a) (5502) 6124a[6]

Acuzio *W M Brisbourne* a52 63
5 b g Mon Tresor—Veni Vici (IRE) (Namaqualand (USA))
882[9] 1194[5] (2242) 2407[3]2522[2] 2788[5] 3192[4] (3270) 3763[6] 4472[5]4764[4] 5174[7] 5531[3] 5725[3]

Adage *David Pinder* 57
3 b f Vettori(IRE) —Aymara (Darshaan)
1374[7] 2113[6] 2584[11] 3440[11] 5057[9]5510[6] 5887[5] 6068[3]

Adagio *Sir Michael Stoute* 112
2 br c Grand Lodge(USA) —Lalindi (IRE) (Cadeaux Genereux)
(5458) 5965[7]

Adalar (IRE) *P W D'Arcy* a44 41
6 br g Grand Lodge(USA) —Adalya (IRE) (Darshaan)
941[5] 1395[4]

Adamantinos *Frau E Mader* 95
2 b c Seattle Dancer(USA) —Aberdeen (GER) (Polish Precedent (USA))
(4857a) 5664a[3]

Adantino *B R Millman* a81 88
7 b g Glory Of Dancer—Sweet Whisper (Petong)
323[2] 441[4]541[3] 949[8] (1188) 1382[2]1939[7] (2189) 2981[5](3486) 3715[7] 4357[5] 5096[11]

Adaptation *M Johnston* 86
2 b f Spectrum(IRE) —Key Academy (Royal Academy (USA))
2375[2] (2999) (3481) 5940[4] 6105[6] 6546a[7]

Adarila (IRE) *James Leavy* a55 73?
5 bb m Mujadil(USA) —Adalya (IRE) (Darshaan)
73[5]

Addictive *S C Williams* 70
2 b f Averti(IRE) —Shadow Bird (Martinmas)
2638[7] (3430) 4146[7] 4761[7] 5503[8] 5866[9]

Adeje Park (IRE) *P W Chapple-Hyam* a98 89+
3 ch f Night Shift(USA) —Iyandas (ITY) (Love The Groom (USA))
1091[5] (1349) 1713a[7] 2744[17] 4172[6] 5990[4]6397[3] 6574a[4]

Adelfia (IRE) *Sir Michael Stoute* a77 77
3 ch f Sinndar(IRE) —Adaiyka (IRE) (Doyoun)
2578[5] 4204[3] (4701) 5109[8]

Adelphos (FR) *Mme N Rossio* 92
2 b c Kendor(FR) —Advalor (FR) (Synefos (USA))
3777a[7]

Adhrhythm (USA) *E Plesa* a100
2 b f Adhocracy(USA) —Relic Rhythm (USA) (Prospector's Halo (USA))
6338a[7]

Adios (GER) *P D Niven* 27
7 b g Lagunas—Aerope (Celestial Storm (USA))
5513[14]

Adjudication (IRE) *P Hughes* 61
4 b g Imperial Ballet(IRE) —Quilting (Mummy's Pet)
4166a[18]

Admiral (IRE) *T J Pitt* 94
5 b g Alhaarth(IRE) —Coast Is Clear (IRE) (Rainbow Quest (USA))
(1584) 2013[6] 2723[28]

Admiral Compton *J R Boyle* a77 72
5 ch g Compton Place—Sunfleet (Red Sunset)
33[9] 135[4]223[9] 764[13]1435[9] 1637[5] 2149[6] 2327[7] 2401[13]2551[7] 2752[7]5621[15]

Admiralofthefleet (USA) *A P O'Brien* 115+
2 b c Danehill(USA) —Rafina (USA) (Mr Prospector (USA))
3492[3] (5521)

Admiral Savannah (IRE) *T D Easterby* 44
2 b g Dilshaan—Valmarana (USA) (Danzig Connection (USA))
3633[4] 4466[8] 5025[7]

Admiral's Cruise (USA) *B J Meehan* 118
4 b h A.P. Indy(USA) —Ladies Cruise (USA) (Fappiano (USA))
1267[6] (1677) 2010[4] (3085) 4096[3] (4595) 5342[3]

Admire Main (JPN) *M Hashida* 122
3 b c Sunday Silence(USA) —Promotion (JPN) (Hector Protector (USA))
6782a[8]

Admire Monarch (JPN) *H Matsuda* 106
5 b h Dream Well(FR) —Split The Night (JPN) (Tony Bin)
1329a[14]

Admire Moon (JPN) *H Matsuda* 125
3 b c End Sweep(USA) —My Katies (JPN) (Sunday Silence (USA))
6785a[2]

Adobe *W M Brisbourne* a46 66
11 b g Green Desert(USA) —Shamshir (Kris)
41[8] 172[9]2482[4] (2702) 2969[13] 3311[6] 3570[9] 3820[10]4518[9] 5166[7] 5450[9] 5954[7] 6232[10]

Adonita *Saeed Bin Suroor* 44
2 b f Singspiel(IRE) —Anna Palariva (IRE) (Caerleon (USA))
6297[10]

Adopted Hero (IRE) *J Howard Johnsona84* 103
6 b g Sadler's Wells(USA) —Lady Liberty (NZ) (Noble Bijou (USA))
5010[11]

Adorabile Fong *M Guarnieri* 99
3 b c Dr Fong(USA) —Divine Secret (Hernando (FR))
1175a[3] 1872a[8]

Adraaj (USA) *E A L Dunlop* a64 87
3 bb f Sahm(USA) —Hachiyah (IRE) (Generous (IRE))
1417[4] (1759) 4555[6] 5895[2] 6202[4] 6411[10]

Ad Valorem (USA) *A P O'Brien* 123
4 b h Danzig(USA) —Classy Women (USA) (Relaunch (USA))
930a[6] (2722) 4416a[5] 5416a[3] 6342a[13]

Advanced *K A Ryan* a105 114
3 b c Night Shift(USA) —Wonderful World (GER) (Dashing Blade)
1083[3] 1404[2] 5358[3]6230a[2]

Advancement *R A Fahey* a73 78
3 b g Second Empire(IRE) —Lambast (Relkino)
2080[2] 2575[U] (3383) 3789[2]4634[8]

Adventuress *B J Meehan* a91 87
3 b f Singspiel(IRE) —Arriving (Most Welcome)
1085[4] (1374) 1819[6] 3491[7] 4808[9] 5150[3]5666[2]

Adversane *J L Dunlop* a58 48
2 ch c Alhaarth(IRE) —Cragreen (Green Desert (USA))
5890[15] 6214[16] 6561[6]

Advice *A Fabre* a85 106
5 b h Seeking The Gold(USA) —Anna Palariva (IRE) (Caerleon (USA))
3662a[5] 5519a[2]

Aegean Dancer *B Smart* a64 85
4 b g Piccolo—Aegean Flame (Anshan)
80[7] 605[3]1297[4] 1496[5] 2380[8] 2784[2] 3170[2](3699) 3938[4] (4453)

Aegean Mist *B P J Baugh* a41 43
6 ch m Prince Sabo—Dizzydaisy (Sharpo)
1396[10] 4054[15]

Aegean Pearl (USA) *J H M Gosden* a64 74
3 b f Lemon Drop Kid(USA) —Reluctant Diva (Sadler's Wells (USA))
2753[5] 3200[4]3901[4] 4396[6] (Dead)

Aegean Prince *R Hannon* a80 67
2 b c Dr Fong(USA) —Dizzydaisy (Sharpo)
5417[3] 5655[21] (6032)

Aegis (IRE) *B W Hills* a74 77
2 b g Beckett(IRE) —Silver Spoon (IRE) (College Chapel)
4028[7] 4295[9] 5125[5] 5585[2] 5783[3]

Aeronaut *J M Bradley* a27 35
3 b g Averti(IRE) —Roufontaine (Rousillon (USA))
2602[12] 3816[4] 5151[8]
Aeroplane *P W Chapple-Hyam* 110
3 b c Danehill Dancer(IRE) —Anita At Dawn (IRE) (Anita's Prince)
(1065) 2031[4] 2721[10] (5116) 5962[13]
Afadan (IRE) *J R Jenkins* a57 57
8 br g Royal Academy(USA) —Afasara (IRE) (Shardari)
125[11] 478[13]700[8] 847[8]1385[3] 1548[7]
Afaf (FR) *M Delzangles* 106
4 b m Spectrum(IRE) —Halawa (IRE) (Dancing Brave (USA))
1398a[7] 4979a[4] 5913a[4] (6454a)
Affiliation (IRE) *R Hannon* 48
2 b f Danehill Dancer(IRE) —Latin Beauty (IRE) (Sadler's Wells (USA))
4964[15] 5371[12]
Affirmed Native (USA) *J A Osborne* a7
3 ch f Machiavellian(USA) —Affirmed Ambience (USA) (Affirmed (USA))
6371[13]
A Foot In Front *N Tinkler* 27
2 b g Sugarfoot—Scoffera (Scottish Reel)
4109[12] 4887[17] 5481[10] 5614[11]
Afrad (FR) *N J Henderson* 96
5 gr g Linamix(FR) —Afragha (IRE) (Darshaan)
2723[23]
Afrashad (USA) *Saeed Bin Suroor* a98+
4 ch h Smoke Glacken(USA) —Flo White (USA) (Whitesburg (USA))
4384a[4]
Afra Tsitsi (FR) *C Lerner* 97
2 b f Belong To Me(USA) —Jafn (Sharpo)
4621a[8] 5471a[4]
African Blues *M R Hoad*
3 ch g College Chapel—Pearl Dawn (IRE) (Jareer (USA))
2131[13] 3006[15] 6801[10]
African Concerto (IRE) *S Kirk* a52 54
3 b c Mozart(IRE) —Out Of Africa (IRE) (Common Grounds)
68[10] 234[11]481[8] 554[DSQ]709[4] 807[9]1312[6] 3226[15] 3646[10]4164[12] 5781[8] 6619[6]6696[7] 6829[7]
African Dream *J Noseda* a104 113
5 b g Mark Of Esteem(IRE) —Fleet Hill (IRE) (Warrshan (USA))
518[4] 666[11]1018[5]
African Gift *J G Given* a77 80
4 b m Cadeaux Genereux—African Light (Kalaglow)
806[8] 1151[7]1413[7] (2211) 2464[7](2856) 3041[14] 3598[3] (Dead)
African Sahara (USA) *Miss D Mountain* a77 83
7 br h El Gran Senor(USA) —Able Money (USA) (Distinctive (USA))
33[7] 1015[2]250[6] 3757[4]21[8] 2088[6] 2982[8]3934[12] (Dead)
African Star *J M Bradley* a40 41
5 b g Mtoto—Pass The Rose (IRE) (Thatching)
1212[10] 1538[7] 1727[10]
Afric Star *P D Evans*
2 b f Woodborough(USA) —America Star (Norwick (USA))
663[8] 877[3] 962[5]1229[6] 2064[4] 2709[8]
Afriketa (IRE) *R Lopez Gallego* 62
3 br f Desert Story(IRE) —Celerite (USA) (Riverman (USA))
6454a[11]
After The Show *Rae Guest* a79 83
5 b g Royal Applause—Tango Teaser (Shareef Dancer (USA))
79[2] 967[6] 1399[9]2340[6] 3199[2]4771[2] 5212[6] 6009[15]6583[11] 6709[4]
After You *B W Hills* a76 96
3 b f Pursuit Of Love—Los Alamos (Keen)
1130[5] (1990) 2744[16] 4808[10] 5525[9]
Against The Grain *M Johnston* 90
3 b g Pivotal—Oh Hebe (IRE) (Night Shift (USA))
(2048) 2650[3] 3079[10] 3889[15]
Agata Laguna (IRE) *R Brogi* 96
3 b f Elnadim(USA) —Tshusick (Dancing Brave (USA))
6005a[4] 6363a[9]
Agent Eleven (IRE) *B J McMath* 45
3 b g Desert Story(IRE) —Elizabethan Air (Elegant Air)
1421[11]
Age Of Kings (USA) *A B Haynes* a62 83
4 b g Kingmambo(USA) —Everhope (USA) (Danzig (USA))
1921[2] 384[9]736[10] 965[7] 1271[11]2070[12]
Aggbag *B P J Baugh* a60 57
2 b g Fath(USA) —Emaura (Dominion)
1639[5] 1884[8] 2145[3] 2179[3] 2346[3]3678[9] 4434[8] (4969) 5208[9] 5738[7]5876[5] 6401[4]6640[3] 6789[U]6926[3]
Aggi Mac *N Bycroft* a44 41
5 b m Defacto(USA) —Giffoine (Timeless Times (USA))
6280[12]
Aggravation *D R C Elsworth* a77 77
4 b g Sure Blade(USA) —Confection (Formidable (USA))
17[7] 416[2](596) 662[8]711[2] 826[3]915[7] 1644[5](2510) (2708) 3044[11] 4209[3] 4565[4] 4879[9] 5444[10]5734[4]
Aggresive *D K Ivory* a49 70
2 ch g Zilzal(USA) —Frankie Fair (IRE) (Red Sunset)
1535[5] 1912[3]2342[8] 4699[9]5043[7] 5262[11] 5871[4]
Agilete *J Pearce* a59 73
4 b g Piccolo—Ingerence (FR) (Akarad (FR))
71[8] 225[11]339[12] 472[7]1201[12] 1265[7] 1572[3]1755[8] 2262[11] 2707[5] 3035[4] 3232[7]3998[3] 4307[6] 4755[3](5033) 5240[2] 5385[9] 5510[2]5683[5] 6037[5]
Agitator *Mrs G S Rees* a56
2 b g Lujain(USA) —Forum Girl (USA) (Sheikh Albadou)
6222[3]
Agnes Gift *Jamie Poulton* a46
3 b f Agnes World(USA) —Evocatrice (Persepolis (FR))
4247[7]
Agnes Jedi (JPN) *Hideyuki Mori* a102
4 b h Agnes World(USA) —Lucky Pisces (CAN) (Crafty Prospector (USA))
740a[6]
Agnes Pearl *B Smart* a11 31
3 b f Agnes World(USA) —Paris Babe (Teenoso (USA))
907[6] 4155[11]
Agnes Raspberry (JPN) *Katsuichi Nishiura* 112
5 b m Air Jihad(JPN) —Agnes Minerva (JPN) (Tony Bin)
6530a[15]
Ahaz *J F Coupland* a40 10
4 b g Zaha(CAN) —Classic Faster (IRE) (Running Steps (USA))
5435[9]
Ahlawy (IRE) *L M Cumani* 82
3 b g Green Desert(USA) —On Call (Alleged (USA))
1336[U] 1684[4] (2146) 2781[6]3301[6]
Ahmedy (IRE) *M R Channon* a80 81
3 b g Polish Precedent(USA) —Nawaji (USA) (Trempolino (USA))
1381[3] 2239[4] 2584[15]3443[9] 3871[4] 3977[3] 4481[4] 4784[8](5236) 5599[8] 6076[5]
Aigle D'Or *H-A Pantall* 108
3 b g Halling(USA) —Epistole (IRE) (Alzao (USA))
5700a[6]
Ai Hawa (IRE) *Eamon Tyrrell* 57
3 b f Indian Danehill(IRE) —Arabian Princess (Taufan (USA))
1736[3] 2195[5] 2746[2] 3115[5]
Ailsa *C W Thornton* a29 51
4 b m Bishop Of Cashel—Mindomica (Dominion)
1126[5] 1589[7] 2019[6] 2418[8]4652[11] 5060[10] 5363[6] 5838[2] 6235[9]
Ailton (GER) *W Baltromei* 95
2 b c Fly To The Stars—Aznavour (GER) (Lagunas)
6000a[3] 6456a[12]
Aimee Vibert *W R Swinburn* a71 75
4 br m Zilzal(USA) —Rose Vibert (Caerleon (USA))
1244[11] 1638[2]2186[6] (3412) (3983) 4528[6]
Ainamaa (USA) *E A L Dunlop* 71
2 bb f Lemon Drop Kid(USA) —Khibrah (IRE) (Lahib (USA))
4084[11] 4830[3]
Aintnecessarilyso *J M Bradley* a35 52
8 ch g So Factual(USA) —Ovideo (Domynsky)
148[2] 261[11]398[7] 529[6]2813[11] 6237[11] 6636[8]
Air Biscuit (IRE) *C F Wall* a61 83
3 b f Galileo(IRE) —Surprise Visitor (IRE) (Be My Guest (USA))
1141[4] 1616[7] 2050[7] 2554[11]3410[3] 4395[6](4671) (5258) (5497) 5888[2] 6333[11]
Airbound (USA) *M Johnston* a73 66
3 ch g Fusaichi Pegasus(USA) —Secrettame (USA) (Secretariat (USA))
1913 2722[4]2409[4] 2809[8] 3167[5]3621[5] 4402[5] (4972) 5610[14]6070[13]
Airbuss (IRE) *M R Channon* a66 86
3 b c Mozart(IRE) —Kardelle (Kalaglow)
16[9] 880[2] (1241) 1615[6]1951[4] 2581[5] 3082[3] (3945)
Airedale Lad (IRE) *R M Whitaker* a48 58
5 b g Charnwood Forest(IRE) —Tamarsiya (USA) (Shahrastani (USA))
974[6] 1560[12] 1757[2] 1852[3] 2286[7]4511[7] 5485[11]
Airgusta (IRE) *C P Morlock* a59 55
5 b g Danehill Dancer(IRE) —Ministerial Model (IRE) (Shalford (IRE))
40[9]
Air Of Supremacy (IRE) *J L Spearing* a56 70
5 gr g Royal Applause—Lap Of Luxury (Sharrood (USA))
3197[7]
Air Twist (IRE) *Edward Lynam* 81
2 b f Barathea(IRE) —Christaleni (Zilzal (USA))
6113a[7]
Aitch (IRE) *J Noseda* 38
3 b f Alhaarth(IRE) —Sevi's Choice (USA) (Sir Ivor (USA))
1191[14]
Aitutaki (IRE) *T D Easterby* 60
2 b g Lend A Hand—Amber Fizz (USA) (Effervescing (USA))
4251[6] 4608[8] 5289[8]
Aizen Myoo (IRE) *Seamus Fahey* a21 70
8 b g Balla Cove—Fly In Amber (IRE) (Doubletour (USA))
6680[9]
Ajaan *H R A Cecil* 76
2 br c Machiavellian(USA) —Alakananda (Hernando (FR))
5088[5] (5730)
Ajhar (USA) *M P Tregoning* 85
2 b c Diesis—Min Alhawa (USA) (Riverman (USA))
5178[2] 5537[2] 5893[2]
Ajigolo *M R Channon* 110
3 ch c Piccolo—Ajig Dancer (Niniski (USA))
2276a[12] 2846[12] 3732[7] 4080[16] 4461[9]
Akarem *K R Burke* 115
5 b h Kingmambo(USA) —Spirit Of Tara (IRE) (Sadler's Wells (USA))
1298[5] (1815) (2010) 2773[10] 3107a[4] 4797[3] 5395a[5]5657[5] 6103[8]
Akash (IRE) *Miss J Feilden* a54 75
6 b g Dr Devious(IRE) —Akilara (IRE) (Kahyasi)
1995[13]
Akimbo (USA) *James Leavy* a89 113
5 b g Kingmambo(USA) —All At Sea (USA) (Riverman (USA))
2471a[5] 2722[7] 3129a[7]
Akinola (IRE) *K A Ryan* a69 73
5 ch h Lil's Boy(USA) —Miss Margaux (IRE) (Royal Academy (USA))
6160[13] 6476[4] 6666[4]6928[9]
Akiyama (IRE) *J Howard Johnson* 68
2 b g Traditionally(USA) —Dark Albatross (USA) (Sheikh Albadou)
4566[3] 5308[4] 5900[2]
Akona Matata (USA) *C E Brittain* a94 100
4 b h Seeking The Gold(USA) —Oh What A Dance (USA) (Nijinsky (CAN))
(720) 826[2] (1262) 1678[4] 2200[5]2742[3] 3493[16]
Akram (IRE) *Jonjo O'Neill* 94+
4 b g Night Shift(USA) —Akdariya (IRE) (Shirley Heights)
3091[5]
Akritas *P F I Cole* a76 82d
5 b g Polish Precedent(USA) —Dazzling Heights (Shirley Heights)
1021[7] 1247[13]1779[4] 1991[8] 2628[11] 3013[4]3452[5] 4981[10]
Alaghiraar (IRE) *J L Dunlop* 69
2 b c Act One—Tarsheeh (USA) (Mr Prospector (USA))
6214[12]
Alambic *Sir Mark Prescott* a36+ 87+
3 gr f Cozzene(USA) —Alexandrine (IRE) (Nashwan (USA))
2539[6] 3140[2] (3352) (3439) (3628) (3674) (4268) 4362[3] (4951) 5069[3]
Alan The Aussie *G Prodromou* 26
3 b g Rossini(USA) —In Ernest (IRE) (Forest Wind (USA))
1386[8] 1613[10] 2291[10]3232[14]
Alarm Call *T D Easterby* a31 34
3 b f Mind Games—Warning Bell (Bustino)
690[7] 874[7]
Alasil (USA) *R J Price* a66 72
6 bb g Swain(IRE) —Asl (USA) (Caro)
(5127) 5769[6] 6189[10] 6503[6]6584[4] 6684[7]
Alasoun (IRE) *Sir Michael Stoute* 79
3 b c Kalanisi(IRE) —Alasana (IRE) (Darshaan)
1139[5] 1613[4] 2261[2] 3231[2]
Alavana (IRE) *D W Barker* 54
2 b f Kyllachy—Grey Galava (Generous (IRE))
1664[11] 2375[6] 2890[7] 3693[4] 5334[8]
Alayan (IRE) *John M Oxx* 118
4 b h Sri Pekan(USA) —Alaya (IRE) (Ela-Mana-Mou)
280a[8] 562a[2] 741a[6] (1365a)
Albert Einstein (IRE) *A P O'Brien* 101
2 b c Danehill(USA) —Sunset Cafe (IRE) (Red Sunset)
5692a[5] 6262a[2]
Albertinelli (IRE) *A P O'Brien* 106
3 b c Danehill(USA) —Sunset Cafe (IRE) (Red Sunset)
3129a[3]
Alberts Story (USA) *R A Fahey* 47
2 b g Tale Of The Cat(USA) —Hazino (USA) (Hazaam (USA))
1807[4] 3830[5] 4260[7]
Alcazar (IRE) *H Morrison* 117
11 b g Alzao(USA) —Sahara Breeze (Ela-Mana-Mou)
1875a[6] 5156[2] 5711a[6]
Alcharinga (IRE) *T J Etherington* a35 35
4 b g Ashkalani(IRE) —Bird In Blue (IRE) (Bluebird (USA))
6389[8]
Alchemist Master *C R Dore* a82 82
7 b g Machiavellian(USA) —Gussy Marlowe (Final Straw)
1561[9] 2614[6] 2787[5] 2974[15] 3213[6]3598[F] (Dead)
Alcyon (IRE) *E A L Dunlop* a78 94
3 b c Alhaarth(IRE) —West Of Eden (Crofter (USA))
850[2] 1741[3] (2366) 3443[3]
Alderney (USA) *M A Jarvis* 95
2 b f Elusive Quality(USA) —Adonesque (IRE) (Sadler's Wells (USA))
(2660) 3415[5] 5672[7]
Al Dhahab (USA) *C E Brittain* 55
3 b f Seeking The Gold(USA) —South Of Saturn (USA) (Seattle Slew (USA))
2350[11] 3017[15] 3412[9]
Aleagueoftheirown (IRE) *David Wachman* 98
2 b f Danehill Dancer(IRE) —Golden Coral (USA) (Slew O'Gold (USA))
3963a[4]
Aleandros (GER) *Mario Hofer* 82
2 b c Big Shuffle(USA) —Atalante (GER) (Alkalde (GER))
5218a[5] 6092a[8] 6546a[4]
Alecia (IRE) *C G Cox* 67
2 gr f Keltos(FR) —Ahliyat (USA) (Irish River (FR))
3700[5] 4824a[19]
Alekhine (IRE) *J R Boyle* a80 84
5 b g Soviet Star(USA) —Alriyaah (Shareef Dancer (USA))
140[4] 214[7]375[10] 463[5]555[9] 983[9]1435[2] 1637[4] 2401[2] 3151[8] 5236[10]5786[9] (6289)
Aleron (IRE) *J J Quinn* 78
8 b g Sadler's Wells(USA) —High Hawk (Shirley Heights)
318[11] (1610) 2018[4] 2326[6]2736[6] 3081[6] 4764[11]
Alessandria *E A L Dunlop* a104+ 91
3 b f Sunday Silence(USA) —Tereshkova (USA) (Mr Prospector (USA))
(1942) 2772[10] 3293[7]
Alessano *G L Moore* a77 101
4 ch g Hernando(FR) —Alessandra (Generous (IRE))
1478[11] 1991[4] (3365) (3853) (4770) 5361[4] 5804[3]5920[2]
Alethia (IRE) *J-C Rouget* 75
3 b f Danehill(USA) —Greek Moon (IRE) (Shirley Heights)
6567a[0]
Aleutian *Doug Watson* a105 91
6 gr g Zafonic(USA) —Baked Alaska (Green Desert (USA))
204a[4] 353a[10]513a[4]
Alevic (IRE) *J R Norton*
2 ch c Tendulkar(USA) —Aster Fields (IRE) (Common Grounds)
2416[10] 3279[7] 5876[11]
Alevisia (FR) *Noel T Chance* 48
3 gr f Emperor Jones(USA) —Alminieh (FR) (Highest Honor (FR))
2188[11] 3017[14]
Alexander Alliance (IRE) *T Stack* 112
3 b f Danetime(IRE) —Geht Schnell (Fairy King (USA))
1508[10]
Alexander Goldrun (IRE) *J S Bolger* 123
5 b m Gold Away(IRE) —Renashaan (FR) (Darshaan)
741a[5] 2053a[2] (3105a) 4127[2] 5193a[3] 5674a[3]6785a[9]
Alexander Sapphire (IRE) *N B King* a56 55
4 gr m Pennekamp(USA) —Beautiful France (IRE) (Sadler's Wells (USA))
55[9] 2707[3]3033
Alexander Tango (IRE) *T Stack* 105
2 ch f Danehill Dancer(IRE) —House In Wood (FR) (Woodman (USA))
3963a[3] 4853a[5] 5522[7]
Alexandrova (IRE) *A P O'Brien* 121+
3 b f Sadler's Wells(USA) —Shouk (Shirley Heights)
1777[2] (2203) (3575a) (4714) 5713a[3]
Alexian *D W P Arbuthnot* a70 71
3 b g Almushtarak(IRE) —Rough Guess (IRE) (Believe It (USA))
365[9] 630[6]823[3] 1052[3] 1350[3]2518[6] 2882[4] 6108[16] 6376[3]6462[9] 6621[4](6828)
Alexia Rose (IRE) *A Berry* a68 60d
4 b m Mujadil(USA) —Meursault (IRE) (Salt Dome (USA))
47[7] 317[7]426[4] 489[2]552[4] 864[17] 3245[11]4636[13] 4834[14] 5493[14] 6274[10]
Alfie Flits *G A Swinbank* 121+
3 b g Machiavellian(USA) —Elhilmeya (IRE) (Unfuwain (USA))
(1854) 2358[2] (2893) 3254[3] 6103[10] (6334)
Alfie Lee (IRE) *D A Nolan* 21
9 ch g Case Law—Nordic Living (IRE) (Nordico (USA))
2928[15] 3334[12] 3781[15]
Alfie Noakes *Mrs A J Perrett* a71 95
4 b g Groom Dancer(USA) —Crimson Rosella (Polar Falcon (USA))
1585[5] 1933[3] (2229) 2848[10] 3533[9]
Alfie Tupper (IRE) *S Kirk* 91
3 ch g Soviet Star(USA) —Walnut Lady (Forzando)
2581[3] 3852[3] 4481[U] 4819[6] 5345[17]5590[8]
Alfonso *I Semple* a84 76
5 ch g Efisio—Winnebago (Kris)
161[4] (412) 611[4]726[10] 1035[3] 1280[15] 2164[5] 3813[4]4350[5] 4692[3] 5031[10]
Alfredian Park *S Kirk* a79+
2 ch g Bertolini(USA) —Ulysses Daughter (IRE) (College Chapel)
(6976)
Alfresco *Pat Eddery* 56
2 b g Mtoto—Maureena (IRE) (Grand Lodge (USA))
3591[13] 5891[10]
Alfridini *D R C Elsworth* a76 75
5 ch g Selkirk(USA) —Vivre En Paix (Nureyev (USA))
36[4] (115) 375[11]4819[5] 5205[7] 6054[7]
Alf Tupper *M H Tompkins* 63
3 b g Atraf—Silvery (Petong)
1182[4] 2243[9] 3231[7] 5316[15]
Algarade *Sir Mark Prescott* a77+
2 b f Green Desert(USA) —Alexandrine (IRE) (Nashwan (USA))
6757[2] (6879)
Algharb *W J Haggas* a99+ 93+
4 bb g Mujahid(USA) —Actress (Known Fact (USA))
(1939) 3077[11] 3986[9] 4796[3]
Algol *J Howard Johnson* 89
2 b g Kyllachy—Heckle (In The Wings)
2191[5] 2827[3] 3080[2] (3830) (4912) 5334[3] (5788)
Algorithm *T D Easterby* a22 59
4 b m Danehill Dancer(IRE) —Dominelle (Domynsky)
2112[16] 2400[9] 2926[7] 3142[10] 3379[9]3635[3] 3749[18]
Alhaajes (USA) *B W Hills* 99
3 b g Bahri(USA) —Mamlakah (IRE) (Unfuwain (USA))
1081[3] 1627[3] 1994[2] 2655 [2] 3987[3]
Alhaitham (USA) *J L Dunlop* 86
3 b c Storm Cat(USA) —Bint Salsabil (USA) (Nashwan (USA))
1065[3] 1640[7] 2174[4] 2815[8] 3711[DSQ]4261[2] (4959) 5266[7]
Al Hazim (IRE) *L M Cumani* a77 78
3 b c Danehill(USA) —Dathiyna (IRE) (Kris)
3871[7] (4483) 5047[4] 5599[11]
Ali Bruce *P A Blockley* a83 79
6 b g Cadeaux Genereux—Actualite (Polish Precedent (USA))
220[8] 348[11]476[3] 611[11]659[3] 1938[5]6814[10]
Alice Amelia *C R Egerton* a43
3 b f Alhaarth(IRE) —Wondrous Maid (GER) (Mondrian (GER))
165[11] 4701[7]
Alice Howe *W R Muir* a41
2 b f Vettori(IRE) —Peacock Alley (IRE) (Salse (USA))
6303[8] 6511[7]6768[10]
Alice Who (IRE) *J S Moore*
2 ch f Spectrum(IRE) —Princesse Sharpo (USA) (Trempolino (USA))
7754 9621[0]
Alicia Higgins (IRE) *M Massimi Jr* 89
4 b m Marju(IRE) —Danzig Times (USA) (Danzig Connection (USA))
1368a[5]
Ali D *G Woodward* a51 69
8 b g Alhijaz—Doppio (Dublin Taxi)
2681[9] 2789[5] 3044[3] 3113[7] 3361[8]3712[4] 4108[6] 5316[3] 5354[11] 5484[7]6289[6]
Alisdanza *N Wilson* a24 57
4 b m Namaqualand(USA) —Enchanting Eve (Risk Me (FR))
1293[2] 1608[3] 2546[3] 2747[5] 3480[4]3762[6] 4404[3] 4954[2] 5242[12] 5837[3]6797[6]

Alistair John *Mrs G S Rees* a58 42
3 b g Komaite(USA) —Young Rosein (Distant Relative)
5077[14] 5432[8] (5873) 6308[10]6541[12]

Alittlebitleft (IRE) *R Hannon* a92+ 65
2 ch c Danehill Dancer(IRE) —Sifaara (IRE) (Caerleon (USA))
4928[9] 5125[11] 5371[9] 6310[3]6506[2] (6582) (6691) 6746[2]6978[3]

Alittleriskie (IRE) *J S Moore* a16 31
2 ch f Rossini(USA) —Riskie Things (Risk Me (FR))
707[8] (877) 1142[7] 2064[5]2145[4] 2346[8] 2916[3]3300[4] 4222[7]

Alix Road (FR) *Mme M Bollack-Badel* 112
3 gr f Linamix(FR) —Life On The Road (IRE) (Persian Heights)
959a[3] 1874a[3] 2491a[5] 4645a[4] 5220a[5]5702a[3] 5999a[2]

Al Ken (FR) *J-M Capitte*
2 ch c Kendor(FR) —Al Duck (FR) (Al Mamoon (USA))
(6528a)

Alkhabar (USA) *J L Dunlop* 31
3 b c Kingmambo(USA) —Ashraakat (USA) (Danzig (USA))
5598[10] 6052[8]

Al Khaleej (IRE) *E A L Dunlop* a79 74
2 b c Sakhee(USA) —Mood Swings (IRE) (Shirley Heights)
1838[7] (3457) 5788[5]

All About Him (USA) *N I M Rossiter* 48
3 ch g Mt. Livermore(USA) —Inscrutable Dancer (USA) (Green Dancer (USA))
2532[13] 3090[14] 4142[6] 4587[8] 4872[13]

All A Dream *Mrs L Williamson* a77
4 br m Desert Story(IRE) —Alioli (Nishapour (FR))
109[8] 319[12]

All Bleevable *Mrs S Lamyman* a53 48
9 b g Presidium—Eve's Treasure (Bustino)
12[5] 287[1]129[5]

All Clued Up (IRE) *Rae Guest* a50 52
3 b f King Charlemagne(USA) —Clunie (Inchinor)
2167[14] 2445[3] 3034[3] 3384[5]3683[10] 4611[7] 5969[8]6129[9] 6440[5]6548[3] 6637[7]

Allegretto (IRE) *Sir Michael Stoute* 111
3 ch f Galileo(IRE) —Alleluia (Caerleon (USA))
1583[6] (2600) (3293) 4714[3] 5155[3]

Alleviate (IRE) *Sir Mark Prescott* a59
2 br f Indian Ridge—Alleluia (Caerleon (USA))
6099[6] 6257[11]6386[6]

Allexina *John M Oxx* 114
4 ch m Barathea(IRE) —Grecian Bride (IRE) (Groom Dancer (USA))
1128[7] 1785a[2] 2689a[3]

Allez Olive (IRE) *F Demets* 116?
8 b g Spectrum(IRE) —Mondsee (Caerleon (USA))
6610a[13]

Allison's Art (IRE) *N A Callaghan* 68
2 b f Rock Of Gibraltar(IRE) —Ibtikar (USA) (Private Account (USA))
5296[7] 5596[4]

All Is Vanity (FR) *W J Cargeeg*
2 ch f Gold Away(IRE) —Castilly (Inchinor)
6528a[3]

All Ivory *R Charlton* 104
4 ch h Halling(USA) —Ivorine (USA) (Blushing Groom (FR))
1086[5] 1667[14] (5523) 5789[8]

All My Life (GER) *N Sauer* 65
2 br c Big Shuffle(USA) —All Saints (GER) (Goofalik (USA))
6092a[7]

All Of Me (IRE) *T G Mills* a74+ 56
2 b c Xaar—Silk Point (IRE) (Barathea (IRE))
6049[9] 6188[4] 6887[2](6998)

Alloro *D J S Ffrench Davis* a48 67
2 ch c Auction House(USA) —Minette (Bishop Of Cashel)
1770[11] 1980[4] 2619[10] 5382[9] 6394[9]

Allouette *W J H Ratcliffe* a12 46
3 b f Largesse—Alo Ez (Alzao (USA))
3001[7] 3355[7] 3941[10] 4734[15]

Alloway *A Fabre* a75 105
3 ch f Rahy(USA) —Always Far (USA) (Alydar (USA))
(1370a) 2491a[10] 4035a[5]

All Quiet *R Hannon* a81+ 85+
5 b m Piccolo—War Shanty (Warrshan (USA))
670[8] 826[5]3121[3] 3590[4] 3953[3] 4660[3] 4965[3]5833[3] 6350[4] 6698[3]

All Rise (GER) *Ian Williams* 2
4 bb m Goofalik(USA) —Astica (GER) (Surumu (GER))
4497[11]

Allroundtheoutside *P R Chamings* a53 55
2 gr g Tomba—Misty Goddess (IRE) (Godswalk (USA))
4895[11] 5126[7] 5780[7]6018[7] 6172[14] 6640[8]

All Spirit (GER) *N Sauer* 111
4 b h Platini(GER) —All Saints (GER) (Goofalik (USA))
(1369a) 2910a[7] 3579a[8] 4414a[6] 5561a[7]

All Square (IRE) *R A Farrant* a41
6 ch g Bahhare(USA) —Intricacy (Formidable (USA))
1911[9] 3013[8]

All Star (GER) *N J Henderson* 82
6 b g Lomitas—Alte Garde (FR) (Garde Royale)
1808[5]

All Talk *Mrs C A Dunnett*
2 b f Muhtarram(USA) —Bron Hilda (IRE) (Namaqualand (USA))
760[8] 877[5] 1248[6]1379[4] 1744[6]2346[6] 2709[5] 3228[7]

All That And More (IRE) *B W Hills* 102+
4 ch h Unfuwain(USA) —Ideal Lady (IRE) (Seattle Slew (USA))
(1239) 2201[14] 2848[19] 4023[16]

All Theatrical (USA) *C Hebeisen* 81
6 b m Theatrical—Slew All (USA) (Seattle Slew (USA))
306a[7]

All The Good (IRE) *G A Butler* a91 100+
3 ch c Diesis—Zarara (USA) (Manila (USA))
1205[6] 4370[7] 4778[4] 5022[2](5644) 5920[4] (6319)

Ally Makbul *Ian Emmerson* a65 54
6 b m Makbul—Clarice Orsini (Common Grounds)
6798[12]

All You Need (IRE) *R Hollinshead* 85
2 b g Iron Mask(USA) —Choice Pickings (IRE) (Among Men (USA))
3553[3] 3958[2] 5645 [8]

Al Maali (IRE) *Doug Watson* a89 107
7 b h Polar Falcon(USA) —Amwag (USA) (El Gran Senor (USA))
353a[13] 494a[3]

Almah (SAF) *Miss Venetia Williams* 92
8 b m Al Mufti(USA) —Jazz Champion (SAF) (Dancing Champ (USA))
1800[5] 3522[3] 4036[10] 4369[4]

Almanshood (USA) *P L Gilligan* a75 76
4 bb g Bahri(USA) —Lahan (Unfuwain (USA))
108[2] 214[8]1992[12] 2322[9] 2647[10]6848[7]

Almaty Express *J R Weymes* a70 62
4 b g Almaty(IRE) —Express Girl (Sylvan Express)
126[2] 317[12]426[8] (532) 824[3] 986[3]1047[5] 1563[8] 5493[10] 5878[10]6162[14] 6325[6] 6622[5]6922[3] 6994[2]

Almerita (GER) *W Hickst* 113
3 ch f Medicean—Averna (Heraldiste (USA))
1328a[2] (2279a) 3993a[3] 6125a[9]

Almisq (USA) *Miss D Mountain* a41 44
5 ch m Diesis—Inscrutable Dancer (USA) (Green Dancer (USA))
6616[14]

Almizan (IRE) *G L Moore* a65 78
6 b g Darshaan—Bint Albaadiya (USA) (Woodman (USA))
2044[7] 2628[3] 3116[6] 6831[5]

Almondillo (IRE) *C F Wall*
2 b g Tagula(IRE) —Almond Flower (IRE) (Alzao (USA))
3253[10]

Almora Guru *W M Brisbourne* 59
2 b f Ishiguru(USA) —Princess Almora (Pivotal)
1046[10] 2026[7] 2394[4] 2517[5] 3476[6]4089[2] 4519[6] 5238[16]

Almowj *C E Brittain* a46 53
3 b g Fasliyev(USA) —Tiriana (Common Grounds)
481[9] 558[6]796[5] 984[7] 1616[14]2210[2] 2535[6] 2645[7]3138[8] 5450[10] 5929[6]6779[7] 6856[6]6961[5]

Almudo (IRE) *B Palling*
2 b g Almutawakel—Doubleuceeone (Compton Place)
4867[13] 5126[11]

Almusa (IRE) *A & G Botti* 87
2 ch f Almutawakel—Susan Bold (IRE) (Persian Bold)
3343a[8]

Alnitak (USA) *B Olsen* 103?
5 br h Nureyev(USA) —Very True (USA) (Proud Truth (USA))
2123a[4] 4189a[6] 5226a[7]

Alnwick *P D Cundell* a48 57
2 b g Kylian(USA) —Cebwob (Rock City)
2572[8] 3701[11] 4074[8]5738[12]

Alocin (IRE) *A D Brown* 75
3 b g Titus Livius(FR) —Poker Dice (Primo Dominie)
755a[7] 5902[13] 6054[16]

Alone He Stands (IRE) *J C Hayden* 99
6 b g Flying Spur(AUS) —Millennium Tale (FR) (Distant Relative)
1156a[15] 3125a[21] 4187a[12]

Alone It Stands (IRE) *D Nicholls* 44
3 b g King Charlemagne(USA) —Golden Concorde (Super Concorde (USA))
4034a[11] 4611[8]

Along The Nile *K G Reveley* 91+
4 b g Desert Prince(IRE) —Golden Fortune (Forzando)
1280[2] 2440[11] (3040) 3413[7] 3937[11] 4379[10]4508[2] 4810[15] 5494[2] 5787[8]

Alonso De Guzman (IRE) *J R Boyle* a47+ 12
2 b g Docksider(USA) —Addaya (IRE) (Persian Bold)
5043[13] 5648[10] 6025[9]

Alost (FR) *A Spanu* 115
6 gr g Highest Honor(FR) —Grey Goddess (Godswalk (USA))
934a[11] 1558a[7]

Alovera (IRE) *M R Channon* 96
2 ch f King's Best(USA) —Angelic Sounds (IRE) (The Noble Player (USA))
(4657) 5257a[4] 5672[9]

Alpacco (IRE) *Mario Hofer* 106
4 b g Desert King(IRE) —Albertville (GER) (Top Ville)
354a[2] 513a[7] 5414a[4]

Alpaga Le Jomage (IRE) *M J Polglase* a69 87
4 b g Orpen(USA) —Miss Bagatelle (Mummy's Pet)
(1) 71[2] 171[4]225[4] 345[7]426[5] 502[3]588[2] 654[5]732[9] 1791[7]

Alpes Maritimes *G Wragg* 76
2 b g Danehill Dancer(IRE) —Miss Riviera (Kris)
4333[16] 5067[5] 5495[2] 5720[4]

Alpha Juliet (IRE) *C J Teague* 46
5 b m Victory Note(USA) —Zara's Birthday (IRE) (Waajib)
2871[14]

Alphun (IRE) *G A Swinbank* a64 62
4 b g Orpen(USA) —Fakhira (IRE) (Jareer (USA))
6959[11]

Alpine Eagle (IRE) *Mrs John Harrington* 55
2 b c Golan(IRE) —Alpine Symphony (Northern Dancer (CAN))
5662a[7]

Alpine Hideaway (IRE) *J S Wainwright* 53
13 b g Tirol—Arbour (USA) (Graustark)
4467[13]

Alpine Reel (IRE) *W R Swinburn* a99+ 87
5 b g Danehill Dancer(IRE) —Alpine Flair (IRE) (Tirol)
5739[2] 6226[3](6418) 6600[2](6744) 6836[4]

Alpino Chileno (ARG) *Rune Haugen* 107
7 gr h Alpino Fitz(ARG) —Fairyland (ARG) (Lode (USA))
1014a[9] 4189a[3] 5226a[10]

Alqaab (USA) *M P Tregoning* 88
3 b g Silver Hawk(USA) —Guerre Et Paix (USA) (Soviet Star (USA))
1120[7] 1374[5] (1670) 2986[11]

Alqaayid *P W Hiatt* a54 76
5 b g Machiavellian(USA) —One So Wonderful (Nashwan (USA))
182[6] 302[11]395[5] 472[2]586[4] 697[9]888[11] 3580a[2] 4332[2]5562a[2] 6238[12]

Al Qasi (IRE) *P W Chapple-Hyam* a85+ 109+
3 b c Elnadim(USA) —Delisha (Salse (USA))
2868[6] (3406) (3879) 4573[2] (4888) (5501)

Al Raahi *M R Channon* a68 73
2 b c Rahy(USA) —Nasmatt (Danehill (USA))
2619[6] 3083[5] 3809[2] 4509[2] 5172[7]5783[8] 6106[9]

Al Rayanah *G Prodromou* a61 68
3 b f Almushtarak(IRE) —Desert Bloom (FR) (Last Tycoon)
30[13] (409) 730[5] 1056[5]1616[5] 1867[4] 2589[2] 2929[11] (3541) 3828[3]4010[4] 4265[5] 4845[2] 5384[4] 5755[3]6060[5] 6206[4]

Alsadaa (USA) *J H M Gosden* a40 79
3 b g Kingmambo(USA) —Aljawza (USA) (Riverman (USA))
2028[6] 2868[4] 5986[10]

Alshawameq (IRE) *Doug Watson* a98 101
5 b g Green Desert(USA) —Azdihaar (USA) (Mr Prospector (USA))
151a[9] 278a[6]

Al Shemali *Sir Michael Stoute* 89
2 ch c Medicean—Bathilde (IRE) (Generous (IRE))
5066[10] (5901)

Altamirano (GER) *W Baltromei* 105
7 b g Law Society(USA) —Azul (GER) (Konigsstuhl (GER))
523a[9]

Altar (IRE) *R Hannon* 74
2 b c Cape Cross(IRE) —Sophrana (IRE) (Polar Falcon (USA))
3025[6] 4781[4] 5293[7]

Altay *R A Fahey* a83+ 83
9 b g Erins Isle—Aliuska (IRE) (Fijar Tango (FR))
(4508) (5506)

Altenburg (FR) *Mrs N Smith* a81 85
4 b g Sadler's Wells(USA) —Anna Of Saxony (Ela-Mana-Mou)
897[5] 1290[2] 2118[3] 3225[2] 3853[5]4560[3] 5429[3]

Alternative *R M Beckett* 85
2 ch c Dr Fong(USA) —Oatey (Master Willie)
961[2] (1203) 1780[7] 4779[5] 5207[3] 5802[6]

Alte Sage (GER) *P Rau* 72
3 b f Goofalik(USA) —Alte Klasse (GER) (Royal Academy (USA))
4649a[8]

Altessa (IRE) *E J Alston* 3
3 b f Desert Style(IRE) —Savona (IRE) (Cyrano De Bergerac)
3039[6]

Al Tharib (USA) *Sir Michael Stoute* 86
2 b c Silver Hawk(USA) —Ameriflora (USA) (Danzig (USA))
5089[3] 5658[3]

Altilhar (USA) *G L Moore* a74 83+
3 b g Dynaformer(USA) —Al Desima (Emperor Jones (USA))
1547[8] 3046[8] 3318[7] 3589[8] 4331[2](4673) (5152) 5260[4]

Altitude Dancer (IRE) *A Crook* a57 57
6 b g Sadler's Wells(USA) —Height Of Passion (Shirley Heights)
2528[6] (Dead)

Altius (IRE) *A P O'Brien* 103+
3 b c Danehill(USA) —Alleged Devotion (USA) (Alleged (USA))
1172a[3] 1708a[7] 5708a[9]

Alucica *D Shaw* a44
3 b f Celtic Swing—Acicula (IRE) (Night Shift (USA))
365[11]

Alugat (IRE) *Mrs A Duffield* a59 75
3 b g Tagula(IRE) —Notley Park (Wolfhound (USA))
1793[4] 2363[13] 2701[7] 3587[4] 3833[2](4056) 4091[3] 4546[4] 5078[3] (5752) (6162) 6315[10]

Alujawill (IRE) *J G M O'Shea* a45 43
3 b c Erhaab(USA) —El-Libaab (Unfuwain (USA))
5669[13] 5830[8] 6053[11]

Alwariah *C E Brittain* a51 61
3 b f Xaar—Signs And Wonders (Danehill (USA))
861[5] 1140[6] 1433[5]2554[10] 3436[3] 3821[6]4141[16] 4690[3] 4927[4] 5327[11]

Always A Story *Miss D Mountain* 44
4 b g Lake Coniston(IRE) —Silk St James (Pas De Seul)
3826[7] 4162[5] 5093[8] 6307[10]

Always Baileys (IRE) *T Wall* a64 76
3 ch g Mister Baileys—Dubiously (USA) (Jolie Jo (USA))
3176[4] 3665[4] 4654[8] 5478[6] 5751[2]5887[4] 6825[4]

Always Best *M Johnston* a59 69
2 b g Best Of The Bests(IRE) —Come To The Point (Pursuit Of Love)
3175[U] 3448[8] (3838) 4250[8] 5113[7] 5482[2]5597[3] 6018[3] 6322[8]

Always Emirates (USA) *Saeed Bin Suroor* 84
3 b c Danzig(USA) —Country Belle (USA) (Seattle Slew (USA))
1513[2] 2587[8]

Always Esteemed (IRE) *K A Ryan* a102 90
6 b g Mark Of Esteem(IRE) —Always Far (USA) (Alydar (USA))
213[4] 452[3]629[3] 726[12] 1280[9]1923[5]

Alwaysforsale (IRE) *J S Moore* a51 47
3 b g City On A Hill(USA) —Prague Spring (Salse (USA))
2131[8] 2861[2] 3439[6]3592[9] (4016)

Always Fruitful *M Johnston* 87
2 b c Fruits Of Love(USA) —Jerre Jo Glanville (USA) (Skywalker (USA))
(1595) 1998[2] 2225[3] 2844[7]

Always Sparkle (CAN) *B Palling* 58
2 ch c Grand Slam(USA) —Dancing All Night (USA) (Nijinsky (CAN))
4867[10] 5381[7]

Always Stylish (IRE) *M Johnston* a53 53
3 b g Nashwan(USA) —Kafezah (FR) (Pennekamp (USA))
3231[5] 5650[5]

Always The Groom (IRE) *Patrick J Flynn* 74+
4 br g Darshaan—Kyka (USA) (Blushing John (USA))
(4166a)

Always Turn Left (IRE) *H S Howe* a27 58
3 b f King's Theatre(IRE) —Light-Flight (IRE) (Brief Truce (USA))
2344[9] 2673[5] 3152[11]5435[4]

Alyzea (IRE) *C Laffon-Parias* 103
3 b f King Charlemagne(USA) —Moivouloirtoi (USA) (Bering)
1717a[5] 2276a[11] 2799a[3] 6547a[12]

Alzarma *J Gallagher* a43 43
4 b g Alzao(USA) —Skimra (Hernando (FR))
257[3] 387[6]581[11] 783[8]1373[11]

Alzerra (UAE) *M R Channon* 109
2 b f Pivotal—Belle Argentine (FR) (Fijar Tango (FR))
1989[3] (2409) 3415[2] 3925[5] 4594[3] (5335) (5802)

Ama De Casa (USA) *J Noseda* a57 57
2 ch f Grand Slam(USA) —Gold Ransom (USA) (Red Ransom (USA))
2442[4] 3645[5] 6512[4]6605[2]

Amadeus Mozart (IRE) *A P O'Brien* 94
3 b c Mozart(IRE) —Lindesberg (Doyoun)
1362a[7]

Amadeus Wolf *K A Ryan* 120
3 b c Mozart(IRE) —Rachelle (IRE) (Mark Of Esteem (IRE))
1486[7] 2846[5] 3494[4] 4191a[3] 4738[2]5011[3] 5712a[5]

Amanda Carter *R A Fahey* 46
2 b f Tobougg(IRE) —Al Guswa (Shernazar)
4424[9] 5495[7]

Amanda's Lad (IRE) *M C Chapman* a51 60
6 b g Danetime(IRE) —Art Duo (Artaius (USA))
24[7] (90) (146) 274[11]605[7] 858[9]3825[10] 3913[8] 4232[14] 5243[6] 5493[6]5684[17] 5752[7] 6464[10]6533[12] 6796[13]6969[3]

Amandus (USA) *Doug Watson* a83 104
6 b g Danehill(USA) —Affection Affirmed (USA) (Affirmed (USA))
149a[6] 282a[9] 437a[15] 509a[9]

Amante Latino *V Caruso* 96
2 b c Mujahid(USA) —Supercharger (Zamindar (USA))
2670a[4] 6003a[5] 6252a[3]

Amaretto Venture *J J Quinn* 37
2 b f Tobougg(IRE) —Cc Canova (Millkom)
3358[11] 4400[11] 5237[13]

Amarjit (IRE) *R J Osborne* 69
5 b h Bahhare(USA) —Dungeon Princess (IRE) (Danehill (USA))
4166a[3]

Amateis (GER) *P Rau* 100
3 b f Tiger Hill(IRE) —Adorea (GER) (Dashing Blade)
1328a[10] 2059a[5] 3661a[4] 5160a[3]

Amazin *N P Littmoden* a70 72
4 b g Primo Dominie—Aegean Blue (Warning)
167[9] 224[6]292[7] 504[4]571[8] 659[5]977[9] 1341[3]

Amazing Charlie (IRE) *Mrs A J Perrett* 67
3 b f King Charlemagne(USA) —Amazonian (CAN) (Geiger Counter (USA))
2532[5] 3032[5] 3676[3]

Amazing King (IRE) *W G M Turner* 58
2 b c King Charlemagne(USA) —Kraemer (USA) (Lyphard (USA))
4928[10] 5111[6] 5379[5] 5933[6]

Amazing Request *R Charlton* 84
2 b c Rainbow Quest(USA) —Maze Garden (USA) (Riverman (USA))
4597[2] (5125) 5828[4]

Amber Glory *K A Ryan* a61 60d
3 b f Foxhound(USA) —Compton Amber (Puissance)
128[4] 248[4]488[5] 673[3]988[5] 1279[10] 5864[6] 6159[9] 6315[17]6464[7] 6719[9]6856[9] 6956[3]

Amber Isle *D Carroll* a67
2 b g Weet-A-Minute(IRE) —Cloudy Reef (Cragador)
6401[3] 6520[4]6662[3]

Amber Nectar Two *A G Newcombe* a43 40
6 b g Bluegrass Prince(IRE) —Another Batchworth (Beveled (USA))
529[13] 772[12]

Ambersong *A W Carroll* a46 43
8 ch g Hernando(FR) —Stygian (USA) (Irish River (FR))
103[4] 284[5]1541[7] 3074[4]3797[11]

Amber Spirit *Peter Grayson* a33
3 ch f Zaha(CAN) —Classic Faster (IRE) (Running Steps (USA))
93[13]

Amber Valley *K A Ryan* 94d
2 b f Foxhound(USA) —Amber Mill (Doulab (USA))
1053[4] (1278) 1831[2] 2309a[3] 2800[13] 4890[5]5356[7]

Ambika (IRE) *H Rogers* 89
3 b f Danehill Dancer(IRE) —Via Verbano (IRE) (Caerleon (USA))
5004a[5]

Ambitious Cat (USA) *E Coatrieux* 115
5 b m Storm Cat(USA) —Lilac Garden (USA) (Roberto (USA))
6125a[4]

Ambrosiano *Miss E C Lavelle* a58 69
2 b g Averti(IRE) —Secret Circle (Magic Ring (IRE))
2579[6] 3407[5] 3892[9]4753[6] 5738[5]

Ameeq (USA) *G L Moore* a84 87+
4 bb g Silver Hawk(USA) —Haniya (IRE) (Caerleon (USA))
(460) (763) 1133[6] 2229[4] 3093[6]

Amelie Brown (IRE) *N Tinkler* 31
2 b f Dr Fong(USA) —Presentation (IRE) (Mujadil (USA))
1342[8] 1863[5] 2321[4] 3720[8] 4887[10]

Ameliore (IRE) *S Woodman* a32 38
3 b f Dansili—Common Consent (IRE) (Common Grounds)
1956[9] 2532[12] 3118[10] 3932[9] 4278[11] 6700[11] 6829[13]

American Gatto (USA) *J Rossi* a88 91
4 b h Lit De Justice(USA) —Cayenne Cat (USA) (Tabasco Cat (USA))
3692a[6]

America Nova (FR) *R Gibson* a64 96
2 gr f Verglas(IRE) —Las Americas (FR) (Linamix (FR))
6228a[5]

American Spin *B J Meehan* 82+
2 ch c Groom Dancer(USA) —Sea Vixen (Machiavellian (USA))
6214[3]

Ames Souer (IRE) *D Carroll* a44 41
3 b f Fayruz—Taispeain (IRE) (Petorius)
6548[6] 6794[8]

Amicus Meus (IRE) *A Bailey* 70
2 b c Danehill Dancer(IRE) —Top Brex (FR) (Top Ville)
5332[6] 6207[2]

Amir Zaman *J R Jenkins* a77 68
8 ch g Salse(USA) —Colorvista (Shirley Heights)
13[4] 131[10]

Amisact *D J S Ffrench Davis* a2 15
4 b m Zaha(CAN) —Valise (Salse (USA))
2260[10] 3074[7]

Amjad (GER) *A Aiello*
2 b c Silvano(GER) —Anna Kalinka (GER) (Lion Cavern (USA))
5771a[5]

Amnesty *G L Moore* a48 65
7 ch g Salse(USA) —Amaranthus (Shirley Heights)
310[3] 394[7] 972[4] 1536[3] 1724[8]

Amongst Amigos (IRE) *Thomas Cleary* a53 78
5 b h Imperial Ballet(IRE) —Red Lory (Bay Express)
815[7] 6497[11] 6503[7]

Amorada *H Morrison* a7 44
3 b f Pursuit Of Love—Duena (Grand Lodge (USA))
122[11] 326[12]

Amorama (FR) *R J Frankel* 112
5 br m Sri Pekan(USA) —Tanzania (IRE) (Alzao (USA))
6368a[9]

Amorist (IRE) *Sir Mark Prescott* a81 58
4 b g Anabaa(USA) —Moivouloirtoi (USA) (Bering)
(223)

Amoroso (GER) *P Rau* 101
5 b h Goofalik(USA) —Abazzia (GER) (Acatenango (GER))
3992a[2]

Amouralis (IRE) *H Rogers* 99
5 b m Dushyantor(USA) —Motley (Rainbow Quest (USA))
3123a[19] 4031a[7] 4187a[7] 4749a[8]

Amour Multiple (IRE) *S Lycett* 50
7 b g Poliglote—Onereuse (Sanglamore (USA))
5792[14]

Amron Hill *R Hollinshead* a62 32
3 b g Polar Prince(IRE) —Maradata (IRE) (Shardari)
4973[8] 5426[9] 5761[8] 6429[6] 6450[5] 6627[5] 6899[10]

Amusing (IRE) *John Joseph Murphy* 91?
2 b f Danehill Dancer(IRE) —Belize Tropical (IRE) (Baillamont (USA))
5464a[8] 6113a[5]

Amwaal (USA) *J L Dunlop* 76
3 b c Seeking The Gold(USA) —Wasnah (USA) (Nijinsky (CAN))
2404[12] 5504[13] (5727)

Amwell Brave *J R Jenkins* a67 66?
5 b g Pyramus(USA) —Passage Creeping (IRE) (Persian Bold)
535[3] 574[3] 652[2] 723[7] 973[5] 1163[5] 1389[4] 1745[6] 1958[3] 2320[10] 3085[3] 3905[4] 4702[6] 5910[7] 6398[4] 6565[3] 6718[2] 6883[2] 6995[6]

Amygdala *M Botti* a68 59
3 b f Royal Applause—Touch And Love (IRE) (Green Desert (USA))
418[7] 645[3] 822[5] 1210[6] 3841[9]

Amy Louise (IRE) *T D Barron* 88
3 ch f Swain(IRE) —Mur Taasha (USA) (Riverman (USA))
(3039) 3418[10] 4567[4] 4844[7] 5317[8] (5861) (6211)

Amy Storm (GER) *P Vovcenko* 93
3 b f Tannenkonig(IRE) —Amanwana (GER) (Platini (GER))
2059a[2] 6248a[6]

Anabaa's Creation (IRE) *A De Royer-Dupre* 104
2 b f Anabaa(USA) —Premiere Creation (FR) (Green Tune (USA))
(6609a)

Anais Filly (FR) *H-A Pantall* a70 82
3 gr f Verglas(IRE) —Elle Est Belle (USA) (Once Wild (USA))
392a[9]

Anani (USA) *A Laird* a113 108
6 ch g Miswaki(USA) —Mystery Rays (USA) (Nijinsky (CAN))
438a[2] (513a)

Anasena *G G Margarson* 58
3 b f Anabaa(USA) —Bolsena (USA) (Red Ransom (USA))
2111[5] 2895[4] 3264[5]

Anatola (GER) *P Schiergen* 105
4 b m Tiger Hill(IRE) —Avocette (GER) (King's Lake (USA))
(5560a)

Anatolian Prince *J M P Eustace* a53 64
2 b c Almutawakel—Flight Soundly (IRE) (Caerleon (USA))
5088[8] 5640[6] 6254[9]

Anchor Date *D Shaw* a66 66
4 b h Zafonic(USA) —Fame At Last (USA) (Quest For Fame)
5117[11] 5391[8] 5593[16] 6227[11] 6390[10]

Ancient Site (USA) *B P J Baugh* a41
2 ch c Distant View(USA) —Victorian Style (Nashwan (USA))
5389[6] 6284[8] 6998[6]

Ancus Martius (FR) *R Biondi* 69
2 b c Almutawakel—White Evening (IRE) (Entitled)
6123a[9]

And Again (USA) *J R Fanshawe* 80
3 b f In The Wings—Garah (Ajdal (USA))
1901[3] (2349) 2781[5] 4159[5] 4610[2] 5152[6] (5935)

And I *M P Tregoning* a73 63
3 b f Inchinor—Fur Will Fly (Petong)
1845[4] 2553[3] 3050[2] 3646[11]

Andorn (GER) *P Schiergen* 78
2 b c Monsun(GER) —Anthyllis (GER) (Lycius (USA))
5763a[6]

Andorran (GER) *A Dickman* 54
3 b g Lando(GER) —Adora (GER) (Danehill (USA))
1345[11] 2379[7] 3785[9] 4734[8]

Andramad (IRE) *Kevin Prendergast* 86
3 b g Fasliyev(USA) —Petite Fantasy (Mansooj)
3123a[22]

Andre Chenier (IRE) *P Monteith* 70+
5 b g Perugino(USA) —Almada (GER) (Lombard (GER))
1610[7] 1756[8] 2549[6] 2812[4]

Andromeda's Hero (USA) *N Zito* a116
4 ch h Fusaichi Pegasus(USA) —Marozia (USA) (Storm Bird (CAN))
5822a[3]

Andronikos *P F I Cole* a104+ 110
4 ch h Dr Fong(USA) —Arctic Air (Polar Falcon (USA))
1979[3] 2303[10] 4158[2] 4803[4] 5358[5] 5812[11] 6335[4] 6514[6] 6692[8]

Anduril *Miss M E Rowland* a78 76
5 ch g Kris—Attribute (Warning)
444[11] 530[7] 578[3] 641[7] 1280[5] 1531[13] 1651[8] 2551[9] 3298[9] 3918[8] (4653) 4871[9] 5362[11] 5974[5] 6189[6] 6503[11] 6818[2]

Anewshade *N Tinkler* 12
2 b f Vettori(IRE) —On Shade (Polar Falcon (USA))
5014[6] 5287[10]

Anfield Dream *J R Jenkins* a87 65
4 b g Lujain(USA) —Fifth Emerald (Formidable (USA))
23[10] 80[10] 224[8] (426) 4573[10] 4771[10] 5212[10] 6035[7] 6174[5] 6496[2] 6585[8] 6720[8] 6882[7]

Angara *W Mott* 117
5 b m Alzao(USA) —Ange Bleu (USA) (Alleged (USA))
5819a[4] 6125a[8]

Angaric (IRE) *B Smart* a77 81
3 ch g Pivotal—Grannys Reluctance (IRE) (Anita's Prince)
978[2] (1441) 1693[2] (2126) 3301[2] 3606[2] 3937[7] 4403[7] 5961[6] 6239[4]

Angel De Madrid (CHI) *R Hagen* 88
5 ch g More Royal(USA) —Labrada (CHI) (Laguardia (USA))
4864a[10]

Angeletta *E S McMahon* a30 73
2 b f Vettori(IRE) —Supreme Angel (Beveled (USA))
908[7] 1181[4] 2026[3] 2500[2] 4427[3] 4895[5] 5527[3] 5866[4] 6007[5]

Angelina Bankes *R A Harris* a56 52
3 b f Observatory(USA) —Cloche Call (Anabaa (USA))
122[3] 286[2] 439[6]

Angeline *H Alexander*
3 b f Atraf—Pawsible (IRE) (Mujadil (USA))
2366[13]

Angelofthenorth *C J Teague* a50 48
4 b m Tomba—Dark Kristal (IRE) (Gorytus (USA))
813[6] 1102[6] 1413[8] 1816[4] 2237[5] 2505[13] 3356[4] 3683[7] 4230[11] 4735[10] 5834[10] 5928[7]

Angel River *J Ryan* a46 53
4 ch m Bold Edge—Riviere Rouge (Forzando)
953[6] 1057[16] 1198[10] 1305[9] 1538[10] 1727[4] 2070[13] 2148[5] 2574[12] 2820[13] 3729[3] 4266[16] 4363[12] 6726[7] 6803[5] 6854[14]

Angel Sprints *C J Down* 88
4 b m Piccolo—Runs In The Family (Distant Relative)
1936[4] 2429[11] 4811[11] 5476[11] 6065[5]

Angel Voices (IRE) *K R Burke* a67 81
3 b f Tagula(IRE) —Lithe Spirit (IRE) (Dancing Dissident (USA))
1100[2] 1404[9] 1836[4] 4155[3]

Angie And Liz (IRE) *Peter Grayson* a59 34
3 b f Spectrum(IRE) —Mary Magdalene (Night Shift (USA))
120[3] (359)

Angus Newz *M Quinn* a34 98
3 ch f Compton Place—Hickleton Lady (IRE) (Kala Shikari)
(896) 1091[2] 1377[5] (1849) 2022[5] 2438[8] (2651) 3414[9] 4345[10] 4832[10] 5171[8] (5405) 5643[10] 5921[4]

Animated *A J McCabe* a25 65
2 b g Averti(IRE) —Anita Marie (IRE) (Anita's Prince)
1499[5] 2623[9] 3351[7] 6920[6]

Annabelle Ja (FR) *D R C Elsworth* a88 81+
3 bb f Singspiel(IRE) —Alamea (IRE) (Ela-Mana-Mou)
1819[10] 3740[4]

Anna Karenina (IRE) *David Wachman* 107
3 b f Green Desert(USA) —Simaat (USA) (Mr Prospector (USA))
4749a[5] 5411a[5]

Annals *R C Guest* a44 40
4 b m Lujain(USA) —Anna Of Brunswick (Rainbow Quest (USA))
640[7] 813[9] 974[9] 1197[6] 1393[11] 1575[8] 3353[8] 4194[10]

Annaly (ITY) *O Pessi* 93
4 ch m Kirkwall—Aloina (ITY) (Ardross)
6362a[9]

Annambo *D Morris* a81 82
6 ch g In The Wings—Anna Matrushka (Mill Reef (USA))
799[4] 1033[11] 2869[3]

Anna Mona (GER) *A De Royer-Dupre* 102
3 ch f Monsun(GER) —Anna Oleanda (IRE) (Old Vic)
2257a[3] 4543a[5] 6171a[4] 6384a[0]

Anna Pavlova *R A Fahey* 110
3 b f Danehill Dancer(IRE) —Wheeler's Wonder (IRE) (Sure Blade (USA))
1832[2] (2024) 2582[6] (4741) 5155[2] (5803) 5917[2]

Anna's Rock (IRE) *J S Bolger* 89
2 b f Rock Of Gibraltar(IRE) —Anna Karenina (USA) (Atticus (USA))
5464a[6]

Annatira (GER) *E Kurdu* 83
5 b m Second Set(IRE) —Anna Diana (GER) (Daun (GER))
3661a[12] 4649a[7] 5710a[15]

Anne Bonney *E J O'Neill* a56
2 b f Jade Robbery(USA) —Sanchez (Wolfhound (USA))
6145[6]

Annenkov (IRE) *E Lellouche* 112
4 b h Danehill(USA) —Agathe (USA) (Manila (USA))
2597a[2] 4417a[3]

Annia Faustina (IRE) *J L Spearing* a61 43
2 ch f Docksider(USA) —Benguela (USA) (Little Current (USA))
4895[8] 6591[4] 6745[4]

Annibale Caro *Sir Mark Prescott* a74 88+
4 b g Mtoto—Isabella Gonzaga (Rock Hopper)
1943[6] 3431[11]

Annies Valentine *J Gallagher* a9 41
3 b f My Best Valentine—Shashi (IRE) (Shaadi (USA))
2951[5] 3451[9] 4982[12] 5870[13] 6495[8]

Annual Event (IRE) *E J O'Neill* 64
2 ch f Traditionally(USA) —Elayoon (USA) (Danzig (USA))
3878[6] 4980[3] 5332[9]

Annunzio *W Baltromei* 96
3 b c Big Shuffle(USA) —Abrakadora (GER) (Aratikos (GER))
1715a[9]

A Nod And A Wink (IRE) *R Hannon* a53 53
2 b f Raise A Grand(IRE) —Earth Charter (Slip Anchor)
4207[10] 4550[5] 4816[5] 6487[4] 6576[3] 6670[2]

Another Bottle (IRE) *R Charlton* 105
5 b g Cape Cross(IRE) —Aster Aweke (IRE) (Alzao (USA))
1129[4] 2742[27] 3493[9] 5675[27]

Another Con (IRE) *P A Blockley* a47 58
5 b m Lake Coniston(IRE) —Sweet Unison (USA) (One For All (USA))
141[2] 284[4] 442[3] 684[6] (2636) (2966) (3115) 3412[4] 3615[5] 4104[8] (Dead)

Another Faux Pas (IRE) *B G Powell* a68 77
5 b m Slip Anchor—Pirie (USA) (Green Dancer (USA))
711[9] 1162[4]

Another Genepi (USA) *J W Hills* a76+ 78+
3 br f Stravinsky(USA) —Dawn Aurora (USA) (Night Shift (USA))
1336[3] 2143[2] 2620[10] 3554[5] 4155[5] 4844[5] 5388[4]

Another Gladiator (USA) *K A Ryan* a61 67
3 br c Danzig(USA) —Scarab Bracelet (USA) (Riverman (USA))
3742[7] 4117[4] 4891[7] 6451[5] 6964[10]

Another Mistress *R M Flower*
4 b m Slip Anchor—Mellow Miss (Danehill (USA))
141[10]

Another True Story *R Hannon* 89
2 b c Piccolo—Lost In Lucca (Inchinor)
3872[7] (4002) 4603[7] (5207) 5829[2]

Anousa (IRE) *P Howling* 85
5 b g Intikhab(USA) —Annaletta (Belmez (USA))
2176[16] 2437[10] 4149[12]

Ans Bach *M A Jarvis* a108+ 97
3 b g Green Desert(USA) —Bezzaaf (Machiavellian (USA))
1016[7] 1404[8] 2033[5] 2824[3] 3317[2] (3852) 5019[2]

Answer Back *Miss J R Tooth* a19 46
2 b f Redback—Martha P Perkins (IRE) (Fayruz)
1744[10] 4971[8] 5448[9] 5766[6] 6175[6] 6491[8]

An Tadh (IRE) *G M Lyons* 111
3 b c Halling(USA) —Tithcar (Cadeaux Genereux)
928a[8] 1362a[5] (2559a) 3129a[5] 3767a[5] 5393a[3]

Antarctica (GER) *M Weber* 35
4 b m Acatenango(GER) —Anna Domani (FR) (Antheus (USA))
6251a[10]

Anthea *B R Millman* a66 68
2 b f Tobougg(IRE) —Blue Indigo (FR) (Pistolet Bleu (IRE))
2958[9] 3448[2] 4394[2] 4897[4] 5349[6]

Anthemion (IRE) *Mrs J C McGregor* 64
9 ch g Night Shift(USA) —New Sensitive (Wattlefield)
1500[9] 2286[11] 2378[7] 2697[10] 3484[3] 3672[4] 3815[3] 4355[5] 4476[2] (4518)

Anthill *I A Wood* 35
2 b f Slickly(FR) —Baddi Heights (FR) (Shirley Heights)
4177[10]

Antica (IRE) *M H Tompkins* 93
3 ch f Raise A Grand(IRE) —Travel Tricks (IRE) (Presidium)
(1097) 1292[4] 1776[2] 1953[3] 4707[5] 5550[7]

Antigel (FR) *W Menuet* 92
3 gr c Verglas(IRE) —Sixtie D'Heyee (FR) (Eymour (FR))
5145a[6]

Antigoni (IRE) *A M Balding* a68 74
3 ch f Grand Lodge(USA) —Butter Knife (IRE) (Sure Blade (USA))
2583[2] 3250[5] 3548[5] 4368[8] 4837[8] 5418[4]

Antigua Bay (IRE) *William Coleman O'Brien* a46 76+
5 b m Turtle Island(IRE) —Vilanika (FR) (Top Ville)
5853a[6]

Antique (IRE) *Saeed Bin Suroor* a64 104
4 ch m Dubai Millennium—Truly Generous (IRE) (Generous (IRE))
6190[12]

Antley Court (IRE) *R Hollinshead* a53
4 ch g Tagula(IRE) —Changed Around (IRE) (Doulab (USA))
974[4] 1665[5]

Anton Chekhov *A P O'Brien* 108+
2 b c Montjeu(IRE) —By Charter (Shirley Heights)
5662a[3] (6357a)

Antrim Rose *J H M Gosden* a65
2 b f Giant's Causeway(USA) —Aunty Rose (IRE) (Caerleon (USA))
6242[7] 6658[8] 6879[5]

Anybody's Guess (IRE) *J S Wainwright* 48
2 b g Iron Mask(USA) —Credibility (Komaite (USA))
5059[7] 5364[8] 5614[15]

A One (IRE) *H J Manners* a53 67
7 b g Alzao(USA) —Anita's Contessa (IRE) (Anita's Prince)
2599[13] 3194[8]

Aoninch *Mrs P N Dutfield* a63 70
6 ch m Inchinor—Willowbank (Gay Fandango (USA))
1800[7]

Apache Chant (USA) *E A L Dunlop* 48
2 b c War Chant(USA) —Sterling Pound (USA) (Seeking The Gold (USA))
4705[16] 5640[12]

Apache Dawn *B W Hills* a75 71
2 ch g Pursuit Of Love—Taza (Persian Bold)
5088[6] 5381[2] 5841[3]

Apache Dream (IRE) *B J Meehan* 75
2 ch f Indian Ridge—Blanche Dubois (Nashwan (USA))
2957[10] 3700[11] (5871) 6201[10]

Apache Fort *T Keddy* a61
3 b g Desert Prince(IRE) —Apogee (Shirley Heights)
6459[9] 6587[6] 6771[8]

Apache Nation (IRE) *M Dods* 69
3 b g Fruits Of Love(USA) —Rachel Green (IRE) (Case Law)
1592[9] 1859[3] (2243) 2923[7] 3355[3] 3760[4] 4069[4] 4255[9] 5015[4] (5312) (5637) 6054[5] 6206[6]

Apache Point (IRE) *N Tinkler* a45 68
9 ch g Indian Ridge—Ausherra (USA) (Diesis)
940[11] 1045[5] 1422[9] 1591[6] 1850[4] 2181[3] 2612[5] (3762) 4381[3] (4467) 4881[10] 5311[2] 5553[9] 5904[13]

Apache Scout (IRE) *R M Beckett* 39
2 ch g Indian Ridge—Salee (IRE) (Caerleon (USA))
6024[8]

Apamea *Mme C Head-Maarek* a78 92
3 ch f Zafonic(USA) —Angelina Ballerina (USA) (Nureyev (USA))
392a[8]

A Peaceful Man *B W Hills* 59
2 b g Tipsy Creek(USA) —My Hearts Desire (Deploy)
5915[11] 6330[11]

Apeiron (GER) *Mario Hofer* a65 109
5 b g Devil River Peek(USA) —Asuma (GER) (Surumu (GER))
1659a[9] 1869a[4] 2692a[4]

Aperitif *D Nicholls* a72+ 75+
5 ch g Pivotal—Art Deco Lady (Master Willie)
726[20] 1041[4] 1124[2] 1186[4] 1382[6] (1561) 4153[9] 4885[12] 5617[12]

Apetite *N Bycroft* 27
4 ch g Timeless Times(USA) —Petite Elite (Anfield)
1447[10] 1791[8] 2077[12]

Apex *N Tinkler* a52 60
5 ch g Efisio—Royal Loft (Homing)
1042[14] 1494[9] 1686[5] 1795[4] 2384[7] 3262[6] 3996[10] 4067[5] 4571[7] 4735[15] 5062[3] 5635[8]

Aphorism *J R Fanshawe* a74+ 77+
3 b f Halling(USA) —Applecross (Glint Of Gold)
3100[6] 3946[8] 4471[3] 4947[5] 5644[3] (6759) 6893[4]

Aphrodisia *S C Williams* 48
2 b f Sakhee(USA) —Aegean Dream (IRE) (Royal Academy (USA))
5456[11]

Apollo Five *D J Coakley* a64 78
2 ch g Auction House(USA) —Dazzling Quintet (Superlative)
1688[3] (2185) 3455[5]

Apollo Star (GER) *Mario Hofer* 98
4 ch g Devil River Peek(USA) —Arwina (GER) (Windwurf (GER))
5856a[3] 6248a[3] 6574a[0]

Apophis (IRE) *A Fabre* 94
2 b c Rainbow Quest(USA) —Aiglonne (USA) (Silver Hawk (USA))
6000a[4]

Appalachian Trail (IRE) *I Semple* a103 109
5 b g Indian Ridge—Karinski (USA) (Palace Music (USA))
57[4] 213[3] 452[2] 2386[7] 2776[2] 3493[8] 3926[4] 4348[3] (4803) 5358[7]

Appealing Zophie (USA) *S Blasi* a113
2 b f Successful Appeal(USA) —Zophie (USA) (Hawkster (USA))
6338a[4]

Appiness (IRE) *John A Quinn* 56
8 b g Be My Native(USA) —Irena (Bold Lad (IRE))
2563a[4]

Apple Annie *M E Sowersby*
3 b f Benny The Dip(USA) —Aneen Alkamanja (Last Tycoon)
5485[17] 5767[14]

Apple Blossom (IRE) *G Wragg* 16
2 b f Danehill Dancer(IRE) —Silk (IRE) (Machiavellian (USA))
5592[15]

Apple Wood *Denis P Quinn* a43 55?
6 b g Woodborough(USA) —Appelania (Star Appeal)
247[13]

Apply Dapply *H Morrison* a60 76
3 b f Pursuit Of Love—Daring Destiny (Daring March)
(868) 1642[2] *3996[8]* 5953[11]6174[2]

Appreciated *W J Haggas* a56
3 b f Most Welcome—Align (Petong)
415[5]

Approval Rating (USA) *M Casse* 85
2 gr c Lemon Drop Kid(USA) —Classic Approval (USA) (With Approval (CAN))
5415a[9]

Approved By Dylan (USA) *Kelly Breen* 75
4 gr h With Approval(CAN) —Remda (USA) (Jade Hunter (USA))
6006a[5]

Apres Ski (IRE) *J F Coupland* a71 67
3 b g Orpen(USA) —Miss Kinabalu (Shirley Heights)
2138[6] 2347[12]2573[7] 2968[7] *3378[4]*(4304) (4845) *(5046) 5739[4]*6054[13]

April Attraction (FR) *C J Down* a35 66
4 b m Mark Of Esteem(IRE) —April Lee (USA) (Lyphard (USA))
4777[11] *5390[10]* 6068[15]

April Fool *J A Geake* 61
2 ch g Pivotal—Palace Affair (Pursuit Of Love)
5339[9] 5867[9] 6298[6]

April Shannon *J E Long*
4 b m Tipsy Creek(USA) —Westering (Auction Ring (USA))
361[10] 573[10]

Apsara *G M Moore* 74
5 br m Groom Dancer(USA) —Ayodhya (IRE) (Astronef)
2540[10] 2761[7] 3283[4] 3361[3] (3716) (4020) 4476[3]4610[3] 4991[4] 5484[3] 5685[8] 5751[5]

Apsis *A Fabre* 116
5 b h Barathea(IRE) —Apogee (Shirley Heights)
(2490a) 3779a[8]

Apt To Run (USA) *E A L Dunlop* a68 75
3 bb c Aptitude(USA) —Tufa (Warning)
1108[9] 1732[2] 1946[2]2498[3] 2990[4] 3310[3]

A. P. Warrior (USA) *J Shirreffs* a115 112
3 bb c A.P. Indy(USA) —Warrior Queen (USA) (Quiet American (USA))
1498a[18] 5985a[3]

Aqaleem *M P Tregoning* 90
2 b c Sinndar(IRE) —Dalayil (IRE) (Sadler's Wells (USA))
4597[3] 5343[2]

Aqmaar *J L Dunlop* 92
2 b c Green Desert(USA) —Hureya (USA) (Woodman (USA))
(3701) 4928[3] 5624[2]

Aqua *P T Midgley* a22 49
4 b m Mister Baileys—Water Well (Sadler's Wells (USA))
609[8] 1032[9] 1252[8]1761[10] 2240[5] 2697[12] 3240[12] *3635[13]*3749[17] 4381[7] 4909[5] 5485[13] (5553) 5838[11]*5926[8]* 6213[5]

Aqua D'Amore (AUS) *Mrs Gai Waterhouse* 113
4 b m Danehill(USA) —Romantic River (USA) (Irish River (FR))
6110a[2] 6347a[3]

Aqualung *D Broad* 90
5 b g Desert King(IRE) —Aquarelle (Kenmare (FR))
1156a[16]

Aquilegia (IRE) *E S McMahon* 72+
2 b f Desert Style(IRE) —Pyatshaw (Common Grounds)
3721[7] 4987[4] 5264[4] 5753[5] 6056[2](6295)

Araafa (IRE) *J Noseda* 126
3 b c Mull Of Kintyre(USA) —Resurgence (Polar Falcon (USA))
1486[4] (2039a) (2721) 4038[5] 5524[2] 6342a[9]

Arabellas Homer *Mrs N Macauley* a51 49
2 b f Mark Of Esteem(IRE) —Rush Hour (IRE) (Night Shift (USA))
3157[5] 4018[4] 4466[6]5482[10] *6422[9] 6520[9]6625[4] 6737[8]6809[5]*

Arabian Breeze *M Mullineaux* a38 61
3 b f Muhtarram(USA) —Dominie Breeze (Primo Dominie)
3916[7] 4708[3] *5248[13]*

Arabian Gulf *Sir Michael Stoute* 74+
2 b c Sadler's Wells(USA) —Wince (Selkirk (USA))
6214[7]

Arabian Moon (IRE) *R Brotherton* a53 61
10 ch g Barathea(IRE) —Excellent Alibi (USA) (Exceller (USA))
1566[4] 2507[7] 2952[4] 3797[5] 3896[4]4239[2]

Arabian Prince (USA) *A P O'Brien* 109
3 b c Fusaichi Pegasus(USA) —Add (USA) (Spectacular Bid (USA))
2039a[11] 2721[11] 3129a[8] 3342a[10] 4641a[3]

Arabian Sea (IRE) *C E Brittain* a81 41
3 b c Sadler's Wells(USA) —Teggiano (IRE) (Mujtahid (USA))
1381[2] 1841[13] *2344[6]*

Arabian Tiger *P W Chapple-Hyam* 70
3 b c Singspiel(IRE) —Um Lardaff (Mill Reef (USA))
3794[17] 4471[5] 5203[7] 5868[15]

Arabian Treasure (USA) *Sir Michael Stoute* 60+
2 b f Danzig(USA) —Very Confidential (USA) (Fappiano (USA))
5638[4]

Arabian Word *Sir Michael Stoute* 67
2 ch c Diesis—Duchcov (Caerleon (USA))
5067[10] 5381[5] 6066[4]

Arabie *Peter Grayson* a47 88
8 b g Polish Precedent(USA) —Always Friendly (High Line)
505[10] 1651[RR] 2387[RR]*5974[10]* 6387[RR]*6531[RR]*

Aragorn (IRE) *N Drysdale* 127
4 ch h Giant's Causeway(USA) —Onaga (USA) (Mr Prospector (USA))
(5825a) 6342a[2]

Aramina (GER) *P Schiergen* 103
3 ch f In The Wings—Akasma (GER) (Windwurf (GER))
2279a[6] 3719a[5]

Arbella *W R Swinburn* a81 100
4 ch m Primo Dominie—Kristal Bridge (Kris)
(1006) 1628[3] (2023)

Arcadio (GER) *P Schiergen* 118
4 b h Monsun(GER) —Assia (IRE) (Royal Academy (USA))
(2061a) (2692a) 3993a[5] 5543a[3] 5982a[5]

Arcangela *J G Given* a44 53
3 b f Galileo(IRE) —Crafty Buzz (USA) (Crafty Prospector (USA))
1421[9] *5247[8]* 5618[10]

Arc Bleu (GER) *Frau Jutta Mayer* 103
5 ch g Monsagem(USA) —Antala (FR) (Antheus (USA))
6252a[10]

Arc De Triomphe (GER) *D Fechner* 102
4 b h Big Shuffle(USA) —Alepha (Celestial Storm (USA))
6093a[13] 6547a[7]

Archange D'Or (IRE) *A Fabre* 115
4 b h Danehill(USA) —Dievotchka (Dancing Brave (USA))
934a[3] 1873a[4] 2597a[3] 3662a[6]

Archduke Ferdinand (FR) *A King* a87 84
8 ch g Dernier Empereur(USA) —Lady Norcliffe (USA) (Norcliffe (CAN))
1247[2] 1690[4] 2723[17]*3203[8] (6075) 6381[3]*

Archerfield Links (USA) *N A Callaghan* a93 89
3 bb g Brahms(USA) —Georgian Bay (USA) (Storm Cat (USA))
(1016) 2774[18] 3121[4]

Arch Folly *R J Price* a51 65
4 b g Silver Patriarch(IRE) —Folly Fox (Alhijaz)
838[4] 1219[5] 1660[5]2219[3] 3291[2] (3896) *4996[8]*5069[9] *6256[12] 6405[11]6540[8]*

Archidona (FR) *M Quinn* a46 53d
3 b f Bluebird(USA) —Gembira (USA) (Alysheba (USA))
422[11] 499[3]642[10] 945[4] 1661[5]

Archie Babe (IRE) *J J Quinn* a55 58
10 ch g Archway(IRE) —Frensham Manor (Le Johnstan)
1187[2] 1590[5] 2075[7] 5581[8]

Archiestown (USA) *J L Dunlop* 75
3 b g Arch(USA) —Second Chorus (IRE) (Scenic)
1087[4] 1680[4] 2175[8]

Archimboldo (USA) *T Wall* a74 80
3 ch g Woodman(USA) —Awesome Strike (USA) (Theatrical)
160[6] 213[9]695[3] 1077[5] *1403[5]*2209[3] 2633[6] *3156[6]3454[3]*

Archirondel *N Wilson* a59 60
8 b g Bin Ajwaad(IRE) —Penang Rose (NZ) (Kingdom Bay (NZ))
*955[4] 1308[7]*1666[5]

Archivist (IRE) *M Blanshard* a56 43
3 b c Kalanisi(IRE) —Mill Rainbow (FR) (Rainbow Quest (USA))
460[8] 2795[7]3388[7] 4556[8] *4972[7]*5298[10]

Arch Of Titus (IRE) *M L W Bell* a61 79
2 ch c Titus Livius(FR) —Cap And Gown (IRE) (Royal Academy (USA))
3385[4] 4566[2] 5283[2]5633[4]

Arch Rebel (USA) *Noel Meade* 114
5 b g Arch(USA) —Sheba's Step (USA) (Alysheba (USA))
(932a) 1365a[4] 3129a[2] 4641a[2] 5004a[2] 5190a[4]

Arch Swing (USA) *John M Oxx* 105+
2 b f Arch(USA) —Gold Pattern (USA) (Slew O'Gold (USA))
(5394a)

Arctic Cove *Micky Hammond* a69 66
5 b g Vettori(IRE) —Sundae Girl (USA) (Green Dancer (USA))
597[10] 2407[11] 2871[7]4072[13]

Arctic Desert *Miss Gay Kelleway* a80 80
6 b g Desert Prince(IRE) —Thamud (IRE) (Lahib (USA))
*(236) 559[5] 764[3]*898[4] 1673[5] *2551[3]*2603[6] *3204[4]* 3543[3]3928[11] 5058[12] *5908[2]6489[2]*

Arctic Wings (IRE) *W R Muir* a69 58
2 b c In The Wings—Arctic Hunt (IRE) (Bering)
5640[9] *6386[2] 6523[5]*

Arculinge *M Blanshard* a59 61
3 b f Paris House—Calamanco (Clantime)
646[5] 1431[5] 1801[2]2316[14] 2987[5] 3950[5] 4305[3] 4690[10]4984[12] *6130[9]*

Ardasnails (IRE) *K G Wingrove* a22 27
4 b g Spectrum(IRE) —Fey Lady (IRE) (Fairy King (USA))
1460[13]

Ardbrae Lady *Joseph G Murphy* 105
3 b f Overbury(IRE) —Gagajulu (Al Hareb (USA))
928a[5] 1363a[2] 2054a[2] 3105a[6] 4502a[3]4749a[4] 5191a[8] 5996a[11] 6356a[4]

Ardea Brave (IRE) *M Botti* a80 72
4 gr m Chester House(USA) —Afto (USA) (Relaunch (USA))
493[4] 596[7]696[3] 972[7] *1152[4]1553[7]* 2133[4] *2577[2]*4104[2] (4331) *(4937) (5671) 5991[6] 6519[3]*

Ardennes (IRE) *M Botti* a42
2 b g Jade Robbery(USA) —Ribbon Glade (UAE) (Zafonic (USA))
6749[6]

Ardent Prince *Heather Dalton* a57 2
3 b g Polar Prince(IRE) —Anthem Flight (USA) (Fly So Free (USA))
2244[7]

Ardglass (IRE) *Mrs P Townsley* a57 61
4 b g Danehill Dancer(IRE) —Leggagh Lady (IRE) (Doubletour (USA))
1748[9] 1769[11]

Ardies *C Laffon-Parias* 88
3 b f Rainbow Quest(USA) —Priena (IRE) (Priolo (USA))
5472a[10]

Ardkeel Lass (IRE) *R A Harris* a51 62
5 ch m Fumo Di Londra(IRE) —Wot-A-Noise (IRE) (Petorius)
24[4] 608[12]681[5] 691[8](1623a) 1645[12] 3863[7] 4675[8]

Ardmaddy (IRE) *J A R Toller* a61
2 b g Generous(IRE) —Yazmin (IRE) (Green Desert (USA))
5780[5] 6145[5]

Arel's Day (FR) *N Branchu* 72
4 gr g Daylami(IRE) —Arel (FR) (Highest Honor (FR))
5562a[0]

Arena's Dream (USA) *R A Fahey* 77
2 rg g Aljabr(USA) —Witching Well (IRE) (Night Shift (USA))
4196[4] 4880[2] 5332[2] 5614[4]

Areyoutalkingtome *C A Cyzer* a115 102
3 b c Singspiel(IRE) —Shot At Love (IRE) (Last Tycoon)
981[3] 1092[4] 1670[2](3162) 4082[14] 4760[2] 5165[3] *5845[5](6192) (6514) (6692) (6849)*

Areyoutalkintome (USA) *Doug O'Neill* a107
5 bb g Smokester(USA) —Andrea Gail (USA) (Storm Bird (CAN))
3134a[5] 6341a[13]

Are You There *Trainer Unknown* a38 36
5 br m Presidium—Scoffera (Scottish Reel)
1625a[5]

Arfinnit (IRE) *Mrs A L M King* a32 55
5 b g College Chapel—Tidal Reach (USA) (Kris S (USA))
1728[10] 2484[8] 3004[9]4365[8] *6233[8]*

Argent *Miss L A Perratt* a44 50
5 b g Barathea(IRE) —Red Tiara (USA) (Mr Prospector (USA))
2808[13]

Argent Danseur *B S Rothwell* 40
2 b g Lujain(USA) —Perfect Pirouette (JPN) (Warning)
1229[4] 1682[5] 2015[5] 2451[4]

Argentina (IRE) *R J Frankel* 113
4 b m Sadler's Wells(USA) —Airline (USA) (Woodman (USA))
5819a[5]

Argentine (IRE) *M Johnston* a75 85
2 b c Fasliyev(USA) —Teller (ARG) (Southern Halo (USA))
1080[3] 1664[4] (3286) 3678[2] 4130[5] *6146[3]*

Argonaut *P Bowen* a72 96
6 b g Rainbow Quest(USA) —Chief Bee (Chief's Crown (USA))
966[14]

Arian's Lad *B Palling* a56 66
5 b g Prince Sabo—Arian Da (Superlative)
*1165[4] 1273[4]*1570[4] 2095[7] 2317[6] 2602[2] *3390[8]*

Ariesanne (IRE) *A C Whillans* a53 35
5 ch m Primo Dominie—Living Legend (ITY) (Archway (IRE))
*9[3] 130[7](145) 411[2]618[9] 691[14]*2811[14] 3166[6]

Ariodante *J M P Eustace* a70 77
4 b g Groom Dancer(USA) —Maestrale (Top Ville)
1186[11] 1591[5] 2149[3] 2360[7] 2822[4]3628[4] 4005[6] (4448) 4900[7] *6766[6]6885[4]*

Arisea (IRE) *R C Guest* a14 39
3 b f Cape Cross(IRE) —Castelfranca (IRE) (Scenic)
*1150[12] 1571[11]*1792[9] 4195[8]

Aristaios (GER) *Bruce Hellier* 89
5 b g Alkalde(GER) —Aerleona (IRE) (Caerleon (USA))
6121a[11]

Aristi (IRE) *M Quinn* a56 62
5 b m Dr Fong(USA) —Edessa (IRE) (Tirol)
*589[8] 643[8]*881[4] 1184[9] 1415[9] *1766[5]3919[11] 4438[7]4929[6]*

Aristofilia *P F I Cole* a51 62
3 b f Bahhare(USA) —Noble Story (Last Tycoon)
916[4] 2458[5] 2727[4]3793[10] 4113[7] 5474[16] *5781[5]*

Arizona Sun (IRE) *A Fabre* 94
3 ch f Spinning World(USA) —Abime (USA) (Woodman (USA))
2799a[11]

Arkadia Honey *J L Spearing* 56
3 ch f Tomba—Arkadia Park (IRE) (Polish Precedent (USA))
969[13] 1378[9]

Arkando (GER) *M Trybuhl* 89
5 ch g Kornado—Advantage (GER) (Glow (USA))
6610a[10]

Arkholme *A M Hales* a28 88
5 b g Robellino(USA) —Free Spirit (IRE) (Caerleon (USA))
3405[6] 3730[13]

Armada (NZ) *J Size* 120
5 ch g Twokay(IRE) —Dance In Time (NZ) (Red Tempo (NZ))
6784a[2]

Armada *Sir Michael Stoute* a79
3 b g Anabaa(USA) —Trevillari (USA) (Riverman (USA))
1336[2] (3100)

Arma Di Taggia (IRE) *Sabrina Ducci* 84
5 b m Lake Coniston(IRE) —Aran Exile (Ahonoora)
1368a[7]

Armagnac *M A Buckley* a78 74
8 b g Young Ern—Arianna Aldini (Habitat)
1662[10]

Armanatta (IRE) *Mrs A M O'Shea* a37 65+
5 b m Spectrum(IRE) —Via Verbano (IRE) (Caerleon (USA))
384[12] 5831[5]

Armand (GER) *P Schiergen* 89
5 b h Winged Love(IRE) —Arpista (GER) (Chief Singer)
456a[3]

Armand *P Bary* a90 101
3 b g Observatory(USA) —Guillem (USA) (Nijinsky (CAN))
5145a[3] 6062a[9]

Armatore (USA) *Ernst Oertel* a64 64
6 b g Gone West(USA) —Awesome Account (USA) (Lyphard (USA))
2414[11] 2790[10]

Arm Candy (IRE) *J A R Toller* a55 100
3 br f Nashwan(USA) —Bedara (Barathea (IRE))
1406[2] 1819[9] 3316[7] 4577[2] 5512[6]5943[4] (6219) *6516[14]*

Armigerent (IRE) *M Johnston* 101d
2 b c In The Wings—Roses From Ridey (IRE) (Petorius)
2778[2] 3143[2] 3442[2] 3924[4] 4344[5]4712[6] 5466a[10]

Armillary *Mrs A J Perrett* 51
2 b f Soviet Star(USA) —Marliana (IRE) (Mtoto)
4558[8] 5068[12] 5454[15]

Arminius (IRE) *R Hannon* 99
3 b g Shinko Forest(IRE) —Tribal Rite (Be My Native (USA))
1358[3] 1990[7] 4740[3] 5520[10] 5943[5]

Arms Acrossthesea *J Balding* a38 45
7 b g Namaqualand(USA) —Zolica (Beveled (USA))
1387[11]

Armus (IRE) *M Ciciarelli*
2 b c Polish Precedent(USA) —Aqua Duce (USA) (St Jovite (USA))
5771a[6]

Army Of Angels (IRE) *Saeed Bin Suroor* 116
4 ch g King's Best(USA) —Angelic Sounds (IRE) (The Noble Player (USA))
(5677) (5789) 6218[2]

Arnie De Burgh *D J Daly* a77 72
4 br h Amfortas(IRE) —Align (Petong)
(170) 292[3] (381) 451[5]644[8] 1188[4] 1885[7]

Arnie's Joint (IRE) *N P Littmoden* a63 73
2 b g Golan(IRE) —Green Green Grass (Green Desert (USA))
(1688) 4766[17] *5017[9]* 5509[6]

Arosa (IRE) *David Wachman* 94
3 b f Sadler's Wells(USA) —Sharata (IRE) (Darshaan)
4212a[5] 5854a[9]

Arpetcheeo (USA) *D Carroll* a49 16
4 bb h Deputy Minister(CAN) —Lizanne (USA) (Theatrical)
1852[10] 2221[13]

Arpino (GER) *P Schiergen* 100
3 b c Protektor(GER) —Arbarine (GER) (Aspros (GER))
2671a[5] 5762a[7]

Arran Scout (IRE) *T G McCourt* a73 78
5 b g Piccolo—Evie Hone (IRE) (Royal Academy (USA))
736[5]

Arras (GER) *A Fabre* 115
3 ch c Monsun(GER) —Avocette (GER) (King's Lake (USA))
2278a[3]

Arravale (USA) *M Benson* 117
3 br f Arch(USA) —Kalosca (FR) (Kaldoun (FR))
(6125a)

Arrears (USA) *R Menichetti* 91
6 br h Barkerville(USA) —Granny Goodrich (USA) (Pool Court (USA))
6252a[8]

Arrivee (FR) *A Fabre* 86
3 br f Anabaa(USA) —Quiet Dream (USA) (Seattle Slew (USA))
1130[10]

Arry Dash *M J Wallace* a74 79
6 b g Fraam—Miletrian Cares (IRE) (Hamas (IRE))
108[9] 1302[7] *5739[9]*6017[11] 6301[3] *6432[5]*

Arsad (IRE) *C E Brittain* a66 63
3 b f Cape Cross(IRE) —Astuti (IRE) (Waajib)
1114[9] *1638[9] (2246)* 2592[7]3249[8] 4687[5] 4944[6] 5445[2] 6068[9]*6435[4] 6565[6]6929[3] 6995[2]*

Art Deco (IRE) *C R Egerton* 115
3 ch c Peintre Celebre(USA) —Sometime (IRE) (Royal Academy (USA))
(1627) 2278a[4] 3517a[5]

Art Elegant *G A Swinbank* a71 73
4 b g Desert Prince(IRE) —Elegant (IRE) (Marju (IRE))
110[2] 162[2]219[3] 1041[15] (2282) 2541[3]2874[6]

Art Eyes (USA) *D R C Elsworth* 113
4 ch m Halling(USA) —Careyes (IRE) (Sadler's Wells (USA))
2085[4] 2430[2] 3085[5] 4079[2] 4797[4]5155[7]

Art Gallery *G L Moore* a38 54
2 ch c Indian Ridge—Party Doll (Be My Guest (USA))
6220[15] 6330[5] *6561[10]*

Art Historian (IRE) *T J Pitt* a63 51
3 b g Barathea(IRE) —Radhwa (FR) (Shining Steel)
5972[13] 6177[3] *6382[3]6509[7] 6571[5]6790[8]*

Arthurs Dream (IRE) *A W Carroll* 51
4 b g Desert Prince(IRE) —Blueprint (USA) (Shadeed (USA))
1204[9] 1772[8] 2186[8] 3614[8] 3898[7]4984[7]

Arthur's Edge *B Palling* 51
2 b g Diktat—Bright Edge (Danehill Dancer (IRE))
5125[12] 5371[16]

Arthurs Legacy *J A R Toller* a58
4 b g Josr Algarhoud(IRE) —Loch Clair (IRE) (Lomond (USA))
217[10] 460[10]696[9]

Articulation *C Byrnes* 88
5 b h Machiavellian(USA) —Stiletta (Dancing Brave (USA))
3128a[14]

Artie *T D Easterby* 91
7 b g Whittingham(IRE) —Calamanco (Clantime)
1076[13] 1597[8]

Artie's Son (IRE) *T D Easterby* a60+ 54
3 b g Mull Of Kintyre(USA) —Eurolink Virago (Charmer)
1147[5] 1564[8] 2016[4] *2939[2]3154[7]* 4069[8] 4199[5]

Artificial *T D Easterby* 12+
2 ch g Bertolini(USA) —Exclusive Davis (USA) (Our Native (USA))
3018[12]

Artimino *J R Fanshawe* 86
2 b c Medicean—Palatial (Green Desert (USA))
4109^{5} (5066) 5546^{2}

Art Investor *D R C Elsworth* a73 76
3 b g Sinndar(IRE) —Maid For Romance (Pursuit Of Love)
3901^{6} 4374^{5} 4945^{8} 5266^{6} *5911^{4}6535^{2} 6680^{2}*

Artistic Lad *Mrs John Harrington* 95
6 ch h Peintre Celebre(USA) —Maid For The Hills (Indian Ridge)
3128a^{11}

Artistic Lady *M A Jarvis* 68
3 br f Jade Robbery(USA) —Noble Lily (USA) (Vaguely Noble)
2261^{4} 2895^{5}

Artistic Liason *G C H Chung* a47
2 ch f Auction House(USA) —Homeoftheclassics (Tate Gallery (USA))
3402^{7}

Artistic Style *B Ellison* a82 97+
6 b g Anabaa(USA) —Fine Detail (IRE) (Shirley Heights)
1017^{12} 1585^{14} 2079^{9}3020^{9} 5310^{6} 5787^{15}

Artist's Muse (USA) *M S Saunders* a2 66
3 b f Royal Academy(USA) —Atelier (Warning)
1516^{4} 2292^{5} 2895^{6} *6828^{6}6987^{12}*

Artists Touch (IRE) *N P Littmoden* a39
3 b g Alhaarth(IRE) —Alla Marcia (IRE) (Marju (IRE))
215^{7}

Art Man *Mrs A J Perrett* 73
3 b g Dansili—Persuasion (Batshoof)
1513^{14} 2028^{5} 2498^{2} 3162^{4}

Art Market (CAN) *P F I Cole* a84 98
3 ch g Giant's Causeway(USA) —Fantasy Lake (USA) (Salt Lake (USA))
665^{7} 2204^{4} 2774^{2}8439^{16} 4988^{9} 5143^{8}

Art Master (USA) *R J Frankel* 113
5 b h Royal Academy(USA) —True Flare (USA) (Capote (USA))
841a^{2} 1371a^{8} 6329a^{7}

Art Modern (IRE) *G L Moore* a75 83
4 ch g Giant's Causeway(USA) —Sinead (USA) (Irish River (FR))
4336^{2} 5295^{8}

Art Museum (USA) *A P O'Brien* 110+
3 b c Storm Cat(USA) —Totemic (USA) (Vanlandingham (USA))
5962^{7}

Art Of Poker (IRE) *B W Hills* a50
2 b c Almutawakel—Poker Dice (Primo Dominie)
5890^{16} *6031^{10}*

Art Success (NZ) *John Collins* 109
5 b g Pentire—Zabelette (NZ) (Zabeel (NZ))
6392a^{16}

Art Trader (USA) *J Moore* 117
5 b g Arch(USA) —Math (USA) (Devil's Bag (USA))
1527a^{10} 6785a^{5}

Arturius (IRE) *P J Rothwell* a103+ 91
4 b h Anabaa(USA) —Steeple (Selkirk (USA))
(377) (572) 666^{12} 2848^{17} 4031a^{17}

Artzola (IRE) *C A Horgan* a58+ 54
6 b m Alzao(USA) —Polistatic (Free State)
1911^{11} 6232^{3}(6373) (6620) (6804)

Aryaamm (IRE) *M A Jarvis* a55 89
3 b f Galileo(IRE) —Zibilene (Rainbow Quest (USA))
3367^{4} *4247^{6}* 4759^{3}(5086) 5502^{6} 5917^{10}

Arzaag *D M Simcock* a69 67
3 b g Bertolini(USA) —Como (USA) (Cozzene (USA))
233^{3} 473^{5}533^{3} 1089^{6} 1589^{4}2222^{4} *2576^{6} (2937)* 3667^{6}

Asaateel (IRE) *G L Moore* a54 70
4 br g Unfuwain(USA) —Alabaq (USA) (Riverman (USA))
905^{7} 1075^{7} *1334^{14}*1755^{7} 1995^{2} (2132) 5734^{10} 6008^{16} *6484^{11}*

Asaawir *M R Channon* 98
3 b f Royal Applause—Triple Joy (Most Welcome)
1023a^{5}

Asafa (IRE) *J S Bolger* 44
2 b f King's Best(USA) —Azra (IRE) (Danehill (USA))
5394a^{9}

Asakusa Den'En *Michifumi Kono* 123
7 ch h Singspiel(IRE) —Whitewater Affair (Machiavellian (USA))
742a^{15} 6850a^{4}

Asarabacca (FR) *E A L Dunlop* a52
3 ch f Halling(USA) —All Our Hope (USA) (Gulch (USA))
337^{5} 515^{8}

Asbury Park *M R Bosley* a55 70
3 b c Primo Valentino(IRE) —Ocean Grove (IRE) (Fairy King (USA))
123^{7} 1052^{4} 1740^{8}5770^{9}

Ascetic Silver (FR) *D Prod'Homme* 101
6 ch h Kendor(FR) —Snowdrop II (FR) (Niniski (USA))
523a^{7}

Ascot Family (IRE) *A Lyon* 88
2 b f Desert Style(IRE) —Family At War (USA) (Explodent (USA))
5048a^{5} 5664a^{5}

Ascot Lady (IRE) *J Balding* 96
3 ch f Spinning World(USA) —Life At The Top (Habitat)
4422^{7} 5535^{15} 5643^{9} 6048^{15}

Ashaawes (USA) *Saeed Bin Suroor* 109+
3 b c Kingmambo(USA) —Crown Of Crimson (USA) (Seattle Slew (USA))
(3681) (4877) 5360^{5}

Asharon *C E Brittain* a88 84
4 b g Efisio—Arriving (Most Welcome)
828^{15} 1112^{12}1410^{9}

Ashburnham (IRE) *N I M Rossiter* a62 45
3 b f Intikhab(USA) —Blu Tamantara (USA) (Miswaki (USA))
266^{8}

Ashdown Express (IRE) *C F Wall* 120
7 ch g Ashkalani(IRE) —Indian Express (Indian Ridge)
1069^{9} 2720^{12} 2846^{4} 3494^{3} 3732^{6}4191a^{8} 5179^{2} 5942^{12}

Ashes (IRE) *K R Burke* a73 76d
4 b m General Monash(USA) —Wakayi (Persian Bold)
*51^{6} 119^{4}225^{5} 486^{2}519^{3} 587^{2}*813^{2} *(954)* 1297^{14} *1338^{2}*1563^{7} 1774^{4} *2462^{5}*(2550) 2661^{16} 3172^{2} 3354^{9} 5309^{18} 5333^{11}6162^{9} 6315^{15}

Ashes Regained *B W Hills* 54
3 b c Galileo(IRE) —Hasty Words (IRE) (Polish Patriot (USA))
6021^{8}

Ashford Castle (IRE) *B J Meehan* 50
3 b g Mujadil(USA) —Lonely Heart (Midyan (USA))
1048^{10} 1134^{10} 5761^{6}

Ashkal Way (IRE) *Saeed Bin Suroor* 120
4 ch g Ashkalani(IRE) —Golden Way (IRE) (Cadeaux Genereux)
513a^{3} (4908a)

Ashlawn (IRE) *H Rogers* 64
6 b g Ashkalani(IRE) —Khaydariya (IRE) (Akarad (FR))
4166a^{4}

Ashmal (USA) *J L Dunlop* 55
2 b f Machiavellian(USA) —Alabaq (USA) (Riverman (USA))
6215^{15}

Ashn Thunder *M Johnston* 69
2 ch c Thunder Gulch(USA) —Ashford Castle (USA) (Bates Motel (USA))
5402^{2} 6049^{5} 6220^{12}

Ashover Rock (IRE) *I W McInnes*
2 b g Danetime(IRE) —Ascoli (Skyliner)
1588^{17}

Ashstanza *R D E Woodhouse* a46 35
5 gr g Ashkalani(IRE) —Poetry In Motion (IRE) (Ballad Rock)
2935^{3} 3382^{11}6623^{9}

Ash The Cash (IRE) *K F Clutterbuck*
4 b g High Roller(IRE) —Angela's Pet (IRE) (Ridgewood Ben)
26^{12}

Ashwell Rose *R T Phillips* a49
4 b m Anabaa(USA) —Finicia (USA) (Miswaki (USA))
*419^{7} 566^{6}*1219^{14} *3597^{5} 3998^{13}*

Asian Alliance (IRE) *K A Ryan* a56 56
5 ch m Soviet Star(USA) —Indian Express (Indian Ridge)
6775^{7} 6936^{9}

Asian Heights *G Wragg* 101
8 b h Hernando(FR) —Miss Rinjani (Shirley Heights)
1677^{3} 4096^{5} 4576^{3}

Asi Siempre (USA) *P L Biancone* a120 113
4 gr m El Prado(IRE) —Siempre Asi (USA) (Silver Hawk (USA))
6343a^{4}

Ask *Sir Michael Stoute* 114
3 b c Sadler's Wells(USA) —Request (Rainbow Quest (USA))
1088^{3} 2304^{2} (2917) 4039^{11} 4742^{2} 5185^{4}

Ask Carol (IRE) *Joseph G Murphy* 92
5 b m Foxhound(USA) —Escape Path (Wolver Hollow)
2840a^{2} 4031a^{15}

Ask Don't Tell (IRE) *Tom Dascombe* a57 61
2 b f Indian Rocket—Cladantom (IRE) (High Estate)
(1223) 1582^{7} 1824^{4} 3216^{5} *3530^{7}*4427^{6} *5687^{5} 5772^{6}*(6064)

Ask Jenny (IRE) *Patrick Morris* a26 64
4 b m Marju(IRE) —Waltzing Matilda (Mujtahid (USA))
6890^{8}

Ask No More *P L Gilligan* a73 30
3 b g Pyramus(USA) —Nordesta (IRE) (Nordico (USA))
(2575) 3055^{3} 3487^{7} *5907^{12}6419^{6} 6898^{3}6952^{9}*

Ask The Clerk (IRE) *Mrs P Sly* a65 79
5 b g Turtle Island(IRE) —Some Fun (Wolverlife)
977^{15} 1186^{3} 1760^{6} 2291^{2}

Ask Yer Dad *Mrs P Sly* a65 59
2 b g Diktat—Heuston Station (IRE) (Fairy King (USA))
2759^{6} 5112^{3} 5496^{8} *6394^{7}6576^{4}*

Asleep At The Back (IRE) *J G Given* a56 11
3 b g Halling(USA) —Molomo (Barathea (IRE))
897^{16} 6052^{11} *6302^{4}6759^{4} 6957^{2}*

Asmaradana *P F I Cole* a23 47
3 b g Groom Dancer(USA) —Nsx (Roi Danzig (USA))
861^{9}

As One Does *K A Ryan* 86
2 b c Lujain(USA) —Night Over Day (Most Welcome)
1090^{5} (1811) 3143^{3} 3735^{7} 4681^{16} 5404^{9}

Aspasias Tizzy (USA) *M Johnston* 86
3 bb f Tiznow(USA) —Ashford Castle (USA) (Bates Motel (USA))
1290^{3} (1492) 2584^{7} 4231^{2} 4631^{8} 4990^{6}

Aspecto (FR) *H-A Pantall*
3 b c Spectrum(IRE) —Astonishing (BRZ) (Vacilante (ARG))
2717a^{4}

Aspectus (IRE) *H Blume* 108
3 ch c Spectrum(IRE) —Anna Thea (IRE) (Turfkonig (GER))
(1176a) 1715a^{2} 2278a^{13} (3131a) 3776a^{6} 4942a^{5}

Aspen Falls (IRE) *Sir Mark Prescott* a75 77
3 ch f Elnadim(USA) —Esquiline (USA) (Gone West (USA))
1617^{4} *1963^{4}* 2620^{8}3606^{7} 3841^{5}

Asperity (USA) *J H M Gosden* 96+
2 b c War Chant(USA) —Another Storm (USA) (Gone West (USA))
5292^{2} (5640)

Assertive *R Hannon* 110
3 ch c Bold Edge—Tart And A Half (Distant Relative)
1131^{3} (1408) 1818^{2} 2303^{9} 2739^{4} 4025^{3}4191a^{9} 4803^{2} 5341^{8} 5549^{4}

Asset (IRE) *R Hannon* a106+ 110
3 b g Marju(IRE) —Snow Peak (Arazi (USA))
(829) 1486^{9} 2739^{2}

Assumption (IRE) *S C Williams* a47 54
3 b f Beckett(IRE) —Native Force (IRE) (Indian Ridge)
20^{5} 676^{3}(779)

Astarte *P R Chamings* a34
2 b f Slip Anchor—Nanouche (Dayjur (USA))
6486^{11}

Aston Lad *Micky Hammond* 56+
5 b g Bijou D'Inde—Fishki (Niniski (USA))
5905^{6} (6161)

Astorygoeswithit *P S McEntee* a46 38
3 b g Foxhound(USA) —La Belle Mystere (Lycius (USA))
*85^{12} 500^{9}*797^{14} *6371^{9} 6550^{6}6707^{8} 6794^{2}6958^{3}*

Astral Charmer *M H Tompkins* a65
2 b g Tobougg(IRE) —Blushing Sunrise (USA) (Cox's Ridge (USA))
6393^{11} 6498^{4}6650^{4}

Astroangel *M H Tompkins* a65 66
2 b f Groom Dancer(USA) —Nutmeg (IRE) (Lake Coniston (IRE))
2638^{16} *3402^{4}* 3799^{2}4547^{4} 5382^{7} 5461^{7} 5721^{3} 6064^{15}*6310^{9}*

Astrobella *M H Tompkins* 80
3 ch f Medicean—Optimistic (Reprimand)
2359^{7} 2679^{7} 5478^{5} 5732^{8}

Astrocharm (IRE) *M H Tompkins* a70 108
7 b m Charnwood Forest(IRE) —Charm The Stars (Roi Danzig (USA))
2453^{4} 2893^{4} 3078^{18}

Astrolibra *M H Tompkins* 43
2 b f Sakhee(USA) —Optimistic (Reprimand)
6050^{8}

Astronomer Royal (USA) *A P O'Brien* 85+
2 b c Danzig(USA) —Sheepscot (USA) (Easy Goer (USA))
(4177)

Astronomia (NZ) *Saeed Bin Suroor* 110
4 ch m King's Best(USA) —Astralita (AUS) (Kenny's Best Pal (AUS))
2011^{5} 2740^{10} 4590^{4}

Astronomical (IRE) *Miss S J Wilton* a67 79
4 b g Mister Baileys—Charm The Stars (Roi Danzig (USA))
3686^{7}

Astronomical Odds (USA) *T D Barron*a71+ 61
3 b g Miswaki(USA) —Perfectly Polish (USA) (Polish Numbers (USA))
(6532) 6762^{4}

Astronomic View *E A L Dunlop* a78
2 b c Observatory(USA) —On Tiptoes (Shareef Dancer (USA))
*2572^{3} 3844^{3}*4323^{P} (Dead)

Astronova *M H Tompkins* a14 53
3 ch f Bahamian Bounty—Astrolove (IRE) (Bigstone (IRE))
*211^{11} 333^{9}*3032^{7} 3611^{5}

Asturias *J W Hills* a68 39
2 b f Anabaa(USA) —Halcyon Daze (Halling (USA))
5424^{5} 5679^{9}

Aswan (IRE) *S R Bowring* a58 47
8 ch g Ashkalani(IRE) —Ghariba (Final Straw)
*56^{11} 121^{2}271^{7} 315^{6}*1443^{5} *1746^{3} 2208^{6}2793^{9} 3155^{2}*

Atakama (GER) *A D Nolan* a27 57
6 b m Platini(GER) —Athene (GER) (Nebos (GER))
358^{8} 636^{8}

Atamane (GER) *Mario Hofer* 98
3 b c Winged Love(IRE) —Adjani (Surumu (GER))
5709a^{5}

A Teen *P Howling* a53 61
8 ch g Presidium—Very Good (Noalto)
90^{4} 130^{4}265^{10} 408^{6}529^{2} 613^{2}633^{12} 766^{6}876^{5} 907^{4}942^{2} 1228^{3}1465^{4} 1534^{2}1722^{5} 1909^{12}3204^{3} 3536^{5}

Athar (IRE) *R Hannon* 80
2 ch c Traditionally(USA) —Lady Nasrana (FR) (Al Nasr (FR))
5890^{3}

Athboy Nights (IRE) *M J Wallace* a62 47
4 b m Night Shift(USA) —Missing Love (IRE) (Thatching)
3389^{4} 3846^{11}

Athea Lad (IRE) *W K Goldsworthy* a37 48
2 b g Indian Danehill(IRE) —Persian Empress (IRE) (Persian Bold)
6757^{11} 6853^{5}6963^{8}

Athena's Dream *C F Wall* 65
3 b f Robellino(USA) —Greek Dream (USA) (Distant View (USA))
1646^{6} 2511^{9} 3931^{6} 4120^{10} 4293^{2}5327^{12}

Athene (DEN) *S Jensen* 28
5 b m Final Appearance(IRE) —Miss Fyns Tivoli (DEN) (Saville Row)
4863a^{7}

Atheneum (IRE) *M Johnston* 75
2 b c Noverre(USA) —Anno Luce (Old Vic)
1811^{5} 2321^{6} 3210^{3} 3623^{6} 4100^{8}5366^{2} 6064^{10}

Athlumney Lad (IRE) *Noel Meade* 88
7 b g Mujadil(USA) —Simouna (Ela-Mana-Mou)
5853a^{11}

A Thousand Smiles (IRE) *M A Jarvis* a71 70
4 b m Sadler's Wells(USA) —Bluffing (IRE) (Darshaan)
(166) 264^{6}

Ath Tiomain (IRE) *D J S Ffrench Davis* 47
3 b g Night Shift(USA) —Broken Spirit (IRE) (Slip Anchor)
4431^{12} 4661^{11} *5429^{13}*

Atlantic Ace *B Smart* a70 71
9 b g First Trump—Risalah (Marju (IRE))
157^{12} 383^{9}734^{6} 1341^{13} 1757^{11}

Atlantic Air (FR) *Y De Nicolay* 107
4 gr h Kaldounevees(FR) —Beg Meil (FR) (Tel Quel (FR))
(4417a) 5704a^{5} 5913a^{5} 6250a^{8}

Atlantic City *Mrs L Richards* a66 66
5 ch g First Trump—Pleasuring (Good Times (ITY))
6435^{11} 6673^{9}6883^{6}

Atlantic Coast (IRE) *M Johnston* a50 8
2 b g In The Wings—Reasonably Devout (CAN) (St Jovite (USA))
5720^{11} 6058^{11} *6447^{3}*

Atlantic Dame (USA) *Mrs A J Perrett* a51
2 ch f Lemon Drop Kid(USA) —While Rome Burns (USA) (Overskate (CAN))
5784^{9} 6073^{10}

Atlantic Gamble (IRE) *K R Burke* a55+ 61
6 b g Darnay—Full Traceability (IRE) (Ron's Victory (USA))
6430^{8} 6509^{3}6540^{4} 6729^{4}6790^{6} 6871^{5}

Atlantic Light *M Johnston* 91
2 gr f Linamix(FR) —Atlantic Destiny (IRE) (Royal Academy (USA))
4830^{7} 5297^{7} 6055^{2} (6271) 6332^{9}

Atlantic Quest (USA) *Miss Venetia Williams* a88 80
7 b g Woodman(USA) —Pleasant Pat (USA) (Pleasant Colony (USA))
*58^{8} 108^{4}161^{2} 404^{6}(444) 542^{8}629^{10} 1111^{9}*1692^{6} *2341^{9}* 2900^{5}*6313^{12} 6607^{5}6752^{2} 6772^{3}6888^{4} 6992^{3}*

Atlantic Story (USA) *M W Easterby* a83 71
4 bb g Stormy Atlantic(USA) —Story Book Girl (USA) (Siberian Express (USA))
3549^{8} 3747^{8} 4087^{4} 4467^{4} 4925^{12}5445^{5} 6300^{7} *(6577) (6642) (6667)*

Atlantic Viking (IRE) *P D Evans* a55+ 70
11 b g Danehill(USA) —Hi Bettina (Henbit (USA))
1886^{3} 2396^{5} 2748^{3} 3832^{4} (4067) 4629^{8}5058^{11} 6061^{12} *6288^{9}6667^{9} 6694^{7}6855^{6} 6906^{4}*

Atlantic Waves (IRE) *M Johnston* 101+
3 b c Sadler's Wells(USA) —Highest Accolade (Shirley Heights)
(1093) 2228^{15}

Atlantique Nord (FR) *D De Watrigant* 111
6 gr g Balleroy(USA) —La Narquoise (FR) (Al Nasr (FR))
5881a^{3} 6786a^{12}

At Once (GER) *Frau E Mader* a87 103
5 gr m Kendor(FR) —Aberdeen (GER) (Polish Precedent (USA))
204a^{8} 431a^{10} *563a^{9}*

Atraas (IRE) *M P Tregoning* 72
2 b g King's Best(USA) —Sundus (USA) (Sadler's Wells (USA))
5340 ^{3} 5892^{4}

Attacca *J R Weymes* a39 61
5 b g Piccolo—Jubilee Place (IRE) (Prince Sabo)
(818) 1253^{5} (1459) 1885^{6} 2135^{10} 2926^{3} 3361^{4}3697^{8} 3786^{6} 4198^{4} 4571^{15} 4729^{4}5636^{5}

Attack Minded *L R James* 18
5 ch g Timeless Times(USA) —French Ginger (Most Welcome)
3141^{12} 4402^{6}

Attentive (IRE) *S Seemar* a89 95
8 ch g Pennekamp(USA) —Snoozeandyoulose (IRE) (Scenic)
437a^{6} *565a^{11}*

At The Bar *A J Chamberlain* a23 32
3 ch c Compton Place—Miss Tress (IRE) (Salse (USA))
1412^{9} *1746^{11}* 3006^{17}

At The Helm (IRE) *W J Knight* a57 50
4 b m Docksider(USA) —Good Reference (IRE) (Reference Point)
770^{4} 917^{2}1553^{5} 2181^{12} *2414^{12}*3095^{7} *3730^{3}* 4276^{4}*(5097) 5609^{8}*

At The Money *J M P Eustace* a68 80
3 b g Robellino(USA) —Coh Sho No (Old Vic)
859^{3} 1221^{2} (1648) 2117^{2}(5952) 6205^{3} *6467^{3} 6495^{2}*

Atticus Kristy (USA) *M Scherer* 110
5 ch g Atticus(USA) —Christy Love (USA) (Unbridled (USA))
6127a^{6}

Atticus Trophies (IRE) *Ms J S Doyle* a60 70
3 b g Mujadil(USA) —Nezool Almatar (IRE) (Last Tycoon)
722^{8} 1261^{8} 1355^{4}2050^{15} 2301^{13} *6810^{3}6918^{11} 6987^{9}*

Attila's Peintre *P C Haslam* 50
2 b g Peintre Celebre(USA) —Atabaa (FR) (Anabaa (USA))
5814^{9}

Attila's Storm (USA) *R Schosberg* a114
4 b h Forest Wildcat(USA) —Sweet Symmetry (USA) (Magesterial (USA))
5820a^{3} 6341a^{5}

Attila The Hun *F Watson* a44+ 47?
7 b g Piccolo—Katya (IRE) (Dancing Dissident (USA))
1391^{4} 2700^{9} 2785^{9}3003^{6} 3635^{7} 4306^{13}

Attilius (BRZ) *I Mohammed* a100 53
4 b h Dodge(USA) —Favorite Blass (BRZ) (Tokatee (USA))
(353a) 619a^{10}

Attima *J Canani* 110
3 b f Zafonic(USA) —Guarded (Eagle Eyed (USA))
6614a^{9}

Attishoe *Miss B Sanders* a24 13
4 b m Atraf—Royal Shoe (Hotfoot)
1723^{10} 2260^{13}

Attitude Annie *S Dow* a56 39
3 b f Josr Algarhoud(IRE) —Eclectic (Emarati (USA))
60^{4} 269^{5}543^{5} 595^{6}902^{13} 3267^{15} *3536^{6}3847^{2}* 4554^{10} *6371^{14}*

Attorney *P D Evans* a59 74
8 ch g Wolfhound(USA) —Princess Sadie (Shavian)
4^{9} 552^{8}608^{6} 862^{11}

Aturo (FR) *C Sprengel* 46
2 br c Big Shuffle(USA) —Avanti Adda (GER) (Law Society (USA))
6092a[10]

Atwirl *D J Daly* a65+ 55
3 b f Pivotal—Amidst (Midyan (USA))
1351[11] 2048[10] 2304[10] 3650[10]4069[2] 5986[2] (6130)

Auburndale *A Crook* 16
4 b g Mind Games—Primitive Gift (Primitive Rising (USA))
1343[12] 3022[9] 4635[9]

Auburn Lodge (IRE) *J J Lambe* a29 40
5 ch m Grand Lodge(USA) —Hadawah (USA) (Riverman (USA))
732[11]

Auchroisk (SWE) *Bruno Nilsson*
3 b f Nicolotte—Fernet-Branca (SWE) (Diligo (FR))
2564a[2] 3326a[5]

Auction Boy *B Palling* a13 56
2 b g Auction House(USA) —Away Win (Common Grounds)
1770[5] 3344[10] 3860[6] 6311[11]6471[8]

Auctioneerscouk (IRE) *P D Evans* a21
2 gr g Desert Style(IRE) —Diamond Waltz (IRE) (Linamix (FR))
701[9] 892[10] (Dead)

Auction Oasis *B Palling* a2 58
2 b f Auction House(USA) —Shining Oasis (IRE) (Mujtahid (USA))
1542[14] 3193[2] 3895[6] (4926) 6388[13]

Auction Room (USA) *B W Hills* 85
3 b f Chester House(USA) —Didina (Nashwan (USA))
1583[8] 2290[3] 2679[8] 3882[4]

Auction Time *J L Spearing* 60
2 b f Auction House(USA) —Sontime (Son Pardo)
962[3] (1142) 1682[6] 3117[12]

Audience *J Akehurst* 99d
6 b g Zilzal(USA) —Only Yours (Aragon)
728[5] 1129[13] 1678[9] 2086[3] 2988[3]3733[2] (4356) 4739[14] 5520[12] 5945[18] 6219[7]

Audit (IRE) *Sir Michael Stoute* 73
2 b g Fusaichi Pegasus(USA) —Amethyst (IRE) (Sadler's Wells (USA))
4107[2] 5297[6] 5886[2] 6058[3]

Auenmoon (GER) *P Monteith* 73
5 ch g Monsun(GER) —Auenlady (GER) (Big Shuffle (USA))
1864[4] 5863[2]

Auenprincess (GER) *U Ostmann* 98
3 ch f Kornado—Auenkronung (GER) (Shareef Dancer (USA))
1714a[5] 2279a[9]

Auentraum (GER) *Ms J S Doyle* a61 57
6 br g Big Shuffle(USA) —Auenglocke (GER) (Surumu (GER))
145[2] 261[6](680) (766) (889) 903[8] 1981[7] 2207[4]3052[13] 6842[9]6984[8]

Augustine *P W Hiatt* a74 84
5 bb g Machiavellian(USA) —Crown Of Light (Mtoto)
134[2] (156) 242[3]324[5] 405[5]462[2] 505[2]603[2] 652[9]706[2] 905[2](965) (1075) 1187[3] 1864[2] 2000[3] 2540[2] 2672[5]2989[7] 3747[4] 3792[3] 4051[2] 4457[2]4626[12]

Augustus John (IRE) *T J Pitt* a39 62
3 gr c Danehill(USA) —Rizerie (FR) (Highest Honor (FR))
6406[6]

Augustus Livius (IRE) *W Storey* a34 49
3 b g Titus Livius(FR) —Regal Fanfare (IRE) (Taufan (USA))
528[5] 690[8]974[4] 1293[4] 1501[3] 2923[10] 3357[9]4881[11]

Auntie Mame *D J Coakley* a48
2 b f Diktat—Mother Molly (USA) (Irish River (FR))
6840[6]

Aunt Julia *R Hannon* 100
4 b m In The Wings—Original (Caerleon (USA))
1398a[6] 2023[2] 5502[7] 5803[6]

Aunty Euro (IRE) *Patrick Morris* a79 82
4 br m Cape Cross(IRE) —Alexander Goddess (IRE) (Alzao (USA))
660[4] 4502a[9] 6226[13]6888[11]

Aura (SWE) *T Gustafsson*
3 b f Richard Of York—Inshallah (SWE) (Diaglyphard (USA))
3326a[4] 4919a[4]

Aurea (GER) *A Trybuhl* 98
3 ch f Silvano(GER) —Alula (GER) (Monsun (GER))
2912a[3] 5543a[8]

Aureate *M Johnston* a79+ 75
2 ch c Jade Robbery(USA) —Anne D'Autriche (IRE) (Rainbow Quest (USA))
5134[2] 5458[3] 5814[3] (6581)

Aurora Jane (FR) *B W Hills* a57 69
3 ch f Distant View(USA) —Alto Jane (The Minstrel (CAN))
692[3] 2171[6] 2518[2]3036[8] 3865[6]

Ausone *Miss J R Gibney* a59
4 b m Singspiel(IRE) —Aristocratique (Cadeaux Genereux)
4931[5] 5429[12]

Aussie Blue (IRE) *R M Whitaker* 41
2 b c Bahamian Bounty—Luanshya (First Trump)
5288[9] 5790[9]

Aussie Cricket (FR) *D J Coakley* a68 67
2 gr f Verglas(IRE) —Coup De Colere (FR) (Pistolet Bleu (IRE))
4221[4] 4980[2] 5389[2]5866[7] 6283[2] 6498[3]

Aussie Rules (USA) *A P O'Brien* 120
3 gr c Danehill(USA) —Last Second (IRE) (Alzao (USA))
1178a[5] (1718a) 2278a[7] 3314[4] 4038[4] 5049a[4](5824a) 6342a[8]

Austriaco (GER) *R Suerland* 92
4 b h Highest Honor(FR) —Autriche (IRE) (Acatenango (GER))
4418a[5] 5856a[7]

Austrian (UAE) *Saeed Bin Suroor* 96
3 ch c Jade Robbery(USA) —Anne D'Autriche (IRE) (Rainbow Quest (USA))
6107[8] 6337[12]

Austrian (GER) *M Sowa* 96
5 br h Second Set(IRE) —Autriche (IRE) (Acatenango (GER))
1869a[5] 3755a[7] 4418a[4] 6121a[7]

Authenticate *E J O'Neill* a67 67
4 b m Dansili—Exact Replica (Darshaan)
3009[8] 3762[5] 4104[6]

Authority (IRE) *Lady Herries* a69 79
6 b g Bluebird(USA) —Persian Tapestry (Tap On Wood)
1995[3] 4149[5] 4604[9]

Authorized (IRE) *P W Chapple-Hyam* 117
2 b c Montjeu(IRE) —Funsie (FR) (Saumarez)
5343[3] (6104)

Autograph Hunter *M Johnston* a87+
2 b g Tobougg(IRE) —Kalindi (Efisio)
1807[7] (6475) 6597[2] 6691[2]

Automation *C W Thornton*
3 b f Tamure(IRE) —Anatomic (Deerhound (USA))
2129[10] 2763[13]

Auto Rouge (IRE) *J-M Capitte*
2 b f Testa Rossa(AUS) —Moonlight Dreams (IRE) (Caerleon (USA))
6528a[8]

Autour Du Monde *P C Haslam* 40
2 ch f Spinning World(USA) —Penang Pearl (FR) (Bering)
1853[7] 2972[3] 3175[5] 5084[10] 5282[6]

Autumn Storm *R Ingram* a48 53
2 b f Auction House(USA) —Cozette (IRE) (Danehill Dancer (IRE))
1242[4] 1743[6]1922[6] (2643) 3120[6] 3409[6]3861[4] 5208[10] 5448[6]

Auwitesweetheart *B R Millman* a78 88d
4 b m Josr Algarhoud(IRE) —Miss Kirsty (USA) (Miswaki (USA))
(947) 1338[5] 2173[3] 3251[8]4343[10] 4598[6] 5627[10] 6020[10]

Auzi (FR) *X Thomas-Demeaulte* a82 102
3 b g Commands(AUS) —Time For Romance (IRE) (Cure The Blues (USA))
1944a[5]

Avalon *Jonjo O'Neill* 103
4 b g Kingmambo(USA) —Lady Carla (Caerleon (USA))
1839[3] 2849[11]

Avanti *Dr J R J Naylor* a50 71
10 gr g Reprimand—Dolly Bevan (Another Realm)
6132[6] 6804[3]6995[8]

Ava's World (IRE) *M Johnston* a60 82
2 b f Desert Prince(IRE) —Taibhseach (USA) (Secreto (USA))
5095[8] (5364) 5748[4] 5940[9]6100[13] 6444[6]

Avelian (IRE) *W J Haggas* 80
3 b g Cape Cross(IRE) —Mashoura (Shareef Dancer (USA))
1674[5] 2448[3] 3066[2] 3911[4] 4931[14]5484[5] 5868[14]

Avening *J E Hammond* 100
6 br g Averti(IRE) —Dependable (Formidable (USA))
5420[7]

Avenlea *G L Moore* a53
5 b g Averti(IRE) —Cloudslea (USA) (Chief's Crown (USA))
310[8] 6817[7](890) 2317[P] (Dead)

Aventura (IRE) *S R Bowring* a74 71
6 b g Sri Pekan(USA) —La Belle Katherine (USA) (Lyphard (USA))
1217[3] 1387[5] 2208[3]2793[5]

Averticus *B W Hills* a60 78
2 b c Averti(IRE) —Santa Vida (USA) (St Jovite (USA))
3588[3] 3930[2] (5326) 5843[7]

Averti Star *Mrs A J Duffield* 49
2 b g Averti(IRE) —Zinzi (Song)
2523[8] 2783[7]

Avertuoso *B Smart* 93
2 b g Averti(IRE) —First Musical (First Trump)
1121[6] (1454) 1780[2] 2127[6] 2724[14] 3239[2](3555) 3734[22] 4736[19]

Avery *R J Hodges* 64
2 gr c Averti(IRE) —Bandanna (Bandmaster (USA))
1770[10] 2185[6] 3110[4] 5162[9] 5419[14]

Avicia *C A Horgan* a72 56
4 ch m Vettori(IRE) —Amarice (Suave Dancer (USA))
3152[9] 3935[13] 5057[14]

Avie Pimiento (IRE) *Eva Olofsson* a93
5 br g Desert Style(IRE) —Run Bonnie (Runnett)
1659a[5]

Avina Laugh *P W Chapple-Hyam* 66
2 ch f Zaha(CAN) —Great Exception (Grundy)
3435[8] 3908[2] 4553[4]

Aviva *J Howard Johnson* 72
2 b g Noverre(USA) —Evangeline (Sadler's Wells (USA))
2680[3] (Dead)

Avoid The Cat *Mrs A J Perrett* a43 61
2 b c Averti(IRE) —Baileys Firecat (Catrail (USA))
3222[12] 3544[4] 4138[8]5647[14]

Avoncreek *B P J Baugh* a52 46
2 b g Tipsy Creek(USA) —Avondale Girl (IRE) (Case Law)
1136[5] 1420[10] 4433[6]4987[10] 5686[9]

Avoriaz (IRE) *L M Cumani* 92
3 gr c Desert Prince(IRE) —Abbatiale (FR) (Kaldoun (FR))
5086[3] 5726[2]

Awaken *Miss Tracy Waggott* 64
5 b m Zafonic(USA) —Dawna (Polish Precedent (USA))
1249[6] 2242[8] 2407[5] (2696) (3527) 3762[4] 4454[5]4944[10] 5403[8]

Awarding *Dr J R J Naylor* a53 41
6 ch g Mark Of Esteem(IRE) —Monaiya (Shareef Dancer (USA))
117[10] 210[8]307[10] 440[8]638[12] 2531[12]

Awatuki (IRE) *A P Jarvis* a79 88
3 b g Distant Music(USA) —Itkan (IRE) (Marju (IRE))
(762) 1108[3] 1515[2] 1781[8]4082[9] 4878[10] 6888[5]

Awe *Mrs C A Dunnett* 38
2 b g Muhtarram(USA) —Fleet Of Light (Spectrum (IRE))
4302[7] 5089[8] 6421[12]

Awelmarduk (IRE) *A & G Botti*
2 b c Almutawakel—Claba Di San Jore (IRE) (Barathea (IRE))
6407a[2]

A Winning Dream (GER) *P Schiergen* 92
4 b m Law Society(USA) —Anna Maria (GER) (Night Shift (USA))
5160a[4]

A Woman In Love *Miss B Sanders* a60 68
7 gr m Muhtarram(USA) —Ma Lumiere (FR) (Niniski (USA))
576[7] 1962[4]2259[9] 2574[8]

Awwal Malika (USA) *C E Brittain* 79
2 b f Kingmambo(USA) —First Night (IRE) (Sadler's Wells (USA))
5638[2] 5966[12]

Axis Mundi (IRE) *T J Etherington* a34 23
2 b f Titus Livius(FR) —Inventive (Sheikh Albadou)
4913[9] 5442[8] 6377[9]

Axis Shield (IRE) *M C Chapman* a53 49
3 b f Shinko Forest(IRE) —La Doyenne (IRE) (Masterclass (USA))
(870) (1762) 2197[6] 2876[4] 2949[4] 3257[10]3913[11] 5928[13] 6548[4]

Ayala Cove (USA) *P C Haslam* a34 37
3 ch f Mt. Livermore(USA) —Kitra (USA) (Woodman (USA))
241[4] 333[12]3357[8]

Ayam Jantan *M Johnston* 64
3 ch g Cadeaux Genereux—Madame Est Sortie (FR) (Longleat (USA))
1444[5] 1616[11] 1888[4] 2198[5] 2698[5](4198) 4961[11]

Ayla (IRE) *John M Oxx* 100
3 bb f Daylami(IRE) —Aliya (IRE) (Darshaan)
4212a[4] 4822a[4]

Aylmer Road (IRE) *P F I Cole* 79
4 b g Groom Dancer(USA) —Pekan's Pride (Sri Pekan (USA))
1132[11] 2357[12] 2902[11]

Aypeeyes (IRE) *S Kirk* a74
2 b g King Charlemagne(USA) —Habaza (IRE) (Shernazar)
(6224) 6506[3] 6824[4]

Aysgarth Flyer (IRE) *James Moffatt*
3 b g Soviet Star(USA) —Why Worry Now (IRE) (College Chapel)
197[6] 347[6]488[7] 6425[13]

Azahara *K G Reveley* 52
4 b m Vettori(IRE) —Branston Express (Bay Express)
1293[9] 2832[8] (Dead)

Azarole (IRE) *J S Moore* a108 113
5 b g Alzao(USA) —Cashew (Sharrood (USA))
149a[2] 278a[3] 370a[3] (625a) 704[3]1299[8] 3563a[3] 4740[6] 4918a[2] 5376[8]

Azerley (IRE) *J D Bethell* 56
3 b f Desert Style(IRE) —Miss Indigo (Indian Ridge)
1126[9] 1684[12] 2080[5] 3379[14]3814[3]

Azime (IRE) *C E Brittain* 63
3 b c Cape Cross(IRE) —Adjisa (IRE) (Doyoun)
1052[14]

Azizam *P W Chapple-Hyam* a29 79
4 ch m Singspiel(IRE) —Perdicula (IRE) (Persian Heights)
1478[8] 2351[10]

Aznavour (NZ) *Danny O'Brien* 99
4 b g Montjeu(IRE) —Sound Of Jazz (NZ) (Sound Reason (CAN))
5817a[2] 6346a[10]

Azreme *P Howling* a51 74
6 ch h Unfuwain(USA) —Mariette (Blushing Scribe (USA))
41[5] (183) 391[9]526[11] 1568[2] 1996[3]

Azul Da Guanabara (BRZ) *Luis Singnoretti* a97
4 b h Aracai(BRZ) —Luz Da Guanabara (BRZ) (Fast Gold (USA))
368a[5] 495a[10]563a[2] 740a[9]

Azurine (IRE) *M Johnston* a48 70
3 b f Spectrum(IRE) —Flamands (IRE) (Sadler's Wells (USA))
668[9] 762[8]1530[3] 1946[6] 2923[2] 3142[6] 3634[4](3911)

Azygous *J Akehurst* a81 90
3 ch g Foxhound(USA) —Flag (Selkirk (USA))
1020[10] 1264[6] 1928[8]2509[3] 3049[3] (3475) 3744[4] 4102[7] 4659[6]4922[3] 5265[4]

Baan (USA) *M Johnston* a95 103
3 ch g Diesis—Madaen (USA) (Nureyev (USA))
1083[6] 1300[3] 1668[3] 2801[7] 4039[8]4359[3] 5310[9] 6468[3]6600[5] 6836[7]

Baaridd *D Selvaratnam* 103
8 b h Halling(USA) —Millstream (USA) (Dayjur (USA))
278a[10] 433a[9] 494a[8]

Baarrij *M R Channon* 50
2 ch f Tobougg(IRE) —Bint Albaadiya (USA) (Woodman (USA))
3796[9] 4566[5]

Baba Ganouge (IRE) *B J Meehan* a53
2 ch f Desert Prince(IRE) —Le Montrachet (Nashwan (USA))
5784[7]

Baba Ghanoush *W Jarvis* a71 51
4 ch m Zaha(CAN) —Vrennan (Suave Dancer (USA))
6483[5]

Babcary *M P Tregoning* a87 91
3 b f Bertolini(USA) —Midnight Break (Night Shift (USA))
112[3] (191) 483[3]558[8] 2404[2] (2608) 2961[3]4040[4] 5016[2] 5164[2]5530[9]

Babe Maccool (IRE) *B W Hills* a87 88
4 ch g Giant's Causeway(USA) —Kotama (USA) (Shahrastani (USA))
4244[8] 5110[3]5299[9]

Babeth (IRE) *A M Balding* a61 63
3 b f Indian Lodge(IRE) —Almond Flower (IRE) (Alzao (USA))
10[3] 85[10] (Dead)

Babieca (USA) *T D Barron* 74+
2 gr c Tactical Cat(USA) —Secret Mountain (USA) (Mt. Livermore (USA))
3175[2] (3940)

Babodana *M H Tompkins* a99 108
6 ch h Bahamian Bounty—Daanat Nawal (Machiavellian (USA))
728[6] 1299[2] 1806[2] 2742[21] 3534[9]4529[7] 4864a[15] 5588[6] 5673[4] 5968[6]6218[7] 6299[2] 6516[8]

Baboosh (IRE) *M Wigham* a60d 73
5 b m Marju(IRE) —Slipper (Suave Dancer (USA))
33[12] 223[14]324[11] 462[9](3803) 4289[7] 4944[5] 5166[2] 5451[12] 5831[8]

Baby Barry *M J Attwater* a50 60
9 b g Komaite(USA) —Malcesine (IRE) (Auction Ring (USA))
2414[8] 3240[2] (3480) (4087) 4381[2]4845[6] 4984[4] 5248[7]5924[10]

Baby Dordan (IRE) *D J Daly* 65
2 b f Desert Prince(IRE) —Three Owls (IRE) (Warning)
2402[6] 5586[4] 5898[9]

Baby First (FR) *J-M Beguigne* 114
3 b c Enrique—First Turn (USA) (Alleged (USA))
5999a[3]

Babylon Sister (IRE) *R Hannon* a64 62
2 b f Val Royal(FR) —Space Travel (Dancing Dissident (USA))
1896[6] 2478[5] (3010) 3641[9]5094[7] 5382[5]

Baby Strange *P A Blockley* 108
2 gr c Superior Premium—The Manx Touch (IRE) (Petardia)
(1770) (2009) 2719[10] 5653[4] (5809) 6229a[2]

Bacharach (IRE) *R F Fisher* a55 69
3 b g Indian Lodge(IRE) —Katherine Gorge (USA) (Hansel (USA))
19[7] 1004[7]1345[9] 1592[12] 1950[11] 6053[10] 6543[12]

Bachelor Party (USA) *J Noseda* 69+
3 bb c Brahms(USA) —Fiancee (USA) (Air Forbes Won (USA))
4162[2] 5093[4] (5571)

Bachnagairn *R Charlton* 68+
2 b g In The Wings—Purple Heather (USA) (Rahy (USA))
4177[4] 4705[7] 5067[7] 5585[4]

Back In The Red (IRE) *M Wellings* a52+ 62+
2 ch c Redback—Fureur De Vivre (IRE) (Bluebird (USA))
2878[6] 4421[8] 4753[8] 5065[5] (5238) 5747[5]6291[8]

Backstreet Lad *Evan Williams* a47 57
4 b g Fraam—Forest Fantasy (Rambo Dancer (CAN))
6435[13] 6553[13]

Back Too Bedlam *Mrs S A Watt* 37
3 b g Petoski—Lutine Royal (Formidable (USA))
2107[8]

Back To Paris (IRE) *Eoin Griffin* 102
4 b g Lil's Boy(USA) —Alisco (IRE) (Shalford (IRE))
4031a[8]

Bad Boy Al (IRE) *D W Barker* 37
2 b g Cape Cross(IRE) —Ladycromby (IRE) (Lycius (USA))
4260[12] 4650[7] 5025[11]

Baddam *M R Channon* 111
4 b h Mujahid(USA) —Aude La Belle (FR) (Ela-Mana-Mou)
1071[15] 1517[5] 2013[9] (2723) (2849) 4081[5] 4677[5]5156[3] 5711a[7] 5963[26]

Badge Of Silver (USA) *R J Frankel* a115 120
6 br h Silver Deputy(CAN) —Silveroo (USA) (Silver Hawk (USA))
6342a[3] 6611a[2]

Bad Habit *M R Channon* 36
2 b c Royal Applause—Waft (USA) (Topsider (USA))
3923[7] 4028[10]

Badou *L Montague Hall* a53 30
6 b g Averti(IRE) —Bint Albadou (IRE) (Green Desert (USA))
6803[8]

Ba Foxtrot *M R Channon* 74
3 b g Foxhound(USA) —Aunt Susan (Distant Relative)
1083[7] 1512[11] (Dead)

Baggio (IRE) *Charles O'Brien* 96
5 b g Foxhound(USA) —Starring Role (IRE) (Glenstal (USA))
3125a[3]

Baghdaria (USA) *T Amoss* a110
3 b f Royal Academy(USA) —Oatsee (USA) (Unbridled (USA))
3757a[8] 6343a[7]

Bahalita (IRE) *L Riccardi* 89
3 b f Bluebird(USA) —Barriyah (Kris)
1713a[8] 6363a[16]

Bahama Mama (IRE) *J Noseda* 104
2 b f Invincible Spirit(IRE) —Nassma (IRE) (Sadler's Wells (USA))
(1675) (2258) 2800[6] (3252) 4026[3] 5154[2] 5373[4]5802[4]

Bahama Reef (IRE) *B Gubby* a59 70
5 b g Sri Pekan(USA) —Caribbean Dancer (Shareef Dancer (USA))
2573[10]

Bahamian Ballet *E S McMahon* a76 78
4 ch g Bahamian Bounty—Plie (Superlative)
1563[12] 2417[2] 3041[18](3593) 4110[3] 5058[5] 5493[2]

Bahamian Bay *M Brittain* a56+ 59
4 b m Bahamian Bounty—Moly (Inchinor)
(782) (873) 3608[9] (4507) 5078[10] 6533[13]

Bahamian Breeze *D M Simcock* a61 78
5 b g Piccolo—Norgabie (Northfields (USA))
51[7] 262[7]474[11] 951[4]1618[10]

Bahamian Duke *K R Burke* a33 67
3 ch g Bahamian Bounty—Madame Sisu (Emarati (USA))
910[6] 1234[4] (2285) (2701) 2976[3]3879[5] 4812[3] 5493[3]

Bahamian Love *B W Hills* a62 67
2 br f Bahamian Bounty—Asian Love (Petong)
1203[6] 1796[6] 2500[3] 3430[4] 4920[4]5231[3] (6278) 6444[5]
Bahamian Pirate (USA) *D Nicholls* a76 108
11 ch g Housebuster(USA) —Shining Through (USA) (Deputy Minister (CAN))
989[2] 1158a[8] 1481[5] 1663[6] 2038a[4]2230[3] 2847[3] 3295[5] 4128[6] 4461[7]4832[3] 5009[6] 5578[5]
Bahar Shumaal (IRE) *C E Brittain* a104 99
4 b h Dubai Millennium—High Spirited (Shirley Heights)
1084[9] 1267[8] 1839[6] 2435[6] 3313[15]3890[11] 4356[5] 4711[17] 5299[12] (6226) 6516[13] 6600[3]6836[6] (6997)
Bahhmirage (IRE) *Stef Liddiard* a49 69
3 ch f Bahhare(USA) —Border Mirage (Selkirk (USA))
69[12] 176[6]326[3] 538[6]651[4] 677[6]779[3] 890[6] 1149[3]1314[4] 1552[4] 1650[8]2069[2] 2167[2] 2415[11]2951[4] 3306[6] 3541[12] 3897[10] 4223[13]
Bahia Breeze *Rae Guest* 107
4 b m Mister Baileys—Ring Of Love (Magic Ring (IRE))
753a[9] 1506[5] 2199[5] (2503) 3086[6] 4808[2]5191a[7] 5968[3] 6218[3]
Bahiano (IRE) *C E Brittain* a103 108
5 ch g Barathea(IRE) —Trystero (Shareef Dancer (USA))
54[7] 282a[5] (367a) 433a[3]494a[2] 1129[20] 1487[3] 2847[18] 3493[12]3926[14] 4593[8] 5523[10]
Bahrain Gold (IRE) *N P McCormack* a58 52
6 b g Great Commotion(USA) —Hassosi (IRE) (High Estate)
242[8] (300) 862[4]2811[9] 3052[4] 3334[14]3617[7] 4233[13] 4401[16]
Baie Des Flamands (USA) *Miss S J Wilton* a41 83
4 b g Kingmambo(USA) —Isle De France (USA) (Nureyev (USA))
6811[10]
Bailador (IRE) *A Laird* a45 110
6 b g Alzao(USA) —Alymatrice (USA) (Alysheba (USA))
153a[9] 208a[8] 370a[8] 511a[6]
Bailamos (GER) *H Hesse* 110
6 b g Lomitas—Bandeira (GER) (Law Society (USA))
1014a[2] 1369a[6] 1860a[7] 2910a[6] 4828a[3]5414a[2] 6109a[12] 6529a[9]
Baileys Encore *M Johnston* 84
3 b g Mister Baileys—Exclusive Life (USA) (Exclusive Native (USA))
1999[5] 4020[3] (4402) 4947[7] 5362[10]
Baileys Hilight (IRE) *M Johnston* 66
2 b c Kyllachy—Como (USA) (Cozzene (USA))
987[8] 1096[5] 1587[5] 3239[4] 3720[7]
Baileys Honour *A G Newcombe* a64 46
4 b m Mark Of Esteem(IRE) —Kanz (USA) (The Minstrel (CAN))
940[13] 1883[8] 2345[5]2998[6]
Baileys Outshine *J G Given* 69
2 ch f Inchinor—Red Ryding Hood (Wolfhound (USA))
5111[3] 5507[3] (5645) 6056[12]
Baileys Polka *J G Given* a50 68
3 b f Polish Precedent(USA) —Mistitled (USA) (Miswaki (USA))
1100[6] 1732[8] 3400[9]3828[6] 4257[11] 4847[9] 5637[11]
Baileysunice (IRE) *Seamus Fahey* 71
4 b g Mister Baileys—Shamneez (IRE) (Pharly (FR))
4166a[2]
Bailieborough (IRE) *B Ellison* a59 92
7 b g Charnwood Forest(IRE) —Sherannda (USA) (Trempolino (USA))
2364[6] 2527[6] 2681[3] 3040[5] 3241[7]3959[2] 4087[3] (4379) (4733) 5301[2] 5680[15]
Baizically (IRE) *J A Osborne* 87
3 ch g Galileo(IRE) —Baize (Efisio)
(1635) 2290[4]
Bajan Parkes *H Candy* 91
3 bb g Zafonic(USA) —My Melody Parkes (Teenoso (USA))
2014[4] 2639[6] 3296[15]
Bajan Pride *R Hannon* a73 72
2 b g Selkirk(USA) —Spry (Suave Dancer (USA))
4794[7] 5622[3] 5893[7] 6458[2]
Bajeel (IRE) *G A Butler* a47
2 b c Traditionally(USA) —Calypso Grant (IRE) (Danehill (USA))
4138[5]
Bakhoor (IRE) *W Jarvis* 73+
3 b f Royal Applause—First Waltz (FR) (Green Dancer (USA))
202a[12] (2704) (3299)
Bakke *B I Case* a44 44
4 b g Danehill(USA) —Valagalore (Generous (IRE))
1227[7] 1538[9]1765[10]
Balakan (IRE) *M Halford* 69
5 b g Selkirk(USA) —Balanka (IRE) (Alzao (USA))
4166a[10]
Balakiref *M Dods* a81 83
7 b g Royal Applause—Pluck (Never So Bold)
(2027) (2074) 3471[12] 3986[8] 4468[3] 4807[4] 4885[15]5117[4] 5336[12] 5476[9] 5765[4] 6048[5]6212[3]
Balanced Budget *J Noseda* a103+ 94+
3 b c Mark Of Esteem(IRE) —Credit-A-Plenty (Generous (IRE))
1134[6] (1421) 2046[6] 2805[11] 3980[3] 4370[5](5430)
Balance Of Power *R Charlton* 89
4 b g Sadler's Wells(USA) —Cattermole (USA) (Roberto (USA))
1051[3] 1206[7] 5479[3]
Balanchine Moon *W J Haggas* a55
2 ch f Zilzal(USA) —Crescent Moon (Mr Prospector (USA))
6290[7]
Balashi (USA) *Saeed Bin Suroor* 62
3 b g Seeking The Gold(USA) —Via Borghese (USA) (Seattle Dancer (USA))
5770[8]

Baldaquin *R Bouresly* a88 82
9 b g Barathea(IRE) —Nibbs Point (IRE) (Sure Blade (USA))
154a[6] 355a[7]371a[10] 497a[9]
Bal De La Rose (IRE) *F Rohaut* 100
2 ch f Cadeaux Genereux—Lady Vettori (Vettori (IRE))
5714a[7]
Baldoria (IRE) *M Delcher-Sanchez* 98
3 b f In The Wings—Prickly Pearl (IRE) (Lahib (USA))
5472a[3]
Baldovina *M Botti* a67 69
2 b f Tale Of The Cat(USA) —Baldwina (FR) (Pistolet Bleu (IRE))
2461[2] 2638[2] 3343a[5]5083[12] 5783[12]
Balearic Star (IRE) *B R Millman* a63 66
5 b g Night Shift(USA) —La Menorquina (USA) (Woodman (USA))
2327[4] 2641[11] 2978[10]3947[5] 4285[6] 5259[2] 5609[6]
Baleegh (USA) *M P Tregoning* 73
3 b c Aljabr(USA) —Awtaan (USA) (Arazi (USA))
(3032) 3546[7]
Balerno *Mrs L J Mongan* a65 67
7 b g Machiavellian(USA) —Balabina (USA) (Nijinsky (CAN))
170[8] 693[12]2317[15] 3014[9] 3933[2]4667[4] 4974[11] 5269[7]
Balfour House *R A Harris* a30 27
3 b g Wizard King—Tymeera (Timeless Times (USA))
293[11] 473[12]2187[10] 3006[11]
Balian *Mrs P Sly* a58 67
3 b g Mujahid(USA) —Imperial Jade (Lochnager)
1355[9] 2105[8] 2652[2] 3118[2] 3349[9]3611[2] 3873[3] 4162[3] 4293[3] 4532[4]5055[6] 5291[13] 6033[3]6129[2] 6492[3]6637[3] 6717[7]
Bali Belony *J R Jenkins* a36
2 b f Erhaab(USA) —Daarat Alayaam (IRE) (Reference Point)
6663[9] 6840[8]
Balik Pearls *N A Callaghan* a75 81
3 b f Xaar—Miss Mercy (IRE) (Law Society (USA))
2864[10] (3453) 3841[8] 3978[6]
Balius (IRE) *C Laffon-Parias* 104
3 b c Mujahid(USA) —Akhla (USA) (Nashwan (USA))
6384a[6]
Balkan Knight *D R C Elsworth* 113
6 b g Selkirk(USA) —Crown Of Light (Mtoto)
1677[4] 1839[2] (2430) 2848[11] 3551[2] 4081[5]5967[3]
Ballare (IRE) *P J Makin* a52 52
7 b g Barathea(IRE) —Raindancing (IRE) (Tirol)
175[10] (770) 792[3]1194[3] 1394[5]3089[8] 3933[12] 5097[13]6128[2] 6545[10]6702[10]
Ballast (IRE) *H G Motion* 110
5 ch g Desert Prince(IRE) —Suedoise (Kris)
5416a[13] 6329a[3]
Ballet Boy (IRE) *Sir Mark Prescott* 53+
2 b g Sadler's Wells(USA) —Happy Landing (FR) (Homing)
5066[13] 5168[8] 5364[4]
Ballet Pacifica (USA) *J-C Rouget* a68+ 105
3 br f Minardi(USA) —Kostroma (Caerleon (USA))
(418) 4645a[3]
Balletto (UAE) *T Albertrani* a118
4 ch m Timber Country(USA) —Destiny Dance (USA) (Nijinsky (CAN))
5818a[2] 6343a[3]
Balliasta (IRE) *B W Hills* 55
2 b f Grand Lodge(USA) —Obeah (Cure The Blues (USA))
5891[5]
Ballinteni *Saeed Bin Suroor* a86 87
4 b h Machiavellian(USA) —Silabteni (USA) (Nureyev (USA))
5739[7] 6226[4]
Balloura (USA) *W J Haggas* a62 78
3 b f Swain(IRE) —Mowaadah (IRE) (Alzao (USA))
(1351) 2961[4] 4224[3] 5109[6]5421[6]
Ballroom Dancer (IRE) *J Noseda* a73
2 b f Danehill Dancer(IRE) —Dwell (USA) (Habitat)
6186[3]
Ballybeg (IRE) *R J Price* a72 70
3 b g Mujadil(USA) —Sabaniya (FR) (Lashkari)
590[2] (709) 848[7]945[3] 1193[5] 1543[5] 1732[6] (2507) 5911[5]6244[7] 6590[7]6712[7] 6848[11]
Ballybunion (IRE) *R A Harris* a63 70
7 ch g Entrepreneur—Clarentia (Ballad Rock)
1689[10] 2571[10] 2632[7] 2949[10] 3863[2](3899) (4141) 4232[6] 4675[5] 4985[12] 5131[6]
Ballycroy Girl (IRE) *A Bailey* a60 65
4 ch m Pennekamp(USA) —Hulm (IRE) (Mujtahid (USA))
133[7] 268[10]582[6] 1201[10]2747[8]
Ballyhooligan (IRE) *Jamie Poulton* a48 22
3 b g Imperial Ballet(IRE) —Cancan Madame (USA) (Mr Prospector (USA))
83[8] 3033[11]
Ballyhurry (USA) *J S Goldie* a66 75
9 b g Rubiano(USA) —Balakhna (FR) (Tyrant (USA))
644[4] 1035[4] 1455[4]3139[3] 3353[4] 4353[5] 4518[2] 4953[15]5553[5] 6241[2]
Ballymena *R A Harris* a31 40
5 b m Saddlers' Hall(IRE) —Ace Gunner (Gunner B)
2063 [11] 2220[11] 2917[6] 3919[7]4282[13] 6685[8]
Ballymore Lady (USA) *Rod Collet* 94
3 b f War Chant(USA) —Basking (USA) (Alydar (USA))
6722a[0]
Ballyrush (IRE) *Miss D A McHale* a41 51
6 ch g Titus Livius(FR) —Mandoline (IRE) (Suave Dancer (USA))
43[7] 240[6]330[6] 386[4]465[10] 527[11]638[8] 689[10]
Ballyshane Spirit (IRE) *N A Callaghan* a49 61
2 b c Distant Music(USA) —Nationalartgallery (IRE) (Tate Gallery (USA))
4572[12] 4897[11] 5646[3] 6653[9]6866[7]

Balmont (USA) *J Noseda* 116
5 b h Stravinsky(USA) —Aldebaran Light (USA) (Seattle Slew (USA))
2115[10] 2675[5]
Balnagore *J L Dunlop* 75
2 bb c Tobougg(IRE) —Bogus Mix (IRE) (Linamix (FR))
3976[7] 4525[5] 5293[6] 5916[5]
Balthazaar's Gift (IRE) *T R George* 120
3 b c Xaar—Thats Your Opinion (Last Tycoon)
1778[15] 2276a[4] 2846[2] 3732[4] 4191a[15]5011[7]
Baltic Belle (IRE) *R Hannon* a70 79
2 b f Redback—Skerries Bell (Taufan (USA))
1542[3] 1930[2] 2800[8] 3402[3]5043[2] 5503[5] 5676[5] 5933[3] 6591[2]
Baltic Gift *M L W Bell* 56
2 b f Cadeaux Genereux—Polish Romance (USA) (Danzig (USA))
6215[13]
Baltic King *H Morrison* 120
6 b h Danetime(IRE) —Lindfield Belle (IRE) (Fairy King (USA))
1069[8] 1485[7] 2303[3] 2720[6] (2847) 3732[5]4191a[14] (4832) 5549[2] 5942[10]
Baltic Princess (FR) *M Johnston* 78+
3 ch f Peintre Celebre(USA) —Snow House (IRE) (Vacarme (USA))
1100[7] 1283[4] 2786[2] (3169) 3452[3] 3748[4]
Baltic Rhapsody *M A Jarvis* a59 57
3 b f Polish Precedent(USA) —Rensaler (USA) (Stop The Music (USA))
123[11]
Baltimore Jack (IRE) *M W Easterby* 80
2 b g Night Shift(USA) —Itsibitsi (IRE) (Brief Truce (USA))
(2159) 2719[18] 4766[9] 4890[4] 5113[6] 5366[4]5681[8] 6271[4]
Balwearie (IRE) *Miss L A Perratt* 65
5 b g Sesaro(USA) —Eight Mile Rock (Dominion)
(1346) 1887[6] 2326[5] 2812[2] 3333[7] 3483[4]3583[4] 3784[6] 4698[7] 5581[12] 5905[4]6158[14]
Balyan (IRE) *J Howard Johnson* 87
5 b g Bahhare(USA) —Balaniya (USA) (Diesis)
1294[7] 1991[5] 2452[5] 2975[14]
Bamalam *C R Wilson*
3 br f Hunting Lion(IRE) —Dragons Daughter (Mandrake Major)
2696[12] 3357[13]
Bamboo Banks (IRE) *J L Dunlop* 69+
3 b g Indian Lodge(IRE) —Emma's Star (ITY) (Darshaan)
1139[4] 1741[9] 2102[7] 5625[6] 5887[6]
Bamzooki *Mrs C A Dunnett* a58 66
4 b m Zilzal(USA) —Cavernista (Lion Cavern (USA))
97[3] 218[15]301[3] 4139[12]4307[11] 4667[8] 5086[16] 5573[15]
Banana Belle *A J Lidderdale* a24 30
2 b f Josr Algarhoud(IRE) —Scurrilous (Sharpo)
663[9] 856[4]1542[10]
Band *E S McMahon* a66 63
6 b g Band On The Run—Little Tich (Great Nephew)
1276[6] 1996[6] 2612[7]3056[2] 3599[4]3999[2] 5285[3] 6059[4](6300) 6451[7] 6628[4]
Bandama (IRE) *Mrs A J Perrett* a78+ 104
3 b c Green Desert(USA) —Orinoco (IRE) (Darshaan)
1335[3] (1823) (2290) 2805[3] 4039[2]4742[6] 5641[5]
Bandari (IRE) *M Johnston* 123
7 b h Alhaarth(IRE) —Miss Audimar (USA) (Mr. Leader (USA))
1507[3] 2116[6] 2845[8] 3444[4]
Bandini (USA) *T Pletcher* a121
4 br h Fusaichi Pegasus(USA) —Divine Dixie (USA) (Dixieland Band (USA))
2093a[4]
Band Of Gold *J Pearce* a57? 51
4 ch m Spectrum(IRE) —Intellectuelle (Caerleon (USA))
2181[14]
Bandos *I Semple* a61 61
6 ch g Cayman Kai(IRE) —Lekuti (Le Coq D'Or)
2926[2] 3786[14] 4456[7] 4729[3]
Banjo Bay (IRE) *Miss Gay Kelleway* a64 71
8 b g Common Grounds—Thirlmere (Cadeaux Genereux)
(708) 845[10] 1054[2] 1150[9]1443[4] 1673[7] 1899[5] (3728) 4141[12] (4365) 4564[14]4894[9] 5081[14] 5232[9] 6833[13]
Banjo Patterson *G A Huffer* 97
4 b h Green Desert(USA) —Rumpipumpy (Shirley Heights)
1262[4] 1487[13] 2047[9] 2323[4] 2732[6]3374[11] 3486[3] 3904[14] 4372[10]
Banknote *A M Balding* a100 99
4 b h Zafonic(USA) —Brand (Shareef Dancer (USA))
1340[2] 2086[7] (3218) 4356[2]5019[5]
Bank On Benny *P W D'Arcy* a72 68
4 b g Benny The Dip(USA) —Green Danube (USA) (Irish River (FR))
52[7] 4845[4] (5621) 6054[4](6878)
Bannaby (FR) *F Rohaut* 113
3 ch c Dyhim Diamond(IRE) —Trelakari (FR) (Lashkari)
4861a[5]
Bantry Bere (IRE) *J R Best* a68 42
2 b c Distant Music(USA) —Tirana (USA) (Fappiano (USA))
6034[6] 6331[11] 6441[3]6651[4] 6699[4]
Barachois Gaudy *Mrs N Smith* a37 43
4 br m Nomination—Barachois Princess (USA) (Barachois (CAN))
84[6] 217[11]462[7] 778[4] 1538[11]1753[13] 2566[7]
Barancella (FR) *R J Frankel* a107 116
5 ch m Acatenango(GER) —Barranciaga (USA) (Bering)
6125a[2]
Baranook (IRE) *D J Wintle* a74+ 66
5 b g Barathea(IRE) —Gull Nook (Mill Reef (USA))
5691[3] 6178[14] (Dead)

Barastraight *J-C Rouget* 110
3 ch c Barathea(IRE) —Straight Lass (IRE) (Machiavellian (USA))
(1179a) 2278a[11] 4623a[3] 5400a[8] 5913a[3]
Barataria *R Bastiman* 55
4 ch g Barathea(IRE) —Aethra (USA) (Trempolino (USA))
992[7] 1500[11] 1947[12] 5285[14] 5839[2]6213[10]
Barathea Blazer *K McAuliffe* a86 106
7 b g Barathea(IRE) —Empty Purse (Pennine Walk)
5520[9] 5808[9] 5963[30] 6337[9] 6602[4]6917[8]
Barathea Dreams (IRE) *J S Moore* a77 87
5 b g Barathea(IRE) —Deyaajeer (USA) (Dayjur (USA))
726[13] 1302[11] 2114[3] 2787[3] 3101[8]3642[5] 4536[7] 4782[8]
Barbaro (USA) *M Matz* a126+ 105
3 br c Dynaformer(USA) —La Ville Rouge (USA) (Carson City (USA))
(1498a) 1861a[P]
Barbilyrifle (IRE) *N B King* a41 58
5 b g Indian Rocket—Age Of Elegance (Troy)
2291[12] 2413[12]
Barbirolli *W M Brisbourne* a68 72
4 b g Machiavellian(USA) —Blushing Barada (USA) (Blushing Groom (FR))
1637[3] 2150[5] 2640[7] 3519[4] 4256[2]4764[5] 4842[4] (5579) 5897[3] 6189[8]6503[5] 6684[9]6837[5] 6954[3]
Barbs Pink Diamond (USA) *Mrs A J Perrett* a64 57
2 b f Johannesburg(USA) —Unsaddled (USA) (Pancho Villa (USA))
4928[8] 5773[6]
Bare Rambler *Stef Liddiard* a30 34
3 ch g Woodborough(USA) —Supreme Rose (Frimley Park)
1513[12] 1646[10] 2573[9]3729[7] 4223[8]
Bargain Hunt (IRE) *W Storey* 46
5 b g Foxhound(USA) —Atisayin (USA) (Al Nasr (FR))
2871[13]
Bar Humbug *R A Fahey* a44 40
2 b c Josr Algarhoud(IRE) —Hi Hoh (IRE) (Fayruz)
5288[7] 5687[2] 5923[8]6401[7] 6534[12]
Bariloche *J R Boyle* a77
3 b c Benny The Dip(USA) —Bella Lambada (Lammtarra (USA))
62[6] 142[4]215[4] (548) 805[6] 5022[7]
Barkass (UAE) *M P Tregoning* a65
2 b c Halling(USA) —Areydha (Cadeaux Genereux)
6254[7]
Barking Mad (USA) *C R Dore* a38 30
8 bb g Dayjur(USA) —Avian Assembly (USA) (General Assembly (USA))
5[7] 230[10]318[8]
Barley Moon *T Keddy* a40 63
2 b f Vettori(IRE) —Trojan Desert (Troy)
4801[8] 5209[9] 5638[3]6332[13] 6840[7]
Barnbrook Empire (IRE) *B J Llewellyn* a57 57
4 b m Second Empire(IRE) —Home Comforts (Most Welcome)
1392[10] 2345[7]2483[3] 2944[5] 3437[10] 3896[3]
Barndeh (IRE) *M A Jarvis* 77
3 b g Marju(IRE) —Sweetest Thing (IRE) (Prince Rupert (FR))
2177[3] 2441[2] 3008[3]
Barney Bubble (IRE) *K J Burke*
5 b g Bahhare(USA) —Barnabas (ITY) (Slip Anchor)
615[9]
Barney McGrew (IRE) *J A R Toller* a79+ 44
3 b g Mark Of Esteem(IRE) —Success Story (Sharrood (USA))
5092[7] (6771)
Barney's Dancer *J Balding* a48
2 b f Iron Mask(USA) —Alcalali (USA) (Septieme Ciel (USA))
6675[4]
Barodine *H R A Cecil* 88
3 ch g Barathea(IRE) —Granted (FR) (Cadeaux Genereux)
1421[2] (1691) 2046[3] 2436[5] 3119[6] 5660[9]6051[9]
Barolo *W R Swinburn* a93 113
7 b g Danehill(USA) —Lydia Maria (Dancing Brave (USA))
2085[3] 2773[7] 3315[4] 4169a[5] 4797[2]5153[4] 6438[3]
Baron De Hoyland *J R Norton* a13 2
3 b g First Trump—Efficacy (Efisio)
193[10] 1293[13] 1576[10]1768[8] 6406[8]6636[10]
Baroness Richter (IRE) *R Hannon* 92
2 b f Montjeu(IRE) —Principium (USA) (Hansel (USA))
(4866) 5187[6]
Baron Rhodes *J S Wainwright* a30 77
5 b m Presidium—Superstream (Superpower)
1297[15] 1686[6] 1795[6] 2293[9] 2780[15]
Barons Spy (IRE) *R J Price* a60 79
5 b g Danzero(AUS) —Princess Accord (USA) (D'Accord (USA))
73[6] 163[5]2170[7] 2482[2] 3089[3] (3311) 3542[3] 3820[2]4390[2] (4706) 5070[3] 5436[3] 6176[6]
Barry Island *D R C Elsworth* a82 73
7 b g Turtle Island(IRE) —Pine Ridge (High Top)
(463) 763[7] 1133[12] 2341[11]3048[9] 5786[11] 6189[11]6566[9] 6889[4]
Barry The Brave *Micky Hammond* a54 61
4 b g Mujadil(USA) —Rakli (Warning)
3398[13] 4068[12] 4456[2] 5285[12] 6404[6]6648[9] 6961[3]
Barshiba (IRE) *D R C Elsworth* a75+
2 ch f Barathea(IRE) —Dashiba (Dashing Blade)
6886[2]
Barton Belle *G A Swinbank* 71
4 b m Barathea(IRE) —Veronica (Persian Bold)
2829[4]
Barton Sands (IRE) *Ernst Oertel* a77 79
9 b g Tenby—Hetty Green (Bay Express)
(35) 113[3] 185[6]324[6] 697[4]904[2] 1164[8]1334[10] 2327[P] 2577[13]3730[11] 5097[14]
Barzak (IRE) *S R Bowring* a54 60
6 b g Barathea(IRE) —Zakuska (Zafonic (USA))
4[7] 163[8]313[9] 358[7]618[5] 1575[4]6134[6] (6282) 6477[5] 6554[5]6756[3] 6897[10]6961[6]

Basaata (USA) *M P Tregoning* a82+ 88
2 b f Dixieland Band(USA) —Asareer (USA) (Gone West (USA))
5344[3] (6886)

Basalt (IRE) *A P O'Brien* 48
2 b c Rock Of Gibraltar(IRE) —Sniffle (IRE) (Shernazar)
5466a[23]

Basiliko (USA) *P W Chapple-Hyam* a53 73
3 ch g Fusaichi Pegasus(USA) —Shootforthestars (USA) (Seattle Slew (USA))
2332[14] 3046[11]

Basinet *J J Quinn* a61 49
8 b g Alzao(USA) —Valiancy (Grundy)
41[2] 172[3]310[2] (469) 586[2]

Baskerville *P W Chapple-Hyam* 95
3 b c Foxhound(USA) —Miss Up N Go (Gorytus (USA))
(1049) (1828) 2024[6] 5301[6] (6051)

Basra (IRE) *J S Bolger* 86
3 b g Soviet Star(USA) —Azra (IRE) (Danehill (USA))
755a[11] 3125a[8]

Bastet (IRE) *E Lellouche* 106
4 b m Giant's Causeway(USA) —Benediction (Day Is Done)
1398a[2] 2092a[4] 6171a[3] 6454a[8]

Batchworth Beau *A M Hales* a35 44
5 ch g Bluegrass Prince(IRE) —Batchworth Belle (Interrex (CAN))
4981[11]

Batchworth Blaise *E A Wheeler* a37 41
3 b g Little Jim—Batchworth Dancer (Ballacashtal (CAN))
4799[10] 5093[7] 5571[7] 5729[6] 5969[9]

Batchworth Fleur *E A Wheeler* a38 45
3 b f Little Jim—Batchworth Belle (Interrex (CAN))
112[10] 233[10]374[10] 540[6]880[15] 1640[10] 2644[4] 3118[12]

Bateleur *M R Channon* 84+
2 b g Fraam—Search Party (Rainbow Quest (USA))
3591[9] (3860) 4377[9] (5349) (5461)

Bathwick Alice *B R Millman* a73 73
3 b f Mark Of Esteem(IRE) —Ciel De Feu (USA) (Blushing John (USA))
851[4] 1208[13] 1693[3]2087[5] 2642[4]

Bathwick Breeze *B R Millman* a63 63
2 ch c Sugarfoot—She's A Breeze (Crofthall)
3025[11] 3448[4] 3843[9]

Bathwick Emma (IRE) *P D Evans* a61 76
3 ch f Raise A Grand(IRE) —Lindas Delight (Batshoof)
717[4] 896[5] 1569[6] 2222[6] 2554[9]4627[7] 4870[3] 5085[3] 5755[8] 6323[8]6493[5] 6538[6]6988[3]

Bathwick Fancy (IRE) *J G Portman* 65d
2 b f Desert Sun—Fleetwood Fancy (Taufan (USA))
1930[5] 4964[8] 5289[10] 5676[14] 5764[4]

Bathwick Finesse (IRE) *B R Millman* a48 80
4 b m Namid—Lace Flower (Old Vic)
3729[5] 4627[12] 4772[8]

Bathwick Leti (IRE) *A M Balding* 44
2 b f Trans Island—Brandon Princess (Waajib)
3344[9]

Bathwick Prince *B R Millman* a61 57
3 b g Superior Premium—Gay Ming (Gay Meadow)
807[6]

Bathwick Princess *P D Evans* a38
2 b f Forzando—Gay Ming (Gay Meadow)
707[9] 962[9] 3915[4]

Bathwick Rox (IRE) *P D Evans* a36 34
3 b g Carrowkeel(IRE) —Byproxy (IRE) (Mujtahid (USA))
69[7] 4871[13] 5733[12]

Bathwick Style *B R Millman* a64 46
2 b f Desert Style(IRE) —Baby Loves (Sadler's Wells (USA))
878[10] 1744[2] 2094[7]3345[10] 4394[3] 4773[5]5947[P] (Dead)

Batian (FR) *E Lellouche* 43
3 b c Desert Prince(IRE) —Blue Cloud (IRE) (Nashwan (USA))
2738a[6]

Batswing *G L Moore* 30
11 b g Batshoof—Magic Milly (Simply Great (FR))
973[11]

Battalion (IRE) *Sir Michael Stoute* a71 64
3 b c Grand Lodge(USA) —The Faraway Tree (Suave Dancer (USA))
3419[9] 5429[6] (Dead)

Battle Green Lad *R F Marvin* 24
9 b g Presidium—Antouna (Clantime)
6490[12]

Battle Paint (USA) *J-C Rouget* 115
2 b c Tale Of The Cat(USA) —Black Speck (USA) (Arch (USA))
5715a[2]

Battle Won (USA) *M Mitchell* a115 103
6 br g Honour And Glory(USA) —Call Her (USA) (Caller I.D. (USA))
3134a[2]

Battling Mac (IRE) *L A Dace* a67 87+
8 ch g Ashkalani(IRE) —Questing Star (Rainbow Quest (USA))
37[RR]

Bauer (IRE) *L M Cumani* a44 100+
3 gr c Halling(USA) —Dali's Grey (Linamix (FR))
952[10] (1533) 1881[2] (2584) (3502) 4197[3](5346)

Bauhaus (IRE) *R T Phillips* 75
5 b g Second Empire(IRE) —Hi Bettina (Henbit (USA))
2653[6]

Bauhinia *J A R Toller* a56 54
4 b m Spectrum(IRE) —Juvenilia (IRE) (Masterclass (USA))
462[8] 1755[10] 2413[7]

Bavarica *Miss J Feilden* a76 66
4 b m Dansili—Blue Gentian (USA) (Known Fact (USA))
73[2] 156[5]252[2] 537[9](697) 905[4]3828[2] 4010[3] 5046[4]5740[10] (5973) 6448[2] 6483[3]6568[3] 6741[3]6942[2]

Bawaader (IRE) *D K Weld* 107
4 b g Indian Ridge—Alyakkh (IRE) (Sadler's Wells (USA))
1171a[4] 5004a[6]

Bayberry King (USA) *J S Goldie* a47 54
3 b c Lear Fan(USA) —Myrtle (Batshoof)
3050[4] 4117[5] 4261[5]

Bay Boy *M Johnston* a74 85
4 b g Tomba—Gay Reign (Lord Gayle (USA))
1156a[2] 6671[8] 6999[8]

Baybshambles (IRE) *R E Barr* 14
2 b g Compton Admiral—Payvashooz (Ballacashtal (CAN))
5753[10] 5956[11] 6157[7]

Bayeux (USA) *G A Butler* a101 110
5 b g Red Ransom(USA) —Elizabeth Bay (USA) (Mr Prospector (USA))
450[3] (541) (627) 1487[12] 2776[4](3482) 3926[5] 4790[12] 5175[2] (6329a)

Bay Hawk *B G Powell* a74 76
4 b g Alhaarth(IRE) —Fleeting Vision (IRE) (Vision (USA))
4206[2] 4432[5] 5506[11] (6408) 6602[5]6766[7]

Baylaw Star *I W McInnes* a54 75d
5 b g Case Law—Caisson (Shaadi (USA))
214[12] 444[3]670[10] 719[7] (1035) 2017[10]2527[8] 3218[7] 4172[15] 4692[DSQ] (4726) 5337[7]5406[6] 5833[13] 5908[10]6160[9] 6273[12]

Baylini *Ms J S Doyle* a85
2 gr f Bertolini(USA) —Bay Of Plenty (FR) (Octagonal (NZ))
3645[3] 4434[2](6187) 6598[3]6866[2]

Baymist *M W Easterby* a34 66
4 b m Mind Games—Milliscent (Primo Dominie)
81[14] 299[8]524[8]

Bay Of Light *P W Chapple-Hyam* 70
2 b f Fantastic Light(USA) —Lady Bankes (IRE) (Alzao (USA))
2638[10] 2958[7] 3868[3] 4897[2] 5380[6]

Bayonyx (IRE) *J Howard Johnson* 72
2 b c Montjeu(IRE) —Dafariyna (IRE) (Nashwan (USA))
5495[5] 5720[5] (6207)

Bayria (IRE) *A De Royer-Dupre* 89
3 b f Kalanisi(IRE) —Bayrika (IRE) (Kahyasi)
5472a[8]

Bay Story (USA) *B Ellison* 107
4 b g Kris S(USA) —Sweeping Story (USA) (End Sweep (USA))
5817a[3] 6391a[2] 6455a[4] 7000a[7]

Baytown Lulu *H S Howe* a27 36
3 b f Timeless Times(USA) —Judys Girl (IRE) (Simply Great (FR))
2068[8] 2190[11] 2678[7] 3195[5] 3839[9]

Baytown Paikea *P S McEntee* a58 60
2 b f Primo Valentino(IRE) —Mystical Song (Mystiko (USA))
856[7] 1229[5] 1248[7]2145[2] (2179) 2346[4] 2538[3]3380[6] 3624[4] 3677[3]3801[7] 4603[4] (4816) 4946[6] 5528[9] 5772[5](6296) 6665[3] 6711[7]6732[3] 6839[8]

Baytown Rosie (IRE) *P S McEntee* a44 30
2 ch f Intikhab(USA) —Masaniya (IRE) (Kris)
856[6] 1922[10]2073[4] 6710[6] 6789[4]6853[7]

Baytown Valentina *R Brotherton* a24 51
3 b f Lugana Beach—Baytown Rhapsody (Emperor Jones (USA))
594[13] 642[11]676[6] 1464[9]2288[13] 2632[14] 3195[2] 3541[13] 4389[10]

Bazelle *D Shaw* a80 58
4 ch m Ashkalani(IRE) —Dona Royale (IRE) (Darshaan)
(167) 384[5] 463[8]

Bazil Des Fieffes (FR) *J M Plasschaert* a58
4 b h Le Balafre(FR) —Aprilca (FR) (April Axe (USA))
4931[12] 6410[11]6459[10] 6779[9]6804[9]

Bazroy (IRE) *P D Evans* a81 95
2 b c Soviet Star(USA) —Kunucu (IRE) (Bluebird (USA))
(707) 1897[3] 2300[8] 2724[15] 3720[3] 4170[4]4824a[3] (5139) 5408a[3] 5681[3] 6096[8]

Beacon Rambler *F Watson* 20
4 ch g Cayman Kai(IRE) —Bunty's Friend (Highlands)
3001[10] 3698[9] 4405[11]

Beamsley Beacon *S T Mason* a57 49
5 ch g Wolfhound(USA) —Petindia (Petong)
29[4] 90[3]145[4] 179[4]686[5] 6959[13]

Bear Essential *Mrs P N Dutfield* a15
2 ch g Rambling Bear—Adar Jane (Ardar)
6891[8]

Beatani *P D Evans* a10 13
2 b f Beat All(USA) —Jerpahni (Distant Relative)
1189[9] 1379[8]

Beat The Bully *I A Wood* a32 55
2 b g Ishiguru(USA) —Edgeaway (Ajdal (USA))
1333[7] 4177[11] 4550[4]5065[14] 5349[15] 5645 [6] 6416[11]6592[9]

Beat The Heat (IRE) *Jedd O'Keeffe* a88 91
8 b g Salse(USA) —Summer Trysting (USA) (Alleged (USA))
2628[8]

Beauchamp Pilot *G A Butler* a68 67
8 ch g Inchinor—Beauchamp Image (Midyan (USA))
3313[17] 3733[12]

Beauchamp Star *Mrs A Duffield* a48 63
5 ch m Pharly(FR) —Beauchamp Cactus (Niniski (USA))
(92) 147[5] 414[6]609[3]

Beauchamp Tiger *J Parkes* a73 62
4 b g Pharly(FR) —Beauchamp Jade (Kalaglow)
414[13] 640[10]

Beauchamp Trump *G A Butler* a70 71
4 b g Pharly(FR) —Beauchamp Kate (Petoski)
237[2] 521[3]628[9] 1213[6] 1457[4]2902[10]

Beauchamp Twist *M R Hoad* a31 51
4 b m Pharly(FR) —Beauchamp Cactus (Niniski (USA))
303[6]

Beauchamp Ultra *G A Butler* a40
3 b f Compton Admiral—Beauchamp Image (Midyan (USA))
191[9] 291[10]904[8]

Beauchamp Unique *James Moffatt* a69+ 58
3 b f Compton Admiral—Beauchamp Jade (Kalaglow)
188[3] 294[5]1634[5] 3411[3] 3637[8] 5365[9]

Beauchamp United *B Palling* a54 46
3 b g Compton Admiral—Beauchamp Kate (Petoski)
515[5] 1350[11] 3264[4]6907[9]

Beauchamp Viceroy *G A Butler* a89 75
2 ch c Compton Admiral—Compton Astoria (USA) (Lion Cavern (USA))
4138[2] (4434) 4804[4] 5372[9]6699[2] (6822) 6834[2] (6978)

Beaufort *D K Ivory* a55 43
4 b g Yaheeb(USA) —Royal Blaze (Scallywag)
3952[11] 4331[9] 5057[11] 5429[8]5910[11] 6256[10]6551[7]

Beau Jazz *W De Best-Turner* a43 44
5 br g Merdon Melody—Ichor (Primo Dominie)
706[12] 2112[12] 2898[8]5938[12] 6372[6] 6774[4]6851[11] 6877[9]

Beau Marche *G G Margarson* a38 57
4 b g My Best Valentine—Beau Dada (IRE) (Pine Circle (USA))
1303[12] 1539[12]1752[6] 2260[2] (2288) 2567[11] 3161[2] 3728[2]3933[11] 4157[18] (4266) 4389[2] 4670[2] 4845[5]5267[9] 5485[10]

Beau Monde *H-A Pantall* 90
3 b f Agnes World(USA) —Somfas (USA) (What A Pleasure (USA))
392a[3] 1177a[8] 1789a[10]

Beaumont (IRE) *M A Jarvis* 48
2 b c Xaar—Belsay (Belmez (USA))
4000[12] 4572[10] 5347[9]

Beaumont Boy *G A Swinbank* 58
2 b g Foxhound(USA) —Play The Game (Mummy's Game)
4151[6] 4421[5] 4731[5] 5307[9]

Beaumont Girl (IRE) *Miss M E Rowland* a41 53
4 ch m Trans Island—Persian Danser (IRE) (Persian Bold)
147[9] 442[4]2935[4] 5033[7]6957[7]

Beau Nash (USA) *P W Chapple-Hyam* 94
3 b g Barathea(IRE) —Style N' Elegance (USA) (Alysheba (USA))
1490[5] 1841[5] 2805[16] 3443[14] 4125[3]5346[2] 5804[15] 6336[18]

Beau Petite *T D Barron* 19
2 b f Kyllachy—Beau Dada (IRE) (Pine Circle (USA))
5288[11]

Beau Sancy *R A Harris* a62 64
2 b g Tobougg(IRE) —Bride's Answer (Anshan) (2524) 3619[3] 4436[6] 5597[15]6322[6] 6518[2](6625) 6824[5]

Beautiful Bets (USA) *G Wismer* a103 86
6 rg m Alphabet Soup(USA) —Sommerfest (USA) (El Prado (IRE))
6368a[10]

Beautiful Madness (IRE) *M G Quinlan* a49 65
2 ch f Shinko Forest(IRE) —Dosha (Touching Wood (USA))
3005[2] 3307[2] 4295[12] 4920[3] 5231[2]5735[8]

Beautiful Mover (USA) *J E Long* a47 47
4 ch m Spinning World(USA) —Dancer's Glamour (USA) (Danzig Connection (USA))
5831[12] 6590[10] 6683[6]6802[6]

Beautiful Reward (FR) *J R Fanshawe* 75+
2 ch f Diesis—Toujours Elle (USA) (Lyphard (USA))
5754[2]

Beautiful South *N Wilson* 36
3 b f Forzando—Fly South (Polar Falcon (USA))
2129[8] 3383[9] 3524[13]

Beautiful Summer (IRE) *R A Fahey* 61
3 br f Zafonic(USA) —Sadler's Song (Saddlers' Hall (IRE))
2734[7] 3146[4] 3909[11] 4470[11] 5637[3]

Beautyandthebeast *N Drysdale* 110
4 ch m Machiavellian(USA) —Nicola Bella (IRE) (Sadler's Wells (USA))
(6253a) 6614a[7]

Beauty Bright (IRE) *A P O'Brien* 111
3 b f Danehill(USA) —Dietrich (USA) (Storm Cat (USA))
1023a[2] 1719a[8] 2054a[15] 3322a[4] 3967a[2]4080[15] 4855a[6] (5393a) 5712a[6]

Beauty Is Truth *Robert Collet* 108
2 b f Pivotal—Zelding (IRE) (Warning)
3777a[4] 3990a[6] 4644a[6] (5122a) 5654[7]

Beaver Patrol (IRE) *R F Johnson Houghton* a97+ 101
4 ch g Tagula(IRE) —Erne Project (IRE) (Project Manager)
1246[3] 1835[14] (2230) 2847[9]3211[4] 3550[2] 3926[8] 4128[24] 5336[16]5667[6] 6192[5]

Bebe Vettori (GER) *A Wohler* 96
4 b h Vettori(IRE) —Bebe Kamira (GER) (Kamiros II)
5543a[6]

Be Bop Aloha *John Berry* a43 49
4 b m Most Welcome—Just Julia (Natroun (FR))
42[12]

Becharm *M A Jarvis* a67
2 b f Singspiel(IRE) —Zuleika Dobson (Cadeaux Genereux)
6433[10] 6886[4]

Beck *M L W Bell* a60 51
2 ch g Cadeaux Genereux—River Cara (USA) (Irish River (FR))
6173[8] 6520[7] 6644[7]

Beckenham's Secret *B R Millman* a71 75
2 b g Foxhound(USA) —Berliese (IRE) (High Estate)
701[6] (1019) 1824[3] 3117[7]3530[8] 4130[4] 4813[10]5447[6]

Beckermet (IRE) *R F Fisher* 113
4 b g Second Empire(IRE) —Razida (IRE) (Last Tycoon)
1069[3] 1145[6] 1485[17] 1778[12] 2303[8]2846[18] 3076[2] 3295[7] 3518[4] 4174[2]4410a[7] 4832[11] 5179[3] 5393a[5] 5682[7]

Beckett Hall (IRE) *R Hannon* a73 76
3 ch c Beckett(IRE) —Date Mate (USA) (Thorn Dance (USA))
1336[5] 1741[2] 1822[3]2805[15] 2986[10] 3794[5] 4838[14] 5045[8]6021[7]

Becrux (ITY) *N Drysdale* a96 113
4 b g Glen Jordan—Rebecca Parisi (IRE) (Persian Heights)
(5416a)

Bective Ranger (IRE) *Peter Casey* 93
4 ch g Barathea(IRE) —Karamiyna (IRE) (Shernazar)
1171a[8]

Bed Fellow (IRE) *A P Jarvis* a62+ 80
2 b c Trans Island—Moonlight Partner (IRE) (Red Sunset)
2979[7] 3498[6] 4794[4]5113[8] (5866) (6106) 6216[5]

Bedizen *Sir Michael Stoute* 59
3 b c Fantastic Light(USA) —Barboukh (Night Shift (USA))
1674[9]

Bedouin Blue (IRE) *P C Haslam* a73 77
3 b g Desert Style(IRE) —Society Fair (FR) (Always Fair (USA))
730[3] (1044) (3156) 4612[4]

Beech Games *E J O'Neill* a74 76
2 b g Mind Games—Dane Dancing (IRE) (Danehill (USA))
3455[4] 3843[4]4829[2] 5126[6] 5933[5] 6285[2]6581[5] 6824[3]6933[3]

Beechside (IRE) *W A Murphy* 28
2 b f Orpen(USA) —Tokurama (IRE) (Mtoto)
6047[9]

Bee Magic *C N Kellett* a46 36
3 ch g Magic Ring(IRE) —Miss Bananas (Risk Me (FR))
1218[7] 1646[11]

Bee Seventeen (USA) *P F I Cole* a25 71
3 b f Chester House(USA) —Stormy Squab (USA) (Storm Bird (CAN))
2583[10] 2987[14] 3410[13]

Bee Stinger *I A Wood* a86 89
4 b g Almaty(IRE) —Nest Egg (Prince Sabo)
(1644) (3121) 3532[3] 3973[5] (4241) 5019[10](5233) 5990[11] 6397[10]6580[7] 6635[2]

Befon (FR) *K Schafflutzel* 84
3 b c Bering—Fontanina (IRE) (Lake Coniston (IRE))
2717a[2]

Before You Go (IRE) *T G Mills* a96+ 107
3 b g Sadler's Wells(USA) —Here On Earth (USA) (Mr Prospector (USA))
19[2] (87) (1237) 1668[4] 2228[13]4818[8] 5142[6] 5657[6] 5808[5] 6337[18]

Beginners Luck (IRE) *D Carroll* a38 40
3 b f Key Of Luck(USA) —Zara's Birthday (IRE) (Waajib)
93[8] 132[9]337[13] 403[11]528[7] 637[7]690[2] 786[3](874) 1226[7]1576[8] 2746[6] 2923[8]3586[5] 3814[9] 4524[6]

Behlaya (IRE) *T D Easterby* 85
5 b m Kahyasi—Behera (Mill Reef (USA))
3019[3] 3522[2] 4204[2] 4549[3] 4792[3](5069)

Being There *P F I Cole* a51 52
3 b g Bien Bien(USA) —Segsbury Belle (Petoski)
62[5] 403[6]2569[6] 4800[5]

Beiramar (IRE) *W Hickst* 99
3 br f Monsun(GER) —Be My Lady (GER) (Be My Guest (USA))
6722a[8]

Bekoning (IRE) *M Quinn* a48 46
3 b c Beckett(IRE) —Echoing (Formidable (USA))
199[6] 286[5]499[6] (687) 790[7] 1768[2]4769[14] 5273[14]

Bel Air Beauty (USA) *F Brothers* a111
2 b f Smart Strike(CAN) —Awe That (USA) (Boundary (USA))
6338a[8]

Belanak (IRE) *Sir Michael Stoute* 83
3 b c Sinndar(IRE) —Balanka (IRE) (Alzao (USA))
948[4] 1343[3] (3376) 4631[6] 5421[5]

Belcantista (FR) *L Urbano-Grajales* 108
4 b g Unfuwain(USA) —Opera Prima (USA) (Alleged (USA))
6786a[4]

Bel Cantor *W J H Ratcliffe* a72 85
3 b c Largesse—Palmstead Belle (IRE) (Wolfhound (USA))
1218[3] 1493[2] (2001) 2896[7] 3287[8] 3718[7]4422[3] 4793[5] 5250[6](6048) (6174) 6425[6]

Beldon Hill (USA) *C E Brittain* a70 70
3 b f Rahy(USA) —Bevel (USA) (Mr Prospector (USA))
2366[5] 3100[2] 3376[3]4010[7] 5388[8] 6260[13]

Belenus (IRE) *Saeed Bin Suroor* 115+
4 ch h Dubai Millennium—Ajhiba (IRE) (Barathea (IRE))
(4145) (4529)

Be Like A Lion *B Palling* a27 55
3 b f Hunting Lion(IRE) —Princess Kelly (Prince Daniel (USA))
1232[13] 2288[17]

Belindas Dream (IRE) *Aidan Anthony Howard* a50 47
5 b m Beneficial—Pretty Beau (IRE) (Beau Charmeur (FR))
573[4] 4929[12]

Belinkin *W P Mullins* 81
6 b g Robellino(USA) —Kintail (Kris)
4166a[16]

Bellabelini (IRE) *S Kirk* a60 47
3 b f Bertolini(USA) —Bethania (Mark Of Esteem (IRE))
722[6] 969[10] 2511[7]2877[10] 3379[12]

Bella Bertolini *T G Mills* a56 65
3 b f Bertolini(USA) —Fly Like The Wind (Cyrano De Bergerac)
1801[16] 2511[12] 3118[7] 5250[4]6632[7]

Bella Fiorella (IRE) *Miss V Haigh* a47 55
3 b f Shinko Forest(IRE) —Phylella (Persian Bold)
211[6] 2876[6]687[7] 2434[9] 2696[2](2814) 3244[7]

Bella Marie *L R James* 47
3 b f Kasakov—Onemoretime (Timeless Times (USA))
4613[8] 5241[3] 5727[6]

Bell Amica *M J Attwater*
2 gr f Weet-A-Minute(IRE) —Capponicus (IRE) (Woodborough (USA))
3915[10]

Bellamont Forest (USA) *O Larsen* 108
10 b g Hermitage(USA) —Teresa's Spirit (USA) (Master Derby (USA))
(5225a)

Bellamy Cay *A Fabre* 118
4 b h Kris—Trellis Bay (Sadler's Wells (USA))
(1558a) 2277a[3] (3516a) 4861a[4] 6119a[2]

Bellanora *R F Johnson Houghton* a43 66
3 b f Inchinor—Barberello (IRE) (Bigstone (IRE))
1565[3] 2602[8] 3204[9]4527[7] 4666[8] 5309[15] 5949[8]

Bellapais Boy *T D Easterby* a50 50
2 b g Spectrum(IRE) —Denice (Night Shift (USA))
1595[10] 3596[4] 4228[8]

Bella Pavlina *R A Harris* a50 58
8 ch m Sure Blade(USA) —Pab's Choice (Telsmoss)
25[12] 103[10]

Belle Chanson *J R Boyle* a48 48
4 b m Kingsinger(IRE) —Tallulah Belle (Crowning Honors (CAN))
311[6] 395[4]469[12]

Belle Encore *A P Jarvis* a43 43
4 b m Prince Sabo—Frisson (Slip Anchor)
121[8] 235[8]

Belle Epine (FR) *C Dufreche* 80
4 ch m Lord Of Men—Belle Muse (FR) (Courtroom (FR))
6786a[16]

Bellehurst *B J Meehan* 58
2 b f King's Best(USA) —Polish Belle (Polish Precedent (USA))
4657[14] 5380[8] 6014[8] 6487[10]

Belleinga (IRE) *T F Lacy* 91
5 b m Orpen(USA) —Bellissi (IRE) (Bluebird (USA))
1158a[7] 3561a[11]

Belle Suisse (FR) *Y De Nicolay* 102
4 b m Hamas(IRE) —Aglaya (FR) (Tropular)
3516a[9] 4169a[9]

Belliflore (FR) *Mlle S-V Tarrou* 96
2 gr f Verglas(IRE) —Truffle (IRE) (Ezzoud (IRE))
4621a[7]

Bellini Star *P D Evans* a49 61
3 b g Fraam—Rewardia (IRE) (Petardia)
880[4] (1622a) 2319[12] 2599[12]4350[10]

Bellsbank (IRE) *A Bailey* a49 57
3 b f Beckett(IRE) —Fag End (IRE) (Treasure Kay)
190[10] 448[6]601[9] 3067[10] 3250[10]3582[7] 4296[11] 5861[5] 6211[9]

Belly Dancer (IRE) *P F I Cole* a79 85
4 gr m Danehill Dancer(IRE) —Persian Mistress (IRE) (Persian Bold)
5212[8] 5670[10]5908[11]

Belrose (IRE) *Mrs C A Dunnett* a49 30
4 b m Robellino(USA) —Blue Bay (GER) (Niniski (USA))
219[12] 460[12]888[14] 1056[8] 1194[11]1618[9] 2319[10]

Beltane *W De Best-Turner* a15 42
8 b g Magic Ring(IRE) —Sally's Trust (IRE) (Classic Secret (USA))
2108[13] 2900[8] 4876[10]

Beltanus (GER) *Tim Gibson* 96
2 ch c Tertullian(USA) —Brighella (GER) (Lomitas)
5218a[2] 6249a[9]

Belton *Ronald Thompson* a33 33
4 b g Lujain(USA) —Efficacious (IRE) (Efisio)
3941[7]

Belvedere Vixen *M J Wallace* a64 63
2 b f Foxhound(USA) —Aunt Susan (Distant Relative)
3838[3] 4238[2] 4445[2] 6927[3]6991[4]

Be My Charm *M Blanshard* a48 59
3 b f Polish Precedent(USA) —Demerger (USA) (Distant View (USA))
2190[9] 2511[13] 3349[15] 3866[5] 4398[2]4710[3] 4962[12] 5350[8] 5480[13] 6371[12]

Be My Queen (IRE) *A P O'Brien* 102
3 b f Sadler's Wells(USA) —Multimara (USA) (Arctic Tern (USA))
1709a[4] 2054a[7] 4502a[4] 5465a[4] 5996a[7]6356a[12]

Be My Wings (SWE) *F Castro*
3 ch g Be My Chief(USA) —Shaa Wing (USA) (Shadeed (USA))
4419a[3]

Benandonner (USA) *E A L Dunlop* a82 88
3 ch g Giant's Causeway(USA) —Cape Verdi (IRE) (Caerleon (USA))
1680[6] 2859[4] 3384[2]3906[3] 4395[2] 4995[3]5249[2] (5599) 5869[2] 6076[8]

Benayoun *M H Tompkins* a55 55
2 b c Inchinor—Sosumi (Be My Chief (USA))
5646[10] 6055[5] (6172) 6394[6]

Ben Bacchus (IRE) *P W Hiatt* a30 27
4 b g Bahhare(USA) —Bodfaridistinction (IRE) (Distinctly North (USA))
1572[2] 2099[9] 2362[9]6375[8]

Benbaun (IRE) *M J Wallace* 119
5 b g Stravinsky(USA) —Escape To Victory (Salse (USA))
2276a[2] 2720[2] 3124a[2] 3312[2] (4855a) 5717a[5]6783a[3]

Benbrook *J L Dunlop* a58 75
3 b c Royal Applause—Muffled (USA) (Mizaaya)
1241[10] 2479[4] 2814[11] (3540) (3816) 4173[2] 4784[4]5236[2] 5568[7] 5911[10]

Ben Casey *B Smart* a62 65
4 b g Whittingham(IRE) —Hot Ice (IRE) (Petardia)
9[10] 144[9]

Benchmark *R Hannon* a75 80
2 b c Mark Of Esteem(IRE) —Tarneem (USA) (Zilzal (USA))
1189[3] 1333[2] 4028[6]4428[4] 5106[13] 5906[7]

Ben Chorley *P W Chapple-Hyam* 77
2 gr g Inchinor—Arantxa (Sharpo)
4600[7] (5614)

Bendarshaan *C A Dwyer* a62 79
6 b g Darshaan—Calypso Run (Lycius (USA))
37[7] 168[9]4848[6] 5235[6] 5725[11]

Benedict *John Berry* 102
4 b g Benny The Dip(USA) —Abbey Strand (USA) (Shadeed (USA))
728[P] (Dead)

Beneking *D Burchell* a60 67
6 bb g Wizard King—Gagajulu (Al Hareb (USA))
(178) 400[3] 486[4]854[2] 903[2]1273[5] 1303[3]2095[5] 2223[5] 6714[2]6869[7]

Benfleet Boy *B J Meehan* a80+ 72+
2 gr g Fasliyev(USA) —Nicely (IRE) (Bustino)
4600[4] (5106)

Bening (FR) *O Pessi* a97 112
6 ch h Shantou(USA) —Bessie Bennett (IRE) (Be My Guest (USA))
393a[7] 1712a[5] 2217a[3]5982a[8]

Benjum *B I Case* a55
3 ch g Benny The Dip(USA) —Boojum (Mujtahid (USA))
2066[6]

Ben Kenobi *Mrs P Ford* a43 50
8 ch g Accondy(IRE) —Nour El Sahar (USA) (Sagace (FR))
2707[12] 4282[8] 4924[9]

Benllech *S Kirk* a84+ 71
2 b c Lujain(USA) —Four Legs Good (IRE) (Be My Guest (USA))
1203[8] 1587[2] 1796[5] 2218[9] 2617[8]5161[4] 5447[4] 5570[4] 6063[2] 6310[2](6591) (6937)

Bennanabaa *S C Burrough* a36 35
7 b g Anabaa(USA) —Arc Empress Jane (IRE) (Rainbow Quest (USA))
396[7] 502[11]1102[17] 1746[10]

Benny The Ball (USA) *N P Littmoden* a58 55
5 bb g Benny The Dip(USA) —Heloise (USA) (Forty Niner (USA))
2141[7] 2936[11]3999[4] 4248[8]4496[7] 6532[3] 6687[5]

Benny The Bat *H Morrison* a73 73
2 gr c Victory Note(USA) —Little Emily (Zafonic (USA))
4103[5] 5105[2] 5730[4](6809)

Benny The Bus *Mrs G S Rees* a72 71
4 b g Komaite(USA) —Amy Leigh (IRE) (Imperial Frontier (USA))
5249[11] 5388[9]5737[2] 5969[4]6286[6] (6490) 6672[4]

Benny The Rascal (IRE) *J Pearce* 42
4 b g Benny The Dip(USA) —Bolshoi Star (Soviet Star (USA))
4549[6]

Bens Georgie (IRE) *D K Ivory* a74 73
4 ch m Opening Verse(USA) —Peperonata (IRE) (Cyrano De Bergerac)
1383[4] 1774[8] (2331) 2417[3]3094[5] 3368[10] 4003[10] 4894[10] 5378[13]5987[7]

Benta Berri (FR) *R Martin-Sanchez* 92
4 ch h Priolo(USA) —Masslama (FR) (No Pass No Sale)
5881a[11] 6786a[14]

Bentley *D Shaw* a46 21
2 b g Piccolo—April Lee (Superpower)
892[9] 987[6] 1333[6]5509[9] 5633[7] 6311[6]6422[5] 6488[6]6653[6] 6760[6]6900[4]

Bentley Brook (IRE) *P A Blockley* a68 74
4 ch g Singspiel(IRE) —Gay Bentley (USA) (Riverman (USA))
167[12] 843[6]3151[5] 3639[6] 5792[13]6301[7] 6415[4] 6571[4]

Bentong (IRE) *P F I Cole* a72+ 108
3 b g Anabaa(USA) —Miss Party Line (USA) (Phone Trick (USA))
1097[2] (1512) 1836[7] (3761) 4128[18] 4601[9]

Benwilt Breeze (IRE) *G M Lyons* 102
4 b h Mujadil(USA) —Image Of Truce (IRE) (Brief Truce (USA))
3125a[9] 3561a[7] 5706a[7]

Beowulf *M Johnston* a60 68
3 b c Green Desert(USA) —Ethelinda (Indian Ridge)
584[3] 658[8]880[14] 978[4] 1441[2] 1592[10] 2109[6]2749[9] (Dead)

Berbatim (USA) *Richard E Mandella* a97 105
4 b m Bernstein(USA) —Word Harvest (USA) (Verbatim (USA))
6253a[6]

Berbatov *Ms Deborah J Evans* a62 52
2 b g Alhaarth(IRE) —Neptunalia (Slip Anchor)
5527[11] 6050[7] 6536[5]

Beresford Boy *J A Pickering* a59 37
5 b g Easycall—Devils Dirge (Song)
1645[16] 2288[14]

Bergonzi (IRE) *J H M Gosden* a79+ 29
2 ch c Indian Ridge—Lady Windley (Baillamont (USA))
5883[12] 6072[5] 6447[2]

Beringoer (FR) *A Fabre* a86 101
3 ch c Bering—Charmgoer (USA) (Nureyev (USA))
1600a[5] 2489a[5]

Berkeley Castle (USA) *Sir Michael Stoute* 76+
2 b c Mizzen Mast(USA) —Bristol Channel (Generous (IRE))
4103[11] 4781[10] 5918[3]

Berkhamsted (IRE) *Tom Dascombe* a81 81d
4 b g Desert Sun—Accounting (Sillery (USA))
213[7] (361) 946[8] 1112[9]1380[8] 1435[8] 1757[5]2447[6] 5815[13] 6108[9]6652[2] 6734[3]

Berlioz (IND) *S Padmanabhan* a70 95
5 b g Sri Pekan(USA) —Innocent Pleasures (IRE) (Night Shift (USA))
149a[4] 438a[10] 560a[12]

Bermuda Beauty (IRE) *J M Bradley* a36 42
3 b f Elnadim(USA) —Believing (Belmez (USA))
53[9] 105[3]248[6] 2190[7] 2704[7]3538[11] 3595[11] 4756[9]6638[10]

Bernardini (USA) *T Albertrani* a128+
3 b c A.P. Indy(USA) —Cara Rafaela (USA) (Quiet American (USA))
(1861a) (5822a) 6345a[2]

Bernardon (GER) *Barry Potts*
10 b g Suave Dancer(USA) —Bejaria (GER) (Konigsstuhl (GER))
816[11]

Bernie's Beau (IRE) *R Hollinshead* a50 46
3 br f Namid—Otter's Field (IRE) (First Trump)
1279[7] 5756[13] 6288[11]6390[11] 6624[11]

Berri Chis (ARG) *Vanja Sandrup* 100
4 b h Strawberry-Li(ARG) —Potrichis (ARG) (Potrillazo (ARG))
5225a[4]

Berti Bertolini *T G Mills* a59 58
3 b g Bertolini(USA) —Cosmic Countess (IRE) (Lahib (USA))
807[12]

Bertie Bear *G G Margarson* a39 39
3 b c Bertolini(USA) —Philarmonique (FR) (Trempolino (USA))
790[2] 874[8]1200[6] 1771[8] 2192[12]3006[3] 3541[8] 4050[7] 4769[11] 5432[14]5733[14]

Berties Brother *D G Bridgwater* a46 32
3 ch g Forzando—Sweets (IRE) (Persian Heights)
110[8] 176[2](308) 595[5]790[3] 1200[3]1576[11] 3612[11] 3821[10]

Bertie Southstreet *J R Best* 82
3 bb g Bertolini(USA) —Salvezza (IRE) (Superpower)
3150[4] 3414[13] 3761[12] 4481[6]

Bertie Swift *J Gallagher* a66 66
2 b g Bertolini(USA) —Hollybell (Beveled (USA))
849[8] 3363[12] 3822[4]4479[4] 5065[10] 6965[2]

Bertoliver *D K Ivory* a66 75
2 b c Bertolini(USA) —Calcavella (Pursuit Of Love)
3363[13] 3591[4] 4428[6] 5262[7](5454) 5655[8] 6332[2]

Bertrada (IRE) *H Morrison* a50 27
2 b f King Charlemagne(USA) —Goldenfort Queen (IRE) (Distinctly North (USA))
2456[15] 3010[4] 3201[11]3727[6]

Bertranicus (FR) *L Urbano-Grajales* 91
3 br g Take Risks(FR) —L'Etoile La Lune (IRE) (Groom Dancer (USA))
392a[5]

Bert's Memory *K A Ryan* a59 67
2 b f Bertolini(USA) —Meg's Memory (IRE) (Superlative)
2791[6] 3307[3] 4251[8]4893[5] 5347[3] 5747[3] 5958[4] 6270[4]6582[5] 6675[2]6891[3]

Berylune (GER) *S Dow* 6
4 ch m Devil River Peek(USA) —Berlanga (GER) (Executive Pride)
1240[10]

Beshairt *D K Ivory* a32
2 b f Silver Wizard(USA) —Irja (Minshaanshu Amad (USA))
5608[10] 6258[9]6441[13]

Bessemer (JPN) *D Carroll* a84 82
5 b g Carnegie(IRE) —Chalna (IRE) (Darshaan)
100[4] (316) 476[10]1220[4] 1561[5] 2681[12] 3097[5]3664[2] 4090[9] 4172[10] 4437[6]5403[7] 5688[8] 6241[5]6417[8] 6573[5](6624) 6938[3]

Best Alibi (IRE) *Sir Michael Stoute* 119+
3 b c King's Best(USA) —Chauncy Lane (IRE) (Sadler's Wells (USA))
1805[2] 2228[6] 3127a[3] (3957)

Best Dancing (GER) *C Von Der Recke* 77
4 br m Keos(USA) —Bergwelt (GER) (Solarstern (FR))
5710a[11]

Best Double *G A Butler* a71 69
3 ch f Compton Place—Bestemor (Selkirk (USA))
533[2] 553[2]901[6] 3000[5] 3406[4]3749[4] 3842[4]

Best Game *D W Thompson* a59 55
4 b g Mister Baileys—Bestemor (Selkirk (USA))
163[11]

Best Gift (NZ) *J Moore* 122
5 b g Bahhare(USA) —Shock Attack (NZ) (Inviting)
1180a[2]

Best Guess (USA) *P W Chapple-Hyam* a77 85
3 bb f Stormin Fever(USA) —Probing (USA) (Brocco (USA))
(2087) 3643[4] (5024) 5895[4]

Best Lady (IRE) *B W Hills* 73
3 b f King's Best(USA) —Sassenach (IRE) (Night Shift (USA))
3794[3] 4661[6] 5567[4]

Best Lead *Ian Emmerson* a69 57
7 b g Distant Relative—Bestemor (Selkirk (USA))
126[9] 317[13]6739[12]

Best Name *Robert Collet* 120+
3 b c King's Best(USA) —Flawly (Old Vic)
2278a[2] 3127a[8] (5400a) 5716a[4]

Best Of The Lot (USA) *R A Fahey* a63 87
4 b g Lear Fan(USA) —Aerosilver (USA) (Relaunch (USA))
3081[9] 3639[7] 4764[3]5242[4] 5513[8] 5815[9]

Best Option *W R Muir* a28
2 b f Best Of The Bests(IRE) —B'Elanna Torres (Entrepreneur)
6927[6]

Best Port (IRE) *J Parkes* a53 67d
10 b g Be My Guest(USA) —Portree (Slip Anchor)
2365[6] 2684[10] 3284[8] 3763[2] 4380[13]4506[4] 5242[15]

Best Prospect (IRE) *M Dods* 102
4 b g Orpen(USA) —Bright Prospect (USA) (Miswaki (USA))
2079[11] 2621[5] 2989[9] (3497) 4259[4] 4676[7]5137[6] 5310[2] 5787[7] (6107) 6337[4]

Best Selection *A P Jarvis* a65
2 ch f Inchinor—Manila Selection (USA) (Manila (USA))
6441[9] 6886[5]

Best Warning *J Ryan* 52
2 br f Best Of The Bests(IRE) —Just Warning (Warning)
3640[14] 4765[13] 5527[12]

Best Woman *P Howling* a47
2 b f Best Of The Bests(IRE) —Business Woman (Primo Dominie)
(1682) 1897[5] 2300[9] 2538[8] 2709[10] 6518[6]

Beta *J E Pease* 101
2 b f Selkirk(USA) —Moonlight's Box (USA) (Nureyev (USA))
3990a[2] 4415a[5] 5122a[3] (5880a)

Bethanys Boy (IRE) *A M Hales* a83 61
5 ch g Docksider(USA) —Daymoon (USA) (Dayjur (USA))
(125) 194[5] 610[6]1187[10] 6871[2]

Betsen (IRE) *D Nicholls* 71d
4 b g Namid—St Clair Star (Sallust)
719[12] 1597[12] 2449[9] 3190[5] 3447[8]3835[3] 4019[5] 4462[8] 5309[16] 5493[15]6162[12]

Better Off Red (USA) *B J Meehan* a32 41
2 bb f Red Ransom(USA) —Unending Love (USA) (Dixieland Band (USA))
2552[11] 3247[9] 4323[9]

Better Talk Now (USA) *H G Motion* 124
7 b g Talkin Man(CAN) —Bendita (USA) (Baldski (USA))
4386a[7] 6344a[2]

Betty Oxo *B P J Baugh*
2 b f Mind Games—Kildine (IRE) (Common Grounds)
6931[4]

Between Friends *A Berry* a19 19
4 b m Slip Anchor—Charisse Dancer (Dancing Dissident (USA))
26[11]

Beverley Beau *Mrs L Stubbs* a51 57
4 b g Inchinor—Oriel Girl (Beveled (USA))
38[6] 307[6]397[8] 772[2]886[4] 1196[8]1447[3] 1722[6] 1909[6]2288[4] (2377) 2928[4] 3524[11] 3608[2] 3825[6]4141[9] 4523[8] 5243[8] 6399[9]6541[4] 6619[8]6805[3]

Beverley Bell *Miss J A Camacho* a30
3 b f Bertolini(USA) —Lowrianna (IRE) (Cyrano De Bergerac)
165[9] 380[8]1126[10]

Beverley Hills (IRE) *J Howard Johnson* 30
3 gr f Mozart(IRE) —Attachment (USA) (Trempolino (USA))
2763[10] 4199[16]

Beverley Polo (IRE) *M W Easterby* 40
3 br c Prince Sabo—Justforthererecord (Forzando)
819[6] 1078[11] 1344[12] 1792[8] 3381[12]

Beverly Hill Billy *A King* a77 73+
2 b g Primo Valentino(IRE) —Miss Beverley (Beveled (USA))
3843[5] 4366[2](4897) 5783[4]

Bevier *T Wall* a15 15
12 b g Nashwan(USA) —Bevel (USA) (Mr Prospector (USA))
1548[10]

Bewildering (IRE) *E J O'Neill* a60
2 b c Tagula(IRE) —Mystic Belle (IRE) (Thatching)
6809[2]

Be Wise Girl *A W Carroll* a61 79?
5 ch m Fleetwood(IRE) —Zabelina (USA) (Diesis)
733[9]

Beyond Belief (IRE) *Charles O'Brien*
3 b f Sadler's Wells(USA) —Adjriyna (Top Ville)
6382[12]

Beyond The Clouds (IRE) *J S Wainwright* 63
10 b g Midhish—Tongabezi (IRE) (Shernazar)
2384[15] 2780[9] 3297[14] 3525[4] 3699[7]4019[10] 4232[13]

Bhutan (IRE) *Jim Best* a49 56
11 b g Polish Patriot(USA) —Bustinetta (Bustino)
694[3] 904[5]1271[6] 1541[12]2566[5] 2935[9] 3437[11]

Bianca Sforza *D Shaw*
4 b m Anabaa(USA) —Caterina Sforza (Machiavellian (USA))
2983[14]

Bianconi (SAF) *A Laird* 105
7 b h Rambo Dancer(CAN) —Coconut Ice (SAF) (Jungle Cove (USA))
207a[4] 356a[6] 513a[8]

Bibi Helen *W M Brisbourne* a26 57
4 b m Robellino(USA) —Tarry (Salse (USA))
2133[7] (Dead)

Bicoastal (USA) *B J Meehan* 103
2 ch f Gone West(USA) —Ocean Queen (USA) (Zilzal (USA))
1675[2] (1989) 2800[17] 4840[2] 5714a[5]

Bidable *B Palling* a66 59
2 b f Auction House(USA) —Dubitable (Formidable (USA))
5348[3] 5563[7] 6257[5]6481[4]

Bidders Itch *A Berry* 11
2 b f Auction House(USA) —Sharp Ego (USA) (Sharpen Up)
1863[9] 3982[11] 4089[6] 4607[5]

Bid For Fame (USA) *J Pearce* a67 69
9 bb g Quest For Fame—Shroud (USA) (Vaguely Noble)
(270) (283) 597[U]

Bid For Glory *H J Collingridge* 91
2 ch c Auction House(USA) —Woodland Steps (Bold Owl)
(3979) 5113[2] 5459[3] 6010[4]

Bid For Gold *Jedd O'Keeffe* 77
2 b c Auction House(USA) —Gold And Blue (IRE) (Bluebird (USA))
2361[8] 2973[4] 3982[5] 4452[4] 5509[3]5788[13]

Bienheureux *Miss Gay Kelleway* a70 59
5 b g Bien Bien(USA) —Rochea (Rock City)
2862[5] 3221[5] (3998) 4606[10](4702) 4924[5] 5213[2]5875[3] 6256[11]6382[5] 6474[5]6565[10] 6718[3]6947[6]

Bien Partie (FR) *Mlle S-V Tarrou* 88
4 ch m Lord Of Men—Zibelina (FR) (Linamix (FR))
6574a[0]

Big Bad Bill (IRE) *P T Midgley*
6 gr g Entrepreneur—Chamonis (USA) (Affirmed (USA))
1385[9]

Big Bertha (GER) *J-C Rouget* 83
2 ch f Tertullian(USA) —Birthday Night (USA) (Southern Halo (USA))
5858a[4] 6528a[7]

Big Bradford *R A Fahey* a73 77
5 b g Tamure(IRE) —Heather Honey (Insan (USA))
2259^7 2603^8 2952^8 3811^6 4119^8 4456^4 4961^8 5285^{13}

Big Bunny (GER) *M Weiss* 83
3 b f Tiger Hill(IRE) —Big Flower (GER) (Big Shuffle (USA))
$925a^5$

Big Easy (NZ) *L Laxon* 90
5 b g Spinning World(USA) —Nicoles Niner (USA) (Forty Niner (USA))
$369a^6$ $513a^9$ $1716a^{11}$

Biggin Hill (IRE) *H R A Cecil* 54
3 b c Alzao(USA) —Fire Of London (Shirley Heights)
3029^{14} 5071^9 5510^{13}

Big Gold (JPN) *T Nakao* 114
8 br h Brian's Time(USA) —Beautiful Gold (USA) (Mr Prospector (USA))
$1329a^{13}$

Big Hassle (IRE) *D Nicholls* 87
4 b h Namid—Night After Night (Night Shift (USA))
718^{11} 1125^8

Big Mistake (USA) *B Cecil* 88
3 b g Broken Vow(USA) —Fly Star (USA) (Fly So Free (USA))
$6613a^9$

Big Moment *Mrs A J Perrett* 98
8 ch g Be My Guest(USA) —Petralona (USA) (Alleged (USA))
1584^{12} 6336^6

Big Mystery (IRE) *S C Williams* a47 20
5 b m Grand Lodge(USA) —Mysterious Plans (IRE) (Last Tycoon)
312^5 398^{11}

Big Player *W J Haggas* 77
2 b c Noverre(USA) —Maxizone (FR) (Linamix (FR))
(4688) 5322^5

Big Ralph *M Wigham* a45
3 ch g Mark Of Esteem(IRE) —Wish Me Luck (IRE) (Lycius (USA))
6901^7

Big Robert *W R Muir* 102
2 b c Medicean—Top Flight Queen (Mark Of Esteem (IRE))
3892^2 (4781) 5176^2 5653^5

Big Smoke (IRE) *J C Tuck* a40 61
6 gr g Perugino(USA) —Lightning Bug (Prince Bee)
6133^9 6373^9

Big Sugar (IRE) *B Grizzetti*
2 b g Mark Of Esteem(IRE) —Finamai (IRE) (Royal Academy (USA))
(6407a)

Big Timer (USA) *I Semple* 105+
2 ch g Street Cry(IRE) —Moonflute (USA) (The Minstrel (CAN))
(3581) (4200) (4680) $5983a^{10}$

Bijli (IRE) *J Noseda* a68 68
3 br g Key Of Luck(USA) —More Magnanimous (King Persian)
1845^7 2859^3 3189^3 3383^2

Bijou Dan *W G Harrison* a76 61
5 ch g Bijou D'Inde—Cal Norma's Lady (IRE) (Lyphard's Special (USA))
106^6 313^5(410) 492^6 568^8 734^{10} 1148^2 (1305) 1947^3 2141^4 (2794) (3101) 3688^8 4355^2 4652^3 5249^7 5403^9 5689^5 6240^{10} 6568^8 6863^6

Bijouterie *G A Swinbank* 69
2 ch f Tobougg(IRE) —Branston Gem (So Factual (USA))
1647^3 2076^9

Billanroy (IRE) *M H Tompkins* 56
3 ch g Inchinor—Charm The Stars (Roi Danzig (USA))
1289^{10} 1738^{13} 2607^{11}

Bill Bennett (FR) *J Jay* a59 70
5 b g Bishop Of Cashel—Concert (Polar Falcon (USA))
28^6 (302) 525^9 882^{10} (973) 1138^5 1562^{10} $1929a^6$ 2104^8 5815^8 5952^5 6158^{11} 6553^6

Billet Express (AUS) *J Moore* 121
5 b g Keltrice(AUS) —Pazzihi (AUS) (Manihi (AUS))
$6783a^6$

Billich *E J O'Neill* a86 81
3 ch c Observatory(USA) —Pomponette (USA) (Rahy (USA))
124^2 2465^3(3231) 3490^6 3748^{10} 3819^3 5164^4 5421^7 6075^4(6381) (6626) 6766^4

Billy Allen (IRE) *F Chappet* a102 104
5 b h Night Shift(USA) —Daintree (IRE) (Tirol)
$152a^{14}$ $354a^4$ $497a^4$ $625a^4$ $1659a^{10}$ $2492a^4$ $5227a^9$

Billy Bathwick (IRE) *J M Bradley* a51 64
9 ch g Fayruz—Cut It Fine (USA) (Big Spruce (USA))
4176^7 4585^9 4869^9 4982^4

Billy Bling (IRE) *R Hannon* a66 56
3 b g Enrique—Shewillifshewants (IRE) (Alzao (USA))
138^6 540^3 577^4 (851) 1208^{14} 1693^6 1801^{11}

Billy Dane (IRE) *B J Meehan* a87 83
2 b g Fayruz—Lomalou (IRE) (Lightning Dealer)
2930^6 3280^2 3663^2 (4436) 4736^7 5843^4

Billy One Punch *G G Margarson* 75+
4 b g Mark Of Esteem(IRE) —Polytess (IRE) (Polish Patriot (USA))
1124^9 1673^9 2112^{14} 2327^5 (2499) 2640^2 3519^2 (3883) 4209^8 5236^4 5484^6 5904^{11}

Billy Red *J R Jenkins* a65 68
2 ch g Dr Fong(USA) —Liberty Bound (Primo Dominie)
2172^4 2710^8 3408^4 3734^{23} 5454^4 5648^3 6409^5

Billy Ruffian *T D Easterby* a70+ 66
2 ch g Kyllachy—Antonia's Folly (Music Boy)
1664^{10} 3596^6 5746^5 6208^5 (6665) 6715^5 6965^3

Billy's Brother *M A Buckley*
4 ch g Wolfhound(USA) —Chili Lass (Chilibang)
173^{13}

Billy The Kid (IRE) *T Clout* 105
8 b g Danehill(USA) —Bleu Cerise (Sadler's Wells (USA))
$523a^5$

Billy Wizz (IRE) *A M Balding* a47
3 b g Namid—Mareha (IRE) (Cadeaux Genereux)
138^9 233^7 373^6 984^9 1149^{10}

Binanti *P R Chamings* a91 94+
6 b g Bin Ajwaad(IRE) —Princess Rosananti (IRE) (Shareef Dancer (USA))
161^7 220^{11}(721) 828^3 1111^3 1301^7 1692^2 1935^3 2435^7 2776^3 3223^3 3493^{11} 3926^{17} 4029^3 4372^8 4535^2 5019^{16} 5175^7

Binary File (USA) *L Kelp* a110 114
8 b h Nureyev(USA) —Binary (Rainbow Quest (USA))
(1659a) $2123a^9$ $3563a^4$ (4864a) $5226a^2$

Bingo One (IRE) *W J H Ratcliffe* 57
3 b f Mujahid(USA) —Barque Bleue (USA) (Steinlen)
1801^{10} 4881^{14}

Biniou (IRE) *Robert Collet* 116
3 b c Mozart(IRE) —Cap Coz (IRE) (Indian Ridge)
$1717a^3$ $2276a^9$ $2941a^4$ $3564a^4$ $4191a^{16}$ $5146a^6$ $5222a^3$ $5712a^4$

Binnion Bay (IRE) *J J Bridger* a59 54
5 b g Fasliyev(USA) —Literary (Woodman (USA))
148^6 265^{11} 576^8 6237^2 6372^7 (6726) (6803) 6855^8

Binocular *B W Hills* 65
2 ch c Observatory(USA) —Well Beyond (IRE) (Don't Forget Me)
5508^4

Bin Rahy (IRE) *M R Channon* a68 88
3 ch c Rahy(USA) —Belle Genius (USA) (Beau Genius (CAN))
188^6 1122^2 (1569) 2024^4 2659^4 3318^{10} 3984^2 4763^2

Bint Il Sultan (IRE) *W M Brisbourne* a50 47
4 b m Xaar—Knight's Place (IRE) (Hamas (IRE))
2362^2 2777^5 3140^{10} 4404^{13} 4755^6 5435^6

Bint Royal (IRE) *Miss V Haigh* a46 65?
8 ch m Royal Abjar(USA) —Living Legend (USA) (Septieme Ciel (USA))
249^{11} 350^{11} 407^6 440^9 2400^{11} 2543^8 2700^{12} 2811^{12}

Binty *A J Chamberlain* 31
4 b m Prince Sabo—Mistral's Dancer (Shareef Dancer (USA))
3155^{11} 3306^9 3356^{13} 3635^8 4670^{14} 6131^{12}

Birbalini *P J McBride* a29 9
3 b f Bertolini(USA) —La Birba (IRE) (Prince Of Birds (USA))
630^9 3647^{12} 3987^6 4556^7

Birdbirdistheword (USA) *K McPeek* a107
2 br c Pure Prize(USA) —Berchta (USA) (Rocky Mountain (USA))
$5823a^4$

Birdie Birdie *R A Fahey* 53
2 b f Superior Premium—Cautious Joe (First Trump)
3787^6 4376^3 4887^2 5238^{18}

Bird Of Paradise (FR) *E Libaud* 103
4 gr m Highest Honor(FR) —Kaldance (FR) (Kaldoun (FR))
$6171a^6$

Bird Over *R M Beckett* a87 89
4 b m Bold Edge—High Bird (IRE) (Polar Falcon (USA))
970^3 (1338) 1820^{11} 2438^{11} 3211^9 3904^{12}

Birdwatch *K G Reveley* a33 22
8 b g Minshaanshu Amad(USA) —Eider (Niniski (USA))
938^8

Birkside *W R Swinburn* a82 79
3 ch g Spinning World(USA) —Bright Hope (IRE) (Danehill (USA))
4431^2 4933^6 5511^5 6206^7 6432^2

Birkspiel (GER) *S Dow* 106
5 b h Singspiel(IRE) —Beaute (GER) (Lord Udo (GER))
(1014a) $1369a^3$ 2010^8 5547^8

Birthday Art (GER) *P Vovcenko* 89
4 b m Areion(GER) —Boucheron (GER) (Turfkonig (GER))
$3661a^{10}$ $5710a^7$

Birthday Star (IRE) *W J Musson* a67 59
4 b g Desert King(IRE) —White Paper (IRE) (Marignan (USA))
115^8 263^3 379^7 478^6(733) 1138^{13} 2345^2 3686^5 4702^8 4972^5 5213^3 5390^2 5725^5

Bisaat (USA) *M S Saunders*
3 b f Bahri(USA) —Tabrir (IRE) (Unfuwain (USA))
5566^{12}

Bischoff's Boy (GER) *P Zollig* 101
5 b h Alkalde(GER) —Bischoffsgorl (Elegant Air)
$305a^7$

Bish Basher (IRE) *P A Blockley* a48 33
2 ch g Zilzal(USA) —Gentle Dame (Kris)
5565^7 6386^{12}

Bishop Auckland (IRE) *Mrs A Duffield* 39
2 b g Docksider(USA) —Chancel (USA) (Al Nasr (FR))
5900^{10} 6318^9

Bishop Court Hill (USA) *T Pletcher* a117
6 ch g Holy Bull(USA) —Just Cuz (USA) (Cormorant (USA))
$4384a^5$

Bishops Finger *Jamie Poulton* a68 63
6 b g Bishop Of Cashel—Bit Of A Tart (Distant Relative)
(113) 187^3 324^{10} 1334^4 1644^8 1926^9 2862^{11}(3411) 3730^9 4332^7 5259^3 5609^2

Bitter Chill *H Morrison* a57 79
3 b c Agnes World(USA) —Azula (Bluebird (USA))
2823^{11} 3381^6 4695^{10}

Biwa (FR) *J-P Gallorini* 93
5 br g Lost World(IRE) —Belle Des Champs (Be My Chief (USA))
$1929a^2$

Biz Bar *M Guarnieri* 95
2 b f Tobougg(IRE) —Ulanova (USA) (Barachois (CAN))
$3343a^2$

Bjorling *M J Gingell* a41
5 ch g Opening Verse(USA) —Pola Star (IRE) (Un Desperado (FR))
180^{14}

Black Beauty *M G Quinlan* a59 87
3 br c Diktat—Euridice (IRE) (Woodman (USA))
112^6 293^7 781^4 (1215) (2128) 2434^4 2622^2 3871^2 4147^4 4833^7 5266^5 5590^4

Blackberry Boy (IRE) *D K Weld* 92
2 b c Desert Prince(IRE) —Summer Crush (USA) (Summer Squall (USA))
$3962a^4$

Black Charmer (IRE) *M Johnston* a32 111
3 b c Black Minnaloushe(USA) —Abla (Robellino (USA))
4896^6 5135^6 5578^8 6192^{14}

Black Chief (SWE) *R A Kvisla* a17 58
5 br g Be My Chief(USA) —La Creole (USA) (Best Turn (USA))
3532^{12} 4001^8 4432^8

Blackcomb Mountain (USA) *M F Harris* a67 66
3 b f Royal Anthem(USA) —Ski Racer (FR) (Ski Chief (USA))
3114^6

Black Falcon (IRE) *P T Midgley* a75 78
6 ch g In The Wings—Muwasim (USA) (Meadowlake (USA))
6313^{10} 6502^{11} 6791^7 6946^3

Blackhall Claw (IRE) *S J Treacy* 69
5 ch g Grand Lodge(USA) —Blue Kestrel (IRE) (Bluebird (USA))
$4094a^{14}$

Blackheath (IRE) *D Nicholls* a72 82
10 ch g Common Grounds—Queen Caroline (USA) (Chief's Crown (USA))
657^6 1102^9 1297^8 1504^2 1686^3 2397^4 (2661) 3170^4 4085^{16} 4834^3 5117^9 5333^2 5493^8

Black Horse (ITY) *L Batzella*
2 b c Bahamian Knight(CAN) —Imco Sun (ITY) (Southern Arrow (USA))
$5771a^{10}$

Black Jade *M A Jarvis* a25 52
3 b c Averti(IRE) —Rivermead (USA) (Irish River (FR))
1218^6 1549^{11}

Black Java (USA) *D Galvin* 98
4 b m Pine Bluff(USA) —Java Drums (USA) (Java Gold (USA))
$6368a^8$

Black Joke (IRE) *P Paciello*
2 b c Dr Devious(IRE) —I Have A Dream (ITY) (Lomond (USA))
$3427a^2$

Blackmail (USA) *P Mitchell* a70 72
8 b g Twining(USA) —Black Penny (USA) (Private Account (USA))
37^3 111^6 237^7 264^2 478^8 521^7 1334^8 1754^4 2455^9 2953^4 3209^6 (3429) 3666^4 4448^3 4704^6 5258^8 5451^9 5587^{12} 6484^9 6565^9 6748^8(6889)

Black Mogul *W R Muir* 47
2 b g Robellino(USA) —Brilliance (Cadeaux Genereux)
4049^5 4774^{11}

Black Moma (IRE) *R Hannon* 76
2 b f Averti(IRE) —Sareb (FR) (Indian Ridge)
3588^4 (3818) 4603^2 (4779) 5234^2

Black Oval *S Parr* a55+ 69?
5 b m Royal Applause—Corniche Quest (IRE) (Salt Dome (USA))
3525^5 3835^7 3912^3 4054^{14} 4267^8 5443^7 5684^{21} 5834^4 6728^2 6856^2 6981^4

Black Profusion (IRE) *P Martometti* 97
3 b f Desert Prince(IRE) —Roman Walk (Petorius)
$2043a^5$ $2694a^{15}$

Blackriver Boy *Niall Moran* 60
3 ch c Muhtarram(USA) —Full Stop (IRE) (Zieten (USA))
$4124a^9$

Black Rock (IRE) *M A Jarvis* a83 70+
2 ch c Rock Of Gibraltar(IRE) —Biraya (Valiyar)
4716^4 5020^2

Black Sea Pearl *P W D'Arcy* a66 67
3 br f Diktat—Made Of Pearl (USA) (Nureyev (USA))
879^{10} 1616^4 2466^{13}(6061) 6293^9 6608^2 6820^3 6897^4

Blacktoft (USA) *S C Williams* a80+ 69
3 bb g Theatrical—Black Truffle (USA) (Mt. Livermore (USA))
1153^3 1386^3 1738^8 2128^3 2823^4 3301^4 4254^5 4930^6 5269^8 5740^4(5992) 6566^3 6712^2

Black Tom (AUS) *F Maynard* 109
5 ch h Langfuhr(CAN) —Narmada (USA) (Blushing Groom (FR))
$7000a^5$

Blackwater Stream (IRE) *Mrs P N Dutfield* 67d
2 b c Shinko Forest(IRE) —Lady Eberspacher (IRE) (Royal Abjar (USA))
2530^{10} 3363^8 3872^3 4377^8 5349^8 5948^5

Blades Girl *K A Ryan* 97
3 ch f Bertolini(USA) —Banningham Blade (Sure Blade (USA))
2650^{13} 3067^3 3418^3 4083^6 4488^2(5143) 5550^5

Blaenavon *D W P Arbuthnot* a48 17
4 b m Cadeaux Genereux—One Of The Family (Alzao (USA))
32^6 311^{12} 399^8

Blaise Hollow (USA) *R Charlton* 94
4 b g Woodman(USA) —Castellina (USA) (Danzig Connection (USA))
1775^{10} 2169^{13} 4805^6 5346^{14} 5678^{12}

Blake Hall Lad (IRE) *P S McEntee* a17 40?
5 b g Cape Cross(IRE) —Queen Of Art (IRE) (Royal Academy (USA))
63^{10}

Blakeshall Boy *A J Chamberlain* a64 83
8 b g Piccolo—Giggleswick Girl (Full Extent (USA))
6983^{10}

Blakeshall Hope *A J Chamberlain* a57 57
4 ch g Piccolo—Elite Hope (USA) (Moment Of Hope (USA))
6544^6

Blakeshall Quest *R Brotherton* a57 56
6 b m Piccolo—Corniche Quest (IRE) (Salt Dome (USA))
145^9 260^2(388) 529^8 608^{11} 858^8(1255) 2096^4 3267^5 3683^3 3847^2 4329^{11} 5928^3 6234^8 6308^2 6470^4(6796)

Blakeshall Rose *A J Chamberlain* a47 44
2 b f Tobougg(IRE) —Giggleswick Girl (Full Extent (USA))
2355^8 3684^4 4109^7 5238^{11} 6422^{14} 6500^5 6582^7

Blanc Visage *Mrs H Sweeting* a60
3 b g Tomba—Trinity Hall (Hallgate)
445^5 531^6 630^2 677^5 823^2 1005^8 1153^6 2209^7 2795^{10} 5690^{12} 6623^8 6743^{10}

Blandford Flyer *W R Swinburn* a64 46
3 b g Soviet Star(USA) —Vento Del Oreno (FR) (Lando (GER))
1416^{11} 5621^{12} 5992^{13}

Blatant *I Mohammed* a115 117
7 ch g Machiavellian(USA) —Negligent (Ahonoora)
(154a) $355a^2$ $738a^8$

Blazing Ability (USA) *Doug Watson* a73 82
7 ch g El Prado(IRE) —Jazzability (USA) (Dixieland Band (USA))
$278a^9$

Blazing Fact (IRE) *Alex Vanderhaeghen* 101
8 b g So Factual(USA) —Gezalle (Shareef Dancer (USA))
$3692a^{12}$

Blazing Heights *J S Goldie* 87
3 b g Compton Place—Harrken Heights (IRE) (Belmez (USA))
1036^5 1529^2 2110^4 2410^2 2855^2 3475^2 3761^6 4717^4 5169^7 5333^{16} 5791^4 (6320)

Blend *J H M Gosden* a72 69
3 b f Zafonic(USA) —Bonash (Rainbow Quest (USA))
5870^5 6026^3 6410^3

Blessed Place *D J S Ffrench Davis* a68 77
6 ch g Compton Place—Cathedra (So Blessed)
2331^{11} 2674^3 2962^7 2971^2 3245^4(3389) 3593^3 3846^2(3988) 4486^5 4598^3 4780^3 4962^3 5058^{14} 6622^4 6672^3 6739^7 6842^6 6858^{12} 6913^8

Blessings Count (USA) *E A L Dunlop* 61
3 ch f Pulpit(USA) —Topicount (USA) (Private Account (USA))
1114^8 1598^5

Blessyourpinksox (IRE) *Peter Casey* 105+
5 ch m Cadeaux Genereux—Kumta (IRE) (Priolo (USA))
$4502a^2$ $5465a^5$ $5996a^{10}$

Bleue Doloise (FR) *A Bonin* 83
2 br f Marchand De Sable(USA) —Ramonda (FR) (Fabulous Dancer (USA))
$6228a^8$ $6609a^8$

Blip *D Smaga* 104
4 ch h Zafonic(USA) —Birdlip (USA) (Sanglamore (USA))
$4417a^5$ $5519a^4$ $5999a^8$

Blissfully *S Parr* 50
2 b f Kyllachy—Bliss (IRE) (Statoblest)
2523^{10} 3605^6 5764^{10}

Blissphilly *M Mullineaux* a19 15
4 b m Primo Dominie—Majalis (Mujadil (USA))
3141^{13} 5865^{14} 6943^6

Blithe *W J Haggas* 85+
2 b f Pivotal—Pious (Bishop Of Cashel)
2890^3 4074^4 4552^2 5133^3 (5676)

Blockley (USA) *Ian Williams* a51
2 b c Johannesburg(USA) —Saintly Manner (USA) (St Jovite (USA))
6662^5 6950^7

Blu Delta Force *V Caruso* 61
4 b h Zafonic(USA) —Carillon Miss (USA) (The Minstrel (CAN))
$6363a^{15}$

Blue Alabama (IRE) *Seamus G O'Donnell* 54
3 b f Ashkalani(IRE) —Alabama (IRE) (Bluebird (USA))
6540^{11}

Blue Army (IRE) *Jane Southcombe* a46 64
3 ch g Titus Livius(FR) —Trojan Tale (USA) (Critique (USA))
710^5 720^{13} 964^4 1352^8 2188^{12} 2465^9 2940^5 3650^{13} (Dead)

Blue Aura (IRE) *R Charlton* 81
3 b g Elnadim(USA) —Absent Beauty (IRE) (Dancing Dissident (USA))
1208^5 1679^3 2329^7 2609^5 3226^{13}(4659) 5148^8 5627^7

Blue Away (IRE) *S Kirk* a33 70
8 b g Blues Traveller(IRE) —Lomond Heights (IRE) (Lomond (USA))
1213^8 1690^{10} 2460^7 $4166a^{11}$ 4777^5 4898^4 5201^4

Blue Bajan (IRE) *Andrew Turnell* a108 103
4 b g Montjeu(IRE) —Gentle Thoughts (Darshaan)
1357^2 2169^3 (2231) 3093^5 (4147) 4810^4 5374^7(5505) 5675^2 6516^2

Blue Bamboo *Mrs A J Perrett* 66
2 b f Green Desert(USA) —Silver Bandana (USA) (Silver Buck (USA))
2957^8 4207^6 5206^4 6024^4

Blue Beacon *K A Ryan* a59 37
3 b f Fantastic Light(USA) —Blue Duster (USA) (Danzig (USA))
70^2 551^3 5036^{11} 5902^8 6193^{11} 6380^3 6647^6 6693^5 6899^{11}

Bluebelle Dancer (IRE) *W R Muir* a65 67
2 b f Danehill Dancer(IRE) —Spring To Light (USA) (Blushing Groom (FR))
1896^7 4559^7 5237^3 6310^7

Blueberry Forest (IRE) *P Hirschberger* 96
8 br h Charnwood Forest(IRE) —Abstraction (Rainbow Quest (USA))
$5856a^5$ $6248a^7$

Blueberry Tart (IRE) *J M P Eustace* a69 76
4 b m Bluebird(USA) —Tart (FR) (Warning)
106^{12} 185^9

Blue Blue Sky (IRE) *Y De Nicolay* 102
3 ch f Anabaa(USA) —Blue Fern (USA) (Woodman (USA))
$773a^6$ $1789a^3$

Bluebok *J M Bradley* a61 89
5 ch g Indian Ridge—Blue Sirocco (Bluebird (USA))
967^{10} 1047^{4} 1643^{2} 1856^{11} 2182^{4}(2449) 2635^{5} 3027^{4} 3449^{2} (3625) 3938^{5} 4085^{4}4360^{5} 4811^{5} 5148^{4} (5275) 5832^{5}

Blue Charm *S Kirk* a77+
2 b g Averti(IRE) —Exotic Forest (Dominion)
6290^{3} (6710) 6881^{3}

Blue Collar Jack (AUS) *K Keys* 94
5 ch g Perugino(USA) —Mellow Chateau (AUS) (Northern Chateau (USA))
6455a^{7}

Blue Coral (IRE) *D K Weld* 85
2 br c Grand Lodge(USA) —Pharmacist (IRE) (Machiavellian (USA))
5466a^{15} 6262a^{5}

Blue Corrig (IRE) *Joseph Crowley* 106
6 gr g Darnay—Myristica (IRE) (Doyoun)
205a^{14} 371a^{11} 435a^{8}

Blue Dakota (IRE) *J S Bolger* 106
4 b h Namid—Touraya (Tap On Wood)
1158a^{12}

Blue Damask (USA) *A Fabre* 109
3 br c Rahy(USA) —Blush Damask (USA) (Green Dancer (USA))
5146a^{4} 5779a^{12}

Blue Danielle (IRE) *A D Brown* a20
3 ch f Blue Ocean(USA) —Imco Lucent (ITY) (Barn Five South (USA))
70^{12} 165^{13}286^{8}

Blue Echo *M A Jarvis* 96
2 b f Kyllachy—Mazarine Blue (Bellypha)
2439^{5} 4657^{2} (5264) 5626^{3} (6201)

Blue Empire (IRE) *C R Dore* a71 72d
5 b g Second Empire(IRE) —Paleria (USA) (Zilzal (USA))
(8) 77^{5} 381^{7}596^{4} 764^{10}985^{11} 1265^{6} 1644^{9}2137^{4} 2541^{2} 2947^{3}3339^{6} 3523^{4} 3820^{3} (3947) 4390^{8} 4831^{9}5269^{12} 6595^{13} 6747^{10}6897^{2} 6934^{11}

Bluegrass Cat (USA) *T Pletcher* a125
3 b c Storm Cat(USA) —She's A Winner (USA) (A.P. Indy (USA))
1498a^{2} 2477a^{2}

Blue Grouse (USA) *Saeed Bin Suroor* a66 70
3 rg f Maria's Mon(USA) —Enrich (USA) (Dynaformer (USA))
202a^{8}

Blue Hedges *H J Collingridge* a67 61
4 b h Polish Precedent(USA) —Palagene (Generous (IRE))
111^{8} (185) 379^{3}461^{2} 972^{5} 1422^{12}2181^{11} 3934^{5} 4307^{2}5072^{7} 5354^{4} 5725^{9} (6378) 6462^{3} (6621)

Blue Hills *P W Hiatt* a65 58
5 br g Vettori(IRE) —Slow Jazz (USA) (Chief's Crown (USA))
28^{2} 129^{2}246^{3} 270^{2}346^{4} (443) 491^{5} 570^{2}643^{11} 2140^{9}3454^{6} 6995^{10}

Blue Java *H Morrison* a61 83
5 ch g Bluegrass Prince(IRE) —Java Bay (Statoblest)
1570^{2} (1802) 1932^{4} (2606) 3928^{13} 4706^{4} 5345^{8}5591^{7} 5896^{12} 6221^{5}

Blue Jet (USA) *R M Whitaker* 44
2 b g Black Minnaloushe(USA) —Clickety Click (USA) (Sovereign Dancer (USA))
5814^{11} 6270^{7}

Blue Knight (IRE) *P Howling* a79 72
7 ch g Bluebird(USA) —Fer De Lance (IRE) (Diesis)
1^{5} 51^{2}(164) 224^{5}316^{6} 639^{11}719^{10} 949^{11} 1151^{9}1504^{14} 2780^{11} 3003^{4} 3817^{13} 4054^{5}4067^{3} 4258^{5} 4324^{6} 4401^{4} 5062^{5}5620^{10} 5878^{8} 5970^{7}6681^{7} 6922^{10}6990^{8}

Blue Ksar (FR) *Saeed Bin Suroor* 114
3 b c Anabaa(USA) —Delicieuse Lady (Trempolino (USA))
1488^{4} 2804^{11} 5142^{2} (5376) (6218)

Blue Line *M Madgwick* a64 66
4 gr m Bluegrass Prince(IRE) —Out Line (Beveled (USA))
902^{5} 1311^{5} 1802^{7}2317^{4} 2574^{4} 3095^{8}3933^{7} 4363^{9} 4795^{6} 5474^{9}

Blue Madeira *Mrs L Stubbs* a77 80
2 b g Auction House(USA) —Queen Of Scotland (IRE) (Mujadil (USA))
1342^{7} (1945) 2586^{2} 3641^{3}4813^{5}

Blue Maeve *A D Brown* a76 81d
6 b g Blue Ocean(USA) —Louisville Belle (IRE) (Ahonoora)
209^{11} 407^{3}1235^{8} 1794^{5} 2376^{2} 2928^{6} 2949^{5}(3171) (3718) (4258) (4352) 4771^{3} 5148^{3} 5493^{11} 5749^{13}5791^{15} 6239^{5} 6478^{8}

Blue Mak *D Shaw* 27
2 b g Makbul—Washm (USA) (Diesis)
3157^{12} 3457^{12}4115^{10}

Blue Mistral (IRE) *W J Knight* 64
2 ch f Spinning World(USA) —Blue Sirocco (Bluebird (USA))
2957^{11} 3700^{10} 4053^{8} 4588^{4} 5262^{12}5419^{4} 5747^{9}

Blue Monday *R Charlton* 120
5 b g Darshaan—Lunda (IRE) (Soviet Star (USA))
1098^{2} (1976) (2597a) 2803^{4} 3314^{3} 4679^{3} (5342)6126a^{4}

Blue Monkey (IRE) *M L W Bell* a71 72
2 b c Orpen(USA) —Resurgence (Polar Falcon (USA))
1284^{3} 2178^{7} 5784^{4}

Blue Moon Hitman (IRE) *R Brotherton* a51 59
5 ch g Blue Ocean(USA) —Miss Kookaburra (IRE) (Namaqualand (USA))
(212) 317^{6} 401^{10}951^{9} 1195^{11}1396^{4} 1762^{9}

Blue On Blues (ARG) *S Seemar* a108 102
5 ch g Lode(USA) —Blue Baby Blue (ARG) (Forever Sparkle (USA))
154a^{4} 369a^{2} 435a^{2}511a^{4} 621a^{4}

Blue Opal *Miss S E Hall* a54 62
4 b m Bold Edge—Second Affair (IRE) (Pursuit Of Love)
131^{6} 549^{5}635^{2} 939^{7}1256^{5} 2242^{10} (6279) 6551^{6} 6795^{2}6972^{6}

Blue Patrick *P A Blockley* a82 70
6 gr g Wizard King—Great Intent (Aragon)
50^{3} (214) 412^{6}498^{4} 640^{2}1051^{14} 1207^{15}

Blue Power (IRE) *K R Burke* a44 49
5 b g Zieten(USA) —La Miserable (USA) (Miswaki (USA))
24^{2} 130^{3}146^{9} 260^{4}388^{8} 686^{6} (Dead)

Blue Quiver (IRE) *C A Horgan* a63 44
6 b g Bluebird(USA) —Paradise Forum (Prince Sabo)
73^{8} 163^{3}6590^{13} 6743^{7}6977^{10}

Blue Rocket (IRE) *T J Pitt* 93
2 ch f Rock Of Gibraltar(IRE) —Champagne Girl (Robellino (USA))
(4323) 4762^{2} 5654^{9}

Blue Shotgun (JPN) *K Take* 111
7 b h Sakura Bakushin O(JPN) —Ogi Blue Venus (JPN) (Super Creek (JPN))
5717a^{10} 6850a^{14}

Blues In The Night (IRE) *P J Makin* a76 87
3 ch g Bluebird(USA) —Always True (USA) (Geiger Counter (USA))
1844^{13} 4045^{2} (4296) 4707^{2}5377^{2} 6221^{8}

Blue Sky Thinking (IRE) *K R Burke* a108 100
7 b g Danehill Dancer(IRE) —Lauretta Blue (IRE) (Bluebird (USA))
1017^{10} 1281^{3}

Blue Spinnaker (IRE) *M W Easterby* 108
7 b g Bluebird(USA) —Suedoise (Kris)
728^{13} 865^{3} (1775) 2803^{10} 3552^{14} 4711^{8}5188^{7} 5675^{13} 6219^{11} 6337^{16}

Blue Tomato *J M Bradley* a76 97
5 b g Orpen(USA) —Ocean Grove (IRE) (Fairy King (USA))
1432^{3} 1570^{8} 1939^{10}2449^{8} 2590^{2} (2813) (3041) (3217) 3486^{2} 3956^{3}4101^{7} 4430^{5} 5044^{9} 5274^{3} 5420^{5}5667^{11}

Blue Tornade (JPN) *Kaneo Ikezoe* 104
5 ch h Jade Robbery(USA) —Blue Savanna (JPN) (Symboli Rudolf (JPN))
1329a^{17}

Blue Train (IRE) *Jonjo O'Neill* a87+ 81
4 b g Sadler's Wells(USA) —Igreja (ARG) (Southern Halo (USA))
946^{13}

Blue Trojan (IRE) *S Kirk* a90 98
6 b g Inzar(USA) —Roman Heights (IRE) (Head For Heights)
946^{3} 1043^{5} 2114^{10} 2510^{12} (2603) 3020^{4}3223^{5} (3679) 3973^{3} 4535^{11}

Blu Manruna *J Akehurst* a61 65
3 ch c Zaha(CAN) —Vrennan (Suave Dancer (USA))
1951^{9} 2620^{5} 3212^{13} 3667^{5} 4076^{3}4332^{5} 4591^{4} 5130^{12} 5590^{11} 6021^{9}6439^{11} 6687^{4}6918^{2}

Blushing Hilary (IRE) *Miss J A Camacho* a74 75
3 ch f City On A Hill(USA) —Trinida (Jaazeiro (USA))
1307^{3} 1732^{3} 2124^{4}3001^{4} 3359^{5} 5284^{3} 5510^{5} 5875^{4}

Blushing King (FR) *J-L Guillochon* 92
4 b h Blush Rambler(USA) —Storm Warning (Tumble Wind)
6786a^{7}

Blushing Light (USA) *M A Magnusson* a62 63
3 bb g Mt. Livermore(USA) —Swan River (USA) (Hennessy (USA))
2343^{10} 2859^{5} 3050^{3}3410^{8}

Blushing Prince (IRE) *R C Guest* a42 46
8 b g Priolo(USA) —Eliade (IRE) (Flash Of Steel)
3352^{9} 4568^{5} 6954^{6}

Blushing Russian (IRE) *J M Bradley* a51 48
4 b g Fasliyev(USA) —Ange Rouge (Priolo (USA))
43^{8} 143^{12}400^{4} 440^{11}6799^{11} 6970^{5}

Blushing Thief (USA) *W Jarvis* a85 45
3 ch c Cat Thief(USA) —Blushing Princess (USA) (Crafty Prospector (USA))
16^{6} 191^{6}418^{3} (551) (725) 1091^{15} 2756^{5}2981^{2} 3403^{9}

Blythe Knight (IRE) *J J Quinn* a107 107
6 ch g Selkirk(USA) —Blushing Barada (USA) (Blushing Groom (FR))
(728) 1129^{11} 1489^{3} 1806^{4} 2742^{29} 4739^{4}5357^{3} 5675^{12}

Blythe Spirit *R A Fahey* a54 55
7 b g Bahamian Bounty—Lithe Spirit (IRE) (Dancing Dissident (USA))
196^{8} 320^{5}401^{4} 6464^{3}6533^{6} 6708^{3}6922^{9} 6974^{6}

Boanerges (IRE) *J M Bradley* a63 66
9 br g Caerleon(USA) —Sea Siren (Slip Anchor)
146^{4} (179) 260^{3}397^{10} 524^{2}679^{10} 772^{4}782^{2} 872^{5}(1150) (1310) 2136^{11} (2376) 2792^{5}2955^{4} 3330^{10}

Bob And John (USA) *B Baffert* a118
3 br c Seeking The Gold(USA) —Minister's Melody (USA) (Deputy Minister (CAN))
1498a^{17} 2477a^{8}

Bobansheil (IRE) *J S Wainwright* 61
2 b f Dushyantor(USA) —Bobanlyn (IRE) (Dance Of Life (USA))
4829^{6} 5187^{9} 5552^{6} 5720^{7}

Bob Baileys *P R Chamings* a49 34
4 b g Mister Baileys—Bob's Princess (Bob's Return (IRE))
350^{9} 527^{6}787^{5} 937^{3}(1197) 1462^{2}1723^{8} 3386^{9}

Bobbish *N A Callaghan* a65 78
2 b g Best Of The Bests(IRE) —Bella Bianca (IRE) (Barathea (IRE))
2619^{13} 3210^{6} 3531^{4}3800^{3} (3902) 4178^{2}

Bobby Charles *Dr J D Scargill* a87 86
5 ch g Polish Precedent(USA) —Dina Line (USA) (Diesis)
140^{3} 463^{3}867^{7} 2201^{13} 2540^{5} 6468^{4}6744^{3}

Bobby Kennard *J A Osborne* a63 60
7 b g Bobinski—Midnight Break (Night Shift (USA))
55^{5} (284)

Bobby Rose *D K Ivory* a71+ 67
3 b g Sanglamore(USA) —Grown At Rowan (Gabitat)
191^{7} 372^{8}479^{4} 590^{4}796^{3} 969^{4} 1825^{2} 2095^{9} 2576^{2}3011^{12} 3406^{3}6842^{2} 6913^{11}

Bobering *B P J Baugh* a49 7
6 b g Bob's Return(IRE) —Ring The Rafters (Batshoof)
(6702) 6980^{5}

Bo Bid (USA) *A Laird* a100
6 ch h Helmsman(USA) —I'm Italian (USA) (Alleged (USA))
277a^{4}

Bobski (IRE) *G A Huffer* a89 89
4 b g Victory Note(USA) —Vivid Impression (Cure The Blues (USA))
476^{6} 798^{3} 1494^{3}1692^{8} 2147^{7} 4338^{5} 4535^{7} 6352^{6}(6461)

Bobsleigh *H S Howe* a63 61
7 b g Robellino(USA) —Do Run Run (Commanche Run)
1339^{4} 1690^{6} 2219^{10}3269^{6} 3723^{6} 3952^{5} 4282^{6} 4530^{7}4996^{3} 5235^{4} 5564^{5}5910^{10}

Bobs Pride (IRE) *D K Weld* 107
4 b g Marju(IRE) —Vyatka (Lion Cavern (USA))
1171a^{5} 4031a^{14} 4187a^{15}

Bob's Your Uncle *J G Portman* a54 71
3 br g Zilzal(USA) —Bob's Princess (Bob's Return (IRE))
538^{4} 859^{9}(945) 1221^{4} (2352) (2933) 3439^{4} 4005^{9} 4432^{2}4702^{13} 5628^{9} 5868^{8}

Boca Dancer (IRE) *Kevin Prendergast* 100+
2 b f Indian Ridge—Rain Dancer (IRE) (Sadler's Wells (USA))
(6113a)

Boccassini (GER) *M Rulec* 108
2 br f Artan(IRE) —Bella Monica (GER) (Big Shuffle (USA))
3132a^{2} (3777a) 4644a^{7}

Bodden Bay *Miss Gay Kelleway* a68 61
4 b g Cayman Kai(IRE) —Badger Bay (IRE) (Salt Dome (USA))
127^{7} 339^{2}407^{2} 514^{9}(2700) 3389^{3} 3682^{7} 4198^{12}5243^{13} 5631^{9} (5885) (6477) (6638) 6721^{13}

Bodes Galaxy (IRE) *N P Littmoden* a79 104
2 b c Marju(IRE) —Prima Centauri (USA) (Distant View (USA))
2130^{5} 2572^{4} (2967) (3372) 4099^{2}4712^{3} 5017^{7} 5802^{7}

Bodfari Dream *M Mullineaux* a11 2
5 ch m Environment Friend—Al Reet (IRE) (Alzao (USA))
103^{8} 615^{8}

Bogaz (IRE) *Mrs H Sweeting* a40 44
4 b g Rossini(USA) —Fastnet (Forzando)
492^{14} 882^{16} 1568^{11}1753^{11} 4389^{4} 4585^{12} 6237^{5}6281^{9} 6726^{9}

Bogside Katie *G M Moore* a50 50
2 b f Hunting Lion(IRE) —Enchanting Eve (Risk Me (FR))
6821^{5} 6925^{6}

Boisdale (IRE) *P S Felgate* a39 45
8 b g Common Grounds—Alstomeria (Petoski)
126^{7} 196^{10}411^{7} 691^{10}1913^{8} 6550^{13}6727^{10} 6962^{13}

Bolckow *J T Stimpson* a67 50
3 b g Marju(IRE) —Stamatina (Warning)
1230^{4} 1564^{9} 2128^{5} 2795^{3}3375^{7} 3790^{5} 4297^{6} 5285^{5} 5485^{4}5683^{6} 5862^{5} (6302) 6754^{8}6936^{3}

Bold Abbott (USA) *Mrs A J Perrett* 82
2 b c Mizzen Mast(USA) —Ms Isadora (USA) (Miswaki (USA))
3701^{9} 4103^{7} 4333^{2} 4572^{3}

Bold Act (IRE) *H Candy* a72 91+
4 b g Brave Act—Banco Solo (Distant Relative)
1401^{5} 1830^{3} 2510^{2}3048^{2} (4209) 4810^{3} 5810^{2}

Bold Adventure *W J Musson* 49
2 ch g Arkadian Hero(USA) —Impatiente (USA) (Vaguely Noble)
3976^{13} 4295^{11} 4920^{11}

Bold Alaska (IRE) *E A L Dunlop* 90
3 b g Cape Cross(IRE) —Dramatic Entry (IRE) (Persian Bold)
(1674) 1990^{6}

Bold Apache (IRE) *A P O'Brien* 79
2 ch c Rock Of Gibraltar(IRE) —Velvet Moon (IRE) (Shaadi (USA))
3962a^{10}

Bold Argument (IRE) *Mrs P N Dutfield* a73 78
3 ch g Shinko Forest(IRE) —Ivory Bride (Domynsky)
916^{5} 1646^{4} 2247^{2}2650^{14} (3368) 3795^{6} 4378^{11} 5377^{15} 5872^{15}

Bold Arrow *B J Llewellyn*
4 bb g Bold Fort—Jubilee Belle (Bell Ringer)
2481^{7}

Bold Bobby Be (IRE) *J L Dunlop* 62
2 br c Bob Back(USA) —Fantasy Girl (IRE) (Marju (IRE))
5659^{11} 5918^{5}

Bold Brownie *Miss Z C Davison* a26 6
4 b m Almaty(IRE) —Polly So Bold (Never So Bold)
2573^{11} 3411^{9} 4755^{14}

Bold Cheverak *Mrs C A Dunnett* a67 71
4 b g Bold Edge—Curlew Calling (IRE) (Pennine Walk)
654^{9} 798^{9} 986^{9}1315^{7} 1618^{7} 2590^{8} 3389^{12}5097^{12}

Bold Cross (IRE) *E G Bevan* 70
3 b g Cape Cross(IRE) —Machikane Akaiito (IRE) (Persian Bold)
1049^{11} 1416^{5} 1851^{12} 2301^{5} 2583^{13}

Bold Crusader *Saeed Bin Suroor* a97 79
3 b c Cape Cross(IRE) —Tee Cee (Lion Cavern (USA))
6424^{3}

Bold Demand *R Bouresly* a98 91
12 b h Rainbow Quest(USA) —Dafrah (USA) (Danzig (USA))
277a^{6} 438a^{8} 495a^{15}

Bold Diktator *Tom Dascombe* a74 80
4 b g Diktat—Madam Bold (Never So Bold)
946^{10} 1302^{9} (2482) (2860) 3113^{6} 3712^{7} 4108^{5}5047^{6} 5345^{18} 5778^{11}(6993)

Bold Finch (FR) *K O Cunningham-Brown*
4 b g Valanour(IRE) —Eagle's Nest (FR) (King Of Macedon)
409^{9} 692^{11}4048^{11}

Bold Havana *T T Clement*
4 b m Bold Edge—Isle Of Sodor (Cyrano De Bergerac)
195^{11}

Bold Haze *Miss S E Hall* 62
4 ch g Bold Edge—Melody Park (Music Boy)
2661^{19} 3217^{11} 3670^{4} 3996^{13}4361^{2} 5062^{7} 5885^{2} 6300^{14}

Bold Indian (IRE) *I Semple* a71 68
2 b g Indian Danehill(IRE) —Desert Gift (Green Desert (USA))
6504^{3} 6751^{2}6963^{3}

Boldinor *N E Berry* a61 69d
3 b g Inchinor—Rambold (Rambo Dancer (CAN))
(449) 725^{5} 1122^{9} 2576^{5}3055^{8} 3349^{2} 3682^{8}5568^{14} 5953^{13} 6193^{12}6288^{13} 6436^{14}

Bold Love *J Balding* a42 48
3 ch f Bold Edge—Noor El Houdah (IRE) (Fayruz)
646^{9} 861^{7}1829^{9} 2192^{7} (4050) 4769^{13} 6306^{5}6538^{8} 6727^{8}6794^{5} 6958^{2}

Bold Maggie *J A Pickering* a49 48
4 ch m Bold Edge—Vera's First (IRE) (Exodal (USA))
179^{12} 360^{10}1397^{10}

Bold Marc (IRE) *K R Burke* a88 86
4 b g Bold Fact(USA) —Zara's Birthday (IRE) (Waajib)
798^{6} 1125^{3} 1496^{7} 1856^{4} 2449^{3}2852^{8} 4453^{8} 4834^{4} 5081^{7} 5384^{6}5861^{4} (5961) 6160^{2} 6273^{2} 6424^{2}6502^{5}

Bold Medicean *T P Tate* 59
3 b g Medicean—Bird Of Time (IRE) (Persian Bold)
1684^{10} 2411^{7} 2829^{6} 3609^{7}

Bold Minstrel (IRE) *M Quinn* a84 84
4 br g Bold Fact(USA) —Ponda Rosa (IRE) (Case Law)
2624^{5} 3447^{12} 3744^{9} (4208) 4952^{6} 5275^{3}5532^{9} 6446^{3}

Bold Nevison (IRE) *B Smart* a58 47
2 b c Danehill Dancer(IRE) —La Pieta (IRE) (Spectrum (IRE))
5614^{9} 6270^{8} 6644^{6}6891^{7}

Bold Phoenix (IRE) *B J Curley* a46 50
5 b g Dr Fong(USA) —Subya (Night Shift (USA))
386^{2} (468) (940) 5740^{13}6294^{10} 6484^{14}6899^{9}

Bold Pioneer (USA) *C P Morlock* a48 23
3 b g Pioneering(USA) —Uber Alyce (USA) (Bold Forbes (USA))
112^{8} 372^{10}2352^{13} 2814^{13}

Bold Saxon (IRE) *M D I Usher* a70 64
2 ch c Desert Sun—Sirdhana (Selkirk (USA))
5890^{7} 6290^{5} 6808^{2}

Bold Start (USA) *K McPeek* a97
2 br c Jump Start(USA) —Dorky (USA) (Flying Paster (USA))
5823a^{6}

Bold Tiger (IRE) *Miss Tracy Waggott* a48 50
3 b g Bold Fact(USA) —Heart Of The Ocean (IRE) (Soviet Lad (USA))
796^{14} 1497^{11} 3138^{5} 3329^{13} 3397^{5}3759^{8} 4057^{12}

Bold Trump *Mrs N S Evans* a51 47
5 b g First Trump—Blue Nile (IRE) (Bluebird (USA))
41^{11} 162^{4}358^{6} 526^{5}939^{5} (1572) 3382^{5} 4282^{9} 6957^{3}

Bollin Billy *R Brotherton* a68 56
4 b g Mind Games—Bollin Ann (Anshan)
(22) 67^{4} 169^{8} (Dead)

Bollin Derek *T D Easterby* a52+ 84+
3 gr c Silver Patriarch(IRE) —Bollin Magdalene (Teenoso (USA))
859^{2} (1221) (1424) (1867) 2102^{2} 4612^{2}5533^{3} (5815)

Bollin Dolly *T D Easterby* 76
3 ch f Bien Bien(USA) —Bollin Roberta (Bob's Return (IRE))
1252^{5} 1598^{6} 3714^{2} 4118^{3} 4402^{3}5284^{5} 5727^{3} 6008^{6}

Bollin Edward *K A Ryan* a51 73
7 b g Timeless Times(USA) —Bollin Harriet (Lochnager)
(1683) (2164) 2541^{6} 2947^{7} 3158^{6}6417^{11} 6624^{7}6814^{7}

Bollin Felix *T D Easterby* 51
2 br c Generous(IRE) —Bollin Magdalene (Teenoso (USA))
3758^{6} 4018^{6} 4566^{6} 5597^{9}

Bollin Fergus *T D Easterby* 68
2 br c Vettori(IRE) —Bollin Harriet (Lochnager)
5059^{4} 5364^{6} 5615^{8}

Bollin Fiona *T D Easterby* 26
2 ch f Silver Patriarch(IRE) —Bollin Nellie (Rock Hopper)
5025^{10} 5536^{9}

Bollin Franny *T D Easterby* 72
2 br c Bertolini(USA) —Bollin Ann (Anshan)
1491^{5} 2281^{2} (2759) 3476^{5} 4088^{6} 4377^{6}4946^{5}

Bollin Freddie *T D Easterby* 41
2 ch g Golden Snake(USA) —Bollin Roberta (Bob's Return (IRE))
2409^{12} 3187^{4} 4466^{9}

Bollin Michael *T D Easterby* a67 72+
4 b h Celtic Swing—Bollin Zola (Alzao (USA))
584^{7} 653^{4}977^{10} 1288^{9} 1531^{5} (1852) 2025^{9} 2794^{10}

Bollin Thomas *R Allan* 77
8 b g Alhijaz—Bollin Magdalene (Teenoso (USA))
990^{5} 1033^{8} 1610^{6}

Bollywood (IRE) *J J Bridger* a50 51
3 ch g Indian Rocket—La Fille De Cirque (Cadeaux Genereux)
31^{2} (139) 211^{7}342^{6} 554^{6}839^{7} 969^{7} 1567^{13}1963^{8} 2316^{10} 2609^{9}3667^{7} 3873^{10} 3932^{4} 4363^{6} 4658^{4}4690^{9} 5291^{11} 6236^{2}6370^{6} 6616^{4}6724^{8} 6802^{9}6854^{12}

Bolodenka (IRE) *R A Fahey* a73 105
4 b g Soviet Star(USA) —My-Lorraine (IRE) (Mac's Imp (USA))
3020^{2} 3413^{8} (4094a) (4187a) 4739^{2} 5188^{4} 5675^{24}

Bolshoi Ballet *Miss J E Foster* a42 49
8 b g Dancing Spree(USA) —Broom Isle (Damister (USA))
283[10] 414[9]2935[5] 3135[2] 3350[7]6495[4] 6685[7]6797[7]

Bolton Hall (IRE) *R A Fahey* 79
4 b g Imperial Ballet(IRE) —Muneera (USA) (Green Dancer (USA))
992[15] 1186[10] 2299[10] 2640[9] 2947[13]3331[7] 4186a[3] 4454[2] (4476) 4518[4] 4953[5]5320[5]

Boluisce (IRE) *M H Tompkins* a53
3 ch f Zilzal(USA) —No Islands (Lomond (USA))
291[9] 479[7]

Bombardier Bush (IRE) *J L Dunlop* 68+
3 b g Desert Prince(IRE) —Fantasy Girl (IRE) (Marju (IRE))
1845[5]

Bomber Command (USA) *J W Hills* a98+ 70
3 b g Stravinsky(USA) —Parish Manor (USA) (Waquoit (USA))
1016[3] 1617[5] 2177[11]5504[12] 5739[6] 6461[4](6580) 6671[2](6830) 6915[3]

Bomber Pilot (IRE) *E Lellouche* 94
2 b c Numerous(USA) —Blue Cloud (IRE) (Nashwan (USA))
4859a[6]

Bo McGinty (IRE) *R A Fahey* a73 90
5 ch g Fayruz—Georges Park Lady (IRE) (Tirol)
413[7] 719[6] 846[11]1042[9] 1285[14] 1487[7] 1858[5] 2194[4]2450[10] 2683[2] (2946) 3281[4] 3561a[3] 3972[7]4360[6] 4468[7] 5333[13] 5532[4] 6009[6]

Bona Dea (GER) *G L Moore* a28
3 br f Tertullian(USA) —Bejaria (GER) (Konigsstuhl (GER))
326[9]

Bonate (IRE) *B Grizzetti*
2 b c Spectrum(IRE) —Rambo Candy (Rambo Dancer (CAN))
6407a[3]

Bond Angel Eyes *G R Oldroyd* 65
3 b f Dr Fong(USA) —Speedybird (IRE) (Danehill (USA))
2109[4] 2399[9] 2896[13] 4402[4] 4835[7]5370[15] 5637[10]

Bond Becks (IRE) *B Smart* a44 64d
6 ch g Tagula(IRE) —At Amal (IRE) (Astronef)
2928[3] 3171[10] 3608[4] (3781) 4091[2] 4523[9]5631[13] 5752[12]

Bond Boy *B Smart* a86 93
9 b g Piccolo—Arabellajill (Aragon)
1031[6] 1285[9] (1856) 2021[3] 2450[7] 3567[4]4085[5] 4682[13] 4771[4] 6009[5] 6320[6]

Bond Casino *G R Oldroyd* 55
2 b f Kyllachy—Songsheet (Dominion)
4510[5] 5237[7]

Bond City (IRE) *B Smart* a97 111
4 b g Trans Island—Where's Charlotte (Sure Blade (USA))
2227[2] 2450[11] 2720[25] 3520[5] 4128[10](4875) 5182[15] 5443[4] 5921[2]

Bond Cruz *G R Oldroyd* a52 46
3 b g King's Best(USA) —Arabis (Arazi (USA))
1259[7] 1501[8] 2198[10]2529[15] 3378[P]

Bond Diamond *P T Midgley* a67 71
9 gr g Prince Sabo—Alsiba (Northfields (USA))
1073[2] 1276[4] 1683[6]2170[2] 2299[4] 2627[15] 2831[2] 3298[8]3500[2] 3789[4] 4116[3] 4602[12] 5320[9]

Bond Free Spirit (IRE) *G R Oldroyd* 53
3 br f Shinko Forest(IRE) —Sawaki (Song)
3285[7] 3909[6] 4155[4] 5243[11]

Bond Millennium *B Smart* a70 71
8 ch g Piccolo—Farmer's Pet (Sharrood (USA))
41[9] 683[7] (Dead)

Bond Platinum Club *B Smart* 57
2 ch f Pivotal—Highland Rowena (Royben)
5753[3]

Bond Playboy *G R Oldroyd* a73+ 62
6 b g Piccolo—Highest Ever (FR) (Highest Honor (FR))
1041[7] 1220[9] 2020[8] 2792[3]3052[2] 3459[7]5635[13] 6288[2] 6465[5]6572[4] 6739[3](6990)

Bond Puccini *G R Oldroyd* a48 61
4 b g Piccolo—Baileys By Name (Nomination)
5834[7] 5969[5] 6308[9]

Bond Sea Breeze (IRE) *G R Oldroyd* 22
3 b f Namid—Gold Prospector (IRE) (Spectrum (IRE))
4611[9] 4948[11] 5363[11]

Bond Silver Strand (IRE) *P D Niven* 14
3 b f Trans Island—Miss Game Plan (IRE) (Hector Protector (USA))
5368[14] 5598[11] 5727[10]

Bonecrusher *M Al Muhairi* a105 114
7 b g Revoque(IRE) —Eurolink Mischief (Be My Chief (USA))
437a[2]

Bongoali *Mrs C A Dunnett* a45 55
4 b m Fraam—Stride Home (Absalom)
5033[11] 5927[11]6305[6] 6373[3]6628[7]

Bongo Bello (DEN) *T Christensen* 96
5 b h Asaasy(USA) —Sypha (FR) (Saumarez)
4189a[7]

Bonnabee (IRE) *C F Wall* a67 65
4 b m Benny The Dip(USA) —Samhat Mtoto (Mtoto)
(111)

Bonne D'Argent (IRE) *J R Boyle* 74
2 b f Almutawakel—Petite-D-Argent (Noalto)
6215[4]

Bonne De Fleur *B Smart* a75 83
5 b m Whittingham(IRE) —L'Estable Fleurie (IRE) (Common Grounds)
362[5] 569[9]954[5] 1125[4] (1448) 1662[16]2194[8] 4135[3] 4468[11] 5286[7] 6223[4]6452[4] 6585[2]6858[8]

Bonnet O'Bonnie *J Mackie* 49
2 br f Makbul—Parkside Prospect (Piccolo)
4731[9]

Bon News (IRE) *J S Bolger* 74
2 ch f Spectrum(IRE) —Princess Nutley (IRE) (Mujtahid (USA))
5850a[4]

Bonnie Belle *J R Boyle* 61
3 b f Imperial Ballet(IRE) —Reel Foyle (USA) (Irish River (FR))
4776[6] 5566[10] 6021[4]

Bonnie Prince Blue *B W Hills* 89
3 ch g Tipsy Creek(USA) —Heart So Blue (Dilum (USA))
1115[4] 1832[5] 2774[30] 4298[4] 4634[25]5150[4] 5504[7] 5833[10]

Bon Nuit (IRE) *G Wragg* a81 105
4 b m Night Shift(USA) —Pray (IRE) (Priolo (USA))
1015[8] 1506[4] 2740[7]4482[7]

Bonny Scotland (IRE) *I W McInnes* 38
2 b f Redback—Muckross Park (Nomination)
1082[12] 2878[3] 3358[12] 3605[7] 3801[8]4115[6] 4334[8] 6951[12]

Bonus (IRE) *G A Butler* a104 102
6 b g Cadeaux Genereux—Khamseh (Thatching)
(238) 1667[5] 3125a[2]

Bon Viveur *R Hannon* 75
3 b g Mozart(IRE) —Fantazia (Zafonic (USA))
1642[7] 2065[8] (2301) 2608[3] 3589[4] (3798) 4490[4]4784[6] 5152[3]

Boo *K R Burke* a103 98
4 b g Namaqualand(USA) —Violet (IRE) (Mukaddamah (USA))
116[2] 222[5]377[4] 572[6]629[6] 666[8]1017[7] 3218[10] 3552[3]3929[5] 4359[8] 5188[11] 5374[20] 6997[5]

Boogie Board *M J Attwater* a50
2 b f Tobougg(IRE) —Royal Gift (Cadeaux Genereux)
2461[5]

Boogie Dancer *H S Howe* a65 65
2 b f Tobougg(IRE) —Bolero (Rainbow Quest (USA))
2456[13] 3545[7] 4084[13] 4866[3] 5676[16]6322[3]

Boogie Magic *T Keddy* a49 51
6 b m Wizard King—Dalby Dancer (Bustiki)
291[6] 417[6]579[9] (1395) 1723[4] 1910[5]2510[11] 3153[10] 3263[9]

Boogie Street *R Hannon* 114d
5 b h Compton Place—Tart And A Half (Distant Relative)
1485[11] 2722[26] 3312[10] 3709[9] 5087[3]

Bookiesindex Boy *J R Jenkins* a73 55
2 b c Piccolo—United Passion (Emarati (USA))
1510[6] 2315[16] 2878[5] 3407[3]3734[14] 3994[DSQ] 5245[2]5735[5] (6255) 6427[2]

Bookman (IRE) *P C Haslam* a61 59
4 b g Barathea(IRE) —Literary (Woodman (USA))
289[5] 460[7]1185[7] 1591[12]

Book Of Days (IRE) *R M Beckett* a39 33
3 b f Barathea(IRE) —Beeper The Great (USA) (Whadjathink (USA))
6019[9] 6450[7] 6792[8]

Book Of Facts (FR) *M Johnston* a80 45
2 ch g Machiavellian(USA) —Historian (IRE) (Pennekamp (USA))
6173[9] (6447) 6634[3]

Book Of Kings (USA) *A Laird* a105 115
5 b h Kingmambo(USA) —Honfleur (IRE) (Sadler's Wells (USA))
370a[10] 512a[11]

Book Of Music (IRE) *Sir Michael Stoute* 107
3 b c Sadler's Wells(USA) —Novelette (Darshaan)
2030[4] 3255[2] 4791[9] 5494[3] (5808) 6336[3]

Boom Or Bust (IRE) *Karen George*
7 ch g Entrepreneur—Classic Affair (USA) (Trempolino (USA))
3862[9]

Boot 'n Toot *C A Cyzer* a90 84
5 b m Mtoto—Raspberry Sauce (Niniski (USA))
65[7] 660[5]1162[3] 2447[8]2706[6] 3028[7] 3412[2] 3853[7] 4448[6](5163) 5671[4] 5991[8]

Boppys Dancer *P T Midgley* a56 40
3 b g Clan Of Roses—Dancing Mary (Sri Pekan (USA))
4613[10] 5244[6] 5726[6] 6177[8] 6852[9]6959[2]

Boppys Dream *P T Midgley* a37 45
4 ch m Clan Of Roses—Laurel Queen (IRE) (Viking (USA))
5949[5] 6557[6] 6702[9]6962[8]

Boppys Pride *R A Fahey* a62 58
3 ch c Clan Of Roses—Joara (FR) (Radetzky)
5363[3] (6213) 6435[2] 6571[3]

Boquilobo *M Johnston* 75
3 b g Rainbow Quest(USA) —Moonlight Paradise (USA) (Irish River (FR))
1034[6] 2081[6] 2622[13] 3283[3]

Boracay Dream (IRE) *Patrick Michael Verling* a70 68
4 ch h Grand Lodge(USA) —Mild Intrigue (USA) (Sir Ivor (USA))
2563a[2] (Dead)

Bordello *B W Hills* 64
3 b g Efisio—Blow Me A Kiss (Kris)
1065[9] 2934[3] 5598[8]

Border Artist *J Pearce* a64 71
7 ch g Selkirk(USA) —Aunt Tate (Tate Gallery (USA))
21[7] 67[8]227[3] 339[3]474[10] 520[5]708[9] 982[21]1196[3] 1539[11]1752[4] 2135[2] 2390[2] 2969[2] 3213[2]3339[2] 3664[3] (4009) (4496) 4795[7] 5085[6] 5617[2]5775[6] 6060[9] 6294[6]6396[9] 6674[4]

Border Edge *J J Bridger* a71 71
8 b g Beveled(USA) —Seymour Ann (Krayyan)
(82) 185[10] 223[10]343[11] 1932[8] 2114[6]2327[9] 3337[4] 3705[11] 3928[16] 4446[7]4565[2] 4879[2] (4968) 5149[7] 5422[6] 5506[7]5897[2] (6069) 6289[3] 6408[7]6590[4] 6635[5]

Borderlescott *R Bastiman* 118
4 b g Compton Place—Jeewan (Touching Wood (USA))
(1835) 2847[4] 3767a[2] (4128) 5358[2] 5779a[6] 5942[2]

Border Music *A M Balding* a109+ 89
5 b g Selkirk(USA) —Mara River (Efisio)
(631) (830) 1220[6] 1561[7] 2302[2] 2429[2]2732[7]

Border News *H R A Cecil* a68 73
3 ch c Selkirk(USA) —Flit (USA) (Lyphard (USA))
1120[13] 3458[2] (3711)

Border Tale *James Moffatt* a70 63
6 b g Selkirk(USA) —Likely Story (IRE) (Night Shift (USA))
535[8] 597[3]3220[7] 3431[8] 3810[7] 6560[6]

Bordonaro (USA) *B Spawr* a118
5 ch g Memo(CHI) —Miss Excitement (USA) (Rajab (USA))
(5827a) 6341a[4]

Boreal Applause *E A L Dunlop* a82 81
2 b f Royal Applause—Rabwah (USA) (Gone West (USA))
(3537) 4322[3] 5672[8] 6201[5] 6563[2]

Boreana *Jedd O'Keeffe* 72
3 ch f Nashwan(USA) —Aliena (IRE) (Grand Lodge (USA))
1191[13] 2350[7] 2587[3] 3044[13] 4108[10]5320[12]

Borehan *M A Jarvis* 105
3 b c Agnes World(USA) —Crime Ofthecentury (Pharly (FR))
(1147) (1482) (2032) 2658[18]

Boris De Deauville (IRE) *S Wattel* 115
3 b c Soviet Star(USA) —Logjam (IRE) (Royal Academy (USA))
(1600a) 3342a[7] 4623a[2] 5704a[3] 6250a[11]

Born Dancing *J G Portman* a27 40
2 b f Groom Dancer(USA) —Birthday Venture (Soviet Star (USA))
5209[11] 5586[9]

Born For Diamonds (IRE) *R E Barr* a41 56
4 b m Night Shift(USA) —Kirri (IRE) (Lycius (USA))
1255[10] 1594[8] 2019[7]2831[6] 3617[12] 3909[10] 4611[6] 5368[9]

Born To Be Bold *R Hannon* 79
4 ch h Bold Edge—Birthday Venture (Soviet Star (USA))
1545[11] 1820[7] 2302[5] 2711[4] 3368[5] (Dead)

Born To Win (CHI) *Annike Bye Nunez* 80
4 b m Special Quest(FR) —Buffonata (CHI) (Broker's Tip (NZ))
4863a[4]

Born West (USA) *P W Chapple-Hyam* a70
2 b c Gone West(USA) —Admirer (USA) (Private Terms (USA))
6386[7] 6570[3]6658[9]

Born Wild (GER) *Sir Michael Stoute* a68 84+
3 b f Sadler's Wells(USA) —Borgia (GER) (Acatenango (GER))
2580[6] 3261[2] (4668)

Borodinsky *R E Barr* a39 59
5 b g Magic Ring(IRE) —Valldemosa (Music Boy)
1041[13] 1683[9] 3398[3] 3697[6] 4059[4]4157[8] 4456[11] 5243[7] 6756[4]6961[14]

Borsch (IRE) *Miss L A Perratt* 22
4 b g Soviet Star(USA) —Cheese Soup (USA) (Spectacular Bid (USA))
1530[7] 1946[9] 4059[14] 4350[13]

Borzoi Maestro *M Wellings* a60 61
5 ch g Wolfhound(USA) —Ashkernazy (IRE) (Salt Dome (USA))
130[2] 225[13]605[12] 951[11]1414[7] 1689[14] 2136[6] 2396[4] 2571[11]3190[7] 3297[16] 5480[11] (6276) 6533[11] 6753[4]6956[6]

Boschendal (IRE) *J W Hills* a37 42
2 b f Zamindar(USA) —My Lass (Elmaamul (USA))
5326[5] 5586[10] 6481[9]

Boscobel *M Johnston* a76+
2 ch c Halling(USA) —Dunnes River (USA) (Danzig (USA))
(6561)

Bosra's Valentine (USA) *R Bouresly* a49
6 b h Sadler's Wells(USA) —Bosra Sham (USA) (Woodman (USA))
565a[12]

Bosset (USA) *J Noseda* 104
3 ch f Stravinsky(USA) —Kadwah (USA) (Mr Prospector (USA))
(1844) 3088[2] (3978) 4593[3] 5159[8]

Boss Mak (IRE) *V Smith* a57 43
3 ch g Shinko Forest(IRE) —Lucky Achievement (USA) (St Jovite (USA))
217[7] 795[12] 1599[11]2591[11] 3454[8]

Botanical (USA) *I Mohammed* a113 97
5 b h Seeking The Gold(USA) —Satin Flower (USA) (Shadeed (USA))
206a[12] 563a[10]

Botham (USA) *T J Pitt* a41 50
2 bb c Cryptoclearance(USA) —Oval (USA) (Kris S (USA))
2821[9] 6072[8] 6295[6]

Botteen *M P Tregoning* 85
3 br c Singspiel(IRE) —Abyaan (IRE) (Ela-Mana-Mou)
1668[F] (Dead)

Bottomless Wallet *F Watson* 48
5 ch m Titus Livius(FR) —Furry Dance (USA) (Nureyev (USA))
2198[14] 2615[13] 3698[7] 4155[10] 4405[12]

Bouboulina *E A L Dunlop* a104 95
3 b f Grand Lodge(USA) —Ideal Lady (IRE) (Seattle Slew (USA))
1094[5] 2204[2] 2880[8] 4343[7] 5785[3]6190[7]

Boucheen *Ms Deborah J Evans* a47 53
3 b g Foxhound(USA) —Anytime Baby (Bairn (USA))
70[11] 524[13]1226[6] 1576[3]2877[13] 4835[4] 5240[7] 5432[2] 5838[7]6543[5] 6701[3]6799[8]

Boule D'Or (IRE) *J Akehurst* a110 112
5 b h Croco Rouge(IRE) —Saffron Crocus (Shareef Dancer (USA))
153a[4] 280a[10] 497a[3] 564a[4] 622a[4]1489[2] 2116[2] 2226[2] 2803[6] 3432[3]3534[8]

Boulevin (IRE) *R J Price* a38 54
6 bb g Perugino(USA) —Samika (IRE) (Bikala)
688[11] (2099) 2360[5] 3270[7]5736[10]

Boumsong (IRE) *R C Guest* 13
3 b g Fasliyev(USA) —Festive Season (USA) (Lypheor)
1791[5] 2243[16] 2923[11] 3288[12] 4195[7]

Boundless Prospect (USA) *Miss Gay Kelleway* a80 91
7 b g Boundary(USA) —Cape (USA) (Mr Prospector (USA))
611[6] 726[5] 800[5]1280[4] (2183) 2819[5] 3413[18] 3928[12] 4241[14]6176[7] (6476) 6818[4]6946[6]

Bouquet *J R Fanshawe* 75+
4 b m Cadeaux Genereux—Bayadere (USA) (Green Dancer (USA))
2104[3] 2822[5] 3215[6]

Bournonville *M Wigham* a47 46
3 b g Machiavellian(USA) —Amellnaa (IRE) (Sadler's Wells (USA))
122[8] 415[7]538[13] 1412[8] 1752[12]2101[9] 5432[6] 6057[11] 6236[5]6378[6]

Bouzouki (USA) *W R Swinburn* a69+ 61
3 bb g Distant Music(USA) —Pamina (IRE) (Perugino (USA))
851[9] 3644[11]

Bowing *J L Spearing* a20 49
6 b g Desert Prince(IRE) —Introducing (Mtoto)
566[7] 734[7]

Bowlander *Karen George* a16 31
3 ch g Zaha(CAN) —Lambeth Belle (USA) (Arazi (USA))
598[8]

Bowled Out (GER) *P J McBride* a71 71
4 b m Dansili—Braissim (Dancing Brave (USA))
1638[6] 2000[7] 2736[7]3009[4] 3388[2] 3686[3]4104[10] 4606[2] 4687[4] 5610[11]5972[3] 6289[2]6430[2] 6666[9]

Bowl Em Over *M E Sowersby* 24
2 ch f Primo Valentino(IRE) —Clansinge (Clantime)
1080[5] 1442[12] 1853[6] 2538[2] 2922[4](3394) 3677[4] 5238[14]

Bowl Of Cherries *I A Wood* a63+ 45
3 b g Vettori(IRE) —Desert Nomad (Green Desert (USA))
4585[4] 4757[7] 5452[7] 5767[10] 6306[3](6552) (6780) 6802[2]6854[2]

Bowman's Boy (IRE) *M W Easterby* 37
2 b g Golan(IRE) —Haut Volee (Top Ville)
1588[16] 3553[6] 4171[10]

Bowman's Crossing (IRE) *C Fownes* 121
7 b g Dolphin Street(FR) —Biraya (Valiyar)
1180a[7] 1716a[3] 6784a[11]

Bowness *J G Given* a65 89?
4 b m Efisio—Dominio (IRE) (Dominion)
1545[13] 2173[5] 3332[3] 3687[8]4468[14]

Bow Wave *H Candy* a64 82+
4 b g Danzero(AUS) —Moxby (Efisio)
1112[13] 1692[9] 1993[13]2603[7]

Boxhall (IRE) *W R Swinburn* 79
4 b g Grand Lodge(USA) —March Hare (Groom Dancer (USA))
1614[9] 2460[5] 3853[2] 4268[2] 4792[5]5383[10] 5963[17]

Boy Dancer (IRE) *D W Barker* 67+
3 ch g Danehill Dancer(IRE) —Mary Gabry (IRE) (Kris)
980[11] 1441[5] 1593[3] 1950[5] (2284) 2896[9]4071[2] 4199[8] 4652[5] 5312[12]

Boysie Brigador (USA) *R A Kvisla* 14
3 ch g Gone West(USA) —Summer Voyage (USA) (Summer Squall (USA))
3090[15] 3436[5] 4239[8]

Brabazon (IRE) *R Charlton* 75
3 b c In The Wings—Azure Lake (USA) (Lac Ouimet (USA))
781[9] 1193[2] 1740[2] 2332[7] 2607[8]

Brabinger (IRE) *B G Powell* a38
3 b g Xaar—Particular Friend (Cadeaux Genereux)
5166[14]

Brace Of Doves *T D Barron* a66 74
4 b g Bahamian Bounty—Overcome (Belmez (USA))
1455[5]

Bracklinn *J R Fanshawe* a68 72
4 b m Deploy—Blane Water (USA) (Lomond (USA))
3095[3] 3703[3] 4279[2]

Braddock (IRE) *T D Barron* 69+
3 b c Pivotal—Sedna (FR) (Bering)
(716) (1141)

Bragadino *Lindsay Woods* a65 92
7 b h Zilzal(USA) —Graecia Magna (USA) (Private Account (USA))
86[5]

Brahminy Kite (USA) *M Johnston* a95 110
4 b g Silver Hawk(USA) —Cope's Light (USA) (Copelan (USA))
1298[4] 1815[6] 3294[16]

Brainy Benny (IRE) *N A Callaghan* a84 83
2 b c Barathea(IRE) —Sonachan (IRE) (Darshaan)
3903[4] 5025[6] (5423) 5783[2]5916[3] 6074[7]

Bramantino (IRE) *T A K Cuthbert* a62 75
6 b g Perugino(USA) —Headrest (Habitat)
1233[9] 1346[14] 2812[8] 5960[13]

Bramcote Lorne *S Parr* a57 67
3 b g Josr Algarhoud(IRE) —Dreamtime Quest (Blakeney)
1055[8] 1269[5] 1345[4] 2124[5] 2379[3]2607[2] 3145[8] 4111[5] 5652[15]5903[7] 6376[7] 6462[4]6630[4]

Brandywell Boy (IRE) *D J S Ffrench Davis* a89 84
3 b g Danetime(IRE) —Alexander Eliott (IRE) (Night Shift (USA))
1020[7] 1604[10] 1848[8]2329[10] 2639[3] 2866[6] 3049[6] 3226[2]3795[7] 3970[6] 5777[4]5842[7] 6352[2]6690[5] 6776[6]

Branston Tiger *Ian Emmerson* a78? 73
7 b g Mark Of Esteem(IRE) —Tuxford Hideaway (Cawston's Clown)
6930[12]

Brass Hat (USA) *W Bradley* a124
5 b g Prized(USA) —Brassy (USA) (Dixie Brass (USA))
743a[DSQ]

Brave Amber *M Blanshard* 21
2 ch f Soviet Star(USA) —Be Brave (FR) (Green Forest (USA))
2328[15] 3545[10]

Brave Bear *T D Easterby* a25 66
4 br m Bold Edge—Sarah Bear (Mansingh (USA))
813[5]

Brave Dane (IRE) *A W Carroll* a66 59
8 b g Danehill(USA) —Nuriva (USA) (Woodman (USA))
(1537) (1723) 1769[5] 2918[10] 3900[7] 4248[7]

Brave Fight *A King* a80 73
3 b g Kalanisi(IRE) —Baalbek (Barathea (IRE))
2290[9] 3202[2] 4249[9]5016[10]

Brave Hiawatha (FR) *J A B Old* 83
4 b g Dansili—Alexandrie (USA) (Val De L'Orne (FR))
3547[9]

Brave Quest (IRE) *C J Down* a44 49
2 b g Indian Danehill(IRE) —Mill Rainbow (FR) (Rainbow Quest (USA))
4434[7] 4897[7] 5623[8]

Brave Tin Soldier (USA) *A P O'Brien* 105
2 b c Storm Cat(USA) —Bless (USA) (Mr Prospector (USA))
4028[2] 4716[2] (5408a) 5656[5]

Bravo Maestro (USA) *N P Littmoden* a110 101
5 b g Stravinsky(USA) —Amaranthus (USA) (Kingmambo (USA))
(161) (222) 377[3] 542[9](629) 666[6]704[5] 1017[4]1678[14] 2079[6] 2848[9] 3552[2] 4359[3]4713[17] 5018[4] 5374[8]

Bravura *G L Moore* a70 59
8 ch g Never So Bold—Sylvan Song (Song)
482[6] 545[6]

Braydeen (IRE) *D K Weld* 83
2 b f Barathea(IRE) —Sparky's Song (Electric)
5464a[25]

Brazilian Bride (IRE) *Kevin Prendergast* 106
2 b f Pivotal—Braziliz (USA) (Kingmambo (USA))
(2309a) 4409a[4] 4853a[4]

Breaker Morant (IRE) *Patrick Morris* a74 74
4 b h Montjeu(IRE) —Arcade (Rousillon (USA))
6239[7]

Breaking Shadow (IRE) *T D Barron* 81
4 br g Danehill Dancer(IRE) —Crimbourne (Mummy's Pet)
1220[3] 1532[2] 2017[3] 2323[8] 2520[10]3079[4] 3500[8] 3937[5] 4090[8] 4569[4]4706[10] 4831[2] 5136[3] 5810[4] 6176[8]6221[3]

Break 'N' Dish *B R Johnson* 7
2 b g Montjoy(USA) —Ship Of Gold (Glint Of Gold)
5423[8] 6016[10]

Brean Dot Com (IRE) *Mrs P N Dutfield* a51 64
2 b g Desert Sun—Anna Elise (IRE) (Nucleon (USA))
4295[7] 6815[5]

Breath Of Love (USA) *J-C Rouget* a97 109
4 ch m Mutakddim(USA) —Breath Taking (FR) (Nureyev (USA))
(6252a)

Breckland Boy *Mrs C A Dunnett* a36 58
2 b g City On A Hill(USA) —Sea Idol (IRE) (Astronef)
2045[4] 2586[6] 2938[10]3903[5] 4302[6] 5245[8]

Brecon Beacon *Doug O'Neill* a96 107
4 b h Spectrum(IRE) —Ffestiniog (IRE) (Efisio)
1721a[2]

Breeder's Folly *T J Fitzgerald* a45 41
4 b m Mujahid(USA) —Wynona (IRE) (Cyrano De Bergerac)
771[12]

Breeze In (IRE) *R A Fahey* a33 40
3 b g Houmayoun(FR) —Breeze Up (Coquelin (USA))
6974[9]

Breezeway (IRE) *B J Meehan* a35 70
2 b f Grand Lodge(USA) —Puck's Castle (Shirley Heights)
3796[7] 4148[13] 5380[3] 6106[8] 6933[8]

Bremen *A Fabre* 106
3 b c Sadler's Wells(USA) —Anka Germania (Malinowski (USA))
1064a[2] 1749a[5] 5221a[6] 6062a[4]

Brendan's Surprise *K J Burke* a56 52
4 b g Faustus(USA) —Primrose Way (Young Generation)
1461[10] 2849[13]

Brenin Gwalia *D M Simcock* a70 67
2 ch c Arkadian Hero(USA) —Princess Aurora (Prince Sabo)
3385[2] 3669[2] 4445[3]5065[3] 5207[2] 5668[2]5835[3]

Brennie (IRE) *V Smith* a50 47
5 ch m Grand Lodge(USA) —Brentsville (USA) (Arctic Tern (USA))
28[3]

Brescello (FR) *J E Pease* a86 93
3 b c Danehill Dancer(IRE) —Balouchina (IRE) (Rainbow Quest (USA))
6547a[8]

Bret Maverick (IRE) *J R Weymes* a50 57
2 b g Josr Algarhoud(IRE) —Shady Street (USA) (Shadeed (USA))
4566[11] 4932[3] 5580[5]

Breuddwyd Lyn *D Burchell* a45
8 br g Awesome—Royal Resort (King Of Spain)
694[10]

Briannie (IRE) *P Butler* a49 49
4 b m Xaar—Annieirwin (IRE) (Perugino (USA))
1313[8]

Briannsta (IRE) *C G Cox* a85+ 60
4 b g Bluebird(USA) —Nacote (IRE) (Mtoto)
1042[15] 1285[11] 1474[11] 1820[14] (6223) (6478) 6740[3]

Briarwood Bear *M Blanshard* a67 23
2 ch g Woodborough(USA) —Bramble Bear (Beveled (USA))
1796[12] 2287[11] 6751[4]6900[8]

Bricks And Porter (IRE) *John A Quinn* 94
6 b g College Chapel—Camassina (IRE) (Taufan (USA))
3123a[17] 4031a[10] 4187a[9]

Bridegroom *D R C Elsworth* a72 60
4 b g Groom Dancer(USA) —La Piaf (FR) (Fabulous Dancer (USA))
1773[10] 2148[15] 3056[6]3366[8] 4248[5] 4702[4](5445) 5625[5] 5831[6]

Brideshead (IRE) *A P O'Brien* 39
3 b c Danehill(USA) —Kanmary (FR) (Kenmare (FR))
1070[10] (Dead)

Bride To Be (USA) *C E Brittain* a60 71
3 b f Dixie Union(USA) —Leading The Way (USA) (Septieme Ciel (USA))
668[3] 1351[13] 2292[7]2781[10] 3030[3] 3731[12]4044[13] 4686[4]

Bridge It Jo *Miss J Feilden* a51 92
2 gr f Josr Algarhoud(IRE) —T G's Girl (Selkirk (USA))
1082[10] 1675[3] 1922[4](2354) 3084[5] 3474[2] 4594[4] 4966[5] 5335[5]

Bridge Loan *Doug Watson* a87 100
4 ch g Giant's Causeway(USA) —Credit-A-Plenty (Generous (IRE))
277a[5]

Bridget's Team *D G Bridgwater* a55 47
2 b f Elnadim(USA) —Overcome (Belmez (USA))
1682[3] 3174[5] 5387[7](6422) 6640[2]6894[3] 6991[6]

Bridgewater Boys *K A Ryan* a71 74
5 b g Atraf—Dunloe (IRE) (Shaadi (USA))
77[7] 156[4](290) 358[3](504) 571[7]736[8] 1002[3](1665) 2170[4] 2627[7] 3159[3]4068[10] 6432[7] 6767[2]

Brief Engagement (IRE) *T D McCarthy*
3 br f Namid—Brief Fairy (IRE) (Brief Truce (USA))
6774[7]

Brief Goodbye *John Berry* 86
6 b g Slip Anchor—Queen Of Silk (IRE) (Brief Truce (USA))
1302[5] 2387[2] 3048[7] (3366) 3876[3] 4370[6]4810[6] (5511)

Brief History *H Candy* 66
3 ch c Galileo(IRE) —Take Liberties (Warning)
2034[9] 2304[11] 3225[7]

Brief Passing (IRE) *Luke Comer* a5
7 b h Karaar—Rose The Brief (IRE) (Barry's Run (IRE))
5650[8]

Brief Statement (IRE) *W M Brisbourne* 68
4 b g Desert Prince(IRE) —Brief Sentiment (IRE) (Brief Truce (USA))
1635[6] 1988[5] (2808) 3333[6] 4205[5] (4836) 5338[7]5506[P] (Dead)

Brierley Lil *J L Spearing* a44 52
2 ch f Intikhab(USA) —Pooka (Dominion)
1688[12] 2456[9] 2816[12] 5094[13] 6951[4]

Briery Blaze *Mrs K Walton* 64
3 b f Dansili—Sabonis (USA) (The Minstrel (CAN))
2171[12] 2699[7] 4071[3] 5577[13]

Briery Lane (IRE) *Mrs K Walton* a65 69
5 ch g Tagula(IRE) —Branston Berry (IRE) (Mukaddamah (USA))
1185[2] 1607[5] 2020[7] (2112) 2504[4] 2737[12]4571[3] 4735[2] 5635[7] 6174[11] 6323[4]

Brigadore (USA) *W R Muir* 80
3 rg c Sandpit(BRZ) —Mersey (Crystal Palace (FR))
2175[5] (2526) 3046[7] 3877[5] 4537[6]

Brigadore *J G Given* a62 79
7 b g Magic Ring(IRE) —Music Mistress (IRE) (Classic Music (USA))
1042[13] 1662[8] 1878[2] 2189[3] 2384[5]2852[6] 2981[10] 3281[9]3715[10] 3936[6] 3988[5] 4258[8] 5327[6](5378) 5577[6] 5635[4] 5872[5] 6060[6]

Bright *Robert Gray*
3 ch g Mister Baileys—Razzle Dazzle (IRE) (Caerleon (USA))
69[9] 333[8]6302[12] 6758[11]

Bright Dance *L M Cumani* a48 49
2 b f Groom Dancer(USA) —Illumination (Saddlers' Hall (IRE))
3640[8] 4150[5] 4553[8]

Brightling (IRE) *Jamie Poulton* a41
2 b f Gorse—Brightside (IRE) (Last Tycoon)
4138[6]

Bright Moon *R Hannon* a69 78
2 b f Compton Place—Mashmoon (USA) (Habitat)
2957[12] 3402[2] 4084[6](4480) 4928[6] 5157[3] 5676[13]

Bright Sparky (GER) *M W Easterby* 49
3 ch g Dashing Blade—Braissim (Dancing Brave (USA))
4069[9] 4734[13]

Bright Sun (IRE) *N Tinkler* a70 76
5 b g Desert Sun—Kealbra Lady (Petong)
1075[9] 1425[9] 2108[4] (2322) 2519[7] 2761[6]3309[2] 3621[4] 3883[4] 4203[7] 5249[5](5484) 5685[9]

Brigydon (IRE) *J R Fanshawe* a54 61
3 b g Fasliyev(USA) —Creme Caramel (USA) (Septieme Ciel (USA))
3458[5] 4899[5]

Briland (IRE) *M Halford* 62
3 b f Namid—Inourhearts (IRE) (Pips Pride)
2308a[10]

Brindabella (AUS) *L Macdonald* 105
5 br m Bellotto(USA) —Poet's Breeze (AUS) (Zephyr Bay (AUS))
5817a[11]

Brindisi *D Selvaratnam* a101 101
5 b m Dr Fong(USA) —Genoa (Zafonic (USA))
155a[4] 351a[2] 510a[3]

Bring It On Home *G L Moore* 54
2 b c Beat Hollow—Dernier Cri (Slip Anchor)
5091[13] 5475[7]

Brisant (GER) *M Trybuhl* 108
4 br g Goofalik(USA) —Beresina (Surumu (GER))
4828a[4] 5561a[5] 6109a[8]

Brisk Breeze (GER) *H R A Cecil* 81
2 ch f Monsun(GER) —Bela-M (IRE) (Ela-Mana-Mou)
4148[3] 4765[5]

Britannic *A Fabre* 102
3 ch g Rainbow Quest(USA) —Anka Britannia (USA) (Irish River (FR))
2738a[3]

British Blue (USA) *J Ruvalcaba* 103
6 ch h Storm Cat(USA) —Memories Of Silver (USA) (Silver Hawk (USA))
5824a[9]

British Isles *A Laird* a88
4 b h Giant's Causeway(USA) —Wildwood Flower (Distant Relative)
495a[4]

Broadfield Lady (IRE) *E J Creighton* a24 36
6 ch m Perugino(USA) —Dama De Noche (Rusticaro (FR))
5576[14] 5970[12] 6274[14]6548[12]

Broadway Calling *M E Sowersby* a59
3 ch g Dr Fong(USA) —Manhattan Sunset (USA) (El Gran Senor (USA))
112[7] 217[12]440[11]

Brocatello (IRE) *M Johnston* a44 70
3 b g Sadler's Wells(USA) —Brocatelle (Green Desert (USA))
4471[3] 5138[2] 6410[10]

Brockhole (IRE) *J G Given* a66 54
4 gr g Daylami(IRE) —Free Spirit (IRE) (Caerleon (USA))
503[4] 603[5]700[2] 882[13] 1436[8]

Brodimix (IRE) *A Chaille-Chaille* 95
3 gr c Linamix(FR) —Broad And High (USA) (Broad Brush (USA))
6062a[7]

Broghill *J H M Gosden* 95
2 ch c Selkirk(USA) —Mystify (Batshoof)
(5457) 5806[3]

Brogue Lanterns (IRE) *E J Creighton* a16 81
4 ch m Dr Devious(IRE) —Landrail (USA) (Storm Bird (CAN))
6787[12] 6897[13]

Broken Spur (FR) *B W Hills* a75 75
3 b c Bahri(USA) —Aerleon Jane (Caerleon (USA))
702[3] 852[5]1349[6] 3644[9] 4143[7]5755[7]

Bronco's Filly (IRE) *J G M O'Shea*
2 bb f Val Royal(FR) —Lady Esther (IRE) (Darnay)
2916[7] 3677[7] 4334[13]

Bronte's Hope *M P Tregoning* a63
2 ch f Gorse—General Jane (Be My Chief (USA))
2980[5]

Bronx Bomber *Dr J D Scargill* a48 46
8 ch g Prince Sabo—Super Yankee (IRE) (Superlative)
181[4] 300[6]

Bronze Dancer (IRE) *G A Swinbank* 78
4 b g Entrepreneur—Scrimshaw (Selkirk (USA))
1560[2] 2018[3] 2381[2] 2828[5] (3483) 3674[3](4231) 6275[6]

Bronze Star *J R Fanshawe* a70 58
3 b f Mark Of Esteem(IRE) —White House (Pursuit Of Love)
5071[4] 5774[9] 6484[2](6775) 6883[4]

Bronzo Di Riace (IRE) *K A Ryan* a38 24
2 b c Montjeu(IRE) —Afreeta (USA) (Afleet (CAN))
4705[14] 5389[8]

Broomielaw *E A L Dunlop* 72+
2 ch c Rock Of Gibraltar(IRE) —Peony (Lion Cavern (USA))
5457[2]

Brosna Cry (IRE) *J G Burns* a81+ 63
2 b c Street Cry(IRE) —Wedding Gift (FR) (Always Fair (USA))
(6644)

Brother Cadfael *John A Harris* a53 32
5 ch g So Factual(USA) —High Habit (Slip Anchor)
91[6] 256[4]

Brother Derek (USA) *Dan L Hendricks* a124
3 b c Benchmark(USA) —Miss Soft Sell (USA) (Siyah Kalem (USA))
1498a[4] 1861a[4]5826a[2] 6345a[5]

Brother's Valcour (FR) *K Schafflutzel* 46
8 b h River Mist(USA) —Lady De Valcour (FR) (Labus (FR))
456a[9]

Broughton Buzzer *A G Newcombe* a50 56
5 b m Rudimentary(USA) —Broughtons Lure (IRE) (Archway (IRE))
2070[2] 3263[11]

Broughtons Folly *W J Musson* a73 55+
3 b f Groom Dancer(USA) —Cressida (Polish Precedent (USA))
5086[11] 5426[4] 6053[7]6432[6] (6601) 6712[3]

Broughtons Revival *W J Musson* a50
4 b m Pivotal—Ella Lamees (Statoblest)
3200[9]

Broughton Treasure *W J Musson*
3 b f Bahamian Bounty—Quite Happy (IRE) (Statoblest)
2415[10]

Brouhaha *Miss Diana Weeden* 64
2 b c Bahhare(USA) —Top Of The Morning (Keen)
5460[9] 5918[7] 6200[5]

Brunel (IRE) *I Mohammed* a75 116
5 b h Marju(IRE) —Castlerahan (IRE) (Thatching)
154a[7] 281a[4] 621a[2]

Brunelleschi *P L Gilligan* a76 78
3 ch g Bertolini(USA) —Petrovna (IRE) (Petardia)
1264[5] 1672[4] 2329[6] 2639[10] 3049[5]3087[6] 3403[8] 5684[18]5842[12]

Brunston Castle *A W Carroll* a27 58
6 b g Hector Protector(USA) —Villella (Sadler's Wells (USA))
182[8]

Brut *D W Barker* a56 70
4 b g Mind Games—Champenoise (Forzando)
1563[3] 1686[15] 2020[14] (2396) 2852[5] 3041[13]3170[7] 3622[3] 3832[5] 4258[12] 5081[9]5309[7] 5487[10] 5620[5] 5752[3]

Brynris *Mrs G S Rees* a32 13
2 gr g Perryston View—Isle Of Mull (Elmaamul (USA))
1535[9] 1744[7]2015[8] 6900[9] 6951[5]

Buachaill Dona (IRE) *D Nicholls* 106
3 b g Namid—Serious Contender (IRE) (Tenby)
(1126) (3636) 4102[2] (4717) 5501[6]

Bu-Ali (USA) *B W Duke* 30
3 b f Silver Hawk(USA) —Mantua (Mtoto)
2352[11] 2933[11] 4111[15]

Bubbling Fun *T Wall* a47 52
5 b m Marju(IRE) —Blushing Barada (USA) (Blushing Groom (FR))
2414[9] 2612[11] 3115[12]3196[6] 3597[6] 4282[11]4709[9] 4869[6] 6312[6]6701[6] 6954[10]

Buccellati *A M Balding* 86
2 ch c Soviet Star(USA) —Susi Wong (IRE) (Selkirk (USA))
3363[9] (4895) 5916[2]

Bucharest *M Wigham* a50 68
3 b g Barathea(IRE) —Zorleni (Zafonic (USA))
702[10] 831[6]1097[16] 1337[10] 1672[7]2050[14] 2864[12] (4325) 6206[17] 6641[11]6819[10] 6949[9]

Buckie Massa *S Kirk* a75+ 68
2 ch c Best Of The Bests(IRE) —Up On Points (Royal Academy (USA))
3222[6] 4129[11] 4766[18] 5647[10] 6562[2]6689[5] (6749)

Buckland Manor (USA) *J Paco Gonzalez* a107 118
6 ch h Bien Bien(USA) —Bags Of Pace (USA) (Shadeed (USA))
5825a[4]

Buckle And Hyde *Mrs A L M King* a54 46
3 ch f Foxhound(USA) —Step On Degas (Superpower)
2353[11] 2704[9] 4052[5] 4329[4]4498[11] 6130[8] 6235[14]

Bucks *Ian Williams* a82 83
9 b g Slip Anchor—Alligram (USA) (Alysheba (USA))
3220[3] 4206[3] 4626[11]

Buckthorn *G Wragg* 54
2 ch c Lomitas—Emma Peel (Emarati (USA))
6220[14]

Buddies Girl (IRE) *R Hannon* a66 69
2 b f Golan(IRE) —Moonlight (IRE) (Night Shift (USA))
1989[2] 2234[3] 2456[4] 4178[5] 4813[4]5503[17] 6290[2] 6332[7]6441[7]

Buddy Brown *J Howard Johnson* a49 66
4 b g Lujain(USA) —Rose Bay (Shareef Dancer (USA))
412[8] 1864[8] 2162[12]3694[4] 5617[11]

Buddy Man (IRE) *Patrick Martin* a41 68
8 ch h Shalford(IRE) —Helen Belle (IRE) (Parliament)
6928[10]

Buds Dilemma *I W McInnes* 27
2 b f Anabaa(USA) —Lady Thynn (FR) (Crystal Glitters (USA))
4109[11]

Buffalo Man (CAN) *C Gambolati* a99
2 b c El Prado(IRE) —Perfect Six (USA) (Saratoga Six (USA))
5983a[8]

Bugatti Royale (USA) *Peter Morgan* 91
6 b h Dynaformer(USA) —Cin Isa Luv (USA) (Private Account (USA))
6391a[7]

Bukit Fraser (IRE) *P F I Cole* a62 87
5 b g Sri Pekan(USA) —London Pride (USA) (Lear Fan (USA))
847[6] 1591[11] 1847[7]3221[3] 3467[6] 4046[9]4331[5] 4898[8]

Bulberry Hill *R W Price* a55 43
5 b g Makbul—Hurtleberry (IRE) (Tirol)
25[2] 147[2]259[3] 389[3]635[6] 3998[7](5927) 6305[7]6495[5] (6797)

Bullish Luck (USA) *A S Cruz* 124
7 b g Royal Academy(USA) —Wild Vintage (USA) (Alysheba (USA))
742a[5] 1180a[5] (1527a) 6784a[4]

Bull Run (IRE) *Saeed Bin Suroor* 91
5 gr g Daylami(IRE) —Bulaxie (Bustino)
6334[6]

Bullseye *J R Boyle* a59 47
4 b g Polish Precedent(USA) —Native Flair (Be My Native (USA))
1163[6] 1334[13]1400[5] 3035[8] 3382[13]3862[6]

Bulwark (IRE) *Mrs A J Perrett* a104 108+
4 b h Montjeu(IRE) —Bulaxie (Bustino)
1071[5] 1584[6] (2437) 3078[9] 3533[3]4081[8] 4677[4] 5551[4] 5967[2]

Bunderos (IRE) *Mrs A Duffield*
2 b f Areion(GER) —Bundheimerin (GER) (Ordos (GER))
5679[15]

Bundy *M Dods* a54 66
10 b g Ezzoud(IRE) —Sanctuary Cove (Habitat)
864[11] 1795[13] 2749[2] 2793[6]

Bungie *Ms Deborah J Evans* a63 59
2 gr g Forzando—Sweet Whisper (Petong)
4986[5] 5168[9] 5508[10] 5645 [4] 5835[6](6788) 6895[4]

Bunood (IRE) *J L Dunlop* 101
3 b f Sadler's Wells(USA) —Azdihaar (USA) (Mr Prospector (USA))
1509[2] 4179[8] 4741[2] 5502[3] 5803[7]

Buon Amici *W J Musson* a22 41
5 b m Pivotal—Supreme Rose (Frimley Park)
304[9]

Burgundy *P Mitchell* a78 77
9 b g Lycius(USA) —Decant (Rousillon (USA))
88[8] 135[5]983[6] 1478[10] 1821[13]1958[5] 2647[11](2752) 3214[8] 3429[6] 3639[3]4073[2] 4244[3] 6070[6]6189[5] 6432[9]6566[6] 6661[6](6843) 6878[6]

Burhaan (IRE) *J R Boyle* a58 33
4 b h Green Desert(USA) —Arjuzah (IRE) (Ahonoora)
764[12] 1164[11]1432[11] 2211[5] 2347[10]2793[10] 5781[10]6234[5] 6619[2]6728[3] 6906[2](6981)

Burley Firebrand *Michael McElhone* a65 79?
6 b g Bahamian Bounty—Vallauris (Faustus (USA))
6595[11]

Burley Flame *J G Given* a93+ 83
5 b g Marju(IRE) —Tarsa (Ballad Rock)
898[9]

Burlington Fayr (IRE) *N Tinkler* 57
2 ch f Fayruz—Fair Princess (Efisio)
1074[5] 2015[2] 2294[6] 4115[5] 4376[7]4724[5] (4887) 5282[3] 5747[8]

Burnbank (IRE) *W Jarvis* a68 74
3 ch c Danehill Dancer(IRE) —Roseau (Nashwan (USA))
981[2] 1241[2] 2224[5]

Burningfold Babe *P Winkworth* a54 2
2 b f Muhtarram(USA) —Laser Light Lady (Tragic Role (USA))
5052[12] 5923[6] 6222[2]6394[13] 6534[7]6736[12]

Burning Incense (IRE) *R Charlton* a67+ 102
3 b g Namid—Night Scent (IRE) (Scenic)
801[6] 1218[2] 1672[2]2014[3] (2931) 3296[2] 4106[3] (4601) 5336[23] 5501[2]

Burning Moon *J Ryan* 48
5 b g Bering—Triple Green (Green Desert (USA))
1847[9] 2104[9] 2820[14]

Burnley Al (IRE) *Peter Grayson* a70 69
4 ch g Desert King(IRE) —Bold Meadows (Persian Bold)
(86) 157^{5} 384^{2}504^{6} 698^{8}955^{7} 1186^{6} 1480^{5}3139^{2} 3168^{3} 3353^{2} 4057^{4} 4133^{2}(4475) 4518^{3} (4692) 4726^{2} 5403^{5} 5510^{8} 5974^{12}6648^{5} 6810^{11}6934^{6} 6977^{4}

Burnt Ember (USA) *S Seemar* a108 94
7 ch h Smoke Glacken(USA) —Castle Gardens (IRE) (Common Grounds)
495a^{12}

Burnt Oak (UAE) *C W Fairhurst* a55 87
4 b g Timber Country(USA) —Anaam (Caerleon (USA))
3261^{4} 4204^{4} (4549)

Burntoakboy *Michael Cunningham* 82
8 b g Sir Harry Lewis(USA) —Sainte Martine (Martinmas)
2723^{29}

Burnt Orange (IRE) *T D McCarthy* 56
3 b g Agnes World(USA) —Orange Walk (IRE) (Alzao (USA))
1845^{10} 2532^{11} 3034^{6} 4141^{17} 4690^{12}5949^{10}

Burton Ash *J G Given* a66 72
4 bb m Diktat—Incendio (Siberian Express (USA))
596^{2} 677^{4}917^{6} 1253^{14} 1852^{4}(2891) 3947^{9} 5316^{9}

Buscador (USA) *W M Brisbourne* a67 52
7 ch g Crafty Prospector(USA) —Fairway Flag (USA) (Fairway Phantom (USA))
163^{10} 231^{3}324^{14} 405^{3}505^{12} 530^{3}(582) 955^{5}1222^{4} 1987^{9} 2522^{7} (6648) 6837^{3} 6924^{3}

Bush Breakfast *P Winkworth* a37 74
2 b c Averti(IRE) —Basbousate Nadia (Wolfhound (USA))
1876^{3} 2759^{3} 3070^{3} 3930^{7} 4284^{7}5668^{11}

Bushfire (USA) *E Kenneally* a117
3 b f Louis Quatorze(USA) —Traki Traki (USA) (Mo Power (USA))
6343a^{11}

Bush Maiden (IRE) *Mrs Seamus Hayes* 100
6 b m Among Men(USA) —Moonbi Range (IRE) (Nordico (USA))
(3123a)

Business Traveller (IRE) *R J Price* 49?
6 ch g Titus Livius(FR) —Dancing Venus (Pursuit Of Love)
881^{8} 966^{10}

Bussel (USA) *W J Haggas* a75 65
2 ch f Royal Academy(USA) —Reigning Princess (USA) (Storm Boot (USA))
5918^{13} 6330^{3} (6575) (6894)

Bussoni (GER) *H Blume* 112
5 br h Goofalik(USA) —Blumme (CHI) (Jadar (CHI))
(1860a) 3516a^{5}

Bustan (IRE) *G C Bravery* a80 103
7 b g Darshaan—Dazzlingly Radiant (Try My Best (USA))
222^{9} 2079^{16} 2364^{2}2742^{19} 3552^{6} 3971^{7} 4348^{4} 5177^{6}5675^{15} 5945^{12} 6299^{4}

Buster Hyvonen (IRE) *J R Fanshawe* a74 80
4 b g Dansili—Serotina (IRE) (Mtoto)
2621^{6} 3401^{4} 4149^{2}(4586) 5479^{11} 5946^{2}

Bustin Justin (USA) *J Noseda* 94
3 b c Forestry(USA) —Designatoree (USA) (Alysheba (USA))
(2458) (3708) (4144) 5942^{9}

Busy Man (IRE) *J R Jenkins* a56+ 6
7 b g Darnay—Make Or Mar (Daring March)
114^{13} 219^{7}291^{3} 576^{6}612^{9} 888^{3}1244^{8} 3014^{5}3706^{12} 3934^{6} 4139^{8}6232^{2}

Busy Shark (IRE) *M R Channon* a67 64
3 gr g Shinko Forest(IRE) —Felicita (IRE) (Catrail (USA))
123^{3}

Butlers Best *E J O'Neill* a64 43
2 b g Best Of The Bests(IRE) —Evening Charm (IRE) (Bering)
5537^{10} 5947^{13} 6570^{6}

Butterfly Bud (IRE) *J O'Reilly* a31 69
3 b g Lend A Hand—Rathbawn Realm (Doulab (USA))
2399^{3} 3154^{9} 3538^{2}3759^{6} 4120^{6} 4834^{18} 5077^{3} 6061^{11}

Buxton *R Ingram* a18
2 b c Auction House(USA) —Dam Certain (IRE) (Damister (USA))
5106^{12}

Buy On The Red *W R Muir* a101 90
5 b g Komaite(USA) —Red Rosein (Red Sunset)
1474^{15} 1820^{17} 2711^{5} 3012^{4}3434^{3} 4106^{11} 4364^{4} 4449^{4} 5021^{9}5453^{5} 5777^{3} 6461^{7}6580^{4} 6690^{3}6835^{2} (6999)

Buzbury Rings *A M Balding* 54
2 b g Piccolo—Mory Kante (USA) (Icecapade (USA))
1796^{7}

Buz Kiri (USA) *A W Carroll* a38 38
8 b g Gulch(USA) —Whitecorners (USA) (Caro)
141^{6}

Buzzin'Boyzee (IRE) *P D Evans* a63 65
3 ch f Monashee Mountain(USA) —Las Bela (Welsh Pageant)
10^{4} 53^{3}83^{3} 226^{8}554^{5} (598) 646^{3} 861^{3}(1232) 1801^{5} 1825^{5} 2316^{3} 2418^{5}6193^{9} 6919^{3}6952^{4} 6964^{7}

Byanita (IRE) *B Palling* a25
2 b f Anita's Prince—Byliny (IRE) (Archway (IRE))
3640^{11} 4657^{16} 5876^{9}6789^{5}

Bygone Days *Saeed Bin Suroor* 119+
5 ch g Desert King(IRE) —May Light (Midyan (USA))
203a^{3} 433a^{2} 506a^{7} 619a^{2} (5578) (5942)

Byo (IRE) *P Howling* a64 64
8 gr g Paris House—Navan Royal (IRE) (Dominion Royale)
146^{2} 212^{2}(299) 401^{2}424^{5} 501^{2}547^{3} 587^{9}674^{3} 1303^{9}1618^{12} 1899^{11} 3683^{6}

Byron *Saeed Bin Suroor* 117
5 b h Green Desert(USA) —Gay Gallanta (USA) (Woodman (USA))
5588^{2} 5962^{16}

Byron Bay *I Semple* a91 91
4 b h My Best Valentine—Candarela (Damister (USA))
108^{5} (276) (632) 865^{2} 1456^{6}1949^{9} 3191^{2} 3881^{4} 4696^{5} 5144^{5}5355^{8} 6678^{5} 6997^{6}

By Storm *John Berry* a39 53
3 b f Largesse—Polar Storm (IRE) (Law Society (USA))
1726^{11} 4304^{2} 4671^{10}5273^{11} (5767) 6128^{8} 6601^{9}

By The Edge (IRE) *T D Barron* 47
2 b f Shinko Forest(IRE) —Magic Annemarie (IRE) (Dancing Dissident (USA))
3878^{7} 4251^{9} 4913^{6}

By The River *P Winkworth*
2 b g Zamindar(USA) —Baby Bunting (Wolfhound (USA))
5348^{11}

Caan *D K Ivory* a24 41
3 br g Averti(IRE) —Bellifontaine (FR) (Bellypha)
85^{11} 199^{9}396^{10}

Cabinet (IRE) *Sir Michael Stoute* a85 85
2 b c Grand Lodge(USA) —Passe Passe (USA) (Lear Fan (USA))
5883^{2} (6188)

Cabo (FR) *C F Swan* 81
3 b f Sagamix(FR) —Debate (High Line)
4124a^{2}

Cabopino Lad (USA) *Miss Tracy Waggott*
4 b g Comic Strip(USA) —Roxanne (USA) (Woodman (USA))
600^{12} 634^{11}

Cabourg (IRE) *R Bastiman* a64 65
3 b g Danehill(USA) —Loire Valley (IRE) (Sadler's Wells (USA))
1192^{13} 1641^{5} 1963^{10}5244^{7} 5553^{5} 6069^{4} 6451^{4}6532^{6} 6762^{13}6977^{3}

Cabrillo (IRE) *John A Quinn* a14 44
4 b m Indian Rocket—Cerosia (Pitskelly)
94^{9} 147^{13}

Cabriole *H R A Cecil* a44 65
3 b f Dansili—Arabesque (Zafonic (USA))
1513^{10} 2167^{8} 2763^{3} 3299^{11} 4045^{6}4613^{3} 5569^{12}

Cacique (IRE) *R J Frankel* 122
5 b h Danehill(USA) —Hasili (IRE) (Kahyasi)
(2476a) 4386a^{2} 6344a^{10}

Cactus King *J H M Gosden* a85 94
3 b g Green Desert(USA) —Apache Star (Arazi (USA))
1505^{5} 2330^{3} 2863^{6} 4160^{3} 5945^{7}6313^{7} 6418^{11}

Cadeaux Des Mages *J G Given* a71 91
6 b g Cadeaux Genereux—On Tiptoes (Shareef Dancer (USA))
3918^{11} 4575^{10} 5249^{10}5553^{12} 6241^{9}

Cadeaux Du Monde *E J O'Neill* a62 83
2 ch c Cadeaux Genereux—La Mondotte (IRE) (Alzao (USA))
1595^{9} 2130^{4} 2416^{8}4246^{4} 4766^{2} 5088^{4}5364^{2} 5867^{3}

Cadi May *W M Brisbourne* 31
2 b f Fasliyev(USA) —Sound Of Sleat (Primo Dominie)
1046^{11} 2166^{9} 4171^{11}

Cadran (FR) *C Lerner* 93
2 b c Poliglote—Brisk Waters (USA) (Saratoga Six (USA))
6609a^{3}

Cadwell *D Nicholls* 53
2 b c Pivotal—Sur Les Pointes (IRE) (Sadler's Wells (USA))
4018^{10} 5495^{4} 5901^{7}

Caernarvon (IRE) *M A Jarvis* a69
2 b g King's Best(USA) —Reloy (USA) (Liloy (FR))
6254^{5} 6447^{7}

Caerphilly Gal *P L Gilligan* a56+ 57
6 b m Averti(IRE) —Noble Lustre (USA) (Lyphard's Wish (FR))
133^{3}

Caesar Beware (IRE) *A Laird* 118
4 b g Daggers Drawn(USA) —Red Shareef (Marju (IRE))
(281a) 496a^{9} 625a^{6}

Caheerloch (IRE) *D K Weld* 88
4 b g Sinndar(IRE) —Pharmacist (IRE) (Machiavellian (USA))
5396a^{17}

Cairdeas (IRE) *D K Weld* 115
5 b h Darshaan—Sabaah (USA) (Nureyev (USA))
932a^{4} 1324a^{4} 2154a^{4}

Caj (IRE) *M Quinn* a24 58
2 b f Tagula(IRE) —Notley Park (Wolfhound (USA))
1046^{5} 1181^{9} 1743^{8}2382^{4} 3300^{2} 4006^{5} 4493^{3} 4950^{2}5238^{8} 5448^{8}

Calabash Cove (USA) *Saeed Bin Suroor* a76
2 ch c Rahy(USA) —I Need A Holiday (USA) (Nureyev (USA))
6254^{2}

Calabaza *W Jarvis* 73
4 ch g Zaha(CAN) —Mo Stopher (Sharpo)
2074^{9} 4338^{3} 4564^{4} 5476^{9} 5593^{15}6174^{14}

Calamari (IRE) *Mrs A Duffield* a35 63
4 ch m Desert King(IRE) —Mrs Fisher (IRE) (Salmon Leap (USA))
1249^{3} 1500^{8} 2293^{6} 2747^{6} 3142^{12}6235^{8} 6543^{9}

Calatagan (IRE) *J M Jefferson* a75 74+
7 ch g Danzig Connection(USA) —Calachuchi (Martinmas)
1033^{4} 2196^{2} 2628^{7} 4252^{3}

Calculating (IRE) *J H M Gosden* 30
2 b c Machiavellian(USA) —Zaheemah (USA) (El Prado (IRE))
5640^{14}

Calcutta *B W Hills* 101
10 b h Indian Ridge—Echoing (Formidable (USA))
1084^{8} 1129^{12} 2440^{13} 2614^{2} 2988^{4}3218^{6} 3733^{10} 3959^{3} 5301^{8}

Calcutta Cup (UAE) *Karen McLintock* a62 76
3 br g Jade Robbery(USA) —Six Nations (USA) (Danzig (USA))
668^{5} 894^{8} 1691^{3}3177^{6} 5284^{12} 5617^{14} 5905^{5} 6317^{2}

Caldra (IRE) *S Kirk* 109+
2 b g Elnadim(USA) —Lady Rachel (IRE) (Priolo (USA))
1980^{2} 2234^{4} (4525) 4809^{2} (5176) (5655) (5805)

Calfraz *Micky Hammond* 51
4 bb g Tamure(IRE) —Pas De Chat (Relko)
1415^{6} 6011^{4}

Caliban (IRE) *Ian Williams* a8
8 ch g Rainbows For Life(CAN) —Amour Toujours (IRE) (Law Society (USA))
6560^{10}

California Laws *T D Barron* a89+ 76d
4 b g Pivotal—Noor El Houdah (IRE) (Fayruz)
2112^{5} 2792^{6} (3263) 3390^{5}4652^{4} (5136) 5406^{5} 5617^{7} 5861^{6} (6425) (6896)

Callahan (FR) *Ms Deborah J Evans* a9 37
2 gr g Verglas(IRE) —Late Night (FR) (Night Shift (USA))
5168^{10} 6534^{11}

Callisto Moon *P A Blockley* a69 60
2 b g Mujahid(USA) —Nursling (IRE) (Kahyasi)
1113^{4} 1912^{2} 2218^{6}2979^{6} 5585^{14} 6224^{3}6284^{2} 6506^{5}6646^{2}

Call Me George *M Johnston* 72
3 ch c Rainbow Quest(USA) —Coretta (IRE) (Caerleon (USA))
897^{12} 1613^{6} (2082) 2592^{2} 2677^{4} 3284^{2}

Call Me Max *E A L Dunlop* a76 87
4 b g Vettori(IRE) —Always Vigilant (USA) (Lear Fan (USA))
1262^{8} 1938^{8} 2508^{6}2983^{11}

Call Me Rosy (IRE) *C F Wall* a66 42
2 ch f Shinko Forest(IRE) —Fanciful (IRE) (Mujtahid (USA))
3043^{11} 4433^{2} 5735^{4}6310^{8} 6488^{8}

Call Me Waki (USA) *A M Balding* 75
3 ch f Miswaki(USA) —S S Capote (USA) (Capote (USA))
3266^{4} 3554^{4} 3950^{4} (4162)

Call My Bluff (FR) *Rae Guest* a72 69
3 b g Highest Honor(FR) —Baino Bluff (Be My Guest (USA))
3639^{2} 6861^{5}

Call My Number (IRE) *M R Channon* a78 86
3 b g Grand Lodge(USA) —Screen Idol (IRE) (Sadler's Wells (USA))
1016^{5} 1250^{2} 2126^{2}2760^{3} 3212^{7}

Calloff The Search *W G M Turner* a59 59
2 b g Piccolo—Unchain My Heart (Pursuit Of Love)
1136^{3} 1420^{4} 2130^{8} 6757^{8}6951^{9}

Callwood Dancer (IRE) *B W Hills* 70
2 ch f Danehill Dancer(IRE) —Ahdaab (USA) (Rahy (USA))
2710^{3} 4000^{2}

Calming Waters *D W P Arbuthnot* a78+
3 ch c Dr Fong(USA) —Faraway Waters (Pharly (FR))
4247^{10} 5611^{2}6459^{2}

Calusa Lady (IRE) *J A Geake* a42 42
6 ch m Titus Livius(FR) —Solas Abu (IRE) (Red Sunset)
6803^{6}

Calypso King *J W Hills* a78 89
3 gr g Agnes World(USA) —T G's Girl (Selkirk (USA))
1091^{16} 1606^{7} 1848^{7} 2658^{10} 3067^{7}4602^{13} 5107^{11} 5427^{2}5782^{8}

Calzaghe (IRE) *A M Balding* a48 38
2 ch g Galileo(IRE) —Novelette (Darshaan)
5339^{12} 5828^{10} 6447^{4}

Cambiocorsa (USA) *Doug O'Neill* 112
4 gr m Avenue Of Flags(USA) —Ultrafleet (USA) (Afleet (CAN))
3109a^{5} 6614a^{13}

Came Back (IRE) *J A Osborne* a69 41
3 ch c Bertolini(USA) —Distant Decree (USA) (Distant View (USA))
165^{3} 233^{4}(266) 601^{8}2263^{7} (5781) 6033^{9}6348^{3} 6833^{5}

Cameo Story *Andrew Oliver* a25 53
3 b f Spectrum(IRE) —Alpine Park (IRE) (Barathea (IRE))
5839^{4} 6545^{11} 6798^{8}6901^{10}

Camissa *D K Ivory* a52 71
2 b f Averti(IRE) —Ambitious (Ardkinglass)
944^{2} 1189^{5} (1542) 1831^{7} 2342^{7}

Campanile *J R Fanshawe* a58 70
3 ch f Zilzal(USA) —High Barn (Shirley Heights)
2325^{8} 2940^{3} 4606^{13}

Camp Attack *S Dow* a71 57
3 b g Fleetwood(IRE) —Queen Of Tides (IRE) (Soviet Star (USA))
1741^{10} 2712^{16} 4210^{8} 4700^{7}5098^{6} 5452^{4} 6459^{5}6601^{2} 6743^{6}6911^{7}

Campbells Lad *Mrs G S Rees* a44 47
5 b g Mind Games—T O O Mamma'S (IRE) (Classic Secret (USA))
1765^{12} 2362^{6} 2696^{5}3139^{4} 3484^{6} 3672^{6} 4404^{4} 6302^{13}6482^{2}

Campbeltown (IRE) *R A Harris* a69 76d
3 b c Mull Of Kintyre(USA) —Jallaissine (IRE) (College Chapel)
665^{5} 829^{6}2022^{7} 4707^{9} 5044^{10} 5087^{7} 5532^{10}5832^{15} 6065^{13}

Camp Commander (IRE) *C R Dore* a95 95
7 gr h Pennekamp(USA) —Khalatara (IRE) (Kalaglow)
44^{12} 167^{13}253^{11}

Campeon (IRE) *J M Bradley* a52 69d
4 b g Monashee Mountain(USA) —Arcticlead (USA) (Arctic Tern (USA))
1243^{4} 1315^{8} 1689^{3}1846^{6} 2136^{10} 3199^{8}3608^{8} 3833^{4} 4872^{8} 6276^{3}6539^{4} 6615^{7}6686^{7} 6755^{3}6956^{5} 6974^{4}

Camphor Best (JPN) *Y Sato* 111
7 b h Amber Shadai(JPN) —Katarina Rabbit (JPN) (Shinzan)
6530a^{10}

Campo Bueno (FR) *A Berry* a54 88
4 b h Septieme Ciel(USA) —Herba Buena (FR) (Fabulous Dancer (USA))
885a^{5} 4988^{7} 5135^{5} 5534^{7} 5749^{4}5957^{6} 6499^{11}

Camps Bay (USA) *Mrs A J Perrett* 68
2 b c Cozzene(USA) —Seewillo (USA) (Pleasant Colony (USA))
4781^{7} 5458^{5} 5886^{3}

Camrose *J L Dunlop* 105
5 ch g Zafonic(USA) —Tularosa (In The Wings)
1511^{2} 2430^{5} 2893^{2} 4576^{2} 5170^{3}5657^{7} 6334^{3}

Canadian Danehill (IRE) *R M H Cowell* a74 76
4 b h Indian Danehill(IRE) —San Jovita (CAN) (St Jovite (USA))
1^{7} 126^{3}137^{4} (227) (320) 532^{7}699^{2} 798^{2} 967^{7}1211^{2} 1432^{8} 2444^{5} 2864^{3} 3004^{2}3281^{8} 3374^{9} 3692a^{5} 5593^{11} 6315^{16}6465^{3} 6688^{6}

Canary Dancer *Miss Z C Davison* a35 45
4 b m Groom Dancer(USA) —Bird Of Time (IRE) (Persian Bold)
181^{8} 331^{5}388^{9} 487^{6}

Canary Girl *Mrs C A Dunnett* a40 41
3 br f Primo Valentino(IRE) —Cumbrian Concerto (Petong)
2146^{10} 2645^{12} 2940^{10}3910^{5} 4304^{11} 5432^{10} 5767^{13} 5873^{4}

Canary Island (IRE) *J M Bradley* a80+ 69
4 b g Polar Falcon(USA) —Yellow Trumpet (Petong)
2340^{7} 2389^{7} 2955^{12}3389^{13} 3728^{16}

Can Can Star *J G Given* a56 67
3 br c Lend A Hand—Carrie Can Can (Green Tune (USA))
2542^{3} 3387^{7} 3638^{3}4154^{5} 4470^{6} 4892^{3} 5258^{4} 5992^{11}

Candarli (IRE) *D R Gandolfo* a63 40
10 ch g Polish Precedent(USA) —Calounia (IRE) (Pharly (FR))
59^{4} 166^{4}545^{4}

Candelabro (USA) *J-C Rouget* 82
2 br c Elusive Quality(USA) —Princess Ellen (Tirol)
4464a^{6}

Candidato Roy (ARG) *M F De Kock* a104 110
5 ch g Roy(USA) —Candila (ARG) (Mariache (ARG))
206a^{9} 352a^{7} 506a^{5}(619a)

Candle *H Candy* a81 87
3 b f Dansili—Celia Brady (Last Tycoon)
2349^{2} (2753) 4125^{11} 4528^{2} 5163^{7} 5533^{2}6202^{11}

Candy Anchor (FR) *R E Peacock* a29 28
7 b m Slip Anchor—Kandavu (Safawan)
400^{10} 771^{7}1467^{7}

Candyland (IRE) *M R Channon* a56 70
2 b f Bubble Gum Fellow(JPN) —Capoeira (USA) (Nureyev (USA))
1817^{6} 2572^{7} 3457^{5}4002^{2} 4444^{2} 4950^{6}

Canina *Ms Deborah J Evans* a68 65
3 b f Foxhound(USA) —Fizzy Fiona (Efisio)
45^{2} 68^{2}364^{3} (380) 601^{3} 702^{9}709^{9} 954^{8}988^{7} 1983^{6} 6478^{12}6572^{10}

Cankara (IRE) *D Carroll* a45
3 b f Daggers Drawn(USA) —Suddenly (Puissance)
3100^{7} 3387^{11}3916^{10} 6618^{11}6960^{8}

Canni Thinkaar (IRE) *P Butler* 1
5 b g Alhaarth(IRE) —Cannikin (IRE) (Lahib (USA))
235^{10} 2636^{16}

Cannon Fire (FR) *Evan Williams* 70
5 ch h Grand Lodge(USA) —Muirfield (FR) (Crystal Glitters (USA))
2219^{8}

Cannygo (IRE) *R M Flower* a2
3 b g Brave Act—Cannylass (IRE) (Brief Truce (USA))
132^{12}

Cantabilly (IRE) *M R Channon* a84 75
3 b g Distant Music(USA) —Cantaloupe (Priolo (USA))
712^{3} 993^{3} 1291^{11}1851^{2} 2065^{11} 2932^{6} 3338^{2} (3665) 3974^{4}4470^{5} 4838^{11} (5879) (5911) 6008^{5} 6070^{4}

Cantabria *Sir Michael Stoute* 102
3 br f Dansili—Valencia (Kenmare (FR))
1130^{2} 4097^{3} 4628^{6} 5159^{4} 5550^{11}

Cantarna (IRE) *J Mackie* a74 75
5 ch m Ashkalani(IRE) —Lancea (IRE) (Generous (IRE))
15^{8} 1830^{7} 2025^{7}3056^{4} (3820) 4390^{3} 4925^{16}

Cantique (IRE) *A G Newcombe* a63 61
2 b f Danetime(IRE) —Bethania (Mark Of Esteem (IRE))
3544^{6} 4221^{7} 4624^{3} 5208^{3}5419^{7} 5876^{2} 6309^{3}6416^{5} 6834^{4}

Cantrip *S Dow* a62 63
6 b m Celtic Swing—Circe (Main Reef)
1313^{10} 2133^{10} 2497^{5} 2822^{8} 3412^{5}4005^{11} 4530^{8} 6729^{12}

Canvas (IRE) *Miss Z C Davison* 45
3 b f Dansili—Sampan (Elmaamul (USA))
2349^{11} 2605^{11} 2937^{8}3161^{7} 4050^{14}

Canyouwin *J H M Gosden* a56 61
3 b f Inchinor—Tharwa (IRE) (Last Tycoon)
372^{6} 460^{3}2961^{7} 4150^{5} 4800^{2}

Capable Guest (IRE) *M R Channon* a97 101
4 bb g Cape Cross(IRE) —Alexander Confranc (IRE) (Magical Wonder (USA))
(542) 728^{3} 1129^{7} 1495^{7} 2742^{9} 3313^{4}3733^{3} 4098^{6} 5188^{6} 5675^{21}

Capahouse *B Palling*
2 b g Auction House(USA) —Perecapa (IRE) (Archway (IRE))
4705^{17}

Capania (IRE) *J W Hills* a55
2 br f Cape Cross(IRE) —Gentle Papoose (Commanche Run)
6433^{8}

Capannacce (IRE) *Francesca Falco* 87
3 ch f Lahib(USA) —Paoenia (IRE) (Pelder (IRE))
1713a^{9}

Capannina *J Noseda* a66+ 77
2 ch f Grand Lodge(USA) —Mauri Moon (Green Desert (USA))
1737^{4} 2638^{3} (3157) 3834^{4} 4335^{3} 5492^{8}

Cape *J R Fanshawe* 92+
3 b f Cape Cross(IRE) —Rubbiyati (Cadeaux Genereux)
1412[3] (2167) (4807) (5643)
Cape Columbine *D R C Elsworth* 106
4 b m Diktat—Cape Merino (Clantime)
1069[15] 1849[3] 2386[3] 3416[7]
Cape Courier (IRE) *I W McInnes* a14 45
3 b g Cape Cross(IRE) —Russian Countess (USA) (Nureyev (USA))
1200[11] 2325[11]
Cape Dancer (IRE) *J S Wainwright* 66
2 b f Cape Cross(IRE) —Yankee Dancer (Groom Dancer (USA))
2854[3] 3878[4] 4424[5] 4766[11] 5271[6]
Cape Diamond (IRE) *W R Swinburn* a82 71
3 b g Cape Cross(IRE) —Jemalina (USA) (Trempolino (USA))
1004[2] 1291[9] 4001[4]4784[5] *(5047)* 5935[6] *6076[12]*
Cape Free *E F Vaughan* a49
2 ch f Mark Of Esteem(IRE) —Cape Cod (IRE) (Unfuwain (USA))
6278[4] 6460[5]
Cape Gigi (IRE) *B J Meehan* a38
3 b f Cape Cross(IRE) —L'Accolade (IRE) (Seattle Dancer (USA))
20[7]
Cape Gold (IRE) *R A Fahey* a16 74
3 b g Cape Cross(IRE) —Filigree (Salse (USA))
1440[7] 1855[11] 2192[8] *2415[9]*
Cape Greko *A M Balding* a92 89
4 ro g Loup Sauvage(USA) —Onefortheditch (USA) (With Approval (CAN))
2988[14] 5520[13] *5845[9]6397[2] 6594[5]6830[11]*
Cape Hawk (IRE) *R Hannon* 68
2 b g Cape Cross(IRE) —Hawksbill Special (IRE) (Taufan (USA))
5659[6]
Cape Jasmine (IRE) *J Howard Johnson* 24
2 b f Danehill(USA) —Oumaldaaya (USA) (Nureyev (USA))
2409[14] 5507[15]
Cape Latina *J R Best* a42 39
3 b f Cape Cross(IRE) —Latina (IRE) (King's Theatre (IRE))
30[11] 5949[7]90[6] 8875[1]226[10] 4671[6]
Capel Island (USA) *R Hannon* 46
2 ch f Royal Academy(USA) —Fight The Question (USA) (Fit To Fight (USA))
4866[9]
Cape Maya *B J Meehan* 68
3 gr f Cape Cross(IRE) —Incatinka (Inca Chief (USA))
1822[6] 2406[9] 2655 [6] 3433[6] 4075[7]
Cape Of Luck (IRE) *P Mitchell* a87 92
3 b c Cape Cross(IRE) —Fledgling (Efisio)
665[6] 1067[16] (2863) *6594[7]6744[9] 6986[10]*
Cape Of Storms *R Brotherton* a67 67
3 b c Cape Cross(IRE) —Lloc (Absalom)
658[3] 716[7] *916[7]*2602[11] 2896[10] 3167[3] 3290[6] 3725[5]*4700[11]* 5936[11] *6721[10]*
Cape Presto (IRE) *Mrs C A Dunnett* a79 78
3 b c Cape Cross(IRE) —Samhat Mtoto (Mtoto)
1115[9] 1505[9] 3223[10] 4160[13] 4605[6]4923[9] 5301[10] *6417[5](6508) 6572[2]6690[6]*
Cape Royal *J M Bradley* a97 102
6 b g Prince Sabo—Indigo (Primo Dominie)
705[8] 989[5] 1116[10]1236[2] 1602[14] 1803[8] 2021[5] 2227[18]2624[4] 2946[3] 3038[6] 3251[7] *3535[5]*3744[7] 4360[4] 4875[2] (5009) 5182[8] 5433[2]5535[6] 5807[11] 5832[3] 5921[6] 5957[11]
Cape Runaway (IRE) *L M Cumani* a35 54
2 b f Cape Cross(IRE) —Secrets Of Honour (Belmez (USA))
3645[8] 4445[4]
Cape Schanck *Jane Chapple-Hyam* a80 77
2 b g Observatory(USA) —Sally Gardens (Alzao (USA))
*2979[2] 3385[3]*4103[2] 4344[6] *5034[2]*
Cape Secret (IRE) *R M Beckett* a56 94
3 b g Cape Cross(IRE) —Baylands Sunshine (IRE) (Classic Secret (USA))
1543[3] 2102[3] (2607) (3249) (3981) 4742[7]
Cape Society (ITY) *M Cicarelli*
2 b c Cape Cross(IRE) —White Society (IRE) (Law Society (USA))
2474a[8]
Cape Sydney (IRE) *D W Barker* a3 46
3 b f Cape Cross(IRE) —Lady At War (Warning)
861[11] 1687[9] 1792[5]2746[8] 3039[2] 4120[11] (5363) 5840[5]
Cape Thea *W R Swinburn* a68
2 b f Cape Cross(IRE) —Pasithea (IRE) (Celtic Swing)
6504[2]
Cape Velvet (IRE) *J W Hills* 80
2 b f Cape Cross(IRE) —Material Lady (IRE) (Barathea (IRE))
4559[8] 5348[2]
Cape Win (IRE) *W J Haggas* a69 69
3 b g Cape Cross(IRE) —Monarchy (IRE) (Common Grounds)
2101[3] *2415[2]* 2727[2]3045[6]
Capistrano *Mrs P Sly* a69 77
3 b g Efisio—Washita (Valiyar)
880[6] (1599) 1881[5] 5889[16]
Capital Exposure (USA) *D K Weld* 103
2 b c Danzig(USA) —Suitably Discreet (USA) (Mr Prospector (USA))
5851a[2]
Capitalise (IRE) *V Smith* a60 55
3 b g City On A Hill(USA) —Prime Interest (IRE) (King's Lake (USA))
123[8] 2299[5] 2479[8]2814[6] 3230[6] 3628[5] 3823[7] 5839[11]*6754[2] 6790[4]6979[2]*
Capital Lass *D K Ivory* a61 53
3 bb f Forzando—Fair Test (Fair Season)
66[9] 5078[13] 5291[15]*6236[7] (6554) 6703[5] 6796[6]6892[4] (6961)*

Capitano Uncino (ITY) *M Marcialis*
2 b c Central Park(IRE) —Seattle Encounter (USA) (Danzig Connection (USA))
2474a[7]
Cappanrush (IRE) *A Ennis* a41
6 gr g Medaaly—Introvert (USA) (Exbourne (USA))
314[6]
Capped For Victory (USA) *W S Cunningham* 91
5 b g Red Ransom(USA) —Nazoo (IRE) (Nijinsky (CAN))
1856[12] 2108[10]
Caprice Meill (FR) *E Leenders* 103
6 b m French Glory—Eria Flore (FR) (Hero's Honor (USA))
5881a[2] 6610a[3]
Capricho (IRE) *J Akehurst* 92
9 gr g Lake Coniston(IRE) —Star Spectacle (Spectacular Bid (USA))
970[5] 1285[7] 1474[9] 2147[6] 2819[3]3413[19] 5765[11] 6054[12]
Capricorn Run (USA) *Saeed Bin Suroor* 84
3 bb c Elusive Quality(USA) —Cercida (USA) (Copelan (USA))
5722[9]
Capriolla *P F I Cole* 64
3 b f In The Wings—Seren Quest (Rainbow Quest (USA))
971[3] 1114[7] 1418[8] 1740[9] 2102[5]
Captain Bolsh *J Pearce* a57 65
3 b g Tagula(IRE) —Bolshoi Star (Soviet Star (USA))
1141[10] 1433[4] *2210[4]*3668[10] 3870[3] 4332[9] *4700[9]*4847[11] *6708[9]*
Captain Darling (IRE) *R W Price* a72 63
6 b g Pennekamp(USA) —Gale Warning (IRE) (Last Tycoon)
*82[8] 1574[1]*170[6] *2688[3]*339[8] *6124(3390)* 3599[5]*(4048) 4368[6]5386[3]* 6060[10] *6624[9]6814[3]*
Captain General *J A R Toller* a79 73
4 br h In The Wings—Sea Quest (IRE) (Rainbow Quest (USA))
(1614) 3256[5] 4604[8] 5276[7] *(5610) (5991)*
Captain Hurricane *P W Chapple-Hyam* 107
4 b g Desert Style(IRE) —Ravine (Indian Ridge)
729[13] 1485[22]
Captain Jacksparra (IRE) *K A Ryan* 69
2 b c Danehill(USA) —Push A Venture (Shirley Heights)
4260[4] 4650[3] 5059[6]
Captain Kurt (NZ) *Melody Conlon* 108
4 b g Volksraad—O'Sequita (NZ) (O'Reilly (NZ))
5416a[9]
Captain Margaret *J Pearce* a78 80
4 b m Royal Applause—Go For Red (IRE) (Thatching)
109[3] 1864[2]64[4] 4214[4]78[2] (557) 800[3] *983[3]* 1419[2]*5786[14] 6189[12]6426[7]*
Captain Marvelous (IRE) *B W Hills* 115+
2 b c Invincible Spirit(IRE) —Shesasmartlady (IRE) (Dolphin Street (FR))
1090[3] (1587) 2144[2] 2719[11] 3924[5] 4789[2](5372) 5656[3] (6229a)
Captain Nemo (USA) *T D Barron* 65
2 b g Officer(USA) —Macarena Macarena (CAN) (Gone West (USA))
3247[5] 5379[9] 6012[3]
Captain Oats (IRE) *Mrs P Ford* a53 51
3 b g Bahhare(USA) —Adarika (King's Lake (USA))
5897[16] *6429[8] 6588[4]6817[6]*
Captain Smoothy *M J Gingell* a14 43
6 b g Charmer—The Lady Captain (Neltino)
5925[11]
Captain Squire (USA) *Jeff Mullins* a114
7 b g Flying Chevron(USA) —Dolly's Back (USA) (At The Threshold (USA))
740a[4]
Captain Torrance (IRE) *P W Chapple-Hyam* 63+
3 b g Titus Livius(FR) —Gay's Flutter (Beldale Flutter (USA))
795[7] 880[16] 1263[13] 1646[9] 2187[4]2570[7]
Captain Xaar (FR) *J R Fanshawe* a65+ 69+
3 b c Xaar—Rabea (USA) (Devil's Bag (USA))
*981[4] 1274[2]*1681[6]
Captivate *A J McCabe* a53 49
3 ch f Hernando(FR) —Catch (USA) (Blushing Groom (FR))
*422[10] 548[5]*979[8] *1259[8]* 1345[12]1661[8] 5497[4] 5955[9] *6133[2]6540[2] 6620[10](6705) 6754[9]*
Carabinieri (IRE) *J Barclay* 48
3 b g Danehill Dancer(IRE) —Cartuccia (IRE) (Doyoun)
3001[8] 3620[4] 4136[P] (Dead)
Caracciola (GER) *N J Henderson* 92
9 b g Lando(GER) —Capitolina (FR) (Empery (USA))
2013[10]
Caracho Directa (GER) *Andreas Lowe* 70
2 ch c Dashing Blade—Capua (GER) (Platini (GER))
6092a[5]
Caradak (IRE) *Saeed Bin Suroor* 118+
5 b h Desert Style(IRE) —Caraiyma (IRE) (Shahrastani (USA))
(3702) 4596[3] (4839) (5701a) 5982a[3]
Caragh Mia (IRE) *G G Margarson* a56 50
4 b m Desert Prince(IRE) —Decant (Rousillon (USA))
6439[13] 6483[6]6577[5] 6693[7]6812[6]
Caraman (IRE) *J J Quinn* a75 72
8 ch h Grand Lodge(USA) —Caraiyma (IRE) (Shahrastani (USA))
(59) 168[2] 2628[10] *3098[2]3388[5]* 4947[4] 5513[9]
Carcinetto (IRE) *P D Evans* a63 64+
4 b m Danetime(IRE) —Dolphin Stamp (IRE) (Dolphin Street (FR))
*38[10] 249[5]465[9] 766[5]*1397[8] 2531[8] (3863) 4223 [2]5131[2] 5480[2] 5631[8] *6325[3](6348) 6521[4]6681[6] 6884[2]6990[3]*

Cardinal Venture (IRE) *K A Ryan* a71 71
8 b g Bishop Of Cashel—Phoenix Venture (IRE) (Thatching)
*7[4] 348[6]542[11] 600[2]*728[20] 1775[14] 3068[7] 4381[5] 5144[9]*6239[10]*
Career Girl (USA) *E A L Dunlop* 63
2 b f Theatrical—Dubai Spirit (USA) (Mt. Livermore (USA))
3796[12] 5068[5] 5352[11] 5748[12]
Carefree *W J Haggas* a54
2 b f Medicean—Hertha (Hernando (FR))
6644[5] 6879[6]
Carefree Girl *E A Wheeler* a40
3 b f Josr Algarhoud(IRE) —Double Fault (IRE) (Zieten (USA))
124[8] 326[10]
Careless Abandon (IRE) *Andrew Oliver* 74
3 b f Mull Of Kintyre(USA) —Ruwy (Soviet Star (USA))
(4124a)
Caressed *J R Fanshawe* 97+
3 b f Medicean—Embraced (Pursuit Of Love)
1418[2] (2129) (2865) (3548)
Caribbean *John M Oxx* 102
3 b g Sadler's Wells(USA) —Quaestio (USA) (Seeking The Gold (USA))
1025a[5] 1708a[4] 2039a[9]
Caribbean Coral *J J Quinn* 95
7 ch g Brief Truce(USA) —Caribbean Star (Soviet Star (USA))
1602[9] 2227[6] 2624[10] 2830[3] 3281[3](3449) 3471[4] 3715[2] 4101[13] 4468[6] 4875[6](5169) 5433[9] 5832[13]
Caribbean Dancer (USA) *M Johnston* a67 74
4 b m Theatrical—Enticed (USA) (Stage Door Johnny (USA))
6947[4]
Caribbean Nights (IRE) *T D Easterby* a60 53
3 b g Night Shift(USA) —Caribbean Knockout (IRE) (Halling (USA))
3910[10] 4120[8] 4262[8]
Caribbean Pearl (USA) *C E Brittain* 77
4 b m Silver Hawk(USA) —Ras Shaikh (USA) (Sheikh Albadou)
799[2]
Carillon (IRE) *M Johnston* 76
2 ch f Desert Prince(IRE) —Steeple (Selkirk (USA))
3780[2] 4228[2] (5237)
Cark *T J Pitt* a50 65
8 b g Farfelu—Precious Girl (Precious Metal)
465[5] 633[11]6704[11]
Carlburg (IRE) *Mrs C A Dunnett* a11 38
5 b g Barathea(IRE) —Ichnusa (Bay Express)
6307[9] 6370[13]
Carlitos Spirit (IRE) *B R Millman* a60 64
2 ch g Redback—Negria (IRE) (Al Hareb (USA))
663[4] 944[5] 2287[6]3117[8] 5041[5] 5382[4]
Carlomagno (IRE) *B Grizzetti* 91
3 b c King Charlemagne(USA) —Streets Of Gold (USA) (Saratoga Six (USA))
1175a[8] 1872a[13]
Carloman *R M Beckett* a64 70
3 ch g King Charlemagne(USA) —Jarrayan (Machiavellian (USA))
1859[8] 2171[4] *2648[2]*3197[2] (3668) 4076[7] 4968[6] *5775[8]*
Carlotamix (FR) *A Fabre* a77 117+
3 gr c Linamix(FR) —Carlitta (USA) (Olympio (USA))
1178a[6] 4168a[2] 4623a[5]
Carlowsantana (IRE) *Adrian Sexton* 67
3 b g Blue Ocean(USA) —Lees First Step (Reprimand)
4034a[3]
Carlton Scroop (FR) *J Jay* a58+ 64
3 ch g Priolo(USA) —Elms Schooldays (Emarati (USA))
(887) 1221[3] *3016[2]* 4777[4]
Carmelixia (IRE) *R Pritchard-Gordon* a82 88
4 gr m Linamix(FR) —Carmel (FR) (Highest Honor (FR))
885a[8]
Carmenero (GER) *W R Muir* a81 79
3 b g Barathea(IRE) —Claire Fraser (USA) (Gone West (USA))
1349[2] 2205[8] 2650[5] 2863[2] 3224[14]3487[6] 4083[7] 4488[5] 5070[6] 5377[7]*5649[2] 6094[6]*
Carmens Girl (IRE) *Daniel Mark Loughnane* 18
3 b f Carrowkeel(IRE) —Still River (King's Lake (USA))
4034a[16]
Carnbridge (IRE) *M J Grassick* 77
4 b h Giant's Causeway(USA) —Mayenne (USA) (Nureyev (USA))
5396a[16]
Carnivore *T D Barron* a54+ 81+
4 ch g Zafonic(USA) —Ermine (IRE) (Cadeaux Genereux)
(2926) 3697[3] (4253) 4378[2] 4521[2] 5144[6] (5345)
Carobene (IRE) *R Mimmocchi* 99
3 b c Distant Music(USA) —Pyjama Girl (USA) (Night Shift (USA))
1872a[7]
Carolina Sky (USA) *M Nicks* 81
4 b m Sky Classic(CAN) —Afleet Summer (USA) (Afleet (CAN))
6368a[11]
Carolines Secret *Mario Hofer* 98
2 ch f Inchinor—Blodwen (USA) (Mister Baileys)
5858a[3]
Carpeting *D Morris* a52 59
3 b g Alhaarth(IRE) —Wigging (Warning)
*254[9] 337[12]*1616[3] 3045[8] 3303[9]
Carpet Ride *B G Powell* a62 70
4 ch g Unfuwain(USA) —Fragrant Oasis (USA) (Rahy (USA))
421[7] 1755[5] *1958[6]*2099[12] 2702[10] *3159[7]*3592[10] 4585[11]
Carr Hall (IRE) *T D Easterby* 61
3 b g Rossini(USA) —Pidgeon Bay (IRE) (Perugino (USA))
1044[5] 1251[5] 1736[15] 2128[4] 2782[3]3290[4] 4943[6]

Carriage Trail (USA) *C McGaughey III* 99
3 b f Giant's Causeway(USA) —Manoa (USA) (Seeking The Gold (USA))
5198a[8]
Carrie McCurry (IRE) *Patrick Martin* a74 47
2 b f Fath(USA) —Simply Devious (IRE) (Dr Devious (IRE))
6505[2] 6925[4]
Carrietau *J G Given* a40 69
3 b g Key Of Luck(USA) —Carreamia (Weldnaas (USA))
2616[11] 3306[12] 3357[2] 4255[5] 4909[2]
Carry On Doc *Ernst Oertel* a64 72
5 b g Dr Devious(IRE) —Florentynna Bay (Aragon)
167[8] 236[10]505[11] 559[11]711[7]
Carson's Spirit (USA) *W S Kittow* a68 81
2 ch c Carson City(USA) —Pascarina (FR) (Exit To Nowhere (USA))
(961) 2719[14] *3641[8]* 5624[6]
Carte Sauvage (USA) *M F Harris* a47 47
5 rg g Kris S(USA) —See You (USA) (Gulch (USA))
306a[2]
Cartimandua *E S McMahon* 74
2 b f Medicean—Agrippina (Timeless Times (USA))
3495[2]
Cartography (IRE) *E Charpy* 104
5 b h Zafonic(USA) —Sans Escale (USA) (Diesis)
(494a) 619a[8]
Cartoonist (IRE) *A King* 58
3 ch g Fruits Of Love(USA) —Verusa (IRE) (Petorius)
1282[3] 2124[12] *2795[12]3017[13]*
Carus (GER) *D K Richardson* 70
7 br h Taishan(GER) —Contessina (FR) (Mistigri)
6610a[12]
Carwell (IRE) *M Johnston* 70+
2 ch f King's Best(USA) —Lady Kestrel (USA) (Theatrical)
(3908) 5884[2]
Casablanca Minx (IRE) *N P Littmoden* a78 60
3 br f Desert Story(IRE) —Conspire (IRE) (Turtle Island (IRE))
31[3] (85) (122) (378) (448) 483[7]724[5] 1190[11] *1381[7]6932[5]*
Casalese *Micky Hammond* a13 31
4 ch g Wolfhound(USA) —Little Redwing (Be My Chief (USA))
4909[13]
Casata (IRE) *F Reuterskiold*
3 b f Kalanisi(IRE) —La Menorquina (USA) (Woodman (USA))
(2564a) *3326a[7]*
Casco Bay (IRE) *P J Prendergast* 62
2 b c Fath(USA) —Montana Miss (IRE) (Earl Of Barking (IRE))
4824a[16]
Cashbar *J R Fanshawe* a64+ 81+
5 b m Bishop Of Cashel—Barford Sovereign (Unfuwain (USA))
660[10]
Cashcade (IRE) *A M Balding* 63
2 br g Raise A Grand(IRE) —Cotton Grace (IRE) (Case Law)
1770[9] 2218[5] 2530[8] 5053[9] 5585[13] (Dead)
Cashel Bay (USA) *Luke Comer* a42 93
8 b g Nureyev(USA) —Madame Premier (USA) (Raja Baba (USA))
3642[10]
Cashel Mead *J L Spearing* a86 96
6 b m Bishop Of Cashel—Island Mead (Pharly (FR))
(119) 320[12] 424[6]608[4] 824[5]858[4] (1243) 1414[5] *1618[3]* 1689[2] (1774) (1846) (1981) (2173) 2189[8]*2340[4]* 3251[10] 4085[19]4180[3] 4468[10] (4598) (4771) 5009[7] 5535[7] 5832[14]
Cashema (IRE) *D R MacLeod* a32 50
5 b m Cape Cross(IRE) —Miss Shema (USA) (Gulch (USA))
818[10] 1530[6] 3139[8]
Cashier *J H M Gosden* 104
4 gr h Alhaarth(IRE) —Cashew (Sharrood (USA))
(278a) 1301[5] 1678[10] (Dead)
Cash Included (USA) *Craig Dollase* a116
2 br f Include(USA) —Henderson Band (USA) (Chimes Band (USA))
6338a[5]
Cash On (IRE) *Karen George* a75 73
4 ch g Spectrum(IRE) —Lady Lucre (IRE) (Last Tycoon)
1927[6]
Casonova (IRE) *T D Easterby* a8 51
3 b g Trans Island—Sherna Girl (IRE) (Desert Story (IRE))
861[13] 1232[7] 1736[9]2284[6] 2782[14]
Caspian Rose *M J Attwater* a35 31
3 b f Paris House—Caspian Morn (Lugana Beach)
5761[14] *6134[13] 6282[7]6492[4]*
Cassiara *J Pearce* 78
2 gr f Diktat—Heaven-Liegh-Grey (Grey Desire)
892[3] 1542[4] 1831[3] 2125[6] 2800[11]4053[3] 5157[7]
Cassie's Choice (IRE) *B Smart* 70
2 b f Fath(USA) —Esteraad (IRE) (Cadeaux Genereux)
2375[4] 2807[3] 3713[2] 4424[2] 5748[5]
Castano *B R Millman* 75
2 br g Makbul—Royal Orchid (IRE) (Shalford (IRE))
987[3] 3308[2] 5147[2] 5645 [7]
Castanza *M Wellings* a58 71
4 b m Bachir(IRE) —Sylhall (Sharpo)
*3[2] 951[2]148[11] 648[9]*1217[10] *1387[4] 1765[11]*
Castara Bay *R Hannon* a82 73
2 b c Sakhee(USA) —Mayaro Bay (Robellino (USA))
2579[7] 3083[3] 5168[3] *6074[5]6599[2]*
Cast In Gold (USA) *B J Meehan* a85+ 91+
2 b f Elusive Quality(USA) —Crystal Crossing (IRE) (Royal Academy (USA))
2958[2] 3707[2] 5344[2] *(6099)*

Castle Caw (IRE) *Miss G Lee* 31
2 b c The West(USA) —Whateveryousay (USA) (Verbatim (USA))
5662a[15]

Castle Howard (IRE) *W J Musson* 94
4 b g Montjeu(IRE) —Termania (IRE) (Shirley Heights)
1842[2] 2850[4] 4027[7] 4631[5] 5010[13]6336[4]

Castleshane (IRE) *S Gollings*
9 b g Kris—Ahbab (IRE) (Ajdal (USA))
4256[10]

Casual Affair *E J O'Neill* a67 70
3 b g Golden Snake(USA) —Fontaine Lady (Millfontaine)
3112[4] 3336[6] 4113[3] 4973[3]5388[7] 6260[8]6572[5] 6738[2]

Casual Glance *A M Balding* a66+ 101?
4 b m Sinndar(IRE) —Spurned (USA) (Robellino (USA))
991[7] 1409[5] 2723[13] 4346[3] 4791[3]

Catabound (USA) *B R Millman* a52 54
3 bb g Black Minnaloushe(USA) —Castellina (USA) (Danzig Connection (USA))
1513[9] 2171[11] 2814[15] 3349[14] 4527[11]

Catbang (IRE) *N A Callaghan* a77 68
3 b c Zafonic(USA) —Silky Dawn (IRE) (Night Shift (USA))
1416[2] 1616[2] 2391[8] 2932[10] (3055)

Cat Belling (IRE) *R Bouresly* a72 102
6 br m Catrail(USA) —Lute And Lyre (IRE) (The Noble Player (USA))
282a[13] 351a[9] 369a[8]

Catch The Cat (IRE) *Robert Gray* a49 72
7 b g Catrail(USA) —Tongabezi (IRE) (Shernazar)
1125[9] 1297[16] 1438[3] 1611[2] 2237[14]3503[6] 3913[9] 3988[16] 4019[6] (4477) 4636[8]4834[7]

Cat De Mille (USA) *P W Chapple-Hyam* 79
2 bb c Stormin Fever(USA) —De Mille (USA) (Nureyev (USA))
5658[5] (5947)

Categorical *K G Reveley* a74 78
3 b g Diktat—Zibet (Kris)
1091[13] 1617[6] 2033[3] 4378[16] 4763[7]5284[8] 6275[5]

Cate Washington *Mrs L Williamson* a13 48
3 b f Superior Premium—Willisa (Polar Falcon (USA))
2095[12] 2554[13] 3245[9]3478[6] 4120[9] 6958[8]

Catherine Medici *R M H Cowell* a56 22
3 ch f Medicean—Fine Honor (FR) (Highest Honor (FR))
835[2] 2019[8] 2244[11]3828[8] 4627[P] 6130[14]

Catherines Cafe (IRE) *Mrs P N Dutfield* a39 52
3 b f Mull Of Kintyre(USA) —Wisecrack (IRE) (Lucky Guest)
851[8] 1801[3] 2190[10]2511[10] 3450[9] 4531[6] 4983[8] 5885[7]6128[13]

Catheriniski (IRE) *P A Blockley* a16 47?
4 b m Danetime(IRE) —Choralli (Inchinor)
180[6] 937[P] (Dead)

Cativo Cavallino *Jamie Poulton* a71 68
3 ch g Bertolini(USA) —Sea Isle (Selkirk (USA))
60[10] 2652[7] 3094[12]3406[7] 3932[8] 4245[11]4591[11] 4800[10] 5426[8]6578[7]

Catlivius (IRE) *K A Ryan* a59 63
2 ch f Titus Livius(FR) —Cat's Tale (IRE) (Catrail (USA))
3358[4] 4421[4] 4920[5] 6271[6] 6679[2]6894[4]

Cat Six (USA) *B J Meehan* 49
2 b f Tale Of The Cat(USA) —Hurricane Warning (USA) (Thunder Gulch (USA))
5592[8]

Catskill *E F Vaughan* a40 77
4 ch g Inchinor—Manhattan Sunset (USA) (El Gran Senor (USA))
1164[12] (2149) 2499[3] 3429[7]3900[6] 4575[7] 6070[12]

Catspraddle (USA) *R Hannon* a65 74
3 ch f High Yield(USA) —Beaux Dorothy (USA) (Dehere (USA))
1241[8] 1411[7] (2511) 2652[11]3150[3] 4562[13] 5350[7] 6508[6]6585[6] 6672[8]

Catweasel *L A Dace* a19 51
2 ch g Auction House(USA) —Gracious Imp (USA) (Imp Society (USA))
701[10] 1429[10] 1862[4]2064[7] 6058[12]

Caught You Looking *W R Swinburn* a65 57
2 b f Observatory(USA) —Corndavon (USA) (Sheikh Albadou)
5871[6] 6377[4]

Cause To Believe (USA) *J Hollendorfer* a104
3 gr c Maria's Mon(USA) —Imaginary Cat (USA) (Storm Cat (USA))
1498a[13]

Caustic Wit (IRE) *M S Saunders* a67 81
8 b g Cadeaux Genereux—Baldemosa (FR) (Lead On Time (USA))
47[11] 532[12]587[10] 693[11]1188[13] 2095[11] 2207[2]2331[7] (2484) (2711) 2792[9] 2971[7]3094[2] 3368[15] (3434) 3898[3] 4172[7] 4364[2]4557[3] 4629[4] (4970) 5476[6]5737[5] 6020[8] 6827[6]6990[5]

Cava Bien *B J Llewellyn* a38 56
4 b g Bien Bien(USA) —Bebe De Cham (Tragic Role (USA))
1219[4] 5587[3] 6161[7]

Cavallini (USA) *G L Moore* 90
4 bb g Bianconi(USA) —Taylor Park (USA) (Sir Gaylord)
2989[10] 3255[8] 4560[9] 5141[5] 5479[10]

Cavallino (USA) *R A Kvisla* 97
6 b g Joyeux Danseur(USA) —Krypto Katie (USA) (Cryptoclearance (USA))
4346[7] 4770[5]

Cavallo Di Ferro (IRE) *J R Boyle* a68 57
2 b g Iron Mask(USA) —Lacinia (Groom Dancer (USA))
1959[10] (2552) 4813[7]

Cavalry Guard (USA) *H R A Cecil* 80
2 ch g Officer(USA) —Leeward City (USA) (Carson City (USA))
3738[2] 4731[2] 5481[4] 5883[10]

Cavalry Twill (IRE) *P F I Cole* a70
2 b c Alhaarth(IRE) —Blue Mantle (IRE) (Barathea (IRE))
6386[8] 6523[2]

Cavan Gael (FR) *P Howling* a62 75
4 b g Dansili—Time Will Show (FR) (Exit To Nowhere (USA))
405[12] 2820[7] 3999[9]4139[2] 4439[5]4575[9] 4974[13] 5609[11]

Cavendish *J M P Eustace* a39 38
2 b g Pursuit Of Love—Bathwick Babe (IRE) (Sri Pekan (USA))
2930[14] 3408[8] 3979[10]6303[7] 6421[6]

Cave Of The Giant (IRE) *T D McCarthy* 81
4 b g Giant's Causeway(USA) —Maroussie (FR) (Saumarez)
4967[3] 5628[8]

Cavewarrior *J Noseda* a82 52
3 b g Arkadian Hero(USA) —Lyna (Slip Anchor)
341[4]

Caviar Heights (IRE) *Miss L A Perratt* 52
2 b c Golan(IRE) —Caviar Queen (USA) (Crafty Prospector (USA))
5632[7] 6316[6]

Cav Okay (IRE) *R Hannon* 96
2 gr g Fasliyev(USA) —Dane's Lane (IRE) (Danehill (USA))
(1113) 1582[2] 2084[2] 2771[3] 3252[8] 3734[18]4026[10]

Cavort (IRE) *Pat Eddery* 76
2 ch f Vettori(IRE) —Face The Storm (IRE) (Barathea (IRE))
1046[13] 1284[2] (1930) 3026[6] 3496[11] 5585[11]

Cavorting *M Kahn* 96
4 ch g Polar Falcon(USA) —Prancing (Prince Sabo)
5225a[7]

Cayman Breeze *J M Bradley* a60 59
6 b g Danzig(USA) —Lady Thynn (FR) (Crystal Glitters (USA))
22[3] 2275[3]336[5] 2567[7] 2898[5]3368[12] 3612[5] 3835[5] 4233[6] 4365[7]4985[6] 5453[4] (6142) 6439[5]6632[6] 6884[3]

Cayman Calypso (IRE) *Mrs P Sly* a54 54
5 ro g Danehill Dancer(IRE) —Warthill Whispers (Grey Desire)
40[4]

Cayman King *R Craggs* a56 58
4 b g Cayman Kai(IRE) —Distinctly Laura (IRE) (Distinctly North (USA))
178[5] 1577[6]

Cayman Mischief *James Moffatt* a12 39
6 b m Cayman Kai(IRE) —Tribal Mischief (Be My Chief (USA))
255[11] 360[11]1272[9]

Caymans Gift *A C Whillans* a21 65
6 ch g Cayman Kai(IRE) —Gymcrak Cyrano (IRE) (Cyrano De Bergerac)
414[12] 1346[3] 1590[2]2078[3] 2751[4] 2998[7] 3810[3] 4351[6]4723[8]

Cd Europe (IRE) *G A Swinbank* a77 64
8 ch g Royal Academy(USA) —Woodland Orchid (IRE) (Woodman (USA))
(1443) 1735[3] (2208)

Cd Flyer (IRE) *R C Guest* a78 77
9 ch g Grand Lodge(USA) —Pretext (Polish Precedent (USA))
1504[12] 1760[13] 3330[12]

Cecchetti (IRE) *Mrs H Sweeting* a47 40
3 b f Imperial Ballet(IRE) —Quiver Tree (Lion Cavern (USA))
543[8] 577[7]676[5] 1149[6]1726[2] 2101[8] 2415[6]3195[10]

Cedarberg (UAE) *R Bouresly* 104
5 b h Cape Cross(IRE) —Crinolette (IRE) (Sadler's Wells (USA))
203a[P]

Cedarlea (IRE) *R A Fahey* 70
2 ch g Shinko Forest(IRE) —Baileys First (IRE) (Alzao (USA))
4251[2] 4693[2] 5959[3]

Cefalu (CHI) *Lee Freedman* 107
5 b g Dushyantor(USA) —Cristal (CHI) (Semenenko (USA))
5817a[4] 6346a[8]

Celebration Song (IRE) *W R Swinburn* a84 85
3 b g Royal Applause—Googoosh (IRE) (Danehill (USA))
724[3] 1617[3] 2330[7]5428[U]

Celebre Vadala (FR) *A Fabre* 102
3 b f Peintre Celebre(USA) —Vadlamixa (FR) (Linamix (FR))
(2374a) 4192a[8] 5702a[8]

Celestial Halo (IRE) *B W Hills* 89
2 b c Galileo(IRE) —Pay The Bank (High Top)
4680[5]

Celtic Carisma *K G Reveley* 60+
4 b m Celtic Swing—Kathryn's Pet (Blakeney)
990[16] (1219) 1758[8] 2196[12] 2871[5] 3019[8]5725[8] 5960[11]

Celtic Change (IRE) *M Dods* 73
2 br c Celtic Swing—Changi (IRE) (Lear Fan (USA))
4424[4] 4880[4]

Celticello (IRE) *Heather Dalton* a26 94+
4 bb g Celtic Swing—Viola Royale (IRE) (Royal Academy (USA))
763[9] 5512[14]

Celtic Empire (IRE) *Jedd O'Keeffe* a42 58
3 b g Second Empire(IRE) —Celtic Guest (IRE) (Be My Guest (USA))
3258[8] 4204[9] 4884[14]5247[9] 6305[5]

Celtic Furrow (IRE) *J S Bolger* 85
3 b g Spectrum(IRE) —Key To Coolcullen (IRE) (Royal Academy (USA))
928a[6]

Celtic Jig (IRE) *T D Easterby*
3 b g Celtic Swing—Ceide Dancer (IRE) (Alzao (USA))
731[8] 1492[5] 1854[8]

Celtic Memories (IRE) *M W Easterby* 62
2 ch f Selkirk(USA) —Memories (IRE) (Don't Forget Me)
4830[5]

Celtic Mill *D W Barker* a107 115
8 b g Celtic Swing—Madam Millie (Milford)
1485[19] 2303[4] 2720[20] 3076[3] 3709[4]3972[16] (4158) (5158) 5375[10] 5642[5]

Celtic Shadow (IRE) *K G Reveley* 48+
4 b g Celtic Swing—Shabby Chic (USA) (Red Ransom (USA))
1233[11] 1591[16]

Celtic Spa (IRE) *P D Evans* a63 76
4 gr m Celtic Swing—Allegorica (IRE) (Alzao (USA))
992[12] 1207[9] 1802[9] 2113[5] 3153[8]3450[3] 3590[5] (3897) (4070) 4286[3] 4602[11] 5590[14]6211[8] 6568[5] 6698[8]6934[10]

Celtic Spirit (IRE) *R M Beckett* a78 90
3 ch g Pivotal—Cavernista (Lion Cavern (USA))
964[6] (2063) 2754[2] (4784) 5511[3]5869[3]

Celtic Star (IRE) *Mrs L Williamson* a53 44
8 b g Celtic Swing—Recherchee (Rainbow Quest (USA))
1748[3]

Celtic Step *M Johnston* 80
2 br c Selkirk(USA) —Inchiri (Sadler's Wells (USA))
4781[9] (5088) 5633[3] (5958) 6106[5]

Celtic Sultan (IRE) *T P Tate* 98
2 b c Celtic Swing—Farjah (IRE) (Charnwood Forest (IRE))
3247[2] (3721) 4561[3] 5183[7] 5809[7]

Celtic Sunset (IRE) *M A Jarvis* a42
3 b f Celtic Swing—Hishmah (Nashwan (USA))
272[8]

Celtic Thunder *T J Etherington* a64 65
5 b g Mind Games—Lake Mistassiu (Tina's Pet)
171[7] 225[9]639[12] 2380[6] 2780[2](3245) 3617[17] 4571[14] 6404[7]

Celtic Warrior (IRE) *Liam Roche* 85
3 b g Celtic Swing—Notable Dear (ITY) (Last Tycoon)
755a[10]

Celtique *M Wigham* a67 77
4 b m Celtic Swing—Heart's Harmony (Blushing Groom (FR))
161[12] 221[11]343[10] 557[8]698[11] (2577) 3152[2] (3706) 3900[3] (4104) 4604[14]

Cemgraft *A J Lidderdale* a52+ 63
5 b m In The Wings—Soviet Maid (IRE) (Soviet Star (USA))
270[P] 328[7]457[2] 1199[6]1415[2] (3894) 4702[9] 4929[8]

Centaurus *Saeed Bin Suroor* 89
4 gr h Daylami(IRE) —Dandanna (IRE) (Linamix (FR))
6334[7]

Centenary (IRE) *J S Wainwright* 70
2 b g Traditionally(USA) —Catherinofaragon (USA) (Chief's Crown (USA))
2733[5] 3187[3] 3619[2] 4250[3] 4509[6]4882[3] 5239[4] (5616) 6007[11]

Centreboard (USA) *R Charlton* 68
2 rg f Mizzen Mast(USA) —Corsini (Machiavellian (USA))
2643[2] 3796[6] 4754[2]

Centreofattention *Mrs A Duffield* 35
3 b f Groom Dancer(USA) —Centre Court (Second Set (IRE))
1218[9] 1445[8] 2001[7] 2874[8] 3306[7]3910[14]

Ceprin (IRE) *A & G Botti* 104
5 b h Desert Prince(IRE) —Black Wood (USA) (Woodman (USA))
2217a[5] 6364a[5]

Cerebus *A J McCabe* a73 73
4 b m Wolfhound(USA) —Bring On The Choir (Chief Singer)
4[8] 80[8]225[6] 332[6]6930[10]

Ceredig *W R Muir* a64 66
3 b g Lujain(USA) —Anneli Rose (Superlative)
1378[3] 2134[5] 2433[7] 2652[13] 3348[10]3842[2] 5874[3] 5969[3]6389[9] 6440[3]

Ceremonial Jade (UAE) *M Botti* a106+ 88+
3 b g Jade Robbery(USA) —Talah (Danehill (USA))
(2948) 4144[2] 4802[11] (5107) (5785)

Ceris Star (IRE) *B R Millman* 47
2 b g Cadeaux Genereux—Midsummernitedream (GER) (Thatching)
2009[10] 4487[8] 5125[13]

Certain Circles (USA) *A M Balding* a72 72
3 b c King Cugat(USA) —Daily Special (USA) (Dayjur (USA))
34[6]

Certain Justice (USA) *Stef Liddiard* a80 78+
8 gr g Lit De Justice(USA) —Pure Misk (Rainbow Quest (USA))
1[8] 100[8](3304) 4114[3] 4602[2] 4706[3]

Cerulean Rose *A W Carroll* a55 65
7 ch m Bluegrass Prince(IRE) —Elegant Rose (Noalto)
1047[11] 1413[5] 1774[10] 2027[2] 2095[2]2962[9] 3267[7] 3368[7] 3899[5] (4780) 5131[3]5378[8] 5756[6] 6556[10]

Cervinio (USA) *J-C Rouget* 92
2 b c Elusive Quality(USA) —Miss Turlington (USA) (Seattle Slew (USA))
5399a[3]

Cesare *J R Fanshawe* a103+ 115
5 b g Machiavellian(USA) —Tromond (Lomond (USA))
728[12] (2742) 3534[10] (4896) 5341[5]

Cesar Manrique (IRE) *A E Jones* a65 74
4 ch g Vettori(IRE) —Norbella (Nordico (USA))
1047[2] 1878[4] 2189[7] 2962[2] 4564[3]4807[7] 5058[13] 5872[6] 6020[7] 6489[10]6762[6]

Cesc *P J Makin* a90+ 79
2 b c Compton Place—Mana Pools (IRE) (Brief Truce (USA))
1203[7] 1429[7] 1737[6] 3544[3] (4178) 4436[2]5783[7] (6458) (6598) (6746)

C'Est Ca *W P Mullins* 73
2 b c Groom Dancer(USA) —Known Class (USA) (Known Fact (USA))
5466a[19]

Cetshwayo *J M P Eustace* a61 66
4 ch g Pursuit Of Love—Induna (Grand Lodge (USA))
3794[9] 4668[9] (5609) 5683[8]

Cezzaro (IRE) *T A K Cuthbert* a42 43
8 ch g Ashkalani(IRE) —Sept Roses (USA) (Septieme Ciel (USA))
2395[5]

Chaco (IRE) *Niall Moran* a20 42
3 b c Cape Cross(IRE) —Carotene (CAN) (Great Nephew)
6729[11]

Chacotero (IRE) *Werner Glanz* 92
3 b c Red Ransom(USA) —Chaguaramas (IRE) (Mujadil (USA))
2671a[6]

Chaibia (IRE) *D Smaga* 108
3 ch f Peintre Celebre(USA) —Mawhiba (USA) (Dayjur (USA))
1330a[5] 1874a[4] 2491a[8] (4035a) 5198a[4]

Chained Emotion (IRE) *Kevin Prendergast* 102
5 b g Danetime(IRE) —Taispeain (IRE) (Petorius)
1469a[9] 2308a[11] 3125a[7] 4187a[10]

Chairman Bobby *D W Barker* a34 61
8 ch g Clantime—Formidable Liz (Formidable (USA))
1563[13] 1735[7] 1794[13] 2376[7] 2505[3]2700[2] 3003[5] 3670[3] (3833) 4232[3] 4477[2]4523[3] 4957[2] 5078[4] 5620[13]

Chairman Rick (IRE) *D Nicholls* a51 62
4 b g Danehill Dancer(IRE) —Come Together (Mtoto)
8[7] 100[13]143[10] 173[7]180[5] (1447) 1594[11] 2544[11]2758[14]

Chaka Zulu *D W Thompson* a46 65
9 b g Muhtarram(USA) —African Dance (USA) (El Gran Senor (USA))
443[P]

Chakra (JPN) *A Adachi* 114
6 b h Mayano Top Gun(JPN) —Carlossa (IRE) (Caerleon (USA))
1329a[16]

Chalentina *P Howling* a62 81
3 b f Primo Valentino(IRE) —Chantilly Myth (Sri Pekan (USA))
1290[5] 1649[2] 2459[5] 3032[2] (3826) 5079[2]5436[12] 5908[8] 6988[4]

Chalice Welcome *C F Wall* a43 36
3 b g Most Welcome—Blue Peru (IRE) (Perugino (USA))
39[2] 176[8]308[3] 594[7]6542[6] 6707[4]

Chalin *S Deledda* 94
6 ch h Efisio—City Centre (IRE) (Be My Guest (USA))
6363a[10]

Challis (IRE) *J Noseda* a66
2 b c Barathea(IRE) —Chalosse (Doyoun)
6658[5] 6887[4]

Champagne Cracker *I Semple* 72
5 ch m Up And At 'Em—Kiveton Komet (Precocious)
813[3] 1031[11] 1611[8] 2925[6] 3190[6]5865[6]

Champagne Moment *V Smith* a53 42
3 ch f Perryston View—Ashleen (Chilibang)
658[6] 796[13] 1272[10]1549[12] 1829[14]

Champagne Perry *V Smith* a21 36
2 ch g Perryston View—Ashleen (Chilibang)
1535[10] 2145[6] 2588[7]3801[9]

Champagne Rossini (IRE) *M C Chapman* 38
4 b g Rossini(USA) —Alpencrocus (IRE) (Waajib)
3[11] 2195[8] 3909[12]

Champagne Shadow (IRE) *K A Ryan* a77 71
5 b g Kahyasi—Moet (IRE) (Mac's Imp (USA))
88[3] 325[4]420[4] (591) 1021[3] 1167[5]2206[4] (2861) 3074[2] (4544) 4935[3]6108[12] 6312[2] 6626[3]6766[3]

Champain Sands (IRE) *E J Alston* a46 71
7 b g Green Desert(USA) —Grecian Bride (IRE) (Groom Dancer (USA))
1123[7] 1422[2] 1996[8] 2378[5] 2697[4]3298[4] (3697) (4154) 4390[4] 4953[4] 5579[13]

Champery (USA) *M Johnston* 95
2 b c Bahri(USA) —Ice Ballet (IRE) (Nureyev (USA))
(3080) (3280) 4775[3]

Champion Lion (IRE) *James Moffatt* a57 66
7 b g Sadler's Wells(USA) —Honey Bun (Unfuwain (USA))
158[3] 379[4]647[3] (715) 857[4]975[6] 1562[6]

Champion Place *R Menichetti* 98
3 b f Compton Place—Villa Via (IRE) (Night Shift (USA))
(6005a) 6363a[11]

Champions Gallery *D R C Elsworth* 107
3 br c Dansili—Pure (Slip Anchor)
1626[5] 1951[5] 2774[20] (3973) 4529[8] (4833)

Championship Point (IRE) *M R Channon* 109+
3 b c Lomitas—Flying Squaw (Be My Chief (USA))
(1473) 2228[11] 4678[9] 5185[9] 5477[3] 5968[9]

Champion's Way (IRE) *B R Millman* a38 27
4 b h Namid—Savage (IRE) (Polish Patriot (USA))
5728[8] 6765[5] 6861[10]

Champlain *M A Jarvis* 107
2 b c Seeking The Gold(USA) —Calando (USA) (Storm Cat (USA))
1838[3] (2844) 3492[7] 5521[4] 6010[2]

Champs Elysees *A Fabre* 109
3 b c Danehill(USA) —Hasili (IRE) (Kahyasi)
2278a[10] 2942a[2] 5400a[2]

Chancellor (IRE) *D K Ivory* a87 102
8 ch h Halling(USA) —Isticanna (USA) (Far North (CAN))
1380[7] (2201) 4818[11] 5374[19]6336[13]

Changeable *T Stack* 97
4 b m Dansili—High And Low (Rainbow Quest (USA))
5854a[15]

Change Course *Sir Michael Stoute* 41
2 b f Sadler's Wells(USA) —Orford Ness (Selkirk (USA))
4084[10]

Change The Grange (AUS) *M C Tam* a100
8 gr g Umatilla(NZ) —Je Reviens (AUS) (The Challenge (AUS))
152a[7] 279a[3]

Changing Wind (USA) *Saeed Bin Suroor* a80
3 bb c Storm Cat(USA) —Miss Caerleona (FR) (Caerleon (USA))
(4247) 4997[6]

Changiz *J A Geake* 54
3 b g Foxhound(USA) —Persia (IRE) (Persian Bold)
1140[4] 1652[12]

Channel Crossing *W M Brisbourne* a47 55
4 b g Deploy—Wave Dancer (Dance In Time (CAN))
4439[11] 4845[12] 5061[7]5581[7] 5837[2] 5925[3]6238[8] 6305[13]

Chantaco (USA) *A M Balding* a80 101
4 b g Bahri(USA) —Dominant Dancer (Primo Dominie)
1133[3] 1484[2] (2079) 2201[7] 2848[8] 3552[5]4347[7] 5374[17]

Chant De Guerre (USA) *P Mitchell* 59
2 b f War Chant(USA) —Fatwa (IRE) (Lahib (USA))
4526[6] 4920[8]

Chantelle's Dream *Ms J S Doyle* a54 59
4 ch m Compton Place—Polar Peak (Polar Falcon (USA))
138[7] 212[8]265[2] 288[12]373[5] 886[8](982) 1645[15] 2347[4]2494[8] 2632[2] 2813[8] 4365[15] 4629[12]

Chanteuse Noire (USA) *J Noseda* 65
3 b f War Chant(USA) —Galeta (ARG) (Southern Halo (USA))
1055[15] 1261[2] 1733[3] 2235[4] 3285[3](4136)

Chantilly Beauty (FR) *R Pritchard-Gordon* a79 105
4 b m Josr Algarhoud(IRE) —Lysabelle (FR) (Lesotho (USA))
1671[2] 2740[8] 3564a[8] 6363a[7]

Chanting (USA) *David Wachman* 98
2 b f Danehill(USA) —Golden Reef (USA) (Mr Prospector (USA))
2309a[5] (3658a)

Chapelizod (IRE) *Liam McAteer* a38 51
3 b g Raphane(USA) —Fulminus Instar (IRE) (Classic Secret (USA))
6755[6]

Chapter (IRE) *Mrs A L M King* 74
4 ch g Sinndar(IRE) —Web Of Intrigue (Machiavellian (USA))
2351[3] 2640[10] 3147[11] 4021[6] 4288[3]4536[8] 4983[6] 5205[9]

Charanne *J M Bradley* a25 22
3 b f Diktat—Mystique (Mystiko (USA))
5055[11] 5272[10] 5874[6]6557[9]

Charles Darwin (IRE) *M Blanshard* a94 95
3 ch c Tagula(IRE) —Seymour (IRE) (Eagle Eyed (USA))
896[4] 1512[9] 2168[7] 2385[3] 2863[3]3414[19] 3722[2] (3970) 4601[5] 4988[2] 5501[3]5807[3] 6243[4]

Charles Parnell (IRE) *M Dods* a76+ 77
3 b g Elnadim(USA) —Titania (Fairy King (USA))
2356[3] (2875) 3761[8] 4262[7] 5313[10] 5593[2]5902[4] 6159[2] 6326[6]6478[4]

Charles Street Lad (IRE) *M R Bosley* a41 57
3 b g Mull Of Kintyre(USA) —Tropicana (IRE) (Imperial Frontier (USA))
692[9] 1355[15] 1923[9]4690[11] 5129[12]

Charley's Aunt (IRE) *Mrs C A Dunnett* a66+
3 ch f King Charlemagne(USA) —Dane's Lady (IRE) (Danehill (USA))
(53) 105[7] 2937[6]3595[9]

Charleys Spirit *T D Barron* 30
2 ch f Presidium—Frilly Front (Aragon)
2759[9]

Charlie Bear *Miss Z C Davison* a67 67
5 ch h Bahamian Bounty—Abi (Chief's Crown (USA))
21[3] 67[5]138[5] 903[9](1057) 1570[5] 2317[5] 2645[4] 3229[3] (3948) 4399[4]4870[6] 5621[14]

Charlie Cool *W J Haggas* a106+ 107
3 ch c Rainbow Quest(USA) —Tigwa (Cadeaux Genereux)
3491[3] (4298) 5374[2] 5675[8] 6516[3]

Charlie Delta *D Carroll* a83 87
3 b g Pennekamp(USA) —Papita (IRE) (Law Society (USA))
1482[7] (2353) 2760[4] 3296[6] 3646[3]4328[8] 4403[2] 4707[8]4888[4] 5842[3] 6009[4]6212[4] 6428[7] 6583[9]6770[4] 6858[5]6896[3] 6943[2]

Charlie Farnsbarns (IRE) *B J Meehan* 114
2 b c Cape Cross(IRE) —Lafleur (IRE) (Grand Lodge (USA))
2579[2] (2821) 3492[5] 5466a[24] (5806) 6104[2]

Charlie George *P Monteith* 63
5 ch g Idris(IRE) —Faithful Beauty (IRE) (Last Tycoon)
3815[9] 4132[10]

Charlie Kennet *Mrs H Sweeting* a63 77
8 b g Pyramus(USA) —Evaporate (Insan (USA))
1288[4] 1821[11] (2104) 2752[5]3401[9] 3934[9]4662[7]

Charlies First (IRE) *Peter Casey* 77+
6 ch g Prince Of Birds(USA) —Royal Cindy (IRE) (Red Sunset)
5853a[14]

Charlies Girl (IRE) *M J Attwater* a38
2 ch f Trans Island—Indian Charm (IRE) (Indian Ridge)
878[9] 2588[11] 2791[8]

Charlie Tango (IRE) *D W Thompson* a60 64+
5 b g Desert Prince(IRE) —Precedence (IRE) (Polish Precedent (USA))
1045[3] 1187[8] 1947[11] 2832[12]

Charlie Tipple *T D Easterby* 72
2 b g Diktat—Swing Of The Tide (Sri Pekan (USA))
2361[6] (3018) 3496[7] 5113[3]

Charlie Tokyo (IRE) *R A Fahey* 89
3 b g Trans Island—Ellistown Lady (IRE) (Red Sunset)
1781[6] 2224[10] 4833[6] 5284[2] 5478[4]5769[2] (5869) 6209[2] 6337[13]

Charlottebutterfly *P J McBride* a52 56
6 b m Millkom—Tee Gee Jay (Northern Tempest (USA))
4265[3] 4554[7] 5370[16] 6130[6]6371[10] 6727[7]6805[2]

Charlotte Grey *C N Allen* a64 50
2 gr f Wizard King—Great Intent (Aragon)
5417[4] 5784[11] 6224[12]6401[5] 6534[2](6706) (6807) 6931[2]

Charlotte O Fraise (IRE) *Rod Collet* 103
2 b f Beat Hollow—Dundel (IRE) (Machiavellian (USA))
3990a[4] (4621a)

Charlotte Vale *Micky Hammond* 81
5 ch m Pivotal—Drying Grass Moon (Be My Chief (USA))
976[2] 1144[2] 1502[5] 2018[2] 2326[4]2850[7] 5634[3] 5792[11] 6275[2]

Charlton *T G Mills* a73 93
3 b g Inchinor—Sabina (Prince Sabo)
717[2] 1016[15] 1924[7]2330[10] 2932[9] 4481[7] 4769[2] 5268[5]5953[8]

Charming Escort *T T Clement* a59?
2 ch g Rossini(USA) —Iktizawa (Entrepreneur)
5665[5]

Charming Princess *J S Wainwright* 30
3 b f Primo Valentino(IRE) —Via Dolorosa (Chaddleworth (IRE))
99[9] 2019[5] 2284[17]2876[10] 3306[17]

Charnock Bates One (IRE) *J J Quinn* a56 56
5 b m Desert Sun—Fleetwood Fancy (Taufan (USA))
109[7] 363[6]

Chart Express *P Howling* 35
2 b c Robellino(USA) —Emerald Angel (IRE) (In The Wings)
5147[11] 5659[14]

Chart Oak *P Howling* a54
3 b g Robellino(USA) —Emerald Angel (IRE) (In The Wings)
531[3] 6588[5]6923[4]

Chasing A Dream *B W Hills* a70 59+
3 b f Pursuit Of Love—Preening (Persian Bold)
1191[11] 2188[9] 5612[3]5844[5] 6314[2]6450[2] 6587[2]6792[2]

Chasing Memories (IRE) *B Smart* a69 61
2 b f Pursuit Of Love—Resemblance (State Diplomacy (USA))
4400[5] 5289[3] 5923[2]6303[6] 6504[4]6639[7] 6815[3]6963[4]

Chastity (IRE) *N Tinkler* 24
2 b f Dilshaan—Fanny Bay (IRE) (Key Of Luck (USA))
3618[3]

Chataway *B J Meehan* 87
2 b g Mujahid(USA) —Copy-Cat (Lion Cavern (USA))
3222[3] (4028) 5655[5]

Chateau (IRE) *G A Swinbank* 63
4 ch g Grand Lodge(USA) —Miniver (IRE) (Mujtahid (USA))
978[6] 1252[9] 1609[6] (2077) 2240[6]

Chateau Nicol *B G Powell* a87 91d
7 b g Distant Relative—Glensara (Petoski)
54[12] 117[4]238[11] 441[9]476[9] 541[9]1932[5] 2757[10] 2981[12]6868[11]

Chater Knight (IRE) *R A Harris* a66
5 b g Night Shift(USA) —Neat Dish (CAN) (Stalwart (USA))
78[4] 273[3]425[4] 607[3](1271) 1548[4]2206[5] 2790[5]3159[8]

Chatila (USA) *J H M Gosden* 95
3 b f Red Ransom(USA) —Silvester Lady (Pivotal)
5300[7]

Chatshow (USA) *A W Carroll* a74 74
5 br g Distant View(USA) —Galanty Show (Danehill (USA))
1297[6] 1496[9] 1662[7] 1846[5] 1878[8]2331[10] 2897[7] (5569) 5938[5] 6020[2] 6437[3]6555[4] 6858[6]

Chavela (IRE) *R Martin-Sanchez* 100
4 b m Second Empire(IRE) —Taysala (IRE) (Akarad (FR))
1398a[8] 6454a[10]

Cheap N Chic *T D Easterby* a79 81
3 ch f Primo Valentino(IRE) —Amber Mill (Doulab (USA))
1146[6] 1482[8]

Cheap Street *J G Portman* 90
2 ch c Compton Place—Anneliina (Cadeaux Genereux)
2432[7] 2967[3] 3363[2] 3872[4] (4161) (4766) 5372[10](5940)

Checkit (IRE) *R Bouresly* a79 113
6 br h Mukaddamah(USA) —Collected (IRE) (Taufan (USA))
560a[10] 621a[9]

Check Tou *P A Blockley* a42 61
2 b f Inchinor—Dramraire Mist (Darshaan)
1347[4] 1743[7] 4552[10]

Cheddar Island (IRE) *Kevin Prendergast* 101
4 b h Trans Island—Poker Dice (Primo Dominie)
1156a[7] 2038a[5]

Cheeky Chi (IRE) *P S McEntee* a31 10
5 gr m Desert Style(IRE) —Grey Patience (IRE) (Common Grounds)
442[11] 821[5]907[7]

Cheeky Girl *Mrs J L Le Brocq* a27 70
6 b m College Chapel—Merry Rous (Rousillon (USA))
1625a[2]

Cheeney Basin (IRE) *M C Chapman* a20 20
8 ch g King's Signet(USA) —Gratclo (Belfort (FR))
81[13] 96[10]143[14] 181[10]388[10] 876[10]

Cheerful Smile (JPN) *Y Ikee* 110
6 b m Sunday Silence(USA) —Golden Colors (USA) (Mr Prospector (USA))
5717a[6] 6850a[7]

Cheery Cat (USA) *D W Barker* a52 55
2 bb g Catienus(USA) —Olinka (USA) (Wolfhound (USA))
5168[11] 5332[3] 5613[9] 5958[8] 6285[7]

Cheese 'n Biscuits *M Wigham* a86 74
6 b m Spectrum(IRE) —Bint Shihama (USA) (Cadeaux Genereux)
36[5]

Chelsea Chelsea *P F I Cole* a68 65
3 ch c Medicean—Shoshone (Be My Chief (USA))
5612[5] 5911[7]

Chelsea Rose (IRE) *C Collins* 117
4 ch m Desert King(IRE) —Cinnamon Rose (USA) (Trempolino (USA))
1785a[4] 2371a[2] 3105a[2] 4127[4] 4407a[2]5702a[7]

Chelsey Jayne (IRE) *M R Channon* 53
3 b f Galileo(IRE) —Lady Lahar (Fraam)
5452[8] 5618[14]

Chenchikova (IRE) *A P O'Brien* 97
3 b f Sadler's Wells(USA) —Kasora (IRE) (Darshaan)
753a[4] 5465a[10] 5996a[9] 6356a[7]

Cheney Hill *H Candy* 73+
3 b g Compton Place—Catriona (Bustino)
1430[2] (1877) 2509[3] 3226[6] 4180[8] 4812[5]5765[12]

Chennai (IRE) *J S Bolger* 80
3 b f Mozart(IRE) —Aeraiocht (IRE) (Tenby)
1023a[7]

Cherie's Dream *D R C Elsworth* 52
2 b f Silver Wizard(USA) —Last Dream (IRE) (Alzao (USA))
5592[5]

Cherished Number *A M Hales* a63 63
7 b g King's Signet(USA) —Pretty Average (Skyliner)
48[6] 107[8]251[4] 498[2]697[2] 833[5]1001[12] 1400[12]3431[7]

Cherokee Nation *P W D'Arcy* a84 74+
5 br g Emperor Jones(USA) —Me Cherokee (Persian Bold)
17[2] 169[10]323[6] 1402[6]1923[3] 2317[7] 2347[3]2590[6] 3004[10] 3389[9]

Cherokee Vision *Miss T Spearing* a56 52
3 b g Primo Valentino(IRE) —Me Cherokee (Persian Bold)
6294[11] 6419[9]6451[11] 6531[13]

Cherri Fosfate *W G M Turner* a67 74d
2 b g Mujahid(USA) —Compradore (Mujtahid (USA))
1664[2] (1912) 5447[8] 5828[8] 6271[5] 6402[5]6491[2] 6894[2]

Cherry Mix (FR) *Saeed Bin Suroor* a103 128
5 gr h Linamix(FR) —Cherry Moon (USA) (Quiet American (USA))
562a[7] 1833[6] 3927[6] (4414a) 4679[6] 6004a[3](6365a)

Cherry Pickings (USA) *A Laird* a115
9 b g Miner's Mark(USA) —Cherry D'Or (USA) (Cassaleria (USA))
154a[2] 560a[15]

Cherub (GER) *Jonjo O'Neill* a54 90
6 b g Winged Love(IRE) —Chalkidiki (GER) (Nebos (GER))
1017[14]

Chervil *Mrs A J Perrett* a76 72
2 b f Dansili—Nashmeel (USA) (Blushing Groom (FR))
2703[3] (3645) 4322[4] 5447[10]

Cheshire Prince *W M Brisbourne* 67
2 br g Desert Prince(IRE) —Bundle Up (USA) (Miner's Mark (USA))
1587[14] (2145) 2586[4] 3246[8] 3481[6] 4170[5]4761[5] 5172[4] 5382[2] 5866[14]

Chess Board *Sir Mark Prescott* a36 68+
3 b c Vettori(IRE) —Cruinn A Bhord (Inchinor)
1648[9] (2569)

Cheveley Flyer *J Pearce* a57 61
3 ch g Forzando—Cavern Breeze (Lion Cavern (USA))
709[6] 984[5]1352[10] 1616[10] 3869[10] 4606[14] 6630[6]

Cheveme (IRE) *B W Duke* 60
2 b f King Charlemagne(USA) —Warusha (GER) (Shareef Dancer (USA))
2328[7] 2800[18] 4897[6]

Cheviot Heights *J S Goldie* a58 63
3 b f Intikhab(USA) —Cheviot Hills (USA) (Gulch (USA))
1598[4] 2526[4] 4610[7] 4814[4] 5284[11]6260[7] 6483[8]6606[10]

Cheyenne Star (IRE) *Ms F M Crowley* 105
3 b f Mujahid(USA) —Charita (IRE) (Lycius (USA))
4187a[6] 4749a[2] 5849a[3] 5996a[2] 6356a[8]

Chia (IRE) *D Haydn Jones* a69 63
3 ch f Ashkalani(IRE) —Motley (Rainbow Quest (USA))
234[7] 558[5]712[4] 2301[10] 2921[7]3364[5] 4291[3] 4933[9]6294[2] 6451[2]6647[3] 6861[2]

Chiado (IRE) *Kevin Prendergast* 94
3 b g Daylami(IRE) —Elegant Bloom (IRE) (Be My Guest (USA))
755a[3] 1172a[5]

Chiave *M A Jarvis* 42
2 ch c Medicean—Fearless Revival (Cozzene (USA))
6220[19]

Chicamia *M Mullineaux* 33
2 b f Kyllachy—Inflation (Primo Dominie)
5507[14] 6013[8]

Chicchirichi (IRE) *M Gasparini*
2 b c Celtic Swing—Velate (USA) (Spend A Buck (USA))
6407a[5]

Chicherova (IRE) *W M Brisbourne* a50 50
3 b f Soviet Star(USA) —Ruby Rose (Red Ransom (USA))
199[4] 430[3]676[2] 1888[11] 2249[9]6967[5]

Chickado (IRE) *D Haydn Jones* a48 38
5 b m Mujadil(USA) —Arcevia (IRE) (Archway (IRE))
44[6] 127[8]315[4] 391[4]602[8] (907) 1255[9] 1463[6]2248[2] 3262[3]5929[7] 6549[3]6624[10] 6721[5]6892[7]

Chicken Soup *T J Pitt* a91 87
4 br g Dansili—Radiancy (IRE) (Mujtahid (USA))
77[4] (200) 504[7]3523[2] 3716[2] (4172) 4325[7] 4760[14] 5877[11](6992)

Chief Argent (IRE) *J Howard Johnson* 72+
3 b c Robellino(USA) —Running Tycoon (IRE) (Last Tycoon)
1759[4]

Chief Commander (FR) *Jane Chapple-Hyam* a84 103
3 bb g Commands(AUS) —Neeran (USA) (Fast Play (USA))
(110) 228[2] 392a[2] 914[6]1358[2] 1715a[4] 1944a[3] 4168a[10] 4740[10]5116[6]

Chief Crazy Horse *A P O'Brien* 100
3 b c Dansili—Dixielake (IRE) (Lake Coniston (IRE))
5393a[6]

Chief Editor *M J Wallace* a76 89+
2 b g Tomba—Princess Zara (Reprimand)
(856) 1066[3] (1780) 1977[2]

Chief Exec *C A Cyzer* a89 71
4 br g Zafonic(USA) —Shot At Love (IRE) (Last Tycoon)
(36) 220[3] 441[3]476[8] 667[12]828[5] 913[2]1112[11] 1246[11]3898[P] 5096[9] 5263[5]6352[11] 6461[13]6633[3]

Chief Export (USA) *W Bradley* 83
4 br g Chief Seattle(USA) —Regal Export (CAN) (Regal Classic (CAN))
6329a[9]

Chief Operator (USA) *Saeed Bin Suroor* a83 87+
2 b c Elusive Quality(USA) —Crimson Conquest (USA) (Diesis)
(5615) 5909[4]

Chief Scout *I Semple* a71 84
4 b g Tomba—Princess Zara (Reprimand)
1532[8] 1985[5] 2810[4] (3168) 4203[6] 4654[4]5579[10] (5863) 6209[4]

Chiff Chaff *M L W Bell* a58 35
2 ch f Mtoto—Hen Harrier (Polar Falcon (USA))
5754[11] 6071[9] 6349[8]

Chifney Rush (IRE) *B W Hills* a19 49
3 b f Grand Lodge(USA) —Don't Rush (USA) (Alleged (USA))
2753[10] 3346[4]

Childish Thoughts *Mrs Norma Pook* a45
2 b f River Falls—Simmie's Special (Precocious)
6187[14] 6778[6]6826[8] 6951[11]

Chillin Out *W Jarvis* a46 30
4 ch h Bahamian Bounty—Steppin Out (First Trump)
21[8] 227[6]293[7] 766[10]4306[9]

Chillipetals *J Balding* a28 37
3 br f Averti(IRE) —Island Mead (Pharly (FR))
2940[9]

Chilly Cracker *John Berry* a68 62
4 ch m Largesse—Polar Storm (IRE) (Law Society (USA))
4294[5] 4691[5] 5569[9]

Chilly Rooster (USA) *D Schettino* a81 89
6 br g Arch(USA) —Chilly Chick (USA) (Raise A Native)
6006a[2]

Chilsdown *Ronald Thompson* 69
3 b g Mozart(IRE) —Goodwood Blizzard (Inchinor)
1230[9] 2366[12] 3835[12] 5368[8] 6473[12]

Chimes At Midnight (USA) *Luke Comer* a44 97?
9 b h Danzig(USA) —Surely Georgies (USA) (Alleged (USA))
2140[8] 2460[9] 2497[4]2822[9] 4929[7] 4996[5]5395a[8] 5853a[15]

China Cherub *H Candy* 78
3 ch f Inchinor—Ashlinn (IRE) (Ashkalani (IRE))
2167[3] (2859) 3299[2] 3841[4] (4484) 4841[5] 5317[3]5896[9]

Chinalea (IRE) *C G Cox* 82
4 b g Danetime(IRE) —Raise-A-Secret (IRE) (Classic Secret (USA))
949[7] 1359[3] 1474[3] 2074[10] 2618[2]2711[7] 3027[3] 3593[6] 3855[2] 4101[12]4486[10] 5333[6] 5575[3] 5791[3] 6020[11]

Chinandega (FR) *P Demercastel* 102
2 ch f Chichicastenango(FR) —European Style (FR) (Ezzoud (IRE))
(6046a)

China Pearl *John Berry* 74
3 ch g Benny The Dip(USA) —Seek The Pearl (Rainbow Quest (USA))
1898[7] 4848[7]

Chinese Whisper (IRE) *A P O'Brien* 107
2 b c Montjeu(IRE) —Majinskaya (FR) (Marignan (USA))
5707a[2] 6003a[3]

Chingford (IRE) *D W P Arbuthnot* a69 45
2 ch f Redback—Beverley Macca (Piccolo)
2456[14] 2984[6] 3588[11] 4326[2]4699[8] 5261[5]5503[12]

Chingola *R M Whitaker* a24 37
4 b m Atraf—Sulaka (Owington)
180[9] (Dead)

Chinkara *Doug Watson* a98 98+
6 ch g Desert Prince(IRE) —You Make Me Real (USA) (Give Me Strength (USA))
208a[3]

Chin Wag (IRE) *E S McMahon* 86
2 b g Iron Mask(USA) —Sweet Chat (IRE) (Common Grounds)
(3005) 3445[3] (3903) 4850a[9] 5373[5]

Chip Leader *R Hannon* a53 62d
2 ch g Kyllachy—Scundes (IRE) (Barathea (IRE))
944[7] 1019[6] 1203[5]1639[7] 5041[12] 5721[13] 5772[9]

Chip N Pin *T D Easterby* 49
2 b f Erhaab(USA) —Vallauris (Faustus (USA))
2943[5]

Chiquitin (ARG) *I Jory* a114 89
6 b h Fitzcarraldo(ARG) —Murias (ARG) (Big Play (USA))
355a[4] 565a[2]743a[5] 1716a[9]

Chiracahua (IRE) *B Smart* a37 49
4 ch g Desert Prince(IRE) —Irish Celebrity (USA) (Irish River (FR))
941[4] 1225[9]1458[5] 1763[6]

Chiron (GER) *Dr A Bolte* 113
5 b h Valanour(IRE) —Corsita (Top Ville)
2061a[5] 6109a[4] 6529a[13]

Chiselled (IRE) *K R Burke* a46 74
4 b g Rossini(USA) —Con Dancer (Shareef Dancer (USA))
978[8] 1272[3] 1886[5]

Chisom *M W Easterby* a24 58
3 b g Averti(IRE) —Cinder Hills (Deploy)
910^{11} 1259^{14}

Chiswick Park *R Brogi* 85
3 b f Daylami(IRE) —Chine (Inchinor)
6251a^{6}

Chivalrous (IRE) *A P O'Brien* 101
2 b c Danehill(USA) —Aspiration (IRE) (Sadler's Wells (USA))
3574a^{3} 4850a^{2}

Chjimes (IRE) *K R Burke* 79
2 b g Fath(USA) —Radiance (IRE) (Thatching)
(987) 2009^{3} 2719^{17} 3126a^{8} 5442^{5} 5681^{17} 5956^{4} 6102^{9}

Chocolate Boy (IRE) *G L Moore* a47 66
7 b g Dolphin Street(FR) —Kawther (Tap On Wood)
55^{6} 141^{5} 379^{10} 484^{7} 888^{7} 1313^{2} 1729^{5} 3797^{10} 4239^{3}

Chocolate Caramel (USA) *Mrs A J Perrett* a94 90
4 b g Storm Creek(USA) —Sandhill (BRZ) (Baynoun)
1842^{5} (2447) 2817^{8}

Choctaw Nation (USA) *Jeff Mullins* a120
6 b g Louis Quatorze(USA) —Melisma (USA) (Well Decorated (USA))
743a^{9}

Chookie Hamilton *I Semple* a70 62
2 ch g Compton Place—Lady Of Windsor (IRE) (Woods Of Windsor (USA))
3328^{7} 3809^{4} 4474^{3} 5013^{7} 5552^{4} 6316^{3} (6522) (6676) 6933^{2}

Chookie Heiton (IRE) *I Semple* 112
8 br g Fumo Di Londra(IRE) —Royal Wolff (Prince Tenderfoot (USA))
1481^{4} 1663^{10} 2450^{6} 2847^{21}

Chookie Windsor *R M Stronge* a47 53
3 b g Lake Coniston(IRE) —Lady Of Windsor (IRE) (Woods Of Windsor (USA))
49^{8} 197^{7} 329^{2} 447^{3} (538) 695^{8} 2131^{11} 2480^{8} 2968^{6} 3161^{5} 3260^{4} 3411^{4} 4282^{10} 5097^{7} 5733^{7}

Choosy (IRE) *R Hannon* a85 94
3 b f Kalanisi(IRE) —Hawksbill Special (IRE) (Taufan (USA))
827^{7}

Choparlas (FR) *M Boutin* 93
4 gr g Verglas(IRE) —Rayonne (Sadler's Wells (USA))
2313a^{9}

Chopastair (FR) *D Soubagne* a107 98
5 b g Astair(FR) —Very Sol (FR) (Solicitor (FR))
393a^{2}

Chord *Sir Michael Stoute* 51
2 ch g Pivotal—Choirgirl (Unfuwain (USA))
5457^{8} 6049^{10}

Choreographic (IRE) *R A Fahey* a7 52+
4 b g Komaite(USA) —Lambast (Relkino)
3334^{9} 4059^{2} 5060^{7} 5244^{3} 5839^{5}

Choreography *D Nicholls* 79
3 ch g Medicean—Stark Ballet (USA) (Nureyev (USA))
716^{3} 1230^{5} 2324^{7} 4058^{4} 4403^{5} (4524) (4695) 4958^{4}

Choristar *J Mackie* a64 67+
5 ch g Inchinor—Star Tulip (Night Shift (USA))
156^{6} 290^{3} 906^{5} 1276^{10} 2641^{8} 4332^{3} (4835) 5072^{2} 5445^{4}

Chorus Beauty *N I M Rossiter* a48 37
5 b m Royal Applause—Happy Lady (FR) (Cadeaux Genereux)
268^{12} 397^{9} 602^{6} 768^{11} 941^{6} 2431^{5} 2632^{10}

Choysia *D W Barker* 78
3 b f Pivotal—Bonica (Rousillon (USA))
1146^{14} 1292^{6} 1836^{5} 2385^{5} 2760^{5} 3568^{4} 3722^{9} 4567^{7} 5619^{8} 6159^{3}

Chris Corsa *M L W Bell* 80
3 b g Mark Of Esteem(IRE) —Risque Lady (Kenmare (FR))
1099^{6} 1681^{15} 4605^{11}

Chrisjen *M W Easterby* 70
4 ch m Wolfhound(USA) —Chadwick's Ginger (Crofthall)
2829^{5} 3750^{5} 4117^{8} 4835^{8} 5240^{16}

Christa Bee *A Berry* a56 71
3 b f Groom Dancer(USA) —Beleza (IRE) (Revoque (IRE))
1604^{8} 1849^{6} 3000^{7} 3568^{7} 3636^{5}

Christalini *J C Fox* 83
2 b g Bertolini(USA) —Jay Tee (IRE) (Charnwood Forest (IRE))
4177^{5} 5340 ^{6} 5624^{4} 6023^{12}

Christavelli *David Marnane* a65 96
7 ch g Machiavellian(USA) —Crystal Cavern (USA) (Be My Guest (USA))
4031a^{12}

Christian Bendix *P Howling* a57 40
4 ch g Presidium—Very Good (Noalto)
29^{3} 145^{5} 195^{6} (260) 388^{2} (411) 489^{11} 552^{11} 1209^{9} 1390^{4} 1645^{9} 2141^{13} 6554^{8} 6719^{4} 6796^{3} 6906^{9} 6974^{8}

Christmas Player (USA) *J H M Gosden* a69 46
3 bb f Theatrical—Christmas Gift (USA) (Green Desert (USA))
460^{6} (735) 1747^{6}

Christmas Tart (IRE) *V Smith* a64 75
2 b f Danetime(IRE) —Missish (Mummy's Pet)
1510^{4} 1817^{4} (2083) 2743^{7} 3084^{11} 3684^{3} 4966^{9} 5788^{9}

Christmas Truce (IRE) *Ms J S Doyle* a62 69
7 b g Brief Truce(USA) —Superflash (Superlative)
186^{14} 284^{6} 458^{2} 514^{5} 582^{10} 770^{5} (853) 889^{11} 1245^{14} 1400^{6} (1753) 2132^{2} 2327^{6} 2499^{7} 2647^{7} 3850^{3} 4565^{7} 4968^{2} 5149^{8} 5236^{6} 5621^{13} 6069^{9} 6848^{8} 6889^{2} 6982^{5}

Chronomatic *M H Tompkins* a60 71
3 gr g Mister Baileys—Sky Red (Night Shift (USA))
731^{2} 1476^{5} 1948^{2} (2646) 5284^{7} 5594^{7} 5815^{6} 5944^{3}

Chrysander *M R Channon* 105
4 b g Cadeaux Genereux—Jumairah Sun (IRE) (Scenic)
728^{26} 1098^{3} 1806^{7} 2226^{7} 3313^{14}

Chunky Bell *P T Midgley* 44
3 b c Easycall—Lady Susan (Petong)
1589^{6} 2285^{8}

Chunky's Choice (IRE) *J Noseda* 70
2 b g Key Of Luck(USA) —Indian Imp (Indian Ridge)
5939^{9} 6214^{10}

Churchtown *K R Burke* a42
2 b g Kyllachy—Manhattan Diamond (Primo Dominie)
6377^{10} 6523^{10} 6749^{8}

Ciao (IRE) *John Joseph Murphy* 86+
3 b f Imperial Ballet(IRE) —White Squall (Caerleon (USA))
2744^{15}

Cicada (IRE) *J R Weymes*
2 b g Tendulkar(USA) —Artic Ocean (IRE) (Spectrum (IRE))
1863^{7} 2733^{13}

Ciccone *G L Moore* a60+ 66
3 ch f Singspiel(IRE) —Untold Riches (USA) (Red Ransom (USA))
1649^{6} 2301^{9} 3072^{3} 4009^{4} 4305^{6} 5907^{5} 6294^{9} 6601^{5} 6657^{2} 6870^{4} 6918^{6} (6982)

Cicerole (FR) *J-C Rouget* 95
2 ch f Barathea(IRE) —Uryale (FR) (Kendor (FR))
5048a^{3} 6046a^{2}

Cimyla (IRE) *C F Wall* a112+ 101
5 b g Lomitas—Coyaima (GER) (Night Shift (USA))
(213) 393a^{4} 666^{5} (6559)

Cinaman (IRE) *R F Fisher* 32
2 b g Key Of Luck(USA) —Madame Nureyev (USA) (Nureyev (USA))
5537^{12}

Cincia (ITY) *G Livraghi*
2 b f Single Empire(IRE) —Muy Loca (Revoque (IRE))
3427a^{5}

Cinder Maid *J G Portman* a37
4 b m Piccolo—Bella Helena (Balidar)
257^{9}

Cinders Spark *G L Moore* a22 16
3 b f Groom Dancer(USA) —Oriel Girl (Beveled (USA))
6177^{10} 6696^{10}

Cindertrack *J A Osborne* a74 87
3 b g Singspiel(IRE) —Beading (Polish Precedent (USA))
2142^{3} 2344^{5} 2881^{3} (3164) (3395) 3453^{3} 3959^{5} 5107^{6} 5649^{10}

Cinematic (IRE) *J R Boyle* a74 75
3 b g Bahhare(USA) —Eastern Star (IRE) (Sri Pekan (USA))
1828^{8} 2642^{5} 2931^{8} 4395^{4}

Cinquante Cinq (IRE) *B J Meehan* 65
2 b f Danehill(USA) —Castilian Queen (USA) (Diesis)
5371^{6}

Cinzia Vegas (IRE) *S Santella* 67
3 ch f Dr Fong(USA) —Itqan (IRE) (Sadler's Wells (USA))
1713a^{16}

Circle Of Love *J L Dunlop* 80
2 b f Sakhee(USA) —Claxon (Caerleon (USA))
2958^{3} 5456^{3}

Circle Of Truth *W G M Turner* a57 45
2 b g Makbul—Jade's Girl (Emarati (USA))
849^{9} 962^{6} 1379^{2} 1744^{3} 2495^{5}

Circuit Dancer (IRE) *D Nicholls* a74 88
6 b g Mujadil(USA) —Trysinger (IRE) (Try My Best (USA))
860^{10} (1235) (1402) 1686^{12} 2397^{2} 2732^{3} 3374^{8} 3904^{2} 4101^{4} 4834^{2} 5169^{6} 5333^{10} (5532)

Circular Quay (USA) *T Pletcher* a118
2 ch c Thunder Gulch(USA) —Circle Of Life (USA) (Belong To Me (USA))
5823a^{2} 6339a^{2}

Circumspect (IRE) *P C Haslam* a50 50
4 b g Spectrum(IRE) —Newala (Royal Academy (USA))
5311^{11} 5922^{3}

Circus Dance *Luke Comer*
9 b h Sadler's Wells(USA) —Dance By Night (Northfields (USA))
6432^{12}

Circus Polka (USA) *P F I Cole* a81+
2 br c Stravinsky(USA) —Far Wiser (USA) (Private Terms (USA))
(6777) (6948)

Cita Verda (FR) *P Monteith* 54
8 b m Take Risks(FR) —Mossita (FR) (Tip Moss (FR))
815^{4}

Citelle (IRE) *Mrs P N Dutfield* a60 58
3 ch f City On A Hill(USA) —La Rochelle (IRE) (Salse (USA))
1052^{5} 1193^{9} 1652^{4} 2246^{3} 2633^{4} 3260^{6}

Cithogue (IRE) *J R Fanshawe* a50 50
3 ch f Machiavellian(USA) —Another Dancer (FR) (Groom Dancer (USA))
6026^{5}

Citoyen (IRE) *Ronald Thompson* 28
2 ch g City On A Hill(USA) —La Doyenne (IRE) (Masterclass (USA))
727^{8} 1074^{10} 1248^{12} 2524^{5}

Citronnade (USA) *R J Frankel* 97
3 b f Lemon Drop Kid(USA) —Primarily (USA) (Lord At War (ARG))
5984a^{9}

Citrus Chief (USA) *R A Harris* a54 61
2 b c Lemon Drop Kid(USA) —Tricky Indy (USA) (A.P. Indy (USA))
5126^{8} 5527^{7} 6523^{7} 6639^{6}

City Affair *J G M O'Shea* a32 39
5 b g Inchinor—Aldevonie (Green Desert (USA))
5609^{7} 6132^{11}

City Bhoy *Tom Dascombe* 49
2 b c Ishiguru(USA) —Magic Moment (Magic Ring (IRE))
2726^{8} 3031^{8} 3930^{5}

City For Conquest (IRE) *T J Pitt* a74 80
3 b f City On A Hill(USA) —Northern Life (IRE) (Distinctly North (USA))
(626) 1146^{8} 1264^{9} 1604^{5} 2110^{5} 2410^{4} 3000^{4} 3873^{8} 4422^{5} 4886^{3} (5250) 5970^{4} 6508^{6} 6585^{5} 6709^{3} 6823^{2} 6844^{7} 6966^{7}

City Minx *S R Bowring* a37 42
4 b m Almaty(IRE) —Marie's Crusader (IRE) (Last Tycoon)
3914^{9} 4708^{6} 5298^{7} 5922^{5} 6302^{5} 6758^{8} 6971^{11}

City Miss *Miss L A Perratt* 31
3 br f Rock City—Miss Pigalle (Good Times (ITY))
4613^{11} 5077^{11} 5368^{7}

City Of Manchester (IRE) *D Nicholls* a36
4 b g Desert Style(IRE) —Nomadic Dancer (IRE) (Nabeel Dancer (USA))
2^{3} 97^{7} 162^{8} 259^{7}

City Of Tribes (IRE) *G M Lyons* 96
2 b c Invincible Spirit(IRE) —Yellow Trumpet (Petong)
2771^{8} 4747a^{4} 5408a^{5}

City Of Troy *Sir Michael Stoute* 106
3 ch c Grand Lodge(USA) —Arazena (USA) (Woodman (USA))
1092^{8} 1627^{4} 4126^{3}

City Well *M Johnston* a73+
3 b g Sadler's Wells(USA) —City Dance (USA) (Seattle Slew (USA))
515^{3} (573)

Clappers (IRE) *T D Easterby* 30
2 b f Royal Applause—Cashmere (Barathea (IRE))
3942^{7} 4510^{9}

Clara Allen (IRE) *John E Kiely* 106+
8 b m Accordion—Deeco Valley (IRE) (Satco (FR))
4212a^{6} 4822a^{3} 5156^{6} 5853a^{3}

Clare Hills (IRE) *K R Burke* a89 98
3 b f Orpen(USA) —Morale (Bluebird (USA))
1020^{8} 1408^{5} 2651^{5} 3332^{4} 5405^{10}

Claret And Amber *R A Fahey* a86 86
4 b g Forzando—Artistic Licence (High Top)
58^{6} 161^{9} 221^{5} 444^{8} 3040^{2} (3241) 3688^{6} 4020^{6} 4521^{6}

Clarricien (IRE) *E J O'Neill* 76
2 br g Key Of Luck(USA) —Tango Two Thousand (IRE) (Sri Pekan (USA))
4867^{7} (5402) 6216^{9}

Clasem Di San Jore (IRE) *A & G Botti* 104
5 b h Second Empire(IRE) —Claw (IRE) (Law Society (USA))
1870a^{4}

Clasp *A Laird* a101 92
4 ch h Singspiel(IRE) —Embrace Me (Nashwan (USA))
152a^{11} 279a^{2} 509a^{3}

Classic Blue (IRE) *E J O'Neill* a58 37
2 b f Tagula(IRE) —Palace Blue (IRE) (Dara Monarch)
5417^{11} 6295^{7} 6504^{8}

Classic Encounter (IRE) *D M Simcock* a99 99
3 b g Lujain(USA) —Licence To Thrill (Wolfhound (USA))
1485^{21} 3535^{7} 4717^{12} 6624^{12} 6776^{3}

Classic Event (IRE) *T D Easterby* 64
5 ch g Croco Rouge(IRE) —Delta Town (USA) (Sanglamore (USA))
2365^{5}

Classic Hall (IRE) *S Kirk* 17
3 b f Saddlers' Hall(IRE) —Classic Mix (IRE) (Classic Secret (USA))
5353^{13}

Classic Punch (IRE) *D R C Elsworth* 105
3 b g Mozart(IRE) —Rum Cay (USA) (Our Native (USA))
(2304) 3127a^{9} 4024^{7} 4877^{2} 5374^{15} 5641^{7}

Classic Siren (IRE) *J W Hills* a35
2 br f Fath(USA) —Vino Veritas (USA) (Chief's Crown (USA))
5773^{10}

Claudia May *Miss Lucinda V Russell* 36
5 gr m Cloudings(IRE) —Princess Maxine (IRE) (Horage)
1814^{4} 2448^{6} 2548^{7} 3352^{11} 3815^{13}

Claws *A J Lidderdale* a58 56
3 b f Marju(IRE) —Paws (IRE) (Brief Truce (USA))
6470^{9} (6708) 6864^{3}

Clear Impression (IRE) *S C Williams* 98
4 b m Danehill(USA) —Shining Hour (USA) (Red Ransom (USA))
1377^{3} 1849^{4} 2438^{3} 3332^{2}

Clearing Sky (IRE) *J R Boyle* a62 62
5 gr m Exploit(USA) —Litchfield Hills (USA) (Relaunch (USA))
22^{7} 216^{10} 486^{3} 580^{5} 2207^{13} 2444^{2} 2858^{3} 3071^{7} (4602) 4962^{11} 5350^{10} 6442^{12} 6713^{11}

Clearing The Water (IRE) *W P Mullins* 90
4 b h Sadler's Wells(USA) —Leave Me Alone (IRE) (Nashwan (USA))
5853a^{10}

Clear Picture *A P Jarvis* 44
3 ch f Observatory(USA) —Defined Feature (IRE) (Nabeel Dancer (USA))
2406^{13}

Clear Sailing *Mrs A J Perrett* 85
3 b g Selkirk(USA) —Welsh Autumn (Tenby)
4686^{3} (5770)

Clear Vision *Mrs A J Perrett* a60
3 b f Observatory(USA) —Claxon (Caerleon (USA))
6668^{3} 6828^{3} 6916^{3}

Cleaver *Lady Herries* a67 81+
5 ch g Kris—Much Too Risky (Bustino)
965^{15} 2088^{11} 2322^{8} 2982^{4} 4698^{4} 5513^{6} (5581) (5905) (6301)

Cleide Da Silva (USA) *J Noseda* a70 67
2 gr f Monarchos(USA) —Sage Cat (USA) (Tabasco Cat (USA))
5297^{2} 5607^{3}

Cleobury *M Meade* 44
2 b f Superior Premium—Nine To Five (Imp Society (USA))
1876^{4} 2478^{6} 2631^{7}

Cleveland *R Hollinshead* a72+ 40
4 b g Pennekamp(USA) —Clerio (Soviet Star (USA))
1570^{11} 4870^{13} 6286^{9} (6493) (6549) 6642^{3} 6938^{7}

Cleveland Way *D Carroll* a44 40
6 b g Forzando—Fallal (IRE) (Fayruz)
11^{5} 330^{7} 387^{4} 529^{12} 638^{9} 876^{4} 942^{7}

Clewer *P A Blockley* a57 59
2 b f Bahamian Bounty—Polisonne (Polish Precedent (USA))
2552^{3} 2980^{8} 3545^{8} 5052^{3} 5162^{4} 5563^{10}

Cliche (IRE) *Sir Michael Stoute* 92
2 b f Diktat—Sweet Kristeen (USA) (Candy Stripes (USA))
4148^{4} 4765^{3} 5464a^{3}

Cliffrose (GER) *Frau E Mader* 103
4 b m Monsun(GER) —Centaine (Royal Academy (USA))
3719a^{2}

Cliffs Of Duneen *T G McCourt* 85
3 b f Dansili—Devils Dirge (Song)
5706a^{10}

Climate (IRE) *K A Ryan* a73 66
7 ch g Catrail(USA) —Burishki (Chilibang)
4706^{8} 5031^{4} 5313^{3} (6227) (6241) 6568^{9} 6892^{3}

Clinet (IRE) *J W Hills* a83 106
4 b m Docksider(USA) —Oiche Mhaith (Night Shift (USA))
(155a) (351a) 564a^{10} 6253a^{2} 6614a^{11}

Clipper Hoy *Mrs H Sweeting* a79+ 56
4 ch g Bahamian Bounty—Indian Flag (IRE) (Indian Ridge)
89^{11} 136^{4} 967^{9} 1047^{8} 1161^{9} 1243^{6}

Cloann (IRE) *E A Wheeler* a55 67
4 b m Danetime(IRE) —Rustic Lawn (Rusticaro (FR))
209^{5} 262^{5} 398^{2} 681^{4} 889^{13} 1310^{12} 1923^{10}

Clod Ber Junior (BRZ) *A Selvaratnam* a66 86
9 b g Clod Ber(BRZ) —Idade De Prata (BRZ) (Mogambo (URU))
366a^{6} 431a^{12}

Clodia (IRE) *B Grizzetti*
2 b f Fasliyev(USA) —Sensazione (Cadeaux Genereux)
3428a^{3}

Close To You (IRE) *T G Mills* a108 112
3 b c Shinko Forest(IRE) —Maritana (USA) (Rahy (USA))
(914) 1486^{10}

Cloud Atlas (IRE) *S Kirk* a76 62+
3 b g Monashee Mountain(USA) —Blue Sioux (Indian Ridge)
776^{2} 1337^{8} 1681^{16} 4249^{10} (4704) 4968^{11} 5377^{16} 5688^{4}

Clouded Leopard (USA) *J H M Gosden* a78
2 b f Danehill(USA) —Golden Cat (USA) (Storm Cat (USA))
6099^{3} 6433^{13}

Cloudor (FR) *P Demercastel* 98
4 b g Kendor(FR) —Glaoutchka (FR) (Glaieul (USA))
5881a^{9}

Club Captain (USA) *G A Butler* 48
3 b g Red Ransom(USA) —Really Fancy (USA) (In Reality (USA))
1212^{12}

Clytha *M L W Bell* 55
2 ch f Mark Of Esteem(IRE) —India Atlanta (Ahonoora)
4148^{10} 5933^{11} 6063^{5}

Cnoc Moy (IRE) *C F Wall* a14
2 b c Mull Of Kintyre(USA) —Ewar Sunrise (Shavian)
6257^{12}

Coalite (IRE) *A D Brown* 53
3 b g Second Empire(IRE) —Municipal Girl (IRE) (Mac's Imp (USA))
893^{4} 1147^{9} 1344^{13} 1564^{5} 2198^{3} 2399^{6} 2782^{13} 3306^{13} 3604^{7} 4232^{12}

Coalpark (IRE) *M Johnston* a77 73
3 b f Titus Livius(FR) —Honey Storm (IRE) (Mujadil (USA))
1099^{7} 2239^{7} 3528^{4} 3724^{6} 4060^{5} (4455) 4953^{2} (5108) 5484^{8} 5879^{12} 6147^{8}

Coalseam (AUS) *Jim Taylor*
5 b g Desert Sun—Crow's Nest (Shirley Heights)
7000a^{10}

Coastal Breeze *J W Hills* a55
3 b c Fasliyev(USA) —Classic Design (Busted)
60^{7} 165^{6} 291^{2}

Coastal Command *R Charlton* a60+
2 b g Sakhee(USA) —Zenith (Shirley Heights)
6826^{4}

Cobra King (IRE) *P Winkworth* a48 20
2 b c Dilshaan—Oiche Mhaith (Night Shift (USA))
5947^{9} 6143^{9}

Cocco (GER) *M Rulec* 72
3 b f Zinaad—Christine Herme (USA) (Nureyev (USA))
2279a^{14}

Cockatoo (USA) *G L Moore* a62 56
3 b c Dynaformer(USA) —Enticed (USA) (Stage Door Johnny (USA))
4931^{10} 5203^{6} 5650^{3}

Cockayne (IRE) *V Valiani* 94
3 b f Barathea(IRE) —Clara House (Shirley Heights)
6362a^{2}

Cockney Rebel (IRE) *G A Huffer* 112
2 b c Val Royal(FR) —Factice (USA) (Known Fact (USA))
(3738) 4736^{2} 5183^{3}

Cocobean *M Appleby*
2 b g Josr Algarhoud(IRE) —Aker Wood (Bin Ajwaad (IRE))
6522^{8}

Cocodrail (IRE) *F Brogi* a84 107
5 b h Croco Rouge(IRE) —Seattle Jey (ITY) (Seattle Dancer (USA))
393a^{10} 1870a^{2} 6365a^{9}

Coconut Moon *E J Alston* a70 81
4 b m Bahamian Bounty—Lunar Ridge (Indian Ridge)
1794[12] 2237[8] (2462) 2521[3] 2897[2] 3069[5]3503[2] 3972[17] 4453[7] (4793) 5169[8] 5405[11]

Coconut Queen (IRE) *Mrs A Duffield* 72
2 b f Alhaarth(IRE) —Royal Bounty (IRE) (Generous (IRE))
3581[4] 3788[3] (4228) 4761[6] 5492[7] 5748[2]

Coconut Squeak *Stef Liddiard* a66 103
4 b m Bahamian Bounty—Creeking (Persian Bold)
729[9] 1287[7] 1671[4] 1849[5] 2199[6]

Coda Agency *D W P Arbuthnot* a62 61
3 b g Agnes World(USA) —The Frog Lady (IRE) (Al Hareb (USA))
422[3] 515[6]762[5] 918[3]1375[5] 2882[5] 3347[11] 3977[6] 5097[3]6027[2] 6398[3] 6630[2]

Codeword (IRE) *M Johnston* a92 92
2 gr c Dansili—Spinamix (Spinning World (USA))
(3553) 4200[4] 5114[2] 5466a[14] 5806[5] 5989[3]

Coeur Courageux (FR) *D Nicholls* a88+ 102
4 b g Xaar—Linoise (FR) (Caerwent)
1487[U] 1835[9] 2649[8] 3079[15]

Coeur De Lionne (IRE) *R Charlton* a76 77
2 b g Invincible Spirit(IRE) —Lionne (Darshaan)
4992[6] 5423[2]5622[2]

Coffin Dodger *C N Allen* a49 44
3 ch f Dracula(AUS) —Karakul (IRE) (Persian Bold)
326[7] 887[4]1226[8] 1726[9]1829[7] 2070[3] 2463[2]2591[2] 3075[7] 3232[2]3628[8] 3823[6] (4263) 4491[7] 4847[7] 5298[8]5757[6] 6057[5] 6423[2]6551[9] 6657[3]

Colchium (IRE) *H Morrison* a71 71
2 br f Elnadim(USA) —Dog Rose (SAF) (Fort Wood (USA))
1514[6] 2354[3] 3344[8] 4773[2] 5322[6]5933[2] (6840)

Cold Climate *Bob Jones* a61 55
11 ch g Pursuit Of Love—Sharpthorne (USA) (Sharpen Up)
86[11]

Colditz (IRE) *D W Barker* a22 68
2 ch g Noverre(USA) —West Escape (Gone West (USA))
1838[14] 2361[2] 2610[8] 2899[6] 3641[12](3831) 4115[3] 4250[7] 4882[2] 5359[7]

Cold Quest (USA) *J H M Gosden* a86 82+
2 b c Seeking The Gold(USA) —Polaire (IRE) (Polish Patriot (USA))
(4705) 5020[3]

Cold Turkey *G L Moore* a99 99
6 bb g Polar Falcon(USA) —South Rock (Rock City)
65[4] 572[5](661) (1021) 1584[7]5678[4] 5963[20] 6336[9] 6515[2]

Cole (IRE) *J Howard Johnson* 50
3 b g Distant Music(USA) —Dark Albatross (USA) (Sheikh Albadou)
2163[7] 3397[10] 3910[16] (Dead)

Coleorton Dancer *K A Ryan* a45 103
4 ch g Danehill Dancer(IRE) —Tayovullin (IRE) (Shalford (IRE))
718[2] 1667[4] 2012[10] 4609[19] 4682[9]5358[4] 5812[16]

Coleorton Dane *K A Ryan* a51 43
4 gr g Danehill Dancer(IRE) —Cloudy Nine (Norton Challenger)
13[12]

Coleridge (AUS) *B G Powell* a80 79
7 ch g Yeats(USA) —Coco Cheval (AUS) (Zephyr Bay (AUS))
(4114) 5070[8] 5345[14] 5428[6]5670[12] 6564[2]6863[5]

Colinca's Lad (IRE) *T T Clement* a67 70
4 b g Lahib(USA) —Real Flame (Cyrano De Bergerac)
1489[6] 2088[9] 2508[8] 4704[4]4879[3] 5205[4] 5422[3]

Colinette *H Candy* 60+
3 b f Groom Dancer(USA) —Collide (High Line)
1289[7] 1797[6] 2332[12] 6052[7]

Colisay *Mrs A J Perrett* a103 112
7 b g Entrepreneur—La Sorrela (IRE) (Cadeaux Genereux)
370a[4] 438a[4] 666[9]1129[2] 1489[5]

Collateral Damage (IRE) *T D Easterby* a62 94
3 b c Orpen(USA) —Jay Gee (IRE) (Second Set (IRE))
1067[9] 1626[2] (1836) 4634[5] 4889[3] 5357[6]5722[2] 5789[3] 6210[2]

Collect *M H Tompkins* 62
4 b m Vettori(IRE) —Ring Fence (Polar Falcon (USA))
2148[10] 3036[6] 3260[RR]

College Land Boy *J J Quinn* 63
2 b g Cois Na Tine(IRE) —Welcome Lu (Most Welcome)
4323[6]

College Queen *S Gollings* a50 60
8 b m Lugana Beach—Eccentric Dancer (Rambo Dancer (CAN))
679[12] 886[12]1195[10] 2949[12] 4551[4]6233[7] 6851[6]

College Rebel *J F Coupland* a48 52
5 b m Defacto(USA) —Eccentric Dancer (Rambo Dancer (CAN))
301[2] 390[5]525[3] 599[5]684[3] 857[5]938[7] 1562[3] 2196[4]2501[5] 3291[10] 3919[10]

College Scholar (GER) *M R Channon* 92
2 ch c Dr Fong(USA) —Colina (GER) (Caerleon (USA))
3738[4] (4292) (4804) 5681[5] (6204)

Collette's Choice *R A Fahey* a41 66
3 b f Royal Applause—Brilliance (Cadeaux Genereux)
1888[9] 2283[2] 2539[3] (3145) 3249[5] 3634[6]

Collier Hill *G A Swinbank* 122
8 ch g Dr Devious(IRE) —Polar Queen (Polish Precedent (USA))
562a[6] 741a[2] 2845[7] 3107a[2] 4414a[3]4967[2] (5226a) (6126a) (6782a)

Colloquial *H Candy* a91 96
5 b g Classic Cliche(IRE) —Celia Brady (Last Tycoon)
2013[7] 2437[2] 3203[6]6205[11]

Colloseum *T J Etherington* a49 51
5 b g Piccolo—Trig Point (Rudimentary (USA))
400[9] 446[8]681[9]

Collow (GER) *M Weiss* 98
6 b g Lando(GER) —Conga (Robellino (USA))
456a[2]

Collusion (FR) *Pat Eddery* a54 57
3 ch g Zafonic(USA) —Chantereine (USA) (Trempolino (USA))
1135[9] 1335[12] 2034[11]

Colmar Supreme *R Hannon* a70 72
3 b f Woodborough(USA) —Child Star (FR) (Bellypha)
34[7] 139[3]

Colonel Bilko (IRE) *J J Bridger* a52 59
4 b g General Monash(USA) —Mari-Ela (IRE) (River Falls)
11[2] 56[5]382[9] 427[2]609[4] 689[7]1387[8] 5625[13] 6462[12]6632[11] 6726[12]6780[6] 6802[4]6854[10]

Colonel Cotton (IRE) *R A Fahey* a55 59
7 b g Royal Applause—Cutpurse Moll (Green Desert (USA))
9[7] 96[9]159[8] 2237[4] 3041[10]3354[4] 3503[3] 3622[4] 4364[6] 4453[10]5309[9] 5577[9] 6162[11] 6442[7]

Colonel Flay *Mrs P N Dutfield* 78
2 ch c Danehill Dancer(IRE) —Bobbie Dee (Blakeney)
3851[2] 4766[15] 5892[9]

Colonel Klink (IRE) *J S Moore* 27
2 b c Monashee Mountain(USA) —Persian Velvet (IRE) (Distinctly North (USA))
2234[10] 2857[6] 5646[15]

Colonial Cross (IRE) *M Halford* 74
2 b g Cape Cross(IRE) —Maytpleasethecourt (IRE) (Persian Heights)
5662a[10]

Colorado Rapid (IRE) *M Johnston* 83
2 b c Barathea(IRE) —Rafting (IRE) (Darshaan)
5125[2]

Color Man *Mrs A J Perrett* a50 52
2 b g Rainbow Quest(USA) —Subya (Night Shift (USA))
2979[11] 3545[12] 3726[5]

Colorus (IRE) *R A Fahey* a63 78
3 b g Night Shift(USA) —Duck Over (Warning)
1606[10] 2385[10] 3761[7] 4403[6] 4717[7]5079[9] 5377[6] 5791[11]

Colour Me Blue (IRE) *J S Bolger* 78
2 b c Spectrum(IRE) —Insijaam (USA) (Secretariat (USA))
5662a[13]

Colourpoint (USA) *C E Brittain* 76d
3 bb f Forest Wildcat(USA) —Farrfesheena (USA) (Rahy (USA))
1137[8] 2050[19]

Coltchester (IRE) *Peter Grayson* a56
3 b g Tagula(IRE) —Eveam (IRE) (Mujadil (USA))
802[5] 984[11]

Colton *J M P Eustace* a79 76
3 b g Zilzal(USA) —Picot (Piccolo)
1355[6] 2583[7] 3329[11] (4257) (4497) 4958[3] 5260[7]5680[4] 6259[4]

Columbus (IRE) *Jennie Candlish* 38
9 b g Sadler's Wells(USA) —Northern Script (USA) (Arts And Letters (USA))
6178[5]

Colway Ritz *W Storey* 54
12 b g Rudimentary(USA) —Million Heiress (Auction Ring (USA))
2242[5] 2788[2] 2871[11] 3192[3]

Comeintothespace (IRE) *Miss Victoria Roberts* a74d 71
4 b g Tagula(IRE) —Playa Del Sol (IRE) (Alzao (USA))
504[10] 1002[4]1152[11] 1560[10] 2221[11]2794[13] 3194[3] 3541[5]4288[8] 4446[8] 5259[6]

Come On *J Hetherton* a53 61
7 b g Aragon—All On (Dunbeath (USA))
792[7] 940[10]1463[8]

Come On Jonny (IRE) *R M Beckett* 109
4 b g Desert King(IRE) —Idle Fancy (Mujtahid (USA))
5804[12] 6336[11]

Come Out Fighting *P A Blockley* a93 102
3 b c Bertolini(USA) —Ulysses Daughter (IRE) (College Chapel)
1020[4] 1438[10] 3360[2]3585[7] (4345) 4601[3] 5116[3] 5501[15]

Come To Daddy (IRE) *F Jordan* 47
4 ch g Fayruz—Forgren (IRE) (Thatching)
2411[8] 3225[9]

Come What Augustus *R M Stronge* a52 52
4 b g Mujahid(USA) —Sky Red (Night Shift (USA))
2305[15]

Come What July (IRE) *D Shaw* a46 65
5 b g Indian Rocket—Persian Sally (IRE) (Persian Bold)
98[6] 200[7]243[6] 6526[9]6621[6] 6687[10]6743[8] 6860[3]6936[10]

Come What May *Rae Guest* 65
2 b f Selkirk(USA) —Portelet (Night Shift (USA))
5645 [10] 6175[3]

Comical Errors (USA) *P C Haslam* 53
4 b g Distorted Humor(USA) —Fallibility (USA) (Tom Rolfe)
3836[3] 4380[15] 4423[2]

Comic Tales *M Mullineaux* a52 40
5 b g Mind Games—Glorious Aragon (Aragon)
29[9] 45[5]126[6] 633[8]686[8] 943[2]1228[2] 1466[4]1607[8] 1762[3] 6548[10]6615[11] 6704[9]6738[3] 6858[11]6944[5]

Comma (USA) *Sir Michael Stoute* 65
2 b f Kingmambo(USA) —Flute (USA) (Seattle Slew (USA))
5596[6] 5898[2] 6215[10]

Commander Wish *P Howling* a25 46
3 ch c Arkadian Hero(USA) —Flighty Dancer (Pivotal)
3089[12] 5210[12] 6378[U]

Commandocourageous (SAF) *D Maroun* a45 72
5 b g National Assembly(CAN) —Enchanted Cove (USA) (Wolf Power (SAF))
206a[14] 494a[10]

Commando Scott (IRE) *I W McInnes* a81 99
5 b g Danetime(IRE) —Faye (Monsanto (FR))
444[10] 726[4] 898[2]1183[2] 1456[3] (1532) 1835[8] (1949) 2012[8] 2230[9]2847[20] 4988[3] 5336[6] 5355[3] 5529[3]5677[8]

Command Respect *E F Vaughan* 27
3 b f Commands(AUS) —The Blade (GER) (Sure Blade (USA))
2304[17] 2951[7] 5571[8]

Commentary *W J Haggas* 85
3 b f Medicean—Eloquent (Polar Falcon (USA))
2735[4]

Commitment Lecture *M Dods* a53 79
6 b m Komaite(USA) —Hurtleberry (IRE) (Tirol)
(1123) (1830) 2170[8] 2853[7] 3331[4] 4153[4] 4660[6]5024[8] 5617[5]

Common Purpose (USA) *J H M Gosden* a72
2 b g Elusive Quality(USA) —Kithira (Danehill (USA))
6188[3]

Common World (USA) *T Hogan* a81 114
7 ch h Spinning World(USA) —Spenderella (FR) (Common Grounds)
728[17] (930a) 1469a[5] 1840[7] 2116[4] 4190a[3]4641a[6] 4864a[13] 5411a[9] 5708a[7]

Competitor *J Akehurst* a63 40
5 b h Danzero(AUS) —Ceanothus (IRE) (Bluebird (USA))
63[2] 185[5]324[7] 484[6](694) 833[3](904) 1163[3]1400[15] 5422[11] 5831[16]6037[14] 6982[3]

Composing (IRE) *H Morrison* 64
2 b f Noverre(USA) —Aqaba (Lake Coniston (IRE))
5623[3]

Compromiznotension (IRE) *I Semple* 84
3 br g Key Of Luck(USA) —Music Khan (Music Boy)
1212[2] 1445[5] 2016[6] (5063) 5312[3] (5724) (6210)

Compton Bay *M Brittain* a43 48
6 b g Compton Place—Silver Sun (Green Desert (USA))
783[9] 3909[5] 4198[14]4548[6] 6277[8]

Compton Bolter (IRE) *G A Butler* a114 114
9 b g Red Sunset—Milk And Honey (So Blessed)
518[7] 666[13]1128[8] 1628[4] 2803[14] 3971[9]

Compton Charlie *J G Portman* a50 66
2 b c Compton Place—Tell Tale Fox (Tel Quel (FR))
5871[11] 6331[5] 6475[3]

Compton Classic *J S Goldie* a59 63
4 b g Compton Place—Ayr Classic (Local Suitor (USA))
680[13] (1228) 1396[2]1611[6] 1794[2] 2449[7] 2550[6] 3171[8](3334) 4232[4] 4477[7] 5078[6] 5309[5] (5631) 5834[3]5865[2] 6315[2] 6521[9]

Compton Commander *E W Tuer* a95 88
8 ch g Barathea(IRE) —Triode (USA) (Sharpen Up)
2018[7] 2196[10] 2871[10] 4960[11]

Compton Court *A M Balding* a75 78+
4 b g Compton Place—Loriner's Lass (Saddlers' Hall (IRE))
905[3] 1821[2] 2401[15]4176[3] 4708[4] 5205[11]

Compton Dragon (USA) *R Johnson* a63 69
7 ch g Woodman(USA) —Vilikaia (USA) (Nureyev (USA))
1500[7] 3037[6]

Compton Drake *G A Butler* a83 83
7 b g Mark Of Esteem(IRE) —Reprocolor (Jimmy Reppin)
250[4]

Compton Earl *J J Lambe* a35 53
6 ch h Efisio—Bay Bay (Bay Express)
680[8] (Dead)

Compton Eclaire (IRE) *B Ellison* a58 63
6 ch m Lycius(USA) —Baylands Sunshine (IRE) (Classic Secret (USA))
482[11] 975[7] 1883[2](2684) 2871[2] 3114[4] 3723[4] 4072[6] 4632[6]4960[7] 5242[3]

Compton Eclipse *J J Lambe* a73 73
6 ch h Singspiel(IRE) —Fatah Flare (USA) (Alydar (USA))
(384) 567[5] 736[9]

Compton Express *Jamie Poulton* a46 29
3 gr f Compton Place—Jilly Woo (Environment Friend)
191[8] 3647[10]4143[9] 6696[9] 6848[13]6918[10]

Compton Fields *R Charlton* 75
2 b g Compton Place—Julia Domna (Dominion)
1796[8] (3110) 3555[3] 4893[4] 5349[10]

Compton Flyer *J M Bradley* a36 37
3 ch c Compton Admiral—Elegantissima (Polish Precedent (USA))
1166[12] 1433[10] 1567[11]2285[9] 3115[U]

Compton Lad *D A Nolan* a46 50
3 b g Compton Place—Kintara (Cyrano De Bergerac)
1612[12] 3479[5] 3526[8] 4056[11] 4354[3]4656[8] 4725[10] 5250[10]5834[13]

Compton Micky *R F Marvin* a38 35
5 ch g Compton Place—Nunthorpe (Mystiko (USA))
3999[13] 4233[10] 4511[9]6282[13] 6307[6]6962[5]

Compton Plume *M W Easterby* a31 76
6 ch g Compton Place—Brockton Flame (Emarati (USA))
1124[12] 1563[10] 2020[9] 2505[15] 2785[11](4157) 4230[4] 4957[6] 5487[4]

Compton's Eleven *M R Channon* a102 106
5 gr g Compton Place—Princess Tara (Prince Sabo)
(201a) 367a[2] 494a[4] 830[4]1086[13] 2012[11] 2776[20] 3079[2] 3493[10]4372[2] 4798[2] 5175[5] 5523[7] 5677[3]

Compton Special *J G Given* a50
2 ch f Compton Place—Spectina (Spectrum (IRE))
6505[8] 6663[7]

Comptonspirit *B P J Baugh*
2 ch f Compton Place—Croeso Cynnes (Most Welcome)
6989[U]

Compton Verney *M W Easterby*
2 b c Compton Admiral—Gipsy Princess (Prince Daniel (USA))
2538[7] 2731[5] 2870[6] 3279[6]

Comrade Cotton *N A Callaghan* a50
2 b c Royal Applause—Cutpurse Moll (Green Desert (USA))
6669[7] 6921[6]

Conceal *R Bouresly* a93 101
8 b g Cadeaux Genereux—Mystery Play (IRE) (Sadler's Wells (USA))
206a[6] 352a[3] 431a[6]506a[3] 563a[6]

Confide (IRE) *G A Swinbank* 74+
4 ch g Namid—Confidential (Generous (IRE))
1683[3] 1996[11] (2195) 2697[2] 2737[4] (3813) 4378[7]

Confident *M A Jarvis* a44
2 b f Machiavellian(USA) —Sweet Willa (USA) (Assert)
6486[9] 6757[10]

Confidential Lady *Sir Mark Prescott* 117
3 b f Singspiel(IRE) —Confidante (USA) (Dayjur (USA))
1508[2] 2054a[6] (2491a) 3575a[5] 5964[5] 6124a[2]

Confuchias (IRE) *Francis Ennis* 103
2 b c Cape Cross(IRE) —Schust Madame (IRE) (Second Set (IRE))
(6262a)

Congestion Charge *E A L Dunlop* a68+ 70
3 b f Diktat—Overdrive (Shirley Heights)
850[5] 1260[2] 1827[4]2607[13]

Congressional (IRE) *M A Jarvis* a66 76
3 b f Grand Lodge(USA) —Gilah (IRE) (Saddlers' Hall (IRE))
4660[10] 5211[9] 5572[5]

Conjecture *R Bastiman* a65 79
4 b g Danzig(USA) —Golden Opinion (USA) (Slew O'Gold (USA))
1297[5] 2449[12] 3004[3] 3354[5] 3802[2]4180[4] 4468[9] 5275[6] 5486[6] 5684[13]6162[2] 6315[6] 6572[6]

Conjuror *A M Balding* a78 82
5 b g Efisio—Princess Athena (Ahonoora)
721[5]

Conkering (USA) *J R Fanshawe* a58 86
3 ch g Horse Chestnut(SAF) —Nunbridled (USA) (Unbridled (USA))
(1100) 3366[10] 5137[7] 5769[4]

Connect *M H Tompkins* a87 99
9 b g Petong—Natchez Trace (Commanche Run)
2303[7] 2683[5] 2847[8] 3077[8] 3550[3]3972[10] 4128[19] 4461[5] 4682[3] 5044[7]5182[7] 5420[9] 5807[5] 5921[9] 6428[5](6499)

Connotation *A G Newcombe* a69 60
4 b m Mujahid(USA) —Seven Wonders (USA) (Rahy (USA))
167[3] 253[5]585[9] 641[11]1220[13] 1773[11] 2464[10]2647[8] 2936[9]4446[5] 6383[4] 6714[11]

Conny Nobel (IRE) *R A Kvisla* a66
2 gr g Marju(IRE) —Beauharnaise (FR) (Linamix (FR))
6561[11] 6778[5]6920[2]

Conquest (IRE) *W J Haggas* 114
2 b c Invincible Spirit(IRE) —Aguinaga (IRE) (Machiavellian (USA))
1510[2] 1838[5] 2724[2] (3308) (4712) 5656[6]

Conrad *R A Fahey* 75
3 b g Royal Applause—Milly-M (Cadeaux Genereux)
2298[3] 2658[17] 3285[5] (4262) 4707[10] 4888[7]5724[3] 6206[9]

Conroy (USA) *A Selvaratnam* a118
8 ch g Gone West(USA) —Crystal Gazing (USA) (El Gran Senor (USA))
206a[2] 563a[5]740a[14]

Consent *A Dickman* 50
3 ch f Groom Dancer(USA) —Preference (Efisio)
2243[14]

Conservation (FR) *P W Chapple-Hyam* 78
3 b c Green Desert(USA) —Lightly Dancing (FR) (Groom Dancer (USA))
880[3] 1055[4] 1375[3] 1738[2] 3347[12]4173[4] 4586[2] 5732[3] 5870[2] 6053[2]

Conservative *P G Murphy* a65 74+
3 bb g Pivotal—Happy Omen (Warning)
4663[2] 5270[2] 6144[3]6489[9]

Considerthelilies (IRE) *Miss L A Perratt* 49
3 b f Mull Of Kintyre(USA) —Gilding The Lily (IRE) (High Estate)
2734[10] 2856[9] 3167[12] 3329[14] 5312[11]

Considine (USA) *C J Mann* a67 74?
5 b g Romanov(IRE) —Libeccio (NZ) (Danzatore (CAN))
2849[8]

Consonant (IRE) *D G Bridgwater* a86 74
9 ch g Barathea(IRE) —Dina Lina (FR) (Top Ville)
135[2] 578[5]763[6] 1051[12] 2186[13]2499[8] 2585[2] 3024[3] 3948[11] 4565[3]5090[4] 5436[5] 5689[2]6313[2] 6418[6]6607[B] 6888[7]6992[9]

Constable Burton *Mrs A Duffield* a75 62
5 b g Foxhound(USA) —Actress (Known Fact (USA))
3583[7] 3918[10]

Constables Art *N A Callaghan* 43
3 b g Royal Applause—Social Storm (USA) (Future Storm (USA))
5298[11] 5441[2] 5733[13]

Constant Cheers (IRE) *W R Swinburn* a55 63
3 b g Royal Applause—Juno Marlowe (IRE) (Danehill (USA))
1141[9] 1375[4] 1925[8]2569[5] 3017[7]

Constructor *C A Cyzer* a69 59
5 b g So Factual(USA) —Love And Kisses (Salse (USA))
3933[15]

Consuelita *B J Meehan* a47 66
3 bb f Singspiel(IRE) —Green Rosy (USA) (Green Dancer (USA))
1191[9] 1798[5] 3146[7] 3793[14] 6810[9]

Consular *M A Jarvis* 102
4 br g Singspiel(IRE) —Language Of Love (Rock City)
1775[11] 2229[3] 2848[7] (3294) 3890[4] 4713[12]

Consul General *D K Weld* 101
2 b c Selkirk(USA) —West Dakota (USA) (Gone West (USA))
(5662a) 6456a[7]

Contact Dancer (IRE) *M Johnston* 96
7 b g Sadler's Wells(USA) —Rain Queen (Rainbow Quest (USA))
1584^{17} 5582^{6} 5963^{29}

Contemplation *G A Swinbank* a67+ 64
3 b c Sunday Silence(USA) —Wood Vine (USA) (Woodman (USA))
1826^{2} 1988^{4} 5368^{2} 5879^{5}6008^{7}

Contented (IRE) *Mrs L C Jewell* a66 65
4 b g Orpen(USA) —Joyfullness (USA) (Dixieland Band (USA))
114^{9} 324^{13}520^{7} 677^{2}693^{4} 862^{2}972^{12} 1390^{2} 1568^{3}2135^{15} 3014^{11}

Contentious (IRE) *D M Simcock* 53
2 b f Danetime(IRE) —Serious Contender (IRE) (Tenby)
4754^{7}

Contentious (USA) *J L Dunlop* 71
2 b f Giant's Causeway(USA) —Illicit (USA) (Mr Prospector (USA))
5292^{4} 5891^{2}

Continent *D Nicholls* 102
9 ch g Lake Coniston(IRE) —Krisia (Kris)
729^{12} 1487^{6} 1835^{12} 2227^{3} 3038^{4}3482^{8} 4128^{16} 4609^{11} 4682^{7} 5355^{2}5534^{10}

Conto Astronomico (ITY) *M Guarnieri*
2 b c Galileo(IRE) —Banque Privee (USA) (Private Account (USA))
6407a^{10}

Contra Mundum (USA) *B J Meehan* a63+ 78
3 ch g Giant's Causeway(USA) —Speak Softly To Me (USA) (Ogygian (USA))
1335^{9} 1823^{3} 2261^{5}

Controvento (IRE) *Eamon Tyrrell* a38 68
4 b m Midhish—La Maya (IRE) (Scenic)
5865^{4} 6315^{7} 6527^{8}

Convallaria (FR) *G Wragg* 57
3 b f Cape Cross(IRE) —Scarlet Davis (FR) (Ti King (FR))
1085^{17} 1674^{8}

Converti *P F I Cole* a45 63
2 b c Averti(IRE) —Conquestadora (Hernando (FR))
2506^{12} 3851^{7} 5105^{10}

Convince (USA) *J M Bradley* a19 61
5 ch g Mt. Livermore(USA) —Conical (Zafonic (USA))
2484^{5} 2897^{10} 3245^{3} 3565^{8} 3899^{3}4211^{11} 4564^{5} 4846^{6} 5131^{10} 5378^{11}5573^{2} 6300^{6}

Convincing *John Joseph Murphy* 80
3 b c Selkirk(USA) —Hot Thong (BRZ) (Jarraar (USA))
5396a^{12}

Convivial Spirit *E F Vaughan* a63 67
2 b g Lake Coniston(IRE) —Ruby Princess (IRE) (Mac's Imp (USA))
3930^{6} 4434^{3} 5315^{2}5655^{23} 6056^{10} 6291^{4}

Cookie Cutter (IRE) *K R Burke* a73 72
4 b m Fasliyev(USA) —Cut The Red Tape (IRE) (Sure Blade (USA))
14^{2} 45^{3}(195) 249^{3}

Cookies Quiff (IRE) *J S Moore* 53
2 b g Iron Mask(USA) —Amy G (IRE) (Common Grounds)
3345^{3} 3799^{4} 4334^{9} 4926^{6} 5282^{9}

Coolaw (IRE) *G G Margarson* a46
3 br f Priolo(USA) —Cool Gales (Lord Gayle (USA))
6578^{6} 6680^{6}

Cool Bathwick (IRE) *G H Yardley* a65 50
7 b g Entrepreneur—Tarafa (Akarad (FR))
229^{12} 283^{11}1566^{9} 2099^{10} 2219^{11} 3998^{12}

Cool Box (USA) *Mrs A J Perrett* a84+ 72
2 b c Grand Slam(USA) —Frigidette (USA) (It's Freezing (USA))
3949^{3} 4525^{6} 5371^{5} 6324^{3}(6444)

Cool Customer (USA) *E A L Dunlop* a81+ 99
3 b c Gone West(USA) —Radu Cool (USA) (Carnivalay (USA))
669^{6} (894) (1403) 1837^{2} 1975^{2}(3589) 4125^{4} 4951^{2} 5325^{4} 5582^{2} 5920^{3}

Cool Ebony *M Dods* 81
3 br g Erhaab(USA) —Monawara (IRE) (Namaqualand (USA))
1034^{5} 1648^{8} 2111^{3} 2622^{5} 3030^{4}(3569) (4225) 4426^{2} 5504^{8} 5833^{9}

Cooleycall Star (IRE) *A G Juckes* a43 44
5 b g Foxhound(USA) —Ozwood (IRE) (Royal Academy (USA))
180^{8} 396^{3}467^{11} 687^{8}

Cool Hunter *W R Swinburn* a62 90
5 ch g Polar Falcon(USA) —Seabound (Prince Sabo)
1133^{10} (1544) 1864^{13} 2387^{16} 3401^{10}4175^{4} 5367^{11}

Cool Isle *P Howling* a56 45
3 b f Polar Prince(IRE) —Fisher Island (IRE) (Sri Pekan (USA))
69^{5} 197^{3}333^{3} 430^{2}543^{6} 676^{4}859^{11} 1259^{10}2463^{5} 2861^{7}3824^{2} 4280^{5} (4491) 4909^{10} 5033^{2}5298^{9} (5441) 6238^{9} 6423^{3}6540^{9} (6584) 6812^{5} 6860^{4}

Cool Panic (IRE) *M L W Bell* a74 98
4 b g Brave Act—Geht Schnell (Fairy King (USA))
828^{12} 1667^{12} 1806^{5}2012^{15} 4372^{9} 4593^{12}

Cool Sands (IRE) *D Shaw* a68 61
4 b g Trans Island—Shalerina (USA) (Shalford (IRE))
4^{5} 47^{5}(575) 977^{6} 1124^{13} 2020^{12}2074^{4} 5246^{12} 5635^{11}5737^{7} 6390^{7}6442^{13} 6590^{14}(6763) 6864^{2}6949^{5}

Cool Sting (IRE) *M G Quinlan* a72 76
3 b g Bluebird(USA) —Honey Bee (Alnasr Alwasheek)
473^{9} 553^{3}801^{2} (916) 1208^{8} 1411^{6} 2553^{9}2863^{4} 3224^{6} 3546^{6} 3708^{5} 4143^{10}4281^{3} 4674^{6} 5054^{3} 5273^{4} (6033) 6061^{10} 6348^{6} 6508^{5}6624^{8} 6913^{6}

Cool Tiger *P Howling* a56 65
3 ch g Vettori(IRE) —Juvenilia (IRE) (Masterclass (USA))
3711^{4} 4247^{9} 4663^{7}5418^{13} 5609^{9} (6550) 6796^{10} (6856)

Cool Touch (IRE) *Peter Casey* 107
3 b g Marju(IRE) —Feather Star (Soviet Star (USA))
5190a^{7}

Cooperstown *J Howard Johnson* 84
3 ch g Dr Fong(USA) —Heckle (In The Wings)
4635^{3} 5727^{2}

Copernican *Sir Mark Prescott* a54+
2 ch g Hernando(FR) —Wonderful World (GER) (Dashing Blade)
5105^{8} 5423^{6}5607^{9}

Copper King *P D Evans* a77 68+
2 ch g Ishiguru(USA) —Dorissio (IRE) (Efisio)
1688^{7} 2094^{3} 2388^{6} 3117^{9} 4893^{6}5065^{7} (5948) 6285^{5} 6525^{2}(6645) 6764^{8}6866^{4}

Coppermalt (USA) *R Curtis* a50 51
8 b g Affirmed(USA) —Poppy Carew (IRE) (Danehill (USA))
309^{3} 574^{12}3035^{13}

Coppington Melody (IRE) *B W Duke* a57 38
3 b f Ordway(USA) —Chorus (USA) (Darshaan)
5830^{7} 6026^{6} 6225^{8}6398^{2} 6560^{8}6831^{10}

Copplestone (IRE) *A C Whillans* 45
10 b g Second Set(IRE) —Queen Of The Brush (Averof)
1883^{3} 2812^{7} 3135^{8}

Coquet Island *G M Moore* a12 61
3 ch g Alhaarth(IRE) —Abir (Soviet Star (USA))
673^{6} 980^{14} 1447^{9}

Coquin D'Alezan (IRE) *W Jarvis* a69
5 ch g Cadeaux Genereux—Nwaahil (IRE) (Nashwan (USA))
653^{5} 806^{5}985^{10}

Coral Gables (IND) *L D'Silva* 43
6 b g Young Senor(USA) —Potsclose (Miswaki (USA))
281a^{11} 507a^{10}

Coranglais *J M Bradley* a62 68
6 ch g Piccolo—Antonia's Folly (Music Boy)
1432^{9} 1528^{8} 1878^{7} 1981^{5} 2331^{8}2484^{7} 2971^{6} 3094^{10} 4361^{4} 4636^{5}

Cora Pearl (IRE) *M J Polglase* 51
3 b f Montjeu(IRE) —Castara Beach (IRE) (Danehill (USA))
528^{10} 1182^{6} 1424^{4}1648^{6} 2124^{11}

Cordage (IRE) *J A Pickering* a35 52
4 ch g Dr Fong(USA) —Flagship (Rainbow Quest (USA))
571^{13} 1455^{7} 2548^{6}2789^{8} 6378^{U} 6532^{13}6621^{8}

Cordelia *B W Hills* a65 69
3 b f Green Desert(USA) —Bint Zamayem (IRE) (Rainbow Quest (USA))
868^{6} 1630^{5} 2734^{5} 3285^{2} 3864^{4}5055^{14} 5728^{5} 6144^{2}6293^{2} 6480^{2}

Cordier *J Mackie* a78 51
4 b g Desert Style(IRE) —Slipper (Suave Dancer (USA))
125^{6} (385) 610^{3}1651^{12} 2000^{6}

Cordwain *J H M Gosden* 80
2 b g Lomitas—Goodie Twosues (Fraam)
5460^{14} 6058^{2} 6216^{4}

Corfu (IRE) *K Borgel* 74
4 ch m Daylami(IRE) —Chania (IRE) (In The Wings)
523a^{8}

Corky (IRE) *I W McInnes* a70 78
5 b g Intikhab(USA) —Khamseh (Thatching)
101^{7} 236^{8}319^{4} 405^{11}571^{10} 777^{2} 992^{10}1186^{12} 1531^{6} 1830^{8} 1932^{10} 2025^{3}

Corlough Mountain *N A Callaghan* a71
2 ch c Inchinor—Two Step (Mujtahid (USA))
6631^{2} 6826^{2}6867^{5}

Cormorant Wharf (IRE) *T E Powell* a74 75
6 b g Alzao(USA) —Mercy Bien (IRE) (Be My Guest (USA))
17^{9} 223^{11}1311^{6} (1769) 2044^{2} 2455^{6} 3141^{2} 3431^{5}5236^{5} 6108^{3} 6462^{2}

Cornell Precedent *J J Quinn* 50
2 ch c Polish Precedent(USA) —Shamwari (USA) (Shahrastani (USA))
5025^{9} 5332^{5} 5900^{6}

Cornflower (USA) *Saeed Bin Suroor* 54
2 b f Seeking The Gold(USA) —Lilium (Nashwan (USA))
5898^{5}

Cornus *A J McCabe* a90 91
4 ch g Inchinor—Demerger (USA) (Distant View (USA))
54^{6} 80^{9}220^{5} 238^{7}362^{8} 441^{8}4085^{11} 4486^{12} 5058^{6} 5391^{4}5593^{4} 5765^{9} 5961^{9}

Coronado Forest (USA) *M R Hoad* a45 56
7 b g Spinning World(USA) —Desert Jewel (USA) (Caerleon (USA))
312^{8} 399^{10}853^{10}

Coronado's Gold (USA) *W R Swinburn* a56 54
5 ch g Coronado's Quest(USA) —Debit My Account (USA) (Classic Account (USA))
185^{8} 498^{5}

Coronation Flight *F P Murtagh* 52
3 b f Missed Flight—Hand On Heart (IRE) (Taufan (USA))
1598^{13} 1814^{5} 2734^{9} 3288^{3} 3785^{5}4195^{6} 4881^{2} 5244^{5} 5726^{3} 5838^{3}6211^{3}

Coronation Queen *S Kirk* 47
3 b f Pivotal—Coffee Ice (Primo Dominie)
1955^{9}

Corran Ard (IRE) *Evan Williams* 93+
5 b g Imperial Ballet(IRE) —Beeper The Great (USA) (Whadjathink (USA))
(1302) (2621) (5494)

Corre Caminos (FR) *M Delzangles* 121
4 b g Montjeu(IRE) —Dibenoise (FR) (Kendor (FR))
934a^{2} (1331a) 1873a^{5} 2741^{6} 5519a^{3}

Correct Time (IRE) *N P Littmoden* a64 54
3 b c Danetime(IRE) —Solo Symphony (IRE) (Fayruz)
68^{5} (239) 359^{4}464^{4} 577^{3}

Corrib (IRE) *B Palling* a77 78
3 b f Lahib(USA) —Montana Miss (IRE) (Earl Of Barking (IRE))
1569^{11} 2318^{12} 3055^{2}(3598) 5079^{11} 6239^{12}6478^{6} 6664^{11}

Corrib Eclipse *Ian Williams* a102 102
7 b g Double Eclipse(IRE) —Last Night's Fun (IRE) (Law Society (USA))
2849^{5} 5318^{5}

Corridor Creeper (FR) *J M Bradley* 106
9 ch g Polish Precedent(USA) —Sonia Rose (USA) (Superbity (USA))
1116^{2} 1485^{10} (1663) 1952^{3} 2227^{7} 2720^{2}1331^{2}9 4080^{14} 4875^{8} 5182^{12} 5274^{5}5642^{4} 5807^{8} 5921^{7} 5957^{3}

Corriolanus (GER) *S Seemar* a108 109
6 b h Zamindar(USA) —Caesarea (GER) (Generous (IRE))
371a^{5} 437a^{4} 562a^{8} 624a^{2}

Corrucaseco *M D I Usher*
2 b f Bertolini(USA) —Konica (Desert King (IRE))
2709^{12} 3054^{7}

Corso Palladio (IRE) *J E Hammond* 101
4 b g Montjeu(IRE) —Falafil (FR) (Fabulous Dancer (USA))
934a^{10}

Cortesia (IRE) *P W Chapple-Hyam* 84
3 ch f Courteous—Cecina (Welsh Saint)
(1114) 1583^{9} 4741^{9} 5869^{11}

Cortina *J Jay* a6 14
3 b f Cigar—Dorothea Sharp (IRE) (Foxhound (USA))
590^{11} 2526^{5} 3261^{9}3836^{6} 4016^{10}

Corum (IRE) *J H M Gosden* 93
3 b c Galileo(IRE) —Vallee Des Reves (USA) (Kingmambo (USA))
(2655) 3980^{6} 4604^{2} 5533^{9} 6337^{17}

Corviglia *J R Fanshawe* 48+
3 b f Nashwan(USA) —Ski Run (Petoski)
5589^{5} 5770^{14}

Coseadrom (IRE) *Peter Henley* 82
4 b h Almutawakel—Madam Lightfoot (USA) (Vice Regent (CAN))
3561a^{4}

Cosimo Primo *J A Geake* 45
2 b g Medicean—Cugina (Distant Relative)
5371^{14} 5891^{16} 6330^{9}

Cosmic Destiny (IRE) *E F Vaughan* a67 64
4 b m Soviet Star(USA) —Cruelle (USA) (Irish River (FR))
986^{8} 1315^{5} 1414^{10}1618^{5} 2571^{3} 2897^{6} 3071^{3} 3348^{4}3825^{12} (3847) 5378^{16} 5480^{5}5575^{5} 5878^{7} 6288^{6}6521^{5} 6688^{9}

Cosmic Girl *H Candy* 48
3 b f Gorse—Lotus Moon (Shareef Dancer (USA))
2985^{10} 3266^{10} 3931^{9}

Cosmic Messenger (FR) *L A Dace* a53 68
3 ch g Septieme Ciel(USA) —Bonnie And Howard (USA) (Fly So Free (USA))
2292^{8} 4708^{7} 5098^{5}5587^{P}

Cosmo Bulk (JPN) *K Tabe* 122
5 b h Zagreb(USA) —Iseno Tosho (JPN) (Tosho Boy (JPN))
(1716a) 6612a^{4}

Cosmoledo (FR) *Mlle A-C Trouve* 69
6 ch g Apple Tree(FR) —Tonic Stream (FR) (Bering)
3580a^{7}

Cosmonaut (USA) *P L Biancone* a103 117
4 rg h Lemon Drop Kid(USA) —Cosmic Fire (USA) (Capote (USA))
4386a^{5} 5824a^{4}

Cosmopolitan Lady *D M Simcock* 81
2 b f Kyllachy—Sunflower Seed (Mummy's Pet)
1082^{6} 2816^{2} 3026^{3} 3430^{3} 4006^{2}4321^{4} 4550^{2} (5234) 5731^{8}

Cosmo Schindler (AUS) *T Kayo* 105
4 b h Green Desert(USA) —Anniegetyourgun (USA) (Gone West (USA))
6850a^{11}

Costume *J H M Gosden* 68
2 b f Danehill(USA) —Dance Dress (USA) (Nureyev (USA))
2867^{3}

Cote D'Argent *M Johnston* 86
3 b g Lujain(USA) —In The Groove (Night Shift (USA))
1115^{11}

Cote Soleil (FR) *R Laplanche* 72
4 b g Dance Brightly(CAN) —Fontaine Guerard (FR) (Homme De Loi (IRE))
5562a^{7}

Cotswold Traveller *Tom Dascombe* 53
2 br f Hunting Lion(IRE) —Perfect Partner (Be My Chief (USA))
1046^{8} 1347^{8}

Cottingham (IRE) *T D Barron* a64 71
5 b g Perugino(USA) —Stately Princess (Robellino (USA))
875^{6} (1461) 1723^{2}2149^{2} (2181) (2414) 3484^{2} (3621)3784^{3} 4068^{6}

Cotton Blossom (USA) *T Pletcher* a111
2 b f Broken Vow(USA) —For Dixie (USA) (Dixieland Band (USA))
6338a^{3}

Cotton Easter *Mrs A J Bowlby* a42 57
5 b m Robellino(USA) —Pluck (Never So Bold)
1723^{11} (1879) 2099^{7} 6280^{5}6423^{7}

Cotton Eyed Joe (IRE) *G A Swinbank* a77 75
5 b g Indian Rocket—Cwm Deri (IRE) (Alzao (USA))
(25) (91) 129^{3} (246) 346^{5}1144^{6} 1502^{3} 1809^{4} 2140^{3}2975^{4} 4156^{5} 4935^{5}

Cottonmouth (IRE) *A Botti* 67
2 b f Noverre(USA) —Nafzira (IRE) (Darshaan)
6123a^{8}

Cougar Bay (IRE) *David Wachman* 113
3 b c Daylami(IRE) —Delimara (IRE) (In The Wings)
1081^{2} 2471a^{2} 3127a^{12} 4358^{4} 5004a^{3}5190a^{2}

Councellor (FR) *Stef Liddiard* a84 83
4 b g Gilded Time(USA) —Sudden Storm Bird (USA) (Storm Bird (CAN))
245^{3} 412^{3}476^{7} (569) 632^{4} 846^{6}946^{4}

Council Member (USA) *Saeed Bin Suroor* a98 112
4 b h Seattle Slew(USA) —Zoe Montana (USA) (Seeking The Gold (USA))
6101^{2}

Counsel's Opinion (IRE) *C F Wall* a111 111
9 ch g Rudimentary(USA) —Fairy Fortune (Rainbow Quest (USA))
518^{3} 666^{7}1239^{5} 1601^{2} 2201^{15} 4818^{9} 5548^{13}5808^{7}

Countback (FR) *A W Carroll* a61
7 b g Anabaa(USA) —Count Me Out (FR) (Kaldoun (FR))
40^{3} 52^{2}129^{4} 231^{4}309^{5} 328^{4}693^{612}

Count Boris *J A Geake* 71
5 b g Groom Dancer(USA) —Bu Hagab (IRE) (Royal Academy (USA))
882^{6} 990^{7} 5954^{8}

Count Ceprano (IRE) *W R Swinburn* a84
2 b c Desert Prince(IRE) —Camerlata (Common Grounds)
5261^{4} (5648) 6100^{2}

Count Cougar (USA) *S P Griffiths* a72d 72
6 b g Sir Cat(USA) —Gold Script (USA) (Seeking The Gold (USA))
1^{12} 317^{9}401^{7} 446^{2}608^{5} (858) 950^{8} 1258^{4}(1388) 5391^{10}6326^{12} 6452^{10}6508^{10} 6642^{4}6827^{8} 6842^{6}6930^{4}

Countdown *T D Easterby* a82 85
4 ch g Pivotal—Quiz Time (Efisio)
362^{2} 441^{5}569^{10} 1125^{2} 1662^{12}2302^{11} 3217^{5} 4357^{2} 4885^{11} 5554^{3}6048^{4} (6160) 6273^{3}

Counterfactual (IRE) *B Smart* a43 56
3 br g Key Of Luck(USA) —Wakayi (Persian Bold)
2325^{5} 2734^{6} 4117^{7} 4426^{8}

Counterpunch *Saeed Bin Suroor* 113+
3 ch g Halling(USA) —Evil Empire (GER) (Acatenango (GER))
(5203) (5732) (5920)

Countess Carmine *P C Haslam* 48
3 b f Royal Applause—Red Ryding Hood (Wolfhound (USA))
1073^{15} 2109^{7}

Countess Majella (IRE) *E J O'Neill* a55 46
2 b f Grand Lodge(USA) —Mrs Moonlight (Ajdal (USA))
6920^{4}

Counting House (IRE) *R Charlton* 85
3 ch g King's Best(USA) —Inforapenny (Deploy)
948^{7} 1192^{9} 2584^{4} 3046^{2} 3974^{5}

Count Kristo *C G Cox* 81
4 br g Dr Fong(USA) —Aryadne (Rainbow Quest (USA))
(1651) 2351^{6} 3248^{5} 3840^{7} 4299^{5}

Count Ricardo (AUS) *S Theodore* 118
5 ch g Principality(AUS) —Shanghai Surprise (AUS) (Imperial Prince)
5817a^{12}

Country Affair (USA) *P R Webber* a73 65
3 ch c Vettori(IRE) —Nany's Affair (USA) (Colonial Affair (USA))
459^{5} 952^{7}

Country Escape *C F Wall* a89 77+
3 b g Zafonic(USA) —Midnight Allure (Aragon)
1055^{3} 4247^{2} 4891^{4}(5384) (5739)

Country Pursuit (USA) *C E Brittain* a91 88
4 ch g Theatrical—Jade Flush (USA) (Jade Hunter (USA))
661^{2} (834) 1511^{3} 6097^{6}6336^{17} 6467^{4} 6515^{8}6917^{3}

Country Rambler (USA) *Doug Watson* a28 93
4 b h Red Ransom(USA) —Country Garden (Selkirk (USA))
435a^{12}

Country Song (USA) *David Wachman* 98
2 b c Fusaichi Pegasus(USA) —Eliza (USA) (Mt. Livermore (USA))
2844^{2} 3962a^{6}

Countrywide Belle *K A Ryan* a57 71d
3 b f Josr Algarhoud(IRE) —Dancing Bluebell (IRE) (Bluebird (USA))
53^{2} 439^{3}(499) 604^{5}642^{2}

Countrywide Luck *N P Littmoden* a78 80
5 b g Inchinor—Thelma (Blakeney)
(186) 283^{2} 420^{10}521^{5}

Countrywide Pride (IRE) *David Evans* a36 47
8 ch g Eagle Eyed(USA) —Lady's Dream (Mazilier (USA))
(1625a)

Countrywide Style (IRE) *N P Littmoden* 46
2 b c Xaar—Nautical Light (Slip Anchor)
4534^{5} 4897^{9}

Count The Trees *W G M Turner* a47 28
3 ch f Woodborough(USA) —Numerate (Bishop Of Cashel)
499^{4} 538^{3}609^{5} 1373^{7} 1661^{9}2568^{8} 6971^{6}

Count Trevisio (IRE) *Saeed Bin Suroor* 102
3 b c Danehill(USA) —Stylish (Anshan)
(2654) 3119^{3} 4298^{2} 5945^{10}

Countyourblessings *I A Wood* a24 31
2 br f Lujain(USA) —To The Woods (IRE) (Woodborough (USA))
2984^{7} 3645^{10} 3915^{8}4485^{5} 4624^{8} 4816^{6}

Coup D'Etat *J L Dunlop* 92
4 b h Diktat—Megdale (IRE) (Waajib)
728^{19} 1129^{14} 1484^{7} 2621^{4} 3255^{3}4023^{9} 4131^{6} 4810^{13} 5346^{5}

Courageous Dove *A Bailey* a15 26
5 gr g Overbury(IRE) —Mazzelmo (Thethingaboutitis (USA))
301^{7}

Courageous Duke (USA) *J Noseda* a66 105
7 b g Spinning World(USA) —Araadh (USA) (Blushing Groom (FR))
207a^{5} 356a^{10} 2803^{8} 3552^{8} 3971^{5}5374^{16}

Court Masterpiece *E A L Dunlop* a115 125
6 b h Polish Precedent(USA) —Easy Option (IRE) (Prince Sabo)
738a^{6} 1840^{3} 2722^{2}(4038) 5524^{3} 6530a^{7} 6850a^{9}

Courtnall (USA) *Craig Dollase* 112
5 br g Cherokee Run(USA) —Brush Runner (USA) (Broad Brush (USA))
5825a^{2} 6329a^{6}

Court Of Appeal *B Ellison* a86d 93d
9 ch g Bering—Hiawatha's Song (USA) (Chief's Crown (USA))
2836 425511448 134613 15605 (2395) 25224 (2788) 311654229 4 45442 59552

Court One *R E Barr* a27 50
8 b g Shareef Dancer(USA) —Fairfields Cone (Celtic Cone)
313511

Cousteau *P W Chapple-Hyam* a81 104
3 ch c Spinning World(USA) —Wavy Up (IRE) (Brustolon)
10925 13352 16275(2028) 27397

Coustou (IRE) *R M Stronge* a42 68
6 b g In Command(IRE) —Carranza (IRE) (Lead On Time (USA))
561013

Cove Mountain (IRE) *S Kirk* a66 81
4 br m Indian Danehill(IRE) —Nordic Pride (Horage)
648410 6687667752 6916469427

Coventgarden (FR) *D Sepulchre* a103 111
6 b g Saumarez—Showgum (FR) (Kadrou (FR))
1558a6

Cover Up (IRE) *Sir Michael Stoute* 112
9 b g Machiavellian(USA) —Sought Out (IRE) (Rainbow Quest (USA))
(1409) 20857 28492 408110

Cow Girl (IRE) *A M Balding* 54
2 b f King's Best(USA) —Reveuse De Jour (IRE) (Sadler's Wells (USA))
370012

Coy Joy (IRE) *M Dods* 24
2 b f Tagula(IRE) —Be Prepared (IRE) (Be My Guest (USA))
16828

Coyote Creek *E F Vaughan* 67
2 b g Zilzal(USA) —High Barn (Shirley Heights)
54176 56164 59473

C P West (USA) *N Zito* a105
2 b c Came Home(USA) —Queen's Legend (USA) (Dynaformer (USA))
6339a6

Crackleando *Mrs J C McGregor* a27 27
5 ch g Forzando—Crackling (Electric)
53388

Craft Fair (IRE) *Saeed Bin Suroor* a78 96
4 b g Danehill(USA) —Brush Strokes (Cadeaux Genereux)
279a5 509a2

Crafty Fox *A P Jarvis* a61 58
3 b g Foxhound(USA) —Surrealist (ITY) (Night Shift (USA))
7224 1166924588 30873 33811058744 60337(6277) 634810

Cragganmore Creek *D Morris* a65+ 48
3 b g Tipsy Creek(USA) —Polish Abbey (Polish Precedent (USA))
615 123979713 14249 165210 2246625911 6 605715 63743(6551) 6718468164

Cragg Lass (IRE) *A Berry*
2 b f King Charlemagne(USA) —Mepa Discovery (USA) (Clever Trick (USA))
64028 658669989

Craic Sa Ceili (IRE) *M S Saunders* a63d 63
6 b m Danehill Dancer(IRE) —Fay's Song (IRE) (Fayruz)
4410

Craig Y Nos *A Berry*
2 ch f Auction House(USA) —Thabeh (Shareef Dancer (USA))
31434

Crail *C F Wall* a85 81
6 b g Vettori(IRE) —Tendency (Ballad Rock)
1087 1408142210 194311 3918345756 524912

Cranworth Blaze *T J Etherington* 47
2 b f Diktat—Julietta Mia (USA) (Woodman (USA))
45108 52379 57468

Crathorne (IRE) *M Todhunter* a69 73
6 b g Alzao(USA) —Shirley Blue (IRE) (Shirley Heights)
(1887) 22424 32205 49543

Crazy Bear (IRE) *K A Ryan* a71 53
3 ch f King Charlemagne(USA) —Specifiedrisk (IRE) (Turtle Island (IRE))
1322 349373541 3072

Creachadoir (IRE) *J S Bolger* 96
2 b c King's Best(USA) —Sadima (IRE) (Sadler's Wells (USA))
3126a4

Creambiscuit *N P Littmoden* a38 56
3 ch g Cadeaux Genereux—Star Ridge (USA) (Storm Bird (CAN))
15499 231617

Cream Of Esteem *M Todhunter* 48
4 b g Mark Of Esteem(IRE) —Chantilly (FR) (Sanglamore (USA))
58377

Creative Mind (IRE) *E J O'Neill* a75 95
3 b f Danehill Dancer(IRE) —Inventive (Sheikh Albadou)
8314 925a6 1440521262 26422 32965 (3487) 40835 4837257104a2

Credential *John A Harris* a66 70
4 b h Dansili—Sabria (USA) (Miswaki (USA))
148010 18507 22862 264110 576886300 4

Credit (IRE) *Jennie Candlish* a81
5 b g Intikhab(USA) —Tycooness (IRE) (Last Tycoon)
64686 6677968116

Credit Slip *J L Dunlop* 56
2 b c Slip Anchor—Credit-A-Plenty (Generous (IRE))
546015 58939 629713

Cree *W R Muir* a66 62
4 b g Indian Ridge—Nightitude (Night Shift (USA))
118811 18789 209514 25675 2898632873 36822 38352 414110 4364749852 52328 55763 630846541 2 67082(6728) (6890) 69222

Creme Brulee *C R Egerton* a61 53
3 b f College Chapel—Balinsky (IRE) (Skyliner)
2662 4494535012 55767 628611651 02 (6738) 692211

Cresta Gold *A Bailey* a105 104
3 b f Halling(USA) —Fleet Hill (IRE) (Warrshan (USA))
16056 (2412) (2975) 32924 37392 40794 474145641 3 61914

Crested *W Dollase* 111
3 ch g Fantastic Light(USA) —Dunnes River (USA) (Danzig (USA))
6613a4

Crime Scene (IRE) *M Johnston* 103
3 b g Royal Applause—Crime (USA) (Gulch (USA))
(1440) 21743 26592 277415 344311 3890943702 467616 (5141) 537414 57583

Criminal Act (USA) *B W Hills* 93
3 b c Bahri(USA) —Captive Island (Northfields (USA))
11173 14885 184110

Crimson And Gold *L Reuterskiold* 100
4 b g Singspiel(IRE) —Rosia (IRE) (Mr Prospector (USA))
4189a4 4864a2 5226a4

Crimson Bow (GER) *J G Given* a18 18
4 ch m Night Shift(USA) —Carma (IRE) (Konigsstuhl (GER))
18214

Crimson Flame (IRE) *A J Chamberlain* a61 77
3 b g Celtic Swing—Wish List (IRE) (Mujadil (USA))
6564 11904 1855621775 262014 303011 34696 3695537256 40092 42576 45242 4757125054 4 52707 547414 6819126995 9

Crimson King (IRE) *T T Clement* a88+
5 ch g Pivotal—Always Happy (Sharrood (USA))
1953 (331) (1258)

Crimson Monarch (USA) *Mrs A J Perrett* 70
2 b c Red Ransom(USA) —Tolltally Light (USA) (Majestic Light (USA))
545710 56236 58824

Crimson Silk *B Smart* 95d
6 ch g Forzando—Sylhall (Sharpo)
10763 420211 460915 533619 60099

Crimson Sun (USA) *I Mohammed* 105
4 b h Danzig(USA) —Crimplene (IRE) (Lion Cavern (USA))
357a8 511a10

Crimson Year (USA) *C E Brittain* 15
4 ch m Dubai Millennium—Crimson Conquest (USA) (Diesis)
126119 16709

Cripsey Brook *K G Reveley* 84
8 ch g Lycius(USA) —Duwon (IRE) (Polish Precedent (USA))
15027 18475 20782 23578 2828430372 34977 39392 41122 43924551115

Cristoforo (IRE) *B J Curley* a101 101
9 b g Perugino(USA) —Red Barons Lady (IRE) (Electric)
653 354a5 437a12

Critic (IRE) *M L W Bell* a85 83
3 b g Fasliyev(USA) —Scruple (IRE) (Catrail (USA))
(70) 14044 17766 2581730074 36674 433810 509614

Critical Stage (IRE) *J D Frost* a71 68
7 b g King's Theatre(IRE) —Zandaka (FR) (Doyoun)
520111 68312

Crocodile Bay (IRE) *Carl Llewellyn* a78 77
3 b g Spectrum(IRE) —Shenkara (IRE) (Night Shift (USA))
33179 385211 67448

Crocodile Dundee (IRE) *L M Cumani* a96 113
5 b g Croco Rouge(IRE) —Miss Salsa Dancer (Salse (USA))
39573 (4817) 53425

Crocodile Kiss (IRE) *J A Osborne* a58 70
4 b m Rossini(USA) —Pipe Opener (Prince Sabo)
262 1431325 75

Crocodile Star (USA) *J A Osborne* a55 50
3 bb g Woodman(USA) —Rhumba Rage (USA) (Nureyev (USA))
495 6171222 2415

Croeso Bach *J L Spearing* 35
2 b f Bertolini(USA) —Croeso-I-Cymru (Welsh Captain)
556313 60249

Croft (IRE) *R M Stronge* a53 70
3 b g Mull Of Kintyre(USA) —Home Comforts (Most Welcome)
88010 104811 14166 17997 25662281412 39515 50988

Cronkyvoddy *Mrs A Malzard* 61
5 b g Groom Dancer(USA) —Miss Pout (Kris)
1622a3

Crooked Throw (IRE) *C F Swan* 99
7 bb g Anshan—Mary's View (IRE) (Phardante (FR))
3125a18 4187a5 6356a10

Crookhaven *John Joseph Murphy* 105?
3 b c Dansili—My Mariam (Salse (USA))
2039a8 277514

Croon *H Morrison* a85 84
4 b g Sinndar(IRE) —Shy Minstrel (USA) (The Minstrel (CAN))
15173 (1927) 24474 30284(3666) 38905 48766

Crosby Hall *N Tinkler* 58
3 b g Compton Place—Alzianah (Alzao (USA))
236312 265814 29768 329614 440384666 7

Crosby Jemma *J R Weymes* 45
2 ch f Lomitas—Gino's Spirits (Perugino (USA))
473112 51118 54956

Crosby Millie *J R Weymes* 57
2 gr f Linamix(FR) —Calling Card (Bering)
48809 55275 58595

Crosby Vision *J R Weymes* 75
3 b c Agnes World(USA) —Aegean Blue (Warning)
12505 15924 19998 37822 4653749536

Crossbow Creek *M G Rimell* a83 70
8 b g Lugana Beach—Roxy River (Ardross)
32256 (4931) 54309

Cross Channel (USA) *E A L Dunlop* a88 98
3 ch f Giant's Causeway(USA) —Sterling Pound (USA) (Seeking The Gold (USA))
8275 16694 25825

Crossing The Line (IRE) *Sir Mark Prescott* a50+ 54
2 b g Cape Cross(IRE) —Tropical Zone (Machiavellian (USA))
53478 55638 56488

Cross My Mind *T Keddy* a86 94
4 b g Cape Cross(IRE) —Dynamic Dream (USA) (Dynaformer (USA))
39732 43723 48899 55236 5945962267

Cross My Shadow (IRE) *M F Harris* a39 51
4 b g Cape Cross(IRE) —Shadowglow (Shaadi (USA))
592610 62377

Crossoffissio (SWE) *L Reuterskiold*
3 b g Diaglyphard(USA) —To The Queen (SWE) (Roi Danzig (USA))
4419a5 4919a14

Cross Of Lorraine (IRE) *I Semple* a72 55
3 b g Pivotal—My-Lorraine (IRE) (Mac's Imp (USA))
55833 57264 6403266372 (6731) 69522

Crosspeace (IRE) *M Johnston* a113 116
4 b h Cape Cross(IRE) —Announcing Peace (Danehill (USA))
512a6 562a9 622a3 9915 1267318394 22018 28033 32544 34324(4023) (4096) 4417a8 50182 5204255477

Cross The Line (IRE) *A P Jarvis* a95 80
4 b g Cape Cross(IRE) —Baalbek (Barathea (IRE))
11642 1382319322 21834 25365 (3202) 40472 437815 51082(5428) 563916 59902

Crossways *Mrs A Malzard* a70 76
8 b g Mister Baileys—Miami Dancer (USA) (Seattle Dancer (USA))
1624a3

Crown Colony *David Wachman* 81
2 b c Royal Applause—Bathe In Light (USA) (Sunshine Forever (USA))
5692a2

Crow's Nest Lad *T D Easterby* 80+
2 b c Komaite(USA) —Miss Fit (IRE) (Hamas (IRE))
24098 33513 (3907)

Crow Wood *J J Quinn* a100 106d
7 b g Halling(USA) —Play With Me (IRE) (Alzao (USA))
5186 14848 2079142656 7 284814 329413 42593 536125678 8

Crucial *Frank Sheridan* 99
6 b g Pivotal—Blessed Honour (Ahonoora)
1871a8 6005a5

Cruise Director *Ian Williams* a86 90
6 b g Zilzal(USA) —Briggsmaid (Elegant Air)
17796 18424 284815 397110 456011

Crumbs Of Comfort (USA) *L M Cumani* a75 81
2 b f Pulpit(USA) —British Columbia (Selkirk (USA))
(3596) 43225 52712 567611 60748

Crusader's Gold (FR) *T D Easterby* a56 63
3 b g Lujain(USA) —Rain And Shine (FR) (Rainbow Quest (USA))
149710 185916 21956 2939331544 3916347106 52507 58738

Crush On You *R Hollinshead* a53 54
3 b f Golden Snake(USA) —Mourir D'Aimer (USA) (Trempolino (USA))
(99) 1939 347787 94 182910 224972877 2 31959 38392 40697 49447(5432) 588514 65244 6814469703

Crusoe (IRE) *A Sadik* a56 59
9 b g Turtle Island(IRE) —Self Reliance (Never So Bold)
811 8112951 0 18432426 26133041 1 386342 33 4404(527) 58276066 (616) 6363 648286 09 9064

Crux *C W Thornton* a40 55
4 b g Pivotal—Penny Dip (Cadeaux Genereux)
17312

Cryfield *N Tinkler* a55 55
9 b g Efisio—Ciboure (Norwick (USA))
18310

Cry Presto (USA) *R Hannon* a78 84
2 b g Street Cry(IRE) —Sabaah Elfull (Kris)
370112 45618 49633 53434 5623558921 1 66342 68246

Cryptic Clue (USA) *D W Chapman* a52 52
2 b g Cryptoclearance(USA) —Nidd (USA) (Known Fact (USA))
20298 29678 51114 54829 5860667152 6760368135 692612

Crystal Air (IRE) *Miss J Feilden* a65 73
3 b f Distant Music(USA) —Columbian Sand (IRE) (Salmon Leap (USA))
11629

Crystal Annie *Heather Dalton* a22 52
3 b f Namaqualand(USA) —Crystal Canyon (Efisio)
535312 55985 58448

Crystal Bay (IRE) *A Berry*
3 b f Carrowkeel(IRE) —Cajo (IRE) (Tirol)
14378 179113 58628

Crystal Gazer (FR) *R Hannon* a79 73
2 b f Elnadim(USA) —Chrysalu (Distant Relative)
12422 1405218173 (2816) 47626 51574 537215

Crystal Ice (IRE) *Mrs L Williamson* a21 58
2 br f Lahib(USA) —Chalfont (IRE) (Common Grounds)
12237 15876 29506

Crystal Ka (FR) *M R Hoad* a7
4 b g Northern Crystal—Kahuna Magic (FR) (Dancing Spree (USA))
11311

Crystal Mystic (IRE) *B Palling* a42 51
4 b g Anita's Prince—Out On Her Own (Superlative)
9504 12357 1645620951 6 29205 41579 613110

Crystal Plum (IRE) *B W Hills* a24 61
2 ch f Rock Of Gibraltar(IRE) —State Crystal (IRE) (High Estate)
408414 47055 509511

Crystal Prince *T P Tate* 40
2 b c Marju(IRE) —Crystal Ring (IRE) (Kris)
581410 617313

Cuban Night *D J S Ffrench Davis*
2 b g Zaha(CAN) —No Candles Tonight (Star Appeal)
562311

Cuccinello (IRE) *K W Hogg* 11
3 b f Makbul—Costa Verde (King Of Spain)
179212 207715

Cuesta Canyon (IRE) *A J McCabe* a38 44
3 b g Indian Ridge—Perfect Plum (IRE) (Darshaan)
6269 7862874 10 14584 1661321959 61316 655411

Culachy Forest *N Tinkler* 27
2 b g Kyllachy—Abscond (USA) (Unbridled (USA))
561315 59019

Culcabock (IRE) *Miss Lucinda V Russell* 49
6 b g Unfuwain(USA) —Evidently (IRE) (Slip Anchor)
333310 38106 43514 50613

Culroy *N Tinkler* 33
2 b g Fath(USA) —Folly Finnesse (Joligeneration)
561310

Cultured *Mrs A J Bowlby* a40 58
5 b m Danzero(AUS) —Seek The Pearl (Rainbow Quest (USA))
88217

Culture Queen *M P Tregoning* 90
3 b f King's Best(USA) —Cultured Pearl (IRE) (Lammtarra (USA))
11307

Cumberland Road *C A Mulhall* a61 59
3 ch g Efisio—Thatcher's Era (IRE) (Never So Bold)
696 536314 69935

Cumbrian Knight (IRE) *J M Jefferson* a71 58
8 b g Presenting—Crashrun (Crash Course)
(52) 2838 643740868 44514 45447 6376566212

Cumin (USA) *B W Hills* 99
2 ch f Fusaichi Pegasus(USA) —User Cat (USA) (Storm Cat (USA))
24092 28446 34982 (4084) 48403 5714a9

Cummiskey (IRE) *J A Osborne* a97 82
4 b g Orpen(USA) —Ansariya (USA) (Shahrastani (USA))
(14) 2452 (275) 348341 33 5163629 11 8364

Cunegonde *G L Moore* 48
3 ch f Observatory(USA) —Brave Princess (Dancing Brave (USA))
240614 26058 292910 36684 4279746712 507213

Cupid's Glory *Sir Mark Prescott* a103 115
4 b g Pursuit Of Love—Doctor's Glory (USA) (Elmaamul (USA))
69143

Cup Of Love (USA) *Rae Guest* a65 63
4 ch m Behrens(USA) —Cup Of Kindness (USA) (Secretariat (USA))
(73) 1877 3832

Cuppacocoa *C G Cox* a49 69
2 b f Bertolini(USA) —Coffee Time (IRE) (Efisio)
16474 19227 31483(4624) (5162) 565510 58294

Curitiba *M G Quinlan*
2 ch f Medicean—Nubile (Pursuit Of Love)
3428a5

Currahee *Miss J A Camacho* 42
2 b c Efisio—Dixie Favor (USA) (Dixieland Band (USA))
550811 59016

Currency *J M Bradley* a85 88
9 b g Sri Pekan(USA) —On Tiptoes (Shareef Dancer (USA))
185811 19616 2189926611 7 30415 336813 35672 3986641196 43615 45649 47726 4870950421 2

Cursum Perficio *W R Muir* a81+ 79
4 b g Tagula(IRE) —Simply Sooty (Absalom)
9152 120712 5108553451 5 54362 5689459086

Curtail (IRE) *I Semple* a95 104
3 b g Namid—Nipitinthebud (USA) (Night Shift (USA))
26517 348211 397010 43458 68474

Curtain Bluff *M R Channon* a85 83
4 b g Dansili—Gayane (Nureyev (USA))
36110 26035 2860532295 33372 (3459) 3542537128 407710 44962 477213 4961453131 1 56883

Curule (USA) *Doug Watson* a116
9 bb h Go For Gin(USA) —Reservation (USA) (Cryptoclearance (USA))
152a3 277a3495a9

Curved Air (IRE) *Stef Liddiard* 24
4 gr m Turtle Island(IRE) —Poetry (IRE) (Treasure Kay)
43308

Curzon Prince (IRE) *C F Wall* 76
2 b c Mujadil(USA) —Smooth Spirit (USA) (Alydar (USA))
41054 (4492)

Cushat Law (IRE) *W Jarvis* 56
2 b f Montjeu(IRE) —Blush With Love (USA) (Mt. Livermore (USA))
353711 545610 60497

Cusoon *G L Moore* a96 82+
4 b g Dansili—Charming Life (Habitat)
16732 25103 (3151) 41608 45364 51496(5786) (6502) (6888)

Custodian (IRE) *H R A Cecil* a72 79
4 gr g Giant's Causeway(USA) —Desert Bluebell (Kalaglow)
1142 (289) 421534010 6 (4051)

Cut Glass *C E Brittain* 59
3 ch f Fantastic Light(USA) —Shady Point (IRE) (Unfuwain (USA))
21469 313710 38235

Cut Ridge (IRE) *J S Wainwright* a36 53
7 b m Indian Ridge—Cutting Ground (IRE) (Common Grounds)
17286 25434 3524739124 40703 44255 47299 (5840) 6130106549 12

Cut The Cake (USA) *J Noseda* 70
2 b f Diesis—Wife For Life (USA) (Dynaformer (USA))
5814[2]

Cut To (USA) *J Akehurst* a18 51
3 b g Red Ransom(USA) —Bubble Club (USA) (Vanlandingham (USA))
4431[11] 5612[10] 5870[14]5986[12]

Cuyamaca (IRE) *C F Wall* a48
4 b m Desert King(IRE) —Surprise Visitor (IRE) (Be My Guest (USA))
289[3] 531[4]

Cyber Santa *J Hetherton* a1 53
8 b g Celtic Swing—Qualitair Ridge (Indian Ridge)
1467[11] 2998[8]

Cyclical *G A Butler* a87 95
4 b g Pivotal—Entwine (Primo Dominie)
3092[11] 3471[14] 3959[4] 5021[3]5096[6]

Cyfrwys (IRE) *B Palling* a56 69
5 b m Foxhound(USA) —Divine Elegance (IRE) (College Chapel)
588[5] 608[9]6174[8] 6477[11] 6541[6]

Cylindree (IRE) *P Bary* 78
2 b f Diktat—Countess Walewska (IRE) (Polish Precedent (USA))
6609a[6]

Cyprus Rose *S Curran* a45 57
2 br f Whittingham(IRE) —Blackpool Belle (The Brianstan)
1347[6] 2178[9] 2346[9]2495[3] 3300[6] 3624[5] 3801[6] 6409[6]6512[8]

Cyr Cry (FR) *C Le Lay* 93
6 b g Freedom Cry—Cinthiana (FR) (Saint Cyrien (FR))
6786a[5]

Daaly Babet (FR) *C Scandella* 98
3 gr f Medaaly—Osmyose (FR) (Sicyos (USA))
1719a[9] 2275a[5]

Daaweitza *B Ellison* a82 81
3 ch g Daawe(USA) —Chichen Itza (Shareef Dancer (USA))
(132) 188[5] 1828[7] 2324[6]2809[2] 3082[2] 3569[3] (3918) 4569[2] (4958) 5680[7] 5810[6]

Dabbers Ridge (IRE) *B W Hills* 109
4 b h Indian Ridge—Much Commended (Most Welcome)
898[3] (1143) (1629) 1806[3] 2742[12] (3926) 4740[5]5135[3]

Dab Hand (IRE) *D M Simcock* a72 69
3 b g Alzao(USA) —Deft Touch (IRE) (Desert Style (IRE))
1546[8] 2188[5] 2940[4]3364[7] 3931[2] 4291[5] 5071[3] (5774) 5992[2]

Dabhani (IRE) *James Leavy* 74
4 gr h Daylami(IRE) —Dabtiya (IRE) (Shirley Heights)
4094a[7]

Da Bookie (IRE) *E J Creighton* a75 70
6 b g Woods Of Windsor(USA) —Hurgill Lady (Emarati (USA))
5845[8] (6147) 6413[6]6564[10] 6741[7]

Daboy (IRE) *John A Quinn* a62
2 b g Indian Danehill(IRE) —Notable Dear (ITY) (Last Tycoon)
6441[8] 6646[6]

Daddy Cool *W G M Turner* a67
2 b c Kyllachy—Addicted To Love (Touching Wood (USA))
3685[6] 4138[3]

Dado Mush *G Prodromou* a50 60
3 b c Almushtarak(IRE) —Princess Of Spain (King Of Spain)
1165[6] 1736[4] (3750) 4052[4]4757[6] 5418[12] 6193[13]6531[8] 6762[12]

Dagola (IRE) *C A Dwyer* a56 56
5 b g Daggers Drawn(USA) —Diabola (USA) (Devil's Bag (USA))
41[12] 172[8]311[3] 395[2]468[10] 591[2]694[4] 891[10](1724) 1911[10]2181[7]

Dahman *Saeed Bin Suroor* 85
4 b g Darshaan—Nuriva (USA) (Woodman (USA))
5163[6] 5769[11]

Daiwa Major (JPN) *H Uehara* 124
5 b h Sunday Silence(USA) —Scarlet Bouquet (JPN) (Northern Taste (CAN))
(6530a)

Daiwa Memphis (JPN) *S Masuzawa* 90
5 b h Warning—Impact (IRE) (Green Desert (USA))
6850a[17]

Daiwa Passion (JPN) *S Masuzawa* 96
3 ch f Forty Niner(USA) —Sun Rouge (JPN) (Shady Heights)
6850a[13]

Daka's Gem (AUS) *A Mathews* 106
7 br g Sedaka(AUS) —Shades Of Jemma (AUS) (Thehool (USA))
(7000a)

Dakota Rain (IRE) *R C Guest* 83
4 br g Indian Ridge—Mill Rainbow (FR) (Rainbow Quest (USA))
815[3] 1532[11] 2900[7] 4090[2] 4253[13]5320[13]

Dalavin (USA) *Audre Cappuccitti* 110
5 br g Native Regent(CAN) —Let's Escape (USA) (Ogygian (USA))
5416a[10]

Dal Cais (IRE) *Francis Ennis* 88
2 b c Noverre(USA) —Annieirwin (IRE) (Perugino (USA))
4824a[12]

Dallma (IRE) *C E Brittain* a62 71
3 b f Daylami(IRE) —Play With Fire (FR) (Priolo (USA))
1418[4] 1630[4] 2383[6] 3250[6] 3477[6]4243[5] 4930[4] 6293[11]

Dalpe *A J Lidderdale* a53 65?
5 ch g Siphon(BRZ) —Double Stake (USA) (Kokand (USA))
1739[5] 2460[12] 4048[10]5267[10]

Dalriath *M C Chapman* a44 44
7 b m Fraam—Alsiba (Northfields (USA))
4104[9]

Daltaya (FR) *A De Royer-Dupre* 112
3 b f Anabaa(USA) —Daltaiyma (IRE) (Doyoun)
(1177a) 1719a[4] 2491a[14] 5400a[7] 6250a[5]

Dalvina *E A L Dunlop* a81+
2 ch f Grand Lodge(USA) —Foodbroker Fancy (IRE) (Halling (USA))
(6186)

Dama'A (IRE) *J H M Gosden* a76+ 80
3 b f Green Desert(USA) —Lady Miletrian (IRE) (Barathea (IRE))
1191[4] 1719a[10] 2587[5] (4045) 4703[10]

Damachida (IRE) *Eva Sundbye* a89 101
7 ch h Mukaddamah(USA) —Lady Loire (Wolverlife)
201a[10] 357a[12] 434a[11]507a[4] 667[13] 1659a[8]

Damascena (GER) *P Schiergen* 94
3 br f Acatenango(GER) —Dance Again (Shareef Dancer (USA))
2694a[9] 5008a[4] 5709a[4]

Damburger Xpress *D M Simcock* a69 66
4 b g Josr Algarhoud(IRE) —Upping The Tempo (Dunbeath (USA))
1288[8] 1591[10] 2221[6] 2577[9]2978[3] 3999[3]4266[13] 4974[12]

Damdam (FR) *J-P Despeyroux* 101
2 gr c Verglas(IRE) —Freeze Frame (FR) (In The Wings)
6546a[2]

Dame Hester (IRE) *E J O'Neill* a68+ 92
3 br f Diktat—Aunt Hester (IRE) (Caerleon (USA))
(372) 1067[4] 1250[4] 2205[9] 2880[5] 3548[3](3871) 4040[5] 4555[3] 4590[10] 5197a[3] 5857a[6]

Damelza (IRE) *T D Easterby* a67 82
3 b f Orpen(USA) —Damezao (Alzao (USA))
1099[4] 1423[5] 1832[4] 2359[3] 2735[6]3176[3] 3687[6] 4567[5]5446[12]

Damhsoir (IRE) *H S Howe* a43 52
2 b f Invincible Spirit(IRE) —Ceide Dancer (IRE) (Alzao (USA))
2703[6] 3148[7] 5773[12]6311[4]

Damika (IRE) *R M Whitaker* 94
3 ch c Namid—Emly Express (IRE) (High Estate)
(1344) (1642) 1983[5] 2363[2] 2760[2] 3317[8] 3761[3](4403) 5501[8]

Damoiselle (USA) *F Head* 103
3 ch f Sky Classic(CAN) —Dariela (USA) (Manila (USA))
1719a[7]

Danaatt (USA) *K R Burke* a24 37
4 b m Gulch(USA) —Agama (USA) (Nureyev (USA))
180[10]

Danacourt (NZ) *J Size* 118
4 ch g Danasinga(AUS) —Frizzie (NZ) (Pompeii Court (USA))
1527a[2]

Danakil *S Dow* a79 81
11 b g Warning—Danilova (USA) (Lyphard (USA))
1926[12] 3209[10] 3429[10]

Danakim *J R Weymes* a28 52
9 b g Emarati(USA) —Kangra Valley (Indian Ridge)
299[11] 502[10]686[13]

Danamour (IRE) *M P Tregoning* a75 88
3 b g Dansili—Love And Affection (USA) (Exclusive Era (USA))
4838[4]

Dana Music (USA) *M R Channon* a58 67
2 br g Silver Hawk(USA) —Inca Princess (USA) (Big Spruce (USA))
5105[7] 5893[8]

Danao (USA) *R Menichetti* 41
2 b c Richter Scale(USA) —Essie's Maid (USA) (Linkage (USA))
6123a[13]

Danaos *J A Osborne* 37
2 b g Danetime(IRE) —Ionian Secret (Mystiko (USA))
4109[10]

Danapali (IRE) *P J Prendergast* a63+ 75
2 b f Danehill(USA) —Taking Liberties (IRE) (Royal Academy (USA))
(6603)

Danawi (IRE) *M R Hoad* a52 63
3 ch c Elnadim(USA) —Just Rainbow (FR) (Rainbow Quest (USA))
692[2] 1355[8] 1565[5]2931[6] 3090[5] 3611[3] 4799[5] 5728[4]5781[7] 6439[9]6618[7]

Dan Buoy (FR) *A King* a54 75
3 b g Slip Anchor—Bramosia (Forzando)
4367[4] 4708[2] 5260[5]5734[2]

Dance A Daydream *J R Fanshawe* a61+ 67
3 b f Daylami(IRE) —Dance A Dream (Sadler's Wells (USA))
1351[10] 1649[10] 2591[6] (3016) 4472[3] 4914[4]5324[6]

Dance In The Mood (JPN) *Kazuo Fujisawa* 119
5 b m Sunday Silence(USA) —Dancing Key (USA) (Nijinsky (CAN))
(3109a) 6530a[2] 6784a[12]

Danceinthevalley (IRE) *G A Swinbank* a55 74
4 b g Imperial Ballet(IRE) —Dancing Willma (IRE) (Dancing Dissident (USA))
2108[11] 3716[12] 4831[12]

Dance Night (IRE) *R Charlton* a56 100
4 b h Danehill Dancer(IRE) —Tiger Wings (IRE) (Thatching)
3535[10] 4811[12]

Dance Of Dreams *N P Littmoden* 65
2 ch c Johannesburg(USA) —Nunatak (USA) (Bering)
4428[7] 5111[2] 5449[6]

Dance Of Light (USA) *Sir Michael Stoute* 68+
2 b f Sadler's Wells(USA) —Flamelight (IRE) (Seattle Slew (USA))
5939[5]

Dance Partner *J H M Gosden* a89 98
4 b m Danzero(AUS) —Dancing Debut (Polar Falcon (USA))
4810[14] (5300)

Dance Party (IRE) *M W Easterby* a62 62
6 b m Charnwood Forest(IRE) —Society Ball (Law Society (USA))
939[9]

Dancer's Serenade (IRE) *T P Tate* 95d
4 b g Almutawakel—Dance Serenade (IRE) (Marju (IRE))
1281[12] 1775[9] 2296[8] 2761[9] 3220[4]3723[3] (4156) 4883[3] 5383[6]

Dance Spiel *J Noseda* a83+
2 b c Singspiel(IRE) —Demure (Machiavellian (USA))
5906[2]

Dance Spirit (IRE) *B J Meehan* a65 72
3 ch g Namid—Phantom Act (USA) (Theatrical)
1822[8] 2605[4] 3266[5] 4249[7]

Dance To My Tune *M W Easterby* a40 82
5 b m Halling(USA) —Stolen Melody (Robellino (USA))
867[3] (Dead)

Dance To The Blues (IRE) *B De Haan* a71 74
5 br m Danehill Dancer(IRE) —Blue Sioux (Indian Ridge)
1315[3] 2962[5] 3612[7] 3936[9] 5167[3]5350[3] 5756[8] 6396[5]6508[8]

Dancewiththestars (USA) *J R Fanshawe* a50
2 b f Cryptoclearance(USA) —Sir Harry's Waltz (IRE) (Sir Harry Lewis (USA))
6591[6]

Dance World *Miss J Feilden* a93 82
6 b g Spectrum(IRE) —Dansara (Dancing Brave (USA))
108[8] 6677[10]6941[6]

Dancing Bay *N J Henderson* a66 109
9 b g Suave Dancer(USA) —Kabayil (Dancing Brave (USA))
991[2] 1584[4] 2849[6] 3533[14]

Dancing Bear *P S McEntee* a51 61
5 b g Groom Dancer(USA) —Sickle Moon (Shirley Heights)
147[8] 1958[10]

Dancing Beauty (IRE) *T T Clement* a39
4 b m Charnwood Forest(IRE) —Viennese Dancer (Prince Sabo)
778[9] 1261[11] 6774[5]6877[6]

Dancing Daisy (IRE) *Mrs P N Dutfield* a42 58
2 br f Bold Fact(USA) —Daisy Dancer (IRE) (Distinctly North (USA))
2185[12] 2631[5] 3344[5] 3860[5] 4327[6]5764[6]

Dancing Deano (IRE) *R M Whitaker* a52 70
4 b g Second Empire(IRE) —Ultimate Beat (USA) (Go And Go)
(1791) 2020[2] 4116[6] 4571[11] 5031[7]5444[3] 5635[14] 6390[9]6719[8]

Dancing Diamonds *D M Simcock* a55 26
3 b f Agnes World(USA) —Aquaba (USA) (Damascus (USA))
4396[7] 4945[9]

Dancing Duo *W J Haggas* a61 58
2 b f Groom Dancer(USA) —Affaire Royale (IRE) (Royal Academy (USA))
4964[11] 5456[13] 5867[6] (6258)

Dancing Edie (USA) *Craig Dollase* 112
4 b m Moscow Ballet(USA) —Duchess Of Ack (USA) (Slewpy (USA))
3109a[4] 6340a[8]

Dancing Flame *E J Alston* a52 51
3 b f Groom Dancer(USA) —Catch The Flame (USA) (Storm Bird (CAN))
1122[10] 1851[7] 2283[4] 2518[3] 2750[5]3250[8] 3695[8] 4297[4] 5510[4] 5862[6]6448[10] 6473[8]6524[3] 6584[5]

Dancing Granny *M L W Bell* 73
2 b f Rock Of Gibraltar(IRE) —Euro Empire (USA) (Bartok (IRE))
2943[3] 3227[5] 3878[2] (4949) 5492[11] 5866[5]

Dancing Guest (IRE) *G G Margarson* a89 93
3 ch f Danehill Dancer(IRE) —Saibhreas (IRE) (Last Tycoon)
1291[13] 2050[9] (2554) 2891[3] (3643) 4249[2]4542a[4] 4802[10] 5019[9]5666[10]

Dancing Jest (IRE) *Rae Guest* 58
2 b f Averti(IRE) —Mezzanine (Sadler's Wells (USA))
5950[5] 6199[8]

Dancing Lyra *R A Fahey* a83 91+
5 b g Alzao(USA) —Badaayer (USA) (Silver Hawk (USA))
(719) (815) 2079[5] 2657[5] 4023[12] 5512[7]

Dancing Melody *J A Geake* 57
3 b f Dr Fong(USA) —Spring Mood (FR) (Nashwan (USA))
1141[6] 1738[11] 2065[7] 4757[9] 5574[11]5897[13]

Dancing Moonlight (IRE) *Mrs N Macauley* a25 13
4 b m Danehill Dancer(IRE) —Silver Moon (Environment Friend)
453[8] 533[11]3383[10] 4382[7] 6490[11]

Dancing Mystery *E A Wheeler* a99 75
12 b g Beveled(USA) —Batchworth Dancer (Ballacashtal (CAN))
6[4] 198[2]295[6] 450[6]664[8] 705[5]947[7] 1211[5] 2536[8] 2858[8] 3593[8]4587[2] (5480) (5938) 6446[4] (6496) 6720[5]

Dancing Reva (IRE) *J J Bridger* 34
2 b g Revoque(IRE) —Brave Dance (IRE) (Kris)
4479[9] 4794[9] 5340 [10] 6066[8]

Dancing Sky (IRE) *D K Weld* 102
3 ch f Polish Precedent(USA) —Foreign Love (USA) (Gulch (USA))
2689a[P]

Dancing Storm *W S Kittow* a54 63
3 b f Trans Island—Stormswell (Persian Bold)
861[6] 1348[9] (3472) 3793[4]4627[5] 4983[14] 5690[9]

Dancing Valentine *L A Dace*
2 b f Primo Valentino(IRE) —Shanuke (IRE) (Contract Law (USA))
4993[11]

Dan Dare (USA) *Sir Michael Stoute* 92
3 b g Dynaformer(USA) —Etheldreda (USA) (Diesis)
1994[3] 2682[5]

Dandy Man (IRE) *C Collins* 118
3 b c Mozart(IRE) —Lady Alexander (IRE) (Night Shift (USA))
1158a[2] (1485) 2720[4] (3124a) 4738[12] 5375[3]

Dandys Hurricane *D Nicholls* 45
3 br g Diktat—Bahamian Rhapsody (IRE) (Fairy King (USA))
5583[4] 5727[8] 6403[12]

Danebank (IRE) *J Mackie* a56 60
6 b g Danehill(USA) —Snow Bank (IRE) (Law Society (USA))
4380[2] 4960[12] 5955[4] 6378[4]6509[4] 6604[7]

Danebury Hill *B J Meehan* 99
2 b c Danehill(USA) —Mackie (USA) (Summer Squall (USA))
(2144) 3442[5] 4099[5] 4809[3] 5653[10]

Danehill Chancer (IRE) *D J Ryan* 65
5 b g Danehill Dancer(IRE) —Tullich Refrain (Petardia)
4186a[15]

Danehill Dazzler (IRE) *Ian Williams* a77 83
4 b m Danehill Dancer(IRE) —Finnegans Dilemma (IRE) (Marktingo)
1162[6] 2071[2] 2892[6]5045[9]

Danehill Kikin (IRE) *B W Hills* 57
2 b f Danehill(USA) —Miletrian (IRE) (Marju (IRE))
5638[7] 6014[5]

Danehill Music (IRE) *David Wachman* 101
3 b f Danehill Dancer(IRE) —Tuesday Morning (Sadler's Wells (USA))
(753a) 928a[3] 5996a[5] 6356a[5]

Danehill Silver *R Hollinshead* 65
2 b g Silver Patriarch(IRE) —Danehill Princess (IRE) (Danehill (USA))
5537[8] 6050[4] 6297[9]

Danehill Stroller (IRE) *A M Hales* a59 61
6 b g Danetime(IRE) —Tuft Hill (Grundy)
1432[5] 2189[6] 2384[10] 2971[5] 3682[6]3995[10] 4223[3] 5232 [7]5453[3] 5755[6] 5937[11] 6442[9]6619[3] 6728[5]6906[6]

Danehillsundance (IRE) *R Hannon* a71 72
2 b c Danehill Dancer(IRE) —Rosie's Guest (IRE) (Be My Guest (USA))
4801[4] 5206[3] 5491[2] 6331[2] 6488[3]6689[4] (6887)

Danehill Willy (IRE) *N A Callaghan* a96 96
4 b g Danehill Dancer(IRE) —Lowtown (Camden Town)
763[2] 867[6] 1071[7]1842[3]

Danelor (IRE) *D Shaw* a54 42
8 b g Danehill(USA) —Formulate (Reform)
48[2] (107) 194[9](273) 843[10]5512[13] 5739[10] 6301[15]6476[7] 6590[12]6674[6] 6762[11]6959[4]

Danescourt (IRE) *J M Bradley* a43 43
4 b g Danetime(IRE) —Faye (Monsanto (FR))
766[12] 951[8]1310[11] 1594[7]

Dane's Rock (IRE) *M S Saunders* a51 46
4 b g Indian Danehill(IRE) —Cutting Ground (IRE) (Common Grounds)
3[6] 600[10]638[5] 734[4]853[6]

Danethorpe (IRE) *D Shaw* a49 20
3 b g Monashee Mountain(USA) —Waroonga (IRE) (Brief Truce (USA))
645[9] 722[9]901[10] 1279[11] 1859[13]6276[12] 6308[3]6549[6] 6707[6]6794[3] 6983[9]

Danethorpe Lady (IRE) *D Shaw* a38 35
4 b m Brave Act—Annie's Travels (IRE) (Mac's Imp (USA))
249[12] 396[5]588[12] 1391[11]1413[11] 1465[5]

Danetime Lady (IRE) *Adrian Sexton* a35 68
6 b m Danetime(IRE) —Hawattef (IRE) (Mujtahid (USA))
449[11]

Danetime Lord (IRE) *K A Ryan* a79 70
3 b g Danetime(IRE) —Seven Sisters (USA) (Shadeed (USA))
211[5] 577[2](646) 819[2] (1004) 1078[6] 1497[5] 3087[5] 4894[4] 5902[9]6770[5] 6858[4]

Danetime Music (IRE) *M J Wallace* a71 71
2 b f Danetime(IRE) —Tuesday Morning (Sadler's Wells (USA))
(3942) 4594[9] 5606[4] 6388[12]

Danetime Panther (IRE) *Carl Llewellyn* 61
2 b c Danetime(IRE) —Annotate (Groom Dancer (USA))
4323[7]

Danettie *W M Brisbourne* a61 59
5 b m Danzero(AUS) —Petite Heritiere (Last Tycoon)
82[3] 157[8]252[6] (285) 327[7]

Daneway *P Howling* a53
3 ch f Danehill Dancer(IRE) —Scylla (Rock City)
6429[4] 6535[4]6911[9]

Danger Alley *E J O'Neill* a61 62
2 b c Bertolini(USA) —My Girl (Mon Tresor)
2234[8] 2610[6] 3110[3] (3624) 4152[6] (4493) 5234[7]5668[4]

Danger Bird (IRE) *R Hollinshead* a47 41
6 ch m Eagle Eyed(USA) —Danger Ahead (Mill Reef (USA))
184[10] 771[11]

Dangermouse *A G Newcombe* a43 46
3 b f Afternoon Deelites(USA) —Ghost Dance (IRE) (Lure (USA))
120[8] 677[8]1768[10]

Dangerous Business (IRE) *H Morrison* a53 60+
5 b m Entrepreneur—Cachet (IRE) (Warning)
4931[6] 5319[7] 5897[14]

Dangerous Dancer (IRE) *R Charlton* 62
2 b f Danehill Dancer(IRE) —Elite Guest (IRE) (Be My Guest (USA))
5344[11]

Dangerously Good *G L Moore* 73
8 b g Shareef Dancer(USA) —Ecologically Kind (Alleged (USA))
5952[13] 6178[15]

Danger Zone *Mrs A J Perrett* a77 77
4 b g Danzero(AUS) —Red Tulle (USA) (A.P. Indy (USA))
115[4] 140[2]186[7] 375[6](421) 530[6]1673[15] 2401[4] 2647[3]3024[2] 3221[6]

Daniella *Rae Guest* 81
4 b m Dansili—Break Point (Reference Point)
(1413) 1686[18] 2233[4] (2818) 3741[2] 4589[9] 5171[3]5588[5] 5919[16]

Danielle's Lad *B Palling* a60d 69
10 b g Emarati(USA) —Cactus Road (FR) (Iron Duke (FR))
169[9] 537[8]606[8] 1273[10]2223[3] 2599[2] 3599[10]4706[13] 4870[7] 5085[7] 5569[10] 5755[4]6726[8] 6793[9]

Daniel Thomas (IRE) *Mrs A J Perrett* a89 86
4 b g Dansili—Last Look (Rainbow Quest (USA))
6868[9] 6986[6]

Dani's Girl (IRE) *P A Fahy* 93
3 bb f Second Empire(IRE) —Quench The Lamp (IRE) (Glow (USA))
4749a[6]

Danish Blues (IRE) *D E Cantillon* a69 61
3 b g Danetime(IRE) —Sing A Song (IRE) (Blues Traveller (IRE))
378[2] 534[5]579[10] 653[7]801[3] 901[7]1272[4] 1937[6]2187[3] 2393[3] 2583[4] 3164[4] 3866[11]4050[12] 4927[7] 5781[4]6033[5] (6129) 6395[7]

Danish Monarch *David Pinder* a38 62
5 b g Great Dane(IRE) —Moly (Inchinor)
682[9] 904[9](1373) 2499[4] 2725[6] 3411[5] 3862[3] 4869[5]5166[12] (5259)

Danish Rebel (IRE) *J I A Charlton* a52
2 b c Danetime(IRE) —Wheatsheaf Lady (IRE) (Red Sunset)
6675[5] 6757[7]

Danjet (IRE) *J M Bradley* a82 82
3 bl f Danehill Dancer(IRE) —Jet Lock (USA) (Crafty Prospector (USA))
665[13] 1146[9] 1482[10]5593[8] 5791[2] 5938[9] 6353[8]

Danjoe *R Brotherton* a53
2 ch c Forzando—Baytown Rhapsody (Emperor Jones (USA))
6386[11] 6523[12]6905[7]

Dannabelle (IRE) *John A Quinn* a56 60
6 b m Danetime(IRE) —Cerosia (Pitskelly)
(4585) 4974[10] 5474[13] 6142[5]6477[12] 6618[10]

Danni Di Guerra (IRE) *P C Haslam* 39
2 b g Soviet Star(USA) —Lina Bella (FR) (Linamix (FR))
1499[6] 4474[5] 5332[12]

Danny Templeton (IRE) *D R C Elsworth* 82
2 ch c Namid—Singing Millie (Millfontaine)
5326[2] 5915[2]

Danny The Dip *J J Bridger* a40 59d
3 b g Prince Sabo—Ann's Pearl (IRE) (Cyrano De Bergerac)
1210[4] 1378[4] 1751[5] 2134[3] 2433[8]2962[4] 3118[8] 3340[5] 3873[2] 4141[15]4532[7] 4874[7] 5181[8] 5576[15] 5781[9]

Dansa Queen *W R Swinburn* 89+
3 gr f Dansili—Pericardia (Petong)
2359[8] 2865[3] 3318[11] (4820) (5294)

Danse Spectre (IRE) *E J O'Neill* a61+
4 b m Spectrum(IRE) —Danse Royale (IRE) (Caerleon (USA))
187[13]

Danseuse *C E Brittain* a64 73
2 b f Dr Fong(USA) —Danemere (IRE) (Danehill (USA))
2572[2] 2800[10]

Dan's Heir *P C Haslam* a63 63
4 b g Dansili—Million Heiress (Auction Ring (USA))
1219[13] 4947[9] 5369[7] (5750) 6011[6] 6735[7]

Dansili Dancer *C G Cox* 106
4 b g Dansili—Magic Slipper (Habitat)
728[9] 1129[24] (2435) 2742[26] (3255) (4359) 5374[4]

Dansil In Distress *S Kirk* a57 48
2 b f Dansili—Just Speculation (IRE) (Ahonoora)
5417[7] 6031[6] 6558[5]

Dansilver *D J Wintle* a58 51
2 b g Dansili—Silver Gyre (IRE) (Silver Hawk (USA))
2598[5] 3193[10] 3677[5] 4115[2] 4509[8]4767[6] 5387[2] 5891[15]6172[11] 6522[7]

Dansimar *M R Channon* 71
2 gr f Daylami(IRE) —Hylandra (USA) (Bering)
4574[3] 5083[11] 5475[5]

Danski *P J Makin* a81+ 93+
3 b c Dansili—Manila Selection (USA) (Manila (USA))
1401[3] 1978[2] 3301[5](4004) 5150[7]

Dante's Diamond (IRE) *G A Swinbank* a63+ 40
4 b g Orpen(USA) —Flower From Heaven (Baptism)
6008[14] 6259[8] 6507[8]6627[3] 6683[2]6810[6]

Dan Tucker *B J Meehan* 55
2 b g Dansili—Shapely (USA) (Alleged (USA))
3701[16] 4428[8] 4873[6]

Danum *R Hollinshead* a49 43
6 b g Perpendicular—Maid Of Essex (Bustino)
390[8] 634[5]791[2] 1198[2]1395[3] 1765[5]2413[9] 6606[8]6701[9]

Danum Dancer *N Bycroft* 88
2 ch c Allied Forces(USA) —Branston Dancer (Rudimentary (USA))
1491[6] 1780[4] 2623[5] 3555[2] 4152[7]4681[8] (4946) 5154[8] (5681) 5809[6]

Danum Diva (IRE) *T J Pitt* 26
2 ch f Danehill Dancer(IRE) —Comprehension (USA) (Diesis)
5507[12] 5679[14]

Danzar *M Brittain* a55 42
4 b g Danzero(AUS) —Tarf (USA) (Diesis)
3909[7] 4974[5] 5285[17]6543[10] 6638[6]6799[14]

Danzare *J L Spearing* a63 59
4 b m Dansili—Shot Of Redemption (Shirley Heights)
596[12] 2636[9] 2725[4]2969[6] 3159[6] 3440[2]3798[8] 4073[7] 4289[5] 4446[6] 4983[13]5450[3] 6775[3]

Danzatrice *C W Thornton* 61
4 b m Tamure(IRE) —Miss Petronella (Petoski)
1850[12] 2362[3] 2684[9] 3352[5] (4086) (4351) 4723[4](4954) 5338[4] 5815[4]

Danzig River (IRE) *D Nicholls* 87
5 b g Green Desert(USA) —Sahara Breeze (Ela-Mana-Mou)
947[12] 1042[7] 1143[4] 1494[4] 1820[18]2661[11] 4569[5] (4834) 4957[14] 5081[8] 5593[10]

Danzili Bay *P W Chapple-Hyam* 93+
4 b h Dansili—Lady Bankes (IRE) (Alzao (USA))
6335[10]

Danzolin *W R Muir* a61 60
5 b m Danzero(AUS) —Howlin' (USA) (Alleged (USA))
163[7] 263[11]361[5]

Danzon (USA) *J-C Rouget* 107
3 br f Royal Academy(USA) —Zappeuse (USA) (Kingmambo (USA))
773a[2] (1330a) 2491a[15] 6366a[2] 6614a[10]

Da Pooch (IRE) *H Rogers* a33 62
3 br f Key Of Luck(USA) —Kinlochewe (Old Vic)
6382[10]

Dapple Dawn (IRE) *D Carroll* a69 74
3 b f Celtic Swing—Lasting Chance (USA) (American Chance (USA))
6863[4]

Dapple Grey (IRE) *T Stack* 82+
3 gr f Aljabr(USA) —Asl (USA) (Caro)
2840a[8]

Dara Mac *M Scudamore* a57 67
7 b g Presidium—Nishara (Nishapour (FR))
242[11] 363[10]3194[10] 6604[8]

Daramsar (FR) *A De Royer-Dupre* 115
3 b c Rainbow Quest(USA) —Daryaba (IRE) (Night Shift (USA))
5400a[3] (5999a)

Darasim (IRE) *M Johnston* a46 119
8 b g Kahyasi—Dararita (IRE) (Halo (USA))
2625[5] 3203[10] 4036[19]

Darcy's Pride (IRE) *D W Barker* 50
2 bb f Danetime(IRE) —Cox's Ridge (IRE) (Indian Ridge)
3018[14] 3830[7] 5746[6] 5835[4]

Dareneur (IRE) *J G M O'Shea* 57
6 ch m Entrepreneur—Darayna (IRE) (Shernazar)
2601[2] 3196[4] 3467[5] 3894[13]

Darenjan (IRE) *Sir Michael Stoute* 71
3 b c Alhaarth(IRE) —Darariyna (IRE) (Shirley Heights)
2118[5] 4471[2] 4776[10]

Darfour *M Johnston* 76
2 b c Inchinor—Gai Bulga (Kris)
2680[6] 3498[7] (3726) 5013[8] 5866[11]

Darghan (IRE) *W J Musson* a54 69
6 b g Air Express(IRE) —Darsannda (IRE) (Kahyasi)
882[5] 1138[10] (1590) 2150[4] 2902[3] 3232[4](3704) 4299[6] 4848[3] 5276[8] 5897[7] 6158[15]

Daring Affair *K R Burke* a85 79
5 b m Bien Bien(USA) —Daring Destiny (Daring March)
50[7] 1094[2]2656[10] 3566[2] (3724) 4160[10] 4911[3] 5538[5](6448) 6607[3](6772)

Daring Heart (JPN) *H Fujiwara* 113
4 b m Sunday Silence(USA) —Daring Danzig (USA) (Danzig (USA))
6530a[13]

Daring Ransom (USA) *J Noseda* 103
4 b g Red Ransom(USA) —Young And Daring (USA) (Woodman (USA))
205a[5] (Dead)

Daring Spirit (IRE) *J C Hayden* 68
2 b g Invincible Spirit(IRE) —Bunker Dolly (USA) (Catrail (USA))
4824a[21]

Daring You *P F I Cole* a43 51
2 b g Mtoto—Sari (Faustus (USA))
2258[3] 2506[7] 2899[8] 5041[8] 5262[8]6016[3]

Dark Champion *R E Barr* a51 67
6 b g Abou Zouz(USA) —Hazy Kay (IRE) (Treasure Kay)
2112[8] 2198[9] (2833) 3190[8] 3617[6] 3913[6]4401[8] 4735[12] 4834[16] (5078) 5486[8] 5684[14]5752[4] 6274[4]

Dark Charm (FR) *R A Fahey* a78 79
7 b g Anabaa(USA) —Wardara (Sharpo)
1043[13] 1280[12] 1494[6] 1830[12] (2025) 2547[5]2853[5] 3528[2] 3792[2] 3900[4] (4256) 4653[2]4730[5] 5137[5]

Dark Cheetah (USA) *R Dutrow Jr* a107 108
4 b h Storm Cat(USA) —Layounne (USA) (Mt. Livermore (USA))
4787a[3] 6127a[9]

Dark Dancer (GER) *W Kelkel* 107
3 gr c Kallisto(GER) —Dark Lady (GER) (Lagunas)
2314a[2] 3776a[5] 4942a[3]

Dark Emotion *W De Best-Turner* 37
3 b g Prince Sabo—Sorrowful (Moorestyle)
1822[10] 3681[6] 5510[15]

Dark Energy *B Smart* 70
2 br c Observatory(USA) —Waterfowl Creek (IRE) (Be My Guest (USA))
6318[3]

Darker Than Blue *B J Meehan* a51 37
3 b f Erhaab(USA) —My Preference (Reference Point)
802[4] 952[13]1139[12] 1350[8] 1731[3] 2101[4] 2573[5]

Dark Islander (IRE) *J W Hills* a99 116
3 br c Singspiel(IRE) —Lamanka Lass (USA) (Woodman (USA))
1094[2] 1924[3] 2774[10](3491) 4126[4] (5165) (5985a) 6613a[8]

Dark Missile *A M Balding* a91 99
3 b f Night Shift(USA) —Exocet (FR) (Selkirk (USA))
1512[7] 1857[4] 2168[2] 2756[2](3414) 4097[9] (4343) 4633[9] 5358[21]

Dark Moon *D Shaw* a51 59
3 b f Observatory(USA) —Lady Donatella (Last Tycoon)
1352[6] 2210[5] 2535[8]2676[3] (4363) 4671[3] 5210[5]5474[15] 6465[9] 6619[10]

Dark Night (IRE) *D W Barker* a37 48
3 b g Night Shift(USA) —Shamaness (USA) (Darshaan)
2243[12] 2746[5] 3145[15]

Dark Parade (ARG) *G L Moore* a73 62
5 b g Parade Marshal(USA) —Charming Dart (ARG) (D'Accord (USA))
973[9] 1339[7] (1958) 2684[4]3098[4] 3649[2]4046[2] 4702[10]4996[2] 5587[6]

Dark Planet *C E Brittain* a67 67
3 ch g Singspiel(IRE) —Warning Shadows (IRE) (Cadeaux Genereux)
918[2] (1251) 1543[6] 1925[4]2209[4] 2622[8] 3075[4]

Dark Society *A W Carroll* a63 69
8 b g Imp Society(USA) —No Candles Tonight (Star Appeal)
3900[9] 4432[6] 4585[18]

Darling Belinda *D K Ivory* a66 64
2 ch f Silver Wizard(USA) —Katyushka (IRE) (Soviet Star (USA))
5095[13] 5261[7]5867[5] 6255[7] 6500[3]6592[3] 6821[2]6905[2]

Darling Deanie (IRE) *K A Ryan* 77
4 ch m Sinndar(IRE) —Blushing Melody (IRE) (Never So Bold)
2305[2] 3028[5] 3547[6] 4991[9]

Darling River (FR) *R Brotherton* a51
7 b m Double Bed(FR) —Oh Lucky Day (Balidar)
172[12] 258[12]442[12] 791[10]

Darrfonah (IRE) *C E Brittain* a65+ 106
2 b f Singspiel(IRE) —Avila (Ajdal (USA))
3201[8] 3495[5] 3893[2]4737[3] (5344) 5714a[2]

Darsi (FR) *A De Royer-Dupre* 117
3 b c Polish Precedent(USA) —Darashandeh (IRE) (Darshaan)
(2278a) 3127a[5]

Dart Along (USA) *Eoin Doyle* a81 80
4 b h Bahri(USA) —Promptly (IRE) (Lead On Time (USA))
4186a[6] 6461[11] 6507[5](6684)

Dartanian *M Scudamore* a49 56
4 b g Jurado(USA) —Blackpool Mamma's (Merdon Melody)
2702[15] 3051[6]

Daruma (IRE) *Peter Grayson* a53 49
2 b g Iron Mask(USA) —Mary's Way (GR) (Night Shift (USA))
1405[5] 2439[9] 2922[5]3246[11] 3521[4] 6400[7]

Darusso *J S Moore* a54 65
3 ch g Daylami(IRE) —Rifada (Ela-Mana-Mou)
6021[6] 6260[9]

Da Schadenfreude (USA) *W G M Turner* a54 61
2 bb g Tale Of The Cat(USA) —Conquistas Jessica (USA) (Boundary (USA))
5020[9] 5289[9] 5527[8]

Dasheena *A J McCabe* a66 50
3 b f Magic Ring(IRE) —Sweet And Lucky (Lucky Wednesday)
851[2] 1004[3]1344[4] 1672[11] 5350[11] 5605[4]5902[11] 6556[3] 6820[6]

Dashfa Baileys *C A Dwyer* a39 46
3 ch g Mark Of Esteem(IRE) —Dahshah (Mujtahid (USA))
83[9]

Dashing Home (IRE) *Noel Meade* 104
7 b g Lahib(USA) —Dashing Rose (Mashhor Dancer (USA))
3128a[4] 4031a[9]

Dash Of Humor (USA) *Hal R Wiggins* 101
6 ch m Distorted Humor(USA) —Dot Dot Dash (USA) (Nureyev (USA))
6368a[6]

Dash Of Lime *J Akehurst* a63 69
4 b m Bold Edge—Green Supreme (Primo Dominie)
1[11] 51[5]

Dash To The Front *J R Fanshawe* a73+ 88
3 b f Diktat—Millennium Dash (Nashwan (USA))
(3387) 4375[2] 4590[7] 5525[7]

Datznyce (IRE) *D R C Elsworth* a40 26
3 b f Cape Cross(IRE) —Sharera (IRE) (Kahyasi)
473[11] 584[9]1006[9]

Daughters World *J R Best* 52
3 b f Agnes World(USA) —Priluki (Lycius (USA))
5210[13] 6234[11]

Davaye *K R Burke* 67
2 b f Bold Edge—Last Impression (Imp Society (USA))
1790[3] 2439[4] 3351[5] 4321[3] (4727) 5860[4]

Davenport (IRE) *B R Millman* a87 87
4 b g Bold Fact(USA) —Semence D'Or (FR) (Kaldoun (FR))
726[7] 1207[4] 1340[4]1957[2] (2114) 2621[7] 2983[3]5639[15] 5833[14] 6176[9] 6424[5]6635[4] 6862[2]6968[4]

Dave's Best *C H Yip* 119
6 b g Bishop Of Cashel—Brightside (IRE) (Last Tycoon)
1527a[11] 6784a[13]

Davidia (IRE) *S Kirk* a66 64
3 b g Barathea(IRE) —Green Life (Green Desert (USA))
710[3] 918[7]1141[5] 1941[4] 2535[2]2648[3] 2814[14] 6694[5]6743[4] 6898[9]

Davidii (IRE) *K J Condon* 91
2 gr c Act One—Magic Cove (USA) (Kingmambo (USA))
5410a[5]

David Junior (USA) *B J Meehan* 127
4 ch h Pleasant Tap(USA) —Paradise River (USA) (Irish River (FR))
(742a) 2741[4] (3314) 6345a[13]

Davids Mark *J R Jenkins* a58 56
6 b g Polar Prince(IRE) —Star Of Flanders (Puissance)
178[2] 288[8]397[3] 524[9]679[4] 772[8]886[6] 1209[8] 1722[4]1914[6] (3825) 4141[7] 4846[5]5569[2] 6539[3] 6615[4](6723)

Davorin (JPN) *R P Burns* a62 98
5 br h Warning—Arvola (Sadler's Wells (USA))
2471a[6] 3128a[6] 5396a[8]

Davoski *Dr P Pritchard* 28
12 b g Niniski(USA) —Pamela Peach (Habitat)
3116[7] 3894[16]

Dawaleeb (IRE) *Jane Chapple-Hyam* a47 65
3 b f Alhaarth(IRE) —Summerhill (Habitat)
1642[9] 4814[6] 5036[8]5418[10] 6241[11]

Dawari (IRE) *R Ford* 100
8 b g In The Wings—Dawala (IRE) (Lashkari)
2140[P]

Dawera (IRE) *Sir Michael Stoute* 79+
3 b f Spinning World(USA) —Dawala (IRE) (Lashkari)
2349[3] (3717)

Daweyrr (USA) *M P Tregoning* 57
2 b c Kingmambo(USA) —With Flair (USA) (Broad Brush (USA))
5125[9]

Dawn Mystery *Rae Guest* a49
2 gr f Daylami(IRE) —Frustration (Salse (USA))
6658[7]

Dawn Sky *M A Jarvis* 66
2 b c Fantastic Light(USA) —Zacheta (Polish Precedent (USA))
6298[2]

Dawn's Last Shot (IRE) *J L Dunlop* 61
4 b g Son Of Sharp Shot(IRE) —Dawn Star (High Line)
894[5] 1138[8] 4836[8]

Dawn Spirit *J R Weymes* 13
3 ch f Barathea(IRE) —Samsung Spirit (Statoblest)
1231[3] 1827[7] 2895[9]

Dawson Creek (IRE) *B Gubby* a48 37
2 ch c Titus Livius(FR) —Particular Friend (Cadeaux Genereux)
2572[9] 3843[11]5730[10]

Daybreaking (IRE) *R F Johnson Houghton* a8
4 br h Daylami(IRE) —Mawhiba (USA) (Dayjur (USA))
218[10] 318[13]

Day By Day *B J Meehan* 33
2 ch f Kyllachy—Dayville (USA) (Dayjur (USA))
5950[10]

Day Flight *J H M Gosden* 119+
5 b h Sadler's Wells(USA) —Bonash (Rainbow Quest (USA))
(1267) 2061a[2] 2845[4]

Daylami Dreams *J S Moore* 69
2 gr g Daylami(IRE) —Kite Mark (Mark Of Esteem (IRE))
3892[7] 4303[4] 5339[8]

Daylami Star *J H M Gosden* a73 90
3 gr c Daylami(IRE) —Ascot Cyclone (USA) (Rahy (USA))
1586[2] 2117[6]

Daylesford *I Semple* 33
3 ch f Golden Snake(USA) —Lady Day (FR) (Lightning (FR))
4300[6]

Dayoff (IRE) *P D Evans* a50 75
5 gr m Daylami(IRE) —Dabtara (IRE) (Kahyasi)
166[2] 318[10]2522[10] 2762[7] 3035[11] 3467[4] (3810) 3894[10]4072[5] 4351[3]

Dayrose *Sir Michael Stoute* 90
3 ch f Daylami(IRE) —Blush Rambler (IRE) (Blushing Groom (FR))
1797[2] 2398[2] (4686) (5538) 6333[9]

Days Of My Life (IRE) *R Charlton* 101+
3 b g Daylami(IRE) —Truly Yours (IRE) (Barathea (IRE))
778[3] 1049[3] (1212) (1954) 2330[4] (2779) (3007) 3040[6]

Daytona (GER) *P Rau* 99
5 br m Lando(GER) —Daytona Beach (GER) (Konigsstuhl (GER))
3719a[6] 5560a[4]

Day To Remember *E F Vaughan* a72 98
5 gr g Daylami(IRE) —Miss Universe (IRE) (Warning)
1357[7] 1544[4] (1992) 3128a[3] 5494[7] 5675[30]5808[10] 6097[11]

Day Walker *Rune Haugen* 110
4 b h Dr Devious(IRE) —Island Race (Common Grounds)
3579a[7] 4864a[6] 5226a[3] 5657[8]

Dazed And Amazed *R Hannon* 97d
2 b c Averti(IRE) —Amazed (Clantime)
1796[3] (2045) 2724[5] (2960) 3442[4] 4026[5] 4099[7]4736[18] 5373[6]

Dazzler Mac *N Bycroft* 68
5 b g Komaite(USA) —Stilvella (Camden Town)
1795[9] 2112[3] 3749[6] 3913[5] (4120) 4405[2]4735[5]

Dazzling Bay *T D Easterby* 107
6 b g Mind Games—Adorable Cherub (USA) (Halo (USA))
(1597) 2323[6] 3956[12] 4202[13] 5534[12] 5957[12]

Dazzling Olivia (IRE) *R A Fahey* a13 44
2 b f Tagula(IRE) —Make Hay (Nomination)
4017[8] 4251[11] 4887[5] 6471[7]

Deadline (UAE) *M Johnston* 74
2 ch c Machiavellian(USA) —Time Changes (USA) (Danzig (USA))
4716[6] 5066[5] 5496[2] 5788[14]

Deadshot Keen (IRE) *B J Meehan* a87 90
2 b g Invincible Spirit(IRE) —Madam Waajib (IRE) (Waajib)
1066[4] (1372) 2719[16] 2960[5] 3531[3]5466a[25] 5989[2]

Dear Gracie (IRE) *J R Fanshawe* a78 70
3 b f In The Wings—Allegheny River (USA) (Lear Fan (USA))
1417[3] 1901[2] 2542[2] (4044)

Dear One (IRE) *P A Blockley* a57
2 b f Montjeu(IRE) —Siamoise (Caerleon (USA))
1019[5] 6751[6]

Dear Sir (IRE) *Mrs P N Dutfield* a30 56
6 ch g Among Men(USA) —Deerussa (IRE) (Jareer (USA))
3437[4] 3896[5] 4380[11]

Deauville (GER) *Frau E Mader* 97
3 b f Dashing Blade—Dea (GER) (Shareef Dancer (USA))
2912a[6] 3661a[7] 4542a[8] (5710a) 6093a[6]

Debbie (SWE) *Catharina Wenell*
3 b f Malvenirco(IRE) —Debonair (Batshoof)
2564a[10]

Debbie *B D Leavy* a51 66
7 b m Deploy—Elita (Sharpo)
(470) 767[5]

Debord (FR) *Jamie Poulton* a59 67d
3 ch c Sendawar(IRE) —Partie De Dames (USA) (Bering)
981[8] 1240[8] 1605[8]1978[4] (2177) 2403[12] 2990[9] 5211[12]6206[16]

De Boxter (FR) *A Trybuhl* 83
6 gr g Medaaly—Deveria (FR) (Lead On Time (USA))
6121a[9]

Debs Broughton *W J Musson* a41 45
4 b m Prince Sabo—Coy Debutante (IRE) (Archway (IRE))
173[8] 312[11]

Debutante *L M Cumani* a67+ 49
3 b f Medicean—Throw Away Line (USA) (Assert)
4431[10] *5669[6]*

Decado (IRE) *Kevin Prendergast* 116+
3 b c Danehill Dancer(IRE) —Pirie (USA) (Green Dancer (USA))
(928a) (1362a) 2039a[3] 2721[9]

Deccan Express (IRE) *R Hannon* 67
2 ch c Grand Lodge(USA) —Harda Arda (USA) (Nureyev (USA))
3253[6] 3498[9] 3851[4] 4767[3] 6007[14]

Decent (IRE) *W J H Ratcliffe* a42 50
3 b f Desert Sun—Guyum (Rousillon (USA))
3609[8] *6554[10]*

Decent Proposal *T D Easterby* 41
2 b f Montjeu(IRE) —Markova's Dance (Mark Of Esteem (IRE))
3908[6]

Dechiper (IRE) *R Johnson* a3 58
4 bb g Almutawakel—Safiya (USA) (Riverman (USA))
3260[9] 3617[4] 4694[4]5063[2]

Decider (USA) *J M Bradley* a63 49
3 ch c High Yield(USA) —Nikita Moon (USA) (Secret Hello (USA))
2445[5] 2763[14] 3090[16] 3538[7] 4120[15]5055[4] 5272[5]
6234[2](6637) (6877)

Decision Day *J A Geake* 41
2 b f Groom Dancer(USA) —Indubitable (Sharpo)
6331[8]

Decree Nisi *Mrs A Duffield* 72
3 ch g Compton Place—Palisandra (USA) (Chief's Crown (USA))
1868[5] (2698) 3082[6] 3695[6] 4257[9] 4943[2]5432[9]

Dee Burgh *J Pearce* a55 47
2 b f Zaha(CAN) —Glensara (Petoski)
4600[11] *4993[6]* 5296[8]

Dee Cee Elle *M Johnston* a54+ 50
2 b f Groom Dancer(USA) —Missouri (Charnwood Forest (IRE))
1647[6] 2026[8] 2924[5] 5492[5] 6007[9]*(6385)*

Dee Jay Wells *R Hannon* 76
2 b g Ishiguru(USA) —Stravaig (IRE) (Sadler's Wells (USA))
1796[9] 2172[2] 2530[5] 3335[2] 3663[4]4485[2] 4779[9]
5231[6] 5647[7]

Deep Cover (IRE) *R M Flower* a57
2 ch c Boundary(USA) —Chibi (USA) (Dynaformer (USA))
4140[11] *6393[8] 6650[6]*

Deeper In Debt *J Akehurst* a83 77
8 ch g Piccolo—Harold's Girl (FR) (Northfields (USA))
(50) 161[10] 2114[9] 2606[5]2969[4] (3153) 3311[2]
3433[4] 4131[7] 4968[5]6054[10] *6397[12] 6580[10]6671[9]
6841[9]*

Deep Impact (JPN) *Y Ikee* 133+
4 b h Sunday Silence(USA) —Wind In Her Hair (IRE) (Alzao (USA))
(1329a) 5716a[DSQ] (6612a)

Deep Purple *A M Balding* 89
5 b g Halling(USA) —Seal Indigo (IRE) (Glenstal (USA))
4160[11] 5346[15]

Deep Sleep *M H Tompkins* a24 67
3 b g Tipsy Creek(USA) —Tiempo (King Of Spain)
969[5] 1851[14] 2184[9]

Deepwater Bay (USA) *A M Balding* a82 101
3 b c Chester House(USA) —Gem Treck (USA) (Java Gold (USA))
(1166) 1953[2] 2775[8]

Deerpark (IRE) *John F Gleeson* 96
4 ch g Orpen(USA) —Early Fin (IRE) (Mukaddamah (USA))
930a[7] 3123a[14]

Deer Park Countess *D A Nolan*
5 ch m Shaddad(USA) —Logani (Domynsky)
3480[9] 4136[8] 5578[9]

Dee Valley Boy (IRE) *J D Bethell* 49
2 b g Val Royal(FR) —Canadian Girl (IRE) (Rainbows For Life (CAN))
2972[7] 4171[7] 4829[11]

Defi (IRE) *I Semple* a76 83
4 b g Rainbow Quest(USA) —Danse Classique (IRE) (Night Shift (USA))
253[3] 381[11]571[4] 1455[3] 2378[9]2547[4] 3040[7] 3287[5]
(3672) (4133) 4521[7] 4953[8]*5249[13]* 6006a[9]
6507[4]6898[7]

Defining *D Hayes* a77 114
7 b g Definite Article—Gooseberry Pie (Green Desert (USA))
6346a[16]

Definite (IRE) *T G McCourt* a46 74
8 b g Definite Article—My Gossip (IRE) (Camden Town)
6540[3]

Definitely Blue *C F Wall* 7
3 b f Definite Article—Atmospheric Blues (IRE) (Double Schwartz)
4776[14] 5598[13]

Definite Rose (SWE) *F Castro*
3 ch f Definite Article—North Cider Rose (IRE) (Goldmark (USA))
2564a[13]

Degas Art (IRE) *D R C Elsworth* 112
3 b g Danehill Dancer(IRE) —Answer (Warning)
1070[2] (1516) 2030[2] 2801[4] 3441[3] 4337[4](5657)

Deira (USA) *C E Brittain* a83+ 77
3 b f Green Desert(USA) —New Sayyedati (USA) (Shadeed (USA))
1078[2] *(1551)* 1843[10] 2403[5] 3072[5] (3841)4241[9]
4689[6] *6461[9]*

Deirdre's Dilemma (IRE) *G C Bravery* a36 30
4 b m Primo Dominie—Sartigila (Efisio)
5363[9] *6694[8]*

Dejeeje (IRE) *D W Chapman* a12 7
5 ch g Grand Lodge(USA) —Christan (IRE) (Al Hareb (USA))
28[9] 7871767[8] 1883[9]

Delamead (IRE) *B Ellison* 23
3 b g King Of Kings(IRE) —Al Saqiya (USA) (Woodman (USA))
1100[10] 1252[11] 1458[7]

Delaporte *M A Buckley* a40
2 ch f Fantastic Light(USA) —Poppadam (Salse (USA))
3942[8] 4207[16] *6457[4]6570[8]*

De La Rue (USA) *M G Quinlan* a81 66
3 b c Louis Quatorze(USA) —Primevere (USA) (Irish River (FR))
(124) 592[3] 4599[8] 5270[6]

Delfinia *Miss Tracy Waggott* 37
5 b m Kingsinger(IRE) —Delvecchia (Glint Of Gold)
5485[15]

Delfos (IRE) *C Laffon-Parias* 116
5 ch h Green Tune(USA) —Akhla (USA) (Nashwan (USA))
934a[12]

Delightfully *Jean-Rene Auvray* a51 51
5 b m Definite Article—Kingpin Delight (Emarati (USA))
6620[13] 6729[10]

Delitme (IRE) *M Gonnelli*
2 b f Val Royal(FR) —Phylella (Persian Bold)
2565a[8]

Delivered (IRE) *Kevin Prendergast* 71
3 b f King Charlemagne(USA) —Run To Jane (IRE) (Doyoun)
4124a[7]

Dellagio (IRE) *R W Price* a63 30
5 b h Fasliyev(USA) —Lady Ounavarra (IRE) (Simply Great (FR))
3683[4]

Della Salute *Miss E C Lavelle* a72 82
4 gr m Dansili—Marie Dora (FR) (Kendor (FR))
1207[13] 1302[6] 2259[8] 2510[8] (3095) 3366[9]3703[4]
4001[2] 4536[5] *5110[9]*5346[10]

Del Mar Sunset *W J Haggas* a87 84+
7 b g Unfuwain(USA) —City Of Angels (Woodman (USA))
4051[5] 4810[5] 5295[2] *5776[9]6226[8] 6418[2]*

Delmarva (USA) *J Kimmel* a96 98
3 b f Unbridled's Song(USA) —Precipice (USA) (Gulch (USA))
5198a[9]

Delora (GER) *M Weber* 106
5 b m Lavirco(GER) —Dissi (GER) (Paris Turf (IRE))
1974a[3] (4649a)

Delorain (IRE) *J A R Toller* 55
3 b g Kalanisi(IRE) —Lady Nasrana (FR) (Al Nasr (FR))
1290[10] 1741[13] 2591[4] 3439[7] 4150[9]4668[3] 5324[3]

Delphia (IRE) *T Hogan* 75
2 ch f Dr Fong(USA) —Calypso Run (Lycius (USA))
5464a[22]

Delphie Queen (IRE) *M Halford* 93
5 ch m Desert Sun—Serious Delight (Lomond (USA))
1156a[13] 3125a[14] 4749a[13]

Delta Blues (JPN) *Katsuhiko Sumii* 122
5 b h Dance In The Dark(JPN) —Dixie Splash (USA) (Dixieland Band (USA))
1329a[10] 6110a[3] (6392a)

Delta Force *P A Blockley* a32 55?
7 b g High Kicker(USA) —Maedaley (Charmer)
270[9] 457[12]570[13] 1436[7] 1660[4]2099[4] 2879[4]

Delta Queen *C N Kellett* 29
2 b f Montjoy(USA) —Full Of Passion (USA) (Blushing Groom (FR))
1587[15] 2072[5] 2355[9] 2731[7] 4545[7]*5686[11]* 6047[12]

Delta Shuttle (IRE) *K R Burke* 62
2 b c Bluebird(USA) —Ibtihal (IRE) (Hamas (IRE))
4716[7] 5613[3] 6157[11]

Delude (IRE) *A Laird* a87
8 ch g Be My Guest(USA) —Deceive (Machiavellian (USA))
204a[14] 434a[6]

Dematraf (IRE) *Ms Deborah J Evans* a64 64
4 gr m Atraf—Demolition Jo (Petong)
159[10] 249[10]315[7] 1393[8]1577[7] 2758[2] 4473[6]

Demerger (AUS) *Danny O'Brien* 111
6 ch m Saithor(USA) —Triattica (AUS) (Centaine (AUS))
6392a[21]

Demi Sec *Dr J D Scargill* a25
3 ch f Bahamian Bounty—Veuve (Tirol)
2575[12]

Democratic Deficit (IRE) *J S Bolger* 112
4 b h Soviet Star(USA) —Grandiose Idea (IRE) (Danehill (USA))
153a[7] 281a[8] 1171a[3] 1299[4] 2371a[7]

Demolition *C A Cyzer*
2 ch g Starborough—Movie Star (IRE) (Barathea (IRE))
6434[12]

Demon Docker (IRE) *P W Chapple-Hyam* a95 97
3 ch c Docksider(USA) —Green Moon (FR) (Shirley Heights)
3648[4] 3978[5] 4605[3](4923) 5150[9]

Denbera Dancer (USA) *M Johnston* 54+
2 b c Danehill(USA) —Monevassia (USA) (Mr Prospector (USA))
4260[5]

Deneuve *M G Quinlan* a32 48
3 ch f Tomba—Princess Sadie (Shavian)
6796[9] 6958[10]

Dennick *P C Haslam* a54 55
4 b g Nicolotte—Branston Dancer (Rudimentary (USA))
86[3]

Den's Gift (IRE) *C G Cox* 73
2 rg g City On A Hill(USA) —Romanylei (IRE) (Blues Traveller (IRE))
2432[3] 5655[12] 6014[4]

Denton Hawk *M Dods* 55
2 b g Mujahid(USA) —Lamasat (USA) (Silver Hawk (USA))
1559[6] 2733[11] 2922[3] 3228[3] 3787[5]4545[5] 4724[4]
5084[4]

Deodatus (USA) *E Charpy* a101
8 b h Darshaan—Intrepidity (Sadler's Wells (USA))
152a[5]

Depp (ITY) *L D'Auria* 93
2 ch c City On A Hill(USA) —Drifa (ITY) (Hamas (IRE))
2474a[3] 6003a[6]

Depraux (IRE) *W J Haggas* a67 66
3 br g Generous(IRE) —Happy Memories (IRE) (Thatching)
5774[6] 6019[3] *6314[4]6578[2] 6758[3]*

Depressed *Ernst Oertel* a69 79
4 ch m Most Welcome—Sure Care (Caerleon (USA))
224[11] 376[5]519[5] 555[7]1961[3] 2637[8] 3095[4]3440[5]

Deputy Glitters (USA) *T Albertrani* a107
3 b c Deputy Commander(USA) —Glitters (USA) (Glitterman (USA))
1498a[8] 2477a[11]

Derison (USA) *H Van De Poele* 97
4 b g Miesque's Son(USA) —Devolli (Saumarez)
6547a[4]

Desabina (GER) *H Blume* 29
2 ch f Big Shuffle(USA) —Despoina (GER) (Aspros (GER))
6122a[12]

Descargo *C G Cox* a49
2 ch f Delta Dancer—Secret Miss (Beveled (USA))
6575[7]

Descartes *Saeed Bin Suroor* a102 82
4 b h Dubai Millennium—Gold's Dance (FR) (Goldneyev (USA))
(5776) 6097[13]

Desert Anger *S Seemar* a83 98
5 b g Cadeaux Genereux—Chere Amie (USA) (Mr Prospector (USA))
207a[3] 513a[6]

Desert Authority (USA) *Saeed Bin Suroor* 110+
3 bb c War Chant(USA) —Tuzla (FR) (Panoramic)
(3875) (5142)

Desert Bounty *G M Moore* 51
3 b f Bahamian Bounty—Aldevonie (Green Desert (USA))
1447[11]

Desert Cactus (IRE) *M Botti*
2 ch f Desert Prince(IRE) —Funun (USA) (Fappiano (USA))
5705a[14]

Desert Chief *Saeed Bin Suroor* 92
4 b h Green Desert(USA) —Oriental Fashion (IRE) (Marju (IRE))
5943[8]

Desert Commander (IRE) *K A Ryan* 105
4 b g Green Desert(USA) —Meadow Pipit (CAN) (Meadowlake (USA))
(1125) 1803[9] (2323) 4128[26] 4609[16] 4682[17]
5358[17]

Desert Cristal (IRE) *J R Boyle* a89 87
5 ch m Desert King(IRE) —Damiana (IRE) (Thatching)
1207[5] *1380[2]* 1992[5]*3490[5]* 5477[7] *5776[6]5895[8]*

Desert Dabby (GER) *J Kozlowski* 65
3 gr f Linamix(FR) —Desert Kaya (FR) (Bikala)
4383a[10]

Desert Destiny *Saeed Bin Suroor* a91 108
6 b g Desert Prince(IRE) —High Savannah (Rousillon (USA))
278a[2] 369a[7] *5845[4]*

Desert Dew (IRE) *B W Hills* 93
2 ch c Indian Ridge—Blue Water (USA) (Bering)
5457[6] (5658) 6102[8]

Desert Dreamer (IRE) *P R Chamings* a89 88
5 b g Green Desert(USA) —Follow That Dream (Darshaan)
*828[4] 1112[10]*1359[7] 1667[7] *1938[2]2232[8]* 2405[2]
*2555[10]*3149[2] (3337) *3532[9]* 4029[11]4535[3] (4658)
5070[4] 5144[7] 5345[5] *5627[13]5877[5] 6397[14]6461[12]*

Desert Dust *R M H Cowell* a58 43
3 b g Vettori(IRE) —Dust (Green Desert (USA))
*331[4] 373[3]*1736[16] 2318[15] 2644[7] 2876[8]
*4710[2]5834[14] 5969[7] 6129[5]6276[2] 6440[4](6539)
6615[5]6686[3] 6753[5]*

Deserted Dane (USA) *G A Swinbank* 87+
2 b c Elusive Quality(USA) —Desertion (IRE) (Danehill (USA))
4801[3] (5288)

Deserted Island (IRE) *N Wilson* 15
3 b f Desert Style(IRE) —Osprey Point (IRE) (Entrepreneur)
1445[10]

Deserted Prince (IRE) *M J Wallace* a58 65
3 b g Desert Prince(IRE) —Pool Party (USA) (Summer Squall (USA))
61[9] 234[5]969[12] 2648[8] 3045[7]3827[6] 4263[3] 4304[13]
4847[4] *5097[11]*

Desert Fantasy (IRE) *M Meade* a5 109
7 b g Desert King(IRE) —Petite Fantasy (Mansooj)
1129[25] *1550[10]* (Dead)

Desert Flair *R Hannon* a52 72
3 b f Desert Style(IRE) —Celtic Cross (Selkirk (USA))
2575[4] 2985[7] 4820[11]

Desert Fury *R Bastiman* a55 77
9 b g Warning—Number One Spot (Reference Point)
94[5] 3044[4](386) 527[9]689[2] (787) 906[13] 1253[8]
1591[14]*2245[9]*

Desert Gold (IRE) *A J Martin* 99
5 b m Desert Prince(IRE) —Brief Sentiment (IRE) (Brief Truce (USA))
2776[24]

Desert Hawk *W M Brisbourne* a56 53
5 b g Cape Cross(IRE) —Milling (IRE) (In The Wings)
72[6] 231[2](363) 469[3]6627[4] 6812[3]6899[3]

Desert Hunter (IRE) *Micky Hammond* a22 55
3 b g Desert Story(IRE) —She-Wolff (IRE) (Pips Pride)
1687[7] 2285[5] 2701[3] (3397) 3814[7] 4199[7]

Desert Image (IRE) *C Tinkler* a71 65
5 b g Desert King(IRE) —Identical (IRE) (Machiavellian (USA))
5213[10] 5910[3] (Dead)

Desertina (IRE) *R M Whitaker* a54 52
4 b m Spectrum(IRE) —Kayanga (Green Desert (USA))
1102[4] 1413[6] 1594[6] 2758[7] 4198[13]4507[13]

Desert Island Disc *Dr J R J Naylor* a53 77
9 b m Turtle Island(IRE) —Distant Music (Darshaan)
(1376) 1690[7] 1931[4] 2067[2] 2534[4] 2672[6]3666[5]
3853[6]

Desert Island Miss *W R Swinburn* a65 60
3 b f Medicean—Miss Castaway (Selkirk (USA))
5353[8] *5611[7]* 6021[5]*6294[5]*

Desert Joy *D R C Elsworth* 48
3 gr f Daylami(IRE) —Russian Rose (IRE) (Soviet Lad (USA))
2673[7] 5151[6]

Desert Leader (IRE) *W M Brisbourne* a85 65
5 b g Green Desert(USA) —Za Aamah (USA) (Mr Prospector (USA))
108[3] 214[11]6426[2] 6677[6]6862[5] 6992[8]

Desert Light (IRE) *D Shaw* a69 47
5 b g Desert Sun—Nacote (IRE) (Mtoto)
*178[3] (288) 400[5]588[6] 608[13](772) 837[4](903)
1383[3]*1795[15] 1981[11] *5246[13]*5631[14] *5737[10]
5878[5]6510[6] 6556[4]6632[4] 6865[4]6922[4]*

Desert Lightning (IRE) *K R Burke* a63 60
4 ch g Desert Prince(IRE) —Saibhreas (IRE) (Last Tycoon)
167[11] 567[7]585[11] 644[9]659[11] 974[2] 1217[2]1447[5]
2077[8] 2240[2] 2546[10] 3353[3]3541[4] 4057[3] 4087[5]
4568[2] 4909[9](5298) 5553[2] *6430[4] 6524[5]6606[7]*

Desert Lord *K A Ryan* a98 123
6 b g Green Desert(USA) —Red Carnival (USA) (Mr Prospector (USA))
761[3] (1031) 1236[7] 1602[5](2227) 3520[2] 4080[2]
4855a[2] 5179[5] (5712a) 6783a[12]

Desert Lover (IRE) *R J Price* a69 62
4 b g Desert Prince(IRE) —Crystal Flute (Lycius (USA))
95[6] (261) (350) (400) 537[3]650[5] (737) 860[8] 977[4]
*1402[2]*1773[6] 2223[9] *6664[12]6820[11]*

Desert Maze (IRE) *J Wade* 26
2 ch g Desert Sun—Allzi (USA) (Zilzal (USA))
3618[2] 3940[6]

Desert Move (IRE) *M R Channon* 85
4 b m Desert King(IRE) —Campestral (USA) (Alleged (USA))
3739[8] 4713[16] 5803[10]

Desert Opal *C R Dore* a79 69
6 ch g Cadeaux Genereux—Nullarbor (Green Desert (USA))
*46[4] 602[5]654[7] (824) 862[6] 1388[7]*1563[2] 1795[5]
*2020[10] 2208[2]3536[9] 3846[7]*4462[2] 4571[12] 4735[3]
4970[4]5032[7] 5386[10]5878[2] 6061[8] *(6325) 6622[3]
(6739)*

Desert Quiet (IRE) *P Giannotti* 107
4 b m Desert Story(IRE) —Quiet Awakening (USA) (Secreto (USA))
(6002a) 6364a[6]

Desert Realm (IRE) *M Johnston* 104+
3 b g Desert Prince(IRE) —Fawaayid (USA) (Vaguely Noble)
2527[2] 2774[29] 3313[13] 3671[2] 3929[2]4082[2] 4711[15]
5165[7] 5374[10] 5808[6]

Desert Reign *A P Jarvis* a76 77
5 ch g Desert King(IRE) —Moondance (Siberian Express (USA))
*375[4] 905[6]*1821[6] 2401[11]

Desert Sea (IRE) *C Tinkler* a90+ 62
3 b g Desert Sun—Sea Of Time (USA) (Gilded Time (USA))
1291[10] 2065[10] *(2795) 3017[2](3935) (5022)*

Desert Secrets (IRE) *J G Portman* a47 52
4 b m Almutawakel—Shaping Up (USA) (Storm Bird (CAN))
521[11]

Desert Soul *M Johnston* 61
2 b c Fantastic Light(USA) —Jalousie (IRE) (Barathea (IRE))
2545[4] 5067[6] 5381[9]

Desert Storm (DEN) *Rae Guest* 76
4 br g Desert Prince(IRE) —Boss Lady (IRE) (Last Tycoon)
5057[2] (5324) 5564[10] (6178)

Desert War (AUS) *Mrs Gai Waterhouse* 121
5 br g Desert King(IRE) —High Heels (AUS) (Canny Lad (AUS))
(6347a)

Desirable Dancer (IRE) *R A Harris* a40 48
2 b f Fath(USA) —Tender Time (Tender King)
5052[9] 5570[7] *5686[8]6401[6] 6471[6]6640[10] 6859[10]*

Desperate Dan *J A Osborne* a94 96
5 b g Danzero(AUS) —Alzianah (Alzao (USA))
79[3] 198[3](244) 275[6]450[7] 1803[11] 2173[14]2635[3]
3027[10] 3449[3] 3956[11] 4180[6]

Desperation (IRE) *B D Leavy* a81 71
4 b g Desert Style(IRE) —Mauras Pride (IRE) (Cadeaux Genereux)
*(48) 113[5] 250[2]361[2] 454[2](535) 628[6]*2522[14]
3098[8] 3388[8]

Destinate (IRE) *I Jory* 100
4 b g Desert Style(IRE) —Double Eight (IRE) (Common Grounds)
153a[11]

Detente *J R Fanshawe* 70
3 b f Medicean—Truce (Nashwan (USA))
2304[8] 4945[4] 5319[4] 6202[8]

Detonate *Ms J S Doyle* a54 63
4 b g Mind Games—Bron Hilda (IRE) (Namaqualand (USA))
*580[6] 806[10]858[6] 1243[5]*1315[9] 1618[4] *1913[10]*2182[3]
2396[9] 2949[5] *3155[7]*3447[7] 3825[5] 4306[14] 4846[2]
6856[3]6983[4]

Detroit City (USA) *P J Hobbs* a77 105
4 rg g Kingmambo(USA) —Seattle Victory (USA) (Seattle Song (USA))
(5963)
Deutschland (USA) *M A Jarvis* a69 83
3 b g Red Ransom(USA) —Rhine Valley (USA) (Danzig (USA))
804^{3} 909^{2}1740^{3} (1946)
Developer (IRE) *G F Bridgwater* a49 49
3 b g Danehill Dancer(IRE) —Via Camp (Kris)
66^{3} 1283^{2}66^{3} 2985^{4}64^{7} 4927^{14} 5291^{8}5781^{11} 6276^{8}6308^{8} 6550^{12}
Deveron (USA) *Saeed Bin Suroor* a80 105
3 bb f Cozzene(USA) —Cruisie (USA) (Assert)
436a^{5} 1472^{6}
Devilfishpoker Com *R C Guest* a31 45
2 ch g Dr Fong(USA) —Midnight Allure (Aragon)
1342^{14} 1790^{7} 2191^{8} 2806^{7} 3286^{10}3780^{4} 4509^{12} 4955^{4} 6951^{8}
Devil's Bite *M C Chapman*
5 ch g Dracula(AUS) —Niggle (Night Shift (USA))
6277^{13}
Devil's Island *Sir Mark Prescott* a69 63
4 b g Green Desert(USA) —Scandalette (Niniski (USA))
15^{11} (163) 236^{9}324^{2} 405^{4}1265^{4} 1644^{4}
Devine Dancer *H Candy* a58 82
3 ch f Woodborough(USA) —Princess Londis (Interrex (CAN))
(801) 1137^{9} (1751) 2329^{12} 2866^{5} 3449^{8}4102^{6} 4226^{3} 4922^{7} 5181^{2}
Devon Flame *R J Hodges* 88
7 b g Whittingham(IRE) —Uaeflame (IRE) (Polish Precedent (USA))
947^{3} 1545^{9} 2189^{2} (2635) 3251^{4} 3471^{15}4223^{6}
Devonia Plains (IRE) *Mrs P N Dutfield* a64 62
4 ch g Danehill Dancer(IRE) —Marlfield Lake (Cadeaux Genereux)
1827^{9} 2118^{12} 2507^{5} 3013^{7}3996^{3}
Devon Ruby *C L Popham* a51 41
3 ch f Zilzal(USA) —Last Result (Northern Park (USA))
1259^{11} 1576^{13}1731^{4} 2187^{5} 2484^{11} 3338^{7} 6134^{11}
Dexileos (IRE) *David Pinder* a56 77
7 b g Danehill(USA) —Theano (IRE) (Thatching)
121^{7} 1485^{2}260^{6} 312^{2}399^{2} 467^{5}616^{3} 649^{6}793^{2} 875^{4}1225^{2} 1462^{5}(1727) 2319^{4}2978^{8} 3933^{6} 4670^{15}6708^{10} 6802^{3}
Dextrous *P T Midgley* a49 77
9 gr g Machiavellian(USA) —Heavenly Cause (USA) (Grey Dawn II)
25^{5} 302^{3}390^{7} 490^{4}525^{5} (615) (788) 871^{6}
Dhanyata (IRE) *B J Meehan* a104 110
2 b f Danetime(IRE) —Preponderance (IRE) (Cyrano De Bergerac)
2166^{10} (2456) 3372^{2} 4736^{5} (5017) 5654^{2}5966^{6}
Dhaular Dhar (IRE) *J S Goldie* a94 99
4 b h Indian Ridge—Pescara (IRE) (Common Grounds)
632^{6} 726^{18} 1143^{5}2194^{2} (2520) 3077^{12} 3482^{5} 3926^{13} 4760^{4}4790^{3} 5357^{8} 5529^{2} (5749) 5812^{6} (5957) 6243^{9}
Dhehdaah *Mrs P Sly* 71
5 b g Alhaarth(IRE) —Carina Clare (Slip Anchor)
990^{2} 1758^{2} 2357^{2}
Dhekraa (IRE) *M A Jarvis* 98
3 b f Fasliyev(USA) —White Heat (Last Tycoon)
1377^{2} 2438^{4} 3520^{6} 3970^{8}
Dhurwah (IRE) *T Keddy* a43 42
3 b f Green Desert(USA) —Bintalbawadi (IRE) (Diesis)
4045^{8} 4948^{5} 5729^{9}
Diable *H Hesse* 101
7 b h Big Shuffle(USA) —Diasprina (GER) (Aspros (GER))
1973a^{8} 3755a^{4} 6093a^{9}
Diabolical (USA) *Steven B Klesaris* a116 91
3 ch c Artax(USA) —Bonnie Byerly (USA) (Dayjur (USA))
1861a^{8}
Dia De La Novia (JPN) *Katsuhiko Sumii* 113
4 b m Sunday Silence(USA) —Potrizaris (ARG) (Potrillazo (ARG))
6785a^{7}
Diafa (USA) *J G M O'Shea* a42 63
4 b m Swain(IRE) —I'm Unapproachable (USA) (Distinctive Pro (USA))
314^{7} 584^{8}647^{7} 882^{12} 5054^{9}5435^{7} 6133^{5} 6551^{10}6620^{9}
Diamondbanker *Jedd O'Keeffe*
3 b c Banker Mason(USA) —Diamante Vii (Damsire Unregistered)
2244^{12} 2895^{10}
Diamond Dan (IRE) *P D Evans* a61 60
4 b g Foxhound(USA) —Kawther (Tap On Wood)
42^{3} 311^{7}684^{8} (771) 1201^{5} 1461^{6}1910^{8} (2262) 2636^{5} 2966^{11}3933^{3} 4276^{2} 4446^{2} 4565^{6} (4974)
Diamond De Triano (USA) *P W Chapple-Hyam* a60+ 82
3 bb f Forest Wildcat(USA) —Hot Princess (Hot Spark)
1551^{7} (1851) (2283) 2823^{6} 3793^{2}4075^{9} 4605^{12}
Diamond Diggins (GER) *V Smith* a62 76
4 ch h Kendor(FR) —Diana Dancer (FR) (Fabulous Dancer (USA))
1051^{10} 1306^{5} 1544^{12}
Diamond Diva *J W Hills* a74+ 81
2 br f Dansili—Vivianna (Indian Ridge)
5344^{5} 5503^{3} (6031)
Diamond Dust (JPN) *H Takaoka* 107
5 b g Lively One(USA) —Shinko Grace (JPN) (Sakura Yutaka O (JPN))
1716a^{5}
Diamond Fire (IRE) *A Wohler* 49
2 b c King Charlemagne(USA) —Diamond Sun (Primo Dominie)
2670a^{8}
Diamond Green (FR) *R J Frankel* 121
5 br h Green Desert(USA) —Diamonaka (FR) (Akarad (FR))
5416a^{8}

Diamond Heritage *S Parr* a15 53
4 ch g Compton Place—Eccolina (Formidable (USA))
1127^{7} 1764^{12} 2137^{14}2358^{8} 2504^{5} 2875^{4} 3112^{7} 3398^{7}3762^{9} 3931^{7} 4113^{11} 5363^{13} 5840^{10}
Diamond Hurricane (IRE) *P D Evans* a65 74
2 b g Mujadil(USA) —Christoph's Girl (Efisio)
1121^{3} (1559) 1824^{5} (4284) 4969^{4}5447^{9}
Diamond Jake (AUS) *B Mayfield-Smith* 99
7 b h Danewin(AUS) —Fine Gem (NZ) (Pevero)
6391a^{5}
Diamond Josh *M Mullineaux* a66 61
4 ch g Primo Dominie—Exit (Exbourne (USA))
67^{2} 137^{8}225^{2} 502^{7}732^{5} 2288^{5} (2632) (2758) 3033 4372^{8}3 4141^{5} 5032^{9}5453^{12} 5970^{3} 6142^{4}6348^{9} 6755^{8}6990^{11}
Diamond Katie (IRE) *N Tinkler* a51 59
4 b m Night Shift(USA) —Fayrooz (USA) (Gulch (USA))
1102^{15} 1297^{17} 1496^{6} 2505^{10} 2856^{6}3297^{9} 3855^{6} 4157^{12} 4507^{2} 4655^{3}5131^{8} 5486^{7} 5569^{3} 6142^{8}
Diamond Light (USA) *M Botti* a41 67
2 ch f Fantastic Light(USA) —Queen Of Women (USA) (Sharpen Up)
2442^{3} 2957^{6} 3537^{4} 3902^{2} 4480^{4}5094^{3} 5382^{12} 6064^{2} 6886^{10}
Diamond Necklace (USA) *A P O'Brien* 95
2 gr f Unbridled's Song(USA) —Helsinki (Machiavellian (USA))
4853a^{10}
Diamonds And Dust *N P Littmoden* a91 91
4 b g Mister Baileys—Dusty Shoes (Shareef Dancer (USA))
1129^{19} 1585^{13} 2232^{3} 2614^{3} (2787) 3218^{5}3973^{12} 5301^{12} 6898^{13}
Diamond Shower (USA) *E A L Dunlop* 79
3 b c Swain(IRE) —Quality Gift (Last Tycoon)
2712^{12} 3029^{2} (3676)
Diamond Tycoon (USA) *B J Meehan* 78
2 b c Johannesburg(USA) —Palacoona (FR) (Last Tycoon)
5939^{2}
Diamond Winnie *Mrs N S Evans* 50
3 b f Komaite(USA) —Winsome Wooster (Primo Dominie)
1126^{3} 1594^{5} 2077^{7} 3472^{12}
Diamond World *C A Horgan* a42 60
3 b f Agnes World(USA) —In A Twinkling (IRE) (Brief Truce (USA))
1513^{3} 1937^{12} 2987^{11}5055^{10}
Dianella (IRE) *David P Myerscough* 86
2 b f Gold Away(IRE) —Dictatrice (FR) (Anabaa (USA))
5408a^{6}
Diane's Choice *J Akehurst* a91 91
3 ch f Komaite(USA) —Ramajana (USA) (Shadeed (USA))
233^{2} 341^{6}(540) 851^{5}(4398) (4922) 5420^{2} 6292^{3}
Diarius (GER) *H Blume* 67
3 b g Ungaro(GER) —Diavolessa (GER) (Subotica (FR))
1872a^{14} 2671a^{10} 3776a^{15}
Dichoh *M A Jarvis* a79+ 16
3 b g Diktat—Hoh Dancer (Indian Ridge)
6052^{10} (6403) 6573^{2} (6781)
Dickens (GER) *H Blume* 112
3 b c Kallisto(GER) —Desidera (IRE) (Shaadi (USA))
3776a^{2} 5051a^{5} 6004a^{6}
Dickensian (IRE) *Saeed Bin Suroor* 102
3 br c Xaar—Cappella (IRE) (College Chapel)
5116^{2} 5813^{6}
Dickie Deano *J M Bradley* a35
2 b g Sooty Tern—Chez Bonito (IRE) (Persian Bold)
6826^{9}
Dickie Le Davoir *K R Burke* 87
2 b g Kyllachy—Downeaster Alexa (USA) (Red Ryder (USA))
1664^{5} (1982) 2127^{4} 2960^{9} 3903^{2} 4146^{10}4789^{4} 4890P 5788^{3}
Dickie's Dream (IRE) *P J McBride* a70 73
3 b c Xaar—Swallowtailed Kite (USA) (Silver Hawk (USA))
5344 735^{2}1077^{3} 5109^{4} 5644^{8}5846^{4} 5971^{5}
Dictation *Mrs Valerie Keatley* a43 68
4 bb m Diktat—Monaiya (Shareef Dancer (USA))
6431^{5} 6756^{9}
Dictator (IRE) *D R Gandolfo* a70 71
5 ch g Machiavellian(USA) —Obsessed (Storm Bird (CAN))
314^{3} 599^{4}
Dictatrix *J M P Eustace* 91
3 gr f Diktat—Apennina (USA) (Gulch (USA))
1130^{6} 1863^{6} 3316^{9} 5143^{9} 5722^{8}
Diction (IRE) *K R Burke* a54 19
4 br m Diktat—Waft (USA) (Topsider (USA))
100^{9} 247^{7}493^{6} 606^{2}618^{4} (648)
Didactic *A J McCabe* a37 48
2 b g Diktat—Scene (IRE) (Scenic)
5111^{7} 5389^{9}
Didifon *Mrs L J Young* 30
11 b g Zafonic(USA) —Didicoy (USA) (Danzig (USA))
2902^{12} 2966^{12} 3305^{11}
Didnt Tell My Wife *P S McEntee* a47 59
7 ch g Aragon—Bee Dee Dancer (Ballacashtal (CAN))
582^{13} 697^{8}1724^{11} 2132^{8} 6232^{12}6549^{U} 6787^{9}6829^{4}
Didn't We (IRE) *T G Mills* a89 94
3 b c Mujadil(USA) —Non Dimenticar Me (IRE) (Don't Forget Me)
70^{4} (138) 269^{2}475^{2} 702^{2}1091^{11} (1672) 2014^{8} (2496) 3795^{4} 4180^{2} 4345^{2}5667^{7} 5832^{7}
Didoe *P W Hiatt* a30 52
7 br m Son Pardo—My Diamond Ring (Sparkling Boy)
1353^{15} 1769^{8} 2262^{12} 2966^{3} 3339^{8}3615^{4} 3862^{4} 4279^{6} 4627^{4} 5259^{8}

Diego Cao (IRE) *Mrs N Smith* a65 89
5 b g Cape Cross(IRE) —Lady Moranbon (USA) (Trempolino (USA))
1239^{6} 1933^{5} 5804^{9}
Dig Deep (IRE) *W J Haggas* a92+ 81
4 b g Entrepreneur—Diamond Quest (Rainbow Quest (USA))
1760^{10} 6654^{11} (6733) 6830^{9}
Digger Boy *M A Jarvis* a69 64
3 b g King's Best(USA) —Chameleon (Green Desert (USA))
658^{7} 802^{2}1641^{11} 2244^{2} 3100^{3}3388^{4} 4044^{9}4491^{2} 5388^{12}
Diggs Lane (IRE) *N A Callaghan* a53 52
2 b g Galileo(IRE) —Desert Bluebell (Kalaglow)
3623^{7} 3976^{11} 4333^{13} 5262^{4}6007^{10} 6385^{10}
Digital *M R Channon* a74 83
9 ch g Safawan—Heavenly Goddess (Soviet Star (USA))
719^{3} 949^{5} 1041^{9} 1474^{7} (1878) 2074^{12}4629^{5} 4885^{7} 5117^{7} 5593^{3} 5782^{6}6048^{2} 6326^{7}
Dijeerr (USA) *M A Jarvis* 106
2 b c Danzig(USA) —Sharp Minister (CAN) (Deputy Minister (CAN))
3923^{2} (5089) 5653^{2} (6102)
Dik Dik *C N Allen* a23 63
3 b g Diktat—Totom (Mtoto)
2028^{12} 3303^{2} 4247^{11}5015^{2} 5574^{12} 5944^{7} 6482^{7}
Diktalex (IRE) *C J Teague* a66 58
3 b f Diktat—Kingdom Royale (IRE) (Royal Academy (USA))
(189) 248^{2} 335^{2}439^{9} 488^{2}598^{5} 646^{8}(861) 907^{2}1003^{2} 1109^{7}2138^{4}
Diktatit *R C Guest* 49
4 b m Diktat—Mystique Smile (Music Boy)
1885^{9} 4355^{8} 4518^{11}
Diktatorial *G A Butler* a87 91
4 br g Diktat—Reason To Dance (Damister (USA))
516^{8} 1111^{14}2819^{6} 3214^{6} 3733^{11} 4029^{7} 4131^{2}4508^{5} 4626^{4} 6097^{7}
Diktatorship (IRE) *Ernst Oertel* a43 59
3 b g Diktat—Polka Dancer (Dancing Brave (USA))
1089^{7} 1640^{8} 1937^{11}2316^{16} 4497^{3} 4847^{2} 5173^{5} 5574^{13}6374^{8} 6627^{U}6700^{10}
Dil *Mrs N Macauley* a19 19
11 b g Primo Dominie—Swellegant (Midyan (USA))
304^{14}
Dilek (FR) *A De Royer-Dupre* 114
3 bl c Sendawar(IRE) —Diyawara (IRE) (Doyoun)
(2942a) 3342a^{3}
Dilshaan's Prize (IRE) *R Pritchard-Gordon* 91
2 b c Dilshaan—Dancing Prize (IRE) (Sadler's Wells (USA))
6456a^{11}
Dilwin (IRE) *D Nicholls* 70
2 b g Dilshaan—Welsh Harp (Mtoto)
4228^{3} 5289^{6}
Diman (IRE) *D K Weld* 67+
3 b g Namid—Bayalika (IRE) (Selkirk (USA))
4034a^{2}
Dimashq *Ronald Thompson* 49
4 b m Mtoto—Agwaas (IRE) (Rainbow Quest (USA))
1590^{7} 2362^{8} 4227^{2} (4506) 4914^{11} 5750^{12}6423^{8}
Dimboola *B W Hills* 86
2 b g Averti(IRE) —Mindomica (Dominion)
892^{2} 1090^{2} 1595^{3} (2321) 2724^{10} 3064^{2}3837^{2}
Dimelight *D R C Elsworth* a69 75
3 b f Fantastic Light(USA) —Dime Bag (High Line)
1797^{4} 2113^{2} 2434P 2533^{2} 2990^{11}3865^{4} 4470^{7} 5446^{7}
Dimenticata (IRE) *Kevin Prendergast* 103
2 b f Danetime(IRE) —Non Dimenticar Me (IRE) (Don't Forget Me)
3963a^{2} 4853a^{6} 5394a^{4}
Diminuto *M D I Usher* a62 57
2 b f Iron Mask(USA) —Thicket (Wolfhound (USA))
760^{3} 856^{3}908^{2} 1107^{5}1379^{5} 2346^{5}2709^{3} 3117^{11} 3345^{6} 3801^{3} (4222) 4699^{7}4971^{4} 5290^{4} 5448^{3}6422^{3} (6715) (6813) 6939^{4}
Dingaan (IRE) *A M Balding* a94 86
3 b g Tagula(IRE) —Boughtbyphone (Warning)
(60) (190) 665^{9} (1404) 1924^{6}2204^{5} 2774^{16} 5116^{5} 5501^{12}
Dinner Dance *W J Haggas* a37
3 b f Groom Dancer(USA) —Misleading Lady (Warning)
409^{6} 5547^{6}42^{6}
Dinner Date *T Keddy* a67 62
4 ch g Groom Dancer(USA) —Misleading Lady (Warning)
1058^{2} (1334) 2982^{3} 3706^{8}3934^{10} 4702^{11}5691^{12} 6435^{5}6565^{8} 6918^{8}
Dionisia (USA) *L M Cumani* 115
3 br f Tejano Run(USA) —Essie's Maid (USA) (Linkage (USA))
1713a^{6} (2043a) (2694a) 5713a^{6}
Dipped Wings (IRE) *J L Dunlop* 54+
3 b f In The Wings—Fantasy Wood (IRE) (Charnwood Forest (IRE))
1070^{12} 1516^{5} 1826^{5} 5587^{13}
Directa (GER) *Andreas Lowe* 99
3 b f Acatenango(GER) —Directa Germania (IRE) (Priolo (USA))
1328a^{4} 2279a^{7} 4383a^{4}
Direct Debit (IRE) *M L W Bell* a87 92
3 b g Dansili—Dimple (Fairy King (USA))
(112) 592^{2} 1268^{3} 1440^{2}2774^{25}
Disco Ball *G Wragg* 77
3 ch f Fantastic Light(USA) —Danceabout (Shareef Dancer (USA))
1680^{7} 2048^{5} 2458^{2} 3226^{14} 5756^{17}
Disco Dan *D M Simcock* a64+ 80
2 b g Danehill Dancer(IRE) —Ghay (USA) (Bahri (USA))
2218^{7} 2572^{6} (2950) 3902^{3}4100^{6} (5447) 5940^{5}
Disco Lights *D J Daly* a67 70
3 b f Spectrum(IRE) —Discomatic (USA) (Roberto (USA))
61^{4} 863^{3} 1193^{7}

Discomania *K F Clutterbuck* a46 50
4 b g Pursuit Of Love—Discomatic (USA) (Roberto (USA))
309^{9} 573^{6}689^{9} 938^{5}6616^{7} 6729^{7}6971^{8}
Disco Queen (IRE) *P C Haslam* a39 65
2 ch f Night Shift(USA) —Fashion (Bin Ajwaad (IRE))
1096^{7} 3246^{4} 3457^{8}(5084) 5323^{2}
Discord *T H Caldwell* a60 57
5 b g Desert King(IRE) —Lead Note (USA) (Nijinsky (CAN))
162^{6} 2894^{4}403^{3} 503^{6}652^{7} 1988^{3}
Discotheque (USA) *P Howling* a65 66
3 ch f Not For Love(USA) —Disco Darlin' (USA) (Citidancer (USA))
835^{3} 1109^{3}2445^{2} 3397^{9} 3538^{4} 4142^{2} 4494^{5}4927^{9} 5302^{6} 5370^{5} 6193^{8}6442^{4} (6608) 6810^{2} 6934^{8}6980^{3}
Discreet Cat (USA) *Saeed Bin Suroor* a131+
3 b c Forestry(USA) —Pretty Discreet (USA) (Private Account (USA))
(620a) (739a) (4787a) (5719a) (6611a)
Disguise *J J Quinn* a65 64
4 b g Pursuit Of Love—Nullarbor (Green Desert (USA))
47^{6} 2396^{10} 3245^{5}3617^{16}
Dishdasha (IRE) *C R Dore* a48
4 b g Desert Prince(IRE) —Counterplot (IRE) (Last Tycoon)
525^{11} 636^{10}682^{3} 891^{8}1395^{5} 1536^{6}
Disintegration (IRE) *A King* 64
2 b g Barathea(IRE) —Leave Me Alone (IRE) (Nashwan (USA))
4525^{12} 5475^{6} 5886^{5}
Diskretion (GER) *W Hickst* 82
3 ch f Acatenango(GER) —Daisy Dance (FR) (Alzao (USA))
5709a^{6}
Dispol Charm (IRE) *D W Chapman* a8 38
4 br m Charnwood Forest(IRE) —Phoenix Venture (IRE) (Thatching)
144^{13}
Dispol Foxtrot *D Nicholls* a56 70
8 ch m Alhijaz—Foxtrot Pie (Shernazar)
5362^{4} 5619^{6} 5863^{9} 6387^{12}
Dispol Isle (IRE) *T D Barron* a65 73
4 gr m Trans Island—Pictina (Petong)
(133) 332^{3} 429^{4}818^{5} (1041) 1531^{9} (1885) 2400^{4} 2737^{9} 3089^{10}4070^{5} 4518^{7} 4729^{11} 5483^{4} 5619^{12}5865^{3} 6054^{2}
Dispol Katie *T D Barron* 81
5 ch m Komaite(USA) —Twilight Time (Aragon)
1035^{5} 1456^{10} 1734^{6} 1865^{2} 2147^{5}2454^{8} 2681^{7} 2851^{2} 2977^{6} 3287^{9}3913^{7} 4230^{10} 4655^{4} 4831^{11} 5313^{7}5635^{3} 5756^{16} 6060^{8}
Dispol Lady *P T Midgley* 44
3 b f Foxhound(USA) —River Of Fortune (IRE) (Lahib (USA))
870^{9}
Dispol Moonlight (IRE) *T D Barron* 17
2 b g Night Shift(USA) —Kiristina (FR) (Royal Academy (USA))
2076^{10} 2626^{8} 2870^{8} 3831^{7} 4115^{13}
Dispol Peto *R Johnson* a62 57
6 gr g Petong—Plie (Superlative)
1341^{10} 1504^{5} 1795^{7} (2137) 3263^{5}4476^{10} 5064^{7} 6317^{5} 6526^{5}6623^{7} 6798^{6}
Dispol Splendid (IRE) *P T Midgley* 39
2 ch f Raise A Grand(IRE) —Somers Heath (IRE) (Definite Article)
2695^{4} 3174^{2} 3878^{9} 4887^{8} 5481^{7}5614^{13}
Dispol Truly (IRE) *A G Newcombe* a27 51
2 b f Bold Fact(USA) —Beautyofthepeace (IRE) (Exactly Sharp (USA))
2015^{6} 2294^{4} 2731^{2} 3174^{4} 6278^{6}
Dispol Valentine *P T Midgley* a9 38
3 b f Whittingham(IRE) —Bint Baddi (FR) (Shareef Dancer (USA))
10^{13} 347^{9}1443^{6} 2192^{6} 2699^{12} 2758^{9} 3538^{10}4050^{11}
Dispol Veleta *Miss T Spearing* a45 70
5 b m Makbul—Foxtrot Pie (Shernazar)
412^{4} 678^{4}1045^{7} 1249^{5} (1500) 1761^{6} 1864^{7} 2747^{3}3168^{8} 5734^{8} 5889^{5} 6289^{11}
Dissitation (IRE) *M Halford* a58 78
3 b f Spectrum(IRE) —Park Charger (Tirol)
6450^{4}
Distant Country (USA) *B D Leavy* a68 63
7 b g Distant View(USA) —Memsahb (USA) (Restless Native)
56^{6} 121^{4}(210) 410^{8}458^{10} 568^{3}(581) 639^{3}662^{6} 734^{3}(953) 1001^{3}1148^{8} 1665^{8} 2211^{9}
Distant Cousin *M A Buckley* a64 64
9 b g Distant Relative—Tinaca (USA) (Manila (USA))
1163^{7} 1385^{5}
Distant Drums (IRE) *B W Hills* a65 56
3 ch f Distant Music(USA) —No Hard Feelings (IRE) (Alzao (USA))
2575^{3} 3931^{4} (4277) 4930^{11}5418^{8}
Distant Flash *G L Moore* 54
2 b f Mujahid(USA) —Fly In Style (Hernando (FR))
3822^{5} (4007) 5419^{11} 6016^{9}
Distant Mind (IRE) *Mrs C A Dunnett*
3 b f Distant Music(USA) —Mind Song (Barathea (IRE))
796^{11} 1101^{10} 1576^{12}5432^{16} 5741^{11}
Distant Prospect (IRE) *A M Balding* 94
9 b g Namaqualand(USA) —Ukraine's Affair (USA) (The Minstrel (CAN))
2723^{12} 4036^{14} 5351^{6}
Distant Stars (IRE) *E S McMahon* 69
2 ch f Distant Music(USA) —Thirlmere (Cadeaux Genereux)
4053^{5} 4657^{6} 5507^{4}
Distant Sun (USA) *R Charlton* a65
2 b g Distant View(USA) —The Great Flora (USA) (Unaccounted For (USA))
6581^{3}

Distant Sunset (IRE) *B W Hills* a47 55
2 b g Distant Music(USA) —Blushing Libra (Perugino (USA))
3591[11] *3844[11]* 4163[8]5482[6]

Distant Times *T D Easterby* 81
5 b g Orpen(USA) —Simply Times (USA) (Dodge (USA))
898[7] 1285[12] 1795[2] 2074[8] 2384[8]2661[12] 3287[6]

Distant Vision (IRE) *A Berry* a23 36
3 br f Distant Music(USA) —Najeyba (Indian Ridge)
3039[3] 3219[6] 4255[10] 5244[8] *6306[11]6490[5]*

Distant Way (USA) *L Brogi* 119
5 b h Distant View(USA) —Grey Way (USA) (Cozzene (USA))
(1712a) 5982a[4] 6365a[3]

Distiller (IRE) *W R Muir* 70
2 b g Invincible Spirit(IRE) —Bobbydazzle (Rock Hopper)
4161[10] 4873[5] 5091[5] 5381[6] 5431[3]5647[4]

Distinction (IRE) *Sir Michael Stoute* 122
7 b g Danehill(USA) —Ivy Leaf (IRE) (Nureyev (USA))
(1839) 2773[3]

Distinctive Look (IRE) *B J Meehan* a82 84
3 b f Danehill(USA) —Magnificient Style (USA) (Silver Hawk (USA))
1118[2] 1423[6] *2446[2]*(2815) 3891[6]

Distinctly Game *K A Ryan* a75 94
4 b g Mind Games—Distinctly Blu (IRE) (Distinctly North (USA))
2450[16] 2847[28] *6496[11]*

Distinctly Jim (IRE) *B Smart* 51
3 ch g City On A Hill(USA) —Bucaramanga (IRE) (Distinctly North (USA))
1593[10] 2282[3] 2782[7] 2923[9] 3288[10]3604[4]

Distinctlythebest *F Watson* 18
6 b g Distinctly North(USA) —Euphyllia (Superpower)
5241[7]

Ditton Dancer *J J Quinn* 63
3 ch f Danehill Dancer(IRE) —Dubai Lady (Kris)
2518[13] 3569[10]

Dium Mac *N Bycroft* 87
5 b g Presidium—Efipetite (Efisio)
1123[4] (1591) (2108) 2540[6] 2975[6] 4570[2] 5685[3](5904) (6008)

Divalini *J Akehurst* a44 49
2 ch f Bertolini(USA) —Divine Grace (IRE) (Definite Article)
5147[9] *5648[9]* 6014[10]

Diverse Forecast (IRE) *Mrs P Sly* 31
2 b g Fasliyev(USA) —Motley (Rainbow Quest (USA))
3083[11] 4103[14] 4630[9]

Divert (IRE) *Edward Lynam* 85
2 b f Averti(IRE) —Dawn Chorus (IRE) (Mukaddamah (USA))
4747a[6]

Divine Design (IRE) *Joseph G Murphy* 78
2 b f Barathea(IRE) —Tortue (IRE) (Turtle Island (IRE))
6357a[9]

Divine Gift *K A Ryan* a100 102
5 b g Groom Dancer(USA) —Child's Play (USA) (Sharpen Up)
*629[2] 1017[13]*1239[3] (1585) 2742[24] 3552[11] 3929[6]

Divine Love (IRE) *E J O'Neill* a68 46
2 b f Barathea(IRE) —Darling (Darshaan)
4866[8] *5608[5] 6073[2]*

Divine Night (IRE) *David Wachman* 81
2 b f Danehill(USA) —Starlight Night (USA) (Distant View (USA))
5850a[6]

Divine Right *B J Meehan* 87
2 ch f Observatory(USA) —Grail (USA) (Quest For Fame)
(2604) 3415[7]

Divine River *A P Jarvis* a75 81
3 b f Lujain(USA) —Berliese (IRE) (High Estate)
(1118) 2961[6] *3489[6]* 3928[19]4838[8] *5109[3]* 5346[6]5644[6]

Divine Spirit *M Dods* a78 78
5 b g Foxhound(USA) —Vocation (IRE) (Royal Academy (USA))
1125[11] 1528[4] (2194) 2618[4] 2852[3] 3041[8]3622[9] 4019[2] 4230[8] 4258[7] 4486[6]4834[15] 5081[6] 5309[8] 5577[5]

Divine Story (FR) *R Pritchard-Gordon* a77 115?
5 ch m Vettori(IRE) —Divine Etoile (USA) (Sanglamore (USA))
5219a[4]

Divine White *Mrs A J Perrett* a57 57
3 ch f College Chapel—Snowy Mantle (Siberian Express (USA))
1110[9] 1431[7] 2190[5]2511[3] 2704[4] 3267[11] 3897[2] *4329[6]*

Divisive *G Wragg* a52 56
3 b f Alhaarth(IRE) —Hakkaniyah (Machiavellian (USA))
*406[8] 538[9]*4489[5] 5724[9] 6059[6]

Divo Nero (IRE) *L M Cumani* a45+ 59+
3 br c Black Minnaloushe(USA) —Backgammon Becky (USA) (Irish River (FR))
1960[5] 2587[12] 3931[5]

Dixie Belle *M G Quinlan* 111
3 br f Diktat—Inspiring (IRE) (Anabaa (USA))
2438[9] 2651[2] 3332[5] 4461[6] 5087[2](5375)

Dixieland Boy (IRE) *P J Makin* a71 71
3 b g Inchinor—Savannah Belle (Green Desert (USA))
3488[5] 4004[4] 4527[4]5621[2] *6406[2] 6593[7]6919[2]*

Dixie Meister (USA) *J Canani* a108
4 b g Holzmeister(USA) —Dixity Do Dah (USA) (Dixieland Band (USA))
6611a[4]

Dixie Storm (USA) *A M Balding* a71 74
3 b c Dixieland Band(USA) —Sweetheart (USA) (Mr Prospector (USA))
1087[5] *2343[6]* 5761[7]

Dixigold (FR) *Frau C Bocskai* 95
5 ch g Gold Away(IRE) —Dixiella (FR) (Fabulous Dancer (USA))
(306a)

Diysem (USA) *B J Meehan* a68 86
2 b c Johannesburg(USA) —Technicolour (IRE) (Rainbow Quest (USA))
4600[2] (5043) 5343[5] *5665[4]*

Dizelle (AUS) *J Hawkes* 117
5 b m Zabeel(NZ) —Danelagh (AUS) (Danehill (USA))
6110a[8] 6392a[17]

Dizzy Dreamer (IRE) *P W Chapple-Hyam* 104
3 b f Spinning World(USA) —Divine Prospect (IRE) (Namaqualand (USA))
1068[8] 3709[6] (4707) 5171[6] 6547a[6]

Dizzy Future *M R Bosley* a60 57
4 b g Fraam—Kara Sea (USA) (River Special (USA))
733[12] 6621[5]6790[11]

Dizzy In The Head *I Semple* a67d 81
7 b g Mind Games—Giddy (Polar Falcon (USA))
1504[4] (1611) 2237[10] (2380) 2550[3] 2830[6] (3170)3482[9] 3584[7] 5333[12] 5749[9]

Django (SWE) *Caroline Stromberg* a88
3 b g Acatenango(GER) —Praeriens Drottning (SWE) (Elmaamul (USA))
4420a[5]

Dockside Dancer (IRE) *P T Midgley*
2 b f Docksider(USA) —Kazimiera (IRE) (Polish Patriot (USA))
1730[9] 2106[15] 3746[5] (Dead)

Docksil *B Grizzetti* 97
2 b f Docksider(USA) —Simil (USA) (Apalachee (USA))
(2062a) 2670a[3]

Docofthebay (IRE) *J A Osborne* a73 74
2 ch c Docksider(USA) —Baize (Efisio)
4794[2] *(6303)*

Doctor Brown *B J Meehan* 113
2 b g Dr Fong(USA) —Molly Brown (Rudimentary (USA))
(4049) 4344[2] (4736) 5373[2]

Doctor Dash *D R C Elsworth* 97
3 ch g Dr Fong(USA) —Dashiba (Dashing Blade)
1268[8] 3889[12] 5165[4] 5660[7]

Doctor David *Ernst Oertel* a64
3 gr g Zilzal(USA) —Arantxa (Sharpo)
372[11] 720[6]1336[7] 3202[10]4395[3] 4930[8]

Doctor Dennis (IRE) *J Pearce* a69 68
9 b g Last Tycoon—Noble Lustre (USA) (Lyphard's Wish (FR))
*(81) 247[5] 274[2]428[7] 552[2]608[2] 654[4]862[8] 4368[11]*5302[14] 5937[13] *6470[5]6532[11] 6629[4]6798[9]*

Doctor Dino (FR) *R Gibson* 113
4 ch h Muhtathir—Logica (IRE) (Priolo (USA))
2490a[4] (5913a)

Doctor Ned *N A Callaghan* 31
2 b g Bahamian Bounty—Sangra (USA) (El Gran Senor (USA))
4801[9]

Doctor's Cave *K O Cunningham-Brown* a61 57
4 b g Night Shift(USA) —Periquitum (Dilum (USA))
*44[2] 170[5]274[4] 383[5]514[11] 587[4]*1050[6] *1243[2]* 1645[10]1878[10] *2207[5] 2792[8]3052[12] 6142[9]*

Doctor Scott *M Johnston* 92
3 b g Medicean—Milly Of The Vally (Caerleon (USA))
1268[6] 1615[4] 2659[6] 2805[6] 3292[5]3483[2] (3877) 4027[9] 4459[6] 4951[7] 5361[6]

Documento Fiscal (BRZ) *C Morgado* a76 82
4 ch h Hibernian Rhapsody(IRE) —Poli Arumba (BRZ) (Executioner (USA))
207a[10] 435a[7] *620a[7]*

Dodaa (USA) *N Wilson* a45
3 b g Dayjur(USA) —Ra'A (USA) (Diesis)
5726[10] *6403[7] 6492[7]6707[7] 6794[12](6958)*

Dodge City (USA) *J Noseda* 94
2 ch c Gone West(USA) —Djebel Amour (USA) (Mt. Livermore (USA))
3923[4] 4492[2] (5206) 5681[22]

Dolcello (IRE) *Mrs P N Dutfield*
2 b f Distant Music(USA) —Mugello (Emarati (USA))
4161[U] (Dead)

Dolce Maria (IRE) *M R Bosley* a50 52
3 bb f Trans Island—The State Of Her (IRE) (Turtle Island (IRE))
*360[7] 466[5]*2632[13]

Dollar Chick (IRE) *M Johnston* 79
2 b f Dansili—Dollar Bird (IRE) (Kris)
2943[2] (3633)

Dollars Rock (IRE) *T J O'Mara* 79
6 bb g Cois Na Tine(IRE) —Pride Rock (IRE) (Ballad Rock)
4186a[14]

Dolly *Tom Dascombe* a43 33
4 b m Thowra(FR) —Sweet Symphony (IRE) (Orchestra)
1462[9] 6026[8] *6801[6]*

Dolly Brown *T D Easterby* 51
3 ch f Bertolini(USA) —Birichino (Dilum (USA))
2249[12] 2543[14]

Dolly Coughdrop (IRE) *K R Burke* a46 74
2 b f Titus Livius(FR) —Fairy Berry (IRE) (Fairy King (USA))
1342[12] *2139[7]* 2759[4]3117[2] 3481[2] 3837[4] 4427[4] (4547) 4912[7]5404[5] 5731[4]

Dolphin Jo (AUS) *Terry & Karina O'Sullivan* 88
4 b g Dolphin Street(FR) —High Rent (AUS) (Belligerent (AUS))
6392a[15]

Domart (POL) *J R Best* 54
6 gr g Baby Bid(USA) —Dominet (POL) (Dixieland (POL))
2114[11]

Domenico (IRE) *J R Jenkins* a53 66
8 b g Sadler's Wells(USA) —Russian Ballet (USA) (Nijinsky (CAN))
1614[10] 2305[7] 3035[12] 3981[5] 4268[4]*6857[3]*

Domesday (UAE) *W G Harrison* a37 38
5 b g Cape Cross(IRE) —Deceive (Machiavellian (USA))
5403[10] 5553[10] *6606[5]*

Dominello *R A Fahey* a30 22
3 b g Primo Valentino(IRE) —Forever Nellie (Sabrehill (USA))
4611[13] 5241[9] *5873[9]*

Dominguin (PER) *D Zanelli* a94 96
4 bb h Domingo(USA) —Paladin's Silver (PER) (Silver Buck (USA))
739a[5]

Domino Dancer (IRE) *J Howard Johnson* 88
2 b g Tagula(IRE) —Hazarama (IRE) (Kahyasi)
1342[3] 1588[2] 2159[5] (2972) 4250[5] 4736[16]

Domirati *J D Bethell* a57 73
6 b g Emarati(USA) —Julia Domna (Dominion)
532[10] 1047[14] *1255[6]1388[9]*

Donaldson (GER) *P Rau* 113
4 b h Lando(GER) —Daytona Beach (GER) (Konigsstuhl (GER))
(2910a) 3579a[6] 4414a[7] 5051a[9] 6365a[6]

Don And Gerry (IRE) *P D Evans* a60 60
5 ch m Vestris Abu—She's No Tourist (IRE) (Doubletour (USA))
*503[3] 566[10]*3376[5]

Donatello (GER) *W Baltromei* 111
5 b h Auenadler(GER) —Devika (Alzao (USA))
885a[3] 1973a[2] 2313a[5] 2941a[9] 4858a[2]6093a[2] (6547a)

Donatessa (GER) *Mario Hofer* 91
3 b f Sternkoenig(IRE) —Donadea (GER) (Dashing Blade)
2279a[12]

Dona Vitoria *S Kirk* a38 67
3 b f Diktat—Salanka (IRE) (Persian Heights)
1431[3] 5937[15] *6293[14]6577[12]*

Donegal Shore (IRE) *Jennie Candlish* a48 40
7 b g Mujadil(USA) —Distant Shore (IRE) (Jareer (USA))
183[5] 258[7]390[9]

Donia Dubai (IRE) *R Bouresly* a65
3 b f Docksider(USA) —Dafrah (USA) (Danzig (USA))
202a[9] 436a[11]623a[8]

Donna Blini *B J Meehan* 110
3 ch f Bertolini(USA) —Cal Norma's Lady (IRE) (Lyphard's Special (USA))
1508[13] 2802[13] 3499[2] (3709) 4080[6] 5375[6]5642[11]

Donna Giovanna *J A Osborne* a72 68
3 b f Mozart(IRE) —Chelsea (USA) (Miswaki (USA))
110[4] (254) 364[4]5689[11] 5907[11]

Donna's Double *Karen McLintock* 58
11 ch g Weldnaas(USA) —Shadha (Shirley Heights)
(974) 1187[5] 1591[4] 1757[3] 2546[6] 3022[2](3333) 4068[4] 4570[4] 4881[3] 5581[10] 5955[8]

Donnaspear (IRE) *J Mackie* a26
3 b f Spectrum(IRE) —Lancea (IRE) (Generous (IRE))
6429[12] 6680[11]6817[7]

Donoma (IRE) *A Botti* 99
2 ch f Beat Hollow—Green Tern (ITY) (Miswaki Tern (USA))
5858a[2]

Don Pasquale *J T Stimpson* a53 50
4 br g Zafonic(USA) —Bedazzling (IRE) (Darshaan)
384[11] 537[13]909[7] 1194[12]2141[11]

Don Pele (IRE) *D Carroll* a93 96
4 b g Monashee Mountain(USA) —Big Fandango (Bigstone (IRE))
2323[5] (2683) 3038[8] 3471[8] 3904[13] 4357[9]*6292[2] 6445[6](6681) 6984[2]*

Don Pietro *D J Coakley* a79 86
3 b g Bertolini(USA) —Silver Spell (Aragon)
1641[2] (2069) 2932[7] *3918[2]*4490[3] *4933[2]* 5504[2]5833[2] *6418[5]*

Don Raphael (AUS) *B Jenkins* 106
7 b g Runyon(IRE) —Rain Queen (AUS) (Been There (AUS))
6391a[13]

Dont Call Me Derek *J J Quinn* a88 95
5 b g Sri Pekan(USA) —Cultural Role (Night Shift (USA))
5963[15]

Don'Tcallmeginger (IRE) *M H Tompkins* 64
3 ch g Fruits Of Love(USA) —Scotia Rose (Tap On Wood)
1424[7]

Don't Desert Me (IRE) *R Charlton* a67
2 b g Desert Style(IRE) —Eye View (USA) (Distant View (USA))
6523[9] 6581[6]6751[5] 6880[2]

Dont Dili Dali *J S Moore* a97 98
3 b f Dansili—Miss Meltemi (IRE) (Miswaki Tern (USA))
202a[5] 436a[6]623a[3] (827) 1093[4] 2054a[12]

Don't Mind Me *T Keddy* 50
3 b f Mutamam—Dynamic Dream (USA) (Dynaformer (USA))
2048[9] 2673[6]

Don't Panic (IRE) *P W Chapple-Hyam* 95
2 ch c Fath(USA) —Torrmana (IRE) (Ela-Mana-Mou)
4129[4] 4824a[4] (5379) 5653[8]

Don't Tell (IRE) *M L W Bell* 53
2 ch f Diesis—Alinga (IRE) (King's Theatre (IRE))
1989[9] (Dead)

Don't Tell Sue *B W Hills* a70 91
3 ch c Bold Edge—Opopmil (IRE) (Pips Pride)
967[3] 1208[16] 1679[6] (2134) (2222) 2329[16] 2639[8]2931[11]

Don't Try It On *M W Easterby*
2 b c Mujahid(USA) —Branston Berry (IRE) (Mukaddamah (USA))
1682[11] 2626[10] 2731[6] (Dead)

Donya One *John A Harris* a39 62
4 b m Cadeaux Genereux—Fadhah (Mukaddamah (USA))
331[7] 466[9]618[13] 634[3]783[10] 3311[7]

Doonigan (IRE) *A M Balding* a48 54
2 b g Val Royal(FR) —Music In My Life (IRE) (Law Society (USA))
6200[8] 6331[6] *6475[4]*

Doorock (IRE) *M Halford* 39
2 b g Redback—Prime Time Girl (Primo Dominie)
5692a[12]

Doraemon (ITY) *Graziano Verricelli*
2 ch f Dr Devious(IRE) —Diamond Change (USA) (Diamond Prospect (USA))
2565a[5]

Dora Explora *P W Chapple-Hyam* 89
2 br f Vettori(IRE) —Fredora (Inchinor)
2816[5] (3435) 3874[5] 4371[6] 5459[8]

Dora's Green *S W Hall* a40 51
3 b f Rambling Bear—Compradore (Mujtahid (USA))
*287[5] 801[5]*980[13] 1378[6] 3869[13] 4306[3] 4554[12]5167[11] *6371[7] 6533[5]*

Dorelia (IRE) *J H M Gosden* a75+ 86
3 b f Efisio—Dominio (IRE) (Dominion)
4495[3] 4799[3] *(5611)* 6328a[9]

Doric (USA) *B Ellison* 94
5 ch g Distant View(USA) —Doree (USA) (Stop The Music (USA))
1532[14] 1835[17] 2405[5] 3020[7] 3079[12]

Doric Charm *B Smart* 92
2 b f Diktat—Cinnamon Lady (Emarati (USA))
5307[2] (5632) (5764) 6201[3]

Dories Dream *Jane Southcombe* a38 36
2 b f Foxhound(USA) —Milliscent (Primo Dominie)
1113[7] *3596[5]* 5052[8]

Dorn Dancer (IRE) *D W Barker* 71
4 b m Danehill Dancer(IRE) —Appledorn (Doulab (USA))
(813) 1102[2] 1413[4] 1504[6] 1686[4] 1795[8]2020[3] 3041[3] 3478[5] 3936[8] 4119[3]4571[8] 5081[2] 5309[4] 5635[6] 5765[6]

Dorn Hill *D G Bridgwater* a47 54
4 b m Lujain(USA) —Benedicite (Lomond (USA))
1310[10] 1594[12] 2288[10] 2599[6] 4425[9]4670[5]

Dorothy's Friend *R Charlton* a87 103
6 b g Grand Lodge(USA) —Isle Of Flame (Shirley Heights)
2437[6] 3078[4] *3533[6]*4036[6] (4346) 4713[11]

Dorset Square (IRE) *John Joseph Murphy* 53
2 b g Fantastic Light(USA) —Albula (FR) (Anabaa (USA))
5662a[11]

Dotty's Daughter *Mrs A Duffield* a59 59
2 ch f Forzando—Colonel's Daughter (Colonel Collins (USA))
*1223[4] 1535[7]*1682[2] 3605[4] 3746[3] 3907[6] *4222[6]*4887[18] 4950[3] 5282[2] (5448) *(5687) 6422[7] 6491[9]*

Double Agent (FR) *J L Dunlop*
3 ch g Sinndar(IRE) —Conspiracy (Rudimentary (USA))
1135[10]

Double Banded (IRE) *J L Dunlop* a44 50
2 b g Mark Of Esteem(IRE) —Bronzewing (Beldale Flutter (USA))
5371[15] 5914[14] *6434[8]*

Double Bay (USA) *Jane Chapple-Hyam* a35 65
3 b f War Chant(USA) —Once To Often (USA) (Raise A Native)
1085[8] 2048[4] 2580[5] 3095[9] *6565[14]6848[12]*

Double Bill (USA) *P F I Cole* 52+
2 bb c Mr Greeley(USA) —Salty Perfume (USA) (Salt Lake (USA))
4716[8]

Double Carpet (IRE) *G Woodward* a48 62
3 b g Lahib(USA) —Cupid Miss (Anita's Prince)
1109[10] 4888[10] 5761[2]*6293[12] 6490[2]6721[9]*

Double Deputy (IRE) *J J Quinn* 91
5 b h Sadler's Wells(USA) —Janaat (Kris)
2169[16] 4990[7]

Double Eagle (FR) *R Gibson* 96
3 br c Anabaa(USA) —Style For Life (IRE) (Law Society (USA))
1557a[7]

Double Exposure *Jamie Poulton* a49 37
2 b c Double Trigger(IRE) —Last Night's Fun (IRE) (Law Society (USA))
6058[7] *6867[9]*

Double Galore (USA) *Myung Kwon Cho* a60
3 b c Grand Slam(USA) —Squall Linda (USA) (Summer Squall (USA))
2477a[12]

Double Helix *B P J Baugh* a21 66
7 b g Marju(IRE) —Totham (Shernazar)
769[7]

Double It (IRE) *P Wahl* a86
3 b g Docksider(USA) —Tilbrook (IRE) (Don't Forget Me)
4420a[6]

Double M *Mrs L Richards* a44 52
9 ch g First Trump—Girton Degree (Balliol)
137[7] 339[11]486[9] 514[4]886[3] 1539[7]1728[4] (1913) 2444[10] 2484[12] 2955[5] *6142[11]6513[12] 6629[7]6805[9] 6855[7]*

Double Mystery (FR) *K J Burke* a71 77
6 ch g Starborough—Chene De Coeur (FR) (Comrade In Arms)
6993[8]

Double Obsession *D Nicholls* 89
6 b g Sadler's Wells(USA) —Obsessive (USA) (Seeking The Gold (USA))
714[4] 1071[16] 1294[11] 1685[3] 1931[12]2452[3] 2723[9] 3396[4] 4469[5]

Double Oh Seven (IRE) *J W Unett* 35
3 ch c Alhaarth(IRE) —Liberi Versi (IRE) (Last Tycoon)
3453[7] 3816[5] 4297[10] *6306[13]*

Double Precedent *M Johnston* 37
2 b f Polish Precedent(USA) —Jolies Eaux (Shirley Heights)
3878[10] 4400[12] 4829[10]

Double Ransom *Mrs L Stubbs* a54 59
7 b g Bahamian Bounty—Secrets Of Honour (Belmez (USA))
394[5] 888[8](1608) 2282[7] 4692[5] 5285[11] 5838[9]

Double Spectre (IRE) *Jean-Rene Auvray* 72
4 b g Spectrum(IRE) —Phantom Ring (Magic Ring (IRE))
1821[3] 2088[5] 2956[10] 3209[3] 4005[12]4483[2] 4982[8] (5267) 5889[3]

Double Valentine *R Ingram* a57 53
3 ch f Primo Valentino(IRE) —Charlottevalentina (IRE) (Perugino (USA))
901[8] 1433[6] 2644[2]2704[6] 3118[11] 6713[2]6869[9]

Double Vodka (IRE) *C Grant* 72
5 bb g Russian Revival(USA) —Silius (Junius (USA))
3019[7]

Doubly Guest *G G Margarson* 72
2 b f Barathea Guest—Countess Guest (IRE) (Spectrum (IRE))
1896[10] 3435[3] 3868[7] 5492[3] (6007)

Doubtful Sound (USA) *T D Barron* a64
2 b c Diesis—Roam Free (USA) (Unbridled (USA))
6963[2]

Douby Douby (IRE) *P Paciello*
2 b f Namid—Doubles (Damister (USA))
2565a[3] 3428a[2]

Doughty *D J Wintle* a43 32
4 b g Bold Edge—Marquante (IRE) (Brief Truce (USA))
387[10] 616[12]791[8] 937[6]

Dove Cottage (IRE) *W S Kittow* a65 75+
4 b g Great Commotion(USA) —Pooka (Dominion)
882[2] 1244[4] (2221) (2601) 3214[7]5295[4]

Dovedale *H S Howe* a60 66
6 b m Groom Dancer(USA) —Peetsie (IRE) (Fairy King (USA))
5506[8] 5846[7] 5971[12]

Dovedon Hero *P J McBride* a76 79
6 ch g Millkom—Hot Topic (IRE) (Desse Zenny (USA))
37[5] (264) 385[6]478[5] 700[5]847[3] 1339[2]1943[5] 2628[2] 2849[9]3116[2] 3446[6] 3748[9] 4268[5] 4937[8]

Dovizioso (IRE) *P Caravati* 84
4 b g Sri Pekan(USA) —Piccola Barbara (ITY) (Scouting Miller)
1870a[9]

Dower House *Andrew Turnell* a87 75
11 ch g Groom Dancer(USA) —Rose Noble (USA) (Vaguely Noble)
65[6] 222[7]325[5] 454[10]556[8] 1380[4]1943[9] 2447[2]3401[7] 4991[6] 5599[6]5889[4] 6176[2] 6313[6]6418[8] 6741[2]6885[3]

Dowlleh *M R Channon* a78 82
2 b g Noverre(USA) —Al Persian (IRE) (Persian Bold)
1811[2] 2185[2] 2660[2] 3080[5] 3685[2]4049[2] (4669) 5334[4] 5829[5]

Downbeat *J L Dunlop* 59
2 b c Fantastic Light(USA) —Green Charter (Green Desert (USA))
2867[6] 5067[9] 5537[6] 6007[13]

Downland (IRE) *N Tinkler* a59 75
10 b g Common Grounds—Boldabsa (Persian Bold)
860[7] 1124[10] 1443[7](1746) 2141[5]2874[7] 3390[7] 3599[8]3999[12] 4425[6]

Down The Brick (IRE) *B R Millman* a58 69
2 b g Daggers Drawn(USA) —Damezao (Alzao (USA))
1107[6] 3265[3] 3844[9]4480[5] 5597[7] 5866[10]

Down The Well (IRE) *J A Osborne* a77+ 77
2 b f Mujadil(USA) —Batchelor's Button (FR) (Kenmare (FR))
1429[8] (1647) 1831[5] 2342[5]3917[4] (4043)

Down To The Woods (USA) *N Wilson* a45 45
8 ch g Woodman(USA) —Riviera Wonder (USA) (Batonnier (USA))
5553[14]

Down Town (AUS) *C H Yip* 115
4 gr g Scenic—Twain (AUS) (Kenvain (AUS))
6783a[4]

Doyles Lodge *H Candy* 69
2 b g Prince Sabo—True Bird (IRE) (In The Wings)
4000[9] 5867[4]

Dracs Back (AUS) *D Weir* 86
5 b g Dracula(AUS) —Clippings (AUS) (Snippets (AUS))
6346a[12]

Dragon Dancer *G Wragg* a66+ 121
3 b c Sadler's Wells(USA) —Alakananda (Hernando (FR))
762[3] 1120[2] 1603[2]2228[2] 3127a[4] 3778a[2] 5221a[4] 6103[6]

Dragon Flame (IRE) *M Quinn* 67
3 b c Tagula(IRE) —Noble Rocket (Reprimand)
1147[4] 1565[4] 1877[4] 2356[5] 5605[12]5949[12]

Dragon Flower (USA) *B W Hills* a64 76
2 b f Gulch(USA) —Rawabi (Sadler's Wells (USA))
4558[2] 5425[2] 5754[10]

Dragon Slayer (IRE) *Ian Williams* a78 85
4 ch g Night Shift(USA) —Arandora Star (USA) (Sagace (FR))
101[6] 167[2]250[3] 385[4]451[8] 571[2]641[3] (800) 2387[3] (3048) 3309[3]3747[7] 4112[5] 5299[8]

Dramatic Review (IRE) *J Barclay* a26 51
4 b g Indian Lodge(IRE) —Dramatic Shift (IRE) (Night Shift (USA))
2407[6] 2808[6] 6213[11]

Dramatic Touch *G Wragg* a51
2 b f Royal Applause—Sismique (Warning)
6821[4]

Dramatic Turn *Mrs A J Perrett* 82+
2 b f Pivotal—Eveningperformance (Night Shift (USA))
5894[6] (6175)

Dramaticus *B Palling* 103
4 b g Indian Ridge—Corinium (IRE) (Turtle Island (IRE))
5476[16] 5677[11] 5896[14]

Drawback (IRE) *R A Harris* a52 65
3 b g Daggers Drawn(USA) —Sacred Heart (IRE) (Catrail (USA))
(76) 1569[9] 1693[7] 2318[5] 3030[10] 5568[8]6069[8] 6260[10] 6473[9]

Drawn Gold *R Hollinshead* 58+
2 b g Daggers Drawn(USA) —Gold Belt (IRE) (Bellypha)
5790[4]

Drawn Out (IRE) *P C Haslam* a32 52
3 ch g Daggers Drawn(USA) —Fastnet (Forzando)
123[12] 193[7]329[5] 3352[10]

Drayton (IRE) *T Stack* 109
2 br c Danetime(IRE) —Exponent (USA) (Exbourne (USA))
(2037a) 3126a[2] 4409a[5] 4747a[5]

Dreadnaught (USA) *T Voss* 115
6 b g Lac Ouimet(USA) —Wings Of Dreams (USA) (Sovereign Dancer (USA))
2476a[7] 4908a[2] 5821a[6]

Dream Again *Sir Michael Stoute* a65 36
2 b f Medicean—Dance A Dream (Sadler's Wells (USA))
5352[12] 6099[5]

Dream Alive *S Curran* 64
5 b g Unfuwain(USA) —Petite Sonnerie (Persian Bold)
3797[8] 4585[8]

Dream Catch (IRE) *Lester Winters* 89
6 ch g Selkirk(USA) —Dream Pursuit (IRE) (Caerleon (USA))
3123a[11]

Dream Catcher (SWE) *R A Kvisla* a95 39
3 b c Songline(SWE) —Queen Ida (SWE) (Diligo (FR))
3224[12] 4420a[4] 4919a[5]6607[6]

Dream Champion *M R Channon* a76+ 86+
3 b c Fraam—Forest Fantasy (Rambo Dancer (CAN))
112[2] 900[2]1216[2] 1503[2] 2081[3] (2398) 2986[2] (3065) 3539[4]4612[8] (5421)

Dream Dance *H Morrison* 59+
3 ch f Diesis—Bella Ballerina (Sadler's Wells (USA))
2934[8] 3367[9]

Dream Eile (IRE) *P D Deegan* a73 37
2 bb c Mull Of Kintyre(USA) —Jayess Elle (Sabrehill (USA))
3457[3]

Dream Factor (IRE) *J O'Reilly* a51 55
3 br f Bold Fact(USA) —Bobby's Dream (Reference Point)
53[4] 120[12]211[10] 3006[16] 3306[16]

Dream Fantasy (IRE) *Sir Mark Prescott* a95+ 101
3 b g Barathea(IRE) —Night Mirage (USA) (Silver Hawk (USA))
5310[3]

Dream Forest (IRE) *M S Saunders* a67 56
3 b g Raise A Grand(IRE) —Theresa Green (IRE) (Charnwood Forest (IRE))
916[3] 1513[11] 1963[7]2583[14] 3011[4] 3854[9]4297[3] 4772[10] 5386[8]5733[9] (5922) 6641[6]6767[11] 6982[4]

Dream Impact (USA) *L Riccardi* a91 104
5 b h Royal Academy(USA) —One Fit Cat (USA) (Storm Cat (USA))
1871a[10] 4080[13]

Dream In Blue (FR) *Robert Collet* a68 106+
3 b c Munir—Kenny Glitters (FR) (Kendor (FR))
(392a) 1178a[3] 1718a[8]

Dreaming Of Anna (USA) *W Catalano* a116 115
2 ch f Rahy(USA) —Justenuffheart (USA) (Broad Brush (USA))
(5415a) (6338a)

Dream Lodge (IRE) *J G Given* a79 73
2 ch c Grand Lodge(USA) —Secret Dream (IRE) (Zafonic (USA))
5105[3] 5537[4] (5841) 6010[6]

Dream Machine (IRE) *Ron Caget* 87
5 b h Machiavellian(USA) —Truly A Dream (IRE) (Darshaan)
3580a[3]

Dream Master (IRE) *J Ryan* 35
3 b g Priolo(USA) —Pip's Dream (Glint Of Gold)
4806[8] 5598[9] 6052[9]

Dream Mountain *Ms J S Doyle* a59 61
3 b g Mozart(IRE) —Statua (IRE) (Statoblest)
3147[12] 4060[9] 5312[8] 6067[2] 6743[6]6911[4]

Dream Of Dubai (IRE) *P Mitchell* a61 60
5 b m Vettori(IRE) —Immortelle (Arazi (USA))
4455[6] 5093[3] 5450[5] 5621[8]

Dream Of Paradise (USA) *Mrs L Williamson* a48 66
3 ch f Atticus(USA) —Scrumptious (USA) (Slew O'Gold (USA))
1259[9] 1605[4] 2128[6]2518[10] 2923[4] 3244[2] 3804[6] (4173) 4847[10]5173[6] 5690[11]

Dream On Dreamers (IRE) *R C Guest* 34
2 b g Iron Mask(USA) —Harifana (FR) (Kahyasi)
5315[10] 5615[11] 6013[9] 6625[9]

Dream Passport (JPN) *H Matsuda* 126
3 b c Fuji Kiseki(JPN) —Grace Land (JPN) (Tony Bin)
6612a[2]

Dream Prize (IRE) *Sir Michael Stoute* 83
3 ch g Peintre Celebre(USA) —Night Teeny (Platini (GER))
948[6] (1296) 5152[4] 5367[9] 5792[16]

Dream Rose (IRE) *M R Channon* 79+
3 b f Anabaa(USA) —Hiddnah (USA) (Affirmed (USA))
1085[14] 1444[8] 2160[2] 2400[8] (3142) 3472[6]3793[3] 4040[12] 4879[8]

Dream Scheme *E A L Dunlop* 85
2 b f Machiavellian(USA) —Dream Ticket (USA) (Danzig (USA))
(5638) 6204[2]

Dream Shared *E A L Dunlop* a73 69
3 ch f Fantastic Light(USA) —Land Of Dreams (Cadeaux Genereux)
1955[7] 2753[4] 3451[6]4118[5] 5651[2] 6301[16]

Dreamshower (IRE) *Kerstin Helander* a38
3 b g Dushyantor(USA) —Dream Fool (IRE) (Fools Holme (USA))
4420a[13]

Dreams Jewel *C Roberts* a47 53
6 b g Dreams End—Jewel Of The Nile (Glenstal (USA))
1006[6] 2220[7]

Dream Theme *B W Hills* a80+ 106+
3 b c Distant Music(USA) —Xaymara (USA) (Sanglamore (USA))
(844) 1505[6] (4083) (4391) 4896[3] 5523[14]

Dream Witness (FR) *W R Muir* a25 61
3 gr f Sagamix(FR) —Dial Dream (Gay Mecene (USA))
1797[5] 2349[8] 2646[8]3347[13] 3791[9] 4280[4] 4755[4]

Dressed To Dance (IRE) *B J Meehan* a63 58
2 b f Namid—Costume Drama (USA) (Alleged (USA))
5507[7] 5760[7] 6015[4] 6653[2]6736[2]

Dress To Impress (IRE) *J R Boyle* a75 77
2 b c Fasliyev(USA) —Dress Code (IRE) (Barathea (IRE))
2084[3] 2517[2] 2827[2] 4699[4](6605) 6732[2]6939[3]

Dr Flight *H Morrison* a42
4 b g Dr Fong(USA) —Bustling Nelly (Bustino)
218[14]

Drifting Gold *C G Cox* a69 61
2 ch f Bold Edge—Driftholme (Safawan)
1743[2] 2166[5] 2791[2]3917[2] 4427[7] 4753[3]6031[5]

Drifting Snow *D K Weld* 83
2 b f Danehill Dancer(IRE) —Ma N'Ieme Biche (USA) (Key To The Kingdom (USA))
5464a[7]

Drink To Me Only *J R Weymes* a53 56
3 b g Pursuit Of Love—Champenoise (Forzando)
(120) 211[8] 335[7]500[7] 1549[6]1792[3] 2284[4] 2873[6] (3138) 4059[9] 4728[8]

Dr Light (IRE) *S Kirk* a57
2 b g Medicean—Allumette (Rainbow Quest (USA))
6283[9] 6658[6]

Dr McFab *J A Osborne* a64
2 ch c Dr Fong(USA) —Barbera (Barathea (IRE))
6520[8] 6662[2]

Drombeg Pride (IRE) *Augustine Leahy*
2 b g High Account(USA) —Proserpina (Most Welcome)
5662a[18]

Drosia (IRE) *C Laffon-Parias* a100 103
3 b f King's Best(USA) —Eriza (Distant Relative)
1789a[7] 6366a[6]

Dr Sharp (IRE) *T P Tate* 93
6 ch g Dr Devious(IRE) —Stoned Imaculate (IRE) (Durgam (USA))
1294[12] 1584[11] 1809[9] 5533[15] 5811[8]5963[3] (6205)

Dr Synn *J Akehurst* a17 74
5 br g Danzero(AUS) —Our Shirley (Shirley Heights)
777[8] 1188[7] 1402[7]2606[2] 3229[2] 3705[7] 4772[11] 5591[9]6060[11]

Dr Thong *P F I Cole* a84 86
5 ch h Dr Fong(USA) —Always On My Mind (Distant Relative)
2440[8] 2708[12] 3202[5]4968[3] (5144) 5345[16] 5670[13]

Drum Dance (IRE) *N Tinkler* a33 56
4 b g Namid—Socialite (IRE) (Alzao (USA))
862[12] 1341[6] 1594[4]1791[2] 2077[3] 2288[3] 4571[9] 4735[4]5631[12] 5885[5]

Drumfergus Boy (IRE) *Andrew Oliver* a38 23
4 b g Josr Algarhoud(IRE) —Care And Comfort (Most Welcome)
6501[3] 6680[5]

Drumfire (IRE) *M Johnston* 101
2 b c Danehill Dancer(IRE) —Witch Of Fife (USA) (Lear Fan (USA))
(2778) 3735[2] (4809) 5466a[3] 6104[11]

Drumming Party (USA) *A M Balding* 70
4 bb g War Chant(USA) —Santaria (USA) (Star De Naskra (USA))
903[11] 1414[2] 1645[3]2331[6] 2536[2] (2962) 3297[5] 3438[8] 4780[4]5167[8]

Drumroll (IRE) *Miss J Feilden* a60 48
4 b g Diktat—Mystic Tempo (USA) (El Gran Senor (USA))
18[5] 157[10]409[3] 493[3]1852[6] 2702[9] 3056[11]

Drury Lane (IRE) *D W Chapman* a52 55
6 bb g Royal Applause—Ghost Tree (IRE) (Caerleon (USA))
2700[14] 3240[14] 3356[12] 3524[4] (3835) 4059[5]4233[9] 6550[8] 6643[6]6962[12]

Dry Ice (IRE) *H Candy* a83 89+
4 b g Desert Sun—Snowspin (Carwhite)
1112[4] 1410[7]2819[2] 3413[3] 4029[6] 4535[8] 5070[7]5591[2] 5833[8]

Dualagi *J S Moore* 55
2 b f Royal Applause—Lady Melbourne (IRE) (Indian Ridge)
5147[7]

Dubai Ace (USA) *Miss Sheena West* a66 71
5 b g Lear Fan(USA) —Arsaan (USA) (Nureyev (USA))
32[3] 218[2]419[2] 478[7]545[5] 2869[2] 3256[6]

Dubai Around (IRE) *Micky Hammond* 59
3 ch g Zinaad—Triple Transe (USA) (Trempolino (USA))
1044[6] 2379[4] 3355[6] 3785[2] 4255[3]4884[7] 5082[3] (Dead)

Dubai Builder *J S Moore* 102
2 b c Tobougg(IRE) —Roseum (Lahib (USA))
2172[7] 3895[3] 4333[9] (4681) 5373[3] (5626) 5965[10]

Dubai Dreams *M Sheppard* a62 56
6 b g Marju(IRE) —Arndilly (Robellino (USA))
4981[13]

Dubai Honor *Doug Watson* a105 74
7 gr h Highest Honor(FR) —Lovely Noor (USA) (Fappiano (USA))
152a[2]

Dubai Magic (USA) *C E Brittain* a79 85
2 ch g Rahy(USA) —Dabaweyaa (Shareef Dancer (USA))
2342[3] 2619[9] (3025) 3442[9]3800[2] 5322[8] 5843[8]6100[5] 6978[2]

Dubai Marina *F Jordan* 16
2 b f Polish Precedent(USA) —Cape Siren (Warning)
5380[11]

Dubai Melody (USA) *J H M Gosden* 73
3 ch f Woodman(USA) —Dabaweyaa (Shareef Dancer (USA))
2825[2] 3146[8] 4159[7]

Dubai On *Saeed Bin Suroor* a101+ 90
3 b f Daylami(IRE) —Cambara (Dancing Brave (USA))
5505[4] (6411)

Dubai's Fairy *R Hannon* a32 45
2 b f Medicean—Fairy Flight (IRE) (Fairy King (USA))
1675[8] 4657[11] 6099[8]

Dubai Shadow (IRE) *C E Brittain* 58
2 b f Cape Cross(IRE) —Farista (USA) (Alleged (USA))
3796[8] 4765[11]

Dubai's Touch *M Johnston* 100
2 b c Dr Fong(USA) —Noble Peregrine (Lomond (USA))
1780[6] 2159[4] (2783) (3143) 3442[3] 4099[3] (4561)6102[10]

Dubai Sunday (JPN) *P S McEntee* a53 70?
5 b g Sunday Silence(USA) —Lotta Lace (USA) (Nureyev (USA))
909[3] 1006[11]2849[12] 3230[11] 3382[7]3706[7] 3900[8] 4139[4]4307[5] 4576[5]

Dubai Twilight *B W Hills* 92
2 b c Alhaarth(IRE) —Eve (Rainbow Quest (USA))
4561[4] 5089[2]

Dubai Typhoon (USA) *C E Brittain* a93 92
3 ch c Thunder Gulch(USA) —Dubian (High Line)
829[3] 1627[7] 2205[12]2774[27]

Dubonai (IRE) *G M Moore* a66 60
6 ch g Peintre Celebre(USA) —Web Of Intrigue (Machiavellian (USA))
906[6]

Dudley Docker (IRE) *D Carroll* a74 66
4 b g Victory Note(USA) —Nordic Abu (IRE) (Nordico (USA))
200[9] 276[7]492[2] 737[2]1002[6] 2947[4] 3820[9]4116[8] 4378[13] 5316[10] 6390[4](6404) 6497[2]6664[4] 6773[6]6930[6]

Dueling B'Anjiz (USA) *E J Creighton* a37 36
7 b g Anjiz(USA) —Stirling Gal (USA) (Huckster (USA))
6132[12] 6857[8]

Duel In The Sands *D Shaw* a54 57
3 ch g Allied Forces(USA) —Kildine (IRE) (Common Grounds)
123[5] 188[9]272[5] 349[7]430[9]

Duelling Banjos *J Akehurst* a73 73
7 ch g Most Welcome—Khadino (Relkino)
37[6] 186[8]723[3] 983[5]1288[13] 1926[8] 6748[4]6878[3]

Due Respect (IRE) *D T Hughes* 100
6 b h Danehill(USA) —Stylish (Anshan)
3123a[23] 5396a[4]

Duff (IRE) *Edward Lynam* 107
3 b c Spinning World(USA) —Shining Prospect (Lycius (USA))
5411a[7] 5682[3]

Duijker (FR) *E Charpy* a34 98
5 ch g Dr Fong(USA) —L'Arrosee (USA) (Woodman (USA))
356a[12]

Dukedom *Sir Michael Stoute* 86+
3 gr c Highest Honor(FR) —Rose Noble (USA) (Vaguely Noble)
2034[3] 2411[2]

Duke Of Marmalade (IRE) *A P O'Brien* 110
2 b c Danehill(USA) —Love Me True (USA) (Kingmambo (USA))
4037[2]

Duke Of Milan (IRE) *G C Bravery* a75 73
3 ch g Desert Prince(IRE) —Abyat (USA) (Shadeed (USA))
4431[3] 4923[6] 5268[8] (5605) 6036[12]6159[10] 6326[3] 6437[10]6579[6] 6656[7]

Duke Of Tuscany *R Hannon* 95
2 b c Medicean—Flawless (Warning)
4177[9] 4525[2] (4794) (5292)

Dukes Bond *M E Sowersby*
3 gr g Paris House—Glowing Lake (IRE) (Lake Coniston (IRE))
4117[10]

Dukestreet *Michael Cunningham* a41 79
5 ch h Cadeaux Genereux—El Rabab (USA) (Roberto (USA))
271[6]

Dulce Sueno *I Semple* 61
3 b f Lahib(USA) —Graceland Lady (IRE) (Kafu)
2161[2] 2855[6] 3587[2] 4136[2] 4477[5]4695[9] 5077[4]

Dumaran (IRE) *W J Musson* a81 82
8 b g Be My Chief(USA) —Pine Needle (Kris)
444[4] 578[6]2088[3] 3639[5] 6301[10]

Dumas (IRE) *A P Jarvis* a57 74
2 b c Iron Mask(USA) —Bucaramanga (IRE) (Distinctly North (USA))
2009[6] 4028[8] 5106[7]5681[23]

Dunaskin (IRE) *Karen McLintock* a96 102
6 b g Bahhare(USA) —Mirwara (IRE) (Darshaan)
572[2] 1017[15]2656[3] 3294[15] 3552[19] 4711[2] 5188[10]5787[12]

Duncanbil (IRE) *J J Bridger*
5 b m Turtle Island(IRE) —Saintly Guest (What A Guest)
84[11] 144[11]

Dundonald *M Appleby* a51 51
7 ch g Magic Ring(IRE) —Cal Norma's Lady (IRE) (Lyphard's Special (USA))
210[6] 315[9]383[10]

Dundry *G L Moore* a80 84
5 b g Bin Ajwaad(IRE) —China's Pearl (Shirley Heights)
1132[3] 2357[7] 5564[8] 5952[6]

Dunelight (IRE) *C G Cox* 111
3 ch c Desert Sun—Badee'A (IRE) (Marju (IRE))
1095[3] (1490) 2774[12] 3491[2] (3889) 4098[2] 5411a[3]5675[33]

Dune Melody (IRE) *J S Moore* a59 82
3 b f Distant Music(USA) —Desert Gift (Green Desert (USA))
896[6] 1843[9] 1954[2] 2642[3] 2818[7]6094[12] 6221[13]

Dunlin *H Morrison* 69
3 ch f Inchinor—Hen Harrier (Polar Falcon (USA))
1191[8] 1649[7] 1955[5] 5751[8]

Dunn Deal (IRE) *W M Brisbourne* a67 76
6 b g Revoque(IRE) —Buddy And Soda (IRE) (Imperial Frontier (USA))
1047[7] 1504[13] (1689) 1878[11] 2074[3] 2920[9]3330[7] 3936[10] 4119[10] 4894[11]
Dunnett Again (IRE) *Mrs C A Dunnett* a41 54
5 b g Petardia—Pat Said No (IRE) (Last Tycoon)
529[4] 618[12]875[8]
Durba (AUS) *R C Guest*
6 ch g Desert Prince(IRE) —Placate (AUS) (Brief Truce (USA))
975[15]
Duroob *K R Burke* a48 69
4 b g Bahhare(USA) —Amaniy (USA) (Dayjur (USA))
(1138) 1346[7] 1809[6] 2408[7] 2812[6] 4848[2]5513[5] 5815[5] 6108[5]
Durova (IRE) *T D Easterby* 75
2 b f Soviet Star(USA) —Taroudannt (IRE) (Danehill (USA))
2827[5] 3188[2] 3521[2] 3745[2] 4089[3]4452[2] (4956) 5528[2] 5956[12]
Dushinka (IRE) *Timothy Doyle* 95
2 b f Titus Livius(FR) —Dusky Virgin (Missed Flight)
4850a[3] 5394a[5]
Duskiness (FR) *M J Wallace* a71 61
2 b f Kyllachy—Johanita (FR) (Johann Quatz (FR))
1675[5] 2355[5] *6099[4]6255[5]*
Dusty Road (GER) *Miss A Casotti*
13 br h Archway(IRE) —Dusty Highway (High Top)
306a[8]
Dutch Art *P W Chapple-Hyam* 121+
2 ch c Medicean—Halland Park Lass (IRE) (Spectrum (IRE))
(2300) (2771) (4644a) (5656)
Dutch Key Card (IRE) *C Smith* a50 80?
5 b g Key Of Luck(USA) —Fanny Blankers (IRE) (Persian Heights)
81[11] 397[7]524[10] *782[8]1228[8]* *1393[6]*5087[4] 5274[6] *5970[10]*
Duty (IRE) *Sir Michael Stoute* a42 99
3 b g Rainbow Quest(USA) —Wendylina (IRE) (In The Wings)
1192[2] (1613) 2436[4] 4560[4] 4770[2] 5325[2]
Duty Free (IRE) *H Morrison* 62
2 b c Rock Of Gibraltar(IRE) —Photographie (USA) (Trempolino (USA))
5828[5] 6023[4]
Duxford *D K Ivory* a63 43
5 ch g Young Ern—Marsara (Never So Bold)
84[10] 537[11]698[6] 854[7]972[11] 1265[10] *1745[10]*2070[11] *2245[7] 2573[6]2978[9]* 3411[7]
Dvinsky (USA) *P Howling* a73 78
5 b g Stravinsky(USA) —Festive Season (USA) (Lypheor)
1422[4] 1665[10] 1882[8] 2020[4] 2223[2](2504) 2603[2] 2864 6 3217[9] 3374[3] 3500[5]3718[8] 4957[4] *5246[3]5778[10]* 5937[9] *6227[3]6326[4] 6417[10]6747[2] 6842[3]6913[4]*
Dwilano (GER) *P Remmert* 107
3 ch c Silvano(GER) —Dwings (IRE) (In The Wings)
3131a[5] 4942a[7] 5762a[5] 6109a[11]
Dyanita *B W Hills* a70 62
3 b f Singspiel(IRE) —Dance Clear (IRE) (Marju (IRE))
850[3] 1214[7] 1823[6]5152[8] 5566[7] *5973[5](6260) 6841[5]6863[3]*
Dyaphora (IRE) *A Mataresi* 70
3 b f Xaar—Miss Caerleon (Caerleon (USA))
6251a[8]
Dylan (IRE) *N Tinkler* a48 53
3 b g Mull Of Kintyre(USA) —Rose Of Shuaib (IRE) (Caerleon (USA))
10[11] 132[8](786) 874[2]1259[12] 1829[13] *2249[11]*
Dylan Thomas (IRE) *A P O'Brien* a70 129
3 b c Danehill(USA) —Lagrion (USA) (Diesis)
(1708a) 2228[3] (3127a) 4679[4] (5193a) *5822a[4]*
Dynacam (USA) *Sir Michael Stoute* a63 87
3 b f Dynaformer(USA) —Najecam (USA) (Trempolino (USA))
1586[4] 4508[3] 4878[3] *5430[7]*
Dynaforce (USA) *A Fabre* 103
3 b f Dynaformer(USA) —Aletta Maria (USA) (Diesis)
6171a[5]
Dynamic Rhythm (USA) *J Noseda* 74
3 b c Kingmambo(USA) —Palme D'Or (IRE) (Sadler's Wells (USA))
3219[2] 4591[9]
Dynamic Saint (USA) *Doug Watson* a84
3 b c Sweetsouthernsaint(USA) —Le Nat (USA) (Dynaformer (USA))
620a[3]
Dynamite Deano *D K Ivory* a53 53
3 b g Dracula(AUS) —Katy Ivory (IRE) (Night Shift (USA))
1141[11] 1314[10] *2246[7]2463[4] 6553[9]*
Dynamo Dancer (IRE) *G M Lyons* 104
3 ch c Danehill Dancer(IRE) —Imperial Graf (USA) (Blushing John (USA))
4187a[2]
Dysonic (USA) *J Balding* a59 43
4 b g Aljabr(USA) —Atyab (USA) (Mr Prospector (USA))
14[7] 121[10]1764[11] 2833[4] *3595[3]3833[6] 6490[3] 6637[5](6704) (6806)*
Dzesmin (POL) *R C Guest* 85
4 b g Professional(IRE) —Dzakarta (POL) (Aprizzo (IRE))
3081[4] 3981[3] 4469[7] (5367) 5678[6]
Dzhani *Jedd O'Keeffe* a53 48
3 b g Singspiel(IRE) —Heuston Station (IRE) (Fairy King (USA))
823[6] 1100[8] *2466[8]3329[9]* 4069[12]
Ea (USA) *Sir Michael Stoute* 72+
2 b c Dynaformer(USA) —Enthused (USA) (Seeking The Gold (USA))
4333[6]

Eager Igor (USA) *R F Johnson Houghton* 72
2 b g Stravinsky(USA) —Danube (USA) (Green Desert (USA))
2506[8] 3363[6] 3907[2] 4766[5] 5307[7]6064[4]
Eager Lover (USA) *B W Hills* a71 95
2 ch c More Than Ready(USA) —True Love (USA) (Affirmed (USA))
961[4] 3701[6] 4037[6]
Eagle Eye *G Wragg* a53+ 61+
3 br g Capote(USA) —Bitwa (USA) (Conquistador Cielo (USA))
844[4] 1055[12] 1640[5]*1941[8]* 2399[11]
Eagle Mountain *A P O'Brien* 117
2 b c Rock Of Gibraltar(IRE) —Masskana (IRE) (Darshaan)
4825a[2] 5183[2] (5851a) 6104[4]
Eamon An Chnoic (IRE) *B W Duke* a54 57
5 gr g Lil's Boy(USA) —Caranina (USA) (Caro)
*371[1] 129[7]*2305[6] 2483[4] *2577[15]*3270[4] 3437[8] 3894[11]
Earl Compton (IRE) *P F I Cole* a52 52
2 b c Compton Place—Noble Story (Last Tycoon)
4815[5] 5645 8 *5784[10]*
Earl Kraul (IRE) *G L Moore* a46 45
3 b g Imperial Ballet(IRE) —Bu Hagab (IRE) (Royal Academy (USA))
4662[11] *5211[13]* 5432[17]5733[4] 6067[3]
Earl Marshal (USA) *Sir Michael Stoute* 62
2 b c Kingmambo(USA) —Fairy Godmother (Fairy King (USA))
6220[10]
Earl Of Spectrum (GER) *J L Spearing* a29 47
5 b g Spectrum(IRE) —Evry (GER) (Torgos)
1724[10]
Earl's Court *I Mohammed* 108
4 b h King's Best(USA) —Reine Wells (IRE) (Sadler's Wells (USA))
207a[2] 354a[3]
Early Evening *H Candy* 84
3 b f Daylami(IRE) —Regent Court (IRE) (Marju (IRE))
2406[2] 3367[2] (3946) (4555) 5164[6] 5538[9]
Early March *Mme C Head-Maarek* 117
4 br h Dansili—Emplane (USA) (Irish River (FR))
2490a[3] 2941a[10]
Early Promise (IRE) *P L Gilligan* a63 57
2 b f Abou Zouz(USA) —Habla Me (IRE) (Fairy King (USA))
1535[4] 2950[2] *3408[2]*5434[8] *5686[2] 5772[7]6032[4]*
Earth And Sky (USA) *Saeed Bin Suroor* 34
3 bb g Dynaformer(USA) —Earthly Angel (USA) (Crafty Prospector (USA))
5870[12]
Earthling *D W Chapman* a38 37
5 b g Rainbow Quest(USA) —Cruising Height (Shirley Heights)
*27[11] 3258[10]*4261[7] 4518[8]
Earth Master (IRE) *S Kirk* a59 76
3 gr g Grand Lodge(USA) —Beautiful France (IRE) (Sadler's Wells (USA))
19[5] 422[8]5558[9] 1350[10] 1740[10]*2466[10] 3016[8]*4052[6] 5054[11]
Easibet Dot Net *I Semple* a64 74
6 gr g Atraf—Silvery (Petong)
1610[3] 1887[4] 2549[4] 3674[4] 4478[4]4723[9] *5971[3] 6256[6]*
Eastborough (IRE) *J R Jenkins* a68 68
7 b g Woodborough(USA) —Easter Girl (Efisio)
33[2] 887[2]37[3] 325[2]420[7] 723[4]832[12] 966[7] 1132[6]1425[2] 1690[2] *1927[7]*2460[11] 2723[6] 2879[3] *3452[6]* 3798[3]4005[8] 4036[16] 4900[3] 5201[6] *5910[6]6256[3] 6415[2]*
East Cape *N Tinkler* a40 40
9 b g Bering—Reine De Danse (USA) (Nureyev (USA))
12[8] 389[7]
Eastern Anthem (IRE) *Saeed Bin Suroor* 85+
2 b c Singspiel(IRE) —Kazzia (GER) (Zinaad) (6050)
Eastern Appeal (IRE) *M Halford* 96+
3 br f Shinko Forest(IRE) —Haut Volee (Top Ville)
5996a[4] 6356a[3]
Eastern Playboy (IRE) *J Jay* a26 52
2 b c Desert Sun—Coolaba Princess (IRE) (Danehill (USA))
3228[5] 3746[9] 4334[12] 5570[8] *6500[10]*
Eastern Premium *R A Fahey*
2 b f Superior Premium—Make Ready (Beveled (USA))
2731[11] (Dead)
Eastern Princess *J A Geake* a51 60
2 b f Almutawakel—Silvereine (FR) (Bering)
3402[6] 3796[4] 4207[9]4773[10] 5419[8] 6014[6] *6487[6]6592[7] 6711[6]6839[4]*
Easter Ogil (IRE) *P G Murphy* a57 61
11 ch g Pips Pride—Piney Pass (Persian Bold)
338[6] 482[10]5914 *833[7]973[12]*
Eastlands (IRE) *Jamie Poulton* a59 69
3 b g Imperial Ballet(IRE) —Blue Dream (USA) (Irish River (FR))
2175[7] 2934[10] 3336[7] *3934[7]*4556[10]
East Riding *A J Chamberlain* a32 39
6 b m Gothenberg(IRE) —Bettynouche (Midyan (USA))
6889[7]
Easy Air *E A L Dunlop* a101+ 101+
3 ch c Zafonic(USA) —Easy Option (IRE) (Prince Sabo)
(852) 1626[4] *1924[2]* 2774[2]3493[5] 3889[2] 4790[7] *6192[4]*
Easy Feeling (IRE) *R Hannon* a57 77
4 b m Night Shift(USA) —Talena (Zafonic (USA))
159[11]
Easy Laughter (IRE) *A King* a73 69
5 b g Danehill(USA) —All To Easy (Alzao (USA))
*603[4] 713[5]*965[10]
Easy Lover *J A Osborne* a83 91
2 ch f Pivotal—Easy To Love (USA) (Diesis)
2328[8] *(2755)* 3496[9] *3997[2]4436[3]* 4775[4] (5013) 5187[8]6105[3] 6217[11]

Eathie *M J Attwater* 53
4 ch g Bluegrass Prince(IRE) —Persian Fortune (Forzando)
1401[12] 1684[9] 2075[15]*2794[12]* 3112[10] *3383[8]*
Eau Good *M C Chapman* a88+ 74
2 ch g Cadeaux Genereux—Girl's Best Friend (Nicolotte)
4987[2] 5307[3] 5790[3] *(6730) 6895[3]6948[2]*
Eau Sauvage *J Akehurst* a16
2 ch f Lake Coniston(IRE) —Mo Stopher (Sharpo)
6826[12]
Ebert *P J Makin* a69 90
3 b g Polish Precedent(USA) —Fanfare (Deploy)
1681[4] 3224[5] (3546) 4076[4] 4481[2] 4838[3]
Ebn Reem *M A Jarvis* a59 88
2 b c Mark Of Esteem(IRE) —Reematna (Sabrehill (USA))
1588[7] 2029[2] *2416[4]*3496[2] (4260) 4804[3] 6204[3]
Ebony Lady *R M Whitaker* 45
3 br f Vettori(IRE) —Keen Melody (USA) (Sharpen Up)
1079[9] 1221[8] 1731[7] 2107[3] 3357[6]4016[7] 4404[7]
Ebony Shades (IRE) *W P Mullins* 74
5 b g Bob Back(USA) —Silks Princess (Prince Tenderfoot (USA))
4166a[14]
Ebraam (USA) *E A L Dunlop* 72+
3 b c Red Ransom(USA) —Futuh (USA) (Diesis)
1641[10] 5093[2] (5368) 5937[7]
Ebtikaar (IRE) *J L Dunlop* 102
4 b h Darshaan—Jawlaat (USA) (Dayjur (USA))
1071[4] (1517) 2013[5] 2849[4] 4081[13] 4677[9]5318[2] 5963[19]
Eccentric *S Seemar* a114 111
5 ch g Most Welcome—Sure Care (Caerleon (USA))
355a[3] 565a[10]
Eccollo (IRE) *T J Pitt* a87+ 47
4 b g Spectrum(IRE) —Taking Liberties (IRE) (Royal Academy (USA))
669[10] 897[15] 2546[8]*6130[2] (6235) (6383) (6436) (6484) (6507) 6564[3]6607[F]* (Dead)
Echelon *Sir Michael Stoute* 112+
4 b m Danehill(USA) —Exclusive (Polar Falcon (USA))
(1671) (2199) 2740[2] 4127[5]
Echoes Rock (GER) *A Fabre* 104
3 ch c Tiger Hill(IRE) —Evening Breeze (GER) (Surumu (GER))
1179a[2]
Echo Of Light *Saeed Bin Suroor* a121 121
4 b h Dubai Millennium—Spirit Of Tara (IRE) (Sadler's Wells (USA))
(3534) 4038[6] (5186) (5703a) 6342a[14]
Eckleberry (IRE) *M Delzangles* 88
4 b g Priolo(USA) —Heavenly Song (FR) (Machiavellian (USA))
(5562a)
Eclipse Park *M J McGrath* a68 40
3 ch g Rainbow Quest(USA) —Gino's Spirits (Perugino (USA))
374[4] 483[8]6684 1543[8] 2065[15]3339[13] *6289[12]*
Eclipse West (ARG) *S Seemar* a30 64
7 bb h Westbridge(USA) —Legitime (ARG) (Southern Halo (USA))
152a[16] 208a[12] 438a[12]
Eclisse (FR) *Y De Nicolay* 89
2 b f Ski Chief(USA) —La Tzingara (FR) (Crystal Glitters (USA))
6046a[7]
Eco Centrism *W J Haggas* 78
2 ch c Selkirk(USA) —Way O'Gold (USA) (Slew O'Gold (USA))
5321 2
Edaara (IRE) *W J Haggas* 82+
3 ch f Pivotal—Green Bonnet (IRE) (Green Desert (USA))
1085[2] 2580[4] (5761)
Edas *J J Quinn* a71 74
4 b h Celtic Swing—Eden (IRE) (Polish Precedent (USA))
2296[7] 2945[6] 3283[6] 3939[6] 4544[5]*5691[2] 6426[5]*
Eddie Jock (IRE) *M L W Bell* 105
2 ch g Almutawakel—Al Euro (FR) (Mujtahid (USA))
1588[9] 1945[5] (2388) (3496) 4100[2] (4344) 4775[2]5806[2]
Eddies Jewel *I W McInnes* a48 50
6 b g Presidium—Superstream (Superpower)
2291[8] 2874[11] 3610[5] 3815[11] 4467[12]
Edelfa (IRE) *C Marinelli* 79
2 b f Fasliyev(USA) —Daziyra (IRE) (Doyoun)
3343a[11]
Eden Rock (IRE) *Pat Eddery* 104
5 b g Danehill(USA) —Marlene-D (Selkirk (USA))
1129[5] 2776[5] 4098[16]
Eden Star (IRE) *D K Ivory* a50 43
4 b m Soviet Star(USA) —Gold Prospector (IRE) (Spectrum (IRE))
27[14]
Ede's Dot Com (IRE) *W J Knight* a80 80
2 b c Trans Island—Kilkee Bay (IRE) (Case Law)
2930[9] *(3408) 3917[3]* 5461[4]5940[10]
Edge Closer *R Hannon* 72
2 b c Bold Edge—Blue Goddess (IRE) (Blues Traveller (IRE))
(6331)
Edged In Gold *P J Makin* a58 53
4 ch m Bold Edge—Piccante (Wolfhound (USA))
119[5] 360[6]4015 480[5]580[10] 951[5]1195[4] (1396) 2444[4] *3155[6] 3847[8]*
Edge End *D J S Ffrench Davis* 39
2 ch g Bold Edge—Rag Time Belle (Raga Navarro (ITY))
6330[6]
Edgefour (IRE) *B I Case* a38 30
2 b f King's Best(USA) —Highshaan (Pistolet Bleu (IRE))
5592[13] *6098[8]*

Edge Fund *Miss Gay Kelleway* a30 57
4 b g Bold Edge—Truly Madly Deeply (Most Welcome)
*157[11] 297[10]398[5] 618[7]*1073[13] 1311[10] 1752[10] 2568[5] 2952[5]
Edin Burgher (FR) *T T Clement* a60 45
5 br g Hamas(IRE) —Jaljuli (Jalmood (USA))
486[4] 1057[7] *1273[3]1644[7] 2936[7]3052[10]*
Edison *N P Littmoden* 78
2 ch c Best Of The Bests(IRE) —Lanciana (IRE) (Acatenango (GER))
4801[6] 5091[3] 5460[4]
Edward (IRE) *A P Jarvis* a55 56
4 b g Namid—Daltak (Night Shift (USA))
373[4] 580[7]858[12]
Eeshee *Miss Diana Weeden* a53d 46
3 b f Distant Music(USA) —Madame Curie (Polish Precedent (USA))
45[8] 212[11]335[6] 687[10]870[4] 1210[7]
Effective *A P Jarvis* a79 85
6 ch g Bahamian Bounty—Efficacy (Efisio)
(323) 541[2] 569[3]761[5] 2302[12] 2405[7]*6882[10]*
Effect Me Not (IRE) *Peter Grayson* 55
4 b m Xaar—Beauty Appeal (USA) (Shadeed (USA))
5033[12]
Effigy *H Candy* 67
2 b c Efisio—Hymne D'Amour (USA) (Dixieland Band (USA))
4987[8] 6331[4]
Efidium *N Bycroft* a54 73
8 b g Presidium—Efipetite (Efisio)
2299[3] 2527[5] 2681[5] 2831[3] 3289[6]3565[6] 4154[7] 4378[4] 4733[10] 5483[3]5680[3] 5961[2] 6160[8]
Efimac *N Bycroft* a43 43
6 b m Presidium—Efipetite (Efisio)
27[12]
Efisio Princess *J E Long* 55
3 br f Efisio—Hardiprincess (Keen)
5093[10] 5729[3] (5951)
Efistorm *J Balding* a87 79
5 b g Efisio—Abundance (Cadeaux Genereux)
*79[10] 244[2]362[11] 424[3](605) 761[4]*1125[5] 1856[6] *6428[10]6496[5] 6682[3]6720[7] (6953)*
Eforetta (GER) *D J Wintle* a68+ 66
4 ch m Dr Fong(USA) —Erminora (GER) (Highest Honor (FR))
*92[13] 261[8]636[2] 794[3]939[10] 1256[3](1766) (2140) 3454[2]*3955[3]
Efrhina (IRE) *Stef Liddiard* a70d 70
6 ch m Woodman(USA) —Eshq Albahr (USA) (Riverman (USA))
414[10]
Egerton (GER) *P Rau* 119
5 b h Groom Dancer(USA) —Enrica (Niniski (USA))
(3579a) 4414a[4] 5051a[4] 5561a[2] 6004a[4] 6782a[6]
Eglevski (IRE) *J L Dunlop* 81
2 b c Danehill Dancer(IRE) —Ski For Gold (Shirley Heights)
3025[5] 3976[2] 4458[3] 5475[2] (5720)
Ego Trip *M W Easterby* a67 71
5 b g Deploy—Boulevard Rouge (USA) (Red Ransom (USA))
869[8] 1144[3] 1756[6] 2075[12] 2812[3]*3382[2]* (6158)
Egyptian (USA) *R Bouresly* a86 97
7 b g Green Desert(USA) —Link River (USA) (Gone West (USA))
149a[9] *204a[7] 353a[9]434a[8]* 511a[8]
Egyptian Lord *Peter Grayson* a73 59
3 ch g Bold Edge—Calypso Lady (IRE) (Priolo (USA))
(66) 1279[9] 1529[8] 2222[3] 2410[8] *2939[6]*3479[3] 4056[8] *5605[8]5878[9] 6521[11]6622[7] 6686[4]*
Eidsfoss (IRE) *T T Clement* a40 49
4 b g Danehill Dancer(IRE) —Alca Egeria (ITY) (Shareef Dancer (USA))
2[7] 6916[7]
Eijaaz (IRE) *Mrs L Stubbs* a62 60
5 b g Green Desert(USA) —Kismah (Machiavellian (USA))
*324[8] 530[4]700[6] 820[6]*1058[11] 1373[2] 2131[10] 2832[6] 3139[6]*3386[11]*
Eilean Ban (USA) *E A L Dunlop* 99
3 ch f Silver Hawk(USA) —Isla Del Rey (USA) (Nureyev (USA))
4808[12]
Eisteddfod *P F I Cole* 116
5 ch g Cadeaux Genereux—Ffestiniog (IRE) (Efisio)
1145[3] 1778[6] 2115[5] 2846[8] 4191a[7]4860a[2] 5375[7] 5578[3] 5942[13] 6335[5]
Ekagra *F & L Camici* 96
3 ch f Barathea(IRE) —Egine (USA) (Irish River (FR))
2043a[6] 2694a[13]
Ekhtiaar *J H M Gosden* a91+ 70
2 b g Elmaamul(USA) —Divina Mia (Dowsing (USA))
5460[6] *(5784) (5989)*
Ektimaal *E A L Dunlop* 73
3 ch g Bahamian Bounty—Secret Circle (Magic Ring (IRE))
4708[10] 5071[6] 5353[4] 5571[3] 6060[2]
Ektishaaf *R McGlinchey* a65+ 61
4 b m Mujahid(USA) —Tahnee (Cadeaux Genereux)
*537[5] 698[12]*837[5] *(985)* 1348[8] 1645[8] *2418[3]6590[11]*
Elaala (USA) *B D Leavy* a54 59
4 ch m Aljabr(USA) —Nufuth (USA) (Nureyev (USA))
(635) 6957[4]
Ela Aleka Mou *M A Jarvis* 82
2 ch f Tobougg(IRE) —Miss Grimm (USA) (Irish River (FR))
(2680) 3216[2] 4146[6]
El Alamein (IRE) *Sir Mark Prescott* a75 67+
3 ch g Nashwan(USA) —El Rabab (USA) (Roberto (USA))
(2591) 2633[3] 3539[6] *3935[2]5022[3]*
Elasos (FR) *D Sepulchre* 109
4 b h Pythios(IRE) —Shikasta (IRE) (Kris)
4861a[6] 6610a[6]

Elated (IRE) *W J Haggas* a67 20
4 b g Erhaab(USA) —Elauyun (IRE) (Muhtarram (USA))
460[9] 566[2]894[12]

El Biba D'Or (IRE) *P Giannotti* 105
7 b h Common Grounds—Quiet Awakening (USA) (Secreto (USA))
3516a[7] 5718a[8]

El Bosque (IRE) *B R Millman* 90
2 b g Elnadim(USA) —In The Woods (You And I (USA))
2617[7] (3247) 3734[4] 4146[9] (4815) 5372[11] 5655[14]

Elcanos (GER) *Mario Hofer* 100
3 ch c Acatenango(GER) —Elisha (GER) (Konigsstuhl (GER))
3776a[10] 5709a[3]

El Capitan (FR) *Miss Gay Kelleway* a50 64
3 b g Danehill Dancer(IRE) —Fille Dansante (IRE) (Dancing Dissident (USA))
2868[9] 3304[6] 3644[12]4533[3] 4847[3] 5868[13]

El Capitano (FR) *C Lerner* 99
3 b c Anabaa(USA) —Guerre De Troie (Risk Me (FR))
4168a[4]

El Chaparral (IRE) *F P Murtagh* a81 74
6 b g Bigstone(IRE) —Low Line (High Line)
331[11] 2628[5] 3141[9]4256[9]

El Coto *K A Ryan* a90 97
6 b g Forzando—Thatcherella (Thatching)
865[12] 1129[21] 2079[4] 2657[4] 2742[23]3552[9] 3985[3] 5310[8] 6226[12]6733[2] 6999[9]

El Dececy (USA) *J L Dunlop* 77
2 b c Seeking The Gold(USA) —Ashraakat (USA) (Danzig (USA))
4129[12] 5088[3] 5623[7]

El Dee (IRE) *D Carroll* a49 46
3 br g Brave Act—Go Flightline (IRE) (Common Grounds)
859[4] 1221[5] 2082[15]2539[8] 4016[2] 4404[5]

Eldon Endeavour *B Storey* 40
2 b g Hunting Lion(IRE) —La Noisette (Rock Hopper)
2159[7] 2972[9] 3173[7] 5402[8]

Eldon Outlaw *B Storey* 46
3 b g Hunting Lion(IRE) —La Noisette (Rock Hopper)
1612[8] 2285[7] 3138[11]

Eldorado *S Kirk* 89
5 b g Hernando(FR) —Catch (USA) (Blushing Groom (FR))
1206[11] 1544[11] 2088[4] 2534[8] (3024) 3365[4]3704[3] 3952[2] 4320[5] 5346[8]

Eldori *M S Saunders* a7
3 b f Vettori(IRE) —Elderberry (Bin Ajwaad (IRE))
835[5] 1355[16] 6019[13]6134[12]

El Dottore *M L W Bell* 53
2 b c Dr Fong(USA) —Edouna (FR) (Doyoun)
5460[12]

Electric Beat *Andreas Lowe* 110
3 b c Shinko Forest(IRE) —Divine Grace (IRE) (Definite Article)
(3755a) 4858a[5]

Electric Storm *R Charlton* 71
3 b c Zafonic(USA) —Rainbow Lake (Rainbow Quest (USA))
1374[6] 2304[13] 2970[6]

Electric Warrior (IRE) *K R Burke* a68+ 86+
3 b g Bold Fact(USA) —Dungeon Princess (IRE) (Danehill (USA))
880[7] 952[6] 1855[7](2441) (2896) (3023) 3304[3] 3852[6] 4298[5] 5722[4]

Electrique (IRE) *A J McCabe* a49 67
6 b g Elmaamul(USA) —Majmu (USA) (Al Nasr (FR))
5775[9] 6037[7]6714[12]

Electrocutionist (USA) *Saeed Bin Suroor* a127 125
5 b h Red Ransom(USA) —Elbaaha (Arazi (USA))
(565a) (743a) 2741[2] 3927[2] (Dead)

Electron Pulse *J S Goldie* a48 64
3 ch f Dr Fong(USA) —Lost In Lucca (Inchinor)
645[8] 1032[7] 1530[5]2109[5] 2856[4] 3582[4]

Elegant Song (SWE) *T Gustafsson*
3 br c Songline(SWE) —Saucy Girl (FR) (Taufan (USA))
4919a[2]

Elegant Times (IRE) *T D Easterby* a64 71
3 b f Dansili—Simply Times (USA) (Dodge (USA))
1230[3] 1734[8] 2019[2] (3050) 3381[8]4058[2] 4116[11] 4524[3] 5036[7]5079[5] 5619[9]

El Faro (FR) *M R Channon* 66
3 b g Fantastic Light(USA) —Pagoda (FR) (Sadler's Wells (USA))
1120[10] 1516[7] 2082[9] 3848[7] 4150[10]

El Gallo (IRE) *F Castro* a39
3 b g Imperial Ballet(IRE) —Klarifi (Habitat)
4420a[12]

Elgin Marbles *A B Haynes* a42 48
4 b g Lujain(USA) —Bold Gem (Never So Bold)
1188[15] 2711[10] 2920[10] 5775[10]6142[12]

Elhamri *S Kirk* 106
2 b c Noverre(USA) —Seamstress (IRE) (Barathea (IRE))
(1189) 1977[6] (2724) (3734) 4712[4] 5154[5] 5802[5]

Elhareer (IRE) *B J Meehan* a76
2 ch f Selkirk(USA) —Ellway Star (IRE) (Night Shift (USA))
5424[3] 5906[10](6921)

El Hogar (IRE) *S Kirk* a37
3 ch g Namid—Fussing (IRE) (Persian Bold)
6144[7]

Elidore *B Palling* a69 76
6 b m Danetime(IRE) —Beveled Edge (Beveled (USA))
2097[8] 2603[9] 2969[15] 4288[4] 4871[2]4983[4] 5130[3] 5384[10] 6054[11]

Eliminator *I W McInnes* a39 69
3 ch g Observatory(USA) —Effie (Royal Academy (USA))
445[8] 583[10]731[5] 993[16] 1345[7] 1444[6] 2299[13]2616[9] 2782[15] 3240[9] 3785[10]

Elise *R Gibson* 91
3 b f Fantastic Light(USA) —Napoleon's Sister (IRE) (Alzao (USA))
5197a[4]

Elisha (IRE) *K A Ryan* a46 62
4 ch m Raise A Grand(IRE) —Social Butterfly (USA) (Sir Ivor (USA))
3172[4] 3912[11] 4157[15] 4507[7]

Elite Land *N Bycroft* 57
3 b g Namaqualand(USA) —Petite Elite (Anfield)
1731[2] 2529[10] 3288[4] 3357[5] 3609[5]3910[4] 4195[4] 4404[2] 4734[12] 4909[8]

Elizabeth Garrett *R M H Cowell* a36 28
2 b f Dr Fong(USA) —Eleonor Sympson (Cadeaux Genereux)
727[4] 1082[11] 1743[3]2538[6] 3380[5] 3801[5]4115[9] 6706[8]

Elizabeth Street (USA) *P F I Cole* a77 70
2 bb f Street Cry(IRE) —Affirmed Ambience (USA) (Affirmed (USA))
1514[3] 2800[15] 3640[2]5157[8] 6254[8]

Eliza May *K A Ryan* 84
2 b f Kyllachy—Elsie Plunkett (Mind Games) (1853) 2191[3] 3084[6] 5503[19] 6105[9]

Elkhorn *Miss J A Camacho* a69 78
4 b g Indian Ridge—Rimba (USA) (Dayjur (USA))
992[13] 1382[7] 1760[11]2417[11] 2749[6] 3171[4]3749[3] 4116[13] 4571[6] (4735) (5243) (5487) (5684) 5791[7]

Ellablue *Rae Guest* a59 58
2 ch f Bahamian Bounty—Elabella (Ela-Mana-Mou)
6025[5] 6409[9] 6838[4]

Ella Woodcock (IRE) *J A Osborne* 55
2 b g Daggers Drawn(USA) —Hollow Haze (USA) (Woodman (USA))
4895[10] 5161[7] 5563[9]

Ella Y Rossa *P D Evans* a52 11
2 ch f Bertolini(USA) —Meandering Rose (USA) (Irish River (FR))
1737[9] 1912[4] 2094[8]5052[11] 5503[21] 6534[5](6853)

Elle Galante (GER) *W Hickst* 98
3 b f Galileo(IRE) —Elle Danzig (GER) (Roi Danzig (USA))
6567a[3]

Elle Nino *Patrick Morris* a72 62
4 b m Inchinor—Robellino Miss (USA) (Robellino (USA))
6526[10]

Ellen Of Doononey (IRE) *G Kussatz* 78
3 gr f Bahhare(USA) —Evening Gold (Linamix (FR))
5008a[7]

Ellens Academy (IRE) *E J Alston* a87 88
11 b g Royal Academy(USA) —Lady Ellen (Horage)
1042[11] 1597[5] 1858[12] 2027[11] 2749[4]3041[4] 3077[6] (3584) 3936[4] 4119[2] (4357) 4885[4]5336[4] 5534[8]

Ellens Princess (IRE) *J S Wainwright* a61 74d
4 b m Desert Prince(IRE) —Lady Ellen (Horage)
1683[13] 2418[9] 2641[7]2891[7] 3142[9] 3947[15] 4455[7]

Elleray (IRE) *J G Given* a38
4 br m Docksider(USA) —Saint Ann (USA) (Geiger Counter (USA))
162[12]

Elle's Angel (IRE) *B R Millman* a27 37
2 b f Tobougg(IRE) —Stamatina (Warning)
849[10] 3005[7] 3838[5]5596[9]

Ellesappelle *G L Moore* a67 75
3 b f Benny The Dip(USA) —Zizi (IRE) (Imp Society (USA))
839[2] 1122[4] 1423[4]1599[5] 2107[5] 2283[6] 4060[6] 4297[2](4567) 4769[10] (5270) 5895[10] 6059[5] 6503[8]6775[14]

Ellies Faith *N Bycroft* 43
2 ch f Sugarfoot—Star Dancer (Groom Dancer (USA))
2106[13] 3174[6] 4376[8] 4630[8] 4887[15]5899[6] 5959[6]

Elli Lewtia *J Jay* a24 33
3 ch f Tomba—Troia (IRE) (Last Tycoon)
1960[9] 2143[10] 3357[7]6758[9] 6860[9]6957[5]

Ellina *J Pearce* a79 70
5 b m Robellino(USA) —Native Flair (Be My Native (USA))
3152[5]

Elliots World (IRE) *I Mohammed* 111
4 b h King's Best(USA) —Morning Welcome (IRE) (Be My Guest (USA))
369a[3] 496a[8]

Ello Lucky (IRE) *C Roberts* a28 36
4 br m Key Of Luck(USA) —Ellopassoff (Librate)
3032[8] 3541[10] 3941[6] 4627[11] 4755[10]6852[10]

El Manx Senorita *C Smith* a3
2 b f Mind Games—L A Touch (Tina's Pet)
6402[7] 6586[5]

Elmasong *J J Bridger* a47 44
2 ch f Elmaamul(USA) —Annie's Song (Farfelu)
4994[8] 5209[10]5570[9] 5933[10] 6441[12]6650[5] 6745[6]

Elms Schoolboy *P Howling* a53 44
4 ch g Komaite(USA) —Elms Schoolgirl (Emarati (USA))
183[6] 427[3]468[11] 527[14]602[3] 613[11]638[7] (793) 875[5] 1227[5]1537[8] 1723[5]2392[6] 2585[6] 2935[6]4280[7] 5097[6] 5926[3]6134[7] 6307[5]

Elmustanser *Doug Watson* a108 103
5 b h Machiavellian(USA) —Elfaslah (IRE) (Green Desert (USA))
152a[6] 355a[5]565a[3] 624a[9]

Elopement (IRE) *W M Brisbourne* a50 58
4 ch m Machiavellian(USA) —Melanzane (Arazi (USA))
1353[3] 5954[5]

Eloquent Knight (USA) *W R Muir* a78 74
4 gr h Aljabr(USA) —Matinee Mimic (USA) (Silent Screen (USA))
223[4] (324) 478[3](652) 983[2]1281[10] 2508[7] 2982[5]3490[8]

Eloquent Rose (IRE) *Mrs A Duffield* 82
2 b f Elnadim(USA) —Quintellina (Robellino (USA))
(1181) (1491) 2125[4] 5133[4] 5681[9] 5956[8]

Elounda (IRE) *H R A Cecil* 62
2 b f Sinndar(IRE) —Gaily Grecian (IRE) (Ela-Mana-Mou)
6215[8]

Elounesse (GER) *Mario Hofer* 72
3 ch f Lando(GER) —Eivissa (GER) (Frontal)
1714a[9]

El Palmar *M J Attwater* a60 58
5 b g Case Law—Aybeegirl (Mazilier (USA))
330[8] 493[10]612[6] 649[2](689) 860[4]906[9] 2137[5]2378[11] 2599[9]

El Paso (GER) *P Schiergen* 83
3 b c Tiger Hill(IRE) —En Vogue (GER) (Dashing Blade)
1526a[5]

El Potro *J R Holt* a71 69+
4 b g Forzando—Gaelic Air (Ballad Rock)
424[9] 532[2]605[4] 1151[13]1297[7] 1689[7] 1846[9] 2207[11]3004[6] 3389[7] 3817[17]6548[2] 6704[8]6727[2] 6851[9]6969[2]

Elrafa Mujahid *Ernst Oertel* a67 49
4 b m Mujahid(USA) —Fancier Bit (Lion Cavern (USA))
101[4] 161[8]252[7] 504[5]641[2] 777[10] 898[10]1015[9] 1164[13]1961[5] 2348[7]2936[8] 3262[4]3731[10] (4329) 4844[6] 5171[13]

El Rey Royale *Micky Hammond* 60
4 b g Royal Applause—Spanish Serenade (Nashwan (USA))
1425[11] 2181[8] 2808[7] 3311[4] 3480[6]3815[8] 4198[10]

El Segundo (NZ) *C Little* 120
5 b g Pins(AUS) —Palos Verdes (NZ) (Oak Ridge (FR))
6347a[4]

Elsie Alderman *J C Fox* 5
4 b m Fumo Di Londra(IRE) —Eastwood Heiress (Known Fact (USA))
2220[14] 4708[11]

Elsie Hart (IRE) *T D Easterby* a66 74d
4 b m Revoque(IRE) —Family At War (USA) (Explodent (USA))
252[10] 492[4]

Elsinora *A G Juckes* a46 51
5 b m Great Dane(IRE) —Deanta In Eirinn (Red Sunset)
43[13]

El Soprano (IRE) *Kevin Prendergast* 86
2 b f Noverre(USA) —Lady Of Kildare (IRE) (Mujadil (USA))
5408a[7]

El Tango (GER) *P Schiergen* 107
4 br h Acatenango(GER) —Elea (GER) (Dschingis Khan)
1369a[4] 2061a[7] 2910a[4] 3775a[2] 4414a[8]5718a[5] (6610a)

Eltanin (IRE) *J Howard Johnson* 69
2 gr g Linamix(FR) —Housatonic (USA) (Riverman (USA))
5025[3] 5790[6]

El Tiger (GER) *B J Curley* a94d 108
5 b g Tiger Hill(IRE) —Elea (GER) (Dschingis Khan)
(135) 377[9] 1779[P] 2341[13]5141[7] 5511[16] 6017[14] 6626[7]

Eltizaam (USA) *B Olsen* a64 93
4 b h Bahri(USA) —Saffaanh (USA) (Shareef Dancer (USA))
2123a[5] 5224a[6]

El Toreador (USA) *G A Butler* 78
2 ch f El Corredor(USA) —Marsha's Dancer (USA) (Northern Dancer (CAN))
3084[10]

Elusive Double (IRE) *Daniel William O'Sullivan* 103
4 ch h Grand Lodge(USA) —Lady Luck (IRE) (Kris)
3129a[9]

Elusive Dream *Sir Mark Prescott* a101 110
5 b g Rainbow Quest(USA) —Dance A Dream (Sadler's Wells (USA))
1584[9] 2013[2] 2723[7] 3533[2](3775a) (4121a) 4713[18]

Elusive Flash (USA) *P F I Cole* a81 80
2 b f Freud(USA) —Giana (USA) (Exclusive Era (USA))
3893[4] 5209[2] (5380) 5783[6]6105[7]

Elusive Warrior (USA) *R A Fahey* a69+ 59d
3 b g Elusive Quality(USA) —Love To Fight (CAN) (Fit To Fight (USA))
981[5] 1241[9] 1430[4]1750[3] 2235[8] 2393[6] (2727) 3164[5] 3879[7]4253[10] 4569[9] 5316[16] 6465[2]6556[8] (6674) (6756) 6919[11]

Elusory *J L Dunlop* 35
2 b c Galileo(IRE) —Elude (Slip Anchor)
6298[8]

Elvard (FR) *D Smaga* 90
3 gr c Highest Honor(FR) —Dame Edith (FR) (Top Ville)
4465a[6]

Elvina *A G Newcombe* a61 60
5 b m Mark Of Esteem(IRE) —Pharaoh's Joy (Robellino (USA))
2207[8] 2494[9] 3172[8]3847[7] 5291[4] 5834[9]

Elvina Hills (IRE) *P Mitchell* a54 60
4 ch m Bluebird(USA) —Women In Love (IRE) (Danehill (USA))
520[6] 917[11]1753[10] 2348[10] 2577[14]

Elyaadi *M R Channon* a68
2 b f Singspiel(IRE) —Abyaan (IRE) (Ela-Mana-Mou)
6071[4]

Emaara *J L Dunlop* 72
2 b f Fasliyev(USA) —Shuruk (Cadeaux Genereux)
4600[3] 5237[2] 5746[2]

Emefdream *Mrs N Macauley* a64+ 62
2 b g Efisio—Alkarida (FR) (Akarad (FR))
987[7] 1107[9] 1982[5]3605[3] 4321[2] 5238[6] 5721[5] 6388[10]6422[13] (6640) 6777[5] 6872[7]

Emerald Bay (IRE) *I Semple* 92+
4 b g King's Best(USA) —Belle Etoile (FR) (Lead On Time (USA))
815[2] 1043[15] 1495[8] 2162[10]

Emerald Beauty (ARG) *M F De Kock* a102 99
6 gr m Equalize(USA) —Emerald Girl (ARG) (Candy Stripes (USA))
155a[8] 351a[6] 508a[2]560a[4]

Emerald Hill (IRE) *M Halford* 99
2 b g Piccolo—Sticky Green (Lion Cavern (USA))
3126a[5] 5466a[4]

Emerald Sky *R Brotherton* a16
2 b f Diktat—Dekelsmary (Komaite (USA))
6278[11] 6414[9]6706[6]

Emerald Wilderness (IRE) *M R Channon* 78
2 b g Green Desert(USA) —Simla Bibi (Indian Ridge)
2867[4] 4466[2] 5293[3] 6023[6]

Emergency Services *Tom Dascombe* a57 58
2 b g Foxhound(USA) —Compact Disc (IRE) (Royal Academy (USA))
707[7] 1688[10] 1838[17]1876[2] 3136[7] 3345[8] 3613[6] 4007[2]4334[5] 4665[2] (6016) 6172[2] 6394[12]6421[2]

Emilio *R A Kvisla* a86 93
5 b g Kris—Easter Moon (FR) (Easter Sun)
2649[12] 3092[15] 3223[7] 3928[6] 4106[10]4535[12] 5021[8] 6671[10]

Emilion *W R Muir* a63+ 67
3 ch f Fantastic Light(USA) —Riberac (Efisio)
963[4] 1252[4] 1747[4]2713[4] 6566[7] 6775[9](6923)

Emily (FR) *Mrs L J Young* a6 62
3 b f Dansili—Palomelle (FR) (Moulin)
598[9] 853[12]

Emily Bronte *Saeed Bin Suroor* a99 101
3 gr f Machiavellian(USA) —Zafadola (IRE) (Darshaan)
6190[2] 6365a[10]

Emily's Pet (IRE) *B W Duke* a41 46
3 ch g Raise A Grand(IRE) —Zaola (IRE) (Alzao (USA))
1274[6] 2479[9] 4176[6]4297[5]

Emily's Place (IRE) *J Pearce* a74 74
3 b f Mujadil(USA) —Dulcinea (Selkirk (USA))
1344[15] 1941[2] 2301[3]2699[3] 4048[7] (4297) (4533) 5568[12]6260[4] 6430[6]6825[3] 6942[4]

Eminence Gift *K R Burke* a54 58
4 b m Cadeaux Genereux—Germane (Distant Relative)
1249[8] 2181[9] 2696[7] 2808[12]

Emirate Isle *J Wade* 69
2 b g Cois Na Tine(IRE) —Emmajoun (Emarati (USA))
3581[5] 4630[7]

Emirates First (IRE) *Saeed Bin Suroor* a68+
3 ch f In The Wings—Genovefa (USA) (Woodman (USA))
6225[2] (6429)

Emirates Gold (IRE) *Saeed Bin Suroor* a66 95
3 b c Royal Applause—Yara (IRE) (Sri Pekan (USA))
150a[11]

Emirates Line (USA) *Saeed Bin Suroor* 88+
3 ch c Kingmambo(USA) —Style Setter (USA) (Manila (USA))
(6052)

Emirates Skyline (USA) *Saeed Bin Suroor* 105
3 b c Sunday Silence(USA) —The Caretaker (Caerleon (USA))
5376[2] 5813[3]

Emma Jean Lad (IRE) *J S Moore* a37 55
2 ch c Intikhab(USA) —Swing City (IRE) (Indian Ridge)
1107[7] 2234[6]

Emma Lilley (USA) *J G M O'Shea* a41 39
4 ch m Theatrical—Changed Tune (USA) (Tunerup (USA))
4011[10]

Emma's Surprise *K A Ryan* a67 74
2 b f Tobougg(IRE) —Selvi (Mummy's Pet)
(2106) 2800[14] 5916[16] 6388[6]6659[4]

Emma Told Lies *M W Easterby* a33 59
2 b f Warningford—Itsanothergirl (Reprimand)
908[8] 1040[6] 1248[9]1862[3] 2015[3] (2294) (2731) 3136[5] 3372[9] 3997[9]5238[9]

Emmpat (IRE) *C F Swan* 96
8 b g Bigstone(IRE) —Nordic Abu (IRE) (Nordico (USA))
3128a[12] 4031a[16]

Emotive *I A Wood* a59 66+
3 b g Pursuit Of Love—Ruby Julie (Clantime)
712[2] 918[10]1241[6] 1314[7] 1736[7] (2101) (2877) 3364[9] 3650[6]4052[2] 4700[10] 5130[11]5210[10] 5435[3] 5621[7]

Emperor Cat (IRE) *Mrs N S Evans* a49 49
5 b g Desert Story(IRE) —Catfoot Lane (Batshoof)
792[4] 941[3]1225[5] 1395[12]3194[2] 3894[12] 4285[8] 5127[2] 6280[7]6552[12]

Emperor's Well *M W Easterby* a53 62
7 ch g First Trump—Catherines Well (Junius (USA))
1666[11] 2702[16] 3056[7]3305[8] 3610[12] 4021[2] 4511[8] 4730[2]5484[10] 6054[6] 6380[10]

Emphasis *Mrs A J Perrett* a67 63
3 ch f Pivotal—Matoaka (USA) (A.P. Indy (USA))
2634[5]

Empire Dancer (IRE) *C N Allen* a73 73
3 b g Second Empire(IRE) —Dance To The Beat (Batshoof)
1260[4] 1552[2] 2174[8](2940) 3871[6] 4395[7]5689[10] 6426[10]

Empire Day (UAE) *M Johnston* 108
2 ch c Lomitas—Evil Empire (GER) (Acatenango (GER))
(5460) 6010[3] (6216) 6456a[3]

Empor Castle (IRE) *Adrian Sexton* a31
4 b g New Frontier(IRE) —Is She A Star (IRE) (Sexton Blake)
6680[7]

Empress Jain *M A Jarvis* 100
3 br f Lujain(USA) —Akhira (Emperor Jones (USA))
(1264) (1604) 2227[11] 3047[6] 4080[18] 5642[10] 5921[11]

Empress Olga (USA) *E A L Dunlop* a72 66
2 b f Kingmambo(USA) —Balistroika (USA) (Nijinsky (CAN))
3645[2] 4041[8]

Empty Gesture *J R Best* a56 48
4 b g Cadeaux Genereux—Broken Spectre (Rainbow Quest (USA))
2317[P] 3845[13]

Emulate *B W Hills* a80 68
2 b f Alhaarth(IRE) —Aquarelle (Kenmare (FR))
(4994) 5672[11]

Encanto (GER) *Carmen Bocskai*
6 b g Dulcero(USA) —Espridoma (Primo Dominie)
305a[3] 455a[3]

Enchanting Times (IRE) *D G Bridgwater* a50 59
3 b f Danetime(IRE) —Enchanted Isle (Mujtahid (USA))
604[13] 1312[10] 1567[12]2260[9] 2494[14]

Enchantment *J M Bradley* 95d
5 b m Compton Place—Tharwa (IRE) (Last Tycoon)
1377[9] 1602[12] 1803[3] 1936[6] 2450[13]3038[11] 3332[7] 5009[5] 5433[8] 6009[13]

Encinas (GER) *P Schiergen* 110
5 br g Lomitas—Epik (GER) (Selkirk (USA))
(205a) 371a[3] 562a[4] 624a[4]

Encircled *D Haydn Jones* a67+ 54
2 b f In The Wings—Ring Of Esteem (Mark Of Esteem (IRE))
5623[9] 6050[5] 6324[12]6558[3] (6737)

Encosta Legend (AUS) *Allison Bennett* 90
8 b m Encosta De Lago(AUS) —Amnykore (NZ) (Wolverton)
6391a[9]

Encrypt (IRE) *O Brennan* a23 58
4 ch m Entrepreneur—Just An Illusion (IRE) (Shernazar)
1827[3] 2357[5] 3919[12]5955[15]

Enda Bu Bu *G Wildgen* 31
3 ch c Bahamian Bounty—Trina's Pet (Efisio)
758a[11]

Endiamo (IRE) *M P Tregoning* 83
2 ch g Indian Ridge—Aldafra (Spectrum (IRE))
1838[4] 2402[4] 5371[4]

Endless Night *H Morrison* a65 65
3 ch g Dracula(AUS) —La Notte (Factual (USA))
475[5] 993[5] 1375[11]2301[8] 3011[3] 3932[2]4531[10] 4930[9] 5474[19]

Endless Summer *A W Carroll* a69 83
9 b g Zafonic(USA) —Well Away (IRE) (Sadler's Wells (USA))
1899[3] 2096[2] 2618[3] (3297) 3593[2] 4211[9](4324) 4793[11] 5058[4] (5291) 5872[10]

Enfield Chase (IRE) *T Stack* 88
5 b g Foxhound(USA) —Melinte (Caerleon (USA))
1487[23] 3125a[24]

Enforcer *W R Muir* 121
4 b h Efisio—Tarneem (USA) (Zilzal (USA))
934a[6] 1267[4] 1507[5] 2202[3] 2845[3]3444[3] 3927[4] 4877[4] 5561a[3]

Enford Princess *Miss B Sanders* a80 86
5 b m Pivotal—Expectation (IRE) (Night Shift (USA))
555[5]

English Archer *J R Weymes* 57
3 b g Rock City—Fire Sprite (Mummy's Game)
1100[5] 2109[10] 2896[11] 3329[8] 4060[10]4728[14] 4959[5]

English Ballet (IRE) *B W Hills* 106
2 ch f Danehill Dancer(IRE) —Stage Presence (IRE) (Selkirk (USA))
(3796) (4371) 5187[2] 5522[3] 5966[5]

English Channel (USA) *T Pletcher* 123
4 ch h Smart Strike(CAN) —Belva (USA) (Theatrical)
2476a[4] 4386a[4] (5821a) 6344a[3]

English City (IRE) *B Smart* a45 61
3 ch c City On A Hill(USA) —Toledana (IRE) (Sure Blade (USA))
1078[10] (1731) 2243[2] 2518[4] 2795[4]3695[3] 3790[3] 4255[4]

Enjoy The Buzz *J M Bradley* a53 62
7 b h Prince Of Birds(USA) —Abaklea (IRE) (Doyoun)
38[12] 119[9]209[6] 260[8]766[13] 1209[7] 1528[5]1645[2] 1981[3] 2136[9] 2376[3] 2494[6]3438[7] 4872[10]

Enjoy The Magic *E J Alston* a29 54
4 br m Namaqualand(USA) —Abaklea (IRE) (Doyoun)
449[7] 844[11]1212[11] 4133[5] (4389) 5285[10]

Enjoy The Moment *J A Osborne* 97+
3 b g Generous(IRE) —Denial (Sadler's Wells (USA))
1741[5] (2261) 2805[2] 4039[6] 4459[5]

Ennobling *E F Vaughan* a50 55
3 b f Mark Of Esteem(IRE) —Noble Dane (IRE) (Danehill (USA))
1240[6] 5992[8] 6387[10]

Ensign's Trick *W M Brisbourne* a25+ 72
2 b f Cayman Kai(IRE) —River Ensign (River God (USA))
908[9] 2294[3] 2731[10]3246[3] (3746) 4170[7] 4762[4] 4912[4] 5509[7]6310[12]

Entailment *Miss Gay Kelleway* a63 75
4 b g Kris—Entail (USA) (Riverman (USA))
1995[10]

Enthusius *M L W Bell* 41
3 b c Generous(IRE) —Edouna (FR) (Doyoun)
1216[7]

Enticing (IRE) *W J Haggas* a95+ 104
2 b f Pivotal—Superstar Leo (IRE) (College Chapel)
(2984) (3684) (4026) 4738[13] 5802[3]

Entranced *Miss J A Camacho* a69 64
3 b f Saddlers' Hall(IRE) —Vent D'Aout (IRE) (Imp Society (USA))
1381[8] 2124[8] 3169[5]6244[5] 6565[7]6718[5]

Envision *R Hannon* a93 94
3 b g Pivotal—Entwine (Primo Dominie)
1115[7] 2024[7] 3045[4] (3213) (3664) (3951) (4429) (4819) 5520[3]5666[3]

Enzed (AUS) *Allison Bennett* 60
8 br g (NZ) — (NZ) (Veloso (NZ))
6391a[16]

Epatha (IRE) *J-C Rouget* 102
3 br f Highest Honor(FR) —Mouriyana (IRE) (Akarad (FR))
(5197a) 6454a[5] 6786a[8]

Epices *R Ingram* a73 47
4 b g Mtoto—French Spice (Cadeaux Genereux)
6841[11] 6982[6]

Epicurean *Mrs K Walton* a46 65
4 ch m Pursuit Of Love—Arminda (Blakeney)
(1997) 2627[14] 3141[8] 5513[10] 5904[5] 6275[7]6571[10]

Epidaurian King (IRE) *D Shaw* a11
3 b g King's Best(USA) —Thurayya (Nashwan (USA))
6944[6]

Epineuse *J R Best* a20 55
3 b f Gorse—Four-Legged Friend (Aragon)
3034[2] 3348[14] (4201) 4551[6] 6688[10]6856[11]

Equal And Approved *R Hannon* 49
2 b c Auction House(USA) —Rave On (ITY) (Barathea (IRE))
2878[4] 3588[14] 4334[7] 4926[12]

Equator *Mrs A J Perrett* a75+ 71
3 ch c Observatory(USA) —Fleet River (USA) (Riverman (USA))
1401[4] 1880[4]

Equilibria (USA) *G L Moore* a48 57
4 b g Gulch(USA) —Julie La Rousse (IRE) (Lomond (USA))
891[6] 2345[6]3437[5] 3616[4] 3894[2] (4282) 5201[7] 6378[5]

Equuleus Pictor *J L Spearing* a63 62
2 br c Piccolo—Vax Rapide (Sharpo)
3344[6] 4002[3] 5245[5]

Erhgent Sea *T M Jones* 11
3 gr g Erhaab(USA) —Gentle Gypsy (Junius (USA))
762[11]

Eridani (IRE) *M L W Bell* a40
2 ch f Daggers Drawn(USA) —Rorkes Drift (IRE) (Royal Abjar (USA))
6697[7] 6840[9]6976[7]

Ermine Grey *A W Carroll* a71 71
5 gr g Wolfhound(USA) —Impulsive Decision (IRE) (Nomination)
404[7] 992[5] 1288[6]1480[6] 1830[2] 2025[4] 2708[5] 3305[2]4001[5] 5621[5] 5954[11] 6300[5] 6497[8]

Ermine Sea *J H M Gosden* a81 100
3 b g Rainbow Quest(USA) —Bint Pasha (USA) (Affirmed (USA))
1613[2] 1940[2] 2412[2]2804[3] (3225) 4465a[5] 5700a[8] 6319[5]

Ernmoor *J R Best* a50 41
4 b g Young Ern—Linpac North Moor (Moorestyle)
32[4] 336[13]472[6] 792[13]

Erra Go On *Adrian McGuinness* a83 85
5 ch g Atraf—Pastelle (Tate Gallery (USA))
6671[7] 6690[10]

Erroneous I D (USA) *P Mouton* 98
5 br h Subordination(USA) —Ten Model Dancers (USA) (Green Dancer (USA))
6329a[8]

Escape Clause (USA) *Sir Michael Stoute* a79+ 87
3 b c Red Ransom(USA) —Promptly (IRE) (Lead On Time (USA))
1166[2] 1984[3] 2615[3]3317[3] 3875[4] 4661[4] 5086[4] (5844) (Dead)

Escape Route (USA) *J H M Gosden* a87
2 b c Elusive Quality(USA) —Away (USA) (Dixieland Band (USA))
(6072)

Escayola (IRE) *Grant Tuer* a85 90
6 b g Revoque(IRE) —First Fling (IRE) (Last Tycoon)
2238[3] 2723[8] 3078[6] 3888[8] 4369[5]5174[3] 6075[5] (6321)

Escobar (POL) *Mrs P Townsley* a48 19
5 b g Royal Court(IRE) —Escola (POL) (Dixieland (POL))
310[6] 398[12]853[3] 2636[14]

Escoffier *Pat Eddery* a64 35
4 b g Entrepreneur—Gooseberry Pie (Green Desert (USA))
218[9] 5513[15] 6037[8](6435) 6843[6]

Eskimo Nell *T D Easterby* a36 16
3 b f Polar Prince(IRE) —We'Re Joken (Statoblest)
1079[10] 1859[15] 2138[8]

Eskimo's Nest *D Shaw* a37 25
4 b m Polar Falcon(USA) —White House (Pursuit Of Love)
231[10] 311[14]407[9]

Esoterica (IRE) *T D Barron* 72
3 b g Bluebird(USA) —Mysterious Plans (IRE) (Last Tycoon)
978[3] 1185[9] 1592[3] 2050[6] 2399[4]2525[4] (2923) 3138[2] 3290[3] 3604[2] 4353[3]5312[9] 5446[6]

Espartano *M J Wallace* a85 87
2 b g Vettori(IRE) —Talighta (USA) (Barathea (IRE))
(944) (1354) 2724[8] 3126a[9] 5655[22] 6146[2]

Espejo (IRE) *K R Burke* 71
2 b g City On A Hill(USA) —Beechwood Quest (IRE) (River Falls)
4424[3] 4897[3] 5614[12]

Esperance (IRE) *J Akehurst* a44 41
6 ch g Bluebird(USA) —Dioscorea (IRE) (Pharly (FR))
484[9] 574[11]

Esplendido (FR) *R Chotard* 82
3 b c Spadoun(FR) —Enti Alamal (Rainbow Quest (USA))
5145a[7]

Esprit D'Amour (IRE) *T D Easterby* 60
2 b f Invincible Spirit(IRE) —Elton Grove (IRE) (Astronef)
1074[6] 1278[3] 1730[4] 2241[5]

Esprit De Corps *Sir Mark Prescott* a56 79+
4 b g Hernando(FR) —Entente Cordiale (USA) (Affirmed (USA))
97[9] 166[8]218[8] (5242) 5369[2] (6011)

Esprit De Nuit (IRE) *Mrs A Duffield* a48
2 b g Invincible Spirit(IRE) —Night Spirit (IRE) (Night Shift (USA))
6512[6] 6605[6]

Esquillon *S Parr* a23 38
4 b m High Estate—Our Aisling (Blakeney)
303[4] 614[6]1826[4] 2196[9] 3763[8] 4227[4] 4451[6]5927[9]

Esquire *Saeed Bin Suroor* 93
4 b h Dubai Millennium—Esperada (ARG) (Equalize (USA))
4782[4] 5523[17]

Essexford (IRE) *John M Oxx* 92
2 ch f Spinning World(USA) —La Rosetta (IRE) (Alzao (USA))
5707a[4] 6113a[3]

Esta Bella (FR) *H Hosselet* 37
4 gr m Astarabad(USA) —Sita Bella (FR) (Freedom Cry)
3580a[5]

Establishment *C A Cyzer* a83 84
9 b g Muhtarram(USA) —Uncharted Waters (Celestial Storm (USA))
(832) 1021[4] 1247[4]1931[3] 2723[14] 2849[7] 3446[4] 4046[3](4792) 5174[2] 5526[5] 6205[5] 6438[7]

Esteem *W Jarvis* a72 75
3 b g Mark Of Esteem(IRE) —Please (Kris)
1335[14] 2034[7] 2587[7]3387[2] 4004[3] (4426)

Esteemed Prince *D Shaw* a52
2 b g Mark Of Esteem(IRE) —Princess Alaska (Northern State (USA))
1333[5] 1824[7]

Est Est Est (IRE) *Kerstin Helander*
3 b f Shinko Forest(IRE) —Bongo Quest (IRE) (Be My Guest (USA))
2564a[8]

Esthlos (FR) *J Jay* a74 74
3 ch g Limnos(JPN) —Cozzie (Cosmonaut)
5353[2] 5879[2] 6240[4]6507[2] (6593)

Estimator *Pat Eddery* a77+
2 b c Auction House(USA) —Fresh Look (IRE) (Alzao (USA))
(6669) (6965)

Estiqraar (IRE) *J L Dunlop* 79+
3 b c Alhaarth(IRE) —Hureya (USA) (Woodman (USA))
(731) 895[6]

Estoille *Mrs S Lamyman* a45 58
5 b m Paris House—Nampara Bay (Emarati (USA))
864[13] 1195[7] (1571) 1762[5]2543[3] 4232[2] 4507[3] 4735[14] 5078[5]5443[9] 5928[4] 6533[10]6956[7]

Estrelle (GER) *H R A Cecil* 79
4 ch m Sternkoenig(IRE) —Enrica (Niniski (USA))
1132[7] 1502[10] 2762[4] 3209[4] 3399[2]

Etaar *C W Fairhurst* 80
4 b g Zafonic(USA) —Hawayah (IRE) (Shareef Dancer (USA))
5320[15] 5617[13]

Eta Draconis (IRE) *Saeed Bin Suroor* 83+
3 ch g Daylami(IRE) —Velvet Moon (IRE) (Shaadi (USA))
(2829) 3819[4]

Et Dona Ferentes *T D Barron* a49 60
3 b f Green Desert(USA) —Sister Golden Hair (IRE) (Glint Of Gold)
6944[2]

Eternal Legacy (IRE) *J Parkes* a4 58
4 b m Monashee Mountain(USA) —Tender Time (Tender King)
1185[4] 1609[5] 2129[5] 3379[11]4198[8] 4961[12]

Eternally *R M H Cowell* a40 33
4 ch g Timeless Times(USA) —Nice Spice (IRE) (Common Grounds)
299[2] 524[12]633[3] 686[3]789[5] 872[4]1228[11] 1571[7]6548[9] 6851[12]

Eternal Path (USA) *Sir Michael Stoute* 80+
2 ch f Theatrical—Houdini's Honey (USA) (Mr Prospector (USA))
6215[3]

Etesaal (USA) *Saeed Bin Suroor* a93+ 114
6 bb h Danzig(USA) —Electric Society (IRE) (Law Society (USA))
280a[6] 622a[2] 4908a[6]

Etijahaat (IRE) *C W Fairhurst* a9 76
4 b g King's Best(USA) —Dance Ahead (Shareef Dancer (USA))
1041[16] 1233[12] 4405[5] 4961[14] 5316[13]5485[9]

Etlaala *B W Hills* 118
4 ch h Selkirk(USA) —Portelet (Night Shift (USA))
(1050) (1287) 1778[13] (2675) 2846[14] 4025[5] 4596[6] (Dead)

Etoile D'Or (IRE) *M H Tompkins* 64+
2 ch f Soviet Star(USA) —Christeningpresent (IRE) (Cadeaux Genereux)
5043[9] 5638[5] 5898[3]

Etoile Russe (IRE) *P C Haslam* a76 67
4 b g Soviet Star(USA) —To The Skies (USA) (Sky Classic (CAN))
1996[17] 5354[2] 6430[12]

Eton (GER) *D Nicholls* a56 59
10 ch g Suave Dancer(USA) —Ermione (Surumu (GER))
48[4] 103[3]158[9]

Ettrick Water *L M Cumani* a104 104
7 ch g Selkirk(USA) —Sadly Sober (IRE) (Roi Danzig (USA))
1676[6] 2435[8] 5639[11]

Eulogize *E A L Dunlop* a68+ 65
2 b f Pivotal—Tantalize (Machiavellian (USA))
5882[3] 6486[3]

Eurana *Jedd O'Keeffe* 40
3 ch f Mark Of Esteem(IRE) —Intervene (Zafonic (USA))
978[9] 1888[6] 2699[5] 3288[8] 4199[15]

European (ARG) *R M Beckett* 80
6 br g Nugget Point—Enfeitada (ARG) (Gem Master (USA))
1280[11] 2302[10] 2531[7] 3149[6]

European Dream (IRE) *R C Guest* 87+
3 br g Kalanisi(IRE) —Tereed Elhawa (Cadeaux Genereux)
993[2] (1345) 1440[4] 1626[3] 1828[3] 3082[5]4108[3] 4298[7] 5810[11]

Evaluator (IRE) *I Mohammed* a64 107
5 b g Ela-Mana-Mou—Summerhill (Habitat)
356a[5] 509a[10]

Eva Soneva So Fast (IRE) *J L Dunlop* a91 78
4 ch g In The Wings—Azyaa (Kris)
5505[8] 5920[12] 6351[5]6602[2] 6661[2]6917[2]

Even Bolder *S Kirk* a70 67
3 ch g Bold Edge—Level Pegging (IRE) (Common Grounds)
1134[12] 1552[3] 2188[7]3055[7] 3406[2]3873[4] 4562[8] 5250[2]5872[13]

Even Hotter *D W P Arbuthnot* a49 44
5 b m Desert Style(IRE) —Level Pegging (IRE) (Common Grounds)
336[7]

Evening *B W Hills* a73+ 66
3 ch f Mark Of Esteem(IRE) —Kind Of Light (Primo Dominie)
1088[7] 2615[11] 3387[4]3934[2] 4173[8] 4660[5]5047[8]

Evening Rushour (IRE) *Brian Nolan* 81
2 b f Mull Of Kintyre(USA) —Tip Tap Toe (USA) (Pleasant Tap (USA))
3060a[6]

Evening Time (IRE) *Kevin Prendergast* 110+
2 gr f Keltos(FR) —Shadow Casting (Warning)
(5692a) (5850a)

Evens And Odds (IRE) *K A Ryan* 91
2 ch c Johannesburg(USA) —Coeur De La Mer (IRE) (Caerleon (USA))
2159[6] (3242) 3777a[8] 5681[4]

Event Music (IRE) *M R Channon* 73
2 ch f Distant Music(USA) —Evening Set (GER) (Second Set (IRE))
4161[2] (4731) 6092a[4]

Ever Cheerful *D G Bridgwater* a75 68
5 b g Atraf—Big Story (Cadeaux Genereux)
(23) 89[2] 220[4]376[4] 5246[9]5688[9] 6223[10]6353[5] 6478[5]6656[4] 6773[5]6919[4]

Everest (IRE) *B Ellison* a76 88
9 ch g Indian Ridge—Reine D'Beaute (Caerleon (USA))
384[6] 530[2]726[6] 3040[3] 3413[11] 3928[14] (4381) 4475[3]

Eversden (USA) *C G Cox* 76
3 b c Red Ransom(USA) —Who Did It And Run (USA) (Polish Numbers (USA))
2609[11] 3226[12] 3873[7] 4532[9] 4927[11]5148[6]

Ever Special (IRE) *P C Haslam* a32 45
3 b g Fruits Of Love(USA) —El Corazon (IRE) (Mujadil (USA))
93[6] 329[7]1293[6] 1501[5] 5838[8]

Every Inch (IRE) *T D Easterby* 27
3 gr g Inchinor—African Light (Kalaglow)
731[6] 1421[12] 1854[6] 2539[11] 3145[14]3791[14] (Dead)

Everyman *P D Evans* a55 62
2 gr c Act One—Maid To Dance (Pyramus (USA))
727[3] 849[5] 961[8]2416[5] 3372[4] 3678[8]4436[9]

Everymanforhimself (IRE) *J G Given* 97
2 b c Fasliyev(USA) —Luisa Demon (IRE) (Barathea (IRE))
(1080) 1824[2] (2127) 2719[12] 3734[10] 4146[5] (4460)4890[2] 5461[3] 5806[7]

Evident Pride (USA) *B R Johnson* a82 69
3 b g Chester House(USA) —Proud Fact (USA) (Known Fact (USA))
703[3] 1212[3] 3053[2](5388) (6652) 6781[2]

Evil Knievel (BRZ) *M F De Kock* a94 109
7 b h Legal Case—Rhana (BRZ) (Sharannpour)
(497a) 622a[5]

Evinado (GER) *P Vovcenko* 83
7 ch h Zinaad—Evry (GER) (Torgos)
3775a[5]

Evita *L M Cumani* 50
2 b f Selkirk(USA) —Darara (Top Ville)
6215[19]

Evolution Ex (USA) *I W McInnes* a55 73
4 bb g Bahri(USA) —Zoe's Gold (USA) (St Jovite (USA))
1544[13] 2169[12] 2621[9] 3309[6] 3694[3]4301[5] (5510) 5955[6] 6748[11]

Evolve (USA) *B W Hills* 39
3 ch f With Approval(CAN) —Conical (Zafonic (USA))
1119[10]

Excalibur (IRE) *M F De Kock* 114
6 b h Danehill(USA) —Sharaniya (USA) (Alleged (USA))
205a[2] 371a[4] 512a[4] 622a[9]

Excellent *Sir Michael Stoute* 62
3 ch f Grand Lodge(USA) —Exclusive (Polar Falcon (USA))
3367[11]

Excellent Art *N A Callaghan* 113
2 b c Pivotal—Obsessive (USA) (Seeking The Gold (USA))
(1090) (2084) 3126a[3] 4644a[3] (5373)

Excellento (USA) *E Charpy* a76 107
6 ch g Rahy(USA) —Golden Opinion (USA) (Slew O'Gold (USA))
153a[10] 282a[6] 438a[11] 513a[11]

Excessive *W Jarvis* 64
2 ch f Cadeaux Genereux—Show Off (Efisio)
5645 [3] 6175[4]

Excusez Moi (USA) *C E Brittain* a78 111+
4 b h Fusaichi Pegasus(USA) —Jiving (Generous (IRE))
2047[6] 2386[4] 2776[17] 3295[2] 4128[4](4609) 5011[6] 5375[2] 5712a[12]

Executive Paddy (IRE) *I A Wood* a65
7 b g Executive Perk—Illbethereforyou (IRE) (Supreme Leader)
6680[3] 6792[4]6861[4]

Exhibit One (USA) *V Valiani* 110
4 b m Silver Hawk(USA) —Tsar's Pride (Sadler's Wells (USA))
(2280a) 4192a[3] 4714[4]

Existence *D Shaw* a22
3 b f Zafonic(USA) —Nullarbor (Green Desert (USA))
6406[11] 6490[7]6637[10] 6731[5]

Exit Smiling *P T Midgley* a77 77
4 ch g Dr Fong(USA) —Away To Me (Exit To Nowhere (USA))
46[2] 121[6]210[U] 297[2]417[8] 458[6](906) 1257[2]1480[7] (1996) 3262[9] 5685[4]5889[8] 6928[7]

Exit Strategy (IRE) *W J Haggas* a55 63
2 b g Cadeaux Genereux—Black Belt Shopper (IRE) (Desert Prince (IRE))
5915[9] 6324[11] 6466[6]

Exit To Luck (GER) *S Gollings* a74
5 b g Exit To Nowhere(USA) —Emy Coasting (USA) (El Gran Senor (USA))
6734[2] 6878[9]

Ex Mill Lady *W De Best-Turner* a47 65
5 br m Bishop Of Cashel—Hickleton Lady (IRE) (Kala Shikari)
806[12]

Exmoor *R Charlton* a77 86
4 b g Cape Cross(IRE) —Royal Jade (Last Tycoon)
970[2] 1183[12] (1820) 2302[14] 4807[11] 5345[12]5670[8] 5896[6] 6020[3]

Exmoor Dancer (IRE) *H S Howe* a30 27
3 b f Mujahid(USA) —Amy G (IRE) (Common Grounds)
2531[11] 3348[11] 3842[6] 4484[8]

Expected Bonus (USA) *Jamie Poulton* a49 46
7 bb g Kris S(USA) —Nidd (USA) (Known Fact (USA))
1536[2] 1911[2]2966[5] 3115[10] 4667[12] 6232[13]6724[9] 6801[4]6852[11] 6904[4]

Expedience (USA) *Sir Michael Stoute* a62
2 gr f With Approval(CAN) —Promptly (IRE) (Lead On Time (USA))
6186[8]

Expensive *C F Wall* 100
3 b f Royal Applause—Vayavaig (Damister (USA))
2744[7] 3316[3] 3627[5] 3891[4] 4808[6]

Expensive Detour (IRE) *Mrs L Stubbs* 75
2 b c Namid—Sail With The Wind (Saddlers' Hall (IRE))
4066[3] 4843[2] 5655[9]

Expensive Dream (GER) *P Vovcenko* 114
7 b g Lomitas—Eurydike (GER) (Anfield)
1369a[2] 2061a[4] 3579a[5]

Experimental (IRE) *John A Harris* a73 78
12 b g Top Of The World—Brun's Toy (FR) (Bruni)
6451[10] 6497[9]6641[10] 6972[2]

Expert Witness (IRE) *M R Channon* 64
3 b f Jade Robbery(USA) —Golden Dancer (IRE) (Sadler's Wells (USA))
6333[12]

Explode *Miss L C Siddall* a40 54
9 b g Zafonic(USA) —Didicoy (USA) (Danzig (USA))
3298[11] 4425[10] 4709[13] 5838[13] 5955[3]6238[11]

Explosive Fox (IRE) *S Curran* a64 66
5 gr g Foxhound(USA) —Grise Mine (FR) (Crystal Palace (FR))
(1308) 1748[8] 3431[13] 5390[11]

Exponential (IRE) *S C Williams* a61 80
4 b g Namid—Exponent (USA) (Exbourne (USA))
316[12] 864[9]

Expression Echo (IRE) *A G Newcombe* a38 47
4 b m Bahhare(USA) —Bint Alreeys (Polish Precedent (USA))
172[11] 2497[7] 3610[7]5625[10] 5837[6]

Express Willy *J R Weymes*
2 b g Hunting Lion(IRE) —Express Girl (Sylvan Express)
3308[4] 3746[8]

Express Wish *J Noseda* 61
2 b c Danehill Dancer(IRE) —Waffle On (Chief Singer)
5658[11]

Extemporise (IRE) *T T Clement* a56 51+
6 ch g Indian Ridge—No Rehearsal (FR) (Baillamont (USA))
940[5] 1390[6](1914)

Extra Cover (IRE) *Miss V Scott* a51 59
5 b g Danehill Dancer(IRE) —Ballycurrane (IRE) (Elbio)
13[8] 783[2]59[6]

Extractor *J L Dunlop* 58
2 b g Siphon(BRZ) —Tri Pac (IRE) (Fairy King (USA))
3726[7] 4526[8] 5091[10]

Extra Mark *J R Best* a65 65
4 b g Mark Of Esteem(IRE) —No Comebacks (Last Tycoon)
35[6] 71[6]

Extraordinary (IRE) *P W Chapple-Hyam*
3 ch f Swain(IRE) —Oumaldaaya (USA) (Nureyev (USA))
1119[14]

Extravagance (IRE) *L M Cumani* a52 77
2 b f King's Best(USA) —Meritxell (IRE) (Thatching)
5296[2] 6073[7]

Extremely Rare (IRE) *M S Saunders* a65 81d
5 b m Mark Of Esteem(IRE) —Colourflash (IRE) (College Chapel)
949[13] 1188[9] 1545[4] 1878[15] 2173[9]2233[8] 2462[9] 3267[8]3593[5] 4003[9] 4985[7] 5378[6] 5756[9]

Eye Candy (IRE) *K A Ryan* a76 70
5 b h Princely Heir(IRE) —Timissa (IRE) (Kahyasi)
521[4] 6288[8]834[8]

Eye Popper (JPN) *I Shimizu* 117
6 b h Soccer Boy(JPN) —Sunday I (JPN) (Sunday Silence (USA))
1329a[4]

Eyjur (USA) *P Nickel Filho* 94
4 b h Dayjur(USA) —Southern Law (USA) (Red Ransom (USA))
497a[12] 621a[8]

Eyshal (IRE) *John M Oxx* 86
2 b c Green Desert(USA) —Ebadiyla (IRE) (Sadler's Wells (USA))
5410a[3] 5662a[2]

Fa A Mezz *A & G Botti* 101
3 b g Halling(USA) —Sispre (FR) (Master Willie)
2671a[2]

Fabine *B J Meehan* a70
2 b f Danehill Dancer(IRE) —Waypoint (Cadeaux Genereux)
6187[3] 6505[4]

Fabrian *R J Price* a76 84
8 b g Danehill(USA) —Dockage (CAN) (Riverman (USA))
1207[8] 1380[6] 1651[6]1830[11] 1995[6] 2510[10] 2708[8] (3197) 3469[3]3854[2] 3973[4] 4392[2] 4536[2] 4810[7]5149[2] 5479[8] (5889) 6221[7]

Fabrigas (IRE) *Kevin Prendergast* 92
2 ch c Catienus(USA) —Night Life (IRE) (Night Shift (USA))
3126a[6] 4824a[8]

Fabuleux Millie (IRE) *R M Beckett* a78 67
2 ch f Noverre(USA) —Flying Millie (IRE) (Flying Spur (AUS))
(3588) 4594[8] (5606)

Fabulous Emperor (IRE) *Jamie Poulton* a66+ 56
4 b g Imperial Ballet(IRE) —Al Cairo (FR) (Vayrann)
18[3] 218[11]

Facchetti (USA) *A P O'Brien* 89+
2 ch c Storm Cat(USA) —Twenty Eight Carat (USA) (Alydar (USA))
5692a[4]

Factual Lad *B R Millman* a64 77
8 b g So Factual(USA) —Surprise Surprise (Robellino (USA))
1152[12] 1754[9] 2351[7]3194[13] (3615) 4240[4] 4673[9] 4982[2] 5127[4]

Fadansil *J Wade* 51
3 b g Dansili—Fatah Flare (USA) (Alydar (USA))
2325[7] 3138[10] 3620[2] 4697[6] 5637[9]

Fade To Grey (IRE) *W G M Turner*
2 gr g Aljabr(USA) —Aly McBear (USA) (Alydeed (CAN))
2530[16] 2588[10] 2870[7]

Fadeyev (IRE) *K A Ryan* 70
2 b g Imperial Ballet(IRE) —Inga (IRE) (Project Manager)
3713[4] 4228[5] 4608[2] 4824a[13] 5364[3]5646[12]

Fair Along (GER) *P J Hobbs* a68 94+
4 b g Alkalde(GER) —Fairy Tango (FR) (Acatenango (GER))
3431[4] (4530) (4777) 5526[4]

Fair Breeze (GER) *P Vovcenko* 107
3 br f Silvano(GER) —Fairwind (GER) (Andrang (GER))
4648a[5]

Fairdonna *D J Coakley* a65+ 67
3 ch f Bertolini(USA) —Shamrock Fair (IRE) (Shavian)
4661[5] 5071[7] 5612[8]5953[9] 6390[6] 6608[3]6771[2] 6901[2]

Fairfield Princess *N A Callaghan* a78 85
2 b f Inchinor—Cool Question (Polar Falcon (USA))
1082[4] (1242) 1405[3] 2300[5]2630[2] 3084[8] 3252[6] 4326[3]4893[3] 5207[4] 5731[2]

Fairgame Man *J S Wainwright* a38 54
8 ch g Clantime—Thalya (Crofthall)
2182[8] 2544[7] 2700[11] 2949[8] 3608[11]3699[8] 3781[12] 3811[3] 4157[14]

Fairlight Express (IRE) *B G Powell* a55 59?
6 ch g Carroll House—Marble Fontaine (Lafontaine (USA))
2261[7] 2917[3] 3258[3]3983[11] 5390[6]

Fairly Honest *D R C Elsworth* a70 64
2 b g Alhaarth(IRE) —Miller's Melody (Chief Singer)
2530[15] 3083[9] 5457[4] 6412[3]6570[5]

Fairmile *W R Swinburn* a98 107+
4 b g Spectrum(IRE) —Juno Marlowe (IRE) (Danehill (USA))
1071[12] 1585[10] (2341) 2989[2] (3552) 4359[2]5675[18]

Fair Nashwan *B Grizzetti* 118
4 b m Nashwan(USA) —Fairy Sensazione (Fairy King (USA))
(5718a) 6004a[2] 6365a[7]

Fairnilee *Sir Mark Prescott* a65+
2 b f Selkirk(USA) —Fantastic Belle (IRE) (Night Shift (USA))
6921[3]

Fair 'n Square (IRE) *J L Spearing* 57
2 b f Fath(USA) —Icefern (Moorestyle)
1542[15] 2355[6] 2631[6] (2726) 3160[4] 4926[4]5162[8] 5747[14]

Fair Rosamond (IRE) *A Laird* a77 75
3 ch f Alhaarth(IRE) —Virgin Stanza (USA) (Opening Verse (USA))
202a[4]

Fair Shake (IRE) *Karen McLintock* a52 81d
6 b g Sheikh Albadou—Shamrock Fair (IRE) (Shavian)
214[10] 567[11]2378[3] 2627[13] 3040[4] 3331[5] 4253[14]4569[8] 5961[8]

Fair Spin *Micky Hammond* 62
6 ch g Pivotal—Frankie Fair (IRE) (Red Sunset)
1187[4] 3333[8] 4764[7] (4914) 5723[9] 6178[8]

Fairy Chief (SWE) *Annike Bye Nunez*
3 b g Be My Chief(USA) —Prussiluskan (Fairy King (USA))
4919a[12]

Fairy Dress (USA) *Robert Collet* a72 99
2 b f Fasliyev(USA) —Sun Spray (USA) (Woodman (USA))
6229a[4]

Fairy Inchinor *E Borromeo* a82
3 b c Inchinor—Fairy Sensazione (Fairy King (USA))
5473a[7]

Fairy Monarch (IRE) *P T Midgley* a51 58
7 b g Ali-Royal(IRE) —Cookawara (IRE) (Fairy King (USA))
1395[11] 2322[10] 2378[4]2697[8] 3147[4] 3283[7] 3716[8] 4511[6]4726[3] 5285[6] 5445[3] 5497[6] (5839) 6232[4]

Fairy Of The Night (IRE) *John M Oxx* 105
4 b m Danehill(USA) —Sassenach (IRE) (Night Shift (USA))
2041a[6] 2371a[5] 3123a[12]

Fairy Slipper *Jedd O'Keeffe* 38
2 b f Singspiel(IRE) —Fairlee Mixa (FR) (Linamix (FR))
4830[11] 5495[8]

Fairytale Of York (IRE) *D Carroll* a30 23
3 b f Imperial Ballet(IRE) —Pekanski (IRE) (Sri Pekan (USA))
2539[13] 3303[11] 4016[6] 4255[11] 4404[9]

Faith And Reason (USA) *Saeed Bin Suroor* a89 84
3 b g Sunday Silence(USA) —Sheer Reason (USA) (Danzig (USA))
2754[4] 3015[2]3589[5]

Faithisflying *D W Chapman* a35 28
4 ch g Wolfhound(USA) —Niggle (Night Shift (USA))
29[5] 1447[6]34[2] 687[2]783[3] (937) 1197[11] 1225[7]1390[8] 1765[7]3240[11]

Fajr (IRE) *Miss Gay Kelleway* a85 88+
4 b g Green Desert(USA) —Ta Rib (USA) (Mr Prospector (USA))
(268) (336) 764[2] (915) (1410) (1676) 1938[7]5428[5] 5639[3]

Fake Left *B P J Baugh*
3 ch c Foxhound(USA) —Ragged Moon (Raga Navarro (ITY))
5988[14] 6225[11]

Falcon Flyer *J R Best* a46 36
2 br f Cape Cross(IRE) —Green Danube (USA) (Irish River (FR))
3408[7] 4525[8] 4774[10]

Falcon's Fire (IRE) *Mrs A Duffield* a50 58
2 b c Orpen(USA) —Tres Chic (USA) (Northern Fashion (USA))
6012[8] 6316[5] 6466[4]

Falimar *Miss J A Camacho* a42 70
2 b f Fasliyev(USA) —Mar Blue (FR) (Marju (IRE))
2461[9] 3878[3] 4400[7]

Falkirk (NZ) *Lee Freedman* 116+
6 br h Tale Of The Cat(USA) —Madam Valeta (NZ) (Palace Music (USA))
2720[4] 3494[13]

Fallal Parc *M F Harris* a47 30
3 ch g Tachyon Park—Fallal (IRE) (Fayruz)
595[8] 1149[9]1576[2] 1799[6] 2249[6]3195[15] 4389[11]

Fallon (SAF) *S Seemar* 76
6 rg g Model Man(SAF) —Miss Pennyfeather (SAF) (Only A Pound)
356a[9]

Falmassim *L M Cumani* a17 74+
3 b c Mozart(IRE) —Scostes (Cadeaux Genereux)
1412[4] 1687[4] (3090) 3646[12]4296[4] 4666[6]

Falpiase (IRE) *L M Cumani* a75 81
4 b g Montjeu(IRE) —Gift Of The Night (USA) (Slewpy (USA))
4300[3] 4931[2] 5768[6]

Falstaff (IRE) *M F De Kock* 117
4 b h Montjeu(IRE) —Dance Of Love (IRE) (Pursuit Of Love)
282a[3] (356a) 562a[3] 741a[3] 1180a[11] 1716a[7]

Famcred *L M Cumani* a84 91
3 b f Inchinor—Sumingasefa (Danehill (USA))
1962[3] 2359[2] 3088[8]3643[5]

Fame *W Jarvis* a76 79
6 ch g Northern Amethyst—First Sapphire (Simply Great (FR))
140[10] 806[6] 1075[11]1425[6] 1821[7]

Familiar Affair *T D Barron* a76 81
5 b g Intikhab(USA) —Familiar (USA) (Diesis)
56[10] 200[13]343[9]

Familiar Territory *Saeed Bin Suroor* 101+
3 br c Cape Cross(IRE) —Forever Fine (USA) (Sunshine Forever (USA))
4082[4] 4805[3]

Fancy Woman *J L Dunlop* 35
2 b f Sakhee(USA) —Fancy Wrap (Kris)
6215[20]

Fancy You (IRE) *A W Carroll* a46 46
3 b f Mull Of Kintyre(USA) —Sunset Park (IRE) (Red Sunset)
1859[14] 3750[6] 3988[7] 4494[7] 5250[5]

Fangorn Forest (IRE) *R A Harris* a72 75
3 b f Shinko Forest(IRE) —Edge Of Darkness (Vaigly Great)
76[2] 1398[8]48[5] 1190[10] 1551[9](1693) 1843[11] 1934[7] 3067[6] 3301[10] 3708[6]

Fanlight Fanny (USA) *P Winkworth* 90
2 b f Lear Fan(USA) —Miss Nureyev (USA) (Nureyev (USA))
3148[2] (4283) 4715[2] 5154[9]

Fann (USA) *C E Brittain* a69 84
3 b f Diesis—Forest Storm (USA) (Woodman (USA))
855[4] 1108[4]1599[2] (2113) 2533[6]

Fantaisiste *P F I Cole* a102+ 89
4 b m Nashwan(USA) —Fantastic Belle (IRE) (Night Shift (USA))
(846) 1086[6] (1246) 2230[14] 2438[10] 3144[5]

Fantastica (GER) *U Ostmann* 101
3 b f Big Shuffle(USA) —Fatal Attraction (GER) (Czaravich (USA))
1328a[14] (6121a)

Fantastic Arts (FR) *Miss Venetia Williams* 69
6 b g Royal Applause—Magic Arts (IRE) (Fairy King (USA))
4792[8]

Fantastic Delight *G M Moore*
3 b f Fantastic Light(USA) —Putout (Dowsing (USA))
4959[8]

Fantastic Love (USA) *Saeed Bin Suroor* 109
6 b g Peintre Celebre(USA) —Moon Flower (IRE) (Sadler's Wells (USA))
205a[15] 624a[10]

Fantastic Mist *M Guarnieri*
2 b f Fantastic Light(USA) —Mistle Thrush (USA) (Storm Bird (CAN))
5705a[12]

Fantastic Promise (USA) *J H M Gosden* a56
3 b f Fantastic Light(USA) —Extra Fancy (USA) (Danzig (USA))
124[5] 4195[5]612[11]

Fantastic Santanyi *Mario Hofer* 98
3 b f Fantastic Light(USA) —Fresher (Fabulous Dancer (USA))
2374a[2] 5472a[11]

Fantastisch (IRE) *H R A Cecil* 84
3 b f Fantastic Light(USA) —Alexandra S (IRE) (Sadler's Wells (USA))
1118[4] (2620) 3088[5] 4838[15]

Fantasy Believer *J J Quinn* 113+
8 b g Sure Blade(USA) —Delicious (Dominion)
1487[25] 1835[13] 2230[6] 2429[9] 2824[5]3077[10] 3211[3] (3374) 3482[4] 3956[8] (4101) 4609[18](4796) (5182) 5358[14] (5642) 5942[8]

Fantasy Crusader *R M H Cowell* a55 61
7 ch g Beveled(USA) —Cranfield Charger (Northern State (USA))
1755[4] (1910) 2401[5] 2499[2] 3014[7]3615[3] 3934[8] (4240) 5205[5]5422[7] 6380[11] 6627[8]6700[8] 6904[9]

Fantasy Defender (IRE) *Ernst Oertel* a51 55d
4 b g Fayruz—Mrs Lucky (Royal Match)
290[7] 1723[7]1915[3] 2291[5] 2702[2]2820[6] 3339[3] 3614[5] (3933) 4276[7] 4585[10]5450[14] 6235[6] 6371[6]6628[3] 6702[2]6780[5]

Fantasy Explorer *J J Quinn* a69 99
3 b g Compton Place—Zinzi (Song)
1304[2] (1937) 2433[2] (2826) (3049) (3585)4717[3] 5535[9]

Fantasy Legend (IRE) *N P Littmoden* a48
3 ch g Beckett(IRE) —Sianiski (Niniski (USA))
124[11] 2159[4]19[10] 6551[12]6812[9]

Fantasy Parkes *K A Ryan* 74+
2 ch f Fantastic Light(USA) —My Melody Parkes (Teenoso (USA))
(5507)

Fantasy Ride *J Pearce* a78 43
4 b g Bahhare(USA) —Grand Splendour (Shirley Heights)
5657[14] 6107[15] 6772[8]

Fanzago (FR) *O Pessi* 86
3 b c Pennekamp(USA) —Fotostacia (FR) (Soviet Star (USA))
2671a[7]

Faraday (IRE) *B J Curley*
3 b g Montjeu(IRE) —Fureau (GER) (Ferdinand (USA))
6980[13]

Farafran (IRE) *E A L Dunlop* 61
3 b f Rainbow Quest(USA) —Sahara Star (Green Desert (USA))
1118[8]

Fara's Kingdom *Miss J A Camacho*
2 ch g Groom Dancer(USA) —Kingdom Ruby (IRE) (Bluebird (USA))
5615[13] 6284[10]

Faraway Echo *James Moffatt* 42
5 gr m Second Empire(IRE) —Salalah (Lion Cavern (USA))
5960[5]

Fardi (IRE) *K W Hogg* 64
4 b g Green Desert(USA) —Shuruk (Cadeaux Genereux)
1041[17] 1075[13] 1233[4] 1887[7] 2078[11]2408[8] 3140[11]

Farefield Lodge (IRE) *C G Cox* 77
2 b c Indian Lodge(IRE) —Fieldfare (Selkirk (USA))
2185[8] 2530[2]

Fares (IRE) *C E Brittain* a86 68
2 b c Mark Of Esteem(IRE) —Iftitan (USA) (Southern Halo (USA))
3485[5] 3844[5] 4107[3]4509[4] 5013[6] 5546[7] 5940[7] 6394[3](6525) (6586) 6881[2]

Farewell Gift *R Hannon* a81 77
5 b g Cadeaux Genereux—Daring Ditty (Daring March)
64[2] (221) 340[3]764[5] 1207[10] 1410[4]2510[9] 2819[4] 5149[10] 5908[7]

Farleigh House (USA) *M H Tompkins* 84
2 b c Lear Fan(USA) —Verasina (USA) (Woodman (USA))
2660[5] 3083[2] 4572[2] (5091)

Farley Star *R Charlton* a68 77
2 b f Alzao(USA) —Girl Of My Dreams (IRE) (Marju (IRE))
3640[3] (4552) 5546[6]

Farnborough (USA) *R J Price* a61 59
5 b g Lear Fan(USA) —Gretel (Hansel (USA))
72[8] 187[12]229[7] 285[2]358[10] 505[6]582[9] 647[2]733[10] 1138[12] 1201[6]1910[14]

Farne Island *J J Quinn* a62 65
3 ch c Arkadian Hero(USA) —Holy Island (Deploy)
1599[9] 1859[10] 2782[4] 3329[4] 3355[2](3609) 3695[4] 4257[8] 4426[7]

Farne Isle *G A Harker* 65
7 ch m Midnight Legend—Biloela (Nicholas Bill)
866[9] 975[10] 1144[9] 3215[7]

Far Note (USA) *S R Bowring* a38 34
8 ch g Distant View(USA) —Descant (USA) (Nureyev (USA))
159[13] 2715[3]30[3] 410[7]3052[11] 3995[7]6308[6]

Farouge (FR) *Mme Pia Brandt* 105
5 gr h Croco Rouge(IRE) —Fablimixa (FR) (Linamix (FR))
1558a[8] 4169a[7]

Farriers Charm *D J Coakley* a61 71
5 b m In Command(IRE) —Carn Maire (Northern Prospect (USA))
106[11] 251[11]

Farringdon *M P Tregoning* 79+
3 b g Sadler's Wells(USA) —Rebecca Sharp (Machiavellian (USA))
(3794) 4392[3] 5163[8]

Far Seeking *Mrs A J Perrett* 58
2 b c Distant Music(USA) —House Hunting (Zafonic (USA))
5914[8]

Fascinatin Rhythm *V Smith* a68
2 br f Fantastic Light(USA) —Marguerite De Vine (Zilzal (USA))
6486[5] 6746[3]

Fashion Chic *Stef Liddiard* a36 27
3 b f Averti(IRE) —Fashion Bride (IRE) (Prince Rupert (FR))
308[7] 477[7]

Fashion Disaster *A Crook* 7
3 b f Weldnaas(USA) —Give Us A Treat (Cree Song)
630[13] 978[12] 1147[12]2285[10]

Fashion Model *M A Jarvis* 75+
2 b f Rainbow Quest(USA) —Gracious Beauty (USA) (Nijinsky (CAN))
5754[3]

Fashion Statement *M A Jarvis* 84
2 b f Rainbow Quest(USA) —Shabby Chic (USA) (Red Ransom (USA))
4084[9] 5083[4] (5859) 6216[3]

Fast Bowler *J M P Eustace* a80 86+
3 b g Intikhab(USA) —Alegria (Night Shift (USA))
(3795) 4144[7] 5143[5] 5666[7]6461[10]

Fast Freddie *T J Pitt* a74
2 b g Agnes World(USA) —Bella Chica (IRE) (Bigstone (IRE))
701[2] 849[3]4026[P]

Fast Heart *R A Harris* a81 89
5 b g Fasliyev(USA) —Heart Of India (IRE) (Try My Best (USA))
1076[6] *1246[10]* 1475[4] 3211[6] 3447[3] 3832[7] 4521[9] 5627[8] *5907[4] 6428[13] 6681[3] 6844[5] 6858[9] 6966[5]*

Fastmambo (USA) *F Head* 94
3 b c Kingmambo(USA) —Slow Down (USA) (Seattle Slew (USA))
4168a[9]

Fast Parade (USA) *Peter Miller* a95 118
3 b g Delineator(USA) —Parade Of Gold (USA) (Prospectors Gamble (USA))
(6127a)

Fastrac Boy *J R Best* a63
3 b g Bold Edge—Nesyred (IRE) (Paris House)
3406[6] (5969) 6521[6] 6686[6]

Fast Tateyama (JPN) *I Yasuda* 114
7 b h Dance In The Dark(JPN) —Main Guest (JPN) (Targowice (USA))
1329a[6]

Fasuby (IRE) *P D Evans* a24 49
2 b f Fasliyev(USA) —Sue's Ruby (USA) (Crafty Prospector (USA))
701[8] 878[6] 1203[9] 2506[10] 2709[4] 3448[6] *4436[8] 4866[6]* 4980[6] 5084[7]

Fasylitator (IRE) *D K Ivory* a87 76
4 b h Fasliyev(USA) —Obsessed (Storm Bird (CAN))
670[4] 826[4] 992[6] 1265[2] 1993[2] 2401[3] 2708[4] *3101[3]* (3712)

Fateful Attraction *I A Wood* a73 58
3 b f Mujahid(USA) —Heavens Above (FR) (Pistolet Bleu (IRE))
(543) 594[3] 712[10] 2050[17] 2535[3] 3869[4] 4363[10] *4930[5] 5605[2] 5987[4] (6293) 6396[7] 6489[8] 6781[5]*

Fath And Furiouth (IRE) *P C Haslam* 22
2 b g Fath(USA) —Bay View (Slip Anchor)
1074[11] 1682[7] 2626[14] 5323[9]

Fathom Five (IRE) *B Smart* 85
2 b c Fath(USA) —Ambria (ITY) (Final Straw)
(1884) 2076[2] 2724[11] 4134[2] 4547[6] 5404[3] 5681[13]

Fauvelia (FR) *Y De Nicolay* 105
3 b f Polish Precedent(USA) —Marion (IRE) (Doyoun)
959a[4] 1874a[5]

Faversham *M A Jarvis* a74 76
3 b g Halling(USA) —Barger (USA) (Riverman (USA))
(897) 1270[4] *2556[7]*

Favouring (IRE) *M C Chapman* a55+ 58
4 ch g Fayruz—Peace Dividend (IRE) (Alzao (USA))
(144) 274[9] 423[7] 612[5] (784) 940[2] 1390[5] 1764[2] 2820[5] 2947[2] 3229[7] 3542[2] 3827[5] 5243[3] 5286[12] *6465[7] 6497[6] 6642[6] 6674[5] 6798[4] 6961[2]*

Favourita *J W Hills* 94
4 b m Diktat—Forthwith (Midyan (USA))
1477[5] 1933[6]

Fay Mayr *Edward Lynam* 57
3 b f Marju(IRE) —Mayfair (Green Desert (USA))
5849a[11]

Fayr Firenze (IRE) *M F Harris* a51 50
5 b g Fayruz—Shillay (Lomond (USA))
417[5] 708[11] 7769[6]

Fayr Jag (IRE) *T D Easterby* 116
7 b g Fayruz—Lominda (IRE) (Lomond (USA))
1778[4] 2303[5] 2846[15] (3076) 3494[10] (3732) 4080[5] 4410a[5] 4738[9] 5158[4] 5549[3] 5942[5]

Fayr Sky (IRE) *J J Quinn* 68
3 b f Fayruz—Dutosky (Doulab (USA))
1137[3] 2784[8] 3042[8] 3943[6] 4507[11]

Fayrz Please (IRE) *M C Chapman* a37 24
5 ch g Fayruz—Castlelue (IRE) (Tremblant)
715[6] *783[6] 870[5]* 974[14] *1763[4]* 2874[10]

Fealeview Lady (USA) *H Morrison* a69
2 b f Red Ransom(USA) —Alice White (USA) (Thunder Gulch (USA))
6031[9] 6187[11] 6481[3] 6646[3] 6832[4]

Fear To Tread (USA) *J L Dunlop* 83
3 ch f Peintre Celebre(USA) —Pleine Lune (IRE) (Alzao (USA))
1205[7] (2882) 3589[6] 4159[6] (4900) 6202[15]

Feast Of Romance *G A Huffer* a59 50
9 b g Pursuit Of Love—June Fayre (Sagaro)
27[2] 148[12] 261[7] 1054[5] *(1575) 1764[4] 2141[2]*

Feathergrass (IRE) *B S Rothwell* a39 65
4 b m Fasliyev(USA) —Jamaican Punch (IRE) (Shareef Dancer (USA))
104[7] 285[12]

Featherlight *J Jay* a52 52
2 b f Fantastic Light(USA) —Feathers Flying (IRE) (Royal Applause)
3495[7] 3707[11] 4400[8] 5053[13] 5492[4] *6322[4] 6421[3] 6518[4]*

Feed The Meter (IRE) *J Ryan* 83
6 b m Desert King(IRE) —Watch The Clock (Mtoto)
1544[3] 1677[6] 1847[3] 2508[9]

Feelin Foxy *D Shaw* a67 72
2 b f Foxhound(USA) —Charlie Girl (Puissance)
1278[2] 1491[3] 1831[6] 1977[3] 2743[12] 4421[3] 4594[6] *6255[4] 6409[3] 6512[3] 6596[2] (6742)*

Feeling Wonderful (IRE) *M Johnston* 67
2 b f Fruits Of Love(USA) —Teodora (IRE) (Fairy King (USA))
(6270)

Feelin Irie (IRE) *J R Boyle* a36 66
3 b g Key Of Luck(USA) —Charlotte's Dancer (Kris)
993[14] 1141[15] 1888[2] 2923[3] 3082[4] 3473[5] 3725[4] 4257[5] 4728[2] 4943[3] *6395[12]*

Fei Mah *J R Jenkins* a2 2
4 b m Vettori(IRE) —Bluewain Lady (Unfuwain (USA))
1348[13] *1571[13]*

Feisty *Rae Guest* a56 60d
2 b f Mujahid(USA) —Fifth Edition (Rock Hopper)
2100[3] 2588[12] *(3054)* (3228) (3834) 5053[14] 5482[16] 5948[13] 6064[11]

Felicitous *Saeed Bin Suroor* a88+ 81
3 b f King's Best(USA) —Embassy (Cadeaux Genereux)
(4663) 5317[6] *(5649) 6350[7]*

Felin Gruvy (IRE) *R F Johnson Houghton* 71
3 b f Tagula(IRE) —Felin Special (Lyphard's Special (USA))
1843[15] 2167[11] 4296[13]

Feminist (IRE) *J M Bradley* a54 67
4 b m Alhaarth(IRE) —Miss Willow Bend (USA) (Willow Hour (USA))
179[9] 212[5] 679[5] 789[3] 951[10]

Fen Dream *E F Vaughan* a50 59
2 b c Tobougg(IRE) —Fred's Dream (Cadeaux Genereux)
3259[4] 3976[10] *4433[11]* 4920[13]

Fen Game (IRE) *J H M Gosden* a79+ 73+
4 b g Montjeu(IRE) —Hatton Gardens (Auction Ring (USA))
264[3] 420[14] 1958[7] 4336[7] *5610[9]*

Fen Guest *Rae Guest* a58 40
3 b f Woodborough(USA) —Crackling (Electric)
3406[8] (3916) 4199[13] 4691[7] *6142[10]*

Fenice (IRE) *Robert Collet* 108
3 gr c Woodman(USA) —Venize (IRE) (Kaldoun (FR))
1718a[10] 1944a[6] 2278a[14]

Fenners (USA) *G P Kelly* 79+
3 ch g Pleasant Tap(USA) —Legal Opinion (IRE) (Polish Precedent (USA))
3359[6] 3637[3] 4022[5] 4472[12] 4884[12]

Fantastic *Rae Guest* a54 39
3 b f Desert Prince(IRE) —Golden Symbol (Wolfhound (USA))
2587[15] *2861[12] 3074[6]* 3264[7] 3411[6]

Fenwicks Pride (IRE) *A Berry* a41 45
8 b g Imperial Frontier(USA) —Stunt Girl (IRE) (Thatching)
29[10] 227[10]

Feolin *H Morrison* 71
2 b f Dr Fong(USA) —Finlaggan (Be My Chief (USA))
4373[9] 5352[3] 5859[4]

Fereeji *M R Channon* 16
2 b g Cape Cross(IRE) —Belle Genius (USA) (Beau Genius (CAN))
3222[11]

Fermion (IRE) *A P O'Brien* 109
3 b f Sadler's Wells(USA) —Pieds De Plume (FR) (Seattle Slew (USA))
(4179) 5220a[6]

Ferneley (IRE) *Francis Ennis* 104
2 b c Ishiguru(USA) —Amber Tide (IRE) (Pursuit Of Love)
4825a[3] 5653[3]

Fern House (IRE) *Peter Grayson* a50 48
4 b g Xaar—Certain Impression (USA) (Forli (ARG))
3199[5] 3356[5] 4551[2] *6233[6]*

Ferrando *G A Swinbank* a58 52
4 b g Hernando(FR) —Oh So Misty (Teenoso (USA))
900[6] 1166[13] 1537[2] 2150[7] 6161[3]

Ferrara Flame (IRE) *R Brotherton* a39 39
4 b m Titus Livius(FR) —Isolette (Wassl)
1002[13] 1276[13] 1723[12] 3161[8]

Ferroli *J Balding* a30 4
3 b g Efisio—Ordained (Mtoto)
1048[13] *1149[8]* 1829[16]

Festive Style (SAF) *H J Brown* a111 111
6 br m Fort Wood(USA) —Fanciful (ARG) (Ringaro (USA))
155a[9] 282a[7] 354a[6] 510a[6]

Festive Tipple (IRE) *P Winkworth* a62 29
2 b c Tipsy Creek(USA) —Gi La High (Rich Charlie)
4550[6] *5261[8] 5608[8]*

Feu D'Artifice (USA) *R Hannon* a74 74
3 b g Stravinsky(USA) —Alashir (USA) (Alysheba (USA))
720[3] 880[11] 1240[4] 1738[4] 2584[10] 2990[8] *3404[7]* 6019[2] *6459[3]*

Fever *R Hannon* a74 65
2 b c Dr Fong(USA) —Follow Flanders (Pursuit Of Love)
3843[3] 4534[3] *4992[5]*

Fez (SAF) *A Laird* a53 74
5 b g National Emblem(SAF) —Saladims Pride (SAF) (Salaadim (USA))
151a[10]

Fianello (ITY) *Gianluca Bietolini*
5 b h Hunting Hawk(IRE) —Speciality Package (USA) (Blushing Groom (FR))
393a[0]

Ficoma *C G Cox* a76 78+
2 b f Piccolo—Hemaca (Distinctly North (USA))
(4221) *4994[4]* 5748[3]

Fictional *E J O'Neill* 102
5 b h Fraam—Manon Lescaut (Then Again)
4461[2] 4855a[7] 5433[5] 5812[15]

Fiction Factory (IRE) *J Pearce* 36
3 b f Alzao(USA) —Nordic Way (IRE) (Nordico (USA))
1741[14]

Fiddlers Creek (IRE) *R Allan* a79 66
7 b g Danehill(USA) —Mythical Creek (USA) (Pleasant Tap (USA))
1251[0] 412[5] 1346[10] 1439[6] 1608[2] 2165[9] 2998[4] 3352[7] 4229[6]

Fiddlers Ford (IRE) *T Keddy* a59 61
5 b g Sadler's Wells(USA) —Old Domesday Book (High Top)
832[9] 1247[9] 1808[6] 2219[6] *3649[P]*

Fiddlers Spirit (IRE) *J G M O'Shea* 45
2 b c Invincible Spirit(IRE) —Coco Ricoh (IRE) (Lycius (USA))
1982[4] 2432[9] 3005[5] 5094[14]

Fiddlers Wood *V Smith* a75 86
3 b g Spectrum(IRE) —Tanasie (Cadeaux Genereux)
*219[2] 374[3](534) 805[5]*1095[4] 1473[5] 1951[8] 2805[18]

Fidelia (IRE) *G Wragg* a76
2 b f Singspiel(IRE) —Rosse (Kris)
6663[2]

Fiefdom (IRE) *I W McInnes* a77 88
4 br g Singspiel(IRE) —Chiquita Linda (IRE) (Mujadil (USA))
728[23] 1301[10] 1629[6] 2147[3] (2443) 2649[4] 2776[21] 3191[6] 3937[10] 4172[8] 4379[11] 4790[9] 5144[3] 5355[12] 5591[5] *5877[8]* 6160[12]

Fields Of Joy (GER) *H Rogers* 90+
5 b m Waky Nao—Flamingo Queen (GER) (Surumu (GER))
1156a[6]

Fields Of Omagh (AUS) *D Hayes* 124
9 b g Rubiton(AUS) —Finneto (AUS) (Cerreto)
742a[7]

Field Sport (FR) *C E Brittain* a23 47
2 b c Sagamix(FR) —Ewar Empress (IRE) (Persian Bold)
3157[10] 4140[9] 5321 [8]5933[9] 6172[8]

Fifty Cents *R Charlton* 84
2 ch c Diesis—Solaia (USA) (Miswaki (USA))
5339[2]

Figaro Flyer (IRE) *P Howling* a86 84
3 b g Mozart(IRE) —Ellway Star (IRE) (Night Shift (USA))
341[2] 1146[7] 1606[3] 2014[9] 2385[12] 2866[8] 3447[9] 3625 [5]4106[9] 4338[7] 4562[4] 4957[8] *5246[2] 5427[7] 5842[4] 6428[8] 6555[6] (6773) 6882[2] 6966[4]*

Figaro's Quest (IRE) *P F I Cole* a63 66
4 b g Singspiel(IRE) —Seren Quest (Rainbow Quest (USA))
973[7] (1313) *(1467)* 1590[4] *2345[3]* 2869[8] 3270[2] 4900[8]

Fight Club (GER) *A Trybuhl* 114
5 b h Lavirco(GER) —Flaming Song (IRE) (Darshaan)
2061a[3] 3993a[4] 4828a[5]

Fighting Mood *A M Balding* 52
2 b c Mujahid(USA) —Dramatic Mood (Jalmood (USA))
5460[13] 5730[9] 6016[4]

Figjam *S Seemar* a76 86
3 b g Groom Dancer(USA) —Sheila's Secret (IRE) (Bluebird (USA))
150a[9] 368a[15]

Figurative (IRE) *G A Swinbank* a60 36
4 b g Machiavellian(USA) —Marble Maiden (Lead On Time (USA))
147[4] 2422[4] 2423[2]

Fikri *T J Pitt* a59 71
3 b g Bertolini(USA) —Welcome Home (Most Welcome)
1153[8] 2247[3] 2550[5] 2833[2] *3154[11]*

Filara *R Menichetti*
2 b f Intikhab(USA) —Cimata Di Castello (ITY) (Lomond (USA))
3428a[8]

Filey Buoy *R M Whitaker* a56 46
4 b g Factual(USA) —Tugra (FR) (Baby Turk)
1258[11] 3159[10] 3240[5] 4381[8] 4467[9] 5483[11] *5929[9] 6280[10]*

Filios (IRE) *L M Cumani* a76 71
2 b c Kutub(IRE) —Karlinaxa (Linamix (FR))
5423[3] 5933[4] *(6284)*

Fillameena *P T Midgley* a44 44
6 b m Robellino(USA) —Lotus Moon (Shareef Dancer (USA))
259[9] 391[6] 468[9]

Filliemou (IRE) *A W Carroll* a38 31
5 gr m Goldmark(USA) —St Louis Lady (Absalom)
5056[8] 5566[11] *6780[7]*

Film Maker (USA) *H G Motion* 119
6 br m Dynaformer(USA) —Miss Du Bois (USA) (Mr Prospector (USA))
4385a[2] 5819a[2] 6340a[2]

Final Award (IRE) *G M Moore* 57
3 b f Grand Lodge(USA) —Never So Fair (Never So Bold)
2542[8] 2948[3] 3362[5] 4253[11] 4961[13] *5986[13]*

Final Bid (IRE) *M G Quinlan* a67 60
3 b g Mujadil(USA) —Dusky Virgin (Missed Flight)
142[5] 269[7] 6060[14] *6578[4]*

Final Contest (USA) *Patrick Morris* 68
6 bb m Grand Slam(USA) —Wild Secret (USA) (Wild Again (USA))
5706a[11]

Final Curtain *M A Magnusson* a61 45
2 b f Royal Applause—Forever Fine (USA) (Sunshine Forever (USA))
5899[5] *6071[7] 6505[9] 6653[10] 6807[5] 6926[11]*

Final Dynasty *Mrs G S Rees* a71 80
2 b f Komaite(USA) —Malcesine (IRE) (Auction Ring (USA))
4434[4] 5076[2] *(5245)* 5528[6] 5809[3] 6201[6]

Final Esteem *I Semple* 68
3 ch g Lomitas—Fame At Last (USA) (Quest For Fame)
1034[10] 3001[5] (3987) 4478[5] 5724[10] 6317[12]

Finalmente *N A Callaghan* a103 101
4 b g Kahyasi—Sudden Spirit (FR) (Esprit Du Nord (USA))
1685[4] (2035) (2231) 3078[11] *(3533)* 5963[27]

Final Promise *J A Geake* 74
4 b g Lujain(USA) —Unerring (Unfuwain (USA))
992[11] 1821[9] 2327[11]

Final Tune (IRE) *Miss M E Rowland* a78 64
3 ch g Grand Lodge(USA) —Jackie's Opera (FR) (Indian Ridge)
716[8] 1344[5] 2399[5] 3137[4] 3395[2] 3668[9] (3839) 4144[6] 4871[4] 5258[5] *(6193) 6323[2]*

Final Verse *Sir Michael Stoute* 113
3 b c Mark Of Esteem(IRE) —Tamassos (Dance In Time (CAN))
1486[6] (1953) 6218[9]

Financial Future *C Roberts* 75
6 b g Barathea(IRE) —In Perpetuity (Great Nephew)
1566[5] 2099[5] 2221[7] 3196[7]

Financial Times (USA) *Stef Liddiard* a82 80
4 b g Awesome Again(CAN) —Investabull (USA) (Holy Bull (USA))
(553) 1399[5] 1643[5] *1928[2] 2298[19]* 3447[13] 4019[7] 4208[8] *6844[2] 6935[2] 6953[2]*

Find It Out (USA) *T D Barron* 56
3 b g Luhuk(USA) —Ursula (VEN) (Phone Trick (USA))
1866[5] 2933[12] 3634[9] 4060[12] 5082[13]

Find Me (USA) *M Johnston* a71 50
2 ch g Point Given(USA) —Island Jamboree (USA) (Explodent (USA))
5537[9] 5730[8] *6145[3]*

Find The King (IRE) *D W P Arbuthnot* a45 49
8 b g King's Theatre(IRE) —Undiscovered (Tap On Wood)
6398[7] 6626[6] 6797[5] 6979[11]

Fine Day *M P Tregoning* 45
2 b f Fantastic Light(USA) —Queen's Gallery (USA) (Forty Niner (USA))
1930[6]

Fine Deed *Ian Williams* a18
5 b g Kadeed(IRE) —Kristis Girl (Ballacashtal (CAN))
6225[12] 6680[10]

Fine Leg *P J McBride* a46 43
2 b f Lujain(USA) —In A Twinkling (IRE) (Brief Truce (USA))
2791[5] 3358[9] *3645[9]* 4688[7] 4926[11] 5323[7]

Fine Ruler (IRE) *M R Channon* 69
2 b g King's Best(USA) —Bint Alajwaad (IRE) (Fairy King (USA))
4479[3] 5297[8]

Finicius (USA) *Eoin Griffin* 99
2 b c Officer(USA) —Glorious Linda (FR) (Le Glorieux)
3574a[5]

Finikas *S Wattel* 101
2 b c Desert Prince(IRE) —Maggi For Margaret (Shavian)
4464a[7] 5471a[2] 6229a[6]

Finished Article (IRE) *P A Blockley* a64 71
9 b g Indian Ridge—Summer Fashion (Moorestyle)
1164[10] 1305[2] 2221[4] 3377[3] *(3594) 4937[5]* 5479[5] *5736[3] 6382[7] 6474[9] 6623[4] 6801[7] 6860[2]*

Finlay's Footsteps *G M Moore* 6
2 ch g Dr Fong(USA) —Bay Shade (USA) (Sharpen Up)
3018[13] 4608[12]

Finnegans Rainbow *M C Chapman* a52 56
4 ch g Spectrum(IRE) —Fairy Story (IRE) (Persian Bold)
2[5] 97[11] 2398[4] 3231[6] 4945[6] *6972[7]*

Finnic Girl (ITY) *B Grizzetti*
2 b f Fasliyev(USA) —Wala (GER) (Acatenango (GER))
(2475a)

Finsbury *Miss J Feilden* a86+ 80
3 gr g Observatory(USA) —Carmela Owen (Owington)
1261[7] *(2553)* 3204[6] *(3644)* 4602[6] *5107[3] 5670[6] 5877[6]* 6580[12] *6830[3] 6999[10]*

Finsceal Beo (IRE) *J S Bolger* 120+
2 ch f Mr Greeley(USA) —Musical Treat (IRE) (Royal Academy (USA))
5466a[6] (5714a) (5966)

Fiona Fox *R Hollinshead* a57
2 b f Foxhound(USA) —First Play (Primo Dominie)
6821[3]

Fiona's Wonder *R A Harris* a40
2 b c Inchinor—Wondrous Maid (GER) (Mondrian (GER))
6290[14] 6891[6]

Fiore Di Bosco (IRE) *T D Barron* a53 59
5 b m Charnwood Forest(IRE) —Carabine (USA) (Dehere (USA))
127[6] 229[6] 350[8] 4931[1](792) 1201[3] 1729[10] 2360[2] 2808[3] 3305[5] 3610[10] 4010[5] *4439[8] 4709[10]*

Fiore Di Marzo (IRE) *M Guarnieri*
2 b f Elnadim(USA) —Splendid Sight (IRE) (Fayruz)
2565a[4]

Fire Alarm *J J Quinn* 38
2 b g Smoke Glacken(USA) —Brandywine Belle (USA) (Trempolino (USA))
1664[7] 3018[10] 3713[10]

Fire And Rain (FR) *A P O'Brien* 105
3 b c Galileo(IRE) —Quatre Saisons (FR) (Homme De Loi (IRE))
4678[6] 5185[10] 5657[9]

Fired Up (GER) *Saeed Bin Suroor* a70
2 b c Rainbow Quest(USA) —Fantastic Flame (IRE) (Generous (IRE))
6523[3]

Fire Finch *T Hogan* 80
5 ch m Halling(USA) —Fly For Fame (Shaadi (USA))
3128a[15]

Fire In Cairo (IRE) *P C Haslam* a12 53
2 b f Barathea(IRE) —Ibiza (GER) (Linamix (FR))
1595[11] 4650[5] 5083[9] 5721[7] *6926[10]*

Firello (NOR) *W Togersen* 76
6 br g Muhab(USA) —Fillippika (NOR) (Dalby Jaguar)
4864a[12]

Firenze *J R Fanshawe* a69 109
5 ch m Efisio—Juliet Bravo (Glow (USA))
2047[3] (2429) 2847[2] 4128[3] 5549[8] (5919)

Fire Of Love *N P Littmoden* a59
3 ch f Allied Forces(USA) —Princess Minnie (Mistertopogigo (IRE))
372[3] 531[7] 669[9] 5774[5] 6442[11]

Fire Path (USA) *J Rogers* 74
4 b h Tale Of The Cat(USA) —Stirling Bridge (USA) (Prized (USA))
6006a[6]

Firesong *Pat Eddery* a64 83
4 b g Dansili—Leaping Flame (USA) (Trempolino (USA))
992[2] 1302[4] 1830[15] 3151[6] *3642[6] 4336[9]*

Firestorm (IRE) *C W Fairhurst* 59
2 b g Celtic Swing—National Ballet (Shareef Dancer (USA))
3758[4] 4466[5] 5014[4] 6007[8]

Fire Two *M R Channon* a47 83
3 b g Cape Cross(IRE) —Reematna (Sabrehill (USA))
1101[4] 1596[4] 2330[9] 2779[2] 3214[2]3760[2] 4125[5] 4778[3]

Fire Up The Band *D Nicholls* a100 114
7 b g Prince Sabo—Green Supreme (Primo Dominie)
664[5] 729[7] 1069[17]1952[4] 2227[20] 2720[24] 2847[27] 5158[9]

Firework *E A Wheeler* a51 50
8 b g Primo Dominie—Prancing (Prince Sabo)
1689[16] 2971[9] 4141[14] 4365[3] *6131[2]6372[3] 6550[4]6632[9] 6727[3]6805[8]*

First Among Equals *D G Bridgwater* a9 37
3 b f Primo Valentino(IRE) —Margarets First (Puissance)
1234[6] 1771[6] 2187[8] 3306[10] 4201[6]4710[5] *6548[13]*

First Approval *B W Hills* a74 74
3 b f Royal Applause—Gaijin (Caerleon (USA))
1240[3] 1956[3] (2298) 3395[6] 3841[6] *5778[7]6489[7]*

First Bloom (USA) *P F I Cole* a65
2 br f Fusaichi Pegasus(USA) —Shy Princess (USA) (Irish River (FR))
6644[2]

First Boy (GER) *D J Wintle* a33
7 b g Bering—First Smile (Surumu (GER))
1257[8] 2137[9]

First Buddy *W J Haggas* a76 57
2 ch g Rock Of Gibraltar(IRE) —Dance Treat (USA) (Nureyev (USA))
5891[8] *6441[2] 6651[2]*

First Byte *Miss D A McHale* a34 44
3 b f Primo Valentino(IRE) —Shark Games (Mind Games)
83[10] 176[11]308[5] 439[8]538[11]

First Centurion *Ian Williams* a60 87
5 b g Peintre Celebre(USA) —Valley Of Hope (USA) (Riverman (USA))
1544[9] 2097[3]

First Charm (FR) *G Cherel* 96
4 b m Anabaa(USA) —First Choice (FR) (Exit To Nowhere (USA))
4979a[2]

First Eclipse (IRE) *G Woodward* 47
5 b m Fayruz—Naked Poser (IRE) (Night Shift (USA))
3912[16]

First Friend (IRE) *P Mitchell* a75 48
5 b h Mark Of Esteem(IRE) —Bustira (Busted)
4337[6] *5016[8] 5428[12]5877[12] 6147[9]6396[10] 6590[3]*

First Frost *M J Gingell* a25
2 ch f Atraf—Bless (Beveled (USA))
6840[10]

First Generation *P D Evans* a9 47
4 b g Primo Dominie—My Cadeaux (Cadeaux Genereux)
6763[11] 6860[12]

First Hostess (IRE) *J-J Boutin* 58
3 gr f Even Top(IRE) —Friendly Hostess (Environment Friend)
3692a[11]

First Look (FR) *P Monteith* 75
6 b g Acatenango(GER) —First Class (GER) (Bustino)
1502[2]

First Mate (IRE) *M Johnston* 82
2 b c Desert Style(IRE) —Sail Away (GER) (Platini (GER))
4066[4] (4349) 4681[3] 5133[5]

First Order *I Semple* a96 92
5 b g Primo Dominie—Unconditional Love (IRE) (Polish Patriot (USA))
*846[8] 1246[8]*1475[7] *1939[2]* 3092[5]3550[4] 4101[14] 4811[3] 5749[8] *6243[3](6583) 6720[9]6849[3]*

First Princess (IRE) *J S Moore* a64
2 b f King's Best(USA) —Try To Catch Me (USA) (Shareef Dancer (USA))
2980[4] 6441[4]6561[5] 6900[2]

First Rhapsody (IRE) *T J Etherington* a54 63
4 b m Rossini(USA) —Tinos Island (IRE) (Alzao (USA))
440[10] 818[4] 1253[15]1795[10] (2020) 2400[3] 2856[8] 4070[9] 4548[4]

First Royal (GER) *P Vovcenko* 52
3 b f Lando(GER) —First Neba (FR) (Nebos (GER))
6248a[8]

First Show *J Noseda* a79+ 82
4 b g Cape Cross(IRE) —Rose Show (Belmez (USA))
559[3] 641[9]946[2] 1957[3] 2510[6]

First Slip *Mrs A J Perrett* a71 26
3 b c Slip Anchor—Nanouche (Dayjur (USA))
4931[9] 5098[4]5478[8]

First To Call *P J Makin* 36
2 ch c First Trump—Scarlett Holly (Red Sunset)
4525[9]

First Valentini *N Bycroft* 50
2 b f Bertolini(USA) —Oscietra (Robellino (USA))
1295[7] 1853[5] 2076[6] 2680[5] 3173[6]3358[7] 4608[9] 4913[4] 5238[10] 5482[12]5790[8] 5956[9]

Fir Tree *S R Bowring* a47 38
6 b g Mistertopogigo(IRE) —Marina's Song (Savahra Sound)
26[5] 144[2]653[6] 687[4]1763[2] 2112[13]

Fisberry *M S Saunders* a61 87
4 gr h Efisio—Elderberry (Bin Ajwaad (IRE))
947[2] 1359[10] 3471[13] 5627[14]

Fisby *K J Burke* a78+ 78
5 ch g Efisio—Trilby (In The Wings)
3098[9]

Fish Called Johnny *B J Meehan* 92
2 b g Kyllachy—Clare Celeste (Coquelin (USA))
3895[4] (4109) 4200[3] 4736[9] 5372[13] 5681[16]

Fisher Bridge (IRE) *W R Swinburn* a62 73
3 ch g Singspiel(IRE) —Kristal Bridge (Kris)
4625[2]

Fishforcompliments *R A Fahey* 105
2 b c Royal Applause—Flyfisher (USA) (Riverman (USA))
3721[2] (4295) 4736[11] 5183[5] 6010[8]

Fisola (IRE) *C G Cox* 82
3 b f Fasliyev(USA) —Afisiak (Efisio)
1264[2] 2329[9] 2639[2] 3049[7] 3802[5]4208[3]

Fistral *M R Channon* a42 52
2 b g Piccolo—Fayre Holly (IRE) (Fayruz)
4177[8] 4688[6] 5570[10] *6258[7]*

Fit The Cove (IRE) *H Rogers* 100
6 b g Balla Cove—Fit The Halo (Dance In Time (CAN))
1171a[7] 5004a[8] 5849a[6]

Fit To Fly (IRE) *C A Mulhall* a32 42
5 b g Lahib(USA) —Maid Of Mourne (Fairy King (USA))
1198[9] 1341[4] *1573[3]*1757[6] 2240[7] 4087[7] 4256[7] *6423[6]*

Fitzsimons (IRE) *A M Hales* a37 46
3 b g Carrowkeel(IRE) —Our Pet (Mummy's Pet)
2861[14]

Fiumicino *M R Channon* 76
2 b f Danehill Dancer(IRE) —Valhalla Moon (USA) (Sadler's Wells (USA))
4552[6] 4866[4] 5178[4] (5492) 6007[4]

Five A Side *M Johnston* 84
2 b c Lomitas—Fifth Emerald (Formidable (USA))
(3663) 4458[2]

Five Two *M R Channon* 74
3 ch g Mark Of Esteem(IRE) —Queen's Gallery (USA) (Forty Niner (USA))
795[3] 1135[5] 1445[2] 2318[9] 3147[10]

Five Wishes *M Dods* 64
2 b f Bahamian Bounty—Due West (Inchinor)
4295[6]

Fizzlephut (IRE) *Miss J R Tooth* a78 86
4 b g Indian Rocket—Cladantom (IRE) (High Estate)
*80[12] 323[9]362[4] 532[5]*947[9] 1047[3] 1211[7] 1297[2] 1475[2]2189[10] 2624[3] 3027[6] 3449[7] 3972[19]4085[15] *4780[9] 6437[7]6555[10] (6585) 6709[7] 6740[2]6823[4] 6953[8]*

Fizzy Lizzy *H E Haynes* a50 50
6 b m Cool Jazz—Formidable Liz (Formidable (USA))
*249[4] 602[11]616[7] (768) 793[7] 1303[13]1463[3] 1764[9]*2599[8] *6694[6] 6803[2]*

Flame Creek (IRE) *E J Creighton* a89+ 76
10 b g Shardari—Sheila's Pet (IRE) (Welsh Term)
5934[2] 6272[2] *6438[6]6626[2] (6718) (6761) 6941[5]*

Flamed Amazement *M Johnston* 63
2 b g Hernando(FR) —Alligram (USA) (Alysheba (USA))
5565[4]

Flamestone *J D Bethell* a33 49
2 b g Piccolo—Renee (Wolfhound (USA))
1080[9] 1442[3] *1912[5]*2731[3] 3246[5] 3619[8] 4376[6] 4887[9]

Flaming Cat (IRE) *J Wade* 49
3 bb g Orpen(USA) —Brave Cat (IRE) (Catrail (USA))
1792[13] 2198[13]

Flamingo Guitar (USA) *David Wachman* 71+
3 ch f Storm Cat(USA) —Lotta Dancing (USA) (Alydar (USA))
1070[11]

Flaming Shot (IRE) *Jennie Candlish*
4 b h Son Of Sharp Shot(IRE) —Brockton Flame (Emarati (USA))
8[14] 5435[10] *6282[14]*

Flaming Weapon *G L Moore* a51 55
4 b g Unfuwain(USA) —Flame Valley (USA) (Gulch (USA))
939[8] 6238[7]

Flamme De Passion (JPN) *Katsuhiko Sumii* a95
3 gr c Kurofune(USA) —Curly Passion (JPN) (Tony Bin)
739a[3]

Flaran *J A R Toller* a63 63
6 b g Emarati(USA) —Fragrance (Mtoto)
1618[14] 2784[10] 3297[12] 3825[15] *6131[8]*

Flash Harry *John Joseph Murphy* 52
2 ch g Fantastic Light(USA) —Woodyousmileforme (USA) (Woodman (USA))
5410a[6]

Flashing Feet (IRE) *R Hannon* a44
2 b c Soviet Star(USA) —Delphini (IRE) (Seattle Dancer (USA))
6658[12] 6768[9]6845[7]

Flashing Floozie *A W Carroll* a49 53
3 ch f Muhtarram(USA) —High Habit (Slip Anchor)
*124[10] 219[5]422[9] 543[4]594[5] 839[5]*1314[5] *2246[9]* 2391[10]2877[7] 3115[4] 3264[3] 4154[8] 4279[3]4455[3] 4944[3] 5637[5] *5929[12]6370[3] 6707[5]*

Flashing Numbers (USA) *Mario Hofer* a98 117
3 bb c Polish Numbers(USA) —Tanwi (Vision (USA))
368a[4] 561a[6](3778a)

Flash McGahon (IRE) *John M Oxx* 99
2 b c Namid—Astuti (IRE) (Waajib)
(4747a) 5408a[4]

Flashy Bull (USA) *K McLaughlin* a112
3 gr c Holy Bull(USA) —Iridescence (USA) (Mt. Livermore (USA))
1498a[14]

Flashy Wings *M R Channon* 112+
3 ch f Zafonic(USA) —Lovealoch (IRE) (Lomond (USA))
1508[11] 2802[2] 5191a[3]

Flaxby *J D Bethell* 63
4 b g Mister Baileys—Harryana (Efisio)
818[6] 1253[2] 2112[7] 2541[10] 2789[7]3361[7] 3697[7] 4467[2] 5285[2] 5683[4]

Fleetfoot Mac *B Storey* a28 27
5 b g Fleetwood(IRE) —Desert Flower (Green Desert (USA))
490[6] 570[10]

Fleet Indian (USA) *T Pletcher* a121
5 b m Indian Charlie(USA) —Hustleeta (USA) (Afleet (CAN))
(5818a) 6343a[P]

Fleeting Memory *Sir Michael Stoute* a58 85
3 b f Danehill(USA) —Flight Of Fancy (Sadler's Wells (USA))
1546[2] 2350[3] (3346) 4159[3] *4997[10]*

Fleeting Passion *N P Littmoden* 78
3 ch g Primo Valentino(IRE) —Rosa Van Fleet (Sallust)
1355[2]

Fleeting Shadow (IRE) *D K Weld* 108
2 b c Danehill(USA) —Rain Flower (IRE) (Indian Ridge)
5715a[5]

Fleetwood Image *J R Weymes* a43 56
2 b g Fleetwood(IRE) —Change Of Image (Spectrum (IRE))
2854[4] *3157[8]*

Fleur A Lay (USA) *Mrs A J Perrett* a51 41
4 br m Mr Greeley(USA) —Toor A Lay (USA) (The Minstrel (CAN))
573[5] 897[13] *1166[5]*2459[14] 2676[5] *3014[12]*

Flexline (IRE) *Daniel Mark Loughnane* 62
3 b g Lend A Hand—Lady Tristram (Miami Springs)
4124a[5]

Flick N Flack *D W Thompson*
3 b g Namaqualand(USA) —Riyoom (USA) (Vaguely Noble)
1866[11] 3288[16] 4195[11]

Flighty Fellow (IRE) *Miss J A Camacho* a69 76
6 ch g Flying Spur(AUS) —Al Theraab (USA) (Roberto (USA))
815[6] 1280[16] 2627[6] 2974[5] *3688[9]3883[6]*

Flint River *H Morrison* a86 86
8 b g Red Ransom(USA) —She's All Class (USA) (Rahy (USA))
*100[2] 276[5]348[10] 489[3]*4573[8] 4807[9] 5233[8] 5572[3] 5937[5]*6493[4] 6696[4]6820[10]*

Flipando (IRE) *T D Barron* 99
5 b g Sri Pekan(USA) —Magic Touch (Fairy King (USA))
1043[7] 1495[2] 2200[4] 2440[3] 2614[4](3020) 3313[9] 5175[6] 5680[5]

Floodlight Fantasy *E S McMahon* a73 71
3 b c Fantastic Light(USA) —Glamadour (IRE) (Sanglamore (USA))
993[7] 1291[4] 1738[7] 2584[9] 2933[4]3347[7] *3650[3]* 4173[3]4892[2] *5388[11] (5972)*

Floral Pegasus (AUS) *A S Cruz* 116
4 ch h Fusaichi Pegasus(USA) —Crown Crest (Mill Reef (USA))
6784a[7]

Flores Sea (USA) *T D Barron* 70
2 ch c Luhuk(USA) —Perceptive (USA) (Capote (USA))
5307[4] (6013)

Florida Legend (IRE) *Miss J Feilden* a20 37
3 ch f Beckett(IRE) —Sunlit Ride (Ahonoora)
1674[10] *4396[10]* 5273[13]

Florimund *Sir Michael Stoute* a89 74
3 b g Sadler's Wells(USA) —Valentine Girl (Alzao (USA))
1055[9] 3451[4] 3794[11] *(5650) 6097[8]*

Floriot (IRE) *Werner Glanz* 117
4 ch m Monsun(GER) —Fureau (GER) (Ferdinand (USA))
2280a[2] (6124a)

Flor Y Nata (USA) *Sir Mark Prescott* a88 99
3 b f Fusaichi Pegasus(USA) —Rose Of Zollern (IRE) (Seattle Dancer (USA))
1789a[6] 2059a[3] 2912a[5] 4383a[2] 5008a[8]

Flotta *B G Powell* a90 88
7 ch g Elmaamul(USA) —Heavenly Goddess (Soviet Star (USA))
834[4]

Flow Chart (UAE) *H-A Pantall* 94
3 ch f Jade Robbery(USA) —Kartajana (Shernazar)
2537a[2] 3515a[13]

Flower Alley (USA) *T Pletcher* a127
4 ch h Distorted Humor(USA) —Princess Olivia (USA) (Lycius (USA))
6345a[11]

Flower Hill (FR) *A Trybuhl* 95
8 b g Esprit Du Nord(USA) —Fleur Du Cap (IRE) (Deep Run)
456a[12]

Flower Of Cork (IRE) *T D Easterby* a61 28
2 b f Noverre(USA) —Scarlet Ribbons (Anabaa (USA))
1295[6] *1743[4] 2139[2]*

Flower Of Kent (USA) *J H M Gosden* a74+
2 b f Diesis—Apple Of Kent (USA) (Kris S (USA))
(6486)

Fluffy *B W Hills* 55
3 b f Efisio—Sirene Bleu Marine (USA) (Secreto (USA))
2028[9]

Fluorescent *L M Cumani* 73+
3 b f Fantastic Light(USA) —Frangy (Sadler's Wells (USA))
1191[3]

Flur Na H Alba *J J Quinn* a71 76
7 b g Atraf—Tyrian Belle (Enchantment)
2504[7] 2784[9] 3297[13] 3503[4] 3988[17]4401[7] 4735[9] 5487[9]

Flushed *A J McCabe* a31 34
2 b g Foxhound(USA) —Sweet And Lucky (Lucky Wednesday)
1454[6] 1807[6] 4290[8] *6839[6]*

Fluted Crystal *H Candy* a41 57
3 b f Alhaarth(IRE) —Crystal Flute (Lycius (USA))
*2343[12] 2753[12]*3303[3] 3804[8]

Fluters House *S Woodman*
2 b g Piccolo—Little Tumbler (IRE) (Cyrano De Bergerac)
6330[15]

Fluttering Rose *R Charlton* a72 52
2 gr f Compton Place—Bethesda (Distant Relative)
6025[7] *6409[2] (6512) 6659[3]*

Fly By Jove (IRE) *Jane Southcombe* a55 22+
3 b g Fasliyev(USA) —Flyleaf (FR) (Persian Bold)
2445[4] *6914[5]*

Fly By Magic (IRE) *Patrick Carey* 71
2 b f Indian Rocket—Travel Tricks (IRE) (Presidium)
5850a[7]

Fly Free *D K Weld* 95
2 b f Halling(USA) —Gipsy Moth (Efisio)
5466a[13]

Flying Bantam (IRE) *R A Fahey* a83 74
5 b g Fayruz—Natural Pearl (Petong)
719[U] 898[8] 3813[5] 4253[5] 4655[6]5085[2] 5313[4] 5961[3] 6212[8] *6932[7]*

Flying Clarets (IRE) *R A Fahey* 83
3 b f Titus Livius(FR) —Sheryl Lynn (Miller's Mate)
(1596) 1851[5] 1999[2] 2324[4] (2679) 2892[4] 3477[4]3954[3] 4612[3] 5361[P] 5538[7] 5792[6]6202[6]

Flying Dancer *R A Harris* a41 57
4 b m Danzero(AUS) —Alzianah (Alzao (USA))
29[7] 144[4]388[4] 402[8]3595[5] 4223[4] 4450[7]5055[8] 5291[10]

Flying Doctor *G M Moore* 50
3 b g Mark Of Esteem(IRE) —Vice Vixen (CAN) (Vice Regent (CAN))
1293[8]

Flying Edge (IRE) *E J Alston* a59 76
6 b g Flying Spur(AUS) —Day Is Dawning (IRE) (Green Forest (USA))
1795[12] *2211[11]* 2504[3]2898[4] 3811[2] (4230) 6160[14] *6323[11]*

Flying Encore (IRE) *W R Swinburn* a75 78
2 b f Royal Applause—Come Fly With Me (Bluebird (USA))
3640[4] 4525[3] *5095[2]*6018[4]

Flying Fraam (SWE) *Mme Pia Brandt* a50 78
3 br c Fraam—Pinkie Rose (FR) (Kenmare (FR))
4420a[9]

Flying Glitter (USA) *R Werner* a107 105
4 b m Glitterman(USA) —American Flier (USA) (Quiet American (USA))
3109a[8]

Flying Goose (IRE) *L M Cumani* a74
2 ch c Danehill Dancer(IRE) —Top Of The Form (IRE) (Masterclass (USA))
6324[2]

Flying Grey (IRE) *P A Blockley* a57 54
2 gr c Desert Prince(IRE) —Grey Goddess (Godswalk (USA))
4920[10] 5112[5] 5379[6] *5738[4]*6064[8] *6291[9] 6322[5]6466[5]*

Flyingit (USA) *K A Ryan* a65 88?
3 b f Lear Fan(USA) —Byre Bird (USA) (Diesis)
3575a[6] *6792[3] (6817)*

Flying Lion *M R Channon*
2 b f Hunting Lion(IRE) —Princess Kelly (Prince Daniel (USA))
727[5] 877[6] 962[8] 2588[3] (2870)

Flying Namid (IRE) *P A Blockley*
2 b f Namid—Palio Flyer (Slip Anchor)
2552[12] 4327[9]

Flying Pass *D J S Ffrench Davis* a69 71
4 b g Alzao(USA) —Complimentary Pass (Danehill (USA))
50[10] 171[6]319[11] 375[5]478[9] 965[11] *1244[2]1334[9] 1400[9]*

Flying Patriarch *G L Moore* a38 37
5 gr g Silver Patriarch(IRE) —Flying Wind (Forzando)
614[4]

Flying Penne *R Curtis* a18 31
3 b f Pennekamp(USA) —Flying Wind (Forzando)
1140[16] 1314[12] 1433[13] *1726[7]*4868[11] 5259[7] 5733[8] 5887[8]

Flying Spirit (IRE) *G L Moore* a60 78
7 b g Flying Spur(AUS) —All Laughter (Vision (USA))
556[9]

Flying Spud *A J Chamberlain* a42
5 ch g Fraam—Lorcanjo (Hallgate)
3[5] 231[12]247[11] 304[10]382[12]

Flying Tackle *I W McInnes* a53 57
8 ch g First Trump—Frighten The Life (King's Lake (USA))
2494[3] 2780[7] 2949[9] 3608[3] 3781[4]3988[8] 4655[7] 4872[2] 5631[7] *6541[8]*

Flying Valentino *G A Swinbank* 74+
2 b f Primo Valentino(IRE) —Flying Romance (IRE) (Flying Spur (AUS))
3188[7] (4251)

Flying Venture (IRE) *B J McMath*
4 b m Mujadil(USA) —Angela's Venture (GER) (Simply Great (FR))
2498[8] 2919[P]

Flying Visitor *J M P Eustace* a39 42
3 b f Magic Ring(IRE) —Just Visiting (Superlative)
1401[11] 1759[9] 2615[12]3472[8] 4450[8]

Flyingwithoutwings *A King* a42 52
7 b g Komaite(USA) —Light Slippers (IRE) (Ela-Mana-Mou)
218[7] 539[9]720[10] 1204[5] *1729[11]*

Flylowflylong (IRE) *I Semple* a70 69
3 b f Danetime(IRE) —Jellybeen (IRE) (Petardia)
448[5] 2525[6] 2977[7]3395[7] 4296[2] 4524[4] *5036[3]*5401[5] 5861[8] *6260[3]6419[4]*

Fly More *J M Bradley* a11 45
9 ch g Lycius(USA) —Double River (USA) (Irish River (FR))
1303[11] 1722[11]

Flyng Teapot (IRE) *J Heloury* 48
2 ch c King Charlemagne(USA) —Joyfullness (USA) (Dixieland Band (USA))
4415a[9]

Flyoff (IRE) *Mrs N Macauley* a14 55
9 b g Mtoto—Flyleaf (FR) (Persian Bold)
6795[13] 6972[10]

Fly Society (DEN) *S Jensen* 107
5 b h Flyinfact(FR) —Pollenca (IRE) (Law Society (USA))
2123a[2] 4864a[5]

Fly So Free (IRE) *D Nicholls* 61
2 b f Fath(USA) —Xania (Mujtahid (USA))
1121[4] 1295[3] 4017[9]

Fly The World *A P Jarvis* a52
2 b f Agnes World(USA) —Focosa (ITY) (In The Wings)
5352[14] 5425[8] 6640[9]

Fly Time *Mrs L Williamson* a52 50
2 b f Fraam—Kissing Time (Lugana Beach)
1853[2] 2125[10] 2478[2] 2643[5] 2759[5]3010[7] 3345[2] 3860[3]4283[5] 4816[2] 5434[12] 5687[3]6255[12] 6401[11]6605[4] 6789[U]

Fly To Dubai (IRE) *T G McCourt* a68 75
4 b g Fly To The Stars—Morna's Fan (FR) (Lear Fan (USA))
4094a[9]

Focus Group (USA) *J J Quinn* 95
5 b g Kris S(USA) —Interim (Sadler's Wells (USA))
8657 1585[3] 1775[3] 2229[10] 3552[17]

Focus Star *J M Jefferson* 51
2 ch g Auction House(USA) —Vida (IRE) (Wolfhound (USA))
1863[8] 2191[7] 2523[6] 3286[8] 5613[14]

Folga *J G Given* a90 99
4 b m Atraf—Desert Dawn (Belfort (FR))
1076[9] 1597[10] 1939[3]2233[2] 2683[4] (2830) (3144) 3482[10] (3741) 4128[2]4343[9] 4633[8]

Folio (USA) *B W Hills* 78
2 b c Langfuhr(CAN) —Foible (USA) (Riverman (USA))
2287[2] 2680[2] 3701[7] 4681[18] 5449[4]

Folio (IRE) *W J Musson* a76 94
6 b g Perugino(USA) —Bayleaf (Efisio)
1544[2] 1992[2] 2508[2] (2761) 3366[4] 4023[3]4359[6] 5299[2] 5787[11] 6107[3] (6337)

Folk Opera (IRE) *M A Jarvis* a77
2 ch f Singspiel(IRE) —Skiphall (Halling (USA))
5906[3]

Folk Tune (IRE) *J-C Rouget* 102
3 b c Danehill(USA) —Musk Lime (USA) (Private Account (USA))
4862a[6]

Folle Biche (FR) *Mme N Rossio* a66 94
3 br f Take Risks(FR) —Folle Garde (FR) (Garde Royale)
773a[4] 1789a[5] 2374a[6]

Follingworth (IRE) *A D Brown* 41
3 ch f Midhish—Pennine Way (IRE) (Waajib)
1226[12] 1343[11]

Following Flow (USA) *R Hollinshead* a81 80
4 bb g King Of Kings(IRE) —Sign Here (USA) (Private Terms (USA))
384[7] (567) 826[15]1280[6] 1830[6] 2170[10] 6741[8]6898[4]

Follow Me In (IRE) *K R Burke* 47
3 b f Elnadim(USA) —Arjan (IRE) (Paris House)
53[RR]

Follow My Trail (IRE) *B Smart* 56+
3 br g Indian Danehill(IRE) —Lady Stalker (Primo Dominie)
859[10] 1073[14] 1217[12]

Follow On *A P Jarvis* a81 71
4 b h Barathea(IRE) —Handora (IRE) (Hernando (FR))
1343[4] 2412[4] 2712[10] 3203[3]3446[9]

Follow The Buzz *J M Bradley*
2 b c Enjoy The Buzz—Moody Madam (Man Among Men (IRE))
5841[12] 6050[13]

Follow The Colours (IRE) *J W Hills* a76 72
3 b g Rainbow Quest(USA) —Gardenia (IRE) (Sadler's Wells (USA))
963[2] 1241[3] 1934[3] 2518[8] 3221[8](3639) 4044[6]4565[5] 6070[10]

Follow The Flag (IRE) *N P Littmoden* a59 72
2 ch g Traditionally(USA) —Iktidar (Green Desert (USA))
2604[3] 3259[3] 3485[2]4100[3] 4766[12]

Folly Lodge *B W Hills* a80 71
2 ch f Grand Lodge(USA) —Marika (Marju (IRE))
4148[7] (5424) 5672[10]

Fondness *D Carroll* a56 74
3 ch f Dr Fong(USA) —Island Story (Shirley Heights)
1118[5] 1741[7] 1940[5]3152[6] 6588[6]

Fongalong *Tom Dascombe* a29+ 73?
2 b f Dr Fong(USA) —Shafir (IRE) (Shaadi (USA))
2631[9] 3026[7] 3407[6]

Fongs Gazelle *M Johnston* 71
2 b f Dr Fong(USA) —Greensand (Green Desert (USA))
1278[4] 1863[3] 2807[5] 3940[2] 4509[5]5322[3] 5492[2] 6007[2]

Fonic Rock (IRE) *M L W Bell* 63
3 b f Zafonic(USA) —Blue Crystal (IRE) (Lure (USA))
1350[6] 2539[2] 3145[11] 3803[2] 4118[9]5057[13] 5451[7] 6057[4]

Font *J R Fanshawe* 87
3 b g Sadler's Wells(USA) —River Saint (USA) (Irish River (FR))
1101[2] 5768[3]

Fontana Amorosa *K A Ryan* 79
2 ch f Cadeaux Genereux—Bella Lambada (Lammtarra (USA))
1082[7] (1824) 5966[14]

Fontanally Springs (IRE) *H Rogers* 93
4 b m Namid—Mary's Way (GR) (Night Shift (USA))
1469a[14] 2308a[4] 3124a[8]

Fonthill Road (IRE) *R A Fahey* a77 109
6 ch g Royal Abjar(USA) —Hannah Huxtable (IRE) (Master Willie)
1663[5] 1778[10] 4609[13] 5009[9] (5358) 5578[2]5921[5]

Foodbroker Founder *D R C Elsworth* 86
6 ch g Groom Dancer(USA) —Nemea (USA) (The Minstrel (CAN))
1992[13] 2229[12] 2989[8]

Food For Thought *J J Quinn* a56 58
3 b f Mind Games—Ladycake (IRE) (Perugino (USA))
2195[12] 3379[3] 3998[11]6431[11] 6549[10]

Foolish Groom *R Hollinshead* a64 67
5 ch g Groom Dancer(USA) —Scared (Royal Academy (USA))
1075[5] 1422[11] 1850[5] 2098[2] 2641[3]3044[2] 3469[9] 4871[5] 4983[9] 6300[12]

Fool Me (IRE) *E S McMahon* 87
2 b c Mull Of Kintyre(USA) —Dawn's Folly (IRE) (Bluebird (USA))
8924 (1284) 4200[2]

Fooram (NZ) *John O'Shea* 105
5 ch g Maroof(USA) —Sinjani (NZ) (Sir Tristram)
6455a[3]

Football Crazy (IRE) *P Bowen* 84
7 b g Mujadil(USA) —Schonbein (IRE) (Persian Heights)
2723[22]

Footstepsinthesnow (IRE) *M A Buckley* a65 47
3 b f Medicean—Charlecote (IRE) (Caerleon (USA))
2383[5] 3090[7] 3554[6] 5761[12] 5988[7]6128[11] 6459[6]6911[8] 6987[10]

Forbidden (IRE) *Daniel Mark Loughnane* 68
3 ch g Singspiel(IRE) —Fragrant Oasis (USA) (Rahy (USA))
4034a[6]

Forced Upon Us *P J McBride* a59 51
2 ch g Allied Forces(USA) —Zing (Zilzal (USA))
4600[9] (5387) 6900[6]

Force Group (IRE) *M H Tompkins* a62 59
2 b c Invincible Spirit(IRE) —Spicebird (IRE) (Ela-Mana-Mou)
5460[8] 5918[11] 6324[8]

Force Nine (AUS) *Cliff Brown* 90
5 b g Zabeel(NZ) —Barents Sea (USA) (Sea Hero (USA))
6455a[9]

Forces Sweetheart *V Smith* a72 86
3 bb f Allied Forces(USA) —Talighta (USA) (Barathea (IRE))
595[11] 1263[8] 2316[11]3299[7] 3866[7] 4164[10] (4494) (4690) (5327) (5756) (5902) 6020[5]6335[9] 6446[6]

Forefathers (USA) *M L W Bell* 63+
2 b c Gone West(USA) —Star Of Goshen (USA) (Lord At War (ARG))
4928[7]

Foreign Affairs *Sir Mark Prescott* 110
8 ch h Hernando(FR) —Entente Cordiale (USA) (Affirmed (USA))
1677[5] 2453[3] (2840a) (3660a) 4081[15] 4639a[2]

Foreign Edition (IRE) *Miss J A Camacho* a84 93
4 b g Anabaa(USA) —Palacegate Episode (IRE) (Drumalis)
4682[16] 5117[3] 5842[5]6499[7]

Foreign Envoy (IRE) *B W Hills* a48 64+
3 ch g Grand Lodge(USA) —Soviet Artic (FR) (Bering)
1049[9] 1240[5] 2434[8] 2882[6] 3046[9]

Foreigner (IRE) *B J Meehan* a61 73
3 b g Montjeu(IRE) —Northumbrian Belle (IRE) (Distinctly North (USA))
4776[4] 5086[5] 5426[6]5651[10]

Foreign Language (USA) *N A Callaghan* a60+
3 ch f Distant View(USA) —Binary (Rainbow Quest (USA))
6593[3] 6765[2](6861)

Foreign Music (FR) *H J Groschel* 72
2 b f Tiger Hill(IRE) —Foreign Affair (GER) (Goofalik (USA))
6122a[8]

For Eileen *M G Quinlan* a53 33
2 b f Dinar(USA) —Dreams Of Zena (Dreams End)
1136[7] 6258[3] 6511[2]6996[7]

Foreland Sands (IRE) *J R Best* 20
2 b g Desert Sun—Penrose (IRE) (Wolfhound (USA))
4550[7] 5043[12] 5231[10]

Forementor *D K Ivory* a17
3 b f Little Jim—Lizzy Cantle (Homing)
3647[11] 4396[12]

Foreplay (IRE) *E A L Dunlop* a83 71
3 b f Lujain(USA) —Watch Me (IRE) (Green Desert (USA))
1551[4] 2293[2] 2554[8]3099[3] 4265[11] 4368[5]4820[8] 6227[2] (6573) 6932[2]

Forest Air (IRE) *B R Johnson* a30 52
6 br m Charnwood Forest(IRE) —Auriga (Belmez (USA))
4077[7] 4278[7]

Forest Dane *Mrs N Smith* a82 79
6 b g Danetime(IRE) —Forest Maid (Thatching)
886[2] (1539) 1728[3](2136) 2813[3] 3199[3] 4208[4](4486) 4780[5] (5148) 5476[2] 5782[2](6035) 6065[9] 6352[5]

Forestelle (IRE) *M Dods* a6 53
3 br f Shinko Forest(IRE) —Machudi (Bluebird (USA))
1127[4] 1687[6] 2129[6] 3166[5] 3378[10]

Forest Lodge (IRE) *D R C Elsworth* 44
3 ch f Indian Lodge(IRE) —Folkboat (Kalaglow)
1955[10] 2678[5] 4944[9]

Forest Machine *J S Wainwright* 57
2 b g Largesse—Polar Storm (IRE) (Law Society (USA))
4452[5] 4956[4]

Forest Of Love *M W Easterby* a72 73
4 br m Charnwood Forest(IRE) —Touch And Love (IRE) (Green Desert (USA))
101[10] 639[10]737[10]

Forever Autumn *B J Meehan* 59
3 b g Sinndar(IRE) —Photo Call (Chief Singer)
1483[6] 2412[5] 2712[14]

Forever Bond (BRZ) *Robert Collet* 73
5 b h Choctaw Ridge(USA) —Flight To Rome (USA) (Storm Bird (CAN))
3692a[8]

Forever Rocky *F Jordan* 10
3 b g Kayf Tara—Song For Jess (IRE) (Accordion)
1290[12] 1726[10] 2968[13]

Forever Thine *J A Geake* 5
3 ch f Groom Dancer(USA) —Indubitable (Sharpo)
4210[13] 4776[13] 5870[15]

Forfeiter (USA) *R Ford* a82 78
4 ch g Petionville(USA) —Picabo (USA) (Wild Again (USA))
6568[11]

Forgery (IRE) *G A Butler* a95 101+
4 ch g Dr Devious(IRE) —Memory Green (USA) (Green Forest (USA))
629[4] (1129) 2742[7] 3552[4]

For Life (IRE) *A P Jarvis* a55 70
4 b g Bachir(IRE) —Zest (USA) (Zilzal (USA))
654[10] 2348[9]2645[2] 3089[5] 3664[9] 3933[16] 4306[5]6473[2] 6619[4]6696[8] 6798[5]

Formal Decree (GER) *G A Swinbank* 114
3 b g Diktat—Formida (FR) (Highest Honor (FR))
1596[2] (1999) (2502) (3443) 4833[4] 5374[3] (5675)

Form And Beauty (IRE) *C Roberts* 58
4 b h Orpen(USA) —Formezza (IRE) (Cyrano De Bergerac)
425[6]

Format *A W Carroll* 20
3 b f Mark Of Esteem(IRE) —Forum (Lion Cavern (USA))
2673[13] 2985[15]

Formidable Will (FR) *D Shaw* a75 52
4 b g Efisio—Shewillifshewants (IRE) (Alzao (USA))
77[13] 3914[2]5316[14] (6473) 6641[4](6814) 6928[4]

For No One (IRE) *M Johnston* 55
3 b g Mozart(IRE) —Dame Laura (IRE) (Royal Academy (USA))
1032[6] 1289[12] 2111[7] 2832[11] 3357[10]

Forrest Flyer (IRE) *Miss L A Perratt* 33
2 b c Daylami(IRE) —Gerante (USA) (Private Account (USA))
6318[10]

Forroger (CAN) *M A Jarvis* 82
3 bb c Black Minnaloushe(USA) —Count On Romance (CAN) (Geiger Counter (USA))
1100[3] 1546[4] 1841[8] 2069[4] (4805) 5869[6]

Forsters Plantin *J J Quinn* 36
2 ch f Muhtarram(USA) —Ischia (Lion Cavern (USA))
5679[10] 5959[10]

Fort Amhurst (IRE) *E A L Dunlop* 75
2 ch c Halling(USA) —Soft Breeze (Zafonic (USA))
5939[3]

Fort Churchill (IRE) *B Ellison* a73 92
5 b g Barathea(IRE) —Brisighella (IRE) (Al Hareb (USA))
385[11] 535[7]723[10] 990[11] 1346[2]1614[6] 2035[5] 2944[2] (3022) 3547[3] (3960) 4626[5]4676[8] (5295) 5346[4] 5769[3] 5787[10]

Forthright *A W Carroll* a81 86
5 b g Cadeaux Genereux—Forthwith (Midyan (USA))
135[10] 1995[8] (2585) 3044[5]3366[2] (3748) 5506[3] 5810[5] 6017[7]

Fortiszamo *A W Carroll* a44 26
4 b g Forzando—Flamingo Times (Good Times (ITY))
1244[13] 1725[11]

Fortress *E J Alston* a62 63
3 b f Generous(IRE) —Imperial Bailiwick (IRE) (Imperial Frontier (USA))
1551[6] 2016[8] 2699[4]3749[2] (4071) 4354[4] 5032[13]

Fortunate Isle (USA) *B W Hills* 95
4 ch h Swain(IRE) —Isla Del Rey (USA) (Nureyev (USA))
(865) 1301[9] 2989[11] 4889[7] 5374[9] 5678[10]6107[4]

Fortune Island (IRE) *D E Pipe* a84 96
7 b g Turtle Island(IRE) —Blue Kestrel (IRE) (Bluebird (USA))
1021[10] 2013[15] 2817[6]3203[9] 4036[15]

Fortune Point (IRE) *A W Carroll* a64 63
8 ch g Cadeaux Genereux—Mountains Of Mist (IRE) (Shirley Heights)
73[9] 825[2]229[8] 472[4]648[5] (2952) 3213[3] 3615[4]2405

Fortunes Favourite *J E Long* a38 38
6 ch m Barathea(IRE) —Golden Fortune (Forzando)
358[11] 888[13]1198[13] 1395[7]1541[10] 4586[7] 5769[15]6373[10]

Fort Worth (IRE) *B Gubby* a64 68
2 b c Mull Of Kintyre(USA) —Raazi (My Generation)
1639[6] 2029[4] 2402[9] 3641[13]4161[4] 4460[7] 6146[9]6331[3]

Forty Hablador (ARG) *S Seemar* a99 86
5 b g Roar(USA) —La Charlatana (ARG) (Kasteel (FR))
279a[4] 437a[16]

Forward Move (IRE) *R Hannon* 111
4 ch h Dr Fong(USA) —Kissing Gate (USA) (Easy Goer (USA))
2803[9] 3091[4]

Forzarzi (IRE) *A Berry* 57
2 b c Forzando—Zarzi (IRE) (Suave Dancer (USA))
4731[15] 5076[5] 5615[3]

Fosroc (USA) *B R Johnson* a37 56
4 ch g Royal Anthem(USA) —Stellar Blush (USA) (Blushing John (USA))
2861[13] 4929[10]

Fossgate *J D Bethell* a81 81
5 ch g Halling(USA) —Peryllys (Warning)
2108[6] (2612) 3037[4] 3621[2] (4205) (4947) 5506[6]6287[3]

Four Amigos (USA) *I A Wood* a52 78
5 b g Southern Halo(USA) —Larentia (Salse (USA))
4[14] 274[6]317[4] 411[3]485[11] 587[6]605[10] 864[5] 6130[3]6234[4] 6308[5]6470[7] 6533[8]6638[7]

Fourfoot Bay (IRE) *J D Bethell* a58 72
2 b g Elnadim(USA) —Zagreb Flyer (Old Vic)
2680[4] 3173[2] 5168[6] 5843[6] (Dead)

Four Kings *R Allan* 24
5 b g Forzando—High Cut (Dashing Blade)
181[11] 3781[11] 4350[12]4546[5] 5063[7]

Four Miracles *M H Tompkins* a65 59
2 b f Vettori(IRE) —North Kildare (USA) (Northjet)
5456[6] 5899[3] 6303[3]

Four Pleasure *A M Hales* 62
4 ch m King's Best(USA) —Please (Kris)
2181[13] 2645[13]

Four Sins (GER) *John M Oxx* 91
2 b f Sinndar(IRE) —Four Roses (IRE) (Darshaan)
5466a[18]

Foursquare Flyer (IRE) *J Mackie* a66+ 76
4 ch g Tagula(IRE) —Isla (IRE) (Turtle Island (IRE))
3009[5] 3220[6] 6967[2]

Four Tel *J H M Gosden* a59
2 gr c Vettori(IRE) —Etienne Lady (IRE) (Imperial Frontier (USA))
6145[7] 6284[3]

Fowey (USA) *Sir Mark Prescott* a48
2 bb f Gone West(USA) —Kumari Continent (USA) (Kris S (USA))
6778[3]

Fox Covert (IRE) *D W Barker* a52 55
5 b g Foxhound(USA) —Serious Contender (IRE) (Tenby)
782[7] 876[8]974[7] 1391[13] 2928[11]3003[8] 3635[5] 3673[3] 3835[9] 4067[4]

Fox Flight (IRE) *D W Barker* 22
3 b g Brave Act—Danz Danz (Efisio)
1661[11] 2107[9] 2398[5] 3022[10]

Foxhaven *P R Chamings* 108
4 ch h Unfuwain(USA) —Dancing Mirage (IRE) (Machiavellian (USA))
3255[6] 4096[2] 4713[7] (5170) 5547[4] 6103[9]

Foxies Firstglance *R D E Woodhouse* a31
2 ch f Zaha(CAN) —Classic Faster (IRE) (Running Steps (USA))
2938[6] 3307[8] 3994[8]

Foxxy *K A Ryan* a51 69
2 b f Foxhound(USA) —Fisher Island (IRE) (Sri Pekan (USA))
908[6] 1248[5] 5237[4](5633) 6007[16] 6322[11] 6421[5]6764[4] 6996[6]

Foxy Games *D J S Ffrench Davis* a27 68+
2 b f Foxhound(USA) —Manderina (Mind Games)
1912[6] 2442[2] 4221[3]4558[7] 4779[2] (5052) 5434[2]

Foxy Gwynne *Patrick J Flynn* a19 69
4 b m Entrepreneur—Nahlin (Slip Anchor)
4186a[13]

Foxy Music *Peter Grayson* a45
2 b g Foxhound(USA) —Primum Tempus (Primo Dominie)
6255[11] 6512[9]6749[9] 6839[7]6939[5] 6985[2]

Foxysox *Carla Gaines* a112 108
3 ch f Foxhound(USA) —Triple Tricks (IRE) (Royal Academy (USA))
5984a[10]

Fracas (IRE) *David Wachman* 114
4 b h In The Wings—Klarifi (Habitat)
4414a[2] 5051a[8] 5395a[4] 6103[7]

Fractured Foxy *J J Quinn* 68
2 b f Foxhound(USA) —Yanomami (USA) (Slew O'Gold (USA))
987[2] 1096[4] 1442[2] 3787[4] (4376) (4545) 4882[5](5366) 5676[2] 5958[5]

Fragrancy (IRE) *M A Jarvis* a70+
2 ch f Singspiel(IRE) —Zibet (Kris)
(6073)

Francescas Boy (IRE) *P D Niven* 41
3 b g Titus Livius(FR) —Mica Male (ITY) (Law Society (USA))
5082[14]

Francesco *M L W Bell* a54 56
2 ch g Vettori(IRE) —Violet (IRE) (Mukaddamah (USA))
5460[10] 6063[7] 6284[5]

Franchoek (IRE) *A King* 56
2 ch c Trempolino(USA) —Snow House (IRE) (Vacarme (USA))
4526[9] 4867[9] 5622[9]

Frank Cartwright (IRE) *A Berry* 45
3 b g Mull Of Kintyre(USA) —Punta Gorda (IRE) (Roi Danzig (USA))
1032[13] 1501[11] 1633[9] 1868[6] 4016[12]

Frank Crow *J S Goldie* 76
3 b g Josr Algarhoud(IRE) —Belle De Nuit (IRE) (Statoblest)
5355[7] 5810[15]

Franklins Gardens *M H Tompkins* 116d
6 b h Halling(USA) —Woodbeck (Terimon)
4677[2] 5223a[7] 5551[8] 5967[5] 6103[11]

Frankly Dancing (HUN) *I Papp* 95
4 b h Satin Stone(USA) —Folklor (HUN) (Komombo (IRE))
3992a[5]

Franksalot (IRE) *I W McInnes* a77 76
6 ch g Desert Story(IRE) —Rosie's Guest (IRE) (Be My Guest (USA))
89[6] 224[4]323[9] 569[7]1432[2] (1899) 2259[2] 2390[4] 3094[6] 3565[4]3789[6] 4116[12] 4350[2] 4652[7] 4729[6]5031[9] 6820[9]6913[7]

Frank Sonata *M G Quinlan* 115
5 b h Opening Verse(USA) —Megdale (IRE) (Waajib)
(991) 1128[6] 1860a[2] 2010[2] 5010[9] 5395a[6]5551[2] (5854a) 6119a[10]

Frank's Quest (IRE) *A B Haynes* a59 67
6 b g Mujadil(USA) —Questuary (IRE) (Rainbow Quest (USA))
297[8] 458[11]734[2] 1305[5]1725[3] 1915[2]2413[3] 3386[5]4139[7] 6543[6]6725[2] 6802[7]6854[4]

Franky'N'Jonny *M J Attwater* a49 47
3 b f Groom Dancer(USA) —Bron Hilda (IRE) (Namaqualand (USA))
193[4] 326[2]422[6] 538[2]604[3] 648[3]879[3] 1293[7] 1829[8] 3378[6]3910[8] 4306[12] 4769[8] 5273[3] 5767[12]5922[6] 6236[3]6306[2] 6552[11]6794[6]

Fraternity *J A Pickering* a44 38
9 b g Grand Lodge(USA) —Catawba (Mill Reef (USA))
200[8] 1001[4]1303[7] 1553[13]2291[11] 2413[6] 3158[12]6282[10] 6307[8]

Fratt'n Park (IRE) *J J Bridger* a65 71
3 b f Tagula(IRE) —Bouffant (High Top)
1241[5] 1547[4] 1801[12] 2403[2] (2583) 3072[8]3364[11] 3852[10] 4143[4] 4838[6] 5211[5]5574[3] 5895[7] 6775[12]

Freda's Choice (IRE) *Patrick Morris* a52 66+
3 b f Shinko Forest(IRE) —Marimar (IRE) (Grand Lodge (USA))
6235[10] (6707)

Freddy (ARG) *Ernst Oertel* a56 71
7 ch h Roy(USA) —Folgada (USA) (Lyphard's Wish (FR))
3093[9] 3533[11]
Frederick Ozanam (IRE) *A P O'Brien* 98
2 b g Traditionally(USA) —Sudden Hope (FR) (Darshaan)
5466a[27] 6262a[3]
Fredrika *F Reuterskiold*
3 ch f Desert Story(IRE) —Hertha (Hernando (FR))
3326a[9]
Free Angel (USA) *M Wigham* a71 56
4 b m Mystery Storm(USA) —No Makeup (USA) (Proud Truth (USA))
(2418) 2574[2] 6396[14]
Freedom At Last (IRE) *W Jarvis* 71
2 ch f Alhaarth(IRE) —Soubrette (USA) (Opening Verse (USA))
3495[4] 4041[11]
Freedonia *J E Hammond* 113
4 b m Selkirk(USA) —Forest Rain (FR) (Caerleon (USA))
(4192a) 5220a[4] 5821a[2] 6612a[7]
Freeloader (IRE) *R A Fahey* a91 92
6 b g Revoque(IRE) —Indian Sand (Indian King (USA))
726[8] 865[6] 2114[5] 2440[9] 2974[7]4379[2] 4696[4] (5362) 6594[3]6678[7]
Free Offer *J L Dunlop* 76
2 b f Generous(IRE) —Proserpine (Robellino (USA))
3707[4] (4238)
Free Roses (IRE) *Edward Lynam* 97
3 b f Fasliyev(USA) —Ghanaj (Caerleon (USA))
(3332) 3561a[10] 4855a[8] 5405[12]
Free Silver (IRE) *Miss K B Boutflower* a54 56
3 b f Lujain(USA) —Joonayh (Warning)
1110[6] 1412[7] 2704[5]2987[13] 3933[9] 4329[8]6130[4] 6235[3]6371[3]
Free Speech *Sir Michael Stoute* 51
3 b c King's Best(USA) —Daring Miss (Sadler's Wells (USA))
1134[9]
Free Style (GER) *Mrs H Sweeting* a49 44
6 ch m Most Welcome—Furiella (Formidable (USA))
309[11] 574[5]684[10]
Free Thinking (USA) *D Danner* a87 116
5 b h Unbridled(USA) —Danka (USA) (Strawberry Road (AUS))
6342a[11]
Free To Air *A M Balding* a80 84
3 b g Generous(IRE) —Petonica (IRE) (Petoski)
(1216) (1543) 1975[3] 2556[5] 2986[8]5141[6] 5594[6] 6108[7]
Free Wheelin (IRE) *T M Jones* a43 54
6 b g Polar Falcon(USA) —Farhana (Fayruz)
1981[6] 4587[9] 6629[12]
Freeze The Flame (GER) *C R Egerton* a56 56
3 b g In The Wings—Fantastic Flame (IRE) (Generous (IRE))
1049[12] 1851[11] 2539[5] 3145[5]
Fregate Island (IRE) *W J Haggas* a84 82
3 gr g Daylami(IRE) —Briery (IRE) (Salse (USA))
1781[12] 2324[2] 2781[7] 3301[3]
Fremen (USA) *D Nicholls* 93
6 ch g Rahy(USA) —Northern Trick (USA) (Northern Dancer (CAN))
2323[10] (3139) (3549) 4031a[11] 4726[5] 5357[5] 5483[2]5680[8] 5810[3]
Frenchgate *I W McInnes* a44 46
5 br g Paris House—Let's Hang On (IRE) (Petorius)
4266[3] 4425[2] 5485[8] 5926[12]6370[5] 6616[9]
French Gigolo *C N Allen*
6 ch g Pursuit Of Love—French Mist (Mystiko (USA))
5922[12]
French Mannequin (IRE) *P A Blockley* a62 53
7 bb m Key Of Luck(USA) —Paris Model (IRE) (Thatching)
2522[11] (2935) (4996) 5069[7] 5736[6]5846[8]
Frenchmans Lodge *L A Dace* a32 32
6 b g Piccolo—St Helena (Monsanto (FR))
1923[11] 2260[15] 2531[16]
French Opera *J A Osborne* a60 63+
3 b g Bering—On Fair Stage (IRE) (Sadler's Wells (USA))
2480[4] 3075[9]
French Transition (USA) *P L Biancone* a49
2 br c Giant's Causeway(USA) —French Manicure (USA) (Hawkster (USA))
5823a[8]
Frescatie (FR) *R Kleparski* 58
4 ch m Septieme Ciel(USA) —Erdijiya (IRE) (Kahyasi)
3692a[10]
Fresh Bread (USA) *R Meichetti* 61
3 b f Mr Greeley(USA) —Lo Cal Bred (USA) (Native Prospector (USA))
758a[6]
Freshwinds *Miss Diana Weeden* a59
4 ch g Bahamian Bounty—La Noisette (Rock Hopper)
45[7] 179[2]299[9] 465[6]6233[4] 6550[10]6727[5] (6851)
Fretwork *R Hannon* 86
2 b f Galileo(IRE) —Celtic Cross (Selkirk (USA))
4373[2] 4964[2] 5595[3]
Freya Tricks *I Semple* 42
2 b f Noverre(USA) —Trick Of Ace (USA) (Clever Trick (USA))
6318[7]
Friarscourt (USA) *R J Osborne* 68
2 ch c Pleasant Tap(USA) —Dance Tempo (CAN) (The Minstrel (CAN))
3962a[11] 4747a[9]
Friendly Island (USA) *T Pletcher* a112 102
5 ch h Crafty Friend(USA) —Island Queen (USA) (Ogygian (USA))
6341a[2]
Friends Hope *P A Blockley* a62 65
5 ch m Docksider(USA) —Stygian (USA) (Irish River (FR))
73[7] 229[2]363[2] 2636[3] 3305[4]3610[4] 4132[5] (4279) 4673[6]
Frill A Minute *Miss L C Siddall*
2 b f Lake Coniston(IRE) —Superfrills (Superpower)
3942[9] 4731[17] 5766[8] 6296[11]
Frimley's Matterry *R E Barr* a50 55
6 b g Bluegrass Prince(IRE) —Lonely Street (Frimley Park)
2700[8] 2874[5] 3137[8] 3240[7] 4057[7]4157[2] (4401) 4694[8] 4957[13] 5243[17] 5839[8]
Fringe *Jane Chapple-Hyam* a60 90
3 ch f In The Wings—El Jazirah (Kris)
6053[3] 6429[2] 6722a[4]
Fringuell *S Iacobelli* 78
3 b c Allied Forces(USA) —Rabadan (IRE) (Warning)
2671a[9]
Frisky Talk (IRE) *B W Hills* a81 77
2 b f Fasliyev(USA) —Happy Talk (IRE) (Hamas (IRE))
1082[8] 1347[2] 1647[2] 2355[4] (2703) 3476[2]3734[12] 4152[2] 4766[6] 5234[3] (5668)
Friston Forest (IRE) *A Fabre* 109
2 ch c Barathea(IRE) —Talented (Bustino)
6249a[4]
Frogs' Gift (IRE) *G M Moore* 52?
4 gr m Danehill Dancer(IRE) —Warthill Whispers (Grey Desire)
1577[10] 2195[15] 2400[6]2789[9] 3333[11] 3610[14] 4154[9]
Froissee *N A Callaghan* a60+ 67
2 b f Polish Precedent(USA) —Crinkle (IRE) (Distant Relative)
2821[3] 4109[6] 6200[11] 6394[5]6569[7]
Fromsong (IRE) *D K Ivory* a103 103
8 b g Fayruz—Lindas Delight (Batshoof)
295[4] 705[2]836[5] 1116[5] 1803[4]2227[16] 2683[8] 6984[7]
Frontlinefinancier *N I M Rossiter* a59 61
6 b g Bluegrass Prince(IRE) —Bunny Gee (Last Tycoon)
1690[8] 3437[12]
Frontline In Focus (IRE) *K R Burke* 86
2 ch f Daggers Drawn(USA) —Christan (IRE) (Al Hareb (USA))
3188[4] (3358) (4006) 4681[5] 5434[14]
Front Rank (IRE) *Mrs Dianne Sayer* a72 66
6 b g Sadler's Wells(USA) —Alignment (IRE) (Alzao (USA))
2998[2] 4451[5]
Frost Giant (USA) *R Dutrow Jr* 114
3 ch c Giant's Causeway(USA) —Takesmybreathaway (USA) (Gone West (USA))
1486[13] (5190a) 5821a[5] 6613a[7]
Frosty Night (IRE) *M Johnston* 90
2 b g Night Shift(USA) —Abla (Robellino (USA))
2619[4] (3328) 4783[2] 5466a[16]
Fruhlingssturm *J-L Salas Molto* a90 111
6 b h Unfuwain(USA) —Fruhlingserwachen (USA) (Irish River (FR))
5913a[8]
Fruits D'Amour (IRE) *S Kirk* a52 21
2 b f Fruits Of Love(USA) —Chatsworth Bay (IRE) (Fairy King (USA))
5894[10] 6309[9] 6575[8]6736[9] 6859[9]
Fubos *Lucinda Featherstone* a65 65
5 b g Atraf—Homebeforemidnight (Fools Holme (USA))
156[13]
Fuel Cell (IRE) *J O'Reilly* a72 65
5 b g Desert Style(IRE) —Tappen Zee (Sandhurst Prince)
1683[10] 1996[16] 2181[10] 5839[8] 6544[8]6790[9]
Fuero Real (FR) *R Brotherton* 7
11 b g Highest Honor(FR) —Highest Pleasure (USA) (Foolish Pleasure (USA))
3896[11]
Fuerta Ventura (IRE) *K J Condon* 101
4 bb m Desert Sun—Cradle Brief (IRE) (Brief Truce (USA))
991[9] 1324a[7]
Fuji (IRE) *M L W Bell* a67 66
2 b c Monashee Mountain(USA) —Yavarro (Raga Navarro (ITY))
(3031) 3531[6] 4178[10]
Fujisan *M Johnston* a54 64
2 b c Fuji Kiseki(JPN) —Appreciation (IRE) (Caerleon (USA))
3242[4] 5841[7]
Fullandby (IRE) *T J Etherington* a90+ 106
4 b g Monashee Mountain(USA) —Ivory Turner (Efisio)
846[3] 1438[9] 1835[7]2450[5] 2683[10] 3038[5] (3904) 4202[5] 4609[2](4988) 5523[2] 5942[7]
Full As A Rocket (IRE) *D Nicholls* 52
5 b g Foxhound(USA) —Taysala (IRE) (Akarad (FR))
2927[10] 4549[8]
Full House (IRE) *P R Webber* 84
7 br g King's Theatre(IRE) —Nirvavita (FR) (Highest Honor (FR))
2176[4] (2501) 2723[4] 5963[25]
Full Of Promise (USA) *Mrs A J Perrett* a65
2 b f Street Cry(IRE) —Believe It Beloved (USA) (Clever Trick (USA))
6071[5]
Full Of Zest *Mrs L J Mongan* a64 53
4 ch m Pivotal—Tangerine (Primo Dominie)
327[5] 706[11]780[6] 1163[4] 1673[11]2044[10] 2320[3] 2862[9]3305[10] 6630[8]
Full Spate *J M Bradley* a46 70
11 ch g Unfuwain(USA) —Double River (USA) (Irish River (FR))
1188[14] 2331[4] 2504[10] (2599) 3094[13] 3245[6]3867[5] 4211[7] 4324[5] 4870[12] 4984[14]5569[4]
Full Speed (IND) *Pesi Shroff* 84
5 b h Burden Of Proof(IRE) —Speedy Beauty (Rousillon (USA))
153a[13] 356a[11]
Full Victory (IRE) *R A Farrant* a82 83
4 b g Imperial Ballet(IRE) —Full Traceability (IRE) (Ron's Victory (USA))
1773[4] (2098) (2327) 2819[7] 3101[4]3459[5] 4209[7] 4429[2]4706[2] 4989[5] 5590[5] 5896[10]
Fulminant (IRE) *W Kujath* 101
5 b g Big Shuffle(USA) —Flagny (FR) (Kaldoun (FR))
6121a[3] 6547a[3]
Fulvio (USA) *P Howling* a61 58
6 b g Sword Dance—One Tuff Gal (USA) (Lac Ouimet (USA))
210[2] (398) 526[3]659[4] 2319[3]2936[3] 3056[3]5031[2] 6439[12]6532[7] 6624[5]6793[2] 6983[3]
Funfair Wane *D Nicholls* a89 93
7 b g Unfuwain(USA) —Ivory Bride (Domynsky)
846[7] 1835[10] 2230[7]2521[4] 2946[10] 4658[U] 5688[11]
Fun In The Sun *Jane Southcombe* 31
2 b g Piccolo—Caught In The Rain (Spectrum (IRE))
2967[9] 3545[11] 3895[8]
Funny Legend (NOR) *Wido Neuroth* 98
5 b m Funambule(USA) —Leap Day Legend (NOR) (Petorius)
2123a[3] 3661a[8] 4864a[4]
Funny Times *N G Richards*
5 b m Silver Patriarch(IRE) —Elegant City (Scallywag)
6272[8]
Funny World (FR) *P Khozian* a61 68
2 ch c Spinning World(USA) —Prostar (FR) (Procida (USA))
5122a[8]
Fun Thai *M R Channon* a37 46
2 ch f Fraam—Thailand (Lycius (USA))
4163[9] 4238[4] 4545[4] 4724[7] 5323[8]6385[7] 6518[7]6576[10] 6859[8]
Fun Time *M R Channon* a57 52
3 br f Fraam—Kissing Time (Lugana Beach)
2589[11] 3195[8] 3866[4] 4494[6] 4728[11]6304[6] 6371[2]6618[3] 6855[2]
Fun To Ride *M W Easterby* 75
5 ch m Desert Prince(IRE) —Zafaaf (Kris)
1183[11] 1285[16] 1856[10]
Furbeseta *L M Cumani* a69
2 b f Danehill Dancer(IRE) —Fafinta (IRE) (Indian Ridge)
6187[6] 6433[3]
Furmigadelagiusta *L M Cumani* a75 64
2 ch c Galileo(IRE) —Sispre (FR) (Master Willie)
3623[8] 4388[9] 4992[3]
Furnace (IRE) *M L W Bell* 91
2 b c Green Desert(USA) —Lyrical Dance (USA) (Lear Fan (USA))
(4333) 4809[7] 5624[3]
Further Outlook (USA) *Miss Gay Kelleway* a71 76
12 gr g Zilzal(USA) —Future Bright (USA) (Lyphard's Wish (FR))
1125[17] 1735[4] (1886) (2748) (3033) (3995) 4602[5] 4780[7]5737[8] 6464[4]6638[4] 6717[6]6961[10]
Fusaichi Dream (IRE) *F Rohaut* 77
3 b f Fusaichi Pegasus(USA) —Royal Ballerina (IRE) (Sadler's Wells (USA))
2537a[8]
Fusaichi Pandora (JPN) *T Shirai* 116
3 ch f Sunday Silence(USA) —Lotta Lace (USA) (Nureyev (USA))
6612a[5]
Fusaichi Richard (JPN) *K Matsuda* a100 117
3 gr c Kurofune(USA) —Fusaichi Airedale (JPN) (Sunday Silence (USA))
(6850a)
Fuschia *R Charlton* a56
2 b f Averti(IRE) —Big Pink (IRE) (Bigstone (IRE))
6187[8]
Fushe Jo *J Howard Johnson* 79
2 gr c Act One—Aristocratique (Cadeaux Genereux)
4716[5] (5332)
Fusijama (USA) *L Brogi* 67
3 b f Fusaichi Pegasus(USA) —Timi (Alzao (USA))
1713a[15]
Fusili (IRE) *N P Littmoden* a98 96
3 ch f Silvano(GER) —Flunder (Nebos (GER))
(19) 87[3] 160[3]294[3] 483[4](592) 805[2]1077[2] 1583[7] 1669[2] 5803[11] 6191[9]6333[8] 6411[3] 6559[4]6744[2]
Fusillade (IRE) *A J Lockwood* 43
6 ch g Grand Lodge(USA) —Lili Cup (FR) (Fabulous Dancer (USA))
4021[11]
Fustaan (IRE) *M P Tregoning* 68
2 b f Royal Applause—Alhufoof (USA) (Dayjur (USA))
4559[6]
Futoo (IRE) *D W Chapman* a34 44
5 b g Foxhound(USA) —Nicola Wynn (Nicholas Bill)
131[9] 820[12]1152[8] 1392[13]1910[11] 2612[15] 3610[9]3941[8] 6280[9] 6852[7]
Futun *L M Cumani* 107+
3 b c In The Wings—Svanzega (USA) (Sharpen Up)
(1289) 1813[2] (3292) 3882[2] 4711[7]
Future Deal *C A Horgan* a69+ 70
5 b m First Trump—Katyushka (IRE) (Soviet Star (USA))
1638[11] 3014[4]4248[10] 4483[6] 5474[10]6435[12]
Future's Dream *K R Burke* a81+ 79
3 b g Bertolini(USA) —Bahawir Pour (USA) (Green Dancer (USA))
(1984) 2142[2] 4833[10] 5512[12]5810[13]
Futuristic Dragon (IRE) *P A Blockley* 49
2 b c Invincible Spirit(IRE) —Calvia Rose (Sharpo)
6024[5]
Fyodor (IRE) *W J Haggas* a107 105
5 b g Fasliyev(USA) —Royale Figurine (IRE) (Dominion Royale)
(6) 295[2] (450) 664[2]1116[13] 3038[9] 3585[10] 3972[4] 4461[3]
Fyvie *E A L Dunlop* a77 80
3 ch f Grand Lodge(USA) —Island Of Silver (USA) (Forty Niner (USA))
1006[2] (2895) 3489[3]4528[8] 5016[9]
Gabor *D W Thompson* a45 45
7 b g Danzig Connection(USA) —Kiomi (Niniski (USA))
1199[13]
Gaburin (AUS) *Hideyuki Mori* a70
4 b h Fusaichi Pegasus(USA) —Dashing Eagle (AUS) (Danehill (USA))
739a[7]
Gadahar (USA) *S Seemar* a58
3 ch c Gilded Time(USA) —Garza (Kris)
150a[13]
Gaelic Games (UAE) *P G Murphy* a59 56
3 b g Jade Robbery(USA) —Colleen (IRE) (Sadler's Wells (USA))
762[6] 1215[P] (Dead)
Gaelic Princess *A G Newcombe* a81 88
6 b m Cois Na Tine(IRE) —Berenice (ITY) (Marouble)
252[8] 2071[5] 2503[4]2735[2] 2892[2] 3020[8] 3953[2] 4241[12]4782[2] (4965) 5523[11] (6483) 6671[3]6791[3]
Gaelic Roulette (IRE) *J Jay* a51 50
6 b m Turtle Island(IRE) —Money Spinner (USA) (Teenoso (USA))
174[7] 891[5]
Gaff (USA) *S Asmussen* a108 107
4 b h Maria's Mon(USA) —Ionlyhaveeyesforu (CAN) (Tunerup (USA))
740a[5]
Gagarin (FR) *Miss L C Siddall* 63
6 b g Quest For Fame—Good To Dance (IRE) (Groom Dancer (USA))
5725[15] 5954[14] 6232[14]
Gainsbury (GER) *P Vovcenko* 80
2 b g Dashing Blade—Glorissima (GER) (Second Set (IRE))
4857a[3]
Gala Casino King (IRE) *M Dods* 60
3 ch g Elnadim(USA) —Fashion Scout (IRE) (Thatching)
1343[6] 2082[4]
Galactic Star *Sir Michael Stoute* 80+
3 ch c Galileo(IRE) —Balisada (Kris)
5768[2] (6053)
Gala Jackpot (USA) *W M Brisbourne* 42
3 bb g Crafty Prospector(USA) —True At Heart (USA) (Storm Cat (USA))
1736[10] 2480[11] 2782[6]
Galandora *Dr J R J Naylor* a24
6 b m Bijou D'Inde—Jelabna (Jalmood (USA))
6537[6] 6857[9]
Galantos (GER) *G L Moore* a63 25
5 b g Winged Love(IRE) —Grey Metal (GER) (Secret 'n Classy (CAN))
684[9] (938) 1219[7] (1540) 3382[8]4046[10] 4929[9](6957)
Gala Sunday (USA) *M W Easterby* a46 77
6 b g Lear Fan(USA) —Sunday Bazaar (USA) (Nureyev (USA))
(1462) 1723[14] 2407[4] 2702[4](3305) (3610) 3939[7] (4021) (4307) 4730[4] 5685[12] 5889[15]
Galatee (FR) *J S Bolger* 113+
3 b f Galileo(IRE) —Altana (USA) (Mountain Cat (USA))
(1785a) 5854a[6]
Galaxie Des Sables (FR) *Mme N Rossio* 79
2 b f Marchand De Sable(USA) —Kruguy Dancer (FR) (Groom Dancer (USA))
6046a[8]
Galaxy Bound (IRE) *D Shaw* a54 63
3 b g Mark Of Esteem(IRE) —Diner De Lune (IRE) (Be My Guest (USA))
188[7] 342[9]406[6] 500[11]594[8] 861[12]1263[12] 5847[10] 6480[11]6629[10] 6726[11]
Galaxy Of Stars *D Shaw* a60 55
2 b f Observatory(USA) —Divine Secret (Hernando (FR))
1278[5] 2791[4] 4913[7]6296[2] 6420[2] (6500) 6592[6] 6750[5]
Galaxy Stars *P J Makin* a68
2 b g Golden Snake(USA) —Moly (Inchinor)
(6905)
Galibard (IRE) *A M Balding* a55 56
3 b g Montjeu(IRE) —His Lady (IRE) (Selkirk (USA))
1516[6] 1940[7]
Galient (IRE) *M A Jarvis* 107
3 b g Galileo(IRE) —Endorsement (Warning)
(1081) (1586) 2804[2] 4595[5] 5185[11]
Galingale (IRE) *Mrs P Sly* 63
2 b f Galileo(IRE) —Urban Sky (FR) (Groom Dancer (USA))
4830[8] 5596[5]
Galipette *H R A Cecil* 78
2 b f Green Desert(USA) —Arabesque (Zafonic (USA))
5894[5]
Gallant Guru (AUS) *Lee Freedman* 105
4 b h Montjeu(IRE) —Proud Halo (AUS) (Don't Say Halo (USA))
(6455a)
Gallantry *D W Barker* 93
4 b g Green Desert(USA) —Gay Gallanta (USA) (Woodman (USA))
1494[2] 1692[11] 2429[8] 2732[8] 3079[5](3500) 3926[7] 4101[11] 4521[8] 5175[11]
Gallant Sir *J R Fanshawe*
3 ch c Grand Lodge(USA) —Gay Gallanta (USA) (Woodman (USA))
1994[12]
Gallas (IRE) *S Lycett* a51 54
5 b g Charnwood Forest(IRE) —Nellie's Away (IRE) (Magical Strike (USA))
6620[2] 6729[5]
Gallego *R J Price* a68 68
4 br g Danzero(AUS) —Shafir (IRE) (Shaadi (USA))
82[9] 240[10]290[11] 469[2](586) (683) 736[7]882[15] 1152[7] 1276[7]1769[3] 2186[4] (2407) 2455[2] 2918[5] 3221[9](3309) 3566[5] 5130[9] 5384[8] 5506[12] 5831[2]5972[12] 6193[3]6323[3] 6451[8]6507[7] 6693[9]

Gallery Breeze *P A Blockley* a73 78
7 b m Zamindar(USA) —Wantage Park (Pas De Seul)
3051[4]

Gallery Girl (IRE) *T D Easterby* 98
3 ch f Namid—September Tide (IRE) (Thatching)
1633[4] 2022[8] 2658[11] 3475[4] 3761[2]4717[8] 5501[11] 5957[8]

Galley Law *R Craggs* a56 40
6 ch g Most Welcome—Miss Blitz (Formidable (USA))
328[3] 414[5]636[5] 939[6]1574[5]

Gallileo Figaro (USA) *W M Brisbourne* a68 68
3 b f Galileo(IRE) —Temperence Gift (USA) (Kingmambo (USA))
3261[8] 4330[5] 4759[4]5174[6] 5618[6] 6027[3] 6415[6]6685[2] 6766[5]

Galloise (IRE) *C G Cox* 31
2 b f Val Royal(FR) —Spring Daffodil (Pharly (FR))
6050[10]

Galloping Gertie *J Hetherton* a28 41
4 b m Aragon—Meltonby (Sayf El Arab (USA))
677[7] 1757[10] 2245[10]2789[16] 5497[7] 5837[8]

Galloway Boy (IRE) *J F Panvert* a30 37
9 ch g Mujtahid(USA) —Supportive (IRE) (Nashamaa)
262[11] 401[13]3728[14] 4551[8] 5291[14]

Gallows Hill (USA) *R A Fahey* 39
2 b g Stravinsky(USA) —Verinha (BRZ) (Baronius (BRZ))
1807[5] 2680[8]

Galma (FR) *E Lellouche* 102
3 br f Goldneyev(USA) —Clarstone (FR) (Bigstone (IRE))
1177a[5] 1789a[4] 3133a[5]

Galway Girl (IRE) *T D Easterby* 43
2 b f Namid—Cherry Falls (IRE) (Ali-Royal (IRE))
4510[7] 5898[7]

Gamble In Gold (IRE) *R Hannon* 89
3 b f Monashee Mountain(USA) —Starisa (IRE) (College Chapel)
896[2] 1512[4] 1671[8] 2022[6] 2651[3]2880[9] 4345[7] 5643[6] 5919[14]

Gambling Spirit *H Candy* a69 81
4 ch m Mister Baileys—Royal Roulette (Risk Me (FR))
965[8] 1244[3] (1754) 2305[13]3152[8] (3440) (4010) (4336)

Game Bertie *N Bycroft*
3 b g Mind Games—Carol Again (Kind Of Hush)
4611[11]

Game Flora *D Shaw* a30 55
5 b m Mind Games—Breakfast Creek (Hallgate)
247[12] 501[9]686[11]

Game Lad *T D Easterby* a55 99
4 b g Mind Games—Catch Me (Rudimentary (USA))
1086[3] 1495[4] 2012[13] 4202[12]

Game Lady *I A Wood* 68
2 b f Mind Games—Highland Gait (Most Welcome)
2045[3] 4053[6] 5347[10]

Gamera (IRE) *Laura Grizzetti* 56
3 gr f Namid—Moonlight Truce (IRE) (Brief Truce (USA))
2493a[7]

Gamesters Lady *W M Brisbourne* a77 82
3 br f Almushtarak(IRE) —Tycoon Tina (Tina's Pet)
2613[5] 3065[4] 3477[7] 4173[9]

Gandalf *J R Fanshawe* a84+ 83
4 b g Sadler's Wells(USA) —Enchant (Lion Cavern (USA))
1132[2] 3098[3] 4469[3]5383[12] 5815[14]

Gandolfino (GER) *W Baltromei*
4 br h Alwuhush(USA) —Gentle Rock (GER) (Archway (IRE))
393a[0]

Gandor (IRE) *J H M Gosden* a97 98
3 b c Cape Cross(IRE) —Daftiyna (IRE) (Darshaan)
(1240) 1627[6] 2774[23] 3681[3] 4936[2]

Ganja (FR) *G Pannier* 94
6 br m Highest Honor(FR) —Repercutionist (USA) (Beaudelaire (USA))
6574a[0]

Ganymede *Mrs L J Mongan* a61 48
5 gr g Daylami(IRE) —Germane (Distant Relative)
314[2] 419[3]599[13] 1163[14]1690[12] 2507[2] 2902[6] 3270[5] 3527[2]3797[6] 4139[3] 4702[5]4929[4] 5451[6] (6132) (6375) 6560[9]

Gap Princess (IRE) *R A Fahey* 66
2 b f Noverre(USA) —Safe Care (IRE) (Caerleon (USA))
2241[3] 4017[2] 4510[3] 5349[2] 5509[4]5748[7]

Garafena *Pat Eddery* 80
3 b f Golden Snake(USA) —Eclipsing (IRE) (Baillamont (USA))
1118[3] 1798[2] 2578[2] 3419[2]

Garden Society (IRE) *T T Clement* a94 68
9 ch g Caerleon(USA) —Eurobird (Ela-Mana-Mou)
5526[7] 6381[5]

Garhoud *Karen George* a62 52
4 b g Grand Lodge(USA) —Puce (Darshaan)
966[13]

Garibaldi (GER) *J O'Reilly* a63 71
4 ch g Acatenango(GER) —Guanhumara (Caerleon (USA))
125[5] 478[10]2351[4] 3024[8] 5904[14] 6382[6]6560[4]

Garlogs *A Bailey* a73 70
3 b g Hunting Lion(IRE) —Fading (Pharly (FR))
(102) (335) 344[2] 359[2]673[2] (819) 988[3] 1279[4]6452[12] 6585[12]6622[8]

Garnica (FR) *J-C Rouget* 114
3 gr c Linamix(FR) —Gueridia (IRE) (Night Shift (USA))
1718a[5] 3342a[5] (6093a)

Garple Burn *Jim Best* a59 51
4 b g Zaha(CAN) —Skedaddle (Formidable (USA))
767[12] 904[7]1540[9]

Garrulous (UAE) *M Johnston* 62
3 b c Lomitas—Friendly (USA) (Lear Fan (USA))
1139[7] 1483[5]

Garrya *R Hannon* a30 47
2 ch c Mark Of Esteem(IRE) —Sherkova (USA) (State Dinner (USA))
3851[10] 4366[7] 4597[8]5323[12] 6016[11]

Garstang *Peter Grayson* a83 75
3 ch g Atraf—Approved Quality (IRE) (Persian Heights)
10[9] 120[2]226[2] (287) 481[7] (577) (595) 709[5]803[3] 980[8] (1411) 1983[2] 2553[6] 3296[4](3646) 4058[6] 4562[9] 5263[9]

Garston Star *J S Moore* a6 50
5 ch g Fleetwood(IRE) —Conquista (Aragon)
1204[12] 1754[7] 2871[12] 3270[6] 3894[4]4176[5] 5451[15] 6068[6]

Gary's Indian (IRE) *B P J Baugh*
3 b f Indian Danehill(IRE) —Martino (Marju (IRE))
5138[7] 5353[14]

Gatecrasher *Pat Eddery*
3 gr g Silver Patriarch(IRE) —Girl At The Gate (Formidable (USA))
1741[17]

Gateland *B J Llewellyn* a63 60
3 br g Dansili—Encorenous (USA) (Diesis)
1165[9] 1738[10] 3730[2]4758[7] 4981[8]

Gates Of Eden (USA) *M L W Bell* 66
3 b f Kingmambo(USA) —Amethyst (IRE) (Sadler's Wells (USA))
2349[9] 2929[7] 3569[5]

Gatorize (USA) *Helen Pitts* a102
2 ch f Exploit(USA) —Cayman Agressor (USA) (Citidancer (USA))
6338a[12]

Gattuso *Ms Deborah J Evans* a63 58
3 b g Zilzal(USA) —Daanat Nawal (Machiavellian (USA))
703[4] 712[5]1078[7] 4426[6] 5035[5]6404[10] 6480[8]6683[8] 6893[5]

Gaudalpin (IRE) *Ernst Oertel* a49 52
4 b m Danetime(IRE) —Lila Pedigo (IRE) (Classic Secret (USA))
22[11] 178[8]265[6] 772[6]889[4] 1538[3]1727[2] 1914[7]2319[7] 2574[10]6372[5] 6851[4]6962[6]

Gaudeamus (USA) *J S Bolger* 100
2 b f Distorted Humor(USA) —Leo's Lucky Lady (USA) (Seattle Slew (USA))
(3060a) 3574a[4] (3963a) 4853a[8] 5522[5]

Gauguin (IRE) *Robert Collet* 100
3 b c Alzao(USA) —Graten (IRE) (Zieten (USA))
5779a[11]

Gautami *L Baldi* a61
3 b c Mtoto—Golden Kendall (IRE) (In The Wings)
5473a[11]

Gavanello *M C Chapman* a44 47
3 bb g Diktat—Possessive Artiste (Shareef Dancer (USA))
1741[11] 2646[7] 4909[12]5485[14] 5618[11] 6973[5]

Gavarnie Beau (IRE) *M Blanshard* a71 89
3 b g Imperial Ballet(IRE) —Mysticism (Mystiko (USA))
481[5] 709[2]851[3] 969[2] 1208[2]1411[5] (1983) (2105) 2756[6]3296[12] 4707[4] 4841[4] 5044[11] 5427[6]6065[8] 6221[12]

Gavioli (IRE) *J M Bradley* a28 60
4 b g Namid—Pamina (IRE) (Perugino (USA))
1209[13] 1689[11] 3094[15] 3245[2] 3728[17]4361[10] 4985[13]

Gavroche (IRE) *J R Boyle* a97 106
5 b h Docksider(USA) —Regal Revolution (Hamas (IRE))
377[6] 572[3]661[7] (1933) 2229[2] 2840a[5]3294[14] 4791[6] 5170[6] 5374[18]

Gawrosz (POL) *G J Smith* a45 23
7 ch g Saphir(GER) —Galarda (POL) (Parysow)
1001[10] 1219[8] 1385[4]1766[6] 2075[11] 2245[5]3260[11]

Gazboolou *K R Burke* 75
2 b c Royal Applause—Warning Star (Warning)
2610[2] 3581[2] 4650[2] 5431[2]

Gaze *W Jarvis* a69 72
3 b f Galileo(IRE) —Gryada (Shirley Heights)
1417[9] 1994[8] 2655 [3] 3215[5] 3911[3]4931[7] 5429[4]5875[5] 6256[9]

Gee Dee Nen *M H Tompkins* 88
3 b g Mister Baileys—Special Beat (Bustino)
730[2] 1286[3] 1586[3] 2117[3] 4259[2]4742[3] 5361[3] 5644[4] 5792[4] 6205[10]

Gee Kel (IRE) *Francis Ennis* 95
2 b f Danehill Dancer(IRE) —Shir Dar (FR) (Lead On Time (USA))
2309a[2] 3658a[3] 5464a[9]

Gegyp (IRE) *L Riccardi* 82
2 b f Orpen(USA) —Peggy Guggenheim (IRE) (Danehill Dancer (IRE))
3343a[10]

Gelder *H Morrison* a73 77
3 b f Grand Lodge(USA) —Purple Heather (USA) (Rahy (USA))
964[5] 1191[5] (2673) 3250[2] 3793[6] 4610[8]5294[8] 5973[2]

Gem Bien (USA) *D W Chapman* a61 60d
8 b g Bien Bien(USA) —Eastern Gem (USA) (Jade Hunter (USA))
8[12] 200[12]612[3] 650[6]1148[4] 1253[16] 1947[6]2245[2] 2413[5]3158[10] 3263[2](3386) 3599[7]3914[4] 4198[9] 4439[6]4974[3] 6431[9]6497[4] 6531[11]

Gemini Gold (IRE) *M J Grassick* 94
3 b f King's Best(USA) —Wakria (IRE) (Sadler's Wells (USA))
753a[3] 1026a[9] 1363a[5]

Gemini Lady *Mrs J C McGregor*
6 b m Emperor Fountain—Raunchy Rita (Brigadier Gerard)
302[12]

Gemology (USA) *Saeed Bin Suroor* 87
2 b c Horse Chestnut(SAF) —Miners Girl (USA) (Miner's Mark (USA))
5901[2]

Genari *P F I Cole* a66 93
3 b g Generous(IRE) —Sari (Faustus (USA))
1268[5] 1813[3] 2224[14] 2988[15] 4082[13]4591[6] 5107[10] 5504[16]

Genau (IRE) *Mrs L Stubbs* a70 71
3 ch g Grand Lodge(USA) —Intizaa (USA) (Mr Prospector (USA))
536[3] 952[9]1182[9]

Genebel (AUS) *M Moroney & A Scott* 97
5 ch m Generous(IRE) —Twinklebelle (NZ) (Star Way)
5817a[6] 6346a[11]

General Feeling (IRE) *M Mullineaux* a81 77
5 b g General Monash(USA) —Kamadara (IRE) (Kahyasi)
159[4] 253[4]569[8] 585[2]632[9] 826[11]1275[7] 1280[13] 2384[13]2520[7] 2947[15] 6739[10]6823[6] 6952[7]6966[6]

General Flumpa *C F Wall* a61 64
5 b g Vettori(IRE) —Macca Luna (IRE) (Kahyasi)
379[6] 574[10]973[3] 2075[3] 2345[4]2956[4] 3934[11] (5072) 5385[4]5652[12]

General Nuisance (IRE) *A J Chamberlain* a12 53
4 ch g General Monash(USA) —Baywood (Emarati (USA))
97[12]

Generator *Dr J D Scargill* a71+ 60
4 ch g Cadeaux Genereux—Billie Blue (Ballad Rock)
653[2] 2184[4] 4606[15]6008[9] 6294[6] (6442) (6747)

Generist *M J Attwater* a50 52
2 b f Generous(IRE) —Amidst (Midyan (USA))
1223[6] 2416[6]2588[4] 2899[4] 3175[3] 4334[4] 4545[6]6172[3] 6258[4] 6421[7]6522[5]

Generosia *A M Balding* 70
3 b f Generous(IRE) —Come On Rosi (Valiyar)
1650[7] 2533[4] 2929[3] (3215) 3703[7] 4159[4]

Generous Jem *G G Margarson* 57
3 b f Generous(IRE) —Top Jem (Damister (USA))
5086[12] 5903[4]

Generous Lad (IRE) *A B Haynes* a72 64
3 b g Generous(IRE) —Tudor Loom (Sallust)
1052[9] 1375[8] 1738[14] 4982[14] (6743) 6878[2]

Genevieve *Mrs C A Dunnett*
4 b m Mtoto—Eternal Flame (Primo Dominie)
1684[15] 2587[16] 3626[6]

Genios (GER) *Dr A Bolte* 101
5 b h Oxalagu(GER) —Glacial Star (Royal Academy (USA))
2492a[5] 4828a[7] 5856a[10]

Genki (IRE) *R Charlton* a55 73
2 ch g Shinko Forest(IRE) —Emma's Star (ITY) (Darshaan)
5780[6] 6015[2]

Genoa Star *T J Pitt* a45 40
3 b f Woodborough(USA) —Naval Dispatch (Slip Anchor)
93[4] 176[4]333[10] 528[4]887[8]

Gentian *Sir Mark Prescott* a58+ 39
3 ch f Generous(IRE) —French Spice (Cadeaux Genereux)
(2463)

Gentle Guru *R T Phillips* 73
2 b f Ishiguru(USA) —Soft Touch (IRE) (Petorius)
5231[5] 5586[2] (5950)

Gentleman Pirate *M H Tompkins* 92
2 ch c Bahamian Bounty—Verdura (Green Desert (USA))
2617[2] 3738[3] 4260[2] 4681[2]

Gentleman's Deal (IRE) *M W Easterby* a115 94
5 b h Danehill(USA) —Sleepytime (IRE) (Royal Academy (USA))
(7) (108) 728[21] 5188[9] 5512[4] 5789[5]6219[4] 6337[7] (6678)

Gentlewave (IRE) *A Fabre* 118
3 b c Monsun(GER) —Saumareine (FR) (Saumarez)
(1064a) 1557a[2] (1872a) 3127a[2]

Genuine Call *C F Wall* a72 73
2 b f Tobougg(IRE) —Gena Ivor (USA) (Sir Ivor (USA))
5296[4] 5773[3] (6034) 6444[10]

Genuine Surprise (IRE) *A P Jarvis* a21 48
4 br m Definite Article—Morning Surprise (Tragic Role (USA))
568[9]

Geojimali *J S Goldie* a78 90+
4 ch g Compton Place—Harrken Heights (IRE) (Belmez (USA))
681[8] 1196[2]1227[2] (1397) 1528[12] (1795) 1816[2] 2504[2] 3097[2]3584[2] (3811) 4119[5] 4357[3] (5336) 6009[3]

Geordie Dancer (IRE) *A Berry* a14 66
4 b g Dansili—Awtaar (USA) (Lyphard (USA))
977[16] 1273[12] 2926[14]3287[11] 3525[6] 3835[11] 4473[5] 6465[10]

Geordieland (FR) *J A Osborne* 118
5 gr h Johann Quatz(FR) —Aerdee (FR) (Highest Honor (FR))
655a[4] 934a[7] 2277a[4] 4081[2] 4713[4]6392a[18]

Geordie's Pool *J W Hills* a62
2 b c Dilshaan—Last Result (Northern Park (USA))
6143[4] 6393[6]

George Henson (IRE) *M H Tompkins* 38
2 bb g Desert Style(IRE) —Alexandria (IRE) (Irish River (FR))
6214[18]

George's Flyer (IRE) *R A Fahey* a70 60
3 b c Daggers Drawn(USA) —Winged Victory (IRE) (Dancing Brave (USA))
(123) 294[7] 2502[7] 3008[6]3621[7] 5446[10] 6158[10] 6503[9]6694[3] 6814[9]6898[11]

Georges Pride *J M Bradley* 49
2 b c Averti(IRE) —Thaw (Cadeaux Genereux)
4753[9] 5161[9] 5563[15]

George The Best (IRE) *Micky Hammond* a38 69
5 b g Imperial Ballet(IRE) —En Retard (IRE) (Petardia)
608[10] 691[12]1102[5] (1504) 1816[7] 2164[6] 3003[7] 3330[6]4253[8] 4571[5] 4735[13] (5577) 5635[17] (5865) 6174[4]

George The Second *Mrs H Sweeting* a67 64
3 b c Josr Algarhoud(IRE) —Pink Champagne (Cosmonaut)
595[3] 879[2] 1263[2](1567) 1801[7] (2576) 3011[13]4562[10] 4703[6] 4927[12]5378[15] 6288[5] 6395[10](6510) 6827[10]

George Washington (IRE) *A P O'Brien* a115 131+
3 b c Danehill(USA) —Bordighera (USA) (Alysheba (USA))
(1486) 2039a[2] 4839[3] (5524) 6345a[6]

Georgie's Lass (IRE) *R J Price* 22
7 gr m Flemensfirth(USA) —Rongai (IRE) (Commanche Run)
5768[10] 6279[13]

Germance (USA) *J-C Rouget* 115+
3 b f Silver Hawk(USA) —Gaily Tiara (USA) (Caerleon (USA))
(959a) (1874a) 2491a[2] (4645a) 5984a[4] 6340a[10]

Gertie (IRE) *E J Creighton* a28
2 b f Redback—Rosalia (USA) (Red Ransom (USA))
6644[8] 6706[4]

Gessecapade *P S McEntee* a3
4 b m Largesse—Muscade (USA) (Spend A Buck (USA))
1460[11] 2180[5]

Getaway (GER) *A Fabre* 110
3 b c Monsun(GER) —Guernica (Unfuwain (USA))
(4465a) (5145a) 5700a[3]

Getbuzzin *M Al Muhairi* a73? 67
3 ch g Bold Edge—Berenice (ITY) (Marouble)
150a[16]

Gettysburg (IRE) *J Howard Johnson* 52
3 b g Imperial Ballet(IRE) —Two Magpies (Doulab (USA))
2082[12] 2529[6] 3399[4] 4111[11] 5618[7]

Ghallab *E A L Dunlop* 70
3 b c Alhaarth(IRE) —Ta Rib (USA) (Mr Prospector (USA))
897[7] 1421[7] 1691[4] 2584[14]

Gharir (IRE) *J E Hammond* 118
4 gr h Machiavellian(USA) —Summer Sonnet (Baillamont (USA))
841a[4] 6250a[6]

Ghost Dancer *L M Cumani* a72 65
2 ch c Danehill Dancer(IRE) —Reservation (IRE) (Common Grounds)
2287[5] 2783[2] 3457[4]4321[7] 4699[6] 5262[2](5843)

Ghostmilk (IRE) *P D Deegan* 73
2 b f Golan(IRE) —Thermopylae (Tenby)
4747a[7]

Ghost Story (JPN) *M A Jarvis* 70
3 ch f Dance In The Dark(JPN) —Pazienza (IRE) (Arazi (USA))
1119[2]

Giacomo (USA) *J Shirreffs* a122
4 gr h Holy Bull(USA) —Set Them Free (USA) (Stop The Music (USA))
5826a[3] 6345a[4]

Giant Slalom *W J Haggas* a73 68
2 b g Tomba—Fallara (FR) (Tropular)
6012[2] 6290[10] (6504)

Giant's Rock (IRE) *B J Llewellyn* a68 66
4 ch g Giant's Causeway(USA) —En Garde (USA) (Irish River (FR))
166[10]

Giardini *Mario Hofer* 77
3 b f Vettori(IRE) —Motto (FR) (Mtoto)
2059a[8]

Gib (IRE) *B W Hills* 53
2 ch f Rock Of Gibraltar(IRE) —Saucy Maid (IRE) (Sure Blade (USA))
2328[14] 2816[11] 5563[6]

Gibbs Camp *E A L Dunlop* a66 55+
3 b f Marju(IRE) —Serengeti Bride (USA) (Lion Cavern (USA))
269[6] 422[2]566[4] 1215[8]

Gibraltar Bay (IRE) *T G Mills* a89 86
4 b m Cape Cross(IRE) —Secrets Of Honour (Belmez (USA))
88[2] 237[6]

Gibsons *Mrs P N Dutfield* a53 24
2 ch g Tipsy Creek(USA) —Amy Leigh (IRE) (Imperial Frontier (USA))
1107[8] 1372[7] 2346[10]2709[11] 3380[2] 3997[7]5065[15] 5735[12] 6278[2]6420[9]

Gidam Gidam (IRE) *J Mackie*
4 b g King's Best(USA) —Flamands (IRE) (Sadler's Wells (USA))
1415[10]

Gift Aid *P J Makin* a54 54
3 b c Generous(IRE) —Sans Diablo (IRE) (Mac's Imp (USA))
1304[4] 2535[4] 3349[5]4690[5] 5092[5] 5873[2]6033[8]

Gifted Flame *J J Quinn* a46 77
7 b g Revoque(IRE) —Littleladyleah (USA) (Shareef Dancer (USA))
1665[5] 2697[3] 3147[2] 4194[7] 4454[4]4831[8] 5320[7] 5617[4]

Gifted Gamble *K A Ryan* a89 97
4 b g Mind Games—Its Another Gift (Primo Dominie)
1183[7] 1597[9] 1835[3] 1939[12]2230[12] 5336[18] 5627[3] 5749[2] 6397[5]6580[3] 6752[3]6999[4]

Gifted Glori *J J Quinn* 47
3 ch g Vettori(IRE) —Azira (Arazi (USA))
1441[6] 1950[13] 3814[5] 4199[4] 4695[5]

Gifted Heir (IRE) *I A Wood* a54 52
2 b c Princely Heir(IRE) —Inzar Lady (IRE) (Inzar (USA))
1912[7] 2530[11] 3408[5]3838[2] 4480[11] 5084[9] 5482[3] 6016[5](6487)

Gifted Lass *J Balding* a69+ 10
4 b m Bold Edge—Meeson Times (Enchantment)
5060[12] 6389[3] 6399[2]6637[4] (6753) 6877[5] (6956)

Gifted Musician *J L Dunlop* 75
4 b g Sadler's Wells(USA) —Photogenic (Midyan (USA))
1132[14] 5628[5] 5815[15]

Gift Horse *D Nicholls* 118
6 ch g Cadeaux Genereux—Careful Dancer (Gorytus (USA))
1778[5] 2846[13] 3494[9] 4738[11] 5158[7]5712a[10]

Gift Range (IRE) *John M Oxx* 103
4 b m Spectrum(IRE) —Highland Gift (IRE) (Generous (IRE))
932a[6] 1785a[3] 3128a[13]

Giganticus (USA) *B W Hills* 95+
3 ch g Giant's Causeway(USA) —Shy Princess (USA) (Irish River (FR))
1067[3] 2774[22] 3491[14] 5639[17]

Gig Harbor *Miss E C Lavelle* a74 49
7 b g Efisio—Petonica (IRE) (Petoski)
2201[16] 2621[13] 3534[11]5430[10] 6097[10]6351[11]

Gigi Glamor *W M Brisbourne* 35
4 b m Secret Appeal—Gilboa (Shirley Heights)
4155[12] 4759[7] 5768[14]

Gigs Magic (USA) *M Johnston* a56 60
3 ch g Gulch(USA) —Magic Of Love (Magic Ring (IRE))
695[6] 993[9] 1215[7]1533[9] 2243[5] (2746) 3355[4] 3615 [2] 3823[2]4205[6] 4478[2] 4651[7] 5129[5] 5581[3]6068[2] 6213[13]

Gilded (IRE) *R Hannon* a48 103
2 b f Redback—Tumbleweed Pearl (Aragon)
760[4] (878) (1066) (1514) (1831) (2743) 3415[3]3734[6]

Gilded Cove *R Hollinshead* a81 77+
6 b h Polar Prince(IRE) —Cloudy Reef (Cragador)
79[5] 245[9]362[3] 569[5](732) 1151[6]1846[2] 2027[3] 2417[6]3097[4] 4894[2] 5246[5]5593[6] 5765[14] 6572[8](6858)

Gilded Youth *H Candy* 75
2 b g Gorse—Nisha (Nishapour (FR))
4600[12] 5206[8] 5890[5]

Gillipops (IRE) *R Hannon* a61 68
3 b f Xaar—Snoozeandyoulose (IRE) (Scenic)
1547[5]

Gilmore (GER) *Mme Pia Brandt* a41 75
3 ch c Acatenango(GER) —Green Water (Suave Dancer (USA))
4420a[11]

Gilt Linked *J S Wainwright* 82
3 b f Compton Place—Copy-Cat (Lion Cavern (USA))
2866[7] 3049[8] 5405[14] 5532[14]

Gimasha *W Jarvis* 102
4 b m Cadeaux Genereux—First Waltz (FR) (Green Dancer (USA))
433a[6] 3047[3] 3499[7] 4128[23] 4811[2](5044) 5405[9] 5642[7]

Ginger Cookie *B Smart* a40 24
4 ch m Bold Edge—Pretty Pollyanna (General Assembly (USA))
875[9]

Ginger Pop *G G Margarson* a62
2 ch g Mark Of Esteem(IRE) —Norcroft Lady (Mujtahid (USA))
6669[4] 6808[6]

Ginger Spice (IRE) *W J Haggas* a70 88
4 ch m Cadeaux Genereux—Pop Queen (Nashwan (USA))
898[13] 3687[5] (4375) 4879[6]5590[15]

Gingko *P R Webber* a81 76
9 b g Pursuit Of Love—Arboretum (IRE) (Green Desert (USA))
108[10] 135[3]375[8] 463[2]556[5] 578[2]843[4] 965[13] 1380[9]1769[6] 2455[8] 2636[2] 2966[6]

Gin Jockey (FR) *R Hannon* 102
3 b c Soviet Star(USA) —Singing Lark (FR) (Pampabird)
1092[3] 1600a[6] 2030[5]

Giocoso (USA) *B Palling* 88
6 b g Bahri(USA) —Wing My Chimes (USA) (Flying Paster (USA))
946[12]

Giovanni D'Oro (IRE) *N A Callaghan* a54 58
2 b g Johannesburg(USA) —Maddie G (USA) (Blush Rambler (USA))
5658[13] 5939[12] 6377[7]

Girandola *R F Johnson Houghton* a40 58d
3 b g Observatory(USA) —Honeyspike (IRE) (Chief's Crown (USA))
2235[7] 3090[10] 4663[3] 4769[6] 5023[5]5729[5] 5774[11] 6019[8]6129[6]

Girardii *R Charlton* 67
3 ch g Sinndar(IRE) —Armeria (USA) (Northern Dancer (CAN))
948[13] 1350[4] 2391[2] 3163[2]

Gist (IRE) *W J Martin* 85
3 b f Namid—Ali Dreamer (IRE) (Ali-Royal (IRE))
1023a[6] 2054a[9] 2308a[9] 5706a[8] 5849a[8]

Giunchiglio *W M Brisbourne* a56 56
7 ch g Millkom—Daffodil Fields (Try My Best (USA))
243[5]

Give Back Calais (IRE) *Miss A Casotti* a74 95
8 b g Brief Truce(USA) —Nichodoula (Doulab (USA))
305a[6]

Give Evidence *A P Jarvis* a69
2 b c Averti(IRE) —Witness (Efisio)
5784[6] 6032[3]6393[7] 6582[4]6699[6]

Give Her A Whirl *B W Hills* a37 64
2 b f Pursuit Of Love—Peggy Spencer (Formidable (USA))
5915[6] 6222[5]

Give It Time *J G Given* a56 67
3 b f Kayf Tara—Startino (Bustino)
1343[5] 4973[9] 5242[13]5618[4] 5960[7] 6178[2] 6495[3]

Give Me The Night (IRE) *B Smart* a84 90
3 b f Night Shift(USA) —There With Me (USA) (Distant View (USA))
202a[3] 436a[4]623a[6] 5171[11] 5405[3]5642[13]

Given A Chance *T J Pitt* a43 51
5 bb g Defacto(USA) —Milly Molly Mango (Mango Express)
4011[11]

Given A Choice (IRE) *R A Fahey* a93 88
4 b g Trans Island—Miss Audimar (USA) (Mr. Leader (USA))
1133[13] 1511[6] 1943[2]2656[8] 2850[10] (3688) 4241[7]5110[8] 5776[5]6148[8]

Giverny Spring *J W Hills* a43 67
3 b f Lujain(USA) —Matisse (Shareef Dancer (USA))
1552[7] 2403[9] 3142[8]3668[3] 3750[2] 4382[3] 4984[5]

Giving *G Wragg* a93 97
3 gr f Generous(IRE) —Madiyla (Darshaan)
1108[2] 4179[9] 4810[2]5110[5] 5917[8] 6411[4]

Gizmo *B Smart*
3 b g Fasliyev(USA) —Sly Baby (IRE) (Dr Devious (IRE))
6861[12]

Gizmondo *M L W Bell* a55 66+
3 ch g Lomitas—India Atlanta (Ahonoora)
669[8] 802[6]3030[6] (3804) 4051[6]

Glad Big (GER) *J A Osborne* a88 81
4 b g Big Shuffle(USA) —Glady Sum (GER) (Surumu (GER))
17[4] (84) 236[2](292) 343[2]451[6] 639[2]721[3] (826) 946[7] 1410[5] 1938[4]2341[8] 3101[9]

Glads Image *S W Hall* a11 31
4 ch m Handsome Ridge—Secret So And So (So Factual (USA))
1434[5] 1765[13] 5741[10]

Glad To Be Fast (IRE) *Mario Hofer* a108 109?
6 ch g Big Shuffle(USA) —Glad To Be Here (IRE) (Waajib)
204a[5] 353a[8]508a[3] 563a[7]5856a[9] 6252a[4] 6574a[6]

Glamaraazi (IRE) *R A Fahey* a57+ 49
3 b f Orpen(USA) —Raazi (My Generation)
4611[3] 4948[10] 5370[14] 6470[3]6538[4]

Glamis Castle (USA) *Sir Michael Stoute* a75+ 66
3 b g Selkirk(USA) —Fairy Godmother (Fairy King (USA))
5669[3] 5870[4]

Glamour Puss (NZ) *Danny O'Brien* 116
6 b m Tale Of The Cat(USA) —Escada (NZ) (Centaine (AUS))
2720[7] 2846[10]

Glaramara *A Bailey* a97 93
5 b g Nicolotte—Digamist Girl (IRE) (Digamist (USA))
198[6] 413[2]718[6] 1949[8]

Glasshoughton *M Dods* 84
3 b g Dansili—Roseum (Lahib (USA))
1032[8] 1482[4] 1983[4] (2652) 2855[5] (2976) 3475[7]4102[10]

Glasson Lodge *A L Forbes* a56 52
4 b m Primo Dominie—Petrikov (IRE) (In The Wings)
243[12]

Glavalcour (FR) *K Schafflutzel* 98
6 b h Glaieul(USA) —Lady De Valcour (FR) (Labus (FR))
456a[10] 6109a[9]

Glazier Mist (IRE) *Ms F M Crowley* 68
3 b f Danehill Dancer(IRE) —Practice (USA) (Diesis)
4124a[8]

Gleaming Spirit (IRE) *A P Jarvis* a64
2 b g Mujadil(USA) —Gleam (Green Desert (USA))
5245[4] 5735[9]

Glenargo (USA) *R A Harris* a58 67
3 ch g Concerto(USA) —Her Gift (USA) (Saint Ballado (CAN))
286[3] 466[3]630[10] 651[6]1750[2] 2134[6] 2570[3] 2937[7]3154[6] (3595) 3821[2] 4164[9] 4398[6] 6234[9]6348[12] 6539[10]6884[10]

Glen Avon Girl (IRE) *T D Easterby* 57
2 b f Mull Of Kintyre(USA) —Sandystones (Selkirk (USA))
4510[4] 5753[6] 5950[6]

Glenbuck (IRE) *A Bailey* a81 91
3 b g Mujadil(USA) —Bryna (IRE) (Ezzoud (IRE))
550[4] 993[11] 1078[9]2050[10] 4296[3] 4352[4] (4769) (5036) (5079) (5355) 5789[4] 5943[17] 6607[10]6733[5]

Glencairn Star *J S Goldie* a66 83
5 b g Selkirk(USA) —Bianca Nera (Salse (USA))
1504[7] 1686[8] (2237) 2449[2] (2852) 3354[2] 3585[8]3972[8] 4258[11] 5336[11] 5791[18] 6223[9]6320[3]

Glencalvie (IRE) *J Akehurst* a87 82
5 ch g Grand Lodge(USA) —Top Of The Form (IRE) (Masterclass (USA))
64[5] 1938[6]2405[4] 2983[2] 3532[7]4029[12] 4429[4] 4819[7] (5301) 5590[9]

Glendale *D K Ivory* a68 67
5 ch g Opening Verse(USA) —Kayartis (Kaytu)
8[9] 172[2](310) 394[3]696[2] 820[3]1152[2] 1400[8]2320[2] 2862[3]3706[3] (3934)

Glendening *D Nicholls* a16 17
3 b g Mark Of Esteem(IRE) —Mistook (USA) (Phone Trick (USA))
797[16] 1791[10]

Glenmuir (IRE) *B R Millman* 86
3 b g Josr Algarhoud(IRE) —Beryl (Bering)
1067[7] 1569[2] 1934[6] (3473) 5504[15] 5833[6]6176[11]

Glen Nevis (USA) *J Noseda* 80+
2 bb c Gulch(USA) —Beating The Buzz (IRE) (Bluebird (USA))
5659[3] (5886)

Glenree *Eamon Tyrrell* a60 53
5 b g Wizard King—The Prussian Queen (Dilum (USA))
86[9]

Glenridding *J G Given* a39
2 b g Averti(IRE) —Appelone (Emperor Jones (USA))
6447[8] 6675[7]

Glentaisie (USA) *J Noseda* a62
3 b f Giant's Causeway(USA) —Successfully (USA) (Affirmed (USA))
215[2] 4034[5]515[4]

Glen Vale Walk (IRE) *Mrs G S Rees* a44 53
9 ch g Balla Cove—Winter Harvest (Grundy)
5925[4] 6280[8]6795[6]

Glenviews Babalou (USA) *Peter Grayson* a53 63
4 ch m Deputy Commander(USA) —Hey Baba Lulu (USA) (Silent Screen (USA))
772[5] 1227[10]1463[2] 1725[12]2418[11] 2926[8]

Glenviews Oldport (USA) *Peter Grayson* a49 64
4 ch m Old Trieste(USA) —Port Plaisance (USA) (Woodman (USA))
59[9] 175[8]311[5] 395[7]546[10] 771[5]2752[8] 3411[10] 4059[13]

Glenviews Youngone (IRE) *Peter Grayson* a75 85
3 b f Namid—Baltic Beach (IRE) (Polish Precedent (USA))
226[4] 464[8]626[3] 1109[2](1304) 1529[4] (2168) 2651[9] 3332[6]3585[13] 4102[8] 4875[6] 5535[12]

Glimmer Of Light (IRE) *S A Brookshaw* 74
6 b g Marju(IRE) —Church Light (Caerleon (USA))
3220[9] 3522[8]

Glistening *L M Cumani* 110
4 b h Sadler's Wells(USA) —Shining Water (Kalaglow)
2229[6] 2848[2] 3890[3] 4713[2] 5547[3]6392a[10]

Glitterati *J S Moore* a10 53
3 b f Observatory(USA) —Stardom (Known Fact (USA))
795[8] 5761[10] 6130[13]

Global Achiever *G C H Chung* a53 32
5 b g Key Of Luck(USA) —Inflation (Primo Dominie)
480[6] 679[8]821[3] 982[6]1762[2] 2208[7]3683[5]

Global Challenge (IRE) *P G Murphy* a69 69
7 b g Sadler's Wells(USA) —Middle Prospect (USA) (Mr Prospector (USA))
591[9] 765[6]1213[7] 1931[8] 2653[5] 3649[6]5201[10] 5587[11]

Global Champion *Mario Hofer* 86
2 b c Elnadim(USA) —Craigmill (Slip Anchor)
5998a[7]

Global Dream (GER) *U Ostmann* 106
2 b c Seattle Dancer(USA) —Goonda (Darshaan)
(5007a) 5998a[2]

Global Guardian *Mrs G S Rees* a37 45
3 ch g Dr Fong(USA) —Penmayne (Inchinor)
5737[12] 5922[9]

Global Guest *M R Channon* a36 71
2 b c Piccolo—By Arrangement (IRE) (Bold Arrangement)
2579[8] 2778[3] 3031[3] 4100[5] 4480[2]4882[11] 5546[11] 5686[7]

Global Leader (AUS) *S Seemar* a60
4 b g Encosta De Lago(AUS) —Northwood Fantasy (AUS) (Bluebird (USA))
150a[15]

Global Strategy *Rae Guest* a46 48
3 b g Rainbow Quest(USA) —Pleasuring (Good Times (ITY))
6771[6] 6861[9]

Global Traffic *P D Evans* a56 53
2 br c Generous(IRE) —Eyes Wide Open (Fraam)
663[7] 2342[6]2626[5] 5041[9] 5482[13] 5948[6] 6016[2]6639[4] 6760[5]6859[2]

Globe *M S Saunders* 2
3 b f Agnes World(USA) —Hoist (IRE) (Bluebird (USA))
3257[11] 3866[12]

Globe Trekker (USA) *Peter Grayson* a18 68
4 gr m Aljabr(USA) —Amazonia (USA) (Deputy Minister (CAN))
4691[8] 4970[13]

Glorious Prince (IRE) *M G Quinlan* 70
2 b c Emperor Jones(USA) —Glorieuse (FR) (Bering)
3031[7] 4008[3] 4302[5] 5094[2] 5322[2]5614[5] 5866[6]

Glorious View *M W Easterby* 49
2 b g Observatory(USA) —Prime Property (IRE) (Tirol)
4260[11] 5025[5] 5495[10]

Glory Be (ITY) *J L Spearing* a50 44
4 ch m Dashing Blade—Hasana (USA) (Private Account (USA))
1568[10] 1852[7] 2360[11] 3592[3] 4289[4]4404[8] 4755[2] 6302[2]6373[2] 6482[4]6553[3] 6620[5]

Gloved Hand *J R Fanshawe* a91 95
4 b m Royal Applause—Fudge (Polar Falcon (USA))
2047[4] 2429[5] 3047[2] 4965[2] 5550[3]

Glowette (IRE) *I W McInnes* 29
4 ch m General Monash(USA) —Why Not Glow (IRE) (Glow (USA))
1224[11]

Gnillah *B W Hills* a54 56
3 b f Halling(USA) —Dimakya (USA) (Dayjur (USA))
710[4] 3419[8] 4245[10]4983[5] 5210[9] 5690[6]

Go Amwell *J R Jenkins* a56 45
3 b g Kayf Tara—Daarat Alayaam (IRE) (Reference Point)
112[11] 329[8]797[11] 2591[12] 2814[5] 3823[13] 4367[12]5741[5] 6132[7]6238[2] (6501) 6729[2] 6972[3]

Go Between (USA) *W Mott* 107
3 ch c Point Given(USA) —Mediation (IRE) (Caerleon (USA))
4387a[6]

Gobi King *L M Cumani* a66+ 68
4 b g Desert King(IRE) —Risarshana (FR) (Darshaan)
1984[4] 2411[5] 3100[5]3724[3] 4393[6]

Go Dancing *P W Chapple-Hyam* a56 39
2 b f Golan(IRE) —Torrid Tango (USA) (Green Dancer (USA))
5638[9] 6433[7] 6558[9]

Go Deputy (USA) *T Pletcher* 118
6 ch h Deputy Minister(CAN) —Partygoer (USA) (Secretariat (USA))
6126a[2] 6344a[7]

Godfrey Street *R Hannon* a85 94
3 ch g Compton Place—Tahara (IRE) (Caerleon (USA))
2115[12] 2720[23] 3414[12] 3970[7] 4717[11]5202[9] 5420[10] 5627[4] 5777[7]5807[2]

Go Dude *J Ryan* a68 52
2 b g Mujahid(USA) —Miss Doody (Gorytus (USA))
5646[7] 5948[14] 6283[6]6421[4] 6576[8]6745[2] 6891[2]6976[5]

Goetot (FR) *J-M Beguigne* a111 107
5 b h Tot Ou Tard(IRE) —La Goetha (FR) (No Lute (FR))
(6574a)

Go Figure (IRE) *B J Meehan* a86 86
3 ch g Desert Prince(IRE) —Interpose (Indian Ridge)
(803) 855[3] 1005[2]1205[2] 1898[6] 5724[2] 5869[9] (6076)

Go For Gold (IRE) *A Laird* 115
5 b h Machiavellian(USA) —Kithanga (IRE) (Darshaan)
371a[2]

Go For Success (USA) *E Hautin* a67 87
6 b g Royal Academy(USA) —Barad (Rainbow Quest (USA))
5562a[3]

Go Free *C J Down* a54 50
5 gr g Easycall—Miss Traxdata (Absalom)
(309) 470[7]

Go Garuda *Miss Gay Kelleway* a65 57
5 b g Air Express(IRE) —Free As A Bird (Robellino (USA))
292[5] 416[5]576[3] 693[5]2936[4] 3914[8]4425[4]

Go Imperial (IRE) *M G Quinlan* a62 28
2 b c Imperial Ballet(IRE) —Miss Divot (IRE) (Petardia)
6047[8] 6562[8] 6710[2]

Going Day (USA) *J E Pease* 101
3 b f Daylami(IRE) —Antics (USA) (Unbridled (USA))
3515a[3]

Going Skint *M Wellings* a62
3 b g Elnadim(USA) —Prospering (Prince Sabo)
331[6] 487[5]653[3] 6944[3]

Going Straight (IRE) *I A Wood* a73 82
2 b f Princely Heir(IRE) —Easy Going (Hamas (IRE))
1347[9] 1535[2] (1922) 2225[2]4344[10] 4594[10] 5234[6] 5668[9]

Going To Work (IRE) *D R C Elsworth* a59
2 b f Night Shift(USA) —Firesteed (IRE) (Common Grounds)
6886[7]

Golano *P R Webber* a83 84
6 gr g Linamix(FR) —Dimakya (USA) (Dayjur (USA))
88[15]

Golan Way *I A Wood* a72 72
2 b c Golan(IRE) —Silk Daisy (Barathea (IRE))
4177[7] 4753[7] 5043[5] 5447[5] 5647[2]6064[3] 6458[5] (6646)

Golband *R F Marvin* a76+ 69
4 b m Cadeaux Genereux—Hatheethah (IRE) (Machiavellian (USA))
3996[12] 4230[13] 4507[12]5487[12] 6325[10] 6956[10]

Golda Seek (USA) *B J Meehan* a51 55
3 b f Seeking The Gold(USA) —Golightly (USA) (Take Me Out (USA))
6430[7] 6767[10]

Golden Acer (IRE) *Doug Watson* a99 95
3 ch c Elnadim(USA) —Shifty Lady (IRE) (Night Shift (USA))
150a[6] 368a[11]620a[2]

Golden Alchemist *M D I Usher* a78 76
3 ch g Woodborough(USA) —Pure Gold (Dilum (USA))
1122[11] 1681[12] 2583[3] 2823[7] 3598[2]4437[7] 6327[3]6568[6] 6698[12]

Golden Applause (FR) *Mrs A L M King* a52 78
4 b m Royal Applause—Golden Circle (USA) (Theatrical)
1993[8] 2457[7] (3036) 3703[5] 4075[3] 4429[5]5689[12] 5833[7]

Golden Arrow (IRE) *D K Weld* 111
3 b c Danehill(USA) —Cheal Rose (IRE) (Dr Devious (IRE))
1172a[2] 1708a[5] 2039a[5] 3129a[4]

Golden Asha *N A Callaghan* a78 92
4 ch m Danehill Dancer(IRE) —Snugfit Annie (Midyan (USA))
1076[4] 1338[4] 1487[4]1858[6] (2233) 2389[4]

Golden Balls (IRE) *R Hannon* 93
2 ch c Danehill Dancer(IRE) —Colourful Cast (IRE) (Nashwan (USA))
2579[3] 2960[6] 3253[3] (3545) 4736[12] 5546[5](5828)

Golden Boot *A Bailey* a61 72
7 ch g Unfuwain(USA) —Sports Delight (Star Appeal)
168[8] 250[8]283[4] 816[10] 1033[7]1138[11] 2522[8] 4320[8] 6509[U]

Golden Cast (JPN) *K Hashiguchi* 110
6 b h Taiki Shuttle(USA) —Return Bandam (JPN) (Niniski (USA))
5717a[12]

Golden Chalice (IRE) *P R Chamings* a85 99
7 ch g Selkirk(USA) —Special Oasis (Green Desert (USA))
6176[13]

Golden Dagger (IRE) *K A Ryan* 85
2 ch f Daggers Drawn(USA) —Santarene (IRE) (Scenic)
4400[3] (4765) 5434[6] 5672[6]

Golden Desert (IRE) *T G Mills* a72 85
2 b c Desert Prince(IRE) —Jules (IRE) (Danehill (USA))
2979[9] 4479[8] 5347[2]5655[15] (6414)

Golden Dixie (USA) *R A Harris* a93 99
7 ch g Dixieland Band(USA) —Beyrouth (USA) (Alleged (USA))
846[2] 1076[8] 1161[2]1399[6] 1474[10] 1936[7](2624) 2946[2] 3251[9] 3471[7] 3972[3] 4101[9]4811[7] 5202[4] 5358[15] 5807[12] 5832[9]

Golden Dynamic (IRE) *G Di Chio* 87
2 b c Danetime(IRE) —Golden Vizcaya (USA) (Alydeed (CAN))
6003a[8]

Golden Event (USA) *M Fratini* 44
2 b c Wild Event(USA) —Tryst Me (USA) (Believe It (USA))
6123a[11]

Golden Folly *Lady Herries* a50 50
2 ch g Polish Precedent(USA) —Height Of Folly (Shirley Heights)
5918[12] 6188[11] 6475[6]

Golden Groom *C W Fairhurst* 55
3 b g Groom Dancer(USA) —Reine De Thebes (FR) (Darshaan)
2948^7 3373^5 3909^9 4470^9 4734^{3}5082^2 5618^3
Golden Iron (IRE) *M Fratini*
2 b f Iron Mask(USA) —Coral Golden (IRE) (Rainbows For Life (CAN))
2062a^8
Golden Knife (IRE) *M Fratini* a84 92
3 b f Cape Cross(IRE) —Coral Golden (IRE) (Rainbows For Life (CAN))
5473a^5
Golden Legacy (IRE) *D K Weld* a88 105
4 b m Rossini(USA) —Dissidentia (IRE) (Dancing Dissident (USA))
3125a^{19}
Golden Measure *G A Swinbank* a21 58
6 b g Rainbow Quest(USA) —Dawna (Polish Precedent (USA))
414^{11}
Golden Prospect *J W Hills* a58 10
2 b c Lujain(USA) —Petonellajill (Petong)
5623^{10} 6034^5 6441^{11}
Golden Quest *M Johnston* a106 120
5 ch g Rainbow Quest(USA) —Souk (IRE) (Ahonoora)
4081^{11} 4677^6
Golden Rahy (USA) *Doug O'Neill* 109
7 ch g Rahy(USA) —Gold Fleece (USA) (Deputed Testamony (USA))
1721a^4
Golden Ribbons *J R Boyle* a36
2 ch f Compton Place—Mim (Midyan (USA))
6034^9 6187^{13}6562^7
Golden Rob'S (IRE) *G Di Chio* 41
2 b c Rob's Spirit(USA) —Lady D'Or (FR) (Kendor (FR))
6123a^{12}
Golden Rose (GER) *H Hesse* 96
6 gr m Winged Love(IRE) —Grey Pearl (GER) (Magic Mirror)
1974a^{10} 6529a^2
Golden Spectrum (IRE) *R A Harris* a63 62
7 ch g Spectrum(IRE) —Plessaya (USA) (Nureyev (USA))
(143) 247^3 391^{2}467^2 (526) 546^7 953^{3}1273^7 1311^3 1553^{2}1753^8 2262^{13} 2936^{12}6897^9 (6955)
Golden Sprite *B R Millman* a63 68
3 b f Bertolini(USA) —Shalad'Or (Golden Heights)
1941^7 2480^2 3865^{5}5566^4 (5831) 6260^6 6474^8
Golden Square *A W Carroll* a65 62
4 ch g Tomba—Cherish Me (Polar Falcon (USA))
(134) 200^4 492^{10}(1353) 1683^4 2098^8 3262^{8}3523^8 3898^2 4281^5
Golden Stravinsky (USA) *A Peraino* a50 98
4 bb h Stravinsky(USA) —Shagadellic (USA) (Devil's Bag (USA))
203a^{11} 434a^{15}
Golden Stud (IRE) *M Fratini* 94
3 b c In The Wings—Susi Wong (IRE) (Selkirk (USA))
1872a^{12} 2671a^{11}
Golden Surf (IRE) *R Hannon* 33
3 b f Gold Away(IRE) —Silvery Surf (USA) (Silver Deputy (CAN))
4162^6
Golden Surfside (USA) *M Fratini* 53
2 b c Bianconi(USA) —Rhonda's Rocket (USA) (Fit To Fight (USA))
2670a^7
Golden System (IRE) *M Fratini* 92
3 ch f Desert Sun—Solid Golden (USA) (Mountain Cat (USA))
1713a^5
Golden Titus (IRE) *A Renzoni* 110
2 ch c Titus Livius(FR) —Oraplata (USA) (Silver Hawk (USA))
(2670a) 3777a^2 4644a^5 6003a^4
Golden Topaz (IRE) *J Howard Johnson* 64
2 b f Almutawakel—Miss Champagne (FR) (Bering)
3188^6 3908^3 4830^4
Golden West (IRE) *G Fratini* 99
3 b c Cape Cross(IRE) —Westside Girl (USA) (Way West (FR))
1871a^4
Gold Express *W A O'Gorman* 74+
3 b g Observatory(USA) —Vanishing Point (USA) (Caller I.D. (USA))
2868^7 3742^9 (4573)
Gold Flame *H Candy* 71
3 b g Gorse—Uaeflame (IRE) (Polish Precedent (USA))
1844^7
Gold For Sale (ARG) *I Jory* a111
4 ch h Not For Sale(ARG) —Lava Gold (USA) (Java Gold (USA))
(368a) 739a^{10}
Gold Guest *P D Evans* a69 61
7 ch g Vettori(IRE) —Cassilis (IRE) (Persian Bold)
4982^5 5354^8
Gold Gun (USA) *K A Ryan* 54
4 b g Seeking The Gold(USA) —Possessive Dancer (Shareef Dancer (USA))
5153^6 5526^9 5920^{13}
Goldhill Prince *Ernst Oertel* a54 51
4 b g Prince Sabo—Lady Mabel (Inchinor)
321^6 520^{11}886^7 982^{3}1310^{16} 1539^9
Gold History (USA) *A Laird* a86 106
5 b h Seeking The Gold(USA) —Battle Hymn (USA) (Danzig (USA))
495a^6
Gold Hush (USA) *Sir Michael Stoute* a78
2 ch f Seeking The Gold(USA) —Meniatarra (USA) (Zilzal (USA))
5095^5 6071^2
Gold Magic (FR) *J-P Gallorini* 108
8 b g Goldneyev(USA) —Djouza (FR) (Djarvis (FR))
5223a^4

Gold Option *J H M Gosden* 93
2 ch c Observatory(USA) —Minskip (USA) (The Minstrel (CAN))
4103^8 (4572) (4783) 5521^5
Gold Response *D Shaw* a55+ 47
2 ch g Intikhab(USA) —Razor Sharp (Bering)
3157^7 3455^{6}3713^9 4115^7 6421^{10}6487^8 6859^4(6996)
Gold Ring *J A Geake* 102
6 ch g Groom Dancer(USA) —Indubitable (Sharpo)
4770^6 5533^{16}
Gold Sound (FR) *C Laffon-Parias* 110
4 ch g Green Tune(USA) —Born Gold (USA) (Blushing Groom (FR))
655a^3 934a^5 2597a^7
Gold Spirit (IRE) *E J O'Neill* a88 101
2 b c Invincible Spirit(IRE) —Butter Knife (IRE) (Sure Blade (USA))
1730^6 2726^4 (3521) 3734^8 4026^7 (4397) (4789)5017^6 5471a^5 5681^{14}
Goldstar Dancer (IRE) *J J Quinn* a49 48
4 b h General Monash(USA) —Ravensdale Rose (IRE) (Henbit (USA))
251^1
Golo Gal *Mrs L J Mongan* a67 59+
4 b g Mark Of Esteem(IRE) —Western Sal (Salse (USA))
1152^9 2088^{12} 6907^{11}
Go Mo (IRE) *S Kirk* a82 82
4 b g Night Shift(USA) —Quiche (Formidable (USA))
1545^{12} 1932^9 4209^{10} 4772^{12} 5302^{7}5573^7
Gone'N'Dunnett (IRE) *Mrs C A Dunnett* a69 68
7 b g Petardia—Skerries Bell (Taufan (USA))
1^4 518^{2}44^3 275^8(424) 532^{6}605^2 798^8 949^{3}1102^7 1151^8 2182^{6}2417^8 2590^3 2784^{3}3094^{14} 3709^8 3846^{3}4267^5 4365^{11} 4846^4 4970^{6}5032^3 5327^8 6513^8
Gone Too Far *P Monteith* 65
8 b g Reprimand—Blue Nile (IRE) (Bluebird (USA))
816^3 1758^6 4522^3 4723^7
Good Article (IRE) *D K Ivory* a65 67
5 b g Definite Article—Good News (IRE) (Ajraas (USA))
291^7 484^{4}769^2 888^{2}1201^8 2577^{8}2861^3 (3074) 3730^4 (4332) (4869) (5166) (5422) 5904^{12}6070^8
Goodbye *B W Hills* 21
2 ch f Efisio—Blow Me A Kiss (Kris)
4559^{10}
Goodbye Cash (IRE) *P D Evans* a51 75
2 b f Danetime(IRE) —Jellybeen (IRE) (Petardia)
2432^2 2800^{12} 3193^3 4824a^6 5125^{3}5735^7 6175^2 (6208) 6332^5
Goodbye Girl (IRE) *Mrs C A Dunnett* a40 48
3 b f Shinko Forest(IRE) —Adieu Cherie (IRE) (Bustino)
613^{12} 1122^8 1312^{7}1571^4 1768^{7}2249^4 2318^6 2589^{10}3229^9 3824^7
Goodbye Mr Bond *E J Alston* a62 99
6 b g Elmaamul(USA) —Fifth Emerald (Formidable (USA))
1281^7 (1864) 1985^2 2079^8 (2657) 3255^5 3985^{4}4356^7 4889^5 5188^8
Good Companion (IRE) *J L Dunlop* 61
3 ch g Elnadim(USA) —Broadway Rosie (Absalom)
1642^6 2353^9 2644^6 3090^2 3538^{13}
Good Effect (USA) *A P Jarvis* a63 55
2 ch c Woodman(USA) —River Dreams (USA) (Riverman (USA))
5914^{10} 6143^3 6581^4
Goodenough Mover *Andrew Turnell* a97 94
10 ch g Beveled(USA) —Rekindled Flame (IRE) (King's Lake (USA))
1359^{14} 2443^2 2776^7 3486^9 4106^{6}5070^{13} 5476^{14} 5627^{11}
Goodenough Prince *Andrew Turnell* a40 53
3 b g Bluegrass Prince(IRE) —Goodenough Girl (Mac's Imp (USA))
3112^9 4367^{10} 5071^{10}5870^{10} 6304^{12}
Good Etiquette *Mrs S Lamyman*
2 b g Tipsy Creek(USA) —Aliuska (IRE) (Fijar Tango (FR))
5491^{11}
Good Intentions *P W Hiatt* a42 26
4 ch m Bien Bien(USA) —Level Headed (Beveled (USA))
894^{11} 6026^{10} 6327^{9}6501^P 6812^{8}6907^4
Good Investment *Miss Tracy Waggott* a43 53
4 b g Silver Patriarch(IRE) —Bundled Up (USA) (Sharpen Up)
5311^4 5683^{10} 5955^{14} 6973^2
Good Luck Chip (IRE) *I A Wood* a28 22
2 b f Princely Heir(IRE) —Surabaya (FR) (Galetto (FR))
6024^{10} 6222^7
Goodricke *Saeed Bin Suroor* 124
4 b h Bahamian Bounty—Star (Most Welcome)
5274^4 5682^9
Good Surprise *J S Bolger* 108
5 b h Halling(USA) —One Way Street (Habitat)
2154a^2 3107a^5 4639a^3 4822a^2
Good Turn *R Hannon* 52
3 b f Royal Applause—Gracious Gift (Cadeaux Genereux)
1119^{11} 1513^6 1733^6 2316^9
Good Wee Girl (IRE) *S Woodman* a39 47
4 b m Tagula(IRE) —Auriga (Belmez (USA))
6726^{14}
Goodwood Belle *J L Dunlop* 35
2 b f Soviet Star(USA) —Waif (Groom Dancer (USA))
2328^{13}
Goodwood March *J L Dunlop* 57
3 b f Foxhound(USA) —Military Tune (IRE) (Nashwan (USA))
1085^{15} 3742^4 4375^6 4799^4 5055^{2}5480^{17} (5729) 6204^7
Goodwood Spirit *J M Bradley* a19 74
4 b g Fraam—Rechanit (IRE) (Local Suitor (USA))
2443^8 3212^{15} 3471^{11} 3679^6 4101^{22}4557^6 6227^{12}

Go On Be A Tiger (USA) *M R Channon* 82
2 br c Machiavellian(USA) —Queen's Logic (IRE) (Grand Lodge (USA))
(5892)
Go On Green (IRE) *E A L Dunlop* a55 82
2 b c Kyllachy—Colouring (IRE) (Catrail (USA))
2234^2 4349^4 5066^4 5608^7
Go On Jessica (IRE) *A G Juckes* a53+ 54
2 ch f Soviet Star(USA) —Peig Sayers (IRE) (Royal Academy (USA))
1142^2 1379^3 1682^{U}2073^3 2731^9 6821^{10}
Goose Chase *A M Hales* a73 61
4 b g Inchinor—Bronzewing (Beldale Flutter (USA))
267^9 480^{4}698^5 (845) 985^{12} 1382^{4}1644^6 6564^{7}6694^4 6898^6
Goose Green (IRE) *M R Channon* a65 69
2 b g Invincible Spirit(IRE) —Narbayda (IRE) (Kahyasi)
775^3 892^7 968^3 3641^{4}3902^6 4436^4 (4520) 5013^{4}5053^5 (5382) 5482^4 5647^8 5948^3
Gopura (USA) *G Martin*
5 b h Atticus(USA) —Dariela (USA) (Manila (USA))
305a^5
Gordonsville *A M Balding* 89
3 b c Generous(IRE) —Kimba (USA) (Kris S (USA))
2970^4 3376^2 4039^5 4374^4
Go Red *M W Easterby* 52
2 b g Best Of The Bests(IRE) —Boulevard Rouge (USA) (Red Ransom (USA))
2733^9 3498^8 4018^5 4466^7 5482^7
Gorella (FR) *P L Biancone* 119
4 ch m Grape Tree Road—Exciting Times (FR) (Jeune Homme (USA))
(4385a) 6342a^7
Gorgeous Boy (IRE) *P L Gilligan* a46 13
4 ch g Forzando—Instil (Rudimentary (USA))
24^{14} 45^{10}
Gorgeous Girl *P W D'Arcy* a45 41
2 b f Generous(IRE) —Zielana Gora (Polish Precedent (USA))
2461^8 3010^{6}3435^9
Gorse *Jamie Poulton* 105
11 b g Sharpo—Pervenche (Latest Model)
2751^2
Go Solo *G A Swinbank* 93
5 b g Primo Dominie—Taza (Persian Bold)
1043^{11} 1494^8 2299^2 (2547) 2975^3 3519^3(4259) (4654) 5115^3 5367^2
Go Tech *T D Easterby* a97 98d
6 b g Gothenberg(IRE) —Bollin Sophie (Efisio)
867^5 1484^9 1775^6 2079^{12} 2657^7(2872) 3552^{10} 4508^{10} 5115^7 5310^7 5494^{5}4578^{16}
Got The Last Laugh (USA) *W Mott* a102
2 br c Distorted Humor(USA) —Theresa's Tizzy (USA) (Cee's Tizzy (USA))
5983a^5 6339a^{13}
Got To Be Cash *W M Brisbourne* a40 38
7 ch m Lake Coniston(IRE) —Rasayel (USA) (Bering)
2407^8 4944^8
Gouranga *H Candy* a49 70
3 b f Robellino(USA) —Hymne D'Amour (USA) (Dixieland Band (USA))
1798^3 2646^4 4181^{4}4687^3 5057^5 5587^7
Government (IRE) *M C Chapman* a42 31
5 b g Great Dane(IRE) —Hidden Agenda (FR) (Machiavellian (USA))
674^4 (783) 5240^{15} 5924^{6}6532^9 6892^{14}
Gower *R Charlton* 84
2 b c Averti(IRE) —Alashaan (Darshaan)
5147^6 5645 ^{2} 6024^2
Gower Song *D R C Elsworth* a69 105
3 b f Singspiel(IRE) —Gleaming Water (Kalaglow)
1955^6 (2391) (2713) (2929) (3046) 3739^4 4039^7 4741^{3}5300^2 5502^2
Gracechurch (IRE) *M R Channon* a55 80
3 b g Marju(IRE) —Saffron Crocus (Shareef Dancer (USA))
(730) (1205) 1781^7 2224^8 2805^{12} 3318^9 3737 ^{5}4051^4 4490^5 4991^3 5152^5 5260^{2}5685^7 6076^{13}
Graceful Flight *P T Midgley* a15 44
4 gr m Cloudings(IRE) —Fantasy Flight (Forzando)
1127^8 1391^{10} 2758^{13}3189^2 3912^{12} 4324^{11}
Graceful Steps (IRE) *E J O'Neill* 58
2 b f Desert Prince(IRE) —Ghassak (IRE) (Persian Bold)
5481^9 5959^5 6270^5
Gracie's Gift (IRE) *A G Newcombe* a68 68
4 b g Imperial Ballet(IRE) —Settle Petal (IRE) (Roi Danzig (USA))
1255^3 1878^3 2792^{2}3996^4 4531^4 (5474) (6060) 6396^{6}6762^3
Gradetime (IRE) *M J Wallace* a81 83
2 b f Danetime(IRE) —Grade A Star (IRE) (Alzao (USA))
878^2 (908) (1405) 2062a^4
Graft *Mrs P Townsley* a61 71
7 b g Entrepreneur—Mariakova (USA) (The Minstrel (CAN))
461^7 596^{11}706^{10} 1244^{10}6870^3 6918^9
Grafton (IRE) *J O'Reilly* a65 62
3 b g Desert Style(IRE) —Gracious Gretclo (Common Grounds)
(500) 601^7 1078^8 1497^{7}2109^{13} 3154^{13} 3378^{11}6721^{11}
Grafty Green (IRE) *T H Caldwell*
3 b g Green Desert(USA) —Banafsajee (USA) (Pleasant Colony (USA))
6923^6
Graham Island *G Wragg* a87 86
5 b g Acatenango(GER) —Gryada (Shirley Heights)
214^4 454^{4}1631^{13}
Grain Of Truth *Sir Michael Stoute* a98+ 101
3 b f Gulch(USA) —Pure Grain (Polish Precedent (USA))
(1598) 2174^6 2679^2 (3489) 4590^2 5300^{3}5525^2 5917^7
Gramada (IRE) *P A Blockley* a64 80?
4 b m Cape Cross(IRE) —Decatur (Deploy)
74^8 252^{4}965^2 (1249) 1376^3 2023^5 2305^{12}

Gramm *L M Cumani* 86
3 b c Fraam—Beacon Silver (Belmez (USA))
5165^8 6219^6
Grammaticus *K A Ryan* 20
3 b c Zaha(CAN) —Autumn Stone (IRE) (Bigstone (IRE))
380^{11}
Granakey (IRE) *M G Quinlan* a62
3 b f Key Of Luck(USA) —Grand Morning (IRE) (King Of Clubs)
3406^{11} 3914^{12}4045^5 5928^{2}6234^3 (6308) 6763^3 6869^{11}
Gran Amor *P D Cundell* 23
3 ch f Piccolo—Sunfleet (Red Sunset)
1214^{10}
Granary Girl *J Pearce* a53 57
4 b m Kingsinger(IRE) —Highland Blue (Never So Bold)
1857 263^{7}382^6 472^{10}683^5 1305^{4}1537^3 2181^6 2728^{6}2935^2 3232^3 3836^{2}4289^3 (4925) 5072^5 5354^{15}
Gran Clicquot *G P Enright* a41 45
11 gr m Gran Alba(USA) —Tina's Beauty (Tina's Pet)
1541^{11} 2952^7 3149^{4}3797^3 4585^{13} 6232^{9}6373^6 6804^7
Grand (IRE) *Dale Romans* a91 85+
6 ch h Grand Lodge(USA) —Easy Pop (IRE) (Shernazar)
6006a^8
Grandad Bill (IRE) *T D Easterby* 67
3 ch g Intikhab(USA) —Matikanehanafubuki (IRE) (Caerleon (USA))
1444^9 2622^{12} 4470^{13}
Gran Dana (IRE) *G Prodromou* a41 41
6 b g Grand Lodge(USA) —Olean (Sadler's Wells (USA))
788^8
Grand Art (IRE) *M H Tompkins* a49 69
2 b g Raise A Grand(IRE) —Mulberry River (IRE) (Bluebird (USA))
3018^5 4251^3 4688^5 6074^9
Grand Assault *P S McEntee* a58
3 b g Mujahid(USA) —As Mustard (Keen)
132^7 445^{7}5986^7 6403^{4}6587^8 6829^{2}6983^{11}
Grand Cherokee (IRE) *B Ellison* a28 68
3 gr c Fayruz—Divine Apsara (Godswalk (USA))
730^8 1005^{11}
Grand Court (IRE) *A W Carroll* 59
3 b f Grand Lodge(USA) —Nice One Clare (IRE) (Mukaddamah (USA))
4004^9 4287^4
Grand Couturier *J-C Rouget* 117
3 b c Grand Lodge(USA) —Lady Elgar (IRE) (Sadler's Wells (USA))
1064a^3 3517a^4
Grand Design *C A Cyzer* a60 56
4 b m Danzero(AUS) —Duende (High Top)
59^5 217^{6}460^5 5035^{7}5267^{12} 5651^8 5988^4
Grand Diamond (IRE) *Mrs A J Perrett* 72
2 b c Grand Lodge(USA) —Winona (IRE) (Alzao (USA))
2619^5 4794^5 5178^7
Grand Dream (IRE) *M Johnston* 49
2 ch c Grand Lodge(USA) —Tamaya (IRE) (Darshaan)
5239^6 5886^7
Grande Caiman (IRE) *R Hannon* a76
2 ch c Grand Lodge(USA) —Sweet Retreat (Indian Ridge)
6324^7 6434^5(6867)
Grand Ekinoks (TUR) *C Kurt* 117
8 b h Barnato(USA) —Violent Girl (TUR) (Aristocrat)
205a^3 512a^3 624a^3
Grande Melody (IRE) *P Bary* 111
3 b f Grand Lodge(USA) —Crystal Melody (Nureyev (USA))
2491a^9
Grand Emporium (SAF) *A Laird* a118 115
6 b g National Assembly(CAN) —Whistling Dixie (SAF) (Raise A Man (USA))
560a^9
Grand Entrance (IRE) *C R Egerton* a73 82
3 b g Grand Lodge(USA) —Alessia (GER) (Warning)
3266^2 (3742) 4114^4 4488^{11} 5042^{13} 5107^{13}
Grande Roche (IRE) *G A Swinbank* a56 73
4 b g Grand Lodge(USA) —Arabian Lass (SAF) (Al Mufti (USA))
231^7 1123^{13} 1334^{6}1500^2 2322^5 2548^2 3675^4
Grande Terre (IRE) *R A Fahey* a51 68+
5 br m Grand Lodge(USA) —Savage (IRE) (Polish Patriot (USA))
1041^2 1123^{15} 1636^5 2286^U 2641^{6}3142^3 3361^6
Grandfield (IRE) *M J Grassick* 67
4 b m Fasliyev(USA) —Vernonhills (Hard Fought)
2369a^7
Grand Heights (IRE) *J L Dunlop* 71
2 br c Grand Lodge(USA) —Height Of Fantasy (IRE) (Shirley Heights)
2867^7 4129^9 4669^3 5585^8
Grand Ideas *G J Smith* a67 67d
7 br g Grand Lodge(USA) —Afrafa (IRE) (Lashkari)
644^{10} 955^{13}
Grand Jour (IRE) *Ms J S Doyle* a86 69
3 b g Grand Lodge(USA) —Reveuse De Jour (IRE) (Sadler's Wells (USA))
(118) (160) 392a^{10} 665^8 914^{7}1016^{14} 1627^9 5150^{13}5666^{13} 6830^{12}6888^{13}
Grand Lucre *E J O'Neill* a58 48
2 b f Grand Slam(USA) —Naughty Crown (USA) (Chief's Crown (USA))
1675^7 3307^5 4394^{4}4932^2 5262^{10}
Grandma Ryta *John Berry* a37 35
4 br m Cyrano De Bergerac—Tamara (Marju (IRE))
304^{12} 659^{7}953^{11} 1460^{5}2248^9
Grandma's Girl *Robert Gray* a41 48
4 b m Desert Style(IRE) —Sakura Queen (IRE) (Woodman (USA))
2242^9 3291^7 4072^{12} 4227^6

Grand Mempari *Mrs C A Dunnett*
3 b f Grand Lodge(USA) —Mempari (IRE) (Fairy King (USA))
1260[7] 1613[11]

Grand Officer (IRE) *D J S Ffrench Davis* a39 51
2 b g Grand Lodge(USA) —Sheer Bliss (IRE) (Sadler's Wells (USA))
4980[10] 5178[14] 6283[7]6670[4]

Grand Opera (IRE) *J Howard Johnson* 74
3 b g City On A Hill(USA) —Victoria's Secret (IRE) (Law Society (USA))
1296[3] 1759[3] (3698)

Grandos (IRE) *Karen George* 62
4 b g Cadeaux Genereux—No Reservations (IRE) (Commanche Run)
1123[14] 1253[6] 1480[8] 2112[10] 2198[7]4285[9] 4755[7] 5625[12]

Grand Palace (IRE) *D Shaw* a56 39
3 b g Grand Lodge(USA) —Pocket Book (IRE) (Reference Point)
1165[14] 1218[8] 1274[5](2249) 2466[6]5637[12] 5936[9] 6537[5]6756[5] 6829[3]6955[2]

Grand Parrot *W De Best-Turner* a42 59?
3 b g Prince Sabo—Silkstone Lady (Puissance)
1818[9] 2080[7] 2897[9] 4045[9]

Grand Passion (IRE) *G Wragg* a109 103
6 b g Grand Lodge(USA) —Lovers' Parlour (Beldale Flutter (USA))
213[6] (518) 666[2]1098[4] 2116[5] 2803[16] 4529[6] 4818[10]5813[5] 6299[3] 6516[5]

Grand Place *R Hannon* a54 79
4 b g Compton Place—Comme Ca (Cyrano De Bergerac)
949[15] 1383[12] 1570[12]2135[12] 2223[15]

Grand Prairie (SWE) *G L Moore* a60 59
10 b g Prairie—Platonica (ITY) (Primo Dominie)
270[8]

Grand Prix *R Hannon* 90
2 ch c Grand Lodge(USA) —Divine Quest (Kris)
1203[3] 1770[2] (2172) (2598) 3026[4] 4344[8] (5172)5806[8]

Grand Rebecca (IRE) *G A Huffer* 35
3 ch f Namid—Krayyalei (IRE) (Krayyan)
5272[6] 5761[13]

Grand Revival (IRE) *David P Myerscough* 80
4 ch g Grand Lodge(USA) —Romancia (USA) (Woodman (USA))
5853a[9]

Grand Sefton *D Shaw* a64 42
3 br g Pivotal—Nahlin (Slip Anchor)
839[6] 2050[18] 6674[13]

Grand Show *W R Swinburn* a96+ 71
4 b g Efisio—Christine Daae (Sadler's Wells (USA))
4706[14] 5021[5] (5263) (5777) 6243[6]6292[4] 6660[6]

Grand Silence (IRE) *W R Swinburn* a48 67
3 ch g Grand Lodge(USA) —Why So Silent (Mill Reef (USA))
4004[6] 5086[7] 5612[9]

Grand Slam Maria (FR) *A J McNamara* 62
3 b f Anabaa(USA) —Kate Marie (USA) (Bering)
4124a[15]

Grand Symphony *W Jarvis* a46
2 ch f Zamindar(USA) —Gitane (FR) (Grand Lodge (USA))
6886[9]

Grand Vadla (FR) *A Fabre* 107
3 b f Grand Lodge(USA) —Vadlava (FR) (Bikala)
3991a[7] 6328a[6]

Grand View *J R Weymes* a53 60
10 ch g Grand Lodge(USA) —Hemline (Sharpo)
680[9] 766[3]873[5] 1391[5](1465) 1728[9]4157[19] 5834[8]

Grand Vista *A Fabre* 96
2 b c Danehill(USA) —Revealing (Halling (USA))
3777a[6] 5399a[6]

Grand Welcome (IRE) *E J Creighton* a55 67
4 b g Indian Lodge(IRE) —Chocolate Box (Most Welcome)
6904[8]

Grand Zulu (AUS) *J Size* 120
5 b g Grand Lodge(USA) —Bravo Zulu (AUS) (Military Plume (NZ))
6110a[11] 6346a[4]

Grangehurst *Miss J R Gibney* a59 57
2 ch f Inchinor—My Way (IRE) (Marju (IRE))
5596[7] 5882[7] 6098[5]

Grange Lili (IRE) *Peter Grayson* a60 71
2 b f Daggers Drawn(USA) —Lili Cup (FR) (Fabulous Dancer (USA))
2552[2] 2755[5]3351[2] 5262[13] 5606[10]6463[2] 6596[4]6670[6] 6813[3]6926[8] 6939[2](6985)

Granny Peel (IRE) *M Brittain* a46 44
2 b f Redback—Bacchanalia (IRE) (Blues Traveller (IRE))
760[5] 877[4] (1040) 1142[3]1229[2] (1744) (2073) (2538) 3136[2]3787[2] 4376[10] 4971[3]6311[10] 6640[11]

Granston (IRE) *J D Bethell* a98 99
5 gr g Revoque(IRE) —Gracious Gretclo (Common Grounds)
726[2] 1111[2] 1495[5]2200[9] 2657[2] 3313[5] (4153) 4889[2] 5019[3]5520[8]

Grantley *H Hesse* a81 79
9 b g Deploy—Matisse (Shareef Dancer (USA))
666[14] 6529a[15]

Grantley Adams *M R Channon* a84 103
3 b g Dansili—Noble Peregrine (Lomond (USA))
1020[9] 3414[5] 3970[3]4345[6] 5044[3] (5202)

Grasp *G L Moore* a62 57
4 b g Kayf Tara—Circe (Main Reef)
5587[14] 6011[12] 6178[3] (6398)

Grasslandik *Miss A Stokell* a31 28
10 b g Ardkinglass—Sophisticated Baby (Bairn (USA))
130[8] 271[8]1571[10] 2396[15]

Grateful *R M Beckett* 58
3 ch f Generous(IRE) —Duende (High Top)
1640[3] 2188[10] 3152[10] 3952[8]

Gravardlax *Miss D A McHale* a39 51
5 ch g Salse(USA) —Rubbiyati (Cadeaux Genereux)
1198[8] 1572[4]1767[7] 2483[8] 2790[7]3013[5] 3260[5]3919[6]

Grave Matters (USA) *T G McCourt* a72 79
3 b g Dynaformer(USA) —Agarita (USA) (Danzig (USA))
1240[7] 2895[3] 3122[5] 3346[3] 6287[8]

Gravinsky (USA) *Mrs A J Perrett* a71 72
3 bb c Theatrical—Prospectress (USA) (Mining (USA))
4776[3] 5151[7] 5669[4]6019[5]

Gravitas *A Fabre* 113
3 ch c Mark Of Esteem(IRE) —Bombazine (IRE) (Generous (IRE))
1179a[4] 3517a[6] 5700a[7]

Graze On *Peter Grayson* a95+ 96
4 b g Factual(USA) —Queens Check (Komaite (USA))
(159) (245) (362) (441) 627[10] 1246[7]1475[3] 1858[9] 2624[6] 2946[7] (3069) 3251[12]3535[6] 3972[12] 4360[12]6243[10] 6496[4]6660[8] 6776[5]

Grazeon Gold Blend *J J Quinn* 91
3 ch g Paris House—Thalya (Crofthall)
1604[6] 1857[2] 2168[8] 2639[7] 3296[8](3360) 3761[5] 3986[5] 4682[8] 4922[2]

Graze On Too (IRE) *J J Quinn* 49
3 b f Rainbow Quest(USA) —Whispering (IRE) (Royal Academy (USA))
1598[8] 2129[7] 3244[8]

Grazie Mille *R Brotherton* a29 59
2 b f Bertolini(USA) —Daintree (IRE) (Tirol)
2827[7] 3908[7] 4376[2] 5592[11] 6322[12]

Great As Gold (IRE) *B Ellison* a58 69
7 b g Goldmark(USA) —Great Land (USA) (Friend's Choice (USA))
52[9] (866) 1184[3] 1808[4]5723[6] 6011[3] 6178[7]

Great Belief (IRE) *T D McCarthy* a24 58
4 b g Namid—Fairy Lore (IRE) (Fairy King (USA))
1261[4] 1430[5] 2136[12] 2494[12] 3071[9]3536[11] (4306) 4872[5] 4985[14]5327[13]

Great Britain *Saeed Bin Suroor* 113
4 b h Green Desert(USA) —Park Appeal (Ahonoora)
5682[6] 5942[4] 6335[3]

Great Chieftain (IRE) *R A Fahey* a64 73
3 b g Lend A Hand—Well Wisher (USA) (Sanglamore (USA))
1493[3] 1855[8] 2163[3] 2297[2] 2698[3]3569[9] 3945[5] 4973[4]5388[5] 5691[10]6060[4] 6323[9] 6473[4]

Great Composer (IRE) *M Wellings* a51 47
3 b g Mozart(IRE) —Talena (Zafonic (USA))
1140[10] 1352[7] 2260[3] 4304[8] 4568[8]6707[9] 6794[10]

Great Explorer (IRE) *E J O'Neill* 60
2 b c Indian Danehill(IRE) —Ninth Wonder (USA) (Forty Niner (USA))
2178[6]

Great Fox (IRE) *P L Gilligan* a80 82
5 b h Foxhound(USA) —Good Enough (IRE) (Simply Great (FR))
4180[10] 5148[13]

Great Hawk (USA) *Sir Michael Stoute* a103+ 88+
3 b c El Prado(IRE) —Laser Hawk (USA) (Silver Hawk (USA))
1087[7] (1483) 2046[4] 2659[5] 4147[5] (5110)

Great Hunter (USA) *Doug O'Neill* a117
2 bb c Aptitude(USA) —Zenith (USA) (Roy (USA))
(5823a) 6339a[3]

Great Orator (USA) *H Candy* 82
4 b g Bahri(USA) —Verbal Intrigue (USA) (Dahar (USA))
2615[5] 3151[2] 3737[6] 4661[3]

Great Plains *Mrs A J Perrett* a96 105
4 b h Halling(USA) —West Dakota (USA) (Gone West (USA))
1678[6] 2341[5] (2989) 3552[13]4359[4] 5374[5] 5808[2]

Great Sphinx (USA) *A P O'Brien* 99
2 b c Giant's Causeway(USA) —Chaposa Springs (USA) (Baldski (USA))
6104[12]

Great Tidings *M Johnston* a69 76
3 b g Fantastic Light(USA) —On The Tide (Slip Anchor)
1421[4] 1867[3] 2607[4] 5284[9] 5594[5]6011[9] 6075[7]

Great Tune (FR) *E Libaud* 104
6 ch g Green Tune(USA) —My Great Hope (Simply Great (FR))
6610a[11]

Great Uncle Ted (USA) *B Grizzetti* 100
3 gr c Running Stag(USA) —One Smooth Dancer (USA) (Vigors (USA))
1175a[10] 1871a[3] 6363a[13]

Great View (IRE) *Mrs A L M King* a71 83
7 b g Great Commotion(USA) —Tara View (IRE) (Wassl)
1666[3] (2044) (2455) 3141[4] (3431) 3960[5] 4876[4]5346[13] 5671[3] (6108) 6336[12]6462[10]

Grecianette (IRE) *W J Musson* a57 54
3 b f Night Shift(USA) —Alexandria (IRE) (Irish River (FR))
190[9] 298[3]477[3] 595[7]709[8] 984[4]1352[4] 4289[9] 4847[5]

Grecian Gold (IRE) *J R Boyle* a40 78
4 b g Lujain(USA) —Falconera (IRE) (Tirol)
1355[3] (2291) 3914[10]

Greek Easter (IRE) *B J Meehan* a76 70+
3 bb f Namid—Easter Heroine (IRE) (Exactly Sharp (USA))
1119[4] 2532[3] 2753[2]3373[3]

Greek Envoy *T P Tate* 86
2 br c Diktat—South Shore (Caerleon (USA))
(4732) 5431[5] 5916[7]

Greek God *W Jarvis* 58
2 b g Grand Lodge(USA) —Cephalonia (Slip Anchor)
3253[7] 4074[7] 4474[4] 5482[17] 5597[11]

Greek Renaissance (IRE) *M P Tregoning* a88 111+
3 b c Machiavellian(USA) —Athene (IRE) (Rousillon (USA))
1844[6] (3053) 3403[2] 4888[2](5476) 5627[2]

Greek Secret *J O'Reilly* a61 72
3 b g Josr Algarhoud(IRE) —Mazurkanova (Song)
(1497) 2363[8] 2760[7] 3296[10] 3604[5] 3943[5]4262[2] 4717[10] 5243[9] 5902[2] 6174[10]6664[9] 6865[7]

Greek Well (IRE) *Sir Michael Stoute* 69+
3 b c Sadler's Wells(USA) —Hellenic (Darshaan)
2304[14] 2712[9] 4549[4]

Greeley's Legacy (USA) *G Weaver* a101
3 b c Mr Greeley(USA) —Deceit Princess (CAN) (Vice Regent (CAN))
1861a[5]

Greenacre Legend *D B Feek* 41
4 br g Faustus(USA) —Alice Holt (Free State)
1434[4] 1826[6]

Greenbelt *G M Moore* a77 80
5 b g Desert Prince(IRE) —Emerald (USA) (El Gran Senor (USA))
15[3] 77[3]131[3] (334) 535[2] 610[4]869[3] 976[14] 1987[2] 2162[7] 5137[8]5617[9] 5904[6] 6240[7]6474[6] 6716[8]

Green Coast (IRE) *Saeed Bin Suroor* 81+
3 b c Green Desert(USA) —Oriental Fashion (IRE) (Marju (IRE))
(5244)

Green Day Packer (IRE) *P C Haslam* a63 65
2 br g Daylami(IRE) —Durrah Green (Green Desert (USA))
2409[5] 2844[10] 4295[8] 6569[10]6736[6] 6872[5]

Green Falcon *Miss S E Forster* a68 55
5 b g Green Desert(USA) —El Jazirah (Kris)
2998[13]

Green Ginger *J T Stimpson* a53 56
10 ch g Ardkinglass—Bella Maggio (Rakaposhi King)
1573[8]

Green Girl (FR) *J E Hammond* 101
4 b m Lord Of Men—Green Sails (IRE) (Slip Anchor)
4417a[4] 6454a[7]

Green Manalishi *D W P Arbuthnot* a108 106
5 b g Green Desert(USA) —Silca-Cisa (Hallgate)
705[6] 989[6] (1116) 1602[3]1952[2] 2227[5] 3124a[6] (3535) 4080[9] 4461[4] 5375[5] 5642[8] 5807[10]

Greenmeadow *S Kirk* a67 64
4 b m Sure Blade(USA) —Pea Green (Try My Best (USA))
1802[8] 2113[7] 3036[4] 3440[6] (4289) 4820[3]4982[3] 5166[6] 5974[3]

Green Park (IRE) *R A Fahey* 91
3 b g Shinko Forest(IRE) —Danccini (IRE) (Dancing Dissident (USA))
1292[8] 1604[2] (1857) 2022[3] 2651[6] 3038[13]3414[16] 3761[13] 4601[6] 5535[10] 5807[4]5957[9]

Green Pirate *W M Brisbourne* a64 61
4 b g Bahamian Bounty—Verdura (Green Desert (USA))
274[8] 428[10]1235[4] 1443[2] 1683[5] 2077[2] 2390[6]3052[9] 3817[8] 6235[11]6703[3] 6787[2](6802) 6955[5]6964[2]

Green Room (FR) *J L Dunlop* 109
3 b f In The Wings—Scarlet Plume (Warning)
1114[6] 2350[2] (2901) 3497[3] 3877[7] (4778) (5758)(6251a)

Greenslades *P J Makin* a97 104
7 ch h Perugino(USA) —Woodfield Rose (Scottish Reel)
1487[10] (2047) 2847[22] 4430[3] 6335[7] 6445[10]

Green Treasure (AUS) *D Cruz* 120
5 b g Danehill(USA) —Sitella (IRE) (Shirley Heights)
1180a[8]

Greenwich Meantime *R A Fahey* a77 101+
6 b g Royal Academy(USA) —Shirley Valentine (Shirley Heights)
(1144) (1294) 1584[3] (2850) 3078[3] 4713[13] 5153[5]

Greenwich Village *W J Knight* a67 73
3 b g Mtoto—D'Azy (Persian Bold)
900[3] 1153[4]2434[3] 3156[9]

Greenwood *P G Murphy* a68 79
8 ch g Emarati(USA) —Charnwood Queen (Cadeaux Genereux)
47[9] 137[3]225[10] 292[2]845[8] 949[4] 1188[12](1673) 2302[13] 2606[3] 2864[8] 3543[4] 3928[2]4573[3] 5042[10] 5233[4] 5591[11] 5896[7]6048[6] 6395[4]

Gremlin *A King* 77
2 b g Mujahid(USA) —Fairy Free (Rousillon (USA))
1688[2] 2287[4] 3895[2] 4146[2] 4766[3]

Grenane (IRE) *P D Evans* a64 49
3 b c Princely Heir(IRE) —Another Rainbow (IRE) (Rainbows For Life (CAN))
(68) 190[8] 6428[12]

Grethel (IRE) *A Berry* 50
2 b f Fruits Of Love(USA) —Stay Sharpe (USA) (Sharpen Up)
5507[10] 5790[5] 6012[6] 6318[8]

Grey Admiral (USA) *B R Johnson* a58 64
5 gr g Cozzene(USA) —Remarkable Style (USA) (Danzig (USA))
162[7] 230[7]

Grey Boy (GER) *R A Fahey* a83 93
5 gr g Medaaly—Grey Perri (Siberian Express (USA))
1561[2] 1760[2] (2147) (2364) 2776[12] 3549[2] 6678[9]6868[8]

Grey Cossack *Mrs L Stubbs* a12 62
9 gr g Kasakov—Royal Rebeka (Grey Desire)
1794[4] 2380[4] 3171[7]

Grey Finale *M Brittain*
4 b m Grey Desire—Tanoda (Tyrnavos)
6759[10]

Greyfriars Abbey *M Johnston* a66 49
2 b c Fasliyev(USA) —Mysistra (FR) (Machiavellian (USA))
6188[5] 6316[7]

Grey Mystique (IRE) *J-C Rouget* 105
3 gr f Linamix(FR) —Atnab (USA) (Riverman (USA))
4465a[2] 5700a[5]

Grey Outlook *Miss L A Perratt* 68+
3 ch f Observatory(USA) —Grey Galava (Generous (IRE))
1032[5] 1458[3] 1530[4] 1946[5] 4835[3]5015[5] 5312[4] 5360[4] 5751[3] (5903) 6321[3]

Grey Paint (USA) *R Hannon* a75 70
3 rg g El Prado(IRE) —Devil's Art (USA) (Devil's Bag (USA))
1569[7] 2290[8] 2584[8] 2933[7] 3649[4]3952[4] 4530[5] 4777[6]

Grey Report (IRE) *R H Buckler* a64
9 gr g Roselier(FR) —Busters Lodge (Antwerp City)
114[6] 573[8]

Grey Rover *R Hannon* a59 73
2 b c Zilzal(USA) —Island Story (Shirley Heights)
5106[6] (6023)

Greyside (USA) *J Howard Johnson* 79
3 gr g Tactical Cat(USA) —Amber Gold (USA) (Mr Prospector (USA))
1635[4] 2682[4] 4549[7]

Greys Inn (USA) *M F De Kock* 124
6 br h Zabeel(NZ) —Great Verdict (AUS) (Christmas Tree (AUS))
280a[2] 741a[13]

Grey Swallow (IRE) *D K Weld* 126
5 gr h Daylami(IRE) —Style Of Life (USA) (The Minstrel (CAN))
(1721a) 2476a[3]

Greyt Big Stuff (USA) *Miss Gay Kelleway* a75 77
2 gr c Aljabr(USA) —Dixie Eyes Blazing (USA) (Gone West (USA))
2178[4] 2506[3] 2733[3] 5655[26] (5923) 6536[2]

Greytown *M A Jarvis* a31 67
3 gr f Daylami(IRE) —Hawayah (IRE) (Shareef Dancer (USA))
5844[6] 6206[19]

Grey Vision *M Brittain*
3 gr f Grey Desire—Brief Star (IRE) (Brief Truce (USA))
6490[9]

Grey Winner (FR) *Rod Collet* 95
2 gr f Take Risks(FR) —Valleeski (FR) (Sky Lawyer (FR))
6546a[6]

Grezie *T D McCarthy* a59 58
4 gr m Mark Of Esteem(IRE) —Lozzie (Siberian Express (USA))
336[2] 440[6]520[2] 693[7]903[4] 1348[11] 2135[6]2317[12] 2574[5] 3817[6]4329[5] 6542[5]

Grigorieva (IRE) *A Fabre* 108
3 ch f Woodman(USA) —Elbaaha (Arazi (USA))
3133a[2] 3991a[6] 4542a[5]

Grigorovitch (IRE) *I Semple* a72 94+
4 b h Fasliyev(USA) —Hasty Words (IRE) (Polish Patriot (USA))
1031[7] 1438[6] 1662[3] 2237[9] 2852[7]3038[2] 3585[12] 3880[3] (3938) 4360[9]

Grimes Faith *R Hannon* a89 90
3 b c Woodborough(USA) —Emma Grimes (IRE) (Nordico (USA))
852[2] 1091[3] 3702[3]3795[8] 4430[6] 4593[5] 5107[7]5211[2] 5504[5] 5590[2]5945[17] 6397[7] 6499[2]6583[8] 6690[8]6830[10]

Grimes Glory *R Hannon* a44 54
2 b c Atraf—Emma Grimes (IRE) (Nordico (USA))
2979[12] 3701[14] 4002[6]4334[6] 4926[8] 5084[3] 5323[3] 6016[7]

Gringo *B W Hills* 94+
4 gr g Alzao(USA) —Glen Falls (Commanche Run)
1051[4] 1631[7] 2169[11] (2822) (3248) 3501[2] 3890[6]4676[4]

Gris De Gris (IRE) *J-M Capitte* 87
2 b c Slickly(FR) —Deesse Grise (FR) (Lead On Time (USA))
6453a[4]

Grisham *Michael John Phillips* 88
8 b g Emarati(USA) —Shibui (Shirley Heights)
4094a[6]

Grizedale (IRE) *J Akehurst* 83d
7 ch g Lake Coniston(IRE) —Zabeta (Diesis)
898[16] 1359[8] 1474[6] 1932[6] 2232[4]2860[2] 3223[2] 3928[5] 4399[3] 4706[11]5345[2] 5591[15] 5943[19] 6221[18]

Grooms Affection *K A Morgan* a83 88
6 b g Groom Dancer(USA) —Love And Affection (USA) (Exclusive Era (USA))
572[4] 765[8]

Groom Tesse *L Camici* 116
5 gr h Groom Dancer(USA) —Vicomtesse Mag (FR) (Highest Honor (FR))
1712a[3] (1870a) 2693a[2] 4861a[2] 5718a[2] 6004a[7]

Ground Patrol *G L Moore* a64 63
5 b g Ashkalani(IRE) —Good Grounds (USA) (Alleged (USA))
115[9] 263[5](379) 461[8]2481[2] 2862[7]

Ground Rules (USA) *V Smith* a81 70
4 b g Boundary(USA) —Gombeen (USA) (Private Account (USA))
267[11] 404[2]567[10] 641[5]777[11] 826[16]

Group Captain *R Charlton* a104 110
4 b g Dr Fong(USA) —Alusha (Soviet Star (USA))
1779[7] 2079[10] (3980) 4711[3] 5548[2] (6336) 6516[7]

Group Force (IRE) *M H Tompkins* a34 56
2 b f Montjeu(IRE) —Allspice (Alzao (USA))
3227[6] 4394[7] 4665[3]5084[16] (5323) 5492[6] 6322[10]

Grove Cherry (IRE) *M H Tompkins* a32 49
3 b f City On A Hill(USA) —Kaliningrad (IRE) (Red Sunset)
69[8] 197[14]

Growl (NZ) *D Hayes* 116
4 b g Montjeu(IRE) —The Lions Roar (NZ) (Western Symphony (USA))
6110a[13] 6347a[2] 6785a[11]

Grub Street *J Parkes* a34 28
10 b g Barathea(IRE) —Broadmara (IRE) (Thatching)
302[9] 688[10]2206[8]

Guacamole *B W Hills* a79 83
2 ch f Inchinor—Popocatepetl (FR) (Nashwan (USA))
2867[5] 3201[4] (3640) 5013[2]5459[4] 6216[6]

Guadalajara (GER) *Saeed Bin Suroor* 114
5 ch m Acatenango(GER) —Guernica (Unfuwain (USA))
2773[6] (3905) 4595[2] 5155[6]

Guadaloup *M Brittain* a60 58
4 ch m Loup Sauvage(USA) —Rash (Pursuit Of Love)
2418[4] 4070[7] 4571[2]5062[10] 6389[6] (6470) 6541[3] 6642[11]6719[12]

Guadiana (GER) *A W Carroll* a47 49
4 b m Dashing Blade—Gamberaia (IRE) (Konigsstuhl (GER))
43[9] 175[13]1460[7] 1767[5]2070[5] 2636[10] 3162[2] 3592[4] 3944[2]4282[3] (4755) 5072[10] (6133)

Guanyin *Ms J S Doyle* a13 24
3 b f Zaha(CAN) —Misty Moon (Polar Falcon (USA))
6277[10] 6657[9]

Guarantia *C E Brittain* a63 90
2 ch f Selkirk(USA) —Maskunah (IRE) (Sadler's Wells (USA))
5425[3] 5672[3]

Guest Connections *M R Channon* a91 91
3 b g Zafonic(USA) —Llyn Gwynant (Persian Bold)
1490[9] 1776[4] 2205[10] 2649[13] 2774[11]3317[5] 3740[6] 4029[10] 4391[3] (4841) 5212[3]5501[13] 5785[12] 6094[13]

Guideline *M W Easterby* a5 64
3 b g Diktat—Polisonne (Polish Precedent (USA))
199[8] 1044[9] (Dead)

Guilded Warrior *W S Kittow* a71 71
3 b g Mujahid(USA) —Pearly River (Elegant Air)
969[3] 1411[3] 1801[4]2496[4] 3349[12] 4368[4]5036[6]

Guildenstern (IRE) *H Morrison* a82 91
4 b g Danetime(IRE) —Lyphard Abu (IRE) (Lyphard's Special (USA))
970[9] 1359[5] 1760[3] 2170[5] (2536) 3217[8](4106) 4573[6] 5420[8]

Guilia *Rae Guest* a101 106
3 ch f Galileo(IRE) —Lesgor (USA) (Irish River (FR))
1819[2] 2203[5] 3293[6] 5502[12] 6191[5]

Guilty Pleasure *G C Bravery* a17 47
2 ch f Inchinor—Idolize (Polish Precedent (USA))
5596[8] 6073[11]

Guiseppe Verdi (USA) *J H M Gosden* a78 69
2 ch c Sky Classic(CAN) —Lovington (USA) (Afleet (CAN))
5658[10] 5890[10] (6143)

Gulf (IRE) *D R C Elsworth* 113
7 ch g Persian Bold—Broken Romance (IRE) (Ela-Mana-Mou)
1128[10] 1507[6]

Gulf Express (USA) *Sir Michael Stoute* 65+
2 b c Langfuhr(CAN) —Wassifa (Sure Blade (USA))
2144[6]

Gulf Of Gold (USA) *Saeed Bin Suroor* 71
3 bb g Seeking The Gold(USA) —Borodislew (USA) (Seattle Slew (USA))
1476[4]

Gulf To Bay (IRE) *Edward Lynam* 51
3 b g Bluebird(USA) —Prosaic Star (IRE) (Common Grounds)
4034a[8] (Dead)

Gull Wing (IRE) *M L W Bell* a76 82
2 ch f In The Wings—Maycocks Bay (Muhtarram (USA))
5083[6] 5595[2] (6242)

Gundula (IRE) *D J S Ffrench Davis* a20 36
3 b f Singspiel(IRE) —Playgirl (IRE) (Caerleon (USA))
4899[10] 5566[8] 6588[8]6795[11]

Gunner's View *B J Meehan* a66+ 54
2 ch c Medicean—Stark Ballet (USA) (Nureyev (USA))
5608[3] 5914[11]

Gus *B W Hills* a66 55
3 b g Dr Fong(USA) —Tender Moment (IRE) (Caerleon (USA))
337[4] 460[2]668[6]

Guto *K A Ryan* a63 99
3 b g Foxhound(USA) —Mujadilly (Mujadil (USA))
(1146) 1604[7] 2022[2] 2651[8] 3970[9] 4717[6]

Gutter Press (IRE) *J S Moore* a29 51
2 b f Raise A Grand(IRE) —Grandel (Owington)
4394[8] 5449[5]

Gweebarra *K A Ryan* 99
2 b c Lomitas—Complimentary Pass (Danehill (USA))
2361[3] 2844[5] 3498[3] (4171) 4680[2] 5176[4]5521[7]

Gwenseb (FR) *C Laffon-Parias* 109
3 ch f Green Tune(USA) —La Popesse (USA) (St Jovite (USA))
(4542a) 5146a[2] 5701a[6] 6250a[2]

Gwilym (GER) *D Haydn Jones* a73 76
3 b c Agnes World(USA) —Glady Rose (GER) (Surumu (GER))
1208[10] 1679[9] 2222[5] 2410[7] 2652[5]3118[4] 3593[4] (3873) 4164[2] 4532[5] 4756[4]5427[3] 6036[5]6485[5] 6585[3]6773[9] 6913[3]

Gwyllion (USA) *J H M Gosden* a71+
2 bb f Red Ransom(USA) —Lady Angharad (IRE) (Tenby)
5773[7] 6098[4]

Gymbolini *N P Littmoden* a43 50
3 b f Bertolini(USA) —Gymcrak Flyer (Aragon)
31[11]

Gypsy Johnny *A Laird* a97 74
4 gr g Bachir(IRE) —Gentle Gypsy (Junius (USA))
152a[12] 353a[16]

Gypsy Royal (IRE) *G Woodward* a30 42
4 b m Desert Prince(IRE) —Menominee (Soviet Star (USA))
2195[14] 2418[12] 3909[8]4425[3] 4909[4] 5240[9] 6279[11]6535[10]

Gypsy's Kiss *B P J Baugh* a49 37
3 b g Cyrano De Bergerac—Reina (Homeboy)
2465[8] 3725[11]

Gyration (IRE) *J G Given*
2 ch c Spinning World(USA) —Tomori (USA) (Royal Academy (USA))
5901[12]

Gyroscope *Sir Michael Stoute* a69
2 b f Spinning World(USA) —Far Across (Common Grounds)
6254[3]

Haatef (USA) *Kevin Prendergast* 116+
2 b c Danzig(USA) —Sayedat Alhadh (USA) (Mr Prospector (USA))
5965[4]

Haatmey *B G Powell* a76 79
4 b g Josr Algarhoud(IRE) —Raneen Alwatar (Sadler's Wells (USA))
800[4] 983[7] 1144[13]1502[4] (2078) 2501[6] (2869) 3220[8] 3607[3] 3743[4]4268[7] 5338[5] 5628[6] 6831[3]6979[6]

Habalwatan (IRE) *C E Brittain* a84+ 69
2 b c In The Wings—Mureefa (USA) (Bahri (USA))
3445[7] 4037[10] 5297[4] 5608[9](6322) (6443) 6599[4](6880)

Habanero *Miss S J Wilton* a71 47
5 b g Cadeaux Genereux—Queen Of Dance (IRE) (Sadler's Wells (USA))
325[7] 404[8]1281[13] 6313[13]

Habanus Livius (IRE) *Joseph Quinn* 50
3 ch g Titus Livius(FR) —Wheatsheaf Lady (IRE) (Red Sunset)
5273[10]

Habitual (IRE) *John A Quinn* a50 71
5 b g Kahyasi—Kick The Habit (Habitat)
5652[5] 6375[9]6398[12]

Habitual Dancer *Jedd O'Keeffe* 68
5 b g Groom Dancer(USA) —Pomorie (IRE) (Be My Guest (USA))
1184[7]

Habshan (USA) *C F Wall* a83 92
6 ch g Swain(IRE) —Cambara (Dancing Brave (USA))
221[10] (559) 2183[2] 2614[5](3113) (3854) 4209[2] 4782[6] 5301[9] 5639[9]

Hadahoo (USA) *M A Jarvis* 81
2 b c War Chant(USA) —Carly's Crown (USA) (Wild Again (USA))
3976[4] 4388[2] (5025) 5585[7]

Hadath (IRE) *B G Powell* a55 59
9 br g Mujtahid(USA) —Al Sylah (Nureyev (USA))
44[9] 262[3]321[3] 474[2]485[4] 575[6]693[10] 708[4]837[6] 903[7]982[4] 1310[2] 1568[13]1752[2] 1923[4] 2135[8]3339[4] 3614[4] 3933[8] 4077[5] (4276) 4674[2]5450[4] 5573[5] 6436[6]

Haenertsburg (IRE) *A L Forbes* a50 59
4 b m Victory Note(USA) —Olivia's Pride (IRE) (Digamist (USA))
56[9] 103[7]243[10]

Hahns Peak *Mrs A L M King* a40 22
3 b g Mujahid(USA) —Fille Genereux (Cadeaux Genereux)
844[7] 2576[8]2644[11] 5733[10] 6236[13]

Haiban *J J Lambe* a41 58
4 b h Barathea(IRE) —Aquarela (Shirley Heights)
6604[3]

Haifa (IRE) *Mrs A Duffield* a70 70
3 ch f Spectrum(IRE) —Mrs Fisher (IRE) (Salmon Leap (USA))
6654[12] 6818[7]6929[5] 6947[3]

Hail The Chief *R Hannon* a102 93
9 b h Be My Chief(USA) —Jade Pet (Petong)
116[4] 213[5](777) (898) (992) (1111) 1301[2] 1676[8]

Hair Of The Dog *J G Given* a40 49
2 b c Foxhound(USA) —Bebe De Cham (Tragic Role (USA))
2139[10] 2523[11] 2695[6]4724[3] 5239[2] 5482[8] 5720[10] 6007[15]6172[5] 6385[6]

Haiti Dancer *C G Cox* a52 61
3 b f Josr Algarhoud(IRE) —Haitienne (FR) (Green Dancer (USA))
879[6] 1141[7] 1652[7] 2814[3] 3400[7]4176[4] 4869[15]

Halabaloo (IRE) *F Reuterskiold* a61 78
5 b m Intikhab(USA) —Outcry (Caerleon (USA))
5160a[7]

Hala Bek (IRE) *M A Jarvis* 121+
3 b c Halling(USA) —Place De L'Opera (Sadler's Wells (USA))
(1120) 2228[4]

Halcyon Magic *M Wigham* a46 57
8 b g Magic Ring(IRE) —Consistent Queen (Queens Hussar)
395[9] 636[7]684[5] 794[10]1995[12] 2132[P] 3044[12] 3469[7] 3712[10]4575[11] 5839[10]

Half Sadlers (SWE) *K P Andersen* a46
3 b g Final Appearance(IRE) —Half And Half (DEN) (Muthhil (IRE))
4420a[10]

Halfsong (SWE) *K P Andersen* a74 98
6 br m Songline(SWE) —Half And Half (DEN) (Muthhil (IRE))
(4189a)

Halfwaytoparadise *W G M Turner* a58 66
3 b f Observatory(USA) —Always On My Mind (Distant Relative)
551[6] 868[5] 1431[9]2210[8] 2574[6]4143[2] 4494[10] 5269[10] 5937[2] 6442[8]6510[8] 6763[9]6855[12]

Halicarnassus (IRE) *M R Channon* 109
2 b c Cape Cross(IRE) —Launch Time (USA) (Relaunch (USA))
(2867) (3492) 5965[14]

Halkerston *C G Cox* 57
2 ch g Medicean—Summer Daze (USA) (Swain (IRE))
5891[8]

Halland *T J Fitzgerald* a71 67
8 ch g Halling(USA) —Northshiel (Northfields (USA))
1247[6] 1808[13] 2357[11]2812[5] 3454[5] 5815[3]6011[10]

Halla San *R A Fahey* 88
4 b g Halling(USA) —St Radegund (Green Desert (USA))
1288[5] (4022) 4544[4] (5479) 5792[10]

Hallhoo (IRE) *D Selvaratnam* a60 94
4 gr h Indian Ridge—Nuit Chaud (USA) (Woodman (USA))
509a[6]

Hallings Overture (USA) *C A Horgan* a61 61
7 b g Halling(USA) —Sonata (Polish Precedent (USA))
383[7] 950[12]1400[14] 1773[9] 1882[6]2401[9] (4139) 5267[7] 6436[11](6693)

Hall Of Fame *Saeed Bin Suroor* a65 64
2 b g Machiavellian(USA) —Petrushka (IRE) (Unfuwain (USA))
6049[6] 6298[4] 6561[4]

Hallucinate *R A Fahey* a12 78
4 b g Spectrum(IRE) —Swift Spring (FR) (Bluebird (USA))
318[12]

Hamaasy *D Nicholls* a72+ 53
5 b g Machiavellian(USA) —Sakha (Wolfhound (USA))
864[10] 2077[5] 2288[8] 2544[2] 2949[15]3617[13] 4157[3] 4233[3] 4511[12] (5928)

Hamilton House *M H Tompkins* 33
2 b g Bahamian Bounty—Grove Dancer (Reprimand)
5659[13]

Hammer Of The Gods (IRE) *P S McEntee* a85 65
6 ch g Tagula(IRE) —Bhama (FR) (Habitat)
320[2] 532[4]657[2] 1645[4] 2136[3](3012) 3368[3] 3728[7] 5212[5]5777[5] 6352[10]6446[2] 6583[10]

Hammers Boy (IRE) *T Stack* 99
2 b c Mujadil(USA) —Majesty's Nurse (Indian King (USA))
2719[19] 3962a[5]

Hamoody (USA) *P W Chapple-Hyam* 104
2 ch c Johannesburg(USA) —Northern Gulch (USA) (Gulch (USA))
(3445) (4099) 5965[13]

Hams (USA) *M Johnston* 62
3 bb f Dixie Union(USA) —Desert Victress (USA) (Desert Wine (USA))
1032[2] 1230[2] 1564[6]

Hanazakari *J A R Toller* a45 39
5 b g Danzero(AUS) —Russian Rose (IRE) (Soviet Lad (USA))
460[13] 688[5]

Hanbrin Bhoy (IRE) *R Dickin* a70 70
2 b c Cape Cross(IRE) —Sea Of Stone (USA) (Sanglamore (USA))
5431[4] 6013[3] (6290)

Hand Chime *Ernst Oertel* a66 56
9 ch g Clantime—Warning Bell (Bustino)
74[3] 157[9]192[6] 268[7]514[2] 575[3]639[6] 698[4]845[5] 985[8]2317[11]

Hand Of Destiny (USA) *N P Littmoden* a55
3 ch g High Yield(USA) —Special Happening (USA) (Relaunch (USA))
406[2] 2210[12]3030[12] 3263[13]

Hands Clean (IRE) *A Candi* 100
3 br f Key Of Luck(USA) —Pre Catelan (Polar Falcon (USA))
1713a[4] 2671a[8] 6124a[7] 6362a[4]

Handset (USA) *H R A Cecil* 57
2 ch f Distant View(USA) —Call Account (USA) (Private Account (USA))
5595[6]

Handsome Cross (IRE) *D Nicholls* a78 92
5 b g Cape Cross(IRE) —Snap Crackle Pop (IRE) (Statoblest)
657[8] 761[11]1125[16] 1496[2] 1662[4] (2450) 2521[2] 3069[4]3447[2] 3585[6] 3972[9] 4101[6] 4468[5]4793[4] 5169[2] 5333[15] 5532[3]

Handsome Falcon *R A Fahey* 77+
2 b g Kyllachy—Bonne Etoile (Diesis)
(5442)

Haneen (USA) *J L Dunlop* 70
3 b f Bahri(USA) —Tamgeed (USA) (Woodman (USA))
963[6] 2608[4]

Hanella (IRE) *R M Beckett* 79
3 b f Galileo(IRE) —Strutting (IRE) (Ela-Mana-Mou)
1845[8] 2406[6] 2919[2] (3865) (4181) 4778[6]

Hanging On *W R Swinburn* a88 86
2 b f Spinning World(USA) —Lydia Maria (Dancing Brave (USA))
(4103) 4840[8] 6074[3]

Hang Loose *S W Hall* a61 47
3 b g Agnes World(USA) —My Cadeaux (Cadeaux Genereux)
901[4] 1430[6] 1801[14]5902[12] 6293[6] 6480[6]

Hannicean *M A Jarvis* 77+
2 ch c Medicean—Hannah's Music (Music Boy)
6214[5]

Hanoona (IRE) *M R Channon* 96
3 ch f Zafonic(USA) —Wedoudah (IRE) (Sadler's Wells (USA))
1237[2] 1819[7]

Hansomelle (IRE) *B Mactaggart* 61
4 b m Titus Livius(FR) —Handsome Anna (IRE) (Bigstone (IRE))
1636[4] 2164[8] 2378[8] 2747[2] 3484[7]4455[4] 4698[11] 5285[7] 5510[12] 5579[6]5636[2] 6211[5]

Hansomis (IRE) *B Mactaggart* 67
2 b f Titus Livius(FR) —Handsome Anna (IRE) (Bigstone (IRE))
3780[6] 5507[5] 5898[4] 6208[2]

Haoin An Bothar (IRE) *Adrian Sexton* a60 16
2 b c Bishop Of Cashel—Drefflane Ann (IRE) (Petorius)
6402[6] 6768[4]

Ha'Penny Beacon *D Carroll* a61 66+
3 ch f Erhaab(USA) —Beacon (High Top)
1866[3] 3258[2] 5741[4]6178[9]

Happening (SWE) *T Gustafsson*
3 b f Duty Time—Tremendous Girl (Rudimentary (USA))
4919a[9]

Happy As Larry (USA) *T J Pitt* a93+ 70
4 bb g Yes It's True(USA) —Don't Be Blue (USA) (Henbane (USA))
340[10] 476[13]541[12] 2547[8] 3459[6]3880[7] 3986[11] 4368[10]6227[9] (6451) (6734) 6791[2]6848[2] (6986)

Happy Diamond (USA) *A Al Raihe* a79 71
9 b h Diesis—Urus (USA) (Kris S (USA))
207a[13]

Happy Go Lily *W R Swinburn* a74+
2 b f In The Wings—Lil's Jessy (IRE) (Kris)
(6349)

Happy Harry (IRE) *B Storey*
3 b g Raphane(USA) —Zalotti (IRE) (Polish Patriot (USA))
2546[13] 3288[15]

Happy Love *M Johnston*
2 b f Royal Applause—Ivory's Joy (Tina's Pet)
1082[9]

Happy Pearl (AUS) *G Moore* a105
6 b g Sri Pekan(USA) —Mosseke (AUS) (Twig Moss (FR))
(204a) 353a[2] 495a[3]560a[7]

Happy Ticket (USA) *A Leggio Jr* a120
5 b m Anet(USA) —Love And Happiness (USA) (Septieme Ciel (USA))
6343a[2]

Harar (GER) *Andreas Lowe* 102
4 ch h Acatenango(GER) —Hosea (GER) (Lagunas)
1369a[8] 1860a[9] 6529a[5]

Harare *R J Price* a63 57+
5 b g Bahhare(USA) —Springs Eternal (Salse (USA))
43[3] 1915[7]2221[5] 2707[3] 2966[4] 3196[3] 3894[9](4439) 4974[7]5474[2] 6683[5] (6793)

Harb (IRE) *Doug Watson* a63 100
6 b h Green Desert(USA) —Ajayib (USA) (Riverman (USA))
149a[12] 433a[8]

Harbour House *J J Bridger* a42 46
7 b g Distant Relative—Double Flutter (Beldale Flutter (USA))
262[8] 321[10]

Harcourt (USA) *M Madgwick* a55 66
6 b g Cozzene(USA) —Ballinamallard (USA) (Tom Rolfe)
33[13] 1478[15] 1772[7]2305[9] 5621[10] 5897[10]

Hard As Iron *M Blanshard* a63
2 b c Iron Mask(USA) —Runs In The Family (Distant Relative)
4525[13] 6188[7] 6441[6]

Hard Gossip (IRE) *T G McCourt* 33
2 br g Desert Style(IRE) —Frisky (IRE) (Hamas (IRE))
5662a[14]

Hard Rock City (USA) *M J Grassick* 108
6 b g Danzig(USA) —All The Moves (USA) (A.P. Indy (USA))
1171a[2]

Hard To Catch (IRE) *D K Ivory* a73 76
8 b g Namaqualand(USA) —Brook's Dilemma (Known Fact (USA))
17[3] 225[8]292[12] 1383[8]1402[5] 2207[6]2331[12]

Hard To Explain (IRE) *L M Cumani* a99 90
3 b c Marju(IRE) —Kesh Kumay (IRE) (Danehill (USA))
213[2] 2046[7] 2805[13]

Hard Top (IRE) *Sir Michael Stoute* 120
4 b g Darshaan—Well Head (IRE) (Sadler's Wells (USA))
1507[7] 2277a[5] 2845[5] 3085[4]

Hardy Norseman (IRE) *W Jarvis* a65 69
3 b g Mull Of Kintyre(USA) —Miss Willow Bend (USA) (Willow Hour (USA))
66[5] 68[6]298[2]

Harland *M A Jarvis* 76
2 b c Halling(USA) —White Star (IRE) (Darshaan)
5883[5]

Harlestone Linn *J L Dunlop* 56
4 ch g Erhaab(USA) —Harlestone Lake (Riboboy (USA))
966[9] 1415[16] 2483[6] 3437[7]

Haroldini (IRE) *J Balding* a65 55
4 b g Orpen(USA) —Ciubanga (IRE) (Arazi (USA))
1196[7] 1447[8] (1763) 1913[4]2793[11] 3617[9] 6549[2](6703) 6763[2]6798[2] (6964)

Harriets Dream *Peter Grayson* 45
2 b f Foxhound(USA) —Rythm N Time (Timeless Times (USA))
1587[10] 2517[P] (Dead)

Harrington (IRE) *Noel Furlong* 92
4 b h Sadler's Wells(USA) —Our Hope (Dancing Brave (USA))
4822a[7]

Harrington Bates *R M Whitaker* a34 52
5 ch g Wolfhound(USA) —Fiddling (Music Boy)
1102[8] 1794[6] 2112[9] 3053[6]3749[9] 4120[7] 4611[4] 4948[3] 5631[6]5865[8] 5928[6] 6274[8]

Harrison's Flyer (IRE) *J M Bradley* a69 75
5 b g Imperial Ballet(IRE) —Smart Pet (Petong)
2173[10] 2449[10] 2618[9] 2962[3] 3297[3]3899[6] 4208[5] 4462[3] 4780[2] 4846[3]5391[11] 5480[3] (5575) 5791[14]5938[3] 6452[8] 6555[8]6585[4] 6622[6]6709[6] 6990[9]

Harrys House *J J Quinn* a59 68
4 gr g Paris House—Rum Lass (Distant Relative)
5078[U] 5620[2] 5684[6] 5865[5] 6162[10]

Harry The Hawk *T D Walford* 63
2 b g Pursuit Of Love—Elora Gorge (IRE) (High Estate)
2409[10] 5289[5] 5814[12]

Harry Tricker *Mrs A J Perrett* 67+
2 b g Hernando(FR) —Katy Nowaitee (Komaite (USA))
6220[8]

Harry Up *K A Ryan* a90 90
5 ch g Piccolo—Faraway Lass (Distant Relative)
79[7] 362[7]1438[2] 2302[8] 2521[6] (3097) 3281[5] 3585[2] 4101[5] 5333[18] 5749[10]6352[7] 6499[8](6776)

Hart Of Gold *M J Wallace* a79 86
2 b g Foxhound(USA) —Bullion (Sabrehill (USA))
912[3] 987[4] 1559[7](2416) 2924[2] 3455[3]3800[5] 4264[2] 4766[8] (5113) 5172[2] 5366[5]

Hartshead *G A Swinbank* a84 103
7 b g Machiavellian(USA) —Zalitzine (USA) (Zilzal (USA))
1495[6] 2017[2] 2364[5] 2657[9] 3020[3](3191) (3937) 4348[5] 5224a[3]

Harvest Joy (IRE) *B R Millman* 90
2 b f Daggers Drawn(USA) —Windomen (IRE) (Forest Wind (USA))
1514[5] 1930[4] 2456[2] (3307) 3874[3] 4840[7]

Harvest Queen (IRE) *P J Makin* a63 99
3 ch f Spinning World(USA) —Royal Bounty (IRE) (Generous (IRE))
(1417) (2359) 2744[5] 3418[8] 5945[4] 6219[5]

Harvest Warrior *T D Easterby* 90
4 gr g Mujahid(USA) —Lammastide (Martinmas)
726[3] 867[4] 1043[4] 1532[9] 1985[8]2627[12] 3500[12] 4253[6] 4602[8] 4706[6]5136[10]

Hasayaz (IRE) *Sir Michael Stoute* a96+ 76+
3 b c Barathea(IRE) —Hasainiya (IRE) (Top Ville)
1070[8] 1421[3] (1940) 6097[2]

Hashbrown (GER) *C Sprengel* 89
2 b f Big Shuffle(USA) —Haraplata (GER) (Platini (GER))
6122a[3]

Hassaad *W J Haggas* a93+ 78
3 b g Danehill(USA) —Ghazal (USA) (Gone West (USA))
1844[11] 2146[5] 3362[4] 4254[4] (5568) 6413[2](6564)

Hatch A Plan (IRE) *Mrs A J Hamilton-Fairley* a71 74+
5 b g Vettori(IRE) —Fast Chick (Henbit (USA))
641[6] 1435[7] 1754[6]2455[4] 2966[U] 3221[2] 3429[8] 3704[2]4005[4] (4432) 4662[4]

Hathaal (IRE) *E J Creighton* a56 79
7 b g Alzao(USA) —Ballet Shoes (IRE) (Ela-Mana-Mou)
6893[6]

Hatherden *Miss E C Lavelle* 56
2 b c Tobougg(IRE) —Million Heiress (Auction Ring (USA))
4781[11] 5178[11]

Hathlen (IRE) *Mrs N Smith* a39 51
5 b g Singspiel(IRE) —Kameez (IRE) (Arazi (USA))
6037[13] 6398[P]

Hattan (IRE) *C E Brittain* 113
4 ch h Halling(USA) —Luana (Shaadi (USA))
622a[8] 1489[4] 2116[3] 2693a[4] 3314[8]3957[2] 4358[3] 4817[6] 5342[6] 6365a[2]

Hatton Flight *A M Balding* a54 58
2 b c Kahyasi—Platonic (Zafonic (USA))
5178[10] 6143[6] 6449[4]

Hat Trick (JPN) *Katsuhiko Sumii* 123
5 b h Sunday Silence(USA) —Tricky Code (USA) (Lost Code (USA))
742a[12] 6530a[8]

Haughton Hope *T J Pitt* a35 38
3 b g Daawe(USA) —Kandymal (IRE) (Prince Of Birds (USA))
1049[10] 3826[8] 5761[11] 6236[11]6373[11]

Haulage Man *Karen McLintock* 53
8 ch g Komaite(USA) —Texita (Young Generation)
818[8] 1341[5] 2376[4] 2544[9] 2700[3]3330[4]

Haut La Vie *R F Johnson Houghton* 50
2 b g Josr Algarhoud(IRE) —Spark Of Life (Rainbows For Life (CAN))
5565[6] 5893[10] 6172[12]

Having A Ball *P D Cundell* a60 40
2 b g Mark Of Esteem(IRE) —All Smiles (Halling (USA))
2552[10] 2938[5]3385[5] 5113[9]

Hawaii Prince *D Nicholls* 70
2 b g Primo Valentino(IRE) —Bollin Rita (Rambo Dancer (CAN))
1491[7] 1884[5] 3080[3] 3555[8] 4088[9]

Hawk Arrow (IRE) *Miss Sheena West* 72
4 ch g In The Wings—Barbizou (FR) (Selkirk (USA))
1478[12] 5952[10]

Hawk Gold (IRE) *M P Sunderland*
2 ch g Tendulkar(USA) —Heiress Of Meath (IRE) (Imperial Frontier (USA))
5662a[17]

Hawkit (USA) *P Monteith* a72 74
5 b g Silver Hawk(USA) —Hey Ghaz (USA) (Ghazi (USA))
78[2] (243) 414[3]535[4] 1075[6] 1281[11]1389[3] 1531[2] 2025[5]2162[5] 2519[6] (2853) 3068[2] 3331[6] 4175[4]4476[4] 4696[8] (5311) 5863[10] 6008[11] 6209[3]

Hawksmoor (IRE) *L A Dace* a1 60
4 b h In The Wings—Moon Cactus (Kris)
6804[10]

Hawkwind (USA) *Patrick O Brady* 89
7 gr h El Prado(IRE) —Pleasantly Quick (USA) (Roanoke (USA))
4166a[8]

Hawridge King *W S Kittow* a62 75
4 b g Erhaab(USA) —Sadaka (USA) (Kingmambo (USA))
2186[3] 2918[3] 3209[2] 4393[3] 4900[2]5506[9]

Hawridge Prince *B R Millman* 112+
6 b g Polar Falcon(USA) —Zahwa (Cadeaux Genereux)
1071[9] 3890[10] 4817[5] (5351) (5551) (5967)

Hawridge Sensation *W S Kittow* a47 61
4 ch g Polish Precedent(USA) —Looks Sensational (USA) (Majestic Light (USA))
2223[12] 2708[13] 2969[7] 3570[10] 3933[13]4285[4] 5054[RR] 5248[6]

Hawridge Star (IRE) *W S Kittow* a42 82
4 b g Alzao(USA) —Serenity (Selkirk (USA))
1051[5] 1943[12] 2097[4]3365[10] 5057[3] 5383[5]

Hayden Grace *M Johnston* 66
3 ch f In The Wings—Original Spin (IRE) (Machiavellian (USA))
3001[3] 3373[4]

Haydock Express (IRE) *Peter Grayson* a52
2 gr g Keltos(FR) —Blusienka (IRE) (Blues Traveller (IRE))
6940[6]

Hayley's Flower (IRE) *J C Fox* a55 48
2 b f Night Shift(USA) —Plastiqueuse (USA) (Quest For Fame)
5894[9] 6290[12] 6504[9]

Hayyani (IRE) *K McAuliffe* a84 82
4 ch g Almutawakel—Just Rainbow (FR) (Rainbow Quest (USA))
89[9] (220) 253[10]476[4] 670[9]843[9] 2705[5] 3048[10]3704[8] 4001[7] 5045[7]5346[17] 5778[4]

Hazelhurst (IRE) *J Howard Johnson* 75
3 b f Night Shift(USA) —Iktidar (Green Desert (USA))
(2400) 2977[8] 4567[9]

Hazelnut *J R Fanshawe* a63+ 68
3 b f Selkirk(USA) —Cashew (Sharrood (USA))
2934[7] 3367[13] 4245[3](5946)

Hazeymm (IRE) *M R Channon* 109
3 b c Marju(IRE) —Shimna (Mr Prospector (USA))
(1117) 1668[2] 2278a[8] 2775[3] 4024[4]

Hazium (IRE) *Patrick Morris* a52 58
3 b f In The Wings—Safe Care (IRE) (Caerleon (USA))
16[5] 337[7]374[9] 1925[10]

Hazzard County (USA) *D M Simcock* 76
2 ch c Grand Slam(USA) —Sweet Lexy May (USA) (Danzig (USA))
4333[3] 5066[3] 5449[2] 6055[3]

Headache (FR) *Robert Collet* 108
3 b c Muhtathir—Psycadelic (FR) (Midyan (USA))
1717a[7]

Headford View (IRE) *James Halpin* 31
2 b f Bold Fact(USA) —Headfort Rose (IRE) (Desert Style (IRE))
5692a[9]

Headland (USA) *D W Chapman* a23 9
8 bb g Distant View(USA) —Fijar Echo (USA) (In Fijar (USA))
3[9] 177[12]196[11] 680[4]768[3] 876[14]1465[10] 4425[14] 4467[16]6638[9]

Heads Turn (IRE) *E J Alston* 41
3 ch f Grand Lodge(USA) —Belle Origine (USA) (Exclusive Native (USA))
2284[8] 3582[5] 4199[10] 4697[8] 5583[8]

Head To Head (IRE) *Peter Grayson* a43
2 gr g Mull Of Kintyre(USA) —Shoka (FR) (Kaldoun (FR))
2416[9] 2938[8]6925[7] 6975[3]

Headturner (AUS) *J Hawkes* 117
4 b g Anabaa(USA) —Monroe Magic (NZ) (Zabeel (NZ))
6110a[14] 6347a[7] 6392a[13]

Health Spa *B R Johnson* a48 40
3 b f King's Theatre(IRE) —Thermal Spring (Zafonic (USA))
419[8] 971[10]

Healthy Addiction (USA) *J W Sadler* a117
5 b m Boston Harbor(USA) —Lady Laika (USA) (Gone West (USA))
6343a[12]

Heart Alone (BRZ) *I Mohammed* a117
5 b h Music Prospector(USA) —Sylicon Purple (BRZ) (Purple Mountain (USA))
(206a) 740a[11]

Heart And Hand (IRE) *M G Quinlan*
2 b f Bertolini(USA) —Alchi (USA) (Alleged (USA))
2145[9] 2294[5] 2588[9] 6900[10]

Heartbeat *I A Wood* a39 39
5 b m Pursuit Of Love—Lyrical Bid (USA) (Lyphard (USA))
113[10]

Heartcrusher (IRE) *G A Swinbank* a56 66
4 ch m Alhaarth(IRE) —Windini (Windjammer (USA))
106[9] 2020[15] 2808[4]3947[11]

Hearthstead Dancer (USA) *M Johnston* 76
3 b f Royal Academy(USA) —Amity (USA) (Afleet (CAN))
1122[12] 1282[4]

Hearthstead Maison (IRE) *M Johnston* 81
2 b c Peintre Celebre(USA) —Pieds De Plume (FR) (Seattle Slew (USA))
(5126) 5805[5]

Hearthstead Wings *M Johnston* 107
4 b g In The Wings—Inishdalla (IRE) (Green Desert (USA))
(1298) 1409[3] 3551[7] 4713[15] 5548[10] 5804[5]6336[16]

Heart Of Cornwall (IRE) *Saeed Bin Suroor* 48
2 ch c Singspiel(IRE) —Kerenza (Seattle Dancer (USA))
6298[7]

Heart Of Glass (IRE) *M L W Bell* 19
2 ch f Peintre Celebre(USA) —Sallanches (USA) (Gone West (USA))
6298[9]

Heart Of Svetlana (IRE) *M Johnston* 90
3 bb f Linamix(FR) —Julius (IRE) (Persian Bold)
(5634) 6202[14] 6319[3]

Heart's Cry (JPN) *K Hashiguchi* 125
5 b h Sunday Silence(USA) —Irish Dance (JPN) (Tony Bin)
(741a) 3927[3] 6612a[10]

Heart Springs *Dr J R J Naylor* a55 66
6 b m Parthian Springs—Metannee (The Brianstan)
3935[7] 4898[7]

Heathcote *G L Moore* 69+
4 b g Unfuwain(USA) —Chere Amie (USA) (Mr Prospector (USA))
1808[7] 2176[11]

Heather Moor (USA) *Sir Michael Stoute* a72+ 80
3 b f Diesis—High Walden (USA) (El Gran Senor (USA))
1418[3] 2129[4] (3336) 3871[5]

Heathers Girl *R Dickin* a51 39
7 ch m Superlative—Kristis Girl (Ballacashtal (CAN))
767[7] (939) 1201[4]1723[9]

Heathyards Joy *R Hollinshead* a54 45
5 ch m Komaite(USA) —Heathyards Lady (USA) (Mining (USA))
634[4] 791[3]1197[4] 1460[3]2725[5]

Heathyards Pride *R Hollinshead* a87 68
6 b g Polar Prince(IRE) —Heathyards Lady (USA) (Mining (USA))
88[6] 194[4]454[9] 832[4]3686[8] (6287) 6468[2] 6677[5]6941[3]

Heat Of The Night *P W Chapple-Hyam* a85+ 99
4 b m Lear Fan(USA) —Hot Thong (BRZ) (Jarraar (USA))
1015[6] 1477[6] 4649a[3](5160a) 6366a[7]

Heaven Knows *W J Haggas* a76 94+
3 ch c Halling(USA) —Rambling Rose (Cadeaux Genereux)
(1855) 2654[2] (4763)

Heaven's Cause (USA) *N Clement* 103
3 b f Giant's Causeway(USA) —Heaven's Command (Priolo (USA))
1789a[2] 2491a[7] 3133a[4]

Heaven Sent *Sir Michael Stoute* 92
3 ch f Pivotal—Heavenly Ray (USA) (Rahy (USA))
(1191) 1834[5] 2851[6] (3418) 4083[3]

Heaven's Gates *K A Ryan* a51
2 ch c Most Welcome—Arcady (Slip Anchor)
6303[11] 6757[9]6950[9]

Heavens Walk *P J Makin* a78 77
5 ch h Compton Place—Ghost Dancing (Lion Cavern (USA))
1414[17] 2494[5] 2955[3] (3071) (3199) 3625[3]4208[7] (4587) 6353[2] 6452[2]6485[3] 6709[2]6844[4]

Heavy Seas *P D Niven* 25
3 b g Foxhound(USA) —Brookhead Lady (Petong)
1493[8] 1866[10]

Hebenus *T A K Cuthbert* a37 40
7 b g Hamas(IRE) —Stinging Nettle (Sharpen Up)
3334[10] 5865[17]

Heidi Hi *J R Turner* 52
2 b f High Estate—Alwal (Pharly (FR))
4376[13] 4731[6] 5076[7]

Height Of Esteem *M Mullineaux* a47 32
3 b g Mark Of Esteem(IRE) —Biscay (Unfuwain (USA))
2948[8] 4899[9] 5368[12] 5865[16] 5969[6]6234[7] 6308[14]

Height Of Fury (IRE) *J L Dunlop* 81+
3 b c Sadler's Wells(USA) —Height Of Fantasy (IRE) (Shirley Heights)
1681[11] 2990[5] 4150[6] 4842[2] 6008[2](6272)

Height Of Spirits *T D McCarthy* a45 52
4 b g Unfuwain(USA) —Kimono (IRE) (Machiavellian (USA))
32[7] 84[3](217) 343[7]596[5] 854[3]1245[7] 1996[12] 2348[5]2862[8] 3642[7]4139[9] 4585[2] 5205[8]6374[11] 6544[7]6617[9] 6829[6]

Heights Of Golan *I A Wood* a75 59
2 br c Golan(IRE) —Nemesia (Mill Reef (USA))
5892[6] 6145[2] 6393[5]

Helena Molony (IRE) *John M Oxx* 99
4 bb m Sadler's Wells(USA) —Kasora (IRE) (Darshaan)
2154a[5] 2471a[4] 2840a[3]

Helen Wood *M D I Usher* a42 65
3 b f Lahib(USA) —Last Ambition (IRE) (Cadeaux Genereux)
1401[10] 2578[10] 2753[9]3405[5] 3932[10] 4367[7]5033[9] 5432[15] (5733)

Helios Quercus (FR) *C Diard* 115
4 bl h Diableneyev(USA) —Criss Cross (FR) (Crystal Palace (FR))
841a[3] 1371a[5] 1873a[8] 2313a[2] 2941a[4]3779a[2] 4416a[9] 5146a[3]

Heliostatic (IRE) *J S Bolger* 112
3 ch c Galileo(IRE) —Affianced (IRE) (Erins Isle)
1025a[2] 1708a[8] 2039a[6] (2471a) 3127a[7] (3964a)4407a[4] 4641a[5] 5190a[6]

Hellbent *M Appleby* a41 43
7 b g Selkirk(USA) —Loure (USA) (Lyphard (USA))
360[8] 524[7]547[6] 633[13]

Hello Deauville (FR) *J Akehurst* a15 37
3 ch f Alhaarth(IRE) —Pulpeuse (IRE) (Pursuit Of Love)
3875[5] 4489[8] 4814[9] 5728[6] 6805[12]

Hello Man (IRE) *Eamon Tyrrell* a80 69
3 b g Princely Heir(IRE) —Mignon (Midyan (USA))
4124a[17] (5874) 6036[2] 6223[5]6654[8] 6773[2](6966)

Hello Molly *E A Wheeler* a14
5 b m Young Ern—Treasurebound (Beldale Flutter (USA))
138[12] 293[9]579[12] 964[10]

Hello Pretty (AUS) *A S Cruz* 117
4 ch g Distorted Humor(USA) —Blazing Aura (AUS) (Blazing Sword (AUS))
6785a[8]

Hello Roberto *R A Harris* a72 80
5 b m Up And At 'Em—Hello Hobson'S (IRE) (Fayruz)
212[4] 360[3](465) (524) 580[8](613) 824[4]954[3] 1402[4]1774[3] 1981[10] 2136[2] (2295) 2462[3]2484[2] 2897[4] (3027) 3447[11] 4003[6] 4085[14]4226[5] 5405[13] 5575[8]

Hello Sunday (FR) *Mme C Head-Maarek* 111
3 b c Poliglote—Hello Molly (FR) (Sillery (USA))
1064a[6] 1749a[3] 2278a[9] 2942a[3] (4862a) 5703a[3]6250a[7]

Hello Tiger *J A Supple*
5 gr g Terimon—Blue Peru (IRE) (Perugino (USA))
591[11] 941[7]1573[9]

Hellvelyn *B Smart* 111
2 gr c Ishiguru(USA) —Cumbrian Melody (Petong)
(892) (1998) (2719) 4409a[2] 5656[4]

He Magic (DEN) *B Olsen*
3 b g Final Appearance(IRE) —Blue Magic (NOR) (Diaglyphard (USA))
4919a[8]

Hemingway's Key (USA) *N Zito* a104
3 ch c Notebook(USA) —Whirl's Girl (USA) (Island Whirl (USA))
757a[6] 1861a[3]2477a[6]

Hemispear *Miss J R Tooth* a63 64
2 ch f Lear Spear(USA) —Milladella (FR) (Nureyev (USA))
2638[15] 3645[7] 4366[5]5105[6] 5596[3] 5947[6]6285[4] 6650[3]

Henchman *Lady Herries* a66 64
3 b g Anabaa(USA) —Gay Heroine (Caerleon (USA))
1215[9] 1851[6] 3055[9]3650[4] 4483[3] 4982[10]5992[12]

Hendrix (USA) *Craig Dollase* 115
5 b h Sultry Song(USA) —Fluttery Danseur (USA) (Wavering Monarch (USA))
5824a[8]

Henny Hughes (USA) *K McLaughlin* a121
3 ch c Hennessy(USA) —Meadow Flyer (USA) (Meadowlake (USA))
(5820a) 6341a[14]

Henry Bernstein (USA) *H R A Cecil* 56
2 bb c Bernstein(USA) —Hidle (USA) (Unbridled (USA))
5918[8]

Henry Hall (IRE) *N Tinkler* 79
10 b h Common Grounds—Sovereign Grace (IRE) (Standaan (FR))
1125[13] 1297[3] 2182[7] 2396[6] 2784[5]3297[2] 3622[8] 3988[3] (4110) 4468[4] 4725[6]5169[10] (5486) 5684[15]

Henry Holmes *Mrs L Richards* a63
3 b g Josr Algarhoud(IRE) —Henrietta Holmes (IRE) (Persian Bold)
62[4] 669[5]918[14] 3650[14]

Henry The Seventh *J W Hills* a67 33
2 b c Royal Applause—Bombalarina (IRE) (Barathea (IRE))
2402[14] 5608[2] 5841[8]6525[3] 6764[3]6933[6]

Henry Tun *J Balding* a48 37
8 b g Chaddleworth(IRE) —B Grade (Lucky Wednesday)
(130) (360) (401) 426[3] 824[9](951) 1150[5]2207[9] 6325[9]6399[10] 6533[9]6755[10] 6956[11]

Hensting House *Dr J R J Naylor* 38
3 b g Slip Anchor—Pallas Athene (Jupiter Island)
2655 [9] 3794[19] 5830[12]

Hephaestus *A J Chamberlain* a72 65
2 b g Piccolo—Fragrant Cloud (Zilzal (USA))
(701) 3544[7] 3734[17] 3861[5] 4178[6] 4460[6]4969[3] 5162[3] 5290[5]5419[5] (5772) 6056[3] 6146[7]6388[5] 6582[9]6732[4]

Herboriste *P Bary* 87
3 b f Hernando(FR) —Helvellyn (USA) (Gone West (USA))
4465a[7]

Herb Paris (FR) *M P Tregoning* a70 68
2 ch f Halling(USA) —Yaya (USA) (Rahy (USA))
3591[2] 4993[3] 5607[4]6388[8]

Here Comes Buster (IRE) *R Hannon* 73
2 b c Alhaarth(IRE) —Blew Her Top (USA) (Blushing John (USA))
5067[8] 5321 [6] 5565[2] 6058[5]

Hereditary *Mrs L C Jewell* a22
4 ch g Hernando(FR) —Eversince (USA) (Foolish Pleasure (USA))
457[10] 6375[10]

Hereford Boy *D K Ivory* a68 62+
2 ch g Tomba—Grown At Rowan (Gabitat)
5645 [13] 5867[11] 6034[4]6295[2] 6427[3] 6742[2]6838[3] (6895)

Here's Blue Chip (IRE) *P W D'Arcy* a9
2 ch c Barathea(IRE) —Blasted Heath (Thatching)
6646[7]

Here She Comes (FR) *Mme C Martens* a93 104
4 gr m Take Risks(FR) —Seule A Paris (FR) (Pistolet Bleu (IRE))
2490a[7] 4646a[6] 6250a[9]

Heriot *S C Burrough* 65
5 br g Hamas(IRE) —Sure Victory (IRE) (Stalker)
2601[8] 3467[8] 3896[9]

Her Majesty (USA) *P L Biancone* a105
2 b f Giant's Causeway(USA) —Slide (USA) (Smarten (USA))
6338a[13]

Hernando Cortes *A P O'Brien* 66
2 b c Sadler's Wells(USA) —Houseproud (USA) (Riverman (USA))
5662a[6]

Hernando Royal *H Morrison* a80 83
3 b c Hernando(FR) —Louis' Queen (IRE) (Tragic Role (USA))
863[2] 2646[3] (3261) 4612[5]5644[5]

Hernando's Boy *K G Reveley* 70
5 b g Hernando(FR) —Leave At Dawn (Slip Anchor)
816[2] 1457[3]

Herninski *M C Chapman* a27 64
3 b f Hernando(FR) —Empress Dagmar (Selkirk (USA))
3634[8] 4307[12] 4471[7] 6959[12]

Heroes *G A Huffer* 87
2 b g Diktat—Wars (IRE) (Green Desert (USA))
5454[3] (5867) 6102[5]

Herons Kiss (IRE) *B S Rothwell*
2 b f Heron Island(IRE) —Kissimmee Bay (IRE) (Brief Truce (USA))
1862[10] 4545[12]

Herotozero (IRE) *Gerard O'Leary* a77 65
2 b g Mull Of Kintyre(USA) —Free To Trade (IRE) (Royal Academy (USA))
5735[2] 6377[2]

Hero Worship (IRE) *M A Jarvis* 94+
3 b c Kalanisi(IRE) —Shesasmartlady (IRE) (Dolphin Street (FR))
(863) (1286) 2436[2]

Herring (IRE) *D J Coakley* a79 76
3 b c Orpen(USA) —Moorfield Daisy (IRE) (Waajib)
(900) 1384[4] 2177[7] 3015[3]3974[6] 4599[7] 5110[13]

He's A Decoy (IRE) *David Wachman* 112
2 b c In The Wings—Allegheny River (USA) (Lear Fan (USA))
(2686a) 3492[2] 5466a[11] 5715a[4] 5965[8]

He's A Diamond *T G Mills* a63 75
4 ch g Vettori(IRE) —Azira (Arazi (USA))
265[5]

Hesaguru (IRE) *J R Norton* 34
2 ch g Ishiguru(USA) —Lady Kinvarrah (IRE) (Brief Truce (USA))
3018[15] 4608[11] 5112[8] 5495[11]

He's A Humbug (IRE) *K A Ryan* 88
2 b c Tagula(IRE) —Acidanthera (Alzao (USA))
(3173) 4712[5] 5455[3]

He's A Rocket (IRE) *K R Burke* a60 57
5 b g Indian Rocket—Dellua (IRE) (Suave Dancer (USA))
126[10] 212[6]320[8] 401[6]480[9] 547[4]951[2] 1150[2]1794[14] 2376[12] 2632[11] 3155[8]3356[11] 6723[5] 6943[4]

He's A Star *B D Leavy* a76 56
4 ch g Mark Of Esteem(IRE) —Sahara Belle (USA) (Sanglamore (USA))
(12) 246[2] 346[3](491) 610[2]652[8] 1808[15] 2206[2]2455[14] (4435) 5213[13]

He's Mine Too *J D Bethell* 64
2 b c Indian Ridge—Screen Idol (IRE) (Sadler's Wells (USA))
5088[7]

Hessian (IRE) *M L W Bell*
2 b f Barathea(IRE) —Red Letter (Sri Pekan (USA))
1675[9]

Hester Brook (IRE) *J G M O'Shea* 59
2 b f Soviet Star(USA) —Keen To Please (Keen)
2166[16] 2631[3] 2878[2] 3160[3] 4006[4]4334[2] 5434[13]

Heureux (USA) *J Howard Johnson* 81
3 b c Stravinsky(USA) —Storm West (USA) (Gone West (USA))
1446[4] 1999[4] 2809[6] 3191[4] 4172[4]4634[P] 5554[12]

Heversham (IRE) *J Hetherton* a34 22
5 b g Octagonal(NZ) —Saint Ann (USA) (Geiger Counter (USA))
94[7] 259[5]302[8]

Hewaraat (IRE) *G A Swinbank* 75
4 b g Fasliyev(USA) —Maraatib (IRE) (Green Desert (USA))
1124[7] (Dead)

Hey Presto *R Rowe* a59 43
6 b g Piccolo—Upping The Tempo (Dunbeath (USA))
17[13] 236[11]1245[12] 1673[17] 2348[11]2860[8] 5937[14]

Heywood *M R Channon* a86 83
2 b g Tobougg(IRE) —Owdbetts (IRE) (High Estate)
2979[10] 3328[5] 3623[3](3843) 4250[6] (4813) (5041) 5459[6]5843[2] 6100[9]

Hezaam (USA) *Mrs A Duffield* a55 75
5 b g Red Ransom(USA) —Ashraakat (USA) (Danzig (USA))
276[11] 1256[8]1590[6] 1758[7] (2362) (2762) 3192[9]

H Harrison (IRE) *I W McInnes* a70 86
6 b g Eagle Eyed(USA) —Penrose (IRE) (Wolfhound (USA))
446[6] 588[6](806) (837) 845[13]1035[11] 1262[10] 2147[4] 2397[6] 2520[4]2705[DSQ] 2946[3] 3191[7] 4090[5] 4172[12]4449[5] 5081[3] 5243[2] 5313[6] 6036[9]

Hialeah *Robert Gray* 34
5 ch g Bal Harbour—Tommys Dream (Le Bavard (FR))
4227[5] 5837[12]

Hiamovi (IRE) *R M H Cowell* a41 33
4 b g Monashee Mountain(USA) —Dunfern (Wolver Hollow)
38[8] 146[6]299[12] 465[12]

Hiats *J O'Reilly* a53 20
4 b g Lujain(USA) —Naulakha (Bustino)
1764[13] 4611[12] 4948[16]5903[9] 6327[6] 6703[4]6796[14]

Hiawatha (IRE) *A M Hales* a56 69
7 b g Danehill(USA) —Hi Bettina (Henbit (USA))
285[7] 358[5]471[4] 683[4]888[4] 6724[6]6904[3]

Hi Calypso (IRE) *Sir Michael Stoute* 76
2 b f In The Wings—Threefold (USA) (Gulch (USA))
5344[9] (5754) 6217[7]

Hiccups *M Dods* 85
6 b g Polar Prince(IRE) —Simmie's Special (Precocious)
798[4] 977[2] 1359[12] 1597[13] 2384[14]2732[9] (4116) 4521[5] (5070) 5355[9] 5749[11] 6160[4](6273)

Hi Dancer *P C Haslam* a56 56
3 b g Medicean—Sea Music (Inchinor)
(199) 430[4] 1859[6] 2379[2]4651[6]

Hidden Ace (IRE) *M W Easterby* a56 26
2 b f Iron Mask(USA) —Kingdom Pearl (Statoblest)
3994[4] 4434[5]4887[14] 5238[13] 5387[8]

Hidden Charm (IRE) *D K Weld* 83
3 b f Big Shuffle(USA) —Polite Reply (IRE) (Be My Guest (USA))
2308a[8]

Hidden Dragon (USA) *J Pearce* a111 98
7 b g Danzig(USA) —Summer Home (USA) (Easy Goer (USA))
151a[3] 204a[10] 366a[5]433a[10] 2230[11] 3077[13] 4106[4] 4338[9]4807[14] 5117[8] 6692[P]

Hiddensee (USA) *M Johnston* a88 88
4 b g Cozzene(USA) —Zarani Sidi Anna (USA) (Danzig (USA))
1021[6] 1167[6]1584[15] 2238[6] 2437[9] (2879) 3098[5]

Hide And Seek (SWE) *H Lundell* a96 104
10 br h Island Reef—Memorabilia (Dominion)
5225a[3]

Hi Friend Try (JPN) *Y Nemoto* 107
6 b h Real Shadai(JPN) —Hi Friend Bird (USA) (Seattle Dancer (USA))
1329a[15]

High (IRE) *W J Musson* a53 33
4 b g Desert Story(IRE) —Sesame Heights (IRE) (High Estate)
26[6] 414[7]615[3] (794) 1199[10] 1467[6]1729[3]

High Action (USA) *Ian Williams* a105 116
6 ch g Theatrical—Secret Imperatrice (USA) (Secretariat (USA))
1839[5] 2773[4] 4081[12] 4677[10]

High Ambition *P W D'Arcy* a53
3 b g High Estate—So Ambitious (Teenoso (USA))
6967[4]

High Arctic *A Bailey* a65 74
4 b g Pivotal—Ladykirk (Slip Anchor)
50[8]

Highband *M Madgwick* 28
3 b f Band On The Run—Barkston Singer (Runnett)
2951[6] 5567[12]

High Bounce (USA) *R J Hodges*
6 ch g Trempolino(USA) —Top Hope (High Top)
5651[11]

High Bray (GER) *D R C Elsworth* 91
5 b g Zieten(USA) —Homing Instinct (Arctic Tern (USA))
4029[14] 4372[4] 5175[9] 5677[10]

High Bullen *M Meade* a42 55
2 ch f Inchinor—Rock Face (Ballad Rock)
1203[12] 3201[13] 3448[5]

High Class Problem (IRE) *P F I Cole* a72 71
3 b c Mozart(IRE) —Sarah-Clare (Reach)
1547[6] 2403[4] 3164[2] 3569[7] (4243) 4933[4]5152[9]

High Command *E A L Dunlop* a93 102
3 b c Galileo(IRE) —Final Shot (Dalsaan)
(895) 1841[3] 1951[7] 3710[4] 4082[8] 4997[3](5299) 5660[4]

High Country (IRE) *Micky Hammond* a51 58
6 b g Danehill(USA) —Dance Date (IRE) (Sadler's Wells (USA))
597[6]

High Curragh *K A Ryan* 96
3 b g Pursuit Of Love—Pretty Poppy (Song)
1091[7] 1292[2] 2658[3] 3414[7] 4083[2]4601[7]

High Dyke *K A Ryan* a79 81
4 b g Mujahid(USA) —Gold Linnet (Nashwan (USA))
632[RR] 726[RR]

Highest Regard *N P McCormack* a84 70
4 b g Mark Of Esteem(IRE) —Free As A Bird (Robellino (USA))
2555[11] 3101[12]3401[11] (3939) 4259[6] 5367[10]5904[17]

High Fidelity (GER) *A Fabre* a83 84
3 ch f Peintre Celebre(USA) —Hold On (GER) (Surumu (GER))
5881a[10]

High Finance (USA) *R Violette* a92
3 ch c Talk Is Money(USA) —Margay (USA) (Conquistador Cielo (USA))
2477a[10]

High Five Society *S R Bowring* a47 69
2 b c Compton Admiral—Sarah Madeline (Pelder (IRE))
5245[9] 5614[2] 5923[7]6285[10]

High Frequency (IRE) *A Crook* a46 50
5 ch g Grand Lodge(USA) —Freak Out (FR) (Bering)
13[6] 75[6]131[2] 231[6]346[2] 443[7]549[6] 688[3]785[2] 1199[12]1256[9] 1436[5] 1766[7](1883) 2528[2] 3919[3] 4423[8]5369[4] 6305[10]

High Heel Sneakers *P F I Cole* a109 107
3 b f Dansili—Sundae Girl (USA) (Green Dancer (USA))
1330a[3] 1777[5] 2582[3] 2772[4] (6191)

High Hope (FR) *G L Moore* a73d 53
8 ch g Lomitas—Highness Lady (GER) (Cagliostro (GER))
556[4] 713[6]1247[10] 2790[2]3013[3] 3935[8]4836[7]

High Intelligent (AUS) *J Size* 115
6 b g Anabaa(USA) —Party Dancer (AUS) (Party Leader (USA))
1527a[8] 6785a[12]

Highland Belle *A M Balding* 61
3 b f Robellino(USA) —Scottish Spice (Selkirk (USA))
1513[8] 2188[8]

Highland Blaze (USA) *Saeed Bin Suroor* 86+
3 ch c Unbridled's Song(USA) —Green Lady (IRE) (Green Desert (USA))
4527[2] (4806) 5504[14]

Highland Cascade *J M P Eustace* a72 85
4 ch m Tipsy Creek(USA) —Highland Hannah (IRE) (Persian Heights)
1183[15] 2233[6] 2590[5] 3041[6] 3478[4]3827[3] 4294[3] 4484[3] 5058[10] 5171[9]5619[11] 5907[3] 6654[9]6770[9] 6833[11]

Highland Harvest *D R C Elsworth* a77 64
2 b c Averti(IRE) —Bee One (IRE) (Catrail (USA))
4600[6] 5206[7] 6298[3] 6689[3]6887[3]

Highland Legacy *M L W Bell* 61
2 ch c Selkirk(USA) —Generous Lady (Generous (IRE))
5882[10] 6173[4]

Highland Song (IRE) *R F Fisher* a69 72
3 ch g Fayruz—Rose 'n Reason (IRE) (Reasonable (FR))
601[4] 1036[3] 1279[3]1453[2] 1793[5] 2237[13] 2855[3] 3297[8]3759[7] (4354) 4834[8] 5181[3] 5864[4] 6159[11]6320[9] 6572[12]

Highland Warrior *J S Goldie* 92
7 b g Makbul—Highland Rowena (Royben)
1031[2] (1438) 2450[8] 3038[10] 3585[5] 3956[10]5009[10] 5336[24] 5535[11] 6009[8] 6320[10]

Highliner *Mrs L Williamson* a60 66
4 b h Robellino(USA) —Bocas Rose (Jalmood (USA))
73[11]

High Lite *M L W Bell* 49
2 ch f Observatory(USA) —Shall We Run (Hotfoot)
5867[13] 6055[6] 6295[8]

High Meadow Girl *J D Bethell* 63
3 b f Pursuit Of Love—Immaculate (Mark Of Esteem (IRE))
4567[12] 5243[16] 5619[14]

High 'n Dry (IRE) *C A Cyzer* a72
2 ch f Halling(USA) —Sisal (IRE) (Danehill (USA))
6186[7] 6433[2]

High Octave (IRE) *B G Powell* a67 70
3 b c Piccolo—Flight Sequence (Polar Falcon (USA))
1048[9] 1642[15] 3011[12]3436[2] 3932[6] 4225[3] 4757[2] 5377[5]5568[6] 5911[8] 6289[7]

High Point (IRE) *G P Enright* a81 79
8 b g Ela-Mana-Mou—Top Lady (IRE) (Shirley Heights)
2377[7] 545[2]628[5] 832[10]1021[5] 1247[3]1584[14] 2219[2] 2723[10] (4046) 5383[8] 5963[14] (6655)

High Reach *W R Muir* a95 103
6 b g Royal Applause—Lady Of Limerick (IRE) (Thatching)
1236[3] 1487[24] 2776[26] 2847[26] 3550[5]3744[3] 4101[20] 4357[8] 4811[4] 5212[12]5777[10]

High Reef (FR) *C F Swan* 92
8 b m Shareef Dancer(USA) —Debate (High Line)
5396a[14]

High Ridge *J M Bradley* a80 81
7 ch g Indian Ridge—Change For A Buck (USA) (Time For A Change (USA))
(1432) 1686[17] (1961) 2302[6] 2661[10] 2981[7]3217[4] 3567[8] 3986[2] 4101[8] 4364[5]4957[3] 5058[3] 5476[13] 5782[3]

High Seasons *B R Millman* a66 70
3 b g Fantastic Light(USA) —El Hakma (Shareef Dancer (USA))
(1375) 1740[5] 2933[5] 3540[2] 6712[5]6878[8]

High Style *R Hannon* a83 84
2 b c Desert Style(IRE) —Gracious Gift (Cadeaux Genereux)
1730[8] 2130[3] 2617[6] 3117[4] 3530[2](4246) 4547[2] 5461[9] 5909[2]6096[11]

High Swainston *R Craggs* a53 55
5 ch g The West(USA) —Reamzafonic (Grand Lodge (USA))
81[4] 177[6]391[3] 526[2]649[4] 787[3]940[8] 2240[3] 2696[9]4059[8]

High Treason (USA) *W J Musson* a70 81+
4 ch g Diesis—Fabula Dancer (USA) (Northern Dancer (CAN))
(1058) 1163[2] 2305[5] (2956) 4662[3](5276) (5897)

High Tribute *Sir Mark Prescott* a66
2 ch c Mark Of Esteem(IRE) —Area Girl (Jareer (USA))
6730[3] 6887[5]6976[6]

High Voltage *K R Burke* 93d
5 ch g Wolfhound(USA) —Real Emotion (USA) (El Prado (IRE))
1042[10] 3584[4] 4230[14] 4655[2] 5136[5]5635[9] 5765[16]

Highway (IRE) *F Castro* a96
3 b g King's Theatre(IRE) —Havinia (Habitat)
4420a[3]

Highway To Glory (IRE) *M Botti* a78 103
3 b f Cape Cross(IRE) —Anita Via (IRE) (Anita's Prince)
3891[2] 4542a[11] 5159[3] 5550[2] 6190[9]

High Window (IRE) *G P Kelly* a32 44
6 b g King's Theatre(IRE) —Kayradja (IRE) (Last Tycoon)
2[4]

Hillbilly Cat (USA) *R Ingram* a66d 56
3 ch g Running Stag(USA) —Flashy Cat (USA) (Mountain Cat (USA))
14[8] 329[3]415[2] 1259[4]1792[11] (2138) (2247) 2937[3] 4703[9]5737[11] 6293[13]6510[9] 6719[7]

Hill Billy Rock (IRE) *G A Swinbank* a46 74
3 b g Halling(USA) —Polska (USA) (Danzig (USA))
2298[6] 2542[7] 3261[5]4060[8] (4884) 5284[4]

Hillfield Flyer (IRE) *Samuel Murphy* a47 60
6 b m Flying Spur(AUS) —Paul's Lass (IRE) (Al Hareb (USA))
183[11] (791) 1392[11]1461[9]

Hillhall (IRE) *W M Brisbourne* a53 54
4 ch g Desert Prince(IRE) —Factice (USA) (Known Fact (USA))
1201[2] 1461[3]1729[8] 2131[7] 2522[12]3068[5] 3305[7] 3944[9]

Hill Of Almhuim (IRE) *Peter Grayson* a49 50
3 b g City On A Hill(USA) —Kitty Kildare (USA) (Seattle Dancer (USA))
848[4] 1099[5] 1547[10]1948[5] 2622[3] 3477[3] 4570[9] 5403 [3]5683[7] 5862[4] 6057[2] 6464[8]6708[6] 6802[5]6856[10]

Hill Of Clare (IRE) *G H Jones* a51 53+
4 gr m Daylami(IRE) —Sarah-Clare (Reach)
1753[7] 1910[3] 2702[14]6621[9]

Hill Of Howth (IRE) *K A Ryan* a46 81
3 b c Danehill Dancer(IRE) —Elton Grove (IRE) (Astronef)
122[9]

Hill Of Lujain *M W Easterby* 70
2 b c Lujain(USA) —Cinder Hills (Deploy)
1074[2] (1499) 1780[5] 2076[4]

Hillside Smoki (IRE) *A Berry*
2 b f Soviet Star(USA) —Najeyba (Indian Ridge)
5496[11]

Hills Of Aran *W K Goldsworthy* 55
4 b h Sadler's Wells(USA) —Danefair (Danehill (USA))
4810[17] 5163[10] 5479[12] 5723[7] 6108[8]

Hill Spirit *D R C Elsworth* a84 89
3 b c Polish Precedent(USA) —Homing Instinct (Arctic Tern (USA))
1115[5] 1680[3] (2143) 2581[8] (4481) 4802[2] 5345[7]5649[8]

Hills Place *J R Best* 53
2 b c Primo Valentino(IRE) —Moxby (Efisio)
4956[8] 5315[5] 5645[11]

Hilltime (IRE) *J S Wainwright* a51 58
6 b g Danetime(IRE) —Ceannanas (IRE) (Magical Wonder (USA))
1748[6] 3377[4] 4256[3]

Hilltop Destiny *V Smith* a86+ 51
3 b c Sure Blade(USA) —Saferjel (Elmaamul (USA))
5879[9] 6177[4] (6735) (6816)

Hilltop Fantasy *V Smith* a43 45
5 b m Danzig Connection(USA) —Hilltop (Absalom)
289[9] 681[11]778[8] 2356[6] 2571[9] 2955[11] 5272[7]6277[3] 6552[5]6726[4] 6779[3]6854[9]

Hilversum *Miss J A Camacho* a42 24
4 ch m Polar Falcon(USA) —Silky Heights (IRE) (Head For Heights)
289[7] 403[10]771[8] 2077[9]

Himba *Mrs A J Perrett* 64+
3 b g Vettori(IRE) —Be My Wish (Be My Chief (USA))
1741[8] 2118[11] 2304[12] 4150[4] 4537[2]4800[7] 5628[12]

Hinterland (SAF) *S Seemar* a85 105
8 ch g Badger Land(USA) —Daunting (SAF) (Raise A Man (USA))
201a[8] 369a[9] 506a[9]

Hinterland (IRE) *M A Jarvis* 110
4 b h Danzig(USA) —Electric Society (IRE) (Law Society (USA))
(2200) 2742[4] (3313) 3926[9] 4358[5] 5675[28]

Hint Of Spring *Saeed Bin Suroor* a53+
2 b f Seeking The Gold(USA) —Cherokee Rose (IRE) (Dancing Brave (USA))
6481[8]

Hinton Admiral *M Johnston* a103 99
2 b c Spectrum(IRE) —Shawanni (Shareef Dancer (USA))
(2745) 3492[6] (5404) 5809[2] (6096)

Hi Perry *M Wellings*
4 b h Meqdaam(USA) —Hi Rock (Hard Fought)
5598[16]

Hippodrome (IRE) *R Simpson* a82 103
4 b g Montjeu(IRE) —Moon Diamond (Unfuwain (USA))
354a[11] 437a[14] 565a[7]4817[8] 5551[9]

Hippodrome Corner *R Hannon* 21
2 br f Mujahid(USA) —Raffelina (USA) (Carson City (USA))
5894[11]

Hippolyte (USA) *J G Given* a48 38
3 b f Monarchos(USA) —Liberty School (USA) (Pine Bluff (USA))
1153[9] 1418[12] 4635[6]5363[16] 5922[2]

Hirvine (FR) *D McCain Jnr* 54
8 ch g Snurge—Guadanella (FR) (Guadanini (FR))
5723[4]

His Honour (IRE) *R Charlton* a82 76
3 ch g Grand Lodge(USA) —Knight's Baroness (Rainbow Quest (USA))
1134[5] 1822[4] 5429[2]

His Master's Voice (IRE) *D W P Arbuthnot* a78 77
3 ch c Distant Music(USA) —Glen Of Imaal (IRE) (Common Grounds)
60[3] 233[5]473[2] 579[3]702[8] 822[7]3487[5] (3845) 4328[4]4802[4] 5377[10] 5649[12]6020[12] 6882[9]

Histoire De Moeurs (FR) *Y De Nicolay* 107
3 b f Kaldounevees(FR) —Vero De Moeurs (FR) (Double Bed (FR))
2913a[6] 4192a[5] 4979a[6] 6454a[4]

Historic Appeal (USA) *M R Channon* 74
3 b g Diesis—Karasavina (IRE) (Sadler's Wells (USA))
817[2] 1077[6] 1881[6] 4892[6] 5513[16]

History Boy *D J Coakley* a84 88
2 b g Dr Fong(USA) —Goldie (Celtic Swing)
4592[4] 5218a[3] 5906[4]6254[4] (6570) 6846[4]

History Prize (IRE) *A G Newcombe* a47
3 b g Celtic Swing—Menominee (Soviet Star (USA))
6524[6] 6792[7]

Hitra (USA) *Mme C Head-Maarek* 92
2 br f Langfuhr(CAN) —Heavenly Spirits (USA) (Southern Halo (USA))
4464a[9] 5880a[5]

Hits Only Cash *J Pearce* a77 76d
4 b g Inchinor—Persian Blue (Persian Bold)
51[4] 569[2]970[12] 1275[3] 1846[12]2074[2] 2981[11] 3598[7]4771[9] 5635[12] 6061[9] 6404[4]

Hits Only Heaven (IRE) *D Nicholls* a92 91
4 ch g Bold Fact(USA) —Algonquin Park (High Line)
64[3] 161[3]1246[9] 1494[11] 2555[9](2983) 3532[6]4796[2] 5019[6] 5175[12]5785[5] 6896[7] (Dead)

Hits Only Jude (IRE) *J Pearce* a63 71
3 gr g Bold Fact(USA) —Grey Goddess (Godswalk (USA))
803[5] 1183[14] 1679[8]1900[5] 2939[9] 4602[10]5036[5] 6060[7] 6390[5]

Hits Only Life (USA) *J Pearce* a54+ 56
3 b g Lemon Drop Kid(USA) —Southern Day (USA) (Dixieland Band (USA))
165[12] 272[7](617) 797[7] 1140[2] 1533[2]1851[10] 2246[10]

Hit's Only Money (IRE) *R A Harris* a71 62
6 br g Hamas(IRE) —Toordillon (IRE) (Contract Law (USA))
253[7] 489[10]644[3] 977[8] 1746[9]3899[10] 4230[7] 4496[6] 4984[13] 5474[20]

Hits Only Vic (USA) *J Pearce* a20 45
2 bb c Lemon Drop Kid(USA) —Royal Family (USA) (Private Terms (USA))
4260[10] 4731[13] 5111[9] 5458[11] 6472[7]

Hit The Road (IRE) *Michael McElhone* a42
2 gr g Carrowkeel(IRE) —Order Of Success (USA) (With Approval (CAN))
6591[10]

Hocinail (FR) *P Winkworth* 51
2 ch c Majorien—Flamme (FR) (Shining Steel)
3031[5] 4008[6] 4980[7]

Hogan's Heroes *G A Butler* a52 63+
3 b g Alhaarth(IRE) —Icicle (Polar Falcon (USA))
801[9] 1232[3] 2648[5]2823[3] 3329[10] 3910[7]

Hogmaneigh (IRE) *S C Williams* a72 106
3 b g Namid—Magical Peace (IRE) (Magical Wonder (USA))
1091[8] (1848) 2032[3] (4811) 5182[3] 5358[13] 5812[13]

Hoh Bla Daa *S Kirk* a62 71
3 b g Cape Cross(IRE) —Monte Calvo (Shirley Heights)
948[8] 1403[3] 1648[4]

Hoh Bleu Dee *T Keddy* a48 66
5 b g Desert Style(IRE) —Ermine (IRE) (Cadeaux Genereux)
229[10] 472[11]568[6] 683[9]

Hoh Hoh Hoh *R J Price* a64 93
4 ch g Piccolo—Nesting (Thatching)
1663[9] 2227[19] 3251[11] 4811[6] 5148[5]5433[4] (5627) 5832[6] 6292[11]

Hohlethelonely *M L W Bell* 80
2 ch c Medicean—Now And Forever (IRE) (Kris)
5580[2] (6318)

Hoh Me Hoh You (IRE) *S Kirk* a48 59
2 ch g Redback—Eastern Aura (IRE) (Ahonoora)
3253[9] 3851[8] 4161[8] 6912[8]

Hoh Mike (IRE) *M L W Bell* 106
2 ch c Intikhab(USA) —Magical Peace (IRE) (Magical Wonder (USA))
1189[2] (1737) (1897) 2771[2] 3442[7] 5154[3] 5681[6]5802[2]

Hoh Wotanite *R Hollinshead* a74 61
3 ch c Stravinsky(USA) —West One (Gone West (USA))
373[2] 2222[7] 2553[2]3154[2] (3410) 5036[2] 5268[11] 5649[11]6664[3] 6928[8]

Holbeck Ghyll (IRE) *A M Balding* a74 91+
4 ch g Titus Livius(FR) —Crimada (IRE) (Mukaddamah (USA))
699[5] 1662[11] 2189[5](4085) 4360[8] 4486[3] 4796[5] 5275[5]

Holdin Foldin (IRE) *K R Burke* a86+ 98
2 b c Fayruz—Escudo (IRE) (Indian Ridge)
(2241) 2771[7] (3618) (4326) 4607[2] 4715[6] 5335[2]5880a[6]

Holding Hands (IRE) *Patrick Morris* 17
5 b m Turtle Island(IRE) —Sakanda (IRE) (Vayrann)
788[9]

Holiday Camp (USA) *M Al Muhairi* a93 109?
4 b h Chester House(USA) —Arewehavingfunyet (USA) (Sham (USA))
496a^{3} 738a^{10}

Holiday Cocktail *Miss J Feilden* a67 58
4 b g Mister Baileys—Bermuda Lily (Dunbeath (USA))
74^{2} 169^{2}223^{8} 375^{3}3149^{3} 3914^{11} 5510^{10}5974^{4}

Hollie Dellamore *A P Jarvis* a6
4 b m Fumo Di Londra(IRE) —Acebo Lyons (IRE) (Waajib)
531^{11} 2411^{9} 2575^{13}4077^{11}

Hollow Jo *J R Jenkins* a77 77
6 b g Most Welcome—Sir Hollow (USA) (Sir Ivor (USA))
(21) 170^{3} (416) 575^{5}698^{3} 845^{4}985^{9} 1644^{3}2331^{13} 3845^{3} 4368^{3}6147^{7} 6396^{2}6595^{5} (6842) (6913)

Hollow Ridge *B W Hills* 91
2 b f Beat Hollow—Bolas (Unfuwain (USA))
(5890) 6105^{2}

Holly Springs *Mrs C A Dunnett* a59 84
4 b m Efisio—Anotheranniversary (Emarati (USA))
45^{4} 255^{9}320^{11}

Hollywood George *W J Haggas* a75
2 b c Royal Applause—Aunt Tate (Tate Gallery (USA))
6669^{3} 6822^{3}(6940)

Hollywood Henry (IRE) *P A Blockley* a51 51
6 b g Bahhare(USA) —Takeshi (IRE) (Cadeaux Genereux)
182^{11} (Dead)

Hollywood Starlet (FR) *Y De Nicolay* a93 89
3 b f Marchand De Sable(USA) —Private Quest (USA) (Quest For Fame)
1874a^{8} 6328a^{8}

Hollywood Story (USA) *J Shirreffs* a115 107
5 br m Wild Rush(USA) —Wife For Life (USA) (Dynaformer (USA))
6343a^{10}

Holocene (USA) *P Bary* 107
2 b c Lemon Drop Kid(USA) —Witching Hour (FR) (Fairy King (USA))
5048a^{2} 5801a^{2} 6249a^{7}

Holy Roman Emperor (IRE) *A P O'Brien* 124+
2 b c Danehill(USA) —L'On Vite (USA) (Secretariat (USA))
2719^{15} (3126a) (4409a) 5410a^{2} (5715a) 5965^{2}

Home Affairs *Sir Michael Stoute* 118+
4 b h Dansili—Orford Ness (Selkirk (USA))
(1739) 2226^{3}

Homebred Star *G P Enright* a49 39
5 ch g Safawan—Celtic Chimes (Celtic Cone)
398^{14} 469^{4}683^{8} 1198^{3}1536^{11} 1911^{12}6620^{12} 6800^{7}

Homecroft Boy *J A Osborne* 49
2 ch g Kyllachy—Quiz Time (Efisio)
3958^{7} 4525^{10} 4897^{8}

Homegrown (IRE) *Patrick Tallis* 104
5 b m Mujadil(USA) —Don't Wary (FR) (Lomond (USA))
4749a^{11}

Homes By Woodford *R A Harris* a72+ 46
2 ch g Tumbleweed Ridge—Partenza (USA) (Red Ransom (USA))
1074^{8} 1342^{11} 1442^{9} 1588^{13} 3994^{6}5282^{4} 5860^{10} 6208^{8} (6471) 6592^{4} 6653^{8}(6736) 6926^{7}(6951)

Home Sweet Home (IRE) *P D Evans* a66 97
3 b f Danehill(USA) —Jungle Moon (IRE) (Sadler's Wells (USA))
2383^{3} (2763) (3150) 3226^{7} 3795^{2} 4633^{2} 4837^{5}5411a^{10} 5550^{4} 6190^{10}

Hometomammy *P W Hiatt* a51
4 b g Diktat—Catania (USA) (Aloma's Ruler (USA))
219^{9} 289^{6}457^{15} 6617^{13}6729^{8} 6995^{12}

Honduras (SWI) *G L Moore* a92 95
5 gr g Daylami(IRE) —High Mare (FR) (Highest Honor (FR))
4096^{7} 5526^{8} 6515^{4}6744^{7}

Honest Danger *J R Best* 80
2 b c Dansili—Allegresse (IRE) (Alzao (USA))
3872^{5} (4550) 4946^{4} 5546^{10} (Dead)

Honest Injun *A G Juckes* a64 66
5 b h Efisio—Sioux (Kris)
50^{11} 167^{10}429^{9}

Honey Bunny *V Caruso* 103
6 b h Zamindar(USA) —Siddharta (USA) (Chief's Crown (USA))
6364a^{8}

Honey Flame *A P Jarvis* a31 44
3 b f Fumo Di Londra(IRE) —Dulzie (Safawan)
248^{9} 326^{11}

Honey Ryder (USA) *T Pletcher* 119
5 gr m Lasting Approval(USA) —Cuando Quiere (USA) (Affirmed (USA))
4385a^{4} (5819a) 6340a^{3}

Honey Ryder *Stef Liddiard* a74? 89
4 b m Compton Place—Urania (Most Welcome)
1338^{6} 1961^{7}

Honey's Gift *G G Margarson* a43 56
7 b m Terimon—Honeycroft (Crofter (USA))
545^{7}

Honor Me (IRE) *J J Quinn* 54
3 b f Beckett(IRE) —Christmas Kiss (Taufan (USA))
2001^{9} 2298^{4} 2704^{11} 3586^{6} 4071^{11}4524^{7}

Hoofbeats Tour *Miss J Feilden* a32
4 b g Vettori(IRE) —Sprite (Fairy King (USA))
5922^{7} 6302^{7}6473^{10} 6758^{6}

Hooplah *J H M Gosden* 47+
3 b f Pivotal—La Piaf (FR) (Fabulous Dancer (USA))
2934^{9}

Ho Pang Yau *J S Goldie* 50
8 bb g Pivotal—La Cabrilla (Carwhite)
4350^{4} 4652^{9} 5840^{9}

Hopeful Isabella (IRE) *Sir Mark Prescott* 46
2 ch f Grand Lodge(USA) —Hopeful Sign (Warning)
5068^{11} 5307^{10} 5507^{13}

Hopeful Purchase (IRE) *W J Haggas* 102
3 ch g Grand Lodge(USA) —Funoon (IRE) (Kris)
1269^{4} (2111) 2775^{7} 4082^{10}

Hope'N'Charity (USA) *C G Cox* 98
2 b f Smart Strike(CAN) —Celestic (USA) (Sky Classic (CAN))
(2638) (3084) 3415^{4} 3925^{7} 4840^{4} 5356^{6}

Hope Road *J R Fanshawe* 71
2 ch g Sakhee(USA) —Bibliotheque (USA) (Woodman (USA))
5883^{7}

Hope's Eternal *J L Dunlop* a2 59
3 ro g Highest Honor(FR) —Tennessee Moon (Darshaan)
1140^{9} 2352^{14} 3017^{12}

Hope Your Safe *J R Best* a54+ 39
2 b f Tobougg(IRE) —Sunday Night (GER) (Bakharoff (USA))
6331^{9} 6457^{3} 6669^{5}

Hoptilludrop (IRE) *Matthieu Palussiere* 50
2 b f Key Of Luck(USA) —Mountain Hop (IRE) (Tirol)
4824a^{18}

Hora *Sir Mark Prescott* a37
2 b f Hernando(FR) —Applecross (Glint Of Gold)
6098^{9} 6254^{10}6475^{7}

Horatio Nelson (IRE) *A P O'Brien* 120+
3 b c Danehill(USA) —Imagine (IRE) (Sadler's Wells (USA))
1486^{8} 2228^{P} (Dead)

Hornpipe *M S Saunders* a59 95
4 b g Danehill(USA) —Dance Sequence (USA) (Mr Prospector (USA))
836^{8} 1475^{10} 2674^{6}3165^{6} 5058^{15} 6823^{9}6935^{4}

Horsley Wiz *E S McMahon* 60
2 b g Wizard King—Breezy Palms (Tragic Role (USA))
5126^{4} 5537^{11}

Hosiva (GER) *M G Quinlan* a14 86
3 b f Silvano(GER) —Hosianna (GER) (Surumu (GER))
1942^{5} 2493a^{6}

Host (CHI) *T Pletcher* a92 118
6 ch h Hussonet(USA) —Colonna Traiana (CHI) (Roy (USA))
742a^{4}

Hostage *M L W Bell* a72+
2 b f Dr Fong(USA) —Catatonic (Zafonic (USA))
6646^{4} (6815)

Hot Agnes *H J Collingridge* a61 61
3 b f Agnes World(USA) —Hot Tin Roof (IRE) (Thatching)
2605^{7} 3053^{5} 3383^{4}4690^{2} 5210^{4} 5936^{6}6439^{4} 6683^{4}6981^{11}

Hot Baby (IRE) *M L W Bell* 39
3 gr f Linamix(FR) —House In Wood (FR) (Woodman (USA))
5567^{11} (Dead)

Hot Cherry *J M P Eustace* 40
2 b f Bertolini(USA) —Cribella (USA) (Robellino (USA))
4207^{15} 4492^{5} 4897^{10}

Hotchpotch (USA) *J R Best* a62 61
3 b g Dayjur(USA) —Anagram (USA) (Farma Way (USA))
3257^{8} (4293) 4524^{5} 4548^{5}5232^{2} 5418^{5} 6442^{3}6632^{5} 6714^{9}6864^{4} (6983)

Hotel Du Cap *G Wragg* a98+ 91
3 br c Grand Lodge(USA) —Miss Riviera Golf (Hernando (FR))
5086^{2} (5429) 6062a^{6}

Hot Fudge (SWE) *L Reuterskiold*
3 ch f Lomitas—Christian Church (IRE) (Linamix (FR))
2564a^{7}

Hotham *N Wilson* a68 73
3 b g Komaite(USA) —Malcesine (IRE) (Auction Ring (USA))
2297^{8} 3042^{10} (3285) 3759^{4} 4262^{3} 4636^{7}5250^{3} 5605^{5}6159^{7}

Hot Shot Hamish (IRE) *B J Meehan* a27 36
2 b c Desert Prince(IRE) —Barbuda (Rainbow Quest (USA))
5918^{15} 6188^{14}

House Arrest *A J McCabe* a47 46
2 ch f Auction House(USA) —Mentro (IRE) (Entrepreneur)
2166^{11} 2552^{6} 2857^{3}3054^{2} 3228^{2} 3613^{2}4222^{2} 4493^{2} 4921^{3} 5282^{5} 5835^{5}6032^{9} 6845^{3}

House Maiden (IRE) *D M Simcock* a61 66+
2 b f Rudimentary(USA) —Dahoar (Charnwood Forest (IRE))
5231^{4} 6031^{3}

House Martin *C R Dore* a42 60
4 bb m Spectrum(IRE) —Guignol (IRE) (Anita's Prince)
84^{4} 242^{7}471^{8} 586^{8}1394^{10} 2181^{2} 3941^{4}6279^{12}

Hout Bay *D W Chapman* a46 49
9 ch g Komaite(USA) —Maiden Pool (Sharpen Up)
3988^{9} 4157^{4} 4401^{15} 4571^{10} 4834^{9}5631^{10} 5684^{11} 5865^{13} 6276^{5}6465^{8} 6548^{5}6638^{5} 6892^{10}

Hovering (IRE) *J S Bolger* 96
3 ch f In The Wings—Orlena (USA) (Gone West (USA))
2689a^{4}

Hovman (DEN) *Ms C Erichsen* a95 91
7 ch g Kateb(IRE) —Skee The Feen (Viking (USA))
1659a^{6}

Howard Le Canard (FR) *F Rohaut* a108 100
5 b g Hamas(IRE) —No Exit (FR) (Exit To Nowhere (USA))
(393a)

Howards Call *W G Harrison* a12
3 b g Easycall—Bouchra (IRE) (Inchinor)
6539^{8}

Howards Dream (IRE) *D A Nolan* 8
8 b g King's Theatre(IRE) —Keiko (Generous (IRE))
1883^{10} 5360^{7}

Howards Prince *I Semple* a6 74
3 gr g Bertolini(USA) —Grey Princess (IRE) (Common Grounds)
1036^{6} 1453^{5} 2855^{4} 3479^{4} 4056^{4}4523^{12} 5250^{11}

Howards Princess *J Hetherton* a61 59
4 gr m Lujain(USA) —Grey Princess (IRE) (Common Grounds)
1865^{5} 2749^{3} 3166^{2} 3354^{8} 3673^{2}4135^{8} 5620^{14} (5970) 6162^{5}6477^{7} 6538^{2}6719^{11} 6922^{12}

Howards Rocket *J S Goldie* a32 46
5 ch g Opening Verse(USA) —Houston Heiress (USA) (Houston (USA))
6482^{6}

Howards Tipple *I Semple* a59 70
2 b c Diktat—Grey Princess (IRE) (Common Grounds)
1632^{6} 2159^{3} 2745^{3} 4452^{3} 5860^{9}6257^{6} 6414^{7}

Howick Falls (USA) *E Charpy* a100 110
5 bb h Stormin Fever(USA) —Hollins (USA) (Roanoke (USA))
431a^{11} 563a^{3} 740a^{13}

Howle Hill (IRE) *A King* a111 105
6 b g Ali-Royal(IRE) —Grandeur And Grace (USA) (Septieme Ciel (USA))
116^{9}

How's She Cuttin' (IRE) *T D Barron* a50+ 69
3 ch f Shinko Forest(IRE) —Magic Annemarie (IRE) (Dancing Dissident (USA))
3916^{4} 4155^{8} (4611) 5631^{2}(5834) 5864^{2} (6315)

Hows That *K R Burke* a52 51
4 ch m Vettori(IRE) —Royalty (IRE) (Fairy King (USA))
11^{4} 95^{14}261^{12} 1387^{9}2248^{8} 2758^{3} 4266^{8}(4881) 5840^{4} 6213^{9}

Howya Now Kid (IRE) *G M Lyons* 94
2 b c Daggers Drawn(USA) —Lear's Crown (USA) (Lear Fan (USA))
2686a^{3} 4824a^{5}

Hoy Soy Usted (BRZ) *C Morgado* a50
5 b h Music Prospector(USA) —Touch Girl (BRZ) (Restless Jet (USA))
204a^{12} 434a^{14}

Hucking Heat (IRE) *J R Best* a25 63
2 b g Desert Sun—Vltava (IRE) (Sri Pekan (USA))
3407^{8} 3872^{8} 4292^{4}

Hucking Hill (IRE) *J R Best* a76 59
2 ch g City On A Hill(USA) —Con Dancer (Shareef Dancer (USA))
707^{4} 912^{2}1053^{2} (1107) 1405^{4}1582^{6} 2127^{10} 3530^{6}3727^{3} 4246^{6} 5606^{9}6074^{10} 6291^{6}6388^{3} (6488) (6592) 6881^{4}

Hucking Hope (IRE) *J R Best* a69 57
2 b f Desert Style(IRE) —Amarapura (FR) (Common Grounds)
1295^{4} (2791) 3120^{7} 4043^{4}4699^{2} 5668^{7}6056^{4} 6400^{4}

Hucking Hot *J R Best* a52+ 82
2 b f Desert Prince(IRE) —True Love (Robellino (USA))
1223^{2} 1429^{6} 2125^{3}(2943)

Hucklebuck (IRE) *T J O'Mara* 75
3 ch c City On A Hill(USA) —Shalstayholy (IRE) (Shalford (IRE))
4034a^{9}

Hue *B Ellison* a65 76
5 ch g Peintre Celebre(USA) —Quandary (USA) (Blushing Groom (FR))
503^{5} 597^{5}976^{9} 1685^{2} (1931)

Huggle *P S McEntee* a41 62
3 b g Groom Dancer(USA) —Perle De Sagesse (Namaqualand (USA))
3906^{9} 6037^{10} 6272^{11}

Hugs Destiny (IRE) *M A Barnes* a56 59
5 b g Victory Note(USA) —Embracing (Reference Point)
1233^{5} 1415^{8} 1562^{5} 3291^{4} (3836) 4072^{3}4380^{7} 4723^{3} 4954^{5} 5369^{11}

Hugs 'n Kisses (IRE) *John Joseph Murphy* 57
2 ch f Noverre(USA) —La Dolores (GER) (Surumu (GER))
6113a^{6} 6357a^{11}

Hula Ballew *M Dods* 85+
6 ch m Weldnaas(USA) —Ballon (Persian Bold)
864^{7} 1124^{3} (1422) 1636^{3} (2299) (2735) 2851^{5}2974^{3} 3289^{4} 3812^{3} 4153^{3} 4653^{4}5024^{4} 5337^{3}

Humble Gift *Mrs L J Mongan* a56
3 ch f Cadeaux Genereux—West Humble (Pharly (FR))
2343^{8}

Humble Opinion *B J Meehan* a75 93
4 br g Singspiel(IRE) —For More (FR) (Sanglamore (USA))
1357^{8} 2200^{8} (2440) 3313^{8} 3737^{3} 4023^{8}

Humility *C A Cyzer* a65 46
5 b m Polar Falcon(USA) —Rich In Love (IRE) (Alzao (USA))
520^{10} 681^{6}(917) 1245^{8}1961^{4} 2348^{6}2574^{3} 3014^{10}3536^{7} 5046^{3}6193^{5} 6439^{3}6747^{9}

Humungous (IRE) *C R Egerton* a96+ 100
3 ch g Giant's Causeway(USA) —Doula (USA) (Gone West (USA))
665^{11} 3091^{3} 3681^{2}4082^{5} 5165^{2} 5374^{11}

Hunaudieres (FR) *Mlle C Cardenne* a78 76
5 b m Take Risks(FR) —Pleasant Bird (USA) (Pampabird)
5562a^{4}

Hunters' Glen (USA) *Saeed Bin Suroor* a99 98
3 b c Bahri(USA) —Hedera (USA) (Woodman (USA))
4117^{2} (4471) 4936^{3} 5813^{4}

Hunting Call *K A Ryan* a54 69
2 b c Foxhound(USA) —Margaret's Gift (Beveled (USA))
1595^{13} 4566^{12} 4895^{4} 5614^{3} 5959^{7}6208^{6} 6401^{9} 6491^{3}

Hunting Haze *Miss S E Hall* 68
3 b g Foxhound(USA) —Second Affair (IRE) (Pursuit Of Love)
2243^{8} 2781^{4} 3359^{3} 3790^{4} 4884^{10}

Hunting Lodge (IRE) *H J Manners* a73 92
5 ch g Grand Lodge(USA) —Vijaya (USA) (Lear Fan (USA))
3203^{12}

Hunting Party (IRE) *B W Hills* a71 74
3 ch c Grand Lodge(USA) —Delilah (IRE) (Bluebird (USA))
952^{3} 1421^{10} 2712^{4}2825^{6} 3419^{10}

Hunting Tower *R Hannon* 80
2 b c Sadler's Wells(USA) —Fictitious (Machiavellian (USA))
2287^{3} 4781^{3} (6066)

Hurlingham *M Johnston* 77
2 b c Halling(USA) —Society (IRE) (Barathea (IRE))
2899^{3} 3253^{2} 5883^{4}

Hurricane Cat (USA) *A P O'Brien* 110
3 b c Storm Cat(USA) —Sky Beauty (USA) (Blushing Groom (FR))
1362a^{3} 2039a^{7} 2278a^{15} 3559a^{5} 5708a^{3}

Hurricane Coast *Ms J S Doyle* a68 75
7 b g Hurricane Sky(AUS) —Tread Carefully (Sharpo)
50^{4} 100^{7}159^{5} (251) 452^{5} 641^{8}1188^{10} 2098^{3} 2259^{5} 2831^{4} 3337^{10}6259^{6} 6413^{12}6652^{11} 6781^{6}

Hurricane Dennis *D K Ivory*
2 ch g Silver Wizard(USA) —Thatcher's Era (IRE) (Never So Bold)
2178^{15} 2588^{13}

Hurricane Flyer *E J O'Neill* 74
2 b c Royal Applause—Cyclone Flyer (College Chapel)
4151^{2} 4630^{2} 5766^{2}

Hurricane James (IRE) *E Charpy* 105
4 bb h Night Shift(USA) —Ginger Candy (USA) (Hilal (IRE))
278a^{8}

Hurricane Mist (IRE) *P Bary* a66 91
3 ch f Spinning World(USA) —Mare Nostrum (Caerleon (USA))
1330a^{6}

Hurricane Run (IRE) *A Fabre* 134+
4 b h Montjeu(IRE) —Hold On (GER) (Surumu (GER))
(2053a) 2914a^{2} (3927) 5219a^{2} 5716a^{3} 5964^{3}6344a^{6}

Hurricane Spirit (IRE) *J R Best* a101+ 68
2 b c Invincible Spirit(IRE) —Gale Warning (IRE) (Last Tycoon)
2623^{6} (6409) (6631) (6659) (6881)

Hurricane Thomas (IRE) *M Johnston* a75 73
2 b g Celtic Swing—Viola Royale (IRE) (Royal Academy (USA))
5640^{7} 6050^{3} 6143^{2}6318^{4}

Hurry Up Helen (IRE) *Mrs L Stubbs* 69
3 b f In The Wings—Imitation (Darshaan)
1283^{7} 2082^{7} 2379^{5} 2607^{12} 3823^{3}4132^{2} 4697^{2} (4847) 5166^{4} (5452) (5574) 5868^{11}

Huw The News *S C Burrough*
7 b g Primo Dominie—Martha Stevens (USA) (Super Concorde (USA))
3194^{14}

Huxley (IRE) *D J Wintle* a42 52
7 b g Danehill Dancer(IRE) —Biddy Mulligan (Ballad Rock)
127^{10} 638^{13}792^{11} 1353^{6} 5838^{4}6552^{13} 6854^{8}

Hyde Park Flight (IRE) *John A Quinn* a67
2 b c Tendulkar(USA) —Quaver (USA) (The Minstrel (CAN))
6651^{5} 6809^{6}6976^{8}

Hyperalert (USA) *M Johnston* 83+
3 ch c Rahy(USA) —Annaba (IRE) (In The Wings)
2829^{2} 3225^{3}

Hypnosis *D W Barker* 77
3 b f Mind Games—Salacious (Sallust)
1344^{14} 1453^{4} 1793^{3} 2016^{2} (2197) 2285^{2}2925^{2} 3042^{2} 3636^{3} 3832^{2} 5309^{3}5684^{2}

Hypnotic *D Nicholls* a71 87
4 ch g Lomitas—Hypnotize (Machiavellian (USA))
1043^{9} 1380^{10} 2299^{11}3147^{8} 3523^{5} 4101^{23} (4456) 4733^{7} (5313) 5554^{5}

Hypocrisy *D Carroll* a85+ 79
3 b f Bertolini(USA) —Glensara (Petoski)
(165) (601) 725^{4} 2049^{4} 2609^{3}3841^{7} 4328^{7} 6773^{3}

Hypoteneuse (IRE) *Sir Michael Stoute* 70
2 b f Sadler's Wells(USA) —Phantom Gold (Machiavellian (USA))
6215^{7}

Hythe Bay *R T Phillips* a79 80d
2 b f Auction House(USA) —Ellway Queen (USA) (Bahri (USA))
1429^{4} 1959^{3} (2234) 2743^{14}3530^{4} 4344^{9} 5041^{11}5909^{7}

Iamback *Miss D A McHale* a53 49
6 b m Perugino(USA) —Smouldering (IRE) (Caerleon (USA))
780^{3} 891^{13} 973^{4}1392^{6} 1540^{6}1766^{3} 2133^{11} 2790^{3}3013^{2} 3260^{3}3803^{11} 4011^{7} 4423^{7} 4929^{3}5324^{11} 6279^{2} 6474^{10}6553^{4} 6657^{6}6795^{9}

Iamtheone (IRE) *Bob Jones* 16
2 b g Soviet Star(USA) —Just Aloof (IRE) (Entrepreneur)
5417^{12} 6145^{10}

Ianina (IRE) *R Rohne* 92
6 b m Eagle Eyed(USA) —Ice Dream (GER) (Mondrian (GER))
(456a) 655a^{6}

Iannis (IRE) *J Noseda* a71 76
3 b c Danehill Dancer(IRE) —Suave Lady (FR) (Suave Dancer (USA))
5761^{9} 5988^{3} (6144)

Iberian Light (USA) *N A Callaghan* a53 63
3 b g Fantastic Light(USA) —Spain Lane (USA) (Seeking The Gold (USA))
16^{7} 291^{8}372^{9} 558^{7}1314^{2} 1634^{3} 2466^{7}2569^{2} 2713^{3} 3017^{9}3163^{3}

Iberus (GER) *S Gollings* a65 61
8 b g Monsun(GER) —Iberica (GER) (Green Dancer (USA))
157^{3} 187^{9}405^{8} 3141^{5}

Ibn Shaqraan (KSA) *I Jory* 77
6 ch h Another Review(USA) —Sparkly Girl (IRE) (Danehill (USA))
207a^{12}

Ibris (GER) *U Ostmann* 85
2 b c Big Shuffle(USA) —Innella (GER) (Lando (GER))
6092a[3]

Icannshift (IRE) *T M Jones* a44 74
6 b g Night Shift(USA) —Cannikin (IRE) (Lahib (USA))
471[10] 973[6] 1313[7]1541[3] 2132[3] 2262[7](2497) 3035[2] 3163[4] 3616[5] 4687[2] 5072[12]5451[16]

Icaros (SWE) *Wido Neuroth*
3 b c Zafonic(USA) —Impetuous Air (Warning)
(4419a) (4919a)

Ice And Fire *J T Stimpson* a61 69
7 b g Cadeaux Genereux—Tanz (IRE) (Sadler's Wells (USA))
91[3] 147[6]182[5] 346[6](767) 825[8]938[4] 1199[4]1392[5] 1766[4]2790[4] (3919) 4438[9] (6305) 6509[6] 6685[3]

Ice Box (IRE) *M Johnston* a56+ 67
2 ch f Pivotal—Thaisy (USA) (Tabasco Cat (USA))
5332[7] 5679[7] 6055[4] 6940[4]

Icecap *W G M Turner* a62 65
6 b m Polar Falcon(USA) —Warning Light (High Top)
882[8] 1194[8] 1394[11]1755[9] 1914[5] 2293[4]2567[6] 2729[5]

Ice Chariot (AUS) *R Maund* 114
4 b g Semipalatinsk(USA) —Snow Chariot (AUS) (Chariot (AUS))
6110a[15] 6346a[14] 6392a[22]

Iced Diamond (IRE) *W M Brisbourne* a66 63
7 b g Petardia—Prime Site (IRE) (Burslem)
227[2] 315[2]520[12] 581[7]693[3] 1057[13] (1273) 2135[4] 2211[4] (2567) 2811[4]2936[6] 3523[3] 3817[7]4116[10] 4456[5]

Iced Tango *F Jordan* a30 45
2 ro g Verglas(IRE) —Tangolania (FR) (Ashkalani (IRE))
2530[14] 3407[7] 4049[8]

Icelandic *Frank Sheridan* 104
4 b h Selkirk(USA) —Icicle (Polar Falcon (USA))
5982a[6] 6364a[9]

Iceman *J H M Gosden* 117
4 b h Polar Falcon(USA) —Virtuous (Exit To Nowhere (USA))
2358[4] 5341[7] 5673[8]

Iceman George *D Morris* 45
2 b g Beat Hollow—Diebiedale (Dominion)
6220[18]

Ice Mountain *B Smart* 90
2 br g Kyllachy—Sulitelma (USA) (The Minstrel (CAN))
2973[8] 3286[2] (3605) 3734[15] 4152[12] 5442[2]5681[21]

Iceni Princess *P Howling* a36
2 b f Victory Note(USA) —Swing Job (Ezzoud (IRE))
6879[9]

Iceni Warrior *P Howling* a46 23
4 b g Lake Coniston(IRE) —Swing Job (Ezzoud (IRE))
900[7] 1225[3]1462[8] 6701[4]6804[5] 6852[4]

Ice Planet *D Nicholls* 98
5 b g Polar Falcon(USA) —Preference (Efisio)
1183[4] 1487[2] 1835[5] 3077[3] 3374[5]3956[2] 4202[4] 4609[3] 5355[6]

Ice Princess (IRE) *David Wachman* 88
3 b f Grand Lodge(USA) —Ghana (IRE) (Lahib (USA))
2840a[6] 3660a[5] 4212a[P] (Dead)

Icy Atlantic (USA) *T Pletcher* 110
5 b h Stormy Atlantic(USA) —Frosty Promise (USA) (Frosty The Snowman (USA))
5821a[7] 6344a[11]

Icy Ridge (IRE) *M Puhich* 109
3 b c Orpen(USA) —Jolly Dale (IRE) (Huntingdale)
5985a[4]

Idarah (USA) *W J Haggas* 95
3 rg c Aljabr(USA) —Fatina (Nashwan (USA))
(1282) 2046[2] 2805[19] 3292[7] 4125[7] 4612[7]6051[3]

Idealist (GER) *P Schiergen* 109
4 b h Tiger Hill(IRE) —I Go Bye (GER) (Don't Forget Me)
(1869a) 6248a[4]

Idealistic (IRE) *L M Cumani* a55 100
5 b m Unfuwain(USA) —L'Ideale (USA) (Alysheba (USA))
1511[5] 2706[5] 4179[4] 4590[8] 5170[5]5803[13] 6191[11]

Ideally (IRE) *B W Hills* a74 70
2 ch g Mark Of Esteem(IRE) —Ideal Lady (IRE) (Seattle Slew (USA))
5020[4] 5340 [4]

Idle Power (IRE) *J R Boyle* a91 100
8 b g Common Grounds—Idle Fancy (Mujtahid (USA))
718[5] (970) 1246[2] 1487[9]1939[4] 2047[2] 2230[4]3092[8] 3211[2] 3486[5] 4101[2] (4430) 4796[7]5807[9] 6292[8]

Ifatfirst (IRE) *M P Tregoning* a61
3 b g Grand Lodge(USA) —Gaily Grecian (IRE) (Ela-Mana-Mou)
5611[10] 5847[7]5986[9] 6479[6]6700[6] (6911)

Iffraaj *Saeed Bin Suroor* 125+
5 b h Zafonic(USA) —Pastorale (Nureyev (USA))
2846[7] 3494[2] (4025) (5184)

If Paradise *R Hannon* a93 105
5 b h Compton Place—Sunley Stars (Sallust)
627[7] 664[6]989[3] 1116[6] 1663[8] 1936[3] 2021[9]3092[13] 3972[18] 4128[25] 5009[4] 5433[3]5535[2] 5832[10]

Iftikhar (USA) *W M Brisbourne* a61 57
7 b g Storm Cat(USA) —Muhbubh (USA) (Blushing Groom (FR))
72[3]

Ignition *W M Brisbourne* a61 64
4 ch m Rock City—Fire Sprite (Mummy's Game)
1636[7] 2113[4] 2634[6] 3331[8] 6387[6]6667[5] 6819[8]6942[6] 6980[6]

Igor Protti *A Wohler* 95
4 b h Opening Verse(USA) —La Busona (IRE) (Broken Hearted)
2217a[6]

I Have Dreamed (IRE) *T G Mills* a83 94+
4 b g Montjeu(IRE) —Diamond Field (USA) (Mr Prospector (USA))
834[6] 3490[3](3876) 4160[9] 4810[11] 5430[8]

Ihla Grande (USA) *E Charpy* a85 72
5 b h Distant View(USA) —Spectatrice (USA) (Nijinsky (CAN))
435a[9] 511a[11]

Ihuru *J G Portman* a54
4 b g Atraf—E Sharp (USA) (Diesis)
18[4] 484[8]615[4]

Ikat (IRE) *D Sepulchre* 101
2 ch f Pivotal—Burning Sunset (Caerleon (USA))
4415a[3] 5257a[2] 5714a[6] 6046a[6]

Ikra (FR) *X Guigand* 94
3 gr f Simon Du Desert(FR) —Sheer Drop (FR) (Kenmare (FR))
1177a[7]

Iktitaf (IRE) *Noel Meade* 88
5 b g Alhaarth(IRE) —Istibshar (USA) (Mr Prospector (USA))
(5853a)

Il Cadetto *L Di Dio* 105
2 b c Zieten(USA) —Nirvana (USA) (Green Dancer (USA))
(6123a)

Il Castagno (IRE) *B Smart* a42 78
3 ch g Night Shift(USA) —Cartesian (Shirley Heights)
1004[11] 1444[2] 1596[5]2297[3] 3067[8] 3395[5]

Il Divo *C Grant*
3 b g Tipsy Creek(USA) —Be My Hattie (Be My Chief (USA))
1731[10]

Ile Michel *Lady Herries* a70 80
9 b g Machiavellian(USA) —Circe's Isle (Be My Guest (USA))
854[9] 2966[7] 6693[10]

I'll Do It Today *J M Jefferson* a62 60
5 b g Mtoto—Knayton Lass (Presidium)
168[4] 318[3]570[6] (825) 3983[6] 4522[7] 5390[5]

Illie Nastase (FR) *R Gibson* 96
2 b c Royal Applause—Flying Diva (Chief Singer)
4859a[5]

Illuminise (IRE) *E A L Dunlop* 89
3 ch f Grand Lodge(USA) —Brief Escapade (IRE) (Brief Truce (USA))
(1085) 1990[5] 2744[6] 3316[6] 4097[6]

Illustrious Blue *W J Knight* a82 109
3 bb c Dansili—Gipsy Moth (Efisio)
(1476) 1954[3] 2344[3] 2754[5](3224) (4029) 4739[6] (4798) (5177) 5675[9] 5808[2]

Il Palio (IRE) *B R Millman* a85 85
2 b c Invincible Spirit(IRE) —Abundance (Cadeaux Genereux)
(760) 1066[7] 1354[5] (1876) 2300[7] (3409) 4043[7](4893)

Ilza *Eamon Tyrrell* a60 53
3 b f Zilzal(USA) —Chimere (FR) (Soviet Lad (USA))
6526[3] 6693[6]6964[12]

I'm A Numbers Guy (USA) *T F Ritchey* a80
2 ch c City Zip(USA) —Midway Gal (USA) (Midway Circle (USA))
5983a[7]

I'm In Love (USA) *M A Magnusson* a83 80
3 bb f Zafonic(USA) —Bank On Her (USA) (Rahy (USA))
1068[9] 2359[10] 3973[9] 4577[8] 4837[3](5096) 5345[9] 6094[9]

Immaculate Red *R Bastiman* a58 47
3 ch g Woodborough(USA) —Primula Bairn (Bairn (USA))
988[6] 1279[6] 1825[8] 2896[15] 3381[3]3749[8] 4306[8] 4690[8] 5929[11]

Imonso (GER) *P Schiergen* 106
3 br c Monsun(GER) —I Go Bye (GER) (Don't Forget Me)
(2314a) 3131a[4] 3776a[13]

Im Ova Ere Dad (IRE) *D E Cantillon* a67 53
3 b g Second Empire(IRE) —Eurolink Profile (Prince Sabo)
2383[9] 2763[6] 3090[8] (3999) 4255[7] 6531[4]6819[5]

Impartial *S J Mahon* a71 82
5 b h Polish Precedent(USA) —Always Friendly (High Line)
4121a[5]

Impeccable Guest (IRE) *P C Haslam* a51 59
3 b f Orpen(USA) —Perfect Guest (What A Guest)
604[6] 1859[4] 2082[3]2246[F] 5581[6] 5960[3]6551[2]

Impeller (IRE) *W R Muir* a102 103
7 ch g Polish Precedent(USA) —Almaaseh (IRE) (Dancing Brave (USA))
452[3] 629[5]666[10] 1239[2] 1484[10]2201[9] 2742[16] 2989[5] (3432) 3552[15] 3929[4]4023[14] (5045) 5204[5] 5477[6]

Imperia (GER) *W Hickst* 95
3 b f Tertullian(USA) —Iberi (GER) (Rainbow Quest (USA))
2059a[4] 2912a[7]

Imperial Beach (USA) *T D Barron* 62
2 b g Coronado's Quest(USA) —Millie's Trick (USA) (Phone Trick (USA))
2623[9] 3018[8]

Imperial Dragon (USA) *W A O'Gorman* a14 28
6 b g Meadowlake(USA) —South Cove (Forli (ARG))
482[14]

Imperial Echo (USA) *T D Barron* 91
5 b g Labeeb—Regal Baby (USA) (Northern Baby (CAN))
1597[11] 2454[2] (2681) (3079) 3493[7] 3937[6] 4172[14]4593[9]

Imperial Gain (USA) *W R Swinburn* a71 81
3 ch g High Yield(USA) —Empress Jackie (USA) (Mount Hagen (FR))
1411[4] 2353[6] 2896[3]3304[2] 3644[5] (3932) 4143[6]4923[7] 5268[3] 5896[13]

Imperial Glory *Mrs P Townsley*
5 b g Imperial Ballet(IRE) —Sally Gardens (Alzao (USA))
6694[10] 6774[8]

Imperial Harry *M R Channon* a71 71
3 b c Alhaarth(IRE) —Serpentara (Kris)
2343[4] 2919[3] 3546[4]3826[4] 4254[6] 6432[10]

Imperial Ice (SAF) *R Simpson* a86 83
4 ch m Western Winter(USA) —Imperial Conquest (SAF) (Royal Chalice (SAF))
155a[10] 202a[7] 351a[4]436a[2] (623a) 5550[10]

Imperialistic (IRE) *K R Burke* a43 98
5 b m Imperial Ballet(IRE) —Shefoog (Kefaah (USA))
412[9] 1806[10] (2017) (2071) 2364[4]2503[3] 2851[4] 3002[3]

Imperial Lucky (IRE) *D K Ivory* a77 64
3 b f Desert Story(IRE) —Irina (IRE) (Polar Falcon (USA))
1551[2] 2400[10] 2589[4]2921[2] 3055[4] 3472[11]6413[3] 6573[3]6664[2] 6781[9]

Imperial Rocket (USA) *W K Goldsworthy* 65
9 bb g Northern Flagship(USA) —Starsawhirl (USA) (Star De Naskra (USA))
2966[14]

Imperial Rose (IRE) *H Rogers* 98?
4 gr m Imperial Ballet(IRE) —Mixwayda (FR) (Linamix (FR))
932a[7] 1026a[10] 1324a[5] 5396a[13]

Imperial Rule (IRE) *W J Knight* a63 75
4 b g Second Empire(IRE) —Alikhlas (Lahib (USA))
737[6]

Imperial Star (IRE) *J H M Gosden* 103+
3 br c Fantastic Light(USA) —Out West (USA) (Gone West (USA))
2034[5] (2712) (3119) 3681[5]

Imperial Stride *Saeed Bin Suroor* 128
5 b h Indian Ridge—Place De L'Opera (Sadler's Wells (USA))
(5477) 6347a[8]

Imperial Style (IRE) *D Shaw* 25
2 b g Imperial Ballet(IRE) —Marinka (Pivotal)
3596[11] 3787[8] 3994[12]6472[9] 6653[12]

Imperial Sword *T D Barron* 94
3 b g Danehill Dancer(IRE) —Hajat (Mujtahid (USA))
1036[2] 1497[4] (1812) 1986[2] 2385[2] 2658[8]3761[10] 4707[7]

Imperioli *P A Blockley* 39
4 b g Fraam—Jussoli (Don)
2548[9]

Imperium *Jean-Rene Auvray* a66 56
5 b g Imperial Ballet(IRE) —Partenza (USA) (Red Ransom (USA))
81[2] 408[5]428[9] 486[10](602) 732[6]821[7] 1054[4] 1310[4]1752[8] 2136[7] 2288[11] (2571) 2955[2] 4675[3](6234) 6442[2](6632) 6827[2]

Impero *G F Bridgwater* 5
8 b g Emperor Jones(USA) —Fight Right (FR) (Crystal Glitters (USA))
857[10]

Impetious *Eamon Tyrrell* 100
2 b f Inchinor—Kauri (USA) (Woodman (USA))
5394a[3] 5714a[8] 5966[9]

Implicita (IRE) *B Grizzetti* 72
3 b f Marju(IRE) —Is Buena (Sri Pekan (USA))
6251a[11]

Impostor (IRE) *J R Fanshawe* a52 77
3 b g In The Wings—Princess Caraboo (IRE) (Alzao (USA))
948[5] 1290[4] 1975[5] 4537[5] 5069[6]5628[7]

Impress *M Johnston*
3 ch g Fantastic Light(USA) —Kissogram (Caerleon (USA))
909[6]

Impressionnante *C Laffon-Parias* 114
3 b f Danehill(USA) —Occupandiste (IRE) (Kaldoun (FR))
1719a[2] (2275a) 3342a[6] 3991a[2] 5701a[8]

Imprimis Tagula (IRE) *A Bailey* a61 57
2 b c Tagula(IRE) —Strelitzia (IRE) (Bluebird (USA))
2439[8] 2517[6] 3521[5] 6736[4]6764[2]

Impromptu *R M Beckett* a46 80
2 b c Mujadil(USA) —Pie In The Sky (Bishop Of Cashel)
2315[2] 3110[2] 3994[5]4774[4] 5509[2]

Impulsive Madam *S Kirk* a36 28
3 b f Diktat—Decorous (IRE) (Runnett)
5625[11] 6616[10]

I'm Right (USA) *M P Tregoning* a79
2 b f Rahy(USA) —Sheer Reason (USA) (Danzig (USA))
(5095) 5783[5] 6412[2]

I'm So Lucky *M Johnston* 107
4 b g Zilzal(USA) —City Of Angels (Woodman (USA))
1484[5] 1815[5] (2803) 3552[18] 4023[11] 4359[11]4739[9] 5177[11]

Im Spartacus *D W Barker* a62 81
4 b g Namaqualand(USA) —Captivating (IRE) (Wolfhound (USA))
2453[6] 2872[5] 3980[9] 4711[12] 5137[4]5511[14]

Imtalkinggibberish *V Smith* a39 57
5 b g Pursuit Of Love—Royal Orchid (IRE) (Shalford (IRE))
608[14] 693[8]903[5] 1245[9]2317[14] 3683[9] 6372[9]

In A Fit *P Howling* a40
5 b m Intikhab(USA) —Millfit (USA) (Blushing Groom (FR))
84[5] 387[7]399[P] (Dead)

Inaminute (IRE) *K R Burke* a76 80
3 ch f Spectrum(IRE) —Phantom Ring (Magic Ring (IRE))
99[5] (197) 241[2](286) 430[5]488[8] (1149) 1549[4] (2050) (2699) 3099[5]3841[2] (4305) 4837[10] 6094[10]6221[4]

Inasus (GER) *M Johnston* 51
2 ch c Kornado—Instinctive Dancer (USA) (Spend A Buck (USA))
4466[4]

Inca Soldier (FR) *R C Guest* a63+ 44
3 br g Intikhab(USA) —Chrysalu (Distant Relative)
645[12] 1529[5] 2109[9]2898[7]

Inch By Inch *P J Makin* a78 80
7 b m Inchinor—Maid Welcome (Mummy's Pet)
2635[4] 3212[5] 3612[4] (4364) 4449[8] 5096[12]6478[3] 6579[11]6999[6]

Inchdhuaig (IRE) *P C Haslam* a53 59
3 ch g Inchinor—Be Thankfull (IRE) (Linamix (FR))
1593[5] 2128[8] 2746[7] 3167[7] 3538[5]5240[3]

Inchdura *N Tinkler* a47 46
8 ch g Inchinor—Sunshine Coast (Posse (USA))
3[7]

Inch Forward *D W Barker* 23
2 b f Inchinor—Lets Be Fair (Efisio)
1295[9] 2015[7] 2294[9]

Inch High *J S Goldie* a50 57
8 ch g Inchinor—Harrken Heights (IRE) (Belmez (USA))
1500[6] (1947) 2165[3] 2811[5] 3333[3] 3583[3]3784[5] 4355[6] 4652[8] 5579[11] 5838[10]

Inchigeelagh (IRE) *H Morrison* a53 52
2 ch f Inchinor—Thank One's Stars (Alzao (USA))
4049[6] 4993[8] 5347[6]

Inchinata (IRE) *B W Hills* 52
2 b f Inchinor—Caviare (Cadeaux Genereux)
6215[17]

Inchinora *M Ciciarelli*
2 b f Inchinor—Maestrale (Top Ville)
5705a[10]

Inchlaggan (IRE) *B W Hills* 59
2 ch c Inchinor—Lakatoi (Saddlers' Hall (IRE))
5659[7] 5918[6]

Inchloch *B G Powell* 91
4 ch g Inchinor—Lake Pleasant (IRE) (Elegant Air)
(2169) 3214[4] (3737) 4676[6] 5505[9] 6107[13]

Inch Lodge *Miss D Mountain* a85 72
4 ch h Grand Lodge(USA) —Legaya (Shirley Heights)
1993[12] 2351[2] 2647[4]3230[5] 3413[17] (5691) 6070[7](6426) 6673[5](6811)

Inchloss (IRE) *C N Kellett* a38 54
5 b g Imperial Ballet(IRE) —Earth Charter (Slip Anchor)
1257[6] 1425[13] 2137[13]3326[10]

Inchmahome *G Wragg* 62
3 b f Galileo(IRE) —Inchmurrin (Lomond (USA))
1418[6] 2034[6]

Inchmarlow (IRE) *T H Caldwell* a41 51
3 b g Cape Cross(IRE) —Glenstal Priory (Glenstal (USA))
1483[9] 2284[5] 2504[9] 3698[5] 5770[13]5924[9] 6480[10]

Inchnacardoch (IRE) *A King* 67
2 b c Marju(IRE) —Inchoate (Machiavellian (USA))
5537[5] 6023[3]

Inchnadamph *T J Fitzgerald* a50 92
6 b g Inchinor—Pelf (USA) (Al Nasr (FR))
1071[11] 3533[12] 4883[7]5963[2]

Incidentally (IRE) *R Hannon* 84
3 ch c Inchinor—Top Sauce (Hector Protector (USA))
1134[3] 1680[2] 1934[2] (2605) 3318[5] 3889[14]4838[10] 5346[11] 5625[3] 5944[2]

Incline (IRE) *R McGlinchey* a76 82+
7 b g Danehill(USA) —Shalwar Kameez (IRE) (Sadler's Wells (USA))
4186a[2]

In Clover *F Head* 110
4 b m Inchinor—Bellarida (FR) (Bellypha)
1398a[4] 2092a[5] 3991a[4] 4646a[4] 6454a[2]

Incony *W R Swinburn* a59 50
2 b f Daggers Drawn(USA) —Illustre Inconnue (USA) (Septieme Ciel (USA))
5867[7] 6222[4] 6481[7]

Incursion *D Nicholls* 84
5 b g Inchinor—Morgannwg (IRE) (Simply Great (FR))
1439[3] 1502[11] 1887[5] 2365[2] 2723[2]3177[5] 4231[3] 4626[2] 4876[2] (5080) 5338[P] (Dead)

Indebted *P W D'Arcy* a82 34
4 b m Royal Applause—Briggsmaid (Elegant Air)
101[13] 252[13]

Indesatchel (IRE) *David Wachman* 119
4 b h Danehill Dancer(IRE) —Floria (IRE) (Petorius)
930a[4] 1171a[6] 5049a[8]

Indian Ballet *M A Jarvis* a63 56
3 ch f Indian Ridge—Bolshaya (Cadeaux Genereux)
2235[5] 3053[4] 3285[6]

Indian Bazaar (IRE) *R A Harris* a45 51
10 ch g Indian Ridge—Bazaar Promise (Native Bazaar)
3863[9] 4223[11]

Indian Chase *Dr J R J Naylor* a54 51
9 b g Terimon—Icy Gunner (Gunner B)
482[13] (614) 635[5]675[5] 966[8] 1339[8]1745[11] 3919[8]4438[13] 5927[8]6797[8] 6857[7]

Indian Dawn (IRE) *T H Caldwell* 50
3 b c Indian Lodge(IRE) —Degree Of Charm (IRE) (Alzao (USA))
4325[10] 4982[16] 5768[12]

Indian Edge *B Palling* a69 79
5 ch g Indian Rocket—Beveled Edge (Beveled (USA))
43[10] 104[5]175[2] 261[9](682) 771[2](1245) (1568) (1773) (1882) 2098[6] 2551[6]3404[12] 5769[10] 5896[2]6176[4] 6259[7] 6507[11]

Indian Fun *F Head* 100
3 b f Poliglote—Follow The Girl (FR) (Saumarez)
773a[5] 1789a[9] 3991a[10]

Indian Gem *A J Chamberlain* a41 41
5 ch m Bijou D'Inde—Cayla (Tumble Wind)
400[8] 768[7]873[8] 951[6]1054[7] 1391[8] 1746[5]2260[4] 2729[6] 3543[12]

Indian Girl *M R Channon* 59
3 b f Erhaab(USA) —Natchez Trace (Commanche Run)
2712[11] 3346[5] 3451[10] 3785[8] 4868[7]5369[6] 6027[9]

Indian Hall (IRE) *U Muntwyler* 49
5 ch g Indian Ridge—Shigeru Summit (Be My Chief (USA))
306a[6]

Indian Ink (IRE) *R Hannon* 111
2 ch f Indian Ridge—Maid Of Killeen (IRE) (Darshaan)
2456[7] (2957) 3925[4] 4737[2] (5503) (5654)

Indian Kate *R Brotherton*
3 b f Komaite(USA) —Indian Nectar (Indian Ridge)
6492[11]

Indian Lady (IRE) *Mrs A L M King* a45 67
3 b f Namid—Lady Eberspacher (IRE) (Royal Abjar (USA))
2190[2] 2652[10] 3004[12] 3349[10] *3846[12]*4365[13] 4690[6] 5131[5] 5576[2] 5756[10]

Indian Maiden (IRE) *M S Saunders* a106 113
6 br m Indian Ridge—Jinsiyah (USA) (Housebuster (USA))
627[3] 885a[2] 1069[16](1377) 1671[6] 1849[2] 2115[6] 2438[6] (3967a) 4174[3]4410a[8] (4633) (4860a) 5171[4] 5393a[4] 5701a[14]5919[3] 6230a[8]

Indian Pride *D J Coakley* 57
4 b m Groom Dancer(USA) —Royal Patron (Royal Academy (USA))
1901[11] 2498[4] 3346[6]

Indian Sabre (IRE) *J Noseda* a81 58
3 ch c Indian Ridge—Kyka (USA) (Blushing John (USA))
2143[9] 2859[7] *(3384) 4703[5]5509[13]*

Indian's Feather (IRE) *N Tinkler* 98?
5 ch m Indian Ridge—Mashmoum (Lycius (USA))
1043[16] 4577[5] 4889[10] 5512[16] 5896[15]

Indianski (IRE) *C Laffon-Parias* 106
3 br c Indian Ridge—Plissetskaia (FR) (Caerleon (USA))
(1944a) 2489a[4]

Indian Sky (IRE) *B R Millman* a54 10
4 b g Indian Lodge(IRE) —Bolero (Rainbow Quest (USA))
4285[10]

Indian Song (IRE) *R F Johnson Houghton* a52+ 67
2 b f Indian Rocket—Canoe Cove (IRE) (Grand Lodge (USA))
2172[9] 2984[4] 3344[4] 3734[19] 3930[4]4460[5] 5052[6] *5208[7]5448[2]*

Indian Spark *J S Goldie* 78
12 ch g Indian Ridge—Annes Gift (Ballymoss)
(1528) 1949[4] 2661[9] 3041[13]

Indian Steppes (FR) *P S McEntee* a95 97
7 b m Indian Ridge—Ukraine Venture (Slip Anchor)
667[4] 1676[4] (2011) 2358[5]2776[11] *3648[2]* 5012[5]5525[6] 5919[13] 6219[13]

Indian Sundance (IRE) *R A Fahey* 37
3 b g Namid—Can't Afford It (IRE) (Glow (USA))
4948[8] 5949[6]

Indian Trail *D Nicholls* a91 111d
6 ch g Indian Ridge—Take Heart (Electric)
830[6] 1086[9] 2230[5]2847[6] (3077) 3295[6] 3926[20] 5182[16] 5812[18]

Indian Wizard (IRE) *P Howling* a69 60
3 b g Indian Ridge—Ragtime Rumble (USA) (Dixieland Band (USA))
(20) 85[8] 197[12]

India Run (IRE) *J L Dunlop* 62
3 b c Hernando(FR) —Sirdhana (Selkirk (USA))
2825[7] 4150[8]

Indication *J H M Gosden* a76 77
3 b f Sadler's Wells(USA) —Insinuate (USA) (Mr Prospector (USA))
4563[2] 4814[2] 5319[11] *(6225) 6411[6]*

Indigo Dancer *C F Wall* a49+ 51
3 b g Groom Dancer(USA) —Violet (IRE) (Mukaddamah (USA))
(1226) 2713[5] *3075[10] 6374[7]6543[4] 6701[7]*

Indigo Nights (IRE) *Mrs A Duffield* 85
3 b f Danehill Dancer(IRE) —Bent Al Fala (IRE) (Green Desert (USA))
1146[3] (Dead)

Indigo Rose (IRE) *J H M Gosden* a65 56
2 b f Cadeaux Genereux—Colourfast (IRE) (Spectrum (IRE))
4373[13] *6071[6]*

Indigo Sky (IRE) *B G Powell* a52 51
5 gr h Adieu Au Roi(IRE) —Urban Sky (FR) (Groom Dancer (USA))
35[10] 867[2]235[4] 310[9]472[3] 888[5]

Indio Sinedo (IRE) *R Feligioni*
2 b c Celtic Swing—Amenity (FR) (Luthier)
2474a[6]

Indonesia *T D Walford* a69 80
4 ch g Lomitas—Idraak (Kris)
1809[14] 2357[3] 2684[3] (4252) 4883[4]

In Dubai (USA) *M P Tregoning* a80 81
3 ch f Giant's Causeway(USA) —Bahr (Generous (IRE))
2174[7] *3489[4]*

Industrial Star (IRE) *Micky Hammond* 72
5 ch g Singspiel(IRE) —Faribole (IRE) (Esprit Du Nord (USA))
1854[5] (2196) 3396[2] 3955[8]

Inescapable (USA) *A W Carroll* a52 54
5 b g Cape Town(USA) —Danyross (IRE) (Danehill (USA))
27[10] 581[10]638[10] 649[9]853[7] (1393) 1538[6] 1914[11]3729[6] 4363[11]

In Fashion *R J Hodges* a44 44
3 b f Bertolini(USA) —Dress Design (IRE) (Brief Truce (USA))
778[7] *936[2]* 1137[4]1623a[2] 1771[10] 2190[8] 2632[15]

Inflagrantedelicto (USA) *D W Chapman* a63
2 ch c Gentlemen(ARG) —Imprudent Love (USA) (Foolish Pleasure (USA))
3385[8] 6284[7]6534[3] 6675[3]6757[3] 6891[4]6948[3]

Inflagranti *J G Portman* a28 69d
2 b f Inchinor—Another Fantasy (IRE) (Danehill (USA))
908[10] 2816[10] (4017) 4427[10]5094[12] 5290[8] 5764[9]

Inflight (IRE) *R M Beckett* a73 72d
2 b f Intikhab(USA) —Red Eagle (IRE) (Eagle Eyed (USA))
1542[9] 2388[4] 2726[2] *3409[2]*3720[5] (4444) *(4699)* 4779[10] 5162[10]6056[13]

In Full Cry *M Johnston* a65 92
3 ch g Grand Lodge(USA) —Red Roses Story (FR) (Pink (FR))
2654[6] 3081[2] 3255[4] 3710[3] 4356[8]5164[8] 5787[9] *6148[9]*

Ingleby Arch (USA) *T D Barron* 100
3 b g Arch(USA) —Inca Dove (USA) (Mr Prospector (USA))
(1091) (1633) 2658[16] 3077[5] 3414[8] 4345[4] 4601[4]5143[7] 5358[23] 5812[8]

Ingleby Flame (IRE) *T D Barron* 55
2 ch g Redback—Boobala (IRE) (General Monash (USA))
3175[4] 3633[3] 4055[3] 4724[6]

Ingleby Hill (IRE) *T D Barron* 43
2 b g Averti(IRE) —Living Daylights (IRE) (Night Shift (USA))
6047[6] 6175[11] 6316[9]

Ingleby Image *T D Barron* 78
2 gr f Averti(IRE) —Miss Mirror (Magic Mirror)
(814) 3734[5] 4152[11] 4727[3] 4910[3] 5334[6]5956[7]

Ingleby Princess *T D Barron* 79
2 br f Bold Edge—Bob's Princess (Bob's Return (IRE))
(1342) (2924) 3496[4] (4134) 5404[2] 5748[6]

Ingleton *G L Moore* a79 80
4 b g Komaite(USA) —Dash Cascade (Absalom)
1545[5] 1820[5] 2173[4] *2555[4](2981)* (Dead)

Ingratitude (IRE) *R M Beckett* 95
3 ch g Inchinor—Merci (IRE) (Cadeaux Genereux)
1048[7] (1547) 1828[2] 3224[11] 5512[3]

Inherit (IRE) *B S Rothwell* a31 56
4 b g Princely Heir(IRE) —Flora Wood (IRE) (Bob Back (USA))
2758[17] 2874[13]

In Hope *D K Ivory* a36 35
3 b f Most Welcome—Frankie Fair (IRE) (Red Sunset)
83[6] 139[4]189[7] 239[5]326[5] 466[4]543[2] 594[4]890[3] 2937[4]5248[10] 5733[6]

Inimical *W S Kittow* a38 56
2 b f Daggers Drawn(USA) —Mara River (Efisio)
3402[8] 5380[9] 5760[5]

Inis Ceithleann (IRE) *Peter Casey* 73d
2 b f Desert Sun—Sylvella (Lear Fan (USA))
4824a[15]

Inka Dancer (IRE) *B Palling* a64 65
4 ch m Intikhab(USA) —Grannys Reluctance (IRE) (Anita's Prince)
1570[3] 2603[3] 3368[2] 4054[6] 4962[7]5078[9] (5350) 5453[2] *6510[3]6556[2] 6672[10]*

Inkjet (IRE) *Ms Deborah J Evans* a40 25
2 b f Beckett(IRE) —Aussie Aisle (IRE) (Godswalk (USA))
2382[5] *2791[7]*

Inmarysfootsteps *N Tinkler*
2 b f Sugarfoot—Mary Jane (Tina's Pet)
1730[10]

Inmom (IRE) *S R Bowring* a29 33
5 b m Barathea(IRE) —Zakuska (Zafonic (USA))
25[9] 616[6]771[9] 6861[11]

Inner Voice (USA) *Sir Michael Stoute* a55
3 gr c Cozzene(USA) —Miss Henderson Co (USA) (Silver Hawk (USA))
2465[6]

Inn For The Dancer *J C Fox* a58 56
4 b g Groom Dancer(USA) —Lady Joyce (FR) (Galetto (FR))
955[10] 1204[11]

Innocent Air *J H M Gosden* 108
3 ch f Galileo(IRE) —Minskip (USA) (The Minstrel (CAN))
1819[5] 3293[5] 4808[4] (5917)

Innpursuit *J M P Eustace* a63 75
4 b g Inchinor—Quest For The Best (Rainbow Quest (USA))
2231[2]

In On The Act (IRE) *Jamie Poulton* a60+ 72
3 b f In The Wings—Mosquera (GER) (Acatenango (GER))
850[7] 1669[9] 2118[14]2349[5] 4029[18] *4395[8]*5235[8] *5992[10]*

Inquisitress *J J Bridger* a69+ 80
2 b f Hernando(FR) —Caribbean Star (Soviet Star (USA))
4148[5] 5083[7] 5679[6] *6074[6]6285[8] (6511) 6653[3] (6670) 6880[3]*

In Return (USA) *A Goldberg* 26
3 ch f Horse Chestnut(SAF) —Bartered Bride (USA) (Shadeed (USA))
5198a[11]

In Rhubarb *P Howling* a46 45
4 ch g Piccolo—Versami (USA) (Riverman (USA))
1947[13] *6795[10] 6907[12]6970[8]*

In Safe Hands (IRE) *Declan Gillespie* 87
2 ch f Intikhab(USA) —Safiya (USA) (Riverman (USA))
5464a[4]

Inscribed (IRE) *G A Huffer* a37
3 b f Fasliyev(USA) —Fay (IRE) (Polish Precedent (USA))
6771[9] 6861[8]

Inside Story (IRE) *G P Kelly* a75 74+
4 b g Rossini(USA) —Sliding (Formidable (USA))
1143[16] 1341[11] 1757[7] 2874[4] *(3159)* (3570)3883[8] 4020[5] 4467[7] (4909) 5311[8] (5435) *6666[3]6748[3]*

Inside Straight (IRE) *R Hannon* a2 52
2 b c Raise A Grand(IRE) —Starisa (IRE) (College Chapel)
2604[8] *5607[12]* 5871[9]

Insignia (IRE) *W M Brisbourne* a52 59
4 b g Royal Applause—Amathea (FR) (Exit To Nowhere (USA))
41[4] 162[11]6232[11] 6543[8]6702[4] 6787[10]6799[4]

In Some Style (IRE) *R A Harris* 44
3 ch f Grand Lodge(USA) —Lovisa (USA) (Gone West (USA))
2063 [12] 2479[14] 2678[11]

Inspainagain (USA) *T D Barron* 59
2 ch c Miswaki(USA) —Counter Cat (USA) (Hennessy (USA))
4196[6] 4956[2]

Inspirina (IRE) *T R George* 74
2 b c Invincible Spirit(IRE) —La Stellina (IRE) (Marju (IRE))
3553[5] 4109[3] 4815[3]

Instinct *Micky Hammond* a52 65
5 b g Zafonic(USA) —Gracious Gift (Cadeaux Genereux)
2550[12] 2700[16] 3334[5] 3781[14] *6723[8]6962[9]*

Instructor *R A Fahey* a89 87
5 ch g Groom Dancer(USA) —Doctor's Glory (USA) (Elmaamul (USA))
867[9] 1043[14] 1281[4] 2162[11] 2627[3]2872[4] 3081[8] (3519) 3840[3] 3890[8] 5810[12]

Insubordinate *J S Goldie* a45 66+
5 ch g Subordination(USA) —Manila Selection (USA) (Manila (USA))
818[2] 1041[5] 1459[3] 1760[12] 1885[5]2384[12] 2546[5] 2808[2] 3333[12] (3484) 3672[5]4137[5] 4476[9] 4692[4] 5311[9] 5579[9]

In Summation (USA) *Christophe Clement* a103 113
3 br c Put It Back(USA) —Fiesta Baby (USA) (Dayjur (USA))
6127a[2]

Intavac Boy *C W Thornton* a61 62
5 ch g Emperor Fountain—Altaia (FR) (Sicyos (USA))
1346[9] 1590[3] 1756[7] 2242[2] 2612[2]2762[2] (3243) 4205[9]

Intavac Girl *C W Thornton* 27
3 b f Sinndar(IRE) —Messila Rose (Darshaan)
1598[14] 1854[9] 3145[16]

Integration *Ronald Thompson* a41
6 b g Piccolo—Discrimination (Efisio)
6302[8] 6971[5]

Intended *A M Balding* a58 64
4 b m Singspiel(IRE) —Introducing (Mtoto)
173[6]

Intensifier (IRE) *P A Blockley*
2 b c Sinndar(IRE) —Licorne (Sadler's Wells (USA))
6757[12]

Interest (USA) *T D Barron* 42
2 ch g Banker's Gold(USA) —Princess Kris (Kris)
4066[8] 4608[7] 5289[7]

Inter Mondo (GER) *P Rau* 105
3 ch c Hondo Mondo(IRE) —In Natura (GER) (Monsun (GER))
4942a[6] 5718a[4] 6109a[13]

Interpatation (USA) *Robert Barbara* 114
4 b g Langfuhr(CAN) —Idealistic Cause (USA) (Habitony)
4908a[3] 5821a[4]

Intersky High (USA) *K A Ryan* 56
4 bb m Royal Anthem(USA) —Worood (USA) (Vaguely Noble)
4204[8] 5319[10]

Intersky Music (USA) *P W Chapple-Hyam* 55+
3 b g Victory Gallop(CAN) —Resounding Grace (USA) (Thunder Gulch (USA))
6019[6]

Intersky Sports (USA) *K A Ryan* a66 65
2 gr g Chester House(USA) —Nightlong (Night Shift (USA))
2139[2] 2523[4] 3018[4]3940[4] *4436[5]* 4882[9]*6569[6] 6736[5](6872)*

Interstice *M J Gingell*
9 b g Never So Bold—Mainmast (Bustino)
25[10]

Inter Vision (USA) *A Dickman* a81 96
6 b g Cryptoclearance(USA) —Fateful (USA) (Topsider (USA))
718[7] 1143[10] 1597[7] 1858[4] 2732[4](4760) 5529[4] 5812[7] 5957[2]

In The Fan (USA) *A Al Raihe* a63 87
4 b g Lear Fan(USA) —Dippers (USA) (Polish Numbers (USA))
367a[7] 435a[6] *563a[12]*

In The Fashion (IRE) *J Noseda* 94
3 b f In The Wings—Tropical Lass (IRE) (Ballad Rock)
1130[9] 2374a[7]

In The Fountain (IRE) *R A Harris* a41
3 b f Mozart(IRE) —Riviere Du Diable (USA) (Irish River (FR))
83[11] 176[10]286[4] 2463[11]

Intiquilla (IRE) *Mrs A J Perrett* 51
2 b f Galileo(IRE) —Orinoco (IRE) (Darshaan)
6050[6] 6297[8]

Into Action *R Hannon* a66 66
2 b c Sendawar(IRE) —Syrian Dancer (IRE) (Groom Dancer (USA))
4103[12] 4867[4] *5389[10]6650[2]*

Into The Breeze (IRE) *J W Hills* a90 95
6 b g Alzao(USA) —Catalane (USA) (Septieme Ciel (USA))
(1112) 1667[13] 2520[2] 4790[8] 5175[10]

Into The Dark *Saeed Bin Suroor* 116
5 ch g Rainbow Quest(USA) —Land Of Dreams (Cadeaux Genereux)
5142[5] 5657[2] (6203)

Into The Shadows *K G Reveley* 92?
6 ch m Safawan—Shadows Of Silver (Carwhite)
(714) 991[6] 5533[14] 5787[3]

Intoxicating *R F Johnson Houghton* a91 107
4 b g Mujahid(USA) —Salalah (Lion Cavern (USA))
238[9] 1487[22] 2649[11]

Intrepid Jack *H Morrison* a113 107
4 b h Compton Place—Maria Theresa (Primo Dominie)
1835[6] 2847[10] 3493[2] 4128[11] 4372[7]4593[11] *5667[2]* (5832) *6095[2]6243[5]*

Intricate Web (IRE) *E J Alston* a62 80
10 b g Warning—In Anticipation (IRE) (Sadler's Wells (USA))
1987[8]

Intrigued *Sir Mark Prescott* 106
4 gr m Darshaan—Last Second (IRE) (Alzao (USA))
2023[3] 4179[3] 4648a[6]

Intriguing Glimpse *Miss B Sanders* a81 99
5 bb m Piccolo—Running Glimpse (IRE) (Runnett)
517[6] 1643[6] *1928[9]*2227[13] (2389) (2674) 3251[5] 3499[6]

Invasian (IRE) *B J McMath* 103
5 ch g Desert Prince(IRE) —Jarrayan (Machiavellian (USA))
3971[8] 4711[9] 5299[3] (5769) 5810[14]

Invasor (ARG) *K McLaughlin* a127+
4 b h Candy Stripes(USA) —Quendom (ARG) (Interprete (ARG))
739a[4] (6345a)

Invention (USA) *J H M Gosden* 95
3 b g Lear Fan(USA) —Carya (USA) (Northern Dancer (CAN))
1087[6] (1994) 2775[15] 4337[5] 5376[10]

Inveraray *P S Felgate* a51
3 ch f Selkirk(USA) —Khalafiya (Darshaan)
5429[11] 5847[6]6545[5] 6617[7]6724[11] 6977[12]

Inverted *Mrs A Duffield* a47
2 b g Averti(IRE) —Indian Silk (IRE) (Dolphin Street (FR))
5753[9] *6222[8] 6895[5]6945[4]*

Invincible Force (IRE) *Ms Deborah J Evans* 101
2 b g Invincible Spirit(IRE) —Highly Respected (IRE) (High Estate)
1982[2] 2439[2] (2878) (3064) 3474[4] (4170) (4824a) 5408a[2]5664a[2] 5802[10]

Invincible Star (IRE) *Peter Casey* 68
2 b f Invincible Spirit(IRE) —Feather Star (Soviet Star (USA))
4824a[17]

Inwaan (IRE) *P R Webber* 71
3 b g King's Best(USA) —Balaabel (USA) (Sadler's Wells (USA))
5734[11]

Ioannina *P Schiergen* 101
3 br f Rainbow Quest(USA) —Iora (GER) (Konigsstuhl (GER))
3515a[5] 4648a[4] 6529a[3]

Iolanthe *B J Meehan* 49
2 ch f Vettori(IRE) —Shakalaka Baby (Nashwan (USA))
5586[11] 5914[12]

Ionian Spring (IRE) *D Carroll* a99 94
11 b g Ela-Mana-Mou—Well Head (IRE) (Sadler's Wells (USA))
1133[5] (1566) 2507[4] 3068[3] 3626[2] *(6871)*

Ioweyou *J S Moore* a53 64
2 ch f Noverre(USA) —Cuore Di Aliante (Alhijaz)
1922[5] 2432[4] 2943[4]4804[8]

I Predict A Riot (IRE) *J W Hills* 59
2 b g Danehill Dancer(IRE) —Manon's Song (IRE) (Sadler's Wells (USA))
5892[7] 6220[17]

Iqte Saab (USA) *Doug Watson* 110
5 b h Bahri(USA) —Shuhrah (USA) (Danzig (USA))
(153a) 370a[4] 497a[11]

Ira Funesta (IRE) *G Angellotti* 57
3 b f Definite Article—Tribal Lady (Absalom)
6124a[11]

Irazu (AUS) *S J Richards* 110
3 br g Encosta De Lago(AUS) —Morrigan Clare (AUS) (Toy Pindarri (NZ))
(5817a) 6346a[2]

Ireland Dancer (IRE) *W R Muir* 68
2 ch g Trans Island—Come Dancing (Suave Dancer (USA))
4028[5] 4588[5] 5091[9]

Ireland's Call (IRE) *Peter Casey* 96+
5 gr g King's Theatre(IRE) —Tarikhana (Mouktar)
6356a[13]

Irish Ballad *W R Swinburn* a65 60
4 b g Singspiel(IRE) —Auenlust (GER) (Surumu (GER))
2320[13] 3035[9] 3437[3]3952[10] *4438[2]* 5369[15]*(5736)*

Irish Dancer *J L Dunlop* 64
2 b f Danehill Dancer(IRE) —Gaelic Swan (IRE) (Nashwan (USA))
3701[8] 4552[4]

Irish Poet (IRE) *E J O'Neill* 53
2 b c Trans Island—Abecedarian (USA) (Barathea (IRE))
4867[11] 5552[5]

Irish Relative (IRE) *T D Barron* 44
2 b g Indian Lodge(IRE) —The Good Life (IRE) (Rainbow Quest (USA))
4251[10]

Irish Wells (FR) *F Rohaut* 120
3 b c Poliglote—Sign Of The Vine (FR) (Kendor (FR))
1179a[3] 2278a[6] (4861a) 5716a[5]

Irish Whispers (IRE) *B G Powell* a60 68
3 b g Marju(IRE) —Muneera (USA) (Green Dancer (USA))
2434[5] 3870[2] *4245[7]4758[4]*

Irish Wolf (FR) *P Bowen* 81+
6 b h Loup Solitaire(USA) —Erins Run (USA) (Irish River (FR))
966[2] 2723[20] (5235)

Iron Dancer (IRE) *P A Blockley* a43 44
2 b c Iron Mask(USA) —Sin Lucha (USA) (Northfields (USA))
4115[14] *4433[9]* 4980[8]*5735[10]*

Iron Fist (IRE) *E J O'Neill* 100
2 b c Desert Style(IRE) —Ricadonna (Kris)
3083[6] (3448) (4859a)

Iron Lips *C Laffon-Parias* 103
2 b f Iron Mask(USA) —Icelips (USA) (Unbridled (USA))
4621a[6] 5122a[2] (5664a) 6229a[3]

Iron Pearl *Jane Chapple-Hyam* a57 55+
2 b f Iron Mask(USA) —Fast Tempo (IRE) (Statoblest)
6562[3] (6912)

Irony (IRE) *A M Balding* a90 93
7 gr g Mujadil(USA) —Cidaris (IRE) (Persian Bold)
1692[3] *1938[3] (2555)* 2776[22](3470) 4029[16] 4535[5] 4790[2]

Irridescence (SAF) *J E Hammond* 119
5 b m Caesour(USA) —Meretricious (SAF) (Dancing Champ (USA))
(510a) (1180a) 5049a[5] 5713a[4]

Is *Rae Guest* a29 58
3 br f Diktat—Blackpool Belle (The Brianstan)
*466[10] 687[13]*2968[10] 3626[3] 3824[6] 4304[6] 4981[7]5441[4] *6604[6]*

Isa'Af (IRE) *P W Hiatt* a76 78d
7 b g Darshaan—Shauna's Honey (IRE) (Danehill (USA))
37[8] (75) 250[9]338[2] 599[3](675) (869) 976[10] *1247[11]*1660[2] 1808[10] 2176[10] 3028[10] 5952[14]6108[13] *6415[5] 6495[7]6604[5] 6761[3]*

Isabella Bay *M Wellings* a22 52
6 b m Meqdaam(USA) —Orchard Bay (Formidable (USA))
6450[9] 6756[13]

Isabella Rossini *A M Hales* a31 13
4 br m Rossini(USA) —Misty Rain (Polar Falcon (USA))
338[8] 484[11]

Isabella's Best (IRE) *E J O'Neill* 47
2 ch f King's Best(USA) —Spanish Quest (Rainbow Quest (USA))
5417[10] 5613[5] 6058[8]

Isharram (IRE) *A Berry* 42
3 ch f Muhtarram(USA) —Ishaam (Selkirk (USA))
1633[8] 3529[6] 4297[15]

Ishetoo *A Dickman* 54
2 b g Ishiguru(USA) —Ticcatoo (IRE) (Dolphin Street (FR))
2523[5] 3018[6] 3940[5] 5613[11]

Ishi Adiva *Tom Dascombe* 85
2 b f Ishiguru(USA) —Nightingale Song (Tina's Pet)
3148[4] 3358[2] 3734[2] 4736[17] (6024)

Ishibee (IRE) *Mrs A Duffield* a62 61
2 b f Ishiguru(USA) —Beauty (IRE) (Alzao (USA))
1442[5] 1664[3] 2394[6] 2827[4] 3096[3]3787[3] 4088[3] (4327) 4727[5]4912[3] 5282[11] 5747[10] 6291[5]6416[6] 6472[6]

Ishimagic *J J Bridger* a53? 43
2 ch f Ishiguru(USA) —Triple Tricks (IRE) (Royal Academy (USA))
5586[7] 5890[11] 6063[8] 6332[8] 6443[4]6777[4] 6853[6]

Ishismart *R Hollinshead* a32
2 ch f Ishiguru(USA) —Smartie Lee (Dominion)
5424[9] 6034[8]6520[10]

Isidore Bonheur (IRE) *G A Swinbank* a83 96
5 b g Mtoto—Way O'Gold (USA) (Slew O'Gold (USA))
1143[6] 1340[5] 1495[10](2527) 2872[2] 4347[6] 4805[7]

Isitloveyourafter (IRE) *G L Moore* 44
4 b m Orpen(USA) —Pericolo (IRE) (Kris)
182[10]

Is It Me (USA) *P A Blockley* a54 74
3 ch c Sky Classic(CAN) —Thea (GER) (Surumu (GER))
952[12] 1052[11] 2518[5]2882[2] 2970[2] 3359[4] (3634)

Is It Time (IRE) *Mrs P N Dutfield* 43
2 b f Danetime(IRE) —Ishaam (Selkirk (USA))
4525[11] 4774[7]

Island Fashion (USA) *J Canani* a117 114
6 ro m Petionville(USA) —Danzigs Fashion (USA) (A Native Danzig (USA))
738a[7]

Island Green (USA) *B J Curley* a50 21
3 b g Cozzene(USA) —Legend Of Spring (Night Shift (USA))
138[11] 291[12]487[7] 3006[10] (6236) 6707[2]

Island Myth (IRE) *M P Tregoning* a70 86
3 ch g Inchinor—Jersey Lillie (IRE) (Hector Protector (USA))
1741[4] 1975[4] 2584[13] 4778[5] (5128) 5478[2]

Island Odyssey *E A L Dunlop* a91 90
3 b f Dansili—Tetravella (IRE) (Groom Dancer (USA))
(1193) 1898[3] (2533) (5109) 5421[3] 5776[7]6202[9]

Island Prince (IRE) *Mrs A Duffield* a51 47
3 b g Mull Of Kintyre(USA) —Green Flower (USA) (Fappiano (USA))
4725[8] 4888[9] 5081[12] 6293[8] (Dead)

Island Rapture *J A R Toller* a79 71
6 b m Royal Applause—Gersey (Generous (IRE))
221[7] 463[7]660[3] 915[4]1275[2] 1962[5]2348[4]

Isn't It Grand (IRE) *Miss V Haigh* a21
2 b f Raise A Grand(IRE) —Fiona March (GER) (Big Shuffle (USA))
6998[7]

Isobel Baillie *H-A Pantall* 80
3 ch f Lomitas—Dubai Soprano (Zafonic (USA))
2537a[9]

Isobel Rose (IRE) *E A L Dunlop* a67 71
2 b f Royal Applause—Total Love (Cadeaux Genereux)
1082[3] 1347[3] 2355[2] 2638[4] 4754[3]5288[3] 5655[25] 6505[3]6575[2] 6730[6]

Isola Madre *M Johnston* a62 49
2 b f Rainbow Quest(USA) —High Standard (Kris)
4866[7] 5898[6] 6298[5] (6518)

Isola Star (IRE) *David P Myerscough* 88
2 bb f Danehill Dancer(IRE) —Ghost Tree (IRE) (Caerleon (USA))
4850a[4] 5464a[17]

Isphahan *A M Balding* a76 79
3 b c Diktat—Waltzing Star (IRE) (Danehill (USA))
118[8] 342[2]483[6] 1115[3] 2177[6]2581[4] 3223[9]

Ista Kareem (NZ) *J Gask* 107
5 ch g Germano—Princesses Touch (NZ) (Touching Wood (USA))
6391a[6]

Italian Girl *A P Jarvis* 94
2 b f Danehill Dancer(IRE) —Little Italy (IRE) (Common Grounds)
(3893) 4840[5] 5672[4]

Italian Mist (FR) *R M H Cowell* a61 46
7 b g Forzando—Digamist Girl (IRE) (Digamist (USA))
1243[11] 2141[10]2494[13] 2571[6] 2955[10]

Italian Romance *J W Unett* a78 45
3 b g Medicean—Polish Romance (USA) (Danzig (USA))
952[5] 1336[4]2177[10] 6588[2] 6741[4]6923[3]

Italian Stallion (IRE) *R Hannon* 79
2 b c Grand Lodge(USA) —Belle Allemande (CAN) (Royal Academy (USA))
3417[12] 4129[8] 4574[2] 5013[5] 5322[4]5866[2] 6018[2]

Italic *Mrs A J Perrett* 74
3 ch f Medicean—Ink Pot (USA) (Green Dancer (USA))
1214[3] 1740[6] 2434[2] 3152[4]

Italstar (IRE) *H Morrison* a46
2 ch f Galileo(IRE) —Jorghinia (FR) (Seattle Slew (USA))
6658[11] 6778[9]6879[8]

Itcanbedone Again (IRE) *Ian Williams* a61 70
7 b g Sri Pekan(USA) —Maradata (IRE) (Shardari)
(41) (358) 505[4] 736[3]1152[10] 2149[8] 4176[8]4925[11]

Itchycoo Park (IRE) *E J O'Neill* 57+
2 b c Rossini(USA) —Queen Molly (Emarati (USA))
4897[5] 5297[9]

It Must Be Speech *S L Keightley* a49 43
5 b g Advise(FR) —Maiden Speech (Pitskelly)
143[3] 258[6]304[2] 394[2]468[6] 526[6]689[12]

Itsabeautifulday (IRE) *M Halford* 68
2 b g King Charlemagne(USA) —Amiela (FR) (Mujtahid (USA))
5662a[9]

It's A Dream (FR) *D R C Elsworth* a79+ 84
3 b g Kaldounevees(FR) —Bahia Mar (USA) (Arctic Tern (USA))
1092[9] 5511[10] 5732[7]

Itsawindup *W J Knight* a54
2 b c Elnadim(USA) —Topwinder (USA) (Topsider (USA))
6591[11] 6689[8]

It's Basil *R M Flower* a58 45
3 b g Foxhound(USA) —Marabela (IRE) (Shernazar)
668[8] 918[9]1314[8] 2352[9] 2646[2]3016[11] 3439[8] 3797[13]4446[12]

It's Gone *J G Given* a34 14
3 b g City On A Hill(USA) —Shafaq (USA) (Dayjur (USA))
2383[10] 3638[6] 4635[11] 6557[7]

Its Moon (IRE) *M R Channon* 65
2 b f Tobougg(IRE) —Shallat (IRE) (Pennekamp (USA))
3796[11] 4089[4] 4788[3]

It's No Problem (IRE) *Jean-Rene Auvray* a39 59
2 b f Averti(IRE) —Polar Rock (Polar Falcon (USA))
663[5] 878[7] 2967[6]3210[5] 3868[5] 4163[7] 5208[11]

It's Rumoured *Jean-Rene Auvray* a48 67
6 ch g Fleetwood(IRE) —Etourdie (USA) (Arctic Tern (USA))
6630[10]

It's Twilight Time *R Hannon* 46
3 b f Royal Applause—Mainly Sunset (Red Sunset)
2458[7] 2985[13]

It's Unbelievable (USA) *P T Midgley* a58 72
3 bb g Stravinsky(USA) —Churn Dat Butter (USA) (Unbridled (USA))
(2325) 3282[4] 4076[6] 4285[5] 4958[6] 5446[4]5879[8]

Iuturna (USA) *R Menichetti* 87
2 b f Intidab(USA) —Samut (IRE) (Danehill (USA))
2062a[5] 3343a[6] 5858a[10]

Ivana Illyich (IRE) *J S Wainwright* a33 41
4 ch m Tipsy Creek(USA) —Tolstoya (Northfields (USA))
2777[6] 3944[15] 4506[7]

Ivan Denisovich (IRE) *A P O'Brien* a35 112
3 b c Danehill(USA) —Hollywood Wildcat (USA) (Kris S (USA))
1178a[8] 1718a[7] 2721[3] 3342a[8] 4387a[2](5411a) 5524[8] 6613a[3]

Ivans Ride (IRE) *J J Quinn* a61 56
3 b g Night Shift(USA) —Ride Bold (USA) (J O Tobin (USA))
5446[13] 6524[9]

Ivorbella (IRE) *M Botti* a48 47
4 gr m Daylami(IRE) —Ivorela (IRE) (Ela-Mana-Mou)
771[3] 1461[7]1724[5]

Ivory Gala (FR) *B J Meehan* 98
3 b f Galileo(IRE) —Rubies From Burma (USA) (Forty Niner (USA))
1994[5] (2292) 3515a[7] 5472a[2]

Ivory Lace *S Woodman* a85 85
5 b m Atraf—Miriam (Forzando)
171[11] 327[11]519[2] 902[2]1432[6] (2390) 2606[6] (2954) 3337[3] 3612[3] (4449)4589[6] 5096[3] 5777[6]6580[8] 6690[9]

Ivorys Song *D K Ivory* a37
2 b f Averti(IRE) —Katy Ivory (IRE) (Night Shift (USA))
701[7] 908[5]

Ivy Creek (USA) *G Wragg* 115+
3 b c Gulch(USA) —Ivy Leaf (IRE) (Nureyev (USA))
(880) (1269) 1627[2] 2775[6]

I Wish *Miss J R Tooth* a51 59
8 ch m Beveled(USA) —Ballystate (Ballacashtal (CAN))
74[5] 137[11]339[10] 837[8]1273[8] 1414[13] 2347[9]6307[2] 6550[7]6726[10] 6798[7]6892[9]

Iwunder (IRE) *Rae Guest* 73
4 b m King's Best(USA) —Sweetest Thing (IRE) (Prince Rupert (FR))
2143[5]

Izabela Hannah *R M Beckett* 68
2 ch f Kyllachy—Papita (IRE) (Law Society (USA))
4657[8] 5563[2] 6025[2]

Iza Coming (IRE) *M G Quinlan* a60
2 b f Fasliyev(USA) —Boiling River (USA) (Dayjur (USA))
6034[3] 6596[3]6749[3]

Izadore (IRE) *E A L Dunlop* a71 69
3 b f In The Wings—Groom Order (Groom Dancer (USA))
2349[7] 2917[4] 3946[3] 4701[4]5056[6] 6588[3] 6792[5]

Izdiham (IRE) *A Manuel* a66 112
7 ch h Nashwan(USA) —Harayir (USA) (Gulch (USA))
207a[11]

Jaad *Christian Wroe* a70 86
3 b c Elnadim(USA) —Off The Blocks (Salse (USA))
1099[3] 1349[3] 2126[8] 3113[2] 3331[5]5627[15] 6397[11]

Jaady (USA) *J H M Gosden* a68
2 b g Coronado's Quest(USA) —Aljawza (USA) (Riverman (USA))
6145[4]

Jaasoos (IRE) *M A Jarvis* 80
2 ch c Noverre(USA) —Nymphs Echo (IRE) (Mujtahid (USA))
4873[3] (5297) 5546[8]

Jaassey *A Crook* a39 65
3 b g Josr Algarhoud(IRE) —Saaryeh (Royal Academy (USA))
1859[5] 2243[4] 2782[2] 3290[8] 3762[7](4943) 5483[8] 5680[11] 6054[8] 6382[11]6531[7]

Jabbara (IRE) *C E Brittain* a63+ 67
3 b f Kingmambo(USA) —Isle De France (USA) (Nureyev (USA))
1777[6] 2406[7] 2587[6] 3440[7] 3793[9]4181[8] 4671[5] 4927[6] 5418[11] (6492) 6608[6] 6994[5]

Jabraan (USA) *D W Chapman* a45 68
4 b g Aljabr(USA) —Miss Zafonic (FR) (Zafonic (USA))
653[11] 4518[13] 4652[12]5241[5] 5363[5] 6282[8]6545[6] 6793[10]

Jack Absolute (IRE) *B J Meehan* 62
3 gr g Fantastic Light(USA) —Crepe Ginger (IRE) (Sadler's Wells (USA))
948[10] 1120[11] 1546[7] 2082[10] 2607[10]

Jack Dawson (IRE) *John Berry* a61 81
9 b g Persian Bold—Dream Of Jenny (Caerleon (USA))
4448[10] (4848) 5069[4] 5531[10] 6075[9]

Jack Durrance (IRE) *G A Ham* a47 47
6 b g Polish Precedent(USA) —Atlantic Desire (IRE) (Ela-Mana-Mou)
771[6] 2206[6]

Jackie Francis (IRE) *R Brotherton* a30 45
3 b g Fasliyev(USA) —Appalachia (IRE) (Imperial Frontier (USA))
653[9] 1304[8]2187[11] 3821[4] 4164[13] 5055[13] 6233[12]

Jackie Kiely *R Brotherton* a77 75
5 ch g Vettori(IRE) —Fudge (Polar Falcon (USA))
12[2] 131[7](259) (389) (414) 491[6] 549[4]652[3] 1058[15] 1256[2]1415[14] 2150[12] 2601[3] 2725[2] 2918[8]2953[5] (4073) 4673[3] (4982) 5314[2] 5935[8] (6947)

Jack Junior (USA) *B J Meehan* 101+
2 bb c Songandaprayer(USA) —Ra Hydee (USA) (Rahy (USA))
5381[4] 5653[6]

Jack Of Trumps (IRE) *G Wragg* a84 95
6 b g King's Theatre(IRE) —Queen Caroline (USA) (Chief's Crown (USA))
1206[5] 1631[2] 3401[5]4023[10] 4631[7] 5299[5]

Jack Oliver *B J Meehan* a71 73
2 ch g Compton Place—Glascoed (Adbass (USA))
2432[8] (4163) 5065[2] 5606[3]

Jack Rackham *B Smart* 84
2 ch c Kyllachy—Hill Welcome (Most Welcome)
1030[3] 1420[2] 1632[2] 1811[4]

Jack Rolfe *G L Moore* a65 55
4 b g Polish Precedent(USA) —Haboobti (Habitat)
(18)

Jacks Delight *C N Kellett* a47 40
6 b g Bettergeton—Impromptu Melody (IRE) (Mac's Imp (USA))
148[8]

Jackson (BRZ) *A Cintra* a89 54
4 ch h Clackson(BRZ) —More Luck (BRZ) (Baynoun)
561a[4] 739a[12]

Jack Sullivan (USA) *G A Butler* a116 117
5 ch g Belong To Me(USA) —Provisions (USA) (Devil's Bag (USA))
(355a) 738a[3]

Jacky Jack (ITY) *P Paciello* 76
4 b h College Chapel—Fashyd (IRE) (Shahrastani (USA))
6252a[5]

Jacobin (USA) *M Scudamore* a15 41
5 b g Tamayaz(CAN) —Simply Follow Me (USA) (Green Dancer (USA))
427[7]

Jadalee (IRE) *M P Tregoning* 113
3 b c Desert Prince(IRE) —Lionne (Darshaan)
1300[5] 3441[2] 4024[2] (4797) 5185[6]

Jadan (IRE) *E J Alston* 59
5 b g Imperial Ballet(IRE) —Sports Post Lady (IRE) (M Double M (USA))
1031[9] 1795[16] 2027[9] 2396[14] 2505[7]2521[8] 3170[5] 3297[15]

Jadeeron *Miss D A McHale* a61 49
7 b g Green Desert(USA) —Rain And Shine (FR) (Rainbow Quest (USA))
40[5] 230[2]309[6] 338[5]470[3] 535[6]599[10] 1392[8]2869[7] 3232[9] 4011[2] 4380[5] (4929) 5324[13] 5971[4] 6132[4](6280) 6375[3]6474[12] 6526[2]

Jade Hill (IRE) *L Riccardi* 66
2 ch c Jade Robbery(USA) —Notting Hill (Lammtarra (USA))
6123a[10]

Jade Queen (USA) *T Pletcher* 117
3 ch f Giant's Causeway(USA) —Jade Flush (USA) (Jade Hunter (USA))
5198a[3] 5819a[3]

Jader (IRE) *S Seemar* a99 103
4 b h Monashee Mountain(USA) —Honey Bee (Alnasr Alwasheek)
282a[8] 565a[9]

Jade Rheinberg (GER) *M Trybuhl* 90
3 b f Platini(GER) —Jade Chequer (Green Desert (USA))
1714a[7]

Jade's Ballet *E A Wheeler* a38 12
2 ch f Ballet Master(USA) —Another Jade (Beveled (USA))
5261[10] 5646[14] 6427[4]6695[5] 6845[8]

Jafaru *G A Butler* a12 41
2 b g Silver Hawk(USA) —Rafha (Kris)
3417[14] 4366[9] 5067[11]

Jagger *D Hayes* a89 110
6 gr g Linamix(FR) —Sweetness Herself (Unfuwain (USA))
6455a[12]

Jagodin (IRE) *B Neuman* 101
6 b g Be My Guest(USA) —Native Joy (IRE) (Be My Native (USA))
5226a[8]

Jahia (NZ) *P T Midgley* a58 53
7 br m Jahafil—Lana (NZ) (Tristram's Heritage (NZ))
686[10] (1391) 2376[9] 2543[6]2780[13] 3297[7] 3988[11] 4401[6] (6233) 6877[7] 6990[12]

Jailamigraine (IRE) *P Bary* 87
2 ch f King Charlemagne(USA) —Moivouloirtoi (USA) (Bering)
4464a[3] 5122a[5] 5880a[4] 6546a[11]

Jaish (USA) *J L Dunlop* 102
3 bb f Seeking The Gold(USA) —Khazayin (USA) (Bahri (USA))
1472[5] 1819[4] 2582[2] 4482[4] 5917[11]

Jakarmi *B Palling* a74 75
5 b g Merdon Melody—Lady Ploy (Deploy)
106[5] 200[2]405[2] 505[3](571) 736[2]965[3] 1148[3] (1204) 1288[10]2186[9] 2794[9] 5599[14]5889[13] 6240[9]

Jakeini (IRE) *E S McMahon* a56 77
3 b c Rossini(USA) —Talita Kumi (IRE) (High Estate)
1549[5] (2016) 2197[4] (2410) 3042[5]3268[2] 3873[5] 4659[7]

Jake The Snake (IRE) *G A Huffer* 75
5 ch g Intikhab(USA) —Tilbrook (IRE) (Don't Forget Me)
1651[DSQ]

Jalamid (IRE) *G C Bravery* 107
4 b g Danehill(USA) —Vignelaure (IRE) (Royal Academy (USA))
282a[10] 511a[12] 1667[10] 2012[14] 2649[6]4348[9] 5677[12]

Jalil (USA) *Saeed Bin Suroor* 72
2 br c Storm Cat(USA) —Tranquility Lake (USA) (Rahy (USA))
5939[6]

Jalissa *R M Beckett* a67 83
4 b m Mister Baileys—Julia Domna (Dominion)
1692[10] 1957[4]

Jalmira (IRE) *C F Swan* 90+
5 b m Danehill Dancer(IRE) —Jaldini (IRE) (Darshaan)
5190a[8]

Jalouhar *J R Best* a54 60
6 b g Victory Note(USA) —Orient Way (IRE) (Danehill (USA))
29[2] 81[5]177[2] 288[6]407[4] (502) 772[3] 889[12]1550[11] (Dead)

Jalta (GER) *H Steinmetz* 97
3 b f Platini(GER) —Juschika (Salse (USA))
3661a[6] 5710a[3]

Jamaahir (USA) *J L Dunlop* 65
3 b c Bahri(USA) —Elrehaan (Sadler's Wells (USA))
1134[7] 1476[6]

Jamaar *C N Kellett* a67 58
4 ch g Nashwan(USA) —Kissogram (Caerleon (USA))
250[11] 443[2]1219[11]

Jamaican (UAE) *M J McGrath* a58 58
4 ch g Timber Country(USA) —Notting Hill (Lammtarra (USA))
1729[13]

Jamaican Flight (USA) *Mrs S Lamyman* a36 41
13 b h Sunshine Forever(USA) —Kalamona (USA) (Hawaii)
28[8] 614[5]688[6] 866[6]

Jambalaya (CAN) *Catherine Day Phillips* 112
4 b g Langfuhr(CAN) —Muskrat Suzie (USA) (Vice Regent (CAN))
6126a[9]

James Caird (IRE) *M H Tompkins* a84 97
6 ch g Catrail(USA) —Polish Saga (Polish Patriot (USA))
2435[3] 3552[16] 6888[8]6992[7]

James Joyce (IRE) *A P O'Brien* 101
3 b c Danehill(USA) —Crumpetsfortea (IRE) (Henbit (USA))
1025a[4] 1718a[11]

James Street (IRE) *J R Best* a75 77
3 b g Fruits Of Love(USA) —Humble Mission (Shack (USA))
3850[7] (4368) 4927[5] 5085[5] 5320[2] 5911[6]6147[4] 6564[6]6654[2] 6781[11]

Jamieson Gold (IRE) *B W Hills* 99+
3 b g Desert Style(IRE) —Princess Of Zurich (IRE) (Law Society (USA))
1490[11] 3317[4] 3889[4] (4593) 4790[16] 5677[9]

Janaah *C E Brittain* a48 49
3 b f In The Wings—Blodwen (USA) (Mister Baileys)
2580[8] 3849[7] 5426[7]

Jane Of Arc (FR) *T D Easterby* 72
2 ch f Trempolino(USA) —Aerleon Jane (Caerleon (USA))
2106[7] (2733) 3265[2] 5157[10]

January *Saeed Bin Suroor* 70
3 gr c Daylami(IRE) —Noushkey (Polish Precedent (USA))
2825[5]

Jardin Bleu *Mme M Bollack-Badel* a92 108?
7 b g Diesis—Cask (Be My Chief (USA))
6547a[10]

Jardines Bazaar *T D Easterby* 52
2 b g Halling(USA) —Alumisiyah (USA) (Danzig (USA))
4880[3] 5239[7] 5615[9]

Jarvo *I W McInnes* a52 52
5 b g Pursuit Of Love—Pinkie Rose (FR) (Kenmare (FR))
6544[4] 6617[8]6800[2]

Jasmine Pearl (IRE) *T M Jones* a44 47
5 b m King Of Kings(IRE) —Tumbleweed Pearl (Aragon)
982[8] 1310[9] 1534[8]2494[7]

Jaufrette *Dr J R J Naylor* 39
3 b f Kayf Tara—Jucinda (Midyan (USA))
5056[7] 5567[9]

Jawaab (IRE) *E A L Dunlop* 74
2 ch g King's Best(USA) —Canis Star (Wolfhound (USA))
3485[4] 4074[9] 4388[4] 4813[2] 5053[4]5585[6] 6066[2]

Jayanjay *P Mitchell* a80 92
7 b g Piccolo—Morica (Moorestyle)
1236[5] 1939[6] 2227[14]2429[14] 3211[8] 4158[5] 4811[10] 4875[3]5021[7] 5782[7]6036[3] 6437[8]6485[7] 6579[2]6709[9] 6842[7]6865[6]
Jayer Gilles *Dr J R J Naylor* a59 66
6 br g Busy Flight—Jadidh (Touching Wood (USA))
3952[9] 4898[3] 5235[2] 5564[6] 6178[16]
Jay Gee's Choice *B G Powell* a63 63
6 b g Barathea(IRE) —Llia (Shirley Heights)
2983[13] 3404[11]
Jay Jay Okocha *James Moffatt*
3 gr g Wizard King—Schatzi (Chilibang)
4451[2] 5981[1]
Jayzee (IRE) *P D Deegan* a34 58
2 b f Iron Mask(USA) —Golden Concorde (Super Concorde (USA))
6808[7] 6815[8]
Jazabelle (IRE) *C Collins* 79
3 gr f Monashee Mountain(USA) —Lingdale Lass (Petong)
4186a[12]
Jazil (USA) *K McLaughlin* a121
3 b c Seeking The Gold(USA) —Better Than Honour (USA) (Deputy Minister (CAN))
1498a[4] (2477a)
Jazrawy *P W Hiatt* a64 59
4 b g Dansili—Dalila Di Mare (IRE) (Bob Back (USA))
416[7] 574[9]1058[16] 1244[7] 2978[11]3411[8] 3680[2] 4072[2] 5080[7] 5451[13]5652[10] 5887[3] 6178[4]6376[9] 6474[3]6553[5] (6758) (6883)
Jazzanova *M W Easterby* 44
2 b g Fasliyev(USA) —Stonegrave (Selkirk (USA))
2321[11] 4987[6] 5059[10] 5790[10] 6421[8]6534[13]
Jazz At The Sands (USA) *D Shaw* a47 42
3 ch g Forest Wildcat(USA) —Dahlia's Krissy (USA) (Kris S (USA))
10[8] 226[6]329[11] 397[12]910[4] 936[4]1200[5] 1464[5]6780[10] 6890[7]
Jazz Festival (USA) *T D Barron* a16 17
2 b g Jambalaya Jazz(USA) —Violets Are Blue (USA) (Full Pocket (USA))
5900[12] 6303[9]
Jazz Princess (IRE) *M Halford* 109
4 br m Bahhare(USA) —Jazz Up (Cadeaux Genereux)
(1363a) 2041a[2] 5708a[8]
Jeanmaire (IRE) *H Morrison* 96
3 b f Dansili—Lovely Lyca (Night Shift (USA))
1512[6] 2205[6] 2744[9] 3418[2] 5919[8]6204[5]
Jebel Ali (IRE) *B Gubby* a81 79
3 b g Fruits Of Love(USA) —Assertive Lass (USA) (Assert)
337[2] 483[2]592[7] (804) 1108[6] 1356[5] 2404[8]3015[6] 3848[2] 4784[9]6076[6] 6206[5]
Jedburgh *J L Dunlop* 109
5 b h Selkirk(USA) —Conspiracy (Rudimentary (USA))
1050[3] (2289) 2776[6] (3572a) 4025[2] 5341[10] 5588[7]5962[9]
Jeepstar *S C Williams* a82 95
6 b g Muhtarram(USA) —Jungle Rose (Shirley Heights)
1071[10] 2013[13] 3028[11] 4259[5] 5531[2]6673[2]
Jeer (IRE) *E A L Dunlop* 79
2 ch c Selkirk(USA) —Purring (USA) (Mountain Cat (USA))
4366[11] 5025[2]
Jeff Le Roi (FR) *K Schafflutzel* 64
4 gr h Balleroy(USA) —Sembrador (FR) (Hours After (USA))
306a[11]
Jellytot (USA) *K A Ryan* a53 70
3 b f Minardi(USA) —Dounine (Kaldoun (FR))
980[10] 1344[8] 1829[2] (2198) 2525[8] (3290) 3782[3]4769[12] 5386[11] 5953[4]
Jember Red *B Smart* a22 39
3 b f Polish Precedent(USA) —Arabellajill (Aragon)
6403[8] 6817[5]
Jemima Godfrey *J Pearce* a31
2 b f Ishiguru(USA) —Quantum Lady (Mujadil (USA))
6751[7]
Jenise (IRE) *Mark Campion* a44 22
3 b f Orpen(USA) —Griqualand (Connaught)
1445[9] 2940[6] 4548[7]6306[7] 6557[5]6794[7] 6901[5]
Jenkins Lane (IRE) *J J Lambe* a8 80
4 b g Revoque(IRE) —Suzy Street (IRE) (Dancing Dissident (USA))
6606[11]
Jenna Stannis *W Storey* 45
4 ch m Wolfhound(USA) —Darling Splodge (Elegant Air)
2362[10] 2696[11] 2832[7] 2926[11]
Jennverse *D K Ivory* a50 50
4 b m Opening Verse(USA) —Jennelle (Nomination)
137[9] 2279[3]336[6] 4866[5]520[8] 6911[3]889[9] 1539[4](1728) 2574[7]3728[9] 3847[5] 4329[7]4554[3] (6131) 6237[4]6477[8] 6541[5]6728[6] 6803[3]
Jennyfromtheblock (IRE) *Samuel Murphy* 56
5 b m General Monash(USA) —Notorious (Auction Ring (USA))
1801[1]
Jenny Geddes (IRE) *R A Fahey* 51
2 b f Intikhab(USA) —Etiquette (Law Society (USA))
4421[7] 4913[5] 5496[9] 5721[14]
Jenny Soba *R M Whitaker* a45 61
3 b f Observatory(USA) —Majalis (Mujadil (USA))
868[7] 1736[6] 2283[7] 3142[2] 3910[2]4257[3] 4567[6] 5446[3] 6314[7]
Jeremy (USA) *Sir Michael Stoute* 115
3 b c Danehill Dancer(IRE) —Glint In Her Eye (USA) (Arazi (USA))
1083[2] (2031) (2739) 4025[6] 4596[2] 5962[12]
Jeritza *S Wattel* a75 95
3 b f Rainbow Quest(USA) —Jade Jewel (USA) (Mr Prospector (USA))
6567a[5]

Jerry Lee (IRE) *M Weiss*
3 b c Orpen(USA) —Vinicky (USA) (Kingmambo (USA))
2717a[9]
Jersey Bounce (IRE) *H J Brown* a62 105
5 b h Septieme Ciel(USA) —Marcotte (Nebos (GER))
204a[9] 356a[4] (512a) 624a[6]
Jessica Wigmo *A W Carroll* a47 46
3 b f Bahamian Bounty—Queen Of Shannon (IRE) (Nordico (USA))
31[8] 120[7]287[9] 2877[15] 3472[10]4164[6] 5055[3] 5729[10]
Je Suis Belle *Miss Gay Kelleway* a66 72
4 ch m Efisio—Blossom (Warning)
1581[0]
Jete (IRE) *D Shaw* a39 60
2 b g Imperial Ballet(IRE) —Jet Lock (USA) (Crafty Prospector (USA))
5735[13] 5915[10] 6047[5]
Jet Express (SAF) *Diego Lowther* a72 100
4 b h Jet Master(SAF) —Outback Romance (SAF) (Sharp Romance (USA))
150a[7] 203a[6] 620a[4]5779a[7]
Jet West (USA) *Ted H West* a111
5 b h Western Fame(USA) —Jetinwith Kennedy (USA) (Kennedy Road (USA))
740a[3]
Jeu D'Esprit (IRE) *J G Given* a63 32
3 b f Montjeu(IRE) —Cielo Vodkamartini (USA) (Conquistador Cielo (USA))
4814[8] 5651[9] 6225[3]6503[10]
Jeudi *Sir Mark Prescott* a34
3 b g Montjeu(IRE) —Portorosa (USA) (Irish River (FR))
16[12] 1041[11]132[11] (Dead)
Jeune Loup *P C Haslam* a44 69
4 b g Loup Sauvage(USA) —Secret Waters (Pharly (FR))
97[10] 3158[11]
Jewaar (USA) *M A Jarvis* 88
3 ch f Diesis—Ringshaan (FR) (Darshaan)
1797[3] 2350[4] 2868[2] 3419[3] 3975[2](4814)
Jewel In The Sand (IRE) *R Hannon* 105
4 b m Bluebird(USA) —Dancing Drop (Green Desert (USA))
1377[11] (3047) 3499[11]
Jewelled Dagger (IRE) *I Semple* a25
2 b g Daggers Drawn(USA) —Cappadoce (IRE) (General Monash (USA))
6523[13] 6859[11]6963[9]
Jewel Of India *Mrs A L M King* a55 57
7 ch g Bijou D'Inde—Low Hill (Rousillon (USA))
235[6] 417[10]640[8] 1353[16] (4511) 5285[9]6532[12]
Jidaar (IRE) *P W Hiatt* a62 76
3 b g Grand Lodge(USA) —Banaadir (USA) (Diesis)
(1458) 6351[12] 6519[8]
Jidiya (IRE) *Mrs H O Graham* a73 67
7 b g Lahib(USA) —Yaqatha (IRE) (Sadler's Wells (USA))
1666[9] 5723[10] 5905[10]
Jiggy Spriggy (IRE) *V Smith* 41
3 b f King Charlemagne(USA) —Amneris (IRE) (Alzao (USA))
880[9] 1048[8] 4806[10]
Jihaaz (IRE) *B W Hills* 87+
3 ch g Elnadim(USA) —Gazar (Kris)
1048[4] 2615[2] (2919) 3224[7] 5512[9] 5722[3]
Jill Dawson (IRE) *John Berry* 60
3 b f Mull Of Kintyre(USA) —Dream Of Jenny (Caerleon (USA))
1355[7] 2034[10] (2678) 3030[2] 3695[7]
Jilly Why (IRE) *Ms Deborah J Evans* a63 78
5 b m Mujadil(USA) —Ruwy (Soviet Star (USA))
343[4] 537[7]950[6] 2027[7] 2384[6]2784[4] 6533[3] 6739[6]
Jimbobalou *T T Clement* 23
2 b c Mujahid(USA) —Barsham (Be My Guest (USA))
5915[14]
Jiminor Mack *W J H Ratcliffe* a35 56
3 bl f Little Jim—Copper Trader (Faustus (USA))
1901[7] 2188[14] 4382[5] 5240[13] 5767[4]6959[10]
Jimmy The Guesser *N P Littmoden* a92 84
3 ch g Piccolo—Brush Away (Ahonoora)
(967) 1146[5] 1482[5] 1529[7] 1963[2]2650[2] 3067[5] 3606[4] 3970[4] 4391[2]4802[3] 5336[20] 5649[6]6094[4] 6352[4]6752[4] 6896[2]
Jinksonthehouse *M D I Usher* a10 47?
5 b m Whittingham(IRE) —Aldwick Colonnade (Kind Of Hush)
1774[11] 2096[6] 2543[11] 2858[6] 3004[14]3348[15] 3863[6] 4223[7] 4585[16]
Jioconda (IRE) *Edward Lynam* 98
3 b f Rossini(USA) —La Joconde (Vettori (IRE))
928a[4] 1172a[6]
Job Done *M W Easterby* 29
2 b f Elmaamul(USA) —Emma Amour (Emarati (USA))
1142[10] 2073[5]
Jo'Burg (USA) *Mrs A J Perrett* a96 97
2 b c Johannesburg(USA) —La Martina (Atraf)
1838[2] 2719[5] (3363) 4037[8] 6100[3]
Joburg Gold (USA) *B W Hills* 28
2 bb c Johannesburg(USA) —Churn Dat Butter (USA) (Unbridled (USA))
1838[16]
Jocheski (IRE) *M J Wallace* a62
2 b c Mull Of Kintyre(USA) —Ludovica (Bustino)
6284[4] 6658[4]
Jockser (IRE) *J W Mullins* 72
5 b g Desert Story(IRE) —Pupa Fiorini (ITY) (Indian Ridge)
5587[2]
Jodrell Bank (IRE) *W Jarvis* 60
3 ch f Observatory(USA) —Aravonian (Night Shift (USA))
4495[2] 4799[6] 5729[11]
Joe Draper *P D Evans* a11
4 ch g Forzando—Shanghai Lil (Petong)
6286[12]

Joe Jo Star *B P J Baugh* a57 54
4 b g Piccolo—Zagreb Flyer (Old Vic)
121[12] 400[2](467) 586[3]697[7] 906[10]1305[7] 6544[11]6667[10] 6787[8]
Joella's Lad *Ms Deborah J Evans* a10 21
2 gr g Bertolini(USA) —Coffee To Go (Environment Friend)
1420[12] 1790[6] 2139[9]5537[13] 6891[9]
Johannes (IRE) *D Nicholls* a85 102
3 b c Mozart(IRE) —Blue Sirocco (Bluebird (USA))
1083[4] 1404[10] 2959[3]3414[11] 3761[4] 5535[16]
Johannesburg Cat (USA) *N P Littmoden* a63 27
2 b f Johannesburg(USA) —High Society (IRE) (Key Of Luck (USA))
4857a[7] 6146[6] 6379[4]6536[6] 6764[7]
Johannesburg Jack (IRE) *H Morrison* a90 88
2 b c Johannesburg(USA) —Out Of Egypt (USA) (Red Ransom (USA))
1420[9] (2130) 2719[13] 3531[2]4344[3] 4775[6] 5466a[22]
Johannian *J M Bradley* a53 78
8 b g Hernando(FR) —Photo Call (Chief Singer)
3948[5] 4288[6] 5130[13] 6054[15]
John Bratby (USA) *P J Makin* a50 32
4 bb h Royal Academy(USA) —Side Saddle (IRE) (Saddlers' Hall (IRE))
1960[4] 3950[8]
John Charles (IRE) *B De Haan* a66 54
4 b g Fraam—Norwegian Queen (IRE) (Affirmed (USA))
(531) 641[12] 1002[8]3221[10] 3798[9]
John Claude (IRE) *Ronald Thompson* a53 67
3 b g Night Shift(USA) —Koukla Mou (Keen)
344[5] 626[8]910[10] 6638[11]
John Falstaff (BRZ) *C Morgado* a72 87
5 b g Burooj—Renata Tebaldi (ARG) (Southern Halo (USA))
149a[10] 513a[10]
John Forbes *B Ellison* a66 75
4 b g High Estate—Mavourneen (USA) (Dynaformer (USA))
250[7] 385[10](816) 1033[6] 1502[6] 1660[6] 2078[7] 2894[3]3446[7]
John Keats *I Semple* 75
3 b g Bertolini(USA) —Nightingale (Night Shift (USA))
1067[8] 1482[2] 1812[5] 2163[5] 2385[11]4725[9] 5079[7] 5554[13] 5902[3] 5961[7]6159[6]
Johnnie Black (IRE) *E J Creighton* 21
4 b g Fayruz—Cunning Kate (IRE) (Roi Danzig (USA))
5573[13] 6237[13]
Johnny Alljays (IRE) *S Lycett* a51 41
5 b g Victory Note(USA) —It's Academic (Royal Academy (USA))
4438[4] 5927[P]
Johnny Alpha (IRE) *P W Chapple-Hyam* 68
3 b g Namid—Green's Maud Earl (Night Shift (USA))
4562[12]
Johnny Jumpup (IRE) *R M Beckett* 101
4 ch g Pivotal—Clarice Orsini (Common Grounds)
930a[8] 1678[8] 2200[15] 5639[10] 5945[16]
John O'Groats (IRE) *W G Harrison* a32 52
8 b g Distinctly North(USA) —Bannons Dream (IRE) (Thatching)
4523[10] 5309[17] 5577[8] 5840[3]
John Stanley (IRE) *D Carroll* a16 52
2 b g Imperial Ballet(IRE) —Pivotable (Pivotal)
4323[11] 4956[5] 5315[8] 6420[8]
Johnston's Diamond (IRE) *E J Alston* a81 96
8 b g Tagula(IRE) —Toshair Flyer (Ballad Rock)
718[10] 1183[5] 1388[11](1858) 2021[6] 3077[7] 4202[10] 4793 [6] 4988[5]5336[25] 5578[7] 5970[5]6326[5] 6478[9]6508[11] 6681[9]
Johnstown Lad (IRE) *Niall Moran* 85
2 b c Invincible Spirit(IRE) —Pretext (Polish Precedent (USA))
4850a[10]
John Terry (IRE) *Mrs A J Perrett* 94
3 b g Grand Lodge(USA) —Kardashina (FR) (Darshaan)
2174[2] 2654[4] 2986[3] 6051[8]
Joint Expectations (IRE) *Mrs C A Dunnett* a36 31
2 b g Indian Rocket—Jenny Spinner (IRE) (Bluebird (USA))
1639[9] 2045[6] 2610[11] 3979[13] 6562[9]6706[7]
Jojesse *S Parr* 44
2 ch g Compton Place—Jodeeka (Fraam)
727[7] 1053[6] 1342[10] 3818[4]
Joking John *C W Fairhurst* a41 44
3 b g Compton Admiral—Bo' Babbity (Strong Gale)
(790) 1200[8] 1768[5]1825[7] 3006[4] 3138[4] 3529[5] 6554[12]
Jolie (IRE) *R Dickin* 67
4 b m Orpen(USA) —Arabian Dream (IRE) (Royal Academy (USA))
1348[12]
Jolizero *John Berry* a58 68
5 br g Danzero(AUS) —Jolis Absent (Primo Dominie)
973[8] 1138[3] 1219[2] 1808[14] 3454[4]5061[8] 5952[4]
Jomelamin *R J Hodges* a36
4 gr m Silver Patriarch(IRE) —Jomel Amou (IRE) (Ela-Mana-Mou)
107[11] 297[12]417[9]
Jomus *L Montague Hall* a64 59
5 b g Soviet Star(USA) —Oatey (Master Willie)
82[4] 185[3]263[6] 379[11]1334[2] 1400[3]2320[9] 2862[4]4139[5] 4248[2]4704[2] 4995[4]6436[2] 6714[3]6841[3]
Jonny Ebeneezer *M Wellings* a56 86
7 b g Hurricane Sky(AUS) —Leap Of Faith (IRE) (Northiam (USA))
1481[3] 1835[16] 2047[8] 2824[9] 3295[8]3845[10] 4368[13]4730[9]
Jools *D K Ivory* a77 71
8 b g Cadeaux Genereux—Madame Crecy (USA) (Al Nasr (FR))
845[6] 950[10]1164[7] 1311[8] 2327[2]2510[5] 2708[6] 3153[4] 3599[6]4073[6] 4446[13] 6855[4]6983[5]
Jopau *G M Lyons* 90
2 ch c Dr Fong(USA) —Kelso Magic (USA) (Distant View (USA))
3962a[8] 4850a[6] 5707a[5]

Jord (IRE) *A J McCabe* a73 53
2 b f Trans Island—Arcevia (IRE) (Archway (IRE))
1040[4] 1248[2] 2626[9] 5738[2]5958[7] (6472) 6525[5]6750[4] 6872[2]
Jordans Elect *T J Pitt* a23 79
6 ch g Fleetwood(IRE) —Cal Norma's Lady (IRE) (Lyphard's Special (USA))
1035[6] 1500[3] 1637[2] 2162[3] 2378[6]2547[6] 2853[4] 3333[9] (3784) 4353[8] 4653[8]5961[14] 6240[11]
Jordan's Light (USA) *T J Pitt* a75 67
3 rg g Aljabr(USA) —Western Friend (USA) (Gone West (USA))
(1888) 1950[6] 4154[6] 5446[8] 6396[4](6497) 6568[2](6590) 6652[8]6946[4]
Jordans Spark *P Monteith* a53 60
5 ch g Opening Verse(USA) —Ribot's Pearl (Indian Ridge)
1947[9] 2165[6] 2546[11] 3480[5] (3815) (4355) 5064[2]5311[3] 5581[9] 6213[7]
Josarty *J J Quinn* a9 55
3 b c Josr Algarhoud(IRE) —Search Party (Rainbow Quest (USA))
1185[5] 1609[3] 2001[8] 2399[10] 2896[6]3290[5] 3749[15] 4262[5] 6304[11]
Jose Bove *R Dickin* a47 23
4 ch g So Factual(USA) —Dark Sirona (Pitskelly)
314[8] 539[6]720[11] 6021[12] 6429[11]
Joseph Henry *M Johnston* 94
4 b g Mujadil(USA) —Iris May (Brief Truce (USA))
2230[15] 2520[8] 2683[9] 3433[5] 3733[4](3812) 4029[5] 4131[4] 5945[6]
Josephine Malines *C G Cox* 53
2 b f Inchinor—Alrisha (IRE) (Persian Bold)
6215[16]
Joseph Locke (IRE) *M Dods* 64
2 b c Indian Rocket—Faypool (IRE) (Fayruz)
814[4] 1096[2] 1454[3] 3994[13]4603[6] 4693[5] (4950) 5334[7] 6296[4]
Josh *K A Ryan* a90 100
4 b g Josr Algarhoud(IRE) —Charlie Girl (Puissance)
627[6] 728[22] 1086[8]1835[15] 4202[6] 4609[14] 4790[4] 5529[8]6733[8]
Joshua's Gold (IRE) *D Carroll* a73 73
5 b g Sesaro(USA) —Lady Of The Night (IRE) (Night Shift (USA))
950[5] 1353[5] 1459[2]1683[8] 1885[3] 2211[3](2936) 3398[4] 3565[2] 4154[2]4325[2] 5249[4] 5436[8]5974[6]
Josh You Are *D E Cantillon* a59 50
3 b g Josr Algarhoud(IRE) —Cibenze (Owington)
5767[5] 6057[3] 6304[7]6553[11] (6907)
Josie Marcus (USA) *J Noseda* a58 83
3 ch f Gone West(USA) —Sheila's Revenge (USA) (Lord Avie (USA))
2587[10] (3554) 3953[6] 4395[9]5345[11]
Josr's Bank *M W Easterby* a8
2 b f Josr Algarhoud(IRE) —Piggy Bank (Emarati (USA))
3994[10] 4510[10] 4887[16]
Josr's Magic (IRE) *Mrs A Duffield* 69
2 b g Josr Algarhoud(IRE) —Just The Trick (USA) (Phone Trick (USA))
1096[3] 1420[3] 1559[4] 3605[5] 3834[2](4196) 4912[5] 5140[7] 5721[15]
Jost Van Dyke *J R Boyle* a64 65
2 b g Foxhound(USA) —Interregnum (Interrex (CAN))
1688[11] 3591[5] (3801) 4284[3] 4779[3] 5162[7]5646[2] 5876[4] 6491[7]6640[5] 6695[4]6845[4]
Jousting *V Smith* a43
2 b g Josr Algarhoud(IRE) —Sweet Wilhelmina (Indian Ridge)
6963[6]
Joy And Pain *R A Harris* a76 74
5 b g Pursuit Of Love—Ice Chocolate (USA) (Icecapade (USA))
17[6] 89[4]192[13] 321[4]502[2] 576[5]950[11] (1645) (2184) (2317) 2864[3]3089[18] 5765[15] 6048[3] 6174[7] 6396[13]
Joybee *B Grizzetti*
2 b c Best Of The Bests(IRE) —Royalcombe (IRE) (Royal Academy (USA))
(3427a)
Joyeaux *J Hetherton* a72 70
4 b m Mark Of Esteem(IRE) —Divine Secret (Hernando (FR))
(51) 441[6] 737[8]977[14] 1686[14] 2020[16] (3052) 3459[3] 3845[5]4437[4] 4694[5] 5081[5]5577[2] 5756[4] 6315[4] 6572[3]6664[6]
Joyful Tears (IRE) *E A L Dunlop* a57+ 71
2 ch f Barathea(IRE) —Perils Of Joy (IRE) (Rainbow Quest (USA))
4705[9] 5425[5] 5754[4]
Joyful Winner (AUS) *J Moore* 119
6 br g El Moxie(USA) —Northern Tycoon (AUS) (Last Tycoon)
1527a[3] 6784a[6]
Joy In The Guild (IRE) *W S Kittow* a41 59
3 b f Mull Of Kintyre(USA) —About Face (Midyan (USA))
1226[4] 1726[5]2968[5] (3264) (3870) 4282[4] 4758[5] 5247[10]
J R Stevenson (USA) *Ernst Oertel* a54 57
10 ch g Lyphard(USA) —While It Lasts (USA) (Foolish Pleasure (USA))
13[7] 158[4]231[9] 471[7]
Juan Bol (IRE) *V Smith* a80 46
2 b g Fayruz—Butterfly Morning (IRE) (Distinctly North (USA))
1053[5] (1535) 1824[6] 3685[7]
Jubilation *F Reuterskiold* a86 115
7 b h Zamindar(USA) —Jubilee Trail (Shareef Dancer (USA))
(2123a) 3563a[5] 4864a[9]
Jubilee Dream *Mrs L J Mongan* a65 64
4 b g Bluebird(USA) —Last Dream (IRE) (Alzao (USA))
324[12] 838[7]1313[6] 1673[13] 2132[7]
Jubilee Street (IRE) *Mrs A Duffield* a42 89
7 b g Dr Devious(IRE) —My Firebird (Rudimentary (USA))
1043[3] (1280) 1532[4] 2787[4] 3241[3] 3549[4]3812[4] (3985) 5680[13]

Jucebabe *J L Spearing* 64
3 b f Zilzal(USA) —Jucea (Bluebird (USA))
1825[13] (2187) 2433[9] 3118[5] 3348[8] 3864[2]4164[3] 4398[3] 4532[3] (4756) 4962[8] 5378[14]

Judd Street *R F Johnson Houghton* a103 103
4 b g Compton Place—Pudding Lane (IRE) (College Chapel)
(1359) 1602[2] 2450[3] 2847[12] 3092[9] 3535[8]5420[6] 5832[2] 6095[3]6243[2] 6445[8]

Judge (USA) *B J Meehan* 94
3 b c Giant's Causeway(USA) —Autumn Leaf (USA) (Gone West (USA))
1093[7]

Judge Neptune *J S Goldie* 54
2 b g Ocean Of Wisdom(USA) —Princess Louise (Efisio)
5332[4] 5632[4] 5900[14]

Judge 'n Jury *C A Cyzer* a43 44
2 ch g Pivotal—Cyclone Connie (Dr Devious (IRE))
5915[13] 6188[13]

Judiths Wild Rush (USA) *Reade Baker* a107 92
5 gr h Wild Rush(USA) —Tie Talk (USA) (Black Tie Affair)
4384a[2]

Judraan *M A Jarvis* 80
3 b c Alhaarth(IRE) —Sakha (Wolfhound (USA))
2650[10] 2988[16]

Juicy Fruits *E A L Dunlop* a62 61
3 b f King's Best(USA) —Fruit Punch (IRE) (Barathea (IRE))
1901[10] 3200[5] 3794[8]

Julatten (IRE) *G A Swinbank* a33 42
2 b f Alhaarth(IRE) —Istibshar (USA) (Mr Prospector (USA))
2500[7] 3596[9] 3994[7]

Julilla *G G Margarson* 37
2 b f Tobougg(IRE) —Kiss Me Again (IRE) (Cyrano De Bergerac)
3799[5] 4920[12] 5613[12]

Jumanji (IRE) *M J Attwater* a51 11
3 b f Imperial Ballet(IRE) —Toshair Flyer (Ballad Rock)
124[9] 364[8]823[5] 1055[14] 1217[14]6406[4] 6549[7]6618[9] 6717[14]6771[7]

Jumbajukiba *Mrs A J Perrett* 94+
3 b c Barathea(IRE) —Danseuse Du Soir (IRE) (Thatching)
2033[3] 2774[6] 3443[13]

Jumeirah Scarer *K A Ryan* a67 67
5 b g Tagula(IRE) —Mountain Harvest (FR) (Shirley Heights)
3147[6] 4205[2] 4423[5] 4632[7] 5242[7]5750[6]

Jump Ship *M P Tregoning* a68+ 61
3 ch f Night Shift(USA) —Flagship (Rainbow Quest (USA))
2578[7] (5098) 5875[12]

Juncea *H Morrison* a73 57
2 b f Elnadim(USA) —Strelitzia (SAF) (Fort Wood (USA))
4207[7] 4657[10] 4993[2]5261[3] (6222)

Junebug Symphony (IRE) *V Smith* a38 64
4 b m Indian Lodge(IRE) —Ladies View (IRE) (Turtle Island (IRE))
43[12] 6855[9]

Jun Fan (USA) *B Ellison* a58 64
4 br g Artax(USA) —Ringside Lady (NZ) (Clay Hero (AUS))
196[9] 290[10]1437[3] 1607[7] 1689[6] 1886[2] 2237[6]2396[3] 3356[9] 6994[11]

Jungle Prince (USA) *J Garcia* a105 108
5 b g Sir Cat(USA) —Wayward Song (USA) (Seattle Song (USA))
5827a[3]

Junior *B J Meehan* a86+ 72+
3 ch g Singspiel(IRE) —For More (FR) (Sanglamore (USA))
4625[5] 5203[3] 5669[9](6244)

Juniper Girl (IRE) *M L W Bell* 101+
3 b f Revoque(IRE) —Shajara (FR) (Kendor (FR))
781[2] 895[3] 1079[2] (1182) 1867[2] 4778[2]4990[2] (5594) (5811)

Junkanoo *K G Reveley* 63
10 ch g Generous(IRE) —Lupescu (Dixieland Band (USA))
5960[P]

Jupiters Moon (IRE) *R Charlton* a22 58
3 b c Galileo(IRE) —Dance Treat (USA) (Nureyev (USA))
4625[7] 5128[6] 5426[11]

Juror (USA) *Sir Michael Stoute* a94+ 83
3 gr c Royal Academy(USA) —Paper Princess (USA) (Flying Paster (USA))
(1274) 5990[5]

Just A Flash (IRE) *B R Johnson* a31
2 b g Redback—Just Deserts (Alhijaz)
6034[10]

Just A Fluke (IRE) *M R Bosley* a45 50
5 b g Darshaan—Star Profile (IRE) (Sadler's Wells (USA))
706[9] 1400[13]

Justalord *A Crook* a59 59
8 b g King's Signet(USA) —Just Lady (Emarati (USA))
5957[13]

Just Beware *Miss Z C Davison* a41 48?
4 b m Makbul—Bewails (IRE) (Caerleon (USA))
1879[5] 3437[13]

Just Bond (IRE) *G R Oldroyd* a86 58
4 b g Namid—Give Warning (IRE) (Warning)
440[5] 1253[4] 2165[10]6286[3] (6431) 6667[3] (6767) (6924) 6968[2]

Just Bonnie *J M Bradley* 39?
4 b h Lujain(USA) —Fairy Flight (IRE) (Fairy King (USA))
1877[7] 2531[15] 2758[19]

Justcallmehandsome *D J S Ffrench Davis* a51 55
4 ch g Handsome Ridge—Pearl Dawn (IRE) (Jareer (USA))
26[4] 143[7](180) 300[2]387[9] 784[9](888) 1334[11]1769[9] 2262[3] 2978[7]5267[3] 5925[2] 6128[7]6544[5]

Just Chrissie *G Fierro*
2 b f Classic Cliche(IRE) —Marsh Marigold (Tina's Pet)
1278[6]

Just Dashing *J E Long* a14 14
7 b g Arrasas(USA) —Smitten (Run The Gantlet (USA))
259[13]

Just Devine (IRE) *B Palling* 73
3 b f Montjeu(IRE) —Shirley Blue (IRE) (Shirley Heights)
948[3] 1118[6] 1823[7] 3472[13] 4661[12]

Just Down The Road (IRE) *R A Harris* a53 69
3 b f Night Shift(USA) —Avigail (USA) (Miswaki (USA))
473[8] 901[9]1109[8] 1567[7] 2068[4](2316) 2511[6] 2543[9] (2987) 3299[8] 3864[7]

Just Dust *D R C Elsworth* 87
2 b g Makbul—Dusty Bankes (Greensmith)
961[7] 1030[7] (1229) 2598[4] (3160) (3619) (4100) 4335[2]4480[3] 4804[7] 5461[2] (5546) 5940[12]

Justenjoy Yourself *R W Price* a48 49
4 b m Tipsy Creek(USA) —Habibi (Alhijaz)
680[11] 1465[3]1534[7]

Just Fly *Dr J R J Naylor* a77 68
6 b g Efisio—Chrysalis (Soviet Star (USA))
33[6] 140[5]214[2] 463[4]556[7] 764[9]1002[11] 6070[5]6419[7] 6590[5]6791[6]

Just Intersky (USA) *K A Ryan* a52 84
3 gr c Distant View(USA) —Hexane (FR) (Kendor (FR))
2809[3] 3224[13] 5554[6] 6418[12]6946[8]

Just James *D Nicholls* a69 99
7 b g Spectrum(IRE) —Fairy Flight (IRE) (Fairy King (USA))
1803[10] 2230[17] 2847[11] 3079[8] 3295[4]3482[12] 3926[15] 4658[2] 5688[10]

Just Jasmin *P D Evans*
3 b f Wizard King—Rose Hill (Sabrehill (USA))
4899[12] 5056[9] 5922[10]

Just Joey *J R Weymes* 85
2 b f Averti(IRE) —Fly South (Polar Falcon (USA))
(1046) 2125[2] 2800[16] 3474[5] (4321) 4946[2]

Just Lille (IRE) *Mrs A Duffield* 78
3 b f Mull Of Kintyre(USA) —Tamasriya (IRE) (Doyoun)
1493[5] 2948[4] 3189[6] (3582) (3725) 4426[3] 4567[8]5320[11]

Just Logic (IRE) *J Noseda* a77 65
3 bb c Desert Prince(IRE) —Tiavanita (USA) (J O Tobin (USA))
191[2] 374[2]630[4] 4661[7] 5611[3]

Just Lovely *M P Tregoning*
2 ch f Inchinor—Just Ice (Polar Falcon (USA))
4657[15] 5348[12]

Just Matty *J G M O'Shea* 32
3 b g Bertolini(USA) —Frisson (Slip Anchor)
2063 [10]

Just Observing *E A L Dunlop* a75 76
3 ch g Observatory(USA) —Just Speculation (IRE) (Ahonoora)
952[2] (1434) 2324[5] 3015[8]

Just Oscar (GER) *W M Brisbourne* a60 66
2 b g Surako(GER) —Jade Chequer (Green Desert (USA))
1588[11] 2130[7] 2416[3]4171[4]

Just Queen *M Nigge* 99
3 b f Dansili—Just Fly (USA) (Capote (USA))
6230a[9]

Just Tallulah *N P Littmoden* a54 51
3 b f Tomba—Tallulah Belle (Crowning Honors (CAN))
645[5] 801[7]1642[10] 2080[6] 2574[14]

Just Tilly *L Montague Hall* a53 36
3 b f Josr Algarhoud(IRE) —Illana Bay (USA) (Manila (USA))
479[5] 710[9]900[10] 1829[6] 2131[6]2463[10] 6236[4]6707[10]

Just Two Numbers *W Jarvis* 58
2 b c Bahamian Bounty—Khadino (Relkino)
5658[12]

Just Waz (USA) *R M Whitaker* a46 65
4 ch g Woodman(USA) —Just Tops (USA) (Topsider (USA))
869[5] 1075[14] 2018[6] 2193[6] 4205[7]4423[6] 4698[8] 4914[3] 5369[9]

Justy (USA) *M L W Bell* 71
2 bb c Danehill(USA) —Saintly Speech (USA) (Southern Halo (USA))
2144[4]

Juvenescent (USA) *R D E Woodhouse* a35 65
2 b f Elusive Quality(USA) —June Moon (IRE) (Sadler's Wells (USA))
3878[8] 4608[5] 5283[7] 5747[12] 6764[6]

Juwwi *J M Bradley* a49 52
12 ch g Mujtahid(USA) —Nouvelle Star (AUS) (Luskin Star (AUS))
145[10] 179[10]216[8]

Juzilla (IRE) *W R Swinburn* a63
2 b f Marju(IRE) —Mizillablack (IRE) (Eagle Eyed (USA))
5424[7]

Kabeer *A J McCabe* a84 47
8 ch g Unfuwain(USA) —Ta Rib (USA) (Mr Prospector (USA))
267[8] 444[9]559[2] 1938[9]2183[7] 2820[10] 3212[14] 5908[9]6147[2] 6469[2](6698) 6986[2]

Kabis Amigos *D Nicholls* 76
4 ch g Nashwan(USA) —River Saint (USA) (Irish River (FR))
1124[11] 1422[17] 1996[18] 3361[5] 4059[7](4233) 4518[5] 4961[2]

Kachgai (IRE) *E Libaud* 104
3 b c Kaldounevees(FR) —Toujours Juste (FR) (Always Fair (USA))
4623a[4] 5519a[6]

Kafuu (IRE) *J Noseda* 77+
2 b c Danehill Dancer(IRE) —Nausicaa (USA) (Diesis)
(5790)

Kahara *L M Cumani* 70
2 b f Sadler's Wells(USA) —Kithanga (IRE) (Darshaan)
5352[6] 6049[3]

Kahlua Bear *Miss K B Boutflower* a56 59
4 b g Mister Baileys—Crystal Magic (Mazilier (USA))
1397[5] 1728[2]2235[10] 2813[4] (3611) 4564[13] 4970[9]5032[6] 5576[12]

Kahlua Kiss *W R Muir* a82 102
3 b f Mister Baileys—Ring Queen (USA) (Fairy King (USA))
1963[6] 2404[10] 2754[3](2961) 3318[3] (3703) (3954) 4482[3] 4818[6] 5188[3]5477[2] 6190[8]

Kahyasola (FR) *G Doleuze* 99
2 b f Kahyasi—Isola D'Elba (USA) (Diesis)
4415a[4] 6046a[3]

Kai Kuri (IRE) *P W Hiatt*
5 br m Carroll House—Lucy's Light (IRE) (Miner's Lamp)
5650[9] 6535[9]

Kailasha (IRE) *C F Wall* 58
2 br f Kalanisi(IRE) —Snow Peak (Arazi (USA))
6215[11]

Kalaam *G P Enright* a16
4 b g Silver Patriarch(IRE) —Phil's Folly (Glasgow Central)
18[8]

Kala Dancer *Lady Herries* 64
3 b g Kalanisi(IRE) —Silly Mid-On (Midyan (USA))
4776[5] 5203[5]

Kaladar (IRE) *K A Ryan* a59 58
2 b g Kalanisi(IRE) —Desert Order (IRE) (Desert King (IRE))
1454[5] 2072[2] 3157[4]4509[13] 4882[8] 5084[5] 5387[9]

Kaladin *G L Moore* 58
3 b g Kalanisi(IRE) —Minstrel's Gift (The Minstrel (CAN))
2332[9] 2569[7] (Dead)

Kalaforte (SAF) *R Simpson* a76 79
4 b m Fort Wood(USA) —Kal Sufi (SAF) (Al Mufti (USA))
351a[5] 510a[10] 623a[4]5550[9] 5895[11]

Kalahari King (FR) *H-A Pantall* 98
5 b g Kahyasi—Queen Of Warsaw (FR) (Assert)
6786a[13]

Kalambari (IRE) *S Dow* 92
7 b g Kahyasi—Kalamba (IRE) (Green Dancer (USA))
1238[6] 4448[LFT]

Kalandara (IRE) *Sir Michael Stoute* a58+ 67+
3 b f Rainbow Quest(USA) —Kalamba (IRE) (Green Dancer (USA))
3200[6] 3901[9] 4759[2]5056[4]

Kalani Star (IRE) *I W McInnes* a34 41
6 b g Ashkalani(IRE) —Bellissi (IRE) (Bluebird (USA))
606[11] 649[8]1073[6] 1341[7] 1462[3]2148[4] 2262[5] 2541[13] 2789[14] 3240[8]3615[9] 3944[5] 4266[7]

Kalankari (IRE) *A M Balding* a103 103
3 b c Kalanisi(IRE) —Stately Princess (Robellino (USA))
(703) 855[2] (1384) 2024[3] 2774[7]3443[8] 4042[2] 5019[4]

Kalantera (IRE) *C L Popham* a56 58
3 b g Kalanisi(IRE) —Tintera (IRE) (King's Theatre (IRE))
372[4] 918[13]2607[9] 3399[3] 5587[10]

Kalasam *W R Muir* 78
2 ch c Noverre(USA) —Spring Sixpence (Dowsing (USA))
4388[7] 4895[3] 5178[3] 5655[27]

Kalatime (IRE) *A M Balding* a73 66
3 bb f Kalanisi(IRE) —Dream Time (Rainbow Quest (USA))
1192[7] 1638[3] 1997[6]2933[3] 3731[4] 4331[6]4842[3] 5388[6] 5733[2]

Kalawoun (FR) *Ferdy Murphy* 59
4 b g Highest Honor(FR) —Kalajana (USA) (Green Dancer (USA))
2206[9]

Kalderon (GER) *T Hogan* 109
6 br g Big Shuffle(USA) —Kreuzdame (GER) (Acatenango (GER))
932a[3] (5004a)

Kaleo *A Wohler* 103
2 ch c Lomitas—Kazoo (Shareef Dancer (USA))
5007a[3]

Kalgoorlie (USA) *J Noseda* 98
2 br c Gone West(USA) —Fair Kris (USA) (Kris S (USA))
2029[5] 2719[4] (3417) 4037[7]

Kalibanos (BRZ) *C Morgado* a83
5 b h Dark Brown(BRZ) —Sharp Profile (USA) (Northern Jove (CAN))
279a[9]

Kalishka (IRE) *R Allan* a44 59
5 b g Fasliyev(USA) —Andromaque (USA) (Woodman (USA))
242[9] 525[6]871[7]

Kalken (FR) *L Planard* 98
3 b c Kendor(FR) —Super Vite (USA) (Septieme Ciel (USA))
6250a[12]

Kallista's Pride *J R Best* a67 73
6 b m Puissance—Clan Scotia (Clantime)
74[6] 119[6](137) 164[6]192[8] 519[7]555[6] 576[2]711[8] 806[7]902[6] 3855[5] 4054[13]4294[4] 4629[7] 4691[4] 4795[10]

Kaluana Court *A W Carroll* a42 57
10 b m Batshoof—Fairfields Cone (Celtic Cone)
881[5] 975[9] 3269[8] 3919[5]4072[8] 4777[7] 4929[11]

Kalush *Miss A Stokell* a44? 28
5 b g Makbul—The Lady Vanishes (Robin Des Pins (USA))
423[10] 526[13]3716[13] 4021[10] 4227[7] 4668[8] 5751[11]6761[4] 6873[6]6957[P]

Kamanda Laugh *K A Ryan* a95 99
5 ch g Most Welcome—Kamada (USA) (Blushing Groom (FR))
631[2] 728[25] 1129[6]1667[9] 2012[20] 3971[3] 4711[5] 5177[10]5675[7] 6678[6]

Kamari Gold *M Mullineaux* 39
3 gr g Cloudings(IRE) —Manse Key Gold (Vaigly Great)
3053[10] 4301[7] 5138[8]

Kamarinskaya (USA) *A P O'Brien* 102
3 br f Storm Cat(USA) —Mr P's Princess (USA) (Mr Prospector (USA))
(1023a) 1719a[11] 2054a[10]

Kames Park (IRE) *I Semple* a68 93
4 b g Desert Sun—Persian Sally (IRE) (Persian Bold)
1281[9] 1585[9] 2162[6] (2452) 2850[3] 3888[7]6677[8]

Kandidate *C E Brittain* a115 113
4 b h Kabool—Valleyrose (IRE) (Royal Academy (USA))
(151a) 281a[6] 353a[7] 496a[7]625a[7] (704) (1017) 1840[5] 2722[6] (3254) 4096[6] 4818[3] (5018) 5547[6]

Kane Hekili (JPN) *Katsuhiko Sumii* a121
4 ch h Fuji Kiseki(JPN) —Life Out There (USA) (Deputy Minister (CAN))
743a[4]

Kaneko (TUR) *K Saglam* a107 108
5 b h Pivotal—Kalimat (Be My Guest (USA))
5227a[2]

Kanonkop *Miss J R Gibney* a57 54
2 b f Observatory(USA) —Camcorder (Nashwan (USA))
5754[7] 5906[8] 6071[10]

Kanpai (IRE) *J G M O'Shea* 62+
4 br g Trans Island—David's Star (Welsh Saint)
3291[3] (5201)

Kansas Gold *W R Muir* a36 72
3 b g Alhaarth(IRE) —Star Tulip (Night Shift (USA))
1960[8] 2458[3] 2859[2]3111[2] (3950) 4296[6] 4841[6]

Kaparolo (USA) *John A Harris*
7 ch g El Prado(IRE) —Parliament House (USA) (General Assembly (USA))
1138[17] 3382[9]

Kapellmeister (IRE) *M S Saunders* a71 86
3 b g Mozart(IRE) —March Hare (Groom Dancer (USA))
254[6] 365[8]2620[9] 2990[6] 3347[8] (3592) (3819) 4005[2]

Kapiolani (USA) *J M P Eustace* a24 30
3 ch f Mr Greeley(USA) —Iolani (Alzao (USA))
1055[10] 1336[11] 1670[8]

Kaptain Kate *R Brotherton* 5
2 ch f First Trump—Done And Dusted (IRE) (Up And At 'Em)
2072[U] 2328[16] 2916[6] 3160[5]

Karashino (IRE) *Mrs L Williamson* a56 65
4 ch m Shinko Forest(IRE) —Karisal (IRE) (Persian Bold)
178[4] 232[6]873[9] 1761[9]

Karathaena (IRE) *M E Sowersby* 27
6 b m Barathea(IRE) —Dabtara (IRE) (Kahyasi)
6272[6]

Karavel (GER) *P Schiergen* 109
3 b f Monsun(GER) —Kittiwake (Barathea (IRE))
1328a[9] 2279a[2] 3133a[7] (5762a)

Karawana (IRE) *John M Oxx* 101+
3 b f King's Best(USA) —Karaliyfa (IRE) (Kahyasi)
5396a[3]

Karayel (IRE) *R Hannon* a88 92
2 b c Fasliyev(USA) —Madamaa (IRE) (Alzao (USA))
1136[2] (1429) 1737[3] (2342) 3026[2] 5466a[7]

Kareeb (FR) *Miss J Feilden* a79 77
9 b g Green Desert(USA) —Braari (USA) (Gulch (USA))
1993[10] 2551[10] 3089[9]3705[6] 4108[7] 4531[5] 5302[11] 6577[3]6714[4] 6793[4]6955[8]

Karijini (IRE) *E A L Dunlop* a36
3 b f Anabaa(USA) —Legaya (Shirley Heights)
703[6]

Karlani (IRE) *G A Swinbank* 78
3 bb g Fantastic Light(USA) —Karliyka (IRE) (Last Tycoon)
1182[3] 1837[9] 2584[2] 3249[3] 5513[7]

Karlo Guitar (BRZ) *M Delzangles* a91 107?
6 gr h Mountain-Lark(BRZ) —La Guita (BRZ) (New Ghadeer (BRZ))
206a[7] 433a[7] 563a[4]2799a[9] 3564a[5]

Karlovy *M A Jarvis* 75
3 b f Halling(USA) —Marienbad (FR) (Darshaan)
1819[8] 2292[2]

Karlu (GER) *Pat Eddery* a76 88
4 ch g Big Shuffle(USA) —Krim (GER) (Lagunas)
1206[9] 2975[11] 3452[4] 4046[8]5533[10] 5935[3]

Karma Llama (IRE) *B Smart* 69
2 b f Intikhab(USA) —Ustka (Lomond (USA))
2924[3] 3328[3] 3758[3] 4377[5]

Karmest *E S McMahon* 50
2 ch f Best Of The Bests(IRE) —Karmafair (IRE) (Always Fair (USA))
5536[6]

Karoo Blue (IRE) *C E Brittain* 82
2 b c Cape Cross(IRE) —Red Conquest (Lycius (USA))
3253[5] 4260[3] 5066[2] (5481) 6102[7]

Karramalu (IRE) *Daniel Mark Loughnane* 72
5 b m Entrepreneur—Bold Feather (Persian Bold)
4166a[6]

Karrnak *Miss J Feilden* a47 77
4 b g Hernando(FR) —Maiden Aunt (IRE) (Distant Relative)
48[8] 174[8]309[12] 1724[4]1911[7] 4206[5] 4764[8]5033[5] 5298[14]

Karshaan (FR) *P Winkworth* a53 69
3 b g Kahyasi—Mon Petitnamour (IRE) (Darshaan)
2332[15] 4800[3] 5022[6]5587[5] 5952[12]

Kartago (GER) *R Suerland* 55
4 ch h Big Shuffle(USA) —Katharina (GER) (Esclavo (FR))
354a[12]

Kartikeya (USA) *J R Fanshawe* a35 43+
3 bb f War Chant(USA) —Egoli (USA) (Seeking The Gold (USA))
2143[8]

Kasarami (IRE) *J S Goldie* 45
3 b g Bluebird(USA) —Masakira (IRE) (Royal Academy (USA))
2243[11] 2746[9] 3167[11]

Kaseema (USA) *Sir Michael Stoute* 92
2 bb f Storm Cat(USA) —Onaga (USA) (Mr Prospector (USA))
(5296) 5966[7]

Kashmir Lady (FR) *H Candy* 69
2 ch f Rock Of Gibraltar(IRE) —Persian Walk (FR) (Persian Bold)
4553[6] 5754[5] 6199[5]

Kashtanka (IRE) *J Balding* a41 43
4 ch g Ashkalani(IRE) —Spark (IRE) (Flash Of Steel)
90[5] 299[6]388[5] 529[7]687[3] 783[4]3749[10] 4019[12] 4293[5]

Kassiopeia (IRE) *M R Channon* a82 99
3 b f Galileo(IRE) —Brush Strokes (Cadeaux Genereux)
(1283) 1669[5] 2203[7] 2804[9] 4079[10] 5641[4]6191[10]

Kassuta *S C Williams* a65
2 b f Kyllachy—Happy Omen (Warning)
4993[7] 5648[2]

Kastan *B Palling* a18
2 ch g Auction House(USA) —Cashiki (IRE) (Case Law)
2938[7]

Kasthari (IRE) *J Howard Johnson* 117
7 gr g Vettori(IRE) —Karliyka (IRE) (Last Tycoon)
4677[11] 5156[4] 5967[7]

Kastoria (IRE) *John M Oxx* 119
5 ch m Selkirk(USA) —Kassana (IRE) (Shernazar)
(1324a) 1833[4] (3107a) (4639a) (5395a) 6126a[8] 6782a[2]

Kasumi *H Morrison* a82 79
3 ch f Inchinor—Raindrop (Primo Dominie)
16[2] 132[4]658[4] 1551[11]2171[3] 2479[7] 3290[2] 4666[2] (4772) (5268) 5504[11]5896[8] 6094[3] 6350[3]

Kasus (GER) *P Vovcenko* 110
8 br g Second Set(IRE) —Kettwig (GER) (Acatenango (GER))
1860a[6]

Kat Act Two *J A Osborne* a60 43
2 gr f Act One—Trempkate (USA) (Trempolino (USA))
2287[8] 2755[4] 2980[9]

Katalog (GER) *Tim Gibson* 82
3 b c Tiger Hill(IRE) —Kapriole (GER) (Surumu (GER))
3776a[11]

Katchit (IRE) *A King* a88 83
3 b g Kalanisi(IRE) —Miracle (Ezzoud (IRE))
34[2] 124[3]160[4] 804[2]1192[4] 1403[2] 1880[2]2066[5] 2608[5] (2990) 4244[2]5016[6]

Katejackiera (IRE) *W M Brisbourne*
3 b f Rossini(USA) —The Merry Widow (IRE) (Brief Truce (USA))
2107[12] 3264[10]

Kathleen Kennet *Mrs H Sweeting* a59 62
6 b m Turtle Island(IRE) —Evaporate (Insan (USA))
897[8] 1289[5] 1797[8] 2221[8] 2647[12]5390[9] 6300[2] 6577[2]6780[3] 6981[6]

Kathryn Janeway (IRE) *W R Muir* 68
4 b m In The Wings—Freak Out (FR) (Bering)
1204[3] 1772[3] 2133[9] 2457[4]

Katie Boo (IRE) *A Berry* a53 21
4 br m Namid—Misty Peak (IRE) (Sri Pekan (USA))
1042[16] 6212[9] 6478[10]6527[7]

Katie Killane *M Wellings* a51 33
4 ch m Komaite(USA) —Efficacy (Efisio)
24[10] 179[7]388[12] 613[14]633[6] 686[4]789[8] 870[3]1272[5] 1466[2]1534[3] (1722) 1909[5] 2897[11] 6704[10]6723[4]

Katie Kingfisher *R M Beckett* a42 42
2 b f Fraam—Sonic Sapphire (Royal Academy (USA))
6015[6] 6330[7] 6912[9]

Katie Lawson (IRE) *D Haydn Jones* a66 26
3 b f Xaar—Idle Chat (USA) (Assert)
49[6] 211[3](333) 415[8]2142[6] (3099) 4757[13]

Katies Tuitor *B W Duke* a74 64
3 b g Kayf Tara—Penny Gold (IRE) (Millfontaine)
592[5] 1193[12] 5109[7]

Katina (FR) *G Lellouche* 78
2 b f Ski Chief(USA) —Hollyhead (FR) (Green Tune (USA))
3990a[8]

Katiypour (IRE) *P Mitchell* a96 92
9 ch g Be My Guest(USA) —Katiyfa (Auction Ring (USA))
54[3] 117[5]238[4] 340[5]516[5] 2555[6]2757[6] 3212[6] 3433[2]3928[9] 4241[2] 5096[2]5263[3] 5523[18]

Katsumoto (IRE) *N P Littmoden* a60 53
3 ch g Muhtarram(USA) —Self Assured (IRE) (Ahonoora)
1533[7] 2124[9] 3169[6] 4069[11] 4304[10]

Katy Carr *M J Wallace* a76
2 b f Machiavellian(USA) —Khalafiya (Darshaan)
6242[2] 6447[6]

Kavachi (IRE) *G L Moore* a67 72
3 b g Cadeaux Genereux—Answered Prayer (Green Desert (USA))
1684[8] 2391[3] 2518[7] 2933[10] 3338[6](4591) 4838[5] 5574[2] 5937[6] 6206[13] 6301[9]

Kavafi (IRE) *C Laffon-Parias* a102 107
4 br h Zafonic(USA) —Loxandra (Last Tycoon)
6574a[3]

Kaveri (USA) *C E Brittain* a86 82
3 bb f War Chant(USA) —Valid Bonnet (USA) (Valid Appeal (USA))
724[2] 1056[2] 1490[8](1962) 2527[3] 3088[7] 3945[6]4577[4] 4965[7] 5377[9] 5643[5] 6065[3]6292[7]

Kavi (IRE) *Simon Earle* a76 61
6 ch g Perugino(USA) —Premier Leap (IRE) (Salmon Leap (USA))
385[9]

Kayah *R M Beckett* 73+
2 b f Kahyasi—Kristina (Kris)
(5596)

Kayf Aramis *J L Spearing* a66+ 80
4 b g Kayf Tara—Ara (Birthright)
(966) 1184[2] (1808) 2894[5] 4046[7]4632[5] 4883[5] 5069[2] 5201[2] 5383[2]5811[5] 6011[2] 6205[2]

Kay Gee Be (IRE) *D J Daly* 79
2 b c Fasliyev(USA) —Pursuit Of Truth (USA) (Irish River (FR))
1945[3] 2821[2] (4424)

Kaylianni *M R Channon* 98
3 b f Kalanisi(IRE) —Vivianna (Indian Ridge)
1583[4] 2203[8] (2578) 4039[12] 5342[7] 5505[5]5803[8]

Kaymich Perfecto *R M Whitaker* a59 82
6 b g Sheikh Albadou—Manhattan Diamond (Primo Dominie)
1041[14] 1996[4] 2299[7] (2831) (3147) 3361[9] 3812[7]4379[4] 4733[4] 5320[14]

Kay Two (IRE) *R J Price* a34 93
4 ch g Monashee Mountain(USA) —Tricky (Song)
206a[13] 1158a[10] 1469a[6]2624[13] 3069[6] 3972[11] 4360[10] 4811[9]5169[11] 5476[5] (5791) (6009)

Keagles (ITY) *J E Long* a5
3 b f Indian Danehill(IRE) —Athens Belle (IRE) (Groom Dancer (USA))
6403[11] 6587[10]

Keel (IRE) *J A Osborne* a77 81+
3 br g Carrowkeel(IRE) —First Degree (Sabrehill (USA))
(104) 228[4] 448[3]592[4] 695[7]2142[4] (3310)

Keel Castle Maine (IRE) *Patrick Joseph Hayes* 86
5 b g Blue Ocean(USA) —Nice Mover (IRE) (Lashkari)
4121a[3]

Keelings Donabate *K R Burke* a63
3 b g Desert Style(IRE) —Sideloader Special (Song)
165[4] 645[4]

Keeneland Swan (USA) *Hideyuki Mori* 114
7 ch h Distant View(USA) —To Act (USA) (Roberto (USA))
5717a[14]

Keen Look (IRE) *Gerard Keane* 90+
7 b h Key Of Luck(USA) —Killone Lady (IRE) (High Estate)
3123a[5] 4187a[14]

Keep A Welcome *S Parr* a25
3 ch g Most Welcome—Celtic Chimes (Celtic Cone)
6177[13] 6403[9]

Keep Bacckinhit (IRE) *G L Moore* a50 67
4 b m Raise A Grand(IRE) —Taispeain (IRE) (Petorius)
2567[2] 2729[2] 2954[3] 3337[7] 4075[6]4281[4] 5046[8] 5474[5]5573[4]

Keepers Knight (IRE) *Karen McLintock* a62 59
5 b g Sri Pekan(USA) —Keepers Dawn (IRE) (Alzao (USA))
570[12] 975[13] 4954[10]

Keep It Cool (IRE) *D K Weld* 87
2 ch c Spinning World(USA) —Sudden Stir (USA) (Woodman (USA))
6357a[6]

Keep Your Distance *K R Burke* a65 64
2 b g Distant Music(USA) —Queen G (USA) (Matty G (USA))
2545[5] 3175[7] 4055[2] 4949[4] 5633[6]6385[5] 6506[4]6625[2] 6872[3]6951[6]

Keidas (FR) *C F Wall* a73 70+
2 b f Lomitas—Kahina (GER) (Warning)
3043[8] 3942[2] 5106[3]6285[6]

Keisha Kayleigh (IRE) *B Ellison* a64 65
3 b f Almutawakel—Awtaar (USA) (Lyphard (USA))
817[7] 1296[6] (1661) 1997[2] 2518[9] 2891[4]3244[6] 4263[2] 4467[5] 5485[3] 5683[2]6648[2] 6767[8]6954[4]

Keladora (USA) *J-C Rouget* a86 87
3 b f Crafty Prospector(USA) —Karmifira (FR) (Always Fair (USA))
2491a[16] 4645a[5]

Kellys Double Gold (IRE) *Mrs H O Graham*
3 ch f Spinning World(USA) —Delighting (USA) (Boundary (USA))
1343[13]

Kellys Dream (IRE) *M Quinn* a61 61
3 br f Bertolini(USA) —Fullfilling (IRE) (Red Ransom (USA))
540[5] 645[2]801[8] 1110[11]1431[4] 2190[6] 2939[11]4495[7]

Kelly's Landing (USA) *E Kenneally* a117
5 b g Patton(USA) —Best Game (USA) (Great Above (USA))
6341a[10]

Keltic Rainbow (IRE) *D Haydn Jones* a48 48
5 b m Spectrum(IRE) —Secrets Of Honour (Belmez (USA))
12[7] 389[6]911[5] 1392[12]6584[11]

Kelucia (IRE) *R M Beckett* a85 97
5 ch m Grand Lodge(USA) —Karachi (SPA) (Zino)
1111[8] 2011[2] 2440[4]2988[2] (3088) 3733[5] 4098[12] 5520[5] 5990[8]

Kempsey *J J Bridger* a80? 73
4 ch g Wolfhound(USA) —Mockingbird (Sharpo)
117[6] 485[9]517[3] 664[9]699[3] 761[10]947[8] 1047[6] 1211[6] 1474[4] 1981[4]2444[3] 2711[9] 4101[24] 6485[6]6709[5] 6913[9]

Kendargent (FR) *Y Fouin* 113
3 b c Kendor(FR) —Pax Bella (FR) (Linamix (FR))
2489a[2] 3342a[4] 4416a[10] 5146a[10]

Kendor Dine (FR) *Eoin Griffin* 111
4 gr g Kendor(FR) —Michellisa (Indian Ridge)
(655a) 934a[4] 1371a[2] 1873a[10] 3964a[3]

Kenmore *D Nicholls* 95
4 b g Compton Place—Watheeqah (USA) (Topsider (USA))
1487[21] 2323[12] 3251[13] 3904[5] 4760[12]5009[2] 5534[11] 5677[5] 5943[7]

Kennington *Mrs C A Dunnett* a74 75
6 ch g Compton Place—Mim (Midyan (USA))
4[4] 47[4]117[9] 224[10]244[5] 1686[10] 1846[3]2182[13] 2417[9] 2611[3]2784[13] 3996[5] 4110[5]4267[2] (4846) 4962[5] 5246[4]5391[7] 5765[8] 6048[9]6452[9]

Ken's Girl *W S Kittow* a52 67
2 ch f Ishiguru(USA) —There's Two (IRE) (Ashkalani (IRE))
3148[10] 4754[5] 5264[2] 5735[6]

Kensington (IRE) *P D Evans* a73 63
5 b g Cape Cross(IRE) —March Star (IRE) (Mac's Imp (USA))
(47) 169[4] 292[9]316[4] 381[4]985[7] 1188[8] 6020[9]6493[2] 6642[9]

Kentavr's Dream *P Howling* a24 28
3 b f Robellino(USA) —Very Good (Noalto)
4045[12] 4806[9] 5092[9]5847[9]

Kentuckian *P W Hiatt* 44
4 b g Kylian(USA) —Snowline (Bay Express)
897[17] 1827[8] 2220[12] 2707[9] 3998[9]4210[10] 4709[14] 4835[2] 5314[8]

Kentucky Boy (IRE) *Jedd O'Keeffe* 43
2 b c Distant Music(USA) —Delta Town (USA) (Sanglamore (USA))
5614[10] 5959[8] 6270[9]

Kentucky Bullet (USA) *A G Newcombe* a51 57
10 b g Housebuster(USA) —Exactly So (Caro)
92[5] 172[10]636[9] 788[2]939[12] 1767[4]6279[5] (6795) 6959[3]

Kentucky Dynamite (USA) *A De Royer-Dupre* 117
3 b c Kingmambo(USA) —Chelsey Flower (USA) (His Majesty (USA))
1557a[5] (2489a) 3342a[2] 5049a[6]

Kentucky Warbler (IRE) *H Morrison* a63 77+
3 b f Spinning World(USA) —Dollar Bird (IRE) (Kris)
1955[4] 2600[4] 3261[3]3731[6] (4698) 5628[13] 6244[9]

Keon (IRE) *R Hollinshead* a60 63
4 b g Rossini(USA) —Lonely Brook (USA) (El Gran Senor (USA))
3944[11] 4276[8] 5035[3]5248[3] (5929) 6130[7] (6545) 6674[8] 6793[3]6934[5] 6964[8]

Kerashan (IRE) *Saeed Bin Suroor* a101 105
4 b g Sinndar(IRE) —Kerataka (IRE) (Doyoun)
512a[8] 3501[8] 4027[10] 4631[4]

Kerdem (IRE) *John M Oxx* 103+
3 b c Rainbow Quest(USA) —Kermiyana (IRE) (Green Desert (USA))
5854a[7]

Keresforth *Mrs L C Jewell* a52 54
4 b g Mind Games—Bullion (Sabrehill (USA))
90[6] 943[5]1310[8] 1534[12] 2260[8]3033[9] 3161[9]

Kerjouanno (FR) *K Schafflutzel* 80
4 ch h Gold Away(IRE) —Star Du Rhuis (FR) (Star Maite (FR))
306a[10]

Kernel Dowery (IRE) *W R Swinburn* a56 56
6 b g Sri Pekan(USA) —Lady Dowery (USA) (Manila (USA))
3270[3] 3616[6] 4139[6]4497[10] 5072[9]

Kerriemuir Lass (IRE) *M A Jarvis* 87
3 b f Celtic Swing—Shabby Chic (USA) (Red Ransom (USA))
1139[2] 2220[2] 3302[3] 3977[2] 4197[2](5056) 5538[2] 6202[10]

Kerry O'Reilly (NZ) *J Gibbs* 111
6 b g O'Reilly(NZ) —Pegarah (NZ) (Grosvenor (NZ))
6392a[11]

Kerry's Blade (IRE) *P C Haslam* a58 56
4 ch g Daggers Drawn(USA) —Treasure (IRE) (Treasure Kay)
91[8] 256[5]

Kerry's Dream *T D Easterby* 81
2 ch f Tobougg(IRE) —Jetbeeah (IRE) (Lomond (USA))
(1096) 1831[4] 2125[5] 3474[3] 4152[9] 4736[14]5335[7]

Kersimon (FR) *J De Roualle* 100
3 ch c Simon Du Desert(FR) —Blue Mary (FR) (Fabulous Dancer (USA))
(4168a)

Kerswell *B R Millman* a57 60
2 b f Komaite(USA) —Polgwynne (Forzando)
1912[8] 2816[4] 3844[7]4427[11] 5349[14]

Keshya *N P Littmoden* a67 56
5 b m Mtoto—Liberatrice (FR) (Assert)
107[3] 251[7]318[2] 2869[9] 3456[6]3686[4] 4351[9] 5691[16]405[5]

Kestrel Cross (IRE) *V Smith* a28 100
4 b g Cape Cross(IRE) —Lady Rachel (IRE) (Priolo (USA))
152a[15] 208a[5] 354a[7]438a[3] 509a[8]

Ketter (BRZ) *Luis Singnoretti* a96 92
5 ch h Much Better(BRZ) —Diana-Bela (BRZ) (Empire Day (BRZ))
371a[7] 565a[5]

Kevkat (IRE) *Eoin Griffin* 101+
5 br g Dushyantor(USA) —Diamond Display (IRE) (Shardari)
5396a[2]

Kew Green (USA) *P R Webber* a111 113
8 bb g Brocco(USA) —Jump With Joy (USA) (Linkage (USA))
518[5] 629[7]1018[2] 1084[2] 1601[3]2803[15] 4818[7] 5360[6] 6516[12]

Kew The Music *M R Channon* a74 66
6 b g Botanic(USA) —Harmonia (Glint Of Gold)
559[6] 639[5]777[4] 845[3] 1057[4]1253[13] 1432[10] 1570[6] 5450[6] 5636[11]

Keyaki (IRE) *C F Wall* a82 79d
5 b m Shinko Forest(IRE) —Woodie Dancer (USA) (Green Dancer (USA))
1432[4] 3229[8] 4378[12] 5233[7] (5778) (6036) 6223[8]

Keyalzao (IRE) *A Crook* 38
4 b m Alzao(USA) —Key Partner (Law Society (USA))
2789[17] 3051[5] 3353[9]3620[5] 3637[7] 3941[9] 4425[11]

Keyed Entry (USA) *T Pletcher* a114
3 br c Honour And Glory(USA) —Ava Knowsthecode (USA) (Cryptoclearance (USA))
1498a[20]

Key In *I W McInnes* a63 51
5 ch m Unfuwain(USA) —Fleet Key (Afleet (CAN))
174[13]

Key Of Destiny (SAF) *M F De Kock* a108 118
8 b g Qui Danzig(USA) —Twist Of Fate (SAF) (Secret Prospector (USA))
153a[12] 280a[9] 369a[4] 512a[12] 621a[6]

Key Of Magic (IRE) *J Hetherton* a17 6
3 b g Key Of Luck(USA) —Desirous Of Peace (Forzando)
39[9] 99[8]

Key Partners (IRE) *B D Leavy* a79 86
5 b g Key Of Luck(USA) —Teacher Preacher (IRE) (Taufan (USA))
6837[7] 6954[2]

Key Time (IRE) *Sir Mark Prescott* a48 95
4 b g Darshaan—Kasota (IRE) (Alzao (USA))
(2828) 3114[2] (3396) (3607) (3696) (4036) 4469[2] 5963[11]

Key To Pleasure (GER) *Mario Hofer* 110
6 b h Sharp Prod(USA) —Key To Love (FR) (Alzao (USA))
1973a[6]

Kezia (FR) *C Laffon-Parias* a93 97
3 b f Spectrum(IRE) —Kresna (FR) (Distant Relative)
6328a[4]

Khadija *R Dickin* a42
5 ch m Kadastrof(FR) —Dark Sirona (Pitskelly)
403[6] 503[9]1006[8]

Khalidia (USA) *M A Magnusson* a69 81
5 b g Boundary(USA) —Maniches Slew (USA) (Slew O'Gold (USA))
3434[9] 3846[8] 4368[9]4735[8]

Khanjar (USA) *J Pearce* a81 79
6 ch g Kris S(USA) —Alyssum (USA) (Storm Cat (USA))
98[3] 194[6]273[2] 338[7]652[10] 2549[2] 2975[5]3022[7] 3248[7] 3680[3] 4229[3] 4544[6]4981[9] 5311[7] 6584[2]6843[9]

Khetaab (IRE) *E J Alston* a54 72
4 b g Alhaarth(IRE) —Liberi Versi (IRE) (Last Tycoon)
955[11] 1124[8] 1390[9]2195[4] 2875[5] 3523[10] 3570[6] 5385[11]5553[11] 6545[2] 6703[2]

Khun John (IRE) *B J Meehan* a85+
3 b g Marju(IRE) —Kathy Caerleon (IRE) (Caerleon (USA))
5612[4] (5847) (6189) (6432)

Khyberie *G Wragg* a49+ 45
3 b f Kahyasi—Reading Habit (USA) (Half A Year (USA))
5774[4] 6177[5]

Khyber Kim *H Candy* 109
4 b g Mujahid(USA) —Jungle Rose (Shirley Heights)
3736[3] 4337[2] 4817[2] 5657[4]

Khyber Knight (IRE) *Jane Southcombe* 59
3 b f Night Shift(USA) —Peshawar (Persian Bold)
1798[9] 2479[12] 2728[3] 2968[4] 3161[4]3472[3] 3668[12] 4627[13] 5054[7] 5129[3]5452[9]

Kiama *M Johnston* a66 70
4 b m Dansili—Catriona (Bustino)
911[9] 1213[11] 1610[4]2326[7] 3714[5] 4668[7]

Kia Ora *J Akehurst* a9 37
3 b g College Chapel—Anastasia Venture (Lion Cavern (USA))
5611[12] 6019[10]

Kia Ora Miss (AUS) *A Durrant*
3 b f Jeune—Precious Stone (AUS) (At Talaq (USA))
7000a[13]

Kibara *L M Cumani* 84
3 b f Sadler's Wells(USA) —Kithanga (IRE) (Darshaan)
2366[3] 3451[2] (3849) 4159[2] 4778[7] 6202[13]

Kickahead (USA) *Ian Williams* a60 65
4 b g Danzig(USA) —Krissante (USA) (Kris)
1148[7] 1773[5] 2360[4]

Kick And Prance *J A Geake* a58 63+
3 ch g Groom Dancer(USA) —Unerring (Unfuwain (USA))
993[13] 1941[11] 3347[16]5247[2] (6068)

Kick Back (GER) *P Schiergen* 88+
2 ch f Royal Dragon(USA) —Kimberly Lake (GER) (Alkalde (GER))
5763a[2]

Kid Creole (IRE) *T M Walsh* 81
8 b g Royal Abjar(USA) —Milly's Song (Millfontaine)
3125a[16]

Kid Mambo (USA) *T G Mills* a77 98
2 b c Lemon Drop Kid(USA) —Spring Pitch (USA) (Storm Cat (USA))
3844[4] 4333[5] (5293) 5805[2]

Kilburn *C G Cox* 84
2 b c Grand Lodge(USA) —Lady Lahar (Fraam)
2402[3] 3222[7] (4129) 5359[5]

Kilcusnin Queen (IRE) *Adrian Sexton* a68 67
2 ch f Indian Rocket—Pip'n Judy (IRE) (Pips Pride)
4630[3] 5237[11] 6047[2] 6377[6]6388[4] 6750[6]

Kildare Sun (IRE) *J Mackie* a82+ 64
4 b g Desert Sun—Megan's Dream (IRE) (Fayruz)
4635[8] 4959[4] 5319[9] (5740) 6240[3](6503) (6607) 6772[9]6992[2]

Kilgary (USA) *J Noseda* a66+ 46+
3 ch f Pleasant Tap(USA) —Fitzy (USA) (A.P. Indy (USA))
3112[5] 5847[3] 6286[8]6743[2] (6967)

Kilimandscharo (USA) *P J McBride* a65+ 51
4 b g Rahy(USA) —Landaria (FR) (Sadler's Wells (USA))
2708[7] (6899)

Kilkenny (ITY) *A Marcialis* 79
2 ch f Spymaster(USA) —Kiska (USA) (Bering)
2475a[2] 3343a[13]

Kill Cat (IRE) *A Peraino* a90 105
5 bb h Catrail(USA) —Feather River (USA) (Strike The Gold (USA))
154a[5] 204a[6]508a[6] 2217a[8] 6364a[7]

Killena Boy (IRE) *W Jarvis* a92 92+
4 b g Imperial Ballet(IRE) —Habaza (IRE) (Shernazar)
2757[3] 2983[9]3973[14] (4782) (5019) 5639[8] 5990[6]

Killer Heels *S Kirk* a45 54
2 b f Kirkwall—High Habit (Slip Anchor)
3201[12] 3868[6] 4552[8]5597[14]

Killing Joke *J J Lambe* a28
6 b h Double Trigger(IRE) —Fleeting Vision (IRE) (Vision (USA))
6604[4]

Killybegs (IRE) *B W Hills* 119
3 b c Orpen(USA) —Belsay (Belmez (USA))
(1092) 1486^{11} 3559a^{4} 4529^{10} 4839^{2} 5524^{4}5962^{2}

Kilmeena Magic *J C Fox* a52 44
4 b m Fumo Di Londra(IRE) —Kilmeena Lady (Inca Chief (USA))
539^{11} 964^{8} 1351^{15}2350^{10} 2531^{9} 3149^{5} 5092^{4} 6059^{9}6134^{5} 6237^{6}6373^{4} 6620^{4}6724^{3} 6800^{5}6852^{2} 6907^{3}

Kilometre Neuf (FR) *F Doumen* 105
3 b c Double Bed(FR) —Mary Astor (FR) (Groom Dancer (USA))
6384a^{10}

Kilvickeon (IRE) *Peter Grayson* a48
2 b g Daggers Drawn(USA) —Queen Of Sweden (IRE) (Solid Illusion (USA))
5686^{10} 5841^{9}6034^{7} 6500^{8}6665^{2} 6711^{4}6951^{3}

Kilworth (IRE) *Saeed Bin Suroor* a104+ 105
3 gr c Kalanisi(IRE) —Perugia (IRE) (Perugino (USA))
368a^{6} 561a^{5}(5845) 6203^{3}

Kimono Kiss (USA) *M P Tregoning* a56
2 ch f Seeking The Gold(USA) —Geisha Girl (Nashwan (USA))
6187^{9}

Kimono My House *J G Given* a55 34
2 ch f Dr Fong(USA) —Roselyn (Efisio)
5898^{8} 6433^{9} 6558^{7}

Kimpton Carer *J A Geake* a40
2 b g Groom Dancer(USA) —So True (So Blessed)
6846^{5} 6950^{11}

Kims Rose (IRE) *R A Harris* 49
3 b f Desert Prince(IRE) —Pinta (IRE) (Ahonoora)
3266^{8} 3436^{6} 3975^{9}

Kincaid *D W Thompson* 36
3 ch g Dr Fong(USA) —Peacock Alley (IRE) (Salse (USA))
5363^{15}

Kindallachan *G C Bravery* a46 44
3 b f Magic Ring(IRE) —Moore Stylish (Moorestyle)
3742^{10} 4489^{6} 5611^{11}6233^{2} 6372^{10}6704^{4}

Kindlelight Blue (IRE) *N P Littmoden* 69
2 gr c Golan(IRE) —Kalimar (IRE) (Bigstone (IRE))
2281^{5} 2844^{9} 3979^{4}

Kindlelight Debut *N P Littmoden* a104 90
6 b m Groom Dancer(USA) —Dancing Debut (Polar Falcon (USA))
(74) (106) (169) 267^{2} 404^{3}(555) 631^{3}660^{2} 704^{6}1015^{7} 1111^{12}(3687) 3928^{15} 4172^{5} 4372 ^{6}4660^{2} 4790^{5} 4965^{4} 5357^{9} 5785^{6}6190^{3} 6516^{4}6600^{4} 6847^{3}6914^{4} 6997^{4}

Kindling *M Johnston* 100
4 br m Dr Fong(USA) —Isle Of Flame (Shirley Heights)
1332a^{8} 5551^{7} 5881a^{8}

Kind Of Fizzy *Rae Guest* 53
2 b f Efisio—Kind Of Light (Primo Dominie)
6055^{9} 6200^{7}

Kineta (USA) *W R Muir* a53 67
3 b f Miswaki(USA) —Kibitzing (USA) (Wild Again (USA))
2406^{12} 2921^{5} 3453^{4} 4045^{3}4494^{8}

Kinetic Power (IRE) *D R C Elsworth* a54+ 50
3 gr g Alhaarth(IRE) —Nichodoula (Doulab (USA))
16^{10} 850^{9}1192^{12} 1925^{11}

Kinetics (JPN) *M Shinkawa* 116
7 ch h Forty Niner(USA) —Incurable Romantic (USA) (Stop The Music (USA))
6530a^{18}

King After *J R Best* a60 67
4 b g Bahamian Bounty—Child Star (FR) (Bellypha)
3820^{11} 4248^{11} 5032^{8}5316^{12} 6793^{6} 6810^{10}6934^{7} 6981^{2}

King And King (AUS) *S Burridge* 117
5 b g Celestial Dancer—Merriang Road (AUS) (Persian Heights)
1716a^{2}

King Charles *E A L Dunlop* a87+ 84
2 b g King's Best(USA) —Charlecote (IRE) (Caerleon (USA))
2619^{12} 2930^{11} 3242^{5} 4000^{7} (5094) (5262) (5459)

King Cugat Kid (USA) *Simon Earle* a43 13
3 bb c King Cugat(USA) —Let's Dance (USA) (Thorn Dance (USA))
5055^{15} 5669^{12} 5830^{10}6375^{7} 6560^{11}

Kingdom Of Dreams (IRE) *J Noseda* a70 87+
4 b g Sadler's Wells(USA) —Regal Portrait (IRE) (Royal Academy (USA))
2440^{6} 3413^{14} 4047^{11}

King Egbert (FR) *A W Carroll* a60 61
5 b g Fasliyev(USA) —Exocet (USA) (Deposit Ticket (USA))
1228^{5} 1466^{7}1722^{2} (1909) 2611^{7} 3071^{4} (3348) 3899^{4} 4208^{2} 4462^{5}4872^{6} 5131^{4} 5480^{7}

King Faz (IRE) *P A Blockley* 62
3 b g Fasliyev(USA) —White Satin (IRE) (Fairy King (USA))
1592^{8} 2109^{12} 4285^{7}

King Forever *D E Cantillon* a60 78
4 b g King's Best(USA) —Elude (Slip Anchor)
180^{3} 251^{9}330^{4} 427^{4}3635^{9} 4227^{3} 5033^{6}5650^{11}

King Gabriel (IRE) *Andrew Turnell* a59 69
4 b g Desert King(IRE) —Broken Spirit (IRE) (Slip Anchor)
6810^{5} 6980^{4}

King Georges (FR) *J C Tuck* a29
8 b g Kadalko(FR) —Djoumi (FR) (Brezzo (FR))
2206^{7}

King Harson *J D Bethell* a66 85
7 b g Greensmith—Safari Park (Absalom)
1143^{11} 1561^{6} 2681^{14} 4116^{14} (4521) 5144^{4}(5554) 5877^{10} 6160^{3} 6273^{8}

King Henrik (USA) *A Crook* 11
4 b g King Of Kings(IRE) —Ma Biche (USA) (Key To The Kingdom (USA))
1594^{14} 3635^{12} 4057^{11}

King In Waiting (IRE) *John M Oxx* 101+
3 b c Sadler's Wells(USA) —Ballerina (IRE) (Dancing Brave (USA))
2055a^{3}

King Jock (USA) *R J Osborne* a60 114
5 bb g Ghazi(USA) —Glen Kate (Glenstal (USA))
(149a) 281a^{5} 496a^{4} 625a^{5} (4641a) 5184^{4} 5588^{3}

King Joshua (IRE) *G A Butler* a61 79
2 b c King's Best(USA) —Lady Joshua (IRE) (Royal Academy (USA))
2821^{8} 3892^{3} 4597^{5} 5648^{5}6066^{5}

King Kasyapa (IRE) *P Bowen* 99
4 b h Darshaan—Ezana (Ela-Mana-Mou)
2220^{6} 2917^{5} 3431^{3}

Kingkohler (IRE) *K A Morgan* a75 76
7 b g King's Theatre(IRE) —Legit (IRE) (Runnett)
250^{10}

King Luna (FR) *A Fabre* 101
3 ch f King's Best(USA) —Luna Caerla (IRE) (Caerleon (USA))
6062a^{3} 6567a^{2}

King Marju (IRE) *K R Burke* a93 106
4 b g Marju(IRE) —Katoushka (IRE) (Hamas (IRE))
151a^{7} 352a^{10} 507a^{3} 667^{3}3926^{19} 4896^{5} 5355^{5} 6192^{11}6830^{6} 6896^{9}6999^{7}

King Marrakech (IRE) *B P J Baugh* a30 19
4 b g King's Best(USA) —Tenue D'Amour (FR) (Pursuit Of Love)
29^{6} 90^{9}145^{13} 402^{11}612^{8} 766^{11}821^{6}

King Nicholas (USA) *J Parkes* a47 36
7 b g Nicholas(USA) —Lifetime Honour (USA) (Kingmambo (USA))
3^{4} 940^{9}2108^{14} 3944^{13} 4194^{8} 5926^{11}

King Nov (ARG) *B Bo* a91 89
4 bl h Romanov(IRE) —Queen Wonder (ARG) (Southern Halo (USA))
5225a^{9} 6514^{10}

King Of Argos *E A L Dunlop* a91 82
3 b g Sadler's Wells(USA) —Wannabe Grand (IRE) (Danehill (USA))
1120^{8} 1823^{2} (2220) 6313^{5}6502^{2} 6772^{2}

King Of Ashford (NZ) *Karen Zimmerman* 106
6 b g His Royal Highness(NZ) —Zena's Wish (NZ) (Super Gray (USA))
6347a^{9}

King Of Charm (IRE) *G L Moore* a44 62
3 ch g King Charlemagne(USA) —Pumpona (USA) (Sharpen Up)
2235^{3} 2859^{10} 3034^{5} 3406^{10}6395^{9} 6869^{12}

King Of Chav's (IRE) *A Bailey* a56 46
3 ch g Beckett(IRE) —La Paola (IRE) (Common Grounds)
1140^{11} 1232^{8} 1950^{12} 3232^{16} 3785^{12}

King Of Diamonds *J R Best* a86 73
5 b g Mtoto—Capricious Lass (Corvaro (USA))
3712^{11} 4365^{10} 4772^{9} 5046^{10}

King Of Knight (IRE) *G Prodromou* a66 56
5 gr g Orpen(USA) —Peace Melody (IRE) (Classic Music (USA))
186^{9} 324^{3}462^{6} 557^{2}574^{13} 696^{4}820^{5} 1058^{10} 1553^{10}6700^{4} 6780^{2}

King Of Magic *W G M Turner* 41
2 b g King O' The Mana(IRE) —Mountain Magic (Magic Ring (IRE))
6016^{8} 6172^{9}

King Of Meze (IRE) *J S Wainwright* a54 50
5 b g Croco Rouge(IRE) —Cossack Princess (IRE) (Lomond (USA))
864^{15} 1227^{3} 1725^{2}2148^{9} 2811^{13} 3637^{4} 3944^{8}

King Of Music (USA) *G Prodromou* a65 58
5 ch g Jade Hunter(USA) —Hail Roberta (USA) (Roberto (USA))
(157) 230^{8} 268^{6}416^{4} 461^{6}537^{4} 650^{12}972^{14} 1265^{8}

King Of Rhythm (IRE) *D Carroll* 62
3 b g Imperial Ballet(IRE) —Sharadja (IRE) (Doyoun)
863^{5} 1216^{4} 1483^{8} 5015^{8} 5446^{2}

King Of Scots *R J Price* a6
5 ch g Halling(USA) —Ink Pot (USA) (Green Dancer (USA))
857^{11} 937^{8}1271^{9}

King Of Swords (IRE) *C Collins* 92
2 b c Desert Prince(IRE) —Okey Dorey (IRE) (Lake Coniston (IRE))
2037a^{2} 3574a^{6} 4026^{8} 4409a^{7}

King Of The Beers (USA) *R A Harris* a57 56
2 rg c Silver Deputy(CAN) —Pracer (USA) (Lyphard (USA))
5088^{9} 5527^{9} 6523^{8}6737^{7} 6950^{10}

King Of The Moors (USA) *T D Barron* 89
3 b g King Of Kings(IRE) —Araza (USA) (Arazi (USA))
(1032) 1440^{3} 2205^{3} 3491^{12} 4605^{7} 4953^{7}5337^{9} 5554^{7}

King Of The Roxy (USA) *T Pletcher* a107
2 b c Littleexpectations(USA) —Marrakesh (USA) (Bold Forbes (USA))
6339a^{8}

King Of Tory (IRE) *Edward Lynam* 93
4 b g Giant's Causeway(USA) —Across The Ice (USA) (General Holme (USA))
4187a^{3}

King Of Tricks *M D I Usher* 54
2 b g First Trump—Antithesis (IRE) (Fairy King (USA))
2617^{10} 3591^{12} 4222^{5} 4816^{7} 5290^{3}5645 ^{5} 6296^{7}

King Orchisios (IRE) *K A Ryan* a107 103
3 ch g Tagula(IRE) —Wildflower (Namaqualand (USA))
1094^{3} 1857^{5} 2032^{8} 2658^{9} 2866^{2}(3296) 4345^{5} 5182^{11} 5501^{7} 6095^{7}(6243)

King's Account (USA) *S Gollings* a54 85
4 ch g King Of Kings(IRE) —Fighting Countess (USA) (Ringside (USA))
6313^{11} 6502^{12}

King's Apostle (IRE) *W J Haggas* 76
2 b c King's Best(USA) —Politesse (USA) (Barathea (IRE))
4260^{6} 5168^{2} 5481^{2}

Kings Art (IRE) *B W Hills* a48 58
2 b g King's Best(USA) —Descant (USA) (Nureyev (USA))
4028^{9} 4705^{8} 5347^{5} 5738^{9}

King's Attitude *B J Meehan* 48
2 b c King's Theatre(IRE) —Sarah's Dream (IRE) (Lion Cavern (USA))
4333^{14}

King's Bastion (IRE) *M L W Bell* 84
2 b g Royal Applause—Aunty Mary (Common Grounds)
1090^{4} (1639) 2009^{5} 2630^{3} 3727^{2} 4146^{11}5372^{12} 5788^{15}

King's Caprice *J A Geake* a95 110
5 ch g Pursuit Of Love—Palace Street (USA) (Secreto (USA))
828^{8} (1086) 2012^{18} 2649^{3}3092^{3} 3223^{4} (3471) 3926^{16} 4798^{7} (5175) 5523^{3}(5943)

King's Causeway (USA) *W J Haggas* a59 77
2 bb c Giant's Causeway(USA) —Dealer's Dream (USA) (A.P. Indy (USA))
3623^{4} 4018^{3} 4388^{3} 5172^{5} 5783^{9}

Kings Cavalier (USA) *I W McInnes* a32 45
3 b g Stormin Fever(USA) —Port Of Silver (USA) (Silver Hawk (USA))
118^{9} 189^{2}380^{9} 1036^{9} 1344^{11}1752^{11} 2284^{14} 2758^{15} 2782^{10} 3604^{6}3910^{9} 4304^{5} 6129^{11}6727^{11}

King's Charter (USA) *S Dow* a49 44
3 b g Red Ransom(USA) —Extry (USA) (Broad Brush (USA))
20^{3} 1652^{15} 2645^{11}

King's College (USA) *P D Evans* a48 44
3 b c Stravinsky(USA) —Talent Quest (IRE) (Rainbow Quest (USA))
138^{10} 191^{11}337^{11} 781^{10} 1314^{9}2352^{7} 4758^{8} 4868^{8} 5127^{11}

Kings College Boy *R A Fahey* 83
6 b g College Chapel—The Kings Daughter (Indian King (USA))
1563^{9} 1846^{7} 2027^{6} 2505^{4} 2550^{2}(2780) 3170^{3} 3190^{2} 3447^{4} (3525) 3715^{4} 3880^{2}3938^{3} 4258^{2} 4453^{5} 4468^{8} 4793^{3}5169^{5} 5286^{4} 5493^{5} 5791^{6}

Kings Confession (IRE) *D Carroll* a67+ 35
3 b g Danetime(IRE) —Night Rhapsody (IRE) (Mujtahid (USA))
2734^{11} 2940^{2}

King's Crest *J J Quinn* a51 67
8 b g Deploy—Classic Beauty (IRE) (Fairy King (USA))
794^{2} 1045^{8} 1256^{6}1666^{2} 1887^{2} 2104^{7} (Dead)

Kingscross *M Blanshard* a81 89
8 ch g King's Signet(USA) —Calamanco (Clantime)
1285^{5} 1474^{12} 1820^{2} 2189^{4} 2520^{11}3471^{10} 3904^{3} 4338^{8} 4593^{10} 4807^{6}5476^{4} 5627^{5} 6499^{5}6583^{7} 6770^{6}6882^{3}

Kingsdale Ocean (IRE) *W M Roper* 102
3 b c Blue Ocean(USA) —Madmosel John (IRE) (Martin John)
1158a^{3} 1362a^{4} 2308a^{3} 3124a^{7}

King's Envoy (USA) *Mrs J C McGregor* a46 46
7 b g Royal Academy(USA) —Island Of Silver (USA) (Forty Niner (USA))
(303) 938^{6} 3350^{6}

King's Fable (USA) *M Johnston* a60 60
3 b g Lear Fan(USA) —Fairy Fable (IRE) (Fairy King (USA))
49^{3} 123^{4}979^{5} 1350^{9} 3145^{12} 3674^{2} 3870^{7}4331^{8} 4734^{10} (5082) 6317^{8}

King's Gait *T D Easterby* 102
4 b g Mujahid(USA) —Miller's Gait (Mill Reef (USA))
718^{3} 1076^{2} 1487^{20} 1803^{5} 4202^{9}4609^{9}

Kingsgate Prince (IRE) *J R Best* a104 109
3 b g Desert Sun—Princess Mood (GER) (Muhtarram (USA))
(233) (269) (341) (665) 829^{4} 914^{2}1408^{2} (1818) 2204^{3} 2739^{3}

King's Head (IRE) *M A Jarvis* a93 103
3 b c King's Best(USA) —Ustka (Lomond (USA))
(1268) 2224^{4} 2659^{3} 3443^{4} 4039^{3} 4936^{4}

Kings Heir (IRE) *Peter Grayson* a53 86
3 b g Princely Heir(IRE) —Unimpeachable (IRE) (Namaqualand (USA))
1190^{7} 1569^{8} 2318^{2} 3337^{8} 4144^{5}4562^{5} 5042^{7} 6478^{11}6647^{9} 6833^{12}6943^{3}

Kingsholm *A M Balding* a78 91
4 ch g Selkirk(USA) —Putuna (Generous (IRE))
1302^{8} 1544^{6} 1957^{5} 3404^{6}3688^{4} 4704^{5}(5590) (5833) 6017^{2} 6337^{14}

King's Jester (IRE) *J J Lambe* a57 71
4 b g King's Best(USA) —Scent Of Success (USA) (Quiet American (USA))
1156a^{14} 5863^{4} 6568^{12}

Kingsmaite *S R Bowring* a86d 45
5 b g Komaite(USA) —Antonias Melody (Rambo Dancer (CAN))
80^{6} 245^{5}611^{10} 1645^{7} 2541^{14}3608^{14} 3995^{4} 5386^{7}6419^{5} 6641^{3}(6762) 6862^{6}

King's Majesty (IRE) *Sir Michael Stoute* a84 93+
4 b h King's Best(USA) —Tiavanita (USA) (J O Tobin (USA))
728^{7}

Kingsmead (USA) *Miss J Feilden* 65
2 b c Kingmambo(USA) —Astor Place (USA) (Deputy Minister (CAN))
3976^{14} 4303^{2} 5321 ^{9}

King's Melody *B R Millman* a51 41
3 b g King Charlemagne(USA) —Anabaa's Music (Anabaa (USA))
70^{8} 254^{11}418^{9} 879^{13} 945^{9}1373^{10} 1726^{6}

Kings Point (IRE) *R A Fahey* a97 109
5 b h Fasliyev(USA) —Rahika Rose (Unfuwain (USA))
1084^{4} 1299^{3} 1806^{6} 2226^{6} 3559a^{7}3881^{2} 4529^{3} 5186^{7} 5673^{6}

Kings Quay *J J Quinn* 105
4 b h Montjeu(IRE) —Glen Rosie (IRE) (Mujtahid (USA))
728^{28} 1129^{22} 1495^{3} 2201^{4} 2803^{13}3313^{7} 4098^{10}

King's Ransom *W R Muir* a66 70
3 b g Daylami(IRE) —Luana (Shaadi (USA))
2532^{4} 3644^{8} 4076^{8}6647^{7} 6825^{P}

King's Regiment (IRE) *M A Jarvis* a57
2 b c King's Best(USA) —Gardenia (IRE) (Sadler's Wells (USA))
3976^{16} 4934^{7}

King's Revenge *T D Easterby* a73 79
3 br g Wizard King—Retaliator (Rudimentary (USA))
1048^{6} (1552) 1948^{4} 2584^{6} 3375^{5} 4833^{11}(5406) 5724^{6} 5810^{9}

Kings Shillings *D Carroll* a51 26
2 br g Superior Premium—The Kings Daughter (Indian King (USA))
5315^{9} 5491^{9} 6173^{11} 6491^{4}6815^{6}

King's Spear (IRE) *P W Chapple-Hyam* a52 66
3 b c Lear Spear(USA) —First Veil (Primo Dominie)
1088^{9} 4899^{6} 5071^{2} 5879^{13}6327^{2}

Kings Square *M W Easterby* 28
6 b g Bal Harbour—Prime Property (IRE) (Tirol)
3135^{6}

King's Thought *S Gollings* a94 96
7 b h King's Theatre(IRE) —Lora's Guest (Be My Guest (USA))
865^{11} 2341^{10} 2752^{3}3639^{4} 4244^{6}4876^{9}

Kings Topic (USA) *A B Haynes* a67 53
6 ch g Kingmambo(USA) —Topicount (USA) (Private Account (USA))
955^{6} 1276^{5}

Kingsword (USA) *O Larsen* 102
5 bl h Dynaformer(USA) —Western Curtsey (USA) (Gone West (USA))
5226a^{9}

King Zafeen (IRE) *M W Easterby* a56 57
4 b h Lend A Hand—Groom Dancing (Groom Dancer (USA))
787^{2} 889^{8}1460^{9}

Kinrande (IRE) *P J Makin* a74 92
4 b g Sri Pekan(USA) —Pipers Pool (IRE) (Mtoto)
2229^{14} 3497^{4}

Kinshasa No Kiseki (AUS) *M Horii* 114
3 b c Fuji Kiseki(JPN) —Keltshaan (USA) (Pleasant Colony (USA))
6530a^{5}

Kinsman (IRE) *T D McCarthy* a51 24
9 b g Distant Relative—Besito (Wassl)
310^{7} 394^{4}1537^{10} 1725^{6}6128^{12} 6370^{7}6616^{3} 6800^{6}

Kinsya *M H Tompkins* 94
3 ch g Mister Baileys—Kimono (IRE) (Machiavellian (USA))
(1099) 1832^{3} 2779^{4} (4605) 5337^{4} 5722^{7} (5810)

Kintbury Cross *P D Cundell* a66 83
4 b g Kylian(USA) —Cebwob (Rock City)
409^{2}

Kinvara Lass (IRE) *L M Cumani* a72 67
3 b f Singspiel(IRE) —Risarshana (FR) (Darshaan)
1351^{12} 2325^{3} 3200^{3}3703^{6} 4044^{4} 4972^{U} (Dead)

Kip Deville (USA) *R Dutrow Jr* 110
3 rg c Kipling(USA) —Klondike Kaytie (USA) (Encino (USA))
6613a^{6}

Kirin *D E Cantillon* a68 69
4 b h Selkirk(USA) —Amaryllis (IRE) (Sadler's Wells (USA))
8^{10}

Kirkbys Belle (IRE) *G A Swinbank* a21 27
3 b f Namid—Saltwood (Mujtahid (USA))
4656^{11}

Kirkby's Treasure *A Berry* a67 80
8 gr g Mind Games—Gem Of Gold (Jellaby)
815^{5} 1561^{8} 1885^{10} 3289^{7}

Kirkhammerton (IRE) *A J McCabe* a62 40
4 ch g Grand Lodge(USA) —Nawara (Welsh Pageant)
230^{5} 334^{4}405^{10} 603^{12}1271^{5} (1573) 1765^{2} 2137^{6}5497^{9} 5840^{8} (5925) 6256^{7}

Kirklees (IRE) *M Johnston* 110
2 b c Jade Robbery(USA) —Moyesii (USA) (Diesis)
2733^{2} (3187) 4037^{3} 5183^{4} 5521^{3} (6003a)

Kirk Michael *H Candy* 82
2 b c Selkirk(USA) —Pervenche (Latest Model)
5089^{4} 5659^{2}

Kirkstall Lane *R Hannon* 47
3 b g Selkirk(USA) —L'Animee (Green Tune (USA))
1823^{10} 2066^{7} 2568^{3} 3264^{8} 3592^{6}

Kirkstone (IRE) *J A Osborne* a73 77
5 b g Alzao(USA) —Night Mirage (USA) (Silver Hawk (USA))
32^{2} 163^{2}185^{2} (314) 478^{12}

Kirstys Lad *M Mullineaux* a40 50
4 b g Lake Coniston(IRE) —Killick (Slip Anchor)
1463^{4} 1764^{10}3050^{6} 3523^{6} 4172^{17}5741^{7} 5927^{7}6279^{14}

Kiss Chase (IRE) *P Mitchell* a52
2 b c Val Royal(FR) —Zurarah (Siberian Express (USA))
6290^{11} 6393^{12}

Kissi Kissi *M J Attwater* a54 44
3 b f Paris House—Miss Whittingham (IRE) (Fayruz)
453^{2} 604^{12}1649^{11} 2210^{3} 2877^{5}3379^{8} 3609^{6} 4113^{10}5873^{5} 5929^{14}6308^{7} 6549^{9}(6649)

Kissimee *N P Littmoden* a31
3 b f Whittingham(IRE) —Shalyah (IRE) (Shalford (IRE))
248^{7} 544^{8}

Kissinthemoonlight *John M Oxx* 86
2 b f Green Desert(USA) —Quaestio (USA) (Seeking The Gold (USA))
5394a^{6} 5850a^{11}

Kiss The Rain *R Brotherton* a56 56
6 b m Forzando—Devils Dirge (Song)
212^{9} 249^{8}315^{8} 2632^{16}

Kiswahili *Sir Mark Prescott* a87 100
4 ch m Selkirk(USA) —Kiliniski (Niniski (USA))
523a^{10} (2563a) 2689a^{6} 3551^{5} (3992a) 4791^{4}5560a^{3} 6438^{4}

Kitabaat (IRE) *E A L Dunlop* 67
3 ch f Halling(USA) —Nabadhaat (USA) (Mr Prospector (USA))
2578^{6} 4204^{10}

Kitara (GER) *P Vovcenko* 100
6 b m Camp David(GER) —Kantilene (GER) (Windwurf (GER))
208a^{6} 510a^{7}

Kitchen Sink (IRE) *P J Makin* a65 62
4 ch g Bold Fact(USA) —Voodoo Rocket (Lycius (USA))
138^{3} 265^{3}485^{10} 1899^{7} 3094^{4}3348^{2} 4629^{2} 4985^{8} 6890^{2}

Kitmaah *R McGlinchey* 36
3 b f Alhaarth(IRE) —Kronengold (USA) (Golden Act (USA))
4034a^{12}

Kiton (GER) *P Rau* 108
5 b g Lando(GER) —Key West (GER) (In The Wings)
3992a^{3} 6109a^{3}

Klassen (USA) *A King* 52
3 bb c Pine Bluff(USA) —One Great Lady (USA) (Fappiano (USA))
2304^{15} 3029^{11} 4210^{7}

Knapton Hill *R Hollinshead* a47 57
2 b f Zamindar(USA) —Torgau (IRE) (Zieten (USA))
5043^{8} 5507^{6} 5950^{7} 6926^{5}

Knead The Dough *A E Price* a56 56
5 b g Wolfhound(USA) —Ridgewood Ruby (IRE) (Indian Ridge)
2636^{15} 2971^{10} 3825^{3} 4306^{2} 5077^{2}5272^{3} 5569^{7} 5729^{7} 6142^{6}

Knickerless (IRE) *N P Littmoden* a36 53
3 b f Fayruz—June Lady (Junius (USA))
2284^{10} 3167^{9} 3604^{8} 4050^{5} 4769^{9}

Knickyknackienoo *T T Clement* a63 66+
5 b g Bin Ajwaad(IRE) —Ring Fence (Polar Falcon (USA))
2141^{12}

Knight Valliant *J Howard Johnson* 62+
3 bl g Dansili—Aristocratique (Cadeaux Genereux)
2366^{9} 3620^{3} 4255^{2} 5082^{8}

Knock Bridge (IRE) *D Carroll* a58 77
4 b m Rossini(USA) —Touraneena (Robellino (USA))
77^{10} 3159^{11}3583^{5} 4133^{4}

Knot In Wood (IRE) *R A Fahey* a22 102
4 b g Shinko Forest(IRE) —Notley Park (Wolfhound (USA))
2027^{4} 2397^{3} 2661^{3} 3217^{2} (3567) 3956^{4}4202^{3} (4682) 5336^{5} 5534^{2} 5812^{2}

Knotted *R Charlton* 59
3 b f Xaar—Ash Glade (Nashwan (USA))
1798^{6}

Koanga (FR) *U Suter* 101
3 b f Orpen(USA) —Karajana (IRE) (Unfuwain (USA))
6328a^{10}

Kocab *A Fabre* 114
4 b h Unfuwain(USA) —Space Quest (Rainbow Quest (USA))
4169a^{3} 5999a^{4}

Kodiac *J L Dunlop* 112
5 b h Danehill(USA) —Rafha (Kris)
203a^{2} (366a) 494a^{6} 621a^{10} 3295^{3} 3732^{2}4191a^{4} 5011^{9} 5712a^{14}

Koening (ITY) *L Camici* 84
2 b c Celtic Swing—Waku Waku (ITY) (Big Reef)
6123a^{6}

Koffibini (IRE) *H J Groschel* 97
4 b m Platini(GER) —Kibla (GER) (Bakharoff (USA))
3719a^{4}

Koffiefontein (USA) *L M Cumani* 39+
2 ch f Diesis—Kimberley Mine (SAF) (Fort Wood (USA))
3537^{9} 4207^{13}

Kokila *M H Tompkins* a59 39
3 b f Indian Danehill(IRE) —Poetry In Motion (IRE) (Ballad Rock)
138^{8} 447^{2}822^{6} 1221^{11} 1387^{6}5741^{8} 6027^{10}

Kolhapur (IRE) *J L Dunlop* 56
3 ch c Barathea(IRE) —Koniya (IRE) (Doyoun)
1375^{13} 1851^{15}

Kompete *V Smith* a78 92
2 b f Komaite(USA) —Competa (Hernando (FR))
1053^{3} 5681^{10} (6047) 6201^{4} 6402^{3}

Komreyev Star *M Mullineaux* a49 56
4 b g Komaite(USA) —L'Ancressaan (Dalsaan)
1198^{7} 2025^{8} 3597^{10}4390^{7} 4709^{17} 4730^{8} (5838) 6213^{2} 6370^{8}6799^{6}

Kondakova (IRE) *M L W Bell* a74 74
2 b f Soviet Star(USA) —Solar Star (USA) (Lear Fan (USA))
5296^{3} (5735)

Kon Tiki *M Johnston* a65 66
2 b f Red Ransom(USA) —First Fleet (USA) (Woodman (USA))
4600^{10} 5089^{5} 5424^{6}6285^{3}

Kool Acclaim *S C Williams* 56
5 b m Royal Applause—Carrie Kool (Prince Sabo)
2590^{9} 2864^{14} 3267^{16} 3825^{8} 4267^{6}

Kool Ovation *A Dickman* 81
4 b g Royal Applause—Carrie Kool (Prince Sabo)
1686^{20} 3041^{16} 3287^{2} 3718^{2} 3936^{3}4253^{2} 4569^{10} 4957^{5}

Korikancha (IRE) *Miss Z C Davison* a63 68
3 b f Fasliyev(USA) —Amravati (IRE) (Project Manager)
132^{3} 234^{12}4288^{9}

Korolieva (IRE) *K A Ryan* a41 69
3 b f Xaar—Dark Hyacinth (IRE) (Darshaan)
4567^{10} 5973^{10} 6387^{11}6756^{11}

Korty *W J Musson* 19
2 b g Averti(IRE) —Promissory (Caerleon (USA))
2623^{13}

Kossies Mate *P W Hiatt*
7 b m Cosmonaut—Pola Star (IRE) (Un Desperado (FR))
3896^{10}

Kostar *C G Cox* a100 101
5 ch g Komaite(USA) —Black And Amber (Weldnaas (USA))
54^{2} (1667) 2847^{7} 3493^{6}4042^{4} 4430^{2} 5358^{16}

Kourka (FR) *J-M Beguigne* 101
4 b m Keos(USA) —Kuneitra (FR) (Lead On Time (USA))
3692a^{2} 5222a^{6} 5779a^{5} 6547a^{2}

Kova Hall (IRE) *B G Powell* 89
4 ch g Halling(USA) —My Micheline (Lion Cavern (USA))
2169^{2} 2621^{8} 2989^{12}

Krakatau (FR) *D J Wintle* a54
2 b c Noverre(USA) —Tomanivi (Caerleon (USA))
6826^{5} 6931^{3}

Krasivi's Boy (USA) *G L Moore* a67 63
4 bb g Swain(IRE) —Krasivi (USA) (Nijinsky (CAN))
5451^{8} 6857^{5} 6959^{7}

Krataios (FR) *C Laffon-Parias* 117
6 b h Sabrehill(USA) —Loxandra (Last Tycoon)
841a^{5} (1371a) 1873a^{3} 2490a^{6} 6250a^{4}

Krikket *W J Haggas* a51+ 50+
2 ch f Sinndar(IRE) —Star Of The Course (USA) (Theatrical)
5095^{9} 5425^{10}5592^{7}

Krischera (USA) *S Seemar* a67 61
3 bb g Kris S(USA) —Torchera (USA) (Pirate's Bounty (USA))
150a^{14}

Krisman (IRE) *M Ciciarelli* 106
7 ch h Kris—Corn Circle (IRE) (Thatching)
1871a^{2} 6005a^{2} 6363a^{5}

Kris Spring *R M H Cowell* a19 14
4 b m Kris S(USA) —Crown Of Spring (USA) (Chief's Crown (USA))
844^{12} 1110^{12}1463^{9} 1763^{5}

Kristalchen *D W Thompson* 44
4 b m Singspiel(IRE) —Crystal Flite (IRE) (Darshaan)
974^{12} 3001^{9} 3353^{11} (3637) 3836^{5} 4227^{8}

Kristensen *Karen McLintock* a85 83
7 ch g Kris S(USA) —Papaha (FR) (Green Desert (USA))
610^{7} 816^{6} 1033^{3}1184^{5} 1584^{16} 2879^{2} 3177^{3} 4036^{7}4522^{2} (4723) 4951^{5}

Kristiansand *P Monteith* 68?
6 b g Halling(USA) —Zonda (Fabulous Dancer (USA))
2808^{9} 3140^{6} 3352^{4} 3810^{5} 4086^{2}4351^{8} 5905^{11} 6209^{6}

Kristinor (FR) *Trainer Unknown* a63 62
4 ch g Inchinor—Kristina (Kris)
301^{8} 1622a^{2}

Kristoffersen *Ian Williams* a63 63
6 ch g Kris—Towaahi (IRE) (Caerleon (USA))
1748^{4} 2357^{10} 3431^{6}

Krugerrand (USA) *W J Musson* a73 94
7 ch g Gulch(USA) —Nasers Pride (USA) (Al Nasr (FR))
1111^{13} 1357^{9} 2200^{7}2657^{3} 3413^{10} 4160^{2} 4359^{10} 4810^{9}(5310) 5787^{5} 6107^{10} 6337^{15}

Kuaicoss (IRE) *A Renzoni* 101
4 br m Lujain(USA) —Silver Queen (Arazi (USA))
(1871a) 3564a^{9} 6005a^{8}

Kudbeme *N Bycroft* 74d
4 b m Forzando—Umbrian Gold (IRE) (Perugino (USA))
1734^{7} 2947^{14} 4733^{8} 5370^{7} 5444^{5}

Kuka *R Hollinshead* a22 22
5 b g Polar Prince(IRE) —Crissem (IRE) (Thatching)
302^{7}

Kumakawa *D K Ivory* a54 29
8 ch g Dancing Spree(USA) —Maria Cappuccini (Siberian Express (USA))
43^{11} 148^{4}184^{9} 386^{5}(423) 527^{8}

Kuniya (NZ) *T Noonan* 88
0 b g (USA) — (USA) (Spectacular Love (USA))
6391a^{11}

Kunte Kinteh *D Nicholls* 66
2 b g Indian Lodge(IRE) —Summer Siren (FR) (Saint Cyrien (FR))
1454^{4} 4228^{6} 5307^{8}

Kurkova (IRE) *John A Quinn* a34 62?
4 b m Fasliyev(USA) —Bellissi (IRE) (Bluebird (USA))
6723^{8}

Kurtiniadis (IRE) *Trainer Unknown* 102
3 br c Mujahid(USA) —Fiddler's Moll (IRE) (Dr Devious (IRE))
5227a^{3}

Kurumda *C R Egerton* a32
2 b g Montjeu(IRE) —Susun Kelapa (USA) (St Jovite (USA))
6434^{11}

Kushnarenkovo *A P O'Brien* 100
3 b f Sadler's Wells(USA) —Eva Luna (USA) (Alleged (USA))
1026a^{3} 2689a^{2} 4212a^{8} 5465a^{6} 5854a^{3}

Kussharro *Mrs L J Young* a24 23
5 ch g Case Law—Risking (Risk Me (FR))
640^{11} 853^{11}1272^{7} 1923^{12}2728^{9}

Kuster *L M Cumani* 97
10 b g Indian Ridge—Ustka (Lomond (USA))
4160^{6} 4626^{14}

Kut (IRE) *J Noseda* a68 60
3 b c Royal Applause—Amber Tide (IRE) (Pursuit Of Love)
110^{3} 254^{4}

Kuwait Tower (IRE) *Joseph Quinn* 68
4 b h Turtle Island(IRE) —Mileeha (USA) (Blushing Groom (FR))
(4186a)

Kyathos (GER) *M F Harris* a46
5 br g Dashing Blade—Kajaana (Esclavo (FR))
6623^{6}

Kykuit (IRE) *L Brogi* 103
4 b m Green Desert(USA) —Cromac (ITY) (Machiavellian (USA))
(1368a) 2280a^{11} 6002a^{4}

Kyle (IRE) *R Hannon* a69 78
2 ch g Kyllachy—Staylily (IRE) (Grand Lodge (USA))
1372^{3} 1587^{3} 5867^{2} 6014^{2} 6330^{2}6457^{2}

Kyle Of Lochalsh *J S Goldie* a55 62
6 gr g Vettori(IRE) —Shaieef (IRE) (Shareef Dancer (USA))
1201^{9} 2242^{3} (2927) 3140^{3}3352^{6} 3675^{2} 4132^{3} (4478) 6256^{5}6317^{6} 6526^{12}

Kyles Prince (IRE) *P J Makin* a86+ 75
4 b g In The Wings—Comprehension (USA) (Diesis)
4206^{7} 4604^{11} 5897^{5} (6148) 6351^{7}

Kylkenny *H Morrison* a82 68
11 b g Kylian(USA) —Fashion Flow (Balidar)
194^{2} 296^{7}(425) (610) 1544^{7}2097^{5} 2508^{10} 2956^{5} 4021^{5} 5314^{3}5581^{5} 5946^{3} 6108^{6} 6351^{13}6633^{7} 6677^{4}6888^{12}

Kyllachy Storm *R J Hodges* a60 61
2 b c Kyllachy—Social Storm (USA) (Future Storm (USA))
3344^{7} 5340^{7} 5563^{5} 6310^{6}6500^{6} 6592^{8}

Kyloe Belle (USA) *Mrs A J Perrett* 57
2 b f Elusive Quality(USA) —Besha (USA) (Turkoman (USA))
4559^{9} 5867^{8} 6055^{8}

Kyoto City *D W Chapman* a29
2 b f Vettori(IRE) —Cominna (Dominion)
2791^{11} 3188^{9} 4971^{19}5835^{9} 6278^{5} 6472^{8}6640^{7} 6706^{5}6789^{6}

Kyoto Summit *L M Cumani* a93+ 97
3 ch c Lomitas—Alligram (USA) (Alysheba (USA))
(1139) 2986^{4} 4082^{7} 5430^{3}

Kyrenia Girl (IRE) *T D Easterby* 46
2 b f King Charlemagne(USA) —Cherry Hills (IRE) (Anabaa (USA))
3286^{6}

Kyrhena *C W Thornton* a21 18
2 b f Desert Prince(IRE) —Kyle Rhea (In The Wings)
6316^{11} 6558^{12} 6737^{10}

Kyshanty *R Hannon* a70 80
2 b c Kyllachy—War Shanty (Warrshan (USA))
2287^{10} (3193) (3544) 4043^{6} 4284^{2}4813^{8} 5788^{16}

La Bandera *B Grizzetti* 95
3 b f Bahhare(USA) —La Calima (GER) (Cadeaux Genereux)
2043a^{7} 2694a^{7}

La Barrique (IRE) *B Grizzetti*
2 br f Indian Ridge—Urmia (Persian Bold)
2565a^{9}

Labelled With Love *J R Boyle* a62 62
6 ch g Zilzal(USA) —Dream Baby (Master Willie)
458^{3} 659^{8}708^{5} 982^{5}(1923) 2319^{2}2793^{3} 6513^{5}6577^{6} 6713^{5}

La Bomba Veloce *Mrs L Williamson* a27 42
3 b f Tomba—Charleigh Keary (Sulaafah (USA))
39^{10}

L A Boy (USA) *R McAnally* 89
2 b c Explicit(USA) —Supreme Silver (USA) (Silver Hawk (USA))
5415a^{7}

La Capitaine (FR) *Y De Nicolay* 92
6 b m Smadoun(FR) —Girka (FR) (Akarad (FR))
6610a^{7}

Lacework *Sir Michael Stoute* a77
2 ch f Pivotal—Entwine (Primo Dominie)
6349^{2} (6663)

La Chesneraie *P C Haslam* a44 33
2 b f Groom Dancer(USA) —Oomph (Shareef Dancer (USA))
6316^{10} 6534^{8} 6768^{6}

La Chunga (USA) *J Noseda* 107
3 br f More Than Ready(USA) —Gypsy Monarch (USA) (Wavering Monarch (USA))
1508^{9} 2720^{13} (3499) 4191a^{11} 5549^{7}

Lac Majeur (FR) *Robert Collet* 98
2 b c Daliapour(IRE) —Charming Quest (USA) (Quest For Fame (USA))
4415a^{7} 4859a^{2}

La Colline (GER) *W J Haggas* a75+ 59
3 ch f Ocean Of Wisdom(USA) —La Laja (GER) (Be My Guest (USA))
5728^{2} (5949) (6465) (6538) (6930)

La Commara (IRE) *Daniel Mark Loughnane* 72
4 ch m Dr Devious(IRE) —Siva (FR) (Bellypha)
6474^{14}

La Conquistadora *J S Bolger* 92
2 b f Pivotal—Camaret (IRE) (Danehill (USA))
6113a^{3}

La Cucaracha *B W Hills* 118
5 b m Piccolo—Peggy Spencer (Formidable (USA))
2720^{9} 3494^{11} (4080)

La Cuvee *R M Beckett* a39 41
2 b f Mark Of Esteem(IRE) —Premiere Cuvee (Formidable (USA))
5586^{8} 6255^{13} 6409^{7}

Ladak *B Grizzetti* 89
2 b c Agnes World(USA) —Lyonette (IRE) (Royal Academy (USA))
2670a^{5}

La Dancia (IRE) *P Rau* 108
3 b f Mull Of Kintyre(USA) —La Constancia (Dominion)
(5008a) (5857a)

Ladas Lad *W G M Turner*
2 ch g Efisio—Ordained (Mtoto)
2916^{5} 3228^{4} 3831^{8}

Laddies Poker (USA) *J Noseda* a63+ 98
2 gr c Stravinsky(USA) —Lady In Waiting (USA) (Woodman (USA))
4768^{10} 5106^{4} 5466a^{5}

Ladies Best *Sir Michael Stoute* 92
2 b c King's Best(USA) —Lady Of The Lake (Caerleon (USA))
4705^{13} (5623) (5916)

Ladies Knight *D Shaw* a49 39
6 b g Among Men(USA) —Lady Silk (Prince Sabo)
320^{6} 402^{6}458^{8} 568^{10}612^{12} 633^{9}

Lady Algarhoud (FR) *M Appleby* a68 63
4 b m Josr Algarhoud(IRE) —Lady Of Limerick (IRE) (Thatching)
4^{6} (1414) 2462^{7}2962^{6} 3595^{2} 3899^{9}4365^{16}

Lady Alize (USA) *R A Kvisla* a63+ 87
2 b f Indian Charlie(USA) —Marina Duff (Caerleon (USA))
4103^{3} 4765^{6} 5894^{2} 6105^{5} 6217^{5}6520^{3}

Lady Althea *Mrs C A Dunnett*
3 ch f Danzig Connection(USA) —Lady Keyser (Le Johnstan)
6052^{12}

Lady Ambitious *D K Ivory* a41 23
3 ch f Pivotal—Ambitious (Ardkinglass)
844^{5} 1166^{8}2048^{11} 6374^{10} 6544^{10}6618^{8}

Lady Bahia (IRE) *Peter Grayson* a73 79
5 b m Orpen(USA) —Do The Right Thing (Busted)
79^{12} 136^{6}225^{12} 480^{7}547^{2} (580) 824^{12} 954^{11}986^{6} 1243^{3}2462^{6} 2521^{5} (2925) 3354^{3}4091^{7} (4135) 4357^{7} 5169^{4} 5791^{20} 6035^{10}6353^{9} 6452^{3}6555^{2} 6740^{7}

Lady Becks (IRE) *C Roberts* a14
3 b f Mull Of Kintyre(USA) —Alca Egeria (ITY) (Shareef Dancer (USA))
645^{6} 835^{6}1218^{14} 2704^{13} 2877^{11} 5733^{11}

Lady Best (IRE) *J R Weymes* 53
2 b f Best Of The Bests(IRE) —Star Of Cayman (IRE) (Unfuwain (USA))
3788^{2} 4424^{10} 4829^{9} 5492^{10}

Lady Cartuccia *J J Quinn* a41
2 b f Fasliyev(USA) —Cartuccia (IRE) (Doyoun)
6998^{5}

Lady Chastity *Mrs L J Young* a42 63
2 b f Iron Mask(USA) —Carati (Selkirk (USA))
4283^{4} 4781^{5} 5112^{6} 5876^{8}6715^{8} 6807^{7}6996^{9}

Lady Cree (IRE) *W R Muir* a45 61
3 b f Medicean—Nightitude (Night Shift (USA))
2344^{8} 2818^{6} 3450^{8}3793^{5} 4225^{9} 4627^{6} 4982^{6} 5166^{11}5574^{9} 6068^{8}

Lady Davali *S Parr*
2 b f Defacto(USA) —Tangalooma (Hotfoot)
2523^{12} 2943^{6} 3228^{6}

Lady Diktat *Mrs A J Hamilton-Fairley* a72 79
4 b m Diktat—Scared (Royal Academy (USA))
894^{9} 1222^{8}

Lady Disdain *G M Moore* 81
3 b f Foxhound(USA) —Much Ado (Mujtahid (USA))
1345^{10} 1855^{12} 2441^{3} 2679^{4} 4203^{8}(4610) (4892) 5115^{5} 5538^{6} 5769^{8} 6051^{11}

Lady Duxyana *M D I Usher* a46 47
3 b f Most Welcome—Duxyana (IRE) (Cyrano De Bergerac)
1110^{8} 1355^{13} 1844^{14}2171^{15} 2459^{9} 2535^{13} 3099^{9}3153^{6} 3668^{13} 4304^{4} 4973^{12}5432^{3} 5733^{3}

Lady Edge (IRE) *A W Carroll* 60
4 ch m Bold Edge—Lady Sheriff (Taufan (USA))
1348^{6} 2676^{6} 2702^{6} 3368^{9} 3749^{7}4070^{10} (5071) 5954^{16}

Lady Enza (IRE) *S Lanteri* 79
2 b f Golan(IRE) —Daymoon (USA) (Dayjur (USA))
3343a^{12}

Lady Evi *D K Ivory* a22
3 ch f Lord Of Men—Clued Up (Beveled (USA))
62^{7} 528^{6}617^{10} 1216^{10}

Lady Firecracker (IRE) *J R Best* a46 55
2 b f Almutawakel—Dazzling Fire (IRE) (Bluebird (USA))
1542^{7} 4774^{9} 5773^{8}

Lady Galadriel (USA) *J M P Eustace* 55
3 ch f Woodman(USA) —Dramatically (USA) (Theatrical)
1901^{8} 2580^{7} 2934^{11} 6053^{8}

Lady Georgette (IRE) *E J O'Neill* a61 64
3 b f Fasliyev(USA) —Georgia Venture (Shirley Heights)
579^{8} 850^{10}1100^{4} 1761^{8} 2400^{7} 3072^{4} 3803^{3}4118^{6} 4556^{3} 5452^{2} 6509^{5}6601^{3} 6911^{3}

Lady Grace (IRE) *W J Haggas* a89 83
2 b f Orpen(USA) —Lady Taufan (IRE) (Taufan (USA))
4993^{5} (5209) 5843^{5}(6074) 6217^{4}

Lady Gregory (IRE) *E J O'Neill* a69 73
4 b m In The Wings—Athlumney Lady (Lycius (USA))
(503)

Lady Grey Bear *R A Fahey* 4
2 gr f Tobougg(IRE) —Southern Psychic (USA) (Alwasmi (USA))
4987^{12} 5287^{11} (Dead)

Lady Gulch (AUS) *G Rogerson* 89
4 ch m (USA) — (USA) (Royal Academy (USA))
6391a^{10}

Lady Hopeful (IRE) *Peter Grayson* a53 57
4 b m Lend A Hand—Treble Term (Lion Cavern (USA))
178^{6} (209) 288^{5}401^{8} 580^{9}1150^{4} 1397^{6}1728^{8} 1913^{6}3356^{7} (4551) 4846^{7} 6539^{7}6688^{8} 6755^{2}6806^{3} 6906^{10}6994^{8}

Lady Kintyre *A W Carroll* a25 8
2 b f Mull Of Kintyre(USA) —Lady Sheriff (Taufan (USA))
5950^{13} 6222^{9} 6427^{P}

Lady Korrianda *B R Johnson* a58 37
5 ch m Dr Fong(USA) —Prima Verde (Leading Counsel (USA))
6779^{4} 6883^{8}

Lady Lafitte (USA) *B W Hills* 67
2 b f Stravinsky(USA) —Ready For Action (USA) (Riverman (USA))
4041^{6} 5068^{4} 5339^{6} 5647^{9}

Lady Lily (IRE) *H R A Cecil* a94 78
2 ch f Desert Sun—Sheila Blige (Zamindar (USA))
1989^{6} 2388^{2} 4053^{4} 4594^{7} (5076) (5434) 6096^{3}

Lady Livius (IRE) *R Hannon* 97
3 b f Titus Livius(FR) —Refined (IRE) (Statoblest)
2032^{10} (2959) 3418^{7} 4343^{2} 5044^{6} 5501^{16}5643^{8}

Lady Lochinver (IRE) *Micky Hammond* a42 54
3 ch f Raise A Grand(IRE) —Opening Day (Day Is Done)
1416^{8} 2283^{5} 4567^{3} 4892^{4} 5581^{13}

Lady Londra *D K Ivory* a65 62
4 b m Fumo Di Londra(IRE) —Lady Phyl (Northiam (USA))
22^{9} 86^{10}196^{12}

Lady Lucas (IRE) *E J Creighton* a2
3 b f Night Shift(USA) —Broadfield Lass (IRE) (Le Bavard (FR))
6649^{9} 6765^{8}

Lady Lucinda *J R Holt* a7 33
5 b m Muhtarram(USA) —Lady Phyl (Northiam (USA))
5768^{9} 6305^{9} 6376^{10}

Lady Luisa (IRE) *Miss A Stokell* a5 18
4 b m Lujain(USA) —Lady Of Dreams (IRE) (Prince Rupert (FR))
28757 30329 326611 33996 390913

Lady Marmelade (ITY) *D Ducci* 94
3 b f Diktat—Ridge Reef (IRE) (Indian Ridge)
6363a4

Lady Misha *Jedd O'Keeffe* a62 65
4 b m Mister Baileys—Hakone (IRE) (Alzao (USA))
*553 2706*30194

Lady Orpen (IRE) *Patrick Morris* a75+ 99+
3 b f Orpen(USA) —Annahala (IRE) (Ridgewood Ben)
(473) 21683 3125a22 46335 (Dead)

Lady Palma Nova *G P Kelly* a40 40
3 b f Danehill Dancer(IRE) —Sangra (USA) (El Gran Senor (USA))
*1010 19711466*6 *4997*17628 254310

Lady Pekan *P Howling* a39 56
7 b m Sri Pekan(USA) —Cloudberry (Night Shift (USA))
*2411 14613216*9 *2997465*7 *52411*

Lady Pickpocket *M H Tompkins* 42
2 b f Benny The Dip(USA) —Circe (Main Reef)
52839 567912

Lady Pilot *Ms J S Doyle* a66 76
4 b m Dansili—Mighty Flyer (IRE) (Mujtahid (USA))
1144 18763795 48235893 (643) 8385 97314
*1163813395 17455*57369 60376*64844* 65668*66873*
*677586843*10 69183

Lady Predominant *Robert Gray* a8 21
5 b m Primo Dominie—Enlisted (IRE) (Sadler's Wells (USA))
310 117

Lady Rocksam *G M Moore*
2 b f Samraan(USA) —Whittle Rock (Rock City)
5237P

Lady Romanov (IRE) *M H Tompkins* a77 58
3 br f Xaar—Mixremember (FR) (Linamix (FR))
21289 *24463 (3075)*

Lady Saffron (IRE) *J Balding* 45
2 b f Distant Music(USA) —Classic Ring (IRE) (Auction Ring (USA))
33083 39588 49209

Lady Shirley Hunt *A D Smith* a35 23
2 ch f Zaha(CAN) —Kathy Fair (IRE) (Nicholas Bill)
506814 *53897*

Lady's Law *G G Margarson* 43
3 b f Diktat—Snugfit Annie (Midyan (USA))
30326 37504 531912

Lady Smock *J R Holt*
2 ch f Elmaamul(USA) —Funky (Classic Music (USA))
50345

Lady Songbird (IRE) *W R Swinburn* 66
3 b f Selkirk(USA) —Firecrest (IRE) (Darshaan)
33678 39466

Lady Stardust *J R Fanshawe* 77
3 b f Spinning World(USA) —Carambola (IRE) (Danehill (USA))
(4563)

Lady Stratagem *E W Tuer* a42 16
7 gr m Mark Of Esteem(IRE) —Grey Angel (Kenmare (FR))
125610

Lady Suesanne (IRE) *M J Attwater* a60 51
4 b m Cape Cross(IRE) —Lady At War (Warning)
(3) 957 13461832 (240) 3504 4298

Lady Suffragette (IRE) *John Berry* a45 45
3 b f Mull Of Kintyre(USA) —Miss Senate (IRE) (Alzao (USA))
374211 42639 57574 *61333*

Lady Synthia *B Palling* a56 63
3 b f Mull Of Kintyre(USA) —Yo-Cando (IRE) (Cyrano De Bergerac)
40528 475611 498415

Lady Taverner *J E Long* a65 66
5 b m Marju(IRE) —Prompting (Primo Dominie)
*2235 26310733*2 9722 *130831879*4 34126
*521365954*12 *64052 67697*

Lady Tilly *W G Harrison* 14
9 b m Puissance—Lady Of Itatiba (BEL) (King Of Macedon)
30025

Lady Toyah (IRE) *Mrs L Williamson* a25 22
2 ch f Titus Livius(FR) —Secur Pac (FR) (Halling (USA))
250010 550717 *5687106278*9

Lady Traill *B W Hills* a55
2 b f Barathea(IRE) —Halska (Unfuwain (USA))
60736 634911

Lady Vee (IRE) *P D Niven* a56 49
4 b m Rossini(USA) —Dama De Noche (Rusticaro (FR))
1789

Lady Warning *W G M Turner* a37
2 b f Averti(IRE) —Ladysmith (Greensmith)
67425 68459

Lady Zanzara (USA) *J W Hills* a62 67
3 ch f Lion Cavern(USA) —Pace (USA) (Indian Ridge)
*667 2399*5442 *98481312*8 *34065*

La Esperanza *T D Barron* 24
2 b f Mind Games—Chantilly Myth (Sri Pekan (USA))
26953 29222 324610 523815

La Estrella (USA) *J G Given* a89 78
3 b c Theatrical—Princess Ellen (Tirol)
8979 10705 60536 *635110(6587) 68112*

Laetare (AUS) *E Martinovich* 102
6 ch g Serheed(USA) —Magdela (AUS) (Is It True (USA))
7000a9

Laeya Star (GER) *U Ostmann* 81
2 b f Royal Dragon(USA) —Linton Bay (GER) (Funambule (USA))
6122a5

La Fanciulla *R Hannon* a55 71
3 b f Robellino(USA) —Molly Brown (Rudimentary (USA))
7764 *155110* (1799) 2068524593 26762 298712
40776

Lafi (IRE) *D Nicholls* 104
7 ch g Indian Ridge—Petal Girl (Caerleon (USA))
11454 16634 397220 48325 5182954433 58077
5957P (Dead)

Lafontaine Bleu *R A Fahey* 64
2 b f Piccolo—Russell Creek (Sandy Creek)
39077 41963 (4608) 49122 578817

La Gessa *John Berry* a46 65
4 gr m Largesse—En Grisaille (Mystiko (USA))
*7310 25211*10584 21503 (2902)

Laggan Bay (IRE) *J S Moore* a40 72
6 b g Alzao(USA) —Green Lucia (Green Dancer (USA))
43693 46268 *4996*1055644 57232 596323 617813

Lagniappe (IRE) *R P Burns* 60
6 b m Definite Article—Cajun Melody (Cajun)
4166a9

Lago D'Orta (IRE) *D Nicholls* 89
6 ch g Bahhare(USA) —Maelalong (IRE) (Maelstrom Lake)
25277 29748 35006

Lagoon Royale *B W Duke* 26
2 b c Lugana Beach—Lutine Royal (Formidable (USA))
442814

La Grande Zoa (IRE) *R M Beckett* 51
3 b f Fantastic Light(USA) —Majestic Sister (IRE) (Last Tycoon)
55669 58707 62729

Laguna Reef *T D Easterby* 48
2 b g Lugana Beach—Trina's Pet (Efisio)
14428

Laheen (IRE) *M H Tompkins* a58 46
3 b f Bluebird(USA) —Ashirah (USA) (Housebuster (USA))
*1125 2545981*9 124111 1997857274 59036 *63148*

Lahiba (IRE) *M Halford* 83
5 b m Lahib(USA) —Eves Temptation (IRE) (Glenstal (USA))
5849a10

Lahob *P Howling* a29 41
6 ch g First Trump—Mystical Song (Mystiko (USA))
3019 6075

Lahudood *J E Hammond* 111
3 b f Singspiel(IRE) —Rahayeb (Arazi (USA))
2913a2 4035a2 5702a2

Laish Ya Hajar (IRE) *M R Channon* a65 73
2 ch g Grand Lodge(USA) —Ya Hajar (Lycius (USA))
32534 *43663*

Laith (IRE) *Miss V Haigh* a63 81
3 b g Royal Applause—Dania (GER) (Night Shift (USA))
12648 23896 *27567*39379 40587 42967 48418
4874652699 548713 *69308*

Laity (USA) *F Brothers* a75
3 b c Pulpit(USA) —Tour (USA) (Forty Niner (USA))
757a10

Lake Andre (IRE) *K A Ryan* a97 96
5 b g Lake Coniston(IRE) —Shadow Casting (Warning)
*5410 238*1010438 15327 185810 252012

Lake Chini (IRE) *M A Jarvis* a81 86
4 b g Raise A Grand(IRE) —Where's The Money (Lochnager)
*1927 2242476*5 *6323*9492 12853 18204

Lake Garda *K A Ryan* a57 84
5 b g Komaite(USA) —Malcesine (IRE) (Auction Ring (USA))
23842 27322 32816 39863 4119943574 48073
539112

Lake Imperial (IRE) *Heather Dalton* a36 49
5 b g Imperial Ballet(IRE) —Lakes Of Killarney (IRE) (Ahonoora)
12908 22208 29569

Lake 'O' Gold *D W Thompson* a55 55
7 ch m Karinga Bay—Ginka (Petoski)
118410

Lake Poet (IRE) *C E Brittain* a81 97
3 ch c Galileo(IRE) —Lyric (Lycius (USA))
*6582 848*3106713 *13845* 16152(2046) 22243
28054 34436 403913 54214554812 60512 63375
6468568117

Lake Pontchartrain (IRE) *S Kirk* a70+ 60
2 b f Invincible Spirit(IRE) —Sunny Slope (Mujtahid (USA))
370014 42215 50525 54196 *5738662913 (6416)*
65222 (6576)

Lake Shabla (USA) *E A L Dunlop* a88 88+
3 b f Silver Hawk(USA) —Miss Zafonic (FR) (Zafonic (USA))
(374) 17774 47842 55388 58955 *6411266078*

Lakeside Guy (IRE) *M Appleby* a46 50
5 b g Revoque(IRE) —Glen Of Imaal (IRE) (Common Grounds)
*248 90814*12 *2274247*9 *3137382*8 *40754671*2

Lake Suprima (IRE) *R M Whitaker* a31 46
3 b f Primo Valentino(IRE) —Sulaka (Owington)
997 374916 465612

Lake Toya (USA) *Saeed Bin Suroor* a106 108
4 b m Darshaan—Shinko Hermes (IRE) (Sadler's Wells (USA))
61913 (6333)

Lake Wakatipu *M Mullineaux* a64 65
4 b m Lake Coniston(IRE) —Lady Broker (Petorius)
*593 17432833 47010599*6 *68367676 (1199) 13922*
1745318476 24086 (2522) 27883 (2998) 35225
57501161084

Lakshmi (IRE) *M R Channon* a71+ 68
2 b f Efisio—Effie (Royal Academy (USA))
29574 *(3407)*

Lalina (GER) *Jane Chapple-Hyam* a47 58
3 ch f Trempolino(USA) —Lanciana (IRE) (Acatenango (GER))
5008a9 *62899 64191165091*0

La Lula (IRE) *Kerstin Helander*
3 b f Lahib(USA) —Lussuria (IRE) (Last Tycoon)
2564a5

Lamargue (GER) *Andreas Lowe* 101
4 b h Mujahid(USA) —Little Movie Star (Risk Me (FR))
1973a10

La Marmotte (IRE) *J W Hills* a62 63
2 b f Mujadil(USA) —Zilayah (USA) (Zilzal (USA))
16478 20832 24787 *34083*39974 (4334) 48133
*520865646*4 *641612 6460*36598*6*

La Matanza *T D Barron* 77
3 b f Hunting Lion(IRE) —Lawless Bridget (Alnasr Alwasheek)
(1445) 23596 26429 30235 40583 50796(5401)

Lambency (IRE) *J S Goldie* a51 59
3 b f Daylami(IRE) —Triomphale (USA) (Nureyev (USA))
15937 188810 25898 33555 38231145683 54016
58648

La Motta (IRE) *Adrian McGuinness* a68 77
6 b g Sesaro(USA) —Cheviot Indian (IRE) (Indian Ridge)
650812 6527466828

La Mottie *J Noseda* 109
3 ch f King's Best(USA) —Bareilly (USA) (Lyphard (USA))
(2330) 27442 33164 48083 5198a6

La Musique *P J McBride* a52 39
4 b g Merdon Melody—Daleside Ladybird (Tolomeo)
*17711 312126008 6382768*9 *8753(941)*
1390315755 224514

Lancaster's Quest *R Ingram* 61
2 ch c Auction House(USA) —Gabibti (IRE) (Dara Monarch)
21728 24325

Land Ahoy *D W P Arbuthnot* 76
2 b c Observatory(USA) —Night Haven (Night Shift (USA))
21726 25303 334411 47797

Land Before Time (IRE) *R J Osborne* a63 77
3 b c Montjeu(IRE) —Last Spin (Unfuwain (USA))
150a10 3127a13

Landela *M A Jarvis* a64
4 ch m Alhaarth(IRE) —Imbabala (Zafonic (USA))
5394 6694

Land 'n Stars *Jamie Poulton* a91 108
6 b g Mtoto—Uncharted Waters (Celestial Storm (USA))
205a8 (371a) 512a5 624a5 24535 (3315)
408166110a18 6392a5 7000a14

Land Of Light *G L Moore* a65 63
3 ch g Fantastic Light(USA) —Russian Snows (IRE) (Sadler's Wells (USA))
43302 *49314*

Land's End (IRE) *J Noseda* 53
2 b c Danehill Dancer(IRE) —Statistic (USA) (Mr Prospector (USA))
591512

Land Sun's Legacy (IRE) *J S Wainwright* 45
5 b g Red Sunset—Almost A Lady (IRE) (Entitled)
451115

Landucci *J W Hills* a86 84
5 b g Averti(IRE) —Divina Luna (Dowsing (USA))
111110 1340626495 30126 33375424113 47609
*(4995) 509645572*2 *(5670) 5778363974*
6594667337

La Neige *M R Channon* a101 97d
2 b c Royal Applause—Mint Royale (IRE) (Cadeaux Genereux)
(1136) 20092 27196 29604 32524 37342040994
46074 *501725292*3 5655U *60969*

Lanfredo *Miss M E Rowland* a55 55
3 b g Fraam—Lana Turrel (USA) (Trempolino (USA))
*1129 219613351*3 173812 2070747008 49815
5625757572 58872 *6302665605 67056681*72

Langford *M H Tompkins* a98 104
6 ch g Compton Place—Sharpening (Sharpo)
16783 274211 30205 331316 40981553104 *65596*
6678867445 69973

Lang Shining (IRE) *Sir Michael Stoute* 78
2 ch c Dr Fong(USA) —Dragnet (IRE) (Rainbow Quest (USA))
59143

Lannleire (IRE) *H Rogers* 57
2 b c Fasliyev(USA) —La Luna (USA) (Lyphard (USA))
5466a26

Lansdown *B Ellison* 46
2 b f Lomitas—Reamzafonic (Grand Lodge (USA))
9687 20643 25242 27318 2870232792 36194

La Nuage *T J Etherington*
2 gr f Tobougg(IRE) —Cole Slaw (Absalom)
589910

La Parrilla (IRE) *H I Larsen*
3 b f Indian Lodge(IRE) —Kilshanny (Groom Dancer (USA))
3326a10

La Petite Chinoise *L Kelp* a64 90
5 ch m Dr Fong(USA) —Susi Wong (IRE) (Selkirk (USA))
4863a3

Laphonic (USA) *T J Etherington* 51
3 b g Labeeb—Speechless (USA) (Hawkin's Special (USA))
144110 16124 22856 31897 (3526)

Lapina (IRE) *Pat Eddery* a53 46+
2 ch f Fath(USA) —Alpina (USA) (El Prado (IRE))
28169 *56084 57848*

Lap Of Honour (IRE) *N A Callaghan* a61 71
2 b g Danehill Dancer(IRE) —Kingsridge (IRE) (King's Theatre (IRE))
41057 53264 54555 57888 *64587*

Lap Of The Gods *Miss Z C Davison*
2 b g Fleetwood(IRE) —Casarabonela (Magic Ring (IRE))
686711

La Presse (USA) *B W Hills* 106
2 b f Gone West(USA) —Journalist (IRE) (Night Shift (USA))
43222 (4716) 53563 56544 62012

Lapwing (IRE) *Christian Wroe* 92
8 b g Tagula(IRE) —Wasaif (IRE) (Lomond (USA))
366a3

Laqataat (IRE) *J L Dunlop* 73
3 b f Alhaarth(IRE) —Jawlaat (USA) (Dayjur (USA))
184314 231811 307210 41819

La Quinta (IRE) *B J Meehan* a65 63
2 ch f Indian Ridge—Peneia (USA) (Nureyev (USA))
24616 26385 307043*40997* *5772364885 67507*

Larad (IRE) *J S Moore* a44 41
5 br g Desert Sun—Glenstal Priory (Glenstal (USA))
*1726 3112597*2 *76721199*3 *17292191*07
*2320625221*3 29669 *6133867299*

Laragh Hill (IRE) *G M Lyons* 50
2 b g Fasliyev(USA) —Marriage (USA) (Affirmed (USA))
5692a11

Laredo Sound (IRE) *Mario Hofer* 106
4 b g Singspiel(IRE) —Lanelly (GER) (Shining Steel)
1014a3 2061a6

Largs *J Balding* a35 35
6 ch m Sheikh Albadou—Madam Zando (Forzando)
*246 146113267*14 382511

Larione (IRE) *M Gasparini* 39
3 b c Bluebird(USA) —Flahuil (Generous (IRE))
2493a9

Larkwing (IRE) *G Wragg* 106
5 b h Ela-Mana-Mou—The Dawn Trader (USA) (Naskra (USA))
9914 14094

Larky's Lob *J O'Reilly* a72 44
7 b g Lugana Beach—Eucharis (Tickled Pink)
*964 2167411*5 *61423(6533) (6719) 69303*

La Roca (IRE) *R M Beckett* 86
2 b f Rock Of Gibraltar(IRE) —Zanella (IRE) (Nordico (USA))
10466 19303 (2328) 28009 47755 56768

Las Beatas *W R Swinburn* 79+
3 b f Green Desert(USA) —Dora Carrington (IRE) (Sri Pekan (USA))
16302

Lascelles *J A Osborne* a70
2 b c Halling(USA) —Poppy's Song (Owington)
19599 69983

Lasira (GER) *P Schiergen* 92
3 ch f Vettori(IRE) —Lupita (GER) (Niniski (USA))
1328a3 2279a10 4383a7 5160a6

La Spezia (IRE) *M L W Bell* 78
2 b f Danehill Dancer(IRE) —Genoa (Zafonic (USA))
43734 48302 52872 56794

Lasser Light (IRE) *D G Bridgwater* a36 56
6 bb g Inchinor—Light Ray (Rainbow Quest (USA))
122410

Last Action Hero (GER) *N Sauer* 86
4 br h Dashing Blade—Lady Lou (GER) (Surumu (GER))
2492a7

Last Answer (CAN) *M Keogh* 110
6 b g Langfuhr(CAN) —Victorious Answer (USA) (Northern Answer (CAN))
6126a6

Last Chapter (IRE) *C A Dwyer* a48 32
4 b g Desert Story(IRE) —Dutosky (Doulab (USA))
*87511 1536121724*3

Last Dog Standing (IRE) *B G Powell* 23
2 b g King Charlemagne(USA) —Rite Of Spring (Niniski (USA))
32229 35459 486712 534913 601613

Last Flight (IRE) *J L Dunlop* 54
2 b f In The Wings—Fantastic Fantasy (IRE) (Lahib (USA))
508310 55958 58864

Lasting Image *S C Williams* 28
4 br m Zilzal(USA) —Minsden's Image (Dancer's Image (USA))
249710

Lasting Love *C R Dore* a55 49
3 ch f Primo Valentino(IRE) —Miss Beverley (Beveled (USA))
*2485 287103596 4661263*73 *69051200*12

Last Pioneer (IRE) *R Ford* 67
4 b g New Frontier(IRE) —Toordillon (IRE) (Contract Law (USA))
20446 49148

Last Sovereign *R Charlton* a58
2 b c Pivotal—Zayala (Royal Applause)
64344 66696

Last Warrior *J H M Gosden* 85
3 ch c Rainbow Quest(USA) —Sena Desert (Green Desert (USA))
31224 43747

Latanazul *J L Dunlop* 87
2 b f Sakhee(USA) —Karamah (Unfuwain (USA))
47658 53522 57602

Late Arrival *Micky Hammond* a46 52
9 b g Emperor Jones(USA) —Try Vickers (USA) (Fuzzbuster (USA))
5510

Late Night Love *K R Burke* a33
3 b f Bluebird(USA) —Syringa (Lure (USA))
937

Lateral *P Schiergen* 115
3 b c Singspiel(IRE) —Ligona (Aragon)
1600a3 2314a3 (3563a) (4190a) 4918a3 (5543a)

Latice (IRE) *J E Sheppard* 121+
5 ch m Inchinor—Laramie (USA) (Gulch (USA))
6125a5

Latif (USA) *Ms Deborah J Evans* a78 79
5 b g Red Ransom(USA) —Awaamir (Green Desert (USA))
(175) 2855 (304) 3582(391) 4932(530) 56737004
(713) 8256 10753 *(1148)* 12883 14802 19876
297410

Latin Express (IRE) *W R Muir* a68 55
4 b g Marju(IRE) —Sea Port (Averof)
21813

Latino Magic (IRE) *R J Osborne* 112
6 ch h Lion Cavern(USA) —Tansy (Shareef Dancer (USA))
280a[3] 496a[12] 564a[9] 3559a[6] 3964a[4] 4031a[4] 4641a[4] 5411a[2] 5708a[4]

Latin Walk (IRE) *J S Bolger* 78
2 b f Lil's Boy(USA) —Via Verbano (IRE) (Caerleon (USA))
2037a[6]

Latona (FR) *J E Pease* 110
4 ch m Kendor(FR) —Silicon Lady (FR) (Mille Balles (FR))
(1717a) 2276a[10] 5222a[8]

Lauder *J Balding* a49
2 ch f First Trump—Madam Zando (Forzando)
6675[6] 6815[7]

Laugh 'n Cry *C A Cyzer* a62 51
5 b m In The Wings—The Kings Daughter (Indian King (USA))
711[10] 4660[7] 4820[9] 5108[8] 5450[13] 5986[8] 6144[6] 6459[8] 6700[5]

Launch It Lily *W G M Turner* 65
2 br f Kyllachy—Bermuda Lily (Dunbeath (USA))
5563[11] 5950[3]

Laura's Best (IRE) *W J Haggas* a78 11
2 b f Green Desert(USA) —Lassie's Gold (USA) (Seeking The Gold (USA))
5773[2] 6201[11]

Laurel Dawn *Miss A Stokell* a53 53
8 gr g Paris House—Madrina (Waajib)
686[7] 782[5] 876[11] (943) 1196[4] 1571[2] 1762[7] 2208[11] 2949[16] 3004[11] 6969[11]

Laureldean Express *E J O'Neill* a80 86
2 ch f Inchinor—Triple Sharp (Selkirk (USA))
2980[3] 3201[2] 4084[3] 5034[3] 6453a[2] 6528a[6]

Laurels Lady *I W McInnes*
2 b f Timeless Times(USA) —Superstream (Superpower)
2703[7] 3188[8] 3787[9]

Lauren Louise *T T Clement* a49 40
4 b m Tagula(IRE) —Movie Star (IRE) (Barathea (IRE))
138[4] 307[5] (396) 1539[5] 1728[7]

Laurentina *B J Meehan* a74 88
2 b f Cadeaux Genereux—Trois Heures Apres (Soviet Star (USA))
4559[4] (4993) (5748) 6217[3]

Lauro (GER) *P Schiergen* 106
3 br c Monsun(GER) —Laurencia (Shirley Heights)
3131a[2] 3776a[7] 6365a[8]

Lauro *Miss J A Camacho* a64 71
6 b m Mukaddamah(USA) —Lapu-Lapu (Prince Sabo)
1553[6] 2108[3] 2747[4] (4068) 4570[6] 5740[9] 5972[11]

Laurollie *B P J Baugh* a53 47
4 b m Makbul—Madonna Da Rossi (Mtoto)
2902[8] 3196[9] 3615[10] 5925[6] 6279[3] 6540[6] 6620[6] 6860[6] 6972[4]

Lava Man (USA) *Doug O'Neill* a127+ 125
5 br g Slew City Slew(USA) —Li'l Ms. Leonard (USA) (Nostalgia's Star (USA))
(5826a) 6345a[7]

Lavarone (ARG) *Diego Lowther* 69
3 ch c Sekari—Siusi (ARG) (Engrillago (ARG))
6121a[10]

La Vecchia Scuola (IRE) *D Nicholls* 65
2 b f Mull Of Kintyre(USA) —Force Divine (FR) (L'Emigrant (USA))
1442[7] 2394[2] 2973[6] 3555[7] 5747[6]

Lavenham (IRE) *R Hannon* 79+
3 b f Kalanisi(IRE) —Antigonel (IRE) (Fairy King (USA))
(1641) 1843[3] 2642[7] 2863[11] 4837[4] 5294[3]

Laverock (IRE) *C Laffon-Parias* 122
4 b h Octagonal(NZ) —Sky Song (IRE) (Sadler's Wells (USA))
1180a[12] (1873a) 2914a[3] 3993a[2] 4679[5] (6004a)

La Via Ferrata (IRE) *A G Newcombe* a73 65
3 ch c Mark Of Esteem(IRE) —Verify (IRE) (Polish Precedent (USA))
(61) (349) 2332[4] 2569[3] 3075[2] (3456) 4537[4] 5628[4] 6027[4] 6378[F] (Dead)

La Viola *K R Burke* a65 60
4 b m Fraam—Arasong (Aragon)
56[13] 2282[2] 2794[2] 3159[P] 3480[2] 3914[7] 4726[6] 4974[8] 5248[4] 6059[7]

La Vriga *B Grizzetti* 99
5 b m Singspiel(IRE) —Juhina (IRE) (Marju (IRE))
1368a[2] 2280a[3] 6124a[9] 6362a[7]

Lawaaheb (IRE) *B R Johnson* a51 57
5 b g Alhaarth(IRE) —Ajayib (USA) (Riverman (USA))
141[8] 457[3] 568[5]

Law Lord *A Fabre* 91
2 br c Diktat—First (Highest Honor (FR))
(5471a)

Law Maker *A Bailey* a83 68
6 b g Case Law—Bo' Babbity (Strong Gale)
23[2] 89[7] (136) 244[8] 362[6] 441[2] 517[8] 657[7] 967[8] 1399[9] 2396[7] 2521[7] 2897[5] 5309[19]

Law Of The Land (IRE) *W R Muir* a63 65
2 b g Trans Island—Bella's Dream (IRE) (Case Law)
1838[18] 3031[2] 3335[5] 4140[3] 4688[8] 5094[9] 5738[3] 6283[5] 6394[10]

Lawood (IRE) *M Scudamore* a34 50
6 gr g Charnwood Forest(IRE) —La Susiane (Persepolis (FR))
990[15] 1772[13] 2641[13] 3115[11] 3196[8] 6797[4]

Lawyer Ron (USA) *T Pletcher* a120
3 ch c Langfuhr(CAN) —Donation (USA) (Lord Avie (USA))
1498a[12] 6345a[9]

Lawyers Choice *Pat Eddery* a68 52+
2 b f Namid—Finger Of Light (Green Desert (USA))
5950[8] 6187[4] 6663[4]

Lawyer To World *N A Callaghan* a64 60
2 gr c Marju(IRE) —Legal Steps (IRE) (Law Society (USA))
3738[6] 5105[4] 5607[6] 6064[5] 6322[7] 6487[2] 6866[6]

Layazaal (IRE) *J L Dunlop* 99
3 b c Mujadil(USA) —Law Review (IRE) (Case Law)
1067[5] 1505[2] (1951) 2774[17] 4833[8] 5660[5] 6107[9]

Layed Back Rocky *M Mullineaux* a50 12
4 ch g Lake Coniston(IRE) —Madam Taylor (Free State)
38[11] 586[10] 684[12] 6281[12] 6765[3] 6861[3] 6901[6]

Layman (USA) *I Mohammed* 121
4 ch h Sunday Silence(USA) —Laiyl (IRE) (Nureyev (USA))
564a[8] 741a[7]

Lay The Cash (USA) *J S Moore* a64 44
2 ch g Include(USA) —Shanade (USA) (Sentimental Slew (USA))
4008[5] 4525[7] 4774[8] 5585[12] 6031[7] (6291) 6525[6]

Lazio (GER) *A Trybuhl* 110
5 b h Dashing Blade—Leontine (GER) (Selkirk (USA))
1869a[3] 2492a[2] 2692a[3] 5227a[8]

Lazy Darren *R Hannon* a77+ 77+
2 b g Largesse—Palmstead Belle (IRE) (Wolfhound (USA))
5658[7] (6950)

Lazzaz *P W Hiatt* a64 59
8 b g Muhtarram(USA) —Astern (USA) (Polish Navy (USA))
1548[9]

Lazzoom (IRE) *Miss Tracy Waggott* 48
3 b g Zilzal(USA) —Bring On The Choir (Chief Singer)
1593[13] 2243[15] 2282[9] 5483[14] 5553[15]

Leadwithyourchin (USA) *M Hushion* 100
4 b h Dynaformer(USA) —Deux Danseuses (USA) (Deputy Minister (CAN))
4908a[5]

Leah's Pride *Miss D A McHale* a54
5 b m Atraf—First Play (Primo Dominie)
38[3] 179[5] 209[2] 502[8] 679[3] 886[5] 982[7] 1150[8] 1195[5]

Leamington Lad (IRE) *J A Geake* a10 69+
3 gr c Beckett(IRE) —Nicea (IRE) (Dominion)
(879) 1078[5] (1352) 2050[8] 2616[7] 3977[4] 5129[4] 5574[5] 5868[3]

Leathaoibh (IRE) *P A Fahy* 69
2 b f Rossini(USA) —Silent Melody (IRE) (Last Tycoon)
4747a[8]

Le Carre (USA) *A De Royer-Dupre* 115
8 gr g Miswaki(USA) —Dibs (USA) (Spectacular Bid (USA))
6610a[16]

Le Chiffre (IRE) *K R Burke* a67 75
4 br g Celtic Swing—Implicit View (Persian Bold)
2282[4] 2531[5] 2947[9] (3158) (3565) 3705[4] 3898[6] 4399[7] 6573[11] (6636) 6720[10]

Le Colombier (IRE) *J W Hills* a85 82
3 ch c Alhaarth(IRE) —Wide Range (IRE) (Spectrum (IRE))
1153[2] 2028[4] (2465) 2986[9] 4244[7] 4604[13]

Le Corvee (IRE) *A King* a94 96
4 b g Rossini(USA) —Elupa (IRE) (Mtoto)
1071[8] 1631[12]

Lee Applause *Edward P Harty* 88?
4 bb m Royal Applause—Ferghana Ma (Mtoto)
6356a[6]

Leeside Music (IRE) *P A Fahy* 88
5 b m Lil's Boy(USA) —Pennine Music (IRE) (Pennine Walk)
4094a[8]

Lefonic *G C H Chung* a67 58
4 ch h Zafonic(USA) —La Adrada (Arazi (USA))
733[5] 1138[15] (2206) 2828[6] (3013) 3628[7] 4011[4] 4996[7] 5736[5]

Left Hand Drive *B W Duke* a58 41
3 b g Erhaab(USA) —Eyelet (IRE) (Satco (FR))
349[2] 781[12] 1350[12] 3017[11]

Left Nostril (IRE) *P S McEntee* a45 42
3 b f Beckett(IRE) —Baywood (Emarati (USA))
105[10] 308[9] 396[12] 1263[4] 5949[3] 6492[2] 6649[7] 6774[2]

Legacy (JPN) *P D Evans* a34 85
6 b g Carnegie(IRE) —Idraak (Kris)
(43) 143[9] 310[5] 358[4] 467[7] 472[8] 770[3] 953[8] 1625a[4] 1911[14] 6370[12]

Legal Approach *R Bouresly* 99
7 b h Zafonic(USA) —Legaya (Shirley Heights)
278a[11] 357a[10]

Legal Call *M Appleby* a26 56
3 b g Easycall—Legal Sound (Legal Eagle)
533[10] 2222[8] 2479[10] 2566[4] 2877[6] 3195[11] 4288[10]

Legal Dram *M Dods* a53 53
5 ch g Case Law—Moonshine Malt (Superlative)
77[8] 183[7] (3240) 3786[11] 4194[6] 4425[7]

Legal Lover (IRE) *R Hollinshead* a66 68
4 b g Woodborough(USA) —Victoria's Secret (IRE) (Law Society (USA))
143[4] 183[4] 648[4] (875) 1073[5] 1574[2] 2245[4] 3263[7] (5054) 5316[5] 6069[2] (6304) 6641[8] 6819[2] 6949[2]

Legally Fast (USA) *S C Burrough* 60
4 b g Deputy Minister(CAN) —Earthly Angel (USA) (Crafty Prospector (USA))
2879[7]

Legal Set (IRE) *Miss A Stokell* a50 44
10 gr g Second Set(IRE) —Tiffany's Case (IRE) (Thatching)
54[11] 212[7] 317[11] 408[10] 1102[16] 1534[5] 1722[8] 1914[10] 5577[14] 6555[11] 6718[P]

Legend House (FR) *M Johnston* a73 47
2 b f Grand Lodge(USA) —Legaya (Shirley Heights)
5595[9] 6242[5] (6536)

Legend Of Dance *J L Spearing* a37 50
4 b m Dansili—Hard Task (Formidable (USA))
91[11] 361[8] 403[9]

Legerete (USA) *A Fabre* 105+
2 b f Rahy(USA) —Sea Hill (USA) (Seattle Slew (USA))
5714a[3]

Legs (NZ) *K Gray* 104
4 b m Pins(AUS) —River Century (NZ) (Centaine (AUS))
6347a[6]

Leg Sweep *D R C Elsworth* a60
2 ch c Compton Place—Radiant Bride (USA) (Blushing Groom (FR))
6887[9]

Leicester Square (IRE) *E Charpy* 109
5 ch g Gone West(USA) —Stage Manner (In The Wings)
151a[8] 511a[5]

Leighton Buzzard *N B King* a53 68
4 b g Cyrano De Bergerac—Winsome Wooster (Primo Dominie)
1253[7] 1683[7] (2286) 2641[5] 2789[2] 3762[8] 5258[2] 5422[5] 6380[7] 6810[7]

Leitmotiv (IRE) *A Fabre* 96
3 b c Sadler's Wells(USA) —Moselle (Mtoto)
6062a[8]

Leitra (IRE) *M Halford* 107
3 b f Danehill Dancer(IRE) —Glenmara (USA) (Known Fact (USA))
2038a[6] 3561a[2] 4855a[3]

Le Marquis (GER) *Frau Jutta Mayer* 94
5 b g Komtur(USA) —Latour (GER) (Goofalik (USA))
3992a[4]

Le Masque *B Smart* a66 57
2 b g Iron Mask(USA) —Red Millennium (IRE) (Tagula (IRE))
4421[12] 4731[7] 5288[5] 5721[6] 6291[7] 6472[2] 6940[2]

Le Miracle (GER) *W Baltromei* 119
5 b g Monsun(GER) —L'Heure Bleue (IRE) (Kendor (FR))
4647a[3] (5223a) 5711a[3]

Lemon Drop Lad (USA) *Sir Michael Stoute* a75 80+
3 ch c Lemon Drop Kid(USA) —April Starlight (USA) (Storm Bird (CAN))
1335[4] (1814)

Lemons Forever (USA) *D Stewart* a118
3 ch f Lemon Drop Kid(USA) —Critikola (ARG) (Tough Critic (USA))
3757a[4] 6343a[5]

Lemon Silk (IRE) *T P Tate* 74
2 ch g Barathea(IRE) —Bois De Citron (USA) (Woodman (USA))
2783[5] 3286[5] 3669[3] (4509) 4882[7] 5633[2] 5958[9]

Lenard Frank (IRE) *M D I Usher* 20
2 b g Daggers Drawn(USA) —Princess Sofie (Efisio)
944[8] 1223[11] 2064[6] 2495[4] 2709[9] 2916[4] 3117[13] 3300[7] 4624[9]

Leningrad (IRE) *M L W Bell* a86+ 97
3 gr c Montjeu(IRE) —Sallanches (USA) (Gone West (USA))
(850) 1805[4] 2775[12] 3491[9] 3978[2] 4298[3] 5639[6]

Lennel *A Bailey* a54 55
8 b g Presidium—Ladykirk (Slip Anchor)
3230[7] 3350[4] 3763[7] 3810[4] 4351[5] 4522[6] 5338[3] 5927[3] 5971[7]

Lennoxtown (IRE) *J Ryan* a62 61
3 ch g Selkirk(USA) —Pump (USA) (Forli (ARG))
1055[11] 1252[6] 1681[13] 5992[4] 6294[7] 6430[5] 6484[6] 6748[10] 6843[2] 6911[6]

Lenoir (GER) *V Smith* a74 66
3 b g Lujain(USA) —Luna De Miel (Shareef Dancer (USA))
19[3] 142[7] 188[2] 342[8] 422[4] 993[15] 1241[7] 2480[9] 3706[9] (4842) 5260[6] 5497[5] 6070[3]

Lenwade *G G Margarson* a41 50
5 gr m Environment Friend—Branitska (Mummy's Pet)
311[8] 792[10] 1313[4] 1755[6] 2132[10] 2497[3] 3035[6] 3437[9] 3803[4] 4011[3] 4423[4] 4960[2] 5324[10] 6132[8]

Leoballero *D J Daly* a81 96
6 ch g Lion Cavern(USA) —Ball Gown (Jalmood (USA))
3202[4] 4108[4] 4429[6]

Leo McGarry (IRE) *N B King* a41 69
3 ch g Fantastic Light(USA) —Lilissa (IRE) (Doyoun)
709[11] 1352[15] 2539[4] 3145[6] (3791) (4111) 4252[4] 4632[4] 5618[2] 6027[5] 6979[7]

Leonard Charles *Sir Mark Prescott* a79+
2 b g Best Of The Bests(IRE) —Iris May (Brief Truce (USA))
(6751) 6991[3]

Leonards Girl (IRE) *P M Mooney*
3 b f Beckett(IRE) —Persian Light (IRE) (Persian Heights)
2247[8]

Leonide *B J Meehan* 81
2 b g Noverre(USA) —Marionetta (USA) (Nijinsky (CAN))
3701[10] 4333[7] 4588[2] 5140[3] (5509)

Leon Knights *G A Butler* a72 66+
2 b c Inchinor—Valnerina (IRE) (Caerleon (USA))
5066[7] 6072[3]

Leopard King (USA) *Sir Michael Stoute* a53+ 89
2 bb c Kingmambo(USA) —Hidden Cat (USA) (Storm Cat (USA))
4105[2] (4843) 5372[3] 5843[10]

Leopoldine *H Morrison* a74 95
3 br f Desert Prince(IRE) —Beaming (Mtoto)
1960[2] (2445) 2651[4] 3499[9] 4102[4] 5643[3] 5919[5]

Leo's Luckyman (USA) *M Johnston* a66 107
7 bb g Woodman(USA) —Leo's Lucky Lady (USA) (Seattle Slew (USA))
4711[11]

Leprechaun's Gold (IRE) *M Johnston* a63
2 ch c Spectrum(IRE) —Ashirah (USA) (Housebuster (USA))
6475[2] 6644[9] 6920[7]

Leprechaun's Maite *B N Pollock* 57?
4 b g Komaite(USA) —Leprechaun Lady (Royal Blend)
4708[8]

Le Prince Charmant (FR) *E Charpy* 105
5 ch h Priolo(USA) —La Petite Danseuse (USA) (Woodman (USA))
497a[2]

Leptis Magna *W J Knight* 65+
2 ch g Danehill Dancer(IRE) —Dark Eyed Lady (IRE) (Exhibitioner)
4479[5] 5125[10] 5496[4]

Lerida *Miss Lucinda V Russell* 24
4 ch g Groom Dancer(USA) —Catalonia (IRE) (Catrail (USA))
5583[7]

Les Arcs (USA) *T J Pitt* a111 123
6 br g Arch(USA) —La Sarto (USA) (Cormorant (USA))
(54) (295) (664) (729) 1069[2] 2115[8] 2720[11] (2846) (3494) 5717a[7]

Les Fazzani (IRE) *M J Wallace* a70+
2 b f Intikhab(USA) —Massada (Most Welcome)
(6697)

Le Singe Noir *D M Simcock* a73 49+
2 b g Averti(IRE) —Prends Ca (IRE) (Reprimand)
5417[9] 5735[3] 6034[2]

Leslingtaylor (IRE) *J J Quinn* 85
4 b g Orpen(USA) —Rite Of Spring (Niniski (USA))
1756[12] 2018[10] 2762[3] 3621[3] 3960[7] 4472[4] (4924) (5132) 5367[7] (5792) 5952[3]

Le Soleil (GER) *B J Curley* a61+ 65+
5 b g Monsun(GER) —La Blue (GER) (Bluebird (USA))
12[9] (972) 4925[14] 5354[7] 5954[13]

Lester Leaps In (USA) *R Hannon* a77 73+
3 bb c Red Ransom(USA) —Rose Aurora (USA) (Majestic Light (USA))
1141[3] 1375[6] 1925[3] (2480) 2713[7] 3816[2] 4044[2] 5260[8] 5911[2]

Lester Quercus (FR) *J Van Handenhove* a78 78
7 ch g Dernier Empereur(USA) —Taboo (FR) (Vitiges (FR))
5562a[0]

Lethal *D K Ivory* a82+ 64
3 ch g Nashwan(USA) —Ipanema Beach (Lion Cavern (USA))
191[10] 4899[4] 5092[3] (6865)

Letham Island (IRE) *M Johnston* a67 53
2 b f Trans Island—Common Cause (Polish Patriot (USA))
6316[4] 6466[2] 6558[2] (6675)

Let It Be *K G Reveley* a60 69
5 ch m Entrepreneur—Noble Dane (IRE) (Danehill (USA))
1346[12] 1756[10] 2078[4] 2408[5] (2871) 3177[4] 3723[5] 4320[3] 4960[5] 5242[8] (5369) 5815[11]

Lets Be Lucky (IRE) *F Jordan* a34
4 b g Desert King(IRE) —Mo Pheata (Petorius)
897[14] 1387[7] 2413[11] 3944[14]

Let's Face It (IRE) *Peter Grayson* a35
2 b g Iron Mask(USA) —Jay And-A (IRE) (Elbio)
4969[7] 5245[10] (Dead)

Lets Get Cracking (FR) *K A Ryan* a72 70
2 b c Anabaa Blue—Queenhood (FR) (Linamix (FR))
4424[6] 5402[3] 5814[5] (6283) 6609a[7]

Let Slip *W Jarvis* a85+ 78
4 b m Second Empire(IRE) —Loose Talk (Thatching)
(1162) 1544[15] 2113[3] 2752[2] (3731) 4610[6] 5110[4]

Lets Roll *C W Thornton* 98
5 b g Tamure(IRE) —Miss Petronella (Petoski)
1071[6] 1294[5] 1779[2] 1991[3] 2850[2] 3294[11] 4027[3] 4713[8] 5010[5] (5361) 5582[5] 5963[21] 6319[4]

Lets Try Again (IRE) *R A Farrant* a39 63
9 b g Barathea(IRE) —Intricacy (Formidable (USA))
966[12] 1415[5] 2483[5] 3196[10] 3597[7] 3894[6] 4438[11]

Level Par (IRE) *J A Supple* a50 64
6 ch g Cadeaux Genereux—Howaida (IRE) (Night Shift (USA))
42[6] 173[10] 311[13] 791[7]

Levera *A King* 109+
3 b c Groom Dancer(USA) —Prancing (Prince Sabo)
(1067) (1505) (1776) 2739[14]

Levin (IRE) *J L Dunlop* 56
3 b g Fantastic Light(USA) —Knight's Place (IRE) (Hamas (IRE))
964[7] 1212[9] 1641[6] 2065[14]

Lewis Island (IRE) *G L Moore* a69 68
7 b g Turtle Island(IRE) —Phyllode (Pharly (FR))
338[4] 589[7] (1772) 1931[9]

Lewis Lloyd (IRE) *I A Wood* a49 52
3 b g Indian Lodge(IRE) —Sandy Fitzgerald (IRE) (Last Tycoon)
604[8] 781[11] 945[7] 1293[5] 1731[6] 2415[4] 2877[12] 2968[9] 3870[8] (4195) 5240[14] 5445[11]

Lewis Michael (USA) *W Catalano* a111 96
3 b c Rahy(USA) —Justenuffheart (USA) (Broad Brush (USA))
6341a[11]

Leyaaly *Miss Z C Davison* a14
7 ch m Night Shift(USA) —Lower The Tone (IRE) (Phone Trick (USA))
328[5] 390[11]

Liability (IRE) *Miss S E Hall* a10 46
4 b m Bluebird(USA) —Madaniyya (USA) (Shahrastani (USA))
386[11]

Liakoura (GER) *Mrs A J Perrett* a71 96
4 b g Royal Academy(USA) —Lady Member (FR) (Saint Estephe (FR))
1133[8] 1544[10] 2440[12] 5149[5] 5590[16] 5908[5]

Liameliss *M A Allen* a20 49
4 ch m Dr Fong(USA) —Ivory Palm (USA) (Sir Ivor (USA))
2497[8] 3803[8] 4011[9] 4239[7]

Liberate *Sir Mark Prescott* a88+ 94+
3 ch g Lomitas—Eversince (USA) (Foolish Pleasure (USA))
1634[4] (2124) 2246[2] (2379) 2677[2] 3502[2] (3649) (3848) 3877[3]

Liberation Square *J S Goldie* 41
3 ch g Compton Place—Class Wan (Safawan)
1612[10] 2928[16]

Liberman (IRE) *R Curtis* a37 70
8 br g Standiford(USA) —Hail To You (USA) (Kirtling)
5318[3] 5846[10]

Liberty Run (IRE) *Mrs A J Hamilton-Fairley* a77 63
4 ch g Grand Lodge(USA) —Bathe In Light (USA) (Sunshine Forever (USA))
1769^{14} 2305^{14} (5451) 5725^{12} 6566^{5}6917^{7}

Liberty Seeker (FR) *G A Swinbank* 74+
7 ch g Machiavellian(USA) —Samara (IRE) (Polish Patriot (USA))
(975) 2196^{3} 2452^{4}

Libor (IRE) *L M Cumani* a84 85
3 b c Lend A Hand—America Lontana (FR) (King's Theatre (IRE))
2080^{3} 2356^{2} 2763^{2} (3349) 3722^{5} 4328^{2}4841^{2} 5265^{2}

Libras Child (IRE) *P Delaney* 90
7 b g Paris House—Butternut (IRE) (Alzao (USA))
3125a^{10} 3561a^{9}

Libre *F Jordan* a75 72
6 b g Bahamian Bounty—Premier Blues (FR) (Law Society (USA))
33^{10} 108^{6}192^{9} 235^{2}313^{2} 641^{4}992^{4} 1288^{11} 1821^{4} 2170^{3} 2585^{7}3311^{3} 5889^{9} 6609^{12}

Librettist (USA) *Saeed Bin Suroor* 124
4 b h Danzig(USA) —Mysterial (USA) (Alleged (USA))
(2358) (3091) (3779a) (4416a) (5049a) 5524^{6} 6342a^{10}

Life (IRE) *J Noseda* 81+
2 b c Sadler's Wells(USA) —Inchyre (Shirley Heights)
5640^{2} 5882^{5}

Life Is Rosie (IRE) *D K Ivory* a39
4 ch m Rossini(USA) —Rachcara (IRE) (Kefaah (USA))
266^{9}

Life Peer *J G Portman* a61 56
3 b g Mark Of Esteem(IRE) —Sadaka (USA) (Kingmambo (USA))
918^{5} 1052^{8} 1543^{9}1925^{6} 3017^{4}6657^{5} (Dead)

Life's A Whirl *Mrs C A Dunnett* a35 62
4 b m Machiavellian(USA) —Spinning Top (Alzao (USA))
1056^{7} 1382^{14} 2148^{7}2645^{9} 3089^{4} 3229^{4} 3679^{3} (3828) 4009^{7}4968^{12} 5302^{10} 6419^{12}

Lifetime Romance (IRE) *John M Oxx* 94
3 b f Mozart(IRE) —Josh's Pearl (IRE) (Sadler's Wells (USA))
1709a^{6}

Lift Cape (IRE) *V Caruso* a94 97
3 br c Cape Cross(IRE) —Lifting (IRE) (Nordance (USA))
1871a^{5} 5473a^{2}

Lifted Way *P R Chamings* a56 76
7 b g In The Wings—Stack Rock (Ballad Rock)
2969^{11} 3642^{13} 4248^{9}4970^{7}

Light Dreams *W J Knight* a35 73
3 b f Fantastic Light(USA) —Dreamawhile (Known Fact (USA))
1374^{8} 2304^{7} 2917^{8} 3412^{8} 4257^{2}4757^{3} 5619^{5} 6406^{5}

Lighted Smile (FR) *C J Gray* 16
3 b f Emperor Jones(USA) —Light The Sky (FR) (Persepolis (FR))
4983^{15} 5273^{12} 5298^{13}

Light Mozart *C E Brittain* a71 67
3 b f Mozart(IRE) —Footlight Fantasy (USA) (Nureyev (USA))
1109^{5} 1431^{2} 1825^{3}1937^{2} 2134^{2} 5480^{9}5605^{6} 5987^{9}

Lightning Flash *J R Fanshawe* a105+ 108
4 b h Docksider(USA) —Threatening (Warning)
(3648) 4740^{2}

Lightning Queen (USA) *B W Hills* 51
2 b f Thunder Gulch(USA) —Fairy Dancer (USA) (Nijinsky (CAN))
5068^{8} 5456^{9} 6023^{7}

Lightning Strike (GER) *T G Mills* a82+ 98
3 ch g Danehill Dancer(IRE) —La Capilla (Machiavellian (USA))
124^{6} (656) (805) 1356^{2} 1898^{4}2804^{5} (3888) 4967^{U} 5351^{5} 5526^{2} 5963^{12}

Light Of Day (IRE) *J R Best* a48
3 b f Mutamam—Top Of The Morning (Keen)
539^{5} 762^{9}1200^{2}

Light Of Joy (FR) *R Pritchard-Gordon* 103
3 b c Mark Of Esteem(IRE) —Silence (IRE) (Alzao (USA))
1178a^{2}

Light Sentence *G A Swinbank* 63
3 b g Fantastic Light(USA) —Almela (IRE) (Akarad (FR))
1230^{7} 1493^{6} 4635^{5} 5082^{4} (5683)

Light Shift (USA) *H R A Cecil* 86
2 b f Kingmambo(USA) —Lingerie (Shirley Heights)
3043^{2} 3707^{3} (5456)

Lights Of Vegas *B J Meehan* 67
2 b c Traditionally(USA) —Catch The Lights (Deploy)
4177^{3} 4592^{7}

Lights Out (DEN) *C A Horgan* a98? 56
6 ch g Kateb(IRE) —Skee The Feen (Viking (USA))
765^{9} 1566^{6}

Ligne D'Eau *P D Evans* a40 38
5 ch g Cadeaux Genereux—Miss Waterline (Rock City)
6638^{6} 6703^{7}6819^{11}

Lihusn Al Haz (USA) *C E Brittain* a32 38
3 bb f King Cugat(USA) —Chaste (USA) (Cozzene (USA))
2578^{9} 3258^{6} 6279^{10}

Lii Najma *C E Brittain* a71 72
3 b f Medicean—Opari (IRE) (Night Shift (USA))
1430^{3} (1941) 2459^{6} 3055^{6}(3827) 4249^{4} 4666^{5} 6036^{11}6227^{4} 6497^{3}6595^{6} 6820^{7}

Like Now (USA) *K McLaughlin* a114
3 b g Jules(USA) —Cant Bluff Me (USA) (Pine Bluff (USA))
1861a^{7}

Like To Golf (USA) *Mrs A J Perrett* 56
2 bb g Bianconi(USA) —Like To Shimmy (USA) (Shimatoree (USA))
4597^{7} 5091^{8} 5460^{11}

Lilac Moon (GER) *Mrs A Duffield* 43
2 b f Dr Fong(USA) —Luna De Miel (Shareef Dancer (USA))
5237^{10}

Lilac Star *Pat Eddery* a53 73
3 ch f Observatory(USA) —La Sorrela (IRE) (Cadeaux Genereux)
1119^{7} 1649^{3} 2985^{2} 3793^{8} 6557^{4}6668^{2}

Lilakiya (IRE) *James Leavy* a41+ 57
3 b f Dr Fong(USA) —Lidakiya (IRE) (Kahyasi)
(6482) 6786a^{11}

Lillebror (GER) *B J Curley* a45 60+
8 b g Top Waltz(FR) —Lady Soliciti (GER) (Solicitor (FR))
3382^{4}

Lillie Lou *T D Easterby* 43
3 b f Tomba—Tread Carefully (Sharpo)
2080^{8} 2325^{12}

Lilly Carson (USA) *Ralph E Nicks* a101
2 ch f Carson City(USA) —Golden Lilly (USA) (Deputy Minister (CAN))
6338a^{14}

Lillyella (IRE) *M J Wallace* a46
3 ch f Raise A Grand(IRE) —Somers Heath (IRE) (Definite Article)
326^{6}

Lilly Hawk (IRE) *Adrian Sexton* 58
5 b m Shernazar—Bloomfield (IRE) (Alzao (USA))
169^{11}

Lily Elsie (IRE) *A P O'Brien* 92
3 b f Danehill(USA) —Toroca (USA) (Nureyev (USA))
4040^{3} 4502a^{7}

Lily On A Hill *B Smart* a15
3 b f City On A Hill(USA) —Gulfstream Park (Barathea (IRE))
11^{6} 197^{13}331^{9}

Limatus (GER) *P Vovcenko* 60
5 br g Law Society(USA) —Limaga (Lagunas)
6786a^{10}

Limbo King *J W Hills* 70
2 b c Barathea(IRE) —Ermine (IRE) (Cadeaux Genereux)
5891^{3} 6214^{11}

Limit Down (IRE) *John Berry* a46 49
5 b g Desert Story(IRE) —Princess Raisa (Indian King (USA))
1393^{5} 1727^{5}2645^{3} 4306^{4} 4667^{10} 6726^{2}6803^{4}

Limited Magician *C Smith* a46 32
5 b m Wizard King—Pretty Scarce (Handsome Sailor)
144^{6} (1272) 2543^{15} 3847^{10}

Limit Up (GR) *Dr A Bolte* a97
8 b h Vamos(GR) —Toccatina (USA) (What A Pleasure (USA))
393a^{6} 1659a^{7}

Limonia (GER) *N P Littmoden* a60 60
4 b m Perugino(USA) —Limoges (GER) (Konigsstuhl (GER))
24^{5} 81^{7}1915^{12} 2136^{5} 2574^{13}(3166) 3368^{11} (3673) 4294^{2} (4554) 4970^{10}5032^{5} 5350^{4} 5576^{6}5752^{8}

Linas Selection *M Johnston* 112+
3 ch c Selkirk(USA) —Lines Of Beauty (USA) (Line In The Sand (USA))
1095^{2} (1270) (2805) (3551) 4024^{3}

Lincoln (JPN) *H Otonashi* 122
6 b h Sunday Silence(USA) —Grace Admire (JPN) (Tony Bin)
1329a^{2}

Lincolneurocruiser *Mrs N Macauley* a77 80
4 b g Spectrum(IRE) —Rush Hour (IRE) (Night Shift (USA))
4^{3} 100^{6}171^{2} 245^{12}(253) 316^{5}384^{4} 451^{2}567^{9} 611^{5}632^{2} 639^{4}826^{8} 1275^{6}1686^{7} 1760^{4} 1993^{11} 2464^{9}2737^{5} 2820^{4} 3044^{4} (3089) 3262^{2}

Linda Green *M R Channon* a78 77
5 b m Victory Note(USA) —Edge Of Darkness (Vaigly Great)
777^{7} 1774^{2} 1878^{5} 2095^{10} 2293^{10}(3094) 3368^{6} 3478^{3} 3718^{4} 3783^{4} 4003^{2}4211^{4} 4294^{7} 5167^{7} 5635^{15} 5872^{4}5987^{2} (6020) 6437^{5}(6579) 6773^{7}6882^{6}

Linda's Colin (IRE) *R A Harris* a77 72
4 b g Xaar—Capable Kate (IRE) (Alzao (USA))
316^{9} 1802^{5} 2170^{9}2499^{5} 3469^{4} (3705) 4009^{3} 4399^{2} 4706^{15}5444^{13} 6654^{6} 6770^{7}6889^{3}

Linda's Lad *A Fabre* 116
3 b c Sadler's Wells(USA) —Colza (USA) (Alleged (USA))
1064a^{4} (1668) 2228^{9} 3778a^{3}

Lindbergh *R Hannon* a89 94
4 b g Bold Edge—Halland Park Girl (IRE) (Primo Dominie)
761^{2} 846^{4}1161^{3} 1399^{7}1475^{6} 2674^{10}

Lindenburgh Way (IRE) *B J Meehan* a55 82
3 b c Red Ransom(USA) —Strange Destiny (Mujadil (USA))
1844^{3} 2244^{4} 4144^{12} (Dead)

Linden Lime *Jamie Poulton* a74 69+
4 ch m Double Trigger(IRE) —Linden Grace (USA) (Mister Baileys)
32^{5} 264^{9}1213^{2} (1339) 1690^{5} 2501^{7}3649^{5} 3935^{4}(4320) 4777^{8} 5201^{3} (5531) 5610^{3}5991^{5} 6602^{6}6831^{4}

Linden's Lady *J R Weymes* a23 62
6 b m Compton Place—Jubilee Place (IRE) (Prince Sabo)
1348^{5} 2164^{2} 2400^{5} 2697^{9} 3137^{7}3353^{6} 3786^{13} 4729^{5}

Lindhoven (USA) *C E Brittain* 55
2 gr c Monarchos(USA) —Bevel (USA) (Mr Prospector (USA))
5882^{8}

Lindus Atenor *M Al Muhairi* a75 74
3 b f Fraam—Nightingale Song (Tina's Pet)
202a^{6} 436a^{8}563a^{11}

Lindy Lou *C A Cyzer* a51 55
2 b f Hernando(FR) —Daylight Dreams (Indian Ridge)
6098^{7} 6215^{14}

Linkslade Lad *W R Muir* 70
2 b g Mujahid(USA) —Goodwood Lass (IRE) (Alzao (USA))
2234^{9} 3031^{6} 3344^{12} 3860^{8} 4163^{2}4445^{LFT} 5065^{13} 5570^{5}

Linlithgow (IRE) *J L Dunlop* a40 52
2 gr c Linamix(FR) —Diarshana (GER) (Darshaan)
6297^{7} 6434^{10} 6778^{8}

Linngari (IRE) *H J Brown* a90 119
4 ch h Indian Ridge—Lidakiya (IRE) (Kahyasi)
(280a) (496a) 742a^{13} 4191a^{6} (4858a) 5701a^{2} 6230a^{4}6784a^{5}

Linning Wine (IRE) *P A Blockley* a76 65
10 b g Scenic—Zallaka (IRE) (Shardari)
313^{4} (417) 600^{7}833^{6} 953^{10}1001^{8} 3730^{5}

Linton Dancer (IRE) *J R Weymes* a51 55
3 b f Mujadil(USA) —Daisy Grey (Nordance (USA))
1533^{6} 1888^{3} 2283^{3} 2529^{5} 2923^{5}3785^{6} 4132^{7} 4892^{10} 6406^{3}6554^{6} 6765^{4}6957^{6}

Lion Sands *L M Cumani* 75
2 b c Montjeu(IRE) —Puce (Darshaan)
4768^{3} 5321 ^{4}

Lion's Domane *K W Hogg* a43 41
9 b g Lion Cavern(USA) —Vilany (Never So Bold)
2546^{14}

Lions Gate (AUS) *T McEvoy* 115
5 b h Danehill(USA) —Kensington Gardens (NZ) (Grosvenor (NZ))
5817a^{7}

Lios Tulcha (IRE) *D T Hughes* 54
2 b c Barathea(IRE) —Ingeburg (Hector Protector (USA))
5466a^{17}

Lipizza (IRE) *N A Callaghan* a72 80
3 b f Spinning World(USA) —Lipica (IRE) (Night Shift (USA))
2864^{7} 3150^{2} 3447^{6} 3904^{10} 4078^{2}4577^{6}

Lipocco *R M Beckett* 92
2 br g Piccolo—Magical Dancer (IRE) (Magical Wonder (USA))
1372^{2} 1770^{3} 2631^{2} (3678) 4736^{6} 5372^{7}

Liquidity (USA) *Doug O'Neill* a106
2 b c Tiznow(USA) —Boa (USA) (Rahy (USA))
5983a^{9}

Liquid Lover (IRE) *W M Brisbourne* a49 50
4 b g Night Shift(USA) —New Tycoon (IRE) (Last Tycoon)
147^{3} 182^{2}302^{2} 390^{4}525^{4} 684^{7}788^{6} 794^{7}6620^{11} 6795^{6}6972^{8}

Liquido (GER) *H Steinmetz* 114?
7 br h Lomitas—Lolli Pop (GER) (Cagliostro (GER))
1860a^{8}

Lirope (GER) *Frau A Glodde* 77
5 b m In A Tiff(IRE) —Lebrija (GER) (Windwurf (GER))
5710a^{13}

Lisathedaddy *B G Powell* a82 59
4 br m Darnay—Erith's Chill Wind (Be My Chief (USA))
692^{4} 900^{4}1165^{3} (1926) 2351^{9} 4660^{8} 5047^{3}(6070) 6351^{2}6566^{2} 6661^{4}

Liscanna (IRE) *David Wachman* 86
2 b f Sadler's Wells(USA) —Lahinch (IRE) (Danehill Dancer (IRE))
3060a^{5} 6357a^{5}

Liset (IRE) *A & G Botti* 89
4 b m Almutawakel—Giselle In Love (IRE) (Law Society (USA))
1368a^{6}

Lisfannon *B W Hills* a48 65+
3 ch f Bahamian Bounty—Amazed (Clantime)
868^{4} 1078^{4} 1616^{6} 2583^{11} 3072^{6}

Li Shih Chen *A P Jarvis* a71 63
3 ch g Dr Fong(USA) —Mad Annie (USA) (Anabaa (USA))
473^{7} (579) 702^{7}1384^{3} 3500^{11}

Liskaveen Beauty *T J Fitzgerald* a35 46
3 gr f Danehill Dancer(IRE) —Smooth Princess (IRE) (Roi Danzig (USA))
2001^{5} 2383^{7} 2763^{8} 6970^{7}

Liss Ard (IRE) *John Joseph Murphy* 98
5 b h In The Wings—Beguine (USA) (Green Dancer (USA))
2154a^{8}

Lisselan Dancer (USA) *Mrs A J Perrett* 29
2 b f Outflanker(USA) —Sambacarioca (USA) (Irish Tower (USA))
4705^{12}

Lisselan Rose (USA) *Mme J Bidgood* 84
3 b f Wild Wonder(USA) —Right Again Rose (USA) (Royal And Regal (USA))
5197a^{7}

Litalia (IRE) *P Schiergen* 98
3 b f Monsun(GER) —Libertad (GER) (Lagunas)
2913a^{3} 3719a^{3} 4543a^{6}

Literato (FR) *J-C Rouget* 95
2 ch c Kendor(FR) —La Cibeles (FR) (Cardoun (FR))
(6453a)

Lit Et Mixe (FR) *Noel T Chance* a58
3 gr g Linamix(FR) —Lit (IRE) (Danehill (USA))
6564^{13} 6673^{8}

Little Biscuit (IRE) *K R Burke* a54 59
4 ro m Indian Lodge(IRE) —Arjan (IRE) (Paris House)
96^{8} 146^{14}

Little Bob *J D Bethell* 64
5 ch g Zilzal(USA) —Hunters Of Brora (IRE) (Sharpo)
992^{8} 1864^{12} 1987^{7} 5863^{3} 6209^{7}6301^{6}

Little Britain (USA) *J Howard Johnson* a33 58
3 b g Stravinsky(USA) —I Don't Know (USA) (Restivo (USA))
1564^{7} 4254^{7} 4884^{15} 5368^{3} 6424^{8}

Little Carmela *S C Williams* 30
2 gr f Beat Hollow—Carmela Owen (Owington)
5867^{12} 6330^{8}

Littledodayno (IRE) *M Wigham* a70 78
3 b f Mujadil(USA) —Perfect Welcome (Taufan (USA))
190^{7} 852^{6}1097^{12} 1337^{12} 2863^{8}3226^{8} 3569^{6} 4199^{3} (4927) (5232) 5350^{2} 5487^{3}

Little Edward *R J Hodges* a92 84
8 gr g King's Signet(USA) —Cedar Lady (Telsmoss)
(3855) 4486^{9} 5021^{10} 5291^{3}6035^{2} (6353) (6446) (6485) 6660^{5}

Little Eskimo *B Smart* a66+ 69
2 b c Johannesburg(USA) —Karla June (Unfuwain (USA))
6199^{4} 6466^{3} (6662)

Little Eye (IRE) *D K Weld* a66 87
5 b g Groom Dancer(USA) —Beaming (Mtoto)
4094a^{2}

Little Eyecatcher (IRE) *T D Easterby* 49
3 b g Beckett(IRE) —Black Jack Girl (IRE) (Ridgewood Ben)
1759^{10} 2082^{14}

Little Gannet *T D McCarthy* a43 37
5 ro m Bien Bien(USA) —Lady Kalliste (Another Realm)
395^{13} 591^{10}

Little Good Bay *A Laird* a101 102
6 b h Danehill(USA) —Brave Kris (IRE) (Kris)
149a^{8} 282a^{4} 357a^{5} 435a^{5} 509a^{7}

Little Hotpotch *J R Jenkins* a15 11
2 b f Erhaab(USA) —Berzoud (Ezzoud (IRE))
1242^{5} 2083^{4} 2588^{8}5923^{9}

Little Iris *L M Cumani* 46+
2 ch f Inchinor—Galanthus (USA) (Rahy (USA))
4657^{13} 5068^{13} 5592^{9}

Little Jim (ARG) *A Laird* a109 103
6 b h Roar(USA) —Clavija (ARG) (Cipayo (ARG))
277a^{2} 434a^{16}508a^{5}

Little Jimbob *R A Fahey* a75+ 88
5 b g Desert Story(IRE) —Artistic Licence (High Top)
214^{3} 375^{12}1864^{9} 2387^{5} 2761^{2} 2945^{5} 3812^{2}6818^{5}

Little Lily Morgan *R Bastiman* 42
3 gr f Kayf Tara—Cool Grey (Absalom)
1101^{8} 1598^{12} 1866^{6}

Littlemadgebob *J R Norton* a14 36
2 b f Primo Valentino(IRE) —Midnight Orchid (IRE) (Petardia)
2890^{9} 4880^{11} 5615^{7} 6278^{10}

Little Miss Daisy *A B Haynes* a43 68
3 br f Zilzal(USA) —Jimgareen (IRE) (Lahib (USA))
993^{12} 1642^{13} (Dead)

Little Miss Gracie *A B Haynes* a83 103
4 gr m Efisio—Circled (USA) (Cozzene (USA))
1477^{4} 2041a^{4} 3002^{2} 3891^{8} 4628^{9}4889^{8}

Little Miss Tara (IRE) *A B Haynes* 74
2 b f Namid—Circled (USA) (Cozzene (USA))
2106^{10} 3735^{5} 4290^{2} 5380^{2} 5624^{5}

Little Miss Verity *J A Geake* a35 46
3 b f Danzig Connection(USA) —Little White Lies (Runnett)
1191^{12} 2532^{8} 3875^{3} 4329^{12}6389^{12} 6714^{8}6800^{9}

Little Miss Wizzy *M L W Bell* a45 70
2 b f Bertolini(USA) —Magical Veil (Majestic Light (USA))
2166^{3} 3010^{5} 3435^{2}(3800) 4335^{4} 4767^{2}

Little Richard (IRE) *M Wellings* a62 57
7 b g Alhaarth(IRE) —Intricacy (Formidable (USA))
(40) (72) 168^{3} 318^{5}482^{2} 570^{3}643^{6} 733^{7}6405^{4} 6526^{6}6729^{6} (6790) 6936^{2} (6995)

Little Ridge (IRE) *H Morrison* a85 66
5 b g Charnwood Forest(IRE) —Princess Natalie (Rudimentary (USA))
79^{11} 424^{4}605^{6} 699^{10}967^{12}

Little Rutland *E J O'Neill* a54
2 ch g Mark Of Esteem(IRE) —Prickly Poppy (Lear Fan (USA))
6072^{10} 6224^{8}6498^{6}

Littlestar (FR) *B D Leavy* 59
5 b g Robellino(USA) —Green Charter (Green Desert (USA))
3382^{12}

Little Task *J S Wainwright* a35 35
8 b g Environment Friend—Lucky Thing (Green Desert (USA))
2788^{9}

Little Tiny Tom *C N Kellett* a28 42
2 b g Tobougg(IRE) —Villa Del Sol (Tagula (IRE))
2416^{7} 2938^{11}3831^{6} 4115^{11} 4545^{3} 5597^{16} 5948^{9}6172^{10} 6471^{5}

Little Tommy Fella *S C Williams* 49
2 b c Diktat—Francia (Legend Of France (USA))
987^{5} 1284^{10} 6050^{12}

Littleton Aldor (IRE) *W G M Turner* a41 36
6 b g Pennekamp(USA) —Belle Etoile (FR) (Lead On Time (USA))
3158^{9} 4670^{10} 5097^{8}5127^{8} 5248^{9}

Littleton Telchar (USA) *S W Hall* a78 83
6 ch g Atticus(USA) —Miss Waikiki (USA) (Miswaki (USA))
1993^{5} 6221^{14} (6654) 6698^{6}6830^{5}

Littleton Zephir (USA) *Mrs P Townsley* a70 64?
7 b m Sandpit(BRZ) —Miss Gorgeous (IRE) (Damister (USA))
17^{12} 327^{12}416^{9}

Littletown Bridge (USA) *Christian Wroe* a109 91
4 b m Stormin Fever(USA) —Fire The Deputy (USA) (Deputy Minister (CAN))
510a^{5} 2430^{6} 4179^{10}

Little Trinket *Mrs C A Dunnett*
3 b f Magic Ring(IRE) —Leen (Distant Relative)
4663^{6} 5023^{10} 5272^{13}

Little White Lie (IRE) *G M Lyons* 87
2 b g Orpen(USA) —Miss Informed (IRE) (Danehill (USA))
2037a^{3}

Little Wishes *S Parr*
3 b f Most Welcome—Zac's Desire (Swing Easy (USA))
5598^{15} 5768^{15}

Livalex *M Dods* 49
2 b f Zamindar(USA) —Evie Hone (IRE) (Royal Academy (USA))
3908^{5}

Live And Dangerous *D Carroll* a40 58
5 b m Mark Of Esteem(IRE) —Mazaya (IRE) (Sadler's Wells (USA))
178^{12}

Live Life (FR) *N Drysdale* 115
4 gr m Linamix(FR) —Reine De La Ciel (USA) (Conquistador Cielo (USA))
4385a[3] 6125a[10]
Liverti *D Carroll*
3 b f Averti(IRE) —Light Of Aragon (Aragon)
6406[12] 6717[13]
Living On A Prayer *J Pearce* a60 42
3 b f Josr Algarhoud(IRE) —Denton Lady (Inchinor)
254[7] 374[6](479) 583[8]781[8] 1307[6] 1616[12]
Livvies Lady (IRE) *D K Ivory* a15
4 b m Opening Verse(USA) —Indian Wardance (ITY) (Indian Ridge)
26[10]
Lizarazu (GER) *R A Harris* a78 85
7 b g Second Set(IRE) —Lilly (GER) (Motley (USA))
1207[6] 1435[10] (1692) 1830[9] 1932[7] 2705[6]3113[4] 3470[5] 4706[12] 5042[4] 5233[6]5572[4] 5765[2] 6048[8] 6595[12]6919[10]
Lizzie Rocket *J O'Reilly* a49 52
6 gr m Paris House—Jane's Affair (Alleging (USA))
24[12] 146[10]2991[0] 2543[17] 2780[14]
Llamadas *C Roberts* a83 67
4 b g Josr Algarhoud(IRE) —Primulette (Mummy's Pet)
375[13] (521) 610[5](765) 832[8]1167[3] 1842[6] 2176[13]6655[5]
Lloret De Mar (NOR) *A Lund*
3 b f Philidor—Top Cat (FR) (Be My Chief (USA))
4919a[13]
Loaded Gun *W Storey* a54 54
6 ch g Highest Honor(FR) —Woodwardia (USA) (El Gran Senor (USA))
1560[13] 2696[8] 3022[4] 3836[7] 5061[5]
Loaderfun (IRE) *N Wilson* a47 80d
4 br g Danehill Dancer(IRE) —Sideloader Special (Song)
1076[12] 1532[10] 1858[13] 2194[5] 2661[18]3041[12] 3598[10] 4831[14]5865[19] 6387[8] 6531[12]
Loa Loa (GER) *A Wohler* 72
2 b f Anabaa Blue—Lorenza (GER) (Top Ville)
5858a[8]
Loanhead (NZ) *P Moody* 112
3 b g I Conquer(NZ) —Just Tuppence (NZ) (Nassipour (USA))
6346a[9]
Lobengula (IRE) *I W McInnes* a61 71
4 b g Spectrum(IRE) —Playwaki (USA) (Miswaki (USA))
74[7] 163[12]3566[4] 4606[3] 5173[2] 5904[16] 6380[4]6436[4] 6577[10]6687[8] 6899[2]6955[3]
Local Fancy *J M P Eustace* a12 78
3 b f Bahamian Bounty—Local Abbey (IRE) (Primo Dominie)
1617[8] 1843[5] 2087[3] 2344[10]4577[3] 5079[3] 5896[16]
Local Poet *I Semple* a83 70
5 b g Robellino(USA) —Laugharne (Known Fact (USA))
(100) 489[5] (585) 719[11] 1949[7]2164[9] 2749[7] 3158[7]4090[10]
Local Spirit (USA) *C E Brittain* a73 97
3 ch f Lion Cavern(USA) —Crimson Conquest (USA) (Diesis)
1254[3] 2343[3](3073) 3293[2] 3627[2] 4179[7]4808[8] 5477[8]
Loch Awe *J G Given* 57
3 b f Inchinor—Lochbelle (Robellino (USA))
1599[12] 1997[5] 2591[7] 3249[6] 4111[13]
Loch Clutha (IRE) *K R Burke* 40
2 b f Averti(IRE) —Loch Fyne (Ardkinglass)
1295[5] 1884[7] 2382[7] 2922[6] 3300[3]3746[2] 4007[6] 4349[5] 5084[8]
Loch Tay *M L W Bell* a70+ 80
2 b g Cape Cross(IRE) —Taysala (IRE) (Akarad (FR))
3976[3] 4873[4] 5607[5]5916[11]
Loch Verdi *A M Balding* 91
3 b f Green Desert(USA) —Lochsong (Song)
1687[3] (2190) 2329[2] (3000) 4102[3] 4717[5]
Lockstock (IRE) *M S Saunders* a65 66
8 b g Inchinor—Risalah (Marju (IRE))
15[10] 77[14]586[12] 697[13]906[8] 1204[14] 1773[12]1882[3] 2098[5] 2327[3] 2414[5]2969[10] 4871[3] 4983[2] (5130) 5621[11] 6069[10]6627[6] 6798[10]
Locombe Hill (IRE) *N Wilson* a67 78
10 b g Barathea(IRE) —Roberts Pride (Roberto (USA))
56[12]
Lodgician (IRE) *J J Quinn* 73
4 b h Grand Lodge(USA) —Dundel (IRE) (Machiavellian (USA))
2871[4] (3291) 3696[2] 3955[2] 4252[8] 5080[8]
Logger Rhythm (USA) *Dr J R J Naylor* a19 28
5 b g Woodman(USA) —Formidable Dancer (USA) (Danzig (USA))
129[6] 256[2]303[2] 614[3]688[4] 5927[10]
Logic (JPN) *K Hashiguchi* 117
3 b c Agnes Tachyon(JPN) —April Drama (JPN) (Sakura Yutaka O (JPN))
6530a[17]
Logsdail *G L Moore* a74 77
6 b g Polish Precedent(USA) —Logic (Slip Anchor)
1382[10] 1820[10] 2173[7]2618[8] 3044[8] 3404[3](3642) 4047[3]4575[2] 4795[9] 5136[2] 5362[5] 5590[12]6189[2] 6301[13]
L'Oiseau De Feu (USA) *E A L Dunlop* 73
2 b g Stravinsky(USA) —Off You Go (USA) (Seattle Slew (USA))
3363[7] 4292[3] 5326[3]
Loitokitok *P D Cundell* a29 62
4 b g Piccolo—Bonita Bee (King Of Spain)
2497[9]
Lol Draper *P D Evans* 49
3 ch f Forzando—Shanghai Lil (Petong)
963[8] 1049[8] 1373[12] 1746[12]
Lolita (GER) *Andreas Lowe* 109
3 b f Lavirco(GER) —Little Movie Star (Risk Me (FR))
(925a) (1328a) 2802[11] 3991a[9]

Lolla's Spirit (IRE) *M L W Bell* a67 64
3 b f Montjeu(IRE) —Glenarff (USA) (Irish River (FR))
2814[7] 3634[3] 4111[14] (4697) (5247) 5652[3]6037[2] 6435[8]
L'Ombrone (ITY) *A Calderone* 32
3 b c Late Parade(IRE) —La Faggeta (ITY) (Horage)
758a[10]
Londolozi (USA) *M A Jarvis* a70
2 bb f Forest Wildcat(USA) —Dearly (Rahy (USA))
5773[4] 6098[3]6505[6] 6872[6]
London Express (IRE) *M Johnston* 99
3 b c King Charlemagne(USA) —Robin (Slip Anchor)
(867) 1231[2] 1473[4] 2224[9] 2805[5] 3971[2]4039[4] (4676)
Londra (IRE) *S Smrczek* 72
5 b m Sadler's Wells(USA) —Lady Ambassador (General Assembly (USA))
(3580a)
Lone Plainsman *P F O'Donnell* 84
5 b g Royal Applause—Suprematie (FR) (Gay Mecene (USA))
4793[2]
Lonesome Tonight *L D'Auria*
2 b f Inchinor—Spirit Of Peace (Singspiel (IRE))
2475a[4] 5705a[3]
Longhill Tiger *G G Margarson* 79
3 b c Tiger Hill(IRE) —Lauren (GER) (Lightning (FR))
3373[2] 3849[6] 5768[5]
Longing For Cindy (USA) *W M Brisbourne* a45 45
4 ch m Belong To Me(USA) —I C Cindy (USA) (Gallapiat (USA))
147[12] 1198[6]1536[8] 1724[9]3291[9]
Longquan (IRE) *P J Makin* 85
2 b g Invincible Spirit(IRE) —Pipers Pool (IRE) (Mtoto)
1189[4] 1796[2] 2185[3] 5371[2] (5508) 5681[11]
Long Weekend (IRE) *D Shaw* a62 49
8 b g Flying Spur(AUS) —Friday Night (USA) (Trempolino (USA))
177[13]
Longy The Lash *K G Reveley* 20
3 b g Contract Law(USA) —Hello Hobson'S (IRE) (Fayruz)
3285[12] 4067[11] 4297[11]
Look Again *R A Fahey* 104
5 ch g Zilzal(USA) —Last Look (Rainbow Quest (USA))
1301[6] 1678[2] 1775[2] 2201[2]
Look At The Stars (IRE) *R Hollinshead* a51 72
4 b g Bachir(IRE) —Pizzazz (Unfuwain (USA))
56[4] 1074[2]433[3] 251[13]382[5] 469[11]683[10]
Looker *J Gallagher* 75
3 b f Barathea(IRE) —Last Look (Rainbow Quest (USA))
1881[3] 2608[8] 2990[10] (5625) 5889[14]
Look Here's May *R Hollinshead* a28 42
4 b m Revoque(IRE) —Where's Carol (Anfield)
1126[8] 1387[P] 2881[5]3266[9] 4278[10] 4948[18]
Looking Great (USA) *R F Johnson Houghton* a36 51
4 b g Gulch(USA) —Shoofha (IRE) (Bluebird (USA))
1540[12]
Look No More *W G M Turner* a44 46
5 ch g First Trump—Jadebelle (Beldale Flutter (USA))
636[13]
Look Of Eagles *P F I Cole* a74 66
4 b m Fraam—Dreamtime Quest (Blakeney)
17[10] 6036[6]6396[11] 6538[5]6656[5] 6781[10]6949[3]
Looks Could Kill (USA) *E J Alston* a91 91
4 bb g Red Ransom(USA) —Mingling Glances (USA) (Woodman (USA))
1532[13] 2323[9] 2520[3] 3077[9] 3567[5]3928[7] 4378[6] 4760[11] 5136[9] 5336[15]
Looks The Business (IRE) *W G M Turner* a69 69
5 b g Marju(IRE) —Business Centre (IRE) (Digamist (USA))
2956[2] (3232) 4005[3] 4432[3] 5422[8]
Look Who's Dancing *J L Dunlop* 66
2 ch f Observatory(USA) —Dust Dancer (Suave Dancer (USA))
2957[9] 3707[6] 4572[5] 5053[8] 5748[9]
Loose Canon *Mrs C A Dunnett* 7
2 b f Josr Algarhoud(IRE) —Trust In Paula (USA) (Arazi (USA))
3908[10] 4302[8] 5095[12]
Lopinot (IRE) *P J Makin* a75 66
3 br g Pursuit Of Love—La Suquet (Puissance)
2581[9] 6593[2] 6841[2]
Lord Admiral (USA) *Charles O'Brien* 116
5 b h El Prado(IRE) —Lady Ilsley (USA) (Trempolino (USA))
496a[2] 564a[2] 2053a[3] 2371a[3] 2559a[2]3964a[2] 5190a[3] 5825a[3] 6329a[2]
Lord Adonis (IRE) *K J Burke* a15 61
3 b g Galileo(IRE) —Flaming June (USA) (Storm Bird (CAN))
909[5] 1283[8] 1826[5]862[9]
Lord Areion (GER) *H J Groschel* 100
4 b h Areion(GER) —Luciana (GER) (Experte (GER))
3563a[6] 4418a[3]
Lord Blue Boy *W G M Turner* a30 51
2 gr g Atraf—Flair Lady (Chilibang)
944[6] 1142[5] 3394[3] 3677[9] 5448[11]5687[8]
Lord Chamberlain *J M Bradley* a69 65
13 b g Be My Chief(USA) —Metaphysique (FR) (Law Society (USA))
44[3] 714[1]06[3] 820[7](950) 1001[2]1245[4] 1353[10] (2135) 2702[3]2978[6] 3194[12] 3817[10]3948[10] 4288[7]
Lord Charles *W G M Turner* a75 84d
2 b g Atraf—Just Run (IRE) (Runnett)
(849) 1066[2] 1582[4] 1897[2] 2225[6] 2724[16]5731[7] 5909[8]
Lord Conyers (IRE) *G Woodward* a35 43
7 b m Inzar(USA) —Primelta (Primo Dominie)
407[7] 501[10]1443[8] 6756[12]

Lord Du Sud (FR) *J-C Rouget* 119+
5 gr h Linamix(FR) —Marseillaise (FR) (Esprit Du Nord (USA))
(523a) 1332a[2] (4647a) 6119a[4]
Lord Erin (NZ) *G Dalziel* 87
7 gr g Lord Ballina(AUS) —Erin Marie (NZ) (Catus (FR))
6346a[15]
Lord Hill (GER) *C Zeitz* 5
2 b c Tiger Hill(IRE) —Lady Fox (GER) (Monsun (GER))
6092a[12]
Lord Lahar *M A Buckley* a58 56
7 b g Fraam—Brigadiers Bird (IRE) (Mujadil (USA))
184[6]
Lord Laing (USA) *H J Collingridge* a64 42
3 bb g Chester House(USA) —Johanna Keene (USA) (Raise A Cup (USA))
337[8] 2403[13] 3977[7]6843[4]
Lord Links (IRE) *D J Daly* a65 65
5 ch g Daggers Drawn(USA) —Lady From Limerick (IRE) (Rainbows For Life (CAN))
101[9] 200[6]429[7] 588[10]837[7]
Lord Mayfair (USA) *Miss A Stokell* a33 74
4 b g Silic(FR) —Spring Wedding (USA) (Prized (USA))
1594[15] 1763[3] 1791[12]2356[4] 2571[5] 2833[5] 3034[7] (3189) 3398[10] (Dead)
Lord Mayor *R M H Cowell* a83 83
5 b g Machiavellian(USA) —Misleading Lady (Warning)
704[7] 1098[5] 1239[9]1495[12] 1667[17] 2012[17] 2341[12]3692a[4] 4106[8] 4573[9] 4881[7] 5259[12]
Lord Nash *M Grassi* 95
4 b h Nashwan(USA) —Freccia D'Oro (GER) (Acatenango (GER))
1870a[7]
Lord Of Adventure (IRE) *Mrs L C Jewell* a56 56
4 b g Inzar(USA) —Highly Fashionable (IRE) (Polish Precedent (USA))
545[8]
Lord Of Beauty (FR) *Noel T Chance* a64
6 ch g Medaaly—Arctic Beauty (USA) (Arctic Tern (USA))
6226[11] 6519[6]
Lord Of Dreams (IRE) *D W P Arbuthnot* a70 52
4 ch h Barathea(IRE) —The Multiyorker (IRE) (Digamist (USA))
1046 162[5]493[9] (820) (955) 1204[15] 1773[13] 2794[7]3918[7] 4871[8] 5249[9]5740[5] 6189[7]6382[9]
Lord Of England (GER) *Mario Hofer* 117
3 ch c Dashing Blade—Loveria (Los Santos (FR))
1176a[2] 1715a[3] (2492a) (3993a)
Lord Of Methley *S Lycett* a46 56
7 gr g Zilzal(USA) —Paradise Waters (Celestial Storm (USA))
4435[6]
Lord Of The East *I W McInnes* a82 95
7 b g Emarati(USA) —Fairy Free (Rousillon (USA))
644[7] 1143[15] 1262[3]1456[8] 1532[12] 2232[2] 2520[6] 2681[13]3813[P] 4437[2] 4760[10]4790[15]
Lord Oroko *K A Ryan* a70 66
2 ch g Lord Of Men—Wannaplantatree (Niniski (USA))
5947[4] 6303[4] 6737[2]6950[2]
Lord Orpheus *B W Hills* 38
2 b g Auction House(USA) —Lady Of The Realm (Prince Daniel (USA))
4597[9] 4801[10] 5206[10]
Lord Raffles *P R Webber* a57
4 b g Zafonic(USA) —Dawna (Polish Precedent (USA))
289[8] 4199[5]591[3]
Lordship (IRE) *M A Jarvis* a59 60+
2 b g King's Best(USA) —Rahika Rose (Unfuwain (USA))
2610[9] 2979[8] 5178[8]
Lord Sunshine (FR) *A Spanu* 99?
4 b h Octagonal(NZ) —Storm And Sunshine (USA) (Star De Naskra (USA))
3516a[8] 4169a[6]
Lordswood (IRE) *A M Balding* a63 63
2 b g Mark Of Esteem(IRE) —Dinwood (Charnwood Forest (IRE))
3222[8] 5371[11] (6460) 6699[3]
Lord Theo *D K Ivory* a74 76
2 b g Averti(IRE) —Love You Too (Be My Chief (USA))
2315[10] 2938[3] (3591)
Loreley (SWE) *P Wahl*
3 b f Nicolotte—Next Information (Chilibang)
2564a[12]
Lorena Wood (USA) *B J Meehan* 71
2 ch f Woodman(USA) —Vilikaia (USA) (Nureyev (USA))
1896[4] 2355[3] (5586)
Loriinae *T G Mills* 43
3 b f Generous(IRE) —Courtain (USA) (Diesis)
1434[3] 1797[7] 2131[5]
Lorikeet *Noel T Chance* a63+ 85
7 b g Rainbow Quest(USA) —Destiny Dance (USA) (Nijinsky (CAN))
6189[14] 6462[11]
Los Bonitos (GER) *L A Berretta* 103
4 br h Waky Nao—La Dolores (GER) (Surumu (GER))
1712a[6]
Los Cabos (IRE) *J H M Gosden* a76 87
3 b g Mozart(IRE) —Limelighting (USA) (Alleged (USA))
2754[6] 3539[2] 3877[6]4459[4] 5022[5]
Los Cristianos *M Brittain* a24
2 b f Atraf—Portite Sophie (Doulab (USA))
6309[10]
Lost All Alone *D M Simcock* a39
2 b c Bertolini(USA) —Wandering Stranger (Petong)
6742[7] 6912[10]6975[4]
Lost Inheritance *P T Midgley* 44
2 b f Bertolini(USA) —Jewel (IRE) (Cyrano De Bergerac)
1559[8] 3713[8] 4017[7] 4376[9] 4630[5]4887[11] 5315[6]

Lost In Wonder (USA) *Sir Michael Stoute* 85
2 b f Galileo(IRE) —Arutua (USA) (Riverman (USA))
4148[9] (4830) 5522[8]
Lost Music (FR) *J-V Toux* 80
4 b m Lost World(IRE) —Natsylda (FR) (Fabulous Dancer (USA))
5562a[6]
Lost Soldier Three (IRE) *L M Cumani* 112
5 b g Barathea(IRE) —Donya (Mill Reef (USA))
2893[3] 3551[3] 4791[5] 5551[3]
Lothaire (FR) *D Allard* 68
5 gr g Baryshnikov(AUS) —Loyalitat (FR) (Tropular)
3692a[9]
Lothian Lass (IRE) *D K Weld* 60?
3 gr f Daylami(IRE) —God Speed (IRE) (Be My Guest (USA))
4124a[12]
Lottie *G Woodward* a42 44
5 b m Robellino(USA) —Montserrat (Aragon)
3749[5] 4467[8] 5244[2] 5483[7] 6277[4]6307[7]
Lough Arrow (IRE) *P S Felgate* a4 8
3 b g Carrowkeel(IRE) —State Of Dream (IRE) (Carmelite House (USA))
528[13] 6371[1]464[8] 6649[10]
Lough Bow (IRE) *M W Easterby* a40 57
8 b g Nicolotte—Gale Force Seven (Strong Gale)
91[7] 182[13]
Louie Louie (IRE) *N A Callaghan* a85 92
3 b c King Charlemagne(USA) —Rose Of Mooncoin (IRE) (Brief Truce (USA))
1091[4] 1490[6] 2033[7] (2650) 3491[6] 3708[3]4144[3] 4488[9] 5150[6] 6094[5]
Louise Dupin (IRE) *R M Beckett* a65 54
3 b f King Of Kings(IRE) —Soubrette (USA) (Opening Verse (USA))
1650[9] 2343[7] 3112[6]3947[10] 4483[7] 4982[7] 5690[5]6057[10]
Louisiade (IRE) *K A Ryan* a73 65
5 b g Tagula(IRE) —Titchwell Lass (Lead On Time (USA))
159[6] 576[4]845[12] 1001[6]1041[11] 1607[4] 1735[8] 6531[2]6674[3] 6855[5]6960[2]
Loulwa (IRE) *J Noseda* a79
2 b f Montjeu(IRE) —Refined (IRE) (Statoblest)
6099[2]
Lounaos (FR) *Eoin Griffin* 110
3 b f Limnos(JPN) —Luanda (IRE) (Bigstone (IRE))
4822a[5]
Loup De Mer (GER) *W Baltromei* 114?
4 b g Law Society(USA) —L'Heure Bleue (IRE) (Kendor (FR))
6119a[6]
Louphole *P J Makin* a79 80
4 ch g Loup Sauvage(USA) —Goodwood Lass (IRE) (Alzao (USA))
44[4] 164[2]501[7] 1383[7]1689[3] 2331[3] 2711[3] (2971) 3434[2] (3682) 6865[2]
Loup Sifflet (IRE) *R A Fahey* a36 50
4 b g Loup Sauvage(USA) —Bee-Bee-Gee (IRE) (Lake Coniston (IRE))
1537[11] 1852[11]
Lourdes (IRE) *J R Fanshawe*
3 b f Spectrum(IRE) —Loure (USA) (Lyphard (USA))
3258[9]
Louve Heureuse (IRE) *B G Powell* a56 61
5 ch m Peintre Celebre(USA) —Louve Sereine (FR) (Sadler's Wells (USA))
940[12] 1373[3] 2482[10]2707[7] 3036[7] 6232[8]6616[8] 6800[3]6959[6]
Love Academy *Luke Comer* a40
11 b g Royal Academy(USA) —Quiet Week-End (Town And Country)
2141[8] 2551[12]4363[14] 6305[14] 6803[9]6829[8]
Love Always *S Dow* 81+
4 b m Piccolo—Lady Isabell (Rambo Dancer (CAN))
1206[12] 2351[5] (2672) 3365[8] 3853[8] 4448[4]4924[2] 5163[3] 5479[7] 5628[3]
Love And Affection *P S McEntee* a50
3 b g Groom Dancer(USA) —Fox Star (IRE) (Foxhound (USA))
6225[7] 6429[10]6668[6]
Love Angel (USA) *J J Bridger* a64 66
4 bb g Woodman(USA) —Omnia (USA) (Green Dancer (USA))
723[11] 1051[11] 1478[14]2097[6] 2534[11] 3256[7] 3649[7]3853[10] 4432[4] 4586[5]
Love Beauty (USA) *M F Harris* 55
4 bb g Seeking The Gold(USA) —Heavenly Rhythm (USA) (Septieme Ciel (USA))
1690[13]
Love Brothers *M R Channon* 77+
2 b g Lomitas—Morning Queen (GER) (Konigsstuhl (GER))
3025[7] 3448[7] 3976[6] 5013[3] 5322[7](5597) 5866[13]
Love Dubai (USA) *M Johnston* a80 73
2 bb c E Dubai(USA) —Omnia (USA) (Green Dancer (USA))
4716[3] 5059[2] 5379[4] 5790[7] 6310[10](6506) (6824)
Love In May (IRE) *J S Moore* a77 62
2 ch f City On A Hill(USA) —May Hinton (Main Reef)
(663) 1066[9] 3280[4] 3678[4] (6834) 6937[2]6978[4]
Lovelace *M Johnston* 79
2 b c Royal Applause—Loveleaves (Polar Falcon (USA))
(1121)
Lovely Hidenka (USA) *C E Brittain* a53 41
3 b f Fusaichi Pegasus(USA) —Eliza (USA) (Mt. Livermore (USA))
1259[2] 1652[11] 2352[10]
Lovely Tiger (GER) *P Schiergen* 91
2 b c Tiger Hill(IRE) —Lupita (GER) (Niniski (USA))
5998a[5]
Love Money (IRE) *B Grizzetti* 95
4 b m Intikhab(USA) —Rivelazione (IRE) (Night Shift (USA))
2280a[9]

Love On Sight *A P Jarvis* 98
2 b f Beat Hollow—Greek Dream (USA) (Distant View (USA))
2456[3] 3925[6] 4400[6]

Love On The Rocks *K A Ryan* 67
2 b c Hernando(FR) —Indian Love Bird (Efisio)
4228[7] 5014[2] 5720[9]

Love Or Money *W J Haggas* a36
3 b f In The Wings—Lafite (Robellino (USA))
3200[12]

Love Profusion (USA) *L Riccardi* 81
2 b f Thunder Gulch(USA) —Clefairy (IRE) (Sri Pekan (USA))
2062a[6] 5858a[5]

Love Ridot (IRE) *M Johnston* a53+ 77
3 b f Fruits Of Love(USA) —Ridotto (Salse (USA))
6987[4]

Lovers Kiss *N Wilson* a49 47d
2 b f Night Shift(USA) —Evening Promise (Aragon)
1295[8] 1664[8] 1853[3] 2375[5] 2806[6]3380[4] 5860[12]
6157[4]6385[12] (6491) 6534[4] 6807[8]6926[9]

Loves Bidding *R Ingram* a55 75
2 b c Auction House(USA) —Charlottevalentina (IRE) (Perugino (USA))
1333[4] 1770[8] 2225[5]2517[4] 2771[11] (3799) 4321[12]

Love's Design (IRE) *Miss J Feilden* a54 48
9 bb g Pursuit Of Love—Cephista (Shirley Heights)
1725[13] 1923[8]2728[2] 2952[6] 3339[11]

Loves Travelling (IRE) *N Wilson* a62 79
6 b g Blues Traveller(IRE) —Fast Love (IRE) (Second Set (IRE))
1233[7] 1666[10] 2196[7]

Love Thirty *M R Channon* a60 93
4 b m Mister Baileys—Polished Up (Polish Precedent (USA))
1477[7] 2011[8] 4577[9] 5428[10]

Love To Boogie (IRE) *David Wachman* 45
2 b f Danehill(USA) —Mabrova (Prince Mab (FR))
5692a[7]

Love You Always (USA) *Miss J Feilden* a46 61
6 ch g Woodman(USA) —Encorenous (USA) (Diesis)
597[9] 706[7]906[11] 2044[12] 2455[5]2585[4] 3116[3]
3900[11] 4307[7] 5205[2]5506[B] 6376[8] 6724[7]6779[6]

Lovingly *W Jarvis* a45 47
3 b f Grand Lodge(USA) —Easy To Love (USA) (Diesis)
3200[10]

Low Cloud *J J Quinn* a73 83
6 b g Danehill(USA) —Raincloud (Rainbow Quest (USA))
319[5] 2761[8]

Lowe Go *Miss J S Davis* a52 77
6 b g First Trump—Hotel California (IRE) (Last Tycoon)
966[11]

Lowestoft Playboy *J Jay* a72 66
4 ch g Pivotal—Red Typhoon (Belfort (FR))
82[2] 268[2]339[4] (461) 537[2] 557[5]

Lowicz *D Carroll* a43 37
4 b m Polish Precedent(USA) —Eldina (Distant Relative)
3480[8]

Loyal Friend (IRE) *Niall Moran*
3 ch g Docksider(USA) —Spartan Girl (IRE) (Ela-Mana-Mou)
658[12]

Loyal Royal (IRE) *D R C Elsworth* 96
3 b c King Charlemagne(USA) —Supportive (IRE) (Nashamaa)
1065[5] (1513) 1818[4] 2032[9] 2675[6] 3223[8]5044[5]

Loyal Tycoon (IRE) *D K Ivory* a90 91
8 br g Royal Abjar(USA) —Rosy Lydgate (Last Tycoon)
1545[6] 6740[6] 6882[8]

Loyalty Lodge (IRE) *M W Easterby* 50d
4 ch g Grand Lodge(USA) —Gaily Grecian (IRE) (Ela-Mana-Mou)
2926[12]

Luas Line (IRE) *David Wachman* 113
4 b m Danehill(USA) —Streetcar (IRE) (In The Wings)
2371a[4] 2740[5] 3109a[3]

Luberon *M Johnston* a80 111+
3 b c Fantastic Light(USA) —Luxurious (USA) (Lyphard (USA))
829[5] 1117[4] (3093) (3501) 4024[5]4576[4] 4791[7]

Lucayan Dancer *D Nicholls* 89
6 b g Zieten(USA) —Tittle Tattle (IRE) (Soviet Lad (USA))
719[2] 800[8] 1220[7] 1610[2] 1864[6]2387[7] (2519) 2975[2]
3748[3] 4023[5] (4131) 4508[9]5115[6]

Lucayos *Mrs H Sweeting* a77 80
3 ch g Bahamian Bounty—Indian Flag (IRE) (Indian Ridge)
673[4] 807[2](910) 1109[6]1378[2] 1751[8] (2263) 2433[3]
2570[5] 2931[3]3268[5] 3568[8] 6740[8]6823[3] 6935[6]6966[2]

Lucefer (IRE) *G C H Chung* a49 51
8 b g Lycius(USA) —Maharani (USA) (Red Ransom (USA))
48[12] 2132[13] 3797[7]

Lucidity Light (IRE) *J D Bethell* a44 62
3 ch f Dr Fong(USA) —Moonlight (IRE) (Night Shift (USA))
1747[7] 2699[11] 4118[10]

Lucidor (GER) *Frau E Mader* 104
3 b c Zafonic(USA) —La Felicita (Shareef Dancer (USA))
1526a[4] 2314a[5] 3563a[7] 5856a[4] (6248a) 6529a[4]

Lucidus *W J Haggas* a62 67
4 b g Danzero(AUS) —Lady In Colour (IRE) (Cadeaux Genereux)
3987[2] 4973[7] 5510[16] (Dead)

Luciferous (USA) *P G Murphy* a48 53?
4 ch m Devil's Bag(USA) —Vital Laser (USA) (Seeking The Gold (USA))
336[9] 471[11]889[3] 1194[10]1394[6] 2350[9] 2636[13]

Lucius Verrus (USA) *D Shaw* a66 48
6 b g Danzig(USA) —Magic Of Life (USA) (Seattle Slew (USA))
67[7] (232) 383[4]429[2] 493[5]650[7] 845[7]950[9]
1276[9]6439[10] 6510[11]6618[4] 6703[6]6798[3]
6897[6]6960[4]

Luck In Running (USA) *M Johnston* a76 69
3 bb g Running Stag(USA) —Mystery Number (USA) (Secret Hello (USA))
817[6] 1296[4] 1503[6] 2750[4] 3101[2]3202[9] 3883[11]

Lucknam (IRE) *M Meade* 36
2 b f Namid—Lady Rushmore (IRE) (Fairy King (USA))
1876[5] 3265[6] 3588[13]

Lucksin (IRE) *N Tinkler* a60+ 78
3 b g Key Of Luck(USA) —Swallowcliffe (Caerleon (USA))
1127[2] 1589[2] 2016[3] 2298[2] 2875[2]3112[3] 3638[2]
(3842) 4262[6] (Dead)

Luck Will Come (IRE) *M J Wallace* a71
2 b f Desert Style(IRE) —Petite Maxine (Sharpo)
6098[2] 6433[11]

Lucky Bamblue (IRE) *P C Haslam* 35
3 b g Key Of Luck(USA) —Bamboo (IRE) (Thatching)
2107[10]

Lucky Bee (IRE) *G A Swinbank* 76
2 b f Indian Danehill(IRE) —All Laughter (Vision (USA))
3982[3] (4510) 5528[5] 5721[8]

Lucky Choice (ITY) *A Candi* 91
2 br c Shantou(USA) —Native Choice (IRE) (Be My Native (USA))
6123a[4]

Lucky Elle (IRE) *Irene J Monaghan* 24
2 b f Key Of Luck(USA) —Lady Ela (IRE) (Ela-Mana-Mou)
5692a[14]

Lucky Emerald (IRE) *B Palling* a18 40
4 b m Lend A Hand—Anita's Love (IRE) (Anita's Prince)
1391[9] 1746[8]2531[13]

Lucky Find (IRE) *M Mullineaux* 44
3 b f Key Of Luck(USA) —Recherchee (Rainbow Quest (USA))
5365[3]

Lucky Galic (GER) *A Trybuhl* 72
3 ch c Galileo(IRE) —La Luganese (IRE) (Surumu (GER))
3131a[7]

Lucky It Is (HOL) *A Trybuhl* 101
2 bl c Dashing Blade—Ballykissangel (GER) (Lagunas)
(5218a) 5998a[3]

Lucky Largo (IRE) *D A Nolan* a5 23
6 bb g Key Of Luck(USA) —Lingering Melody (IRE) (Nordico (USA))
734[8] 1608[7] 1814[7]2546[12] 2927[11]

Lucky Lark *M Johnston* a67 84
3 b g Key Of Luck(USA) —Meadow Pipit (CAN) (Meadowlake (USA))
(630) 730[7] 1948[7] 2882[3] (3163) 3243[3]

Lucky Leo *Ian Williams* a56 78
6 b g Muhtarram(USA) —Wrong Bride (Reprimand)
2305[10] 2902[2] 3248[2] 3704[5]

Lucky Lil *R M Whitaker* a23 44
4 ch m Cadeaux Genereux—Amalia (IRE) (Danehill (USA))
1217[9] 2160[3] 3158[8]5363[8] 5922[8]

Luckylover *M G Quinlan* a73 74
3 b c Key Of Luck(USA) —Hang Fire (Marju (IRE))
880[5] (1416) 1681[9] 2823[10] 4048[9]4968[4] 5617[3]
6878[4]

Lucky Lucioni (IRE) *G A Butler* a51 83
3 b g Key Of Luck(USA) —Fanny Blankers (IRE) (Persian Heights)
592[8] 2509[7] 2573[3]3155[12]

Lucky Millionaire (IRE) *A Trybuhl* 93
2 b f Indian Rocket—Triple Tie (USA) (The Minstrel (CAN))
5007a[4]

Lucky Strike *A Trybuhl* 115
8 br g Petong—Urania (Most Welcome)
1973a[3] 2941a[6] 3755a[3] 4418a[2]

Lucky Tern *J M Bradley* 10
3 b g Sooty Tern—Miss Money Spider (IRE) (Statoblest)
5598[14] 5847[11] 5951[8]

Lucky Token (IRE) *E A L Dunlop* a76 77
3 gr f Key Of Luck(USA) —Shawanni (Shareef Dancer (USA))
579[2] (823) 1934[4] 2865[2]3400[3]

Lucky Uno *C Smith*
10 b g Rock City—Free Skip (Free State)
257[10]

Lucy Babe *G Prodromou* a39 55
3 ch f Groom Dancer(USA) —La Puce Volante (Grand Lodge (USA))
2070[U] 2291[9] 2498[5] 3264[6] 3823[10]6057[7] 6907[7]

Lucy Rebecca *M R Channon* 61
2 b f Diktat—Crown Water (USA) (Chief's Crown (USA))
6215[9]

Lucys Lady *K R Burke* a41 49
3 b f Primo Valentino(IRE) —Sandblaster (Most Welcome)
53[10] 1057[2]48[8] 893[5] 1263[9]1501[2] 2101[2] 3006[9]
3839[7] 5273[9]

Ludovico *K A Ryan* a90 74
3 b c Zilzal(USA) —Devastating (Bluebird (USA))
254[3] (550) (831) 1016[10]1836[8] 5666[14]
6397[8](6694)

Luferton Lane (IRE) *R F Marvin* 13
9 b m Ela-Mana-Mou—Saddle 'Er Up (IRE) (Sadler's Wells (USA))
4229[9] 4506[6] 6376[11]

Luisant *F Doumen* 113
3 ch c Pivotal—La Legere (USA) (Lit De Justice (USA))
6230a[3] 6547a[5]

Luis Melendez (USA) *Tom Dascombe* a82 76
4 ch g Horse Chestnut(SAF) —Egoli (USA) (Seeking The Gold (USA))
267[5] 711[3]915[10] 1769[U] 2455[3]3139[5] (3626)
(3914) (4176) 4457[7](5689)

Lujain Rose *N M Babbage* a47 56
4 b m Lujain(USA) —Rose Chime (IRE) (Tirol)
147[7]

Luke After Me (IRE) *Miss Tracy Waggott* a37 37
6 b g Victory Note(USA) —Summit Talk (Head For Heights)
974[13] 1443[11] 2198[11] 4456[9]

Luloah *P S McEntee* a56 55
3 b f Mujahid(USA) —Bangles (Chilibang)
66[2] (83) 189[8]344[3] 477[4]488[4] 577[9]626[5] 673[7]807[7]
910[8]1003[6] 6755[9]6856[7] 6884[8]

Lumen (FR) *O Larsen* 83
4 gr m Verglas(IRE) —La Le Lu (FR) (Exit To Nowhere (USA))
4863a[5]

Luminous One (IRE) *J S Bolger* 91
2 b f Galileo(IRE) —Smaoineamh (Tap On Wood)
6357a[3]

Luna Landing *Jedd O'Keeffe* a44 87
3 ch g Allied Forces(USA) —Macca Luna (IRE) (Kahyasi)
2239[3] 2779[3] 3375[6] (3984) 4784[3] 5266[4](5751)
5792[9] 6319[7]

Lunar Exit (IRE) *Lady Herries* a84 93
5 gr g Exit To Nowhere(USA) —Moon Magic (Polish Precedent (USA))
765[5] 1247[12]

Lunar Express (USA) *W J Haggas* a88 85
3 b f Giant's Causeway(USA) —June Moon (IRE) (Sadler's Wells (USA))
1337[2] 2330[6] 3067[2]3643[3] 3889[8] 4837[7]

Lunar Landscape (USA) *Saeed Bin Suroor* a73+ 65
3 ch c Giant's Causeway(USA) —Melikah (IRE) (Lammtarra (USA))
5669[5] 5934[3]

Lunar Promise (IRE) *Ian Williams* a75 67
4 b g Mujadil(USA) —Lunadine (FR) (Bering)
6684[5]

Lunar River (FR) *E A L Dunlop* a71 74+
3 b f Muhtathir—Moon Gorge (Pursuit Of Love)
2929[5] 3731[2] 4044[3]4836[2] 5260[3] 5574[6] (5830)

Lunar Sovereign (USA) *D E Pipe* a76 119
7 bb g Cobra King(USA) —January Moon (CAN) (Apalachee (USA))
5045[6]

Luna Tacumana (IRE) *J J Lambe* a71+ 71
6 b m Bahhare(USA) —Orange And Blue (Prince Sabo)
171[5] 236[3](327) 384[8]

Lunces Lad (IRE) *M R Channon* a79 83
2 gr g Xaar—Bridelina (FR) (Linamix (FR))
4129[10] (4597) 5007a[6] 5546[12] 5989[4]

Lundy's Lane (IRE) *S Seemar* a98 107
6 b g Darshaan—Lunda (IRE) (Soviet Star (USA))
153a[5] 278a[4] 370a[6] 497a[6]

Lundy's Liability (BRZ) *M F De Kock* a112 109
6 b h Candy Stripes(USA) —Emerald Counter (USA) (Geiger Counter (USA))
154a[3] 355a[6]564a[6] 738a[9]

Lurifux (SWE) *Maria ANdersson* 43
7 ch m Regal Parade I—Luperca Valeria (FR) (Dom Racine (FR))
4863a[6]

Luscivious *A J McCabe* a66 93+
2 ch g Kyllachy—Lloc (Absalom)
1442[6] 1587[8] 2139[5]5349[7] 5496[5] (5753) (5956)

Lusolly *M G Quinlan* 73
2 br c Lujain(USA) —Speak (Barathea (IRE))
2474a[4] 3448[3] 5613[7] 6013[6]

Luxi River (USA) *Michael McElhone* a58 62
6 b g Diesis—Mariella (USA) (Roberto (USA))
4166a[12]

Luxstar (FR) *Mme I T Oakes-Cottin* 75
2 b g Starborough—Luxukarada (FR) (Akarad (FR))
4415a[8]

Luzdeluna (IRE) *Patrick J Flynn* 75
2 b g Desert Sun—Stroll (IRE) (Pennekamp (USA))
5662a[16]

Lygeton Lad *Miss Gay Kelleway* a98 70
8 b g Shaamit(IRE) —Smartie Lee (Dominion)
238[5] 377[7]516[6] 542[12]2820[11] 3648[6]

Lykios (IRE) *C Laffon-Parias* 100
2 b c Night Shift(USA) —Shot Of Redemption (Shirley Heights)
5048a[4] 6000a[5]

Lyndalee (IRE) *P D Evans* a65 71
3 b f Fasliyev(USA) —Itsibitsi (IRE) (Brief Truce (USA))
1448[4] 2295[5] 2701[8] 3759[2] 4135[6]6320[8] 6452[7]
6585[10]6773[11] 6935[9]

Lynford Lady *D J S Ffrench Davis* a54 50
3 b f Zaha(CAN) —Little Miss Rocker (Rock Hopper)
573[3] 1079[7] 1221[7]5129[9] 5690[8]

Lyrical Blues (IRE) *B R Millman* a75 45
3 ch g Namid—Latest (IRE) (Bob Back (USA))
852[7] 2353[10] 3453[6]4050[13]

Lyrical Girl (USA) *H J Manners* a12 26
5 b m Orpen(USA) —Lyric Theatre (USA) (Seeking The Gold (USA))
530[9] 906[12]

Lyrical Sound (IRE) *B W Hills* 84
3 ch f Distant Music(USA) —Unscathed (Warning)
1241[12] (2642) 3067[9] 3708[2] 4481[5] 4923[5]5504[4]

Lyric Dances (FR) *J Jay* a42 44
4 ch m Sendawar(IRE) —Romanche (FR) (Galetto (FR))
25[7]

Lysander's Quest (IRE) *R Ingram* a54 59
8 br g King's Theatre(IRE) —Haramayda (FR) (Doyoun)
174[4] 309[4]570[7] 891[2]1392[3] 1540[4]2320[12] 2497[6]
3035[7]3437[2] (4011) 4438[10] 5235[5]5587[8] 6132[2]
6375[2]6630[3] 6857[2]

Lysandra (IRE) *N Tinkler* 81
4 b m Danehill(USA) —Oriane (Nashwan (USA))
1419[6] 1779[13] 2540[7] 2777[2] 3037[8]3429[4] 3724[2]
3954[4] 4455[5] (5090) (5314) 5511[9]5792[12]

Ma'Am (USA) *I A Wood* a76 72
4 ch m Royal Anthem(USA) —Hide The Bride (USA) (Runaway Groom (CAN))
780[5] (1164) 1804[5] 2457[8] 4662[8] 5599[12]6791[8]

Maarees *G P Enright* a2
5 b m Groom Dancer(USA) —Shemaleyah (Lomond (USA))
18[9]

Maayafushi *Micky Hammond* 50
3 ch f Fraam—Pastelle (Tate Gallery (USA))
1234[7] 1413[14] 3397[11] 4201[11]

Mabadi (USA) *B W Hills* 83
3 b f Sahm(USA) —Barakat (Bustino)
2578[3] (3066) 5538[3] 5758[6]

Mabella (IRE) *B J Llewellyn* 69
4 b m Brave Act—Wee Merkin (IRE) (Thatching)
2966[13] 3194[11] 3862[8]

Macademy Royal (USA) *H Morrison* a71 22
3 b g Royal Academy(USA) —Garden Folly (USA) (Pine Bluff (USA))
916[2] 1412[10]

Macaroni Gin (IRE) *J Howard Johnson* 68
2 b g Grand Slam(USA) —Polyandry (IRE) (Pennekamp (USA))
4880[8] 5481[5] 5616[2]

Macaroni Gold (IRE) *D J Daly* a74+ 69
6 b g Rock Hopper—Strike It Rich (FR) (Rheingold)
(78) 246[6]

Macedon *J S Moore* 89+
3 b g Dansili—Hypnotize (Machiavellian (USA))
(3436) (4143) 4802[5] 5150[5]

Mac Gille Eoin *J Gallagher* a73 65
2 b c Bertolini(USA) —Peruvian Jade (Petong)
961[6] 1107[4] 2967[7]3588[8] 4043[5] (4753)
5140[6]5349[4] 5772[2] 6146[5](6388)

Mac Han (IRE) *Eamon Tyrrell* a55 63
7 ch g Pennekamp(USA) —Ryazana (IRE) (Fairy King (USA))
838[6]

Machhapuchhare *W M Brisbourne* a52 36
3 ch g Most Welcome—Spring Flyer (IRE) (Waajib)
1732[5] 2246[5] 2814[10]4150[7] 5452[12] 5926[2]

Machinate (USA) *W M Brisbourne* a59 67
4 bb g Machiavellian(USA) —Dancing Sea (USA) (Storm Cat (USA))
2149[7] 2612[14]

Machinist (IRE) *D Nicholls* a90 101
6 br g Machiavellian(USA) —Athene (IRE) (Rousillon (USA))
846[5] 1183[9] 2230[10]3482[2] (3972) 4609[17] 5202[2]
5534[9]

Macho Dancer (IRE) *K J Burke* a52 67
3 ch f Desert Prince(IRE) —Mynador (USA) (Forty Niner (USA))
374[8] 554[3]651[5] 2103[4] 2463[3]2901[5] 3066[3]
3456[4]4280[6] 4759[6] 4877[5]

Macky Max (JPN) *H Fujiwara* 114
6 b h Dance In The Dark(JPN) —Clear Chance (JPN) (Dictus (FR))
1329a[7]

Macleod's (SWE) *L Reuterskiold*
3 b g Nicolotte—Miss Ponnelle (Crofter (USA))
4419a[2]

Macleya (GER) *A Fabre* 106
4 b m Winged Love(IRE) —Minaccia (GER) (Platini (GER))
4979a[3] (5881a)

Mac Love *R Charlton* a95 113
5 b g Cape Cross(IRE) —My Lass (Elmaamul (USA))
1050[2] 2289[3] 3086[2] 3518[3] 4025[7]4596[4] 5184[5]
5341[9]

Macorville (USA) *G M Moore* 98
3 b g Diesis—Desert Jewel (USA) (Caerleon (USA))
1296[2] 1781[4] (1868) 2081[4] (4911) (5137) (5582)
5804[10]

Macs All Heart (IRE) *A B Coogan* a43 45
3 ch f Alhaarth(IRE) —Top Of The Form (IRE) (Masterclass (USA))
1576[7] 1771[4] 2288[16]

Macs Ransom (USA) *S C Williams* a44 57
3 b f Red Ransom(USA) —Gaye's Express (USA) (Timeless Native (USA))
2050[13] 2823[8] 3161[3] 3614[3] 3839[3]4556[6]

Mac Zanna (ITY) *M G Quinlan*
2 b c Fay Breeze(IRE) —Serenity Bay (USA) (Mukaddamah (USA))
3427a[8]

Mad *Ernst Oertel* a55 40
5 br m Pursuit Of Love—Emily-Mou (IRE) (Cadeaux Genereux)
854[6] 917[3]1245[5] 1537[6]2348[12]

Madaarek (USA) *E A L Dunlop* 71
2 b c Kingmambo(USA) —Hachiyah (IRE) (Generous (IRE))
5939[7] 6220[11]

Madaares (USA) *M Johnston* 81
3 ch c Rahy(USA) —Tajannub (USA) (Dixieland Band (USA))
978[5] 1252[2] 1596[3] 2948[2] 3191[8]

Madame Constanze (IRE) *Miss Gay Kelleway* a44 52?
3 b f Mozart(IRE) —Darbela (IRE) (Doyoun)
291[11] 797[15] 3906[8]4291[6] 5082[9] 5276[9]
5651[6]6279[9]

Madame Diktatit *Ms Deborah J Evans* 29
3 b f Diktat—Madame Jones (IRE) (Lycius (USA))
3288[9] 3839[8] 4297[12]

Madame Guillotine *P T Midgley* a34 33
4 b m Sure Blade(USA) —Delicious (Dominion)
14[3] 145[8]195[9] 387[5]618[10] 3189[8] 3749[13]

Madame Medusa (IRE) *J A R Toller* a70 75
3 b f Mozart(IRE) —Belize Tropical (IRE) (Baillamont (USA))
1094[6] 1681[7] 2146[2] 2587[2] 3144[3]3826[2] (4495)
5317[5] 5919[9] 6204[4] 6353[7]

Madam Gaffer *B J Meehan* a66 49
2 ch f Tobougg(IRE) —True Precision (Presidium)
3407[4] 3640[5]4433[3] 5349[9] 5646[9](5876)
6416[3]6582[3]

Madam Mac (IRE) *B J Meehan* a50 42
3 b f Royal Applause—Wild Woman (Polar Falcon (USA))
981^{10} 1736^{12} 2249^{3} 2877^{3} 3824^{8} 5033^{10}

Madam Moschata *D W Barker* 55
3 b f Muhtarram(USA) —Casaque Rose (USA) (Lord Avie (USA))
1592^{11} 2019^{9} 2195^{13} 2399^{12} 3172^{9} 3814^{P} 5368^{11}

Madam Patti *B Palling* a42 41
3 b f Monashee Mountain(USA) —Thabeh (Shareef Dancer (USA))
3897^{8} 4756^{8} 4984^{10} 5928^{5} 6470^{10} 6545^{9} 6702^{8}

Madan Di San Jore (IRE) *M Marcialis*
3 b c Danehill Dancer(IRE) —Mar (ITY) (Roakarad (IRE))
2493a^{10}

Mad Carew (USA) *J R Boyle* a80 83
7 ch g Rahy(USA) —Poppy Carew (IRE) (Danehill (USA))
48^{3} 113^{2} 325^{3} (Dead)

Mad Dog Slew (USA) *F Reuterskiold* a101
3 br c Slew City Slew(USA) —Skep (USA) (Fappiano (USA))
(4420a)

Maddox (POL) *Mrs P Townsley* a49 44
4 b g Upper Heights(GER) —Muddy's Girl (SWE) (Muddy Blues)
312^{6}

Mademoiselle *R Curtis* a22 22
4 b m Efisio—Shall We Dance (Rambo Dancer (CAN))
127^{3} 240^{4} 5354^{16} 6068^{13}

Mademoiselle Louna (FR) *J-M Beguigne* 84
3 b f Broadway Flyer(USA) —Ma Sonate (USA) (Val De L'Orne (FR))
2537a^{6} 6384a^{9}

Madge *W Storey* a65 64
4 br m Marju(IRE) —Aymara (Darshaan)
3379^{7}

Madhavi *B S Rothwell* a65 72
4 gr m Diktat—Grey Galava (Generous (IRE))
115^{5} (252) 327^{6} 557^{4} 696^{12} 1334^{12} 1772^{4} (2481) 2953^{2}(3152) 3666^{2} 4104^{11} 4528^{7} 6448^{7}

Madiba *P Howling* a69 62
7 b g Emperor Jones(USA) —Priluki (Lycius (USA))
643^{4} 675^{3} 911^{3} 1219^{10} 1339^{3}(1758) 2219^{4} 3203^{7} (3454) 4046^{5} 4252^{5} 4914^{6} 4996^{9} 5963^{18} 6831^{9} 6873^{4}

Madison Avenue (GER) *T M Jones*
9 b g Mondrian(GER) —Madly Noble (GER) (Irish River (FR))
6132^{14}

Mad Marty Wildcard *R Brotherton* a35 39
4 b g Komaite(USA) —Done And Dusted (IRE) (Up And At 'Em)
104^{10} 144^{8} 783^{7}

Mad Maurice *B J Curley* a53+ 57+
5 ch g Grand Lodge(USA) —Amarella (FR) (Balleroy (USA))
(258) 1256^{7} 2181^{15} 6627^{F} (Dead)

Mad Professor (IRE) *D J S Ffrench Davis* a49 64
3 b g Mull Of Kintyre(USA) —Fancy Theory (USA) (Quest For Fame)
1547^{9} 2131^{9}

Madrasee *N E Berry* a58 50
8 b m Beveled(USA) —Pendona (Blue Cashmere)
265^{7} 401^{9} 474^{6} 480^{2} 580^{4} 806^{8} 837^{9} 1150^{11} 1243^{10} 1913^{11} 2347^{5} 2632^{4} 2955^{8}

Madresal (GER) *P Schiergen* a103 107
7 gr h Lomitas—Midnight Society (USA) (Imp Society (USA))
2692a^{6} 6248a^{2} 6574a^{5}

Madrigale *G L Moore* 62
2 b f Averti(IRE) —Shy Minstrel (USA) (The Minstrel (CAN))
5161^{3} 5586^{5}

Madroos *J L Dunlop* a86 86
3 ch c Medicean—Soolaimon (IRE) (Shareef Dancer (USA))
(1975) 2556^{3} 2986^{6} 4604^{3} 5533^{5}

Madura (GER) *Mario Hofer* 98
3 ch f Dashing Blade—Mandellicht (IRE) (Be My Guest (USA))
1328a^{7} 2059a^{6} 3661a^{5} 4542a^{12} 5160a^{5}

Mae Cigan (FR) *M Blanshard* a59 74+
3 gr g Medaaly—Concert (Polar Falcon (USA))
123^{2} 604^{4} 781^{3} 1005^{12} (1881) 2518^{12} 3650^{9} 4301^{4} 4606^{8}(5015) 5513^{3} 5769^{9}

Maeve (IRE) *E J Creighton* a54
2 b f Tomba—Boozy (Absalom)
6324^{10} 6505^{10} 6778^{7}

Mafeking (UAE) *M R Hoad* a79+
2 b c Jade Robbery(USA) —Melisendra (FR) (Highest Honor (FR))
6145^{8} (6393) 6599^{3}

Magadar (USA) *C E Brittain* a62 78
3 bb f Lujain(USA) —Slow Jazz (USA) (Chief's Crown (USA))
4488^{7} 4807^{15} 6564^{12}

Magadino (FR) *Brigitte Renk* 107
5 b g Solon(GER) —Madeleina (FR) (Top Waltz (FR))
523a^{3} (4169a)

Magdalene *Rae Guest* 59
2 ch f Act One—Three Terns (USA) (Arctic Tern (USA))
5352^{10} 6297^{6}

Magena Gold *R Charlton* a53
2 b g Bertolini(USA) —Linens Girl (Thowra (FR))
3844^{8} 4934^{8} 5261^{11}

Mageniken (USA) *J Howard Johnson*
2 ch g Giant's Causeway(USA) —Freshwater Pearl (IRE) (Alzao (USA))
4228^{RR}

Maggies Farm (USA) *M Johnston* a78 71
3 ch f Forest Wildcat(USA) —Moss (USA) (Woodman (USA))
1781^{9} 5299^{10} 6209^{8} 6564^{5} 6607^{7}

Magical Mimi *K G Wingrove* a55 48
5 b m Magic Ring(IRE) —Naval Dispatch (Slip Anchor)
(821) 1196^{6} 1397^{7} 2208^{12} 2288^{12}

Magical Music *J Pearce* a91 62
3 b f Fraam—Magical Flute (Piccolo)
(604) 712^{6} 822^{2} 1005^{7} (1307) 1681^{10} 2301^{6} 2823^{9} 4249^{3} 4933^{8} 5689^{3} 6671^{4} (6741) (6862) (6968)

Magicalmysterytour (IRE) *A P O'Brien* 94+
3 b c Sadler's Wells(USA) —Jude (Darshaan)
4039^{9} 5854a^{11}

Magical World *J M Bradley* a8 27
3 b f Agnes World(USA) —Otaru (IRE) (Indian Ridge)
3538^{12} 4120^{14}

Magic America (USA) *Mme C Head-Maarek* 111
2 b f High Yield(USA) —Shoofha (IRE) (Bluebird (USA))
3132a^{6} 3777a^{3} 4644a^{2} 5654^{6} (6228a)

Magic Amigo *J R Jenkins* a66 79
5 ch g Zilzal(USA) —Emaline (FR) (Empery (USA))
799^{6} 1614^{3} 2088^{10} 3009^{6} 4848^{5} 6590^{8} 6843^{3}

Magic Amour *P A Blockley* a67 60
8 ch g Sanglamore(USA) —Rakli (Warning)
11^{3} (38) (95) 119^{3} 127^{2} 271^{4}(315) 402^{4} 492^{12}

Magic Box (ITY) *F & L Brogi* 101
3 ch c Namid—Bodiniyeh (IRE) (Persian Heights)
(758a) 1175a^{5}

Magic Charm *K G Wingrove* a34 45
8 b m Magic Ring(IRE) —Loch Clair (IRE) (Lomond (USA))
1461^{8}

Magic Dancer (GER) *D Ronge* 89
5 b h Big Shuffle(USA) —Montrastani (IRE) (Shahrastani (USA))
6093a^{10}

Magic Echo *M Dods* 70
2 b f Wizard King—Sunday News'N'Echo (USA) (Trempolino (USA))
(5898) 6106^{6}

Magic Glade *Tom Dascombe* a93 96
7 b g Magic Ring(IRE) —Ash Glade (Nashwan (USA))
6^{6} 79^{6} 244^{6} 761^{8} 989^{9} 2173^{6} (2521) 3027^{7} 5832^{8} 6953^{3}

Magic Instinct *P Moody* 97
4 b g Entrepreneur—Passe Passe (USA) (Lear Fan (USA))
6346a^{5} 6455a^{2}

Magic Merlin *W R Swinburn* a71 78
5 b g Magic Ring(IRE) —St James's Antigua (IRE) (Law Society (USA))
167^{7}

Magic Moth *M Johnston* a65+
3 b c Mtoto—Majoune (FR) (Take Risks (FR))
(403)

Magic Mountain (IRE) *R Hannon* 83
2 b c Dr Fong(USA) —Hard Task (Formidable (USA))
3222^{4} 3591^{7} (3949)

Magic Peak (IRE) *Sir Michael Stoute* a65 79+
3 b f Danehill(USA) —Magic Cove (USA) (Kingmambo (USA))
1351^{2} (1901) 2359^{11} 3088^{4} 4209^{9}

Magic Red *J Ryan* a52 51
6 ch g Magic Ring(IRE) —Jacquelina (USA) (Private Account (USA))
28^{5} 174^{11}

Magic Rush *Mrs Norma Pook* a89 83
4 b g Almaty(IRE) —Magic Legs (Reprimand)
844^{3} 3647^{2} 3931^{3} (4437) 4807^{5} 5591^{6} 5785^{10} 6733^{3} 6986^{9}

Magic Sting *M L W Bell* a43 88
5 ch g Magic Ring(IRE) —Ground Game (Gildoran)
867^{10} 1051^{9} 2079^{15} 2640^{6} (3214) 3429^{2} 4023^{4} 4203^{3} 4878^{6} 5403^{2}

Magic Tango (ITY) *L D'Auria*
2 b c Stuck(USA) —Mademoiselle Lili (FR) (Cadoudal (FR))
6407a^{6}

Magic Warrior *J C Fox* a72 65
6 b g Magic Ring(IRE) —Clarista (USA) (Riva Ridge (USA))
82^{6} 972^{10} 1194^{2}(1394) 1461^{2} 1753^{4} (2641) 2862^{3} 3820^{4}(4248) 4709^{7} 5267^{5} 5974^{7}(6294) 6451^{12} 6652^{4} (6841)

Magna Graduate (USA) *T Pletcher* a117
4 bb h Honor Grades(USA) —Peacock Alley (USA) (Fast Play (USA))
743a^{3}

Magnificent Song (USA) *T Pletcher* 111
3 gr f Unbridled's Song(USA) —Song To Remember (USA) (Storm Cat (USA))
(5198a) 5984a^{6}

Magnum (ARG) *Darrell Vienna* a117
5 br h El Compinche(ARG) —Merrymaker (ARG) (Rainbow Corner)
5826a^{6}

Magnum Force (NZ) *L Laxon* a58
7 ch g Turbulent Dancer(USA) —Otehi Opal (NZ) (Otehi Bay (AUS))
353a^{11} 495a^{11}

Magnum Opus (IRE) *T J Pitt* 88
4 b g Sadler's Wells(USA) —Summer Breeze (Rainbow Quest (USA))
1585^{12} 1827^{5} 2549^{5} 2656^{11} 5513^{12}

Maguire (GER) *M F Harris* a49 59
5 gr g Medaaly—Mayada (USA) (The Minstrel (CAN))
5385^{13}

Mahmjra *C N Allen* a36 69
4 b g Josr Algarhoud(IRE) —Jamrat Samya (IRE) (Sadler's Wells (USA))
5324^{16} 5610^{15} 6979^{8}

Mahrajaan (USA) *J H M Gosden* a65 78
3 bb c Machiavellian(USA) —Karen S (USA) (Kris S (USA))
1135^{3} 2143^{3} (2881) 3473^{8} 5107^{12}

Mahtoum (AUS) *K Waugh* 118
7 b g Suave Dancer(USA) —Egyptian Secret (AUS) (Sir Tristram)
6392a^{6}

Maiden Investor *Stef Liddiard* 50
3 b f Orpen(USA) —Actress (Known Fact (USA))
4799^{7}

Maidford (IRE) *M Meade* a63 59+
3 ch f Singspiel(IRE) —Milde (USA) (Desert Wine (USA))
971^{7} 1274^{4} (1726) 2403^{6}(2479) 2921^{3} (3650) 4173^{7} 4758^{6}

Maid In England *G A Ham* a46 45
3 b f Mujadil(USA) —Lalique (IRE) (Lahib (USA))
(3006) 4533^{8} 5054^{13}

Maid Of Ale (IRE) *B J Meehan* 60
2 b f Barathea(IRE) —Borders Belle (IRE) (Pursuit Of Love)
1896^{9} 2816^{6} 4207^{11} 5041^{4} 5382^{10} 5503^{13}

Maid To Believe *J L Dunlop* 68
2 b f Galileo(IRE) —Maid For The Hills (Indian Ridge)
5456^{7} (5882) 6217^{8}

Mail Express (IRE) *L M Cumani* 87+
3 b f Cape Cross(IRE) —Mystic Tempo (USA) (El Gran Senor (USA))
2859^{6} 3554^{3} (4142)

Maisha (GER) *D Smaga* 95
3 b f Platini(GER) —Myth And Reality (Linamix (FR))
6722a^{10}

Maison Dieu *E J Alston* 71
3 bb g King Charlemagne(USA) —Shining Desert (IRE) (Green Desert (USA))
1127^{9} (1594) 2109^{2} 2873^{2} 2976^{7} 3879^{9} 4296^{5} 5401^{14}

Majaales (USA) *M P Tregoning* 88
3 b g Diesis—Roseate Tern (Blakeney)
2655 ^{5} (3029) 4125^{6}

Majehar *A G Newcombe* a57+ 50
4 b g Marju(IRE) —Joonayh (Warning)
399^{3} 471^{2} 546^{3} 582^{2} 888^{10} 1461^{5} 2221^{9} 5838^{5} (6232) 6617^{3}(6854) 6955^{4}

Majestas (IRE) *J G M O'Shea* 64
2 b c Val Royal(FR) —Pantera Piceno (IRE) (College Chapel)
3193^{13} 4129^{13} 5067^{4} 5402^{5} 5828^{9}

Majestical (IRE) *J M Bradley* a71 64
4 b g Fayruz—Haraabah (USA) (Topsider (USA))
51^{10} 137^{2}(225) 292^{4} 323^{5} 986^{10} 1151^{11} 2182^{14} 2484^{9} 2571^{8} 2858^{7} 6827^{9} 6913^{10} 6990^{10}

Majestic Cheer *M R Channon* a75 59
2 b g Royal Applause—Muwasim (USA) (Meadowlake (USA))
5020^{6} 5371^{13} 5891^{6}(6324)

Majestic Chief *K A Ryan* 29
2 b c Xaar—Grand Splendour (Shirley Heights)
5900^{7} 6173^{12}

Majestic Concorde (IRE) *D K Weld* 93+
3 b g Definite Article—Talina's Law (IRE) (Law Society (USA))
5853a^{2}

Majestic Halo *E A L Dunlop* a73+ 76
3 b f Royal Applause—Circle Of Light (Anshan)
2028^{2} 2673^{3} 3946^{2} 4396^{2} 5024^{11} 6225^{5} (6459)

Majestic Missile (IRE) *W J Haggas* 117
5 b h Royal Applause—Tshusick (Dancing Brave (USA))
1485^{14} 2720^{18} 3709^{2} 4080^{12} (5222a) 5712a^{7}

Majestic Roi (USA) *M R Channon* 79
2 ch f Street Cry(IRE) —L'Extra Honor (USA) (Hero's Honor (USA))
1930^{7} (2375)

Majestic Times (IRE) *Liam McAteer* a57 109
6 b g Bluebird(USA) —Simply Times (USA) (Dodge (USA))
1158a^{6} 1469a^{3} 2308a^{5} 3124a^{4}

Majik *P T Midgley* a58 30
7 ch g Pivotal—Revoke (USA) (Riverman (USA))
80^{2} 245^{7} 271^{2} 345^{5} 1102^{14} 1255^{8} 1388^{4} 3995^{12} 6464^{6} 6636^{3} 6719^{2}

Majofils (FR) *M Weiss*
3 ch c Majorien—Lias Creek (Lahib (USA))
(2717a)

Majolica *N P Littmoden* 43
2 br f Lujain(USA) —Marjorie's Memory (IRE) (Fairy King (USA))
3043^{10}

Major Blade (GER) *Heather Dalton* a53 40
8 b g Dashing Blade—Misniniski (Niniski (USA))
1353^{8} (1553) 1724^{2} 3597^{9} 4282^{12}

Major Cadeaux *R Hannon* 103+
2 ch c Cadeaux Genereux—Maine Lobster (USA) (Woodman (USA))
(1838) 2719^{2}

Major Grace (FR) *Y De Nicolay* 105
3 b c Majorien—Grace Royale (IRE) (Marignan (USA))
1178a^{10} 1944a^{2} 4168a^{5} 5400a^{5}

Major Gunn's (SWE) *L Reuterskiold*
3 b g Nicolotte—Porla (SWE) (Miami Springs)
4419a^{9}

Major League (USA) *K Bishop* a71?
4 b g Magic Cat(USA) —Quick Grey (USA) (El Prado (IRE))
828^{14} 1340^{8}

Major Magpie (IRE) *M Dods* 81+
4 b g Rossini(USA) —Picnic Basket (Pharly (FR))
1123^{6} (1186) 1455^{6} 2299^{3} 2627^{8} 3147^{7} 3331^{2} 3583^{2} 4154^{3} 4653^{6} (5320) 5810^{8}

Major Rhythm (USA) *Ed Beam* 111
7 b h Rhythm(USA) —Specifically (USA) (Sky Classic (CAN))
4386a^{9}

Majors Cast (IRE) *J Noseda* a100 122
5 b h Victory Note(USA) —Ziffany (Taufan (USA))
(1479) 1840^{2} (Dead)

Major Speculation (IRE) *J M Bradley* a48 53
6 b g Spectrum(IRE) —Pacific Grove (Persian Bold)
143^{11}

Major Third (IRE) *T D Easterby* 68
2 b c Daggers Drawn(USA) —Red Rosie (USA) (Red Ransom (USA))
1080^{6} (1442) 2076^{7} 3136^{6} 4321^{11} 5655^{11}

Major Title (IRE) *M J Grassick* 95
7 b g Brief Truce(USA) —Dariyba (IRE) (Kahyasi)
4094a^{U}

Majounes Song *M Johnston* 85
2 gr f Singspiel(IRE) —Majoune (FR) (Take Risks (FR))
2409^{3} 2660^{3} (3227) 3874^{6}

Majuro (IRE) *M R Channon* a91 87+
2 b c Danetime(IRE) —First Fling (IRE) (Last Tycoon)
3892^{8} (4290) 4732^{2} (5034) 5665^{3}(5884)

Maka (FR) *F Cohen* 94
2 b f Slickly(FR) —Carneia (FR) (Funambule (USA))
4464a^{2} 5122a^{6}

Makaan (USA) *F Head* 109
2 b c Swain(IRE) —Khassah (Green Desert (USA))
(5801a) 6249a^{6}

Makabul *B R Millman* 86
3 b g Makbul—Victoria Sioux (Ron's Victory (USA))
1512^{8} 1900^{6} 2329^{4} 2931^{9} 3150^{6} 4922^{8}

Makai *J J Bridger* a71 54
3 ch g Cayman Kai(IRE) —Young Sue (Local Suitor (USA))
1599^{10} (2142) 2616^{6} 2947^{5} 3194^{15} 3914^{6} 4195^{3} 4728^{9} 5259^{5} 5767^{8} (6067) 6408^{3} 6462^{7}

Makarim (IRE) *M R Bosley* a38 30
10 ch g Generous(IRE) —Emmaline (USA) (Affirmed (USA))
52^{5} 174^{5}(256) 270^{3} 389^{2} 549^{6} 635^{4} 938^{3} 1392^{7} 1766^{2} 5929^{5} 6305^{8} 6630^{11} 6973^{P}

Makderah (IRE) *M P Tregoning* 106
3 b f Danehill(USA) —Wijdan (USA) (Mr Prospector (USA))
(1134) 1819^{3} 2744^{3} 4097^{2} (5550) 5962^{15}

Make Haste (IRE) *R Charlton* 57
2 b c Sadler's Wells(USA) —Mosaique Bleue (Shirley Heights)
5892^{8}

Make It Happen Now *P A Blockley* a27 21
4 bb m Octagonal(NZ) —Whittle Woods Girl (Emarati (USA))
255^{10} 4629^{13} 5938^{14}

Make Me An Offer (IRE) *B W Hills* 78
2 b c Fasliyev(USA) —Rafif (USA) (Riverman (USA))
1113^{3} 1838^{13} 2185^{4} 2517^{7}

Make My Dream *J Gallagher* a59 64
3 b g My Best Valentine—Sandkatoon (IRE) (Archway (IRE))
2644^{3} 3011^{9} 3612^{2} 3936^{7} 4242^{3} 4985^{9} 5453^{10} 6389^{2} 6510^{7} 6649^{2} 6884^{5}

Make My Hay *J Gallagher* a49 55
7 b g Bluegrass Prince(IRE) —Shashi (IRE) (Shaadi (USA))
767^{11} 6553^{14}

Makena (FR) *B Dutruel*
4 b m Sky Swallow(FR) —Maiakovskaia (FR) (Bikala)
5562a^{0}

Maker's Mark (IRE) *H Candy* 79
2 b g Invincible Spirit(IRE) —Certain Impression (USA) (Forli (ARG))
3591^{3} 4177^{2} 4774^{2} (5563) 5829^{9}

Makeusabuck *A Berry*
2 ch f Foxhound(USA) —Just A Gem (Superlative)
1030^{8} 1499^{8} 1862^{7} 4545^{11} 4724^{11}

Make Us Flush *A Berry* a22 39
4 b m Mind Games—Pearls (Mon Tresor)
974^{11} 1594^{9} 4070^{12} 5483^{13}

Makfly *R Hollinshead* a52 80
3 b g Makbul—Flying Flip (Rolfe (USA))
1606^{9} 1983^{3} 5079^{12} 5724^{4} 6221^{9} 6417^{12} 6735^{8}

Making Moves *Miss J A Camacho* a54
3 b f Afternoon Deelites(USA) —Simona (CHI) (Dancing Groom (USA))
1149^{7}

Making Music *T D Easterby* 72
3 b f Makbul—Crofters Ceilidh (Scottish Reel)
1097^{13} 1497^{9} 1793^{2} 2109^{3} 3042^{3} 3299^{3} 3722^{6} 3912^{6} 4507^{6} 5902^{7} 6159^{5}

Makshoof (IRE) *M A Jarvis* 77
2 b g Kyllachy—Tres Sage (Reprimand)
3242^{2} 4028^{3} (4987) 5829^{11}

Maktavish *R Brotherton* a70 56
7 b g Makbul—La Belle Vie (Indian King (USA))
(96) 198^{9} 450^{4}(547) 1150^{13} 4468^{12} 4793^{12} 5791^{17} 6555^{9} 6585^{9} 6740^{5} 6823^{5}

Maktu *P G Murphy* a51 46
4 ch g Bien Bien(USA) —Shalateeno (Teenoso (USA))
5385^{10} 6405^{6} 6560^{7}

Maktub (ITY) *Ernst Oertel* 113
7 b h Love The Groom(USA) —Carmen The Best (IRE) (Waajib)
2010^{P}

Malaaq *M A Jarvis* a63 72
2 b f Green Desert(USA) —Izwah (USA) (Bahri (USA))
2144^{3} 2890^{4} 3188^{3} 4292^{2} 5112^{2} 5668^{6} (6056)

Malaath (IRE) *Saeed Bin Suroor* a74+
2 b f Green Desert(USA) —Mouwadh (USA) (Nureyev (USA))
(6098)

Malacara *A P O'Brien* 93
2 b c Rock Of Gibraltar(IRE) —Treacle (USA) (Seeking The Gold (USA))
5851a^{4} 6104^{13}

Malahide Express (IRE) *E J Alston* a71 58
6 gr g Compton Place—Gracious Gretclo (Common Grounds)
38^{4} 46^{6}

Malakiya (IRE) *G A Butler* a57 73
3 b g Sadler's Wells(USA) —State Crystal (IRE) (High Estate)
1032^{10} 3347^{3} 4470^{3} 4586^{4} 5057^{6}(6027)

Malameeze (USA) *B Barnett* a108
3 ch c Saint Ballado(CAN) —Valentine Magic (USA) (Knight (USA))
757a^{3}

Malapropism *M R Channon* a84 90d
6 ch g Compton Place—Mrs Malaprop (Night Shift (USA))
705^{7} 947^{6} 1076^{10} 1820^{8} 2237^{11} (2618) 2674^{4} 2858^{2} 3027^{3} 3165^{4} 3447^{5} (3503) 3625^{2} 3715^{4} 3938^{2} 4085^{18} 4180^{5} 4771^{8} 5169^{9} 5532^{13} 6009^{14}

Malcheek (IRE) *T D Easterby* a92+ 94
4 br g Lend A Hand—Russland (GER) (Surumu (GER))
1143[2] (1494) 1629[9] 3079[3] 3493[17] 3937[14]4682[15] 5070[5] 5529[10] (5877) 6192[8]

Malech (IRE) *M L W Bell* 75
3 b g Bahhare(USA) —Choral Sundown (Night Shift (USA))
(797) 1444[7] 1681[2] 3542[4] 3977[5] 4575[12]5270[3] 5568[13]

Malelane (IRE) *A Dickman* 44+
3 b f Prince Sabo—Indigo (Primo Dominie)
2167[12] 2876[3] 3749[11] 4056[2] 4656[10]

Malibu (IRE) *M Appleby* a53 44
5 b g Second Empire(IRE) —Tootle (Main Reef)
88[12] 521[9]591[8] 694[5]4709[12] 5390[7] 5609[4]6128[5] 6238[5]6705[2] 6857[4]6995[11]

Malibu Mint (USA) *Jim Chapman* a118
4 ch m Malibu Moon(USA) —Ivory Mint (USA) (Key To The Mint (USA))
6341a[12]

Malinsa Blue (IRE) *S Parr* 84?
4 b m Desert Style(IRE) —Talina's Law (IRE) (Law Society (USA))
2503[5] 2977[9] 3542[7] 3789[5] 4267[10]5317[9]

Maltese Falcon *P F I Cole* a104+ 99
6 b g Mark Of Esteem(IRE) —Crime Ofthecentury (Pharly (FR))
3972[15] 4080[11] 4461[8] 5087[6] 5158[10]5443[8] 5832[4] 6095[4]6292[9] (6445) (6660) 6849[5]

Malt Lios (IRE) *John Joseph Murphy* 75?
3 b f Lil's Boy(USA) —Maltesse (IRE) (Never So Bold)
4212a[10]

Malt Magic (USA) *B Baffert* a90
2 bb c Cherokee Run(USA) —La Cucina (IRE) (Last Tycoon)
6339a[12]

Malt Or Mash (USA) *R Hannon* 81
2 gr c Black Minnaloushe(USA) —Southern Tradition (USA) (Family Doctor (USA))
5091[6] 5381[3] 5893[3]

Maluti *Rae Guest* a23 33
5 ch g Piccolo—Persian Blue (Persian Bold)
1722[10] 2700[17]

Malyana *M A Jarvis* a74 74
2 b f Mtoto—Pass The Peace (Alzao (USA))
4373[6] 5106[2] 5536[2](5933)

Mamalini *P D Cundell* a36 58
2 b f Bertolini(USA) —Mamalama (Nishapour (FR))
877[8] 4163[5] 4327[8]5052[10]

Mambazo *S C Williams* a81 44
4 b g Dansili—Kalindi (Efisio)
22[2] 67[6](126) 317[5]532[3] (699) 1161[4] 1209[10] 1414[16]2340[5] 3012[5]4846[11] (5246) 5263[2]5391[2] 5778[12]5782[5] 5842[10]6966[10]

Mambo King (DEN) *L Kelp* 92
4 b h Diktat—Gypsy Singer (USA) (Kingmambo (USA))
2123a[7] 4189a[8]

Mambomoon *T D Easterby* 33
2 b c Zaha(CAN) —Moontime (FR) (Habitat)
3080[7] 4066[11] 6157[13]

Mambonow (USA) *J Noseda* a61 75+
3 b c Kingmambo(USA) —Easy Now (USA) (Danzig (USA))
1844[12] 2662[4] 3742[6] 4287[3] 5986[5]

Mambo Spirit (IRE) *J G Given* 84
2 b g Invincible Spirit(IRE) —Mambodorga (USA) (Kingmambo (USA))
2623[12] 4151[4] 4421[2] 4766[13] (5065) (5528) 5829[7]

Mambo Sun *P A Blockley* a68 70
3 b g Superior Premium—The Manx Touch (IRE) (Petardia)
349[4] 475[4]583[3] 1005[3]1052[2] 1251[2] 2124[10] 2633[5] 3609[2]3695[2]

Mamela (GER) *L M Cumani* a95 102
5 b m Protektor(GER) —My Rita (IRE) (Brief Truce (USA))
1506[6] 2503[2] 3627[6] 5159[6] 5525[3]6190[4]

Mamichor *J R Boyle* a54 65
3 br g Mamalik(USA) —Ichor (Primo Dominie)
969[14] 1241[13] 2210[10]2576[7] 2644[9] 3016[7]3804[5]

Mamonta *M J Wallace* a61 61
3 b f Fantastic Light(USA) —Mamoura (IRE) (Lomond (USA))
1613[8] 5567[6] 6026[7] 6911[5]

Mamora Reef *J R Weymes* a48 79
2 b f Primo Valentino(IRE) —Aubrieta (USA) (Dayjur (USA))
2500[9] 2973[3] 3351[6] 4969[5]5245[6]

Manaal (USA) *Sir Michael Stoute* 73
2 b f Bahri(USA) —Muwakleh (Machiavellian (USA))
(6063)

Manbala (FR) *J L Dunlop* 100
3 gr f Linamix(FR) —Do The Mambo (USA) (Kingmambo (USA))
773a[7] 6333[14]

Manchurian *M J Wallace* a86+ 79
2 b c Singspiel(IRE) —Royal Passion (Ahonoora)
4323[3] (4934) 5805[6]

Manda Honor (GER) *Mario Hofer* 88
3 gr f Highest Honor(FR) —Mandamou (GER) (Ela-Mana-Mou)
925a[4] 1328a[12] 2912a[10]

Mandarin Dancer (IRE) *Miss L A Perratt* 38
3 gr f King Charlemagne(USA) —Shamneez (IRE) (Pharly (FR))
1501[9] 2192[11] 2379[10]

Mandarin Grand (IRE) *Miss L A Perratt* 45?
3 b f Raise A Grand(IRE) —Playa Del Sol (IRE) (Alzao (USA))
1501[10] 2192[4] 3288[13] 3353[7] 3586[7]3814[6] 4059[11] 4350[11] 4524[10]

Mandarin Lady *Miss J A Camacho* a49 57
3 ch f Timeless Times(USA) —Lapu-Lapu (Prince Sabo)
645[7] 2080[4] 2763[12]4494[4] 5062[6]

Mandarin Rocket (IRE) *Miss L A Perratt* 58
3 ch c Titus Livius(FR) —Two Thousand (IRE) (Polish Patriot (USA))
1609[2] 2161[6] 2923[6] 3138[6] 3355[9]

Mandarin Spirit (IRE) *G C H Chung* a84 74
6 b g Primo Dominie—Lithe Spirit (IRE) (Dancing Dissident (USA))
575[11] (644) 721[9]1275[12] 2184[11] 2464[5]3664[8] 3846[5] 4230[2]4629[6] 5096[7] 5246[6]6036[4] 6227[6](6437) 6579[3](6770) 6999[2]

Mandatum *L M Cumani* a90 87
5 b g Mtoto—Reamur (Top Ville)
1927[2] 2447[5]3723[DSQ] 4299[2] 5163[2]

Mandela (NZ) *R Yuill* 108
5 br g Ebony Grosve(NZ) —Wairongoa Belle (NZ) (Sea Anchor)
6392a[9]

Mandesha (FR) *A De Royer-Dupre* 122+
3 b f Desert Style(IRE) —Mandalara (IRE) (Lahib (USA))
(2537a) 3133a[DSQ] (3991a) (5220a) (5713a)

Mandinka *J F Coupland* a76+ 33
6 b g Distinctly North(USA) —Primo Panache (Primo Dominie)
334[7]

Mandobi (IRE) *D Selvaratnam* a100 108
5 ch h Mark Of Esteem(IRE) —Miss Queen (USA) (Miswaki (USA))
151a[11] (357a) 497a[10]

Mandragola *B W Hills* 37
2 b c Machiavellian(USA) —Viz (USA) (Kris S (USA))
4768[13]

Mandriano (ITY) *D W Barker* a48 21
2 b g Averti(IRE) —My Penny (USA) (Gulch (USA))
5332[14] 5615[14] 5900[11] 6157[5] 6463[3]6500[7]

Mandurah (IRE) *D Nicholls* 48
2 b g Tagula(IRE) —Fearfully Grand (Grand Lodge (USA))
1587[13] 3830[3] 4055[6]

Manduro (GER) *A Fabre* 122
4 br h Monsun(GER) —Mandellicht (IRE) (Be My Guest (USA))
(934a) 1331a[3] 1873a[2] 2741[3] 3779a[3] 4416a[2]5049a[3] 5704a[2]

Mandy's Maestro (USA) *R M Whitaker* 66
2 br c Brahms(USA) —Belle Masque (USA) (Devil's Bag (USA))
3018[7] 3958[5] 4607[3] 5681[24]

Maneki Neko (IRE) *E W Tuer* a75 79
4 b g Rudimentary(USA) —Ardbess (Balla Cove)
(976) 1144[5] 1809[11] 2365[4] (2736) 3960[9] 4231[5]

Mangano *A Berry* a37 48
2 b g Mujadil(USA) —Secret Dance (Sadler's Wells (USA))
5364[5] 5753[7] 6295[9] 6463[6]6730[5]

Mango Mischief (IRE) *J L Dunlop* 106
5 ch m Desert King(IRE) —Eurolink Mischief (Be My Chief (USA))
1506[3] 1804[2] 2706[2] 4417a[6] 5342[9]5917[4] 6333[2] 6567a[4]

Mango Music *M R Channon* 91
3 ch f Distant Music(USA) —Eurolink Sundance (Night Shift (USA))
(776) 1097[6] 1843[6] 2049[2] 2609[2] 2931[10]4078[5] (4242) 4589[7] (5265) 5643[7] 5919[4]

Manhasset Indian (USA) *J Noseda* 75
2 b c Johannesburg(USA) —Half A Scent (USA) (Judge Smells (USA))
4428[3] 4986[6]

Manhattan Jack *G A Swinbank* a25 42
5 ch g Forzando—Manhattan Diamond (Primo Dominie)
5837[5] 6280[11]

Manic *Ernst Oertel* a62 53
4 br m Polar Falcon(USA) —Gentle Irony (Mazilier (USA))
262[2]

Manipulate *L M Cumani* 84
3 b c Machiavellian(USA) —Balalaika (Sadler's Wells (USA))
2825[9] 3711[3] 4661[2]

Mankanja (IRE) *W Jarvis* a69+
2 b f Orpen(USA) —Whispered Melody (Primo Dominie)
6309[2] 6710[7](6927)

Mannello *B Palling* 62
3 b f Mamalik(USA) —Isle Of Sodor (Cyrano De Bergerac)
1567[6] 2068[2] 2602[5] 2987[2] 4985[16]

Mannico (GER) *Mario Hofer* 99
3 b c Banyumanik(IRE) —Manon (Alzao (USA))
1176a[4] 1526a[U] 5543a[7] 5856a[6]

Mannikko (IRE) *G Wragg* 80
3 gr g Green Desert(USA) —Cassandra Go (IRE) (Indian Ridge)
988[2] (1378) 1672[3] 2329[5] 3802[3] 4562[7]

Man Of Fortune (IRE) *D Shaw*
2 b g Trans Island—Missfortuna (Priolo (USA))
4572[13] 4829[12]

Man Of Illusion (AUS) *P L Biancone* 104
5 b h Encosta De Lago(AUS) —Raunchy Ruler (AUS) (Rancho Ruler (AUS))
6127a[10]

Man Of Vision (USA) *M R Channon* a70
2 b c Kingmambo(USA) —Nalani (IRE) (Sadler's Wells (USA))
6867[3]

Man On Fire (IRE) *C Von Der Recke* 44
2 b c Spectrum(IRE) —Medina (IRE) (Pennekamp (USA))
6092a[11]

Man On The Nile (IRE) *W P Mullins* 85+
6 b g Snurge—Spirit Of The Nile (FR) (Generous (IRE))
5853a[4]

Manor Law (IRE) *C Collins* 87
4 b g Night Shift(USA) —Flush Rush (Zilzal (USA))
1156a[11]

Manouche *K A Ryan* a65 73
3 b g Highest Honor(FR) —Green Charter (Green Desert (USA))
445[3] 584[2](817) 1005[5] 1855[10] 2324[10]

Mansiya *C E Brittain* a62 63
4 ch m Vettori(IRE) —Bay Shade (USA) (Sharpen Up)
252[3] 462[10]693[14] 1645[14] 2248[10]

Manston (IRE) *B J Meehan* a96 97
3 ch g Indian Ridge—Bye Bold Aileen (IRE) (Warning)
1083[5] 1404[6] 1818[8]2739[13] 6101[3]

Mantle *J R Fanshawe* a76 61
4 b m Loup Sauvage(USA) —Kyle Rhea (In The Wings)
4973[2] 5426[3]5741[2] 6108[11] 6501[P]

Mantolini *Pat Eddery* a42 39
3 b g Bertolini(USA) —Leading Princess (IRE) (Double Schwartz)
4247[8] 5353[11] 5774[10]6619[11]

Many Volumes (USA) *H R A Cecil* 86
2 b c Chester House(USA) —Reams Of Verse (USA) (Nureyev (USA))
3417[3] 4768[6]

Maona (IRE) *G Miliani*
2 b f Cape Cross(IRE) —Miss Mimosa (IRE) (Salmon Leap (USA))
2475a[11]

Maraagel (USA) *Saeed Bin Suroor* 61+
3 b c Danzig(USA) —Hasnaael Reef (USA) (Seattle Slew (USA))
5272[9]

Maraahel (IRE) *Sir Michael Stoute* a100 125
5 b h Alzao(USA) —Nasanice (IRE) (Nashwan (USA))
743a[6] 1128[3] (1601) (2845) 3927[5]4679[2] 5964[6] 6782a[5]

Maraakez *J H M Gosden* 70+
3 b g Kalanisi(IRE) —Questabelle (Rainbow Quest (USA))
5203[4] 6053[9]

Marabout Directa (GER) *Andreas Lowe* 104
5 b h Big Shuffle(USA) —Musique (Hamas (IRE))
2941a[7] 4418a[6]

Maraca (IRE) *J H M Gosden* a76+ 26
2 b c Danehill Dancer(IRE) —Marasem (Cadeaux Genereux)
6214[19] (6386)

Marachi Band (USA) *E J O'Neill* a73 86
3 b f Dixieland Band(USA) —Khamsin (USA) (Mr Prospector (USA))
199[2] 544[3]859[8] (918) (1079) 1162[2] 1251[3] 1583[5]1837[7] 2537a[3] 3293[8]

Marahute (ITY) *L Camici*
2 ch f Wixim(USA) —Ormsby County (USA) (Carson City (USA))
5705a[2]

Marajaa (IRE) *W J Musson* a95 88
4 b g Green Desert(USA) —Ghyraan (IRE) (Cadeaux Genereux)
828[10] 1262[6] 1667[8]5877[9] 6221[17] (6397) 6692[2]

Marajel (IRE) *P W Chapple-Hyam* 70
3 b c Marju(IRE) —Idilic Calm (IRE) (Indian Ridge)
1087[9] 2146[4] (5023) 5755[10] 5872[14]

Maraseel (USA) *C E Brittain* 52
3 bb f Machiavellian(USA) —Cymbala (FR) (Assert)
4967[4]

Mara Spectrum (IRE) *B Grizzetti* 103
3 b f Spectrum(IRE) —Mara Dancer (Shareef Dancer (USA))
2694a[5]

Maraval *M Wellings* a42 58
3 b g Mark Of Esteem(IRE) —Mayaro Bay (Robellino (USA))
1652[14] 3074[8]

Marbaa (IRE) *S Dow* a70 76
3 b c Peintre Celebre(USA) —Bahareeya (USA) (Riverman (USA))
1674[4] 2343[5] 2919[5]5611[4] 6413[7]6635[8] 6848[6]6987[2]

Marbush (IRE) *D Selvaratnam* a117 89
5 ro h Linamix(FR) —Fig Tree Drive (USA) (Miswaki (USA))
204a[3] 353a[6](495a) (560a) 738a[4]

Marcavelly (USA) *W Mott* 111
2 b c Johannesburg(USA) —Darkjewel (USA) (Majestic Light (USA))
5415a[2]

Marcello *P F I Cole* a59 60
3 b c Diktat—Girl From Ipanema (Salse (USA))
630[7] 710[2]900[5] 1052[7] 1291[14]4245[9] 5035[11]5474[11] 5885[6]

Marchand D'Argent (FR) *N Clement* 92
3 b c Marchand De Sable(USA) —Masslama (FR) (No Pass No Sale)
3342a[11]

Marchand D'Or (FR) *F Head* 121
3 gr g Marchand De Sable(USA) —Fedora (FR) (Kendor (FR))
(2941a) 3564a[6] (4191a) 5701a[7]

March Gold (IRE) *H Morrison* a55 45
3 ch f Rich Man's Gold(USA) —Dog Wood (SAF) (Fort Wood (USA))
669[7] 971[5] 1114[10]2535[10] 2929[14]

Marching Song *R Hannon* a95 104
4 b g Royal Applause—Marl (Lycius (USA))
667[5] 2012[2] 2776[8]3493[3] 3926[3] 4529[5] 5175[8] 5523[8]

Marc Of Brilliance (USA) *G L Moore* 75
3 ch g Sunday Silence(USA) —Rahcak (IRE) (Generous (IRE))
5934[4]

Marcosdream (IRE) *Jarlath P Fahey* 52
5 ch m Lord Of Appeal—Lady Taleca (IRE) (Exhibitioner)
6648[10]

Marcus Andronicus (USA) *A P O'Brien* 116
3 b c Danehill(USA) —Fiji (Rainbow Quest (USA))
1131[2] 1718a[2] 2721[4] 3494[14]

Mardi *W J Haggas* a73 60
2 b g Montjeu(IRE) —Portorosa (USA) (Irish River (FR))
5892[5] 6644[3] (6757)

Mardus Di San Jore *M Marcialis*
2 b f Dushyantor(USA) —Mar (ITY) (Roakarad (IRE))
5705a[6]

Marend (FR) *D Sepulchre* 119
5 ch g Green Tune(USA) —Marende (FR) (Panoramic)
1558a[4] 2277a[8] 4169a[4] 4861a[3]

Margaret's Dream (IRE) *D Carroll* a49 62
5 b m Muhtarram(USA) —Acidanthera (Alzao (USA))
184[8] 312[7]399[7] 768[2]1393[3] 1727[8]1914[13] 2195[3] 2811[7]3786[8] 4363[3]

Margarets Wish *T Wall* a38 43
6 gr m Cloudings(IRE) —Gentle Gain (Final Straw)
55[7] 361[9]

Margine Rosso (IRE) *R Brogi* 103
3 b c Night Shift(USA) —Elisa War (Warning)
1175a[7] 6364a[4]

Maria Antonia (IRE) *P A Blockley* a66+ 59
3 ch f King's Best(USA) —Annieirwin (IRE) (Perugino (USA))
1351[7] 1733[8] 2465[5]5567[8] (5757) (5955) 6068[14] (6423) 6758[5]

Maria Gabriella (IRE) *C Laffon-Parias* 94
2 ch f Rock Of Gibraltar(IRE) —Celestial Lagoon (JPN) (Sunday Silence (USA))
6228a[4]

Maria Luisa (IRE) *David P Myerscough* 85
4 b m King's Best(USA) —Miss Amy R (USA) (Deputy Minister (CAN))
2011[7]

Maria Maria (IRE) *Mrs N Macauley* 47
5 ch m Among Men(USA) —Yiayia's Girl (Smackover)
301[13]

Mariaverdi *B J Meehan* a50
2 b f Diktat—Belinda (Mizoram (USA))
6186[10] 6710[4]

Ma Ridge *T D McCarthy* 32
2 ch c Tumbleweed Ridge—Ma Barnicle (IRE) (Al Hareb (USA))
2315[17] 4705[15] 5206[11]

Marikhar (IRE) *Seamus Fahey* a73 71
4 b g Alzao(USA) —Marilaya (IRE) (Shernazar)
6766[2]

Marina Gamba (IRE) *E A L Dunlop* 59
3 b f Galileo(IRE) —Appreciatively (USA) (Affirmed (USA))
2366[8] 4004[10]

Marine Parade *R Hannon* a69 74
2 b c Royal Applause—Ipanema Beach (Lion Cavern (USA))
1838[6] 2029[6] 3193[4] 4000[4] 4600[5]5655[19] 6460[2]

Mariotto (USA) *M Johnston* 87+
2 b c Swain(IRE) —Shamaat Hayaaty (IRE) (Sadler's Wells (USA))
4129[2] (4534)

Marist Madame *D K Ivory* a52 7
2 ch f Tomba—Linda's Schoolgirl (IRE) (Grand Lodge (USA))
2145[8] 3915[3] 4327[5]5084[17]

Marju's Gold *E J O'Neill* a51
2 b c Marju(IRE) —Dubious (Darshaan)
6950[8]

Marker *J A Geake* a48 74
6 ch g Pivotal—Palace Street (USA) (Secreto (USA))
777[5] 1188[5] 1474[13] 3094[8] 4211[5]4564[7] 5765[5] 6293[10]6595[14]

Markestino *T D Easterby* a50 54
3 b g Mark Of Esteem(IRE) —Mademoiselle Chloe (Night Shift (USA))
(1576) 2249[2] 2746[10] 3609[3]3785[11] (4199) 4695[3] 5062[11]

Market Day *L M Cumani* a100 92
2 b f Tobougg(IRE) —Makhsusah (IRE) (Darshaan)
2166[6] 2755[2] (3096) (3530) 4146[4]5157[5] 5503[11] (6100)

Market Forces *H R A Cecil* a70
2 b f Lomitas—Quota (Rainbow Quest (USA))
6349[4]

Market Watcher (USA) *Seamus Fahey* a80+ 58
5 b g Boundary(USA) —Trading (USA) (A.P. Indy (USA))
(6560) (6685)

Markington *J D Bethell* a74 78
3 b g Medicean—Nemesia (Mill Reef (USA))
536[2] 731[4] 1005[4]1605[5] 2324[3] 2786[3] 3310[2] (3760) 4173[5]5284[10]

Marko Jadeo (IRE) *R A Harris* a88d 80
8 b g Eagle Eyed(USA) —Fleeting Quest (Rainbow Quest (USA))
36[2] 89[10]192[2] (321) 340[4] (476) 541[6] 667[11]1545[10] 2405[3] 2531[3] 6352[8]6446[8] 6696[2]6835[5] (6858) 6932[3] 6938[4]

Markovitch *P W Chapple-Hyam* 107
3 b c Mark Of Esteem(IRE) —Perdicula (IRE) (Persian Heights)
(1070) 2030[3] 3778a[4] 4358[8] 5400a[6] 6203[6]

Markusha *Jamie Poulton* a32 46
8 b g Alhijaz—Shafir (IRE) (Shaadi (USA))
35[12] 394[9]

Marlion (FR) *B R Johnson* 17
4 gr g Linamix(FR) —Marzipan (IRE) (Green Desert (USA))
1670[10]

Marlyn Ridge *D K Ivory* a66 47
2 b g Tumbleweed Ridge—Kayartis (Kaytu)
2315[12] 5091[12] 5261[6]5655[24]

Marmaida (IRE) *W J Knight* 82
2 b f Danetime(IRE) —Marathon Maid (Kalaglow)
(2178) 2598[2] 3084[7] 4006[3] 4427[5] 4815[6]5655[13]

Marmooq *A M Hales* a73 80
3 ch g Cadeaux Genereux—Portelet (Night Shift (USA))
1049[2] 1345[15] (2160) 2525[3] 2831[5] 3212[3]4573[4] (5031) 5688[6]5907[9]

Marmota (IRE) *M Johnston* a64 45
3 b c King's Best(USA) —Reloy (USA) (Liloy (FR))
(566) 1182[7] 2209[10] 3156[5]

Maromito (IRE) *R Bastiman* a50 60
9 b g Up And At 'Em—Amtico (Bairn (USA))
864[16] 943[3] 1228[4]1466[3] 1722[3]1909[11]

Maroussies Wings (IRE) *P C Haslam* 108
3 b f In The Wings—Maroussie (FR) (Saumarez)
1423[2] 1777[3] 2772[3] (4543a) 5155[4]

Marozi (USA) *M A Jarvis* 80+
2 ch c Forest Wildcat(USA) —Chitka (USA) (Jade Hunter (USA))
6200[2]

Marquee (IRE) *P A Blockley* 52
2 b c Mark Of Esteem(IRE) —Queen's Ransom (IRE) (Last Tycoon)
5111[5] 5883[11]

Marriage Value (IRE) *J A Osborne* a58 79
3 b f Marju(IRE) —Braari (USA) (Gulch (USA))
717[3] 1067[15] 1843[13] 2329[13] 2756[8]5756[15]

Marriaj (USA) *B Smart* 78
2 bb c Giant's Causeway(USA) —Be My Sweetheart (USA) (No Robbery)
5901[3] 6173[2]

Marron Flore *A J Lidderdale* a41
3 ch f Compton Place—Flore Fair (Polar Falcon (USA))
60[9] 533[7]790[5] 6233[5]6440[7] 6533[4]6649[6]
6794[4]6958[6]

Marronnier (IRE) *T D Easterby* 68
3 ch g Vettori(IRE) —Reservation (IRE) (Common Grounds)
730[6] 1182[8]

Marryl *M W Easterby*
2 b g Warningford—Nordico Princess (Nordico (USA))
1080[10] 1420[11] 1595[12] 3385[11]3831[9]

Marsad (IRE) *J Akehurst* a62 64
12 ch g Fayruz—Broad Haven (IRE) (Be My Guest (USA))
22[10] 171[9]336[11]

Marshall (FR) *S Jensen* 115
6 b h Anabaa(USA) —Monitrice (FR) (Groom Dancer (USA))
2492a[6]

Marshallspark (IRE) *R A Fahey* a63 74
7 b g Fayruz—Lindas Delight (Batshoof)
67[11] 288[7]408[8] 1102[10] 1397[2]1539[3]

Marshman (IRE) *M H Tompkins* a93 96d
7 ch g College Chapel—Gold Fly (IRE) (Be My Guest (USA))
1935[6] 2681[2] 3079[9] 3926[18] 4760[8]5355[10] 5943[11]
6221[16] 6397[13]

Martharum *J J Quinn* a23 50
3 ch f Muhtarram(USA) —Needwood Truffle (IRE) (Brief Truce (USA))
2543[19] 3257[7] 3759[9]4201[4] 4656[6] 5060[11]

Martian Mystery *M Madgwick* 31
3 ch f Bluegrass Prince(IRE) —Martian Melody (Enchantment)
3090[12] 4162[7]

Martines (FR) *B Grizzetti* 94
4 gr m Linamix(FR) —Fracci (Raise A Cup (USA))
6002a[6]

Maruka Shenck (JPN) *T Setoguchi* 118
3 b c Sunday Silence(USA) —Shenck (Zafonic (USA))
6530a[12]

Marvin Gardens *P S McEntee* a33 43
3 b g Largesse—En Grisaille (Mystiko (USA))
776[6] 2070[10] 3378[8]4304[3] 5273[8] 5728[11]

Marvo *M H Tompkins* 76
2 b c Bahamian Bounty—Mega (IRE) (Petardia)
5454[8] (5900)

Mary Anastatia (USA) *Eamon Tyrrell* a31 66
4 ch m Lion Cavern(USA) —Vannozza (Kris)
84[8]

Mary Delaney (USA) *M J Wallace* a81 68
3 b f Hennessy(USA) —Crafty Emerald (USA) (Crafty Prospector (USA))
(981) 1208[15] 2353[2]

Mary Gray *M Johnston* a54 69
4 gr m Mujahid(USA) —Ancestry (Persepolis (FR))
825[5] 990[10] 1138[14]1436[3] 1748[7] 2242[7]2751[2]
2927[6] 3135[5]

Mary Louhana *M Delzangles* 106
3 b f Loup Solitaire(USA) —Miss Daisy (FR) (Shirley Heights)
3515a[6] 4543a[2] 5220a[10] 5700a[4]

Mary Pekan (IRE) *V Valiani* 91
4 b m Sri Pekan(USA) —Mary Rose (ITY) (Royal Academy (USA))
1368a[3]

Masai Moon *B R Millman* 79
2 b c Lujain(USA) —Easy To Imagine (USA) (Cozzene (USA))
2530[9] 3363[4] 4161[5] 4774[3] 5133[2]5546[4] 5788[2]

Maseem *Rae Guest* a54 59
3 ch c Generous(IRE) —Entail (USA) (Riverman (USA))
3073[8] 3717[4]

Mashaahed *B W Hills* 112+
3 b c In The Wings—Patacake Patacake (USA) (Bahri (USA))
1070[3] 1603[3] (2175) 2775[5] (5360) 5657[3] 5968[4]

Mashaair (IRE) *B W Hills* a61 73
3 ch c King's Best(USA) —Al Bahathri (USA) (Blushing Groom (FR))
1845[3] 3909[3] 4287[2] 4891[5] 5611[8]

Maskaraid *B R Millman* a18 19
2 b g Iron Mask(USA) —Radiant Sky (IRE) (Spectrum (IRE))
4163[10] 5387[12] 5646[13]

Maslak (IRE) *E A L Dunlop* a81 82
2 b g In The Wings—Jeed (IRE) (Mujtahid (USA))
3417[5] 4458[5] 4992[2]

Mason Ette *C G Cox* 78
2 br f Grand Lodge(USA) —Karlaska (Lashkari)
2816[3] 3796[2] 4295[2]

Masquerader (USA) *I Mohammed* a99 73
4 ch h Unbridled(USA) —Guise (USA) (Believe It (USA))
204a[13]

Massaro Pape (IRE) *L M Cumani* a74+ 83+
4 b h Intikhab(USA) —Megeve (IRE) (Ahonoora)
(1165) 1673[3] (Dead)

Massenzio (IRE) *J H M Gosden* a59 72
2 b c Green Desert(USA) —Monnavanna (IRE) (Machiavellian (USA))
2144[5] 2409[4] 4934[6]5449[3] 5940[6]

Massey *C R Dore* a49 9
10 br g Machiavellian(USA) —Massaraat (USA) (Nureyev (USA))
196[5] 274[12]288[13] 408[4]613[10] 784[7]876[9]
6799[13](6962)

Massif Centrale *D R C Elsworth* 103
5 ch g Selkirk(USA) —Madame Dubois (Legend Of France (USA))
1511[7] 1933[4] 2229[13] 4770[7] 5325[8]

Massive (IRE) *M R Channon* 100
2 b c Marju(IRE) —Khatela (IRE) (Shernazar)
3976[12] (4650) 5308[2] 5759[2] 6000a[2] 6456a[13]

Mass Media (USA) *R J Frankel* a117
5 br h Touch Gold(USA) —Sultry Allure (USA) (Forty Niner (USA))
2093a[3] 4384a[3]

Masta Plasta (IRE) *J Howard Johnson* 105
3 b c Mujadil(USA) —Silver Arrow (USA) (Shadeed (USA))
3076[5] 3585[9] 4174[5] 4803[6] 5182[13]

Master Ben (IRE) *S R Bowring* a49 41
3 b g Carrowkeel(IRE) —Java Jive (Hotfoot)
69[11] 193[6]1216[8] 1576[9]

Master Cobbler (IRE) *J Akehurst* 81
4 b g Alhaarth(IRE) —Lady Joshua (IRE) (Royal Academy (USA))
1847[4] 2176[12] (3028) 4036[3]

Master Golfer (USA) *B W Hills* 27
2 br g Mr Greeley(USA) —Princess Leia (USA) (Skywalker (USA))
3222[14] 3417[13] 4000[11]

Master Mahogany *R J Hodges* a80 82
5 b g Bandmaster(USA) —Impropriety (Law Society (USA))
5833[4] 6259[5] 6417[3]6502[10]

Master Malarkey *Mrs C A Dunnett* a41 44
3 b g Tipsy Creek(USA) —Girl Next Door (Local Suitor (USA))
795[10] 1100[12] 1261[6] 1534[4]1768[11] 2263[4]
2644[10]3821[5] 4462[11] 4663[5] 5874[10]

Master Mark *P D Evans* 49
3 b g Mark Of Esteem(IRE) —Sur Le Fil (IRE) (Funambule (USA))
948[14] 1141[8] 1652[9]

Master Marvel (IRE) *T J O'Mara* 96
5 ch h Selkirk(USA) —Insijaam (USA) (Secretariat (USA))
1156a[3] 3123a[6] 4031a[5]

Master'n Commander *C A Cyzer* a73 69
4 ch g Zafonic(USA) —Magical Retreat (USA) (Sir Ivor (USA))
114[5] 218[3]443[12] 557[3]713[3] 1163[13]1334[5] 2132[12]
2647[2]

Master Nimbus *J J Quinn* 52
6 b g Cloudings(IRE) —Miss Charlie (Pharly (FR))
2707[6] 3941[2] (4380)

Master Of Destiny (IRE) *H J Collingridge* a55 45
2 ch g Compton Place—Memo (Groom Dancer (USA))
4485[6] 5066[12] 5608[6]

Masterofthecourt (USA) *H Morrison* 79+
3 ch g Horse Chestnut(SAF) —Great Verdict (AUS) (Christmas Tree (AUS))
1135[7] (1741) 2174[5] 3589[7]

Master Of The Race *Tom Dascombe* a77 91
4 ch g Selkirk(USA) —Dust Dancer (Suave Dancer (USA))
2114[2] 2657[11] 3401[8]4112[7] 6992[4]

Master Pegasus *C F Wall* a68 90
3 b g Lujain(USA) —Seeking Utopia (Wolfhound (USA))
(1845) 2774[9] 4298[6] 4819[3]

Master Pip *T H Caldwell* 7
4 b g Wizard King—Tachelle (IRE) (Elbio)
1492[6] 4431[13]

Master Rattle *Jane Southcombe* a52 45
7 b g Sabrehill(USA) —Miss Primula (Dominion)
1623a[3]

Master Robbie *R Bouresly* a74 81
7 b g Piccolo—Victoria's Secret (IRE) (Law Society (USA))
204a[11] 353a[14]434a[9]

Mastership (IRE) *C E Brittain* a80+ 66
2 ch c Best Of The Bests(IRE) —Shady Point (IRE) (Unfuwain (USA))
2586[5] 2979[5] 4366[8]4829[7] (5482) 6106[2]
6569[2](6933)

Master Theo (USA) *Lucinda Featherstone* a93 79
5 b g Southern Halo(USA) —Lilian Bayliss (IRE) (Sadler's Wells (USA))
57[5]

Master William *W G M Turner* 14
2 b g Hello Mister—Grecian Melody (Heroic Air)
6175[12]

Mataram (USA) *W Jarvis* a81+ 59
3 b g Matty G(USA) —Kalinka (USA) (Mr Prospector (USA))
(3011) 3644[2] 4144[9] (5211) 6206[15]6502[3] 6868[4]

Materialize (USA) *H R A Cecil* a69 75
3 b f Chester House(USA) —A La Mode (USA) (Known Fact (USA))
1260[3] 1669[10] 3451[3] 4375[5] 4945[7]5889[10]

Material Witness (IRE) *W R Muir* a89 97
9 b g Barathea(IRE) —Dial Dream (Gay Mecene (USA))
1935[2] 2555[5] 2776[2]3470[2] 4042[7] 4535[9] 4798[4]
5591[8]6239[11]

Mathoor *Sir Michael Stoute* 58+
3 ch c Fantastic Light(USA) —Madame Dubois (Legend Of France (USA))
1680[9]

Maticochina *Laura Grizzetti*
2 b f Zamindar(USA) —Savignano (Polish Precedent (USA))
2475a[3]

Matinee Idol *Mrs S Lamyman* a1 63
3 ch f In The Wings—Bibliotheque (USA) (Woodman (USA))
2350[5] 2970[5] 3303[3] 4263[6] 4734[9]5318[4] 6790[12]
6957[9]

Matispingo (IRE) *Laura Grizzetti*
2 ch f Mark Of Esteem(IRE) —Celestial Bold (IRE) (Persian Bold)
5705a[9]

Matrix (GER) *W Baltromei* 110
5 b h Big Shuffle(USA) —Massena (GER) (Konigsstuhl (GER))
(885a) 1717a[2] 1973a[5] 2799a[10] 3755a[2]
4858a[4]5779a[9] 6230a[7]

Matsunosuke *A B Coogan* 85+
4 b g Magic Ring(IRE) —Lon Isa (Grey Desire)
1211[4] (1496) 1662[15] 2182[9] 2618[7] (3447)
3715[3]3880[6] 3972[U] 4486[2] 4811[8] 5148[2]

Matterofact (IRE) *Mrs P N Dutfield* 77
3 b f Bold Fact(USA) —Willow Dale (IRE) (Danehill (USA))
1672[10] 2189[11] 2509[6] 2987[6] 3349[8]3864[3] 4164[7]
4756[5] 5167[6]

Matty Tun *J Balding* a61 77
7 b g Lugana Beach—B Grade (Lucky Wednesday)
3038[12] 4598[4] 4771[7] 5333[5] 5535[13]6009[17]

Maturus Ardor (GER) *Mario Hofer* 101
3 b c Silvano(GER) —Marousskia (GER) (Feenpark (GER))
2493a[2]

Matuza (IRE) *W R Muir* a95+ 85
3 ch c Cadeaux Genereux—Aoife (IRE) (Thatching)
2014[7] 2329[3] 2509[2] 3403[4]3795[3] 4102[12] (6352)
6496[3]6583[5] 6720[4]

Maud's Cat (IRE) *A P Jarvis* a54 59
3 b f Black Minnaloushe(USA) —Tree House (USA) (Woodman (USA))
2753[6] 4382[2] 4489[4]5015[7] 6476[6] 6870[7]

Maunby Reveller *P C Haslam* a47 47
4 b g Benny The Dip(USA) —Aunt Tate (Tate Gallery (USA))
28[4] 303[5]688[9]

Mauralakana (FR) *P L Biancone* 112
3 b f Muhtathir—Jimkana (FR) (Double Bed (FR))
1719a[5] 2491a[6] 4035a[3] 5984a[2] 6340a[7]

Mawazeen (IRE) *N I M Rossiter* 68
5 b m Unfuwain(USA) —Atnab (USA) (Riverman (USA))
1798[4] 2533[5] 4104[13] 4528[9]

Maxemull *D J Wintle* a7
3 b f Mull Of Kintyre(USA) —Silver Gyre (IRE) (Silver Hawk (USA))
132[10] 215[10]380[10] 617[9]

Maxima (ITY) *M Bebbu*
2 ch f Spymaster(USA) —Melara (Manila (USA))
2475a[9]

Maximix *B W Hills* a70 63+
3 gr g Linamix(FR) —Time Will Show (FR) (Exit To Nowhere (USA))
590[5] 720[12]2713[9] 2933[6] 4847[8] (6037)

Maxim's (ARG) *R A Kvisla* a90
5 b h Lode(USA) —Mari's Ballerina (USA) (Mari's Book (USA))
3535[9]

Maxolini *J J Quinn* 21
3 ch g Bertolini(USA) —Evening Falls (Beveled (USA))
1218[13]

Max Scal (IRE) *P J Rothwell* a49 69
5 b g Danehill Dancer(IRE) —Slightly Latin (Ahonoora)
567[8]

Maxxi Arte (IRE) *J Cassidy* 101
3 ch f Danehill Dancer(IRE) —Liyana (IRE) (Shardari)
5198a[5] 5984a[8]

Mayadeen (IRE) *J G M O'Shea* 77d
4 b g King's Best(USA) —Inaaq (Lammtarra (USA))
3289[5] 3528[5] 4149[11] 4871[10] 6008[15]

Maya's Prince *M D I Usher* a45
4 b g Easycall—Delciana (IRE) (Danehill (USA))
778[11] 900[8] 1166[10]1753[14] 3073[10] 3386[10]3595[6]

Maybach *B Bo* a98 96
5 gr h Machiavellian(USA) —Capote Line (USA) (Capote (USA))
1659a[4] 2123a[6] (5224a) 6516[10]

Maybe Better (AUS) *B Mayfield-Smith* 115
4 b g Intergaze(AUS) —Amarula (AUS) (Rubiton (AUS))
(6346a) 6392a[3]

Mayden Dawn *Miss E C Lavelle* a60 51
3 ch f Silver Wizard(USA) —Delight Of Dawn (Never So Bold)
3849[8] 4245[12] 4757[8]5450[15] 5576[11] 6632[8]

Mayden Dream *D K Ivory* a5
4 b m Silver Wizard(USA) —I Have A Dream (SWE) (Mango Express)
293[10]

Mayireneyrbel *R Ingram* a49 60
2 ch f Auction House(USA) —Travel Secret (Blakeney)
3210[9] 3851[5] 4394[5]6650[7]

Maylea Gold (IRE) *Miss J Feilden* 43
3 b g Fasliyev(USA) —Clipping (Kris)
1430[9] 2235[9] 2587[14] 3045[9] 3306[15]

May Night (USA) *Frederick J Seitz* a100 105
3 ch f Gulch(USA) —Riverjinsky (USA) (Riverman (USA))
5198a[10]

Maynooth Prince (IRE) *A Dickman* a12 23
4 b g Spectrum(IRE) —Muffle (Sadler's Wells (USA))
6304[10]

Mayonga (IRE) *Sir Mark Prescott* a104 81
3 ch f Dr Fong(USA) —Mayara (IRE) (Ashkalani (IRE))
(5988) (6190) 6574a[2]

Mayoress *A Fabre* 96
3 b f Machiavellian(USA) —Minister Wife (USA) (Deputy Minister (CAN))
1874a[6]

Mayor Of London (USA) *M Johnston* a54 80
2 b c Carson City(USA) —Lustre (USA) (Halo (USA))
4109[4] (4566) 4882[10] 5459[7] 6074[11]

Maysarah (IRE) *G A Butler* a77 56
2 b f Green Desert(USA) —Royale (IRE) (Royal Academy (USA))
4994[2] 5464a[20]

Maysoor *M Johnston* 67
3 ch c Selkirk(USA) —Just Dreams (Salse (USA))
1283[6] 1854[4]

Maystock *B G Powell* a86 77
6 ch m Magic Ring(IRE) —Stockline (Capricorn Line)
420[13] 1247[7](1690) 1800[2] 2067[4] 2653[4] 3028[3]
3743[2]4104[3] 4530[4] 5383[11] (5564) 6075[2]6438[5]

Mayyas *C C Bealby* a54
6 b g Robellino(USA) —Amidst (Midyan (USA))
6680[4] 6971[2]

Mazindar (USA) *P T Midgley* a48 43
4 bb g Zamindar(USA) —Fantastic Bloom (VEN) (Imperial Ballet (IRE))
1197[12] 1393[10]

Mazin Lady *Miss J A Camacho* a68 67
2 b f Kyllachy—Amazing Bay (Mazilier (USA))
2972[6] 3745[5] 3982[4] 4519[2] 5065[4]5238[2] 5753[2]
6255[2]6400[2]

Mazoran (FR) *D G Bridgwater* 11
2 ch g Majorien—Isgala (FR) (Galetto (FR))
5067[13] 5347[12]

Mccormack (IRE) *Micky Hammond* a7 55
4 b g Desert Story(IRE) —La Loba (IRE) (Treasure Kay)
612[10] 1252[7] 1503[5]2108[7] 2707[8] 3377[7] 3484[9]

Mceldowney *M Johnston* a76 95
4 b g Zafonic(USA) —Ayodhya (IRE) (Astronef)
869[4] 976[8] 1233[2] (1389) 1756[11] (2018)(2193)
2238[4] 2452[2] 2723[5] 3533[8]3888[5] 4036[4] 4346[2]
4883[6] 5010[4]5325[5] 5811[7]

Mcnairobi *P D Cundell* a91 86
3 b f Josr Algarhoud(IRE) —Bonita Bee (King Of Spain)
1640[6] 2575[2] 3367[6](3647) (4249) (4395) 5019[11]
5294[4] 5666[11]

Mcqueen (IRE) *B D Leavy* a66 66
6 ch g Barathea(IRE) —Bibliotheque (USA) (Woodman (USA))
955[12] 3454[7]

Me *P W Chapple-Hyam* 70
3 b f Green Desert(USA) —Myself (Nashwan (USA))
1085[12] 2864[13] 3864[5]

Mea Domina (USA) *R McAnally* 115
5 b m Dance Brightly(CAN) —Madame Pandit (USA) (Wild Again (USA))
6614a[4]

Meadow Floss *S Kirk* a37 58+
3 b f Cyrano De Bergerac—Pea Green (Try My Best (USA))
2575[8] 3032[3]

Meadow Mischief (FR) *E A L Dunlop* a75 90+
3 ch c Halling(USA) —Moonlight Saunter (USA) (Woodman (USA))
453[5] 515[2]695[2] (909) 1648[2] 2677[3] 3539[3] (4537)
4770[3] 5531[12]

Meadow Soprano (IRE) *M P Sunderland* 49
4 b m Imperial Ballet(IRE) —Good Aim (IRE) (Priolo (USA))
4944[2]

Meancog (IRE) *Peter Henley* 68
2 ch f Monashee Mountain(USA) —Mislead (IRE) (Distinctly North (USA))
5692a[8]

Me And Mine (USA) *T D Barron*
2 b g Belong To Me(USA) —Iron Miss (USA) (Fit To Fight (USA))
1136[6] 2451[2] 2806[4] 3394[2] (Dead)

Meantime (USA) *G Prodromou* a34 74
3 b g Point Given(USA) —Interim (Sadler's Wells (USA))
1260[5] 1613[9] 2142[7]2933[8] 4268[6] 5770[12]

Measured Response *J G M O'Shea* a67 64
4 ch g Inchinor—Seal Indigo (IRE) (Glenstal (USA))
114[3] 319[9]421[9] 965[12] 1568[4]2223[6] 2567[10] 4287[6]
6294[12]

Measured Tempo *Saeed Bin Suroor* 89+
2 b f Sadler's Wells(USA) —Allez Les Trois (USA) (Riverman (USA))
(6215)

Meathop (IRE) *R F Fisher* a33 38
2 b g Imperial Ballet(IRE) —Jacobina (Magic Ring (IRE))
6012[7] 6570[7] 6730[7]

Mecca's Mate *D W Barker* a67 107
5 gr m Paris House—Clancassie (Clantime)
1778[9] 2115[3] 2369a[3] 2720[14] 3076[6]4738[10] 4832[7]
5158[5] 5358[8] 5534[6]5812[5] (5921) 5957[4]

Medalla (FR) *M Brittain* a34 76
6 gr h Medaaly—Sharp Cracker (IRE) (Hamas (IRE))
4068[11] 4972[8]

Meddle *J Jay* a40 58
3 b f Diktat—Ingerence (FR) (Akarad (FR))
722[7] 984[12]2529[14] 4734[14] 6237[10]

Medfae (KSA) *C F Wall* a67 57
3 b c Florida's Son(ARG) —Maureen's Hope (USA) (Northern Baby (CAN))
669[11] 2934[5] (3730)

Media Puzzle (USA) *D K Weld* 114
9 ch g Theatrical—Market Slide (USA) (Gulch (USA))
932a[5] (2154a) 2773[P] (Dead)

Medici Code *H Morrison* a61 48
2 ch c Medicean—Fiveofive (IRE) (Fairy King (USA))
4074[10] 5106[5] 5379[8]

Medicine Path *E J O'Neill* 110
2 b c Danehill Dancer(IRE) —Indian Mystery (IRE) (Indian Ridge)
(3498) 4037[5] 5521[2] 6104[3]

Medieval Maiden *W J Musson* a49 70
3 gr f Zaha(CAN) —Brillante (FR) (Green Dancer (USA))
3045[2] 4661[9] 4973[10]

Meditation *I A Wood* a77 88
4 ch m Inchinor—Trojan Desert (Troy)
327[4] 555[2](576) 662[2]1057[2] 1348[4] 1673[6] 1802[3] 2184[7]2293[3] (2459) (2705) 2860[6] (3450) (3953) 4343[6] 4593[4]4965[9] 5345[13] 6868[10]

Medley *R Hannon* 91+
2 ch f Danehill Dancer(IRE) —Marl (Lycius (USA))
2328[2] 2800[4] (3495)

Mednaya (IRE) *R Gibson* 105
3 b f Anabaa(USA) —Sopran Dandy (IRE) (Doyoun)
2739[12] 4860a[5]

Medora Leigh (USA) *J A R Toller* a57 57
4 ch m Swain(IRE) —Gaily Tiara (USA) (Caerleon (USA))
218[12] 318[9]

Meelup (IRE) *P G Murphy* a61 70
6 ch g Night Shift(USA) —Centella (IRE) (Thatching)
596[9] 826[14]965[9] 1204[10] 1400[11]2401[6] 2612[4] 2862[6]3115[2] 3616[2] 4005[5] 4448[7] 4673[5]5276[12] 5652[7]

Meerlust *E F Vaughan* a36 38
2 ch f Compton Place—Le Pin (Persian Bold)
4753[10] 5638[10] 5876[7]

Meeting Of Minds *W Jarvis* a46
2 b f Mind Games—Turn Back (Pivotal)
6821[6] 6905[5]

Me Fein *B J Curley* 33
2 gr g Desert Prince(IRE) —Attachment (USA) (Trempolino (USA))
5067[12] 5297[11] 5915[15]

Megalala (IRE) *J J Bridger* a59 59
5 b g Petardia—Avionne (Derrylin)
84[9] 217[8]291[4] 459[7]557[7] 1753[9] 2132[6]2262[4] 2956[DSQ] 3705[10] 3933[10] 4450[4](5573)

Megalo Maniac *R A Fahey* 50+
3 b g Efisio—Sharanella (Shareef Dancer (USA))
817[8] 1032[12] 1252[10] 2284[13] 2529[13]3586[9] 4199[2] 4354[2] 4656[4]

Megaton *P Bowen* 71
5 ch g Nashwan(USA) —Pan Galactic (USA) (Lear Fan (USA))
1213[5]

Megavegas *P T Midgley* a33 36
3 b f Erhaab(USA) —Jade Pet (Petong)
3759[10] 5023[9] 5077[6] 5873[7]5951[4] 6306[9] 6557[8]

Meikle Barfil *J M Bradley* a69 79+
4 b g Compton Place—Oare Sparrow (Night Shift (USA))
1545[14] 2302[15] 2674[8] 3855[7] 4110[9]4462[7] 4587[5] (4962) 5131[7] 5378[9] 5878[11]

Meikle Beoch *Mrs H Sweeting*
4 b m Magic Ring(IRE) —Portvasco (Sharpo)
3919[13]

Meiner Scherzi (JPN) *R Inaba* 117
3 b c Grass Wonder(USA) —Aladeya (Machiavellian (USA))
6530a[4] 6850a[3]

Meisho Bowler (JPN) *T Shirai* a73 118
5 b h Taiki Shuttle(USA) —Nice Raise (USA) (Storm Cat (USA))
5717a[2] 6783a[RR]

Meisho Samson (JPN) *T Setoguchi* 124+
3 b c Opera House—My Vivien (JPN) (Dancing Brave (USA))
6612a[6]

Melaaya (USA) *M Johnston* 91
3 b f Aljabr(USA) —Saint Emilia (PER) (Saint Ballado (CAN))
2103[3] 3418[9]

Melalchrist *J J Quinn* a53 84d
4 b g Almaty(IRE) —Lawless Bridget (Alnasr Alwasheek)
1076[5] 1285[13] 1662[14] 2194[6] 3097[6]6223[12]

Melandre *M Brittain* a46 74
4 b m Lujain(USA) —Talighta (USA) (Barathea (IRE))
6773[12]

Melee *J Jay* a59 46
4 ch m Cadeaux Genereux—Nashmeel (USA) (Blushing Groom (FR))
84[2] 162[3]285[4]

Meliksah (IRE) *Mrs D Smith* 104
12 ch g Thatching—Lady Of Shalott (King's Lake (USA))
1717a[8] 2799a[13] 5712a[11]

Mellanie Surprise (HOL) *J Pubben* 65
3 bb f Platini(GER) —Sunday Surprise (HOL) (All Wins (USA))
2059a[9] 4383a[8]

Melmott *R Ingram* a54 40
6 ch g Piccolo—Time For Tea (IRE) (Imperial Frontier (USA))
419[11] 1240[9] 1513[13]

Melodian *M Brittain* a44 72
11 b h Grey Desire—Mere Melody (Dunphy)
869[7] 1187[9] 4205[12] 4570[3] 5064[3]5905[8]

Melograno (IRE) *Mark Campion* a51 51
6 ch g Hector Protector(USA) —Just A Treat (IRE) (Glenstal (USA))
182[4] 684[11]

Melpomene *M Johnston* a87 84
3 ch f Peintre Celebre(USA) —Lady Joyce (FR) (Galetto (FR))
4549[2] 5583[2] (6535) (6917)

Melrose Avenue (USA) *Saeed Bin Suroor* 109
4 b h Kris S(USA) —Sham Street (USA) (Sham (USA))
4096[8]

Mel's Moment (USA) *R J Price* a71 78
4 b g Storm Creek(USA) —One Moment In Time (USA) (Magesterial (USA))
2935[11] 3116[8] 3390[10]3817[18]

Melvino *T D Barron* a68 68
4 b g Josr Algarhoud(IRE) —Safe Secret (Seclude (USA))
1144[11] 1346[6] 1756[9] 2150[8] 2612[10]2736[5] 2927[5] 3192[2] 3431[2] 3983[3]4022[3] 4478[3] 4698[9] 4723[5] 5276[4]5451[4] 6158[6] 6317[10] 6571[6]6693[2] (6769) 6883[5] (6954)

Memorette (USA) *W Currin* a109 112
4 br m Memo(CHI) —Forever Fondre (USA) (Shahrastani (USA))
6614a[8]

Memphis Belle *G A Swinbank* a56 50
3 gr f Linamix(FR) —Clipper (Salse (USA))
5086[13] 5770[10] 6474[7]6871[3]

Memphis Man *D G Bridgwater* a76 82
3 b g Bertolini(USA) —Something Blue (Petong)
341[5] 550[5]831[3] 1250[6] 1617[9]2138[7] 2616[10] (4812) 5265 5540[12] 5476[3] 5684[5] 6033[10]6348[8] 6833[6]6892[8]

Memphis Marie *C N Allen* 44
2 b f Desert Sun—Spirito Libro (USA) (Lear Fan (USA))
4373[14]

Menestrol (FR) *D Prod'Homme* a99 102
4 ch h Dyhim Diamond(IRE) —Magaletta (FR) (Galetto (FR))
393a[5]

Me No Puppet *E J Alston* a41
2 b f Mtoto—Puppet Play (IRE) (Broken Hearted)
6257[9]

Mentik (RUS) *W Hickst* 97
4 ch h Tormount(USA) —Mugan (SU) (Mistnk)
5762a[8]

Menwaal (FR) *Kevin Prendergast* 104+
4 b g Montjeu(IRE) —Mythical Creek (USA) (Pleasant Tap (USA))
5853a[12]

Meohmy *M R Channon* a30 55+
3 b f Marju(IRE) —Meshhed (USA) (Gulch (USA))
1351[14] 1823[8] 2352[6] 2539[7] 3145[10]3378[9] 3592[11]

Mephistos Kick *Jean-Rene Auvray* a47
5 b g Kingmambo(USA) —Mempari (IRE) (Fairy King (USA))
459[8]

Mercari *Mrs J C McGregor* a47 48
4 ch m Bahamian Bounty—Aonach Mor (Anabaa (USA))
1608[5] 1947[10]

Merchant Bankes *W G M Turner* a70 68
3 b c Observatory(USA) —Lady Bankes (IRE) (Alzao (USA))
188[4] 403[5]1034[3] 2065[4] 2990[7] 4243[6] 5211[10]5741[6]

Mercury Chief (SAF) *Diego Lowther* a91 86
5 ch g London News(SAF) —Ivor's Girl (SAF) (Northern Guest (USA))
151a[6] 357a[7] 6093a[11]

Merdiff *W M Brisbourne* a48 30
7 b g Machiavellian(USA) —Balwa (USA) (Danzig (USA))
74[9] 171[3]381[10] 501[6]588[7] 602[10](734) 953[7]1001[7] 1305[3]1550[9] 1746[2]2260[6] 2413[4] 2793[8]2936[10] 6606[3]6793[5] 6955[7]

Meridia (GER) *Mario Hofer* 94
2 b f Monsun(GER) —Montserrat (GER) (Zilzal (USA))
6456a[6]

Meridian Grey (USA) *K A Ryan* 62
2 gr c More Than Ready(USA) —Love Rhythm (CAN) (Seeking The Gold (USA))
2733[7] 3328[8]

Merioneth (IRE) *W Kujath* 5
6 b h Key Of Luck(USA) —Mithl Al Hawa (Salse (USA))
456a[11]

Merlerault (USA) *P Demercastel* a89 88
3 b c Royal Anthem(USA) —Jungle Rhythm (USA) (Rhythm (USA))
392a[6]

Merlin's Dancer *D Nicholls* a94 105
6 b g Magic Ring(IRE) —La Piaf (FR) (Fabulous Dancer (USA))
705[4] 1438[4] (1602) 2227[8]2450[4] 2847[17] 3038[15] 4128[27] 5182[17]

Merlins Dreams *S Parr*
3 b c Dansili—Red Leggings (Shareef Dancer (USA))
6177[16]

Merlins Profit *G A Swinbank* a60 65
6 b g Wizard King—Quick Profit (Formidable (USA))
1194[4] (1227) 1394[4]2737[8]

Merlins Quest *J M Bradley* 61
2 b c Wizard King—Wonderland (IRE) (Dolphin Street (FR))
1284[8] 1770[6] 2185[11] 3031[9] 5065[11]5161[5] 5747[2] 6296[8]

Mermaid's Cry *R Brotherton*
4 b m Danzero(AUS) —Little Tramp (Trempolino (USA))
1763[9]

Merrymadcap (IRE) *M Blanshard* a84 81
4 b g Lujain(USA) —Carina Clare (Slip Anchor)
(405) (505) (641) 826[7] 1207[3]1410[3] 1773[2] 1882[2]2510[13] 3532[8] 3854[4]4209[5] 4575[3] 4989[6] 5108[4]5739[5] 6259[3]

Merrymaker *W M Brisbourne* a86 80
6 b g Machiavellian(USA) —Wild Pavane (Dancing Brave (USA))
1631[3] 2018[5] 2326[3] 2762[6] 2850[8](3522) 3955[11] 4175[6] 4792[4] 5174[4] 5531[9]

Merry Moon (IRE) *M Dods* a50 55
2 b f Night Shift(USA) —Adaja (Cadeaux Genereux)
2166[2] 2807[7] (3246) 3917[6]4509[10] 5747[7] 5860[7]

Merryvale Man *Miss Kariana Key*
9 b g Rudimentary(USA) —Salu (Ardross)
303[7]

Mersey Sound (IRE) *D R C Elsworth* a79 86
8 b g Ela-Mana-Mou—Coral Sound (IRE) (Glow (USA))
2460[3] 3114[3] (3446) (3743) 4036[11] 4369[2] 4560[8]6075[6] 6205[12]

Meru Camp (IRE) *P Winkworth* 57
2 ch g Loup Sauvage(USA) —Morgan Le Fay (Magic Ring (IRE))
2073[2] 2617[9] 3345[4] 3801[2] 4007[3]4926[9] 5323[11]

Merveilles *J H M Gosden* 90
3 b g Vettori(IRE) —Finlaggan (Be My Chief (USA))
1615[3] 2224[11] 2786[4] 3318[4]

Mesbaah (IRE) *M A Jarvis* 92
2 b g Noverre(USA) —Deyaajeer (USA) (Dayjur (USA))
3083[4] 3892[6] (4466) 5176[5]

Mescalera (GER) *B G Powell* a52
5 b m Alkalde(GER) —Miskinissa (GER) (Esclavo (FR))
1305[6] 1393[2]1538[13] 1914[14]2573[4]

Mesmeric (IRE) *B G Powell* a62 83
8 b g Sadler's Wells(USA) —Mesmerize (Mill Reef (USA))
420[12]

Messaia (GER) *S Smrczek*
3 b f Kornado—Mellinia (GER) (Dashing Blade)
2279a[15]

Messiah Garvey *M R Channon* a74+ 70
2 b c Lear Fan(USA) —Maid Of Camelot (Caerleon (USA))
3545[4] 4487[5] 4829[8] 5914[4] (6826)

Metal Guru *R Hollinshead* 58
2 ch f Ishiguru(USA) —Gemtastic (Tagula (IRE))
5076[5] 5563[4]

Metaphoric (IRE) *M L W Bell* 80
2 b c Montjeu(IRE) —Virgin Hawk (USA) (Silver Hawk (USA))
(6049)

Meteor Storm *W Dollase* 116
7 b h Bigstone(IRE) —Hunt The Sun (Rainbow Quest (USA))
6126a[5]

Methaaly (IRE) *W J Haggas* 77+
3 b g Red Ransom(USA) —Santorini (USA) (Spinning World (USA))
(2383) 5902[6]

Methodical *B G Powell* a58 61
4 b m Lujain(USA) —Simple Logic (Aragon)
230[9]

Methusaleh (IRE) *D Shaw* a70 79
3 b g Mutamam—Madamaa (IRE) (Alzao (USA))
7317[7] 1122[3] (1444) 2239[5] 2502[5] 3945[4]5483[6] 6733[6] 6898[10]

Metro Meteor (USA) *Linda Rice* 88
3 b g City Zip(USA) —Here Comes Nikki (USA) (The Prime Minister (USA))
6127a[7]

Metropolitan Chief *D M Simcock* 55
2 b c Compton Place—Miss Up N Go (Gorytus (USA))
5454[11] 5918[16]

Metropolitan Man *D M Simcock* 107
3 ch c Dr Fong(USA) —Preceder (Polish Precedent (USA))
1092[2] 1990[2] 2721[5] (3671) 4126[2] 5186[4]

Mexican (USA) *Micky Hammond* a53 58
7 b g Pine Bluff(USA) —Cuando Quiere (USA) (Affirmed (USA))
689[8]

Mexican Bob *Heather Dalton* a51 71
3 b g Atraf—Eskimo Nel (IRE) (Shy Groom (USA))
1552[6] 2411[4] 2919[6]3311[5] 4001[3] 4402[2] 4842[6]

Mexican Pete *A W Carroll* a74 84
6 b g Atraf—Eskimo Nel (IRE) (Shy Groom (USA))
2534[9] 2953[3] (3116) 3497[8]

Mezel (USA) *J-C Rouget* 95
3 b c Grand Slam(USA) —Spankin' (USA) (A.P. Indy (USA))
4168a[6]

Mezereon *D Carroll* a31 27
6 b m Alzao(USA) —Blown-Over (Ron's Victory (USA))
469[9]

Mezuzah *M W Easterby* 92
6 b g Barathea(IRE) —Mezzogiorno (Unfuwain (USA))
(726) 1043[12] 1280[8] 1985[6] 3040[8] 3937[2]4153[5] 4760[6] 4989[8] (5554) 5680[12] (6176) 6210[3]

Mezzo *L M Cumani* a34
3 b f Singspiel(IRE) —Real Time (Polish Precedent (USA))
2753[8]

Mezzolino (FR) *D Fechner* 82
2 b c Marchand De Sable(USA) —Lamboghina (GER) (Alkalde (GER))
5399a[5]

Mharadono (GER) *P Hirschberger* 97
3 b c Sharp Prod(USA) —Monalind (GER) (Park Romeo)
1176a[6] 1715a[8] 5856a[2] 6248a[5] 6529a[8]

Mia (POL) *Mrs P Townsley* a45
5 b m Llandaff(USA) —Mykos Dream (SWI) (Mykonos)
394[8] 458[12]

Miacarla *A Berry* 44
3 b f Forzando—Zarzi (IRE) (Suave Dancer (USA))
3383[11] 4136[3] 4948[6]

Mia Kross (IRE) *B Grizzetti* 93
3 b f Cape Cross(IRE) —Waku Waku (ITY) (Big Reef)
6362a[5]

Miami Tallyce (IRE) *E J O'Neill* a58
2 b f Montjeu(IRE) —Altishaan (Darshaan)
6441[10] 6558[11]6879[4]

Mia's Boy *P W Chapple-Hyam* 68
2 b c Pivotal—Bint Zamayem (IRE) (Rainbow Quest (USA))
5458[6]

Mica's Island (IRE) *Andrew Oliver* 88
2 b c Trans Island—Mica Male (ITY) (Law Society (USA))
5851a[6]

Michabo (IRE) *H Morrison* a77 94
5 b g Robellino(USA) —Mole Creek (Unfuwain (USA))
1021[8] 1517[2] 2176[2]2723[19] 4027[8] 4560[6]

Michaels Dream (IRE) *N Wilson* a49 47
7 b g Spectrum(IRE) —Stormswept (USA) (Storm Bird (CAN))
1199[8] 4086[7] 4380[14]4960[10]

Michaels Pride (IRE) *M Johnston* a54 73
4 b m Distant View(USA) —Ruacana Falls (USA) (Storm Bird (CAN))
1419[5] 3168[9]

Michikabu (IRE) *D K Weld* 96
3 b f Grand Lodge(USA) —Mood Indigo (IRE) (Indian Ridge)
5996a[13]

Mick Is Back *P D Evans* 50
2 b g Diktat—Classy Cleo (IRE) (Mujadil (USA))
3721[4] 4171[6] 4323[10]

Mick Jerome (IRE) *Rune Haugen* 101
5 b h Kahyasi—Acquilata (USA) (Irish River (FR))
1014a[8] 4189a[5] 5226a[6]

Mickleberry (IRE) *J D Bethell* a48 64
2 b f Desert Style(IRE) —Miss Indigo (Indian Ridge)
2139[6] 2500[4] 3358[5]4017[5]

Mickledo *A Bailey* a44 45
4 b g Perryston View—Ever So Lonely (Headin' Up)
789[13] 1465[11]

Micky Mac (IRE) *I W McInnes* 46
2 b g Lend A Hand—Gazette It Tonight (Merdon Melody)
1096[9] 2281[10] 3830[4] 4228[9]

Midas Way *P R Chamings* 106
6 ch g Halling(USA) —Arietta's Way (IRE) (Darshaan)
5551[6] 5967[6] 6334[5]

Middle Eastern *P A Blockley* a71 66
4 b g Mujahid(USA) —Swissmatic (Petong)
276[6] 489[8]3089[13] 3598[6] 4629[9]5286[3] 5684[9] 6061[4] 6288[3]6395[3] 6642[5]

Middleham (IRE) *M Johnston* 98
2 ch c Best Of The Bests(IRE) —Taalluf (USA) (Hansel (USA))
1588[5] (1790) 2127[7] 2844[3] 3962a[2] 5176[6]

Middlemarch (IRE) *J S Goldie* a81 78
6 ch g Grand Lodge(USA) —Blanche Dubois (Nashwan (USA))
726[19] 2378[2] 2853[2] 3168[5] 4068[2]4379[5] 4653[3] (4696) 5406[3] 5680[6] 6239[2](6259) 6502[6]

Middlethorpe *M W Easterby* a15 64
9 b g Noble Patriarch—Prime Property (IRE) (Tirol)
869[2] 990[9] 1144[12] 1729[12]1850[6]

Middleton Grey *A G Newcombe* a93 85
8 gr g Ashkalani(IRE) —Petula (Petong)
54[8] 238[12]632[8] 846[9]1220[14] 3434[10] 4602[4] 5167[10] (5755) 5937[4]6580[9]

Midge's Girl (IRE) *Mrs A Duffield* a46 44
3 b f Indian Lodge(IRE) —Blue Sky Lady (IRE) (Bluebird (USA))
53[8] 145[11]528[2] 637[5](690) 1447[4] 4881[12] 5840[12]

Midmaar (IRE) *M Wigham* a59 69
5 b g Cape Cross(IRE) —Khazinat El Dar (USA) (Slew O'Gold (USA))
95[5] 793[3]1393[4] 1465[2]1534[9] 1913[9](6372) 6884[6](6906) 6983[2]

Midnight Beauty (IRE) *M Delcher-Sanchez* 100
2 b c Celtic Swing—Thoroughly (IRE) (Woodman (USA))
(6000a)

Midnight Creek *A Sadik* a57 54
8 br g Tragic Role(USA) —Greek Night Out (IRE) (Ela-Mana-Mou)
688[7] 911[8]

Midnight Diamond (IRE) *Mrs L Williamson* a34 51
3 b c Alzao(USA) —Derena (FR) (Crystal Palace (FR))
1759[6] 2366[11] 3387[12]

Midnight Lace *J R Boyle* a56 51
4 ch m Tomba—Royal Passion (Ahonoora)
106[13] 659[2]678[2] 853[8]1746[6]

Midnight Moonlight *C F Wall* a69 32
3 ro f Bahamian Bounty—Magnolia (Petong)
2580[9] 3073[2]

Midnight Pearl (USA) *J Howard Johnson* 57
3 bb f Woodman(USA) —Elegant Ridge (IRE) (Indian Ridge)
1437[7] 3759[11]

Midnight Sky *Rae Guest* a51
2 b f Desert Prince(IRE) —Midnight Shift (IRE) (Night Shift (USA))
6575[6]

Midnight Traveller *L M Cumani* a54 84
3 b c Daylami(IRE) —Swift Dispersal (Shareef Dancer (USA))
1640[2] 1999[3] 2608[2] 3318[6] 5266[2]5869[5]

Mid Ocean *P W D'Arcy* a61 50
2 ch f Sakhee(USA) —Wavy Up (IRE) (Brustolon)
4765[14] 5095[7] 6298[12]

Midshipman *T Keddy* a73 65
8 b h Executive Man—Midler (Comedy Star (USA))
50[2] 1067[3]19[7] 571[9]882[7] 1164[4] 1553[11]4575[13] 5213[7] 5385[14]6059[11]

Mid Valley *J R Jenkins* a50 53
3 ch c Zilzal(USA) —Isabella D'Este (IRE) (Irish River (FR))
120[9] (528) 617[3]1215[5] 1888[8] 2479[6] 3164[7] 3932[3]4291[7] 5924[8] 6236[6]6542[2] 6725[6]

Miesque's Approval (USA) *M D Wolfson* 125
7 b h Miesque's Son(USA) —Win Approval (USA) (With Approval (CAN))
5824a[4] (6342a)

Mighty *Sir Michael Stoute* 75+
3 ch c Pivotal—Miswaki Belle (USA) (Miswaki (USA))
2028[3] 2662[3]

Mighty Dancer (IRE) *S Kirk* a64 62
3 b g Danehill Dancer(IRE) —K S Sunshine (USA) (Sunshine Forever (USA))
604[2] 984[2]1140[8] 1215[2] 1925[7]2101[7] 2480[3] 2795[8]3804[4] (4280) 5247[5]

Mighty Duel *J R Norton* 37
3 b g Daggers Drawn(USA) —Runs In The Family (Distant Relative)
2195[7] 2615[16] 3638[5] 3762[14] 6799[12]6957[10]

Mighty Kitchener (USA) *P Howling* a61 47
3 br g Mighty(USA) —Libeccio (NZ) (Danzatore (CAN))
4097 58446565 2246112895 7 68284 69673

Mighty Missouri (IRE) *W R Swinburn* 65
2 b g Danehill(USA) —Pietra Dura (Cadeaux Genereux)
359116 39496 41058

Mighty Moon *J O'Reilly* a91 86
3 gr g Daylami(IRE) —Moon Magic (Polish Precedent (USA))
17389 260714 (3900) 47232 52763 (6275) 6515666772 68365

Mighty Observer (IRE) *M H Tompkins* a48 48
3 b g Observatory(USA) —Staff Approved (Teenoso (USA))
22446 25915 33037

Mighty Splash *R Charlton* a45 59+
3 b f Cape Cross(IRE) —Serotina (IRE) (Mtoto)
38239 (4672) 63809

Migration *Mrs S Lamyman*
10 b g Rainbow Quest(USA) —Armeria (USA) (Northern Dancer (CAN))
(1222) 16147 18478 20444 261212

Mikao (IRE) *M H Tompkins* a55 94
5 b g Tagula(IRE) —Oumaladia (IRE) (Waajib)
(1071) 158413 307814 38886 43473 4676145325 3 (5678) 59207

Mika's Fable (FR) *Miss Tor Sturgis* 44
3 ch f Muhtathir—Baie Des Anges (Pas De Seul)
119214 16917 617714

Mikes Mate *C J Teague* a32 7
5 b g Komaite(USA) —Pitcairn Princess (Capricorn Line)
176710

Mike Stone *F Fuhrmann* 58
6 b g Factual(USA) —Perpetual Tiara (Green Desert (USA))
305a8 455a5 6121a13

Mikey (IRE) *Edgar Byrne* a69 56
3 b g Danetime(IRE) —Sharp Hint (Sharpo)
66379 67713

Mikimoto (IRE) *S C Williams* a50 47
4 b m Enrique—Etiquette (Law Society (USA))
66203 6705568525 69713

Miles Gloriosus (USA) *R Menichetti* 108
3 b c Repriced(USA) —Treasure Coast (CAN) (Foolish Pleasure (USA))
1872a5 2671a4 5718a3 6004a8

Military Cross *W J Haggas* 102+
3 b g Cape Cross(IRE) —Tipsy (Kris)
15057 22242 277421 34435 3889343563

Milk And Sultana *G A Ham* a58 52
6 b m Millkom—Premier Princess (Hard Fought)
1134 1587310 10 (382) 3946 (484) 6833 770624815 26367 31153 34112 3730838625 50974 60678(6128) 6238663744 6544266172 677513

Milky Bar Kid (IRE) *C F Wall* a37 52
3 ch c Night Shift(USA) —Baileys Cream (Mister Baileys)
2396

Millachy *B W Hills* 66
2 b f Kyllachy—Millazure (USA) (Dayjur (USA))
50522

Millagros (IRE) *I Semple* a70 76
6 b m Pennekamp(USA) —Grey Galava (Generous (IRE))
(109) 6038 57517 6321464797

Milla's Rocket (IRE) *D J Daly* a61 46
2 b f Galileo(IRE) —Tenable (Polish Precedent (USA))
545612 62428

Millbag (IRE) *D Selvaratnam* 107
5 bb h Cape Cross(IRE) —Play With Fire (FR) (Priolo (USA))
201a8 511a3

Millbrook Star (IRE) *M C Chapman* a42? 45
3 b g Orpen(USA) —Lady Bodmin (IRE) (Law Society (USA))
6177 12169 13866219213 33837 35411139103 52449 57279 58731068921 2 697010

Mill By The Stream *R Brotherton* a59 47
4 b g Lujain(USA) —Lonesome (Night Shift (USA))
8623 13035179415 250414 270010 27855 32403361710 39953 43891349708 503112

Mill End (IRE) *R M H Cowell* a57 61
4 br g Trans Island—Tumble (Mtoto)
33879 50715 5598762864 66488

Mill End Chateau *D K Ivory* a45 34
4 ch g Paris House—Mill End Quest (King's Signet (USA))
33836 39161164406 65488

Millennium Force *M R Channon* a82 94
8 b g Bin Ajwaad(IRE) —Jumairah Sun (IRE) (Scenic)
149a7 357a3 511a7 7189 1086142776 16 322311 39378 41729 4706953452 55914 58773

Millennium Hall *Miss Lucinda V Russell* 69
7 b g Saddlers' Hall(IRE) —Millazure (USA) (Dayjur (USA))
23817 27513 299810 36746 40721144787 469810 (Dead)

Millestan (IRE) *H R A Cecil* 88
2 b f Invincible Spirit(IRE) —Atnab (USA) (Riverman (USA))
26388 32272 (5083) 56725 621710

Millfield (IRE) *J Howard Johnson* 81
3 br g Elnadim(USA) —Eschasse (USA) (Zilzal (USA))
236311 27325 35846 437814 48311053092 0 568419

Millfields Dreams *M G Quinlan* a65 63
7 b g Dreams End—Millfields Lady (Sayf El Arab (USA))
(2494) 28135 29202 34383 3683239362 41412 448611 456412 52121153274 55764 6439664776 (6713) 69904

Milliegait *T D Easterby* 74
2 b f Tobougg(IRE) —Miller's Gait (Mill Reef (USA))
20264 40666 52838 (5613)

Millinsky (USA) *Rae Guest* a79+ 81
5 ch m Stravinsky(USA) —Millyant (Primo Dominie)
14482 22952 28584 344710 3913347252 52752 6035366825 69534

Million All Day (IRE) *W R Muir* a53 58
3 gr f Daylami(IRE) —Madame Nureyev (USA) (Nureyev (USA))
21719 23523 3016331567

Million Percent *C R Dore* a75 69
7 b g Ashkalani(IRE) —Royal Jade (Last Tycoon)
3238 (402) 60277328 12353 (1550) 16072 17352 (2319) 2347238466 405410 44011148468 49702 5032452692 53865 57752624012 (6396) 65952 68414

Million Waves (IRE) *Kevin Prendergast* 92+
3 b f Mull Of Kintyre(USA) —Multicolour Wave (IRE) (Rainbow Quest (USA))
1026a5 1785a6

Millisecond *M A Jarvis* a65 75
2 b f Royal Applause—Milligram (Mill Reef (USA))
49643 57603 61875

Millistar *M A Jarvis* a71+ 82
3 b f Galileo(IRE) —Milligram (Mill Reef (USA))
18234 23044 (3200) 40408 (4599)

Millkom Elegance *G A Ham* a45 51
7 b m Millkom—Premier Princess (Hard Fought)
154811

Millsini *Rae Guest* 43
2 b f Rossini(USA) —Millyant (Primo Dominie)
60246

Millsy *J L Spearing* 49d
4 b m Pursuit Of Love—Jucea (Bluebird (USA))
179511 213613 450715 57298

Millville *M A Jarvis* a112 102
6 ch g Millkom—Miss Topville (FR) (Top Ville)
(1779) 30933 467619 55485 (6097) 6516668362

Millwood Lad (IRE) *B S Rothwell*
3 ch g Most Welcome—Triple Concerto (Grand Lodge (USA))
156410 175911 18689

Milly Beat *C Grant* 13
2 b f Beat All(USA) —Keep Ikis (Anshan)
10408 124811

Millyjean *John Berry* a48 34
2 ch f Whittingham(IRE) —Taken Aback (IRE) (Robellino (USA))
619910 69054

Milongo (FR) *Brigitte Renk* 108
4 b h Blush Rambler(USA) —Madeleina (FR) (Top Waltz (FR))
523a4 5881a6

Milord Du Bourg (FR) *K Schafflutzel* 95
3 br c Nombre Premier—Milady Du Bourg (FR) (Mister Sicy (FR))
522a3 2717a6

Milson's Point (IRE) *I Semple* a69 49
2 b g Fasliyev(USA) —Hilbys Brite Flite (USA) (Cormorant (USA))
49879 530711 62073 65693(6764) (6931)

Miltons Choice *J M Bradley* 64
3 b g Diktat—Starosta (Soviet Star (USA))
(988) 120811 156714 164212 228416

Milton's Keen *P S McEntee* a38 57
3 gr g Largesse—Not A Word (Batshoof)
20488 301114 4602949271 0 57292

Milton Star (IRE) *John A Harris* a67 86
7 ch g Mukaddamah(USA) —Bajan Girl (IRE) (Pips Pride)
56918 5875859053

Mimetico (IRE) *B Grizzetti* 44
2 b f Monsun(GER) —Liza (IRE) (Lycius (USA))
5858a11

Mimi Mouse *T D Easterby* 93
4 br m Diktat—Shifty Mouse (Night Shift (USA))
18563 245015 26249 38804 44681551693 55326

Mimisel *Rae Guest* 85
2 ch f Selkirk(USA) —Milly-M (Cadeaux Genereux)
42073 45593 49664 55072 (5899) 62019

Mimita (IRE) *M Cicarelli*
2 b f Cape Cross(IRE) —Marania (IRE) (Marju (IRE))
2475a10 5705a7

Mimiteh (USA) *R M Beckett* a36 78
3 ch f Maria's Mon(USA) —Green Minstrel (FR) (Green Tune (USA))
16934 (2393) 28184 40034 42424 562712

Mina *Rae Guest* a72 68
4 ch m Selkirk(USA) —Midnight Shift (IRE) (Night Shift (USA))
12092 16455 21604 60612 62935(6395) 6513366432 66721268424 69309

Mina A Salem *C E Brittain* a96 81
4 b g Singspiel(IRE) —Amber Fizz (USA) (Effervescing (USA))
4447 (578) 113314 1629321148 24434 3532243995 59909 (6868) 69864

Minaash (USA) *J Noseda* a83 84
2 b c Dixie Union(USA) —Metanoia (USA) (Seeking The Gold (USA))
23422 26604 (3070) 3474647276

Minatlya (FR) *A Fabre* 106
3 gr f Linamix(FR) —Mintly Fresh (USA) (Rubiano (USA))
(2257a) 2913a5

Mind Alert *D Shaw* a62 42
5 b g Mind Games—Bombay Sapphire (Be My Chief (USA))
8110 19642882 31734089 (485) 5876 83710 9036 179514 22071030525 3389239951 1 66321067136 683310 68905 69742

Mind Out (USA) *J T Stimpson* a65
3 b g Minardi(USA) —Tapped Twice (USA) (Pleasant Tap (USA))
1325 21583472 44985512 12542 (Dead)

Mind That Fox *T Wall* a49?
4 b g Mind Games—Foxie Lady (Wolfhound (USA))
69210 1150712728 1571831551 0 65241066818

Mind The Style *W G M Turner* 86d
2 b g Mind Games—Sioux Lady (Petong)
10802 (1309) 15823 19775 30645 4397444443 54427

Mine (IRE) *J D Bethell* 116
8 b h Primo Dominie—Ellebanna (Tina's Pet)
7288 112923 20127 27428 (3493) 39261051352 552312

Mine Behind *J R Best* a83 94
6 b g Sheikh Albadou—Arapi (IRE) (Arazi (USA))
16024 223016 24294 309210 3471339282 0 410117

Mineral Rights (USA) *I Semple* a65 39
2 ch g Gulch(USA) —Long Vacation (IRE) (Thatching)
533210 56138 6224665205 66465

Mineral Star (IRE) *M H Tompkins* a80 92
4 b g Monashee Mountain(USA) —Summit Talk (Head For Heights)
13407 21478 26211229741 6 47067 532010

Mine The Balance (IRE) *J R Best* a59 43
3 b g Desert Style(IRE) —Dia (IRE) (Astronef)
317 239228 78 46454813 59527128 7966 64397657713 6629367137 (6884)

Minge Cove (USA) *S Blasi* 107
5 b m Sandpit(BRZ) —Gypsy Miss (USA) (Raise A Bid (USA))
4385a9

Ming Vase *P T Midgley* a47 50
4 b g Vettori(IRE) —Minstrel's Dance (CAN) (Pleasant Colony (USA))
84 242103505 470125267 875211239 11946 1573517656 20776 2137835416 (3944) 44046 45686 49093 5240559259

Minimum Bid *B Smart* a80 75
5 b m First Trump—La Noisette (Rock Hopper)
36705 391213 411912

Minimum Fuss (IRE) *M C Chapman* a57 59
2 b f Second Empire(IRE) —Jamis (IRE) (Be My Guest (USA))
8147 9084 1142618626 22942 25243 262612 (3380) 41074 49104 52387 54343 57211260568 67153

Minister Of State *M A Jarvis* 95+
3 ch c Machiavellian(USA) —Mystic Goddess (USA) (Storm Bird (CAN))
10882 16743 (2615) (3176) 39784 515012

Minivet *R Allan* 45
11 b g Midyan(USA) —Bronzewing (Beldale Flutter (USA))
97512 14366 313512

Minnie Magician *C Grant* 40
2 b f Wizard King—Moving Princess (Prince Sabo)
11429 12293 16824 18628 2294833944 408810

Minnie Mill *B P J Baugh* a60
2 b f Mind Games—Sometime Never (IRE) (College Chapel)
68217 69403

Minnis Bay (CAN) *E F Vaughan* a78 66+
2 b g Royal Academy(USA) —Aly's Daylite (USA) (Dayjur (USA))
54545 58412 60314

Minnow *S C Williams* a67+ 50
2 b f Averti(IRE) —Tharwa (IRE) (Last Tycoon)
34356 44216 50598 65004(6839) (6939)

Minority Report *L M Cumani* 106
6 b g Rainbow Quest(USA) —Queen Sceptre (IRE) (Fairy King (USA))
(1495) 274215 (4042) 47983 56777 594313

Minos (IRE) *R Hannon* 83
2 ch c Grand Lodge(USA) —Miniver (IRE) (Mujtahid (USA))
38925 47882 (5178) 5466a21 59412

Mint *D W Barker* 77
3 b f Bahamian Bounty—Tick Tack (Primo Dominie)
23633 26529 30426 372211 5081115486 10 562012

Minthare (IRE) *C Grant* 67
3 br g Bahhare(USA) —Mintaka (IRE) (Fairy King (USA))
19882 27502 31693 46985 4884650809

Mint State *D R C Elsworth* 69
2 b g Zilzal(USA) —Pure (Slip Anchor)
20455 25795 30838 34177 4572659391 3

Mi Odds *Mrs N Macauley* a74 38
10 b g Sure Blade(USA) —Vado Via (Ardross)
2469 33484252 5491213897 29351064741 1 68719

Miola (IRE) *V Caruso* 86
3 b f In The Wings—River Hill I (IRE) (Danehill (USA))
6251a5

Mirabilis (USA) *R J Frankel* 112
4 b m Lear Fan(USA) —Media Nox (Lycius (USA))
6614a12

Miracle Baby *A J Chamberlain* a30 38
4 b m Atraf—Musica (Primo Dominie)
122511 297111 37301266578

Miracle Ridge (IRE) *Adrian McGuinness* a57 76
11 ch g Indian Ridge—Highly Delighted (USA) (Verbatim (USA))
94 (24) 1791350 13

Mirage Prince (IRE) *D Shaw* a20 53
4 ch g Desert Prince(IRE) —Belle Bijou (Midyan (USA))
127311 135313 15909177215 24079 261114

Mirasol Princess *D K Ivory* a60 68
5 ch m Ali-Royal(IRE) —Yanomami (USA) (Slew O'Gold (USA))
215 14631779 30783972 22089(2347) 26326 3155537286 38474 (4211) 43656

Mirin *G Wragg* a65 15
2 b f Generous(IRE) —Musetta (IRE) (Cadeaux Genereux)
595012 68404

Mirjan (IRE) *L Lungo* 98
10 b g Tenby—Mirana (IRE) (Ela-Mana-Mou)
17795 24374 30788 38883 (4883) 59631063198

Mirko *Pat Eddery* a44
2 b c Dansili—Marithea (IRE) (Barathea (IRE))
61459

Mirth *R Hannon* a45 71
3 b f Alhaarth(IRE) —Justine Au Jardin (USA) (Black Tie Affair)
7627 107912 (Dead)

Mirthful (USA) *B W Hills* 79
2 b f Miswaki(USA) —Musicanti (USA) (Nijinsky (CAN))
53447

Misaine (IRE) *T J Etherington* a22 51
2 b g Fasliyev(USA) —Rose Paille (FR) (General Holme (USA))
297312 35968 4986752886

Misaro (GER) *R A Harris* a76+ 79
5 b g Acambaro(GER) —Misniniski (Niniski (USA))
3453 654811513 (1209) (1315) 14327 2189122417 5 (2858) 31652 38554462911 50587 55759 65851167391 1 6844669357

Misbehaviour *G L Moore* a44+ 36
7 b g Tragic Role(USA) —Exotic Forest (Dominion)
15414 67973

Mis Chicaf (IRE) *Robert Gray* 49
5 b m Prince Sabo—Champagne Season (USA) (Vaguely Noble)
141310 184610 239613 250511 3245836081 5 391214 472913

Miskina *W M Brisbourne* a63 55
5 b m Mark Of Esteem(IRE) —Najmat Alshemaal (IRE) (Dancing Brave (USA))
110 71523 24 44675146 69329024 1273634787 43292 4970358401 1 64048 65561166085

Misphire *M Dods* 84
3 b f Mister Baileys—Bombay Sapphire (Be My Chief (USA))
41448 460112 53774 56432 62125

Miss A Bargain (IRE) *K R Burke* a44
3 ch f Bahamian Bounty—Miss Clarinet (Pharly (FR))
1894 466859810

Miss Apricot *J D Bethell* a43
3 ch f Indian Ridge—Mora (IRE) (Second Set (IRE))
64036 67314

Missatacama (IRE) *D J Daly* a83 84
4 b m Desert Style(IRE) —Delta Town (USA) (Sanglamore (USA))
1357

Miss Autumnal (IRE) *N A Callaghan* a68 39
2 b f Night Shift(USA) —Autumnal (IRE) (Indian Ridge)
514710 57735 6024763111 3

Miss Bear (IRE) *B Smart* a53 38
4 b m Orpen(USA) —The Poachers Lady (IRE) (Salmon Leap (USA))
1310 9210

Miss Beatrix (IRE) *Kevin Prendergast* 109
2 b f Danehill Dancer(IRE) —Miss Beabea (IRE) (Catrail (USA))
3060a7 3658a2 4409a3 (4853a) (5466a)

Miss Brush *J R Fanshawe* a73+ 59
3 b f Foxhound(USA) —Tattinger (Prince Sabo)
14318 24336

Miss Capricorn *K A Ryan* 19
2 b f Forzando—Miss Flirtatious (Piccolo)
35216 41518

Miss Champagne (IRE) *M Quinn* a53 48
3 b f Tagula(IRE) —Champagne Lady (IRE) (Turtle Island (IRE))
315 6942269 32644662 (544) 7968 8936 11492

Miss Charismatic *Eamon Tyrrell* a48
2 br f Kalanisi(IRE) —Mild Deception (IRE) (Glow (USA))
624212

Miss Cue *J Pearce* a28
4 b m Polish Precedent(USA) —Sharp Girl (FR) (Sharpman)
90410

Miss Daawe *S Parr* 19
2 b f Daawe(USA) —Feiticeira (USA) (Deposit Ticket (USA))
550716 576411

Miss Dagger (IRE) *J R Best* a61 31
3 b f Daggers Drawn(USA) —Royal Rumpus (Prince Tenderfoot (USA))
5444 (594) 709RR8075 902RR

Missdevina (IRE) *M G Quinlan* a34 63
3 b f Namid—Vintage Escape (IRE) (Cyrano De Bergerac)
21299 255412 34535

Miss Dixie *T D Easterby* a54 67
3 b f Bertolini(USA) —Dixie Favor (USA) (Dixieland Band (USA))
13047 21977 2873849481 3

Miss Donovan *Declan Gillespie* 99
3 b f Royal Applause—Cumbrian Melody (Petong)
5706a3 591910

Miss Double Daisy *B Smart* a38
3 ch f Compton Place—Stealthy (Kind Of Hush)
63895 66498

Missed A Beat *M Blanshard* a77 78
4 b m Mister Baileys—Lonely Heart (Midyan (USA))
138212 24597 2865532982 (3542) 37125 40754 424110 5046953014

Missed Turn *J M P Eustace* a54 42
4 b m Mind Games—Miss Beverley (Beveled (USA))
358 2359

Miss Fancy Pants *M Johnston* a62
2 gr f Act One—Sweetness Herself (Unfuwain (USA))
62834 6449267373

Miss Glory Be *Ernst Oertel* a56 44
8 b m Glory Of Dancer—Miss Blondie (USA) (Stop The Music (USA))
944 148101755 68227693 88812(1198) 1723319101 2 213211 38036

Miss Gorica (IRE) *Ms Joanna Morgan* 47
2 b f Mull Of Kintyre(USA) —Allegorica (IRE) (Alzao (USA))
5692a15

Miss Havisham (IRE) *J R Weymes* 48
2 b f Josr Algarhoud(IRE) —Agony Aunt (Formidable (USA))
401811 45668 51394 54916

Miss Highjinks (USA) *E J O'Neill* a93 79
3 ch f Stravinsky(USA) —Ready For Action (USA) (Riverman (USA))
(16) 392a7 8279 1205966353

Miss Holly *D Carroll* a66+ 36
7 b m Makbul—Seraphim (FR) (Lashkari)
4947^{11} 5314^{10} 5751^{10} 6158^{12} (6972)

Miss Hoolie *W R Swinburn* 39
2 b f Danehill Dancer(IRE) —Silky Dawn (IRE) (Night Shift (USA))
6015^{7}

Missie Baileys *Mrs L J Mongan* a63 63
4 ch m Mister Baileys—Jilly Woo (Environment Friend)
48^{10} (263) 379^{12}5744^{4} 697^{5}3035^{3} 3412^{7} 3935^{12}4702^{2} 5213^{9}5652^{8} 6037^{3}6405^{3} (6571) 6693^{8} 6769^{5}

Miss Imperious *B Smart* a48 49+
3 b f Imperial Ballet(IRE) —Birthday Belle (Lycius (USA))
3053^{8} 3916^{U}4155^{6} 4891^{6} 6667^{11}6799^{3} 6970^{4}

Miss Inch *G Wragg* a54 63
4 b m Inchinor—Twitcher's Delight (Polar Falcon (USA))
289^{F} 453^{3}596^{10}

Missin Margot *P D Evans* a38 49
4 b m Fraam—Abstone Queen (Presidium)
144^{5} 300^{9}315^{11}

Mission Affirmed (USA) *Peter Grayson* a79 67
5 ch g Stravinsky(USA) —Affirmed Legacy (USA) (Affirmed (USA))
100^{3} 276^{12}410^{3} 640^{3}732^{3} 1002^{5}1275^{11} 1550^{2}1752^{9} 2208^{4} 2793^{7}6477^{LFT}

Miss Ippolita *J R Jenkins* a62 76
2 b f Diktat—Isabella D'Este (IRE) (Irish River (FR))
878^{4} 1989^{5} 3402^{5}4737^{7} (5592)

Missisipi Star (IRE) *Eamon Tyrrell* 98
3 b f Mujahid(USA) —Kicka (Shirley Heights)
(1650) 2582^{7} 3021^{3}

Miss Jenny (IRE) *B J Meehan* a80 84
2 b f Desert Prince(IRE) —Please Believe Me (Try My Best (USA))
3148^{6} 4559^{2} 4737^{6} (5261) 5676^{15} 6100^{6}

Misskinta (IRE) *M J Grassick* 82
3 b f Desert Sun—Darabaka (IRE) (Doyoun)
755a^{2}

Miss Kitty *T D Easterby* a18
2 br f Monsieur Cat(USA) —Upstream (Prince Sabo)
6420^{7}

Miss Kool Kat (USA) *K A Ryan* a56 54
2 bb f Exploit(USA) —Pristine (USA) (Gone West (USA))
849^{4} 1080^{4} 1587^{9}5528^{10} 6025^{6}

Miss Lacey (IRE) *J A Osborne* 45
3 b f Diktat—Launch Time (USA) (Relaunch (USA))
329^{12}

Miss Lemon (IRE) *J Hetherton* 38
3 b f Tagula(IRE) —Sesame Heights (IRE) (High Estate)
1493^{7} 2019^{10}

Miss Lips (GER) *P Hirschberger* 104
5 ch m Big Shuffle(USA) —Massada (Most Welcome)
1973a^{11}

Miss Lopez (IRE) *K R Burke* a61 65
3 br f Key Of Luck(USA) —Legit (IRE) (Runnett)
110^{5} 380^{3}(653) 2856^{10} 3154^{8}3290^{9} 4524^{9} 4927^{3} 5401^{3}

Miss Lorella (IRE) *M Grassi* 84
3 b f Orpen(USA) —Lodema (IRE) (Lycius (USA))
1713a^{10} 2493a^{3}

Miss Lucifer (FR) *B W Hills* 81
2 b f Noverre(USA) —Devil's Imp (IRE) (Cadeaux Genereux)
5894^{3} (6200)

Miss Madame (IRE) *T G Mills* a55 64
5 b m Cape Cross(IRE) —Cosmic Countess (IRE) (Lahib (USA))
327^{10} 596^{8}696^{8} 1753^{6} 2645^{5}3044^{7} 3728^{10} 4447^{3} 4674^{7}

Miss Marlene *B G Powell*
3 ch f Shahrastani(USA) —Harlequin Walk (IRE) (Pennine Walk)
3200^{14} 3729^{8}

Miss Marvellous (USA) *J R Fanshawe* a39+
2 ch f Diesis—Sue Warner (USA) (Forli (ARG))
5095^{10}

Miss McGuire *G L Moore* 73
3 b f Averti(IRE) —Friend For Life (Lahib (USA))
2188^{2} (2951) 3667^{DSQ} 4040^{10}

Miss Meggy *Miss J A Camacho* a80 85
4 b m Pivotal—Selkirk Rose (IRE) (Pips Pride)
1275^{8} (1734) 2851^{3} 3450^{6}3687^{9}

Miss Monica (IRE) *P W Hiatt* a34 50
5 ch m Grand Lodge(USA) —Bea's Ruby (IRE) (Fairy King (USA))
175^{7} 240^{7}311^{11} 363^{5}468^{4} 1755^{2} 2070^{4}2262^{9} (2392) 2725^{3} 2952^{2} 3305^{9} 4279^{4}4568^{4} 4673^{4} 4709^{8} 5072^{3}

Miss Mujahid Times *A D Brown* a52 52
3 b f Mujahid(USA) —Stealthy Times (Timeless Times (USA))
1571^{9} 1791^{6} 2138^{3}(3257) 4201^{7} (4710) 5062^{8} 5752^{6}6274^{12}

Miss Odd Sox *R Ingram* a62
3 ch f Primo Valentino(IRE) —Dam Certain (IRE) (Damister (USA))
266^{7} 418^{6}536^{4} 918^{8}

Miss Otis *P Winkworth* 76
2 b f Danetime(IRE) —Nesting (Thatching)
(1896) 2125^{7} 3120^{4}

Missoula (IRE) *M H Tompkins* 78
3 b f Kalanisi(IRE) —Medway (IRE) (Shernazar)
1423^{3}

Missouri (USA) *G M Moore* a52 46
3 b g Gulch(USA) —Coco (USA) (Storm Bird (CAN))
1147^{11} 1687^{8} 4651^{5} 5082^{10} 6279^{4}6754^{12} 6871^{8}(6971)

Miss Patricia *J G Portman* a68 82
4 b m Mister Baileys—Zoena (Emarati (USA))
(692)

Miss Pebbles (IRE) *R Dickin* a22 22
6 ch m Lake Coniston(IRE) —Sea Of Stone (USA) (Sanglamore (USA))
6008^{13}

Miss Percy *R A Fahey* 65
2 b f Mark Of Esteem(IRE) —Anabaa's Music (Anabaa (USA))
4731^{8} 5059^{3} 5507^{8}

Missperon (IRE) *K A Ryan* a61 65
4 b m Orpen(USA) —Secret Hideaway (USA) (Key To The Mint (USA))
126^{8} 249^{9}(332) 429^{10}608^{8} 2637^{7} 3172^{7}4070^{3} 4401^{2} 4571^{13}

Miss Phuket *G Wragg* 70
2 bb f Hernando(FR) —Miss Amanpuri (Alzao (USA))
4041^{7} 5068^{6} 5679^{5} (Dead)

Miss Porcia *P A Blockley* a58 60
5 ch m Inchinor—Krista (Kris)
119^{7} 249^{6}446^{10} 3543^{2} 3897^{6}4294^{6} 4554^{6} 6371^{4}6448^{6} (6543) 6608^{12} 6955^{10}

Miss Provence *G Wragg* a71 92
3 b f Hernando(FR) —Miss Beaulieu (Northfields (USA))
5727^{7} 6052^{4} (6314) 6567a^{6}

Miss Provvidence (IRE) *W R Swinburn* a96 95
4 b m Grand Lodge(USA) —My Southern Love (ITY) (Southern Arrow (USA))
(1357) 1775^{5} 2892^{3} 3255^{9} 4676^{12}

Miss Puffle *S Parr*
2 b f Superior Premium—Selkirk Rose (IRE) (Pips Pride)
3618^{4} 5347^{13}

Miss Redactive *M D I Usher* a20 62
3 b f Whittingham(IRE) —Gold And Blue (IRE) (Bluebird (USA))
1049^{6} 1431^{10} 1801^{13} 2458^{6} 2535^{7}3072^{9} 4306^{11} 5259^{11}

Miss Ruby *Rae Guest* a22 40
4 ch m Tagula(IRE) —Ruby Heights (Shirley Heights)
2167^{13} 2587^{13} 3387^{13}4497^{7} 5949^{4}

Miss Saafend Plaza (IRE) *R Hannon* a74 81
2 b f Danetime(IRE) —Coup De Coeur (IRE) (Kahyasi)
1989^{10} 2619^{2} 2958^{6} 3496^{3} 3902^{4}5041^{2} 5271^{3} 5676^{9} 6309^{4}6598^{2} 6697^{2}6840^{2}

Miss Sally (IRE) *M Halford* 115
4 b m Danetime(IRE) —Evictress (IRE) (Sharp Victor (USA))
(1469a) 2038a^{3} 2369a^{4} 4410a^{6} 5011^{8} 5849a^{4}

Miss Salvador (FR) *S Wattel* a97 108
3 ro f Smadoun(FR) —Miss Recif (IRE) (Exit To Nowhere (USA))
1370a^{4} (6171a)

Miss Shontaine *B G Powell* a36+
4 b m Fumo Di Londra(IRE) —Stockline (Capricorn Line)
387^{8}

Miss Shop (USA) *H A Jerkens* a113 95
3 b f Deputy Minister(CAN) —Shopping (USA) (Private Account (USA))
3757a^{3}

Miss Silver Spurs *M D I Usher* a36 40
2 gr f Mujahid(USA) —Wakeful Night (FR) (Linamix (FR))
2899^{7} 3640^{12} 5083^{14}5423^{7}

Miss Sissy (FR) *H-A Pantall* 90
3 ch f Sicyos(USA) —Vinon (FR) (Son Of Silver)
6328a^{7}

Miss Sudbrook (IRE) *A W Carroll* a46 58
4 ch m Daggers Drawn(USA) —Missed Opportunity (IRE) (Exhibitioner)
2223^{16} 3749^{20} 4054^{11} 6314^{6}6542^{12} 6803^{10}6907^{8}

Miss Sure Bond (IRE) *B Smart* a25 65
3 ch f Danehill Dancer(IRE) —Desert Rose (Green Desert (USA))
5401^{15} 5619^{4} 5902^{5} 6061^{13}

Miss Taboo (IRE) *Miss V Haigh* a6 20
2 b f Tobougg(IRE) —Miss Croisette (Hernando (FR))
4572^{11} 5287^{9} 6421^{9}

Miss Thailand *G Wragg* 81+
3 b f Grand Lodge(USA) —Miss Amanpuri (Alzao (USA))
1417^{6} 4563^{4} 5241^{2} 5768^{7}

Miss The Boat *A Lund* 97
4 b m Mtoto—Missed Again (High Top)
(4863a)

Miss Tocqueville (FR) *P Van De Poele* a76 71
5 ch m Volochine(IRE) —Miss Bonfosse (FR) (Hard Leaf (FR))
5562a^{9}

Miss Trinidad (USA) *B J Meehan* 79
3 b f Kingmambo(USA) —Miznah (IRE) (Sadler's Wells (USA))
1994^{6} 2600^{3} 3794^{2} 4204^{5} 5152^{2}5895^{9}

Missvinski (USA) *J-C Rouget* 98
2 b f Stravinsky(USA) —Miss U Fran (USA) (Brocco (USA))
4621a^{5} (6546a)

Miss Wedge *T G Mills* a63 69
3 b f Fraam—Tough Nell (IRE) (Archway (IRE))
781^{7} 1241^{4} 1547^{3} 1941^{5}2554^{5}

Miss Zoe *V Caruso* 72
3 b f Diktat—Painter's Palet (Royal Academy (USA))
2493a^{5}

Mist And Stone (IRE) *G M Lyons* 94
3 b f Xaar—Daunting Lady (IRE) (Mujadil (USA))
3125a^{17}

Mister Always *Ms J S Doyle* a45
2 b g Titus Livius(FR) —Pieta (IRE) (Perugino (USA))
4433^{10} 4843^{7} 6845^{5}

Mister Arjay (USA) *B Ellison* a62 73
6 b g Mister Baileys—Crystal Stepper (USA) (Fred Astaire (USA))
1756^{13} 2326^{8} 2501^{3} 2828^{3} (3019) 3607^{2}3696^{3} 3955^{4} 4252^{2} (4632) 5080^{2} 5723^{3}6011^{5} 6321^{11}

Mister Aziz (IRE) *J R Jenkins* a48 59
4 b g Mister Baileys—Aziz Presenting (IRE) (Charnwood Forest (IRE))
293^{8} 398^{3}529^{5} 618^{3}638^{4} 691^{3}766^{4} 890^{10}

Mister Becks (IRE) *M C Chapman* a51 49
3 b g Beckett(IRE) —Cappuchino (IRE) (Roi Danzig (USA))
617^{6} 716^{6} 936^{3}1147^{7} 1218^{10} (1768) 2247^{4}2876^{9} 3381^{9} 3538^{15}5724^{8}

Mister Bell *J G M O'Shea*
4 gr g Lujain(USA) —Zaragossa (Paris House)
613^{13} 789^{12}

Mister Benedictine *W R Muir* a83 83
3 b g Mister Baileys—Cultural Role (Night Shift (USA))
1115^{10} 1515^{5} 2205^{2} 2642^{6} 3317^{6}3667^{3} 4078^{6} 5096^{5}5377^{11}

Mister Benji *B P J Baugh* a67 67
7 b g Catrail(USA) —Katy-Q (IRE) (Taufan (USA))
8^{5} 77^{2}134^{3} 383^{3}(537) 571^{6}650^{8} 736^{4}1002^{9} 1276^{8}2141^{3} 2378^{10} 2794^{8}6934^{4}

Misterbianco (IRE) *B J Meehan* a52
3 b g Danehill Dancer(IRE) —Price Of Passion (Dolphin Street (FR))
1094^{7} 1336^{9} 3030^{13}3195^{13}

Mister Charm (FR) *J-C Rouget* a115 100
6 gr g Linamix(FR) —Miss Sacha (IRE) (Last Tycoon)
4862a^{7} 6574a^{7}

Mister Chocolate (IRE) *Robert Collet* a80 102
3 br g Night Shift(USA) —Terracotta Hut (Habitat)
2276a^{8} 2799a^{5} 5222a^{5} 5712a^{13}

Mister Completely (IRE) *Ms J S Doyle* a58 58
5 b g Princely Heir(IRE) —Blue Goose (Belmez (USA))
52^{4} 92^{3}(141) (174) 443^{3}482^{5} (1415) 1754^{8} 3454^{10}5652^{6} 5897^{8} 6037^{9}6256^{13} 6804^{6}(6857)

Mister Conway (FR) *P Van De Poele* 109
5 b h Exit To Nowhere(USA) —Cordial Lady (USA) (The Minstrel (CAN))
5913a^{6} (6786a)

Mister Cricket (IRE) *M E Sowersby*
2 b c Tendulkar(USA) —Fire Reply (IRE) (Royal Academy (USA))
1142^{11} 1862^{9} 2524^{4} 2870^{9}

Mister Des Aigles (FR) *Mme C Barande-Barbe* 92
3 b c Sendawar(IRE) —Baliyna (USA) (Woodman (USA))
522a^{6}

Mister Elegant *J L Spearing* a64 61
4 b h Fraam—Risky Valentine (Risk Me (FR))
121^{3} (247) 440^{3}606^{3} 1245^{10}2135^{9} 2599^{10} (2793) 3158^{4}(3405) 4795^{5} 4870^{14} 5031^{5}6642^{10} 6820^{4}6919^{9}

Mister Fasliyev (IRE) *G Colella* 83
4 b h Fasliyev(USA) —Carisheba (USA) (Alysheba (USA))
6364a^{10}

Mister Fizzbomb (IRE) *J S Wainwright* 62
3 b g Lend A Hand—Crocus (IRE) (Mister Baileys)
1293^{14} 1661^{2} 2107^{2} (2539) 3145^{4}

Mister Incredible *V Smith* a59 56
3 b c Wizard King—Judiam (Primo Dominie)
(10) 102^{3} 481^{11}646^{7} 861^{4}910^{2} 1304^{3}5631^{15} 5938^{11} 6288^{7}6395^{8} 6964^{6}

Mister Jingles *R M Whitaker* a48 44
3 ch g Desert Story(IRE) —Fairy Free (Rousillon (USA))
1101^{9} 2080^{9} 3050^{5}4199^{9} 4695^{7} 6282^{2}6490^{6}

Mister Jungle (FR) *Mrs S C Bradburne* 33
4 b g Saint Cyrien(FR) —Fabuleuse Histoire (FR) (Fabulous Dancer (USA))
4549^{9}

Mister Lucky (FR) *Sir Michael Stoute* 62
2 bb c Key Of Luck(USA) —Ma Paloma (FR) (Highest Honor (FR))
3591^{8} 4049^{4} 4669^{4} 5366^{12}

Mister Maq *A Crook* a54 58
3 b g Namaqualand(USA) —Nordico Princess (Nordico (USA))
1345^{5} 1732^{4} 2128^{7} 2698^{4} 3303^{5}(3910) 4195^{2} 4533^{4} 5757^{7} 6387^{7}6571^{9} 6716^{6}6758^{7}

Mister Marmaduke *D A Nolan* a24 37
5 b g Marju(IRE) —Lalique (IRE) (Lahib (USA))
1031^{12} 1504^{16} 1886^{8} 2550^{11} 2928^{9}3003^{10} 3356^{14}

Mister Minty (IRE) *J O'Reilly* 45
4 b g Fasliyev(USA) —Sorb Apple (IRE) (Kris)
1684^{14}

Mister Pennekamp (IRE) *G Colella* 41
4 ch h Pennekamp(USA) —My-O-My (IRE) (Waajib)
6252a^{12}

Mister Pete (IRE) *D W Barker*
3 b g Piccolo—Whistfilly (First Trump)
1100^{11}

Mister Regent *W M Brisbourne* a17 14
5 b g Mind Games—River Of Fortune (IRE) (Lahib (USA))
772^{11} 783^{5}

Mister Right (IRE) *D J S Ffrench Davis* a78 84
5 ch g Barathea(IRE) —Broken Spirit (IRE) (Slip Anchor)
723^{6} 1033^{12} 1478^{3}1927^{4} (2460) 2723^{6} 3256^{3}3853^{3} 4626^{10}

Mistongo (URU) *S Seemar* a83 93
6 br h Mantle Rock(USA) —Dona Guapa (URU) (Don Omar (ARG))
208a^{4} 565a^{8}

Mist Opportunity (IRE) *P C Haslam* a13 43
4 b g Danetime(IRE) —Lady Of The Mist (IRE) (Digamist (USA))
256^{7}

Mistral Sky *Stef Liddiard* a83 75
7 b g Hurricane Sky(AUS) —Dusk In Daytona (Beveled (USA))
253^{8} 316^{7}451^{4} 585^{4}631^{5} 737^{3}985^{6} 1057^{3} 1151^{4}2223^{13} 2464^{2} 3565^{7}3827^{4} 4437^{12} 6938^{5}(6984)

Mistress Bailey (IRE) *R Pritchard-Gordon* 90
3 b f Mister Baileys—Carson Dancer (USA) (Carson City (USA))
6384a^{0}

Mistress Twister *T D Barron* 81
5 b m Pivotal—Foreign Mistress (Darshaan)
(1636) 2627^{11} (2892) (3528) 3954^{2} 4476^{6} 4654^{5}5362^{8}

Misty Princess *M J Attwater* a53 44
4 gr m Paris House—Miss Whittingham (IRE) (Fayruz)
487^{3} 633^{4}680^{7} 766^{2}(876) 942^{4}(1196) 1539^{8}3608^{5} 3835^{8}

Misu Bond (IRE) *B Smart* 114
3 b c Danehill Dancer(IRE) —Hawala (IRE) (Warning)
(1083) 1486^{5} 2559a^{3}

Miswadah (IRE) *Kevin F O'Donnell* a59 56
3 b f Machiavellian(USA) —Khulan (USA) (Bahri (USA))
1119^{8} 2985^{6} 6587^{9}6721^{8} 6827^{5}

Mitanni (USA) *Mrs A J Perrett* a61 68
3 b g Lear Fan(USA) —Maria Dolores (USA) (Prized (USA))
5353^{5} 6021^{3} 6144^{4}

Mitchelland *E J Alston* a68 72d
4 b m Namaqualand(USA) —Precious Girl (Precious Metal)
290^{13}

Mixing *W Jarvis* 65
4 gr g Linamix(FR) —Tuning (Rainbow Quest (USA))
1187^{6} 1478^{7} 1987^{4} 2647^{13}3221^{4} 4073^{5} 4565^{8} 5954^{6} 6300^{13}

Mizzle (USA) *Saeed Bin Suroor* a54 61+
2 ch f Rahy(USA) —Loving Claim (USA) (Hansel (USA))
3227^{3} 3640^{6}

Mizz Tee (IRE) *T D Easterby* a92 86
4 b m Orpen(USA) —D D's Jakette (USA) (Deputy Minister (CAN))
116^{6} 214^{9}

Mkuzi *John M Oxx* 113
7 ch g Halling(USA) —African Peace (USA) (Roberto (USA))
2154a^{3} 3107a^{3} 3660a^{2} 4822a^{8}

Mo (USA) *R A Kvisla* a66 70
2 br c Cherokee Run(USA) —Mambo Mate (USA) (Kingmambo (USA))
3923^{6} 4768^{4} 5891^{7} 6025^{4} 6561^{3}6669^{2} 6921^{5}

Moayed *N P Littmoden* a102 87
7 b g Selkirk(USA) —Song Of Years (IRE) (Shareef Dancer (USA))
7^{3} (117) 238^{6}295^{5} 413^{10}516^{2} 629^{13}667^{6} 704^{4}828^{6} 1487^{18} 1667^{10}2047^{7} 2649^{9} 2776^{9}

Mobaasher (USA) *Sir Michael Stoute* 89
3 ch c Rahy(USA) —Balistroika (USA) (Nijinsky (CAN))
1289^{3} 1605^{2} 2829^{3} 4175^{2} 4625^{3}(5319) 5758^{5}

Mobane Flyer *R A Fahey* a12 70
5 b g Groom Dancer(USA) —Enchant (Lion Cavern (USA))
(1757) 2108^{15} 2790^{9} 4467^{10}5090^{8} 5955^{11}

Mobsir *E A L Dunlop* a89 87
3 b c Mozart(IRE) —Pretty Sharp (Interrex (CAN))
(1640) 2031^{6} 5143^{2} 5666^{4}

Mocairde (USA) *J R Best*
3 ch f Royal Academy(USA) —White Wisteria (Ahonoora)
3436^{7} 3711^{5}

Mocha Java *Mrs L J Mongan* a67 74
3 b c Bertolini(USA) —Coffee Cream (Common Grounds)
993^{4} 1693^{5} 1799^{4} 2101^{6} (3195) 3869^{2}(4666) 5268^{7} 5765^{10} 6568^{13}6747^{14}

Mo Chroi *C G Cox* a30 24
3 ch f Observatory(USA) —Away To Me (Exit To Nowhere (USA))
122^{10}

Modaffaa *P R Webber* a85 84
6 b g Darshaan—Irish Valley (USA) (Irish River (FR))
454^{3} 628^{4}834^{5} 1206^{3} 1809^{3}1943^{4} 2672^{4}

Moddlij (IRE) *M R Channon* 11
2 b g Cape Cross(IRE) —Moet (IRE) (Mac's Imp (USA))
3222^{13}

Modeeroch (IRE) *J S Bolger* 108
3 gr f Mozart(IRE) —Majinskaya (FR) (Marignan (USA))
1709a^{2} 2369a^{5} 3322a^{3} 3559a^{3} 3967a^{7}(4749a) 5004a^{4} 5708a^{5} (6356a)

Modern Tate (IRE) *R Brogi* a69
3 gr c Titus Livius(FR) —Rofan (IRE) (Cozzene (USA))
5473a^{9}

Mofarij *Saeed Bin Suroor* 86+
2 ch c Bering—Pastorale (Nureyev (USA))
6220^{2}

Moffied (IRE) *J Barclay*
6 b g Nashwan(USA) —Del Deya (IRE) (Caerleon (USA))
301^{10}

Mogaamer (USA) *S Seemar* a98 97
4 b h Dixieland Band(USA) —Dolly Talbo (USA) (Capote (USA))
434a^{10} 619a^{9}

Mogok Ruby *L Montague Hall* a68 71
2 gr c Bertolini(USA) —Days Of Grace (Wolfhound (USA))
1107^{3} 2172^{15} 3588^{6}3930^{3} 4246^{3} 4699^{3}5065^{16} (5290) 5606^{5}

Mohandas (FR) *W Hefter* 109
5 b h Lomitas—Mille Espoir (FR) (Mille Balles (FR))
2597a^{5} 3662a^{3} 4828a^{2} 5519a^{7} 6109a^{2}6529a^{11}

Mohawk Star (IRE) *I A Wood* a75 74
5 ch g Indian Ridge—Searching Star (Rainbow Quest (USA))
3121^{9} 3642^{4} 4048^{4}4575^{4} 5042^{9} 5590^{7} 6762^{5}

Moheebb (IRE) *M P Tregoning* 51
2 b g Machiavellian(USA) —Rockerlong (Deploy)
3701^{15}

Mohtarres (USA) *M A Jarvis* 70
3 b c Kingmambo(USA) —Adored Slew (USA) (Seattle Slew (USA))
1994^{10} 3029^{4}

Moi Aussi (USA) *Sir Mark Prescott* a88 79
3 ch f Mt. Livermore(USA) —Acquiesce (Generous (IRE))
34^{3} 160^{2} 2522a^{7} 3489^{5} 3648^{5} 4047^{9} 4989^{4} 5337^{5} 6424^{9}

Moist *Jedd O'Keeffe* a18 19
2 b f Mark Of Esteem(IRE) —Native Ring (FR) (Bering)
1989^{11} 2388^{7} 2588^{6} 3054^{3} 3279^{4} 3613^{7} 4724^{8}

Mokabra (IRE) *D Selvaratnam* a55 104
5 b h Cape Cross(IRE) —Pacific Grove (Persian Bold)
203a^{10} 431a^{5} 507a^{9}

Molem *Lady Herries* a77 76
4 br g Green Desert(USA) —Injaad (Machiavellian (USA))
(854) 1311^{2} 2348^{2} 2647^{14} 3213^{4} 3706^{6} 4288^{5} (5775) 6147^{6}

Mollyanko *W G M Turner* a37 54
2 gr f Komaite(USA) —Molly Malone (Formidable (USA))
2015^{4} (2064) 2294^{7} 3054^{6} 6172^{7} 6258^{8}

Molly Art (GER) *U Ostmann* 110
4 br m Big Shuffle(USA) —Molly Dancer (GER) (Shareef Dancer (USA))
(1974a) 2912a^{2} (3661a) (4383a) 6366a^{3}

Molly Max (GER) *Frau K Haustein* 105
2 ch c Big Shuffle(USA) —Molly Dancer (GER) (Shareef Dancer (USA))
(5998a)

Molly Pitcher (IRE) *M A Jarvis* a60 65+
2 ch f Halling(USA) —American Queen (FR) (Fairy King (USA))
2958^{8} 6242^{9} 6558^{13}

Mollyputtheketelon (USA) *M J Wallace* a68 68
5 b m Rainbow Quest(USA) —Nemea (USA) (The Minstrel (CAN))
109^{11} 186^{16}

Molly's Secret *Miss S J Wilton* a51 38
8 b m Minshaanshu Amad(USA) —Secret Miss (Beveled (USA))
273^{5} 442^{6} 715^{3} 794^{4} 857^{7} 1271^{3} 1385^{6} 3260^{7} 3594^{2} 4435^{4}

Molotov (AUS) *J Conlan* 112
4 ch g Grand Lodge(USA) —Admit Anywhere (AUS) (Zabeel (NZ))
6347a^{14}

Molotov *M Dods* a43 49
6 b g Efisio—Mindomica (Dominion)
5834^{6} 6233^{10}

Molto Duro (IRE) *N Wilson* a36 37
2 b f Tagula(IRE) —Dieci Anno (IRE) (Classic Music (USA))
4510^{11} 4731^{14} 5076^{9} 6157^{10} 6296^{6} 6463^{4} 6640^{6} 6945^{5}

Mombassa (IRE) *Edward Lynam* 108
6 b g Mujadil(USA) —Twilight Tango (Groom Dancer (USA))
3123a^{3}

Momtic (IRE) *W Jarvis* a88 113
5 ch h Shinko Forest(IRE) —Uffizi (IRE) (Royal Academy (USA))
1299^{7} 1739^{2} 2226^{4} 2803^{11} 3313^{3} (3881) 4145^{5} 4529^{4} 5227a^{6} 5845^{7}

Monachello (USA) *Mrs A J Perrett* a58 77
2 b g Lemon Drop Kid(USA) —Antoniette (USA) (Nicholas (USA))
(2899) 3735^{6} 6074^{12}

Monachesi (IRE) *F & L Camici* 102
3 b c Key Of Luck(USA) —O'Keefe (IRE) (Be My Guest (USA))
1872a^{4}

Monaco Prince (IRE) *G A Huffer* 52
3 ch g King Charlemagne(USA) —Maytpleasethecourt (IRE) (Persian Heights)
3090^{6}

Monahullan Prince *Gerard Keane* 65
5 b g Pyramus(USA) —Classic Artiste (USA) (Arctic Tern (USA))
4166a^{5}

Monashee Brave (IRE) *J J Quinn* 78
3 b g Monashee Mountain(USA) —Miss Butterfield (Cure The Blues (USA))
1147^{3} 1589^{3} (4948) 5532^{5}

Monashee Express (IRE) *G H Yardley* a59 53
4 ch g Monashee Mountain(USA) —Curie Express (IRE) (Fayruz)
3056^{12} 4288^{11}

Monashee Grey (IRE) *R A Fahey* 39
3 gr g Monashee Mountain(USA) —Ex-Imager (Exhibitioner)
3140^{7} 3791^{4} 4111^{8}

Monashee Prince (IRE) *J R Best* a73 73
4 ch g Monashee Mountain(USA) —Lodema (IRE) (Lycius (USA))
115^{2} 236^{7} 416^{3} 575^{3} 698^{9} 806^{3} 4211^{2} 4564^{10} 5232^{3} 5480^{14} 6656^{9} 6781^{3} 6870^{5}

Monashee River (IRE) *Miss V Haigh* a60 22
3 b f Monashee Mountain(USA) —Dixie Jazz (Mtoto)
6177^{6} 6403^{3} 6450^{3} 6565^{13} 6666^{10} 6899^{12}

Monash Lad (IRE) *Mrs K Waldron* a62 77
4 ch g General Monash(USA) —Story Time (IRE) (Mansooj)
50^{9} 114^{10} 992^{9} 1187^{7} 1425^{4} 2401^{14} 2499^{6} 2696^{3} 3022^{6} (3616) (3797) 4393^{8}

Monda *Miss J A Camacho* a51 60
4 b m Danzig Connection(USA) —Fairey Firefly (Hallgate)
2856^{5}

Monet's Lady (IRE) *R A Fahey* 38
2 gr f Daylami(IRE) —Wide Range (IRE) (Spectrum (IRE))
3830^{6} 4260^{8}

Monets Masterpiece (USA) *G L Moore* a79 77
3 b c Quiet American(USA) —Math (USA) (Devil's Bag (USA))
1940^{3} 2261^{3} 2825^{4} 4125^{10} 6828^{2} 6916^{2}

Moneyforcredit (IRE) *Jarlath P Fahey* a25
6 b g Charente River(IRE) —Bridesglen (Paddy's Stream)
6680^{8}

Money For Fun *J S Moore* a62 64
2 b f Whittingham(IRE) —Urban Dancer (IRE) (Generous (IRE))
4774^{6} 5686^{4} 6024^{3} 6255^{3} 6420^{4} 6665^{5} 6789^{F} (Dead)

Money Hills *Mrs C A Dunnett* a26 38?
4 b g Vettori(IRE) —Starfida (Soviet Star (USA))
871^{8}

Money Mate (IRE) *J O'Reilly* a62 58
3 ch g Titus Livius(FR) —Xania (Mujtahid (USA))
10^{5} 128^{2} 2275^{11} 344^{3} 601^{10} 980^{6} 1736^{11} (2876) 3257^{5} 3608^{13} 3821^{3} 4071^{5} 4710^{9} (Dead)

Money Penny (ITY) *B Grizzetti*
2 b f Montjeu(IRE) —Miss Marisa (Beldale Flutter (USA))
5705a^{5}

Monkey Glas (IRE) *K R Burke* a73 74
2 b c Mull Of Kintyre(USA) —Maura's Pet (IRE) (Prince Of Birds (USA))
1019^{3} 2178^{5} (2523) 3372^{3} (4250) 5366^{7} 5843^{3}

Monkey Madge *B Smart* a48 56
4 br m Cape Cross(IRE) —Runelia (Runnett)
95^{4} 181^{2} 247^{8} 391^{8} 592^{4} 630^{8} 6554^{4} 6961^{8}

Monkshill *Miss Tor Sturgis*
2 b f Fraam—Fatah Flare (USA) (Alydar (USA))
6023^{15} 6172^{13}

Monkstown Road *C N Kellett* a58 73
4 b g Makbul—Carolside (Music Maestro)
157^{7} 493^{8} 706^{6} 857^{12} 1058^{9} 4176^{11} 4390^{9} 4457^{8} 6936^{8}

Mon Michel (IRE) *Kevin Prendergast* 102
3 b g Montjeu(IRE) —Miniver (IRE) (Mujtahid (USA))
2055a^{2} 2471a^{7} 4641a^{7}

Monmouthshire *M L W Bell* a48 51
3 b g Singspiel(IRE) —Croeso Cariad (Most Welcome)
1260^{6} 1546^{6} 1994^{11} 4225^{7} 5298^{6} 5690^{10} 6383^{10}

Monolith *L Lungo* 89
8 b g Bigstone(IRE) —Ancara (Dancing Brave (USA))
1808^{3} (2894) 5533^{13} 5963^{16}

Mon Petite Amour *D W P Arbuthnot* a55+ 50
3 b f Efisio—Food Of Love (Music Boy)
298^{7} 373^{7} 543^{7} 595^{4} 642^{5} 1549^{10} (1752) 1923^{2} 2293^{5} 3488^{4} 5885^{4} 6554^{3} 6708^{4} 6756^{7} (6855) 6981^{8}

Monreale (GER) *T Horwart* 87
2 b c Literat(GER) —Maratea (USA) (Fast Play (USA))
5998a^{6}

Monsieur Dumas (IRE) *T P Tate* a67 65
2 b c Iron Mask(USA) —Serenity (Selkirk (USA))
4066^{10} 4732^{3} 5239^{3} 5597^{8} 6224^{5}

Monsieur Henri (USA) *J C Hayden* 101?
3 b c Chester House(USA) —Lady Of Vision (Vision (USA))
3127a^{11} 5396a^{15}

Monsignor Fred *H Candy* 71
4 b g Fraam—Monsoon (Royal Palace)
2118^{13} 2815^{5} 3346^{8} 5436^{11}

Monsoon Wedding *M Johnston* 71
2 b f Monsun(GER) —Hyabella (Shirley Heights)
5352^{9} 5536^{3}

Montage (IRE) *J Akehurst* a65 51
4 b g Montjeu(IRE) —Ocean View (USA) (Gone West (USA))
1670^{5} 2320^{5} 2577^{7} 3209^{9} (3597) 3919^{2} 4046^{6} 4777^{12} 5201^{8} 5736^{2} 5971^{2} 6509^{F} (Dead)

Montalegre (IRE) *A & G Botti* 108
4 b h Montjeu(IRE) —Alma Alegre (IRE) (Lahib (USA))
2693a^{5}

Montalembert (USA) *J S Moore* a83+ 86
2 b c Kalanisi(IRE) —Garendare (Vacarme (USA))
1838^{9} 2844^{8} 4824a^{11} (5283) 5763a^{4} (6599)

Montana *C W Fairhurst* a54 68
6 b g Puissance—Mistral's Dancer (Shareef Dancer (USA))
1235^{9} 1687^{5} 2112^{15} 2833^{7} 3398^{14} 4120^{4} 4613^{5}

Montanah Jet *C N Kellett* a37
4 b g Montjoy(USA) —Nashwanah (Nashwan (USA))
539^{10} 634^{9} 715^{5}

Montana Sky (IRE) *R A Harris* a7 61
3 b c Peintre Celebre(USA) —Catch The Lights (Deploy)
2304^{16} 2917^{7} 4625^{6} 5057^{8} 5589^{7} 6178^{11} 6398^{9}

Montara (IRE) *Barry Potts* a55 59
7 b h Perugino(USA) —Tatra (Niniski (USA))
818^{7} 2808^{10} 4132^{8}

Montare (IRE) *J E Pease* 117
4 b m Montjeu(IRE) —Contare (Shirley Heights)
1331a^{5} 1875a^{2} 3516a^{2} 4192a^{2} 5220a^{2} (5702a) (6119a)

Montchara (IRE) *G Wragg* 58+
3 b g Montjeu(IRE) —Mochara (Last Fandango)
5589^{4} 5870^{9}

Monte Alto (IRE) *L M Cumani* 79
2 b c Danehill Dancer(IRE) —Peruvian Witch (IRE) (Perugino (USA))
5297^{3} 5883^{3}

Monte Carrio *C Drew* a3
3 ch g Observatory(USA) —Kundalini (USA) (El Gran Senor (USA))
5426^{13} 6971^{12}

Montecristo *Rae Guest* a46 69
13 br g Warning—Sutosky (Great Nephew)
5652^{14} 6068^{10} 6685^{4}

Monte Cristo (FR) *Mrs L C Taylor* a75 69
8 ch g Bigstone(IRE) —El Quahirah (FR) (Cadoudal (FR))
168^{7} 237^{4} 420^{5} (589) 838^{2} 966^{5} 1247^{5} 1339^{10}

Monte Major (GER) *D J Daly* a46 28
3 ch g Trempolino(USA) —Monbijou (GER) (Dashing Blade)
887^{2} 6133^{7} 6375^{5} 6501^{2}

Monte Major (IRE) *D Shaw* a60 59
5 b g Docksider(USA) —Danalia (IRE) (Danehill (USA))
209^{9} (317) 401^{12} 426^{7} 580^{3} 824^{8} 1414^{8} 1611^{14} 1794^{3} 2611^{15} 6629^{8} 6713^{3} 6884^{4} 6994^{3}

Monte Mayor Boy *D Haydn Jones* a71d 66
4 b g First Trump—Risalah (Marju (IRE))
15^{5} 236^{4} 319^{6} 504^{U} 1002^{12} 1257^{5} 1773^{7} 2098^{15} 2482^{9} 3388^{6} 3999^{11}

Monte Mayor Junior *D Haydn Jones* a58 54
3 b g Mull Of Kintyre(USA) —Monte Mayor Golf (IRE) (Case Law)
193^{3} (329) 604^{9} 1052^{13} 1259^{3} 3263^{6} 4662^{5} 4982^{13} 6430^{11} 6769^{8}

Montemayorprincess (IRE) *D Haydn Jones* a50 60
2 b f Fath(USA) —Blonde Goddess (IRE) (Godswalk (USA))
1203^{11} 1347^{7} 2094^{2} 2478^{4} 3117^{6} 3997^{6} 6257^{8}

Mont Etoile (IRE) *W J Haggas* a64 108+
3 b f Montjeu(IRE) —Troyes (Troy)
(1260) 1583^{2} (2772) 3575a^{4} 5185^{8}

Montevideo *Jonjo O'Neill* 92
6 b g Sadler's Wells(USA) —Montessori (Akarad (FR))
3093^{7} 3547^{7}

Montgomery's Arch (USA) *J Noseda* 118
4 bb h Arch(USA) —Inny River (USA) (Seattle Slew (USA))
201a^{7} (433a) 619a^{7}

Monthly Medal *Charles O'Brien* 85
3 b g Danehill Dancer(IRE) —Sovereign Abbey (IRE) (Royal Academy (USA))
755a^{9}

Montillia (IRE) *J W Unett* a51 56
4 b m Monashee Mountain(USA) —Steel Tap (IRE) (Flash Of Steel)
21^{11} 216^{6} 2494^{2} 2928^{2} 3356^{3} 3847^{6} 6539^{12} 6739^{13} 6753^{8}

Montjeu Baby (IRE) *B J Meehan* a63 67
4 b m Montjeu(IRE) —Catch The Lights (Deploy)
1926^{11} 2186^{14} 2601^{5} 4709^{2}

Montjeu Boy (IRE) *M Botti*
2 b c Montjeu(IRE) —Annie Girl (IRE) (Danehill (USA))
5771a^{7}

Montjeu Man *E A L Dunlop* a83 78+
3 b c Montjeu(IRE) —Camp Fire (IRE) (Lahib (USA))
1684^{3} 2465^{2} 3794^{7} 5128^{4} (Dead)

Montjeu's Melody (IRE) *E J O'Neill* 46
2 b f Montjeu(IRE) —Pride Of Place (IRE) (Caerleon (USA))
4400^{9}

Montosari *P Mitchell* a72 65
7 ch g Persian Bold—Sartigila (Efisio)
521^{2} 589^{4} (838) 1167^{4} 1339^{12} 3013^{6} 3894^{3} (4451) 4764^{10} 5910^{8} 6408^{6} (6630)

Mon Tour *I A Wood* 43
2 b g Montjeu(IRE) —Flamingo Queen (GER) (Surumu (GER))
5893^{12}

Montpellier (IRE) *E A L Dunlop* a91 88
3 b g Montjeu(IRE) —Ring Of Esteem (Mark Of Esteem (IRE))
1192^{3} 1670^{3} 2304^{3} 3419^{7} 4004^{2} (5583) 6226^{6}

Montrachet Belle *R Johnson* 38
4 b m Kadeed(IRE) —Swiss Hat (Hatim (USA))
3039^{7} 3258^{11}

Montrose Man *B J Meehan* 54
2 ch g Foxhound(USA) —Don't Jump (IRE) (Entitled)
5890^{8}

Montzando *B R Millman* 74
3 b g Forzando—Clashfern (Smackover)
1208^{9} 1801^{9} 2065^{13} 2535^{11} 3118^{3} (3864) 4164^{5} 4532^{6} 5167^{5} 5569^{8}

Monzante (USA) *R Charlton* a97 82
2 gr g Maria's Mon(USA) —Danzante (USA) (Danzig (USA))
3701^{3} (4992) 5665^{2}

Mood Music *E J O'Neill* 99
2 b c Kyllachy—Something Blue (Petong)
1203^{2} (1632) 2127^{2} 2771^{6} 3252^{2} 4099^{6} 4747a^{3} 5335^{3} 5880a^{2}

Moody Goose *M Meade*
2 b f Beat Hollow—Brecon Beacons (IRE) (Shirley Heights)
1379^{7} 3054^{5}

Moody Tunes *K R Burke* a45 85
3 b g Merdon Melody—Lady-Love (Pursuit Of Love)
879^{9} (1593) (1859) (1950) 2087^{2} 2809^{4} 5639^{13} 6160^{11}

Moohimm (IRE) *M P Tregoning* a77 75
3 b c Sadler's Wells(USA) —Lurina (IRE) (Lure (USA))
1120^{5} 2175^{4} 3015^{4} 4911^{6}

Mookerr (IRE) *M P Tregoning* a53 64
3 b g Mtoto—Seyooll (IRE) (Danehill (USA))
1088^{10} 4367^{6}

Moon At Midnight *R J Osborne* 81
6 b g Night Shift(USA) —Mashmoon (USA) (Habitat)
4186a^{11}

Moon Bird *C A Cyzer* a69 57
4 b m Primo Dominie—Time For Tea (IRE) (Imperial Frontier (USA))
519^{10} 555^{8} 902^{10} (2574) 3099^{10} 3845^{7} 4003^{8} 5032^{10} 5474^{18} 6442^{6} (6696) 6869^{2} 6984^{4}

Moondancer (GER) *B G Powell* a52
7 br g General Assembly(USA) —Miskinissa (GER) (Esclavo (FR))
113^{9} 258^{10}

Moondine (IRE) *B S Rothwell* 15
2 b f Princely Heir(IRE) —Second Dream (IRE) (Second Set (IRE))
5283^{11} 6012^{9}

Moone Cross (IRE) *Mrs John Harrington* 96
3 b f Cape Cross(IRE) —Cannikin (IRE) (Lahib (USA))
755a^{5} 1469a^{11} 2369a^{6} 3125a^{12} 4174^{4} 5171^{6}

Moon Emperor *J R Jenkins* a78 50
9 b g Emperor Jones(USA) —Sir Hollow (USA) (Sir Ivor (USA))
12^{4} (129) (168) 237^{5} 420^{8} 545^{3} 675^{4} 832^{7} 1213^{9} 3935^{6} 4996^{4} 5324^{9} 5971^{8} 6398^{6}

Moon Empress (FR) *W R Muir* a60 69+
3 gr f Rainbow Quest(USA) —Diamoona (FR) (Last Tycoon)
2753^{7} 3367^{7} 4210^{3} 6929^{6} 6987^{3}

Moon Forest (IRE) *J M Bradley* a62 62
4 br g Woodborough(USA) —Ma Bella Luna (Jalmood (USA))
1124^{14} 1570^{10} 1752^{3} 2317^{8} 2611^{5} 3988^{10} 4157^{13} (4984) 5302^{3} 5327^{2} 5576^{8} 5937^{3} 6294^{8} 6390^{2} 6556^{13}

Moonhawk *J Howard Johnson* 76
3 b g Montjeu(IRE) —Enclave (USA) (Woodman (USA))
1283^{5} 1837^{4} 2111^{2} 4197^{5}

Moonlight (GER) *Dr J R J Naylor* a43 39
3 b f Kornado—Miskinissa (GER) (Esclavo (FR))
1165^{8} 1552^{8} 2070^{6} 2790^{8}

Moonlight Applause *T D Easterby* 40
2 b f Royal Applause—Antonia's Choice (Music Boy)
1853^{4} 2166^{14}

Moonlight Fantasy (IRE) *N Tinkler* a4 55
3 b g Night Shift(USA) —County Girl (IRE) (Prince Rupert (FR))
861^{14} 1232^{4} 1433^{8} 2195^{11} 2758^{8} 3006^{5} (3357) 3785^{3} (4255) 4651^{4} 5082^{11}

Moonlight Man *R Hannon* a71 104
5 ch g Night Shift(USA) —Fleeting Rainbow (Rainbow Quest (USA))
828^{13} 1086^{12}

Moonlight Music (IRE) *E J O'Neill* a64 76
3 ch f Rossini(USA) —Jarmar Moon (Unfuwain (USA))
1759^{2} 2188^{3} 2446^{5} 3073^{3} 3848^{4} 4279^{8} 5903^{2}

Moonlight Safari (IRE) *P Winkworth* 31
3 b f Desert Prince(IRE) —Moon Masquerade (IRE) (Darshaan)
5870^{11} 6535^{8}

Moonlit Skies *Saeed Bin Suroor* 83+
3 b c Singspiel(IRE) —Truly Special (Caerleon (USA))
(5589) 6051^{10}

Moon Melody (GER) *M L W Bell* 62
3 b g Montjeu(IRE) —Midnight Fever (IRE) (Sure Blade (USA))
1120^{12} 1343^{10} 1691^{5} 2171^{14}

Moon Mix (FR) *A Fabre* 100
3 gr c Linamix(FR) —Cherry Moon (USA) (Quiet American (USA))
1749a^{6}

Moon On A Spoon *J R Fanshawe* a77 84
3 b f Dansili—Tinashaan (IRE) (Darshaan)
1401^{8} (2324) 2622^{4} 4911^{2} 5610^{2} 6017^{13}

Moon Prospect (IRE) *F Head* 103
3 b c Sadler's Wells(USA) —North Of Neptune (USA) (Mr Prospector (USA))
1179a^{4} 2942a^{5}

Moonshadow *H R A Cecil* a56 75
3 ch f Diesis—La Sky (IRE) (Law Society (USA))
1613^{3} 2292^{3} 5128^{2} 5429^{7} 5594^{8} 6272^{4} 6410^{6}

Moonshine Beach *P W Hiatt* a69 84
8 b g Lugana Beach—Monongelia (Welsh Pageant)
2219^{12} 2501^{8}

Moonshine Bill *P W Hiatt* a46 52
7 ch g Master Willie—Monongelia (Welsh Pageant)
4709^{11} (4981) 5314^{7}

Moonshine Creek *P W Hiatt* 51
4 b g Pyramus(USA) —Monongelia (Welsh Pageant)
1290^{7} 1826^{7} 2220^{13}

Moon Shot *A G Juckes* a60 58
10 gr g Pistolet Bleu(IRE) —La Luna (USA) (Lyphard (USA))
40^{2} 103^{2} (147) 259^{2} 389^{4} 490^{3} 694^{8} 6860^{11}

Moonstreaker *R M Whitaker* a64 65
3 b g Foxhound(USA) —Ling Lane (Slip Anchor)
1592^{5} 2297^{4} 2873^{5} 3569^{8} 5444^{8} 6286^{10} 6819^{3} (6897)

Moon Unit (IRE) *H Rogers* 113
5 b m Intikhab(USA) —Chapka (IRE) (Green Desert (USA))
(1158a) 1469a^{4} 2038a^{2} 2308a^{2}

Moon Valley *M P Tregoning* 82+
3 ch f Halling(USA) —Crescent Moon (Mr Prospector (USA))
3975^{3} 4814^{3} 5567^{2}

Moonwalking *Jedd O'Keeffe* 80
2 b c Danehill Dancer(IRE) —Macca Luna (IRE) (Kahyasi)
2409^{9} (2807) 3481^{5} 4250^{2} 4509^{7} 5359^{6} 5916^{15}

Mooretown Boy (IRE) *F Oakes* 89
6 b g Lapierre—Tender Always (Tender King)
3123a^{8}

Moorhouse Lad *G Woodward* a91+ 87
3 b g Bertolini(USA) —Record Time (Clantime)
1147^{10} (1589) 2363^{4} 2639^{4} (2866) 3475^{5} 4422^{6} 6583^{6} 6720^{2}

Moorlander (USA) *Mrs A J Perrett* 66
2 ch g Cozzene(USA) —Forest Key (USA) (Green Forest (USA))
4479^{6} 5067^{3} 6023^{8}

Moors Myth *B G Powell* a7 24
5 b g Anabaa(USA) —West Devon (USA) (Gone West (USA))
343^{8} 458^{7} 606^{9} 6955^{13}

Mootamaress (IRE) *Kevin Prendergast* 83
2 b c Fath(USA) —Perle D'Irlande (FR) (Top Ville)
5662a^{5}

Moraadi *D W Chapman* a32 5
3 b f Lujain(USA) —Saleyma (Mtoto)
102^{8} 637^{10} 690^{6} 786^{6} 870^{7} 936^{7} 1576^{4} 2192^{10}

Moral Code (IRE) *E J O'Neill* a62
2 ch c Danehill Dancer(IRE) —Scruple (IRE) (Catrail (USA))
6737^{6}

Moral Fibre (IRE) *M Johnston* a61 48
2 b c Green Desert(USA) —Mellow Park (IRE) (In The Wings)
5615[10] 5901[5] *6386[9]*

More Than Promised (USA) *S Blasi* 109
4 ch m More Than Ready(USA) —Sacred Promise (USA) (Blushing John (USA))
6368a[5]

More Than Regal (USA) *S Asmussen* a103
3 br c More Than Ready(USA) —Reina Victoriosa (ARG) (Interprete (ARG))
757a[4]

Morgan Lewis (IRE) *J A Geake* a51 72
5 b g Orpen(USA) —Party Piece (Thatch (USA))
1570[7] 1882[9] *3845[9]4248[13]* 4795[3] 6300[10]

Morghim (IRE) *J L Dunlop* a84 101
3 b c Machiavellian(USA) —Saleela (USA) (Nureyev (USA))
1093[6] 1488[3] 2801[6] 3441[5] 4337[3]

Morinqua (IRE) *K A Ryan* a37+ 80
2 b f Cadeaux Genereux—Victoria Regia (IRE) (Lomond (USA))
2166[8] *2461[10]* (4913) 5676[17]5956[10]

Moriwood (ITY) *A Botti* 88
2 b c Morigi—Black Wood (USA) (Woodman (USA))
6003a[7]

Mormeatmic *M W Easterby* 83
3 b g Orpen(USA) —Mimining (Tower Walk)
819[4] (980) 1344[7] (1793) (2161) 2410[10] (2855) 3568[6]4468[13] 6320[7]

Morna (FR) *S Wattel* 100
3 b f Spectrum(IRE) —More Magic (GER) (Dashing Blade)
(6062a)

Morning Farewell *P W Chapple-Hyam* 71
2 br c Daylami(IRE) —Got To Go (Shareef Dancer (USA))
3976[8] 5457[5] 5939[8]

Morning Song (IRE) *N P Littmoden* a41 36
2 b f Fath(USA) —John's Ballad (IRE) (Ballad Rock)
3148[8] 4053[9] *4993[9]*

Morristown Music (IRE) *J S Wainwright* 66
2 b f Distant Music(USA) —Tongabezi (IRE) (Shernazar)
5288[2] 5632[2] 5956[6]

Morse (IRE) *J A Osborne* a83 83
5 b g Shinko Forest(IRE) —Auriga (Belmez (USA))
*5212[2] 5670[7]*6048[10] *6527[5] 6579[7](6882)*

Morshdi *D Selvaratnam* 97
8 b g Slip Anchor—Reem Albaraari (Sadler's Wells (USA))
438a[5] 513a[5] 624a[7]

Mortarboard *E J O'Neill* 78
3 gr c Daylami(IRE) —Miss University (USA) (Beau Genius (CAN))
2220[3] 3347[6]

Mosharref (IRE) *B W Hills* a73 94+
3 b g Alhaarth(IRE) —Murjana (IRE) (Pleasant Colony (USA))
1087[2] *4247[3]* (4635) (5150) 5660[8]

Mosquera's Rock (IRE) *M Johnston* 31
2 ch f Rock Of Gibraltar(IRE) —Mosquera (GER) (Acatenango (GER))
5899[8]

Mossmann Gorge *M Wellings* a63+ 66
4 b g Lujain(USA) —North Pine (Import)
13[3] 131[11]231[5] 361[6]442[7] (490) (609) 647[4]1389[5] 1560[8] 1772[5]1850[2] 2099[2] 2221[3] 2612[3] 2956[8]*6474[13] 6571[7]6758[2] 6871[4]*

Moss Vale (IRE) *D Nicholls* 123
5 b h Shinko Forest(IRE) —Wolf Cleugh (IRE) (Last Tycoon)
1485[13] 1778[11] (2038a) (2276a) 2720[8] 3494[5](4410a) 4738[14] 5712a[3] 6127a[5]

Mostakbel (USA) *M D I Usher* a54
7 bb g Saint Ballado(CAN) —Shamlegh (USA) (Flying Paster (USA))
390[3] 442[2]

Mostanad *J M Bradley* a45 59
4 b g Alhaarth(IRE) —Jeed (IRE) (Mujtahid (USA))
1196[11] 1877[3] 2377[2]2602[10] 3438[4] 3749[12] 4120[2] 4985[10]5131[12] *6619[9] 6713[4]6728[7]*

Mostaqeleh (USA) *J L Dunlop* 108
3 ch f Rahy(USA) —Istiqlal (USA) (Diesis)
1068[5] 2275a[2] 2802[14]

Mostarsil (USA) *G L Moore* a65 77
8 ch g Kingmambo(USA) —Naazeq (Nashwan (USA))
37[9] 168[5]186[3] 1958[8](2320) (2483) (2953) (3209)

Mostashaar (FR) *Sir Michael Stoute* a104+ 107
4 b h Intikhab(USA) —Nasanice (IRE) (Nashwan (USA))
1407[4] 2431[4] 4740[8] 4896[2] 5376[5]*(6101)*

Most Definitely (IRE) *R M Stronge* a82 86
6 b g Definite Article—Unbidden Melody (USA) (Chieftain)
1294[6] 1779[11] 2238[5] 2850[6] 3078[20]3501[7] 3748[8] *4231[6]* 4631[2] 4676[13]5383[3] *5991[9]* 6205[6]*6467[2] 6677[7]*

Motafarred (IRE) *Micky Hammond* 86
4 ch g Machiavellian(USA) —Thurayya (Nashwan (USA))
1298[6] 1809[13] 2387[6] 2773[11] 3483[7]3960[6] 4203[9]

Motaraqeb *Sir Michael Stoute* 91
3 b g Grand Lodge(USA) —Pink Cristal (Dilum (USA))
1088[5] (1684) 2033[2] 2774[26] 2988[13] 5639[4]5945[8]

Mother's Day *Martin Browne* 73
3 b f Foxhound(USA) —Compact Disc (IRE) (Royal Academy (USA))
1158a[9]

Motive (FR) *J Howard Johnson* 100
5 ch g Machiavellian(USA) —Mistle Song (Nashwan (USA))
1298[3] 3552[12]

Motu (IRE) *I W McInnes* a40 69
5 b g Desert Style(IRE) —Pink Cashmere (IRE) (Polar Falcon (USA))
440[7] 1057[8] 1073[3]1253[11] 1753[3] 2148[6] 2390[7] 2541[5]2641[12] 3240[4] 3716[6] (3786) 4059[3] 4233[2](4652) 4729[2] 5269[3] 5444[9]

Mouchoir *P J Makin* a35 74
3 b g Bahamian Bounty—Mouchez Le Nez (IRE) (Cyrano De Bergerac)
1279[5] 2652[8] *3055[11]*4927[8]

Moudez (IRE) *D M Simcock* 91
2 b c Xaar—Summer Dreams (IRE) (Sadler's Wells (USA))
(4768) 5805[3]

Mountain (IRE) *A P O'Brien* 113
3 b g Montjeu(IRE) —Skidmore Girl (USA) (Vaguely Noble)
1172a[4] 1708a[2] 2228[8] 3127a[6] 3517a[7]5185[7] 6103[2]

Mountain Call (IRE) *Mrs A J Perrett* a18 16
2 b c Monashee Mountain(USA) —Amazonian (CAN) (Geiger Counter (USA))
5457[9] *6284[9]*

Mountain Cat (IRE) *W J Musson* 53
2 b g Red Ransom(USA) —Timewee (USA) (Romanov (IRE))
5867[10] 6200[9]

Mountain High (IRE) *Sir Michael Stoute* 120
4 b h Danehill(USA) —Hellenic (Darshaan)
(1489) 1976[2] 2845[2] 3444[2]

Mountain Pass (USA) *S Dow* a64 64
4 b g Stravinsky(USA) —Ribbony (USA) (Dayjur (USA))
(373) 532[9] 947[11] 1211[9]2331[9] *2792[4] 3052[6]3204[5] 3390[4]*3825[4] 4141[4] 4564[11] (4670) (5302) 5573[3] *6193[7]6348[4] 6439[2]6531[5] 6624[3]6864[7] 6984[5]*

Mount Benger *Mrs A J Hamilton-Fairley* a75 69
6 ch g Selkirk(USA) —Vice Vixen (CAN) (Vice Regent (CAN))
643[9]

Mount Eliza (IRE) *J E Hammond* 99
4 b m Danehill(USA) —Siamoise (Caerleon (USA))
(6362a)

Mount George (IRE) *Evan Williams* 45
8 bb g Greensmith—Baylands Sunshine (IRE) (Classic Secret (USA))
4239[RR]

Mount Hadley (USA) *E A L Dunlop* 88
2 b c Elusive Quality(USA) —Fly To The Moon (USA) (Blushing Groom (FR))
5658[9] (5883)

Mount Hermon (IRE) *H Morrison* 75
2 b c Golan(IRE) —Machudi (Bluebird (USA))
4526[3] 5091[2] 5655[18]

Mount Kilimanjaro (IRE) *J L Dunlop* 95
3 b c Sadler's Wells(USA) —Hill Of Snow (Reference Point)
1120[6] (2066) 2804[8]

Mount Nelson *A P O'Brien* 115
2 b c Rock Of Gibraltar(IRE) —Independence (Selkirk (USA))
(6249a)

Mount Parnassus *A P O'Brien* 91
2 bb c Rock Of Gibraltar(IRE) —Qui Liz (USA) (Benny The Dip (USA))
5658[6] 5965[12]

Mount Royale (IRE) *N Tinkler* a55 49
8 ch g Wolfhound(USA) —Mahabba (USA) (Elocutionist (USA))
95[9] 181[3]247[2] 300[4]410[2] (618) *681[2] 784[3]873[3] 1227[6]*

Mount Sinai *W J Knight* a67 62
3 b g Green Desert(USA) —Apache Song (USA) (Dynaformer (USA))
1335[7] 1684[13] 2605[6]3030[7] *3644[10]* 4211[12]5232[5] *5605[10]*

Mount Street (NZ) *L Laxon* 104
5 br g Kilimanjaro—Real Trier (AUS) (Turf Ruler (NZ))
1716a[12]

Mount Usher *G A Swinbank* a71 81
4 br g Polar Falcon(USA) —Division Bell (Warning)
(1253) 1422[5] 2020[6] 2540[4] (3037) 3283[2] 3747[5]4508[4] *4937[6]*

Mouseen (IRE) *R A Harris* a50 67
3 ch g Alhaarth(IRE) —Marah (Machiavellian (USA))
6721[6] 6898[12]

Move On (IRE) *B Ellison* 47
3 b f Night Shift(USA) —Beaufort Lady (IRE) (Alhaarth (IRE))
1140[15] 1293[10] 4726[7] 4881[13]

Moverra (IRE) *M J Grassick* 86
2 ch f Noverre(USA) —Muneera (USA) (Green Dancer (USA))
3060a[8] 5464a[27]

Moves Goodenough *Andrew Turnell* a71 70
3 ch g Woodborough(USA) —Rekindled Flame (IRE) (King's Lake (USA))
1641[3] 2188[4] 2919[7] 5830[3] *6314[3]6564[9]*

Movethegoalposts *M Johnston* a47 68
2 ch c Dr Fong(USA) —Rohita (IRE) (Waajib)
2783[8] 3193[11] (3669) 4134[3] 4547[8] 5721[16]*6291[10]*

Movie King (IRE) *S R Bowring* a65 47
7 ch g Catrail(USA) —Marilyn (IRE) (King's Lake (USA))
81[3]

Movie Star (BRZ) *R J Frankel* 100
5 b m Royal Academy(USA) —Femme Fatale (BRZ) (Clackson (BRZ))
6253a[4]

Moving Story *T J Fitzgerald* 52
3 b g Desert Story(IRE) —Arianna Aldini (Habitat)
1759[7] 2366[10] *2940[8]*

Moving Target (IRE) *Luke Comer* 32
7 ch g Karaar—Lucky Noire (Aragon)
5092[8]

Mowazana (IRE) *M P Tregoning* 78
3 ch f Galileo(IRE) —Taqreem (IRE) (Nashwan (USA))
5151[3] 5566[2] (6026)

Moyenne (IRE) *Timothy Doyle* 106
4 b m Trans Island—Mica Male (ITY) (Law Society (USA))
1469a[12] 1973a[9] 5996a[8]

Moyne Pleasure (IRE) *R Johnson*
8 b g Exit To Nowhere(USA) —Ilanga (IRE) (Common Grounds)
6797[10]

Moyoko (IRE) *M Blanshard* a55+ 55
3 b f Mozart(IRE) —Kayoko (IRE) (Shalford (IRE))
2678[6] *3016[10]* 4531[2]4772[4] 5936[2] *6648[3](6779) 6899[6]*

Mozakhraf (USA) *K A Ryan* a77 66
4 b g Miswaki(USA) —Anakid (USA) (Danzig (USA))
1275[10] 1437[4] 2611[8]3171[9] 3287[4] 3543[10] 4154[4] *6390[3]6404[3] 6642[2](6721) 6781[7]*

Mozayada (USA) *M Johnston* 62
2 ch f Street Cry(IRE) —Fatina (Nashwan (USA))
4084[8] 4788[5] 5287[4]

Mozie Cat (IRE) *John Berry* a63 57
3 b f Mozart(IRE) —Golden Cat (USA) (Storm Cat (USA))
1085[13] 1680[10] 4495[4] *(6787) 6934[9]*

Mpumalanga *R Gibson* 95
2 b f Observatory(USA) —Dimakya (USA) (Dayjur (USA))
4621a[3] 5257a[5] 5664a[6] 6228a[9]

Mr Aitch (IRE) *R T Phillips* a78 84+
4 b g Soviet Star(USA) —Welsh Mist (Damister (USA))
1631[11] 2387[8] 2519[4] (3009) 3724[5] (4175) 4299[3]4876[8]

Mr Aviator (USA) *R Hannon* a76+
2 bb c Lear Fan(USA) —In Bloom (USA) (Clever Trick (USA))
6561[8] (6778)

Mr Belvedere *A J Lidderdale* a53 41
5 b g Royal Applause—Alarming Motown (Warning)
175[3] 312[3](399) 1769[10] *1915[6]*

Mr Bilbo Baggins *J S Moore* a19 34
3 ch g Magic Ring(IRE) —I'll Try (Try My Best (USA))
4210[12] 4776[11] 5618[15]

Mr Cellophane *J R Jenkins* a81 74
3 ch g Pursuit Of Love—Fresh Fruit Daily (Reprimand)
969[6] 1263[6] 1642[3] 2050[2] 2316[2]2896[2] 4666[4] 4927[2] (5272) 5418[2] 5872[3]*6326[2] (6452) 6555[3]*

Mr Chad *E J O'Neill* a72
3 b c Mujahid(USA) —Robanna (Robellino (USA))
3647[3]

Mr Cheers *C A Dwyer* a61 55
3 b g Bertolini(USA) —Plie (Superlative)
*120[10] 329[6](466) (554) 594[6]651[7] 839[8]*1829[15] 2678[12] *6541[9]*

Mr Chocolate Drop (IRE) *M J Attwater* a49 36
2 b g Danetime(IRE) —Forest Blade (IRE) (Charnwood Forest (IRE))
3157[11] 3448[11] *6757[13]6891[5]*

Mr Crystal (FR) *Micky Hammond* a41
2 ch c Trempolino(USA) —Iyrbila (FR) (Lashkari)
6581[8] 6815[9]

Mr Dip *L A Dace* a45 65
6 b g Reprimand—Scottish Lady (Dunbeath (USA))
3013[10]

Mr Ed (IRE) *P Bowen* 89
8 ch g In The Wings—Center Moriches (IRE) (Magical Wonder (USA))
5383[9] 5678[14] 5963[22]

Mr Excel (IRE) *J A Osborne* a80+ 59
3 b g Orpen(USA) —Collected (IRE) (Taufan (USA))
(6494) 6655[3]

Mr Fast (ARG) *J Gallagher*
9 ch g Numerous(USA) —Speediness (ARG) (Etienne Gerard)
549[13]

Mr Floodlight (IRE) *R Hannon* a81 76
3 b g Bertolini(USA) —French River (Bering)
(34) 118[4]

Mr Forthright *J M Bradley* 56
2 b c Fraam—Form At Last (Formidable (USA))
5043[10] 5161[6] 5570[6] 5947[11]

Mr Garston *M P Tregoning* a89 74
3 b g Mull Of Kintyre(USA) —Ninfa Of Cisterna (Polish Patriot (USA))
6292[5]

Mr Hicks (IRE) *F & L Brogi* 84
3 b c Desert Prince(IRE) —Michelle Hicks (Ballad Rock)
1175a[9]

Mr Jack Daniells (IRE) *Anthony Mullins* a81 95
5 b g Mujadil(USA) —Neat Shilling (IRE) (Bob Back (USA))
5396a[9] *6811[8]*

Mr Jawbreaker (IRE) *J T Stimpson* a49
7 b g Sadler's Wells(USA) —Abury (IRE) (Law Society (USA))
166[7] 314[10]

Mr Kayos *Mrs G S Rees* a26
4 b g Kayf Tara—Highland Heights (IRE) (Lomond (USA))
6305[11] 6501[4]

Mr Kennedy (IRE) *B Grizzetti*
2 b c Cape Cross(IRE) —Catch A Smile (USA) (Silver Hawk (USA))
6407a[7]

Mr Kings Best (IRE) *G Colella* a91
3 b c King's Best(USA) —Matilda Bay (IRE) (Indian Ridge)
5473a[3]

Mr Klick (IRE) *N Wilson* 85
2 b g Tendulkar(USA) —Lake Poopo (IRE) (Persian Heights)
968[8] 1096[6] (1248) 1780[3] 2009[7] 3555[5]4152[3] 4321[6] 4464a[5] 5788[18]

Mr Lambros *A M Balding* a101 88
5 ch g Pivotal—Magical Veil (Majestic Light (USA))
58[10] (340) 667[2](913) 1262[11] 5523[13] *6192[9]6514[5]*

Mr Loire *R Charlton* a71 70
2 b g Bertolini(USA) —Miss Sancerre (Last Tycoon)
3861[3] 4753[2] *5245[3]*5647[15] *(6562) 6750[3]6834[3]*

Mr Majestic *R M Whitaker* 66
4 b g Vettori(IRE) —Alacrity (Alzao (USA))
1045[4] 1346[5] 2078[5] (2365) 2828[2] 3763[5]3955[10]

Mr Marucci (USA) *B Ellison* a44 38
4 b g Miner's Mark(USA) —Appealing Style (USA) (Valid Appeal (USA))
498[7] 568[7]1001[9] 1341[16]

Mr Maxim *R M Whitaker* 60
4 ch g Lake Coniston(IRE) —White Hare (Indian Ridge)
2381[5] 2684[6] 2944[3] 4229[5] 4506[2]

Mr Mini Scule *A B Haynes* a47 55
2 b g Piccolo—Courtisane (Persepolis (FR))
962[7] *1223[5]* 2179[5]3300[5] 3613[3] 4178[12] 4926[3] 5448[4]*6311[9] 6401[10]*

Mr Napper Tandy *M R Channon* 84
2 ch c Bahamian Bounty—Starfleet (Inchinor)
5890[2] (6214)

Mr Rein (IRE) *J Parkes* a38
4 b g Indian Danehill(IRE) —Lady's Vision (IRE) (Vision (USA))
549[14] 640[9]

Mr Rigsby *P Howling* a66
3 gr g Forzando—Rain Splash (Petong)
68[12] 189[3]439[2] 500[4]554[8] 646[12]2415[7] 2793[12]

Mr Rooney (IRE) *M Johnston* a34 87
3 b c Mujadil(USA) —Desert Bride (USA) (Key To The Kingdom (USA))
2363[6] 2760[8] *3404[9]*4058[5] 4888[11]

Mr Sandicliffe *C N Allen* 95
3 b c Mujahid(USA) —Crinkle (IRE) (Distant Relative)
1089[2] (1412) 1836[6] (2363) 2658[12] 3414[18] 3926[11]

Mrs Backshoe (IRE) *F Poulsen* 90
3 ch f Vettori(IRE) —Personal Best (IRE) (Kris)
2913a[7] 6567a[0]

Mrs Crossy (IRE) *A W Carroll* a60 57
2 b f Alhaarth(IRE) —God Speed (IRE) (Be My Guest (USA))
912[5] 1046[7] 1309[4]*(1379) 1744[5](2346)* 2709[2] *3641[10]*3837[5] 4284[4] 4779[8] 5065[12] *5772[8]6311[8] 6500[11]*

Mrs Gillow (IRE) *J S Bolger* 96
5 b m Danzero(AUS) —Belladera (IRE) (Alzao (USA))
5853a[5]

Mrs Miskovsky (SWE) *Ewa Breitholtz*
3 b f Duty Time—Senza Una Donna (SWE) (Steve's Friend (USA))
3326a[12]

Mrs Moneybags (IRE) *L Kelp*
3 b f Exit To Nowhere(USA) —Christopherssister (Timeless Times (USA))
3326a[3]

Mrs Mooney (IRE) *E J O'Neill* a11 37
3 b f Vettori(IRE) —Mrs Moonlight (Ajdal (USA))
6540[10]

Mrs Philip *P J Hobbs* 50
7 b m Puissance—Lightning Legacy (USA) (Super Concorde (USA))
3894[15]

Mr Spliffy (IRE) *M C Chapman* a43 28
7 b g Fayruz—Johns Conquerer (IRE) (Conquering Hero (USA))
260[13] 388[11]782[4] 872[9]

Mrs Quince *F Watson* 43
4 b m Mark Of Esteem(IRE) —T G's Girl (Selkirk (USA))
3039[4] 4155[9] 5368[4]

Mrs Snaffles (IRE) *Francis Ennis* 99
3 b f Indian Danehill(IRE) —Lake Nyasa (IRE) (Lake Coniston (IRE))
1023a[4] 4502a[5] 5004a[9]

Mrs Snow *Mario Hofer* 100
3 ch f Singspiel(IRE) —Shining Vale (USA) (Twilight Agenda (USA))
925a[2] 1328a[5] 1713a[F] 2279a[8] 6002a[3]6366a[5]

Mrs Solese (IRE) *J R Boyle* a59 64
3 b f Imperial Ballet(IRE) —Sugar (Hernando (FR))
1336[12] 2118[7] *3073[5]*5830[5]

Mr Stroger *S Curran* a38 39
5 b g Dancing Spree(USA) —Matoaka (Be My Chief (USA))
484[10] 788[5]4435[5]

Mr Velocity (IRE) *E F Vaughan* a69 86+
6 b g Tagula(IRE) —Miss Rusty (IRE) (Mukaddamah (USA))
915[9]

Mr Wall Street *Mrs L Williamson* a47 52
2 b g Efisio—La Suquet (Puissance)
1080[7] 2999[3] *3385[7]*6157[14] *6283[10] 6480[9]*

Mr Whizz *A P Jones* a38 38
9 ch g Manhal—Panienka (POL) (Dom Racine (FR))
259[4]

Mr Wiseguy *G C Bravery* a65 63d
3 b c Groom Dancer(USA) —Tassagh Bridge (IRE) (Double Schwartz)
2028[7] 2655[7] *3073[4]4044[10]* 4662[9] 5129[8]5725[10] *5910[5]* 6161[6]*6378[3]*

Mr Wolf *D W Barker* a90 100
5 b g Wolfhound(USA) —Madam Millie (Milford)
1042[8] 1183[13] 1438[7] (2397) 2683[7] 2830[7](3715) (3986) 4174[7] 4609[5] 4832[6] 5158[8] 5443[6]*6095[8]*

Mr Wong (IRE) *M Sheppard* a59 85
10 br g Be My Native(USA) —Adare Boreen (Boreen (FR))
857[2] (Dead)

Ms Polly Garter *J M Bradley* a17 37
4 br m Petong—Utopia (Primo Dominie)
1413[15] 2632[9] 2758[16] 3863[10]

Ms Rainbow Runner *P Butler* a58 58
3 b f Josr Algarhoud(IRE) —Silk Law (IRE) (Barathea (IRE))
*30[2] 85[3]142[6] 234[6]342[5] 422[5]544[6] 918[12]*1314[14] 4585[14]

Ms Victoria (IRE) *B J Meehan* 80
2 b f Fasliyev(USA) —Musical Refrain (IRE) (Dancing Dissident (USA))
2984[5] 4657[3]

Mt Desert *C J Mann* 81
4 b g Rainbow Quest(USA) —Chief Bee (Chief's Crown (USA))
1690[11]

Mtilly *K G Reveley* a59 50
5 br m Mtoto—Corn Lily (Aragon)
4944[11]

Muara *D W Barker* a61 61
4 ch m Wolfhound(USA) —Darussalam (Tina's Pet)
424[8] 552[6]813[4] 1235[6] 2376[10] (2543) 3003[3] 3781[7]5684[16] 6465[6] 6533[2](6615) 6922[8]

Mubaashir (IRE) *E A L Dunlop* a93 96
2 ch c Noverre(USA) —Birdsong (IRE) (Dolphin Street (FR))
(1333) (1582) 2225[4] 2719[7] 3442[8] 5681[15]6100[4]

Mubtaker (USA) *M P Tregoning* 119
9 ch h Silver Hawk(USA) —Gazayil (USA) (Irish River (FR))
(1128) 1628[5] 2085[6] (Dead)

Muccia (IRE) *G Miliani* 72
2 b f Fasliyev(USA) —Mesenzana (IRE) (Mac's Imp (USA))
(3428a) 5858a[9]

Mucho Loco (IRE) *J G Portman* a59 59
3 ch g Tagula(IRE) —Mousseux (IRE) (Jareer (USA))
4157[10] 1799[2] 2065[2]2583[6] 3364[4] 4050[2] 4297[9] 4533[6]4769[5] 5474[7] 5885[3] 6277[2]

Muckle *S C Williams* a59 51
3 gr f Muhtarram(USA) —Crackle (Anshan)
692[7] 1925[5]2591[13] 3017[10] 3379[13]

Mudawin (IRE) *Jane Chapple-Hyam* a99 100
5 b g Intikhab(USA) —Fida (IRE) (Persian Heights)
714[3] 1098[6] 1357[11] (1943) 2817[3] (3256)3888[9] (4713) 5153[3] 5853a[7] 6438[2]

Mud Monkey *B G Powell* a65+ 60
2 ch c Muhtarram(USA) —Tenderfoot (Be My Chief (USA))
5178[9] 5423[5] 5622[7]6385[2]

Muffett's Dream *J A Geake* a59 62
2 b f Fraam—Loveless Carla (Pursuit Of Love)
5344[10] 6023[9] 6349[7]

Mugeba *Miss Gay Kelleway* a57 65
5 b m Primo Dominie—Ella Lamees (Statoblest)
2184[6] 2233[7] 2590[10] 4265[8] (4844) 5302[4]5327[5] 5756[3] 6061[5]

Muhannak (IRE) *G A Butler* 28
2 b c Chester House(USA) —Opera (Forzando)
4140[10]

Muhareb (USA) *Doug Watson* a100 100
7 ch g Thunder Gulch(USA) —Queen Of Spirit (USA) (Deputy Minister (CAN))
(279a)

Mujahaz (IRE) *J L Dunlop* 68
2 b c Act One—Sayedati Eljamilah (USA) (Mr Prospector (USA))
4592[8] 5178[12] 5622[6] 6066[3]

Mujamead *P C Haslam* a53
2 b c Mujahid(USA) —Island Mead (Pharly (FR))
6815[4] 6925[6]6963[7]

Mujarad (USA) *P M Mooney* a24 81
6 ch g King Of Kings(IRE) —Happy Result (USA) (Diesis)
285[13] 2245[13]

Mujart *J A Pickering* a58 57
2 b f Mujahid(USA) —Artifact (So Factual (USA))
3157[9] 3596[10]5348[7] 5592[6] 5764[5] 6296[3] 6414[3]6500[2] 6788[4]

Mujazaf *D Burchell* a49 59
4 b g Grand Lodge(USA) —Decision Maid (USA) (Diesis)
141[3] 3098[3]338[3] 4429[6]94[2] 2413[10]2861[8] (Dead)

Mujeak (IRE) *J J Quinn* a39 72d
3 b g Mujadil(USA) —Break For Peace (IRE) (Brief Truce (USA))
1127[5] 2763[7] 4886[2] 5060[3] 5401[12]5951[5] 6389[7]

Mujelle *D K Ivory* a65 65
3 b g Mujahid(USA) —Jennelle (Nomination)
1312[9] 2050[16] 2247[7]2678[10] 3410[12] 3999[5]4491[6] 5054[8] 5248[8]

Mujimac (IRE) *P A Blockley* a38 32
4 b g Mujadil(USA) —Cross Dall (IRE) (Blues Traveller (IRE))
41[7] 92[7]259[12] 394[10]

Mujma *Sir Michael Stoute* a65 62
2 gb c Indian Ridge—Farfala (FR) (Linamix (FR))
5883[9] 6188[6]

Mujobliged (IRE) *Seamus G O'Donnell* a40 68
3 b c Mujadil(USA) —Festival Of Light (High Top)
6545[8]

Mujood *R F Johnson Houghton* a84 91
3 b g Mujahid(USA) —Waqood (USA) (Riverman (USA))
1016[12] 1515[4] 1615[5]2344[2] 2620[11] 3202[3]3404[5] 3906[4] 4076[2]4241[4] (4557) 4831[5] 5211[6]5670[3] (6065) 6204[6]

Mukaaber *M P Tregoning* 22
3 ch c Pivotal—Placement (Kris)
1134[13] 1374[9]

Mukafeh (USA) *E Charpy* a101 111
5 b h Danzig(USA) —Bint Salsabil (USA) (Nashwan (USA))
434a[5] 507a[8]

Muktasb (USA) *D Shaw* a59 52
5 b g Bahri(USA) —Maghaarb (Machiavellian (USA))
146[5] 1787[1]95[7] 299[3]465[2] 487[4]679[2] 886[9](1195) 1396[5]1611[7] 1794[9] 6615[2]6688[7] 6723[2]6753[2] 6994[4]

Mulaazem *M P Tregoning* 85
3 b g King's Best(USA) —Harayir (USA) (Gulch (USA))
3875[2] (4300)

Mulaqat *M P Tregoning* a80 119
3 b c Singspiel(IRE) —Atamana (IRE) (Lahib (USA))
1092[6] (1488) 2226[8] 2775[4] 3254[5] 3736[4](4358) 4818[5]

Mulberry Lad (IRE) *P W Hiatt* a63 54
4 b g Entrepreneur—Taisho (IRE) (Namaqualand (USA))
81[8] 126[4]177[4] 247[4](265) 288[11]307[4] 502[5]546[4] 613[4]708[12] 1310[5] (1463) 1594[13] 1752[13] 2288[7] 2702[12] 6493[7]6549[11] (6632) 6713[10] (6727)

Mullady Penelope *Mrs A Duffield* 62+
3 b f Mull Of Kintyre(USA) —Gracious Imp (USA) (Imp Society (USA))
1733[5] 2833[6] 2876[2] (3340) 3538[6] 3608[10]4201[9] 4226[6]

Mulligan's Gold (IRE) *T D Easterby* 73
3 b g Fasliyev(USA) —Magic Lady (IRE) (Bigstone (IRE))
(978) 1344[2] 1857[7] 2110[3] 2410[5] 2976[4]3397[2] 3879[6] 4403[4] 4888[8] 5401[10]

Mulligan's Pride (IRE) *G A Swinbank* 61
5 b g Kahyasi—Babs Mulligan (IRE) (Le Bavard (FR))
(2528) 3019[6] 3284[6] 3696[4] 4252[6] 4506[3]4914[7]

Mulligans Pursuit (IRE) *M P Sunderland* 56
2 b g Musical Pursuit—Anna Mong Men (Man Among Men (IRE))
5692a[13]

Mullins Bay *J E Hammond* 119
5 b h Machiavellian(USA) —Bella Colora (Bellypha)
6364a[2]

Mull Of Dubai *J S Moore* a49 75
3 b g Mull Of Kintyre(USA) —Enlisted (IRE) (Sadler's Wells (USA))
1567[4] 1801[6] 2065[3] 2535[5] 2814[2](3347) 3589[3] 4197[4] 4672[2] (5284) 5644[7] (5868)5935[4]

Mullzima (IRE) *P D Evans* a43 50?
3 b f Mull Of Kintyre(USA) —Habaza (IRE) (Shernazar)
945[11]

Multahab *Miss D A McHale* a36 72
7 bb g Zafonic(USA) —Alumisiyah (USA) (Danzig (USA))
1727[11] (2955) 3165[5] 3825[7](4232) (4675) 5275[8] 5987[12]

Multakka (IRE) *M P Tregoning* a88 90
3 b c Alhaarth(IRE) —Elfaslah (IRE) (Green Desert (USA))
964[3] 1337[3] 1951[2]2605[2] 3491[10] 4083[4]

Multidimensional (IRE) *H R A Cecil* 110
3 b c Danehill(USA) —Sacred Song (USA) (Diesis) (2868) (3740) 4126[8] (4623a)

Multiplex *A Fabre* 108
3 b c Danehill(USA) —Shirley Valentine (Shirley Heights)
3778a[5]

Multitude (IRE) *T D Easterby* 65
2 b g Mull Of Kintyre(USA) —Sea Modena (IRE) (Mac's Imp (USA))
5076[8] 5491[3] 5766[3] 6013[4]

Mulvany (IRE) *B J Meehan* a48 61
2 b c Mull Of Kintyre(USA) —Flamanda (Niniski (USA))
2579[9] 3417[11] 3949[4] 4284[6] 5084[6]5876[6]

Mumaathel (IRE) *M P Tregoning* a83+ 86
3 b g Alhaarth(IRE) —Alhufoof (USA) (Dayjur (USA))
1048[3] 1476[2] 2343[2]3317[7] 4899[3] 5988[2]

Mumbleswerve (IRE) *W Jarvis* a65 49
2 b c City On A Hill(USA) —Dolcezza (FR) (Lichine (USA))
6214[15] 6887[7]

Mum's Memories *Jedd O'Keeffe* 33
2 ch g Zaha(CAN) —Trevorsninepoints (Jester)
1080[8] 2145[7] 2178[11]

Munaa (IRE) *K R Burke* a63 79
3 b f Alhaarth(IRE) —Beseeching (IRE) (Hamas (IRE))
2613[4] 3250[9] (4052) 4426[4] 4820[2] 5724[7]

Munaddam (USA) *E A L Dunlop* 105
4 ch g Aljabr(USA) —Etizaaz (USA) (Diesis)
1667[2] 2012[19] 2776[10] 4128[9] 4682[12](5420)

Muncaster Castle (IRE) *R F Fisher* 55
2 b g Johannesburg(USA) —Eubee (FR) (Common Grounds)
1790[5] 2854[5] 4066[5] 4724[2] 5860[8]6007[6]

Mundo's Magic *D W Barker* 79
2 b g Foxhound(USA) —Amber's Bluff (Mind Games)
1342[13] 1588[15] (3713) 4134[5] 4547[9] 5334[5]

Mungo Jerry (GER) *B N Pollock* a57 64
5 b g Tannenkonig(IRE) —Mostly Sure (IRE) (Sure Blade (USA))
318[7] 3382[10]

Munsef *J L Dunlop* 117
4 b g Zafonic(USA) —Mazaya (IRE) (Sadler's Wells (USA))
1128[2] 1507[2] 2277a[7] 4595[3] 5547[2]6103[5]

Munster Mountain (IRE) *P A Blockley* a33 55
2 ch c Monashee Mountain(USA) —The Voice (ITY) (Catrail (USA))
2778[5] 4109[U] 5066[11] 5381[8] 6416[10]6534[10]

Muntada *M P Tregoning* a67 77
3 b f King's Best(USA) —Inaaq (Lammtarra (USA))
1335[10] 1955[3] 2815[2]4489[3] 4945[5] 5589[2] 6459[4]

Muntami (IRE) *S Donohoe* a52 73
5 gr g Daylami(IRE) —Bashashah (IRE) (Kris)
98[5] 4121a[4]

Muqarrar (IRE) *T J Fitzgerald* a59 49
7 ch g Alhaarth(IRE) —Narjis (USA) (Blushing Groom (FR))
147[10]

Muqtadi (IRE) *Mrs Barbara Waring*
8 b g Marju(IRE) —Kadwah (USA) (Mr Prospector (USA))
6133[14]

Murbek (IRE) *M A Jarvis* 83
2 b c Dansili—Flagship (Rainbow Quest (USA))
4487[2] 5658[4]

Murdoch *E S McMahon* 71
2 b c Mutamarkiz(IRE) —Miss Pharly (Pharly (FR))
6023[2]

Muree Queen *R Hollinshead* 50
2 b f Diktat—Bright Future (FR) (Akarad (FR))
5134[3] 5283[3] 5614[6]

Murfreesboro *J H M Gosden* 95
3 b c Bahamian Bounty—Merry Rous (Rousillon (USA))
1818[10] 2959[2] 3494[15] 5642[12]

Murrieta *Miss J R Gibney* a52? 54
4 ch m Docksider(USA) —Lafleur (IRE) (Grand Lodge (USA))
1373[4] 1548[3] 1754[5]1879[7] 2133[6]

Murrin (IRE) *T G Mills* a75 66
2 bb g Trans Island—Flimmering (Dancing Brave (USA))
4781[6] 5178[5] (5608) 5989[5]6412[4]

Murrisk *Eamon Tyrrell* a72
2 ch c Groom Dancer(USA) —Food Of Love (Music Boy)
6032[5] 6224[4]6520[2]

Murrumbidgee (IRE) *J W Hills* a61 68
3 gr g Bluebird(USA) —Blanche Neige (USA) (Lit De Justice (USA))
85[5] 234[4]1352[2] 1652[6] 1941[6]2479[13] 2678[2] (3030) 3542[6] 3906[5] 4243[3]4757[11] 5205[3] 5621[6] 6206[11]

Murts Magic (IRE) *M J McGrath* a31
3 ch c Rossini(USA) —Clover Tina (IRE) (Coquelin (USA))
538[12] 762[10] (Dead)

Musadif (USA) *R A Kvisla* 105
8 ch g Shadeed(USA) —Tadwin (Never So Bold)
3312[8] 4128[22] 4875[10]

Musa Golosa *B Grizzetti* 104
3 b f Mujahid(USA) —Maid In The Shade (Forzando)
1713a[2] 2694a[14] 6002a[2] 6252a[7]

Musango *B R Johnson* a57
3 b g Night Shift(USA) —Imbabala (Zafonic (USA))
6593[6] 6828[5]6987[5]

Musardiere *J Balding* a47 57
4 b m Montjeu(IRE) —Majestic Image (Niniski (USA))
4925[8] 5954[15] 6280[4]6729[14]

Musca (IRE) *J Howard Johnson* 83+
2 b g Tendulkar(USA) —Canary Bird (IRE) (Catrail (USA))
2854[2] (5959)

Muscari *S Woodman* a65 66
4 ch m Indian Ridge—Desert Serenade (USA) (Green Desert (USA))
720[8] 2349[6] 2712[7]3260[10] 3703[9] 4077[3]4381[6] 5031[3] (5316) 5474[4]5973[7] 6694[2]6827[4] 6913[2]

Musette (IRE) *R E Barr* a32 46
3 b f Mujadil(USA) —Repique (USA) (Sharpen Up)
544[10] 637[6]2876[6] 3397[6] 3526[4] 4613[9] 5077[12]

Musheed (IRE) *E A L Dunlop* 36
2 b c King's Best(USA) —Khulan (USA) (Bahri (USA))
5458[10]

Musical Affair *F Jordan* a28 53
2 b f Alflora(IRE) —Song For Jess (IRE) (Accordion)
2610[7] 3096[5] 5068[10]5948[8] 6296[9]

Musical Award (IRE) *M G Quinlan* 67
2 b c Tobougg(IRE) —Emy's Girl (USA) (Prospect Bay (CAN))
4103[10] 4333[12] 4829[5] 5597[13] 5655[16]5933[7]

Musical Beat *Miss V Haigh* a71
2 ch f Beat Hollow—Warbler (Warning)
6663[3] 6840[3]6927[2]

Musical Chimes *W M Brisbourne* a47 3
3 br f Josr Algarhoud(IRE) —Sally Slade (Dowsing (USA))
710[8] 971[11] 1110[7]2318[14] 2575[5] 3016[13]3488[6] 5951[9] 6542[11]

Musical City *B Smart* a44 44
3 ch f City On A Hill(USA) —Royal Musical (Royal Abjar (USA))
39[7] 99[6]347[8]

Musical Echo *G C H Chung* a72 67
3 b f Distant Music(USA) —Distant Music (Darshaan)
1901[9] 3011[5] 3410[4]4248[4] (4700)

Musical Giant (USA) *J Howard Johnson* 42
3 ch g Giant's Causeway(USA) —Music House (USA) (Sadler's Wells (USA))
2662[5] 3001[6] 3620[6]

Musical Gift *P A Blockley* a51
6 ch g Cadeaux Genereux—Kazoo (Shareef Dancer (USA))
258[2] 285[11]410[4] 1148[U](1194) 1387[2]1915[8] 2245[8]6067[12] 6544[12] 6725[5]6799[7] 6855[3]

Musical Guest (IRE) *G G Margarson* a68 85
3 b g Mozart(IRE) —Hoh Dear (IRE) (Sri Pekan (USA))
803[6] 1349[8] 5765[17]

Musical Land (IRE) *J R Weymes* 72
2 ch c Distant Music(USA) —Esquiline (USA) (Gone West (USA))
2924[4] 3328[4] 4018[7] 4949[2] 5552[2]6318[6]

Musical Magic *J Noseda* 66
3 b f Mozart(IRE) —Kirk (Selkirk (USA))
1085[9] 2325[4] 2712[13] 3230[4] 3540[3]4697[3] 5875[11]

Musical Mirage (USA) *G A Swinbank* 84
2 b f Royal Anthem(USA) —Fantasy (Cadeaux Genereux)
3982[8] (4400) 4732[4] 5187[7]

Musical Romance (IRE) *B J Meehan* a63 75
3 b f Mozart(IRE) —Dear Girl (IRE) (Fairy King (USA))
1004[5] 1551[8]1937[9] 2190[3] (2433) 2652[4]2826[7] (3118) 3349[4] 3873[6] 4226[2] 5181[5]

Musical Script (USA) *Mrs A J Hamilton-Fairley* a68 64
3 b g Stravinsky(USA) —Cyrillic (USA) (Irish River (FR))
418[5] 778[2] 963[3]2050[12] 2583[8] 3094[3] 3866[3] 4054[8]4365[9] 5938[2] (6288) 6395[2]

Musical Way (FR) *P Van De Poele* a80 112
4 ch m Gold Away(IRE) —Mulika (FR) (Procida (USA))
(5519a) 6124a[3] 6785a[10]

Musicanna *J R Fanshawe* 113
5 b m Cape Cross(IRE) —Upend (Main Reef)
1506[7] 2199[2] 3416[3] 5674[4] 5968[10]

Music By Mozart *P W Chapple-Hyam* a70 80
3 b c Mozart(IRE) —Dayville (USA) (Dayjur (USA))
1089[4] 1476[3] 2383[8] 3646[7]

Music Celebre (IRE) *S Curran* a66 79
6 b g Peintre Celebre(USA) —Marwell (Habitat)
6968[5]

Musicmaestroplease (IRE) *S Parr* a68 70
3 b c Rossini(USA) —Who Told Vicky (IRE) (Anita's Prince)
195[6] 646[4](796) 1232[2] 1616[9] 2441[4] 2698[2] 3089[2]3906[6] 4325[5] 5384[9] 6101[8]6387[2]

Music Note (IRE) *M R Channon* 88
3 b c Indian Ridge—Samara Middle East (FR) (Marju (IRE))
(2033) 3224[9] 4805[8]

Music Teacher *N A Callaghan* a56 40
4 ch m Piccolo—Duena (Grand Lodge (USA))
485[7] 679[8]782[9] 1195[6]

Musiotal *P A Blockley* a51 53
5 ch g Pivotal—Bemuse (Forzando)
43[6] 81[6]181[5] 315[3]399[6] 467[3]1148[5] 1394[3]1746[4] 2546[9] 3729[4]

Musketier (GER) *P Bary* 108
4 gr h Acatenango(GER) —Myth And Reality (Linamix (FR))
4417a[2] 5519a[5]

Mussoorie (FR) *R Gibson* 110
3 gr f Linamix(FR) —Fascinating Hill (FR) (Danehill (USA))
2491a[4] 4035a[9]

Mustajed *B R Millman* 90
5 b g Alhaarth(IRE) —Jasarah (IRE) (Green Desert (USA))
1357[3]

Mustakhlas (USA) *B P J Baugh* a50 47
5 ch g Diesis—Katiba (USA) (Gulch (USA))
403[7] 566[5](684) 794[9]1467[8] 2522[9] 2788[7]3270[10] 6754[5] 6995[4]

Mustamad *Sir Michael Stoute* 77
3 b c Anabaa(USA) —Nasanice (IRE) (Nashwan (USA))
1421[6] 1691[2] 2366[6]

Mustameet (USA) *Kevin Prendergast* 123+
5 b h Sahm(USA) —Hamasah (USA) (Irish River (FR))
930a[2] (1171a) (2371a) (3129a) (3559a) (4407a) 5193a[4] 6784a[14]

Mustammer *D Shaw* a53 42
3 b g Fasliyev(USA) —Alazima (USA) (Riverman (USA))
1336[8] 1823[11] 4806[6]6439[8] 6477[10]6619[7] 6728[9]6755[5] 6833[2]6856[5]

Mustaneer (USA) *Doug Watson* 107
6 b h Gone West(USA) —Market Booster (USA) (Green Dancer (USA))
207a[8]

Mustanfar (USA) *K McLaughlin* a93 115
5 ch h Unbridled(USA) —Manwah (USA) (Lyphard (USA))
741a[9]

Mustang Ali (IRE) *Dr J R J Naylor* a53 60
5 ch g Ali-Royal(IRE) —Classic Queen (IRE) (Classic Secret (USA))
116[7] 174[2]309[10] 443[5](3437) 4777[10]

Mustang Lil *Ms J S Doyle* a51
5 b m Mark Of Esteem(IRE) —Quivira (Rainbow Quest (USA))
1750[7]

Must Be Keen *Ernst Oertel* a46 56
7 b g Emperor Jones(USA) —As Mustard (Keen)
97[13] 897[10] 1166[6]1644[12] 4248[12]4845[13] 5035[8] 6128[4]6235[12]

Musthav (IRE) *T Stack* 90
2 b f Fasliyev(USA) —Stellar Empress (USA) (Star De Naskra (USA))
2686a[5] 3658a[4] 4850a[7] 5464a[11]

Mutadarek *Eoin Griffin* 89+
5 b g Machiavellian(USA) —Nasheed (USA) (Riverman (USA))
3128a[10]

Mutadarrej (IRE) *J L Dunlop* 72
2 ch c Fantastic Light(USA) —Najayeb (USA) (Silver Hawk (USA))
4333[11] (4867)

Mutafanen *E Charpy* a68 112
5 gr h Linamix(FR) —Doomna (IRE) (Machiavellian (USA))
208a[2] 354a[10] 509a[4]

Mutajarred *W J Haggas* 72
2 ch g Alhaarth(IRE) —Bedara (Barathea (IRE))
6200[4]

Mutakarrim *D K Weld* 111
9 ch g Mujtahid(USA) —Alyakkh (IRE) (Sadler's Wells (USA))
3107a[7]

Mutamaasek (USA) *Lady Herries* a67 68+
4 bb g Swain(IRE) —Tamgeed (USA) (Woodman (USA))
1288[7] 2305[16] 3365[6] 4149[6] 4702[12]5652[2]

Mutamared (USA) *K A Ryan* a110+ 109+
6 ch g Nureyev(USA) —Alydariel (USA) (Alydar (USA))
(836) (1487) 2227[9] 2847[25] 4128[2] (5667)

Mutamarres *Sir Michael Stoute* a75 101
3 b g Green Desert(USA) —Injaad (Machiavellian (USA))
1016[9] 1404[11](2760) 3414[2] 3761[8] 4601[2] 4875[11]

Mutanaseb (USA) *M A Jarvis* 81
2 b c Mr Greeley(USA) —Rose Rhapsody (USA) (Pleasant Colony (USA))
5915[5] 6220[3]

Mutared (IRE) *N P Littmoden* a48 46
8 b g Marju(IRE) —Shahaada (USA) (Private Account (USA))
143[5] 311[10]467[8]

Mutasallil (USA) *Doug Watson* a98 110+
6 bb h Gone West(USA) —Min Alhawa (USA) (Riverman (USA))
371a[8] 512a[10]

Mutawaffer *R A Fahey* 100
5 b g Marju(IRE) —Absaar (USA) (Alleged (USA))
1835[4] 2520[5] 3218[2] 3549[5] 3980[2]4711[10] 5188[5] 5787[4]

Mutawajid (IRE) *R Hannon* 100
3 b c Zafonic(USA) —Zeiting (IRE) (Zieten (USA))
1818[5] 2204[6] 2959[5]

Mutawaqed (IRE) *M A Magnusson* a78 85
8 ch g Zafonic(USA) —Waqood (USA) (Riverman (USA))
1820^{9} 2173^{12}

Mutayam *D A Nolan* 44
6 b g Compton Place—Final Shot (Dalsaan)
1611^{10} 2928^{14} 3356^{15} 3781^{13} 4091^{9}

Mutoon (IRE) *E A L Dunlop* a46
2 b f Erhaab(USA) —Nafhaat (USA) (Roberto (USA))
6073^{8}

Mutual Friend (USA) *E A L Dunlop* 72
2 gr c Aljabr(USA) —Dubai Visit (USA) (Quiet American (USA))
6214^{9}

Muzher (IRE) *B W Hills* a84 95
3 ch g Indian Ridge—Almurooj (Zafonic (USA))
1065^{4} (2034) 4047^{10} (4802) 5677^{4}5943^{3}

My Amalie (IRE) *C E Brittain* a87 91
3 b f Galileo(IRE) —Princess Amalie (USA) (Rahy (USA))
(835) 1130^{8} 1671^{7} 1990^{4} 3316^{8} 3891^{7}5666^{8}

My Arch *K A Ryan* 86
4 b g Silver Patriarch(IRE) —My Desire (Grey Desire)
1814^{3} 2366^{4} 3362^{3} 4203^{2} 4635^{2}(4945) 5678^{9}

My Beautaful *Miss J S Davis* a54
2 ch f Classic Cliche(IRE) —Ginger Rogers (Gildoran)
6809^{3}

My Best Secret *L Lungo* 9
7 ch g Secret Appeal—Mohibbah (USA) (Conquistador Cielo (USA))
3353^{12}

My Boo *T Keddy* a51 59
4 b m Sri Pekan(USA) —Malwiya (USA) (Shahrastani (USA))
109^{10} 309^{7}684^{7} 1562^{12} 2497^{12}3013^{9}

Mycenean Prince (USA) *R C Guest* a43 43
3 b g Swain(IRE) —Nijinsky's Beauty (USA) (Nijinsky (CAN))
1122^{14} 1345^{16} 1441^{11} 3785^{7} 5838^{6}6281^{11} 6799^{5}

My Dock (IRE) *Jan-Erik Pettersson*
3 ch f Docksider(USA) —Acquilata (USA) (Irish River (FR))
2564a^{11}

My Drop (IRE) *E J O'Neill* a51
2 b c Danetime(IRE) —Notluckytochange (IRE) (King Of Clubs)
6912^{4}

Myfrenchconnection (IRE) *P T Midgley* 63
2 b g Tendulkar(USA) —Papinette (IRE) (Maelstrom Lake)
4566^{9} 5289^{4} 5613^{6}

My Gacho (IRE) *T D Barron* a78 93
4 b g Shinko Forest(IRE) —Floralia (Auction Ring (USA))
100^{10} (2384) 2661^{20} (2732) 2830^{2}3077^{4} 3482^{6} 3956^{5} 5420^{3}

My Girl Pearl (IRE) *M S Saunders* a40 50
6 b m Sri Pekan(USA) —Desert Bloom (FR) (Last Tycoon)
581^{9} 2135^{13} 2233^{9}2531^{2} 2599^{5} 3033^{3} 3094^{9} 3267^{3}3543^{11} 3682^{9} 3867^{6} 4484^{6} 4554^{5}6131^{5} 6542^{10}

My Golden Opinion (USA) *E G Harty* a89
2 ch c High Yield(USA) —Distant Breeze (CHI) (Distant View (USA))
5983a^{4}

My Jeanie (IRE) *J C Fox* a60 26
2 ch f King Charlemagne(USA) —Home Comforts (Most Welcome)
4177^{12} 6486^{8} 6597^{3}6853^{2}

Mykeyta *J G Given* a43 32
3 b f Key Of Luck(USA) —Mylania (Midyan (USA))
93^{2} 329^{4}617^{4} 887^{6}

My Learned Friend (IRE) *A M Balding* 84
2 b c Marju(IRE) —Stately Princess (Robellino (USA))
3417^{8} 4129^{5} (4928) 5546^{3}

My Legal Eagle (IRE) *E G Bevan* a39 60
12 b g Law Society(USA) —Majestic Nurse (On Your Mark)
881^{3} 1138^{4} 1415^{11} 2099^{3} 2408^{4}5836^{5}

My Lovely Lady (IRE) *M L W Bell* 75
3 b f Cape Cross(IRE) —Lace Flower (Old Vic)
1055^{2} 1419^{4} 1946^{4} 2359^{4} (2729) 3088^{3}3472^{2} 3548^{6} 3828^{9} 4243^{7}

My Lovely Lesley (USA) *B J Meehan* a74 89
2 ch f Hennessy(USA) —My Cherie (USA) (Woodman (USA))
2125^{8} (2572) 3084^{3}

My Love Thomas (IRE) *E A L Dunlop* a67+
2 b f Cadeaux Genereux—Flanders (IRE) (Common Grounds)
(6457)

My Maite Mickey *R C Guest* a31 43
2 b g Komaite(USA) —Mrs Plum (Emarati (USA))
5315^{7} 5835^{7} 6278^{8}

My Man (FR) *C Laffon-Parias* a96 107?
4 b h Anabaa(USA) —Monitrice (FR) (Groom Dancer (USA))
2313a^{4}

My Michelle *B Palling* a50 64
5 b m Ali-Royal(IRE) —April Magic (Magic Ring (IRE))
1568^{9} 3405^{4} 4772^{5}4870^{5} 4983^{7}

My Mirasol *K A Ryan* a58 67
2 ch f Primo Valentino(IRE) —Distinctly Blu (IRE) (Distinctly North (USA))
814^{2} 1030^{2} 1499^{3} 5237^{14} 5681^{20}6639^{5} 6760^{4}(6859)

My Monna *Miss Sheena West* a51 36
2 b f Josr Algarhoud(IRE) —Albarsha (Mtoto)
2733^{10} 6879^{7}

My Mystic (USA) *L Brogi* 82
3 b f Machiavellian(USA) —Sehna (USA) (Dixieland Band (USA))
2493a^{4}

Mynd *B Palling* a56 67
6 b g Atraf—Prim Lass (Reprimand)
96^{7} 864^{2} 1102^{3}1414^{11} 1528^{3} 2027^{12} (2096) 5878^{12}6399^{5}

My Obsession (IRE) *John Berry* 60d
4 b g Spectrum(IRE) —Little Love (Warrshan (USA))
(778) 1041^{12} 1996^{14} 5042^{15} 6008^{12}

My Only Sunshine *M J Wallace* a44 69
7 b g First Trump—Fiveofive (IRE) (Fairy King (USA))
1047^{12} 2074^{6} 5765^{3} 5872^{12} 6174^{15}

My Paris *K A Ryan* a104 109
5 b g Paris House—My Desire (Grey Desire)
629^{8} 728^{15} 1479^{3}1678^{5} 2358^{3} 3313^{12} 4098^{7} 5520^{11}5675^{17}

My Pension (FR) *B Grizzetti* 89
3 gr f Kendor(FR) —Third Dimension (FR) (Suave Dancer (USA))
758a^{3}

My Pension (IRE) *P Howling* a68 50
5 b g Orpen(USA) —Woodenitbenice (USA) (Nasty And Bold (USA))
106^{4} 187^{8}383^{6} 462^{4}582^{8} 6787^{11}6863^{P}

My Petra *A King* a12 83
3 b f Midnight Legend—Lac Marmot (FR) (Marju (IRE))
1483^{3} 1898^{2} 2446^{6}2917^{2} (4159) 4528^{3} 5421^{2} 5732^{5}

My Princess (IRE) *N A Callaghan* a68 83
4 b m Danehill Dancer(IRE) —Shanoora (IRE) (Don't Forget Me)
1056^{4} 1636^{6} 1993^{6} 2400^{12} 2865^{6}3433^{3} 3712^{2} 3828^{4} 4447^{5} 5301^{3}(5572) 6148^{6}

My Putra (USA) *P F I Cole* a56 83
4 bb g Silver Hawk(USA) —Petite Triomphe (USA) (Wild Again (USA))
1006^{5} 1289^{11} 2044^{14}

My Quentin (FR) *F Demets* 90
2 ch c Medaaly—Nekhtabet (FR) (Fast Topaze (USA))
6609a^{4}

My Rascal (IRE) *J Balding* a54 61
4 b g Imperial Ballet(IRE) —Derena (FR) (Crystal Palace (FR))
1414^{12} 3171^{11} 3608^{16} 4232^{9}

My Reflection *D Shaw* a45 5+
3 b g Cape Cross(IRE) —There's Two (IRE) (Ashkalani (IRE))
(39) 102^{5} 176^{5}308^{2} 415^{9}577^{5} 637^{8}1200^{9} 1464^{6}1612^{9}

My Royal Captain (NZ) *L Laxon* a106
4 b g Zabeel(NZ) —Kiwi Magic (NZ) (Vice Regal (NZ))
368a^{3} 739a^{9}

Myrtle Bay (IRE) *K R Burke* a70 68
3 bl g Pennekamp(USA) —Moneypenny (GER) (Neshad (USA))
1296^{5} 1837^{10} 2332^{10} 2548^{4} 3249^{7}3527^{3} 3791^{3} 4111^{12} 5365^{2}

My Sara *R A Fahey* a48 20
2 b f Mujahid(USA) —Ancestry (Persepolis (FR))
2178^{12} 2552^{7} 2938^{4}6991^{5}

My Sea Of Love *A & G Botti* 101
3 b f King's Best(USA) —Scent Of Success (USA) (Quiet American (USA))
(2493a)

My Secrets *M Johnston* a76 65
2 b c Fantastic Light(USA) —St Radegund (Green Desert (USA))
3247^{7} 3713^{3} 6207^{5} (6394) (6569)

My Silver Monarch (IRE) *H S Howe* a20
2 b f Bertolini(USA) —April View (USA) (Distant View (USA))
5773^{11}

Mysteriosa *B R Millman* a54 46
4 b m Mujahid(USA) —Mrs Gray (Red Sunset)
6899^{13}

Mysterious Lina (FR) *P Demercastel* a97 107
3 gr f Linamix(FR) —Mysterious Guest (FR) (Barathea (IRE))
4645a^{2} 5220a^{9}

Mystery Cat (IRE) *Miss S Collins* 77
3 ch c Night Shift(USA) —Milly's Song (Millfontaine)
4034a^{4}

Mystery Ocean *R M Beckett* 86
2 b f Dr Fong(USA) —Tiriana (Common Grounds)
(4754) 5434^{10} 5940^{2} 6201^{7}

Mystery Pips *N Tinkler* a67 65d
6 b m Bin Ajwaad(IRE) —Le Shuttle (Presidium)
299^{13} 524^{4}(633) 686^{2}782^{6} (1618) (2207) 2462^{2} 2780^{10} 2925^{4}3172^{5} 4636^{14} 5078^{12} 5752^{9} 5878^{4}6325^{8} 6521^{3}

Mystery River (USA) *B J Meehan* a70 70
2 ch f Dr Fong(USA) —Bacinella (USA) (El Gran Senor (USA))
4558^{9} 4964^{6} 5730^{3} 6071^{3}

Mystery World *M Johnston* 66
2 b g Agnes World(USA) —Dahshah (Mujtahid (USA))
1074^{7} 1284^{5} 1688^{4} 1884^{6} 5094^{8}

Mystic *D W Barker* 19
2 ch f Bahamian Bounty—Sweet Myrtle (USA) (Mutakddim (USA))
1664^{9} 3745^{7}

Mystical Ayr (IRE) *Miss L A Perratt* 63
4 br m Namid—Scanno's Choice (IRE) (Pennine Walk)
1531^{12} 1947^{2} 2165^{2} 5636^{7} 5861^{7}5904^{3} 6158^{8}

Mystical Moon *Lady Herries* 66+
2 b g Medicean—Moon Carnival (Be My Guest (USA))
4794^{8} 5178^{6} 5622^{5}

Mystic Dancer *Sir Michael Stoute* a80 69+
2 ch c Machiavellian(USA) —Mystic Goddess (USA) (Storm Bird (CAN))
5659^{5} 6072^{2}

Mystic Forest *Miss J A Camacho* a33
7 b g Charnwood Forest(IRE) —Mystic Beauty (IRE) (Alzao (USA))
129^{8}

Mystic Man (FR) *I W McInnes* a84 75+
8 b g Cadeaux Genereux—Shawanni (Shareef Dancer (USA))
(44) 107^{2} (235) 321^{2}559^{8} 585^{3}(639) 826^{12}1455^{8} 1531^{10} 3298^{12} 4116^{5} 4496^{5}4831^{15} 5085^{10} 5573^{11} 5688^{12}6696^{6} 6938^{6}

Mystic Promise (IRE) *Mrs N Macauley* a31 12
5 gr g Among Men(USA) —Ivory's Promise (Pursuit Of Love)
18^{10}

Mystic Queen (IRE) *A P Jarvis* a61 18
3 b f Woodborough(USA) —Speed Queen (IRE) (Goldmark (USA))
536^{9} 1254^{5}2138^{2} 2576^{4}3154^{5} 3257^{2}5620^{16} 5970^{8} 6129^{3}6477^{4} 6642^{12}6713^{9}

Mystic Roll *Jane Chapple-Hyam* a56 65d
3 br g Medicean—Pain Perdu (IRE) (Waajib)
1190^{8} 1681^{14} 2318^{10} 5755^{13} 6021^{10}6526^{8} 6693^{4}

Mystic Storm *Lady Herries* a79+ 75
3 b g Medicean—Mrs Nash (Night Shift (USA))
1165^{10} 1736^{2} (1925) 2404^{3}3318^{8} 4125^{8} 4634^{7}

Mystified (IRE) *R F Fisher* a65 54
3 b g Raise A Grand(IRE) —Sunrise (IRE) (Sri Pekan (USA))
(406) 712^{9} 1005^{10}1345^{13} 2240^{8} 2795^{5}3456^{5} 5836^{2} 6161^{8}6509^{8}

My Super Bird (USA) *M Johnston* 65
2 b g Gulch(USA) —Tadwiga (Fairy King (USA))
5491^{4} 5882^{6} 6066^{6}

Mytass *J A Pickering* a36 34
3 b g Averti(IRE) —Emerald Dream (IRE) (Vision (USA))
197^{10} 466^{7}1221^{9} 2070^{9} 2291^{7} 2415^{8}3006^{7} 3839^{10}

Mythical Charm *J J Bridger* a65+ 64
7 b m Charnwood Forest(IRE) —Triple Tricks (IRE) (Royal Academy (USA))
86^{6} 2860^{3} 3153^{3}3590^{8} 3854^{8} 4795^{8} 5267^{2} 5937^{10}6069^{5} 6130^{5} 6235^{2}(6618) 6652^{6}(6725) 6841^{8}

Mythical Echo (USA) *David Wachman* 89
2 ch f Stravinsky(USA) —Fabulous Fairy (USA) (Alydar (USA))
4853a^{11} 5408a^{9} 5850a^{12}

Mythical Kid (USA) *Sir Michael Stoute* 106
2 bb c Lemon Drop Kid(USA) —Myth To Reality (FR) (Sadler's Wells (USA))
(5891) 6102^{2}

Mythical King (IRE) *R Lee*
9 b g Fairy King(USA) —Whatcombe (USA) (Alleged (USA))
881^{6}

Mythological (USA) *Luke Comer* a39
9 b g El Gran Senor(USA) —Finance Charge (USA) (Pretense)
2345^{10}

Myths And Verses *K A Ryan* a64 61
3 b f Primo Valentino(IRE) —Romantic Myth (Mind Games)
1137^{6} 2353^{5} 3138^{3} 3250^{3} 3725^{3}4071^{9} 4728^{5} 5312^{6} 5637^{7} 6436^{3}6608^{4} 6934^{2}

My Tiger Lilly *W J Knight* a52 61
2 ch f Tobougg(IRE) —Ashantiana (Ashkalani (IRE))
2816^{8} 3645^{6} 4163^{3}4480^{6} 5419^{3}

Mytori *D Shaw* a46 37
4 ch m Vettori(IRE) —Markievicz (IRE) (Doyoun)
252^{12}

My Trip (IRE) *Kieran P Cotter* a49 55
4 bb g Midhish—Crissy (IRE) (Entitled)
263^{9}

Mytton's Dream *R Brotherton* a56 56
4 br m Diktat—Courtisane (Persepolis (FR))
42^{11} 121^{11}261^{10} 793^{5}1197^{9} 1393^{9}1465^{6}

Mytton's Pride *A Bailey* a50 66
3 b g Tagula(IRE) —Pictina (Petong)
1036^{7} 1529^{3} 1751^{4} 2027^{10} 2161^{7}2521^{10} 2939^{4} 3587^{6}4354^{8}

My Two Girls (IRE) *P T Midgley* 62
2 b f Danetime(IRE) —Sanctuary Line (IRE) (Lake Coniston (IRE))
3745^{6} 3907^{5} 4421^{10} 5238^{12}

My Typhoon (IRE) *W Mott* 118
4 ch m Giant's Causeway(USA) —Urban Sea (USA) (Miswaki (USA))
6340a^{6}

My Valerina (IRE) *Mrs A Duffield* a66 73
2 b f Danehill Dancer(IRE) —Witching Hour (IRE) (Alzao (USA))
1790^{2} 2026^{5} 2191^{2} 2623^{2} (2695) 3481^{3}(3720) 4152^{4} 4326^{4} 4912^{6}5404^{4} 5958^{6}

Naaddey *D Selvaratnam* a93 92
5 b h Seeking The Gold(USA) —Bahr (Generous (IRE))
434a^{13}

Naayla (IRE) *B J Meehan* a83 81
2 br f Invincible Spirit(IRE) —Pink Cashmere (IRE) (Polar Falcon (USA))
2506^{5} 2957^{2} (3259) 3925^{8} 4152^{5} 4460^{4}5503^{20} 5668^{3} 5829^{8}

Nabir (FR) *P D Niven* a63 90
6 gr g Linamix(FR) —Nabagha (FR) (Fabulous Dancer (USA))
505^{9} 1591^{7} 2286^{13}

Nabra *J H M Gosden* a49 54
2 b f Kyllachy—Muja Farewell (Mujtahid (USA))
4492^{3} 6055^{7} 6186^{11}

Nadawat (USA) *J L Dunlop* 81
2 bb f Kingmambo(USA) —Tashawak (IRE) (Night Shift (USA))
3700^{9} 4373^{3} 5206^{2} 5679^{3}

Nadine (GER) *H Hiller* 92
3 b f Perugino(USA) —Night Music (GER) (Acatenango (GER))
2279a^{11}

Naemi (GER) *S L Keightley* a22
4 b m Tannenkonig(IRE) —Noanah (GER) (Konigsstuhl (GER))
2^{6}

Nahaar (IRE) *M P Tregoning* 61
3 b g Royal Applause—Elhida (IRE) (Mujtahid (USA))
1641^{9} 2393^{4}

Nahlass *Ms J S Doyle* a49 22
3 ch f Bluegrass Prince(IRE) —Nahla (Wassl)
3647^{9} 5127^{10} 5510^{14}6987^{8}

Naigani (USA) *A P O'Brien* 83
2 ch c Storm Cat(USA) —Fiji (Rainbow Quest (USA))
5965^{15}

Naini Tal *D R C Elsworth* a69 67
3 ch f Inchinor—Royal Patron (Royal Academy (USA))
2615^{7} 3029^{8} 3794^{6} 4330^{4} 4701^{5}5510^{9}

Naissance Royale (IRE) *Christophe Clement* 115
4 ch m Giant's Causeway(USA) —Net Worth (USA) (Forty Niner (USA))
6125a^{3}

Nakheel *M Johnston* 106
3 b c Sadler's Wells(USA) —Matiya (IRE) (Alzao (USA))
5186^{5} 5477^{5} 6203^{5}

Nakwa (IRE) *E J Alston* a45 52
8 b g Namaqualand(USA) —Cajo (IRE) (Tirol)
318^{6} 537^{10}1590^{12} 2381^{9} 2790^{6}2927^{3} 3140^{4} 3675^{3} 3810^{2} 4132^{4}4320^{6} 4954^{9} 5925^{8}6279^{7}

Namarian (IRE) *T D Easterby* 56
2 b f Namid—Zalamera (Rambo Dancer (CAN))
2500^{5} 3307^{6} 4017^{6} 5366^{8}

Namaya (IRE) *J S Bolger* 62
3 ch c Namid—Touraya (Tap On Wood)
1362a^{9} 3561a^{13}

Namibian Pink (IRE) *R M Beckett* a58
2 b f Cape Cross(IRE) —Sky Pink (Warning)
6879^{3}

Namid Reprobate (IRE) *P F I Cole* a91 84
3 br g Namid—Morning Surprise (Tragic Role (USA))
848^{2} 1016^{4}(1337) 1986^{3} 4083^{8} 4488^{8}4802^{6} 5019^{13} 5943^{9}

Namir (IRE) *D Shaw* a64 72
4 b g Namid—Danalia (IRE) (Danehill (USA))
23^{5} 317^{8}480^{3} 532^{8}588^{9} 824^{7}986^{5} 1414^{6} (2505) 2550^{4}3004^{8} (3306) 3988^{2} 4258^{4} 4636^{11} 5378^{5}(5493) 5620^{11} 5938^{10} 6048^{14}

Namoos (USA) *J L Dunlop* 68
3 bb f Sahm(USA) —Shuhrah (USA) (Danzig (USA))
1646^{3} 1956^{6} 2583^{12} 4563^{6}

Namroc (IRE) *N A Callaghan* 95
5 b g Indian Ridge—Hesperia (Slip Anchor)
800^{2} 1043^{2} 1262^{9} 1992^{8} 2824^{4}3413^{9}

Namroud (USA) *R A Fahey* a83 91
7 b g Irish River(FR) —Top Line (FR) (Top Ville)
(2810) 3733^{9} 3985^{2} 4790^{10} 5337^{13} 5789^{10}6059^{13} 6241^{7}

Namu *B W Hills* a71 76
3 b f Mujahid(USA) —Sheraton Heights (Deploy)
2167^{4} 2763^{4} (3111) 3349^{6} (3866) 3943^{3} 4242^{6}4841^{3} (5317) 5427^{5} 5782^{12}

Nando's Dream *J Noseda* a78+
3 ch f Hernando(FR) —Dream Quest (Rainbow Quest (USA))
4367^{3} 5098^{3}(5741) 6287^{2}(6602)

Nan Jan *R Ingram* a81d 57
4 b m Komaite(USA) —Dam Certain (IRE) (Damister (USA))
644^{5} 721^{11}1258^{7} 1993^{15} 3262^{5}3642^{9} 4820^{10}

Nannina *J H M Gosden* 119
3 b f Medicean—Hill Hopper (IRE) (Danehill (USA))
1508^{12} (2802) 3416^{2} 4127^{3} 5191a^{4} 5713a^{5}

Nanny State (IRE) *P C Haslam* 49
2 b f Averti(IRE) —Roxy (Rock City)
2973^{10} 3188^{5}

Nanosecond (USA) *J H M Gosden* 59
3 ch g Kingmambo(USA) —Easyngold (USA) (Slew O'Gold (USA))
2825^{11} 5086^{9}

Nantes (GER) *A Fabre* 92
3 b f Night Shift(USA) —Nevskij Prospect (IRE) (Acatenango (GER))
1789a^{8}

Nanton (USA) *N Wilson* a85 89
4 rg g Spinning World(USA) —Grab The Green (USA) (Cozzene (USA))
3213^{5} 3688^{7} 3951^{4}4209^{6} 4819^{2} 5149^{3} (5483) (5680) 5945^{11} 6313^{8}

Nantyglo *M L W Bell* 103
3 b f Mark Of Esteem(IRE) —Bright Halo (IRE) (Bigstone (IRE))
(1477) 2199^{10} 2802^{12} 3499^{10}

Naomia (GER) *P Rau* 75
2 br f Monsun(GER) —Nagoya (GER) (Goofalik (USA))
6122a^{7}

Napapijri (FR) *W G M Turner* a38 58
4 gr m Highest Honor(FR) —Les Marettes (FR) (Baillamont (USA))
94^{13} 600^{11}

Napoleon Dynamite (IRE) *J W Hills* a67 67
2 b c Danetime(IRE) —Anita's Contessa (IRE) (Anita's Prince)
1510^{8} 2130^{6} 5648^{4}6055^{11} 6291^{2} 6414^{2}6603^{2}

Napoletano (GER) *S Dow* a62 101
5 b h Soviet Star(USA) —Noble House (GER) (Siberian Express (USA))
6564^{11} 6652^{10}6747^{8}

Nar (USA) *N Zito* a77
3 gr c Northern Afleet(USA) —Country Morning (USA) (Country Pine (USA))
5719a^{3}

Narita Century (JPN) *N Fujisawa* 118
7 b h Tony Bin—Princess Liebe (JPN) (Northern Taste (CAN))
1329a^{12}

Narratrice (IRE) *M Gasparini*
2 b f Night Shift(USA) —Northgate Raver (Absalom)
3428a^{7}

Narrjoo (USA) *M R Channon* 91
2 ch c Elusive Quality(USA) —Edhkerini (Lammtarra (USA))
(2545) 3442^6 4026^9 4789^3 5404^8

Narvik (IRE) *Saeed Bin Suroor* 99
3 ch c Galileo(IRE) —Arctic Hunt (IRE) (Bering)
6337^6

Nashaab (USA) *P D Evans* a90 96
9 b g Zafonic(USA) —Tajannub (USA) (Dixieland Band (USA))
1629^7 2435^9 2627^{16} 3068^4 (3194) 3519^{5}3812^5 4871^6 5130^2 5974^{8}6059^8

Nasheej (USA) *R Hannon* 109
3 b f Swain(IRE) —El Nafis (USA) (Kingmambo (USA))
(1130) 1508^3 2054a^{14} 2802^3 3416^5 4127^7

Nashharry (IRE) *R Hannon* a59 58
2 b f Ishiguru(USA) —Abbey Park (USA) (Known Fact (USA))
4657^7 5209^4 5570^3

Nashida (DEN) *Eva Olofsson*
3 b f Richard Of York—Natalja (DEN) (Niniski (USA))
2564a^{14}

Nassar (IRE) *G Prodromou* a45 63
3 b c Danehill(USA) —Regent Gold (USA) (Seeking The Gold (USA))
1055^7 1674^6 2587^9 2932^8 3230^{9}3540^4 3804^7 4697^5 4847^6 5247^{6}5929^8

Nassmaan (IRE) *P W Chapple-Hyam* a68 45
2 b c Alhaarth(IRE) —Just In Love (FR) (Highest Honor (FR))
5640^{13} 6297^{11} 6434^3

Nastrelli (IRE) *M Halford* 92
3 b g Mozart(IRE) —Dawnsio (IRE) (Tate Gallery (USA))
1362a^6

Natacha Rostow *C A Dwyer* a43 43
3 b f Pursuit Of Love—Piroshka (Soviet Star (USA))
5353^9 5774^7 5988^{12}

National Captain (SAF) *A Laird* a80 98
4 b h Captain Al(SAF) —National Secret (SAF) (Secret Prospector (USA))
150a^5 368a^{13}507a^2

National Express (IRE) *David Marnane* a39 70
4 b g Nashwan(USA) —National Portrait (IRE) (Royal Academy (USA))
571^{12}

National Icon (SAF) *D Maroun* a101 110
6 ch g National Emblem(SAF) —Royal Fields (SAF) (Northfields (USA))
281a^9 506a^8 619a^5

Nation State *G L Moore* a68
5 b g Sadler's Wells(USA) —Native Justice (USA) (Alleged (USA))
6205^{16}

Native American *T D McCarthy* a58 70
4 b g Indian Lodge(IRE) —Summer Siren (FR) (Saint Cyrien (FR))
1435^{11} 1821^{12} 2150^{11} 2345^{9}3035^{10} 3798^6 4497^6 4709^6 4869^{2}5954^{10}

Native Tiptoes *Miss Gay Kelleway* a41 56
3 b f Arkadian Hero(USA) —Waltham Skylark (Puissance)
233^8 298^{8}543^{10} 687^9

Native Title *D Nicholls* a84 94d
8 b g Pivotal—Bermuda Lily (Dunbeath (USA))
9^9 96^{2}159^3 (480) (761) 947^4 1031^8

Natural Blitz I (AUS) *D Cruz* 121
6 br g Maroof(USA) —Miiharo (NZ) (Bletchingly (AUS))
6783a^{11}

Natural Force (IRE) *Saeed Bin Suroor* a90+ 76
3 b c King's Best(USA) —Wolf Cleugh (IRE) (Last Tycoon)
3176^7 6051^{13}

Naughty By Nature *Sir Michael Stoute* 68
3 b g Machiavellian(USA) —Rumpipumpy (Shirley Heights)
1270^5 2087^6

Naughty Girl (IRE) *John A Harris* a45 75
6 b m Dr Devious(IRE) —Mary Magdalene (Night Shift (USA))
94^{10} 304^{6}410^6 616^{2}648^8

Naughty Thoughts (IRE) *K A Ryan* 67
2 b f Grand Lodge(USA) —Gentle Thoughts (Darshaan)
3721^3 4657^9 5503^6 5859^3

Nautical *A W Carroll* a76 86
8 gr g Lion Cavern(USA) —Russian Royal (USA) (Nureyev (USA))
64^7 167^{5}253^2 316^{3}569^4 726^9 (949) 1188^{3}1545^2 1820^3 2711^2 2981^{4}3204^2 4085^7 4101^{16}4602^3 5336^7 5682^{10}

Nautico *Miss L A Perratt* 42
3 ch f Compton Place—Sabre Lady (Sabrehill (USA))
1609^8 2377^9 3526^7 3587^5 3814^{10}4201^{10} 4524^8 4656^2 5363^7

Navajo Warrior (IRE) *T D Easterby* 27
3 b g Namid—Nassma (IRE) (Sadler's Wells (USA))
1386^9 3145^{13} 3791^{12} (Dead)

Naval Attache *P A Blockley* a55 58
4 b g Slip Anchor—Cayla (Tumble Wind)
42^5 2348^{3}3014^3 3386^{2}3698^3 4120^{13}

Naval Hero (IRE) *Mrs L Williamson* 48
3 b g Arkadian Hero(USA) —Isla Negra (IRE) (Last Tycoon)
1483^7 1868^4 2412^8 4111^{10} 4868^9

Navette (GER) *P Schiergen* a70 88
3 br f Highest Honor(FR) —Nouvelle Fortune (IRE) (Alzao (USA))
2059a^7

Navigation (IRE) *T J Etherington* a65 71
4 ch g Bahamian Bounty—Bridge Pool (First Trump)
1611^9 2505^8 2661^{15} 3398^{15} 4361^{9}6431^{10}

Nawaadi *M P Tregoning* a81 78+
3 b g Intikhab(USA) —Elhilmeya (IRE) (Unfuwain (USA))
1135^6 5612^2 6052^3

Nawamees (IRE) *G L Moore* a93 96
8 b g Darshaan—Truly Generous (IRE) (Generous (IRE))
661^3 765^{4}1071^2 1933^2 2656^4 4027^6 4347^{9}4997^5 5430^{4}5991^2

Nawaqees *J L Dunlop* 76
3 b c Danehill(USA) —Elrafa Ah (USA) (Storm Cat (USA))
1569^5

Nawassi (CHI) *M Al Darmaki*
4 b m Columbus Day(USA) —Basteza (CHI) (Razors Edge (CHI))
623a^{10}

Nawayea *C N Allen* a44 44
3 b f Lujain(USA) —Shallat (IRE) (Pennekamp (USA))
5270^9 6389^4 6774^3

Nawow *P D Cundell* a79 74+
6 b g Blushing Flame(USA) —Fair Test (Fair Season)
88^{10} 2647^{4}420^2 5895^{6}628^7 2460^4 3935^{5}5935^2 (6885)

Naxon (GER) *W Baltromei* 92
3 b c Big Shuffle(USA) —Nikitria (GER) (Miller's Mate)
1176a^7

Nayyir *G A Butler* a112 121
8 ch g Indian Ridge—Pearl Kite (USA) (Silver Hawk (USA))
(452) 666^3 1018^4(2226) 3086^4 4025^4 4098^{13} 5186^6 6218^8(6516)

Nazaaha (USA) *A G Newcombe* a59 50
4 gr m Elnadim(USA) —Taatof (IRE) (Lahib (USA))
110^6 164^{8}1774^5 2112^6 2602^6 2833^8

Nazdaq (IRE) *M Halford* 81
2 b c Danehill Dancer(IRE) —Dance Date (IRE) (Sadler's Wells (USA))
5466a^9

Nazlia (FR) *A De Royer-Dupre* 79
3 ch f Polish Precedent(USA) —Nasriyda (FR) (Darshaan)
6567a^{10}

Ndola *B J Curley* a50+ 30
7 b g Emperor Jones(USA) —Lykoa (Shirley Heights)
310^{12} 469^{10}(1541) 1910^{6}6238^{10} 6551^4

Near Dock (GER) *K R Burke* a107 112
5 b h Docksider(USA) —Night Year (IRE) (Jareer (USA))
154a^9 280a^7 496a^{5}621a^3 1018^3 1365a^{3}1601^4

Neardown Beauty (IRE) *I A Wood* a86 81
3 br f Bahhare(USA) —Habla Me (IRE) (Fairy King (USA))
1312^2 1592^6 2050^3 (2318) 2554^{4}2880^6 3176^5 3644^{3}3667^2 4144^4 4305^2 5619^3 5778^{2}5896^3 6350^2 (6413) 6594^2

Neardown Queen *I A Wood* a48 52
3 b f Lugana Beach—Polgwynne (Forzando)
1166^4 1771^9 2859^{8}3340^2 3595^8 4223^{10}

Near Honor (GER) *A Fabre* 107
8 ro h Highest Honor(FR) —Night Year (IRE) (Jareer (USA))
1014a^4 1331a^7 2914a^6 5219a^5

Neat 'n Tidy *C A Cyzer* a25 55
2 b f Josr Algarhoud(IRE) —Raspberry Sauce (Niniski (USA))
4624^6 4934^{10} 5231^{7}5563^{14}

Nebdi (IRE) *E J Alston* a58 90
5 b g Fayruz—Miss Nutwood (IRE) (Prince Rupert (FR))
6241^{10} 6624^{6}6796^2 6833^4

Nebraska City *D W Thompson* a47 47
5 b g Piccolo—Scarlet Veil (Tyrnavos)
173^9 783^{11}974^{10} 1443^{10} 4350^8

Nebraska Lady (IRE) *E J O'Neill* a77 85
4 b m Lujain(USA) —Montana Lady (IRE) (Be My Guest (USA))
2851^7 3687^3 3953^{8}4649a^6

Ned Kelly (SAF) *D Maroun* a85 93
5 b h Goldkeeper(USA) —Assemblance (SAF) (Complete Warrior (USA))
201a^5 355a^8 511a^{9}560a^8

Ned Ludd (IRE) *R Hannon* 83
3 b g Montjeu(IRE) —Zanella (IRE) (Nordico (USA))
2712^6 3665^2 4125^{12} 6017^{12}

Needle Rock (FR) *J-M Beguigne* 83
5 b g Verglas(IRE) —Black Dalhia (FR) (Sanglamore (USA))
2277a^{10}

Nee Lemon Left *M Mullineaux* a21 35
4 b m Puissance—Via Dolorosa (Chaddleworth (IRE))
4759^9

Nefski Alexander (USA) *P F I Cole* a63 74
3 b c Minardi(USA) —Reluctant Guest (USA) (Hostage (USA))
1065^7 1335^8 1741^{6}2118^4 (2498) 3008^7 3665^3 4490^7 5625^8

Negra Del Oro (GER) *A Lund* a49 93
3 br f Danehill Dancer(IRE) —Notenqueen (GER) (Turfkonig (GER))
2564a^3 3326a^2 4420a^{8}6722a^7

Negrito (GER) *Dagmar Wernli*
7 br h Protektor(GER) —Nordsee (IRE) (King's Lake (USA))
306a^5

Neideen (IRE) *J Akehurst* 67
4 ch m Elnadim(USA) —Mynador (USA) (Forty Niner (USA))
2317^{10}

Neila (GER) *W Hickst* 87
3 br f Diktat—Nigella (GER) (Limbo (GER))
4649a^5

Neil's Legacy (IRE) *Miss L A Perratt* a61 61
4 br m Second Empire(IRE) —Eliade (IRE) (Flash Of Steel)
3333^5 3480^3 4132^6 4692^2 5064^9(5403)

Nell Gwyn (IRE) *A P O'Brien* 78
2 b f Danehill(USA) —Offshore Boom (Be My Guest (USA))
5394a^7 5714a^{12}

Nellie *R M Whitaker*
2 b f Lake Coniston(IRE) —Boomerang Blade (Sure Blade (USA))
6295^{10}

Nellie Gwyn *J G Given* 30
4 b m King's Best(USA) —On Tiptoes (Shareef Dancer (USA))
1261^{10} 1733^{10} 2543^{13} 2833^9

Nellie Soprano (IRE) *K R Burke* 61
2 br f Key Of Luck(USA) —Danalia (IRE) (Danehill (USA))
4428^{13} 5287^3 5595^5

Nell Tupp *G Woodward* a2 55
3 b g Killer Instinct—Eternal Triangle (USA) (Barachois (CAN))
4403^{10} 5023^{11} 6944^8

Nelson (POL) *Jean-Rene Auvray* 18
4 br g Fourth Of June(USA) —Neustria (POL) (Who Knows)
309^{14} (Dead)

Nelsons Column (IRE) *G M Moore* 96
3 b g Benny The Dip(USA) —Sahara Rose (Green Desert (USA))
1139^6 1421^8 2325^2 3007^3 (3282) (3747) (4203)4508^8 4833^5 5758^4

Nelson Vettori *R M Beckett* 16
2 ch c Vettori(IRE) —Eskimo Nel (IRE) (Shy Groom (USA))
4774^{12}

Neon *J R Fanshawe* 65
2 b f Fantastic Light(USA) —River Saint (USA) (Irish River (FR))
4830^{10} 5352^7

Neon Blue *R M Whitaker* a55 79
5 bb g Atraf—Desert Lynx (IRE) (Green Desert (USA))
2681^8 3212^{16} 3813^2 (3959) 4253^3 4961^{6}5313^8 6425^8 6507^{10}

Nephetriti Way (IRE) *P R Chamings* a77 84
5 b m Docksider(USA) —Velvet Appeal (IRE) (Petorius)
1382^{13} 3450^5 3953^{5}4294^8 4894^8 5269^6

Nepos *A J McCabe* a59 60
2 b g Piccolo—Blushing Victoria (Weldnaas (USA))
3588^{10} 3860^2 4434^{6}4893^8 5162^6 5738^8

Nepro (IRE) *E J Creighton* a75 61
4 b g Orpen(USA) —My Gray (FR) (Danehill (USA))
424^2 489^{4}517^5

Neptune *J C Fox* a35 33
10 b g Dolphin Street(FR) —Seal Indigo (IRE) (Glenstal (USA))
599^{11} 706^{5}857^9 2044^{13}

Nerone (GER) *P Monteith* 51
5 gr g Sternkoenig(IRE) —Nordwahl (GER) (Waajib)
1502^{14}

Nero's Return (IRE) *M Johnston* 88
5 b g Mujadil(USA) —Snappy Dresser (Nishapour (FR))
728^{16} 865^8 1043^6 1357^6 1775^{12}2086^4 2201^{11} 2435^5 3748^2 3840^{2}4347^5 (4876) 5367^5

Neshla *C E Brittain* a42+
3 ch f Singspiel(IRE) —Nordica (Northfields (USA))
6817^3 6987^{11}

Nesno (USA) *J D Bethell* a70 83
3 ch c Royal Academy(USA) —Cognac Lady (USA) (Olympio (USA))
1108^8 2081^2 2502^3(3375) 4203^{10} 5115^{11}

Nessen Dorma (IRE) *J G Given* a76 84
5 b g Entrepreneur—Goldilocks (IRE) (Caerleon (USA))
976^6 1631^9 2000^5 2326^2 2975^{15}

Networker *P J McBride* a68+ 49
3 ch g Danzig Connection(USA) —Trevorsninepoints (Jester)
1126^6 1612^{11} 2876^7 3759^5 4056^{6}5844^3 (6901) 6964^4

Neuf Trois (FR) *Robert Collet* 72
2 ch f Pennekamp(USA) —Louve Solitaire (FR) (Loup Solitaire (USA))
4415a^6

Neutrino *P C Haslam* a58 80
4 b g Mtoto—Fair Seas (General Assembly (USA))
3248^8 4299^4 4698^2 4935^{6}5815^{10}

Nevada Desert (IRE) *R M Whitaker* a91 83
6 b g Desert King(IRE) —Kayanga (Green Desert (USA))
1280^{10} 1531^7 1987^5 (2378) 2627^9 3241^{4}4020^2 4153^7 4696^2 (4989) 5337^2 5680^{10}6313^4 (6424) 6678^3

Never Cross (IRE) *B Storey*
2 b f Cape Cross(IRE) —Itsy Bitsy Betsy (USA) (Beau Genius (CAN))
5859^7

Neverletme Go (IRE) *G Wragg* 84+
4 b m Green Desert(USA) —Cassandra Go (IRE) (Indian Ridge)
989^8 1377^{12}

Neveronamonday (IRE) *A Berry*
2 br f Night Shift(USA) —Appalachia (IRE) (Imperial Frontier (USA))
3693^5 4956^7

Never Say Deya *M R Channon* a50 55
3 b f Dansili—Dream On Deya (IRE) (Dolphin Street (FR))
2210^7 2529^{12} 3815^{4}4052^3 4277^2 4671^7 5571^2 5637^{14}5936^{10} 6235^4 6497^{10}

Never Will *K A Ryan* a70 81
5 b g Cadeaux Genereux—Answered Prayer (Green Desert (USA))
5810^{16} 6226^{10} 6469^{8}6684^6

Never Without Me *J F Coupland* a75 72
6 ch g Mark Of Esteem(IRE) —Festival Sister (Belmez (USA))
1414^3 1563^6 2182^2 2505^5 (2784) 3190^{10}3913^4 4230^9 4846^9 5286^6

Nevinstown (IRE) *C Grant* a58+ 64
6 b g Lahib(USA) —Moon Tango (IRE) (Last Tycoon)
134^{10} 3786^5 5062^{4}5839^{12}

New Beginning (IRE) *Mrs S Lamyman* a75+ 82
2 b c Keltos(FR) —Goldthroat (IRE) (Zafonic (USA))
4572^8 5114^4 5720^6 6010^5 (6498) 6824^8

New Blood (IRE) *J M Bradley* 10
3 b g Beckett(IRE) —Utmost (IRE) (Most Welcome)
1640^{12} 2730^8 3006^{13}

Newcastles Owen (IRE) *R Johnson* 29
3 b g Elnadim(USA) —Brittas Blues (IRE) (Blues Traveller (IRE))
3698^{11} 4382^8 4656^7

Newcorp Lad *Mrs G S Rees* a61 51
6 b g Komaite(USA) —Gleam Of Gold (Crested Lark)
1276^{11} 4974^{2}5285^{15} 5725^{16} 6383^{12}6899^8

New Destiny (IRE) *J Howard Johnson*
2 b c Xaar—Order Of The Day (USA) (Dayjur (USA))
1632^P (Dead)

New Diamond *Mrs P Ford* a76 41
7 ch g Bijou D'Inde—Nannie Annie (Persian Bold)
3894^8

New England *W M Brisbourne* a66 69
4 ch g Bachir(IRE) —West Escape (Gone West (USA))
43^2 157^{2}290^2 (383) 504^2 571^{3}3918^{12} 4565^{10} 4991^8(5173) 5740^6 5972^{4}6240^5

Newgate Lodge (IRE) *M Halford* 96
2 b f Namid—Oh'Cecilia (IRE) (Scenic)
5850a^3

New Girlfriend (IRE) *Robert Collet* 114
3 b f Diesis—New Story (USA) (Dynaformer (USA))
1719a^6 2275a^3 4191a^{12} 4416a^8 5701a^5(6230a)

New Guinea *M A Jarvis* a93+ 101+
3 b g Fantastic Light(USA) —Isle Of Spice (USA) (Diesis)
1192^5 1483^2 2175^2 2682^3 (3258) 4125^2(4631) (4791)

New Inspiration (GER) *W Kujath* 99
5 ch m Big Shuffle(USA) —Newhaven (Waajib)
1974a^4 2912a^4 4383a^6 6529a^{12}

Newkeylets *I Semple* a58 62
3 b f Diktat—Jay Gee Ell (Vaigly Great)
1279^8 1612^2 2161^5 2285^3 2856^{7}3526^5 3814^2 4354^5 4695^2 5060^{2}5577^3 5631^4 5864^5 6315^{13} 6480^{3}6649^4 6901^3

New Light *R F Johnson Houghton* 52
2 ch f Generous(IRE) —May Light (Midyan (USA))
5622^8

Newnham (IRE) *J R Boyle* a77 76
5 ch g Theatrical—Brief Escapade (IRE) (Brief Truce (USA))
59^2 (114) (250) (404) (454) 556^{6}5786^7 6148^{7}6287^4 6408^{5}6494^5

New Options *Peter Grayson* a63 52
9 b g Formidable(USA) —No Comebacks (Last Tycoon)
679^7 782^{10}1195^2 1396^{3}1539^{10} 1909^{10}2928^{10} 3356^8 4462^{10} 4551^{10} 6555^{12}6682^6 6739^{2}6755^4 6806^{2}6877^2 6994^{10}

Newport Boy (IRE) *R A Harris* a62+ 62
3 b g Montjeu(IRE) —Dream Chaser (Record Token)
762^4 894^4 3075^{8}5128^5 5258^3 5574^7 5875^{10}6526^7

Newport Lass (IRE) *K R Burke* a38 53
2 b f Mull Of Kintyre(USA) —Mari-Ela (IRE) (River Falls)
3096^4 4053^7 5364^7

New Proposal (IRE) *A P Jarvis* 57
4 b g Orpen(USA) —Woodenitbenice (USA) (Nasty And Bold (USA))
1402^8

News At Ten (IRE) *Declan Gillespie* 58
3 b g Almutawakel—Peak Viewing (IRE) (Sri Pekan (USA))
4124a^{14}

New Seeker *P F I Cole* 118
6 b g Green Desert(USA) —Ahbab (IRE) (Ajdal (USA))
1287^5 1840^8 2386^2 3086^3 3926^{12}(5682) 6252a^9

News Of The Day (IRE) *M Johnston* a55 56
2 ch f Diesis—Etoile Ascendante (USA) (Arctic Tern (USA))
5760^6 6012^4 6290^{6}6576^9

New Spirit (IRE) *John Joseph Murphy* 80
2 b f Invincible Spirit(IRE) —Rainbow Java (IRE) (Fairy King (USA))
2037a^4 2309a^4

Newsround *D W Chapman* a49 80
4 ch g Cadeaux Genereux—Ring The Relatives (Bering)
6^{10} 860^{12}1042^{17} 1258^{10} 1762^{4}1913^5 2505^{16} 2811^{2}3330^3 6549^{13}

New Very (JPN) *H Otonashi* 115
8 b h Fuji Kiseki(JPN) —Brilliant Very (JPN) (Northern Taste (CAN))
6530a^{16} 6850a^6

New World Order (IRE) *Declan Gillespie* 85
2 b c Night Shift(USA) —Kama Tashoof (Mtoto)
5466a^8 5851a^7

New York Hero (USA) *R Dutrow Jr* a93
6 br h Partner's Hero(USA) —Nin Two (USA) (John Alden (USA))
2093a^7

New York Oscar (IRE) *A J McCabe* a62
2 b g Tobougg(IRE) —Special Dissident (Dancing Dissident (USA))
6695^2 6838^5(6925) 6945^2

Next Flight (IRE) *R E Barr* a35 45
7 b g Woodborough(USA) —Sans Ceriph (IRE) (Thatching)
389^5 5750^8 5836^6

Next King (ITY) *A Botti* 94
2 gr c Shantou(USA) —Native Choice (IRE) (Be My Native (USA))
6123a^3

Next Ness (IRE) *R F Fisher* a55 58
3 b g Indian Lodge(IRE) —Fauna (IRE) (Taufan (USA))
31^4 500^{3}604^7 1274^{11}1950^8 (2192) 2377^7 2926^{10} (Dead)

Next Time Around (IRE) *Mrs L Stubbs* 92
4 bb g Namid—In Due Course (USA) (A.P. Indy (USA))
9897 20217

Niagara Causeway (USA) *Ron Sticka* a75 105
3 br c Giants Causeway—Theoretically (USA) (Theatrical)
4387a5

Nicada (IRE) *Miss Gay Kelleway* a70 65
2 ch c Titus Livius(FR) —Rhapsani (IRE) (Persian Bold)
12488 17444 198052726³ 29504 340953800⁴ 39975 49207(5738) 628596525⁷ 66393(6760) 68724

Nicaron (GER) *H Steinmetz* 116
4 b h Acatenango(GER) —Nicol's Girl (Dunbeath (USA))
1369a7 2693a6

Nice Applause (IRE) *Mme J Laurent-Joye Rossi* 103
3 b c Royal Applause—Mona Em (IRE) (Catrail (USA))
522a5 2942a6

Nice One *J R Turner*
2 b f Almaty(IRE) —Roecliffe (Totem (USA))
33807 37467 488719

Nice To Know (FR) *E A L Dunlop* 61
2 ch f Machiavellian(USA) —Entice (FR) (Selkirk (USA))
52975

Nice Tune *C E Brittain* a94 97
4 b m Diktat—Military Tune (IRE) (Nashwan (USA))
(451) 5554 (660) 843210153 15852 234143489² (4040) 45906

Nick's Nikita (IRE) *M Halford* 104+
3 ch f Pivotal—Elaine's Honor (USA) (Chief's Crown (USA))
5854a5

Nicofonte (ITY) *P Caravati*
2 b c Crisos Il Monaco(IRE) —Nigel's Lucky Girl (Belfort (FR))
3427a7

Nicomedia (IRE) *R Hannon* a67 79
2 br f Key Of Luck(USA) —Ladylishandra (IRE) (Mujadil (USA))
29585 37075 499345464a19 68863

Niconero (AUS) *D Hayes* 115
4 b g Danzero(AUS) —Nicola Lass (AUS) (Scenic)
1527a12

Nicozetto (FR) *N Wilson* a53 51
6 b g Nicolotte—Arcizette (FR) (Sarhoob (USA))
4235 (871) 9393314110 31925

Nid D'Abeilles (IRE) *P Bary* 105
4 b h Green Desert(USA) —Massarossa (Mr Prospector (USA))
2313a3 4862a8 5146a8

Nidhaal (IRE) *E A L Dunlop* 97
3 ch f Observatory(USA) —Jeed (IRE) (Mujtahid (USA))
24382 34998 40977 54052 591911

Nigella *E S McMahon* a75 85
3 b f Band On The Run—Yabint El Sham (Sizzling Melody)
13778 16044

Night Crescendo (USA) *Mrs A J Perrett* a85 98+
3 bb g Diesis—Night Fax (USA) (Known Fact (USA))
(1115) 19513

Night Cru *C F Wall* a74 76
3 b g Night Shift(USA) —Jouet (Reprimand)
12918 16813 23916 (3364) (3906) 49335550410

Night Cruise (IRE) *J A Osborne* a82
3 b g Docksider(USA) —Addaya (IRE) (Persian Bold)
(6578) 68252

Night Explosion (IRE) *D J S Ffrench Davis* a48 25
8 ch g Night Shift(USA) —Voodoo Rocket (Lycius (USA))
636

Night Falcon *H Morrison* a52 19
2 b f Act One—Original Spin (IRE) (Machiavellian (USA))
589113 624211

Night Groove (IRE) *N P Littmoden* a62 63
3 b g Night Shift(USA) —Taysala (IRE) (Akarad (FR))
612 122618813 54839452 10442 131411 69885

Nightime (IRE) *D K Weld* 116
3 ch f Galileo(IRE) —Caumshinaun (IRE) (Indian Ridge)
(2054a) 280215

Night In (IRE) *N Tinkler* a72+ 76
3 b g Night Shift(USA) —Sherannda (USA) (Trempolino (USA))
114612 16068 21106 23533 304293879³ 42968 50798 531210 590210

Nightinshining (IRE) *A King* a72 92
2 ch c Night Shift(USA) —Malthouse Mistress (IRE) (Peintre Celebre (USA))
302510 38442 (4388) 48096

Nightmare Affair (USA) *M J Azpurua* a121
5 rg h Out Of Place(USA) —Beaux Arts Ball (USA) (Black Tie Affair)
6341a3

Night Market *Ronald Thompson* a53 53
8 ch g Inchinor—Night Transaction (Tina's Pet)
2713

Night Prayers (IRE) *B Smart* a29 91
4 ch g Night Shift(USA) —Eleanor Antoinette (IRE) (Double Schwartz)
71913 36736 391413

Night Prospector *R A Harris* a93+ 89
6 b g Night Shift(USA) —Pride Of My Heart (Lion Cavern (USA))
84610 116171475⁹ 19362 222710 30279 408534796⁶ 48754 52027 547615 606546399³ (6527) (6643) (6682) 672066896⁸

Night Rainbow (IRE) *C Tinkler* a41 61
3 ch f Night Shift(USA) —Teresita (Rainbow Quest (USA))
234010 26486³2994 35383 37288 471010 497012

Night Reveller (IRE) *M C Chapman* a31? 33
3 b f Night Shift(USA) —Tir-An-Oir (IRE) (Law Society (USA))
2912 52891386⁷ 168710 4050104227⁹ 430412 494312 58747605713 67316

Night Rocket (IRE) *A M Balding* a58
2 b f Night Shift(USA) —Exorcet (FR) (Selkirk (USA))
65753

Night Spot *B R Millman* a69 89
5 ch g Night Shift(USA) —Rash Gift (Cadeaux Genereux)
220117 262111 29186 33665 38545416012

Night Storm *S Dow* a71 81
5 b m Night Shift(USA) —Monte Calvo (Shirley Heights)
1114 18752365 32721926⁷ (2401) (2634) 28654 2900 240409 42415 45366 48795 510865436⁸ 63506 641396635⁷ 66985

Nightstrike (IRE) *H Candy* a64 70
3 b f Night Shift(USA) —Come Together (Mtoto)
216710 25326 305333381⁴ 39506 (4287) 45575483712 575614

Night Warrior (IRE) *N P Littmoden* a59 49
6 b g Alhaarth(IRE) —Miniver (IRE) (Mujtahid (USA))
754 (230) 263883791³ 549112413⁸

Night Wolf (IRE) *Jamie Poulton* a60 61
6 gr g Indian Ridge—Nicer (IRE) (Pennine Walk)
864 343667471³ 68649

Nihal (IRE) *M Johnston* 93+
3 b f Singspiel(IRE) —Katie McLain (USA) (Java Gold (USA))
14462 16157 222415 34775 (3882) 4039104833⁹ 567815

Nihil Petere (IRE) *P T Midgley* 46
2 b f Xaar—Forest Berries (IRE) (Thatching)
32426 34489 387811 44248 4830125084¹⁴

Nikki Bea (IRE) *Jamie Poulton* a64 64+
3 ch f Titus Livius(FR) —Strong Feeling (USA) (Devil's Bag (USA))
2172 119110 163841925² 24049 (2648) 29299 33384 3731P52108 68489

Nilsatisoptimum (USA) *M Mullineaux* a42 44
3 ch c Gilded Time(USA) —Fluid Emotion (USA) (Rhythm (USA))
316 104912321⁰ 12749 154983821⁸ 40716 429612 46563 471075840⁷ 61314 628211630610 64069

Nimble Star *C W Fairhurst* a11 40
3 b f Foxhound(USA) —Deerlet (Darshaan)
9368 14457 219222616⁸ 269910

Nimello (USA) *A G Newcombe* a78 75
10 b g Kingmambo(USA) —Zakota (IRE) (Polish Precedent (USA))
10710 25156404 953410011 155386819⁴ 698010

Nimra (USA) *G A Butler* a74 82
3 rg f Cozzene(USA) —Purity (USA) (Fappiano (USA))
15162 16696 26002 31223 43742470125650/

Nimrana Fort *G A Swinbank* a45 65
3 b g Indian Ridge—Ninotchka (USA) (Nijinsky (CAN))
10447 19467 531110 626011

Nina Blini *B J Meehan* a79 91
2 b f Bertolini(USA) —Film Buff (Midyan (USA))
11896 (1347) 27433 34159 373421 414685234⁵ 68222

Nina Fontenail (FR) *B R Millman* a65+ 67
5 gr m Kaldounevees(FR) —Ninon Fontenail (FR) (Turgeon (USA))
6973 12042 177262902⁵ 31527 373134282²

Ninetails (IRE) *E J O'Neill* a56 72
3 b f Rainbow Quest(USA) —Minerva (IRE) (Caerleon (USA))
32007 39015

Ninifee (GER) *W Hickst* 76
5 b m Alkalde(GER) —Nee Au Vent (GER) (Baylis)
5710a12

Ninth House (USA) *N P Littmoden* a91 81
4 b h Chester House(USA) —Ninette (USA) (Alleged (USA))
341313 (4047) 43799 501975045⁴ 54287(5688) 646186594⁸ 67726

Niqaab *B W Hills* a68 58+
2 ch f Alhaarth(IRE) —Shanty (Selkirk (USA))
295810 59065

Nisr *Miss Gay Kelleway* a56 64
9 b g Grand Lodge(USA) —Tharwa (IRE) (Last Tycoon)
(172) 2584 (297) 41724579

Nistaki (USA) *D Shaw* a71 70
5 ch g Miswaki(USA) —Brandywine Belle (USA) (Trempolino (USA))
29818 3199635361⁰ 3846104573⁵ 48947 52865 54875 6556765951⁰ 667226773⁸

Niteowl Lad (IRE) *J Balding* 84+
4 ch g Tagula(IRE) —Mareha (IRE) (Cadeaux Genereux)
232311 262411 34496 36226 411010

Niza D'Alm (FR) *Miss Suzy Smith* a8
5 bb m Passing Sale(FR) —Bekaa II (FR) (Djarvis (FR))
275313

Noah Jameel *A G Newcombe* 68
4 ch h Mark Of Esteem(IRE) —Subtle One (IRE) (Polish Patriot (USA))
56259

Nobbler *N A Callaghan* a48 64
4 br g Classic Cliche(IRE) —Nicely (IRE) (Bustino)
990014 13139

Nobelix (IRE) *J R Fanshawe* a83 87+
4 gr g Linamix(FR) —Nataliana (Surumu (GER))
19433 24473(3220) 402712 56787

Nobelmann (GER) *A W Carroll* a46
7 ch g Lomitas—Ninova (GER) (Esclavo (FR))
8914 122431536⁵ 1724P (Dead)

Nobileo *Wido Neuroth* a100 73
3 ch c Galileo(IRE) —Nataliana (Surumu (GER))
3776a14 4420a2

Nobilissima (IRE) *J L Spearing* 65
2 b f Orpen(USA) —Shadow Smile (IRE) (Slip Anchor)
35916 (3930) 46035 58296

Nobiz Like Shobiz (USA) *B Tagg* a112
2 b c Albert The Great(USA) —Nightstorm (USA) (Storm Cat (USA))
5983a2

Noble Calling (FR) *R J Hodges* a46 40
9 b g Caller I.D.(USA) —Specificity (USA) (Alleged (USA))
433212 54229 613213

Noble Edge *Robert Gray* a57 67
3 ch g Bold Edge—Noble Soul (Sayf El Arab (USA))
693 9921975 241360928595979² 12216 14242 21246 402244362⁷ 488413 544515

Noble Gent (IRE) *Saeed Bin Suroor* 104+
3 b c Danehill(USA) —Blanche Dubois (Nashwan (USA))
33182 37102 (4370) 48333 55308

Noble Locks (IRE) *J W Unett* a25 21
8 ch g Night Shift(USA) —Imperial Graf (USA) (Blushing John (USA))
654111

Noble Mind *P G Murphy* a49 49
5 b g Mind Games—Lady Annabel (Alhijaz)
785 17353014 457489171199111392⁹

Noble Minstrel *S C Williams* a63+ 55
3 ch g Fantastic Light(USA) —Sweetness Herself (Unfuwain (USA))
3807 21718 (6526) 67355

Noble Mount *A B Haynes* a46 48
5 b g Muhtarram(USA) —Our Poppet (IRE) (Warning)
3077 397679381228942782 637211 672766805⁶

Noble Nova *M R Channon* a58 67
3 br f Fraam—Noble Destiny (Dancing Brave (USA))
7976 13523 159311 19504 206592782⁹ (3329) (3529) (3586) 36723 37824 49957556815 56197

Noble Purpose (IRE) *J C Hayden* 69
3 b f Carrowkeel(IRE) —Roundstone Dancer (IRE) (Dancing Dissident (USA))
4186a9

Noble Tiger (IRE) *Mrs S C Bradburne*
5 b m Tiger Hill(IRE) —Noble Conquest (USA) (Vaguely Noble)
313910

Noble Twining (USA) *R Menichetti* 49
3 ch c Twining(USA) —Rhonda's Rocket (USA) (Fit To Fight (USA))
2493a8

No Commission (IRE) *R F Fisher* a45 45
4 b g General Monash(USA) —Price Of Passion (Dolphin Street (FR))
37847 662310

Noddies Way *J F Panvert* a61 73
3 b c Nomadic Way(USA) —Sharway Lady (Shareef Dancer (USA))
222817 38495 43303 48006 5057105651³ 591046398¹¹

Noddledoddle (IRE) *J Ryan* a52 42
2 b f Daggers Drawn(USA) —En Retard (IRE) (Petardia)
56388 60327 651136853⁴ 69635

Nod's Star *Mrs L C Jewell* a45 47
5 ch m Starborough—Barsham (Be My Guest (USA))
68044

Noelani (IRE) *John M Oxx* 109
4 b m Indian Ridge—Dawnsio (IRE) (Tate Gallery (USA))
1469a13 2369a2 28469 3572a2 4749a95393a²
(5708a)

No Frontier (IRE) *T Hogan* a60 74
8 ch m Imperial Frontier(USA) —Poly Dancer (Suave Dancer (USA))
4186a4

No Grouse *E J Alston* a69 69
6 b g Pursuit Of Love—Lady Joyce (FR) (Galetto (FR))
20205 23844 26615 32173 411674456⁸ 53864 548776390¹² 640456595⁴ 67474

No Inkling (IRE) *John A Harris* a35 35
3 b f Xaar—No Tippling (IRE) (Unblest)
1024 120113354 47108 4943954321³ 576711 630646958⁴

Noisy Silence (IRE) *P W Chapple-Hyam* 74
2 b c Giant's Causeway(USA) —Golightly (USA) (Take Me Out (USA))
59394 62206

Nommo (FR) *R Martens* 95
2 ch c Lahint(USA) —Noemie (FR) (Beaudelaire (USA))
6456a9

Nomoreblondes *P T Midgley* 52
2 ch f Ishiguru(USA) —Statuette (Statoblest)
27597 33586

Nomoretaxes (BRZ) *M F De Kock* a90
4 b h First American(USA) —Raghida (BRZ) (Roi Normand (USA))
150a3 368a105561a⁸ 620a6

Nona *Jedd O'Keeffe* a13 57
3 ch f Halling(USA) —Zarma (FR) (Machiavellian (USA))
279511 46979

Non Compliant *J W Hills* a84 84
2 b c Lujain(USA) —Flourish (Selkirk (USA))
24022 29382 4934454372⁶ (5686) 61464

Nonno Carlo (IRE) *M Grassi* 115
6 ch h Alhaarth(IRE) —Most Of People (Horage)
1712a7 1870a6

Noojoom (IRE) *M P Tregoning* 79
2 ch f Machiavellian(USA) —Abeyr (Unfuwain (USA))
53446

Noonmark (USA) *S Blasi* a111
3 br c Unbridled's Song(USA) —In The Storm (USA) (Storm Cat (USA))
5719a5

Noora (IRE) *C G Cox* a76 87
5 ch m Bahhare(USA) —Esteraad (IRE) (Cadeaux Genereux)
6606 24572 289253703² 45557 589512

Noorain *A M Hales* a51 46
4 ch m Kabool—Abeyr (Unfuwain (USA))
139412 157521725⁷ 22914 272843158³ 3263124389⁷ 661712 672510

Noplacelikehome (IRE) *Thomas Mullins* 96+
3 ch g Distant Music(USA) —Far From Home (Habitat)
4187a16

Nopleazinu *Mrs N S Evans* a42 42
6 ch m Sure Blade(USA) —Vado Via (Ardross)
30111

Norakit *M R Channon* 57
3 b f Mull Of Kintyre(USA) —Thailand (Lycius (USA))
298514 32195 336712 42773

Norcroft *Mrs C A Dunnett* a78 78
4 b g Fasliyev(USA) —Norcroft Joy (Rock Hopper)
445 11781647 253610543 (1151) 138281686¹³ 259011 273210 29816(3204) 353683709⁷ 40544 (4267) 436514 524685391⁵ 578296048¹² 63268

Nord (FR) *Stall Passy* 76
6 ch g Kadounor(FR) —Lake Annecy (USA) (Capote (USA))
5562a0

Nordhal *B Grizzetti* 108
7 br g Halling(USA) —Nord's Lucy (IRE) (Nordico (USA))
2217a4 5982a7

Nordic Affair *D R C Elsworth* a79 37
2 b c Halling(USA) —Affair Of State (IRE) (Tate Gallery (USA))
54589 589012 (6689) 68462

Nordic Light (USA) *P W Chapple-Hyam* 66
2 bb g Belong To Me(USA) —Midriff (USA) (Naevus (USA))
26238 429513

Nordic Thunder (GER) *A Fabre* 105
3 b c Singspiel(IRE) —Navona (GER) (Leone (GER))
1557a4

Nordtanzerin (GER) *P Schiergen* 105
3 gr f Danehill Dancer(IRE) —Nona (GER) (Cortez (GER))
1714a2 2279a3 3579a3 4648a3 (5414a) 5857a2

Nordwind (IRE) *W R Swinburn* a75 94
5 b g Acatenango(GER) —Narola (GER) (Nebos (GER))
12387 177912 (2296) 32947 38882

No Recollection (IRE) *M J Wallace* a67 45
3 b g Mozart(IRE) —Good Standing (USA) (Distant View (USA))
42452 4700551273 (Dead)

Norisan *R Hannon* a92 97
2 ch c Inchinor—Dream On Deya (IRE) (Dolphin Street (FR))
240211 (2867) (3531) 39243 48094 517635805⁷

Norman Beckett *I Semple* a64 74
3 b g Beckett(IRE) —Classic Coral (USA) (Seattle Dancer (USA))
194 1231014²⁴ 7816 (1948) 265973065² 34836 41736 50156 54034(5862)

Norman Norman *W S Kittow* a54
4 b g Double Trigger(IRE) —Nour El Sahar (USA) (Sagace (FR))
146710

Norman The Great *Jane Chapple-Hyam* a56
2 b c Night Shift(USA) —Encore Du Cristal (USA) (Quiet American (USA))
622411 63939

Norman Tradition *A M Balding* a28
2 ch f Traditionally(USA) —Normandy (CHI) (Great Regent (CAN))
510610

Norse Dancer (IRE) *D R C Elsworth* 125
6 b h Halling(USA) —River Patrol (Rousillon (USA))
741a8 1180a13 5051a7 53424 56737

Northern Boy (USA) *T D Barron* 85
3 ch g Lure(USA) —Catala (USA) (Northern Park (USA))
19842 (2448) 31766 36068 49897 540645863⁵

Northern Candy *A Dickman*
2 ch g Sugarfoot—Thalya (Crofthall)
507610 583510

Northern Chorus (IRE) *A Dickman* 76
3 ch g Distant Music(USA) —Nationalartgallery (IRE) (Tate Gallery (USA))
9803 134410 21972 23992 270123042⁴ 33978 (3759) 48865

Northern Dare (IRE) *D Nicholls* 50
2 b g Fath(USA) —Farmers Swing (IRE) (River Falls)
56148

Northern Desert (IRE) *P W Hiatt* a92 72
7 b g Desert Style(IRE) —Rosie's Guest (IRE) (Be My Guest (USA))
(64) 2213 (267) 542563256705843⁷ 130212 578595990¹² 663596830⁷ 69867

Northern Dune (IRE) *B J Curley*
2 b c Dilshaan—Zoudie (Ezzoud (IRE))
691211

Northern Empire (IRE) *B J Meehan* 103
3 ch g Namid—Bumble (Rainbow Quest (USA))
14084 29594

Northerner (IRE) *J R Norton* a55 63
3 b c Mark Of Esteem(IRE) —Ensorceleuse (FR) (Fabulous Dancer (USA))
3496 548611822 14243

Northern Fling *D Nicholls* a82 85
2 b g Mujadil(USA) —Donna Anna (Be My Chief (USA))
15877 (2517) 30644 40433(4130) 4824a9

Northern Jem *G G Margarson* 88
2 b c Mark Of Esteem(IRE) —Top Jem (Damister (USA))
43023 58066

Northern Promise (IRE) *J Parkes* 23
3 b g Brief Truce(USA) —Sudden Hope (FR) (Darshaan)
12967 210711 490911 53658 57579

Northern Rock (JPN) *A Laird* a102 91
8 ch g Northern Taste(CAN) —Special Jade (USA) (Cox's Ridge (USA))
353a[3] 434a[7]

Northern Splendour (USA) *Saeed Bin Suroor* 104
4 ch h Giant's Causeway(USA) —Ribbonwood (USA) (Diesis)
5813[2] 6203[7]

Northern Svengali (IRE) *D A Nolan* a17 55
10 b g Distinctly North(USA) —Trilby's Dream (IRE) (Mansooj)
1886[7] 2748[8] 2928[13] 3003[11] 3482[13]4091[6]

North Fleet *J M Bradley* a53 63
3 b g Bertolini(USA) —Rhiann (Anshan)
1048[12] 1355[5] 1751[10] 2316[8] 4120[12]4690[7] (5728) 5936[14] 6442[10]6556[12]

North Landing (IRE) *R C Guest* 8
6 b g Storm Bird(CAN) —Tirol Hope (IRE) (Tirol)
3350[9]

North Lodge (GER) *A King* a77 86
6 b g Grand Lodge(USA) —Nona (GER) (Cortez (GER))
1167[7] 1478[9]

Northside Lodge (IRE) *W R Swinburn* a77 69
8 b g Grand Lodge(USA) —Alongside (Slip Anchor)
88[11] 140[9]375[9] 2149[9] 3151[7]3798[5] 5047[2] 5258[6]5610[4] 6070[2]

North Walk (IRE) *K A Ryan* a79 85
3 b g Monashee Mountain(USA) —Celtic Link (IRE) (Toca Madera)
1097[14] 1596[9] 1855[2] 3176[2] 3473[4]3945[3] 4802[8] 5649[7]6160[10] 6424[6] 6698[11]6898[2]

Norton (IRE) *T G Mills* a107 101
9 ch g Barathea(IRE) —Primrose Valley (Mill Reef (USA))
1676[7] 2086[5] 2988[7] 3413[5] 3973[11]4819[4] 5428[2] 5833[12]6671[5]

Norwegian *Ian Williams* a52 20
5 b g Halling(USA) —Chicarica (USA) (The Minstrel (CAN))
2360[8] 4301[8] 6067[11] 6383[13]6524[7] (6701)

Norwegian Pride (FR) *P Schiergen* 106
4 b m Diktat—Tricorne (Green Desert (USA))
1974a[6] (2912a) 3661a[9] 4383a[9]

Nor'Wester *J R Fanshawe* a68 69
4 br g Inchinor—Princess Nawaal (USA) (Seattle Slew (USA))
2555[12] 3101[11]

Nosferatu (IRE) *Mrs A J Perrett* 83
3 b c In The Wings—Gothic Dream (IRE) (Nashwan (USA))
2175[3] (5870)

No Supper (IRE) *M G Quinlan* a55
2 ch c Inchinor—Be Thankfull (IRE) (Linamix (FR))
6950[5]

Nota Bene *D R C Elsworth* 116+
4 b g Zafonic(USA) —Dodo (IRE) (Alzao (USA))
1116[12] 1485[12]

Notability (IRE) *M A Jarvis* a111 115
4 b h King's Best(USA) —Noble Rose (IRE) (Caerleon (USA))
2012[6] 2776[19] 3534[3]4529[2] (4918a) 5703a[4] 5982a[2]

Notable Guest (USA) *Sir Michael Stoute* a100 117
5 b h Kingmambo(USA) —Yenda (Dancing Brave (USA))
1267[2] 2202[5] 3314[9] 4358[2] 5018[6]

Nota Liberata *G M Moore* 69
2 b g Spinning World(USA) —Kyda (USA) (Gulch (USA))
1595[8] 1884[2] 2076[5] 2623[11] 3372[5]4250[4] 4882[6] 4955[2] 5366[3] 5721[2]5788[7] 5958[2] 6270[2]

Not Another Cat (USA) *K R Burke* a72
2 ch c Hennessy(USA) —Isle Be Loving You (USA) (Stuka (USA))
4934[5] 6257[3]

Not For Me (IRE) *T J Pitt* a78+ 100
2 b c Mull Of Kintyre(USA) —Floral Hall (IRE) (Tagula (IRE))
1587[12] 2416[2] (2938) (3474) 3777a[5](4715) 5154[7]

Nothing Is Forever (IRE) *Mrs A J Perrett* a63 58
2 b g Daylami(IRE) —Bequeath (USA) (Lyphard (USA))
4534[4] 5105[5] 6058[9]

No Time (IRE) *A J McCabe* a79 66
6 b h Danetime(IRE) —Muckross Park (Nomination)
664[10] 761[9]1047[15] 1161[5] 1297[13]1399[4] 1795[17] 1928[7]4110[4] 4267[3] 4531[7] 5782[11](6709) 6823[8]

Notnowcato *Sir Michael Stoute* 125
4 ch h Inchinor—Rambling Rose (Cadeaux Genereux)
(1084) (2116) 2741[5] 3314[2] (4679) 5964[8]

Notte Italiana (IRE) *H J Koll* 55
4 b m Mtoto—Nordic Way (IRE) (Nordico (USA))
1860a[11]

Nottingham (SWE) *L Reuterskiold*
3 b g Richard Of York—Ibri (IRE) (Ore)
4919a[3]

Not To Know *John A Quinn* a68
2 b g Mujahid(USA) —Little Tramp (Trempolino (USA))
6662[4] 6808[3]

Not Too Taxing *R Hannon* a64
2 b g Forzando—Areish (IRE) (Keen)
6826[3] 6905[3]

Notturno Di Chopin (IRE) *J Heloury* 88
2 b c Desert Style(IRE) —Be Magic (Persian Bold)
(2474a) 6003a[11]

N'Oubliez Jamais (GER) *H Blume* 100
3 br c Poliglote—Night Green (GER) (Green Forest (USA))
5709a[2]

Nou Camp *N A Callaghan* a58 51
2 ch c Compton Place—Real Popcorn (IRE) (Jareer (USA))
3738[7] 4138[4] 4428[11]4921[2] 6388[9] 6488[4]6592[2] 6711[2]6839[3]

Noul (USA) *J S Moore* a49 43
7 ch g Miswaki(USA) —Water Course (USA) (Irish River (FR))
258[8] 581[6]616[4]

Nova Tor (IRE) *Peter Grayson* a57 72
4 b m Trans Island—Nordic Living (IRE) (Nordico (USA))
177[3] 216[2]320[3] 401[11]501[4] 588[11]806[4] 1150[6]1528[10]

Novellara *H R A Cecil* 103
3 b f Sadler's Wells(USA) —Modena (USA) (Roberto (USA))
(1797) 2772[8] 4079[7] (5641)

Noverenzi (IRE) *M Ciciarelli*
2 ch c Noverre(USA) —Luciana Massenzi (ITY) (Salmon Leap (USA))
6407a[11]

Noverfancy (IRE) *M Botti* a46 45
2 b f Noverre(USA) —Fair McLain (IRE) (Fairy King (USA))
2475a[5] 3385[6] 6172[4]

Novista (IRE) *M H Tompkins* 78
2 b g Anabaa Blue—Bistranova (USA) (Torrential (USA))
2604[2] 4264[4] 4895[9]

Nowisza (FR) *Ron Caget* a78 97
3 ch f Ocean Of Wisdom(USA) —Byanozza (Mtoto)
2374a[3] 6384a[0]

Now Look Out *E S McMahon* 74
2 gr c Bahamian Bounty—Where's Carol (Anfield)
(5766) 6332[6]

No Worries Yet (IRE) *J L Spearing* 70
2 b f Orpen(USA) —Charming Victoria (IRE) (Mujadil (USA))
(962) 1354[2] 1737[7] 2076[3] 3468[4] 5509[5]

Now Tell Me This *I Semple* 38
3 b g Mister Baileys—Inimitable (Polish Precedent (USA))
1034[9] 1503[4] 1814[6] 2548[8]

Nudrah *J L Dunlop* 74
3 b f Green Desert(USA) —Sayedati Eljamilah (USA) (Mr Prospector (USA))
1672[6] 2459[13]

Nufoudh (IRE) *M Johnston* 67d
2 b g Key Of Luck(USA) —Limpopo (Green Desert (USA))
1632[4] 2094[4] 2827[6] 4955[6]

Nuit Sombre (IRE) *J G M O'Shea* a62 88
6 b g Night Shift(USA) —Belair Princess (USA) (Mr Prospector (USA))
417[3] 659[6]1566[2] (2566) 3068[8] 4001[6]

Numeric (GER) *J H M Gosden* 95
3 br g Singspiel(IRE) —Narola (GER) (Nebos (GER))
1134[4] (1605) 1841[4] 2805[9] 3292[3] (4125) 4742[5]5530[6] 5920[9]

Numerical (IRE) *J L Dunlop* 56
2 ch g Numerous(USA) —Conspiracy (Rudimentary (USA))
2402[12] 3025[9] 3663[8] 4290[6]

Numerieus (FR) *Y De Nicolay* 97
2 br f Numerous(USA) —Northern Mixa (Linamix (FR))
(4464a) 5122a[4] 5880a[3]

Numero Due *G M Moore* 96+
4 b g Sinndar(IRE) —Kindle (Selkirk (USA))
976[3] 1294[2] (1685) 2437[7] 2723[24] 4883[2](5174) (5383)

Numidas (POL) *Mrs A L M King* a22
4 bl h Duke Valentino—Numata (POL) (Freedom's Choice (USA))
982[12] 1353[17]

Numide (FR) *J-C Rouget* 115+
3 b c Highest Honor(FR) —Numidie (FR) (Baillamont (USA))
(1557a) 2278a[5] 3517a[8] 5999a[6]

Nuqoosh *F Head* 100
2 ch f Machiavellian(USA) —Al Ishq (FR) (Nureyev (USA))
6228a[2]

Nurenberg (IRE) *M Halford* 84
4 b g Giant's Causeway(USA) —Peneia (USA) (Nureyev (USA))
(5396a)

Nur Tau (IRE) *M P Tregoning* 78
2 b g Peintre Celebre(USA) —Litchfield Hills (USA) (Relaunch (USA))
2402[10] (3253) 4037[9] 4773[8]

Nusoor (IRE) *Peter Grayson* a72 83
3 b g Fasliyev(USA) —Zulfaa (USA) (Bahri (USA))
(1687) 3296[3] 5107[14] 5476[7]5896[4] 6499[10] 6555[7]

Nut (IRE) *J W Hills* a48 65
3 b f Fasliyev(USA) —La Rosetta (IRE) (Alzao (USA))
104[4] 269[8]

Nutley Queen (IRE) *M Appleby* a45 53
7 b m Eagle Eyed(USA) —Secret Hideaway (USA) (Key To The Mint (USA))
59[6] 3594[7]3862[7]

Nyarhini *G Wragg* a92 96
3 b f Fantastic Light(USA) —Nuryana (Nureyev (USA))
827[3] 1472[3] 2744[18]

Oakbridge (IRE) *D J Wintle* a52 55
4 b g Indian Ridge—Chauncy Lane (IRE) (Sadler's Wells (USA))
22[12] 6708[5]

Oakley Absolute *R Hannon* a74 60
4 ch g Bluegrass Prince(IRE) —Susie Oakley VII (Damsire Unregistered)
(698) 915[5] 1288[12] 1665[4]1821[15] 2327[10] 2401[8] 3024[9] 3900[5]4332[8] 4869[4] 5166[8] 5474[3] 5831[10]6189[13]

Oakley Heffert (IRE) *R Hannon* a77 80
2 b c Titus Livius(FR) —Daftiyna (IRE) (Darshaan)
4428[5] 4873[7] 5091[4] 5647[6] (6018) 6458[3]

Oasis Flower *J R Fanshawe* 49
3 b f Green Desert(USA) —Carpet Of Leaves (USA) (Green Forest (USA))
2615[9] 2948[5] 3373[6]

Oasis Sun (IRE) *J R Best* a50 46
3 ch f Desert Sun—Albaiyda (IRE) (Brief Truce (USA))
422[7] 543[3]797[9] 2678[9] 6829[11]

Obe Bold (IRE) *A Berry* a50 55
5 b m Orpen(USA) —Capable Kate (IRE) (Alzao (USA))
360[2] 465[3]680[2] 789[7]876[6] (1303) (1607) 2749[8] 3004[13] 3330[11] 3673[7] 3783[2]4059[10] 4157[5] 4655[8] 4957[11] 5486[14]6308[13] 6719[14]

Obe Brave *M R Channon* 105
3 b g Agnes World(USA) —Pass The Rose (IRE) (Thatching)
1067[2] (1292) 1633[2] 2032[4] 4083[9] 4593[7]5044[2] 5501[9] 5812[12]

Obe Gold *M R Channon* a98 109
4 b g Namaqualand(USA) —Gagajulu (Al Hareb (USA))
(203a) 352a[6] 431a[3] (506a) 619a[6] 729[11] 830[5]2847[16] 3092[4] 3471[9] 3956[7] 4128[8]4430[4] 4609[6] 5358[18]

Obe One *D Nicholls* a62 70
6 b g Puissance—Plum Bold (Be My Guest (USA))
864[4] 1459[6] 2505[9] 2700[7] 3171[2]3398[2] 3524[8] 5309[13]

Obergurgl (IRE) *Mrs A Duffield* a62 46
3 br g Titus Livius(FR) —Lorella (IRE) (Fayruz)
1793[6] 2197[5] 2939[7]

Oberon's Prize *V Smith* 53?
4 b g King's Theatre(IRE) —Taj Victory (Final Straw)
1271[12] 1572[P]

Obe Royal *M R Channon* 70
2 b g Wizard King—Gagajulu (Al Hareb (USA))
3498[5] 3982[6] 4151[7] 5014[3] 5366[9]5866[12]

Obezyana (USA) *G A Huffer* a90 79
4 ch g Rahy(USA) —Polish Treaty (USA) (Danzig (USA))
140[6] 5990[7]

Obrigado (GER) *M Sowa* 102
5 br h Lavirco(GER) —Osina (GER) (Wise Money)
5762a[6] 6529a[14]

Obrigado (FR) *N Drysdale* 115
3 b c Enrique—Banakill (FR) (Funambule (USA))
5985a[2] 6613a[2]

Obrigado (USA) *Karen George* a96 93
6 b g Bahri(USA) —Glorious Diamond (USA) (His Majesty (USA))
444[5] 542[2]670[6] (843) 1017[5] 2341[3]2848[12] 3401[2] 3876[2]3971[4] 5045[2] 5430[5]5990[10]

Obscene *A J McCabe* a71 66
3 b g Key Of Luck(USA) —Scene (IRE) (Scenic)
730[10] 1185[8] 1337[7]1441[9] 1859[9] 6901[8]

Observatory Star (IRE) *T D Easterby* 69
3 br g Observatory(USA) —Pink Sovietstaia (FR) (Soviet Star (USA))
1983[7] 2363[7] 2947[12] 3473[7] 4735[7]5487[6] 6061[3] (6159)

Obstreperous Way *Miss Tracy Waggott* a54 37
4 ch g Dr Fong(USA) —Fleet Key (Afleet (CAN))
1293[11] 6973[6]

Obstructive *D K Ivory* a77
2 ch g Zilzal(USA) —Emily-Mou (IRE) (Cadeaux Genereux)
2979[4] 5261[2]5607[10]

Oceana Gold *A M Balding* 72
2 ch g Primo Valentino(IRE) —Silken Dalliance (Rambo Dancer (CAN))
4774[5] (5289) 5866[8]

Ocean Avenue (IRE) *C A Horgan* a70 84
7 b g Dolphin Street(FR) —Trinity Hall (Hallgate)
1478[2] 1943[7] 2534[3]3365[2] 4560[10] 5346[7]

Ocean Blaze *B R Millman* 68
2 b f Polar Prince(IRE) —La Belle Vie (Indian King (USA))
2957[13] 4559[5] 5592[14] 6025[3]

Oceancookie (IRE) *A M Balding* a59 77
4 b m Dashing Blade—Sankaty Light (USA) (Summer Squall (USA))
(1348) 2818[5]

Ocean Gift *Patrick J Flynn* 82
4 b g Cadeaux Genereux—Sea Drift (FR) (Warning)
3125a[6]

Oceanico Dot Com (IRE) *A Berry* a63 74
4 br m Hernando(FR) —Karen Blixen (Kris)
126[11] 320[10]362[10] 813[8] 1846[14]2784[12] 4091[10] 5078[7] 5631[16]

Ocean King (USA) *M G Quinlan* a63 64
5 ch g Sky Classic(CAN) —From Sea To Sea (CAN) (Gregorian (USA))
168[6] 607[4]

Ocean Of Champagne *A Dickman* 60
2 ch f Arkadian Hero(USA) —Champagne Grandy (Vaigly Great)
2106[5] 2745[5] 3713[7] 5860[2]

Ocean Of Dreams (FR) *J D Bethell* a81 59
3 b g Ocean Of Wisdom(USA) —Tifosa (USA) (Hickman Creek (USA))
118[7] 2363[9] 2756[9]3708[P] 3879[10]

Ocean Of Storms (IRE) *N I M Rossiter* 69?
11 bb g Arazi(USA) —Moon Cactus (Kris)
1517[4] 1931[13] 2013[14] 3952[3] 4036[20]4530[12]

Ocean Pride (IRE) *D E Pipe* a81 88
3 b g Lend A Hand—Irish Understudy (ITY) (In The Wings)
895[5] 1016[13] 1490[10]1569[4] 1828[4] (2232) 2650[9] 3212[11] 5150[11]5591[12] 6352[12] (6657) 6811[5] 6917[5]

Ocean Rock *C A Horgan* a59+ 35
5 b g Perugino(USA) —Polistatic (Free State)
1308[6] 1748[10]2577[5] 3597[4](6238) 6374[6](6729) 6936[4]

Oceans Apart *P F I Cole* 89
3 ch f Desert Prince(IRE) —Ffestiniog (IRE) (Efisio)
2880[7] 3418[4] 3852[5] 4083[13] 4837[6]5294[2]

Ocean Sunrise (IRE) *M Johnston* 63
3 b f Danehill(USA) —Wind Silence (USA) (A.P. Indy (USA))
2160[7] 3361[12]

Ocean Tide *R Ford* a45 67
9 b g Deploy—Dancing Tide (Pharly (FR))
866[3] 1184[6]

Ocean Valentine *B R Millman* a45 58
3 gr g King Charlemagne(USA) —Dolly Bevan (Another Realm)
844[6] 1355[12] 1851[9]

Ochil Hills Dancer (IRE) *A Crook* a31 31
4 b m Bluebird(USA) —Classic Dilemma (Sandhurst Prince)
3554[9] 4059[12] 4655[10] 5241[6] 5577[15]

Ochre Bay *R Hollinshead* a78 72
3 b c Polar Prince(IRE) —Cloudy Reef (Cragador)
1097[11] 1679[7] 2353[7] 2896[8] 6425[5]6573[4] (6919)

Ockums Razor (IRE) *C A Dwyer* a66 67
3 b g Mozart(IRE) —Merlannah (IRE) (Shy Groom (USA))
104[3] 195[2](248) 344[8](364) 550[8]592[6] 665[12]1923[7] 2208[5]3055[10] 3646[6]3708[7] 4930[12] (5273) 5781[2]6033[4]

Octave (USA) *T Pletcher* a113
2 gr f Unbridled's Song(USA) —Belle Nuit (USA) (Dr Carter (USA))
6338a[2]

October Ben *M D I Usher* a71 66
3 b f Killer Instinct—Birmania (IRE) (Rainbow Quest (USA))
1401[7] 1845[9] 2171[2]2589[7] (2978) 3400[8]3643[2] 4048[3]4660[9] 4995[2] 5211[3]

October Mist (IRE) *K G Reveley* 74
12 gr g Roselier(FR) —Bonny Joe (Derring Rose)
869[9] 2196[11]

October Sun *Miss D Mountain* a38 28
3 b c Dansili—Autumn Pride (USA) (Lear Fan (USA))
735[6] 874[4]1576[5] 2244[8]2463[8]

Oddsmaker (IRE) *M A Barnes* a77 77
5 b g Barathea(IRE) —Archipova (IRE) (Ela-Mana-Mou)
2020[13] 2164[7] 2387[4] 2407[2] 2684[7]2736[3] 2853[3] 3019[2] 3566[3] (3723) 4036[17](4299) 4448[8] 5132[2] 5513[2] 5533[11]

Odessa Star (USA) *J G Portman* a74 69
3 gr f Stravinsky(USA) —Cryptocari (USA) (Cryptoclearance (USA))
(2415) 2729[3] 2921[6] 3224[10] (3400) 4181[6]6244[8] 6432[8]6566[10] 6878[7](6942)

Odiham *H Morrison* a101 101
5 b g Deploy—Hug Me (Shareef Dancer (USA))
2013[3] 3078[15] 3533[4]4713[10] 5548[11] 5963[8] (6438) 6610a[17]

Odin Dawn *R Hannon* 78
2 b c Desert Style(IRE) —Desert Dawn (Belfort (FR))
5043[4] 5339[5] (5496) (Dead)

O'Dwyer (IRE) *A D Brown* a51 53
2 ch g Namid—Leopardess (IRE) (Ela-Mana-Mou)
5746[7] 6047[11] 6175[9] 6736[11]6845[2] 6945[7]

Oedipuss (IRE) *K J Burke* 45
2 b c Mujadil(USA) —Evrobi (IRE) (Grand Lodge (USA))
2218[10] 3838[4] 4161[9] 5759[4] 5884[3]

Oeuf A La Neige *Miss L A Perratt* a50 61
6 b g Danehill(USA) —Reine De Neige (Kris)
159[12] 262[10]485[12] 514[12]1528[14] 4091[5] (4655) 5062[9] 5078[2] 5309[11]5577[7] 5631[11] 5865[10]

Ofaraby *M A Jarvis* a105 106
6 b g Sheikh Albadou—Maristax (Reprimand)
1239[7] 1585[4] 2079[7] 4711[13] 5374[12]5675[11] (5813) 6203[2] 6337[3]

Off Hire *C Smith* a43 43
10 b g Clantime—Lady Pennington (Blue Cashmere)
179[6] 260[9]872[6] 942[5]1577[5]

Off Message (IRE) *E A L Dunlop* a78 79
3 b f In The Wings—Independence (Selkirk (USA))
(445) 1583[10] 1942[3] 2961[5]

Off Minor (FR) *J S O Arthur*
9 ch g Lomitas—La Hoya (IRE) (Darshaan)
1624a[2]

Off The Record *J G Given* a70+ 63
2 b c Desert Style(IRE) —Record Time (Clantime)
6047[4] (6463)

Ogee *Sir Michael Stoute* a70 93+
3 ch g Generous(IRE) —Aethra (USA) (Trempolino (USA))
1205[3] (1740) (1898) 2804[10]

Ogmore Vale (GER) *P Rau* 92
3 ch f Silvano(GER) —Ocotal (Vitiges (FR))
5008a[3]

Ohana *Miss Gay Kelleway* a60 46
3 b g Mark Of Esteem(IRE) —Subya (Night Shift (USA))
19[6] (241) 378[4]447[5] 550[7]554[2] 651[8]4923[8] 5740[7] 6069[11]6383[6] 6484[7]6628[6]

Oh Boy (IRE) *J M Bradley* a49 57
6 b g Tagula(IRE) —Pretty Sally (IRE) (Polish Patriot (USA))
1311[4] 1753[5] 2135[3] 2390[5] (Dead)

Oh Danny Boy *Jane Chapple-Hyam* a75 67
5 b g Cadeaux Genereux—Final Shot (Dalsaan)
3044[15] 3642[8] 3914[5]4307[4] (4606) 4925[9] 5354[10]

Oh Dara (USA) *M J Attwater* a60 74
4 b m Aljabr(USA) —Sabaah Elfull (Kris)
605[11] 732[7]

Oh Glory Be (USA) *R Hannon* a45 89+
3 b f Dixieland Band(USA) —Long View (USA) (Damascus (USA))
(1798) 2404[7] (2986) 4039[15]

Oh Golly Gosh *N P Littmoden* a67 62
5 ch g Exit To Nowhere(USA) —Guerre De Troie (Risk Me (FR))
3056[9] 4511[14]

Oh Gracious Me (IRE) *P A Blockley* 42
2 b c Traditionally(USA) —Classic Jenny (IRE) (Green Desert (USA))
3080[6] 5959[13]

Oh So Awesome (USA) *J Jerkens* a106 84
3 b c Awesome Again(CAN) —Identify (IRE) (Persian Bold)
2477a[5]

Oh So Saucy *C F Wall* 59
2 b f Imperial Ballet(IRE) —Almasi (IRE) (Petorius)
2930[13] 3796[5] 4550[3] 5419[12]

Oi Vay Joe (IRE) *W Jarvis* 87
2 b c Namid—Nuit Des Temps (Sadler's Wells (USA))
944[3] (2930) 4130[2] 4766[14] 5372[2] 5546[14]

Okikoki *W R Muir* a42 80
2 b g Ishiguru(USA) —Crofters Ceilidh (Scottish Reel)
2506[11] 2930[2] 3286[4] (3895) 4246[9]4766[10] 5372[4] 5940[8]

Ok Pal *T G Mills* a102 87
6 b g Primo Dominie—Sheila's Secret (IRE) (Bluebird (USA))
(198)

Oktaj (GER) *A Savujev* 93
2 ch c Seattle Dancer(USA) —Orletta (GER) (Platini (GER))
5007a[5]

Oktis Morilious (IRE) *A W Carroll* a44 44
5 b g Octagonal(NZ) —Nottash (IRE) (Royal Academy (USA))
78[9]

Old Bailey (USA) *G L Moore* a50 41
6 gr g Lit De Justice(USA) —Olden Lek (USA) (Cozzene (USA))
181[6] 258[3]300[5] 398[13]

Old Dodge (BRZ) *R Horgan* 113
5 b h Dodge(USA) —Ojeada Fighter (BRZ) (Irish Fighter (USA))
5824a[3] 6127a[3]

Oldenway *R A Fahey* a77 81
7 b g Most Welcome—Sickle Moon (Shirley Heights)
(98) 125[3] 264[8]491[3] 1222[6] (1560) 1887[3](2180) 2548[3] 2944[4] 3022[3] 3483[5] 3680[4]

Old Golden Grey *M Wellings*
9 gr g Thethingaboutitis(USA) —Modina April (New Member)
5934[5]

Oldjoesaid *H Candy* 95+
2 b g Royal Applause—Border Minstral (IRE) (Sri Pekan (USA))
3895[7] 4428[2] (5147) (5731)

Old Romney *M Johnston* 88
2 br c Halling(USA) —Zaeema (Zafonic (USA))
3417[4] (3851) (4474) 4680[6]

Old Time Dancing *M J Wallace* a51 57
3 b f Danehill Dancer(IRE) —Rare Old Times (IRE) (Inzar (USA))
30[8]

Olgarena (IRE) *T D Easterby* 48
2 b f Xaar—Copine (Selkirk (USA))
3175[6] 4830[9] 5237[8]

Oligarchica (GER) *R Rohne* 94
5 b m Desert King(IRE) —Ostwahlerin (GER) (Waajib)
2280a[6]

Olimpo (FR) *B R Millman* 83
5 ch g Starborough—Emily Allan (IRE) (Shirley Heights)
1651[4] (2097) (2305) 3365[5] 3876[5] 4160[7] 4900[6]

Olivair (IRE) *M E Sowersby* 7
3 b f Daggers Drawn(USA) —Exhibit Air (IRE) (Exhibitioner)
2529[16] 2874[12]

Olivino (GER) *B J Llewellyn* a58 52
5 ch g Second Set(IRE) —Osdemona (GER) (Solarstern (FR))
52[3] 231[8]482[8] 1540[2]1729[6] 3196[5]

Ollie George (IRE) *A M Balding* a69 88+
3 ch g Fruits Of Love(USA) —The Iron Lady (IRE) (Polish Patriot (USA))
880[12] 2069[5] 2678[3] 2990[2] (3221) 3439[2]3974[2] (4224) 4626[9]

Olympian Odyssey *B W Hills* 117
3 b c Sadler's Wells(USA) —Field Of Hope (IRE) (Selkirk (USA))
1093[2] 1486[3] 2278a[12] 5186[3] 5673[5]5964[4]

Oman Gulf (USA) *Micky Hammond* a36 57
5 b g Diesis—Dabaweyaa (Shareef Dancer (USA))
1346[15] 5354[13] 5905[9] 6584[9]

Omasheriff (IRE) *W Baltromei* 108
4 ch h Shinko Forest(IRE) —Lady Of Leisure (USA) (Diesis)
885a[6] 1973a[7] 2799a[4] 3755a[6] 4858a[7]6121a[2] 6230a[6]

Omikron (IRE) *I Jory* 117
5 b h Germany(USA) —Ost Tycoon (GER) (Last Tycoon)
205a[11] 370a[9]

Ommadawn (IRE) *J R Fanshawe* 69
2 b f Montjeu(IRE) —Bonheur (IRE) (Royal Academy (USA))
5380[4]

Ommraan (IRE) *M A Jarvis* 77
2 ch c King's Best(USA) —Auntie Maureen (IRE) (Roi Danzig (USA))
(5495)

Omoto Sando (FR) *A Lund*
3 b c Trempolino(USA) —Mayreau (Slip Anchor)
4419a[7]

On A Cloud (USA) *A Fabre* 102+
3 ch f Silver Hawk(USA) —Be Exclusive (IRE) (Be My Guest (USA))
(773a) 1177a[6]

On Air (USA) *E J O'Neill* a44 72+
3 rg f Cozzene(USA) —Cumulate (USA) (Gone West (USA))
948[11] 1251[4] 1648[12] 3008[4] 3347[14]4671[4] 5035[10]

On A Jeune (AUS) *P Montgomerie* 115
6 b g Jeune—Chandada Rose (AUS) (King's High (AUS))
5817a[5] 6392a[20]

Onatopp (IRE) *T D Easterby* a53 62
2 b f Soviet Star(USA) —Blueprint (USA) (Shadeed (USA))
3878[5] 5496[10] 5899[2] 6157[2] 6309[7]

Once In A Bluemoon (IRE) *A Berry*
3 ch f Beckett(IRE) —Ma Bella Luna (Jalmood (USA))
1437[9]

One Alone *Jean-Rene Auvray* a53d 40
5 b m Atraf—Songsheet (Dominion)
694[7] 794[8]1541[5]

One And Gone (IRE) *R A Fahey* 62
2 b g Machiavellian(USA) —Bright Smile (IRE) (Caerleon (USA))
5283[4] 5616[7] 5900[5]

One And Only (GER) *D W Thompson*
5 ch m Kornado—On My Guest (IRE) (Be My Guest (USA))
469[13] 4227[12]

One Good Thing (USA) *Christian Wroe* a12 70
4 b g Touch Gold(USA) —Once To Often (USA) (Raise A Native)
5621[16]

Oneiro Way (IRE) *P R Chamings* a69 67
4 b g King's Best(USA) —Koumiss (Unfuwain (USA))
225[7] 449[2]1261[3] 2095[13] 2567[9]

One Last Time *Miss B Sanders* a61 67
6 b g Primo Dominie—Leap Of Faith (IRE) (Northiam (USA))
2136[8] 2645[14]

One Little David (GER) *P Vovcenko* 107
6 bb g Camp David(GER) —Open Heart (GER) (Sure Blade (USA))
205a[10] 512a[2] 1014a[6]

One More Round (USA) *N P Littmoden* a101 106+
8 b g Ghazi(USA) —Life Of The Party (USA) (Pleasant Colony (USA))
7[7] 57[6]213[8] 295[3]450[5] 627[8]664[3] 705[3]836[7] 1116[7] 1487[8]2012[12] (3092) 3972[2] 4128[12] 5182[14] 5358[2]6849[4]

One More Than Ten *T D Easterby* a46 20
3 b g Piccolo—Julietta Mia (USA) (Woodman (USA))
2763[11] 3053[7] 3916[5]4656[13] 4948[15]

Onenightinlisbon (IRE) *K R Burke* a88 82
2 br f Bold Fact(USA) —Mickey Towbar (IRE) (Mujadil (USA))
1142[4] 1342[4] 2125[9] 2890[5] 3173[5](3787) (4088) 4681[4] 4946[3] 6096[6]6402[2] 6444[2]6631[4] 6846[3]

One Night In Paris (IRE) *M J Wallace* a71 49
3 bb f Danetime(IRE) —Forget Paris (IRE) (Broken Hearted)
969[9] 5874[2] (6286) 6448[4]6666[2]

One Off *N Drysdale* a66 106
6 b g Barathea(IRE) —On Call (Alleged (USA))
1721a[5]

One Putra (IRE) *M A Jarvis* 114
4 b h Indian Ridge—Triomphale (USA) (Nureyev (USA))
1069[6] (1481) (2303) 2847[13] 3312[11] 4128[15] 4803[5]5182[5] 5779a[2] 6005a[6]

Onerous *J-C Rouget* 106
3 b c Groom Dancer(USA) —Baileys On Line (Shareef Dancer (USA))
1749a[2] 6062a[2]

One To Follow *C G Cox* 80
2 b g Mtoto—Becalmed (Dilum (USA))
(3892) 6216[7]

One To Win (IRE) *J Noseda* a73 96
4 b m Cape Cross(IRE) —Safe Exit (FR) (Exit To Nowhere (USA))
438a[9]

One Trick Pony *Karen McLintock* 33
3 ch g Timeless Times(USA) —Lavernock Lady (Don't Forget Me)
980[12] 1344[16]

On Every Street *R Bastiman* a42 81
5 b g Singspiel(IRE) —Nekhbet (Artaius (USA))
1573[7] 1767[3]4307[10] 4544[8]

One Way Ticket *J M Bradley* a60 90d
6 ch h Pursuit Of Love—Prima Cominna (Unfuwain (USA))
2389[3] 2624[8] (3165) 3449[9] 3832[6] 4085[17]4793[10] 5148[7] 5275[9] 5791[19] 6533[14]6629[2] 6688[2]6753[3] 6890[4]

One White Sock *J L Spearing* a42 52
2 b f Compton Admiral—Night Gypsy (Mind Games)
4283[6] 5348[4] 6222[11]6487[9] 6711[5]6905[6]

Onida (IRE) *C G Cox* 90
2 b f Noverre(USA) —Molomo (Barathea (IRE))
3043[5] 3874[4] 4765[2] 5464a[12] (5760) 5966[13]

Online Investor *C Smith* a70 79
7 b g Puissance—Anytime Baby (Bairn (USA))
130[5]

Only A Grand *R Bastiman* 60
2 b f Cloudings(IRE) —Magic Orb (Primo Dominie)
1223[9] 1863[6] 2680[9]3831[2] 4509[11] 5238[4] (5835) 6056[5] 6208[4]

Only A Splash *D W Chapman* a45 47
2 b g Primo Valentino(IRE) —Water Well (Sadler's Wells (USA))
3259[6] 3780[5] 4433[8]4545[2] 4955[5] 5113[13] 5843[11]6172[6] 6278[12] 6518[8]

Onlybayinvillage (IRE) *A Berry* 45
3 b g Monashee Mountain(USA) —Hierarchy (Sabrehill (USA))
1633[7] 3671[3]

Only For Sue *W S Kittow* a52 54
7 ch g Pivotal—Barbary Court (Grundy)
1138[9] 1745[13] 2099[6]

Only Him *A Fabre* 90
3 b c Seeking The Gold(USA) —Only Seule (USA) (Lyphard (USA))
5703a[7]

Only Hope *Ernst Oertel* a52 65
2 b f Marju(IRE) —Sellette (IRE) (Selkirk (USA))
3193[8] 3713[5] 4794[3] 5094[5] 5387[4]5676[10] 5941[3] 6217[12] 6394[11]6518[5] 6625[8]

Only If I Laugh *R A Harris* a65 62
5 ch g Piccolo—Agony Aunt (Formidable (USA))
(181) 300[3] 391[7](681) 784[2]1057[5] 2317[2] 2645[6] 2936[5]4363[2] 4984[2] (5032) 5302[8]6193[10] 6470[8]

Onlytime Will Tell *D Nicholls* a72 81
8 ch g Efisio—Prejudice (Young Generation)
253[9] 381[3]585[7] 644[6]974[3] (1217) 1341[2] 1504[11] (1735) 1885[2] 2020[11]5861[14]

Only Words (USA) *A J Lockwood* 23
9 ch g Shuailaan(USA) —Conversation Piece (USA) (Seeking The Gold (USA))
3610[11]

On The Go *M A Jarvis* 61
2 b f Tobougg(IRE) —Altaweelah (IRE) (Fairy King (USA))
3707[9] 4552[9]

On The Map *A P Jarvis* a63
2 b f Agnes World(USA) —Noor El Houdah (IRE) (Fayruz)
6071[11] 6349[6]

On The Trail *D W Chapman* a46 39
9 ch g Catrail(USA) —From The Rooftops (IRE) (Thatching)
24[3] 90[2]146[12] 633[7]679[11] 943[7]1391[12] 1466[9]1909[7] 3334 [7] 3356[10]3833[5] 4523[4] 6636[9]6753[7] 6943[5]6969[5]

On The Up (AUS) *J Hawkes* 74
5 b g Peintre Celebre(USA) —Incline (AUS) (Century (AUS))
6346a[13]

On Watch *H Candy* 36
2 b f Josr Algarhoud(IRE) —Sole Control (Jupiter Island)
5352[13]

Onyergo (IRE) *J R Weymes* 66
4 b g Polish Precedent(USA) —Trick (IRE) (Shirley Heights)
1590[13] 3352[3] 4072[4] (4522) 4954[4] 5369[8]5750[2] 5960[2] 6158[2] 6321[5]

Ooh Aah Camara (IRE) *T J Pitt* a66 93
3 b f Danehill Dancer(IRE) —Simla Bibi (Indian Ridge)
665[10] 827[11]1292[9] 1448[3] (1606) 1848[3] 2385[7] 2880[3]3144[6] 3520[3] 4174[9] 5171[5]

Opal Noir *J Howard Johnson* 84
2 b g Lujain(USA) —Wrong Bride (Reprimand)
(1730) 2127[5] 3239[3] 4681[14] 5788[6]

Opal's Helmsman (USA) *W S Coltherd* 40
6 b g Helmsman(USA) —Opal's Notebook (USA) (Notebook (USA))
1034[12]

Opal Warrior *Jane Southcombe* a61 50
3 b f Orpen(USA) —Indian Wardance (ITY) (Indian Ridge)
68[4] 6672[10]6827[11] 6977[7]

Opatja *L Camici* 93
4 b m Nashwan(USA) —Thundercloud (Electric)
1368a[4] 2280a[7] 6124a[8] 6362a[11]

Open Arms *Mrs A L M King* a49 54
10 ch g Most Welcome—Amber Fizz (USA) (Effervescing (USA))
186[10] 457[6]

Openide *B W Duke* a55 69
5 b g Key Of Luck(USA) —Eyelet (IRE) (Satco (FR))
1409[7] 1826[3] 2118[9] 2501[4] 2894[4]3269[5] 3522[6] 3955[9]

Opening Line *Ernst Oertel*
4 ch g Opening Verse(USA) —Denton Lady (Inchinor)
14[10] 110[9]

Open Loop (IRE) *Edgar Byrne* a62 67
4 b h Danehill(USA) —Last Exit (Dominion)
6451[6] 6767[6]

Opera Belle *Miss Gay Kelleway* a33 57?
4 b m Dr Fong(USA) —Opera Lover (IRE) (Sadler's Wells (USA))
115[6] 231[11]350[10] 1911[13]2261[6] 3379[5] 4450[6]4667[6]

Opera Cape *Saeed Bin Suroor* 114
3 b c Barathea(IRE) —Optaria (Song)
1486[14]

Opera Comica *J H M Gosden* a59 76
3 b f Dr Fong(USA) —Comic (IRE) (Be My Chief (USA))
62[3] 188[12]403[2] 573[2]695[5] 5652[13]

Opera Crown (IRE) *P F I Cole* 80
2 b g Grand Lodge(USA) —Silly Goose (IRE) (Sadler's Wells (USA))
5340 [?] (5565) 5916[8] 6106[7]

Opera Knight *A W Carroll* a31 47
6 ch g In The Wings—Sans Escale (USA) (Diesis)
(42) 181[7] 310[4]468[5] 682[8]1198[5] 1541[2]1729[4] (1911) 2636[12] 4282[5] 5072[4] 6133[11]

Opera Music *S Kirk* 93
2 b c Kirkwall—Optaria (Song)
4479[2] (5339) 6102[4]

Opera Writer (IRE) *R Hollinshead* a74 69
3 b g Rossini(USA) —Miss Flite (IRE) (Law Society (USA))
1589[5] 2001[6] 2383[4] 2734[4] 3055[5](3378) (3729) 4249[11]4533[5] 4933[11] 5248[11]6276[9] 6893[2]6929[2]

Oporto (UAE) *D M Fogarty* a69 54
3 b f Jade Robbery(USA) —Potentille (IRE) (Caerleon (USA))
949[8] 1306[3] (1747) 2332[13]2729[7] 5973[12]

Opportunist (IRE) *Doug Watson* a111
7 b h Machiavellian(USA) —Fatefully (USA) (Private Account (USA))
560a[3]

Optari (USA) *J-C Rouget* 101
2 ch c Diesis—Desert Sky (IRE) (Green Desert (USA))
3990a[3]

Optical Illusion (USA) *E A L Dunlop* 71
2 b c Theatrical—Paradise River (USA) (Irish River (FR))
5883[8]

Optical Seclusion (IRE) *T J Etherington* a39 58d
3 b g Second Empire(IRE) —Theda (Mummy's Pet)
2284[3] 2701[5] 2873[7] 3842[5] 4071[10]5874[5] 6403[10]

Optimum (IRE) *J T Stimpson* a67 56
4 br g King's Best(USA) —Colour Dance (Rainbow Quest (USA))
1222[7] 2221[14] 2862[14](3382) 4632[9] 5390[8]6718[6] 6873[5]6979[10]

Optimus (USA) *B G Powell* a85 85
4 ch g Elnadim(USA) —Ajfan (USA) (Woodman (USA))
1355[10] 2405[6] 2708[2] (3044) 3413[4] 3973[7]5428[3] 5625[4] 6017[5]6148[3] 6418[10]

Opus Magnus (IRE) *P J Makin* a60 31
3 b g Mozart(IRE) —Bold As Love (Lomond (USA))
1430[8] 5611[9] 5988[6]

Oracle West (SAF) *J E Hammond* 112
5 b g Western Winter(USA) —Noble Prophet (SAF) (Noble Ambition (USA))
(207a) (354a) (562a) 741a[11] 5999a[5]

Orange *W J Haggas* 58
2 ch f Giant's Causeway(USA) —Shopping For Love (USA) (Not For Love (USA))
4373[11]

Orange Blue (GER) *C Von Der Recke* a52+ 94
4 b h Laroche(GER) —Onanga (GER) (Acatenango (GER))
97[5] 6529a[10]

Orange Dancer (IRE) *H Morrison* a76 73+
3 b f Danehill Dancer(IRE) —Strelitzia (SAF) (Fort Wood (USA))
1004[4] (2068) 2511[5] 3299[5]3846[4]

Orange Lady (IRE) *M L W Bell* 29
2 b f Montjeu(IRE) —Young Affair (IRE) (Mukaddamah (USA))
5760[8]

Orange Lily *M A Jarvis* 36
2 b f Royal Applause—Tarsa (Ballad Rock)
4843[5]

Orange Pekoe (USA) *P Mitchell* a60 77
2 b c Miswaki(USA) —Rascal Lass (USA) (Ack Ack (USA))
3531[5] 4292[5] 4928[5]5262[9]

Oranges And Lemons (FR) *C E Brittain* a33 31
3 b f Zafonic(USA) —Tarte Aux Pommes (USA) (Local Talent (USA))
6652[12] 6952[10]

Orange Stravinsky *P C Haslam* a17 72
3 b g Stravinsky(USA) —Orange Sunset (IRE) (Roanoke (USA))
1596[10] 1948[8] 3169[4] 4697[7] 5690[13]

Orange Touch (GER) *Mrs A J Perrett* a86 102
6 b g Lando(GER) —Orange Bowl (General Assembly (USA))
2430[4] 4096[4] 4797[5] 5920[8] 6334[8]6438[6]

Orangino *J S Haldane* 42
8 b g Primo Dominie—Sweet Jaffa (Never So Bold)
4086[10]

Oranmore Castle (IRE) *D Nicholls* 86
4 b g Giant's Causeway(USA) —Twice The Ease (Green Desert (USA))
1474[8] 1820[6] 2302[3] 2661[2] 2864[9](3281) 4085[8] 5333[3] 6009[7]

Oratory (SAF) *A Laird* 104
9 b g Centenary(USA) —Leah The Lark (USA) (Lear Fan (USA))
205a[13] 371a[9]

Orcadian *J M P Eustace* a83 113
5 b g Kirkwall—Rosy Outlook (USA) (Trempolino (USA))
1267[7] 1628[2] 1833[3] 2010[6] 6103[3]6334[2] 6515[7]

Orchard House (FR) *J Jay* a50 38
3 b g Medaaly—Louisa May (IRE) (Royal Abjar (USA))
3916[8] 4635[10] 5071[14]5830[6] 6236[12] 6907[5]6973[3]

Orchard Supreme *R Hannon* a103 87
3 ch c Titus Livius(FR) —Bogus Penny (IRE) (Pennekamp (USA))
269[3] (475) (558) 1337[5](1924) 2330[11] 3852[4] 4083[15]5345[6] 5990[3] 6192[6]6514[2] (6594) 6692[5] (6915)

Orchestration (IRE) *M J Attwater* a57 44
5 ch g Stravinsky(USA) —Mora (IRE) (Second Set (IRE))
96[5] 196[3]411[4] 424[10]858[2] 1054[9] 1255[2]2207[3] 2376 [8] 2792[7]3389[8] 5928[11]6276[4] 6477[3]6533[7] 6619[5]6719[6] 6906[7]6956[2] (6969)

Orchestrator (IRE) *T G Mills* a46
2 b g Docksider(USA) —Summerhill (Habitat)
6826[7]

Ordnance Row *R Hannon* 97
3 b c Mark Of Esteem(IRE) —Language Of Love (Rock City)
3889[10] 4029[9] 4760[5] (4790)

Orenay (USA) *M J Wallace* a50 76
4 ch g Grand Slam(USA) —Moonfire (Sadler's Wells (USA))
63[7]

Orewa Matteruze (JPN) *H Otonashi* 119
6 b h Sunday Silence(USA) —Curly Angel (JPN) (Judge Angelucci (USA))
5717a[9] 6850a[15]

Organizer (NOR) *E Charpy* a97 98
6 b g Zafonic(USA) —Orange Walk (IRE) (Alzao (USA))
497a[5] 622a[10]

Oriental Dance *Saeed Bin Suroor* a52
2 b f Fantastic Light(USA) —Oriental Fashion (IRE) (Marju (IRE))
6187[10]

Oriental Lady (IRE) *E Lellouche* 89
3 b f King's Best(USA) —Otaiti (IRE) (Sadler's Wells (USA))
5472a[9]

Oriental Tiger (GER) *U Ostmann* 115
3 b c Tiger Hill(IRE) —Oriental Flower (GER) (Big Shuffle (USA))
1176a[3] 2314a[4] 3131a[3] 3776a[3] 5051a[2]5561a[4]

Oriental Warrior *S Al Salloom* 46
5 b h Alhaarth(IRE) —Oriental Fashion (IRE) (Marju (IRE))
507a[11]

Orientor *J S Goldie* a87 112
8 b h Inchinor—Orient (Bay Express)
627[9] 729[6] 1116[4]1803[2] 2115[4] 2720[8] 3585[3] 3972[14]4738[8] 5158[2] 5358[9]

Original Empire (IRE) *F Costello* 58
3 b g Second Empire(IRE) —Originality (Godswalk (USA))
4034a[5]

Orissa (GER) *W Hickst* 57
4 b m Platini(GER) —Ordina (GER) (Zampano (GER))
6366a[8]

Orlano (FR) *D Baillif* 38
4 u g (USA) — (USA) (King's Lake (USA))
3580a[6]

Orna (USA) *Michael J Doyle* 100
2 b c Tethra(CAN) —Heavenly Lark (CAN) (Septieme Ciel (USA))
5415a[3]

Orotund *T D Easterby* 49
2 b g Orpen(USA) —Soyalang (FR) (Alydeed (CAN))
4731[10] 5283[10] 5753[8]

Orpailleur *Ms Joanna Morgan* 97
5 gr g Mon Tresor—African Light (Kalaglow)
3125a[4] 4187a[8]

Orpendonna (IRE) *K A Ryan* a62 51
4 b m Orpen(USA) —Tetradonna (IRE) (Teenoso (USA))
(162) 505[5] 644[11]

Orpenlina (IRE) *R A Fahey* 60
3 b f Orpen(USA) —Westlife (IRE) (Mind Games)
2016[7] 2356[7] (4613) 4886[7] 5631[17]

Orpen Prince (IRE) *K A Ryan* a48 72
2 b g Orpen(USA) —She's The Tops (Shernazar)
1945[2] 2610[10] 2972[2] (4761) 5113[11] 5843[9]

Orpen Quest (IRE) *M J Attwater* a63 56
4 b g Orpen(USA) —Pursuit Of Truth (USA) (Irish River (FR))
41[6] 92[6]1538[8] 1852[2] 2789[10](3112) 3305[3] (3599) 3947[12] 4845[8]4983[11]

Orpen's Astaire (IRE) *Jedd O'Keeffe* 59
3 b g Orpen(USA) —Rhythm And Style (USA) (Keen)
1101[6] 2325[14] 4961[7] 5316[7]

Orpen Wide (IRE) *M C Chapman* a83 81
4 b g Orpen(USA) —Melba (IRE) (Namaqualand (USA))
80[11] 101[3]276[10] 426[9]1123[12] 2820[9] (2947) 3230[10] 5314[4] 5444[2](5617) (6946)

Orphan (IRE) *K R Burke* 78
4 b g Orpen(USA) —Ballinlee (IRE) (Skyliner)
3217[7] 3567[9] 4885[5] 5529[11] 5791[8]6048[11]

Orphina (IRE) *B G Powell* a55 65
3 b f Orpen(USA) —Keralba (USA) (Sheikh Albadou)
1291[12] 2065[5] 2301[7] 3011[10]3364[12] 3472[9] 3869[9] 5936[7] 6618[6]6724[12] 6801[3]

Orphir (IRE) *Mrs N Macauley* a37
3 b g Orpen(USA) —Silver Moon (Environment Friend)
6535[7] 6759[7]

Orpsie Boy (IRE) *N P Littmoden* a86 94
3 b g Orpen(USA) —Nordicolini (IRE) (Nordico (USA))
1606[2] 2032[7] 2658[4] 3414[6] 3740[3]3970[5] 4083[11] 4601[11] 4807[10]

Orvietan (IRE) *M Johnston* a69 62
3 b c Sadler's Wells(USA) —Fiamma (IRE) (Irish River (FR))
(419) 548[2] 804[4]1052[6] 1381[5] 1732[7]

Oscarshall (IRE) *M H Tompkins* a20 53
2 ch g Halling(USA) —Mafaatin (IRE) (Royal Academy (USA))
2680[7] 5457[7] 5814[8] 6285[13]

Oscar Snowman *M P Tregoning* 58
3 b g Selkirk(USA) —Chilly Start (IRE) (Caerleon (USA))
6019[4]

Oscillator *G A Butler* a77+ 74
3 b g Pivotal—Craigmill (Slip Anchor)
(1306) 2502[8] 4599[4] 5109[5]

Osiris Way *P R Chamings* a43 43
4 ch g Indian Ridge—Heady (Rousillon (USA))
3458[9] 6019[7]

Osolomio (IRE) *G A Swinbank* a72 70
3 b g Singspiel(IRE) —Inanna (Persian Bold)
1153[7] 1343[8] 2529[2]2814[4] 3634[2] 4150[2] 4362[2] 4668[4]6244[2] (6382)

Ostankino (FR) *E Lellouche* 117
5 b h Zieten(USA) —Otaiti (IRE) (Sadler's Wells (USA))
1332a[6] 1875a[4] 3516a[3]

Osteopathic Remedy (IRE) *M Dods* 86
2 ch g Inchinor—Dolce Vita (IRE) (Ela-Mana-Mou)
(5307) 5788[4]

Osterhase (IRE) *J E Mulhern* 119
7 b g Flying Spur(AUS) —Ostrusa (AUT) (Rustan (HUN))
1158a[11] (2308a) 3124a[3] (3561a) (3767a) 5706a[2] 5849a[9]

Ostfanni (IRE) *M Todhunter* 73
6 b m Spectrum(IRE) —Ostwahl (IRE) (Waajib)
2196[5] (3135) (3350) 3955[6]

Otaki (IRE) *Sir Mark Prescott* a28
2 gr f King's Best(USA) —On Call (Alleged (USA))
6826[10]

O'Tara (IRE) *M H Tompkins* 84
3 b c Danehill(USA) —Utr (USA) (Mr Prospector (USA))
1101[3] 1814[2] 2662[2] (4261) 4763[3] 5512[10]

Otelcaliforni (USA) *J Noseda* a54 74+
3 b f Gulch(USA) —Ive Gota Bad Liver (USA) (Mt. Livermore (USA))
1191[2] 1458[2] (3001) 3984[5]

Otis B Driftwood *Miss J R Tooth* a60 57
3 b g Tipsy Creek(USA) —Gi La High (Rich Charlie)
322[5] 359[3]477[2] 593[6]626[4] 910[3]1003[7] 1210[2] 1549[7]1771[3] 2187[6] 6541[10]6615[10] 6723[11]6753[6]

Otranto (USA) *M Johnston* a67 72
4 ch h Rahy(USA) —Tethkar (Machiavellian (USA))
2918[9] 3377[2] (3583) 3960[3] 4073[4]

Ouija Board *E A L Dunlop* 126
5 b m Cape Cross(IRE) —Selection Board (Welsh Pageant)
741a[4] 1180a[3] 2202[2] (2741) 3314[5] (4127) 5193a[2](6340a) 6612a[3]

Oulan Bator (FR) *R A Fahey* 61
6 b g Astair(FR) —Scarieuse (FR) (Crackao (FR))
4353[7] 4692[6] 5080[5] 5369[13]

Ouninpohja (IRE) *I Semple* 116
5 b g Imperial Ballet(IRE) —Daziyra (IRE) (Doyoun)
1815[2] 2453[2] 3085[2] 3294[2] 3905[2]4817[3] 5360[2]

Our Archie *M J Attwater* 19
2 b c Kyllachy—Oriel Girl (Beveled (USA))
3193[14] 3457[13]

Our Blessing (IRE) *A P Jarvis* a73 72
2 b c Lujain(USA) —Berenice (ITY) (Marouble)
701[4] 5348[8] 5613[4]5681[18] (6012) 6310[5] 6488[2]6866[5]

Our Chelsea Blue (USA) *J R Jenkins* a49 49
8 ch m Distant View(USA) —Eastern Connection (USA) (Danzig Connection (USA))
633[10] 686[9]1228[12]

Our Choice (IRE) *N P Littmoden* a73 73
4 b g Indian Danehill(IRE) —Spring Daffodil (Pharly (FR))
597[4] 628[3]832[6] 976[7] 1346[4]2044[3] 2150[2] 2460[10] 2822[11] 4451[10]5971[9]

Our Faye *S Kirk* a72 71
3 b f College Chapel—Tamara (Marju (IRE))
3387[3] 3647[4](4708) 5294[6] 5619[10] 5973[3]6189[9]

Our Fugitive (IRE) *A W Carroll* 85
4 gr g Titus Livius(FR) —Mystical Jumbo (Mystiko (USA))
1856[2] 2674[2] 5333[4] 5532[12] 5791[10]

Our Georgia *T D Barron* a6
3 b f Mind Games—Our Krissie (Kris)
6637[12] 6738[6]

Our Glenard *J E Long* a47 41
7 b g Royal Applause—Loucoum (FR) (Iron Duke (FR))
1541[8] 2861[11](4239) 6132[10] 6657[4]6804[2]

Our Herbie *J W Hills* a78 74
2 b g Tobougg(IRE) —Trevillari (USA) (Riverman (USA))
2506[13] 3157[2] 3663[5]4773[6] 5262[5] (5647) 5916[13]6310[4] 6458[6]

Our Jaffa (IRE) *H Rogers* a82 89
5 br m Bin Ajwaad(IRE) —Griddle Cake (IRE) (Be My Guest (USA))
5396a[7]

Our Kes (IRE) *P Howling* a74 49
4 gr m Revoque(IRE) —Gracious Gretclo (Common Grounds)
6448[8] 6684[3]6741[6] 6924[5]

Our Little Secret (IRE) *A Berry* a57 75
4 ch m Rossini(USA) —Sports Post Lady (IRE) (M Double M (USA))
(1102) (1563) 2925[3] 3715[9] 4135[5] 4546[3] 5309[2]5684[3] 5970[9]

Our Mary (IRE) *Robert Gray* a60 59
3 b f Mujadil(USA) —Desert Gem (Green Desert (USA))
2504[8] 2873[3] 3262[11]3381[11] 3912[15] 4071[4]4473[2] 4728[6] 5637[13] 5885[15]

Our Mona (USA) *M R Channon* 38
2 b f Diesis—Buckeye Gal (USA) (Good Counsel (USA))
4754[8]

Our Monogram *R M Beckett* a50 81
10 b g Deploy—Darling Splodge (Elegant Air)
1339[9] (2219) 2894[2] 3446[2]4036[9] 5069[8] 5564[7]

Our Putra *M A Jarvis* a85 69
3 b g King's Best(USA) —Prima Volta (Primo Dominie)
2001[3] (2934) 3404[2] 4047[8]4429[7] 5512[11]

Our Ruby *P W Chapple-Hyam* 71
2 b f Diktat—Almost Amber (USA) (Mt. Livermore (USA))
1542[6] 1989[7] 4552[7] (4920)

Ours (IRE) *J D Bethell* a66 65
3 b g Mark Of Esteem(IRE) —Ellebanna (Tina's Pet)
1825[10] 2525[2] 3023[6] 3582[3] 4069[3]5316[11] 5847[4] 6286[2](6557)

Our Serendipity *K G Reveley* 25
3 ch f Presidium—Berl's Gift (Prince Sabo)
1593[14] 1761[13] 2874[9] 3288[14] 4297[13]

Our Sheila *B Smart* a48 82
3 ch f Bahamian Bounty—Shifting Mist (Night Shift (USA))
1445[3] 1733[2] (2019) (2399) (2873) (3287) 3783[7]

Our Smoking Joe (AUS) *Lee Freedman* 117
6 b g Encosta De Lago(AUS) —Dalzing (AUS) (Blazing Sword (AUS))
6110a[6]

Our Susie (IRE) *M D I Usher* a49 57
2 b f Bold Fact(USA) —Paris Model (IRE) (Thatching)
878[5] 1046[3] 1223[3]1535[6] (Dead)

Our Teddy (IRE) *P A Blockley* a76 91
6 ch g Grand Lodge(USA) —Lady Windley (Baillamont (USA))
2351[8] 2640[5] (3283) (3547) 3748[6] (4149) 4626[7]5163[4] 5367[8]

Our Toy Soldier *B Smart* a53 59
2 gr g Forzando—The Wild Widow (Saddlers' Hall (IRE))
814[6] 1074[3] 1284[12] 2139[7]2999[2] 3351[8]

Out After Dark *C G Cox* 106
5 b g Cadeaux Genereux—Midnight Shift (IRE) (Night Shift (USA))
1069[12] 1663[3] 2115[7] 2675[7] 4128[14]5358[6] 5812[3]

Outer Hebrides *Stef Liddiard* a89 81
5 b g Efisio—Reuval (Sharpen Up)
58[11] 220[2]340[6] 444[6]542[6] 726[14] 913[3]1112[2] 1340[3]1938[11] 2232[5] 2757[2]2983[5] 4047[7]4658[3] 5345[4] 5670[2]6059[3] 6397[6] 6580[6]6696[3]

Out For A Stroll *S C Williams* a73 78
7 b g Zamindar(USA) —The Jotter (Night Shift (USA))
267[10] 381[8]567[6] 737[9]1057[15] 1164[5] 1993[16]2211[8] 2645[8] (3339) 3404[4](3523) 3570[3] 4879[4] 4995[6]6684[8]

Outlook *N P Littmoden* a76 67
3 ch c Observatory(USA) —Area Girl (Jareer (USA))
76[4] 139[5]294[8] (447) 550[3] (583)

Out Of India *B Smart* a73 71+
4 b m Marju(IRE) —Tide Of Fortune (Soviet Star (USA))
15[2] 100[11]381[9] 1760[8] 3697[5]

Out Of This Way *I A Wood* a58
3 b c Spectrum(IRE) —Pirouette (Sadler's Wells (USA))
6225[9] 6314[5]6429[5] 6716[9]6860[10]

Out Of Time (FR) *J-C Rouget* 100
2 b f Panis(USA) —Manettia (FR) (Midyan (USA))
(3990a) 5664a[4] 6229a[5]

Out Of Town *Ronald Thompson* a34
2 ch g Namid—Superstore (USA) (Blushing Groom (FR))
6675[9]

Outrageous Flirt (IRE) *A Dickman* a57 57
4 b m Indian Lodge(IRE) —Sofia Aurora (USA) (Chief Honcho (USA))
2248[5] (2544) 2926[6] 3398[12]3617[14] 3786[4] 4157[6] 4198[7] 5062[2]5370[3]

Overdrawn (IRE) *A J McCabe* a49 52
5 b g Daggers Drawn(USA) —In Denial (IRE) (Maelstrom Lake)
6130[11] 6551[13]6617[6]

Over Ice *Karen George* a18 67
3 b f Mister Baileys—Oublier L'Ennui (FR) (Bellman (FR))
1049[4] 2188[6] 2753[11]4286[5] 5567[3]

Overjoy Way *P R Chamings* a60 62
4 b m Cadeaux Genereux—May Light (Midyan (USA))
268[11] 917[4]1638[5] 2063 [4]

Overlook *A M Balding* a30 63+
3 b f Generous(IRE) —Spurned (USA) (Robellino (USA))
1942[4] 4005[10] 4330[7]4868[3] 5057[12]

Overlord Way (GR) *P R Chamings* a82
4 br g Tony Galvin(GR) —Fortunate Way (GR) (Wadood (USA))
2555[8] 2983[8]3202[6] 4937[2]5610[7]

Overrule (USA) *J Noseda* 45
2 b c Diesis—Her Own Way (USA) (Danzig (USA))
5616[9]

Oversighted (GER) *Mrs Y Dunleavy* 92
5 b h Selkirk(USA) —Obvious Appeal (IRE) (Danehill (USA))
1156a[8] 4094a[12]

Overstayed (IRE) *P A Blockley* 90
3 ch g Titus Livius(FR) —Look Nonchalant (IRE) (Fayruz)
1146[4]

Overstrand (IRE) *Robert Gray* a63 74
7 b g In The Wings—Vaison La Romaine (Arctic Tern (USA))
1808[2] 2625[3] 2894[6] 3284[7]

Over Tipsy *R Hannon* 46
4 b g Tipsy Creek(USA) —Over Keen (Keen)
4363[8] 5127[6] 5259[10]

Over To You Bert *R J Hodges* a35 28
7 b g Overbury(IRE) —Silvers Era (Balidar)
6370[10]

Overturn (IRE) *W R Swinburn* 91+
2 b c Barathea(IRE) —Kristal Bridge (Kris)
3976[5] (4487) 5805[4]

Overwing (IRE) *R M H Cowell* a77 77
3 b f Fasliyev(USA) —Sierva (GER) (Darshaan)
136[5] 1679[4] 2134[4]2433[4] 2826[3] 3049[4] 3866[6] (4226) 4691[2](4874) 5317[7] 6035[5] 6353[4]

Owed *B Ellison* a75d 54
4 b g Lujain(USA) —Nightingale (Night Shift (USA))
(4) 15[9] 245[4]275[9] 345[9]489[9] 737[11]

Owners Biscuits *M Johnston* a57 48
3 gr f Diktat—Delta Tempo (IRE) (Bluebird (USA))
4909[7] 5127[13] 6133[13]6281[5] (6370)

Pab Special (IRE) *K R Burke* a79 75
3 b g City On A Hill(USA) —Tinos Island (IRE) (Alzao (USA))
104[2] 219[4]378[3] 459[6]795[5] 2160[6] 3266[3] 3569[4] 4634[4](4891) 5301[5] 5863[6] 6240[2]

Paceman (USA) *R Hannon* 81
2 b c Diesis—Innes (USA) (A.P. Indy (USA))
3923[5] 4597[4] (5321) 5916[10]

Pace Shot (IRE) *G L Moore* a77 80
4 b g Montjeu(IRE) —Pacific Grove (Persian Bold)
419[6]

Pace Telecom Flyer (IRE) *J W Hills* 53
2 b c Fath(USA) —Contravene (IRE) (Contract Law (USA))
2185[9] 4171[5] 4566[13] 4980[9] 5527[6]5933[8]

Pachello (IRE) *J M Bradley* a29 100
4 b g Priolo(USA) —Most Charming (FR) (Darshaan)
1246[12] 1858[14] 2624[14]3212[12] 3434[4] 3682[10] 4101[21] 4486[13]5453[11]

Pacific Pride *J Howard Johnson* 106
3 b g Compton Place—Only Yours (Aragon)
1633[3] 2031[5] 3079[14] 4682[2] 5116[4]5578[6] 5812[17]

Pacific Sun (GER) *P Rau* 48
2 br f Dashing Blade—Prairie Flame (IRE) (Marju (IRE))
6122a[9]

Packers Hill (IRE) *G A Swinbank* 69
2 b c Mull Of Kintyre(USA) —Head For The Stars (IRE) (Head For Heights)
2972[8] 4260[B] 4829[4] 5289[2] 5614[7]

Pacolet (IRE) *Patrick J Flynn* 76
7 b g Revoque(IRE) —Elupa (IRE) (Mtoto)
2723[16] 5853a[13]

Pactolos Way *P R Chamings* a70 56
3 b g Docksider(USA) —Arietta's Way (IRE) (Darshaan)
583[7] 984[10]1259[5] 3016[6]3650[5] 4367[2](4973) 5786[10]

Paddy Moon *J G Given* a45 52
3 b g Lujain(USA) —Tara Moon (Pivotal)
1141[17] 1416[10] 1950[9] 3378[5]

Paddy's Day (IRE) *T J O'Mara* 68
3 b c Imperial Ballet(IRE) —Shifting Shadow (IRE) (Mujadil (USA))
4124a[6]

Paddy's Place (IRE) *M Blanshard* a31 49
3 b f Compton Place—Lamarita (Emarati (USA))
544[9] 1433[11]

Paddys Tern *N M Babbage* a63 49
4 b g Fraam—Great Tern (Simply Great (FR))
194[8] 2483[9]

Paddywack (IRE) *D W Chapman* a69 67
9 b g Bigstone(IRE) —Millie's Return (IRE) (Ballad Rock)
2700[6] (2949) 3137[5] 3524[2] (3608) 3913[2] (4019)4157[17] 4258[6] 4834[5] 4957[10] 5243[14]5286[2] 5493[7] 5577[4] 5620[6] (5878) 6174[13]

Padre Nostro (IRE) *J R Holt* a57 63
7 ch g Grand Lodge(USA) —Meglio Che Posso (IRE) (Try My Best (USA))
(13) 246[8] 334[3]414[4] 549[7]1850[8] 2075[13] (3196) 3706[2] 3850[8] 4282[7]4924[7] 5090[6] 5725[6] 5960[12] 6305[4]6553[7] (6959)

Pagan Crest *Mrs A J Perrett* 78+
3 ch g Indian Ridge—Maria Theresa (Primo Dominie)
1291[5] 2171[7] (2403) 2713[2] (3008) 3665[5] (4490)4838[12]

Pagan Game (IRE) *David Marnane*
4 b m Montjeu(IRE) —Pagan Rhythm (USA) (Joanie's Chief (USA))
566[9]

Pagan Island *J A R Toller* 44
3 b c Polish Precedent(USA) —Dodo (IRE) (Alzao (USA))
4708[12] 5071[13] 5353[10]

Pagano (IRE) *W R Swinburn* a81 68+
3 b g Night Shift(USA) —Frippet (IRE) (Ela-Mana-Mou)
4004[5] 4431[8] 6327[4]6590[6] (6712) (6825)

Pagan Prince *J Gallagher* a82 87
9 br g Primo Dominie—Mory Kante (USA) (Icecapade (USA))
101[12] 185[12]

Pagan Rules (IRE) *Mrs A J Perrett* 67
2 b g Desert Prince(IRE) —Fernanda (Be My Chief (USA))
2604[6] 3210[7] 3663[7] 5053[11]

Pagan Starprincess *G M Moore* 64
2 b f Robertico—Pagan Star (Carlitin)
4228[4]

Pagan Sword *Mrs A J Perrett* a73 95+
4 ch g Selkirk(USA) —Vanessa Bell (IRE) (Lahib (USA))
2169[8] 2848[18] 4023[6] 4359[5] 4810[12]

Pain In The Neck (IRE) *M J Wallace* a60
3 br g Orpen(USA) —Ravishing (IRE) (Bigstone (IRE))
590[7] 6557[3]6649[5]

Paint For Pleasure (IRE) *P W Chapple-Hyam* 60
2 ch g Namid—Kyra Crown (IRE) (Astronef)
2409[6]

Paint In Green (IRE) *A Botti* 79
2 b f Invincible Spirit(IRE) —Theory Of Law (Generous (IRE))
5858a[6]

Paint The Lily (IRE) *F Watson* 40
5 b m Barathea(IRE) —Chocolate Box (Most Welcome)
2111[9] 2998[11] 3350[11]

Pair Of Kings (USA) *W Bradley* a96
3 gr g K One King(USA) —Little Symphony (USA) (Theatrical)
757a[7]

Pairumani Princess (IRE) *E A L Dunlop* a70 70
2 b f Pairumani Star(IRE) —Persian Fantasy (Persian Bold)
4140[6] 5595[4] (6145)

Pairumani's Girl (IRE) *J L Dunlop* 77
3 b f Pairumani Star(IRE) —Persian Fantasia (Alzao (USA))
1569[10] 2359[12]

Paita *E Lellouche* 111
4 b m Intikhab(USA) —Prada (GER) (Lagunas)
(1398a) 2092a[2]

Pajada *M D I Usher* a53 17
2 b f Bertolini(USA) —Last Ambition (IRE) (Cadeaux Genereux)
5894[12] 6433[11] 6591[8]

Pakama (GER) *Mario Hofer* 87
2 br f Kalatos(GER) —Puntilla (GER) (Acatenango (GER))
5763a[3] 6122a[4]

Palace Episode (USA) *Saeed Bin Suroor* 114
3 bb c Machiavellian(USA) —Palace Weekend (USA) (Seattle Dancer (USA))
1805[6]

Palace Walk (FR) *B G Powell* a51 65
4 b g Sinndar(IRE) —Page Bleue (Sadler's Wells (USA))
2497[2] 2902[4] 3035[14]

Palais Polaire *J A Geake* a60 60
4 ch m Polar Falcon(USA) —Palace Street (USA) (Secreto (USA))
1110[5] 1212[4] 2095[8]2459[4] 4531[3] 4820[4] 6538[3]6674[7]

Palais Tiff (GER) *Frau M Fechner* 102
7 ch g In A Tiff(IRE) —Palais (GER) (Wise Money)
1014a[7] 1860a[10] 3775a[4]

Palamoun *B W Hills* 80
2 b c Mtoto—Princess Minnie (Mistertopogigo (IRE))
5343[7] 5640[3] 5914[2]

Palatinate (FR) *C G Cox* 81
4 b g Desert Prince(IRE) —Dead Certain (Absalom)
2508[11] 3121[8] 3679[9] 4325[9]

Palin *F Folco* 98
2 b c Averti(IRE) —Painter's Palet (Royal Academy (USA))
3132a[3] 4464a[4]

Palm Desert (IRE) *M H Tompkins* a40
3 b g Spectrum(IRE) —Dixieline City (USA) (Dixieland Band (USA))
70[10] 215[11]

Palmetto Point *H Morrison* a57 21
2 ch c Bahamian Bounty—Forum (Lion Cavern (USA))
5890[14] 6032[6] 6188[12]

Palmiro *W J Haggas* a53
2 ch g Medicean—Tolyatti (Green Desert (USA))
3844[14] 5106[9]

Palmistry *A M Balding* 53+
3 br g Lend A Hand—Divina Mia (Dowsing (USA))
5728[7] 5951[3]

Palomar (USA) *R Charlton* 108
4 bb g Chester House(USA) —Ball Gown (USA) (Silver Hawk (USA))
1298[2] 1677[2] 2013[8] 2848[3] 3551[4]4711[4] 5374[13] 5548[9]

Palosanto (FR) *J-C Rouget*
2 b c Starborough—Ephemeride (USA) (Al Nasr (FR))
6528a^{2}
Palo Verde *M Johnston* a83 84
2 b c Green Desert(USA) —Aquaba (USA) (Damascus (USA))
3581^{3} 3982^{2} (4151) 4460^{2} 4681^{12} 5140^{4}5788^{10} (6146)
Pamir (IRE) *P R Chamings* a76d 72
4 b g Namid—Mijouter (IRE) (Coquelin (USA))
245^{8} 340^{7}559^{10} 639^{7}721^{10} 949^{10} 1258^{6}2095^{3} 2417^{10} (5872) 6174^{3}6485^{2} 6579^{5}6709^{10}
Pampamee *M Wellings*
4 b m Meqdaam(USA) —Running For You (FR) (Pampabird)
591^{11} 243^{13}
Pandim (GER) *W Hickst* 100
3 b c Tiger Hill(IRE) —Panagia (USA) (Diesis)
5414a^{5}
Panfield Belle (IRE) *R Allan* 12
5 b m Danetime(IRE) —Make Hay (Nomination)
3139^{9} 3833^{10}
Pango *H Morrison* a77 104
7 ch g Bluegrass Prince(IRE) —Riverine (Risk Me (FR))
151a^{4} 278a^{12} (Dead)
Pango's Legacy *H Morrison* a62 73
2 ch c Bertolini(USA) —Sans Egale (FR) (Lashkari)
2506^{6} 3430^{2} 3895^{5} 4603^{3} 5606^{7}5871^{7}
Panic Stations *M L W Bell* a75 63
3 ch f Singspiel(IRE) —Fiddle-Dee-Dee (IRE) (Mujtahid (USA))
981^{7} 1417^{5} 1641^{7}2198^{2} 2648^{4} 3099^{2}3410^{7} 3947^{2} 4375^{4}5035^{2} 5210^{3}(6387)
Panshir (FR) *Mrs C A Dunnett* a52 56+
5 ch g Unfuwain(USA) —Jalcamin (IRE) (Jalmood (USA))
330^{5} 474^{8}1058^{7} 1265^{5} 2149^{10} 2789^{6} 3229^{6}3817^{15} 4266^{2} (4667) 4845^{3}
Pantani (NZ) *R Laing* 107
7 gr g Pentire—Dewamar (AUS) (Marscay (AUS))
6455a^{11}
Pantomime Prince *C A Dwyer* a55 68
3 b g Royal Applause—Floppie (FR) (Law Society (USA))
1550^{3} 1941^{14}2316^{7} 2730^{6} 6234^{12}6606^{9}
Papal Bull *Sir Michael Stoute* 117+
3 b c Montjeu(IRE) —Mialuna (Zafonic (USA))
(1095) (1603) 2228^{10} (2801) 4678^{8} 5221a^{5}
Paparaazi (IRE) *R A Fahey* a69 78
4 b g Victory Note(USA) —Raazi (My Generation)
88^{13} 223^{6}3519^{6} 3883^{2} 4137^{2} 4508^{6} 5137^{3}5579^{2} 5810^{7} 6696^{5}6889^{5}
Papeete (GER) *Miss B Sanders* a69 74
5 b m Alzao(USA) —Prairie Vela (Persian Bold)
1339^{6} 2460^{6} 2653^{3}2982^{6} 3431^{12} 3853^{9}4046^{4} 4530^{10} 4996^{6}
Paper Doll *B P J Baugh* a47
4 ch m Mister Baileys—Grand Coronet (Grand Lodge (USA))
27^{6} 148^{3}312^{9} 527^{10}768^{6} 1197^{8}1395^{6}
Paper Maite *S R Bowring* a20
5 b m Komaite(USA) —Cliburnel News (IRE) (Horage)
6389^{10} 6637^{11}6814^{8} 6971^{10}
Paper Profits *A De Royer-Dupre*
2 b f Kendor(FR) —Cas Royaux (USA) (Woodman (USA))
6528a^{5}
Paper Talk (USA) *B W Hills* 105
4 br h Unbridled's Song(USA) —Journalist (IRE) (Night Shift (USA))
1086^{11} 2012^{5} 2776^{18} (3223) 4098^{17} (4372) 5523^{9}
Papillon Rose (IRE) *H-A Pantall* 100
3 b c Indian Danehill(IRE) —English Rose (FR) (Caerleon (USA))
522a^{2}
Pappas Image *A J McCabe* a53
2 b g Arkadian Hero(USA) —Fair Attempt (IRE) (Try My Best (USA))
5906^{11} 6706^{3}6921^{4}
Pappas Ruby (USA) *J S Goldie* 41
3 b f Red Ransom(USA) —Pappa Reale (Indian Ridge)
1458^{6} 1950^{3} 3355^{11} 3586^{8} 3785^{13}
Papradon *J R Best* a46
2 b g Tobougg(IRE) —Salvezza (IRE) (Superpower)
6330^{14} 6457^{5} 6562^{6}
Paradise Expected *P W Chapple-Hyam* a62 47
3 ch f North Briton—Phenomenon (Unfuwain (USA))
(219) 3706^{10} 6147^{10}
Paradise Flight (IRE) *K A Ryan* a63 72
5 ch m In The Wings—Aloft (IRE) (Ela-Mana-Mou)
2044^{11} 2365^{3} 2894^{7} 3284^{5} 4036^{18}
Paradise Isle *C F Wall* 109
5 b m Bahamian Bounty—Merry Rous (Rousillon (USA))
(1069) 1485^{20} (2438) 3499^{3} 4174^{8} 5179^{4}
Paradise Street (IRE) *J R Fanshawe* 66
3 b f Machiavellian(USA) —Tani (USA) (Theatrical)
1070^{9} 3044^{14}
Paradise Valley *Stef Liddiard* a55 57
6 b g Groom Dancer(USA) —Rose De Reve (IRE) (Persian Heights)
40^{8}
Paradise Walk *R Charlton* 65
2 b f Sakhee(USA) —Enclave (USA) (Woodman (USA))
4964^{9} 5890^{6}
Paraguay (USA) *Miss V Haigh* a82 89
3 b c Pivotal—Grisonnante (FR) (Kaldoun (FR))
1978^{3} 2304^{9} 2781^{9} (3045) 3282^{2} (3433) 3740 ^{2}3928^{10} 4356^{9} 4605^{9} 6678^{4}6830^{8} 6915^{5}6997^{8}
Para Siempre *B Smart* a75 56
2 b f Mujahid(USA) —Miriam (Forzando)
4608^{6} 5307^{5} 6414^{5}6749^{2} (6926)
Parasol (IRE) *Doug Watson* a112+ 114
7 br g Halling(USA) —Bunting (Shaadi (USA))
152a^{4} 565a^{4}
Parazone *E J O'Neill* a58
3 b c Superior Premium—Instinction (Never So Bold)
53^{6}
Parched (IRE) *Robert Collet* 71
2 b f Coronado's Quest(USA) —Desert Drama (IRE) (Green Desert (USA))
4464a^{8}
Parchment (IRE) *A J Lockwood* 67
4 ch g Singspiel(IRE) —Hannalou (FR) (Shareef Dancer (USA))
1253^{10} 1996^{13} 2832^{3} 3240^{6} 3610^{2}3762^{2} 4021^{4} 4229^{2} (4472) 4960^{3} 5369^{3}5750^{9}
Par Excellence *W G M Turner* a53 51
3 gr f Wizard King—Great Intent (Aragon)
239^{8} 322^{2}481^{6} 595^{9}1378^{8} 1567^{8} 2138^{9}
Paris Bell *T D Easterby* 83
4 gr g Paris House—Warning Bell (Bustino)
898^{15} (1042) 1597^{3} 1858^{3} 1949^{6} 2397^{8}2661^{8} 2830^{5} 4602^{7} 4885^{13} (5117) 5749^{3}6160^{6}
Parisette *A J Lidderdale* a39 64
4 b m Dansili—Moulin Rouge (Shareef Dancer (USA))
5525^{10} 6259^{11}
Paris Heights *R M Whitaker* 57
4 gr g Paris House—Petra Nova (First Trump)
1253^{12} 1665^{7} 2077^{11} 4467^{15} 4652^{2}
Parisian Dream *B W Hills* 42
2 b c Sakhee(USA) —Boojum (Mujtahid (USA))
4987^{7}
Parisian Playboy *A D Brown* a40 44
6 gr g Paris House—Exordium (Exorbitant)
616^{13} 792^{6}1395^{10} 1573^{10}5497^{10} 6552^{14}
Parisi Princess *D L Williams* a21 45?
5 ch m Shaddad(USA) —Crambella (IRE) (Red Sunset)
2860^{7} 3664^{5} 4077^{9} 4450^{5} 4627^{9}
Paris Power *D Morris* a43 32
3 b g Superpower—Gables Turner (Paris House)
30^{5} 93^{2}176^{7} 286^{7}528^{3} 617^{8}
Paris Winds (IRE) *David Wachman* 108
3 ch f Galileo(IRE) —Lil's Jessy (IRE) (Kris)
5465a^{3} 5996a^{3}
Park Esteem (IRE) *J Noseda* a97 97
3 b f Singspiel(IRE) —Park Special (Relkino)
1509^{3} 1942^{2} 2772^{9}
Park Lane Princess (IRE) *D M Simcock* a53 58
3 ch f King Of Kings(IRE) —Heated Debate (USA) (Woodman (USA))
2406^{16} 2929^{8} 3594^{3}4280^{3} 4556^{2} 4884^{3} 5767^{2}
Park's Girl *P C Haslam* a54 76
2 b f Averti(IRE) —Halland Park Girl (IRE) (Primo Dominie)
3216^{6} 3596^{3} 3958^{3}
Parkside Pursuit *J M Bradley* a63 72
8 b g Pursuit Of Love—Ivory Bride (Domynsky)
1689^{15} 2444^{9} (2897) 3071^{6} 3348^{13} 3438^{2}3699^{4} 3899^{7} 4110^{7} 4365^{4} 4629^{3}4894^{12} 5167^{9} 5327^{7} 5453^{13}
Park Star *D Shaw* a49 49
6 b m Gothenberg(IRE) —Miriam (Forzando)
81^{3} 177^{5}255^{5} 307^{3}397^{5} 411^{6}
Parkview Love (USA) *D Shaw* a77 69
5 bb g Mister Baileys—Jerre Jo Glanville (USA) (Skywalker (USA))
(319) 567^{4} 611^{7}764^{4} 1123^{3} (1275) 2170^{6} 2752^{6} 3202^{8}3459^{8} 6476^{8}6652^{5} 6767^{9}6919^{8}
Parnassian *J A Geake* a65 76
6 ch g Sabrehill(USA) —Delphic Way (Warning)
826^{9} 1051^{7} 1544^{8}1993^{7} 4575^{5} 4968^{10} 5384^{7} (5734) 6176^{5}6301^{8}
Parnassus (SAF) *A Laird* a98 98
4 b g Baroon—Belle Of Athens (SAF) (Foveros)
357a^{2} 507a^{6}
Parole Board (USA) *A Laird* a106+
4 bb g Dynaformer(USA) —Forget About It (IRE) (Be My Guest (USA))
495a^{13} 560a^{11}
Parthenope *J A Geake* 45
3 gr f Namid—Twosixtythreewest (FR) (Kris)
2458^{9} 2985^{11} 3950^{7}
Participation *M J Wallace* a78 75
3 b g Dansili—Andaleeb (USA) (Lyphard (USA))
1016^{8} 1446^{3} 1841^{12}2608^{9} 3045^{3} (3303) 3488^{3}
Particle (IRE) *M Johnston* a93 78
3 ch g Selkirk(USA) —Bernique (USA) (Affirmed (USA))
2901^{2} 3376^{4} 5319^{3} (5651) 5991^{4}6205^{15}
Partly Sunny *J E Pease* 91
3 b f Alhaarth(IRE) —Fleeting Rainbow (Rainbow Quest (USA))
6722a^{9}
Partners In Jazz (USA) *T D Barron* 105
5 gr g Jambalaya Jazz(USA) —Just About Enough (USA) (Danzig (USA))
1086^{10} (2012)
Part Timer (IRE) *M R Channon* a63 86
2 b c Mujadil(USA) —Dame Laura (IRE) (Royal Academy (USA))
2234^{5} (2439) 3903^{3} 4130^{3} 4761^{4} 5139^{2}5372^{5} 5809^{9} 6100^{12}
Party (IRE) *R Hannon* a69 92
2 ch f Cadeaux Genereux—Forty Belles (USA) (Forty Niner (USA))
2755^{3} 3043^{6} 3700^{2}4084^{4} 5592^{2} (5894) (6105)
Party Belle *C E Brittain* a64 43
3 b f Silver Patriarch(IRE) —Third Party (Terimon)
85^{2} 500^{2}
Party Best *C E Brittain* a50 58
2 gb f Best Of The Bests(IRE) —Third Party (Terimon)
2315^{6} 6591^{5} 6689^{9}
Party Boss *C E Brittain* a108 101
4 gr h Silver Patriarch(IRE) —Third Party (Terimon)
154a^{10} 357a^{11} 508a^{8}5341^{13} 5845^{2} 6101^{9}6514^{13} 6559^{3}
Party Boy (IRE) *Edgar Byrne* a32 35
4 b g Indian Rocket—Bajan Girl (IRE) (Pips Pride)
5830^{9} 6423^{5}
Party Palace *J A Osborne* a52 42
2 b f Auction House(USA) —Lady-Love (Pursuit Of Love)
1542^{12} 1688^{9} 2478^{3} (2626) 3678^{7} 4178^{11}6291^{11} 6522^{3}6768^{4} 6859^{3}6996^{4}
Party Princess (IRE) *S Parr* a40 37
5 b m Orpen(USA) —Summer Queen (Robellino (USA))
46^{5} 177^{8}212^{10} 288^{10}402^{10}
Pas De Trois *J Pearce* a25 46
2 b g Victory Note(USA) —Maziere (Mazilier (USA))
1796^{10} 3005^{4} 3448^{10} 4246^{10}4665^{6} 5084^{11} 5323^{5} 6064^{13} 6385^{9}6471^{4}
Paso Doble *D K Ivory* a59 46
8 b g Dancing Spree(USA) —Delta Tempo (IRE) (Bluebird (USA))
101^{8} 345^{6}429^{6} 600^{9}708^{7} 853^{4}904^{3} 1271^{7}1550^{5} 2245^{3}2413^{2} 3386^{6}3730^{10} 3948^{6} 6304^{2}6473^{6} 6532^{2}6780^{4} 6892^{5}
Passage Of Time *H R A Cecil* 112
2 b f Dansili—Clepsydra (Sadler's Wells (USA))
3623^{5} (4373) (6217) (6456a)
Passager (FR) *Mme C Head-Maarek* 113
3 b g Anabaa(USA) —Passionnee (USA) (Woodman (USA))
(6250a)
Passarelle (USA) *R M Beckett* 57
2 b f In The Wings—Kitza (IRE) (Danehill (USA))
6297^{4}
Pass Go *J J Lambe* a68 65
5 b g Kris—Celt Song (IRE) (Unfuwain (USA))
680^{12}
Passified *D R C Elsworth* 86
2 ch f Compton Place—Passiflora (Night Shift (USA))
(5491) 5655^{4} 5966^{8}
Passing Hour (USA) *G A Butler* 65
2 b f Red Ransom(USA) —Timely (King's Lake (USA))
3893^{5}
Passionately Royal *R A Fahey* a51 76
4 b g Royal Applause—Passionelle (Nashwan (USA))
2681^{13} 3716^{10}
Passion Fruit *C W Fairhurst* a74 86
5 b m Pursuit Of Love—Reine De Thebes (FR) (Darshaan)
1734^{5} 2299^{8} 2541^{4} (2977) 3598^{5}4090^{7} 5024^{9} 5144^{2} 5317^{4} (5619) 5919^{6}6221^{15}
Passport (SWE) *L Reuterskiold* a64 90
5 b g Caerwent—Skyline (SWE) (Jimmy Reppin)
2123a^{8}
Passport (USA) *F Brothers* a104
2 b c Pulpit(USA) —Trip (USA) (Lord At War (ARG))
5823a^{5}
Pass The Port *D Haydn Jones* a84 81
5 ch g Docksider(USA) —One Of The Family (Alzao (USA))
88^{9} (194) 454^{6}5430^{6} 5792^{18} 6287^{5}6426^{4} 6519^{2}6661^{3} 6811^{3}6917^{6}
Pastel Rose (USA) *M R Channon* 19
2 b f Diesis—Seba (Alzao (USA))
5595^{11}
Patapan (USA) *R Brogi* 106
4 b h Stravinsky(USA) —Pappa Reale (Indian Ridge)
1871a^{9} (6363a)
Patavellian (IRE) *R Charlton* a51 115
8 bb g Machiavellian(USA) —Alessia (Caerleon (USA))
1485^{6}
Patavian (IRE) *M R Channon* 69
2 b g Titus Livius(FR) —Five Of Wands (Caerleon (USA))
4592^{6} 5126^{5}
Patavium (IRE) *E W Tuer* a62 51
3 b g Titus Livius(FR) —Arcevia (IRE) (Archway (IRE))
1216^{5} 1648^{10} 2592^{6} 3159^{5}3869^{7} 6275^{4}
Patavium Prince (IRE) *J R Best* a65 78
3 ch g Titus Livius(FR) —Hoyland Common (IRE) (Common Grounds)
269^{4} 481^{5}540^{4} 1642^{8} (1801) 2318^{3}2496^{3} 2826^{2} 2931^{4} 3004^{4} 3543^{5}3708^{4} 3866^{2} 4116^{4} 4291^{4} 4562^{2}4874^{5} 4957^{12} 5872^{9} 6020^{4} 6325^{5}6390^{8}
Path To Glory *Miss Z C Davison* a50 42
2 b c Makbul—Just Glory (Glory Of Dancer)
5292^{5} 5947^{5} 6330^{12} 6488^{7}6742^{3} 6912^{5}
Patitiri (USA) *M G Quinlan* a29 36
3 ch f Rahy(USA) —Dharma (USA) (Zilzal (USA))
2859^{9} 3436^{8}
Patrixprial *M H Tompkins* 79
4 gr g Linamix(FR) —Magnificent Star (USA) (Silver Hawk (USA))
990^{3} 1132^{9}
Patternmaker (USA) *A M Hales* a67 44
4 bb g Elnadim(USA) —Attasliyah (IRE) (Marju (IRE))
23^{7} 169^{7}271^{3} (474) 514^{10} 806^{9}1383^{6} 1689^{12} 6288^{12}6399^{12} 6513^{7}6629^{6} 6856^{4}
Pat Will (IRE) *P D Evans* a38 60
2 b f Danetime(IRE) —Northern Tara (IRE) (Fayruz)
1587^{11} 1896^{8} 2315^{4} 2517^{3} 3117^{10}(3300) 4222^{8} 6951^{10} 6965^{6}
Patxaran (IRE) *P C Haslam* 80
4 b m Revoque(IRE) —Stargard (Polish Precedent (USA))
3215^{2} 3396^{5}
Pauillac (GER) *U Suter* a52 87
5 b g Machiavellian(USA) —Pelagic (Rainbow Quest (USA))
456a^{5}
Pauline's Prince *R Hollinshead* a68 64
4 b h Polar Prince(IRE) —Etma Rose (IRE) (Fairy King (USA))
227^{P} (546) 650^{9}(736) 1002^{7}1148^{9} 2025^{6} 3361^{11}3570^{7} 3947^{4} 4405^{9} 5072^{8} 5316^{4}5740^{8}
Pauvic (IRE) *Mrs A Duffield* a74 67
3 b g Fayruz—Turntable (IRE) (Dolphin Street (FR))
105^{6} (226) (322) 464^{2}(481) 593^{2}1097^{5}
Pavlovia *T D Easterby* a61 75
2 b f Diktat—Waseyla (IRE) (Sri Pekan (USA))
2973^{5} 3247^{6} 3994^{2}
Pawan (IRE) *Miss A Stokell* a91 83?
6 ch g Cadeaux Genereux—Born To Glamour (Ajdal (USA))
6^{5} 58^{4}198^{4} 244^{4}275^{5} 348^{5}413^{6} 541^{10}569^{11} 1145^{5} 1220^{10}1663^{7} 2236^{4} 2358^{6} 2618^{10} 2898^{2}2946^{5} 3281^{2} 3449^{4} 3880^{5} 3937^{12}(4468) 4598^{5} 4832^{12} 5443^{5} 5578^{4} 5749^{12}6496^{9} 6720^{3}
Pawn Broker *Miss J R Tooth* 24
9 ch g Selkirk(USA) —Dime Bag (High Line)
2879^{6}
Pawn In Life (IRE) *M J Attwater* a63d 54
8 b g Midhish—Lady-Mumtaz (Martin John)
94^{11} 143^{8}184^{5} 261^{2}387^{2} (492) 527^{3} 546^{5}649^{5} 860^{6}906^{3} 1050^{5} 1258^{3}(1390) 1644^{10}2141^{9} 6380^{8}6532^{8} 6642^{7}
Pax *D Nicholls* 76
9 ch g Brief Truce(USA) —Child's Play (USA) (Sharpen Up)
974^{16}
Pay Attention *T D Easterby* 67
5 b m Revoque(IRE) —Catch Me (Rudimentary (USA))
2078^{6}
Paymaster General (IRE) *M D I Usher* 69
2 b g Desert Style(IRE) —Khawafi (Kris)
1980^{3} 2604^{5} 2930^{5}
Pay On (IRE) *W Jarvis* a37 58+
3 ch g Danehill Dancer(IRE) —Richly Deserved (IRE) (King's Lake (USA))
2048^{7} 2622^{10} 3156^{8}3626^{4}
Pays D'Amour (IRE) *D A Nolan* a43 44
9 b g Pursuit Of Love—Lady Of The Land (Wollow)
732^{12} 974^{15} 1607^{10}
Pay Time *R E Barr* a26 67
7 ch m Timeless Times(USA) —Payvashooz (Ballacashtal (CAN))
2874^{2} (3137) (3398) 3697^{2} 3912^{9} 4405^{10} (4961)
Peace Emblem (IRE) *J W Unett* a47 46
5 b m Bahhare(USA) —Beseeching (IRE) (Hamas (IRE))
42^{10}
Peace Lily *R F Johnson Houghton* a35 67+
4 b m Dansili—Shall We Run (Hotfoot)
1348^{2} 1683^{2} 2148^{8} 2459^{8} (2676) 3450^{7}3845^{11} 3953^{7}
Peace Offering (IRE) *D Nicholls* a99 113
6 b g Victory Note(USA) —Amnesty Bay (Thatching)
664^{4} 830^{3}1158a^{4} 1481^{2} 1602^{11} 2227^{12} 2450^{2}2847^{14} (3038) 3585^{4} 3972^{6} 4128^{17} (4461) 4875^{9}5222a^{2} (5706a) 6127a^{12}
Peachy Pear *Mrs L J Young* 29
3 b f Mark Of Esteem(IRE) —Sea Quest (IRE) (Rainbow Quest (USA))
2970^{7} 4981^{12} 5128^{7}
Peak Of Perfection (IRE) *P Hughes* a73 92
5 b g Deploy—Nsx (Roi Danzig (USA))
4121a^{2}
Peak Park (USA) *P L Gilligan* a77 60
6 br g Dynaformer(USA) —Play Po (USA) (Play On (USA))
5^{2} 168^{12}1808^{16} 2140^{6}
Peak Seasons (IRE) *M C Chapman* a52 64
3 ch g Raise A Grand(IRE) —Teresian Girl (IRE) (Glenstal (USA))
807^{11} 1166^{11}1741^{12} 2034^{8} 2415^{5}2646^{5} 2901^{4} 3650^{7}(3824) 4470^{12} 5082^{15} 5316^{17} 5724^{12}
Pearl (IRE) *W J Haggas* a66+
2 b f Daylami(IRE) —Briery (IRE) (Salse (USA))
6481^{5}
Pearl Farm *C A Horgan* a61 57
5 b m Foxhound(USA) —Trinity Hall (Hallgate)
2574^{9} 3933^{4} 4329^{3}
Pearl Fisher (IRE) *D Carroll* a45 58
5 ch m Foxhound(USA) —Naivity (IRE) (Auction Ring (USA))
104^{8} 313^{6}525^{7} 1219^{9}
Pearl Island (USA) *D J Wintle* a51 11
5 b g Kingmambo(USA) —Mother Of Pearl (IRE) (Sadler's Wells (USA))
180^{2} (257) 350^{7}386^{10} 940^{3}
Pearl Of Esteem *J Pearce* 53
3 ch f Mark Of Esteem(IRE) —Ribot's Pearl (Indian Ridge)
4686^{5} 5086^{10} 5566^{6} 6289^{13}
Pearl Oyster *D J Wintle* a26
4 ch g Spectrum(IRE) —Upper Strata (Shirley Heights)
2^{8} 314^{9}442^{10}
Pearl's Girl *W J Haggas* 83
3 gr f King's Best(USA) —Karsiyaka (IRE) (Kahyasi)
2143^{4} 2406^{4} 3554^{2} (3975) 5024^{6}
Pearl Sky (FR) *Y De Nicolay* 97
3 b f Kahyasi—Patissima (FR) (Lightning (FR))
1370a^{6} 2491a^{11} 3515a^{9} (6722a)
Pearls Of Wisdom *J H M Gosden* 40
2 b f Kyllachy—Placement (Kris)
6055^{10}
Pearly King (USA) *Sir Michael Stoute* 108
3 br c Kingmambo(USA) —Mother Of Pearl (IRE) (Sadler's Wells (USA))
(1055) (1446) (1841) 2805^{7} 4082^{3} 4833^{2} 5374^{6}5675^{19}
Pearly Poll *R M Beckett* a68 78+
3 ch f Prince Sabo—Bit Of A Tart (Distant Relative)
1843^{16} 2609^{10} 3150^{5} 3349^{11} 5593^{12}5872^{16}
Pearly Wey *C G Cox* 102
3 b g Lujain(USA) —Dunkellin (USA) (Irish River (FR))
(1089) 1512^{2} 2014^{2} 2658^{13} 3414^{17} 4083^{12}4391^{4} 5202^{6}
Pearson Glen (IRE) *James Moffatt* a61 65
7 ch g Dolphin Street(FR) —Glendora (Glenstal (USA))
1467^{9}

Peas 'n Beans (IRE) *T Keddy* a60 64
3 ch g Medicean—No Sugar Baby (FR) (Crystal Glitters (USA))
2082[11] 2591[3] 3115[6] 3870[4] 4255[8]4734[4] 5082[6] 5581[2] 6410[8]6509[2] 6754[7]6790[7] 6973[4]

Pecoiquen (CHI) *F Castro* a81 71
5 ch g Hussonet(USA) —Tonguie (ARG) (Big Play (USA))
2123a[11] 4864a[14]

Peculiar Prince (IRE) *Liam McAteer* 84
4 b h Desert Prince(IRE) —Lady Peculiar (CAN) (Sunshine Forever (USA))
3123a[4] 4094a[4]

Pedlar Of Luck *A G Newcombe* a32
3 ch c Zaha(CAN) —Victoriet (Hamas (IRE))
165[10] 233[11]

Pee Jay's Dream *M W Easterby* a58 63
4 ch g Vettori(IRE) —Langtry Lady (Pas De Seul)
975[2] 1138[6] 1745[5]3998[4] (5725) 5905[2] 5960[4]6275[3]

Peephole *A Bailey* a52 61
3 ch g Pursuit Of Love—Goodwood Lass (IRE) (Alzao (USA))
30[10] 500[6]984[3] 1259[6](1829) 2641[9] 2746[4] 4173[10] 6057[12]

Peeress *Sir Michael Stoute* a89 122
5 ch m Pivotal—Noble One (Primo Dominie)
(1840) 2722[4] 3416[4] 4416a[3] 5191a[2]

Pegase Jem (FR) *P Bary* a93 100
3 b c Deputy Commander(USA) —Reine Amandine (FR) (Marignan (USA))
1179a[8] 1600a[7]

Pegasus Dancer (FR) *K A Ryan* 76
2 b g Danehill Dancer(IRE) —Maruru (IRE) (Fairy King (USA))
(4630) 5139[3] 5788[12]

Pegasus Prince (USA) *Miss J A Camacho* 37
2 b g Fusaichi Pegasus(USA) —Avian Eden (USA) (Storm Bird (CAN))
4880[7] 5481[6]

Pegasus Wind (USA) *D Wayne Lukas* a109
2 b c Fusaichi Pegasus(USA) —Ride The Wind (USA) (Meadowlake (USA))
5983a[3] 6339a[11]

Peggys First *D E Cantillon* a51 32
4 b g Wolfhound(USA) —Peggys Rose (IRE) (Shalford (IRE))
553[5] 687[6]890[2] 1054[10] 1194[13]1728[5] 1913[3]2551[8] 2758[12] 6727[12]6851[7] 6962[3]

Peggys Flower *N A Callaghan* a58 45
2 b f Arkadian Hero(USA) —Peggys Rose (IRE) (Shalford (IRE))
1333[3] 2315[8] 2495[2](2709) 3160[2] 3409[9] 3624[2]4007[5] 4493[5] 5448[10]

Peggy's Pearl *J S Moore* a53 43
2 ch f Ishiguru(USA) —Sweet Compliance (Safawan)
3796[13] 4138[7] 4926[7](4971)

Peintre Modern (FR) *R Gibson* a85 99
3 ch g Peintre Celebre(USA) —Spring Haven (USA) (Lear Fan (USA))
4420a[7]

Peintre's Wonder (IRE) *E J O'Neill* 65
2 b f Peintre Celebre(USA) —Ring The Relatives (Bering)
5083[8] 5859[2]

Pelham Crescent (IRE) *B Palling* a75 76
3 ch g Giant's Causeway(USA) —Sweet Times (Riverman (USA))
118[6] 3197[9] 4483[9]

Pelican Hill (IRE) *T H Caldwell*
3 b g Black Minnaloushe(USA) —Perusha (USA) (Southern Halo (USA))
1674[11] 1984[9]

Pelican Key (IRE) *D M Simcock* a77 81
2 b f Mujadil(USA) —Guana Bay (Cadeaux Genereux)
(3120) 3925[10] 4594[5] 6096[7]

Pelican Waters (IRE) *Mrs John Harrington* 87d
2 b f Key Of Luck(USA) —Orlena (USA) (Gone West (USA))
3060a[4] 5464a[16]

Pelleas *R Charlton*
2 b g Mark Of Esteem(IRE) —Questabelle (Rainbow Quest (USA))
6023[14]

Penalty Clause (IRE) *P Howling* 9
6 b g Namaqualand(USA) —Lady Be Lucky (IRE) (Taufan (USA))
5564[9] 5927[12]

Penang Cinta *A J Chamberlain* a56 55
3 b g Halling(USA) —Penang Pearl (FR) (Bering)
(211) 430[7] 1314[3] 1593[12]2968[2] 3338[5] 3730[14]6436[12] 6787[3]

Penchee *Mme C Head-Maarek* 99
3 b f Grand Lodge(USA) —Light Ballet (Sadler's Wells (USA))
2257a[6] 2913a[4] 4035a[10]

Pending (IRE) *J R Boyle* a53 65
5 b g Pennekamp(USA) —Dolcezza (FR) (Lichine (USA))
8[8] 156[2]290[6] 382[2]606[4] 649[3]734[5] 862[10]953[9] 1394[8]1575[7]

Penel (IRE) *P T Midgley* a58 57
5 b g Orpen(USA) —Jayess Elle (Sabrehill (USA))
27[5] 148[9]184[4] 261[5](387) 526[8]618[2] 784[10](873) 1255[5]1764[8] (2141)

Penelope Star (GER) *H Blume* 106
3 b f Acatenango(GER) —Prairie Queen (GER) (Konigsstuhl (GER))
5560a[2] 6251a[2]

Penfection (IRE) *M Botti* a87 97
3 b f Orpen(USA) —Pharfetched (Phardante (FR))
2043a[4] 3021[5] 3548[4] 4555[2] 5666[5]5888[3] 6362a[3]

Penmara *M H Tompkins* 60
3 b f Mtoto—Pendulum (Pursuit Of Love)
2124[7] 2622[7] 2929[13] 3230[3] 3440[12]3804[3] 4263[4]

Penne (FR) *J-C Rouget* 102
3 b f Sevres Rose(IRE) —Une Pensee (FR) (Kenmare (FR))
1370a[5] 2257a[4] 3515a[2] 4543a[8] 5197a[2]

Penny From Heaven (IRE) *E A L Dunlop* a70
2 b f Machiavellian(USA) —Flying Kiss (IRE) (Sadler's Wells (USA))
6242[6] 6349[3]

Penny Glitters *S Parr* a50 63
3 br f Benny The Dip(USA) —Lucy Glitters (USA) (Cryptoclearance (USA))
795[4] 1085[16] 1441[8] 2324[12] 2699[2]2947[8] 3142[5] 3933[14] 4306[10] 5988[10]6130[12] 6480[7](6542) 6703[9]6725[8]

Penny Post (IRE) *M Johnston* a83+
2 b f Green Desert(USA) —Blue Note (FR) (Habitat)
6187[7] (6377) (6563)

Penny Rich (IRE) *T Hogan* a41 85
12 br g Little Bighorn—Musical Puss (Orchestra)
6435[10]

Pennyrock (IRE) *K A Ryan* 64
2 b c Rock Of Gibraltar(IRE) —Inforapenny (Deploy)
3280[3] 4466[3] 4880[12]

Penny Thoughts *E S McMahon* a30 56
3 b f Prince Sabo—United Passion (Emarati (USA))
1003[4] 1150[10]

Penny Whisper (IRE) *I W McInnes* a12 48d
3 b f Orpen(USA) —Ionian Secret (Mystiko (USA))
993[8] 1693[8] 2109[11] 5636[8] 5928[12]

Penryn *D R C Elsworth* 74
3 ch g Selkirk(USA) —Camcorder (Nashwan (USA))
4806[7] (5353) 5944[4]

Pensata *Miss L A Perratt* 40
3 b f Compton Place—Artistic Merit (Alhaarth (IRE))
1234[9] 1437[6] 4056[10] 4136[6] 4354[7]5077[10] 5309[21] 5864[10]

Pentatonic *L M Cumani* 73+
3 b f Giant's Causeway(USA) —Fascinating Rhythm (Slip Anchor)
4814[5] 5203[2] (5567)

Pentecost *A M Balding* a75 108
7 ch g Tagula(IRE) —Boughtbyphone (Warning)
149a[3] (282a) 370a[7] 1806[9] 2742[5] 3313[11]4348[6] 5520[6]

Penway *A Sadik* a62
5 b g Groom Dancer(USA) —Imani (Danehill (USA))
35[11] 78[8]247[10] 257[7]331[8]

Penwell Hill (USA) *Miss M E Rowland* a54
7 b g Distant View(USA) —Avie's Jill (USA) (Lord Avie (USA))
9[6] 100[12]125[12] 200[3]276[8] 492[13]606[10] 6380[12]6814[2]

Penzo (IRE) *J Howard Johnson* 73
3 gr g Shinko Forest(IRE) —Thatchabella (IRE) (Thatching)
1564[4] 2001[2] 2448[2] 5312[13]

Peopleton Brook *J M Bradley* a80 93d
4 b h Compton Place—Merch Rhyd-Y-Grug (Sabrehill (USA))
1125[7] (1475) (1643) 1936[8] 2450[14] 2946[11] 5433[6]5832[12] 6009[16] 6446[5]

Pep In Her Step (IRE) *Eamon Tyrrell* a64 64
3 b f Cape Cross(IRE) —Monzitta (GER) (Monsun (GER))
839[4]

Peppermint Green *L M Cumani* 76
2 b f Green Desert(USA) —One So Wonderful (Nashwan (USA))
4765[12] 5344[8]

Pepper Road *R Bastiman* a44 44
7 ch g Elmaamul(USA) —Floral Spark (Forzando)
940[6] 1227[4]4154[11] 4511[10] 4729[10] 5483[9]

Peppertree *J R Fanshawe* 92
3 b f Fantastic Light(USA) —Delauncy (Machiavellian (USA))
1650[6] (3122) 3974[3] 5803[12]

Peppertree Lane (IRE) *M Johnston* 112+
3 ch c Peintre Celebre(USA) —Salonrolle (IRE) (Tirol)
(1101) (1832) 2024[5] 2774[24] 3292[9] (4612) (5010) 5548[3](5804) 6336[15]

Peppin's Gold (IRE) *B R Millman* a47 54
2 b f King Charlemagne(USA) —Miss Senate (IRE) (Alzao (USA))
849[7] 1046[2] 1347[10]2980[7] 4178[8] 4926[5]5387[10] 5948[2] 6258[5]6422[4]

Percristina (IRE) *B Grizzetti* 82
3 b f Orpen(USA) —Donna Marzia (USA) (Farma Way (USA))
1713a[11]

Percussionist (IRE) *J Howard Johnson* 121
5 b g Sadler's Wells(USA) —Magnificient Style (USA) (Silver Hawk (USA))
(1833) 5395a[7]

Percy Douglas *Miss A Stokell* a54 56
6 b g Elmaamul(USA) —Qualitair Dream (Dreams To Reality (USA))
24[13] 90[11]216[4] 299[4]320[7] 465[11]524[6] 633[2](686) 782[3](789) 858[5]872[2] 1102[13] 1243[8]1794[8] 2928[7] 3190[9] 3356[2] 3608[7]3913[10] 3988[13] 6539[11]

Percy's Pearl (USA) *D R C Elsworth* 82+
4 ch g Rainbow Quest(USA) —Ridgewood Pearl (Indian Ridge)
2114[4] 3121[5]

Perdono (USA) *A Wohler* 94
2 b c Lear Fan(USA) —Chateaumist (USA) (Trempolino (USA))
(5771a) 6456a[10]

Peregrine Falcon *M Johnston* a74+
2 b c In The Wings—Island Race (Common Grounds)
6386[4] (6523) 6599[5]

Perez (IRE) *W Storey* a79 69
4 b g Mujadil(USA) —Kahla (Green Desert (USA))
343[3] 504[3]711[6] 1002[2]1288[14] (2413) 4733[11] 4911[9]5249[8] 5403[6] 5510[11]

Perfect Courtesy (IRE) *P W Chapple-Hyam* a1 76
2 ch g Danehill Dancer(IRE) —Kate Maher (IRE) (Rainbow Quest (USA))
3417[9] 3851[3] 4366[10]4767[5]

Perfect Cover (IRE) *J A R Toller* a40 40
3 b f Royal Applause—See You Later (Emarati (USA))
1261[5] 4045[7] 5272[11]

Perfect Drift (USA) *Murray W Johnson* a124 115
7 b g Dynaformer(USA) —Nice Gal (USA) (Naskra (USA))
6345a[8]

Perfect Hedge *John M Oxx* 109
4 ch m Unfuwain(USA) —Via Saleria (IRE) (Arazi (USA))
(1026a) 2689a[5] 3105a[7]

Perfectionist *Mrs C A Dunnett* a47 50
4 b m In The Wings—Lady Donatella (Last Tycoon)
2944[8] 3230[8] 3594[5]3998[8] 4104[5] 4668[5]4848[4] 5033[8] 5298[12]

Perfectly Ready (AUS) *Mick Price* a74 113
4 br h More Than Ready(USA) —Elle Duccio (AUS) (Danehill (USA))
740a[8]

Perfect Order (USA) *N A Callaghan* a52 53
3 bb f Red Ransom(USA) —Ideal Index (USA) (Copelan (USA))
30[9] 193[2]430[8] 548[8]797[4] 879[7] 2727[6] 3016[9]3668[11] 4446[3] 4667[13] 6304[3]6543[7] 6617[10]

Perfect Partner (AUS) *A S Cruz* 120
6 b g Quest For Fame(USA) —Stockings (AUS) (Whiskey Road (USA))
1527a[13]

Perfectperformance (USA) *Saeed Bin Suroor* 112
4 ch h Rahy(USA) —Balistroika (USA) (Nijinsky (CAN))
(4576)

Perfect Practice *J A R Toller* a54
2 ch f Medicean—Giusina Mia (USA) (Diesis)
6689[6] 6886[8]

Perfect Promise (SAF) *Lee Freedman* 114
7 b m Caesour(USA) —Meretricious (SAF) (Dancing Champ (USA))
742a[6]

Perfect Punch *K G Reveley* a71 73
7 b g Reprimand—Aliuska (IRE) (Fijar Tango (FR))
1045[9] 1138[16] 2684[11] 2871[9]

Perfect Reflection *A Berry*
2 b f Josr Algarhoud(IRE) —Surrealist (ITY) (Night Shift (USA))
1454[7] 2999[4] 3780[7]

Perfect Reward *Mrs A J Perrett* 60
2 b c Cadeaux Genereux—Maid To Perfection (Sadler's Wells (USA))
3253[8] 5891[11] 6173[5]

Perfect Solution (IRE) *J A R Toller* a60 64
4 ch m Entrepreneur—Pearl Barley (IRE) (Polish Precedent (USA))
1383[9] 2331[14] 2978[12]

Perfect Star *C G Cox* 79
2 b f Act One—Granted (FR) (Cadeaux Genereux)
4084[2] (5914)

Perfect Story (IRE) *J A R Toller* a89 81
4 b m Desert Story(IRE) —Shore Lark (USA) (Storm Bird (CAN))
220[6] 555[3]657[4] 5643[4] 6461[5](6690) 6849[7]

Perfect Style (IRE) *M Blanshard* a48 51
2 b f Desert Style(IRE) —Seymour (IRE) (Eagle Eyed (USA))
2638[13] 3247[10] 3872[6] 4433[5]

Perfect Treasure (IRE) *J A R Toller* a68 73
3 ch f Night Shift(USA) —Pitrizza (IRE) (Machiavellian (USA))
60[5] (1750) 2263[3] 2987[15]4242[2] 5649[13] 6227[10]6865[5]

Perfidious (USA) *J R Boyle* a79 71
8 b g Lear Fan(USA) —Perfolia (USA) (Nodouble (USA))
1163[11] 2320[11]

Perianth (IRE) *J G M O'Shea* a51 61
4 ch g Bluebird(USA) —Meandering Rose (USA) (Irish River (FR))
3[12]

Perilore (IRE) *A Berry* 9
2 b f Traditionally(USA) —Titania (Fairy King (USA))
1499[7] 1884[9] 4055[5] 4520[4] 4724[9]5860[11] 6157[8]

Perlachy *Mrs N Macauley* a60 75
2 b g Kyllachy—Perfect Dream (Emperor Jones (USA))
1121[5] 1863[4] 2321[3] 2523[2] 3242[3]3605[2] 3958[4] 4151[3] 5307[6] 6715[6]6940[5]

Perle Noire (IRE) *F Rohaut* 89
3 b f Dansili—Batchelor's Button (FR) (Kenmare (FR))
5197a[5]

Permanent Way (IRE) *B J Meehan* a94 71
3 b c Fantastic Light(USA) —Itab (USA) (Dayjur (USA))
215[6] 337[3](515) 1095[9] (2556)

Pernomente (IRE) *J S Moore* a63 76
2 b g Orpen(USA) —Tread Softly (IRE) (Roi Danzig (USA))
707[3] 849[2]961[5] 1897[4] 2315[13] 3907[3] 4196[7]5161[2] 5668[5] (6025)

Persian Carpet *B I Case* a43 66
4 b m Desert Style(IRE) —Kuwah (IRE) (Be My Guest (USA))
1308[8]

Persian Conqueror (IRE) *J L Dunlop* 48
3 b g Sinndar(IRE) —Persian Fantasy (Persian Bold)
1140[5] 2082[13] 4111[4] 4868[4]

Persian Express (USA) *B W Hills* a94 78+
3 b f Bahri(USA) —Istikbal (USA) (Kingmambo (USA))
2613[3] 3046[10] 4181[4] 4591[5] (4933) 5211[4](5666) (6350)

Persian Fox (IRE) *G A Huffer* 74d
2 b g King Charlemagne(USA) —Persian Mistress (IRE) (Persian Bold)
1284[7] 1688[8] 4008[2] (4303) 4767[7] 5053[12]5461[8]

Persian Majesty (IRE) *H J Brown* 103
6 b g Grand Lodge(USA) —Spa (Sadler's Wells (USA))
278a[5] 438a[7]

Persian Peril *G A Swinbank* a80 73
2 br g Erhaab(USA) —Brush Away (Ahonoora)
2241[4] 2610[4] 2807[2] 3259[2](4055)

Persian Storm (GER) *P Schiergen* 99
2 ch c Monsun(GER) —Private Life (FR) (Bering)
5998a[4]

Persian Warrior (IRE) *W R Swinburn* a16 58
3 b g Desert Prince(IRE) —Viscaria (IRE) (Barathea (IRE))
3794[14] 4210[11] 4931[13]5452[13]

Persona (IRE) *B J McMath* a65 65
4 b m Night Shift(USA) —Alonsa (IRE) (Trempolino (USA))
186[13] 5422[10] 5954[2]6158[5] 6484[8]

Personal Column *T G Mills* a71+
2 ch g Pursuit Of Love—Tromond (Lomond (USA))
6393[3] (6650)

Personify *C G Cox* 80
4 ch g Zafonic(USA) —Dignify (IRE) (Rainbow Quest (USA))
1207[14] 1651[10] 2510[7] (2969) 3469[2] 4536[2](5149) 5833[11]

Perstrovka (IRE) *E Lellouche* 95
3 b f Sadler's Wells(USA) —Palmeraie (USA) (Lear Fan (USA))
3515a[10]

Pertemps Green *Stef Liddiard* 74
3 b g Green Desert(USA) —Pure Misk (Rainbow Quest (USA))
3742[5] 4527[10]

Pertemps Heroine *A G Newcombe* a42 46
3 b f Arkadian Hero(USA) —Watheeqah (USA) (Topsider (USA))
595[12] 4563[8] 5873[6]6236[9] 6707[12]

Pertemps Networks *M W Easterby* a51 53
2 b g Golden Snake(USA) —Society Girl (Shavian)
2287[7] 3457[9] 3830[8]4433[7]

Pertinence (IRE) *C Lerner* 82
2 b f Fasliyev(USA) —Peace Signal (USA) (Time For A Change (USA))
3990a[7]

Peruginos Flyer (IRE) *F Reuterskiold* 82
7 br g Perugino(USA) —Kriva (Reference Point)
3775a[6]

Peruvian Prince (USA) *R A Fahey* a89 84
4 b g Silver Hawk(USA) —Inca Dove (USA) (Mr Prospector (USA))
1265[3] 4108[9] 4673[2] 5236[3] 5479[6]5972[2] 6469[3](6791) (6837) (6863) 6924[2]

Peruvian Princess *J T Stimpson*
7 gr m Missed Flight—Misty View (Absalom)
615[10]

Peruvian Style (IRE) *J M Bradley* a56 66
5 b g Desert Style(IRE) —Lady's Vision (IRE) (Vision (USA))
845[9] 1209[4] 1570[9]1683[12] 2599[4] 2785[2] 3389[6](4223) 4324[2] 4551[9] 4985[4] 5167[2] 5327[3]5576[10] 5878[6] 6399[7]

Pescatorio (USA) *A P O'Brien* 80
3 b c Storm Cat(USA) —Morning Devotion (USA) (Affirmed (USA))
1065[8]

Petana *Peter Grayson* a41 41
6 gr m Petong—Duxyana (IRE) (Cyrano De Bergerac)
789[6] 951[7]1228[10] 1391[7]1466[6] 1722[7]

Petara Bay (IRE) *T G Mills* 90
2 b c Peintre Celebre(USA) —Magnificient Style (USA) (Silver Hawk (USA))
5126[10] (5537) 6104[10]

Peter Island (FR) *J Gallagher* a82 81
3 b g Dansili—Catania (USA) (Aloma's Ruler (USA))
475[10] 601[5]807[4] 1004[8](1109) 1497[2] 1606[4] 2105[7]2363[5] 2756[4] 3449[5]3568[5] 3943[2] 4158[3] (4703) 5021[6] 5427[10]

Peters Delite *R A Fahey* a59 72d
4 b g Makbul—Steadfast Elite (IRE) (Glenstal (USA))
1885[8] 2541[11] 2947[10] 3283[5] 3566[9]3947[6] 4198[5] 4585[5] 5035[6]5240[4] 5485[12]

Peter's Imp (IRE) *A Berry* 29
11 b g Imp Society(USA) —Catherine Clare (Sallust)
2998[12] 4086[9] 4451[9]

Petit Colibri (FR) *P Baudry* 101
5 br g Kaldou Star—Manesta (FR) (Gay Mecene (USA))
655a[5]

Petite Boulangere (IRE) *S Kirk* a31+
3 b f Namid—Preponderance (IRE) (Cyrano De Bergerac)
2985[16] 4045[10] 5969[13]

Petite Cherie (IRE) *G M Lyons* 94+
2 b f Fasliyev(USA) —Diamant (IRE) (Bigstone (IRE))
3963a[5] 5464a[10]

Petite Mac *N Bycroft* a55 71
6 b m Timeless Times(USA) —Petite Elite (Anfield)
1443[3] (1794) 2661[6] 2700[5] 2977[2] 3912[7]4116[9] 4401[3] (4571) 4885[10] 5487[2] 5620[4]

Petite Paramour (IRE) *Miss Gay Kelleway* a63 64
5 b m Malmsey(USA) —Fleet Petite (IRE) (Posen (USA))
156[3] 187[2]

Petite Speciale (USA) *E Lecoiffier* 110
7 br m Atticus(USA) —Petite Sonnerie (Persian Bold)
(1332a) 1875a[5] 5223a[6] 5711a[5] 6119a[9] 6610a[8]

Petito (IRE) *Ian Williams* 63
3 b g Imperial Ballet(IRE) —Fallacy (Selkirk (USA))
1290[6] 1546[5] 1741[16]

Petit Paris (CHI) *I Jory* a111
6 ch h Hussonet(USA) —Petite France (CHI) (Roy (USA))
154a[8]

Petrichan (IRE) *K A Ryan* a68 43
3 b g Medicean—Numancia (IRE) (Alzao (USA))
(93) (193) 406[5] 822[3]2128[11] 3156[10]

Petroglyph *Saeed Bin Suroor* 64+
2 ch c Indian Ridge—Madame Dubois (Legend Of France (USA))
6297[3]

Petrograd (IRE) *E Lellouche* 89
5 b h Peintre Celebre(USA) —Palmeraie (USA) (Lear Fan (USA))
2277a9 2914a5

Petrosian *M Johnston* a42 69
2 b g Sakhee(USA) —Arabis (Arazi (USA))
37884 43033 60586 628511

Petross *R M Whitaker* 61
3 b g Efisio—Zoena (Emarati (USA))
21636 289614 40696 46559 531225637 2 58613 (Dead)

Petrovich (USA) *J Noseda* 109+
3 ch c Giant's Causeway(USA) —Pharma (USA) (Theatrical)
(1088) 27752

Petrula *K A Ryan* 80
7 ch g Tagula(IRE) —Bouffant (High Top)
16318 20448

Pevensey (IRE) *M A Buckley* a91 96
4 b g Danehill(USA) —Champaka (IRE) (Caerleon (USA))
8438 112916 1357421691O 238712 30932 35013 (3840) 416044347 4 52994 (5548) 58046 60975

Phantom Rose (USA) *A Fabre* 105
3 b f Danzig(USA) —Honest Lady (USA) (Seattle Slew (USA))
(1789a) 2275a4 5701a13

Phantom Whisper *B R Millman* a82 94
3 br g Makbul—La Belle Vie (Indian King (USA))
7253 1020618482 (2329) 263911 341415 43453 550110

Pharaoh Prince *G Prodromou* a52 42
5 b g Desert Prince(IRE) —Kinlochewe (Old Vic)
7210 229537915 683288861 120171467 3 69046

Pharoah's Gold (IRE) *Mrs N S Evans* a35 35
8 b g Namaqualand(USA) —Queen Nefertiti (IRE) (Fairy King (USA))
38 240930210

Phebe *L M Cumani* 69+
3 b f Sadler's Wells(USA) —Puce (Darshaan)
37944 42046

Pheckless *J M Bradley* a51 53
7 ch g Be My Guest(USA) —Phlirty (Pharly (FR))
385 2321028593393398 8 44656811 2 175312

Philandering *R F Johnson Houghton* a39
2 b c Robellino(USA) —Just My Hobby (Kris)
589017 60729

Philanthropy *M Johnston* 84
2 ch c Generous(IRE) —Clerio (Soviet Star (USA))
488010 (5475) (5759) 62168

Philharmonic *R A Fahey* 109
5 b g Victory Note(USA) —Lambast (Relkino)
(718) 12872 14792 17787 22892 2675230764 501110 (5443) 56429 59218

Phills Pearl *D Burchell* a14
3 gr f Piccolo—Cole Slaw (Absalom)
59010 179710

Phinerine *R A Harris* a70 69
3 ch g Bahamian Bounty—Golden Panda (Music Boy)
2984 3805473 3 55156262 90151150 3 12086 17506(1771) 20965 29398 311893821 7 43985 67171167398 68333699O 7 69946

Phlaunt *R F Johnson Houghton* a45 49
4 b m Faustus(USA) —Phlirty (Pharly (FR))
45544 55738 58304 627966373 8

Phluke *R F Johnson Houghton* a90 91
5 b g Most Welcome—Phlirty (Pharly (FR))
76411 (1220) 16925 270832954 2 (3212) 35324 (3789) 45354507010 (5529) 578511 5943146221 6 658014

Phoebe Woodstock (IRE) *W R Swinburn* 76
4 ch m Grand Lodge(USA) —Why So Silent (Mill Reef (USA))
11869 16519 25347 30955 36283393514 48364 52357

Phoenix Eye *M Mullineaux* a54 59?
5 b h Tragic Role(USA) —Eye Sight (Roscoe Blake)
14614 1553416105 240710 661714

Phoenix Hill (IRE) *D R Gandolfo* a62 71
4 b g Montjeu(IRE) —Cielo Vodkamartini (USA) (Conquistador Cielo (USA))
58757 62564

Phoenix Nights (IRE) *A Berry* a33 52
6 b g General Monash(USA) —Beauty Appeal (USA) (Shadeed (USA))
36757 40579 45689

Phoenix Reach (IRE) *A M Balding* 121
6 b h Alhaarth(IRE) —Carroll's Canyon (IRE) (Hatim (USA))
4386a10 53428

Phoenix Tower (USA) *H R A Cecil* a80+
2 b c Chester House(USA) —Bionic (Zafonic (USA))
(6254)

Phone In *R Brotherton* a75 70
3 b g Sinndar(IRE) —Patria (USA) (Mr Prospector (USA))
13814 2556227952 3156434562 38192 42047475 82 50574 5875663985 65718674 89

Physical (IRE) *Mrs A J Perrett* a66 54
4 b g Efisio—St Clair (Distant Relative)
36111 137122683 4161152O4 6982(711) 854591 53 12451313537 (Dead)

Pianoforte (USA) *E J Alston* a64 69d
4 b g Grand Slam(USA) —Far Too Loud (CAN) (No Louder (CAN))
7648 8601111441O 18509 22868 31687 (3361) 357023716 7

Piano Key *R Charlton* a35
2 ch f Distant Music(USA) —Ivorine (USA) (Blushing Groom (FR))
618614

Piano Man *J C Fox* a64 78
4 b g Atraf—Pinup (Risk Me (FR))
19266 39489

Piano Player (IRE) *J A Osborne* a87 71
3 b g Mozart(IRE) —Got To Go (Shareef Dancer (USA))
3654 (590) (839) 14444 26086(3488) 39512 4225U 47043

Picacho (IRE) *J L Dunlop* 70+
3 b f Sinndar(IRE) —Gentle Thoughts (Darshaan)
20663 26075 (4800) 60277

Picador *Sir Mark Prescott* a61 39
3 b g Pivotal—Candescent (Machiavellian (USA))
66272 (6700) 67435

Picaresque Coat (JPN) *Y Ikee* 113
4 b h Jade Robbery(USA) —Fujino Taka Komachi (JPN) (Kolymsky (USA))
5703a2

Piccled *E J Alston* a88 69
8 b g Piccolo—Creme De Menthe (IRE) (Green Desert (USA))
761RR 95112

Piccleyes *M J Polglase* a57 56
5 b g Piccolo—Dark Eyed Lady (IRE) (Exhibitioner)
9077 3605501 5 5875(862) 10546 13032150415 179411 22077

Piccolena Boy *P Winkworth* a34 70
2 b c Piccolo—Bella Helena (Balidar)
21857 29674 33442 37993 475355234 9 566812

Piccolini *Mrs G S Rees* a6 27
2 b f Bertolini(USA) —Piccolo Cativo (Komaite (USA))
279110 32869 36696

Piccolo Diamante (USA) *T J Pitt* a58
2 bb c Three Wonders(USA) —Bafooz (USA) (Clever Trick (USA))
62556 64148

Piccolomini *E W Tuer* a63 63
4 b g Diktat—La Dama Bonita (USA) (El Gran Senor (USA))
25019 28329 398314 42297

Piccolo Prezzo *I A Wood* a40 21
2 ch f Piccolo—Bon Marche (Definite Article)
7607 9083164710 22871 2 23467295O5 34079

Piccolo Prince *P A Blockley* a60 66
5 ch g Piccolo—Aegean Flame (Anshan)
16 47867 12 3155408 2 (864) 12655 1528931715 45714 46946 58659 6477266382 66815685810

Piccostar *A B Haynes* a68 75
3 b f Piccolo—Anneliina (Cadeaux Genereux)
8073 954614316 22632 25702 (2730) 29874 329993646 8 54539 560595987 6 657211

Pick A Nice Name *R M Whitaker* 75
4 ch m Polar Falcon(USA) —Opuntia (Rousillon (USA))
(1733) 21947 28642 35676

Pickering *E J Alston* a67 34
2 br c Prince Sabo—On The Wagon (Then Again)
619911 63244 63778

Pickled Again *S Dow* 37
2 br f Piccolo—Queen Of Tides (IRE) (Soviet Star (USA))
420714

Pick Of The Crop *J R Jenkins* a41 45
5 ch g Fraam—Fresh Fruit Daily (Reprimand)
682 12

Pickwick Miss (USA) *D M Simcock* a39 47
3 b f Repriced(USA) —Sihasapa (USA) (Diesis)
25759 33871041138 57573 60579

Picot De Say *C Roberts* a13 50
4 b g Largesse—Facsimile (Superlative)
37916 32709

Pictavia (IRE) *Saeed Bin Suroor* 114+
4 ch m Sinndar(IRE) —Insijaam (USA) (Secretariat (USA))
(3021) 37393 (4482) (5204) 6124a5

Picture Frame *J T Stimpson* 69
2 ch g Fraam—Floral Spark (Forzando)
10403 12483 14992 18843 (2382) 49128

Picture Show (USA) *C E Brittain* a65 65
3 b f Swain(IRE) —Impetuous Image (USA) (Mr Prospector (USA))
6692 8508 23935 30118 333683804 10 48457 5690364368

Pic Up Sticks *B G Powell* a92 96
7 gr g Piccolo—Between The Sticks (Pharly (FR))
14742 182016 242912 26745 2983632117 (3251) (3744) 468214 52023 54337 5667858321 1 64454

Piddies Pride (IRE) *Miss Gay Kelleway* a57 63
4 b m Indian Lodge(IRE) —Fairybird (FR) (Pampabird)
105712 18996 26119 (3867) (4294) 52324 5350559289

Pieter Brueghel (USA) *D Nicholls* a87 98
7 b g Citidancer(USA) —Smart Tally (USA) (Smarten (USA))
7184 8366 1487518351 1 20178 23233 30387 460944796 8 55345 6292664993

Pietersen (IRE) *T D Barron* a52 55
2 ch g Redback—Faye (Monsanto (FR))
109O6 158814 59014 62O83 64221264725 67367

Piety (IRE) *M Johnston* 95+
3 b f Danehill(USA) —Quest Of Passion (FR) (Saumarez)
31462 34515 49452 (5151) 57697 (6202) 631926567a9

Pigeon Flight *M L W Bell* 66
2 ch g Compton Admiral—Fervent Fan (IRE) (Soviet Lad (USA))
59478 61733

Pigeon Island *H Candy* a77 72
3 gr g Daylami(IRE) —Morina (USA) (Lyphard (USA))
15463 25026 40518 45917 526865568 9 587910

Pikaboo *S C Williams* a46 61
3 ch f Pivotal—Gleam Of Light (IRE) (Danehill (USA))
44316 59888 69444

Pillars Of Wisdom *J L Dunlop* a82 90
4 ch h Desert Prince(IRE) —Eurolink Mischief (Be My Chief (USA))
120711 22329 33376 36792 424185108 3 56709

Pinafore *P Winkworth* a63 53
4 ch m Fleetwood(IRE) —Shi Shi (Alnasr Alwasheek)
372813 414111

Pinchbeck *M A Jarvis* a91 83
7 b g Petong—Veuve Hoornaert (IRE) (Standaan (FR))
(80) 2753 413482 89 9706 11838669O 7 68354

Pinch Of Salt (IRE) *A M Balding* 80
3 b g Hussonet(USA) —Granita (CHI) (Roy (USA))
12696 16842 18416 24366 52846

Pindar (GER) *B J Curley*
2 b g Tertullian(USA) —Pierette (GER) (Local Suitor (USA))
69769

Pineapple Poll *P L Gilligan* 9
2 b f Josr Algarhoud(IRE) —Petrovna (IRE) (Petardia)
246112 304312 34029

Pine Cone (IRE) *A King* 92
4 ch m Dr Fong(USA) —Pine Needle (Kris)
18008 (2457) 27064 36274 40798 58039

Pine Island (USA) *C McGaughey III* a117
3 br f Arch(USA) —Matlacha Pass (USA) (Seeking The Gold (USA))
3757a2 6343aF

Pinkabout (IRE) *J H M Gosden* a76+ 59
2 br f Desert Style(IRE) —Dinka Raja (USA) (Woodman (USA))
(3402) 39259

Pink Bay *W S Kittow* a61 71
4 b m Forzando—Singer On The Roof (Chief Singer)
902 12 180212 2223112676 4 36824 38973 44845 4984954746

Pink Notes *R J Hodges* 22
2 ch c Bandmaster(USA) —Pink Petal (Northern Game)
537910

Pink Pyjamas *J A R Toller* a35 19
3 ch f Compton Place—Pagan Princess (Mujtahid (USA))
154913 27307 33407

Pink Salmon *Mrs L J Mongan* a39
2 ch f Dr Fong(USA) —West Humble (Pharly (FR))
634912

Pinky *B J McMath*
3 ro f Bluebird(USA) —Lost Dream (Niniski (USA))
24987

Pinky Tinky (ITY) *A Peraino*
2 br f College Chapel—Pay Me More (IRE) (Doyoun)
2062a7

Pinpoint (IRE) *W R Swinburn* a80+ 105
4 b g Pivotal—Alessia (GER) (Warning)
20124 27426 (5374) 56753 63378

Pinson (IRE) *Saeed Bin Suroor* 120
4 gr h Halling(USA) —Tadorne (FR) (Inchinor)
56732 596811

Pintle *J L Spearing* a64 93d
6 b m Pivotal—Boozy (Absalom)
14076 21472 24407 (2900) 31212 3493194628 10 496510 619011

Piper General (IRE) *J Mackie* a79 36
4 br g General Monash(USA) —Pipewell (IRE) (Lake Coniston (IRE))
2467 5999

Piper Lily *M Blanshard* a51 54
4 b m Piccolo—Polly Golightly (Weldnaas (USA))
14665 281312

Piper's Song (IRE) *H Candy* a63 71
3 gr g Distant Music(USA) —Dane's Lane (IRE) (Danehill (USA))
218813 29194 36476(5269) 57345

Pipoldchap (CHI) *F Castro* a75 106
6 bb g The Great Shark(USA) —Tiquitiquiti (CHI) (Cresta Rider (USA))
5225a5

Pippa's Dancer (IRE) *W R Muir* a75 83
4 b m Desert Style(IRE) —Soreze (IRE) (Gallic League)
9028 (1383) 1961222335 (2637) (2898) 33328

Pips Assertive Way *A W Carroll* a8 39
5 ch m Nomadic Way(USA) —Return To Brighton (Then Again)
598 16611

Pip's Baby *S Kirk* a63 57
3 ch g Groom Dancer(USA) —Captivating (IRE) (Wolfhound (USA))
293313 470013 5992146241 13

Pipssalio (SPA) *Jamie Poulton* a46 47
9 b g Pips Pride—Tesalia (SPA) (Finissimo (SPA))
180811

Piquet *J J Bridger* a51 49
8 br m Mind Games—Petonellajill (Petong)
1137 3951047155576780 7 9046 137351536 9 17276234 88 240112 613486232 6 6462868018 685236904 5

Pires *M R Channon* 97
2 br g Generous(IRE) —Kaydee Queen (IRE) (Bob's Return (IRE))
22582 23883 28444 31872 (3758) 39242456 15

Pirner's Brig *M W Easterby* a61 49
2 b c Warningford—Loch Maree (Primo Dominie)
124810 17449 238233997 10 528210 (6789) 69262

Pirouetting *B W Hills* a75+ 79
3 b f Pivotal—Jitterbug (IRE) (Marju (IRE))
10853 18444 25322 28812 32193(4489) 52663 591713 64117

Pistol Dawn *J J Quinn* 63
3 b f Primo Valentino(IRE) —Pearls (Mon Tresor)
489211 537011

Pitbull *Mrs G S Rees* a61 65
3 b g Makbul—Piccolo Cativo (Komaite (USA))
24417 28965 32907 34732 3725850316

Pitch Up (IRE) *T G Mills* a95 83
4 b g Cape Cross(IRE) —Uhud (IRE) (Mujtahid (USA))
135911 16434 278514

Pititana (IRE) *R Hannon* a69 72
3 b f Xaar—Jet Cat (IRE) (Catrail (USA))
7223 9012108 93 (1430) 16725 38739 42086

Pitsi Kahtoh *P W Hiatt* a31 45
4 b m Petoski—Plectrum (Adonijah)
12246 1460617679 20756 2362529529 323211 327011 36806

Pitton Justice *W G M Turner* a20
4 ch h Compton Place—Blind Justice (Mystiko (USA))
48010

Pittsburgh *A M Balding* a65+ 78
4 ch g Nashwan(USA) —Oatey (Master Willie)
15688 19265 2305425346 29567

Pivotal Flame *E S McMahon* 115
4 b h Pivotal—Reddening (Blushing Flame (USA))
7294 10694 14852 2276a5 267533312 7 40803 47383 53754 5712a8

Pivotalia (IRE) *W R Swinburn* a63
3 b f Pivotal—Viscaria (IRE) (Barathea (IRE))
618712 64334

Pivotal Point *P J Makin* 117
6 b g Pivotal—True Precision (Presidium)
14858 2276a6 27203 284611 (3312) 349484410a3

Pivotal's Princess (IRE) *E S McMahon* 105
4 ch m Pivotal—Art Princess (IRE) (Fairy King (USA))
16027 20218 43602 48322 51821054053 56423

Pix *S Kirk* a54 46
3 b f Bertolini(USA) —Fair Kai (IRE) (Fayruz)
3012 834

Pixie Ring *Sir Mark Prescott* a77
2 b f Pivotal—Ard Na Sighe (IRE) (Kenmare (FR))
(6821) (6989)

Place Vendome (FR) *Mlle S-V Tarrou* 90
2 ch f Dr Fong(USA) —Mediaeval (FR) (Medaaly)
6546a5

Plain Champagne (IRE) *Dr J R J Naylor* a41 58d
4 b m Victory Note(USA) —Paddys Cocktail (IRE) (Tremblant)
12148 154116 191114(2133) 22622 28226 31962 361610 410412545114 60687 61329

Plane Painter (IRE) *M Johnston* a64 79
2 b g Orpen(USA) —Flight Sequence (Polar Falcon (USA))
44873 (5168) 610011

Planters Punch (IRE) *G M Moore* 65
5 b g Cape Cross(IRE) —Jamaican Punch (IRE) (Shareef Dancer (USA))
39394 42564 49252 52425 558145750 7

Plateau *C R Dore* a83 91
7 b g Zamindar(USA) —Painted Desert (Green Desert (USA))
6573 7188 79851236 6 14964 16625 24509 3069233547 39725 410119 47939 52915635310 652766568 (6952)

Platinum Charmer (IRE) *K R Burke* a65 58
6 b g Kahyasi—Mystic Charm (Nashwan (USA))
8696 10452 12222 14394 16666176912 27886 31928 36282 3763340866 57519 61584 63174

Platinum Couple (IRE) *J Lostritto* a98
3 gr c Tale Of The Cat(USA) —Ingot's Dance Away (USA) (Gate Dancer (USA))
1861a6 2477a7

Platinum Hound (IRE) *H Morrison* 57
3 b f Vettori(IRE) —Dog Rose (SAF) (Fort Wood (USA))
141710 17988

Plato's Republic (USA) *C Collins* 71
2 b c Catienus(USA) —Life Of The Party (USA) (Pleasant Colony (USA))
5408a8

Plausabelle *G G Margarson* a61 46
5 b m Royal Applause—Sipsi Fach (Prince Sabo)
641910 66676681O8 69934

Playing Games *M W Easterby*
2 b c Mind Games—Contradictory (Reprimand)
23826 262611 (Dead)

Play Master (IRE) *R A Harris* a69 69
5 b g Second Empire(IRE) —Madam Waajib (IRE) (Waajib)
2512 319134983 (600) 65010 9055

Play Me *P W Chapple-Hyam* a100 98
4 b m Nashwan(USA) —Mrs Moonlight (Ajdal (USA))
27063 32934 45903 50185

Play Straight *R M Beckett* a62
2 ch f Piccolo—Align (Petong)
64415 67108(6963)

Play The Ball (USA) *J J Lambe* a77 59
4 ch g Boundary(USA) —Copper Play (USA) (Fast Play (USA))
6327 1275414559 25514 275786573 8

Playtotheaudience *R A Fahey* 73
3 b g Royal Applause—Flyfisher (USA) (Riverman (USA))
331710 388913 42989 49588 568515

Play Truant (SWE) *J Malmborg*
3 br c Diaglyphard(USA) —College Camp (College Chapel)
4919a10

Play Up Pompey *J J Bridger* a58 54
4 b g Dansili—Search For Love (FR) (Groom Dancer (USA))
97213 12445 140010222628 240110 29566 32097 3429 959101 2 623576374 9 66207(6668) 672469185

Pleasant *D P Keane* a44 74
5 b m Topanoora—Devon Peasant (Deploy)
116312

Please The King (IRE) *T Hogan* 64
2 b c King Charlemagne(USA) —Placate (Rainbow Quest (USA))
4824a24

Pleasing *J L Dunlop* a62 98?
3 b f Dr Fong(USA) —Trounce (Barathea (IRE))
(1291) 18514 25546 4660451301 4 60693 (6206) 63337

Pleasing Gift *J M P Eustace* a59 53
3 b f Largesse—Pleasure Dome (Most Welcome)
48998 50718 5611659361 2 63275 65847

Pleasure Pursuit *B W Hills* 26
2 b g Pursuit Of Love—Glen Falls (Commanche Run)
619912 633116

Plemont Bay *M L W Bell* a66 73+
3 b g Robellino(USA) —Jezyah (USA) (Chief's Crown (USA))
3745 453659O9 23525 3017332494 (4150) 46044 48844

Plenty Cried Wolf *R A Fahey* a63 65
4 b g Wolfhound(USA) —Plentitude (FR) (Ela-Mana-Mou)
1389[6] 2150[10] 3388[3]3686[9] 4320[4] 4947[10]5954[4] 6158[7]

Plough Maite *D E Cantillon* a39 41
3 b g Komaite(USA) —Plough Hill (North Briton)
4016[9] 4263[7] 4668[6] 5365[5] 5887[7]

Plum Blossom *S A Brookshaw* a30 43
3 br f Beat All(USA) —Plum Bold (Be My Guest (USA))
2462[12]

Plum Pudding (IRE) *R Hannon* a83 102
3 b g Elnadim(USA) —Karayb (IRE) (Last Tycoon)
1401[2] 1547[2] (1681) 2774[14]3413[2] 5376[9] (5639) 5677[6] 5945[15] 6219[9]

Plush *Sir Mark Prescott* a57 38
3 ch c Medicean—Glorious (Nashwan (USA))
1274[8] 1386[2]2244[3] 2754[8]

Plusvite (SWI) *Karin Suter* 53
3 ch f Silvano(GER) —Pacanda (SWI) (Acatenango (GER))
5008a[11]

Pochard *J M P Eustace* a68 58
3 br f Inchinor—Pomorie (IRE) (Be My Guest (USA))
3146[6] 3717[2] 4396[3]5276[11] 5650[4]

Pocket Too *M Salaman* a60 23
3 b g Fleetwood(IRE) —Pocket Venus (IRE) (King's Theatre (IRE))
61[8] 515[7]1193[11] 5897[7] 6995[3]

Pocketwood *Jean-Rene Auvray* a72 83
4 b g Fleetwood(IRE) —Pocket Venus (IRE) (King's Theatre (IRE))
6205[14] 6381[4]

Poderoso Kike (ARG) *M Grassi* 73
3 ch c Iberique(ARG) —Miss Ponderosa (ARG) (Numerous (USA))
6364a[11]

Poetical (IRE) *D J Daly* 101
5 ch m Croco Rouge(IRE) —Abyat (USA) (Shadeed (USA))
2824[7] 4502a[6]

Point Calimere (IRE) *Liam McAteer* a65 87
5 b g Fasliyev(USA) —Mountain Ash (Dominion)
3125a[11] 3561a[8]

Point Determined (USA) *B Baffert* a116 100
3 b c Point Given(USA) —Merengue (USA) (Broad Brush (USA))
1498a[9]

Poirot *J Howard Johnson* a51 66
4 b g Montjeu(IRE) —Opari (IRE) (Night Shift (USA))
258[11] 4544[9]

Poisiedon (IRE) *Liam McAteer* a69
2 b c King's Best(USA) —Lizanne (USA) (Theatrical)
6751[3] 6920[5]

Poker Player (IRE) *G C Bravery* a81 75
4 ch g Raise A Grand(IRE) —Look Nonchalant (IRE) (Fayruz)
80[4] 245[11]340[9] 476[12]569[6] 699[7]949[12] 2184[2] 2737[7] 3089[15] 3304[5]4009[8]

Polar Ben *J R Fanshawe* 117
7 b g Polar Falcon(USA) —Woodbeck (Terimon)
1287[4] (1979) 4145[3] 5135[4] 5341[4] 5588[4]5962[6] 6218[5]

Polar Force *Mrs C A Dunnett* a72 61
6 ch g Polar Falcon(USA) —Irish Light (USA) (Irish River (FR))
23[6] 117[3]224[9] 2864[15] 3447[14]5737[9] 5987[10]6061[6] 6325[2] 6395[5](6556) 6622[10]6966[9]

Polar Haze *J Pearce* a37 44
9 ch g Polar Falcon(USA) —Sky Music (Absalom)
29[8] 260[5]388[6] 529[11]

Polar Magic *J R Fanshawe* a85 110
5 ch g Polar Falcon(USA) —Enchant (Lion Cavern (USA))
(1935) 2289[4] 3926[6] 4593[2] 5523[4]

Polar Wind (ITY) *R Menichetti* 84
2 ch c Rob's Spirit(USA) —Miss Buffy (Polar Falcon (USA))
6003a[10]

Polesworth *C N Kellett* a51 44
4 b m Wizard King—Nicholas Mistress (Beveled (USA))
145[6] 300[7]

Poliama *Evan Williams* 17
4 b m Polish Precedent(USA) —Amal (Top Ville)
5830[11] 6021[13]

Policy Maker (IRE) *E Lellouche* 121
6 b h Sadler's Wells(USA) —Palmeraie (USA) (Lear Fan (USA))
1558a[5] (2277a) 2914a[4] 4647a[2] 5223a[5] 5999a[7]

Polished Gem (IRE) *D K Weld* 84
3 b f Danehill(USA) —Trusted Partner (USA) (Affirmed (USA))
1363a[4] 2744[11]

Polish Effigy *B W Duke* a41
3 b g Bertolini(USA) —Corn Dolly (IRE) (Thatching)
447[6]

Polish Emperor (USA) *D W Barker* a83 76
6 ch g Polish Precedent(USA) —Empress Jackie (USA) (Mount Hagen (FR))
1236[8] 2389[5] 2674[9] 3802[6] 4338[6]4598[2] 4793[7] 5148[11] 5593[13] 6065[2]6320[13] 6496[10] 6953[7]

Polish Index *J R Jenkins* a52 74
4 b g Polish Precedent(USA) —Glossary (Reference Point)
972[9] (1265) 1993[9] 2443[5] 3642[11]4496[4] (4894) 5593[14]

Polish Magic *A Wohler* 98
6 gr h Magic Ring(IRE) —Petitesse (Petong)
1871a[7] 6093a[4]

Polish Power (GER) *J S Moore* a85 83
6 br h Halling(USA) —Polish Queen (Polish Precedent (USA))
13[5] 283[5]414[2] (457) 549[2] (574) (706) (847) 983[4]1439[2] (1756) 2231[3] 2656[9] 6148[4]6351[8] (6661) 6917[4]

Polish Prospect (IRE) *H S Howe* 13
2 ch f Elnadim(USA) —Always True (USA) (Geiger Counter (USA))
6023[13]

Polish Red *G G Margarson* 73
2 b c Polish Precedent(USA) —Norcroft Joy (Rock Hopper)
4388[5] 4867[6] 5321 [5]

Polish Star *R Hannon* 55
2 b g Polish Precedent(USA) —Apennina (USA) (Gulch (USA))
5340 [9]

Polish Welcome *S C Williams* a54 54
3 ch f Polish Precedent(USA) —Three White Sox (Most Welcome)
1085[18] 1351[8] 2391[7] 3016[4]3823[4] 3870[6] 4279[5] 4944[4] 5445[7]

Polish World (USA) *E A L Dunlop* a55 50
2 b c Danzig(USA) —Welcometotheworld (USA) (Woodman (USA))
5890[9] 6072[6]

Polite Reply (USA) *D M Simcock* a46
3 gr f With Approval(CAN) —Tsar's Pride (Sadler's Wells (USA))
1552[5]

Politkovskaya *T H Caldwell*
3 ch f Medicean—Soluce (Junius (USA))
6177[15]

Polliwilline (IRE) *R Hannon* 82
3 b f Mull Of Kintyre(USA) —Zelah (IRE) (Alzao (USA))
(1190) 1734[4] 2581[10] 2818[3] 3418[6] 4481[3]5164[7] 5591[10] 6020[13]

Polly Jones (USA) *G L Moore* a50 38
2 b f Lear Fan(USA) —Polly's Link (USA) (Phone Trick (USA))
3591[14] 3893[8] 5947[10] 6143[8](6695) 6845[6]

Polly Rocket *P D Niven*
2 ch f Tendulkar(USA) —Celts Dawn (Celtic Swing)
6789[B]

Polonius *P R Webber* a85 93
4 b g Great Dane(IRE) —Bridge Pool (First Trump)
64[8] 340[8]578[7]

Poltava (FR) *D Smaga* 104
2 b f Victory Note(USA) —Passiflore (FR) (Sillery (USA))
3132a[5] 4621a[2] (5257a) 5714a[4]

Poly Dance (FR) *J-C Rouget* 109
5 b h Le Triton(USA) —Dancing Machine (FR) (Kaldoun (FR))
2313a[8]

Polygonal (FR) *Ernst Oertel* a101 97
6 b g Octagonal(NZ) —Sectarine (FR) (Maelstrom Lake)
(65) 222[3] 296[3]518[8] 728[18] 2201[12]2848[4] 3294[9]

Polyquest (IRE) *P F I Cole* a53 45
2 b f Poliglote—Seren Quest (Rainbow Quest (USA))
4866[10] 6349[9] 6498[5]

Polysheba (FR) *A Fabre* 98
3 b f Poliglote—Ganasheba (USA) (Alysheba (USA))
6328a[3]

Pomeroy (USA) *M D Wolfson* a116
5 b h Boundary(USA) —Questress (USA) (Seeking The Gold (USA))
6341a[9]

Pomfret Lad *J J Quinn* a54 86
8 b g Cyrano De Bergerac—Lucky Flinders (Free State)
1125[6] (1297) 1597[6] 1856[9] 2397[9] (2785) 3217[10]3673[4] 4085[9] 4636[10] 4881[5]

Pommes Frites (USA) *W Mott* a87 114
4 br m Dynaformer(USA) —Dolce Amore (USA) (Relaunch (USA))
6614a[3]

Pommes Frites *W R Muir* a70 77
3 b f Bertolini(USA) —Picolette (Piccolo)
2330[8] 3643[6] 4437[9]4933[10] 5384[2] 5724[11]6259[10] 6350[8]6489[12] 6624[2]

Pompeus (GER) *T Howart* 100
3 gr c Acambaro(GER) —Pompeju (GER) (Cagliostro (GER))
4942a[4]

Poniard (IRE) *D W Barker* 58
2 b g Daggers Drawn(USA) —It's Academic (Royal Academy (USA))
1142[8] 1342[5] 1682[10] 3746[4] 4321[13]4887[3] 5632[8]

Pontefract Glory *M Dods* 47
3 b g Lujain(USA) —Final Glory (Midyan (USA))
1232[12] 1736[14] 2192[9] 2758[5] 3006[2]3288[5] 3814[8] 4389[6] 4695[6] 5432[4]

Ponte Tresa (FR) *Y De Nicolay* 107
3 gr f Sicyos(USA) —Ponte Brolla (FR) (Highest Honor (FR))
2257a[2] 3515a[8] 4543a[3] 5220a[8] 5700a[2](6567a)

Ponte Vecchio (IRE) *J R Boyle* a44 39
2 b g Trans Island—Gino Lady (IRE) (Perugino (USA))
4992[9] 5659[12] 6603[4]6746[4]

Ponticello (GER) *Mario Hofer* 76
3 b c Law Society(USA) —Pretty Su (IRE) (Surumu (GER))
1526a[8]

Pont Neuf (IRE) *A Crook* a60d 74
6 b m Revoque(IRE) —Petite Maxine (Sharpo)
869[10] 1045[14] 5955[12]

Pont Wood *M Blanshard* a59
2 b c Iron Mask(USA) —Bajan Rose (Dashing Blade)
6603[3] 6749[5]

Ponty Carlo (IRE) *T D Easterby* 47
3 b g Mujadil(USA) —Distant Shore (IRE) (Jareer (USA))
4613[6] 4948[14] 5077[13]

Ponty Rossa (IRE) *T D Easterby* a78 96
2 ch f Distant Music(USA) —Danish Gem (Danehill (USA))
2106[2] (2973) (3685) (4146) 4681[10] 5356[5]

Pool Land (USA) *T Pletcher* a115
4 ch m Silver Deputy(CAN) —Slew City Slicker (USA) (Slew City Slew (USA))
6343a[9]

Poor Nelly *J L Dunlop* a45 49
2 ch f King's Best(USA) —Kootenay (IRE) (Selkirk (USA))
2638[12] 3537[8] 4292[6] 5906[12]

Pop Music (IRE) *Miss J Feilden* a68 55
3 b g Tagula(IRE) —Easy Pop (IRE) (Shernazar)
365[3] 534[3]630[3] 720[5]1055[6] 1254[4] 3387[8]4113[6] 5035[9] 5847[6](6628) 6767[3]6977[2]

Popolo (IRE) *M L W Bell* 65
2 b f Fasliyev(USA) —Delisha (Salse (USA))
3588[7] 3979[3] 4283[3] 4804[5] 5434[4]

Poppys Footprint (IRE) *K A Ryan* a74 85
5 ch m Titus Livius(FR) —Mica Male (ITY) (Law Society (USA))
252[9] 384[3]567[2] 660[8]3598[11] 3789[8]

Pop Rock (JPN) *Katsuhiko Sumii* 125
5 b h Helissio(FR) —Pops (JPN) (Sunday Silence (USA))
6110a[7] 6392a[2]

Poquelin (FR) *F-X de Chevigny* 103
3 bl g Lahint(USA) —Babolna (FR) (Tropular)
1600a[2]

Porcelain (IRE) *A Dickman* 74
2 ch f Peintre Celebre(USA) —Clunie (Inchinor)
3908[4] (5527) 6217[9]

Porjenski *A B Haynes* a47 36
2 ch f Piccolo—Stygian (USA) (Irish River (FR))
3915[5] 4327[3]4971[6] 5448[7] 6401[13]

Portacarron (IRE) *Eamon Tyrrell* a54 67
4 b m Rossini(USA) —Night Patrol (IRE) (Night Shift (USA))
3841[0] 1645[11]

Portal *J R Fanshawe* 103
3 b f Hernando(FR) —White Palace (Shirley Heights)
(2404) 3929[3] (4590) 5917[5]

Portant Fella *Ms Joanna Morgan* 86
7 b g Greensmith—Jubilata (USA) (The Minstrel (CAN))
3123a[18] 5396a[11]

Porters (USA) *R Hannon* a93+ 98
3 bb g Minardi(USA) —Time For The Show (USA) (Academy Award (USA))
(724) 831[2] 1404[7]2774[13] 3443[2] 3710[5] 4082[12] 5724[5]

Portland *B W Hills* 78
3 b c Zafonic(USA) —Bayswater (Caerleon (USA))
(1048)

Port Luanda (IRE) *R M Flower* a22
2 ch g Docksider(USA) —Lady Angola (USA) (Lord At War (ARG))
3408[10] 3843[12]

Port Macquairie (IRE) *R M Beckett* a58
2 b g Val Royal(FR) —Hishmah (Nashwan (USA))
6581[9] 6809[4]

Portmeirion *S C Williams* a73 87
5 b m Polish Precedent(USA) —India Atlanta (Ahonoora)
1413[12] 3097[3] (3846) 4633[7]5171[2] 5405[6] 6121a[6]

Port 'n Starboard *C A Cyzer* a70 67
5 ch g Polar Falcon(USA) —Sally Slade (Dowsing (USA))
(32) 111[2] 223[3]375[14] 6967[7]820[2] (1244) 6503[4] 6590[9]6848[4]

Porto Santo (FR) *P Demercastel* 110
3 b c Kingsalsa(USA) —Exciting Times (FR) (Jeune Homme (USA))
1178a[7] 1718a[6]

Portrayal (USA) *Saeed Bin Suroor* 111+
4 b m Saint Ballado(CAN) —True Glory (IRE) (In The Wings)
1804[3]

Poseidon Adventure (IRE) *A P O'Brien* 105
3 b c Sadler's Wells(USA) —Fanny Cerrito (USA) (Gulch (USA))
1179a[9]

Poseidon's Bride (USA) *A Fabre* a85 90
3 ch f Seeking The Gold(USA) —Neptune's Bride (USA) (Bering)
5779a[10]

Poseidon's Secret (IRE) *Pat Eddery* a65 68
3 b c Night Shift(USA) —Chita Rivera (Chief Singer)
1088[8] 6578[3]

Possessed *T D McCarthy* a74 71
3 b f Desert Prince(IRE) —Obsessive (USA) (Seeking The Gold (USA))
188[8] 342[4]475[8] 855[8]1681[8] 2589[3] 3364[10] 3932[7] 4248[6]4700[6] 5210[2]

Postage (USA) *K A Morgan* a51
3 bb g Chester House(USA) —Nimble Mind (USA) (Lyphard (USA))
254[10] 710[6]1274[3] 1950[14] 2573[12]

Postage Stampe *D M Simcock* a90+ 74+
3 b f Singspiel(IRE) —Jaljuli (Jalmood (USA))
(2446) 3627[8] 6411[9] 6515[5]

Postgraduate (IRE) *W J Knight* a92 97+
4 b g Almutawakel—Institutrice (IRE) (College Chapel)
728[27] 1111[7] 2364[7]3223[B]

Postmaster *R Ingram* a56 61
4 b g Dansili—Post Modern (USA) (Nureyev (USA))
114[11] 218[5]379[9] 482[9]1204[16] 1725[5] 2135[14]2599[3] 3213[8] 3817[14] 3933[5] 4332[6]4667[11] 5035[4]

Postsprofit (IRE) *N A Callaghan* a65 65
2 b c Marju(IRE) —Housekeeper (IRE) (Common Grounds)
5914[6] 6066[7] 6324[6]

Potential (USA) *Laura Wohlers* a103 102
3 bb c General Royal(USA) —Crack Willow (USA) (Wolf Power (SAF))
5985a[5]

Potentiale (IRE) *J W Hills* a57 51
2 ch g Singspiel(IRE) —No Frills (IRE) (Darshaan)
5339[11] 5607[8] 6434[9]

Pothos Way (GR) *P R Chamings* a65 49
3 ch g Wadood(USA) —Evropi's Way (Sanglamore (USA))
3387[6] (4367) 4700[4]5129[7] 5992[7]

Pound Sign *M L W Bell* a81+ 78
3 ch g Singspiel(IRE) —Profit Alert (IRE) (Alzao (USA))
(668) 1108[7]

Pout (IRE) *John Joseph Murphy* a96 105
4 b m Namid—Symphony (IRE) (Cyrano De Bergerac)
753a[7] 1469a[7] (2041a)

Poutu (FR) *A Berry* 27
3 b f Acteur Francais(USA) —Sanctus Lady (IRE) (High Estate)
4651[9] 4943[15]

Power Alert *B R Millman* a45 39
2 b g Averti(IRE) —Crystal Power (USA) (Pleasant Colony (USA))
5348[6] 5891[12] 6669[9]6859[5] 6996[5]

Power And Demand *C W Thornton* a9
9 b g Formidable(USA) —Mazurkanova (Song)
3610[13]

Power Assisted *C F Wall* a72 72
3 ch f Observatory(USA) —Caribbean Star (Soviet Star (USA))
118[3] 269[9]475[9]

Power Ballad *W J Knight* 63
2 ch f Titus Livius(FR) —Sea Music (Inchinor)
3868[4]

Power Broker *P F I Cole* a39 74
3 b c Mark Of Esteem(IRE) —Galatrix (Be My Guest (USA))
720[9] 2069[6]

Power Elite (IRE) *Noel Meade* 105
6 b g Linamix(FR) —Hawas (Mujtahid (USA))
4639a[5]

Power Girl (GER) *P F I Cole* 102
4 b m Dashing Blade—Picara (GER) (Prince Ippi (GER))
(2706) 3739[6] 4079[6] 4741[5] 5502[10]

Power Glory *M J Gingell* a6 10
4 b g Namaqualand(USA) —Belamcanda (Belmez (USA))
243[4] 3900[13] 5925[14]

Power Of Future (GER) *H R A Cecil* a85 81
3 ch f Definite Article—Pik Konigin (GER) (Konigsstuhl (GER))
(1503) 2117[5] 3046[6] 4459[3] 5383[13] 6202[5](6415)

Power Politics (USA) *Saeed Bin Suroor* a31 93
3 b c Seeking The Gold(USA) —Stormy Pick (USA) (Storm Creek (USA))
5143[3] 5722[6] 6192[13]

Power Strike (USA) *Mrs L B Normile* a43 51
5 b g Coronado's Quest(USA) —Galega (Sure Blade (USA))
40[7] 1034[11]

Poyle Josh *H J Manners* a23 50
6 b g Danzig Connection(USA) —Poyle Jezebelle (Sharpo)
6492[8] 6606[12]

Poyle Kiera *M Blanshard* a48 51
2 b f Diktat—Poyle Amber (Sharrood (USA))
3435[5] 3838[5] 4394[6]4980[4] 6284[6]

Poyle Ruby *M Blanshard* a28
2 b f Josr Algarhoud(IRE) —Poyle Jezebelle (Sharpo)
6853[8]

Practicallyperfect (IRE) *H R A Cecil* 80
2 b f King Charlemagne(USA) —Morningsurprice (USA) (Future Storm (USA))
1442[10] (5287) 5828[3]

Pragmatica *R M H Cowell* a59 57
5 b m Inchinor—Isabella Gonzaga (Rock Hopper)
42[9] 3614[10] 4266[10]

Prairie Sun (GER) *Mrs A Duffield* a45 80
5 b m Law Society(USA) —Prairie Flame (IRE) (Marju (IRE))
976[12] 1184[8] (1562) (1660) 1758[4] 2501[2]

Pray For Sun (IRE) *F Rohaut* 83
3 b f Fantastic Light(USA) —Karakia (IRE) (Sadler's Wells (USA))
2537a[7] 6567a[8]

Preachinatthebar (USA) *B Baffert* a116 116
5 gr h Silver Charm(USA) —Holy Nola (USA) (Silver Deputy (CAN))
5826a[4]

Precautionary *Miss J Feilden* a57 47
3 b f Green Desert(USA) —Well Warned (Warning)
579[7] 630[11]722[5] 902[9]3869[8] 4305[4] 5055[9] 5273[7] 5969[10]

Precious Bunny (FR) *R Chotard* a78 85
3 ch c Peintre Celebre(USA) —Viking's Cove (USA) (Miswaki (USA))
392a[11]

Precious Dancer *W R Muir* a46 67
3 b c Sinndar(IRE) —Crodelle (IRE) (Formidable (USA))
963[7] (1314) 1740[4]

Precious Lucy (FR) *G F Bridgwater* 13
7 gr m Kadrou(FR) —Teardrops Fall (FR) (Law Society (USA))
2901[7]

Precious Mystery (IRE) *A King* a66 75
6 ch m Titus Livius(FR) —Ascoli (Skyliner)
(881) 966[4] 5952[8]

Precise Machine (JPN) *K Hagiwara* 118
7 b h Mayano Top Gun(JPN) —Be Silent (JPN) (Sunday Silence (USA))
6530a[6] 6850a[2]

Precocious Star (IRE) *K R Burke* 92
2 ch f Bold Fact(USA) —Flames (Blushing Flame (USA))
8925 (2890) (3216) 3874[2] 4371[4]

Premier Cru *Andrew Turnell* a55 31
3 b g King's Best(USA) —No Rehearsal (FR) (Baillamont (USA))
1567[10] 2535[14] 6371[8]6616[11]

Premier Dane (IRE) *N G Richards* 96
4 b g Indian Danehill(IRE) —Crystal Blue (IRE) (Bluebird (USA))
2657[6] 3501[4] 4359[7]

Premiere Note *A Fabre* 95
3 b f Alhaarth(IRE) —Good To Dance (IRE) (Groom Dancer (USA))
4979a[5] 6567a[0]

Premier Escalon *F Jordan*
2 ch g Alflora(IRE) —Premiere Foulee (FR) (Sillery (USA))
5379[11]

Premier Fantasy *T J Pitt* a84 75
4 b g Pivotal—Hemaca (Distinctly North (USA))
(2259) 2705[7] 6223[6] (6326) 6428[3]6527[2] 6583[3]
Premio Loco (USA) *C F Wall* a58
2 ch c Prized(USA) —Crazee Mental (Magic Ring (IRE))
6254[8]
Premium Tap (USA) *J Kimmel* a125
4 b h Pleasant Tap(USA) —Premium Red (USA) (Thirty Six Red (USA))
6345a[3]
Present *D Morris* 48
2 ch f Generous(IRE) —Miss Picol (Exit To Nowhere (USA))
2867[8] 4705[10] 5321 [7]
Presently Blessed (IRE) *K A Ryan* a17 53
3 ch f Inchinor—Present Imperfect (Cadeaux Genereux)
6954[12]
Preskani *Mrs N Macauley* a58 38
4 b g Sri Pekan(USA) —Lamarita (Emarati (USA))
8[6] 779[4]29[3] 492[11]612[2] 650[4]860[5] 950[7]1276[12] 1683[11] 1915[11]2137[3] 5926[5]6281[2] (6307) 6425[3] 6470[2]6642[8] 6819[9]
Presque Perdre *K G Reveley* 35
2 ch g Desert Prince(IRE) —Kindle (Selkirk (USA))
5615[12] 5959[9]
Press Express (IRE) *R A Fahey* 70
4 ch g Entrepreneur—Nawaji (USA) (Trempolino (USA))
1651[2] 2162[9] 3309[5] 3980[8] 4662[6]5236[7] 5599[9] 6301[12]
Pressing (IRE) *R Feligioni* 96
3 b c Soviet Star(USA) —Rafif (USA) (Riverman (USA))
758a[7] 1872a[9] 2671a[3]
Press The Button (GER) *J R Boyle* a82 91
3 b g Dansili—Play Around (IRE) (Niniski (USA))
1165[7] 1978[5] 2605[3]2932[12] 3644[4] 4029[2](4076) 4605[2] 5107[4]
Pressure Putt *W J Haggas* a78 89
3 ch g Tipsy Creek(USA) —Carnbrea Belle (IRE) (Kefaah (USA))
(1312) (2239)
Presto Shinko (IRE) *R Hannon* a108 117
5 b g Shinko Forest(IRE) —Swift Chorus (Music Boy)
830[2] 1069[10] 2303[2]2675[4] (3564a) 4191a[10] 5549[10] 5942[6] 6335[2]
Presumptive (IRE) *R Charlton* a92 92
6 b g Danehill(USA) —Demure (Machiavellian (USA))
828[2]
Pret A Porter (UAE) *P D Evans* a66 64
2 br f Jade Robbery(USA) —Velour (Mtoto)
3796[10] 4400[4] 4830[6] 5748[8] 6581[7](6768) 6933[4]
Prettilini *R Brotherton* a62 66
3 ch f Bertolini(USA) —Pretiosa (IRE) (Royal Abjar (USA))
68[8] (128) 248[3](439) (488) 550[6]1004[10] 3598[8]3897[7] 4265[4] 5036[10]5350[13] 6323[6] 6465[4]6608[11] 6756[2]6964[9]
Pretty Game *K A Ryan* 39
2 b g Mind Games—Catwalk Girl (Skyliner)
4066[7] 4566[7]
Pretty In Pink (IRE) *Anthony Moloney* 45
7 b m Teamster—Jewell For A King (IRE) (King's Ride)
4121a[8]
Pretty Majestic (IRE) *M R Channon* 91
2 b f Invincible Spirit(IRE) —Cheeky Weeky (Cadeaux Genereux)
1514[2] 2106[4] (2500) 4146[3] (4762) 5503[10]
Pretty Miss *H Candy* 74
2 b f Averti(IRE) —Pretty Poppy (Song)
3588[9] 4283[2] 4510[2] 5234[8]
Pretty Posh (IRE) *Timothy Doyle* 61
5 b m Desert Style(IRE) —Petticoat Rose (IRE) (Salt Dome (USA))
4186a[10]
Pretty Selma *R M H Cowell* a35
2 b f Diktat—Brave Vanessa (USA) (Private Account (USA))
6222[6] 6463[5]6749[7]
Pretty Sister *W J Haggas* a63
3 ch f Groom Dancer(USA) —Remarkable (Wolfhound (USA))
70[3] 365[10]445[6]
Pretty Star (GER) *A King* 98
6 b g Lando(GER) —Pretty Ballerina (Sadler's Wells (USA))
1511[4] 1931[7] 2817[4]
Prianca (GER) *Mario Hofer* 48
2 br f Diktat—Palanca (Inchinor)
5880a[8]
Priceless Melody (USA) *Mrs A J Perrett* a42 39
2 bb c Orientate(USA) —Regatta Queen (USA) (Danzig Connection (USA))
4292[7] 4526[11] 4774[13] 6487[5]6653[11]
Priceoflove (IRE) *P J Makin* a53 65
3 ch f Inchinor—Piaf (Pursuit Of Love)
6771[4]
Price Tag *R J Frankel* 116
3 b f Dansili—Tarocchi (USA) (Affirmed (USA))
1177a[3] 1719a[3] 2802[8] 3991a[5] (5146a) 5701a[12](6614a)
Pride (FR) *A De Royer-Dupre* a67 126
6 b m Peintre Celebre(USA) —Specificity (USA) (Alleged (USA))
1331a[4] (2092a) (2914a) 5219a[3] 5716a[2] (5964) (6785a)
Pride Of Joy *D K Ivory* a70 33
3 ch f Pursuit Of Love—Ivory's Joy (Tina's Pet)
901[3] 1110[4]1378[7] 2340[3] 2939[5]3199[7]
Pride Of Kinloch *N Wilson* a43 58
6 ch m Dr Devious(IRE) —Stormswept (USA) (Storm Bird (CAN))
1465[7] 1947[5] 2811[3]3330[5] 3786[10] 4233[5] 4548[9]
Pride Of Nation (IRE) *L M Cumani* 108+
4 b h Danehill Dancer(IRE) —Anita Via (IRE) (Anita's Prince)
(1207) (1985) 2742[13] 4739[3]
Pride Of Westbury (AUS) *Danny O'Brien* 84
3 b c Octagonal(NZ) —Taittinger (NZ) (Al Akbar (AUS))
6391a[15]
Priere *N Clement* 107
4 b m Machiavellian(USA) —Play Around (IRE) (Niniski (USA))
2799a[6] 4649a[2] 5710a[4] 6547a[9]
Prima Luna *K R Burke* a48 36
2 b f Primo Valentino(IRE) —Ash Moon (IRE) (General Monash (USA))
4327[7] 5387[6]5876[10] 5948[10]
Prima Markova *J Jay* a37 46
3 b f Mark Of Esteem(IRE) —Ball Gown (Jalmood (USA))
1417[12] 3073[9] 3742[12]4489[7] 4973[11] 5435[8]6144[8] 6794[13]
Prima Patrona *Mrs H Sweeting* 66d
6 b m Hector Protector(USA) —Ballet Rambert (Rambo Dancer (CAN))
363[11]
Primarily *Peter Grayson* a55 71
4 b g Mind Games—Prim N Proper (Tragic Role (USA))
1127[3] 1504[3] 1816[5] 2875[3] 3003[9]4133[3] 4456[10] 5023[3] 5243[15] 5368[6]5865[20] 6649[3] 6704[3]6806[5]
Primary (USA) *W J Haggas* 116
3 b c Giant's Causeway(USA) —Prospective (USA) (Mr Prospector (USA))
(1300) 1603[5] (2671a) 4387a[3] 5204[4]
Prime Contender *G L Moore* a81 76
4 b g Efisio—Gecko Rouge (Rousillon (USA))
834[3] 1132[13] 1478[4]2035[6] 2519[2] 3214[3] 5935[7] (6566) (6673)
Prime Defender *B W Hills* a105+ 105
2 ch c Bertolini(USA) —Arian Da (Superlative)
3222[2] (3872) 4736[3] 5965[11] (6402)
Primed Up (IRE) *R M Beckett* a34 73
4 b g Rainbow Quest(USA) —Cape Mist (USA) (Lure (USA))
82[11] (2131) 2455[11] 2725[8]4139[10] 4755[5] 5127[9]
Prime Number (IRE) *G A Butler* 97+
4 gr g King's Best(USA) —Majinskaya (FR) (Marignan (USA))
1129[18] 1484[6] 4112[6]
Prime Powered (IRE) *R M Beckett* a82 80
5 b g Barathea(IRE) —Caribbean Quest (Rainbow Quest (USA))
37[10] 1478[5] (1821) (1995) (2982) 4244[11]
Prime Recreation *P S Felgate* a53 43
9 b g Primo Dominie—Night Transaction (Tina's Pet)
633[5] 789[2](886) 1195[12]1396[8] 1618[11] 6539[6]6615[6] 6723[12]6851[5]
Primeshade Promise *J M Bradley* a60 63
5 ch m Opening Verse(USA) —Bonnie Lassie (Efisio)
697[11] 1204[13] 1276[2]1882[7] 2098[4] 2414[7]3159[4] 3197[6] 4845[10](4983) 5302[9] 5450[11] 6054[14] 6436[10]
Primitive Academy *H R A Cecil* a67 64
4 b h Primitive Rising(USA) —Royal Fontaine (IRE) (Royal Academy (USA))
2901[3] 3376[6] 5426[5]5651[4] 5952[7] 6633[6]6684[10]
Primo Gold *W R Swinburn* a69+ 55
3 b g Primo Valentino(IRE) —Bullion (Sabrehill (USA))
3642[3] 4405[4] (5210) 5974[2]
Primondo (IRE) *A W Carroll* a68 68
4 b g Montjeu(IRE) —Tagiki (IRE) (Doyoun)
1415[13] 2408[2] 3935[3]4423[3] (4898) 5587[4] 6630[9]
Primo Way *I Semple* a79 87d
5 b g Primo Dominie—Waypoint (Cadeaux Genereux)
1143[12] 2017[4] 2454[9] (3331) 3812[8] 4989[3]5337[8] 5512[8] 6273[7] 6418[9]6643[8] 6752[6]6862[3] 6938[2]
Primrose Queen *D R C Elsworth* 43
3 b f Lear Fan(USA) —Primrose Place (USA) (Dayjur (USA))
2673[11]
Primus Inter Pares (IRE) *D Nicholls* a63 96
5 b g Sadler's Wells(USA) —Life At The Top (Habitat)
728[24] 8651[0]
Princeable Lady (IRE) *J A Pickering* a42 40
4 b m Desert Prince(IRE) —Saucy Maid (IRE) (Sure Blade (USA))
363[8] 469[8]
Prince Ary *B W Hills* a67 87
3 b g Desert Prince(IRE) —Aryaf (CAN) (Vice Regent (CAN))
802[3] (4210) 4599[2] 5504[3]5869[4] 6017[3]
Prince Charlemagne (IRE) *N P Littmoden* a81 87
3 br g King Charlemagne(USA) —Ciubanga (IRE) (Arazi (USA))
30[3] (142) (188) (422) (483) 1205[4]1841[9] (2081) 2805[10] 6992[6]
Prince Charming *R Bouresly* a58 104
4 b h Royal Applause—Miss Primula (Dominion)
201a[11] 352a[8] 366a[8] 433a[11]
Prince Cyrano *W J Musson* a81+ 79
7 b g Cyrano De Bergerac—Odilese (Mummy's Pet)
949[14] 1545[8] (2417) 2864[5] 3904[7] 4101[18]4771[5] 5246[10] 5391[6]5765[13] 6437[9]
Prince Darius *P W Chapple-Hyam* a50
3 br g Efisio—Celt Song (IRE) (Unfuwain (USA))
2175 3371[0]
Prince Dayjur (USA) *J Pearce* a81 83
7 bb g Dayjur(USA) —Distinct Beauty (USA) (Phone Trick (USA))
1550[6] 5031[8]5688[2] (5907) (6239) 6770[2]6932[4]
Prince De Conde (USA) *Robert Collet* 92
2 b c Sadler's Wells(USA) —Reach For The Moon (USA) (Pulpit (USA))
5399a[4]
Prince Duval (IRE) *D Carroll* a49 55
3 b g Desert Prince(IRE) —Ladylishandra (IRE) (Mujadil (USA))
2198[6] 2525[7] 3329[6] 4050[6] 5241[4]
Prince Egor (IRE) *M Dods* 74
3 b g Imperial Ballet(IRE) —Harifana (FR) (Kahyasi)
1101[5] 1530[2] 1759[5] 2441[9]
Prince Evelith (GER) *G A Swinbank* 87+
3 b g Dashing Blade—Peace Time (GER) (Surumu (GER))
2243[7] (2616) (3082) 3298[3] (5446)
Prince Flori (GER) *S Smrczek* 119
3 br c Lando(GER) —Princess Liberte (GER) (Nebos (GER))
(1526a) 2738a[4] 3776a[9] (5051a)
Prince Forever (IRE) *M A Jarvis* 88
2 b c Giant's Causeway(USA) —Routilante (IRE) (Rousillon (USA))
(4592) 5183[8]
Prince Golan (IRE) *K A Ryan* 94
2 b c Golan(IRE) —Mohican Princess (Shirley Heights)
1595[4] (1863) 2719[9] 4809[8] 6104[14]
Princekris *M Ciciarelli*
2 ch c Desert Prince(IRE) —Tipsy (Kris)
5771a[9]
Princely Royal *J J Bridger* a28 58d
2 b g Prince Sabo—Premium Princess (Distant Relative)
968[4] 1189[8] 1535[8]1977[4] 2094[6] 3641[11]3727[5] 5829[12]
Princely Ted (IRE) *E J Creighton* a51 50
5 b g Princely Heir(IRE) —Just Out (IRE) (Bluebird (USA))
5572[8] 5972[10] 6067[5]6405[8] 6628[9]
Princely Vale (IRE) *W G M Turner* a45 57
4 b g Princely Heir(IRE) —Lomalou (IRE) (Lightning Dealer)
2390[8] 2536[9] 2955[7] 3306[5] 3867[2]4389[3] 5569[11]
Princely Venture (IRE) *R Bouresly* a31 116
7 ch h Entrepreneur—Sun Princess (English Prince)
560a[13]
Prince Marju (IRE) *P A Blockley* a30 29
3 b g Marju(IRE) —Playwaki (USA) (Miswaki (USA))
630[12] 735[8]1049[13] 2746[13] 3111[5]
Prince Namid *Mrs A Duffield* a80 100
4 b g Namid—Fen Princess (IRE) (Trojan Fen)
1125[14] (1662) 1856[5] (2021) 2230[2] 2683[3] 4832[9]5358[19] 5807[6] 5957[5] 6292[10]
Prince Noel *N Wilson* 60
2 b g Dr Fong(USA) —Baileys On Line (Shareef Dancer (USA))
4260[9] 4731[4] 5614[14] 5958[10]
Prince Of Blues (IRE) *M Mullineaux* a29 66
8 b g Prince Of Birds(USA) —Reshift (Night Shift (USA))
3069[10]
Prince Of Charm (USA) *P Mitchell* a67+ 58
2 ch c Mizzen Mast(USA) —Pretty Clear (USA) (Mr Prospector (USA))
3408[6] 3851[9] 4397[3]4813[9] 5208[8] 5585[5]6106[11] 6394[4] 6576[2](6653)
Prince Of Delphi *H Candy* 67
3 b c Royal Applause—Princess Athena (Ahonoora)
2235[2] 2458[4]
Prince Of Elegance *Mrs A J Perrett* a76 90
2 b c Cape Cross(IRE) —Elegant Lady (Selkirk (USA))
1959[5] (2402) 2960[3] 3924[6]
Prince Of Gold *R Hollinshead* a54 48
6 b g Polar Prince(IRE) —Gold Belt (IRE) (Bellypha)
134[4] 240[2]285[10] 350[3]400[6] 612[7]681[3] 784[6]889[6] 1353[9] 4467[11]6493[3] 6554[2]6638[3] 6763[6]6961[9]
Prince Of Light (IRE) *M Johnston* 111
3 ch c Fantastic Light(USA) —Miss Queen (USA) (Miswaki (USA))
3091[2] (3518) 4025[9] (4126) 4529[9] 5341[6] 5682[8]
Prince Of Love (IRE) *Jedd O'Keeffe* a72 64
3 b c Fruits Of Love(USA) —Teodora (IRE) (Fairy King (USA))
5685[16] 5889[12] 6206[10] 6474[2]6716[4] 6816[2]
Prince Of Medina *J R Best* a63 62
3 ch g Fraam—Medina De Rioseco (Puissance)
4483[8] 4929[2] 5235[3]5910[9]
Prince Of Thebes (IRE) *J Akehurst* a71 105
5 b g Desert Prince(IRE) —Persian Walk (FR) (Persian Bold)
828[11] 1086[2] 2012[3]2742[22] 3493[14] 4098[3] (4348) 5175[3] 5523[15]6093a[8]
Prince Of The May *H Morrison* a28 59
4 ch g Bluegrass Prince(IRE) —Maytime (Pivotal)
1353[4] 1850[10] 2482[6] 3948[4] 4497[4]
Prince Picasso *Sir Mark Prescott* 88
3 b g Lomitas—Auspicious (Shirley Heights)
(1616) 1736[5] (3338) (3695) 3871[3] 5115[8]
Prince Richard *B Smart* 45
3 b g Diktat—Princess Latifa (Wolfhound (USA))
1736[17] 3357[12] 4016[11]
Prince Rossi (IRE) *J D Bethell* 78
2 b c Royal Applause—Miss Rossi (Artaius (USA))
1863[2] (2361) 2960[8] 4681[13] 5172[6] 5366[10]
Prince Sabaah (IRE) *R Hannon* 78
2 b c Spectrum(IRE) —Princess Sabaah (IRE) (Desert King (IRE))
5126[3] 5475[3] 5720[2]
Prince Sakhee *E Borromeo*
2 b c Sakhee(USA) —Princess Manila (CAN) (Manila (USA))
6407a[8]
Prince Samos (IRE) *R Hannon* a86 94
4 b h Mujadil(USA) —Sabaniya (FR) (Lashkari)
670[7] 946[5] (1133) 1281[2]1678[16] 2169[5]
Princess Arwen *Mrs Barbara Waring* a35 40
4 b m Magic Ring(IRE) —Absolutelystunning (Aragon)
95[11] 1819[7]66[8] 876[7]1391[6] 1727[13]6131[7] 6550[9]6728[8]
Princess Cleo *T D Easterby* a73 78
3 ch f Mark Of Esteem(IRE) —Classy Cleo (IRE) (Mujadil (USA))
1292[7] 1865[4] 3087[9] 4507[5] 5081[4]5493[9]
Princess Cocoa (IRE) *R A Fahey* 80
3 b f Desert Sun—Daily Double (FR) (Unfuwain (USA))
1230[6] 1599[4] 2124[3] (2518) 2781[2] 3359[2](3790) 4040[2]
Princess Danah (IRE) *W R Swinburn* a68 64
3 b f Danehill(USA) —Thaidah (CAN) (Vice Regent (CAN))
1901[6] 2406[11] 3266[6] 3650[11]4289[2] 5166[9] (5690) 5992[6]
Princesse Dansante (IRE) *F Doumen* 107
3 b f King's Best(USA) —Vallee Dansante (USA) (Lyphard (USA))
(5472a) 5702a[4]
Princess Ellis *E J Alston* 60
2 ch f Compton Place—Star Cast (IRE) (In The Wings)
3982[9] 4196[2] 4510[U] 4693[4] 4986[4]5528[3] 5956[5]
Princess Galadriel *J M P Eustace* a60 67
5 b m Magic Ring(IRE) —Prim Lass (Reprimand)
1761[12] 2184[13] 2317[16]
Princess Georgina *S C Williams* 82
2 b f Royal Applause—Degree (Warning)
2610[3] 3084[9] 3745[3] (3822) 5122a[7]
Princess Ileana (IRE) *K R Burke* a68 78d
2 b f Danetime(IRE) —Uhud (IRE) (Mujtahid (USA))
1542[2] 2791[3] 3120[2]3693[2] 4913[3] 5528[8]
Princess Iris (IRE) *E J O'Neill* 104
2 ch f Desert Prince(IRE) —Athlumney Lady (Lycius (USA))
(2355) 2743[13] 4840[6] (5356)
Princess Jones *J-L Guillochon* 98
6 b m Emperor Jones(USA) —Nationalvelvetgirl (Alhijaz)
6171a[7] 6454a[9]
Princess Kai (IRE) *R Ingram* a53 58
5 b m Cayman Kai(IRE) —City Princess (Rock City)
886[11] 1397[9]1752[5] 2571[2] 2955[6] 3664[10] 4670[13]6723[10] 6984[6]
Princess Lavinia *G Wragg* a54 75
3 ch f Fraam—Affaire De Coeur (Imperial Fling (USA))
1085[7] 1630[3] 3224[8] 5320[8] 5953[5]6652[9]
Princess Nada *L M Cumani* 105
3 b f Barathea(IRE) —Zomaradah (Deploy)
(1418) (2582) 3293[3] 4482[2] 5917[6] 6333[6]
Princess Nala (IRE) *M Halford* 100
4 b m In The Wings—Adjisa (IRE) (Doyoun)
3128a[7]
Princess Of Aeneas (IRE) *I Semple* a48 60
3 b f Beckett(IRE) —Romangoddess (IRE) (Rhoman Rule (USA))
2448[5] 3167[6] 4060[7] 4651[3] 5247[7]5553[7] (5837)
Princess Palatine (IRE) *K R Burke* 71
2 b f Iron Mask(USA) —Kitty Kildare (USA) (Seattle Dancer (USA))
2106[3] 2807[4] 5536[4] 5959[2]
Princess Rioja *J M Bradley*
6 b m Man Among Men(IRE) —Miss Gruntled (Arctic Lord)
184[13] 1305[10]
Princess Society (IRE) *E A L Dunlop* a64 64
3 b f Desert Prince(IRE) —Ballet Society (FR) (Sadler's Wells (USA))
293[2] 406[3]548[11] 979[7]
Princess Taise (USA) *M Johnston* 99
2 gr f Cozzene(USA) —Cumulate (USA) (Gone West (USA))
(3707) 4371[2] 4840[10] 5714a[13]
Princess Taylor *M Botti* a76 72+
2 ch f Singspiel(IRE) —Tapas En Bal (FR) (Mille Balles (FR))
4148[6] 4994[3] 5424[4]6558[4]
Princess Toto *P C Haslam* a26 55
3 b f Mtoto—Flower Princess (Slip Anchor)
1598[7] 3717[3] 5683[9] 6971[9]
Princess Valerina *B W Hills* 89+
2 ch f Beat Hollow—Heart So Blue (Dilum (USA))
5871[2] (6199)
Princess Woodman (BRZ) *C Morgado* a72
4 ch m Roi Normand(USA) —Shoo Bee Doo (USA) (Woodman (USA))
202a[10] 436a[9]623a[5]
Princess Zada *B R Millman* 58
2 ch f Best Of The Bests(IRE) —Barnacla (IRE) (Bluebird (USA))
2456[10] 4000[10] 4221[6] 4895[7] 5764[3]
Prince Tamino *H Morrison* a88 113
3 b g Mozart(IRE) —Premiere Dance (IRE) (Loup Solitaire (USA))
1020[2] 2168[4] (2509) (2658) 3414[3]5642[2]
Princeton (IRE) *M R Channon* a76 84
2 ch c Maria's Mon(USA) —Enrich (USA) (Dynaformer (USA))
3025[4] (3455) 3735[4] 4178[4] 4474[2] 4963[2]5359[2] 5633[5]
Prince Tum Tum (USA) *D Shaw* a92+ 83
6 b g Capote(USA) —La Grande Epoque (USA) (Lyphard (USA))
54[4] 220[10]1143[13] 1456[4] 1597[2] 1939[8]2017[9] 2323[7] 2681[10] 3567[7] 4202[8]5246[7] 5391[3]5842[8] 6223[7](6417) (6489) 6583[2]6915[6]
Prince Valentine *G L Moore* a47 62+
5 b g My Best Valentine—Affaire De Coeur (Imperial Fling (USA))
259[8] 395[6]1537[4] 1723[6]2131[2] 2392[2] 2568[2] (2728) 3614[2] (4446) 5450[8]5937[12]
Prince Vector *A King* a93 89
4 b g Vettori(IRE) —The In-Laws (IRE) (Be My Guest (USA))
1206[2] 1927[3] 3028[6]4560[7]
Prince Vettori *D J Coakley* a67 51
4 b g Vettori(IRE) —Bombalarina (IRE) (Barathea (IRE))
6606[4] 6814[5]6982[2]
Prince Zafonic *M W Easterby* 68
3 ch c Zafonic(USA) —Kite Mark (Mark Of Esteem (IRE))
1065[10] 1680[8] 2620[7] 6321[10]
Principal Witness (IRE) *Evan Williams* a74 79
5 b g Definite Article—Double Eight (IRE) (Common Grounds)
(37) 186[2] 264[11]1548[2] 1745[7]

Principle Secret (USA) *C S Paasch* a112
2 b c Sea Of Secrets(USA) —Beright (USA) (Gray Slewpy (USA))
6339a[14]

Prinquet (USA) *C E Brittain* 46
3 ch f Marquetry(USA) —Princess Kris (Kris)
4495[6] 4959[7]

Prins Willem (IRE) *J R Fanshawe* a96 97
7 b g Alzao(USA) —American Gardens (USA) (Alleged (USA))
(420) 2723[18] (3203) 3533[5]

Prinsycios (FR) *J Fonzo* 84
11 br g Sicyos(USA) —Princesse Gege (FR) (Dom Racine (FR))
3692a[3]

Printsmith (IRE) *J R Norton* a39 39
9 br m Petardia—Black And Blaze (Taufan (USA))
304[13] 1395[9]

Priorina (IRE) *D Haydn Jones* a54 56
4 b m Priolo(USA) —Strina (IRE) (Indian Ridge)
290[8] (330) 648[6]708[6] 889[10]1574[4] 2141[6]2245[6]
3194[7] 3541[2]3817[12] 5054[5] 5924[2]

Priors Dale *Miss E C Lavelle* a70 73
6 br g Lahib(USA) —Mathaayl (USA) (Shadeed (USA))
5213[11]

Priors Hill (IRE) *Saeed Bin Suroor* 103+
3 b c Danehill(USA) —Lailati (USA) (Mr Prospector (USA))
5660[2] 5787[6] 6319[9]

Prior Warning *D Smaga* 88
2 ch c Barathea(IRE) —Well Warned (Warning)
6453a[3]

Priory Bay (USA) *E A L Dunlop* a72 72
2 b c Lear Fan(USA) —Isla Del Rey (USA) (Nureyev (USA))
3417[6] 3726[6] 5780[2]6049[8]

Private Benjamin *M R Hoad* a64 58
6 gr g Ridgewood Ben—Jilly Woo (Environment Friend)
186[15]

Private Business (USA) *B W Hills* 105
3 rg c Cozzene(USA) —Privity (USA) (Private Account (USA))
1300[4] 2804[7] 3441[4] 4791[8] 5945[3]

Private Dancer (FR) *Y De Nicolay* 94
3 gr f Green Tune(USA) —Ideale Dancing (FR) (Shining Steel)
2374a[5] 3133a[6]

Private Peachey (IRE) *B R Millman* 50
2 b g Shinko Forest(IRE) —Adamas (IRE) (Fairy King (USA))
961[10] 1372[4] 3843[13]4480[8]

Private Reason (USA) *R Hannon* 71
2 b c Red Ransom(USA) —Sultry Lass (USA) (Private Account (USA))
4592[9] 5293[4] 6023[5]

Private Vow (USA) *S Asmussen* a115
3 bb c Broken Vow(USA) —Smooth As Silk (USA) (Deputy Minister (CAN))
1498a[15]

Privy Seal (IRE) *R Dutrow Jr* 112
5 b g Cape Cross(IRE) —Lady Joshua (IRE) (Royal Academy (USA))
6006a[4]

Prix Masque (IRE) *B Smart* 57
2 b c Iron Mask(USA) —Prima Marta (Primo Dominie)
2409[7] 2745[4]

Proclamation (IRE) *Saeed Bin Suroor* 131
4 gr h King's Best(USA) —Shamarra (FR) (Zayyani)
2722[3] 5524[5]

Procrastinate (IRE) *R F Fisher* a35 35
4 ch g Rossini(USA) —May Hinton (Main Reef)
4723[10] 5837[9]

Professor Twinkle *W J Knight* 61
2 ch c Dr Fong(USA) —Shining High (Shirley Heights)
4781[8] 5293[8] 5730[5]

Profitable *B W Hills* a79 71
3 b f Daylami(IRE) —Manuetti (IRE) (Sadler's Wells (USA))
1081[5] 4959[2] (5426) 5644[9] 6075[11]

Profit's Reality (IRE) *P A Blockley* a90 105
4 br g Key Of Luck(USA) —Teacher Preacher (IRE) (Taufan (USA))
1017[8] (1098) 1239[4] 1815[3]2010[3] 2201[10] 5360[3]
5547[5] 5657[12]

Project Sunshine (GER) *J A Osborne* a59+ 58
3 b g Xaar—Prada (GER) (Lagunas)
1192[10] 1691[6] 1940[8]4044[11]

Pro Ken (FR) *Rod Collet* a94 103
6 gr g Kendor(FR) —Premier Amour (IRE) (Salmon Leap (USA))
393a[8] 523a[6]

Prokopios (GER) *H Blume* a99 65
4 b g Kallisto(GER) —Princess Taufan (Taufan (USA))
6574a[8]

Pronto Vende (IRE) *G A Butler* a45
3 b g Fasliyev(USA) —Hilbys Brite Flite (USA) (Cormorant (USA))
2343[14] 3050[8]3384[7]

Proper (IRE) *M R Channon* 73
2 b g Rossini(USA) —Pardoned (IRE) (Mujadil (USA))
1838[10] 2178[3] (2432) 2630[4] 3734[16] 4170[6]

Proper Article (IRE) *Miss J E Foster* a52 85
4 b g Definite Article—Feather 'n Lace (IRE) (Green Desert (USA))
4166a[15] 6873[7]

Prophet Preacher (IRE) *M Wellings* a47 50
3 b f Imperial Ballet(IRE) —Teacher Preacher (IRE) (Taufan (USA))
1101[7] 1417[11] 1598[9] 2246[P]2379[9] 3261[6]
3456[3]3791[10] 6759[8]

Propinquity *W R Swinburn* 101
4 b g Primo Dominie—Lydia Maria (Dancing Brave (USA))
2358[7]

Proponent (IRE) *R Charlton* 93+
2 b c Peintre Celebre(USA) —Pont Audemer (USA) (Chief's Crown (USA))
(5340) (5941)

Proposal *C E Brittain* a51 57
2 b f Tobougg(IRE) —Patiala (IRE) (Nashwan (USA))
4994[7] 5287[5] 5595[10]

Proprioception (IRE) *W K Goldsworthy* a34 59
4 ch m Danehill Dancer(IRE) —Pepper And Salt (IRE) (Double Schwartz)
2918[4] 3467[7] 6626[5]6685[6]

Prorunner (USA) *Molly Pearson* a101
4 ch g Tejano Run(USA) —Perfect Wings (USA) (Quest For Fame (USA))
3134a[8]

Prospect Court *A C Whillans* a52 75
4 ch g Pivotal—Scierpan (USA) (Sharpen Up)
2376[13] 2811[10] 3137[3] 3330[2] (3617) 3811[5]4352[7]
4729[7] (5062)

Prospect Place *M Dods* 84
2 b c Compton Place—Encore My Love (Royal Applause)
(1074) 2127[8] 3026[5] 4681[7] (5133)

Protective *J G Given* 92
5 ch g Hector Protector(USA) —You Make Me Real (USA) (Give Me Strength (USA))
1033[10] 1502[9]

Protector (SAF) *Diego Lowther* a85 95
5 b g Kilconnel(USA) —Mufski (SAF) (Al Mufti (USA))
367a[3] 431a[4] 563a[13](3692a) 4860a[8] 5222a[9]

Pro Tempore *David Pinder* a38 52d
4 b m Fraam—Record Time (Clantime)
903[10] 954[7]1414[14] 1689[8] 1913[12]2494[4] 2637[5]
3348[6] 3438[5] 3899[8]4226[7] 4675[9] 4984[8] 6282[9]

Protettore (GER) *Frau D Breuer* 81
3 ch c Zinaad—Party Bloom (FR) (Baillamont (USA))
1526a[6]

Protocol (IRE) *Mrs S Lamyman* a41 33
12 b g Taufan(USA) —Ukraine's Affair (USA) (The Minstrel (CAN))
2395[4] 4506[5]

Prototype *P Bary* 90
2 b f Beat Hollow—Tuning (Rainbow Quest (USA))
6000a[6]

Proud *M L W Bell* 69
2 b f Kyllachy—Precious (Danehill (USA))
2354[7] 3537[3] 3942[3] 4321[5] 4603[8]

Proudance (GER) *R Suerland* 107
4 b h Tannenkonig(IRE) —Proudeyes (GER) (Dashing Blade)
369a[5] 511a[2] 625a[2] 2217a[7] 3563a[10]

Proudinsky (GER) *R J Frankel* 103
3 b c Silvano(GER) —Proudeyes (GER) (Dashing Blade)
4387a[4]

Proud Killer *J R Jenkins* a19 78
3 b g Killer Instinct—Thewaari (USA) (Eskimo (USA))
776[3] (1565) 2739[11] 3644[14]

Proud Ruler (IRE) *Niall Moran* a49 45
6 b h Spectrum(IRE) —La Pellegrina (IRE) (Be My Guest (USA))
6724[5]

Proud Scholar (USA) *R A Kvisla* a59+ 78
4 br m Royal Academy(USA) —Proud Fact (USA) (Known Fact (USA))
3440[8] 4005[13] 6775[6]6812[7]

Proud Tower Too (USA) *S Gonzalez* a116
4 b h Proud Irish(USA) —Dora's Tower (USA) (Irish Tower (USA))
(740a)

Proud Western (USA) *B Ellison* a36 52
8 bb g Gone West(USA) —Proud Lou (USA) (Proud Clarion)
1459[5] 1914[4] 2240[4]2544[4] 2780[6] 2926[9]

Providence Farm *M W Easterby* 44
2 b c Best Of The Bests(IRE) —Aneen Alkamanja (Last Tycoon)
2073[7] 2321[9] 2626[4] 3174[3] 3619[6]3831[4] 4115[8]
4520[3] (Dead)

Provost *M Johnston* 65
2 b c Danehill Dancer(IRE) —Dixielake (IRE) (Lake Coniston (IRE))
5616[5]

Prowess (IRE) *R Gibson* 95
3 ch f Peintre Celebre(USA) —Yawl (Rainbow Quest (USA))
1583[3] 2203[9] (2682) 3292[2] 4039[14] 4179[11]6384a[0]

Pseudonym (IRE) *M F Harris* a65 68
4 ch g Daylami(IRE) —Stage Struck (IRE) (Sadler's Wells (USA))
2879[DSQ]

Psychiatrist *Miss J R Tooth* a99 95
5 ch g Dr Devious(IRE) —Zahwa (Cadeaux Genereux)
57[3] 6600[7]6915[7] 6997[9]

Psychic Star *W R Swinburn* a72 88
3 b f Diktat—Southern Psychic (USA) (Alwasmi (USA))
2744[8] 3119[5] 4555[4] 4997[9]5346[9] 5732[6]

Psycho Cat *P A Blockley* a64 71
3 b g Hunting Lion(IRE) —Canadian Capers (Ballacashtal (CAN))
347[3] 488[3]651[2] 893[2] 969[8]3839[6]

Ptarmigan Ridge *Miss L A Perratt* 84
10 b h Sea Raven(IRE) —Panayr (Faraway Times (USA))
1438[5] 1856[8] 2237[3] 2449[4] 2852[2]3281[10] 3585[11]
4725[3] 4952[3] 5309[12](5333) 5532[2] 6212[13] 6320[5]

Publication (USA) *V Cerin* a119
7 br g Petionville(USA) —Cat News (USA) (Storm Cat (USA))
3134a[4]

Public Forum *Sir Michael Stoute* 101
4 b h Rainbow Quest(USA) —Valentine Girl (Alzao (USA))
(1301) 2803[12] 3552[20] 4713[14] 6107[5]

Puerto Rico (IRE) *A P O'Brien* 111+
3 b c Sadler's Wells(USA) —Commanche Belle (Shirley Heights)
(2055a) 3127a[10] 3517a[9] 4678[3]

Puggy (IRE) *R A Kvisla* 99
2 b f Mark Of Esteem(IRE) —Jakarta (IRE) (Machiavellian (USA))
(4964) 5672[2] 5966[3]

Pugilist *B J Meehan* a81 89
4 b g Fraam—Travel Mystery (Godswalk (USA))
5787[14] 6418[7]

Puissant Princess (IRE) *E J O'Neill* 53
2 bb f Rock Of Gibraltar(IRE) —Toroca (USA) (Nureyev (USA))
5595[7]

Pukka Tique *R Hollinshead* a63 70
3 b g Groom Dancer(USA) —Surf Bird (Shareef Dancer (USA))
1182[5] 1286[4] 2209[6]5618[13] 5815[12] 6037[15]

Punch Punch (BRZ) *C Morgado* 109
5 b h Aksar(USA) —By The Law (BRZ) (Minstrel Glory (USA))
205a[12] (437a) (624a) 741a[10]

Punisher (FR) *S Loeuillet* 90
2 ch c Until Sundown(USA) —Fitness Queen (USA) (Gilded Time (USA))
6546a[8]

Punjabi *Mrs G S Rees* a86+ 80
3 b g Komaite(USA) —Competa (Hernando (FR))
1141[13] (1593) (2171) 2344[4] (2809) 3301[6]5446[11]
5689[7] 5908[3]

Punta Galera (IRE) *R Hannon* a91 91
3 br g Zafonic(USA) —Kobalt Sea (FR) (Akarad (FR))
1951[6] 2224[13] 3401[3]4763[4] 4997[8] (5266)
5530[7]6107[12] 6337[10] 6515[3]6600[6]

Purde (NZ) *P Gatt* 109
3 br f Bahhare(USA) —Dupre (NZ) (Masterclass (USA))
6347a[12] 7000a[6]

Pure As Gold (USA) *J Carava* a112 112
4 ch g Stolen Gold(USA) —Pure Wool (USA) (Relaunch (USA))
5827a[4]

Pure Fiction *R Hannon* a56 73
3 b f Zilzal(USA) —Once Upon A Time (Teenoso (USA))
1349[5] 1963[9]

Pure Illusion (IRE) *Saeed Bin Suroor* a90 86
3 b f Danehill(USA) —Saintly Speech (USA) (Southern Halo (USA))
(5888) 6190[6]

Pure Imagination (IRE) *J M Bradley* a77 79
5 ch g Royal Academy(USA) —Ivory Bride (Domynsky)
970[11] 1285[6] 1532[6] 1820[13] 2454[5]2603[4] 3101[5]
3470 [3]3705[8] 3937[3] 4961[5] 5042[6] 5212[7]5688[5]
5937[8] (6054) 6240[6]6301[11]

Pure Velvet (IRE) *S Kirk* 39+
2 b f Mull Of Kintyre(USA) —Velvet Slipper (Muhtafal (USA))
5091[11]

Purity (GER) *Werner Glanz* 83
3 ch f Peintre Celebre(USA) —Pariana (USA) (Bering)
2279a[13]

Purple Dancer (FR) *J P L Ewart* 61
4 b g Daylami(IRE) —Stage Manner (In The Wings)
1425[7] 2242[6] 2612[9] 5314[11]

Purple Moon (IRE) *Sir Michael Stoute* 103
3 ch g Galileo(IRE) —Vanishing Prairie (USA) (Alysheba (USA))
(1135) 1488[2] 2775[10] 4676[11] 5530[3] 5804[4]

Purple Night *Doris Schonherr*
2 b c Night Shift(USA) —Tessara (GER) (Big Shuffle (USA))
5771a[4]

Purple Sands (IRE) *B J Meehan* a55 43
2 b g Desert Prince(IRE) —Violet Spring (IRE) (Exactly Sharp (USA))
3157[6] 3591[15] 4428[9]5261[9] 6015[9]

Purus (IRE) *P Mitchell* a89d 87
4 b g Night Shift(USA) —Pariana (USA) (Bering)
238[8] 1112[8]1475[5] 1939[5] 2405[8](2757) 3211[5]
3532[11]5777[11] 6397[9]6580[13] 6654[4]6770[3]

Pusey Street Lady *J Gallagher* 53
2 b f Averti(IRE) —Pusey Street Girl (Gildoran)
2703[5]

Puskas (IRE) *M R Channon* 96
3 b g King's Best(USA) —Chiquita Linda (IRE) (Mujadil (USA))
896[3] 1091[9] 1512[5] 1848[6] 2014[12]

Pussy Galore (ITY) *M Innocenti* 87
2 b f Mutamam—Pasionaria (IRE) (Celtic Swing)
3343a[7]

Puteri Sas (IRE) *P F I Cole* 37
3 b f Fasliyev(USA) —Puteri Wentworth (Sadler's Wells (USA))
971[9] 1118[10] 1416[13]

Put It On The Card *P D Evans* a59 59
2 ch g Bertolini(USA) —Madame Jones (IRE) (Lycius (USA))
1744[8] 2145[5] 2626[2]3246[7] 6258[6] 6401[2]6491[5]
6789[U]

Putra Kuantan *M A Jarvis* 97
6 b g Grand Lodge(USA) —Fade (Persepolis (FR))
1676[2] 2201[6] 2440[14]

Putra Laju (IRE) *J W Hills* a72
2 b c Trans Island—El Corazon (IRE) (Mujadil (USA))
5648[11] 5784[5]6324[5] 6645[3](6808)

Putra Sas (IRE) *P F I Cole* a96 103
5 b h Sri Pekan(USA) —Puteri Wentworth (Sadler's Wells (USA))
(57)

Putra Square *P F I Cole* 90
2 b c Cadeaux Genereux—Razzle (IRE) (Green Desert (USA))
3701[2] 4680[4] 5339[3] 5893[4]

Puya *H Candy* a84 90
4 b m Kris—Pervenche (Latest Model)
898[5] 1692[7] 2555[3]2983[7] 3470[4] 4108[2](4577)
4965[6]

Pyramid *A J Lidderdale* a55 55
4 ch g Pivotal—Mary Cornwallis (Primo Dominie)
1165[12] 1414[9] 1794[16]2347[7] 3053[9]3386[13] 5573[14]
6134[9]6233[11]

Qaasi (USA) *M Brittain* a62 70d
4 ch g Rahy(USA) —Recording (USA) (Danzig (USA))
1280[17] 1651[7] 2322[7] 2627[17] 2947[11]3749[19] 6383[3]
(6405) 6571[11] 6769[4]6980[9]

Qadar (IRE) *N P Littmoden* a106 100
4 b g Xaar—Iktidar (Green Desert (USA))
116[8] 2757[4]13[5] 450[2](517) 6314[6]64[7] (705) 836[3]
1116[11] 1602[6]5182[19] 5667[10] 6095[5]6243[8]
6445[3]6514[3] 6660[3]6849[2]

Qasbah (GER) *H Rogers* 74
5 ch g Waky Nao—Queen Of Heart (GER) (Acatenango (GER))
2563a[3]

Qik Dip (IRE) *P D Evans* a58 60
3 b g Desert Style(IRE) —Noble Clare (IRE) (The Noble Player (USA))
3798[4] 5129[10] 5690[4]6383[5] 6524[8]6907[10]

Qobtaan (USA) *M R Bosley* a65d 49
7 b g Capote(USA) —Queen's Gallery (USA) (Forty Niner (USA))
77[12] 416[10]582[12] 681[10]1197[10] 1225[6]1394[9]

Quadrophenia *J G Given* a23 50
3 b f College Chapel—Truly Madly Deeply (Most Welcome)
1137[5] 1612[3] 1792[4] 2284[15] 2896[12]4507[10] 4710[4]
5636[12] 5756[12] 6276[11]

Quadrupa (GER) *C Von Der Recke* a51 104
4 ch m Big Shuffle(USA) —Queen's Diamond (GER) (Konigsstuhl (GER))
1015[10] 1974a[9] 4649a[4]

Quaich *Saeed Bin Suroor* 75
3 b f Danehill(USA) —Quecha (IRE) (Indian Ridge)
(4155) 4555[5]

Quaker Boy *M Dods* 61
3 b g Agnes World(USA) —La Brise (IRE) (Llandaff (USA))
988[8] 1232[9] 1441[4] 1792[2] 2284[12]3023[4]

Qualify *M R Channon* a71 75
3 b g Mark Of Esteem(IRE) —Raneen Alwatar (Sadler's Wells (USA))
1251[6] 1867[6]

Qualinka Royale (FR) *Andreas Lowe* 40
2 b f Tiger Hill(IRE) —Gleneagles (GER) (Platini (GER))
4857a[5]

Qualitair Wings *J Hetherton* a68 68
7 b g Colonel Collins(USA) —Semperflorens (Don)
1075[8] 1425[14] 1637[6] 1996[7] 3168[2]3429[5] 3706[4]
3900[2] 4336[3] 4606[6]4925[5] 5314[5] 5579[5] 5725[7]
6037[11]6431[2] (6627) 6666[5] 6767[4]

Quality Special (BRZ) *P Bary* a84 99
4 b m Burooj—Lady Be Special (USA) (Bering)
155a[5] 351a[8] 510a[9] 623a[2]2490a[8] 5913a[7]

Quality Street *P Butler* a71 83
4 ch m Fraam—Pusey Street Girl (Gildoran)
947[5] 2389[2] 2858[5] 3251[3] 3715[6]4085[13] 4158[4]
4780[8] 5791[13] 6353[3]6485[9] 6656[3]6844[8] 6865[3]

Quantica (IRE) *N Tinkler* a32 60
7 b g Sri Pekan(USA) —Touche-A-Tout (IRE) (Royal Academy (USA))
1528[2] 1794[10] 2380[7] 2785[10] 3617[8]3786[3] 4401[9]
5243[5] 5636[10]

Quantum (IRE) *J H M Gosden* 90
3 b f Alhaarth(IRE) —Frappe (IRE) (Inchinor)
2587[4] 3440[3] (3977) 5478[3] 5644[2] 6202[3]

Quantum Leap *S Dow* a78 78d
9 b g Efisio—Prejudice (Young Generation)
17[5] 192[3]267[6] 559[7](662) 721[4]985[4] (1382)
1938[12] 2555[13]3212[2] 3854[7] 4879[10] 5096[10]5778[5]
6489[6]6654[3] 6781[8]

Quasimodo (IRE) *A W Carroll* 66
4 b g Night Shift(USA) —Daziyra (IRE) (Doyoun)
946[14] 1480[12]

Quebecois *P D Evans* 25
3 b g Zaha(CAN) —Fanciful (FR) (Gay Mecene (USA))
4755[13]

Queen Cleopatra (IRE) *A P O'Brien* 114
3 b f Kingmambo(USA) —Sequoyah (IRE) (Sadler's Wells (USA))
928a[2] 1177a[4] (1709a) 2054a[3] 2491a[3] 3105a[5]

Queen Cobra (IRE) *H Morrison* a66 80
3 b f Indian Rocket—Miss Sabre (Sabrehill (USA))
1900[3] 3268[3] 4398[4] 4659[2] 4886[6]5427[9] 5791[12]

Queen Isabella *J R Fanshawe* 71+
3 gr f El Prado(IRE) —Ausherra (USA) (Diesis)
1289[9] 1822[5] 2825[8]

Queen Jean *J G Given* 67
3 ch f Pivotal—Composition (Wolfhound (USA))
(1736) 2171[10] 2746[11] 3329[5] 3355[8]

Queenly Bearing *H-A Pantall* 87
3 b f Night Shift(USA) —Queen Of Warsaw (FR) (Assert)
5197a[6]

Queen Meabh (IRE) *P J Rothwell* 29
6 ch m Eagle Eyed(USA) —Wide Outside (IRE) (Don't Forget Me)
787[7]

Queen Noverre (IRE) *E J O'Neill* a77 76
2 b f Noverre(USA) —Tafrah (IRE) (Sadler's Wells (USA))
3096[2] 4041[3] 4552[3]5464a[23] 5906[6]

Queen Of Diamonds (IRE) *Mrs P N Dutfield* a38 45
3 b f Fruits Of Love(USA) —Royal Jubilee (IRE) (King's Theatre (IRE))
850[11] 1079[8] 1648[11]4868[10] 5757[4] 6133[10]6302[3]

Queen Of Fire *D R C Elsworth* a71 85
3 b f Dr Fong(USA) —Sonic Sapphire (Royal Academy (USA))
1834[3] 2582[8] 3418[11] 5945[14] 6411[8]

Queen Of Fools (IRE) *R Hannon* 52
2 b f Xaar—Foolish Fun (Fools Holme (USA))
3700^13 4559^11 5760^10 *6385^13*
Queen Of France (USA) *David Wachman* 88
2 b f Danehill(USA) —Hidden Storm (USA) (Storm Cat (USA))
5966^10
Queen Of Iceni *J L Dunlop* 78
4 b m Erhaab(USA) —Princess Genista (Ile De Bourbon (USA))
1132^4 1800^3 2460^8 3024^5
Queen Of Narnia *M R Channon* a57 68
2 b f Hunting Lion(IRE) —Fading (Pharly (FR))
878^3 968^5 1514^4 2315^7 (2495) 4857a^4 5065^9 *5207^5* 5234^4 5434^5 *5668^10* 5731^6 6056^7 *6311^3* 6488^U *6592^5* *6665^6*
Queen Of Night *D W Chapman* a59 59
6 b m Piccolo—Cardinal Press (Sharrood (USA))
2462^10 2550^7 2925^7
Queen Of Rap (IRE) *D K Weld* 90
3 b f Alhaarth(IRE) —Sudden Stir (USA) (Woodman (USA))
1709a^7 6356a^15
Queen Of Saba *M Weiss* 91
3 gr f Daylami(IRE) —Flourishing Way (Sadler's Wells (USA))
2717a^7 5008a^P
Queen Of Song *G L Moore* a19 25
4 b m Singspiel(IRE) —Fascination Waltz (Shy Groom (USA))
2261^8 3122^9 *4396^11*
Queen's Best *Sir Michael Stoute* 92+
3 b f King's Best(USA) —Cloud Castle (In The Wings)
2330^2 (5504) 5789^11
Queens Bounty *B Ellison* a4 46
3 b f Bahamian Bounty—Queen Shirley (IRE) (Fairy King (USA))
1234^8
Queen's Composer (IRE) *B Smart* a75 81
3 b g Mozart(IRE) —Queen Leonor (IRE) (Caerleon (USA))
952^11 1855^4 1999^7(2525) 3113^3 3813^3 4153^8
Queens Destiny *P W Hiatt* 49
3 b f First Trump—Eventuality (Petoski)
5870^8
Queen's Echo *M Dods* a36 68
5 b m Wizard King—Sunday News'N'Echo (USA) (Trempolino (USA))
1041^8 1531^4 1761^5 2165^5 *2794^11* 5316^6 5636^3 6211^4
Queen's Entry (IRE) *Patrick Carey* 51
3 b f King Charlemagne(USA) —Eliade (IRE) (Flash Of Steel)
4124a^16
Queen's Fortune (IRE) *M R Channon* 40
2 b f Iron Mask(USA) —No Shame (Formidable (USA))
3700^15 (Dead)
Queensgate *M Blanshard* a58 58
2 b f Compton Place—Ring Queen (USA) (Fairy King (USA))
1639^8 2185^10 2710^4 3148^9 4480^7 4779^6 5065^8 5162^2 5419^2 *5772^4* *6291^12*
Queen's Lodge (IRE) *J S Wainwright* 82
6 ch m Grand Lodge(USA) —Manilia (FR) (Kris)
1949^10
Queen's Pudding (IRE) *J R Fanshawe* 84+
3 b f Royal Applause—Gooseberry Pie (Green Desert (USA))
2824^8 4577^7
Queens Quay *R Hannon* 44
2 b f Grand Lodge(USA) —Nirvana (Marju (IRE))
5344^12
Queens Rhapsody *A Bailey* a81 78
6 gr g Baryshnikov(AUS) —Digamist Girl (IRE) (Digamist (USA))
36^8 *192^11* *245^6* *316^11* *585^10* 1528^13 3523^7
Queenstown (IRE) *J E Long* a34 35
5 b g Desert Style(IRE) —Fanciful (IRE) (Mujtahid (USA))
5926^9 *6370^11* *6473^11*
Queen Tara *Mrs C A Dunnett* a34 26
4 b m Kayf Tara—Lucy Tufty (Vin St Benet)
531^8 894^10 1222^9 *1536^13*
Quel Ange (FR) *R J Hodges* 75
4 b h Tel Quel(FR) —Corrossol (FR) (Kaldounevees (FR))
2063 ^5 2220^5 2615^8 2918^2 3469^10 4331^7
Queleden Candela (ARG) *I Jory* a102 76
5 b m West By West(USA) —Celia La Rumbera (ARG) (Robin Des Bois (USA))
155a^11 431a^13
Quelle Amore (GER) *A Wohler* 106
3 b f Monsun(GER) —Qelle Amie (CAN) (Beau Genius (CAN))
(1714a) 2279a^4 3776a^8 4648a^2 5561a^6
Quelle Beaute (FR) *H Hosselet* a69 82
6 b m Mansonnien(FR) —Quelle Horreur (FR) (Hero's Honor (USA))
5562a^5
Quemar (NZ) *Roger Stein* 101
4 b m Haafiz(IRE) —Quedar (NZ) (Clay Hero (AUS))
6253a^3
Quenched *J H M Gosden* 108
3 br f Dansili—Love The Rain (Rainbow Quest (USA))
1955^2 (2350) 2772^6 (3739) 4192a^6 5155^5 5502^9
Question (USA) *J M Bradley* 49
3 ch f Coronado's Quest(USA) —Royal Shyness (Royal Academy (USA))
2763^5 3090^9 3950^9
Questive *E A L Dunlop* a66 72
3 b g Rainbow Quest(USA) —Hawait Al Barr (Green Desert (USA))
16^4 *191^5* *337^6* *460^4*(781)
Quest On Air *J R Jenkins* a53 50
7 b g Star Quest—Stormy Heights (Golden Heights)
767^10

Quest Star (USA) *N J Howard* 111
7 br h Broad Brush(USA) —Tinaca (USA) (Manila (USA))
4908a^7
Queue Up *A G Newcombe* a43 53
4 b g Royal Applause—Faraway Lass (Distant Relative)
92^9 *395^8* *527^7* *634^6* *791^4* *937^4* *1224^4* *1460^4* 2636^6 4276^9
Quezon Sun (GER) *S Wattel* 92
3 br f Monsun(GER) —Quezon City (GER) (Law Society (USA))
6384a^5 6722a^3
Quick Little Miss (USA) *M Stute* a102
2 b f Freud(USA) —Swift Girl (USA) (Unbridled (USA))
6338a^10
Quicksharp (IRE) *Daniel Mark Loughnane* a41 76
3 br g Imperial Ballet(IRE) —Jack-N-Jilly (IRE) (Anita's Prince)
5911^12
Quicks The Word *T A K Cuthbert* a55 74
6 b g Sri Pekan(USA) —Fast Tempo (IRE) (Statoblest)
1341^15 1607^3 2544^5 3398^5 3786^2
Quiddity (IRE) *E J O'Neill* a55 69
2 ch f Diesis—The Strand (Gone West (USA))
3685^3 4669^2 5352^5
Quietly Go (USA) *B Baffert* a96
3 br c Real Quiet(USA) —Leah's Promise (USA) (Fit To Fight (USA))
5719a^4
Quiet Reading (USA) *M R Bosley* a62 56
9 b g Northern Flagship(USA) —Forlis Key (USA) (Forli (ARG))
8^2 *77^6*(242) *423^6* *650^13* *906^2* *1257^4* *2137^7* *6531^6* *6641^7* *6960^6*
Quiet Royal (USA) *T Pletcher* 110
3 ch f Royal Academy(USA) —Wakigoer (USA) (Miswaki (USA))
1177a^2 4191a^5 5049a^7 5984a^3 6340a^9
Quiet Times (IRE) *K A Ryan* a94 61
7 ch g Dolphin Street(FR) —Super Times (Sayf El Arab (USA))
6^9 *54^13* *413^9* *541^11* *6690^2* *(6835)*
Quincannon (USA) *W M Brisbourne* a63 50
5 b g Kayrawan(USA) —Sulalat (Hamas (IRE))
581^4 *649^7*
Quince (IRE) *J Pearce* a86 89
3 b g Fruits Of Love(USA) —Where's Charlotte (Sure Blade (USA))
1095^6 1781^2 2046^5 2290^2 5511^6 5660^6 6051^7 *(6519)* *6811^4* *6941^2*
Quinmaster (USA) *M Halford* 116
4 gr h Linamix(FR) —Sherkiya (IRE) (Goldneyev (USA))
(4031a) 5411a^4
Quintin *T D Easterby* 49
3 ch f Spinning World(USA) —Quadri (Polish Precedent (USA))
1866^9 2412^7 3244^5 4155^7 4728^7 5368^5 *6306^14*
Quintrell *H Candy* 90
3 b f Royal Applause—Peryllys (Warning)
1640^4 1956^2 3336^2 3975^5 4527^8(5092) 5590^3 (5896)
Quiron (IRE) *Carmen Bocskai* 70
5 b g Desert King(IRE) —Quebra (GER) (Surumu (GER))
456a^8
Quite A Bride (USA) *W Mott* 109
3 ch f Stormy Atlantic(USA) —Wise Bride (USA) (Blushing Groom (FR))
5198a^7
Quito (IRE) *D W Chapman* a107 119
9 b r Machiavellian(USA) —Qirmazi (USA) (Riverman (USA))
627^2 *729^2* 1069^7 1287^3 1778^2 (2386) 2846^17 3494^6 4025^10(4740) 4832^8 5011^2 (5135) 5184^7 5588^8 5942^14 5962^8 6218^6
Quizzene (USA) *M Johnston* 91
4 gr g Cozzene(USA) —Company Binness (USA) (Seattle Dancer (USA))
1238^5 1631^6 2035^2 2176^7 4676^18 5010^2 5533^7 5963^24
Quizzical Question (IRE) *L M Cumani* a74 75
4 ch m Bob Back(USA) —Quality Of Life (Auction Ring (USA))
1162^8 1376^4
Quote Unquote *M Brittain* a48 42
3 ch f Allied Forces(USA) —Quiz Time (Efisio)
10^12 3285^11 3759^12 4401^12 5432^5 *6129^7* *6282^3* *6548^7* *6794^9*
Qusoor (IRE) *J L Dunlop* 89
3 b f Fasliyev(USA) —Winsa (USA) (Riverman (USA))
1091^12 2639^9 3144^4 3741^6 4589^8
Rabatash (USA) *David Wachman* 108+
2 bb c Johannesburg(USA) —Attasliyah (IRE) (Marju (IRE))
2724^7 4409a^6 (4850a)
Rabbit Fighter (IRE) *P A Blockley* 93
2 ch c Observatory(USA) —Furnish (Green Desert (USA))
4103^6 4349^2 4809^5 5114^3
Rabshih (IRE) *Sir Michael Stoute* 60
2 b f Green Desert(USA) —Kylemore (IRE) (Sadler's Wells (USA))
4302^4 5347^7
Raccoon (IRE) *D W Chapman* 75
6 b g Raphane(USA) —Kunucu (IRE) (Bluebird (USA))
1496^3 1563^4 2237^7 2380^3 2449^5 2748^6 3525^3 3584^3 3938^7 4258^13 4834^12 5309^6
Race For The Stars (USA) *A P O'Brien* 110
3 b f Fusaichi Pegasus(USA) —La Lorgnette (CAN) (Val De L'Orne (FR))
1508^8 2054a^4 2802^4 4127^6 (4502a) 5191a^5 5465a^7
Racer Forever (USA) *J H M Gosden* 107
3 b g Rahy(USA) —Ras Shaikh (USA) (Sheikh Albadou)
1818^6 (2204) 2739^8 4174^6

Racinger (FR) *F Head* 109
3 b c Spectrum(IRE) —Dibenoise (FR) (Kendor (FR))
1600a^4 2489a^3 3779a^4 4862a^2
Racing Stripes (IRE) *Miss E C Lavelle* a65 77
2 ch g Night Shift(USA) —Swan Lake (IRE) (Waajib)
775^2 1429^3 (2710) 3468^3 4026^12 *4246^8* 6332^11
Racing Times *B J Meehan* a76 76
2 b g Danetime(IRE) —Cartesian (Shirley Heights)
4105^5 4525^4 *4992^4* *6764^5* *6866^3*
Rada (IRE) *R Hannon* 58
3 b f Danehill(USA) —Old Domesday Book (High Top)
1119^9 1418^10 2175^10 2591^15
Radiant Bride *P A Blockley* a47 43
6 ch m Groom Dancer(USA) —Radiancy (IRE) (Mujtahid (USA))
55^11 *91^13* *256^8*
Radiator Rooney (IRE) *Patrick Morris* a73+ 71
3 br g Elnadim(USA) —Queen Of The May (IRE) (Nicolotte)
10^2 *138^2* *275^10* *(298)* *464^6* *481^2*
Radical Attraction (USA) *R Hannon* a49
3 bb f Silver Hawk(USA) —Running Flame (IND) (Steinbeck (USA))
479^9 *668^10*
Radical Views *B W Hills* 66
2 ch c Machiavellian(USA) —Nawaiet (USA) (Zilzal (USA))
4600^8 5066^6 5379^2
Radius *H Morrison* a74 65
3 b g Lujain(USA) —Georgianna (IRE) (Petardia)
60^8 *645^10* 1208^12 1799^3 2531^6
Radlett Lady *D K Ivory* a42 51
5 ch m Wolfhound(USA) —Royal Dream (Ardkinglass)
145^7 *307^9* *388^3* *529^10*
Raetihi *P S Felgate* a21 29
5 b m Wizard King—Foreno (Formidable (USA))
45^11
Rafelite *Lady Herries* a56 64
4 b m Fraam—Megan's Flight (Welsh Pageant)
1163^9 1879^2 2751^7 3270^12
Raffaas *M P Tregoning* 68
2 b g Green Desert(USA) —Felawnah (USA) (Mr Prospector (USA))
3025^3 3545^6 4129^14 5647^12
Rafferty (IRE) *T D Barron* a97d 83
7 ch g Lion Cavern(USA) —Badawi (USA) (Diesis)
58^2 *275^4* *348^4* 719^5 *6892^2*
Raffiene (IRE) *E J O'Neill* a54 25
3 ch f Spectrum(IRE) —Alcove (USA) (Valdez (USA))
1940^6 2350^12 *3100^11*
Raffish *M Scudamore* a71 72
4 ch g Atraf—Valadon (High Line)
2585^8
Ragad *W Jarvis* a69 8
3 b c Alhaarth(IRE) —Waafiah (Anabaa (USA))
5951^7 *6480^5* *6731^2* *(6944)*
Ragasah *Ernst Oertel* a49 39
8 b m Glory Of Dancer—Slight Risk (Risk Me (FR))
232^8 *917^P*
Ragazza Mio (IRE) *N Clement* 93
3 b f Generous(IRE) —Via Saleria (IRE) (Arazi (USA))
6567a^7 6722a^2
Rageman *M Cheno* 112
6 b g Desert King(IRE) —Subasta (FR) (Kendor (FR))
841a^6 1371a^9 2941a^8
Raging Creek (USA) *D Selvaratnam* a101
7 b h Storm Creek(USA) —Yardstick (USA) (Sunny Clime (USA))
740a^15
Raglan Copenhagen *B R Millman* 49
2 b g Lahib(USA) —Peperonata (IRE) (Cyrano De Bergerac)
4781^12
Rag Tag (IRE) *A M Balding* 87
3 b g Tagula(IRE) —Lovat Spring (USA) (Storm Bird (CAN))
2329^11 3027^8 3568^3 3802^7 4223^9
Rahiyah (USA) *J Noseda* 108
2 ch f Rahy(USA) —Meiosis (USA) (Danzig (USA))
4041^2 (4588) 5966^2
Rahy's Crown (USA) *G L Moore* a71 70
3 b c Rahy(USA) —Inca Princess (USA) (Big Spruce (USA))
918^4 (1052) 2332^6 2592^4*(3017)* 4224^2 4448^9
Railings (AUS) *J Hawkes* 120
5 b g Zabeel(NZ) —La Suffragette (NZ) (Palace Music (USA))
6110a^10 6347a^10 6392a^12
Rail Link *A Fabre* 129
3 b c Dansili—Docklands (USA) (Theatrical)
(2738a) (3517a) (5221a) (5716a)
Rain And Shade *M Johnston* a52
2 ch c Rainbow Quest(USA) —Coretta (IRE) (Caerleon (USA))
6950^6
Rainbow Bay *R A Fahey* a48 77d
3 b g Komaite(USA) —Bollin Victoria (Jalmood (USA))
1218^4 (1529) 1812^6 2363^10 3296^9 3360^4 3722^4 4422^10 4888^6 5401^7 5635^16 *6399^8*
Rainbow Fox *R A Fahey* a67 80
2 b g Foxhound(USA) —Bollin Victoria (Jalmood (USA))
2517^8 2973^2 (3351) *3685^4* 4170^2 4377^4 4547^3 4681^9 5113^4
Rainbow Mirage (IRE) *E S McMahon* 92
2 b c Spectrum(IRE) —Embers Of Fame (IRE) (Sadler's Wells (USA))
1595^5 (2218) (3026) 4890^3 5681^2 5809^8
Rainbow Prince *A Dickman* 43
3 b g Desert Prince(IRE) —Eve (Rainbow Quest (USA))
716^9 1100^9 1252^12 2298^8 2734^8 4199^11 4656^5 5060^6

Rainbow Promises (USA) *B J Meehan* a96+
2 bb f Came Home(USA) —To Be A Lover (USA) (The Minstrel (CAN))
(5773)
Rainbow Rising (IRE) *J Howard Johnson* 93
4 bb g Desert King(IRE) —Fantastic Bid (USA) (Auction Ring (USA))
2017^5 4202^2 4988^8 5536^10 6009^2
Rainbow's Classic *K A Ryan* 70
3 b g Muhtarram(USA) —Legend Of Aragon (Aragon)
1122^7 1866^4 2616^5 3082^7 4426^9 4892^5 5446^5
Rainbow's Edge *R Charlton* 81
3 b f Rainbow Quest(USA) —Film Script (Unfuwain (USA))
1283^3 (1988) 5594^3
Rainbows Guest (IRE) *A M Balding* a70 55
3 ch f Indian Lodge(IRE) —Maura's Guest (IRE) (Be My Guest (USA))
6417^9 *6635^10* *6928^6*
Rainbow Treasure (IRE) *R M Beckett* a32 32
4 ch m Rainbow Quest(USA) —Gaily Royal (IRE) (Royal Academy (USA))
1198^11
Rainbow Zest *P W Chapple-Hyam* 78
3 b c Rainbow Quest(USA) —Original (Caerleon (USA))
2412^6 3419^5 4806^3 5138^5
Raincoat *J H M Gosden* 82+
2 b c Barathea(IRE) —Love The Rain (Rainbow Quest (USA))
(2619)
Rain Holly (IRE) *R A Harris* a19 65
4 b m Indian Rocket—Holly Bird (Runnett)
26^9
Rainstar (IRE) *M Weiss* 59
4 b h Real Quiet(USA) —Restikarada (FR) (Akarad (FR))
306a^3
Rain Stops Play (IRE) *M Quinn* a49 96
4 b g Desert Prince(IRE) —Pinta (IRE) (Ahonoora)
719^9 898^12 1186^7 (1993) (2170) 2440^10 2810^7 3413^16 4108^8 (4879) 5406^9 5639^2 (5945) 6219^3 *6424^7*
Raise The Goblet (IRE) *W J Haggas* a40 56
2 b g Almutawakel—Saninka (IRE) (Doyoun)
5914^9 6331^14 *6603^5*
Raise The Heights (IRE) *C Tinkler* a63 62
3 b g Orpen(USA) —Blue Heights (IRE) (Persian Heights)
219^8 *918^6*(1140) 1543^7 2102^8 *4245^5* *5652^9* *6435^7*
Rajaall *M R Channon* a79 76
3 b g Royal Applause—Gorgeous Dancer (IRE) (Nordico (USA))
1356^3 2332^5 2607^6 *3156^2* 3704^6 4224^6
Rajam *G A Harker* 82
8 b g Sadler's Wells(USA) —Rafif (USA) (Riverman (USA))
1756^14 2193^10 2628^6 3674^7 3983^8 4472^10 4960^8 5080^6 5960^6
Rajayoga *M H Tompkins* a50 57
5 ch g Kris—Optimistic (Reprimand)
4011^5 4252^7 *6754^4* *6857^6* *6979^4*
Rajeef Ashog *L M Cumani* 66
2 ch c Dr Fong(USA) —Dakhla Oasis (IRE) (Night Shift (USA))
4428^15 5089^6 5508^5 6064^6
Rajeem *C E Brittain* a86 114
3 b f Diktat—Magic Sister (Cadeaux Genereux)
827^8 1093^5 1328a^8 2802^5 (3416)
Rakata (USA) *P F I Cole* a80 82
4 b m Quiet American(USA) —Haleakala (IRE) (Kris)
1056^6 1348^3 1802^4 2071^4 2457^5 3590^3 *4048^8* (4286) (4660) 5436^4*(5908)*
Rallying Cry (USA) *J H M Gosden* a98 113
2 br c War Chant(USA) —Turning Wheel (USA) (Seeking The Gold (USA))
(3083) 3492^4 *(5665)* 5965^6 6249a^5
Rambling Light *A M Balding* 64
2 b c Fantastic Light(USA) —Rambler (Selkirk (USA))
5939^10
Rambling Socks *S R Bowring* a42 35
3 ch f Rambling Bear—Cledeschamps (Doc Marten)
5885^16 *6129^4* *6476^9* *6637^8* *6719^10* *6956^13*
Rambo Blue *G J Smith* a52 64
6 b g Elmaamul(USA) —Copper Trader (Faustus (USA))
257^8 *328^9*
Rambo Honours (IRE) *K A Ryan* a44 67
2 b g Dilshaan—Rousselino (USA) (Silver Hawk (USA))
3544^2 4140^7 *6447^5* *6670^5*
Ramiro (AUS) *M Dillon*
4 br g Iglesia(AUS) —Anne (AUS) (Kaoru Star (AUS))
7000a^3
Ramonti (FR) *A & G Botti* 120
4 b h Martino Alonso(IRE) —Fosca (USA) (El Gran Senor (USA))
(2217a) 4416a^7 (5982a) (6364a) 6784a^3
Rampage *W J Haggas* a83+ 75+
5 ch m Pivotal—Noor El Houdah (IRE) (Fayruz)
348^7
Rampallion *Saeed Bin Suroor* 105+
3 b c Daylami(IRE) —Minute Waltz (Sadler's Wells (USA))
(5660) 6337^2
Ramsgill (USA) *J Pearce* a74+ 74
4 b g Prized(USA) —Crazee Mental (Magic Ring (IRE))
187^4 *324^9* *535^5* *652^6* *706^3* *833^2**(1748)* 2585^3 3116^4 3900^10 4544^3 (4764)
Ranavalona *A M Balding* a54 52
2 br f Diktat—Syrian Queen (Slip Anchor)
4002^5 4161^7 5586^6 *6807^10*

Rancho Cucamonga (IRE) *T D Barron* a61 63
4 ch m Raphane(USA) —Kunucu (IRE) (Bluebird (USA))
813[7] 1102[12] 1413[9] 1528[6] 2574[11]2856[2] 3171[6] (3524) 3670[2] 3835[6] 3996[7]4352[5] (4473) 4694[3] 5032[11]5243[4] 5350[14] 6719[3]6964[3]

Randall's Diana (IRE) *Daniel Mark Loughnane* 60
3 b f Monashee Mountain(USA) —Altiyna (Troy)
6497[13]

Random Call (USA) *Sir Michael Stoute* 82
3 b f War Chant(USA) —Lignify (ARG) (Confidental Talk (USA))
2582[9]

Rangali Belle *C A Horgan* 62
2 b f Diktat—Dalaauna (Cadeaux Genereux)
5340 [5]

Rann Na Cille (IRE) *K A Ryan* a63 62
2 b f Agnes World(USA) —Omanah (USA) (Kayrawan (USA))
6697[4] 6927[4]

Ransom Captive (USA) *M A Magnusson* 89
2 b f Red Ransom(USA) —Cap Rouge (USA) (Summer Squall (USA))
(5679) 6105[4]

Ransom Strip (USA) *M Brittain* a63 69
3 b g Red Ransom(USA) —L'Extra Honor (USA) (Hero's Honor (USA))
380[6] (453) 583[9]1044[3] 1948[10] 3081[7] 3939[3] 4256[5]5815[7] 6244[6]

Rapid City *Miss J Feilden* a80+ 55
3 b g Dansili—West Dakota (USA) (Gone West (USA))
(6765) (6848)

Rapid Flow *J W Unett* a64 64
4 b g Fasliyev(USA) —Fleet River (USA) (Riverman (USA))
209[8] 533[4]587[11] 1235[10] 1852[5]2148[11] 4324[9]

Rapscallion (GER) *Heather Dalton* a77 84
7 b g Robellino(USA) —Rosy Outlook (USA) (Trempolino (USA))
600[3] 4244[9]4604[12]

Rapsgate (IRE) *R Hannon* a70 79
3 b f Mozart(IRE) —Lady Rushmore (IRE) (Fairy King (USA))
66[6] 190[5]464[3] 593[4](1137) 2049[8] 2105[4] 2609[6] 3087[2] 3403[7]

Raptor (GER) *Mario Hofer* 101
3 b c Auenadler(GER) —Royal Cat (Royal Academy (USA))
4918a[4] 5543a[4] 6093a[5]

Raquel White *P D Evans* a71 47
2 b f Robellino(USA) —Spinella (Teenoso (USA))
5646[6] 5948[4] 6242[4]6582[6] 6760[7]6920[3]

Raratomba *P D Evans* 7
3 b c Tomba—Bit On The Side (IRE) (Vision (USA))
4899[11] 5128[8]

Rare Breed *Mrs L Stubbs* 89
3 b g Foxhound(USA) —Rare Indigo (Timeless Times (USA))
(2110) 2651[10] 4102[9] 4422[8]

Rare Coincidence *R F Fisher* a62 66
5 ch g Atraf—Green Seed (IRE) (Lead On Time (USA))
75[7] 603[3]643[2] 733[3]816[5] 975[3] 2193[5] 2381[4] (2751) 3140[5]3454[9] (4072) 4351[2] 4522[5]5736[11] 6011[11] 6321[9]

Rare Cross (IRE) *P Mitchell* a78 91
4 b m Cape Cross(IRE) —Hebrides (Gone West (USA))
1236[4] 6095[10] 6446[7]6776[7]

Rasaman (IRE) *M A Jarvis* 74
2 b g Namid—Rasana (Royal Academy (USA))
5371[7] 5915[4]

Rascacio (GER) *C Von Der Recke*
4 br h Big Shuffle(USA) —Royal Wind (GER) (Windwurf (GER))
305a[2] 455a[2]

Rashida *M Appleby* a67 61
4 b m King's Best(USA) —Nimble Lady (AUS) (Fairy King (USA))
385[7] 505[7]5384[15] 5973[8] 6380[6]

Rasid (USA) *C A Dwyer* a46 63
8 b g Bahri(USA) —Makadir (USA) (Woodman (USA))
158[6] 311[9]3951[2] 5915[6]694[6]

Raslan *M Johnston* a80 91+
3 b g Lomitas—Rosia (IRE) (Mr Prospector (USA))
656[2] 863[6] 1006[4]2556[4] (3114) (3269)

Rathnait *M J Attwater*
2 b f Weet-A-Minute(IRE) —Dahlidya (Midyan (USA))
3915[12]

Ratio *J E Hammond* 114
8 ch g Pivotal—Owdbetts (IRE) (High Estate)
2799a[8] 4860a[3] 5549[5] 5779a[4]

Rationale (IRE) *S C Williams* a56 91
3 b g Singspiel(IRE) —Logic (Slip Anchor)
579[5] 778[5] 1218[5]2616[3] (3301) (4392) (4626) (5325) 5804[14]

Rattle And Hum (ITY) *F & L Camici* 106
3 b c Celtic Swing—Scuola Genovese (IRE) (Ela-Mana-Mou)
(1175a) 1872a[10]

Ratzia (IRE) *C E Brittain* a56 11
3 b f Sinndar(IRE) —Imelda (USA) (Manila (USA))
6177[11] 6587[5]

Raucous (GER) *T P Tate* 85
3 b g Zinaad—Roseola (GER) (Acatenango (GER))
3676[2] (4204)

Raul Sahara *J W Unett* a55 55
4 b g Makbul—Sheraton Heights (Deploy)
41[10] 3680[7] 4325[8]4439[10]

Ravarino (USA) *Sir Michael Stoute* 53+
2 ch f Unbridled's Song(USA) —Sous Entendu (USA) (Shadeed (USA))
5068[7]

Raven (IRE) *Mark Campion*
4 b m Alzao(USA) —Eman's Joy (Lion Cavern (USA))
449[9] 616[11]

Ravenna *M P Tregoning* a49
2 ch f Compton Place—Cultural Role (Night Shift (USA))
6912[3]

Raven Rascal *J F Coupland* a19 23
2 b f Zaha(CAN) —Eccentric Dancer (Rambo Dancer (CAN))
2178[14] 2461[11] 2759[10]

Rave Reviews (IRE) *A Wohler* 110
5 b m Sadler's Wells(USA) —Pieds De Plume (FR) (Seattle Slew (USA))
5560a[5] 6124a[10]

Ravinia (USA) *B J Meehan* a68+ 60+
2 ch f Rahy(USA) —Reverie (USA) (Nijinsky (CAN))
5371[8] (6520)

Ravi River (IRE) *B W Hills* 85
2 ch c Barathea(IRE) —Echo River (USA) (Irish River (FR))
4592[3] (4788) 5172[3]

Ravish *W J Haggas* a38 59+
3 b f Efisio—Looks Sensational (USA) (Majestic Light (USA))
2069[3] 2589[12] 4567[11] 4799[8] 5250[8]5569[14]

Rawaabet (IRE) *P W Hiatt* a79 75
4 b g Bahhare(USA) —Haddeyah (USA) (Dayjur (USA))
223[13] 1051[8] 1164[9]1257[7] 2327[12] 2708[11]

Rawdon (IRE) *M L W Bell* a76 93
5 b g Singspiel(IRE) —Rebecca Sharp (Machiavellian (USA))
1071[14] 1992[10] 2387[9] 3048[6] 3366[6]4147[3] 4805[10] 5137[2] 5511[7] 5769[14]

Rayhani (USA) *M P Tregoning* a91 96+
3 b g Theatrical—Bahr Alsalaam (USA) (Riverman (USA))
1095[8] 3490[2] (3974) 4560[5]4951[8]

Raymond's Pride *K A Ryan* a70 89d
6 b g Mind Games—Northern Sal (Aragon)
1042[4] 1285[10] 1858[2] 1949[3] 3069[3]5117[10] 5336[22] 6009[12] 6212[10]

Raza Cab (IRE) *Karen George* a81 68
4 b g Intikhab(USA) —Laraissa (Machiavellian (USA))
(192) 316[2] 451[9](659) (764) 1938[10]2510[14] 2983[12]

Razed *P L Gilligan* a58 61
3 b g King's Best(USA) —Key Academy (Royal Academy (USA))
1005[9] 2324[13] 5484[5]5751[6] 5992[9] 6949[7]

Razzano (IRE) *P D Evans* a52 58+
2 b f Fasliyev(USA) —Shewillifshewants (IRE) (Alzao (USA))
6808[5] 6950[4]

Reaching Out (IRE) *N P Littmoden* a70 82
4 b g Desert Prince(IRE) —Alwiyda (USA) (Trempolino (USA))
1992[4] 2540[8] 3048[11] 3404[13]3900[12] 4454[7] 5046[7]5450[12] (6918) 6980[2]

Readyforone *P D Evans* a8 40
2 b g Mutamarkiz(IRE) —Blackpool Mamma's (Merdon Melody)
856[5] 1040[5] 1223[8]2064[2] 2626[13] 6016[12]

Ready For Spring (USA) *J Noseda* a95 99
2 b c More Than Ready(USA) —Maybe In May (USA) (Miswaki (USA))
(4105) 4680[3] 5017[4] (5431)

Ready's Gal (USA) *T Pletcher* 114
4 ch m More Than Ready(USA) —Exquisite Mistress (USA) (Nasty And Bold (USA))
6125a[7]

Ready Teddy Go *J Ryan* a42 16
4 b g Danzig Connection(USA) —Mariette (Blushing Scribe (USA))
94[12] 461[9]767[9] 1224[5]1313[11] 1540[11]

Ready To Please (USA) *T Pletcher* a115 111
3 br f More Than Ready(USA) —Guilty Pleasure (USA) (Pine Bluff (USA))
6614a[6]

Real Chief (IRE) *Miss M E Rowland* a50 25
8 b g Caerleon(USA) —Greek Air (IRE) (Ela-Mana-Mou)
166[6] 314[4]503[10] 675[6]1415[15]

Realism (FR) *R A Fahey* a95 104
6 b g Machiavellian(USA) —Kissing Cousin (IRE) (Danehill (USA))
208a[10] 356a[8] 437a[5] 513a[2] 728[29]1017[9]

Reality Time (IRE) *W J Knight* a57 60
3 b f Daggers Drawn(USA) —Vitality (Young Generation)
68[11] 139[6]189[6] 2704[10] 3195[4]3867[8] 4670[8]

Realy Naughty (IRE) *B G Powell* a65
2 b c Night Shift(USA) —Naughty Reputation (IRE) (Shalford (IRE))
6887[6] 6998[4]

Reballo (IRE) *J R Fanshawe* a65+
3 b c King's Best(USA) —Lyrical Dance (USA) (Lear Fan (USA))
1165[2]

Re Barolo (IRE) *A & G Botti* 94
3 b c Cape Cross(IRE) —Dalaiya (USA) (Irish River (FR))
1175a[6]

Rebel Duke (IRE) *M G Quinlan* a69+ 75
2 ch c Namid—Edwina (IRE) (Caerleon (USA))
2315[3] 2821[4] (6975)

Rebelling (IRE) *M F Harris* 67
3 ch g Peintre Celebre(USA) —El Divino (IRE) (Halling (USA))
1052[10] 1837[3] 2082[8] 3347[10] 5564[12]

Rebellion *M Johnston* a77 84
3 b c Mozart(IRE) —Last Resort (Lahib (USA))
418[2] (459) (702) 831[5]1250[3]

Rebellious Spirit *P W Hiatt* a77 74+
3 b g Mark Of Esteem(IRE) —Robellino Miss (USA) (Robellino (USA))
380[2] 473[4]673[5] 890[7]1141[2] 1416[3] 1599[3] 1999[6] 2301[11]6928[3]

Rebel Pearl (IRE) *M G Quinlan* a67
2 b f Barathea(IRE) —Rebel Clan (IRE) (Tagula (IRE))
6283[8] 6504[5]

Rebel Rebel (IRE) *R Dutrow Jr* 117
4 b h Revoque(IRE) —French Quarter (Ile De Bourbon (USA))
5416a[2] 6784a[8]

Recalcitrant *S Dow* a61 59
3 b g Josr Algarhoud(IRE) —Lady Isabell (Rambo Dancer (CAN))
1193[10] 6435[9] 6565[4]6712[6] 6748[6]6911[2]

Recoaro (IRE) *B Grizzetti* 53
2 b c Regal Archive(IRE) —Melting Gold (USA) (Cadeaux Genereux)
2670a[6]

Record Breaker (IRE) *M Johnston* 74
2 b c In The Wings—Overruled (IRE) (Last Tycoon)
3892[4]

Recruit *R Hannon* a70 73
2 b g Mujahid(USA) —Georgianna (IRE) (Petardia)
1959[8] 2432[6] 4074[3]4773[4] 5423[4] 5783[10]

Rectangle (IRE) *Micky Hammond* 65
6 ch g Fayruz—Moona (USA) (Lear Fan (USA))
2504[15] 2780[8] 3245[10] 3988[14] 4258[10]4636[16]

Rectangle Blue *Micky Hammond* a4
4 b g Atraf—Golden Decoy (Decoy Boy)
330[9]

Red *R M Beckett* a63 63
2 ch f Fraam—Great Tern (Simply Great (FR))
1647[9] 2530[7] 3468[5] 5053[2] 5597[6]6385[3]

Red Admiral (USA) *Saeed Bin Suroor* 98
4 b g Red Ransom(USA) —Ausherra (USA) (Diesis)
5141[3] 5582[7] 6107[2] 6336[19]

Red Apache (IRE) *H J Collingridge* 21
4 b g Namid—Special Dissident (Dancing Dissident (USA))
2182[15] 4531[9]

Red Birr (IRE) *P R Webber* a83 78
5 b g Bahhare(USA) —Cappella (IRE) (College Chapel)
106[2] 223[2]375[2] 1051[6] 1380[5]5786[2] 6633[4]

Red Blooded Woman (USA) *E A L Dunlop* 71
2 b f Red Ransom(USA) —Maskaya (IRE) (Machiavellian (USA))
5296[5]

Red Bloom *Sir Michael Stoute* 118
5 b m Selkirk(USA) —Red Camellia (Polar Falcon (USA))
1804[4] 3105a[3] 4646a[3] (5465a) 6125a[6]

Red Cape (FR) *Jane Chapple-Hyam* a91 91
3 b g Cape Cross(IRE) —Muirfield (FR) (Crystal Glitters (USA))
1067[17] (2824) 2988[10] 3414[20] 4391[5] 4782[5]5143[4] 5785[8] 6101[4]

Red Chairman *R Johnson* a82 78
4 br g Red Ransom(USA) —Chine (Inchinor)
1887[8] 2547[7] 3081[5] 3621[6] 4253[7]4401[5] 4569[6] 4697[4] 5060[4] 5240[8]5483[5]

Redcliff (GER) *M W Easterby* 73
2 ch g Lomitas—Rhode Island (GER) (Waajib)
4140[8] (4445) 5041[6] 6208[7] 6332[14]

Red Clubs (IRE) *B W Hills* 118
3 bl c Red Ransom(USA) —Two Clubs (First Trump)
(1131) 1486[12] 2739[6] 3494[12] 4410a[2] 4738[5]5011[5] (5549) 5712a[9]

Red Contact (USA) *A Dickman* a86 46
5 b g Sahm(USA) —Basma (USA) (Grey Dawn II)
412[7] 763[4]1882[13] 2752[4] 2983[10]3469[8] 6417[2] (6469) 6772[10]

Red Coronet *W J Haggas* a63
2 br f Singspiel(IRE) —Red Tiara (USA) (Mr Prospector (USA))
6433[5] 6558[6]

Red Countess *Mrs A J Perrett* a57+ 72
3 b f Pivotal—Red Empress (Nashwan (USA))
1114[3] 2578[4] 5844[2]6301[14]

Red Crescent (SAF) *A Selvaratnam* a38 85
9 b g Northern Guest(NZ) —Salaadims Pride (SAF) (Salaadim (USA))
149a[5] 278a[7] 367a[6]

Red Current *J R Fanshawe* a53 66
2 b f Soviet Star(USA) —Fleet Amour (USA) (Afleet (CAN))
5068[3] 6309[8]

Red Diadem *W J Haggas* a67 65+
3 b f Pivotal—Red Tiara (USA) (Mr Prospector (USA))
844[2] 1386[4]2511[8] 2987[8]

Red Dress On (SWE) *T Gustafsson*
3 ch f Loup Solitaire(USA) —See Me (SWE) (Spectrum (IRE))
2564a[9] (3326a)

Red Evie (IRE) *M L W Bell* 114
3 b f Intikhab(USA) —Malafemmena (IRE) (Nordico (USA))
(795) (1056) (1843) (2103) (2744) (4097) (5191a) 5674[5]

Redeye Special *M L W Bell* a73+ 68
4 b m Efisio—Red May (IRE) (Persian Bold)
(902) 1245[3] 1568[7] 2148[3]3014[2] 4048[2]4248[3] 4925[3]

Red Fama *N Bycroft* 11
2 ch g Fraam—Carol Again (Kind Of Hush)
5900[13]

Red Finesse *M A Jarvis* a55 63
4 b m Soviet Star(USA) —Jouet (Reprimand)
21[9] 133[4]235[7]

Red Flare (IRE) *M R Channon* 48
2 b g Redback—Cwm Deri (IRE) (Alzao (USA))
1372[6] 1945[8] 2402[13]

Redflo *Ms J S Doyle* a52
2 b f Redback—Button Hole Flower (IRE) (Fairy King (USA))
6742[6] 6838[6]

Red Forest (IRE) *J Mackie* a65 74
7 b g Charnwood Forest(IRE) —High Atlas (Shirley Heights)
2140[5] 2408[3] 2871[3]3952[7] 4320[2] 4924[3]

Red Gala *Sir Michael Stoute* a84 86+
3 b c Sinndar(IRE) —Red Camellia (Polar Falcon (USA))
5151[5] 5426[2] 5770[2](5934)

Red Hot Jazz (IRE) *Mrs P N Dutfield* 58
2 bb f Danetime(IRE) —That's Jazz (Cool Jazz)
2172[13] 2456[5] 3544[5] 5290[9]

Redi (ITY) *A M Balding* a78 65
5 b g Danehill Dancer(IRE) —Rossella (Shareef Dancer (USA))
700[7]

Red Iris (IRE) *G A Swinbank* 37
3 ch f Soviet Star(USA) —Last Rolo (Mark Of Esteem (IRE))
1230[8] 1501[7]

Red Lancer *R A Fahey* a94 102d
5 ch g Deploy—Miss Bussell (Sabrehill (USA))
2201[5] 3294[10] 4713[9] 5010[12] 5494[5]5505[6] 5804[13] 5920[10]

Red Lantern *M J Attwater* a42 45?
5 ch g Young Ern—Croft Sally (Crofthall)
1852[14] 2789[15] 3679[10] 4114[6] 6327[8]6524[11]

Red Oog (AUS) *J Pride* 117
6 b g Brief Truce(USA) —Mary Julia (AUS) (Zoffany (USA))
6783a[9]

Redouble *N B King* a34 68
10 b g First Trump—Sunflower Seed (Mummy's Pet)
857[14]

Red Petal *Sir Mark Prescott* a67
2 ch f Medicean—Red Garland (Selkirk (USA))
6832[3] 6950[3]

Red Pride (IRE) *Miss J Feilden* a39 52
3 b g Fasliyev(USA) —True Love (Robellino (USA))
797[12] 5844[9] 5986[11]6302[10]

Red Racketeer (USA) *E A L Dunlop* a97 101
4 b h Red Ransom(USA) —Furajet (USA) (The Minstrel (CAN))
1017[6] 1238[2] 1775[8]

Red Raptor *J A Geake* a38 57
5 ch g Polar Falcon(USA) —Star Precision (Shavian)
778[6] 1212[7] 2063 [8] 6955[6]

Red River Rebel *J R Norton* a62 55
8 b g Inchinor—Bidweaya (USA) (Lear Fan (USA))
1392[4] 1590[11] 2788[10]3243[4] 4022[2] 4472[6] 4924[6] 5927[2]6305[2] (6553) 6797[2] (6973)

Red River Rock (IRE) *T J Fitzgerald* a52 52
4 b g Spectrum(IRE) —Ann's Annie (IRE) (Alzao (USA))
1591[15] 2165[11] 5838[12] 5925[5]6280[2] 6553[2]6705[7]

Red Rock Canyon (IRE) *A P O'Brien* 106
2 b c Rock Of Gibraltar(IRE) —Imagine (IRE) (Sadler's Wells (USA))
4129[3] 6104[8] 6456a[5]

Red Rocks (IRE) *B J Meehan* 124
3 b c Galileo(IRE) —Pharmacist (IRE) (Machiavellian (USA))
(1192) (2030) 2801[2] 3517a[2] 4678[2] 5185[3] (6344a)

Red Romeo *G A Swinbank* a91 91
5 ch g Case Law—Enchanting Eve (Risk Me (FR))
220[9] 2454[3] 2830[4]3223[6] 3986[7] 4379[3] 5070[2]

Red Rudy *A W Carroll* a69 75
4 ch g Pivotal—Piroshka (Soviet Star (USA))
845[2] 972[3] 1245[2]4772[2] (4870) 5384[5] 6568[10]

Red Ruth Lady *D L Williams* a16
4 ch m Karinga Bay—Equilibrium (Statoblest)
783[12] 890[11]1460[12]

Red Sail *Dr J D Scargill* a62 60
5 ch m Dr Fong(USA) —Manhattan Sunset (USA) (El Gran Senor (USA))
185[4] 461[3]1334[3] (1638) 2133[8] 3036[3] 3803[10] 5354[3] 6383[11]6775[5]

Red Sans *P Mitchell* a62
4 b g Rainbow Quest(USA) —Sarah Georgina (Persian Bold)
111[7]

Red Somerset (USA) *R Hannon* a82+ 98
3 b c Red Ransom(USA) —Bielska (USA) (Deposit Ticket (USA))
1087[3] (1335) 1953[4] 4805[5] 5376[6] 5660[10]

Red Sovereign *D G Bridgwater* a59 77
5 b m Danzig Connection(USA) —Ruby Princess (IRE) (Mac's Imp (USA))
46[8] 130[6](679) 951[3]1315[2] 1774[9] 2207[12]4691[3] 5350[15]

Red Spell (IRE) *R Hannon* a108 101
5 ch g Soviet Star(USA) —A-To-Z (IRE) (Ahonoora)
238[2] 377[2]518[2] 666[4]1129[3] 1301[4] 1659a[2]1935[4] 2435[2] 2742[10] 2988[8] 4098[5]4348[7] 5177[9] 5376[4] 5675[10] 6692[6]6847[2] 6914[2]

Redspin (IRE) *J S Moore* a54 54
6 ch g Spectrum(IRE) —Trendy Indian (IRE) (Indian Ridge)
2483[2] 2871[8] 3437[6] 3628[6] 4011[6]

Red Spinel *E A L Dunlop* a42
2 ch f Fantastic Light(USA) —Golden Digger (USA) (Mr Prospector (USA))
5424[8]

Redstone Dancer (IRE) *Miss S Collins* 102+
4 ch m Namid—Red Affair (IRE) (Generous (IRE))
932a[8]

Red Sun *J Mackie* a71 68
9 b g Foxhound(USA) —Superetta (Superlative)
(55) 168[10] 270[5]3522[7]

Red Tsarina *V Smith* a21
3 b f Russian Red—Tudor Bay Lady (Faustus (USA))
124[12] 333[11]

Red Vixen (IRE) *C N Allen* a63 58
3 b f Agnes World(USA) —West Escape (Gone West (USA))
226[7] 322[6]796[12] (1200) 1464[2]2576[3] 2826[4] 2987[10]3299[6] 3869[3] 4329[5]5636[13] 5885[8] 6541[7]6707[11] 6958[5]

Redwood Rocks (IRE) *B Smart* a73+ 71
5 b g Blush Rambler(USA) —Crisp And Cool (USA) (Ogygian (USA))
504[9] 585[8]736[6] 1035[10] 2697[11]3289[8] 4475[2] 5444[4] 6060[3] (6390) 6573[7] 6930[7]

Redwood Star *P L Gilligan* a60 75
6 b m Piccolo—Thewaari (USA) (Eskimo (USA))
967[11] 1315[4]

Reebal *B J Meehan* 83
2 b c Danehill(USA) —Applaud (USA) (Rahy (USA))
3193^6 3445^6 3738^5 (4910) 5731^3 5940^11 6332^4

Reefscape *A Fabre* 119
5 gr h Linamix(FR) —Coraline (Sadler's Wells (USA))
1332a^3 1875a^3 2773^2 4081^7 4647a^5 5711a^4

Reeling N' Rocking (IRE) *B W Hills* a75+ 71
3 b f Mr Greeley(USA) —Mystic Lure (Green Desert (USA))
1085^19 1844^10 4814^7 5568^3 (5986) 6396^3 (6595)

Reem Al Fallah (IRE) *M R Channon* 72
2 br f Cape Cross(IRE) —Hanna Dome (IRE) (Salt Dome (USA))
2394^3 2703^4 4221^2 4608^4 4949^3 5271^4 6013^7

Reem Three *L M Cumani* a71 101
3 b f Mark Of Esteem(IRE) —Jumaireyah (Fairy King (USA))
(1153) (1781) (2659) 3021^2 3739^7 6337^11

Refinery (USA) *Richard E Mandella* a90 100
3 b c Victory Gallop(CAN) —Sugar Is Gold (USA) (Slew O'Gold (USA))
5985a^6

Reflecting (IRE) *J W Hills* a70 66
3 gr f Daylami(IRE) —Church Light (Caerleon (USA))
1649^4 2411^3 2929^12 3731^7 4286^6 4704^U 5270^8

Reflective Glory (IRE) *J J Quinn* a28 53
2 ch f City On A Hill(USA) —Sheznice (IRE) (Try My Best (USA))
1181^6 1664^6 2538^4 2731^4 2870^4 6422^10 6582^8

Reform Act (USA) *D K Weld* 107
3 b f Lemon Drop Kid(USA) —Solar Colony (USA) (Pleasant Colony (USA))
2471a^3 2840a^4 (4212a) 5502^4

Regal Ali (IRE) *Mrs A Malzard* a3 48
7 ch g Ali-Royal(IRE) —Depeche (FR) (King's Lake (USA))
1625a^3

Regal Connection (USA) *M Johnston* 76
3 b f Deputy Commander(USA) —Clever Empress (Crafty Prospector (USA))
1837^5 2290^7 2679^6 3375^4 3784^4 (4197) 4672^3 4991^5 5868^12

Regal Curtsy *P R Chamings* a57 66
2 b f Royal Applause—Giant Nipper (Nashwan (USA))
4992^8 5894^7 6575^4

Regal Dream (IRE) *J W Hills* a75 79
4 b h Namid—Lovely Me (IRE) (Vision (USA))
985^5 1382^11 2259^3 2606^4 2954^5 3612^9 4267^4 4674^8 5233^5 5386^6 5573^10

Regal Fantasy (IRE) *P A Blockley* a12 52
6 b m King's Theatre(IRE) —Threesome (USA) (Seattle Dancer (USA))
2751^5

Regal Flush *Sir Michael Stoute* 81
2 b c Sakhee(USA) —Ruthless Rose (USA) (Conquistador Cielo (USA))
3701^4 4781^2 (6298)

Regal Lass *J G Given* a14 42
3 b f Royal Applause—Faraway Lass (Distant Relative)
5368^10 5924^11

Regal Ovation *W R Muir* 61
2 b g Royal Applause—Briggsmaid (Elegant Air)
1770^7 2530^12 2950^3 3496^6 4178^9 4773^7 5094^6 5597^2

Regal Quest (IRE) *S Kirk* a75 79
2 b f Marju(IRE) —Princess Sceptre (Cadeaux Genereux)
3700^6 4084^7 (5425) 5676^6

Regal Raider (IRE) *I Semple* a81 70
3 b g King's Best(USA) —Alegranza (IRE) (Lake Coniston (IRE))
1065^11 1493^4 2662^7 (6664) 6770^8 6999^3

Regal Riband *Sir Mark Prescott* a76+
2 b f Fantastic Light(USA) —Regal Rose (Danehill (USA))
6808^4 (6920) 6937^3

Regal Royale *Peter Grayson* a89 100
3 b g Medicean—Regal Rose (Danehill (USA))
1067^10 1490^2 2224^12 2774^5 3491^11 3985^5 6101^6 6514^12 6600^8

Regal Setting (IRE) *J Howard Johnson* a71 93
5 br g King's Theatre(IRE) —Cartier Bijoux (Ahonoora)
2238^8

Regal Sunset (IRE) *W R Swinburn* a74 58
3 b g Desert Prince(IRE) —Sunsetter (USA) (Diesis)
1335^6 2465^4 2934^4 5211^11 5391^13 5953^12

Regal Velvet *J H M Gosden* 87
3 b f Halling(USA) —Ruthless Rose (USA) (Conquistador Cielo (USA))
3367^3 3975^6 4489^2 (5566) 5917^12

Regency Red (IRE) *W M Brisbourne* a60 61
8 ch g Dolphin Street(FR) —Future Romance (Distant Relative)
42^2 (158) 2306^4 4425^6 4756^3 3637^2 3694^2 4086^3 4451^3 5451^2 5531^5 6376^4 6526^4 6571^2 6769^3 (6812) 6936^6

Regent's Park *R Charlton* a71 81
3 b f Green Desert(USA) —New Assembly (IRE) (Machiavellian (USA))
1119^5 1650^4 2753^3 3347^4 4181^2 4686^2 (5260)

Regent's Secret (USA) *J S Goldie* a83 88
6 br g Cryptoclearance(USA) —Misty Regent (CAN) (Vice Regent (CAN))
1035^7 1456^5 2162^8 2547^3 (2974) 3289^2 3971^6 4356^6 4696^7 5406^2 6226^5 6418^3 6607^4

Reggae Rhythm (IRE) *A J Lidderdale* a79 62
12 b g Be My Native(USA) —Invery Lady (Sharpen Up)
(237) 420^3 589^2 1931^10

Regime (IRE) *M L W Bell* 105
2 b c Golan(IRE) —Juno Madonna (IRE) (Sadler's Wells (USA))
4574^4 (4829) 5466a^2 6104^7

Regional Counsel *Kevin Prendergast* 103
2 b c Medicean—Regency Rose (Danehill (USA))
(3574a) 4825a^5

Rehearsal *L Lungo* a98 98
5 b g Singspiel(IRE) —Daralaka (IRE) (The Minstrel (CAN))
65^2 296^4 1815^4 2848^6 3501^6 4346^4 5361^5

Rehearsed (IRE) *H Morrison* a74 70
3 ch f In The Wings—Emilia Romagna (USA) (Acatenango (GER))
1543^4 2082^5 2607^7 (3952) 4530^3 4777^2 5324^12 (5971) (6312)

Reina De Mexico *E Russo* 75
3 b f Zafonic(USA) —Dom Pennion (Dominion)
1713a^13

Reinstated (IRE) *B W Hills* a77 75+
3 b f Galileo(IRE) —Miletrian (IRE) (Marju (IRE))
1845^12 2580^3 2970^3 3225^4 4537^3 4931^3 5594^2 5846^6 6381^2 6535^5

Rekaab (IRE) *Kevin Prendergast* 106
3 b g In The Wings—Za Aamah (USA) (Mr Prospector (USA))
1025a^3 1708a^6 5004a^7

Relaxed Gesture (IRE) *Christophe Clement* a79 123
5 ch h Indian Ridge—Token Gesture (IRE) (Alzao (USA))
741a^12 2476a^2 6126a^10

Relkida *M R Channon* 75
2 b f Bertolini(USA) —Roofer (IRE) (Barathea (IRE))
1896^3 2328^3 (3148) 3468^2 3861^2 4178^7 4779^4 5140^5

Reload (IRE) *J Noseda* a69+
3 b c Minardi(USA) —Rapid Action (USA) (Quest For Fame)
4247^4 5612^7

Relocation (IRE) *J J Lambe*
5 b g Grand Lodge(USA) —Olean (Sadler's Wells (USA))
570^11

Reluctant Suitor *J S Goldie* 77
4 b g Singspiel(IRE) —Belle Esprit (Warning)
(1033) 1457^2 1809^5 3483^3 3960^2 4951^3 5362^6 5531^4 5634^2 6312^2

Remaadd (USA) *D Selvaratnam* a104 111
5 gr g Daylami(IRE) —Bint Albaadiya (USA) (Woodman (USA))
205a^4 437a^3 512a^7

Remark (IRE) *M W Easterby* 71
2 b g Machiavellian(USA) —Remuria (USA) (Theatrical)
6295^5 6331^15

Remarkable News (VEN) *A Penna Jr* 118
4 ch h Chayim(USA) —Unreachable (VEN) (Alhajras (USA))
5416a^5 5824a^2

Rembrandt Quality (USA) *N A Callaghan* a71 72
3 b c Elusive Quality(USA) —My Sister Sarah (USA) (Dr Geo Adams (USA))
2650^12 2863^10 4142^5 5054^2 5273^2 5444^7

Remember Ramon (USA) *M J Wallace* a75 95
3 ch g Diesis—Future Act (USA) (Known Fact (USA))
(1034) (1356) 1586^6 2717a^5 6205^4

Reminiscent (IRE) *B P J Baugh* a62 60
7 b g Kahyasi—Eliza Orzeszkowa (IRE) (Polish Patriot (USA))
48^5 246^10 (599) 733^4 1308^10 2381^6 2684^12 6936^7

Rem Time (IRE) *John Berry* a53 47
6 b m Fraam—Any Dream (IRE) (Shernazar)
3817^5 4439^3 4667^7

Renderoc (USA) *J S Moore* a82+ 88
3 ch g Mt. Livermore(USA) —Rewarding (USA) (Storm Bird (CAN))
150a^12 368a^14 1953^5 3007^5 3491^13 3606^6 3889^16 5270^4 5907^8

Renee Lard (IRE) *A Berry* 31
3 ch f Titus Livius(FR) —Miss Body (IRE) (Hamas (IRE))
3002^6 5365^10

Renegade (IRE) *Mrs L J Mongan* a43 56
5 b g Fasliyev(USA) —Arcade (Rousillon (USA))
886^10 1310^3 1725^10 1899^10 (2260) 2536^7 3033^6 3664^4 4077^4 4564^15 4970^11 6779^10

Requested Pleasure (IRE) *J S Bolger* 84
4 b m Rainbow Quest(USA) —Aminata (Glenstal (USA))
1026a^7

Rescue (USA) *M R Channon* 50
2 b c Red Ransom(USA) —Distinct Beauty (USA) (Phone Trick (USA))
2029^7

Resignation (IRE) *R Hannon* a95 97
2 b c Invincible Spirit(IRE) —Madrina (Waajib)
1066^6 (2630) 3252^7 3734^11 4715^4 5455^2 5626^2 6096^4

Resleon (FR) *H-A Pantall* 60
3 b c Sendawar(IRE) —Resleona (Caerleon (USA))
6786a^15

Resonance *S Lycett*
5 b m Slip Anchor—Music In My Life (IRE) (Law Society (USA))
5174^8 5628^11

Resonate (IRE) *A G Newcombe* a78 89
8 b h Erins Isle—Petronelli (USA) (Sir Ivor (USA))
33^5 2169^9 2974^9 3850^2 4626^6 (4878) 5115^4 5548^6 6107^6 6336^2 6673^3

Respect (NZ) *P Cave* 105
7 b g Zabeel(NZ) —Kindness (NZ) (Star Way)
7000a^8

Respect My Wishes *R Ingram* a29 29
2 b f Dansili—Snow Shoes (Sri Pekan (USA))
2930^16 3588^15 6575^9 6853^9

Resplendent Ace (IRE) *P Howling* a73
2 b c Trans Island—Persian Polly (Persian Bold)
6689^2

Resplendent Alpha *P Howling* a99 89
2 ch c Best Of The Bests(IRE) —Sunley Scent (Wolfhound (USA))
(4138) 4815^2 5455^4 (5909) 6096^2

Resplendent Glory (IRE) *T G Mills* a96+ 114
4 ch h Namid—Aoife (IRE) (Thatching)
2115^11 2720^17

Resplendent Nova *P Howling* a90 85
4 b g Pivotal—Santiburi Girl (Casteddu)
777^3 898^6 1188^2 2302^9 5739^8 (5937) 6221^2 6461^2 6580^2

Resplendent Prince *P Howling* a65 45
4 ch g Primo Dominie—Last Result (Northern Park (USA))
(11) 100^5 3218^4 410^5 492^8 568^12 1217^11 1550^4 1746^7 (2245) 2793^2 3390^11

Ressource (FR) *G L Moore* a41
7 b g Broadway Flyer(USA) —Rayonne (Sadler's Wells (USA))
52^10

Restless Soul *C A Cyzer* a34
2 b f Singspiel(IRE) —Seasonal Splendour (IRE) (Prince Rupert (FR))
6486^10

Retaliate *M Quinn* 73
2 br f Wizard King—Retaliator (Rudimentary (USA))
2354^5 2806^5 3822^3 4221^8 (4665) 5271^7 (5646) 5940^3 6271^2

Retirement *R M Stronge* a44 43
7 b g Zilzal(USA) —Adeptation (USA) (Exceller (USA))
5384^14 5609^10

Return In Style (IRE) *J W Hills* a77 49
5 b h Desert Style(IRE) —Silver Echo (Caerleon (USA))
1410^8 1993^14 2392^3 2862^13

Reunite (IRE) *Saeed Bin Suroor* 110
3 ch f Kingmambo(USA) —Allez Les Trois (USA) (Riverman (USA))
(2613) 2772^5 (3627) 4179^2 4818^2

Reve D'Ailleur (FR) *J-M Sauve* 80
2 b f Panis(USA) —O'Tango (FR) (Fijar Tango (FR))
6609a^5

Reve De Rose *W P Mullins* 68
7 b m Emperor Jones(USA) —Rose De Reve (IRE) (Persian Heights)
4166a^19 (Dead)

Reve Lunaire (USA) *A Fabre* a104 103
3 b c Hennessy(USA) —My Dream Castles (USA) (Woodman (USA))
1131^4 1944a^4

Reverence *E J Alston* 122
5 ch g Mark Of Esteem(IRE) —Imperial Bailiwick (IRE) (Imperial Frontier (USA))
729^3 (989) 1485^4 (2115) 2720^16 3312^5 (4738)(5011) 5712a^2

Reveur *M Mullineaux* a73+ 69
3 b f Rossini(USA) —Without Warning (IRE) (Warning)
(49) 160^5 1282^2 1586^5 1851^8 2209^12 2518^11 6942^8 6993^7

Revien (IRE) *Miss J R Tooth* a53 64
4 b g Rossini(USA) —Kazimiera (IRE) (Polish Patriot (USA))
51^9 119^8 400^7 446^9 1310^7 2288^6 2544^12 3833^8 4324^10

Revisionist (IRE) *R Hannon* a44 66
2 b g Indian Danehill(IRE) —Lady Of Dreams (IRE) (Prince Rupert (FR))
2009^9 3210^8 3663^6 5041^7 5597^4 6007^3 6322^9

Reviving (IRE) *R F Johnson Houghton* a46 78
3 b g Fasliyev(USA) —Hartstown House (IRE) (Primo Dominie)
4731^0 1954^7 2301^14 2955^9 3306^14

Revolve *Mrs L J Mongan* a61 52
6 b g Pivotal—Alpine Time (IRE) (Tirol)
(395) (1536) 1910^2 3934^4 6128^6 6238^4 6374^5 6617^4 6700^2 (6801) (6904)

Revolving World (IRE) *T J Fitzgerald* a34 49
3 b c Spinning World(USA) —Mannakea (USA) (Fairy King (USA))
1343^7 1866^7 2243^10 4884^9 6601^8 6972^11

Reyadi (IRE) *T D Easterby* 88+
6 b g Peintre Celebre(USA) —Valley Of Hope (USA) (Riverman (USA))
5961^12

Rezeez (USA) *W J Haggas* 16
2 bb c Seeking The Gold(USA) —Mehthaaf (USA) (Nureyev (USA))
5066^14

Rezzago (USA) *W R Swinburn* a83+ 86+
6 b g Night Shift(USA) —Western Friend (USA) (Gone West (USA))
376^3 541^5 1939^11 2302^4 2555^2 3679^5 5021^4 5670^5 5877^4 6239^3 6489^5 6654^5

Rhaam *B W Hills* 70+
2 b c Fantastic Light(USA) —Elhilmeya (IRE) (Unfuwain (USA))
5659^4

Rhetorical *P Butler* a17 9
5 b g Unfuwain(USA) —Miswaki Belle (USA) (Miswaki (USA))
338^10 545^10 1313^12

Rhinebird *J R Fanshawe* a78 87
3 b g Lomitas—Twitcher's Delight (Polar Falcon (USA))
1192^8 (2825) 4508^7 4997^7

Rhodagna (IRE) *V Valiani* 97
4 b m Mark Of Esteem(IRE) —Rainbow Mountain (Rainbow Quest (USA))
6362a^6

Rhodesian Winner (GER) *Frau Marion Rotering* 112
7 ch h Snurge—Rhodesia (GER) (Solo Dancer (GER))
1870a^8

Rhuepunzel *P F I Cole* 58
2 b f Elnadim(USA) —Fairy Story (IRE) (Persian Bold)
5592^4

Rhyming Slang (USA) *J Noseda* 63
2 bb c Street Cry(IRE) —Purr Pleasure (USA) (El Gran Senor (USA))
5871^5

Rhythm 'N' Blues (IRE) *John M Oxx* 77+
3 b f Sinndar(IRE) —Cadence (Cadeaux Genereux)
5853a^8

Rhythm'n Roots (IRE) *J S Bolger* 107+
3 b c Daggers Drawn(USA) —Saana (IRE) (Erins Isle)
(1172a) 2055a^4

Riabouchinska *E Borromeo* 85
3 b f Fantastic Light(USA) —Reine Wells (IRE) (Sadler's Wells (USA))
2043a^10 6251a^9

Ribald *T Hogan* 66
3 b f Alhaarth(IRE) —Reactress (USA) (Sharpen Up)
4124a^11

Ribella (IRE) *O Isgoren* 107
7 b m Revoque(IRE) —Tajarib (IRE) (Last Tycoon) (5227a)

Ribh *C E Brittain* a79 50
3 b f Zafonic(USA) —Torgau (IRE) (Zieten (USA))
5023^8 5272^4 5649^4 5986^3 6259^6 6654^10

Richards Claire (IRE) *D P Keane* a22 54
5 b m Darazari(IRE) —Loquacious (IRE) (Distinctly North (USA))
6852^12

Richelieu *J J Lambe* a64 72
4 b h Machiavellian(USA) —Darling Flame (USA) (Capote (USA))
5861^11 6572^7

Richie Boy *Jennie Candlish* 16
5 b h Dr Fong(USA) —Alathezal (USA) (Zilzal (USA))
1560^15 1850^14

Rich In Spirit (USA) *T Proctor* 111
4 b m Repriced(USA) —Qualative (USA) (Woodman (USA))
4385a^5 6368a^4

Richtee (IRE) *R A Fahey* 78
5 ch m Desert Sun—Santarene (IRE) (Scenic)
1666^7 2193^8 (2628) 3009^7 3714^3 3960^8 4451^8 4991^7 5445^9 5725^13

Ricine (IRE) *F Rohaut* 108
4 b m Titus Livius(FR) —Rince Deas (IRE) (Alzao (USA))
885a^4 4860a^6 6252a^2

Ridaar (FR) *J-P Gallorini* 108
6 ch g Starborough—Ridiyara (IRE) (Persian Bold)
2941a^2

Ridgeway Cross (IRE) *Ernst Oertel* a61 49
3 gr f Cape Cross(IRE) —Karatisa (IRE) (Nishapour (FR))
31^10 3339^15

Rifaat *C A Horgan* 56
3 ch g Nashwan(USA) —Swame (USA) (Jade Hunter (USA))
1823^9

Riff Raff *W Jarvis* a66 77
3 b f Daylami(IRE) —Rafiya (Halling (USA))
1421^5 1613^5 2292^6 3256^4 3974^9 (4330) 4792^5 5022^4

Rifleman (IRE) *B Ellison* a51 38
6 ch g Starborough—En Garde (USA) (Irish River (FR))
5755^12 5972^7

Rigat *T D Barron* 74
3 b g Dansili—Fudge (Polar Falcon (USA))
2734^12 3285^4 (3909) 4958^7 5961^5

Right Answer *T D Easterby* 92
4 b m Lujain(USA) —Quiz Show (Primo Dominie)
1076^11 1377^14 1602^15

Right Option (IRE) *J R Weymes* a62 62
2 b g Daylami(IRE) —Option (IRE) (Red Ransom (USA))
707^5 1838^11 2619^11 4303^5 5387^3 6224^7 6322^2 6518^3 6625^3 6676^4 6768^2

Right Or Wrong (IRE) *Kevin Prendergast* 86
2 b c Key Of Luck(USA) —Sarifa (IRE) (Kahyasi)
5851a^5

Right Place (FR) *Robert Collet* a63 99
2 ch c Compton Place—Djayapura (FR) (Fabulous Dancer (USA))
5471a^6 5664a^7 6229a^7 6546a^10

Right Ted (IRE) *T Wall* a63 73d
3 b f Mujadil(USA) —Islandagore (IRE) (Indian Ridge)
1843^7 2620^4 2932^5 (3149) 3469^5 3945^10 4286^8 4871^12 5386^9 6054^9 6380^2 6387^9 6648^4 6837^8

Right To Play (USA) *J H M Gosden* a71+ 58
3 bb c Kingmambo(USA) —Possibly Perfect (USA) (Northern Baby (CAN))
5669^7 6052^6

Riguez Dancer *P C Haslam* a51
2 b g Dansili—Tricoteuse (Kris)
6757^6

Rikochet *Mrs A J Perrett* a46 65
2 ch c Generous(IRE) —Narva (Nashwan (USA))
4129^15 4487^7 5066^8 5597^12 6285^12

Riley Boys (IRE) *J G Given* a61 94
5 ch g Most Welcome—Scarlett Holly (Red Sunset)
1220^12 1830^10 (2540) (2945) 2974^2 3241^2 3876^4 4508^11

Rileys Dream *C J Price* a30 44
7 b m Rudimentary(USA) —Dorazine (Kalaglow)
3348^16

Ringarooma *C N Allen* a52 51
4 b m Erhaab(USA) —Tatouma (USA) (The Minstrel (CAN))
175^6 (311) 682^7 833^4 917^5 1537^12 1958^9 2131^4 2392^5

Ring Hill *Mme C Head-Maarek* 38
3 ch f Bering—Sound Hill (FR) (Green Tune (USA))
1177a^9

Ringsider (IRE) *G A Butler* a94 98
5 ch g Docksider(USA) —Red Comes Up (USA) (Blushing Groom (FR))
572^7 1017^16 1357^12 3748^12

Rinty (NZ) *C G Cox* a54
4 ch g Istidaad(USA) —Nearco Gold (NZ) (Virginia Privateer (USA))
6429^7 6714^6

Riodan (IRE) *J J Quinn* 77
4 ch m Desert King(IRE) —Spirit Of The Nile (FR) (Generous (IRE))
1854^2 (2750) 4156^3 4469^4 5338^6

Rio De Janeiro (IRE) *Miss E C Lavelle* a74 76
5 b g Sadler's Wells(USA) —Alleged Devotion (USA) (Alleged (USA))
713^4 847^6 3256^2

Riolo (IRE) *K F Clutterbuck* a58 65
4 ch g Priolo(USA) —Ostrusa (AUT) (Rustan (HUN))
692^6 849^11 1166^14 1750^4 2390^9 2611^4 2820^8 3111^3 3728^12 4306^6 (4674) 5302^5 5576^9

Rio Riva *Miss J A Camacho* a91 104
4 b g Pivotal—Dixie Favor (USA) (Dixieland Band (USA))
(1043) 2657^12 3020^6 (4889) 5357^4 5680^2 6219^2

Riotous (IRE) *A Dickman* 70
2 b g Royal Applause—Takarna (IRE) (Mark Of Esteem (IRE))
1442^4 2321^2 2695^2 3476^3 4519^5

Riotous Applause *J R Fanshawe* 98+
3 b f Royal Applause—Wiener Wald (USA) (Woodman (USA))
(5274)

Riotous Assembly *B Smart* 53
3 b g Dansili—Pretty Pollyanna (General Assembly (USA))
2615^14

Ripping *P Bary* 72
2 b f Green Desert(USA) —Zooming (IRE) (Indian Ridge)
2300^4 2743^10 2984^3 3796^3 5471a^7

Ripples Maid *J A Geake* a68 99
3 b f Dansili—Rivers Rhapsody (Dominion)
(901) (1208) (2049) 2168^5 2658^6 3414^4 3967a^5 4633^3 (5171) 5501^4 5919^2

Rippling River *W Jarvis* a69 72
2 b c Foxhound(USA) —Mylania (Midyan (USA))
968^2 1107^2 1309^2 6047^7

Riquewihr *J S Wainwright* a71 79
6 ch m Compton Place—Juvenilia (IRE) (Masterclass (USA))
315^10 402^2 (520) 588^3 (693) 902^3 1124^4 1413^2 1686^2 1774^6 2417^7 2637^2 2977^4 3144^2 3783^3 3811^4 4135^9 4507^4 4885^2 5317^2 5756^5

Rising Cross *J R Best* a91 114
3 b f Cape Cross(IRE) —Woodrising (Nomination)
665^3 827^6 914^5 (1472) 2203^2 2694a^8 3575a^3 4385a^10 (5155) 5702a^5 6119a^5

Rising Shadow (IRE) *T D Barron* a81 112
5 b g Efisio—Jouet (Reprimand)
1183^10 1487^15 1835^2 1949^2 2230^8 3125a^15 3471^6 (4202) 4609^10 4682^4 5336^3 5534^4 (5812) (6335)

Riska King *P A Blockley* a58 58
6 b g Forzando—Artistic Licence (High Top)
44^8 183^12 290^9 1217^4 3386^7

Risk Challenge (USA) *C J Price* a37
4 ch g Mt. Livermore(USA) —Substance (USA) (Diesis)
6771^11 6923^5

Risk Free *P D Evans* a61 42
9 ch g Risk Me(FR) —Princess Lily (Blakeney)
(56) 73^4 107^7 156^10 251^3 285^3 (313) 5740^12 6241^3 6380^5 6419^13

Risk Runner (IRE) *A King* 83
3 b g Mull Of Kintyre(USA) —Fizzygig (Efisio)
1193^8 1881^4 2332^2 2584^5 3365^9 5599^2 5869^7

Risque Heights *G A Butler* a70 73
2 b g Mark Of Esteem(IRE) —Risque Lady (Kenmare (FR))
6214^8 6316^2 6778^2 6976^3

Ritsi *Mrs A J Perrett* a56 77
3 b g Marju(IRE) —Anna Comnena (IRE) (Shareef Dancer (USA))
1193^3 1424^6 2332^8 2607^3 3269^3 3649^8 4777^3

River Alhaarth (IRE) *P W Chapple-Hyam* 99
4 b h Alhaarth(IRE) —Sudden Interest (FR) (Highest Honor (FR))
1133^2 1631^4 1991^2 3078^2 4713^5 5010^8

River Beau (IRE) *E J O'Neill* a41 26
3 ch f Galileo(IRE) —Dafariyna (IRE) (Nashwan (USA))
6133^6 6373^13 6616^13

River Biscuit (USA) *M J Polglase* a66 71
4 ch g Diesis—Elle Est Revenue (IRE) (Night Shift (USA))
662^10 726^17 1058^13

River Bravo (IRE) *P W Chapple-Hyam* 97+
3 b c Indian Ridge—Sheer Spirit (IRE) (Caerleon (USA))
(1986) 2658^15

River City (IRE) *Noel T Chance* a62 70
9 b g Norwich—Shuil Na Lee (IRE) (Phardante (FR))
566^3 2220^4 3100^10 3743^6 6735^6

River Club *A Dickman* 26
2 ch g Kyllachy—Amused (Prince Sabo)
6175^10

River Crossing *T D Easterby* 73
3 b f Zafonic(USA) —Vax Star (Petong)
1592^13

River Dancer (IRE) *J Size* 118
7 b g Sadler's Wells(USA) —Darara (Top Ville)
1180a^10

River Deuce *M H Tompkins* a71 56
2 b c Zaha(CAN) —Light Hand (Star Appeal)
4572^7 5640^10 6303^2

River Falcon *J S Goldie* a94 98
6 b g Pivotal—Pearly River (Elegant Air)
1145^2 4682^6 5336^17 5535^4 5812^4 6243^7

River Gypsy *D R C Elsworth* a65 69
5 b g In The Wings—River Erne (USA) (Irish River (FR))
218^4 419^4 503^11 965^5 1339^11 1926^4 2305^11 2507^8 4483^4 5267^6

Riverhill (IRE) *J Howard Johnson* a38 49
3 b g Mull Of Kintyre(USA) —Thrill Seeker (IRE) (Treasure Kay)
1868^2 2750^3 3398^16 4198^6 4835^5 5510^7 6213^4 6425^9

River Kintyre *B W Hills* 74
3 b c Mull Of Kintyre(USA) —Our Pleasure (IRE) (Lake Coniston (IRE))
2205^13 2760^6 3226^11 4488^3 4958^9 5377^12 5953^2

River Kirov (IRE) *P W Chapple-Hyam* 84+
3 b c Soviet Star(USA) —Night Shifter (IRE) (Night Shift (USA))
795^2 1048^5 (2080) 3226^4 (3943) 4422^4 5117^6

River Logic (IRE) *A D Brown* 64
3 b g Fasliyev(USA) —Grey Again (Unfuwain (USA))
1232^5 2195^10 (3288) 3610^3 3716^3 (3785) (4132) 4353^4 4651^2 5129^6 5173^7 5497^11

River Melody (GER) *Mario Hofer* 101
4 b m Keos(USA) —River Pearl (GER) (Turfkonig (GER))
4383a^3

River Mist Image (USA) *J R Fanshawe* a60 71
4 ch m Swain(IRE) —Cat's Image (CAN) (Storm Cat (USA))
503^7 3706^11 4010^6 6060^12

River Of Babylon *M L W Bell* a77 87
5 b m Marju(IRE) —Isle Of Flame (Shirley Heights)
2011^9 2606^8 3113^5 (Dead)

River Of Diamonds *R A Harris* a46 55
5 b g Muhtarram(USA) —City Gambler (Rock City)
243^9

River Prince *W G M Turner* 49
2 br g Riverwise(USA) —Princess Penny (King's Signet (USA))
1136^4 1309^5

River Rosie (IRE) *J G Portman* a36 51
2 b f Bertolini(USA) —Young Rosein (Distant Relative)
1542^8 1922^9 3010^8 (3345) 3677^6 4816^9

River Royale *P W Chapple-Hyam* 96
4 b g Royal Applause—Trundley Wood (Wassl)
1086^7 2364^9 2742^25 (Dead)

Riverside Dancer (USA) *K A Ryan* a70 82
2 ch f Stravinsky(USA) —Odori (USA) (The Minstrel (CAN))
1019^4 (1295) 2800^7 3734^7 4152^8 4736^15 5503^9 6400^3

River's Prayer (USA) *Paula Capestro* a109 97
3 gr f Devon Lane(USA) —Cozzy Flyer (USA) (Cozzene (USA))
6614a^14

River Tarrant *P W Chapple-Hyam* 63
2 b f Compton Place—Altizaf (Zafonic (USA))
2821^5 3942^6 5264^6 6063^6 6311^12

River Thames *J A R Toller* a83 86
3 b c Efisio—Dashing Water (Dashing Blade)
1069^14 1818^7 4601^10 4922^6 5777^9 6065^7

River Tiber *A P O'Brien* 108?
3 b c Danehill(USA) —Heavenly Whisper (IRE) (Halling (USA))
2039a^10 4839^4 5524^7

Riverweld *J R Holt* a27 50
4 ch g Weldnaas(USA) —Riverain (Bustino)
4925^15 6374^12

Rivetting *Sir Mark Prescott* a33 50
3 b g Vettori(IRE) —Frog (Akarad (FR))
1533^5 2082^6 2592^3

Riviera Red (IRE) *L Montague Hall* a43
6 b g Rainbow Quest(USA) —Banquise (IRE) (Last Tycoon)
310^11 398^9 1725^8

Riyalma (IRE) *Sir Michael Stoute* 108
3 b f Selkirk(USA) —Riyafa (IRE) (Kahyasi)
(1509) 2203^10

Road Home *G Wragg* 77+
3 ch g Grand Lodge(USA) —Lady In Waiting (Kylian (USA))
2825^3 3419^6

Road To Love (IRE) *M Johnston* 115+
3 ch g Fruits Of Love(USA) —Alpine Flair (IRE) (Tirol)
2224^6 2502^2 2805^14 (3318) 3443^12 (3971) (4082) 4358^6 4877^3 5204^3 5673^3

Road To Mandalay (IRE) *A P O'Brien* 104
3 b c Galileo(IRE) —Child Prodigy (IRE) (Ballad Rock)
2804^4 3660a^7 4639a^4

Road To Recovery *A M Balding* 66
2 b g Mujahid(USA) —Legend Of Aragon (Aragon)
1737^5 2617^5 3193^9 5162^5

Roanoke (AUS) *A Cummings* 56
4 b g Danehill(USA) —Lakab (USA) (Manila (USA))
6346a^17

Robbie Can Can *A W Carroll* a68 69
7 b g Robellino(USA) —Can Can Lady (Anshan)
13^2 37^2 131^8 574^8 973^2 1138^2 1415^12 2075^9 (3467) 3894^5 5952^11 6435^6

Robbie Scott *M Johnston* a26 62
2 b g Robellino(USA) —Milly Of The Vally (Caerleon (USA))
4932^5 5402^4 5552^3

Robbie Will *F Jordan* a42 57d
5 b g Robellino(USA) —Life's Too Short (IRE) (Astronef)
91^5 256^6 614^9

Robbo *K G Reveley* 57
12 b g Robellino(USA) —Basha (USA) (Chief's Crown (USA))
866^4

Robema *J J Quinn* 81
3 b f Cadeaux Genereux—Germane (Distant Relative)
2129^2 (2542) (3250)

Robert The Brave *A J McCabe* a67 27
2 b c Primo Valentino(IRE) —Sandicliffe (USA) (Imp Society (USA))
5389^3 5900^8 6224^2 6569^4

Robeson *D M Simcock* a66 73
3 br g Primo Dominie—Montserrat (Aragon)
4945^10 5435^5 5837^4

Robin Sharp *J Akehurst* a44? 20
8 ch h First Trump—Mo Stopher (Sharpo)
576^9 2551^11 6802^12

Robinzal *C J Mann* 70
3 b g Zilzal(USA) —Sulitelma (USA) (The Minstrel (CAN))
5734^3

Rob Roy (USA) *Sir Michael Stoute* 120
4 b h Lear Fan(USA) —Camanoe (USA) (Gone West (USA))
(1299) 1840^6 4038^3 4839^6 5964^2 6342a^5

Rob's Love (ITY) *R Menichetti* 94
2 b c Rob's Spirit(USA) —Eros Love (ITY) (Love The Groom (USA))
6123a^2

Robustian *R F Johnson Houghton* a63 87
3 b g Robellino(USA) —Pontressina (USA) (St Jovite (USA))
1190^3 2177^2 2581^2 2781^3 3119^4 3589^2 3911^2 4810^8 5164^5 (5478) 6097^12

Rocamadour *M R Channon* 115
4 b h Celtic Swing—Watch Me (IRE) (Green Desert (USA))
1084^6 1712a^4 1840^9 3881^3 4145^4 4828a^8 5142^4 5675^31

Roca Redonda (IRE) *D J Daly* 69
2 b f Fasliyev(USA) —Devil's Crown (USA) (Chief's Crown (USA))
4552^5 5296^6

Rochdale *M A Jarvis* a106 94
3 ch g Bertolini(USA) —Owdbetts (IRE) (High Estate)
1097^4 (1679) 2329^8 2866^3 3296^7 (3722) 4357^6 5785^2

Rochesis *Miss K B Boutflower* 72
3 b f Mujahid(USA) —Northern Bird (Interrex (CAN))
4003^5

Rockall Blizzard (USA) *Noel Meade* 104
3 gr c Cozzene(USA) —Kentucky Storm (USA) (Dynaformer (USA))
5396a^5 5854a^8

Rock Anthem (IRE) *J L Dunlop* 77
2 ch c Rock Of Gibraltar(IRE) —Regal Portrait (IRE) (Royal Academy (USA))
4768^9 5339^4 5939^11

Rockatorri *G G Margarson* 37
3 b f Vettori(IRE) —Lady Rockstar (Rock Hopper)
1822^9 1955^12 2349^13 3870^9 4263^5 4491^4 4868^5 5365^6 5441^3 5757^8 6057^6

Rockazar *G M Lyons* 96
5 b g Opening Verse(USA) —Final Rush (Final Straw)
(1156a) 3123a^21 4031a^18

Rockbranglen (USA) *F Reuterskiold*
3 b g Sandpit(BRZ) —Medicine Path (USA) (Strawberry Road (AUS))
4419a^6

Rockburst *K R Burke* 64
4 b m Xaar—Topwinder (USA) (Topsider (USA))
2377^5 2737^10 2891^5

Rock Concert *I W McInnes* a39 30
8 b m Bishop Of Cashel—Summer Pageant (Chief's Crown (USA))
172^13 390^10 527^13

Rock Diva (IRE) *P C Haslam* a34
2 ch f Rock Of Gibraltar(IRE) —Merlannah (IRE) (Shy Groom (USA))
6481^11

Rocker *B R Johnson* a68 70
2 b g Rock Of Gibraltar(IRE) —Jessica's Dream (IRE) (Desert Style (IRE))
2402^8 5147^3 5496^3 5753^4 (6838)

Rocket (IRE) *H J Manners* a12 27
5 ch g Cadeaux Genereux—Prends Ca (IRE) (Reprimand)
1460^10 3948^13 6019^12

Rocket Force (USA) *N Wilson* a49 81
6 ch g Spinning World(USA) —Pat Us (USA) (Caucasus (USA))
1144^4 1756^2 2000^2 2296^3 2850^9 3686^10

Rockets 'n Rollers (IRE) *M Al Muhairi* a98 109
6 b h Victory Note(USA) —Holly Bird (Runnett)
203a^8 353a^5 563a^8

Rock Fever (IRE) *Peter Grayson* a51 43
4 ch m Desert Sun—Icefern (Moorestyle)
216^11 307^11 532^11 789^11 (1466) 1534^10 1909^9

Rockfonic *J R Weymes* 52
2 br c Rock Of Gibraltar(IRE) —Procession (Zafonic (USA))
4055^4 4650^6 5402^7 5613^16

Rock Haven (IRE) *J Mackie* a24 68
4 b g Danehill Dancer(IRE) —Mahabba (USA) (Elocutionist (USA))
162^10 405^13 3944^6 (4404) 4709^15 5485^5

Rockie *T Hogan* 98+
3 b c Bertolini(USA) —Breezy Louise (Dilum (USA))
755a^4

Rock Lily *Charles O'Brien* 82
2 b f Rock Of Gibraltar(IRE) —Persian Song (Persian Bold)
6357a^7

Rockmaster (IRE) *F Brogi* 104
3 b c Galileo(IRE) —Cromac (ITY) (Machiavellian (USA))
1872a^3

Rock Music *Saeed Bin Suroor* a102 87
4 ch h Singspiel(IRE) —Stack Rock (Ballad Rock)
(277a) (434a) 560a^6

Rock 'N' Roller (FR) *W R Muir* 68
2 bb c Sagacity(FR) —Diamond Dance (FR) (Dancehall (USA))
5340 8 5623^4

Rock Of Cloonavery (IRE) *S C Williams* a53 66
3 b g Desert Prince(IRE) —Mackla (Caerleon (USA))
234^8 475^11 642^4 984^6 1141^12 1829^4 2101^11 2566^8

Rock Opera (SAF) *A Laird* a82 93
4 b m Lecture(USA) —Drummer Girl (SAF) (Al Mufti (USA))
155a^3 436a^3 494a^11 623a^9

Rockpiler *D W Thompson* 42
4 b g Halling(USA) —Emma Peel (Emarati (USA))
2829^7 3192^10 4252^9 4960^13

Rocksham (IRE) *J J Lennon* 56
6 b m Bluebird(USA) —Kates Choice (IRE) (Taufan (USA))
3660a^8

Rocky Reppin *J Balding* a48 37
6 b g Rock City—Tino Reppin (Neltino)
27^8 616^8 638^3 689^3 941^2 1225^12 1575^6 1765^9 6554^9 6814^6 6970^6

Roclette (USA) *B W Hills* 79
2 ch f Rock Of Gibraltar(IRE) —Rose Bourbon (USA) (Woodman (USA))
2638^6 2958^4 4260^F 4843^3

Rodeo *B W Hills* 82
3 ch g Pivotal—Flossy (Efisio)
1134^2 4117^6 4806^4

Roehampton *H J Brown* a97 103
5 b h Machiavellian(USA) —Come On Rosi (Valiyar)
152a^10

Rogers Lodger *J Akehurst* 16
2 b g Cyrano De Bergerac—Bertrade (Homeboy)
6330^13

Rogue *Jane Southcombe* a50 74
4 b m Royal Applause—Mystique (Mystiko (USA))
1513^7 2383^2 3090^3 3950^2 4484^5 5055^7

Rohaani (USA) *Sir Michael Stoute* a103 108
4 ch h High Yield(USA) —Strawberry's Charm (USA) (Strawberry Road (AUS))
1017^2 1267^10 4098^14 4739^7 (5188) 5675^25

Roheryn (IRE) *John A Quinn* a41 75
2 b g Efisio—Special One (Aragon)
(5315) 5528^3 5788^11 6400^6

Roisin's Star (IRE) *M M Lynch* 95
6 b m Accordion—Lightning Bolt (IRE) (Magical Strike (USA))
4094a^16

Roko *S R Bowring* a43 30
4 b g Komaite(USA) —Robert's Daughter (Robellino (USA))
674^5 876^13 943^6 1397^12 1577^4 2245^11 2758^11 3595^7 4389^12 6962^11

Rokocoko (IRE) *John A Quinn* 67?
4 b h Fasliyev(USA) —Early Memory (USA) (Devil's Bag (USA))
4636^6

Rollerbird *T Hogan* a54 64
4 b m Sinndar(IRE) —Speedybird (IRE) (Danehill (USA))
6448^11

Rolling Home (GER) *A Wohler* 94+
2 b c Dashing Blade—Roma Libera (GER) (Pharly (FR))
(5763a)

Rolons Advice *V Smith* a17
5 ch g Weldnaas(USA) —Clova (Move Off)
6314^9 6482^8

Rol'Over Beethoven (FR) *A P O'Brien* 92+
3 b c Mozart(IRE) —Don't Worry Me (IRE) (Dancing Dissident (USA))
4083^10

Romanae Memento (ITY) *F & L Camici* 70
3 b c Diktat—Talikota (ITY) (Fire Of Life (USA))
758a^4

Roman Arch (AUS) *R Laing* 113
7 b g Archway(IRE) —Celestial Option (AUS) (Clear Choice (USA))
6110a^16 6347a^5

Roman Boy (ARG) *Stef Liddiard* a53 71
7 ch g Roy(USA) —Roman Red (USA) (Blushing Groom (FR))
3995^6 6897^8

Roman Empire *P A Blockley* a65 52
6 b g Efisio—Gena Ivor (USA) (Sir Ivor (USA))
9^8 67^3 (127) 274^10 492^3 581^2 602^2 650^3 1152^5 1258^5

Roman History (IRE) *Miss Tracy Waggott* a35 58
3 b g Titus Livius(FR) —Tetradonna (IRE) (Teenoso (USA))
347^10 1073^10 2192^5 2696^6 3288^2 3762^12 4057^6 (4350) 4456^6 4943^4 (5240)

Roman Maze *W M Brisbourne* a91 102
6 ch g Lycius(USA) —Maze Garden (USA) (Riverman (USA))
627^5 1050^4 1629^4 2017^11 3550^6 3928^3 4172^3 4760^7 4790^11 5336^21 5529^7 5877^7

Romanoff (GER) *M Weiss*
3 br c Silvano(GER) —Royal Army (GER) (Pirate Army (USA))
2717a^3

Romanova (IRE) *Dr J R J Naylor* a50 69
4 b m Grand Lodge(USA) —Millitrix (Doyoun)
660^9 854^12 1214^6 1772^12 2460^13 3798^10 4289^8 4755^9 5259^9

Romanov Dynasty (IRE) *R Hannon* 79
2 br c Green Desert(USA) —Russian Rebel (Machiavellian (USA))
3445^2 4129^7 4479^7 5125^4 5466a^20 5916^12

Roman Quest *H Morrison* a65 85+
3 b g Lujain(USA) —Roma (Second Set (IRE))
658^5 (969) 1109^4 1825^11 (2609) 3226^3 3487^4 5476^12

Roman Quintet (IRE) *D W P Arbuthnot* a76 79
6 ch g Titus Livius(FR) —Quintellina (Robellino (USA))
541^4 721^7 949^6 1545^3 2074^11 3012^2 3486^8 4564^6 4807^8 5263^4 5778^13 6036^7

Romany Nights (IRE) *Miss Gay Kelleway* a69 93
6 b g Night Shift(USA) —Gipsy Moth (Efisio)
1359^6 (1474) 1667^3 2047^10 2824^2 3486^4 3904^8 4106^2 5420^12

Rome (IRE) *G P Enright* a77 56
7 br g Singspiel(IRE) —Ela Romara (Ela-Mana-Mou)
264^12

Romeo Plus (ARG) *P Gallagher* a91 84
6 b h Alpha Plus(USA) —Helen Toss (ARG) (Egg Toss (USA))
5826a^7

Romil Star (GER) *M Wellings* a64 52
9 b g Chief's Crown(USA) —Romelia (USA) (Woodman (USA))
5^4 126^7 52^2 243^2 273^4 425^3 490^2 549^3 607^2 625^2 (857) 975^11 1385^2 1560^4 2140^4 2395^3 2528^5 3260^2 3382^3 3998^6 6551^3

Ronaldo *A M Hales* a25 55
3 b g Tomba—Satiric (IRE) (Doyoun)
880[17] 964[9] 1049[5] 1352[11] 1616[13]4363[15] 4672[4] 4869[13] 5097[10]

Ronaldsay *R Hannon* a60+ 79
2 gr f Kirkwall—Crackling (Electric)
2980[6] 3868[2] 4553[2](5157)

Ronannis *J Jay* 31
2 b c Efisio—Blown-Over (Ron's Victory (USA))
3979[11] 4843[6] 5348[9]

Rondo *T D Barron* 76
3 b g Piccolo—Flourish (Selkirk (USA))
(1127) 1482[11] 2855[7] 2976[6] 3360[7] 3722[10]3943[7] 4296[9] 4695[4] 5418[6] 5637[8]5865[15]

Ron In Ernest *J A Geake* 62
2 ch g Medicean—Viewfinder (USA) (Boundary (USA))
2530[6] 3025[8] 3485[3] 4480[10] 5372[14]

Ronnie From Donny (IRE) *C J Teague* a7
6 b g Eagle Eyed(USA) —New Rochelle (IRE) (Lafontaine (USA))
1762[10] 2874[14] 6943[7]

Ronnie Howe *M Dods* 73
2 b g Hunting Lion(IRE) —Arasong (Aragon)
2361[7] 2759[2] 3351[4] 3907[4] 4251[7]5076[3] 5746[3]

Ronnies Lad *J R Norton* a55 41
4 b g Lake Coniston(IRE) —Lycius Touch (Lycius (USA))
2291[6] 2832[10] 3022[8] 3762[13] 4467[14]5929[10] 6552[8]6898[5]

Ronsard (IRE) *J C Tuck* a57 59
4 b g Spectrum(IRE) —Touche-A-Tout (IRE) (Royal Academy (USA))
115[10] 319[8]504[8] 571[11]965[16] 3390[6] 3947[7]4389[5] 4709[5] 4982[15] 5609[3]6405[12]

Roodolph *R F Johnson Houghton* 74+
2 ch g Primo Valentino(IRE) —Roo (Rudimentary (USA))
(5417)

Rooftop Protest (IRE) *T Hogan* 87
9 b g Thatching—Seattle Siren (USA) (Seattle Slew (USA))
1033[5]

Rookwith (IRE) *T G McCourt* a69 71
6 b g Revoque(IRE) —Resume (IRE) (Lahib (USA))
4094a[11]

Roonah (FR) *Karen McLintock* a10 44
3 b f Xaar—Caer Mecene (FR) (Caerwent)
76[7] 211[12]3023[8] 3330[9] 6272[10]

Rosa Chester (IRE) *R J Osborne* 42
2 b f Chester House(USA) —Nunatall (Night Shift (USA))
4824a[22]

Rosada (ITY) *M Innocenti*
2 b f Rossini(USA) —Foresta Verde (USA) (Green Forest (USA))
3427a[6]

Rosalie *C F Wall* a38 66
3 ch f Fantastic Light(USA) —Tularosa (In The Wings)
2434[12] 3400[10]

Rosamixa (FR) *A Fabre* 95
2 gr f Linamix(FR) —Rose Quartz (Lammtarra (USA))
4621a[4]

Rosapenna (IRE) *C F Wall* a72 83
4 b m Spectrum(IRE) —Blaine (USA) (Lyphard's Wish (FR))
1188[6] 2233[3] (2590) 3217[12] (4003)

Rosbay (IRE) *T D Easterby* 85
2 b c Desert Prince(IRE) —Dark Rosaleen (IRE) (Darshaan)
1595[6] 1945[4] 2361[5] (3175) 3633[2] (4882) 5359[4]5958[11]

Roscommon *I Semple* 65
3 br g Fraam—Gaelic Air (Ballad Rock)
2239[8] 3782[5] 4353[9] 4652[10]

Rose Amber *J J Bridger* a28
5 ch m Double Trigger(IRE) —Sun Follower (Relkino)
35[9] 114[14]

Rose Bien *P J McBride* a59 69
4 bb m Bien Bien(USA) —Madame Bovary (Ile De Bourbon (USA))
574[7] 733[8]1058[5] 1199[2] (1392) 1745[4] (3035) (3284) (3763) 3955[5]4632[2] 5069[5] 5324[2] 5875[9]

Rose Briar (IRE) *R Charlton* a37 62
3 b f Grand Lodge(USA) —My Branch (Distant Relative)
1085[10] 1649[5] 1956[7] 2301[12] 4044[14]

Rosecliff *Heather Dalton* a67 76
4 b g Montjeu(IRE) —Dance Clear (IRE) (Marju (IRE))
5792[19]

Rose Court *K G Reveley* 28
2 b f Celtic Swing—Smart Spirit (IRE) (Persian Bold)
1121[7] 2523[9] 3246[9] 3619[9] 4376[11]5679[13]

Rose Germany *M R Channon* 60
2 ch f Inchinor—Hoist (IRE) (Bluebird (USA))
4964[14] 5380[7] 5894[8]

Rosein *Mrs G S Rees* a82 66
4 b m Komaite(USA) —Red Rosein (Red Sunset)
(2248) 2417[12] 3217[6] 3459[2]3996[2] 4437[5]5246[11] (5391) 5593[5] (5842) 6428[4]6499[4]

Rose Lady (IRE) *M R Channon* a44 67
3 ch f King Of Kings(IRE) —Shamisen (Diesis)
1417[2] 1844[15] 2406[15] 5036[9]

Rosemarkie *J L Spearing* a6
2 br f Diktat—Sparkling Isle (Inchinor)
6486[12]

Rose Muwasim *M J Attwater* a68 67
3 ch f In The Wings—Muwasim (USA) (Meadowlake (USA))
372[2] 539[2]855[5] 1599[6] 1997[9]6643[7] 6771[5]6988[2]

Rosencrans (USA) *Saeed Bin Suroor* a106 84
5 b g Forest Wildcat(USA) —General's Mistress (USA) (General Meeting (USA))
431a[8]

Rosenkreuz (JPN) *K Hashiguchi* 114
4 br h Sunday Silence(USA) —Rose Colour (USA) (Shirley Heights)
1329a[8]

Rose Of Battle *M Halford* 78
2 b f Averti(IRE) —Sky Red (Night Shift (USA))
2309a[6]

Rose Of Inchinor *R E Barr* 69
3 b f Inchinor—Rosa Canina (Bustino)
2177[9] 3055[12] 4527[3]4943[8] 5902[14]

Rose Of Petra (IRE) *Sir Michael Stoute* a81 81
2 b f Golan(IRE) —Desert Beauty (IRE) (Green Desert (USA))
4373[10] 5083[2] (5449) 6074[4]

Rose Thistle (UAE) *John A Quinn* a49 65
4 b m Timber Country(USA) —Ines Bloom (IRE) (Sadler's Wells (USA))
59[7] 170[10]358[9]

Roshanak (IRE) *B J Meehan* 81
2 b f Spinning World(USA) —Desert Bloom (IRE) (Pilsudski (IRE))
3700[7] (4053)

Rosie Cross (IRE) *R F Johnson Houghton* a65 52
2 b f Cape Cross(IRE) —Professional Mom (USA) (Spinning World (USA))
1959[4] 2456[6] 3201[7]4427[9] 5738[10]

Rosiella *M Appleby* a46 46
4 b m Tagula(IRE) —Queen Of Silk (IRE) (Brief Truce (USA))
209[10] 321[11]501[8] 2568[4] 3024[7]3161[6] 3592[8] 3896[6]

Rosie's Glory (USA) *B J Meehan* 76
2 bb f More Than Ready(USA) —Cukee (USA) (Langfuhr (CAN))
4373[8] 5460[3] 5828[6]

Rosie's Result *M Todhunter* a40 53
6 ch g Case Law—Precious Girl (Precious Metal)
1396[7] 1886[6] 2780[3]2928[8] 3334[6] 3781[2] 4477[6] (4523)

Rosinka (IRE) *J L Dunlop* 89+
3 b f Soviet Star(USA) —Last Drama (IRE) (Last Tycoon)
3702[4] 4808[7]

Rosita Mia (IRE) *D W Barker* a37 64
3 ch f Dr Fong(USA) —Intercede (Pursuit Of Love)
1497[6] 2019[3] 2399[8] 2758[6]

Roslea Lady (IRE) *Liam McAteer* a61 61
3 b f Alhaarth(IRE) —Aguinaga (IRE) (Machiavellian (USA))
4034a[10]

Rossin Gold (IRE) *P Monteith* a66 55?
4 b g Rossini(USA) —Sacred Heart (IRE) (Catrail (USA))
1608[6] 5061[2]

Ross Is Boss *C J Teague* a8 16
4 gr g Paris House—Billie Grey (Chilibang)
6944[7] 6974[10]

Ross Moor *N P Littmoden* a74 67
4 b g Dansili—Snipe Hall (Crofthall)
(6916)

Rosthwaite (IRE) *Ronald Thompson* a57 71
3 b f Desert Style(IRE) —Thirlmere (Cadeaux Genereux)
76[5] 730[9] 1122[13]2525[9] 4548[8] 5370[13] 6674[11]

Rotation (IRE) *J W Hills* 41
2 b g Galileo(IRE) —Termania (IRE) (Shirley Heights)
5043[11] 5347[11] 5871[10]

Rothesay Dancer *J S Goldie* a66 67
3 b f Lujain(USA) —Rhinefield Beauty (IRE) (Shalford (IRE))
1036[11] 1448[7] 2161[3] 2449[11] 2925[5]3000[3] 3479[2] (3587) 3636[2] 4135[4] 4725[7]5309[14] 5333[14] 5684[8] 6162[8] 6315[12]6521[2] 6622[11]

Rotuma (IRE) *M Dods* a57 67
7 b g Tagula(IRE) —Cross Question (USA) (Alleged (USA))
229[11] 1075[10] 1591[2]1850[3] 2149[5] 2181[4] 2808[11] 3784[2](4570) 5445[6] 5954[9]

Rouen (IRE) *M R Channon* 86
2 b c Noverre(USA) —Sheezalady (Zafonic (USA))
727[2] 944[4] 1595[2] 1770[P] (Dead)

Rouge (FR) *C Laffon-Parias* 93
3 b f Red Ransom(USA) —Natural Gold (FR) (Mr Prospector (USA))
5472a[4]

Rouge Et Noir *P Monteith* a49 56
8 b g Hernando(FR) —Bayrouge (IRE) (Gorytus (USA))
1560[11] 2528[3] 3135[7] 3350[3] 3810[9]4954[8] 5836[9]

Round Pond (USA) *M Matz* a121
4 b m Awesome Again(CAN) —Gift Of Dance (USA) (Trempolino (USA))
5818a[3] (6343a)

Rovana Jowe (GER) *A Wohler* 99
3 b f Silvano(GER) —Rovana (GER) (Dashing Blade)
2043a[3]

Rowanberry *R M H Cowell* a57+ 53
4 b m Bishop Of Cashel—Raintree Venture (Good Times (ITY))
1195[3] 1539[2]1913[2] 2376[6] 2611[11]3334[3] 3825[14] 6704[2]6805[7]

Rowan Lodge (IRE) *M H Tompkins* a79 80
4 ch g Indian Lodge(IRE) —Tirol Hope (IRE) (Tirol)
1302[3] 2983[4] 3404[8]4457[3] 4990[5] 5362[7] 5599[3] 5734[6]5904[9] (6059) 6176[12]

Rowan Pursuit *J Akehurst* a57? 43
5 b m Pursuit Of Love—Golden Seattle (IRE) (Seattle Dancer (USA))
235[3] 297[4]458[5] 575[7]708[8] 853[5]

Rowan River *M H Tompkins* 60
2 b f Invincible Spirit(IRE) —Lemon Tree (USA) (Zilzal (USA))
2643[6] 4553[5] 5380[10]

Rowan Venture *M H Tompkins* a54 59
2 b g Vettori(IRE) —Golden Seattle (IRE) (Seattle Dancer (USA))
2178[13] 2979[13] 3844[12]4987[5] 5646[11] 5738[11]6016[6]

Rowan Warning *J R Boyle* a65 67
4 b g Diktat—Golden Seattle (IRE) (Seattle Dancer (USA))
74[4] 163[4]268[5] 440[2]2184[10] 2317[3] 2645[10] 3153[7] 5474[17]5885[11] 6779[2] (6829)

Rowe Park *Mrs L C Jewell* a74 51
3 b g Dancing Spree(USA) —Magic Legs (Reprimand)
3122[8] 3647[8] 5093[6]6348[7] (6440) (6688) (6994)

Roxan (IRE) *K A Ryan* 102+
2 b f Rock Of Gibraltar(IRE) —Gamra (IRE) (Green Desert (USA))
(2125) 2743[11] 5356[2]

Roxy Singer *W J Musson* a30 33
2 b f Erhaab(USA) —Rainy Day Song (Persian Bold)
2626[7] 3640[10] 3915[7]4334[10]

Roya *R Hannon* 70
3 b c Daylami(IRE) —Aegean Dream (IRE) (Royal Academy (USA))
1880[5] 2434[7] 3347[5] 3849[4] 4533[2]4982[9]

Royal Agreement *B G Powell* 56
3 b g Royal Applause—Another Fantasy (IRE) (Danehill (USA))
1433[9] 2479[3] 2877[8] 3164[8]

Royal Alchemist *B J Meehan* a101 108
4 b m Kingsinger(IRE) —Pure Gold (Dilum (USA))
(1015) 1506[2] 2041a[3] 2740[3] 3314[7] 3534[7]5675[14]

Royal Amnesty *G C H Chung* a82 53
3 br c Desert Prince(IRE) —Regal Peace (Known Fact (USA))
(642) (822) (1005) (1381) 1841[15] (2344) 2754[7]3973[13] 4249[6] 5016[4]6076[3] 6351[4]6661[5] 6968[3]

Royal Approach *J R Norton* a25 58
5 b m Royal Applause—Passionelle (Nashwan (USA))
5683[13] 5922[4] 6302[9]

Royal Auditon *T T Clement* a68 65
5 ch m First Trump—Loriner's Lass (Saddlers' Hall (IRE))
503[12] 1436[12] 1879[6]

Royal Axminster *Mrs P N Dutfield* a56 50
11 b g Alzao(USA) —Number One Spot (Reference Point)
230[11] 379[14](636) 911[4]1256[4] 2481[3] 3998[10]

Royal Bandit *N A Callaghan* a76 56
3 b c King Charlemagne(USA) —Cutpurse Moll (Green Desert (USA))
722[2] 801[4]916[6] 1609[4] 2864[11]5432[11]

Royal Beacon *Christian Wroe* a37 107
6 b h Royal Applause—Tenderetta (Tender King)
278a[P]

Royal Borough *R M Beckett* 48
3 ch g Compton Place—Norpella (Northfields (USA))
4799[9] 5092[11]

Royal Challenge *M H Tompkins* 89
5 b g Royal Applause—Anotheranniversary (Emarati (USA))
970[10] 1183[3] 1474[5] 1949[5] (2302) 2661[7]3251[2] (3880)

Royal Choir *C E Brittain* a73
2 ch f King's Best(USA) —Harmonic Sound (IRE) (Grand Lodge (USA))
6186[4]

Royal Citadel (IRE) *C G Cox* a10 72
3 b f City On A Hill(USA) —Royal Baldini (USA) (Green Dancer (USA))
1646[2] 2050[4] 2583[9] 3349[7] 3793[12]4870[10] 5418[7] 5874[9]

Royal Composer (IRE) *T D Easterby* 72
3 b g Mozart(IRE) —Susun Kelapa (USA) (St Jovite (USA))
1185[6] 1592[2] 2126[4] 2441[5] 3282[3]3606[9] 4257[10] 5446[9]

Royal Copenhagen (FR) *C Block* 110
4 b m Inchinor—Amnesia (USA) (Septieme Ciel (USA))
4385a[6] 6368a[3]

Royal Crescent (IRE) *Sir Mark Prescott* a39+
3 b f Spectrum(IRE) —Marling (IRE) (Lomond (USA))
45[6] 195[10]

Royal Curtsy *Sir Mark Prescott* a66+ 54
3 b f Pivotal—Fen Princess (IRE) (Trojan Fen)
2466[2]

Royal Dignitary (USA) *D Nicholls* a90 91
6 br g Saint Ballado(CAN) —Star Actress (USA) (Star De Naskra (USA))
719[8] 1143[14] (1455) 1629[8] (2454) 3079[6] 3500[3]3928[8] 4379[6] (4953) 5355[13]

Royal Embrace *D Shaw* a57 50
3 b g Bertolini(USA) —Tight Spin (High Top)
49[7] 123[6]211[2] 364[2]2210[11] 6624[4]6901[4]

Royal Envoy (IRE) *B W Hills* 79d
3 b g Royal Applause—Seven Notes (Zafonic (USA))
1135[2] (1493) 2205[11] 2863[9] 6065[11]

Royal Fantasy (IRE) *J R Fanshawe* 67+
3 bb f King's Best(USA) —Dreams (Rainbow Quest (USA))
1351[5] 2673[2]

Royal Fire (GER) *Miss A Casotti*
7 b h Bin Ajwaad(IRE) —Royal Future (IRE) (Royal Academy (USA))
306a[4]

Royal Flynn *M Dods* 67
4 b g Royal Applause—Shamriyna (IRE) (Darshaan)
1233[6] 1756[5] 2075[4] 2193[7] 3037[3]3333[2] 3792[4] 4606[12] 4709[3] 5064[4](5385) 5904[8] (5954) 6301[4]

Royal Glen (IRE) *W S Coltherd* 49
8 b m Royal Abjar(USA) —Sea Glen (IRE) (Glenstal (USA))
1034[7] 1436[9] 3815[10]

Royal Guest *M R Channon* a54 39
2 b g Royal Applause—Bajan Blue (Lycius (USA))
5508[7] 6257[7]

Royal Highness (GER) *P Bary* 115
4 b m Monsun(GER) —Reem Dubai (IRE) (Nashwan (USA))
1331a[2] 2277a[6] 4192a[4] 5220a[3] 5821a[3]

Royal Indulgence *W M Brisbourne* a43 69
6 b g Royal Applause—Silent Indulgence (USA) (Woodman (USA))
1462[4] 1724[6]2482[7] (2697) 2789[13] 3484[8] 3716[4] 3947[3]4068[7] 4355[4] (4565) 5173[3] 5354[6] 5579[8]

Royal Intrigue (IRE) *D K Weld* 106
3 b c Royal Applause—Congress (IRE) (Dancing Brave (USA))
928a[7] 5190a[5]

Royal Island (IRE) *M Johnston* a105 110
4 b h Trans Island—Royal House (FR) (Royal Academy (USA))
116[3] 456a[4] 629[9]728[2] 1017[11] 1678[13]2200[13] 4348[8] 4739[12] 5675[22]

Royal Jet *M R Channon* a98 92
4 b g Royal Applause—Red Bouquet (Reference Point)
3294[8] 3501[5] 3890[2] 4259[7] 4997[2]5430[2] 5776[3]6097[3]

Royal Lass *Rae Guest* a28
3 b f Fraam—Sabotini (Prince Sabo)
308[6] 528[11]

Royal Lustre *Robert Gray* a50 19
5 b g Deputy Minister(CAN) —Snow Bride (USA) (Blushing Groom (FR))
615[7] 635[8]857[8] 1460[2]

Royal Master *P C Haslam* a70 64
4 b g Royal Applause—High Sevens (Master Willie)
1075[P] 2108[9] 5497[2]

Royal Melbourne (IRE) *Miss J A Camacho* a57 66
6 ch g Among Men(USA) —Calachuchi (Martinmas)
767[8] 1346[11] 4947[2]5750[5] 6158[9]

Royal Millennium (IRE) *M R Channon* 106
8 b g Royal Academy(USA) —Galatrix (Be My Guest (USA))
1069[11] 1778[16] 3076[7]

Royal Mirage (FR) *P Bary* a100 95
3 b g Zafonic(USA) —Tiara (Risk Me (FR))
1178a[9]

Royal Moon (USA) *T D Barron* a55 50
3 ch g Royal Academy(USA) —Wedding Gift (FR) (Always Fair (USA))
10[6] 445[4]979[9] 1149[5] 1501[6]

Royal Oath (USA) *J H M Gosden* a101+ 87
3 b c Kingmambo(USA) —Sherkiya (IRE) (Goldneyev (USA))
1844[9] (2411) (3532) 3889[5] 6192[10]

Royal Obsession (IRE) *J G M O'Shea* 28
2 b f Val Royal(FR) —Britique (USA) (Critique (USA))
6025[10] 6330[10]

Royal Orissa *D Haydn Jones* a69 92d
4 b g Royal Applause—Ling Lane (Slip Anchor)
846[13] 1285[15] 1545[7]1820[12] 2189[14] 2384[9] 3368[16] 6572[9]

Royal Pardon *R C Guest* 58
4 b m Royal Applause—Miss Mercy (IRE) (Law Society (USA))
1123[16] 1500[5] 1636[2] 1761[3] 2198[8]2544[14] 2891[8] 3484[5] 3786[9] 4070[2]4198[3] 4455[8]

Royal Pennekamp (FR) *H-A Pantall* 95
3 b c Pennekamp(USA) —Lead Cora (FR) (Lead On Time (USA))
1557a[6] 6384a[7]

Royal Power (IRE) *M R Channon* a95 107
3 b c Xaar—Magic Touch (Fairy King (USA))
829[2] 1175a[2] (1715a) 2721[7]3342a[9] 4596[5] 5341[12]

Royal Premier (IRE) *H J Collingridge* a62 61
3 b c King's Theatre(IRE) —Mystic Shadow (IRE) (Mtoto)
1052[12] 1652[8] 2102[6] (5129) 5385[8] 6383[8]6565[12] 6812[2]

Royal Prince *Doug Watson* a70 107
5 gr h Royal Applause—Onefortheditch (USA) (With Approval (CAN))
(438a)

Royal Prodigy (USA) *R J Hodges* a74 74
7 ch g Royal Academy(USA) —Prospector's Queen (USA) (Mr Prospector (USA))
(1624a)

Royal Rationale (IRE) *W J Haggas* a76 61
2 b g Desert Prince(IRE) —Logic (Slip Anchor)
4801[5] 5297[10] 5648[6]6257[2]

Royal Reservation *P W Chapple-Hyam* a84 70
3 b c Royal Applause—Wig Wam (IRE) (Indian Ridge)
(294) 1095[7] 1384[9] 5428[9]6076[9]

Royal Rumble (IRE) *G Miliani*
2 ch c Shantou(USA) —Fedina (Shaamit (IRE))
2474a[9]

Royal Sailor (IRE) *J Ryan* a56 61
4 b g Bahhare(USA) —Old Tradition (IRE) (Royal Academy (USA))
2935[12] 3339[12] 3614[13]3933[18] 4009[9] 4266[12] 4667[9] 6800[8]6971[4]

Royal Senga *C A Horgan* a19 54
3 b f Agnes World(USA) —Katyushka (IRE) (Soviet Star (USA))
1960[10] 3090[4] 4162[4]5055[5]

Royal Song *D Shaw* a32 32
3 b c Royal Applause—La Caprice (USA) (Housebuster (USA))
790[12] 874[6]4426[10] 4943[13]

Royal Spell *M Appleby*
4 b m Wizard King—Manadel (Governor General)
289[10]

Royal Storm (IRE) *Mrs A J Perrett* a94 106
7 b h Royal Applause—Wakayi (Persian Bold)
366a[2] 431a[2] 506a[4] 1069[5] 1407[7]1487[19] 2846[16]

Royal Supremacy (IRE) *J M Bradley* 39
5 ch m Desert Prince(IRE) —Saucy Maid (IRE) (Sure Blade (USA))
2494[10] 3267[12] 3348[9] 4226[8] 4675[10]

Royal Tavira Girl (IRE) *M G Quinlan* a57 63
3 b f Orpen(USA) —Just Like Annie (IRE) (Mujadil (USA))
590[3] 776[5] 1263[5]2648[7] 3072[2] 3453[2]3668[2] 3869[5] 4052[7] 5690[7]

Royal Tender (IRE) *V Smith* a50
2 gr f Woods Of Windsor(USA) —Tender Guest (IRE) (Be My Guest (USA))
6143[11] 6737[9]

Royal Tiara (UAE) *Saeed Bin Suroor* a45
2 br f Machiavellian(USA) —Crown Of Light (Mtoto)
6099[7]

Royalties *M A Allen* a13
4 b m Mujahid(USA) —Rock Face (Ballad Rock)
3261[10] 5741[9]
Royle Dancer *R Hollinshead* a63 64
3 b g Makbul—Foxtrot Pie (Shernazar)
4470[8] 4757[4] 5384[3] *6314[P]6451[9] 6871[7]6977[5]*
Rubber (IRE) *R Hannon* a66 85
3 b f Namid—Bold Fashion (FR) (Nashwan (USA))
1110[3]
Rubber Duck (IRE) *Peter Grayson* a25
2 b f Daggers Drawn(USA) —Dhuhook (USA) (Dixieland Band (USA))
3408[9] 3645[11]4138[9] 4971[7]6975[6]
Rubenstar (IRE) *M H Tompkins* a84 85
3 b g Soviet Star(USA) —Ansariya (USA) (Shahrastani (USA))
1067[14] *1337[6]* 2126[3]2620[2] 2809[5] 3740[5] 3889[7] 5504[6]5833[5] *(6094)*
Rubilini *M R Channon* 55
2 ch f Bertolini(USA) —Aunt Ruby (USA) (Rubiano (USA))
2957[7] 3335[4]
Ruby Hill (GER) *W Baltromei* 99
4 b m Tiger Hill(IRE) —Ruby Lady (GER) (Master Willie)
1974a[11] 4383a[5]
Ruby Legend *K G Reveley* 63
8 b g Perpendicular—Singing High (Julio Mariner)
1757[9] 2282[6] 2696[10] 2832[2] 3333[4](3566) 3941[5] 4301[6] 4568[U] 5064[5] (5354) 5497[3]6008[17]
Ruby Muja *T G McCourt* a48 58
4 b m Mujahid(USA) —Ruby Julie (Clantime)
7321[3]
Ruby Rubble *K R Burke* 50
3 b f Distant Music(USA) —Topwinder (USA) (Topsider (USA))
2699[6] 3329[7] 3910[13]
Ruby's Dream *J M Bradley* a49 60
4 b m Tipsy Creek(USA) —Sure Flyer (IRE) (Sure Blade (USA))
*954[10] 1243[7]*1413[13] 1774[7] 2897[3] (3004) 3267[2] 3728[11]3897[9] 4484[7] 4985[15]
Ruby Sunrise (IRE) *B P J Baugh* a48 23
4 ch m Polish Precedent(USA) —Kinlochewe (Old Vic)
467[9] 793[11]1225[10] 5844[7]6277[9] 6429[9]6616[12] 6701[8]6792[6] 6898[8]
Ruby Wine *J M P Eustace* 105
4 b m Kayf Tara—Cribella (USA) (Robellino (USA))
3627[3] 4179[5] 4741[P]
Rudaki *M E Sowersby* a56 57
4 ch g Opening Verse(USA) —Persian Fountain (IRE) (Persian Heights)
2360[10] 2789[11] 2832[4] 3377[6] 3762[10]3944[3] 4381[4] 4467[6] 4909[6] 5240[12]
Rudi's Pet (IRE) *D Nicholls* a50 79
12 ch g Don't Forget Me—Pink Fondant (Northfields (USA))
1886[4] 2396[11] 2748[5] *3155[4]*(3354) 3699[3] 3833[3]
Rudry Dragon (IRE) *P A Blockley* a27 74
2 b c Princely Heir(IRE) —Jazz Up (Cadeaux Genereux)
4105[6] 5665[8] *5841[11]*
Rudry World (IRE) *P A Blockley* a54
3 ch g Spinning World(USA) —Fancy Boots (IRE) (Salt Dome (USA))
70[7] 1247[7]272[4] 604[11]
Rue D'Alsace *B Olsen* 92
4 b m Danehill Dancer(IRE) —Dim Ofan (Petong)
4863a[8]
Rue Soleil *J R Weymes* a29 64
2 ch f Zaha(CAN) —Maria Cappuccini (Siberian Express (USA))
2973[9] 3358[10] 3758[7] 4376[4] 4693[3]4893[7] 5404[6] 5721[4] 6157[3] *6278[7]*
Ruffie (IRE) *Miss Gay Kelleway* a68 52
3 b f Medicean—Darling Lover (USA) (Dare And Go (USA))
*1747[2] 2415[3]3378[3] 4044[12]*4491[8] *6260[5] 6641[2]6762[10]*
Rule For Ever *M Johnston* 75
4 br g Diktat—Tous Les Jours (USA) (Dayjur (USA))
1033[9] 1502[12] 1685[7] 1883[5] 2219[13]3019[5] 3696[5] 4156[9]
Rule Of Life *B W Hills* a79+ 79
2 br c Dansili—Prophecy (IRE) (Warning)
3445[8] 6200[3] *6434[2]*
Ruling Reef *M D I Usher* a42 57
4 b m Diktat—Horseshoe Reef (Mill Reef (USA))
1204[4] 1415[7] *1910[13]*2636[8] 3803[5] 3944[4] 4497[2] 4869[3]5166[13]
Ruman (IRE) *M J Attwater* a65 62
4 b g Fayruz—Starway To Heaven (ITY) (Nordance (USA))
4[2] (67) 274[7]428[6] 3052[7]
Rumbled *J A Geake* 58
2 b f Halling(USA) —Tatanka (IRE) (Lear Fan (USA))
4207[8] 4964[13] 5592[3] 6064[12]
Rumplestiltskin (IRE) *A P O'Brien* 112
3 b f Danehill(USA) —Monevassia (USA) (Mr Prospector (USA))
1508[7]
Rumsfeld (ITY) *A & G Botti* a104 104
3 b c Martino Alonso(IRE) —Radura (Brook)
1117[2] 1872a[11] 4082[16] 4805[4] *(5473a)* 6364a[3]
Runaway *A Fabre* 116+
4 b h King's Best(USA) —Anasazi (IRE) (Sadler's Wells (USA))
5913a[2]
Runaway Dancer (USA) *Dan L Hendricks* 115
7 gr g Runaway Groom(CAN) —Salsa Dancer (USA) (Dahar (USA))
1721a[3]
Runaway Ruby *B J McMath* a25 27
12 ch m Respect—Chrislim VII (Damsire Unregistered)
1261[12]
Run For Ede'S *R M Beckett* 67
2 b f Peintre Celebre(USA) —Raincloud (Rainbow Quest (USA))
5380[5]
Run Free *N Wilson* 67
2 b g Agnes World(USA) —Ellie Ardensky (Slip Anchor)
5491[8] 5790[2] 5959[4]
Ruse *J R Fanshawe* a62 62
3 b f Diktat—Reuval (Sharpen Up)
1445[4] 4113[4] *5046[5]5830[2] 6748[7] 6916[5]*
Rush Bay (USA) *T Amoss* 115
4 b h Cozzene(USA) —Seoul (USA) (Deputy Minister (CAN))
6344a[4]
Rushing Dasher (GER) *A Wohler* 89
4 ch h Dashing Blade—Roma Libera (GER) (Pharly (FR))
3563a[8]
Ruskin *K McAuliffe*
3 ch g Bluebird(USA) —Scenic Venture (IRE) (Desert King (IRE))
5071[15]
Rusky Dusky (USA) *R Hannon* a14 74
4 b g Stravinsky(USA) —Celtic Shade (Lomond (USA))
2319[11] 2599[11]
Russalka *M Wigham* a41 47
5 b m Opening Verse(USA) —Philarmonique (FR) (Trempolino (USA))
1995[9]
Russian Cafe (IRE) *N Tinkler* a28 64+
5 b m Stravinsky(USA) —Bistro (USA) (Strawberry Road (AUS))
937[9]
Russian Consort (IRE) *A King* a94+ 85
4 ch g Groom Dancer(USA) —Ukraine Venture (Slip Anchor)
2614[7] 2989[4] 3980[5]
Russian Desert (IRE) *A Fabre* 104
2 ch c Desert Prince(IRE) —Dievotchka (Dancing Brave (USA))
5801a[3]
Russian Dream (IRE) *W R Swinburn* a75 65
3 b g Xaar—Summer Dreams (IRE) (Sadler's Wells (USA))
1336[6] 2175[9] 2712[15]*3156[3]* 3686[11]5691[7] *6312[4]6479[8] 6893[3]*
Russian Gift (IRE) *C G Cox* 64
2 b f Soviet Star(USA) —Birthday Present (Cadeaux Genereux)
2328[4] 4207[5] 4754[4]
Russian Mist (IRE) *M J Wallace* a65+ 60
3 gr g Xaar—Cape Mist (USA) (Lure (USA))
*112[4] 215[5]*1049[7] 1599[8] *2209[11]*
Russian Pearl (NZ) *A S Cruz* 122
6 b g Soviet Star(USA) —Velinda (NZ) (Veloso (NZ))
742a[9] 1180a[9] 1527a[4] 6784a[10]
Russian Rocket (IRE) *Mrs C A Dunnett* a81 78
4 b g Indian Rocket—Soviet Girl (IRE) (Soviet Star (USA))
*23[9] 605[5]*1211[8] 1618[6] 1846[4] 2182[5] 2331[2](2611) 3094[11] *(3536)* 3709[5] 4807[12]*5263[8] 6882[4]6966[8]*
Russian Rosie (IRE) *J G Portman* 86
2 b f Traditionally(USA) —Pink Sovietstaia (FR) (Soviet Star (USA))
3700[4] 4053[2] (4558) 4966[3] 5503[7]
Russian Servana (IRE) *J Pearce*
4 b m Rossini(USA) —Ring Of Light (Auction Ring (USA))
1763[7]
Russian Silk *Jedd O'Keeffe* 74
2 b f Fasliyev(USA) —Queen Of Silk (IRE) (Brief Truce (USA))
(2281) 5442[3] 6056[9]
Russian Symphony (USA) *C R Egerton* a98 95
5 ch g Stravinsky(USA) —Backwoods Teacher (USA) (Woodman (USA))
54[9] 3092[16] 3904[9]
Russki (IRE) *Mrs A J Perrett* a76+
2 b c Fasliyev(USA) —Rose Of Mooncoin (IRE) (Brief Truce (USA))
6188[8] (6434)
Rust En Vrede *J J Quinn* a33 33
7 b g Royal Applause—Souveniers (Relko)
4511[11]
Rustic Gold *J R Best* a64
2 ch c Tobougg(IRE) —Suave Shot (Suave Dancer (USA))
6591[9] 6689[7]6887[8]
Ruthles Philly *D W Barker* 59
2 b f Primo Valentino(IRE) —Compton Amber (Puissance)
1664[12] 3018[11] 3553[7] 4630[6] 5237[6]
Ruwi *J-C Rouget* 120
4 b h Unfuwain(USA) —Ma Paloma (FR) (Highest Honor (FR))
934a[8] 3662a[2] 4417a[7]
Ryan's Future (IRE) *Miss L A Perratt* a87 92
6 b h Danetime(IRE) —Era (Dalsaan)
(2162)
Rychter (ITY) *F & L Brogi* 94
5 b h Stuck(USA) —Fire Play (ITY) (Don Orazio)
1871a[13]
Rydal (USA) *E J Alston* a96 80
5 ch g Gilded Time(USA) —Tennis Partner (USA) (Northern Dancer (CAN))
6[7]
Rydal Mount (IRE) *W S Kittow* 82
3 b f Cape Cross(IRE) —Pooka (Dominion)
1119[3] (1956) 2739[10] 3722[8] 4589[5] 4837[11]6020[14]
Ryedale Ovation (IRE) *T D Easterby* 83
3 b g Royal Applause—Passe Passe (USA) (Lear Fan (USA))
1097[3] 1292[3] 1848[4] 2385[8] 3296[11]4119[4] 4378[3] 4958[5]
Ryedane (IRE) *T D Easterby* a81 80
4 b g Danetime(IRE) —Miss Valediction (IRE) (Petardia)
*79[8] 362[9]*1125[18] 1496[11] 1662[6] 2194[9] 2504[11](3190) (3622) 3715[8] 3832[3] 4453[6] 4834[11] 5309[10]5486[4] 5684[4] 6315[5]
Ryhope Chief (IRE) *M F Harris* a36 46
3 b g Indian Danehill(IRE) —Rachel Pringle (IRE) (Doulab (USA))
538[8] 945[10]
Ryono (USA) *S Smrczek* a108 118?
7 ch h Mountain Cat(USA) —Racing Blue (Reference Point)
1371a[6] 2217a[2] 3779a[5] 5227a[5] *6574a[10]*
Rythm N Rhyme (IRE) *John A Harris* a44
7 ch g Danehill Dancer(IRE) —Valley Heigh (IRE) (Head For Heights)
97[14] 166[9]314[5] 526[9]791[9] 1271[8]1572[5]
Saabiq (USA) *C E Brittain* a95 95
3 br f Grand Slam(USA) —Lucky Lineage (USA) (Storm Cat (USA))
665[2] 1068[6] 1509[4]2199[8] 2744[13] *3535[4]*3761[11] *5667[9]*
Saameq (IRE) *D W Thompson* a59 49
5 b g Bahhare(USA) —Tajawuz (Kris)
470[9] 767[4]1199[7] 1590[10] *(6860)*
Saaratt *M P Tregoning* a61
2 ch f Mark Of Esteem(IRE) —Cambara (Dancing Brave (USA))
6433[6]
Sabah *A M Balding* 87
3 ch f Nashwan(USA) —Massorah (FR) (Habitat)
1358[4] 2712[2] (3367) 4628[3]
Sabana Perdida (IRE) *A De Royer-Dupre* 104
3 b f Cape Cross(IRE) —Capriola (USA) (Mr Prospector (USA))
1713a[3] 2694a[4] 4542a[3]
Sabasha (FR) *F Rohaut* 104
3 b f Xaar—Saba (ITY) (Kris)
5701a[10] 6230a[5]
Sabbeeh (USA) *Saeed Bin Suroor* a96 114
5 b h Red Ransom(USA) —Capistrano Day (USA) (Diesis)
281a[3] *508a[4]*
Sabbiosa (IRE) *J L Dunlop* a70 80+
4 b m Desert Prince(IRE) —Alla Marcia (IRE) (Marju (IRE))
780[2] 990[6] 1772[2] (2067) *2982[7]*
Sabellina (USA) *C Simon* 107
5 br m Langfuhr(CAN) —Restored Hope (USA) (He's Bad (USA))
(6368a)
Sabirli (TUR) *C Kurt* 111
5 b h Strike The Gold(USA) —Free Trade (TUR) (Shareef Dancer (USA))
151a[5] (369a) 5227a[4]
Sable D'Olonne (IRE) *A Savujev* 85
3 b f Brave Act—Silver Venture (USA) (Silver Hawk (USA))
2840a[7] 3660a[6] 5008a[10]
Sabo Prince *J M Bradley* a48 47
4 ch g Atraf—Moving Princess (Prince Sabo)
210[7] 793[4]875[10] 982[10]
Sabre D'Argent (USA) *T Albertrani* 119
6 br h Kris S(USA) —Sterling Pound (USA) (Seeking The Gold (USA))
2476a[6]
Sabrina Brown *J A Geake* a44 71
5 br m Polar Falcon(USA) —So True (So Blessed)
898[14] 1285[17] 2074[5] 4807[13] 5756[7]5872[8] 6174[9]
Sacho (GER) *W Kujath* 100
8 br g Dashing Blade—She's His Guest (IRE) (Be My Guest (USA))
455a[4] 6005a[3]
Sacranun *L M Cumani* a79 91
4 ch h Pivotal—Spanish Craft (IRE) (Jareer (USA))
2621[10] 5511[3] *6097[9]*
Sacre Coeur *J L Dunlop* 83+
2 b f Compton Place—Take Heart (Electric)
3588[5] (4041)
Sacred Light (USA) *D Hofmans* a103
3 rg c Holy Bull(USA) —Summer Glimmer (USA) (Summer Squall (USA))
2477a[9]
Sacrosanct (IRE) *A P O'Brien* 96
3 b f Sadler's Wells(USA) —Tambora (Darshaan)
1785a[5] 4212a[7] 5465a[8] 5854a[4] 5996a[6]6356a[9]
Saddex *P Rau* 114
3 b c Sadler's Wells(USA) —Remote Romance (USA) (Irish River (FR))
1526a[3] 3776a[4] 5051a[3] 5762a[2]
Saddler's Quest *B P J Baugh* a40 37
9 b g Saddlers' Hall(IRE) —Seren Quest (Rainbow Quest (USA))
6860[7] 6979[9]
Sadeek *K A Ryan* 102
2 ch c Kyllachy—Miss Mercy (IRE) (Law Society (USA))
(1807) (2225) 2719[8] 3574a[2] 4736[13] 5653[9]
Sadler's Hill (IRE) *N A Callaghan* a50 27
2 b g Sadler's Wells(USA) —Dedicated Lady (IRE) (Pennine Walk)
5293[9] 5495[9] *5906[13]*
Sadler's Star (GER) *H J Groschel* 82
3 b g Alwuhush(USA) —Sadlerella (IRE) (King's Theatre (IRE))
3776a[12]
Sad Times (IRE) *W G M Turner* a61 58
2 b f Tendulkar(USA) —Mrs Kanning (Distant View (USA))
*707[6] 760[6]*877[2] 962[4] 1229[7] 1862[5] (2588) 2870[3]3613[RR] *(3915)*
Safaah *G Prodromou* a38
3 b g Almushtarak(IRE) —Lawn Order (Efisio)
62[8] 487[9]687[12] 887[9]
Safanya (IRE) *A & G Botti* 90
4 b m Indian Lodge(IRE) —Silvia Puca (IRE) (Nebos (GER))
1368a[8]
Safari *R J Hodges* a24 36
3 b f Namaqualand(USA) —Breakfast Creek (Hallgate)
779[2] *1226[11]* 1771[5]2187[7]
Safariknight (IRE) *Kerstin Helander*
3 b f Night Shift(USA) —Selous (IRE) (Second Set (IRE))
3326a[11]
Safari Mischief *P Winkworth* 76
3 b g Primo Valentino(IRE) —Night Gypsy (Mind Games)
(3034) 3349[3] 4164[11] 4532[2] 4756[2] (5181) 5575[6]
Safari Sundowner (IRE) *P Winkworth* 69
2 b c Daggers Drawn(USA) —Acadelli (IRE) (Royal Academy (USA))
2234[7] 2930[12] 4103[9] 5349[12]
Safari Sunset (IRE) *P Winkworth* a75 82
4 b g Fayruz—Umlani (IRE) (Great Commotion (USA))
2429[10] 3486[6] 3904[11] *6223[11]6489[4] 6564[8]6664[7]*
Safe Investment (USA) *J H M Gosden* 89
2 b c Gone West(USA) —Fully Invested (USA) (Irish River (FR))
3417[2] (3976) 4928[2]
Safe Shot *Mrs J C McGregor* 47?
7 b g Salse(USA) —Optaria (Song)
939[13] 2927[8] 3140[8]3352[8]
Safe Structure (SAF) *D Maroun* a53 109
6 ch g National Assembly(CAN) —Thatch Umbrella (SAF) (Golden Thatch I (IRE))
203a[9] (352a) 433a[5] *563a[14]*
Safin (GER) *Carmen Bocskai* 74
6 b g Pennekamp(USA) —Sankt Johanna (GER) (High Game)
456a[7]
Safqa *B W Hills* 93
3 b f Singspiel(IRE) —Shamah (Unfuwain (USA))
1114[2] 1650[2] (2662) 3945[2] 4838[2] 5164[3]5530[4] 5895[3]
Safranine (IRE) *Miss A Stokell* a50 63
9 b m Dolphin Street(FR) —Webbiana (African Sky)
1448[8] *1762[6] 1909[3]*2295[6] *2462[11]* 2897[8]3172[3] (3267) 3478[2] 3682[3] 3783[5] 3912[10]4230[6] 4401[13] 4636[4] 5171[10] 5370[6]5487[11]
Safsoof (USA) *I Mohammed* a92 93
4 b h Gilded Time(USA) —Halcyon Bird (IRE) (Storm Bird (CAN))
206a[4] 434a[3]495a[7]
Sagassa *W De Best-Turner* a36 46
2 b f Largesse—Sally's Trust (IRE) (Classic Secret (USA))
1737[8] 2106[11] 5507[9] 5586[12] 5899[4]*6143[10] 6597[4]*
Sagemacca (IRE) *J J Quinn*
4 ch m Danehill Dancer(IRE) —Aubretia (USA) (Hatchet Man (USA))
3373[7]
Sagredo (USA) *Sir Mark Prescott* a84 86+
2 b g Diesis—Eternity (Suave Dancer (USA))
5841[4] 6050[2] (6297) *6379[2]*
Sagunt (GER) *W Hickst* 64
3 ch c Tertullian(USA) —Suva (GER) (Arazi (USA))
1526a[9]
Sahara Crystal *H Candy* 58
2 b f Desert Prince(IRE) —Laser Crystal (IRE) (King's Theatre (IRE))
3537[5] 4207[12] 5168[5]
Sahara Dawn (IRE) *C G Cox* a3 51
2 b f Desert Sun—Sharadja (IRE) (Doyoun)
2166[12] 3942[4] 4295[14] *5923[10]*
Sahara Prince (IRE) *K A Morgan* a54 75
6 b g Desert King(IRE) —Chehana (Posse (USA))
235[5] 321[9]458[9] 1217[13] *6983[7]*
Sahara Secret (IRE) *D Shaw* a32
3 b f Revoque(IRE) —Buddy And Soda (IRE) (Imperial Frontier (USA))
122[7] 199[7]333[7]
Sahara Silk (IRE) *D Shaw* a79 69
5 b m Desert Style(IRE) —Buddy And Soda (IRE) (Imperial Frontier (USA))
1[9] 119[2](249) 332[4]424[7] 519[6]587[3] 824[2]954[2] 1161[8]1338[2] 1774[12] *2462[4]*3267[10] 4507[8] *6527[3]6656[10] (6740) 6896[4] 6953[5]*
Sahara Sphinx (USA) *Saeed Bin Suroor* 74
3 ch c Giant's Causeway(USA) —Sculpture (USA) (Deputy Minister (CAN))
6053[4] 6177[9]
Sahara Style *R Hollinshead* a42 37
3 b g Desert Style(IRE) —Scapavia (FR) (Alzao (USA))
*349[5] 447[7]566[8] 859[6]*1216[6] 1424[10] 1661[4] *2463[9]3264[9]*
Sahara Sun (IRE) *A King* a34 49
3 b f Desert Sun—Perfect Rainbow (Rainbow Quest (USA))
5567[10] *6133[12] 6373[12]*
Sahem (IRE) *Robert Gray* 60
9 b g Sadler's Wells(USA) —Sumava (IRE) (Sure Blade (USA))
1294[9] 1502[13] 2528[4] 3284[10]
Sahf London *G L Moore* a45 37
3 b g Vettori(IRE) —Lumiere D'Espoir (FR) (Saumarez)
1546[10] *2246[8] 6133[4]*
Sahrati *C E Brittain* a56 78
2 ch c In The Wings—Shimna (Mr Prospector (USA))
3623[2] 4129[6] 5457[11] (6173) *6948[4]*
Saif Sareea *N G Richards* a21 81+
6 b g Atraf—Slipperose (Persepolis (FR))
1075[2] (1233) (1439) 2656[5]
Sailing Days *C A Cyzer* a55 63
4 b m Kris—Uncharted Waters (Celestial Storm (USA))
2262[P]
Sailor King (IRE) *D K Ivory* a85 104
4 b g King's Best(USA) —Manureva (USA) (Nureyev (USA))
6219[15] *6445[9] 6514[11]6660[7] 6896[6]*
Sainara (IRE) *J M Bradley*
2 b f Fasliyev(USA) —Reem Al Fala (Green Desert (USA))
878[11] 1046[15] 1647[12] 2073[6] 2179[6]
Saint Alebe *D R C Elsworth* 102
7 b g Bishop Of Cashel—Soba Up (Persian Heights)
5325[6] 5551[5] 5963[13]
Saint Andrew (IRE) *Peter Casey* 90
2 b c Desert Prince(IRE) —Champs Elysees (USA) (Distant Relative)
2686a[4] 4850a[5] 5408a[10]
Saint Bernadette *P T Midgley* 21
3 b f Bertolini(USA) —Primulette (Mummy's Pet)
1218[11]

Saintly Place *A W Carroll* a55 57
5 ch g Compton Place—Always On A Sunday (Star Appeal)
1909^8 4278^4 4551^3 5291^9

Saintly Rachel (IRE) *C F Swan* 101?
8 b m Religiously(USA) —Ursha (IRE) (Shardari)
371a^6 437a^13 753a^8 1026a^4 1785a^7

Saint Nick *J J Bridger* 6
3 b g Delta Dancer—Queen's Hat (Cadeaux Genereux)
1121^2 4142^7

Saint Remus (IRE) *Peter Grayson* a42
2 b g Diktat—Fur Will Fly (Petong)
4932^6 5735^11

Saishu (IRE) *E Libaud* 101
4 b m Indian Ridge—Sagar Pride (IRE) (Jareer (USA))
1398a^5 2313a^7 6002a^5

Saitama *A M Hales* a17 63
4 b m Pursuit Of Love—Sea Ballad (USA) (Bering)
6754^13

Sajaaya (AUS) *Sir Michael Stoute* a37 66+
3 b f Secret Savings(USA) —Million In Mind (AUS) (Snaadee (USA))
1956^5 2673^12 3826^6

Sakabula (USA) *G C Bravery* 67
3 b f King Of Kings(IRE) —Sianema (Persian Bold)
3364^8 3977^8 5130^15

Sake (IRE) *N Tinkler* 78
4 b g Shinko Forest(IRE) —Drosera (IRE) (Thatching)
1041^3 1480^9 (1760) 1996^2 (2541) 2974^14 3549^6 4114^2 4378^5 4653^5

Sakhee's Secret *H Morrison* 94
2 ch c Sakhee(USA) —Palace Street (USA) (Secreto (USA))
3363^3 (4428) 5806^4

Sakkara Star (IRE) *M Halford* 94
3 b f Mozart(IRE) —Sun Silk (USA) (Gone West (USA))
5465a^11

Salaasa (USA) *M Johnston* 73+
2 ch c Swain(IRE) —Jawla (Wolfhound (USA))
5640^4 6318^2

Salamanca *S Kirk* a92 101
4 ch m Pivotal—Salanka (IRE) (Persian Heights)
1015^5 1477^3 2011^6 2803^7 4023^15 4590^9 5177^3 5300^5 5494^6

Salar Violet (IRE) *R Feligioni* 43
3 b f Orpen(USA) —Sopran Lawka (ITY) (Catrail (USA))
1713a^17

Salawat *G Prodromou*
3 b f Tomba—Galadriel (Fairy King (USA))
1254^7 3399^5 5098^9

Salazaar (IRE) *David Wachman* 79
2 b c Xaar—Dance Ahead (Shareef Dancer (USA))
5662a^4

Saldenblatt *Mario Hofer* 101
3 b c Dashing Blade—Salde (GER) (Alkalde (GER))
1715a^6

Salesin *L M Cumani* 96
3 ch c Lomitas—Elisita (ARG) (Ride The Rails (USA))
1374^3 (1880) 2436^3 4742^4 5533^12

Salford City (IRE) *Noel Meade* 119
5 b h Desert Sun—Summer Fashion (Moorestyle)
4121a^7

Salford Mill (IRE) *D R C Elsworth* a74+
2 b c Peintre Celebre(USA) —Razana (IRE) (Kahyasi)
6867^2

Salient *J Akehurst* a82 60
2 b c Fasliyev(USA) —Savannah Belle (Green Desert (USA))
4597^6 5206^9 (5607) (6412) 6586^3 6634^4

Salila (IRE) *R Gibson* 75
3 b f Sadler's Wells(USA) —Love For Ever (IRE) (Darshaan)
6567a^0

Salinger (USA) *Mrs L J Mongan* a49 50
4 b g Lear Fan(USA) —Sharp Flick (USA) (Sharpen Up)
187^11 268^9 297^6 2131^12 2319^8 2861^6 3074^5 3730^7 4278^5 4670^3 5259^4

Salinja (USA) *Mrs A J Perrett* 102
4 b g Boundary(USA) —Lasha (USA) (Rahy (USA))
2988^12 (3733) 4023^13 4711^14 5177^5 5675^20 5945^2 6219^10

Salisbury Plain *N I M Rossiter* a56 71
5 b h Mark Of Esteem(IRE) —Wild Pavane (Dancing Brave (USA))
847^7 1772^11

Salisbury World (IRE) *J F Coupland* a59d 48
3 ch g Spinning World(USA) —Dinka Raja (USA) (Woodman (USA))
16^3 219^11 293^6 378^5 1416^9 2001^10 2504^13 2782^5 3288^11 3910^11 4304^9 4943^11 5432^12

Salonga (IRE) *C F Wall* a63 62
3 b f Shinko Forest(IRE) —Alongside (Slip Anchor)
1674^7 2118^10 3073^6 4118^8 4700^3 5452^11 5831^4 (6450)

Salon Prive *C A Cyzer* a76 67
6 b g Green Desert(USA) —Shot At Love (IRE) (Last Tycoon)
23^4 824^10 986^4 3825^9

Saloon (USA) *Sir Michael Stoute* 46
2 b c Sadler's Wells(USA) —Fire The Groom (USA) (Blushing Groom (FR))
4768^11

Salsalava (FR) *P Demercastel* 105
3 b c Kingsalsa(USA) —Lavayssiere (FR) (Sicyos (USA))
392a^4 (522a) 1064a^5 2489a^8 2942a^4 4168a^8

Salsa Steps (USA) *H Morrison* a76 78
2 ch f Giant's Causeway(USA) —Dance Design (IRE) (Sadler's Wells (USA))
5894^4 6186^2

Salthill (IRE) *Jarlath P Fahey* a37 43
3 ch f Fruits Of Love(USA) —Ambria (ITY) (Final Straw)
6648^6 6705^9

Salt Man *M P Tregoning* a77 93
3 b c Mtoto—Romaneh (Lahib (USA))
1093^8 2654^3 4082^15 4810^10

Salto Chico *W M Brisbourne* 58
2 b g Fraam—Miss Tango (Batshoof)
2854^7 3328^6 4171^9 5482^11 6007^7

Saltrio *W M Brisbourne* a80 108
8 b g Slip Anchor—Hills' Presidium (Presidium)
1385^7 6382^2 (6623) 6735^3

Salt Track (ARG) *Niels Petersen* a97 95
6 b h Salt Lake(USA) —Astralisima (ARG) (Fitzcarraldo (ARG))
1659a^3 4864a^7 5224a^2

Salty Humor (USA) *S McCarthy* 101
4 br g Distorted Humor(USA) —Salt Loch (USA) (Salt Lake (USA))
5825a^6

Saluscraggie *K G Reveley* 56
4 b m Most Welcome—Upper Caen (High Top)
1997^7 2360^3 2808^8 4072^9 4380^3 4924^10 5903^5 (5960)

Salut D'Amour (IRE) *J Noseda* 99
3 ch f Danehill Dancer(IRE) —Juno Madonna (IRE) (Sadler's Wells (USA))
1068^3 1834^2

Salute (IRE) *P G Murphy* a79 85
7 b g Muhtarram(USA) —Alasib (Siberian Express (USA))
88^14 237^9 832^3 1247^8 1690^3 1931^5 (2176) 2817^7 3203^5 4036^13 4937^3 5383^4 5846^2 6205^9 6479^3 (6766) (6831)

Salute Him (IRE) *M R Channon* 97
3 b g Mull Of Kintyre(USA) —Living Legend (ITY) (Archway (IRE))
755a^12 1115^6 1505^8 (2174) 3119^2 3443^7 4082^11 (4810) 5530^2

Salute The General *W R Muir* a79 86
3 ch c Mark Of Esteem(IRE) —Oiselina (FR) (Linamix (FR))
1270^2 1841^2 2224^7 2805^8 3292^6

Salutino (GER) *A Fabre* 116
4 ch h Monsun(GER) —Saderlina (IRE) (Sadler's Wells (USA))
1558a^2 2277a^2 2910a^3 5223a^2

Salut Saint Cloud *G L Moore* a71 55
5 b g Primo Dominie—Tiriana (Common Grounds)
(570) 2140^2 6630^7 (6873)

Salvestro *Mrs A J Perrett* a65 65
3 b g Medicean—Katy Nowaitee (Komaite (USA))
1215^3 1738^6 2480^5 3338^3 3650^12 4076^5 4243^2 4757^5 5210^11 5474^8 5936^8

Salvia *R Charlton* 29
3 ch f Pivotal—Satin Bell (Midyan (USA))
1119^12

Salviati (USA) *J M Bradley* a70 59
9 b g Lahib(USA) —Mother Courage (Busted)
1161^6 1297^10 1662^18 2618^5 2784^7 2962^8 3004^7 3330^8 3543^6 3855^9 3988^6 4636^15 4962^9 5480^6 5752^13

Salym (FR) *D J S Ffrench Davis* 82
5 ch g Limnos(JPN) —Tina's Crest (FR) (Ocean Falls)
4777^9

Sama (IRE) *C E Brittain* 73
2 gr f Machiavellian(USA) —Amellnaa (IRE) (Sadler's Wells (USA))
4966^6

Sama Dubai (AUS) *Sir Michael Stoute* a32 79+
3 b f Secret Savings(USA) —Eajaab (Tragic Role (USA))
(2532) 3590^6

Samahir (USA) *M A Jarvis* 68+
2 b f Forest Wildcat(USA) —Saabga (USA) (Woodman (USA))
1896^5

Samantha Queen (IRE) *S Postiglione* a86
3 ch f King Charlemagne(USA) —Argus Gal (IRE) (Alzao (USA))
5473a^6

Samarinda (USA) *Mrs P Sly* a67 68
3 ch g Rahy(USA) —Munnaya (USA) (Nijinsky (CAN))
2034^12 2712^8 3100^4 5727^5 6841^6 (6987)

Sambaprinz (GER) *H Horwart* 111
7 br h Big Shuffle(USA) —Samambaia (GER) (Ti Amo (GER))
1869a^6

Samdaniya *C E Brittain* a51 84
2 b f Machiavellian(USA) —Cloud Castle (In The Wings)
4041^10 4840^9 5648^7

Same Old Scene (IRE) *J R Best* a16
3 b g Orpen(USA) —Saratoga Scene (USA) (Grey Dawn II)
5781^12

Samerous (FR) *H Blume* 99
3 ch f Generous(IRE) —Samshu (Nashwan (USA))
1714a^4 2694a^12

Sam Lord *J H M Gosden* a69 80
2 ch g Observatory(USA) —My Mariam (Salse (USA))
5020^5 5454^6 (5939)

Samorra (IRE) *M P Tregoning* 70+
2 b f In The Wings—Walesiana (GER) (Star Appeal)
(1980)

Samsa (FR) *R Gibson* a98 100?
3 b f Zafonic(USA) —Everlasting Love (Pursuit Of Love)
4542a^7 6328a^2

Samson Quest *G F Bridgwater* a60 51
4 b g Cyrano De Bergerac—Zenita (IRE) (Zieten (USA))
35^2 86^2 268^4 297^5 (458) 568^4 820^9 906^7 1353^11 3056^8 3386^4 3730^6 4585^15

Samsouma (IRE) *C E Brittain* a50 53
3 b f Marju(IRE) —St Bride's Bay (Caerleon (USA))
544^7 859^7 2249^10 2529^9

Sam's Secret *G A Swinbank* a69 69
4 b m Josr Algarhoud(IRE) —Twilight Time (Aragon)
3500^4 3883^10 4265^9 5301^7 5444^12 6273^9

Sam The Sorcerer *J R Norton* a42 28
5 b g Wizard King—Awham (USA) (Lear Fan (USA))
300^8 3835^13

Samuel *J L Dunlop* 53
2 ch c Sakhee(USA) —Dolores (Danehill (USA))
6220^16

Samuel Charles *C R Dore* a86 84
8 b g Green Desert(USA) —Hejraan (USA) (Alydar (USA))
(71) (101) 276^4 381^2 611^9 721^8 1220^11 1644^2 (2348) 2464^8 (2551) (2614) 3532^5 3688^2 3973^6 4241^6 5149^11 6580^5 6671^6 6999^5

Samuel John Peploe (IRE) *G L Moore* a34 14
4 b g Intikhab(USA) —Sadalsud (IRE) (Shaadi (USA))
32^9

Samurai Jack (IRE) *John A Quinn* a64 71
3 b g Mark Of Esteem(IRE) —Kasota (IRE) (Alzao (USA))
(584) 822^4 1837^6 2391^5 2633^7

Samurai Prince (USA) *G Aimonetti* 86
2 b c War Chant(USA) —Elle (USA) (Mr Prospector (USA))
5415a^8

Samurai Way *L M Cumani* 85
4 b h Darshaan—Truly Special (Caerleon (USA))
4945^3 5319^2 5792^6

San Antonio *Mrs P Sly* a96 94
6 b g Efisio—Winnebago (Kris)
238^2 516^4 865^4 1183^6 2086^6 3121^7 4819^8 5785^7

Sa Nau *T Keddy* a48 64
3 b g Generous(IRE) —Trellis Bay (Sadler's Wells (USA))
1336^10 2028^13 2465^10 2933^9 3870^5 4380^10 (4734) 5242^2 (5618)

Sanaya (IRE) *A De Royer-Dupre* 109
3 b f Barathea(IRE) —Sanariya (IRE) (Darshaan)
959a^2 1370a^2 1874a^2 2491a^12 4543a^4 6454a^3

Sanbuch *L M Cumani* a81+ 33+
2 b c Tobougg(IRE) —Monte Calvo (Shirley Heights)
2178^10 (2979)

Sanchi (IRE) *Saeed Bin Suroor* 101
4 b h Darshaan—Samara (IRE) (Polish Patriot (USA))
(5115) 5310^5 5920^6

Sanctity *J R Fanshawe* a70+ 66+
3 ch f Pivotal—Blessed Honour (Ahonoora)
1212^5 2171^13 2418^2 3410^11 (4470) 5740^2 5992^3

Sand And Stars (IRE) *M H Tompkins* 84
5 ch m Dr Devious(IRE) —Charm The Stars (Roi Danzig (USA))
1376^7 2238^7 2628^9 3152^3 3412^3 (Dead)

San Dany (IRE) *M Massimi Jr* 92
6 b h Danetime(IRE) —Pharmacy (Mtoto)
1871a^11 6363a^12

Sand Cat *Doug Watson* a89 89
3 b c Cadeaux Genereux—Desert Lynx (IRE) (Green Desert (USA))
620a^5

San Deng *Micky Hammond* a68 70
4 gr g Averti(IRE) —Miss Mirror (Magic Mirror)
1045^6 1591^8 2193^2 2549^3 2736^2 3983^5 4205^10 5751^4

Sander Camillo (USA) *J Noseda* 116
2 b f Dixie Union(USA) —Staraway (USA) (Star De Naskra (USA))
1989^4 (2800) (3415)

Sanders Boy *J R Norton* a48 39
3 gr g Arkadian Hero(USA) —Rising Of The Moon (IRE) (Warning)
39^4 176^9 790^8 893^8 1464^3 1768^6 6550^11 6704^7 6833^9

Sandglass *Mrs A J Perrett* 99
3 b f Zafonic(USA) —Clepsydra (Sadler's Wells (USA))
(2580) 4035a^6 4741^10 5917^14

Sandhill Dancer *S Parr* a1
4 b m Perryston View—Just Like You (Sandhurst Prince)
243^11 427^8 498^8

Sandie (IRE) *J S Bolger* 98
3 b f Lil's Boy(USA) —Sukeena (IRE) (Brief Truce (USA))
753a^10 1363a^3 1709a^5 4031a^13 5396a^10

Sand Iron (IRE) *John Allen* a59 67
4 b m Desert Style(IRE) —Mettlesome (Lomond (USA))
4^13 2098^13 2551^5 2978^4 6431^6 6532^10 6775^11

San Domenico *P Bary* 97
2 b c Zamindar(USA) —Guarded (Eagle Eyed (USA))
5399a^2

Sandra's Rose (USA) *M Machowsky* 99
4 b m Old Trieste(USA) —St Lucinda (CAN) (St Jovite (USA))
6253a^8

Sand Repeal (IRE) *Miss J Feilden* a76 69
4 b g Revoque(IRE) —Columbian Sand (IRE) (Salmon Leap (USA))
2^2 (97) (231) 334^2 603^7 723^8 (911) 1222^5 1389^2 1847^11 2140^7 6718^7 6947^5

Sandrey (IRE) *P W Chapple-Hyam* 78
2 b c Noverre(USA) —Boudica (IRE) (Alhaarth (IRE))
5168^4 5454^7 (6014)

Sands Crooner (IRE) *D Shaw* a78 78
3 b c Imperial Ballet(IRE) —Kurfuffle (Bluebird (USA))
(45) 190^4 341^3 (464) (593) 1146^10 1604^12 6583^12 6709^8 6935^5

Sands Of Barra (IRE) *I W McInnes* a71 76
3 gr g Marju(IRE) —Purple Risks (FR) (Take Risks (FR))
702^5 803^4 1312^4 (1617) 1855^9 2863^12 3679^7 4143^5 4769^7 5377^13 5778^9 6147^5 6573^12 6595^7 6747^7 6952^8

Sand Sprite (IRE) *Sir Michael Stoute* 51
3 b f Green Desert(USA) —Fleet Amour (USA) (Afleet (CAN))
2028^10 2542^9

Sandton City (IRE) *Francis Ennis* 97
3 ch c Daggers Drawn(USA) —Inter Madera (IRE) (Toca Madera)
1627^8

Sandwaki (USA) *C Laffon-Parias* 106
2 b c Dixieland Band(USA) —Wakigoer (USA) (Miswaki (USA))
(3132a) 4644a^4 5715a^8

Sandwith *I Semple* a58 70
3 ch g Perryston View—Bodfari Times (Clantime)
(1036) 1529^6

Sandy's Legend (USA) *Mrs L Williamson* a59 49
4 ch g Tale Of The Cat(USA) —Avasand (USA) (Avatar (USA))
186^6 264^10 443^4 570^5 4914^10

Sanfrancullinan (IRE) *M Halford* 85
4 b m Bluebird(USA) —Harir (Kris)
3125a^25 5849a^7

Sangfroid *Sir Mark Prescott* a34 20
2 gr g With Approval(CAN) —Affaire D'Amour (Hernando (FR))
5261^12 5389^11 5570^11

Sangreal *K R Burke* a65 64
2 ch f Medicean—La Belle Dominique (Dominion)
5592^10 6175^5 6505^5 6679^3

San Hernando *Miss E C Lavelle* a69 79
6 b g Hernando(FR) —Sandrella (IRE) (Darshaan)
1931^2 3028^9

San Langfuhr (ITY) *M Massimi Jr* a77
3 b c Langfuhr(CAN) —Crafty Sarre (USA) (Crafty Prospector (USA))
5473a^8

San Marco (IRE) *M Sheppard* a20 20
8 b g Brief Truce(USA) —Nuit Des Temps (Sadler's Wells (USA))
91^10

Sansel *J Ryan* 9
3 b f Well Beloved—Abbisluckystar (IRE) (Soughaan (USA))
1940^10 2146^11 2261^9 4263^10 5061^9

Sans Reward (IRE) *B J Meehan* a72 101
2 b f Barathea(IRE) —Fritta Mista (IRE) (Linamix (FR))
1688^5 1922^2 (2530) (3265) 4371^5 5187^3 6046a^9

Santando *C E Brittain* a78 72d
6 b g Hernando(FR) —Santarem (USA) (El Gran Senor (USA))
454^7 521^8 847^4 1614^8 1926^3 1958^2 2647^5 3490^7 4457^5 (5875) 6075^10

Sant Elena *G Wragg* a85 74
3 ch f Efisio—Argent Du Bois (USA) (Silver Hawk (USA))
852^3 1056^3 2865^7 (3403) 4328^3 5107^2 5627^9 6352^9

Santera (IRE) *Mrs A Duffield* a16
2 br f Gold Away(IRE) —Sainte Gig (FR) (Saint Cyrien (FR))
6523^11

Santiago (GER) *U Ostmann* 113
4 gr h Highest Honor(FR) —Serenata (GER) (Lomitas)
4190a^4 5856a^8

Santiago Atitlan *A Wohler* 102
4 gr h Stravinsky(USA) —Sylvette (USA) (Silver Hawk (USA))
6363a^3

Sanvic (IRE) *J-C Rouget* 86
2 b c Green Desert(USA) —Puzzled Look (USA) (Gulch (USA))
5801a^6 6453a^5

Sapienza *C E Brittain* a45 67+
3 ch f Singspiel(IRE) —Kameez (IRE) (Arazi (USA))
1215^4 (Dead)

Sapphire Dream *A Bailey* a41 69d
4 b m Mind Games—Bombay Sapphire (Be My Chief (USA))
288^9 524^5 613^6 680^10 691^11 1465^8

Sapphire Storm (IRE) *P T Midgley* a35 60
3 b f Elnadim(USA) —Blu Tu Miami (USA) (Robin Des Pins (USA))
554^4 598^7 642^8 1341^9 1791^4 2192^3 (2644) 3299^12 3604^3 (4728) (5370)

Sapucai (ARG) *S Seemar* a83 91
6 b g Lode(USA) —Saint Donatila (ARG) (Saint Sever (FR))
152a^8 207a^7 507a^7

Sarabanda Heat *B Grizzetti*
2 b c Agnes World(USA) —Tuscania (USA) (Woodman (USA))
2474a^2

Sarah's Art (IRE) *Miss D A McHale* a63 73
3 gr g City On A Hill(USA) —Treasure Bleue (IRE) (Treasure Kay)
39^5 779^6 1272^2 (1464) (1612) 1937^3 2393^2 (2570) 2730^2 2931^7 3049^2 3612^10 6865^9

Sarah's Prince (IRE) *D K Ivory* a48 45
3 b g Royal Applause—Peaceful Sarah (Sharpo)
1937^8 2535^18 2937^2 3257^4 3995^9 5924^5 6129^12

Sara Mana Mou *J G Portman* a45 36
3 b f Medicean—Sarabah (IRE) (Ela-Mana-Mou)
1118^9 3258^4 4111^7 4556^5 4734^7

Saratoga *Sir Michael Stoute* 42
3 b c Danehill(USA) —Rockerlong (Deploy)
1680^11

Sardis Road *W G M Turner* 64
2 ch c Daggers Drawn(USA) —Ave Atque Vale (FR) (Most Welcome)
877^7 962^2

Sarenne *John Berry* a34 45
5 b m Desert Sun—Fabulous Pet (Somethingfabulous (USA))
302^6 525^8 614^8

Sarraaf (IRE) *I Semple* a75 69
10 ch g Perugino(USA) —Blue Vista (IRE) (Pennine Walk)
56^3 170^4 2546^4

Sarrera (AUS) *M Moroney* 99
6 b g Quest For Fame—Zamsong (NZ) (Zabeel (NZ))
6346a^7

Sarwin (USA) *W J Musson* a69 59
3 rg g Holy Bull(USA) —Olive The Twist (USA) (Theatrical)
1140[12] 1652[3] (2466) 2713[6] 5868[10] 6289[5]6484[3] 6735[2]6878[5]

Sasetti (IRE) *J R Fanshawe* a46 58
3 ch f Selkirk(USA) —My Potters (USA) (Irish River (FR))
2868[8] 3458[6] 3946[9]4556[4] 5452[6]

Sasphee (GER) *E Kurdu* 45
2 b f Lomitas—Suanita (GER) (Big Shuffle (USA))
6122a[10]

Sass Cafe (IRE) *T J Pitt* a41
2 gr f Sendawar(IRE) —Ashtarka (Dalsaan)
5209[7]

Satchem (IRE) *Saeed Bin Suroor* a114 119
4 br h Inchinor—Mohican Princess (Shirley Heights)
(2431) 3534[2] 5341[3] (5673) 5962[3]

Satchmo Bay (FR) *C Boutin* a82 104
5 b g Alamo Bay(USA) —Royale Aube (FR) (Garde Royale)
885a[7]

Satin Braid *B J Meehan* a63 71
2 b f Diktat—Beading (Polish Precedent (USA))
4964[5] 5456[5] 6073[4]6309[5]

Satin Doll *M P Tregoning* a64 53
3 b f Diktat—Unconditional Love (IRE) (Polish Patriot (USA))
1335[5] 2403[11] 3073[7]3644[13]

Satin Rose *K J Burke* a6 6
4 b m Lujain(USA) —Shamwari (USA) (Shahrastani (USA))
309[13] 338[9]

Satintheslip (IRE) *Mrs P Ford* 23
5 b m Idris(IRE) —Gauloise Bleue (USA) (Lyphard's Wish (FR))
6026[11] 6241[12]

Satisfaction (IRE) *E J O'Neill* a44 61
3 b c Dansili—Presentation (IRE) (Mujadil (USA))
3100[9] 4300[4] 5302[12]

Sativa (IRE) *Noel Meade* 76
4 b m Docksider(USA) —Nightlark (IRE) (Night Shift (USA))
4094a[15]

Satri (IRE) *J-M Beguigne* 114
4 b h Mujadil(USA) —Laramie (USA) (Gulch (USA))
(2313a) 3564a[2] 4191a[2]

Satulagi (USA) *J S Moore* a72 100
2 b f Officer(USA) —Shawgatny (USA) (Danzig Connection (USA))
701[3] (1053) 2800[5] 3084[2]3734[9] (3924) 4371[3] 5522[4] 6338a[11]

Saturn (IRE) *C Fownes* 115
6 b g Marju(IRE) —Delphinus (Soviet Star (USA))
6782a[9]

Satwa Queen (FR) *J De Roualle* 120
4 ch m Muhtathir—Tolga (USA) (Irish River (FR))
155a[2] 510a[2] (4646a) 5713a[2] 6340a[5] 6785a[6]

Satyricon *M Botti* a67
2 b c Dr Fong(USA) —Belladera (IRE) (Alzao (USA))
3843[6] 4366[4]4932[4]

Saucepot *Miss J R Tooth* a48 53
4 ch m Bold Edge—Apple Sauce (Prince Sabo)
1310[13] 2096[9]

Saucy *A W Carroll* a61+ 58
5 b m Muhtarram(USA) —So Saucy (Teenoso (USA))
1400[16] 2148[12] 3731[11]4289[6] 6232[7] 6693[3](6800)

Savanagh Forest (IRE) *M Quinn* a46 29
2 b f Shinko Forest(IRE) —Adieu Cherie (IRE) (Bustino)
5773[9] 6055[12]

Savannah *Luke Comer* a55 103
3 b c Sadler's Wells(USA) —La Papagena (Habitat)
4024[6] 4822a[6] 5657[11] 6914[6]

Savannah Bay *B Ellison* a85 92
7 ch g In The Wings—High Savannah (Rousillon (USA))
1021[9] 1294[10] 2229[9]2723[25] 3078[7]

Savannah Pride (IRE) *Ernst Oertel* a43 64
3 b f Namid—Milady Lillie (IRE) (Distinctly North (USA))
2554[14] 4143[11] 4494[11]

Savernake Blue *M R Channon* a73 85
3 b g Mtoto—Mrs Malaprop (Night Shift (USA))
1067[11] 1349[7] 1812[7] (3087) 3150[7] 3722[7]4144[11] 4449[7] 4888[12] 5427[8]5649[9] 5842[U]

Savernake Brave (IRE) *Mrs H Sweeting* a59 45
5 b g Charnwood Forest(IRE) —Jordinda (IRE) (Indian Ridge)
682[10] 1538[12]3614[12]

Save The Secret (AUS) *Sir Michael Stoute* 33
3 b c Secret Savings(USA) —Nothing To Do (USA) (Nijinsky (CAN))
3794[18]

Savile's Delight (IRE) *R Brotherton* a71 83
7 b g Cadeaux Genereux—Across The Ice (USA) (General Holme (USA))
1[3] 47[3]119[10] 225[3]320[9] 588[4]1878[14] 2331[5] 2792[10]

Saville Road *D J Daly* 101
3 br c Mozart(IRE) —In Full Cry (USA) (Seattle Slew (USA))
(1094) 2739[9] 3702[2] 4740[9]

Saviour Sand (IRE) *D R C Elsworth* a75+
2 b c Desert Sun—Teacher Preacher (IRE) (Taufan (USA))
6658[2] 6867[6]

Saviours Spirit *T G Mills* a95 77
5 ch g Komaite(USA) —Greenway Lady (Prince Daniel (USA))
89[3] (224) (376) 517[9](657) 836[2]970[8] 1246[4] 5476[8]5627[6] (6292) 6445[5]6660[4]

Savoy Chapel *A W Carroll* a49 27
4 br g Xaar—Royal Gift (Cadeaux Genereux)
71[9] 121[5]232[5] 290[12]350[6] 382[7]1915[10] 2137[11]5926[7] 6134[2]6370[4]

Sawwaah (IRE) *D Nicholls* a73 81
9 b g Marju(IRE) —Just A Mirage (Green Desert (USA))
764[6] 946[9] 1035[2]1220[8] 1455[2] 2282[5] 2454[6] 2696[4](2874) 3158[5] (3353) 4057[2] 4087[2]4467[3] 4692[7] 5313[12] 5553[4]

Saxenberg *Miss J R Gibney* a49 48
2 b f Foxhound(USA) —Latour (Sri Pekan (USA))
908[11] 2388[5] 3435[7]3844[13] 6016[14]

Saxon Lil (IRE) *J L Spearing* a60 80
4 b m Second Empire(IRE) —Salva (Grand Lodge (USA))
898[11] 977[12] 1962[7]2232[6] 2459[10] 2818[2] 2947[6] 3450[2]3679[8] 4116[2] 4399[6] (4831) 5436[7] 5896[11]

Saxon Saint *M D I Usher* a30 77
3 b g Josr Algarhoud(IRE) —Antithesis (IRE) (Fairy King (USA))
2329[14] 2756[11]

Saxon Star (IRE) *P Howling* a40 45
3 b g Vettori(IRE) —Thicket (Wolfhound (USA))
39[3] 83[7]176[12] 239[7]396[11] 779[5] 870[2]936[6] 1200[10]2968[8] 3804[9] 4050[8] 4278[8] 6057[14]6236[8] 6553[12]6584[10]

Say Great (IRE) *V Smith* 18
2 ch c Beckett(IRE) —Say Wonderful (IRE) (Roi Danzig (USA))
3417[15] (Dead)

Scamperdale *B P J Baugh* a66 46
4 br g Compton Place—Miss Up N Go (Gorytus (USA))
600[5] 820[4]953[12] (1460) 2414[2] 3196[11] 3599[3]4439[2] (6977)

Scandal Keeper (USA) *Saeed Bin Suroor* a92 84+
3 bb c Danzig(USA) —Canny Miss (AUS) (Marscay (AUS))
6192[7]

Scantlebury *S Kirk* 48
2 b g Mark Of Esteem(IRE) —Krameria (Kris)
5454[13]

Scaramoushca *P S McEntee* a59
3 gr g Most Welcome—Kinraddie (Wuzo (USA))
6916[6]

Scarface *J L Spearing* 15
9 ch g Hernando(FR) —Scarlatine (IRE) (Alzao (USA))
3896[8]

Scarlet Baby *K A Ryan* 19
2 ch g Elmaamul(USA) —Eastern Ruby (Be My Chief (USA))
2409[13] 4732[5]

Scarlet Flyer (USA) *G L Moore* a53 83
3 b g Gilded Time(USA) —Tennis Partner (USA) (Northern Dancer (CAN))
1016[16] 2205[5] 2650[4]3212[4] 3487[2] 4078[4] 4242[5] 5265[3]5377[3] 5591[14]

Scarlet Ibis *Saeed Bin Suroor* a79
2 b f Machiavellian(USA) —Flagbird (USA) (Nureyev (USA))
6186[5] 6481[2]

Scarlet Knight *P Mitchell* a89 87
3 b g Lujain(USA) —Gem (Most Welcome)
725[2] 1091[6] 1512[10]1954[5] 2014[11] 3015[5]4591[3]

Scarlet Romance *M W Easterby* a46
4 ch m Pursuit Of Love—Scarlet Livery (Saddlers' Hall (IRE))
653[8] 817[9] 937[5]

Scarlet Runner *J L Dunlop* 106
2 b f Night Shift(USA) —Sweet Pea (Persian Bold)
1989[8] (2506) 2800[3] (3925) 4737[5] 5654[8]

Scarlett Heart (IRE) *P J Makin* a54
2 b f Lujain(USA) —Scarlett Ribbon (Most Welcome)
6575[5] 6788[2]

Scarrabus (IRE) *A Crook* 53
5 b g Charnwood Forest(IRE) —Errazuriz (IRE) (Classic Music (USA))
1034[8] 1233[8] 1660[7]

Scar Tissue *Tom Dascombe* a46
2 ch f Medicean—Possessive Lady (Dara Monarch)
6745[3]

Scat Daddy (USA) *T Pletcher* a112
2 b c Johannesburg(USA) —Love Style (USA) (Mr Prospector (USA))
(5983a) 6339a[4]

Scene Three *J J Quinn* 45
2 gr f Act One—Ferber's Follies (USA) (Saratoga Six (USA))
5496[7] 5899[7]

Scenic Shot (AUS) *D Morton* 107
4 b g Scenic—Sweepshot (AUS) (Dr Grace (NZ))
(7000a)

Scented Present *B J Meehan* a78 96
2 b c Foxhound(USA) —Its Another Gift (Primo Dominie)
1354[4] 1737[2] (2315) 2724[17] 2771[9] 3252[3](3468) 3734[13] 4026[6] 5626[4] 6096[10]

Scherzo A La Russe (USA) *A G Newcombe* a36 57
3 bb f Stravinsky(USA) —Zadracarta (CAN) (Bold Ruckus (USA))
178[11] 308[10] (Dead)

Schiaparelli (GER) *P Schiergen* 113
3 ch c Monsun(GER) —Sacarina (Old Vic)
2910a[2] (3776a) 5051a[6] (5709a)

Schinken Otto (IRE) *J M Jefferson* a46 45
5 ch g Shinko Forest(IRE) —Athassel Rose (IRE) (Reasonable (FR))
42[4] 242[4]405[9] 469[6]

Schooner (GER) *Lady Herries* a69 65
6 b g Slip Anchor—Sweet Enough (Caerleon (USA))
2035[8] 3269[4]

Sciatin (IRE) *L M Cumani* 89
3 b c Alhaarth(IRE) —Robalana (USA) (Wild Again (USA))
6051[12]

Scintillation (AUS) *C S Shum* 121
6 b g Danehill(USA) —Subterfuge (Machiavellian (USA))
6783a[8]

Scipione Borghese *L Camici* 13
3 b c Anabaa(USA) —Sharenara (USA) (Vaguely Noble)
2671a[12]

Sconced (USA) *R C Guest* a40 49
11 ch g Affirmed(USA) —Quaff (USA) (Raise A Cup (USA))
816[4] 1436[11]

Scooby Dude (IRE) *Ms Deborah J Evans* a82 83
3 b g Tagula(IRE) —Miraculous (IRE) (Marju (IRE))
341[7] 1146[2] 1279[2]1604[3] 1857[3] 2021[4] 2168[6] 3475[3]6682[4] 6740[4]

Scorch *V Smith* a39 57d
5 b g Mark Of Esteem(IRE) —Red Hot Dancer (USA) (Seattle Dancer (USA))
6237[12] 6542[9]6701[10]

Scorchio (IRE) *B Smart* a38 31
5 b g Desert Sun—White-Wash (Final Straw)
6281[7] 6795[7]6957[8]

Scorpion (IRE) *A P O'Brien* 123
4 b h Montjeu(IRE) —Ardmelody (Law Society (USA))
5854a[2] 6344a[5] 6782a[7]

Scotch Pancake *D R C Elsworth* a73 81
3 ch f Selkirk(USA) —Galette (Caerleon (USA))
5151[9] 5669[2] 6410[5]6633[8]

Scotland The Brave *J D Bethell* 75
6 ch m Zilzal(USA) —Hunters Of Brora (IRE) (Sharpo)
2977[5] 4020[4] 4569[7] 4831[16] (5636) 5861[2]6211[2]

Scotland Yard (UAE) *D E Pipe* a76 93
3 b g Jade Robbery(USA) —Aqraba (Polish Precedent (USA))
850[4] 952[4]1306[2] (2786) 2975[12] (3359) 3882[3]

Scot Love (IRE) *J Noseda* a85 82
3 b c Dansili—Fashion (Bin Ajwaad (IRE))
720[2] 1016[2](1401) 1781[5] 2330[5] 2757[9]3202[7]

Scott *J Jay* a69 66
5 gr g Polar Falcon(USA) —Circled (USA) (Cozzene (USA))
443[11]

Scottish River (USA) *M D I Usher* a68d 69
7 b g Thunder Gulch(USA) —Overbrook (Storm Cat (USA))
50[5] 115[7]223[7] 319[10]530[8] 706[4]955[2] (1152) 1308[9] 2097[7] 2455[10]2708[9] 3798[7] 4005[7] 4160[5] 4432[7]4606[7] 4991[2] 5213[12]5506[13] 5897[6] 6376[6]6462[6] 6531[3]

Scottish Spirit (IRE) *J S Haldane*
2 b g Invincible Spirit(IRE) —Triphibious (Zafonic (USA))
5059[11] 5615[15]

Scottish Stage (IRE) *Sir Michael Stoute* a70+ 110
3 ch f Selkirk(USA) —Drama Class (IRE) (Caerleon (USA))
(1819) 2772[2] 3575a[2] 4079[5] 5502[8]

Scott's Mill *M Johnston* a28 37
4 ch g Unfuwain(USA) —Mill On The Floss (Mill Reef (USA))
785[3] 911[7]1199[9]

Scotty's Future (IRE) *A Berry* a35 56
8 b g Namaqualand(USA) —Persian Empress (IRE) (Persian Bold)
50[6] 107[5]251[10] 427[6]484[3] 582[3]640[5] 715[4] (1073) 1217[5]1500[4] (1666) 2788[8] 3519[7] 4068[3] 4194[4]4654[7] 4730[6] 5311[5] 5579[12] 5955[7]6158[3] 6213[6] 6317[11] 6551[11]

Scoubidou (GER) *H Blume* 100
2 b f Johan Cruyff—Simply Red (GER) (Dashing Blade)
(5858a)

Scratch The Dove *A E Price* 42
9 b m Henbit(USA) —Coney Dove (Celtic Cone)
2219[9] 3291[6]

Screenplay *Miss Sheena West* a72 73
5 ch g In The Wings—Erudite (Generous (IRE))
420[9]

Screen Test *B G Powell* a64 64
4 b m Danzero(AUS) —Audition (Machiavellian (USA))
574[6] 643[3]881[2] 1745[8] 2133[5]2483[7] 3196[RR]

Screwdriver *Miss J R Tooth* a80 84
4 b g Entrepreneur—Lust (Pursuit Of Love)
58[3] 192[5]316[8] 504[11]4020[7]

Scriptwriter (IRE) *Saeed Bin Suroor* 110+
4 b g Sadler's Wells(USA) —Dayanata (Shirley Heights)
(5787) 6336[7]

Scroll *P Howling* a73 59
3 b g Mark Of Esteem(IRE) —Bella Bellisimo (IRE) (Alzao (USA))
34[4] 118[5]234[2] 342[3]459[3] 539[3]558[3] 630[5](658) 702[4]855[6] 4395[5]4757[10] 5211[7] 5775[5]6698[7] 6820[5]6964[5]

Scrummage *Sir Michael Stoute* a84 84
3 b c Sinndar(IRE) —Ghariba (Final Straw)
1192[11] 2532[9] (3229) (3667) 3852[2] 4760[3] 5268[2]6094[2]

Scrunch *Miss J R Tooth* a52 70
5 b m Royal Applause—Antonia's Folly (Music Boy)
2637[9]

Scuba (IRE) *H Morrison* a74 72
4 b g Indian Danehill(IRE) —March Star (IRE) (Mac's Imp (USA))
1[2] (440) 492[5]1383[11] 1673[10] 2211[7](2792) 3543[9] 3598[4](3996) (4694) 5593[7] 5861[13] 6425[2]6595[9] 6747[6]6952[6]

Sculastic *L M Cumani* 81
3 b g Galileo(IRE) —Mutual Consent (IRE) (Reference Point)
4806[2] 5770[4] 6052[2]

Sculpted (FR) *H Steguweit* 104
5 b m Orpen(USA) —Wenge (USA) (Housebuster (USA))
4862a[4]

Scurra *A C Whillans* a37 46
7 b g Spectrum(IRE) —Tamnia (Green Desert (USA))
614[2] 688[8]2381[8] 4072[7] 4438[8]5061[4] 6161[5]

Scutch Mill (IRE) *Karen George* a73 64
4 ch g Alhaarth(IRE) —Bumble (Rainbow Quest (USA))
1380[11] 1926[2]2508[12] 3024[6] 3951[3] 4704[7]5621[4] 5972[9] 6323[7]6687[7] (6714) (6810)

Scuzme (IRE) *Miss Sheena West* a56 58+
3 br g Xaar—Decatur (Deploy)
796[4] (1501) 1829[3] 2568[6] 6027[8] 6889[6]

Scylla Cadeaux (IRE) *Sir Michael Stoute* a59 66
3 ch f Cadeaux Genereux—She's Classy (USA) (Boundary (USA))
1191[6] 2063 [3] 2985[5] 4070[8] 4703[4]

Seabow (USA) *Saeed Bin Suroor* 80+
3 b c Rainbow Quest(USA) —Dream Bay (USA) (Mr Prospector (USA))
5598[2] (5768)

Sea Cookie *W De Best-Turner* a48 31
2 b f Largesse—Maylan (IRE) (Lashkari)
6331[13] 6596[5] 6691[3]

Seaflower Reef (IRE) *A M Balding* a63 69
2 b f Robellino(USA) —Sankaty Light (USA) (Summer Squall (USA))
2328[9] 3120[5] 3684[2]4246[7]

Sea Frolic (IRE) *Jennie Candlish* a48 46
5 b m Shinko Forest(IRE) —Centre Travel (Godswalk (USA))
95[13] 1390[7]1574[6] 4114[5] 4405[3]5085[9] 5926[4] 6281[10]6307[3] 6552[9]6627[7] 6702[3]6799[9]

Sea Grain (IRE) *Robert Gray* 56
3 b g Beckett(IRE) —Tara View (IRE) (Wassl)
1441[7] 1736[13] 2539[9] 3303[6] 3983[4]

Sea Holly (IRE) *G G Margarson* a60 60
6 b g Barathea(IRE) —Mountain Holly (Shirley Heights)
4307[9] 4925[10] 5090[5] 6108[14]

Sea Hunter *I Mohammed* a104 101
4 b h Lend A Hand—Ocean Grove (IRE) (Fairy King (USA))
204a[2] 353a[4]495a[5] 560a[14]

Sea Land (FR) *M P Tregoning* a76
2 ch c King's Best(USA) —Green Bonnet (IRE) (Green Desert (USA))
6188[2]

Sealed Bid *M W Easterby* 41
3 b g Zilzal(USA) —Thea (USA) (Marju (IRE))
409[8]

Seallarain *A Berry* 1
3 ch f Perryston View—Bergliot (Governor General)
2928[17] 4136[7] 5862[7]

Seal Of Hope *M P Tregoning* a50 67
3 b g Cape Cross(IRE) —Heavenly Waters (Celestial Storm (USA))
2343[11] 2605[10] 2815[6]3347[15] 4800[9]

Seal Point (USA) *Christian Wroe* 79
2 ch c Point Given(USA) —Maudie May (USA) (Gilded Time (USA))
5893[5] 6220[7]

Seamount (GER) *W Figge* 100
5 ch h Sternkoenig(IRE) —Santa Clara (Star Appeal)
5718a[7]

Seamus Shindig *H Candy* a84 89
4 b g Aragon—Sheesha (USA) (Shadeed (USA))
2047[5] 2429[6] 3012[3]3904[4] 4338[4] 4771[6] 5148[9]

Sean Og (IRE) *E J Creighton* a31 53
4 gr g Definite Article—Miss Goodbody (Castle Keep)
6375[11] 6551[8]6852[8]

Sea Of Calm (USA) *E A L Dunlop* a56 58
3 b f Quiet American(USA) —Ocean Ridge (USA) (Storm Bird (CAN))
1055[5] 1351[6] 5619[13] 5992[5]6244[10] 6482[3]6601[4]

Sea Of Serenity (IRE) *P A Blockley* a31 47
3 b f Namid—Serenity (Selkirk (USA))
165[8] 322[7]

Sea Salt *T D Barron* 81+
3 b g Titus Livius(FR) —Carati (Selkirk (USA))
1147[2] (1437) 1857[6] 3879[8] (4886) 5333[8] 6009[10]6320[4]

Seaside Links (CAN) *M Casse* 97
2 b c Street Cry(IRE) —Miami Vacation (USA) (Far North (CAN))
5415a[5]

Seaside Retreat (USA) *M Casse* a111 107
3 b c King Cugat(USA) —Shes Like Rio (USA) (Boundary (USA))
757a[2] 1498a[10]

Sea Sprite (IRE) *S Kirk*
3 ch g Bahhare(USA) —Khawater (USA) (Silver Hawk (USA))
2463[12]

Sea Storm (IRE) *D R MacLeod* a87 89
8 b g Dolphin Street(FR) —Prime Interest (IRE) (King's Lake (USA))
1035[8] 1280[14] 1531[8]

Seaton Snooks *T D Easterby* 64
2 b g Diktat—Buck's Fizz (Kris)
1588[10] 1982[3] 2321[6] 4251[5] 4912[9]

Seattle Buddy (USA) *George P Frousiakis* a88 93
4 bb h Seattle Slew(USA) —Bad Pussycat (USA) (Distinctive Pro (USA))
3134a[7]

Seattle Robber *P A Blockley* a63 67
4 b g Robellino(USA) —Seattle Ribbon (USA) (Seattle Dancer (USA))
56[2] 107[6]285[6] 405[7]603[6] 955[3]1152[3] 1400[2]1666[4] 1769[2] 2044[5] (2725) 3141[3] 3616[8](3862) 4137[3] 5485[7]

Seattle Spy (USA) *G A Huffer* a51 56
3 bb g Catienus(USA) —Theyrplayinoursong (USA) (Seattle Dancer (USA))
49[9]

Sebaaq (USA) *M E Sowersby* 59
3 ch g Rahy(USA) —Malibu Karen (USA) (Seeking The Gold (USA))
1314[6] 2535[12] 4404[10]

Secam (POL) *Mrs P Townsley* a56 42
7 gr g Alywar(USA) —Scytia (POL) (Euro Star)
336[4] 416[6]520[9] 693[6]854[3] 1002[10]1245[11] 6779[5]6829[9] 6864[8]

Second City *E J Alston* a14
3 ch f Mark Of Esteem(IRE) —Trefoil (FR) (Blakeney)
6327^10 6482^9 6680^12

Second Reef *E J Alston* a61 58
4 b g Second Empire(IRE) —Vax Lady (Millfontaine)
4^11 71^3 1041^18 1258^12 2025^10 2211^6 2792^11 2926^4 3137^2 3398^3 3786^7 4233^7 4881^4 5248^2 (5485) 6383^9 6405^9 6524^2 6606^2 6667^4 6837^2

Second Wind *D A Nolan*
11 ch g Kris—Rimosa's Pet (Petingo)
3673^8

Secretary General (IRE) *P F I Cole* a84 85
5 b g Fasliyev(USA) —Katie McLain (USA) (Java Gold (USA))
843^5 (1435) 1995^7 (2351) 2640^4 3214^5 3686^6 4244^5 5045^5 5110^10

Secret Assassin (IRE) *W R Muir* a77 77
3 b g Daggers Drawn(USA) —Lypharden (IRE) (Lyphard's Special (USA))
2525^5 3112^2 3436^4 (3638) 4689^2 5042^3 5268^4 5778^6

Secret Cavern (USA) *Mrs Barbara Waring* a32 52
4 b g Lion Cavern(USA) —River Dyna (USA) (Dynaformer (USA))
5988^13

Secret Liaison *Sir Mark Prescott* a74 87+
3 gr g Medicean—Courting (Pursuit Of Love)
1384^8 (1530) 1948^3 2142^5 3310^4 3688^5 (4058) (4281) (4689) 5070^9

Secret Moment *C G Cox* a47 59
4 b g Polar Prince(IRE) —Inchtina (Inchinor)
1670^6 2220^9 3029^9 6289^10 6767^13

Secret Night *J A R Toller* a93 88
3 gr f Dansili—Night Haven (Night Shift (USA))
117^2 665^4 914^4 1404^3 1924^5 2880^2 3741^3 4343^5 4798^5 6192^3 6514^9 6915^2

Secret Pact (IRE) *A M Hales* 89
4 br g Lend A Hand—Schust Madame (IRE) (Second Set (IRE))
2176^14

Secret Place *M Al Muhairi* a104 96
5 ch g Compton Place—Secret Circle (Magic Ring (IRE))
353a^12 508a^7 560a^16

Secret Tender (IRE) *J R Weymes* a51 57
3 ch g Beckett(IRE) —Mystery Bid (Auction Ring (USA))
69^10 (676) 1293^15 1731^8 4943^14

Secret Vision (USA) *R M H Cowell* a44 44
5 ch m Distant View(USA) —Secret Angel (Halo (USA))
24^9 216^5 255^8 943^4 1209^6 (1534) 2611^13 3683^11 6131^9 6233^6 6723^9 6851^10

Secret World (IRE) *J Noseda* 107
3 ch c Spinning World(USA) —Classic Park (Robellino (USA))
(1087) 2739^5

Security Tiger (IRE) *M R Channon* 66
2 b f Desert Prince(IRE) —Nuit Chaud (USA) (Woodman (USA))
2958^11 3707^8 4018^2 4526^5 5157^9 5527^4

Sedge (USA) *P T Midgley* a68 68
6 b g Lure(USA) —First Flyer (USA) (Riverman (USA))
606^5 1258^2 2541^7 2789^3 3361^2 3817^2 4198^2 4961^3 5386^2 5974^9

Sedgwick *J G Given* a51
4 b g Nashwan(USA) —Imperial Bailiwick (IRE) (Imperial Frontier (USA))
365^6

See In The Dark (IRE) *B J Meehan* a74 79
2 b g Night Shift(USA) —Ms Mary C (IRE) (Dolphin Street (FR))
1113^2 1429^2 1639^2 2724^12 (3117) 3496^8 4766^20 5461^5 5909^5

Seejay *B R Johnson* a55 49
6 b m Bahamian Bounty—Grand Splendour (Shirley Heights)
4075^8 4670^11 5258^9

Seeking Kali (IRE) *Sir Michael Stoute* a66 64
3 br f Kalanisi(IRE) —Sought Out (IRE) (Rainbow Quest (USA))
1290^9 4396^4 5567^5

Seeking Straight (IRE) *Sir Michael Stoute* 76+
3 b g Rainbow Quest(USA) —Alignment (IRE) (Alzao (USA))
1070^7

Seeking The Buck (USA) *M A Magnusson* 46
2 b c Seeking The Gold(USA) —Cuanto Es (USA) (Exbourne (USA))
4333^15

Seesawmilu (IRE) *E J Alston* a57 53
3 b g Almutawakel—Clos De Tart (IRE) (Indian Ridge)
861^10 1226^9 (1549) 1792^10 3397^4 3814^4 4695^8 5928^8

Segoria (IRE) *A M Hales* a65 77+
4 b m Shinko Forest(IRE) —Moon Tango (IRE) (Last Tycoon)
22^6 (255) 485^3 519^8

Sehoya (IRE) *Eoin Doyle* a41 50
4 bb m Second Empire(IRE) —Blue Jazz (IRE) (Bluebird (USA))
6448^12 6627^9

Seihali (IRE) *D Selvaratnam* 118
7 b h Alzao(USA) —Edwina (IRE) (Caerleon (USA))
370a^2 564a^3 (621a) 742a^3 1527a^6

Sekula Pata (NZ) *Christian Wroe* a73 83
7 b g Pompeii Court(USA) —Torquay (NZ) (Wharf (USA))
207a^9 279a^7 509a^12 2988^6 3433^7 3973^15 5149^9 5590^10 6189^3 6432^3 6661^8

Selam (GER) *U Suter* 72
2 ch f Tertullian(USA) —Sparkling Star (FR) (Art Sebal (ITY))
5880a^7

Se La Vie (FR) *P Demercastel* a76 70
3 b f Highest Honor(FR) —Lady Winner (FR) (Fabulous Dancer (USA))
2537a^10

Seldemosa *M S Saunders* a64 51
5 br m Selkirk(USA) —Baldemosa (FR) (Lead On Time (USA))
1152^13 2113^8 2186^11 4363^5 4585^6 4869^14 4974^6 6829^5 6955^11

Selective *A W Carroll* a66 80
7 b g Selkirk(USA) —Portelet (Night Shift (USA))
135^9 267^7 451^12 1220^2 1422^7 1932^3 2510^4 2705^3

Self Defense *Miss E C Lavelle* a111 114
9 b g Warning—Dansara (Dancing Brave (USA))
1507^4 2010^5 2845^6 4595^4 5018^3

Self Discipline *Mrs L B Normile* 55
4 b g Dansili—Cosh (USA) (A.P. Indy (USA))
6473^14

Self Respect (USA) *A King* a19 88
4 b g Lear Fan(USA) —Cap Of Dignity (Shirley Heights)
1779^14 2176^9 4149^4 4676^5

Selinea (FR) *D Prod'Homme* 85
2 b f Keltos(FR) —Plenilunium (FR) (Zafonic (USA))
6228a^7

Selinka *R Hannon* 95
2 b f Selkirk(USA) —Lady Links (Bahamian Bounty)
3893^6 4558^3 (5347) (5672)

Selkirk Lady *W R Swinburn* a66 65
3 ch f Selkirk(USA) —Dubious (Darshaan)
1901^5 3200^8 3946^10 5247^4 5725^4

Sell Out *G Wragg* a75 45
2 gr f Act One—Nordica (Northfields (USA))
5914^15 (6433)

Selmis *V Caruso* 82
2 ch c Selkirk(USA) —Nokomis (Caerleon (USA))
6123a^7

Semahs Holly *J O'Reilly* 21
2 b f Beat All(USA) —Semah's Dream (Gunner B)
3908^8 4251^13 5076^11 6385^11

Semenovskii *Mrs N Smith* a73 74
6 b g Fraam—Country Spirit (Sayf El Arab (USA))
4085^6 4211^6 4780^6 5575^7 5938^6 6672^7 6827^7

Semi Detached (IRE) *J R Boyle* a68 75
3 b c Distant Music(USA) —Relankina (IRE) (Broken Hearted)
1401^6 1934^5 2403^14 4490^6 4973^5

Seminole Sun (IRE) *Martin Browne* 60
2 b f Invincible Spirit(IRE) —Moneypenny (IRE) (In The Wings)
5692a^16

Semper Paratus (USA) *V Smith* a5 24
7 b g Foxhound(USA) —Bletcha Lass (AUS) (Bletchingly (AUS))
3^3 258^5 1724^13

Senator's Alibi *T J O'Mara* a68 98
8 b h Caerleon(USA) —Salul (Soviet Star (USA))
2776^25 3125a^13 4094a^3 4187a^11

Sendalam (FR) *Y Fouin* a101 106
4 ch h Sendawar(IRE) —Alamea (IRE) (Ela-Mana-Mou)
5146a^7 5703a^8

Sendali (FR) *J D Bethell* 71
2 b c Daliapour(IRE) —Lady Senk (FR) (Pink (FR))
3758^5 4788^4 5616^6

Sendinpost *S C Williams* a72 67+
3 b f Dansili—Colleville (Pharly (FR))
373^8 (4005) 4604^5 5531^16 6479^4 6748^2

Send Me Home (IRE) *Adrian McGuinness* a55 52
4 b g Victory Note(USA) —Purty Dancer (IRE) (Foxhound (USA))
6683^3 6708^8

Seneschal *A B Haynes* a76 83
5 b g Polar Falcon(USA) —Broughton Singer (IRE) (Common Grounds)
292^6 777^6 1151^5 1383^2 1402^DSQ 1760^5 1878^6 2417^13 2444^7 2971^8 3405^2 3536^4 3846^9

Senex (GER) *H Blume* 117
6 b h Pelder(IRE) —Septima (GER) (Touching Wood (USA))
1870a^5

Senora Lenorah *D A Nolan*
2 ch f Tumbleweed Ridge—Blue Diamond (First Trump)
5835^11 6207^6 6316^12

Senora Thatcher (CHI) *M Nygard* 84
5 ch m Sam M(USA) —Lorenza (CHI) (Putifar (CHI))
5225a^10

Senor Benny (USA) *M McDonagh* 111+
7 br h Benny The Dip(USA) —Senora Tippy (USA) (El Gran Senor (USA))
1158a^5 1469a^2 4855a^10 5393a^8 5706a^6 5849a^2 6356a^11

Senor Dali (IRE) *J L Dunlop* 106
3 ch c Peintre Celebre(USA) —Far Fetched (IRE) (Distant Relative)
1070^4 1473^3 (2118) 2775^11 (3929) 4942a^2 5400a^4

Senor Eduardo *S Gollings* a57 50
9 gr g Terimon—Jasmin Path (Warpath)
1198^12

Senor Mac *B J Meehan*
3 b g Fraam—Annie Hall (Saddlers' Hall (IRE))
1073^16

Senor Set (GER) *J Pearce* a66 63
5 b g Second Set(IRE) —Shine Share (IRE) (El Gran Senor (USA))
1219^3 1415^4 1562^2 (1745) 2869^4 3350^2 3935^9

Sensible Lady *C Collins* 93
2 b f Tobougg(IRE) —Be Practical (Tragic Role (USA))
6113a^2 6357a^8

Sensuous *R Hannon* 77
3 b f Royal Applause—Zafaaf (Kris)
1406^3 1565^2 1750^5 2511^11 2987^9 4077^2 4769^4 (Dead)

Sentiero Rosso (USA) *B Ellison* a74 75d
4 b g Intidab(USA) —Kheyrah (USA) (Dayjur (USA))
1438^11 1662^9 1858^7 2173^11 2504^12 3041^9 3389^5 3543^8 (4059) 4090^3 4548^2 4831^6 5313^9 5961^10 6227^7 6273^4 6425^4 (6641) 6762^2 6818^6

Sentire (NZ) *R Laing* 97
5 br g Pentire—Sent To War (NZ) (Centaine (AUS))
5817a^8

Sentry Duty (FR) *E Libaud* 103
4 b h Kahyasi—Standing Around (FR) (Garde Royale)
5881a^4 6610a^5 6786a^6

Sepia Print (IRE) *W J Knight* a53 53
2 b f Tagula(IRE) —Photo Flash (IRE) (Bahamian Bounty)
2604^7 3335^6 4327^2 5084^12

Septimus (IRE) *A P O'Brien* 119
3 b c Sadler's Wells(USA) —Caladira (IRE) (Darshaan)
1179a^7 (1805) 2228^12

Seracina *P Bary* 80
3 ch f Nashwan(USA) —Seralia (FR) (Royal Academy (USA))
3515a^11

Serampour (FR) *A De Royer-Dupre* a91 75
3 gr c Monsun(GER) —Serasia (FR) (Linamix (FR))
6384a^8

Serenade Rose (AUS) *Lee Freedman* 114
4 b m Stravinsky(USA) —Rose Of Tralee (AUS) (Sadler's Wells (USA))
6110a^9

Serene Dancer *Mrs P N Dutfield* 55
3 b f Danehill Dancer(IRE) —Bliss (IRE) (Statoblest)
1119^13 1513^5

Serene Highness (IRE) *J L Dunlop* 66
2 b f Highest Honor(FR) —Dollysister (FR) (Alydar (USA))
3726^3 4553^7

Serengeti *M Johnston* a80+
2 b c Singspiel(IRE) —Tanzania (USA) (Darshaan)
(6832)

Serevi (IRE) *J Noseda* a60 70
3 b c Cape Cross(IRE) —Winter Tern (USA) (Arctic Tern (USA))
449^3 553^4 1065^6

Sergeant Cecil *B R Millman* a66 120
7 ch g King's Signet(USA) —Jadidh (Touching Wood (USA))
1128^4 1833^2 2773^5 3315^2 4081^4 (4677) (5156) (5711a) 6119a^3

Sergeant Lewis *R M Flower* a68 36
4 gr g Mind Games—Silver Blessings (Statoblest)
1383^10 1899^12 2347^6

Sergeant Slipper *C Smith* a44 40
9 ch g Never So Bold—Pretty Scarce (Handsome Sailor)
179^8 388^7 529^3 876^3 907^3 1054^14 1393^7 1577^2 1764^5 1914^12

Serieux *D Nicholls* a87 87
7 b g Cadeaux Genereux—Seranda (IRE) (Petoski)
662^7 719^4 826^6 977^3 1382^5 1629^5 2454^4 2737^2 3191^5 3664^6 4029^4 4230^5 5688^7

Seriously Lucky (IRE) *D Nicholls* 29
2 b g Key Of Luck(USA) —Serious Delight (Lomond (USA))
1420^8 2660^6 3581^6

Serramanna *Ms J S Doyle* a66 63
5 ch m Grand Lodge(USA) —Spry (Suave Dancer (USA))
1334^7 1772^9 2305^8 2577^3 2956^3 3221^7 3467^3 4331^3 4702^7 4836^3 5201^U 5506^5 (5587) 5897^4 5935^5 6178^10 6408^2 6565^2 6673^7 6831^11 6883^3

Servillia (IRE) *W R Swinburn* a62 56
3 b f Dansili—Housekeeper (IRE) (Common Grounds)
1191^7 2143^11 (Dead)

Sesmen *M Botti* a80 104
2 bg f Inchinor—Poetry In Motion (IRE) (Ballad Rock)
(3201) (4458) (4840) 5522^6

Sessile (USA) *J H M Gosden* a57 60
3 b f Forestry(USA) —Madam Lagonza (USA) (Kingmambo (USA))
2406^8 4004^8 4930^7

Set Alight *Mrs C A Dunnett* a74 58
5 b m Forzando—Me Spede (Valiyar)
276^3 316^10 (429) 492^7 662^5 721^13 860^3 1057^6 2184^12 6425^11 6642^13

Seteem (USA) *M P Tregoning* 70
2 ch g Diesis—Inscrutable Dancer (USA) (Green Dancer (USA))
4867^8 5293^5

Setembro Chove (BRZ) *P Nickel Filho* a99 95
5 b h Fast Gold(USA) —Setting Trends (BRZ) (Knifebox (USA))
282a^12 438a^6 495a^2

Set Fire (IRE) *M Halford* 91
3 b f Bertolini(USA) —Incendio (Siberian Express (USA))
755a^8 4749a^7

Set The Scene (IRE) *J H M Gosden* a69+
2 b f Sadler's Wells(USA) —Margarula (IRE) (Doyoun)
6349^5

Settle (IRE) *W M Brisbourne* a43 45
7 b g Ali-Royal(IRE) —Airport (Warpath)
259^14 469^7

Seulement (USA) *L M Cumani* 98
4 ch g Rahy(USA) —Only Seule (USA) (Lyphard (USA))
2200^10 3313^10 3733^7 4372^5 4790^6 5175^4 5675^6 5945^5

Seven No Trumps *J M Bradley* a32 63
9 ch g Pips Pride—Classic Ring (IRE) (Auction Ring (USA))
967^5 1211^3 1563^5 1846^11 1981^9 2505^6 2949^3 3334^8 3608^6 3863^3 4232^8 4872^3 4962^4 6276^7

Seven Shirt *E G Bevan* a30 59
5 b g Great Dane(IRE) —Bride's Answer (Anshan)
180^12

Seven Steps (IRE) *J W Hills* a71 58
2 b f Best Of The Bests(IRE) —Seven Wonders (USA) (Rahy (USA))
4487^6 5209^3 5503^14 6032^2

Sevillano *A Laird* a72 109+
5 b g Nicolotte—Nashville Blues (IRE) (Try My Best (USA))
203a^4 431a^7 506a^2

Sew In Character *M Blanshard* a34 33
2 ch g Woodborough(USA) —Elegant Rose (Noalto)
4934^9 5381^10

Sew'N'So Character (IRE) *M Blanshard* a98 94
5 b g Imperial Ballet(IRE) —Hope And Glory (USA) (Well Decorated (USA))
542^2 728^10 1111^6 1585^6 1985^4 2440^5 (2988) 3218^4 3413^6 3973^8 4889^4 5299^6 5787^17 6772^5 6992^5

Sexy Lady (GER) *P Rau* 105
3 ch f Danehill Dancer(IRE) —Sky Dancing (IRE) (Exit To Nowhere (USA))
(2059a) (3133a) 3661a^2

Seyaadi *Robert Gray* 32
4 b g Intikhab(USA) —Sioux Chef (Be My Chief (USA))
1779^15 2079^17

Sforzando *Mrs L Stubbs* a66 79
5 b m Robellino(USA) —Mory Kante (USA) (Icecapade (USA))
106^10 252^5 1123^8 1422^16 1761^4 2108^2 2457^3 2777^4 3037^5 (4301) (4457) 4606^4 5090^7 (5513) 5685^2 5792^15 5897^11

Sgiaff *A & G Botti* 94
3 b c Spinning World(USA) —Belladera (IRE) (Alzao (USA))
758a^2 1175a^4

Sgt. Bert (USA) *Gary Montgomery* 98
5 b g Confide(USA) —Another Good Thing (USA) (Crafty Prospector (USA))
6127a^11

Sgt Pepper (IRE) *P L Gilligan* a60 60
5 b g Fasliyev(USA) —Amandine (IRE) (Darshaan)
632^10 670^12 847^10

Sgt Schultz (IRE) *J S Moore* a74 74
3 b g In The Wings—Ann's Annie (IRE) (Alzao (USA))
702^6 1004^6 1441^3 1616^15 2616^2 3364^3 3569^2 4225^6 4730^3 4972^2 6244^4 6415^3

Shaaban (IRE) *R J Price* a55 55
5 b g Woodman(USA) —Ashbilya (USA) (Nureyev (USA))
2702^17 3051^3 3386^12

Shabernak (IRE) *M L W Bell* 113
7 gr g Akarad(FR) —Salinova (FR) (Linamix (FR))
991^3

Shade Cozy (USA) *A M Balding* a82+ 60
4 gr g Cozzene(USA) —Fire And Shade (USA) (Shadeed (USA))
47^2 4180^7 6036^8 (6572) 6622^2 6656^2

Shaded Edge *D W P Arbuthnot* a49
2 b g Bold Edge—Twilight Mistress (Bin Ajwaad (IRE))
6710^9 6912^7

Shadow Aspect *Sir Michael Stoute* 63+
3 b c Nashwan(USA) —Hedonic (Gone West (USA))
1289^8

Shadow Jumper (IRE) *J T Stimpson* a67 70
5 b g Dayjur(USA) —Specifically (USA) (Sky Classic (CAN))
9^2 (46) (196) 345^4 428^2 552^5 608^7 824^11 1255^7 1388^10

Shady Green (IRE) *M W Easterby* a31 63
2 b g Kalanisi(IRE) —Albacora (IRE) (Fairy King (USA))
5720^8 6207^4 6475^8

Shahdawar (FR) *M Pimbonnet* 95
3 b g Sendawar(IRE) —Shahrazad (FR) (Bering)
6062a^5

Shaheen (GER) *P Vovcenko* 67
3 b f Tertullian(USA) —Sweety (GER) (Sir Felix (FR))
1328a^13

Shaheer (IRE) *J Gallagher* a60 56
4 b g Shahrastani(USA) —Atmospheric Blues (IRE) (Double Schwartz)
78^6 173^3 (301) 470^6 609^9 2362^4 2902^7 3592^5 3862^2 4280^2 4755^8 6423^4 6540^7 (6617) (6724) 6918^7

Shahin (USA) *M P Tregoning* 103
3 b c Kingmambo(USA) —String Quartet (IRE) (Sadler's Wells (USA))
5204^6

Shahm (IRE) *B J Curley* a51 66
7 b g Marju(IRE) —Istibshar (USA) (Mr Prospector (USA))
6370^2

Shahmina (IRE) *J H M Gosden* a73 68
3 b f Danehill(USA) —My Ballerina (USA) (Sir Ivor (USA))
3946^4 4374^3 4701^3 5650^2 6410^4

Shahzan House (IRE) *P G Murphy* a60 67
7 b g Sri Pekan(USA) —Nsx (Roi Danzig (USA))
65^8 296^8 591^6 1239^8 1484^11 2169^14 5016^11 5236^9 5513^13

Shaika *G Prodromou* a41 56
3 b f Almushtarak(IRE) —Subtle Girl (Selkirk (USA))
653^10 795^9 971^6 1387^10 (2070) 2463^7 2591^9 3232^10 3824^4 5298^3 5767^6 (6057) 6279^8 6373^7 6804^8

Shake On It *R F Johnson Houghton* 75
2 b c Lomitas—Decision Maid (USA) (Diesis)
3222^10 4895^2 5527^2

Shakerattleandroll (IRE) *Mrs L Richards* a69 71+
5 b g Dr Fong(USA) —Speedybird (IRE) (Danehill (USA))
556^10 713^7 1213^10 2088^13 2577^12 5201^12

Shake The Spear (IRE) *Miss J R Tooth* a52 41
3 b g Lear Spear(USA) —Milladella (FR) (Nureyev (USA))
4204^11

Shakis (IRE) *Doug Watson* a87 116
6 b h Machiavellian(USA) —Tawaaded (IRE) (Nashwan (USA))
153a^3 280a^5 497a^8 (622a) 743a^10

Shalapour (IRE) *M Johnston* 116
4 b h Darshaan—Shalama (IRE) (Kahyasi)
714[2]

Shamarkanda (FR) *Y De Nicolay* 93
3 ch f Kahyasi—Sharakanda (USA) (Alydar (USA))
4035a[11] 5472a[6]

Shamayoun (FR) *C R Egerton* 83
4 b g Kahyasi—Shamanara (IRE) (Danehill (USA))
2723[3] (Dead)

Shambar (IRE) *Miss E C Lavelle* 98?
7 gr g Linamix(FR)—Shamawna (IRE) (Darshaan)
6336[20]

Shamdala (IRE) *A De Royer-Dupre* 117
4 b m Grand Lodge(USA)—Shamadara (IRE) (Kahyasi)
1332a[4] (1875a) (2693a) 3516a[4] 4714[6] 5711a[2]6119a[7] 6782a[3]

Shamhoota (USA) *Sir Michael Stoute* 81+
2 bb c Danzig(USA)—Lucky Rainbow (USA) (Rainbow Quest (USA))
4105[3] (4664)

Shami *D W Chapman* a49 49
7 ch h Rainbow Quest(USA)—Bosra Sham (USA) (Woodman (USA))
72[5] 259[11]636[6] 1765[3]1911[6]

Shamila *G A Butler* a76 79
3 b f Green Desert(USA)—Shamaiel (IRE) (Lycius (USA))
459[2] 1635[5] 2533[3]3036[2] *3400[2] 3731[5]*

Shamoan (IRE) *E G Harty* a107 79
4 ch g Monashee Mountain(USA)—Fable (Absalom)
738a[5]

Shamrock Bay *C R Dore* a25 67
4 b m Celtic Swing—Kabayil (Dancing Brave (USA))
1560[3] 1754[3] 1847[2] 2078[12] 4393[5]5369[10] *5736[12]* 5960[10]

Shamrock Tea *M E Sowersby* a13 62
5 b g Imperial Ballet(IRE)—Yellow Ribbon (IRE) (Hamas (IRE))
782[11] 875[12]

Sham Ruby *M R Bosley* a29 33
4 ch m Tagula(IRE)—Bistro (USA) (Strawberry Road (AUS))
2575[10] 3306[8] 4670[7]5272[8]

Shamsalmaidan (IRE) *C E Brittain* a48 62+
3 ch f Fantastic Light(USA)—Maggi For Margaret (Shavian)
2293[8] 2391[9] 3803[7] 5056[5] 5451[5]*5651[5]* 5725[17]

Shamwari Fire (IRE) *I W McInnes* a32 41
6 ch g Idris(IRE)—Bobby's Dream (Reference Point)
2392[4] 2789[12] 3240[10] 3614[7] 3815[5]3941[3] 4087[6] 4266[5]

Shanagolden Juan (IRE) *M R Bosley* a30
3 ch g King Charlemagne(USA)—Ida Lupino (IRE) (Statoblest)
4931[11]

Shanawa (IRE) *M R Channon* 60
2 b f Cape Cross(IRE)—Yulara (IRE) (Night Shift (USA))
3707[10] 5287[6]

Shandelight (IRE) *Mrs A Duffield* 43
2 b f Dilshaan—By Candlelight (IRE) (Roi Danzig (USA))
4566[14] 4731[11] 5615[6]

Shane (GER) *Andreas Lowe* 98
2 ch f Kornado—Semplice (IRE) (Common Grounds)
(6122a)

Shangazi (USA) *B W Hills* 64
3 ch f Miswaki(USA)—Gran Ole Flag (USA) (El Gran Senor (USA))
1087[8] 1956[4] 2406[10] 4759[8] 5726[7]

Shankly Bond (IRE) *B Smart* a76 70
4 b g Danehill Dancer(IRE)—Fanellan (Try My Best (USA))
108[11]

Shank On Fourteen (IRE) *K R Burke* a68 67
5 b g Fayruz—Hever Rosina (Efisio)
1125[15] 1496[13] 2785[8] 3287[10] 3622[7]3863[8] (3913) 4587[6]

Shannon Arms (USA) *R Brotherton* a70 78
5 b g Wolf Power(SAF)—Crestasbest (USA) (Cresta Rider (USA))
1[13] 171[10]428[8] (498) 568[2] 650[11]737[5] 864[14] 1057[10]*1273[9] 1553[3]2137[10]* 2702[7] *3056[5]3599[9]* 3817[16] *6431[4]6618[5] 6708[7]*

Shannon House *M J McGrath* a58 61
3 ch g Inchinor—Sulitelma (USA) (The Minstrel (CAN))
479[6] 712[11]797[5] 1212[6] 1312[5] 1567[5] 2316[5]2730[5] *3016[12]*

Shannon Springs (IRE) *Andrew Turnell* a73
4 b g Darshaan—Our Queen Of Kings (Arazi (USA))
6888[9]

Shantell (ITY) *M Guarnieri*
2 ch f Shantou(USA)—Tally Cold (IRE) (Tate Gallery (USA))
2475a[6]

Shantina's Dream (USA) *H Morrison* 57
2 b f Smoke Glacken(USA)—J'Aime Jeblis (USA) (Jeblar (USA))
3193[5] 4558[6] 5264[7]

Shanty Star (IRE) *R Bouresly* a92 109
6 gr g Hector Protector(USA)—Shawanni (Shareef Dancer (USA))
153a[2] 205a[6] 356a[2] 437a[7] (509a) 562a[5]622a[6] 741a[14]

Shape Up (IRE) *R Craggs* a86 83
6 b g Octagonal(NZ)—Bint Kaldoun (IRE) (Kaldoun (FR))
867[2] 1281[6] 2387[11] 5115[10] 5367[4]5685[10] 5905[7] *6494[4]*

Shapira (GER) *Andreas Lowe* 109
5 ch m Kornado—Semplice (IRE) (Common Grounds)
2740[9] 4190a[5]

Sharaab (USA) *D E Cantillon* a50 52
5 bb g Erhaab(USA)—Ghashtah (USA) (Nijinsky (CAN))
2345[8] (4423) *6132[5]*

Sharapova (IRE) *M J Grassick* 83
3 b f Elusive Quality(USA)—Naazeq (Nashwan (USA))
2744[12] 5996a[17]

Shardda *F Watson* a2 69
6 b m Barathea(IRE)—Kronengold (USA) (Golden Act (USA))
1574[7]

Shardia (IRE) *J Jay* a50 52
3 b f Marju(IRE)—Shabarana (FR) (Nishapour (FR))
*70[6] 630[8]*1140[3] 1648[5] 4150[11] 4944[12] 5768[4]6213[14]

Shares (IRE) *P Monteith* a50 65
6 b g Turtle Island(IRE)—Glendora (Glenstal (USA))
1346[8]

Share The Feeling (IRE) *J W Unett* a68 65
4 b m Desert King(IRE)—Antapoura (IRE) (Bustino)
(6754) 6790[2] (6979)

Shariki (USA) *Saeed Bin Suroor* a81 81
3 bb c Spectrum(IRE)—Zahrat Dubai (Unfuwain (USA))
5016[5]

Sharmy (IRE) *Ian Williams* 90
10 b g Caerleon(USA)—Petticoat Lane (Ela-Mana-Mou)
3547[8] 4393[7]

Sharp Attack (USA) *D Wayne Lukas* a92
3 b c Storm Cat(USA)—Foppy Dancer (USA) (Fappiano (USA))
757a[8]

Sharpazmax (IRE) *P J Makin* a83 59
2 b c Daggers Drawn(USA)—Amour Toujours (IRE) (Law Society (USA))
3949[5] *(6441) (6597) (6866)*

Sharp Dresser (USA) *Mrs A J Perrett* a71
2 ch f Diesis—A La Mode (USA) (Known Fact (USA))
6187[2]

Sharp Duo (IRE) *M S Saunders* a26 59
3 ch g Daggers Drawn(USA)—Fay's Song (IRE) (Fayruz)
531[10] 4870[15] 5054[10]5885[10]

Sharpe Image (IRE) *G Woodward* 54
3 b f Bluebird(USA)—Silvretta (IRE) (Tirol)
1649[8] 2542[11] 3145[17]

Sharp Hat *D W Chapman* a48 57
12 b g Shavian—Madam Trilby (Grundy)
*(872) 1195[8] 1397[4]1571[5] 1909[4]*2700[13] (2928) 3190[4] 3617[3] 3781[5] 4091[8]4232[7] 4523[7] 5631[3] 5834[2] *6276[13]6539[5] 6851[2]6969[6]*

Sharp Humor (USA) *Dale Romans* a118
3 b c Distorted Humor(USA)—Bellona (USA) (Hansel (USA))
1498a[19] 6611a[5]

Sharplaw Autumn (USA) *W J Haggas* a71 84
3 b f Red Ransom(USA)—Hawzah (Green Desert (USA))
(1252) 2290[6] 3007[2] 3546[3] 4040[7] *6076[10]*

Sharp Lisa (USA) *Doug O'Neill* a110 110
4 ch m Dixieland Band(USA)—Winter's Gone (USA) (Dynaformer (USA))
4385a[7] *6343a[6]*

Sharp N Frosty *W M Brisbourne* a54 62
4 b g Somayda(IRE)—Wily Miss (Teenoso (USA))
2075[10] (2408) 4156[7] 4320[9]

Sharp Reply (USA) *R M Whitaker* 96+
4 b g Diesis—Questonia (Rainbow Quest (USA))
1281[8] 2079[13] 2736[4] 2975[8] 3748[11]4457[6] 5115[9] 5533[6] 5815[2]

Sharpsburg (USA) *Saeed Bin Suroor* 85+
3 b c Giant's Causeway(USA)—Sofitina (USA) (Alydar (USA))
(4776)

Sharp's Queen (IRE) *C Adaldo* 78
6 ch m Spinning World(USA)—Sharp Sass (USA) (Sharpen Up)
6362a[8]

Sharp Thrust (IRE) *A P Jarvis* a66 74
3 b g Daggers Drawn(USA)—Oumaladia (IRE) (Waajib)
233[9] 342[10] (Dead)

Sharp Tune (USA) *J D Frost* a26 51
4 ch g Diesis—Moonflute (USA) (The Minstrel (CAN))
6829[10]

Sharstar (ITY) *B Grizzetti*
2 b c Lando(GER)—Sharfire (IRE) (Shareef Dancer (USA))
6407a[4]

Shatin Leader *Miss L A Perratt* 49
4 b m Atraf—Star Dancer (Groom Dancer (USA))
1886[9] 2377[5] 2550[10] 2928[12] 3166[4]3334[4] 3356[6] 3673[5]

Shaunas Vision (IRE) *D K Ivory* a83 84
7 b m Dolphin Street(FR)—In Behind (IRE) (Entitled)
(700) (780) *847[2] (983)* 1376[5]*1927[5] 3098[7]3686[2]*

Shava *H J Evans* a55 58
6 b g Atraf—Anita Marie (IRE) (Anita's Prince)
6237[3] 6542[7]6726[3] (6805)

Shavoulin (USA) *Christian Wroe* 76
2 bb c Johannesburg(USA)—Hello Josephine (USA) (Take Me Out (USA))
5508[8] 5890[4]

Shawl *B J Meehan* 29
3 ch f Shahrastani(USA)—Circlet (Lion Cavern (USA))
971[8] 1214[9]

Shaydreambeliever *R A Fahey* 73
3 ch g Daggers Drawn(USA)—Aunt Sadie (Pursuit Of Love)
1948[6] 2290[11] 3477[2] 3760[3] 4173[11]4892[9] 5868[9] *6929[7]*

Shayrazan (IRE) *James Leavy* 92
5 ch g Zilzal(USA)—Shayraz (Darshaan)
1156a[4] 3123a[15] 4031a[6]

Shazand (FR) *A De Royer-Dupre* 98
3 b c Daylami(IRE)—Shawara (IRE) (Barathea (IRE))
4465a[3]

Shea's Round *G L Moore* a48
2 b c Josr Algarhoud(IRE)—Elms Schoolgirl (Emarati (USA))
6777[6] 6867[10]

Shebang (IRE) *M G Quinlan* a70 71
2 b f Trans Island—Mystery Hill (USA) (Danehill (USA))
4140[2] 4688[2] *5095[4]*(5570) 6064[7] *6402[4]*

She Cat (IRE) *V Caruso* 41
2 b f Noverre(USA)—She Bat (Batshoof)
5858a[13]

Sheer Tenby (IRE) *Paul A Roche* 99
9 b h Tenby—Take My Pledge (IRE) (Ahonoora)
3123a[9] 4187a[13]

Sheikh Shakey *R Hannon* a13 46
5 b g Muhtarram(USA)—Princesse Zelda (FR) (Defensive Play (USA))
1006[10] 1289[13]

She Is Tosho (JPN) *A Tsurudome* 109
6 b m Sakura Bakushin O(JPN)—Jane Tosho (JPN) (Tosho Fleet (JPN))
5717a[8] 6783a[10]

Shekan Star *K G Reveley* a51 62
4 b m Sri Pekan(USA)—Celestial Welcome (Most Welcome)
(891) 1249[2] 1590[8] *1729[7]*1997[3] (2381) 2998[5] 3243[2] 3983[2] 4393[2]4698[3] 4947[6] 5581[11]

She Knows Too Much *G A Butler* a32
2 ch f Tobougg(IRE)—How Do I Know (Petong)
6433[14]

Shelhom *Saeed Bin Suroor* a83 89
3 b g Green Desert(USA)—Felawnah (USA) (Mr Prospector (USA))
5845[6] 6107[11]

Shepherdess (USA) *D M Simcock* a54
2 ch f Stravinsky(USA)—Hushi (USA) (Riverman (USA))
6409[4] 6505[7]6605[5]

Sherafey (IRE) *Edgar Byrne* a13 13
2 br f Celtic Swing—Babolna (Generous (IRE))
6447[9]

Shergael (IRE) *J L Spearing* a53 53
5 b g Barathea(IRE)—Shergress (Siberian Express (USA))
6780[9] 6906[11]

Sheriff's Deputy *C N Kellett* a49 47
6 b g Atraf—Forest Fantasy (Rambo Dancer (CAN))
4709[16] 5831[14] *6419[8]6544[13]*

Sheriff's Silk *B Smart* a62 22
2 b c Forzando—Sylhall (Sharpo)
5481[8] *5923[3] 6303[5](6534) 6760[8]*

Sheriff Star *N Tinkler* 6
3 b f Killer Instinct—Westcourt Ruby (Petong)
5368[13] 5726[8]

Sherjawy (IRE) *Miss Z C Davison* a54 62
2 b c Diktat—Arruhan (IRE) (Mujtahid (USA))
3721[6] 4163[6] *5106[8]*6063[4] 6332[12]

Shersha (IRE) *Kevin F O'Donnell* 103
7 b m Priolo(USA)—Sheriya (USA) (Green Dancer (USA))
155a[7] 203a[7] 351a[3] 496a[10] 510a[4]753a[6] 1671[5] 2199[4] 2776[14] 3322a[6]

She's A Softie (IRE) *C F Wall* 38
2 b f Invincible Spirit(IRE)—New Tycoon (IRE) (Last Tycoon)
6331[10]

She's Dunnett *Mrs C A Dunnett* a22 53
3 b f Diktat—College Night (IRE) (Night Shift (USA))
528[8] 796[2] 1126[2]*6510[12]*

She's Included (USA) *C S Paasch* a100
2 b f Include(USA)—Dancingonice (USA) (Robyn Dancer (USA))
6338a[6]

Shes Millie *J G M O'Shea* 54
2 b f Auction House(USA)—Wintzig (Piccolo)
1136[8] 1688[6] 3307[7] (3677) 4134[4] 5094[11]5323[4]

Shes Minnie *J G M O'Shea* a70 83
3 b f Bertolini(USA)—Wintzig (Piccolo)
868[3] *(1110)* 1482[6] 1900[2] 2222[2] *2553[7]*3000[2] (3568) 4135[2] 4659[4] 5532[8] 6009[18]

She's My Dream (IRE) *A J Lidderdale* a34 20
4 ch m General Monash(USA)—She's My Love (Most Welcome)
59[10]

She's My Outsider *I A Wood* a82 83
4 b m Docksider(USA)—Solar Flare (IRE) (Danehill (USA))
3737[4] 4097[8] *5021[2](5212) 5670[11]*5919[7]

She's Our Beauty (IRE) *S T Mason* a51 9
3 b f Imperial Ballet(IRE)—Eleonora D'Arborea (Prince Sabo)
128[5] 2550[13] 2701[9]*3154[12]* 3608[17] 4056[5]4201[3] 4523[5] 5078[11] 5834[15] 6274[11]*(6548) 6755[7]6956[12]*

She's Our Lass (IRE) *D Carroll* a66 81
5 b m Orpen(USA)—Sharadja (IRE) (Doyoun)
1761[7] 2627[2] (3298) 3570[4] 3883[3] (4575) 5024[2]5320[4] 5810[10]

She's So Pretty (IRE) *W R Swinburn* 62
2 ch f Grand Lodge(USA)—Plymsole (USA) (Diesis)
4148[11] 4765[9] 5352[8]

Shesthebiscuit *J Parkes* a11 72
4 b m Diktat—Selvi (Mummy's Pet)
13[13]

Shevchenko (IRE) *J Noseda* 84+
2 bb c Rock Of Gibraltar(IRE)—Hula Angel (USA) (Woodman (USA))
5457[3] 6199[3]

She Whispers (IRE) *W M Brisbourne* a53 60
3 b f Royal Applause—Zariyba (IRE) (In The Wings)
69[2] 1224[2]86[6] 5445598[3] 6423[8]79[5] 1149[4] 5432[7]5839[6]

She Who Dares Wins *L R James* a9 14
6 b m Atraf—Mirani (IRE) (Danehill (USA))
487[10] 1763[8]

She Wont Wait *T M Jones* a47 60
2 b f Piccolo—Who Goes There (Wolfhound (USA))
849[6] 1046[4] 1309[3]1639[4] 2643[7] 3070[5] *3409[10]*

Shibumi *P A Trueman* a31 55
5 ch m Cigar—Hurricane Rose (Windjammer (USA))
2221[15] *2978[P] 3099[11]*4289[11]

Shifty *D Carroll* a74 69
7 b g Night Shift(USA)—Crodelle (IRE) (Formidable (USA))
1123[5] 1422[8] 1830[5] 2025[11] *2137[2]*2286[10] 2360[6] 2702[13] *(3262) 6425[7] 6476[3]6818[3] 6928[5]6946[5]*

Shifty Night (IRE) *Mrs C A Dunnett* a67d 58?
5 b m Night Shift(USA)—Bean Island (USA) (Afleet (CAN))
*332[2] 428[4]489[7] 519[4]608[3] 654[2]*798[10] *862[7] 1258[8]1388[6]* 1849[7] 3047[5]

Shiitake *Miss L A Perratt* 56+
3 b f Cayman Kai(IRE)—Petticoat Rule (Stanford)
2734[3] 4155[2] 5063[6]

Shimoni *W J Knight* 73
2 b f Mark Of Esteem(IRE)—Limuru (Salse (USA))
5456[8] (6058)

Shine And Rise (IRE) *C G Cox* a52
2 b c Marju(IRE)—Ela Cassini (IRE) (Ela-Mana-Mou)
6434[7]

Shingle Street (IRE) *I A Wood* a64 65
4 b g Bahhare(USA)—Sandystones (Selkirk (USA))
825[4] 966[6] *1385[8]*1690[9] 2219[7] 3269[7] *3597[8]4046[11] 4438[12]5033[4]*

Shining Energy (USA) *J Canani* 114
4 ch m Rahy(USA)—Miss Universal (IRE) (Lycius (USA))
3109a[6]

Shinko (IRE) *Miss J Feilden* a58 64
3 b f Shinko Forest(IRE)—Sharp Circle (IRE) (Sure Blade (USA))
*1307[5] 1551[5]*2293[11] 2727[3] 2951[3] 3336[5] 3668[8]4293[4] (4450) 4671[8] 5453[15]

Shinko Dancer (IRE) *H Rogers* 83
3 bb f Shinko Forest(IRE)—Bobbydazzle (Rock Hopper)
4855a[9] 5706a[9]

Shinko Femme (IRE) *J O'Reilly* a19 51
5 b m Shinko Forest(IRE)—Kilshanny (Groom Dancer (USA))
4067[7] 4198[11]

Shinko's Best (IRE) *A Kleinkorres* 107
5 ch g Shinko Forest(IRE)—Sail Away (GER) (Platini (GER))
1973a[4] (4418a) 6093a[7]

Shipmaster *A King* 98
3 b g Slip Anchor—Cover Look (SAF) (Fort Wood (USA))
1283[2] (1826) 2804[6]

Ship Mate (IRE) *Eamon Tyrrell* a61+ 67
3 b f Docksider(USA)—Universal Star (Unfuwain (USA))
1940[4] 2747[9]

Shiraz (GER) *M Weiss* 75
6 br h Bigstone(IRE)—Sintenis (GER) (Polish Precedent (USA))
456a[6]

Shirazi *D R Gandolfo* a81 84
8 b g Mtoto—Al Shadeedah (USA) (Nureyev (USA))
1115 186[11]

Shirley Oaks (IRE) *Miss Z C Davison* a53 56
8 b m Sri Pekan(USA)—Duly Elected (Persian Bold)
179[3] 255[7](262) 397[4]708[10] 858[11]872[3] 6728[10]6869[8]

Shirocco (GER) *A Fabre* 127
5 b h Monsun(GER)—So Sedulous (USA) (The Minstrel (CAN))
(1507) (2202) (5219a) 5716a[7]

Shmookh (USA) *J L Dunlop* 85+
2 b c Green Desert(USA)—Elrafa Ah (USA) (Storm Cat (USA))
3083[10] 5915[3] 6199[2]

Shoal Water (CAN) *M Frostad* 109
6 b g Smart Strike(CAN)—Puffin Island (CAN) (Pleasant Colony (USA))
5416a[11]

Shoeshine Boy (IRE) *Mlle A De Clerck* 91
8 br g Prince Sabo—Susie Sunshine (IRE) (Waajib)
2799a[12]

Shogun Prince (IRE) *A King* a81 87
3 b g Shinko Forest(IRE)—Lady Of Dreams (IRE) (Prince Rupert (FR))
1828[9] 2232[7] 2932[2] 3224[3] 4051[3]4599[5] *5110[6] 5428[8]*

Sholto *J O'Reilly* a58 54
8 b g Tragic Role(USA)—Rose Mill (Puissance)
2949[7] 3171[12]

Shoof (USA) *M J Gingell* 74
7 bb m Dayjur(USA)—Shemaq (USA) (Blushing John (USA))
240[11] 301[12]

Shopfitter *Mrs C A Dunnett* a44 40
3 b c Sugarfoot—Madam Wurlitzer (Noble Patriarch)
39[8] 1054[12] 1127[6]*1571[3] 1768[3]*1825[6] *2247[5]* 2644[8]

Shore Thing (IRE) *M H Tompkins* 79
3 b c Docksider(USA)—Spicebird (IRE) (Ela-Mana-Mou)
795[6] 1345[8] (2592) 3249[2] 3502[3] 4268[3]4530[2] 5479[9]

Shortbread *M Salaman* 69
4 ch g Selkirk(USA)—Breadcrumb (Final Straw)
2098[14] 2585[10] 3221[12] 3797[14] 4389[9]

Short Dance (USA) *B W Hills* 107
3 b f Hennessy(USA)—Clog Dance (Pursuit Of Love)
1130[3] (1834) 2054a[13] 4097[4] 5184[9] 5708a[6]

Shortest Day *Sir Michael Stoute* 102
3 b f Zafonic(USA)—Winter Solstice (Unfuwain (USA))
(1423) 1669[8] 2744[4] 4590[11]

Shorthand *Sir Michael Stoute* 98
2 b f Diktat—Much Too Risky (Bustino)
(5595) 5966[4]

Short Pause *D Hayes* 116
7 b h Sadler's Wells(USA) —Interval (Habitat)
6110a[17] 6392a[14]

Short Skirt *Sir Michael Stoute* 116
3 bl f Diktat—Much Too Risky (Bustino)
(1777) 2203[3] 4714[2] 5702a[6] (6103)

Short Stuff *R J Hodges* a47
2 b g Atraf—Cedar Lady (Telsmoss)
6258[10] 6511[6]6695[6]

Shoshiba (IRE) *P Martometti* 61
3 b f Plumbird—Magic Surprise (Bluebird (USA))
6363a[14]

Shoshoni *M A Jarvis* 40+
3 ch f Indian Ridge—Vituisa (Bering)
1640[11] 2146[7] 3111[4]

Shosolosa (IRE) *Mrs A L M King* a59 74
4 b m Dansili—Hajat (Mujtahid (USA))
1821[14] 2248[4] 2634[3]3142[7] 4176[2] 4730[7] 5205[12]
5831[13]

Shotfire Ridge *E F Vaughan* 78
3 ch g Grand Lodge(USA) —Darya (USA) (Gulch (USA))
(5598)

Shotley Dancer *N Bycroft* a38 46
7 ch m Danehill Dancer(IRE) —Hayhurst (Sandhurst Prince)
25[4]

Shotley Mac *N Bycroft* 65
2 ch g Abou Zouz(USA) —Julie's Gift (Presidium)
2281[4] 4421[11] 4731[16]

Shot To Fame (USA) *D Nicholls* 102
7 b g Quest For Fame—Exocet (USA) (Deposit Ticket (USA))
728[14] 1129[10] 1495[11] 1629[2] 1935[5]2200[3] 2742[30]
4029[13] 4098[11] 4739[16]5337[10] 5529[12]

Shouldntbethere (IRE) *Mrs P N Dutfield* a64 43
2 ch g Soviet Star(USA) —Octomone (USA) (Hennessy (USA))
4526[12] 5348[10] 5622[11] 6278[3](6421) 6639[2]

Shout (IRE) *R Charlton* a80 77
3 ch f Halling(USA) —Spout (Salse (USA))
1114[4] 1583[11] 5566[3] 6272[7] (6410) 6519[5]

Show Barry (AUS) *J Rattle* 106
6 b g Baryshnikov(AUS) —Tantinet (AUS) (Snippets (AUS))
6455a[6]

Show Business (IRE) *Sir Mark Prescott* a31
2 ch g Distant Music(USA) —Gertie Laurie (Lomond (USA))
6789[3]

Show House (USA) *Mrs A J Perrett* 58
2 b f Chester House(USA) —Galanty Show (Danehill (USA))
4161[6] 4553[10]

Showing Up (USA) *B Tagg* a111 122
3 ch c Strategic Mission(USA) —Miss Alethia (USA) (T V Commercial (USA))
1498a[6] (4387a) (6613a)

Show Me The Lolly (FR) *P J McBride* a57 54
6 b m Sri Pekan(USA) —Sugar Lolly (USA) (Irish River (FR))
6648[7] 6801[5]

Show No Fear *G M Moore* a54 74
5 b g Groom Dancer(USA) —La Piaf (FR) (Fabulous Dancer (USA))
911[6] 5080[10]

Show Thyme *K A Ryan* a35+ 57
3 ch g Compton Place—Souadah (USA) (General Holme (USA))
199[10]

Showtime Annie *A Bailey* a30 42
5 b m Wizard King—Rebel County (IRE) (Maelstrom Lake)
5925[10]

Showtime Faye *A Bailey* a42 21
4 b m Overbury(IRE) —Rebel County (IRE) (Maelstrom Lake)
182[12] 771[10]

Show Trial (IRE) *D J S Ffrench Davis* a61 59
2 b f Jade Robbery(USA) —Court Lane (USA) (Machiavellian (USA))
3537[10] 4041[12] 4664[2] 5282[7] 5780[3]6015[5] (6316)
6422[6] 6653[4]6807[3] 6900[3]

Show Winner *J Noseda* a63 86
3 b c Mtoto—Rose Show (Belmez (USA))
4973[6] 5151[2] 5589[3]5870[3] (6177)

Shreddy Shrimpster *A B Haynes* a56 48
2 ch f Zilzal(USA) —Empress Dagmar (Selkirk (USA))
2354[6] 2643[3] 2916[2] 3409[3]3678[5] 5419[10] 6311[7]

Shrewd Dude *Carl Llewellyn* a48 48
2 bb c Val Royal(FR) —Lily Dale (IRE) (Distinctly North (USA))
5766[7] 6014[9] 6409[8]6653[5]

Shrine Mountain (USA) *R A Harris* a70 60
4 b g Distorted Humor(USA) —Fancy Ruler (USA) (Half A Year (USA))
56[7] 1275[4]29[2] 546[2]696[10] 940[4]1073[11] (1387)
(1574) 2291[3] 2641[4] 2820[3] 4925[7] 5385[5]6059[12]
6419[3] 6641[5]6762[7] (6892) 6964[11]

Shrink *M Dods* a69 79+
5 b m Mind Games—Miss Mercy (IRE) (Law Society (USA))
2295[3] 2784[11] 3170[6]

Shrogginet (NZ) *Tom Hughes* 91
6 br g (USA) — (USA) (Silver Hawk (USA))
6391a[8]

Shropshirelass *Mrs Norma Pook* a51 53
3 b f Beat All(USA) —Emma-Lyne (Emarati (USA))
5032[12] 5567[7] 5936[3]6700[9]

Shumookh (IRE) *M A Jarvis* 109
3 b g Mujahid(USA) —Midway Lady (USA) (Alleged (USA))
3676[4] (4113) (4634) 4923[2] (5722) 6299[5]

Shunkawakhan (IRE) *G C H Chung* a62 54
3 b g Indian Danehill(IRE) —Special Park (USA) (Trempolino (USA))
1937[5] 2833[3] 3154[10]3866[8] 4930[3] 5210[6]5273[5]
5781[6] 6033[6]6348[2] 6510[4]6688[5] 6906[8]

Shustraya *P J Makin* a75 69
2 b f Dansili—Nimble Fan (USA) (Lear Fan (USA))
4207[4] 4558[4] 4920[2] 6512[2](6596) (6750) 6989[2]

Shy Glance (USA) *G A Swinbank* a74 69
4 b g Red Ransom(USA) —Royal Shyness (Royal Academy (USA))
2111[4] 2298[5] 3168[4] 4068[5] 4301[3]4698[6] 5388[3]
5579[7](6323)

Siakira *I A Wood* a67 71
3 ch f Golden Snake(USA) —Minette (Bishop Of Cashel)
2403[10] 2929[6] 3467[2] 3848[5] 4245[4]4836[6] 5129[2]
5574[4] 5911[9]

Siamese Cat (IRE) *B J Meehan* 100
2 ch f Rock Of Gibraltar(IRE) —Real Cat (USA) (Storm Cat (USA))
5371[3] 5503[2] 6215[2]

Siamun (AUS) *T Vasil* 102
6 gr g Desert King(IRE) —Walch's Lane (AUS) (Delgado (USA))
6391a[3]

Sibelius (SWE) *Caroline Stromberg* 47
5 h Night Shift(USA) — (Doyoun)
5226a[11]

Sicilian (IRE) *B W Hills* 84
3 b g Sadler's Wells(USA) —Hula Angel (USA) (Woodman (USA))
1291[3] 1596[8] (2932) 4249[13]4605[10]

Sidonius (GER) *P Vovcenko* 94
7 br h Sharp Prod(USA) —Sitmarie (GER) (Chief Singer)
6121a[5]

Siegfrieds Night (IRE) *M C Chapman* a68 55
5 ch g Night Shift(USA) —Shelbiana (USA) (Chieftain)
975[5] 1808[8] 2196[6]

Siena Gold *J G Given* a73 95
4 bb m Key Of Luck(USA) —Corn Futures (Nomination)
1377[13] 2851[10] 3687[7]4573[7] 4885[14]

Siena Star (IRE) *Stef Liddiard* a67 67
8 b g Brief Truce(USA) —Gooseberry Pie (Green Desert (USA))
610[8] 1560[7] 1757[4]2262[6] 2320[4] 2612[6](2707)
3115 [7] 4307[3] 4925[6] 5422[2] 5691[9]6289[4]
6484[5]6590[2] 6687[2]6848[5] (6870) 6954[7]

Sienna Storm (IRE) *M H Tompkins* 99
3 b g Peintre Celebre(USA) —Saint Ann (USA) (Geiger Counter (USA))
1237[3] 1473[2] 2228[14] 4678[10] 5186[8]5641[6]

Sierra *A W Carroll* a59 56
5 ch m Dr Fong(USA) —Warning Belle (Warning)
27[3] (94) (148) 1833[4]29[5]

Sierra Vista *D W Barker* a77 109
6 ch m Atraf—Park Vista (Taufan (USA))
1377[4] 1663[2] 2227[4] 3038[3] 3520[9]4080[8] 4343[8]
5171[12] 5405[8] (5535) 5921[3]

Siesta (IRE) *J R Fanshawe* 41
2 ch f King Charlemagne(USA) —Quiescent (Primo Dominie)
5231[9]

Si Foo (USA) *A M Balding* a75 76
2 ch c Fusaichi Pegasus(USA) —Ascension (IRE) (Night Shift (USA))
3457[2] (4000)

Sights On Gold (IRE) *Saeed Bin Suroor* 119
7 ch g Indian Ridge—Summer Trysting (USA) (Alleged (USA))
562a[10]

Sigismundus (IRE) *J R Boyle* a72 52
3 b g Mozart(IRE) —Bella Vie (IRE) (Sadler's Wells (USA))
34[8] 1182[1906] (228) 803[7] 1411[8]1954[6] 2318[7]
2553[8]5263[6] 5755[14] 5907[7]

Signal Hill *W J Haggas* a78 69
3 ch g Observatory(USA) —Rose Des Andes (IRE) (Royal Academy (USA))
3329[2] 3586[4] 4225[2] 4933[3]5388[2] 5879[7]

Signatory (USA) *J H M Gosden* 105
4 b h Kris S(USA) —Escrow Agent (USA) (El Gran Senor (USA))
(1991) 3294[4] 4713[19]

Sign Of The Cross *J R Fanshawe* a79+
2 b c Mark Of Esteem(IRE) —Thea (USA) (Marju (IRE))
6393[2]

Signor Albertini (IRE) *P C Haslam* a31 28
3 b g Bertolini(USA) —Snow Eagle (IRE) (Polar Falcon (USA))
2077[10] 4909[14]

Signor Panettiere *R J Smith* 82
5 b g Night Shift(USA) —Christmas Kiss (Taufan (USA))
3069[9]

Signor Peltro *H Candy* a86 91
3 b g Bertolini(USA) —Pewter Lass (Dowsing (USA))
1482[3] 2032[2] 2981[3](4488) 5943[6]

Signor Whippee *A Berry* a47 54
3 ch g Observatory(USA) —Revoltosa (IRE) (Catrail (USA))
487[8] 1612[6] 1792[7]2876[5] 2939[10] 3526[2]3833[7]
4056[3] 4296[10] 4611[5] 4948[4](5060) 5864[7] 6994[12]

Silaah *E A L Dunlop* 61
2 b c Mind Games—Ocean Grove (IRE) (Fairy King (USA))
5454[9]

Silca Chiave *M R Channon* 109
2 ch f Pivotal—Silca-Cisa (Hallgate)
3893[3] (4559) 4853a[2] 5654[3]

Silca Key *M R Channon* a71 77
2 ch f Inchinor—Baalbek (Barathea (IRE))
4553[3] 4873[2] 4994[4]5676[3] 5916[4]

Silca Soprano *M R Channon* a70 70
2 br f Kyllachy—Broughton Singer (IRE) (Common Grounds)
1817[2] 2026[6] 2523[3] 2890[6] 3210[4](3997) 4767[4]
5053[10]

Silca's Sister *Saeed Bin Suroor* 111
3 ch f Inchinor—Silca-Cisa (Hallgate)
1508[4] 2802[6] 6368a[2]

Silenia (USA) *R Menichetti*
2 ch f Ecton Park(USA) —Star On My Flag (USA) (Personal Flag (USA))
2062a[2]

Silent Applause *Dr J D Scargill* a67 82
3 b c Royal Applause—Billie Blue (Ballad Rock)
2542[6] 3742[2] 3826[3] 4249[8]4923[3] 5504[9]

Silent Beauty (IRE) *S C Williams* 37
2 b f Intikhab(USA) —Precedence (IRE) (Polish Precedent (USA))
5899[9] 6331[12]

Silent Name (JPN) *G Mandella* 117
4 b h Sunday Silence(USA) —Danzigaway (USA) (Danehill (USA))
5824a[7] 6342a[6]

Silent Storm *C A Cyzer* a80 75
6 ch g Zafonic(USA) —Nanda (Nashwan (USA))
(89) 221[9] 376[6]721[6] 1474[14] 1939[2]2464[3]
2757[7]3827[2] 4496[3] 4674[5] 5233[2] 5689[8]

Silent Times (IRE) *E J O'Neill* a69 112
3 bb c Danehill Dancer(IRE) —Recoleta (USA) (Wild Again (USA))
757a[11] 1362a[8]

Silent Waves (USA) *M Johnston* 103
2 gr c Cozzene(USA) —Michelle's Monarch (USA) (Wavering Monarch (USA))
(2854) (3788) 4037[4] 5851a[3]

Silent Willow (IRE) *D Nicholls* 46
5 b g Gothenberg(IRE) —Ardee Flo Jo (IRE) (Horage)
4059[6] 4694[9]

Silent Witness (AUS) *A S Cruz* 130
7 b g El Moxie(USA) —Jade Tiara (AUS) (Bureaucracy (NZ))
1527a[9] 5717a[4] 6783a[2]

Silex (GER) *P Schiergen* 99
3 b c Zilzal(USA) —Shine (GER) (Sanglamore (USA))
1176a[8] 1715a[7] 3563a[9]

Silidan *T P Tate* 90
3 b g Dansili—In Love Again (IRE) (Prince Rupert (FR))
1626[6] 2779[5] 3079[13] 3937[13]

Silk Blossom (IRE) *B W Hills* 110
2 ch f Barathea(IRE) —Lovely Blossom (FR) (Spinning World (USA))
(1082) 2800[2] 3415[6] (4737) (5464a)

Silk Dress (IRE) *John Joseph Murphy* 96
2 b f Gulch(USA) —Zvezda (USA) (Nureyev (USA))
4853a[9] 5394a[2]

Silken Act (CAN) *Mrs A J Perrett* a69 69
3 b f Theatrical—Silca Key Service (Bering)
2712[3] 3029[3] 3731[9]5056[3] 5868[5] 6448[9]

Silken Dance (IRE) *G L Moore* 14
3 b g Kalanisi(IRE) —Lady Ela (IRE) (Ela-Mana-Mou)
3029[13]

Silk Famous (JPN) *I Sameshima* 118
7 b h Marvelous Sunday(JPN) —Saint Sailor (JPN) (Caerleon (USA))
1329a[11]

Silkie Smooth (IRE) *B W Hills* a66 75
2 b f Barathea(IRE) —Whassup (FR) (Midyan (USA))
1807[3] 3495[3] 4171[2] 5157[6] 5676[12]6332[10] 6377[3]

Silk Merchant (IRE) *J Howard Johnson* 61
3 b g Distant Music(USA) —Space Travel (Dancing Dissident (USA))
978[7] 1344[3] 2160[5] 3582[6] 5636[14]

Silk Purse *M Madgwick* 50
3 b f Mujahid(USA) —Cieladeed (USA) (Shadeed (USA))
1901[13] 2753[14] 3794[15]4289[10] 4755[11]

Silk Topper (IRE) *R A Fahey* 52
3 b g Spectrum(IRE) —Dances With Dreams (Be My Chief (USA))
2542[10] 2948[6] 3750[3] 4382[4]

Silloth Spirit *Mrs A M Naughton* 19
6 b g Atraf—Gaelic Air (Ballad Rock)
144[12] 634[12]

Silly Gilly (IRE) *A Berry* a51 51
2 b f Mull Of Kintyre(USA) —Richly Deserved (IRE) (King's Lake (USA))
1442[11] 3247[11] 4066[9] 4196[5] 4608[10]4762[7] 5315[4]
5528[7] 6013[5] 6296[5]6679[4]

Silmi *E A L Dunlop* a69 57
2 gr c Daylami(IRE) —Intimaa (IRE) (Caerleon (USA))
6214[13] 6561[2]

Silsong (USA) *Miss Gay Kelleway* a49 59
4 ch m Stephen Got Even(USA) —Silver Trainor (USA) (Silver Hawk (USA))
173[4] 257[2]301[6] 615[2](634)

Silva (FR) *C Laffon-Parias* 104
3 b f Anabaa(USA) —Silverqueen (FR) (Alydar (USA))
1719a[12]

Silvaani (USA) *B Forsey* a49 56
8 gr g Dumaani(USA) —Ruby Silver (USA) (Silver Hawk (USA))
6375[4] 6630[5]

Silvabella (IRE) *D Haydn Jones* a14 54
3 gr f Monashee Mountain(USA) —Siva (FR) (Bellypha)
215[12] 534[10]1417[8] 2968[14] 3195[7]

Silvanella (IRE) *M S Saunders* a23 54
3 gb f Namid—Mystical (Mystiko (USA))
533[8] 1565[6] 1877[6]2235[6] 2602[9] 5728[9] 5874[8]

Silver Appraisal *B Smart* a46 59
2 gr f Royal Applause—Arinaga (Warning)
2500[6] 2783[3] 4424[11] 5349[3] 5747[13]6388[11] 6422[8]

Silver Bank *M W Easterby* 39
3 b f Silver Patriarch(IRE) —Piggy Bank (Emarati (USA))
1221[13] 1661[6] 1868[3] 2107[6]

Silver Blue (IRE) *R Hannon* a77 88
3 ch g Indian Lodge(IRE) —Silver Echo (Caerleon (USA))
1093[3] 1268[4] 1488[6] 2775[9] 2988[9]3443[10] 3737[7]
4782[9] 5869[8] 6017[8]6107[7] 6633[5]

Silver Bolt (IRE) *N P Littmoden*
2 gr c Night Shift(USA) —Missie Madam (IRE) (Kenmare (FR))
4664[3] 4969[8] 5646[16]

Silver Chariot *B W Hills* a71 55
3 gr g Silver Patriarch(IRE) —Asian Love (Petong)
724[4] 1205[8] 2177[8]4599[6]

Silver Court *A W Carroll* a38 52
4 b g Silver Patriarch(IRE) —Double Stake (USA) (Kokand (USA))
386[9] 894[13] 1225[8]1434[2] 1910[9] 2149[11]2601[9]
3153[9] 3798[2] 4068[8] 4497[5]4869[12]

Silver Cross (FR) *D Prod'Homme* 109
4 b h Kahyasi—Snowdrop II (FR) (Niniski (USA))
523a[2]

Silver Dane (IRE) *Mrs C A Dunnett* a80 81
4 b g Danetime(IRE) —Silver Prairie (IRE) (Common Grounds)
517[7] 605[13](798) 1125[12] (1161) 1399[8]1643[3]
1928[6] 2182[12]2711[6] 3625[4] (3802) 4110[6] 5275[7]
5782[10]6035[9]

Silver Dip *B W Hills* 90
3 gr f Gulch(USA) —Silver Bandana (USA) (Silver Buck (USA))
1843[8] (2297) 2650[8] 3418[5] 3852[8] (4837)
5529[6]5945[20]

Silver Flame *B J Meehan* 48
2 ch f Dr Fong(USA) —Pastel (Lion Cavern (USA))
1989[12] 2638[9] 3495[6]

Silverfoot (USA) *D Stewart* 114
6 rg g With Approval(CAN) —Northern Silver (USA) (Silver Ghost (USA))
6344a[9]

Silverhay *T D Barron* 79
5 b g Inchinor—Moon Spin (Night Shift (USA))
1075[4] 1425[8] 1480[4] 1631[5] 2193[4]2540[3] 2640[3]
(3141) 3724[4] 4021[8] (4730) 5599[4]

Silver Hotspur *M Wigham* a41 77
2 b g Royal Applause—Noble View (USA) (Distant View (USA))
1510[9] 2617[3] 3070[2] 4002[4] 5290[7]6866[8]

Silver Mitzva (IRE) *M Botti* a52
2 b f Almutawakel—Ribblesdale (Northern Park (USA))
6840[5]

Silver Mont (IRE) *S R Bowring* a54 53
3 b g Montjeu(IRE) —Silvernus (Machiavellian (USA))
2379[6] 3329[12] 3355[10] 3791[7] 4111[6]4380[6] 4734[5]
4884[8] 5618[9] (5926) 6128[10] 6305[3]

Silver Nun *T D Easterby* a43 28
3 gr f Mind Games—Sapphire Mill (Petong)
637[2] 690[3]874[3] 1200[4]1594[16] 1768[9] 1791[9]

Silver Pivotal (IRE) *G A Butler* 72
2 br f Pivotal—Silver Colours (USA) (Silver Hawk (USA))
6215[5]

Silver Prelude *D K Ivory* a67 91
5 gr g Prince Sabo—Silver Blessings (Statoblest)
1161[10] 1359[13] 1643[7]2182[10] 2444[6] 3593[7]

Silver Prophet (IRE) *M R Bosley* a74 69
7 gr g Idris(IRE) —Silver Heart (Yankee Gold)
1467[5]

Silver Reign *J J Bridger* a41 50
5 gr g Prince Sabo—Primo Donna Magna (Primo Dominie)
321[12] 396[8]553[6] 890[12]1310[14]

Silver Sail *J S Wainwright* 46
3 gr f Daylami(IRE) —Fiveofive (IRE) (Fairy King (USA))
2699[9] 3138[7] 3586[3] 4651[8] 5063[4]5583[6] 5726[5]

Silver Snipe *John Joseph Murphy* 30
2 b c Piccolo—Baileys Silver (USA) (Marlin (USA))
5692a[10]

Silver Timber (USA) *Linda Rice* 85
3 gr c Prime Timber(USA) —River Princess (CAN) (Alwuhush (USA))
6127a[8]

Silver Touch (IRE) *M R Channon* 109
3 b f Dansili—Sanpala (Sanglamore (USA))
(1119) 1719a[13] 3316[2] (5159) 5701a[9] 5962[5]

Silvertown *L Lungo* 87
11 b g Danehill(USA) —Docklands (USA) (Theatrical)
(1457) (2238) 2850[5] 4231[7] 4951[6] 6321[8]

Silvertown Sky (IRE) *P L Gilligan* a42 42
3 b f Lahib(USA) —Miss Verity (Factual (USA))
453[7] 687[5]1771[2] 2138[5] 2249[5]

Silver Train (USA) *R Dutrow Jr* a120
4 br h Old Trieste(USA) —Ridden In Thestars (USA) (Cormorant (USA))
(2093a) 5820a[5] 6611a[3]

Silver Visage (IRE) *Miss J Feilden* a57 57
4 b g Lujain(USA) —About Face (Midyan (USA))
4[10] 164[10]1303[10] 1673[18] 2288[9]3033[10] (3161)
3541[9] 4266[15] 4670[6]

Silver Whistle (USA) *W Mott* 110
4 rg h Alphabet Soup(USA) —Polish Polka (USA) (Polish Numbers (USA))
2476a[5] 6329a[5]

Silvo (NZ) *M F Harris* a49 34
7 gr g Lowell(USA) —Silvadella (NZ) (Silver Prospector (USA))
697[12] 1163[10]1311[9] 1723[13]

Simba Sun (IRE) *R M Beckett* 85
2 b g Intikhab(USA) —Lions Den (IRE) (Desert Style (IRE))
2218[3] (2857) 4824a[10] 5546[9]

Simlet *E W Tuer* 45
11 b g Forzando—Besito (Wassl)
346[8]

Simnel (IRE) *S L Keightley*
7 b m Turtle Island(IRE) —Caca Milis (IRE) (Taufan (USA))
546[11] 787[6]

Simonas (IRE) *A Wohler* 122
7 gr g Sternkoenig(IRE) —Sistadari (Shardari)
2910a[5] 3579a[4] 4828a[6] 5718a[6] (6109a)

Simonda *Mrs A J Perrett* 91
5 ch m Singspiel(IRE) —Jetbeeah (IRE) (Lomond (USA))
1376[2] 1931[11] 2231[5] 4604[7] 6202[12]

Simondiun *Mrs A J Perrett* 95
3 b g Hernando(FR) —Jetbeeah (IRE) (Lomond (USA))
(1822) 2986[7] 4125[9] 4459[2]

Simonetta (IRE) *J S Bolger* 87
2 br f Lil's Boy(USA) —Zavaleta (IRE) (Kahyasi)
3060a[3] 3658a[6] 4853a[12]

Simon Magus (GER) *U Ostmann* 77
2 br c Golan(IRE) —S'Il Vous Plait (GER) (Dashing Blade)
6092a[2]

Simpatica (ITY) *G Avvisati*
2 ch f Central Park(IRE) —Woody Prospect (USA) (Woodman (USA))
3428a[10]

Simpatico Bribon (CHI) *I Jory* a109
4 b h Election Day(IRE) —Saca La Mano (CHI) (Savaret (USA))
(561a) 739a[6]

Simple Exchange (IRE) *D K Weld* a109 111
5 b h Danehill(USA) —Summer Trysting (USA) (Alleged (USA))
(1018) 1365a[5] 2371a[6] 3660a[3] 3964a[6] 6516[9]

Simplified *N B King* a53 47
3 b f Lend A Hand—Houston Heiress (USA) (Houston (USA))
372[5] 479[8]579[4] 709[12]1642[11] 1829[12] 2589[5] 2968[12] 3264[2]3824[3] 4016[5] 4491[3] 5298[4] 6724[10]6801[9] 6907[2]

Simplify *T M Jones* a68 69
4 b g Fasliyev(USA) —Simplicity (Polish Precedent (USA))
576[10] 698[7]854[10] 972[8] 1802[6]2708[10] 3014[6] 3820[12]4332[10] 4842[5] 5267[4]

Simply Perfect *J Noseda* 111
2 gr f Danehill(USA) —Hotelgenie Dot Com (Selkirk (USA))
2300[2] 2743[2] (3485) 3925[3] 4853a[7] (5187) (5522)

Simply St Lucia *J R Weymes* a68 68
4 b m Charnwood Forest(IRE) —Mubadara (IRE) (Lahib (USA))
15[6] 109[9]334[5] 443[8]3263[8]

Simply The Guest (IRE) *N Tinkler* a46 39
7 b g Mujadil(USA) —Ned's Contessa (IRE) (Persian Heights)
92[12] 182[7]243[7] 302[4]390[6] 788[3]871[3] 939[2]

Simpsons Gamble (IRE) *R M Flower* a59 29
3 b g Tagula(IRE) —Kiva (Indian Ridge)
5092[10] 5427[11] 6019[11]6144[5] 6442[5]6577[4]

Simpsons Ross (IRE) *R M Flower* a64 67
3 br g Imperial Ballet(IRE) —Brunswick (Warning)
60[6] 142[2]234[9] 342[7]422[12] 1433[2] 1642[5]2318[4] 2978[5] 3410[6]3705[9] 3869[11] 4143[8] 5774[2]6593[4]

Sina Cova (IRE) *Peter Casey* 115
4 b m Barathea(IRE) —Kumta (IRE) (Priolo (USA))
1026a[2] (2689a) 4212a[2] 4714[5] 5465a[2] (5996a)

Sincerely *B W Hills* a74 68
4 b m Singspiel(IRE) —Noble Form (Double Form)
3099[12] 3398[8] 4557[2]5130[10] 5302[2] 5450[2] 5775[3]6069[7] 6294[3] (6439) 6564[4] 6747[3]

Sin City *R A Fahey* 78+
3 b g Sinndar(IRE) —Turn Of A Century (Halling (USA))
2986[5] 3502[5]

Sindirana (IRE) *Sir Michael Stoute* 101
3 br f Kalanisi(IRE) —Sinndiya (IRE) (Pharly (FR))
(1669) 2772[11] 3739[5] 4179[6]

Singalong *P Gallagher* 104
4 b m Singspiel(IRE) —No Frills (IRE) (Darshaan)
6253a[7]

Singalullaby (IRE) *D K Weld* 64
2 b g Singspiel(IRE) —Brief Lullaby (IRE) (Brief Truce (USA))
5692a[17]

Singapore Pearl (FR) *S Wattel* a83 93
4 b m Kendor(FR) —Beijaflor (FR) (Pampabird)
393a[9]

Singhalongtasveer *W Storey* 54
4 b g Namaqualand(USA) —Felinwen (White Mill)
1562[4] 2196[8] 4914[9] 5061[6]

Sinister Minister (USA) *B Baffert* a119
3 b c Old Trieste(USA) —Sweet Minister (USA) (The Prime Minister (USA))
1498a[16]

Sinjaree *Mrs S Lamyman*
8 b g Mark Of Esteem(IRE) —Forthwith (Midyan (USA))
616[14]

Sinner Or Saint (IRE) *T D Easterby* a41 67
3 ch g Sinndar(IRE) —Hillquest (Rainbow Quest (USA))
1077[7] 1855[13] 2698[6] 4117[3] 4254[3]4892[8] 5312[7] 6260[12]6469[7]

Siobhans Pearl (IRE) *Miss Martina Anne Doran* 80
2 ch f Fasliyev(USA) —Venetian Pearl (IRE) (Generous (IRE))
5850a[10]

Sion Hill (IRE) *Mrs N Macauley* a51 66
5 b g Desert Prince(IRE) —Mobilia (Last Tycoon)
26[3] 3947[14] 6277[6]6492[6] 6550[2]6637[6] 6717[2]6796[5] 6892[11]6962[10]

Si O No (CHI) *Patrick L Reynolds* 86
4 ch h Special Quest(FR) —A Mi Ciudad (CHI) (Sweeping Change (CAN))
6006a[3]

Siraj *J Ryan* a71 54
7 b g Piccolo—Masuri Kabisa (USA) (Ascot Knight (CAN))
21[6] 336[10]408[7] 3204[8]3728[4] 3835[4] 4054[7] 4141[3] 4365[5]6371[5] (6541) (6619) (6672) 6728[4](6827)

Sir Arthur (IRE) *M Johnston* 86
3 ch c Desert Prince(IRE) —Park Express (Ahonoora)
1635[3] (1866) 2324[9] (2781) 3214[9] 3737[8] 3984[6]

Sir Bond (IRE) *G R Oldroyd* a71 59
5 ch g Desert Sun—In Tranquility (IRE) (Shalford (IRE))
860[2] 950[2](1002) 1257[3]3262[7] 4068[9] 4518[10]6993[3]

Sirbrit *W J Musson* 41
3 b g Cadeaux Genereux—Evening Promise (Aragon)
1141[16] 2814[9] 3145[9] 5767[9] 6068[5]

Sirce (IRE) *D J Coakley* a94+ 103
4 b m Josr Algarhoud(IRE) —Trading Aces (Be My Chief (USA))
799[3] (1167) 2013[4] (2453) 4079[3]

Sir Charles *M Dods* 68+
2 b g Mujahid(USA) —Chocolate (IRE) (Brief Truce (USA))
2623[7] 3018[2] 4066[2]

Sir Desmond *Rae Guest* a86 86
8 gr g Petong—I'm Your Lady (Risk Me (FR))
80[3] 245[10]970[13] 1285[4] (1545)

Sir Don (IRE) *E S McMahon* a59 59
7 b g Lake Coniston(IRE) —New Sensitive (Wattlefield)
2397[7] 2611[2] 3398[6] 3682[5] 4054[2]4361[7] (6521) 6739[4]6922[7]

Sir Douglas *J A Osborne* a77 62
3 ch c Desert Sun—Daintree (IRE) (Tirol)
(533) 725[6] 1963[5]2863[7] 6206[20]

Sir Duke (IRE) *P W D'Arcy*
2 b c Danehill(USA) —Dimanche (IRE) (Sadler's Wells (USA))
5640[15]

Sir Edwin Landseer (USA) *Christian Wroe* a95 100
6 gr h Lit De Justice(USA) —Wildcat Blue (USA) (Cure The Blues (USA))
367a[5] (431a) 2429[7] 2847[24] 5535[5] 5667[4]

Sirene Doloise (FR) *A Bonin* a97 104
3 br f Marchand De Sable(USA) —Ramonda (FR) (Fabulous Dancer (USA))
773a[3] 1330a[2] 2491a[13] 4035a[8] 4542a[6]

Siren Lure (USA) *Art Sherman* a124 110
5 b g Joyeux Danseur(USA) —Cantamar (USA) (Gulch (USA))
(3134a) 6341a[8]

Siren's Gift *A M Balding* 99
2 ch f Cadeaux Genereux—Blue Siren (Bluebird (USA))
2300[6] 2984[2] (3239) 4026[4] 4737[4] 5154[4]

Sir Ernesto (AUS) *D Cruz* 116
5 b g Danehill(USA) —Brise De Mer (USA) (Bering)
6784a[9]

Sir Gerard *J R Fanshawe* a80+ 108
3 b c Marju(IRE) —Chapeau (Zafonic (USA))
(1250) 2024[2] (2774) 4098[4]

Sir Greeley (USA) *J Jerkens* a117
4 br g Mr Greeley(USA) —Worry Not (USA) (Concern (USA))
2093a[6]

Sir Haydn *J R Jenkins* a83 75
6 ch g Definite Article—Snowscape (Niniski (USA))
(33)

Sir Laughalot *Miss E C Lavelle* a80 77
6 b g Alzao(USA) —Funny Hilarious (USA) (Sir Ivor (USA))
2647[6] 3014[8]3431[10]

Sir Liam (USA) *P Mitchell* a58 73
2 b c Monarchos(USA) —Tears (USA) (Red Ransom (USA))
5020[7] 5417[2] 5893[11]

Sir Loin *N Tinkler* a59 65
5 ch g Compton Place—Charnwood Queen (Cadeaux Genereux)
2376[5] 2949[14] 3155[3]3523[9] (3683) 4232[11] 4462[4](4636) 4872[4] 5286[13]

Sir Mikeale *G Prodromou* a50
3 b c Easycall—Sleep Standing (IRE) (Standaan (FR))
45[9] 298[6]

Sir Monty (USA) *Mrs A J Perrett* 86
4 ch g Cat's Career(USA) —Lady Of Meadowlane (USA) (Pancho Jay (USA))
(2534) 3028[13] 4036[5] (4369) 5180[3] 5963[28] 6205[7]

Sir Nod *Miss J A Camacho* a87 84
4 b g Tagula(IRE) —Nordan Raider (Domynsky)
1042[5] 3567[3] 3986[10] 4885[9] 5117[2](5286) 6009[11] 6428[2]

Sir Orpen (IRE) *T D Barron* 79
3 gr g Orpen(USA) —Yalciyna (Nishapour (FR))
(1564) 1855[5] 2032[5] 2863[5] 3087[4] 3395[4]3879[4] 4885[3] 5079[4] 5765[7] 6048[7]

Sir Percy *M P Tregoning* 121
3 b c Mark Of Esteem(IRE) —Percy's Lass (Blakeney)
1486[2] (2228) 5964[7]

Sir Sandicliffe (IRE) *B W Hills* 73
2 b g Distant Music(USA) —Desert Rose (Green Desert (USA))
4049[3] 4295[5] 4705[4]

Sir Sandrovitch (IRE) *R W Price* a50 64
10 b g Polish Patriot(USA) —Old Downie (Be My Guest (USA))
96[3] 209[4]262[6] 485[8]547[5] 613[5]674[6]

Sir Xaar (IRE) *B Smart* 107
3 b c Xaar—Cradle Brief (IRE) (Brief Truce (USA))
1092[7] 1362a[2] 3086[5] 4596[7] 4896[4]5341[11]

Sismix (IRE) *C Laffon-Parias* 97
2 ch f Diesis—Goldamix (IRE) (Linamix (FR))
5257a[3] 5714a[10] 6046a[5]

Sissy So Lucky (GER) *A Trybuhl* 86
3 b f Raintrap—Scamander (GER) (Primo Dominie)
2912a[8]

Sister Etienne (IRE) *T D Barron* a66 67
2 b f Lend A Hand—Final Favour (IRE) (Unblest)
2791[9] 3358[3] 3745[4]4088[4] 4377[7] 4950[4] (5282) 6400[5]6813[2] (6945)

Sister Gee (IRE) *R Hollinshead* a38 31
4 b m Desert Story(IRE) —My Gloria (IRE) (Saint Estephe (FR))
1594[3] 2288[15] 3379[6]4155[13] 6129[10] 6277[5]

Sister Maria (USA) *E A L Dunlop* a72 76
2 bb f Kingmambo(USA) —Fraulein (Acatenango (GER))
4765[7] 6658[3] 6832[2]

Sister Sox (IRE) *M Halford* 95
6 b m Elbio—Eves Temptation (IRE) (Glenstal (USA))
5706a[4]

Sister Trouble (FR) *F Head* a81 100
3 b f Spectrum(IRE) —Messoeurs (FR) (Anabaa (USA))
959a[5] 1330a[4] 2257a[7] 5519a[8]

Situla (IRE) *H J L Dunlop* a72 69
2 ch f Pairumani Star(IRE) —Suspiria (IRE) (Glenstal (USA))
(6309) 6582[2] 6777[3]

Sivivatu (USA) *J Noseda* a75 81
3 b g Stravinsky(USA) —Belle Sultane (USA) (Seattle Slew (USA))
1067[12] 1381[6]

Sivota (IRE) *T P Tate* 73
2 b g Sakhee(USA) —Mamara Reef (Salse (USA))
5616[3] 5900[3] 6297[2]

Siwa *E A L Dunlop* a70
3 b f Green Desert(USA) —Criquette (Shirley Heights)
254[2] 365[2]533[5] 902[11]1638[8]

Six Mile Bottom (IRE) *Bruce Hellier* 72
2 b f Mull Of Kintyre(USA) —Nizamiya (Darshaan)
4766[16]

Six Of Trumps (IRE) *J A Osborne* 16
2 b g Fasliyev(USA) —Run To Jane (IRE) (Doyoun)
3892[10]

Six Shots *J A Osborne* 64
2 b c Josr Algarhoud(IRE) —Captive Heart (Conquistador Cielo (USA))
1838[15] 4290[7] 4526[7]

Sixties Icon *J Noseda* 123+
3 b c Galileo(IRE) —Love Divine (Diesis)
1070[6] (1546) 2228[7] 2801[3] (4024) (5185) 5716a[6]

Skelligs Rock (IRE) *A W Carroll* a48 72
6 b g Key Of Luck(USA) —Drew (IRE) (Double Schwartz)
18[6] 582[11]2707[11] 3896[7] 4239[4]

Skerries (IRE) *H Rogers* 89
5 ch m Dr Fong(USA) —Spanker (Suave Dancer (USA))
5996a[12]

Skezahra *T M Jones* a13
3 b f Zaha(CAN) —Skedaddle (Formidable (USA))
20[6]

Skhilling Spirit *T D Barron* 101
3 b g Most Welcome—Calcavella (Pursuit Of Love)
1292[5] 1836[2] (2022) 4601[8] 5358[12] 5677[2]5812[10]

Skiddaw Fox *Mrs L Williamson* a5
2 ch c Foxhound(USA) —Stealthy Times (Timeless Times (USA))
6480[13]

Skidmark *Miss J R Tooth* a84 72
5 b g Pennekamp(USA) —Flourishing (IRE) (Trojan Fen)
135[6] 214[6]454[11] 843[11]

Skidrow *M L W Bell* 98
4 b g Bachir(IRE) —Flourishing (IRE) (Trojan Fen)
1129[15] 1676[3] 1985[3] 2200[2] 2787[2]2988[5] 4739[8] 5512[2] 5789[9]

Ski For Luck (IRE) *J L Dunlop* 54+
2 br g Key Of Luck(USA) —Ski For Me (IRE) (Barathea (IRE))
3976[15] 4574[5] 5178[13]

Ski Jump (USA) *R A Fahey* a60 90
6 gr g El Prado(IRE) —Skiable (IRE) (Niniski (USA))
799[7] 976[13] 1809[7] 2238[2] (2625) 3533[10]4036[8] 4676[15] 5351[3] 5811[4] 5963[4]

Skin Sure Thing *D G Bridgwater* a40 39
3 b f Zaha(CAN) —Bay Bianca (IRE) (Law Society (USA))
93[12] 499[2]642[7] 1226[5]1726[8] 3797[9] 4239[6]4435[7]

Skip Code (USA) *M Casse* a103
2 rg c Skip Away(USA) —Heavenly Note (USA) (Sunny's Halo (CAN))
6339a[9]

Skip Of Colour *P A Blockley* a65 61
6 b g Rainbow Quest(USA) —Minskip (USA) (The Minstrel (CAN))
5842[11] (6717) 6858[7]

Skit *W M Brisbourne* 51
3 b g In The Wings—Skew (Niniski (USA))
1605[7] 3066[4] 4362[8] (4868)

Skodger (IRE) *G Woodward* 8
3 b c Nashwan(USA) —Ghay (USA) (Bahri (USA))
4635[12] 4891[8]

Sky At Night (IRE) *P Mitchell* a50 50
3 b g Beckett(IRE) —Grade A Star (IRE) (Alzao (USA))
31[9] 1401[9]1829[5] 2507[6] 2861[5]3016[5] 3797[12] 4367[13]4556[9]

Sky Beam (USA) *J L Dunlop* 38
2 bb f Kingmambo(USA) —Weekend In Seattle (USA) (Seattle Slew (USA))
4148[14] 4866[11] 5886[8]

Sky Conqueror (CAN) *Darwin D Banach* 113
4 ch h Sky Classic(CAN) —Heavenly Ballerina (CAN) (Conquistador Cielo (USA))
6126a[3]

Sky Crusader *R Ingram* a93 98
4 b g Mujahid(USA) —Red Cloud (IRE) (Taufan (USA))
1129[8] 1456[7] 2200[12] 2649[7] 2776[15]3212[10]

Skye Boat Song *J Jay* a40
3 b c Inchinor—Nebulae (IRE) (Unfuwain (USA))
272[10] 850[12]1226[3] 1726[13]

Skye But N Ben *T D Barron* a42 48
2 b g Auction House(USA) —Island Colony (USA) (Pleasant Colony (USA))
1420[6] 2361[9] 5959[11] 6316[8] 6625[6]

Skyelady *Miss J A Camacho* a70 88
3 b f Dansili—Song Of Skye (Warning)
1384[7] 4634[6] 5024[3]5590[13] 6176[10]

Sky High Guy (IRE) *S Kirk* a69 71
3 b g Galileo(IRE) —Well Bought (IRE) (Auction Ring (USA))
62[2] 479[3]668[2] 735[3]1375[7] 1740[7] 1898[5] 2990[3] 4124a[4]4884[2]

Sky Quest (IRE) *J R Boyle* a91 85
8 b g Spectrum(IRE) —Rose Vibert (Caerleon (USA))
2169[7] 2508[5] 2945[4] 3840[5] 4244[4]4900[5] 5163[5] 6841[7]

Skyscape *Thomas Cooper* 90
4 b m Zafonic(USA) —Aquarelle (Kenmare (FR))
3123a[13]

Sky Walk *Jamie Poulton* a40
3 b g Josr Algarhoud(IRE) —Jamrat Samya (IRE) (Sadler's Wells (USA))
4367[9] 5426[14]

Slade (GER) *Andreas Lowe* 90
4 b m Big Shuffle(USA) —Semplice (IRE) (Common Grounds)
5710a[5]

Slalom (IRE) *D Burchell* a77 74
6 b g Royal Applause—Skisette (Malinowski (USA))
825[7]

Slaney Time (IRE) *J S Bolger* 82
2 b c Rock Of Gibraltar(IRE) —Aretha (IRE) (Indian Ridge)
5410a[4] 5692a[3]

Slapper (ITY) *R Brogi* 96
4 b h Indian Ridge—Daniela Grassi (Bound For Honour (USA))
1871a[12]

Slate (IRE) *J A Osborne* 69
2 b c Rock Of Gibraltar(IRE) —Sharp Catch (IRE) (Common Grounds)
(5067) 5546[13]

Slavonic (USA) *B Storey* a67 69
5 ch g Royal Academy(USA) —Cyrillic (USA) (Irish River (FR))
2020[17] 3139[7]

Slavonic Lake *I A Wood* 58d
2 b c Lake Coniston(IRE) —Slavonic Dance (Muhtarram (USA))
(3174) 5053[15] 5482[15] 6007[12]

Sleeping Indian *J H M Gosden* 122
5 b h Indian Ridge—Las Flores (IRE) (Sadler's Wells (USA))
(5341) 5701a[11] (5962) 6342a[4]

Sleeping Storm (IRE) *B J Meehan* a78 79
3 b f Danehill Dancer(IRE) —Caribbean Escape (Pivotal)
827[10] 1091[10] 1482[9]1900[9] 2650[11] 2932[4] (3226) 3741[4] 4328[5]4562[3] 4874[4] 5377[14] 6094[7]

Sleeping Weapon (USA) *Doug Watson* a102
7 b h Gulch(USA) —Beating The Buzz (IRE) (Bluebird (USA))
206a[8] 434a[12]

Sleipner (BRZ) *A Selvaratnam* a81
5 b h Roi Normand(USA) —Iasmin Edge (BRZ) (Ghadeer (FR))
201a[P]

Slickly Royal (FR) *P Demercastel* 100
2 bl c Slickly(FR) —Royal Bride (FR) (Garde Royale)
4859a[3] 5801a[4]

Sling Back (IRE) *Eamon Tyrrell* a70 84
5 b m Desert Style(IRE) —Arabian Princess (Taufan (USA))
381[5] 4343[3] 5345[10]

Slipasearcher (IRE) *P D Evans* a67 86d
2 b f Danetime(IRE) —Imperialist (IRE) (Imperial Frontier (USA))
2218[4] (2478) 2743[5] 3120[3] 3415[8] 3874[7]4344[4] 4966[8] 5447[7] 6100[7]6569[5] 6586[4]6699[5] 6822[4]6939[6]

Slip Dance (IRE) *Eamon Tyrrell* a94 102
4 br m Celtic Swing—Hawala (IRE) (Warning)
201a[2] 352a[5] 506a[6] 1485[16]

Slipperfoot *J J Quinn* a27 61d
3 ch f Sugarfoot—She's A Breeze (Crofthall)
2543[2] 2701[4] 3526[6] 4056[7] 4201[2]4611[10] 5486[11] 5752[11]

Slip Star *T J Etherington* a24
3 b f Slip Anchor—Shiny Kay (Star Appeal)
5244[10] 6450[8]

Slo Mo Shun *B R Millman* a27 48
2 b f Polish Precedent(USA) —Malvadilla (IRE) (Doyoun)
5950[9] 6331[7] 6558[10]

Small Fortune *R Charlton* 69
2 b f Anabaa(USA) —New Assembly (IRE) (Machiavellian (USA))
3700[3]

Small Stakes (IRE) *P J Makin* a74 70
4 b g Pennekamp(USA) —Poker Chip (Bluebird (USA))
4564[2] 4799[2] 5378[3] 5729[4] 5987[3](6389) (6656) 6842[5]

Small Time Blues (IRE) *J Parkes* a34 3
4 b m Danetime(IRE) —Barinia (Corvaro (USA))
28[P] 103[9]

Smart Angus *R A Fahey* 24
2 gr g Agnes World(USA) —She's Smart (Absalom)
4987[11] 5288[10]

Smart Ass (IRE) *J S Moore* a84 71
3 b f Shinko Forest(IRE) —Jayess Elle (Sabrehill (USA))
10[7] 120[4]287[3] (347) (415) 583[2]3590[7] 3906[7] 4144[10] 4844[2] 5619[2]5953[6] 6239[6] 6652[3](6818) (6928) 6946[2]

Smart Boy Prince (IRE) *C Smith* a53 45
5 b g Princely Heir(IRE) —Miss Mulaz (FR) (Luthier)
(28) 938[2] 1766[8]3135[4]

Smart Cassie *D Shaw* a28 69d
3 ch f Allied Forces(USA) —Katy-Q (IRE) (Taufan (USA))
1264[7] 2410[9] 2826[9] 3268[6] 3821[9]5250[9]

Smart Cat (IRE) *A P Jarvis* 60
3 ch f Barathea(IRE) —Lioness (Lion Cavern (USA))
5319[6]

Smart Enough *M A Magnusson* 111+
3 gr c Cadeaux Genereux—Good Enough (FR) (Mukaddamah (USA))
1674[2] (1978) 2774[4] (3413) (4739) 5675[5]

Smart Gal (IRE) *J L Dunlop* 74
3 ch f Galileo(IRE) —Spring Easy (IRE) (Alzao (USA))
1515[3] 2117[7] 3256[8] 5057[15]

Smart Golden Boy (IRE) *Mrs L C Jewell* a52 4
3 ch g Raise A Grand(IRE) —Stoneware (Bigstone (IRE))
16[8] 188[14]595[10] 1433[12] 3073[11]6374[13] 6805[11]

Smart Guy (DEN) *B Olsen*
3 b c Grape Tree Road—Tower Of Menga (USA) (Afleet (USA))
4419a[4]

Smart Instinct (USA) *R A Fahey* 98
2 ch f Smart Strike(CAN) —Smile N Molly (USA) (Dixieland Band (USA))
(3982) (4607) 4715[3]

Smart John *D Shaw* 75
6 b g Bin Ajwaad(IRE) —Katy-Q (IRE) (Taufan (USA))
4575[8] 4900[9] 5132[4]

Smart Move (GER) *H Blume* 100
4 br m Monsun(GER) —Septima (GER) (Touching Wood (USA))
2280a[4] 4648a[7] 5857a[5]

Smart Tiger (GER) *N P Littmoden* a74
4 b g Tiger Hill(IRE) —Smoke Signal (IRE) (College Chapel)
530[5] 557[9]

Smash N'Grab (IRE) *K A Ryan* 61
2 ch f Jade Robbery(USA) —Sallwa (IRE) (Entrepreneur)
1647[7] (5111) 5747[11]

Smemi An Nada *P Bowen* 62
4 b g Selkirk(USA) —One Way Street (Habitat)
963[5] 1212[8]

Smiddy Hill *R Bastiman* a68 75
4 b m Factual(USA) —Hello Hobson'S (IRE) (Fayruz)
1618[2] 2295[4] 3825[2] (4091) 4691[6] (4952) 6353[6]6452[11]

Smile For Us *C Drew* a68 73
3 b g Whittingham(IRE) —Don't Smile (Sizzling Melody)
30[6] 139[10]287[2] 502[6]598[2] 646[2]861[2] 910[5](1263) 1825[12] 2247[6] 2896[4]3089[6] 3932[5] 6930[13]

Smirfys Diamond *D Nicholls* 76
2 b g Mujahid(USA) —Jade Pet (Petong)
1342[2] 4028[4] (4421) 4766[4] (Dead)

Smirfys Gold (IRE) *E S McMahon* 52
2 ch c Bad As I Wanna Be(IRE) —Golden Jorden (IRE) (Cadeaux Genereux)
5161[11] 5508[9] 5766[5]

Smirfys Night *E S McMahon* a55 55
7 b g Tina's Pet—Nightmare Lady (Celestial Storm (USA))
2544[3] 3682[P] 4233[8]

Smirfys Party *W M Brisbourne* a53 56
8 ch g Clantime—Party Scenes (Most Welcome)
38[7] 175[11]680[6] 768[5]793[9] 1481[6] 2484[6]3003[2] 3524[14] 4361[8]

Smirfy's Silver *W M Brisbourne* a45 69
2 b g Desert Prince(IRE) —Goodwood Blizzard (Inchinor)
1074[4] 1582[5] 2432[12] 2807[9] 3917[9]4321[10]

Smirfys Systems *W M Brisbourne* a54 53
7 b g Safawan—Saint Systems (Uncle Pokey)
1151[12] 4119[11] 4735[11]5453[6] 5752[14]

Smith N Allan Oils *C Smith* a65 65
7 b g Bahamian Bounty—Grand Splendour (Shirley Heights)
134[9]

Smoke It (IRE) *A Berry* 23
3 b g Carrowkeel(IRE) —Deerussa (IRE) (Jareer (USA))
1866[12] 1984[8] 3066[5] 4195[9]

Smokejumper (GER) *Frau E Mader* 79
2 b c Big Shuffle(USA) —Shikoku (Green Desert (USA))
(6092a)

Smokey Blue *M J Wallace* a66 13
3 gr g Tomba—Misty Goddess (IRE) (Godswalk (USA))
372[7] 536[5]993[17] 1941[13] 2466[4]3075[12]

Smokey Oakey (IRE) *M H Tompkins* a75 86
2 b c Tendulkar(USA) —Veronica (Persian Bold)
2930[3] 3407[2] 4295[3]4824a[20] (5359) 5916[9] 6100[8]

Smokin Beau *N P Littmoden* a109 95
9 b g Cigar—Beau Dada (IRE) (Pine Circle (USA))
1597[4] 1936[5] 2189[13] 3027[11] 3069[7]4085[2] 4101[3] 4453[2] (4725) 5009[8] 5333[9]5535[3] 6776[4] 6849[8]

Smokincanon *W G M Turner* a54 54
4 ch g Fumo Di Londra(IRE) —Secret Miss (Beveled (USA))
262[9] 321[7]402[5] 474[3]602[9] 2208[8]2319[5] 2531[4] 2785[7]3306[3] 3635[2] 3867[7] 4223[12]

Smoking Star *N I M Rossiter* 16
3 b f Observatory(USA) —Gitane (FR) (Grand Lodge (USA))
2479[15] 2673[9] 2968[11] 3975[7] 4585[17]5127[12] 5564[11]

Smokin Joe *J R Best* a76 51
5 b g Cigar—Beau Dada (IRE) (Pine Circle (USA))
36[3] 89[8]5391[9] 5778[8]5908[4] 6147[3]6652[7] 6698[4]6781[4] 6848[3]6878[10]

Smooch *R M H Cowell* a65 82
3 b f Inchinor—Two Step (Mujtahid (USA))
117[11] 344[6]954[9] 1264[3] 1448[6]2049[10] 2496[6] 3000[6] 4812[6]

Smoothie (IRE) *Ian Williams* a55 55
8 gr g Definite Article—Limpopo (Green Desert (USA))
52[8] 318[4]603[9] 733[6]1204[6] 1415[3] 2150[6] 3894[14]

Smooth Jazz *R M Beckett* a74 81
4 b g Zafonic(USA) —Halska (Unfuwain (USA))
1651[3] (2186) 2387[15] 3048[4] 3365[11] 4149[10]5786[6] 6070[11]

Smoothly Does It *Mrs A J Bowlby* a70 73
5 b g Efisio—Exotic Forest (Dominion)
1882[5] 2098[11] 2862[12]5831[7]

Smorfia *V Valiani* 79
3 b f Mtoto—Fragrant Belle (USA) (Al Nasr (FR))
2043a[11]

Smugglers Bay (IRE) *T D Easterby* 69
2 b g Celtic Swing—Princess Mood (GER) (Muhtarram (USA))
2733[8] 3940[3] 4566[10]

Snaafy (USA) *B W Hills* 61
2 b c Kingmambo(USA) —Nafisah (IRE) (Lahib (USA))
4768[8]

Snaefell (IRE) *M Halford* 96
2 gr g Danehill Dancer(IRE) —Sovereign Grace (IRE) (Standaan (FR))
2037a[5] 2724[4]

Snake Dancer (IRE) *N Clement* 100
3 ch f Golden Snake(USA) —Moidart (Electric)
2537a[5]

Snake's Head *J L Dunlop* 80
2 b f Golden Snake(USA) —Satin Bell (Midyan (USA))
3545[2] 4084[5] 4866[5]

Snake Skin *J Gallagher* a58 56
3 ch f Golden Snake(USA) —Silken Dalliance (Rambo Dancer (CAN))
85[6] 2480[6] 2929[4]3400[4] 3828[7] 5767[3]6430[9] 6627[10]

Snap *Liam McAteer* 70
5 ch g Dr Fong(USA) —Reactress (USA) (Sharpen Up)
3123a[20]

Snark (IRE) *P J Makin* a79 79
3 b g Cape Cross(IRE) —Agoer (Hadeer)
1190[9] 1738[3] 3046[5] 3547[4] 5889[11]6076[7] 6432[4]

Snoqualmie Boy *D R C Elsworth* a77+ 115
3 b c Montjeu(IRE) —Seattle Ribbon (USA) (Seattle Dancer (USA))
1120[3] (1515) 1805[3] 2228[16] (2775) 3314[6] 4126[7]4679[7] 5376[3] 5968[5]

Snow Ballerina *E A L Dunlop* 57
2 b f Sadler's Wells(USA) —Snow Bride (USA) (Blushing Groom (FR))
4964[12]

Snowberry Hill (USA) *P Howling* a59 68
3 b g Woodman(USA) —Class Skipper (USA) (Skip Trial (USA))
1345[14] 1867[7] 4044[8]4700[12] 5650[6]

Snow Bunting *Jedd O'Keeffe* a66 64
8 ch g Polar Falcon(USA) —Marl (Lycius (USA))
1717[8] 2504[6] (2811) 3287[7]3817[4] 4253[9] (4729) 5085[8] 5269[11] 6404[2]6820[2] 6919[7]

Snow Crystal (IRE) *J H M Gosden* 75
3 ch f Kingmambo(USA) —Crystal Spray (Beldale Flutter (USA))
4634[9]

Snow Dancer (IRE) *A Berry* a71 64
2 b f Desert Style(IRE) —Bella Vie (IRE) (Sadler's Wells (USA))
5632[3] 6013[2] 6270[3] 6481[6]6581[2] 6976[2]

Snowed Under *J D Bethell* a79 86
5 gr g Most Welcome—Snowy Mantle (Siberian Express (USA))
1051[2] 1380[3] 2088[8](2640) 3497[5] 3980[4] 4392[6] 4911[7] 5346[16]

Snowflight *R A Fahey* 69
2 b c Danehill Dancer(IRE) —Sadler's Song (Saddlers' Hall (IRE))
3080[4] 3809[5] 4171[3]

Snow Symphony (IRE) *D M Simcock* a46 65
3 b g Distant Music(USA) —Snowspin (Carwhite)
2951[2] 3668[5] 4243[4] 4930[13]5298[5] 5571[4] 6059[14]

Snow Wolf *J M Bradley* a67 72
5 ch g Wolfhound(USA) —Christmas Rose (Absalom)
1563[11] 1846[15] 2380[9] 2571[7] 2632[5]3033[5] 3867[4] 4278[6] 4872[11]

Snowy Day (FR) *W J Haggas* a72+
3 b g Pennekamp(USA) —Snow White (Polar Falcon (USA))
677[3] (1254) 6647[2]

Snugfit *G G Margarson* 26
2 b f Agnes World(USA) —Snugfit Annie (Midyan (USA))
5754[12] 5898[10]

Snugfit Dubarry *M W Easterby*
6 ch m Ali-Royal(IRE) —Spanish Serenade (Nashwan (USA))
412[10] 650[14]1249[9]

Soapy Danger *M Johnston* a80 120
3 b c Danzig(USA) —On A Soapbox (USA) (Mi Cielo (USA))
445[2] (536) 895[2] (1077) 1286[2](2436) (2804) (3444) 4678[5]

Soar With Eagles (USA) *A P O'Brien* 115
3 b c Kingmambo(USA) —Bound (USA) (Nijinsky (CAN))
1135[8] 4407a[3]

Soave (GER) *A Trybuhl* 114
7 ch h Dashing Blade—She's His Guest (IRE) (Be My Guest (USA))
(1973a) 4858a[3] 6093a[3]

Soba Fella *P T Midgley*
3 b g Puissance—Cedar Jeneva (Muhtarram (USA))
1687[11] 2001[11] 2325[13] 2944[9]

Soba Jones *J Balding* a71 69
9 b g Emperor Jones(USA) —Soba (Most Secret)
(9) 67[9] 196[2]274[5] (408) (674) 1255[4]1388[3] 3297[4] 3995[5]6930[5]

Social Rhythm *H J Collingridge* a76
2 b f Beat All(USA) —Highly Sociable (Puissance)
(4433) 6379[3] 6563[3]6750[2] 6991[2]

Society Hostess (USA) *Christophe Clement* 113
4 b m Seeking The Gold(USA) —Touch Of Truth (USA) (Storm Cat (USA))
6614a[5]

Society Music (IRE) *M Dods* 84
4 b m Almutawakel—Society Fair (FR) (Always Fair (USA))
1043[17] 1280[7] 1531[14] 2071[3] 2164[3]2810[5] 4253[12] 4831[4] 5384[12]

Socrepes (ITY) *F Contu*
2 br c Celtic Swing—Scorribanda (ITY) (Law Society (USA))
5771a[3]

So Elegant (IRE) *J Jay* a57 50
4 b m Bahhare(USA) —Soignee (Night Shift (USA))
72[11] 471[6]2483[10] 3597[3] 3836[4]4104[7] 4929[13]

Soffooh (USA) *W J Musson* a25 52
2 b c Elusive Quality(USA) —United Kingdom (USA) (Danzig (USA))
3193[12] 3830[2] 4007[4] 4436[7]5948[11]

Sofia Royale *B Palling* 50
2 b f Royal Applause—Once In My Life (IRE) (Lomond (USA))
6330[4]

Sofinella (IRE) *A W Carroll* a60 71
3 gr f Titus Livius(FR) —Mystical Jumbo (Mystiko (USA))
1900[8] 2826[8] 4078[7] 4587[4] 5181[6]6485[8] 6521[8]6686[8]

Soft Centre *Mrs A J Perrett* 102+
3 ch f Zafonic(USA) —Foodbroker Fancy (IRE) (Halling (USA))
(1472) 5502[13]

Soft Focus (IRE) *J A Osborne* a65 56
4 b m Spectrum(IRE) —Creme Caramel (USA) (Septieme Ciel (USA))
21[2] 133[2]170[2] 255[4]262[4] 345[8]474[5] (Dead)

Softlanding (IRE) *J E Hammond* 84
3 b f Nashwan(USA) —Forest Rain (FR) (Caerleon (USA))
4543a[9]

Soft Morning *Sir Mark Prescott* a69
2 b f Pivotal—Summer Night (Nashwan (USA))
6886[6] 6998[2]

Soho Square *M Johnston* a79 78
3 ch g Generous(IRE) —Stardance (USA) (Rahy (USA))
(337) 805[3] 1356[4] 2117[8]3248[6]

Sohraab *H Morrison* 67
2 b c Erhaab(USA) —Riverine (Risk Me (FR))
4000[6]

Soizic (NZ) *C G Cox* a72
4 ch m Istidaad(USA) —Nellie May (NZ) (Babarooom (USA))
6448[5] 6684[11]

Sokoke *D A Nolan* a22 68
5 ch g Compton Place—Sally Green (IRE) (Common Grounds)
1437[5] 1816[5] 5577[10] 6320[12]

Solarias Quest *A King* a71 82
4 b g Pursuit Of Love—Persuasion (Batshoof)
6811[9]

Soldier Field *A M Balding* a51
2 b g Fantastic Light(USA) —Khambani (IRE) (Royal Academy (USA))
6658[10]

Soldier Hollow *P Schiergen* 119
6 b h In The Wings—Island Race (Common Grounds)
1014a[5] 1712a[2] 2692a[2] 4386a[3] (5704a) 6365a[4]

Soldier Of Fortune (IRE) *A P O'Brien* 114
2 b c Galileo(IRE) —Affianced (IRE) (Erins Isle)
6456a[2]

Soldiers Romance *T D Easterby* a58
3 b g Allied Forces(USA) —Still In Love (Emarati (USA))
823[3]

Sole Agent (IRE) *G L Moore* 56
4 b g Trans Island—Seattle Siren (USA) (Seattle Slew (USA))
6108[10]

Soledad (IRE) *G Cherel* 113
6 b g Priolo(USA) —True (FR) (Common Grounds)
4647a[4] 5223a[3] 6119a[8]

Solent (IRE) *R Hannon* a93 104
4 b g Montjeu(IRE) —Stylish (Anshan)
1357[5] (1842) 2229[11] 2817[2] 3533[7]4027[4] 4713[6] 5010[3] 5678[5]

Solicitude *D Haydn Jones* a57 38
3 ch f Bertolini(USA) —Sibilant (Selkirk (USA))
1642[14] 2583[15] 3101[10]4533[7] 5781[3] 6033[2]6608[7] 6721[3]6897[3]

Solid Rock (IRE) *T G Mills* a94+ 80+
2 b c Rock Of Gibraltar(IRE) —Sheer Spirit (IRE) (Caerleon (USA))
5147[5] 5458[4] 5841[6](6332) 6444[4] (6634) (6699)

Solipsist (IRE) *N I M Rossiter* a43 53
5 ch g Grand Lodge(USA) —Mijouter (IRE) (Coquelin (USA))
470[11] 573[7]785[5] 973[13]

Solis Obitus *B R Millman*
2 b g Foxhound(USA) —Tramonto (Sri Pekan (USA))
2218[11]

Solo City *P A Blockley* a33 37
2 b g Averti(IRE) —Surakarta (Bin Ajwaad (IRE))
5886[9] 6023[11] 6675[8]

Solo Flight *H Morrison* a87 95
9 gr g Mtoto—Silver Singer (Pharly (FR))
1206[4] 1992[11] 2672[7] 4112[3] 4878[8]5511[12] 6351[3] (6633) 6888[6]

Solomans Prospect *Miss D A McHale*
3 b c Hazaaf(USA) —Our Stella (Petong)
658[11] 735[7]4263[11]

Solomon's Mine (USA) *M J Polglase* a68 74
7 b g Rahy(USA) —Shes A Sheba (USA) (Alysheba (USA))
1184[P]

Solo Star *Miss J A Camacho* a36 54
3 ch f Observatory(USA) —Aura Of Grace (USA) (Southern Halo (USA))
406[7] 609[7]642[9]

Sol Rojo *J Pearce* a75 65
4 b g Efisio—Shining Cloud (Indian Ridge)
13[9] 73[3]158[8] 229[3]251[12] 382[3](568) 820[10]857[3] 1058[3] 1293[3](2148) 2327[8] 2702[8] (3056) 3948[7]4511[4] (4991) 6378[2] (6568) 6621[3]

Solva *B J Meehan* 93?
3 b f Singspiel(IRE) —Annapurna (IRE) (Brief Truce (USA))
(1419) 2613[2] 2961[2] 3292[8] 4040[6] 4482[6](5164) 5300[4]

Solvana (IRE) *Wido Neuroth* 102
4 b m Selkirk(USA) —Simmering (Mas Media)
5225a[2]

Solwind (USA) *B Smart* a47 60
2 b f Johannesburg(USA) —For Love (USA) (Sultry Song (USA))
4151[5] 5237[5] 5679[8] 6416[9]6592[10]

Some Diva *W R Swinburn* a72 62
3 ch f Dr Fong(USA) —Dorothea Brooke (IRE) (Dancing Brave (USA))
1641[8] 2167[6] 2704[2] 2987[3] 3410[5]4930[10] 5370[4] 5936[4](6380) 6503[3]

Somersault *Sir Michael Stoute* a61 69
3 ch f Pivotal—Rash (Pursuit Of Love)
3029[7] 3711[2] (4117) 4610[4] 5108[7]

Something (IRE) *T G Mills* a108+ 99
4 b g Trans Island—Persian Polly (Persian Bold)
(516) (667) 1299[6] 1487[16]

Something Exciting *D R C Elsworth* 115
4 ch m Halling(USA) —Faraway Waters (Pharly (FR))
2202[6] 3905[3] 4817[7]

Something Simple (IRE) *R Ford* a46 67
3 ch g Raise A Grand(IRE) —Baccara (IRE) (Sri Pekan (USA))
6623[5]

Sommertag (GER) *P Schiergen* 103
3 b c Tiger Hill(IRE) —Sommernacht (GER) (Monsun (GER))
1526a[2] 2314a[6] 3131a[6] 5414a[3]

Somnus *T D Easterby* 115
6 b g Pivotal—Midnight's Reward (Night Shift (USA))
1778[3] 2386[5] (3295) 4191a[13] 4740[4] 5011[4]5184[2] 5549[6] 5962[4] 6218[4]

Som Tala *M R Channon* 91
3 ch c Fantastic Light(USA) —One Of The Family (Alzao (USA))
894[3] 1120[4] 1492[2] 2117[4] (2677) 3502[4]3877[4] (4469) (5318) 5811[6]

Sonara (IRE) *M H Tompkins* 59
2 b g Peintre Celebre(USA) —Fay (IRE) (Polish Precedent (USA))
4768[12] 5332[11] 5640[8]

Sonar Sound (GER) *T P Tate* 47
2 b c Slickly(FR) —Samothrace (IRE) (Arazi (USA))
4018[8] 4458[4] 5402[6]

Sonderborg *J Mackie* a52 50
5 b m Great Dane(IRE) —Nordico Princess (Nordico (USA))
(94) 183[9] 3947[13] 4405[7]4974[9] 5929[5]6473[5] 6606[6]6701[5] (6799) 6960[7]

Song Huntress *A G Newcombe* a55 50
3 b f Foxhound(USA) —Eastern Lyric (Petong)
287[12] 1771[7] 2208[13]3340[4] 4278[9] 5840[6] 6236[10]

Songmaster (USA) *Mrs A J Perrett*
3 b g Singspiel(IRE) —One Beautiful Lady (USA) (Broad Brush (USA))
2655 [10]

Song Of Kintyre (FR) *A Couetil* 92
3 b f Mull Of Kintyre(USA) —Opera Song (IRE) (In The Wings)
2537a[4]

Song Of Passion (IRE) *R Hannon* a88 99
3 b f Orpen(USA) —Bint Al Balad (IRE) (Ahonoora)
(1626) (2205) 2744[19] 3687[4] 4042[3]5525[4]

Song Of Silence (USA) *E A L Dunlop* a92 67
3 b f Unbridled's Song(USA) —State Secret (Green Desert (USA))
(234) 294[2] (342) 448[4]827[2] 1130[11] 4083[14]

Song Of Wind (JPN) *Hidekazu Asami* 122
3 b c El Condor Pasa(USA) —Memorial Summer (JPN) (Sunday Silence (USA))
6782a[4]

Song Writer (GER) *Carmen Bocskai* 110
6 b h Monsun(GER) —Song Maker (IRE) (Sadler's Wells (USA))
3579a[2] 4414a[5]

Sonic Anthem (USA) *D Nicholls* a73 54
4 b g Royal Anthem(USA) —Whisperifyoudare (USA) (Red Ransom (USA))
(2) 131[5] 383[8]1123[10]

Sonning Star (IRE) *D R C Elsworth* 52
2 b g Desert Prince(IRE) —Fantazia (Zafonic (USA))
5454[12] 5914[13]

Sonnium (IRE) *W P Mullins* 59
2 ch c Lomitas—Cutting Glance (USA) (Woodman (USA))
5662a[12]

Sonntag Blue (IRE) *Miss J Feilden* a59 55
4 b g Bluebird(USA) —Laura Margaret (Persian Bold)
82[7] 363[7]520[3] 693[9]1057[9]

Sonny Mac *B J Meehan* a73 62
3 b c Pivotal—Sea Drift (FR) (Warning)
2825[10] 3029[6] 4044[5]4842[7]

Sonny Parkin *G A Huffer* a78 85
4 b g Spinning World(USA) —No Miss Kris (USA) (Capote (USA))
33[8] 3044[6] 3712[3](4108) 4336[4] 4604[6] 4805[2] 5110[11]5299[11]

Sonny Red (IRE) *R Hannon* 98
2 b c Redback—Magic Melody (Petong)
(1510) (1977) 2771[4]

Sono *P D Niven* a54 54
9 b g Robellino(USA) —Sweet Holland (USA) (Alydar (USA))
168[11] 443[9]643[13]

Son Of Bathwick (IRE) *Mrs Norma Pook* a8 57
4 b g Dr Fong(USA) —Bathwick Babe (IRE) (Sri Pekan (USA))
5426[12]

Son Of Greek Myth (USA) *G L Moore* a67 80
5 b g Silver Hawk(USA) —Greek Myth (IRE) (Sadler's Wells (USA))
521[12]

Son Of Samson (IRE) *R J Price*
5 ch g Diesis—Delilah (IRE) (Bluebird (USA))
403[12]

Son Of Sophie *C N Kellett* a35 39
4 b g Band On The Run—Fair Enchantress (Enchantment)
26[8] 180[7]302[5] 615[6]

Son Of Thunder (IRE) *M Dods* a44 62
5 ch g Dr Fong(USA) —Sakura Queen (IRE) (Woodman (USA))
1045^{11} 2286^{3} 2697^{6} 3353^{5} $3570^{8}$$3815^{7}$ 4194^{5} (4568) 5311^{6} 5683^{3} 5831^{3}

Sonovishi *E J O'Neill* a46
2 b g Ishiguru(USA) —Kastaway (Distant Relative)
4366^{6}

Sophia Gardens *D W P Arbuthnot* 69
2 ch f Barathea(IRE) —Lovely Lyca (Night Shift (USA))
4558^{5} 5068^{2} 5754^{6} 6018^{6}

Sophie James *M G Quinlan* a33 45
3 b f Mujahid(USA) —Night Trader (USA) (Melyno)
1417^{13} *4045^{11} 4396^{9}*

Sophie'Jo *Miss J Feilden* a47 69
3 b f Agnes World(USA) —Maureena (IRE) (Grand Lodge (USA))
2615^{6} 2990^{13} *$3400^{11}$$5973^{9}$ $6476^{5}$$6759^{5}$ 6907^{6}*

Sophie's Dream *J G Given* a53 60
2 b g Averti(IRE) —Sophielu (Rudimentary (USA))
1730^{5} 2281^{9} 3351^{9} *$6416^{4}$$6653^{7}$ 6807^{9}*

Sopran Nyda (ITY) *V Ficara*
2 br c Daro Sopran(GER) —Sopranyn (IRE) (Nordico (USA))
$3427a^{3}$

Sopran Promo (IRE) *B Grizzetti* 89
2 b c Montjeu(IRE) —Middle Prospect (USA) (Mr Prospector (USA))
$5771a^{2}$ $6123a^{5}$

Sopran Slam (IRE) *B Grizzetti* 89
2 b f Grand Slam(USA) —Sopran Londa (IRE) (Danehill (USA))
$3343a^{4}$ (5705a)

Sorbiesharry (IRE) *Mrs N Macauley* a44 16
7 gr g Sorbie Tower(IRE) —Silver Moon (Environment Friend)
15^{7} $405^{6}$$493^{7}$ $505^{6}$$537^{6}$ $586^{5}$$820^{8}$ $955^{8}$$1244^{12}$ $1553^{9}$$1574^{3}$ $1910^{10}$$2345^{11}$ $3998^{5}$$6280^{6}$ $6552^{7}$$6795^{4}$

Sorrel Point *H J Collingridge* a60+ 61
3 b c Bertolini(USA) —Lightning Princess (Puissance)
165^{7} $380^{4}$$1430^{7}$ 3410^{9} $4113^{5}$$4666^{3}$

Sorrent (GER) *P Schiergen* 106+
4 br m Monsun(GER) —Salka (GER) (Doyoun)
$1974a^{P}$

So Shy (IRE) *J R Boyle* a24 60
2 ch f Fath(USA) —Mytilene (IRE) (Soviet Star (USA))
2354^{4} 6015^{8} *6409^{10}*

So Sober (IRE) *D Shaw* a41 38
8 b g Common Grounds—Femme Savante (Glenstal (USA))
789^{4} $872^{8}$$1466^{8}$

So Stream (ITY) *B Grizzetti* 93
3 b f Elmaamul(USA) —Snug Dinner (IRE) (Jareer (USA))
$2043a^{8}$

Sosueme Now *A B Haynes* a47 46
2 ch f Foxhound(USA) —So Discreet (Tragic Role (USA))
4980^{5} 5565^{5} *6224^{10}*

So Sweet (IRE) *M R Channon* 87+
2 b f Cape Cross(IRE) —Announcing Peace (Danehill (USA))
3851^{6} (4148) (4955) $5464a^{18}$

Sotanna (IRE) *P R Webber* 54
4 b m Stravinsky(USA) —Festive Season (USA) (Lypheor)
4447^{4} *5035^{12}*

Soterio (GER) *W Baltromei* 114
6 b h Lavirco(GER) —So Rarely (USA) (Arctic Tern (USA))
$1860a^{5}$ $3775a^{3}$ $5881a^{7}$ $6109a^{5}$ $6610a^{15}$

Sotik Star (IRE) *P J Makin* a85+ 78
3 b c Elnadim(USA) —Crystal Springs (IRE) (Kahyasi)
4605^{4} *(5612) (6635) 6868^{7}*

Soto *M W Easterby* a59 78
3 b g Averti(IRE) —Belle Of The Blues (IRE) (Blues Traveller (IRE))
1097^{7} 1497^{8} 1812^{3} 2163^{2} $2661^{13}$$3041^{7}$ 3360^{3} 3722^{3} (3936) 4262^{4} 5401^{4}

Soubriquet (IRE) *T G Mills* a48 74+
3 b g Daylami(IRE) —Green Lucia (Green Dancer (USA))
1670^{4} 2118^{8} 3029^{10} *$3935^{11}$$4537^{7}$ 5609^{5}*

Soudaine (GER) *P Schiergen* 101
3 b f Monsun(GER) —Suivez (FR) (Fioravanti (USA))
$5008a^{2}$

Soudelor (IRE) *Rune Haugen* 95
5 b g Orpen(USA) —Desert Place (Green Desert (USA))
$5225a^{8}$

Soufah (IRE) *J L Dunlop* 75
4 b g Desert Style(IRE) —Entracte (Henbit (USA))
897^{11} 1288^{2} 2104^{2} 2822^{2} 3547^{2}

Souffleur *M L W Bell* 79
3 b c In The Wings—Salinova (FR) (Linamix (FR))
897^{2} 1081^{4} (1827) (2117) 3981^{4}

Soulacroix *L M Cumani* 108+
5 b g Kylian(USA) —California Dreamin (Slip Anchor)
(2656) (4027) 5170^{2} 5548^{7} $6346a^{6}$

Soulard (USA) *J Noseda* 75
3 b c Arch(USA) —Bourbon Blues (USA) (Seeking The Gold (USA))
1192^{6} 1483^{4} 1827^{6} 2526^{2} 3231^{3}(3399)

Soul Blazer (USA) *A M Balding* a66
3 b g Honour And Glory(USA) —See You (USA) (Gulch (USA))
5986^{4} $6429^{3}$$6587^{3}$ 6841^{10}

Soul Of Magic (IRE) *Karin Suter* 102
7 b m Definite Article—Blazing Soul (IRE) (Common Grounds)
$6251a^{3}$

Soul Provider (IRE) *G Prodromou* a48 61
5 ch m Danehill Dancer(IRE) —Wing And A Prayer (IRE) (Shalford (IRE))
29^{11} $312^{4}$$399^{11}$

Sound And Vision (IRE) *M Dods* a61 62
4 b g Fayruz—Lyrical Vision (IRE) (Vision (USA))
(26)

Soundasapound *I W McInnes* 19
2 b f Pursuit Of Love—Blue Nile (IRE) (Bluebird (USA))
1074^{9} 1588^{8} 2106^{12} 2890^{8} $4115^{12}$$5084^{15}$ *6576^{14}*

Sound Of Nature (USA) *H R A Cecil* 74+
3 b c Chester House(USA) —Yashmak (USA) (Danzig (USA))
5598^{6} (6019)

Sounds Simla (IRE) *R A Harris* a55 80
3 b f Indian Rocket—Evocative (IRE) (Double Schwartz)
53^{7} $83^{5}$$139^{7}$ 326^{8}(477) $598^{4}$$626^{7}$ $2462^{8}$$2758^{4}$ 3912^{U} 4401^{10} 4546^{2} $4756^{10}$$5291^{6}$ 5480^{15} *$5970^{6}$$6325^{7}$ $6541^{13}$$6717^{9}$ $6833^{7}$$6969^{8}$*

Sound That Alarm *P D Evans* a38 52
4 b g Groom Dancer(USA) —Warning Star (Warning)
*691^{7} 1465^{9}*1882^{11} 2221^{12}

Southandwest (IRE) *J S Moore* 91
2 ch g Titus Livius(FR) —Cheviot Indian (IRE) (Indian Ridge)
2218^{2} (2631) 3252^{5} (3861) $4824a^{2}$ 5335^{8}

Southborough Lad *Mrs C A Dunnett* 27
3 ch g Woodborough(USA) —Caribbee Beach (IRE) (Magical Strike (USA))
795^{11} 893^{7}

South Cape *M R Channon* a95 98
3 b g Cape Cross(IRE) —Aunt Ruby (USA) (Rubiano (USA))
(717) 1268^{7} 1776^{5} 2988^{11} 3491^{4} *3648^{3}*3978^{3} 4379^{7} 5150^{2} 5520^{2} $5639^{7}$$5943^{12}$

Southern Bazaar (USA) *M C Chapman* a60 60
5 ch g Southern Halo(USA) —Sunday Bazaar (USA) (Nureyev (USA))
4229^{8}

Southern Courage (NZ) *Mick Price* 103
4 b g Bahhare(USA) —Calm Courage (NZ) (Spectacular Love (USA))
(6391a)

Southern Shore (IRE) *D Burchell* 62
4 ch g Erhaab(USA) —Intisab (Green Desert (USA))
103^{11}

Southern Tide (USA) *J Pearce* a38 43
4 b h Southern Halo(USA) —My Own Lovely Lee (USA) (Bucksplasher (USA))
1910^{4} 2262^{10} 2820^{15}*3999^{7} $6134^{10}$$6552^{6}$ 6726^{5}*

Southgate Lady (IRE) *N P Littmoden* a25 36
3 b f Night Shift(USA) —German Lady (Mon Tresor)
93^{10}

South Hill *R J Price* a42 45
3 b f Marju(IRE) —Briggsmaid (Elegant Air)
1375^{12} 2569^{8} *6701^{12}*

South O'The Border *T G Mills* a79 86
4 b g Wolfhound(USA) —Abbey's Gal (Efisio)
843^{3} 1133^{9} $1435^{3}$$2088^{2}$ 2621^{3} 3366^{7} (4536) 5295^{3} 5625^{2}

Southport Star (IRE) *J R Fanshawe* a83 80
3 b g King's Best(USA) —Danzig's Girl (USA) (Danzig (USA))
*1166^{7} 1963^{3}*2403^{3} 2823^{5} (3266) 4689^{7} *$5249^{3}$$5778^{14}$ 6076^{11}*

Souvenance *Sir Mark Prescott* 106
3 b f Hernando(FR) —Summer Night (Nashwan (USA))
$1714a^{3}$ $2694a^{3}$ $3515a^{4}$ $4212a^{3}$ $4863a^{2}$$5156^{5}$

Sovereign Dancer (GER) *Mario Hofer* 103
5 b c Dashing Blade—Selana (GER) (Lomitas)
$1715a^{4}$ $2489a^{6}$

Sovereign Dreamer (USA) *P F I Cole* a2 64
6 b g Kingmambo(USA) —Spend A Dream (USA) (Spend A Buck (USA))
1566^{10} *2320^{16}* 2507^{9}

Sovereign Spirit (IRE) *W R Swinburn* a74 61
4 b g Desert Prince(IRE) —Sheer Spirit (IRE) (Caerleon (USA))
*(131) (318) 491^{4} 4972^{4}*5324^{7} *6256^{2} $6560^{3}$$6754^{6}$*

Sovereign State (IRE) *D W Thompson* a50 55
9 b g Soviet Lad(USA) —Portree (Slip Anchor)
1184^{11} 1560^{9} 3637^{5} 5836^{7}

Sovereignty (JPN) *D K Ivory* a71 67
4 b g King's Best(USA) —Calando (USA) (Storm Cat (USA))
1531^{11} 1760^{7} 2377^{8} 2748^{4} *(3155)* 3612^{8}*3845^{4} $4368^{2}$$5046^{6}$ (5386) 5775^{4} $5907^{6}$$6293^{3}$ $6478^{7}$$6489^{3}$ 6747^{5}(6820) 6919^{6}*

Soviet Joy (IRE) *J J Quinn* a28 49
5 b g Russian Revival(USA) —Danny's Joy (IRE) (Maelstrom Lake)
715^{2} 1073^{9}

Soviet Kiri (IRE) *S Ibido*
2 b f Soviet Star(USA) —Kiriyaki (USA) (Secretariat (USA))
$3427a^{4}$

Soviet Legend (IRE) *T J Etherington* a51 47
3 b c Soviet Star(USA) —Another Legend (USA) (Lyphard's Wish (FR))
*359^{5} 646^{10}*1234^{2} 1612^{7} 3397^{7} 3821^{11} $4056^{9}$$5486^{12}$

Soviet Palace (IRE) *K A Ryan* 82
2 b g Jade Robbery(USA) —Daisy Hill (Indian Ridge)
1588^{6} (2287) 4100^{9} 4912^{10}

Soviet Promise (IRE) *G G Margarson* 39
3 b f Soviet Star(USA) —Akarita (IRE) (Akarad (FR))
2498^{6} 3006^{8} 3541^{7} 3824^{5}

Soviet Sceptre (IRE) *R T Phillips* a56 60
5 ch g Soviet Star(USA) —Princess Sceptre (Cadeaux Genereux)
*379^{2} 457^{7}*882^{4} *1199^{5} 1548^{6}*

Soviet Song (IRE) *J R Fanshawe* 124
6 b m Marju(IRE) —Kalinka (IRE) (Soviet Star (USA))
1840^{4} (2740) 3416^{6} 4038^{2} 4839^{5} 5674^{2}

Soviet Sound (IRE) *Jedd O'Keeffe* 48
2 ch c Soviet Star(USA) —Orange Grouse (IRE) (Taufan (USA))
2409^{11} 3018^{9} 4421^{9} 5860^{5}

Sovietta (IRE) *A G Newcombe* a52 65
5 b m Soviet Star(USA) —La Riveraine (USA) (Riverman (USA))
780^{4} 1222^{3} 1772^{10} 1879^{2} (2075) *6843^{8}*

Soviet Threat (IRE) *A G Juckes* a72 54
5 ch g Soviet Star(USA) —Veiled Threat (IRE) (Be My Guest (USA))
*169^{6} 381^{6}*1830^{14} *2319^{9}*

Sowdrey *M R Channon* 76
2 b c In The Wings—Baaderah (IRE) (Cadeaux Genereux)
3701^{5}

Sowerby *M Brittain* a35 60
4 b g Grey Desire—Brief Star (IRE) (Brief Truce (USA))
872^{7}

So Will I *Doug Watson* 112
5 ch g Inchinor—Fur Will Fly (Petong)
$201a^{3}$ $281a^{10}$ $431a^{9}$

Soylent Green *S Parr* 3
2 b f Primo Valentino(IRE) —Slipperose (Persepolis (FR))
5491^{10} 6012^{10}

Space Cowboy (IRE) *G L Moore* a55 78
6 b g Anabaa(USA) —Lady Moranbon (USA) (Trempolino (USA))
3209^{8}

Spaceman *L M Cumani* a62 66
3 b c In The Wings—Souk (IRE) (Ahonoora)
1055^{13} 1652^{16} 2569^{4} 3232^{6} (3823) $4224^{4}$$5276^{6}$ *5736^{4}*

Spainnash (IRE) *J J Lambe* 97
6 b g Nashwan(USA) —Agreed (Green Desert (USA))
$1156a^{5}$ $4094a^{13}$ *6607^{11}*

Spanish Ace *J M Bradley* a60 94
5 b g First Trump—Spanish Heart (King Of Spain)
(1047) (1211) 1487^{11} 1662^{2} 2450^{12} 2674^{7} $3625^{6}$$4085^{10}$ 4486^{8} 5148^{12}

Spanish Affair *Jedd O'Keeffe* a12 24
2 b c Pursuit Of Love—Catalonia (IRE) (Catrail (USA))
5900^{9} *6303^{10}*

Spanish Air *J W Hills* a56 40
2 b f Muhtarram(USA) —Spanish Heart (King Of Spain)
1930^{8} *2461^{4} $2755^{6}$$3385^{9}$*

Spanish Conquest *Sir Mark Prescott* a23 31
2 b g Hernando(FR) —Sirena (GER) (Tejano (USA))
5106^{11} 5332^{8} *5608^{11}*

Spanish Don *D R C Elsworth* a97 103
8 b g Zafonic(USA) —Spanish Wells (IRE) (Sadler's Wells (USA))
1084^{7} 1678^{15} 2742^{28} 4739^{13}

Spanish Hidalgo (IRE) *J L Dunlop* 94
2 b c Night Shift(USA) —Spanish Lady (IRE) (Bering)
2899^{2} 3545^{3} (4140) (4767) 5805^{8}

Spanish Lace *Miss J A Camacho* a64 62
3 b f Hernando(FR) —Kabayil (Dancing Brave (USA))
(215) 2081^{5} 3249^{10}

Spanish Law *M Dods* 61
4 b g Zaha(CAN) —Misty Moon (Polar Falcon (USA))
1253^{9} 2165^{4} 2641^{2} 2811^{6} $2926^{5}$$3361^{10}$ 4425^{12}

Spanish Moon (USA) *Sir Michael Stoute* 90+
2 b c El Prado(IRE) —Shining Bright (Rainbow Quest (USA))
(6220)

Spanish Music *R Ingram* a45 64
4 b m Piccolo—Raffelina (USA) (Carson City (USA))
266^{5} $293^{4}$$399^{9}$ $534^{6}$$890^{4}$ $1165^{11}$$1391^{3}$ $1538^{5}$$1727^{7}$

Spanish Rainbow (IRE) *J L Dunlop* 67
3 ch f Rainbow Quest(USA) —Spanish Lady (IRE) (Bering)
1118^{7}

Spanish Ridge (IRE) *J L Dunlop* 79d
4 b g Indian Ridge—Spanish Lady (IRE) (Bering)
1132^{10} 1685^{8} 2078^{9} 2869^{6} $3743^{P}$$4320^{7}$

Spanish Star *Mrs N Macauley* a29 14
9 b g Hernando(FR) —Desert Girl (Green Desert (USA))
182^{9} 490^{7}

Spanish Story *J G Portman* a31 27
3 br f Vettori(IRE) —Spanish Heart (King Of Spain)
1165^{5} 2293^{12} *3458^{7}*4531^{8} *6304^{13}*

Sparkbridge (IRE) *R F Fisher* a40 60
3 b g Mull Of Kintyre(USA) —Persian Velvet (IRE) (Distinctly North (USA))
709^{10} 817^{4} $1593^{8}$$1888^{7}$ 1946^{8} 2379^{11} 3815^{12} 5836^{8}

Sparkling Eyes *C E Brittain* a64 82
2 b f Lujain(USA) —Lady Georgia (Arazi (USA))
2328^{11} 2617^{4} 2743^{4} *3259^{5}*4130^{6} (4485) 4910^{2} 5442^{6} 6105^{8} *$6332^{5}$$6563^{4}$*

Spark Up *J W Unett* a62 68
6 b m Lahib(USA) —Catch The Flame (USA) (Storm Bird (CAN))
229^{4} 290^{4}(407) $446^{4}$$586^{11}$ $2418^{6}$$2794^{6}$ $3099^{4}$$3390^{3}$ $3599^{2}$$4974^{4}$ 5370^{10} *$6387^{3}$$6483^{4}$ (6683) 6934^{3} 6993^{2}*

Sparkwell *D Shaw* a69 77
4 b h Dansili—West Devon (USA) (Gone West (USA))
2737^{11} 3041^{15} 4957^{9} 5243^{10} *$5878^{3}$$6672^{6}$ 6739^{5}(6823) $6865^{8}$$6953^{6}$*

Sparky Vixen *S Parr* 10
2 b f Mujahid(USA) —Lucy Glitters (USA) (Cryptoclearance (USA))
4053^{10} 6157^{9} 6298^{11}

Spartan Dance *J A Geake* a69 61
2 ch g Groom Dancer(USA) —Delphic Way (Warning)
6173^{10} 6297^{5} *$6536^{3}$$6676^{3}$*

Spartan Odyssey *A Bailey* a49 31
5 b g Overbury(IRE) —Spartan Native (Native Bazaar)
3810^{8} *6535^{6}*

Spasiba *Mrs L Williamson* a46 42
3 b f Pivotal—Skimra (Hernando (FR))
199^{5} $584^{10}$$874^{9}$

Spatzolita (GER) *D K Richardson* 96
7 br m Goofalik(USA) —Santa Clara (Star Appeal)
$4828a^{9}$ $5857a^{4}$ $6109a^{10}$ $6529a^{6}$

Speagle (IRE) *D Carroll* a85 72
4 ch h Desert Sun—Pohutakawa (FR) (Affirmed (USA))
6241^{8} (6524) (6666) (6893)

Speakerboxxx *P F I Cole* a59 60
4 ch g Zafonic(USA) —Trounce (Barathea (IRE))
44^{7} 134^{8}

Spearit (IRE) *D R C Elsworth* a78 79
3 ch c Lear Spear(USA) —French Gift (Cadeaux Genereux)
1900^{7} 2105^{6} 2385^{4} 2931^{5} $3226^{9}$$3904^{6}$ (4338) *4703^{2}* 4874^{2} (Dead)

Spear Thistle *Mrs N Smith* a87 85
4 ch g Selkirk(USA) —Ardisia (USA) (Affirmed (USA))
*765^{3} 1021^{11}*2013^{12} 5678^{3} 6107^{14}

Special Ballot (IRE) *G A Swinbank* a40 30
5 br m Perugino(USA) —Election Special (Chief Singer)
1503^{7} 4948^{17} 5077^{8} *$6327^{7}$$6482^{5}$ 6553^{8}*

Special Day *B W Hills* 80+
2 b f Fasliyev(USA) —Mustique Dream (Don't Forget Me)
(2617)

Special Envoy (FR) *N Clement* 108
4 gr g Linamix(FR) —Pawnee Dancer (IRE) (Dancing Brave (USA))
$3662a^{4}$ $4864a^{3}$

Special Gold *A D Brown* a71 62
4 b g Josr Algarhoud(IRE) —Inya Lake (Whittingham (IRE))
1496^{12} 1846^{8} 2396^{12} 2785^{3} $3166^{3}$$3306^{2}$ 4230^{12} *4324^{8}* 4636^{3} (5620) *$5970^{2}$$6325^{4}$ 6513^{6}(6686) 6844^{3}*

Special Kaldoun (IRE) *D Smaga* 121
7 b h Alzao(USA) —Special Lady (FR) (Kaldoun (FR))
$655a^{2}$ $1371a^{7}$ $1873a^{9}$ $3779a^{7}$ $4416a^{6}$$5703a^{6}$

Special Lad *P F I Cole* a95+ 89+
4 b g Spectrum(IRE) —Oh Hebe (IRE) (Night Shift (USA))
4682^{11} *(5021) 5212^{4} 5777^{2}*

Special Moment (IRE) *B W Hills* a70 70
3 b f Sadler's Wells(USA) —Upper Circle (Shirley Heights)
656^{6} 1079^{3} 1424^{5}*2209^{8}* 5015^{3} 5868^{2}*6426^{8} 6537^{3}*

Special Place *J A R Toller* a66 48
3 b g Compton Place—Petarga (Petong)
1065^{12} *2575^{6} 4367^{11}*5093^{5} *5774^{3} 5988^{5}(6869)*

Special Reggae (IRE) *L Lannoo* 73
4 b m Xaar—Special Dancer (Shareef Dancer (USA))
$3580a^{4}$

Special Scene (AUS) *Dan O'Sullivan* 102
7 b g Scenic—Georgia Jean (NZ) (Dahar (USA))
$6391a^{12}$

Speciosa (IRE) *Mrs P Sly* 114
3 b f Danehill Dancer(IRE) —Specifically (USA) (Sky Classic (CAN))
(1068) (1508) 2203^{4} 2802^{9} 5184^{6}

Speckled Hen (IRE) *D Haydn Jones* a19 76
3 b f Titus Livius(FR) —Colouring (IRE) (Catrail (USA))
6652^{13} 6820^{12}

Spectaculaire *A Fabre* 100
3 ch c Spectrum(IRE) —Gold Round (IRE) (Caerleon (USA))
$5145a^{5}$ $6384a^{3}$

Spectacular Dancer (IRE) *Heather Dalton* a81 36
4 b g Fasliyev(USA) —Committal (USA) (Chief's Crown (USA))
449^{10}

Spectacular Joy (IRE) *Mrs A Duffield* a51 58
2 b g Spectrum(IRE) —Great Joy (IRE) (Grand Lodge (USA))
2806^{3} *5245^{7}*

Spectacular Show (IRE) *M Quinn* a69 74
3 ch f Spectrum(IRE) —Stage Presence (IRE) (Selkirk (USA))
717^{5} *851^{6}* $1312^{3}$$2049^{3}$ 2441^{6} 3047^{4} 3299^{10} $3741^{5}$$4305^{5}$

Spectait *Sir Mark Prescott* a109 109
4 b g Spectrum(IRE) —Shanghai Girl (Distant Relative)
(1938) 2086^{2} *3534^{5}* (4098) 5675^{16}

Spectested (IRE) *A W Carroll* a64 64
5 ch g Spectrum(IRE) —Nisibis (In The Wings)
55^{4} 346^{7}

Spectral Star *J R Fanshawe* a72 79
4 b m Unfuwain(USA) —Hyperspectra (Rainbow Quest (USA))
1162^{7} 2067^{3} (4393) $4900^{4}$$5897^{12}$

Speed Dial Harry (IRE) *K R Burke* a87 83
4 b g General Monash(USA) —Jacobina (Magic Ring (IRE))
(15) (77) 101^{2} $1674^{2}$$276^{2}$ (348) 542^{10} $611^{3}$$826^{13}$ 1143^{3} $1280^{3}$$1864^{3}$ 2657^{10} 4696^{3} 4790^{13} $5337^{12}$$6176^{3}$ *6424^{4} $6716^{3}$$6791^{5}$ 6947^{2}*

Speedfit World *G G Margarson* a47 62
2 ch c Spinning World(USA) —Petomi (Presidium)
4103^{13} 4424^{7} *5105^{9}*5721^{11} 5958^{12}

Speedie Rossini (IRE) *Miss J R Tooth* a18 20
4 b g Rossini(USA) —Skatt (Caerleon (USA))
407^{8} 493^{12}

Speed Of Sound *A M Balding* a32 56
4 ch m Zafonic(USA) —Blue Siren (Bluebird (USA))
3267^{13} 4003^{7}

Speedy Sam *K R Burke* a104 93
3 b c Medicean—Warning Star (Warning)
1866^{2} *(2244)* 4634^{3} (4838) 5505^{3} 6051^{5}*6559^{2} (6600)*

Speedy Spirit *M Salaman* a33 24
4 ch m Wolfhound(USA) —Ansellady (Absalom)
180[13]

Speedy Suzanne (USA) *B J Meehan* a55+ 38
2 b f Forest Camp(USA) —Gilded Image (USA) (Gilded Time (USA))
5326[6] (6480)

Spellbinder (USA) *Richard E Mandella* a106
5 br h Tale Of The Cat(USA) —Thorough Fair (USA) (Quiet American (USA))
5827a[5]

Spellbinding (IRE) *J M P Eustace* 30
2 b f Kirkwall—Ancient Secret (Warrshan (USA))
5882[9] 6058[10]

Spell Casting (USA) *M H Tompkins* 89
3 b g Kingmambo(USA) —Copper Play (USA) (Fast Play (USA))
1343[2] 1813[4] 2682[2] 3901[3] 5319[5]

Spence Appeal (IRE) *C Roberts* a73 59
4 b g Nicolotte—It's All Academic (IRE) (Mazaad)
6735[9]

Spence's Choice (IRE) *M W Easterby* a53 57
2 b g Desert Sun—Late Night Lady (IRE) (Mujadil (USA))
2321[10] 2783[4] 3457[7]3834[5] 5482[14] 6576[11]6926[4]

Sphenophyta (NZ) *Lee Freedman* 116
6 b g Groom Dancer(USA) —Ballermoss (NZ) (Lord Ballina (AUS))
6110a[5] 6347a[13]

Sphinx (FR) *Jamie Poulton* a72 89+
8 b g Snurge—Egyptale (Crystal Glitters (USA))
37[12] 111[10](990) 1132[5] (1809) (1847) 2035[4] 4560[P]

Spice Bar *A M Balding* a67 47
2 b c Barathea(IRE) —Scottish Spice (Selkirk (USA))
6214[17] 6434[6] 6536[4]

Spice Gardens (IRE) *W Jarvis* 55
2 ch f Indian Ridge—Lime Gardens (Sadler's Wells (USA))
6200[6]

Spicy Wings (FR) *P Bary* 95
3 b c In The Wings—Spicy Girl (FR) (Marignan (USA))
2738a[5]

Spiderback (IRE) *R Hannon* a64 71
2 ch g Redback—Geht Schnell (Fairy King (USA))
2530[13] 2930[10] 3843[7]5053[3] 5585[3] 5866[3] 6106[3]

Spin Dancer *W M Brisbourne* a9 21
2 b f Muhtarram(USA) —Rosa Canina (Bustino)
3246[12] 3915[9] 5527[10]

Spinetail Rufous (IRE) *Miss Z C Davison* a50 53
8 b g Prince Of Birds(USA) —Miss Kinabalu (Shirley Heights)
3438[9] 4054[12] 4462[9] 5291[7] 6282[6]6372[4] 6615[3]6704[6] 6723[3]6806[4] 6906[5]

Spinney (AUS) *J Hawkes* 110
3 b g Octagonal(NZ) —Ochiltree (AUS) (Twig Moss (FR))
6455a[10]

Spinning *T D Barron* a59 70+
3 ch g Pivotal—Starring (FR) (Ashkalani (IRE))
331[3] 1412[5] 1687[2]2001[4] 3384[3] 3698[2]4257[4] 5060[8] (5241)

Spinning Coin *J G Portman* a56 83
4 b m Mujahid(USA) —Cointosser (IRE) (Nordico (USA))
834[7] 1132[8] 1376[6]2869[5] 3365[3] 3714[4] 4528[4] 4876[3](5628) 6202[7]

Spinning Crystal (IRE) *B W Hills* a63 65
2 b f Spinning World(USA) —Crystal Valkyrie (IRE) (Danehill (USA))
2354[9] 3363[11] 4000[5] 5208[2](5419) 5721[9] 6064[9]

Spinning Dancer (IRE) *J R Holt* a18 10
3 b f Spinning World(USA) —Fair McLain (IRE) (Fairy King (USA))
1901[12] 2304[18] 5951[6] 6450[10]6765[7] 6958[7]

Spinning Game *D W Chapman* a42 45
2 b f Mind Games—Spindara (IRE) (Spinning World (USA))
1682[9] (1862) 2538[5] 2626[6] 3372[8] 3917[8]4436[10] 4887[7] 5084[13]6296[10] 6472[3] 6506[7]6534[6] 6569[8]6639[8]

Spinning Gold *Miss Gay Kelleway* a32 46
3 ch f Spinning World(USA) —Blue Birds Fly (Rainbow Quest (USA))
6588[7] 6759[6]

Spinning Queen *B W Hills* 119
3 ch f Spinning World(USA) —Our Queen Of Kings (Arazi (USA))
1068[2] 1508[6] 2031[3] (2880) (3322a) 4097[5] 5341[2](5674)

Spinning Reel *W R Swinburn* a60+ 57
3 ch f Spinning World(USA) —Glenross (IRE) (Warning)
5353[6] 5847[2] 6668[4]6792[10]

Spinning Ruby *R M Beckett* 94
3 b f Pivotal—Red Rabbit (Suave Dancer (USA))
(1406) 1834[4] 4042[6] 4628[7] 4965[8]

Spirited Speedfit (IRE) *G G Margarson* 62
2 b c Invincible Spirit(IRE) —Winsome Girl (Music Boy)
2178[8] 2610[5] 3979[7] 5041[10] 5647[5]5958[3]

Spirit Guide (FR) *R C Guest* a17 36
4 b g Anabaa(USA) —Shining Molly (FR) (Shining Steel)
977[13] 1148[10] 1422[14]2926[13] 5926[13]

Spirito Del Vento (FR) *J-M Beguigne* a97 107
3 b g Indian Lodge(IRE) —Heavenly Song (FR) (Machiavellian (USA))
1178a[4] 2489a[7]

Spirit Of Adjisa (IRE) *Pat Eddery* a69
2 b c Invincible Spirit(IRE) —Adjisa (IRE) (Doyoun)
6826[6] 6976[4]

Spirit Of Arosa (IRE) *J Akehurst* a68 84
3 b f Dansili—Vettorina (IRE) (Vettori (IRE))
1110[2] (1431) 1843[2] 2205[4]

Spirit Of Coniston *Peter Grayson* a64 64
3 b g Lake Coniston(IRE) —Kigema (IRE) (Case Law)
68[9] 322[3]481[10] 577[6]626[6] 1003[3](1210) 1549[3] 1751[3] 2187[2](2340) 3199[4]3587[3] 3864[6] 4201[12] 6399[13]6521[10] 6686[10]6877[4] (6943)

Spirit Of Ecstacy *G M Moore* 38
2 b f Val Royal(FR) —Isla Negra (IRE) (Last Tycoon)
4880[5] 5536[7]

Spirit Of France (IRE) *Christian Wroe* 98
4 b g Anabaa(USA) —Les Planches (Tropular)
282a[2] 435a[3] 507a[5] 3733[8] 4098[8]

Spirit Of Pearl (IRE) *R Pritchard-Gordon* 95
2 b f Invincible Spirit(IRE) —Aguilas Perla (IRE) (Indian Ridge)
4747a[2] 6546a[9]

Spirit Of The Fen (IRE) *J H M Gosden* a96 75
3 b f Pivotal—Malabarista (FR) (Assert)
2406[5] 3367[5] 3946[7] (4396) 5300[8] 6191[8]

Spirit Of The Mist (IRE) *T J Pitt* 77
2 ch c Trans Island—Exciting (Mill Reef (USA))
4487[4] (4873) 5466a[28]

Spirit Of Venus (FR) *E A L Dunlop* a47 57+
2 b f Invincible Spirit(IRE) —Trazando (Forzando)
1647[5] 1922[8]

Spirit One (FR) *P Demercastel* 115
2 b c Anabaa Blue—Lavayssiere (FR) (Sicyos (USA))
(5399a) 6249a[2] 6456a[4]

Spirit Rising *J M Bradley* 47
2 gr g Zilzal(USA) —River's Rising (FR) (Mendez (FR))
1688[14] 2072[4] 2631[10] 3678[6] 4624[7]

Spiritual Peace (IRE) *K A Ryan* a79 85
3 b g Cadeaux Genereux—Emerald Peace (IRE) (Green Desert (USA))
(1218) 1848[5] 2553[5] 3403[6]4403[9] 4422[2] 5532[11] 6212[11]

Spiritwind (IRE) *W R Swinburn* a52 25
3 ch g In The Wings—Tallahassee Spirit (THA) (Presidential (USA))
1880[7] 5319[14] 5669[11]6068[12]

Spitfire Bob (USA) *M E Sowersby* a58 49
7 b g Mister Baileys—Gulf Cyclone (USA) (Sheikh Albadou)
240[8] 328[2]457[5] 599[7]647[6] 857[6]1666[8]

Spittal Point *J J Quinn* 36
4 b m Tagula(IRE) —Ring Side (IRE) (Alzao (USA))
3362[6]

Spitting Image (IRE) *M Johnston* a80 58
6 ch m Spectrum(IRE) —Decrescendo (IRE) (Polish Precedent (USA))
(5) 98[2] 420[11]

Splendidio *D K Ivory* a51 43
2 b f Zamindar(USA) —Diddymu (IRE) (Revoque (IRE))
1046[9] 1372[5] 2179[4] 2346[2]2709[7] 3148[5] 3380[3]3624[3] 6742[4] 6788[5]6945[3]

Splendored Love (USA) *R Hannon* a54 62
2 rg f Buddha(USA) —Starcrossed Affair (USA) (Black Tie Affair)
2957[5] 3201[9] 3700[8]4558[11] 5492[9]

Spliff *M S Saunders* a31 58
5 b g Royal Applause—Snipe Hall (Crofthall)
2173[13] 2711[8] 5970[11]

Split Briefs (IRE) *D J Daly* 72
2 b f Mull Of Kintyre(USA) —Jay Gee (IRE) (Second Set (IRE))
2456[8] 3707[7] 4373[5]

Split The Wind (USA) *R F Johnson Houghton* a37 43
2 ch f Just A Cat(USA) —Maple Hill Jill (USA) (Executive Pride)
5161[10] 5780[10]

Splodger Mac (IRE) *N Bycroft* 55
7 b g Lahib(USA) —Little Love (Warrshan (USA))
1443[9] 1665[2] 2286[15] 2541[12] (3377) 3610[8]3716[5] 4256[6] 4425[8] 5285[4]

Spoilsport *P D Evans* a54 63
3 b f Muhtarram(USA) —Spoilt Again (Mummy's Pet)
6286[5] 6587[7]6837[4] 6899[5]6955[9]

Spoof Master (IRE) *W G M Turner* a72 87
2 b g Invincible Spirit(IRE) —Talbiya (IRE) (Mujtahid (USA))
663[2] (727) 1121[2] 1354[3]2300[3] 3026[8] 3476[4] 5956[2]

Sporting Gesture *M W Easterby* 89
9 ch g Safawan—Polly Packer (Reform)
976[11] 1238[3] 1631[10] 1779[9] 2296[5]2656[6] 2975[7] 3960[4] 4175[3] 4626[13]5367[3] 5531[6] 5792[8] 6317[3]

Spotoncon *A J Lidderdale* a35
5 b g Contract Law(USA) —Emma Victoria (Dominion)
6938[8]

Spot The Subbie (IRE) *Jamie Poulton* a56 56
3 b g Tagula(IRE) —Agent Scully (IRE) (Simply Great (FR))
6869[3]

Spriggan *C G Cox* 72
2 b c Ishiguru(USA) —Hope Chest (Kris)
4588[3]

Spring Dream (IRE) *M R Channon* a79 75
3 gr f Kalanisi(IRE) —Zest (USA) (Zilzal (USA))
1079[6] (1350) (2209) 3215[3] 3666[6] 4159[8]

Spring Glory *Sir Mark Prescott* a62
2 b f Dr Fong(USA) —Doctor Bid (USA) (Spectacular Bid (USA))
6697[5] 6867[4]

Spring Goddess (IRE) *A P Jarvis* a89 87
5 b m Daggers Drawn(USA) —Easter Girl (Efisio)
221[2] 340[2]476[2] 670[3]1112[5] 3088[6] 4379[8]5680[9] 6226[9] 6350[5]6698[9]

Spring Is Here (FR) *R Hannon* 76+
2 ch c King's Best(USA) —Aube D'Irlande (FR) (Selkirk (USA))
3025[2]

Spring Snowdrop (IRE) *D K Weld* 87
3 b f Danehill Dancer(IRE) —Sao Gabriel (IRE) (Persian Bold)
(755a)

Spring Time Girl *B Ellison* a46 49
4 b m Timeless Times(USA) —Daira (Daring March)
706[8] 1341[12] 1757[8]2077[4] 2546[7] 2966[8] 3541[3] 4057[5]4266[4] 4667[2] 6134[3]6281[8]

Springtime Parkes *K A Ryan* 39
2 ch f Medicean—Summerhill Spruce (Windjammer (USA))
1046[12] 2026[9] 2355[7]

Springwood Blues (IRE) *I W McInnes* 38
3 b f Bluebird(USA) —Fun Board (FR) (Saumarez)
2412[10] 2895[8] 4835[9]

Sprinkle *B R Johnson* a42 64+
3 b f Selkirk(USA) —Showery (Rainbow Quest (USA))
2985[12] 3458[8] 3950[3]4286[7] 4820[7] 5350[9] 5885[12] 6780[8]

Spritza (IRE) *M L W Bell* a51 72
2 b f Spectrum(IRE) —Starlight Smile (USA) (Green Dancer (USA))
2026[2] 2506[2] 3640[7]5464a[21]

Sprouston (FR) *J S Moore* a39 64
3 ch g Grand Lodge(USA) —River Fantasy (USA) (Irish River (FR))
1109[11] 1801[15] 3869[12]4199[12] 6802[10] 6855[13]

Spume (IRE) *Sir Michael Stoute* a64 79+
2 b g Alhaarth(IRE) —Sea Spray (IRE) (Royal Academy (USA))
4388[8] 4992[7] (5622)

Spunger *H J L Dunlop* a49 67
3 b f Fraam—Complimentary Pass (Danehill (USA))
6494[6] 6712[8]

Spun Sugar (USA) *T Pletcher* a117
4 b m Awesome Again(CAN) —Irish Cherry (USA) (Irish Open (USA))
6343a[8]

Spurron (IRE) *Gerard Keane* a46 56?
6 b m Flying Spur(AUS) —The Realtour (Warning)
6545[7]

Spy Game (IRE) *Jennie Candlish* 55
6 b g Definite Article—Postie (Sharpo)
589[10] 1562[9] 1772[14]

Spy Gun (USA) *T Wall* a50 42
6 ch g Mt. Livermore(USA) —Takeover Target (USA) (Nodouble (USA))
43[4] 95[8]143[2] 261[4]469[5] 792[2]1198[4] 1573[4]3194[9] 3944[10]

Spyros (FR) *H Gelhay* 89
8 ch g Sicyos(USA) —Arche Perdue (FR) (Groom Dancer (USA))
3692a[7]

Squadron *Mrs A J Perrett* a65 56
2 b g Sakhee(USA) —Machaera (Machiavellian (USA))
6173[7] 6449[3] 6737[5]

Squadron Leader (IRE) *R Hannon* a67 71
3 b g Imperial Ballet(IRE) —Tancholo (So Factual (USA))
900[9] 1355[11] 1751[9]1825[4] 2318[13] 2531[10] 3614[15]

Squaw Dance *W J Haggas* 106
4 ch m Indian Ridge—Likely Story (IRE) (Night Shift (USA))
1979[4] (3002) 3661a[3] 3891[3] 4628[8]

Squiffy *P D Cundell* 66
3 b g Kylian(USA) —Cebwob (Rock City)
3794[13] 4004[7] 4431[9] 5057[7] 5574[10]

Squire Street (USA) *C Collins* 61
3 ch c Catienus(USA) —Glen Kate (Glenstal (USA))
4124a[10]

Squirrel Tail *E S McMahon* a35
3 ch c Band On The Run—Crees Sqaw (Cree Song)
1274[10]

Squirtle (IRE) *W M Brisbourne* a72+ 76
3 ch f In The Wings—Manilia (FR) (Kris)
1079[5] 1350[2] 1634[2] 2124[13] 4118[2](4362) 4758[3] 5174[5] 5531[7] 5952[2] 6244[3]6415[7]

Sri Diamond *S Kirk* a110 89
6 b g Sri Pekan(USA) —Hana Marie (Formidable (USA))
(296) (666) 1128[11]

Sriology (IRE) *J Pearce* a47 52
5 b g Sri Pekan(USA) —Sinology (Rainbow Quest (USA))
72[9] 113[8]242[5] 350[2]471[9] 546[6]689[6] 1915[5]4266[6] 4511[2] 5097[5]6067[6] 6552[3] 6616[5]6795[8]

Sri Pekan Two *P F I Cole* a81 74
2 b c Montjeu(IRE) —Brigadiers Bird (IRE) (Mujadil (USA))
2402[5] 3363[5] (4366) 4882[4] 5459[5]

Staceymac (IRE) *B R Johnson* a54
3 ch f Elnadim(USA) —Neat Shilling (IRE) (Bob Back (USA))
6440[2] (6774) 6981[9]

Staff Nurse (IRE) *N Wilson* a51 51
6 b m Night Shift(USA) —Akebia (USA) (Trempolino (USA))
6623[11] 6795[12]

Stagbury Hill (USA) *J W Hills* a74 100
4 ch g Woodman(USA) —Shalabia (Fast Topaze (USA))
1935[7] 2429[13] 2776[13] 3218[8] 4244[10]4810[16]

Stagecoach Emerald *R W Price* a62 65
4 ch g Spectrum(IRE) —Musician (Shirley Heights)
453[4] 603[11]882[11] 6759[2] 6923[2]

Stage Flight *B J Meehan* 98d
3 b f In The Wings—Midsummernitedream (GER) (Thatching)
1509[5] 2744[14] 3316[10]

Stage Gift (IRE) *Sir Michael Stoute* a80+ 115+
3 ch g Cadeaux Genereux—Stage Struck (IRE) (Sadler's Wells (USA))
(1108) (1615) (2224) 4678[7] 5186[2] (5968)

Stagehand (IRE) *B R Millman* a75 77
2 b g Lend A Hand—Ridotto (Salse (USA))
1189[7] 2530[4] 2857[2] (3641) 4178[3] 4773[3]5382[6] 5783[11]

Stagelight (IRE) *J Noseda* a103 108
4 b h Montjeu(IRE) —Zivania (IRE) (Shernazar)
2742[20] 3313[6] 5675[26]

Stage Manager (IRE) *M J Wallace* a76 76
4 ch h In The Wings—Evangola (Persian Bold)
114[8] (218) 385[8]478[4] 521[6]1425[5]

Stagnite *Karen George* a58 41
6 ch g Compton Place—Superspring (Superlative)
86[8] 210[5]307[2] 679[9]772[7] 821[2]1310[6] 1539[6] 1899[4]2096[3] 2347[11] (3543) 3635[6]3867[9] 3948[8] 4670[9] (6371) 6513[9] 6713[8]6869[6]

Stainley (IRE) *J D Bethell* 71
3 b g Elnadim(USA) —Fizz Up (Alzao (USA))
730[4] 1044[4] 1596[6] 1851[3] 2171[5]3473[3] 4426[5] 5173[8]

Staked A Claim (IRE) *T D Barron* 57
2 ch c Danehill Dancer(IRE) —Twany Angel (Double Form)
5288[4]

Stallone *N Wilson* a79 79
9 ch g Brief Truce(USA) —Bering Honneur (USA) (Bering)
6860[8]

Stamford Blue *R A Harris* a48 69
5 b g Bluegrass Prince(IRE) —Fayre Holly (IRE) (Fayruz)
772[10] 1073[7] 1217[7]1568[6] (2095) 2135[7] 2567[3] 2860[4] (2920) 3565[10]4054[3] 4364[3] 4870[4] 4985[3] (5131) 5378[10]5480[16] 5755[9]

Stamford Street (IRE) *J S Moore* a62 6
3 ch c Distant Music(USA) —Exemplaire (FR) (Polish Precedent (USA))
83[2] 217[9]579[6] 645[11]779[7] 982[11]

Stance *G L Moore*
7 b g Salse(USA) —De Stael (USA) (Nijinsky (CAN))
589[6]

Stand By Me *M A Jarvis* 49
3 b g Tomba—Princess Zara (Reprimand)
4899[7] 5071[11]

St Andrews (IRE) *M A Jarvis* a99 113
6 b g Celtic Swing—Viola Royale (IRE) (Royal Academy (USA))
1407[3] 1678[17] 2236[3] 4529[11] 5012[4]5376[7] 5845[3] 5968[12]

Stanley Bay (IRE) *T D Easterby* 53
3 ch f Namid—Joy St Clair (IRE) (Try My Best (USA))
2873[4] 3725[10] 3910[6] 4195[5] 4943[10]

Stanley George (IRE) *M A Jarvis* a81 72
2 b c Noverre(USA) —Quinzey (JPN) (Carnegie (IRE))
4705[3] 5381[11] 5841[5]6283[3] 6570[2](6891)

Stanley Goodspeed *J W Hills* a78 92
3 ch g Inchinor—Flying Carpet (Barathea (IRE))
1335[11] (1646) 2087[4] 2650[6]3301[11] 3918[4] (4562) 4807[2](5534)

Stanley Wolfe (IRE) *Peter Grayson* a30 52
3 b g City On A Hill(USA) —Quatredil (IRE) (Mujadil (USA))
790[11] 980[9] 1234[3]1464[7] 1612[5] (1792) 2284[7]2701[6] 6234[10]

St Anna Arresi (IRE) *M Halford* 68
2 ch f Namid—Silver Hut (USA) (Silver Hawk (USA))
5464a[13]

Staramix (FR) *E Lellouche* a77 113
5 gr h Linamix(FR) —Sectarine (FR) (Maelstrom Lake)
1929a[4]

Star Berry *B J Meehan* a47 58
3 b f Mtoto—Star Entry (In The Wings)
3647[7] 4004[11] 4210[6]5574[8]

Starboard Light *R M Beckett* a70 65
3 b f Mark Of Esteem(IRE) —Light Ship (Warning)
1747[3] 2210[9]2634[2] 3472[4] 4075[2] 4627[2] (5035) 5568[4]

Starbougg *B Smart* 70
2 b f Tobougg(IRE) —Celestial Welcome (Most Welcome)
4400[2] 5332[13]

Star Cluster *H R A Cecil* 101
3 b f Observatory(USA) —Didicoy (USA) (Danzig (USA))
2103[2] 2582[4] (3316) 3891[5]

Starcross Maid *J F Coupland* a56 52
4 ch m Zaha(CAN) —Maculatus (USA) (Sharpen Up)
304[3] 386[8]527[5] 600[6]682[5] 871[5]939[4] (1385) 1560[6] 2180[2] 2362[7] 2777[3] (3260)

Star Crowned (USA) *B J Meehan* a91+ 97
3 b c Kingmambo(USA) —Fashion Star (USA) (Chief's Crown (USA))
952[8] 1065[2] 1505[4]1990[3] 2304[5] 3346[2] 4047[6](4661)

Starduster *B R Millman* 71
4 gr m Paris House—To The Stars (IRE) (Zieten (USA))
1047[13] 1689[5] 1981[12] (2444)

Star Fern *M J Attwater* a49 24
5 br g Young Ern—Christening (IRE) (Lahib (USA))
172[7] 2789[18] 4114[7]4496[10] 5924[13] 6304[9]6545[4] 6701[11]

Stargazer Jim (FR) *W J Haggas* a87 73
4 br g Fly To The Stars—L'Americaine (USA) (Verbatim (USA))
5685[14] (6313) 6519[4] 6772[4]6888[3]

Stargazy *R Charlton* a58 75
2 b c Observatory(USA) —Romantic Myth (Mind Games)
2402[7] 2724[18] 3588[2] 3822[2] 6255[10]6444[9] 6736[8]6965[4]

Stargem *J Pearce* a75 74
5 b m Compton Place—Holy Smoke (Statoblest)
89[12] 332[8]

Star Inside (IRE) *Kevin Prendergast* 100
2 b g Key Of Luck(USA) —Zara's Birthday (IRE) (Waajib)
6357a[2]

Star Jasmine *M L W Bell* 56
3 b f Grand Lodge(USA) —Shalimar (IRE) (Indian Ridge)
971[4] 1418[7] 1649[9] 1851[13]

Stark Contrast (USA) *G A Butler* 74
2 ch c Gulch(USA) —A Stark Is Born (USA) (Graustark)
3498[4] 4333[4]

Star King Man (USA) *Hideyuki Mori* a115
7 ch h Kingmambo(USA) —Princesse Timide (USA) (Blushing Groom (FR))
743a[7]

Starlight Gazer *J A Geake* 79
3 b g Observatory(USA) —Dancing Fire (USA) (Dayjur (USA))
1089[5] (1355) 2014[5] 2609[4] 3226[5] 6221[10]

Starling (IRE) *D Nicholls* a37 71
4 ch m Cadeaux Genereux—Warrior Wings (Indian Ridge)
149 1079
Star Magnitude (USA) *S Dow* a88 85
5 ch g Distant View(USA) —Stellaria (USA) (Roberto (USA))
369 2365(343) 42127635 (905) 113311 *14102* 211472508 3 29893 41472 48789 *511012*
Star Member (IRE) *Ian Williams* a83 91
7 b g Hernando(FR) —Constellation (IRE) (Kaldoun (FR))
24378
Starmix *G A Harker* a42 67
5 br g Linamix(FR) —Danlu (USA) (Danzig (USA))
97517 29446 31409 45068
Starnevees (FR) *L M Cumani* a89 103
5 b g Kaldounevees(FR) —Stadia (FR) (Star Maite (FR))
27876 37372 *51107*
Star Of Canterbury (IRE) *A P Jarvis* a65 77
3 ch g Beckett(IRE) —Villa Nova (IRE) (Petardia)
33794757 6589 (859) (2434) 37047
Star Of Erhaab *E A Wheeler* a3 21
3 b g Erhaab(USA) —Star Glade (Charnwood Forest (IRE))
119216 18269
Star Of India (GER) *R Rohne* 43
3 ch f Tertullian(USA) —Suguta (GER) (Lagunas)
925a7
Star Of Light *B J Meehan* a87 109
5 b g Mtoto—Star Entry (In The Wings)
(1678) 22013 28035 32943 35527 435912
Star Of Night *C Grant* 10
2 ch f River Falls—Gemma's Choice (Beveled (USA))
39089 440013
Star Of Russia (IRE) *V Smith* a67 67
4 ch m Soviet Star(USA) —Shakanda (IRE) (Shernazar)
66566 678113
Star Of Siam (IRE) *J D Bethell* 42
3 ch f Elnadim(USA) —Thoroughly (IRE) (Woodman (USA))
32858 36387
Star Of The Desert (IRE) *C G Cox* a63 74
3 bb g Desert Story(IRE) —Cindy's Star (IRE) (Dancing Dissident (USA))
7204 11354 188062404 5 32244 42254 48389 *58796*
Starofthemorning (IRE) *A W Carroll* a38 45
5 ch m Foxhound(USA) —Leggagh Lady (IRE) (Doubletour (USA))
31927 *66879*
Starparty (USA) *Mrs A J Perrett* a70 52
2 gr f Cozzene(USA) —Cherie Yvonne (USA) (Vice Regent (CAN))
621518 *64864 66513*
Starpix (FR) *Diego Lowther* a66 111
4 gr h Linamix(FR) —Star's Proud Penny (USA) (Proud Birdie (USA))
206a11 281a7 494a5622a7 4918a5 5146a9
Star Rising *N B King* a57 59
4 ch m Most Welcome—My Greatest Star (Great Nephew)
6966 1308415375 20752 *232082684 5 35972* 41044 44383 46682 532485 7367 *5910P*
Starry Mary *R J Price* a48 64
8 b m Deploy—Darling Splodge (Elegant Air)
9110
Starry Messenger *M P Tregoning* 72
2 b f Galileo(IRE) —The Faraway Tree (Suave Dancer (USA))
50833 54754
Stars Above *Sir Mark Prescott* a46 51
2 b f Observatory(USA) —Skimra (Hernando (FR))
58718 60147 61576 *63854 65066 676836859 6*
Starship (IRE) *W J Haggas* a75 85+
3 b f Galileo(IRE) —Council Rock (General Assembly (USA))
(2823) (3590) 39545 48387
Star Sign *D W Barker* 61
4 b m Robellino(USA) —Amid The Stars (Midyan (USA))
19478 39874 42613 (4382) 45186 544514615813
Starspangled Gator (USA) *W G Gowan* a63
3 b c Editor's Note(USA) —Ever A Lady (USA) (Lord At War (ARG))
757a12
Star Strider *A M Balding* a60 70
2 gr c Royal Applause—Onefortheditch (USA) (With Approval (CAN))
120310 26314 33443 41007 44603509410 54616 *560665829 3*
Startengo (IRE) *D R C Elsworth* a58 55
3 ch g Nashwan(USA) —Virgin Hawk (USA) (Silver Hawk (USA))
1611 10816
Start Of Authority *J Gallagher* a56 55
5 ch g Muhtarram(USA) —Heiden's Delight (USA) (Shadeed (USA))
*17273 19143*296914 (3614) 42765 46673 54507 *5929365451 2*
Startolini *B Smart* 69
2 ch f Bertolini(USA) —Ragged Moon (Raga Navarro (ITY))
11813 17303 210614 (3693) 45193 47274
Startori *B Smart* a69 84
3 b f Vettori(IRE) —Celestial Welcome (Most Welcome)
39459 46966 502410 553810 *64695 66648 686326946 7*
Star Welcome *W J Musson* a58 59
5 ch m Most Welcome—My Greatest Star (Great Nephew)
722 4578(472)
State Dilemma (IRE) *D Shaw* a79d 72d
5 b g Green Desert(USA) —Nuriva (USA) (Woodman (USA))
1645 274133435 4614(6513) 6577116827 3 69906
State Shinto (USA) *R Bouresly* a115 90
10 bb g Pleasant Colony(USA) —Sha Tha (USA) (Mr Prospector (USA))
152a13 208a9 435a11*565a13*
Statute *F J Bowles* 61
4 b h Fasliyev(USA) —Unopposed (Sadler's Wells (USA))
4121a6
Stay Active (USA) *I Semple* 64
2 gr c Johannesburg(USA) —Mature Miss (USA) (Mi Cielo (USA))
28076 36694 43493 53349
Stay Quiet (USA) *T D Barron*
2 b g Quiet American(USA) —Serene Nobility (USA) (His Majesty (USA))
550813
Steady As A Rock (FR) *M Johnston* 81+
2 ch c Rock Of Gibraltar(IRE) —Metisse (USA) (Kingmambo (USA))
(1420)
Steady Rain *P S McEntee* a45 11
4 br m Zafonic(USA) —Love The Rain (Rainbow Quest (USA))
*2892 5038*167011 *24187*
Steam Cuisine *M G Quinlan* a74 85
2 ch f Mark Of Esteem(IRE) —Sauce Tartar (Salse (USA))
33282 *(4394)* (5271) 56764
Steel Blue *R M Whitaker* a66 90
6 b g Atraf—Something Blue (Petong)
104212 15325 159714 20176 26614(3211) 39569 *44682* 46825 511712 53368 55358 594318 *632696508 4*
Steel City Boy (IRE) *D Carroll* a73 56
3 b g Bold Fact(USA) —Balgren (IRE) (Ballad Rock)
11478 20165 *(2939) 315436452 5*
Steelcut *R A Fahey* 90
2 b g Iron Mask(USA) —Apple Sauce (Prince Sabo)
16323 (2076) 21273
Steel Grey *M Brittain* a40
5 gr g Grey Desire—Call Me Lucky (Magic Ring (IRE))
118511 *66367*
Steel Silk (IRE) *G Woodward*
2 b c Desert Style(IRE) —Dear Catch (IRE) (Bluebird (USA))
581413
Steely Dan *J R Best* a92 74
7 b g Danzig Connection(USA) —No Comebacks (Last Tycoon)
5418 (670) 7638
Steenberg (IRE) *M H Tompkins* 118
7 ch g Flying Spur(AUS) —Kip's Sister (Cawston's Clown)
7295 930a5 (1778) 47387 501111 554995682 5
Stella Celtica (ITY) *A Botti* 81
3 b f Celtic Swing—Kanun (Dancing Brave (USA))
1713a14 6002a7
Stellenbosch (USA) *J W Hills* a68 76
3 b g Cape Town(USA) —New Account (USA) (Private Account (USA))
1423 40644835 13759 173852391 4 (2633) 30464 35475 42245 48365
Stellite *J S Goldie* a73+ 83
6 ch g Pivotal—Donation (Generous (IRE))
(1124) 15313 21644 28102 *310164090* 4 43522 (4569) 533626 55544 6212 *664999*
Stepaside (IRE) *M Johnston* 68
2 gr g Fasliyev(USA) —Felicita (IRE) (Catrail (USA))
10305 19829 22813
Stephanie's Mind *M Quinn* a43 55
4 b m Mind Games—Adorable Cherub (USA) (Halo (USA))
228 46581534 6 172292543 18 382513
Stephenson (FR) *W Baltromei* 106
5 br g Platini(GER) —Sternina (IRE) (Runnett)
6610a9
Steppe Dancer (IRE) *D J Coakley* a99 106
3 b c Fasliyev(USA) —Exemina (USA) (Slip Anchor)
(1336) 24044 28018 (3710) 43703 *(4936)* 51704
Steppenwolfer (USA) *D Peitz* a114
3 gr c Aptitude(USA) —Wolfer (USA) (Wolf Power (SAF))
1498a3 2477a4
Step Perfect (USA) *G M Moore* a49 52
5 b g Royal Academy(USA) —Gossiping (USA) (Chati (USA))
6353 68828667 975 14 41568 *44385*49609 *59276*
Stepping Stones *H R A Cecil* 81
3 ch f Selkirk(USA) —Light Step (USA) (Nureyev (USA))
13513 16503 (2587) 30477
Stepping Up (IRE) *Saeed Bin Suroor* 102
3 ch c Soviet Star(USA) —Rise And Fall (Mill Reef (USA))
56824
Step To The Stars (IRE) *M Johnston* 53
2 b f Galileo(IRE) —Tudor Loom (Sallust)
57548 620012
Sterling Moll *W De Best-Turner* 50
3 gr f Lord Of Men—Princess Maud (USA) (Irish River (FR))
417912 55896 59038
Sternenkonigin (IRE) *W Hickst* 41
2 ch f Samum(GER) —Soljanka (GER) (Halling (USA))
6122a11
Stetchworth Prince *Saeed Bin Suroor* a11 108
4 b h Cadeaux Genereux—Elfin Laughter (Alzao (USA))
201a6 *353a15* (511a) 621a5
Stevedore (IRE) *J R Boyle* a79 66
5 ch g Docksider(USA) —La Belle Katherine (USA) (Lyphard (USA))
49955 57347 *6413116476 2 65684 6871 6 69282*
Steve's Champ (CHI) *Rune Haugen* 110
6 b h Foxhound(USA) —Emigracion (CHI) (Semenenko (USA))
5225a11
Stevie Gee (IRE) *G A Swinbank* a80+ 101
2 b c Invincible Spirit(IRE) —Margaree Mary (CAN) (Seeking The Gold (USA))
30808 *36855 (3994)* (4377) (4890) 568112
St Fris *J A R Toller* a57
3 gr g Silver Patriarch(IRE) —Fragrance (Mtoto)
50987 5669106410 12
Sticky Mint (IRE) *M Blanshard* a34 47
3 b f Inchinor—Creme De Menthe (IRE) (Green Desert (USA))
661813 6714768001 0
Still Calm *B W Hills* 58
2 b c Zamindar(USA) —Shining Water (Kalaglow)
51687
Still Going On *Miss Martina Anne Doran* 70
9 b g Prince Sabo—Floppie (FR) (Law Society (USA))
5854a14
Sting Like A Bee (IRE) *J S Goldie* a64 51
7 b g Ali-Royal(IRE) —Hidden Agenda (FR) (Machiavellian (USA))
7312 15672229
Stingray (IRE) *N I M Rossiter*
4 b h Danehill(USA) —Music And Dance (USA) (Northern Dancer (CAN))
151315 209610
Stir Crazy (IRE) *M R Channon* a65 65
2 b g Fath(USA) —La Captive (IRE) (Selkirk (USA))
8143 *(912)* 10668 31175 31364 34961036783 (3727) *39175* 40888415210 46654 54472 56468 58291060561 1 *(6401) 65009*
St Ivian *Mrs N Macauley* a49 49
6 b g Inchinor—Lamarita (Emarati (USA))
95 81928843604502 4 52436133 7729139 12 27805 3089143635P (Dead)
Stock Exchange (IRE) *P Bowen*
4 b g King's Best(USA) —Queen's Ransom (IRE) (Last Tycoon)
121213
Stockholder *C A Cyzer* a52 31
3 b g Hernando(FR) —Springs Welcome (Blakeney)
*24657 32617*36765 38499
Stoic Leader (IRE) *R F Fisher* a77 87
6 b g Danehill Dancer(IRE) —Starlust (Sallust)
*(17) 367 64427115 7374*10359 *12759* 145621561 3 *24174 24646*25274 *27944* 307973218 9 38126 *39374* (4090) 45215 5554105680 14 *64177 650836573 6 67339*
Stokesies Luck (IRE) *J L Spearing* 41d
3 gr c King Charlemagne(USA) —Lesley's Fashion (Dominion)
26059 28818 440117 572812
Stokesies Wish *J L Spearing* a44 53
6 ch m Fumo Di Londra(IRE) —Jess Rebec (Kala Shikari)
29206 336814 34348 41418 43651249851 1 62749 *630811*
Stolen *W R Muir* a44 45
4 b g Groom Dancer(USA) —Jezyah (USA) (Chief's Crown (USA))
187
Stolen Glance *M W Easterby* a65 77
3 b f Mujahid(USA) —Stolen Melody (Robellino (USA))
(1259) 15934 (1761) 18592 212810 28099419 76 58622 60083 *647446716 5*
Stolen Hours (USA) *J Akehurst* 87+
6 bb h Silver Deputy(CAN) —Fasta (USA) (Seattle Song (USA))
154416 22314 253410 34319 3840443314 562810
Stolen Light (IRE) *A Crook* a78 75
5 ch g Grand Lodge(USA) —Spring To Light (USA) (Blushing Groom (FR))
632112 *(6537) 67189 67612*
Stolen Song *J Ryan* a60 32
6 b g Sheikh Albadou—Sparky's Song (Electric)
56 29357320311 33826
Stolen Summer (IRE) *B S Rothwell* a27 69d
3 ch g Spectrum(IRE) —Touche-A-Tout (IRE) (Royal Academy (USA))
551215 572210 617614 627310 *646966497 12*
Stolt (IRE) *N Wilson* 88
2 b g Tagula(IRE) —Cabcharge Princess (IRE) (Rambo Dancer (CAN))
(1030) 14914 21279 27249 30643 37202
Stoneacre Boy (IRE) *Peter Grayson* a75 36
3 ch g City On A Hill(USA) —Sans Ceriph (IRE) (Thatching)
*2263 3647(487) 6012(673) (807) 10205*114613 *19284 275610309 77 3595126446 9 6555136682 7 (6844) 69353*
Stoneacre Fred (IRE) *Peter Grayson* a52+ 51
3 br g Lend A Hand—Election Special (Chief Singer)
1022 23933353 325763916 9 43546 469046276 10 *67073(6794) 69838*
Stoneacre Gareth (IRE) *Peter Grayson* a75
2 b c Grand Lodge(USA) —Tidal Reach (USA) (Kris S (USA))
25725 642066504 6 65985(6645) 682476880 4 69655
Stoneacre Girl (IRE) *Peter Grayson* a38 8
3 ch f Rossini(USA) —Ring Of Light (Auction Ring (USA))
1059 308847756379790 4 93651464 4
Stoneacre Lad (IRE) *Peter Grayson* a92+ 93
3 b c Bluebird(USA) —Jay And-A (IRE) (Elbio)
*(344) 5933 10203*160411 20212 25219 (2639) 34758 4360134717 9 50093 *64966(6720)*
Stoneacre Lil (IRE) *Peter Grayson* a49 25
3 b f Fasliyev(USA) —Lady Ounavarra (IRE) (Simply Great (FR))
3498
Stone Arch (IRE) *Jarlath P Fahey* a51 58
6 bb g Turtle Island(IRE) —Broadway Royal (Royal Match)
19092 670412
Stonecrabstomorrow (IRE) *P F I Cole* a88 87
3 b g Fasliyev(USA) —Tordasia (IRE) (Dr Devious (IRE))
1652 (293) 5502(4328) 48883 *510795649 4 58772*
Stonehaugh (IRE) *J Howard Johnson* 83+
3 b g King Charlemagne(USA) —Canary Bird (IRE) (Catrail (USA))
(1230) 22396 27373 (3606) 507910
Stoop To Conquer *J L Dunlop* 89
6 b g Polar Falcon(USA) —Princess Genista (Ile De Bourbon (USA))
12943 180812 21768 (4560) 50106 55266
Stormburst (IRE) *M Dods* 55
2 b f Mujadil(USA) —Isca (Caerleon (USA))
11815 216613
Storm Centre *Miss J S Davis* a66 70
4 ch g Pivotal—Long View (Persian Bold)
*7110 5963*777P 296912 *38458*4870P
Storm Chase (USA) *A P Jarvis* a62 67
4 bb g Awad(USA) —Night Duja (USA) (Dayjur (USA))
1695 5751069313
Stormello (USA) *W Currin* a113
2 ch c Stormy Atlantic(USA) —Wilshewed (USA) (Carson City (USA))
6339a5
Stormiano (GER) *Dr A Bolte* 94
4 b h Big Shuffle(USA) —Storm Weaver (USA) (Storm Bird (CAN))
2799a7 3755a5
Stormina (USA) *T Pletcher* 104
4 br m Gulch(USA) —Brooklyn's Storm (USA) (Storm Cat (USA))
6368a7
Stormingmichaelori *N Wilson* 49
3 b g Vettori(IRE) —Stormswept (USA) (Storm Bird (CAN))
185911 22987 278212 352410 3909444056 49619 536312
Storm Mission (USA) *Miss V Haigh* a42 67
2 bb g Storm Creek(USA) —Bemissed (USA) (Nijinsky (CAN))
243211 30183 *3457103800*7 40887 468117 *64221164724 657612*
Storm Mountain (IRE) *B Grizzetti* 110
3 b c Montjeu(IRE) —Lady Storm (IRE) (Mujadil (USA))
1872a2
Storm Of Arabia (IRE) *W R Swinburn* a66 71
3 b g Intikhab(USA) —Mauradell (IRE) (Mujadil (USA))
19419 26229 293323347 2 *(6687) 68437*
Storm On The Run (IRE) *R Hannon* a81 87
3 b c Desert Prince(IRE) —Happy Dancer (USA) (Seattle Dancer (USA))
14122 *(1960)* 24433 35462 39458
Storm Path (IRE) *C E Brittain* 40
2 gr c Giant's Causeway(USA) —Sianema (Persian Bold)
433317 57593
Storm Petrel *N P Littmoden* a51+ 58
2 b f Xaar—Vitesse (IRE) (Royal Academy (USA))
621512 *64804*
Storm Prospect *C Tinkler* a62 75
3 b g Mujahid(USA) —Bajan Blue (Lycius (USA))
2063 9 43324 (5057)
Storm Treasure (USA) *S Asmussen* a106 106
3 ch c Storm Boot(USA) —Boogie Beach Blues (USA) (Cure The Blues (USA))
1498a11
Storm Trooper (GER) *P Schiergen* 112
6 ch h Monsun(GER) —So Sedulous (USA) (The Minstrel (CAN))
4864a11 5226a5 565710 6109a7 6529a7
Stormy Love (IRE) *M Johnston* 65
4 ch h Giant's Causeway(USA) —Hula Angel (USA) (Woodman (USA))
18148 216512
Stormy Monday *J W Hills* a77 78
3 b f Cadeaux Genereux—Hasta (USA) (Theatrical)
19626 2554232047 364653845 6 (4531) 47723 49651155911 3 60592 620612
Stormy River (FR) *N Clement* 124
3 gr c Verglas(IRE) —Miss Bio (FR) (River Mist (USA))
(1178a) 1718a3 27212 (3342a) 4416a4 5049a25701a4
Stotsfold *W R Swinburn* a93+ 105
3 b g Barathea(IRE) —Eliza Acton (Shirley Heights)
18227 23046 26055 *(3015)* (3477) 45993*(5016)* (5530) 58048
St Petersburg *M H Tompkins* a96? 104d
6 ch g Polar Falcon(USA) —First Law (Primo Dominie)
47395 50123 53572 578912 59451962191 2 *69863*
St Philip (USA) *R M Beckett* 96
2 b c Dance Brightly(CAN) —Tender Moment (USA) (Torrential (USA))
39492 (4479) (5114) 56537
Strabinios King *P C Haslam* a60
2 b g King's Best(USA) —Strawberry Morn (CAN) (Travelling Victor (CAN))
67574
Stradivari (USA) *D Bressou* 77
4 b h Silver Hawk(USA) —Vibrant (Machiavellian (USA))
1929a5
Straffan (IRE) *J Hetherton* a49 43
4 bb m Shinko Forest(IRE) —Katherine Gorge (USA) (Hansel (USA))
(29) 1468 24974083 (529) 5529 69198737 10548 *14476*415720 44733 472912 549313 58651262824 *649365550 3 67279* (Dead)
Straight As A Die *R J Hodges* a35 36
3 b f Pyramus(USA) —Tenderetta (Tender King)
1055 189532910 529112 *61298*
Straight Face (IRE) *W J Knight* a75 69
2 b g Princely Heir(IRE) —Dakota Sioux (IRE) (College Chapel)
158812 21782 27336 *297933641*7 42904 5094455082 55702 572110
Straight Gal (IRE) *G A Huffer* 49+
3 br f Namid—Kazimiera (IRE) (Polish Patriot (USA))
21677 300612

Stratagem (JPN) *O Hirata* 117
5 b h Sunday Silence(USA) —Muncie (IRE) (Sadler's Wells (USA))
1329a^{3}

Strategic Mount *P F I Cole* 99
3 b c Montjeu(IRE) —Danlu (USA) (Danzig (USA))
897^{3} 1193^{4} 1543^{2} 2066^{4} (2970) (3539) (4039)5153^{7}

Strategic Prince *P F I Cole* 117
2 b c Dansili—Ausherra (USA) (Diesis)
(1796) 2771^{5} (3442) (4037) 5965^{3}

Strathaird (IRE) *P C Haslam* a47
2 b g Medicean—Heed My Warning (IRE) (Second Set (IRE))
6504^{10} 6730^{4}

Strathclyde (IRE) *A M Hales* a51 45
7 b g Petong—It's Academic (Royal Academy (USA))
209^{7} 680^{5}982^{9}

Strathmore (IRE) *R A Fahey* 62
2 gr g Fath(USA) —In The Highlands (Petong)
2281^{7} 4545^{8} 4956^{3}

Strathtay *M Appleby* a34 58
4 ch m Pivotal—Cressida (Polish Precedent (USA))
63^{9} 103^{5}243^{8}

Stravara *R Hollinshead* a65 76
3 b g Kayf Tara—Stravsea (Handsome Sailor)
6494^{3} 6716^{7}6862^{8}

Stravinsky's Art (USA) *D R C Elsworth*
2 b c Stravinsky(USA) —Halo's Gleam (USA) (Halo (USA))
2029^{10}

Stravita *R Hollinshead* a62
2 b f Weet-A-Minute(IRE) —Stravsea (Handsome Sailor)
(6558)

Strawberry Dale (IRE) *J D Bethell* 109
4 b m Bering—Manchaca (FR) (Highest Honor (FR))
(1804) 4646a^{5} 5465a^{9}

Strawberry Leaf *R Charlton* a74 87+
4 ch m Unfuwain(USA) —Satin Bell (Midyan (USA))
1133^{15}

Strawberry Lolly *Sir Michael Stoute* a87 83
3 b f Lomitas—Strawberry Morn (CAN) (Travelling Victor (CAN))
1306^{6} (3458) (4244) 4763^{6}

Strawberry Patch (IRE) *J S Goldie* 69
7 b g Woodborough(USA) —Okino (USA) (Strawberry Road (AUS))
2376^{11} 2544^{10} 2928^{5} (3356) 3525^{2} 3781^{9}4091^{4} 4352^{6} 4523^{2} 4952^{2} 5078^{8}5577^{11} 6315^{8}

Straw Boy *R Brotherton* 57
2 br g Hunting Lion(IRE) —Sky Light Dreams (Dreams To Reality (USA))
3701^{17} 3860^{4} 4177^{13} 4887^{4} 5084^{2}5730^{11}

Streamer *M Johnston* a50 59
2 b f Elnadim(USA) —Noble Water (FR) (Noblequest (FR))
2106^{6} 6270^{6} 6393^{10} (Dead)

Street Life (IRE) *W J Musson* a71 74
8 ch g Dolphin Street(FR) —Wolf Cleugh (IRE) (Last Tycoon)
478^{11} 723^{5}990^{8} 1144^{7} 1591^{9} 2149^{4} 6289^{8}6767^{7} (6980)

Streetofchampions (USA) *T J O'Mara* 90
2 b c Street Cry(IRE) —Becky's Ransom (USA) (Red Ransom (USA))
3962a^{9} 4850a^{8}

Streets Ahead *A M Balding* 99
2 b c Beat Hollow—Frond (Alzao (USA))
3545^{5} 4074^{2} (4526) (4775) 5415a^{4}

Street Sense (USA) *C Nafzger* a125+
2 b c Street Cry(IRE) —Bedazzle (USA) (Dixieland Band (USA))
5823a^{3} (6339a)

Street Warrior (IRE) *M Johnston* a82 85
3 b g Royal Applause—Anne Bonny (Ajdal (USA))
716^{5} 1048^{2} 1185^{3} 5144^{8} (5436) 6076^{4}6313^{9} 6502^{9}6661^{7}

Strensall *R E Barr* a67 76
9 b g Beveled(USA) —Payvashooz (Ballacashtal (CAN))
1563^{14} 2396^{2} 2784^{6} 3190^{3} 3354^{6}3622^{5} (3832) 3938^{6} 4453^{9} 4725^{4} 5486^{3}5684^{10}

Stretton (IRE) *J D Bethell* a74 88
8 br g Doyoun—Awayil (USA) (Woodman (USA))
(1631) 1943^{8} 2296^{6} 3748^{5}4175^{7} 4676^{2} 5141^{4} 5792^{5} 6287^{7}

Strident (USA) *J J Lambe* 66
5 ch g Deputy Commander(USA) —Regrets Only (USA) (Black Tie Affair)
570^{9} 733^{11}

Strife (IRE) *W M Brisbourne* a28 58
3 b g Stravinsky(USA) —Fife (IRE) (Lomond (USA))
(1433) 1736^{8} 2403^{8} 2479^{5} 6628^{10}6812^{4}

Strike *John Charles McConnell* 88
5 b h Silver Hawk(USA) —Shemozzle (IRE) (Shirley Heights)
4166a^{13}

Strikeen (IRE) *T G Mills* a88 74+
2 ch c Intikhab(USA) —Sheen Falls (IRE) (Prince Rupert (FR))
5622^{4} 5947^{2} 6257^{4}(6639) 6760^{2}

Strike Force *M Wellings* a58 72
2 b g Dansili—Miswaki Belle (USA) (Miswaki (USA))
2029^{9} (2442) 4335^{5} 6933^{5}

Strike Up The Band *D Nicholls* 114
3 b c Cyrano De Bergerac—Green Supreme (Primo Dominie)
1083^{8} 1408^{3} 1818^{3} 2847^{15} 3520^{4}4080^{10} 5158^{3} 5443^{2} (5779a)

Striking Force (IRE) *D Broad* 74
4 b h Danehill(USA) —Trusted Partner (USA) (Affirmed (USA))
1156a^{9}

String Serenade (IRE) *V Smith* a36 52
5 b m Key Of Luck(USA) —Bubbly Dancer (USA) (Crafty Prospector (USA))
227^{7} 682^{6}854^{11} (2568) 2952^{3} 3232^{5}3616^{3} 3803^{9} 5097^{9}5925^{12}

Stringsofmyheart *Sir Michael Stoute* 35
2 b f Halling(USA) —Heart's Harmony (Blushing Groom (FR))
4373^{15}

Strive *D Smaga* 99
3 gr c Dr Fong(USA) —Silver Pursuit (Rainbow Quest (USA))
4168a^{7}

Striving Storm (USA) *P W Chapple-Hyam* 100
2 bb c Stormin Fever(USA) —Sugars For Nanny (USA) (Brocco (USA))
3735^{3} 4415a^{2} (5014) 6102^{3}

Strobe *J A Osborne* 48
2 ch g Fantastic Light(USA) —Sadaka (USA) (Kingmambo (USA))
5112^{7} 5563^{12} 5645 ^{14}

Strobilus *M A Jarvis* a97+ 110
2 b c Mark Of Esteem(IRE) —Mount Elbrus (Barathea (IRE))
4768^{2} (5134) (5783) 6003a^{2}

Strobinia (IRE) *R M Beckett* a41
4 b m Soviet Star(USA) —Robinia (USA) (Roberto (USA))
14^{6}

Strokestown Percy (IRE) *Niall Moran* 23
2 b c Danetime(IRE) —Annaduff (IRE) (Indian Ridge)
5692a^{18}

Stroll In The Park (IRE) *D R C Elsworth* 45
3 b g Galileo(IRE) —Highshaan (Pistolet Bleu (IRE))
1087^{10} 2146^{6}

Strong Approach (IRE) *T D Barron* a67 69
3 ch g Fruits Of Love(USA) —Shragraddy Lass (IRE) (Jareer (USA))
1592^{7} 2297^{6} 2809^{7} 3189^{4} 3383^{3}3638^{4} 4060^{11}

Strong Faith (USA) *Darrell Vienna* a99 100
5 br m Pioneering(USA) —Let's Eat Out (USA) (Banquet Table (USA))
6253a^{5}

Stronghold *J H M Gosden* a110+ 121
4 b h Danehill(USA) —Insinuate (USA) (Mr Prospector (USA))
(1407) 1806^{12} 2431^{2} 2742^{2} 3534^{4}(5588) 5962^{14}

Strong Survivor (USA) *L M Cumani* 65
3 b g Kingmambo(USA) —Summer Solstice (IRE) (Caerleon (USA))
2662^{6} 3794^{10} 5138^{6}

Strut *R Charlton* 99
3 ch f Danehill Dancer(IRE) —Boast (Most Welcome)
1130^{4} 1671^{3} 2032^{6} 2438^{7} 5159^{5}

St Savarin (FR) *R A Fahey* a91 95
5 ch g Highest Honor(FR) —Sacara (GER) (Monsagem (USA))
221^{12} 404^{4}763^{3} 2982^{2}4631^{3} (4990) 5115^{2} 5533^{8} 5804^{2} 6336^{8}(6468) 6677^{3}

Stuck Of Caffeina (ITY) *R Brogi* a58 85
3 b c Stuck(USA) —Caffeina (Chief Singer)
5473a^{12}

Stumped *W J Haggas* a70 73+
3 b g Bertolini(USA) —So Saucy (Teenoso (USA))
1680^{5} 2325^{9} 3387^{5}4708^{5} 5098^{2}

Stunningjo *J L Spearing* 44
2 gr f Pursuit Of Love—Dolly Bevan (Another Realm)
961^{9} 1181^{11} 3345^{5} 4545^{9} 4665^{7}

Style Sunday (IRE) *B W Hills* 64
2 b c Alhaarth(IRE) —March Star (IRE) (Mac's Imp (USA))
4333^{10} 4768^{7} 5348^{5}

Stylish Sunrise (IRE) *A J Chamberlain* a52 66
5 b g Desert Style(IRE) —Anita At Dawn (IRE) (Anita's Prince)
1572^{6}

Stylistic (IRE) *J J Lambe* a65 64
5 b m Daggers Drawn(USA) —Treasure (IRE) (Treasure Kay)
14^{5} 137^{5}292^{8} 5865^{18} 6608^{8}

Sualda (IRE) *D Carroll* 84
7 b g Idris(IRE) —Winning Heart (Horage)
1809^{8} 2296^{2} (2549) 2975^{9} 3248^{4} (3694) 4604^{10}

Suave (USA) *P McGee* a122
5 b h A.P. Indy(USA) —Urbane (USA) (Citidancer (USA))
6345a^{12}

Subadar *R Charlton* a74
2 b c Zamindar(USA) —Valencia (Kenmare (FR))
5784^{3} 6072^{4}

Subpoena *Saeed Bin Suroor* 98
4 b h Diktat—Trefoil (Kris)
357a^{6}

Subsidise (IRE) *F P Murtagh* a61 48
3 br g Key Of Luck(USA) —Haysong (IRE) (Ballad Rock)
123^{13} 333^{2}(430) 548^{4}1044^{8} 1533^{8} 2107^{U} 2282^{8} 3999^{8}

Subtle Affair (IRE) *P F Cashman* a48 82
4 b m Barathea(IRE) —Uncertain Affair (IRE) (Darshaan)
1026a^{8} 1324a^{6} 2840a^{9}

Succeed (IRE) *Mrs H Sweeting* a59+ 50
3 b f Elnadim(USA) —Pico (Piccolo)
66^{4} 239^{4}322^{4} 487^{2}3349^{13} 3847^{9} 4164^{8}5480^{8} 6399^{6} 6539^{2}6615^{9} 6686^{2}(6755) 6877^{3}

Successor *M D I Usher*
6 ch g Entrepreneur—Petralona (USA) (Alleged (USA))
63^{3} 310^{P} (Dead)

Sudan (IRE) *E Lellouche* 117
3 ch c Peintre Celebre(USA) —Sarabande (USA) (Woodman (USA))
1557a^{3} 2738a^{2} 3517a^{3} 4623a^{6} 5221a^{3}5704a^{4}

Sudden Edge *H Candy* 61
4 b g Bold Edge—Surprise Surprise (Robellino (USA))
2611^{12} 3090^{13}

Sudden Impulse *A D Brown* a43 69
5 b m Silver Patriarch(IRE) —Sanshang (FR) (Astronef)
788^{4} 1224^{2}1767^{6} 1911^{3}2320^{7} 2927^{2} (3140) 3352^{2}4205^{4} 4380^{12} (4709) (4944) 5725^{2} 5904^{2} 6008^{10}6317^{9}

Su Doku (USA) *N P Littmoden* a61 67
2 ch f Lemon Drop Kid(USA) —Bellehop (USA) (Hennessy (USA))
2083^{3} 2743^{9} 3942^{5} 4767^{8} 5017^{8}6444^{8}

Sudoor *J L Dunlop* 100
2 b f Fantastic Light(USA) —Wissal (USA) (Woodman (USA))
(2958) (3874) 5187^{5} 5966^{11}

Sue Princesse (IRE) *K J Condon* 69
3 ch f Alhaarth(IRE) —Princesse Sharpo (USA) (Trempolino (USA))
4124a^{3}

Suesam *B R Millman* 69
3 b f Piccolo—Barnacla (IRE) (Bluebird (USA))
3793^{7} 4627^{8} 4820^{5} 5350^{6} 5568^{11}

Sues Surprise (IRE) *B W Hills* 89+
2 b f Montjeu(IRE) —My Micheline (Lion Cavern (USA))
5344^{4} 6217^{2}

Suffolk House *M Brittain* a48
4 b g Paris House—Suffolk Girl (Statoblest)
77^{11} 196^{13}5929^{4} 6304^{5}6628^{5} 6959^{9}

Sugar Baby Love (GER) *Mario Hofer* 102
2 b f Second Empire(IRE) —Salzgitter (Salse (USA))
5007a^{2} 5714a^{11}

Sugar Ray (IRE) *Sir Michael Stoute* 70
2 b c Danehill(USA) —Akuna Bay (USA) (Mr Prospector (USA))
5339^{7}

Sugar Shake (USA) *R J Frankel* a73
3 b f Awesome Again(CAN) —Skipping Around (USA) (Skip Trial (USA))
3757a^{7}

Suggestive *W J Haggas* a117 115
8 b g Reprimand—Pleasuring (Good Times (ITY))
281a^{2} 619a^{4} 2386^{6} (3086) 3534^{6}4025^{8} 5146a^{5} 5682^{2} 5962^{11}

Sugitani (USA) *N B King* a73+ 60
4 b g Kingmambo(USA) —Lady Reiko (IRE) (Sadler's Wells (USA))
97^{2} 131^{4}218^{6} 482^{4}(549) 574^{2}(597) 652^{4}881^{7}

Suhayl Star (IRE) *W J Musson* a69+ 72
2 b g Trans Island—Miss Odlum (IRE) (Mtoto)
1019^{2} 1113^{5} 1284^{9}2733^{4} 3372^{7} 3800^{6} 3834^{6} (4115) 4761^{2}5647^{13} 6064^{14}

Suhezy (IRE) *J S Wainwright* a47 54
3 b f Orpen(USA) —Ervedya (IRE) (Doyoun)
287^{11} 415^{4}613^{7} 861^{8}980^{4} 1234^{5} 1447^{2} 1594^{10} 2284 ^{2}2543^{5} 2782^{8} 3306^{4} 3582^{2} 4199^{6}4548^{3} 4728^{4} 4943^{7}

Suits Me *J J Quinn* a17 73
3 ch g Bertolini(USA) —Fancier Bit (Lion Cavern (USA))
848^{6} 1097^{15} 1444^{3}2781^{8} 3375^{3} 3883^{5} 4378^{9}

Suivez Moi (IRE) *M F Harris* a79 72
4 ch g Daggers Drawn(USA) —Pamiers (Huntercombe)
3948^{12} 4073^{P} (Dead)

Sujana (USA) *B J Meehan* 61
3 bb f Grand Slam(USA) —Indian Fashion (USA) (General Holme (USA))
1085^{11} 1418^{11}

Suki Bear *W R Muir* 72
2 br f Xaar—Dominion Rose (USA) (Spinning World (USA))
(4207) 4966^{7} 5503^{18}

Sularina (IRE) *L M Cumani* 77+
3 br f Alhaarth(IRE) —Quiet Counsel (IRE) (Law Society (USA))
3975^{4}

Sularno *H Morrison* a65 30
2 ch c Medicean—Star Precision (Shavian)
5892^{10} 6188^{10} (6466)

Sullivan's Cascade (IRE) *E G Bevan* a23 30
7 b g Spectrum(IRE) —Sombre Lady (Sharpen Up)
55^{12}

Sumi Girl (IRE) *R A Fahey* 75
2 b f Tiger Hill(IRE) —Allonia (GER) (Surumu (GER))
(5059)

Summer Bounty *F Jordan* a39 61
10 b g Lugana Beach—Tender Moment (IRE) (Caerleon (USA))
363^{9} 794^{5}(882) 965^{4} 1204^{7} 1729^{9}2221^{10} 2601^{4} 3270^{8} 5354^{12} 5954^{3}6067^{10}

Summer Celebrity (IRE) *D R C Elsworth* 59
3 ch f Spinning World(USA) —Summer Style (IRE) (Indian Ridge)
4527^{9} 5272^{2} 5728^{3}

Summer Charm *W Jarvis* a77 84
4 b m Dansili—Regent's Folly (IRE) (Touching Wood (USA))
109^{6} 521^{10}(1045) 1614^{2} (2088) 2457^{6} 5016^{7}5479^{13} 5897^{9}

Summer Dancer (IRE) *D R C Elsworth* a67+ 67
2 br g Fasliyev(USA) —Summer Style (IRE) (Indian Ridge)
5458^{7} 5918^{4} 6220^{9} (6745)

Summer Force *C N Kellett* a43 37
4 ch g Tina's Pet—Hustle An Bustle (USA) (Lomond (USA))
4835^{6}

Summer Lodge *A J McCabe* a74 74
3 b g Indian Lodge(IRE) —Summer Siren (FR) (Saint Cyrien (FR))
1291^{7} 1681^{5} 1946^{3} 4254^{2} 4470^{2}5090^{3} 5435^{2} 5510^{3} 5741^{3}5903^{3} 6225^{6} 6791^{4}6929^{4}

Summer Of Love (IRE) *P F I Cole* a63 47
2 b f Fasliyev(USA) —Overboard (IRE) (Rainbow Quest (USA))
3707^{12} 6242^{10} 6386^{5}6498^{2}

Summer Recluse (USA) *J M Bradley* a74 76
7 gr g Cozzene(USA) —Summer Retreat (USA) (Gone West (USA))
1686^{9} 2340^{2} 2536^{3}2590^{7} 2898^{3} 2971^{4} 3434^{5} 4101^{15}4449^{3} (4629) 4894^{6} 5058^{9} 5167^{4} 5480^{10}5575^{2} 5842^{9} 5938^{6}6326^{10} 6437^{4}6579^{10}

Summer's Eve *H Candy* 102
3 gr f Singspiel(IRE) —Early Rising (USA) (Grey Dawn II)
948^{2} 1214^{2} 1669^{3} (1955) 3133a^{3} 4035a^{4}4482^{DSQ} 5300^{6} 5917^{3}

Summer Shades *W M Brisbourne* a43 70
8 b m Green Desert(USA) —Sally Slade (Dowsing (USA))
467^{4} 648^{7}

Summer Shower *A Fabre* 97
3 b f Sadler's Wells(USA) —Summer Breeze (Rainbow Quest (USA))
5472a^{7} 6610a^{2}

Summertime Parkes *H Candy* a62 57
3 ch f Silver Patriarch(IRE) —Summerhill Spruce (Windjammer (USA))
1956^{8}

Summerville Star (IRE) *Michael McElhone* a46+ 31
2 b f Fruits Of Love(USA) —Alexandra Fair (USA) (Green Dancer (USA))
6591^{7}

Summoner *A Al Raihe* a87 122
9 b h Inchinor—Sumoto (Mtoto)
149a^{11} 496a^{11}

Sumner (IRE) *M H Tompkins* a61+ 61+
2 b c Xaar—Black Jack Girl (IRE) (Ridgewood Ben)
5659^{10} 5914^{7} 6290^{9}

Sun Bian *L P Grassick* a71 28
4 br h Makbul—Silken Dalliance (Rambo Dancer (CAN))
992^{14}

Sunbolt (IRE) *T D Barron* a54 68
3 b g Barathea(IRE) —Sunset (IRE) (Polish Precedent (USA))
817^{3} 1251^{7} 1599^{7} 1867^{5} 2795^{6}3167^{8} 3378^{7} 3695^{9}4111^{9}

Sunburn (IRE) *Mrs A J Perrett* 49
2 b g Mark Of Esteem(IRE) —Sundrenched (IRE) (Desert King (IRE))
5918^{14}

Sun Catcher (IRE) *R Hannon* a83 81
3 b g Cape Cross(IRE) —Taalluf (USA) (Hansel (USA))
2620^{12} 3644^{6} (4078) 4703^{8}6221^{11} 6461^{6} 6579^{4}6882^{11}

Sundae *C F Wall* a57
2 b g Bahamian Bounty—Merry Rous (Rousillon (USA))
3457^{6}

Sundance (IRE) *H J Collingridge* a72 73
4 ch g Namid—Titchwell Lass (Lead On Time (USA))
4486^{7} 5070^{12} 5791^{9} 6174^{12} 6579^{12}

Sunday Symphony *Saeed Bin Suroor* 114
4 br g Sunday Silence(USA) —Darrery (Darshaan)
4791^{2} (5153) 5325^{7}

Sunderland Echo (IRE) *B Ellison* a42 91+
3 ch f Tagula(IRE) —La Alla Wa Asa (IRE) (Alzao (USA))
548^{10} 797^{8} 868^{2}(1185) 1344^{9} (1825) 2022^{4} 2105^{5} 4633^{6} 4803^{3}

Sundried Tomato *D W Chapman* a76 76
7 b g Lugana Beach—Little Scarlett (Mazilier (USA))
127^{9} 178^{13}638^{6} (691) 766^{9} 1196^{12}1577^{3} 2544^{6} 2700^{15}3334^{13} 3524^{5} 4157^{7} 5834^{12}

Sundrive (IRE) *Eamon Tyrrell* a52 25
2 ch f Dr Fong(USA) —Wood Sorrel (IRE) (Woodman (USA))
6523^{6}

Sungio *B P J Baugh* a42 47
8 b g Halling(USA) —Time Or Never (FR) (Dowsing (USA))
141^{4} 361^{7}614^{7} 694^{9}

Sun Hill *C W Fairhurst* a69 57
6 b g Robellino(USA) —Manhattan Sunset (USA) (El Gran Senor (USA))
12^{3} 98^{4}549^{8} (607)

Sunisa (IRE) *J Mackie* a73 86
5 b m Daggers Drawn(USA) —Winged Victory (IRE) (Dancing Brave (USA))
1281^{5} (1800) 1991^{7} 5769^{5}

Sunken Rags *K R Burke* a49 42
2 b f Superior Premium—Mise En Scene (Lugana Beach)
1559^{3} (1743) 2125^{11} 2451^{3} 5687^{6}

Sun King *K G Reveley* 67
9 ch g Zilzal(USA) —Opus One (Slip Anchor)
1562^{7} 3022^{5} 4380^{4} 4960^{4} 5242^{6}

Sun King (USA) *N Zito* a120
4 bb h Charismatic(USA) —Clever But Costly (USA) (Clever Trick (USA))
2093a^{2} 6345a^{10}

Sunley Gift *M R Channon* 72
2 b f Cadeaux Genereux—Thracian (Green Desert (USA))
(1817) 2743^{15} 5434^{11}

Sunley Peace *D R C Elsworth* 73
2 ch c Lomitas—Messila Rose (Darshaan)
5460^{7} 5640^{5} 5892^{3} 6106^{4}

Sunley Song *B G Powell* a43 44
3 b f Fleetwood(IRE) —Sunley Sinner (Try My Best (USA))
3200^{11} 3451^{8} 4367^{8}4687^{6}

Sunley Sovereign *M R Channon* a42 68
2 b g Josr Algarhoud(IRE) —Pharsical (Pharly (FR))
2506^{9} 2710^{5} 3335^{3} 5382^{8} 5686^{6}

Sunlight (IRE) *M A Jarvis* a81+ 85
2 ch f Sinndar(IRE) —Church Light (Caerleon (USA))
5456^{2} (6071)

Sunny Afternoon *Miss E C Lavelle* a59 87
6 ch m Atraf—Pinup (Risk Me (FR))
336[12] 474[7]485[2] 514[8]

Sunny Disposition (IRE) *E F Vaughan* a38 39
3 b c Desert Sun—Madam Waajib (IRE) (Waajib)
887[10] 1648[7] 4111[16]

Sunny Haze *Mrs P N Dutfield* a6
3 ch f Compton Place—Sunrise Girl (King's Signet (USA))
1768[4] 2531[14] 5272[12]5728[13] 6492[9] 6641[12]

Sunny Parkes *M Mullineaux* a48 56
3 ch f Arkadian Hero(USA) —Janette Parkes (Pursuit Of Love)
2210[6] 3100[8]3725[7] 4362[5] 4734[11] 5082[7] 5618[12]

Sunnyside Tom (IRE) *R A Fahey* 78
2 b g Danetime(IRE) —So Kind (Kind Of Hush)
3958[6] (4452)

Sunny Sing (IRE) *J Moore* 115
4 b h Sri Pekan(USA) —Sagrada (GER) (Primo Dominie)
1527a[7] 6783a[5]

Sun Of The Glen (IRE) *B D Leavy* 5
4 b m Key Of Luck(USA) —Gaelic Foray (IRE) (Unblest)
534[7] 634[10]2077[13]

Sun Of The Sea *N P Littmoden* a57 59
2 b g Best Of The Bests(IRE) —Gem (Most Welcome)
2315[9] 6175[8] 6255[8]

Sunoverregun *J R Boyle* 79
2 b c Noverre(USA) —Jumairah Sun (IRE) (Scenic)
6014[3] (6330)

Sunquest *R Hannon* 65
2 b c Groom Dancer(USA) —Icaressa (Anabaa (USA))
4163[4] 4445[6]

Sunrise Safari (IRE) *I Semple* 87
3 b g Mozart(IRE) —Lady Scarlett (Woodman (USA))
1032[3] (1609) 2658[7]

Sunriver (USA) *T Pletcher* a116
3 br c Saint Ballado(CAN) —Goulash (USA) (Mari's Book (USA))
2477a[3]

Sunsemperchi *E Borromeo* 96
4 b m Montjeu(IRE) —Sharp Terms (Kris)
2280a[8] 6362a[12]

Sunset Boulevard (IRE) *J Noseda* a73 65
3 b g Montjeu(IRE) —Lucy In The Sky (IRE) (Lycius (USA))
4374[6] 5429[5] 5870[6]

Sunset Dreamer (USA) *P Mitchell* a43 43
5 ch m Boundary(USA) —Quaff (USA) (Raise A Cup (USA))
35[7] 1727[12]1914[8] 2131[3] 2725[7]6302[11] 6373[5]

Sunset Ridge (IRE) *Rae Guest* 59
3 b f Indian Ridge—Barbara Frietchie (IRE) (Try My Best (USA))
969[11] 1378[5] 2285[4] 3164[3] 4450[3]5273[6]

Sunshine Kid (USA) *J H M Gosden* 95
2 b c Lemon Drop Kid(USA) —Nepenthe (USA) (Broad Brush (USA))
5460[2] (5893) 6104[6]

Sunstroke (IRE) *M G Quinlan* a33 60
2 b f Raphane(USA) —Wish List (IRE) (Mujadil (USA))
1223[10] 1429[9] 2643[4](3613) 3801[4] 4334[3] (4724) 5053[7] 5482[5] 5948[7]6522[6]

Suntan Lady (IRE) *Miss V Haigh* a46 26
2 b f Redback—Scarletta (USA) (Red Ransom (USA))
1181[10] 1647[11] 3994[9]4327[4] 4630[4] 4727[7]5238[17] 5448[12] 6665[7]6715[4] 6807[2]6813[4] 6900[5]6926[6]

Supa Sal *P F I Cole* a72
2 b f King's Best(USA) —Supamova (USA) (Seattle Slew (USA))
(3385)

Supaseus *H Morrison* 99
3 b g Spinning World(USA) —Supamova (USA) (Seattle Slew (USA))
(1680) 2774[8] 3491[8] (5520) 5722[5] 6219[14]

Supa Tramp *J R Fanshawe* a51 61+
3 b g Kayf Tara—Shirley Superstar (Shirley Heights)
531[5] 1216[3]

Superbisli (IRE) *S Ibido*
2 br f Orpen(USA) —Beaufort Lady (IRE) (Alhaarth (IRE))
2565a[7]

Super Canyon *J Pearce* a34 34
8 ch g Gulch(USA) —Marina Park (Local Suitor (USA))
638[14] 1463[7]1765[14]

Supercast (IRE) *W M Brisbourne* a70 78
3 b g Alhaarth(IRE) —Al Euro (FR) (Mujtahid (USA))
1020[11] 1146[11] 1900[4]2329[15] 3268[4] 4532[8] 4659[3] 4922[5]5872[7] 5938[7] 6681[4]6919[5] 6952[3]

Super Cross (IRE) *E A L Dunlop* 72
2 b c Cape Cross(IRE) —Super Trouper (FR) (Nashwan (USA))
5089[7] 5537[3]

Super Dominion *R Hollinshead* a47 50
9 ch g Superpower—Smartie Lee (Dominion)
41[3] 258[13]290[5] 395[11]468[7] 682[4]792[12] 1197[7]2728[7] 6799[10]

Super Eagle (GER) *S Wegner* 47
2 b c Auenadler(GER) —Superlove (IRE) (Hector Protector (USA))
6092a[9]

Superfling *H J Manners* a34 56
5 ch g Superpower—Jobiska (Dunbeath (USA))
1460[8] 2099[11]

Superfly (USA) *N Zito* a102
3 bb c Fusaichi Pegasus(USA) —Marozia (USA) (Storm Bird (CAN))
757a[5]

Super Frank (IRE) *J Akehurst* a64 48
3 b g Cape Cross(IRE) —Lady Joshua (IRE) (Royal Academy (USA))
(30) 558[4] 1215[10] 1616[16]3011[7] 3650[8]4245[8] 5129[11] (6864)

Super Frolic (USA) *S Blasi* a122 102
6 ch h Pine Bluff(USA) —Lindsay Frolic (USA) (Mt. Livermore (USA))
743a[8] 5826a[5]6342a[12]

Super Hornet (JPN) *Y Yahagi* 112
3 b c Rodrigo De Triano(USA) —You Sun Polish (JPN) (El Senor (USA))
6530a[9]

Superior Dream *J W Unett*
4 b g Superpower—California Dreamin (Slip Anchor)
162[13]

Superior Point *P Howling* a6
3 b f Superior Premium—Raisa Point (Raised Socially (USA))
233[12]

Superior Star *R A Fahey* 76+
3 b g Superior Premium—Lindfield Belle (IRE) (Fairy King (USA))
819[5] 1345[2] 3023[7] 3282[6] 3725[2](4060) 4257[7]

Superjain *J M Jefferson* a45 62
2 b f Lujain(USA) —Plie (Superlative)
5686[5] 6047[3] 6420[5]6750[8]

Super Kid (NZ) *J Moore* 121
7 b h Gaius—Pompeii Pride (NZ) (Pompeii Court (USA))
1180a[4]

Super Nebula *P L Gilligan* a31
2 b c Fantastic Light(USA) —It Girl (Robellino (USA))
5841[10]

Supershot (IRE) *O Brennan* 65
8 b g Son Of Sharp Shot(IRE) —One To Two (IRE) (Astronef)
5553[13]

Super Sifted (GER) *H R A Cecil* a36
2 b f Saddlers' Hall(IRE) —Sun Moon Stars (IRE) (Shahrastani (USA))
6558[8]

Supersonic Dave (USA) *B J Meehan* 84+
2 bb c Swain(IRE) —Vickey's Echo (CAN) (Clever Trick (USA))
(5659)

Support Fund (IRE) *R F Johnson Houghton* 60
2 ch f Intikhab(USA) —Almost A Lady (IRE) (Entitled)
5043[3] 5563[3]

Suppose (USA) *A P O'Brien* 70
2 b f Danehill(USA) —Sophisticat (USA) (Storm Cat (USA))
4041[5]

Supposition *D K Weld* 106
2 b f Dansili—Topicality (USA) (Topsider (USA))
4853a[3] 5394a[8]

Supreme Charter *M Johnston* a71 83
3 b g Diktat—Alchi (USA) (Alleged (USA))
5511[8] 5671[7] 5869[10]6287[6] 6647[8]

Supreme Kiss *Mrs N Smith* a61 62
3 b f Barathea Guest—Kiss Me Again (IRE) (Cyrano De Bergerac)
1937[10] 2190[4] 2433[5]2652[12] 4164[4] 4398[7] 4756[3] 5569[5]6142[2] 6440[9]6513[2] 6632[3]

Supreme Salutation *D K Ivory* a29 40
10 ch g Most Welcome—Cardinal Press (Sharrood (USA))
240[5] 297[3]391[5] 423[8]689[11] 1227[8]1373[8] 1724[12]

Supreme Speedster *T R George* 77
2 br c Superior Premium—Effervescent (Efisio)
(1664) 2127[11] 4603[9]

Surangi *Gianfranco Verricelli*
2 b c Best Of The Bests(IRE) —Joe's Dancer (Shareef Dancer (USA))
5771a[12]

Surbiton (USA) *A Al Raihe* a92 110
6 ch h El Prado(IRE) —Mastina (USA) (Gulch (USA))
152a[9] 205a[9] 495a[8]565a[6]

Surdoue *P Howling* a52 39
6 b g Bishop Of Cashel—Chatter's Princess (Cadeaux Genereux)
25[6] 92[2](182) (390) 525[12]696[13]

Surely Truly (IRE) *A E Jones* a81 79
3 b f Trans Island—Londubh (Tumble Wind)
1097[17] 1337[11] 2049[6]2760[9] 3488[2] 6672[9]6833[8]

Sureyya (GER) *E Lellouche* 97
3 br f Monsun(GER) —Sankt Johanna (GER) (High Game)
6384a[2] 6722a[0]

Surf City *R A Harris* a55 67
3 ch c Distant Music(USA) —Tolyatti (Green Desert (USA))
1078[12]

Surprise Pension (IRE) *J J Quinn* 51
2 b g Fruits Of Love(USA) —Sheryl Lynn (Miller's Mate)
4608[13] 5491[7] 5901[8]

Surrey Spinner *Mrs A J Perrett* 54
2 ch c Intikhab(USA) —Markievicz (IRE) (Doyoun)
2579[10]

Surwaki (USA) *R M H Cowell* a69 85
4 b g Miswaki(USA) —Quinella (Generous (IRE))
826[10] 1262[2] 2183[3]2606[7] 3223[B] 3928[4] (4390) 5337[11] 6580[11]

Susanna's Prospect (IRE) *B J Meehan* a56 64+
2 ch f Namid—Substantive (USA) (Distant View (USA))
2328[10] 2930[7] 3201[8]4815[4] 5747[4] 6394[8]

Susi Applause *B Grizzetti* 21
2 b f Royal Applause—Scisciabubu (IRE) (Danehill (USA))
5858a[14]

Susiedil (IRE) *D Nicholls* a37 40
5 b m Mujadil(USA) —Don't Take Me (IRE) (Don't Forget Me)
183[8] 616[10]

Susie May *C A Cyzer* a53
2 ch f Hernando(FR) —Mohican Girl (Dancing Brave (USA))
6071[8] 6349[10]

Suteki Shinsukekun (USA) *Hideyuki Mori* 107
3 b c Danzig(USA) —Autumn Moon (USA) (Mr Prospector (USA))
5717a[16] 6530a[14]

Sutra (USA) *M Stidham* a109
2 bb f Meadowlake(USA) —Desert Liaison (USA) (Woodman (USA))
6338a[9]

Suzieblue (IRE) *J S Moore* a57 49
2 b f Redback—Blue Holly (IRE) (Blues Traveller (IRE))
1542[13] 2315[15] 2709[6] (2916) 3345[9] 3624[6]4222[4] 4971[2] 5687[12]

Suzuki (IRE) *H Morrison* a14 57
3 ch f Barathea(IRE) —Nishan (Nashwan (USA))
2350[8] 3258[7] 4210[9]4868[6] 5451[10]

Suzy Bliss *W R Swinburn* a88 100
3 b f Spinning World(USA) —Poppy Carew (IRE) (Danehill (USA))
827[4] 1472[4] 2199[7]2772[7]

Svedov (FR) *E Lellouche* 111
5 ch h Exit To Nowhere(USA) —Carla (FR) (Cardoun (FR))
(841a) 1371a[3] 2490a[5] 4862a[3] 5703a[5] 6250a[3]

Sven (SWE) *B I Case* 34
2 b g Duty Time—Last Romance (IRE) (Last Tycoon)
6050[11]

Svenson *J S Wainwright*
5 ch h Dancing Spree(USA) —Bella Bambola (IRE) (Tate Gallery (USA))
2077[14]

Swains Bridge (USA) *L M Cumani* 86+
4 b h Swain(IRE) —Saraa Ree (USA) (Caro)
2143[6] (3230) 3377[5] 4392[5]

Swainson (USA) *P Mitchell* a70 77
5 br g Swain(IRE) —Lyphard's Delta (USA) (Lyphard (USA))
37[4] 125[9]186[5] 700[3]1213[3] 6565[11] 6831[6]

Swallow Senora (IRE) *M C Chapman* a44 54
4 b m Entrepreneur—Sangra (USA) (El Gran Senor (USA))
3635[10] 4306[15] 4507[14] 4948[12] 5077[9]6490[4] 6636[5]6962[7]

Swan Maiden (USA) *A Laird* a87 68
3 ch f Swain(IRE) —Robust (USA) (Conquistador Cielo (USA))
202a[2] 436a[10]

Swan Of Raunds *J R Norton* a9
2 b g Fraam—Persian Fortune (Forzando)
3385[10] 4566[15] 5537[14]

Swan Queen *J L Dunlop* a43 83+
3 b f In The Wings—Bronzewing (Beldale Flutter (USA))
897[4] (1214) (1837) 4997[11]

Swayze (IRE) *N P Littmoden* a59 69
3 b g Marju(IRE) —Dance Of Love (IRE) (Pursuit Of Love)
993[10] (1732) 2209[9] 3977[9]

Sweeney (IRE) *M A Jarvis* a85+
2 ch c Jade Robbery(USA) —Arduine (Diesis)
(6658) (6846)

Sweet Afton (IRE) *Eamon Tyrrell* 98
3 b f Mujadil(USA) —Victory Peak (Shirley Heights)
1377[7] 2438[5] 2744[10] 3767a[4] 3967a[6]4345[9] 4749a[12]

Sweet Boulangere *R Hannon* a60 68
3 ch f Grand Lodge(USA) —Cybinka (Selkirk (USA))
712[7] 1162[11]1282[5] 1638[10] 2352[12]3615[8]

Sweet Candy *K A Ryan* a76 63
2 ch f Cadeaux Genereux—Hajat (Mujtahid (USA))
1884[4] 2076[8] 3201[5](3917) 4246[5]4766[7] 5140[8] 5503[16] 5860[3]

Sweet Cherokee *C N Kellett* a38 19
3 b f Mind Games—Sioux Lady (Petong)
105[4] 308[4]396[6] 528[12]790[9] 874[5]936[9]

Sweet Emily *Patrick J Flynn* a74+ 69
4 ch m Inchinor—Thamud (IRE) (Lahib (USA))
2293[7] 3099[7] 3304[4]4186a[5]

Sweetest Revenge (IRE) *M D I Usher* a74+ 59
5 ch m Daggers Drawn(USA) —Joza (Marju (IRE))
71[11] 164[3]249[2] 486[7](519) (587) 657[5]699[6] 761[7]2223[14] 2459[12] 2813[7] 3094[7] 3368[8]4462[6] 4985[5] 5480[12] 5737[3](5987)

Sweet Georgie Bee (IRE) *R A Fahey* 56+
2 b c Titus Livius(FR) —Duck Over (Warning)
2191[6] (Dead)

Sweetheart *M A Jarvis* a60
2 b f Sinndar(IRE) —Love And Adventure (USA) (Halling (USA))
6486[6] 6737[4]

Sweet Indulgence (IRE) *W J Musson* a98 89
5 ch g Inchinor—Silent Indulgence (USA) (Woodman (USA))
1991[6] 3048[3] 3497[6] (4604) 5010[10] 5548[8]5792[3] (6351) (6515) (6836)

Sweet Lavinia *J D Bethell* 51
3 ch f Lomitas—Latch Key Lady (USA) (Tejano (USA))
2325[10] 3357[4] 4471[6] 5240[6] 5618[5]5960[9] 6305[12]

Sweet Lilly *M R Channon* a74 103+
2 b f Tobougg(IRE) —Maristax (Reprimand)
2456[12] 3201[3] 3663[3](4008) (4264) (4773) 5187[4] (6010)

Sweetly Sharp (IRE) *A Berry* a39 50
3 ch f Daggers Drawn(USA) —Pecan Pie (IRE) (Sri Pekan (USA))
980[7] 1447[7] 1791[3] 4201[8] 4324[12]5864[9] 6717[12]

Sweet Medicine *P Howling* a71 74
4 ch m Dr Devious(IRE) —Crimley Crumb (Rainbow Quest (USA))
503[2] 669[3]1006[3] 1213[4] 3231[4]4104[14] 6861[7] 6967[6]

Sweet Namibia (IRE) *J W Hills* a61 62
4 ch m Namid—Almond Flower (IRE) (Alzao (USA))
47[10] 170[7]327[8]

Sweetnorthernsaint (USA) *M Trombetta* a120
3 br g Sweetsouthernsaint(USA) —Ice Beauty (USA) (Waquoit (USA))
1498a[7] 1861a[2]

Sweet Peak (IRE) *Eamon Tyrrell* 83
2 b f Desert Style(IRE) —Victory Peak (Shirley Heights)
5850a[8]

Sweet Petite (IRE) *Kevin F O'Donnell* 89
3 b f Mark Of Esteem(IRE) —Zagaleta (Sri Pekan (USA))
4502a[8] 5996a[16]

Sweet Pickle *J R Boyle* a76 72
5 b m Piccolo—Sweet Wilhelmina (Indian Ridge)
21[4] 133[5]265[9] 474[4]519[11] (552) (608) 654[6]732[4] 2248[3]2637[3] 3033[2] 3434[7] 3995[2](4077) 4449[2] 4589[4] 5232[6] 5453[7] 6464[2]6643[3] 6930[11]

Sweet Request *R M Beckett* a56
2 ch f Best Of The Bests(IRE) —Sweet Revival (Claude Monet (USA))
5425[6]

Sweet Return *R McAnally* 121
6 ch h Elmaamul(USA) —Sweet Revival (Claude Monet (USA))
5416a[4]

Sweet Rosella *G M Moore* a36
3 b f Alhaarth(IRE) —Thamud (IRE) (Lahib (USA))
76[6] 488[9]

Sweet Seville (FR) *Mrs G S Rees* 50
2 b f Agnes World(USA) —Hispalis (IRE) (Barathea (IRE))
4323[8]

Sweet Shop *A Fabre* 92
3 b f Grand Lodge(USA) —Candice (IRE) (Caerleon (USA))
3515a[12]

Sweet Soul Diva *Miss V Haigh* 33
2 b f Cadeaux Genereux—Alarming Motown (Warning)
3640[13] 4049[7] 4665[5]5323[13]

Sweet Spot *Eamon Tyrrell* 87
3 ch f Generous(IRE) —Cutting Glance (USA) (Woodman (USA))
1374[2] 2578[8]

Sweet Stream (ITY) *J E Hammond* 115
6 b m Shantou(USA) —Snug Dinner (IRE) (Jareer (USA))
4646a[2] 6004a[5]

Sweet Symphony (USA) *W Mott* a122
4 bb m A.P. Indy(USA) —Brandy Rose (USA) (Distinctive Pro (USA))
5818a[5]

Sweet Talker (USA) *H G Motion* 115
4 b m Stormin Fever(USA) —Another Vegetarian (USA) (Stalwart (USA))
3109a[2]

Sweet Travel (IRE) *A Fabre* 101
3 b f Danzig(USA) —Raise A Beauty (USA) (Alydar (USA))
1068[4] 5222a[10]

Sweet Treat (IRE) *J R Fanshawe* 103
4 b m Orpen(USA) —Canton Lightning (Rheingold)
1477[2] 2041a[5] 4628[2] 5159[9] 5525[8]

Sweet Venture (FR) *M Weiss* 102
4 gr h Verglas(IRE) —Bitter Sweet (FR) (Esprit Du Nord (USA))
(305a) (455a)

Sweet Wind Music *B Grizzetti* 98
2 ch f Zamindar(USA) —Sadhya (FR) (Prince Sabo)
(3343a) 5858a[12]

Sweet World *A P Jarvis* a60
2 b g Agnes World(USA) —Douce Maison (IRE) (Fools Holme (USA))
5780[4] 6031[8]6224[9] 6487[3]6576[7] 6711[3]

Swell Lad *S Gollings* a52 68
4 b g Sadler's Wells(USA) —Lydara (USA) (Alydar (USA))
163[6] 185[11]482[12] 683[13]

Swift Current (JPN) *Hideyuki Mori* 121
5 ch h Sunday Silence(USA) —Whitewater Affair (Machiavellian (USA))
6612a[8]

Swift Cut (IRE) *A P Jarvis* a76 75
2 ch c Daggers Drawn(USA) —Jugendliebe (IRE) (Persian Bold)
5111[10] 5454[2] 5615[2] (5780) 6146[8]

Swift Image *S C Williams* 75
2 gr f Act One—Swift Dispersal (Shareef Dancer (USA))
4302[2] (5068)

Swiftly Addicted (IRE) *A King* a50 59
2 ch f King's Best(USA) —Swiftly (Cadeaux Genereux)
2456[11] 4084[15] 4993[10]5290[2] 5668[8]

Swift Oscar *J W Hills* a88 82
4 b g Mark Of Esteem(IRE) —Surf Bird (Shareef Dancer (USA))
64[4] 2214[2]67[4]

Swift Princess (IRE) *K R Burke* 29
2 b f Namid—Swift Chorus (Music Boy)
5764[8]

Swift Sailor *G L Moore* a104 103
5 gr g Slip Anchor—New Wind (GER) (Windwurf (GER))
1128[9]

Swinbrook (USA) *J A R Toller* a91 96
5 ch g Stravinsky(USA) —Dance Diane (USA) (Affirmed (USA))
970[4] (1285) 1803[7] 2230[13] 3092[6] 3493[4]4106[7] 5420[4] 5785[4]

Swindon (USA) *P F I Cole* a51 72
4 b m Kingmambo(USA) —Dance Design (IRE) (Sadler's Wells (USA))
3302[5] 3704[4] 3952[12] 6484[12]

Swing On A Star (IRE) *W R Swinburn* a61+
2 br f Celtic Swing—Lady Stalker (Primo Dominie)
6290[4]

Swing The Ring (IRE) *Bruce Hellier* 99
3 b c Rossini(USA) —Sharkiyah (IRE) (Polish Precedent (USA))
4740[7] 6093a[12]

Swing Wing *P F I Cole* a78 113
7 b g In The Wings—Swift Spring (FR) (Bluebird (USA))
3078[13]

Swinton *M Brittain*
5 gr g Grey Desire—Portite Sophie (Doulab (USA))
4205[11] 6280[14]

Swiper Hill (IRE) *B Ellison* a76+
3 b g City On A Hill(USA) —Alkariyh (USA) (Alydar (USA))
(722) 1004[9] 1529[9]

Swiss Act *M Johnston* 81+
2 ch c Act One—Dancing Mirage (IRE) (Machiavellian (USA))
5025[4] 5321 [3] (5580)

Swords *Heather Dalton* a66 57
4 b g Vettori(IRE) —Pomorie (IRE) (Be My Guest (USA))
63[8] 173[2]257[6] 3998[2](4438) 4914[5] (5213) 5691[4] 5971[10]6426[3]

Sword's Edge (IRE) *W A Murphy* a48 68
5 b g Pennekamp(USA) —Scimitarra (Kris)
5972[8] 6405[10]6526[11]

Swordsman (GER) *M L W Bell* 98
4 b h Acatenango(GER) —Saiga (Windwurf (GER))
4027[5] 4346[8] 4876[7] 5533[4]

Sworn In (USA) *N I M Rossiter* 101?
5 ch h Kingmambo(USA) —Under Oath (USA) (Deputed Testamony (USA))
991[8] 1409[6]

Sybelio (FR) *W Hefter* 37
2 b c Lord Of Men—Trueville (GER) (Top Ville)
4857a[6]

Sybella *J L Dunlop* a56 83
3 ch f In The Wings—Samara (IRE) (Polish Patriot (USA))
1516[3] 2292[4] 3122[2] 3539[5] 5128[3]5594[4] 6205[8] 6410[7]

Sybilia (GER) *Mario Hofer* 80
2 b f Spectrum(IRE) —Slawa (GER) (Polish Precedent (USA))
6122a[6]

Syllable *Mario Hofer* 79
2 b f Halling(USA) —Quarter Note (USA) (Danehill (USA))
5763a[5]

Sylvan (IRE) *S Kirk* 73
2 bb f Shinko Forest(IRE) —Auriga (Belmez (USA))
4041[9] (4774) 5372[8]

Symboli Escape (JPN) *T Kubota* 107
5 b h Sakura Bakushin(JPN) —Sweet Kenmare (JPN) (Kenmare (FR))
5717a[13]

Symboli Gran (IRE) *Y Hatakeyama* 119
4 gr h Grand Lodge(USA) —Valixa (FR) (Linamix (FR))
6530a[3] 6850a[5]

Symbol Of Peace (IRE) *J W Unett* a72 71
3 b f Desert Sun—Rosy Lydgate (Last Tycoon)
6507[6] 6666[7](6792) 6942[3]

Synonymy *M Blanshard* a67 64
3 b g Sinndar(IRE) —Peony (Lion Cavern (USA))
656[3] 979[3] 1350[7]2622[6] 3075[11] 3347[9]4111[3] 4362[4] 4800[4] 5564[2] (5846) 6027[6] 6560[2]

Syrakus (GER) *H Blume* 101
8 b h Kris—Sistadari (Shardari)
456a[13]

Szuma (SWE) *Elisabeth Gautier*
3 b g Richard Of York—Santa Clara (Star Appeal)
4919a[7]

Tabadul (IRE) *E A L Dunlop* a105 96
5 b g Cadeaux Genereux—Amaniy (USA) (Dayjur (USA))
(1380) 1678[12] 2341[2] 4023[2]5177[4] 5505[7]

Tabaret *R M Whitaker* 101
3 ch c Bertolini(USA) —Luanshya (First Trump)
1485[9] 2720[F] 3312[12]

Tableau (USA) *R Bouresly* a77 89
5 ch g Marquetry(USA) —Model Bride (USA) (Blushing Groom (FR))
206a[10] 355a[9]

Taboor (IRE) *R M H Cowell* a73 73
8 b g Mujadil(USA) —Christoph's Girl (Efisio)
22[4] 216[3]317[2] 401[3]837[3] 986[7]1235[2] (1816) (2182) 6035[6] 6320[11]6485[4] 6585[7]6656[11]

Tabulate *P L Gilligan* a65 59
3 b f Dansili—Let Alone (Warning)
1153[5] 1386[5]1747[5] 2554[3]2987[7] 3099[8] 3379[2]5690[2] 6026[4]

Tacid *Dr J D Scargill* a50+ 39
4 b m Diktat—Defined Feature (IRE) (Nabeel Dancer (USA))
(184) 304[7] (493) 678[3]917[9] 2248[6]3263[3] 4497[8] 6281[4]6799[2] 6960[5]

Tackcoat (IRE) *Eoin Doyle* a53 40
6 b g Sesaro(USA) —Damaslin (Camden Town)
1764[6] 6854[3]6961[7] (6970)

Tadlil *J M Bradley* 78
4 b g Pivotal—Pretty Poppy (Song)
1414[4] 1618[8] 1878[12] 2602[7] (3749) 4054[9](4361) 4894[3] (4957)

Tafilah *P W D'Arcy* a56 54
3 b f Foxhound(USA) —Petra Nova (First Trump)
85[4] 139[2]1974[4] (326)

Tafis Beach *J R Jenkins* a11 18
2 b f Lugana Beach—Sifat (Marju (IRE))
3148[11] 3979[12] 6034[11]6463[8]

Tafiya *G A Butler* a62 73
3 b f Bahri(USA) —Fickle (Danehill (USA))
479[2] 668[7]3362[2] 3865[3] 4040[13] 4759[5] 6225[4]

Tagano Bastille (JPN) *Kaneo Ikezoe* 114
3 b c Brian's Time(USA) —Wien Concert (JPN) (Sakura Yutaka O (JPN))
5717a[3] 6850a[12]

Tagart *J J Quinn* 43
3 b g Triple Hay—Clancassie (Clantime)
3987[5] 4261[6] 5363[4]

Tag Team (IRE) *John A Harris* a74 63
5 ch g Tagula(IRE) —Okay Baby (IRE) (Treasure Kay)
96[6] 320[4]426[2] 605[9]858[7] 4846[10] 5032[2](5737) 6452[6]6508[7] 6930[2]

Tagula Bay (IRE) *T D Easterby* a24 66
4 b m Tagula(IRE) —Nezool Almatar (IRE) (Last Tycoon)
864[12] 1413[3] 1735[6] 2112[4] 4735[6]5060[9] 5370[9] 5620[9] 5951[2] 6276[9]

Tagula Blue (IRE) *Ian Williams* a66 76
6 b g Tagula(IRE) —Palace Blue (IRE) (Dara Monarch)
882[3] (1187) (1288) 1821[8] 2104[5]

Tagula Music (IRE) *B Palling* 39
2 ch f Tagula(IRE) —Mandolin (IRE) (Sabrehill (USA))
961[12] 1284[11] 2094[5] 3345[7] 4926[10]5084[18]

Tagula Sunrise (IRE) *R A Fahey* 100
4 ch m Tagula(IRE) —Lady From Limerick (IRE) (Rainbows For Life (CAN))
1143[7] 1532[3] 1667[15] (1865) 2017[7] (2851) 3499[5]4343[4] 4609[8] 4988[4] 5159[7]

Tahafut *W J Haggas* 52
2 b f Marju(IRE) —Farha (USA) (Nureyev (USA))
5147[8] 5454[10]

Tahoe Warrior (USA) *T Pletcher* a75 97
3 b c Carson City(USA) —Amy's Gold (USA) (Strike The Gold (USA))
757a[9]

Tahreeb (FR) *D Selvaratnam* a85 115
5 ch h Indian Ridge—Native Twine (Be My Native (USA))
153a[15] 367a[8] 494a[9]

Taili *D A Nolan* 9
5 b m Taipan(IRE) —Doubtfire (Jalmood (USA))
3350[10] 3675[5] 4132[11] 4351[10] 5581[14]

Taita (GER) *H J Groschel* 82
2 ch f Big Shuffle(USA) —Tamarita (GER) (Acatenango (GER))
4857a[2]

Tajaathub (USA) *M Johnston* 83
4 ch m Aljabr(USA) —Tajannub (USA) (Dixieland Band (USA))
1865[3] 2454[7] 2851[9] 4521[4] 4879[7]5554[9]

Tajjree *Miss K B Boutflower* a54 27
3 b f Lujain(USA) —Rateeba (IRE) (Green Desert (USA))
1960[6] 3112[8] 3406[9]5969[2] 6440[8]

Tajseed (IRE) *A Manuel* 100
6 b g Bahhare(USA) —Dublah (USA) (Private Account (USA))
151a[2] 357a[4]

Takafu (USA) *W S Kittow* a68 83
4 b g Lemon Drop Kid(USA) —Proper Protocol (USA) (Deputy Minister (CAN))
1206[10] 1544[14] 2088[7] 2534[5] 3028[2](3452) 3853[4] 4369[6] 5564[3] 6075[8]

Takanewa (IRE) *J Howard Johnson* 70
3 b f Danetime(IRE) —Lady Ingabelle (IRE) (Catrail (USA))
1598[3] 2129[3] 2699[8] 3189[5] 3604[9]4881[6] 5370[12]

Take A Bow *P R Chamings* 110
5 b h Royal Applause—Giant Nipper (Nashwan (USA))
1299[5] 1739[3] 2236[2] 2431[3] 5142[3]5477[4] 5675[4] 6203[4] 6334[4]

Take A Mile (IRE) *B G Powell* a70 67
4 ch g Inchinor—Bu Hagab (IRE) (Royal Academy (USA))
3615[7] 4073[3] 4240[6] 5422[4]

Take Blood (FR) *Mlle S-V Tarrou* 93
2 gr f Take Risks(FR) —Young Blood (FR) (Northern Crystal)
3132a[4] 3990a[5]

Take D'Tour (USA) *D Fawkes* a122
5 ch m Tour D'Or(USA) —Cherry Flare (USA) (Mr Washington)
5818a[6]

Take Grace (FR) *Y De Nicolay* a99 100
4 b m Take Risks(FR) —Grace Royale (IRE) (Marignan (USA))
6574a[0]

Take It There *A J Lidderdale* a62 47
4 ch m Cadeaux Genereux—Feel Free (IRE) (Generous (IRE))
5388[10] 5756[11] 5988[9]6404[9] (6531) 6641[9]

Take My Turn *M Blanshard* a45 50
2 b c Josr Algarhoud(IRE) —Swizzle (Efisio)
2172[14] 2552[8] 3246[6]4334[11] 4526[13] 4816[8]

Take No Notice (IRE) *K R Burke* a40 40
3 b f Imperial Ballet(IRE) —North Telstar (Sallust)
93[9] 241[6]

Takeover Target (AUS) *J Janiak* a116 126
7 b g Celtic Swing—Shady Stream (AUS) (Archregent (CAN))
(2720) 2846[3] 3494[7] (5717a)

Takes Tutu (USA) *C R Dore* a71 76
7 b g Afternoon Deelites(USA) —Lady Affirmed (USA) (Affirmed (USA))
7[6] 161[6]251[6] 313[3]377[5] 484[2]596[6] 1075[12] (1311) 1422[3](1480) 2820[12] 3147[3] 3298[6] 3565[5] 3642[2]4048[5] 4241[11] 5149[12]5436[10] 6573[10] 6747[11]6918[4]

Take The Ribbon (USA) *W Dollase* 105
3 b f Chester House(USA) —Magical Flash (USA) (Miswaki (USA))
5198a[2] 5984a[5]

Take To The Skies (IRE) *A P Jarvis* 48
2 b c Lujain(USA) —To The Skies (USA) (Sky Classic (CAN))
2771[10]

Taking The Gold (ITY) *M Innocenti*
2 ch c Spymaster(USA) —Themis Mou (IRE) (Ela-Mana-Mou)
5771a[13]

Takitwo *P D Cundell* a49 75
3 b g Delta Dancer—Tiama (IRE) (Last Tycoon)
(2535) 2678[8] 3011[11] (3869) (4291) 4689[4]5042[8] 5568[10]

Talbot Avenue *M Blanshard* a97 108
8 b g Puissance—Dancing Daughter (Dance In Time (CAN))
367a[4] 433a[4] 494a[7] 2624[2] 3520[7]4128[20] 4360[11] 6776[2]6849[9]

Talbot Street *Robert Gray*
3 ch c Compton Place—Roxy (Rock City)
2298[10] 3288[17]

Talcen Gwyn (IRE) *M F Harris* a69 74
4 b g Fayruz—Cheerful Knight (IRE) (Mac's Imp (USA))
136[3] 305a[4] 455a[6]3683[8] 3988[4] 4110[2]4258[3] 4587[3] 4675[2] (4872) (5167) 5378[4] 5486[5]5575[10]

Talenti (IRE) *A P O'Brien* 85+
3 b g Sadler's Wells(USA) —Sumoto (Mtoto)
2055a[5]

Talisker Rock (IRE) *B Storey* 4
6 gr g Tagula(IRE) —Hallatte (USA) (Trempolino (USA))
2398[6] 4117[9]

Tally (IRE) *D G Bridgwater* a64 54
6 ch g Tagula(IRE) —Sally Chase (Sallust)
27[7] 148[7]261[13] 312[10]793[10] 904[11]2260[7] 3614[14]

Tallyhobye *M E Sowersby* a41 56
3 b g Foxhound(USA) —Bebe De Cham (Tragic Role (USA))
272[9] 500[8]817[5] 1352[13] 1609[9] (2107) 2539[10] 2832[5]3303[10] 3983[9] 4404[12] (Dead)

Talpour (IRE) *M C Chapman* 45
6 ch g Ashkalani(IRE) —Talwara (USA) (Diesis)
2682[6] 4945[12] 5922[11]

Talwin (IRE) *Kevin Prendergast* 100
3 b f Alhaarth(IRE) —Lady Windley (Baillamont (USA))
2054a[8] 5854a[13]

Tamagin (USA) *P D Evans* a92 76+
3 b c Stravinsky(USA) —Luia (USA) (Forty Niner (USA))
228[5] (291) 500[10]558[2] 583[5](712) 803[2](855) 1122[5] 1337[4]1384[6] (1963) 6094[8] 6461[3]6514[7] 6692[4]6830[4] 6868[2]6986[8]

Tamamo Hot Play (JPN) *K Minai* 110
5 b h Fuji Kiseki(JPN) —Hot Play (JPN) (Northern Taste (CAN))
5717a[15] 6850a[10]

Tamatave (IRE) *K A Ryan* a73 66
4 b g Darshaan—Manuetti (IRE) (Sadler's Wells (USA))
1032[11] 1492[3] 1864[11] 3298[5] 3565[9]6323[5] 6721[2]6977[8]

Tamazug *Kevin Prendergast* 102+
3 b f Machiavellian(USA) —Nasheed (USA) (Riverman (USA))
1709a[3] 5996a[14]

Tamino (IRE) *H Morrison* a58 70
3 b c Mozart(IRE) —Stop Out (Rudimentary (USA))
1801[8] 2602[3] 3118[6] (4532) 4962[2] 5378[2]5987[8]

Taminoula (IRE) *J G Given* a59 69
5 b m Tagula(IRE) —Taormina (IRE) (Ela-Mana-Mou)
170[11] 265[4]327[9] 336[3]582[4] 917[8]1353[12] 2286[12]

Tam Lin *Sir Michael Stoute* 118
3 b c Selkirk(USA) —La Nuit Rose (FR) (Rainbow Quest (USA))
(1290) (1813) 2801[5] (3736) (4818) 5342[2]

Tammy *C W Thornton* 45
3 b f Tamure(IRE) —Heather Honey (Insan (USA))
1296[8] 1598[11] 1854[7] 2107[7] 4227[10]

Tamora *A P Jarvis* a57 54
4 ch m Dr Fong(USA) —Tahara (IRE) (Caerleon (USA))
917[7] 1197[3](1538) 1727[9]3099[6] 3339[14]

Tamworth (IRE) *E J Creighton* a69 54
4 b g Perugino(USA) —Faiblesse (Welsh Saint)
6069[6] 6193[2] 6396[12]6464[5] 6721[7]6864[6] 6938[10]

Tancredi (SWE) *N B King* a48
4 b g Rossini(USA) —Begine (IRE) (Germany (USA))
6977[9]

Tancred Times *D W Barker* a35 14
11 ch m Clantime—Mischievous Miss (Niniski (USA))
5752[15] 6308[12] 6464[9]6851[8]

Tanforan *Ms J S Doyle* a77 87
4 b g Mujahid(USA) —Florentynna Bay (Aragon)
64[6] 192[4]221[6] 451[10]721[2] 1042[2] 1262[7]1359[2] 1487 [17] 2047[11] 4172[11] 4378[10]4760[13] 5144[10] 5554[11] 5685[5] 6437[2]6579[8] 6654[7]

Tang *W G M Turner* a52 67
2 ch f Bahamian Bounty—Hymne (FR) (Saumarez)
1587[4] 1743[5] 6605[3]6715[7]

Tangarita *A M Balding* a51 64
3 b f Tagula(IRE) —Santa Isobel (Nashwan (USA))
1375[2] 1652[2] 1925[9]2480[7] 3244[3] 3804[2] 4021[7] 5072[6]

Tanmeya *R C Guest* 42
5 gr m Linamix(FR) —Ta Awun (USA) (Housebuster (USA))
2901[6] 3376[7]

Tannenberg (IRE) *G A Swinbank* 91
5 b g Polish Precedent(USA) —Upper Strata (Shirley Heights)
1756[4] (2000) 2176[5]

Tanning *M Appleby* a47 49
4 b m Atraf—Gerundive (USA) (Twilight Agenda (USA))
63[4] 3594[8]

Tantien *T Keddy* a35 4
4 b m Diktat—Tahilla (Moorestyle)
1573[6] 1852[9] 3089[16]3541[14] 5728[10] 6696[11]6800[11] 6971[7]

Tanzanite (IRE) *D W P Arbuthnot* 100
4 b m Revoque(IRE) —Resume (IRE) (Lahib (USA))
1301[3] 1678[11] 2011[3] (2086) 3123a[10] 4590[5]4808[11] 5012[5] 5675[29]

Tapa *C A Dwyer* a59 66
4 b m Tagula(IRE) —Tweed Mill (Selkirk (USA))
46[10] 137[10]327[3] 416[8]581[8] 659[10]

Tapau (IRE) *J M Bradley* a40 57
8 b m Nicolotte—Urtica (IRE) (Cyrano De Bergerac)
4365[2] 4484[2] 4844[8] 5302[13] 5569[6]

Tapping Toes (IRE) *J R Best* a30
3 b f Danehill Dancer(IRE) —It's A Gift (IRE) (Brief Truce (USA))
6033[11]

Tappit (IRE) *L R James* a32 30
7 b g Mujadil(USA) —Green Life (Green Desert (USA))
1607[9]

Tapsalteerie *M J Attwater* a30
3 b f Tipsy Creek(USA) —Croft Sally (Crofthall)
365[12] 536[10]6327[11] 6490[10]

Taqseem (IRE) *Kevin Prendergast* 105
3 b g Fantastic Light(USA) —Elshamms (Zafonic (USA))
755a[6] (3125a) 4031a[3]

Tarabut *E A L Dunlop* 83
4 b m Green Desert(USA) —Nabadhaat (USA) (Mr Prospector (USA))
2296[4] 2723[21] 4231[8]

Tara King *A B Haynes* a48
4 b m Deploy—Trinity Hall (Hallgate)
166[3] 1006[7]

Taranaki *P D Cundell* a68 77
8 b g Delta Dancer—Miss Ticklepenny (Distant Relative)
71[7] 137[6]232[2] 339[7]777[9] 1209[3] 1273[2]1673[8] 2211[2] 2390[3]2567[4] 2936[2] 3153[5]3390[2] 3705[5] (4399) 4446[11](4795) (5042) 5233[3] 5591[3] 5896[5]

Tarandot (IRE) *G G Margarson* 99
5 b m Singspiel(IRE) —Rifada (Ela-Mana-Mou)
1804[6] 2023[4] 3078[5] 4079[9] 4346[9]5963[31]

Taranis *Sir Mark Prescott* a51 56
3 b g Lomitas—Woodbeck (Terimon)
2529[8] 3075[5] 3586[2]4728[13] 5637[4] 5936[5] 6068[4]

Taranto *Saeed Bin Suroor* a109 102
3 b f Machiavellian(USA) —Magna Graecia (IRE) (Warning)
6191[2] 6333[5]

Taran Tregarth *A Bailey* a33 31
2 b f Tobougg(IRE) —Little Change (Grundy)
2439[10] 2938[9] 3915[6]4171[8] 5720[12] 6049[11] 6471[2]6534[9] 6625[7]6768[7]

Taras Tornado *J J Quinn* a41 56
3 b f Distant Music(USA) —Yellow Ribbon (IRE) (Hamas (IRE))
177[10] (893) 1232[6] 1792[6]2284[11] 5885[9] (Dead)

Tara Too (IRE) *D W P Arbuthnot* 93
3 b f Danetime(IRE) —Gone With The Wind (IRE) (Common Grounds)
1843[4] 2205[7] 2650[7] 2880[4] 3316[5]3852[9] (4589) 4841[7] 5550[8] 5919[15]

Tarfah (USA) *G A Butler* 109+
5 b m Kingmambo(USA) —Fickle (Danehill (USA))
2199[9]

Targer Place *T T Clement* a62 44
3 ch g Compton Place—Floral Spark (Forzando)
1147[6] 5060[5] 5969[11]

Tarif (IRE) *Mrs P Sly* a61 60
2 b c Fath(USA) —Tarrifa (IRE) (Mujtahid (USA))
1284[6] 2139[4] 2857[5]3997[3] 4509[5]

Tariq *P W Chapple-Hyam* 100+
2 ch c Kyllachy—Tatora (Selkirk (USA))
(2029) 2719[3]

Tarkamara (IRE) *P F I Cole* 68
2 ch f Medicean—Tarakana (USA) (Shahrastani (USA))
1082[2] 1675[4] 2743[8]

Tarraburn (USA) *J Howard Johnson* 73
2 ch g Eltish(USA) —Rahy's Wish (USA) (Rahy (USA))
2439[7] 3173[4] 4987[3] (5721)

Tarrjoo *M R Channon* 42
2 b f Diktat—Maid Of Kashmir (IRE) (Dancing Brave (USA))
4964[16]

Tartan Special *K R Burke* a54 50
4 b g Fasliyev(USA) —Colchica (Machiavellian (USA))
1396[6] 2112[11] 3524[9]4120[3] 4157[11] (6134) 6281[6]6545[3] 6725[4]

Tartan Tie *M Johnston* 67
2 b c Grand Lodge(USA) —Trois Graces (USA) (Alysheba (USA))
3809[3] 4650[4]

Tartatartufata *D Shaw* a85 68
4 b m Tagula(IRE) —It's So Easy (Shaadi (USA))
6[8] 517[10]699[8] 4598[8] 4834[10]6162[6] 6315[3] (6555) (6622) 6682[2] 6776[8]

Tarteel (USA) *J L Dunlop* 88
2 b f Bahri(USA) —Elrehaan (Sadler's Wells (USA))
4148[8] 4964[4] (5536) 6217[6]

Tartouche *Lady Herries* 109
5 b m Pursuit Of Love—Megan's Flight (Welsh Pageant)
(1511) 1860a[4] (4079) 4861a[7] 5803[4]

Tartu (IRE) *Patrick J Flynn*
3 ch f Tagula(IRE) —No Way (IRE) (Rainbows For Life (CAN))
4034a[15]

Tashkandi (IRE) *P Bowen* a40 84
6 gr g Polish Precedent(USA) —Tashiriya (IRE) (Kenmare (FR))
107[12] (2918) 3255[10]

Tasjeel (USA) *W J Haggas* 83
3 b f Aljabr(USA) —Siyadah (USA) (Mr Prospector (USA))
1598[2] (2188) 2679[3] 3302[4]

Task Complete *Jean-Rene Auvray* a52+ 46
3 ch f Bahamian Bounty—Taskone (Be My Chief (USA))
2316[15] 2535[15] 2704[8] 4287[5] 4872[9]6372[2] 6726[6]

Tasleem (IRE) *B W Hills* 54
2 b f Alhaarth(IRE) —Almurooj (Zafonic (USA))
5638[6] 6025[8]

Tastahil (IRE) *B W Hills* a76 88
2 ch c Singspiel(IRE) —Luana (Shaadi (USA))
4561[6] (5105) 5343[6]

Tasweet (IRE) *T G Mills* a47 66
2 b g Mujahid(USA) —Injaad (Machiavellian (USA))
5659[9] 5914[5] 6689[10]

Tata Naka *Mrs C A Dunnett* a56 74?
6 ch m Nashwan(USA) —Overcast (IRE) (Caerleon (USA))
800[7] 1058[12] 1162[10]1614[5] 1850[11] 2181[5] (2360) 3095[6] 3232[8]3627[7] 4010[2] 4336[6] 4606[5] 4925[13]5300[9]

Tatillius (IRE) *J M Bradley* 11
3 ch g King Charlemagne(USA) —Aunty Eileen (Ahonoora)
5055[12] 5729[13] 5951[10]

Tatstheticket *J Balding* a48 29
3 b g Diktat—Dekelsmary (Komaite (USA))
105[2] 910[9]3257[12] 3538[14] 3916[6]

Tatsuya (FR) *J-C Rouget* 96
2 b c Night Shift(USA) —Lamballe (USA) (Woodman (USA))
4859a[4]

Tau Ceti *R M Beckett* 113
7 b h Hernando(FR) —Napoli (Baillamont (USA))
1267[9] 1976[5] 4818[4] 5968[7] 6203[8]

Tavalu (USA) *G L Moore* 68
4 b g Kingmambo(USA) —Larrocha (IRE) (Sadler's Wells (USA))
966[3] 3035[5] 3666[3]

Tawaaf *P W Chapple-Hyam* a76
3 b c Medicean—Yasalam (IRE) (Fairy King (USA))
228[3]

Tawaafud *B W Hills* 78
3 b f Nashwan(USA) —Intimaa (IRE) (Caerleon (USA))
1418[9] 2673[4] (3362) 3984[3] 4763[5]

Tawaagg *M A Jarvis* a58
2 b g Kyllachy—Ascendancy (Sadler's Wells (USA))
6188[9]

Tawaajud (USA) *B W Hills* a67 82+
3 ch f Dixieland Band(USA) —Tabheej (IRE) (Mujtahid (USA))
1119[6] (1630) 2581[6] 5294[5] 6350[10]

Tawaassol (USA) *Sir Michael Stoute* 111
3 b c War Chant(USA) —Montecito (USA) (Seeking The Gold (USA))
(1261) 1617[2] (2385) 2658[2] 3312[4] 3732[3] 4803[7]5942[11]

Tawnybrack (IRE) *E J O'Neill* 66
2 b g Rossini(USA) —Ceannanas (IRE) (Magical Wonder (USA))
4251[4]

Tawqeet (USA) *D Hayes* 117
5 ch h Kingmambo(USA) —Caerless (IRE) (Caerleon (USA))
(6110a) 6392a[19]

Tax Free (IRE) *D Nicholls* 117
4 b g Tagula(IRE) —Grandel (Owington)
1485[3] 2276a[3] 2720[15] 4128[5] 4832[4](5087) (5179) 5942[3]

Taxman (IRE) *C E Brittain* a77 77
4 ch g Singspiel(IRE) —Love Of Silver (USA) (Arctic Tern (USA))
(478) 589[9] 713[2]838[3] 1745[2]2035[7] (2150) 2460[2] (3098) 3743[5]4393[4] 5276[5] 5610[5]5846[3] 6479[5]6602[7]

Tay Bridge (IRE) *G F Bridgwater* a10 48
3 ch g Tagula(IRE) —Wild Liffey (USA) (Irish River (FR))
1221[12] 2101[5] 3264[11] 4389[8] 5949[11]6306[8] 6584[12]

Taylor Maid *G A Ham* a44 42
4 b m First Trump—Island Maid (Forzando)
148[13] 791[12]

Tayman (IRE) *G Wragg* a69+ 70
4 bb g Sinndar(IRE) —Sweet Emotion (IRE) (Bering)
894[6] 1400[7] 2822[3]3983[12] (4687) 5276[10] 5691[5]

T-Bird (SAF) *E Charpy* 112
5 ch h Special Preview(SAF) —Lady Greystoke (SAF) (Lords (SAF))
201a[4] 352a[2] 496a[6] 619a[3]

Tcherina (IRE) *T D Easterby* 85
4 b m Danehill Dancer(IRE) —Forget Paris (IRE) (Broken Hearted)
976[4] 1779[3] 2000[4] 2975[10] 4149[8]5538[4] 5792[7] 6202[16]

T. D. Vance (USA) *H G Motion* 109
4 b g Rahy(USA) —Freedom Of Speech (USA) (Danzig (USA))
4908a[4]

Teach To Preach (USA) *B W Hills* 74
3 ch c Pulpit(USA) —Chateaubaby (USA) (Nureyev (USA))
(964) 2324[11] 3065[5]

Team-Mate (IRE) *Miss J Feilden* a71 88
8 b g Nashwan(USA) —Ustka (Lomond (USA))
55[8] 158[11]

Teammate (USA) *H A Jerkens* a112
3 gr f A.P. Indy(USA) —Starry Dreamer (USA) (Rubiano (USA))
3757a[5] 5818a[4]

Tears Of A Clown (IRE) *J A Osborne* a85+ 89+
3 b g Galileo(IRE) —Mood Swings (IRE) (Shirley Heights)
(1386) 1781[3]

Teasing *J Pearce* a76 61
2 b f Lujain(USA) —Movieland (USA) (Nureyev (USA))
5915[7] 6199[7] (6505) 6631[3]6659[2]

Tebee *J H M Gosden* a70+
2 ch f Selkirk(USA) —Massarra (Danehill (USA))
6073[5]

Tech Engine (GER) *P Schiergen* 95
3 b f Enrique—Technik (GER) (Nebos (GER))
925a[3] 1328a[11] 5160a[2] 6251a[4] 6722a[0]

Tecktal (FR) *P M Phelan* a62 61
3 ch f Pivotal—Wenge (USA) (Housebuster (USA))
4225[8] 6775[10]

Teddy Monty (IRE) *R E Barr* a19 30
3 b g Bold Fact(USA) —Mount Soufriere (IRE) (Maledetto (IRE))
20[4] 193[8]466[11] 594[10](637) 690[10]893[9] 1263[14] 1771[11] 3257[9]3821[12] 4263[8] 6763[12]6958[9]

Tedsdale Mac *N Bycroft* 69
7 ch g Presidium—Stilvella (Camden Town)
2627[4] 2697[5] 2945[2] 3243[5] 3500[9]3747[6] 3883[7] 4454[6] 4947[8] 5314[6]5445[10]

Tedstale (USA) *K A Ryan* a84 90
8 ch g Irish River(FR) —Carefree Kate (USA) (Lyphard (USA))
5[3] 125[7]2975[13] (3680) (4229) 4475[4] 5955[5]

Tee Jay Kassidy *P S McEntee* a61 9
6 b g Petong—Priceless Fantasy (Dunbeath (USA))
6193[14] 6531[10](6798) 6949[6]

Teen Ager (FR) *J S Moore* 41+
2 b c Invincible Spirit(IRE) —Tarwiya (IRE) (Dominion)
3005[6]

Teenage Rampage *W M Brisbourne* a33 33
4 b g Prince Sabo—Sorridar (Puissance)
260[12] 531[9]734[9] 768[8]791[11]

Tee Off (IRE) *B W Hills* a67 72
2 ch f Barathea(IRE) —Forget Me Not (IRE) (Danehill Dancer (IRE))
2328[5] 2957[3] 3893[7] 5434[7] 5950[2]6271[3] 6598[4]

Tees Components *K G Reveley* 101
11 b g Risk Me(FR) —Lady Warninglid (Ela-Mana-Mou)
(5533) 5811[2]

Teide Lady *Rae Guest* a71 65
3 ch f Nashwan(USA) —Oshiponga (Barathea (IRE))
1079[11] 1761[11] 2466[3]3263[4] 3650[2](4254) 4565[9] 5502[11] 5525[11] 5879[3]6448[3]

Tejareb (IRE) *C E Brittain* 47
3 b f Sadler's Wells(USA) —La Pepite (USA) (Mr Prospector (USA))
1650[10]

T E Lawrence (USA) *A Renzoni* 104
6 b h Charnwood Forest(IRE) —Only Gossip (USA) (Trempolino (USA))
1871a[6]

Telegnosis (JPN) *H Sugiura* 123
7 b h Tony Bin—Make A Wish (JPN) (Northern Taste (CAN))
6530a[11]

Telegonus *C E Longsdon* a73 44
3 b g Fantastic Light(USA) —Circe's Isle (Be My Guest (USA))
850[6] 5429[9]

Telemachus *Noel Meade* a78 96
6 b g Bishop Of Cashel—Indian Imp (Indian Ridge)
(3128a)

Telepathic (IRE) *A Berry* a34 56
6 b g Mind Games—Madrina (Waajib)
1611[5] 3334[11] 3670[6] 4067[10] 4352[8]

Tell *J L Dunlop* 100
3 b c Green Desert(USA) —Cephalonie (USA) (Kris S (USA))
1269[2] 2030[6] 2775[13] 3681[4] 4168a[3]

Telling *Mrs A Duffield* 56
2 b g Josr Algarhoud(IRE) —Crystal Canyon (Efisio)
5315[3] 5835[8] 6013[10]

Tellitlikeitis *Miss Kariana Key*
5 b g Defacto(USA) —Chimes Of Peace (Magic Ring (IRE))
6814[11]

Telltime (IRE) *A M Balding* a62+
2 b f Danetime(IRE) —Tesla (IRE) (Fayruz)
6838[2]

Tembanee (IRE) *R Hannon* 90
2 b c Selkirk(USA) —Rivana (Green Desert (USA))
(4980) (5624)

Tembladora (IRE) *J W Hills* a52 61
3 b f Docksider(USA) —Oiche Mhaith (Night Shift (USA))
2167[5] 5873[3] 6884[7]

Tempelstern (GER) *H R A Cecil* 76
2 gr c Sternkoenig(IRE) —Temple Esprit (Esprit Du Nord (USA))
4829[3] 5495[3]

Temperance (IRE) *S Kirk* 82
3 b f Orpen(USA) —Alberjas (IRE) (Sure Blade (USA))
1114[5] 1416[4] 2301[2] 2616[4] 2929[2]

Temper Tantrum *J R Best* a49 46
8 b g Pursuit Of Love—Queenbird (Warning)
35[5] 635[1]87[10] 398[6]

Tempestuous Sea (IRE) *T D Barron* 56
3 ch f Tagula(IRE) —Mrs Siddons (IRE) (Royal Academy (USA))
4120[16]

Temple Air (IRE) *W G M Turner* a23 31
2 ch g Abou Zouz(USA) —Regal Air (IRE) (Distinctly North (USA))
3345[11] 5687[11] 6401[12]

Temple Belle Xpres *S R Bowring* a34 34
4 b m Overbury(IRE) —Kustom Kit Xpres (Absalom)
647[8] 769[8]870[6]

Temple Hills (NZ) *P Moody* 105
4 br g Marju(IRE) —Soltanto (NZ) (Tights)
6347a[11]

Temple Place (IRE) *D McCain Jnr* 98
5 b g Sadler's Wells(USA) —Puzzled Look (USA) (Gulch (USA))
1585[8] 2848[16]

Templet (USA) *W G Harrison* a68 52
6 b g Souvenir Copy(USA) —Two Step Trudy (USA) (Capote (USA))
1608[4] 1883[6] 2165[8] 2548[5] 6241[4]6382[4] 6604[2]6860[5]

Tempsford Flyer (IRE) *J W Hills* a84+ 87
3 b g Fasliyev(USA) —Castellane (FR) (Danehill (USA))
(952) 1384[2] 1832[6] (2581) 3546[5]4029[8] 5666[9] 6502[7]

Temtation (IRE) *J R Boyle* a58 70
2 b f Trans Island—Ish (IRE) (Danehill (USA))
968[6] 2461[3] 4657[4]4913[2] 5052[4] 5655[20]

Tenancy (IRE) *J A Osborne* a67 66
2 b c Rock Of Gibraltar(IRE) —Brush Strokes (Cadeaux Genereux)
5379[3] 5814[7] 6523[4]6644[4]

Ten Black *R Brotherton* a55 53
2 ch g Dr Fong(USA) —Pulau Pinang (IRE) (Dolphin Street (FR))
4109[9] 4445[5] 4969[6]5387[5] 6670[3]

Ten Carat *M Todhunter* 97
6 ch g Grand Lodge(USA) —Emerald (USA) (El Gran Senor (USA))
1294[8] 2013[11] 2625[4] 3078[16] 3396[3]4036[12] 5811[10]

Tencendur (IRE) *D Nicholls* 79
2 ch c King Charlemagne(USA) —Jallaissine (IRE) (College Chapel)
1203[4] 1454[2] 1730[2] (3335) 3834[2] 4100[4]4509[3] (5308)

Ten-Cents *C F Wall* a60 64
4 b m Dansili—Daylight Dreams (Indian Ridge)
172[4] (394) 471[3]1754[2] 2133[3] 2822[10] 3230[2]

Ten Commandments (IRE) *K J Burke* a43 43
3 br f Key Of Luck(USA) —Zoudie (Ezzoud (IRE))
1226[13] 1576[6]1768[12] 2463[6]2646[6] 2861[9]3162[3]

Tender Falcon *R J Hodges* 95
6 br g Polar Falcon(USA) —Tendresse (IRE) (Tender King)
1238[4] 1517[6]

Tender Moments *K A Ryan* 73+
2 br f Tomba—Cherish Me (Polar Falcon (USA))
(2026) 3216[3] 5359[8]

Tender Process (IRE) *E S McMahon* 83
3 b g Monashee Mountain(USA) —Appledorn (Doulab (USA))
1412[6] 1646[5] 1877[2] (4422) 4922[4] 5286[11](5864)

Tender The Great (IRE) *V Smith* a69 69
3 br f Indian Lodge(IRE) —Tender Guest (IRE) (Be My Guest (USA))
1598[10] 2128[2] 2589[6] (2820) 3044[9] 5314[9]5590[6] 6260[2] 6430[3]6483[2] 6647[4]6752[6]

Tender Trap (IRE) *T G Mills* a88 100
8 b g Sadler's Wells(USA) —Shamiyda (USA) (Sir Ivor (USA))
420[6] 628[P]2653[2] 3028[8]

Ten Dollars More (IRE) *J A Osborne* a76 70
2 b c Elnadim(USA) —Saltaire (IRE) (Idris (IRE))
1429[5] 1588[3] 1811[3] (2139) 3265[4] 3455[2]3641[5] 4264[3] 5034[4]5113[5] 5382[11] 5646[5]

Ten For Tosca (IRE) *J A Osborne* 57
2 b c Distant Music(USA) —Errazuriz (IRE) (Classic Music (USA))
1559[5] 2315[14] 4222[3] 4624[4] 4816[4]5448[5]

Tenini *J A Osborne* a55
3 ch g Bertolini(USA) —River Abouali (Bluebird (USA))
272[3]

Tennessee Belle (IRE) *C N Allen* a48 38
4 b m Lahib(USA) —Spirito Libro (USA) (Lear Fan (USA))
255[6] 398[10]793[12] 2180[4] 2568[7]2861[10] 3051[2]3260[8] 3456[7]

Tennessee Sun (IRE) *R Menichetti*
2 b f Desert Sun—Tennessee Valley (USA) (Quiet American (USA))
2565a[2]

Tennis Star (IRE) *R Charlton* a78 76
3 b g Montjeu(IRE) —Fabled Lifestyle (King's Lake (USA))
1374[4] 4249[5] 5770[6]6021[2]

Ten Prophets (IRE) *J A Osborne* a63
3 b g Namid—Mrs Evans (IRE) (College Chapel)
165[5] 195[8]

Ten Shun *P D Evans* a79+ 82
3 ch g Pivotal—Mint Royale (IRE) (Cadeaux Genereux)
20[2] (69) 122[5]197[2] 855[7]1941[3] 2920[3] 3030[5]3898[5] 4870[11] (4985) (5309) 5872[2] 6212[2] 6579[9]6858[3] 6932[8]

Tension Point *J A Osborne* a66 71+
2 b c Hernando(FR) —Blessed (IRE) (Jurado (USA))
2619[3] 2844[11] 3844[6]4773[9] 5389[4] 5565[3]

Ten Tenors (IRE) *J A Osborne* a57
3 b f Rossini(USA) —Prima (Primo Dominie)
254[8] 331[2]473[6] 646[11]

Tenterhooks (IRE) *J A Osborne* a54
2 b f Orpen(USA) —Punta Gorda (IRE) (Roi Danzig (USA))
2552[9] 3010[2]3096[6]

Ten To The Dozen *P W Hiatt* a58 68
3 b g Royal Applause—Almost Amber (USA) (Mt. Livermore (USA))
2366[7] 2542[4] 5388[13]6406[7] 6508[13]6667[8] 6674[9]

Teodora Adivina *H R A Cecil* 67
2 b f Fantastic Light(USA) —Omara (USA) (Storm Cat (USA))
6049[4]

Teofilo (IRE) *J S Bolger* 124+
2 b c Galileo(IRE) —Speirbhean (IRE) (Danehill (USA))
(3962a) (4825a) (5410a) (5965)

Teorban (POL) *Mrs N S Evans* a58 60
7 b g Don Corleone—Tabaka (POL) (Pyjama Hunt)
443[10] 832[11]6831[8] 6979[5]

Teorea (ITY) *R Menichetti*
2 b f Tendulkar(USA) —Titorea (IRE) (Blakeney)
5705a[13]

Te Quiero *Miss Gay Kelleway* a89 55
8 gr g Bering—Ma Lumiere (FR) (Niniski (USA))
7[5] 348[9]412[2] 611[2]1112[14] 1938[13]

Tequila Brown (FR) *M Delzangles* a86 92
3 gr f Kendor(FR) —La Tirana (FR) (Akarad (FR))
6384a[4] 6722a[5]

Tequila Rose (IRE) *A Bailey* a44 47
3 b f Danehill Dancer(IRE) —Enthrone (USA) (Diesis)
120[5] 551[4]690[4] 790[10]

Tequila Sheila (IRE) *K R Burke* a63 61
4 ch m Raise A Grand(IRE) —Hever Rosina (Efisio)
133[6] 227[8]1594[2] 2165[7] 2544[13] 2811[11] 4070[6](4425) (4548) 4844[3] 4983[3] 5636[4] 6211[6]

Teratai (IRE) *M A Jarvis* 22
2 b f Shinko Forest(IRE) —London Pride (USA) (Lear Fan (USA))
4553[9]

Terentia *E S McMahon* 107
3 br f Diktat—Agrippina (Timeless Times (USA))
(1279) (1900) 2639[5] (4102) 4717[2] 5405[7] 5919[12]

Terenzium (IRE) *L M Cumani* a61 63
4 br g Cape Cross(IRE) —Tatanka (ITY) (Luge)
1276[3] (1915) 2702[5] 2978[2]4048[6] 4446[9]

Terfel *Daniel J Murphy* 105
7 ch g Lion Cavern(USA) —Montserrat (Aragon)
153a[8] 208a[7] 354a[9] 509a[5] 1716a[6]

Terlan (GER) *P Monteith* 2
8 b g Medicus(GER) —Taxodium (GER) (Blakeney)
6210[5]

Terminate (GER) *N P Littmoden* a75 79
4 ch g Acatenango(GER) —Taghareed (USA) (Shadeed (USA))
1051[13] 1357[10] 1992[9] 2299[12] 2455[13](3792) 4353[10] 4606[9] 5047[7]

Terraquin (IRE) *J J Bridger* a44 53
6 b g Turtle Island(IRE) —Play The Queen (IRE) (King Of Clubs)
891[14] (Dead)

Terra Verde (IRE) *I Mohammed* 108
4 ch h Indian Ridge—Vituisa (Bering)
435a[4]

Terrific Challenge (USA) *S Hough* 105
4 ch h Royal Academy(USA) —Clever Empress (Crafty Prospector (USA))
6127a[4]

Terrific Storm (USA) *T Pletcher* 79
5 bb h Storm Cat(USA) — (IRE) (Second Set (IRE))
4908a[8]

Terry Molloy (IRE) *K R Burke* 71
2 b g Xaar—Pile (USA) (Shadeed (USA))
3247[8] (4066) 4813[6] 5366[6]

Terrys Alfie *N P Littmoden* a38
3 b g Compton Place—Loveless Carla (Pursuit Of Love)
1006[12] 1552[9]1960[7] 2576[9]

Teslin (IRE) *M Johnston* 92
2 b c In The Wings—Yukon Hope (USA) (Forty Niner (USA))
4534[2] 4867[2] (5343) 6104[9] 6249a[10]

Tesoro *P A Blockley* a44 9
3 b g Compton Place—Zenita (IRE) (Zieten (USA))
70[9] 333[5]415[6] 1661[7] (Dead)

Testama (FR) *J De Roualle* a68 92
2 gr f Testa Rossa(AUS) —Maid Of Honor (FR) (Highest Honor (FR))
5471a[3] 6228a[6]

Testimony (USA) *Saeed Bin Suroor* a99
3 b c Yes It's True(USA) —Kit Kat Kitty (USA) (Pentelicus (USA))
150a[2] 368a[8]739a[2]

Tetouan *R Charlton* 56+
2 b c Danehill Dancer(IRE) —Souk (IRE) (Ahonoora)
5066[9] 5659[8]

Tetragon (IRE) *D Carroll* a62 66
6 b g Octagonal(NZ) —Viva Verdi (IRE) (Green Desert (USA))
3068[6] 3797[4] 4137[4] 4472[2] 4709[4]4924[8] 5925[13]

Tetrode (USA) *R M H Cowell* a39 59
4 b g Quiet American(USA) —Mother Courage (Busted)
3384[6] 4142[4] 4663[4]5081[13] 5576[13]

Teuflesberg (USA) *Jamie Sanders* a98
2 b c Johannesburg(USA) —St. Michele (USA) (Devil's Bag (USA))
5823a[7] 6339a[10]

Teutonic (IRE) *R F Fisher* a44 41
5 b m Revoque(IRE) —Classic Ring (IRE) (Auction Ring (USA))
1271[4] 1767[2]1883[4] 3135[9]

Texas Gold *W R Muir* a108 106
8 ch g Cadeaux Genereux—Star Tulip (Night Shift (USA))
1485[18] 2227[15] 2720[19] 2847[19] 3535[2]3972[13] 4128[13] 4360[3] 4875[5] 5044[8]5182[4] 5202[5] 5535[14] 5667[5](6095) 6243[11]6445[7]

Teyaar *M Wellings* a48+ 46
10 b g Polar Falcon(USA) —Music In My Life (IRE) (Law Society (USA))
145[3] 260[7]397[11] 465[4]613[9] 766[7]789[9] 907[5]4324[4] 5243[12] 6131[3]6237[9] 6542[4]6727[4] 6805[4]

Thabaat *B W Hills* 85+
2 ch c Pivotal—Maraatib (IRE) (Green Desert (USA))
4592[2] 5067[2]

Thajja (IRE) *Doug Watson* a105 105
5 b h Daylami(IRE) —Jawlaat (USA) (Dayjur (USA))
206a[3] 366a[7] 434a[2]560a[5] 740a[10]

Thalberg *M A Jarvis* 87
3 gr g Highest Honor(FR) —Stage Manner (In The Wings)
1289[2] 2366[2] 2815[3]

T. H. Approval (USA) *E Inda* a110 115
5 gr h With Approval(CAN) —Potrichal (ARG) (Potrillazo (ARG))
6344a[8]

Tharua (IRE) *Ernst Oertel* a59 55
4 b m Indian Danehill(IRE) —Peig Sayers (IRE) (Royal Academy (USA))
91[2] 174[6]256[3] 3919[9]

Thathshan (ITY) *S Billeri*
2 gr f Shantou(USA) —Thatchprincesse (IRE) (Love The Groom (USA))
2475a[7] 3428a[6]

That Look *D E Cantillon* a58 57
3 b g Compton Admiral—Mudflap (Slip Anchor)
1263[11] 2591[8] 4734[2] 6979[3]

That's An Outrage (USA) *M Puhich* a105 98
5 b h Quiet American(USA) —Cable News (USA) (Known Fact (USA))
5825a[7]

That's Blue Chip *P W D'Arcy* a56+ 67+
3 b g Namid—Star Cast (IRE) (In The Wings)
3285[9] (4164)

That's Hot (IRE) *G M Lyons* 100
3 b f Namid—Smoke Lady (IRE) (Barathea (IRE))
3125a[23] 3767a[3] 3967a[3] 4749a[10]

That's Racing *J Hetherton* a33
6 ch g Classic Cliche(IRE) —All On (Dunbeath (USA))
938[9]

The Alamo *Malachy J Ryan* 70
8 b g Supreme Leader—Culinary (Tower Walk)
4166a[17]

The Aldbury Flyer *W R Swinburn* 72
3 b g Royal Applause—Fantasy Ridge (Indian Ridge)
5086[6] 5353[3] 5770[5] 6076[14]

Theann *A P O'Brien* 102
2 b f Rock Of Gibraltar(IRE) —Cassandra Go (IRE) (Indian Ridge)
5464a[5] 5654[5] 5850a[2]

Theatre (USA) *Jamie Poulton* a88 88
7 b g Theatrical—Fasta (USA) (Seattle Song (USA))
1931[6] 2219[5] 3203[4]3649[3] 4036[2] 5180[2](5526) 5963[7]

Theatre Groom (USA) *M R Bosley* a48
7 ch g Theatrical—Model Bride (USA) (Blushing Groom (FR))
4931[8]

Theatre Royal *A M Balding* a59 71
3 b f Royal Applause—Rada's Daughter (Robellino (USA))
2048[6] 2932[3] 3400[5]3865[2] 4181[5] 4627[3] 4838[13]

Theatre Tinka (IRE) *R Hollinshead* a52 55
7 b g King's Theatre(IRE) —Orange Grouse (IRE) (Taufan (USA))
470[4]

The Bavarian (AUS) *C Little* 108
4 b g Grand Lodge(USA) —Kachina (AUS) (El Qahira (NZ))
6391a[14]

The Bear *I Semple* 93
3 ch g Rambling Bear—Precious Girl (Precious Metal)
1633[6]

The Beduth Navi *D G Bridgwater* a24 19
6 b g Forzando—Sweets (IRE) (Persian Heights)
25[8] 174[10]597[11]

Thebestisyettocome *T G Mills* a62 57+
4 b g Montjeu(IRE) —French Quartet (IRE) (Lycius (USA))
263[4] 379[8]462[5] 2132[9] 2577[11]5385[3] 5652[4]

The Bonus King *J Jay* a70 70
6 b g Royal Applause—Selvi (Mummy's Pet)
698[10] 950[3]1186[5] (1276) 1665[6] 1996[15]2317[9] 3159[9] 3947[8]

The Brat *James Moffatt* 37
2 b f Perryston View—Kalarram (Muhtarram (USA))
2759[8] 3394[5] 3721[5] 4089[5] 4452[6]4545[10] 5238[5]

The Bronx *M J Wallace* a61 52
2 b c Dansili—Carradale (Pursuit Of Love)
3843[10] 6295[3] 6838[7]

The Carbon Unit (USA) *C Collins* a78 98
4 bb h Catienus(USA) —Glen Kate (Glenstal (USA))
207a[6] 356a[3] 509a[11] 2840a[10]

The Carlton Cannes *G Wragg* 74
2 b c Grand Lodge(USA) —Miss Riviera Golf (Hernando (FR))
5883[6] 6214[6]

The Cayterers *J M Bradley* 78+
4 b g Cayman Kai(IRE) —Silky Smooth (IRE) (Thatching)
1877[5] (3817) (4054) 4157[16] (5058) (5453)

The City Kid (IRE) *P D Evans* a66 49
3 b f Danetime(IRE) —Unfortunate (Komaite (USA))
76[3] 1799[8] 2068[6]3381[5] 3995[8]5636[9] 6636[2] 6717[4]6892[6] (6988)

The Combo *M Blanshard* a29 47
3 gr c Selkirk(USA) —Snowing (Tate Gallery (USA))
3100[12] 4776[9]

The Composer *M Blanshard* a68 78
4 b g Royal Applause—Superspring (Superlative)
723[9] 1132[12] (1987) 2989[6]3248[3] 4299[7] 4990[4] 5599[13] 5889[6]

The Cool Sandpiper *P Winkworth* 64
2 ch g Piccolo—The Dark Eider (Superlative)
4624[2]

The Crooked Ring *P D Evans* a69 75
4 b g Magic Ring(IRE) —My Bonus (Cyrano De Bergerac)
2520[9] 3069[8] 3543[7] 4211[8] 4437[8]4894[5] 5737[6] 6060[13]6293[4] 6396[8]

The Crunch (IRE) *Daniel Mark Loughnane* a28 44
5 b m College Chapel—Lady Tristram (Miami Springs)
6473[13]

The Cute Won (USA) *N Dooly* a52 61
8 b g Defensive Play(USA) —Alzabella (USA) (Top Command (USA))
6936[5]

The Dagger *J R Best* a12
2 ch g Daggers Drawn(USA) —Highland Blue (Never So Bold)
6034[12]

The Dandy Fox *R Bastiman* a39 41
2 b f Foxhound(USA) —Classic Storm (Belfort (FR))
1181[12] 2321[5] 3619[7] 3831[3] 4115[4]4547[10] 4887[13] 5687[7]6012[5]

The Devil (GER) *U Suter* 102
4 b h Goofalik(USA) —Tascalina (GER) (Big Shuffle (USA))
1929a[3] 4169a[8]

The Diamond Bond *G R Oldroyd* 54
2 bl g Josr Algarhoud(IRE) —Alsiba (Northfields (USA))
4566[4] 4880[6]

The Duke (AUS) *C Fownes* 120
6 b g Danehill(USA) —Mer Du Sud (IRE) (Bluebird (USA))
(6784a)

The Dunion *Miss L A Perratt* 43?
3 br g Beckett(IRE) —Dacian (USA) (Diesis)
1635[7] 1950[7] 2243[13] 2746[12] 4132[9]4478[6] 4954[6]

The Ethiopian (IRE) *A P O'Brien* 91
2 b c Sadler's Wells(USA) —Kasora (IRE) (Darshaan)
6357a[4]

The Fifth Member (IRE) *R M Flower* a69
2 b c Bishop Of Cashel—Palace Soy (IRE) (Tagula (IRE))
6143[5] 6393[4]6651[7]

The Fisio *S Gollings* a69 61
6 b g Efisio—Misellina (FR) (Polish Precedent (USA))
23[8] 126[5]6162[13] 6485[10] 6688[3]6877[8]

The Flying Cowboy (IRE) *N P Littmoden*
2 b g Tagula(IRE) —Sesame Heights (IRE) (High Estate)
5460[16]

The Flying Peach *W M Brisbourne* a22 37
3 ch f Observatory(USA) —Taffeta (IRE) (Barathea (IRE))
1351[9] 1726[12] 2101[10]3288[6] 3529[2] 3910[12] 4297[14]

The Fonze (IRE) *Eoin Doyle* a67+ 71
5 br g Desert Sun—Ultimate Beat (USA) (Go And Go)
2221[2] (2647) (2862)

The French (FR) *F Legros* 102
4 b h French Glory—Sibertie (FR) (Pebble (FR))
5881a[5]

The Gaikwar (IRE) *R A Harris* a68 78
7 b g Indian Ridge—Broadmara (IRE) (Thatching)
905[8] 1148[6]1435[5] 1773[8] 2098[7] 2186[5] 2482[11]2969[3] 3197[3] (3469) 3712[6] 3854[3] 4131[3]4390[5] 5149[4] 5236[8] 5572[6] 5974[11]6387[4] 6497[5]6683[10] 6787[7]

The Geester *S R Bowring* a55 50
2 b c Rambling Bear—Cledeschamps (Doc Marten)
4815[7] 5283[5] 5613[13] 5923[5]6420[3] 6679[5]6807[11] 6925[2]

The Geezer *Saeed Bin Suroor* a74 119
4 ch h Halling(USA) —Polygueza (FR) (Be My Guest (USA))
1833[5]

The God Of Love (USA) *G M Lyons* 98+
3 ch g Stravinsky(USA) —Miss Dyna Chris (USA) (Dynaformer (USA))
3128a[6]

The Graig *C Drew* 52
2 b c Josr Algarhoud(IRE) —Souadah (USA) (General Holme (USA))
3713[6] 3979[8] 4588[6]

The Great Delaney *Ms J S Doyle* a54 64
3 b g Inchinor—Top (Shirley Heights)
241[7] 887[7](2065) 2243[6] 4060[4] 4405[8] 4983[12] 6870[6]

The Grey Bam Bam *R J Hodges* 48
2 gr f Baryshnikov(AUS) – Leonie Samual (Safawan)
2984[8] 3949[7] 4487[10]

The Grey Berry *C Grant* 65
2 gr c Observatory(USA) —Elderberry (Bin Ajwaad (IRE))
3780[3] 5059[5] 5632[5]

The Grey Man *J W Mullins* a31 71
5 gr g Muhtarram(USA) —Lavender Della (IRE) (Shernazar)
909[4] 1289[6] 1492[4]1847[10] 2357[6] 3284[4] 4156[2] 4898[2]5383[7]

The Grey One (IRE) *J M Bradley* 64
3 gr g Dansili—Marie Dora (FR) (Kendor (FR))
879[14] 1433[3] 1567[2] 1859[7] 2284[9]2727[5] 5453[16] 5949[2] 6177[2] 6300[11]

The History Man (IRE) *M W Easterby* 77
3 b g Titus Livius(FR) —Handsome Anna (IRE) (Bigstone (IRE))
1097[8] 1812[4] 1983[8] 2105[2] 2976[5]3296[13] 3550[7] 3879[2] 4119[14] 4888[5]5401[11] 5864[3]

The Illies (IRE) *B W Hills* 83
2 b c Fasliyev(USA) —Velvet Appeal (IRE) (Petorius)
1113[6] 1510[5] 4000[8] (5053) (5322) 5916[14]

The Iron Giant (IRE) *B G Powell* a64 61
4 b g Giant's Causeway(USA) —Shalimar (IRE) (Indian Ridge)
3451[7] 3952[6] 4530[11] 4702[3]5213[5] 5451[3] 5831[9]6037[12] 6700[3]6769[6]

The Italian Job *T D Easterby* a63+ 57
2 b f Bertolini(USA) —Charming Lotte (Nicolotte)
1181[7] 1559[2] 2394[5] 3358[8] 3720[6]4017[4] 5238[3] 5860[13] 6311[2](6420)

The Jailer *J G M O'Shea* a41 43
3 b f Mujahid(USA) —Once Removed (Distant Relative)
499[5] 617[2]887[3] 945[6] 1226[2]1501[4] 1726[3] 2968[3]3195[6]

The Jay Factor (IRE) *Pat Eddery* a56 67+
2 b c Bold Fact(USA) —Corn Futures (Nomination)
2172[5] 3588[12] 6562[4]

The Jewel (FR) *H Vanderdussen* 86
4 b m Octagonal(NZ) —The Blade (GER) (Sure Blade (USA))
5562a[8]

The Job *A D Smith* a54 43
5 ch g Dancing Spree(USA) —Bay Bianca (IRE) (Law Society (USA))
95[2] 143[6]247[6] 618[8]1725[9] 1915[4]4585[3]

The Jobber (IRE) *M Blanshard* a93 107
5 b g Foxhound(USA) —Clairification (IRE) (Shernazar)
295[8] (1928) 2173[15] 2624[7]3092[12] 3251[6] 3744[6] 4085[12] (4180) (4360) 5182[18](5433)

The Keep *R E Barr* a36 44
4 ch m Shinko Forest(IRE) —Poyle Amber (Sharrood (USA))
2377[4] 3189[9] 3524[6] 3749[14] 4613[4]4694[10] 6274[5] 6492[10]

The Khamsin (DEN) *Ms C Erichsen* 101
7 b h Kateb(IRE) —Medinova (Mas Media)
4189a[9]

The Kiddykid (IRE) *P D Evans* 110
6 b g Danetime(IRE) —Mezzanine (Sadler's Wells (USA))
729[8] 1778[8] 2303[6] 3092[2] (4174) 5358[11]5812[14]

The King And I (IRE) *Miss E C Lavelle* 72
2 b g Monashee Mountain(USA) —Scrimshaw (Selkirk (USA))
2172[3] 5508[6]

The Lady Caster *R M Beckett* a18 56
3 ch f City On A Hill(USA) —Cinnamon Lady (Emarati (USA))
477[6] 2068[7] 2704[3]3267[9] 3866[9] 4710[11]

The Lady Ermyn *T G Mills* a29
3 b f Mull Of Kintyre(USA) —Corniche Quest (IRE) (Salt Dome (USA))
191[12] 337[14]

The Lady Mandarin *G Wragg* a21 28
3 b f Groom Dancer(USA) —Lonely Shore (Blakeney)
3200[13] 3946[11] 4701[8]

The Last Drop (IRE) *B W Hills* 116
3 b c Galileo(IRE) —Epping (Charnwood Forest (IRE))
(948) 1300[2] 1805[5] 2805[17] 4678[4] 5185[2]6126a[7]

The Last Hurrah (IRE) *Mrs John Harrington* 95
6 b h In The Wings—Last Exit (Dominion)
3128a[2]

The Leather Wedge (IRE) *R Johnson* a74 70
7 b g Hamas(IRE) —Wallflower (Polar Falcon (USA))
1031[10] 1438[8] 1816[3] 2237[12] 4477[4]4725[11] 4952[4] 5486[2] 5620[7] 5684[7]6162[7] 6315[9] 6521[7]6622[12]

The Light Fandango *R A Harris* a49 49
2 ch f Kyllachy—Alifandango (IRE) (Alzao (USA))
2631[11] 4492[4] 4657[12] 5586[13] 6471[3]6522[4] 6996[2]

The London Gang *P D Evans* a68 72
3 b c Mind Games—Nom Francais (First Trump)
344[7] 475[3]601[6] 709[7]807[8] 851[7]1109[9] 1642[4] 1899[2]2318[8] 3381[7] (3814) 3959[6]4067[8] 5635[5] 5953[3] 6493[10]6717[8] (6833) 6864[5] (6938)

The Loose Screw (IRE) *C W Thornton* a38
8 b g Bigstone(IRE) —Princess Of Dance (IRE) (Dancing Dissident (USA))
5837[10] 6694[9] 6993[6]

The Lord (ARG) *S Seemar* a49
6 b h Southern Halo(USA) —Lourdes (ARG) (Ringaro (USA))
740a[12]

The Lord *W G M Turner* a92 108
6 b g Averti(IRE) —Lady Longmead (Crimson Beau)
(79) 198[8] 989[4] 1116[8]1602[8] (1936) (1952) 4080[17] 5158[11] 5957[7] 6095[6]6243[13]

Theme Time (USA) *D Morris* a43 38
10 b g Stop The Music(USA) —Ranales (USA) (Majestic Light (USA))
4881[15] 6469[9] 6763[10]

The Mighty Ogmore *R C Guest* 61
2 ch f Dr Fong(USA) —Welsh Dawn (Zafonic (USA))
1342[9] 1790[4] 2241[2] (2451) 3136[3] 3372[6]3481[4] 4547[7] 5748[11]

The Music Queen *G A Swinbank* 45
5 ch m Halling(USA) —Sadly Sober (IRE) (Roi Danzig (USA))
4549[5]

The Nawab (IRE) *J L Dunlop* a95+ 94+
4 ch h Almutawakel—Eschasse (USA) (Zilzal (USA))
1167[2] 1584[8] 2625[2]

The Nifty Fox *T D Easterby* 79
2 b g Foxhound(USA) —Nifty Alice (First Trump)
1030[4] 1342[6] 1632[5] 2623[3] 3555[6]4321[8] 4547[5] 4727[2] 5076[4] 5335[6](5746) 5956[3]

The Old Fella *R Hannon* a93 98
2 ch c Compton Place—Centre Court (Second Set (IRE))
2009[4] 2724[3] (3210) 3445[5] 4397[2] 4736[10]5017[5] 5802[9]

The Old Soldier *A Dickman* a57 59
8 b g Magic Ring(IRE) —Grecian Belle (Ilium)
2700[4] 2874[3] (3635) 4233[4]

Theologicum *Miss J R Gibney* a66 51
3 b f King's Best(USA) —Valnerina (IRE) (Caerleon (USA))
4396[5] 4776[8] 4945[11]5954[17] 6601[6] 6700[7]6911[10]

Theoretical *A J McCabe* a64 58
2 b f Marju(IRE) —Relativity (IRE) (Distant Relative)
1853[8] 5347[4] 5503[22] 6520[6](6711) 6926[13]

The Osteopath (IRE) *M Dods* 79
3 ch g Danehill Dancer(IRE) —Miss Margate (IRE) (Don't Forget Me)
1855[3] (2163) 2620[6] 4605[5] 4802[7] 5863[8]6206[8]

The Pen *C W Fairhurst* a50 64
4 ch m Lake Coniston(IRE) —Come To The Point (Pursuit Of Love)
(2777) 3141[6] (3675) 3983[10] 4205[3] 4472[8]

The Perfect Plan (IRE) *Tom Dascombe* a18 50
3 b g Kalanisi(IRE) —Talbiya (IRE) (Mujtahid (USA))
6980[11]

The Plainsman *P W Hiatt* a31 22
4 b g Atraf—Mylania (Midyan (USA))
97[8] 141[9]184[7] 301[5]525[10] 615[5]634[7]

The Power Of Phil *R Brotherton*
2 b c Komaite(USA) —Starboard Tack (FR) (Saddlers' Hall (IRE))
3860[7]

The Preacher *J S Wainwright* 50
3 b g Namaqualand(USA) —Bustling Around (Bustino)
863[7] 1139[11] 2529[11] 4016[3] 5441[5]

The Quantum Kid *T J Etherington* 50
2 b c Desert Prince(IRE) —Al Hasnaa (Zafonic (USA))
5239[5]

The Real Thing (IRE) *C Collins* 89
2 b f Traditionally(USA) —Mad Madam Mym (Hernando (FR))
3060a[2] 3962a[7] 5466a[12]

The Rebound Kid *G A Huffer* a61 61
4 b g Royal Applause—Hayhurst (Sandhurst Prince)
217[3] 365[5]504[12] 897[6] 1057[11]1265[9]

Therecomesatiger (USA) *T Proctor* 110
4 br g Tiger Ridge(USA) —Come Tight (USA) (Artistry (SAF))
5416a[6]

There's A Light (IRE) *C Collins* 61
2 b f Fantastic Light(USA) —Last Spin (Unfuwain (USA))
5464a[24]

The Rip *R M Stronge* a37 62
5 ch g Definite Article—Polgwynne (Forzando)
2455[15] 4483[10] 6904[7]

The Salwick Flyer (IRE) *A Berry* a43 55
3 b g Tagula(IRE) —Shimla (IRE) (Rudimentary (USA))
1126[4] 1272[6] 3526[3]3814[11] 4120[5] 4613[2] 4656[9] (5077) 5401[9]5752[10] 6159[4] 6521[12]

The Skerret *P Winkworth* 58
2 ch c Loup Sauvage(USA) —Cosmic Star (Siberian Express (USA))
2857[4] 4794[6] 5417[8]

The Slider *P A Blockley* a58 54
2 b f Erhaab(USA) —Cottage Maid (Inchinor)
3054[4] (3279) 3613[4] 3915[2]

The Snatcher (IRE) *R Hannon* 97
3 b c Indian Danehill(IRE) —Saninka (IRE) (Doyoun)
1067[6] 1505[3] 1836[3] 2014[6] (3317) 4042[5]4707[3] 5501[14]

The Spread *M Blanshard* a52 57
3 ch f Alhaarth(IRE) —Evie Hone (IRE) (Royal Academy (USA))
2220[10] 3017[5] 3439[5]4530[6] 4868[2] 5324[5]

The Spring Flower (GER) *Andreas Lowe* 99
4 b m Kornado—The Dashing Lady (GER) (Dashing Blade)
1974a[5] 6366a[4]

The Stafford (IRE) *L Wells* a43
5 b g Selkirk(USA) —Bint Zamayem (IRE) (Rainbow Quest (USA))
539[8] 778[10]

The Struie *E F Vaughan* a46 71
3 b f Observatory(USA) —My Way (IRE) (Marju (IRE))
1547[7] 1925[12] 3017[8]

Theta *H R A Cecil* a33
2 b f Rainbow Quest(USA) —Self Esteem (Suave Dancer (USA))
6481[12]

The Tatling (IRE) *J M Bradley* 116
9 bb g Perugino(USA) —Aunty Eileen (Ahonoora)
1069[13] 1485[5] 1717a[4] 2115[9] 2720[10]2846[6] 3312[6] 4080[4] 4738[6] 5158[6]5375[8] 5642[6] 5921[10]

The Terminator (IRE) *M Mullineaux* a45 49
4 b g Night Shift(USA) —Surmise (USA) (Alleged (USA))
4518[12] 4959[6] 6629[9]6726[13] 6861[6]6949[8]

The Terrier *G A Swinbank* 76+
3 b f Foxhound(USA) —Branston Gem (So Factual (USA))
1497[3] 1812[8] 3023[3] 3718[3] 4403[3]4957[17] 5079[P]

The Thrifty Bear *C W Fairhurst* 69
3 ch g Rambling Bear—Prudent Pet (Distant Relative)
1097[9] 1497[12] 2109[8] 3042[7] 3395[8]4071[7] 4886[4] 5250[12]5839[7]

The Tin Man (USA) *Richard E Mandella* 122
8 br g Affirmed(USA) —Lizzie Rolfe (USA) (Tom Rolfe (USA))
742a[2] (4386a)

The Trader (IRE) *M Blanshard* 117
8 ch g Selkirk(USA) —Snowing (Tate Gallery (USA))
1485[15] 2115[2] 2720[22] 3312[3] 3709[3]4410a[4] 4738[4] 5087[5]

The Tyke *C G Cox* a65
3 gr g Cloudings(IRE) —Vonispet (Cotation)
6557[2] 6738[5]

The Violin Player (USA) *H J Collingridge* a90 89
5 b g King Of Kings(IRE) —Silk Masque (USA) (Woodman (USA))
88[5] 135[8](325) 454[5]556[2] 661[4]765[7] 1478[13] 2447[7]3209[5] 4149[9] 4448[5] 4937[7]5610[8] 5875[2]

Thewhirlingdervish (IRE) *T D Easterby* 73
8 ch g Definite Article—Nomadic Dancer (IRE) (Nabeel Dancer (USA))
2018[8] 2828[7] 3284[3] 3723[2] 3955[7]4156[4] 4451[2] 4632[8] 5080[3] 5338[2](5723) 6011[8] 6161[2] 6321[6]

The Whistling Teal *G Wragg* a90 110
10 b g Rudimentary(USA) —Lonely Shore (Blakeney)
1128[5] (1628) 3516a[6] 4677[3] 5395a[3] 6103[4]

The Wily Woodcock *G Wragg* a54+ 28
2 b c Mark Of Esteem(IRE) —Lonely Shore (Blakeney)
5326[7] 6561[9]

The Wizard Mul *W Storey* a27 55
6 br g Wizard King—Longden Pride (Superpower)
1560[14] 3999[10] 4692[8]

The Wizened Apple (USA) *N A Callaghan* 80
2 b g Gulch(USA) —Lakabi (USA) (Nureyev (USA))
4705[2]

They All Laughed *P W Hiatt* a62 60
3 ch g Zafonic(USA) —Royal Future (IRE) (Royal Academy (USA))
536[6] 579[11]658[10] 890[13]1352[5] 1652[5] (2210) 2479[11]2678[4] 3030[8] 4069[5] 4511[5] 5205[6]5452[5]

The Yellow (GER) *M Sowa* 76
3 br f Big Shuffle(USA) —The Green (FR) (Greinton)
6121a[8]

Thignon Boy (BRZ) *C Morgado* 100
6 ch h Thignon Lafre(BRZ) —Betina Girl (ARG) (Mat-Boy (ARG))
513a[12]

Thinking Positive *J H M Gosden* 72+
2 b f Rainbow Quest(USA) —Midnight Air (USA) (Green Dancer (USA))
5456[4]

Thinking Robins (IRE) *P Martometti* 92
3 b c Plumbird—Rose Jasmine (ITY) (Sikeston (USA))
1175a[11] 6363a[6]

Third Set (IRE) *R Charlton* a89 92
3 b g Royal Applause—Khamseh (Thatching)
1844[2] (2343) 2757[5] 3970[2]

Thistimesforgood (IRE) *Adrian Sexton* a60
3 ch g Rossini(USA) —Midsummer Night (IRE) (Fairy King (USA))
6389[11] (6406) 6767[12]

Thistle *J Howard Johnson* 77
5 ch g Selkirk(USA) —Ardisia (USA) (Affirmed (USA))
1439[5] 2761[5] 3241[6] 4154[12]

Thistle Suite *M Delzangles* 96
8 b h Unfuwain(USA) —Chepstow Vale (USA) (Key To The Mint (USA))
1873a[11] 5519a[9]

Thomas A Beckett (IRE) *P R Chamings* a37 49
3 b g Beckett(IRE) —Kenema (IRE) (Petardia)
1416[12] 2065[12] 2466[12]5071[12] 6067[4] 6544[9]

Thomas Of Bathwick *B G Powell* a36 64
3 b g Beckett(IRE) —Bathwick Babe (IRE) (Sri Pekan (USA))
5911[13] 6206[18]

Thornaby Green *T D Barron* a57 53
5 b g Whittingham(IRE) —Dona Filipa (Precocious)
1764[3] 1947[4] 2286[9]2789[4] 3672[2] 3762[3] (3941) 4355[7] 4570[8]5064[10] 5240[11] 5485[2] 5683[11] 5924[3]6304[4] (6544) 6683[9] 6899[4]

Thornbill *H Candy*
3 ch g Gorse—Red Hot Dancer (USA) (Seattle Dancer (USA))
5949[9] 6406[10]

Thornfield Clo (IRE) *R Hannon* 57
3 gr f Zafonic(USA) —Flounce (Unfuwain (USA))
(2968) 3440[4] 3793[11] 3869[14] 4285[3]

Thornton Princess *B S Rothwell* 53
3 b f Most Welcome—Princess Emily (IRE) (Dolphin Street (FR))
2019[4] 2782[11] 3138[9] 3357[11] 3529[4]

Thornton Welcome *B S Rothwell* 12
3 ch g Most Welcome—Lindrick Lady (IRE) (Broken Hearted)
1493[9]

Thornylee *M Johnston*
2 b c Selkirk(USA) —Sound Asleep (USA) (Woodman (USA))
6207[7]

Thorny Mandate *R F Johnson Houghton* a63 71
4 b g Diktat—Rosa Canina (Bustino)
965[14] (1425) 1926[13] 2455[12]2707[4] 3024[4] 4205[8]

Thorpeness (IRE) *P D Cundell* a47 63
7 b g Barathea(IRE) —Brisighella (IRE) (Al Hareb (USA))
40[6]

Thor's Echo (USA) *Doug O'Neill* a124
4 ch g Swiss Yodeler(USA) —Helen Of Troy (USA) (Mr. Integrity (USA))
740a[2] 5827a[2](6341a)

Thoughtsofstardom *P S McEntee* a68 59
3 b g Mind Games—Alustar (Emarati (USA))
(105) 190[2] 226[5]439[4] 475[6]807[10] 988[4] 1210[3] 1304[5] 1751[7] 1937[7]2263[5] 2316[6] 2826[5] 3340[3] 3397[3]3866[10] 4927[13] 6713[12]6856[8] 6890[6]

Thousand Words *B W Hills* 110
2 b c Dansili—Verbose (USA) (Storm Bird (CAN))
(2579) (3735) 5183[6] (5653) 6104[5]

Thou Shalt Not *P S Felgate* 17
3 bb g Commands(AUS) —Soyalang (FR) (Alydeed (CAN))
5598[12] 5768[13] 6177[12]

Thoutmosis (USA) *L Lungo* 59
6 ch g Woodman(USA) —Toujours Elle (USA) (Lyphard (USA))
1436[4] 1758[5]

Three Boars *S Gollings* a63+ 54
4 ch g Most Welcome—Precious Poppy (Polish Precedent (USA))
284[2] 482[7]570[8] 696[5]1436[10] 2788[4] 3680[5] 4380[8] 5750[3]6238[3] (6374) (6540) 6870[2]

Three Counties (IRE) *N I M Rossiter* 80?
5 b h Danehill(USA) —Royal Show (IRE) (Sadler's Wells (USA))
2430[7] 2849[10] 3114[7] 3905[5]

Three Decades (IRE) *C A Cyzer* a85 87
2 b f Invincible Spirit(IRE) —Parvenue (FR) (Ezzoud (IRE))
1242[3] 1542[11] 1922[3](2461) 3084[4] 3415[10] 3530[5]5909[3] 6096[5]

Three Degrees (IRE) *P Gallagher* a75 114
4 gr m Singspiel(IRE) —Miss University (USA) (Beau Genius (CAN))
6614a[2]

Three Feathers *M Salaman* a41 53?
3 b g Averti(IRE) —Jane Grey (Tragic Role (USA))
39[6] 176[3]329[9] 779[4] 890[8]1726[4] 2570[4] 2730[3]3006[6] 3195[3] 3614[6] 4450[2]

Three Graces (GER) *I Mohammed* 112
6 ch g Peintre Celebre(USA) —Trefoil (Kris)
203a[5] 352a[9]

Three Half Crowns (IRE) *P Howling* a42
2 b c Barathea(IRE) —My-Lorraine (IRE) (Mac's Imp (USA))
6072[7]

Three Mates *W G M Turner* a29 38
2 b f Auction House(USA) —Great Aim (Great Nephew)
878[8] 1040[7] 1379[6]

Three No Trumps *D Morris* a48 49
2 ch f First Trump—Renaissance Lady (IRE) (Imp Society (USA))
2588[5] 3031[4] 4008[4] 5323[10] 5923[4]6172[15] 6385[8] 6511[4]

Three Ships *Miss J Feilden* a63 65
5 ch g Dr Fong(USA) —River Lullaby (USA) (Riverman (USA))
72[7] (328) 3232[15] 4206[6]

Three Strings (USA) *P D Niven* a32 69?
3 b g Stravinsky(USA) —Just Cause (Law Society (USA))
1684[5] 2249[8] 2529[4]3329[3] (3355) 3716[9] 3790[2] 4470[10] 5082[5]

Three Thieves (UAE) *M S Saunders* a68 77
3 ch g Jade Robbery(USA) —Melisendra (FR) (Highest Honor (FR))
5164[10] 5478[7] 5786[13]6647[5] 6825[5]6954[5]

Three Valleys (USA) *R J Frankel* 119
5 ch h Diesis—Skiable (IRE) (Niniski (USA))
5416a[7] 5824a[6]

Three Welshmen *D Burchell* a48 59
5 b g Muhtarram(USA) —Merch Rhyd-Y-Grug (Sabrehill (USA))
882[14] 1204[8] 1882[4] 2647[9]

Three Wrens (IRE) *D J Daly* a94 97
4 b m Second Empire(IRE) —Three Terns (USA) (Arctic Tern (USA))
1015[4] 1407[5] 1974a[12](4628) 5550[6] 6190[5]

Threezedzz *R A Harris* a59 79
8 ch g Emarati(USA) —Exotic Forest (Dominion)
1480[11] 1802[10] 2098[12] 5302[16] 5621[9]5755[15]

Throw The Dice *D W Barker* 69
4 b g Lujain(USA) —Euridice (IRE) (Woodman (USA))
1035[12] 1496[8] 1858[8] 2302[7] 3041[19]3718[6] 4324[3] 4636[2] 4834[6] 5286[8]5865[11] 6162[3] 6274[7] 6315[14]

Thumpers Dream *H R A Cecil* 86
3 b f Cape Cross(IRE) —Perfect Peach (Lycius (USA))
1994[4] 2349[4] 3146[3] 3901[7] (4759) 5530[5]5895[6]

Thunderousapplause *K A Ryan* a58 82+
2 b f Royal Applause—Trustthunder (Selkirk (USA))
5679[2] 6098[6]

Thunder Road (IRE) *P A Fahy* 70+
6 b m Mtoto—Shefoog (Kefaah (USA))
4166a[7]

Thunder Rock (IRE) *Sir Michael Stoute* 97
4 b g King's Best(USA) —Park Express (Ahonoora)
1484[3] 2848[5] 3294[12] 4711[6] 5548[4]5920[5]

Thunder S (USA) *L M Cumani* a24 49
3 ch f Kris S(USA) —Thunder Maid (USA) (Alydar (USA))
3458[10] 4300[5]

Thunder Storm Cat (USA) *P F I Cole* a79 89
2 b c Storm Cat(USA) —Tenga (USA) (Mr Prospector (USA))
4934[2] (5371)

Thunder Touch (USA) *K McLaughlin* a102
5 ch h Gulch(USA) —Highland Vixen (USA) (Highland Ruckus (USA))
3134a[10] 4384a[6]

Thunderwing (IRE) *K R Burke* a73 89
4 bb g Indian Danehill(IRE) —Scandisk (IRE) (Kenmare (FR))
865[9] 1043[18] 2974[12] 3374[10] 3918[6]4437[11] 4831[3] 5249[6]5689[9]

Thurlestone Rock *B J Meehan* a77 86
6 ch g Sheikh Albadou—Don't Smile (Sizzling Melody)
323[3] 541[7]1359[4] 2302[16]

Thyolo (IRE) *C G Cox* a75 91
5 ch g Bering—Topline (GER) (Acatenango (GER))
667[10] 1133[7] 2200[11]2387[14] 2656[2] 3093[8] 4626[3] 5346[12]

Ti Adora (IRE) *P W D'Arcy* a98 99
4 b m Montjeu(IRE) —Wavy Up (IRE) (Brustolon)
1800[6] (2357) (2653) 3220[2] 3446[3] 4149[3] 4347[2]4676[3] 5010[7] 5678[2] 5803[3] 6191[7]

Tiana *J H M Gosden* 97
3 b f Diktat—Hill Welcome (Most Welcome)
4808[5] 5525[5]

Tiara Boom De Ay (IRE) *R Hannon* 58+
2 b f Fasliyev(USA) —Fez (Mujtahid (USA))
1347[5]

Tiberius Caesar (FR) *F Reuterskiold* a98 111
6 b h Zieten(USA) —Thekla (GER) (Prince Ippi (GER))
1659a[11] 2123a[10] 4864a[8]6121a[12]

Tiber Tiger (IRE) *N P Littmoden* a62 76
6 b g Titus Livius(FR) —Genetta (Green Desert (USA))
1041[10] 1673[4] 1993[4] 2820[2] 3044[10]3712[9] 4288[2] 4456[3] 5130[5]

Tiber Tilly *N P Littmoden* a69 77
3 b f King Charlemagne(USA) —Clarice Orsini (Common Grounds)
1679[11] 2049[11] 2609[7] 3250[4] 4070[11](4265) 4494[3] 5268[10] 5973[11]

Tibinta *P D Evans* a46 58
2 b f Averti(IRE) —Bint Albadou (IRE) (Green Desert (USA))
4492[6] 4816[3] 4926[2] 5366[11] 6416[7]6576[13]

Tibroso (ITY) *A & G Botti*
2 ch c Tibullo(USA) —Calabrosa (IRE) (Barathea (IRE))
2474a[5]

Tiburon *H Morrison* a58 62
2 b c Xaar—Sahara Rose (Green Desert (USA))
3591[10] 4074[6] 4485[4] 5208[4]

Ticina (GER) *G Sybrecht* 86
6 b m Royal Solo(IRE) —Tannenprima (GER) (Sure Blade (USA))
1974a[8]

Ticinella (GER) *C Brandstatter* 103
3 ch f Hernando(FR) —Triclaria (GER) (Surumu (GER))
2279a[5]

Ticking *T Keddy* a49 15
3 ch g Barathea(IRE) —Tuning (Rainbow Quest (USA))
2343[9] 2934[12] 6225[10]

Ticki Tori (IRE) *G C H Chung* a62 81
4 b m Vettori(IRE) —Lamees (USA) (Lomond (USA))
1821[10] 2044[9]

Tidal Chorus *J G Given* 66
3 ch f Singspiel(IRE) —South Shore (Caerleon (USA))
3946[5] 5086[15]

Tidy (IRE) *Micky Hammond* a66 74
6 b g Mujadil(USA) —Neat Shilling (IRE) (Bob Back (USA))
611[12] 1422[13] 1996[9](2165) 2810[3] 4108[11] 4733[6] 4911[5] 5362[3]5904[10] 6008[8]

Tie Black (IRE) *F Rohaut* 113
3 b f Machiavellian(USA) —Tender Is Thenight (IRE) (Barathea (IRE))
(1719a) 3991a[3]

Tiegs (IRE) *P W Hiatt* a52 57
4 ch m Desert Prince(IRE) —Helianthus (Groom Dancer (USA))
91[4] 259[10](647) 785[4]6959[8]

Tifernati *W J Haggas* 59+
2 b g Dansili—Pain Perdu (IRE) (Waajib)
3979[6]

Tiffany Gardens (IRE) *T Hogan* 78
4 b m Desert Sun—Hoyland Common (IRE) (Common Grounds)
3125a[5]

Tiffin Deano (IRE) *H J Manners* a48 48
4 b g Mujadil(USA) —Xania (Mujtahid (USA))
2096[8] 2536[10]

Tiger Dance (USA) *A P O'Brien* 100
4 b h Storm Cat(USA) —Mariah's Storm (USA) (Rahy (USA))
2559a[4] 3572a[3]

Tiger Frog (USA) *J Mackie* 53
7 b g French Deputy(USA) —Woodyoubelieveit (USA) (Woodman (USA))
1233[10]

Tiger Hunter *P Howling* a57 45
4 b g Lake Coniston(IRE) —Daynabee (Common Grounds)
27[9] 184[11]

Tiger King (GER) *P Monteith* 64
5 b g Tiger Hill(IRE) —Tennessee Girl (GER) (Big Shuffle (USA))
976[15]

Tiger Royal (IRE) *C A Murphy* 110
10 gr g Royal Academy(USA) —Lady Redford (Bold Lad (IRE))
3125a[20]

Tiger Shark (SAF) *H J Brown* 102
5 b g Spaceship(ARG) —Dolphin Coast (SAF) (Dolpour)
352a[4] (435a) 625a[3]

Tiger Tango (USA) *W J Haggas* 52
2 b f Johannesburg(USA) —Sweet Little Lies (USA) (Raise A Native)
3537[6]

Tiger Tiger (FR) *Jamie Poulton* a96 99
5 b h Tiger Hill(IRE) —Adorable Emilie (FR) (Iron Duke (FR))
(116) 222[8] 296[5]1585[11] 1775[7] 1976[4] 4676[10] 5657[13]5804[11]

Tigim (IRE) *Peter Henley* 96
7 b g Fayruz—Rousalong (Rousillon (USA))
3561a[12]

Tignasse (FR) *Karen George* a44 50
5 b m Double Bed(FR) —Off Guard (FR) (Bakharoff (USA))
(338) 457[13] 597[7]891[12]

Tigron (USA) *Mme C Barande-Barbe* a106 102
5 ch h Lion Cavern(USA) —Tidy Tune (USA) (The Minstrel (CAN))
393a[3] 6574a[0]

Tikram *G L Moore* a81 87
9 ch g Lycius(USA) —Black Fighter (USA) (Secretariat (USA))
2723[11]

Tilapia (IRE) *Sir Mark Prescott* a55
2 ch c Daggers Drawn(USA) —Mrs Fisher (IRE) (Salmon Leap (USA))
6749[4] 6912[2]6940[7]

Tilbury *H R A Cecil* 73+
3 ch f Peintre Celebre(USA) —Dockage (CAN) (Riverman (USA))
2985[4] 3554[7]

Tilen (IRE) *V Smith* a34 16
3 ch g Bluebird(USA) —New Sensitive (Wattlefield)
93[11] (176) 364[6]604[10] 796[9] 1441[12]2539[12] 3115[13] 5840[13] 6281[13]6306[6] 6852[6]6979[12]

Tilla *Mrs A J Hamilton-Fairley* a34 42
6 b m Bin Ajwaad(IRE) —Tosca (Be My Guest (USA))
545[9] 643[12]973[10] 2935[8] 4530[9]

Tilly's Dream *G C H Chung* a72 77
3 ch f Arkadian Hero(USA) —Dunloe (IRE) (Shaadi (USA))
2049[5] 2353[8] 2554[7]3381[2] 3996[6]4494[2] (4691)

Tilsworth Charlie *J R Jenkins* a59 53
3 bl f Dansili—Glossary (Reference Point)
418[8] 703[7]835[4] 1352[9] 2589[13]3668[7] 3865[7] 4447[2] (5055) 5576[5] 6325[11]

Tilt *B Ellison* a80 95+
4 b g Daylami(IRE) —Tromond (Lomond (USA))
976[5] (1502) 1756[3] 2176[3] 3078[10] 5582[3]6319[6]

Tiltili (IRE) *P C Haslam* 50
3 ch f Spectrum(IRE) —Alexander Confranc (IRE) (Magical Wonder (USA))
1866[8] 3791[6] 5365[4]

Timbalada (GER) *U Ostmann* 86
3 b f Big Shuffle(USA) —Tennessee Waltz (Caerleon (USA))
5710a[6]

Timberlake *Miss E C Lavelle* a59 55
4 b m Bluegrass Prince(IRE) —Ambience Lady (Batshoof)
6484[13]

Timber Treasure (USA) *H R A Cecil* 65
2 bb c Forest Wildcat(USA) —Lady Ilsley (USA) (Trempolino (USA))
2821[6]

Time Dancer (IRE) *A Berry* a35
2 ch g Desert Sun—With Finesse (Be My Guest (USA))
6157[12] 6297[14] 6504[11]6581[10] 6996[10]

Time For Change (IRE) *B W Hills* a44+ 51
2 ch g Elnadim(USA) —Dance Lesson (In The Wings)
4002[7] 4428[10] 5161[8]

Time For Life (USA) *H J Collingridge* a85 86
3 bb c Woodman(USA) —Marie's Star (USA) (Risen Star (USA))
87[2] 294[4]448[2] 1569[3] 2033[6]2608[7] 5301[11]

Time For You *J M Bradley* a37 37
4 b m Vettori(IRE) —La Fija (USA) (Dixieland Band (USA))
2133[12] 2707[10]

Time Marches On *K G Reveley* a22 54
8 b g Timeless Times(USA) —Tees Gazette Girl (Kalaglow)
4381[9] 4568[7] 4954[7]

Time N Time Again *Peter Grayson* a60 61
8 b g Timeless Times(USA) —Primum Tempus (Primo Dominie)
292[11] 381[12]486[8] 552[7]587[7] 732[10]1196[9] 6796[11]6969[10]

Time On *J L Dunlop* 109
3 b f Sadler's Wells(USA) —Time Away (IRE) (Darshaan)
(971) (1583) 2203[6] (2913a) 4192a[7] 5220a[7] 6124a[4]

Time Out (IRE) *A M Balding* 68
3 b g Alhaarth(IRE) —Waif (Groom Dancer (USA))
1134[8] 1841[14] 2332[11] 3030[9]

Times Review (USA) *C A Dwyer* a68 68
5 b g Crafty Prospector(USA) —Previewed (USA) (Ogygian (USA))
67[10] 159[7](216) 426[6]485[6] 580[2]824[6] 986[2]1243[9] 1383[5]2182[11] 2505[12]

Time To Regret *I W McInnes* a51 42
6 b g Presidium—Scoffera (Scottish Reel)
1123[2] 1422[6] 1480[3] 1947[7] 2108[12]4325[6] 4845[11] 6213[8]

Time To Shine *Mrs L J Mongan* a17 18
7 b m Pivotal—Sweet Jaffa (Never So Bold)
6108[15]

Time Upon Time *W J Knight* a45
2 b f Groom Dancer(USA) —Watchkeeper (IRE) (Rudimentary (USA))
6073[9]

Timore Tiger (IRE) *Martin Browne* 68
3 b g Elnadim(USA) —Granza (FR) (Saumarez)
4034a[14]

Tina's Magic *Mrs G S Rees*
3 ch f Primitive Rising(USA) —Night Transaction (Tina's Pet)
1731[9]

Tinian *Miss Tracy Waggott* a46 46
8 b g Mtoto—Housefull (Habitat)
147[11] 974[5] 1073[12]4057[8]

Tinnarinka *R Hannon* a77 59
2 ch f Observatory(USA) —Dancing Fire (USA) (Dayjur (USA))
4994[5] 5424[2]5891[4]

Tintac *E J O'Neill* a52 44
5 b m Intikhab(USA) —Susquehanna Days (USA) (Chief's Crown (USA))
42[8] 174[9]

Tintawn Gold (IRE) *S Woodman* a31 31
6 b m Rudimentary(USA) —Clear Ahead (Primo Dominie)
141[7]

Tinted View (USA) *B W Hills* a54 55+
2 ch f Distant View(USA) —Gombeen (USA) (Private Account (USA))
5206[6] 6309[6]

Tiny Tim (IRE) *A M Balding* a49 47
8 b g Brief Truce(USA) —Nonnita (Welsh Saint)
876[12] 4278[2] 4670[12]6805[5]

Tioga Gold (IRE) *L R James* a51 24
7 b g Goldmark(USA) —Coffee Bean (Doulab (USA))
490[5] 5723[11]

Tio Poppy (IRE) *R Gibson* 84
2 b f Grand Lodge(USA) —Virgin Stanza (USA) (Opening Verse (USA))
6453a[6]

Tipolino (GER) *H Rogers* 68d
4 ch g Trempolino(USA) —Tintina (USA) (General Assembly (USA))
4094a[10]

Tipperary (GER) *P Vovcenko* 66
2 b c Areion(GER) —Tipsy (GER) (Konigsstuhl (GER))
6092a[6]

Tipperary All Star (FR) *M Halford* 107
6 b g Highest Honor(FR) —Moucha (FR) (Fabulous Dancer (USA))
208a[11] 354a[8] 437a[11]

Tipsy Lad *D J S Ffrench Davis* a61 49+
4 b g Tipsy Creek(USA) —Perfidy (FR) (Persian Bold)
985[13] 1245[6]1303[6] 1644[11]3390[12]

Tipsy Lillie *P S McEntee* a45 50
4 ch m Tipsy Creek(USA) —Belle De Nuit (IRE) (Statoblest)
4554[2] 6274[13] 6538[7]6763[4] 6854[5]6970[9]

Tipsy Me *M L W Bell* a67 66+
3 b f Selkirk(USA) —Time Saved (Green Desert (USA))
4661[8] 5138[4] 5598[3] 5973[4]6430[10] 6664[5]

Tipsy Prince *Mrs G S Rees* a70 72
2 b g Tipsy Creek(USA) —Princess Of Garda (Komaite (USA))
3596[2] 3818[3] 4433[4]5065[6] 5349[5] (5747) (5860)

Tiptoeing *M H Tompkins* a48 48
3 b f Tipsy Creek(USA) —Grove Dancer (Reprimand)
1416[7] 1950[10] 2573[8]3232[13] 3823[8] 4016[8] 5097[2]5298[2] 5733[5]

Tip Toes (IRE) *P Howling* a48 52
4 b m Bianconi(USA) —Tip Tap Toe (USA) (Pleasant Tap (USA))
2260[11] 2861[4] 3074[3]3592[2] 3896[2] 4330[6] 4929[5]5324[4] 6623[3] 6797[9]6995[7]

Tip Top Style *J Mackie* a54 29
3 b g Tipsy Creek(USA) —Eliza Jane (Mistertopogigo (IRE))
132[6] 272[6]536[8] 4069[10] 5319[13]6793[7] 6819[6]6970[2]

Tipu Sultan *Micky Hammond* 51
6 ch g Kris—Eye Witness (IRE) (Don't Forget Me)
1500[10] 2395[2] 3291[8] 3637[9] 4072[14]

Tirade *J H M Gosden* 51
2 b g Vettori(IRE) —Elfin Laughter (Alzao (USA))
6214[14]

Tirailleur (IRE) *J R Boyle* a44 40
6 b m Eagle Eyed(USA) —Tiralle (IRE) (Tirol)
304[8] 468[8]689[4] 875[7]939[11]

Tirol Livit (IRE) *N Wilson* a46 50
3 ch g Titus Livius(FR) —Orange Royale (IRE) (Exit To Nowhere (USA))
193[5] 333[4]716[4] 1221[10] 1533[4] 3258[5]

Tirwanako (FR) *J-L Pelletan* 108
4 b g Sin Kiang(FR) —Alhena (FR) (Kaldoun (FR))
1860a[3] 6610a[4]
Tirzia (IRE) *R Feligioni*
2 b f Fasliyev(USA) —Indian Walkin (IRE) (Indian Ridge)
2475a[8] 5705a[4]
Titan Triumph *W J Knight* 73
2 b c Zamindar(USA) —Triple Green (Green Desert (USA))
4333[8] 4928[4]
Titian Dancer *W R Swinburn* a78 79
3 ch c Danehill Dancer(IRE) —La Limite (IRE) (Dr Devious (IRE))
1166[3] 1640[9] 1960[3]2757[4] 3906[2] 4782[7]5362[9]
Titian Saga (IRE) *D Nicholls* a53 57
3 ch f Titus Livius(FR) —Nordic Living (IRE) (Nordico (USA))
2049[12] 2866[9] 3087[8] 3841[10] 4267[7]4703[7] 5577[12] 5752[5]
Titinius (IRE) *Micky Hammond* 77
6 ch g Titus Livius(FR) —Maiyria (IRE) (Shernazar)
1042[3] 1124[5] 1561[4] 2184[3] 2749[5]3374[6] 3986[4] 4338[2] 4885[6] 6160[5]6273[11]
Titus Alone (IRE) *B Smart* 101
3 ch g Titus Livius(FR) —Swan Sea (USA) (Sea Hero (USA))
1633[5] 3038[14] 3475[6] 3761[14]
Titus Lumpus (IRE) *R M Flower* a65 62
3 b g Titus Livius(FR) —Carabosse (Salse (USA))
307 857[7]703[5] 853[2](984) 1941[12]3011[6] 3364[6] 3869[6]5046[2]
Titus Maximus (IRE) *H J Manners* a63 72
3 ch g Titus Livius(FR) —Haraabah (USA) (Topsider (USA))
593[5] 1036[10] 2263[6]4587[7] 6348[11]
Titus Shadow (IRE) *B Grizzetti* 85
2 ch c Titus Livius(FR) —Mujadil Shadow (IRE) (Mujadil (USA))
6363a[8]
Titus Wonder (IRE) *P A Blockley* a45 52
3 ch f Titus Livius(FR) —Morcote (IRE) (Magical Wonder (USA))
287[7] 396[2]543[9] 598[6]890[5] (936) 1003[5] 4554[9]
Tivers Jewel (USA) *Mrs A J Perrett* 64
2 bb g Tiznow(USA) —Box Of Jewels (USA) (Half A Year (USA))
5371[10] 5891[14]
Tivers Song (USA) *Mrs A J Perrett* a69 31
2 gr c Buddha(USA) —Rousing (USA) (Alydar (USA))
5890[13] 6254[6] 6386[3]6569[9]
Tiverton (USA) *D Donk* 93
4 b g Unaccounted For(USA) —Big Band Singer (USA) (Dixieland Band (USA))
(6006a)
Tiviski (IRE) *Miss Gay Kelleway* a55 56
4 b m Desert Style(IRE) —Mummys Best (Bustino)
46[3] 255[2]402[3] (486) 519[5] 587[12]711[11] 806[11]903[3] 1209[5] 1348[7]4554[11] 5327[9] 5987[11]6288[8] 6513[10]6719[5] 6974[7]
Tiyoun (IRE) *Jedd O'Keeffe* a69 88
8 b g Kahyasi—Taysala (IRE) (Akarad (FR))
3078[19] 3743[3]
Tizi Ouzou (IRE) *M C Pipe* a38 52
5 ch m Desert Prince(IRE) —Tresor (USA) (Pleasant Tap (USA))
457[11]
Tiz Timely (USA) *A M Balding* a58 54
3 b f Tiznow(USA) —Delivery Day (USA) (Dayjur (USA))
1798[7] 3458[4] 4247[5]5046[12] 6069[13]
Tizzydore (IRE) *A M Balding* a17 26
2 b f Shinko Forest(IRE) —Shannon Dore (IRE) (Turtle Island (IRE))
5424[10] 5760[9]
Toamasina (FR) *M Rulec* 108
5 b m Marju(IRE) —Top Speed (IRE) (Wolfhound (USA))
1974a[2]
To Arms *T D Easterby* 65
4 b g Mujahid(USA) —Toffee (Midyan (USA))
1425[3] 2104[6] 2612[8] 2762[5]
Tobago Reef *Mrs L Stubbs* a75 58
2 b g Tobougg(IRE) —Silly Mid-On (Midyan (USA))
2545[3] 2973[7] 3669[5] 4949[6] 5282[8]5876[3] 6416[2]6706[2] (6900) (6991)
To Be Fare (IRE) *J Pearce* a52 57
6 ch g Eagle Eyed(USA) —Petrolea Girl (Connaught)
184[2] 3045[5]390[2] 525[2]635[7]
Tobermory (IRE) *M A Jarvis* 86
2 b f Green Desert(USA) —Kerrera (Diesis)
(5348) 5731[5]
Toberogan (IRE) *W A Murphy* a39 67
5 b g Docksider(USA) —Beltisaal (FR) (Belmez (USA))
4186a[16] 5865[7]
Toboggan Lady *Mrs A Duffield* a46
2 b f Tobougg(IRE) —Northbend (Shirley Heights)
6498[7] 6697[6]
Tobosa *W Jarvis* 106
2 b c Tobougg(IRE) —Sovereign Abbey (IRE) (Royal Academy (USA))
2821[7] (3623) (4107) (4335) 5655[2] 6102[6]
Tobougg Welcome (IRE) *S C Williams* a22
2 ch c Tobougg(IRE) —Three White Sox (Most Welcome)
6826[11]
Toccata (IRE) *D M Simcock* a53 74
2 b f Cape Cross(IRE) —Sopran Marida (IRE) (Darshaan)
5425[7] 6049[2]
Todlea (IRE) *Jean-Rene Auvray* a55 73
6 b g Desert Prince(IRE) —Imelda (USA) (Manila (USA))
(4285) 4968[9] (5205) 5436[6] 6387[5]
Todman Avenue (USA) *A Al Raihe* a61 90
4 bb g Lear Fan(USA) —Three Wishes (Sadler's Wells (USA))
565a[14]
Tod Sloan (IRE) *J M Bradley* a51 44
4 ch g Titus Livius(FR) —Poscimur (IRE) (Prince Rupert (FR))
293[4] 399[4]527[12] 584[6]682[11] 1852[13] 2566[6]
To Dubai *M A Jarvis* 59
3 ch f Daylami(IRE) —Albertville (USA) (Polish Precedent (USA))
894[7] 1214[5]
Todwick Owl *J G Given* a59 55
2 b g Namid—Blinding Mission (IRE) (Marju (IRE))
1945[7] 2552[5] 4295[10]5208[5] 5647[3]
Toffee Vodka (IRE) *J W Hills* a84+ 82+
4 b m Danehill Dancer(IRE) —Vieux Carre (Pas De Seul)
1673[12] 2011[4] 2459[11] 3212[9] 3450[4]3687[2] 4075[5] 4281[2](4447) 4965[5] 5428[11]
Tofta Tilly *L R James* a4
6 ch m Muhtarram(USA) —Budding Prospect (Rudimentary (USA))
937[7]
Toga (ITY) *M Bebbu*
2 b f Kalanisi(IRE) —Tesana (Saddlers' Hall (IRE))
5705a[11]
Togambo (FR) *P Chatelain* 72
4 b g Le Triton(USA) —Movin' Meghan (USA) (Mogambo (USA))
5562a[10]
Together (FR) *Mme C Vergne* a98 105
6 b m Valanour(IRE) —Toomixa (FR) (Linamix (FR))
2313a[6] 2941a[3] 3779a[6] 3991a[8] 4862a[5]6250a[10] 6574a[9]
Toggle *R Hannon* a53 68
2 b g Tobougg(IRE) —Niggle (Night Shift (USA))
3701[13] 4290[5] 4895[6] 5780[8]
Togher Castle (IRE) *T J O'Mara* 67
6 b h Among Men(USA) —Soul Fire (IRE) (Exactly Sharp (USA))
4186a[7]
To Green (GER) *Mario Hofer* a76 82
3 br f Greinton—The Mood (GER) (Mondrian (GER))
2912a[9]
To Hatta (IRE) *M R Channon*
2 b g Shinko Forest(IRE) —Monarchy (IRE) (Common Grounds)
4880[13]
Tojoneski *I W McInnes* a46+ 51
7 b g Emperor Jones(USA) —Sampower Lady (Rock City)
2497[11] 2927[7] 3637[6] 4086[5] 4351[7]
Tokai Come Come (JPN) *H Tadokoro* 115
5 b h Tokai Teio(JPN) —Tokai Pastel (JPN) (Sunday Silence (USA))
1329a[5]
Tokai Trick (JPN) *S Matsumoto* 116
4 b h El Condor Pasa(USA) —Zoonaqua (USA) (Silver Hawk (USA))
1329a[9]
Tokewanna *W M Brisbourne* a67 58
6 b m Danehill(USA) —High Atlas (Shirley Heights)
109[5]
Tokyo Jo (IRE) *T T Clement* a58 60
2 b f Raise A Grand(IRE) —Wakayi (Persian Bold)
814[5] 1040[2] 1248[4] 1862[2] (2015) 2179[2]2626[3] 3997[11] 4887[6]4969[2] 6258[2]6736[10] 6777[2]
Tokyo Rose (UAE) *H-A Pantall* 94
3 b f Jade Robbery(USA) —Sawara (Danzig (USA))
6328a[5]
Tokyo Rose *R Hannon* 70
2 b f Agnes World(USA) —Wildwood Flower (Distant Relative)
5043[6] 5264[3] 5586[3]
Toldo (IRE) *G M Moore* 97
4 gr g Tagula(IRE) —Mystic Belle (IRE) (Thatching)
867[8] 1294[4] 1685[5] (2013) 2437[5] (3078)
Tolinis Girl *B Smart* a32 52
3 b f Bertolini(USA) —Skiddaw Bird (Bold Owl)
197[8]
Tolpuddle (IRE) *T Stack* 115
6 b g College Chapel—Tabdea (USA) (Topsider (USA))
932a[2] 1084[3] 5411a[8]
Tombalina *C J Teague* a50 50
3 ch f Tomba—Ashkernazy (IRE) (Salt Dome (USA))
335[5] 605[8]910[7] 980[5] 1137[7]1234[10] 4232[15]
Tom Bell (IRE) *J G M O'Shea* a44 59+
6 b g King's Theatre(IRE) —Nordic Display (IRE) (Nordico (USA))
2099[8] 2998[9]
Tombi (USA) *J Howard Johnson* 85
2 b g Johannesburg(USA) —Tune In To The Cat (USA) (Tunerup (USA))
1998[3] 2361[4] 5114[5] 5681[7]
Tom Forest *K A Ryan* a62 72
4 b g Forest Wildcat(USA) —Silk Masque (USA) (Woodman (USA))
1830[13] 2737[6] 4116[15] 4350[3] 5445[16]
Tommifrancs (AUS) *Lee Freedman* 96
5 br g Real Quiet(USA) —Schwarzkoff (AUS) (Centaine (AUS))
5817a[10]
Tommy Tobougg *I Semple* 55
2 ch g Tobougg(IRE) —Celebrate (IRE) (Generous (IRE))
6318[5]
Tommy Toogood (IRE) *B W Hills* a86 84
3 b c Danehill(USA) —On The Nile (IRE) (Sadler's Wells (USA))
(669) 1190[2] 5428[4] 5639[5](6076)
Tommytyler (IRE) *D Carroll* a53 22
7 b g Goldmark(USA) —John's Ballad (IRE) (Ballad Rock)
386[7] 527[2]616[5] 634[13]783[2] 937[2]1462[7] 1573[2]1765[4] 1852[8] 6552[10]6960[11]
Tomorrow's Dancer *K A Ryan* 55
2 b g Danehill Dancer(IRE) —Today (IRE) (Royal Academy (USA))
4716[10] 5615[4] 6200[10]
Tom Paris *W R Muir* a74 70
2 b g Bertolini(USA) —Nom Francais (First Trump)
892[8] 1284[4] 2315[11] 3117[3] 3530[3](3837) 4284[5] 4766[19] 5290[6] 5447[3] 5909[6](6285) 6458[4]
Tomthevic *J M Bradley* a47 51
8 ch g Emarati(USA) —Madame Bovary (Ile De Bourbon (USA))
2571[4] 3071[5] 3348[3] 3699[5] 3863[4]4223[5] 4551[5] 4675[4]
Tom Tower (IRE) *M R Channon* 72
2 b g Cape Cross(IRE) —La Belle Katherine (USA) (Lyphard (USA))
961[11] 1420[5] (2094) 2598[3] 5113[12] 5509[8]
Tom Tun *J Balding* a93 93
11 b g Bold Arrangement—B Grade (Lucky Wednesday)
729[10] 1145[7]
Toni Alcala *R F Fisher* a57 67
7 b g Ezzoud(IRE) —Etourdie (USA) (Arctic Tern (USA))
6540[5] 6705[4]
Tonic Star (FR) *E Lellouche* 98
3 b f Enrique—Tonic Stream (FR) (Bering)
2374a[4] 4542a[2]
Tonight (IRE) *W M Brisbourne* a29 50
4 b g Imperial Ballet(IRE) —No Tomorrow (IRE) (Night Shift (USA))
792[8] 1197[13]1225[13] 2070[8]
Tonnante *Sir Mark Prescott* a63+ 53
2 b f Hernando(FR) —Thunder Queen (USA) (Thunder Gulch (USA))
5095[6] 5287[7] 5580[4]
Tony The Tap *B Palling* a86 95
5 b g Most Welcome—Laleston (Junius (USA))
2683[6] 3092[7] 3471[5] 3744[5] 4682[10]5420[11]
Too Keen *J M Jefferson*
5 ch m Keen—Janie-O (Hittite Glory)
313[10]
Too Much Bling (USA) *B Baffert* a111
3 gr c Rubiano(USA) —Rose Colored Lady (USA) (Formal Dinner (USA))
6341a[6]
Too Nice (FR) *Robert Collet* 99
4 gr h Kaldounevees(FR) —Toomixa (FR) (Linamix (FR))
393a[0]
Toorah Laura La (USA) *N Clement* 92
3 ch f Black Minnaloushe(USA) —Zuppa (USA) (Woodman (USA))
522a[4]
To Party (IRE) *M P Tregoning* a68 70
2 ch f Elusive Quality(USA) —Magongo (Be My Chief (USA))
2980[2] 4041[4] 5206[5]
Toparudi *M H Tompkins* a50 78
5 b g Rudimentary(USA) —Topatori (IRE) (Topanoora)
33[14]
Topatoo *M H Tompkins* 107
4 ch m Bahamian Bounty—Topatori (IRE) (Topanoora)
1186[2] 1830[4] (2627) 2810[8] (4711) 5188[2] 5787[2]5917[9]
Top Award *J R Fanshawe* 37
3 b g Mark Of Esteem(IRE) —First Fantasy (Be My Chief (USA))
1741[15] 1994[9] (Dead)
Topazleo (IRE) *J Howard Johnson* 67
2 ch g Peintre Celebre(USA) —Mer Noire (IRE) (Marju (IRE))
5814[6]
Top Bid *T D Easterby* 87
2 b c Auction House(USA) —Trump Street (First Trump)
1588[4] (2072) 3445[4] 4200[5]
Top Dirham *M W Easterby* 86
8 ch g Night Shift(USA) —Miller's Melody (Chief Singer)
1143[9] 2681[4] 2974[17] 3549[7] 4172[16]4350[6] 4881[8] 5617[8] 5861[9]
Topflight Wildbird *Mrs G S Rees* a43 71
3 br f Diktat—Jamarj (Tyrnavos)
1726[14] 2244[9]2411[6] (2747) 3215[4] 5173[9]
Topiary Ted *H Morrison* a68 46
4 ch g Zafonic(USA) —Lovely Lyca (Night Shift (USA))
6300[8] 6470[6] (6606) 6683[7](6934)
Topic (IRE) *J W Hills* 16
2 b f Stravinsky(USA) —Lyric Fantasy (IRE) (Tate Gallery (USA))
2172[12]
Top Jaro (FR) *T P Tate* 83
3 b g Marathon(USA) —Shahmy (USA) (Lear Fan (USA))
1099[2] 1596[7] 5362[2] 5685[13] 6051[6](6209)
Topjeu (IRE) *L M Cumani* 89
3 b c Montjeu(IRE) —Arabian Lass (SAF) (Al Mufti (USA))
1823[5] 3901[2] (4625) 5920[11]
Top Level (IRE) *M G Quinlan* a55 51
3 b f Fasliyev(USA) —Aiming Upwards (Blushing Flame (USA))
1306[7] 4050[3] 4297[8]4491[5] 5767[7] 6067[7] 6281[3](6306) 6549[5]
Top Man Tee *D J Daly* a76 79
4 gr g Vettori(IRE) —Etienne Lady (IRE) (Imperial Frontier (USA))
1809[12]
Top Mark *J R Boyle* a82 81
4 b g Mark Of Esteem(IRE) —Red White And Blue (Zafonic (USA))
1112[7] (2223) 2443[7] 4047[4]5096[8] 5670[4]5907[2] 6239[6]6469[4] (6898)
Topple *P W Hiatt* 38
5 b m Master Willie—Top Cover (High Top)
42[13]
Top Royelle *R Hannon* a63 76
2 b f Royal Applause—Colchica (Machiavellian (USA))
1082[5] 1896[2] (2100) 4427[8] 4804[2] 5434[9]5764[7] 6100[10]
Top Seed (IRE) *A J Chamberlain* a83 87
5 b g Cadeaux Genereux—Midnight Heights (Persian Heights)
799[5] (1206) (1478) 1779[10] 2229[7] 3093[4] 3497[2]3748[7] 4027[11] 4347[8] 4676[17] 5163[9]5479[4] 5671[2] 6351[9]6602[8] 6761[5]6885[6]
Top Shot *M H Tompkins* a67 77
3 ch g College Chapel—Topatori (IRE) (Topanoora)
233[6] 3657[4]459[4] 583[6](993) (1122)
Top Spec (IRE) *J Pearce* a78 80
5 b g Spectrum(IRE) —Pearl Marine (IRE) (Bluebird (USA))
250[4] 385[5]1435[4] 1995[5] 2322[2] 2628[4] 3009[2]3706[5] 4256[8] 4924[4] 5242[14] 5513[4](5944) 6301[2] 6673[4]
Top Style (IRE) *G A Harker* a44 66
8 ch g Topanoora—Kept In Style (Castle Keep)
599[12] 975[16]
Topsy Maite *R Curtis*
2 b f Komaite(USA) —Noble Soul (Sayf El Arab (USA))
961[13]
Top The Charts *A J Martin* 93
4 b g Singspiel(IRE) —On The Tide (Slip Anchor)
2723[2]
Top Tier *Peter Grayson* a32 52
2 gr f Best Of The Bests(IRE) —Ladycake (IRE) (Perugino (USA))
1030[6] 1499[4] 2375[3] (2922) (3136) 3409[8]4088[5] 4493[4] 5282[12] 5687[9]6258[11] 6945[6]
Top Tiger *M H Tompkins* 73+
2 b c Mtoto—Topatori (IRE) (Topanoora)
5814[4]
Top Trees *W S Kittow* a56 56
8 b g Charnwood Forest(IRE) —Low Line (High Line)
1541[9] 2879[5] 5201[5]
Top Wave (FR) *Mme M Bollack-Badel* 94
3 b f Medaaly—Top Aster (FR) (Assert)
1874a[7]
Tora Petcha (IRE) *R Hollinshead* a44 76
3 b g Bahhare(USA) —Magdalene (FR) (College Chapel)
1349[4] 2163[4] 2642[10] 3008[5] 3303[8]5247[11]
Tora Warning *John A Harris*
2 b c Warningford—Torrecilla (General Monash (USA))
3677[8]
Torgiano (IRE) *P Monteith* 64
5 b g Cadeaux Genereux—Delimara (IRE) (In The Wings)
1032[4] 1343[9] 1635[8] (Dead)
Tornadodancer (IRE) *T G McCourt* a48 60
3 b g Princely Heir(IRE) —Purty Dancer (IRE) (Foxhound (USA))
6286[7]
Torquemada (IRE) *W Jarvis* a69 71+
5 ch g Desert Sun—Gaelic's Fantasy (IRE) (Statoblest)
711[3] 1164[6]1665[3] 2148[16] (2645) 3089[7] 3679[4] 4795[2](5085) 5444[11] 6489[13]
Torrens (IRE) *R A Fahey* a69 88
4 b g Royal Anthem(USA) —Azure Lake (USA) (Lac Ouimet (USA))
1775[13] 2169[4] 2519[5] 4203[5] 4654[2]4911[8] 5367[6] 5792[17]
Torrent *J M Saville* a35 37
11 ch g Prince Sabo—Maiden Pool (Sharpen Up)
90[10] 686[12]1228[7] 1396[9]3245[12] 3635[11] 3833[9] 4546[6] 6969[9]
Torrid Kentavr (USA) *B Ellison* a75 81
9 b g Trempolino(USA) —Torrid Tango (USA) (Green Dancer (USA))
194[7] 3853[5]454[8]
Torver *Dr J D Scargill* a46 53
2 br f Lake Coniston(IRE) —Billie Blue (Ballad Rock)
4105[9] 4572[9] 5112[4] 5419[9] 6416[8]
Tosen Shana O (JPN) *Hideyuki Mori* 112
3 b c Sunday Silence(USA) —Jono Angel (JPN) (Tosho Boy (JPN))
6612a[9]
Toshi (USA) *I Semple* a77 88
4 b g Kingmambo(USA) —Majestic Role (FR) (Theatrical)
2547[2] 2872[3] 3413[15] 4175[8] 4476[8]4726[4] 5406[7] 6241[6]
Toss The Caber (IRE) *K G Reveley* 64
4 ch g Dr Devious(IRE) —Celtic Fling (Lion Cavern (USA))
1045[13] 1436[2] 2193[3] 2927[9] 3763[4]4072[10] 4570[7]
Total Impact *C A Cyzer* a89 92
3 ch g Pivotal—Rise 'n Shine (Night Shift (USA))
540[2] (645) (1020) 1404[5]1924[4] 2866[4] 3414[10]4102[5] 5202[8]
Totally Free *M D I Usher* a52 57
2 ch g Woodborough(USA) —Barefooted Flyer (USA) (Fly So Free (USA))
2572[10] 2967[5] 3246[13]3677[2] 5290[10] 6311[5]6388[7] 6487[6]6789[2] 6807[6](6845) 6951[7]
Totally Scottish *K G Reveley* 49
10 b g Mtoto—Glenfinlass (Lomond (USA))
866[5] 975[4] 1184[4] 3291[5] 5836[3]6011[7]
To The Max (IRE) *R Hannon* 94
2 b c Spectrum(IRE) —Pray (IRE) (Priolo (USA))
(3923) 5715a[9]
To Tiger (GER) *P Monteith* 69
5 b g Tiger Hill(IRE) —The Mood (GER) (Mondrian (GER))
(5338)
Toucantini *R Charlton* a62
2 b f Inchinor—French Quartet (IRE) (Lycius (USA))
6031[2] 6290[8]
Touched By Madness (USA) *E Allard* 105
4 b g Sword Dance(USA) —Marilyn's Madness (USA) (Shananie (USA))
6006a[7]
Touch My Soul (FR) *P Schiergen* 93
2 b f Tiger Hill(IRE) —Topline (GER) (Acatenango (GER))
6122a[2]

Touch Of Ivory (IRE) *P Monteith* 70
3 b f Rossini(USA) —Windomen (IRE) (Forest Wind (USA))
1593[6] 1888[5] 2243[3] (2529) (3167) 3244[4] (3604)4060[2] 4353[2] 4476[7] 6211[7]
Touch Of Land (FR) *H-A Pantall* 123
6 b h Lando(GER) —Touch Of Class (GER) (Be My Guest (USA))
(564a) 742a[8] (3662a) 4386a[8] 5704a[6]
Touch Of Style (IRE) *J R Boyle* 81
2 b g Desert Style(IRE) —No Hard Feelings (IRE) (Alzao (USA))
2579[4] 2960[7]
Tough Love *T D Easterby* 85
7 ch g Pursuit Of Love—Food Of Love (Music Boy)
1220[5] 1494[10] 2299[6] 2681[6] (2737) 2974[11]3191[3] 3500[7] 3549[3] 3789[7] 4153[6]4733[9] 4957[7] 5313[5] 5444[6]
Toupie *C B Greely* 108
4 ch m Intikhab(USA) —Turpitude (Caerleon (USA))
3109a[7]
Tour D'Amour (IRE) *R Craggs* a65 71
3 b f Fruits Of Love(USA) —Touraneena (Robellino (USA))
(651) 1078[3] 1551[3] 1734[2]2735[3] 2977[3] 4567[2] 4733[3] 5024[7]5312[5] 5484[12] 6497[7]
Tournedos (IRE) *R Charlton* 111
4 b h Rossini(USA) —Don't Care (IRE) (Nordico (USA))
1116[9] 3124a[5] (3520) 4080[7] 4855a[5] 5222a[4]5375[9]
Tous Les Deux *Peter Grayson* a82 71
3 b g Efisio—Caerosa (Caerleon (USA))
1208[3] 1411[2] 2014[10]2509[5] 4562[6] 5107[5]5268[9] 5605[7] 5872[11]6419[2] 6503[2]6507[3] (6647) 6684[4] 6734[5]6941[4]
Tower Hill (IRE) *M A Jarvis* a71+ 64
3 b g Grand Lodge(USA) —Champaka (IRE) (Caerleon (USA))
1193[6]
Towerofcharlemagne (IRE) *Miss Gay Kelleway* 71
3 ch c King Charlemagne(USA) —Nozet (Nishapour (FR))
1845[11] 4431[4] 4708[9]
Town House *B P J Baugh* a37 54
4 gr m Paris House—Avondale Girl (IRE) (Case Law)
209[3] 299[5]679[13] 789[10]1228[6] 1466[10]3004[5] 3297[6] 4110[8]
Townsville (IRE) *E J O'Neill* a55 33
4 b g Soviet Star(USA) —Valmarana (USA) (Danzig Connection (USA))
574[14] 6431[0]
Towy Girl (IRE) *I A Wood* a71 50
2 b f Second Empire(IRE) —Solar Flare (IRE) (Danehill (USA))
5828[7] 6073[3] 6486[2]6697[3]
Toy Top (USA) *M Dods* a14 87
3 rg f Tactical Cat(USA) —I'll Flutter By (USA) (Concorde's Tune (USA))
980[2] 1137[2] (1234) 1453[3] 2161[4] 2410[3](3042) (3268) 3568[2] 3636[4] 4422[9] 4659[5] 5532[7]5749[7]
Trace Clip *N I M Rossiter* a68 56
8 b g Zafonic(USA) —Illusory (King's Lake (USA))
1689[4] 1802[11] 1981[8] 2484[3] 2813[10]2962[10] 3438[6] 3728[15]
Tracer *R Hannon* 69
2 b c Kyllachy—Western Sal (Salse (USA))
2710[6] 3222[5] 5915[8]
Trackattack *P Howling* a46 50
4 ch g Atraf—Verbena (IRE) (Don't Forget Me)
92[11] 609[6]636[12] 3591[3]
Trademark (SAF) *A Laird* a78 113
10 b g Goldmark(SAF) —Popular (SAF) (Elliodor (FR))
153a[6] 280a[4] 497a[7] 621a[7]
Traditionalist (IRE) *G A Butler* a56 72
2 ch c Traditionally(USA) —Rouberia (IRE) (Alhaarth (IRE))
4592[5] 5020[8]
Trafalgar Bay (IRE) *S Kirk* 99
3 b g Fruits Of Love(USA) —Chatsworth Bay (IRE) (Fairy King (USA))
1512[3] (2014) 2658[5] 3414[14] 4593[6] 5143[6]5501[5] 5943[10]
Trafalgar Day *W M Brisbourne* 64
3 b g Mark Of Esteem(IRE) —Rosy Sunset (IRE) (Red Sunset)
3065[3] 4150[3] 4884[5]
Trafalgar Square *J Akehurst* 92
4 b h King's Best(USA) —Pat Or Else (Alzao (USA))
946[6] 1262[5] 1667[6] (1957) 2210[4] 2776[7]5523[16]
Traffic Guard (USA) *J S Moore* 98
2 b c More Than Ready(USA) —Street Scene (IRE) (Zafonic (USA))
(3222) (5455) 5965[9]
Trailmix (FR) *D R C Elsworth* a61 67
3 gr g Linamix(FR) —Yield To Maturity (USA) (Conquistador Cielo (USA))
6052[5] 6587[4]
Tralanza (IRE) *P J Prendergast* 77
2 ch f Traditionally(USA) —Alegranza (IRE) (Lake Coniston (IRE))
5464a[14]
Trance (IRE) *T D Barron* a86 88
6 ch g Bahhare(USA) —Lady Of Dreams (IRE) (Prince Rupert (FR))
48[7] 1943[4]491[2] 816[8] 1033[2](1132) 1584[10] 2035[3] 2723[15] 3177[2] 3446[8]4346[6] 4951[4] 5351[2] 5811[3] 5963[5]6205[13]
Tranos (USA) *L M Cumani* a65 68+
3 b c Bahri(USA) —Balancoire (USA) (Diesis)
1274[7] 1641[4] 2063 [6]2990[12] 3725[9] 4245[6]4884[11] 5452[3]
Tranquility *J Pearce* a38 39
2 b f Barathea(IRE) —Immortelle (Arazi (USA))
2638[14] 3201[14] 6669[8]
Tranquilizer *D J Coakley* a82 62
4 b m Dr Fong(USA) —Tranquillity (Night Shift (USA))
109[2] 385[2]628[2] 832[5]5610[12] 6312[3]6479[2] (6941)

Tranquil Tiger *H R A Cecil* 74
2 ch c Selkirk(USA) —Serene View (USA) (Distant View (USA))
5893[6]
Transaction (IRE) *J M P Eustace* a44 73
4 ch g Trans Island—Meranie Girl (IRE) (Mujadil (USA))
22[5] 232[11]402[7] 474[9]
Transcend *J H M Gosden* 80
2 ch c Beat Hollow—Pleasuring (Good Times (ITY))
5918[9] 6220[4]
Trans Gold (IRE) *A Renzoni* 95
2 b f Dushyantor(USA) —Sweetwater Run (USA) (Rahy (USA))
2062a[3] 3343a[3]
Transit *B Ellison* a54 53
7 b g Lion Cavern(USA) —Black Fighter (USA) (Secretariat (USA))
270[4] 570[4]2684[14] 2871[6] 3135[3] 3350[5] 3919[4]4086[4] 4451[7] 4723[6]
Transpique (IRE) *C G Cox* 81
2 b c Trans Island—Repique (USA) (Sharpen Up)
2930[4] 3247[3] 3872[2] 4736[8]
Transponder *W R Muir* a49
3 b g Piccolo—Miletrian Cares (IRE) (Hamas (IRE))
981[11]
Trans Sonic *A P Jarvis* a83 76
3 ch g Trans Island—Sankaty Light (USA) (Summer Squall (USA))
60[2] (539) (848) 1016[11]1115[8] 3473[6] 4029[17] 4488[10] 5107[8]5427[4] 5617[6] 6008[4]6351[6]
Transvestite (IRE) *J W Hills* a93 90
4 b g Trans Island—Christoph's Girl (Efisio)
1133[4] 1544[5] 1992[3] 2519[8] 2918[7]3429[3] (3850) 4112[4] 4448[2] 4876[5] 5346[3]5776[2] 6097[4]6336[5]
Trappeto (IRE) *C Smith* a65 57
4 b h Barathea(IRE) —Campiglia (IRE) (Fairy King (USA))
25[3] (Dead)
Travelling Band (IRE) *J Mackie* a68 91
8 b g Blues Traveller(IRE) —Kind Of Cute (Prince Sabo)
955[9] 1422[15]
Travelling Fox *H Morrison* 42
3 b g Slip Anchor—Lola Mora (Nearly A Hand)
1192[15] 1759[8]
Travel Team (USA) *J-C Rouget* 95
3 b f Danzig(USA) —Lady Upstage (IRE) (Alzao (USA))
4542a[10]
Travolta *C G Cox* a49 60
3 b g Dansili—Generous Diana (Generous (IRE))
880[13] 1139[10] 2352[2] 3017[6]3791[11]
Traytonic *D Nicholls* a93 95
5 b g Botanic(USA) —Lady Parker (IRE) (Nordico (USA))
667[8] 1098[7] 1495[13]1806[11] 3079[11] 3493[18] 4101[10] (4378) 4609[12]4798[6] 5355[11]
Treason Trial *W M Brisbourne* a61 73
5 b g Peintre Celebre(USA) —Pampabella (IRE) (High Estate)
990[13] 5952[9] 6972[9]
Treasure Cay *P W D'Arcy* a96 101
5 ch h Bahamian Bounty—Madame Sisu (Emarati (USA))
433a[12] 627[4] 1116[3]2308a[7] 2799a[2] 3520[8] 4360[7] 5182[6]5433[10] 6095[9]
Treasure House (IRE) *M Blanshard* a92 77
5 b g Grand Lodge(USA) —Royal Wolff (Prince Tenderfoot (USA))
1151[10] 1802[2] 2184[8]2464[4] 2794[3]3101[7] 3459[4]4325[3] 4968[7] 5269[5] (5444)
Treat *M R Channon* 110+
2 b f Barathea(IRE) —Cream Tease (Pursuit Of Love)
2958[12] (5352) 5522[2]
Trebello *J R Boyle* a3 5
5 b g Robellino(USA) —Trempkate (USA) (Trempolino (USA))
(688) 6375[13]
Tredegar *P F I Cole* a87 83
2 ch c Inchinor—Ffestiniog (IRE) (Efisio)
4323[5] 5607[2] (5918) (6379)
Treetops Hotel (IRE) *B R Johnson* a72 59
7 ch g Grand Lodge(USA) —Rousinette (Rousillon (USA))
113[6] (471) 586[6]1244[6] 1400[4]1755[3] 2455[7] 2707[2] 3928[18] (5652) (5910) 6037[4]6748[5]
Tregarron *P A Blockley* a58 72
5 br g Efisio—Language Of Love (Rock City)
35[4] 157[6]251[8] 321[5]461[5] 514[7]586[9] 1201[11]4870[8] 4983[10]
Trepa (USA) *W Jarvis* 70+
2 ch c Hennessy(USA) —Ball Gown (USA) (Silver Hawk (USA))
(5112)
Tres Hombres *Tom Dascombe* a39 52
2 ch g Tobougg(IRE) —Duena (Grand Lodge (USA))
1510[7] 3005[3] 3265[5] 3902[5] 4480[9]6745[5]
Tresor Secret (FR) *J Gallagher* a65 76
6 b g Green Desert(USA) —Tresor (USA) (Pleasant Tap (USA))
6954[11]
Trevian *J M Bradley* a54 61
5 ch g Atraf—Ascend (IRE) (Glint Of Gold)
1882[12] 2135[5] 2286[4] 2482[3] (2789) 3197[4]3298[10] 3820[8] 4363[7] (5450) 6436[5]6577[9]
Trew Flight (USA) *M H Tompkins* a53 44
4 b g Rahy(USA) —Magdala (IRE) (Sadler's Wells (USA))
461[10] 552[10]1058[6] 1293[12] 1373[9]
Trew Style *M H Tompkins* a73 80
4 ch g Desert King(IRE) —Southern Psychic (USA) (Alwasmi (USA))
246[4] 334[6](1213)
Trezene (USA) *D Smaga* 106
4 b h Atticus(USA) —Trevilla (USA) (Lyphard (USA))
(1929a) 6610a[14]

Trials 'n Tribs *C A Cyzer* a47 71?
4 b m Rainbow Quest(USA) —Seasonal Splendour (IRE) (Prince Rupert (FR))
1058[14] 1540[10] 2577[4]3269[2] 4011[8] 4438[6]4898[6] 5201[9] 5847[5]6333[10]
Tribe *Sir Michael Stoute* 76
4 b g Danehill(USA) —Leo Girl (USA) (Seattle Slew (USA))
1206[8] 1651[5] 1821[5] 2357[4]
Tribiani (IRE) *Gerard Cully* 58
2 b f Alzao(USA) —Suzette (Zilzal (USA))
5464a[26]
Tribute (IRE) *John A Harris* a38 74
5 b g Green Desert(USA) —Zooming (IRE) (Indian Ridge)
1611[3] 1878[13] 2550[8] 2780[12] 3390[6]6956[4]
Trick Cyclist *M W Easterby* a62 70
5 b g Mind Games—Sabonis (USA) (The Minstrel (CAN))
798[11] 1102[18] 1297[11] 1528[7] 2505[2]2852[4] 3699[6] 3988[15] 4019[9] 4523[11]5620[3] 5752[2]
Trickey Trevor (USA) *J Hollendorfer* a111
7 bb h Demaloot Demashoot(CAN) —Show Your Pride (USA) (Silver Deputy (CAN))
3134a[9]
Trickle (USA) *Miss D Mountain* a67 61
2 ch f Rahy(USA) —Avitrix (USA) (Storm Bird (CAN))
2328[12] 6199[6] 6377[5]6576[6] 6736[3]6951[2]
Trick Or Treat *J G Given* a100 99
3 b f Lomitas—Trick Of Ace (USA) (Clever Trick (USA))
2246[4] (3244) (3714) (4118) (4528) (4742) 5141[2]5758[2] 5803[2] 6191[6]
Trick's Pic (USA) *P L Biancone* a85 77
3 bb f Favorite Trick(USA) —Nice Pic (USA) (Piccolino (USA))
5984a[11]
Trickstep *D McCain Jnr* a37 37
5 b g Imperial Ballet(IRE) —Trick Of Ace (USA) (Clever Trick (USA))
4227[11] (Dead)
Tricky Venture *Mrs L C Jewell* a69 71
6 gr g Linamix(FR) —Ukraine Venture (Slip Anchor)
73[13] 111[9]659[9] 833[9]4139[11]
Triennale (FR) *Mme C Head-Maarek* 91
3 br f War Chant(USA) —Tresoriere (FR) (Lyphard (USA))
4542a[9]
Triffid *R A Fahey* a58
4 b g Dracula(AUS) —Rockfest (USA) (Stage Door Johnny (USA))
92[8] (Dead)
Trifti *C A Cyzer* a92 60
5 b g Vettori(IRE) —Time For Tea (IRE) (Imperial Frontier (USA))
57[2] 161[11]2226[8] 444[2]542[7] 670[2]828[7] 1111[11]1410[6] 3532[10]3850[5] 4047[5] 4937[4]5258[7] 5739[11] 6502[8]6698[2] 6986[5]
Trim Image *K R Burke* 71
4 br m Averti(IRE) —Altizaf (Zafonic (USA))
5333[17] 5684[20]
Trimlestown (IRE) *H Candy* a61 89
3 b g Orpen(USA) —Courtier (Saddlers' Hall (IRE))
2868[5] 3546[8] 3742[3] (3931) 4689[3] 5042[2](5377) (6221)
Trinculo (IRE) *D Nicholls* a96 99d
9 b g Anita's Prince—Fandangerina (USA) (Grey Dawn II)
6[3] 545[19]81[0] 2449(1076) 1399[2] 1602[13] (1803) 1936[9]3535[3] 3972[21] (4546) (6274) 6399[4]6681[2]
Trinity College (USA) *A P O'Brien* 100
2 ch c Giant's Causeway(USA) —City College (USA) (Carson City (USA))
4825a[4] 5715a[7]
Trinity Rose *M Johnston* a86 71
3 ch f Generous(IRE) —Stylish Rose (IRE) (Don't Forget Me)
1034[2] 1214[4] 2102[4] 6321[7] 6408[4](6495) 6537[2]6655[4]
Triple Bend *Mrs A J Perrett* 55
3 b c Singspiel(IRE) —Triple Green (Green Desert (USA))
2655 [8] (Dead)
Triple Bluff *Mrs A J Perrett* a42 70
3 b c Medicean—Trinity Reef (Bustino)
1994[7] 2412[9] 2815[7] 5152[7] 5479[14]5911[11]
Triple Jump *K A Ryan*
5 ch g Inchinor—Meteoric (High Line)
200[5] 383[11]6067[7] 683[12]
Triple Point (IRE) *J M Plasschaert*
4 b g Perugino(USA) —Quench The Lamp (IRE) (Glow (USA))
6440[10]
Triple Shadow *T D Barron* 73
2 ch g Compton Place—Arctic High (Polar Falcon (USA))
3286[7] (4693) 5404[7] 5681[19]
Triple Zero (IRE) *A P Jarvis* a61 64
4 b m Raise A Grand(IRE) —Locorotondo (IRE) (Broken Hearted)
232[3] 255[3]336[8] 485[5]708[3] 902[7]1341[8]
Trip To The Moon *Y Durepaire* 103
3 b f Fasliyev(USA) —Sparkling Isle (Inchinor) (6328a)
Triskaidekaphobia *Miss J R Tooth* a58 92
3 b g Bertolini(USA) —Seren Teg (Timeless Times (USA))
1604[9] 2168[9] 3503[5] 3744[8] 4102[11]4562[11] 5181[7] 5286[10] 6844[6]6994[7]
Troialini *S W Hall* a83 51
2 b c Bertolini(USA) —Troia (IRE) (Last Tycoon)
5918[10] (6449) 6824[2]
Trojan Flight *D W Chapman* 80
5 ch g Hector Protector(USA) —Fairywings (Kris)
1042[6] 1297[9] 1494[7] 1561[10] 2194[3]2384[3] 2397[5] 2661[14] 3041[11] 3281[7]3374[7] 3789[3] 4119[7] 4230[3] 4831[7](5081) 5749[6] 6160[7]
Trombone Tom *J R Norton* a59 58
3 b g Superior Premium—Nine To Five (Imp Society (USA))
68[3] 646[6]1344[6] 2197[3] 2399[7] 2937[5]3759[3] 4019[3] 4232[5] 5486[9] 5620[15]6276[6]

Tromp *D J Coakley* a79 78
5 ch g Zilzal(USA) —Sulitelma (USA) (The Minstrel (CAN))
125[2] 264[5]556[3] 6148[5]6426[6]
Trompette (USA) *N J Henderson* 81+
4 b m Bahri(USA) —Bold Bold (IRE) (Sadler's Wells (USA))
1800[4] 2067[5]
Troodos Jet *K W Hogg* a25 25
5 b g Atraf—Costa Verde (King Of Spain)
3137[9]
Tropical Climate (USA) *B W Hills* 62
3 b f Lear Fan(USA) —Navarene (USA) (Known Fact (USA))
1088[6] 3266[7]
Tropical Lady (IRE) *J S Bolger* 113
6 b m Sri Pekan(USA) —Tropical Lake (IRE) (Lomond (USA))
1365a[6] 3105a[4] 4212a[9]
Tropical Star (IRE) *A Al Raihe* a116 94
6 b g Machiavellian(USA) —Tropical (Green Desert (USA))
206a[5] (508a) (563a) 740a[7]
Troppo Bello (IRE) *L Polito* 77
2 b f Daggers Drawn(USA) —Cool Chron (Polar Falcon (USA))
5858a[7]
Troque (FR) *F Doumen* 100
2 b g Enrique—The Trollop (FR) (Double Bed (FR))
5801a[5]
Trouble Maker *A M Balding* a58 60
5 b g Green Desert(USA) —River Abouali (Bluebird (USA))
38[2] (177) 339[5]514[3] 854[8]1913[7]
Trouble Mountain (USA) *M W Easterby* a57 80
9 br g Mt. Livermore(USA) —Trouble Free (USA) (Nodouble (USA))
1045[10] 1591[3] (1850) 2097[2] 2162[2] (2387) 3081[3]3566[6] 4203[4] 4570[5] (5685) 5889[2] 6017[4]6301[5]
Trouville (IRE) *Gerard O'Leary* a45 59
7 b m Mukaddamah(USA) —Trouville Lass (IRE) (Be My Native (USA))
5736[8]
Truckle *C W Fairhurst* a70 66
4 b g Vettori(IRE) —Proud Titania (IRE) (Fairy King (USA))
6871[10]
True (IRE) *Mrs S Lamyman* a54 53
5 ch m Barathea(IRE) —Bibliotheque (USA) (Woodman (USA))
94[6] 2398[3] (2832) 3232[12]3944[7] (4227) 4632[3] 5080[4] 5369[5] 5750[4]5927[4] 6161[4] 6553[10]6790[10]
True Cause (USA) *Saeed Bin Suroor* 102
3 ch c Storm Cat(USA) —Dearly (Rahy (USA))
3432[2] 4126[5]
True Companion *N P Littmoden* a83 84
7 b g Brief Truce(USA) —Comanche Companion (Commanche Run)
88[4] 3490[9]4370[4] 5132[3] 5786[8]
True Magic *J D Bethell* a74 75
5 b m Magic Ring(IRE) —True Precision (Presidium)
(588) 954[4] 1448[5] 1686[16]2295[7] 2637[4] 3097[8]3622[2] 3699[2] 3912[8] 4453[4] 4957[15]6508[2] 6773[10]6966[3]
True Night *D Nicholls* a71 77
9 b g Night Shift(USA) —Dead Certain (Absalom)
15[4] 276[13]585[6] 641[10]662[4] 708[2]833[8] 953[5](977) 1124[6] 1341[14] 3718[5] 4090[6] 4194[3]4569[3] 4795[4] 4881[9] 5311[12]
True Ruby *S Kirk* a33 56
3 b f Josr Algarhoud(IRE) —St James's Antigua (IRE) (Law Society (USA))
4004[12]
True To Yourself (USA) *J G Given* a51 37
5 b g Royal Academy(USA) —Romilly (Machiavellian (USA))
91[12] (525) 636[4] (Dead)
True Valentine *A Berry*
3 br f Primo Valentino(IRE) —Prim N Proper (Tragic Role (USA))
870[8] 1791[11] 3290[10]
True West (USA) *Miss Gay Kelleway* a53 68
3 b f Gulch(USA) —True Life (USA) (El Gran Senor (USA))
1418[5] 2028[11] 3336[3] 4336[8] 4673[10]5046[11] 6608[6]6714[5]
Truly Fruitful (IRE) *K R Burke* a71 78
3 ch g Fruits Of Love(USA) —Truly Flattering (Hard Fought)
1005[6] 1403[4]2324[8] 2502[4] 3375[2] 3984[4] 4586[3]4784[7] 5599[5]
Truly Genuine (IRE) *K A Ryan*
2 ch f Hernando(FR) —Truly Generous (IRE) (Generous (IRE))
6832[5]
Truly Royal *Saeed Bin Suroor* 91+
2 b c Noverre(USA) —Her Ladyship (Polish Precedent (USA))
(5915)
Truman *John A Harris* a60 64
5 b g Entrepreneur—Sabria (USA) (Miswaki (USA))
3115[P] (Dead)
Trump Call (IRE) *R M Beckett* a70
2 b c Mull Of Kintyre(USA) —Trumped (IRE) (Last Tycoon)
6591[3] 6867[7]
Trumpita *T D Easterby* 49
3 b g Bertolini(USA) —Trump Street (First Trump)
716[2] 978[10] 1126[7] 1593[9] 3167[10]3538[8] 4199[14] (4656) 5631[5] 5834[10]
Trumps (IRE) *M Blanshard*
2 ch c Raise A Grand(IRE) —Manuka Too (IRE) (First Trump)
2506[14]
Trusted Mole (IRE) *W M Brisbourne* a57 65
8 b g Eagle Eyed(USA) —Orient Air (Prince Sabo)
4439[12] 5072[11]

Trym (SWE) *B Olsen*
3 b c Lorofino(NOR) —Star Speeder (IRE) (Nomination)
4919a[6]

Trysting Grove (IRE) *E G Bevan* a36 36
5 b m Cape Cross(IRE) —Elton Grove (IRE) (Astronef)
871[2] 2345[12]5925[7] 6280[13]

Tsaroxy (IRE) *J Howard Johnson* 86
4 b g Xaar—Belsay (Belmez (USA))
2364[3] 2810[6] 4153[10] 4911[4] 5396a[6]

Tschaikowskij (GER) *W Kujath* 77
3 b c Dashing Blade—Trikolore (GER) (Konigsstuhl (GER))
1526a[7]

Tsini *Patrick J Flynn* 32
3 b f Alhaarth(IRE) —Susquehanna Days (USA) (Chief's Crown (USA))
4034a[13]

Tsurugaoka Hayate (JPN) *M Ito* 96
6 b g Air Dublin(JPN) —Air Passion (USA) (Halo (USA))
6850a[16]

Tucker *W R Swinburn* 109
4 b g Inchinor—Tender Moment (IRE) (Caerleon (USA))
1084[5] 1806[8] 2435[3] 2742[18] 4348[2]5177[2] 5808[8]

Tuckerman *F J Bowles* a46 75
5 b g Gulch(USA) —Remuria (USA) (Theatrical)
173[11]

Tuckers Point (IRE) *J A Osborne* a56 67
3 b f Mujadil(USA) —Romanovna (Mummy's Pet)
195[4] 291[5]415[3]

Tudor Bell (IRE) *J G M O'Shea* 89
5 b g Definite Article—Late Night Lady (IRE) (Mujadil (USA))
1987[3] 4001[9] 4764[9] 5069[P]

Tudor Prince (IRE) *B J Meehan* a89 92
2 bb c Cape Cross(IRE) —Savona (IRE) (Cyrano De Bergerac)
1838[8] 2029[3] 2719[20] 3210[2] *3641[2]4323[2]* (4801) 5655[6]

Tullochrome *E J O'Neill* a51 31
3 b f Foxhound(USA) —Choire Mhor (Dominion)
904[4] 1073[8] *1259[13]*

Tullyorior Promise (IRE) *Emmanuel Hughes* 69
3 b g Imperial Ballet(IRE) —Selkirk Flyer (Selkirk (USA))
4124a[13]

Tullythered (IRE) *A Berry*
2 ch c Docksider(USA) —Marjie (IRE) (Desert Style (IRE))
1982[8] 4171[12]

Tumbelini *C F Wall* 39
2 b f Pivotal—Kundalini (USA) (El Gran Senor (USA))
5592[12]

Tumble Jill (IRE) *J J Bridger* a51 55
2 b f Dilshaan—Jack-N-Jilly (IRE) (Anita's Prince)
2432[10] 2588[2] 2870[5] 3279[3] 3613[5]5344[13] 5730[12] *5780[9]6032[8] 6576[5]6853[3]*

Tumbleweed Glory (IRE) *B J Meehan* a87 84
3 b g Marju(IRE) —Tathkara (USA) (Alydar (USA))
1108[5] 1270[3] 1951[10]2654[5] 3008[2] *(3404)* 3889[6]4209[4]

Tumblin Rosie *M Blanshard* a47 13
2 ch f Tumbleweed Ridge—Myhat (Factual (USA))
2166[15] *6562[5] 6710[5]*

Tumby Lawn (USA) *E A L Dunlop* 66
2 ch g Rahy(USA) —Dharma (USA) (Zilzal (USA))
3976[9]

Tumpuluna (IRE) *G Prodromou* 60
3 b f Marju(IRE) —Tarhhib (Danzig (USA))
4142[3] 5093[9] 5761[U]

Tunduru (IRE) *R Martin-Sanchez* 108
5 ch h Croco Rouge(IRE) —Spring Daffodil (Pharly (FR))
1332a[5] 6786a[9]

Tune Up The Band *R J Hodges* 66
2 b c Bandmaster(USA) —Name That Tune (Fayruz)
961[3]

Tungsten Strike (USA) *Mrs A J Perrett* 120
5 ch g Smart Strike(CAN) —Bathilde (IRE) (Generous (IRE))
1409[2] (2085) 2773[8] 4081[3] 4677[7] 5156[7]

Tuning Fork *T M Jones* a47 64
6 b g Alzao(USA) —Tuning (Rainbow Quest (USA))
1353[2] 2148[2] 2401[7] 2969[5] 3339[10]3933[17] 5267[13]

Turcci (FR) *R Avial Lopez* 87
3 b c Vettori(IRE) —Neriella (Darshaan)
1600a[8]

Turibius *T E Powell* a62 64
7 b g Puissance—Compact Disc (IRE) (Royal Academy (USA))
136[7] 4675[7] 4962[13](5576) *6395[6] 6513[4]6688[4] 6913[5]*

Turkish Sultan (IRE) *T D Easterby* 76
3 b g Anabaa(USA) —Odalisque (IRE) (Machiavellian (USA))
3909[2] 5023[2] 5077[5] 5761[3] 5953[7]

Turkus Quercus (USA) *J L Dunlop* 77
2 rg f Tactical Cat(USA) —Antipodes (USA) (Pleasant Colony (USA))
2354[2]

Turn Around *J Pearce* a77 58
6 b g Pivotal—Bemuse (Forzando)
3459[9] 3996[11]4735[16] 5248[12]

Turner *W M Brisbourne* a63 67
5 gr g El Prado(IRE) —Gaily Royal (IRE) (Royal Academy (USA))
1308[11] 1769[13] 2522[5]2902[9] 3114[5] 3522[4] 3983[7] 4175[10]4764[6] 4898[5] 5385[12] 5836[4]

Turner's Touch *G L Moore* a79 49
4 ch g Compton Place—Chairmans Daughter (Unfuwain (USA))
363[3] (462) (696) 965[6] *(1163) 1958[4] 6408[6]6566[11] (6748) 6885[2]*

Turning Light (GER) *Mario Hofer* 108
3 b f Fantastic Light(USA) —Turning Leaf (IRE) (Last Tycoon)
1714a[6] 2694a[10] (6366a)

Turnkey *M R Channon* 106
4 br g Pivotal—Persian Air (Persian Bold)
930a[3] 1469a[10] 1979[2]

Turn Me On (IRE) *M L W Bell* a60+ 74
3 b g Tagula(IRE) —Jacobina (Magic Ring (IRE))
2575[7] 3611[4] 3867[3]4201[5]

Turn 'n Burn *C A Cyzer* a73 71
5 b g Unfuwain(USA) —Seasonal Splendour (IRE) (Prince Rupert (FR))
5295[7] *5786[5] 6075[3]6566[4] 6602[3]6831[7]*

Turn Of Phrase (IRE) *B Ellison* a67 67
7 b g Cadeaux Genereux—Token Gesture (IRE) (Alzao (USA))
4472[9] 4947[3] (5064) *5390[3]5484[2]* 5904[7]

Turn On The Style *J Balding* a75 83
4 ch g Pivotal—Elegant Rose (Noalto)
5842[6] 6428[6]6496[7]

Turtle Bowl (IRE) *F Rohaut* a113 113
4 b h Dyhim Diamond(IRE) —Clara Bow (FR) (Top Ville)
1873a[7] 2490a[2]

Turtle Magic (IRE) *Miss J S Davis* a1 39
4 b m Turtle Island(IRE) —Theda (Mummy's Pet)
360[12] 534[8]

Turtle Soup (IRE) *T R George* 76
10 b g Turtle Island(IRE) —Lisa's Favourite (Gorytus (USA))
866[2]

Tuscan Flyer *R Bastiman* a51 52
8 b g Clantime—Excavator Lady (Most Secret)
1196[13] 1577[8]1914[9] 2785[6] 3617[2]4157[10] (4278) *6796[12] 6892[13]*

Tuscan Treaty *P J McBride* a49 66
6 b m Brief Truce(USA) —Fiorenz (USA) (Chromite (USA))
42[7] 311[4]395[3] 582[5]771[4] 888[9]1197[2] 1395[8]

Tuscany Queen (IRE) *R Hannon* a60 51
3 b f Titus Livius(FR) —Queen Molly (Emarati (USA))
692[5] 1263[7] 1433[7]1799[5] 1899[9] *(2573) 3410[10]4329[10]*

Tuscany Rose *W R Muir* a47 47
3 ch f Medicean—Rosewood Belle (USA) (Woodman (USA))
2480[10] 2877[9] 3839[5] 4239[5] *4435[3]4981[4]* (5365) 5618[8]

Tuscarora (IRE) *A W Carroll* a72 65
7 b m Revoque(IRE) —Fresh Look (IRE) (Alzao (USA))
17[8] (171) 332[7]4511[1] 3197[5] 3897[4]4286[2] (4627) 5130[8] 5572[7] *6227[8]6483[7] 6573[9]6767[5]*

Tusculum (IRE) *A P O'Brien* 113
3 b c Sadler's Wells(USA) —Turbaine (USA) (Trempolino (USA))
(4822a) 5185[5]

Tu Sei Romantica (IRE) *K A Ryan* a22
2 b f Agnes World(USA) —Akamantis (Kris)
2565a[6] *3457[11] 6663[8]*

Tuxedomoon (GER) *Frau Jutta Mayer* 69
5 b g Waky Nao—Tiputip (GER) (Nebos (GER))
6252a[6]

Twardowska (ITY) *F Losani* 105
3 gr f Daylami(IRE) —Todeschina (Sure Blade (USA))
2694a[2]

Twentyfirst Dansar *A D Smith* a57 42
3 b g Zahran(IRE) —Joker's Luck (Desert Splendour)
241[8] 1352[12] 1799[9]

Twenty Percent *P R Chamings*
2 ch g Auction House(USA) —Truly Madly Deeply (Most Welcome)
4525[14]

Twentytwosilver (IRE) *D B Feek* a54 46
6 rg g Emarati(USA) —St Louis Lady (Absalom)
309[2] 5917[6]84[2] 767[3]891[3] 1540[3](1729) 2577[10]3616[9]

Twilight Avenger (IRE) *W M Brisbourne* a56 59
3 b g Dr Fong(USA) —Asterita (Rainbow Quest (USA))
30[4] 53[8]99[3] 139[9]211[4] 287[4]347[4] 418[4]500[5] 577[8]594[11] 2198[12] 3609[4]4060[3] 4255[6] 4892[7]

Twilight Dawn *M Johnston* 34
2 ch f Muhtarram(USA) —Indigo Dawn (Rainbow Quest (USA))
5014[5] 5596[10]

Twill (IRE) *H Morrison* a80 84
3 ch g Barathea(IRE) —Khafaya (Unfuwain (USA))
895[4] 1781[11] 2584[12] 3877[2] 4459[7]4792[7] (5180) 5582[4] 5811[9]

Twindego *T D Barron* 66
3 b g Komaite(USA) —On The Wagon (Then Again)
1097[10]

Twinned (IRE) *Karen George* a58 46
3 ch g Soviet Star(USA) —Identical (IRE) (Machiavellian (USA))
(1003) 1304[6] 1937[4]2187[9] 3155[9] 3595[4]3863[5] 4756[6] *6234[6](6399) 6615[8]6686[4] 6723[7]6994[9]*

Twist Bookie (IRE) *S Lycett* a57 41
6 br g Perugino(USA) —Twist Scarlett (GER) (Lagunas)
4176[9] 4845[14] *6705[3]6790[3] (6936)*

Twitch Hill *H Candy* 60
2 ch f Piccolo—Whittle Woods Girl (Emarati (USA))
4986[2] 5264[5] 5950[4]

Two Acres (IRE) *A G Newcombe* a35 59+
3 b g Danetime(IRE) —Raise-A-Secret (IRE) (Classic Secret (USA))
844[10] 1218[12] 1646[7](3821) 4756[7]

Two Chimneys (USA) *K A Ryan* a54 50
4 b m Deputy Commander(USA) —Take Heart (USA) (Secretariat (USA))
91[9]

Two Dreamers *A Crook* 41
2 ch f Best Of The Bests(IRE) —Mossy Rose (King Of Spain)
5237[12] 5536[8]

Two Sips Sue *P D Evans* 49
2 b f Zamindar(USA) —Miss Waterline (Rock City)
1796[11] 2382[2]

Tybalt (USA) *J H M Gosden* a88 89
2 b c Storm Cat(USA) —Tuzla (FR) (Panoramic)
5458[2] *(5906)*

Tycheros *S C Williams* a65 50
4 b g Polar Falcon(USA) —Marie De Flandre (FR) (Crystal Palace (FR))
55[2] (482) (545) 832[2]866[8] 3935[10]

Tycoon Hall (IRE) *P Bowen* 65
6 ch h Halling(USA) —Tycooness (IRE) (Last Tycoon)
3256[9] 4175[9]

Tycoon's Hill (IRE) *Robert Collet* 111
7 b g Danehill(USA) —Tycoon's Drama (IRE) (Last Tycoon)
1717a[6] 2276a[7] (2799a) 3564a[3] 4191a[17] 4860a[7]5222a[7] 5779a[3] 6547a[11]

Tykie Two *E J O'Neill* 43
2 ch f Primo Valentino(IRE) —Tycoon's Last (Nalchik (USA))
5231[8]

Typhoon Ginger (IRE) *G Woodward* 70
11 ch m Archway(IRE) —Pallas Viking (Viking (USA))
1864[10] 2627[10] 2891[9] 3115[8] 3762[11]3883[9] (4405) 4733[5] 5024[5] 5320[3] 5354[9]

Typhoon Tilly *C R Egerton* a73 72
9 b g Hernando(FR) —Meavy (Kalaglow)
48[11]

Tyreless Endeavour (IRE) *Peter Casey* 71
2 b g Mull Of Kintyre(USA) —Rebecca's Girl (IRE) (Nashamaa)
4824a[14]

Tyrone Lady (IRE) *J J Quinn* 5
3 b f Key Of Luck(USA) —Kutaisi (IRE) (Soviet Star (USA))
4613[12]

Tyrone Sam *K A Ryan* a72 72
4 b g Mind Games—Crystal Sand (GER) (Forzando)
164[4] 276[9]639[9] 737[6]762[9] 6897[11]

Tyson (SAF) *M F De Kock* 118
6 b g Silvino(USA) —Telle Belle (SAF) (Sledgehammer (NZ))
(208a) (370a) 564a[5] 742a[10]

Tyspane *S Kirk* 5
3 bb f Zilzal(USA) —Simply Sooty (Absalom)
2188[15]

Tyzack (IRE) *Stef Liddiard* a90 89
5 b g Fasliyev(USA) —Rabea (USA) (Devil's Bag (USA))
(606) (650) (860) (1257) 1985[7] 2440[2] 2900[4] 3413[12]3928[17]

Uace Mac *N Bycroft* 27
2 b f Compton Place—Umbrian Gold (IRE) (Perugino (USA))
4196[9]

U D Ghetto (USA) *A Reinstedler* a105
2 b g Honour And Glory(USA) —Legend Of Seattle (USA) (Silver Hawk (USA))
6339a[7]

Ugenius *R A Harris* a36
2 b c Killer Instinct—I'm Sophie (IRE) (Shalford (IRE))
6640[4] 6768[8]6996[8]

Ugo Fire (IRE) *Kevin Prendergast* 110
3 b f Bluebird(USA) —Quiet Mouse (USA) (Quiet American (USA))
1023a[3] 2054a[11] 3322a[5] 4749a[3] 5191a[6]5411a[6] 5708a[2] (5849a) 6356a[2]

Uhoomagoo *K A Ryan* a99 106
8 b g Namaqualand(USA) —Point Of Law (Law Society (USA))
516[7] 667[7]1111[5] 1495[9] 2200[16](2776) 3926[2] 4187a[4] *5019[15]*

Uhuru Peak *M W Easterby* a61 62
5 ch g Bal Harbour—Catherines Well (Junius (USA))
1253[3] 1353[14] 1665[9] 2541[9] 3298[7]3697[4] (4194) 5354[5] *6383[2]6532[4] 6810[4]6980[8]*

Uig *H S Howe* a68 78
5 ch m Bien Bien(USA) —Madam Zando (Forzando)
660[7] 1162[5]1638[7] 2067[6] 3703[8]4040[11]

Ullah Pendragon (IRE) *A J McCabe* a51 44
3 gr g Beckett(IRE) —Marathon Maid (Kalaglow)
61[6] 181[11]548[9] 5955[13] *6617[11]*

Ulshaw *J M Bradley* a50 44
9 ch g Salse(USA) —Kintail (Kris)
794[6] 1313[3] *1540[8]2075[8]* 2481[4] 3616[7] 4981[6] *5846[9]6584[6] 6754[10]6795[3]*

Uluru (IRE) *A P O'Brien* 64
2 ch f Rock Of Gibraltar(IRE) —Dajarra (IRE) (Blushing Groom (FR))
6113a[8] 6357a[10]

Ulysees (IRE) *I Semple* a51 67
7 b g Turtle Island(IRE) —Tamasriya (IRE) (Doyoun)
1459[4] (1637) 1885[4] (2240) (2546) 2853[6] 3168 6348[4]4137[6] 4475[5] 5553[3] 5579[4]5904[4] 6209[5] 6317[7] *6405[7]*

Uma King (AUS) *Mick Price* 91
6 ch g Umatilla(NZ) —Suspicious Minds (NZ) (Le Grand Seigneur (CAN))
5817a[9]

Umlilo *Mrs A J Perrett* 59
4 b m Mtoto—Ingozi (Warning)
2186[12] 2729[4] 3036[5]

Umpa Loompa (IRE) *D Nicholls* 61
2 ch c Indian Lodge(IRE) —Bold Fashion (FR) (Nashwan (USA))
1595[7] 2523[7] 4129[16] 5615[5]

Umthoulah (IRE) *K R Burke* 75
4 br m Unfuwain(USA) —Susquehanna Days (USA) (Chief's Crown (USA))
1804[7]

Unasuming (IRE) *J Pearce* a53 58d
3 b f Orpen(USA) —Untold (Final Straw)
49[10] (1652) 2352[8] 2529[17]6068[11] *6509[9] 6705[10]*

Unbridled Belle (USA) *T Pletcher* a94
3 b f Broken Vow(USA) —Little Bold Belle (USA) (Silver Buck (USA))
3757a[6]

Unbridled Storm (IRE) *G A Swinbank* 58
3 b g Aljabr(USA) —Afkaar (USA) (Unbridled (USA))
2111[6]

Uncle Max (IRE) *N A Twiston-Davies* a30 22
6 b g Victory Note(USA) —Sunset Park (IRE) (Red Sunset)
1566[8] *1745[12]*

Under Fire (IRE) *A W Carroll* a56 59
3 b g Lear Spear(USA) —Kahyasi Moll (IRE) (Brief Truce (USA))
364[9] 1352[14] 2069[7]2877[4] 3221[11] 3538[9] 3839[4] 4050[4](4757) (5936) *6436[7] 6787[5]6897[7]*

Underscore (USA) *R A Harris* a78 87
4 ch g Spinning World(USA) —Speed Dialer (USA) (Phone Trick (USA))
2169[15] 2705[4] 2900[6] 3664[7] *3914[3]4437[10]* 5205[10]

Underthemistletoe (IRE) *R E Barr* a35 46
4 b m Lujain(USA) —Christmas Kiss (Taufan (USA))
1733[7] 2019[11] 2377[3] 2758[10] 3039[5]3524[12] 3635[4] 3835[10] 5023[7]

Under The Rainbow *P W Chapple-Hyam* 104+
3 gr f Fantastic Light(USA) —Farfala (FR) (Linamix (FR))
1509[6] 5502[5] 5803[5] 6333[3] 6722a[6]

Undertone (IRE) *C E Brittain* 79
2 ch f Noverre(USA) —Shadow Roll (IRE) (Mark Of Esteem (IRE))
(6055)

Undeterred *K J Burke* a80 84
10 ch g Zafonic(USA) —Mint Crisp (IRE) (Green Desert (USA))
212[3] 295[9]323[4] 451[7]602[4] 726[21] *(1001)* 1302[2] *1673[16]* 1739[4] 2180[3] 3854[6]3948[2] (4206) 5506[10] *5671[8]*

Une Pivoine (FR) *J E Pease* 104
2 b f Pivotal—Motzki (FR) (Le Glorieux)
6609a[2]

Unfurl The Flag (USA) *D Bernstein* a119
6 b g Bertrando(USA) —Escape The Storm (USA) (Storm Cat (USA))
3134a[3]

Unicorn Reward (IRE) *Mrs L C Jewell* a58 77
6 b h Turtle Island(IRE) —Kingdom Pearl (Statoblest)
4094a[5] *5786[12] 6240[8]6497[14] 6743[9]*

Unification (CAN) *I Mohammed* a94
3 bb c Dixie Union(USA) —Devil's Orchid (USA) (Devil's Bag (USA))
368a[7] 561a[3]739a[13]

Union Jack Jackson (IRE) *J G Given* a56 63
4 b g Daggers Drawn(USA) —Beechwood Quest (IRE) (River Falls)
101[11] 200[11]383[12] 618[6]691[2] 876[2](942) 1196[5](1577) 1764[7]3171[3] 3996[9] 6622[9]6787[13] 6974[3]

Unique Moment *D J S Ffrench Davis* 75
3 ch f Vettori(IRE) —Lonesome (Night Shift (USA))
(979) 1079[4] 1837[8] 2507[3] (2548) (2944) 3974[8]4118[7] 5324[15]

United Nations *N Wilson* a81 77
5 ch g Halling(USA) —Congress (IRE) (Dancing Brave (USA))
*3688[3] 3918[5]*4301[2] 4733[2] *(5249)* 5689[6]5810[17]

United Spirit (IRE) *Jedd O'Keeffe* a71 65
5 b m Fasliyev(USA) —Atlantic Desire (IRE) (Ela-Mana-Mou)
3527[4]

Unleash (USA) *P J Hobbs* a79 105
7 ch g Benny The Dip(USA) —Lemhi Go (USA) (Lemhi Gold (USA))
3533[13]

Unlimited *R Simpson* a67 67
4 b g Bold Edge—Cabcharge Blue (Midyan (USA))
1102[11] *1388[5]* 1504[9]1794[7] 2027[8] 2396[8] 2748[2] 2785[4]4870[2] 5130[6] 5269[4] *5987[4]6193[4]*

Unlock (IRE) *D K Weld* 81
2 b f Key Of Luck(USA) —Lock's Heath (CAN) (Topsider (USA))
3658a[5] 5464a[15]

Uno *B W Hills* a83 80
3 b f Efisio—Glen Falls (Commanche Run)
1085[6] 2034[2] 2868[3] 4113[2] 4899[2](5138) 5512[5] *5739[3]*

Unprecedented (IRE) *T T Clement* a35 40
5 br g Primo Dominie—Misellina (FR) (Polish Precedent (USA))
179[11] 266[6]449[6] 1727[14]4575[14]

Unquenchable (USA) *Saeed Bin Suroor* a64
3 b f Kingmambo(USA) —First Night (IRE) (Sadler's Wells (USA))
6459[7]

Unreachable Star *Mrs A J Perrett* 65
2 ch f Halling(USA) —Spinning The Yarn (Barathea (IRE))
4964[7]

Unrestricted *C F Wall* a61 58
4 ch m Mark Of Esteem(IRE) —Generous Lady (Generous (IRE))
115[3] 263[13]462[3] 586[7]6383[7]

Unshakable (IRE) *Bob Jones* 99
7 b g Eagle Eyed(USA) —Pepper And Salt (IRE) (Double Schwartz)
2742[17] 4535[6] 4782[3] 5177[7] 5520[7]5789[6] 6219[8]

Unsuited *J E Long* a43 63
7 b m Revoque(IRE) —Nagnagnag (IRE) (Red Sunset)
1850[13] 5769[13]

Until When (USA) *B Smart* a67 73
2 b g Grand Slam(USA) —Chez Cherie (Wolfhound (USA))
4018[9] 4843[4] 5481[3] 5900[4] *6525[4]*

Up At Dawn *C F Wall* a38 49
3 b f Inchinor—Up And About (Barathea (IRE))
4661[10] *6128[9]*

Up In Arms (IRE) *P Winkworth* 75
2 b c Daggers Drawn(USA) —Queenliness (Exit To Nowhere (USA))
2172[11] 3193[7] 3726[2] 4688[4] 5125[8]5585[9]

Upper Hand *M R Channon* 109
3 ch c Mark Of Esteem(IRE) —Pelagia (IRE) (Lycius (USA))
1094^{4} (1358) 1776^{3} 2774^{3}

Up Tempo (IRE) *C R Dore* a78 72
8 b g Flying Spur(AUS) —Musical Essence (Song)
345^{2} (501) 639^{8}674^{2} 732^{2}864^{8} (1054) (1341) (1570) 1993^{3} 3012^{7}3536^{2} 3845^{2}4831^{13} 5263^{7} 5961^{13}6174^{6} 6273^{6} 6413^{5}6568^{7} 6820^{8}

Upthedowns (IRE) *T D Barron* a51 63
3 b g Beckett(IRE) —Golden Charm (IRE) (Common Grounds)
197^{9}

Up The Pole *M W Easterby* a46+ 53
2 ch f Polish Precedent(USA) —Arletty (Rainbow Quest (USA))
2106^{8} 2461^{7} 2733^{12}3619^{5} 6760^{9} 6859^{7}

Uptown Rosie (IRE) *John Monroe* a32
3 ch f Desert Sun—Downtown Rosie (IRE) (Good Thyne (USA))
6901^{9}

Urban Calm *J W Unett* a40 60
5 b m Cadeaux Genereux—Silver Sun (Green Desert (USA))
402^{9} 6542^{8}

Urban Freeway (IRE) *Robert Gray* 39
7 b g Dr Devious(IRE) —Coupe D'Hebe (Ile De Bourbon (USA))
4511^{13} 5369^{12} 5750^{13} 5836^{11}

Urban Rose *J W Unett* a52 59
5 b m Piccolo—Blue Lamp (USA) (Shadeed (USA))
38^{9}

Urban Spirit *B W Hills* 89
2 b c Dansili—Tenuous (Generous (IRE))
5658^{2}

Urban Tiger (GER) *A King* 89
3 b g Marju(IRE) —Ukraine Venture (Slip Anchor)
1190^{6} 1476^{8} 2332^{3} (2622) 3366^{3} (4160)

Urban Warrior *Mrs Norma Pook* a69 67
2 b g Zilzal(USA) —Perfect Poppy (Shareef Dancer (USA))
707^{2} 760^{2}856^{2} (968) 1066^{5} 1998^{4}2084^{4} 3496^{12} 3727^{4} 3997^{8}5053^{6} 5176^{7} 5382^{3} 5585^{10} 5989^{6}

Urbe Condita (IRE) *T J Etherington* 92+
3 b g Titus Livius(FR) —Kayanga (Green Desert (USA))
1437^{2} (2356) (3479)

Urgente *L Brogi* 106
4 b h Halling(USA) —Persian Filly (IRE) (Persian Bold)
1870a^{3}

Ursis (FR) *Jonjo O'Neill* 80
5 b g Trempolino(USA) —Bold Virgin (USA) (Sadler's Wells (USA))
6336^{10}

Useful *A W Carroll* a48 54+
3 ch f Nashwan(USA) —Tarf (USA) (Diesis)
2673^{10} 2985^{8} 3975^{8} 5210^{7}6765^{6}

Usk Melody *B J Meehan* a75 67
2 ch f Singspiel(IRE) —One Of The Family (Alzao (USA))
4373^{7} 5095^{3} 6242^{3}

Usk Poppy *D R C Elsworth* a52 84
3 b f Mark Of Esteem(IRE) —Wars (IRE) (Green Desert (USA))
1845^{2} 2406^{3} (2985) 3548^{2} 4375^{3} 4837^{9}

Utmost Respect *R A Fahey* 88+
2 b c Danetime(IRE) —Utmost (IRE) (Most Welcome)
(4986) (5334)

Utopia (JPN) *K Hashiguchi* a120 119
6 ch h Forty Niner(USA) —Dream Vision (JPN) (Northern Taste (CAN))
(738a)

Utterly Heaven (IRE) *D K Weld* 102
4 b m Danehill(USA) —Epicure's Garden (USA) (Affirmed (USA))
753a^{2} 1026a^{6} 3322a^{7}

Uva Fragola *J S Bolger* 90
3 ch f Nashwan(USA) —Revival (Sadler's Wells (USA))
3128a^{9}

Vacare (USA) *C Block* 113
3 b f Lear Fan(USA) —Appealing Storm (USA) (Valid Appeal (USA))
(5984a)

Vacation (IRE) *V Smith* a95+ 80
3 b c King Charlemagne(USA) —Lady Peculiar (CAN) (Sunshine Forever (USA))
215^{3} 1844^{5} 2126^{5}4802^{9} 5761^{5} 6054^{3} 6206^{3} (6327) 6607^{2} (6671) 6868^{3} 6997^{2}

Vadapolina (FR) *A Fabre* 98
2 ch f Trempolino(USA) —Vadaza (FR) (Zafonic (USA))
6046a^{4}

Vadinka *N Tinkler* a73 73
2 b c Averti(IRE) —Inchalong (Inchinor)
1770^{4} 2315^{5} 2726^{5} 3641^{6}4246^{2} 5262^{3}5606^{2} 5871^{3} 6388^{2}6504^{7} 6710^{3}6815^{2} 6925^{3}

Vague (USA) *J Noseda* a104 104
3 b f Elusive Quality(USA) —April In Kentucky (USA) (Palace Music (USA))
(202a) (436a) 2802^{7} 3757a^{9} 5984a^{7}

Vague Star (ITY) *R Ingram* a68d 74
4 b h Soviet Star(USA) —Simova (USA) (Vaguely Noble)
317^{10} 858^{3}1414^{15} 1899^{8} 2173^{8}

Valance (IRE) *C R Egerton* a89 88
6 br g Bahhare(USA) —Glowlamp (IRE) (Glow (USA))
1021^{2} 2437^{11} 4231^{4}(4935) 6655^{2}

Valart *Ms J S Doyle* a57 66
3 ch f Bien Bien(USA) —Riverine (Risk Me (FR))
3029^{5} 3849^{3} 4625^{4} 5056^{2} 5566^{5}6601^{7}

Valbenny (IRE) *G A Swinbank* 67
2 b f Val Royal(FR) —Dark Indian (IRE) (Indian Ridge)
2281^{6} 2806^{2} (3809)

Valdan (IRE) *P D Evans* 92
2 b g Val Royal(FR) —Danedrop (IRE) (Danehill (USA))
3247^{4} (3958) 4561^{7} 5140^{2}

Val De Maal (IRE) *Miss J A Camacho* a65 65
6 ch g Eagle Eyed(USA) —Miss Bojangles (Gay Fandango (USA))
862^{5} 1645^{13} 2792^{12}3052^{3} 3245^{7} 4067^{2}4401^{14} 4970^{5} 6288^{4}6556^{6} 6719^{13}6922^{6}

Valdemosa *B I Case* 64
3 ch f Mark Of Esteem(IRE) —Valagalore (Generous (IRE))
1901^{4} 2673^{8} 4701^{9}

Val D'Ham (FR) *F Forneron*
2 b c Hamas(IRE) —Vallee D'Aube (FR) (Baillamont (USA))
6528a^{4}

Vale De Lobo *B R Millman* a78 77
4 b m Loup Sauvage(USA) —Frog (Akarad (FR))
(3068) 4528^{5} 5016^{3} 5295^{6}6017^{9} 6432^{11}

Valeesha *W G M Turner* a38 49
2 b f Erhaab(USA) —Miss Laetitia (IRE) (Entitled)
4238^{3} 4552^{11} 5209^{8}

Valentina Guest (IRE) *Peter Casey* 97
5 b m Be My Guest(USA) —Karamiyna (IRE) (Shernazar)
1324a^{3} 2154a^{6} 3964a^{5} 4741^{7} 5996a^{15}

Valentine's Pet *A W Carroll* a31 65
6 b m My Best Valentine—Fabulous Pet (Somethingfabulous (USA))
26^{7}

Valentino (FR) *A De Royer-Dupre* 116
7 b g Valanour(IRE) —Rotina (FR) (Crystal Glitters (USA))
1371a^{4}

Valentino Swing (IRE) *J L Spearing* a74 74
3 ch g Titus Livius(FR) —Farmers Swing (IRE) (River Falls)
1208^{17} 2353^{4} 2609^{8} 2931^{2} 3226^{10}3795^{5} 3943^{8} 4143^{3} 4496^{9} 5036^{4}5568^{5} (5953) 6239^{8} 6417^{4}6489^{11}

Valentino Taffi *S C Williams* a60
3 b g Primo Valentino(IRE) —Drudwen (Sayf El Arab (USA))
70^{5} 439^{7}594^{12} 1140^{13} 1661^{10}

Vale Of Belvoir (IRE) *K R Burke* 97
2 b f Mull Of Kintyre(USA) —Sunrise (IRE) (Sri Pekan (USA))
2100^{2} (2394) (3476) (4152) 4594^{2}

Valerie *L M Cumani* a60 55
3 b f Sadler's Wells(USA) —Horatia (IRE) (Machiavellian (USA))
1417^{7} 2209^{5} 2592^{5}

Valerius (IRE) *David P Myerscough* 61
2 b c Galileo(IRE) —Rainbow Dream (Rainbow Quest (USA))
5662a^{8}

Valery Borzov (IRE) *D Nicholls* 68
2 b c Iron Mask(USA) —Fay's Song (IRE) (Fayruz)
(6157)

Valet *J G M O'Shea* 15
4 b g Kayf Tara—Val De Fleurie (GER) (Mondrian (GER))
1540^{13} 1766^{10}

Valeureux *J Hetherton* a54 60
8 ch g Cadeaux Genereux—La Strada (Niniski (USA))
470^{5} 549^{10}599^{2} 825^{2}990^{4} 1308^{5} 5242^{11}5750^{14} 5836^{10}

Valhar *D W Thompson* a49 45
3 b f Diktat—Diamond Jayne (IRE) (Royal Abjar (USA))
796^{7} 879^{11} 1210^{5} 2535^{16} 4067^{12}

Valiance (USA) *J H M Gosden* a80 97
2 ch c Horse Chestnut(SAF) —Victoria Cross (IRE) (Mark Of Esteem (IRE))
(3844) 4561^{2} 6443^{3}

Valiant Romeo *R Bastiman* a35 63
6 b g Primo Dominie—Desert Lynx (IRE) (Green Desert (USA))
858^{10} 1195^{9}1571^{12} 3608^{12} 5131^{9}6548^{11}

Valiant Shadow (GER) *W Jarvis* a8 46
4 b g Winged Love(IRE) —Vangelis (Gorytus (USA))
6272^{5} 6398^{10}

Valid Notebook (USA) *Patrick L Reynolds* a98
3 b c Notebook(USA) —Silk Appeal (USA) (Valid Appeal (USA))
5719a^{2}

Valixir (IRE) *Saeed Bin Suroor* 129
5 b h Trempolino(USA) —Vadlamixa (FR) (Linamix (FR))
564a^{7} 742a^{14} 1716a^{13}

Vallemeldee (IRE) *P W D'Arcy* a60
2 b f Bering—Vassiana (FR) (Anabaa (USA))
5425^{4} 5947^{12}

Valley Observer (FR) *W R Swinburn* 36
2 ch c Observatory(USA) —Valleyrose (IRE) (Royal Academy (USA))
2287^{9}

Valley Of The Moon (IRE) *R A Fahey* 74
2 b f Monashee Mountain(USA) —Unaria (Prince Tenderfoot (USA))
2106^{9} 2623^{4} (3188) 3555^{4} 4377^{3} 4681^{11}5133^{6}

Valrhona (IRE) *J Noseda* 71
2 bb f Spectrum(IRE) —Minerva (IRE) (Caerleon (USA))
6215^{6}

Value Plus (IRE) *S Parr* a36 72
4 b m Mujadil(USA) —Brittas Blues (IRE) (Blues Traveller (IRE))
331^{10} 449^{5}533^{9} 612^{11}1733^{9} 2112^{17} 2543^{16} 3111^{P} (Dead)

Valuta (USA) *R A Kvisla* a71 77
3 rg c Silver Charm(USA) —Misleading Miss (USA) (Miswaki (USA))
2815^{4} 3225^{8} 3849^{2} 4419a^{10}5260^{9} 5911^{3} 6565^{5}6668^{5} 6712^{4}

Valverde (IRE) *J L Dunlop* 85
3 b c Sinndar(IRE) —Vert Val (USA) (Septieme Ciel (USA))
1088^{4} 1822^{2} 4210^{2} 6053^{5}

Vampyrus *H Candy* a22 74+
3 ch g Dracula(AUS) —Anna Karietta (Precocious)
2063 ^{2} 2940^{7} 4806^{5}5726^{9} 6177^{7}

Vanadium *J G Given* a80 82
4 b g Dansili—Musianica (Music Boy)
3040^{9} 3500^{10} 4119^{13} (4885) 5136^{4} 5749^{5}6048^{13} 6223^{3} 6437^{6}6773^{4}

Vanatina (IRE) *A Bailey* 48
2 b f Tagula(IRE) —Final Trick (Primo Dominie)
1347^{11} 2807^{8} 3096^{8}4986^{3}

Vancouver Gold (IRE) *K R Burke* a67+ 76
4 b m Monashee Mountain(USA) —Forest Berries (IRE) (Thatching)
(121) 210^{3} 330^{2}(427) 546^{9}(649) (678) 818^{3}953^{2} 1001^{5}

Vandal *M Appleby* a52 44
6 b g Entrepreneur—Vax Star (Petong)
44^{11} 170^{9}446^{11} 1001^{13}1303^{8} 1769^{7} 1911^{8}2360^{9} 2481^{6} 2636^{11}

Vanderlin *A M Balding* a113 116
7 ch g Halling(USA) —Massorah (FR) (Habitat)
(704) 1527a^{5} 3518^{2} 4038^{7} 5416a^{12}

Vanilla Delight (IRE) *J Howard Johnson* 75
3 b f Orpen(USA) —Fantastic Bid (USA) (Auction Ring (USA))
2126^{7} 3082^{8} 4989^{2} 5961^{4}

Vanishing Dancer (SWI) *B Ellison* a60 58
9 ch g Llandaff(USA) —Vanishing Prairie (USA) (Alysheba (USA))
443^{6}

Vanitosa (IRE) *L Brogi* 69
3 ch f Spectrum(IRE) —Luna D'Estate (IRE) (Alzao (USA))
6362a^{10}

Vanquished (AUS) *B Murray* 113
6 br g Hector Protector(USA) —Exuberance (AUS) (Last Tycoon)
6346a^{3} 6455a^{8}

Vanquisher (IRE) *W J Haggas* 73
2 b g Xaar—Naziriya (FR) (Darshaan)
4768^{5} 5460^{5} 5730^{2}

Varevees *J Boisnard* 97
3 b f Kahyasi—Danse Bretonne (FR) (Exit To Nowhere (USA))
4465a^{4} 5472a^{5} 6786a^{3}

Varro *M G Quinlan*
2 b c Machiavellian(USA) —Valleria (Sadler's Wells (USA))
6407a^{9}

Varsity *H-A Pantall* 75
3 b f Lomitas—Renowned (IRE) (Darshaan)
6567a^{0}

Varsity Blues (IRE) *T Stack* 91
2 b c Fasliyev(USA) —Basin Street Blues (IRE) (Dolphin Street (FR))
2037a^{7} 2686a^{2}

Vatori (FR) *P Demercastel* 112
4 ch h Vettori(IRE) —High Mecene (FR) (Highest Honor (FR))
1331a^{6} 1873a^{6} 2597a^{6} 4861a^{8}

Vaudevire *Peter Grayson* a43 42?
5 b g Dancing Spree(USA) —Approved Quality (IRE) (Persian Heights)
90^{12} 126^{12}

Vaunt *R Charlton* 91
2 b g Averti(IRE) —Boast (Most Welcome)
2185^{5} 2506^{4} 2967^{2} 4109^{2} (5161) (5829)

Vauquelin (IRE) *E S McMahon* 97
2 b c Xaar—Beryl (Bering)
2545^{2} 2960^{2} 3553^{2}

Veba (USA) *M D I Usher* a62 64+
3 ch g Black Minnaloushe(USA) —Make Over (USA) (Time For A Change (USA))
2244^{10} 2570^{6} 6593^{8}6714^{13}

Veenwouden *J R Fanshawe* a60 76
2 b f Desert Prince(IRE) —Delauncy (Machiavellian (USA))
3645^{4} (4553) 5041^{3} 5655^{17}

Vegas Boys *M Wigham* a72 76
3 b g Royal Applause—Brief Glimpse (IRE) (Taufan (USA))
1337^{9} 2496^{5} 3434^{6}3612^{6} 4077^{8} 4324^{7} 5684^{12} 5938^{13}6315^{11} (6922) 6990^{2}

Vega's Lord (GER) *P Rau* 103
3 ch c Lord Of Men—Vega Sicilia (Environment Friend)
5543a^{2} 6613a^{10}

Vehari *M Scudamore* a35 66
3 ch g Tomba—Nannie Annie (Persian Bold)
445^{10} 894^{2} 2066^{2}

Veiled Applause *R M Beckett* a72 72
3 b g Royal Applause—Scarlet Veil (Tyrnavos)
3820^{5} 4591^{2} (4871) 5130^{4} 5879^{4}6189^{4}

Veils Of Salome *A J McCabe* a38
2 ch f Arkadian Hero(USA) —Helen Bradley (IRE) (Indian Ridge)
5959^{12} 6821^{9} 6927^{7}

Velodrome (BRZ) *E Charpy* 97
7 b h Booming(FR) —Licena (BRZ) (Derek (BRZ))
205a^{16} 437a^{8} 512a^{9} 624a^{8}

Velvet Heights (IRE) *J L Dunlop* a104+ 91
4 b h Barathea(IRE) —Height Of Fantasy (IRE) (Shirley Heights)
(1247) 1809^{15} 2176^{6} 3203^{2}4792^{2} 5351^{4} 5634^{4} 6148^{2}(6467) (6677) 6836^{3}

Velvet Revolver (IRE) *L Riccardi* 103
3 b f Mujahid(USA) —Noble Kara (FR) (Noblequest (FR))
6005a^{7} 6363a^{2}

Velvet Touch *D M Simcock* a52 46
5 b m Danzig Connection(USA) —Soft Touch (GER) (Horst-Herbert)
144^{3} 180^{4}

Velvet Valley (USA) *C E Longsdon* a60+ 69+
3 ch g Gone West(USA) —Velvet Morning (USA) (Broad Brush (USA))
981^{6} 1252^{3} 2654^{7}4662^{10} 6987^{6}

Velvet Waters *R F Johnson Houghton* a68 74
5 b m Unfuwain(USA) —Gleaming Water (Kalaglow)
1614^{4} 2186^{7} 2305^{3} 2534^{2} 2672^{3}3009^{3} 3365^{12}

Vendangeur (IRE) *E Lellouche* 110
3 b c Galileo(IRE) —Vahine (USA) (Alysheba (USA))
4169a^{2} 5145a^{2} (5700a)

Veneer (IRE) *Miss Gay Kelleway* a52 76
4 b g Woodborough(USA) —Sweet Lass (Belmez (USA))
467^{10} 857^{13}972^{6} 1073^{4} 1217^{6} 1387^{3}1538^{2} 1765^{8}1914^{2}

Venerable *J H M Gosden* 55
2 b c Danehill(USA) —Fragrant View (USA) (Distant View (USA))
6220^{13}

Venetian Dancer (IRE) *M J Wallace* a62 60
2 gr c Danehill Dancer(IRE) —Venize (IRE) (Kaldoun (FR))
3994^{3} 4705^{6} 5496^{6}

Venetian Princess (IRE) *P Howling* a38 38
4 b m Desert Style(IRE) —Dance With Care (Arazi (USA))
94^{8} 184^{12}386^{6} 427^{5}638^{11}

Venetian Romance (IRE) *M R Bosley* a39 53
5 ch m Desert Story(IRE) —Cipriani (Habitat)
361^{4} 1224^{7}1271^{10}

Veneto (IRE) *K G Reveley* 49
3 ch g Spinning World(USA) —Padua (IRE) (Cadeaux Genereux)
859^{12}

Vengeance *S Dow* 101
6 b g Fleetwood(IRE) —Lady Isabell (Rambo Dancer (CAN))
(1238) 2229^{8} 2848^{13} 3294^{5}

Vengeance Of Rain (NZ) *D Ferraris* 127
5 b g Zabeel(NZ) —Danelagh (AUS) (Danehill (USA))
6785a^{3}

Vengo (NZ) *Lee Freedman* 96
5 b g — (Busted)
6391a^{4}

Venir Rouge *M Salaman* a70 68
2 ch c Dancing Spree(USA) —Al Awaalah (Mukaddamah (USA))
1838^{12} 2009^{8} 2619^{8} 3083^{7} 3726^{4}5125^{7} 6106^{10} 6394^{2}

Ventura (USA) *Mrs A J Perrett* a71
2 bb f Chester House(USA) —Estala (Be My Guest (USA))
6186^{6}

Venus Arising (IND) *V Gaekwad* 89
5 ch m Steinbeck(USA) —Lei (IND) (Razeen (USA))
155a^{6} 351a^{7} 510a^{8}

Venus Line (JPN) *N Hori* 107
5 b h Fuji Kiseki(JPN) —Hokuto Pendant (JPN) (Park Regent (CAN))
5717a^{11} 6850a^{8}

Veracity *M A Jarvis* 57
2 ch c Lomitas—Vituisa (Bering)
5730^{7}

Verbatim *A M Balding* a49
2 b f Vettori(IRE) —Brand (Shareef Dancer (USA))
5209^{5}

Veronica Franco (ITY) *E Borromeo* 95
3 ch f Lomitas—Gravette (Kris)
2694a^{6}

Veronica's Girl *W J Knight* a70 50
3 b f Desert Prince(IRE) —Veronica Franco (Darshaan)
34^{5} 190^{3}234^{3} 3400^{6}3848^{8} 4399^{8}

Versatile *G A Ham* a43
3 b g Vettori(IRE) —Direcvil (Top Ville)
4249^{12} 4784^{10} 5651^{7}

Version Originale (FR) *Mme N Rossio* a58 68
5 b m Poliglote—Any Colour (Anshan)
5562a^{0}

Verstone (IRE) *R F Fisher* a19 36
4 b m Brave Act—Golden Charm (IRE) (Common Grounds)
1766^{9}

Vert Helice (SPA) *M Rolland* a96 102
4 b g Helissio(FR) —New Vert (SPA) (Vert Amande (FR))
6786a^{2}

Very Agreeable *W R Swinburn* a68 86+
3 b f Pursuit Of Love—Oomph (Shareef Dancer (USA))
3200^{2} (3901)

Very Clear *R M H Cowell* a46
4 b m Loup Sauvage(USA) —Shoot Clear (Bay Express)
692^{8} 1110^{10}1254^{6} 2418^{10}

Very Far (USA) *Saeed Bin Suroor* 89
3 b c Forestry(USA) —Hail Atlantis (USA) (Seattle Slew (USA))
(4431) 4958^{2} 5150^{8}

Very Wise *W J Haggas* a90+ 92
4 b g Pursuit Of Love—With Care (Warning)
2440^{15} 2657^{8} 3218^{3} (6752)

Vesozchi (IRE) *B Grizzetti*
2 b c Hernando(FR) —Very Speed (USA) (Silver Hawk (USA))
5771a^{8}

Vesuvio *B W Hills* a59 64
2 br c Efisio—Polo (Warning)
6015^{3} 6324^{9}

Vettori Dancer *G G Margarson* a44 37
3 b f Vettori(IRE) —Assertive Dancer (USA) (Assert)
1351^{17} 1613^{7} 1940^{9}2592^{8}

Veverka *J C Fox* a30 71
5 b m King's Theatre(IRE) —Once Smitten (IRE) (Caerleon (USA))
1334^{15} 2186^{10}

Viable *Mrs P Sly* a37 71
4 b g Vettori(IRE) —Danseuse Davis (FR) (Glow (USA))
905^{9} 2104^{3} 2540^{9}3141^{7} 4457^{4} 5090^{2} 5497^{8}

Viapervita (IRE) *H Blume* 100
3 b f Spectrum(IRE) —Way For Life (GER) (Platini (GER))
5008a^{5}

Vibe *A W Carroll* a54 69
5 gr g Danzero(AUS) —Courting (Pursuit Of Love)
2148^{13} (2602) 2920^{4} 3405^{3}4141^{6} 4211^{10} 4984^{6}

Vibrato (USA) *C J Teague* a60+ 49
4 b g Stravinsky(USA) —She's Fine (USA) (Private Account (USA))
3384[9] 4136[5] 4613[7]4948[7] 5023[4] 5840[2] 5949[7] (6281) 6307[4] 6532[5]6787[6] 6899[7](6949)

Vice Admiral *M W Easterby* a39 70
3 ch g Vettori(IRE) —Queen Of Scotland (IRE) (Mujadil (USA))
1140[7] 1350[13] 2529[7] 3145[2] 3634[5]3791[2] 4111[2] 4380[16] (4960) (5061) 5242[9] 5723[8]5971[11] 6161[9]

Vicious Knight *D Nicholls* a79 93
8 b g Night Shift(USA) —Myth (Troy)
(640) 1156a[10] 1456[9]

Vicious Prince (IRE) *R M Whitaker* a52 76
7 b g Sadler's Wells(USA) —Sunny Flower (FR) (Dom Racine (FR))
454[12] 816[7] 4469[6]

Vicious Warrior *R M Whitaker* a86 92
7 b g Elmaamul(USA) —Ling Lane (Slip Anchor)
(1531) 2364[8] 2974[4] 3289[3] 3747[2] 3939[5]4654[3] 4889[6] (5357) 5789[7] 6888[10]

Vicky Pollard *P Howling* a46 47
3 b f King Charlemagne(USA) —Day Star (Dayjur (USA))
2316[18] 3034[4] 3257[3]3842[3] 6539[9] 6704[5]6805[10] 6851[3]6969[7]

Victimised (IRE) *R J Price* a12 17
4 b g Victory Note(USA) —Eurolink Virago (Charmer)
402[12] 584[11]687[11] 942[9]

Victor Buckwell *G L Moore* a45 48
4 br g Pivotal—Lonely Shore (Blakeney)
1313[5] 1540[7] 3592[12]

Victoriana *H J Collingridge* a39 56
5 b m Wolfhound(USA) —Silk St James (Pas De Seul)
396[4] 1228[13]1534[11] 1618[13] 2785[13]

Victorian Prince (IRE) *E J O'Neill* 81+
2 b c Desert Prince(IRE) —Miss Lorilaw (FR) (Homme De Loi (IRE))
(5814)

Victors Prize (IRE) *T J Pitt*
4 b m Dr Devious(IRE) —Spoken Word (IRE) (Perugino (USA))
6213[12]

Victor Trumper *P W Chapple-Hyam* a81 73
2 b g First Trump—Not So Generous (IRE) (Fayruz)
4895[12] (5381) 6018[5] 6443[2]6586[2] 6645[4]6676[2]

Victory Design (IRE) *P L Biancone* 100
4 b h Danehill(USA) —Sun Silk (USA) (Gone West (USA))
6329a[4]

Victory Quest (IRE) *Mrs S Lamyman* a71 53
6 b g Victory Note(USA) —Marade (USA) (Dahar (USA))
5[5] 98[7]246[5] (346) 491[7] 628[10]675[2] 6495[6]6626[4] 6718[8]6873[2]

Victory Spirit *J L Dunlop* 73
2 b c Invincible Spirit(IRE) —Tanouma (USA) (Miswaki (USA))
2604[4] 3005[8] 3979[2] (5231) 5647[11]

Vienna's Boy (IRE) *W J Musson* a77 77
5 b g Victory Note(USA) —Shinkoh Rose (FR) (Warning)
292[10] 451[3]575[8] 1388[2]2223[4] (2464) 3598[9]4437[3] 4706[5] 5085[4]

Vietnam *S Kirk* a56 56
2 ch g Compton Place—Mosca (Most Welcome)
3363[14] 5105[11] 5389[5]5597[10]

Viewforth *M A Buckley* a59 70
8 b g Emarati(USA) —Miriam (Forzando)
1504[10] 1816[8] 2748[7] 3334[2] 3524[3](3670) 3781[3] 4352[3] 4477[3] 4694[7] 5081[10]5635[2] 6162[4] 6274[6] 6510[5]6629[5] 6869[4]

View From The Top *Sir Mark Prescott* a37 73
2 b c Mujahid(USA) —Aethra (USA) (Trempolino (USA))
4103[4] 4487[9] 5091[7] 6933[7]

Vigata (IRE) *V Valiani* 105
5 b m Orpen(USA) —Welsh Dawn (Zafonic (USA))
2280a[10]

Vijay (IRE) *Mrs J C McGregor* a60 59
7 ch g Eagle Eyed(USA) —Foolish Fun (Fools Holme (USA))
1611[11] (Dead)

Viking Spirit *W R Swinburn* a104 96
4 b g Mind Games—Dane Dancing (IRE) (Danehill (USA))
1246[5] 5358[10] 5667[3]6192[2] 6445[2]

Viking Star (IRE) *A D Brown*
5 b g Indian Rocket—Nordic Flavour (IRE) (Nordico (USA))
230[12]

Villa Bianca's (IRE) *J A Osborne* a47
3 ch f Priolo(USA) —Ostrusa (AUT) (Rustan (HUN))
6492[5] 6731[3]

Villa Chigi (IRE) *G R Oldroyd* a42 32
4 ch g Pistolet Bleu(IRE) —Musical Refrain (IRE) (Dancing Dissident (USA))
2875[6] 3384[10] 4381[10]

Village Fete *D Smaga* 102
3 b f Singspiel(IRE) —Danefair (Danehill (USA))
(3515a) 4543a[7]

Village Storm (IRE) *C J Teague* 5
3 b g Mujadil(USA) —First Nadia (Auction Ring (USA))
6792[9]

Villago (GER) *E W Tuer* 70
6 b g Laroche(GER) —Village (GER) (Acatenango (GER))
975[8] (1184) 1808[9] (Dead)

Villarosi (IRE) *J R Best* a53 75
4 b m Rossini(USA) —Trinida (Jaazeiro (USA))
3705[2] 4265[6] 4627[10] 5236[11] 5599[10]5755[11]

Villa Sciarra (IRE) *A Peraino* a88 53
3 b c Elnadim(USA) —Villafranca (IRE) (In The Wings)
150a[8] 758a[8] 5473a[4]6252a[11]

Villa Sonata *J R Fanshawe* a62 80
3 b f Mozart(IRE) —Villa Carlotta (Rainbow Quest (USA))
2048[2] 2615[4] 3301[8] 4336[5] (4662) 5478[9]5732[4] 5944[5]

Vinando *C R Egerton* 108
5 ch h Hernando(FR) —Sirena (GER) (Tejano (USA))
1584[2] 2085[5] 2849[3] 3315[5] 3551[6]5963[9]

Vincennes *M A Jarvis* a75+
2 bb f King's Best(USA) —Park Appeal (Ahonoora)
6663[5] 6879[2]

Vincent Vegas *Mrs S Lamyman* a17 16
3 b g Foxhound(USA) —Annie's Song (Farfelu)
1768[13] 1988[6] 2542[12]4227[P]

Vindication *R M H Cowell* a68 69
6 ch g Compton Place—Prince's Feather (IRE) (Cadeaux Genereux)
1402[3] 2259[4] 2443[6]2590[4] 3089[11] 3536[3]3802[4] 4267[9] 4674[4] 5327[10] 5573[6]6142[7]

Viniyoga *M H Tompkins* a11 33
4 b g Cadeaux Genereux—Optimistic (Reprimand)
129[9]

Vino *B W Hills* a72 72
3 b f Efisio—Polo (Warning)
1351[4] 2985[3] (4527) 6227[5]6413[8]

Vinska (USA) *J W Hills* a35 53
3 br f Stravinsky(USA) —Konvincha (USA) (Cormorant (USA))
2349[10] 2814[8] 3016[14]3440[10] 4181[3]

Vintage (IRE) *P Mitchell* a68
2 b c Danetime(IRE) —Katherine Gorge (USA) (Hansel (USA))
1959[7]

Vintage Times (IRE) *R A Fahey* a44 37
4 bb g Namid—Vintage Escape (IRE) (Cyrano De Bergerac)
94[14] (Dead)

Vintage Year (IRE) *T J O'Mara* 79+
4 b h Tagula(IRE) —Shalstayholy (IRE) (Shalford (IRE))
3561a[5]

Violent Velocity (IRE) *J J Quinn* a79 63
3 b c Namid—Lear's Crown (USA) (Lear Fan (USA))
(365) 1091[14] 1812[9] 5791[16] 6428[9]6896[10]

Violet Ballerina (IRE) *B J Meehan* a82 56
3 b f Namid—Violet Spring (IRE) (Exactly Sharp (USA))
1843[12] 3403[5] 3646[4]4703[3] (5427) 6065[12]

Violet Park *B J Meehan* a97 104+
5 b m Pivotal—Petonellajill (Petong)
1015[2] (1506) 2740[6]

Violet's Pride *S Parr* a47 58
2 b f Kyllachy—Majalis (Mujadil (USA))
2695[5] 3110[0] 3307[4] 3818[2] 4321[9]5835[2] 6056[6] 6255[9]

Violette *Sir Mark Prescott* a87 98
3 b f Observatory(USA) —Odette (Pursuit Of Love)
1328a[6] 3322a[8] 6101[5]6335[6] 6559[7]

Virginia Key (IRE) *F Head* a70 76
3 ch f Mark Of Esteem(IRE) —Bellarida (FR) (Bellypha)
4192a[9]

Virginia Plain *Miss Diana Weeden* 40
3 ch f Vettori(IRE) —Iyavaya (USA) (Valiant Nature (USA))
1139[9] 1955[8] 2600[5] 3115[9] 3627[9]3823[12] 4276[6] 5092[6] 5244[4] 5550[12]5926[14]

Virginia Reel *M Johnston* a36 59
2 b f King's Best(USA) —Golden Dancer (IRE) (Sadler's Wells (USA))
5068[9] 5760[4] 6186[13]6639[9]

Virginia Rose (IRE) *J G Given* a69 64
3 b f Galileo(IRE) —Rispoto (Mtoto)
1684[6] 1984[6] 2466[11]3169[2] 3791[8] 4362[6] 4734[6] 5445[8](5836) (6317) 6435[3] 6537[4]

Virginia Woolf *John M Oxx* 101
4 gr m Daylami(IRE) —Vice Vixen (CAN) (Vice Regent (CAN))
1324a[2] 2154a[7] 3107a[6] 3660a[3] 4822a[9]

Virgin Islands (IRE) *M A Jarvis* a64+ 71
3 b f Sadler's Wells(USA) —Antiguan Jane (Shirley Heights)
762[2] 971[2] 1854[3]

Virtuosity *Sir Michael Stoute* a75 85
3 ch f Pivotal—Virtuous (Exit To Nowhere (USA))
(3373) 3954[6] 5164[9] 5769[12] 6350[9]

Vi's Boy *W M Brisbourne* a34
3 b g Almushtarak(IRE) —Risk The Witch (Risk Me (FR))
254[12] 445[11]534[9]

Viscount Rossini *A W Carroll* a43 38
4 bb g Rossini(USA) —Spain (Polar Falcon (USA))
174[12] 791[5]1225[4] 1462[6]3192[11] 3944[12] 4266[9] 5127[5]

Visindar *A Fabre* 117
3 ch c Sinndar(IRE) —Visor (USA) (Mr Prospector (USA))
(1749a) 2228[5]

Visionario (IRE) *A Fabre* 110+
2 b c Spinning World(USA) —Visionnaire (FR) (Linamix (FR))
(4415a) (5048a) 5715a[6]

Visionist (IRE) *Pat Eddery* a103+ 88
4 b g Orpen(USA) —Lady Taufan (IRE) (Taufan (USA))
(828) 1667[16] 5943[16]

Visit Wexford (IRE) *John E Kiely* 91
5 b h Entrepreneur—Elida (IRE) (Royal Academy (USA))
3128a[5]

Vital Equine (IRE) *E J O'Neill* 115
2 b c Danetime(IRE) —Bayalika (IRE) (Selkirk (USA))
(1588) (2586) (5183) 5715a[3] 5965[5] 6249a[8]

Vital Statistics *D R C Elsworth* 105
2 br f Indian Ridge—Emerald Peace (IRE) (Green Desert (USA))
1796[4] 2045[2] 2743[6] 3043[4] (3700) 3925[2](4966) 5654[10]

Vital Tryst *J G Given* 25
2 ch g Pivotal—Splicing (Sharpo)
5883[13]

Vitznau (IRE) *R Hannon* a62 75
2 b c Val Royal(FR) —Neat Dish (CAN) (Stalwart (USA))
2552[4] 2930[8] 4000[3]4681[6] 5147[4] (6015)

Viva Pataca *J Moore* a84+ 121
4 b g Marju(IRE) —Comic (IRE) (Be My Chief (USA))
1180a[6] 6785a[4]

Viva Volta *T D Easterby* 78
3 b g Superior Premium—La Volta (Komaite (USA))
(1078) 1345[6] 2105[3] 2297[5] 3023[2] 3395[3]5961[11]

Vivi Belle *M L W Bell* a38
2 b f Cadeaux Genereux—Locharia (Wolfhound (USA))
6821[8]

Vixen Virago *Jane Southcombe* a29 50
3 ch f Foxhound(USA) —Le Pin (Persian Bold)
2068[9] 2575[11] 6026[9]6501[5] 6725[9]6779[8]

Vizionary *Mrs P Sly* a23 43
2 b f Observatory(USA) —Zietunzeen (IRE) (Zieten (USA))
1046[14] 2354[10] 4109[8] 4510[6] 4913[8]6491[6]

Vizulize *A W Carroll* a52 60
7 b m Robellino(USA) —Euridice (IRE) (Woodman (USA))
172[5] 467[6]1227[11] 1536[10]

Vlasta Weiner *J M Bradley* a64d 59
6 b g Magic Ring(IRE) —Armaiti (Sayf El Arab (USA))
74[10] 4551[7] 5386[12]6288[10] 6395[11]6629[11] 6796[8]6906[3] 6974[5]

Vodka Luge *J W Hills* a46 43
2 ch f Inchinor—Turn To Vodka (FR) (Polish Precedent (USA))
3640[9] 4074[5] 4394[9]5323[6] 6460[4]

Vodkat *N Tinkler* 27
2 ch f Kyllachy—Ebba (Elmaamul (USA))
1420[7] 1982[7] 2973[11] 3746[5] 4887[12]

Vodkatini *P J Makin* a70 73
3 b g Bertolini(USA) —Cold Blow (Posse (USA))
228[6] 1291[6] 1828[5]2301[4] 2620[13] 3310[5] 4044[7]4933[7]

Voice *H R A Cecil* a58
2 b f Zamindar(USA) —Seven Sing (USA) (Machiavellian (USA))
6414[4]

Voice Mail *P Howling* a65 79
7 b g So Factual(USA) —Wizardry (Shirley Heights)
915[8] 1207[7] 2186[2]2482[5] 2640[8] 2969[8] 3309[4] 3566[7]3850[4] 4241[3] 4483[5] 4673[8] 6667[7]6883[7]

Volaire *A J Lidderdale* a59 41
4 b m Zaha(CAN) —Appelania (Star Appeal)
1306[4] 1670[7] 1797[9]2320[15]

Vola Vola (IRE) *R Feligioni* 82
2 br f Danehill Dancer(IRE) —Mistress Thames (Sharpo)
(2565a) 3343a[9]

Vol De Nuit *L M Cumani* 116
5 gr h Linamix(FR) —Bedside Story (Mtoto)
1976[3] 2693a[3] 4358[7] 6365a[5]

Voleris Pearl *C F Wall* a56
2 b f Voleris(FR) —Maureen's Hope (USA) (Northern Baby (CAN))
6561[7]

Vondova *D A Nolan* 60
4 b m Efisio—Well Proud (IRE) (Sadler's Wells (USA))
3002[4] 3332[9] 3783[6] 4135[7] 4352[9]4477[8]

Vonnies Night Out *C J Teague*
3 ch c Night Shift(USA) —Mountain Bluebird (USA) (Clever Trick (USA))
5023[12] 6971[P]

Von Wessex *W G M Turner* a46 49
4 b g Wizard King—Gay Da Cheen (IRE) (Tenby)
2096[7] 2288[2] 2347[8]2632[8] 3033[7] 3306[11]

Voodoo Moon *M Johnston* 88
2 b f Efisio—Lunasa (IRE) (Don't Forget Me)
1181[2] 1295[2] 1945[6] (3780) 3837[3] 4377[2]4761[3] 5157[2] 5503[15]

Vorteeva (USA) *John M Oxx* 94
2 b g Bahri(USA) —Super Supreme (IND) (Zafonic (USA))
4825a[6]

Vortex *Miss Gay Kelleway* a108 113
7 b g Danehill(USA) —Roupala (USA) (Vaguely Noble)
1407[2] 2722[5] 3134a[6]3881[5] 5274[2] 5682[11] 6101[7]6514[4] 6692[3](6847) (6914)

Voss *M Johnston* a48 39
2 b f Halling(USA) —Valdara (Darshaan)
5859[6] 6297[12] 6867[8]

Votive Daniel (IRE) *Simon Earle* a47
3 b c Dansili—Volte Face (Polar Falcon (USA))
5055[16] 5729[12] 5774[8]6128[14]

Vroom Vroom (ARG) *D Hayes* 113
5 br g Fitzcarraldo(ARG) —Disneyland (ARG) (Ringaro (USA))
1716a[4]

Vrubel (IRE) *J R Holt*
7 ch g Entrepreneur—Renzola (Dragonara Palace (USA))
52[11] 328[10]

Waajeb (USA) *A Al Raihe* a91? 73
6 b h Silver Deputy(CAN) —Bridal Tea (USA) (Gulch (USA))
357a[9] 434a[4]

Wabra (USA) *C E Brittain* 81
3 ch f Diesis—Min Elreeh (USA) (Danzig (USA))
1087[11] 1669[7]

Wachiwi (IRE) *A P Jarvis* a63 57
2 ch f Namid—Carpet Lady (IRE) (Night Shift (USA))
3096[7] 4485[3] 4753[4](5208)

Waddon (IRE) *C G Cox* a41 70
3 b g Green Desert(USA) —Baldemara (FR) (Sanglamore (USA))
1208[4] 1672[9] 4689[5] 5418[9] 5988[11]

Wadnagin (IRE) *I A Wood* a59 48+
2 b f Princely Heir(IRE) —Band Of Colour (IRE) (Spectrum (IRE))
4177[6] 6414[6] 6663[6]6807[4] 6839[5]

Waggledance (IRE) *D Carroll* a39 53
4 b g Mujadil(USA) —Assertive Lass (USA) (Assert)
862[9] 1196[10]2611[10] 2780[4] 3285[10] 3781[6] 4232[10]4948[9] 6233[9] 6399[11]

Wagtail *E A L Dunlop* a89 98+
3 b f Cape Cross(IRE) —Dancing Feather (Suave Dancer (USA))
(710) 1419[3] 2344[7] (3793) (4075) 4628[4]5019[12] (5525)

Wahchi (IRE) *M W Easterby* a42 64
7 ch g Nashwan(USA) —Nafhaat (USA) (Roberto (USA))
3141[11] 4021[9] 4194[9] 4307[8] 4730[10]6667[12]

Wahoo Sam (USA) *K A Ryan* a83 83
6 ch g Sandpit(BRZ) —Good Reputation (USA) (Gran Zar (MEX))
(58) 161[5] 611[8]2974[13] 3528[3] 4029[15] 4153[2] 5406[8]5554[8] 6418[4] 6772[7]6938[9]

Waiheke Island *B Mactaggart* 61
2 b f Winged Love(IRE) —West Of Warsaw (Danzig Connection (USA))
2159[2] 2854[6] 5507[11] 5632[6]

Wainwright (IRE) *P A Blockley* a73 58
6 b g Victory Note(USA) —Double Opus (IRE) (Petorius)
51[3] 164[9]1607[6] 5269[13] 5737[4]6065[10] 6323[10] 6556[9]6643[4]

Wait A While (USA) *T Pletcher* a115 119
3 gr f Maria's Mon(USA) —Flirtatious (USA) (A.P. Indy (USA))
6340a[4]

Wait For The Light *E A L Dunlop* a77 53
2 b c Fantastic Light(USA) —Lady In Waiting (Kylian (USA))
5886[6] (6257)

Wait For The Will (USA) *G L Moore* a78 78
10 ch g Seeking The Gold(USA) —You'd Be Surprised (USA) (Blushing Groom (FR))
1247[14] 2447[9]5213[8] 5910[2](6376) 6462[5]

Waiting For Mary (IRE) *J G M O'Shea* 62
3 b f Tagula(IRE) —Lady Abigail (IRE) (Royal Academy (USA))
1141[14] 1567[9] 2535[17] 3897[5] 4286[9]5054[6]

Wait Watcher (IRE) *P A Blockley* 96
2 b f Fath(USA) —Campestral (USA) (Alleged (USA))
2745[2] 4290[3] (4600) 5464a[2]

Wake Up Maggie (IRE) *C F Wall* a90 109
3 b f Xaar—Kalagold (IRE) (Magical Strike (USA))
1508[5] 2031[2] 2802[10] 3322a[2] 5159[2]

Wakeys Wizzard *M E Sowersby* 24
2 ch f Piccolo—Golden Ciel (USA) (Septieme Ciel (USA))
2500[8] 2778[4] 3279[5] 3831[5] 4376[12]

Wakita (IRE) *Gerard Keane* 64
3 b f Bold Fact(USA) —Pleasant Outlook (USA) (El Gran Senor (USA))
4034a[7]

Waleria (GER) *H J Groschel* 106
3 br f Artan(IRE) —Wiolante (GER) (Lagunas)
(4942a) 5762a[3]

Walharer *B Grizzetti* 86
2 ch c Cadeaux Genereux—Love Roi (ITY) (Roi Danzig (USA))
6003a[9]

Walking Talking *H R A Cecil* 83+
2 b c Rainbow Quest(USA) —Wooden Doll (USA) (Woodman (USA))
6214[2]

Walk In The Park (IRE) *J E Hammond* 121
4 b h Montjeu(IRE) —Classic Park (Robellino (USA))
934a[9] 1558a[3]

Walk With Kings (CAN) *M Frostad* 94
2 gr c Monarchos(USA) —Go First Class (CAN) (Easy Goer (USA))
5415a[6]

Wally Barge *D K Ivory* a56 44
3 b g Reprimand—Linda's Schoolgirl (IRE) (Grand Lodge (USA))
374[7] 479[11]590[8] 797[10] 5210[14]

Walmooh *D Selvaratnam* a91 110
10 b h In The Wings—Walimu (IRE) (Top Ville)
282a[14] 435a[10]

Walnut Grove *T D Barron* 60
3 b f Forzando—Final Rush (Final Straw)
1859[12] (2782) 3529[3] 3786[12] 4728[3] 5370[2]

Waltzing Wizard *A Berry* a55 61
7 b g Magic Ring(IRE) —Legendary Dancer (Shareef Dancer (USA))
134[11]

Wanchai Lad *T D Easterby* 86
5 b g Danzero(AUS) —Frisson (Slip Anchor)
1031[3] 1236[9] 1602[10] 1856[7] 2624[12]3715[P] 3972[22] 4725[5] 5333[7] (5593) (5765) 5791[5]6212[7]

Wanchai Night *T D Easterby* 59
2 b g Night Shift(USA) —Hot Tin Roof (IRE) (Thatching)
2439[6] 2972[5] 3693[3] 3982[7] 4196[8]4955[3] 5113[10]

Wanderin Boy (USA) *N Zito* a116
5 ch h Seeking The Gold(USA) —Vid Kid (CAN) (Pleasant Colony (USA))
5822a[2]

Wandle *T G Mills* 75
2 b c Galileo(IRE) —Artistic Blue (USA) (Diesis)
6220[5]

Wanessa Tiger (IRE) *M R Channon* a43 58
2 ch f Titus Livius(FR) —Lominda (IRE) (Lomond (USA))
4765[10] 5209[6] 5580[3]

Wannabe Posh (IRE) *J L Dunlop* 94
3 b f Grand Lodge(USA) —Wannabe (Shirley Heights)
993[6] 1375[10] (2332) 2584[3] (3302) 4990[3] 5479[2]5732[2] 6202[2]

Wanna Shout *R Dickin* a58 49
8 b m Missed Flight—Lulu (Polar Falcon (USA))
175[12] 258[9](769) 1194[9]1394[2] (1725) 1915[9] 2414[10]2891[6] 3142[11] 6235[5]6431[8] 6543[11]6702[11] 6854[11]

Waquaas *B Bo* a94 100
10 b g Green Desert(USA) —Hamaya (USA) (Mr Prospector (USA))
5225a[6]

War At Sea (IRE) *A W Carroll* a72 84
4 b g Bering—Naval Affair (IRE) (Last Tycoon)
(5887) 6519[7] 6673[6]6862[7]

War Dancer *E A Wheeler* a40 40
4 b g Wolfhound(USA) —Batchworth Dancer (Ballacashtal (CAN))
219[10] 553[7]

Warden Rose *D R C Elsworth* 59
3 ch f Compton Place—Miss Rimex (IRE) (Ezzoud (IRE))
2985[9] 3367[10] 3742[8] 4527[5] 4820[6]

Warden Warren *Mrs C A Dunnett* a53 53
8 b g Petong—Silver Spell (Aragon)
17[14] 185[13]200[10] 3089[17] 3262[10]3827[8] 4009[6] 4233[12] 4496[8] 5573[9]6134[4] (6237) 6477[9] 6543[3]6618[12] 6703[10]6855[11]

War Feather *T D McCarthy* a55 44
4 b h Selkirk(USA) —Sit Alkul (USA) (Mr Prospector (USA))
696[11] 891[9]1540[5] 5650[10]6375[12] 6410[9]6578[5] 6729[13]

War Front (USA) *H A Jerkens* a114 102
4 b h Danzig(USA) —Starry Dreamer (USA) (Rubiano (USA))
(4384a) 5820a[2] 6341a[7]

War Horn (ARG) *P Shaw* 90
4 b g Festin(ARG) —Forli Vous (ARG) (Forlitano (ARG))
1716a[8]

Warlingham (IRE) *P Howling*
8 b g Catrail(USA) —Tadjnama (USA) (Exceller (USA))
606[12] 768[10]853[9]

Warm Tribute (USA) *W G Harrison* 67
2 ch c Royal Anthem(USA) —Gentle Mind (USA) (Seattle Slew (USA))
5746[4] 5901[11]

Warne's Way (IRE) *R Hannon* a61 67
3 ch g Spinning World(USA) —Kafayef (USA) (Secreto (USA))
720[7] 948[12] 1120[9]2434[11]

War Of The Roses (IRE) *R Brotherton*
3 b c Singspiel(IRE) —Calvia Rose (Sharpo)
6588[9]

War Pennant *G L Moore* a69 69
4 b g Selkirk(USA) —Bunting (Shaadi (USA))
4206[8]

Warren Place *A D Brown* a44 51
6 ch g Presidium—Coney Hills (Beverley Boy)
1185[10] 1393[12] 1577[9]2298[9] 3050[9] 3698[8]

Warriors Key (IRE) *Kevin Prendergast* 90
2 b c Key Of Luck(USA) —Warrior Wings (Indian Ridge)
5707a[3] 6262a[4]

Warsaw Pact (IRE) *Sir Mark Prescott* a93 93+
3 b g Polish Precedent(USA) —Always Friendly (High Line)
(2102) 2209[2] (3388) (3490) (3686) 3981[2]4935[2] 4997[4]

Wasalat (USA) *D W Barker* a76 72
4 b m Bahri(USA) —Saabga (USA) (Woodman (USA))
1685[6] 2018[9] 4476[5] 4610[9] 5173[4]5484[4] 5685[6] 5973[6]6259[2] (6430) 6684[2]

Wasseema (USA) *Sir Michael Stoute* 110+
3 br f Danzig(USA) —Vantive (USA) (Mr Prospector (USA))
1068[7] (2406) (3891) (4808) 5184[3]

Wassfa *C E Brittain* a74 76
3 b f Mark Of Esteem(IRE) —Mistle Song (Nashwan (USA))
1583[12] 2556[6] 3419[4]3974[7] 5294[7] 5611[5]5879[11] 6206[2] 6593[5]6775[4] 6954[8]

Watamu (IRE) *P J Makin* a88 97+
5 b g Groom Dancer(USA) —Miss Golden Sands (Kris)
6888[2]

Watching *R A Fahey* a76 92
9 ch g Indian Ridge—Sweeping (Indian King (USA))
1561[11] 2384[16] 2573[2]

Watchmaker *W J Knight* 28
3 b g Bering—Watchkeeper (IRE) (Rudimentary (USA))
5203[9]

Watch Out *M W Easterby* 48
2 b g Observatory(USA) —Ballet Fame (USA) (Quest For Fame)
4260[U] 4520[2] 5239[8] 5901[10]

Watch Out Jess *M Madgwick* 52
3 gr f Averti(IRE) —Out Line (Beveled (USA))
1751[6] 2316[12] 2730[4] 3340[8] 5131[14]

Wateera (IRE) *J L Dunlop* 70
2 b f Sakhee(USA) —Azdihaar (USA) (Mr Prospector (USA))
4373[12] 5083[5] 5596[2]

Waterline Twenty (IRE) *P D Evans* a86 86
3 b f Indian Danehill(IRE) —Taisho (IRE) (Namaqualand (USA))
1020[12] 1377[10] 1606[5]2385[6] 2824[6] (3067) 3374[4] 3487[3] 4172[2]4628[5] 4790[14] 5165[6] 6868[5]

Waterloo Corner *R Craggs* a67 71
4 b g Cayman Kai(IRE) —Rasin Luck (Primitive Rising (USA))
97[6] 2322[6] 2526[3]2975[16]

Water Margin (IRE) *T G Mills* a46
2 b c Shinko Forest(IRE) —Tribal Rite (Be My Native (USA))
5607[11]

Water Mill (USA) *A M Balding* a83+
2 gr c Unbridled's Song(USA) —Capote Miss (USA) (Capote (USA))
(5020)

Watermill (IRE) *D W Chapman* a30
3 b g Daylami(IRE) —Brogan's Well (IRE) (Caerleon (USA))
6759[9] 6817[4]

Water Pistol *M C Chapman* 63
4 b g Double Trigger(IRE) —Water Flower (Environment Friend)
1219[12]

Waterside (IRE) *G L Moore* a94 96
7 ch g Lake Coniston(IRE) —Classic Ring (IRE) (Auction Ring (USA))
7[2] 80[5]140[7] 221[8]348[8] 542[4](611) 667[9]1111[4] (1340) (2405) 2649[2] (2819) 4131[5] (4535) 5019[8]5357[7]

Waterways (IRE) *P J Prendergast* 96
3 b f Alhaarth(IRE) —Buckle (IRE) (Common Grounds)
1469a[8] 2308a[6] 3561a[6] 5405[5] 5706a[5]

Wavertree Boy (IRE) *D R C Elsworth* 110
6 ch g Hector Protector(USA) —Lust (Pursuit Of Love)
1991[9] 3028[12]

Wavertree One Off *D R C Elsworth* a62 55
4 b g Diktat—Miss Clarinet (Pharly (FR))
32[8]

Wavertree Warrior (IRE) *N P Littmoden* a93 98
4 br g Indian Lodge(IRE) —Karamana (Habitat)
58[9] 267[3]559[4] 662[3]726[11] (946) 1207[2] (1932) 2200[6] (2649) 3493[15]5789[2] 5943[15] 6594[4]6830[2] 6915[4]

Wax Eloquent *C G Cox* 64
3 ch f Zaha(CAN) —Wax Lyrical (Safawan)
4563[5]

Waymark (IRE) *M A Jarvis* 72
2 ch c Halling(USA) —Uncharted Haven (Turtle Island (IRE))
5882[2]

Way To The Stars *A M Balding* a64 74+
3 gr f Dansili—Reason To Dance (Damister (USA))
1355[14] 1844[8] 2459[2] 2735[5] 3953[4]4591[10] 5755[2] 5953[10] 6595[8]

Wayward Shot (IRE) *G P Kelly* a54 67
4 b g Desert Prince(IRE) —Style Parade (USA) (Diesis)
818[9] 1041[6] 1422[18] 2299[14] 3147[9]4154[10] 5285[8] 6725[3]6756[6]

Wazir (USA) *J H M Gosden* a86+ 96+
4 bb h Pulpit(USA) —Top Order (USA) (Dayjur (USA))
282a[11] 366a[4] 495a[14]

Weakest Link *E J Alston* a56 56
5 b g Mind Games—Sky Music (Absalom)
288[3] 411[8]1397[3] 2112[2] 2544[8]3524[15] 4067[6] 4361[2] 4611[2] 4636[12]5486[13] 5969[12] 6277[11]

Webbow (IRE) *T D Easterby* a69 75
4 b g Dr Devious(IRE) —Ower (IRE) (Lomond (USA))
534[2] (677) 992[3] 1186[8]1864[5]

Webbswood Lad (IRE) *Stef Liddiard* a64 65
5 b g Robellino(USA) —Poleaxe (Selkirk (USA))
18[2] 324[4]421[6] 603[10]

Wednesdays Boy (IRE) *P D Niven* a61 61+
3 b g Alhaarth(IRE) —Sheen Falls (IRE) (Prince Rupert (FR))
1549[2] 1950[2] 2466[9]2746[3] 3167[4] (4651) 5064[6]

Wee Charlie Castle (IRE) *G C H Chung* a71 73
3 b g Sinndar(IRE) —Seasonal Blossom (IRE) (Fairy King (USA))
49[2] 2050[5] 2466[5]2823[2] 3045[5] (4245) 4702[14]5270[5] 5740[11] (6565) 6843[5]

Wee Ellie Coburn *A Bailey* a58 54
2 ch f Bold Edge—Wathbat Mtoto (Mtoto)
4949[5] 5616[8] 6050[9] 6422[2]6730[2] 6927[5]

Weekend Escape (IRE) *K J Condon* 82
2 b g Mujahid(USA) —Sakha (Wolfhound (USA))
4824a[7]

Weekend Fling (USA) *M Johnston* 70
2 bb f Forest Wildcat(USA) —Woodman's Dancer (USA) (Woodman (USA))
2890[2] 3173[3]

Weet A Head (IRE) *R Hollinshead* a70 75
5 b g Foxhound(USA) —Morale (Bluebird (USA))
48[9] 640[6]820[11] 990[12] 1566[3]4869[11] 5127[7]

Weet An Haul *T Wall* a42 42
5 b g Danzero(AUS) —Island Ruler (Ile De Bourbon (USA))
2260[14]

Weet For Ever (USA) *P A Blockley* a59 59
3 bb g High Yield(USA) —Wild Classy Lady (USA) (Wild Again (USA))
1868[8] 2881[6] 3219[4] 4871[14] 5070[11]5844[4] 6403[5]6450[6] 6535[3]6621[7] 6759[3]6980[12]

Weet In Line *K J Burke* a51
2 gr f Weet-A-Minute(IRE) —Weet Ees Girl (IRE) (Common Grounds)
4971[5] 5687[4]6015[11]

Weet N Measures *T Wall* a50 54
4 b g Weet-A-Minute(IRE) —Weet Ees Girl (IRE) (Common Grounds)
46[9] 144[10]260[10] 382[10]

Weet Watchers *T Wall* a36 38
6 b g Polar Prince(IRE) —Weet Ees Girl (IRE) (Common Grounds)
442[8] 2260[5] 2632[12]

Weet Yer Tern (IRE) *W M Brisbourne* a52 60
4 b g Brave Act—Maxime (IRE) (Mac's Imp (USA))
14[4] 46[7]257[4] 382[4]468[3] 573[9]769[5] 793[6]6616[2] 6701[2]6800[4] 6960[9]6977[6]

Wee Ziggy *D Nicholls* 36
3 b g Ziggy's Dancer(USA) —Midnight Arrow (Robellino (USA))
978[11] 1230[10] 3698[10]

Weightless *N P Littmoden* a95 110
6 ch g In The Wings—Orford Ness (Selkirk (USA))
1267[5] 1976[6] (2236) 2597a[4] 3254[6] 5968[8]6516[11] 6559[5]6997[7]

Weingeist (GER) *T Stauffer*
12 b h Goofalik(USA) —Weinrebe (GDR) (Immer (HUN))
306a[9]

Welcome Approach *J R Weymes* a12 76
3 b g Most Welcome—Lucky Thing (Green Desert (USA))
1036[4] (1453) 2110[2] 2410[6] 2976[2] 3360[6]4812[2] 5265[6] 5593[9] 6159[8]

Welcome Releaf *G C H Chung* a57 54
3 ch g Most Welcome—Mint Leaf (IRE) (Sri Pekan (USA))
445[9] 531[2]735[5] 1941[10]2143[7] 2644[5] 3087[7] 3378[2]3999[6]

Welcome Spirit *J S Haldane* 1
3 b g Most Welcome—Valadon (High Line)
5485[16] 5837[11]

Weld Il Balad (IRE) *M Johnston* 78
2 b c Alhaarth(IRE) —Claustra (FR) (Green Desert (USA))
(4018) 5916[6]

Well Armed (USA) *C E Brittain* a108 77
3 b c Tiznow(USA) —Well Dressed (USA) (Notebook (USA))
(150a) 368a[9] 739a[11]

We'll Come *M A Jarvis* 81
2 b g Elnadim(USA) —Off The Blocks (Salse (USA))
4801[2] 5655[7] 5918[2]

We'll Confer *K A Ryan* a99 99
2 b c Piccolo—Medina De Rioseco (Puissance)
1491[2] (1959) 2724[6] 3734[3] 4736[4] 5017[3]5335[4] 6229a[8]

Well Established (IRE) *M A Jarvis* a84 84
4 b g Sadler's Wells(USA) —Riveryev (USA) (Irish River (FR))
4878[4] 5299[7] 5671[5]5944[6]

Well Guarded (IRE) *C R Egerton* a75 70+
3 b g Sadler's Wells(USA) —En Garde (USA) (Irish River (FR))
4431[5] (Dead)

Well Hidden *Sir Michael Stoute* 88
3 b f Sadler's Wells(USA) —Phantom Gold (Machiavellian (USA))
2412[3] 3225[5] (4374) 4741[8]

Wellington Hall (GER) *P W Chapple-Hyam* a85 87
8 b g Halling(USA) —Wells Whisper (FR) (Sadler's Wells (USA))
325[6] 2621[2] 3048[5]3497[9] 3980[7] 4149[7] 5506[2] 6017[10]

Wellola (IRE) *H Blume* 103
4 b m Lomitas—Well Known (GER) (Konigsstuhl (GER))
5857a[3]

Well Versed *C F Wall* a35 53+
3 b f Most Welcome—Versatility (Teenoso (USA))
4776[7] 5429[10] 5589[P]

Welsh Auction *G A Huffer* 42
2 ch c Auction House(USA) —Anneli Rose (Superlative)
5454[14] 5645 [12]

Welsh Cake *Mrs A J Perrett* a60 70
3 b f Fantastic Light(USA) —Khubza (Green Desert (USA))
1307[4] 1616[8] 2535[9]5092[2] (5418) 5568[2]

Welsh Dragon *A M Balding* a64 56
3 b g Cape Cross(IRE) —Blorenge (Prince Sabo)
(31) 594[2] 709[3]839[3] 2050[11] 3339[7]

Welsh Emperor (IRE) *T P Tate* a89 117
7 b g Emperor Jones(USA) —Simply Times (USA) (Dodge (USA))
(1145) 1778[14] (4596) 5184[8] 5701a[2] 5962[10]

Welsh Whisper *S A Brookshaw* a47 47
7 b m Overbury(IRE) —Grugiar (Red Sunset)
232[9] 502[9]769[4] 792[5]1197[5] (1225) 2098[10] 2702[11] 3386[8]3594[6]

Welsh Wind (IRE) *M Wigham* a64 65
10 b g Tenby—Bavaria (Top Ville)
35[3] 297[11]

Wend (USA) *W Mott* 116
5 b m Pulpit(USA) —Thread (USA) (Topsider (USA))
4385a[8]

Wendals *Rae Guest* 67
3 br f Xaar—Runelia (Runnett)
1646[8] 2167[9] 2589[9] 4495[5] 4872[12]

Wendy's Boy *R Hannon* 18
2 b c Elnadim(USA) —Tatouma (USA) (The Minstrel (CAN))
1688[13]

Wensleydale Star *T D Barron* a21 42
3 b g Alzao(USA) —Janiceland (IRE) (Foxhound (USA))
347[5] 430[6]1232[11] 1731[5] 2107[4] 2379[8] 3288[7]3357[3] 3785[4] 4016[4]

Wessex (USA) *P A Blockley* a100 83
6 ch g Gone West(USA) —Satin Velvet (USA) (El Gran Senor (USA))
58[5] 275[2]348[2] (413) 629[12] 1246[6]6678[2]

Westbrook Blue *W G M Turner* a66 84
4 b h Kingsinger(IRE) —Gold And Blue (IRE) (Bluebird (USA))
1031[4] 1076[7] 4598[7] 4793[8] 5957[10]6274[2] 6682[9]

Westcourt Dream *M W Easterby* a57 60
6 ch m Bal Harbour—Katie's Kitty (Noble Patriarch)
1249[4] 2322[4] 2407[7] 2891[2] 3142[4]4455[2]

Westcourt Phoenix *M W Easterby* 10
3 b f Josr Algarhoud(IRE) —Boulevard Rouge (USA) (Red Ransom (USA))
3261[11] 4195[10] 5241[8]6758[10]

Westering Home (IRE) *J Mackie* a62 68
3 b f Mull Of Kintyre(USA) —Glympse (IRE) (Spectrum (IRE))
3007[6] 3250[11] 3816[3] 4118[4] 4470[4]5484[11] 6942[5]

Wester Lodge (IRE) *J M P Eustace* a70 77
4 ch g Fraam—Reamzafonic (Grand Lodge (USA))
2183[5] 2519[3] 2761[4] 3037[7] 3840[6]4240[2] 4673[7] 5047[5]5610[10] 6070[9]6256[8]

Western Adventure (USA) *E A L Dunlop* 78
2 b c Gone West(USA) —Larrocha (IRE) (Sadler's Wells (USA))
5088[2]

Western Roots *M Appleby* a69 55
5 ch g Dr Fong(USA) —Chrysalis (Soviet Star (USA))
111[3] 214[5]319[3] 571[5]723[12] 3566[8] 3820[13]3918[9] 4368[12]4972[6] 5385[6] 5740[3]5972[6] (6419) 6451[3] 6666[6]6734[4]

Western Sky *J Noseda* a47
3 ch f Barathea(IRE) —Western Heights (Shirley Heights)
266[4] 460[11]

Wester Ross (IRE) *J M P Eustace* 78+
2 b c Fruits Of Love(USA) —Diabaig (Precocious)
6214[4]

West Highland Way (IRE) *Mrs H O Graham* a71 80
5 b g Foxhound(USA) —Gilding The Lily (IRE) (High Estate)
5685[11] 5904[15]

Westlake Bond (IRE) *G R Oldroyd* a13 44
4 b m Josr Algarhoud(IRE) —Rania (Aragon)
232[7] 1728[11]3379[10] 3912[5] 4507[9]6490[8]

West Of Amarillo (USA) *J H M Gosden* 113
3 b g Gone West(USA) —Navarra (USA) (El Gran Senor (USA))
1269[3] 1718a[4]

Westport *K A Ryan* a73+ 86
3 b g Xaar—Connemara (IRE) (Mujadil (USA))
191[4] (272) 852[4]1812[2] (2109) 2385[9] 3360[5] 4707[6] 5401[8]6320[2]

West Warning *M W Easterby* 34
2 b g Warningford—Westcourt Pearl (Emarati (USA))
2973[13] 3787[7] 5746[9] (Dead)

Weyba Downs (IRE) *J R Best* a65 62
2 b g Daggers Drawn(USA) —Jarmar Moon (Unfuwain (USA))
701[5] 912[4]2172[10] 2710[7] 4043[2]4519[4] 4699[5] 6310[11]

Whaleef *B J Llewellyn* a78 83
8 br g Darshaan—Wilayif (USA) (Danzig (USA))
2944[7]

What-A-Dancer (IRE) *R A Harris* a69 68
9 b g Dancing Dissident(USA) —Cool Gales (Lord Gayle (USA))
1275[5] 1673[14] 1923[6]2223[7] 2319[6] 3194[5]3570[5] 3820[6] (3898) 4368[7]4674[3] 4871[7] 5130[7] 5269[14] 5907[10]6293[7] 6493[8]

Whatatodo *M L W Bell* 60
4 b m Compton Place—Emerald Dream (IRE) (Vision (USA))
1753[2] 2135[11] 2634[4] 3339[9] 3827[7]4266[14]

What A Treasure (IRE) *L M Cumani* a55 68
2 ch f Cadeaux Genereux—Treasure Trove (USA) (The Minstrel (CAN))
3537[7] 4323[4] 4754[6] 5606[8]

What Budget *B J Meehan* a56 51
2 br f Halling(USA) —Baked Alaska (Green Desert (USA))
4558[10] 5339[10] 5906[9]

What Do You Know *G A Butler* a76 70
3 b g Compton Place—How Do I Know (Petong)
1672[8] 2553[4] 2652[6]3646[9] 4591[8] 4943[5]6348[5]

Whatizzit *E A L Dunlop* a86 83
3 b f Galileo(IRE) —Wosaita (Generous (IRE))
2446[4] 3095[2] 4490[2]5109[2]

Whatsthescript (IRE) *David Wachman* a97 98
2 b c Royal Applause—Grizel (Lion Cavern (USA))
3962a[3]

Whats Your Game (IRE) *A Berry*
2 ch g Namid—Tahlil (Cadeaux Genereux)
3247[12]

Whaxaar (IRE) *S Kirk* a66 37
2 b c Xaar—Sheriyna (FR) (Darshaan)
5126[9] 6143[7] 6651[6]

Whazzat *P W Chapple-Hyam* a65 100
4 b m Daylami(IRE) —Wosaita (Generous (IRE))
356a[7] 3021[4]

Whazzis *W J Haggas* a81 81
2 br f Desert Prince(IRE) —Wosaita (Generous (IRE))
4762[3] 5503[4] 5784[2](6481)

Wheelavit (IRE) *B G Powell* a73 74+
3 b g Elnadim(USA) —Storm River (USA) (Riverman (USA))
2343[13] 2532[7] 2934[6](3538) 4078[3] 5042[16] 6986[12]

Wheels In Motion (IRE) *T P Tate* 81
2 b c Daylami(IRE) —Tarziyana (USA) (Danzig (USA))
(4880) 5308[3]

Whenwillitwin *J S Moore* a53 50
5 b g Bluegrass Prince(IRE) —Madam Marash (IRE) (Astronef)
(63) 472[5] 636[11]1201[13]

Where's Broughton *W J Musson* a75 61
3 ch f Cadeaux Genereux—Tuxford Hideaway (Cawston's Clown)
(6588) 6862[4]

Where's Sally *J Mackie* a27
6 b m Polar Prince(IRE) —Mustang Scally (Makbul)
382[11] 634[8]791[6]

Where's That Tiger (USA) *M F De Kock* a102 98
3 ch c Storm Cat(USA) —Blissful (USA) (Mr Prospector (USA))
368a[2] 561a[2]739a[8]

Whiffle (USA) *M Johnston* 71+
2 b f Red Ransom(USA) —Whist (Mr Prospector (USA))
2191[4] (2610)

Whilly (IRE) *Doug O'Neill* 117
5 b h Sri Pekan(USA) —Santa Rosa (IRE) (Lahib (USA))
742a[11]

Whinhill House *D W Barker* a69 92d
6 ch g Paris House—Darussalam (Tina's Pet)
79[9] 198[7]569[12] 1031[5] 1125[10]1496[10] 1686[19] 2237[2] 2449[5] 2624[15]3584[5] 3988[12] 4453[3] 4636[17] 4957[16]5487[8] 5620[8]

Whipchord (IRE) *R Hannon* 62
2 ch f Distant Music(USA) —Spanker (Suave Dancer (USA))
1542[5] 2166[7] 2631[8] 3435[4] 4427[2]5419[13]

Whipper In *P C Haslam* a49 61
3 ch f Foxhound(USA) —Come To The Point (Pursuit Of Love)
120[6] 335[8]

Whiskey Junction *A M Balding* a73 38
2 b g Bold Edge—Victoria Mill (Free State)
1535[3] 1959[2]2281[8] 3409[4] 3917[7]

Whispering Death *W J Haggas* 89
4 br g Pivotal—Lucky Arrow (Indian Ridge)
1756[15] 2035[9] 2357[9] 2684[2] (3177) 3452[2](3955) 4770[4] 5678[11] 5963[6]

Whisper Inthe Wind (IRE) *Miss J Feilden* a43 55
3 ch f King Charlemagne(USA) —Persian Mistress (IRE) (Persian Bold)
1431[11] 2316[13] 2583[5] 3072[7] 3379[4]3668[6] 4265[7] 4494[9] 5453[14] 5924[12]

Whist Drive *Mrs N Smith* a27 65
6 ch g First Trump—Fine Quill (Unfuwain (USA))
6398[8]

Whistle Away *W R Swinburn* a58 55
3 b g Piccolo—Miss Dangerous (Komaite (USA))
3050[7] 3916[2]4527[6]

Whistler *Miss J R Tooth* a71 68
9 ch g Selkirk(USA) —French Gift (Cadeaux Genereux)
947[10] 1047[10] 1297[12] 1475[8] 1662[13]1846[13] 2027[5] 2136[4] 2505[14] 2550[9]2618[6] 3297[11] 3348[5] 3449[10] 4019[8]4180[9] (4462) 4780[10] 4962[6] 5131[11] 5286[9]5378[12] 5493[12]

Whistleupthewind *J M P Eustace* a66 64
3 b f Piccolo—The Frog Queen (Bin Ajwaad (IRE))
868[8] 1200[7] 1955[11]2198[4] 2479[2] (2589) (3072) 3250[7] 3828[5] 4265[2]4930[2] 6608[10]6672[5] 6869[10]

Whiston Lad (IRE) *S R Bowring* 48
3 b g Barathea(IRE) —Fille De Bucheron (USA) (Woodman (USA))
1290[11] 2111[8] 2615[15] 3791[13]

Whitbarrow (IRE) *B R Millman* a60 67
7 b g Royal Abjar(USA) —Danccini (IRE) (Dancing Dissident (USA))
36[6] 587[7]159[2] 224[7]480[8] 2444[8] 2813[6]3071[2] 3297[10] 3348[7] 3899[2] 4211[3]4361[6] 4962[10] 5378[7] 5755[5] 6193[6]

Whitby Echo (IRE) *R Hollinshead* a54 61
4 b g Entrepreneur—Nom De Plume (USA) (Nodouble (USA))
597[8] 770[2]891[11] 2193[9] (Dead)

White Bear (FR) *C R Dore* a71 63
4 ch g Gold Away(IRE) —Danaide (FR) (Polish Precedent (USA))
240[3] (339) (514) 575[2]985[3] 1164[3]2464[11] 3404[10]

White Deer (USA) *M Johnston* 87
2 bb c Stravinsky(USA) —Brookshield Baby (IRE) (Sadler's Wells (USA))
2972[4] 3758[2] (4074) 5359[3]

White Gables (IRE) *M Halford* 71
2 b g Invincible Spirit(IRE) —Redeem (IRE) (Doyoun)
5692a[6]

White Heather *A M Balding* a33 18
3 br f Selkirk(USA) —Durrah Green (Green Desert (USA))
479[12] 963[10]

White Ladder (IRE) *P F I Cole* a54+ 66
3 gr c Marju(IRE) —Lady Rachel (IRE) (Priolo (USA))
4045[4] 4769[15] 5031[11]5605[11]

White Ledger (IRE) *R E Peacock* a52 41
7 ch g Ali-Royal(IRE) —Boranwood (IRE) (Exhibitioner)
119[11] 164[11]3052[8] 3389[10]6739[9] 6922[5]

White Lightening (IRE) *J Howard Johnson* 78
3 ch g Indian Ridge—Mille Miglia (IRE) (Caerleon (USA))
3001[2] 5063[5]

White Lightning (GER) *U Stech* 111
4 gr h Sternkoenig(IRE) —Whispering Grass (GER) (Konigsstuhl (GER))
(4828a) 5414a[6] 5762a[4] 6109a[6]

White On Black (GER) *G L Moore* a56
5 b h Lomitas—White On Red (GER) (Konigsstuhl (GER))
983[10]

Whitethorne *R A Fahey* a48 83
4 b m Mujadil(USA) —Sharpthorne (USA) (Sharpen Up)
(2293) 2705[2] 2851[8] (3289) 3891[P] (Dead)

White Visor (IRE) *A Angelelli*
2 ch f Dr Fong(USA) —Imco Cracking (IRE) (Piccolo)
3428a[9]

White Wingo (SAF) *R Simpson* a40 18
6 gr g Al Mufti(USA) —Glib Talk (SAF) (Mr Justice (USA))
4625[8]

Whitgift Rock *S Dow* a78 76
5 b g Piccolo—Fly South (Polar Falcon (USA))
764[7] 915[6]1244[9] 1926[10]

Whitsbury Common *D R C Elsworth* a40 61
4 b m Lujain(USA) —Vallauris (Faustus (USA))
114[12] 457[14]917[10]

Whittinghamvillage *D W Whillans* a35 63
5 b m Whittingham(IRE) —Shaa Spin (Shaadi (USA))
1761[2] 2286[6] 2747[7] 3137[6] 3617[11]3815[6] 4355[3] 4729[8] 5063[3] 5285[16]5839[3]

Whole Grain *B R Millman* a43 72
5 b m Polish Precedent(USA) —Mill Line (Mill Reef (USA))
13[11]

Whoopee (USA) *M Johnston* 41
3 bb f Mozart(IRE) —Time For A Wedding (USA) (Manila (USA))
3554[8] 3826[5] 4473[4] 4944[14]

Whoopsie *S Parr* a51 59
4 b m Unfuwain(USA) —Oops Pettie (Machiavellian (USA))
1138[7] (1436) 1660[3] 2078[8] 4156[6] 5324[14]5750[10] 6132[3] 6375[6]6620[8]

Whos Counting *R J Hodges* a47
2 ch f Woodborough(USA) —Hard To Follow (Dilum (USA))
6254[11] 6511[5]6695[3]

Who's The Cowboy (USA) *K Sleeter* a103
4 b g Intensity(USA) —Image's Image (USA) (Better Arbitor (USA))
5820a[4]

Who's Winning (IRE) *B G Powell* a84 82
5 ch g Docksider(USA) —Quintellina (Robellino (USA))
117[7] 220[7]376[2] 476[11]970[7] 1112[6] 1359[6]2384[11] 2635[6] 3368[4] (3612) 3855[3] 4106[5]4486[4] 5058[2] 5148[10] 5575[3] 6065[6]6437[11] 6690[4]6835[3] 6984[3]

Whozart (IRE) *A Dickman* a37
3 b g Mozart(IRE) —Hertford Castle (Reference Point)
6480[12] 6771[10]

Why Harry *J J Quinn* a65 58
4 b g Cyrano De Bergerac—Golden Ciel (USA) (Septieme Ciel (USA))
46[11]

Why Now *K A Ryan* a78 81
4 b m Dansili—Questionable (Rainbow Quest (USA))
245[13]

Wibbadune (IRE) *Peter Grayson* a58
2 ch f Daggers Drawn(USA) —Becada (GER) (Cadeaux Genereux)
6222[10] 6463[7]6512[5] 6605[7]6665[4] 6788[3]6839[2] 6921[2]6975[2]

Wickedish *P Howling* 54
2 b f Medicean—Sleave Silk (IRE) (Unfuwain (USA))
3043[9] 3417[16] 4148[12] 5271[5]

Wicked Lady (UAE) *B R Johnson* a50
3 b f Jade Robbery(USA) —Kinsfolk (Distant Relative)
6987[7]

Wicked Uncle *S Gollings* a87 73
7 b g Distant Relative—The Kings Daughter (Indian King (USA))
23[3] 136[2]517[4] 699[4](986) 1047[9] (1399) 1662[17] 1928[5] 2946[8]3281[11]

Wicked Wilma (IRE) *A Berry* 63
2 b f Tagula(IRE) —Wicked (Common Grounds)
3286[3] 3521[3] 4017[3] (4089)

Wickwing *A & G Botti* 102
3 b f In The Wings—Chetwynd (IRE) (Exit To Nowhere (USA))
2043a[2] 2694a[11] 6251a[7]

Wid (USA) *J L Dunlop* 101
2 rg f Elusive Quality(USA) —Alshadiyah (USA) (Danzig (USA))
(3043) (4322) 4966[2] 5654[11]

Widow Blach *Nicola De Chirico*
2 b f Bertolini(USA) —Trieste (GER) (Law Society (USA))
5705a[8]

Wi Dud *K A Ryan* 114
2 b c Elnadim(USA) —Hopesay (Warning)
(2623) 4026[2] 4712[2] (5154) 5656[2]

Wiesenpfad (FR) *W Hickst* 109
3 ch c Waky Nao—Waldbeere (Mark Of Esteem (IRE))
(5856a) (6529a)

Wiggy Smith *O Sherwood* a72 84
7 ch g Master Willie—Monsoon (Royal Palace)
1779[8] 2169[6]

Wig Wam Bam (IRE) *R A Fahey* 50
3 b f Indian Rocket—Almasa (Faustus (USA))
2704[12]

Wigwam Willie (IRE) *K A Ryan* 90
4 b g Indian Rocket—Sweet Nature (IRE) (Classic Secret (USA))
865[5] 1143[8] 1676[5] 2162[4] 2974[6](5337) 5639[12] 6210[4]

Wild Academy (IRE) *G C Bravery* a67 73
3 b f Royal Academy(USA) —Wild Vintage (USA) (Alysheba (USA))
2146[3] 2587[11] 4563[7] 5211[8]5734[9] 6147[12]

Wild Buddy (USA) *Steve Knapp* 114
7 b g Line In The Sand(USA) —Island Capitol (USA) (Manila (USA))
5825a[5]

Wilde Jasmine (IRE) *J R Weymes* a26 37
2 ch f Daggers Drawn(USA) —No Tomorrow (IRE) (Night Shift (USA))
3745[8] 3982[10] 4251[12] 4950[5] 6257[10]

Wilderness Bay (IRE) *M R Bosley* a57 70+
4 bb m Fasliyev(USA) —Pleine Lune (IRE) (Alzao (USA))
2601[7] 3440[9] 3731[8]4005[14] 5831[11]

Wilde Thing *S Curran* 21
2 b f Muhtarram(USA) —Lochbelle (Robellino (USA))
5947[7] 6298[10] 6570[9]

Wild Fell Hall (IRE) *W R Swinburn* 72
3 ch c Grand Lodge(USA) —Genoa (Zafonic (USA))
1868[7]

Wild Gardenia *J H M Gosden* a57
2 b f Alhaarth(IRE) —Frappe (IRE) (Inchinor)
6486[7]

Wild Groove (USA) *Gianluigi Bietolini* a64 96
3 br c Wild Event(USA) —Groovy Babe (USA) (Image Of Greatness (USA))
5473a[10]

Wild Lass *J C Fox* a41 56d
5 ch m Bluegrass Prince(IRE) —Pink Pumpkin (Tickled Pink)
539[7] 963[9] 1351[16]2349[12] (2531) 3194[6] 3817[9] 4332[11] 4667[5]6059[10] 6370[9] 6725[7]6802[8] 6904[10]

Wild Pitch *P Mitchell* a79+ 73
5 ch g Piccolo—Western Horizon (USA) (Gone West (USA))
(1400) 1995[4] (2345) 2585[5] 5991[7]6885[5]

Wild Savannah *J H M Gosden* a106 112+
4 b h Singspiel(IRE) —Apache Star (Arazi (USA))
(1484) 2803[2]

Wild Thyme *R Hannon* 69
2 ch f Desert Prince(IRE) —Once Upon A Time (Teenoso (USA))
4866[2] 5352[4] 5536[5]

Wildwish (IRE) *Enda Kelly* 65
2 b f Alhaarth(IRE) —Wish (Danehill (USA))
5850a[5]

Wilford Maverick (IRE) *M J Attwater* a54 28
4 b g Fasliyev(USA) —Lioness (Lion Cavern (USA))
43[5] 121[9]175[9] 210[4]315[12] 613[8](638) 680[3]784[5] 940[7]5929[13] 6554[7]6618[2] 6702[6]6756[10] 6961[11]

Wilko (USA) *J Noseda* a120 112
4 ch h Awesome Again(CAN) —Native Roots (IRE) (Indian Ridge)
743a[2] 2093a[5]

Will Be (IRE) *R A Kvisla* a69 67
3 bb f In The Wings—Bintalshaati (Kris)
2564a[4] 3326a[6] 3848[6]4240[3] 4700[2] 4972[3]5868[4]

Will Doo *M E Sowersby* a19
2 b c Elmaamul(USA) —Perpetuo (Mtoto)
4018[12] 4829[13] 5387[11]

Willheconquertoo *I W McInnes* a73 73
6 ch g Primo Dominie—Sure Care (Caerleon (USA))
89[5] 192[10]224[3] 323[6]441[7] 569[P]

Willhego *J R Best* a87 73
5 ch g Pivotal—Woodrising (Nomination)
33[4] (88) (140) 222[2]296[9] 377[8]

Will He Rock (IRE) *John A Quinn* a72 80
5 b g Diesis—Recoleta (USA) (Wild Again (USA))
825[3]

Will He Wish *S Gollings* a94 97
10 b g Winning Gallery—More To Life (Northern Tempest (USA))
1112[3] (1456) 2289[5] 2649[10]3121[6] 3518[5] 4172[13] 4535[10] 6192[12]6499[6] 6733[4]6868[6]

Willhewiz *M S Saunders* a79 83
6 b g Wizard King—Leave It To Lib (Tender King)
79[4] 244[7]967[2] 1285[8] 2189[15] 2536[4] 2635[2]3027[5] 3165[3] 3486[7] 3855[8] 4449[6]4629[10]

William John *B Ellison* a58? 61
3 b g Foxhound(USA) —Classy Relation (Puissance)
979[6] 1345[3] 1533[3] 2529[3] 3145[7](4069) 4454[3] 4845[9]

William's Way *I A Wood* a77 75
4 b g Fraam—Silk Daisy (Barathea (IRE))
3122[7] 3458[3] 3647[5](4001) 4586[6] 4662[2] 5295[5] 5599[7] 5786[4]5889[7] 6426[9] 6494[2]6716[2]

William Tell (IRE) *Micky Hammond* a63 67
4 b g Rossini(USA) —Livry (USA) (Lyphard (USA))
599[8] 1045[12] 1562[8]4380[9] 5369[14]

Willingly (GER) *M Trybuhl* 108
7 b h Second Set(IRE) —Winara (GER) (Konigsstuhl (GER))
1869a[2] 2492a[3] 2692a[5] 3563a[2] 4190a[2]5227a[7] 5543a[5]

Willofcourse *H Candy* a35 72+
5 b g Aragon—Willyet (Nicholas Bill)
1689[13] 2223[10] 2602[4] 2920[8] 3389[11]

Will The Till *J M Bradley* 69
4 b g Fraam—Prim Ajwaad (Bin Ajwaad (IRE))
1568[12] 1773[3] 1882[10] 2223[8] 2601[10]3542[8] 3948[3] 4325[4] 4869[8] 5166[5]5385[7]

Willy (SWE) *R Brotherton* a55 30
4 ch g Heart Of Oak(USA) —Kawa-Ib (IRE) (Nashwan (USA))
5897[15] 6584[3] 6758[4]6936[11]

Wilman (IRE) *M Halford* 97
3 b g Alhaarth(IRE) —Shadowglow (Shaadi (USA))
5853a[16]

Wilmas Gal *R Bastiman* a17 30
3 ch f Compton Place—Malthouse Girl (IRE) (Barathea (IRE))
1501[12] 1868[10] 2763[9] 3006[14] 3384[8]3910[15]

Wilmington *N P Littmoden* a68 72
2 ch g Compton Place—Bahawir Pour (USA) (Green Dancer (USA))
3363[10] 3844[10] 4161[2]4681[15] 5262[6] 6063[3]6475[5]

Wiltshire (IRE) *P T Midgley* a58 63
4 br g Spectrum(IRE) —Mary Magdalene (Night Shift (USA))
56[8] 297[7]398[4] 458[4]581[3] 889[2]1550[7] 2546[2] 2728[8]5885[13] 6431[3] 6577[7]6787[4] 6955[12]

Windbeneathmywings (IRE) *J W Hills* a50 53
2 b f In The Wings—Moneefa (Darshaan)
5425[9] 5730[6] 6449[5]

Wind Chime (IRE) *A G Newcombe* a62 74
9 ch h Arazi(USA) —Shamisen (Diesis)
792[9] 1769[4] 2482[8]2969[9] 3820[7] (4288) 4772[7] 5166[10] 6232[5]6616[6] (6852)

Wind Flow *E A L Dunlop* a64 69
2 b c Dr Fong(USA) —Spring (Sadler's Wells (USA))
3843[8] 4388[6]

Windhuk (GER) *P Giannotti* 106
3 b f Platini(GER) —Waconda (GER) (Pursuit Of Love)
758a[9] (1713a)

Windjammer *T D Easterby* 50
2 b g Kyllachy—Absolve (USA) (Diesis)
1982[6] 2783[6] 3994[11]

Wind Shuffle (GER) *T P Tate* 68+
3 b g Big Shuffle(USA) —Wiesensturmerin (GER) (Lagunas)
1564[2] 5761[4]

Winds Of Change *M Johnston* a53 76+
3 gr f King's Best(USA) —New Wind (GER) (Windwurf (GER))
797[3] 918[11] (1634) 2124[2]2633[2] 3046[3] 3302[2]

Windsor Knot (IRE) *Saeed Bin Suroor* 115
4 ch h Pivotal—Triple Tie (USA) (The Minstrel (CAN))
3254[2] 3736[2] (4337) 4817[4] 5968[2]

Wind Star *G A Swinbank* 94+
3 ch g Piccolo—Starfleet (Inchinor)
2325[6] 2448[4] 2734[2] 3167[2] (3782) (4137) 4298[8]5579[3]

Windy Prospect *P A Blockley* a67 77
4 ch g Intikhab(USA) —Yellow Ribbon (IRE) (Hamas (IRE))
75[5] 334[9]2317[13] 2541[8] 2567[8] 2728[5] 4439[9]5267[8] (6464) 6549[4]6674[2] 6721[4]6949[4]

Winga (IRE) *B Grizzetti* 93
3 b f In The Wings—Bog (USA) (Majestic Light (USA))
1713a[12] 2043a[9]

Wing Collar *T D Easterby* 93
5 b g In The Wings—Riyoom (USA) (Vaguely Noble)
1809[2] 2437[3] 3078[12]

Wing Commander *I W McInnes* a32 76
7 b g Royal Applause—Southern Psychic (USA) (Alwasmi (USA))
726[16] 1043[10] 1302[10] 1651[11] 2108[5]2322[3] 2627[5] 2945[3] 3147[5] 3241[5]3716[11] (4353) (4454) 4654[6]

Winged D'Argent (IRE) *M Johnston* 114
5 b g In The Wings—Petite-D-Argent (Noalto)
1332a[7] 1584[5] 1833[7] 2085[2] 2773[9]3315[3] 4081[14] 4677[8] 5156[8] 5526[3]

Winged Farasi *Miss J Feilden* 69
2 b c Desert Style(IRE) —Clara Vale (IRE) (In The Wings)
3979[5] 4688[3]

Winged Flight (USA) *M Johnston* 87
2 b c Fusaichi Pegasus(USA) —Tobaranama (IRE) (Sadler's Wells (USA))
3923[3] (4302) 4680[7]

Wingman (IRE) *J W Hills* a88 91
4 b g In The Wings—Precedence (IRE) (Polish Precedent (USA))
1071[3] 1775[4] 2229[5] 2817[5] 3490[4]3890[7] 4347[10] 5671[6]

Wingsinmotion (IRE) *K R Burke*
2 b f Indian Lodge(IRE) —Coulisse (IRE) (In The Wings)
3915[11] 4724[10]

Wings Of Dawn *M P Tregoning* 58
3 b f In The Wings—Petit Point (IRE) (Petorius)
1652[13] 2434[6] 3145[3] (4758) 5587[9]

Wings Of Morning (IRE) *D Carroll* a55 56
5 ch g Fumo Di Londra(IRE) —Hay Knot (Main Reef)
(27) 526[10] 784[4]1463[5] 1575[3](1764) 2208[10]3158[2] 6431[7]6703[8] 6961[13]6981[7]

Wingspan (USA) *A Fabre* 108
3 b f Silver Hawk(USA) —Broad Pennant (USA) (Broad Brush (USA))
1370a[3] 2257a[5] 6171a[2] 6454a[6]

Winisk River (IRE) *E Charpy* a100+ 111
6 b h Barathea(IRE) —Brisighella (IRE) (Al Hareb (USA))
(507a)

Winners Delight *C F Wall* a88 86
5 ch g First Trump—Real Popcorn (IRE) (Jareer (USA))
670[11] 1992[6] (2508) 3048[8]3365[7] 4051[7] 5786[3]

Winning Connection (IRE) *P A Blockley* 36
3 b g Beckett(IRE) —Schiranna (Seymour Hicks (FR))
3112[11] 3346[7] 4113[9]

Winning Pleasure (IRE) *J Balding* a68 35
8 b g Ashkalani(IRE) —Karamana (Habitat)
4[12] 159[9](271) (345) 428[3](654) 6428[11]6643[5] 6896[5]

Winning Smile (USA) *P W Chapple-Hyam* 24
2 ch f With Approval(CAN) —Acquiesce (Generous (IRE))
5950[11]

Winning Spirit (IRE) *J Noseda* 81
2 b g Invincible Spirit(IRE) —Taisho (IRE) (Namaqualand (USA))
1510[3] 2130[2] 2439[3] (2827) 4026[11] 4910[5]

Winning Venture *A W Carroll* a57 69
9 b g Owington—Push A Button (Bold Lad (IRE))
265[8] 360[9](446) 526[12]581[5] 821[4]1303[4] 1550[8]

Win River Win (USA) *C Kurt* a112
7 b h Virginia Rapids(USA) —Thirty Zip (USA) (Tri Jet (USA))
(152a) 560a[2] 738a[2]

Winslow Boy (USA) *P Monteith* a19 65
5 bb g Expelled(USA) —Acusteal (USA) (Acaroid (USA))
3583[6]

Winthorpe (IRE) *J J Quinn* a73 70
6 b g Tagula(IRE) —Zazu (Cure The Blues (USA))
169[3] 274[3](428) (489) 585[5]654[3] 967[4] 1151[2]1686[11] 2380[5] 4019[4] 4694[2] 4885[8]5493[4] 6326[11] 6664[10]

Wisdom's Kiss *J D Bethell* a50
2 b g Ocean Of Wisdom(USA) —April Magic (Magic Ring (IRE))
6290[13]

Wise Choice *N P Littmoden* a60 59
3 b g Green Desert(USA) —Ballykett Lady (USA) (Sir Ivor (USA))
548[7] 584[5]695[4] 979[4] 1350[5]1648[3] 2082[2] 2591[10] 3075[6]3791[5] (4556) 5247[3]

Wise Decision (IRE) *E J O'Neill*
2 b f Redback—Eleanor Rigby (IRE) (Turtle Island (IRE))
5780[11]

Wise Dennis *A P Jarvis* a77 103
4 b g Polar Falcon(USA) —Bowden Rose (Dashing Blade)
1129[9] 4098[9] 4356[4] 4739[11] 5520[4]5675[32]

Wise Kid *P T Midgley* a2 2
3 b g Cloudings(IRE) —Samana Cay (Pharly (FR))
102[7] 335[9]

Wise Owl *J Pearce* a90 90
4 b g Danehill(USA) —Mistle Thrush (USA) (Storm Bird (CAN))
65[5] 296[6]463[6] (628) 765[2] 3098[6]3446[5] 3888[4] 4346[5] 4935[4]5506[4] 5678[13] 5991[3]

Wise Tale *P D Niven* a49 49
7 b g Nashwan(USA) —Wilayif (USA) (Danzig (USA))
1562[11]

Wiseton Dancer (IRE) *Miss V Haigh* a26 7
2 b c Danehill Dancer(IRE) —Your Village (IRE) (Be My Guest (USA))
727[6] 6998[8]

Wise Wager (IRE) *Miss Z C Davison* a72 75
4 b m Titus Livius(FR) —Londubh (Tumble Wind)
699[9] 1315[6] 1643[8]2858[10] (Dead)

Wishfully Tropical (IRE) *C Collins* 40
2 ch f Desert Prince(IRE) —Bean Island (USA) (Afleet (CAN))
4824a[23]

Wishing On A Star *E J O'Neill* 79
2 b f Fantastic Light(USA) —Sephala (USA) (Mr Prospector (USA))
4765[4] 5287[8]

Wistman (UAE) *D Nicholls* a29 62
5 br g Woodman(USA) —Saik (USA) (Riverman (USA))
101[14] 161[13]977[7] 1057[14] 1123[17]

Witchelle *R Craggs* a66 65
5 br m Wizard King—Tachelle (IRE) (Elbio)
332[5] 864[6] 2400[2]2637[6] 3142[13] 3398[11] 6470[11]

Witchry *A G Newcombe* a79+ 78
4 gr g Green Desert(USA) —Indian Skimmer (USA) (Storm Bird (CAN))
224[12] 2484[4] 2536[6]2971[3] (3438) 4258[9] 5058[8] 5291[2] 6274[3]6478[2] 6555[5]6882[5]

With A City (USA) *Michael J Maker* a114
3 ch c City Zip(USA) —With A Princess (USA) (With Approval (CAN))
(757a)

With Admiration *C Drew* 25
3 ch g Whittingham(IRE) —Admire (Last Tycoon)
1546[11] 2048[12] (Dead)

With Interest *Saeed Bin Suroor* 108
3 b c Selkirk(USA) —With Fascination (USA) (Dayjur (USA))
(6299)

Without A Paddle *Daniel Mark Loughnane* a44 71
3 ch g Woodborough(USA) —Sandra Dee (IRE) (Be My Guest (USA))
5834[5]

With Style *E A L Dunlop* 77
3 b f Grand Lodge(USA) —Coyote (Indian Ridge)
2350[6] 3336[4] 4286[4]

Wizard Looking *J S Wainwright* a47 68+
5 b g Wizard King—High Stepping (IRE) (Taufan (USA))
1425[10] 2150[9] 2612[13]

Wizardmicktee (IRE) *A Bailey* a13 22
4 b g Monashee Mountain(USA) —Epsilon (Environment Friend)
3240[13]

Wizard Of Us *M Mullineaux* a40 63
6 b g Wizard King—Sian's Girl (Mystiko (USA))
2025[2] 3724[7] 4511[2] 5136[7] 5316[8]6300[3]

Wizard Prince *J G M O'Shea* a45 50
3 b g Wizard King—Choral Dancer (USA) (Night Shift (USA))
1003[8] 3195[12]

Wizard Quay *W K Goldsworthy* 49
3 b g Wizard King—Roonah Quay (IRE) (Soviet Lad (USA))
2599[7] 2813[9] 2920[7]

Wizards Dream *D R C Elsworth* 72+
3 b c Silver Wizard(USA) —Last Dream (IRE) (Alzao (USA))
2028[8] 2712[5] 5598[4] 5868[6]

Wizby *P D Evans* a47 58
3 b f Wizard King—Diamond Vanessa (IRE) (Distinctly North (USA))
879[8] 1567[3] 2068[3] 2095[4] 2511[4]2676[U] (2921) 3197[8] 3472[7] 5637[6] 6213[3]6300[9] 6762[8]

Wodhill Be *D Morris* a55 50
6 b m Danzig Connection(USA) —Muarij (Star Appeal)
95[3] 134[7]446[3] 889[7]1227[9] 1538[14]2248[7] 4009[5] 4265[10]4844[4] 5573[12] 5926[6]6425[10] 6542[3]6961[4]

Wodhill Gold *D Morris* a57 46
5 ch g Dancing Spree(USA) —Golden Filigree (Faustus (USA))
468[12] 1536[7](1765) 2148[14] 3626[5] 4266[11]5248[5] 5929[2]6473[3] 6543[2]6854[6]

Wodhill Schnaps *D Morris* a55 65
5 b g Danzig Connection(USA) —Muarij (Star Appeal)
2146[8] 2615[10] 3032[4] 3642[12]3931[8] 5302[15] 5571[6] 6237[8]6552[2] 6897[5]6960[3]

Wolds Dancer *T D Easterby* 54
4 b m Fraam—Dancing Em (Rambo Dancer (CAN))
1997[4] 2193[11] 5445[13]

Wolfman *D W Barker* a49 47
4 ch g Wolfhound(USA) —Madam Millie (Milford)
533[6] 873[6]1397[11] 2949[13] 3617[15]3781[10] 5023[6] 5077[7] 5363[2]

Wolf Pack *R W Price* a23 38
4 b g Green Desert(USA) —Warning Shadows (IRE) (Cadeaux Genereux)
3090[11] 3383[5] 3999[14]5768[11] 6059[15]

Wolf River (USA) *D M Simcock* a71
2 b c Mr Greeley(USA) —Beal Street Blues (USA) (Dixieland Band (USA))
4934[3] 5607[7]

Wolf Whistle (SAF) *M F De Kock* a64 116
8 ch g Badger Land(USA) —Certainly (SAF) (Foveros)
153a[14]

Wonderful Day (GER) *C Brandstatter* 91
4 b m Kahyasi—Wonderful Dreams (GER) (Dashing Blade)
1974a[7]

Wonderful Desert *L M Cumani* 57
3 b f Green Desert(USA) —One So Wonderful (Nashwan (USA))
3164[6]

Wonderful One (IRE) *J H M Gosden* a57 69
3 ch f Nashwan(USA) —Ring The Relatives (Bering)
5612[6] 6026[2] 6448[13]

Wonder Lady Anne L (USA) *R Dutrow Jr* a115
3 b f Real Quiet(USA) —Ancho (USA) (Wild Zone (USA))
(3757a)

Woodala (AUS) *A Mathews* 90
5 b m Woodman(USA) —Darmala (NZ) (Danehill (USA))
7000a[11]

Woodcote (IRE) *C G Cox* 103
4 b g Monashee Mountain(USA) —Tootle (Main Reef)
1487[14] 2429[3] 2946[6] 3077[2] 3471[2]4128[7] 4796[4] 5182[5] 5358[20] (5807)

Woodcote Place *P R Chamings* a70 96
3 b c Lujain(USA) —Giant Nipper (Nashwan (USA))
1845[6] 2642[8] 3153[2] 3364[2] 3852[7]4488[6] (4899) (5591) 5785[13] 5943[2]

Wood Dalling (USA) *Mrs J C McGregor* a44 44
8 b g Woodman(USA) —Cloelia (USA) (Lyphard (USA))
1637[7] 3137[11] 3353[10] 4057[10] 4350[9]4475[6]

Wood Fern (UAE) *W M Brisbourne* a54 54
6 b g Green Desert(USA) —Woodsia (Woodman (USA))
787[4] (1224) 1395[2]1467[4] 2075[5] 2132[4]2414[6] 2522[6] 2636[4]2966[2] 3305[6] 3610[6] 4497[9] 5166[3]6128[3] 6544[3]6617[5] 6724[2]6801[2] 6904[2]

Woodford Consult *M W Easterby* a60 59
4 b m Benny The Dip(USA) —Chicodove (In The Wings)
1219[6] 6178[6]

Woodlands Belle *B G Powell* 36
3 ch f Woodborough(USA) —Blushing Belle (Local Suitor (USA))
4280[8]

Woodland Symphony *N Tinkler* a37 54
2 b g Auction House(USA) —Red Symphony (Merdon Melody)
1730[7] 5508[12] 6047[10] 6401[8]

Woodland Traveller (USA) *N Tinkler* 64
2 b g Gone West(USA) —Iftiraas (Distant Relative)
4295[15] 4608[3] 5283[6]

Woodnook *J A R Toller* a90 82
3 b f Cadeaux Genereux—Corndavon (USA) (Sheikh Albadou)
1264[4] 1679[2] 2049[9] 2756[3]3403[3] 3744[2] 4812[4]5275[4] (5782) 6352[3]6660[2] 6849[6]

Woodsley House (IRE) *Miss Gay Kelleway* a59 86
4 b g Orpen(USA) —Flame And Shadow (IRE) (Turtle Island (IRE))
(4799) 5263[10] 6781[12]

Woodwee *J R Weymes* a51 36
3 ch g Woodborough(USA) —Evaporate (Insan (USA))
99[4] 199[3]439[5] 488[6]651[3] 819[3] 893[3]5401[13] 5865[21] 6425[12]6493[9] 6636[4]6717[10] 6796[4]6961[12]

Woodwool *H Candy* a57
4 br m Benny The Dip(USA) —Woodcrest (Niniski (USA))
114[7] 263[12]

Woolfall Blue (IRE) *G G Margarson* a86 69
3 gr c Bluebird(USA) —Diamond Waltz (IRE) (Linamix (FR))
1048[14] 1289[4] 1617[7] 4959[3] (5669) 6313[3]6607[9] 6744[4]

Woolfall King (IRE) *G G Margarson* 46
3 b g King Charlemagne(USA) —Bazaar Promise (Native Bazaar)
796[10] 1263[10] 2591[14] 3804[11] 4050[9]4304[7] 4909[15]

Woolly Back (IRE) *A C Whillans* a63 81
5 b g Alzao(USA) —Hopping Higgins (IRE) (Brief Truce (USA))
1591[13] 2808[5] 3159[2]4435[2] 5064[8] 5553[8]

Woolly Bully *G A Huffer* 81
3 b c Robellino(USA) —Belle Ile (USA) (Diesis)
797[2] 1291[2] (5726) 6051[4] 6206[14]

Wool Mart *M Blanshard* a37 71
2 ch g Auction House(USA) —Worsted (Whittingham (IRE))
2930[15] 3596[7] 4295[4]4804[6] 5349[11]

Woolsey *M Blanshard* 55
3 b g Kingsinger(IRE) —Worsted (Whittingham (IRE))
1546[9] 2063 [7] 3029[12] 4297[7] 4755[12]

Woolstone Boy (USA) *K C Bailey* a61 68?
5 ch g Will's Way(USA) —My Pleasure (USA) (Marfa (USA))
3382[14]

Woqoodd *M A Jarvis* 65
2 b g Royal Applause—Intervene (Zafonic (USA))
4428[12] 5508[3] 5766[4]

Worcester Lodge *Mrs L Richards* a62 78+
5 ch g Grand Lodge(USA) —Borgia (Machiavellian (USA))
847[9]

Word Perfect *M W Easterby* 81
4 b m Diktat—Better Still (IRE) (Glenstal (USA))
864[3] 977[11] 1795[3] 2095[6] 4610[5]5136[8] (5635) 5756[2] 6020[6] 6212[12]

Worlaby Dale *Mrs S Lamyman* a10 21
10 b g Terimon—Restandbethankful (Random Shot)
6626[8] 6718[10]

World At My Feet *N Bycroft* 50
4 b m Wolfhound(USA) —Rehaab (Mtoto)
1249[7] 2543[7] 2758[18] 4636[9] 4834[17]4944[13] 5240[10] 5485[6]

World In Action (IRE) *A P Jarvis* 65
3 bb g Spinning World(USA) —Pretty Procida (USA) (Procida (USA))
1684[7] 2404[11]

Worldly *S Kirk* a70+ 77
2 gr g Selkirk(USA) —Miss Universe (IRE) (Warning)
4526[2] (4932) 5459[9]

Worldly Pursuit *B Smart* a33 50
3 ch f Spinning World(USA) —Final Pursuit (Pursuit Of Love)
211[9] 1232[14]

World's Heroine (IRE) *G A Butler* 82
2 ch f Spinning World(USA) —Metaphor (USA) (Woodman (USA))
2816[7] 3553[4] (3878) 5676[7]

World's Mission (GER) *Mario Hofer* 99
3 b c Fasliyev(USA) —World's Vision (GER) (Platini (GER))
1176a[5] 1715a[10] 6121a[4]

World Spirit *Rae Guest* a68 66
2 b f Agnes World(USA) —Belle Esprit (Warning)
4801[7] 5613[2] (6651)

World Supremacy (IRE) *Gerard O'Leary* a37 38
3 b g Spinning World(USA) —Cream Jug (IRE) (Spectrum (IRE))
6584[8]

Worth Abbey *M Appleby* a16 5
4 b g Mujadil(USA) —Housefull (Habitat)
537[12] 568[11]640[12]

Wotavadun (IRE) *Ms J S Doyle* a41 22
3 ch g King Of Kings(IRE) —Blush With Love (USA) (Mt. Livermore (USA))
66[8] 102[6]177[7] 3340[6] 3595[10]6774[6] 6806[6]

Wotchalike (IRE) *R J Price* a81 71
4 ch h Spectrum(IRE) —Juno Madonna (IRE) (Sadler's Wells (USA))
125[8] 4390[6] 4968[8]5213[4] 5610[6]5691[6] 5846[5]

Wovoka (IRE) *M R Channon* a81 99
3 b g Mujadil(USA) —Common Cause (Polish Patriot (USA))
150a[4] 368a[12]561a[7] 758a[5] 1490[3]1841[11] 2046[8] 3710[6]

Wraith *H R A Cecil* 54
2 b c Maria's Mon(USA) —Really Polish (USA) (Polish Numbers (USA))
5537[7]

Wrecking Crew (IRE) *B R Millman* a41 72
2 b c Invincible Spirit(IRE) —Rushing (Deploy)
663[6] 892[6] 1639[3]2218[8]

Wrenlane *J J Quinn* a71 70
5 ch g Fraam—Hi Hoh (IRE) (Fayruz)
8[3] 163[9]285[8] 363[4]2108[8] 2286[14] 4914[2] 5242[10]

Wrighty Almighty (IRE) *P R Chamings* a78 74
4 b g Danehill Dancer(IRE) —Persian Empress (IRE) (Persian Bold)
1820[15] 2555[7] 3404[14]3898[4] 4557[4] 5042[14] 5453[8] 6147[11]

Writ (IRE) *I Semple* a80 25
4 ch g Indian Lodge(IRE) —Carnelly (IRE) (Priolo (USA))
297[9] 2793[4](3014) 3729[2]3934[3] 5311[13] 5636[6](5974) (6240) 6502[4]6741[5] (6932)

Wrynoes Pass (IRE) *R F Fisher*
2 b g Bold Fact(USA) —Home To Reality (IRE) (Imperial Frontier (USA))
2922[7] 3758[8]

Wujood *H Morrison* a64 79
4 b g Alzao(USA) —Rahayeb (Arazi (USA))
946[11] 1373[6]

Wulimaster (USA) *Sir Michael Stoute* 71
3 br g Silver Hawk(USA) —Kamaina (USA) (Mr Prospector (USA))
1880[3] 2934[2]

Wunderwood (USA) *D R C Elsworth* a103 111+
7 b g Faltaat(USA) —Jasoorah (IRE) (Sadler's Wells (USA))
1018[6] 1511[8] 2430[3](2817) 4027[2] (4967) (Dead)

Wurfscheibe (GER) *P Rau* 112
4 b m Tiger Hill(IRE) —Wurfbahn (GER) (Frontal)
1369a[5] 2280a[5] (3719a) (4648a) 5220a[11]

Wyatt Earp (IRE) *R A Fahey* a89 98
5 b g Piccolo—Tribal Lady (Absalom)
2946[4] 3374[2] (3550) (3956) 5336[9] 5523[5] 5812[9]

Wyeth *J R Fanshawe* 57
2 ch c Grand Lodge(USA) —Bordighera (USA) (Alysheba (USA))
6173[6]

Xaara (SWE) *M Kahn*
3 gr f Xaar—Angel Rose (IRE) (Definite Article)
2564a[6] 3326a[8] 4419a[8]

Xaar Breeze *Mrs P Townsley* a30 50
3 br f Xaar—Dicentra (Rambo Dancer (CAN))
690[9] 786[4]2494[11] 2632[3] 3033[8] 3348[12] 3867[10]

Xaaretta (IRE) *R Hannon*
2 b f Xaar—Hello Mary (IRE) (Dolphin Street (FR))
3222[P]

Xaar Too Busy *Mrs A Duffield* 58
2 b f Xaar—Desert Serenade (USA) (Green Desert (USA))
2638[11] 4400[10] 4731[3] 5748[10]

Xacobeo (IRE) *R Hannon* a28 62
4 b g Montjeu(IRE) —Afisiak (Efisio)
1204[17] 1548[8] 3196[12]

Xaloc Bay (IRE) *R A Harris* a46 43
8 br g Charnwood Forest(IRE) —Royal Jade (Last Tycoon)
313[8] 387[3]527[4] 546[8]616[9] 691[4]768[4]

Xalted *S C Williams* 35
2 b f Xaar—Joonayh (Warning)
3979[9] 5059[9] 5288[8]

Xaluna Bay (IRE) *W R Muir* a81 76
3 br f Xaar—Lunadine (FR) (Bering)
1208[7] 1679[10] 2049[7] 2511[2] (2756) 3646[2]3841[3] 4328[6] 4589[3]4874[3] 5181[4] 5782[4]5842[2] 6035[4]

Xchanger (USA) *M Shuman* a102
2 gr c Exchange Rate(USA) —Saragoza (USA) (Crafty Prospector (USA))
5983a[6]

Xenes *R Menichetti* 101
2 b c Xaar—Lucia Tarditi (FR) (Crystal Glitters (USA))
2670a[2]

Xenia *T J Etherington* a33 31
3 b f Labeeb—Known Class (USA) (Known Fact (USA))
93[5] 3146[9] 4382[6]5082[12]

Xeniam (IRE) *A King* 32
3 b g Rossini(USA) —Rose Tint (IRE) (Salse (USA))
4776[12] 5203[8]

Xenophile *J L Dunlop* 44
3 ch g Elnadim(USA) —Femme Femme (USA) (Lyphard (USA))
1978[6] 2532[10]

Xocolatl *Peter Grayson* a33
3 b f Elnadim(USA) —Chocolate (IRE) (Brief Truce (USA))
6738[4]

Xpres Boy (IRE) *S R Bowring* a58 11
3 b g Tagula(IRE) —Highly Motivated (Midyan (USA))
68[7] 364[5]1140[14] 1825[9] 2877[14] 3378[12]6674[10] 6956[9]

Xpres Digital *S R Bowring* a84 73
5 b g Komaite(USA) —Kustom Kit Xpres (Absalom)
1[14]

Xpres Maite *S R Bowring* a80 73
3 b g Komaite(USA) —Antonias Melody (Rambo Dancer (CAN))
1445[6] 2244[5] 2542[5](3154) (3381) 3606[5]3943[4] 5617[10] 6417[6]

Xtra Torrential (USA) *D M Simcock* a97 100
4 b g Torrential(USA) —Offering (USA) (Majestic Light (USA))
1287[6] 1806[13] 6514[8]6692[7] 6915[9]

Yakimov (USA) *D J Wintle* a88 91
7 ch g Affirmed(USA) —Ballet Troupe (USA) (Nureyev (USA))
726[15] (1051) 1206[6] 1585[7] 2387[10] 2672[2]3255[7]

Ya Late Maite *E S McMahon* 57
3 ch f Komaite(USA) —Plentitude (FR) (Ela-Mana-Mou)
1564[3] 2195[2]

Yandina (IRE) *B W Hills* a68 70
3 b f Danehill(USA) —Lughz (USA) (Housebuster (USA))
4563[3] (5093) 5649[14]

Yankeedoodledandy (IRE) *C Roberts* a75 86
5 b g Orpen(USA) —Laura Margaret (Persian Bold)
1943[10] 2176[15] 4046[12]

Yaqeen *M A Jarvis* 82
2 b f Green Desert(USA) —Lady Elgar (IRE) (Sadler's Wells (USA))
3043[3]

Yaria (IRE) *Kevin Prendergast* 94?
4 b m Danehill(USA) —Yara (IRE) (Sri Pekan (USA))
753a[5]

Yarqus *C E Brittain* a84 100
3 b g Diktat—Will You Dance (Shareef Dancer (USA))
1016[6] (1268) 1603[4] 1872a[6]2721[8] 3889[9] 4126[6] 4739[17] 5019[14]6915[8]

Yashin (IRE) *P A Blockley* a50 64
5 b g Soviet Star(USA) —My Mariam (Salse (USA))
92[4] 182[3]468[2] 770[7](1767) 1911[5]

Yasoodd *M R Channon* 112
3 br c Inchinor—Needwood Epic (Midyan (USA))
(1025a) 1718a[9] 2039a[4] 2721[6] 3957[4]

Yassooma (IRE) *T J Pitt* a38 50
3 b g King Of Kings(IRE) —Statistic (USA) (Mr Prospector (USA))
415[11] 617[5]637[4] 690[11]890[9] 974[8]

Yawmi *B D Leavy* a76 67
6 ch h Zafonic(USA) —Reine Wells (IRE) (Sadler's Wells (USA))
125[4]

Yazamaan *J H M Gosden* 100+
2 b c Galileo(IRE) —Moon's Whisper (USA) (Storm Cat (USA))
(4574) (4963)

Yeaman's Hall *A M Balding* 79
2 b c Galileo(IRE) —Rimba (USA) (Dayjur (USA))
5892[2]

Yearning (IRE) *J G Portman* 51
2 b f Danetime(IRE) —Hiraeth (Petong)
4221[9] 4624[5] 5052[7] 5948[12]

Yeats (IRE) *A P O'Brien* 126+
5 b h Sadler's Wells(USA) —Lyndonville (IRE) (Top Ville)
(2773) (4081) 5395a[2] 6392a[7]

Yeldham Lady *A J Chamberlain* a50 48
4 b m Mujahid(USA) —Future Options (Lomond (USA))
1224[8] 5054[12] 6657[7]6852[13]

Yellow Card *N A Callaghan* a69 78
3 ch g Inchinor—Tranquillity (Night Shift (USA))
1679[5] 1751[2] (2235) 2496[2] 2652[3] 2826[6]

Yellow Mane (IRE) *Luke Comer* a42 56
3 ch c On The Ridge(IRE) —Mother Nellie (USA) (Al Nasr (FR))
6531[9] 6884[9]

Yellow Ridge (IRE) *Luke Comer* a56 76
3 ch c On The Ridge(IRE) —Jonathan's Rose (IRE) (Law Society (USA))
(4034a) 5708a[10] 5854a[12] 6356a[14] 6986[11]

Yellowstone (IRE) *A P O'Brien* 111
2 b c Rock Of Gibraltar(IRE) —Love And Affection (USA) (Exclusive Era (USA))
4825a[7] 6249a[3]

Yemen Desert (IRE) *M Johnston* 76+
3 b f Sadler's Wells(USA) —Humble Fifteen (USA) (Feather Ridge (USA))
2895[2] 3146[5]

Yenaled *J M Bradley* a53 59
9 gr g Rambo Dancer(CAN) —Fancy Flight (FR) (Arctic Tern (USA))
75[3] 106[8]186[12] 1058[8] 2601[6]2862[10] 3797[2] 3894[7]4869[7] 4981[2] 5385[2] 5725[14] 5955[10]6382[8]

Yeoman Leap *A M Balding* 53
2 b c Val Royal(FR) —Chandni (IRE) (Ahonoora)
6023[10]

Yeoman Spirit (IRE) *A M Balding* a42 74
3 ch c Soviet Star(USA) —Hollywood Pearl (USA) (Phone Trick (USA))
710[7] 964[2] 1139[3]5511[13]

Yerevan *R T Phillips* a67 71
2 b f Iron Mask(USA) —Unfuwaanah (Unfuwain (USA))
1817[5] (2166) 2342[4] 2586[3]3246[2] 3720[4] 4170[3] (4427) 4762[5] (4921) 5207[6]

Yes Dear *W M Brisbourne* 62
3 ch f Fantastic Light(USA) —Abeyr (Unfuwain (USA))
1605[9]

Yokoran (SWI) *Karin Suter*
3 gr c Rainbows For Life(CAN) —Yokohama (IRE) (Hello Gorgeous (USA))
2717a[8]

Yomalo (IRE) *Rae Guest* a99+ 105
6 ch m Woodborough(USA) —Alkariyh (USA) (Alydar (USA))
6[2] 1377[6] (2369a) 2847[5]3499[4] 3956[6]

Yo Pedro (IRE) *J R Fanshawe* a82 86
4 b g Mark Of Esteem(IRE) —Morina (USA) (Lyphard (USA))
1435[6] 2508[4] 2900[3] 3212[8]

York Cliff *W M Brisbourne* a64 69
8 b g Marju(IRE) —Azm (Unfuwain (USA))
72[4] 103[6]158[5] 230[4]361[3] (442) 470[8] 600[4]643[5] (785) 871[4] 911[2]1271[2] 1308[2]1548[5] 1748[5]2206[3] 2522[3] (2812) 2998[3]

Yorke's Folly (USA) *C W Fairhurst* a36 54
5 b m Stravinsky(USA) —Tommelise (USA) (Dayjur (USA))
1733[4] 2543[12] 2949[2] 3172[6] 3617[5]3912[2] 4306[7] 4948[2]

Yorkie *J Pearce* a40 59
7 b g Aragon—Light The Way (Nicholas Bill)
1528[11] 2074[7] 2211[10]2611[6] 2811[8] 3817[11] 4233[11] 5924[7]6372[8]

Yorkies Boy *N E Berry* a28 46
11 gr g Clantime—Slipperose (Persepolis (FR))
1802[13] 2573[13] 3543[13]4531[11]

Yorkshire Blue *J S Goldie* a68 89
7 b g Atraf—Something Blue (Petong)
818[11] 1124[15] 1504[8] 2380[2] (2749) (3003) 3041[2](3330) 3482[3] 3936[5] 4378[8] 5336[14] 5355[4](6212)

Yorkshire Lad (IRE) *Miss Gay Kelleway* a68 77
4 b g Second Empire(IRE) —Villaminta (IRE) (Grand Lodge (USA))
798[7] 1054[11] 1209[11] 1310[15]

Yossi (IRE) *M H Tompkins* 77
2 b c Montjeu(IRE) —Raindancing (IRE) (Tirol)
5293[2] 5720[3] 6058[4]

Youbetterbegood (IRE) *Adrian Sexton* a60 12
2 b c Indian Rocket—Milain (IRE) (Unfuwain (USA))
6379[5] 6386[10]

You Call That Art (USA) *R Hannon* a68 79
3 b f Royal Academy(USA) —Support The Arts (USA) (Taylor's Falls (USA))
1085[5] 1513[4] 2458[10] 3644[7]4225[5]

Youko (SWE) *B Bo*
3 ch g Diaglyphard(USA) —Orange Wave (SWE) (Jalmood (USA))
4919a[11]

You Live And Learn *H Morrison* 59+
3 ch f Galileo(IRE) —Anniversary (Salse (USA))
3794[12] 4210[5] 4431[7] 5451[11]

Youmzain (IRE) *M R Channon* 120
3 b c Sinndar(IRE) —Sadima (IRE) (Sadler's Wells (USA))
(1231) 1708a[3] 2801[9] (3441) (4678) 5221a[2] (5561a)

Young Bertie *H Morrison* a76 70
3 ch g Bertolini(USA) —Urania (Most Welcome)
1263[3] 2316[4] 3410[2]3705[3] 4291[2] (4930) 5042[5]5605[3] 6036[10]

Young Emma *G G Margarson*
3 b f Vettori(IRE) —Just Warning (Warning)
6482[10]

Young Flavio *J M Bradley* a48 67
3 ch g Mark Of Esteem(IRE) —Flavian (Catrail (USA))
2730[9] 3195[14] 3538[16] 3821[13] 4690[13]5273[15]

Young Kate *J R Best* a51 55
5 b m Desert King(IRE) —Stardyn (Star Appeal)
94[3] 175[4](312) 399[5]683[11]

Young Mick *G G Margarson* a95 116+
4 br g King's Theatre(IRE) —Just Warning (Warning)
162[9] (173) (187) (229) 263[2]319[2] (603) (723) (799) 834[2]1017[3] 1484[4] 2341[6](2848) 3294[6] (3890) (4347) 4713[3] (5547)

Young Mr Grace (IRE) *B S Rothwell* a51 73
6 b g Danetime(IRE) —Maid Of Mourne (Fairy King (USA))
1123[18] 1760[9] 1996[10] 4652[6] 4729[14]5483[12]

Young Poli (FR) *A Couetil* 101
3 b c Poliglote—Yole (FR) (Dancing Spree (USA))
5145a[4] 5700a[9]

Young Scotton *J Howard Johnson* a34 63
6 b g Cadeaux Genereux—Broken Wave (Bustino)
409[5] 1123[11]

Young Thomas (IRE) *B Storey* a18 67
4 ch g Inchinor—Splicing (Sharpo)
6277[7]

Young Valentino *A W Carroll* a39 51
4 ch g Komaite(USA) —Caprice (Mystiko (USA))
5569[13] 6282[12] 6372[12]6702[7] 6829[12]

Youralittlemiller *P G Murphy* a53 52
3 b f Kalanisi(IRE) —Jam (IRE) (Arazi (USA))
49[4] 333[6]538[7]

Your Amount (IRE) *W J Musson* a78 76
3 b g Beckett(IRE) —Sin Lucha (USA) (Northfields (USA))
1349[9] 1828[6] 2290[10] 3015[7]4606[11] 5868[7] (6479) 6754[3]

You're My Son *A B Haynes* a59 39
4 b g Bold Edge—Sheer Nectar (Piaffer (USA))
4367[5] 5354[14] 5986[6]6436[9] 6793[8]

You Too *M Johnston* 68+
4 b m Monsun(GER) —You Are The One (Unfuwain (USA))
2078[10] 3607[4]

Ysoldina (FR) *A De Royer-Dupre* 106
4 b m Kendor(FR) —Rotina (FR) (Crystal Glitters (USA))
841a[7] 1398a[3] 2092a[3]

Yukino Sun Royal (JPN) *S Masuzawa* 110
9 br h Sunday Silence(USA) —Miami Gulch (USA) (Gulch (USA))
6612a[11]

Yungaburra (IRE) *T J Pitt* a95+ 56
2 b g Fath(USA) —Nordic Living (IRE) (Nordico (USA))
2973[14] 5491[5] 5686[3](6311) (6400) (6427) 6444[3] (6732)

Yve Sam La Champ *A W Carroll* 26
2 b c Tomba—Dona Krista (King Of Spain)
1189[10] 2072[6] 5871[12] 6015[10]

Zaafira (SPA) *E J Creighton* a47
2 b f Limpid—Hot Doris (IRE) (Fayruz)
6186[12] 6471[9]6778[4] 6996[3]

Zaafran *M A Jarvis* 84
3 b f Singspiel(IRE) —Roshani (IRE) (Kris)
1240[2] 1650[5] (3590) (4112) 4878[2]

Zaahid (IRE) *B W Hills* 55
2 ch c Sakhee(USA) —Murjana (IRE) (Pleasant Colony (USA))
3417[10]

Zaajel (IRE) *E Charpy* a9 90
7 b h Nashwan(USA) —Mehthaaf (USA) (Nureyev (USA))
205a[7] 437a[10]

Zabeat (NZ) *Donna Logan* 114
7 b g Rhythm(USA) —Zabest (NZ) (Zabeel (NZ))
6346a[18] 6392a[23]

Zabeel House *J A R Toller* a79 83
3 b g Anabaa(USA) —Divine Quest (Kris)
1095[5] 1440[6] 1954[4] 2620[3] 2932[11]4605[8] 5150[10] 5649[3]6413[4] 6635[6]

Zabeel Palace *Saeed Bin Suroor* a77 87
4 b g Grand Lodge(USA) —Applecross (Glint Of Gold)
279a[8] 5776[10]6017[6]

Zabeel Tower *James Moffatt* 72
3 b g Anabaa(USA) —Bint Kaldoun (IRE) (Kaldoun (FR))
945[5] (1293) 1634[6] 2441[8] 3634[7]

Zacatecas (GER) *A J Chamberlain* a68 91
6 gr g Grand Lodge(USA) —Zephyrine (IRE) (Highest Honor (FR))
5383[14] 6381[6] 6626[9]6816[5]

Zacharova (IRE) *J S Bolger* 95+
3 b g Lil's Boy(USA) —Voronova (IRE) (Sadler's Wells (USA))
3123a[7]

Zackmunde (GER) *Frau A Glodde* 55
3 br f Lavirco(GER) —Zermatt (GER) (Tirol)
3661a[11] 5710a[14]

Zadalla *Andrew Oliver* a64 63d
2 b f Zaha(CAN) —Inishdalla (IRE) (Green Desert (USA))
5850a[9] (6679) 6895[2]

Zafantage *S Kirk* 69
3 ch f Zafonic(USA) —Up On Points (Royal Academy (USA))
1348[10] 2403[7] 2622[11] 2921[4] 3472[5]3793[13] 4671[9] 4984[3] 5418[3] 5936[13]

Zafarilla (IRE) *Pat Eddery* 46+
3 b f Zafonic(USA) —Claustra (FR) (Green Desert (USA))
3614[9] 4198[15] 5452[10]

Zafarshah (IRE) *R A Harris* a50 51
7 b g Danehill(USA) —Zafarana (FR) (Shernazar)
1311[7] 1568[5] 1752[7] 2098[9] 2260[12]2566[3] 3194[4] 3817[3] 4285[2] 4363[4]4446[4] 4670[4] 5267[11] 6235[13]6371[11] 6493[11]

Zaffeu *A G Juckes* a56 62
5 ch g Zafonic(USA) —Leaping Flame (USA) (Trempolino (USA))
158[2] 230[3]284[3] 470[2]1467[2] 1748[2]2320[14] 5033[3](6604) 6790[5]6995[5]

Zafonical Storm (USA) *B W Duke* a66 102
2 ch c Aljabr(USA) —Fonage (Zafonic (USA))
663[3] (775) 2719[21] 3126a[7]3496[5] 4344[7] 5459[2] (5707a) 6010[7]

Zagreus (GER) *H J Manners* a25 58
4 gr g Fasliyev(USA) —Zephyrine (IRE) (Highest Honor (FR))
5844[10] 6021[11] 6378[7]

Zahara Joy *D W Thompson* 59d
3 ch f Cayman Kai(IRE) —Enjoy (IRE) (Mazaad)
4070[13] 4425[13] 4728[12] 5365[7]

Zaharath Al Bustan *M R Channon* 74
3 ch f Gulch(USA) —Cayman Sunset (IRE) (Night Shift (USA))
1099[8] 1635[2] 1948[9] 2359[9]

Zahour Al Yasmeen *M R Channon* a72 40
2 b f Cadeaux Genereux—Bareilly (USA) (Lyphard (USA))
2354[8] (2980)

Zah Reef *P A Blockley*
3 b f Zaha(CAN) —Cuban Reef (Dowsing (USA))
2600[6]

Zaif (IRE) *D R C Elsworth* 94
3 b g Almutawakel—Colourful (FR) (Gay Mecene (USA))
1134[11] 2034[4] (3419) 4082[6] 4878[5] 5505[2]5804[7]

Zain (IRE) *J G Given* a48 48
2 b c Alhaarth(IRE) —Karenaragon (Aragon)
6199[9] 6295[4] 6512[7]6625[5] 6900[7]

Zakfree (IRE) *Liam McAteer* a63 71
5 b g Danetime(IRE) —Clipper Queen (Balidar)
4186a[8] 6924[4]

Zakopane (GER) *P Schiergen* 87
3 b f Monsun(GER) —Zayraba (IRE) (Doyoun)
1714a[8] 5008a[6]

Zalkani (IRE) *J Pearce* a74 35
6 ch g Cadeaux Genereux—Zallaka (IRE) (Shardari)
33[3] 167[6]283[9] (375) 421[3] 463[9]578[4] 723[2](833) 983[8](1548) (2790) (3051) 3594[4] 5390[4]5652[11] 5971[5]6376[2] (6462)

Zalzaar (IRE) *C G Cox* 55
4 b g Xaar—Zalamalec (USA) (Septieme Ciel (USA))
2881[4] 3794[16] 4871[11] 5831[15]

Zamala *J L Dunlop* 82
3 b f King's Best(USA) —Ajayib (USA) (Riverman (USA))
880[8] (1934) 2359[5] 3301[9]

Zambezi River *J M Bradley* a45? 45
7 ch g Zamindar(USA) —Double River (USA) (Irish River (FR))
84[7] 110[7]396[9] 844[8]1165[13] 1852[12]

Zamboozle (IRE) *D R C Elsworth* a84+ 78
4 ch g Halling(USA) —Blue Sirocco (Bluebird (USA))
404[5] (556) 661[5]1071[13] 1478[6] 2341[7]

Zameliana *Dr J R J Naylor*
2 ch f Zaha(CAN) —Amelia's Field (Distant Relative)
1912[9]

Zamhrear *C E Brittain* a69 55
3 b f Singspiel(IRE) —Lunda (IRE) (Soviet Star (USA))
4261[4] 4396[8] 5353[7]5571[5] (5924) 6333[13] 6667[2](6819)

Zando *E G Bevan* a60 51
4 b g Forzando—Rockin' Rosie (Song)
1553[12] 2414[3]2794[5] 3056[10]3263[14] 6980[7]

Zangeal *C F Wall* a76 79
5 ch g Selkirk(USA) —Generous Lady (Generous (IRE))
2551[2]

Zanida (IRE) *K R Burke* 98
2 b f Mujadil(USA) —Haraabah (USA) (Topsider (USA))
2166[4] (2806) 4715[5] 5356[4] 5809[4] 6201[8]

Zankel (NZ) *D Koh* 111
4 b h Carnegie(IRE) —Happiness (NZ) (Bluebird (USA))
1716a[10]

Zann (USA) *M Machowsky* 110
3 b c Dynaformer(USA) —Moments Of Magic (USA) (Danzig (USA))
6613a[5]

Zantero *W M Brisbourne* a46 54
4 b g Danzero(AUS) —Cruinn A Bhord (Inchinor)
1538[4] 2112[18] 2641[14]2881[7] 3480[7] 3698[4] 4067[9] 4136[4]4523[6]

Zanzibar (ARG) *J W Sadler* a113
5 b h Luhuk(USA) —Zebra (ARG) (Southern Halo (USA))
5827a[6]

Zap Attack *J Parkes* a40 52
6 b g Zafonic(USA) —Rappa Tap Tap (FR) (Tap On Wood)
942[8] 1217[8] 1571[6]1735[5] 2785[12] 3781[8] 4019[11] 5483[10]5865[22]

Zarabad (IRE) *K R Burke* a80+ 82
4 b g King's Best(USA) —Zarannda (IRE) (Last Tycoon)
64[9] 1494[5] 2183[6]4961[10] 5320[6] 5861[12] 6932[6]6952[5]

Zarakash (IRE) *Jonjo O'Neill* a77? 58
6 b g Darshaan—Zarannda (IRE) (Last Tycoon)
913[4] 1692[12] 1995[11]

Zarandja (IRE) *Patrick Martin* 76
4 b m King's Best(USA) —Zarlana (IRE) (Darshaan)
1156a[12]

Zariano *T D Barron* a52 61
6 b g Emperor Jones(USA) —Douce Maison (IRE) (Fools Holme (USA))
134[5] 196[6]526[4] 689[5]1305[8] 1394[7]

Zarina Caterina *B Grizzetti*
2 b f Mark Of Esteem(IRE) —Fabulous Charm (ITY) (Fabulous Dancer (USA))
3428a[4]

Zarnitza (USA) *E A L Dunlop* 36
2 b f Quiet American(USA) —Zawaahy (USA) (El Gran Senor (USA))
5679[11]

Zarova (IRE) *M W Easterby* a58+ 65+
4 gr g Zafonic(USA) —Estarova (FR) (Saint Estephe (FR))
1233[3] 1425[15] (2326) 2684[13] 2927[4] 3377[8]3983[13] 4021[3] 4355[3]5445[12] 5836[12]

Zar Solitario *M Johnston* a69
2 b c Singspiel(IRE) —Ginevra Di Camelot (FR) (Alzao (USA))
6570[4]

Zarwala (IRE) *John M Oxx* 88+
3 b f Polish Precedent(USA) —Zarlana (IRE) (Darshaan)
4741[6]

Zarzu *C R Dore* a88 83
7 b g Magic Ring(IRE) —Rivers Rhapsody (Dominion)
198[5] 295[7]517[2] 761[6]1928[3] 2173[2] 3012[8]4834[13] 5212[9] 5777[8]6035[8] 6223[2](6428) 6583[4]6690[11]

Zastra's Pride *W G M Turner* a17 31
3 ch f Zaha(CAN) —Strath Kitten (Scottish Reel)
786[5] 4491[U] 5127[14]

Zato (IRE) *M R Channon* a99 99
3 ch g Zafonic(USA) —Top Table (Shirley Heights)
914[3] 1131[5] 2774[19]3491[5] 3889[11] 5165[5] 5666[6](5990) 6226[2]

Zatonic (FR) *P Demercastel* 105
3 gr c Zafonic(USA) —Marie De Ken (FR) (Kendor (FR))
1179a[6] 1749a[4]

Zaville *J O'Reilly* a71 51
4 gr m Zafonic(USA) —Colleville (Pharly (FR))
1809[10] 2133[2] 2822[7] 5513[11] 5683[12]5971[6] (6256) (6509) 6754[11]

Zavite (NZ) *A Cummings* 94
4 b h Zabeel(NZ) —Miss Vita (USA) (Alleged (USA))
6455a[5]

Zawariq (IRE) *M P Tregoning* a61
2 b f Marju(IRE) —Alikhlas (Lahib (USA))
6186[9]

Zayafa (FR) *A De Royer-Dupre* 99
3 b f Kalanisi(IRE) —Zayannda (IRE) (Alzao (USA))
4035a[7]

Zayanida (IRE) *A De Royer-Dupre* a78 91
3 b f King's Best(USA) —Zayana (IRE) (Darshaan)
4979a[7]

Zayn Zen *M A Jarvis* a104 105
4 ch m Singspiel(IRE) —Roshani (IRE) (Kris)
1506[8] 2199[3] 2740[4] 3957[5]

Zayyir (IRE) *G A Butler* 51
2 b c Indian Ridge—Lurina (IRE) (Lure (USA))
4716[9]

Zazous *J J Bridger* a67+ 67
5 b g Zafonic(USA) —Confidentiality (USA) (Lyphard (USA))
146[7] (307) 339[6](397) 806[2]837[2] 1209[12] 1981[2]2095[15] 2813[2] 3071[8] (4564) 5480[4] 5938[4]6061[7] 6510[10] 6595[3](6629)

Zed Candy (FR) *J T Stimpson* a68 60
3 b g Medicean—Intrum Morshaan (IRE) (Darshaan)
536[7] 731[3] 863[4]1139[8] 2065[6] 2795[9]4635[4] 4982[11] 5960[8] 6272[3] (6474) (6716) 6816[3]

Zeena *C A Horgan* a47 56
4 b m Unfuwain(USA) —Forest Fire (SWE) (Never So Bold)
1224[9] 1536[4]1724[7]

Zeeuw (IRE) *D J Coakley* a71 54
2 b g Xaar—Lucky Bet (IRE) (Lucky Guest)
1959[6] 2899[5]

Zefooha (FR) *M R Channon* 71
2 ch f Lomitas—Bezzaaf (Machiavellian (USA))
3227[4] (3868)

Zeina Of Arabia *Doug Watson* a76
3 b f Capote(USA) —Heaven's Echo (USA) (Woodman (USA))
202a[11] 436a[7]623a[7]

Zell (IRE) *E J Alston* 61
3 b f Lend A Hand—Skisette (Malinowski (USA))
4382[F] 4635[7] 4891[2] 5370[8] 5583[5]

Zell Am See *M H Tompkins* 46
2 b g Averti(IRE) —Pretty Pollyanna (General Assembly (USA))
5458[8] 5658[14]

Zelos (IRE) *J A Osborne* a68 70
2 b g Mujadil(USA) —First Degree (Sabrehill (USA))
2619[7] 3157[3] 4140[4]

Zeloso *M F Harris* a53 53
8 b g Alzao(USA) —Silk Petal (Petorius)
1758[3] 1883[7]

Zenato (GER) *F Reuterskiold* a77 102
5 ch h Acatenango(GER) —Zephyrine (IRE) (Highest Honor (FR))
279a[6] 437a[9] 4189a[2]

Zendaro *W M Brisbourne* a63 68
4 b g Danzero(AUS) —Countess Maud (Mtoto)
2184[5] 2853[8] (4057) 4350[7] (5248) 5384[11]5775[7]

Zennerman (IRE) *W M Brisbourne* a70 83
3 b g Observatory(USA) —Precocious Miss (USA) (Diesis)
1606[6] 2239[2] 3067[4] 3606[3] 3945[7]4488[4] 4769[3] 5337[6] 5529[5] 6094[11]

Zero (IRE) *M A Jarvis* a72 84+
3 b c Halling(USA) —Zonda (Fabulous Dancer (USA))
1605[3] (3451)

Zero Engagement (AUS) *T Roney* 102
6 b g Woodman(USA) —Dateless (NZ) (Grosvenor (NZ))
7000a[4]

Zero Tolerance (IRE) *T D Barron* a77 112
6 ch g Nashwan(USA) —Place De L'Opera (Sadler's Wells (USA))
728[4] 1371a[10] (1806) 2226[5] 3123a[16] 4739[10](5012) 5808[4] 6333[14]

Zeydnaa (IRE) *C R Wilson* a40 56
6 b g Bahhare(USA) —Hadawah (USA) (Riverman (USA))
2381[3] 2684[8] 3192[6] 3284[9] 5080[11]5750[15]

Zhitomir *M Dods* a52 69
8 ch g Lion Cavern(USA) —Treasure Trove (USA) (The Minstrel (CAN))
977[5] 1561[12] 4655[5] 5136[6] 5313[2]5635[10] 5861[10] 6273[5]

Zibeline (IRE) *B Ellison* 79
9 b g Cadeaux Genereux—Zia (USA) (Shareef Dancer (USA))
4231[9] 4676[9] 4981[3]

Zidane *J R Fanshawe* 96+
4 b g Danzero(AUS) —Juliet Bravo (Glow (USA))
949[9] 1285[2] (1686) 2323[2] (2864) 3493[13] 5044[4]

Zilcash *A King* a76 76
3 b g Mujahid(USA) —Empty Purse (Pennine Walk)
1205[5] 1781[10] 2404[6] 3151[4] 3848[3]4206[4] 5732[9]

Zilli *N P Littmoden* a45
2 ch f Zilzal(USA) —Zizi (IRE) (Imp Society (USA))
6481[10] 6912[6]6975[5]

Zimbali *J M Bradley* a41 59
4 ch m Lahib(USA) —Dawn (Owington)
2484[10] 2858[9] 2949[11] 3267[6] 3728[5]4226[4] 4554[8] 4675[6] 4872[7] 5131[13]

Zingbat (IRE) *J G Given* 48d
3 b g Rainbow Quest(USA) —Shastri (USA) (Alleged (USA))
1684[11] 1984[7] 2539[14] 3249[9]

Zinging *J J Bridger* a20 40
7 b g Fraam—Hi Hoh (IRE) (Fayruz)
417[4] 472[9]484[5] 575[9]889[14] 1566[7] (1755) 2132[5]2585[9] 3213[7] 3339[5] 3614[11] 4073[8]4276[3] 4446[10] 4585[7] 6067[9] 6800[12]6852[14]

Zipping (AUS) *G Rogerson* 113
5 b g Danehill(USA) —Social Scene (IRE) (Grand Lodge (USA))
6110a[12] 6392a[4]

Ziride (FR) *H-A Pantall* a94 95
3 b f Valanour(IRE) —Zircon Lady (FR) (King's Lake (USA))
1370a[7]

Zirkel (IRE) *Mrs A L M King* 72
3 br g Highest Honor(FR) —Mythical Creek (USA) (Pleasant Tap (USA))
2175[6] 2655[4] 3901[8] 5770[11]

Zita (GER) *P Bradik* 96
4 b m Tannenkonig(IRE) —Zizi Top (Robellino (USA))
4858a[6] 5710a[10]

Zizou (IRE) *J J Bridger* a46 51
3 b g Fantastic Light(USA) —Search Committee (USA) (Roberto (USA))
61[3] 85[9]188[10] 479[10]538[10] 781[5] 879[12]1215[6] 1314[13] 2352[4] 2434[10] 2713[8]3075[3] 3439[3] 3592[7]4800[8] 6057[8]

Zohar (USA) *B J Meehan* 95
4 b g Aljabr(USA) —Dafnah (USA) (Housebuster (USA))
1086[4] 1301[8] 2012[16] (Dead)

Zoltano (GER) *M Todhunter* 32
8 b g In The Wings—Zarella (GER) (Anatas)
816[9] 1758[9]

Zomerlust *J J Quinn* 101
4 b g Josr Algarhoud(IRE) —Passiflora (Night Shift (USA))
728^{11} (1183) 2012^{9} 2847^{23} 3482^{7} $4202^{7}4609^{7}$ 4988^{6} 5336^{2} 5529^{9}

Zonergem *Lady Herries* a100 101
8 ch g Zafonic(USA) —Anasazi (IRE) (Sadler's Wells (USA))
296^{2} $661^{6}5045^{3}$ 5776^{4}

Zonic Boom (FR) *Heather Dalton* a61 66
6 bb g Zafonic(USA) —Rosi Zambotti (IRE) (Law Society (USA))
156^{9} 6954^{9}

Zonta Zitkala *R M Beckett* 83
2 b f Daylami(IRE) —Sioux Chef (Be My Chief (USA))
3043^{7} 3537^{2} 4148^{2}

Zoom (GER) *Tim Gibson* 75
3 ch f Lomitas—Zizi Top (Robellino (USA))
$5710a^{9}$

Zoometric (AUS) *G Webster Snr* 105
6 b g Unbridled's Song(USA) —What A Joy (AUS) (Bluebird (USA))
$7000a^{12}$

Zoom One *M P Tregoning* 80+
2 ch c In The Wings—Seyooll (IRE) (Danehill (USA))
4867^{5} (5239) (5585)

Zoorina *M P Tregoning* a48 52
2 b f Xaar—Saeedah (Bustino)
3201^{10} 4084^{12} 5754^{9}

Zoripp (IRE) *J G Given* a59 54
4 b g Spectrum(IRE) —Allspice (Alzao (USA))
(1256) 1590^{14} 2075^{14} *$2414^{4}2577^{6}$*

Zorn (GER) *M F Harris* 31
7 b g Lavirco(GER) —Zypern (GER) (Acatenango (GER))
4176^{10} 4687^{7}

Zorn *P Howling* a68 60
7 br g Dilum(USA) —Very Good (Noalto)
21^{10} $127^{4}178^{10}$ 196^{7}(274) $413^{8}428^{5}$ $489^{6}552^{3}$ (612) 650^{2} $845^{11}1258^{9}$ 1388^{8}

Zorooni *M A Jarvis* a60
3 b f Josr Algarhoud(IRE) —Zeyaarah (USA) (Rahy (USA))
217^{4}

Zowington *C F Wall* a76 98
4 gr h Zafonic(USA) —Carmela Owen (Owington)
(1236) 1803^{6} 2227^{17} 3092^{14} 4875^{12} $5534^{3}6335^{8}$ *6496^{8}*

Zuccarella (GER) *J Warren* 78
3 ch f Banyumanik(IRE) —Zigeunerin (GER) (Nebos (GER))
$5710a^{8}$

Zulu Queen (IRE) *David Wachman* 84+
3 b f Sadler's Wells(USA) —Jaya (USA) (Ela-Mana-Mou)
$5854a^{10}$

Zumrah (IRE) *P Bowen*
5 b g Machiavellian(USA) —The Perfect Life (IRE) (Try My Best (USA))
1212^{14}

Zurbaran (IRE) *B J Meehan* 108
3 ch c Alhaarth(IRE) —Broken Romance (IRE) (Ela-Mana-Mou)
1984^{5} 2290^{5} (4459) 4560^{2} 5153^{2} $5641^{2}5967^{4}$

Zut Alors (IRE) *Robert Collet* 96
2 b f Pivotal—Zeiting (IRE) (Zieten (USA))
$6228a^{3}$ $6546a^{3}$

Leading Flat Trainers - Turf 2006

NAME	WINS-RUNS	2nd	3rd	4th	WIN £	TOTAL £	£1 STAKE
Sir Michael Stoute	107-486 (22%)	74	57	45	1,842,582	3,026,215	-63.68
M Johnston	157-1005 (16%)	126	110	108	1,239,246	1,863,648	-92.90
B W Hills	103-733 (14%)	96	102	68	1,101,091	1,823,167	-135.32
R Hannon	127-1067 (12%)	128	133	109	1,043,024	1,753,411	-261.36
A P O'Brien	11-74 (15%)	9	7	9	1,247,461	1,741,362	-21.08
Saeed Bin Suroor	70-247 (28%)	40	21	22	935,406	1,610,204	+13.17
M R Channon	127-1027 (12%)	121	107	118	878,649	1,548,587	-106.84
B J Meehan	74-532 (14%)	59	61	54	892,694	1,471,770	-85.89
K A Ryan	95-828 (11%)	86	93	73	621,913	1,315,560	-198.74
J Noseda	47-249 (19%)	37	40	30	923,559	1,266,539	-41.92
E A L Dunlop	55-437 (13%)	79	56	48	778,103	1,201,303	-68.13
M P Tregoning	29-210 (14%)	32	27	21	957,939	1,162,051	-27.59
R A Fahey	87-734 (12%)	96	71	75	677,880	1,098,407	-99.25
M A Jarvis	72-395 (18%)	67	50	44	631,845	1,028,253	-50.51
J H M Gosden	56-298 (19%)	34	32	30	605,237	848,469	-21.98
A Fabre	4-13 (31%)	1	2	2	653,374	823,498	-4.66
J R Fanshawe	46-285 (16%)	40	35	33	437,772	785,411	-43.33
W J Haggas	59-334 (18%)	55	38	30	531,547	771,051	+0.96
C E Brittain	48-480 (10%)	51	43	46	467,565	768,365	-13.83
D Nicholls	58-674 (9%)	57	66	65	417,914	732,415	-170.43
J L Dunlop	53-467 (11%)	65	43	38	381,423	716,012	-122.04
T J Pitt	31-154 (20%)	13	13	8	654,501	692,596	+42.24
T D Barron	76-555 (14%)	60	58	70	484,602	683,039	+10.75
R Charlton	37-263 (14%)	44	32	26	357,488	641,810	-91.41
K R Burke	82-703 (12%)	96	91	81	361,484	638,068	-118.11
P W Chapple-Hyam	40-252 (16%)	22	26	22	467,448	609,723	+8.59
T D Easterby	54-719 (8%)	59	83	64	312,565	582,443	-220.39
A M Balding	49-467 (10%)	54	52	40	360,348	565,318	-156.97
P F I Cole	44-324 (14%)	26	23	36	410,015	539,782	-61.64
G A Swinbank	50-276 (18%)	34	40	26	397,642	537,768	+41.19
W R Swinburn	37-338 (11%)	39	29	39	355,027	525,786	-44.09
E J Alston	20-269 (7%)	28	16	35	465,890	522,049	-45.90
H Morrison	46-381 (12%)	42	37	41	331,242	517,940	-73.00
S Kirk	30-292 (10%)	23	29	29	434,908	516,019	-98.17
D R C Elsworth	37-344 (11%)	39	25	39	278,581	516,006	-26.90
N P Littmoden	43-451 (10%)	39	49	52	269,745	506,386	-118.13
G Wragg	10-138 (7%)	15	16	16	94,191	498,800	-43.25
L M Cumani	39-293 (13%)	38	40	27	270,792	497,652	-92.53
Sir Mark Prescott	44-210 (21%)	29	24	22	323,330	494,172	-32.05
M L W Bell	46-348 (13%)	48	34	39	289,240	458,167	-93.05
C G Cox	25-239 (10%)	31	24	24	278,095	447,133	+15.65
M H Tompkins	31-394 (8%)	39	53	27	227,296	444,104	-126.48
Mrs A J Perrett	32-376 (9%)	24	47	33	270,282	442,691	-129.23
J R Best	31-302 (10%)	29	27	42	228,326	418,469	-87.94
B R Millman	29-347 (8%)	32	27	32	287,330	413,913	-105.54
J J Quinn	37-362 (10%)	35	27	30	306,117	411,900	-86.46
W R Muir	30-377 (8%)	40	47	34	143,708	383,167	-119.20
I Semple	49-388 (13%)	31	51	50	238,078	366,678	-80.09
G L Moore	58-429 (14%)	47	36	42	248,873	365,853	-18.42
C F Wall	32-225 (14%)	20	27	17	160,900	345,168	+27.19

Leading Flat Jockeys 2006

NAME	WIN-RIDES	1st	2nd	3rd	WIN £	TOTAL £	£1 STAKE
Ryan Moore	182-1174 (16%)	147	141	127	1,842,605	2,720,806	-152.90
Jamie Spencer	157-839 (19%)	112	98	88	1,668,838	2,588,700	-65.67
Eddie Ahern	140-1155 (12%)	128	108	130	828,570	1,247,037	-266.57
Robert Winston	136-981 (14%)	121	104	100	841,078	1,379,965	-184.48
L Dettori	131-592 (22%)	81	72	58	2,205,289	3,353,591	-55.92
N Callan	129-1028 (13%)	126	129	94	827,473	1,521,070	-98.38
Seb Sanders	117-834 (14%)	105	79	80	795,251	1,251,785	-193.81
Richard Hughes	113-804 (14%)	95	107	76	1,156,435	1,854,740	-73.74
Paul Hanagan	107-1039 (10%)	118	101	123	694,156	1,132,646	-264.86
Joe Fanning	107-937 (11%)	95	98	98	617,855	1,049,121	-256.05
Dane O'Neill	94-944 (10%)	94	115	103	385,780	722,692	-201.10
John Egan	91-841 (11%)	81	95	80	1,235,259	1,727,501	+45.66
Martin Dwyer	90-863 (10%)	93	93	78	1,427,555	2,035,811	-281.69
Tony Culhane	88-870 (10%)	94	75	85	539,588	855,663	-246.29
Tom Eaves	87-911 (10%)	68	86	79	443,447	666,928	-183.33
Steve Drowne	84-1052 (8%)	134	92	119	523,825	1,069,253	-446.24
Francis Norton	83-786 (11%)	91	90	78	452,706	705,314	-38.66
Jimmy Fortune	77-659 (12%)	98	57	54	1,006,185	1,494,263	-155.40
K Darley	75-604 (12%)	64	61	54	1,054,460	1,396,144	-61.09
Philip Robinson	75-428 (18%)	81	49	40	697,706	1,173,924	-6.35
Kerrin McEvoy	74-464 (16%)	57	44	39	844,501	1,335,220	+121.13
Chris Catlin	73-1172 (6%)	89	97	99	320,347	572,333	-528.91
James Doyle	73-757 (10%)	85	82	73	329,221	571,590	-168.18
Darryll Holland	73-689 (11%)	79	78	65	648,915	1,221,175	-175.67
Ted Durcan	71-731 (10%)	65	69	74	519,692	928,100	-229.34
Jimmy Quinn	70-928 (8%)	85	93	81	409,273	674,791	-346.79
George Baker	70-508 (14%)	52	52	55	288,846	563,223	-74.90
Michael Hills	69-513 (13%)	72	62	46	994,300	1,475,823	-83.35
Royston Ffrench	63-570 (11%)	38	50	46	421,199	616,328	-73.59
Robbie Fitzpatrick	61-629 (10%)	57	41	39	232,007	379,183	-25.44
T P Queally	59-584 (10%)	50	58	53	308,004	464,811	-11.41
Adam Kirby	58-677 (9%)	64	59	73	376,749	559,112	-164.85
Shane Kelly	58-586 (10%)	51	53	66	244,318	401,315	-174.91
Phillip Makin	58-505 (11%)	36	57	65	223,312	358,229	-56.78
Nicky Mackay	57-494 (12%)	53	52	53	465,207	705,543	-108.29
Micky Fenton	56-906 (6%)	66	71	80	410,508	637,031	-358.97
David Allan	56-665 (8%)	63	71	69	350,797	538,293	-143.75
J-P Guillambert	56-546 (10%)	45	60	45	243,776	350,921	-34.54
Dean McKeown	54-590 (9%)	55	47	49	232,128	379,584	-158.66
R Hills	54-429 (13%)	72	64	41	569,000	1,192,393	-198.05
Graham Gibbons	53-565 (9%)	55	47	67	269,730	434,527	-158.72
Daniel Tudhope	53-470 (11%)	60	24	58	174,952	290,199	-126.43
Oscar Urbina	52-373 (14%)	48	45	48	232,242	437,012	+19.78
Fergus Sweeney	49-625 (8%)	52	53	59	193,938	316,089	-182.80
Alan Munro	49-473 (10%)	53	48	57	487,083	952,039	-119.67
Pat Cosgrave	48-522 (9%)	58	46	49	210,635	371,542	-172.92
Stephen Donohoe	47-395 (12%)	33	37	35	197,312	302,308	-36.26
Ian Mongan	44-470 (9%)	47	43	43	314,657	457,699	-149.39
Dale Gibson	41-593 (7%)	49	55	48	157,172	270,684	-43.26
Liam Jones	40-412 (10%)	40	41	37	153,484	235,275	-29.37

Leading Flat Owners 2006

NAME	WINS-RUNS	2nd	3rd	4th	WIN £	TOTAL £
Godolphin	70-247 (28%)	40	21	22	935,406	1,610,204
Hamdan Al Maktoum	83-556 (15%)	87	81	57	672,734	1,310,455
Gainsborough Stud	51-318 (16%)	62	36	27	613,392	1,045,393
Cheveley Park Stud	34-192 (18%)	28	27	22	617,724	964,005
A E Pakenham	1-4 (25%)	1	0	1	740,695	811,952
Mrs Magnier, Tabor, Smith	4-10 (40%)	2	1	1	736,096	767,480
K Abdulla	49-237 (21%)	29	26	25	496,503	756,919
Sheikh A Al Maktoum	39-229 (17%)	39	21	31	333,142	624,185
Michael Tabor	3-27 (11%)	4	3	3	453,815	534,234
Mrs Susan Roy	7-20 (35%)	1	2	1	461,440	530,313
Willie McKay	9-43 (21%)	2	5	3	483,223	500,241
Nigel Shields	34-270 (13%)	30	38	28	272,182	464,005
A & D de Rothschild	3-6 (50%)	1	0	0	340,680	449,463
Jaber Abdullah	28-144 (19%)	26	15	11	278,355	436,489
Mr & Mrs G Middlebrook	10-74 (14%)	7	6	9	393,661	417,522
S Al Homaizi & I Al Sagar	10-32 (31%)	3	5	4	316,373	413,380
Lord Derby	4-13 (31%)	4	1	0	331,892	402,182
Mountgrange Stud	22-124 (18%)	16	14	18	154,232	341,673
Mrs P W Harris	21-141 (15%)	18	13	17	233,564	327,875
Raymond Tooth	7-92 (8%)	8	6	8	263,760	320,979
Sheikh Mohammed	17-87 (20%)	11	12	9	204,826	320,351
J L C Pearce	2-26 (8%)	6	3	3	7,247	313,492
Saeed Manana	18-176 (10%)	11	14	19	209,971	309,200
Norman Ormiston	7-28 (25%)	3	0	3	276,294	298,660
Roldvale Limited	3-10 (30%)	0	0	2	270,012	290,989
Elite Racing Club	7-64 (11%)	8	5	7	108,820	284,243
Jumeirah Racing	41-231 (18%)	34	24	25	186,549	266,959
J C Smith	13-101 (13%)	12	8	10	150,069	261,227
Mrs J Magnier & M Tabor	1-12 (8%)	4	1	2	12,464	253,241
M H Sly, Dr T Davies Mrs P Sly	2-11 (18%)	0	0	1	215,764	240,817
H R H Sultan A Shah	11-66 (17%)	7	6	4	181,110	239,335
Baron G Von Ullmann	2-3 (67%)	0	1	0	193,052	233,114
Ballymacoll Stud	11-44 (25%)	7	1	4	158,829	225,881
Matthew Green	20-115 (17%)	16	7	13	143,593	207,582
R J Arculli	6-43 (14%)	7	5	2	112,642	205,193
D Smith, M Tabor, Mrs J Magnier	4-8 (50%)	1	1	0	184,434	204,344
Transcend Bloodstock LLP	18-176 (10%)	17	23	17	148,023	204,101
N P Bloodstock	1-1 (100%)	0	0	0	198,730	198,730
Mrs J Magnier & Mrs D Nagle	2-4 (50%)	0	0	0	193,733	193,733
J M Greetham	6-24 (25%)	3	2	3	79,622	193,504
P D Savill	14-86 (16%)	5	15	7	159,212	185,229
J S Threadwell	2-8 (25%)	2	0	0	164,308	184,544
M F Kentish	11-25 (44%)	3	3	2	153,963	183,728
Franconson Partners	7-45 (16%)	5	6	4	155,378	179,146
Terry Cooper	2-12 (17%)	2	0	2	127,755	178,452
Philip Newton	2-16 (13%)	1	3	0	54,988	169,802
Mrs J Magnier, D Smith, M Tabor	3-5 (60%)	0	0	0	168,370	168,370
Mrs J Wood	14-68 (21%)	4	12	8	118,275	168,285
Mrs M Gittins	9-77 (12%)	12	8	3	85,927	163,155
Mrs Charles Cyzer	18-209 (9%)	18	22	18	105,612	163,010

Racing Post top rated 2006

(Best performance figures recorded between 6th November 2005 and 31st December 2006)

Deep Impact (JPN)	133
Discreet Cat (USA)	131
George Washington (IRE)	131
Absolute Champion (AUS)	129
Barbaro (USA)	129
Rail Link	129
Shirocco (GER)	129
Bernardini (USA)	128
Hurricane Run (IRE)	128
Aragorn (IRE)	127
David Junior (USA)	127
Dylan Thomas (IRE)	127
Invasor (ARG)	127
Lava Man (USA)	127
Araafa (IRE)	126
Dream Passport (JPN)	126
Electrocutionist (USA)	126
Pride (FR)	126
Takeover Target (AUS)	126
Yeats (IRE)	126
Admire Moon (JPN)	125
Alkaased (USA)	125
Heart s Cry (JPN)	125
Iffraaj	125
Maraahel (IRE)	125
Notnowcato	125
Pop Rock (JPN)	125
Premium Tap (USA)	125
Vengeance Of Rain (NZ)	125
Artie Schiller (USA)	124
Brass Hat (USA)	124
Court Masterpiece	124
Daiwa Major (JPN)	124
Grey Swallow (IRE)	124
Holy Roman Emperor (IRE)	124
Meisho Samson (JPN)	124
Miesque s Approval (USA)	124
Ouija Board	124
Red Rocks (IRE)	124
Siren Lure (USA)	124
Teofilo (IRE)	124
Thor s Echo (USA)	124
Alexander Goldrun (IRE)	123
Bluegrass Cat (USA)	123
Buzzards Bay (USA)	123
Commentator (USA)	123
Kane Hekili (JPN)	123
Librettist (USA)	123
Manduro (GER)	123
Moss Vale (IRE)	123
Sixties Icon	123
Street Sense (USA)	123
Admire Main (JPN)	122
Balance Of Game (JPN)	122
Brother Derek (USA)	122
Bullish Luck (USA)	122
Collier Hill	122
Delta Blues (JPN)	122
Hat Trick (JPN)	122
Helene Pillaging (AUS)	122
I m The Tiger (USA)	122
Laverock (IRE)	122
Les Arcs (USA)	122
Lincoln (JPN)	122
Peeress	122
Reverence	122
Showing Up (USA)	122
Song Of Wind (JPN)	122
Stormy River (FR)	122
The Tin Man (USA)	122
Zenno Rob Roy (JPN)	122
Ad Valorem (USA)	121
Alexandrova (IRE)	121
Best Gift (NZ)	121
Better Talk Now (USA)	121
Cherry Mix (FR)	121
Corre Caminos (FR)	121
Cosmo Bulk (JPN)	121
Distinction (IRE)	121
Dragon Dancer	121
Dubai Escapade (USA)	121
Echo Of Light	121
Enforcer	121
Eremein (AUS)	121
King s Drama (IRE)	121
Majors Cast (IRE)	121
Mountain High (IRE)	121
Mustameet (USA)	121
Narita Century (JPN)	121
Pussycat Doll (USA)	121
Ramonti (FR)	121
Round Pond (USA)	121
Scintillation (AUS)	121
Sir Percy	121
Sleeping Indian	121
Stronghold	121

Raceform median times 2006

ASCOT

(BASED ON OLD TRACK AS INSUFFICIENT DATA SINCE COURSE REALIGNED IN 2006)

5f	1m 1.40
6f	1m 14.90
6f 110y	1m 21.50
7f	1m 28.10
1m Rnd	1m 42.10
1m Str	1m 41.80
1m 2f	2m 8.00
1m 4f	2m 33.00
2m 4f	4m 24.60

AYR

5f	1m 0.44
6f	1m 13.67
7f 50y	1m 32.72
1m	1m 43.49
1m 1f 20y	2m 0.00
1m 2f	2m 11.72
1m 2f 192y	2m 23.64
1m 5f 13y	2m 56.61
1m 7f	3m 22.47
2m 1f 105y	3m 54.77

BATH

5f 11y	1m 2.50
5f 161y	1m 11.20
1m 5y	1m 41.10
1m 2f 46y	2m 11.00
1m 3f 144y	2m 30.30
1m 5f 22y	2m 51.50
2m 1f 34y	3m 49.60

BEVERLEY

5f	1m 4.00
7f 100y	1m 34.31
1m 100y	1m 47.40
1m 1f 207y	2m 7.30
1m 4f 16y	2m 40.21
2m 35y	3m 39.50

BRIGHTON

5f 59y	1m 2.30
5f 213y	1m 10.10
6f 209y	1m 22.70
7f 214y	1m 35.04
1m 1f 209y	2m 2.60
1m 3f 196y	2m 32.20

CARLISLE

5f	1m 1.50
5f 193y	1m 13.61
6f 192y	1m 27.10
7f 200y	1m 40.09
1m 1f 61y	1m 57.56
1m 3f 206y	2m 32.40
1m 6f 32y	3m 7.30
2m 1f 52y	3m 49.90

CATTERICK

5f	1m 0.60
5f 212y	1m 14.00
7f	1m 27.36
1m 3f 214y	2m 39.00
1m 5f 175y	3m 4.50
1m 7f 177y	3m 31.40

CHEPSTOW

5f 16y	59.60
6f 16y	1m 12.40
7f 16y	1m 23.30
1m 14y	1m 36.00
1m 2f 36y	2m 9.90
1m 4f 23y	2m 38.72
2m 49y	3m 39.40
2m 2f	4m 0.62

CHESTER

5f 16y	1m 2.05
6f 18y	1m 15.65
7f 2y	1m 28.47
7f 122y	1m 34.75
1m 2f 75y	2m 13.14
1m 3f 79y	2m 25.79
1m 4f 66y	2m 40.65
1m 5f 89y	2m 55.42
1m 7f 195y	3m 33.60
2m 2f 147y	4m 5.57

DONCASTER

(TRACK CLOSED IN 2006 DUE TO REFURBISHMENT)

5f	1m 1.42
5f 140y	1m 7.94
6f .	1m 14.30
6f 110y	1m 20.48
7f .	1m 27.77
1m Rnd	1m 40.61
1m Str	1m 41.51
1m 2f 60y	2m 11.83
1m 4f	2m 35.53
1m 6f 132y	3m 9.74
2m 110y	3m 41.96
2m 2f	3m 57.93

EPSOM

5f	55.68
6f	1m 10.63
7f	1m 23.95
1m 114y	1m 45.74
1m 2f 18y	2m 9.04
1m 4f 10y	2m 38.73

FOLKESTONE

5f	1m 0.80
6f	1m 13.60
7f	1m 27.90
1m 1f 149y	2m 5.23
1m 4f	2m 40.50
1m 7f 92y	3m 27.20
2m 93y	3m 40.70

GOODWOOD

5f	59.05
6f	1m 12.85
7f	1m 28.04
1m	1m 40.27
1m 1f	1m 56.86
1m 1f 192y	2m 7.75
1m 3f	2m 27.21
1m 4f	2m 38.92
1m 6f	3m 3.97
2m	3m 30.79
2m 4f	4m 20.89

HAMILTON

5f 4y	1m 1.20
6f 5y	1m 13.10
1m 65y	1m 49.30
1m 1f 36y	1m 59.66
1m 3f 16y	2m 26.26
1m 4f 17y	2m 39.18
1m 5f 9y	2m 53.40

HAYDOCK

5f	1m 2.07
6f	1m 14.90
7f 30y	1m 32.06
1m 30y	1m 45.51
1m 2f 120y	2m 17.73
1m 3f 200y	2m 34.99
1m 6f	3m 6.29
2m 45y	3m 37.90

KEMPTON

5f	1m 0.40
6f	1m 13.70
7f	1m 26.80
1m	1m 40.80
1m 1f	1m 54.55
1m 2f	2m 9.00
1m 4f	2m 36.90
2m	3m 31.40

LEICESTER

5f 2y	1m 0.90
5f 218y	1m 13.20
7f 9y	1m 26.10
1m 60y	1m 45.30
1m 1f 218y	2m 8.30
1m 3f 183y	2m 34.50

LINGFIELD (TURF)

5f	58.94
6f	1m 11.67
7f	1m 24.21
7f 140y	1m 31.46
1m 1f	1m 55.29
1m 2f	2m 9.72
1m 3f 106y	2m 29.92
1m 6f	3m 6.92
2m	3m 33.26

LINGFIELD (A.W)

5f	59.78
6f	1m 12.81
7f	1m 25.89
1m	1m 39.43
1m 2f	2m 7.79
1m 4f	2m 34.39
1m 5f	2m 48.30
2m	3m 28.79

MUSSELBURGH

5f	1m 0.50
7f 30y	1m 29.94
1m	1m 42.50
1m 1f	1m 53.86
1m 4f	2m 36.90
1m 6f	3m 5.70
2m	3m 33.90

NEWBURY

5f 34y	1m 2.56
6f 8y	1m 14.32
7f .	1m 27.00
1m Str	1m 40.62
1m 1f	1m 54.59
1m 2f 6y	2m 8.71
1m 3f 5y	2m 22.27
1m 4f 5y	2m 35.99
1m 5f 61y	2m 50.99
2m	3m 36.15

NEWCASTLE

5f	1m 1.50
6f	1m 15.09
7f	1m 28.02
1m	1m 43.48
1m 3y Str	1m 41.90
1m 1f 9y	1m 57.81
1m 2f 32y	2m 11.80
1m 4f 93y	2m 43.55
1m 6f 97y	3m 12.60
2m 19y	3m 35.20

NEWMARKET (ROWLEY)

5f	1m 0.47
6f	1m 13.10
7f	1m 26.50
1m	1m 39.37
1m 1f	1m 51.95
1m 2f	2m 5.71
1m 4f	2m 33.50
1m 6f	3m 0.13
2m	3m 26.92
2m 2f	3m 54.80

NEWMARKET (JULY)

5f	59.56
6f	1m 13.35
7f	1m 26.78
1m	1m 40.43
1m 2f	2m 6.44
1m 4f	2m 32.91
1m 6f 175y	3m 11.04
2m 24y	3m 26.99

NOTTINGHAM

5f 13y	1m 1.80
6f 15y	1m 15.00
1m 54y	1m 46.40
1m 1f 213y	2m 9.70
1m 6f 15y	3m 7.10
2m 9y	3m 33.50

PONTEFRACT

5f 1m 3.80
6f 1m 17.40
1m 4y 1m 45.70
1m 2f 6y 2m 14.08
1m 4f 8y 2m 40.30
2m 1f 22y 3m 50.50
2m 1f 216y 4m 3.00
2m 5f 122y 5m 0.80

REDCAR

5f 58.70
6f 1m 11.70
7f 1m 24.90
1m 1m 37.80
1m 1f 1m 53.40
1m 2f 2m 6.80
1m 3f 2m 21.00
1m 6f 19y 3m 5.02
2m 4y 3m 31.50

RIPON

5f 1m 0.20
6f 1m 13.00
1m 1m 41.10
1m 1f 1m 53.85
1m 1f 170y.................2m 5.00
1m 4f 10y 2m 37.00
2m 3m 33.00

SALISBURY

5f 1m 1.59
6f 1m 14.98
6f 212y 1m 29.06
1m 1m 43.09
1m 1f 198y 2m 8.46
1m 4f 2m 36.36
1m 6f 15y 3m 6.23

SANDOWN

5f 6y 1m 2.21
7f 16y 1m 31.09
1m 14y 1m 43.95
1m 1f 1m 56.11
1m 2f 7y 2m 10.24
1m 3f 91y 2m 28.07
1m 6f 3m 4.51
2m 78y 3m 38.23

SOUTHWELL (TURF)

6f 1m 16.10
7f 1m 29.20
1m 2f 2m 13.70
1m 3f 2m 28.0
1m 4f 2m 40.30
2m 3m 41.50

SOUTHWELL (A.W)

5f 1m 0.30
6f 1m 16.90
7f 1m 30.80
1m 1m 44.60
1m 3f 2m 28.90
1m 4f 2m 42.09
1m 6f 3m 9.60
2m 3m 44.54

THIRSK

5f 59.90
6f 1m 12.50
7f 1m 27.10
1m 1m 39.70
1m 4f 2m 35.20
2m 3m 31.20

WARWICK

5f 59.40
5f 110y 1m 5.50
6f 21y 1m 12.10
7f 26y 1m 25.00
1m 22y 1m 39.60
1m 2f 188y 2m 19.40
1m 4f 134y 2m 43.60
1m 6f 213y.................3m 15.90
2m 39y 3m 32.70

WINDSOR

5f 10y 1m 1.10
6f 1m 13.67
1m 67y 1m 45.60
1m 2f 7y 2m 8.30
1m 3f 135y 2m 30.10

WOLVERHAMPTON (A.W)

5f 20y 1m 2.82
5f 216y 1m 15.81
7f 32y.........................1m 30.40
1m 141y 1m 51.76
1m 1f 103y 2m 2.62
1m 4f 50y 2m 42.42
1m 5f 194y 3m 7.37
2m 119y 3m 43.13

YARMOUTH

5f 43y 1m 2.80
6f 3y 1m 13.70
7f 3y 1m 26.60
1m 3y 1m 39.90
1m 2f 21y...................2m 8.10
1m 3f 101y 2m 27.50
1m 6f 17y 3m 5.30
2m 3m 31.41
2m 2f 51y 4m 6.90

YORK

5f 3y 59.25
6f 3y...........................1m 11.50
6f 217y 1m 24.31
7f 205y 1m 38.74
1m 208y.....................1m 50.99
1m 2f 88y 2m 10.48
1m 3f 198y 2m 31.11
1m 5f 197y 2m 58.44
1m 7f 198y 3m 23.25

Raceform Flat speed figures 2006

(Best time performances achieved 1st January - 31st December 2006 (min. rating 110, two-year-olds 105)

THREE YEAR OLDS AND UPWARDS - Turf

Abundance 111 (6f,Dea,VS,Aug 27)
Ace 110 (10f,Leo,GF,Sep 9)
Ad Valorem 112 (8f,Dea,VS,Aug 13)
Adoration 112 (8f,Cur,HY,May 27)
Aigle D Or 112 (15f,Lon,G,Sep 30)
Airbuss 111 (8f,Not,GF,Jly 29)
Akarem 110 (12f,Ham,G,May 19)
Al Maali 111 (6 1/2f,Nad,G,Feb 23)
Alayan 115 (12f,Nad,GF,Mar 2)
Alexander Goldrun 114 (10f,Cur,G,Jly 1)
Alexandrova 111 (12f,Cur,GF,Jly 16)
Alfie Flits 113 (11 1/2f,Wdr,GS,Nov 4)
Alix Road 112 (12f,Lon,G,Oct 15)
All The Good 110 (14f,Mus,GS,Nov 3)
Allegretto 111 (12f,Hay,GF,Jly 8)
Along The Nile 110 (10f,Pon,GF,Sep 21)
Alpacco 112 (10f,Nad,GF,Feb 9)
Amadeus Wolf 114 (6f,Nmk,GF,Jly 14)
Anani 111 (10f,Nad,GS,Feb 24)
Angus Newz 111 (5f,Ham,GS,Sep 17)
Anna Karenina 112 (8f,Cur,G,Sep 17)
Anna Pavlova 111 (14f,Yor,G,Sep 8)
Ans Bach 112 (7f,San,GF,Jly 26)
Appalachian Trail 110 (8f,Asc,GF,Aug 12)
Apsis 115 (8f,Cha,G,Jun 11)
Araafa 116 (8f,Cur,HY,May 27)
Arabian Prince 110 (8f,Leo,GY,Aug 20)
Arch Rebel 111 (8f,Leo,Y,May 14)
Areyoutalkingtome 111 (7f,Chs,G,Aug 25)
Ariodante 110 (12f,Bri,F,Aug 15)
Arm Candy 110 (8f,Nmk,S,Oct 28)
Army Of Angels 112 (8f,Yor,S,Oct 6)
Art Master 113 (8f,Sai,HY,Apr 1)
Ashdown Express 114 (6f,Nmk,GF,Jly 14)
Assertive 112 (6f,Lin,G,May 3)
Asset 111 (7f,Asc,GF,Jun 21)
Atlantic Air 111 (10f,Dea,VS,Aug 13)
Aussie Rules 113 (8f,Lon,GS,May 14)
Azarole 110 (7 1/2f,Nad,GF,Jan 19)

Babodana 112 (8f,San,G,Apr 29)
Baby First 112 (12f,Lon,G,Oct 15)
Bahamian Pirate 113 (6f,Goo,GF,Aug 5)
Bahiano 114 (6 1/2f,Nad,GF,Feb 10)
Ballet Pacifica 111 (10f,Dea,VS,Aug 20)
Balthazaar s Gift 111 (6f,Asc,GF,Jun 24)
Baltic King 112 (6f,Asc,GF,Jun 24)
Bandama 110 (12f,Asc,GF,Jun 23)
Banknote 111 (8f,Hay,GF,Jly 6)
Bannaby 112 (12 1/2f,Dea,VS,Aug 27)
Barastraight 110 (10f,Dea,S,Aug 19)
Bauer 111 (11f,Nby,G,Sep 15)
Bawaader 110 (8f,Cur,SH,Mar 26)
Beau Nash 110 (11f,Nby,G,Sep 15)
Beaver Patrol 112 (6f,Eps,GF,Jun 3)
Beckermet 111 (6f,Ncs,GF,Jly 1)
Belenus 111 (8f,Sal,GS,Aug 17)
Bellamy Cay 112 (12f,Cha,G,Jun 4)
Benbaun 113 (5f,Cur,GF,Jly 2)
Best Alibi 111 (12f,Cur,G,Jly 2)
Billich 111 (11 1/2f,Yar,F,Jly 6)
Binanti 111 (8f,Goo,G,Aug 1)
Biniou 110 (5f,Lon,GS,May 14)
Blessyourpinksox 110 (9f,Cur,GF,Aug 27)
Blue Ksar 112 (10f,Sth,GF,Sep 7)
Blue Monday 113 (11f,Nby,G,Sep 15)
Blue On Blues 111 (8f,Nad,GF,Feb 10)
Blythe Knight 111 (8f,Yor,S,Aug 24)
Bo McGinty 110 (5f,Bev,GF,Jun 27)
Bold Act 110 (9f,Yor,S,Oct 7)
Bolodenka 112 (8f,Yor,S,Aug 24)
Bond Boy 110 (5f,Thi,HY,May 20)
Bond City 111 (6f,Goo,GF,Aug 5)
Borderlescott 115 (6f,Goo,GF,Aug 5)
Boris De Deauville 111 (10f,Dea,S,Aug 19)
Boule D Or 112 (10f,San,GS,May 30)
Brunel 112 (7 1/2f,Nad,GF,Feb 2)
Bullish Luck 110 (9f,Nad,GF,Mar 25)
Burning Incense 111 (6f,Nmk,G,Aug 19)
Bygone Days 115 (6f,Nmk,GS,Oct 13)

Caesar Beware 117 (7 1/2f,Nad,GF,Feb 2)
Candidato Roy 112 (6 1/2f,Nad,GF,Mar 9)
Cape Royal 110 (5f,Lei,GF,Sep 18)
Caradak 111 (7f,Nby,GF,Jly 21)
Cartography 115 (6 1/2f,Nad,G,Feb 23)
Cashier 110 (8f,San,G,Apr 29)
Celtic Mill 113 (5f,Nmk,G,Sep 28)
Cesare 111 (8f,Asc,GF,Jun 21)
Chained Emotion 110 (5f,Cur,YS,Sep 19)
Chancellor 111 (10f,Eps,G,Jun 2)
Chantaco 110 (10f,Red,G,May 29)
Charlie Cool 111 (8f,Nmk,GF,Jly 14)
Chelsea Rose 113 (10f,Cur,G,Jly 1)
Cherry Mix 110 (12f,Nad,GF,Mar 2)
Chief Crazy Horse 111 (6f,Cur,Y,Sep 19)
Clinet 110 (8f,Nad,GF,Feb 9)
Colisay 111 (8f,Nby,G,Apr 22)
Collier Hill 113 (12f,Nad,GF,Mar 25)
Common World 114 (7f,Cur,YS,Apr 9)
Compton s Eleven 110 (6 1/2f,Nad,GF,Feb 10)
Conceal 112 (6 1/2f,Nad,GF,Feb 9)
Confidential Lady 112 (8f,Nmk,S,May 7)
Consular 110 (12f,Hay,GF,Jly 8)
Continent 110 (6f,Goo,GF,Aug 5)
Corran Ard 111 (10f,Pon,GF,Sep 21)
Corre Caminos 111 (10 1/2f,Lon,GS,Apr 30)
Corridor Creeper 114 (5f,Nmk,G,Sep 28)
Corriolanus 111 (12f,Nad,GF,Feb 10)
Cougar Bay 115 (10 1/2f,Hay,GF,Aug 12)
Court Masterpiece 116 (8f,Goo,GF,Aug 2)
Crossing 112 (12f,Leo,GF,Sep 9)
Crosspeace 112 (10f,Goo,GF,Sep 10)

Dabbers Ridge 112 (7f,Asc,GF,Jly 29)
Daltaya 116 (8f,Lon,GS,May 14)
Damoiselle 111 (8f,Lon,GS,May 14)
Danak 114 (9f,Fai,GF,Jly 23)
Dandy Man 115 (5f,Nmk,GF,May 6)
Daramsar 113 (12f,Lon,G,Oct 15)
Dark Islander 113 (8f,Nmk,GF,Jly 14)
Dark Missile 111 (6f,Nmk,GF,Jly 12)
Darsi 110 (12f,Cur,G,Jly 2)
David Junior 117 (9f,Nad,GF,Mar 25)
Day Flight 111 (10f,San,G,Apr 28)
Daylami Star 112 (12f,Chs,GF,May 10)
Days Of My Life 110 (8 1/2f,Bev,GF,Jun 22)
Decado 113 (8f,Cur,HY,May 27)
Deep Impact 110 (12f,Lon,G,Oct 1)
Defi 110 (8f,Ham,GF,Jly 20)
Degas Art 111 (12f,Nmk,S,Sep 29)
Democratic Deficit 110 (8f,San,G,Apr 29)
Desert Authority 113 (10f,Sth,GF,Sep 7)
Desert Lord 114 (5f,Lon,G,Oct 1)
Dhaular Dhar 111 (7f,Chs,G,Jun 13)
Dilek 112 (8f,Cha,GS,Jly 9)
Dixie Belle 110 (5f,Nby,G,Sep 16)
Dizzy Dreamer 110 (6f,Lei,GS,Aug 23)
Doctor Dino 113 (8f,Cha,G,Jun 11)
Dolphin Bay 113 (12f,Leo,Y,May 14)
Dragon Dancer 112(12f,Eps,GF,Jun 3)
Dream Catch 111 (8f,Cur,HY,May 27)
Dry Ice 110 (8f,Goo,G,Aug 1)
Duff 110 (8f,Cur,G,Sep 17)
Dunelight 113 (8f,Goo,GF,Aug 4)
Dylan Thomas 116 (10f,Leo,GF,Sep 9)

Earl s Court 112 (10f,Nad,GF,Feb 9)
Early March 114 (8f,Cha,G,Jun 11)
Easy Air 110 (7f,Nmk,GF,Jly 14)
Echelon 110 (7f,Lin,G,May 13)
Echo Of Light 115 (8f,Lon,G,Sep 30)
Eisteddfod 112 (6 1/2f,Dea,G,Aug 6)
Elasos 110 (12 1/2f,Dea,VS,Aug 27)
Electrocutionist 111 (10f,Asc,GF,Jun 21)
Emmpat 111 (9f,Leo,GF,Sep 9)
Encinas 113 (12f,Nad,GF,Mar 2)
Enforcer 111 (12f,Asc,GF,Jun 24)
Enjoy The Moment 111 (12f,Asc,GF,Jun 23)
Etesaal 111 (10f,Nad,GF,Mar 9)
Etlaala 114 (6f,Sal,GF,Jun 18)
Excalibur 111 (12f,Nad,GF,Feb 10)
Excusez Moi 113 (6f,Goo,GF,Aug 5)
Exmoor 111 (6f,Nby,G,May 19)

Fairmile 110 (10 1/2f,Yor,GF,Jly 15)
Falkirk 110 (5f,Asc,GF,Jun 20)
Falstaff 115 (12f,Nad,GF,Mar 2)
Fantasy Believer 117 (5f,Nmk,G,Sep 28)
Fayr Jag 112 (6f,Ncs,GF,Jly 1)
Fermion 110 (12f,Lon,G,Sep 10)
Fields Of Omagh 110 (9f,Nad,GF,Mar 25)
Firenze 114 (6f,Goo,GF,Aug 5)
Flashy Wings 113 (8f,Leo,GF,Sep 9)
Foreign Affairs 114 (12f,Leo,GY,Aug 20)
Forgery 112 (8f,Nby,G,Apr 22)
Formal Decree 110 (10f,Pon,GF,Jun 12)
Fortunate Isle 111 (8f,Pon,HY,Apr 4)
Foxhaven 110 (12f,Asc,GS,Sep 24)
Frank Sonata 112 (12f,Cur,SH,Oct 8)
Freedonia 111 (12f,Lon,G,Sep 10)
Fremen 110 (9f,Yor,S,Oct 7)
Fullandby 110 (6f,Rip,S,Aug 19)

Gaelic Princess 110 (7f,Sal,GF,Aug 31)
Galient 113 (12f,Chs,GF,May 10)
Gandor 112 (8 1/2f,Eps,G,Apr 26)
Garnica 111 (8f,Cha,GS,Jly 9)
Gee Dee Nen 111 (12f,Chs,GF,May 10)
Gentlewave 112 (12f,Cur,G,Jly 2)
Geordieland 112 (12f,Cha,G,Jun 4)
George Washington 115 (8f,Asc,GS,Sep 23)
Germance 114 (10f,Dea,VS,Aug 20)
Getaway 113 (15f,Lon,G,Sep 30)
Gharir 111 (8f,Sai,HY,Apr 1)
Gift Horse 110 (6f,Nmk,GF,Jly 14)
Gimasha 112 (5f,Nmk,G,Sep 28)
Glistening 112 (14f,Yor,GS,Aug 23)
Global Wings 111 (12f,Leo,GF,Sep 9)
Go For Gold 112 (12f,Nad,GF,Feb 10)
Golden Arrow 111 (8f,Cur,HY,May 27)
Golden Cross 111 (16f,Leo,SH,Nov 6)
Golden Grimshaw 110 (12f,Leo,Y,May 14)
Good Surprise 114 (12f,Leo,Y,May 14)
Goodbye Mr Bond 110 (8f,Hay,HY,May 26)
Grand Entrance 111 (7f,Nmk,GF,Jly 22)
Great Britain 112 (6f,Nmk,GS,Oct 13)
Grecian Dancer 111 (7f,Cur,GY,Sep 17)
Greek Renaissance 114 (6f,Goo, G, Sep 20)
Green Manalishi 110 (5f,Nby,G,Apr 21)
Greenslades 110 (6f,Nmk,GS,May 28)
Greenwich Meantime 110 (16f,Ncs,GF,Jly 1)
Grey Mystique 112 (15f,Lon,G,Sep 30)
Groom Tesse 113 (12 1/2f,Dea,VS,Aug 27)

Hail The Chief 112 (8f,San,G,Apr 29)
Hala Bek 112 (12f,Eps,GF,Jun 3)
Halla San 112 (12f,Goo,G,Sep 20)
Hard Rock City 110 (8f,Leo,Y,May 14)
Hard Top 110 (12f,Cha,G,Jun 4)
Hattan 115 (10 1/2f,Hay,GF,Aug 12)
Heart s Cry 116 (12f,Nad,GF,Mar 25)
Hearthstead Wings 113 (12f,Rip,G,Apr 29)
Helios Quercus 112 (8f,Sai,HY,Apr 1)
Heliostatic 110 (12f,Cur,G,Jly 2)
Hello Sunday 113 (8f,Dea,VS,Aug 27)
Here She Comes 110 (8f,Cha,G,Jun 11)
Hidden Dragon 111 (6 1/2f,Nad,GF,Feb 10)
Hinterland 113 (10 1/2f,Hay,GF,Aug 12)
Hoh Hoh Hoh 110 (6f,Sal,GS,Sep 27)
Holiday Camp 110 (8f,Nad,G,Feb 23)
Home Affairs 111 (8 1/2f,Eps,GF,Jun 3)
Host 111 (9f,Nad,GF,Mar 25)
Hurricane Run 118 (12f,Sai,GS,Jun 25)

I m So Lucky 110 (10f,Asc,GF,Jun 23)
Ice Planet 110 (6f,Rip,S,Aug 19)
Iffraaj 117 (7f,Goo,G,Aug 1)
Illustrious Blue 114 (8f,Goo,G,Aug 1)
Imperial Rose 111 (12f,Leo,Y,May 14)
Impressionnante 117 (8f,Lon,GS,May 14)
Indian Maiden 113 (6f,Dea,VS,Aug 27)
Indian Trail 112 (6f,Ncs,GF,Jly 1)
Inter Vision 112 (7f,Chs,G,Aug 25)
Into The Breeze 110 (7f,Chs,G,Jun 13)
Intrepid Jack 113 (7f,Nmk,GF,Jly 14)
Intriguing Glimpse 111 (5f,Sal,GF,Jun 18)
Invasian 110 (10f,Not,S,Oct 4)
Ireland s Call 110 (6f,Cur,Y,Sep 19)
Irish Wells 115 (12 1/2f,Dea,VS,Aug 27)
Irridescence 113 (9f,Nad,GS,Feb 24)
Ivan Denisovich 113 (8f,Cur,G,Sep 17)

Jedburgh 112 (7f,Goo,G,Aug 1)
Jeremy 114 (7f,Asc,GF,Jun 21)
Jersey Bounce 111(10f,Nad,GF,Feb 9)
Joseph Henry 111 (8f,Goo,G,Aug 1)
Jubilee Street 110 (8f,Pon,GF,Jly 30)

Kandidate 113 (10f,San,GF,Jly 7)
Karawana 112 (12f,Leo,GF,Sep 9)
Kastoria 116 (12f,Leo,GY,Aug 20)
Keen Look 111 (9f,Leo,G,Jly 19)
Kendargent 111 (8f,Cha,GS,Jly 9)
Kentucky Dynamite 113 (8f,Cha,GS,Jly 9)
Khyber Kim 112 (10f,Nby,G,Jly 22)
Killybegs 113 (7f,Nmk,GS,Oct 14)
King Jock 114 (7 1/2f,Nad,GF,Jan 19)
King Of Tory 110 (7f,Leo,GF,Sep 9)
King s Caprice 110(7f,Nmk,GF,Apr 19)
Kings Point 110 (8f,San,G,Apr 29)
Kingscross 110 (6f,Nby,G,May 19)
Kingsgate Prince 111 (7f,Asc,GF,Jun 21)
Kinsya 111 (9f,Yor,S,Oct 7)
Kocab 111 (12f,Lon,G,Oct 15)
Kodiac 115 (6 1/2f,Nad,GF,Feb 10)
Krataios 111 (8f,Sai,HY,Apr 1)
Kristensen 110 (14f,Mus,GF,Apr 16)

Lafi 111 (5f,Bev,GF,Sep 19)
Lake Poet 110 (12f,Asc,GF,Jun 23)
Land n Stars 113 (12f,Nad,GF,Feb 10)
Lapwing 112 (6^1/2f,Nad,GF,Feb 10)
Latino Magic 112 (8f,Cur,G,Sep 17)
Latona 113 (5f,Lon,GS,May 14)
Laverock 117 (12f,Sai,GS,Jun 25)
Le Carre 110 (15^1/2f,Sai,HY,Apr 1)
Le Miracle 113 (15^1/2f,Lon,G,Sep 10)
Lee Applause 110 (9f,Leo,GY,Aug 20)
Les Arcs 116 (6f,Nmk,GF,Jly 14)
Lets Roll 111 (14f,Goo,G,Aug 1)
Librettist 117 (8f,Dea,VS,Aug 13)
Lightning Flash 111 (7f,Yor,S,Aug 24)
Linas Selection 114 (12f,Asc,GF,Jun 23)
Linngari 114 (8f,Nad,G,Feb 23)
Little Eye 111 (9f,Leo,G,Jly 19)
London Express 111 (12f,Yor,GS,Aug 22)
Lone Plainsman 111 (5f,Cur,YS,Sep 19)
Look Again 110 (10f,Eps,G,Jun 2)
Lord Admiral 113 (9f,Nad,GF,Mar 2)
Lord Du Sud 114 (15f,Dea,VS,Aug 20)
Loup De Mer 110 (15^1/2f,Lon,G,Oct 22)
Lundy s Liability 110 (9f,Nad,GF,Mar 2)

Mac Love 114 (7f,Nmk,F,Jly 1)
Majestic Missile 113 (5f,Lon,G,Sep 10)
Majestic Times 111 (5f,Cur,GF,Jly 2)
Major Magpie 110 (8f,Pon,GS,Sep 14)
Mandesha 114 (12f,Lon,G,Sep 10)
Mandobi 112 (7^1/2f,Nad,GF,Feb 9)
Manduro 116 (8f,Dea,VS,Aug 13)
Mango Mischief 110 (10f,Dea,VS,Aug 13)
Maraahel 113 (12f,Asc,GF,Jun 24)
Marchand D Or 117 (6^1/2f,Dea,G,Aug 6)
Marching Song 113(7f,Nmk,GF,Jly 14)
Marcus Andronicus 112 (8f,Lon,GS,May 14)
Marend 112 (12^1/2f,Dea,VS,Aug 27)
Maroussies Wings 110 (12f,Asc,GF,Jun 22)
Mary Louhana 113 (15f,Lon,G,Sep 30)
Mashaahed 111 (10f,Ayr,GS,Sep 16)
Master Marvel 114 (8f,Cur,HY,May 27)
Matrix 110 (5f,Lon,GS,May 14)
Mauralakana 116 (8f,Lon,GS,May 14)
Mecca s Mate 111 (5f,San,S,May 30)
Medico 113 (9f,Leo,G,Jly 19)
Menwaal 113 (12f,Leo,Y,May 14)
Mersey Sound 112 (15f,Nmk,GF,Jly 22)
Military Cross 110 (10f,Eps,GF,Jun 3)
Millbag 110 (7^1/2f,Nad,GS,Feb 24)
Millennium Force 111 (7^1/2f,Nad,GF, Feb 9)
Millville 111 (12f,Yor,GS,May 17)
Mine 116 (7f,Nmk,GF,Jly 14)
Minister Of State 110 (8f,Thi,F,Jly 4)
Minority Report 110(7f,Goo,GF,Aug 2)
Miss Sally 111 (6f,Cur,HY,May 27)
Miss Una 110 (7f,Cur,GY,Sep 17)
Mkuzi 111 (14f,Cur,G,Jly 1)
Momtic 111 (8^1/2f,Eps,GF,Jun 3)
Mont Etoile 111 (12f,Asc,GF,Jun 22)
Montare 113 (12f,Lon,G,Sep 10)
Montgomery s Arch 110 (6f,Nad,F,Feb 16)
Moon Unit 113 (6f,Cur,HY,May 27)
Mosharref 113 (8f,San,GF,Sep 8)
Moss Vale 115 (6f,Cur,HY,May 27)
Motive 110 (12f,Rip,G,Apr 29)
Mountain 111 (12f,Nby,HY,Oct 21)
Mountain High 112 (12f,Asc,GF,Jun 24)
Mudawin 113 (14f,Yor,GS,Aug 23)
Mulaqat 118 (10^1/2f,Hay,GF,Aug 12)
Multidimensional 112 (10f,Dea,S,Aug 19)
Munaddam 112 (6f,Goo,GF,Aug 5)
Munsef 112 (12f,Asc,GS,Sep 24)
Musketier 110 (10f,Dea,VS,Aug 13)
Mustameet 115 (10f,Cur,GF,Aug 13)
Mutakarrim 115 (12f,Cur,S,May 28)
Mutamared 114 (6f,Goo,GF,Aug 5)
Mutamarres 110 (6f,Nmk,GF,Jly 12)

Mysterious Lina 111 (10f,Dea,VS,Aug 20)
Nakiska 111 (12f,Leo,Y,May 14)
Namroud 111 (8f,Ayr,G,Jun 23)
Nannina 112 (8f,Leo,GF,Sep 9)
Nasheej 111 (8f,Nmk,S,May 7)
National Captain 111 (7^1/2f,Nad,GS,Feb 24)
Nautical 110 (6f,Nby,G,May 19)
Nawamees 110 (14f,Goo,G,Aug 1)
Nayyir 113 (7f,Nmk,F,Jly 1)
Nelsons Column 110 (10f,Rip,GF,Jly 22)
New Girlfriend 112(8f,Lon,GS,May 14)
New Seeker 113 (7f,Nmk,F,Jly 1)
Nice Tune 110 (9f,Goo,GF,Aug 2)
Nick s Nikita 114 (12f,Leo,GF,Sep 9)
Nidhaal 110 (5f,Ham,GS,Sep 17)
Nightime 113 (8f,Cur,HY,May 28)
Notability 112 (8f,Lon,G,Sep 30)
Notable Guest 116 (10^1/2f,Hay,GF, Aug 12)
Notnowcato 113 (10f,San,GS,May 30)
Numero Due 110 (16f,Chs,GF,Sep 9)

Obe Gold 112 (6f,Goo,GF,Aug 5)
One More Round 111 (6f,Goo,GF,Aug 5)
One Putra 110 (6f,Goo,GF,Aug 5)
Oracle West 117 (12f,Nad,GF,Mar 2)
Orcadian 111 (12f,Nby,HY,Oct 21)
Orientor 111 (5f,San,S,May 30)
Osterhase 112 (5f,Cur,GF,Jly 2)
Ouija Board 115 (10f,Leo,GF,Sep 9)
Out After Dark 110 (6f,Goo,GF,Aug 5)

Palomar 111 (12f,Rip,G,Apr 29)
Papal Bull 111 (12f,Asc,GF,Jun 23)
Paper Talk 111 (7f,Nmk,S,Aug 12)
Parnassus 111 (7^1/2f,Nad,GF,Feb 9)
Patavellian 111 (5f,Nmk,GF,May 6)
Peace Offering 111 (5f,Lon,G,Sep 10)
Peeress 116 (8f,Dea,VS,Aug 13)
Percussionist 114 (14f,Yor,S,May 19)
Perfect Promise 110 (9f,Nad,GF,Mar 25)
Petite Speciale 113 (15^1/2f,Lon,GS, Apr 30)
Philharmonic 112 (5f,Bev,GF,Sep 19)
Picaresque Coat 113(8f,Lon,G,Sep 30)
Pictavia 113 (10f,Goo,GF,Sep 10)
Pieter Brueghel 110 (6f,Rip,S,Aug 19)
Pivotal Flame 113 (5f,Nmk,GF,May 6)
Pivotal Point 111 (5f,Asc,GF,Jun 20)
Pivotal s Princess 115 (5f,Nmk,G,Sep 28)
Polar Magic 110 (7f,Goo,GS,May 24)
Policy Maker 116 (12f,Sai,GS,Jun 25)
Polygonal 110 (12f,Asc,GF,Jun 24)
Ponte Tresa 113 (15f,Lon,G,Sep 30)
Porto Santo 110 (8f,Lon,GS,May 14)
Press The Button 112 (8f,Goo,G,Aug 1)
Presto Shinko 110 (6^1/2f,Dea,G,Aug 6)
Price Tag 119 (8f,Lon,GS,May 14)
Pride 119 (12f,Sai,GS,Jun 25)
Pride Of Nation 112 (8f,Hay,HY,May 26)
Primary 111 (10f,Goo,GF,Sep 10)
Prince Namid 111 (6f,Eps,GF,Jun 3)
Prince Of Thebes 112 (8f,Goo,GF,Aug 4)
Prince Tamino 116 (5f,Nmk,G,Sep 28)
Princess Nala 113 (12f,Leo,Y,May 14)
Proudance 112 (7^1/2f,Nad,GS,Feb 24)
Public Forum 113 (8f,San,G,Apr 29)
Puya 111 (7f,Nmk,G,Aug 18)

Quenched 110 (14f,Yor,G,Sep 8)
Quiet Royal 113 (6^1/2f,Dea,G,Aug 6)
Quinmaster 112 (8f,Cur,G,Sep 17)
Quito 114 (6f,Yor,GS,May 17)

Race For The Stars 112 (8f,Leo,GF,Sep 9)
Racinger 112 (8f,Dea,VS,Aug 27)
Rageman 110 (8f,Sai,HY,Apr 1)
Rail Link 111 (12f,Lon,G,Oct 1)
Rain Stops Play 111 (8f,Nmk,S,May 26)
Ratio 111 (6f,Dea,VS,Aug 27)
Realism 110 (10f,Nad,GS,Feb 24)
Rebel Rover 110 (12f,Fai,GF,Jly 23)
Red Bloom 112 (10f,Cur,G,Jly 1)
Red Clubs 111 (6f,Asc,GS,Sep 24)
Red Evie 114 (8f,Leo,GF,Sep 9)
Red Rocks 110 (12f,Asc,GF,Jun 23)
Red Spell 111 (8f,Nby,G,Apr 22)
Reluctant Suitor 112 (14f,Mus,GF,Apr 16)
Reunite 110 (10f,Yar,F,Jly 18)
Reverence 115 (5f,San,S,May 30)
Rio Riva 111 (8f,Red,GF,Apr 17)
Ripples Maid 110 (6f,Nmk,GF,Jly 12)
Rising Cross 112 (14f,Yor,G,Sep 8)
Rising Shadow 110 (6f,Yor,S,Oct 7)
River Alhaarth 110 (16f,Ncs,GF,Jly 1)
Road To Love 112 (10^1/2f,Hay,GF,Aug 12)
Road To Mandalay 113 (12f,Leo,GY,Aug 20)
Rob Roy 113 (8f,San,G,Apr 29)
Rocamadour 110 (10f,Sth,GF,Sep 7)
Rockie 112 (6f,Cur,HY,Oct 22)
Royal Highness 112 (12f,Lon,G,Sep 10)
Royal Storm 114(6^1/2f,Nad,GF,Feb 10)

Sabbeeh 112 (7^1/2f,Nad,GF,Feb 2)
Sabirli 112 (8f,Nad,GF,Feb 10)
Safe Structure 115 (6^1/2f,Nad,GF,Feb 9)
Safqa 110 (8f,Not,GF,Jly 29)
Saintly Rachel 111 (12f,Nad,GF,Feb 10)
Salute Him 110(10^1/2f,Chs,GF,Sep 23)
Salutino 113 (12f,Cha,G,Jun 4)
Sanchi 110 (11f,Sth,G,Sep 6)
Satchem 114 (8f,Goo,GF,Jun 10)
Satri 114 (6^1/2f,Dea,G,Aug 6)
Satwa Queen 111 (9f,Nad,GS,Feb 24)
Saville Road 110 (7f,Nby,GF,Jly 21)
Scorpion 111 (12f,Cur,SH,Oct 8)
Scottish Stage 110 (12f,Asc,GF,Jun 22)
Scrummage 111 (7f,San,GF,Jly 26)
Secret World 110 (7f,Asc,GF,Jun 21)
Seihali 112 (9f,Nad,GF,Mar 2)
Septimus 111 (10^1/2f,Yor,S,May 18)
Sergeant Cecil 112 (14f,Yor,S,May 19)
Serieux 111 (8f,Goo,G,Aug 1)
Shakis 113 (10f,Nad,GF,Mar 9)
Shamdala 110 (15^1/2f,Lon,G,Oct 22)
Shanty Star 113 (10f,Nad,GF,Feb 9)
Shayrazan 117 (8f,Cur,HY,May 27)
Shinko Dancer 110 (5f,Cur,YS,Sep 19)
Shirocco 111 (12f,Nmk,S,May 7)
Short Skirt 113 (12f,Nby,HY,Oct 21)
Shumookh 110 (8f,Pon,GS,Oct 2)
Sierra Vista 112 (5f,Hay,G,Sep 23)
Signatory 111 (12f,Nmk,S,May 26)
Silca s Sister 110 (8f,Nmk,S,May 7)
Silent Applause 110 (7f,Nmk,GF,Jly 22)
Silver Touch 110 (7f,Yor,G,Sep 8)
Sina Cova 110 (10f,Cur,YS,Sep 19)
Sir Edwin Landseer 113 (6f,Nad,F,Feb 16)
Sir Gerard 110 (8f,Asc,GF,Jun 22)
Sir Percy 113 (12f,Eps,GF,Jun 3)
Sleeping Indian 115 (7f,Nmk,GS,Oct 14)
Slip Dance 111 (6^1/2f,Nad,GF,Feb 9)
Smart Enough 115 (8f,Yor,S,Aug 24)
Soar With Eagles 111 (10f,Cur,GF,Aug 13)
Soldier Hollow 112 (10f,Lon,G,Sep 30)
Soledad 110 (15^1/2f,Lon,G,Oct 22)
Solent 111 (12f,Nby,S,May 20)
Solerina 110 (16f,Leo,SH,Nov 6)
Somnus 113 (7f,Yor,G,Sep 9)
Song Of Passion 113 (7f,Eps,G,Jun 2)
Soulacroix 112 (14f,Goo,G,Aug 1)
South Cape 111 (8f,San,GF,Sep 8)
Soviet Song 114 (8f,Goo,GF,Aug 2)
Special Kaldoun 110 (8f,Dea,VS,Aug 13)
Speciosa 115 (8f,Nmk,S,May 7)
Spectait 114 (8f,Goo,GF,Aug 4)
Speedy Sam 110 (9f,Goo,G,Aug 27)
Sphinx 112 (14f,Yor,S,May 18)
Spinning Queen 116 (8f,Nmk,GS,Sep 30)
St Petersburg 110 (8f,Yor,S,Aug 24)
Stage Gift 111 (10f,Eps,GF,Jun 3)
Steenberg 115 (6f,Yor,GS,May 17)
Stellite 110 (8f,Ayr,G,Jun 23)
Stetchworth Prince 113 (7^1/2f,Nad,GS, Feb 24)
Stormy River 115 (8f,Dea,VS,Aug 13)
Stotsfold 112 (10^1/2f,Chs,GF,Sep 23)
Strategic Mount 110 (12f,Goo,GF,Aug 2)
Stretton 110 (12f,Yor,GS,Aug 22)
Strike Up The Band 111 (5f,Bev,GF, Sep 19)
Stronghold 113 (8f,Goo,GF,Jun 10)
Sugarhoneybaby 110 (7f,Leo,SH,Nov 6)
Suggestive 115 (7f,Nmk,F,Jly 1)
Sunday Symphony 112 (14f,Yor,G, Sep 8)
Svedov 115 (8f,Sai,HY,Apr 1)
Swinbrook 112 (7f,Nmk,GF,Jly 14)
Swordsman 110 (14f,Goo,G,Aug 1)

T-Bird 113 (6^1/2f,Nad,GF,Feb 9)
Tajneed 113 (6f,Cur,HY,Oct 22)
Tajseed 111 (7^1/2f,Nad,GF,Feb 9)
Take A Bow 111 (10f,Sth,GF,Sep 7)
Takeover Target 113 (6f,Nmk,GF,Jly 14)
Tam Lin 114 (10f,Nby,G,Jly 22)
Tanzanite 111 (8f,San,G,Apr 29)
Taqseem 110 (9f,Fai,GF,Jly 23)
Tax Free 113 (6f,Goo,GF,Aug 5)
Telemachus 113 (12f,Leo,Y,May 14)
Texas Gold 110 (6f,Goo,GF,Aug 5)
The Carbon Unit 111 (10f,Nad,GF,Feb 9)
The Jobber 112 (5f,Lei,GF,Sep 18)
The Lord 111 (5f,Goo,GS,May 24)
The Tatling 113 (5f,Nmk,G,Sep 28)
The Tin Man 113 (9f,Nad,GF,Mar 25)
The Trader 113 (5f,San,S,May 30)
Theatre 110 (16f,Asc,GS,Sep 23)
Thunder Rock 110 (12f,Asc,GF,Jun 24)
Ti Adora 110 (12f,Yor,GS,Aug 22)
Tie Black 117 (8f,Lon,GS,May 14)
Tiger Shark 112 (6^1/2f,Nad,GF,Feb 9)
Time On 110 (12f,Lon,G,Sep 10)
Tipper Road 110 (12f,Cur,YS,Apr 9)
Toldo 111 (16f,Ncs,GF,Jly 1)
Touch Of Land 115 (9f,Nad,GF,Mar 2)
Toufan Express 110 (9f,Leo,GF,Jun 21)
Tournedos 111 (5f,Cur,GF,Jly 2)
Trance 111 (14f,Mus,GF,Apr 16)
Traytonic 110 (7f,Red,GF,Aug 12)
Trinculo 111 (5f,Yor,S,May 18)
Tropical Lady 112 (10f,Cur,G,Jly 1)
Tucker 110 (8f,Asc,GF,Aug 12)
Tungsten Strike 110 (16^1/2f,San,S, May 29)
Turtle Bowl 114 (8f,Cha,G,Jun 11)
Tyson 111 (9f,Nad,GF,Feb 10)

Ugo Fire 111 (8f,Leo,GF,Sep 9)
Uhoomagoo 111 (7f,Asc,GF,Jly 29)

Valentina Guest 110 (12f,Leo,Y,May 14)
Valixir 110 (9f,Nad,GF,Mar 2)
Vendangeur 114 (15f,Lon,G,Sep 30)
Violet Park 110 (9f,Nmk,S,May 7)
Virginia Woolf 110 (16f,Leo,SH,Nov 6)
Visindar 111 (12f,Eps,GF,Jun 3)

Wagtail 110 (8f,Asc,GS,Sep 23)
Wannabe Posh 111 (12f,Goo,G,Sep 20)
Warrens Castle 110 (14f,Leo,GF,Jun 21)
Wasseema 112 (8f,Asc,G,Jly 28)
Wavertree Warrior 110(8f,Yor,S,Oct 6)
Wazir 111 (6^1/2f,Nad,GF,Feb 10)
West Of Amarillo 111 (8f,Lon,GS,May 14)

Windsor Knot 113 (10f,Nby,G,Jly 22)
Winisk River 114 (7 1/2f,Nad,GS,Feb 24)
With Interest 110 (8f,Not,S,Nov 1)
Woodcote 113 (6f,Goo,GF,Aug 5)
Wunderwood 111 (14f,Goo,G,Aug 1)

Yasoodd 112 (8f,Cur,HY,May 27)
Yeats 114 (16f,Goo,GF,Aug 3)
Yomalo 110 (6f,Leo,G,Jun 7)
Youmzain 110 (12f,Yor,GS,Aug 22)
Young Mick 114 (12f,Asc,GS,Sep 24)
Ysoldina 110 (8f,Sai,HY,Apr 1)

Zero Tolerance 111 (8f,Yor,S,May 18)
Zomerlust 111 (6f,Pon,G,Apr 24)

THREE YEAR-OLDS AND UPWARDS - Sand

Acrobatic 112 (11f,Kem,SD,Sep 1)
Activo 112 (10f,Lin,SD,Jan 14)
African Dream 110 (10f,Lin,SD,Feb 25)
Akona Matata 111 (8f,Kem,SD,Mar 25)
Alpine Reel 111 (12f,Wol,SS,Dec 15)
Amorist 115 (10f,Lin,SD,Jan 28)
Amwell Brave 110 (12f,Sth,SD,Mar 16)
Appalachian Trail 111 (9f,Wol,SD,Nov 11)
Areyoutalkingtome 114 (6f,Lin,SD, Dec 16)
Atlantic Quest 114(10f,Lin,SD,Dec 20)
Atlantic Story 110 (7f,Sth,SD,Nov 28)
Attilius 117 (7f,Nad,FT,Feb 9)
Awatuki 110 (10f,Lin,SD,Dec 20)

Babcary 110 (10f,Kem,SD,Sep 2)
Bahar Shumaal 113 (9 1/2f,Wol,SD,Oct 28)
Balanced Budget 113 (12f,Kem,SD,Sep 18)
Bavarica 110 (9 1/2f,Wol,SD,Dec 7)
Bayeux 110 (5f,Wol,SD,Feb 18)
Blatant 110 (9f,Nad,FT,Feb 9)
Blue On Blues 110 (9f,Nad,FT,Feb 2)
Blue Sky Thinking 111 (10f,Kem,SD,Apr 15)
Bobski 111 (7f,Lin,SD,Nov 13)
Bomber Command 113 (7f,Kem,SD,Dec 15)
Bonus 112 (6f,Wol,SD,Dec 2)
Boo 114 (10f,Lin,SD,Jan 14)
Bouboulina 110 (7f,Lin,SD,Oct 6)
Brandywell Boy 110 (6f,Lin,SD,Nov 5)
Brass Hat 113 (10f,Nad,FT,Mar 25)
Bravo Maestro 114 (10f,Kem,SD,Apr 15)
Brindisi 110 (9f,Wol,SD,Nov 11)
Bulwark 113 (16f,Lin,SD,Jly 15)

Captain Squire 110 (6f,Nad,FT,Mar 25)
Ceremonial Jade 112 (7f,Lin,SD,Oct 6)
Cimyla 114 (9f,Wol,SD,Nov 11)
Claret And Amber 111 (8f,Lin,SD,Jan 28)
Counsel s Opinion 111 (10f,Lin,SD, Feb 25)
Country Pursuit 113(12f,Lin,SD,Apr 1)
Crow Wood 110 (10f,Lin,SD,Feb 25)
Cusoon 117 (10f,Lin,SD,Dec 20)

Descartes 110 (12f,Lin,SD,Oct 5)
Dinner Date 110 (10f,Kem,SD,May 1)
Discreet Cat 119 (8f,Nad,FT,Mar 9)
Dower House 110(9 1/2f,Wol,SD,Dec 7)
Dubai Honor 112 (9f,Nad,FT,Feb 2)

Eccentric 110 (9f,Nad,FT,Feb 9)
Echo Of Light 115 (8f,Lin,SD,Jly 15)
Electrocutionist 115 (10f,Nad,FT,Mar 2)
Eloquent Knight 111 (12f,Sth,SD,Mar 16)
Elusive Dream 114 (16f,Lin,SD,Jly 15)
Emerald Beauty 111 (7f,Nad,SY,Feb 24)
Evident Pride 111 (8f,Kem,SD,Nov 29)

Fantaisiste 112 (6f,Kem,SD,Apr 26)
Farewell Gift 114 (8f,Lin,SD,Jan 28)
Finalmente 115 (16f,Lin,SD,Jly 15)
Finsbury 112 (7f,Kem,SD,Dec 15)
First Order 111 (6f,Lin,SD,Dec 16)
Flamme De Passion 113 (9f,Nad,FT, Mar 25)
Flotta 110 (12f,Lin,SD,Apr 1)
Fyodor 113 (5f,Wol,SD,Feb 18)

Gentleman s Deal 113 (8f,Sth,SD,Dec 2)
Glencalvie 110 (8f,Kem,SD,Jun 28)
Glenviews Youngone 110 (5f,Wol,SD, Apr 29)
Gold For Sale 114 (8f,Nad,FT,Feb 10)
Golden Acer 115 (8f,Nad,FT,Mar 9)
Grand Passion 112(10f,Lin,SD,Feb 25)
Great Hawk 110 (10f,Kem,SD,Sep 6)
Greenbelt 114 (11f,Sth,SD,Feb 7)

Hail The Chief 112 (10f,Lin,SD,Jan 14)
Happy Pearl 115 (7f,Nad,FT,Feb 9)
High Command 110 (11f,Kem,SD,Sep 1)
Hits Only Heaven 112 (8f,Kem,SD,Jun 28)

Indian Steppes 110 (7f,Lin,SD,Mar 18)
Invasor 112 (9f,Nad,FT,Mar 25)
Island Rapture 111 (8f,Lin,SD,Jan 28)

Jack Sullivan 112 (8f,Nad,FT,Mar 25)
Jet West 111 (6f,Nad,FT,Mar 25)

Kalankari 110 (8f,Kem,SD,May 2)
Kandidate 116 (10f,Kem,SD,Apr 15)
Kew Green 110 (10f,Lin,SD,Feb 25)
Khanjar 114 (12f,Sth,SD,Dec 15)
Kilworth 110 (9f,Wol,SD,Oct 8)
Kindlelight Debut 111 (9 1/2f,Wol,SD, Jan 13)
King Marju 111 (7f,Lin,SD,Mar 18)
King Of Argos 110 (9f,Wol,SD,Nov 16)
King s Caprice 112 (7f,Lin,SD,Nov 19)
Kostar 111 (6f,Wol,SD,Dec 2)

La Colline 111 (6f,Sth,SD,Nov 13)
Les Arcs 112 (6f,Wol,SD,Jan 6)
Little Jim 113 (8f,Nad,FT,Feb 2)

Magical Music 111 (9 1/2f,Wol,SD,Dec 7)
Maltese Falcon 112 (6f,Lin,SD,Nov 11)
Marbush 117 (8f,Nad,FT,Mar 2)
Marching Song 110 (7f,Lin,SD,Mar 18)
Master Theo 110 (9f,Wol,SD,Nov 11)
Matuza 111 (6f,Lin,SD,Nov 5)
Melpomene 110 (12f,Sth,SD,Nov 20)
Millville 113 (12f,Wol,SS,Dec 15)
Mizz Tee 110 (10f,Lin,SD,Jan 14)
Mr Lambros 112 (7f,Lin,SD,Mar 18)
Mutamared 110 (6f,Lin,SD,Apr 1)
My Royal Captain 111 (8f,Nad,FT,Feb 10)

Nayyir 110 (10f,Lin,SD,Mar 18)
New Guinea 113 (11f,Sth,SD,Jly 7)
Nice Tune 111 (8f,Kem,SD,Apr 15)
Northern Desert 112(8f,Lin,SD,Jan 28)
Northern Rock 111 (7f,Nad,FT,Feb 9)
Notability 111 (8f,Lin,SD,Jly 15)

Obrigado 114 (10f,Kem,SD,Apr 15)
Odiham 113 (16f,Lin,SD,Jly 15)
Oldenway 114 (12f,Sth,SD,Dec 15)
One More Round 111 (6f,Lin,SD,Dec 16)
Orchard Supreme 112 (8f,Lin,SD,Dec 22)

Parasol 113 (9f,Nad,FT,Feb 2)
Piper General 115 (12f,Sth,SD,Dec 15)
Prime Contender 110 (12f,Lin,SD,Apr 1)
Profit s Reality 112 (10f,Kem,SD,Apr 15)
Proud Tower Too 114 (6f,Nad,FT,Mar 25)

Qadar 112 (5f,Wol,SD,Feb 18)

Rafferty 110 (7f,Wol,SD,Jan 6)
Raza Cab 111 (8f,Kem,SD,Mar 27)
Realism 111 (10f,Kem,SD,Apr 15)
Red Birr 112 (10f,Lin,SD,Jan 28)
Red Racketeer 114 (10f,Kem,SD,Apr 15)
Red Spell 114 (7f,Lin,SD,Nov 19)
Resplendent Nova 110 (7f,Lin,SD,Nov 13)
Rochdale 111 (7f,Lin,SD,Oct 6)
Rock Music 116 (8f,Nad,FT,Feb 2)
Rohaani 115 (10f,Kem,SD,Apr 15)
Royal Alchemist 113 (8f,Kem,SD,Apr 15)
Royal Island 114 (10f,Lin,SD,Jan 14)
Royal Jet 111 (11f,Kem,SD,Sep 1)

Safsoof 112 (7f,Nad,FT,Feb 16)
Sand Repeal 111 (11f,Sth,SD,Feb 7)
Satchem 112 (8f,Lin,SD,Jly 15)
Sea Hunter 110 (7f,Nad,FT,Jan 26)
Secret Night 111 (8f,Lin,SD,Dec 22)
Setembro Chove 112 (8f,Nad,SY,Feb 23)
Shamoan 110 (8f,Nad,FT,Mar 25)
Simpatico Bribon 116 (9f,Nad,FT,Mar 2)
Solo Flight 110 (10f,Lin,SD,Nov 28)
Something 114 (7f,Lin,SD,Mar 18)
Spectait 110 (8f,Lin,SD,Jly 15)
Speedy Sam 112 (10f,Lin,SD,Nov 25)
Spring Goddess 113 (8f,Lin,SD,Jan 28)
Sri Diamond 111 (10f,Lin,SD,Mar 18)
Stargazer Jim 114 (10f,Lin,SD,Dec 20)
Stoneacre Lad 111 (5f,Sth,SD,Dec 5)
Stotsfold 114 (10f,Kem,SD,Sep 2)
Stronghold 110 (8f,Lin,SD,Jly 15)
Sweet Indulgence 114 (12f,Wol,SS, Dec 15)
Swift Oscar 112 (8f,Lin,SD,Jan 28)

Tamagin 111 (7f,Kem,SD,Dec 15)
Tanforan 111 (8f,Lin,SD,Jan 28)
Te Quiero 113 (8f,Sth,SD,Mar 7)
Testimony 113 (9f,Nad,FT,Mar 25)
Texas Gold 110 (5f,Lin,SD,Oct 21)
Thajja 114 (7f,Nad,FT,Feb 16)
Thor s Echo 112 (6f,Nad,FT,Mar 25)
Three Wrens 111 (8f,Kem,SD,Apr 15)
Tiger Tiger 115 (10f,Lin,SD,Jan 14)
Tropical Star 115 (7f,Nad,SY,Feb 24)

Utopia 117 (8f,Nad,FT,Mar 25)

Velvet Heights 112 (12f,Wol,SS,Dec 15)
Viking Spirit 110 (6f,Lin,SD,Nov 11)
Violet Park 112 (8f,Kem,SD,Apr 15)

Wahoo Sam 111 (7f,Wol,SD,Jan 6)
Watamu 115 (10f,Lin,SD,Dec 20)
Waterside 115 (8f,Sth,SD,Mar 7)
Wavertree Warrior 112 (7f,Kem,SD, Dec 15)
Well Armed 110 (7f,Nad,FT,Jan 19)
Where s That Tiger 113 (8f,Nad,FT, Feb 10)
Wilko 111 (10f,Nad,FT,Mar 25)
Win River Win 113 (8f,Nad,FT,Mar 25)
Woodnook 110 (6f,Lin,SD,Nov 5)

Young Mick 114 (10f,Kem,SD,Apr 15)

Zalkani 111 (10f,Lin,SD,Feb 11)

TWO YEAR-OLDS - Turf

Abby Road 111 (5f,Nby,GS,Aug 19)
Adagio 110 (7f,Nmk,GS,Oct 14)
Admiralofthefleet 110 (8f,Asc,GS,Sep 23)
Albert Einstein 105 (7f,Leo,S,Oct 30)
Alexander Tango 105 (7f,Cur,GF,Aug 27)
Alzerra 107 (5f,Nby,GS,Aug 19)
Arch Swing 107 (7f,Cur,GY,Sep 16)
Archipenko 110 (7f,Leo,S,Oct 30)
Armigerent 107 (6f,Nmk,GF,Jly 13)
Authorized 109 (8f,Nby,HY,Oct 21)

Bahama Mama 107 (5f,Yor,G,Sep 8)
Bal De La Rose 107 (8f,Lon,G,Oct 1)
Bazroy 106 (6f,Cur,GY,Sep 17)
Bicoastal 108 (7f,Goo,G,Aug 27)
Big Robert 105 (8f,Goo,G,Sep 9)
Blue Echo 106 (6f,Nmk,GS,Oct 27)
Boca Dancer 105 (8f,Cur,SH,Oct 22)
Brave Tin Soldier 111 (6f,Cur,GY,Sep 17)
Brazilian Bride 108(6f,Cur,GF,Aug 13)
Bridge It Jo 107 (5f,Nby,GS,Aug 19)

Caldra 108 (6f,Nmk,S,Sep 29)
Captain Marvelous 107 (6f,Nmk,S,Sep 29)
Champlain 105 (8f,Asc,GS,Sep 23)
Charlie Farnsbarns 107 (8f,Nby,HY, Oct 21)
Cockney Rebel 106 (7f,Yor,G,Sep 9)
College Scholar 105 (6f,Nmk,GS,Oct 27)
Confuchias 106 (7f,Leo,S,Oct 30)
Conquest 105 (5f,Not,F,Jly 8)
Cumin 107 (7f,Goo,GF,Aug 3)

Dal Cais 110 (6f,Cur,GF,Jly 16)
Danebury Hill 105 (6f,Nmk,GF,Jly 13)
Darrfonah 110 (8f,Lon,G,Oct 1)
Dazed And Amazed 105 (6f,Nmk,GF, Jly 13)
Dhanyata 106 (6f,Nmk,S,Sep 29)
Dijeerr 105 (7f,Nmk,S,Sep 29)
Dimenticata 105 (8f,Leo,G,Jly 19)
Doctor Brown 107 (6f,Nby,G,Sep 16)
Drayton 108 (6f,Cur,GF,Aug 13)
Drumfire 105 (7f,San,G,Aug 26)
Dubai Builder 106 (6f,Yor,GS,Aug 22)
Dubai s Touch 106 (6f,Nmk,GF,Jly 13)
Duke Of Marmalade 106 (7f,Goo,GF, Aug 2)
Dutch Art 112 (6f,Nmk,S,Sep 29)

Eagle Mountain 111 (8f,Cur,SH,Oct 8)
El Soprano 105 (6f,Leo,G,Jun 7)
Elhamri 106 (5f,Nby,G,Jly 22)
English Ballet 109 (7f,Nmk,S,Aug 12)
Essexford 105 (7f,Cur,GY,Sep 17)
Evening Time 108 (6f,Cur,SH,Oct 8)
Excellent Art 108 (6f,Nby,G,Sep 16)

Ferneley 106 (7f,Cur,GF,Aug 26)
Finsceal Beo 115 (8f,Lon,G,Oct 1)
Flash McGahon 105 (6f,Cur,GY,Sep 17)
Friston Forest 106 (8f,Sai,GS,Oct 29)

Golden Balls 105 (7f,Sal,GF,Jly 15)

Haatef 112 (7f,Nmk,GS,Oct 14)
Halicarnassus 106 (7f,Nmk,GF,Jly 14)
Hamoody 105 (6f,Goo,GF,Aug 4)
He s A Decoy 106 (7f,Nmk,GS,Oct 14)
Hellvelyn 109 (6f,Asc,GF,Jun 20)
Hoh Mike 107 (5f,Yor,G,Sep 8)
Holocene 105 (8f,Sai,GS,Oct 29)
Holy Roman Emperor 115 (7f,Nmk,GS, Oct 14)
Hope N Charity 105 (7f,Goo,G,Aug 27)

Ikat 108 (8f,Lon,G,Oct 1)
Impetious 107 (8f,Lon,G,Oct 1)
Indian Ink 107 (6f,Nmk,S,Sep 29)
Invincible Force 107 (6f,Cur,GY,Sep 17)

Jo Burg 105 (6f,Asc,GF,Jun 20)
Just Dust 106 (7f,Goo,GF,Aug 4)

Kalgoorlie 106 (6f,Asc,GF,Jun 20)
Kirklees 105 (8f,Asc,GS,Sep 23)

La Neige 105 (6f,Asc,GF,Jun 20)
La Presse 105 (6f,Nmk,GS,Oct 27)
Legerete 109 (8f,Lon,G,Oct 1)
Lucky Kyllachy 107(6f,Cur,GY,Sep 17)

Magic America 106(6f,Dea,VS,Aug 20)
Major Cadeaux 108(6f,Asc,GF,Jun 20)
Makaan 106 (8f,Sai,GS,Oct 29)
Medicine Path 107 (8f,Asc,GS,Sep 23)
Mesbaah 105 (7 1/2f,Bev,G,Aug 16)
Midnight Beauty 105(9f,Lon,G,Oct 15)
Miss Beatrix 109 (6f,Cur,GF,Aug 13)
Mount Nelson 109 (7f,Cur,SH,Oct 22)
Mubaashir 105 (5f,Chs,GF,May 10)
Musthav 109 (6f,Cur,GF,Jly 16)

Passage Of Time 105 (7f,Nmk,S,Aug 12)
Poltava 108 (8f,Lon,G,Oct 1)
Princess Iris 105 (6f,Ayr,GS,Sep 16)
Princess Taise 107 (7f,Nmk,S,Aug 12)

Rabatash 106 (6f,Cur,GF,Aug 13)
Rahiyah 106 (7f,Nmk,GS,Oct 14)
Rallying Cry 111 (7f,Nmk,GS,Oct 14)
Ravi River 105 (7f,Chs,G,Aug 26)
Resignation 105 (6f,Nmk,GF,Sep 19)

Sans Reward 105 (8f,Yor,G,Sep 9)
Satulagi 105 (7f,Nmk,S,Aug 12)
Sesmen 109 (7f,Goo,G,Aug 27)
Silca Chiave 106 (7f,Cur,GF,Aug 27)
Simply Perfect 107 (8f,Yor,G,Sep 9)
Siren s Gift 105 (5f,Yor,G,Sep 8)
Spirit Of Pearl 109 (6f,Cur,GF,Jly 16)
Spirit One 108 (8f,Sai,GS,Oct 29)
Strategic Prince 112 (7f,Nmk,GS,Oct 14)
Sudoor 106 (7f,San,GF,Jly 27)
Sunshine Kid 107 (8f,Nby,S,Oct 10)
Supposition 105 (7f,Cur,GF,Aug 27)
Sweet Lilly 105 (8f,Pon,GS,Oct 16)

Tariq 106 (6f,Asc,GF,Jun 20)
Teofilo 116 (7f,Nmk,GS,Oct 14)
Thousand Words 108 (7f,Nmk,S,Sep 29)
Tobosa 107 (6f,Nmk,S,Sep 29)
Traffic Guard 106 (6f,Nmk,GF,Sep 19)

Uimhir A Haon 106 (7f,Leo,S,Oct 30)

Vale Of Belvoir 109 (5f,Nby,GS,Aug 19)
Visionario 106 (7f,Lon,GS,Sep 3)
Vital Equine 112 (7f,Nmk,GS,Oct 14)
Vital Statistics 105 (6f,Sal,GF,Aug 31)

Wi Dud 110 (5f,Yor,G,Sep 8)

Yellowstone 107 (8f,Sai,GS,Oct 29)

TWO YEAR-OLDS - Sand

Beverly Hill Billy 105 (8f,Lin,SD,Aug 12)

Cesc 106 (8f,Kem,SD,Dec 8)

Dhanyata 105 (6f,Kem,SD,Sep 2)

Hinton Admiral 105 (6f,Lin,SD,Oct 21)

Love Dubai 106 (9 1/2f,Wol,SD,Dec 14)

Montalembert 105 (10f,Lin,SD,Nov 25)
Monzante 105 (8f,Kem,SD,Sep 30)

Onenightinlisbon 106 (6f,Wol,SF,Nov 8)

Prime Defender 110 (6f,Wol,SF,Nov 8)

Rallying Cry 106 (8f,Kem,SD,Sep 30)

Sri Pekan Two 107 (8f,Lin,SD,Aug 12)
Strobilus 106 (8f,Lin,SD,Oct 6)

Troialini 105 (9 1/2f,Wol,SD,Dec 14)

Raceform Flat record times

ASCOT

Distance	Time	Age	Weight	Going	Horse	Date
5f	60.82 sec	2	9-3	Gd To Firm	Elhamri	Jun 20 2006
5f	59.79 sec	7	9-7	Gd To Firm	TakeoverTarget(AUS)	Jun 20 2006
6f	1m 14.16	2	8-12	Gd To Firm	Scarlet Runner	Jly 29 2006
6f	1m 13.12	6	9-4	Gd To Firm	Les Arcs (USA)	Jun 24 2006
7f	1m 27.90	2	9-3	Gd To Firm	Champlain	Jun 24 2006
7f	1m 25.89	4	8-9	Gd To Firm	Dabbers Ridge (IRE)	Jly 29 2006
1m	1m 39.14	3	9-0	Gd To Firm	Nannina	Jun 23 2006
1m	1m 39.83	3	9-2	Good	Dunelight (IRE)	Jly 28 2006
1m 2f	2m 4.150	4	8-7	Gd To Firm	I m So Lucky	Jun 23 2006
1m 4f	2m 27.24	3	8-9	Gd To Firm	Linas Selection	Jun 23 2006
2m	3m 25.60	3	9-1	Gd To Firm	Soapy Danger	Jun 23 2006
2m 4f	4m 20.45	5	9-2	Gd To Firm	Yeats (IRE)	Jun 22 2006
2m 5f	5m 4.600	4	9-0	Gd To Firm	Baddam	Jun 24 2006

AYR

Distance	Time	Age	Weight	Going	Horse	Date
5f	56.9 secs	2	8-11	Good	Boogie Street	Sep 18 2003
5f	57.2 secs	4	9-5	Gd to Firm	Sir Joey	Sep 16 1993
6f	69.7 secs	2	7-10	Good	Sir Bert	Sep 17 1969
6f	68.9 secs	7	8-8	Gd to Firm	Sobering Thoughts	Sep 18 1993
7f	1m 25.7	2	9-0	Gd to Firm	Jazeel	Sep 16 1993
7f	1m 24.9	5	7-11	Firm	Sir Arthur Hobbs	Jun 19 1992
7f 50y	1m 28.9	2	9-0	Good	Tafaahum (USA)	Sep 19 2003
7f 50y	1m 28.2	4	9-2	Gd to Firm	Flur Na H Alba	Jun 21 2003
1m	1m 39.2	2	9-0	Gd to Firm	Kribensis	Sep 17 1986
1m	1m 36.0	4	7-13	Firm	Sufi	Sep 16 1959
1m 1f 20y	1m 50.3	4	9-3	Good	Retirement	Sep 19 2003
1m 2f	2m 4.0	4	9-9	Gd to Firm	Endless Hall	Jly 17 2000
1m 2f192y	2m 13.3	4	9-0	Gd to Firm	Azzaam	Sep 18 1991
1m 5f 13y	2m 45.8	4	9-7	Gd to Firm	Eden s Close	Sep 18 1993
1m 7f	3m 13.1	3	9-4	Good	Romany Rye	Sep 19 1991
2m 1f105y	3m 45.0	4	6-13	Good	Curry	Sep 16 1955

BATH

Distance	Time	Age	Weight	Going	Horse	Date
5f 11y	60.1 secs	2	8-11	Firm	Double Fantasy	Aug 25 2000
5f 11y	59.9 secs	6	9-2	Firm	Cauda Equina	Aug 25 2000
5f 161y	69.1 secs	2	8-7	Firm	Sibla	Aug 25 2000
5f 161y	68.1 secs	6	9-0	Firm	Madraco	May 22 1989
1m 5y	1m 39.7	2	8-9	Firm	Casual Look	Sep 16 2002
1m 5y	1m 37.2	5	8-12	Gd to Firm	Adobe	Jun 17 2000
1m 5y	1m 37.2	3	8-7	Firm	Alasha (IRE)	Aug 18 2002
1m 2f 46y	2m 5.8	3	9-0	Gd to Firm	Connoisseur Bay(USA)	May 29 1998
1m 3f144y	2m 25.74	3	9-0	Hard	Top Of The Charts	Sep 8 2005
1m 5f 22y	2m 47.2	4	10-0	Firm	Flown	Aug 13 1991
2m 1f 34y	3m 43.4	6	7-9	Firm	Yaheska (IRE)	Jun 14 2003

BEVERLEY

Distance	Time	Age	Weight	Going	Horse	Date
5f	61.0 secs	2	8-2	Gd to Firm	Addo (IRE)	Jly 17 2001
5f	60.1 secs	4	9-5	Firm	Pic Up Sticks	Apr 16 2003
7f 100y	1m 31.1	2	9-7	Gd to Firm	Champagne Prince	Aug 10 1995
7f 100y	1m 31.1	2	9-0	Firm	Majal (IRE)	Jly 30 1991
7f 100y	1m 29.5	3	7-8	Firm	Who s Tef	Jly 30 1991
1m 100y	1m 43.3	2	9-0	Firm	Arden	Sep 24 1986
1m 100y	1m 42.2	3	8-4	Firm	Legal Case	Jun 14 1989
1m 1f 207y	2m 1.8	3	9-7	Firm	Rose Alto	Jly 5 1991
1m 3f 216y	2m 30.8	3	8-1	Hard	Coinage	Jun 18 1986
1m 4f 16y	2m 35.8	4	9-3	Gd to Firm	Red River Rebel	Aug 25 2002
2m 35y	3m 29.5	4	9-2	Gd to Firm	Rushen Raider	Aug 14 1996

BRIGHTON

Distance	Time	Age	Weight	Going	Horse	Date
5f 59y	60.1 secs	2	9-0	Firm	Bid for Blue	May 6 1993
5f 59y	59.3 secs	3	8-9	Firm	Play Hever Golf	May 26 1993
5f 213y	68.1 secs	2	8-9	Firm	Song Mist (IRE)	Jly 16 1996
5f 213y	67.3 secs	3	8-9	Firm	Third Party	Jun 3 1997
5f 213y	67.3 secs	5	9-1	Gd to Firm	Blundell Lane	May 4 2000
6f 209y	1m 19.9	2	8-11	Hard	Rain Burst	Sep 15 1988
6f 209y	1m 19.4	4	9-3	Gd to Firm	Sawaki	Sep 3 1991
7f 214y	1m 32.8	2	9-7	Firm	Asian Pete	Oct 3 1989
7f 214y	1m 30.5	5	8-11	Firm	Mystic Ridge	May 27 1999
1m 1f 209y	2m 4.7	2	9-0	Gd to Soft	Esteemed Master	Nov 2 2001
1m 1f 209y	1m 57.2	3	9-0	Firm	Get The Message	Apr 30 1984
1m 3f 196y	2m 25.8	4	8-2	Firm	New Zealand	Jly 4 1985

CARLISLE

Distance	Time	Age	Weight	Going	Horse	Date
5f	60.1 secs	2	8-5	Firm	La Tortuga	Aug 2 1999
5f	58.8 secs	3	9-8	Gd to Firm	Esatto	Aug 21 2002
5f 193y	1m 12.45	2	9-6	Gd to Firm	Musical Guest (IRE)	Sep 11 2005
5f 193y	1m 10.83	4	9-0	Gd to Firm	Bo McGinty (IRE)	Sep 11 2005
6f 192y	1m 24.3	3	8-9	Gd to Firm	Marjurita (IRE)	Aug 21 2002
6f 206y	1m 26.5	2	9-4	Hard	Sense of Priority	Sep 10 1991
6f 206y	1m 25.3	4	9-1	Firm	Move With Edes	Jly 6 1996
7f 200y	1m 37.34	5	9-7	Gd to Firm	Hula Ballew	Aug 17 2005
7f 214y	1m 44.6	2	8-8	Firm	Blue Garter	Sep 9 1980
7f 214y	1m 37.3	5	7-12	Hard	Thatched (IRE)	Aug 21 1995
1m 1f 61y	1m 53.8	3	9-0	Firm	Little Jimbob	Jun 14 2004
1m 3f 206y	2m 29.13	5	9-8	Gd to Firm	Tempsford (USA)	Sep 19 2005
1m 4f	2m 28.8	3	8-5	Firm	Desert Frolic (IRE)	Jun 27 1996
1m 6f 32y	3m 2.2	6	8-10	Firm	Explosive Speed	May 26 1994
2m 1f 52y	3m 46.2	3	7-10	Gd to Firm	Warring Kingdom	Aug 25 1999

CATTERICK

Distance	Time	Age	Weight	Going	Horse	Date
5f	57.6 secs	2	9-0	Firm	H Harrison	Oct 8 2002
5f	57.1 secs	4	8-7	Fast	Kabcast	Jly 7 1989
5f 212y	1m 11.4	2	9-4	Firm	Captain Nick	Jly 11 1978
5f 212y	69.8 secs	9	8-13	Gd to Firm	Sharp Hat	May 30 2003
7f	1m 24.1	2	8-11	Firm	Lindas Fantasy	Sep 18 1982
7f	1m 22.5	6	8-7	Firm	Differential (USA)	May 31 2003
1m 3f 214y	2m 30.5	3	8-8	Gd to Firm	Rahaf	May 30 2003
1m 5f 175y	2m 54.8	3	8-5	Firm	Geryon	May 31 1984
1m 7f 177y	3m 20.8	4	7-11	Firm	Bean Boy	Jly 8 1982

CHEPSTOW

Distance	Time	Age	Weight	Going	Horse	Date
5f 16y	57.6 secs	2	8-11	Firm	Micro Love	Jly 8 1986
5f 16y	56.8 secs	3	8-4	Firm	Torbay Express	Sep 15 1979
6f 16y	69.4 secs	2	9-0	Fast	Royal Fifi	Sep 9 1989
6f 16y	68.1 secs	3	9-7	Firm	America Calling (USA)	Sep 18 2001
7f 16y	1m 20.8	2	9-0	Gd to Firm	Royal Amaretto (IRE)	Sep 12 1996
7f 16y	1m 19.3	3	9-0	Firm	Taranaki	Sep 18 2001
1m 14y	1m 33.1	2	8-11	Gd to Firm	Ski Academy (IRE)	Aug 28 1995
1m 14y	1m 31.6	3	8-13	Firm	Stoli (IRE)	Sep 18 2001
1m 2f 36y	2m 4.1	5	8-9	Hard	Leonidas	Jly 5 1983
1m 2f 36y	2m 4.1	5	7-8	Gd to Firm	It s Varadan	Sep 9 1989
1m 2f 36y	2m 4.1	3	8-5	Gd to Firm	Ela Athena	Jly 23 1999
1m 4f 23y	2m 31.0	3	8-9	Gd to Firm	Spritsail	Jly 13 1989
1m 4f 23y	2m 31.0	7	9-6	Hard	Maintop	Aug 27 1984
2m 49y	3m 27.7	4	9-0	Gd to Firm	Wizzard Artist	Jly 1 1989
2m 2f	3m 56.4	5	8-7	Gd to Firm	Laffah	Jly 8 2000

CHESTER

Distance	Time	Age	Weight	Going	Horse	Date
5f 16y	60.06 secs	2	8-9	Gd to Firm	Not For Me (IRE)	Jly 14 2006
5f 16y	59.2 secs	3	10-0	Firm	Althrey Don	Jly 10 1964
6f 18y	1m 12.8	2	8-10	Gd to Firm	Flying Express	Aug 31 2002
6f 18y	1m 12.7	3	8-3	Gd to Firm	Play Hever Golf	May 4 1993
6f 18y	1m 12.7	6	9-2	Good	Stack Rock	Jun 23 1993
7f 2y	1m 25.2	2	9-0	Gd to Firm	Due Respect (IRE)	Sep 25 2002
7f 2y	1m 23.75	5	8-13	Gd to Firm	Three Graces (GER)	Jly 9 2005
7f 122y	1m 32.2	2	9-0	Gd to Firm	Big Bad Bob (IRE)	Sep 25 2002
7f 122y	1m 30.91	3	8-12	Gd to Firm	Cupid's Glory	Aug 18 2005
1m 2f 75y	2m 7.15	3	8-8	Gd to Firm	Stotsfold	May 7 2002
1m 3f 79y	2m 22.5	3	8-9	Gd to Firm	Rockerlong	Sep 23 2006
1m 4f 66y	2m 33.7	3	8-10	Gd to Firm	Fight Your Corner	May 7 2002
1m 5f 89y	2m 45.4	5	8-11	Firm	Rakaposhi King	May 7 1987
1m 7f 195y	3m 20.3	4	9-0	Gd to Firm	Grand Fromage (IRE)	Jly 13 2002
2m 2f 147y	4m 0.2	6	8-9	Gd to Firm	Fantasy Hill (IRE)	May 8 2002

DONCASTER

Distance	Time	Age	Weight	Going	Horse	Date
5f	58.4 secs	2	9-5	Firm	Sing Sing	Sep 11 1959
5f	58.4 secs	2	9-0	Good	D Urberville	Sep 13 1967
5f	57.2 secs	6	9-12	Gd to Firm	Celtic Mill	Sep 9 2004
5f 140y	67.2 secs	2	9-0	Gd to Firm	Cartography (IRE)	Jun 29 2003
5f 140y	65.6 secs	9	9-10	Good	Halmahera (IRE)	Sep 8 2004
6f	69.6 secs	2	8-11	Good	Caesar Beware (IRE)	Sep 8 2004
6f	69.6 secs	2	8-11	Good	Caesar Beware (IRE)	Sep 8 2004
6f 110y	1m 17.9	2	8-13	Good	Swan Nebula (USA)	Sep 8 2004
7f	1m 22.6	2	9-1	Good	Librettist (USA)	Sep 8 2004
7f	1m 21.6	3	8-10	Gd to Firm	Pastoral Pursuits	Sep 9 2004
1m	1m 36.5	2	8-6	Gd to Firm	Singhalese	Sep 9 2004
1m (R)	1m 35.4	2	8-10	Good	Playful Act (IRE)	Sep 9 2004
1m	1m 35.3	3	9-0	Gd to Firm	Gneiss	May 2 1994
1m (R)	1m 36.6	7	9-9	Gd to Firm	Invader	Jun 29 2003
1m 2f 60y	2m 13.4	2	8-8	Good	Yard Bird	Nov 6 1981
1m 2f 60y	2m 5.4	3	8-8	Gd to Firm	Carlito Brigante	Jly 26 1995
1m 4f	2m 27.7	3	8-12	Gd to Firm	Takwin (IRE)	Sep 9 2000
1m 6f 132y	3m 2.2	3	8-3	Gd to Firm	Brier Creek	Sep 10 1992
2m 110y	3m 34.4	4	9-12	Gd to Firm	Farsi	Jun 12 1992
2m 2f	3m 50.2	7	9-1	Gd to Firm	Boreas	Sep 12 2002

EPSOM

Distance	Time	Age	Weight	Going	Horse	Date
5f	55.0 secs	2	8-9	Gd to Firm	Prince Aslia	Jun 9 1995
5f	53.6 secs	4	9-5	Firm	Indigenous	Jun 2 1960
6f	67.8 secs	2	8-11	Gd to Firm	Showbrook	Jun 5 1991
6f	67.3 secs	5	8-12	Good	Loyal Tycoon (IRE)	Jun 7 2003
7f	1m 21.3	2	8-9	Gd to Firm	Red Peony	Jul 29 2004
7f	1m 20.1	4	8-7	Firm	Capistrano	Jun 7 1972
1m 114y	1m 42.8	2	8-5	Gd to Firm	Nightstalker	Aug 30 1988

1m 114y	1m 40.7	3	8-6	Gd to Firm	Sylva Honda	Jun 5 1991
1m 2f 18y	2m 3.5	5	7-13	Good	Crossbow	Jun 7 1967
1m 4f 10y	2m 32.3	3	9-0	Gd to Firm	Lammtarra	Jun 10 1995

FOLKESTONE

Distance	Time	Age	Weight	Going	Horse	Date
5f	58.4 secs	2	9-2	Gd to Firm	Pivotal	Nov 6 1995
5f	58.59 secs	5	9-10	Gd to Firm	Spanish Ace	Apr 25 2006
6f	1m 10.8	2	8-9	Good	Boomerang Blade	Jly 16 1998
6f	69.38 secs	4	9-8	Gd to Firm	Munaddam (USA)	Sep 18 2006
6f 189y	1m 23.7	2	8-11	Good	Hen Harrier	Jly 3 1996
6f 189y	1m 21.4	3	8-9	Firm	Cielamour (USA)	Aug 9 1988
7f	1m 25.2	2	8-11	Gd to Firm	Persian Jasmine	Aug 12 2002
7f	1m 23.76	3	8-11	Gd to Firm	Welsh Cake	Sep 18 2006
1m 1f 149y	1m 59.7	3	8-6	Gd to Firm	Dizzy	Jly 23 1991
1m 4f	2m 33.2	4	8-8	Hard	Snow Blizzard	Jun 30 1992
1m 7f 92y	3m 23.1	3	9-11	Firm	Mata Askari	Sep 12 1991
2m 93y	3m 34.9	3	8-12	Gd to Firm	Candle Smoke (USA)	Aug 20 1996

GOODWOOD

Distance	Time	Age	Weight	Going	Horse	Date
5f	57.5 secs	2	8-12	Gd to Firm	Poets Cove	Aug 3 1990
5f	56.0 secs	5	9-0	Gd to Firm	Rudi s Pet	Jly 27 1999
6f	69.8 secs	2	8-11	Gd to Firm	Bachir (IRE)	Jly 28 1999
6f	69.18 secs	4	9-0	Good	Tax Free (IRE)	Sep 9 2006
7f	1m 24.9	2	8-11	Gd to Firm	Ekraar	Jly 29 1999
7f	1m 23.8	3	8-7	Firm	Brief Glimpse (IRE)	Jly 25 1995
1m	1m 37.21	2	9-0	Good	Caldra (IRE)	Sep 9 2006
1m	1m 35.6	3	8-13	Gd to Firm	Aljabr (USA)	Jly 28 1999
1m 1f	1m 52.8	3	9-6	Good	Vena (IRE)	Jly 27 1995
1m 1f 192y	2m 2.81	3	9-3	Gd to Firm	Road To Love (IRE)	Aug 3 2006
1m 3f	2m 23.0	3	8-8	Gd to Firm	Asian Heights	May 22 2001
1m 4f	2m 31.5	3	8-10	Firm	Presenting	Jly 25 1995
1m 6f	2m 58.5	4	9-2	Gd to Firm	Mowbray	Jly 27 1999
2m	3m 21.55	5	9-10	Gd to Firm	Yeats (IRE)	Aug 3 2006
2m 4f	4m 11.7	3	7-10	Firm	Lucky Moon	Aug 2 1990

HAMILTON

Distance	Time	Age	Weight	Going	Horse	Date
5f 4y	58.0 secs	3	7-8	Firm	Fair Dandy	Sep 25 1972
5f 4y	58.0 secs	5	8-6	Firm	Golden Sleigh	Sep 6 1972
6f 5y	1m 10.0	2	8-12	Gd to Firm	Break The Code	Aug 24 1999
6f 5y	69.3 secs	4	8-7	Firm	Marcus Game	Jly 11 1974
1m 65y	1m 45.8	2	8-11	Firm	Hopeful Subject	Sep 24 1973
1m 65y	1m 42.7	6	7-7	Firm	Cranley	Sep 25 1972
1m 1f 36y	1m 53.6	5	9-6	Gd to Firm	Regent's Secret	Aug 10 2005
1m 3f 16y	2m 19.8	3	8-1	Gd to Firm	McEldowney	Aug 22 2005
1m 4f 17y	2m 32.0	4	10-0	Firm	Hold Tight	Aug 22 1983
1m 4f 17y	2m 32.0	4	7-4	Firm	Fine Point	Aug 24 1981
1m 5f 9y	2m 45.1	6	9-6	Firm	Mentalasanythin	Jun 14 1995

HAYDOCK

Distance	Time	Age	Weight	Going	Horse	Date
5f	59.2 secs	2	9-4	Firm	Money For Nothing	Aug 21 1964
5f	58.2 secs	5	8-9	Good	Sierra Vista	Sep 3 2005
6f	1m 10.9	4	9-9	Gd to Firm	Wolfhound (USA)	Sep 4 1993
6f	69.9 secs	4	9-0	Gd to Firm	Iktamal (USA)	Sep 7 1996
7f 30y	1m 29.4	2	9-0	Gd to Firm	Apprehension	Sep 7 1996
7f 30y	1m 26.8	3	8-7	Gd to Firm	Lady Zonda	Sep 28 2002
1m 30y	1m 40.6	2	8-12	Gd to Firm	Besiege	Sep 7 1996
1m 30y	1m 40.1	3	9-2	Firm	Untold Riches (USA)	Jly 11 1999
1m 2f 120y	2m 22.2	2	8-11	Soft	Persian Haze	Oct 9 1994
1m 2f 120y	2m 8.5	3	8-7	Gd to Firm	Fahal (USA)	Aug 5 1995
1m 3f 200y	2m 26.4	5	8-2	Firm	New Member	Jly 4 1970
1m 6f	2m 59.5	3	8-3	Gd to Firm	Castle Secret	Sep 30 1989
2m 45y	3m 27.0	4	8-13	Firm	Prince of Peace	May 26 1984
2m 1f 130y	3m 55.0	3	8-12	Good	Crystal Spirit	Sep 8 1990

KEMPTON (A.W)

Distance	Time	Age	Weight	Going	Horse	Date
5f	60.29 sec	2	9-1	Standard	Inflight (IRE)	Aug 23 2006
5f	59.77 sec	5	8-7	Standard	Harry Up	Dec 10 2006
6f	1m 12.22	2	8-11	Standard	Dhanyata (IRE)	Sep 2 2006
6f	1m 11.49	5	9-0	Standard	Saviours Spirit	Nov 1 2006
7f	1m 25.93	2	9-0	Standard	Boscobel	Nov 22 2006
7f	1m 23.91	3	8-4	Standard	BomberCommand(US)	Nov 24 2006
1m	1m 38.56	2	9-0	Standard	Rallying Cry (USA)	Sep 30 2006
1m	1m 37.47	3	9-1	Standard	Evident Pride (USA)	Nov 29 2006
1m 2f	2m 4.44	3	8-11	Standard	Stotsfold	Sep 2 2006
1m 3f	2m 19.08	3	9-8	Standard	Acrobatic (USA)	Sep 1 2006
1m 4f	2m 32.69	4	9-4	Standard	Kandidate	Sep 2 2006
2m	3m 27.49	4	9-2	Standard	Velvet Heights (IRE)	Apr 26 2006

LEICESTER

Distance	Time	Age	Weight	Going	Horse	Date
5f 2y	58.4 secs	2	9-0	Firm	Cutting Blade	Jun 9 1986
5f 2y	59.85 secs	5	9-5	Gd to Firm	The Jobber (IRE)	Sep 18 2006
5f 218y	1m 10.1	2	9-0	Firm	Thordis (IRE)	Oct 24 1995
5f 218y	69.4 secs	3	8-12	Gd to Firm	Lakeland Beauty	May 29 1990
7f 9y	1m 22.8	2	8-6	Good	Miss Dragonfly (IRE)	Sep 22 1997
7f 9y	1m 20.8	3	8-7	Firm	Flower Bowl	Jun 9 1986
1m 60y	1m 44.05	2	8-11	Gd to Firm	Congressional (IRE)	Sep 6 2005
1m 60y	1m 42.49	3	9-2	Gd to Firm	Street Warrior (IRE)	Sep 18 2006
1m 1f 218y	2m 5.3	2	9-1	Gd to Firm	Windsor Castle	Oct 14 1996
1m 1f 218y	2m 2.4	3	8-11	Firm	Effigy	Nov 4 1985
1m 1f 218y	2m 2.4	4	9-6	Gd to Firm	Lady Angharad (IRE)	Jun 18 2000
1m 3f 183y	2m 27.1	5	8-12	Gd to Firm	Murghem (IRE)	Jun 18 2000

LINGFIELD (TURF)

Distance	Time	Age	Weight	Going	Horse	Date
5f	57.1 secs	2	8-9	Good	Emerald Peace	Aug 6 1999
5f	56.2 secs	3	9-1	Gd to Firm	Eveningperformance	Jly 25 1994
6f	68.6 secs	2	9-3	Firm	The Ritz	Jun 11 1965
6f	68.2 secs	6	9-10	Firm	Al Amead	Jly 2 1986
7f	1m 21.3	2	7-6	Firm	Mandav	Oct 3 1980
7f	1m 20.1	3	8-7	Gd to Firm	Zelah (IRE)	May 13 1998
7f 140y	1m 29.9	2	8-12	Firm	Rather Warm	Nov 7 1978
7f 140y	1m 26.7	3	8-6	Fast	Hiaam	Nov 7 1978
1m 1f	1m 52.4	4	9-2	Gd to Firm	Quandary (USA)	Jly 15 1995
1m 2f	2m 4.6	3	9-3	Firm	Usran	Jly 15 1989
1m 3f 106y	2m 23.9	3	8-5	Firm	Night-Shirt	Jly 14 1990
1m 6f	2m 59.1	5	9-5	Firm	Ibn Bey	Jly 1 1989
2m	3m 23.7	3	9-5	Gd to Firm	Lauries Crusader	Aug 13 1988

LINGFIELD (A.W)

Distance	Time	Age	Weight	Going	Horse	Date
5f	58.6 secs	2	9-7	Standard	Classy Cleo (IRE)	Nov 28 1997
5f	57.3 secs	4	9-5	Standard	No Time (IRE)	Mar 20 2004
6f	1m 11.03	2	9-0	Standard	RainbowPromises(USA)	Oct 5 2006
6f	1m 10.06	6	8-4	Standard	Maltese Falcon	Nov 11 2006
7f	1m 24.0	2	8-12	Standard	Scottish Castle	Nov 2 1990
7f	1m 22.19	4	8-7	Standard	Red Spell	Nov 19 2005
1m	1m 36.5	2	9-5	Standard	San Pier Niceto	Nov 30 1989
1m	1m 35.40	4	9-1	Standard	Mina A Salem	Dec 19 2006
1m 2f	2m 2.19	4	9-4	Standard	Cusoon	Dec 20 2006
1m 4f	2m 28.22	4	9-5	Standard	Descartes	Oct 5 2006
1m 5f	2m 42.9	3	9-7	Standard	Global Dancer	Dec 7 1994
2m	3m 20.0	3	9-0	Standard	Yenoora	Aug 8 1992

MUSSELBURGH

Distance	Time	Age	Weight	Going	Horse	Date
5f	57.7 secs	2	8-2	Firm	Arasong	May 16 1994
5f	57.3 secs	3	8-12	Firm	Corunna	Jun 3 2000
7f 30y	1m 28.4	2	8-8	Firm	Sand Bankes	Jun 26 2000
7f 30y	1m 26.3	3	9-5	Firm	Waltzing Wizard	Aug 22 2002
1m	1m 40.3	2	8-12	Gd to Firm	Succession	Sep 26 2004
1m	1m 38.8	6	9-4	Gd to Firm	Sea Storm (IRE)	May 29 2004
1m 1f	1m 50.8	3	9-2	Firm	Short Respite	Aug 22 2002
1m 4f	2m 33.7	3	9-11	Firm	Alexandrine	Jun 26 2000
1m 5f	2m 48.9	6	8-10	Gd to Firm	Tojoneski	July 27 2005
1m 6f	2m 59.2	3	9-7	Firm	Forum Chris	Jly 3 2000
2m	3m 26.6	5	9-6	Gd to Firm	Jack Dawson (IRE)	Jun 1 2002

NEWBURY

Distance	Time	Age	Weight	Going	Horse	Date
5f 34y	59.1 secs	2	8-6	Gd to Firm	Superstar Leo	Jly 22 2000
5f 34y	59.2 secs	3	9-5	Gd to Firm	The Trader (IRE)	Aug 18 2001
6f 8y	1m 11.19	2	8-9	Gd to Firm	Mixed Blessing	Jly 23 2005
6f 8y	69.42 secs	3	8-11	Gd to Firm	Nota Bene	May 13 2005
7f	1m 23.0	2	8-11	Gd to Firm	Haafhd	Aug 15 2003
7f	1m 21.5	3	8-4	Gd to Firm	Three Points	Jly 21 2000
1m	1m 37.5	2	9-1	Gd to firm	Winged Cupid (IRE)	Sep 16 2005
1m	1m 33.59	6	9-0	Firm	Rakti	May 14 2005
1m 1f	1m 49.6	3	8-0	Gd to Firm	Holtye	May 21 1995
1m 2f 6y	2m 1.2	3	8-7	Gd to Firm	Wall Street (USA)	Jly 20 1996
1m 3f 5y	2m 16.5	3	8-9	Gd to Firm	Grandera (IRE)	Sep 22 2001
1m 4f 5y	2m 28.26	4	9-7	Gd to Firm	Azamour (IRE)	Jul 23 2005
1m 5f 61y	2m 44.9	5	10-0	Gd to Firm	Mystic Hill	Jly 20 1996
2m	3m 25.4	8	9-12	Gd to Firm	Moonlight Quest	Jly 19 1996

NEWCASTLE

Distance	Time	Age	Weight	Going	Horse	Date
5f	58.8 secs	2	9-0	Firm	Atlantic Viking (IRE)	Jun 4 1997
5f	58.0 secs	4	9-2	Firm	Princess Oberon	Jly 23 1994
6f	1m 12.18	2	9-0	Gd to Firm	Stepping Up (IRE)	Sep 5 2005
6f	1m 10.6	8	9-5	Firm	Tedburrow	Jly 1 2000
7f	1m 24.2	2	9-0	Gd to Firm	Iscan (IRE)	Aug 31 1998
7f	1m 23.3	4	9-2	Gd to Firm	Quiet Venture	Aug 31 1998
1m	1m 38.9	2	9-0	Gd to Firm	Stowaway	Oct 2 1996
1m	1m 38.9	3	8-12	Firm	Jacamar	Jly 22 1989
1m 3y	1m 37.1	2	8-3	Gd to Firm	Hoh Steamer (IRE)	Aug 31 1998
1m 3y	1m 37.3	3	8-8	Gd to Firm	Its Magic	May 27 1999
1m 1f 9y	2m 3.2	2	8-13	Soft	Response	Oct 30 1993
1m 1f 9y	1m 52.3	3	6-3	Good	Ferniehurst	Jun 23 1936
1m 2f 32y	2m 6.5	4	8-9	Fast	Missionary Ridge	Jly 29 1990
1m 4f 93y	2m 37.3	5	8-12	Firm	Retender	Jun 25 1994
1m 6f 97y	3m 6.4	3	9-6	Gd to Firm	One Off	Aug 6 2003
2m 19y	3m 24.3	4	8-10	Good	Far Cry (IRE)	Jun 26 1999

NEWMARKET (ROWLEY)

Distance	Time	Age	Weight	Going	Horse	Date
5f	58.7 secs	2	8-5	Gd to Firm	Valiant Romeo	Oct 3 2002
5f	56.8 secs	6	9-2	Gd to Firm	Lochsong	Apr 30 1994
6f	69.6 secs	2	8-11	Gd to Firm	Oasis Dream	Oct 3 2002
6f	69.9 secs	5	8-6	Gd to Firm	Indian Trail	Apr 30 2005
7f	1m 22.9	2	8-11	Gd to Firm	Grosvenor Square(IRE)	Sep 21 2004
7f	1m 22.2	4	9-5	Gd to Firm	Perfolia	Oct 17 1991
1m	1m 35.7	2	9-0	Gd to Firm	Forward Move (IRE)	Sep 21 2004
1m	1m 34.5	4	9-0	Gd to Firm	Desert Deer	Oct 3 2002
1m 1f	1m 47.2	4	9-5	Firm	Beauchamp Pilot	Oct 5 2002
1m 2f	2m 4.6	2	9-4	Good	Highland Chieftain	Nov 2 1985
1m 2f	2m 1.0	3	8-10	Good	Palace Music	Oct 20 1984
1m 4f	2m 27.1	5	8-12	Gd to Firm	Eastern Breeze	Oct 3 2003
1m 6f	2m 51.59	3	8-7	Good	Art Eyes (USA)	Sep 29 2005
2m	3m 19.5	5	9-5	Gd to Firm	Grey Shot	Oct 4 1997
2m 2f	3m 47.5	3	7-12	Hard	Whiteway	Oct 15 1947

NEWMARKET (JULY)

Distance	Time	Age	Weight	Going	Horse	Date
5f	58.5 secs	2	8-10	Good	Seductress	Jly 10 1990
5f	57.3 secs	6	8-12	Gd to Firm	Rambling Bear	Jan 1 1999
6f	1m 10.6	2	8-10	Gd to Firm	Mujtahid	Jly 11 1990
6f	69.5 secs	3	8-13	Gd to Firm	Stravinsky (USA)	Jly 8 1999
7f	1m 24.1	2	8-11	Good	My Hansel	Aug 27 1999
7f	1m 22.5	3	9-7	Firm	Ho Leng (IRE)	Jly 9 1998
1m	1m 39.0	2	8-11	Good	Traceability	Aug 25 1995
1m	1m 35.5	3	8-6	Gd to Firm	Lovers Knot	Jly 8 1998
1m 110y	1m 44.1	3	8-11	Good	Golden Snake	Apr 15 1999
1m 2f	2m 0.9	4	9-3	Gd to Firm	Elhayq (IRE)	May 1 1999
1m 4f	2m 25.2	4	9-2	Good	Craigsteel	Jly 6 1999
1m 6f 175y	3m 4.2	3	8-5	Good	Arrive	Jly 11 2001
2m 24y	3m 20.2	7	9-10	Good	Yorkshire	Jly 11 2001

NOTTINGHAM

Distance	Time	Age	Weight	Going	Horse	Date
5f 13y	57.9 secs	2	8-9	Firm	Hoh Magic	May 13 1994
5f 13y	57.6 secs	6	9-2	Gd to firm	Catch The Cat (IRE)	May 14 2005
6f 15y	1m 11.4	2	811	Firm	Jameelapi	Aug 8 1983
6f 15y	1m 10.0	4	9-2	Firm	Ajanac	Aug 8 1988
1m 54y	1m 40.8	2	9-0	Gd to Firm	King s Loch	Sep 2 1991
1m 54y	1m 39.6	4	8-2	Gd to Firm	Blake s Treasure	Sep 2 1991
1m 1f 213y	2m 5.6	2	9-0	Firm	Al Salite	Oct 28 1985
1m 1f 213y	2m 2.3	2	9-0	Firm	Ayaabi	Jly 21 1984
1m 6f 15y	2m 57.8	3	8-10	Firm	Buster Jo	Oct 1 1985
2m 9y	3m 24.0	5	7-7	Firm	Fet	Oct 5 2036
2m 2f 18y	3m 55.1	9	9-10	Gd to Firm	Pearl Run	May 1 1990

PONTEFRACT

Distance	Time	Age	Weight	Going	Horse	Date
5f	61.1 secs	2	9-0	Firm	Golden Bounty	Sep 20 2001
5f	60.8 secs	4	8-9	Firm	Blue Maeve	Sep 29 2004
6f	1m 14.0	2	9-3	Firm	Fawzi	Sep 6 1983
6f	1m 12.6	3	7-13	Firm	Merry One	Aug 29 1970
1m 4y	1m 42.8	2	9-13	Firm	Star Spray	Sep 6 1983
1m 4y	1m 42.8	2	9-0	Firm	Alasil (USA)	Sep 26 2002
1m 4y	1m 40.6	4	9-10	Gd to Firm	Island Light	Apr 13 2002
1m 2f 6y	2m 10.1	2	9-0	Firm	Shanty Star	Oct 7 2002
1m 2f 6y	2m 8.2	4	7-8	Hard	Happy Hector	Jly 9 1979
1m 2f 6y	2m 8.2	3	7-13	Hard	Tom Noddy	Aug 21 1972
1m 4f 8y	2m 34.1	3	9-5	Gd to Firm	High Action	Aug 6 2003
2m 1f 22y	3m 40.67	4	8-7	Gd to Firm	Paradise Flight	June 6 2005
2m 1f 216y	3m 51.1	3	8-8	Firm	Kudz	Sep 9 1986
2m 5f 122y	4m 47.8	4	8-4	Firm	Physical	May 14 1984

REDCAR

Distance	Time	Age	Weight	Going	Horse	Date
5f	56.9 secs	2	9-0	Firm	Mister Joel	Oct 24 1995
5f	56.01 secs	10	9-3	Firm	Henry Hall	Sep 20 2006
6f	68.8 secs	2	8-3	Gd to Firm	Obe Gold	Oct 2 2004
6f	68.6 secs	3	9-2	Gd to Firm	Sizzling Saga	Jun 21 1991
7f	1m 21.28	2	9-3	Firm	Karoo Blue	Sep 20 2006
7f	1m 21.0	3	9-1	Firm	Empty Quarter	Oct 3 1995
1m	1m 34.37	2	9-0	Firm	Mastership	Sep 20 2006
1m	1m 32.42	4	10-0	Firm	Nanton	Sep 20 2006
1m 1f	1m 52.4	2	9-0	Firm	Spear (IRE)	Sep 13 2004
1m 1f	1m 48.5	5	8-12	Firm	Mellottie	Jly 25 1990
1m 2f	2m 10.1	2	8-11	Good	Adding	Nov 10 1989
1m 2f	2m 1.4	5	9-2	Firm	Eradicate	May 28 1990
1m 3f	2m 17.2	3	8-9	Firm	Photo Call	Aug 7 1990
1m 5f 135y	2m 54.7	6	9-10	Firm	Brodessa	Jun 20 1992
1m 6f 19y	2m 59.81	4	9-1	Gd to Firm	Esprit De Corps	Sep 11 2006
2m 4y	3m 24.9	3	9-3	Gd to Firm	Subsonic	Oct 8 1991
2m 3f	4m 10.1	5	7-4	Gd to Firm	Seldom In	Aug 9 1991

RIPON

Distance	Time	Age	Weight	Going	Horse	Date
5f	57.8 secs	2	8-8	Firm	Super Rocky	Jly 5 1991
5f	57.6 secs	5	8-5	Good	Broadstairs Beauty	May 21 1995
6f	1m 10.4	2	9-2	Good	Cumbrian Venture	Aug 17 2002
6f	69.8 secs	4	9-8	Gd to Firm	Tadeo	Aug 16 1997
6f	69.8 secs	5	7-10	Firm	Quoit	Jly
1m	1m 39.79	2	8-6	Good	Top Jaro (FR)	Sep 2
1m	1m 36.62	4	8-11	Gd to Firm	Granston (IRE)	Aug 29
1m 1f 170y	1m 59.12	5	8-9	Gd to Firm	Wahoo Sam (USA)	Aug 30 20
1m 2f	2m 2.6	3	9-4	Firm	Swift Sword	Jly 20 1990
1m 4f 10y	2m 32.06	4	8-8	Good	Hearthstead Wings	Apr 29 2006
2m	3m 27.07	5	9-12	Gd to Firm	Greenwich Meantime	Aug 30 2005

SALISBURY

Distance	Time	Age	Weight	Going	Horse	Date
5f	59.3 secs	2	9-0	Gd to Firm	Ajigolo	May 12 2005
5f	59.3 secs	2	9-0	Gd to Firm	Ajigolo	May 12 2005
6f	1m 12.1	2	8-0	Gd to Firm	Parisian Lady (IRE)	Jun 10 1997
6f	1m 11.3	3	8-1	Firm	Bentong (IRE)	May 7 2006
6f 212y	1m 25.9	2	9-0	Firm	More Royal (USA)	Jun 29 1995
6f 212y	1m 24.9	3	9-7	Firm	High Summer (USA)	Sep 5 1996
1m	1m 40.4	2	8-13	Firm	Choir Master (USA)	Sep 17 2002
1m	1m 38.29	3	8-7	Gd to Firm	Layman (USA)	Aug 11 2005
1m 1f 198y	2m 4.9	3	8-6	Gd to Firm	Zante	Aug 12 1998
1m 4f	2m 31.6	3	9-5	Gd to Firm	Arrive	Jun 27 2001
1m 6f 15y	2m 59.4	3	8-6	Gd to Firm	Tabareeh	Sep 2 1999

SANDOWN

Distance	Time	Age	Weight	Going	Horse	Date
5f 6y	59.4 secs	2	9-3	Firm	Times Time	Jly 22 1982
5f 6y	58.8 secs	6	8-9	Gd to Firm	Palacegate Touch	Sep 17 1996
7f 16y	1m 27.8	2	8-12	Gd to Firm	Red Camellia	Jly 25 1996
7f 16y	1m 26.3	3	9-0	Firm	Mawsuff	Jun 14 1983
1m 14y	1m 41.1	2	8-11	Fast	Reference Point	Sep 23 1986
1m 14y	1m 39.0	3	8-8	Firm	Linda s Fantasy	Aug 19 1983
1m 1f	1m 54.6	2	8-8	Gd to Firm	French Pretender	Sep 20 1988
1m 1f	1m 52.4	7	9-3	Gd to Firm	Bourgainville	Aug 11 2005
1m 2f 7y	2m 2.1	4	8-11	Firm	Kalaglow	May 31 1982
1m 3f 91y	2m 21.6	4	8-3	Fast	Aylesfield	Jly 7 1984
1m 6f	2m 56.9	4	8-7	Gd to Firm	Lady Rosanna	Jly 19 1989
2m 78y	3m 29.9	6	9-2	Firm	Sadeem	May 29 1989

SOUTHWELL (TURF)

Distance	Time	Age	Weight	Going	Horse	Date
6f	1m 15.03	2	9-3	Good	Trepa	Sep 6 2006
6f	1m 13.48	4	8-10	Good	Paris Bell	Sep 6 2006
7f	1m 27.56	2	9-7	Good	Hart Of Gold	Sep 6 2006
7f	1m 25.95	3	9-0	Good	Aeroplane	Sep 6 2006
1m 2f	2m 7.470	3	8-11	Good	Desert Authority(USA)	Sep 6 2006
1m 3f	2m 20.13	4	9-12	Good	Sanchi	Sep 6 2006
1m 4f	2m 34.4	5	9-3	Gd to Firm	Corn Lily	Aug 10 1991
2m	3m 34.1	5	9-1	Gd to Firm	Triplicate	Sep 20 1991

SOUTHWELL (A.W)

Distance	Time	Age	Weight	Going	Horse	Date
5f	58.89 secs	2	8-6	Standard	Egyptian Lord	Dec 15 2005
5f	57.35 secs	5	9-2	Std to Fast	Fyodor (IRE)	Jan 1 2006
6f	1m 14.00	2	8-5	Standard	Panalo	Nov 8 1989
6f	1m 13.50	4	10-02	Standard	Saladan Knight	Dec 30 1989
7f	1m 27.10	2	8-2	Standard	Mystic Crystal	Nov 20 1990
7f	1m 26.80	5	8-4	Standard	Amenable	Dec 13 1990
1m	1m 38.00	2	8-9	Standard	Alpha Rascal	Nov 13 1990
1m	1m 38.00	2	8-10	Standard	Andrew s First	Dec 30 1989
1m	1m 37.25	3	8-6	Standard	Valira	Nov 3 1990
1m 3f	2m 21.50	4	9-7	Standard	Tempering	Dec 5 1990
1m 4f	2m 33.90	4	9-12	Standard	Fast Chick	Nov 8 1989
1m 6f	3m 1.60	3	7-8	Standard	Erevnon	Dec 29 1990
2m	3m 37.60	9	8-12	Standard	Old Hubert	Dec 5 1990

THIRSK

Distance	Time	Age	Weight	Going	Horse	Date
5f	57.2 secs	2	9-7	Gd to Firm	Proud Boast	Aug 5 2000
5f	56.9 secs	5	9-6	Firm	Charlie Parkes	April 11 2003
6f	69.2 secs	2	9-6	Gd to Firm	Westcourt Magic	Aug 25 1995
6f	68.8 secs	6	9-4	Firm	Johayro	Jly 23 1999
7f	1m 23.7	2	8-9	Firm	Courting	Jly 23 1999
7f	1m 22.8	4	8-5	Firm	Silver Haze	May 21 1988
1m	1m 37.9	2	9-0	Firm	Sunday Symphony	Sep 4 2004
1m	1m 34.8	4	8-13	Firm	Yearsley	May 5 1990
1m 4f	2m 29.9	5	9-12	Firm	Gallery God	Jun 4 2001
2m	3m 22.3	3	8-11	Firm	Tomaschek	Jul 17 1981

WARWICK

Distance	Time	Age	Weight	Going	Horse	Date
5f	58.4 secs	2	9-7	Gd to Firm	Prenonamoss	Oct 9 1990
5f	57.7 secs	4	9-6	Gd to Firm	Little Edward	Jly 7 2002
5f 110y	63.6 secs	5	8-6	Gd to Firm	Dizzy In The Head	Jun 27 2004
6f 21y	1m 10.6	2	9-0	Gd to Firm	Viking Spirit	Sep 6 2004
6f 21y	69.6 secs	6	9-2	Firm	Parkside Pursuit	Jun 20 2004
7f 26y	1m 22.9	2	9-0	Firm	Country Rambler(USA)	Jun 20 2004
7f 26y	1m 20.7	4	8-8	Good	Etlaala	Apr 17 2006
1m 22y	1m 37.1	3	8-11	Firm	Orinocovsky (IRE)	Jun 26 2002
1m 2f 188y	2m 16.2	6	7-12	Gd to Firm	Scented Air	Apr 21 2003
1m 4f 134y	2m 39.5	3	8-13	Gd to Firm	Maimana (IRE)	Jun 22 2002
1m 6f 135y	3m 7.5	3	9-7	Gd to Firm	Burma Baby (USA)	Jly 2 1999
2m 39y	3m 27.9	3	8-1	Firm	Decoy	Jun 26 2002

WINDSOR

Distance	Time	Age	Weight	Going	Horse	Date
[illegible]	[illegible]	2	8-12	Gd to Firm	Hoh Mike (IRE)	May 15 2006
[illegible]	[illegible]	5	7-10	Gd to Firm	Beyond The Clouds	Jun 2 2001
[illegible]	[illegible]	2	9-5	Gd to Firm	Cubism (USA)	Aug 17 1998
[illegible]	[illegible]	[illegible]	9-1	Gd to Firm	Baltic King	May 23 2005
[illegible]	[illegible]	[illegible]	9-0	Good	Genre	Oct 3 2005
[illegible]	[illegible].27	4	9-3	Gd to Firm	Librettist (USA)	Jul 1 2006
[illegible]y	2m 3.0	2	9-1	Firm	Moomba Masquerade	May 19 1990
1m 3f 135y	2m 21.5	3	9-2	Firm	Double Florin	May 19 1980

WOLVERHAMPTON (A.W.)

Distance	Time	Age	Weight	Going	Horse	Date
5f 20y	61.13 sec	2	8-8	Std to Fast	Yungaburra (IRE)	Nov 8 2006
5f 20y	60.56 sec	3	8-10	Standard	King Orchisios (IRE)	Oct 29 2006
5f 216y	1m 12.61	2	9-0	Std to Fast	Prime Defender	Nov 8 2006
5f 216y	1m 13.32	5	8-12	Standard	Desert Opal	Sep 17 2005
7f 32y	1m 27.70	2	9-5	Standard	Billy Dane	Aug 14 2006
7f 32y	1m 27.44	7	9-12	Standard	Suggestive	Dec 9 2005
1m 141y	1m 48.08	2	8-9	Std to Fast	Worldly	Aug 30 2006
1m 141y	1m 46.71	4	8-12	Standard	Cimyla	Nov 11 2005
1m 1f 103y	2m 0.76	2	9-0	Standard	Mr Excel (IRE)	Nov 14 2005
1m 1f 103y	1m 57.34	4	8-13	Standard	Bahar Shumaal (IRE)	Aug 31 2006
1m 4f 50y	2m 35.71	3	9-2	Std to Fast	Steppe Dancer (IRE)	Aug 30 2006
1m 5f 194y	2m 59.85	6	9-12	Std to Fast	Valance (IRE)	Aug 30 2006
2m 119y	3m 35.85	5	8-11	Std to Fast	Market Watcher (USA)	Nov 21 2006

YARMOUTH

Distance	Time	Age	Weight	Going	Horse	Date
5f 43y	60.4 secs	2	8-6	Gd to Firm	Ebba	Jly 26 1999
5f 43y	59.8 secs	4	8-13	Gd to Firm	Roxanne Mill	Aug 25 2002
6f 3y	1m 10.4	2	9-0	Fast	Lanchester	Aug 15 1988
6f 3y	69.9 secs	4	8-9	Firm	Malhub (USA)	Jun 13 2002
7f 3y	1m 22.2	2	9-0	Gd to Firm	Warrshan	Sep 14 1988
7f 3y	1m 22.2	3	8-7	Firm	Cielamour	Sep 15 1988
1m 3y	1m 36.3	2	8-2	Gd to Firm	Outrun	Sep 15 1988
1m 3y	1m 33.9	3	8-8	Firm	Bonne Etoile	Jun 27 1995
1m 2f 21y	2m 2.83	3	8-8	Firm	Reunite (IRE)	Jul 18 2006
1m 3f 101y	2m 23.1	3	8-9	Firm	Rahil	Jly 1 1993
1m 6f 17y	2m 57.8	3	8-2	Gd to Firm	Barakat	Jly 24 1990
2m	3m 26.7	4	8-2	Gd to Firm	Alhesn (USA)	Jly 26 1999
2m 2f 51y	3m 56.8	4	9-10	Firm	Provence	Sep 19 1991

YORK

Distance	Time	Age	Weight	Going	Horse	Date
5f	57.3 secs	2	7-8	Gd to Firm	Lyric Fantasy	Aug 20 1992
5f	56.1 secs	3	9-3	Gd to Firm	Dayjur	Aug 23 1990
6f	69.5 secs	2	9-0	Gd to Firm	Indiscreet (CAN)	Aug 22 1996
6f	68.58 secs	7	9-4	Firm	Cape Of Good Hope	Jun 16 2005
6f 214y	1m 22.9	2	8-10	Gd to Firm	Options Open	Aug 16 1994
6f 214y	1m 21.3	3	9-0	Firm	Bold Fact (USA)	Aug 20 1998
7f 202y	1m 37.2	2	9-4	Gd to Firm	The Wife	Sep 2 1999
7f 202y	1m 34.8	4	8-10	Gd to Firm	Concer Un	Aug 22 1996
1m 205y	1m 52.4	2	8-1	Gd to Firm	Oral Evidence	Oct 6 1988
1m 205y	1m 47.0	3	8-10	Gd to Firm	Gold Academy	Sep 2 1999
1m 2f 88y	2m 6.09	4	8-11	Gd to Firm	Imperial Stride	Jun 17 2005
1m 3f 195y	2m 25.1	3	8-9	Gd to Firm	Sea Wave (IRE)	Aug 18 1998
1m 5f 194y	2m 51.8	3	8-7	Gd to Firm	Tuning	Aug 19 1998
1m 7f 195y	3m 18.4	3	8-0	Gd to Firm	Dam Busters	Aug 16 1988